CWS104 6
OP -

MW00355106

FOURTH EDITION

MEDICINE
FOR THE
PRACTICING
PHYSICIAN

Editor-in-Chief
J. Willis Hurst, M.D.

Section Editors

Edmund Bourke, M.D.
Louis R. Caplan, M.D.
William H. Coles, M.D., M.S.
Suzanne S. P. Gebhart, M.D.
Sam D. Graham, Jr., M.D.
John B. Griffin, Jr., M.D.
Gerald S. Gussack, M.D.
W. Dallas Hall, M.D.
Stephan L. Kamholz, M.D.
James T.C. Li, M.D., Ph.D.
Alan E. Lichtin, M.D.
Maurie Markman, M.D.
Marilynne McKay, M.D.

Stephen B. Miller, M.D.
Dorothy E. Mitchell-Leef, M.D.
Robert L. Rietschel, M.D.
Robert C. Schlant, M.D.
Jonas A. Shulman, M.D.
Corey M. Slovis, M.D.
David S. Stephens, M.D.
Eugene Straus, M.D.
John S. Turner, Jr., M.D.
Nelson B. Watts, M.D.
Roland L. Weinsier, M.D., Dr.P.H.
Randolph Martin York, M.D.

Appleton & Lange
Stamford, Connecticut

Notice: The authors and the publisher of this volume have taken care to make certain that the doses of drugs and schedules of treatment are correct and compatible with the standards generally accepted at the time of publication. Nevertheless, as new information becomes available, changes in treatment and in the use of drugs become necessary. The reader is advised to carefully consult the instruction and information material included in the package insert of each drug or therapeutic agent before administration. This advice is especially important when using, administering, or recommending new and infrequently used drugs. The authors and publisher disclaim all responsibility for any liability, loss, injury, or damage incurred as a consequence, directly or indirectly, of the use and application of any of the contents of this volume.

Copyright © 1996 by Appleton & Lange
A Simon & Schuster Company
Copyright © 1992 by Butterworth-Heinemann

All rights reserved. This book, or any parts thereof, may not be used or reproduced in any manner without written permission. For information, address Appleton & Lange, Four Stamford Plaza, PO Box 120041, Stamford, Connecticut 06912-0041.

97 98 99 00 / 10 9 8 7 6 5 4 3 2

Prentice Hall International (UK) Limited, *London*
Prentice Hall of Australia Pty. Limited, *Sydney*
Prentice Hall Canada, Inc., *Toronto*
Prentice Hall Hispanoamericana, S.A., *Mexico*
Prentice Hall of India Private Limited, *New Delhi*
Prentice Hall of Japan, Inc., *Tokyo*
Simon and Schuster Asia Pte. Ltd., *Singapore*
Editora Prentice Hall do Brasil Ltda., *Rio de Janeiro*
Prentice Hall, *Upper Saddle River, New Jersey*

Library of Congress Cataloging–in–Publication Data

Medicine for the practicing physician / [edited by] J. Willis Hurst. –
- 4th ed.
        p.   cm.
    Includes bibliographical references and index.
    ISBN 0–8385–6317–1 (case : alk. paper)
    1. Family medicine.   I. Hurst, J. Willis (John Willis), 1920–   .
    [DNLM: 1. Medicine. 2. Diagnosis. 3. Therapeutics.   WB 100
M49053 1996]
    RC46.M4776   1996
    616—dc20
    DNLM/DLC   96–1711
    for Library of Congress   CIP

Developmental Editor: Kathleen McCullough
Production Editor: Elizabeth C. Ryan
Designer: Janice Barsevich Bielawa

PRINTED IN THE UNITED STATES OF AMERICA

0-8385-6317-1

90000

9 780838 563175

This book is dedicated to the noble profession of medicine and the practicing physician whose "face is marred by the dust and sweat and blood, who knows the great enthusiasms, the great devotions, and spends himself [and herself] in a worthy cause."*

---

*The quotation is from a speech made by President John F. Kennedy about Theodore Roosevelt on December 5, 1961. The word *herself* has been added to the quotation in courteous respect for the women who will soon make up 50 percent or more of the practicing physicians in the United States.

Contents

viii   Contents

Contributors

Cynthia K. Aaron, M.D.
Assistant Professor of Emergency Medicine
Director, Toxicology Services
University of Massachusetts Medical Center
Worcester, Massachusetts

Walter H. Abelmann, M.D.
Professor of Medicine, Emeritus
Harvard Medical School

Senior Physician
Beth Israel Hospital
Boston, Massachusetts

David J. Adelstein, M.D.
Vice Chairman
Department of Hematology and Medical
　Oncology
Cleveland Clinic Foundation
Cleveland, Ohio

Sheldon Adler, M.D.
Professor of Medicine
University of Pittsburgh School of Medicine
Pittsburgh, Pennsylvania

Carlos A. Agudelo, M.D.
Professor of Medicine
Acting Chief, Rheumatology Section
Emory University School of Medicine

Chief, Rheumatology
Veterans Affairs Medical Center
Atlanta, Georgia

Michael J. H. Akerman, M.D.
Assistant Professor of Medicine
Director of the Asthma Service
State University of New York-Health Science
　Center at Brooklyn
Brooklyn, New York

Toshio Akiyama, M.D.
Professor of Medicine
University of Rochester School
　of Medicine

Director of Arrhythmia and Pacemaker
　Service
University of Rochester Medical Center
Rochester, New York

Richard K. Albert, M.D.
Professor of Medicine
Section Head, Pulmonary and Critical Care
　Medicine
University of Washington Medical Center
Seattle, Washington

Dewitt C. Alfred Jr., M.D.
Chair and Professor of Psychiatry
Morehouse School of Medicine

Chief Psychiatrist
Morehouse Medical Associates, Inc.
Atlanta, Georgia

Michael Allon, M.D.
Associate Professor of Medicine
University of Alabama at Birmingham
Birmingham, Alabama

Joseph S. Alpert, M.D.
Flinn Professor of Medicine
Head, Department of Medicine
University of Arizona College of
　Medicine
Tucson, Arizona

Samuel S. Ambrose, M.D.
Professor of Surgery (Urology) Emeritus
Emory University School of Medicine
Atlanta, Georgia

Steven W. Andresen, D.O.
Staff Physician
Cleveland Clinic Foundation
Cleveland, Ohio

Theodore J. Anfinson, M.D.
Assistant Professor of Psychiatry and
　Behavioral Sciences
Instructor of Medicine
Emory University School of Medicine

Director, Medical Psychiatry Unit
Emory University Hospitals
Atlanta, Georgia

Frederick J. Angulo, D.V.M., Ph.D.
Medical Epidemioilogist
Division of Bacterial and Mycotic Diseases
National Center for Infectious Disease
Centers for Disease Control and
　Prevention
Atlanta, Georgia

Joseph D. Ansley, M.D.
Associate Professor of Surgery
Emory University School of Medicine
Atlanta, Georgia

Dominique M. Anwar-Bruni, M.D.
Research Fellow in Infectious Diseases
Department of Medicine
Emory University School of Medicine
Atlanta, Georgia

Daniel Arensberg, M.D.
Associate Professor of Medicine
Emory University School of Medicine

Director of Coronary Care Unit
Grady Memorial Hospital
Altlanta, Georgia

Kathryn E. Arnold, M.D.
Infectious Diseases Fellow
Emory University School of Medicine
Atlanta, Georgia

Michael E. Assey, M.D.
Professor of Medicine
Director, Adult Cardiac Catheterization
　Laboratories
Medical University of South Carolina
Charleston, South Carolina

Howard A. Austin III, M.D.
Chief, Clinical Nephrology Service
National Institutes of Health
Bethesda, Maryland

James E. Balow, M.D.
Professor of Medicine
Uniformed Services University of the Health
　Sciences

Clinical Director, NIDDK
National Institutes of Health
Bethesda, Maryland

George D. Baquis, M.D.
Assistant Professor of Neurology
Tufts University School of Medicine
Boston, Massachusetts

Robert H. Barth, M.D.
Associate Professor of Clinical
　Medicine
State University of New York–Health Science
　Center at Brooklyn

Chief, Hemodialysis
Veterans Administration Medical Center
Brooklyn, New York

John R. Bartholomew, M.D.
Staff Physician
Cleveland Clinic Foundation
Cleveland, Ohio

Patrick M. Battey, M.D.
Clinical Assistant Professor of Surgery
Emory University School of Medicine
Atlanta, Georgia

Alice Beal, M.D.
Assistant Professor of Clinical
　Medicine
State University of New York–Health Science
　Center at Brooklyn

Chief, MICU
Brooklyn Veterans Administration Medical
　Center
Brooklyn, New York

John R. Belden, M.D.
Stroke Fellow, 1994–1995
New England Medical Center
Boston, Massachusetts

Nora Valeria Bergasa, M.D.
Assistant Professor
Clinical Scholar
The Rockefeller University
New York, New York

Geoffrey M. Berlyne, M.D.
Associate Professor of Medicine
State University of New York–Health Science
    Center at Brooklyn

Chief, Hemodialysis
Brooklyn Veterans Administration Medical
    Center
Brooklyn, New York

William G. Blackard, M.D.
Professor of Medicine
Chairman, Division of Endocrinology
    and Metabolism
Medical College of Virginia
Richmond, Virginia

Lewis S. Blevins, Jr., M.D.
Assistant Professor of Medicine
Section of Endocrinology and
    Metabolism
Emory University School of Medicine
Atlanta, Georgia

Henry M. Blumberg, M.D.
Assistant Professor of Medicine
Division of Infectious Diseases
Emory University School of Medicine

Hospital Epidemiologist
Grady Memorial Hospital
Atlanta, Georgia

Naomi Bock, M.D.
Assistant Professor of Medicine
Division of Infectious Diseases
Emory University School of Medicine
Atlanta, Georgia

Henry C. Bodenheimer, Jr., M.D.
Professor of Medicine
Clinical Director of Liver Diseases
Mount Sinai Medical Center
New York, New York

Brian J. Bolwell, M.D.
Director
Bone Marrow Transplant Program
The Cleveland Clinic Foundation
Cleveland, Ohio

Darwin R. Boor, M.D.
Assistant Professor
Department of Neurology
Emory University School of Medicine
Atlanta, Georgia

Arthur Boshnack, M.D.
Associate Attending Physician
Mercy Medical Center
Rockville Center, New York

Edmund Bourke, M.D.
Professor of Medicine
Vice Chairman
Department of Medicine
State University of New York–Health Science
    Center at Brooklyn

Chief, Medical Service
Brooklyn Veterans Administration
    Medical Center
Brooklyn, New York

William Boyer, M.D.
Assistant Professor of Psychiatry
Emory University

Director of Clinical Psychiatric Research
Atlanta Veterans Administration Medical
    Center
Atlanta, Georgia

Roger Boykin, M.D.
Assistant Professor of Medicine
State University of New York–Health Science
    Center at Brooklyn
Brooklyn, New York

Associate Chief of Staff for Extended Care
St. Albans Veterans Administration Extended
    Care Center
St. Albans, New York

Emmanuel L. Bravo, M.D.
Professor of Medicine
Departments of Nephrology and Hypertension
    and Molecular Cardiology
Cleveland Clinic Foundation
Cleveland, Ohio

Stephen M. Brenner, M.D.
Assistant Clinical Professor of Medicine
Albert Einstein College of Medicine
Bronx, New York

Sue Anne Brenner, M.D.
Fellow in Infectious Diseases
Emory University School of Medicine
Atlanta, Georgia

Jeffrey Brent, M.D., Ph.D.
Assistant Clinical Professor of Surgery and
    Pediatrics
University of Colorado Health Sciences
    Center
Denver, Colorado

Steven L. Brody, M.D.
Assistant Professor of Medicine
Washington University School of Medicine
St Louis, Missouri

Neil M. Brodsky, M.D.
Clinical Instructor of Internal Medicine
State University of New York–Health Science
    Center at Brooklyn
Brooklyn, New York

Bruce H. Broecker, M.D.
Clinical Associate Professor of Surgery
    (Urology)
Emory University School of Medicine
Atlanta, Georgia

Frank W. Brown, M.D.
Assistant Professor of Psychiatry
Emory University School of Medicine
Atlanta, Georgia

Paul C. Browne, M.D.
Director, Maternal-Fetal Medicine
DeKalb Medical Center
Decatur, Georgia

G. Thomas Budd, M.D.
Staff Physician
Cleveland Clinic Foundation
Cleveland, Ohio

Ronald M. Bukowski, M.D.
Director
Experimental Therapeutics Program
The Cleveland Clinic Cancer Center
Cleveland, Ohio

Warner M. Burch, M.D.
Associate Professor of Medicine
Assistant Professor of Pharmacology
Duke University School of Medicine
Durham, North Carolina

Jay C. Butler, M.D.
Assistant Chief, Respiratory Diseases
Epidemiology Section
Division of Bacterial and Mycotic
    Diseases
Centers for Disease Control and
    Prevention
Atlanta, Georgia

Khalid Butt, M.D.
Professor and Vice Chairman
Department of Surgery
New York Medical College
New York, New York

Michael L. Callaham, M.D.
Professor of Medicine
University of California San Francisco
    School of Medicine

Chief
Division of Emergency Medicine
University of California San Francisco
    Medical Center
San Francisco, California

Quinton C. Callies, M.D.
Consultant in Allergic Diseases and
    Internal Medicine (Emeritus)
Mayo Medical School
Scottsdale, Arizona

Louis R. Caplan, M.D.
Professor of Neurology
Chairman, Department of Neurology
New England Medical Center Hospitals–Tufts
    University
Boston, Massachusetts

Rafael A. Caputi, M.D.
Fellow, Infectious Diseases
Division of Infectious Diseases
Emory University School of Medicine
Atlanta, Georgia

Hugh J. Carroll, M.D.
Distinguished Teaching Professor of
    Medicine
Director, Electrolyte-Hypertension
    Division
State University of New York
Health Science Center at Brooklyn
Brooklyn, New York

C. Michael Cawley, M.D.
Senior Resident
Department of Neurosurgery
Emory University School of Medicine
Atlanta, Georgia

Claudia Jacob Chaves, M.D.
Resident in Neurology
Tufts University School of Medicine
Boston, Massachsetts

David J. Clain, M.D.
Associate Professor of Medicine
Albert Einstein College of Medicine
Bronx, New York

Head, Liver Disease
Beth Israel Medical Center
New York, New York

Richard V. Clark, M.D., Ph.D.
Associate Professor of Medicine
Clinical Director
Division of Endocrinology and
  Metabolism
Duke University Medical Center
Durham, North Carolina

Harry S. Clarke, Jr., M.D., Ph.D.
Assistant Professor of Surgery
  (Urology)
Emory University School of Medicine
Atlanta, Georgia

Leonard A. Cobb, M.D.
Professor Emeritus of Medicine
University of Washington
Seattle, Washington

Peter F. Cohn, M.D.
Professor of Medicine
Chief of Cardiology
State University of New York
Stony Brook, New York

Steven A. Cole, M.D.
Professor of Psychiatry
Albert Einstein College of Medicine
Bronx, New York

Director
Managed Care and Service System
  Development
Hillside Hospital
Glen Oaks, New York

Claire D. Coles, Ph.D.
Associate Professor of Psychiatry
Emory University School of Medicine

Director, Psychological Services
Marcus Center at Emory University
Atlanta, Georgia

William H. Coles, M.D., M.S.
Professor and Chairman
Department of Ophthalmology
State University of New York at Buffalo
Buffalo, New York

Donal A. Costigan, M.B., B. Ch., B.A.O.
Associate Professor
Department of Neurology
Emory University School of Medicine
Atlanta, Georgia

Robert B. Couch, M.D.
Professor and Chairman
Department of Microbiology and Immunology
Director of the Acute Viral Respiratory
  Diseases Unit
Baylor College of Medicine
Houston, Texas

Philip E. Cryer, M.D.
Professor of Medicine
Director, Division of Endocrinology, Diabetes
  and Metabolism
Washington University School of Medicine
St. Louis, Missouri

Gordon B. Cutler, Jr., M.D.
Chief, Section on Developmental
  Endocrinology, Developmental
  Endocrinology Branch National Institute
  of Child Health and Human Development
National Institutes of Health
Bethesda, Maryland

Vera Delaney, M.D. Ph.D.
Associate Professor of Medicine
  and Surgery
New York Medical College
New York, New York

Barbara G. Delano, M.D.
Professor of Clinical Medicine
State University of New York Brooklyn
Brooklyn, New York

Mary Lynn Dell, M.D., M.T.S., Th.M.
Assistant Professor of Psychiatry and
  Pediatrics
Emory University School of Medicine
Atlanta, Georgia

Carlos del Rio, M.D.
Associate Professor
Department of Medicine, Infectious Diseases
  Section
Hospital Angeles del Pedregal and
  Universidad La Salle

Director, National AIDS Program
  (CONASIDA)
Mexico
Mexico City, Mexico

Spiro Demetis, M.D.
Assistant Professor of Medicine
State University of New York–Health
  Sciences Center at Brooklyn

Director of Medical Firm
Kings County Hospital
Brooklyn, New York

Mario DiGirolamo, M.D.
Professor of Medicine and Physiology
Director, Division of Gerontology and
  Geriatric Medicine, Department of
  Medicine
Emory University School of Medicine
Atlanta, Georgia

William E. Dismukes, M.D.
Professor of Medicine
Vice Chairman, Department of Medicine
Director, Division of Infectious Diseases
Director, Internal Medicine Residency
  Training Program
The University of Alabama
  at Birmingham
Birmingham, Alabama

Thomas F. Dodson, M.D.
Associate Professor of Surgery
Emory University School of Medicine

Associate Program Director, Emory
  University Affiliated Hospitals Program in
  Surgery
Atlanta, Georgia

Ronald E. Domen, M.D.
Section of Blood Banking and Transfusion
  Medicine
Department of Clinical Pathology
The Cleveland Clinic Foundation
Cleveland, Ohio

James V. Donadio, Jr., M.D.
Professor of Medicine
Mayo Medical School

Consultant, Internal Medicine and
  Nephrology
Mayo Clinic and Foundation
Rochester, Minnesota

Robert Downs, Jr., M.D.
Associate Professor of Medicine
Medical College of Virginia/Virginia
  Commonwealth University
Richmond, Virginia

A. Gatewood Dudley, M.D.
Clinical Professor of Obstetrics and
  Gynecology
Mercer University School of Medicine
Macon, Georgia

Francis Dumler, M.D.
Chief, Division of Nephrology
William Beaumont Hospital
Royal Oak, Michigan

Molly E. Eaton, M.D.
Assistant Professor
Division of Infectious Diseases
Emory University School of Medicine
Atlanta, Georgia

James R. Eckman, M.D.
Professor of Medicine
Division of Hematology/Oncology
Assistant Professor Pediatrics
Division of Human Genetics
Emory University School of Medicine
Atlanta, Georgia

Linda S. Efferen, M.D.
Assistant Professor of Medicine
Acting Chief, Division of Pulmonary and
  Critical Care Medicine
State University of New York–Health
  Sciences Center at Brooklyn
Brooklyn, New York

Thomas Eglin, M.D.
Attending Physician
Emergency Department
Yakima Valley Memorial Hospital
Yakima, Washington

Bruce L. Ehrenberg, M.D.
Assistant Professor of Neurology
Tufts University School of Medicine

Senior Neurologist
New England Medical Center
Boston, Massachusetts

R. E. S. El-Galley, M.B., B. Ch.
Fellow
Department of Surgery (Urology)
Emory University School of
  Medicine
Atlanta, Georgia

Imad M. El-Kebbi, M.D.
Assistant Professor of Medicine
Emory University School of
  Medicine
Atlanta, Georgia

Carlene W. Elsner, M.D.
Reproductive Endocrinologist
Reproductive Biology Associates
Atlanta, Georgia

Mark D. Faber, M.D.
Clinical Instructor
University of Michigan
Ann Arbor, Michigan

Senior Staff Physician
Department of Nephrology
    and Hypertension
Henry Ford Hospital
Detroit, Michigan

Arthur Falek, Ph.D.
Professor of Psychiatry
Emory University School of Medicine
Atlanta, Georgia

Monica M. Farley, M.D.
Associate Professor of Medicine
Emory University School of Medicine
Atlanta, Georgia

Staff Physician
Veterans Administration Medical Center
Decatur, Georgia

W. Edmund Farrar, M.D.
Professor Emeritus of Medicine
Medical University of South Carolina
Charleston, South Carolina

Joel M. Felner, M.D.
Associate Dean, Clinical Education
Professor of Medicine (Cardiology)
Emory University School of
    Medicine
Atlanta, Georgia

Sidney M. Fierst, M.D., M.S.
Professor of Clinical Medicine
State University of New York–Health Science
    Center at Brooklyn

Director Emeritus Gastroenterology
Brookdale Hospital Center
Brooklyn, New York

Peter J. P. Finch, M.D.
Director, Pulmonary Rehabilitation
Brooklyn Veterans Administration Medical
    Center

Assistant Professor of Medicine
State University of New York–Health Science
    Center at Brooklyn
Brooklyn, New York

Adrian Fine, M.D.
Professor of Medicine
Department of Medicine
University of Manitoba

St. Boniface General Hospital
Winnipeg, Manitoba, Canada

Andrew J. Fishleder, M.D.
Staff, Section of Laboratory
    Hematology
The Cleveland Clinic Foundation
Cleveland, Ohio

Carmen M. Fonseca, M.D.
Assistant Staff, Department of Vascular
    Medicine
Cleveland Clinic Foundation
Cleveland, Ohio

Clinical Assistant Professor of
    Medicine
College of Medicine of the Pennsylvania State
    University
Hershey, Pennsylvania

Ethan D. Fried, M.D.
Assistant Professor of Medicine
Division of Pulmonary and Critical Care
    Medicine
State University of New York–Health
    Sciences Center at Brooklyn
Brooklyn, New York

Eli A. Friedman, M.D.
Distinguished Teaching Professor of
    Medicine
Chief, Division of Renal Diseases
Department of Medicine
State University of New York Health Science
    Center at Brooklyn
Brooklyn, New York

Evangelos Frigas, M.D.
Associate Professor of Medicine
Mayo Medical School
Rochester, Minnesota

Gerald Fruchter, M.D.
Associate Clinical Professor of Medicine
State University of New York Health Science
    Center at Brooklyn

Associate Chief of Gastroenterology
Brooklyn Veterans Administration Medical
    Center
Brooklyn, New York

J. Timothy Fulenwider, M.D.
Clinical Assistant Professor of Surgery
Emory University School of Medicine
Atlanta, Georgia

Thomas E. Fulmer, M.D.
Associate Professor of Psychiatry
Emory University School of Medicine

Chief, Psychiatry Service (Retired)
Atlanta Veterans Administration Center
Atlanta, Georgia

Niall T. M. Galloway, M.B., B. Ch.
Assistant Professor of Surgery (Urology)
Emory University School of Medicne
Atlanta, Georgia

R. Don Gambrell, Jr., M.D.
Clinical Professor of Endocrinology and
    Obstetrics and Gynecology
Medical College of Georgia
Augusta, Georgia

George K. Ganaway, M.D.
Clinical Assistant Professor of Psychiatry
Emory University School of Medicine
Atlanta, Georgia

Stuart M. Garay, M.D.
Clinical Professor of Medicine
Department of Pulmonary and Critical Care
    Medicine
New York University Medical Center
New York, New York

David F. Gardner, M.D.
Professor of Medicine
Division of Endocrinology
Medical College of Virginia
Richmond, Virginia

Kenneth D. Gardner, Jr., M.D.
Emeritus Professor of Medicine
University of New Mexico Health Sciences
    Center
Albuquerque, New Mexico

Renee Garrick, M.D.
Associate Professor of Medicine
New York Medical College
New York, New York

Attending Physician
Westchester County Medical Center
Valhalla, New York

Suzanne S. P. Gebhart, M.D.
Associate Professor (Endocrinology and
    Metabolism)
Department of Medicine
Emory University School of Medicine
Atlanta, Georgia

Charles D. Gerson, M.D.
Associate Clinical Professor of Medicine
Mount Sinai School of Medicine
New York, New York

Amy S. Gewirtz, M.D.
Fellow, Section of Laboratory
    Hematology
Cleveland Clinic Foundation
Cleveland, Ohio

Ray W. Gifford, Jr., M.D.
Professor of Internal Medicine
Ohio State University College of
    Medicine
Columbus, Ohio

Consultant, Department of Nephrology and
    Hypertension
Cleveland Clinic Foundation
Cleveland, Ohio

Lawrence Glaubiger, M.D.
Assistant Professor of Medicine
State University of New York–Health Science
    Center at Brooklyn
Section of Pulmonary and Critical Care
    Medicine
Department of Veterans Affairs Medical
    Center
Brooklyn, New York

Lewis Goldfrank, M.D.
Associate Professor of Clinical Medicine
New York University

Director, Department of Emergency
    Medicine
Bellevue Hospital and New York
    University
New York, New York

Lynn Goldowski, M.D.
Clinical Assistant Instructor
Pulmonary Division, Department of
    Medicine
State University of New York–Health Science
    Center at Brooklyn
Brooklyn, New York

Emilio B. Gonzalez, M.D.
Associate Professor of Medicine
Emory University School of Medicine

Chief, Rheumatology Service
Grady Memorial Hospital
Atlanta, Georgia

Louis W. Goolsby, M.D.
Assistant Professor of Obstetrics and
    Gynecology
Mercer University School of Medicine
Macon, Georgia

Kenneth C. Gorson, M.D.
Assistant Professor of Neurology
Tufts University School of Medicine

Attending Neurologist
St. Elizabeth's Medical Center
Boston, Massachusetts

Antonio M. Gotto, Jr., M.D., D.Phil.
Chairman, Department of Medicine
Baylor College of Medicine

Chief, Internal Medicine Service
The Methodist Hospital
Houston, Texas

André Gougoux, M.D.
Professor of Medicine and Physiology
University of Montreal

Nephrologist
Notre-Dame Hospital
Montreal, Canada

Sam D. Graham, Jr., M.D.
Professor of Surgery (Urology)
Emory University School of Medicine
Atlanta, Georgia

Michael D. Graubert, M.D.
Fellow, Reproductive Endocrinology
Beth Israel Hospital
Boston, Massachusetts

Ralph Green, M.B., B. Ch., M.D.
Professor of Pathology
Ohio State University

Associate Clinical Professor of Medicine
Case Western Reserve University

Departments of Clinical Pathology and Cell
Biology
The Cleveland Clinic Foundation
Cleveland, Ohio

John B. Griffin, Jr., M.D.
Professor of Psychiatry
Emory University School of Medicine

Member, Emory Clinic
Atlanta, Georgia

Ronald F. Grossman, M.D.
Associate Professor of Medicine
University of Toronto
Head, Division of Respiratory Medicine
Mount Sinai Hospital
Toronto, Canada

Richard L. Guerrant, M.D.
Thomas H Hunter Professor of International
Medicine
Chief, Division of Geographic and
International Medicine
Director, Office of International Health
University of Virginia School of
Medicine
Charlottesville, Virginia

Clifford J. Gunthel, M.D.
Assistant Professor of Medicine
Emory University School of Medicine
Atlanta, Georgia

Gerald S. Gussack, M.D.
Associate Professor of Otolaryngology, Head
and Neck Surgery
Director of Residency Education
Emory University School of Medicine
Atlanta, Georgia

Paul S. Haber, M.B., B.S., B.Med.Sc., M.D.
Fellow in Gastroenterology
Prince of Wales Hospital
Randwick, New South Wales, Australia

George C. Haidet, M.D.
Associate Professor of Medicine and
Radiology
University of Minnesota School of Medicine

Director, Exercise Laboratories and
Cardiovascular Rehabilitation
Director (Cardiology) of Nuclear
Cardiology
University of Minnesota Hospital and Clinic
Minneapolis, Minnesota

Rana A. Hajjeh, M.D.
Medical Epidemiologist
National Center for Infectious Diseases
Center for Disease Control
Atlanta, Georgia

W. Dallas Hall, M.D.
Professor of Medicine
Director, Division of Hypertension
Emory University School of Medicine
Atlanta, Georgia

Lewis H. Hamner III, M.D.
Director, Perinatology
Kaiser Permanente
Atlanta, Georgia

W. Lee Hand, M.D.
Professor and Regional Chairman
Department of Medicine
Texas Tech University Health Sciences
Center
El Paso, Texas

Joe G. Hardin, M.D.
Professor of Medicine
Director, Division of Rheumatology
University of South Alabama
Mobile, Alabama

John T. Harrington, M.D.
Dean for Academic Affairs
Professor of Medicine
Tufts University School of Medicine
Boston, Massachusetts

Mary Elizabeth Hartnett, M.D.
Clinical Instructor
Harvard Medical School

Associate in Ophthalmology
Massachusetts Eye & Ear Infirmary
Boston, Massachusetts

Robert A. Hatcher, M.D., M.P.H.
Professor of Gynecology and Obstetrics
Emory University School of Medicine
Atlanta, Georgia

Ian D. Hay, M.B., Ph.D.
Professor of Medicine
Mayo Medical School

Consultant in Endocrinology
May Clinic
Rochester, Minnesota

Michael T. Hayes, M.D.
Assistant Professor of Neurology
Tufts University Medical School

Division of Neurology
St. Elizabeth's Hospital
Boston, Masachusetts

Robert P. Heaney, M.D.
John A Creighton University Professor
Professor of Medicine (Department of Internal
Medicine)
Creighton University
Omaha, Nebraska

Douglas C. Heimburger, M.D., M.S.
Associate Professor of Nutrition Sciences
and Medicine
Director, Division of Clinical Nutrition
University of Alabama at Birmingham
Birmingham, Alabama

Richard L. Hengel, M.D.
Fellow in Infectious Diseases
Emory University School of Medicine
Atlanta, Georgia

Deborah O. Heros, M.D.
Clinical Neuro-oncologist
Neurosciences
Park Nicollet Medical Center
St. Louis Park, Minnesota

Steven M. Hersch, M.D., Ph.D.
Assistant Professor of Neurology
Director, Emory Huntington's Disease
Program
Emory University School of Medicine
Atlanta, Georgia

Albert E. Heurich, M.D.
Associate Professor of Clinical Medicine
State University of New York–Health Science
Center at Brooklyn
Brooklyn, New York

A. Ross Hill, M.D., C.M.
Associate Professor of Clinical Medicine
State University of New York–Health Science
Center at Brooklyn
Brooklyn, New York

Judith A. Hinchey, M.D.
Fellow in Neurophysiology
Harvard Medical School
Beth Israel Hospital
Boston, Massachusetts

Gerald A. Hoeltge, M.D.
Head, Section of Blood Banking and
Transfusion Medicine
Cleveland Clinic Foundation
Cleveland, Ohio

Robert S. Hoffman, M.D.
Clinical Assistant Professor of Surgery and
Emergency Medicine
Director, New York City Poison Center
New York University School of Medicine
New York, New York

Dave Hollander, M.D.
Assistant Professor of Neurology
Tufts University School of Medicine

Associate Director, Neuromuscular Research
Unit
Tufts-New England Medical Center
Boston, Massachusetts

Peter R. Holt, M.D.
Professor of Medicine
Columbia University

Chief, Gastrointestinal Division
St. Luke's Hospital Center
New York, New York

Thomas M. Hooten, M.D.
Associate Professor of Medicine
University of Washington School
    of Medicine
Seattle, Washington

Sarah L. Hosford, M.D.
Assistant Clinical Professor of Obstetrics and
    Gynecology
Medical College of Georgia
Augusta, Georgia

Assistant Clinical Professor of Obstetrics and
    Gynecology
Morehouse School of Medicine

Assistant Director, Gynecologic Oncology
Georgia Baptist Medical Center–Cancer
    Center of Georgia
Atlanta, Georgia

George F. Howard III, M.D.
Assistant Professor of Neurology
Tufts University School of Medicine
Boston, Massachusetts

Division of Neurology
Baystate Medical Center
Springfield, Massachusetts

James M. Hughes, M.D.
Clinical Associate Professor of Medicine
Division of Infectious Diseases
Emory University School of Medicine

Director, National Center for Infectious
    Diseases
Centers for Disease Control and Prevention
Atlanta, Georgia

Charles M. Huguley, Jr., M.D.
Professor of Medicine, Emeritus
Emory University School of Medicine
Atlanta, Georgia

Loren W. Hunt, M.D.
Assistant Professor of Medicine
Mayo Clinic
Rochester, Minnesota

J. Willis Hurst, M.D.
Consultant to the Division of Cardiology
Department of Medicine
Emory University School of Medicine

Former Professor and Chairman
Department of Medicine
Emory University School of Medicine,
    1957–1986
Atlanta, Georgia

Mohamad A. Hussein, M.B., B. Ch., M.D.
Staff, Hematology/Oncology
Cleveland Clinic Foundation
Cleveland, Ohio

Charles L. Hyman, M.D.
Assistant Professor of Medicine
Division of Infectious Diseases
State University of New York–Health
    Sciences Center at Brooklyn

Director for Clinical Affairs
Department of Medicine
Kings County Hospital Center
Brooklyn, New York

Daniel H. Jacobs, M.D.
Assistant Professor of Neurology
Tufts University School of Medicine
Boston, Massachusetts

Ghassan W. Jamaleddine, M.D.
Former Assistant Professor of Medicine
State University of New York–Health
    Sciences Center at Brooklyn
Brooklyn, New York

Current Chief of Pulmonary Medicine
American University of Beirut Medical
    School
Beirut, Lebanon

John A. Jernigan, M.D.
Assistant Professor of Medicine
Division of Infectious Diseases
Emory University School of Medicine
Atlanta, Georgia

Karen A. Johnson, M.D., Ph.D., M.P.H.
Program Director
Community Oncology and Rehabilitation
    Branch
Division of Cancer Prevention and Control
National Cancer Institute
Bethesda, Maryland

Mark E. Jonas, M.D.
Chief Gastroenterology Fellow
University of Medicine and Dentistry of New
    Jersey
New Jersey Medical School
Newark, New Jersey

Peter H. Jones, M.D.
Director, Lipid Metabolism and
    Atherosclerosis Clinic
Section of Atherosclerosis and Lipid
    Research
Baylor College of Medicine
Houston, Texas

Randi Jones, Ph.D.
Faculty Member, Department of
    Neurology
Emory University School of Medicine
Atlanta, Georgia

Robert N. Jones, M.D.
Professor of Medicine
Tulane University School of Medicine
New Orleans, Louisiana

Stevo Julius, M.D., Sc.D.
Professor of Internal Medicine and
    Physiology
University of Michigan School of Medicine

Chief, Division of Hypertension
University of Michigan Medical Center
Ann Arbor, Michigan

Rafael L. Jurado, M.D.
Associate Professor of Medicine
Emory University School of Medicine

Assistant Chief, Medical Service
Veterans Administration Medical Center
Atlanta, Georgia

Matt E. Kalaycioglu, M.D.
Staff Physician
Hematology/Oncology
Cleveland Clinic Foundation
Cleveland, Ohio

Stephan L. Kamholz, M.D.
Professor and Chairman
Department of Medicine
State University of New York–Health Science
    Center at Brooklyn

Chief of Service
Department of Medicine
Kings County Hospital Center
Brooklyn, New York

Sotirios Kassapidis, M.D.
Clinical Assistant Instructor
State University of New York–Health Science
    Center at Brooklyn
Brooklyn, New York

Harold P. Katner, M.D.
Chief of Infectious Diseases
Department of Internal Medicine
Mercer University School of Medicine
Macon, Georgia

Paul Katz, M.D.
Vice Chairman, Department of Medicine
Professor of Medicine, Microbiology and
    Immunology
Chief, Division of Rheumatology,
    Immunology and Allergy
Georgetown University
Washington, DC

Pratibha Kaul, M.D.
Assistant Professor of Clinical
    Medicine
State University of New York Health Science
    Center at Brooklyn

Medical Director, Respiratory Care
Brooklyn Veterans Administration Medical
    Center
Brooklyn, New York

David T. Kawanishi, M.D.
Associate Professor of Medicine
Director, Griffith Laboratories
University of Southern California

Director, Cardiac Catheterization
    Laboratory
Los Angeles County and University of
    Southern California Medical Center
Los Angeles, California

Thomas E. Keane, M.B., B. Ch., B.A.O.
Assistant Professor of Surgery
    (Urology)
Emory University School of Medicine
Atlanta, Georgia

David A. Khan, M.D.
Assistant Professor
Division of Allergy and Immunology
Department of Internal Medicine
University of Texas Medical Center at
    Dallas
Dallas, Texas

George G. Klee, M.D., Ph.D.
Professor of Laboratory Medicine
Mayo Medical School
Rochester, Minnesota

Joel S. Klein, M.D.
Aaronson Asthma Allergy Associates, Ltd.
Des Plaines, Illinois

Mark A. Korsten, M.D.
Professor of Medicine
Mount Sinai School of Medicine

Associate Chief of Medical Service
Bronx Veterans Administration Medical
    Center
Bronx, New York

Kandice Kottke-Marchant, M.D., Ph.D.
Adjunct Assistant Professor
Department of Biomedical Engineering
Case Western Reserve University

Director, Hemostasis and Thrombosis
 Laboratory
Department of Clinical Pathology
Cleveland Clinic Foundation
Cleveland, Ohio

László Kovács, M.D., D.Sc.
Associate Professor of Pediatrics
Department of Pediatrics
Comenius University Medical School
Bratislava, Slovakia

Alan M. Kozarsky, M.D.
Clinical Assistant Professor
Emory University School of Medicine
Atlanta, Georgia

Phyllis E. Kozarsky, M.D.
Associate Professor of Medicine (Infectious
 Diseases)
Emory University School of Medicine
Atlanta, Georgia

Barnett S. Kramer, M.D., M.P.H.
Associate Director, Early Detection and
 Community Oncology Program
Division of Cancer Prevention and Control
National Cancer Institute
Bethesda, Maryland

Martin Kramer, M.D.
Assistant Professor of Medicine
Director, AIDS Unit
University Hospital of Brooklyn

Director of Infection Control
Kings County Hospital Center
State University of New York–Health Science
 Center at Brooklyn
Brooklyn, New York

Ken Kulig, M.D.
Associate Clinical Professor
University of Colorado Health Sciences
 Center
Denver, Colorado

Director, Porter Regional Toxicology
 Center
Morrison, Colorado

Rajiv Kumar, M.B., B.S.
Ruth and Vernon Taylor Professor of
 Medicine, Biochemistry and Molecular
 Biology
Chair, Division of Nephrology
Mayo Medical School
Rochester, Minnesota

James P. Kushner, M.D.
MM Wintrobe Professor of Medicine
Chief, Division of Hematology-Oncology
University of Utah School of Medicine
Salt Lake City, Utah

Douglas M. Landwehr, M.D., Ph.D.
Associate Professor of Medicine
The Medical College of Pennsylvania
Hahnemann University

Director, Division of Nephrology and
 Hypertension
Allegheny General Hospital
Pittsburgh, Pennsylvania

Steven A. Lauter, M.D.
Assistant Professor of Clinical Medicine
Washington University School of
 Medicine,
St. Louis, Missouri

R. Allen Lawhead, Jr., M.D.
Associate Clinical Professor of Obstetrics
 and Gynecology
Medical College of Georgia
Augusta, Georgia

Associate Clinical Professor of Obstretrics
 and Gynecology
Director, Gynecologic Oncology
Morehouse School of Medicine

Director, Gynecologic Oncology
Chairman, Department of Obstetrics
 and Gynecology
Georgia Baptist Medical Center
Atlanta, Georgia

Terri E. Lawless, M.D.
Unit Physician
Gracewood State School and Hospital
Augusta (Greenwood), Georgia

Laurie M. Lawrence, M.D.
Clinical Instructor
Department of Emergency Medicine
Fellow, Division of Toxicology
Vanderbilt University Medical Center
Nashville, Tennessee

David H. Lawson, M.D.
Associate Professor of Medicine
Emory University School of Medicine
Atlanta, Georgia

Carroll B. Leevy, M.D.
Assistant Professor of Medicine
Associate Director for Clinical Affairs
New Jersey Medical School Liver Center
Sammy Davis, Jr. National Liver Institute
Newark, New Jersey

Jeffrey L. Lennox, M.D.
Assistant Professor of Medicine
Division of Infectious Diseases
Emory University School of Medicine
Atlanta, Georgia

Walfredo J. Leon, M.D.
Assistant Professor of Medicine
State University of New York Health Science
 Center at Brooklyn
Brooklyn, New York

E. Carwile LeRoy, M.D.
Professor of Medicine
Director, Division of Rheumatology and
 Immunology
University of South Carolina
Charleston, South Carolina

Nathan W. Levin, M.D.
Professor of Medicine
Albert Einstein College of Medicine of
 Yeshiva University
New York, New York

Hulya Levendoglu, M.D.
Associate Professor of Clinical
 Medicine
State University of New York–Health
 Sciences Center at Brooklyn
Brooklyn, New York

Steven T. Levy, M.D.
Professor of Psychiatry
Vice-Chairman for Academic Affairs
Department of Psychiatry and Behavioral
 Sciences
Emory University School of Medicine

Chief of Psychiatry
Grady Health System
Atlanta, Georgia

Richard P. Lewis, M.D.
Professor of Internal Medicine
Ohio State University College of
 Medicine
Columbus, Ohio

James T. C. Li, M.D., Ph.D.
Associate Professor of Medicine
Mayo Clinic Foundation
Rochester, Minnesota

Alan E. Lichtin, M.D.
Staff Physician
Cleveland Clinic Foundation
Cleveland, Ohio

Joseph Lindsay, Jr., M.D.
Professor of Medicine
The George Washington University
 School of Medicine

Director, Section of Cardiology
Washington Hospital Center
Washington, DC

Brian N. Ling, M.D.
Associate Professor of Medicine
Co-Director, Center for Cell and Molecular
 Signalling
Emory University School of
 Medicine
Atlanta, Georgia

Earl A. Loomis, Jr., M.D.
Professor of Psychiatry (Retired)
Medical College of Georgia
Augusta, Georgia

D. Lynn Loriaux, M.D., Ph.D.
Professor of Medicine
Chairman, Department of Medicine
Oregon Health Sciences University
Portland, Oregon

A. Peter Lundin, M.D.
Professor of Clinical Medicine
State University of New York-Health Science
 Center at Brooklyn
Brooklyn, New York

John A. Lust, M.D., Ph.D.
Assistant Professor of Medicine
Mayo Medical School

Consultant, Division of Hematology and
 Internal Medicine and Laboratory
 Genetics
Mayo Clinic and Foundation
Rochester, Minnesota

Jerre F. Lutz, M.D.
Assistant Professor of Medicine
 (Cardiology)
Emory University School of Medicine

Director, Coronary Care Unit
Emory University Hospital
Atlanta, Georgia

Kathy Lynn, M.D.
Assistant Professor of Medicine
Mercer University School of Medicine
Macon, Georgia

Edward J. MacInerney, M.D.
Assistant Professor of Medicine
University of Texas Medical Branch
    Galveston
Galveston, Texas

Daniel E. Maddox, M.D.
Assistant Professor of Medicine
Mayo Medical School

Consultant in Allergic Diseases and
    Internal Medicine
The Mayo Clinic
Rochester, Minnesota

William P. Maier, M.D.
Clinical Assistant Professor of Medicine
Oregon Health Sciences University
Portland, Oregon

Laura J. Mandel, M.D.
Associate Professor of Medicine
    (Infectious Diseases)
Associate Dean for Education
State University of New York–Health Science
    Center at Brooklyn
Brooklyn, New York

William Muir Manger, M.D., Ph.D.
Professor of Clinical Medicine
New York University Medical Center

Chairman, National Hypertension
    Association, Inc.
New York, New York

Maurie Markman, M.D.
Chairman, Department of Hematology
    and Medical Oncology
Cleveland Clinic Foundation

Director, Cleveland Clinic Cancer Center
Cleveland, Ohio

Jennifer B. Marks, M.D.
Assistant Professor of Medicine
Division of Endocrinology
University of Miami School of Medicine
Miami, Florida

J. Jeffrey Marshall, M.D.
Assistant Professor of Medicine
Emory University School of Medicine

Chief of Cardiology
Atlanta VA Medical Center
Atlanta, Georgia

Barbara J. Marston, M.D.
Assistant Professor of Medicine
Division of Infectious Diseases
Emory University School of Medicine
Atlanta, Georgia

David E. Mathis, M.D.
Assistant Professor of Medicine
Ambulatory Care Co-ordinator
Mercer University School of Medicine
Macon, Georgia

W. Brem Mayer, Jr., M.D.
Peachtree Neurological Clinic, P.C.
Clinical Professor of Neurology
Emory University School of Medicine
Atlanta, Georgia

Ernest L. Mazzaferri, M.D.
Professor of Internal Medicine and
    Physiology
Chairman of Internal Medicine
The Ohio State University
Columbus, Ohio

D. Robert McCaffree, M.D.
Professor of Medicine
Department of Medicine (Pulmonary and
    Critical Care Medicine)
University of Oklahoma Health Sciences
    Center

Chief of Staff
Veterans Administration Medical Center
Oklahoma City, Oklahoma

J. Stephen McDaniel, M.D.
Assistant Professor of Psychiatry and
    Behavioral Sciences
Emory University School of Medicine

Medical Director, Mental Health
    Services
Grady Infectious Disease Program
Atlanta, Georgia

John E. McGowan, Jr., M.D.
Professor of Pathology and Laboratory
    Medicine
Professor of Medicine (Infectious
    Diseases)
Emory University School of Medicine
Atlanta, Georgia

Marilynne McKay, M.D.
Professor of Dermatology and
    Gynecology/Obstetrics
Director of Continuing Medical Education
    and Medical Television
Emory University School of Medicine
Atlanta, Georgia

Patrick E. McKinney, M.D.
Assistant Professor of Emergency Medicine
    and Pharmacy
University of New Mexico Health Sciences
    Center

Medical Director
New Mexico Poison and Drug Information
    Center
Albuquerque, New Mexico

Susan L. F. McLellan, M.D.
Fellow in Medicine
Division of Infectious Diseases
Emory University School of Medicine
Atlanta, Georgia

David B. McMicken, M.D.
Director, Emergency Services
The Medical Center
Columbus, Georgia

Associate Clinical Professor
Department of Medicine, Division of
    Ambulatory and Community Medicine
University of California School of
    Medicine
San Francisco, California

Brian R. McMurray, M.D.
Assistant Professor of Emergency Medicine
    and Medicine
Vanderbilt University Medical Center
Nashville, Tennessee

John R. Meadows, M.D.
Assistant Professor of Internal Medicine
Section of General Internal Medicine
Mercer University School of Medicine
Macon, Georgia

Lincoln P. Miller, M.D.
Research Associate
Department of Microbiology and Immunology
Albert Einstein College of Medicine
Bronx, New York

Michael L. Miller, D.O.
Section Head, Section of Laboratory
    Hematology
Cleveland Clinic Foundation
Cleveland, Ohio

Stephen B. Miller, M.D.
Professor and Vice Chairman
Department of Medicine
Mercer University School of Medicine
Macon, Georgia

Albert D. Min, M.D.
Assistant Professor of Medicine
Division of Liver Diseases
Mount Sinai Medical Center
New York, New York

Jere H. Mitchell, M.D.
Professor of Internal Medicine and Physiology
Director, Harry S. Moss Heart Center
University of Texas Southwest Medical
    Center
Dallas, Texas

Dorothy E. Mitchell-Leef, M.D.
Clinical Associate Professor of Obstetrics–
    Gynecology
Emory University School of Medicine

Reproductive Biology Associates
Southeastern Fertility Institute
Atlanta, Georgia

Harvey Moldofsky, M.D.
Professor of Psychiatry and Medicine
Director, University of Toronto Centre for
    Sleep and Chronobiology
University of Toronto
Toronto, Ontario, Canada

Melvin R. Moore, M.D.
Clinical Professor of Medicine
Emory University School of Medicine
Atlanta, Georgia

Juliette Morgan, M.D.
Fellow in Medicine (Infectious Diseases)
Emory University School of Medicine
Atlanta, Georgia

Sarah L. Morgan, M.D., M.S., R.D.
Associate Professor of Nutrition Sciences
    and Medicine
University of Alabama at Birmingham
Birmingham, Alabama

Mark W. Moritz, M.D.
Clinical Assistant Professor of Surgery
College of Physicians and Surgeons
Columbia University
New York, New York

Douglas C. Morris, M.D.
Associate Professor of Medicine
Emory University School of Medicine
Atlanta, Georgia

Roland W. Moskowitz, M.D.
Professor of Medicine
Case Western Reserve University

Director, Division of Rheumatic
  Diseases
University Hospitals of Cleveland
Cleveland, Ohio

Steven F. Moss, M.B., B.S., M.D.
Assistant Professor of Medicine
Gastroenterology Division
St Luke's/Roosevelt Hospital Center
Columbia University
New York, New York

John T. Murphy, M.D., Ph.D.
Professor Emeritus
Departments of Physiology and Medicine
  (Neurology)
University of Toronto Medical School
Toronto, Ontario, Canada

Lindsay Murray, M.B., B.S.
Fellow in Clinical Toxicology
Departments of Medicine and
  Emergency Medicine
Vanderbilt University Medical Center
Nashville, Tennessee

Victoria C. Musey, M.D.
Associate Professor of Medicine
Emory University School of Medicine
Atlanta, Georgia

Jonathan L. Myles, M.D.
Staff Pathologist
Cleveland Clinic Foundation
Cleveland, Ohio

Robert G. Narins, M.D.
Division Head, Division of Nephrology
  and Hypertension
Henry Ford Hospital
Detroit, Michigan

Paul F. Nassab, B.S.E.
Boston University School of Medicine
Boston, Massachusetts

Charles B. Nemeroff, M.D., Ph.D.
Runette W. Harris Professor and Chairman,
  Department of Psychiatry and Behavorial
  Sciences
Emory University School of Medicine
Atlanta, Georgia

Samuel R. Newcom, M.D.
Associate Professor of Medicine
Emory University School of Medicine

Chief, Hematology/Oncology
Veterans Affairs Medical Center
Atlanta, Georgia

John T. Nicoloff, M.D.
Professor of Medicine
Director of the Clinical Research
  Center
University of Southern California Medical
  School
Los Angeles, California

Ira W. Nierenberg, M.D.
Assistant Professor of Medicine
Division of Digestive Diseases
State University of New York–Health Science
  Center at Brooklyn
Brooklyn, New York

Philip T. Ninan, M.D.
Associate Professor of Psychiatry
Director, Anxiety Disorders Program
Emory University School of Medicine
Atlanta, Georgia

Vincent James Notar-Francesco, M.D.
Assistant Professor of Medicine
Division of Digestive Diseases
State University of New York–Health Science
  Center at Brooklyn
Brooklyn, New York

David P. O'Brien III, M.D.
Associate Professor of Surgery
  (Urology)
Emory University School of Medicine
Atlanta, Georgia

Margaret E. O'Donoghue, M.D.
Assistant Professor of Neurology
Division of Neurology
Tufts University School of Medicine
St. Elizabeth's Medical Center
Boston, Massachusetts

Man S. Oh, M.D.
Professor of Medicine
State University of New York–Health
  Sciences Center at Brooklyn
Brooklyn, New York

Thomas E. Olencki, D.O.
Associate Staff, Hematology/Oncology
The Cleveland Clinic
Cleveland, Ohio

Babatunde Olutade, M.D.
Assistant Professor of Medicine
Division of Hypertension
Emory University School of Medicine
Atlanta, Georgia

George A. Omura, M.D.
Professor of Medicine
Professor of Obstetrics and Gynecology
University of Alabama at Birmingham
Birmingham, Alabama

Michael Orenstein, M.D.
Attending Physician
Morristown Memorial Hospital
Morristown, New Jersey

Beth A. Overmoyer, M.D.
Staff, Hematology and Medical
  Oncology
Cleveland Clinic Foundation
Cleveland, Ohio

Charles Y. C. Pak, M.D.
Professor of Internal Medicine
Distinguished Chair in Mineral
  Metabolism
Director, General Clinical Research
  Center
University of Texas Southwestern Medical
  Center
Dallas, Texas

Melody Pratt Palmore, M.D.
Senior Associate in Medicine
Emory University School of Medicine
Atlanta, Georgia

John S. Parks, M.D., Ph.D.
Professor of Pediatrics
Emory University School of Medicine
Atlanta, Georgia

David Paydarfar, M.D.
Assistant Professor of Neurology
Tufts University School of Medicine
  St. Elizabeth's Medical Center
Boston, Massachusetts

David M. Peereboom, M.D.
Staff Physician
Cleveland Clinic Foundation
Cleveland, Ohio

Robert J. Pelley, M.D.
Staff Physician
Cleveland Clinic Foundation
Cleveland, Ohio

Eric A. Peña, M.D.
Fellow in Cardiology
Emory University School of Medicine
Atlanta, Georgia

Bradley A. Perkins, M.D.
Medical Epidemiologist
Childhood and Respiratory Diseases
  Branch
Division of Bacterial and Mycotic
  Diseases
National Center for Infectious
  Diseases
Centers for Disease Control and
  Prevention
Altanta, Georgia

Carl A. Perlino, M.D.
Associate Professor of Medicine
Emory University School of Medicine
Atlanta, Georgia

Mark G. Perlroth, M.D.
Professor of Medicine
Division of Cardiovascular Disease
Stanford University School of
  Medicine
Stanford, California

John A. Petros, M.D.
Assistant Professor of Surgery
Emory University School of Medicine
Atlanta, Georgia

Scott D. Phillips, M.D.
Assistant Clinical Professor
University of Colorado Health Sciences
  Center

Toxicology Associates
Denver, Colorado

Robert W. Pinner, M.D.
Medical Epidemiologist
National Center for Infectious Disease
Center for Disease Control and
  Prevention
Atlanta, Georgia

Romano C. Pirola, M.D.
Senior Staff Gastroenterologist
Associate Professor of Medicine
Prince Henry Hospital
Little Bay, New South Wales, Australia

A. Bernard Pleet, M.D.
Professor of Neurology
Tufts University School of Medicine
Boston, Massachusetts

Chief of Neurology
Baystate Medical Center
Springfield, Massachusetts

Robert H. Poe, M.D.
Professor of Medicine
University of Rochester School of Medicine
  and Dentistry
Chief, Pulmonary Medicine
Highland Hospital
Rochester, New York

Brad Pohlman, M.D.
Staff Physician
Hematology and Medical Oncology
Cleveland Clinic Foundation
Cleveland, Ohio

Veronica Prego, M.D.
Assistant Professor of Medicine
State University of New York–Health Science
  Center at Brooklyn
Section of Gastroenterology
Brooklyn Veterans Administration Medical
  Center
Brooklyn, New York

Harry G. Preuss, M.D.
Professor of Medicine and Pathology
Georgetown University Medical
  Center
Washington, DC

C. Elizabeth Pringle, M.D.
Assistant Professor of Medicine
Division of Neurology
University of Ottawa
Director, EmG Laboratory
Ottawa General Hospital
Ottawa, Ontario, Canada

David W. Purcell, J.D., Ph.D.
Clinical Psychology Postdoctoral Fellow and
  Instructor
Department of Psychiatry and Behavioral
  Sciences
Emory University School of
  Medicine
Atlanta, Georgia

Simon S. Rabinowitz, M.D., Ph.D.
Clinical Associate Professor of
  Pediatrics
State University of New York–Health Science
  Center at Brooklyn
Chief, Pediatric Gastroenterology and
  Nutrition
Children's Medical Center of
  Brooklyn
Brooklyn, New York

Shahbudin H. Rahimtoola, M.D.
Distinguished Professor
George C. Griffith Professor of
  Cardiology
Chairman, Griffith Center
Professor of Medicine
University of Southern California
Los Angeles, California

C. Venkata S. Ram, M.D.
Professor of Internal Medicine
University of Texas Southwestern Medical
  Center
Director, Hypertension Clinic, Parkland
  Memorial Hospital
Director, Hypertension Unit, St. Paul Medical
  Center
Dallas, Texas

Jean-Pierre Raufman, M.D.
Professor of Medicine
State University of New York–Health Science
  Center at Brooklyn
Director of Medicine
University Hospital of Brooklyn
Brooklyn, New York

Susan M. Ray, M.D.
Senior Associate
Department of Medicine
Emory University School of Medicine
Atlanta, Georgia

Nigel J. Raymond, M.D.
Fellow in Medicine
Division of Infectious Diseases
Emory University School of Medicine
Atlanta, Georgia

Charles E. Reed, M.D.
Professor of Medicine (Emeritus)
Mayo Clinic
Rochester, Minnesota

Robert L. Rietschel, M.D.
Clinical Associate Professor of Dermatology
Louisiana State University School
  of Medicine
Tulane University Medical Center
Chairman, Department of Dermatology
Ochsner Clinic
New Orleans, Louisiana

David Rimland, M.D.
Professor of Medicine
Emory University School of Medicine
Chief, Infectious Diseases
Director, HIV Program
Veterans Administration Medical Center
Decatur, Georgia

Roger S. Rittmaster, M.D.
Professor of Medicine
Dalhousie University
Attending Physician
Queen Elizabeth II Health Science Center
Halifax, Nova Scotia, Canada

Gary L. Robertson, M.D.
Professor of Medicine and Neurology
Northwestern University Medical School
Chicago, Illinois

Aymarah M. Robles, M.D.
Assistant Professor of Medicine
State University of New York–Health Science
  Center at Brooklyn
Assistant Director, AIDS Unit
University Hospital of Brooklyn
Brooklyn, New York

Patricia M. Romano, M.D.
Former Visiting Associate Professor of
  Medicine
State University of New York–Health Science
  Center
Downstate Medical Center
Attending Physician, Department
  of Medicine
Director, Pulmonary Procedure Service
Director, Pulmonary Function Laboratory
Brooklyn Veterans Administration Medical
  Center
Brooklyn, New York

John L. Rombeau, M.D.
Professor of Surgery
University of Pennsylvania School of
  Medicine
Philadelphia, Pennsylvania

Ralph E. Roughton, M.D.
Clinical Professor of Psychiatry
Emory University School of Medicine
Atlanta, Georgia

Jack Rudick, M.D.
Professor of Surgery
Mount Sinai School of Medicine
New York, New York

Michael S. Saag, M.D.
Associate Professor of Medicine
University of Alabama at Birmingham
Director, University of Alabama at
  Birmingham AIDS Outpatient Clinic
Associate Director for Clinical Care and
  Therapeutics
University of Alabama at Birmingham AIDS
  Center
Birmingham, Alabama

David B. Sachar, M.D.
The Dr. Burrill B. Crohn Professor of Medicine
Director of the Dr. Henry D. Janowitz
  Division of Gastroenterology
Mount Sinai Medical Center
New York, New York

Atef A. Salam, M.D.
Professor of Surgery
Emory University School of Medicine
Atlanta, Georgia

Aida Y. Saldivia, M.D.
Assistant Professor of Psychiatry
Emory University
Chief, Inpatient Psychiatry Unit
Atlanta Veterans Administration Medical
  Center
Atlanta, Georgia

Amiram Samin, M.D.
Assistant Professor of Radiology
Director of Gastrointestinal Radiology
State University of New York–Health Science
  Center at Brooklyn
Brooklyn, New York

Abraham Sanders, M.D.
Associate Professor of Clinical Medicine
Cornell University Medical College
New York, New York

W. Holt Sanders, M.D.
Assistant Professor of Surgery (Urology)
Emory University School of Medicine
Atlanta, Georgia

Harold H. Sandstead, M.D.
Professor of Preventive Medicine and
  Community Health, Human Nutrition,
  Internal Medicine, Human Biological
  Chemistry and Genetics
The University of Texas Medical Branch
Galveston, Texas

P. Ravi Sarma, M.D.
Associate Professor of Medicine
  (Hematology/Oncology)
Emory University School of Medicine
The Winship Cancer Center
Atlanta, Georgia

Sithiporn Sastrasinh, M.D.
Chief, Renal-Hypertension Section
Department of Veterans Affairs Medical
  Center
East Orange, New Jersey

Associate Professor of Medicine
  (Hematology/Oncology)
University of Medicine and Dentistry
  of New Jersey
Newark, New Jersey

Howerde E. Sauberlich, Ph.D.
Professor, Division of Experimental Nutrition,
  Department of Nutrition Sciences
University of Alabama at Birmingham
Birmingham, Alabama

Philip S. Schein, M.D.
Chairman and Chief Executive Officer
US Bioscience, Inc.
West Conshohocken, Pennsylvania

Adjunct Professor of Medicine and
  Pharmacology
University of Pennsylvania School
  of Medicine
Philadelphia, Pennsylvania

Robert C. Schlant, M.D.
Professor of Medicine (Cardiology)
Emory University School of Medicine

Chief of Cardiology
Grady Memorial Hospital
Atlanta, Georgia

David Schlossberg, M.D.
Professor of Medicine
Medical College of Pennsylvania
Professor of Medicine
Hahnemann University

Director, Department of Medicine
Episcopal Hospital
Philadelphia, Pennsylvania

Leona Kim Schluger, M.D.
Instructor of Liver Diseases
Mount Sinai Medical Center
New York, New York

Sidney H. Schnoll, M.D., Ph.D.
Professor of Internal Medicine and
  Psychiatry
Chairman, Division of Substance Abuse
  Medicine
Medical College of Virginia–Virginia
  Commonwealth University
Richmond, Virginia

George F. Schreiner, M.D., Ph.D.
Vice President, Medical Science
CV Therapeutics, Inc.
Palo Alto, California

John S. Schroeder, M.D.
Professor of Medicine
Division of Cardiovascular Medicine
Stanford University School of Medicine
Stanford, California

David E. Schteingart, M.D.
Professor of Internal Medicine
Division of Endocrinology and
  Metabolism
Associate Division Chief for Clinical
  Affairs
University of Michigan School of Medicine
Ann Arbor, Michigan

Stephen W. Schwarzmann, M.D.
Associate Professor of Medicine
  (Infectious Diseases)
Emory University School of Medicine
Atlanta, Georgia

Curtis E. Scott, M.D.
Former Fellow
Division of Gastroenterology
State University of New York–Health Science
  Center at Brooklyn
Brooklyn, New York

Donna L. Seger, M.D., A.B.M.T.
Assistant Professor of Emergency Medicine
  and Medicine
Medical Director, Middle Tennessee Poison
  Center
Nashville, Tennessee

Thomas F. Sellers Jr., M.D.
Professor Emeritus
Emory University School of Medicine
Atlanta, Georgia

Sandra B. Sexson, M.D.
Associate Professor of Psychiatry
Chief, Division of Child and Adolescent
  Psychiatry
Emory University School of Medicine
Atlanta, Georgia

Susan B. Shelton, M.D.
Assistant Professor of Psychiatry
Emory University School of Medicine
Atlanta, Georgia

Alex Sherman, M.D.
Clinical Instructor in Medicine
New York University School of Medicine
New York, New York

Urmila Shivaram, M.D.
Associate Professor of Clinical Medicine
State University of New York–Health Science
  Center at Brooklyn

Chief, Pulmonary Section
Brooklyn Veterans Administration Medical
  Center
Brooklyn, New York

Jonas A. Shulman, M.D.
Professor of Medicine (Infectious
  Diseases)
Executive Associate Dean, Medical Education
  and Student Affairs
Emory University School of Medicine
Atlanta, Georgia

Peter T. Singleton, M.D.
Professor of Medicine
Chief, Rheumatology–Immunology
Morehouse School of Medicine
Atlanta, Georgia

Jay S. Skyler, M.D.
Professor of Medicine, Pediatrics and
  Psychology
University of Miami School of Medicine
Miami, Florida

Corey M. Slovis, M.D.
Professor of Emergency Medicine and
  Medicine
Chairman, Department of Emergency
  Medicine
Vanderbilt University School of Medicine
Nashville, Tennessee

Martin J. Smilkstein, M.D.
Assistant Professor of Emergency
  Medicine
Oregon Health Sciences University

Medical Director and Medical Toxicology
  Fellowship
Oregon Poison Center
Portland, Oregon

Iris E. Smith, M.P.H.
Senior Research Associate
Department of Psychiatry
Emory Schools of Medicine and Public
  Health
Atlanta, Georgia

James W. Smith, M.D.
Professor of Internal Medicine
The University of Texas Southwestern
  Medical School at Dallas

Infectious Diseases Section
Department of Veterans Affairs Medical
  Center
Dallas, Texas

Peter R. Smith, M.D.
Clinical Associate Professor of
  Medicine
State University of New York–Health
  Science Center at Brooklyn

Chief, Pulmonary Medicine
The Long Island College Hospital
Brooklyn, New York

Robert B. Smith III, M.D.
Professor of Surgery
Head, General Vascular Surgery
Emory University School of
  Medicine

Associate Medical Director
Emory University Hospital
Atlanta, Georgia

William McFate Smith, M.D., M.P.H.
Clinical Professor of Medicine
University of California at
  San Francisco
San Francisco, California

William B. Solomon, M.D.
Assistant Professor of Medicine,
  Division of Hematology/Oncology
Assistant Professor of
  Microbiology/Immunology
Morse Institute for Molecular Biology and
  Genetics
State University of New York–Health
  Science Center at Brooklyn
Brooklyn, New York

Cyril O. Spann, M.D.
Associate Professor
Department of Obstetrics and
  Gynecology
Emory University School of Medicine
Atlanta, Georgia

James F. Spann, Jr., M.D.
Professor of Medicine
Director, Cardiology Division
Medical University of South Carolina
Charleston, South Carolina

Thomas J. Spira, M.D.
Clinical Associate Professor of Medicine
Clinical Assistant Professor of Pediatrics
Emory University School of Medicine

Chief, Clinical Immunology Laboratory,
Division of HIV/AIDS
National Center for Infectious Diseases
Centers for Disease Control and Prevention
Atlanta, Georgia

David H. Spodick, M.D., D.Sc.
Professor of Medicine
University of Massachusetts Medical School
Worcester, Massachusetts

Lecturer in Medicine
Tufts and Boston Universities Schools of
Medicine
Boston, Massachusetts

Walter E. Stamm, M.D.
Professor of Medicine
Head, Division of Allergy and Infectious
Diseases
University of Washington
Seattle, Washington

James P. Steinberg, M.D.
Assistant Professor of Medicine
Division of Infectious Diseases
Emory University School of Medicine

Associate Chief of Medicine
Crawford Long Hospital of Emory University
Atlanta, Georgia

David S. Stephens, M.D.
Professor of Medicine
Director, Division of Infectious Diseases
Department of Medicine
Emory University School of Medicine
Atlanta, Georgia

Jeffrey L. Stephens, M.D.
Assistant Professor of Medicine (Infectious
Diseases)
Mercer Unversity School of Medicine
Macon, Georgia

Irmin Sternlieb, M.D.
Professor of Medicine Emeritus
Albert Einstein College of Medicine
Bronx, New York

Senior Lecturer in Medicine
Columbia University College of Physicians
and Surgeons
New York, New York

Alan Stoudemire, M.D.
Professor of Psychiatry and Behavorial Sciences
Emory University School of Medicine
Atlanta, Georgia

Eugene Straus, M.D.
Professor of Medicine
Chief, Digestive Diseases
State University of New York–Health Science
Center at Brooklyn
Brooklyn, New York

Amy A. Swartz, M.D.
Instructor in Medicine
Emory University School of Medicine
Atlanta, Georgia

Harry A. Swedlund, M.D.
Assistant Professor of Medicine
Mayo Medical School

Consultant in Internal Medicine and Allergic
Diseases
Mayo Clinic
Rochester, Minnesota

Panagiotis N. Symbas, M.D.
Professor of Thoracic and Cardiovascular
Surgery
Emory University School of Medicine

Director, Thoracic and Cardiovascular
Surgery
Grady Memorial Hospital
Atlanta, Georgia

J. David Talley, M.D.
Professor of Internal Medicine
Associate Director, Division of Cardiology
University of Arkansas for Medical
Sciences

Chief, Cardiology Section
John L. McClellan Memorial Veterans
Hospital
Little Rock, Arkansas

Abdelghani I. Tbakhi, M.D.
Special Fellow, Immunopathology Section
Department of Clinical Pathology
Cleveland Clinic Foundation
Cleveland, Ohio

George T. Tindall, M.D.
Professor of Neurosurgery
Department of Neurosurgery
Emory University School of Medicine
Atlanta, Georgia

Hillel Tobias, M.D., Ph.D.
Associate Professor of Clinical Medicine
Department of Medicine
New York University School of Medicine
New York, New York

Richard E. Toran, M.D.
Assistant Professor of Medicine and
Neurology
Tufts University School of Medicine
Newton-Wellesley Hospital
Boston, Massachusetts

Teresa A. Tran, M.D.
Assistant Professor of Neurology
Division of Neurology
Tufts University School of Medicine
St. Elizabeth Medical Center
New England Medical Center
Boston, Massachusetts

Bruce W. Trotman, M.D.
Professor of Medicine
Director, Gastroenterology Division
University of Medicine and Dentistry of
New Jersey/New Jersey Medical School
Newark, New Jersey

Raymond R. Tubbs, D.O.
Head, Immunopathology Section
Department of Clinical Pathology
Cleveland Clinic Foundation
Cleveland, Ohio

Larry E. Tune, M.D., M.A.S.
Professor of Psychiatry and Behavioral
Sciences
Professor of Geriatrics
Chief, Division of Geriatric Psychiatry
Emory University School of Medicine
Atlanta, Georgia

John S. Turner, Jr., M.D.
Professor and Chief
Division of Otolaryngology
Emory University School of
Medicine
Atlanta, Georgia

Guillermo E. Umpierrez, M.D.
Assistant Professor of Medicine
Division of Endocrinology
Emory University School of
Medicine
Atlanta, Georgia

Jaime Uribarri, M.D.
Assistant Professor of Medicine
Mount Sinai Medical Center
One Gustave Levy Place
New York, New York

Richard G. Van Dellen, M.D.
Associate Professor of Medicine
Consultant, Division of Allergic Diseases and
Internal Medicine
Mayo Medical School
Rochester, Minnesota

Patrick Vinay, M.D.
Professor of Medicine and Physiology
University of Montreal

Nephrologist
Notre-Dame Hospital
Montreal, Canada

Tamara Vokes, M.D.
Department of Internal Medicine
Hammond Clinic
Munster, Indiana

Robert Volpé, M.D.
Professor Emeritus of Medicine
University of Toronto

Director, Endocrine Research
Laboratory
Wellesley Hospital
Toronto, Ontario, Canada

Jacob S. Walfish, M.D.
Assistant Clinical Professor of
Medicine
Mount Sinai School of Medicine
New York, New York

Jonathan Waltuck, M.D.
Assistant Professor of Medicine
Emory University School of
Medicine
Atlanta, Georgia

Christine A. Wanke, M.D.
Assistant Professor of Medicine
Harvard Medical School

Division of Infectious Diseases
New England Deaconess Hospital
Boston, Massachusetts

David Waters, M.D.
Professor of Medicine
University of Connecticut

Director of Cardiology
Hartford Hospital
Hartford, Connecticut

Nelson B. Watts, M.D.
Associate Professor of Medicine
Emory University School of Medicine
Atlanta, Georgia

John G. Weg, M.D.
Professor of Internal Medicine
Pulmonary and Critical Care Medicine
  Division
University of Michigan
Ann Arbor, Michigan

David H. Weinberg, M.D.
Director, Neurophysiology Laboratory
St. Elizabeth's Medical Center

Assistant Professor of Neurology
Tufts University School of Medicine
Boston, Massachusetts

Roland L. Weinsier, M.D., Dr.P.H.
Professor of Nutrition Sciences and Medicine
Chair, Department of Nutrition Sciences
University of Alabama at Birmingham
Birmingham, Alabama

Richard S. Weisman, Pharm.D., A.B.A.T.
Research Associate Professor of Pediatrics
University of Miami School of Medicine

Director
Florida Poison Information Center–Miami
Miami, Florida

Nanette K. Wenger, M.D.
Professor of Medicine (Cardiology)
Emory University School of Medicine
Consultant, Emory Heart Center
Director, Cardiac Clinics
Grady Memorial Hospital
Atlanta, Georgia

John D. Whelchel, M.D.
Livingston Professor of Surgery
Emory University School of Medicine
Atlanta, Georgia

Steven J. White, M.D.
Assistant Professor of Emergency Medicine
Vanderbilt University Medical Center
Nashville, Tennessee

John F. Wilber, M.D.
Professor of Medicine
Head, Division of Endocrinology
University of Maryland School of Medicine
Baltimore, Maryland

Jeremy S. Wilson, M.D.
Senior Staff Gastroenterologist
Senior Lecturer in Medicine
Prince of Wales Hospital
Randwick, New South Wales, Australia

Harry A. Winters, M.D.
Assistant Professor of Medicine
Chief, Gastrointestinal Endoscopy
State University of New York-Health
  Sciences Center
Brooklyn, New York

Michael A. Witt, M.D.
Assistant Professor of Surgery (Urology)
Emory University School of Medicine
Atlanta, Georgia

Kimberly A. Workowski, M.D.
Assistant Professor of Medicine
Division of Infectious Diseases
Emory University School of Medicine
Atlanta, Georgia

Keith D. Wrenn, M.D.
Professor of Emergency Medicine and
  Medicine
Vice Chairman, Department of Emergency
  Medicine
Residency Director, Department of
  Emergency Medicine
Vanderbilt University School of Medicine
Nashville, Tennessee

Susan Rudd Wynn, M.D.
Fort Worth Allergy and Asthma
  Associates
Fort Worth, Texas

Henry M. Yager, M.D.
Associate Professor of Medicine
Tufts University School of Medicine
Associate Chair of Medicine

Chief of Renal Service
Newton-Wellesley Hospital
Newton, Massachusetts

Stanley R. Yancovitz, M.D.
Associate Professor of Medicine
Albert Einstein college of Medicine
Director of Clinical AIDS Activities

Chief of Chemical Dependency
Beth Israel Medical Center
New York, New York

Michael W. Yocum, M.D.
Assistant Professor of Medicine
Mayo School of Medicine
Mayo Clinic
Rochester, Minnesota

Randolph Martin York, M.D.
Former Clinical Director, Medical Oncology
Emory Clinic
Atlanta, Georgia

John W. Yunginger, M.D.
Professor of Pediatrics
Mayo Medical School

Consultant in Pediatric and Adolescent
  Medicine
Mayo Clinic and Foundation
Rochester, Minnesota

Christine A. Zurawski, M.D.
Fellow in Medicine
Division of Infectious Diseases
Emory University School of Medicine
Atlanta, Georgia

Preface

System, or as I shall term it, the virture of method, is the
harness without which only the horses of genius travel.

Sir William Osler[1]

Sir William Osler's book, *The Principles and Practice of Medicine
(Designed for the use of Practitioners and Students of Medicine)* was
published by D. Appleton and Company in 1892. Now, more than 100
years later, I am honored that Appleton & Lange will publish *Medicine
for the Practicing Physician,* fourth edition.

Medicine has changed since Osler. Although brilliant and talented
physicians have influenced the practice of medicine, the greatest advance has been in the technological field. Osler, if he were alive, would
stand in awe at the number of diagnostic procedures and therapeutic options that are available today. He would, I believe, emphasize that the
diagnosis, or a differential diagnosis, should be based on the data collected from the initial examination of the patient. He would, I believe,
emphasize that high-tech procedures should be used to refine a diagnosis or to identify the diagnosis when several possibilities are considered. Osler would, I believe, call attention to his aphorism (see quotation above) and point out again that a *system* is needed that recognizes
how the busy practitioner functions, assists in the transfer of medical
knowledge to patient care, enables the physician to record the proper
items, and communicates to others who are involved in the care of the
patient.

THE BUSY PRACTITIONER AND THIS BOOK

Primary care physicians and practicing subspecialists are busy people.
Their work is never done. Their reading time is limited. They want to
know what is wrong with the patient and what to do about it. They are
interested in the basic science related to the patient's problem but, because of the press of time, may not wish to read about that when another patient is waiting to be seen. When time permits they will read
about the basic science that is linked to their patients' problems.

As discussed in Chapter 1, the format of each chapter has been designed to follow the approach Weed (1969)[2] suggested when he created
the problem-oriented record. The objective is to capitalize on the behavioral pattern of busy practitioners. Practicing physicians usually
have an idea what is wrong with a patient. At times they make a definitive diagnosis based on the clues found on the initial examination. At
other times they may be able to identify the organ system that is ailing
and, in such cases, they are able to create a differential diagnosis. The
titles of the chapters of this book were chosen to match the medical
problems that are commonly encountered.

When the practicing physician looks up the medical problem in this
book he or she will encounter quickly the *Definition,* the *Etiology,* and
the *Criteria for Diagnoses.* Within seconds the practioner can determine if he or she is on the appropriate diagnostic track or not. If the
physician believes, after reading the *Criteria for Diagnosis* and the
Clinical Manifestations, that he or she is on the correct diagnostic track,
he or she can then review the *Plans* suggested for the condition that is
thought to be present. The *Differential Diagnosis* can be reviewed
quickly. The practicing physician reviews the *Diagnostic Plans* and
discovers, at times, that there are several options. They are discussed

under the heading of *Diagnostic Options.* This is followed by a discussion of *Recommended Approach* in which the author gives his or her diagnostic preference. When the *Diagnostic Options* and *Recommended
Approach* are similar, the two descriptive headings are combined.

The busy practitioner then reviews the *Therapeutic Options* for specific instructions regarding treatment. When several methods of treatment are available the author's choice is discussed under *Recommended Approach.* When the *Therapeutic Options* and *Recommended
Approach* are similar, the two descriptive headings are combined.

The next important item is the matter of follow-up of the patient.
When should the patient be seen again and what does one look for?
These subjects are discussed under the heading of *Follow-up.*

The final heading is labeled *Discussion.* The subjects discussed there
are linked specifically to the medical problem. This linkage enables the
practitioner to remember material covered in the *Discussion.* This linkage is very important because practicing physicians learn best when
they can link the information to their patients' problem. Practitioners
remember patients; they have more difficulty remembering abstract information that is not specifically linked to the patient in front of them.

The *Discussion* includes *Prevalence and Incidence, Related Basic
Science, Natural History and its Modification with Treatment, Prevention,* and *Cost Containment.* Whereas all of these subjects are important, the discussion of *Prevention* and *Cost Containment* are considered
extremely important.

The problem-oriented record as designed by Weed is discussed in
Chapter 1. Ideally, every practitioner should create a problem-oriented
record on each patient he or she sees. The *Defined Data Base, Problem
List, Plans,* and *Follow-up* are the steps needed to transfer medical
knowledge to patient care. This book is designed to assist the busy
practitioner accomplish that objective. In the end, the discussion of the
behavioral pattern of physicians, the problem-oriented record, and the
chapters of this book become united. When this is accomplished the editor-in-chief of this book believes that patient care improves, physicians
learn more from what they do, and communication improves to others
involved in the patient's care.

WHO SHOULD USE THIS BOOK?

This book will be useful to two different groups of physicians:

- Primary care physicians including internists, family practitioners,
  and house officers in training for internal medicine or family practice.
- Subspecialists of all types. This is not a book to be used by the subspecialist to look up information related to their subspecialty. It is a
  book that the subspecialist should use to look up information that is
  not related directly to their subspecialty.

HOW THIS BOOK WAS CREATED

This fourth edition contains 679 chapters. The chapters were written by
411 authors. There are 24 sections in the book. The section editors were
chosen with care. The first order of business was to create a table of
contents that encompasses most (but not all) of the medical conditions
that the practicing physician might encounter. The section editors ad-

dressed this problem and in a few weeks the first tentative table of contents was ready. It was later altered because actually working on the book stimulated the section editors to add more chapters to their sections. The authors were then selected and multiple mailings of information followed their acceptance. The format for the fourth edition of this book is slightly different from the format used in the first three editions of the book. The additions were added because of the feedback information given to the editor-in-chief regarding the earlier editions.

Each author was asked to adhere rigidly to the format that was designed to be used in each chapter. This is not an easy task. I thank the authors for their mighty effort in this regard. It is terribly tempting to add a heading here and there, to omit headings, to combine headings, and to discuss subjects under a heading that should be discussed under some other heading (failing to be germane). When modifications of the format occurred the authors were asked to try again. They did so and I, as editor-in-chief, am grateful to them.

Each manuscript was reviewed and edited by the section editors and sent to me. Every line of every manuscript was reviewed by the editor-in-chief. Carol Miller in my office also reviewed each manuscript before it was sent to the publisher. The copy editor did her job well. The corrected manuscript was checked by the author and editor-in-chief. The first page proofs were checked by the authors, section editors, and editor-in-chief. The final page proofs were reviewed by the editor-in-chief and appropriate calls to the authors were made when needed.

A great effort was made to be certain that the text, figures, and tables were original or, when used from other sources, that permission was obtained from the original publisher and author to use the material. Although the authors are responsible for their work—including citing the source and obtaining the permission to use material that has been published elsewhere—this editor-in-chief is obsessed with the need to give credit where credit is due. Accordingly, the letters to the publishers and authors to use previously published material were obtained by the authors and sent to me. I, in turn, sent a copy of the permission letter to Appleton & Lange along with each chapter. An independent "auditor," Cynthia Shepard, was recruited to check the tables and figures in every chapter and determine if appropriate permissions had been obtained. In addition to this, Carol Miller and Mary Cotton in my office made a final check to be certain that appropriate permissions had been obtained for the use of material from other sources. So, if by inadvertent omission we have not identified any material that was published elsewhere, we offer our deep apologies.

When specific numbers and percentages were used in the text the authors were asked to cite the source by placing the author's name and year in the text. In such cases the brief reference list contains the reference. When numbers and percentages are believed to be common knowledge the credit is not shown in the text. At times it is a judgment call as to whether a number or percentage is common knowledge or not. In such instances we did the best we could but leaned on the side of citing this source.

ACKNOWLEDGMENTS

I thank the section editors and authors. They are busy. They tried out a new format. They put up with my letters, numerous faxes, and calls. I thank them. I thank them.

I thank Carol Miller who was the major organizer. She wrote hundreds of letters, sent numerous faxes, reviewed and kept up with manuscripts, galleys, page proofs, copyright releases, and permission letters, and answered numerous phone calls regarding the book. The book could not have been produced without her. When overwhelmed with paper she asked her sister, Mary Cotton, to help. Mary saved us both a time or two.

I thank Appleton & Lange for their intense interest in the book. They believe, as I do, that it is time to change the organizational structure of a textbook of medicine in order to meet the needs of practicing physicians. I especially thank Eric Newman, President of Appleton & Lange, and Edward Wickland, Vice-President of Appleton & Lange, for their faith in the book and me. The copy editor, Josephine Della Peruta, was magnificent. I also thank Kathleen McCullough, Elizabeth Ryan, and Janice Bielawa at Appleton & Lange. What professionals they are!

Finally, I thank my wife Nelie. No Nelie, no book. She has tolerated manuscripts and books in every room of our house—on the floor near my work chairs, on tables, and on beds. Now, in deference to her and in recognition of the increasing loudness of the ticking clock, I will, in the future, turn over the editorship of the book to someone else who has an itch that he or she wishes to scratch. Appleton & Lange, I am happy to state, will continue to publish the book as *Hurst's Medicine for the Practicing Physician*.

J. Willis Hurst, M.D.
Editor-in-Chief
Emory University

REFERENCES

1. Osler W. Aphorisms from his Bedside Teaching and Writing. Collected by Robert Bennett Bean (1874–1944). Edited by William Bennett Bean. New York: Henry Schuman, Inc., 1950, p 72.
2. Weed LL. Medical Records, Medical Education, and Patient Care. Chicago: Yearbook Medical Publishers, 1969.

Special Instructions
The Identification of Sections, Chapters, Tables and Figures

This book is divided into numbered sections. Each section is divided into numbered chapters. The chapters are identified by the number of the section followed by the number of the chapter. For example, the number 8–6 identifies Chapter 6 in Section 8. Tables and figures are identified with three numbers. For example, Table 2 in Chapter 8–6 is identified by the number 8–6–2.

The Purpose of This Book and How to Use It

The Evolution of the Format

J. Willis Hurst, M.D.

The discussion in this introductory chapter emphasizes the thought process and actions of busy practicing physicians, the Problem-Oriented Record, and the unique format used in the chapters of this book.

THE THOUGHT PROCESS AND ACTIONS OF PRACTICING PHYSICIANS

The excellent practice of medicine entails the transfer of medical knowledge to the care of patients. This is accomplished by compassionate practicing physicians who realize that the more they know about medicine, the more they can improve the patient care they deliver. But practitioners are busy and the day's work is never finished. They learn as much as possible from their experiences, which include identifying and managing their patients' medical problems, and from their reading. Because reading time is limited, *the material they read must be relevant to the problems they encounter and must be immediately accessible.* Accordingly, the format of each chapter of this book parallels the thought process and actions of practicing physicians whose major objectives are to determine what is medically wrong with their patients, what can (or should) be done about it, and why did it happen.

When physicians know which information to collect, have the skill to collect it, and look up a discussion of the abnormalities they find in a well-organized textbook, they learn *clinical medicine* and improve the care of their patients.

Students in medical school study basic science in abstract and later set out to use their knowledge to understand the medical problems in the patients assigned to them.

Busy practitioners learn basic science when the discussion of it is linked directly to the medical problems they have identified in their patients; they rarely have time to study basic science in abstract.

The preceding statements can be summarized as follows:

- Students in medical school employ the following learning sequence:

  basic science → clinical problems

  Students are exposed initially to basic science courses and then to textbooks of medicine that emphasize basic science.
- Practicing physicians (including house officers) use the following learning sequence:

  clinical problems → basic science

The authors of the chapters of this book discuss what really matters in the immediate care of patients. The format of each chapter enables the busy practitioner to find quickly what he or she is looking for. The relevant basic science discussion and other important discussions are then linked to the clinical problem.

THE PROBLEM-ORIENTED RECORD

Practicing physicians must translate what they know to the care of the patient. Therefore, they consider and respond to the following questions.

- What medical data should be collected initially on a patient?
- What does one do with the medical data that are collected on a patient?
- How does one organize his or her views regarding the medical conditions or disorders that are thought to exist in the patient?
- What are the medical goals for each of the patient's medical disorders?
- Are other diagnostic procedures indicated?
- What medical questions are the additional diagnostic procedures supposed to answer?
- What medical therapy should be used, and why?
- What surgical procedures are indicated, and why?
- Does the patient understand the illness, including its cause? Do the appropriate family members understand the patient's illness?
- What specific items should be observed in the patient's follow-up to determine if the treatment plan is succeeding?
- Can the illness be prevented?
- Can money be saved without decreasing the quality of medical care?
- Does the written record communicate the proper information to others?

Weed (1969) created and popularized the Problem-Oriented Record as a tool that permits one to deal with the questions listed above. The four elements of the Problem-Oriented Record are illustrated in Figure 1–1–1. His approach is discussed below because some of the headings used in the format of the chapters of this book are similar to the headings used in the Problem-Oriented Record.

Elements of the Problem-Oriented Record

Defined Data Base*

The defined Data-Base consists of the medical information that is collected initially. The physician defines in advance the type of information he or she should collect on every new patient. Accordingly, no items are placed in a defined Data Base that the physician cannot justify collecting. The exact content of a Data Base varies form physician to physician. This is true because the factors that determine the content of an initial defined Data Base include (1) the goal of the physician

---

*See Appendix 1 for a complete Data Base.

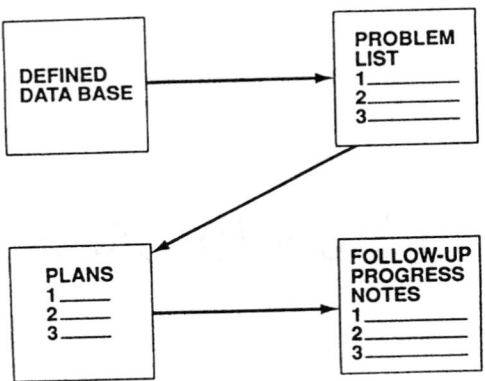

Figure 1-1-1. The Problem-Oriented Record created by Larry Weed. The four steps illustrate the steps required to translate medical information to the care of patients. Each of the four steps should be viewed as a red flag, where the clinician should stop and think and before moving forward (see text).

who collects the information (an ophthalmologist does not collect the same information collected by the general internist); (2) the prevalence of diseases in the population of patients the physician examines (the Data Base should be different for patients in a nursing home and for young recruits for the Armed Forces); (3) the amount of time the physician has to collect the information (the physician who examines 100 patients each day must set his or her priorities of data gathering so it is possible to examine the 100 patients; on the other hand, the physician who sees 2 patients a day can collect more information); (4) the number of assistants the physician uses (physicians who use physicians' assistants can collect more information than those who do not); and (5) the cost of data collection (expensive laboratory work and procedures that give a low yield of positive results per patient should not be done initially).

The Data Base shown in the Appendix of this book can be viewed as a model; it may be too long for many physicians (see Appendix 1, Data Base). It was originally designed for use in one of the teaching hospitals of the Department of Medicine of Emory University School of Medicine (Grady Memorial Hospital) with the assumption that we wished to give comprehensive medical care to the patients who go there. The patients are usually quite ill, with multiple serious diseases. There were adequate personnel to collect the information (students, interns, residents, fellows, and senior staff members). This Data Base worked for our purposes but it is obvious that physicians should create their own Data Base form to meet the needs of their patients.

Problem List

The physician should identify every abnormality in the Data Base. Having done so, he or she may be able to perceive a cluster of abnormalities that suggest a diagnosis. For example, the physician may be able to recognize that in a 55-year-old man, the combination of anterior chest pain and electrocardiographic evidence of new abnormal Q waves and a shift in the ST segments indicates myocardial infarction resulting from atherosclerotic coronary heart disease. The statement of the problem is numbered and placed on the Problem List. On the other hand, there might be no evidence of infarction on the electrocardiogram, or the physician might be unable to interpret the electrocardiogram. Should this be the case, the medical problem would then be stated as chest pain. The first designation would require no differential diagnoses; the second condition would require the consideration of myocardial infarction, dissection of the aorta, pericarditis, and so on. In the second example a differential diagnosis would be carefully thought out and recorded in the Diagnostic section of the record known as the *Initial Plans* (discussed below).

The physician should create a *Problem List, that is, a numbered listing of all the diseases, disorders, and abnormalities that he or she has identified after surveying the completed defined Data Base. A disease is defined as an abnormal disease process, such as rheumatic heart disease with mitral stenosis. A disorder is defined as a consequence of a* disease process, such as heart failure. An *abnormality* is defined as a deviation from the normal range, such as edema or an elevated hematocrit. *The Problem List should be placed at the front of the record. The date each problem is entered on the list is recorded by the side of the problem statement.* The Problem List must be updated in follow-up when new problems are identified or when previously listed problems are viewed in a different way. The Problem List should be signed by the physician who created it.

The thinking skills that are sharpened by being required to survey the abnormalities and then create a Problem List are as follows:

- Attention is devoted to identifying what is normal and what is abnormal.
- Considerable attention is directed toward stating the problem as precisely as possible. The physician must never overstate or understate the problem; the problem statement must be supported by the data that are available. *The first step in problem solving is to state the problem as precisely as possible.*
- The Problem List can be surveyed easily and should stimulate new thoughts. It may be possible to recognize the influence one problem has on another problem, and this, at times, leads to a clearer understanding of the patient's illnesses. For example, the patient may have fever and a heart murmur. The rushed physician might not initially consider bacterial endocarditis; however, the training acquired by using the Problem List demands that the physician realize that any item on the Problem List that is poorly resolved should force one to stop, think, and wonder if it is related to another problem on the list. Most physicians who are given the chance to think will recognize that the presence of fever and a heart murmur might imply bacterial endocarditis, and such a possibility would be included in the differential diagnosis of the cause of the fever. The latter is recorded in the Diagnostic portion of the problem-oriented record that is labeled *Plans*.
- The Problem List should also enable one to perceive the patient as a whole. The parts of a whole must, by definition, add up to the whole. One should not investigate or manage one problem without determining the impact of the investigation and management on the other problems. For example, one should not use propranolol for angina pectoris without considering its affect on bronchial asthma. One should not state that the operative risk of coronary bypass surgery is 1 to 2% (as it is in many large series) in patients who also have severe lung diseases and carotid artery disease.

Plans

Plans should be written for all active problems and for those problems that require follow-up observation. The Plans should be numbered and titled just as they are on the Problem List. It is useful to consider *three types of planning* for each problem.

Diagnostic Plans. If the problem is clearly understood (perceived to be at a high level of resolution), very little diagnostic work is needed. If the problem is poorly understood (perceived to be at a low level of resolution), it is proper to make a list of possibilities, called a *differential diagnosis*. It is also useful to list the possibilities according to the priority of the projected workup and determine which possibility should be worked on first. It is desirable to record the investigation that is planned for each possibility listed in the differential diagnosis.

Therapeutic Plans. The physician should determine what therapy is needed for the problem at that point. This should be stated in the record. One should especially consider the therapeutic goals that should be achieved for each problem.

The orders physicians write are a part of the Diagnostic and Therapeutic Plans. All orders should be numbered and titled just as they are numbered and titled on the Problem List and in the Plans. Accordingly, anyone who uses the chart (nurse or physician) can identify the problems for which the orders were issued.

Educational Plans. One should record what the patient has been told about the risk of the diagnostic or therapeutic procedure and why the procedure is necessary. This enables other physicians and nurses to know what the responsible physician has told the patient. This portion of a medical record is becoming increasingly important.

Follow-up (Progress Notes)

Follow-up Notes (Progress Notes) should be written for each active problem and for other problems one wishes to follow. The Follow-up Notes should be numbered and titled, as are the Problem List and the Plans. The components of the Progress Notes are new Subjective data, new Objective data, the Assessment of the new data, and new Plans that are determined by the new data (SOAP). Any new *orders* generated during the follow-up are numbered and titled to match the problem number and title as listed on the Problem List and in the Plans.

As stated earlier, new perceptions of problems emerge from observations made during the follow-up of patients. Accordingly, a problem on the Problem List should be updated to match the new perceptions. When this occurs, the date of the Follow-up note that indicates the clarification of the problem should be placed adjacent to the revised problem statement.

Value of the Problem-Oriented Record

Improved Thinking

The motivated and compassionate practicing physician makes every effort to learn medicine and tries to link what he or she learns to the care of patients. In the rush of a busy day it is useful to have *red flags* positioned at proper points to emphasize that one should pause and think. The system we are now discussing places *four red flags* at very strategic points in the workup and follow-up of a patient: the defined Data Base, the Problem List, the Plans with their components, and the Follow-up notes with their components.

These *red flags* represent thinking posts. Attention to them will encourage physicians to think about the *data they collect;* refine their analytic thought process as they state a *problem* based on the available data; think carefully about the *plans* for each problem because this is the active transfer of knowledge to the care of the patient; *Follow-up* the problems because the results of therapy, good and bad, must be identified; develop clinical judgment as one learns how to view and manage each problem within the context of all other problems; and *read about the perceived problems* in an appropriate textbook. The last is necessary for the self-learning process that all physicians try to develop.

Improved Communication (with Physicians, Nurses, and Other Health Care Personnel)

The system makes it possible for other physicians, nurses, and other health care professionals to identify quickly what is considered to be wrong with the patient and what is being done about it. This form of communication is essential today because medical practice is more complex now than it was in the past; there is more information to communicate to more people than in years past; nurses must know what is happening; physicians often work in group practices and one partner should know exactly what another partner is trying to accomplish if they both see the same patient; and third-party payers and lawyers require that physicians record their actions as clearly as possible.

Improved Discrimination

Everyone is familiar with the medical record that has so little in it that it communicates nothing. Everyone is also familiar with the medical record that has so much in it that it is equally useless. The Problem-Oriented Record can be used to teach *pertinence* by defining some of the essential elements of patient care and encouraging physicians to record them in a terse and careful manner.

Advantages of the System to Patients

A well-conceived Problem List can be used for many purposes. The physician finds the list very useful in the follow-up of patients. In fact, many patients are astonished when their physicians inquire about each problem on their Problem List. Some physicians give their patients a copy of the Problem List and update it when new problems are discovered. This permits patients to be fully informed about the problems they

have. They, in turn, may ask their physician appropriate questions about their problems. In this way, the patient becomes a partner in his or her quest for "good" medical care.

THE UNIQUENESS OF THIS BOOK AND HOW TO USE IT

The preceding discussion considers the thought process and actions of practicing physicians and points out the value of the Problem-Oriented Record. It is apparent that the two subjects have much in common. This stimulated the development of the format used in each chapter of this book—a format that capitalizes on the physician's thought process and actions and the problem-oriented record. *It guarantees physicians that the reading they have time to do is relevant to the patient's problems and that the information is easily accessible.*

The format for each chapter in the book is shown in Table 1–1–1. Note that a great deal of the format for the chapters is based on the Problem-Oriented Record of Weed. Accordingly, in several instances, the headings used in the record the physician creates and the headings used to organize the chapters of this book are identical. Note also that headings are designed to answer the questions practitioners have about the medical problems they encounter. The *chapter title* may be consid-

TABLE 1–1–1. FORMAT FOR EACH CHAPTER

Chapter Title
Definition
Etiology
Criteria for Diagnosis
Suggestive
Definitive
Clinical Manifestations
Subjective
Objective
Physical Examination
Routine Laboratory Abnormalities
Plans
Diagnostic
Differential Diagnosis
Diagnostic Options
Recommended Approach
Therapeutic
Therapeutic Options
Recommended Approach
Follow-up
Discussion
Prevalence and Incidence
Related Basic Science
Genetics   ⎫ The heading
Altered Molecular Biology   ⎬ that is
Physiologic or Metabolic Derangement ⎪ appropriate
Anatomic Derangement   ⎭ is used
Natural History and its Modification with Treatment
Prevention
Cost Containment
References

Some of the headings that constitute the format for each chapter of this book parallel the headings used to create the problem-oriented record. The *chapter title* represents the medical *Problem*. The section labeled *Clinical Manifestations* contains the type of data that should be collected in the Data Base. The section labeled *Criteria for Diagnosis* is not one of the headings in the problem-oriented record, but is useful to the practitioner as he or she analyzes the data base and formulates a problem. The *Plans* discussed in each chapter parallel the plans used in the Problem-Oriented Record. *Diagnostic* and *Therapeutic* Plans are highlighted in the chapter just as they are in the problem-oriented record. *Educational Plans* are omitted from the chapter because, as we learned from the first three editions of this book, the physician who is managing the patient's medical problems should write the *Educational Plans* for the patient. Accordingly, *Educational Plans* are not discussed in each chapter of the book, but *should be written in the problem-oriented record*. The heading *Follow-up* is used in the book and in the Problem-Oriented Record.

The headings used in the remainder of the format of each chapter are designed to link the discussion of the relevant basic science, and the discussion of other important aspects of medical knowledge and patient care, to the patient's problem.

ered to be a statement of the problem that might be recorded on a Problem List. This is followed by the *Definition* and *Etiology* of the problem. The section entitled *Criteria for Diagnosis* is especially important because this information is needed to state the problems precisely. The section *Clinical Manifestations* contains the type of data that might be in the Data Base. The headings in the text entitled *Plans* are similar to those recorded in the problem-oriented record. *The format may be altered slightly in some chapters to prevent redundancy.* For example, if there is no differential diagnosis, it is omitted. If there is only one diagnostic or therapeutic approach to a problem, then diagnostic and therapeutic options and recommended approaches may be omitted. Although the Educational Plan has been omitted from the text that relates to plans, *it should be included in the patient's record.* It is left out of the text because the Educational Plan should be determined by the physician who is responsible for the patient's care rather than someone who has not seen the patient and is only writing about the subject. The information needed to Follow-up the patient's problems is always discussed.

The *Discussion* at the end of the format includes discussions of *Prevalence and Incidence, Related Basic Science, Natural History and Its Modification with Treatment, Prevention,* and *Cost Containment.* These headings, too, may be altered slightly so that the discussion is always germane to the heading. This arrangement makes it possible for the practitioner to link these important related issues to the clinical problems they have identified in their patients.

This book is divided into sections devoted to disorders of the bodily systems (e.g., Renal Disorders) or to disease states (e.g., Neoplastic Diseases). The sections are, in turn, divided into chapters dealing with a particular condition or presenting problem. Some chapter titles (problems) are at a low level of resolution (such as anemia), where the bulk of diagnostic work remains to be done, whereas other chapter titles are at a high level of resolution (e.g., rheumatoid arthritis), where a specific clinical entity is discussed. Thus, the reader can enter the text at whatever level is appropriate to his or her immediate understanding of the patient's condition. Entering at a low level of understanding suggests that he or she will be guided to other chapters in the search for a definitive diagnosis and regimen of treatment.

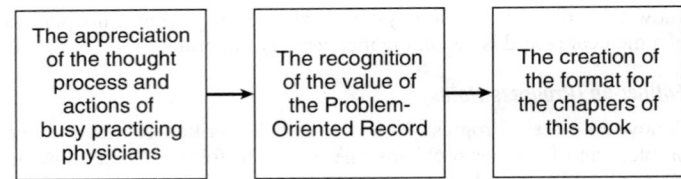

Figure 1–1–2. The format for the chapters of this book evolved according to the diagram shown here.

The figures and tables are identified by the number of the section, the number of the chapter within the section, and the number of the figure or table within the chapter. So, Table 1–1–1 indicates it is Table 1 in Chapter 1 of Section 1.

SUMMARY

The format for the chapters of this book evolved as shown in Figure 1–1–2. What physicians think, what they say, what they write, and what they do should be the same. This book is designed to help the physician achieve this goal.

ACKNOWLEDGMENT

Portions of this chapter are from the Preface and Chapters 1–1 and 1–3 of the third edition of *Medicine for the Practicing Physician.*

REFERENCES

Hurst JW, Walker HK. The problem-oriented system. Baltimore: Williams & Wilkins, 1972.

Weed LL. Medical records, medical education, and patient care. Chicago: Year Book Medical Publishers, Inc., 1969.

Behavioral Problems

John B. Griffin, Jr., M.D.

CHAPTER 2–1

Reaction to Physical Illness

Aida Y. Saldivia, M.D., and Thomas E. Fulmer, M.D.

DEFINITION

Reaction to physical illness refers to a series of emotional reactions experienced by patients when confronted with the suspicion or diagnosis of an illness. Although an emotional reaction must be regarded as an integral part of any physical illness, the reaction may vary in presentation, intensity, and duration depending on several factors. Biological factors include the nature and severity of the illness, the extent of the loss, and the presence of disability after the acute phase has subsided. Psychological factors, including the patient's personality organization, defense mechanisms used, coping abilities, existence of previous psychiatric disorders, and unique significance and personal implications of the illness for each patient, are of serious importance. The social factors are the availability of social and emotional support to provide the pa-

tient with adequate care, the existence of information to help understand the illness, and the availability of resources to solve problems generated by the illness.

ETIOLOGY

To react to illness is innate. The emotional response to illness was first defined in relation to death and dying; however, similar stages of reaction can be seen in relation to physical illness. Persons affected by physical illness are confronted with a disruption in the balance of their life that threatens their integrity (e.g., loss of body function, loss of body parts, as well as loss of independence). The severity of the threat depends on the acuteness, intensity, and duration of the illness and the possibility of temporary or permanent disability. Once confronted with a threat, a person initiates a reaction that is determined by the implications of the illness to him or her and his or her psychological structure, coping abilities, and quality of social support. Understanding an individual's adaptive or coping style to previous stresses can be of great value in understanding subsequent responses.

CRITERIA FOR DIAGNOSIS
Suggestive

An emotional reaction should be considered in every patient afflicted with a physical illness. This is particularly important when working with the chronically and severely ill. Intense anxiety during the diagnostic period, demands for immediate answers to complex situations, or lack of concern in the presence of severe illness are suggestive of a reaction. Particular attention should be given to withdrawn and helpless patients and to those with behavioral changes that may be indicative of pathologic responses complicating the underlying illness.

Definitive

The predominant symptoms at the time the patient presents for care vary with each stage in the reaction process. These stages include (1) shock and denial, (2) anger and depression, and (3) acceptance and recovery. In the stage of shock and denial, various degrees of fear and anxiety may develop. Some patients, however, present no obvious feelings or reaction in relation to the illness, regardless of its severity. In these cases, the patient is using denial to protect against disorganization in response to overwhelming emotions. The individual may appear unaware or unconcerned and may even disagree with the physician's diagnosis. The stage of anger and depression is characterized by irritability and anger directed at situations, circumstances, and individuals, including those close to the patient. The patient may use criticism and defiance, blame others or self, and ruminate about the unfairness of the illness. Eventually, the patient experiences depressed mood often accompanied by difficulty sleeping, somatic symptoms, decreased tolerance to pain, and crying episodes. In the stage of acceptance and recovery, awareness of the illness evolves as denial is relinquished. The patient develops a more realistic view of the illness and is willing to participate in the process of treatment. It is important to know that although an individual may go through some or even all of the various stages, the process is rarely sequential. For example while denying one aspect of the illness, the patient may simultaneously experience anger at or adaptation to other aspects of the situation. An individual generally reacts to the stress of illness as he or she has reacted to stressful situations throughout life. The magnitude and intensity of the response are characteristic for a given patient.

CLINICAL MANIFESTATIONS
Subjective

The subjective manifestations may begin with anxiety over the uncertainty of diagnosis or the possible losses the illness may bring. Many patients fear loss of body parts or function, intolerable pain, loss of physical independence, and inability to provide for their dependents. Denial of the illness, or certain aspects of it, is frequently present early in the process. Patients may deny the loss of a limb or its function, deny the need for treatment, or develop unrealistic hope. Patients suffering with anger frequently perceive the illness as unjust, unfair, undeserved. They often blame themselves for the illness on the basis of moral, religious, hygienic, or other grounds. Other patients displace their anger onto others and may be defiant, rebellious, and difficult to work with or treat, leading to severe conflicts with caretakers. Such behavior may be quite uncharacteristic of these individuals and, thus, puzzling to the physician and family. Some patients are unable to express anger even when it is justified. Somatic symptoms and/or depression are common in these instances; patients may complain of headache, backache, lack of energy, sleep disturbance, change in appetite, anhedonia, crying episodes, sadness, hopelessness, and emotional withdrawal.

Patients in the stage of bargaining present with increasing acceptance

of the illness and willingness to participate in the process of diagnosis and treatment. During this period, patients usually make efforts to lessen disappointments and frustrations that have emerged with the illness and develop a new interest in life. External events assume major significance and serve as markers or goals toward which the patient aims, for example, hoping to be well or better by the time of graduation, a wedding, or a special visit. Patients suffering with prolonged, severe, or life-threatening illnesses may also complain of a deterioration of their social support, including rejection and abandonment by significant others, inadequate financial resources, lack of insurance, and negative reactions from health care providers because of repeated hospitalizations. Patients who seek treatment as the result of acute trauma may complain of distressing memories or nightmares of the traumatic event as well as inability to recall the event. They often present with startle response, hypervigilance, and disturbance in sleep.

Objective

The physician must rely on a comprehensive clinical history and mental status examination to elicit pertinent symptoms when suspecting an emotional reaction to illness, as the physical examination and laboratory findings are usually nonspecific. Anxiety may manifest as restlessness, tachycardia, dry mouth, sweating, dilated pupils, insomnia, difficulty concentrating and thinking, or hyperventilation. There may be a history of similar symptoms in response to previous stressful situations. Patients in denial may refuse to accept the diagnosis when discussing the illness with the physician and may refuse to undergo necessary diagnostic procedures or prescribed treatment; for example, a patient diagnosed with laryngeal carcinoma insists he only suffers from bronchitis, continues to smoke heavily, and refuses therapy. Anger may be observed as dissatisfaction with the care providers, overt or covert hostility toward the health care team, uncooperativeness, and noncompliance. It is not uncommon for significant others and health care providers to become overwhelmed by the patient's anger (which has been directed at them instead of the original target—the disturbance in health) and react with the wish to abandon the patient. Depressed patients may present as indifferent, isolative, withdrawn, with psychomotor slowing and inability to concentrate. It is not unusual for patients with depression to become suicidal and "wish to give up fighting the illness." Suicide potential should be investigated in every patient who presents with depression.

PLANS
Diagnostic
Differential Diagnosis

Health care providers should realize when patients are having an emotional reaction and not attribute all the symptoms to the physical illness if appropriate care is to be rendered. Other illnesses, however, need to be considered in the differential diagnosis, including hypo- or hyperthyroidism, alcohol and benzodiazepine withdrawal, drug interactions and side effects to medications (e.g., aminophylline, steroids, chemotherapy agents), and exacerbation of preexisting psychiatric disorders.

Diagnostic Options

The most important diagnostic tool is the ability of the physician to obtain a detailed history and mental status examination and to carefully evaluate the patient as she or he reacts to the illness. Cross-history from family members can be invaluable when the patient is unable or unwilling to provide information. A physical examination and pertinent laboratory tests can help differentiate emotional reactions from organically based symptoms.

Recommended Approach

- Elicit symptoms employing an empathic approach while encouraging the patient to express his or her concerns.
- Perform a comprehensive clinical interview, mental status examination, and physical examination, giving special attention to the pa-

tient's perception, knowledge, and expectations of the illness and to the history of preexisting psychiatric and substance abuse disorders.

- When patients have a psychiatric history or present with atypical symptoms, exacerbation of preexisting psychiatric disorders must be considered and the manifestations integrated into the evaluation.
- Consider organic disorders presenting with emotional symptoms when patients have endocrinologic abnormalities (e.g., hypo- or hyperthyroidism), electrolyte imbalances (e.g., hyponatremia), metabolic or systemic disorders (uremia, hepatic encephalopathy, hypoxia, etc.), drug or alcohol withdrawal, and medication side effects (e.g., steroid therapy, chemotherapy).
- Evaluate the patient's support system and its relevance in relation to the symptoms.

Therapeutic

Therapeutic Options

The therapeutic measures required depend on the severity of the reaction, the support system available to the patient, and the ability of the patient to use healthy coping mechanisms. With any significant illness (the emotional significance is determined by the patient), some form of support is always necessary. A caring, sympathetic, understanding physician who has a good relationship with the patient may be sufficient. In more difficult situations, consultation with a psychiatrist is recommended, as the patient may require psychotherapy and medication.

Concomitant psychiatric disorders, especially those with suicidal or homicidal potential, as well as alcohol or drug dependence issues, need to be addressed when developing a treatment plan.

Recommended Approach

- Maintain an empathic relationship with the patient; acknowledge the feelings as appropriate and understandable, offering an open discussion of the patient's concerns. The patient should be told the physician is aware that the patient is upset. When this is done in an accepting manner, patients often feel relieved.
- Evaluate the patient's perception of the illness and educate him or her about the illness, its course, possible outcomes, and treatment options. It is not uncommon for patients to feel overwhelmed by certain diagnoses regardless of physical symptoms at the time. Restoring their self-esteem can put the patient back in control and prevent further emotional damage.
- Include significant others early in treatment to provide the social support the patient will need. Family members often go through similar phases of distress if the illness is severe or chronic.
- Include rehabilitation services in the treatment of patients requiring prolonged bed rest to prevent weakness, whenever appropriate.
- Refer the patient and significant others to social services if the support system is limited or insufficient to take care of the patient's needs when discharge from the hospital is anticipated.
- Refer the patient to a psychiatrist if the symptoms are severe or complicate the clinical course and treatment of the illness.
- Consider the patient's cultural background and religious faith when developing the treatment plan. Considerable inner strength is often derived from internalized value systems.

FOLLOW-UP

The follow-up and frequency of visits are usually determined by the severity of the illness and the psychological reaction to it. During periods of acute distress or depression, patients require closer observation and supportive intervention. It must be emphasized that the stages of reaction do not always occur sequentially, nor is one phase completed before the next begins. Patients who experience exacerbations of a chronic illness or new loss of function may not return to previous levels of coping even after achieving the acceptance phase. Patients who seem to have more severe problems with depression or an exacerbation of preexisting psychiatric disorders will require close follow-up and treatment by a psychiatrist. Use of community resources when dealing with disabling or life-threatening diseases (e.g., AIDS) can facilitate the ac-

ceptance of the illness and adaptation to the losses imposed on the patient and family. Self-help groups, home care programs for homebound patients, family support groups, and other groups should be included in the follow-up plan for all patients who are ill for prolonged periods, especially those with permanent or significant impairment. The clinician needs to feel comfortable treating terminally ill patients and helping them make final arrangements. These include issues of comfort and dignity, aspects of bereavement, decisions about life support so that care can be provided according to the patient's wishes, family and social concerns, as well as legal issues related to dying.

DISCUSSION

Prevalence and Incidence

Assessing prevalence and incidence is complicated by the wide range and nonspecificity of symptoms. Although emotional reactions to the loss of health are expected to be intense in patients with severe or prolonged illnesses, they occur with every episode of illness and should be considered in every patient.

Related Basic Science

The body's response to stress can be explored from several aspects. Among the neurobiologic mechanisms involved in the brain's response to stress, activation of the hypothalamic–pituitary–adrenal axis plays an important role. Through the release of corticotropin-releasing factor, the hypothalamus stimulates the secretion of adrenocorticotropic hormone by the anterior pituitary. Adrenocorticotropic hormone, in turn, stimulates the release of glucocorticoids by the adrenal cortex cells. The hypothalamic–pituitary-adrenal axis also raises levels of β-endorphins, enhances release of norepinephrine and epinephrine from the adrenal medulla, and increases the synthesis of serotonin under acute stress. Severe uncontrollable stress, however, may lead to depletion of neurotransmitters, resulting in exhaustion of adaptive responses. It has been noted that stressors like bereavement and depression can impair the immune response and decrease natural killer cell activity. Genetic and environmental factors also play an important role in the psychological development and the adaptation responses of an individual. Integrating our current knowledge of the genetic, environmental, neurobiologic, and psychological factors involved in the reactions to stress may allow us to develop a better understanding of these reactions and contribute to effective treatment.

Natural History and Its Modifications with Treatment

There is invariably an emotional reaction to every episode of physical illness. The intensity of the reaction varies in relation to the nature, severity, and course of the illness, maturity of ego function, coping skills, and extent of social support in response to the particular illness. In times of excessive stress, patients are often able to ask for and receive support. Most patients go through the phases of reaction in a matter of days or weeks, are able to accept the reality of having an illness, and cooperate with the physician in the process of diagnosis and treatment without much intervention on the part of the clinician other than a receptive, compassionate attitude. Patients with severe or chronic disorders may have a slower course, eventually overcoming their loss if provided with a supportive environment.

Unfortunately, in some cases, the progression through the various stages of reaction may be incomplete because of inability to resolve feelings precipitated by the loss, leading to the development of pathologic reactions that complicate the course of the illness and alter the outcome of treatment. Some of these complications include severe depressive disorders, suicidal behavior, disabling anxiety, chronic somatization, unresolved anger leading to an adversarial attitude toward health care providers and significant others, dissolution of long-term relationships, maladaptive denial leading to noncompliance, and pathologic dependency resulting in erosion of support systems. The treatment of pathologic reactions should be undertaken as soon as a diagnosis is made. Early intervention (as soon as a reaction is detected by health care providers) can decrease the time required by patients to work through the stages of mourning their loss of health. Patients who are able to reach the acceptance and resolution phase are able to cooperate and achieve the previous or a new level of functioning.

Prevention

Good coping skills and an ability to adapt under stress are perhaps the most important preventive measures. A good working relationship with the physician providing the care is also of considerable importance. A biopsychosocial approach to patient care will provide the treating physician with a better understanding of his or her patients and facilitate the patients' psychological adjustment to the loss of health. Early interventions to prevent the onset of pathologic responses include educating the patient and family members about the illness, providing a safe environment for the expression of emotions, and consulting with social workers, chaplains, rehabilitation services, psychiatrists, community-based organizations, and others, when indicated, to ensure a comprehensive approach to patient care.

Cost Containment

The need for repeated and even unnecessary diagnostic tests and procedures may be avoided through good communication and a compassionate relationship between physician and patient. Reassurance and educa-

tion play an important role in reducing the patient's anxiety in the early stages of the reaction. When patients reach the stage of acceptance, treatment time may be reduced as they take an active role in the recovery process. Perhaps the greatest cost is in the suffering of the patient and his or her family who struggle to adapt to the pain and losses caused by the illness.

REFERENCES

Cassem NH. Massachusetts General Hospital handbook of general hospital psychiatry. St. Louis: Mosby-Year Book, 1991:309.

Holland JC, Tross S. Psychosocial aspects: The psychosocial and neuropsychiatric sequelae of the acquired immunodeficiency syndrome and related disorders. Ann Intern Med 1985;103:760.

Hyman SE, Nestler EJ. The molecular foundations of psychiatry. Washington, DC: American Psychiatric Press, 1993:135, 198.

Krueger DW. Emotional rehabilitation of physical trauma and disability. Wallingford, CT: Spectrum, 1984:3.

Stoudemire A. Human behavior: An introduction for medical students. Philadelphia: JB Lippincott, 1990.

CHAPTER 2–2

The Difficult Patient

John B. Griffin, Jr., M.D.

DEFINITION

The *difficult patient* may be defined as one whose behavior disrupts the relationship with health care personnel and the expected cooperation toward mutually shared goals for recovery.

ETIOLOGY

The doctor–patient relationship includes a strongly implied assumption that the expectations of the physician and of the patient are congruent. It is assumed that the patient has the goal of being healed and will cooperate in achieving health and that the physician has the goal of effecting a cure. In the difficult patient, this congruence is disrupted. The patient comes to the doctor–patient relationship with an occult agenda. In such patients, some need, usually an emotional one, is served by being ill. Such patients typically present with numerous physical complaints that do not have an organic basis. They frequently fail to cooperate with prescribed treatment. In general, their symptoms do not respond to usual medical management.

CRITERIA FOR DIAGNOSIS

Suggestive

The difficult patient frequently shows behavior or attitudes that suggest the diagnosis in the early interactions with the physician. When the physician has the first inkling that something is not going smoothly between himself or herself and the patient, he or she should immediately investigate what is wrong. Clues suggesting that a patient may be difficult include the following: problems with or litigation against former physicians; unusual requests or demands; hostility, complaining, or suspiciousness; exaggeration or inconsistency in reporting complaints; failure to improve despite apparently adequate previous treatment.

Definitive

When the physician has clearly identified that a patient's attitudes and behavior have caused a significant disruption in the doctor–patient relation, the identification of a patient as difficult can be done with certainty.

CLINICAL MANIFESTATIONS
Subjective

The key subjective manifestation of the difficult patient is chronic dissatisfaction with the medical care received, despite the fact that the treatment given has been adequate. Such patients typically complain bitterly to others, if not directly to their physician, that their doctor is not helping them. These patients manifest their dissatisfaction in many direct and indirect ways, as will be described below. Characteristically, they do not regard themselves as having emotional problems, and they strongly resent any implication that they might need psychiatric care. Furthermore, they do not see themselves as being difficult patients.

Patients who are malingering or have a factitious disorder may not complain about the care they are receiving as long as it meets their occult agenda. No matter how hard the physician tries, their physical complaints characteristically never subside until the physician identifies the falsification of illness.

Subjective reactions of health care personnel are very useful in diagnosing the difficult patient. Typically, several members of the health care team will verbalize negative reactions to the patient with such remarks as "Oh, no! Not him [or her] again." When the physician experiences a sense of dread in contemplating a particular patient's visit, he or she should regard this feeling as a signal that the interaction with the patient should be carefully examined.

Objective

Difficult patients can be divided into four major clinical categories: (1) oppositional, (2) manipulative, (3) hostile, and (4) malingering or factitious.

The *oppositional category* includes those patients who could follow directions but do not. Thus, patients who do not follow a prescribed regimen for reasons beyond their control, such as senility, are not included in this category. Oppositional patients often seem bent on self-destruction. Examples of such patients abound: the diabetic who fails to follow his or her prescribed diet, the hypertensive patient who fails to take the prescribed medication, the postcoronary patient who does not keep follow-up appointments, the heroin addict who is detoxified only to return immediately to the addiction.

The *manipulative patient* is one who maneuvers the physician into a position that makes it difficult for the physician to avoid gratifying some pathologic emotional need of the patient. This definition implies that an element of coercion is involved, although the physician may not recognize it at the time he or she is being coerced. Patients become manipulative because they are attempting to achieve some end that they feel will not be gratified by direct request. Some manipulative patients use flattery, gifts, or sexually seductive behavior as a means of obtaining special favors from physicians. Frequently, they become highly dependent and clinging. They often seek so much reassurance that the physician feels exhausted. They tend to telephone too often and to prolong office visits interminably. Some highly dependent patients receive such emotional gratification from being ill that nothing appears to help them. To the enormous frustration of their physicians, they no sooner lose one symptom than they develop another. They convey intense pessimism, as if they know that nothing will help them. Some manipulative patients who are receiving disability payments accept the sick role so completely that they pressure their physician to confirm illness long after the actual physical impairment has subsided.

The *hostile patient* is one who, despite being given adequate treatment, is chronically dissatisfied with the services rendered. These patients often indicate such a lack of confidence in their physician that the physician wonders why they keep coming for treatment. They may criticize the doctor's office, receptionist, charges, and so on. These patients are often experts in producing guilt in others. Even when one of their symptoms is cured, they tend to attribute the improvement to something other than the physician's efforts. It is maddening to have such a patient smugly announce after a course of penicillin that his or her sore throat did not disappear until a neighbor gave him or her some proprietary lozenges. Such patients seem to delight in enraging their physicians. Many physicians themselves feel intimidated by the extreme demands of these patients. Hostile patients often indicate directly or indirectly that they may retaliate in some way if their demands are not met. Some even instigate litigation against their physicians. More often they change endlessly from one doctor to another, expecting that each new physician will be the "right one." At times they are propelled on this odyssey by the direct or indirect refusal of their physician to continue treatment. Hostile patients are prone, sooner or later, to become involved with useless treatment procedures rendered by quacks.

The *malingering patient* is one who deliberately attempts to deceive the physician by pretending illness. Such patients frequently show antisocial behavior in other areas of their lives. Examples include persons feigning illness to obtain drugs, criminals seeking transfer from prison to a hospital facility, and persons seeking benefits through litigation in injury cases.

Techniques used by malingering patients may be quite sophisticated. Hematuria is sometimes simulated by pricking a finger and then urinating over the bleeding finger to collect a specimen. Other patients may bring x-rays, purportedly their own, that show pathologic changes such as degenerative spinal lesions. Some persons with antisocial personality disorder are skillful impostors with sufficient medical knowledge to pass as physicians. The modus operandi of one such fraudulent physician was as follows: The imposter sent a friend to a hospital emergency room. The friend then faked illness and asked that his private physician be called. The friend gave the emergency room nurse a telephone number where the imposter would be waiting. After being called, the imposter went to the emergency room, "examined" the friend, and wrote a prescription for a narcotic drug.

Patients with *factitious disorder* intentionally produce or pretend illness out of a deep-seated need to assume the sick role. This condition is differentiated from malingering by the fact that the motivation in malingering is external (e.g., obtaining narcotic drugs), whereas the motivation in factitious disorder is an internal desire for the sick role. Münchausen's syndrome is one class of factitious illness in which patients repeatedly present themselves to hospitals with a plausible history and symptoms of acute illness that result in admission. Münchausen syndrome by proxy is similar, except the symptoms are produced in the child by a parent or caretaker, most often the mother. Typically, these parents exhibit concern and caring toward the child while at the same time they are deliberately causing the symptoms.

PLANS

Diagnostic

Differential Diagnosis and Diagnostic Options

Problems with the Physician. The physician should examine himself or herself carefully for negative feelings that are wholly or partially to blame for the problem in the relationship with the patient.

Undiagnosed Physical Illness in the Patient. Some patients become difficult to treat because of frustration related to their inability to obtain proper diagnosis and treatment of a legitimate physical problem. The physician must not allow a patient's difficult behavior to compromise an adequate medical evaluation.

Problems in the Medical Environment. The physician is responsible not only for his or her own behavior with the patient but also for that of his or her employees. Employees who are inconsiderate of patients can cause many difficulties in the doctor–patient relationship. It is very important that the physician make certain that patients are treated in a pleasant, efficient atmosphere.

Nonmedical Problems in the Patient's Life. Troublesome behavior on the part of a patient may arise as a carryover from conflicts in many other areas of the patient's life. Such patients often overreact to minor difficulties in their medical therapy. Pointing out that the patient seems unusually upset can, if done tactfully, often provide an opportunity for the patient to discuss such areas as marital or occupational conflicts.

Recommended Approach

Although psychological tests such as the Rorschach test or the Minnesota Multiphasic Personality Inventory can identify some of the personality characteristics found in difficult patients, these are not readily available in most medical settings. For practical purposes, the diagnosis must be made on the basis of clinical observations. The clinician should remember that a single episode of difficult behavior is not sufficient to make a diagnosis. Patients should be classified as difficult only when they show a repeated pattern of the behaviors described under Clinical Manifestations.

When malingering or factitious disorder is a significant possibility, the physician is forced into the position of distrusting the patient. In these situations, the physician must carefully check the patient's statements with outside sources for truthfulness and at times arrange for surreptitious observations of the patient's activities.

Therapeutic

Therapeutic Options

Once the physician clearly understands the reasons for the patient's difficult behavior, therapeutic options can be chosen effectively. The following case illustrates such a situation:

J., a 15-year-old high school student from a lower-middle-class family, became pregnant out of wedlock. The father was a 35-year old married man who had no intention of leaving his family. The pregnancy was confirmed at approximately 7 weeks' gestation. Shortly thereafter, J. began complaining of severe epigastric pain accompanied at times by nausea but only occasionally by vomiting. Physical examination, laboratory studies, and radiologic evaluations were all negative. During each of two hospitalizations her symptoms became somewhat better, only to return with their original intensity after her discharge. J. was also noted to be showing unusual behavior consisting of taking 10 to 12 baths daily and washing her hands over and over again throughout her waking hours.

Investigation of the family situation revealed that the parents were very angry with J. and repeatedly reminded her of the disgrace and financial burden that her pregnancy had brought upon them. Exploration of J.'s feelings about the pregnancy quickly confirmed that she felt enormously guilty about what had happened.

The parents were told that their behavior might be contributing to J.'s illness, and they were able to see that recriminations at this point were serving no useful purpose. As the parents became less angry and more supportive, J.'s symptoms improved. The abdominal pain and the compulsive washing stopped and J. eventually gave birth to a healthy infant.

With oppositional patients who persistently fail to follow medical plans, it is generally useful for the physician to shift from discussing whether the prescribed regimen is being carried out to discussing why the patient is not carrying out the plan. With many of these patients, the emotional conflicts underlying their extensive use of denial are quite complex. In such cases, psychiatric referral is appropriate.

Hostile patients who have paranoid tendencies are among the most troublesome of all difficult patients; however, as the following case illustrates, even these patients can often be dealt with successfully if the boundaries of the doctor–patient relationship are clearly established.

Mr. L., a 42 year-old businessman, brought his 10-year-old son for a psychiatric evaluation because of rebelliousness, vandalism, and academic problems. Mr. L.'s son had been previously hospitalized because he was so unmanageable. Mr. L. was dissatisfied with almost everyone who had treated his son and had instituted litigation against some of them.

The physician agreed to see Mr. L.'s son only with very definite guidelines being understood and accepted from the beginning by the patient:

- All the physician's time would be paid for at the regular hourly rate, including time spent writing letters, preparing reports, and talking on the telephone.
- The patient's bill must be kept current at all times.
- No letters or reports would be sent concerning Mr. L.'s son until Mr. L. had first had a chance to review them.

By establishing at the beginning that charges would be made according to the amount of time spent, the physician introduced a reality factor that was very useful in controlling Mr. L.'s tendency to make excessive demands. Mr. L. made a more carefully considered judgment about requesting the doctor to make a lengthy report when he knew that the report would be a significant expense. The physician's scrupulous attention to the details of letting Mr. L. know everything that was done, including reading reports that were sent out, was effective in decreasing Mr. L.'s suspiciousness. Mr. L. continued the relationship with the doctor for several years without the contentiousness that had been present in his other medical relationships. Termination of treatment did not occur until Mr. L. lost custody of his son.

The hostile patient is usually benefited most by an approach that focuses directly on his or her hostility. As the physician explores the reasons for the patient's hostility, it is often possible to shift the doctor–patient interaction from an adversary relationship to a cooperative one.

When treating the patient who is malingering or has factitious disorder, it is important to provide adequate control of the deceptive behavior. Frequently, this is best done within the framework of special programs, such as those in drug abuse treatment centers, psychiatric units, or, in some cases, prison facilities. Primary care physicians should not be hesitant to refer such patients, as they are extremely difficult to treat even in the best circumstances.

Recommended Approach

Physicians should not attempt to treat the difficult patient by ignoring the troublesome behavior. When such a course of action is attempted, the physician typically experiences a feeling of martyrdom and the patient's behavior tends to worsen.

Changes in health care delivery such as patient rights legislation, increased emphasis on consumerism, and efforts at cost containment through managed care have resulted in changes in the doctor–patient relationship. Many patients now have only limited input into the decision regarding choice of their physicians and may have to change physicians much more often than in the past. Patients often feel less personally attached to their physicians and much more empowered to make decisions about their own medical care. In many cases this leads to useful participation by the patient in the decision-making process. On the other hand, some difficult patients unfortunately pressure physicians to initiate treatment that is not medically sound, such as prescribing antibiotics for the common cold. Physicians should listen to such requests and explain clearly why they cannot comply. If all efforts to reach a negotiated consensus fail, the physician should stand firm even if it becomes necessary to resign as the patient's physician.

A team approach is often very useful in treating the difficult patient. Meetings of hospital, clinic, or office staff to discuss the demands of these patients make it possible to identify clearly the major problem areas. Once these are identified, the staff can develop a program to ensure that all persons involved in treating the patient do so in a consistent manner. A clear, consistent approach has been one of the most valuable ways of teaching difficult patients more useful behavior.

The difficult patient should be informed clearly that his or her behavior is causing difficulty. This should be expressed to the patient in the sense that "we have a problem" rather than the patient is causing a problem. If a patient is disrupting hospital routine by constant demands, is disrupting the physician's schedule by prolonging office visits, is embarrassing the physician by hostile remarks, or is showing any of the other behaviors already described, the physician can respond by pointing out the behavior and expressing the desire to understand it. For example, Groves (1978) has pointed out that the demanding patient is often masking feelings of terror about his or her illness. Such patients seem by their demands to be emphasizing the fact that they are entitled to special treatment. Groves suggests that such patients may be best approached by supporting the entitlement but rechanneling it in the direction of proper treatment. In essence, the physician can say to the patient, "I understand your anger, and you have every right to it because you are fighting a tough disease. You don't want to give up. You're entitled to the very best care that I can give you, but if you fight me instead of the disease, we'll both have a hard time dealing with your problem."

FOLLOW-UP

Because the difficult patient usually incites negative feelings in others, a frequent response to such patients is withdrawal on the part of medical personnel. Initially, it is advisable to provide follow-up at short intervals for these patients, as resolution of the problem in the doctor–patient relationship is most likely to occur if adequate time is available for discussing the issues involved. As the relationship improves, the difficult behavior tends to decrease.

It is important that difficult patients feel that medical care is accessible to them. They should be encouraged to express directly to the physician any concerns they may have. If they are dissatisfied, they should understand that the physician is willing to discuss this openly with them and that it is appropriate for them to make additional follow-up visits as needed to discuss these concerns.

DISCUSSION
Prevalence and Incidence

The conditions described here are common, but the exact prevalence and incidence are not known.

Related Basic Science

Many sociologic studies of medical settings have been carried out. Lorber (1975) has pointed out that hospital rules and regulations are, in general, designed for efficient delivery of care by medical personnel rather than the convenience of patients. In general, "good" patients are patients who fit smoothly into the hospital routine, whereas problem patients are those who require an extraordinary amount of time. If the extraordinary amount of time is caused by physical illness, the hospital staff tends to be relatively supportive of the patient. When, however, the hospital staff receives what they consider to be unnecessary requests, there is a strong tendency for hostility toward the patient. Unless the difficulty involved in working with the patient is carefully analyzed and dealt with, the hostility engendered can seriously compromise medical care. In such cases, hospital personnel tend to become defensive and rejecting toward the patient. These reactions can lead to early discharge and failure to respond to legitimate medical needs.

With the exception of the malingering patient, who usually shows antisocial behavior, the psychological processes of patients who are labeled as difficult vary considerably. The antisocial personality is extremely difficult to change and must usually be handled with great care if the physician is to avoid being deceived. In essence, when treating the patient with antisocial personality disorder, such as the one who is attempting to obtain abusable drugs, the physician must first make certain that devious behavior is exposed and prevented from becoming successful. After this has been done, appropriate ways of solving the patient's problems can be sought.

In the other categories of difficult patients described above, the difficult behaviors represent underlying, unmet emotional needs. These needs can often be satisfied within the usual medical or surgical setting by physicians who are warm and caring. For example, patients at times conceal information from the physician out of a fear that the physician may find some fatal disease. Patients find it much easier to be self-revealing if their trust in the physician is strong. Physicians can promote the development of trust by focusing on the patient's fears and taking care to avoid being critical or authoritarian. This may lead to sufficient trust to overcome initial concealment. Other patients, however, may have a more generalized lack of trust in others. In these cases, the lack of trust may go back to early experiences, such as having undergone marked deprivation during childhood. In these cases, referral for psychotherapy to repair this long-standing emotional damage is appropriate.

Many difficult patients have psychiatric disorders. Frequently occurring psychiatric diagnoses include personality disorders (particularly borderline personality, paranoid personality, antisocial personality, and narcissistic personality), psychogenic pain disorder, major depression, conversion disorder, and panic disorder. Resolving the problems of these patients usually requires referral to mental health professionals.

Natural History and Its Modification with Treatment

The natural history of the difficult patient is often an unhappy one. Some of these patients eventually so negate efforts to help them that a potentially curable illness results in death. For example, the chronic alcoholic patient who continues to drink heavily in the face of cirrhosis and esophageal varices may eventually commit suicide as surely as a person who takes an overdose of sleeping pills. Many difficult patients go from one medical facility to another on an endless round of unsatisfactory relationships. Patients who refuse to discuss the difficulties in the doctor–patient relationship or who, despite all efforts to give them understanding, do not show changes in their behavior have a very poor prognosis. Fortunately, other patients, given the help of an understanding physician, can comprehend the emotional factors in their difficult behavior. They then use this knowledge to work with the physician in bettering their joint relationship. For these patients, the prognosis is usually quite good.

Prevention

In discussing the difficult patient, it must be emphasized that there are also difficult physicians. Some physicians, by brusqueness, tactless-

ness, and lack of concern about their patients' needs, can change good patients into difficult ones. The first step in preventing the development of the difficult patient syndrome is a careful examination of the physician's own behavior and that of his or her medical team toward patients. Elimination of persons who are not thoughtful of patients can go a long way toward prevention of many difficulties. This process can be primary prevention at its best.

Secondary prevention involves early recognition of the meaning of noncompliant, manipulative, demanding, or malingering behavior on the part of patients. It also involves instituting the procedures already described for helping difficult patients change their behavior. Tertiary prevention relates principally to those difficult patients who cannot entirely change their behavior. These include some who have been unable to cope with their feelings about having a chronic or terminal illness. Even with psychiatric help, such patients may never be entirely free of difficult behavior. In these cases, treatment personnel must give particular attention to providing sufficient environmental control of the patient's behavior to avoid serious disruption of medical activities.

Cost Containment

Difficult patients are among the most costly groups in the health care field. They often insist on expensive and useless diagnostic and treatment efforts. Unless the basic underlying emotional issues are recognized, cost containment is very difficult. Direct focus on the relationship between the doctor and the difficult patient is the most economical way of treating these patients. Even when long-term psychotherapy is required to correct the patient's problems, this is still much more economical than continued fruitless efforts to treat nonexistent or exaggerated physical illness on a purely medical basis.

REFERENCES

Groves JE. Taking care of the hateful patient. N Engl J Med 1978; 298:883.
Lerner AM, Luby Ed. Error of accommodation in the care of the difficult patient in the 1990s. Psychiatry Law 1992;20:191.
Lorber J. Good patients and problem patients: Conformity and deviance in a general hospital. J Health Soc Behav 1975;16:213.
Novack DH, Landau C. Psychiatric diagnoses in problem patients. *Psychosomatics* 1985;26:853.
Quill TE. Recognizing and adjusting to barriers in doctor–patient communication. Ann Intern Med 1989;111:51.
Schwenk TL, Romano SE. Managing the difficult physician–patient relationship. Am Fam Physician 1992;46:1503.

CHAPTER 2–3

Suicide

William Boyer, M.D., and Charles B. Nemeroff, M.D., Ph.D.

DEFINITION

For the purpose of this chapter the definition of a suicidal patient is one who has a desire for his or her life to end in the near future. This definition includes patients who are aware of and admit to suicidal intent; patients who wish to die but are constrained by family or religious concerns (these constraints may fail); and patients who deny suicidal intent, but whose behavior (e.g., recent overdose, wristcutting) may suggest otherwise. This definition excludes patients whose behavior may shorten their life in the long run (e.g., excessive drinking, dangerous behavior) but who have no conscious desire to die in the near future.

ETIOLOGY

Suicide is usually an attempt to end or avoid pain. This pain is most often psychological (e.g., depression) but may also be physical. Although the decision to commit suicide is a supremely emotional act, its preconditions can be expressed in a quasi-mathematical fashion:

$$\text{stress (subjective)} > \text{coping ability (subjective)} \rightarrow \text{suicide}$$

Stress may represent the patient's current situation or the situation she or he expects to encounter in the near future. Often it represents the assumption that the current stress will continue, unabated, forever. The patient's subjective assessment of the present and future, as well as his or her ability to cope, is rarely fully rational. Instead a pathologic state such as depression or alcohol or drug intoxication (or withdrawal) makes the stress seem magnified and coping abilities diminished.

CRITERIA FOR DIAGNOSIS
Suggestive

Some behaviors suggest that a person may be considering suicide. These include the signs and symptoms of major depression (see Chapter 2–6). In addition to lowered mood there may be insomnia, significant weight loss (or gain), crying spells, and psychomotor agitation or retardation. Statements that convey a sense of hopelessness or helplessness should prompt the physician to inquire about suicidal ideation. Studies suggest that 50% or more of patients who commit suicide see a physician within the month prior to death (Roy, 1989).

A suicidal patient may be noted to go about securing the means of suicide, such as purchasing a weapon or stockpiling medicines. A patient may behave in ways that suggest "putting one's affairs in order." These include checking on insurance policies, writing or updating a will, giving away belongings, or telling others what the patient would like them to have after she or he dies. Patients may hint at or even confide their wish to die to some family or friends. Premeditated suicide attempts such as these are very often successful.

Definitive

A person's statement that they want to commit suicide or a recent potentially lethal suicide attempt establishes the diagnosis.

CLINICAL MANIFESTATIONS
Subjective

Symptoms

The particular symptoms of a suicidal patient depend on his or her associated disorder(s). Depression and/or alcoholism are present in the majority of cases of completed suicide. Other frequent comorbid disorders include situational adjustment reactions, bipolar affective disorder ("manic–depressive" illness), schizophrenia, and personality disorders (Roy, 1989).

The symptoms of depression were reviewed previously and in Chapter 2–6. Alcoholism may be associated with suicidality either during acute intoxication or as a result of a loss (e.g., divorce, unemployment) suffered as result of the alcoholism. Losses may also precipitate a situational adjustment reaction in nonalcoholic individuals. Schizophrenia is typified by hallucinations (usually auditory), delusions (often persecutory or of the "command" type), and bizarre delusions. Such symptoms may also occur as a result of acute or chronic drug abuse.

It is impossible to summarize personality disorders succinctly, because the term covers a broad range of heterogenous conditions. It is also rare to be able to make the firm diagnosis of a personality disorder without knowing the patient over a period of time; however, the presence of a personality disorder can be suspected on the basis of intense, inappropriate anger, relating to people as either "all good" or "all bad" (one's category may change abruptly), and highly labile, dramatic, but shallow mood.

Past History

The most important historical predictor of death by suicide is a previous suicide attempt. Although most suicide attempters do *not* ultimately die by suicide, their risk is still far above that of the general population.

The first few months following psychiatric hospitalization for depression carry a high risk of relapse and therefore a higher-than-average suicide risk (Roy, 1989). There may also be a history suggestive of schizophrenia (hallucinations, delusions, social withdrawal), substance abuse (arrests for driving while intoxicated, arguments or loss of relationships or employment because of substance use), or other psychiatric disturbance. Patients with personality disorders may have histories of tumultuous relationships, multiple suicide attempts, and substance abuse.

Clusters of suicides sometimes occur among adolescents. The recent suicide of a peer may be a risk factor in this age group.

Family History

The family history may disclose suicide or suicide attempts. There may also be a family history of depression, bipolar (manic–depressive) disorder, and/or substance abuse. Patients with personality disorders often have a history of being abused as children.

Objective
Physical Examination

Physical examination may reveal evidence of clinical depression such as a lowered mood, weight loss, poor personal hygiene, and psychomotor agitation or retardation. Evidence of acute or chronic substance abuse may also be noted.

Routine Laboratory Abnormalities

There are currently no routine laboratory studies to aid in the assessment of suicidality, though research suggests that suicidal patients differ from nonsuicidal patients on a variety of neurochemical and neurophysiologic measures (see Discussion). Routine laboratory examination may help to corroborate an underlying disorder such as substance abuse.

PLANS
Diagnostic
Differential Diagnosis

The disorders most commonly associated with completed suicide are depression, bipolar disorder, and alcoholism. Others include schizophrenia, personality disorder, and acute situational adjustment reactions. The risk of suicide is also increased in some medical disorders, including epilepsy, Huntington's chorea, multiple sclerosis, head injury, cardiovascular disease, dementia, acquired immune deficiency syndrome, peptic ulcer, cirrhosis, Cushing's disease, porphyria, and Klinefelter's syndrome (Roy, 1989). All of these disorders are associated with a greater than expected prevalence of major depression.

Because suicidality is a condition that is defined on the basis of behavior, verbal or physical, there is no true "differential" diagnosis. A patient who says or shows that she or he is self-destructive has the condition; however, suicidal patients vary widely in their intent to die. At one extreme are those whose minds are firmly resolved and at the other are those who threaten suicide or commit a nonlethal suicide gesture with no intent, or have merely passive suicidal ideation, for example, the wish to have a fatal myocardial infarction. The characteristics of more lethal suicide ideation or attempts are premeditation, lethality of means, minimal or no possibility of rescue, and disappointment at being rescued.

It is important to emphasize that all suicide attempts or statements of suicidal intent should be taken seriously until thorough evaluation is possible. A patient whose suicide attempt is not viewed as serious by health care professionals may feel challenged to make a serious attempt.

Diagnostic Options

The diagnostic options for assessment of suicidality include the mental status examination, medical and psychiatric history (including substance abuse disorders), and family history of psychiatric disorders and suicide attempts. Psychological testing may occasionally be of value.

Recommended Approach

There is no method of determining suicidality that is always successful. A person who is determined to die may be able to convince the physician that he or she is really all right. Fortunately, these cases are very rare. Most suicidal patients have mixed feelings. They want an end to their suffering but also want to keep on living, if possible. Physicians depend on this ambivalence for the patient's cooperation.

The first question in managing a potentially suicidal patient is whether protective hospitalization is required. Much of this decision depends on the answer to the question, "Do you want to kill yourself?" The physician should no more shrink from asking this question than any of the other very personal questions required in a medical workup. Patients may be reluctant to bring up their suicidal feelings spontaneously for fear of a scornful response, and there is certainly no truth to the folklore that asking about suicidality will cause someone to be suicidal.

Patients who answer the question with "Yes, I want to kill myself" require protective hospitalization with suicide precautions. Patients who answer "No, I don't want to" are usually being truthful. They should then be asked whether they feel in control of their suicidal impulses, if any. If they say "No" they should also be hospitalized. If they say they do feel in control the physician should, if she or he has not already, try to find whether there are historical data that suggest the patient should not be trusted, such as multiple previous attempts. If not, the patient usually does not require immediate hospitalization, but rapid entry into psychiatric treatment or elective hospitalization should be considered. If the patient is released home prior to psychiatric consultation, it is best to provide him or her with the name, location, telephone number, and time and date of the initial psychiatric appointment as well as a way to contact the referring physician if there are problems with or before the initial consultation.

Therapeutic

Therapeutic Options

The therapeutic options in the treatment of the suicidal patient are as wide as the number of conditions associated with suicidality. For example, the depressed patient may be treated with antidepressant medication and/or psychotherapy, the alcoholic may be referred to Alcoholics Anonymous and offered Antabuse, and the noncompliant schizophrenic patient may be restarted on his or her antipsychotic medication.

Recommended Approach

The equation that described the conditions that lead to suicide, high subjective stress and low subjective coping, also suggests a way of managing these patients. At one end, efforts should be made to reduce current levels of stress. Therapy should be aimed at alleviating the cause(s) of the patient's suicidality, whether it is depression, substance abuse, marital problems, or chronic pain. The primary physician may need to work with one or more specialists, including psychiatrists, recovery programs, family counselors, and specialists in pain or rehabilitation.

The clinician may occasionally see a case in which the patient's wish to die seems "rational." This is most common in the face of incurable illness. The physician should, however, remember that the desire to survive is a *non*rational drive ingrained deeply in all organisms. The loss of this drive usually indicates a pathologic mental state. Most patients with incurable illness are *not* depressed and do *not* want to further shorten their lives.

The following describes the basic approach in conditions frequently associated with suicide.

Depression. Patients who are depressed typically see the future as bleak and hopeless: their subjective stress levels are high. Therefore, suicidal patients will profit from reassurance that their current level of distress will *not* extend indefinitely into the future. Similarly, these patients see themselves as overly weak, hopeless, and helpless (low subjective coping). Reminding them of times when they overcame other stresses may be useful. The treatment of depression, including the use of antidepressant medication, is covered in detail in Chapter 2–6.

Schizophrenia. The acute treatment of schizophrenia centers on the use of antipsychotic medication. If the patient has stopped taking his or her maintenance antipsychotic, it should be restarted at the same or slightly higher dosage. If this history is unavailable, a high-potency antipsychotic such as haloperidol or fluphenazine (5–20 mg/d) may be used. Treatment of schizophrenia beyond the acute phase should usually involve a psychiatrist.

Alcoholism/Substance Abuse. The goal of treatment for alcoholism or other substance abuse is abstinence. Controlled use has not been shown to be a viable option. Relapses are very frequent but should not discourage the patient or physician from pursuing sobriety.

The main intervention is to strongly encourage involvement in Alcoholics Anonymous. People who object to the religious overtones of Alcoholics Anonymous may be encouraged to investigate Rational Recovery. Although the occasional patient stops using alcohol on his or her own, this is very rare. Attempts to become "clean" or "sober" by oneself should not be encouraged.

Personality Disorders. A common scenario is the recently suicidal patient who tries to convince the physician to release him or her immediately from the emergency department or hospital and reacts with intense anger if unsuccessful. It is best to treat such a patient as though she or he is a serious threat to herself or himself, at least until psychiatric consultation can be obtained. This management may, at the most, save a life and, at the least, impress a patient with the consequences of impulsive behavior and help the patient exert control in the future.

Suicide Attempt by an Adolescent. The rising rate of adolescent suicide deaths, particularly among males (Figure 2–3–1), dictates that suicide attempts in this age group be taken very seriously. Family members are often caught between feelings of anger and guilt toward the suicide attempter. Therefore, family therapy is often a recommended component of treatment. If so, the family members should not conclude that they are to blame, but rather that the family needs attention and that they may be a tremendous asset in the adolescent's recovery.

Suicide Attempt in the Elderly. The elderly represent the group most at risk for completed suicide (Figure 2–3–2). An elderly patient who survives a suicide attempt is at very high risk of ultimate death by suicide. Male sex, physical illness, and lack of social supports further increase the risk; however, the latter two may also be therapeutic targets. The physician is in a position to maximally treat physical illness and to disabuse the elderly patient of the notion that living with severe illness or pain is "just part of being old." Social supports can be garnered from

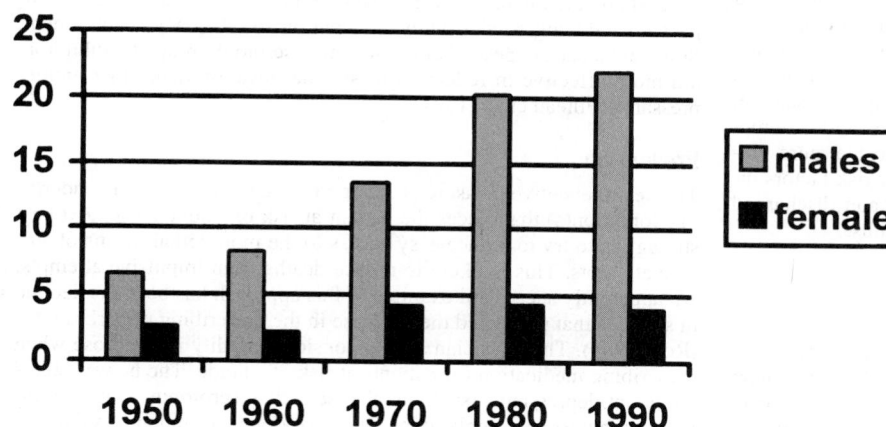

Figure 2–3–1. Suicides per 100,000 population, ages 15 to 24. (*Source: O'Carroll and Potter (1994).*)

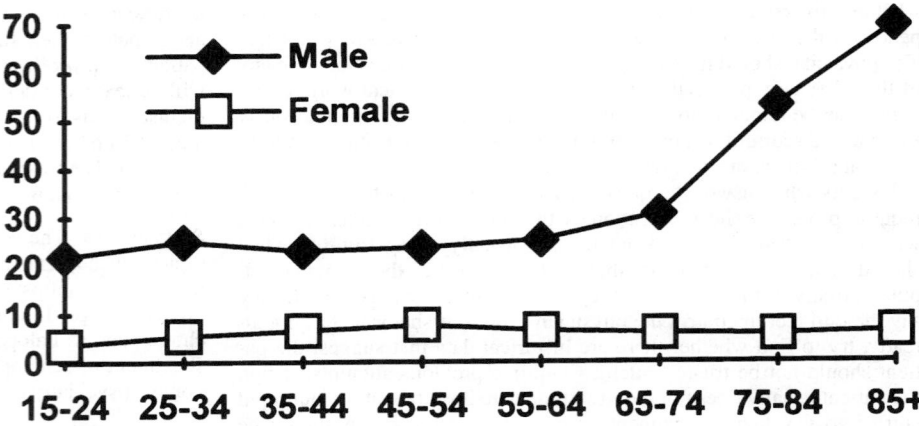

Figure 2–3–2. U.S. suicides per 100,000 population, 1991. (*Source: O'Carroll and Potter (1994).*)

family, church, and community organizations. Often the help of a social worker and/or visiting nurse can be invaluable.

The Terminally Ill Patient. Suicidality among terminally ill patients may be due to a number of factors. These include depression, fear of how they will die (e.g., alone, with pain, without dignity because of inability for self-care), and fear of being a burden to others. The primary physician should assess these concerns and allay them whenever possible. Suicidality is usually not a "rational" reaction in the terminally ill. Suicidality, in fact, was quite rare in our experience with a large number of cancer patients. Terminal illness is by no means a contraindication to antidepressant treatment and/or psychotherapy.

FOLLOW-UP

Many of the conditions associated with suicidality, such as depression and substance abuse, are chronic, recurrent disorders. Therefore, suicidality is often recurrent. Up to 35% of suicide attempters make another attempt within the next 2 years. Unfortunately, many physicians who treat patients who committed suicide are unaware of this aspect of their patients' histories.

The goal of follow-up care is to try to make certain that the conditions that presaged the suicide attempt are adequately addressed, usually through psychiatric treatment. A patient who has attempted suicide is often ashamed and frightened that she or he lost control to such an extent. Therefore, some patients may gloss over the significance of the attempt or try to convince themselves that things have "completely changed." The physician should be aware of this anxiety and/or shame and consistently but gently reinforce the need to address the underlying problem(s). Follow-up care should also extend to family members, who may require therapy to deal with their reactions to the suicide attempt.

DISCUSSION
Prevalence and Incidence

The incidence of suicide is between 11 and 12 per 100,000 population in the United States (Masica et al., 1992). The incidence of attempted suicide is at least 10 times as great (Roy, 1989). The rate of completed suicide increases with age (Figure 2–3–2), although the rate of suicide among young males has been increasing (Figure 2–3–1) (O'Carroll and Potter, 1994). Male sex is itself a risk factor for completed suicide, though women are significantly more likely to make a suicide attempt (Appleby, 1992). This difference may in part be due to the more violent, and therefore lethal, means chosen by males. Other risk factors include being Caucasian, single, divorced or separated, and discharged from a psychiatric hospital within the previous few months.

Related Basic Science
Genetics

The incidence of suicide appears to be genetically influenced. The most powerful evidence is that monozygotic twins are significantly more often concordant for suicide than dizygotic twins. Some family pedigrees are heavily loaded for suicide. Although this might be attributed

to environmental influences, it also holds true if the family member is raised in an adopted family (Roy, 1989).

Physiologic or Metabolic Derangement

A large body of evidence links reductions in the efficacy of serotonergic neurotransmission with suicidality. These abnormalities tend to occur in suicidal patients regardless of their primary psychiatric diagnosis, and especially characterize patients who attempt suicide by more violent, that is, lethal, means. These findings include reduced cerebrospinal fluid levels of 5-hydroxyindoleacetic acid, the primary metabolite of serotonin, reduced prolactin response to serotonergic probes, and increased numbers of 5HT-2 receptors in the brains of suicide victims (Coccaro et al., 1989; Owens et al., 1994). Some evidence also suggests altered function of noradrenergic and dopaminergic systems, which, with serotonin, are most closely involved in the regulation of mood (Roy et al., 1989; Virkunnen et al., 1989; Lonnqvist et al., 1994).

Natural History and Its Modification with Treatment

There are few direct data available that show the efficacy of interventions intended to decrease suicide. Epidemiologic evidence suggests that the presence of a suicide prevention center in the community is associated with a decreased rate of suicide (Lester, 1993). Several studies suggest that patients who receive maintenance lithium therapy are significantly less likely to commit suicide than those in the general population (Schifano and DeLeo, 1991; Hanus and Tuma, 1992).

Malone and colleagues categorized depressed hospital inpatients according to whether they had made a suicide attempt in their present episode of depression (recent attempter), during a previous episode (remote attempter), or never. There was no significant difference between the three groups in the percentage of patients who received antidepressants within the 3 months prior to hospitalization; however, only 6% of recent attempters versus 55% of remote attempters and 85% of never attempters were on a *therapeutic* dose of antidepressant drugs in the 3 months prior to hospitalization ($P = 0.02$). (Malone et al., 1994). This suggests that antidepressant treatment alone may have a negligible impact on reducing suicide without attention to adequacy of treatment. Some evidence suggests that the selective serotonin reuptake inhibitors are more effective in reduction of suicidal ideation than other antidepressants (Filteau et al., 1993).

Prevention

The best preventive measure is the aggressive treatment of the underlying condition(s) that places the patient at risk of suicide. The next best strategy is to try to reduce easy access to the more lethal means of suicide attempts. This is likely to reduce deaths from impulsive attempts. An apparently successful example of this approach has been the decline in suicides that paralleled the decrease in the prescribing of barbiturates (Roy, 1989). The physician should consider lethality in overdose when prescribing medication for patients at risk of suicide. The newer-generation antidepressants, such as the selective serotonin reuptake inhibitors, bupropion, venlafaxine, and trazodone, are much less dangerous in overdose than the tricyclic antidepressants. It has been estimated that the routine first-line use of selective serotonin reuptake inhibitors would save 300 to 450 lives a year in a country the size of Great Britain (Freemantle et al., 1994). If a tricyclic antidepressant is prescribed, care should be taken that the patient not receive more than 1 week of medicine at a time, because as little as 10 days' supply may be deadly if taken at once.

Easy access to firearms in the United States contributes to fatal impulsive suicide attempts. Sixty-six percent of suicides are committed by firearms in the United States compared with only 6% in Britain, where access is much more restricted. If someone is a potential suicide risk, it is important to ask about the availability of firearms and to strongly recommend that they be placed out of easy reach.

"Copycat" suicides may sometimes occur among adolescents, especially if the deaths or deceased are glorified in news reports. Guidelines are available for handling such cases (O'Carroll and Potter, 1994). Physicians may wish to make themselves available to families, schools, or the media in such cases to reduce the risk of further deaths.

Cost Containment

The emotional cost of suicide is, of course, devastating. The financial costs incurred in the medical and psychiatric management of suicide attempters, especially those who make multiple attempts, can be devastating as well. Therefore, the best avenue to cost containment is prevention.

REFERENCES

Appleby L. Suicide in psychiatric patients: Risk and prevention. Br J Psychiatry 1992;161:749.

Coccaro EF, Siever LJ, Klar HM, et al. Serotonergic studies in patients with af- fective and personality disorders: Correlates with suicidal and impulsive ag- gressive behavior. Arch Gen Psychiatry 1989;46:587.

Filteau MJ, Lapierre YD, Bakish D, Blanchard A. Reduction in suicidal ideation with SSRIs: A review of 459 depressed patients. J Psychiatry Neurosci 1993;18:114.

Freemantle N, House A, Song F, et al. Prescribing selective serotonin reuptake inhibitors as strategy for prevention of suicide. Br Med J 1994;309:249.

Hanus H, Tuma I. [Prevention of suicidal activity in patients with affective dis- orders by treatment with lithium] [Czech]. Cesk Psychiatrie 1992;88:113.

Lester D. The effectiveness of suicide prevention centers. Suicide Life-Threat- ening Behav 1993;23:263.

Lonnqvist J, Sintonen H, Syvalahti E, et al. Antidepressant efficacy and quality of life in depression: A double-blind study with moclobemide and fluoxetine. Acta Psychiatr Scand 1994;89:363.

Malone KM, Corbitt EM, Szanto K, Mann JJ. Antidepressant pharmacotherapy and suicidal behavior during major depression. Psychopharmacol Bull 1994;30(4):634.

Masica DN, Kotsanos JG, Beasley CM Jr, Potvin JH. Trend in suicide rates since fluoxetine introduction (letter). Am J Public Health 1992;82:1295.

O'Carroll PW, Potter LB. Programs for the prevention of suicide among adoles- cents and young adults. MMWR 1994;43(RR-6):3.

Owens MJ, Nemeroff CB. Role of serotonin in the pathophysiology of depres- sion: Focus on the serotonin transporter. Clin Chem 1994;40:288.

Roy A. Suicide. In: Kaplan HI, Sadock BJ, eds. Comprehensive textbook of psy- chiatry. Baltimore: Williams & Wilkins, 1989:1414.

Roy A, De Jong J, Linnoila M. Cerebrospinal fluid monoamine metabolites and suicidal behavior in depressed patients. Arch Gen Psychiatry 1989;46:609.

Schifano F, De Leo D. Can pharmacological intervention aid in the prevention of suicidal behavior? Pharmacopsychiatry 1991;24:113.

Statistical abstract of the United States. 114th ed. Washington, DC: U.S. Depart- ment of Commerce, 1994.

Virkunnen M, De Jong J, Bartko J, Linnoila M. Psychobiological concomitants of history of suicide attempts among violent offenders and impulsive fire set- ters. Arch Gen Psychiatry 1989;46:604.

CHAPTER 2–4

Schizophrenia

Dewitt C. Alfred, Jr., M.D.

DEFINITION

Schizophrenia is a group of psychotic disorders with similar clinical features involving multiple psychological processes but with possibly varying etiologies. The most common denominator of this group of disorder is the *classic schizophrenic thought disorder* characterized by loosened associations of thought, autistic thought, ambivalence, and impairment of affect.

ETIOLOGY

The etiology of schizophrenia is unknown, but current speculation involves the possibility of multiple causes for the different individual diagnostic entities that exist within the group of disorders known as schizophrenia.

CRITERIA FOR DIAGNOSIS
Subjective

Subjective criteria include the onset of a psychotic illness before the age 45. It is important to determine that the disturbance is not due to an organic mental disorder, affective disorder, substance use disorder, or mental retardation. There must be a clear history of continuous signs of the illness for at least 6 months at some time during the patient's life, with some of these signs existing at the time of diagnosis. There is almost always deterioration from a previous level of functioning (i.e., social, vocational, self-care) during some phase of the illness. Also, at some point, schizophrenia involves delusions and/or certain disturbances in the form of thought ("thought disorder").

Definitive

The definitive criteria are essentially the same as the clinical manifestations and include perceptual disorders, cognitive disorders, disturbances of thinking, disorders of verbal behavior, behavioral disorders, disorders of affect, and somatic disturbances.

CLINICAL MANIFESTATIONS
Subjective

Behavioral Disorders. Schizophrenic patients are often described as having reduced energy. There is a disturbance in self-initiated goal-directed activity, with inadequate interest or drive, and the loss of ability to follow a course of action to its logical conclusion. Ambivalence, previously described under Disturbances of Thinking, can lead to immobility and cessation of goal-directed activity. Patients are often described as seemingly awkward.

Cognitive Disorders. Delusions or false ideas not amenable to logical refutation represent the major disturbance in content of thought. The delusions are often bizarre and absurd; the themes are often persecution, jealousy, grandiosity, religiosity, nihilism, and somatic preoccupation. The delusions often incorporate hallucinatory perceptions.

Disorders of Affect. In schizophrenia, emotional responses are universally reduced, with decreased intensity and decreased range of emotional display. The patient's affect is also described as apathetic, blunted, constricted, or flat. Another aspect of schizophrenic affect is its inappropriateness, which refers to the incongruous responses shown by many patients.

In fact, it is this classic "splitting of the psychic functions" that is the origin of the name *schizophrenia*. An apparent split between the functions of thinking and feeling causes an individual to verbalize a preoccupation with death and despair while his or her emotional display is one of happiness. Many patients experience anhedonia, the inability to feel or even imagine a pleasant emotion. These patients are emotionally barren; they are not depressed, but rather they have no feelings except of emptiness and of a terrible hopeless void. This may lead to suicide. Other abnormal emotions sometimes seen in schizophrenia are exaltation and omnipotence, or even oceanic feelings of oneness with the universe or religious ecstasies. Some patients feel a terror of disintegration of personality and body, and others have anxiety or even panic over their perception of the imminent catastrophic destruction of the universe.

Disorders of Verbal Behavior. Verbal behavior demonstrates the paradox referred to under Disturbances of Thinking. The patient is simultaneously overly concrete and overly symbolic in speech patterns. Patients are often incoherent; it is said that schizophrenics use language for self-expression, not for communication. Production of speech encompasses the entire spectrum from mutism to verbigeration, which is the senseless repetition of words or phrases for hours or even days.

Disturbances of Thinking. One of the most typical disturbances of schizophrenic thought is autism, which is characterized by private rules of logic in which two things are similar if they have a similar property, no matter how trivial or obscure. There is much in the way of magical and mystical thought involved, including extreme perplexity about one's own identity and the meaning of existence. This is sometimes referred to as the *loss of ego boundaries*. Paradoxically, although preoccupied with mystical, magical, and symbolic phenomena, the patient loses the capacity for abstract thought and is very concrete in the recognition of relationships in reality. The patient is markedly ambivalent. His or her thinking may be made up of exactly equal and opposing thoughts, multiple simultaneous thoughts, or jumbled thoughts. The association or sequence of ideas or thoughts is illogical. It becomes loosened with the intrusion of many side or secondary thoughts and ideas, so that the original train of logic is often lost to the individual. This is referred to as *tangential thinking*.

Perceptual Disorders. The major disturbances in perception are hallucinations, which may occur in all sensory modalities. The most common are auditory and usually involve solitary or multiple voices that provide an ongoing commentary on the patient's thoughts or behavior. The voices may be "familiar" and may criticize, ridicule, threaten, or urge the patient to do something he or she believes is wrong. Occasionally, hallucinations occur in other sensory spheres. Visual hallucinations may occur, and the perceptions are usually life-sized, three-dimensional, and moving. Visual hallucinations seldom occur alone; they usually occur in combination with one or more of the sensory modalities (auditory, haptic or tactile, olfactory, or gustatory). Cenesthesic hallucinations, which involve the perception of an altered state of an internal organ, are often noted.

Somatic Disturbances. Of course, the schizophrenic patient is just as susceptible to disease, infection, and trauma as any other person, but many schizophrenics are inordinately concerned or preoccupied with health and bodily functions. These patients are frequently hypochondriacal and often have somatic delusions that are associated with cenesthesic hallucinations. In contrast to the symptoms of affective disorders, the complaint of insomnia is not as frequent.

Objective

Behavioral Disorders. Psychomotor phenomena encompass the entire spectrum from the cerea flexibilitas (waxy posturing) of catatonia, which may last hours or even days, to agitated and excited behavior, which may be threatening to the patient or to others. Frequently, highly stylized mannerisms of hand motions, facial grimacing, and speech patterns are noted. In many instances, the patient demonstrates automatic obedience, which is robotlike compliance to a command, or stereotyped behavior, which is the repetitive pattern of a sequence of motions or behaviors day after day. This may take the form of walking in a circle or some other more intricate pattern, making the same comments, or asking the same questions day after day. Also noted are echopraxia, the mimicry or repetition of the movements of others, and negativism, the failure to cooperate with any command. The chronic schizophrenic demonstrates a deteriorated appearance, with diminished grooming and self-care and poor regard for manners and the social amenities.

Cognitive Disorders. The patient may freely verbalize delusional material or, conversely, may be very secretive and mysterious. Some of the more bizarre delusional symptoms involve ideas of thought control, thought broadcasting, thought insertion or withdrawal, depersonalization, and ideas of reference (in which the patient perceives any and every event, no matter how trivial, as being related to, or in reference to, himself or herself). Sometimes the patient formulates an elaborate construction of intrigue and conspiracy that involves all those with whom he or she has contact, no matter how casually. This is called the *paranoid pseudocommunity*.

Disorders of Affect. Disorders of affect are recognized via verbalization and other behavior produced by the particular affect, as described above. A particular affect may determine whether an individual is withdrawn or excited or potentially dangerous to self or others.

Disorders of Verbal Behavior. Verbal behavior is the prime modality by which the examiner may objectively assess the multiple psychological impairments in the schizophrenic patient. In addition to the verbalization of hallucinations, delusions, and disturbances of thinking, there are other interesting aspects of typical schizophrenic verbal behavior. These include mutism, incoherence, and verbigeration (described above), plus such phenomena as neologism (the creation of new words, which are sometimes bizarre and have private definitions) and echolalia (the repetition of the words of another). Schizophrenic speech is often described as stilted, that is, having a grotesquely quaint, pseudoformal, or perhaps pseudointellectual style or form.

Disturbances of Thinking. Disturbances of thinking are elicited in the patient interview, particularly in the structured interview.

Perceptual Disorders. The patient may verbalize perceptual distortion or may assume certain facial expressions, postures, and behaviors that are clearly indicative of the perceptual disorders (e.g., a vigilant listening posture).

Somatic Disturbances. The "autonomic triad" has been described in most schizophrenic patients as consisting of dilated pupils, moist palms, and tachycardia. Frequently, systolic blood pressure is elevated 10 to 20 mm Hg. Voluntary retention of feces may lead to leakage or encopresis. Chronic constipation may lead to psychogenic megacolon. The combination of somatic delusions and cenesthesic hallucinations may lead to such complaints as "my brain is burning" or "a snake is eating my insides." Schizophrenics seem to be hypersensitive to all stimuli: noise, odor, touch, light, and so on. The individual experiencing psychotic exhaustion, such as the excited catatonic patient, may be hyperpyrexic with leukocytosis. Self-mutilation, such as amputation, enucleation of an eye, or castration, known as the van Gogh syndrome, does occur, but it is relatively rare. Self-mutilation is usually associated with dysmorphic delusions or disturbances of the body image.

PLANS
Diagnostic
Differential Diagnosis

Affective Disorder. In those affective disorders that develop a psychotic picture similar to schizophrenia, the onset of delusions and hallucinations follows a period of affective disturbance (depression or euphoria). A manic episode with anger and paranoid delusions may need to be distinguished from paranoid schizophrenia. Therefore, the historical sequence of the development of symptoms is of critical significance in the diagnosis.

Atypical Psychosis. The diagnosis of atypical psychosis is made when there is a nonaffective psychotic disorder with insufficient criteria to diagnose schizophrenia. It is also diagnosed in unusual instances, such as in the presence of a classic schizophrenic delusion of bodily change without the other criteria of schizophrenia.

Brief Reactive Psychosis. The psychotic symptoms of a brief reaction appear immediately after a recognizable and significant psychosocial stress. These include varying combinations of incoherence, loose associations, delusions, hallucinations, and disorganized or catatonic behavior. These psychotic symptoms last more than a few hours but less than 2 weeks, and there is a return to premorbid functioning. There is no period of increasing psychopathology preceding the precipitating stress.

Developmental Disorders. Although there may be a resemblance to schizophrenia, there is no history of delusions, hallucinations, or incoherence with developmental disorders.

Mental Retardation. Although the impoverished affect and cognition, low level of social functioning, and oddities of behavior may suggest schizophrenia, the history and absence of other criteria will distinguish mentally retarded patients.

Obsessive–Compulsive Disorder, Phobic Disorder, and Hypochondriasis. These psychoneurotic disorders are sometimes characterized by such extremely overvalued ideational symptoms that it is difficult to distinguish them from delusions; however, the patients with these disorders recognize to some degree that their symptoms and thinking are irrational, even though they are dominated by their symptoms. None of the other criteria of schizophrenia are present.

Organic Mental Disorder. Organic mental disorder may present a cross-sectional picture indistinguishable from schizophrenia except for the presence of disorientation and memory impairment, which differentiates organic mental disorder. Some toxic organic psychoses, such as those resulting from phencyclidine and amphetamine, may not be differentiated except in retrospect unless a positive history is elicited early or unless the disorder is detected via laboratory diagnosis. To further complicate matters, it must be noted that it is possible for a schizophrenic to have a superimposed organic mental disorder.

Paranoid Disorder. Paranoid disorder is distinguished from schizophrenia by the absence of prominent hallucinations, incoherence, loosening of associations, or bizarre delusions.

Personality Disorder. Certain personality disorders, especially schizotypal, borderline, schizoid, and paranoid, may present transient psychotic symptoms, but these last only a few hours or days.

Subcultural and Religious Sect Beliefs. Subcultural and religious beliefs may be difficult to differentiate from delusions, but when shared and accepted by a group, they should not in and of themselves be considered evidence of psychosis.

Schizophreniform Disorder. The cross-sectional symptom picture for schizophreniform disorder is indistinguishable from any one of the other types of schizophrenia. By definition, however, the duration of the illness is less than 6 continuous months. The duration of illness required to warrant the diagnosis schizophrenia is 6 continuous months. A person may have several episodes of schizophreniform disorder, with each lasting less than 6 months.

Schizoaffective Disorder. The diagnosis of schizoaffective disorder has no specific criteria but is used when the clinician is unable to differentiate between schizophrenia and affective disorder.

Diagnostic Options and Recommended Approach

Although the limits of the concept of schizophrenia are lacking in absolute precision, it is customary to attempt to define as nearly as possible the particular subtype of the disorder to be treated.

Catatonic Type. The essential features of catatonic schizophrenia are any one or more of the following: catatonic stupor and mutism, catatonic negativism, catatonic rigidity, catatonic posturing.

Disorganized Type (Hebephrenia). The essential features of the disorganized type of schizophrenia are marked incoherence, absence of systematized delusions, and a flat, inappropriate, incongruous, silly affect.

Paranoid Type. Paranoid schizophrenia is dominated by one or more of the following: persecutory delusions, grandiose delusions, delusional jealously, hallucinations with persecutory or grandiose content.

Residual Type. In the residual type, there are no prominent psychotic symptoms as in the other types, but there is continuing evidence of the illness, such as blunted or inappropriate affect, social withdrawal, eccentric behavior, illogical thinking, or loosening of associations. There is a history of at least one previous episode of schizophrenia with prominent psychotic symptoms.

Undifferentiated Type. In the undifferentiated type of schizophrenia there are prominent delusions, hallucinations, and incoherence or grossly disorganized behavior. The clinical picture does not meet the criteria of any of the other types, or it meets the criteria of more than one.

Therapeutic

Therapeutic Options

It has been established by well-controlled and replicated studies that the neuroleptic antipsychotic drugs are of real value in the treatment of schizophrenia. There is no great difference in effectiveness among the currently available antipsychotic agents. The major differences are in side effects and potency per milligram. Although there are numerous chemical families of neuroleptics, about five categories have real significance currently. These are the phenothiazines, thioxanthenes, dihydroindolones, dibenzoxazepines, and butyrophenones. The phenothiazines are most numerous, with four important subfamilies, the thioxanthenes have two subfamilies, and the others each have a single representative. Potency is usually measured in comparison to the first neuroleptic, chlorpromazine (Thorazine) (Table 2–4–1).

In general, it is best to use only one drug at a time. It is probably wiser to treat side effects when and if they occur and not with the traditional "prophylactic" use of an antiparkinsonism drug.

Side effects include drowsiness, dizziness, dry mouth, constipation, hypotension, blurred vision, weight gain, and breast engorgement. Extrapyramidal side effects include rigidity, akathisia, dystonia, dyskinesia, and pseudoparkinsonism. Much less common are such side effects as agranulocytosis, obstructive hepatitis, and allergic cutaneous rashes. Chorioretinopathy is reported in some cases with a daily dose of thioridazine above 800 mg.

The typically effective antipsychotic dose range is 200 to 2000 mg chlorpromazine, or the "equivalent" dose of the other drugs as expressed in Table 2–4–1. The higher-dose neuroleptics, such as chlorpromazine, tend to have a greater sedative and hypotensive effect, whereas the lower-dose drugs, such as fluphenazine, tend to cause more extrapyramidal effects. In 1990, an atypical neuroleptic antipsychotic agent, clozapine, was released from restricted experimental status. This "new" drug is a dibenzodiazepine derivative and is proving to be very useful in the 10 to 20% of chronic schizophrenics who have been in-

TABLE 2–4–1. DRUGS USED TO TREAT SCHIZOPHRENIA

Chemical Group	Drug	Approximate Oral Dose Equivalency (mg)
Phenothiazines		
Aliphatic Series	Chlorpromazine	100
Piperidine Series	Thioridazine	100
	Mesoridazine	50
Piperazine Series	Trifluoperazine	10
Phenazine Series	Perphenazine	4
	Fluphenazine	3
Thioxanthenes		
Aliphatic Series	Chlorprothixene	100
Piperazine Series	Thiothixene	10
Dihydroindolone	Molindone	25
Dibenzoxazepine	Loxapine Succinate	25
Butyrophenone	Haloperidol	2

tractable in their therapeutic responses to other medications or who have developed serious dyskinetic side effects from other drugs. Clozapine is a very low potency drug such that the approximate equivalency to 100 mg of chlorpromazine is 150 mg of clozapine. Unfortunately, bone marrow suppression with severe agranulocytosis is a not-infrequent complication. Thus, risk–benefit ratios must be carefully measured. Clozapine is also extraordinarily expensive, requiring equal concern about cost–benefit issues.

The uncooperative patient may require parenteral medication. The usual rule of thumb is to use half the standard oral dose. Although conservative administration of medication dictates that one begin with low doses and gradually titrate upward, it is becoming increasingly useful to employ the technique of rapid neuroleptization to decrease hospital costs and length of stay. In this procedure, high doses of neuroleptics are administered parenterally during the first 1 or 2 days of hospitalization. Then the switch to oral medication is made, still in high doses, and the dose is gradually titrated downward to a less than sedative level. This procedure should be followed with caution after a thorough physical examination with close monitoring of the vital signs.

On rare occasions, electroconvulsive therapy still has a place in the treatment of schizophrenia and other psychotic disorders, especially in the presence of severe catatonic and/or affective features.

Whereas initial treatment is usually done in the inpatient setting, later stages of treatment may continue on an inpatient or outpatient basis. The various modalities include milieu therapy and combined behavioral therapy and drug therapy. For the chronic patient who is noncompliant with maintenance oral medication, long-acting, depot-injectable neuroleptics may be used, such as fluphenazine decanoate and fluphenazine enanthate (Prolixin). These provide antipsychotic activity of 2 to 3 weeks' duration after a single intramuscular injection in a usual dose, which varies between 25 and 100 mg. Long-acting depot-injectable haloperidol (Haldol) decanoate is also available and provides antipsychotic activity of 3 to 4 weeks' duration per single injection in a dose range of 10 to 50 mg.

Recommended Approach

The patient and family should be informed of all aspects of the diagnostic impression and treatment plan at a level that is most easily comprehensible to them. One should try to avoid excessively technical jargon and euphemisms; however, the unsophisticated listener might better understand a comment such as "Mr. Doe is having a serious nervous breakdown. He is talking out of his head and his imagination is playing tricks on him. I think we can help him to get better soon, but he needs to be in the hospital." In another setting, one might describe a similar patient by saying, "Your husband has had a psychotic breakdown. Right now he is incoherent with auditory hallucinations and delusions of persecution. He needs to be hospitalized, and with some potent medicine he should be much better in a few weeks."

Psychotherapy itself is a highly specialized technique of investigation and education. It can be used to varying degrees of effectiveness depending on the patient's condition and psychological mindedness. The techniques of psychotherapy with psychotic patients are significantly different from those with neurotic patients. With psychotic patients, the therapist is more supportive and directive.

Because the genetic basis of schizophrenia is established, although not clearly defined, genetic counseling is an important educational factor.

The recovering schizophrenic patient should receive thorough instruction concerning his or her medication, possible side effects, and the necessity for compliance.

FOLLOW-UP

Follow-up is a complex phenomenon and can involve many different professions and agencies. It includes various combinations of maintenance drug therapy, group or individual psychotherapy, sheltered living, partial hospitalization, sheltered work situations, vocational rehabilitation, behavioral modification, and rehospitalization when necessary.

DISCUSSION
Prevalence and Incidence

Prevalence in Europe and Asia, with narrow diagnostic criteria, is reported to be from 0.2 to 1% of the population (Cancro, 1989). In the United States, with broader diagnostic criteria, studies still report a low prevalence, usually less than 2.5% (Karno et al., 1989).

All investigators have found an increased prevalence of schizophrenia among the close relatives of schizophrenic patients. The prevalence is reported as between 10 and 15%, compared with under 1% in the general population. Twin studies consistently show three to six times higher rates for schizophrenia in monozygotic twins, whereas the concordance rate for dizygotic twins is about the same as that for ordinary siblings. In summary, the data indicate the likelihood of a hereditary predisposition to schizophrenia.

Related Basic Science

To date, no biochemical abnormalities or neurophysiologic correlates have been consistently identified in schizophrenia. There are, however, several viable hypotheses with contradictory and/or incomplete evidence. Tolerance to histamine is found consistently in schizophrenic patients. Elevated levels of plasma creatinine phosphokinase are found consistently in acute psychotic patients, although not exclusively in schizophrenia. Phenothiazines seem to work by blocking dopaminergic receptors, and recent studies consistently report decreased dopamine β-hydroxylase levels. Schizophrenia and amphetamine psychosis may produce a hyperactive dopaminergic system or some imbalance in the dopamine–norepinephrine regulatory system. Other hypotheses speculate on abnormalities in neuropeptides or suggest possible imbalances of neuroregulators that work in tandem. One of the more exciting hypotheses involves the possible excessive methylation of a norepinephrine precursor such as dimethyltryptamine, which could produce a "natural mescaline-like substance" in the central nervous system. Recent findings of decreased monoamine oxidase and increased N-methyltransferase in the platelets of schizophrenic patients are supportive of this theory. Currently, it is possible to study brain structure and basic brain metabolic processes in living human beings using computerized axial tomography, positron emission tomography, and magnetic resonance imaging, the last having the advantage of not exposing persons to ionizing radiation. The work is at an early stage, but it does suggest that schizophrenic patients may experience a decrease in brain volume and metabolic deficiencies in specific brain regions as compared with normal control subjects. We appear now to be on the brink of either confirming or disproving a number of long-standing hypotheses.

Natural History and Its Modification with Treatment

The onset of schizophrenia is usually in adolescence or early adulthood. As the onset is insidious, it is difficult to know with certainty when the disorder actually started; however, the history will usually reveal lifelong personality traits such as excessive shyness, social awkwardness, and difficulty in forming close relationships. Often the family has been "concerned" about the patient for months or years before psychotic symptoms become manifest. The history is also likely to reveal academic and achievement difficulties in the patient's childhood and adolescence and occasional antisocial or delinquent behavior.

The development of the active phase of illness may be preceded by a prodromal phase, in which deterioration in the level of functioning is clear. The change is noted by friends and relatives. The prodromal phase is of variable length, but in general, the more insidious the onset, the poorer the prognosis.

Next is the active phase of psychotic symptoms: delusions, hallucinations, and so on. The onset of the active phase, either initially or in exacerbation, may be associated with a psychosocial stressor. If no external stress is obvious, the prognosis is poor.

Usually, the residual phase follows the active phase. The clinical picture is similar to that of the prodromal phase, although the affect may be more impoverished. One could say that in the prodromal and residual phases, the patient is schizophrenic but not psychotic.

A complete return to premorbid functioning is rare; however, there is the slim possibility of full recovery. The most common course is that of remission and recurrent acute exacerbation, with increasing residual impairment between episodes.

Factors associated with a "good" prognosis are absent premorbid schizoid personality, adequate premorbid social functioning, a definite precipitating stress, abrupt onset, onset in midlife, clinical symptoms of confusion, and a family history of affective disorders.

As a description of the course of the illness has prognostic and treatment implications, it is useful to describe schizophrenia as subchronic (6 months to 2 years from the prodromal to the residual phase), chronic (greater than 2 years from the prodromal to the residual phase), subchronic with acute exacerbation, chronic with acute exacerbation, and in remission. In current terminology, there is no acute schizophrenia, as any episode less than 6 months is by definition a schizophreniform disorder.

Some of the major complications of schizophrenia should be noted. The violence of schizophrenic patients gains much public and media attention, but the data are not clear as to whether schizophrenic patients commit more violent acts than the general population. The life expectancy of schizophrenic patients is shorter than that of the general population because of an increased suicide rate and death from a variety of other causes, including accidents, diminished self-care, inadequate institutional care, and the deprived environments in which many of these individuals live.

The diagnosis of schizophrenia appears to be equally common in men and women. It is more common in lower socioeconomic groups for reasons that are unclear, but that may involve downward social drift and the lack of upward social mobility inherent in the personality features associated with the disorder. Certain patterns of family interaction are described as predisposing to onset, relapse, and chronicity of schizophrenia.

Prevention

Because of the low level of resolution concerning the etiology and diagnostic criteria of schizophrenic disorders, comment on prevention has an equally low level of resolution; however, we may describe several stages of prevention.

Primary Prevention

Genetic counseling is probably the only available means of reducing incidence and prevalence. Early identification of individuals at high risk and the initiation of special programs to reduce risk are advocated, but such policies carry the possibility for abuse of civil liberties and even political and social atrocities.

Secondary Prevention

Active early intervention using all known successful modalities, especially chemotherapy, can shorten the active phase considerably.

Tertiary Prevention

Vigorous efforts toward educational, vocational, and individual rehabilitation and maintenance and aggressive follow-up programs can prevent relapse, exacerbation, and chronicity in some cases.

Cost Containment
Research

The ultimate cost containment plan involves the apparent paradox of increased funding for research in schizophrenia. Discoveries in bio-

chemistry and neurophysiology, which seem imminent, may lead to a cure or treatment far more effective than anything now available.

Cost-Effectiveness Analysis

Many techniques and procedures of treatment are based on theory and tradition. There is a need to collect hard data on their impact on morbidity, recidivism, rehabilitation, and so on, and there is a need for subsequent funding of those that actually work.

Reexamination of the Community Mental Health Center Concept

The community mental health center concept, a popular concept of social activists, may in fact be far more expensive in the delivery of care than the psychiatric service of the general hospital or even more expensive than private psychiatric care. Many studies suggest this alarming possibility. If community mental health centers have failed qualitatively, quantitatively, and economically, as many believe, they should be studied quickly, and if ineffective, they should be abandoned for cost-effective measures. Since the late 1980s, public mental health agencies at the state and federal levels have abandoned the somewhat arbitrary concept of the "catchment area" and have focused more on staff-utilization cost-effectiveness issues such that the economic merit of community mental health centers is becoming increasingly pragmatic.

Medical Audit and Utilization Review

There should be universal implementation of audit and review in the public and private sectors to examine justifications for admissions and treatment, duration of hospital stay, length of therapy, and cost-effectiveness of all procedures and techniques.

Cost–Benefit Analysis of Specific Treatment Factors

It seems obvious that there is a need for individualized service plans in the treatment of schizophrenia. Depending on the individual and the level of illness, it seems clear that all patients cannot benefit from verbal therapies or milieu therapy at certain points in the course of the disorder. These treatments should not be routinely prescribed. The least expensive therapy and form of medication appropriate to the clinical situation should be used.

REFERENCES

Alfred DC. Schizophrenia. In: Hurst JW, ed. Medicine for the practicing physician. 3rd ed. Boston: Butterworth–Heinemann, 1992:23.
Bleuler E. Dementia praecox or the group of schizophrenias. New York: International Universities Press, 1911; translated by Joseph Zinkin, 1950.
Cancro R. Schizophrenia. In: Karasu TB, et al., eds. Treatments of psychiatric disorders. Washington, DC: American Psychiatric Association, 1989; 2:1485.
Cancro R, Babigian HM, Weiner H, et al. Schizophrenic disorders. In: Kaplan HI, Sadock BJ, eds. Comprehensive textbook of psychiatry IV. Baltimore: Williams & Wilkins, 1985:631.
Diagnostic and statistical manual of mental disorders. 4th ed. Washington, DC: American Psychiatric Association, 1994:274.
Karno M, Norquist GS, Berman KF, et al. Schizophrenia. In: Kaplan HI, Sadock BJ, eds. Comprehensive textbook of psychiatry V. Baltimore: Williams & Wilkins, 1989:699.
Weinberger DR, sec. ed. Schizophrenia. In: Tasman and Goldfinger review of psychiatry. Washington, DC: American Psychiatric Press, 1991; 10:sect. I.

Paranoid Disorders

Dewitt C. Alfred, Jr., M.D.

DEFINITION

Paranoid disorders are a group of rare psychotic disorders characterized by the sole central feature or symptom of a nonbizarre delusion or delusional system. A *delusion* is a false belief that is firmly held even in the face of contradictory facts. The delusion is not amenable to refutation by logic, reason, or overwhelming evidence to the contrary.

ETIOLOGY

The etiology of paranoid or delusional disorders is unknown. The delusional symptoms occur in a wide variety of medical and psychiatric conditions. Differences in definition and classification of these disorders add to the problem.

CRITERIA FOR DIAGNOSIS

Suggestive

The suggestive criterion for diagnosis is the presence of a nonbizarre delusion or delusional system that involves situations that may occur in real life.

Definitive

Unfortunately the most definitive criteria for diagnosis are criteria of exclusion. That is, the diagnostician must rule out other psychiatric conditions that may be associated with paranoid symptomatology, especially schizophrenia. The emphases in the definition of the presence of a nonbizarre delusional system can create further problems, particularly of a cultural nature, in the definition of what is or is not bizarre. Though older and younger ages have been reported, the usual age of onset between 40 and 55 years is relatively late in life compared with schizophrenia and the bipolar disorders.

CLINICAL MANIFESTATIONS

Subjective

The nonbizarre delusional system involves situations that can and do happen in real life. The delusional content may focus, for example, on being poisoned, infected, followed, deceived, or loved at a distance.

It is equally important to note what is not present, for the presence of other psychiatric symptoms casts serious doubt on the diagnosis of delusional disorder. Thus, there should be no disturbance of thinking or disturbance of behavior. Very rarely visual or auditory hallucinations may be present, but they are not bizarre and not prominent. Such perceptual distortion is brief and transitory. Likewise, a mood disorder may be superimposed on a delusional disorder. Careful history reveals that the mood aberration began after the delusion was present; such disturbances of affect also are likely to be brief and transitory.

Objective

The patient usually freely verbalizes the delusional material, but is sometimes secretive and mysterious if the content focuses on conspiracy. Verbalizations of affective impairment and perceptual distortion are rare, as previously noted. There should be no evidence of serious disorder of thinking and verbal behavior and no unusual psychomotor phenomena. Apart from the delusion or its ramifications, the behavior is not obviously odd or bizarre.

Somatic complaints pose the most serious clinical dilemma. On the one hand, somatic delusions are not uncommon as the central theme; on the other hand, any illness or injury that can cause an organic brain syndrome may have associated paranoid systems. The list is comprehensive and includes head trauma, endocrinopathy, infection, anoxia, anesthesia, toxins (including medications, drugs, and alcohol), and nu-

tritional disorders. Thus, one must carefully exclude possible somatogenesis of paranoid disorder.

PLANS

Diagnostic

Differential Diagnosis

Almost every category of mental or emotional disorder may display some aspect of the paranoid spectrum of symptoms. The early recognition of the underlying condition or disorder precludes the diagnosis of paranoid disorder. Other diagnostic possibilities include the following categories.

Acute Paranoid Reaction. The cross-sectional clinical picture of acute paranoid reaction is identical to that of paranoid disorder, except that the duration is less than 1 month, there is a very clear and obvious psychosocial stressor, and there is no premorbid disposition and no persistent sequelae. This clinical picture may occur after a natural catastrophe (e.g., earthquake, hurricane); after some types of traumatic stress (e.g., combat, although these problems become chronic in about a third of cases); after surgery (from the experience of the operation, perceived as mutilation, not from anesthesia, which is a different category); and with prolonged social isolation. (Culture shock arising from sudden transition into an alien culture may also fit into this category.)

Organic Delusional Disorder. Any illness leading to impairment of brain tissue functioning, resulting in the organic brain syndrome (characterized by impairment of orientation, memory, intellectual functioning, judgment, and affect), may have associated paranoid symptoms. This includes but is not limited to the following:

- *Infectious diseases,* such as trypanosomiasis, encephalitic syndromes, the paretic syndrome of central nervous system syphilis, and AIDS dementia associated with HIV infection.
- *Metabolic disorders,* such as degenerative neurologic disease, collagen disease, endocrinopathy, nutritional disease (e.g., pellagra, pernicious anemia).
- *Primary dementia,* such as Alzheimer's disease, Pick's disease, Creutzfeldt–Jakob disease (also infectious), and senility.
- *Secondary dementia,* associated with anoxia or a more general pathophysiology, for example, congestive heart failure, malignant hypertension with encephalopathy, hepatic failure, renal failure, and a mild postanesthetic syndrome.
- *Delirium and/or toxin-induced paranoia* caused by all medications, illegal drugs, and other substances that change consciousness, including alcohol. Nearly all of the psychotomimetic drugs, including some of the more potent strains of cannabis, can cause a significant incidence of paranoid reactions and paranoid "flashbacks."

Paranoid Schizophrenia and the Group of Schizophrenias and Schizophreniform Disorders. This group of disorders represents the major differential diagnostic issue. Any or all of the symptoms that should not be present to diagnose paranoia are likely to be present if the diagnosis is schizophrenia. Thus, the presence of prominent bizarre hallucinations, bizarre delusions, bizarre behavior, unusual psychomotor phenomena, constricted or flattened affect, disordered and disorganized thought processes, and so on will lead to the strong presumptive diagnosis of schizophrenia or schizophreniform disorder.

Affective Psychosis with Paranoia. Delusions may be quite prominent in either the manic or the depressive phase of bipolar affective psychosis or in psychotic depression. The careful history will delineate the characteristic course of the affective disorder with subsequent onset of delusional thought. In mania the delusions are typically grandiose and omnipotent, whereas the depressive delusions are typically focused on derogation of the evil or worthless self and perhaps the destruction of the evil self, such as somatic delusions of a terminal or fatal condition.

Severe Anxiety with "Pseudoparanoia." Several psychiatric conditions associated with extreme anxiety are sometimes characterized by such extremely overvalued ideational symptoms that it is difficult to distinguish them from delusions; however, these patients recognize to some degree that their symptoms and thinking are irrational, even though they may be dominated by their symptoms. These anxiety states are obsessive–compulsive disorder, anxiety with phobia, anxiety with panic, and hypochondriasis.

Personality Disorders. Personality is defined as the characteristic and largely predictable behavior response pattern evolved consciously and unconsciously as one's unique style of life. Thus, personality may be conceptualized as the sum of an individual's psychological mechanisms of defense and the ensuing behavior derived from said defense mechanisms. When these enduring patterns or traits are inflexible or maladaptive, one is defined as having a personality disorder. Persons with certain personality disorders, such as the paranoid, schizoid, schizotypal, and borderline personality disorders, have very little room to maneuver under stress, and may become briefly and transiently psychotic and manifest persecutory delusions. Such delusions last only hours or days but can recur. Most of the time, these persons are merely perceived as odd, eccentric, aloof, cold, rigid, unsocial, easily slighted, exquisitely sensitive, and so on.

Diagnostic Options and Recommended Approach

Although the vast spectrum of paranoid symptoms is found throughout the practice of medicine, delusion is seldom the primary or presenting symptom. Once the diagnosis is seriously entertained, however, it is customary to categorize the type or subtype of the paranoia based on the predominant delusional theme. The following six subtypes of delusional disorder are traditionally defined.

Persecutory Delusional Disorder. The predominant theme of the delusion is that the patient or a significant other is being malevolently treated in some way. Such patients frequently take their complaints to legal authorities and may be frequently involved in litigation. Often one thing leads to another, such that an elaborate conspiracy of intrigue and secrecy is formulated until the patient has created a "paranoid pseudocommunity." This type of paranoia is most likely to involve violence when the individual feels trapped and defensively arms and barricades himself. Violence is rare in paranoid disorders as compared with paranoid schizophrenia.

Grandiose Delusional Disorder. The predominant delusional theme is one of inflated worth, power, or knowledge. The patient may assume a powerful identity or believe that he or she has a special relationship to a famous person or a deity.

Erotomanic Delusional Disorder. The predominant delusional theme is that a person, usually of higher status or fame, is in love with the patient. The patient may be indignant over the alleged love interest or become a nuisance in efforts to reciprocate.

Jealous Delusional Disorder. The predominant delusional theme is that of unfaithfulness or infidelity of the patient's spouse, sexual partner, or love interest. Though violence is rare among paranoid disorders in general, it is this subtype that is most likely to result in murder–suicide tragedies.

Somatic Delusional Disorder. The predominant delusional theme is that the patient has a physical disease, defect, or disorder. This subtype is most likely to have an associated mood disorder (depression), which, if severe enough, can lead to the decision to kill one's self to avoid dying.

Unspecified Delusional Disorder. The predominant delusional theme does not fit clearly into one of the other five subtypes; more commonly, it manifests a mixture of two or more subtype themes. Common mixtures involve the persecutory–somatic theme (e.g., the patient has abdominal pain because someone is poisoning him) or the erotomanic–grandiose or erotomanic–jealousy theme.

Therapeutic
Therapeutic Options

A major aspect of treatment in any medical condition is the correctness of diagnosis. This is especially true in the case of paranoia, because if there is an underlying condition, treatment of the primary condition is paramount and will lead to resolution of the paranoia. This is true even if the underlying condition is one of the other psychoses. Lithium is a definitive therapy for mania, psychotic depression responds dramatically to antidepressant medication, and neuroleptic antipsychotic agents are of real value in the vast majority of schizophrenia patients. In fact, paranoid schizophrenia patients are most likely to show an effective response to antipsychotic medicines.

Unfortunately, little is available in the way of definitive treatment for the uncommon and rare paranoid disorder or delusional disorder. The clinician is always justified in employing a trial of an antipsychotic or a combination of an antipsychotic and an antidepressant (e.g., perphenazine and amitriptyline); however, in the true delusional disorder the results may be disappointing.

As one might expect, these patients are likely to be the least compliant with appropriate doses and the most sensitive to the least side effects. Often, the best results are obtained with a combination of symptom management and brief crisis intervention. Symptom management of anxiety and tension with anxiolytics (i.e., benzodiazepines) or of nocturnal agitation, restlessness, and insomnia with sedative–hypnotics may be efficacious. Crisis intervention, including brief hospitalizations (which may have to be involuntary), can be used to protect the patient and others. This, of course, must be associated with constant and consistent interpretation of the realities of the environment as consensually validated by others in the patient's environment.

Long-term supportive and ventilative psychotherapy may provide the patient with relief of recurring social crises and allow the patient to function within acceptable social boundaries despite his or her delusion.

Recommended Approach

One should be kind and warm, but firm, dignified, and very professional with the paranoid patient. The patient will always focus on the slightest differences in any two similar statements; therefore, one should be carefully specific and honest with the patient, and decline to argue or debate his or her paranoid misinterpretations. Maintaining confidentiality often means that family and significant others cannot be counseled because the patient refuses permission. When faced with the dilemma of confidentiality versus the safety of others, the physician must often confront the patient with the absolute necessity of protecting both the patient and others.

Therefore, at best, patient education is difficult. By definition, the primary symptom—delusional thought—is not amenable to refutation by contrary evidence, logic, or reason. Though it is difficult, the kind, firm, caring, no-nonsense physician can frequently establish a trusting and confident relationship with paranoid patients; even though the patient knows you are wrong, he or she knows that you mean well and that you are sincere.

FOLLOW-UP

It is presumed that in the initial evaluation, the physician has done a thorough differential screening to exclude organic and other disorders that may produce paranoia. Thereafter, the physician should avoid unnecessary, repetitious, expensive tests and reevaluations.

The physician should be accessible but within a well-defined appointment system; otherwise, the paranoid patient, exercising his or her sense of special privilege, can become a disruptive nuisance.

The kind but firm no-nonsense physician is quickly recognized by the patient as a major support system though he or she may never overtly acknowledge this fact.

Contact with significant others and/or environmental manipulation should be used judiciously, but without hesitation, when it is the physician's best professional judgment.

DISCUSSION
Prevalence and Incidence

Various reports agree that incidence is less than 3 per 100,000, and most place the incidence at less than 1 per 100,000. The gender differential data indicate that the disorder occurs only slightly more often in women (male:female ratio = 0.85:1.00).

Related Basic Science

Many theories attempting to explain the etiology are found in the literature but supporting evidence is quite limited. At this level of uncertainty, the best assertion is that paranoid (delusional) disorder is extremely rare, if in fact it does exist as a separate diagnostic category distinct from schizophrenia, bipolar disorder, pathologic personality, or organic brain syndrome. This questioning of the validity of the diagnosis has existed since the concept of the disorder was introduced by Kahlbaum in 1863. There are no distinctive psychophysiologic, genetic, biochemical, or neuroanatomic measures of paranoid (delusional) disorder.

Natural History and Its Modification with Treatment

Paranoid (delusional) disorder has been diagnosed (in accordance with current American Psychiatric Association standards [*Diagnostic and Statistical Manual,* 1994]) in persons from age 18 to 80, but the vast majority of documented cases have an onset between ages 40 and 55.

About two thirds of patients have an acute onset at earlier ages, and the evidence confirms that the more acute and earlier the onset, the more favorable the prognosis. Half of younger (45 years), more acute cases experience a lasting remission, and 10% become chronic. In older, more chronic cases with insidious onset, the condition changes little over time for more than one third of patients, whereas another third fall into a relapsing pattern.

The presence of clear and obvious precipitating factors is associated with favorable prognosis, whereas insidious onset at older ages, without clear and obvious precipitating stress, has the worst prognosis.

Delusional patients seldom present as a self-referral, but are cajoled into an evaluation by a significant other or come to the attention of authorities via various incidents such as seeking protection or quarreling. The patient will usually deny a psychiatric problem, and is likely to be uncooperative, hostile, angry, and/or sarcastic. The physician is surprised after hearing an obvious delusion that the patient's thinking, orientation, memory, attention, affect, perception, and personality are all clear and intact except for the obvious delusion. The intensity of the delusion and its content give the examiner clear clues as to possible dangerousness to self or others. Unlike other psychotic patients (schizophrenics, manics, and organic psychotics), the paranoid patient is very predictable within the framework of his or her delusional perspective. If dangerousness and impulsivity are obvious possibilities, the physician must not hesitate with involuntary hospitalization, though surprisingly, many of these patients will accept the medical decision voluntarily.

The psychodynamic and psychoanalytic theories concerning paranoia are varied and complex. The most widely accepted scenario is found in Freud's 1911 opus on "Dementia Paranoides" and Sullivan's later "The Paranoid Dynamism" in the 1940s. In this symbolic paradigm, paranoia is seen as arising out of denial of unacceptable negative belief about the self ("I am unlovable"), followed by projection of the negation to others ("No, it is not I who am unlovable, it is *they* who do not love me"), followed by irrational rationalization to protect the self from even worse undesirable self-images ("*They* don't love me because . . ." [here one inserts the delusion]; otherwise the dynamic would become "they don't love me because I am . . . different, strange, queer, etc.") Thus, paranoia is seen as a defense against unacceptable homosexual impulses.

Assuming the validity of this useful paradigm we can perhaps understand why the younger person with acute onset arising from an obvious environmental stress has a better prognosis than the older individual with insidious onset arising from internal stresses against which the individual has struggled for years.

Prevention

There is no known specific prevention of these disorders. A caring physician–patient relationship may be supportive to the patient and assist in prevention of relapse and/or prolonged chronicity.

Cost Containment

As previously noted, the physician should avoid unnecessary repetitious examinations, laboratory tests, or invasive medical procedures. The use of placebo medication will almost certainly be discovered by the patient and interpreted as hostile deceit; thus, avoid this temptation. The best cost containment is also excellent practice of medicine, that is, a thorough medical history, a thorough physical examination, and a comprehensive mental status examination.

REFERENCES

Alfred DC. Paranoid disorders. In: Hurst JW, ed. Medicine for the practicing physician. 3rd ed, Boston: Butterworth-Heinemann, 1992:28.
Diagnostic and statistical manual of mental disorders. 4th ed. Washington, DC: American Psychiatric Association, 1994:296.
Freud S. Psychoanalytic notes upon an autobiographical account of a case of paranoia (dementia paranoides). In: Collected papers, vol. 3. London: Hogarth Press, 1950; originally published in 1911.
Manschreck TC. Delusional (paranoid) disorders. In: Kaplan HI, Sadock BJ, eds. Comprehensive textbook of psychiatry V. Baltimore: Williams & Wilkins, 1989:816.
Pattison EM. Paranoid disorders. In: Hurst JW, ed. Medicine for the practicing physician. 2nd ed. Boston: Butterworths, 1988:27.
Sullivan HS. The paranoid dynamism. In: Perry SW, Gawel ML, Gibbon M, eds. The collected works of Harry Stack Sullivan. New York: WW Norton, 1956:145.

CHAPTER 2–6

Mood Disorders • Depression and Mania

William Boyer, M.D., and Charles B. Nemeroff, M.D., Ph.D.

DEFINITION: DEPRESSION

It is important to distinguish the everyday meaning of the word *depression* from its meaning in clinical medicine. Clinical depression is a syndrome consisting of a relatively sustained disturbance in mood, psychological functions such as memory and concentration, and physical symptoms may include disturbed sleep, appetite, energy level, and sex drive.

DEFINITION: MANIA

Mania is a syndrome that consists of a sustained, abnormal, and distinct elevation of mood (euphoria, often with irritability), extreme and unrealistic confidence, and a generalized acceleration of psychomotor function. The last typically includes a markedly decreased need for sleep, rapid thoughts, and rapid speech.

ETIOLOGY

The etiologies of both depression and mania are unclear. Most affective (mood) disorders, which include depression and mania, are thought to occur in individuals who are genetically predisposed. This is especially true for manic–depressive (bipolar) disorder. The person's life experiences and current stressors also determine who becomes ill. One or more discrete psychological stressors, especially an actual or threatened loss of relationship or status, commonly (but not always) occur before the onset of an affective disorder. In some individuals the stress may be chronic rather than discrete, such as the cumulative effects of parental abuse or neglect.

CRITERIA FOR DIAGNOSIS: DEPRESSION
Suggestive

Common chief complaints of patients in primary care settings with major depressive disorder include the following:

- Pain, including headaches, abdominal pain, and other body aches
- Low energy, excessive tiredness, or a reduced capacity for enjoyment
- A mood of apathy, irritability, or anxiety
- Sexual complaints, including problems with sexual functioning or desire

Definitive

For a diagnosis of major depression according to the official (DSM-IV) nomenclature, several criteria must be met (Table 2–6–1). At least five of the symptoms in the table must be present during the same 2-week period, the symptoms must represent a change from previous functioning, there must be significant distress or impairment, and at least one of the symptoms must be (1) depressed mood or (2) loss of interest or pleasure.

Note that presence or absence of a precipitating stress is *not* mentioned. Although a depressed mood in response to stress is normal, the persistent syndrome of clinical depression is not.

Psychotic depression is a particularly severe form. It is characterized by the presence of delusions that reflect the dramatically poor self-image (e.g., "I am the Antichrist").

CRITERIA FOR DIAGNOSIS: MANIA
Suggestive

Patients with mania may not feel that they are ill and it may be the family that contacts the physician for help. The family may say that the patient is not sleeping, is active all of the time, is spending lots of money, is driving fast, is hypersexual, is impatient, and feels that nothing is wrong.

Definitive

The official diagnostic criteria are listed in Table 2–6–2.

Hypomania ("below mania") is a somewhat less severe state that does not meet the criteria of marked impairment in functioning, need for hospitalization, or psychotic features. It is, however, "an unequivocal change in functioning that is uncharacteristic of the person when not symptomatic."

CLINICAL MANIFESTATIONS: DEPRESSION
Subjective
Symptoms

The subjective symptoms follow from the diagnostic criteria, above. Patients may complain of a depressed mood, but in some anhedonia, or lack of enjoyment, is the prominent mood disturbance. Many patients who complain of chronic anxiety in fact have a depressive disorder.

Many depressed patients present with somatic complaints, which are either excessive for the underlying pathology or for which no pathology can be found. Frequent examples include fatigue, insomnia, headache, and other painful conditions. Missed diagnoses of depression occur most often when patients complain of such organic symptoms and their mood is not addressed.

Past History

The history may disclose previous episodes of treated or untreated depression. Because some patients early in their disorder do not think of themselves as "depressed," it may be helpful to ask whether they have had episodes in which they felt "like this" rather than times in which they felt "depressed." The history usually shows complete recovery between episodes, but about 20% of patients have a continuous, waxing/waning course.

TABLE 2–6–1. AMERICAN PSYCHIATRIC ASSOCIATION CRITERIA FOR DIAGNOSIS OF MAJOR DEPRESSION

(1) Depressed mood most of the day, nearly every day, as indicated by either subjective report (e.g., feels sad or empty) or observation made by others (e.g., appears tearful). Note: In children and adolescents, this can be irritable mood.

(2) Markedly diminished interest or pleasure in all, or almost all, activities most of the day, nearly every day (as indicated by either subjective account or observation made by others).

(3) Significant weight loss (when not dieting) or weight gain (e.g., a change of more than 5% of body weight in a month), or decrease or increase in appetite nearly every day. Note: In children, consider failure to make expected weight gains.

(4) Insomnia or hypersomnia nearly every day.

(5) Psychomotor agitation or retardation nearly every day (observable by others, not merely subjective feelings of restlessness or being slowed down).

(6) Fatigue or loss of energy nearly every day.

(7) Feelings of worthlessness or excessive or inappropriate guilt (which may be delusional) nearly every day (not merely self-reproach or guilt about being sick).

(8) Diminished ability to think or concentrate, or indecisiveness, nearly every day.

(9) Recurrent thoughts of death (not just fear of dying), recurrent suicidal ideation without a specific plan, or a suicide attempt or a specific plan for committing suicide.

Source: Diagnostic and statistical manual of mental disorders. 4th ed. Washington, DC: American Psychiatric Association, 1994. Reproduced with permission.

TABLE 2–6–2. AMERICAN PSYCHIATRIC ASSOCIATION CRITERIA FOR DIAGNOSIS OF MANIA

- A distinct period of abnormally and persistently elevated, expansive, or irritable mood, lasting at least 1 week (or any duration if hospitalization is necessary).
- During the period of mood disturbance, three (or more) of the following symptoms have persisted (four if the mood is only irritable) and have been present to a significant degree:
  (1) Inflated self-esteem or grandiosity.
  (2) Decreased need for sleep (e.g., feels rested after only 3 hours of sleep).
  (3) More talkative than usual or pressure to keep talking.
  (4) Flight of ideas or subjective experience that thoughts are racing.
  (5) Distractibility.
  (6) Increase in goal-directed activity (either socially, at work or school, or sexually) or psychomotor agitation.
  (7) Excessive involvement in pleasurable activities that have a high potential for painful consequences (e.g., engaging in unrestrained buying sprees, sexual indiscretions, or foolish business investments).
- The mood disturbance is sufficiently severe to cause marked impairment in occupational functioning or in usual social activities or relationships with others, or to necessitate hospitalization to prevent harm to self or others, or there are psychotic features.

Source: Diagnostic and statistical manual of mental disorders. 4th ed. Washington, DC: American Psychiatric Association, 1994. Reproduced with permission.

Family History

The family history often discloses one or more relatives with depression and/or alcoholism. One or more family members may have a history of attempted or completed suicide, "nervous breakdown," or "shock therapy."

Objective

Physical Examination

There are no typical abnormalities on physical examination. A distressed mood may be apparent in facial expressions or expressed verbally. Some patients may show uncharacteristic disregard for their appearance or evidence of recent weight loss or gain. Psychomotor retardation or agitation may also be observed.

Routine Laboratory Abnormalities

No routine laboratory abnormalities characterize major depression. Very severely ill patients may show evidence of poor nutrition and even dehydration.

CLINICAL MANIFESTATIONS: MANIA
Subjective

Symptoms

The symptoms of mania are also related to the diagnostic criteria. The patient may feel that nothing is wrong, but admit to an enhanced feeling of well-being, increased sexual interest, racing thoughts, one or more grandiose schemes with universal implications (e.g., fixing the federal deficit, replenishing the ozone layer), and little need for sleep.

Past History

A history of a clinically significant depression in a patient who is currently manic is highly suggestive of bipolar disorder. A history of one or more manic episodes is diagnostic. There may be a history of excessive alcohol or illicit drug use during previous episodes when the patient could not sleep.

Family History

The family history often discloses another member with bipolar or "manic–depressive" disorder. Family members with a history of "nervous breakdowns" requiring hospitalization, treatment with "shock therapy," and reasonably good function between episodes may have bipolar disorder. Before the advent of lithium therapy many bipolar patients were misdiagnosed as schizophrenic.

Objective

Physical Examination

Physical examination is usually normal except for psychomotor acceleration. The patient talks rapidly and excessively, is distractible, and has difficulty sitting still. Vital signs may be mildly elevated.

Routine Laboratory Abnormalities

No characteristic routine laboratory abnormalities are found in mania. There may be a slight leukocytosis, and some patients may show ketonuria and evidence of dehydration. If the patient has been very physically active, creatine phosphokinase may be mildly elevated.

PLANS: DEPRESSION
Diagnostic

Differential Diagnosis

The differential diagnosis includes the following:

Medical Conditions
- Neurologic: stroke, tumor, head injury, infection, inflammation, dementia
- Endocrine: abnormalities of thyroid, parathyroid, or adrenal function; pancreatic tumor

External Substances
- Prescription drugs
- Antihypertensives, narcotics
- Illicit substances
- Alcohol or other sedatives, withdrawal from stimulants

Depression should not be diagnosed immediately after the death of a loved one, *unless* the symptoms persist for more than 2 months or include marked functional impairment, morbid preoccupation with worthlessness, suicidal ideation, psychotic symptoms, or psychomotor retardation.

Diagnostic Options

Several diagnostic methods can be used:

- Mental status examination
- Interviews with family, friends, employer, and/or co-workers
- Psychological testing
- Complete physical examination
- Complete blood count, thyroid and liver functions, electrolytes, sedimentation rate, rapid plasma reagin, urinalysis and urine toxicology, hepatitis antigens, and HIV testing
- Computed tomography or magnetic resonance imaging scan of the head
- Chest x-ray
- Electroencephalogram (sleep deprived with nasopharyngeal leads)
- Ultrasound or computed tomography scan of the abdomen

Approximately one half of depressed patients may fail to show cortisol suppression after a 1-mg dexamethasone suppression test or have an abnormal response on the thyrotropin-releasing hormone stimulation test (Loosen, 1988; Sharma et al., 1988); however, normal results on these tests in no way rules out a major depressive episode.

Recommended Approach

The diagnosis of depression can usually be made by clinical examination with corroborating information from family or friends. The history should include recent changes in drug use (prescription or otherwise) and a general review of systems. A physical examination should be conducted with special attention to the neurologic, cardiopulmonary, and abdominal examinations. Laboratory testing for most patients should include general chemistries with liver functions, blood count, thyroid functions (minimum of thyroid-stimulating hormone and thyroxine), urinalysis, and urine toxicology screen. A chest x-ray, computed tomography or magnetic resonance imaging scan of the brain, electroencephalogram, and HIV screening should be considered in patients presenting in their first or second episode.

Efforts to rule out systemic disease should be greater in late-onset depression (over age 50), both because of the relative rarity of first-episode depression in this age group and the increased risk of serious medical illnesses. Abdominal imaging should be included in the workup of these patients because there is evidence that malignant tumors, especially of the head of the pancreas, can have depression as their sole presenting symptom.

Therapeutic

Therapeutic Options

The therapeutic options for depression can be divided into the following categories:

- Antidepressant medication
- Psychotherapy
  - Individual
    - Short-term (supportive, cognitive–behavioral, interpersonal)
    - Long-term (psychodynamic, psychoanalytic)
  - Group
  - Marital/family

- Electroconvulsive therapy
- Other options
  - Exercise
  - Light therapy

Antidepressant Medication. Currently, 18 drugs that have an official Food and Drug Administration indication for the treatment of depression are marketed in the United States (Table 2–6–3). In addition, clomipramine (Anafranil) and fluvoxamine (Luvox) carry indications for obsessive–compulsive disorder but are widely used around the world as antidepressants.

Psychotherapy. A variety of psychotherapies are also used in the treatment of depression. Supportive psychotherapy is practiced to some extent with virtually all patients and may be very helpful. Two of the most rigorously studied specific psychotherapies are cognitive–behavioral therapy and interpersonal therapy.

Supportive psychotherapy consists of several activities. The establishment and maintenance of a supportive therapeutic relationship in which the doctor or a colleague is available in times of crisis are crucial. Other features include the following:

- Providing an explanation for the patient's symptoms and an acceptable prescription for relief
- Observing for suicidal impulses
- Providing ongoing education and feedback concerning the patient's illness, prognosis, and treatment
- Advising the patient in life issues, including relationships, work, living conditions, and other medical needs
- Assisting the patient in scheduling absences from work or other responsibilities as required
- Discouraging the patient from major life changes that might be predicated on the depression
- Helping to bolster the patient's morale by strengthening expectations of help and hope for the future
- Enlisting the support of others in the patient's social network and supporting them as well, if need be
- Setting realistic, attainable, and tangible goals
- Encouraging the patient to seek new successes, however small, including greater engagement with the outside world (e.g., vocational, social, and religious activities)

Cognitive–behavioral psychotherapy holds that irrational or unrealistic negative beliefs and attitudes toward the self, environment, and future cause or perpetuate depression. Therapy consists of identifying and modifying these beliefs.

Interpersonal therapy seeks to recognize and explore events that involve interpersonal losses, role disputes and transitions, social isolation, or deficits in social skills. Important activities include mourning losses, resolving role disputes or transitions, and overcoming deficits in social skills. ("Practice Guideline for Major," 1993).

Electroconvulsive Therapy. Modern electroconvulsive therapy is nothing like the sadistic procedure often portrayed in the media. The patient is anesthetized with a short-acting general anesthetic and paralyzed (to prevent injury) with a muscle blocker. Electroconvulsive therapy is most often employed in patients with psychotic, life-threatening, or treatment-resistant depression.

Recommended Approach

The mainstays of treatment are antidepressant medication and psychotherapy. With the large number of antidepressants available, the choice of agent may be confusing. There is no conclusive evidence that any antidepressant is faster acting or significantly more effective than the others. Therefore, the guiding principles in choosing an antidepressant include side effects, danger of interaction with alcohol or other drugs, potential interaction with underlying illnesses, toxicity in overdose, and dosing schedules.

In general, second-generation antidepressants have an advantage in each of these areas. These include the selective serotonin reuptake inhibitors, trazodone, bupropion, venlafaxine, and the soon-to-be-released nefazodone. Bupropion, nefazodone, and venlafaxine, however, require divided dosing. A sustained-release form of bupropion is likely to be released in the near future.

Most depressed patients should be started on one of the newer agents, usually one of the selective serotonin reuptake inhibitors, because of their advantages in terms of side effects, lack of toxicity in overdose, and minimal drug–drug and drug–disease interactions. The patient can usually start with an average therapeutic dose (Table 2–6–1). Exceptions include the very old or very young, the physically infirm, and patients with panic attacks. These patients should be started on one-quarter to one-half the usual therapeutic dose, which should be increased over the course of 1 to 2 weeks depending on the patient's tolerance for and response to treatment. Some patients do not require an average therapeutic dose to respond fully, but the routine use of low doses should be discouraged.

Although standard psychiatric texts often advocate waiting 6 to 8 weeks before judging a treatment trial to be a failure, some improvement is usually seen by week 3 and may occur within the first week (Boyer and Feighner, 1994). An early sign of improvement is often the patient's report that their life stresses no longer feel completely overwhelming and that their patience is improved. A patient's spouse sometimes notices improvement before the patient.

The primary physician is well situated to practice supportive psychotherapy as outlined above. The need to provide the patient information, reassurance and a contact point in case of crisis cannot be overstated.

The decision to modify the treatment plan depends on whether the depression is improving, stable, or deteriorating. Improvement argues for a longer trial of the same agent, perhaps as long as 8 to 12 weeks. A stable condition (i.e., no improvement) suggests a change by 4 to 6 weeks. A reasonable first modification of antidepressant treatment is to increase the dose to the higher end of the therapeutic range. The dosage increase may induce a response and the risks of increased dosage are minimal, provided the patient has tolerated it well to that point.

Deterioration argues for more aggressive treatment, including referral to a psychiatrist. Consultation with or referral to a mental health specialist is also indicated for patients who fail to respond fully to one or two trials of medication, for those who are at special risk for suicide (see Chapter 2–3), for those suffering very severe psychotic or bipolar depression, and for patients who require hospitalization ("Depression in Primary Care," 1993).

TABLE 2–6–3. FDA-APPROVED ANTIDEPRESSANTS

Classification	Generic Name	Brand Name	Usual Minimum–Maximum Daily Therapeutic Dose
Tricyclics	Doxepin	Sinequan, Adapin	100–300
	Amitriptyline	Elavil, Endep	100–300
	Imipramine	Tofranil	100–300*
	Desipramine	Norpramin, Pertofrane	100–300
	Nortriptyline	Pamelor, Aventyl	75–150†
	Trimipramine	Surmontil	150–300
	Protriptyline	Vivactil	10–40
Tetracyclics	Maprotiline	Ludiomil	75–225
	Amoxapine	Asendin	100–300
Triazolopyridine	Trazodone	Desyrel	200–400
	Nefazodone	Serzone	200–500
Selective serotonin reuptake inhibitors	Fluoxetine	Prozac	20–80
	Sertraline	Zoloft	50–200
	Paroxetine	Paxil	20–50
Monoamine oxidase inhibitors	Phenelzine	Nardil	45–90
	Tranylcypromine	Parnate	30–60
Phenylaminoketones	Bupropion	Wellbutrin	225–450
	Venlafaxine	Effexor	75–375

*Usual therapeutic blood level, >225 ng/mL imipramine + desipramine.
†Usual therapeutic blood level, 50–150 ng/mL.

PLANS: MANIA

Diagnostic

Differential Diagnosis

A manic episode must be distinguished from a mood disorder secondary to a medical condition. Late onset of a first manic episode (e.g., after age 50 years) is relatively uncommon and should alert the clinician to the possibility of a medical problem or substance abuse disorder. Manic symptoms may be precipitated by antidepressant treatment or by drugs of abuse, especially psychostimulants. It is important to note that abuse of sedatives, including alcohol, is not unusual among bipolar patients and may be an attempt at self-medication.

Hyperthyroidism or Cushing's disease may present with psychomotor agitation. Multiple sclerosis can, at times, present with euphoria. Patients with central nervous system injury, tumors, and atypical seizure disorders rarely present with mania, but these conditions must be ruled out.

Diagnostic Options

Several diagnostic methods are available:

- Mental status examination
- Interviews with family, friends, employer, and/or co-workers
- Psychological testing
- Complete physical examination
- Complete blood count, thyroid and liver functions, electrolytes, sedimentation rate, rapid plasma reagin, urinalysis and urine toxicology, hepatitis antigens, and HIV testing
- Computed tomography or magnetic resonance imaging scan of the head
- Chest x-ray
- Electroencephalogram (sleep deprived with nasopharyngeal leads)

Recommended Approach

The signs and symptoms of a manic episode are usually easy to see in the clinical examination. Family members or close acquaintances can usually corroborate the history.

Physical examination and laboratory tests should center on ruling out other causes of psychomotor acceleration and euphoria. Appropriate tests would include general chemistries and blood count, thyroid evaluation, and urine toxicology. The physician should also consider tests to rule out neurologic disorders, such as an electroencephalogram or a computed tomography or magnetic resonance imaging scan of the head.

Therapeutic

Therapeutic Options

The therapeutic options for mania include the following:

- Mood-stabilizing medication (lithium, valproic acid, carbamazepine)
- Antipsychotic medication (haloperidol, trifluoperazine, perphenazine)
- Benzodiazepines (clonazepam, lorazepam)
- Electroconvulsive therapy

Recommended Approach

Like depression, the approach to mania should be divided into phases. The goals of the acute phase should be to ensure the patient's safety. Almost all patients with fully developed mania require hospitalization on a psychiatric unit. This will help prevent dehydration and exhaustion as well as protect the patient from the consequences of his or her impaired judgment (e.g., bankruptcy, disruption of relationships).

Lithium remains the mainstay of treatment. The dose is adjusted to attain a serum level of approximately 0.8 to 1.2 mEq/L 12 hours following the last dose. Patients may require treatment with adjunctive medications during the initial phase, because significant clinical response to lithium typically takes several days or longer. These adjunctive medications may include a high-potency antipsychotic such as haloperidol (5–20 mg/d) and/or a benzodiazepine such as clonazepam (2–6 mg/d). The dosage of these adjunctive medications may need to be

titrated above or below these suggested ranges to help the patient sleep and diminish agitation.

Patients who do not adequately respond to lithium, perhaps 30% of cases, may respond to one of the other mood stabilizers, valproic acid or carbamazepine. Valproic acid is as effective as lithium in the treatment of acute mania and was recently approved by the Food and Drug Administration for this indication. Dosage of either valproic acid or carbamazepine is typically adjusted to attain blood levels similar to those for treatment of seizures. In severe cases a second mood stabilizer is added to lithium. In less severe cases it is used instead of lithium. Treatment-refractory patients or those at risk of severe exhaustion usually respond to a course of electroconvulsive therapy.

FOLLOW-UP: DEPRESSION

The patient should understand that depression is an illness prone to relapse and recurrence. It is vital to continue the antidepressant medication for a period following recovery. The optimum length of continuation treatment varies from one individual to another. Some patients require very long-term treatment. The World Health Organization recommends that prophylaxis be started in all patients who have had more than one severe episode and that the medication be reviewed after 2 years without depression ("Consensus Statement: WHO Mental," 1989). Other criteria include a first-degree relative with bipolar disorder or recurrent major depression, a history of recurrence within 1 year of completing treatment, a first episode that occurred early in life (before 20 years of age), or occurrence of two episodes within the past 3 years that were severe, sudden, or life-threatening.

Although maintenance psychotherapy has not been shown to prevent recurrence, it may help delay the onset of a future episode. In selected situations it can be especially useful, for example, for women who want to become pregnant and bear a child in a drug-free condition; however, women whose maintenance antidepressant treatment was discontinued during pregnancy appear to be particularly at risk for recurrence of depression; such individuals should have their medications restored after delivery, in the absence of a contraindication.

Discontinuation studies suggest that patients who are still slightly symptomatic are at higher risk of relapse than those who are not. The patient should also be discouraged from discontinuing medication around the time of a major life change, such as marriage or a new job. Discontinuation of all antidepressants should be gradual, over a course of at least a few weeks. The physician should review with the patient his or her experience with depression, to be better able to identify a recurrence as quickly as possible. Office visits should again be somewhat more frequent for the first few months after discontinuation.

FOLLOW-UP: MANIA

The necessity of maintenance treatment is well established in bipolar disorder. Patients should be maintained indefinitely on a dose of their mood-stabilizing medication sufficient to produce a therapeutic blood level. In most individuals this prophylactic treatment reduces, but does not eliminate, clinically significant episodes of depression or mania. Antidepressant treatment of depression in bipolar patients can be complicated by induction of mania or hypomania. Therefore, bipolar patients who require antidepressant treatment must be maintained on their mood-stabilizing medication and be followed carefully for early signs of hypomania or mania. These may include a distinct upturn in mood or insomnia without fatigue over the course of a few days. Consultation should be considered for these patients.

Hypomania or mania occurring in the course of mood stabilizer treatment should be rapidly and aggressively treated in the hopes of aborting a more serious attack. Antidepressants, if currently prescribed, must be rapidly discontinued. A blood level of lithium or other mood stabilizer should be determined and the dose adjusted, if necessary. The need for medication compliance should be reviewed with the patient. A high priority is to help the patient sleep, as sustained insominia may convert hypomania to full mania (Kasper and Wehr, 1992). Psychiatric consultation should be obtained in most cases.

DISCUSSION

Prevalence and Incidence

Depression

Studies of the incidence and prevalence of major depressive disorder have reported a wide range of values. The point prevalence of major depressive disorder in adults in community samples has varied from 5 to 9% for women and from 2 to 3% for men. The lifetime risk for major depressive disorder in community samples has varied from 10 to 25% for women and from 5 to 12% for men. The risk of developing major depressive disorder appears to be unrelated to ethnicity, education, income, or marital status (*Diagnostic and Statistical Manual,* 1994).

Mania

The lifetime prevalence of bipolar I disorder in community samples has varied from 0.4 to 1.6%. Community studies suggest a lifetime prevalence of bipolar II disorder of approximately 0.5% (*Diagnostic and Statistical Manual,* 1994).

Related Basic Science

Major depressive disorder is 1.5 to 3 times more common among first-degree biological relatives of persons with this disorder than among the general population. There is evidence for an increased risk of alcohol dependence in adult first-degree biological relatives, and there may be an increased incidence of attention deficit/hyperactivity disorder in the children of adults with this disorder.

First-degree biological relatives of individuals with bipolar I disorder have elevated rates of bipolar I disorder (4–24%), bipolar II disorder (1–5%), and major depressive disorder (4–24%). Twin and adoption studies provide strong evidence of a genetic influence for bipolar I disorder (*Diagnostic and Statistical Manual,* 1994).

Natural History and Its Modification with Treatment

Depression

As with many other chronic illnesses, the best predictor of the course of depressive illness is the patient's own history. Patients who have had previous episodes of depression and more severe depressive episodes face a high (>50%) chance of recurrence (Giles et al., 1989; Coryell et al., 1991; Maj et al., 1992; Winokur et al., 1993). Prophylactic antidepressant medication reduces the chance of recurrence from two to three (Kupfer 1991; Maj et al., 1992; Montgomery and Montgomery, 1992).

Mania

The recurrent nature of bipolar disorder is even better established than that of unipolar depression. Goodwin and Jamison (1990) reviewed 10 placebo-controlled maintenance studies of lithium in bipolar illness between 1970 and 1978. The studies ranged from 5 to 30 months in duration. Placebo treatment was associated with an average relapse rate of 81%, which was more than twice the average relapse rate on lithium, 34%.

Prevention

Individuals who have had one or more episodes of depression and mania may be offered genetic counseling concerning the risk of passing their illness onto their children. Research into "at risk" children of affectively disordered parents is being conducted, but there are currently no paradigms for primary prevention of depression and mania. The only practical efforts at prevention at present are those, already described, aimed at prophylaxis of future episodes in individuals who have had one or more previous episodes.

Cost Containment

One recurrent theme in economic studies of psychiatric treatment is that the most effective treatment is also the most *cost*-effective. Second-generation antidepressants, such as the selective serotonin reuptake inhibitors, are considerably more expensive than tricyclic antidepressants on a per-pill basis, but appear to cost less on a per-patient basis primarily because of improved compliance and less risk of underdosing. These factors lead, in turn, to a higher success rate, fewer recurrences, less hospitalization, and fewer physician visits.

Lithium, too has been shown to be an effective means of cost containment. Ten years after its introduction into the United States, the use of lithium as a treatment for bipolar disorder was conservatively estimated to have saved $2.88 billion and resulted in a $1.28 billion gain in production (Reifman and Wyatt, 1980).

REFERENCES

Boyer WF, Feighner JP. Clinical significance of early non-response in depressed patients. Depression 1994;2:32.

Consensus statement: WHO Mental Health Collaborating Centres. J Affect Disord 1989;17:197.

Coryell W, Endicott J, Keller MB. Predictors of relapse into major depressive disorder in a nonclinical population. Am J Psychiatry 1991;148:1353.

Depression in primary care. JAMA 1993;270:172.

Diagnostic and statistical manual of mental disorders. 4th ed. Washington, DC: American Psychiatric Association, 1994.

Giles DE, Jarrett RB, Biggs MM, et al. Clinical predictors of recurrence in depression. Am J Psychiatry 1989;146:764.

Goodwin FK, Jamison KR. Manic–depressive illness. New York: Oxford University Press, 1990.

Kasper S, Wehr TA. The role of sleep and wakefulness in the genesis of depression and mania. Encephale 1992;18:45.

Kupfer DJ. Long-term treatment of depression. J Clin Psychiatry 1991;52 (suppl.):28.

Loosen PT. TRH: Behavioral and endocrine effects in man. Prog Neuropsychopharmacol Biol Psychiatry 1988;12:587.

Maj M, Veltro F, Pirozzi R, et al. Pattern of recurrence of illness after recovery from an episode of major depression: A prospective study. Am J Psychiatry 1992;149:795.

Montgomery SA, Montgomery DB. Prophylactic treatment in recurrent unipolar depression. In: Montgomery SA, Rouillon F, eds. Long-term treatment of depression. Chichester: John Wiley and Sons, 1992:53.

Practice guideline for major depressive disorder in adults. Am J Psychiatry 1993;150(suppl. 1):1.

Reifman A, Wyatt RJ. Lithium: A brake in the rising cost of mental illness. Arch Gen Psychiatry 1980;37:385.

Sharma RP, Pandey GN, Janicak PG, et al. The effect of diagnosis and age on the DST: A metaanalytic approach. Biol Psychiatry 1988;24:555.

Winokur G, Coryell W, Keller M, et al. A prospective follow-up of patients with bipolar and primary unipolar affective disorder. Arch Gen Psychiatry 1993;50:457.

Anxiety Disorders

Philip T. Ninan, M.D.

DEFINITION

The anxiety disorders are a group of major psychiatric disorders in which the predominant symptom is pathologic anxiety. The diagnosis is established by the clinical presentation of subjective emotional anxiety and/or somatic manifestations, within the framework of specific clustering of symptoms seen in the different anxiety disorders. Objective evidence of anxiety may or may not be present. Significant distress and/or dysfunction must be present for the diagnosis of an anxiety disorder.

ETIOLOGY

The etiology of anxiety disorders, like most psychiatric disorders, is largely unknown. Familial aggregation is often present in anxiety disorders. Twin studies suggest the heritability of various anxiety disorders is modest, generally around 30%, with environmental factors being largely responsible for the remainder.

CRITERIA FOR DIAGNOSIS

Suggestive

The symptoms of an anxiety disorder include excessive anxiety which can be described as worry, tension, nervousness, fear, and so on. Many patients with anxiety disorders present with somatic complaints. Persistent somatic complaints that are physiologically inconsistent or lack objective validation should raise the suspicion of an anxiety disorder. These symptoms must cause significant distress and/or dysfunction to be labeled an anxiety disorder. Presentation of certain symptom clusters (e.g., phobias, compulsive rituals) is also suggestive of the diagnosis. Objective signs of anxiety include facial and bodily expressions of nervousness, and physiologic manifestations of autonomic arousal (e.g., tachycardia, tachypnea).

Definitive

Diagnostic confirmation in psychiatry is limited by the lack of validating tests. Further evidence supporting the diagnosis of an anxiety disorder would include the longitudinal course of symptoms, a positive family history, and appropriate treatment response.

CLINICAL MANIFESTATIONS

Subjective

Generalized anxiety disorder is characterized by excessive and pathologic worry over a number of routine matters lasting for at least 6 months. The worry can manifest as somatic symptoms including muscle tension, dry mouth, cold and clammy hands, and trouble swallowing. Generalized anxiety disorder can be associated with tension, fatigue, difficulty concentrating, irritability, and insomnia. Patients must have significant distress or impairment in social, occupational, or other areas to be given the diagnosis.

Panic disorder is characterized by unexpected attacks of intense anxiety called *panic attacks*. Panic attacks are characterized by a rapid crescendo of anxiety which peaks relatively quickly. The panic attacks are associated with an intense fear of death, feelings of unreality, fear of losing control, and a need to flee. Somatic symptoms seen in panic attacks include chest pain, palpitations, smothering or choking sensations associated with hyperventilation, dizziness, and tingling sensations. The panic attacks can occur in clusters and are associated with the development of anticipatory anxiety and avoidance of situations where the panic attacks are more likely (phobias). The phobias can involve several situations, including driving, crowded or open spaces, closed spaces like elevators, and heights. If the avoidance behavior is

extensive or develops into a fear of being alone, with resulting constriction of activities, the diagnosis of *agoraphobia* is given. Twenty percent of patients with panic disorder have made suicidal attempts, pointing to the severity and morbidity associated with the illness.

Social phobia is characterized by an excessive fear of being the focus of attention in social or performance situations, leading to avoidance or endurance of such situations with intense anxiety. The patient recognizes the anxiety as unreasonable and excessive. The diagnosis of social phobia requires significant distress or impairment of normal functioning.

Specific phobia is characterized by intense anxiety or avoidance of a specific situation, entity, or object, such as heights, animals, or blood. This is in contrast to social phobia, where the fear is scrutiny by others, or panic disorder, where the fear is of panic attacks.

Obsessive–compulsive disorder is characterized by obsessional ideas, images, or impulses that intrude into an individual's mind much against their will and is associated with anxiety. Obsessional ideas include irrational fears of contamination with dirt or germs (including HIV infections), fear of harming someone, distressing sexual or religious ideas, and desire to hoard or have exactness and symmetry. Compulsions are rituals that are performed to reduce the anxiety associated with obsessions. Common compulsions include repetitive cleaning, checking, counting, hoarding, and mental rituals that might not be behaviorally obvious. Mental rituals can include reviewing, list making, recreating a mental image to neutralize a thought, and counting (Table 2–7–1).

Posttraumatic stress disorder results from life–threatening stressful events that cause episodic reexperiencing of the trauma in the form of intrusive recollections, flashbacks, or recurrent nightmares. This is associated with numbing of emotional responses, excessive autonomic arousal, and survival guilt. The onset of the disorder can be immediately following the trauma or it can be delayed for a considerable period, sometimes years. The disorder can be seen at any age, including in childhood. If the symptoms start immediately after the traumatic event and last less than a month, the label of *acute stress disorder* is given.

Anxiety disorder caused by a general medical condition is pathologic anxiety resulting from the direct physiologic effects of a general medical condition, such as endocrine (e.g., hyperthyroidism), cardiovascular, and respiratory conditions.

Substance-induced anxiety disorder is the presentation of pathologic anxiety resulting from the direct physiologic effects of a substance (e.g., drug of abuse, medication).

Objective

Physical Examination

Patients with an anxiety disorder do not necessarily have any physically overt manifestations of their anxiety. Intense anxiety may evince autonomic arousal such as elevations in heart rate, blood pressure, and res-

TABLE 2–7–1. COMMON OBSESSIONS AND COMPULSIONS

Obsessions	Compulsions
Contamination	Checking
Doubt	Cleaning/washing
Aggression	Repeating
Sexual	Counting
Hoarding/saving	Ordering/arranging
Religious	Hoarding/collecting
Exactness, symmetry	Mental
Somatic	

piration; increased perspiration; and fine tremors. The absence of such symptoms, however, does not rule out an anxiety disorder.

Panic disorder is, at times, associated with mitral valve prolapse. In the presence of a click and systolic murmur at the apex of the heart, a two-dimensional echocardiogram may be considered for the diagnosis. The significance of the association between panic disorder and mitral valve prolapse is unclear. In some patients with panic disorder, mitral valve prolapse might be a functional state caused by hemodynamic factors that regress when the panic attacks are under control. True comorbid mitral valve prolapse should be treated appropriately, including the use of prophylactic antibiotics during medical and dental procedures.

Obsessive–compulsive disorder can be associated with Tourette's syndrome, as well as with motor tics, both chronic and transient. About 5 to 7% of patients with obsessive–compulsive disorder also meet criteria for Tourette's syndrome and about 50 to 70% of patients with Tourette's syndrome have obsessive–compulsive symptoms. Chronic multiple motor tics and obsessive–convulsive disorder might be the result of incomplete penetrance of a gene that is associated with Tourette's syndrome.

Routine Laboratory Abnormalities

Routine laboratory tests such as chest x-ray, electrocardiogram, urinalysis, hemogram, SMA 18, and thyroid studies are generally normal in patients with anxiety disorders.

PLANS
Diagnostic
Differential Diagnosis

The anxiety disorders are diagnosed predominantly from the patient's subjective report and the constellation of specific symptom clusters. Lack of consistent objective signs and confirmatory laboratory tests do not decrease the reliability of the diagnosis but make the evaluation more difficult. Other medical conditions that could present as anxiety, such as thyroid abnormalities and pheochromocytoma, should be routinely ruled out (Table 2–7–2).

TABLE 2–7–2. DIFFERENTIAL DIAGNOSIS OF ANXIETY DISORDERS

Endocrine
    Hyperthyroidism
    Hypothyroidism
    Hyperparathyroidism
    Pheochromocytoma
    Hypoglycemia
    Hyperadrenocorticism
Cardiovascular
    Mitral valve prolapse
    Cardiac arrythmia
    Coronary insufficiency
    Pulmonary embolus
Respiratory
    Chronic obstructive pulmonary disease
    Pneumonia
    Hyperventilation
Metabolic
    Vitamin B_{12} deficiency
    Porphyria
Neurologic
    Neoplasms
    Vestibular dysfunction
    Encephalitis
    Complex partial seizures
    Sympathomimetic toxicity
Psychiatric
    Symptoms of withdrawal from alcohol and other substances
    Drug abuse and dependence
    Affective disorders

Diagnostic Options and Recommended Approach

Every clinician should be aware of the high incidence of anxiety disorders. A thorough history is the critical step in making the diagnosis of an anxiety disorder. If routine physical examination and laboratory tests do not show any evidence of an abnormality, or any abnormality discovered is minor and not adequate to explain the clinical symptomatology, an anxiety disorder diagnosis should be considered. The use of additional diagnostic tests should be based on need and clinical judgment. Response to treatment can provide indirect confirmation of an anxiety disorder.

Therapeutic
Therapeutic Options

The therapeutic approaches to the treatment of anxiety disorders include psychotherapy, pharmacologic treatment, and, rarely, neurosurgery.

Psychotherapy. Can be divided into supportive counseling, cognitive behavior therapy, and the insight–oriented psychoanalytic form of psychotherapy. The aim of *supportive counseling* is to provide education about the nature of the illness, reassurance, and emotional support. Education about the illness includes describing its varying presentations, characteristics, age of onset, natural course, and treatment response. Reassurance that there is nothing significantly abnormal from a general medical perspective is important. Emotional support through individual sessions or through support groups of other patients suffering from the same condition can be of valuable help.

The clinician should be aware that subtle negative attitudes are common responses to anxiety disorders among the lay public, family members, and clinicians who misunderstand an anxiety disorder as a "weakness." Providing an open channel for patients to discuss their feelings about others' responses to their illness is important. *Cognitive and behavioral techniques* are often combined and have been shown to be effective in each of the anxiety disorders. Cognitive therapy is based on the concept that appraisal of a situation is distorted by past experiences and faulty cognitive assumptions leading to anxiety and depression. Cognitive therapy is a structured, directive, and time-limited therapy (i.e., problem-oriented). Exploration of illogical cognitive assumptions through images and automatic thoughts provides a framework for restructuring the appraisal of situations and correcting distortions of reality. This leads to behavioral and emotional modification. Thus, phobias are defined as a fear of the anxiety response itself, and cognitive modification reduces the fear of panic attacks.

Behavior therapy focuses on behaviors and the factors that maintain them. Behavior therapy uses the principles of learning theory (classic and operant conditioning, social learning) to explain the development of psychopathology such as phobias and obsessive–compulsive symptoms. Treatment techniques use the relaxation response induced by the progressive tensing and relaxing of various voluntary muscles to approach the behavioral symptoms. *Systematic desensitization* uses a relaxation response in a series of hierarchically graded steps that induce anxiety moving from imagery to in vivo challenges. *Flooding* uses prolonged in vivo exposure to intense anxiety, inducing stimuli that initially increase anxiety but are followed by extinction. *Implosion* is flooding using imagery.

Exposure to phobic situations is often essential for successful treatment of avoidance behavior. The presence of continued unexpected panic attacks and depressive symptomatology can limit successful treatment of phobic disorders with cognitive–behavioral strategies.

In treating obsessive–convulsive disorder, cognitive–behavioral therapy uses *exposure and response prevention* techniques to prevent the performance of rituals following exposure. On exposure, there is an initial surge of anxiety followed by habituation and extinction. Thus, the reinforcing cycle of the rituals is broken. Response prevention techniques have a remarkable degree of success in patients who are willing to go through the rigors of treatment and are compliant. Cognitive techniques aimed at thought stopping for obsessions have shown some degree of success.

The advantages of cognitive–behavioral therapy are considerable efficacy and lack of significant side effects (excepting a transient increase in anxiety). Follow-up studies suggest that long-term maintenance of benefits is likely even after treatment is discontinued.

The insight-oriented psychoanalytic form of psychotherapy is based on the Freudian concept that anxiety is a signal from the ego that unacceptable repressed conflicts are threatening to rise to the conscious level. The ego uses anxiety to marshal defense mechanism to aid in continuing the repression. The disturbing conflicts are reflections of infantile wishes and early developmental experiences that shape the patient's character and neurotic symptoms. Through free association and exploration of resistance, defenses, and the transference neurosis, the nuclear conflict is brought into awareness by clarification and interpretation. Conscious awareness and working through are followed by symptom resolution. The neurotic conflicts associated with phobias and obsessive–compulsive disorder were thought to be related to oedipal conflicts, though psychoanalytic treatments have been less than successful in controlling the symptoms of these disorders.

Psychoanalytic views on posttraumatic stress disorder see the catastophic trauma as being internalized and repeated within the personality structure in an attempt to gain psychic control. A cathartic revisitation of the trauma within the framework of a supportive relationship potentially allows some healing.

Pharmacologic Treatment. The pharmacologic agents used in the treatment of anxiety disorders can be classified into the following categories:

- Benzodiazepines
- Azapirones
- Antidepressants
- Beta-adrenergic blockers
- Other agents

Benzodiazepines such as diazepam (Valium) have essentially replaced other sedative–hypnotic compounds (e.g., barbiturates, meprobamate) because of their remarkable efficacy and excellent therapeutic index (Table 2–7–3). The pharmacologic properties of benzodiazepines include reduction of anxiety, sedation, muscle relaxation, and anticonvulsant and amnestic effects. Their effect on anxiety is palliative.

Studies suggest that three quarters of patients with generalized anxiety disorder respond moderately or better to benzodiazepines. There is no evidence suggesting superiority of one benzodiazepine over another in this disorder.

High-potency benzodiazepines (e.g., alprazolam [Xanax], clonazepam [Klonopin], and lorazepam [Ativan]) have great affinity for the benzodiazepine receptor. These benzodiazepines have been particularly effective in controlling panic attacks and anticipatory anxiety in panic disorder. Whether their effectiveness is merely quantitatively or also

qualitatively different from that of low-potency benzodiazepines is unclear. Relapse rates are high on discontinuation of benzodiazepine therapy in panic disorder, partly because of benzodiazepine withdrawal symptoms, which are difficult to distinguish from anxiety and panic.

The length of action of a benzodiazepine is determined by a number of factors including elimination half-life, volume of distribution, and lipophilicity. The elimination half-life of a benzodiazepine reflects the rate of metabolism and excretion of the drug. Accumulation of the benzodiazepine occurs from one dose to another if the drug has a long half-life. Ultrashort-acting benzodiazepines do not accumulate. Those with intermediate half-lives (5–24 hours) accumulate to some degree, but reach a steady-state level relatively quickly and are eliminated rapidly when the medication is discontinued. Long-acting benzodiazepines take a longer time to reach steady-state levels, are removed more slowly, and cause greater side effects (e.g., sedation), but reduce the likelihood and intensity of withdrawal symptoms when discontinued. High lipid solubility results in faster absorption, greater distribution in tissues, and faster entrance and exit from brain sites of action. Diazepam (Valium), midazolam (Versed), and flurazepam (Dalmane) have high lipid solubility.

Tolerance for the sedating effects of benzodiazepines develops at moderate doses, but tolerance does not seem to develop for anxiolytic effects. Common side effects include sedation, impaired psychomotor performance, and impaired learning of new information. Transient global anterograde amnesia has been reported with high-potency benzodiazepines such as triazolam (Halcion), especially when combined with alcohol. The abuse potential for benzodiazepines does not appear prominent in patients who do not abuse alcohol or other substances.

Because of their capacity to cause dependence if used continuously for more than a few weeks at a time, benzodiazepines are a mixed blessing in the treatment of anxiety disorders. In the disorders in which the anxiety is episodic, episodic use of benzodiazepines may effectively control the symptoms. In situations in which anxiety is not episodic, benzodiazepines may control the symptoms, but their therapeutic benefits should be balanced against their capacity to cause dependence. Patients which otherwise untreatable and chronic anxiety may require long-term treatment with benzodiazepines despite the potential for dependence.

Benzodiazepines not only are effective in pathologic anxiety, but also have a calming effect in nonpathologic states ("normal" anxiety). There is a risk that patients in benzodiazepines come to expect normality as experiencing not only an absence of pathologic anxiety but also a pharmacologically induced calmness. Subsequent to the discontinuation of the benzodiazepine, they are at risk for interpreting any anxiety as being pathologic.

Buspirone (BuSpar) is an anxiolytic medication chemically belonging to the *azapirone class* and is a partial agonist of the 5-hydroxytryptamine 1A receptor. It is as effective in the treatment of generalized anxiety disorder as benzodiazepines. Preliminary data suggest that it is not effective in controlling unexpected panic attacks. Buspirone has a 1- to 2-week delay in the onset of its therapeutic action. The starting dose is 15 to 30 mg daily. Doses above 70 mg tend to cause jitteriness and dysphoria. It does not cause sedation, psychomotor impairment, physical dependence, or withdrawal symptoms. It does not have abuse potential. Patients taking buspirone do not develop cross-tolerance for alcohol or benzodiazepines; therefore, buspirone is not effective in the treatment of withdrawal from these substances. It is generally well tolerated, so that relatively few people have side effects. Side effects, when they do occur, include nausea, dizziness, headaches, and nervousness.

Antidepressants, though traditionally thought of as specific for the treatment of depression, are also effective in all of the anxiety disorders evaluated. Antidepressants used in the management of anxiety disorders come in three categories: cyclic antidepressants, serotonin transport inhibitors, and monoamine oxidase inhibitors (Table 2–7–4).

Cyclic antidepressants are commonly used drugs. Imipramine (Tofranil) is the prototypic tricyclic antidepressant. It is effective in controlling panic attacks seen in patients with panic disorder, but it does not have any direct effects on anticipatory anxiety or phobic avoidance behavior. The dose of imipramine needed to control panic attacks in the average nonelderly adult is between 150 and 300 mg

TABLE 2–7–3. CLASSIFICATION OF BENZODIAZEPINES

Generic Name	Brand Name	Usual Dose (mg)
Long-acting		
Chlorazepate	Tranxene	15–60
Chlordiazepoxide	Librium	15–100
Clonazepam	Klonopin	0.5–4
Diazepam	Valium	4–40
Estazolam	Prosom	0.5–2
Flurazepam	Dalmane	15–30
Halazepam	Paxipam	40–160
Prazepam	Centrax	20–40
Quazepam	Doral	7.5–15
Intermediate-acting		
Alprazolam	Xanax	0.5–40
Lorazepam	Ativan	1.5–6
Oxazepam	Serax	30–120
Temazepam	Restoril	15–30
Ultrashort-acting		
Triazolam	Halcion	0.125–0.5
Midazolam	Versed	Injectable

TABLE 2–7–4. CLASSIFICATION OF ANTIDEPRESSANTS

Generic Name	Brand Name	Inital Dose (mg)	Usual Dose (mg)
Serotonin Transport Inhibitors			
Fluoxetine	Prozac	10–20	10–80
Fluvoxamine	Luvox	25–50	100–300
Nefazodone	Serzone	50–100	200–500
Paroxetine	Paxil	10–20	20–50
Sertraline	Zoloft	25–50	75–200
Venlafaxine	Effexor	12.5–50	50–375
Cyclic Antidepressants			
Amitriptyline	Elavil	10–50	150–300
Amoxapine	Asendin	25–50	150–450
Clomipramine	Anafranil*	25–50	150–250
Desipramine	Norpramin	10–25	100–250
Doxepin	Sinequan, Adapin	10–25	150–300
Imipramine	Tofranil	10–50	150–300
Maprotiline	Ludiomil	25–50	150–200
Nortriptyline	Pamelor	10–25	75–125
Protriptyline	Vivactil	5–10	15–60
Trimipramine	Surmontil	25–50	150–300
Monoamine Oxidase Inhibitors			
Phenelzine	Nardil	15	45–90
Tranylcypromine	Parnate	10	30–50
Other			
Trazadone	Desyrel	25–50	150–300
Buproprion	Wellbutrin	75–100	300–450

*Also a serotonin transport inhibitor.

daily, though some patients respond at lower doses. The response is gradual over a period of weeks. About two thirds of the patients have at least a moderate response. Clinical experience has indicated that other tricyclic antidepressants are equally effective for panic disorder.

In panic disorder, about one third of the patients feel overstimulated on initiating cyclic antidepressant therapy, with feelings of jitteriness, irritability, and insomnia often associated with an exacerbation of the anxiety symptoms. To overcome this problem cyclic antidepressant should be initiated at the lowest dose possible in panic disorder, and the dose built up to a therapeutic range gradually. Benzodiazepines can also be used on a short-term basis to cover this initial period of symptom exacerbation. About one third of patients discontinue cyclic antidepressants because of their inability to tolerate side effects.

Cyclic antidepressants can cause anticholinergic side effects such as dryness of the mouth and other mucosal surfaces, blurred vision, tachycardia, constipation, and urinary hesitancy. Because of these side effects, cyclic antidepressants should not be used in patients with narrow-angle glaucoma or urinary retention. Other side effects are postural hypotension, which is particularly dangerous in the elderly; carbohydrate craving, which can result in significant weight gain; excessive perspiration; and sexual dysfunction. Cyclic antidepressants have a quinidine-like effect on the cardiac conduction system and, therefore, should be used with caution in patients with conduction abnormalities. Cyclic antidepressants can lower the seizure threshold, particularly at higher doses. Patients should be warned that cyclic antidepressants enhance the central nervous system effects of alcohol. Side effects of cyclic antidepressants often limit the capacity to achieve a therapeutic dose to get optimal benefits, resulting in residual symptomatology. Plasma measurements of tricyclic antidepressants are possible and should be performed in selected situations as needed.

With growing evidence that panic disorder is an episodic disorder with a chronic course, long-term management of the disorder is gaining increasing attention. A significant number of patients need to be continued indefinitely on their medication for effective control, just as in the management of conditions like hypertension.

Serotonin transport inhibitors are effective in controlling symptoms of anxiety in all of the anxiety disorders evaluated. A significant advantage of serotonin transport inhibitors is their more benign side effect profile, which makes them more acceptable to patients compared with other classes of antidepressants. They can be classified into *nonselective serotonin transport inhibitors* like clomipramine (Anafranil), which is structurally a cyclic antidepressant whose metabolite inhibits norepinephrine transport, and venlafaxine (Effexor); and *selective serotonin transport inhibitors* like fluoxetine (Prozac), fluvoxamine (Luvox), paroxetine (Paxil), and sertraline (Zoloft). Nefazodone (Serzone) has serotonin transport inhibitor properties, but also blocks 5-hydroxytryptamine receptors.

Clomipramine and selective serotonin transport inhibitors are the only effective medications known that control the symptoms of obsessive–compulsive disorder. More than half the patients treated with clomipramine have the intensity of their symptoms completely controlled or become subclinical (i.e., minimal distress and no dysfunction). Others' symptoms are reduced in intensity. The effective oral dose of clomipramine for obsessive–compulsive disorder is generally 150 to 250 mg daily. The selective serotonin transport inhibitors also have to be used in relatively high doses to be effective in obsessive–compulsive disorder. It takes 4 to 6 weeks for the antiobsessional effects to become evident and sometimes more than 12 weeks to achieve full benefit. Serotonin transport inhibitors are a palliative treatment, not a cure, for obsessive–compulsive disorder, as the vast majority of patients relapse on discontinuation of medication.

Controlled studies have also demonstrated the efficacy of selective serotonin transport inhibitors in panic disorder, generalized anxiety disorder, social phobia, and posttraumatic stress disorder. The side effect profile of selective serotonin transport inhibitors like fluoxetine comprises few if any anticholinergic effects. Common side effects include nausea, headache, insomnia and drowsiness, nervous jitteriness, sexual difficulties, diarrhea, rash–urticaria, and weight loss. Roughly 15% of patients treated with selective serotonin transport inhibitors discontinue treatment because of side effects. Preliminary data suggest that the effects of overdose of selective serotonin transport inhibitors are relatively benign and fatality is rare. Selective serotonin transport inhibitors can inhibit one or more of the liver microsomal enzymes and therefore should be combined with certain medications (e.g., cyclic antidepressants, terfenadine, astemizole) with great caution. Combination of serotonin transport inhibitors with monoamine oxidase inhibitors has resulted in reactions marked by hyperthermia, rigidity, and autonomic dysregulation that are potentially lethal.

Monoamine oxidase inhibitors are dramatically effective in controlling panic attacks in the vast majority of patients suffering from panic disorder. Apart from controlling the panic attacks, monoamine oxidase inhibitors have an activating effect that can secondarily aid patients to challenge their phobias. Monoamine oxidase inhibitors are also useful in patients with posttraumatic stress disorder and social phobia.

The monoamine oxidase inhibitor most commonly used is phenelzine (Nardil) between 45 and 90 mg daily. Monoamine oxidase inhibitors have anticholinergic side effects: blurred vision, dryness of the mouth and other mucosal surfaces, constipation, urinary hesitancy, and tachycardia. In addition, weight gain, agitation, and sexual dysfunction occur frequently. Another common side effect is hypotension, which is aggravated by postural changes. This effect seems to develop over time but generally diminishes in a few weeks. Palliative measures such as increased fluid intake, salt tablets, and, if necessary, low-dose florinef can be used to counteract hypotension. The biggest danger with monoamine oxidase inhibitors is the possible development of hypertensive crises caused by food or drug interactions, which can result in cerebral hemorrhage and death. As monoamine oxidase inhibitors prevent the breakdown of monoamines, sympathomimetic substances and foods containing tyramine (such as cheese and liver) must be avoided.

Propranolol (Inderal) and other *beta blockers* block somatic symptoms like tachycardia that are often a part of anxiety; however, they do not seem to have an effect on the emotion of anxiety. They are potentially useful in the management of discreet specific forms of social phobia. Their usefulness in the management of panic disorder is limited.

Side effects of propranolol include bradycardia, hypotension, and depression. They are contraindicated in patients with a history of asthma and diabetes as they prevent the expression of the adrenergic rebound seen with hypoglycemia.

Other agents include clonidine (Catapres), an alpha-2-adrenergic agonist. Clonidine has some benefits in controlling panic attacks, but preliminary evidence suggests that tolerance to this effect develops in a few weeks.

Neurosurgery. Neurosurgical procedures are an option in patients with anxiety disorders, specifically obsessive-compulsive disorder, who are severely dysfunctional and in whom all other treatment options have failed. Current surgical procedures are different from the controversial prefrontal leucotomy that fell into disrepute in the 1950s. The surgical procedures practiced today include cingulotomy, also called modified leucotomy, limbic leucotomy, and capsulotomy. Overall, between 60 and 85% of patients show improvement with neurosurgical procedures, with the average level of symptomatic improvement between 30 and 60%. The rate of surgical complications is low. Thus, in highly selected patients, neurosurgery should be considered a treatment option.

Recommended Approach

The two treatments favored for anxiety disorders are cognitive–behavioral therapy and pharmacologic therapy. If a cognitive–behavioral therapist is available, patients can be referred to him or her for specific cognitive–behavioral therapy for the anxiety disorder. It is important to recognize that cognitive–behavioral therapy is different from counseling, which focuses on stressful life situations and strategies to cope with them.

Pharmacologically the treatment of choice today is serotonin transport inhibitors because of their effectiveness, more benign side effect profile, lack of dependence, and general safety from overdoses compared with other antidepressants.

FOLLOW-UP

Follow-up is important because after initiating treatment with medications, optimizing treatment to attain the maximum benefits is critical. Treatment should be continued for a minimum of another 6 months to consolidate the gains. At that point, an active decision is required either to discontinue treatment gradually or to switch to a maintenance strategy. Maintenance treatment aims at controlling symptoms and preventing relapse. Thus, if the anxiety disorder is initially well controlled with an antidepressant, the patient should be continued on the same dose for roughly 6 to 9 months to consolidate the gains; then gradual discontinuation should be considered. A significant number of patients with an anxiety disorder need to be maintained on medication indefinitely because of their tendency to relapse when the medication is discontinued. Previous unsuccessful attempts to discontinue medications should be an indication to continue the medication indefinitely. Because obsessive–compulsive disorder is a continuous illness, the majority of patients are likely to require medications continuously. Current data do not raise significant concerns about indefinite treatment of patients with antidepressants.

DISCUSSION
Prevalence and Incidence

The 1-year incidence of generalized anxiety disorder is 3%; the lifetime prevalence 5%. Familiar aggravation of generalized anxiety disorder is common. The age of onset of generalized anxiety disorder is relatively early, with a significant proportion developing it in their teens or early twenties. The majority of patients have other comorbid anxiety and affective disorders. Half of patients with generalized anxiety disorder are not working, and 25% are on disability.

The 1-year prevalence of panic disorder (with and without agoraphobia) is 1 to 2%; the lifetime prevalence, 1.5 to 3.5%. These figures are reported to be similar in several cultures and countries. There is a 3.5:1 female: male ratio. Median age of onset is 24 years. The risk of developing panic disorder is highest between ages 25 and 34 for women and ages 30 and 44 for men. Familial aggregation of panic disorder is common. Exit events (interpersonal loss, recent move, etc.) are present to a greater degree in the 6 months prior to the onset of unexpected panic attacks.

The prevalence rate of social phobia is about 2%. The disorder usually starts in childhood or early adolescence. It is often continuous and lifelong. The gender ratio is roughly equal. Familial aggregation is common.

The 6-month prevalence rate of specific phobias is between 4.5 and 11.8%. The female: male ratio is greater than 2:1. Median age of onset for phobias is 13 years, and the highest hazard rates for the development of specific phobias occur between the ages of 5 and 9.

The 1-year prevalence of obsessive–compulsive disorder is about 1.5 to 2.1%. Median age of onset is 23 years, with the highest hazard rates occurring between 15 and 39. Men have a slightly earlier age of onset, though the gender ratio is roughly equal. The illness shows some familial aggregation.

The prevalence of posttraumatic stress disorder varies tremendously based on the type of assessment. About 20% of wounded veterans from the Vietnam War and 3.5% of civilians attacked physically meet criteria for posttraumatic stress disorder. Sudden unexpected and life-threatening calamities result in significant emotional sequalae. The majority of such individuals will meet the criteria for acute stress disorder, but only one third go on to develop it for longer periods. The liability for development of such chronic responses to potentially life-threatening trauma might have some genetic mediation.

Related Basic Science

A number of neurotransmitter systems have been implicated in the pathophysiology of anxiety disorders. A fruitful approach has been to understand the mechanism of action of effective medications and use them as tools to explore the underlying pathophysiologic processes.

The site of action of the benzodiazepines is the benzodiazepine receptor, a membrane receptor that is the focus of much molecular biology research. The benzodiazepine receptor is functionally and structurally connected to the γ-aminobutyric acid receptor and a chloride ionophore to form a supramolecular complex. This complex seems to mediate the pharmacologic effects of benzodiazepines. Drugs bind to the benzodiazepine receptor in a stereospecific saturable and reversible manner and set forth a cascade of events that ultimately results in the pharmacologic effects of anxiolysis.

Abnormalities in the norepinephrine and serotonin systems have also been postulated in a number of anxiety disorders like panic disorder and obsessive–compulsive disorder. The noradrenergic system, particularly its principal nucleus, the locus ceruleus, has been postulated as an essential part of the anatomic substrate of fear and anxiety. Biochemical and pharmacologic data would suggest that the noradrenergic system is involved in the pathophysiology of panic and various other anxiety disorders, although the evidence to suggest an etiologic relationship is lacking. Serotonin has been implicated in the pathophysiology of obsessive–compulsive disorder, partly because all the effective antiobsessional agents known so far are powerful serotonin transport inhibitors.

The noradrenergic and serotonin systems are regulatory systems in the brain that have an impact on a variety of physiologic functions. Antidepressants have a general effect in making these systems more efficient, which might explain the clinical nonspecificity of their therapeutic effects in different anxiety and affective disorders.

Functional brain imaging studies have implicated various anatomic sites with altered metabolic activity or blood flow in various anxiety disorders. Advances in such techniques open windows to the functioning brain and will lead to a better understanding of the pathophysiology of a variety of psychiatric illnesses including anxiety disorders.

Natural History and Its Modification with Treatment

All of the anxiety disorders are likely to increase the likelihood of the development of depression later in life. Major depression should be considered a risk factor for significant complications, including disability and increased risk for suicide. The development of depression in patients with anxiety disorders should result in aggressive management and would indicate a greater need for pharmacologic strategies.

Prevention

Prevention of the development of an anxiety disorder in a patient prior to its symptomatic development is difficult because of our poor understanding of the vulnerabilities specific to each condition. First-degree family members of patients with certain anxiety disorders are at greater risk for the development of anxiety and affective disorders compared with the general population and can be monitored for such development.

New and unfamiliar situations can result in what has been termed *behavioral inhibition* in certain children. Such children can show sleeplessness, irritability, a tendency to colic, and marked physiologic symptoms including sympathetic arousal in unfamiliar situations. These children may be a risk for the later development of anxiety disorders. Childhood conditions such as separation anxiety disorder and school phobia might be a precursor or an indication of predisposition to anxiety disorders later in life. Hence, these conditions should be dealt with aggressively in the hope that adult pathology can be prevented.

Physiologic study suggests that some individuals have an exaggerated arousal mechanism to novel situations that takes time to habituate. Cognitive–behavioral strategies to enhance a person's capacity to deal with the arousal from unexpected situations and new environments might allow greater mastery of novel challenges. Successes can breed greater confidence and possibly mitigate the individual's constitutional vulnerability toward the development of an anxiety disorder.

Once they are diagnosed, aggressive and quick management of anxiety disorders results in a reduced likelihood of continued dysfunction. Partial or undertreatment can result in unnecessary residual symptomatology, which results in distress, dysfunction, and greater utilization of medical services. Chronic symptomatology has a pervasive influence on the patient's world view, making full recovery less likely. Hence, appropriate management of an individual early in the illness is critical.

Many anxiety disorders have a fluctuating course with periodic exacerbation in remissions. The recognition of relapse is an important part of the management of anxiety disorders. Treatment early in relapse can prevent a full episode and allow easier control of symptoms.

Cost Containment

A significant number of patients with anxiety disorders feel that they have an undiagnosed, serious medical illness; however, medical procedures can be reinforcing and therefore should be held to a minimum in patients with anxiety disorders who present with a variety of somatic symptoms. This is particularly true of panic disorder and obsessive–compulsive disorder. Once organic causes for the cause of their symptoms are ruled out, the focus should be on treating the anxiety disorder.

One of the major reasons patients are not given appropriate treatment for anxiety disorders is the hesitancy of the clinician to diagnose and make appropriate decisions to treat or refer for treatment. Sociocultural norms often stigmatize psychiatric disorders and imply that conditions such as anxiety disorders are failures of morality or will power rather than genetically predisposed, environmentally influenced disorders. The important point is that specific and effective treatments are now available for the majority of patients with anxiety disorders and it is a shame that effective treatments are not delivered because of prejudice.

REFERENCES

Ballenger JC (ed). Clinical aspects of panic disorder. Frontiers of clinical neuroscience, vol 9. New York: Wiley–Liss, 1990.

Benzodiazepine dependence, toxicity and abuse: A task force report of the American Psychiatric Association. Washington, DC: American Psychiatric Association, 1990.

Diagnostic and statistical manual of mental disorders. 4th ed. Washington, DC: American Psychiatric Association, 1994.

Jenike MA, Baer L, Minichiello W. Obsessive compulsive disorder: Theory and management. 2nd ed. Littleton, MA: PSG, 1990.

Treatment of psychiatric disorders: A task report of the American Psychiatric Association. Washington, DC: American Psychiatric Association, 1989.

CHAPTER 2–8

Somatoform Disorders, Including Somatization Disorder, Conversion Disorder, and Hypochondriasis

Theodore J. Anfinson, M.D., and Alan Stoudemire, M.D.

DEFINITION

Somatoform disorders are a group of psychiatric conditions characterized by symptoms that suggest a physical disease process in the absence of a demonstrable organic cause. Psychological processes are judged to be etiologically important for the development of the symptoms, which are not voluntarily produced, unlike those in malingering or factitious disorder. Diagnoses included among the somatoform disorders are somatization disorder, undifferentiated somatoform disorder, conversion disorder, pain disorder, hypochondriasis, and body dysmorphic disorder.

Somatization disorder is a chronic relapsing condition characterized by multiple, unexplained physical complaints in multiple organ systems for which no clear organic etiology can be found. *Undifferentiated somatoform disorder* is a chronic disorder related to somatization disorder, but requiring fewer symptoms to make the diagnosis. *Hypochondriasis* is a disorder characterized by fears of serious illness, based on the misinterpretation of bodily symptoms. No clear identifiable organic etiology can be found to fully account for the patient's concerns, which persist despite reassurance. *Conversion disorder* is a disorder affecting voluntary motor or sensory dysfunction that suggests a neurologic cause, but for which no clear organic etiology can be found. Psycholog-

ical factors are presumed to be involved in the etiology of the disturbance. *Pain disorder* (previously referred to as somatoform pain disorder and psychogenic pain) is a chronic condition of 6 months' or longer duration dominated by complaints of pain where appropriate investigation is unsuccessful at determining the etiology of the pain, or if the pain complaints are grossly disproportionate to the objective physical findings. *Body dysmorphic disorder* is a condition characterized by a preoccupation with an imagined or exaggerated defect in physical appearance.

ETIOLOGY

The etiology of somatization disorder is unknown. Several potential contributing factors have been implicated, however, including genetic, familial, neuropsychological, and cultural. A high prevalence of the disorder among first-degree relatives is the most compelling genetic evidence, whereas impaired information processing on neuropsychological testing suggests subtle frontal lobe dysfunction and impairments in distinguishing target from nontarget stimuli. Lower socioeconomic status is the dominant environmental factor associated with somatization disorder. Somatization of anxiety and depressed affect with positive reinforcement in the family system is a likely contributing factor in perpetuating the behavioral syndrome.

The dominant etiologic theory of conversion disorder is a psychodynamic model that suggests that the development of conversion symptoms is a direct symbolic expression of repressed psychological conflict. Affect related to the conflict is converted into a somatic symptom; the function of the physical symptom is to alleviate anxiety caused by the conflict and to derive "secondary gain" (attention or emotional support). Babinski advocated a theory of suggestion, known as pithiatism, which states that the symptom was suggested to the patient in some way (e.g., a model for the symptom in the environment) and, by extension, could be treated through the use of suggestion. Modern neurophysiologic studies have revealed evidence of impaired descending inhibitory relationships between the cerebral cortex and the reticular activating system in some conversion disorder patients (Cloninger, 1986).

Several etiologic theories have been advanced for hypochondriasis, including psychological developmental arrest, a heightened awareness of bodily sensations, and learned sick-role behavior (Barsky and Klerman, 1983). Some psychiatrists consider hypochondriasis as a variant of an anxiety disorder with marked obsessional features.

CRITERIA FOR DIAGNOSIS
Suggestive

The typical patient with somatization disorder offers a polysymptomatic presentation characterized by vague complaints, multiple medical encounters often involving numerous procedures, chronic duration, and a chaotic life history. Conversion disorder is suggested by a monosymptomatic presentation that suggests neurologic dysfunction, but is not consistent with known neuroanatomic functioning (e.g., sharply demarcated glove anesthesia) or the natural history of neurologic phenomena (e.g., clear sensorium immediately following apparent tonic–clonic seizure). In patients with hypochondriasis, less attention may be given to individual symptoms; rather, the patient may appear to be in a relentless if not obsessive pursuit of a diagnosis to confirm their fears about a specific illness being present (e.g., AIDS, cancer). A striking feature of this disorder is the ineffectiveness of medical reassurance and persistence of anxiety related to the fear of disease.

Definitive

Full formal diagnostic criteria for somatization disorder, conversion disorder, and hypochondriasis are listed in Tables 2–8–1, 2–8–2, and 2–8–3.

CLINICAL MANIFESTATIONS
Subjective

There is considerable overlap between the somatoform disorders, so careful attention must be given to the nature of the patient's subjective complaints. Conversion disorder should be considered when the symptoms mimic neurologic dysfunction. Gastrointestinal and urologic symptoms, such as difficulty swallowing and urinary retention, should be evaluated as possible conversion symptoms. Patients with conversion symptoms and multiple pain complaints should be evaluated for somatization disorder. Vague historical detail or an inability to identify a chief complaint characterize the somatization disorder patient, as do historical details that are at odds with the medical record. Burning pains in the mouth, rectum, or genitalia and vomiting throughout pregnancy are particularly characteristic of somatization disorder.

Objective
Physical Examination

The physical examination is seldom revealing in patients with somatoform disorders. It is important to note, however, that the diagnosis of the somatoform illnesses is based on the exclusion of physical illness that could explain the symptoms. Therefore, it is essential to perform a directed physical examination in these patients. Furthermore, the presence of a somatoform disorder does not preclude a comorbid physical

TABLE 2–8–1. AMERICAN PSYCHIATRIC ASSOCIATION CRITERIA FOR DIAGNOSIS OF SOMATIZATION DISORDER

A. A history of many physical complaints beginning before age 30 that occur over a period of several years and result in treatment being sought or significant impairment in social, occupational, or other important areas of functioning.

B. Each of the following criteria must have been met, with individual symptoms occurring at any time during the course of the disturbance:

(1) Four pain symptoms: a history of pain related to at least four different sites or functions (e.g., head, abdomen, back, joints, extremities, chest, rectum, during menstruation, during sexual intercourse, or during urination).

(2) Two gastrointestinal symptoms: a history of at least two gastrointestinal symptoms other than pain (e.g., nausea, bloating, vomiting other than during pregnancy, diarrhea, or intolerance of several foods).

(3) One sexual symptom: a history of at least one sexual or reproductive symptom other than pain (e.g., sexual indifference, erectile or ejaculatory dysfunction, irregular menses, excessive menstrual bleeding, vomiting throughout pregnancy).

(4) One pseudoneurologic symptom: a history of at least one symptom or deficit suggesting a neurologic condition not limited to pain (conversion symptoms such as impaired coordination or balance, paralysis or localized weakness, difficulty swallowing or lump in throat, aphonia, urinary retention, hallucinations, loss of touch or pain sensation, double vision, blindness, deafness, seizures; dissociative symptoms such as amnesia; or loss of consciousness other than fainting).

C. Either (1) or (2):

(1) After appropriate investigation, each of the symptoms in criterion B cannot be fully explained by a known general medical condition or the direct effects of a substance (e.g., a drug of abuse, a medication).

(2) When there is a related general medical condition, the physical complaints or resulting social or occupational impairment are in excess of what would be expected from the history, physical examination, or laboratory findings.

D. The symptoms are not intentionally produced or feigned (as in factitious disorder or malingering).

Source: American Psychiatric Association. Diagnostic and statistical manual of mental disorders. 4th ed. Washington, DC: American Psychiatric Association, 1994. Reproduced with permission.

illness, again emphasizing the need for a thorough medical assessment of the patient. Some findings are helpful, however. The absence of atrophic or reflexive changes in a patient complaining of weakness can suggest a conversion diagnosis, as does breakaway weakness. Conversion disorders commonly present with a nonphysiologic sensory examination. Overly dramatic presentations of gait disturbances (astasia–abasia) or convulsive episodes also suggest the diagnosis of conversion disorder. The presence of multiple abdominal scars may be reflective of a somatization patient's persistent complaints in spite of (or because of) multiple surgical procedures directed at alleviating the complaints.

TABLE 2–8–2. AMERICAN PSYCHIATRIC ASSOCIATION CRITERIA FOR DIAGNOSIS OF CONVERSION DISORDER

A. One or more symptoms or deficits affecting voluntary motor or sensory function that suggest a neurologic or other general medical condition.

B. Psychological factors are judged to be associated with the symptom or deficit because the initiation or exacerbation of the symptom or deficit is preceded by conflicts or other stressors.

C. The symptom or deficit is not intentionally produced or feigned (as in factitious disorder or malingering).

D. The symptom or deficit cannot, after appropriate investigation, be fully explained by a general medical condition, or by the direct effects of a substance, or as a culturally sanctioned behavior or experience.

E. The symptom or deficit causes clinically significant distress or impairment in social, occupational, or other important areas of functioning or warrants medical evaluation.

F. The symptom or deficit is not limited to pain or sexual dysfunction, does not occur exclusively during the course of somatization disorder, and is not better accounted for by another mental disorder.

Source: American Psychiatric Association. Diagnostic and statistical manual of mental disorders. 4th ed. Washington, DC: American Psychiatric Association, 1994. Reproduced with permission.

TABLE 2–8–3. AMERICAN PSYCHIATRIC ASSOCIATION CRITERIA FOR DIAGNOSIS OF HYPOCHONDRIASIS

A. Preoccupation with fears of having, or the idea that one has, a serious disease based on the person's misinterpretation of bodily symptoms.

B. The preoccupation persists despite appropriate medical evaluation and reassurance.

C. The belief in criterion A is not of delusional intensity (as in delusional disorder, somatic type) and is not restricted to a circumscribed concern about appearance (as in body dysmorphic disorder).

D. The preoccupation causes clinically significant distress or impairment in social, occupational, or other important areas of functioning.

E. The duration of the disturbance is at least 6 months.

F. The preoccupation is not better accounted for by generalized anxiety disorder, obsessive–compulsive disorder, panic disorder, a major depressive episode, separation anxiety, or another somatoform disorder.

Source: American Psychiatric Association. Diagnostic and statistical manual of mental disorders. 4th ed. Washington, DC: American Psychiatric Association, 1994. Reproduced with permission.

Routine Laboratory Abnormalities

Like the physical examination, laboratory investigations seldom reveal clinically meaningful abnormalities. Iron deficiency anemia may be encountered in the metromenorrhagic somatization patient or in the patient taking multiple nonsteroidal antiinflammatory agents.

PLANS
Diagnostic
Differential Diagnosis

The differential diagnosis of all the somatoform disorders includes any physical illness that could account for the patient's symptoms. Particular attention must be given to exclude those disorders associated with a fluctuating clinical course and psychological symptoms, such as multiple sclerosis and systemic lupus erythematosus. Rigorous attention should be given to ruling out a primary psychiatric disorder, such as major depression. Psychiatric diagnoses that may mimic a somatoform disorder include panic disorder, somatized major depression, and obsessive–compulsive disorder. Panic disorder is manifest by numerous cardiopulmonary, gastrointestinal, and neurologic complaints that occur during episodes of panic anxiety. Somatization is a common clinical presentation of depression, especially in the elderly, wherein the patient complains of multiple physical complaints and hypochondriacal concerns. Patients may or may not acknowledge a depressed mood. Major depression and panic disorder are common in patients with somatization disorder, so careful attention must be given to the longitudinal history of the patient's symptoms to delineate these disorders. The patient with obsessive–compulsive disorder manifest primarily by somatic obsessions may be mistaken for a patient with hypochondriasis; evidence for other obsessions and compulsions assists in this differential diagnosis. Finally, longitudinal data indicate that a substantial fraction (13–21%) of patients diagnosed with conversion disorder eventually develop objective evidence of neurologic disease, such as multiple sclerosis, seizure disorder, or head injury (Stoudemire, 1988). Close, long-term nonperjorative medical monitoring is essential whenever this diagnosis is being considered.

Diagnostic Options

The primary initial diagnostic procedures for the evaluation of somatorm illness involve the gathering of historical data. In addition to a careful history of the chief complaint, the clinician should consider old medical records, operative and pathologic reports, and collateral history from family to be valuable adjuncts to the patient's reported history. A careful, directed physical examination, with emphasis on the neurologic examination, completes the bedside diagnostic procedure. Hypnosedative interviews (amobarbital interviews) are occasionally helpful in revealing the nature of a conversion symptom, arriving at psychologically

important conflicts in the patient's life, or facilitating suggestive treatment directed at resolution of the symptom.

Recommended Approach

A careful history and physical examination are the most important diagnostic procedures in the evaluation of the somatoform patient. Attention to the longitudinal history is important, as is a complete review of systems. Sometimes it is not possible to complete this evaluation in one office visit. It is perfectly reasonable to schedule the patient for a timely return to complete the information-gathering process. Judicious application of the laboratory, avoiding invasive tests whenever possible, and directing the laboratory inquiry toward objective findings constitute the most beneficial approach. False-positive laboratory results can result in a cascade of unnecessary and potentially harmful investigations in these patients. Hypnosedative interviews should be conducted only by clinicians familiar with this procedure.

Therapeutic
Therapeutic Options

The primary therapeutic options involve chronic management by a primary care provider, with or without the assistance of a psychiatric consultant.

Recommended Approach

It is important to emphasize that the office visit serves as the most potent therapeutic element in the treatment of somatoform disorder patients, particularly those with somatization disorder and hypochondriasis. Therefore, regularly scheduled office visits are the cornerstone to treatment. In the treatment of somatization disorder and hypochondriasis, it will prove useful to keep in mind the following principles:

- Consider the symptoms in the context of the psychosocial stressors and exclude coexistent psychopathology such as depression and panic disorder.
- Take the patient's concerns seriously while avoiding unnecessary medical tests, procedures, and surgery.
- Perform a directed physical examination at each visit.
- Assess for the presence of "somatized" depression or panic disorder. A trial of an antidepressant may be effective in eliminating or greatly diminishing somatic symptoms in such patients.
- Schedule brief, regular follow-up visits that are time contingent (e.g., monthly visits for 15–30 minutes) and not contingent on the production of new symptoms. Emphasize to the patient that although his or her symptoms may be distressing, they are not life-threatening, and you will continue to monitor them.
- Refer the patient for marital or family therapy based on the social situation.
- Do not attempt to prove to the patient that his or her illness is purely "psychological," but gradually focus the conversation during office visits to emotional issues or stresses in the patient's life that may be exacerbating the somatization.
- Monitor the patient for concurrent medical illness.

Psychotropic medications, particularly those with an addiction potential, should be avoided if at all possible in patients with somatoform illnesses. It is possible for patients to have both a somatoform disorder and comorbid depression and anxiety disorders. When they become depressed, however, these patients tend to respond less well to antidepressant therapy than patients with affective illness without somatoform disorders. If psychotropic agents are to be employed, identification of target symptoms can facilitate the measurement of a response to treatment. In addition, informing the patient in advance that the medication may be discontinued in the future if it proves to be ineffective may circumvent an exacerbation of symptoms due to feelings of abandonment within the patient.

FOLLOW-UP

Recognizing that patients with somatoform disorders typically have strong unmet emotional dependency needs, follow-up should be pre-arranged and not contingent on the generation of new symptoms. The patient and physician should work out a mutually acceptable plan for regular brief visits. The clinician should avoid the temptation to delay or postpone the visits, as this may result in an exacerbation of symptoms. In fact, multiple visits to the emergency room or to other facilities may be an indication that the frequency of visits with the primary care provider is insufficient. If the patient is referred to a psychiatrist for consultation, brief regular follow-up should continue with the primary care physician, as few of these patients will continue in long-term psychiatric care.

DISCUSSION

Prevalence and Incidence

Of all the somatoform disorders, the best epidemiologic data exist regarding somatization disorder. It is primarily a disorder of women, with a female: male ratio of 10:1. Community samples reveal a prevalence of 0.1% using a structured interview and up to 0.5% using careful clinical assessment. Primary care outpatient samples reveal a prevalence of 0.2 to 5.0%, whereas inpatient samples reveal a prevalence of 2.0 to 9.0%. An even higher prevalence is noted in certain subpopulations, such as in patients with irritable bowel syndrome or chronic pain or in those undergoing non-cancer-related hysterectomies (Smith, 1991).

The prevalence of conversion disorder is variable depending on the methodology employed. Five to fourteen percent of psychiatric consultations in the general hospital involve conversion disorder (Ford and Folks, 1985). It is more common in women and those from rural or psychologically unsophisticated backgrounds (Stoudemire, 1988).

Related Basic Science

Few data are available concerning the basic science aspects of the somatoform disorders. Genetic data concerning somatization disorder reveal a ten fold increase in somatization disorder in first-degree female relatives (Cloninger, 1986). Other psychiatric diagnoses common in the families of somatization disorder patients include antisocial personality disorder and alcoholism. Neuropsychologic data in patients with somatization disorder reveal evidence for lowered pain thresholds, distractibility, difficulty distinguishing target form nontarget stimuli, and impaired verbal communication. Neurophysiologic studies of some conversion patients have revealed abnormalites in somatosensory and visual evoked potentials, suggesting reactive inhibition in sensorimotor pathways between the cerebral cortex and the brainstem reticular formation (Cloginger, 1986).

Natural History and Its Modification with Treatment

Somatization disorder is a chronic relapsing condition, beginning early in life, usually by adolescence. It has diagnostic stability over time, with a pattern of multiple unexplained somatic complaints persisting for decades after initial presentation. Physical complaints tend to increase during periods of life stress. Proper identification of the patient with somatization disorder, coupled with the development of a therapeutic relationship with a primary care provider, can result in an improvement in symptoms, with less utilization of emergency services. Conversion disorder tends to be a more acute disorder and time limited, although some patients with conversion disorder have relapsing conversion symptoms (Kent, et al., 1995). Hypochondriasis is typically a chronic disorder, beginning in the twenties and thirties, and tends to run a more benign course than somatization disorder.

Prevention

No data are available on the prevention of somatoform disorders. Given the importance of learned behavior and modeling in many of the disorders, however, an emphasis on education and intervention may have beneficial effects in somatizing families. Appropriate recognition and noninvasive monitoring of such patients are likely to reduce morbidity related to testing and invasive diagnostic procedures.

Cost Containment

Unnecessary laboratory investigations, invasive procedures with their attendant complications, and overutilization of emergency services contribute to the high cost of care of somatoform patients, particularly those with somatization disorder. Clinician anxiety over missing a potentially life-threatening illness or over medicolegal concerns can result in overutilization of diagnostic procedures. Data now exist that reveal that accurate diagnosis of somatization disorder, followed by regularly scheduled visits to a primary care physician, substantially reduces the cost of care without compromising the medical well-being of these patients (Smith et al., 1986).

REFERENCES

Barsky A, Klerman G. Overview: Hypochondriasis, bodily complaints, and somatic styles. Am J Psychiatry 1983;140:273.

Cloninger CR. Somatoform and dissociative disorders. In: Winokur G, Clayton P, eds. The medical basis of psychiatry. Philadelphia: Saunders, 1986:123.

Ford CV, Folks DG. Conversion disorders: An overview. Psychosomatics 1985;26:371.

Kent D, Tomasson K, Coryell W. Course and outcome of conversion and somatization disorders. A four year follow-up. Psychosomatics 1995;36:2:138.

Smith GR Jr. Somatization in the medical setting. Washington, DC: American Psychiatric Press, 1991.

Smith GR, Monson RA, Ray DC. Psychiatric consultation in somatization disorder: A randomized controlled study. N Engl J Med 1986;314:1407.

Stoudemire A. Somatoform disorders, factitious disorders, and malingering. In: Talbott JA, Hales RE, Yudofsky SC, eds. The American Psychiatric Press textbook of psychiatry. Washington, DC: American Psychiatric Press,1988: 533.

CHAPTER 2–9

Dissociative Disorders

George K. Ganaway, M.D., Steven T. Levy, M.D., and Susan B. Shelton, M.D.

DEFINITION

The group of dissociative disorders is characterized by disturbances in the normally integrated functions of consciousness, memory, identity, or perception of the environment. Onset may be acute or gradual, and the course transient, episodic, or chronic.

ETIOLOGY

The underlying causes of dissociative disorders are unknown, although much is known about the psychological processes that lead to symptom formation. Dissociative reactions may occur as a protective response to perceived *external* dangers (such as overwhelming traumatic life experiences) or *internal* dangers (such as frightening sexual or aggressive wishes and impulses).

CRITERIA FOR DIAGNOSIS

Suggestive

Patients with dissociative disorders may appear in many clinical settings, but often first come to medical attention in emergency rooms when their bizarre and perplexing symptomatology interferes with their ability to fit in with their home and work environments. They are frequently brought for evaluation by others who are concerned about their behavior. Exceptions are patients with depersonalization disorder, who experience their symptoms as ego-alien and may seek psychiatric help of their own accord. Acute-onset dissociative disorders are usually associated with sudden, severe, and overwhelming stress (e.g., military combat, natural disasters, physical and sexual assaults, divorce, financial setbacks) and occur in the absence of evidence of organic mental impairment. Chronic dissociative syndromes appear to be more related to character pathology and overall defensive style.

Symptoms and signs suggestive of a dissociative disorder would include evidence of depersonalization, derealization, functional amnesia, identity confusion, and/or identity alterations in the absence of demonstrable organic causes.

Definitive

Definitive diagnosis depends on the identification of the specific clinical manifestations that distinguish dissociative identity disorder, dissociative fugue, dissociative amnesia, and depersonalization disorder as described below.

CLINICAL MANIFESTATIONS
Subjective

Dissociative Identity Disorder

Previously known as multiple personality disorder, dissociative identity disorder remains a controversial diagnosis; some believe it to be overdiagnosed and others to be underdiagnosed. Originally considered to be rare, it is being reported increasingly in North American psychiatric literature. The disorder is believed to originate in childhood, although the diagnosis is rarely made before adolescence or early adult life. Nine of ten newly diagnosed cases are female. Nearly all diagnosed patients in treatment eventually disclose a history of childhood abuse or severe emotional trauma.

Dissociative identity disorder is characterized by the presence of two or more distinct identities or personality states in a single individual, with some degree of amnesia that is frequently asymmetric. At least two of these identities recurrently take control of behavior. Transitions among identities usually are triggered by psychosocial stress or role requirements, and may be sudden or gradual, subtle or dramatic.

As the name suggests, dissociative identity disorder is distinguished by a failure to integrate various aspects of identity, memory, and consciousness. Identities or personality states may be experienced as if each has a distinct personal history and a unique manner of perceiving, thinking about, and relating to the self and the environment. Alternate identities may have different names and characteristics that contrast sharply with the "primary" identity. Different personality states may vary in their knowledge of each other. Consequently, these individuals suffer a lack of continuity in their sense of time and experience, with selective memory gaps for recent and remote events. First awareness of amnesia may come through reports from others of behaviors disavowed or disremembered by the patient or by the patient's discovery of clothing or other possessions he or she does not remember acquiring.

Patients with dissociative identity disorder often present with a wide variety of symptoms that do not initially betray the presence of the disorder. Common presenting symptoms include depression, anxiety, conversion symptoms, and headaches or other physical complaints that are often diagnosed as somatoform disorders. Occasionally there is frank awareness of amnesia. Patients may report hallucinations or a sense of being influenced or controlled by unknown others, suggestive of a schizophrenic disorder. Fluctuation in symptoms and level of function may vary markedly over time, reflecting the different levels of adaptive functioning of the experienced identities. Most patients receive several alternative psychiatric diagnoses before being diagnosed with dissociative identity disorder.

Dissociative Fugue

Dissociative fugue is an infrequently reported disorder that is more commonly seen in wartime and in the wake of a natural disaster. No data are available regarding age, sex, racial, or familial patterns.

The essential feature of dissociative fugue is amnesia associated with sudden and unexplained travel to a new location, accompanied by confusion about personal identity or sometimes the assumption of a new identity. Typically the patient has no recall of his or her previous life and, following recovery, no recall of events that took place during the fugue. Fugue states may occur in which sudden travel with amnesia occurs without the assumption of a totally new identity. Likewise, amnesia for the events during the fugue may not be complete. When a new identity is assumed and the fugue lasts for days or weeks, the new identity typically involves elements significantly different from the patient's premorbid personality.

Usually the patient lives a quiet, withdrawn life with very few interpersonal contacts. Travel and subsequent behavior during the fugue are more purposeful than the aimless and confused wandering observed in patients with dissociative amnesia. As with the latter condition, dissociative fugue is usually seen following an extremely stressful environmental event, for example, marital quarrels, military conflict, or natural disaster. Other symptoms sometimes observed are violent outbursts against people or property that the patient cannot explain and that occur suddenly and without obvious provocation, and often are culture specific (e.g., *amok*).

Dissociative Amnesia

Dissociative amnesia can present in any age group, but is more commonly seen in young adults, both male and female. Episodes are most frequent during times of severe environmental stress. There are no reliable data about familial patterns or age or sex ratio. Once thought to be apparently rare, recently in the United States there has been a marked increase in reported cases of dissociative amnesia involving previously forgotten early childhood traumas.

Patients with dissociative amnesia most commonly present with a retrospectively reported gap or series of gaps in recall for aspects of their life history. These memory gaps usually are related to traumatic or extremely stressful events. For example, an individual may have amnesia for episodes of violence toward others or toward the self, such as a suicide attempt. A less common form of dissociative amnesia is marked by the acute onset of a florid episode of localized amnesia for a circumscribed period or selective amnesia for some but not all events during a given period. For example, following a car accident, the patient might remember a wrecker towing away his damaged car but have no recall of an ambulance arriving to take his seriously injured passenger to a hospital. The events remembered are usually less emotionally upsetting than those that are forgotten. This acute form of amnesia is more likely to occur during wartime or in response to a natural disaster. Rarely, a patient will present with total or generalized amnesia, with no recall for any aspect of his or her previous life, or with continuous amnesia dating from a particular time and continuing to the time of clinical presentation. Patients with dissociative amnesia often feel perplexed and may wander about purposelessly. Most patients are distressed at being amnestic, but patients occasionally are seen who appear almost indifferent or casual about obvious and significant gaps in their memory. Some patients will make up details to "fill in the gaps" in their memory, but do so in a manner that shows gross lack of concern for logical consistency or sequence. Some individuals will additionally report depressive symptoms, depersonalization, trance states, and spontaneous age regressions.

Depersonalization Disorder

Depersonalization disorder involves a subjective alteration in self-experience characterized by a feeling of detachment or estrangement from one's self. Patients report feeling different, changed, unreal, mechanical, lifeless, or as if living in a dream or movie. Many have difficulty describing how they feel. They may perceive some change in their appearance or feel they are viewing themselves from a distance. Various sensory anesthesias may be present. Depersonalization is often accompanied by derealization, a sense that the external world is strange or unreal. These symptoms are very distressing to the patient, often producing anxiety and depression. There is no gross loss of reality testing. Although transient depersonalization experiences occur in nearly one third of individuals exposed to life-threatening danger, the diagnosis of depersonalization disorder requires significant social or occupational impairment owing to episodes of depersonalization that are not secondary to other mental or physical disorders. The disorder usually begins in adolescence or early adult life and may have a chronic, fluctuating course with remissions and exacerbations. No data are available regarding sex ratio or familial pattern.

Dissociative Disorder Not Otherwise Specified

Dissociative disorder not otherwise specified is a residual category for patients who have dissociative symptoms but do not fulfill the diagnostic criteria for a specific dissociative disorder. Included in this category is an entity called Ganser syndrome in which patients give "approximate" (illogical) answers to questions in the context of other cognitive disturbances. Also included in this category are various trancelike states, derealization in the absence of depersonalization, and lasting changes in conscious experience associated with prolonged and intense psychological coercion (e.g., brainwashing). Cases in which full diagnostic criteria for dissociative identity disorder are not met are also included in this category.

Objective

There are no consistent abnormal physical or laboratory findings in patients with dissociative disorders other than anxiety-related phenomena during acute episodes of depersonalization or distressing amnesia (e.g., tachycardia, profuse perspiration). As a group, dissociative disorder patients skew toward the high end of objective scales of hypnotizability; however, it has not been demonstrated that high hypnotizability alone predisposes individuals to dissociative syndromes.

PLANS
Diagnostic
Differential Diagnosis

Malingering involving purposefully feigned amnesia and identity change can be difficult to distinguish from a genuine dissociative disorder. Hypnosis and drug-facilitated interviews have not proven reliable in ruling out malingering. Moreover, even in cases where malingering is not likely, some authorities implicate sociocultural shaping influences fueled by media attention and/or therapists' beliefs and expectations as important determinants of the unfolding symptom picture seen in many newly diagnosed cases of dissociative identity disorder and dissociative amnesia.

Schizophrenia may be a difficult diagnosis to differentiate from dissociative identity disorder. Patients may complain of hearing voices or of being passively influenced. Typically, however, dissociative identity disorder patients demonstrate a full range of appropriate affective responses to their environment, and reality testing remains generally intact. Voices almost always are heard inside the head. Additionally, thought broadcasting, common in schizophrenia, rarely is reported by these patients.

Diagnostic Options and Recommended Approach

The diagnosis of dissociative disorder is made by clinical interview, including careful evaluation of the patient's mental status together with historical information provided by the patient and others. The SCID-D, a semistructured interview focusing on dissociative disorder symptoms, recently has become available as a differential diagnostic tool, but is too time consuming for practical clinical applications. Hypnosis and amobarbital interviews have been promoted as helpful diagnostic procedures; however, some authorities contend that misuse and overuse of these procedures in recent years have led to an inordinately large number of false-positive diagnoses of dissociative identity disorder or dissociative amnesia in suggestible individuals. On the other hand, hypnosis and amobarbital used cautiously and conservatively in selected situations of acute and subacute amnesia for recent events may result in the prompt recovery of lost memory, suggesting a psychogenic rather than an organic basis for the amnesia. In dissociative fugue, these procedures likewise may be helpful in recovering lost identity based on psychogenic causes. Organic causes of amnesia with or without fugue

(e.g., alcohol or other intoxicants, head trauma, epilepsy) can usually be ruled out by careful history taking, detailed evaluation of the memory impairment, and physical examination for signs of physical illness. Electroencephalogram and computed tomography or magnetic resonance imaging scans, when indicated by other findings, may be helpful in ruling out organic disease.

Therapeutic
Therapeutic Options and Recommended Approach

Dissociative disorders result from a breakdown in the integration of mental functions when the patient is faced with overwhelming anxiety owing to internal or environmental threat. Acute treatment is based on removing the patient from the threatening situation. This often includes psychiatric hospitalization and an exploration of the patient's emotional distress in a supportive psychotherapeutic relationship. The memory disturbance in dissociative amnesia and dissociative fugue usually clears rapidly, but not always completely, if the patient and therapist explore precipitant events and current stresses in the patient's life. Hospitalization, which temporarily removes the patient from environmental stresses, often is sufficient to ameliorate acute symptoms. Hypnosis and narcosynthesis may be helpful in recovering lost memory in acute dissociative amnesias and dissociative fugues, but these procedures are of equivocal value and remain controversial as adjuncts in the treatment of dissociative identity disorder and dissociative amnesias where the memory gaps in question are suspected to involve alleged early childhood traumas. These patients are at high risk for confabulation under such conditions. Psychopharmacologic interventions to date have not been shown effective for dissociative disorders involving loss of memory.

Psychotherapy to alleviate psychological conflict that has led to dissociative phenomena may be helpful in preventing recurrence. Experience, however, is limited with more intensive psychotherapy to resolve long-standing unconscious conflict in patients with dissociative disorders to protect them against relapse. Its effectiveness cannot be documented with any certainty.

Various psychotherapeutic treatment approaches have been described for dissociative identity disorder, but data are insufficient to support any one treatment as superior to others. Most authorities recommend psychodynamic psychotherapy with adjunctive cognitive techniques. A cautious approach is warranted given these patients' often very primitive psychic organization.

Depersonalization disorder has been usually approached psychologically. Hospitalization is rarely necessary. Supportive and more insight-oriented psychotherapeutic approaches have been used with varying success. Psychotropic drugs have been tried in some patients, but no pattern of effectiveness has been established.

FOLLOW-UP

No general plan of follow-up can be recommended for patients with dissociative disorders. Dissociative amnesia and dissociative fugue are believed to recur only rarely. Thus, follow-up after the acute episode may not be necessary. In patients who experience recurrence, extensive psychotherapeutic intervention should be strongly recommended.

Patients with dissociative identity disorder require individualized long-term treatment and follow-up, in view of the chronic and somewhat ego-syntonic nature of the dissociative pathology. Relapses of dissociative symptoms are not uncommon, even in allegedly "fully integrated" patients. Patients with depersonalization disorder, if they take psychotropic medications, require follow-up at least every 3 months once they have been stabilized on the medication.

DISCUSSION
Prevalence and Incidence

The lifetime prevalence of depersonalization disorder is unknown. Approximately half of all adults may have experienced a brief single episode at some time in their lives, usually triggered by severe stress. Dissociative fugue is considered to be a rare disorder. Dissociative amnesia and dissociative identity disorder were once considered rare. In recent years in the United States, a marked increase in the number of newly diagnosed cases has become the subject of considerable controversy. Some believe that a greater awareness of the diagnosis among mental health professionals has resulted in the identification of previously undiagnosed cases. Others believe that these syndromes are being overdiagnosed in individuals who are highly hypnotizable, suggestible, and fantasy-prone.

Related Basic Science

Dissociative disorders have, because of their dramatic nature, been important in the development of psychiatric thinking about unconscious mental processes. Recognition of the capacity to block from conscious awareness painful thoughts, feelings, wishes, and memories has been a cornerstone of modern psychiatry's understanding of mental illness. Dissociative phenomena, which appear closely linked to repression, primitive denial, and other unconscious defense mechanisms, are powerfully persuasive arguments for the existence of unconscious mental processes. Although repression, some dissociative experiences, and other associated phenomena are ubiquitous and in many situations normal mental processes, the tendency in some individuals toward grossly maladaptive dissociation such as is seen in dissociative disorders is poorly understood. No structural or substructural physical or chemical abnormalities have been demonstrated in patients who have dissociative disorders. A perhaps constitutionally derived trance proneness, or high hypnotizability, appears in some manner to be related to a propensity for dissociative experiences, but hypnosis and dissociation have been shown experimentally to be different, albeit related, phenomena. Many developmental influences, both environmental and psychological, have been anecdotally associated with the later development of dissociative disorders, but reliable data are lacking to support any particular theory of etiology.

Natural History and Its Modification with Treatment

Dissociative disorders tend to occur most frequently in adolescence and early adulthood. As mentioned earlier, most cases are associated with extremely stressful environmental events, are nonprogressive and time limited, and do not recur. There is believed to be no lasting morbidity in such cases. During amnestic episodes and fugues, although purposeful behavior can and does occur, from the standpoint of consciously integrated wishes, goals, and usual behaviors the patient is seriously incapacitated. Patients with dissociative identity disorder usually become symptomatic during late adolescence or early adulthood and have extremely variable courses. Some patients have periods of productivity and generally stable and rewarding personal relationships interrupted by stress-related episodes of dissociation. Others are chronically debilitated and frequently hospitalized for psychiatric and somatic complaints. Response to treatment often depends more on the degree of character pathology than on the severity of dissociative symptoms. Depersonalization phenomena may occur in mild form in normal individuals, persist as a chronic disabling disorder with frequent remissions and exacerbations, or appear as part of the symptomatic picture in other mental illnesses.

There are no available data on the mortality of these disorders. Suicide attempts may occur in this patient population, but they are generally not thought to be characteristic of the dissociative disorders. Certain patients with dissociative identity disorder at times appear particularly prone to reckless and self-destructive behavior that may result in death or disfigurement.

Prevention

No preventive measures are currently available.

Cost Containment

Patients with dissociative fugue and dissociative amnesia may require brief (1–3 weeks) psychiatric hospitalizations to establish the diagnosis and to undergo treatment designed to restore their memory and reestablish their previous life pattern. Costly workups for organic causes can usually be avoided by careful characterization of the memory loss, fugue, identity confusion or alteration, and the setting in which such changes occurred. Likewise, careful history taking and physical examination will usually rule out organic impairment (e.g., epilepsy, acute and chronic drug and alcohol abuse, head trauma) without the need for extensive and expensive neurologic workup. In a typical clinical presentation of dissociative disorder with no overt evidence by history, physical examination, or routine laboratory studies of organic impairment, a drug screen for intoxicants is the only special laboratory procedure indicated to rule out underlying organic causes. In cases of acute dissociative amnesia or dissociative fugue, hypnosis or amobarbital interview leading to temporary recall of lost memories supports the diagnosis of dissociative disorder. An electroencephalogram, computed tomography scan, or magnetic resonance imaging scan should not be ordered unless there is particular reason to suspect neurologic impairment (e.g., abnormal neurologic examination, history of head trauma, or history of seizurelike symptoms).

Hospitalization in most cases can be brief. Memory usually returns quickly and completely in dissociative amnesia and dissociative fugue. Psychotherapeutic exploration of underlying problems can occur in an outpatient setting. It is difficult to persuade most patients with amnesia and fugue to undertake intense, long-term psychotherapy, an expensive and time-consuming treatment that may or may not prove useful to the patient. Patients with dissociative identity disorder can usually be best managed as outpatients. They have a chronic course, and treatment cost will depend on their particular symptomatic picture and severity of underlying character pathology. Because conversion disorder is a commonly associated problem in these patients, care should be taken to avoid costly and unnecessary medical and surgical interventions.

REFERENCES

Diagnostic and statistical manual of mental disorders. 4th ed. Washington, DC: American Psychiatric Association, 1994.

Gabbard GO. Psychodynamic psychiatry in clinical practice: The DSM-IV edition. Washington, DC: American Psychiatric Press, 1994:291.

Ganaway GK. Transference and countertransference shaping influences on dissociative syndromes. In: Lynn S, Rhue J, eds. Dissociation: Clinical and theoretical perspectives. New York: Guilford Press, 1994:317.

Loewenstein RJ. Psychogenic amnesia and psychogenic fugue: A comprehensive review. In: Tasman A, Goldfinger S, eds. American Psychiatric Press review of psychiatry. Washington, DC: American Psychiatric Press. 1991;10:189.

Steinberg M. The spectrum of depersonalization: Assessment and treatment. In: Tasman A, Goldfinger S, eds. American Psychiatric Press review of psychiatry. Washington, DC: American Psychiatric Press, 1991;10:223.

Eating Disorders

Mary Lynn Dell, M.D., M.T.S., Th.M.

DEFINITION

Eating disorders are disturbances of attitudes and behaviors that may have significant physiologic and psychiatric morbidities. Obesity, described as 120% or more of ideal body weight, is the most prevalent eating disorder, although anorexia nervosa and bulimia nervosa are the main topics of this chapter. *Anorexia nervosa* is characterized by a distorted body image, a great fear of gaining weight, and failure to maintain body weight at a healthy minimum. *Bulimia nervosa* also consists of a distorted body image, with alternating binging and purging behaviors.

ETIOLOGY

A variety of biological, individual, family, and sociocultural factors contribute to the onset of eating disorders. A genetic predisposition exists for anorexia, with half of monozygotic twins but only 5% of dizygotic twins concordant for the condition. Hypothalamic dysfunction is hypothesized to be both a cause and a result of anorexia. Hypothalamic–pituitary–adrenal, hypothalamic–pituitary–thyroid, and hypothalamic–pituitary–gonadal axes are all affected. Homeostasis and regulatory mechanisms are reset in starvation, contributing to symptom perpetuation. Psychodynamic theories have postulated a fear or inhibition of sexual instincts, blurring of ego boundaries with mother, poorly formed sense of self, and highly entrenched traits of perfectionism, dependence, and excessive compliance. Controlling oral intake becomes a patient's way of dealing with stereotypically enmeshed, rigid, overprotective, conflicted families with poor communication skills. These factors are further affected by modern culture's emphasis on achievement, cosmetic attractiveness, and physical fitness.

Bulimia nervosa shares many possible etiologic factors with anorexia nervosa. Biologically, binging may be associated with α_2–noradrenergic overactivity, serotonergic underactivity, or both. Twin concordance is demonstrable, but not as clearly for bulimics as for anorexics. Psychodynamically, bulimic patients are viewed as highly neurotic, less disciplined and self-controlled than anorexics, and have families of origin that are more openly chaotic and hostile. Sexual abuse, depression, and substance abuse may be both partially etiologic and associated with bulimia.

CRITERIA FOR DIAGNOSIS

Suggestive

Anorexia nervosa should be suspected in individuals, especially adolescent or young adult women, who present with unexplained weight loss over a relatively brief period, amenorrhea, or electrolyte or vital sign instability. Bulimia nervosa is less obvious when the individual is normal weight or overweight, but should be suspected in the presence of objective signs of vomiting, diarrhea, bowel problem, or other gastrointestinal abnormalities. Additional associated medical and psychiatric features of eating disorders are discussed below.

Definitive

The American Psychiatric Association criteria for anorexia nervosa are listed in Table 2–10–1, and those for bulimia nervosa are listed in Table 2–10–2

CLINICAL MANIFESTATIONS

Subjective

Eating disorders frequently have an insidious onset, beginning with the elimination of snacks and increased physical exercise. The list of restricted foods may expand to include all or most carbohydrates, dairy products, and any item with measurable fat and sodium content. Preferred fluids are water, diet sodas, tea, and coffee. The patient skips meals and avoids eating in public or with the family. Time devoted to exercise increases, and sometimes secretive workouts are done at night. More time is spent in the bathroom, especially after meals, if vomiting and laxative abuse are occurring. "Anorexia" is actually a misnomer, as patients still have an appetite and are preoccupied with thoughts of food. Many spend hours in the kitchen preparing food for others, but refuse to eat themselves. The anorexic often dresses in such a way that the amount of weight loss is camouflaged. Rigidity and perfectionism increase in many other areas, including schoolwork, extracurricular activities, housekeeping, and interpersonal relationships. Friends and relatives often notice a sad mood, depressed affect, and diminished self-esteem and confidence.

Most bulimics vomit and many abuse laxatives. Depression frequently accompanies bulimia. Anxiety, loneliness, impulsivity, emotional lability, and needs for external behavioral limits are common. Binging episodes are preceded by boredom, anxiety, and tension relieved by overeating. Guilt, shame, and anger follow the binge, prompting purging and/or laxative abuse in efforts to relieve uncomfortable feelings and prevent weight gain. Bulimics subjectively experience the urges to binge eat and vomit as being out of their control.

There is some evidence that individuals who develop anorexia nervosa have a higher incidence of feeding disorders and colic as infants and young children. They may have always been "picky eaters." Patients who initially present with bulimia may have had previous episodes of anorexia nervosa.

Objective

Physical Examination

On physical examination (Table 2–10–3), the anorexic will be below 85% of ideal body weight for height, occasionally down to 70% of ideal body weight. Many individuals will have significant medical and psychiatric symptoms at 90% of ideal body weight. Adolescents and preadolescents may fall off their growth curves for both height and weight. Patients will be hypothermic and hypotensive, and can demonstrate im-

---

TABLE 2–10–1. AMERICAN PSYCHIATRIC ASSOCIATION CRITERIA FOR DIAGNOSIS OF ANOREXIA NERVOSA

A. Refusal to maintain body weight at or above a minimally normal weight for age and height (e.g., weight loss leading to maintenance of body weight less than 85% of that expected; or failure to make expected weight gain during period of growth, leading to body weight less than 85% of that expected).

B. Intense fear of gaining weight or becoming fat, even though underweight.

C. Disturbance in the way in which one's body weight or shape is experienced, undue influence of body weight or shape on self-evaluation, or denial of the seriousness of the current low body weight.

D. In postmenarcheal females, amenorrhea, i.e., the absence of at least three consecutive menstrual cycles (a woman is considered to have amenorrhea if her periods occur only following hormone, e.g., estrogen, administration).

Specify type:

Restricting type: During the current episode of anorexia nervosa, the person has not regularly engaged in binge-eating or purging behavior (i.e., self-induced vomiting or the misuse of laxatives, diuretics, or enemas).

Binge eating/purging type: During the current episode of anorexia nervosa, the person has regularly engaged in binge-eating or purging behavior (i.e., self-induced vomiting or the misuse of laxatives, diuretics, or enemas).

Source: Diagnostic and statistical manual of mental disorders. 4th ed. Washington, DC: American Psychiatric Association, 1994. Reproduced with permission.

TABLE 2–10–2. AMERICAN PSYCHIATRIC ASSOCIATION CRITERIA FOR DIAGNOSIS OF BULIMIA NERVOSA

A. Recurrent episodes of binge eating. An episode of binge eating is characterized by both of the following:
  (1) Eating, in a discrete period of time (e.g., within any 2-hour period), an amount of food that is definitely larger than most people would eat during a similar period of time and under similar circumstances.
  (2) A sense of lack of control over eating during the episode (e.g., a feeling that one cannot stop eating or control what or how much one is eating).
B. Recurrent inappropriate compensatory behavior in order to prevent weight gain, such as self-induced vomiting; misuse of laxatives, diuretics, enemas, or other medications; fasting; or excessive exercise.
C. The binge eating and inappropriate compensatory behaviors both occur, on average, at least twice a week for 3 months.
D. Self-evaluation is unduly influenced by body shape and weight.
E. The disturbance does not occur exclusively during episodes of anorexia nervosa.

Specify type:

Purging type: During the current episode of bulimia nervosa, the person has regularly engaged in self-induced vomiting or the misuse of laxatives, diuretics, or enemas.

Nonpurging type: During the current episode of bulimia nervosa, the person has used other inappropriate compensatory behaviors, such as fasting or excessive exercise, but has not regularly engaged in self-induced vomiting or the misuse of laxatives, diuretics, or enemas.

Source: Diagnostic and statistical manual of mental disorders. 4th ed. Washington, DC: American Psychiatric Association, 1994. Reproduced with permission.

pressive orthostatic hypotension. Bradycardia may be extreme, and pulse difficult to detect. Vital sign instability, especially hypothermia, is typically more pronounced in the mornings and can improve later in the day. Scalp and genital hair may be thinning, dry, brittle, and falling out. Soft, downy lanugo hair may be evident on the shoulders, back, cheeks, and extremities. Skin becomes mottled, dry, and desquamated. Obviously, there is significant loss of subcutaneous body fat stores. Peripheral edema, cyanosis, and cold hands and feet are common. Muscle is decreased in mass, tone, and strength. Menstrual irregularities range from complete amenorrhea to sporadic spotting, and the cervix and uterus may be smaller than expected on bimanual pelvic examination.

Bulimics may exhibit many of the same physical findings as anorexics, depending on past history (Table 2–10–4). Other prominent findings include hypertrophy of the parotid glands, erosion of dental enamel, pyorrhea, and excessive cavities secondary to purging. Self-induced vomiters may have calluses over the dorsum of their knuckles called *Russell's sign.* Muscle tone is decreased, with peripheral edema, hyporeflexia, and peripheral neuropathy possible. The abdomen may be distended and tender to palpation, or dilated bowel loops may be palpable if an ileus exists. Occasionally, bulimics present emergently vomiting bright red blood if a Mallory–Weiss tear has occurred.

Routine Laboratory Abnormalities

Routine laboratory tests for anorexia include complete blood count with differential, urinalysis, an SMA-20 or the equivalent, thyroid functions, and electrocardiogram. The results frequently show anemia, thrombocytopenia, leukopenia, elevated blood urea nitrogen, and hypo-

TABLE 2–10–3. PHYSICAL FINDINGS IN ANOREXIA NERVOSA

Vital sign instability: orthostasis, bradycardia, hypotension, hypothermia
Thinning scalp and genital hair
Lanugo hair (shoulders, face, extremities)
Dry skin
Minimal subcutaneous fat
Peripheral edema
Cyanosis and mottling (especially hands and feet)
Decreased muscle mass
Loss of muscle tone and strength

TABLE 2–10–4 PHYSICAL FINDINGS IN BULIMIA NERVOSA

Vital sign instability: orthostasis, bradycardia, hypotension, hypothermia
Thinning of brittle scalp and genital hair
Dry skin
Calluses on knuckles (Russell's sign)
Muscle weakness, decreased tone
Hyporeflexia
Peripheral neuropathy
Peripheral edema
Abdominal distension
Esophogeal tears
Ileus
Parotid gland hypertrophy
Dental enamel erosion and caries
Pyorrhea

glycemia. Serum cholesterol will be elevated early in the disease course, but decreased later. An electrocardiogram is essential to define the extent of bradycardia and possible arrhythmias (Table 2–10–5).

The same routine laboratory testing should be done for bulimics, but the results may be more variable and require more careful interpretation. Bulimics are frequently anemic. Blood urea nitrogen and creatinine may both be elevated, for a certain degree of renal failure may be seen. An SMA-20 may reveal hyponatremia, hypokalemia, hyperkalemia, hypochloremia, hypocalcemia, or hypercalcemia. A metabolic alkalosis with elevated serum bicarbonate is seen with vomiting, and a metabolic acidosis is seen with frequent laxative abuse. Stool speci-

TABLE 2–10–5. LABORATORY AND TEST FINDINGS IN ANOREXIA NERVOSA

Cardiovascular	Bradycardia
	Low-voltage electrocardiogram
	Decreased cardiac diameter, narrowed left ventricular wall, pericardial effusion on echocardiogram
	Diminished cardiac compensation during exercise
Neuroendocrine	Low luteinizing hormone
	Low follicle-stimulating hormone
	Low estrogen and testosterone
	Low triiodothyronine
	Elevated reverse triiodothyronine
	Low to normal thyroxine
	Elevated growth hormone
	Erratic vasopressin secretion with partial diabetes insipidus
	Elevated serum cortisol
Hematologic	Leukopenia
	Thrombocytopenia
	Anemia
	Hypocellular bone marrow
Renal	Elevated blood urea nitrogen
	Decreased glomerular filtration rate
	Prerenal azotemia
Metabolic	Hypoglycemia
	Elevated cholesterol (early)
	Decreased cholesterol (late)
	Decreased zinc
	Elevated sweat chloride
Gastrointestinal	Gastric dilation
	Delayed gastric emptying
	Elevated liver enzymes
	Decreased intestinal lipase and lactase
Radiology	Generalized atrophy on head computed tomography or magnetic resonance imaging scan
	Osteopenia on bone films
	Diminished cardiac silhouette on chest x-ray

mens should be submitted for a guaiac test for occult blood. An electrocardiogram is essential to identify any cardiac arrhythmias (Table 2–10–6).

PLANS
Diagnostic
Differential Diagnosis

The differential diagnosis for anorexia nervosa includes any malignancy that may result in radical weight loss and malnutrition. Inflammatory bowel disease should be accompanied by other gastrointestinal symptoms. Thyroid abnormalities are easily detected and reversible. Intracranial disease usually presents with other neurologic symptoms, such as headache, nausea, vomiting, seizures, eye ground changes, and visual field deficits. Anterior pituitary disorders, Addison's disease, diabetes mellitus, and hyperparathyroidism can be ruled out by appropriate laboratory testing. In overweight bulimics, the diagnosis of Cushing's disease must be entertained.

Psychiatric differential diagnosis must also be considered. Depression can lead to appetite disturbance with weight gain or loss. Bizarre food preferences and eating patterns are also seen in obsessive–compulsive disorder and psychotic illnesses.

Diagnostic Options

Beyond the basic laboratory studies discussed above, the following additional studies may be necessary or helpful. There may be low serum triiodothyronine, elevated reserve triiodothyronine, and low to normal thyroxine. Serum amylase is elevated if vomiting has occurred. When bradycardia or arrhythmias are noted, a 24-hour Holter monitor, echocardiogram, and stress testing can further define cardiac status. Abdominal ultrasound and radiographic imaging studies can answer questions about esophageal, gastric, and intestinal size and integrity. Bone films provide estimates of osteopenia and risk of fracture. Serum levels of hormones, such as estrogen, testosterone, vasopressin, and luteinizing, follicle-stimulating, and growth hormones, can aid in endocrinologic evaluation and treatment. Head computed tomography and magnetic resonance imaging and electroencephalogram should be

ordered in cases of seizures, encephalopathy, delirium, or other mental status changes. Electromyography is helpful in some instances of muscle weakness, cramping, or peripheral neuropathy.

Recommended Approach

Most cases of eating disorders can be accurately diagnosed by history, physical examination and routine laboratory assessment. Weight, height, and orthostatic vital signs are necessary, preferably on several occasions. Complete blood count with differential to assess extent of anemia and SMA-20 to screen for electrolyte imbalances, renal and liver abnormalities, diabetes, and metabolic derangements are necessary. An electrocardiogram is essential to detect bradycardia and/or arrhythmias. If either is questionable or of concern, a 24-hour Holter monitor should be obtained. If the clinical cardiac examination is similarly borderline or abnormal, an echocardiogram with a cardiology consult is indicated. Many physicians require patients with a resting pulse rate less than 45 beats per minute to use a cardiac monitor while sleeping. A pregnancy test should be obtained in all amenorrheic adolescents and adults. A gynecologic exam and HIV testing may be indicated, especially if the girl or woman with the eating disorder has a history of sexual abuse. Head computed tomography and magnetic resonance imaging and electroencephalogram have low yields and are not routine, unless the history or physical examination indicates the possibility of an anatomic lesion or seizure disorder.

Any person seriously suspected of having an eating disorder should be referred to a psychiatrist or other mental health professional with training and expertise in this area. In addition to a diagnostic psychiatric interview, psychological testing is helpful. Several scales and questionnaires have been developed for the diagnosis and assessment of eating disorders. The Eating Disorders Inventory is one of the more commonly used instruments. Personality inventories and self-report measures for depression, anxiety, and obsessive–compulsive disorder aid in the identification of comorbid psychiatric conditions. Optimal evaluation and treatment comprises both medical and psychiatric attention, with fluent communication between all involved caregivers, the patient, and family members.

Therapeutics
Therapeutic Options

The first decision to be made is whether or not to hospitalize a patient. Medical indications for hospitalization include cardiac compromise, significant vital sign instability, electrolyte or metabolic disturbances not amenable to outpatient treatment, encephalopathy, seizures, continued weight loss despite outpatient intervention, gastrointestinal immotility, and ileus. Esophageal or gastric hemorrhage or rupture should be treated as a medical emergency. Even if outpatient treatment is medically possible, depression, anxiety, psychosis, obsessive–compulsive disorder, or suicidality may necessitate psychiatric hospitalization, either as a full-time inpatient or as a day patient in a partial treatment program.

Gradual weight gain to 90% or more of ideal body weight is the key to restoring normal physiologic functioning in the anorexic. Nasogastric tube feedings or total parenteral nutrition may be necessary when behavioral programs are unsuccessful in the refeeding process. This should be coordinated by the physician and nutritionist. Electrolytes and trace elements such as zinc and magnesium may need correction or supplementation. Bed rest is indicated when vital signs are so unstable that syncope or injury is likely with unrestricted activity. Warm clothing, heating pads, or warming blankets may be needed for hypothermic patients.

Behavioral treatment is the cornerstone of eating disorder management. Increases in daily caloric intake and/or weight gain should be positively reinforced. Loss of privileges, work and exercise restrictions, or other measures serve as negative reinforcers when incremental goals are not met or the patient's condition worsens. Behavioral programs that address binge eating, purging, and excessive exercise can also be designed. Often, changes in environment and schedule effectively reduce forbidden bulimic behaviors.

Individual psychotherapy is essential to try to understand the psychodynamic aspects of each individual as they relate to the predisposition,

TABLE 2–10–6. LABORATORY AND TEST FINDINGS IN BULIMIA NERVOSA

Cardiovascular	Arrhythmias on electrocardiogram
	Toxicity (if ipecac abused)
Neuroendocrine	Variable, depending on history of anorexia nervosa
Hematologic	Anemia
Renal	Prerenal azotemia
	Acute renal failure
	Chronic renal failure
Metabolic	Dehydration
	Metabolic alkalosis with elevated serum bicarbonate secondary to vomiting
	Metabolic acidosis secondary to laxative use
	Hypokalemia
	Hypochloremia
	Hyponatremia
	Hypocalcemia
	Hypercalcemia
	Hypomagnesemia
Gastrointestinal	Hyperamylasemia
	Gastric distension
	Gastric dilation
	Irritable bowel syndrome
	Melanosis coli secondary to laxative abuse
Neurologic and musculoskeletal	Seizures
	Abnormal electroencephalogram
	Muscle cramps
	Tetany
Radiology	Esophageal or gastric rupture
	Bowel distension or atony

etiology, perpetuation, and recovery of his or her eating disorder. Insight-oriented psychodynamic psychotherapy, cognitive–behavioral therapy, interpersonal therapy, and psychoanalysis have all been used successfully, as long as the patient is not too encephalopathic or cognitively impaired due to catabolic state. Individual therapy may be conducted by a psychiatrist, psychologist, clinical nurse specialist, or other mental health practitioner experienced in this area. Nonmedical therapists must work closely with or under the supervision of a psychiatrist. All families of children or adolescents with eating disorders should be engaged in family therapy, as should older patients for whom family or origin of current family issues figures in the psychodynamics of the condition. Couples therapy is highly recommended with patients with spouses and significant others. Group therapy is especially helpful during inpatient hospitalization, and may remain so for bulimics and patients with comorbid personality and conduct problems or histories of sexual abuse. Overeaters Anonymous is a 12-step program that has helped many bulimics, especially those with accompanying substance abuse. Group therapy tends to be less beneficial for younger, nonpurging, restrictor anorexics.

Pharmacologic management of eating disorders should first focus on reversing medical complications of starvation. As mentioned previously, potassium levels should be monitored closely and supplements prescribed as indicated. Cholinergic and antidopaminergic agents, such as metoclopramide, have been advocated when gastric motility is delayed, although efficacy of such treatment has not been proven consistently. Gynecologic consultation regarding hormonal therapy may be considered. Certainly, concomitant psychiatric disorders should be treated with the appropriate psychopharmacologic agents. For the rare delirious patient, a very low dose of benzodiazepine or neuroleptic may be used very cautiously. Appropriate medications may include lorazepam 0.5 to 1.0 mg orally or intramuscularly every 4 to 6 hours and/or haloperidol 0.5 to 2 mg orally one to four times daily. Depression and anxiety disorders are essentially treated ideally with antidepressant agents. Historically, tricyclic antidepressants have been the most prescribed and studied, with varying degrees of success. Drawbacks of imipramine, desipramine, amitriptyline, nortriptyline, clomipramine, and others are their cardiac arrhythmic potentials and lethality in overdose. Monoamine oxidase inhibitors are seldom prescribed for anorexics because of their extensive side effect profiles, but efficacy has been demonstrated in bulimics. Several multicenter clinical trials support the efficacy of selective serotonin reuptake inhibitors in the treatment of eating disorders. Fluoxetine has been studied most extensively, although many clinicians are also prescribing sertraline and paroxetine. The medications are most helpful when the patient has discernible depression or depressive features. Overall, antidepressant treatment has shown more promise and success in bulimia than anorexia.

Recommended Approach

The following strategy follows logically from the preceding discussion of treatment options:

- Decide appropriate level of care: inpatient medical, inpatient psychiatric, partial hospitalization, outpatient.
- If inpatient care is indicated, immediate assessment and treatment of electrolyte, fluid, and cardiac abnormalities are begun. Institute gradual refeeding with nutrition consultation. Obtain psychiatric consultation for appropriate psychotherapy and behavioral management.
- Inquire regularly about suicidality or other intentions of harming self or others. Patients with eating disorders have been known to become more depressed and/or suicidal as treatment begins and they gain weight.
- Establish the patient's ideal body weight. Ninety percent of the ideal body weight should be the target or goal maintenance weight. The patient should be expected to gain weight in slow increments, usually 1 pound per week, until the target weight is reached.
- Collaborative treatment with a knowledgeable nutritionist is invaluable.
- Refer to a psychiatrist or appropriate therapist(s) for individual, family, behavioral, and group therapies.
- Treat comorbid psychiatric disorders, such as depression, anxiety,

obsessive–compulsive disorder, personality disorders, and substance abuse.
- Continue to follow the patient for months to years after treatment goals are met. Eating disorders are chronic and relapsing, and distorted body images and disturbed eating patterns continue long after weight is stabilized.
- Consultation and second opinions are advisable when working with this patient population.

DISCUSSION

Prevalence and Incidence

Estimates of prevalence of eating disorders range from 1 to 5%, of which 5 to 10% are males. Affected individuals are typically from industrialized societies, middle and upper socioeconomic brackets, white, and above-average education and intelligence. This stereotypic picture is gradually changing to include more ethnic minorities, greater cultural and socioeconomic diversity, and less intellectually gifted individuals. Researchers and clinicians agree that bulimia is much more common than anorexia, especially in the college and young adult populations.

Related Basic Science

See Etiology.

Natural History and Its Modification with Treatment

The medical and psychiatric morbidities of anorexia nervosa can be progressive, with 20% mortality rate from complications of starvation and suicide. Factors related to poor prognosis in anorexia include older age of onset, bulimic symptoms, laxative and ipecac abuse, vomiting, being married, lower socioeconomic background, family psychiatric illness, extreme family dysfunction, and obsessive–compulsive personality traits.

Morbidity in bulimia nervosa tends to be related to complications of concurrent psychiatric disorders, especially substance abuse, personality disorders, and depression. Factors associated with good treatment outcomes are early detection and age of onset, stable interpersonal relationships, and desire for treatment. Poor prognostic indicators include a history of anorexia nervosa, low body weight, impulsivity, and delay in diagnosis and institution of treatment.

As discussed previously, multiple therapeutic modalities applied over months to years are usually necessary to ensure good treatment outcomes.

Prevention

Eating disorders are quite difficult to prevent. Patients and their families should be referred to appropriate mental health professionals as soon as problems are suspected to minimize morbidity. Cultural attitudes about thinness and attractiveness need to be addressed on a grand scale as a public health issue.

Cost Containment

Responsible economic management of eating disorders begins with a thorough, comprehensive history taking and examination. For example, emaciation in the young, energetic, professional adult woman with amenorrhea, lanugo hair, cold intolerance, and Tanner IV pubic hair is highly consistent with anorexia nervosa; however, comparable sudden weight loss, despite a reasonable diet, and extensive loss of public hair in a postpartum borderline intellectually functioning young woman raises the possibility of Sheehan's syndrome and hypopituitarism. A head computed tomography or magnetic resonance imaging scan and extensive endocrine laboratory testing are indicated in the second patient, but not the first. After the diagnosis of an eating disorder is suspected or confirmed, early aggressive management is indicated. The longer the anorexic remains at 85% or less of ideal body weight, or the more the bulimic abuses laxatives, ipecac, and alcohol, the greater the immediate and long-term morbidities and economic burdens. Referrals for psychiatric care, behavioral management, and group and family therapies may initially appear expensive and unnecessary, but are wise investments of time and money for patients and health care professionals because of the chronicity of these disorders. In short, early detection and prompt, rigorous, multidisciplinary treatment strategies can limit the severity of physiologic damage and psychiatric dysfunction, decrease acute and chronic morbidity and mortality, and limit the financial liabilities of the patients, families, health care system, and society at large.

REFERENCES

Diagnostic and statistical manual of mental disorders. 4th ed. Washington, DC: American Psychiatric Association, 1994.

Joffe A. Eating disorders. In: Oski FA, (editor-in-chief). Principles and practice of pediatrics. 2nd ed. Philadelphia: Lippincott, 1994:797.
Practice guidelines for eating disorders. Washington, DC: American Psychiatric Association, 1993.
Woolston JA, ed. Eating and growth disorders. Child and Adolescent Psychiatric Clinics of North America. Philadelphia: Saunders, 1993; 1.
Yager J, Gwirtsman HE, Edelstein CK, eds. Special problems in managing eating disorders. Washington, DC: American Psychiatric Press, 1992.

CHAPTER 2–11

Psychosomatic Symptoms

Steven A. Cole, M.D., and Frank W. Brown, M.D.

DEFINITION

The term *psychosomatic symptoms* refers to a heterogeneous group of poorly defined clinical presentations characterized by a preponderance of psychologically induced physical complaints.

ETIOLOGY

These symptoms can appear in the context of virtually any true physical condition, as a mixed biological–psychological problem (e.g., "psychological overlay"), or in the absence of any documentable physical illness, as in a somatoform disorder (e.g., conversion disorder, hypochondriasis, or somatization disorder). The most common situation in which psychosomatic symptoms appear is as part of a group of rather vague physical conditions that possess some degree of observable pathophysiology, but often to a degree insufficient to explain the intensity of patients' subjective complaints, for example, irritable bowel syndrome, lower back strain, fibromyositis, and tension headache.

CRITERIA FOR DIAGNOSIS

The only observable cues that suggest psychosomatic symptoms consist of physical complaints that appear out of proportion to the objective physical findings. These cues can, of course, be very misleading, as the style and intensity of patients' complaints vary greatly according to social, cultural, and individual differences, and many true physical illnesses can routinely cause substantial subjective distress with little demonstrable physical pathology. Negative or "insufficient" physical findings, therefore, should never lead convincingly to an assumption of psychogenic etiology. The impression of psychogenicity should result only from a careful psychological and social history that demonstrates positive psychological conflicts and social stresses that can help explain symptom production or intensity.

CLINICAL MANIFESTATIONS
Subjective

No occupational, family history, or other environmental factors are known to relate etiologically to the development of psychogenic physical complaints. A past history of such symptoms may be a predisposing factor.

Psychosomatic complaints are nonspecific and universal. No physical symptoms can be excluded from the universe of pathogenicity. Common psychosomatic symptoms include ill-defined pains, unusual bodily sensations, fatigue, and "spells." Of course, these symptoms may well indicate serious physical illness, so no presumption of psychogenicity can be reasonably made on the basis of symptom profile alone.

Objective

The routine physical and laboratory findings are negative or insufficient to adequately explain the patient's problem(s). Furthermore, no specific mental status findings can confirm the presence of psychosomatic symptoms. Unusual degrees of psychological distress, emotional intensity, or demanding behaviors often suggest psychogenicity; however, it must be remembered that any type of psychological problem or personality configuration can also be consistent with true physical illness.

PLANS
Diagnostic

The diagnostic tests indicated by the specific presenting symptoms must be completed. Once a patient has a demonstrated history of previous psychosomatic symptoms, physicians should emphasize the use of diagnostic tests indicated by objective signs of illness rather than by subjective symptoms alone.

Therapeutic

The treatment of psychosomatic symptoms differs depending on whether the problem is acute or chronic. Acute problems require appropriate reassurance that no serious physical disease is present and no further diagnostic or therapeutic measures are necessary.

Chronic psychosomatic symptoms, on the other hand, require psychosocial management based on the following basic principles.

- Emphasize coping, not curing. Chronic psychosomatic symptoms cannot, in general, be cured completely. They should be viewed by the physician and patient as ongoing problems requiring medical attention. The physician and patient together should develop strategies to enhance coping with the symptoms.
- Schedule regular, not as-needed, visits. Patients with psychosomatic symptoms demonstrate a psychological need for medical attention. They should never be discharged from the office or hospital with the message, "Come back when you have more trouble." This encourages illness behavior. Rather, they should be given regular appointments for follow-up, *whether or not* they are having acute physical complaints. This allows such patients to get medical attention without requiring symptomatic exacerbations. Regular visits can encourage more adaptive behavior and less "illness behavior."
- Communicate with patients, emphasizing relationship, emotional, and psychosocial issues. Patients with psychosomatic symptoms generally experience distressing emotional issues in their lives or in relation to the uncertainties of their physical problems. By using basic relationship and emotional support skills, doctors can increase rapport, decrease patient suffering, and facilitate exploration of psychosocial issues.
- The most important of such interventions include naming the pa-

tient's emotion or reflection (e.g., "You seem very distressed by my inability to find any clear physical cause for your pain") and legitimation (e.g., "I can certainly understand why you would be upset when you hurt so badly and I cannot find any good explanation for it"). Other such interventions include expressions of personal support ("I'm here to do what I can to help you with this"), partnership ("Maybe you and I together can come up with some ideas to help you cope better with these problems"), and respect ("I think you've done a good job handling this problem so far, given the extent of your suffering, and I'm impressed by your determination to keep working in spite of your problems").

By using such supportive interventions, which help develop rapport, physicians can generally encourage patients to discuss relevant psychosocial issues and stresses. This psychosocial discussion can be instrumental in helping patients make more adaptive adjustments to life stresses instead of focusing on somatic symptoms. It should be emphasized that this type of psychosocial discussion does not need to take more than 5 to 10 minutes to be appreciated and helpful for patients.

- Emphasize having one doctor, not a committee. These patients should be discouraged from "doctor shopping," as this increases the likelihood of multiple invasive procedures.
- Perform a brief physical examination. This conveys to the patient that the doctor cares, and is reassuring to the patient. When no objective evidence of disease is found, the patient can be reassured that the symptoms will be followed.
- "Don't just do something, stand there." Doctors often feel the need to "fix" patients as quickly as possible, and patients often demand rapid relief. Thus, doctors often feel great pressure to "do something" when faced with psychosomatic symptoms. It is best for physicians to "buy time," however, and offer a longer-term management plan instead of ineffective acute interventions or diagnostic procedures that have previously been unproductive. Short-term acute medical interventions may not work and may even be counterproductive (e.g., iatrogenic injury). The "standing there" part of the plan encourages the patient to see that the doctor has not deserted him or her emotionally or medically and will continue to see him or her regularly and responsibly.
- Avoid unnecessary medications if possible. Patients with chronic psychosomatic symptoms usually have a long history of multiple prescription and over-the-counter medications. A wide variety of antihistamines, analgesics, sedatives, hypnotics, anxiolytics, and antidepressants have been used to try to help such patients cope. In the absence of specific indications, these medications, especially habituating ones, should be avoided. Occasionally, such medications (especially the antidepressants) may be quite helpful if used in an adjunctive and not necessarily curative way.
- Encourage alternative "stress reduction" therapies if acceptable to patients. Relaxation, yoga, meditation, biofeedback, exercise, and massage have all been used as adjunctive treatments for psychosomatic symptoms with good and occasionally excellent results. Again, these should be used as adjunctive treatments to general supportive management, rather than as primary or curative treatments in themselves.

Proper education is essential for the treatment success. Patients can be told:

You have some physical complaints that I cannot fully explain by my physical examination and the laboratory studies I have done. This is not so unusual because many patients have various symptoms that doctors are unable to explain. I realize that you are suffering with this pain; I know you're not imagining it; and I want to discuss some ways that I may be able to help.

First of all, you and I both need to understand that you've had this problem, on and off now, for a long time and that you've had multiple studies and multiple medications. You've been evaluated by the best specialists I know. So we need to understand that we probably cannot cure the problem entirely. I care about you and your pain, so I'm going to keep trying to help you, but we need to realize that our goal needs to be to help you cope with the pain rather than eliminate it entirely. If we focus on eliminating it entirely, you and I may both fail.

I also want to see you regularly so I can get a better idea of what you're like even when you don't have this pain, or when it is less severe. One of the things we can try to understand better is how you're coping with the stresses in your life. We all have stress, and we know that physical problems get worse when we feel stress. If we find a way to help you with your life stresses, your pain may be a bit less severe and you may be able to cope with it better.

These educational interventions should be documented in the progress notes.

FOLLOW-UP

The frequency of follow-up should be roughly equivalent to the patient's previous history of seeking medical attention. Patients who seem to go to a doctor at least once a month need to be followed by scheduled appointments at least that frequently. Patients should be cautioned not to focus on any particular physical problem, but to focus instead on more general issues of coping. They should come for regular and, if necessary, frequent follow-up.

DISCUSSION
Prevalence and Incidence

The incidence, prevalence, and demographic characteristics of psychosomatic symptoms are generally unknown. Suffice it to say that at least 10 to 20% of most physicians' practices (more in primary care settings) concern management of psychosomatic symptoms.

Natural History and Its Modification with Treatment

The morbidity of psychosomatic symptoms is unknown. The major complications, however, are iatrogenic surgical complications (e.g., exploratory laparotomies resulting in adhesions) and drug effects (e.g., addiction to analgesics, drug side effects, overdoses).

Mortality is quite low, other than for unpredictable surgical accidents or drug overdoses. Coryell (1981) found no evidence of excess mortality after a 42-year follow-up of 76 women with somatization disorder.

Prevention

Prevention of iatrogenic complications and "doctor shopping" is extremely important. The therapeutic approach described above has been shown to decrease hospitalizations.

Avoiding unnecessary medications and surgical procedures is the key to prevention of iatrogenic injury. Relying primarily on the presence of objective signs rather than subjective symptoms for surgery or medication is a good principle for a responsible prevention approach.

Psychiatric referral is often indicated. Affective disorders (depression), anxiety disorders (panic), and dissociative disorders often present with psychogenic physical complaints. Such disorders may be readily treatable and reversible with psychotropic medications and/or psychotherapy. Psychiatric evaluation also may reveal prominent stresses or conflicts that were not readily apparent to the primary care physician or patient. In addition, when the conservative management described above is not successful or leads to the revelation of psychological difficulties beyond the expertise of the primary care physician, psychiatric referral is also indicated. Recent evidence suggests that psychotherapy, especially group therapy, is effective as an adjunct to the treatment of chronic physical illness and leads to decreased medical costs for the physical illness itself.

When making the referral to a psychiatrist, it is generally best to indicate to the patient that you refer many of your patients to psychiatrists, that you do not think your patient is "crazy," and that you want to keep your relationship with the patient intact. You simply want a psychiatric evaluation to help you understand or manage the patient better, just as you would seek a consultation from any other expert.

Cost Containment

Even though regular and occasionally frequent outpatient visits are encouraged for this type of illness behavior, such conservative management is generally cost-effective. It encourages adaptive patient coping rather than focusing on physical distress. It helps avoid unnecessary diagnostic tests, medications, hospitalizations, and "doctor shopping." Research in this area demonstrates a long-term cost-effectiveness of about 50% reduction in quarterly health care charges.

REFERENCES

Borus JF, Olendjki MC, Kessler L, et al. The offset effect of mental health treatment on ambulatory medical care utilization. Arch Gen Psychiatry 1985;42:573.
Brown, FW, Golding JM, Smith GR Jr. Psychiatric comorbidity in primary care somatization disorder. Psychosom Med 1990;52:445.
Cohen-Cole S. The medical interview: The three function approach. St. Louis: Mosby-Year Book, 1991.
Coryell W. Diagnosis-specific mortality: Primary unipolar depression and Briquet's syndrome (somatization disorder). Arch Gen Psychiatry 1981;38:939.
Drossman D. The problem patient: Evaluation and care of medical patients with psychosocial disturbances. Ann Intern Med 1978;86:366.
Ford CV. The somatizing disorders. Psychosomatics 1986;277:337.
Rics R, Bokan JA, Katow W, Kleinman A. The medical care abuser: Differential diagnosis and management. J Fam Pract 1981;13:257.
Smith GR, Manson RA, Ray DC. Psychiatric consultation in somatization disorders: A randomized controlled study. N Engl J Med 1986;314:1407.

CHAPTER 2–12
Loss of Cognitive Function (See Section 20, Chapter 19)

CHAPTER 2–13
Mental Retardation
Earl A. Loomis, Jr., M.D., and Terri E. Lawless, M.D.

DEFINITION

Mental retardation is defined as significantly subaverage intellectual functioning (IQ approximately 70 or below), with onset before 18 years and with concurrent deficits or impairments in at least two significant areas of adaptive functioning (e.g., communication, self-care, home living, social/interpersonal skills, use of community resources, self-direction, work, leisure, health, or safety).

ETIOLOGY

The predisposing factors vary with the varieties of the disorder. They have been divided into several broad categories: biological, psychological, or a combination (nature/nurture). Despite extensive diagnostic evaluation, no clear etiology can be determined in 30 to 40% of individuals seen in clinical settings. In other cases, chromosomal abnormalities, inborn errors of metabolism, physical trauma, infection, or exposure to toxins may account for the mental retardation.

CRITERIA FOR DIAGNOSIS
Suggestive

Impairments in adaptive functioning, rather than low IQ scores, tend to be the presenting signs and symptoms, especially in mildly impaired individuals. Severely impaired persons are often identified at birth by physical stigmata associated with phenotypic abnormalities or by atypical results of routine newborn laboratory screening. Delays in development of motor and/or speech skills are the hallmark of less severe (moderate) mental retardation, whereas the mildest forms are often heralded only by poor school performance.

Phenotypic abnormalities, congenital cataracts, persistent jaundice, seizures, hypotonia, hypertonia, or failure to thrive should alert one to the possibility of mental retardation. Delays or abnormalities in bonding, delays in attainment of age-appropriate motor milestones, absence of or delayed acquisition of speech, or learning difficulties in school constitute later manifestations of mental retardation. The individual and/or caretaker should be queried regarding a history of special school placement, academic difficulties, problems in social and occupational endeavors, gaps in breadth and depth of knowledge, and difficulties in adapting to novel situations.

Definitive

A definitive diagnosis of mental retardation is based on documented evidence of significantly subaverage intelligence and of deficiencies in adaptive behavior manifested prior to age 18. After this age, a similar clinical picture would be classified as an organic mental disorder (dementia).

Level of intelligence is ascertained via standardized tests administered by a qualified clinical psychologist. Individuals scoring two standard deviations or more below the mean (IQ of 70 or below) are considered to be significantly intellectually impaired. Presently accepted classifications include *mild* (IQ 50–70), *moderate* (IQ 35–49), *severe* (IQ 20–34), and *profound* (IQ less than 20). The current American Psychiatric Association classification (*Diagnostic and Statistical Manual,* 1994) also includes *borderline intellectual functioning* (IQ 71–84) to indicate subaverage intellectual functioning not meeting the criteria for mental retardation.

CLINICAL MANIFESTATIONS
Subjective

Medical history begins not just at conception but must include family history and must continue until the individual's 18th year. Despite in-depth data, a review of epidemiologic studies concluded that in approximately 30% of cases classified as severe mental retardation and approximately 50% of cases classified as mild, no known cause can be identified (McClaren and Bryson, 1987). Family members and/or caretakers may note behavior problems, poor peer interactions, impaired social skills, and delays in various areas of development. These characteristics may or may not be associated with mental retardation and alone are not sufficient for diagnosis.

Objective
Physical Examination

In many cases, the physical examination will be unremarkable. In others, when familial or genetic disorders are present, specific physical findings may prove to be helpful clues in diagnosis. Appropriate head size for age is an important indicator of brain growth, and microcephaly may indicate impaired growth or function of the brain. Eye examination may reveal evidence of corneal clouding and/or lens dislocation (mucopolysaccharidoses), lens dislocation (homocystinuria), or congenital cataracts (congenital rubella and others). Hypopigmented macules on the skin may suggest tuberous sclerosis, and café-au-lait spots are indicative of neurofibromatosis. Characteristic facies are seen in many disorders associated with mental retardation, including Down syndrome, myotonic muscular dystrophy, fetal alcohol syndrome, and Hurler syndrome. Hypertonia, hypotonia, or seizure disorder may be noted on neurologic history or examination.

The mental status examination may reveal absent or unusual speech (with abnormalities of tempo, rhythm, or tone), concrete thinking, decreased alertness, increased distractibility, and limitations in vocabulary and fund of knowledge, or "headline intelligence." This term describes superficial access to vocabulary and general knowledge without accompanying depth of comprehension, a phenomenon commonly seen in mild mental retardation.

Routine Laboratory Abnormalities

Laboratory screening in newborns has permitted the early diagnosis of disorders that may lead to mental retardation, most notably congenital hypothyroidism and phenylketonuria. Several laboratory tests may prove to be useful in attempting to delineate the etiology of mental retardation (see Plans, Diagnostic).

PLANS
Diagnostic
Differential Diagnosis

The diagnostic criteria for mental retardation remain very specific and do not contain exclusion parameters. The diagnosis is made when the criteria of age of onset and significantly subaverage abilities in intellectual functioning, existing concurrently with limitations in two or more adaptive skill areas, are met. The differential diagnosis of disorders occurring in conjunction with mental retardation remains very extensive and includes prenatal, perinatal, and postnatal causes. Yet, the correlation between the two fails to be 100% (patients with phenylketonuria or who have had meningitis do not always manifest mental retardation).

Diagnostic Options

Helpful tests may include thyroid function tests; assessment of speech, hearing, and vision; electroencephalogram; heavy metal screening; chromosome analysis; cranial magnetic resonance imaging or computed tomography scan; blood and urine screening for amino acids; and urine screening for organic acids. A variety of psychological tests are available. These include tests for ages from birth through adulthood: tests for verbal and nonverbal subjects. Instruments of assessments for sensory/perception, affect/impulse, memory, judgment, and adaptation are readily available for persons of various ethnic and cultural backgrounds. Environmentally appropriate standards and instruments are currently replacing monolithic measures. Current American Association on Mental Retardation (AAMR) standards are calling for *levels of support* as more appropriate indices of incapability or limitation than the old IQ. For example, is the necessary level of support *intermittent, limited, extensive,* or *pervasive?*

Adaptive behavior refers to an individual's ability to master age-appropriate interpersonal and social skills in various aspects of social functioning compared with what is expected developmentally for a same-age person. Tests commonly used in obtaining such a maturity index include the Adaptive Behavior Scale (ABS) and the Vineland Social Maturity Scale.

It is important to be mindful of cultural bias, which has been described in psychological testing. Minority groups and individuals from foreign countries should have access to tests that compensate for these cultural differences.

Recommended Approach

No specific approach can be recommended. Each individual has different problems and presents in an unique way. Signs and symptoms may develop any time from prior to birth up to 18 years of age. A multidisciplinary team approach is conducive to formulating the correct diagnosis.

Therapeutic
Therapeutic Options

Clinical management of the mentally retarded can be time consuming and difficult. Some potential obstacles were identified recently in a questionnaire presented to practicing physicians in Maine and can be generalized to any community. It was found that medical history, medical records, and pertinent data concerning a presenting health issue tend to be the most significant sources of problems identified. As the person ages, the number of family members able to provide family history decreases, the number of caretakers from whom to obtain pertinent health history increases, and the number of places in which the person has lived is probably large. The person's presentation alone can be very deceptive. The physician sees a 35-year-old, well-dressed individual who may have excellent expressive speech and no phenotypic stigmata of mental retardation. But, this same patient, with a moderate degree of mental retardation, has the "mental age" of a 5- to 8-year-old. Failing to recognize the cognitive capabilities of this patient may severely compromise medical care. The patient may be unable to adequately describe his signs and symptoms of illness or may not associate them with illness. Some patients tend to be uncooperative during an examination. Only 20% of physicians felt "very prepared" to cope with this behavior according to the questionnaires.

The mentally retarded person and/or caretaker should be alerted to new developments, such as seizure disorder or side effects of medications, and to changes in mental state that may indicate an underlying or overlying psychiatric disorder.

Recommended Approach

Current practices and standards point to a consensus: a multidisplinary approach is in order, perhaps both indispensible and inevitable. What continues to plague many professionals is (1) learning to work with such a team and (2) maintaining professional medical standards in the face of political pressure to yield medical responsibility and authority to protocols, procedures, and bureaucratic regulations, often as interpreted or enforced by nonprofessional administrators or other functionaries. Notwithstanding current pressures, even crises, the experience of many physicians has been of mutual enrichment of themselves and other professionals through harmonious teamwork planning and care.

FOLLOW-UP

Frequency of follow-up is determined on an individual basis. A team approach is often most helpful to the mentally retarded person and his or her family, with various health care personnel available. The treatment team might consist of the physician, psychologist, retardation and behavior specialist, occupational and vocational therapists, special education specialist, social worker, speech therapist, home health care nurse, and others as needed. At times, consultation with various medical specialists may be needed, as in follow-up of congenital heart malformations in Down syndrome or for treatment of seizures or psychiatric disorders that may impair the mentally retarded person's functioning. But a physician who is thoroughly familiar with and experienced with treating mentally retarded individuals on a regular basis may not be within one's referral list.

DISCUSSION
Prevalence and Incidence

It is estimated that approximately 1% of the population is mentally retarded, with mild mental retardation being the most prevalent classification (about 85%). More severely affected individuals tend to be diagnosed earlier, often as infants, have a higher frequency of phenotypic abnormalities, manifest organic aberrations, and have a higher mortality rate. The mildly mentally retarded most often show no remarkable physical characteristics, but show varying degrees of developmental delay and are prone to behavior problems, school failure, difficulties in occupational endeavors, poor interpersonal relationships, and sexual vulnerability.

Related Basic Science

Chromosomal Abnormalities

Down syndrome is the most common chromosomal disorder associated with mental retardation. The incidence of Down syndrome is estimated to be between 1 per 800 and 1 per 1200 live births. Down syndrome typically presents with hypotonia, mild face flattening, oblique palpebral fissures, epicanthal folds, and Brushfield spots on the irides. Approximately 50% show a unilateral or bilateral single palmar crease. Thirty to forty percent of persons with Down syndrome have congenital heart malformations (such as ostium primum atrial septal defect), and one tenth have gastrointestinal abnormalities. A seizure disorder occurs in 5 to 10%.

Other chromosomal etiologies of mental retardation include the fragile-X syndrome (a syndrome of X-linked mental retardation with a family history of mentally retarded male offspring of normal maternal relatives), and Klinefelter's syndrome (XXY karyotype), and Turner's syndrome (XO karyotype).

Inborn Errors of Metabolism

Inborn errors of metabolism are marked by specific genetically determined enzyme deficiencies that interrupt or distort a metabolic process. These alterations may disturb the metabolism of carbohydrates, mucopolysaccharides, and amino acids, among others. Amino acids are most commonly involved, as in the case of phenylketonuria, which has an incidence of approximately 1 per 14,000. Early diagnosis via newborn screening is imperative in phenylketonuria, as appropriate dietary manipulation may reduce progressive disability.

Physical Trauma

Head injuries during the developmental years may produce mental retardation. Household accidents, motor vehicle accidents, and child abuse are frequent causes of such injuries.

Infections and Toxins

Intrauterine infection with herpes simplex, rubella, toxoplasmosis, cytomegalovirus, syphilis, and other agents may produce mental retardation in the newborn. Postnatal infections causing encephalitis or meningitis may likewise cause irreversible brain damage.

A wide variety of toxins, including lead, mercury, and radioactive substances, and maternal ingestion of prescription and illicit drugs and alcohol have been implicated as etiologic agents in mental retardation. Notable among these is the fetal alcohol syndrome (see Chapter 2–15), a result of maternal ingestion of alcoholic beverages.

The recent surge in the use of cocaine and its derivatives is currently causing increasing concern about infants born to cocaine-addicted mothers. Although at this time some evidence links maternal cocaine use with mental retardation in offspring, ongoing prospective studies are needed to clarify and verify this connection and mechanisms. This syndrome is characterized by growth retardation, hypoplasia of the midface and jaw, short palpebral fissures, and skeletal and cardiac anomalies.

Environmental Factors

As stated previously, sociocultural factors are believed to play a role in the development of mild mental retardation. Although as yet poorly understood, it is believed that environmental circumstances, including poverty, deprivation, poor nutrition, poor medical care, and lack of appropriate stimulation, may culminate in what is often referred to as "familial" mental retardation. In such families there may be evidence of faulty infant bonding, severe parental mental illness, multiple caretakers, physical trauma, and child abuse and neglect. The interplay of heredity and physical and social factors appears to be complex in such cases, and further research is needed to delineate the "nature versus nurture" question of causality.

Natural History and Its Modification With Treatment

Mentally retarded persons are particularly vulnerable to psychiatric disorders, a factor that is frequently overlooked but may cause significant impairment. Communication difficulties, low self-esteem, isolation from the mainstream of society, troubled peer relationships, forced dependence on others, and impaired cognitive control over emotions and behavior all play a role in placing the individual at risk for affective disorders, personality disorders, and psychotic disorders. Symptoms of attention deficit disorder are frequently seen in mentally retarded persons. These and other overlying psychiatric disorders may further impair the person's cognitive and adaptive ability, which may lead to overestimation of the role of the retardation. It has been consistently estimated that about a quarter of noninstitutionalized retarded individuals also suffer from mental illness, compared with less than a fifth of the general population. Ongoing research also suggests that mentally retarded persons may be at increased risk for alcohol abuse, drug abuse, or both.

It has been reported that persons with Down syndrome have a higher risk of developing Alzheimer's disease. In addition, the mentally retarded appear to be more susceptible than the population to infection and injury. Those in institutional or residential placement have an increased risk of exposure to hepatitis and other infectious processes. Studies of some institutionalized populations have also revealed unsatisfactory seizure control in mentally retarded residents, which may be accounted for in part by unavailability of adequate laboratory facilities to assess anticonvulsant levels, insufficient numbers or training of staff, and multiple caretakers. The prevalence of convulsive disorders is estimated to be greatly increased in the mentally retarded as compared with control populations (more than 50% in some institutionalized populations). But the mentally retarded person's general health for his or her age may be no different than that of the general population. Some studies show that the cardiovascular risk factor levels in adults with mental retardation are similar to those of the general population. Knowledge of health problems associated with individual syndromes becomes increasingly important as the population of retarded individuals is surviving longer due to advances in medical care.

It is possible for mentally retarded persons to have offspring with normal intelligence, and some mentally retarded persons can have satisfactory marriages. In many cases, however, pregnancy in the mentally retarded woman adds a burden to the individual, her family, and society.

Severe and profound levels of mental retardation are associated with high mortality rates, in part due to cardiac and other physical malformations incompatible with life. It has also been suggested that death rates are higher in institutional populations than in comparable mentally retarded populations in the community.

Prevention

Primary prevention of mental retardation involves such diverse services as genetic counseling, public education, emphasis on adequate maternal nutrition and medical care, proper immunizations, efforts to decrease the incidence of child abuse and neglect, use of automobile seat belts and bicycle helmets, and reduction in the pregnancy rates of teenagers and retarded females.

Secondary preventive measures include amniocentesis for the prenatal diagnosis of chromosomal aberrations, routine newborn screening for treatable metabolic disease, and identification of carriers of genetic conditions associated with mental retardation, such as Tay–Sachs disease.

Tertiary prevention makes use of community resources, special education, respite care (for the temporary respite of both the family and the mentally retarded individual), support of ongoing developmental momentum, and avoidance of regressive pressure by the merely average environment.

Cost Containment

Many programs at the state and federal levels offer financial assistance to aid families of mentally retarded persons. Families should be cautioned against "doctor shopping," in which families who have prolonged difficulty in accepting the diagnosis sometimes engage in an effort to find a "cure." Family members may become well versed in providing physical therapy and other treatment procedures at home, thereby decreasing the need for frequent follow-up visits. Vocational training may prove more beneficial than prolonged academic placement for many mentally retarded individuals, who may use their skills in community workshops, apprenticeships, or other sheltered environments and become positively involved in the community. This type of involvement and support often leads to better functioning, and may alleviate the necessity for financial subsidization. Prompt recognition and treatment of coexisting psychiatric disorders are rewarding for the mentally retarded person and his or her family, and are cost-effective for the community. In general, primary or secondary prevention is less costly than tertiary prevention, both from a financial perspective and in terms of providing the highest possible quality of life for the mentally retarded person and his or her family.

REFERENCES

Diagnostic and statistical manual of mental disorders. 4th ed. Washington, DC: American Psychiatric Association, 1994.

Grossman HJ. Classification in mental retardation, American Association on Mental Deficiency. Baltimore: Garamond-Pridemark Press, 1983.
McLaren J, Bryson SE. Review of recent epidemiological studies of mental retardation: Prevalence, associated disorders, and etiology. Am Ment Retard 1987;92:243.
Menolascino FJ, Stark JA, eds. The handbook of mental illness in the mentally retarded. New York: Plenum Press, 1984.
Mental retardation: Definition, classification and systems of supports. 9th ed. Washington, DC: American Association on Mental Retardation, 1992.
Minihan PM, Dean DH, Lyons CM. Managing the care of patients with mental retardation: A survey of physicians. Ment Retard 1990;31(4):239.
Rimmer JH, Graddock D, Fujura G. Cardiovascular risk factor levels in adults with mental retardation. Am J Ment Retard 1994;98(4):510.
Szymanski L, Tanguay P. Emotional disorders of mentally retarded persons: Assessment, treatment, and consultation. Baltimore: University Park Press, 1980.

CHAPTER 2–14
Alcoholism (See Section 24, Chapter 1)

CHAPTER 2–15
Fetal Alcohol Syndrome and Alcohol-Related Birth Defects

Claire D. Coles, Ph.D., Iris E. Smith, M.P.H., and Arthur Falek, Ph.D.

DEFINITION

Fetal alcohol syndrome is a constellation of birth defects found in individuals who were exposed to alcohol prenatally in sufficient quantities to produce a teratogenic effect. Usually included in the criteria for diagnosis are facial dysmorphisms, growth retardation, and central nervous system deficits (Jones et al., 1973).

ETIOLOGY

Children with fetal alcohol syndrome are born only to women who drink heavily during pregnancy. The majority of these women are multigravid, are "older," and have a diagnosis of alcoholism, but this condition can certainly occur in the offspring of younger women. Although there are many associated factors (i.e., cigarette smoking, poor prenatal care, other drug use, low socioeconomic status) that may contribute to negative outcomes, both clinical studies in human samples and experimental work with animal models confirm the etiologic significance of the teratogenic effects of alcohol. The mechanism by which these toxic effects occur is unknown at present.

CRITERIA FOR DIAGNOSIS

The diagnosis of fetal alcohol syndrome is made when a patient is affected in three primary areas:

- *Face:* In addition to microcephaly, the characteristic facies of a fetal alcohol syndrome patient may include hypoplasia of the midface, which manifests as a flattened nasal bridge, shortened palpebral fissures (less than 1.8 cm in the neonate or greater than 2 standard deviations [SD] below the mean in older patients), hypoplastic (absent) philtrum, and upper lip with thinned vermilion. In addition, there may be low-set ears, retrognathia in infancy, and, occasionally, mi-

crognathia in adolescence. Oral cavity and dental abnormalities may also occur.
- *Growth retardation:* Infants with the fetal alcohol syndrome are usually small at birth (more than 2 SD below the mean), and growth deficits may persist into adolescence despite normalization of size in some individuals over childhood.
- *Neurologic impairment:* The majority of patients with fetal alcohol syndrome are deficient to some degree in intellectual functioning or in adaptive behavior. Although mental retardation is the most serious cognitive consequence, learning deficits, behavioral disorders, and attentional problems have been observed in alcohol-affected children with intelligence quotients within the normal range. In clinical samples, these disorders may be accompanied by hyperactivity, varying degrees of fine and gross motor dysfunction, and/or evidence of dysfunction in some of the attentional processes or in executive functions like judgment and planning. Social functioning is often impaired in clinically referred samples, particularly in older children, adolescents, and adults. There appears to be an increased risk for substance abuse and addiction in adolescents and adults.

In addition to the defining facial dysmorphisms, patients with fetal alcohol syndrome may exhibit a wide range of birth defects including congenital heart defects, liver and kidney abnormalities, and musculoskeletal defects. Impairments in vision and hearing are common.

Suggestive

Individuals who display some but not all of the constellation of primary deficits are considered to exhibit alcohol-related birth defects or fetal alcohol effects. These children may display varying degrees of dysfunction, including learning and behavioral disorders, growth deficiency, and other organic defects. Other defects thought to be associated with prenatal alcohol exposure but not included in those defining the syndrome are called *alcohol-related birth defects* (e.g., cleft palate, cardiac problems). To receive a diagnosis of fetal alcohol syndrome, deficits must be present in all three primary areas; deficits in only two areas are indicative of fetal alcohol effects.

To give the diagnosis of fetal alcohol syndrome or alcohol-related birth defects, the family history must include maternal alcohol use during pregnancy. Behavioral and learning problems in children with a known history of prenatal alcohol exposure, as well as characteristic dysmorphisms and/or growth retardation, when maternal history is absent, are suggestive of fetal alcohol effects.

Definitive

There are no laboratory tests for fetal alcohol syndrome or alcohol-related birth defects at this time.

CLINICAL MANIFESTATIONS
Subjective
Behavioral Abnormalities in Infancy

During the neonatal period, alcohol-affected infants may display an unusual degree of irritability, hypertonia, tremulousness, and a generally increased activity level. In the first few months, infants may have abnormal sleeping patterns, and sucking or feeding difficulties may be reported by the caretaker. Although some of these abnormalities may be the transient manifestations of neonatal withdrawal syndrome, deficits in autonomic regulation and abnormal reflexive behavior may persist through the first 30 days of life. These behavioral abnormalities may occur even in the absence of the other morphologic characteristics of the full fetal alcohol syndrome.

Developmental Delay and Behavioral Abnormalities

Many, but not all, children with the full fetal alcohol syndrome are intellectually retarded, usually in the mild to moderate range. Many, however, have IQ scores in the borderline to low average range, and a few score within the average range. Children with IQ scores within the normal range may show evidence of learning and attentional problems or other behavioral disorders. Developmental delay can occur in children prenatally exposed to alcohol even in the absence of the dysmorphic features characteristic of fetal alcohol syndrome.

Developmental delays and learning problems may be relatively subtle in infants who are less affected physically and, because of the nature of the developmental process, may not manifest completely until the preschool period or later. Recent research (Streissguth et al., 1993) suggests that academic deficits may follow a characteristic pattern that includes relatively preserved vocabulary and verbal fluency, with deficits in mathematical and visual/spatial abilities as well as in abstract skills and metacognitive functioning.

Unusual Appearance

As a result of the minor facial birth defects associated with fetal alcohol syndrome, affected children may not resemble other family members or may have an unusual appearance. In other children, physical characteristics may be subtle and easily overlooked.

Family History

Family history is usually positive for alcoholism, alcohol abuse, and, frequently, other drug abuse. When a maternal reproductive history is obtained, there is often more than one affected child, with evidence of effects becoming more prominent with each successive birth. Fetal wastage is also common.

Many children also have a history of abuse and neglect, often leading to foster care placement or adoption. For this reason, there is a high risk for comorbidity with attachment disorders and conduct disorders.

Objective
Prenatal and Postnatal Growth Deficiency

Alcohol-affected patients are frequently more than 2 SD below the mean for both height and weight. Even full-term infants are often small for gestational age, with symmetric growth retardation including weight, length, and head circumference. Failure to thrive in infancy is often associated with prenatal alcohol exposure, particularly when maternal addiction is present.

Reduction in head circumference or microcephaly is the most significant growth problem when persistent. In some children, retardation in weight and height persists throughout childhood, and a disproportionate reduction in adipose tissue may also be observed in these patients. At puberty, girls may gain weight while maintaining a short stature. With increasing public knowledge about this disorder, extremes in growth retardation appear to be less common, apparently as a result of reduction in exposure during the later parts of pregnancy.

Intellectual Retardation

The majority of patients with full fetal alcohol syndrome are mentally retarded, with the degree of retardation ranging from mild to severe. Most are in the mild to moderate range. In infancy, scores on developmental tests are often in the low average to borderline range, which may disguise the eventual seriousness of the intellectual deficit.

Behavioral Abnormalities

Patients with fetal alcohol syndrome may display a wide range of behavioral and learning problems consistent with a diagnosis of mental retardation (e.g., poor social skills, lack of judgment). Other behavioral abnormalities that have been reported include hyperactivity, attention deficit disorder, and specific learning disabilities in individuals in the average to low average intellectual range. Deficits in arithmetic and sequential processing appear to be most common.

Associated Problems

A number of physical problems are associated with fetal alcohol syndrome or alcohol-related birth defects. These may include problems related to the characteristic dysmorphology (e.g., otitis media) or those associated with exposure (e.g., complications of cleft palate or heart defects). The incidence of infectious disease or immune-related problems may also be increased.

Physical Examination

The facial features and growth retardation associated with fetal alcohol syndrome can be identified on physical examination.

Routine Laboratory Abnormalities

None have been identified.

PLANS
Diagnostic
Differential Diagnosis

When signs from each of the three diagnostic categories are present and maternal alcohol abuse during pregnancy is confirmed, the diagnosis is appropriate. A much more difficult situation arises when the physical and clinical features are present but alcohol exposure is not confirmed. In that situation, judgment is called for in deciding whether the label should be used; however, the individual symptoms (e.g., cardiac defects, learning problems) associated with the syndrome can be identified and treated.

The growth retardation and dysmorphisms associated with fetal alcohol syndrome and alcohol-related birth defects may be similar to that seen in other syndromes caused by genetic anomalies or exposure to other teratogenic substances. Therefore, conditions like fetal hydantoin syndrome and maternal phenylketonuria should be ruled out.

Behavioral deficits associated with fetal alcohol syndrome and alcohol-related birth defects are not specific to this disorder. Nor are there unique treatments at present. For that reason, behavioral and intellectual problems should be identified and treated symptomatically. Behavioral disorders often identified in children with fetal alcohol syndrome are also commonly seen in children with attachment disorder, particularly when the child has been the victim of abuse and neglect or of frequent changes in caregiving.

Diagnostic Options

Children suspected of having fetal alcohol syndrome or alcohol-related birth defects should receive a complete physical evaluation as well as developmental and educational testing. In those experiencing behavior problems, psychological evaluation is recommended.

Recommended Approach

Because fetal alcohol exposure can affect many different systems, it is often necessary to evaluate and rule out many physical and functional problems in these individuals. In addition, because the effects of prenatal exposure may manifest differently at different points during development, examinations may have to be repeated over time. Medical issues are most likely to be observed during infancy, and behavioral and educational problems, during later childhood. During adolescence, problems in social and adaptive functioning frequently develop and may be complicated by a higher risk for substance abuse or mental health problems.

Therapeutic

Therapeutic Options

Due to the complexity of the teratogenic effects of alcohol, many different systems may be affected, necessitating a wide range of therapeutic responses. Affected systems may include vision, hearing, cardiac function, and nervous system integrity. Therapies must be specific to the problems noted.

Recommended Approach

Because of the wide range and varying severity of symptoms observed in patients with fetal alcohol syndrome or alcohol-related birth defects, the needs of each patient must be evaluated on an individual basis. Every effort should be made to ensure that the patient with fetal alcohol syndrome is able to achieve his or her full potential on both physical (organic) and intellectual levels. Infants whose health is adequate benefit from early intervention and preschool, and school-age children benefit from special education services.

FOLLOW-UP

Patients identified with fetal alcohol syndrome should be followed over development both to ensure that specific problems are identified as they occur, monitored, and treated and to allow caregivers a resource for information and help as needed.

DISCUSSION
Prevalence

It is now believed that the incidence of fetal alcohol syndrome in the general population in the United States is between 0.3 and 1 per 1000 (Abel and Sokol, 1987), and that of milder manifestations (alcohol-related birth defects), much higher. However, there appears to be a much higher reported incidence among minorities and in individuals of low socioeconomic status. The reasons for this discrepancy are unknown, but similar effects of social class on the reported incidence have been noted in other countries.

Related Basic Science
Genetics

Although a genetic contribution to vulnerability to fetal alcohol syndrome is suspected, this hypothesis has not yet been confirmed.

Anatomic Derangement

The anatomic anomalies associated with fetal alcohol syndrome and fetal alcohol effects have been discussed in the description of this disorder.

Natural History and Its Modifications with Treatment

Relatively few of the children with fetal alcohol syndrome who have been identified in prospective studies have reached adulthood, and, as a result, knowledge about longevity, fecundity, and long-term functional abnormalities in these individuals is inadequate. Clinical follow-up of individuals with fetal alcohol syndrome, however, indicates that these patients are at risk for a number of structural and organic problems. Chronic otitis media with sustained conductive hearing loss, vision problems, dental hypoplasia, and severe malocclusion have been reported. Deficits have been seen in speech and language, including difficulties in articulation and fluency secondary to malformations of the midfacial area. In addition, these children may be at higher risk for viral and bacterial infections as a result of the prenatal insult to the developing immune system.

Academic performance appears to be affected even in children without mental retardation, with math and reading skills most impaired. Problems with vigilance and reaction time have been reported in alcohol-exposed children without the full fetal alcohol syndrome. Behavior and social problems are commonly reported. In long-term studies, severity of medical, intellectual, and social outcome is related to several factors, including severity of facial and physical dysmorphia and degree of environmental disruption, suggesting both biological and environmental etiologies (Lemoine and Lemoine, 1992).

No systematic studies of treatment have been done.

Prevention

Women who consume alcoholic beverages on a regular basis throughout pregnancy are at higher risk for bearing alcohol-affected offspring. Although children with full fetal alcohol syndrome are usually the offspring of chronically alcoholic women, those who consume as few as one to two drinks (a drink is defined as one 12-oz beer, one cocktail containing 1.5 oz of distilled liquor, or one 5-oz glass of wine) daily are at increased risk for stillbirths, small-for-date infants, and infants who experience neonatal withdrawal syndrome during the newborn period. Although less is known about the negative effects of sporadic or binge drinking, present evidence indicates that blood alcohol levels are related to severity of outcome, suggesting that binge drinking may be particularly harmful. Although available data suggest that the severity of fetal alcohol effect is roughly dose-responsive, no safe level of alcohol consumption can be assumed.

The facial and other dysmorphisms associated with fetal alcohol syndrome have been demonstrated to be related to first-trimester exposure; however, drinking after the first trimester is also damaging to the fetus, and reduction of use or abstinence from alcoholic beverages even as late as the second trimester reduces the risk of growth deficits and neurobehavioral alterations in offspring. Neurobehavioral deficits are consistently found in the offspring of women who continue alcohol use into the third trimester. Women who are pregnant or contemplating pregnancy in the near future should be advised of the risk associated with alcohol use during pregnancy and should be encouraged to discontinue the use of alcoholic beverages during pregnancy.

No information is available about the prevention of secondary disabilities in affected individuals.

Cost Containment

The most efficient approach to the treatment of fetal alcohol syndrome and fetal alcohol effects is primary prevention, that is, encouraging abstention from alcohol during pregnancy or avoidance of pregnancy by addicted women. An educational approach, through either public education or individual counseling, is effective with nonaddicted women; however, this approach is not always effective with those most at risk who will often require referral to alcohol and drug treatment programs.

When an affected child has been born, early identification and treatment are very important to avoid the development of secondary disabilities. If the child is living with the biological parents, intervention with the child will often require that the parent receive treatment for her addiction as well. Consistent follow-up and screening will identify problems early and prevent secondary disabilities. For instance, because otitis media is common in children with fetal alcohol syndrome, attention to the problem of ear infections will prevent associated problems with hearing and language development.

REFERENCES

Abel EL, Sokol RJ. Incidence of fetal alcohol syndrome and economic impact of FAS-related anomalies. Drug Alcohol Depend 1987;19(1):51.

Coles CD, Platzman KA. Behavioral development in children prenatally exposed to drugs and alcohol. Int J Addict 1993;28:1393.

Jones KL, Smith DW, Ulleland CN, Streissguth AP. Pattern of malformations in offspring of chronic alcoholic mothers. Lancet 1973;1:1267.

Lemoine P, Lemoine Ph. Avenir des enfants de meres alcooliques (Etude de 105 Cas retrouves a l'age adulte) et quelques constatations d'interet prophylactique. Ann Pediat 1992;39:226.

Streissguth AP, Bookstein FL, Sampson PD, Barr HM. *The enduring effects of prenatal alcohol exposure on child development: Birth through seven years: A partial least squares solution.* International Academy of Research in Learning Disabilities, Monograph Series, No. 10. Ann Arbor: University of Michigan Press, 1993.

CHAPTER 2–16

Adjustment Disorders

Sandra B. Sexson, M.D.

DEFINITION

An adjustment disorder is a clinically significant psychological or behavioral reaction to a recent (within 3 months) identifiable stressor. The reaction is considered maladaptive either because the distress experienced is greater than that usually expected in response to a particular stressor or because functioning in the workplace (school) or within the social environment is significantly impaired. The response must not be an exacerbation of another diagnosable psychiatric disorder.

ETIOLOGY

An adjustment disorder is, by definition, precipitated by a stressor or stressors to which the patient is exposed. The stressor does not need to be catastrophic to evoke an adjustment disorder response, nor is the severity of the stressor necessarily predictive of the extent of the adjustment disorder. In fact, the most frequently identified stressors are relatively common life experiences such as school problems, interpersonal difficulties, job stresses or changes, and family moves.

CRITERIA FOR DIAGNOSIS

Suggestive

The diagnosis of an adjustment disorder is suggested when a person of any age develops symptoms of emotional distress such as depression, anxiety, and behavioral dysfunction that are a departure from the usual personality style of the patient. According to the *Diagnostic and Statistical Manual of Mental Disorders,* 4th edition. (1994), the maladaptive response must be associated with an identified stressor and must become symptomatic within 3 months of the onset of the stressor. The symptoms expressed must either be disproportionate to the stressor or cause significant impairment in the social or occupational (academic) functioning of the patient. The clinical diagnosis of an adjustment disorder requires the evaluation of two components: the precipitant or stressor and the maladaptive reaction or disorder.

Identification of the precipitating stressor requires a thorough clinical search. Not only must one consider the first-hand report from the patient, but it is necessary to augment the information by feedback from persons within the environment. The first-reported or seemingly obvious stressor often may not be the crucial one. For example, a 33-year-old mother of twins developed symptoms of depression and overwhelming guilt when the second of her premature twins was terminally ill in the neonatal intensive care unit. The immediate assumption was that her symptoms were related to concerns about something she might have done during the pregnancy to cause the prematurity and, thus, the impending death of her child, but when interviewed carefully, she revealed that she felt guilty because she had been uncooperative with her child's nurses several weeks earlier and feared his illness had worsened because the nurses may not have given him as good care after she had angered them. A wide range of stressors have been associated with the diagnosis of an adjustment disorder. The stressor may be single, such as the death of a significant friend or relative, or multiple, such as a divorce with concomitant changes in economic stability, friends, or the need to move into a different residence. Stressors may be acute and time limited (such as a tangible loss), recurrent (such as seasonally increased job demands), or continuous (such as coping with a chronic illness).

Establishing that a response to an identified stressor is maladaptive and disproportionate to what might be expected from the particular stressor can be very difficult. Consideration must be given to the psychosocial developmental level of the patient (whether child, adolescent, or adult), as symptoms may be expectable at certain developmental levels but considered maladaptive at others. For example, bedwetting may be expectable for a recently toilet-trained 3-year-old child whose parents are divorcing, but would be considered a maladaptive response for a 10-year-old who was toilet-trained years before. Additionally, cultural or group norms and values as well as the environmental and interpersonal context within which the stressor occurs may contribute to the disproportionate response to stressors. Finally, stressor variables such as intensity, quantity, duration, and reversibility must be considered.

The disorder may involve a disruption of adaptive functioning. Accurate assessment of academic, occupational, and social impairment requires an evaluation of the patient within the context of the home, the school or work environment, and the social milieu.

Definitive

Definitive diagnosis of an adjustment disorder relies solely on the diagnostic criteria outlined in Table 2–16–1 and depends on the clinical evaluation of the patient and his or her presenting symptoms.

TABLE 2–16–1. AMERICAN PSYCHIATRIC ASSOCIATION CRITERIA FOR DIAGNOSIS OF ADJUSTMENT DISORDERS

A. The development of emotional or behavioral symptoms in response to an identifiable stressor(s) occurring within 3 months of the onset of the stressor(s).

B. These symptoms or behaviors are clinically significant as evidenced by either of the following:
   (1) Marked distress that is in excess of what would be expected from exposure to the stressor.
   (2) Significant impairment in social or occupational (academic) functioning.

C. The stress-related disturbance does not meet the criteria for another specific Axis I disorder and is not merely an exacerbation of a preexisting Axis I or Axis II disorder.

D. The symptoms do not represent bereavement.

E. Once the stressor (or its consequences) has terminated, the symptoms do not persist for more than an additional 6 months.

Specify if:

Acute: if the disturbance lasts less than 6 months

Chronic: if the disturbance lasts for 6 months or longer

Source: Diagnostic and statistical manual of mental disorders. 4th ed. Washington, DC: American Psychiatric Association, 1994. Reproduced with permission.

CLINICAL MANIFESTATIONS
Subjective

An adjustment disorder can develop in a patient at any age who is confronted with a particular stressor during a period of vulnerability to that stress. Similar stresses have the capacity to produce a wide range of reactions in different individuals and little is known about predisposing factors. The stressful life events may exert their negative impact on the patient, the patient's family, and/or the patient's community. Additionally, normative life crises associated with specific developmental stages such as beginning school, graduating from high school, leaving home, getting married, becoming a parent, and retiring are often associated with adjustment disorders. The symptoms do not always develop immediately after the onset of the stressor, nor do they subside as soon as the stressor remits. Chronic stressors may lead to a chronic adjustment disorder.

Symptoms of adjustment disorder may vary considerably. Depression and anxiety are most common in adults. Adolescents are more likely to develop behavioral symptoms such as persistent lying, stealing, physical fighting, and temper outbursts. Physical symptoms are more frequent in children and the elderly but may occur at any time. The American Psychiatric Association delineates five subtypes of adjustment disorders classified according to the predominant symptom. A sixth category of adjustment disorder unspecified allows for even more variability in symptom development (Table 2–16–2). Because of the wide range of potential presentations, a description of symptoms specific to the disorder according to expected frequency is impossible. An adjustment disorder should not be viewed as a mild or trivial condition by either the physician or family of the patient. Such an error can be catastrophic, as suicidal or homicidal thinking may be present and can be acted on as impulsively as when it is a part of a seemingly more serious psychiatric disorder. The emotional pain experienced by the patient with an adjustment disorder may be very severe and is never trivial.

Objective

Objective data to support the diagnosis of adjustment disorder are dependent on objective evidence of the identified stressor and evidence of the dysfunction or symptomatology. No specific abnormal physical findings or laboratory abnormalities are characteristic of this disorder.

PLANS
Diagnostic
Differential Diagnosis

Adjustment disorders must be differentiated from reactions to stress that are considered nonpathologic, reactions that do not lead to disproportionate responses or do not impact significantly on social or occupational functioning. As absolute criteria for what constitutes an excessive response are not available, careful clinical judgment is necessary.

Adjustment disorders share the diagnostic criteria of a psychosocial stressor with both posttraumatic stress disorder and acute stress disorder. These latter categories require that the stressor be extreme and that a specific cluster of symptoms develop, whereas an adjustment disorder can be precipitated by a stressor of any severity and may present with any variety of symptoms.

Frequently the physician will be faced with patients who present with physical complaints in response to psychosocial stressors. These may include gastrointestinal distress or pain syndromes and must be differentiated from a specific medical illness, as well as from psychiatric disorders that have major physical symptomatology. Usually in an adjustment disorder the psychologically determined symptoms develop in response to the stressor. Patients diagnosed with chronic medical conditions may develop adjustment disorders in response to the stress of having a serious medical condition.

During the process of bereavement, people are generally expected to experience distress and potentially some work or social inhibition. These persons would not be diagnosed with an adjustment disorder unless the reaction is prolonged or excessively exaggerated.

Finally, an adjustment disorder must be differentiated from other psychiatric disorders such as depressive or anxiety disorders. If an individual develops symptoms that meet the criteria (*Diagnostic and Statistical Manual*, 1994) for another psychiatric diagnosis in response to a stressor, the other specific diagnosis is applicable. Additionally, some patients may develop symptoms that do not meet the full criteria for a specific psychiatric diagnosis such as major depressive episode without an identifiable stressor. The physician should diagnose such patients with the atypical category of "not otherwise specified" rather than use the adjustment disorder definition. On the other hand, patients with a primary psychiatric diagnosis (e.g., depression) may develop symptoms when stressed that are not a part of their psychiatric disorder and, therefore, may meet criteria for both their primary psychiatric disorder and an adjustment disorder. When a patient has a personality disorder that worsens in the face of an acute stressor, the adjustment disorder diagnosis is not appropriate; however, patients with personality disorders can develop an adjustment disorder when exposed to a stressor with symptoms not characteristic of their personality diagnosis. In such cases, the adjustment disorder designation is appropriate.

Diagnostic Options

No specific tests are available that will confirm the diagnosis of adjustment disorder. Please refer to Recommended Approach.

Recommended Approach

The diagnosis of an adjustment disorder is based on the clinical evaluation of the patient and his or her presenting symptoms and is dependent on meeting the criteria outlined in Table 2–16–1, as discussed under Criteria for Diagnosis. Assessment of both the precipitant stressor and the maladaptive response in the context of other potential psychiatric disorders is imperative as outlined previously.

Therapeutics
Therapeutic Options

The treatment of choice for adjustment disorders continues to be psychotherapeutic interventions aimed at relieving the patient's emotional distress and reestablishing the patient's premorbid level of functioning in a timely manner. Various psychotherapeutic options may be employed depending on the type of adjustment disorder and the specific symptomatology. Psychotropic medications may occupy a very limited place in the treatment of adjustment disorders.

Recommended Approach

Once the diagnosis of an adjustment disorder is made the physician must consider carefully an appropriate intervention. It is unwise to delay treatment, thinking that the disorder will remit spontaneously once the identified stressor is alleviated. Immediate treatment serves to relieve the emotional distress and prevent further psychiatric morbidity.

TABLE 2–16–2. SUBTYPES OF ADJUSTMENT DISORDER ACCORDING TO THE AMERICAN PSYCHIATRIC ASSOCIATION

Subtype	Predominant Manifestation
With depressed mood	Depressed mood, tearfulness, or feelings of hopelessness
With anxiety	Nervousness, worry, jitteriness, or, in children, fear of separation from primary caretakers
With mixed anxiety and depressed mood	Combination of depression and anxiety
With disturbance of conduct	Violation of rights of others or age-appropriate societal norms and rules (e.g., vandalism, reckless driving, fighting, defaulting on legal responsibilities)
With mixed disturbance of emotions and conduct	Both emotional (depression or anxiety) and conduct symptoms
Unspecified	Those reactions unclassifiable under the other subtypes (physical complaints)

Source: Diagnostic and statistical manual of mental disorders. 4th ed. Washington, DC: American Psychiatric Association, 1994: 623–624. Adapted and reproduced with permission.

Whenever possible, environmental manipulation to eliminate the stressor or to mobilize support systems is the first act of intervention. Psychotherapeutic endeavors are the treatment of choice and may follow a number of pathways. Techniques of crisis intervention and time-limited psychotherapy may be useful early interventions. Patients who have experienced common stressors (e.g., divorce, retirement, a chronic illness) may respond to group therapy with others in similar situations. Cognitive–behavioral therapy techniques may be helpful to improve problem-solving abilities and to alter dysfunctional beliefs that contribute to the reaction to the stressor. Brief psychiatric hospitalization may be necessary if active suicidal or homicidal behavior develops. In cases where the symptomatology involves significant behavioral manifestations, such as legal difficulties, the physician must consider very carefully any attempts to rescue the patient from the consequences of the behavior, as such rescue may inadvertently reinforce such socially unacceptable behavior as a means of coping with the stressor and delay the development of more adaptive methods of coping. In any case, active intervention in an expedient manner is necessary to prevent the development of more intrinsic psychopathology or to facilitate a more adaptive response if the stressor becomes chronic.

Psychotropic medication may occupy a limited place in the treatment of adjustment disorders. Severe anxiety may be treated on a short-term basis with anxiolytic agents. Occasionally, the transient use of hypnotic agents may be helpful for severe and prolonged sleep disturbances. A more specific diagnosis should be entertained, however, should anxiolytic agents or antidepressants be needed for extended periods or considered as the primary treatment. Adequate treatment of adjustment disorders is unlikely to be achieved with the use of medication alone.

FOLLOW-UP

Follow-up of the patient with an adjustment disorder is determined by the active treatment of the disorder. The physician should consider an assessment of the coping skills of the patient and the status of the stressor when planning follow-up after the symptoms have abated. Reevaluation within 6 months after the stressor has subsided is indicated, as symptomatology that persists should be evaluated within the context of a different diagnosis. Once an adjustment disorder has resolved, it is advisable to encourage the patient to seek help immediately should symptoms reappear or new symptoms develop.

DISCUSSION
Prevalence and Incidence

Adjustment disorders are presumed to be common in human experience, although specific epidemiologic data vary widely. Among psychiatric patients the incidence of adjustment disorder ranges from 5 to 20%. The disorder may be even more common in general medical patients. Many, perhaps even most, cases may not come to professional attention. Adjustment disorders are diagnosed more commonly in children and adolescents and in single women, although overall males and females are equally affected. Individuals living in high-stress situations and in disadvantaged life circumstances may be at increased risk for the disorder.

Related Basic Science

The specific biological mechanism through which adjustment disorder symptomatology develops is unknown. Despite the fact that the diagnosis of adjustment disorder has low reliability, in part because of the difficulty in operationalizing what symptoms are "excessive" or "maladaptive," it is considered a valid subthreshold diagnosis for patients who exhibit a variety of emotional symptoms in the context of situational stress and whose symptoms do not meet the criteria for a more specific psychiatric disorder.

Natural History and Its Modification with Treatment

There are insufficient data to delineate accurately the natural history of adjustment disorder. It is presumed to have a relatively good prognosis, with a 70 to 90% recovery rate when comorbid psychiatric diagnoses are controlled. By definition, the disorder must remit within 6 months of alleviation of the stressor and another disorder must be considered at that time if symptoms persist. It is recognized that chronic stressors may lead to chronic adjustment disorders as defined by the new American Psychiatric Association criteria. Variables that predict a poorer prognosis in adolescents and adults include more behavioral symptoms, more stressor precipitants, and chronicity. Early intervention and specific treatment have the potential to decrease the morbidity significantly, often allowing the patients to resume their previous level of functioning despite the persistence of the precipitating stressor.

Prevention

Prevention measures specific to adjustment disorders have not been identified; however, general measures to address stress reduction and management may be helpful. Early intervention aimed at resolution of the symptoms as well as development of new levels of successful adaptation may improve the long-term prognosis and prevent recurrent symptomatology.

Cost Containment

Cost-effectiveness may best be addressed by aggressive early intervention and anticipatory management of identified stressors.

REFERENCES

Diagnostic and statistical manual of mental disorders. 4th ed. Washington, DC: American Psychiatric Association, 1994.

Enzer NB, Cunningham SD. Adjustment and reactive disorder. In: Wiener JM, ed. Textbook of child and adolescent psychiatry. Washington, DC: American Psychiatric Press, 1991:43:468.

Kaplan H, Sadock BJ. Synopsis of psychiatry. Behavioral sciences and clinical psychiatry. 5th ed. Baltimore: Williams & Wilkins, 1988.

Newcorn JH, Strain J. Adjustment disorder in children and adolescents. J Am Acad Child Adolesc Psychiatry 1992;31:318.

Strain JJ, Newcorn J, Wolf D, et al. Considering changes in adjustment disorder. Hosp Community Psychiatry 1993;44:13.

CHAPTER 2–17

Psychoactive Substance Use Disorders

Sidney H. Schnoll, M.D., Ph.D.

DEFINITION

Psychoactive substance use disorders can broadly be defined as use of licit substances in a manner outside of common accepted use or use of illicit substances. More specifically, they can be divided into two categories: (1) addiction—a chronic disease characterized by compulsive use of substances resulting in physical, psychological, or social harm with continued use despite evidence of that harm; and (2) dependence—an adaptation of cells in the body to the presence of a drug resulting in a characteristic withdrawal syndrome when the drug is stopped.

Addiction and dependence frequently coexist; however, each can occur independently. Physicians must recognize the difference between these conditions. Addiction is a behavioral disorder, whereas dependence is a physiologic response to certain classes of drugs.

ETIOLOGY

The etiology of psychoactive substance use disorders is not known, but they cannot be manifested without exposure to the substances. Genetic, psychological, social, and environmental factors play important roles in the etiology of the disorders.

CRITERIA FOR DIAGNOSIS
Suggestive

The basic clue to the diagnosis is suspicion of the problem. Patients presenting unusual symptoms that cannot be readily diagnosed, displaying evidence of drug-seeking behavior by losing prescriptions, requesting specific medications, failing to respond to medical treatment for simple disorders, becoming annoyed at questions about alcohol or drug use, having a family history of addiction, having unreported drugs detected on a urine toxicology screen, or having a blood alcohol concentration of 150 mg/kL or greater without showing signs of intoxication should be suspected of addiction. Reports of drug or alcohol use from family members, employer, or school are also important potential identifying characteristics.

Definitive

Signs of withdrawal from drugs make the diagnosis of dependence, but further investigation is necessary to diagnose addiction. Patients who have negative sequelae of their psychoactive drug use, but continue to use the drugs and deny the relationship to the problems they are experiencing are suffering from addiction. It is important to recognize that addiction is like a chameleon and may be very difficult to diagnose.

CLINICAL MANIFESTATIONS
Subjective

A positive family history of addiction is important in identifying patients who are at high risk. The history should include inquiries about parents, siblings, aunts, uncles, and grandparents. Addiction often skips a generation. Addiction is most common in young adults (18–25 years), but can occur at any time during life. It also occurs in the elderly who are prescribed numerous drugs. Individuals with chronic illnesses and personality disorders are also prone to addiction.

Patients suffering from addiction often have complaints about their families, employers, or legal matters (e.g., driving under the influence convictions). They complain about vague symptoms for which there are no objective findings and often request a specific mood-altering drug for the complaints.

Objective
Physical Examination

Intoxication and drug withdrawal are strong clues to the presence of a psychoactive substance use disorder. Intoxication with depressant drugs causes decreased respirations, bradycardia, hypotension, sleepiness, ataxia, and dysarthria. Opioid drugs cause miosis (except for meperidine, which causes mydriasis), constipation, pruritus, decreased libido, and slowed mentation. There may be little change in vital signs until doses are quite high. Stimulant drugs cause hyperactivity, hypertension, tachycardia, hyperpyrexia, and seizures. The most severe withdrawal occurs with sedative–hypnotic drugs and alcohol, during which patients present with tachycardia, hypertension, agitation, hallucinations, and seizures. In its most severe state, major withdrawal (delirium tremens), death can occur from cardiovascular collapse. Narcotic withdrawal is characterized by mydriasis, piloerection (goose flesh), rhinorrhea, lacrimation, uncontrolled yawning, and strong drug-seeking behavior. Withdrawal from stimulants is characterized by an immediate prolonged episode of sleeping, lasting up to 24 hours, followed by depression, agitation, and insomnia.

Other physical findings include "tracks" in the intravenous drug user,

enlarged liver from chronic alcohol use, and/or hepatitis associated with intravenous drug use, peripheral neuropathies from poor nutrition, and degeneration of the central nervous system. Presence of HIV infection or manifestation of AIDS should increase suspicion of injection drug use and other forms of substance use. Two or more non-sports-related episodes of physical trauma in a person over the age of 18 are highly correlated with psychoactive substance use disorders.

Routine Laboratory Abnormalities

Routine laboratory tests are not helpful in making the diagnosis. It is necessary to obtain liver function tests to determine the presence of liver abnormalities occurring with alcohol and intravenous drug use; however, these abnormalities could be secondary to nonpsychoactive drug use. Alcoholics may show a macrocytic anemia and elevated uric acid. Those who abuse or are addicted to other drugs do not show any specific abnormalities on routine laboratory tests.

PLANS
Diagnostic
Differential Diagnosis

The diagnostic possibilities are enormous. Psychoactive substance use disorders can mimic many different disorders. Most commonly they present as other psychiatric disorders like anxiety, depression, or mania. They can also present as hypertension, thyroid disease, and cardiac disease.

Diagnostic Options and Recommended Approach

The best approach to diagnosis is taking a careful history in a nonthreatening manner. The diagnosis may not be made in one visit but may require repeated visits to put the pieces of the puzzle into place. Helpful information can be gained from the *CAGE* questions: Have you ever tried to *c*ut down on your alcohol and/or drug use? Have you ever been *a*nnoyed when others talk about your alcohol and/or drug use? Do you feel *g*uilty about anything you have done while intoxicated? Do you need an *e*ye opener in the morning? Asking questions about non-sports-related injuries can also provide an important clue to drug use problems. Two or more injuries are highly correlated with abuse problems.

The best diagnostic screening test for suspected substance use disorders is a urine drug toxicology screen. Tests are currently available for opioids, benzodiazepines and barbiturates, amphetamines, cocaine, and phencyclidine (PCP). It is more difficult to determine the presence of hallucinogens. Blood tests for drugs are less helpful, as the concentration of drug in the blood is often lower than that found in the urine. In patients suspected of opioid dependence, naloxone (Narcan) 0.4 mg intravenously should produce withdrawal signs. In patients suspected of sedative–hypnotic drug or alcohol dependence who are not intoxicated, a test dose of pentobarbital (Nembutal) 200 mg orally will make the naive patient become somnolent or intoxicated. The dependent patient will show no, or minimal, effects.

Therapeutic

There is no single best approach to the treatment of psychoactive substance use disorders. Treatment of addiction and treatment of dependence are quite different, and there are different treatment options depending on the specific substance or substances being used. When medicating for withdrawal, do not rely on the patient's subjective complaints. Base medication decisions on objective signs of withdrawal.

Dependence is most frequently and effectively treated with chemotherapy. Long-acting drugs displaying cross-dependence and cross-tolerance with the abused drugs should be administered. For opioids, the treatment of choice is methadone. Once a dose of methadone is found that suppresses withdrawal without producing intoxication, the dose of methadone can be reduced at a rate of 5 mg a day. If methadone is to be used in an outpatient setting for the treatment of addiction, a special license is required. An alternative approach is to give clonidine (Catapres) to block some of the withdrawal signs and symptoms. Start with clonidine 0.1 mg three times daily and increase the dose until maximum relief is provided without causing hypotension. If the patient is taking a prescribed amount of opioid, reduce the daily dose 10% a day from the original dose while maintaining the dosing interval. Increasing the interval between doses will create more problems for the patient and result in a less satisfactory outcome.

Sedative–hypnotic drug or alcohol withdrawal can be treated with phenobarbital or long-acting benzodiazepines. Once the dose of medication necessary to control withdrawal without excessive sedation is reached, it can be reduced daily by 20% of the maximum 24-hour dose. Major withdrawal (delirium tremens) should be treated with lorazepam (Ativan) 2 mg intravenously, with repeated doses until the patient's tachycardia drops below 120. Then phenobarbital or another long-acting sedative–hypnotic drug should be administered, as the effects of lorazepam wear off in 2 hours.

Currently there are no specific medications that have been demonstrated to be efficacious in the treatment of withdrawal from psychostimulants (including cocaine), phencyclidine, or marijuana. Supportive therapy is very important in ensuring a successful withdrawal from these drugs as well as from drugs for which medication is available.

In all withdrawals, the dose of medication should be titrated to control the withdrawal symptoms without producing intoxication. In treating acute withdrawal syndromes, medication should be administered in a liquid, with the dose being blind to the patient. The volume of liquid should be held constant so the patient is not aware of decreasing dosage schedules. This reduces the anxiety associated with withdrawal. Clonidine 0.1 mg two to three times daily is useful in reducing some of the peripheral manifestations associated with withdrawal from both opioid and sedative–hypnotic drugs.

Once a drug-free state has been achieved, it is possible to start treatment for the addiction. The treatment of addiction is primarily psychosocial, behavioral, or both. It can be initiated in an inpatient setting or an outpatient setting, where the individual can deal with all the environmental, social, and psychological cues associated with addiction. An important adjunct to treatment is participation in 12-step/peer support groups modeled after Alcoholics Anonymous. Twelve-step programs are available for alcohol, narcotics, cocaine, and other drugs. These groups provide support and guidance to patients during recovery. Family, friends, and employers should be included in the treatment process to assist in making and supporting the behavior changes necessary for recovery.

Medications used during recovery include methadone maintenance, l-α-acetylmethadol, and naltrexone (ReVia) for opioid addiction and disulfiram (Antabuse) for alcohol addiction. Recent studies have shown that naltrexone also reduces alcohol consumption. Methadone and l-α-acetylmethadol maintenance can be administered only in specially licensed clinics. Naltrexone 50 mg daily will block the effects of opioids for 24 hours; its usefulness has been demonstrated especially for health care professionals. It can also be used in similar doses to reduce alcohol craving and alcohol consumption in alcoholics. Disulfiram 250 to 500 mg daily has been helpful in assisting alcoholics to maintain sobriety. In patients suffering from nicotine dependence, nicotine substitutes in the form of chewing gum or patch have been shown to have some effect when used in conjunction with behavioral treatment. The combination of behavioral and chemotherapeutic treatments appears to be the most effective when treating psychoactive substance use disorders. Although other drugs have been studied for these and other addiction problems, none have proven to be effective at this time.

Physicians should educate patients regarding the differences between addiction and dependence: addiction is progressive, leading to deterioration in functioning. The physician should be nonjudgmental in discussing addiction with the patient, explaining that recovery is possible. Short-term recovery (6 months) occurs in 60 to 70% of treated cases, and prolonged recovery occurs in about 35% of treated cases. The education should include a warning that all future physicians should be told about the problem with addiction so that appropriate prescribing practices can be initiated to reduce the potential for relapse.

FOLLOW-UP

Treatment of addiction, like that of other chronic disease, is a lifelong process. Chronic diseases are characterized by periodic remissions and exacerbations. Addiction is no different. To expect lifelong sobriety after a single treatment is like expecting a diabetic to maintain a normal blood sugar once placed on an appropriate diet and insulin. It just does not happen. Failure to follow up after treatment can lead to relapse. Intensive treatment can last 1 year, with gradually reduced follow-up over time. The patient should be encouraged to use peer and/or 12-step support groups as part of the recovery process.

The physician must continue to monitor the patient's progress in treatment after a referral is made. This requires at least monthly visits during the first year, with less frequent visits later depending on the status of the patient's recovery. Follow-up should include random urine drug screens and breath tests to determine if the patient is using unauthorized licit or illicit substances and if the patient is taking prescribed medications. The testing of hair and other tissues is not recommended at this time because of expense and technical problems. It is also prudent to check with significant others (family, friends, employers, and others) to see if there are any behavioral changes that may indicate a return to addictive behaviors.

DISCUSSION
Prevalence and Incidence

It is estimated that there are about 40 million nicotine addicts, 12 million alcoholics, 1 million cocaine addicts, and 600,000 heroin addicts in the United States. The number of addicts addicted to prescribed drugs is not known. More than 350,000 deaths a year are attributed to nicotine and 125,000 to alcohol. About 20,000 deaths a year are attributed to all other drugs of abuse combined. Although there is considerable fear that prescribing drugs with abuse potential will result in addiction, there is little evidence to support this contention. Patients may become dependent on the prescribed medication and require careful withdrawal, but less than 0.1% become addicted.

It is often believed that the incidence of addiction is higher because addicts are frequent users of medical care. Approximately 25 to 40% of hospital admissions are addicts, with most being admitted for the treatment of sequelae of their addiction. This rate may be higher in some settings. In an outpatient practice it is estimated that 8 to 16% of patients are suffering from addiction. The majority of these cases are related to nicotine and alcohol use.

Related Basic Science

The etiology of addiction is not known. Evidence indicates a strong genetic component, but psychological, social, and environmental factors also play important roles. Studies to determine defects in specific neurotransmitter systems leading to addiction have not proven successful. It is estimated that approximately 10% of the population is susceptible to the problems of addiction.

Natural History and Its Modification with Treatment

Addiction usually begins in early adolescence and progresses through the late teens and early twenties. Those with early onset have a strong family history of addiction and also present with an array of personality disorders, particularly antisocial and borderline personality disorders. As drug use becomes daily, the secondary complications of addiction occur, including psychiatric, medical, and social problems.

There is a late-onset addiction usually beginning after the third decade, although it may not appear until the sixth or seventh decade of life. This late-onset disorder is less progressive. Usually evidence of family history is lacking and the prevalence of psychiatric disorders, particularly personality disorders, is less frequent.

It is estimated that less than 10% of patients suffering from addiction ever seek treatment. There is some evidence that 20 to 25% of patients suffering from addiction will spontaneously remit without any specific treatment. Mortality rates are highest with nicotine and alcohol addiction, with approximately 350,000 and 125,000 deaths a year, respectively. Total mortality rates for the illicit drugs are less than 20,000 per year.

Treatment can reduce or stop the progression of the disease. Although sobriety may not be lifelong in all cases, interruption can have significant effects on the life of the patient and significant others. There is a reduction in medical sequelae and significant societal cost savings. For every dollar spent on treatment, it is estimated that $5 to $7 is saved in future health and related costs.

Prevention

Prevention of substance use disorders falls into two general categories: (1) The general prevention approach tries to reduce initiation of substance use in the general population. This approach uses school education programs, television advertising, and scare tactics. The approach has yet to be proven effective. (2) The targeted approach aims to direct specific strategies at high-risk groups, those with a family history of addiction or those living in high-risk areas. Targeted prevention efforts are relatively new, and little evidence is available regarding their effectiveness.

Cost Containment

Treatment of addiction can occur in many different settings. It used to be believed that all addicts required treatment in a 28-day inpatient setting. This is no longer true. Recent studies have shown that for many patients, the results of outpatient treatment are similar to those of inpatient treatment. Intensive outpatient programs (day hospitals) provide many of the services found in the residential setting. Outpatient withdrawals can also be safely performed.

The inpatient setting should be reserved for those patients who have severe addictions complicated by the presence of medical or psychiatric problems. For uncomplicated cases, outpatient treatment along with a 12-step or peer support group can be cost-effective. Many different types of ambulatory treatments are currently available, ranging form very intensive settings like partial hospital or intensive outpatient programs to weekly or less frequent therapy sessions.

The decision about the most appropriate clinical setting should be based on the severity of illness. Patients who have failed at outpatient treatments may require inpatient treatment. The decision on the most appropriate treatment setting can be made only after a careful evaluation of the patient and the environment. A patient with a severe addiction but with good support systems may require less intensive treatment than a patient with less severe disease but no or inappropriate support systems. Treatment should be based on a variable rather than a fixed length of stay, with criteria used to judge progress in treatment.

Because addicts are such frequent users of medical care, treatment is extremely cost-effective; however, the treatment should be based on the severity of the patient's problem and not some fixed approach. If you do not feel qualified to make the decision about the type and intensity of treatment needed, referral to a colleague trained in addictions can be helpful in reducing long-term costs. When making the referral, choose someone who is not connected with a single treatment program or modality so the best options can be presented to the patient.

REFERENCES

Jaffee JH. Drug addiction and drug abuse. In: Gilman AG, Goodman LS, Rall TW, Murad F, eds. Goodman and Gilman's the pharmacological basis of therapeutics. 7th ed. New York: MacMillan, 1985:532.

Lowinson JH, Ruiz P, Millman RB, Langrod JG. Substance abuse: A comprehensive textbook. 2nd ed. Baltimore: Williams & Wilkins, 1992.

Miller NS. Principles of addiction medicine. Chevy Chase, MD: American Society of Addiction Medicine, 1994.

Schnoll SH. Aiding the drug abuser. Hosp Med 1983;19(8):116.

Trachtenberg AI, Fleming MF. Diagnosis and treatment of drug abuse in family practice. Am Fam Physician Monogr 1994.

CHAPTER 2–18

Sleep Disorders (See Section 13, Chapter 1; Section 20, Chapter 26; and Section 21, Chapter 37)

CHAPTER 2–19

Personality Disorders

Ralph E. Roughton, M.D.

DEFINITION

Personality *traits* are enduring patterns of perception, attitude, and behavior that are manifest in all aspects of one's life. These traits make up a major portion of what we think of as the "personality." When these traits become so exaggerated or inflexible as to result in significant maladaptation or subjective distress, then the diagnosis of personality disorder may be made.

ETIOLOGY

The etiology of personality disorder is best understood in a biopsychosocial model. A biological predisposition, in the form of general temperament or more specific biological factors, in combination with psychological and social risk factors, results in the organization of a pervasive pattern of psychological defensive operations.

CRITERIA FOR DIAGNOSIS
Suggestive

Personality disorder should be considered when (1) a pattern of inner experience and/or outward behavior results in persistent distress or dis-

ruptive behavior, is inflexible and pervasive, and has persisted since adolescence or early adulthood; (2) the individual fails to recognize the difficulties as a problem within himself or herself but blames external factors or other people; and (3) symptoms of psychosis are either absent or transient. In addition, these individuals tend to be self-centered, easily offended, chronically dissatisfied, and immature. They either shun close relationships or repeatedly establish ones that are characterized by instability or by interlocking pathology. On the other hand, some people with relatively mild personality pathology may be highly successful in fields in which those traits are adaptive up to a point, for example, an obsessive-compulsive bookkeeper, a narcissistic actress, or a schizoid lighthouse keeper.

Because one meets every life situation in one's own characteristic way of being, one's personality (or, when present, one's personality disorder) will manifest in any visit for medical care and will influence one's manner of presenting symptoms of unrelated illnesses, one's relationship with caretakers, and one's compliance with treatment. Thus, behavioral manifestations of personality disorders may be encountered in any clinical setting. In addition, the personality disorder itself is often a significant background factor in patients who present with anxiety, depression, or somatic symptoms, as well as in populations found in substance abuse clinics, in prisons, and among the chronic homeless.

Definitive

Unfortunately, because of the diversity of types of personality disorder and the lack of clear boundaries with those traits in normal people, the diagnostic criteria for the general category of personality disorder can only be suggestive. The American Psychiatric Association (*Diagnostic and Statistical Manual, 1994*) describes 10 categories of personality disorder. Diagnostic specificity is often difficult, however, because criteria to delineate the boundary between normality and impairment, between the different types of personality disorders, and between personality disorder and other psychiatric entities have not been clearly defined.

CLINICAL MANIFESTATIONS

Subjective

Although disturbance in early parent–child relationships is typical of the family history of patients with personality disorder, problems of research methodology and of diagnostic criteria have hampered the establishment of typical family histories for most of the personality disorders. Definitive criteria for the different types of personality disorders have been established by the American Psychiatric Association. The categories are necessarily somewhat arbitrary but useful for systematic study and clinical classification.

Patients with *paranoid personality disorder* expect to be harmed or exploited by others, are unable to trust even friends, read threatening meanings into benign events, are jealous, bear grudges, easily feel slighted, and react quickly with anger. Other people usually see them as stubborn and hostile, overly concerned with power and rank, and avoidant of intimacy.

Patients with *schizoid personality disorder* show an indifference to social contact and a preference for solitary activities, have a restricted emotional life and little facial expressiveness, are indifferent to praise or criticism, and have no close friends and little desire for sexual experience. They are seen by others as cold and aloof, odd, and emotionally vacant. They may, however, function at a high level in an occupation that permits social isolation.

Patients with *schizotypal personality disorder* exhibit more severe pathology, including disturbance in thought content (odd beliefs, magical thinking, ideas of reference), excessive social anxiety, eccentric behavior, lack of close friends, and inappropriate affect. In contrast to the schizoid person, who appears merely odd and emotionally limited, the schizotypal person seems disturbed, although to a lesser degree than those diagnosed as schizophrenic.

Antisocial personality disorder manifests early as conduct disorder in childhood and later as irresponsible and lawless behavior, including inability to keep a job, exploitation of others, criminal behavior, irritability and aggressive outbursts, impulsivity, financial irresponsibility, habitual lying, and lack of remorse. They rarely are able to sustain lasting, close relationships and repeatedly disregard or violate the rights of other people. Their distress is usually masked and channeled into action, and they are more likely to come to the attention of law officers than physicians. Some people of the antisocial type have the charm of the con artist, but repeated exploitation eventually turns most people against them.

Borderline personality disorder is characterized by intense but unstable relationships; intolerance of being alone, with frantic efforts to forestall real or imagined abandonment; disturbances of identity; self-damaging impulsivity; chronic feelings of emptiness, punctuated by brief shifts in mood to anxiety, depression, or inappropriate outbursts of temper; and recurrent suicidal or self-mutilating behavior. These individuals are experienced by others as leading chaotic lives, constantly attempting to manipulate and control others, and persistently unhappy.

Histrionic personality disorder describes a pattern of excessive emotionality and attention-seeking behavior. Emotions are expressed with inappropriate exaggeration but appear shallow. These people strive to be the center of attention, using physical attractiveness, self-dramatization, and sexual seductiveness to manipulate others or to get dependency needs met. They feel helpless, demand repeated reassurance, and are easily influenced. They are often seen as charming, impressionistic, and creative but have difficulty establishing deep relationships.

Those people with *narcissistic personality disorder* have a grandiose sense of self-importance, believe themselves to be special and unique, and require excessive admiration. They are overly sensitive to criticism, excessively vulnerable to humiliation, and may respond with rage to perceived slights. A sense of entitlement and grandiosity coexists with envy and shame. Their lack of empathy makes it difficult for them to identify with the needs or feelings of others, and so they are seen as cold, aloof, and self-absorbed. This makes for difficulties in relationships, and friends and lovers tend to be treated as objects without feelings.

Avoidant personality disorder describes a person who shows a predominant pattern of social discomfort, who fears being criticized or shamed, and who feels inadequate and timid. The result is painful social inhibitions, avoidance of social contacts, lack of friends, and fear of embarrassment. These people yearn for, but fear, social involvement, in contrast to the schizoid person, who appears indifferent. Depression, anxiety, and specific phobias may be associated.

Those with *dependent personality disorder* show a pervasive pattern of submissive and dependent behavior, characterized by inability to make decisions, catering to others, difficulty taking initiative, and fear of rejection. They feel helpless when alone, try to make themselves agreeable to avoid abandonment, and are easily hurt by criticism but may suffer in silence. They function poorly in roles that require initiative and assertiveness. They often form pathologic, but relatively stable, relationships with partners having one of the exploitive personality disorders.

The *obsessive–compulsive personality disorder* is characterized by inflexibility, perfectionism, and a need for control. They are so preoccupied with rules and details that the major point of an activity or discussion gets lost. Indecision, doubting, and the need for perfection interfere with completing anything. These people constantly feel judged, obligated, and in danger of failing. Spontaneity and emotional experience are blunted, and pleasure, if permitted at all, is pursued as a task. They are experienced by other as formal and serious, conscientious, and dedicated, but they may also become obstructionists and boring companions. The personality disorder is to be distinguished from obsessive–compulsive disorder, in which daily life becomes dominated by obsessive thoughts or compulsive rituals.

The descriptive *passive-aggressive personality* was removed from the *Diagnostic and Statistical Manual* (1994) as a diagnostic category and relegated to further study. This term describes individuals with a pattern of resistance to ordinary social and occupational demands using passive tactics to carry out aggressive and negativistic aims. Examples include forgetting, procrastination, argumentativeness, obstructing the efforts of others, intentional inefficiency, and criticizing authority figures for requiring that they do their job. They tend not to realize that their behavior is responsible for their difficulties, and they are frequently in conflicts with others, who see them as unpleasant and difficult to work or live with.

Objective

Physical Examination

Patients with personality disorders have no characteristic physical findings. Diagnosis is based on a history of the present pattern of difficulties beginning in adolescence or early adulthood and extending throughout adult life, on the physician's observation of the patient's pattern in interaction with himself or herself, and on the physician's subjective reaction to the patient's interactive personality characteristics.

Routine Laboratory Abnormalities

The routine laboratory test results are normal.

PLANS

Diagnostic

Differential Diagnosis

To distinguish personality disorders from personality traits, there should be significant personal distress and exaggeration to the level of dysfunction across a broad range of situations. Many of the features of personality disorders are also characteristic of other mental disorders, such as anxiety and depressive disorders, social phobias, and obsessive–compulsive disorder. The diagnosis of personality disorder should be based on the presence of a stable and enduring pattern since early adulthood, on its being typical of the person's routine functioning and not on its occurrence exclusively during episodes of other psychiatric disorders, and on the absence of the more specific criteria for the other diagnosis. Some of the personality disorders may have blurred boundaries with other diagnostic categories with which they share a spectrum relationship, for example, schizotypal personality disorder and schizophrenia.

Diagnostic Options and Recommended Approach

Psychological tests, such as the Minnesota Multiphasic Personality Inventory or more specific instruments for personality disorders, may be used but are rarely necessary for experienced clinicians. Diagnosis is based on history and observation in the clinical interview.

Therapeutic

No psychopharmacologic agents have been demonstrated to have a specific effect on the personality disorder itself. Rather, psychoactive medications are used, if at all, as symptomatic treatment for anxiety, depression, psychic disorganization, panic attacks, impulsivity, and so on. Hospitalization is sometimes necessary in an acute affective or disorganizational crisis (primarily in patients with borderline or paranoid personality disorders) or when the patient becomes a suicide risk. Hospitalization may also be indicated for long-term, dynamic psychotherapeutic treatment of certain borderline patients.

In less severe cases, the overwhelming majority of patients seen, the optimal treatment of personality disorder is outpatient psychoanalytic psychotherapy or psychoanalysis in those patients who are able to form a workable therapeutic relationship and who have the motivation to sustain a prolonged endeavor. This usually is not possible in the antisocial type and may be limited in some of the more severe cases of paranoid, schizoid, schizotypal, and borderline disorders. Because patients with personality disorders often do not initially experience their difficulties as something that needs to be changed in themselves, it may be difficult to interest them in this type of therapy. One must determine whether the patient can best be served by strengthening his or her current level of functioning or by attempting fundamental change in the personality structure. The latter would be the goal of the psychoanalytic approach. For the former, a supportive psychotherapy approach would be indicated and might, in some cases, include group therapy or various behavioral techniques, such as assertiveness training for dependent types. The practicing physician in any specialty can provide a stable, supportive relationship that may be helpful to many of these patients, even without more formal psychotherapy.

FOLLOW-UP

Assuming that the patient has been referred for some form of psychotherapy, follow-up is determined by the working agreement between patient and therapist. The referring physician should make it clear that he or she is available for continued general medical care and support. No laboratory data are required. The therapist should continue to monitor overlapping symptoms that may be the result of physical illness or other psychiatric diagnoses. If medication is used, patient compliance and side effects should be monitored.

DISCUSSION
Prevalence and Incidence

Epidemiologic data are difficult to gather because of the imprecise nature of the diagnostic criteria and noncomparable patient populations in different studies. Overall lifetime rates for all personality disorders based on pooled studies are about 10 to 13%, with wide variability for the different categories of disorder, ranging from less than 1% for paranoid and schizoid disorders to as high as 5% for the more common obsessive–compulsive and borderline disorders. Prevalence is fairly

consistent across sex and age groups and seems higher in poor, urban populations. Although sex differences even out when diagnostic categories are grouped, the antisocial type is more frequently diagnosed in men and the histrionic type more frequently in women.

Related Basic Science

Some studies suggest that there is an important genetic component in development of personality disorders, although exactly what is inherited and how it is manifest are still unknown. It is now widely accepted that a person's basic temperament is present at birth, although how much might be genetic and how much related to other prenatal factors are unclear. This predisposition (which may influence such personality features as level of activity, degree of shyness, and tolerance for frustration) forms the substrate on which life experiences exert their influence. Early relationships with parents, as well as accidental and traumatic experiences, and the way the specific individual responds to these circumstances are the important factors in personality development. Data from twin and adoptive studies should prove more useful now that criteria for the subtypes of personality disorder have been standardized.

Natural History and Its Modification with Treatment

By definition, personality disorder has a chronic course, usually beginning in adolescence (often preceded by associated conduct disorders in childhood) and continuing throughout adult life. With about one in every ten adults affected, this group constitutes a major cause of psychological impairment in the population. Besides their specific manifestations, personality disorders contribute to the morbidity of other emotional and physical conditions. Stressful life events often precipitate crises in the personality trait disturbances, and, in turn, personality disorder conflicts often produce stressful life situations and interpersonal difficulties and contribute to comorbidity (e.g., a passive-aggressive type who undermines the treatment of his diabetes). As the person ages, manifestations seem to decline in some categories (antisocial, narcissistic, histrionic), whereas other types seem to remain steady (schizoid, borderline) or to increase (dependent, paranoid, obsessive–compulsive).

Personality disorders in themselves are not a cause of death, but they may be considered a contributing cause in some cases (suicide in histrionic and borderline types, homicide and alcoholism in antisocial types, increased coronary risk factors in the lifestyle of an obsessive–compulsive type).

Significant modification through psychoanalytic psychotherapy or psychoanalysis can often be achieved in obsessive–compulsive, histrionic, avoidant, and dependent personality disorders. A modified form of analytic therapy may result in significant improvement for borderline and paranoid disorders. Supportive therapy for schizotypal and schizoid types may lead to better functioning, but no form of psychotherapy has been very effective with antisocial personality disorders.

Prevention

No preventive measures are known for constitutional risk factors. Better parent training and availability of counseling services for abusive and inadequate parents, as well as earlier detection and treatment of children with emotional and behavioral problems, should reduce experiential factors. Earlier treatment of adolescents and young adults with personality disorders can prevent some of the accumulated trauma of years of repetitive dysfunctional patterns and emotional pain.

Cost Containment

Cost containment in personality disorders consists primarily of early diagnosis and institution of effective psychotherapy at whatever level the patient is able to use. Although individual psychotherapy is expensive, at least for some patients it will be cost-effective in the reduction of repetitive utilization of other noneffective medical services, in the patient's greater productivity, and in the reduction of utilization of social services. Diagnostic tests are not needed, medications do not play a major role, and hospitalization is rarely indicated.

REFERENCES

Diagnostic and statistical manual of mental disorders. 4th ed. Washington, DC: American Psychiatric Association, 1994.

Giovacchini P. Borderline patients, the psychosomatic focus, and the therapeutic process. Northvale, NJ: J. Aronson, 1993.

Paris J. Personality disorders: A biopsychosocial model. J Pers Disorders 1993;7:255.

Reich J, Green A. Effect of personality disorders on outcome of treatment. J Nerv Ment Dis 1991;179:74.

Siever LJ, Steinberg BJ, Trestman RL, Intrator J. Biological markers in personality disorders. In Oldham JM, Riba MB, eds. Review of psychiatry, vol. 13. Washington, DC: American Psychiatric Association, 1994.

CHAPTER 2–20

Neuropsychiatric Disorders in HIV and AIDS

J. Stephen McDaniel, M.D., and David W. Purcell, J.D., Ph.D.

DEFINITION

The neuropsychiatric aspects of HIV infection present diagnostic as well as treatment challenges. HIV is a neurotropic virus with both organic and psychological complications including HIV-associated dementia, delirium, depressive disorders, anxiety disorders, and adjustment disorders. Although substance abuse is a common complicating factor for both HIV transmission and disease progression, it is not covered in this chapter.

ETIOLOGY

The primary etiologies of neuropsychiatric disorders in HIV infection are direct central nervous system involvement (e.g., HIV-associated dementia), complications of systemic and/or central nervous system disease (e.g., delirium), and psychological reactions sometimes in combination with central nervous system disease or altered central nervous system neurochemistry (e.g., depression, anxiety, adjustment disorders).

CRITERIA FOR DIAGNOSIS

Suggestive

HIV-associated Dementia. Although early signs may suggest mild neurocognitive impairment, later presentations show marked cognitive, motor, behavioral, and emotional impairments.

Delirium. New onset changes in sensorium, often accompanied by sleep–wake cycle changes in medically ill HIV seropositive patients, are typically suggestive of an acute change in mental status, such as delirium.

Major Depression. Psychological signs such as pervasive sadness, behavioral signs such as social withdrawal, and somatic signs such as impaired sleep are important early symptoms.

Anxiety Disorders. The spectrum of anxiety disorders may manifest in autonomic and somatic symptoms, including hyperventilation, palpitations, tremor, tachycardia, flushing, and diarrhea.

Adjustment Disorders. Adjustment disorders generally present with early signs of anxiety and/or depression, but are milder than those symptoms seen in anxiety disorders or major depression.

Definitive

HIV-associated Dementia. The essential feature of dementia is the gradual development of multiple cognitive deficits that include memory impairment *and* at least one of the following cognitive disturbances: aphasia, apraxia, agnosia, or a disturbance in executive functioning. The cognitive deficits must be sufficiently severe to cause impairment in occupational or social functioning and must represent a decline from a previously higher level of functioning.

Delirium. The primary distinguishing features of delirium are (1) disturbance of consciousness, typically an inability to maintain attention; (2) change in cognition or the development of a perceptual disturbance, such as illusions and hallucinations; and (3) symptom onset occurring over hours to days, often with daily fluctuations.

Major Depression. A diagnosis of major depression is made if a patient has experienced pervasive dysphoria and/or loss of pleasure (anhedonia) for at least 2 weeks. In addition, the patient must have four of the following symptoms (three if experiencing both dysphoria *and* anhedonia): sleep disorder, appetite changes, fatigue, psychomotor agitation or retardation, feelings of low self-esteem or guilt, impaired concentration, thoughts of death or suicidal ideation. Even though some of the preceding somatic symptoms may be attributed to physical illness (e.g., fatigue, appetite changes), they should be included in the symptom profile of patients presenting with depression. Although sadness may be a normal response to the stresses of HIV infection, when the sadness is accompanied by the constellation of symptoms described above, a major depressive syndrome has developed that requires treatment.

Anxiety Disorders. A number of diagnostic categories constitute the group of anxiety disorders: panic disorder, social phobia, simple phobia, obsessive–compulsive disorder, posttraumatic stress disorder, and generalized anxiety disorder. For the practicing physician, recognition of symptom presentations is of paramount importance, as specialized psychiatric treatment is indicated.

Adjustment Disorders. The essential feature of an adjustment disorder is the development of an emotional or behavioral symptom in response to an identifiable stressor(s) occurring within 3 months of the onset of the stressor(s). The stressor generally causes marked distress that is in excess of what would be expected from exposure to the stressor and is accompanied by significant impairment in social or occupational functioning. Importantly, the stress-related disturbance cannot meet criteria for another disorder, such as major depression or generalized anxiety disorder. Adjustment disorders in HIV seropositive patients usually present with depressed mood, anxiety, or a combination of depression and anxiety.

CLINICAL MANIFESTATIONS

Subjective

HIV-associated Dementia. Usual subjective symptoms are memory loss, usually short-term, often accompanied by patient complaints of mental slowing and concentration problems. Motor symptoms may include complaints of poor balance or incoordination. Symptoms usually become more severe as the disease progresses.

Delirium. Because delirium typically occurs in medically ill, hospitalized patients, they may not be aware of their condition at the time prominent symptoms present. Anxiety, however, is a frequent accompanying symptom and may be the primary patient complaint.

Major Depression. Common subjective symptoms of major depression include sadness or blue feelings, crying spells, loss of motivation and interest, difficulty making decisions, feelings of hopelessness, and thoughts of suicide or preoccupation with death.

Anxiety Disorders. Usual subjective symptoms of anxiety disorders include complaints of nervous tension accompanied by autonomic and/or somatic symptoms.

Adjustment Disorders. The most common symptom of adjustment disorders is subjective distress accompanied by anxiety and/or depression which may manifest as decreased occupational performance and temporary changes in social relationships.

Objective

Physical Examination/Mental Status Examination

HIV-associated Dementia. Because symptoms of motor dysfunction usually lag behind those of cognitive impairment, the mental status examination is an important objective tool for diagnosis. Although the mental status examination can be normal early in the evolution of HIV-associated dementia, verbal responses are characteristically slow. Patients may perform poorly on tasks requiring concentration and attention, such as word and digit reversals and serial 7s. With increasing severity, affected individuals may appear apathetic, with poor insight and indifference to their illness.

Physical examination, even when motor symptoms are lacking, often reveals slowing of rapid successive and alternating movements of the extremities, impaired ocular smooth pursuits, and saccadic eye movements. Abnormal reflexes may also be present, with generalized hyperreflexia and development of release signs such as snout, glabellar, and, less commonly, grasp responses. As the disease evolves, findings may include ataxia, bladder and bowel incontinence, and, in the final stages, a nearly vegetative state, however, with level of arousal preserved.

Delirium. Classic mental status examination abnormalities in delirious patients include disorientation (time, place, situation) and inattentiveness (inability to do serial subtractions or spell the word *world* backward). Motor system abnormalities may also be present and include tremor, myoclonus, or symmetric reflex and muscle tone changes.

Major Depression. The most prominent finding on mental status examination in patients with major depression is that of a sad affect, often accompanied by tearfulness, slowed speech, and depressed facial expression. Patients may also exhibit psychomotor agitation (e.g., inability to sit still, handwringing) or psychomotor retardation (e.g., slowed body movements, sluggish speech). Cognitive deficits may also be apparent, including poor memory, decreased attention and concentration, and indecisiveness.

Anxiety Disorders. Patients with anxiety disorders present with unique mental status findings characteristic of the specific disorder (e.g., pervasive anxiety for generalized anxiety disorder, discrete panic attacks for panic disorder, and obsessions and compulsions for obsessive–compulsive disorder).

Adjustment Disorders. On mental status examination, patients with adjustment disorders primarily manifest with mild anxiety and/or depression. A specific stressor should be identifiable within 6 months of the onset of symptoms. For many patients with HIV disease, these stressors may include initial knowledge of seroconversion, change in health status (e.g., decrease in CD4 count), occupational change, or any of a number of psychosocial stressors related to HIV and AIDS.

Routine Laboratory Abnormalities

With the exception of delirium, routine laboratory examination yields few if any abnormalities specific to neuropsychiatric abnormalities in HIV infection. For all patients presenting with delirium, baseline screening labs should access blood chemistries for metabolic disturbances.

PLANS
Diagnostic

Differential Diagnosis

HIV-associated Dementia. This diagnosis should be made only after a complete examination rules out other central nervous system abnormalities, such as opportunistic infections, neoplasms, and delirium. Because depression may also present with impaired concentration and apathy, major depression should be ruled out.

Delirium. Rule out any organic disturbances of the central nervous system. In HIV seropositive patients, always consider HIV-associated dementia, central nervous system opportunistic infections, neoplasms, metabolic and toxic (medication-induced) abnormalities, and psychoactive substance intoxication or withdrawal.

Major Depression. The differential diagnosis in persons with HIV infection includes normal sadness, bereavement, adjustment disorders, substance use disorders, and organic central nervous system complications which may first present with alterations in mood (e.g., HIV-associated dementia, opportunistic infections). Other organic conditions such as endocrine disorders, anemia, and B_{12} deficiency, as well as toxic medication side effects, may contribute to a major depressive syndrome.

Anxiety Disorders. Distinguish possible organic causes of anxiety, particularly complications of the cardiovascular, endocrine, or respiratory systems. Other psychiatric disorders with comorbid anxiety, such as adjustment disorders, depression, and delirium, should be ruled out.

Adjustment Disorders. All organic etiologies and all other psychiatric diagnoses should be excluded. Specifically, if symptoms of depression or anxiety are prominent, they should not meet diagnostic criteria for other mood or anxiety disorders.

Diagnostic Options

HIV-associated Dementia. Formal neuropsychological testing can quantitatively support the clinical findings of HIV-associated dementia and is useful in serially following the course of disease or response to therapy. Neuroradiologic procedures and cerebrospinal fluid examination are essential diagnostic components for all patients with suspected HIV-related central nervous system dysfunction. Neuroradiologic findings include the nearly universal finding of cerebral atrophy (widened cortical sulci and enlarged ventricles) clearly evident on either computed tomography or magnetic resonance imaging. Additionally, some patients have patchy or diffuse T2-weighted abnormalities on magnetic resonance imaging scans in the hemispheric white matter. Examination of the cerebrospinal fluid is usually nondiagnostic for HIV-associated dementia, as it is confounded by abnormalities seen in patients with asymptomatic HIV infection (e.g., elevated immunoglobulin G levels, HIV-specific antibodies, mononuclear cells, and oliogoclonal bands). The lumbar puncture, however, is useful in ruling out other treatable central nervous system conditions (e.g., cryptococcal meningitis, tuberculosis).

Delirium. A thorough diagnostic evaluation includes blood chemistries (metabolic abnormalities), complete blood count, arterial blood gases, urinalysis, drug levels, computed tomography or magnetic resonance imaging, lumbar puncture, and electroencephalogram. The electroencephalogram usually shows slowing consistent with delirium.

Major Depression. Rule out organic etiologies such as B_{12} deficiency, anemia, endocrine disorders (e.g., Addison's disease secondary to HIV, cytomegalovirus, or ketoconazole therapy), central nervous system opportunistic infections, HIV-associated dementia, and medication side effects (e.g., corticosteroids, interferon).

Anxiety Disorders. A baseline evaluation for anxiety disorders depends heavily on clinical presentation and the mental status examination. A detailed drug and alcohol history should be completed, as anxiety is a frequent characteristic of psychoactive substance withdrawal. Laboratory evaluation should include thyroid function tests to rule out hyperthyroidism, a toxicology screen to rule out psychoactive substance use, electrocardiogram to evaluate for cardiac disease, and arterial blood gases for those patients in whom respiratory compromise is a complication.

Adjustment Disorders. Like other neuropsychiatric manifestations of HIV disease, routine laboratory evaluation should rule out organic etiologies. The most useful tool for diagnosing adjustment disorders is a detailed mental status examination and history of psychosocial stressors.

Recommended Approach

HIV-associated Dementia. The diagnostic evaluation for all patients with suspected HIV-associated dementia should include routine laboratory examination, B_{12} levels, VDRL, computed tomography or magnetic resonance imaging of the brain, and lumbar puncture. If available, neuropsychological testing should be administered.

Delirium. The most conservative approach for most patients with delirium would include routine laboratory assessments including a toxicology screen. If the delirium persists beyond correction of metabolic abnormalities, further investigation is warranted, including computed tomography or magnetic resonance imaging, electroencephalogram, and lumbar puncture.

Major Depression. For all persons with AIDS and most persons with symptomatic HIV disease, a diagnostic evaluation should include routine laboratory examination, thyroid function tests, B_{12} levels, computed tomography or magnetic resonance imaging of the brain in more advanced cases of HIV infection, and a thorough review of all medications for potential toxic interactions.

Anxiety Disorders. For all HIV seropositive patients with prominent symptoms of anxiety, thyroid function tests and urine or serum toxicology screens should be performed.

Adjustment Disorders. Pertinent tests to rule out organic causes of depression and anxiety should accompany a detailed psychosocial history and mental status examination.

Therapeutic

For most neuropsychiatric complications of HIV infection, a combination of psychopharmacologic and psychotherapeutic management is optimal for all patients.

HIV-associated Dementia. First-line pharmacotherapy uses antiretroviral medications to affect the primary pathophysiology. High-dose zidovudine (AZT, 2000 mg/d) has been shown to reduce neuropsychological symptoms; however, this dose is much higher than that generally used clinically (100–200 mg PO tid). Limited data exist on other antiretroviral agents such as dideoxycytidine, dideoxyinosine, or stavudine which are thought to less effectively cross the blood–brain barrier. Second-line pharmacotherapy consists of those agents used for palliative treatment of specific symptoms. Psychostimulants (methylphenidate 5–60 mg/d, usually bid or tid; dextroamphetamine 5–45 mg/d bid) have been used extensively to treat psychomotor slowing and attention deficits; however, as these medications are dopamine agonists, side effects such as paranoid psychosis and tics must be monitored closely and mandate discontinuation. Neuroleptic agents (e.g., haloperidol 0.5–2.0 mg/d) may be helpful for psychotic symptoms or behavioral dyscontrol in advanced disease. Patients with HIV infection are especially sensitive to extrapyramidal symptoms and should be monitored closely. Nonpharmacologic treatment for HIV-associated dementia can include cognitive skills training/rehabilitation and should always address appropriate education about guardianship and advance directives. Supportive psychotherapy can be extremely beneficial for both patients and loved ones.

Delirium. The primary rule of treatment for delirium is to reverse any metabolic abnormalities found during evaluation. Although there is no consensus on the pharmacologic treatment of confusional states, clinical experience indicates that neuroleptic medication is helpful and that haloperidol is the drug of choice. It can be given orally, intramuscularly, or intravenously. A starting dose of 0.5 to 1.0 mg should be administered and then repeated every 30 minutes until the patient is calm/sedated. The cumulative dose required to reach a calm state is then administered over the next 24-hour period. After the confusion has cleared, the medication is tapered over a 3- to 5-day period by a 50% dosage reduction per day. The patient is monitored closely for extrapyramidal symptoms. In patients with AIDS, benzodiazepines typically worsen the disorientation and inattention of delirium.

Psychosocial interventions are also important for delirious patients.

A calm friend or family member can reassure the patient during confusional episodes. Environmental interventions such as placing a clock, calendar, and familiar objects in the room and ensuring adequate light during the night to decrease frightening illusions may be helpful.

Major Depression. Pharmacotherapy for patients with HIV infection should be targeted toward aggressive treatment because of the known complications of untreated depression (e.g., medical noncompliance, increased medical morbidity, decreased functioning and quality of life, and suicide). In general, lower doses of antidepressant agents are used in patients with symptomatic HIV disease and medication side effect profiles are matched with patient symptoms, such that more sedating agents may be used in those patients with severe insomnia or anxiety. Because of their favorable side effect profile in medically ill populations and lack of lethality in overdose, selective serotonin reuptake inhibitors are frequently used (fluoxetine 10–20 mg/d, sertraline 50–150 mg/d, paroxetine 10–20 mg/d). Tricyclic agents are equally efficacious (nortriptyline 50–150 mg/d, desipramine 50–150 mg/d); however, side effects such as orthostasis, sedation, and anticholinergic complications must be monitored closely. For refractory cases of depression, adding psychostimulant agents may be helpful and electroconvulsive therapy remains a safe, effective treatment, particularly for those patients who are unable to take antidepressant medications or in whom medications have not proven helpful. Nonpharmacologic treatment includes numerous types of psychotherapy which may be administered in both individual and group formats. Psychotherapy in combination with pharmacotherapy generally offers the optimal treatment regimen for most HIV seropositive patients with major depression.

Anxiety Disorders. Pharmacotherapy for HIV seropositive patients with anxiety disorders is driven by symptom severity, disorder-specific treatment, and complicating substance abuse. Benzodiazepines remain the most effective anxiolytic therapy available; however, for most patients benzodiazepines should be used on a time-limited basis due to the development of tolerance and possible complications of cognitive impairment. Lorazepam (0.5–2.0 mg/d), a long-acting benzodiazepine, is an optimal agent, particularly for persons with advanced HIV infection, as it is primarily conjugated in the liver, rather than oxidatively metabolized like most benzodiazepines, and is therefore less likely to accumulate. Buspirone (5–15 mg PO tid), a nonbenzodiazepine anxiolytic without the side effects of sedation or tolerance, is particularly useful for those patients requiring more long-term treatment or for those patients with substance abuse histories. Psychotherapeutic treatment strategies include psychotherapy, muscle relaxation therapies, biofeedback, meditation techniques, behavioral techniques, and hypnosis.

Adjustment Disorders. Most adjustment disorders do not require psychopharmacologic intervention; however, brief (e.g., less than 1 week) trials of anxiolytic agents (e.g., alprazolam 0.25–0.5 mg/d) may be helpful. The treatment of choice is supportive psychotherapy which usually will bring about resolution of symptoms. Importantly, if adjustment disorders are not treated, they may rapidly progress to a more serious disorder, such as major depression.

FOLLOW-UP

HIV-associated Dementia. Patients should be followed closely for disease progression and medication response. Because dementia usually occurs in more advanced disease stages, these patients are vulnerable to a host of central nervous system opportunistic complications, which may co-occur with dementia. A brief cognitive screen should be repeated on *every* visit.

Delirium. Patients suffering from delirium should be followed daily. If hospitalized, rounding on the patients more than once daily may be helpful as the condition tends to wax and wane.

Major Depression. Patients should be followed particularly closely during their initial phase of treatment for major depression, as suicide risk often increases during the window of initial treatment response. Weekly appointments can be transitioned to less frequent appointments once the depression has resolved. Medications should be continued for at least 6 months beyond resolution of symptoms.

Anxiety Disorders. These patients should be followed closely during the initial phases of treatment. Weekly appointments are often necessary to monitor symptom response. Symptoms may progress rapidly, requiring aggressive treatment.

Adjustment Disorders. Patients with adjustment disorders should receive weekly supportive psychotherapy during the period of prominent distress. Less frequent therapy may follow as symptoms resolve.

DISCUSSION

Prevalence and Incidence

HIV-associated Dementia. Seven to sixteen percent of AIDS patients are affected, but autopsies have shown brain tissue damage associated with HIV-associated dementia in up to 66% of AIDS patients.

Delirium. Delirium has been estimated to occur in 43 to 65% of patients in late stages of infection and is the most common neuropsychiatric diagnosis in hospitalized, critically ill AIDS patients. Patients at highest risk are those with preexisting brain pathology or advanced HIV disease or those on psychoactive medications.

Major Depression. The prevalence of major depression in HIV seropositive patients has been studied extensively and ranges from 8 to 42% depending on disease stage. Major depression may present throughout the spectrum of HIV disease and particularly as the disease progresses.

Anxiety Disorders. Considering all anxiety disorders, researchers have documented a prevalence of 2 to 38% in HIV seropositive patients, depending on illness stage. There is a general trend of increased prevalence with disease progression.

Adjustment Disorders. Adjustment disorders are common throughout the spectrum of HIV disease; however, an adjustment disorder with anxious mood is the most frequent psychiatric condition described after serostatus notification.

Related Basic Science

HIV-associated Dementia. Pathogenesis begins with HIV infection and viral entry into the brain through HIV-infected monocytes. Numerous hypotheses are currently under study to ascertain the pathophysiology of HIV-associated dementia, including direct infection of neurons, cytokine effects on central nervous system macrophages, infectious cofactors, autoimmune responses, neurotransmitters, oxidative free radicals, central nervous system viral load, and increased central nervous system free calcium.

Delirium. Delirium is nearly always attributable to underlying metabolic, infectious, or toxic etiologies.

Major Depression. Alterations in neurotransmitter systems (e.g., reduction in synaptic neurotransmitter availability, alterations in receptor site sensitivity) have been studied extensively in mood disorders. More recent research and pharmacologic interventions focus on replenishing norepinephrine and serotonin.

Anxiety Disorders. Although milder symptoms of anxiety may be direct emotional responses to stressful life experiences, actual anxiety disorders are felt to result from abnormalities of central neurotransmitter systems, including the noradrenergic and serotonin systems, and the γ-aminobutyric acid receptor.

Adjustment Disorders. These disorders are thought to be emotional reactions to psychosocial stressors; therefore, no pathophysiologic changes are described.

Natural History and Its Modification with Treatment

HIV-associated Dementia. Although treatment may improve symptoms and, in some patients, disease progression, it remains unclear whether any current treatment strategies affect the natural history.

Delirium. Delirium, although a serious condition, is completely reversible in most cases by treating the underlying medical etiology. If left untreated, however, delirium significantly increases the risk of medical morbidity.

Major Depression. As in the general population, most HIV seropositive patients with major depression, even those with an organic mood disorder, respond to treatment. Little information is known about recurrence rates in patients with HIV infection. Prognostically, those patients who have depression as a component of HIV-associated dementia appear less likely to respond to treatment.

Anxiety Disorders. Most anxiety disorders respond to therapy; however, a number are chronic illnesses with a fluctuating course (e.g., panic disorder, obsessive–compulsive disorder).

Adjustment Disorders. These disorders are generally very responsive to treatment. Without intervention they often progress to more serious psychiatric conditions.

Prevention

HIV-associated Dementia. Current research does not yet support definitive preventive measures for patients with HIV-associated dementia. Recent evidence has shown that although therapy with antimicrobial drugs has protected HIV-infected patients against certain central nervous system infections, the more widespread and earlier use of antiretroviral agents has not been shown to protect against the development of HIV-associated dementia.

Delirium. Prevention of delirium requires maintaining physical health and normal laboratory values and being cautious of medication side effects and interactions as persons progress with HIV disease.

Major Depression. Although there are no current measures for the prevention of initial episodes of major depression, recurrent episodes may be prevented by maintenance antidepressant treatment. Because patients with previous histories of mood disorders or family histories of depression or suicide are at increased risk of developing depression, they should be monitored for early intervention.

Anxiety Disorders. Prevention of anxiety disorders may be difficult in patients with HIV infection. For patients who appear vulnerable to anxiety responses or who have family histories of anxiety disorders, early supportive psychotherapy or cognitive–behavioral strategies may be useful.

Adjustment Disorders. As these disorders are reactions to unplanned stressful events, preventive measures are not pertinent. Facilitating the maintenance of a strong social support system may be an important preventive intervention for all persons with HIV disease.

Cost Containment

For most neuropsychiatric complications of HIV infection, cost containment is best achieved by early diagnosis and treatment. Because of host vulnerability to numerous opportunistic complications that may mimic neurospsychiatric disorders, a thorough diagnostic evaluation is always essential. Most conditions respond to combinations of pharmacotherapy and psychotherapy. If left untreated, however, neuropsychiatric complications not only impair life quality, but they may place HIV seropositive patients at substantially increased risk of medical morbidity.

REFERENCES

Beckett A, Fernandez F, Goodkin K, McDaniel JS. HIV-related neuropsychiatric complications and their treatment (AIDS Training Curriculum). Washington, DC: American Psychiatric Association, 1994.

Diagnostic and statistical manual of mental disorders. 4th ed. Washington, DC: American Psychiatric Association, 1994.

Forstein M. The neuropsychiatric aspects of HIV infection. Primary Care 1992;19(1):97.

Wise MG, Rundell JR. Consultation psychiatry. Washington, DC: American Psychiatric Press, 1988.

Worley JM, Price RW. Management of neurologic complications of HIV-1 infection and AIDS. In: Sande MA, Volberding PA, eds. The medical management of AIDS. 3rd ed. Philadelphia: Saunders, 1992:193.

CHAPTER 2–21
....
Psychological Disorders in the Geriatric Population
Larry E. Tune, M.D., M.A.S.

As our population ages, it is likely that common psychiatric syndromes, including depressive disorders, anxiety disorders, and dementia, will pose increasingly significant challenges to the primary care physician. This chapter examines two exemplary psychological disorders: (1) grief/bereavement and (2) adjustment disorders with associated depression and anxiety. The focus is on distinguishing these "syndromes" from major depressive and anxiety disorders and from dementing illnesses.

DEFINITION

Grief Bereavement. Uncomplicated grief/bereavement is a ubiquitous experience that most individuals face many times in their lives. Usually it does not require psychiatric intervention. The typical "stages" of uncomplicated grief are listed in Table 2–21–1. It is an important disorder for several reasons. First, it is common. Second, it often goes unrecognized, and frequently unnecessary medical workups/interventions are conducted in response to somatic complaints associated with this syndrome. Third, it can easily complicate the psychiatric assessment of coexisting depressive disorders. Lastly, in some instances, the grieving process can itself become pathologic and require specific psychiatric intervention.

Adjustment Disorders with Depressed or Anxious Mood. "The essential feature of an Adjustment Disorder is the development of clinically significant emotional or behavioral symptoms in response to an identifiable psychosocial stressor or stressors. The symptoms must develop within three months after the onset of the stressor" (*Diagnostic and Statistical Manual,* 1994). In general, the syndrome will resolve within 6 months, though symptoms may be prolonged, particularly if the stressor becomes chronic. The subtypes of psychological reactions include depression, anxiety, a mixture of both anxiety and depression, disturbances of conduct, social withdrawal, or work-related impairments.

CLINICAL MANIFESTATIONS
Subjective

Grief/Bereavement. The grieving process is not simply confined to the death of a loved one. Grief can occur in response to a host of significant life events: job losses, with associated financial insecurity, loss of social and/or physical functioning (e.g., a stroke). Based on this broader definition, the incidence in the elderly population can be as high as 9% (Cohen-Cole et al., 1993).

The typical grief process (Table 2–21–1) incorporates a threefold response to loss: (1) intellectual acceptance of the loss, (2) emotional acceptance of the loss, and (3) a change in the individual's concept of the self and the world that incorporates the loss. It is common for the grieving individual to identify or understand the stage of grief he or she is experiencing. Typically, within the first 6 months of the loss, there is at least the clear sense that the subjective symptoms are improving. Table 2–21–2 lists the concomitant psychiatric symptoms that should alert the physician of co-occurring major depression in grief reactions (and adjustment disorders). This is especially important in assessing the grieving individual because "a full depressive syndrome is frequently a normal reaction to the loss of a loved one, with feelings of depression and such associated feelings as poor appetite, weight loss, and insomnia. However, morbid preoccupation with self-worthlessness, prolonged and marked functional impairment, and marked psychomotor impairment are uncommon and suggest that the bereavement process is complicated by the development of major depression" (*Diagnostic and Statistical Manual,* 1994).

Adjustment Disorders. The subjective diagnostic criteria for adjustment disorders were discussed in Chapter 2–16 (see Table 2–16–1). Of importance is that the disorder may manifest itself in a variety of ways, including diminished job performance and a significant change in relationships. At times "an adjustment disorder may complicate the course of illness in individuals who have a general medical condition" (*Diagnostic and Stastical Manual,* 1994).

Objective

Grief/Bereavement. The physical examination and routine laboratory findings are usually negative in patients with grief reactions.

Adjustment Disorders. The physical examination and routine laboratory findings are negative in patients with adjustment disorders with anxious and depressed moods.

TABLE 2–21–1. PHASES OF BEREAVEMENT IN THE ELDERLY

Stage	Symptoms	Psychiatric Symptoms	Usual Duration	Concerns in the Elderly
I. Denial	• Shock, disbelief • Emotional numbness	• Intense anxiety, emotional lability • Somatic symptoms (especially if preexisting medical condition exists) • Insomnia, loss of appetite	Weeks to months	Symptoms may be misidentified as or confounded by major depression or anxiety disorder.
II. Depression, Yearning, and Protest	• Sense of grief possibly intensified • Search for meaning of loved one's death	• Persistent somatic symptoms • Possible auditory/visual hallucinations of loved one • Symptoms of major depression • "Vegetative" symptoms • Depressed mood seen as normal by patient	Typically 2–4 months, may last 6–12 months	Losses may "bring out" preexisting dementia; 1-year anniversary may exacerbate symptoms.
III. Recovery, Identity Reconstruction	• Acceptance of finality of loss • Coping with loneliness	• Fewer somatic symptoms • Acknowledgment by patient of improvement in clinical symptoms	6–12 months	Prolonged symptoms may indicate pathologic or incomplete grieving process.

Source: Constructed from data in Gallagher D, Thompson LW. Bereavement and adjustment disorders. In: Busse EW, Blazer DG, eds. Geriatric psychiatry. Washington, DC: American Psychiatric Press, 1989.

TABLE 2–21–2. PSYCHIATRIC SYMPTOMS THAT SUGGEST BEREAVEMENT/GRIEF COMPLICATED BY MAJOR DEPRESSION

Preoccupation with self-worthlessness	The bereaved individual may think his or her life has been diminished by the loss or that the meaning of life is gone. They usually see this as an understandable phase in reaction to their loss. Typically, they do not focus on their own *self*-worthlessness.
Prolonged functional impairment	Usually, functional impairment—inability to return to work, care for oneself, and so on—begins to improve in the first 3 months.
Preoccupation with thoughts of death	Bereaved patients may view death as a relief or that dying by natural causes would be an acceptable outcome. Typically, they do not dwell on the topic of death. Nor do they develop plans, actively or passively (e.g., stopping medication), to die.
Psychomotor retardation	The critical variable may be the extent and duration of these symptoms. A typical bereaved individual may lose interest in food, activities, and so on, but within the first several months these "vegetative" symptoms begin to improve. These symptoms are usually not associated with significant weight loss. In major depression, appetite disturbance with significant weight loss is not uncommon.

PLANS

Diagnostic

The psychological reactions listed in this chapter are diagnosed primarily from the patient's subjective reports of stressful life events and the report of symptom clusters. There are no specific diagnostic tests that serve to validate the diagnosis.

Therapeutic

Pharmacologic Treatment

Grief/Bereavement. Although controversial, the use of antidepressant medications has proven beneficial, especially in more complicated instances where neurovegetative symptoms or the full blown depressive syndrome develops early in the course of the grief process (Cohen-Cole et al., 1993).

Adjustment Disorders. The general clinical experience is that many patients with adjustment disorders who do not satisfy diagnostic criteria for major depressive disorder, but who do suffer clinically significant disability (primarily with neurovegetative symptoms), will often respond, especially in the short run (3–6 months), to antidepressant therapy. Many patients respond to low doses of sedating tricyclic antidepressants, including trazodone and nortriptyline (Cohen-Cole et al., 1993).

Psychotherapy

Grief/Bereavement. A variety of preventive mental health strategies, ranging from self-help programs to more comprehensive counseling programs, have been created to assist the bereaved individual to work through the process of grieving and to identify those individuals who develop pathologic grief reactions. Often, the patient's primary care physician serves in the role of counselor. The format (i.e., self-help, pastoral counseling, group counseling, psychoeducational or individual counseling with a mental health professional) of counseling and support depends on the individual's needs and progress in the grieving process. The methods employed (e.g., cognitive, behavioral, and affective) tend to focus on successful completion of the grief process.

Adjustment Disorders. The focus should be on supportive and psychosocial interventions. Careful attention should be paid throughout the expected recovery period to the development of symptoms of major depression. For individuals who are, by history, chronically depressed, special care should be taken to observe for the development of major depression.

DISCUSSION

Prevalence and Incidence

The conditions discussed in this chapter are common. The exact prevalence and incidence are not known.

Related Basic Science

Little is known about the basic science related to the conditions discussed here.

Natural History and Its Modification with Treatment

Grief/Bereavement. One reason that recognizing both pathologic grief reactions and severe adjustment disorders in the elderly is important lies in the potential increased morbidity and mortality. Most prospective studies, however, have found modest, if any, direct effects on physical health. It is important to appreciate the dual effect of the grieving process on the elderly: it can confound an assessment of major depression (thus delaying treatment), and it can also exaggerate or exacerbate preexisting physical symptoms. Distinguishing normal grief reactions, which can resemble major depression, from major depression is difficult, especially in the first month. At 6 to 12 months, however, neurovegetative symptoms are uncommon, and there is a clear sense that somatic symptoms, if present, are improving. Assessing symptoms of grief may be harder in elderly patients (Gallagher and Thompson, 1989). First, the bereaved elderly may have a more difficult time with the bereavement process. They have been found to be more likely to suffer from increased somatic (especially cardiovascular) symptoms. Delayed, prolonged, or absent grief reactions also can have significant adverse effects on the survivor's physical and mental health. This may result in increased physician visits and a decreased sense of physical well-being. Grief has often been associated with increased mortality, especially in men.

Adjustment Disorders. Less attention has been paid to adjustment disorders in the elderly. Epidemiologic samples show that the prevalence of depressive symptoms can range widely, and may incorporate at least 4% of the population. This group likely includes patients with adjustment disorder with depressed mood. Although the number of adverse life events decreases in the elderly, the severity of these events is typically more serious. For example, loss of a job or retirement often results in the loss of the concept of a work role. Declining health may often result in a significant loss in physical and social function. Physical health problems, economic deprivation, and social isolation have all been associated with various psychological disorders and diminished subjective sense of well-being. Of these, ill health is consistently the most important source of strain leading to distress.

Prevention

No preventive measures have been developed. The support of family and friends is obviously important.

Cost Containment

These clinical syndromes are generally self-contained and are associated with increased somatic symptoms, particularly if the patient has preexisting medical conditions. Although little research is available to support the cost containment benefits of appropriate diagnosis and treatment, unnecessary medical procedures and workups in patients with these disorders are often the costly outcome of the failure to appreciate these syndromes.

REFERENCES

Cohen-Cole SA, Brown F, McDaniel S. Assessment of depression and grief reactions in the medically ill. In: Stoudemire and Fogel. Principles of medical psychiatry. Stratton, 1993.

Diagnostic and statistical manual of mental disorders, 4th ed. Washington, DC: American Psychiatric Association, 1994.

Gallagher D, Thompson LW. Bereavement and adjustment disorders. In: Busse EW, Blazer DG, eds. Geriatric psychiatry. Washington, DC: American Psychiatric Press, 1989.

Neoplastic Diseases

Randolph Martin York, M.D.

CHAPTER 3–1

Carcinoma of the Lung   (See Section 13, Chapter 39)

CHAPTER 3–2

Carcinoma of the Esophagus

Samuel R. Newcom, M.D.

DEFINITION

Carcinoma of the esophagus arises from the mucosa and is usually squamous (epidermoid) carcinoma, but adenocarcinoma of the esophagus is increasing in frequency. In one recent series adenocarcinoma accounted for 75% of the entrants, and 50% arose in Barrett's esophagus (Urba et al., 1995).

ETIOLOGY

The cause of esophageal carcinoma is incompletely understood. Squamous carcinoma usually occurs in persons who smoke tobacco and consume alcohol. When gastric reflux induces columnar epithelium to replace squamous epithelium in the distal esophagus (Barrett's esophagus), the incidence of adenocarcinoma is 8 to 15% (Hesketh et al., 1989; Cameron et al., 1985)

CRITERIA FOR DIAGNOSIS
Suggestive

Dysphagia and pain on swallowing should alert one to the possibility of carcinoma of the esophagus.

Definitive

The diagnosis of carcinoma of the esophagus requires a tissue biopsy, usually from the primary site. Esophagoscopy is the most direct procedure. Squamous cell carcinoma is found 93 to 98% of the time (Rosai, 1981; Moertel, 1982). A diagnosis may also occur because of distant metastases of squamous cell carcinoma, with a characteristic lesion found on barium esophagram or at endoscopy.

Adenocarcinomas of the esophagus are recognized in 2.3 to 6.9% of the cases. Tumor registries report that adenocarcinoma is increasing in frequency, particularly in Caucasian patients. Fifty-nine to 86% of adenocarcinomas of the esophagus arise in Barrett's esophagus. Barrett's esophagus has been found in 8 to 20% of patients who undergo esophagoscopy for evaluation of esophagitis (Hesketh et al., 1989; Cameron et al., 1985).

CLINICAL MANIFESTATIONS
Subjective

The patient is usually a smoker, is likely to consume alcohol regularly, and may have a history of previous episodes of poor nutrition. The risk of developing esophageal cancer in smokers is increased 10-fold for beer drinkers and about 25-fold for whiskey drinkers compared with smoking, matched nondrinkers. African-Americans have 3.5 times the incidence and mortality from squamous cell carcinoma of the esophagus as do white Americans. Over the past 25 years, the incidence and mortality rates for esophageal cancer in African-Americans have increased 105%. In contrast to the higher incidence of squamous cell carcinoma of the esophagus in blacks is the increasing incidence of adenocarcinomas of the esophagus in whites (Schottenfield, 1984; American Cancer Society, 1994).

Certain conditions are known to predispose the patient to esophageal carcinoma:

- *Tylosis:* This is the only congenital condition associated with an increased incidence of carcinoma of the esophagus. An autosomal dominant gene results in hyperkeratosis palmaris et plantaris as well as papillomata of the esophagus. In some families, 95% of afflicted patients develop squamous cell carcinoma of the esophagus (Harper et al., 1970).
- *Achalasia:* This neurologic disorder manifests as an upper esophageal sphincter that does not function properly. The esophagus is partially obstructed and squamous cell carcinoma occurs 5 to 7% of the time. Achalasia must usually be present for 20 years or longer before the carcinoma arises (MacFarlane, 1988).
- *Diverticula:* A few case reports have been assembled (35–40 patients) describing carcinomas in pharyngoesophageal or epiphrenic diverticula.
- *Lye stricture:* Strictures secondary to lye ingestion are usually located in the esophagus adjacent to the tracheal bifurcation. Squamous cell carcinomas have been noted to arise in strictures, usually 30 to 45 years after onset. The incidence of squamous cell carcinoma in a lye stricture is estimated at 5 to 33% (Appelqvist and Salmo, 1980; Hopkins and Postlewait, 1992).
- *Plummer–Vinson syndrome:* Iron deficiency anemia associated with glossitis, esophagitis, and eventually esophageal "webs" is associated with esophageal carcinoma in approximately 10% of patients. The cervical esophagus is affected most frequently, and the patients are usually women. With the improved diagnosis and treatment of iron deficiency, the incidence of this syndrome is decreasing.

Symptoms of esophageal carcinoma are usually present for 3 to 4 months prior to diagnosis. Dysphagia and weight loss are present in 80 to 90% of patients at presentation. Pain on swallowing (odynophagia) is seen in about half the patients with cancer of the esophagus. As the cancer advances, pain may radiate to the back, on swallowing, and should alert the clinician to the possibility of vertebral body involvement. Other signs of advanced disease include recurrent laryngeal nerve involvement, phrenic nerve paralysis, tracheoesophageal fistula with cough productive of food particles after eating, superior vena cava obstruction, metastases in supraclavicular and cervical lymph nodes, malignant pleural effusion, malignant ascites, and bone pain.

The most common paraneoplastic syndrome associated with esophageal carcinoma is hypercalcemia secondary to secreted mediators (e.g., peptide growth factors such as transforming growth factor α) that mimic parathormone.

Objective

Physical Examination

Physical examination seldom helps in establishing the diagnosis of esophageal carcinoma. Supraclavicular and cervical lymphadenopathy, hepatic enlargement, and pleural effusion are all late findings.

Routine Laboratory Abnormalities

Hemoglobin (anemia commonly results from folate deficiency, iron deficiency, ethanol suppression, or inflammatory blockade), liver function tests, and calcium levels are important to evaluate.

PLANS

Diagnostic

Differential Diagnosis

Benign lesions may masquerade as malignancy, for example, esophageal reflux with esophagitis and fibrotic stricture, squamous cell papillomata, or the most common benign neoplasm of the esophagus, a leiomyoma. Other malignancies, particularly squamous cell carcinoma and small cell carcinoma of the lung, may occasionally present with dysphagia secondary to extrinsic esophageal involvement by metastatic hilar and mediastinal lymph nodes.

Diagnostic Options

Identification and measurement of the primary neoplasm are best accomplished by barium swallow. Esophagoscopy with biopsy establishes the diagnosis in approximately 90% of patients with the first procedure. Occasional patients are symptomatic with negative findings and require repeat esophageal studies for an accurate diagnosis. Falsely negative studies are most likely to occur with small esophageal carcinomas (< 3.5 cm long) that are noted on barium esophagram only 60% of the time. Posterior carcinomas are best seen on the lateral chest x-ray with barium swallow, usually as a result of periesophageal lymphatic involvement. These may be found up to 6 months before the development of symptoms (Moertel, 1982).

Recommended Approach

Staging of esophageal carcinoma for surgical resection should include a barium esophagram, routine chest x-ray, and thoracoabdominal computed tomography scan. Bronchoscopy and upper airway evaluation are usually performed and are most important when the primary site is in the upper two thirds of the esophagus. Bronchoscopy allows the detection of synchronous primary lung lesions and can reveal direct invasion by the esophageal carcinoma into the tracheobronchial tree. Special attention is given to the posterior wall of the left main-stem bronchus and trachea where the esophagus crosses these structures. Narrowing in this area or infiltration of tumor, as evidenced by edema, prominent longitudinal folds, and bleeding on contact are findings that preclude surgical cure. Celiac lymph nodes are routinely sampled at surgery and have a 10% yield in patients with upper esophageal malignancies. Fine-needle aspiration cytology under computed tomographic guidance is used to assess enlarged celiac nodes or other sites of possible involvement that preclude the usefulness of surgical resection. Brain scans and bone scans have too low a yield and are too nonspecific to be included unless the patient has symptoms or laboratory findings to suggest involvement of these sites.

Esophageal carcinoma is staged according to the TNM classification as outlined in Tables 3–2–1 and 3–2–2.

TABLE 3–2–1. TNM STAGING SYSTEM FOR ESOPHAGEAL CARCINOMA

T1	Invasion of lamina propria or submucosa
T2	Invasion of muscularis propria
T3	Invasion of adventitia
T4	Invasion of adjacent structures
N0	No regional metastases
N1	Regional lymph node metastases
M0	No distant metastases
M1	Distant metastases

Source: American Joint Committee for Cancer. Manual for staging of cancer, 4th ed. Philadelphia: Lippincott, 1992. Reproduced with permission of the publisher.

Therapeutic

Therapeutic Options

Patients with stage I and II disease should be assessed for operability in conjunction with the thoracic surgeon. Some patients with stage III disease may be technically resectable, although the prognosis is poor. Debilitation from nutritional deficits should be corrected before considering surgery. At least 5 days of nutritional support is usually required. Electrolyte derangements require immediate attention. Pulmonary function should be maximized by eliminating smoking and instituting vigorous pulmonary physiotherapy. Prophylactic antibiotics are frequently used to decrease the flora of the diseased esophagus. Electrocardiogram, arterial blood gases, and pulmonary function tests are part of an appropriate preoperative evaluation for these patients.

Approximately 50% of patients with thoracic esophageal carcinoma are found to be eligible for attempted resection. The operative mortality is reported to be 0 to 14% (mean, 5.7%) (Roth et al., 1993). The esophagogastrectomy is usually performed through an upper midline laparotomy and a separate right anterior thoracotomy in the fourth intercostal space (Ivor–Lewis procedure). Rarely, a lateral neck incision is used. The laparotomy is performed first and the status of the celiac lymph nodes and liver assessed. When the liver contains metastases or there is gross celiac axis node involvement, the operative procedure is terminated and the patient is declared unresectable. If the laparotomy is negative, then a thoracotomy is performed to assess the resectability of the thoracic esophagus. If the carcinoma is found densely adherent to the great vessels, the operative procedure is terminated. If all staging studies support resectability as the best treatment, an abdominal esophagectomy and esophagogastrostomy procedure is completed, followed by dissection of the thoracic esophagus. The esophagus is removed and frozen sections of the two ends are performed to determine the sterility of the surgical margins. End-to-end anastomosis (esophagogastrostomy) is performed by stapling the esophagus to the fundus of the stomach.

Of those patients resected, the 5-year survival rate in 18 series (4109 patients) was 9.65% (Moertel, 1982) and, in 21 more recent series (1773 patients), 19.5% (Roth et al., 1993). The overall 5-year survival of all patients with esophageal cancer, based on 8024 patients described in the literature, is still extremely low at 3%; however, tumor registries report improvement in this outcome in the past decade (see Discussion).

TABLE 3–2–2. STAGE GROUPING OF ESOPHAGEAL CARCINOMA

Stage I	T1 (invasion of submucosa), N0, M0
Stage IIA	T2 or T3 (invasion of adventitia), N0, M0
Stage IIB	T1 (invasion of submucosa), N1, M0
	T2 (invasion of muscularis), N1, M0
Stage III	T3 (invasion of adventitia), N1
	T4 (invasion of adjacent structures), N0, N1, M0
Stage IV	M1

Source: American Joint Committee for Cancer. Manual for staging of cancer, 4th ed. Philadelphia: Lippincott, 1992. Reproduced with permission of the publisher.

Recommended Approach

No other therapy has been proven to be superior to surgery. Several phase II studies have been completed that suggest that some patients with stage I primary carcinomas of the thoracic esophagus may be cured by radiotherapy or radiotherapy plus chemotherapy. Primary radiotherapy has been effective in producing 5-year cures of esophageal cancer presenting in the cervical esophagus (13–17%) (Moertel, 1982). The radiation tolerance of the esophageal mucosa is 6000–6500 cGy.

When radiation therapy is used for palliation of unresectable esophageal carcinoma, 60 to 80% of irradiated patients have dysphagia partially or completely relieved. Similar frequencies of relief may be obtained by esophageal dilation or rigid tube placement (e.g., Celestin tube) depending on the expertise of the institutional consultants. YAG laser therapy has been used in some centers.

Increasingly, chemotherapy is employed as a useful component of therapy. A broad experience with single-agent chemotherapy, combination chemotherapy, and combination chemotherapy and radiotherapy has developed. Single agents with objective activity include taxol, bleomycin, cisplatin, 5-fluorouracil, mitomycin C, adriamycin, and methotrexate, with response rates of 6 to 28% in small series. Combination chemotherapy using these "active" agents has produced response rates of 17 to 63% and median survival times of 4 to 7.5 months (Roth et al., 1993).

Two randomized studies of preoperative radiotherapy demonstrated the feasibility of delivering this therapy but did not demonstrate an advantage in resectability or survival when compared with surgery only (Launois et al., 1981; Gignoux et al., 1987). The evaluation of postoperative radiotherapy has been less extensive; however, improvements in survival for stage III patients given postoperative radiotherapy has been reported to be 13 months versus 7 months (Hankins et al., 1982).

Recently, combination chemotherapy and radiotherapy have been evaluated either as primary therapy or as preoperative treatment of thoracic esophageal carcinoma. In three phase II studies, 24 of 111 patients who were resected (21.6%) were found to have no viable tumor cells visible in the resected specimens after combined radiotherapy/chemotherapy. A similar result (17% pathologic complete remission) was obtained for adenocarcinoma of the esophagus (Keller, et al., 1995). Two studies have shown that giving chemotherapy prior to surgery does not improve survival and is rarely associated with pathologic complete remission. Postoperative chemotherapy has not been adequately studied and cannot be recommended (Roth et al., 1993). A randomized phase III study of preoperative chemotherapy/radiotherapy shows that, in spite of a 23% pathologic complete remission, there was no improvement in 2-year survival when compared to surgery alone (Urba et al., 1995).

For unresectable disease, no therapy has been convincingly proven to be better than symptomatic treatment only. Radiation therapy alone has been used to treat 4465 patients in 13 reported studies; 671 patients were alive at 2 years (15%) and 305 patients were alive at 5 years (6.8%). These apparent cures usually occur in patients with resectable disease who refuse surgery or cannot tolerate surgery because of other medical problems. In one small series of patients receiving primary radiation therapy for stage I disease, 46% survived 1 year and 14% were alive at 5 years (Earlam and Johnson, 1990).

Three phase III studies have been completed that compared radiotherapy with chemotherapy/radiotherapy. One study showed no survival advantage (Araujo et al., 1991). An Eastern Cooperative Oncology Group study of 130 patients demonstrated a survival advantage of 14.9 months versus 9 months by adding mitomycin C and 5-fluorouracil (Sischy et al., 1990). A Radiation Therapy Oncology Group study of 121 patients showed a survival advantage of 12.5 months versus 8.9 months when four cycles of 5-fluorouracil and cisplatin were given concurrently with 50 Gy. In the combined modality group, 38% of the patients were alive at 2 years compared with 10% of those treated only with radiotherapy (64 GY) (Herskovic et al., 1992).

Patients with proven metastatic disease are not candidates for resection. Radiation therapy may be used for palliation of local or distant symptoms, but does not change survival. Chemotherapy is not curative at this stage and should be considered experimental if employed. All patients with esophageal cancer, including those with nonresectable

and metastatic tumors, may become candidates for palliative measures for the common problems associated with esophageal cancer, such as dysphagia, chest pain, tracheoesophageal fistula, and malnutrition. Survival is not meaningfully prolonged by these measures but symptoms may be significantly alleviated. Dysphagia may be addressed by peroral dilation. A variety of techniques and instruments may be used, including simple inflatable catheters. YAG laser therapy is another useful technique but more expensive and occasionally associated with perforation.

Adequate doses and schedules of analgesics should be employed as necessary for controlling pain. Sustained-release oral morphine sulfate every 12 hours (e.g., 30–60 mg MS Contin) with additional morphine sulfate solution as necessary may be effective and should be initiated if simple narcotics such as codeine and oxycodone are ineffective or poorly tolerated. Dosing of morphine should be aggressive and continuous if pain persists as a complaint. Radiation therapy may be transiently effective to relieve hemorrhage, superior vena cava obstruction, unrelenting chest pain, complete obstruction, and so on. Tracheoesophageal fistulas are rarely improved by radiation therapy and are best treated with a prosthesis placed in the least invasive manner possible. The prognosis is poor at this stage of the patient's illness and aggressive intervention does more harm than good. Malnutrition is a common problem in esophageal carcinoma and can only be partially overcome with the aggressive relief of pain and obstruction. Cancer cachexia is also present in the late stages of this disease, and local therapy is not usually effective. A feeding gastrostomy or nasogastric tube is rarely required and may significantly add to the adversity and discomfort of this disease.

FOLLOW-UP

The successfully resected patient should be scheduled for weekly, and then monthly, visits in the outpatient setting, and routine laboratory studies should be performed. Dehydration, hemorrhage, and infection should be attended to vigorously in these fragile and, sometimes, debilitated patients. Tumor recurrence, which will develop in the majority of resected patients, should be evaluated by history and physical examination. Chest x-ray, liver function tests, repeat barium swallows, computed tomography scans, and repeat endoscopy may all become necessary both for explaining symptoms and for investigating the possibility of a second primary squamous cell carcinoma. Each patient is at increased risk for synchronous and metachronous carcinomas of the aerodigestive tract. Any opportunity presented to the physician to curtail the patient's alcohol and tobacco use should be taken.

Patients with recurrent or unresectable disease require active intervention for the palliation of symptoms and for the support required by a dying patient with an incurable and symptomatic disease. The doctor's outpatient office setting may not be the optimal arrangement because of the patient's weakness, debility, and desire for privacy. Home visits, when available, allow the necessary medication adjustment and review of symptoms and physical examination to take place. A home hospice program with clerical, social service, pastoral, and medical input has been very successful in some settings and should be considered for the patient with a stable home situation and motivated family members. An inpatient hospice program, although expensive, may be an alternative when more intensive nursing care is desired.

DISCUSSION
Prevalence and Incidence

With an annual incidence over 10,000 and increasing each year, esophageal carcinoma has become an important public health problem. The incidence and mortality of this disease are higher in blacks than in whites in the United States. In an analysis of the 5-year survival rates of white versus black patients, the most recent data available (1985–1986) show a statistically significant improvement in the survival of white patients when compared with the 1974–1976 data (8% versus 6%), but nonsignificant improvement for black patients (6% versus 4%) (American Cancer Society, 1994). The reason for the increased incidence and decreased survival in blacks is probably multifold and most likely reflects primarily differences in socioeconomic levels. The incidence of smoking has been greater among blacks (40%) than among whites (30%), but there is no significant difference in the reported consumption of ethanol. There is evidence suggesting that black men may be more sensitive to the potentiating effects of alcohol. Pointing out the likely differences in etiology between squamous cell carcinomas and adenocarcinomas of the esophagus is the fact that adenocarcinomas are significantly more frequent in white as compared with black patients (American Cancer Society, 1994).

Related Basic Science

Investigation of alcohol and tobacco as the primary risk factors for the induction of squamous cell carcinoma of the esophagus has suggested that concentrated alcohol is more effective in inducing carcinoma than dilute and that the risk can increase to 40 times baseline when more than 120 g of ethanol is consumed per day. Cigarette, cigar, and pipe smoking are all associated with relative risk ratios of 5 or more. In the United States, poor nutrition, as characterized by low levels of consumption of fresh or frozen meat, fish, fruits, vegetables, and dairy products, has been associated with an increased risk of esophageal carcinoma in urban blacks. In endemic areas of esophageal carcinoma, high levels of N-nitroso compounds may play a major role in esophageal carcinogenesis. Highly carcinogenic N-nitroso compounds are produced by such events as contamination of food (particularly with fungus), low soil content of molybdenum, and zinc deficiency (Moertel, 1982; Roth et al., 1993).

There is a 4:1 male predominance in the incidence of esophageal carcinoma in this country, but not in high-incidence areas. The distal thoracic esophagus is more commonly involved in men, whereas in the cervical esophageal patients, women predominate. Ten to 20% of esophageal carcinomas are seen in the cervical esophagus, about 50% in the upper thoracic esophagus, and 30 to 40% in the lower thoracic esophagus (Rosai, 1981).

Several studies of the cells from esophageal carcinoma indicate that 30 to 50% of esophageal carcinoma neoplasms are aneuploid. As in breast cancer, aneuploidy has a strong correlation with lymph node metastases. Therefore, DNA analysis by flow cytometry may become clinically useful in selecting low- and high-risk patients for future clinical trials.

Chromosome abnormalities have also been identified in patients with adenocarcinoma related to Barrett's mucosa (Garewal et al., 1989). Nine of ten short-term cell cultures had clonal chromosome rearrangements. In 15 patients with Barrett's mucosa there was increased ornithine decarboxylase, suggesting altered polyamine metabolism (Garewal et al., 1988). 13-cis-Retinoic acid did not change the extent of the Barrett's mucosa.

No alterations in c-RAS or p53 gene expression have been found in esophageal carcinomas; however, p53 mutations have been identified in four of seven Barrett's mucosa cells adjacent to adenocarcinoma. This finding suggests that a p53 mutation is a premalignant alteration that is lost in the clonal malignant transformation (Roth et al., 1993).

Natural History and Its Modification with Treatment

The mean survival for all patients with esophageal carcinoma is poor, ranging from 2.3 to 8.7 months (Moertel, 1982; Roth et al., 1993, American Cancer Society, 1994). Curative resection of an upper-third esophageal carcinoma is associated with a mean survival of 21.6 months. A lower-third resection yields a 35.7-month mean survival. Patients receiving radiotherapy or radiotherapy/chemotherapy for unresectable disease have median survivals of approximately 12 months.

Prevention

Primary prevention in the United States requires decreased levels of exposure to tobacco, alcohol, and possibly, packaged food. In endemic areas, improvements or changes in the ecology of the production and storage of food stuffs and the prevention of zinc deficiency may be effective primary preventive measures. Early diagnosis through the screening of high-risk populations has been attempted in a few foreign countries but has not been evaluated in the United States. The cost-effectiveness of this approach is not likely to be proven. Aspirin, taken regularly, may reduce the incidence of esophageal carcinoma.

Cost Containment

The prevention of tobacco and alcohol abuse is the most effective means of decreasing the cost of esophageal carcinoma. Both the National Cancer Institute and the American Cancer Society recognize this fact and have begun to shift funds from clinical trials of treatment of disease to cancer control methods. Once a diagnosis of esophageal carcinoma has been established, vigorous maintenance of esophageal patency using dilation can usually replace expensive and ineffective surgical and radiotherapy treatments in those patients clearly beyond cure. Careful preoperative evaluation for resectability with mediastinal and abdominal computed tomography scanning will help eliminate unnecessary and expensive surgery. Replacing expensive prostheses, feeding gastrostomies, and YAG laser therapy with simple dilation will eliminate unnecessary procedures in the majority of dying patients. Home hospice care is the least expensive care and, for many patients, provides the most comfortable care site. Attention to the full postoperative recovery of the rare cured patient is also important and should include attention to postthoracotomy pain and cessation of tobacco and alcohol use.

REFERENCES

American Cancer Society. Cancer statistics. *Ca Cancer J Clin* 1994;44:1.

Appelqvist P, Salmo M. Lye corrosion carcinoma of the esophagus: A review of 63 cases. Cancer 1980;45:2655.

Araujo C, Souhami L, Gil R, et al. A randomized trial comparing radiation therapy versus concomitant radiation therapy and chemotherapy in carcinoma of the thoracic esophagus. Cancer 1991;67:2258.

Boyce, HW. Palliation of advanced esophageal cancer. Semin Oncol 1984;11:186.

Cameron AJ, Ott BJ, Payne WS. The incidence of adenocarcinoma in columnar-lined (Barrett's) esophagus. *N Engl J Med* 1985;313:857.

Earlam R, Johnson L. 101 oesophageal cancers: A surgeon uses radiotherapy. Ann R Coll Surg Engl 1990;72:32.

Garewal HS, Gerner EW, Sampliner RE, Roe D. Ornithine decarboxylase and polyamine levels in columnar upper gastrointestinal mucosae in patients with Barrett's esophagus. *Cancer Res* 1988;48:3288.

Garewal HS, Sampliner R, Liu Y, Trent JM. Chromosomal rearrangements in Barrett's esophagus: A premalignant lesion of esophageal adenocarcinoma. Cancer Genet Cytogenet 1989;42:281.

Gignoux M, Roussel A, Paillot B. The value of preoperative radiotherapy in esophageal cancer: Results of a study of the EORTC. World J Surg 1987;11:426.

Hankins JR, Cole FN, Ahar S, et al. Carcinoma of the esophagus: Twelve years' experience with a philosophy for palliation. Ann Thorac Surg 1982;33:464.

Harper PS, Parper RMJ, Howel-Evans AW. Carcinoma of the oesophagus with tylosis. Q J Med 1970;34:317.

Herskovic A, Martz MS, Al-Sarraf M, et al. Combined chemotherapy and radiotherapy compared with radiotherapy alone in patients with cancer of the esophagus. N Engl J Med 1992;326:1593.

Hesketh PJ, Clapp RW, Doos WG, Spechler SJ. The increasing frequency of adenocarcinoma of the esophagus. Cancer 1989;64:526.

Hopkins JRA, Postlethwait RW. Caustic burns and carcinoma of the esophagus. Ann Surg 1992;194:146.

Keller SM, Coia LR, Ryan L, et al. Chemoradiation followed by esophagectomy for adenocarcinoma of the esophagus and gastroesophageal junction: Results of a phase II study of the Eastern Cooperative Oncology Group (abstract). *Proc Am Soc Clin Oncol* 1995;14:196.

Launois B, DeLaRue D, Campion J, et al. Preoperative radiotherapy for carcinoma of the esophagus. Surg Gynecol Obstet 1981;153:690.

MacFarlane SD. Carcinoma of the esophagus. In: Hill L, Kozarek R, McCallum R, Mercer CD, eds. The esophagus: Medical and surgical management. Philadephia: Saunders, 1988.

Moertel CG. The esophagus. In: Holland JF, Frei E, eds. Cancer medicine. 2nd ed. Philadelphia: Lea & Febiger, 1982.

Philip PA, Ajani JA. Has combined modality therapy improved the outlook in carcinoma of the esophagus? Oncology 1994;8:37.

Rosai J. Gastrointestinal tract. In: Rosai J, ed. Ackerman's surgical pathology. 6th ed. St. Louis: Mosby, 1981.

Roth JA, Putnam JB, Lichter AS, Forastiere AA: Cancer of the esophagus. In: DeVita VT, Hellman S, Rosenberg SA, eds. Cancer, principles and practice of oncology. 4th ed. Philadelphia: Lippincott, 1993.

Schottenfield D. Epidemiology of cancer of the esophagus. Semin Oncol 1984;11:92.

Sischy B, Ryan L, Heller D, et al. Interim report of EST 1282 phase III protocol for the evaluation of combined modalities in the treatment of patients with carcinoma of the esophagus, stage I and II (abstract). Proc Am Soc Clin Oncol 1990;9:105.

Urba S, Orringer M, Turris A, et al. A randomized trial comparing transhiatal

esophagectomy to preoperative concurrent chemoradiation followed by esophagectomy in locoregional esophageal carcinoma (abstract). *Proc Am Soc Clin Oncol* 1995;14:199.

Carcinoma of the Head and Neck • The Role of Medical Therapy

Melvin R. Moore, M.D.

DEFINITION

Squamous cell carcinomas of the larynx, oral cavity, and pharynx are grouped under the heading carcinoma of the head and neck (see Chapters 21–23, 21–24, and 21–25, respectively).

ETIOLOGY

Cigarette smoking is the major etiologic agent in these cancers, conferring a relative risk of 5- to 25-fold based on the intensity of exposure. Alcohol consumption increases risk in a more than additive fashion, with a relative risk of 17-fold in heavy drinkers when adjusted for cigarette smoking. Additional etiologic agents include other forms of tobacco products; diets lacking in vitamin A and carotene; human papillomavirus types 16 and 18; and genetic phenotypes that result in increased metabolic activation of tobacco-related carcinogens or decreased efficiency of DNA repair.

CRITERIA FOR DIAGNOSIS

See Chapters 21–23, 21–24, and 21–25.

CLINICAL MANIFESTATIONS

See Chapters 21–23, 21–24, and 21–25.

PLANS
Diagnostic

See Chapters 21–23, 21–24, and 21–25.

Therapeutic
Therapeutic Options

Early-stage head and neck cancers can be cured with surgery and/or radiotherapy; however, patients presenting with more advanced primary tumors or with regional lymph node involvement experience local treatment failure rate greater than 50% and very low long term survival rates. The definition of advanced stage differs by primary site. For oral cancers, including that of the oropharynx, a tumor more than 4 cm in diameter (T3) or invading adjacent structures (T4) or the presence of lymph node metastases (N1–N3) confers a poor prognosis. For cancers of the nasopharynx, a tumor that invades the nasal cavity or oropharynx (T3) or invades the skull or cranial nerves (T4) or the presence of lymph node metastases (N1–N3) confers a poor prognosis. T3 and T4 lesions in the hypopharynx are defined by fixation of the hemilarynx and invasion of adjacent structures, respectively. T3 and T4 lesions of the larynx are defined primarily by vocal cord fixation and invasion of adjacent structures, respectively. Either T3/T4 or involvement of any lymph node confers a poor prognosis. The majority of head and neck cancers present in these advanced stages (stages III and IV), with more than 50% of patients dying of local/regional recurrence and more than 25% with distant metastases. Thus, both local and systemic failures are significant when local treatment modalities are used alone.

The integration of systemic chemotherapy into treatment strategies employing radiation therapy and/or surgery is an important approach to the problem of managing late-stage nonmetastatic head and neck cancer. The optimal chemotherapy regimen is not yet worked out, but cis-

platin (100 mg/m^2) given along with infusional 5-fluorouracil (800 mg/m^2/d × 5 days) with or without leucovorin (either oral or by infusion) has been widely reported as an effective regimen with an objective response rate of about 80% in patients with recurrent or metastatic disease. Studies have used chemotherapy followed by local therapy, chemotherapy given concurrently with radiation, and local therapy followed by chemotherapy.

Induction chemotherapy may have a role in laryngeal preservation in patients presenting with advanced carcinoma of the larynx, but has not been shown to be effective in improving survival when compared with local therapy alone despite high initial response rates including many complete pathologic responses.

Chemoradiotherapy has been the most successful of the combined modality approaches to date. Despite the use of suboptimal chemotherapy or radiation in most of the completed randomized clinical trials, reproducible clinical benefits have been observed in the form of significant improvements in local control and trends toward better survival. Regimens that alternate courses of chemotherapy and radiation as well as regimens that deliver combined chemotherapy and radiation in split courses to decrease toxicity have had promising initial results.

Recommended Approach

For stage III and IV patients with head and neck cancer who are not participating in clinical trials, a combined chemotherapy/radiation therapy approach is recommended with the addition of surgery for resectable residual disease. The use of platinum and 5-fluorouracil (60 mg/m^2 cisplatin on day 1 and 800 mg/m^2/d by continuous intravenous infusion on days 1–5) with concomitant radiotherapy during days 1 to 21, with a 3-week break, followed by two additional cycles of chemotherapy and then either surgery and/or additional radiation therapy is an acceptable approach. Refinements in chemotherapy and radiation techniques are occurring continually, and the preceding strategy may be quickly replaced when the results of ongoing trials become available.

For metastatic and recurrent head and neck cancer, chemotherapy with cisplatin and infusional 5-fluorouracil provides high response rates but equivocal gains in survival. Data on quality of life with and without chemotherapy are not available. Single-agent chemotherapy is not recommended. An acceptable schedule is cisplatin 33 mg/m^2/d on days 1 to 3 and continuous infusion of 5-fluorouracil (200 mg/m^2/d) and leucovorin (20 mg/m^2/d) on days 1 to 14 repeated every 21 days. An excellent baseline performance status and a clear understanding on the part of the patient of the palliative nature of treatment are required prior to starting chemotherapy in this setting.

FOLLOW-UP

Patients who have been successfully treated for primary head and neck cancer have a high incidence of local relapse. Distant metastases occur in more than 25% of patients with stage III and IV tumors, with distant metastases found at autopsy in up to 50%. Second primary tumors of the upper aerodigestive tract (head and neck, esophagus, and lung) occur at a constant annual rate of more than 5%. Patient follow-up is based on the above data with an emphasis on local relapse and second primary tumors as clinical situations where curative treatment is still possible. Patients should be encouraged to stop using tobacco and alcohol. The suggested frequency of follow-up visits is every 3 months for 2 years followed by every 6 months for life. Clinical examinations including the oral cavity and nasopharynx should be done at each visit and a careful history taken. Dysphagia, weight loss, and respiratory and oral symptoms demand a full evaluation. Chemoprevention using 50 mg/m^2/d 13-*cis*-retinoic acid should be instituted. Chest x-rays should be obtained every 6 months. Patients on active therapy demand much closer supervision with weekly complete blood count and blood chemistries prior to each cycle of therapy. Patients should be seen and examined prior to each cycle of therapy. More intensive scrutiny may be required in this population of patients who are often suffering from comorbidity related to smoking- and alcohol-induced pathology and who will experience major toxic effects during these complicated combined modality treatments.

DISCUSSION
Prevalence and Incidence
More than 40,000 new cases of head and neck cancer with almost 12,000 deaths are expected in the United States in 1995. Incidence and mortality are highest among African-American men. There is a 3:1 male predominance in incidence. Mortality for Caucasian men has been steadily declining since 1975, but has been increasing among African-American men.

Related Basic Science
See Chapters 21–23, 21–24, and 21–25.

Natural History and Its Modification with Treatment
Untreated, squamous cell carcinomas of the head and neck are uniformly fatal. Cure rates are dependent on stage at diagnosis and are quite good for early tumors. Four-year survival rates in excess of 40% have been reported for combined modality regimens for stage III and IV patients. Approximately 10% of patients present with distant metastases at the time of diagnosis.

Prevention
Head and neck cancer provides many opportunities for prevention. Any reduction in the use of tobacco products and alcohol will have a major impact on this disease. A diet high in vitamin A and retinoid is reasonable based on epidemiologic studies, but is not of proven benefit. Chemoprevention with 50 mg/m^2/d 13 -*cis*-retinoic acid is of proven benefit in the prevention of second malignancies of the upper aerodigestive tract and in the therapy of leukoplakia, a precursor of oral cancer. Primary chemoprevention is not of established benefit.

Cost Containment
The most effective strategy to contain the costs of this malignancy is reduction of tobacco and alcohol consumption.

REFERENCES
Beahrs OH, Henson DE, Hutter RV, Myers MH, eds. Manual for staging of cancer. 3rd ed. Philadelphia: Lippincott, 1988:27.

Browman GP, Cronin L. Standard chemotherapy in squamous cell head and neck cancer: What we have learned from randomized trials. Semin Oncol 1994;21:311.

Huber MH, Lippman SM, Hong WK. Chemoprevention of head and neck cancer. Semin Oncol 1994;21:366.

Spitz MR. Epidemiology and risk factors for head and neck cancer. Semin Oncol 1994;21:281.

Stupp R, Weichselbaum RR, Vokes EE. Combined modality therapy of head and neck cancer. Semin Oncol 1994;21:349.

CHAPTER 3–4
Carcinoma of the Oral Cavity (See Section 21, Chapter 24)

CHAPTER 3–5
Carcinoma of the Pharynx (See Section 21, Chapter 25)

CHAPTER 3–6
Nasal and Sinus Tumors (See Section 21, Chapter 26)

CHAPTER 3–7
Carcinoma of the Larynx (See Section 21, Chapter 23)

CHAPTER 3–8

Carcinoma of the Stomach

Barnett S. Kramer, M.D., M.P.H., and Karen A. Johnson, M.D., Ph.D., M.P.H.

DEFINITION

Although a variety of neoplasms may occur in the stomach, including squamous cell carcinoma, carcinoid tumors, and lymphomas, 95% of gastric carcinomas are adenocarcinomas; the term *gastric carcinoma* nearly always refers to the latter. Gastric adenocarcinoma is a malignant neoplasm originating from cells in mucosal glands of the stomach. As such, these malignant gastric cells, when they are well differentiated, almost always take on one of two characteristic appearances: metaplastic intestinal cells or mucus-secreting (signet ring) cells. Usually one of these two cell types predominates, but a mixture is sometimes seen. The histologic features of these cells are absent in poorly differentiated carcinomas.

ETIOLOGY

In 1965, a concept was introduced that has provided a long-standing theoretical construct for gastric cancer etiology. Gastric adenocarcinomas may be characterized as representing either an epidemic or endemic form of the disease. The epidemic form of gastric cancer is said to be well differentiated with intestinal features and sometimes observed to occur in approximation with intestinal metaplasia, a possible precursor of the malignancy. The endemic form of gastric carcinoma is an undifferentiated tumor in which there is a lack of cell cohesion and a diffuse infiltration by the tumor. This nomenclature is based on the observation that the endemic form of the disease occurs around the world at a relatively constant, but low, rate. In geographic areas where the rates of gastric cancer are high, however, the preponderance of cases are of the epidemic variety.

Some of the environmental factors that have been associated with the development of gastric cancer include a lack of refrigeration; a diet poor in fresh fruits, vegetables, and vitamins A and C, but high in preserved foods (salted, smoked, or pickled); cigarette smoking; and certain exposures to high doses of ionizing radiation. Recently, there has been intense interest in the role of *Helicobacter pylori* infection in the development of gastric cancers. Three nested case–control studies have shown that *H. pylori* infection is associated with the subsequent development of gastric adenocarcinoma, with a relative risk reported to range from 2.7 to 6.0. This evidence is buttressed by other epidemiologic studies showing the following:

- An association between *Helicobacter* infection, atrophic gastritis, intestinal metaplasia, and intestinal type gastric carcinoma
- Either a higher prevalence of *Helicobacter* infection or an early age of infection in geographic areas, populations, and families with high rates of gastric cancer
- The correlation of *H. pylori* seroprevalence with gastric cancer incidence and mortality

Additional preliminary investigations have enlarged the possible role of *H. pylori* infection in malignant disease of the stomach, by establishing a relationship between it and gastric lymphoma. Perhaps the most remarkable evidence of this connection has been the remission of low-grade gastric lymphomas following the eradication of *Helicobacter* infection with antibiotic therapy. Although the prevalence of *Helicobacter* infection increases with age, involving 50% of the U.S. population by age 50, and the great majority of these individuals do not develop a gastric malignancy, there is increasing evidence that *Helicobacter* infection is an important cofactor in the pathogenesis of gastric cancer.

CRITERIA FOR DIAGNOSIS

Suggestive

As gastric cancer occurs relatively infrequently and symptoms at presentation are usually nonspecific, diagnostic acumen must be sharpened by a heightened awareness of the significance of certain clinical details and their pattern. It is easy to overlook vague complaints related to epigastric discomfort, anorexia, easy fatigability, and/or indigestion. When a gastric mass or ulceration has been documented in the presence of these symptoms, then the suspicion of malignancy is increased.

Definitive

The definitive diagnosis of gastric carcinoma is made on the basis of the pathology examination of cells or tissue removed from a gastric lesion. Most often, the material for examination is obtained from brushings and/or biopsy performed at the time of an upper endoscopy.

CLINICAL MANIFESTATIONS

Subjective

Symptoms

At presentation, the most common symptom of gastric carcinoma is weight loss, followed in frequency by abdominal pain, diminished appetite, vomiting, and an alteration in bowel habit. Esophageal regurgitation may occur if the tumor is near the esophagogastric junction. Symptoms of weakness, hematemesis, and early satiety are reflective of more advanced disease. Rarely, patients may present with symptoms caused by metastatic disease, such as bowel obstruction problems or pulmonary symptoms.

Past History

A variety of preexisting conditions are associated with the subsequent development of gastric carcinoma. Individuals with a history of pernicious anemia, hypochlorhydria, achlorhydria, and previous gastric surgery have an elevated risk of developing gastric cancer. These conditions have low gastric acidity in common, a condition that may favor carcinogenic events. In an individual who has been diagnosed with atrophic gastritis or intestinal metaplasia, there is increased risk of subsequently developing gastric carcinoma. Infection with *H. pylori* frequently accompanies these conditions.

Family History

A family history of gastric cancer in a first-degree relative doubles the risk of a patient's being diagnosed with gastric carcinoma. Clustering of gastric carcinoma in families appears to be related more to a shared environmental factor like *Helicobacter* infection than to an underlying genetic predisposition to gastric cancer. One heritable factor that has been related to a slight increase in gastric cancer is blood type A. In the rare situation when there is a family history of Peutz–Jeghers syndrome (multiple hamartomas and buccal melanosis), the risk of gastric carcinoma is increased if gastric hamartomas are present.

Objective

Physical Examination

Physical findings associated with gastric carcinoma occur late in the natural history of the tumor and denote incurability. Most patients do not have physical signs at initial presentation. One may occasionally find a palpable supraclavicular node, usually on the left side, due to metastasis (Virchow's node). Even less frequently, a palpable umbilical nodule (Sister Mary Joseph's nodule) or left axillary node (Irish's node) is a sign of metastatic spread. A right upper quadrant or epigastric mass signifies spread to the liver or massive enlargement of the gastric tumor locally. Rectal examination may reveal an extrinsic mass due to a rectal shelf metastasis, whereas ovarian metastasis in women may be detected on bimanual examination of the pelvis. Rarely an abnormal neurologic examination may suggest the presence of carcinomatous meningitis. Also rare is the presentation of a patient with the paraneoplastic syndrome of acanthosis nigricans, which is manifested by development of "velvety" pigmented hypertrophic skin lesions, especially in the axilla. Other rare paraneoplastic syndromes that may herald the disease are migratory superficial and deep venous thromboses (Trousseau's syndrome) and thrombotic thrombocytopenic purpura.

Routine Laboratory Abnormalities

At the onset of symptoms, the routine laboratory workup is usually normal. The most frequent abnormality is a mild anemia. This may be microcytic and hypochromic from blood loss or, more frequently, the nonspecific normochromic, normocytic anemia of chronic disease. In the former case, the stool may be hematest-positive. Rarely, there may be fragmented red cells and thrombocytopenia signifying the microangiopathic hemolytic anemia of thrombotic thrombocytopenic purpura. Blood chemistries are nearly always normal at diagnosis, but abnormal liver function tests may signify hepatic metastases.

PLANS
Diagnostic
Differential Diagnosis

An ulcerative lesion in the stomach may reflect the presence of any of several disease processes including adenocarcinoma, lymphoma, metastatic melanoma, and peptic ulcer disease. If the initial evaluation shows no evidence of cancer, the ulcer should be treated medically and reassessed in several weeks to confirm that it is resolving. Ulcers that fail to resolve are surgically resected. When a gastric mass is identified, then polyp, leiomyoma, or enlarged ruggal folds may become a consideration in the differential diagnosis. Multiple polyps are associated with polyposis–achlorhydria syndrome and also lymphoma. Solitary polyps are evaluated with endoscopy. An adenomatous polyp is much more likely to be associated with carcinoma than is a hyperplastic polyp. Enlarged ruggae are seen with superficial spreading gastric cancer, hypertrophic gastritis, lymphoma, and sarcoidosis.

Diagnostic Options and Recommended Approach

It is still common to investigate symptoms that suggest an upper gastrointestinal disorder by obtaining a barium upper gastrointestinal series; however, upper endoscopy with biopsy and exfoliative cytology, which carries a diagnostic accuracy of greater than 95%, is increasing as the initial procedure of choice. Findings on barium upper gastrointestinal series that should lead to immediate endoscopy are poor stomach distensibility, a mass effect, obstruction, and/or enlarged gastric folds. Even benign-appearing ulcers on gastrointestinal series may be due to carcinoma in as many as 3 to 15% of patients. Hence, in many centers, early endoscopy with biopsy is performed in almost every patient with a gastric ulcer seen on upper gastrointestinal series.

As part of the diagnostic process, if gastric carcinoma is found by cytology and/or histology, the next step is to determine the extent of disease, because this information will play a major part in deciding on how to proceed with subsequent therapy. Pulmonary metastases are occasionally seen at diagnosis on routine chest roentgenogram as intraparenchymal or pleura-based nodules, mediastinal node enlargement, or a pattern consistent with lymphangitic spread. Malignant pleural effusions or, rarely, a chylous effusion due to lymphatic obstruction may develop. Computed tomography scan of the abdomen and pelvis may alert the surgeon to the possibility of extragastric extension, liver metastases, peritoneal spread, or the occasional ovarian metastasis (Krukenberg's tumor). A new staging technique using endoscopic ultrasonography is complementary to computed tomography scanning. Nevertheless, patients with findings on physical or radiologic examination should not be judged inoperable unless the presence of distant metastases is confirmed with biopsy.

Therapeutic

Once the diagnosis of gastric carcinoma is documented by histology or cytology, a frank discussion about therapeutic options is in order. If staging workup suggests that the tumor is resectable, then surgery should be recommended. The patient should be told that the goal is complete removal of tumor, which depends on the operative findings (e.g., invasion through the stomach wall, lymph node spread, spread to other organs). This goal is not consistent with widely metastatic disease or malignant ascites. After surgery, another discussion should cover the operative findings and whether residual tumor was known to be left behind. If all gross tumor is removed, the risk of recurrence is still significant, but there is no recognized adjuvant therapy at present that can reliably change this risk.

If the disease is unresectable, the patient can be offered palliative chemotherapy. Such treatment does not offer cure, but it has a 30 to 40% chance of shrinking the tumor temporarily. Because it is not definitively proven that chemotherapy extends survival, the patient with minimal or no symptoms may choose to forego therapy until symptoms occur or progress.

Chemotherapy. Curative surgery is the therapy of choice. At most medical centers, the current role for medical management using cytotoxic chemotherapy is focused on patients with gross disease, whether residual after surgery or recurrent. Whether a single agent or combination chemotherapy is used, the median survival of these patients is similarly short, so no single treatment has been identified as the therapy of choice. Nevertheless, at least some patients appear to benefit from chemotherapy, when their symptoms abate on the therapy in conjunction with tumor shrinkage. Hence, all newly diagnosed patients who are not surgically curable are candidates for clinical trials when circumstances and inclination permit. Otherwise, 5-fluorouracil has been given as a single agent for 5 days at a daily dose of 500 mg/m^2 every 4 weeks for 8 weeks, and then every 5 weeks thereafter. Recently, promising response rates have been obtained with several combination chemotherapy regimens.

Of three commonly used multidrug chemotherapy regimens, all employ 5-fluorouracil and doxorubicin. One of these treatments is the 4-week FAMTX regimen with 5-fluorouracil, doxorubicin (Adriamycin), and high-dose methotrexate. An integral part of this regimen is leucovorin rescue from days 2 to 5. Two other regimens are FAM (an 8-week cycle with 5-fluorouracil, doxorubicin, and mitomycin C) and FAP (a 5-week regimen with 5-fluorouracil, doxorubicin, and cisplatin). Essentially all patients who respond to any of these regimens do so within the first 2 months. Responders are continued on therapy until disease progression occurs. Virtually all responses are partial. There is ongoing controversy over whether any chemotherapy significantly extends survival, leaving much room for improvement.

A sobering backdrop to any discussion of chemotherapy for gastric carcinoma is its very narrow therapeutic index. Common toxic effects that limit dose and tolerance are bone marrow suppression and mucositis. Methotrexate, mitomycin C, and cisplatin all may have substantial renal toxicity, depending on dose, treatment schedule, and host factors.

If an optimal chemotherapy regimen were identified, it would become a candidate for adjuvant therapy, an additional treatment to be used after complete resection of all gross disease for the purpose of extending survival. None of the regimens that have been used to test this concept have provided convincing evidence that survival can be extended in this way. Neoadjuvant chemotherapy, given before definitive surgical resection is attempted, also remains a theoretical issue for future investigation.

Surgery. Surgery may be applied with either curative or palliative intent. The extent of curative surgery depends on the location and regional spread of the primary tumor. A complete discussion of the various procedures is beyond the scope of this chapter, but a few principles are outlined here:

- A gross tumor-free margin of at least 5 cm is considered the standard. This often requires a total gastrectomy, except in the case of tumors of the pyloris, cardia, or esophagogastric junction.
- Routine splenectomy does not improve survival; however, splenectomy is performed in the case of tumors that are adjacent to or directly invading the spleen.
- The first echelon of draining nodes is removed.
- En bloc resection of all gross tumor is attempted. This includes con-

tiguous spread to the liver and pancreas, which mandates caudal pancreatectomy.

The operative and perioperative mortality of radical gastric surgery is about 10 to 12%. Palliative surgery is generally offered to patients with local tumor-related problems such as perforation, bleeding, or obstruction.

Radiation. Gastric cancer is considered to be a relatively radioresistant tumor, because the low tolerance of surrounding structures interferes with the delivery of a dose adequate for response. Consequently, radiotherapy is generally reserved for patients with unresectable tumors for control of bleeding or pain. Some centers are using intraoperative electron beam therapy at the time of gastrectomy as an investigative modality. Such an approach allows the reduction of radiation exposure to the bowel and other organs, eliminating one of the main impediments to the use of external beam radiation.

FOLLOW-UP

At 4 to 5 years after "curative" surgery, the hazard function of death becomes relatively stable, so patients are at a lower risk of recurrence after this point. In the early years, the goal of follow-up is the detection of recurrence so that palliative interventions can be provided for symptomatic patients. One approach is to have a history and physical, chest x-ray, and blood work every 3 to 4 months for the first year, with the same evaluations at 6-month intervals for the next 3 to 4 years. Lifetime parenteral replacement of vitamin B_{12} at about monthly intervals will be needed. Items of particular interest should include recurrence of the symptoms outlined previously. Diarrhea may be due to a dumping syndrome in patients who have undergone gastric resection, but the onset of diarrhea months to years after surgery may also be due to partial gastrointestinal obstruction from peritoneal metastases. Occurrence of any of these symptoms between routine visits should prompt the patient to contact the physician. The physician should perform a careful examination for the presence of peripheral adenopathy, pleural effusions, hepatomegaly, an abdominal mass, and occult blood in the stool. Laboratory abnormalities that may be due to disease recurrence are abnormal liver function tests, anemia, and chest roentgenogram abnormalities.

Patients who are receiving palliative chemotherapy are necessarily seen more frequently by the physician for their treatments. Any disturbing symptoms must be brought to the attention of the physician, who must differentiate between tumor-related and chemotherapy-induced problems.

DISCUSSION

Prevalence and Incidence

In the United States, there were an estimated 22,800 new cases of gastric carcinoma in 1995, corresponding to an overall age-adjusted incidence of about 7 to 8 per 100,000 population. The male-to-female ratio is around 2:1, with rates approximately 60% higher for African-Americans. For unknown reasons, the death rate from gastric carcinoma has been dropping steadily since before 1930, when it was the most common cause of cancer-related death in the United States. The dramatic 75% decline in gastric cancer deaths has been due primarily to decreasing incidence rather than an improvement in early detection or therapy; however, one subset of this disease, adenocarcinoma of the gastric cardia, is now on the increase. Although an overall drop in gastric cancer incidence has been observed in the United States and several similar Western nations, the worldwide incidence of stomach cancer is estimated to be second only to lung cancer. In many countries, gastric carcinoma is still a leading cause of cancer, with rates higher than 100 per 100,000 in certain areas of Japan and South America.

Related Basic Science

In recent years, the intestinal form of gastric carcinoma has been postulated to develop through a sequence of phenotypic tissue changes that are characterized by related genetic events. It is thought that atrophic gastritis develops in normal gastric mucosa preceding the occurrence of intestinal metaplasia, which subsequently gives rise to premalignant dysplasia. As early changes in tissue occur, some of the corresponding genetic alterations may involve the translocated promoter region MET and the K-*ras* proto-oncogene. Later in the carcinogenesis sequence, further genetic alterations in genes like p53 and C-*erb*-B2 are thought to contribute.

Natural History and Its Modification with Treatment

Gastric carcinoma commonly spreads by any of the following four routes: direct extension, seeding and implantation on serosal surfaces, lymphatic invasion, and hematogenous spread. Any organ that abuts on the stomach may be involved by direct extension: liver, diaphragm, transverse colon, spleen, pancreas, left adrenal and kidney, splenic flexure of the colon, greater omentum, and small bowel. Tumor cell implantation may involve any organ in the peritoneal cavity, leading to such complications as small bowel, colonic, or rectal obstruction. The stomach has three major lymphatic draining systems: the left gastric chain, the splenic chain, and the hepatic chain; however, there are extensive interconnections, making prediction of the lymphatic route of spread in any individual patient virtually impossible. The most common sites of distant hematogenous spread are, in decreasing order, liver, lungs and/or pleura, adrenal glands, and bone. Of these, the least likely to produce clinical signs or symptoms are the adrenal glands, as the observation of Addison's syndrome is rare even when there is extensive adrenal involvement by metastases.

Because even the earliest symptoms of stomach carcinoma are often those of an extensive tumor, and because systemic therapy for extensive disease does not effect cure, the disease carries a high mortality rate. According to Surveillance, Epidemiology and End Results (SEER) data from the National Cancer Institute, the overall 5-year survival rate in the United States for 1986 to 1991 was 19.9%. This result represents at best a slight improvement compared with the 5-year survival rate in 1973, which was 13.9%, and could be due at least in part to increasing use of endoscopy, which can advance the date of diagnosis without changing the outcome. As shown in Table 3–8–1, survival is strongly correlated with initial stage at diagnosis.

TABLE 3–8–1. 5-YEAR SURVIVAL BY INITIAL STAGE OF GASTRIC CARCINOMA

Stage	Criteria*	5-Year Survival† (%)
0	Carcinoma in situ	>90
I	Disease limited to the lamina propria/submucosa ± perigastric lymph nodes within 3 cm of the primary tumor or tumor invading the muscularis propria/subserosa without spread to lymph nodes	50–85 (distal) 10–15 (proximal)
II	Tumor penetrating serosa without invasion of adjacent structures and without node involvement; tumor limited to muscularis propria/subserosa + perigastric nodes within 3 cm; or tumor limited to lamina propria/submucosa + regional nodes > 3 cm from the primary	~20 (distal)
III	Tumor invading adjacent structures + perigastric nodes within 3 cm; or tumor penetrating serosa and involving regional nodes but not adjacent structures; or tumor invading the muscularis propria/subserosa ± regional lymph nodes > 3 cm from the primary	~15 (distal)
IV	Tumor invading adjacent structures and involving regional nodes > 3 cm from the primary; or distant metastases	<5

*Staging criteria adapted from *Stomach.* In: Beahrs OH, Henson DE, Hutter RV, Kennedy BY, eds. American Joint Committee on Cancer. Manual for staging of cancer. 4th ed. Philadelphia: Lippincott, 1992:63. Reproduced with permission.
†5-Year survival adapted from Physician's data query information for health care professionals, gastric cancer file. Bethesda, April 1995.

Prevention

Dramatic geographic variation in gastric carcinoma incidence and mortality, as well as migrant studies, suggest an environmental (and therefore correctable) etiology for a large proportion of gastric cancer. With this vantage point, the prospects for gastric cancer prevention seem bright, as several etiologic leads have provided the basis for large-scale prevention studies. One of these, a nutrition intervention trial in Linxian, China, demonstrated that a combination of β-carotene, vitamin E, and selenium led to a relative risk of gastric cancer mortality of 0.79 (95% confidence interval of 0.64–0.99). In this trial, risk reduction started 1 to 2 years after beginning the intervention, which was assessed for the 5-year period from 1986 to 1991 (Blot et al., 1993). Continued observation is expected to provide additional information about the study participants, which may be most representative of a population that has a critical deficiency in dietary micronutrients like β-carotene, vitamin E, and selenium. Generalizability to the better-nourished American population is uncertain, and results from this study must be considered preliminary until there is confirmation by an independent replication of the result.

Following the lead provided by studies of intestinal metaplasia as it relates to *H. pylori* infection and dietary factors, the European Cancer Prevention Organization has launched a trial to evaluate antibiotic versus placebo at startup for *Helicobacter* carriers followed by a 3-year intervention with placebo versus vitamin C. The endpoint will be the status of intestinal metaplasia at the end of the intervention. Because there has been concern about the potential effectiveness of using antibiotic therapy to eradicate *H. pylori* infection due to the high probability of subsequent reinfection, there is the expectation that in the future, public health considerations will support the development of a vaccine, as this intervention could be expected to have a huge impact worldwide, affecting not only rates of gastric cancer but also reducing the incidence of gastric and duodenal ulcers.

Cost Containment

Numerous tests have been reported to be of some use in the diagnosis or follow-up of gastric carcinoma. These include carcinoembryonic antigen determinations and measurement of gastric acidity, serum gastrin, and various tumor markers. It is rare that any of these tests is useful in either diagnosis or management, and so in the opinion of the authors, it is prudent to avoid them.

REFERENCES

Blot WJ, Li J-Y, Taylor PR, et al. Nutrition intervention trials in Linxian, China: Supplementation with specific vitamin/mineral combinations, cancer incidence, and disease-specific mortality in the general population. J Natl Cancer Inst 1993;85:1483.

Correa P, Shiao Y-H. Phenotypic and genotypic events in gastric carcinogenesis. Cancer Res 1994;54:1941s.

De Koster E, Buset M, Fernandes E, Deltenre M. *Helicobacter pylori:* The link with gastric cancer. Eur J Cancer Prev 1994;3:247.

Findlay M, Cunningham D. Chemotherapy of carcinoma of the stomach. Cancer Treat Rev 1993;19:29.

Isaacson PG. Gastric lymphoma and *Helicobacter pylori.* N Engl J Med 1994;330:1310.

CHAPTER 3–9

Carcinoma of the Gallbladder (See Section 19, Chapter 95)

CHAPTER 3–10

Carcinoma of the Pancreas

Philip S. Schein, M.D.

DEFINITION

Pancreatic carcinoma is a rapidly progressive and almost universally fatal cancer. Although a number of histologic forms are recognized, approximately 90% are classified as adenocarcinomas, with duct cell adenocarcinoma predominating. Acinar carcinoma accounts for approximately 1% of all pancreatic tumors and arises from the pancreatic exocrine cell; it may present with a unique clinical syndrome of subcutaneous fat necrosis, polyarthralgia, and eosinophilia as well as an increased serum lipase. Functional and nonfunctional islet cell tumors originating from the cells of the islets of Langerhans are rare.

Tumors of the pancreas are divided into those involving the head versus the body and tail region, with the former predominating. Approximately 15% of all newly diagnosed cases have a tumor confined to the pancreas. Twenty percent have invasion of regional lymph nodes, whereas the remainder have distant metastases at the time the tumor is first detected. Tumors of the head region may be diagnosed earlier because of obstruction of the common bile duct and jaundice, whereas tumors of the body and tail have a more insidious course and are typically detected at a later stage of the disease. Tumors of the head region are also capable of invading the second portion of the duodenum, causing obstruction. In addition to regional lymph node involvement, the cancer invades outside the pancreas to encase or occlude major abdominal vessels including the portal vein, splenic vein, and superior mesenteric artery, which can be diagnosed by angiography. Invasion into the nerves of the retroperitoneum is a prominent cause of tumor-related pain. Obstruction of the pancreatic duct, as well as the bile duct, is an important contributing factor in the overall syndrome of cachexia associated with this tumor.

ETIOLOGY

In past surveys, pancreatic cancer is more prevalent in men than in women, with a ratio of 2:1. More recent estimates have suggested a male-to-female ratio of essentially 1:1, the equalization attributed to the increased use of tobacco products in women.

Several risk factors have been identified for pancreatic cancer, such as cigarette smoking and occupational exposure to specific chemicals. It is estimated that approximately 30% of cases of pancreatic cancer can be attributed to cigarette smoking, but the majority of patients present without any identifiable history that would suggest they were predisposed to this cancer. There are, however, rare familial forms of this tumor, including a syndrome of relapsing pancreatitis which has been associated with a significantly increased risk for this tumor.

CRITERIA FOR DIAGNOSIS

Suggestive

The diagnosis must be suspected in an individual 45 years of age or older (typically 60 years of age) presenting with symptoms of progressive abdominal pain, weight loss, and jaundice. The presence of an abdominal mass or an enlarged liver mandates a search for metastatic tumor, which is typically found by the time the symptoms are sufficiently severe to bring the patient to the attention of a physician. Biopsy of a hepatic mass revealing histology consistent with a pancreatic adenocarcinoma supports, but does not definitely make, the diagnosis.

Definitive

The diagnosis is made by biopsy of a pancreatic mass at surgery, or by fine-needle aspiration with ultrasound or computed axial tomography scan guidance. Alternatively, specimens may be obtained by exfoliative brush cytology during a diagnostic endoscopic retrograde cholangiopancreatography.

CLINICAL MANIFESTATIONS

Subjective

The tumor invades out of the pancreas into surrounding structures in the retroperitoneum and abdomen, producing a constellation of symptoms. Pain is the most common presenting complaint and, initially, may be difficult to localize. Pain may present in the epigastrium with radiation into the midback, or less commonly, it may be confined to the back region. Patients may describe paroxysms of discomfort associated with meals, with exacerbations at night relieved by assuming a sitting position. Weight loss is also an important presenting sign, which in some cases can be explained by a profound state of anorexia, as well as the metabolic entity of cachexia of malignancy. Patients may describe abnormalities in smell and taste sensation, and the development of aversions to particular foods, especially meat. With progressive destruction of the pancreas and occlusion of the pancreatic duct, relative degrees of pancreatic insufficiency may contribute to the malnourished condition. Jaundice is a common feature of pancreatic cancer, and its mechanism is related to the location of the tumor within the head or body–tail region. Tumors of the head may present early with obstruction of the common bile duct as it traverses through the organ, whereas jaundice in the presence of a tumor in the body or tail section is often associated with advanced stage of hepatic metastases. Less common symptoms include nausea, vomiting, and diarrhea.

Objective

Physical Examination

On physical examination, patients may demonstrate signs of weight loss and icterus. An upper abdominal mass representing tumor in the body of the pancreas may be present in as many as 25% of patients. Additionally, the liver may be enlarged as a result of metastases. Obstruction of the splenic vein by cancer may be associated with splenomegaly, whereas occlusion of the portal veins can result in esophageal varices and the development of ascites.

Routine Laboratory Abnormalities

Routine laboratory examinations may demonstrate the presence of anemia, which may be significant if there has been invasion of the duodenum and gastrointestinal bleeding. Liver function tests may demonstrate abnormalities, particularly in alkaline phosphatase as well as in serum bilirubin, and the gallbladder may be palpable in the absence of cholangitis.

Chest x-ray films may disclose the presence of either pleural infusion or overt pulmonary metastases.

PLANS

Diagnostic

Differential Diagnosis

The vague initial symptoms of early pancreatic cancer may be attributed to "indigestion" or "dyspepsia"; however, as the disease follows its unrelenting course, a number of conditions must be considered in the differential diagnosis, including benign pancreatitis, peptic ulcer disease, cholelithiasis, and specific benign and neoplastic causes of obstruction of the biliary tract.

Diagnostic Options

The initial approach to diagnosis typically involves the use of noninvasive tests. The symptoms often lead to an upper gastrointestinal tract barium series, which may suggest the presence of pancreatic cancer because of displacement or invasion of the stomach or duodenum. Institutional preferences and relative expertise often dictate the selection of ultrasonography or computed tomography. These tests are employed to detect the presence of an enlargement of the region of the pancreas, dilation of biliary ducts, and the presence of hepatic metastases. Neither test is specific and cannot discriminate between enlargement of the pancreas as a result of cancer and enlargement caused by benign pancreatitis. Fine-needle aspiration cytology can be performed with either computed tomography or ultrasonography guidance. Accuracy is estimated to be approximately 90%, and is recommended for patients with tumors in the body and tail of the pancreas who are usually not candidates for resection for cure. There is controversy as to whether small tumors in the head region should be aspirated, as seeding along the aspiration track represents a possible complication.

Endoscopic retrograde cholangiopancreatography can provide useful radiologic imaging of the pancreatic duct, which may be narrowed or compressed by a tumor mass. Specificity for pancreatic cancer is estimated to be 90% with a low complication rate. Importantly, this procedure provides the opportunity to obtain material for cytologic analysis from the periampullary region, by either brushing or aspiration of pancreatic juice. Endoscopic ultrasonography is a new modality that is being evaluated for its ability to detect tumors smaller than 2.5 cm. Angiography is rarely used as a primary diagnostic aid in patients with symptomatic tumors. Its role, to delineate the vascular anatomy, has been largely relegated to preoperative assessment of resectability; encasement or obstruction of the portal, splenic, or superior mesenteric veins provides evidence that the tumor has invaded regionally and confirms that the patient is not a candidate for an operation with curative intent.

Several tumor markers have been assessed for their utility in pancreatic cancer. None has demonstrated sufficient specificity or sensitivity so as to be applicable as a cancer diagnostic test. Nevertheless, these tests may have applicability in following patients who have undergone resection or other forms of treatment to determine the progress of disease. In addition to the carcinoembryonic antigen (CEA), the pancreatic oncofetal antigen (POA) and α-fetoprotein have also demonstrated some utility. More recently, attention has been addressed to the CA 19-9 antigen, using monoclonal antibodies against this sialylated Lewis antigen as a general gastrointestinal cancer-associated antigen. An improved specificity has been reported when the levels of both CA 19-9 and CA 242 are used.

Recommended Approach

Because the diagnosis of pancreatic cancer carries such a dire prognosis, it is important that it be made definitively, where feasible. The following sequence is recommended: upper gastrointestinal tract series, computed tomography of the upper abdomen with guided aspiration biopsies of lesions suspicious for primary pancreatic cancer and/or liver metastases, and endoscopic retrograde cholangiopancreatography with exfoliative cytology.

Therapeutic

Pancreaticobiliary resection, either a Wipple procedure (partial pancreatectomy) or total pancreatectomy, is reserved for patients with small tumors in the head region of the organ, with no evidence of regional invasion of the bowel, lymph nodes, or abdominal vessels. The probability that a tumor arising in the body and tail region has not metastasized at time of diagnosis is extremely low. It is estimated that only 15% of patients with pancreatic cancer are candidates for an operation with curative intent. Historically, there has been a 20% perioperative mortality, but improvements have been recognized in referral centers that have gained extensive experience in surgical technique and postoperative care. In most series, only 5% of patients undergoing resection survive 5 years longer. Therefore, patient selection is essential, recognizing that only a minority of patients have an opportunity to benefit from such radical surgery. Patients with regional metastatic involvement should, nevertheless, be considered for an operation with palliative intent to diminish or delay the onset of symptoms. This may include decompression of the biliary tract with a choledochojejunostomy, as well as bypass of the stomach with a gastrojejunostomy. Relief of biliary obstruction can also be achieved in some patients by the endoscopic placement of a stent; occlusion of a stent from biliary debris, however, is a concern and can precipitate cholangitis. Further palliation can be achieved by the injection of splanchnic nerves with phenol (intraoperative chemical splanchnicectomy) to reduce narcotic requirements, as well as by placement of radiopaque surgical clips in areas of locally advanced tumor to define a postoperative radiation field for cases where this modality is applicable. Percutaneous chemical splanchnicectomy also serves as a useful adjunct for the nonsurgical reduction of pain.

Radiation therapy for pancreatic cancer is restricted largely to patients with locally advanced (regional) tumor. A number of regimens have been described; in general, doses around 6000 rad are recommended. This dose may be administered in three 2000-rad increments over 2 weeks, separated by an intervening 2-week rest, and combined with 5-fluorouracil, 350 mg/m^2 of body surface area, on the first 3 days of radiation. Interstitial radiation, with the direct placement of ^{125}I into a small tumor mass, is recommended in selected cases; approximately 15,000 rad can be delivered locally using this technique, which can be followed by additional external radiotherapy. The use of intraoperative radiation with high single doses of electrons is an experimental approach that is undergoing further evaluation.

The majority of patients diagnosed with pancreatic cancer have advanced disease. As a result, they are potential candidates for systemic management with chemotherapy. Once again, patient selection is essential, as chemotherapy can be toxic and only a portion of patients have an opportunity of responding to such treatment. At present, there is no consensus as to the optimal approach to the management of patients with pancreatic cancer with chemotherapy, and many investigators feel that therapy in general is ineffective. In the past, patients were treated with single-agent 5-fluorouracil; the drug was administered for 5 consecutive days every 3 to 4 weeks using a daily dose of 500 mg/m^2 of body surface area. More recently, attempts have been made to design an effective form of combination chemotherapy, and, although there is no standard and universally adopted regimen, the SMF combination of streptozotocin, mitomycin-C, and 5-fluorouracil has gained some acceptance, as 30 to 40% of patients have responded in several series. In general, chemotherapy for advanced pancreatic cancer is regarded as investigational and should be undertaken by specialists who are attempting to evaluate the efficacy and safety of new regimens.

In recognition of the relatively poor survival results with surgery, postoperative programs of adjuvant therapy have undergone limited study. The combined use of radiation therapy, 4000 rad in two split courses, and 5-fluorouracil, 500 mg/m^2 on the first 3 consecutive days of each radiation course, can result in an improvement in survival in patients who have been resected for cure but nevertheless remain at a high probability for relapse and death. In one control trial there was significant improvement in median survival; however, relatively few patients ultimately survived 5 or more years.

It should be recognized that the physician has an important role in the overall management of the complications of pancreatic cancer even if tumor-specific therapy is not indicated. Nutritional debilitation is a major contributing factor for morbidity and mortality, and should be dealt with aggressively with the combined use of pancreatic enzyme replacement and careful attention to diet. Because of protein degradation by acid exposure in the stomach, as many as 8 tablets of oral pancreatic enzyme preparations may be required, in addition to the coadministration of H$_2$ antihistamine receptor inhibitors, to deliver sufficient enzyme activity to the small intestine. Patients may also require supplements in the form of medium-chain triglycerides as well as fat-soluble vitamins. Many patients will have, in addition to exocrine deficiency, the loss of endocrine function and diabetes mellitus, which can be managed with insulin to ensure that glucose is effectively used. The control

of pain is an essential part of overall management with liberal use of narcotics and the possible role of nerve blocks during laparotomy or percutaneously to reduce requirements.

FOLLOW-UP

The patient's contribution to care consists of personal efforts to maintain an adequate caloric intake and to report promptly new symptoms to the physician for management. The physician has the responsibility to determine whether the patient is a suitable candidate for tumor-directed treatment, recognizing that surgery, radiation therapy, and chemotherapy can be associated with important complications that may not be tolerated by a patient who is already debilitated by disease and cachexia. In addition, the physician has a critical role in attempting to prevent or delay the recognized symptoms of pancreatic cancer, by paying careful attention to nutrition management, including the use of pancreatic enzyme replacement therapy, and promptly and aggressively using analgesics and percutaneous chemical splanchnicectomy for the management of pain. Percutaneous biliary drainage procedures, and specifically the endoscopic placement of a stent, may be indicated to relieve the symptoms of obstructive jaundice.

DISCUSSION
Prevalence and Incidence

It is currently estimated that 27,000 new cases of pancreatic cancer will be diagnosed in the United States this year, with approximately 25,000 deaths. This tumor currently ranks as the fifth most common cause of cancer death in the United States. The incidence of pancreatic cancer has been increasing over the past several decades, and disproportionately so in African-Americans, in whom it occurs approximately 1.5 times more frequently than in whites. Recent estimates indicate that the cancer occurs in females as often as it does in males. During the past three decades, the death rate for pancreatic cancer in the United States has risen by approximately 12% in men and 26% in women.

Related Basic Science
Genetics and Altered Molecular Biology

Genetic predispositions to adenocarcinoma of the pancreas, although rare, have been described. In addition, an inherited syndrome of relapsing pancreatitis has been associated with an increased risk for the development of this tumor. Pancreatic adenocarcinomas have been frequently shown to contain mutations in the p53 tumor suppressor gene. Abnormal karyocytes and nuclear aneuploidy are also described.

Physiologic or Metabolic Derangement

Glucose intolerance, which may antedate the diagnosis of pancreatic cancer by 6 to 12 months, is a frequently cited metabolic complication. The presence of newly diagnosed diabetes in an elderly person may herald the presence of an underlying pancreatic carcinoma. Occlusion of the pancreatic duct, typically with a tumor in the head region, with destruction of pancreatic parenchyma by tumor or concurrent pancreatitis may result in pancreatic enzyme deficiencies. It is for this reason that pancreatic enzyme replacement may represent an important adjunct to the overall management of the weight loss commonly associated with this tumor. Obstruction of the common bile duct may require bypass by either a stent or a surgical procedure.

Anatomic Derangement

Pancreatic cancer typically invades into local structures and organs, including the stomach or duodenum. The latter may cause obstruction of the common bile duct and a palpable gallbladder (Courvoisier's sign).

Natural History and Its Modification with Treatment

Pancreatic cancer is a relatively rapidly fatal disease with a median survival of approximately 4 to 6 months. Modestly longer survivals are expected with limited stages of disease. Preventive measures, other than stopping smoking and limiting exposure to chemicals, such as β-naphthylamine and benzidine, are currently not available.

Prevention

Although reduced exposure to organic chemicals and smoking cessation can be offered as general measures to reduce risk for pancreatic cancer, more specific approaches for prevention have not as yet been identified.

Cost Containment

Although a wide range of diagnostic and treatment modalities are available for pancreatic cancer, in reality both can be used sparingly given the probable advanced nature of the tumor at diagnosis, as well as the limited prospect for achieving tumor control. In general, the systemic management of pancreatic cancer with chemotherapy represents clinical investigation; patients should be, when possible, enrolled into well-designed clinical trials of new therapies for which some base of support is ordinarily provided.

REFERENCES

Gastrointestinal Tumor Study Group. Treatment of locally unresectable carcinoma of the pancreas: Comparison of combined-modality therapy (chemotherapy plus radiotherapy) to chemotherapy alone. J Natl Cancer Inst 1988;80:751.

Lynch HT, Fusaro L, Lynch JF. Familial pancreatic cancer: A family study. Pancreas 1992;7:511.

Niederau C, Grendell JH. Diagnosis of pancreatic carcinoma: Imaging techniques and tumor markers. Pancreas 1992;7:66.

Schein PS. The role of chemotherapy in the management of gastric and pancreatic carcinomas. Semin Oncol 1985;12:49.

Silverman DT, Dunn JA, Hoover RN, et al. Cigarette smoking and pancreatic cancer: A case–control study based on direct interviews. J Natl Cancer Inst 1994;86:1510.

Steinberg WM, Gelfand R, Anderson KK, et al. Comparison of the sensitivity and specificity of the CA19-9 and carcinoembryonic antigen assays in detecting cancer of the pancreas. Gastroenterology 1986;90:343.

CHAPTER 3–11

Hepatocellular Carcinoma (Hepatoma)

Melvin R. Moore, M.D.

DEFINITION

Hepatocellular carcinoma is a primary malignancy of the liver arising from adult hepatocytes.

ETIOLOGY

Hepatitis B virus (HBV) infection is highly correlated with increased risk for hepatocellular carcinoma. In areas of the world where the carrier state for HBV is endemic, 50% of hepatocellular carcinoma patients are HBsAg positive as compared with 10% of matched controls. In the United States and Western Europe, roughly 25% of hepatocellular carcinoma patients are HBsAg positive, with background rates of well below 1%. In areas endemic for HBV carrier state such as Taiwan, the relative risk of HBsAg-positive individuals for developing hepatocellular carcinoma is 200:1, whereas relative risk is closer to 10:1 in nonendemic areas such as the United States. The association of hepadenovirus infection with hepatocellular carcinoma is seen in humans, woodchucks, and ground squirrels. Several possible oncogenic mechanisms have been proposed. Among these possible mechanisms is the transactivation of transcription regulated by certain *cis*-acting sequences of the hepadenovirus x gene (*hbx*). The potential for *hbx* oncogenesis is supported by the development of hepatocellular carcinoma in *hbx* transgenic mice and the malignant transformation of cultured cells expressing *hbx*. The oncogenes c-*myc* and c-*jun* are transactivated by *hbx*.

Necroinflammatory disease of the liver, cirrhosis of any etiology, may cause hepatocellular carcinoma regardless of the inciting agent. Hepatitis C virus (HCV) infection confers a risk of developing hepatocellular carcinoma that is similar to that of HBV, but with a later onset and a different geographic distribution. In areas endemic for HCV (Japan, Spain, Italy), the relative risk of developing hepatocellular carcinoma is well above 50. In nonendemic areas, the relative risk is closer to 10. The pathogenesis of hepatocellular carcinoma is unknown, but the invariable association of cirrhosis or chronic hepatitis with HCV-associated malignancy suggests that malignant transformation is a result of the chronic necroinflammatory disease. Exposure to other hepatotoxins such as alcohol, aflatoxin, and iron overload that lead to cirrhosis is also associated with increased risk for developing hepatocellular carcinoma.

Estrogen exposure (oral contraceptive) is associated with a small, but reproducible risk of hepatocellular carcinoma in younger women.

CRITERIA FOR DIAGNOSIS

Suggestive

Clinical or laboratory deterioration in a patient with known cirrhosis or a patient with known HBV or HCV chronic infection should suggest the diagnosis of hepatocellular carcinoma. Imaging studies (computed tomography [CT] scan of the liver) and α-fetoprotein determination are required to confirm space-occupying liver disease.

Definitive

The definitive diagnosis of hepatocellular carcinoma requires a tissue biopsy from the liver or from a metastatic site.

CLINICAL MANIFESTATIONS

Subjective

The most common presenting signs and symptoms of hepatocellular carcinoma and their approximate frequencies are abdominal pain (50%), abdominal mass (35%), anorexia/weight loss (30%), and ascites (20%). Other symptoms associated with primary tumor growth include gastrointestinal bleeding associated with portal hypertension, nausea/vomiting, and altered mental status due to hepatic encephalopathy. Symptoms secondary to metastatic disease such as bone pain and respiratory complaints are seen at presentation in less than 10% of patients. Paraneoplastic manifestations reported with hepatocellular carcinoma include hypercalcemia, anemia, polycythemia, hypoglycemia, and recurrent thrombophlebitis. Rarely, patients present with an acute abdomen secondary to tumor rupture and hemorrhage.

Objective

Physical Examination

Physical findings in order of prevalence include hepatomegaly or mass (90%), tenderness over the liver (60%), jaundice (25%), ascites (20%), and, less commonly, splenomegaly, edema, and hepatic bruit or friction rub. None of the preceding findings is specific for hepatocellular carcinoma.

Routine Laboratory Abnormalities

Routine laboratory abnormalities commonly encountered include elevated liver chemistries or bilirubin (90%), anemia (50%), hypercalcemia or polycythemia (2%), and metastatic disease on chest x-ray film (30%).

PLANS
Diagnostic
Differential Diagnosis

Other benign and malignant space-occupying lesions of the liver must be differentiated from primary hepatocellular carcinoma. Benign conditions include hemangiomas, cysts, and regenerating nodules. Fifteen percent of primary hepatic neoplasms are cholangiocarcinomas. Metastatic carcinomas make up the bulk of malignancies involving the liver.

Diagnostic Options

Diagnostic options include imaging of the liver with ultrasound, CT scan, magnetic resonance imaging, and technetium–sulfur colloid liver scan. A tagged red blood cell liver scan may help in the differential diagnosis of hemangioma versus tumor. Arteriography of the liver is used primarily in planning hepatic resection after the diagnosis has been established. Laboratory evaluation should include screening for HBV and HCV as well as serum α-fetoprotein. The serum level of α-fetoprotein is greater than 25 ng/mL in 75% of patients and greater than 1000 ng/mL in more than 60%. Biopsy procedures include percutaneous blind liver biopsy, CT- or peritoneoscopy-guided biopsy, or open biopsy at laparotomy. Up to 5% of patients may have hemorrhagic complications of closed biopsy procedures. Hemorrhagic complications have been greatly reduced with CT-guided fine-needle aspiration.

The recommended approach consists of serum α-fetoprotein determination, HBV/HCV serologies, CT scan of the abdomen, and CT-directed fine-needle aspiration of suspected liver lesions.

Therapeutic
Therapeutic Options

The rapid and certain mortality of unresected hepatoma provides a strong rationale for resection of hepatocellular carcinoma whenever possible. Surgical approaches range from local tumor excision to hepatic resection and transplant. Tumors that are small (<5 cm), well differentiated or fibrolamellar, unifocal, lacking in vascular invasion, and occurring in the absence of cirrhosis are associated with 5-year survivals approaching 50%; however, fewer than 20% of patients present with these features.

Nonsurgical local therapy consisting of alcohol injection into lesions that are less than 5 cm may provide local control for several years. Gelfoam embolization and chemoembolization with Gelfoam and a variety of agents have caused local tumor regression but have not been documented to extend life expectancy. Intraarterial chemotherapy with a variety of agents (fluorodeoxyuridine, doxorubicin, mitomycin C) has also been associated with rates of tumor regression approaching 50%, but without documented impact on survival.

Systemic chemotherapy has been associated with response rates of 20% or less and has had minimal impact on survival (<4 months). Tamoxifen, an antiestrogenic agent, has been associated with decreases in serum α-fetaprotein and periods of clinical stability that are unusual in untreated patients. Larger trials of this hormonal approach are needed.

Recommended Approach

Surgical evaluation for resectability should include CT scan of the liver and a biochemical profile of liver tests and prothrombin time. Patients who have small single tumors and who do not have evidence of hepatic decompensation should be considered for resection, sparing as much normal liver as possible. Patients with fibrolamellar histology who have more extensive hepatic involvement and are negative for HBV and HCV carrier states should be considered for hepatic resection and liver transplantation. Local alcohol injection is reasonable for patients with small tumors. Tamoxifen in a dose of 30 mg/d is also reasonable, but requires further study. Other more aggressive chemotherapy, local infusional, or surgical procedures should be considered experimental at the present time.

FOLLOW-UP

Patients on active therapy require close clinical and laboratory follow-up, as hepatic dysfunction increases the toxicity of all of the approaches described above.

DISCUSSION
Prevalence and Incidence

Hepatocellular carcinoma is one of the most common malignant tumors worldwide and is responsible for more than one million deaths each year. The incidence of hepatocellular carcinoma varies markedly by geographic area. The incidence is as high as 150 cases per 100,000 population per year in parts of China, Korea, Taiwan, and sub-Saharan Africa. The incidence is less than 4 per 100,000 in the United States. There is a 3:1 male predominance. The peak age incidence in endemic areas is the fourth decade, as compared with the sixth decade in the United States.

Related Basic Science

See Etiology.

Natural History and Its Modification with Treatment

Hepatocellular carcinoma is often multicentric. Hepatocellular carcinoma occurring in the absence of cirrhosis has a much better outlook than when diagnosed in the presence of major necroinflammatory liver disease. Most patients die from hepatic failure without distant metastases. More than half of patients presenting with a clinical picture leading to the diagnostis die in 1 to 2 months. Only 3% survive beyond 1 year. Up to 50% of patients with resectable lesions meeting the good prognostic criteria described above survive 5 years from surgical resection. Major modification in mortality and morbidity will come only with effective screening and prevention (see below).

Prevention

Primary prevention through vaccination against the hepatitis B virus in regions where it is endemic should reduce the incidence of hepatocellular carcinoma. The control of hepatitis C virus infection also provides an opportunity for primary prevention. Prevention through altered lifestyle (alcohol) and decreased exposures (aflatoxin) should also impact on the incidence of this malignancy. Secondary prevention in the form of α-fetoprotein and ultrasound screening at 3-month to 1-year intervals in HBsAg carriers has resulted in the detection of smaller tumors. An impact on survival has been documented in endemic areas.

Cost Containment

The use of expensive and frequent diagnostic tests such as nuclear scans, CT scans, α-fetoprotein determination, and routine x-rays and blood tests should be minimized in patients with known unresectable or metastatic hepatocellular carcinoma unless under active treatment.

REFERENCES

DiBisceglie AM, Rustgi VK, Hoofnagle JH, et al. NIH Conference: Hepatocellular carcinoma. Ann Intern Med 1988;108:390.

McMahon DJ, London T. Workshop on screening for hepatocellular carcinoma. J Natl Cancer Inst 1991;83:916.

Okuda K, Ohtsuki T, Obata H, et al. Natural history of hepatocellular carcinoma and prognosis in relation to treatment: Study of 850 patients. Cancer 1985;56:918.

Prince AM. Hepatitis B virus and primary liver cancer. In: Fortner JG, Rhoads JE, eds. Accomplishments in cancer research 1984. Philadelphia: Lippincott, 1985:110.

Ravoet C, Bleiberg H, Gerard B. Non-surgical treatment of hepatocarcinoma. J Surg Oncol 1993;3:104.

Robinson WS. Molecular events in the pathogenesis of hepadnavirus-associated hepatocellular carcinoma. Annu Rev Med 1994;45:297.

Sallie R, DiBisceglie AM. Viral hepatitis and hepatocellular carcinoma. Clin North Am 1994;23:567.

CHAPTER 3–12

Malignant Carcinoid Tumor

Melvin R. Moore, M.D.

DEFINITION

Carcinoid tumors are neoplasms of enterochromaffin cell origin. These cells are widely distributed throughout the body. Malignant behavior is determined by size and location rather than by histologic criteria. The majority of carcinoid tumors originate in the appendix, rectum, and small intestine. The bronchus is the next most common site of origin. The malignant carcinoid syndrome, a manifestation of advanced disease, is characterized by facial flushing and/or diarrhea in the presence of an elevated urinary 5-hydroxyindoleacetic acid (5-HIAA) level.

ETIOLOGY

The etiology of carcinoid tumors is unknown.

CRITERIA FOR DIAGNOSIS
Suggestive

The patient with persistent abdominal pain of obscure etiology should be suspected of harboring a small bowel carcinoid. Abdominal symptoms may be present for many years. Routine contrast studies of the bowel may be negative, and physical findings may be absent. Thus, a high index of suspicion is required to establish the diagnosis prior to the appearance of a palpable abdominal mass, hepatic enlargement, or malignant carcinoid syndrome. Symptoms of bowel obstruction and ischemia may be due to a small bowel or appendiceal carcinoid. Bronchial carcinoids most often present as a coin lesion on chest x-ray films. Massive hepatic enlargement due to tumor invasion in a relatively intact patient is characteristic of carcinoid or islet cell tumor.

Definitive

Histologic documentation is required for a definitive diagnosis. An elevated urinary 5-HIAA or platelet serotonin assay is required to confirm the diagnosis of malignant carcinoid syndrome. Rectal and appendiceal carcinoids are most often incidental findings encountered during sigmoidoscopy (approximately 1 in 3000 procedures) or appendectomy (approximately 1 in 300).

CLINICAL MANIFESTATIONS
Subjective

Many patients with small carcinoids are completely asymptomatic. Chronic, episodic, nondescript abdominal pain is the most frequent presentation for small bowel carcinoid. Symptoms of ischemia and obstruction of the bowel often herald more advanced carcinoids with locoregional fibrosis or tumor infiltration. The chronicity of symptoms and the absence of other diagnoses to explain persistent abdominal complaints should raise the suspicion of a small bowel carcinoid. Facial flushing progressing to chronic erythema and telangiectasia and diarrhea occur either separately or together in about two thirds of patients with carcinoid tumors and elevated urinary levels of 5-HIAA. Less than 25% of patients with carcinoid tumor develop the carcinoid syndrome. Bone pain, malnutrition and weight loss, symptomatic anemia, and wheezing are uncommon symptoms encountered in patients with carcinoid tumor.

Objective
Physical Examination

Physical findings are most often absent. A palpable abdominal mass is encountered in roughly 20% of patients with small bowel carcinoid. Wheezing may be encountered in patients with bronchial carcinoid. Late in the course of metastatic carcinoid, hepatomegaly and signs of malnutrition or niacin deficiency may be seen. In patients with carcinoid syndrome, acute and chronic skin changes (erythema, hives, telangiectasia), cardiac enlargement, neck vein abnormality consistent with tricuspid regurgitation, and the murmurs of valvular heart disease (tricuspid regurgitation and/or pulmonic stenosis) may be encountered. Rectal carcinoids are found on sigmoidoscopy as yellow–gray nodules between 4 and 13 cm above the dentate line.

Routine Laboratory Abnormalities

Routine laboratory tests are normal in patients with early carcinoid tumors, with the exception of chest x-ray abnormalities in patients with bronchial carcinoids. In advanced metastatic carcinoid, involvement of liver, bone, and bone marrow will be reflected in the routine chemistries and hemogram. The electrocardiogram may show right ventricular conduction delay.

PLANS
Diagnostic

The list of conditions in the differential diagnosis of obscure abdominal pain is immense. Routine diagnostic studies (upper gastrointestinal series with small bowel follow-through, barium enema, computed tomography scan of the abdomen, gallbladder imaging) should be performed to rule out other gastrointestinal disorders, but are usually negative in early small bowel carcinoid.

Diagnostic Options

Diagnostic options include gastrointestinal and gallbladder imaging studies as listed above and upper and lower gastrointestinal endoscopy. Magnetic resonance imaging and whole-body scintigraphy with radio-labeled analogs of somatostatin have added to the diagnostic accuracy in cases of suspected carcinoid tumor. Twenty-four-hour urinary 5-HIAA assay is critical in the diagnosis of malignant carcinoid syndrome. Minor elevation of the urinary level of 5-HIAA is associated with the ingestion of certain foods (walnuts, pecans, bananas, tomatoes, avocados, pineapple) and, depending on the assay used, certain medications (guaifenesin, acetaminophen, salicylate, L-dopa). Urinary levels above 25 mg per 24 hours, however, have a diagnostic accuracy of almost 100%. Serotonin measured in blood platelets is unaffected by food intake and, in addition, is found to be more sensitive in establishing a diagnosis of malignant carcinoid syndrome.

Recommended Approach

The recommended approach to the diagnosis depends on the presentation. Small tumors (<1 cm) found incidentally at appendectomy or endoscopy of the rectum require no additional diagnostic evaluation beyond histologic confirmation. In patients suspected of having a small bowel carcinoid because of persistent nonspecific abdominal complaints, the full gamut of noninvasive diagnostic procedures alluded to above may be required to lead to a site for biopsy confirmation. Other neuroendocrine tumors may appear similar by histology and require assays for various peptide hormones. Anaplastic small cell tumors are variants of carcinoid malignancy that will be detected by histologic appearance. This distinction has important implications for prognosis and therapy. Assays for 24-hour urine 5-HIAA and/or platelet serotonin are required in the presence of symptoms suggestive of the carcinoid syndrome or metastatic spread.

Therapeutic

Carcinoid tumors less than 1 cm in diameter that are found in the rectum and appendix may be adequately treated by simple excision. More extensive surgery is required for local carcinoids larger than 2 cm in diameter or tumors originating in the small bowel. Small bowel carcinoids are multicentric in about one quarter of patients. Patients with tumors that have spread beyond the primary site are seldom cured by surgery, although the median time to recurrence is well over 10 years from the time of resection. Thus, resection and debulking are important in the management of all patients with carcinoid tumors.

Patients with malignant carcinoid syndrome may be treated with the long-acting analog of somatostatin, octreotide. Subcutaneous injection of 150 μg three times daily will effectively control carcinoid syndrome symptoms in almost all patients. Symptomatic responses to octreotide therapy are accompanied by significant decreases in urinary 5-HIAA levels that last for a median of about 1 year. Objective tumor regressions are not usually seen with these doses of octreotide, but have been reported in a small series of patients receiving 2000 μg three times daily. Interferon alfa has also been shown to be effective in managing the symptoms of carcinoid syndrome and, rarely, in causing tumor regression. Other measures to control symptoms of carcinoid syndrome include cyproheptadine, 8 mg orally three times daily, for diarrhea and niacin to prevent niacin deficiency (see below).

Percutaneous hepatic artery embolization at intervals of one or more months has been effective in controlling the endocrine manifestations of carcinoid tumor and is associated with major tumor regressions lasting a median of 24 months. Patients with metastatic carcinoid syndrome who are to undergo surgical interventions or hepatic artery embolization should receive intravenous somatostatin analog (100 μg) to prevent carcinoid crisis. Systemic chemotherapy using streptozotocin and 5-fluorouracil has had limited success in producing objective tumor responses in about one third of patients treated. These responses last a median of slightly more than 6 months. Anaplastic small cell carcinoids are responsive to chemotherapy using etoposide plus cisplatin and such treatment should be tried in this group of patients.

Carcinoid of the ovary may be cured by surgical removal of the ovary because the full syndrome, including severe carcinoid heart disease, may be present without liver metastasis.

FOLLOW-UP

Carcinoids of the rectum and appendix smaller than 1 cm require no additional postoperative follow-up. All other patients should be evaluated for symptoms suggesting small bowel obstruction or carcinoid syndrome at 1-year intervals following surgical excision. Urinary 5-HIAA levels should be determined to evaluate symptoms suggestive of carcinoid syndrome. Recurrences should be managed surgically whenever possible. Metastatic carcinoid patients may be followed off therapy at intervals of 4 to 6 months until symptoms related to tumor growth or to carcinoid syndrome occur. Patients requiring hepatic artery embolization, chemotherapy, or medical management for carcinoid syndrome should be seen every 1 to 2 months. Symptoms, physical findings, and levels of urinary 5-HIAA should be carefully assessed at each visit.

DISCUSSION
Prevalence and Incidence

Carcinoid tumors are rare, with an annual incidence rate of approximately 0.3 per 100,000 population, or just over 600 new cases per year in the United States. With its protracted natural history, the prevalence of carcinoid is obviously much higher than the incidence; however, precise figures for prevalence are not available. There is a slight male predominance in incidence, with a broad age range peaking in the seventh decade. The small bowel is the most common site for primary carcinoid tumors, with more than 40% occurring within 2 feet of the ileocecal valve.

Related Basic Science

The metabolism of L-tryptophan is deranged in the carcinoid syndrome, with more than 90% of this amino acid being shunted to serotonin production. Tryptophan hydroxylase catalyzes the conversion of trypto-

phan to 5-hydroxytryptophan as the rate-limiting step in the production of serotonin. Tumor dopa decarboxylase rapidly converts 5-hydroxytryptophan to serotonin, which is either stored in neurosecretory granules or secreted into the vascular compartment. The majority of intravascular serotonin is taken up and stored in the dense granules of platelets. Monoamine oxidase and aldehyde dehydrogenase convert serotonin to 5-HIAA in the plasma and kidney. Although the carcinoid syndrome is clearly associated with elevated serotonin production, some symptoms, flushing in particular, are not well correlated with serotonin levels. The overproduction and interaction of serotonin and bradykinin probably explain the majority of carcinoid syndrome symptoms. The loss of available L-tryptophan to form nicotinic acid may lead to clinical niacin deficiency late in the course of severe carcinoid syndrome. Other neurohumors such as tachykinins (substance P), gastrointestinal peptides, prostaglandin, and histamine may play minor roles in carcinoid syndrome symptoms. The preponderance of other peptide hormones in the tumor (e.g., insulin, gastrin, glucagon, vasoactive intestinal polypeptide, parathormone) suggests that one is dealing with a noncarcinoid type of neuroendocrine tumor.

Obstructive symptoms in carcinoid patients occur as the result of intense fibrotic reaction to tumor invasion into the mesentery of the small bowel. Fibrotic involvement of the mesenteric artery is associated with bowel ischemia and infarction. Metastatic spread beyond the mesentery is almost invariably to the liver. Less commonly, bone and bone marrow are involved. An ovarian carcinoid delivers its toxic substances into the ovarian vein and azygos system without the substances being detoxified by the liver. Therefore, ovarian carcinoid heart disease can occur without liver metastasis.

Natural History and Its Modification with Treatment

The malignant potential of carcinoid tumors is directly related to tumor size and location. Carcinoids of the small intestine have about a 15% incidence of metastasis when between 0.5 and 1 cm. The risk for metastasis increases with size to more than 60% for tumors between 1 and 1.5 cm and more than 80% for tumors exceeding 1.5 cm (Moertel, 1987). The carcinoid syndrome is not seen in patients with rectal carcinoids. Patients with widely metastatic carcinoid tumors in whom the carcinoid syndrome is controlled or is not present may be remarkably asymptomatic despite large tumor volumes. The survival of patients with carcinoid tumors that are localized to the site of origin does not differ from that of an age-matched population cohort. Patients presenting with regional resectable disease have a median survival of more than 15 years, and those with regional unresectable disease have a median survival of more than 5 years. Even patients presenting with hepatic metastasis have a median survival longer than 3 years.

Prevention

At present there is no proven method for the prevention of carcinoid tumor.

Cost Containment

Follow-up care should rely on careful history taking and physical assessment rather than on laboratory tests and x-ray in asymptomatic patients.

REFERENCES

DeVries EG, Kema IP, Slooff MJ, et al. Recent developments in diagnosis and treatment of metastatic carcinoid tumours. Scand J Gastroenterol Suppl 1993;200:87.
Feldman JM. Carcinoid tumors and syndrome. Semin Oncol 1987;14:237.
Kvols LK, Reubi JC. Metastatic carcinoid tumors and the malignant carcinoid syndrome. Acta Oncol 1993;32(2):197.
Moertel CG. An odyssey in the land of small tumors. J Clin Oncol 1987;5:1503.
Moertel CG, Rubin J, Kvols LK. Therapy of metastatic carcinoid tumor and the malignant carcinoid syndrome with recombinant leukocyte A interferon. J Clin Oncol 1989;7:865.

CHAPTER 3–13

Carcinoma of the Colon

Samuel R. Newcom, M.D.

DEFINITION

Carcinoma of the colon arises from the mucosa and is usually adenocarcinoma. Unless identified by screening asymptomatic patients, the carcinoma presents with symptoms such as local pain, hemorrhage, and obstruction.

ETIOLOGY

Although the etiology of colon cancer is unknown, there is extensive epidemiologic and animal data to suggest that environmental carcinogens are partially responsible. Fourteen case–control studies have explored the association of cancer risk with meat or fat consumption and a smaller number have examined protein and energy intake (Potter, 1992). Taken together, these data strongly suggest that some aspect(s) of a diet high in meat, fat, protein, and total energy (all of which are highly correlated) are important in the etiology of colon cancer. A role for dietary fiber in colon carcinogenesis was first proposed by Burkitt in 1969. A meta-analysis of 13 case–control studies shows an inverse dose response for fiber. The more impressive and consistent lower risk has been associated with the consumption of vegetables. Eleven of 14 analytic studies report an inverse effect: more consistent with fiber, cereals, or fruit and a finding not confined to specific vegetables or vegetable groups (Potter, 1992). Other aspects of diet appear to be related, particularly calcium intake and perhaps alcohol consumption. There are also data to suggest a role for physical activity, gender, and reproduction. Carcinogens contained in human feces include fecapentaenes produced by gastrointestinal microflora. Also, 3-ketosteroids from cholesterol metabolism have been shown to be tumor promoters or initiators. Benzopyrene and other pyrolysis products produced by broiling or frying meat at high temperatures are found in the stool of ingesters. Free bile acids produce epithelial proliferation and are increased by high fat intake, inadequate calcium salts, and an alkaline pH (the bile acid/volatile fatty acid hypothesis).

Familial polyposis is eventually associated with colon cancer 100% of the time and demonstrates the strong influence that genetic predisposition may play in some patients (Erbe, 1976). There is accumulating evidence that a series of specific chromosomal and genetic changes accompany the transition from normal colonic mucosa to metastatic carcinoma (Stanbridge, 1990). Further, some of these changes, such as the identification of the deletion site on chromosome 18q as a cell adhesion molecule, fit well with expectation. The familial adenomatous polyposis (FAP) gene is found at 5q21, but there is no known homology and it is not the MCC gene frequently mutated in colon cancer (Kinzler et al., 1991). DNA hypomethylation is also an early step in colon carcinogenesis and methylation is controlled at the genetic level. Although the molecular genetic work is incomplete, it is now a very exciting time in the understanding of the etiology of colon cancer as coherence begins to form between the various lines of investigation.

CRITERIA FOR DIAGNOSIS

Suggestive

Abdominal pain and/or blood in the stool should alert one to the possibility of neoplastic disease of the colon or rectum.

Definitive

Radiographic examination or colonoscopy may reveal the colon mass and lead one to a biopsy for pathologic diagnosis.

The diagnosis of colon carcinoma requires a tissue biopsy, usually from the primary site. The colon is defined here as extending from the ileocecal valve to the upper valve of Houston (15 cm from the anal verge). In some patients presenting with metastatic adenocarcinoma, the diagnosis must be inferred from the constellation of pathologic findings and clinical signs and symptoms. Rare malignancies presenting as primary colon cancers include, in order of frequency, lymphoma (0.1–0.5%), leiomyosarcoma (0.1%), and squamous cell carcinoma (fewer than 100 cases reported) (Spjut, 1984). Two to three percent of carcinoid tumors arise in the colon, and approximately 50% are metastatic at surgery. The discussion in the remainder of this chapter is limited to adenocarcinoma of the colon.

CLINICAL MANIFESTATIONS

Subjective

Adenocarcinoma of the colon is predominantly a disease found in patients over 50 years of age, but all ages are affected. In recent studies of adjuvant chemotherapy involving 1697 patients (Laurie et al., 1989; Moertel et al., 1990), more than 50% of the patients were below age 65 and several patients in their twenties were entered on the studies. The growth rate of adenocarcinoma of the colon is slow, and spontaneous regression has not been reported. The average doubling time of the tumor volume is greater than 1 year, and symptoms are usually present for 6 to 18 months before the diagnosis is made. These observations suggest that an earlier diagnosis is possible and that earlier lesions will be smaller and more likely to be resectable. Early-stage colon carcinoma has a mortality of approximately 20%, as compared with a mortality of almost 60% for the entire population with colon carcinoma (Table 3–13–1). Therefore, early detection of asymptomatic persons could prove to be important.

The symptoms of primary colon carcinoma are usually referable to the primary site. Left-sided lesions present with abdominal pain (72%), blood in the stool (53%), change in bowel habits, nausea, and/or vomiting. Right-sided carcinomas present predominantly with abdominal pain (75%); only a minority of patients report weakness secondary to anemia, visible blood in the stool, or nausea (Ackerman and del Regato, 1970; Moertel and Thynne, 1982).

Left-sided lesions produce lower abdominal cramping, which may be relieved by a bowel movement or flatulence. Right-sided lesions produce less specific abdominal complaints, and other gastrointestinal or urinary tract lesions may be suggested by the history. Colon carcinoma should be considered in any patient with nonspecific abdominal pain for which a satisfactory explanation is not apparent.

Twenty to thirty percent of colon carcinoma patients present with locally advanced disease. A few patients have distant metastases at presentation and may have nonspecific symptoms such as weight loss,

TABLE 3–13–1. SIMPLE DUKES' STAGING SYSTEM FOR COLORECTAL CARCINOMA

Dukes' Stage	Definition	5-Year Survival (%)
A	Disease limited to bowel wall without penetration through serosa	75–93
B	Penetration through serosa	65–75
C	Regional lymph node metastases	35–60
D	Unresectable metastases	<5

Source: Based on data published in: Eisenberg B, DeCosse JJ, Harford E, Michalek J. Carcinoma of the colon and rectum: The natural history reviewed in 1704 patients. Cancer 1982;49:1131. Fisher ER, Sass R, Palekar A, et al. Dukes' classification revisited: Findings from the national surgical adjuvant breast and bowel projects. Cancer 1989;64:2354. Mayer RJ, O'Connell MJ, Tepper JE, Wolmark N. Status of adjuvant therapy for colorectal cancer. J Natl Cancer Inst 1989;81:1359. McDermott FT, Hughes EST, Pihl EU, et al. Changing survival prospects in rectal carcinoma: A series of 1,306 patients managed by one surgeon. Dis Colon Rectum 1986;29:798.

malaise, and anorexia or specific complaints with reference to metastases in liver, peritoneum, lung, or brain.

Several disorders are associated with an increased risk of colon carcinoma:

- After 15 years of poorly controlled active chronic ulcerative colitis, 3 to 5% develop carcinoma; after 20 years of disease, 5% develop carcinoma; and after 25 years of disease, 9% develop colon carcinoma (Ekbom et al., 1990; Moertel and Thynne, 1982).
- A past history of colon carcinoma increases the incidence of a second primary colon cancer by three times.
- Familial polyposis (multiple polyposis, Gardner's syndrome, Oldfield's syndrome, Turcot's syndrome) results in carcinoma in 100% of patients (Erbe, 1976).
- Villous adenomas are malignant 29 to 70% of the time (Ackerman and del Regato, 1970).

Disorders with a suspected but unproven association with colon carcinoma include granulomatous disease (Crohn's disease, regional enteritis) with onset before age 21; colon adenomas; family history of carcinoma, particularly colon carcinoma; past history of genital or breast carcinoma; and history of radiation to the colon.

Objective

Physical Examination

Approximately one third of patients with a left-sided colonic carcinoma have a palpable mass, which must be distinguished from enlargement of other left-sided structures such as the spleen and the left kidney. Approximately three quarters of right-sided lesions are palpable and may be confused with abnormalities of the right kidney. The primary mass is usually fixed, and the presence of a movable ballottable mass, several masses, or ascites suggests metastatic disease. Other sites of metastases are suggested by an enlarged liver, a pleural effusion, a left-sided supraclavicular node (Virchow's node), skin nodules, bone pain, or focal neurologic abnormalities. A careful rectal examination may allow bimanual examination of a colonic mass in both males and females and usually supplies a stool specimen for evaluation for occult blood.

Routine Laboratory Abnormalities

Of symptomatic patients with colorectal cancer, 72 to 82% have been found to have a positive Hemoccult (Allison et al., 1990). Thirty-five percent of patients with adenomas were found to have a positive Hemoccult. Only 10 to 12% of asymptomatic patients with a positive Hemoccult are found to have a colonic carcinoma. Overall, one in three patients with a positive Hemoccult will be found to have either a carcinoma or an adenomatous polyp. An asymptomatic patient with a negative Hemoccult has only a 0.5% chance of having a colorectal carcinoma diagnosed within 4 years of testing and a 1.5% chance of having an adenomatous polyp. With chronic blood loss, microcytic anemia of iron deficiency may be present.

PLANS

Diagnostic

Laboratory studies for suspected colon carcinoma should include a complete blood count and reticulocyte count as well as routine measurements of liver and renal function. A chest x-ray should be performed. Flexible sigmoidoscopy is a reasonable first diagnostic step for suspected left-sided colonic carcinomas. An air-contrast (double-contrast) barium enema is a well-established diagnostic technique for identifying colon carcinoma. Complete colonoscopy is needed in most patients prior to surgery for a colonic carcinoma, both to reach right-sided lesions for histologic confirmation and to rule out synchronous primaries not discovered by the other diagnostic studies. Once a tissue diagnosis is established, a carcinoembryonic antigen (CEA) level should be determined (Miller, 1974; Sugarbaker et al., 1976; Holyoke, 1975). An elevated level correlates with extent of disease and survival. In one series, only 28% of early-stage patients had a level greater than 2.5 ng/mL and only 4% had a level greater than 9.9 ng/mL, whereas more than 80% with advanced disease had a level greater than 2.5 ng/mL and

60% had a level greater than 9.9 ng/mL. In addition, the level should fall to normal after complete resection and not rise unless there is recurrence or a second primary carcinoma.

The approach to the evaluation of the patient for sites of metastatic disease must be guided by the preceding findings. In general, no other evaluation is indicated prior to surgery. Suspected metastases should usually be proven by biopsy of at least one distant site. No patient's carcinoma should be declared unresectable on the basis of abnormal laboratory tests or vague radiographic studies. Routine bone scans, liver–spleen scans, and ultrasounds have not proved helpful and may delay necessary surgery. Although abdominal computed tomography scans are performed routinely in most hospitals prior to colectomy, their value in influencing survival, treatment, and staging remains to be established. Patients with suspicious abnormalities on barium enema and negative biopsies will usually be taken to surgery for a definitive diagnosis. Patients with metastatic disease will benefit from a palliative resection, colostomy, or bypass of the obstructing lesion.

Staging has been confusing because of the proposal of at least nine different systems, many using similar terms for a different extent of disease. The original Dukes (1932, 1940) staging system for rectal carcinoma has been shown to be as discriminatory as any other system and is the most widely used (Table 3–13–1). The TNM classification proposed by the American Joint Committee on Cancer is able to subclassify Dukes' B and C categories into better and worse prognostic groups (Tables 3–13–2 and 3–13–3).

Therapeutics

Invasive adenocarcinoma of the colon can be cured only by surgical resection. Left or right hemicolectomy is performed with primary end-to-end reanastomosis. Resection of isolated lymph node metastases is routine by an en bloc technique. Resection of isolated liver metastases has been successful in a few selected patients. Many infectious complications of hemicolectomy have been eliminated by thorough mechanical cleansing of the bowel prior to surgery. This is usually accomplished using a clear liquid diet and magnesium citrate. Lavage and enemas are sometimes used. The addition of oral antibiotics remains controversial, although oral neomycin and erythromycin can reduce the wound infection rate from 35% (placebo) to 9% (antibiotics) (Nichols et al., 1973).

Postoperatively, nasogastric suction is employed until the paralytic ileus has resolved. Fluid and electrolytes must be replaced. A urinary catheter is frequently necessary for several days, and narcotics are indicated until the pain of the wound has resolved. Urinary tract infection, cardiac disease, pneumonia, liver dysfunction, thromboembolism, and renal failure are all potential complications occurring in as many as 50% of hemicolectomy patients. Large series have reported mortality rates as high as 6.7 to 9.6% (Moertel and Thynne, 1982), but, more re-

TABLE 3–13–2. DEFINITION OF TNM STAGING SYSTEM FOR COLON AND RECTUM

Primary Tumor (T)	
TX	Cannot be assessed
T0	No evidence of primary
Tis	Carcinoma in situ
T1	Invades submocosa
T2	Invades muscularis propria
T3	Invades into subserosa or retroperitoneum
T4	Invades visceral peritoneum or other organs
Regional Lymph Nodes (N)	
NX	Cannot be assessed
N0	No nodal metastases
N1	1 to 3 pericolic or perirectal nodes
N2	4 or more nodes
N3	A positive node along a named vascular trunk
Distant Metastasis (M)	
MX	Metastases cannot be assessed
M0	No distant metastasis
M1	Distant metastasis

Source: American Joint Committee on Cancer manual for staging of cancer. Philadelphia: Lippincott, 1992:81. Reproduced with permission.

TABLE 3–13–3. STAGE GROUPING FOR TNM CLASSIFICATION OF COLORECTAL CANCER

Stage	TNM			Dukes
0	Tis	N0	M0	
I	T1	N0	M0	A
	T2	N0	M0	
II	T3	N0	M0	B
	T4	N0	M0	
III	Any T	N1	M0	C
	Any T	N2,N3	M0	
IV	Any T	Any N	M1	NA

Source: American Joint Committee on Cancer manual for staging of cancer. Philadelphia: Lippincott, 92:81. Reproduced with permission.

cently, the mortality rate has averaged 3.5% in most hospitals (Cohen et al., 1993). Patients over the age of 70 have higher mortality rates and may be better managed using a more conservative surgical approach. Close cooperation between the patient's surgeon and internist is necessary during this postoperative period to prevent complications of therapy and to maximize diagnostic and therapeutic interventions when needed.

There is no established role for radiation therapy in the cure of colon carcinoma. Radiation therapy (50 Gy in 5 weeks) may be useful in the palliation of brain metastases, as may a high dose of a glucocorticoid (e.g., dexamethasone, 6 mg orally every 6 hours). Local radiotherapy to painful bone metastases or a site of spinal cord compression by extradural metastasis may also offer significant palliation if metastatic colon carcinoma involves these sites.

It has been shown in two prospective randomized trials (Laurie et al., 1989; Moertel et al., 1990) that Dukes' C patients receiving levamisole (50 mg orally every 8 hours for 3 days, every 2 weeks for 1 year) and 5-fluorouracil (450 mg/m^2 intravenously daily for 5 days, followed at 4 weeks by weekly 5-fluorouracil for 48 weeks) reduced their risk of cancer recurrence by 31 and 41% after median follow-up periods of 7 years 9 months and 3 years, respectively. Levamisole, an immunomodulating agent, is commercially available as Ergamisol. The use of levamisole has been associated with rare episodes of agranulocytosis, an Antabuse-like effect when taken with ethanol, and increased plasma levels of phenytoin when taken in conjunction with phenytoins. Other, less serious, adverse reactions are almost never reported and include nausea, vomiting, diarrhea, stomatitis, dermatitis, altered taste perception, arthralgia, myalgia, dizziness, headache, paresthesias, and somnolence.

Although no combination of chemotherapeutic agents has been proven to be more effective than 5-fluorouracil alone, the combination of leucovorin (folinic acid) and 5-fluorouracil has recently been extensively tested in at least nine phase III randomized prospective trials (Einhorn, 1989). In three studies of weekly 5-fluorouracil/leucovorin, all three showed superior response rates but did not significantly alter survival. In six studies of 5-day courses of 5-fluorouracil/leucovorin, three showed superior response rates and two showed significant improvements in survival (53 versus 34 weeks, 54 versus 41 weeks). These studies also confirmed the known poor results with 5-fluorouracil as a single agent with response rates of 5 to 17.3%. One inexpensive and effective regimen is 5-fluorouracil 425 mg/m^2 plus leucovorin 20 mg/m^2 given by intravenous injection daily for 5 days every 4 weeks. Ice chips held in the mouth tend to reduce stomatitis. Chemotherapy is usually best reserved for patients with good performance status and tumor measurements that allow cessation of treatment when there is a greater than 25% progression of the carcinoma. 5-Fluorouracil and leucovorin are being tested in adjuvant trials with and without levamisole.

Several studies have shown that intrahepatic arterial administration of 5-fluorouracil or floxuridine is superior to intravenous 5-fluorouracil in producing regression of liver metastases. There is little survival advantage, however. Some patients decline palliative chemotherapy, and many are found to be inappropriate candidates. Entry into an experi-

mental protocol of one of the large cooperative cancer chemotherapy study groups is usually the best approach for the patient with metastatic colorectal cancer who desires palliative chemotherapy.

An important aspect of the care of patients with incurable colon carcinoma is attention to the patient's need for information about prognosis and therapeutic options, as well as regular counseling of the patient and family with respect to diet, analgesics, and exercise. Also, the physician should provide, as necessary, therapeutic paracentesis, thoracentesis, and blood transfusions. Most patients can be made comfortable through the duration of their life. Hospitalization should not be necessary for most complications. A home hospice program provides the necessary support for a comfortable confinement at home in many cases. In summary, the continued presence of a compassionate physician can provide significant palliation even if specific therapy is not available, and the patient should not feel that he or she is being abandoned or neglected when metastatic disease is present and not being treated by specific anticarcinoma measures.

Most series have reported a 45 to 46% cure rate of all patients by surgery alone (Cohen et al., 1993; Moertel and Thynne, 1982; Ackerman and del Regato, 1970). Survival times in three different series of patients with incurable or recurrent colon carcinoma were 9.0, 7.8, and 11.4 months. Aggressive resection of local recurrence and liver metastasis may cure an additional 2 to 5%. Adjuvant 5-fluorouracil and levamisole for the 20% of cases with Dukes' stage C may change the survival of that group from 20–35% to as high as 40–50%. The remaining 45 to 48% die of their disease or its complications. Recurrences become apparent within 5 years in 90 to 95% of those patients destined to die of colon cancer.

FOLLOW-UP

The focus of attention should be postoperative complications, recurrent carcinoma, second colorectal primaries, and general medical care. Monthly carcinoembryonic antigen determinations for the first 6 months to be followed by progressively lengthening intervals (every 2–4 months) for 5 years after resection is recommended by some authorities. The goal of this close follow-up is resection and cure of solitary metastases, as well as the discovery of second, curable primaries. There is no evidence that early discovery of incurable metastatic disease is beneficial. History, physical examination, complete blood count, and a stool guaiac should be done at each of these visits. A chest x-ray and a chemistry profile should be obtained every 3 to 6 months for the first 2 to 3 years and then every 6 months or as indicated by symptoms for 5 years. Air-contrast barium enemas are performed annually, and colonoscopy is performed to evaluated abnormalities. Reexploration may be indicated if evidence of recurrent carcinoma becomes apparent. The surgery is done in an effort to salvage patients by resecting involved lymph nodes, isolated liver metastases, or, perhaps, solitary pulmonary nodules. (It is unusual, in colon carcinoma, to have pulmonary metastases without simultaneous liver metastases.)

DISCUSSION

Prevalence and Incidence

The American Cancer Society (1994) predicted that approximately 107,000 people in the United States would be afflicted with cancer of the colon in 1994, and approximately 49,000 would die of colon carcinoma. Because of the marked rise in lung cancer in women and the significant increase in prostate cancer in men, colorectal cancer has fallen to the third leading cause of cancer death for each sex. Since 1945 there has been a steady decline in the age-adjusted death rate among women with colon cancer. The death rate among men has fallen less dramatically. Among 46 countries, the United States ranks 19th and 20th for female and male death rates, well behind Ecuador and Mexico, the countries with the lowest colon carcinoma death rates.

Related Basic Science

Approximately 24% of colon cancers are found in the sigmoid colon, with an even distribution throughout the rest of the colon (12.5% in the cecum, 9% in the ascending colon, 11% in the transverse colon, 6.1%

in the descending colon). Women are affected slightly more frequently than men (1.2:1). The mean age at diagnosis is 69 years.

The suspected etiology of colon carcinoma has been reviewed above. Colorectal cancer is one of the most extensively characterized human malignancies in terms of the molecular genetic alterations associated with its progression. Tissues that represent the progression from normal mucosa through hyperplasia, that is, benign adenoma to carcinoma in situ and finally metastasis, are readily accessible in the same patient. Therefore, by studying the DNA from these lesions in a single patient, investigators have been able to determine which oncogenes are activated and which "tumor suppressor genes" are lost. The following changes are reproducibly observed in sporadic colorectal carcinoma: activation of the Ki-*ras* oncogene in 40 to 50% and loss of genetic information from chromosomes 5q21–q22 in 35%, 17p12–p13 in more than 70%, and 18q21–qter in more than 70% (Stanbridge, 1990). Current work is being directed at the functional effect of these genetic alterations.

Natural History and Its Modification with Treatment

The early diagnosis of colon carcinoma in asymptomatic patients is possible. The least morbid and least expensive method is the use of impregnated guaiac slides (Hemoccult) prepared at home by the patient on three consecutive days while eating a high-roughage diet free of meat, horseradish (guaiac measures peroxidase activity), beets, vitamins, and aspirin. One to two percent of subjects are found to have a positive Hemoccult test. Air-contrast barium enema and colonoscopy identify carcinoma in 5 to 10% and polyps in 25%. Approximately 60% of these asymptomatic carcinomas are Dukes' stage A as compared with 15% of control patients.

The American Cancer Society recommends a digital rectal examination for all people over the age of 40 on an annual basis and flexible sigmoidoscopy every 3 to 5 years after age 50. The economy and ease of the stool guaiac suggest that it should be performed anytime a rectal examination is performed and perhaps more liberally. The motivation of the patient and the patient's risk factors for colon carcinoma should guide the physician's recommendations with respect to a sigmoidoscopy when the stool guaiac is negative. The yield will be low in asymptomatic patients (less than 0.2% in patients over 40).

Prevention

Prophylactic total colectomy in high-risk patients with multiple polyposis or long-standing ulcerative colitis is recommended. The compromise of an iliorectal anastomosis has been unsuccessful in some hands despite monthly proctoscopic examinations for carcinoma. A diet high in fiber (bran, psyllium hydrophilic mucilloid, legumes, etc.) and low in fat appears healthy in several aspects and should be encouraged in the population in general, although proof of the prevention of colon carcinoma is still lacking. Regular exercise and the avoidance of abdominal adiposity should be encouraged (Giovannucci et al., 1995). Aspirin, taken regularly, may reduce the incidence of colon cancer.

Cost Containment

Prevention of colon carcinoma and identification of early asymptomatic disease, as outlined above, are approaches that may avoid the loss of income and medical costs of caring for a patient with colon cancer. Economy is also accomplished through the prudent use of diagnostic studies, particularly with critical attention to expensive and nonspecific isotope scans. Computed tomography scans and too frequent laboratory testing should be avoided. Ineffective chemotherapy and unskillful postoperative care both generate unnecessary medical costs. Home hospice care of the dying patient with significant help from family and volunteers markedly reduces the patient's financial burden and usually improves the quality of remaining life.

REFERENCES

Ackerman LV, del Regato JA. Cancer: Diagnosis, treatment, and prognosis. 4th ed. St. Louis: Mosby, 1970.
Allison JE, Feldman R, Tekawa IS. Hemoccult screening in detecting colorectal neoplasm: sensitivity, specificity, and predictive value: Long-term follow-up in a large group practice setting. Ann Intern Med 1990;112:328.
American Cancer Society. Cancer statistics. Ca Cancer J Clin 1994;44:1.
Burkitt D. Related disease-related cause? Lancet 1969;2:1229.
Cohen AM, Minsky BD, Schilsky RL. Colon cancer. In: DeVita VT, Hellman S, Rosenberg SA, eds. Cancer: Principles and practice of oncology. 4th ed. Philadelphia: Lippincott, 1993.
Einhorn LH. Improvements in fluorouracil chemotherapy? J Clin Oncol 1989;7:1377.
Ekbom A, Helmick C, Zack M, Adami H-O. Ulcerative colitis and colorectal cancer: A population based study. N Engl J Med 1990;323:1228.
Erbe RW. Inherited gastrointestinal–polyposis syndromes. N Engl J Med 1976;294:1101.
Fisher ER, Sass R, Palekar A, et al. Dukes' classification revisited: Findings from the national surgical adjuvant breast and bowel projects. Cancer 1989;64:2354.
Fletcher RH. Carcinoembryonic antigen. Ann Intern Med 1986;104:66.
Giovannucci E, Ascherio A, Rimm EB, et al. Physical activity, obesity, and risk for colon cancer and adenoma in men. Ann Intern Med 1995;122:327.
Holyoke ED. Present and probable uses of CEA. Cancer 1975;25:22.
Kinzler KW, Nilbert MC, Li-Kuo S, et al. Identification of FAP locus genes from chromosomes 5q21. Science 1991;253:661.
Laurie JA, Moertel CG, Fleming TR, et al. Surgical adjuvant therapy of large-bowel carcinoma: An evaluation of levamisole and the combination of levamisole and fluorouracil. J Clin Oncol 1989;7:1447.
Miller AB. The joint National Cancer Institute/American Cancer Society study of a test for carcinoembryonic antigen (CEA). Cancer 1974;34:932.
Moertel CG. Chemotherapy for colorectal cancer. N Engl J Med 1994;330:1136.
Moertel CG, Fleming TR, MacDonald JS, et al. Levamisole and fluorouracil for adjuvant therapy of resected colon carcinoma. N Engl J Med 1990;322:352.
Moertel CG, Thynne GS. Large bowel. In: Holland JF, Frei E, eds. Cancer medicine. 2nd ed. Philadelphia: Lea & Febiger, 1982.
Nichols RL, Broido P, Condon RE, et al. Effect of preoperative neomycin–erythromycin intestinal preparation on the incidence of infectious complications following colon surgery. Ann Surg 1973;178:453.
Potter JD. Reconciling the epidemiology, physiology, and molecular biology of colon cancer. JAMA 1992;268:1573.
Spjut HJ. Pathology of neoplasms. In: Spratt JS, ed. Neoplasms of the colon, rectum and anus: Mucosal and epithelial. Philadelphia: Saunders, 1984.
Stanbridge EJ. Identifying tumor suppressor genes in human colorectal cancer. Science 1990;247:12.
Sugarbaker PH, Zamcheck N, Moore FD. Assessment of serial carcinoembryonic antigen (CEA) assays in postoperative detection of recurrent colorectal cancer. Cancer 1976;38:2310.

CHAPTER 3–14

Carcinoma of the Rectum

Samuel R. Newcom, M.D.

DEFINITION

Carcinoma of the rectum arises from the mucosa and is usually adenocarcinoma. Unless identified by screening asymptomatic patients, the carcinoma presents with symptoms such as hemorrhage and partial obstruction.

ETIOLOGY

Although the etiology of rectal cancer is unknown, there are extensive epidemiologic and animal data to suggest that environmental carcinogens are partially responsible. There is clearly an association of cancer risk with meat or fat consumption and, perhaps, protein and total energy intake. Taken together, these strongly suggest that some aspect (s) of a diet high in meat, fat, protein, and total energy (all of which are highly correlated) are important in the etiology of rectal cancer. A role for dietary fiber has also been proposed and the most consistent low risk appears to correlate with the consumption of vegetables: more consistent than fiber, cereals, or fruit and a finding not confined to specific vegetables or vegetable groups. Other aspects of diet may be related, particularly calcium intake and perhaps alcohol consumption. There are also data to suggest a role for physical activity, gender, and reproduction. Carcinogens contained in human feces include fecapentaenes produced by gastrointestinal microflora. Also, 3-ketosteroids from cholesterol metabolism have been shown to be tumor promoters or initiators. Benzopyrene and other pyrolysis products produced by broiling or frying meat at high temperatures are found in the stool of ingesters. Free bile acids produce epithelial proliferation and are increased by high fat intake, inadequate calcium salts, and an alkaline pH (the bile acid/volatile fatty acid hypothesis).

Familial polyposis is eventually associated with colorectal cancer 100% of the time and demonstrates the strong influence that genetic predisposition may play in some patients. Evidence is accumulating that a series of specific chromosomal and genetic changes accompany the transition from normal rectal mucosa to metastatic carcinoma. Further, some of these changes, such as the identification of the deletion site on chromosome 18q as a cell adhesion molecule, fit well with expectation. The familial adenomatous polyposis (FAP) gene is found at 5q21, but there is no known homology and it is not the MCC gene frequently mutated in colorectal cancer. DNA hypomethylation is also an early step in colorectal carcinogenesis and methylation is controlled at the genetic level. Although the molecular genetic work is incomplete, it is now a very exciting time in the understanding of the etiology of colorectal cancer as coherence begins to form between the various lines of investigation.

CRITERIA FOR DIAGNOSIS
Suggestive

Rectal bleeding and/or the palpation of a rectal mass should alert one to the possibility of cancer of the rectum.

Definitive

The diagnosis of rectal carcinoma requires a tissue biopsy, usually from the primary site. The rectum extends from the pectinate line (1 to 2 cm below the anorectal muscular ring) to the upper valve of Houston (approximately 15 cm). Lesions distal to the pectinate line are usually squamous cell carcinomas of the anus or, infrequently (0.6%), malignant melanomas. Ninety-eight percent of rectal carcinomas are adenocarcinomas. Primary lymphoma (1%), leiomyosarcoma (0.2%), and squamous cell carcinomas (0.1%) all occur about twice as frequently in the rectum as in the colon. Similarly, carcinoid tumors tend to cluster in the rectum and, unlike those in the colon, are usually asymptomatic and small when identified (Spjut, 1984; Dukes, 1940).

CLINICAL MANIFESTATIONS
Subjective

Adenocarcinoma of the rectum is reported in all ages, but most frequently in patients over the age of 40. Rectal carcinoma has a worse prognosis than colon carcinoma in some but not in all series.

The majority of symptomatic patients present with blood in the stool (approximately 85%) and less frequently with constipation or a sense of incomplete evacuation (50%). Other symptoms may include tenesmus (30%), diarrhea (30%), and abdominal pain (25%). A delay in diagnosis of 6 to 9 months after symptoms begin is common.

Several conditions are unquestionably associated with an increased risk of rectal carcinoma:

- Chronic ulcerative colitis, particularly after 10 years of active disease, poses a significant risk of carcinoma. The extent of involvement is important in that the incidence of carcinoma is only 0 to 1% when inflammatory disease is limited to the rectal area, but it ap-

proaches 50% or greater in patients with extensive disease of three or four decades' duration (Ekbom et al., 1990).
- Multiple polyposis is an inherited disorder in which there is an abnormal mitotic potential of the rectal mucosa eventually resulting in carcinoma in 100% of patients. Carcinoma usually develops between the ages of 35 and 40.
- Patients with a prior large bowel carcinoma are at an increased risk for developing a second primary carcinoma.
- The benign lesion villous adenoma has a reported 29 to 70% incidence of malignancy (Ackerman and del Regato, 1970).

Other facts obtained in the patient's history that indicate a possible increased risk of rectal carcinoma are granulomatous colitis, particularly with onset before age 21; tubulovillous adenomas (adenomatous polyps), particularly if large or multiple (Atkin et al., 1992); a family history of carcinoma, particularly colon carcinoma (Miller et., 1976); a past history of genital or breast carcinoma; and a history of pelvic irradiation (Castro et al., 1973).

Objective
Physical Examination

About 75% of rectal carcinomas can be palpated by digital examination. Some findings that are confused with a primary carcinoma include a fecal impaction (which can be separated digitally from the mucosa), a polyp (which may be on a stalk), an enlarged prostate or prostatic carcinoma, the retroverted cervix, and a thrombosed hemorrhoid. A gentle, careful, methodical rectal examination is required to avoid overlooking a rectal carcinoma. A stool guaiac test (Hemoccult) should be performed on all available specimens.

In addition to the rectal examination, a complete physical examination is indicated with special attention to subcutaneous metastases, supraclavicular adenopathy (90% left, 10% right), pleural effusion, bone tenderness, liver enlargement, ballottable intraabdominal metastases, and ascites. A neurologic examination will identify metastases in the brain or extradural spinal cord. The most common early metastases of rectal carcinoma occur in regional lymph nodes. Lesions of the cutaneous part of the anus may drain to inguinal nodes, but the middle and superior lymphatic collecting trunks are more commonly the draining sites and fill nodes of the hypogastric, presacral, perirectal, and superior hemorrhoidal blood vessel areas. These latter lymph nodes, even when involved, are not usually palpable and do not produce symptoms until they are unresectable.

Routine Laboratory Abnormalities

Anemia may be present but is nonspecific and the test for blood in the stool may be positive but may be caused by other benign and malignant gastrointestinal lesions.

PLANS
Diagnostic
Differential Diagnosis

It is necessary to consider all neoplasms of the colon and rectum as well as vascular and inflammatory abnormalities in a patient with rectal bleeding. Hemostatic deficiencies may precipitate bleeding from the normal rectal mucosa as well.

Diagnostic Options and Recommended Approach

Laboratory studies to be obtained in the evaluation of suspected rectal carcinoma should include a complete blood count, reticulocyte count, and liver and renal function tests. Hypercalcemia has been reported.

A chest film should be obtained to identify pulmonary metastases.

A proctoscopic examination should be performed to obtain tissue and examine as much of the primary lesion as possible. Barium should not be instilled into the colon if the patient will not be able to evacuate the contrast material after the examination. An air-contrast (double-contrast) barium enema will delineate small lesions, and a single-contrast barium enema will delineate a large constricting lesion. Low-lying rectal lesions may require special views for visualization and are one reason proctoscopy should be the first step in evaluating a patient for rectal carcinoma.

Some investigators have found computed tomography scanning or magnetic resonance imaging studies to be useful in planning the surgical procedure. These studies appear useful in identifying enlarged lymph nodes and bone erosion. They should be obtained if this information will change the patient's management. Frequently, however, a diverting colostomy is necessary even if the patient's carcinoma is unresectable. Isotope scans and other contrast studies have not been helpful.

A carcinoembryonic antigen determination should be performed prior to surgery. An elevated level correlates with the extent of disease and survival. The level should return to less than 2.5 ng/mL after surgery and not rise unless there is recurrent cancer.

The *staging* of rectal carcinoma was first undertaken by Dukes in 1932 and extensively correlated with prognosis in 1940. Although many staging systems have been proposed, a slight modification of the original system is used by most clinicians and is adequate for determining the therapy and prognosis of patients with rectal carcinoma. Both Dukes' staging system and the TNM system are outlined in Chapter 3–13 and may be applied to rectal cancer (Table 3-14-1).

Therapeutic

Invasive rectal carcinoma is best treated by surgical resection; however, because of the regional lymphatic drainage, the early identification in some patients, the refusal of some patients with low-lying lesions to undergo surgery, and the contraindication to surgery for some elderly or fragile patients, other local procedures have been performed in the treatment of rectal carcinoma.

Radical surgical resection should be preceded by careful evaluation of the patient for cardiorespiratory or other medical illness making surgery more difficult or dangerous. Careful bowel cleansing through the use of a liquid diet, cathartics, and enemas is routine. Antibiotics may be employed.

In general, lesions within 5 cm of the pectinate line require permanent colostomy and perineal resection of the anus and rectum as well as abdominal resection of the primary carcinoma.

Abdominoperineal resection carries a higher mortality (approximately 4–10%) than hemicolectomy (3.5%) and greater morbidity (e.g., urinary infection, impotence, prostatic obstruction, abnormal bladder emptying). The overall morbidity of 30 to 50% includes postoperative complications such as wound infection, pneumonia, cardiac decompensation, thrombophlebitis, and pulmonary embolus. Close cooperation between the internist and the surgeon during this period may help decrease these complications as well as hasten the diagnosis and treatment of each (Cohen et al., 1993).

The use of staplers and anastomotic clamps, as well as careful selec-

tion of properly staged patients, has allowed a reduction in the number in whom the anal sphincter must be sacrificed.

The substitution of electrocoagulation, cryosurgery, and radiation techniques for abdominoperineal resection has demonstrated that patients with early, mobile, well-differentiated tumors may achieve 5-year survivals of 68 to 78% with local procedures only (Moertel and Thynne, 1982). These techniques, however, must be considered secondary at this time and used only for those patients unwilling or unable to withstand radical resection.

The localized lymph node drainage and the fact that as many as 50% of patients with rectal carcinoma who die still have disease confined to the pelvic area suggest that radiotherapy has the potential to enhance the cure of rectal carcinoma, particularly Dukes' B or C lesions. Both preoperative and postoperative regimens have been reported in a anecdotal fashion. To date, most trials have indicated that radiotherapy significantly decreases the local recurrence rate but does not change overall survival. These series demonstrate that pelvic recurrences can be reduced from an expected incidence of 37 to 48% with surgery alone to 6 to 12% with postoperative irradiation of Dukes' B and C patients with 40 to 50 Gy (Cohen et al., 1993). This experience suggests that postoperative radiotherapy is a reasonable consideration in Dukes' B and C patients.

Recently, both the GI Tumor Study Group (Douglass et al., 1985) and the North Central Treatment Group (Krook et al., 1991) have shown that a combination of chemotherapy and radiotherapy can improve the results in resected high-risk rectal cancer as compared with treatment with radiotherapy alone. In the North Central study both disease-free survival and overall survival were significantly improved. All patients had a poor prognosis as indicated by invasion of the primary cancer into adjacent tissue (T3) or adjacent organs (T4) or regional lymph nodes (N1, N2). These Dukes' B and C patients were treated either with radiotherapy or with chemotherapy with methyl-CCNU (semustine) and 5-fluorouracil followed by radiotherapy with 5-fluorouracil sensitization and then a cycle of methyl-CCNU plus 5-fluorouracil. After more than 7 years of follow-up, this short course of chemotherapy had reduced the recurrence of rectal cancer by 34% (P = .0016), the rate of cancer-related death by 36% (P = .0071), and the overall death rate by 29% (P = .025). On the basis of the two studies, a National Institutes of Health Consensus Conference (1990) has recommended combined therapy for rectal cancer with regional nodal metastasis or invasion of perirectal fat or adjacent organs.

A recent large Intergroup Trial has shown that methyl-CCNU (semustine) is not more effective that a higher dose of systemic 5-fluorouracil (O'Connell et al., 1994). Currently, it is recommended that Dukes' B and C rectal cancer patients receive postoperative chemotherapy with 2 cycles of 5-fluorouracil 500 mg/m^2 for 5 days (day 1-5 and day 36-40). On approximately day 64 the patient should begin pelvic irradiation. The best results are achieved in patients who also receive a continuous 5-flourouracil infusion (225 mg/m^2) during the entire period of radiotherapy. After irradiation the patient receives two more cycles of 5-fluorouracil. After 4 years of follow-up 70% of these patients are surviving (P = 0.005) and 60% are free of relapse (P = 0.01).

External radiation alone has been reported to yield a 79% 5-year survival for anal canal carcinoma (usually squamous cell carcinomas) (Papillon and Chassard, 1992). Regimens using combination chemotherapy, for example, mitomycin C and 5-fluorouracil, coupled with radiotherapy have been effective and have allowed the preservation of fecal continence in the majority of patients. Surgery is reserved for those patients failing sterilization of disease in the radiotherapy field (Shank et al., 1993).

A solitary pulmonary nodule may be a resectable rectal carcinoma metastasis or a primary lung carcinoma (ratio approximately 50:50). Such lesions should be approached as potentially curable lesions. Similarly, isolated liver metastases have been shown to be surgically curable. Because of the lymphatic drainage, it is more likely that rectal carcinoma patients will have isolated pulmonary metastases without liver involvement as compared with colon carcinoma patients, in whom pulmonary metastases are usually secondary to liver involvement.

Palliation of incurable metastatic rectal carcinoma requires attention to the predominant sites of disease. Local pelvic pain, sacral plexus invasion, and venous obstruction may be relieved by radiotherapy. In one

TABLE 3–14–1. SIMPLE DUKES' STAGING SYSTEM FOR COLORECTAL CARCINOMA

Stage	Definition	5-Year Survival (%)
Dukes' A	Disease limited to bowel wall without penetration through serosa	75 – 93
Dukes' B	Penetration through serosa	65 – 75
Dukes' C	Regional lymph node metastases	35 – 60
Dukes' D	Unresectable metastases	< 5

Based on data published in Eisenberg B, DeCosse JJ, Harford E, Michalek J. Carcinoma of the colon and rectum: The natural history reviewed in 1704 patients. Cancer 1982;49:1131.
Fisher ER, Sass R, Palekar A, et al. Dukes' classification revisited: Findings from the national surgical adjuvant breast and bowel projects. Cancer 1989;64:2354.
Mayer RJ, O'Connell MJ, Tepper JE, Wolmark N: Status of adjuvant therapy for colorectal cancer. J Natl Cancer Inst. 1989;81:1359.
McDermott FT, Hughes EST, Pihl EU, et al. Changing survival prospects in rectal carcinoma: A series of 1306 patients managed by one surgeon. Dis Colon Rectum 1986;29:798.

study, 40 Gy induced symptomatic improvement for 11 months. The addition of 3 days of 5-fluorouracil (15 mg/kg) as a radiopotentiator yielded 18 months of palliation (Moertel et al., 1969). Brain metastases, spinal cord compression, and painful bone metastases may all benefit from radiotherapy. Systemic 5-fluorouracil has a low response rate (10 – 20%), but may be considered in selected patients. The combination of 5-fluorouracil and leucovorin has been compared with 5-fluorouracil alone and found to give superior response rates in some studies and not in others (Einhorn, 1989). In two of six studies of 5-day leucovorin/5-fluorouracil, there was a statistically significant improvement in survival from 34 to 53 weeks in one study and from 41 to 54 weeks in the second. Leucovorin plus 5-fluorouracil is significantly more toxic than 5-fluorouracil alone as well as more expensive and time consuming for the patient. A regimen employing low-dose leucovorin (20 mg/m^2) and 5-fluorouracil (425 mg/m^2) intravenously for 5 days every 4 to 5 weeks has been proposed as the least expensive equivalent regimen for palliation of metastatic or locally recurrent adenocarcinoma of the rectum.

The liver is the primary site of 5-fluorouracil metabolism. Metastatic neoplasms in the liver obtain the majority of their oxygen supply from the hepatic artery, whereas the hepatocyte receives oxygen from the dual sources of the portal vein and hepatic artery. Therefore, 5-fluorouracil or floxuridine may be infused directly into the hepatic artery and a high drug level achieved at the metastatic rectal cancer site. Because the 5-fluorouracil is metabolized immediately, much larger concentrations can be delivered without producing systemic toxicity. This concept has been tested and there is evidence that, in some hands, this approach is superior to systemic 5-fluorouracil for inducing regression of liver metastases.

Adjuvant chemotherapy with levamisole (Ergamisol) and 5-fluorouracil for Dukes' C adenocarcinoma of the colon and rectum has recently been studied and shown to be effective in reducing the recurrence rate of this stage of tumor by 31 to 41% after median follow-up periods of 7 years 9 months (Laurie et al., 1989), and 3 years (Moertel et al., 1990), respectively. Levamisole is an immunomodulating agent also used in the treatment of animal helminths. The use of levamisole has only rarely been associated with agranulocytosis, an Antabuse-like effect when taken with ethanol, and increased plasma levels of phenytoins when taken in conjunction with diphenylhydantoin. Other, less serious, adverse reactions include nausea, vomiting, diarrhea, stomatitis, dermatitis, altered taste perception, arthralgia, myalgia, dizziness, headache, paresthesias, and somnolence.

In rectal Dukes' C patients who cannot receive combined pelvic radiotherapy and 5-fluorouracil, a 1-year course of 5-fluorouracil and levamisole is indicated. For both rectal Dukes' B and C patients who can receive pelvic radiotherapy, combined 5-fluorouracil and radiotherapy is an excellent choice but not proven to be superior to 5-fluorouracil and levamisole alone.

Important secondary aspects of the care of patients with rectal carcinoma include attention to the preoperative discussion of colostomy care and the informed consent for such a procedure if necessary. In addition, patients with incurable rectal carcinoma need information about the diagnosis and, most likely, prognosis and therapeutic options for advanced rectal carcinoma. The physician should provide regular counseling of the patient and family with respect to dietary needs, analgesics, antiemetics, stool softeners, and antibiotics. Throughout the illness, palliation of symptoms may usually be achieved, when necessary, by therapeutic paracentesis, thoracentesis, or blood transfusion.

Regional pain is a more distinct problem with incurable rectal carcinoma than with colon carcinoma. The opioid analgesics, particularly morphine, are the main agents used. Codeine, oxycodone, and methadone may be adequate for moderate pain, but escalating doses of oral solutions or sustained-release forms of morphine sulfate should be used for severe pain. Ten to seventeen percent of the oral dose is absorbed, and starting doses are 20 to 30 mg orally every 4 to 6 hours (30 mg orally every 12 hours for the sustained-release forms). Regular dosing of adequate amounts is necessary and should be encouraged rather than as-needed dosing. The addition of aspirin may be helpful in some patients, as may hydroxyzine (100 mg intramuscularly) or dextroamphetamine (10 mg intramuscularly). Intrathecal or epidural administration of morphine (1 – 2 mg) or a local anesthetic has been advocated by

some. For severe sacral pain, neurosurgical procedures should be considered if the patient has a long anticipated survival, that is, several months. Transcutaneous stimulation has not been effective for severe pain of this nature.

Most series indicate a surgical 5-year cure rate of 45%. Adjuvant chemotherapy/radiotherapy has improved the 5-year cure rate of Dukes' B and C patients to approximately 58%. The median survival of those with unresectable disease is less than 1 year (Cohen et al., 1993; Moertel et al., 1982).

A policy of honesty on the part of the physician cannot be overemphasized. If a suspicious lesion is noted at proctoscopy, the patient will want to know the physician's opinion and will understand the uncertainty of the visual impression. When available, biopsy results (official reading) should be reported to the patient with a plan of treatment. The physician should be prepared to address many questions: "Will I need surgery?" "Will I have a colostomy?" "Am I going to die?" "Is it contagious?"

If the physician is not confident of his or her knowledge in this area, then he or she should provide the diagnostic information and indicate that he or she is uncertain of the proper therapy and has asked a consultant to see the patient. (The consultant should not be asked to see a new patient to discuss the therapy of a newly diagnosed carcinoma without the patient being aware of the diagnosis.) Frequently, the patient wants his or her family present during this discussion of options and prognosis.

Preparation for surgery provides a good time for the transition of primary care from the internist or family physician to the surgeon. After surgery, the results should be explained to the patient (the findings at surgery), as should the pathology report, when available.

Patients with incurable rectal carcinoma should be so informed and assured of vigilant medical care. Questions may arise concerning unorthodox, ineffective, or unproven treatment, and the physician must be knowledgeable in this area or provide appropriate consultation. The discussant should be honest but not destructive and should attempt to alleviate a feeling of helplessness, isolation, or abandonment. It is far preferable to provide answers to the patient's questions and to create an unhurried atmosphere in which they can be asked than to provide a rushed, didactic presentation of medical facts.

FOLLOW-UP

For the resected patient, the focus of the physician's attention should be postoperative complications, recurrent carcinoma, second colorectal primaries, and general medical care. Monthly carcinoembryonic antigen determinations are useful for at least 6 months, to be followed by determinations every 3 to 4 months. A complete blood count and stool guaiac should be done at each visit. A chest x-ray and chemistries should be obtained every 3 to 6 months for the first 2 to 3 years and then every 6 months for 5 years. Barium enemas are performed annually, and colonoscopy is performed, as necessary, to explain abnormal findings. Reexploration may be indicated, if evidence of carcinoma recurrence becomes apparent. An effort to salvage patients by resecting involved lymph nodes, isolated liver metastases, or perhaps solitary pulmonary nodules is sometimes successfully undertaken by experienced surgeons.

DISCUSSION

Prevalence and Incidence

According to the 1994 American Cancer Society survey, colorectal carcinoma is the second most common visceral carcinoma in the United States. Approximately 30% are found in the rectum, and approximately 42,000 cases are expected in 1994. Men are affected somewhat more frequently than women (1.3:1), and the mean age is 67 years. The mortality rate has been falling since 1950, and 7000 deaths from rectal cancer are expected in 1994. The incidence in African-Americans has slowly increased, and the very poor survival of African-Americans in the 1950s (5-year survival of 22%) has improved somewhat (current 5-year survival is 30 – 35%) (American Cancer Society, 1994).

Related Basic Science

The geographic variation in incidence, the increase in migrant populations moving from low- to high-incidence areas, and the presence of low-incidence populations in this country (Seventh Day Adventists and Mormons) suggest an environmental carcinogen or carcinogens related to dietary habits. The dietary habits may include ingestion of the carcinogens, increased exposure of the bowel mucosa to carcinogens because of slow transit, or a combination. Epidemiologic studies suggest that diets high in fat, high in beef, or low in fiber are associated with an increased incidence of rectal carcinoma. Animal models and stool analyses for carcinogens suggest neutral sterols, epoxides of cholesterol, bile acids, and nitrosamines as possible carcinogens or tumor promoters. The exciting work in molecular genetics has been briefly reviewed.

Natural History and Its Modification with Treatment

The diagnosis of rectal carcinoma in asymptomatic patients is more feasible than colon carcinoma. The least morbid and least expensive method is the use of impregnated guaiac slides (hemoccult) prepared at home by the patient on 3 consecutive days while eating a high-roughage diet free of meat, horseradish, beets, vitamins, and aspirin. One to two percent of asymptomatic subjects are found to have a positive hemoccult test. Air-contrast barium enema and colonoscopy then identify a carcinoma in 5 to 10% and polyps in 25%. Approximately 60% of these asymptomatic carcinomas are Dukes' A, as compared with 15% in control patients (Allison et al., 1990; Hardcastle et al., 1989).

The American Cancer Society recommends an annual digital examination to begin at age 40 and stool guaiac tests and sigmoidoscopy at age 50. The economy and ease of a stool guaiac test suggest that it should be performed anytime a rectal examination is performed and perhaps more liberally. The sigmoidoscopic examination remains controversial with respect to the age at which screening examinations should begin and whether screening of asymptomatic individuals is a productive undertaking. The motivation of the patient and the physician and the patient's risk factors should guide the physician's recommendations about sigmoidoscopy when the stool guaiacs are negative.

Prevention

Prophylactic total colectomy in high-risk patients with multiple polyposis or long-standing pancolitis is recommended. A diet high in fiber (bran, psyllium hydrophilic mucilloid, legumes, etc.) and low in fat is healthy in several aspects and should be encouraged in the general population, although proof of the prevention of rectal carcinoma is lacking. Aspirin, taken regularly, may reduce the incidence of colorectal cancer.

Cost Containment

Prevention of rectal carcinoma and identification of asymptomatic resectable disease are approaches that can reduce the loss of income and the medical cost of caring for a patient with metastatic rectal carcinoma. The prudent use of diagnostic studies with critical attention to expensive and nonspecific isotope scans, computed tomography scans, and too frequent laboratory testing in follow-up can reduce costs. The avoidance of ineffective chemotherapy and unskilled postoperative care markedly reduces medical costs. Home hospice care of the dying patient with significant help from family and volunteers reduces the patient's financial burden and usually improves the quality of the remaining life.

REFERENCES

Ackerman LV, del Regato JA. Cancer: Diagnosis, treatment, and prognosis. 4th ed. St. Louis: Mosby, 1970.

Allison JE, Feldman R, Tekawa IS. Hemoccult screening in detecting colorectal neoplasm: Sensitivity, specificity, and predictive value. Ann Intern Med 1990;112:328.

American Cancer Society. Cancer statistics. Ca Cancer J Clin 1994;44:1.

Atkin WS, Morson BC, Cuzick J. Long-term risk of colorectal cancer after excision of rectosigmoid adenomas. N Engl J Med 1992;326:658.

Castro EB, Rosen PP, Quan SH: Carcinoma of large intestine in patients irradiated for carcinoma of cervix and uterus. Cancer 1973;31:45.

Cohen AM, Minsky BD, Friedman MA. Rectal cancer. In: DeVita VT, Hellman S, Rosenberg SA, eds. Cancer: Principles and practice of oncology. 4th ed. Philadelphia: Lippincott, 1993.

Douglass HO, Moertel CG, Mayer RJ, et al. Prolongation of the disease-free interval in surgically treated rectal carcinoma. N Engl J Med 1985;315:1294.

Dukes CE. Cancer of the rectum: An analysis of 1000 cases. J Pathol Bacteriol 1940;50:527.

Einhorn LH. Improvements in fluorouracil chemotherapy? J Clin Oncol 1989;7:1377.

Ekbom A, Helmick C, Zack M, Adami H-O. Ulceratvie colitis and colorectal cancer: A population based study. N Engl J Med 1990;323:1228.

Grinnell RS. The lymphatic and venous spread of carcinoma of the rectum. Ann Surg 1942;50:527.

Hardcastle JD, Chamberlain J, Sheffield J, et al. Randomized controlled trial of faecal occult blood screening for colorectal cancer. Lancet 1989;1:1160.

Hoskins RB, Gunderson LL, Dosoretz DE, et al. Adjuvant postoperative radiotherapy in carcinoma of the rectum and rectosigmoid. Cancer 1985;55:61.

Krook JE, Moertel CG, Gunderson LL, et al. Effective surgical adjuvant therapy for high-risk rectal carcinoma. N Engl J Med 1991;324:709.

Laurie JA, Moertel CG, Fleming TR, et al. Surgical adjuvant therapy of large-bowel carcinoma: An evaluation of levamisole and the combination of levamisole and fluorouracil. J Clin Oncol 1989;7:1447.

Miller AB. The joint National Cancer Institute/American Cancer Society study of a test for carcinoembryonic antigen (CEA). Cancer 1974;34:932.

Miller MS, Costanza ME, Li FP, et al. Familial colon cancer. Cancer 1976;37:946.

Moertel CG, Childs DS, Reitemeier RJ, et al. Combined 5-fluorouracil and supervotage radiation therapy of locally unresectable gastrointestinal cancer. Lancet 1969;2:865.

Moertel CG, Fleming TR, MacDonald JS, et al. Levamisole and fluorouracil for adjuvant therapy of resected colon carcinoma. N Engl J Med 1990;322:352.

Moertel CG, Thynne GS. Large bowel. In: Holland JF, Frei E, eds. Cancer medicine. 2nd ed. Philadelphia: Lea & Febiger, 1982.

National Institutes of Health Consensus Conference. Adjuvant therapy for patients with colon and rectal cancer. JAMA 1990;264:1444.

O'Connell MJ, Martenson JA, Wieland HS et al. Improving adjuvant therapy for rectal cancer by combining protracted infusion fluorouracil with radiation therapy after curative surgery. N Engl J Med 1994; 331:502.

Papillon J, Chassard JL. Respective role of radiotherapy and surgery in the management of epidermoid carcinoma of the anal margin: A series of 57 patients. Dis Colon Rectum 1992;35:422.

Shank B, Cohen AM, Delsen D. Cancer of the anal region. In: DeVita VT, Hellman S, Rosenberg SA, eds. Cancer: Principles and practice of oncology. 4th ed. Philadelphia: Lippincott, 1993.

Spjut HJ. Pathology of neoplasms. In: Spratt JS, ed. Neoplasms of the colon, rectum and anus: Mucosal and epithelial. Philadelphia: Saunders, 1984.

CHAPTER 3–15

Zollinger–Ellison Syndrome (See Section 19, Chapter 29)

Carcinoma of the Breast

Melvin R. Moore, M.D.

DEFINITION

Carcinoma of the breast, or breast cancer, is a malignant proliferation of cells originating from breast epithelium.

ETIOLOGY

Although the precise etiology of breast cancer is elusive, there are many hypotheses that are supported by epidemiologic and experimental data.

Genetic

Approximately 5% of breast cancer occurring in women is hereditary. A personal history of breast cancer confers a 1% per year risk of developing a second primary breast cancer. A marked increased risk is also observed among women with a positive family history of breast cancer. Risk increases with multiple first-degree relatives affected, early age of onset, and bilateral involvement.

Germline mutations in a breast cancer susceptibility gene located on chromosome 17, *BRCA1,* account for roughly 50% of these hereditary cancers. A second breast cancer susceptibility gene mapped to chromosome 13, *BRCA2,* is responsible for an additional 30 to 35% of hereditary breast cancer. Women with germline mutations of either *BRCA1* or *BRCA2* have a greater than 80% lifetime risk of developing breast cancer. Up to one third of breast cancers diagnosed before the age of 45 are linked to *BRCA1* mutations. *BRCA1* mutations are also linked to an increased risk of ovarian cancer that may be as high as 60%. *BRCA2* mutations may confer a smaller excess risk of male breast cancer.

Women who have germline mutations in *TP53,* the gene that causes Li–Fraumeni syndrome, have a markedly elevated risk of developing breast cancer.

Hormonal

Endogenous endocrine factors seemingly related to prolonged uninterrupted menstruation elevate the relative risk of developing breast cancer. Late first pregnancy (after age 30), late menopause (after age 55), and early menarche (before age 14) all are associated with a reproducible relative risk of more than 1.3 times baseline of developing breast cancer.

Postmenopausal estrogens taken for more than 15 years and oral contraceptives taken for more than 10 years are associated with a slight increase in breast cancer incidence.

Environmental

Worldwide variations in breast cancer incidence and the experiences of migrant populations suggest an environmental or lifestyle factor in the etiology of breast cancer. Links between dietary fat and breast cancer risk observed in population studies have not been supported by case–control data. An elevated risk for developing breast cancer has been reported to be associated with alcohol intake, especially early in life.

CRITERIA FOR DIAGNOSIS

Suggestive

Physical findings include palpable mass in the breast; diffuse breast thickening; inflammation or enlargement of the nonlactating breast; and crusting, scaling, or skin erosion around the nipple (Paget's disease). Mammographic findings include a spiculated mass, microcalcifications, and distorted breast architecture.

Definitive

Histopathologic confirmation of breast cancer is always required for a definitive diagnosis. Biopsy material may be obtained by fine-needle aspiration providing cytology and cell block, excisional biopsy of a palpable mass or wire-guided excisional biopsy of a suspicious finding on mammography, incisional biopsy of larger masses within the breast or draining lymph nodes, and, rarely, biopsy of a suspected metastatic lesion in the appropriate clinical setting.

Ductal carcinoma accounts for approximately 80% of breast cancers, lobular carcinoma for approximately 10%, medullary carcinoma for approximately 5%, and other histologies for the remaining 5%. All of the preceding cell types are adenocarcinomas of breast epithelial origin.

CLINICAL MANIFESTATIONS

Subjective

The most common presenting complaint is that of an asymptomatic mass in the breast. The increased use of mammography screening in asymptomatic women has altered the presentation of breast carcinoma in recent years. More than 50% of newly diagnosed breast cancers are now smaller than 2 cm.

Signs or symptoms of metastatic cancer in a woman with no known primary site should prompt a search for primary breast cancer. Metastases to skin, bone, pleura, lung, and liver are suggestive of primary breast cancer.

Objective

Physical Examination

Physical findings are often absent or are limited to the involved breast at the time of diagnosis. A careful description of the location, size, and associated local findings, such as fixation and skin changes, determines stage and prognosis. Particular attention should be directed to examination of the ipsilateral axillary contents, supraclavicular area, and contralateral breast. Distant lymph node enlargement, subcutaneous or intradermal skin nodules, pulmonary findings, hepatomegaly, bone tenderness, neurologic dysfunction, and choroidal masses in a patient with suspected or known breast carcinoma are indicative of metastatic disease and require further evaluation.

Routine Laboratory Abnormalities

Routine blood counts and chemistries are most often normal.

PLANS

Diagnostic

Differential Diagnosis

Benign breast disease, such as cystic mastopathy, adenofibroma, intraductal papilloma, and cystosarcoma phylloides, can be distinguished from breast carcinoma with certainty only by histologic examination.

Diagnostic Options

Tumor markers such as carcinoembryonic antigen and CA 15-3 may be elevated. An elevated alkaline phosphatase level or bone pain should prompt a bone scan followed by x-ray films of abnormal areas.

Radiologic evaluation of the breast is abnormal in the vast majority of patients and should be performed prior to biopsy.

Excisional biopsy of small breast masses or incisional biopsy of large breast masses should be done in all postmenopausal women with noncystic masses, postmenopausal women with persistence of mass following cyst aspiration and cytology, premenopausal women with persistence of mass for 2 weeks, and asymptomatic women with suspicious lesions on mammogram. Fine-needle aspiration and wire-guided biopsy are increasingly used to evaluate palpable and nonpalpable breast lesions, respectively. It must be emphasized that a palpable breast mass with no abnormality on mammogram requires a biopsy.

Recommended Approach

All patients should have a careful history and physical examination, histologic confirmation of breast cancer (see above), complete blood count, liver chemistries, mammography, and chest radiogram. An immunochemical or biochemical assay for estrogen and progesterone receptors should be obtained on all malignant breast biopsies. The use of tumor markers such as carcinoembryonic antigen and CA 15-3 remains controversial. Additional testing such as bone scan; computed tomography scans of chest, abdomen, and pelvis; imaging studies of the brain; and bone radiographs should be obtained only in cases where initial findings support further evaluation. Additional prognostic indices performed on biopsy material such as S-phase fraction, ploidy, and DNA index may also be obtained.

Therapeutic

Therapeutic Options

The loco-regional management of invasive breast cancer has evolved greatly over the past few decades. The results achieved with local excision, axillary dissection, and postoperative radiation to the breast are equivalent to the results achieved by modified radical mastectomy in terms of long-term survival. Size of the primary breast tumor, location, and anatomy of the breast should be considered along with the wishes of the patient in choosing the initial approach to locoregional therapy. Patients who are not candidates for breast conservation or who choose mastectomy should be considered for primary reconstructive surgery using an implant or autologous tissue reconstruction.

Carcinoma in situ constitutes about 20% of breast malignancies. Lobular carcinoma in situ is a marker for high risk of invasive carcinoma in both breasts. Either of two therapeutic options, close observation or bilateral total mastectomy, is reasonable. Ductal carcinoma in situ is a lesion with local malignant potential that requires local excision. The use of total mastectomy for the treatment of ductal carcinoma in situ, which is associated with eventual metastases in fewer than 2% of patients, has been largely replaced by local excision alone if the tumor is smaller than 2.5 cm, it is not comedo carcinoma, and no residual microcalcifications remain in the breast. If the tumor does not meet these criteria, postoperative breast irradiation or total mastectomy should be considered.

Advanced local breast carcinomas include inflammatory cancers, tumors that involve the skin of the breast, tumors that are fixed to the chest wall, and tumors associated with fixed or matted axillary nodes. These lesions require systemic chemotherapy (see below) prior to definitive locoregional treatment with either surgery or radiation therapy.

Local and systemic recurrence of breast cancer can be decreased by the use of systemic therapy consisting of hormonal manipulation or chemotherapy following locoregional therapy. This use of systemic therapy as part of initial treatment is termed *adjuvant therapy.* Hormonal adjuvant therapies include oral antiestrogen therapy (tamoxifen), oophorectomy, and luteinizing hormone-releasing hormone super agonist. Chemotherapeutic programs used in the adjuvant setting almost always include multiple drugs used together for periods ranging from 12 weeks to 12 months. No clearly superior regimen has emerged from current and completed clinical trials. Controversies surrounding dose intensity, number of cycles of therapy, drug selection, and combination of chemotherapy with hormonal therapy are unresolved. Some consensus exists that a minimum of two active agents (e.g., doxorubicin and cyclophosphamide) given at full doses and continued for at least four cycles of treatment are required for maximal benefit. More details regarding patient selection for adjuvant therapy are given below. Adjuvant chemotherapy and/or hormonal therapy reduces the annual death rate among women with breast cancer by approximately 15% and reduces overall mortality at 10 years by approximately 6% when compared with no adjuvant systemic therapy. Active research in this area is continuing.

The myriad approaches to the treatment of metastatic breast cancer reflect the responsiveness of this tumor to systemic treatment and the often protracted course of the disease after metastatic spread has occurred. Specific recommendations for therapy are discussed below.

Recommended Approach

The general principles of breast cancer management are broken down into locoregional treatment, adjuvant treatment, and treatment for metastatic disease.

Locoregional Treatment. Locoregional treatment is further broken down into noninvasive cancer and invasive cancer with and without locally advanced disease.

NON-INVASIVE BREAST CANCER. For lobular in situ cancer, observation and annual mammography are recommended. The option of bilateral mastectomy and reconstruction may be considered based on risk factors and patient preference. Tamoxifen prophylaxis or primary prevention is being studied, but definitive results of this trial will not be available for many years.

With respect to intraductal carcinoma, for lesions smaller that 2.5 cm and noncomedo carcinoma, local excision with postoperative breast radiation is recommended. Studies to date do not confirm a survival advantage when the above strategy is compared with lumpectomy alone. Lesions larger than 2.5 cm and comedo histology may also be managed by lumpectomy with postoperative breast irradiation. Alternatively, total mastectomy may still be used for intraductal breast cancer.

INVASIVE BREAST CANCER WITHOUT ADVANCED LOCAL DISEASE OR CLINICALLY APPARENT METASTASES. Lumpectomy, axillary lymph node dissection, and postoperative breast irradiation are the recommended treatment for invasive breast cancer. Large tumors (>5 cm), local anatomic considerations, and patient preference may tip the balance in favor of modified radical mastectomy. Postoperative radiation therapy to the chest wall should be considered when more than four axillary nodes are involved at the time of modified radical mastectomy.

INVASIVE BREAST CANCER WITH LOCALLY ADVANCED DISEASE AT PRESENTATION. When the primary tumor is inflammatory, invades the skin or chest wall, or is larger than 2 cm, or the axillary nodes are fixed or matted, systemic therapy should be administered before local surgery or radiation is begun. Multiagent chemotherapy consisting of three or four cycles of cyclophosphamide (600 mg/m^2), doxorubicin (60 mg/m^2), and 5-fluorouracil (600 mg/m^2) is given once every 21 days or continued until tumor regression is maximal. Modified radical mastectomy and postoperative radiation therapy should than be used if the tumor is deemed resectable. Lumpectomy and radiation therapy or radiation therapy alone may be considered. Additional chemotherapy using only 5-fluorouracil and cyclophosphamide as described above should be administered during radiation therapy, as should additional cycles of three-drug chemotherapy, until the cumulative dose of doxorubicin reaches 450 mg/m^2. Hormonal therapy consisting of tamoxifen, 20 mg orally every day at bedtime, is then begun in patients whose tumors were estrogen receptor positive and is continued until relapse or for 5 years. The use of marrow-ablative doses of chemotherapy followed by autologous stem cell infusion is experimental, and its efficacy and optimal timing are unknown.

Postoperative Adjuvant Systemic Therapy. The type, timing, and efficacy of adjuvant systemic therapy for breast cancer are perhaps the most intensively researched topics in oncology today. Despite overview analyses of 133 randomized clinical trials involving almost 75,000 women, few definitive conclusions are available. Adjuvant therapy is effective in reducing annual recurrence rate, annual death rate, and total mortality from breast cancer, but the benefit to an individual with breast cancer is hard to quantify and varies with age, hormonal receptor status, and stage (lymph node involvement and tumor size). No woman with breast cancer is free of the risk of recurrence and no woman with breast cancer has an absolute certainty of metastases after locoregional therapy. Adjuvant therapy should be discussed with every patient with breast cancer and decisions based on individual risk–benefit analyses.

LOW RISK. Women with small primary tumors (<2 cm) and negative axillary lymph nodes have a less than 10% risk of recurrence and may be followed without additional adjuvant therapy. Recent data suggest that one to three positive lymph nodes in women with tumors smaller than 2 cm may not increase the risk of relapse. The use of tamoxifen to decrease the risk of developing second primary breast carcinomas in this group is supported by some studies, but is still considered experimental.

HIGH RISK. Women with primary tumors larger than 2 cm or with positive axillary lymph nodes have a 25% to more than 75% risk of relapse and are candidates for systemic adjuvant therapy. The groups displayed in Table 3–16–1 are somewhat arbitrary and definitive recommendations require individual patient evaluation. When possible, adjuvant treatment should be given as part of ongoing clinical research protocols.

Women with more than 10 positive lymph nodes or with advanced local disease at presentation are candidates for studies evaluating bone marrow-ablative doses of chemotherapy followed by autologous stem cell infusion.

Combined or sequential use of chemotherapy and hormonal therapy, optimal duration of chemotherapy, optimal dose of chemotherapy, and optimal regimen of chemotherapy are all issues under active investigation.

Treatment for Metastatic Disease. Systemic hormonal therapy and systemic chemotherapy together provide the cornerstones for the management of metastatic breast cancer. As systemic treatment, although very effective in reducing tumor size and symptoms, is not curative, the toxicity of treatment must be carefully considered and local or supportive treatment modalities optimally used. Local and supportive treatments include the optimal use of radiation therapy for symptomatic sites of disease (bone, spinal cord, central nervous system, and skin) and the use of bisphosphonates to control hypercalcemia.

HORMONAL THERAPY. Tamoxifen given at a daily dose of 20 mg orally should be the first line of therapy for metastatic breast cancer in women with positive estrogen receptors, long intervals between diagnosis and recurrence, and non-life-threatening sites of metastases, such as bone, skin, and lymph nodes. Responses are often not seen for 1 to 2 months following the initiation of therapy. An increase in bone pain, hypercalcemia, and increase in alkaline phosphatase termed a *tumor flare* is seen in less than 5% of women started on tamoxifen. A tamoxifen-induced flare is often associated with eventual good response to the drug and should be managed medically while tamoxifen therapy is continued. Roughly 50% of patients meeting the criteria listed above will have an objective response to tamoxifen therapy (>50% decrease in measurable tumor). These responses last approximately 1 year. Women who respond favorably to initial hormonal therapy may also respond to subsequent hormonal treatment (megestrol acetate or aromatase inhibitors such as aminoglutethimide). Premenopausal women may receive a trial of ovarian ablation (oophorectomy or leuteinizing hormone-releasing hormone agonist) prior to or along with tamoxifen.

SYSTEMIC CHEMOTHERAPY. First-line therapy for metastatic breast cancer among estrogen receptor-negative patients or patients with life-threatening sites of metastases consists of multiagent treatment (see above under advanced local breast cancer). Methotrexate may be substituted for doxorubicin in patients with cardiac disease or patients with prior exposure (>300 mg/m²) to anthracyclines. Paclitaxel is a new agent with good initial efficacy in the treatment of metastatic breast cancer. Paclitaxel as first-line chemotherapy or in combination with other first-line agents is now in active clinical trials. The use of bone marrow-ablative doses of chemotherapy and stem cell infusion is being evaluated

only in patients who have responded well to standard chemotherapy and is of unproven benefit. Other second- and third-line chemotherapy regimens are of questionable benefit in achieving objective remissions and improving quality of life. Initial chemotherapy response rates in excess of 50% are observed with median response durations of 9 to 12 months in most series.

FOLLOW-UP

Patients with resectable breast carcinoma who receive no adjuvant therapy should be seen at intervals of 3 months for the first year, 6 months for the second year, and annually thereafter. Patients should be instructed in and told to practice breast self-examination. History and physical examination should be performed at each visit. Mammography should be done annually. The utility of complete blood count, liver chemistries, chest x-ray films, and bone scans is doubtful, and these should be performed only to evaluate specific complaints or physical findings. Tumor markers such as carcinoembryonic antigen and CA 15-3 are often evaluated in this setting at each visit, but their value in improving quality of life or survival has not been demonstrated.

Patents receiving adjuvant chemotherapy should have weekly complete blood counts and platelet counts while on treatment. History and physical examination should be done prior to each cycle of therapy along with liver chemistries. Patients receiving doxorubicin or other anthracycline therapy should be monitored clinically for signs and symptoms of congestive heart failure and should have ejection fractions determined at baseline and before each cycle after a cumulative dose of 450 mg/m² of doxorubicin.

DISCUSSION
Prevalence and Incidence

In the United States, more than 180,000 new cases of breast cancer were reported in 1993. The incidence has been increasing at a rate of 4% per year since 1982. Annual mortality among women with breast cancer is approaching 50,000. Estimates of lifetime risk of developing breast cancer must take into account age and a variety of risk factors (see above). It should be stressed that the vast majority of breast cancers are diagnosed in women with no particular risk factor.

Related Basic Science

See Etiology

Natural History and Its Modification with Treatment

Breast cancer occurs as a spectrum of diseases with various potentials for metastatic spread and mortality. Malignant potential ranges from noninvasive lesions, such as lobular carcinoma in situ, to breast cancers that are systemic at the time of initial clinical detection, such as inflammatory breast carcinoma. The documented efficacy of mammographic screening in detecting smaller breast cancers has been responsible not only for some of the observed increase in breast cancer incidence, but also for a 30% reduction in breast cancer mortality among screened women. Mortality reduction has not been definitively demonstrated for women under age 50 or over age 75. The use of adjuvant therapy has resulted in a modest reduction in breast cancer mortality of about 6%.

Prevention

Chemoprevention of breast cancer using tamoxifen therapy is currently undergoing large-scale clinical investigation. Data on decreased risk for second breast cancers among women enrolled in clinical trials of tamoxifen as adjuvant therapy support this concept. Tamoxifen side effects and the potential for inducing uterine malignancies (similar to conjugated estrogen use among postmenopausal women) demand clear efficacy data prior to widespread use of tamoxifen in women without a diagnosis of breast cancer. Use of the vitamin A analog fenritinide in chemoprevention, either alone or in combination with tamoxifen, has been proposed.

Modifying diet and modifying environmental exposures are approaches to prevention that are under investigation. A diet consisting of less than 20% of calories from fat is currently being evaluated.

TABLE 3–16–1. RECOMMENDED THERAPY WITH RESPECT TO AGE AND ESTROGEN RECEPTOR STATUS FOR HIGH-RISK WOMEN

Age	Estrogen Receptor Status	Recommended Therapy
<50	Positive	Chemotherapy* and/or ovarian ablation†
	Negative	Chemotherapy
>50	Positive	Tamoxifen‡ and/or chemotherapy
	Negative	Chemotherapy

*Chemotherapy consists of cycolophosphamide 600 mg/m² plus doxorubicin 60 mg/m² intravenously every 21 days for 4 cycles.
†Surgical oophorectomy or luteinizing hormone-releasing hormone agonist.
‡Dose is 20 mg orally every day for 5 years.

Cost Containment

Tamoxifen chemoprevention should be used on a nonexperimental basis only after more data on its efficacy become available.

Mammography screening has been of proven efficacy among women between ages 50 and 75. The use of mammography in other age groups should be individualized based on risk analysis and individual physician and patient preference.

An ever-increasing role for limited surgery in breast cancer management not only decreases patient morbidity but also impacts favorably on cost. This savings is balanced by an increased use of radiation therapy.

Limiting the use of adjuvant chemotherapy to situations where it is of proven benefit is important. Adjuvant therapy also decreases cost by decreasing metastatic spread and mortality. Diagnostic and follow-up tests should be used judiciously so as to improve quality of life and duration of survival.

REFERENCES

Early Breast Cancer Trialists' Collaborative Group. Systemic treatment of early breast cancer by hormonal, cytotoxic, or immune therapy: 133 randomized trials involving 31,000 recurrences and 24,000 deaths among 75,000 women. Lancet 1992;339:1.

Eddy DM. Screening for breast cancer. Ann Intern Med. 1989;111:389.

Harris JR, Lipman ME, Veronesi U, Willett W. Breast cancer. N Engl J Med. 1992;327:319.

Hellman S. Natural history of small breast cancers. Karnofsky Memorial Lecture. J Clin Oncol 1994;12:2229.

Sledge GW, Antman KH. Progress in chemotherapy for metastatic breast cancer. Semin Oncol 1992;19:317.

Weber BL. Susceptibility genes for breast cancer: Clinical implications of basic research. N Engl J Med 1994;331:1523.

CHAPTER 3–17

Carcinoma of the Ovary

George A. Omura, M.D.

DEFINITION

Carcinoma of the ovary is a malignant neoplasm of the female gonad. Most cases arise in the epithelial component of the ovary, but germ cell tumors, sarcomas, and other cell types are sometimes encountered.

ETIOLOGY

The cause is unknown, although a small fraction of cases have a genetic link and there is some epidemiologic evidence that reproductive factors and excess dietary fat may play a role in the sporadic cases.

CRITERIA FOR DIAGNOSIS
Suggestive

This lesion may be found incidentally at the time of a routine pelvic examination or as part of the evaluation of vague abdominal or pelvic pain or abdominal swelling. There are very few clues other than a pelvic mass.

Definitive

The definitive diagnosis requires the demonstration of a malignant tumor arising in an ovary (pathologic examination). Adenocarcinoma from another site, such as pleural fluid or the omentum in a patient with a pelvic mass, may be consistent, but should not be regarded as diagnostic. Most ovarian carcinomas are of epithelial origin (Table 3–17–1).

CLINICAL MANIFESTATIONS
Subjective

Symptoms

The symptoms of early ovarian carcinoma are not specific. As the mass enlarges, vague lower abdominal pain may be noted. Late symptoms are abdominal swelling from ascites or large masses and cramps from intestinal obstruction. Vaginal bleeding sometimes occurs, but it is much more likely to be secondary to other female pelvic lesions.

Past History

Occupational exposure has not been defined. Nulliparity is a risk factor for ovarian cancer.

Family History

The family history is not usually helpful, but there is a small subset of patients who have a strong family history of ovarian cancer or ovarian and breast cancer, with or without other types of cancer.

Objective

Physical Examination

In a postmenopausal woman a "palpable ovary" is almost certainly abnormal and deserves evaluation. Abdominal masses or ascites are late signs.

Routine Laboratory Abnormalities

The chest x-ray may show a pleural effusion in advanced disease or, rarely, parenchymal lung involvement.

PLANS
Diagnostic

Diagnosis requires a laparotomy; as surgical staging ideally is part of the same procedure, a gynecologic oncologist or other experienced pelvic surgeon should, if possible, perform the initial surgery. In addition to general physical and pelvic examination, the preoperative workup should include blood counts, a chemistry profile, and a chest x-ray; however, additional studies such as intravenous pyelogram, barium enema, sigmoidoscopy, and computed tomography scanning of the abdomen and pelvis are not clearly indicated unless the medical history is complex.

TABLE 3–17–1. ABBREVIATED CLASSIFICATIONS OF OVARIAN TUMORS

I. Epithelial tumors
A. Benign
B. Borderline
C. Malignant (carcinoma)
II. Germ cell tumors
A. Dysgerminoma
B. Carcinoma (embryonal, chorio-, terato-)
C. Endodermal sinus tumor
D. Other
III. Stromal tumors
A. Granulosa cell
B. Sertoli cell
C. Other
IV. Sarcomas
V. Other ovarian tumors
VI. Metastatic to ovary

Differential Diagnosis

The differential diagnosis of an ovarian mass preoperatively includes colon carcinoma, diverticulitis, pelvic inflammatory disease, pelvic kidney, fibroids, and endometriosis. Carcinoma involving the ovary is not always primary in the ovary; metastases from stomach, breast, or colon carcinoma sometimes cause confusion. Occasionally, a clinical and histologic picture resembling ovarian carcinoma is found in the abdomen and pelvis without evidence of the carcinoma originating in the ovary and without evidence of another primary site (primary peritoneal carcinoma, extraovarian carcinomatosis). The distinction between benign and borderline tumors of the ovary and carcinoma may require expert pathology consultation; borderline tumors may trouble both the pathologist and the surgeon because of the diffuse intrabdominal spread that is sometimes noted, despite the indolent nature of the process.

Diagnostic Options

Laparoscopic staging is being studied.

Recommended Approach

As discussed above, a careful staging laparotomy is indicated.

Therapeutic

Therapeutic Options

The primary treatment is surgical. The staging system is based on the surgical findings (Table 3–17–2). The surgical procedure should include removal of the ovaries, uterus, omentum, and as much carcinoma as possible, as well as a systematic exploration of the abdominal cavity and peritoneal contents with multiple biopsies. Biopsy of the undersurface of the diaphragm should be performed, as tumor cells may spread to that location, even in a case that grossly appears to be limited to the pelvis. If the initial resection and staging procedures are incomplete, reexploration by a gynecologic oncologist is usually indicated.

As ovarian carcinoma is more often than not in an advanced stage at the time of diagnosis, the question of adjunctive chemotherapy or radiotherapy frequently arises. With carcinoma confined to the ovaries and well differentiated in histology, the surgical cure rate is in excess of 90%, so that adjunctive treatment with its side effects and toxicity is not clearly indicated. With less well differentiated or poorly differentiated carcinomas, or with spread of small tumor deposits in the pelvis, there is at least a 20% chance of fatal spread despite the use of intraperitoneal radioactive phosphorus. Thus, drug therapy is being evaluated for such cases. With stage III and IV cases, platinum-based chemotherapy is employed.

Combination chemotherapy, including cisplatin or carboplatin, is indicated in most cases. Recently, paclitaxel has been identified as one of the most active drugs in this disease. The combination of paclitaxel and cisplatin is more active than that of cyclophosphamide and cisplatin (McGuire et al., 1993). The chemotherapy is highly toxic. Skill and attention to detail are necessary to minimize the risk of drug treatment. "Second-look" laparotomy is sometimes recommended after 6 months of combination chemotherapy if there are no clinical, radiographic or serologic signs of persistent carcinoma. Occasionally, such surgery is therapeutic, by virtue of removing a solitary residual metastasis or by debulking lesions from an incomplete first operation. More often, the surgery demonstrates multiple macroscopic and/or microscopic foci of residual carcinoma, documenting the need for additional treatment. Unfortunately, other agents such as hexamethylmelamine, methotrexate, fluorouracil, and interferon or other approaches such as radioactive phosphorus, intraperitoneal cisplatin, and whole-abdomen radiotherapy are not of predictable usefulness for patients with a "positive" second look. High-dose chemotherapy with autologous bone marrow rescue is being investigated.

The major value of second-look surgery is to document complete response (negative second look); unfortunately, a substantial percentage of these pathologically confirmed complete responses relapse sooner or later, so that additional adjunctive therapy needs to be studied in such patients. Some women with negative second looks are cured, but further follow-up of current and recent trials will be needed to determine the frequency. Debulking surgery, both at the time of the original diagnosis and at the time of second-look surgery, is usually advocated. Women with small (< 1 cm) residual lesions appear to do better than those with larger lesions. It is unclear, however, exactly how much benefit is obtained from radical surgery.

The postoperative treatment of ovarian sarcomas is unsatisfactory. The management of germ cell tumors is reviewed elsewhere (Williams et al., 1994).

Recommended Approach

Several questions about management remain unanswered, so eligible, consenting patients should be referred to clinical trials. In the absence of a study, the following recommendations can be made, with the understanding that the choice of drugs and duration of treatment remain controversial.

- *Stage 1A and 1B* cases with well-differentiated histology do not require postoperative adjuvant treatment.
- *Stage 1C* or poorly differentiated, cases, or clear cell carcinoma (stage 1), should be considered for three courses of cisplatin and paclitaxel.
- *Stage II, III, and IV* cases should receive six courses of chemotherapy. A second-look laparotomy is not routinely recommended. A late relapse can be re-treated with the same drugs. An early relapse or nonresponder should be considered for experimental protocols.

FOLLOW-UP

Once treatment has been completed, the optimal frequency of follow-up is unclear, but general physical examination, pelvic examination, and possibly determination in blood samples of the tumor-associated antigen CA-125 should be done every 3 or 4 months for the first 2 or 3 years, with gradually decreasing follow-up thereafter. Follow-up computed tomography scans of the abdomen and pelvis also should be considered, although the value of early diagnosis of recurrence is limited.

Early symptoms of recurrence are nonspecific, as in the case of the original diagnosis. Pelvic or abdominal discomfort or increased abdominal girth should prompt careful evaluation. Signs and symptoms of distant metastatic disease outside the peritoneal cavity are uncommon.

TABLE 3–17–2. ABBREVIATED STAGING OF PRIMARY OVARIAN CARCINOMA

IA	Growth limited to one ovary; no malignant ascites, no tumor on the external surface, capsule intact.
IB	Growth limited to both ovaries; no malignant ascites, no tumor on the external surfaces, capsules intact.
IC	Tumor either stage IA or IB, but with tumor on the surface of one or both ovaries, or with capsule ruptured, or with ascites containing malignant cells, or with positive peritoneal washings.
II	Growth involving one or both ovaries with pelvic extension.
IIA	Extension and/or metastases to the uterus and/or tubes.
IIB	Extension to other pelvic tissues.
IIC	Tumor either stage IIA or IIB, but with tumor on the surface of one or both ovaries, or with capsule(s) ruptured, or with malignant ascites, or with positive washings.
III	Tumor involving one or both ovaries with peritoneal implants outside the pelvis and/or positive retroperitoneal or inguinal nodes. Superficial liver metastasis equals stage III.
IIIA	Tumor grossly limited to the true pelvis with negative nodes, but with histologically confirmed microscopic seeding of abdominal peritoneal surfaces.
IIIB	Tumor of one or both ovaries with histologically confirmed implants of abdominal peritoneal surfaces, none exceeding 2 cm in diameter. Nodes negative.
IIIC	Abdominal implants greater than 2 cm in diameter and/or positive retroperitoneal or inguinal nodes.
IV	Growth involving one or both ovaries with distant metastasis. If pleural effusion is present, there must be positive cytology to equal stage IV. Parenchymal liver metastasis equals stage IV.

DISCUSSION

Prevalence and Incidence

Currently, there are about 24,000 new cases of ovarian cancer per year in the United States, with 13,600 deaths. It is the fourth leading cause of cancer deaths among women in this country and causes almost half of all gynecologic carcinoma deaths. The median age at diagnosis for the usual epithelial types is about 57 years. It is a much less common disease in Japan than in the United States, but the incidence increases in Japanese women who move to the United States. This cancer is more common in single women and nulliparous married women. Ovarian carcinoma has on occasion been reported to affect members of the same family. Women with breast carcinoma have an increased incidence of ovarian carcinoma. The use of oral contraceptives does not increase the risk of ovarian carcinoma.

Related Basic Science

Genetic

In most cases no inherited or acquired genetic defect has been identified; however, there is increasing appreciation of a small subset of familial cases, either multiple cases of ovarian cancer, or breast and ovarian cancer, or colorectal, breast, endometrial, and ovarian cancer. The pattern is consistent with autosomal dominant inheritance. Cancer-associated genes are currently being identified. This is a rapidly developing area of research.

Altered Molecular Biology

Activation of oncogenes and tumor suppressor genes is being identified in some ovarian carcinomas, but the molecular pathology is still incompletely understood.

Anatomic Derangement

Ovarian carcinoma is a disease of the peritoneal surface that may involve the peritoneal lymphatics, the omentum, and the undersurface of the diaphragm. The pleura may be involved. Periaortic lymph nodes may be affected in a minority of patients. Hematogenous spread is uncommon.

Natural History and Its Modification with Treatment

Untreated ovarian carcinoma causes progressive local and regional problems in the pelvis and abdomen by invasion of normal structures and lymphatic obstruction, leading to intestinal obstruction, ascites, and cachexia. The surface of the liver may be studded with tumor nodules, but parenchymal liver involvement and dysfunction are uncommon. Ureteral obstruction is also uncommon. Pleural effusions, with or without demonstrable malignant cells, may embarrass respiratory function.

With recurrence after initial therapy, similar problems may be observed. Survival depends on the stage of disease at the time of diagnosis, as well as grade, amount of tumor left after surgery, performance status, and type of postoperative therapy. The 5-year survival for completely resected IA and IB grade 1 carcinomas is about 90 to 95% without chemotherapy, whereas 5-year survival for other stage I lesions is about 50 to 80% and that for stage II lesions ranges from about 40 to 80% with chemotherapy. For stage III carcinoma, the 2-year survival with chemotherapy ranges from about 35 to 70% for those women whose tumors are thought to be completely resected, to about 25 to 40% for those with residual tumor; a few survive 5 years after combination chemotherapy. In stage IV, about 5% survive 2 years and 0 to 4% live 5 years after chemotherapy. (Omura and Stiller, 1994).

Prevention

No preventive measures are currently available, other than removal of the ovaries at the time of elective hysterectomy or other pelvic surgery, but the premature elimination of endogenous estrogen creates its own problems. More research is needed in this field. Women with one of the hereditary ovarian cancer syndromes need to consider prophylactic oophorectomy.

Cost Containment

The diagnosis and treatment of this disease are expensive, with few economies available. Second-look surgery is widely practiced and very useful to the investigator but of value only to selected patients. Regarding chemotherapy, melphalan is relatively inexpensive but inferior therapeutically to cisplatin-based combination chemotherapy.

In contrast to the use of abdominal and pelvic scans, scans of bone and brain are seldom indicated, as these sites are rarely affected.

REFERENCES

Advanced Ovarian Cancer Trialists Group. Chemotherapy in advanced ovarian cancer: An overview of randomized clinical trials. Br Med J 1991;303:884.

McGuire WP, Hoskins WJ, Brady MF, et al. A phase III trial comparing cisplatin/cytoxan (PC) and cisplatin/taxol (PT) in advanced ovarian cancer (AOC). Proc Am Soc Clin Oncol 12:255, 1993 (abst 808).

Omura GA, Brady MF, Homesley HD, et al. Long-term follow-up and prognostic factor analysis in advanced ovarian carcinoma: The Gynecologic Oncology Group experience. J Clin Oncol 1991;9:1138.

Omura GA, Siller BS. Primary chemotherapy of epithelial ovarian carcinoma. Semin Surg Oncol 1994;10:283.

Williams S, Blessing JA, Liao S-Y, et al. Adjuvant therapy of ovarian germ cell tumors with cisplatin, etoposide, and bleomycin: A trial of the Gynecologic Oncology Group. J Clin Oncol 1994;12:701.

CHAPTER 3–18

Cervical Carcinoma (See Section 10, Chapter 8)

CHAPTER 3–19

Uterine Carcinoma (See Section 10, Chapter 9)

CHAPTER 3–20

Carcinoma of the Vulva (See Section 10, Chapter 12)

CHAPTER 3–21
....
Carcinoma of the Vagina (See Section 10, Chapter 14)

CHAPTER 3–22
....
Carcinoma of the Prostate
W. Holt Sanders, M.D., and Sam D. Graham, Jr., M.D.

DEFINITION

The definition is self-evident: neoplastic cells are found in the prostate gland.

ETIOLOGY

The etiology of carcinoma of the prostate is unknown.

CRITERIA FOR DIAGNOSIS
Suggestive

A highly elevated serum prostate-specific antigen, the presence of osteoblastic bone lesions, and a nodular or irregular prostate are suggestive of the diagnosis of prostate cancer.

Definitive

The diagnosis of prostate cancer is made by identifying histopathologic evidence of adenocarcinoma in tissue obtained from a biopsy of the prostate.

CLINICAL MANIFESTATIONS
Subjective

Localized, early-stage prostate cancer is usually asymptomatic. Rarely, a small carcinoma will contribute to symptoms of bladder outlet obstruction, irritation, or bleeding. These symptoms are more likely to accompany locally extensive disease. Extension toward the base of the bladder can cause bilateral ureteral obstruction and renal failure, manifested by anemia, weakness, and gastrointestinal complaints. Edema of the legs and genitalia may result from pelvic, lymphatic, or venous obstruction by locally extensive or metastatic disease. Bone metastases may produce local pain or, if the spinal canal is involved, progressive paralysis. Patients with a family history of prostate cancer are at increased risk for development of the disease.

Objective
Physical Examination

The digital rectal exam should be performed with the patient either standing and leaning forward so that his abdomen rests on the examining table or, alternatively, in the knee–chest position. The normal prostate feels similar to the thenar eminence when the thumb and fifth finger are opposed. A carcinoma feels more like the bent knuckle of the thumb, and is nontender. The physical exam is frequently normal, but may reveal prostatic induration, enlargement, asymmetry, or nodularity. In locally advanced cases, there may be extension to the pelvic side wall with obliteration of the sulcus, which marks the lateral edge of the prostate.

Routine Laboratory Abnormalities

The routine blood and urine examination is usually normal.

The American Urologic Association and the American Cancer Society have indicated that a serum prostate-specific antigen (PSA) determination should be performed annually in men between the ages of 50 and 70 years. For African-American men and men with a positive family history, the PSA determination should be made annually after age 40.

Prostate-specific antigen is a molecule made only by the epithelial cells of the prostate. An elevation in the serum PSA level above 4.0 ng/mL is a very sensitive indicator of disease in the prostate. The PSA is elevated in the majority of patients with prostate cancer, but an elevated PSA is not specific for cancer; it is also elevated in benign prostatic hyperplasia and in acute and chronic prostatis. The serum acid phosphatase level has been eclipsed by the serum PSA and now has a very limited role in the detection of prostate cancer.

PLANS
Diagnostic
Differential Diagnosis

The differential diagnosis of an elevation in serum PSA or of an abnormal digital rectal exam includes adenocarcinoma of the prostate, benign prostatic hyperplasia, and prostatitis.

Diagnostic Options

The diagnostic options include transrectal ultrasound with directed biopsy, digitally guided transrectal biopsy, prostate aspiration, and transperineal biopsy with either digital or ultrasound guidance.

Recommended Approach

Any man with an elevated serum PSA or an abnormal digital rectal exam should have a transrectal ultrasound with biopsy of any palpable or visible abnormality plus systematic biopsies of the entire gland. This transrectal ultrasound with biopsy is performed by the urologist in most communities.

The extent of the tumor (staging) and its grade are important prognostic indicators with important therapeutic implications. The Gleason scale of grading ranges from a low grade of 2 up to a maximum grade of 10. Low-grade tumors are more likely curable, whereas high-grade tumors are more likely to cause symptomatic disease from progression. The TNM (International Union Against Cancer) system has superseded the classic Jewett system. The two systems are compared in Table 3–22–1.

If the PSA is elevated above 10 ng/mL, a radionuclide bone scan is performed to determine the presence of bone metastases. A bone scan is not necessary if the PSA is less than 10 ng/mL. Other staging tests, such as computed tomography of the abdomen and pelvis, magnetic resonance imaging, and cystoscopy are useful in only a few select circumstances. A pelvic lymph node dissection may be helpful to determine extent of disease if definitive local therapy is planned.

Therapeutic
Therapeutic Options

The therapeutic modalities available for prostatic carcinoma include radical prostatectomy, external-beam radiation therapy, cryotherapy, interstitial radiation therapy, and hormonal therapy. The patient's life expectancy, as predicted by his age and general medical condition, must be taken into account in deciding on optimal treatment. A tumor that requires definitive local therapy in a healthy 55-year-old man may require

TABLE 3–22–1. COMPARISON OF TNM AND JEWETT STAGING SYSTEMS FOR PROSTATE CANCER

Pathology	TNM	Jewett (1975)
Digitally unrecognizable cancer	T1	A
≤ 5% of TURP specimen, low to medium grade	T1A	A1
> 5% of TURP specimen, or high-grade tumor	T1B	A2
Tumor detected by elevated PSA	T1C	
Digitally palpable cancer, organ confined	T2	B
≤ 1/2 of one lobe	T2A	B1
> 1/2 of one lobe	T2B	B2
Cancer extending beyond prostate capsule	T3	C
Metastases	N or M	D
To lymph nodes	N1–3	D1
Distant	M1–2	D2

only watchful waiting with palliation, if necessary, in a 65-year-old man with severe heart disease or in a moderately healthy 75-year-old man. Because low-grade adenocarcinoma in patients older than 70 carries only a 13% 10-year disease-specific mortality rate, it is completely reasonable in many cases to defer local therapy, with the expectation that the patient is more likely to die of some other medical problem.

Radical prostatectomy can be performed by the perineal, retropubic, or transcoccygeal approach. Complications include severe incontinence (2%) and impotence (40–50%). Most men have some transient incontinence, which resolves spontaneously over the first few weeks to months after the prostatectomy. Recent alterations in surgical techniques have improved the potency results by sparing the neurovascular bundles lateral to the prostate. Although there is no evidence that nerve-sparing techniques alter the cure rates, there is concern that these techniques may not completely excise locally extensive tumors, so they are reserved for patients with small local tumors.

Cryotherapy, or liquid nitrogen freezing of the entire prostate, is an increasingly common method of treatment for localized prostate cancer. Early results of this form of treatment, even in patients who have previously failed radiation therapy, have been encouraging. Because most series have follow-up periods shorter than 2 years, the durability of cryosurgery's early success is unknown.

Radiation therapy is performed as either external-beam or interstitial implants (brachytherapy). The maximum dose with external radiation is 7000 cGy (centigray) with side effects of vesical and rectal irritability. Brachytherapy delivers 15,000 or more cGy and has fewer side effects than external therapy. Both forms of radiation therapy are associated with positive prostate biopsies in up to 50% of patients at 12 months after therapy, yet the 5-year survival rates are comparable to those with surgery. There has been a resurgence of interest in brachytherapy now that improved ultrasound techniques allow more precise placement of the radioactive seeds.

Hormonal therapy is usually reserved for the symptomatic patient with systemic disease. The forms of hormonal treatment include orchiectomy, oral estrogens, antiandrogens, progestational agents, and luteinizing hormone-releasing hormone agonists. Frequently, an antiandrogen is combined with either orchiectomy or a luteinizing hormone-releasing hormone agonist to accomplish total androgen ablation. Each method has a 70 to 90% response rate. Oral estrogens are inexpensive, but are seldom used because of their association with cardiovascular and thromboembolic side effects. Orchiectomy, which is somewhat more expensive but much less appealing to patients, and luteinizing hormone-releasing hormone agonists, which are very expensive, have minimal cardiovascular or thromboembolic side effects. Use of a second form of hormonal manipulation following failure of primary therapy occasionally results in an objective response, and subjective responses have been reported in a significant number of patients.

Recommended Approach

Stage T1. Historically, stage T1 cancers were found on examination of prostate chips after a transurethral resection for benign disease. Low-

grade cancers involving less than 5% of the tissue were observed without definitive treatment, whereas all others were treated with either radical prostatectomy or radiation therapy. Currently, most stage TA cancers are found as a result of PSA-driven detection strategies rather than incidentally at transurethral resection of the prostate. The distinction between stage T1 and stage T2 tumors is one of prognosis rather than of therapeutic implication. Treatment is essentially the same for both T1 and T2 tumors, with the following guideline: younger patients receive aggressive treatment in the form of radical prostatectomy for smaller tumors, while aggressive treatment is reserved for larger tumors in older patients.

Stage T2. In true stage T2 tumors, radical prostatectomy results in a 15-year survival rate that closely approximates actuarial life expectancy for the general population. In many cases, a pelvic lymph node dissection is performed at the time of radical prostatectomy to ensure that no lymph node metastases are present. Most urologists defer prostatectomy if the lymph nodes are positive on frozen-section examination. The incidence of positive lymph nodes has decreased from approximately 30%, when all tumors were discovered as a palpable nodule, to approximately 5%, now that most tumors are not palpable when they are discovered. Survival rates of 50% at 10 years and 33% at 15 years were achieved with radical prostatectomy in clinical stage T2A lesions prior to the advent of better staging modalities, including the pelvic lymph node dissection. More recent reports indicate that 50–80% of patients with T2A disease have an undetectable PSA 5 years after radical prostatectomy. Radical prostatectomy can be performed through the perineal or retropubic approach. The retropubic approach allows simultaneous staging pelvic lymphadenectomy, but the perineal approach allows an easier anastomosis and a quicker recovery.

Patients who are considered poor candidates for radical surgery may be best managed with watchful waiting. Those patients who prefer not to have radical surgery may be offered cryosurgery, with the warning that long-term results are not yet known, or radiation therapy, with the caveat that positive biopsy rates in patients after radiation are very high.

Stage T3. There are two categories of stage T3 prostate cancer: (1) clinical stage T3, determined prior to definitive treatment, and (2) pathologic stage T3, found on pathologic examination of the radical prostatectomy specimen. Because the optimal treatment for stage T3 disease is controversial, factors such as patient age, voiding symptoms, and interest in maintaining sexual activity are important considerations in determining the best treatment for a particular patient.

External-beam radiation is advocated on the basis that local control is achieved in 85% of patients and is the most commonly recommended treatment for locally advanced disease. If obstructive voiding symptoms ensue, however, a channel transurethral resection of the prostate after radiation carries a risk of incontinence as high as 30%. For this reason, men with obstructive voiding symptoms are frequently offered hormonal therapy, followed by transurethral resection if symptoms are not relieved. There is some promise that cryosurgical ablation of the prostate may allow eradication even of locally extensive tumors, but longterm follow-up data are not yet available.

Stage TXN$_{1-3}$M$_0$. Pelvic lymphadenectomy has revealed nodal disease in patients whose cancer was thought clinically to be confined to the prostate. Therapeutic options include radical prostatectomy with immediate or delayed hormonal therapy, immediate hormonal therapy without prostatectomy, and watchful waiting with delayed hormonal therapy, but there is no consensus as to the best approach. There is no definite evidence that radical prostatectomy in patients with nodal disease increases survival, but many argue that local control can be achieved with this strategy. This argument is most compelling in the case of a patient who is already impotent and has severe obstructive voiding symptoms. Several studies have suggested that early hormonal therapy in patients with lymph node metastases increases their survival, but none of these studies were randomized, and the Kaplan–Meier curves were constructed before half of the patients had died. Nevertheless, most patients with nodal disease receive hormonal therapy.

Stage TXNXM$_{1-2}$. Treatment is directed at palliation. Hormonal therapy is the preferred modality, and the PSA level falls in 80% of patients treated. The average survival with hormonal therapy is 3 years, with

10% of patients dying within 6 months and 10% living more than 10 years. The options for hormonal therapy as listed above are oral estrogens, orchiectomy, luteinizing hormone-releasing hormone agonists, and antiandrogens. Despite their expense, luteinizing hormone-releasing hormone agonists are the most commonly used form of hormonal therapy because of their low complication rate and ready patient acceptance. There has been good evidence that total androgen ablation, achieved by combining antiandrogens with either luteinizing hormone-releasing hormone agonists or orchiectomy, prolongs survival by several months, and this effect is especially marked in those patients with minimal skeletal metastases.

Local symptoms can be relieved with local palliation. Obstructive voiding symptoms that persist after hormonal therapy can be alleviated with a channel transurethral resection of the prostate. External-beam radiation therapy is efficacious in relieving localized bone pain. Strontium-89 has been useful even for those patients whose bone pain has been resistant to radiation therapy.

Disseminated prostate cancer that progresses despite hormonal therapy has a very grim prognosis. There is no good chemotherapy or immunotherapy. Gene therapy trials using cytoreductive strategies are in their infancy. It may be many years before an effective therapy is developed for prostate cancers that have escaped hormonal control.

FOLLOW-UP

Measurement of serum PSA levels has been the most important development for the follow-up of treatments for prostate cancer. After radical prostatectomy, the PSA should fall to less than 0.2 ng/mL. The PSA falls to undetectable levels after hormonal therapy as well. Radiation therapy is less likely to result in an undetectable PSA, and the PSA level will continue to fall for up to 12 months after the completion of radiation therapy. The recommended follow-up is a serum PSA at 6 months and at 1 year, followed by annual PSA determinations. Any increase in the PSA after definitive local therapy should be evaluated with a transrectal ultrasound with biopsy. Local recurrence after radical prostatectomy can be treated with external-beam radiation therapy, whereas local recurrence after radiation may be treated with cryotherapy.

DISCUSSION
Prevalence and Incidence

In 1994, 200,000 men will be diagnosed with prostate cancer, and 38,000 will die of their disease. It is now the most common cancer in men, and the second most common cause of cancer death in males.

Related Basic Science
Epidemiology

The differences between countries in the incidence and mortality rate for prostate cancer are striking. The United States has a very high incidence, whereas Japan has a very low incidence and mortality rate. The prevalence of incidental cancers discovered at autopsy, however, is identical in the two countries. In addition, immigrants from Japan to the United States and their offspring acquire incidence rates and mortality rates similar to those of the general U.S. population. These observations suggest that the factors causing initiation of prostate cancer are universal, whereas the factors responsible for promotion differ with the environment.

Risk Factors

The most important risk factor for prostate cancer is age. A man is more likely to develop prostate cancer as he ages. Total fat consumption has been associated with mortality from prostate cancer both in questionnaire studies and in comparisons of prostate cancer mortality rates among countries with differing total fat consumption per capita. Recent evidence has suggested that ultraviolet radiation may be protective. Benign prostatic hyperplasia and prostatitis do not increase the risk of prostate cancer. Recent suggestions that men who undergo vasectomy have a higher risk of prostate cancer have not been substantiated, and vasectomy is not currently considered a risk factor.

Natural History and Its Modification with Treatment

The strange biology and natural history of prostate cancer have led to a heated discussion of the efficacy of diagnosing and treating this disease. In its early stages, prostate cancer has a very long doubling time, between 2 and 4 years. Autopsy studies have shown that approximately 30% of men over the age of 50 have at least a small focus of prostate cancer. In contrast, the lifetime risk of developing clinically significant prostate cancer is about 13%, and the risk of dying from prostate cancer is about 3%. In addition, there have been recent studies in which the survival for untreated prostate cancer was reported to be excellent. These factors have led to the common misconception that prostrate cancer is a relatively benign disease and that aggressive therapy is unwarranted. In fact, about 25% of men with prostate cancer die from their disease, a proportion that is similar to that of women with breast cancer who die from their disease.

The studies suggesting that prostate cancer rarely kills and that treatment is rarely necessary are based on studies of older men with low-grade, low-stage tumors. This population does not represent the group of men in the United States presenting with prostate cancer. Although it is true that older men with small, low-grade tumors will be more likely to die of some other illness, younger men with the same tumor are likely to die of prostate cancer. Every 70-year-old man with incurable stage D2 prostate cancer was once a 50-year-old man with curable stage B prostate cancer.

Prevention

Because there is no known prevention for prostate cancer, efforts are concentrated on prevention of advanced disease by the early detection of prostate cancer while it is still localized. The American Urologic Association and the National Cancer Institute recommend an annual digital rectal exam and a serum PSA determination for every man between the ages of 50 and 70. For African-American men and for men with positive family histories, detection efforts begin at age 40.

Cost Containment

Because men over the age of 70 are unlikely to be candidates for aggressive local treatment of their prostate cancer, and because early hormonal therapy for asymptomatic prostate cancer is still somewhat controversial, men over 70 do not need annual serum PSA determinations. This guideline will eliminate many transrectal ultrasounds with biopsies in the patients who are unlikely to benefit from early detection.

REFERENCES

Jewett NJ. Present status of radical prostatectomy for stages A & B prostatic cancer. Urol Clin North Am 1975;2:105.

Partin AW, Pound CR, Clemens JQ, et al. Serum PSA after anatomic radical prostatectomy: The Johns Hopkins experience after 10 years. Urol Clin North Am 1993;20:713.

Resnick MI. Carcinoma of the prostate. In: Resnick MI, Caldamone AA, Spirnak JP, eds. Decision making in urology. 2nd ed. Philadelphia: Decker, 1991:114.

Stamey TA, McNeal JE. Adenocarcinoma of the prostate. In: Walsh PC, Retik AB, Stamey TA, Vaughan ED, eds. Campbell's urology. 6th ed. Philadelphia: Saunders, 1992:1159.

Walsh PC. Prostate cancer kills: Strategy to reduce deaths. Urology 1994;44:463.

CHAPTER 3–23

Carcinoma of the Testis

Thomas E. Keane, M.B., B. Ch., B.A.O.

DEFINITION

Testicular carcinoma is a malignant neoplasm of the testis that is primarily of germ cell origin. A tumor that is biologically and pathologically similar may originate in the retroperitoneum or mediastinum or in embryologic nests of germ cell tissue that have persisted in these areas.

Testicular tumors account for 1 to 2% of all neoplasms in males. In the age range 20 to 35 years, testicular tumors are the most common malignancy excluding leukemia.

Primary neoplasms of the testis fall into two groups. The majority are tumors arising from germ cells; these account for 94 to 97% of cases. The remaining primary testicular neoplasms are tumors arising from nongerminal elements; these account for 3 to 6% of all testicular neoplasms.

There are two classifications of testis tumors: American and British. The American classification is based on the premise that seminomatous and nonseminomatous tumors originate from germ cells. The British scheme is based on the concept that nonseminomatous tumors develop from teratoma. Embryonal cell carcinoma fits into this scheme as a single cell-type tumor developing from teratoma. As does the American system, the British system agrees that seminoma develops from germ cells. A further discussion of these differences is beyond the scope of this chapter, and for all practical purposes the American classification system is used herein.

ETIOLOGY

Chemicals and viral exposure have been postulated as possible etiologic agents for testicular cancer. Trauma, atrophy, and cryptorchism are also factors taught to be associated with testicular cancer.

A history of testicular trauma has been reported in 8 to 25% of all patients with testicular cancer; however, trauma may not have a definitive role in the etiology of testicular cancer, but perhaps provides the mechanism for discovery of the testicular mass in the patient. Atrophy is thought to be a possible etiologic factor in a small percentage of patients presenting with testicular cancer. An orchiectomy should be performed immediately if any suspicious mass is noted in an atrophic testis. Data from several series indicate that even after orchiopexy is successfully performed for a cryptorchid testis, there is a persistently elevated risk of development of a subsequent tumor in the same testis. In approximately one fifth of patients with a history of cryptorchid testis and the subsequent development of testicular cancer, however, the tumor occurs in the contralateral, normally descended testis.

It is critical that self-examination of the scrotal contents be encouraged as soon as the patient is old enough to thoroughly understand the procedure.

CRITERIA FOR DIAGNOSIS

Suggestive

Testicular tumors are diseases primarily of young men. The majority of patients are between 25 and 35 years of age, although, occasionally, the diagnosis of germ cell tumor should be considered in male patients who present with a scrotal, retroperitoneal, or mediastinal mass.

Definitive

Diagnosis of retroperitoneal or mediastinal mass may occasionally require biopsy, although the diagnosis is almost always confirmed pathologically through tissue obtained by radical inguinal orchiectomy.

We wish to thank Dr. Steven D. Williams and Dr. Sam D. Graham, Jr., for their contribution to this chapter in the third edition of this book.

A scrotal mass that is thought to represent a malignant tumor of the testis should *never* be biopsied through the scrotum. In such cases, an inguinal approach should be used, and the testicle with its associated cord should be resected in a radical fashion up to the level of the deep inguinal ring. In a critically ill patient, an elevated level of a serum marker (human chorionic gonadotropin and α-fetoprotein) may be considered confirmatory, obviating the need for a tissue diagnosis.

CLINICAL MANIFESTATIONS

Subjective

The first symptom of testicular cancer is frequently a scrotal mass, which may or may not be painful. This mass has often been present for weeks or months before the patient seeks medical attention. Some patients present with significant back or abdominal pain made worse with recumbency, which is related to retroperitoneal nodal involvement. Gynecomastia may occasionally be present. This finding is related to human chorionic gonadotropin production. The manifestations of testicular cancer may range from an asymptomatic nodule to catastrophic medical emergencies, such as life-threatening dyspnea from massive pulmonary metastatic tumor burden, acute intracerebral bleeding from a metastatic intracranial deposit, and ascites from symptomatic liver metastases.

Objective

Physical Examination

The most important and frequent physical finding is a scrotal mass. The mass should involve the testis, although at times, identification of the exact anatomy is difficult. Whether or not the lesion transilluminates is critical, as a transilluminable lesion does not represent a testicular tumor. Other physical findings may include an abdominal mass, hepatomegaly, supraclavicular lymphadenopathy, and gynecomastia.

Routine Laboratory Abnormalities

Most routine laboratory studies are nondiagnostic. A mild anemia may be present or the lactate dehydrogenase level may be mildly or markedly elevated. A chest x-ray is mandatory, as the lung is a common area of metastatic spread.

PLANS

Diagnostic

Differential Diagnosis

Testicular ultrasound examination may prove useful in excluding other causes of scrotal masses.

Diagnostic Options and Recommended Approach

A mass that is thought to be a malignant tumor of the testis must never be biopsied. If neoplasm is suspected, direct testicular extirpation via a high inguinal incision should be performed; a blood sample to determine levels of α-fetoprotein and the β subunit of human chorionic gonadotropin should be drawn prior to the surgery. If an intraparenchymal solid lesion is confirmed, a radical orchiectomy with high ligation at the internal ring should be performed. Other approaches (especially transscrotal) should still be considered inappropriate because of the potential for local recurrence with metastasis to the inguinal lymphatics (not otherwise involved except in patients with massive tumor burden); changes in anticipated sites of recurrence could be important if surveillance approaches are contemplated during the follow-up period. Once the testicle is removed, the pathologic diagnosis is the initial critical factor in determining subsequent treatment of the tumor. Multiple sections through the mass are mandatory to identify the various histologic patterns present within the tumor. The clinically relevant issue is whether the pathology is pure seminoma or not (nonseminomatous germ cell carcinoma). It is my belief that therapeutic decisions of more extensive treatment should not be made on the basis of a frozen-section interpretation alone.

The tumor markers α-fetoprotein and human chorionic gonadotropin β subunit are also critical components essential in the choice of therapy. One or both are raised in more than 90% of patients with disseminated nonseminomatous germ cell tumors. α-Fetoprotein is secreted by yolk sac elements within the tumor; it has a half-life of 5 days. Complete resection of the primary tumor leads to a fall in marker levels. Human chorionic gonadotropin is a product of syncytiotrophoblastic cells; its α subunit is common to follicle-stimulating, luteinizing, and thyroid-stimulating hormones. Consequently, only assays specific for β subunit should be used; its half-life is 24 hours. Modest elevation (defined variously by different authors) may occur with true testicular seminomas, but this marker is associated principally with trophoblastic neoplasms. Other markers have failed to provide any substantive additional clinical benefit.

Germ cell tumors of the testis account for more than 90% of testicular neoplasms and can be broadly divided in seminomatous and nonseminomatous germ cell tumors. The latter are frequently composed of mixtures of cell types. During the brief recuperative period following orchiectomy, further clinical staging should be completed. Accurate clinical staging is critical; newer imaging modalities provide a precise assessment of extensive disease. Computed tomography scanning has essentially replaced lymphangiography as the imaging modality of choice for staging. The chief drawback of this investigation is its criterion for abnormality: nodule size. Its limit of sensitivity for involved nodes is a lesion of about 1.5 cm. Consequently, nodes at this limit must be scrutinized critically, particularly if they are ipsilateral to the primary (contralateral early spread is very rare). Both abdominal and usually chest computed tomography scans are now obtained by this author. Particular attention is given to such areas associated with early nodal involvement (the anterior niche between the inferior vena cava and aorta for right-sided tumors, and the posterior lateral paraaortic region for left-sided lesions). Computed tomography scanning of the retroperitoneal lymphatics is only 75% sensitive (25% false negative). Likewise, if the plain chest x-ray is normal, a computed tomography scan is recommended.

For the purposes of defining the extent of disease, the clinical data obtained above can be used to assign the patient to a particular clinical stage. A commonly used staging system for germ cell tumors comprises three stages: Stage I disease is limited to the testis, stage II disease involves the retroperitoneal nodes, and stage III disease involves the area above the diaphragmatic or the viscera. These stages have subdivisions within them, discussion of which is beyond the scope of this chapter.

Therapeutic

The management of patients with testicular carcinoma is a complex topic. Tumors are broadly divided into seminomatous and nonseminomatous germ cell tumors. Most patients with seminomatous tumors have stage I or limited stage II involvement at diagnosis. This cell type is extremely sensitive to radiation therapy, and more than 95% of stage I and early stage II patients are cured with radiation therapy to the retroperitoneal lymphatics. Such patients are usually treated with abdominal radiotherapy delivering 25 to 30 Gy (3000 rad) to the subdiaphragmatic lymph nodes and ipsilateral groin and a 6-Gy (600-rad) boost in areas of known disease.

Prophylactic, mediastinal and supraclavicular radiation therapy is not recommended, as the risk of mediastinal relapse with low-tumor-burden infradiaphragmatic disease is extremely low (1.5%). Furthermore, such extended-field irradiation may compromise the efficiency of subsequent chemotherapy, if required at a later stage, by lessening tolerance to high-dose myelotoxic regimens. Radiotherapy is no longer considered the sole or necessarily even the best treatment of advanced seminoma, which is exquisitely sensitive to cisplatin-based chemotherapy (see below).

The situation is considerably different for nonseminomatous germ cell tumors. About 40% of these patients have clinical stage I disease; the abdominal computed tomography scan would reveal a false-negative test in 15 to 25%. For this reason, the optimal management of patients with low-stage metastatic disease (stage I unlimited, stage II) is retroperitoneal lymph node dissection. This is a major surgical procedure, but it cures up to 60% of patients with positive nodes. The major morbidity of this treatment is loss of ejaculatory function as a result of interference with the retroperitoneal autonomic system. Sexual function is otherwise unaffected. More recently, the optimal management of patients with such low-stage metastatic disease has become controversial. As mentioned, the cure rate with surgery alone for low-stage disease is about 60%. A major breakthrough in the treatment of low-stage disease has been the addition of two cycles of adjuvant chemotherapy following surgery, which has resulted in a 100% cure rate. Whether adjuvant therapy should be implemented immediately in all or only in those who relapse is subject to debate. Current anatomic dissections specifically focus on sparing the critical sympathetic nerve pathways, and excellent early results have been achieved. These approaches appear well suited for limited disease, and this surgical technique allows the continued use of the strategy of immediate adjuvant therapy with a limited number of cycles (two) while retaining ejaculatory function.

It is now recognized that selected patients with disease limited to the testis after careful staging can be observed after orchiectomy. About 35% will have a recurrence, but chemotherapy and sometimes surgery will cure virtually all patients. Although this strategy will certainly preserve ejaculatory function, at least three or four cycles of chemotherapy are required with all the additional cumulative toxicity. Moreover, should a retroperitoneal node dissection subsequently become necessary after chemotherapy, it is widely recognized to be substantially more difficult as a result of fibrotic scarring, and nerve-sparing approaches are substantially less successful in this setting. In patients with true clinical stage I disease, the choice between observation and surgery is a difficult one based on the unique circumstances of the particular patient. If there are obvious small-volume, radiographically positive retroperitoneal lymph nodes, the patient should undergo surgery.

After retroperitoneal lymph node dissection, about 10% of patients with negative nodes and 40 to 60% of those with positive nodes develop a recurrence unless adjuvant (two cycles) chemotherapy is used.

In summary, there are essentially two different approaches to the treatment of early-stage nonseminomatous germ cell tumors. Either approach (surgery and adjuvant chemotherapy or observation with treatment at relapse) leads to cure in virtually all patients; however, an observation protocol does demand a compliant patient and is probably likely to result in the use of more resources, which is a significant consideration in the modern health care era. Patients with bulky stage II or stage III disease should be treated initially with chemotherapy. As mentioned above, disseminated testicular carcinoma is extremely chemosensitive, and modern chemotherapy regimens have dramatically improved the results of treatment in the past decade. The history of this evolution is beyond the scope of this chapter; however, modern chemotherapy regimens are based on cisplatin, bleomycin, and VP-16 (etoposide). Overall, about 70 to 80% of patients treated with this or similar regimens survive. Although the majority of these patients are complete responders to chemotherapy, a few require surgical resection of residual disease. Prognosis is strongly related to the amount of metastatic disease present at the initiation of chemotherapy. Patients with a very small volume of disease almost always attain a complete response, whereas those with massive metastatic disease do so about 60% of the time. Biological markers frequently normalize after 12 weeks of such therapy. If a residual mass persists and the markers are normal, surgical resection should be undertaken in patients with nonseminomatous germ cell tumors. If residual masses persist following chemotherapeutic management of advanced seminoma, radiation can be used if necessary. Surgical therapy is not recommended in such cases. In dealing with nonseminomatous germ cell tumors, if a residual mass persists and markers are normal, surgical resection should be undertaken for two reasons:

- It is critical to evaluate the residual disease site histologically to assess the extent of response to chemotherapy.

• It is important to resect potential areas of residual teratoma even without carcinomatous elements.

If the markers are elevated, additional chemotherapy should be undertaken. Surgery (retroperitoneal node dissection, teratotomy, etc., depending on site of disease) should not be attempted until markers normalize. Slow diminution of markers is a poor prognostic sign and may signal the need to consider a salvage protocol; surgical resection is unlikely to be of substantial benefit in these cases. The presence of a residual mass after normalization of tumor markers demands surgical dissection of disease, as 25 to 35% of such elements contain viable carcinoma (despite normal markers); further salvage chemotherapy is clearly necessary. In another 30 to 35% of patients, the pathology reveals only fibrosis or necrosis, whereas the remaining specimens show mature teratomatous elements. If either fibrosis/necrosis or teratoma is present, additional chemotherapy is not necessary. There are two reasons for resection of teratoma: First, even benign mature teratoma will continue to grow and cause problems. Second, several reports of malignant generation, metaplastic change, and unresected foci of teratoma have been published. In such cases, recurrent tumor is commonly refractory to chemotherapy.

A brief history and physical examination should include careful palpation of the remaining testicle, examination of the breasts, lymph node palpation, and abdominal examination. Tumor marker levels and chest x-ray should be obtained at each monthly visit.

FOLLOW-UP

Following removal of the testicle, the patient should be seen once a month for the first year and every other month for the second.

Follow-up may be less intense after the first 2 years, but prolonged surveillance is needed. Patients should be instructed in testicular self-examination and should be aware of the significance of gynecomastia.

If the patient is on an observation protocol, repeated computed tomography scans are necessary.

DISCUSSION

Prevalence and Incidence

The classic article by Dickson and Moore (1952) on testis cancer cited an incidence of 2.88 cases per year per 100,000 men in the U.S. Army between 1940 and 1947.

Testicular tumors are relatively uncommon in blacks (one-sixth to one-tenth those of whites.

Related Basic Science

Almost all testicular neoplasms are of germ cell origin; a very small percentage are of non-germ cell origin. Seminoma is the predominant cell type, followed by embryonal cell carcinoma, teratocarcinoma, teratoma, and finally choriocarcinoma. Testicular tumors have been reported from infancy to 89 years of age. Seminomas tend to appear later; however, three age groups experience an increased incidence:

• *Young adults* (ages 20–40): most common; all tumor types seen.
• *Infants:* mostly embryonal cell and yolk-sac types; seminoma exceedingly rare.
• *Older than 50 years:* seminoma most common type.

Natural History and Its Modification with Treatment

Great strides have been made in the treatment of germ cell tumors with the development of multiagent, cisplatin-based chemotherapy. Nearly 100% of patients with stage I and II disease are cured. Patients presenting with advanced pulmonary disease, palpable abdominal masses, hepatic bone metastases, and even central nervous system metastases have a cure rate of more than 60%. Postchemotherapy surgery is sometimes required to evaluate and treat residual pulmonary or abdominal

disease. Two additional courses of chemotherapy are given to the group with residual viable tumor; later relapses, through quite uncommon, occasionally occur.

Many advances have been made in the treatment of germ cell malignancy; however, clinicians should not become complacent. Although patients with early- and intermediate-stage testicular cancer are for the most part cured, patients with advanced disease or huge tumor burdens (i.e., poor risks) continue to relapse with their disease. Further study of the pathogenesis of these unique tumors is required; the genetic and microenvironmental factors controlling differentiation are poorly understood. New and innovative approaches to the treatment of patients with advanced disease include evaluation of dose intensity and integration of other active agents such as new cisplatin analogs. Newer compounds, particularly those that overcome drug resistance (particularly cisplatin chemosensitizers), are presently undergoing preclinical evaluation. Bone marrow transplantation might hold promise with the use of almost purely myelotoxic drugs. Modifying tolerance with bone marrow cytokines may play a role by allowing the intensification of therapy in the refractory patient with relapsing disease.

Prevention

The neoplasm cannot be prevented.

The general consensus, at this time, is that orchiopexy should be performed between the ages of 1 and 2 years. Orchiopexy prior to age 1 is contraindicated because of the possibility of spontaneous descent of the testicle within the first year of life. If the testis has not been treated by the time the patient reaches puberty, it should be removed instead of being relocated in the scrotum, as this testicle has more than likely lost the capacity for spermatogenesis. Even in patients who have undergone early orchiopexy, long-term follow-up is required because of the increased incidence of subsequent development of testis tumor in this patient population.

Cost Containment

Early aggressive treatment and studies to determine the optimal treatment protocol should minimize redundant or unnecessary studies or treatment and optimize savings. Experience of other countries with observation protocols may provide some insight into the potential cost of this form of therapy.

REFERENCES

Blandy JP, Hope-Stone HF, Dyan AD. Tumors of the testicle. New York: Grune & Stratton, 1970.

Dickson FJ, Moore RA. Tumors of the male sex organs. In: Atlas of tumor pathology. Section 8: Fascicles 31B and 32. Washington, DC: Armed Forces Institute of Pathology, 1952:127.

Dow JA, Mestoffie FK. Testicular tumors following orchiopexy. South Med J 1967;60:193.

Einhorn LH. Radiotherapy in seminoma: More is not better. Int J Radiat Oncol Biol Phys 1982;8:309.

Einhorn LH, Donohue JP, Peckham MJ. Cancer of the testis. In: DeVito VT, Hammond S, Rosenberg SA, eds. Cancer: Principles and practice of oncology. Philadelphia: Lippincott, 1989:1071.

Hogan JM, Johnson DE. Etiology of testicular tumors. In: Johnson DE, eds. Testicular tumors. 2nd ed. Flushing, NY: Medical Examination Pub. Co. Inc., 1976:31.

Lang PH, Fraley E. Controversies in the management of low volume stage II nonseminomatous germ cell testicular cancer. Semin Oncol 1988;15:324.

Loehrer PJ, Williams ST, Einhorn LH. Testicular cancer: The quest continues. J Natl Cancer Inst 1988;80:1373.

Patton JF, Hewitt CB, Mallis N. Diagnosis and treatment of tumors of the testis. JAMA 1959;171:2194.

Roland RG, Donohue JP. Scrotum and testis. In: Gillenwater JY, et al, eds. Adult and pediatric urology. St. Louis: Mosby Yearbook, 1991:1565.

Walter PJ, Paulsen DF. Testicular seminoma revisited: Time for a multimodal therapeutic approach. World J Urol 1984;2:68.

Carcinoma of the Bladder (See Section 18, Chapter 31)

Renal Carcinoma (See Section 18, Chapter 32)

Soft Tissue Sarcomas

P. Ravi Sarma, M.D.

DEFINITION

Soft tissue sarcomas are malignant mesenchymal tumors that arise from the various connective tissue elements in the body. Sarcomas of bone and cartilage are generally considered separately from soft tissue sarcomas.

ETIOLOGY

The etiology of most soft tissue sarcomas is not known. Identifiable risk factors, genetic or environmental, are rare. About 10 to 15% of individuals with hereditary neurofibromatosis (von Recklinghausen's disease) develop neurofibrosarcomas. Asbestos exposure, both occupational and environmental, increases the risk of mesotheliomas, especially in smokers. The earlier concern about an increased risk of soft tissue sarcomas among individuals exposed to phenoxy herbicides (Swedish rail road workers, Vietnam veterans exposed to agent orange) has not been borne out by later case–control studies (Kang et al., 1987).

Postradiation bone or soft tissue sarcomas may be seen in a small number of patients following treatment for conditions such as Hodgkin's disease and breast cancer. Patients with a history of the inherited form of retinoblastoma are at increased risk of developing sarcomas, even in the absence of radiation or chemotherapy. Deletion of the protective *Rb* gene from the 13q14 locus is considered essential for this susceptibility.

An excess incidence of the nonendemic form of Kaposi's sarcoma (a hemangiosarcoma) was first noted in renal transplant recipients and subsequently in patients with the AIDS. Nearly 95% of all cases of epidemic Kaposi's sarcoma occur in homosexual or bisexual men. Cases are seen among injection drug users but not in individuals with hemophilia who have become HIV positive from transfusion of factor VIII concentrates. It is not clear if the human immunodeficiency virus has any etiologic role at all in the development of AIDS-related Kaposi's sarcoma.

CRITERIA FOR DIAGNOSIS

Suggestive

Most often, patients seek medical attention because of an asymptomatic mass lesion. Although the majority of soft tissue sarcomas occur in the extremities or retroperitoneum, they also occur in the head and neck area, trunk, viscera, and occasionally bone. These tumors are usually seen in children and in adults between the third and seventh decades of life.

Definitive

The diagnosis of soft tissue sarcoma is established by a biopsy of the mass lesion.

CLINICAL MANIFESTATIONS

Subjective

Symptoms

Patients commonly seek medical attention because of a lump or swelling that is generally painless but may be associated with pain. Some deep-seated lesions and those with slow growth may reach considerable proportions before a physician is consulted. Kaposi's sarcoma often presents as an indolent skin lesion(s). Rapidly growing tumors may be accompanied by fever and weight loss. Pain in sarcomas may be due to the rapidity of growth or pressure on nerves and surrounding structures. Retroperitoneal sarcomas give rise to vague abdominal pain, flank pain, back pain, or obstructive symptoms. Occasionally, symptoms from metastatic disease may bring an individual to a physician. Hemoptysis and chest pain from lung metastases or back pain and leg weakness from extradural metastases are two such examples. Although many patients relate the development of the mass to recent trauma, no causal effect has been established between the two.

Past History

Most patients with sarcomas do not have any past history of predisposition to soft tissue sarcomas. Previous history of radiation therapy to the area in question, exposure to asbestos, or occupational exposure to chemicals may be obtained in a small number of individuals. Lymphangiosarcoma may be seen in areas of long-standing lymphedema, as in women who develop lymphedema following radical mastectomy.

Family History

The inherited form of retinoblastoma is a rare tumor. Most of the affected individuals are children under the age of 2. Individuals with hereditary neurofibromatosis are at risk for the development of malignant schwannomas (neurofibrosarcomas).

Objective

Physical Examination

A palpable mass in an otherwise asymptomatic individual is the most common finding. It may be vague or well defined. Rapidly growing tumors may be associated with signs of inflammation such as erythema, warmth, and tenderness. Regional node involvement is not common, occurring in about 5% of patients; however, in certain histologic types like synovial cell sarcoma, regional node involvement may be as high as 30%. Multiple skin and mucous membrane lesions are characteristically seen in epidemic Kaposi's sarcoma.

Routine Laboratory Abnormalities

Routine laboratory tests may be entirely normal or may reveal nonspecific abnormalities such as anemia, leukocytosis, and thrombocytosis due to the malignancy and the associated reactive state. Lactate dehydrogenase, alkaline phosphatase, and calcium levels may be elevated. Retroperitoneal sarcomas and some rapidly growing tumors in other locations may be associated with symptomatic hypoglycemia. Lung metastases may be noted on chest x-ray, and an x-ray of the involved region may show the relation of the soft tissue mass to bone.

PLANS
Diagnostic
Differential Diagnosis

An undifferentiated tumor can be a carcinoma, lymphoma, sarcoma, or melanoma. Immunohistochemistry may be required to establish the tumor as a sarcoma. Sometimes it may be difficult to tell whether one is dealing with a benign or malignant mesenchymal tumor. Lipoma versus low-grade liposarcoma is one such example. Mesotheliomas can be "benign" or malignant. Desmoid tumors are often of "borderline" malignancy. They tend to recur locally but only rarely do they metastasize.

Diagnostic Options

Definitive diagnosis is established by a biopsy of the suspected lesion, generally by an incisional biopsy. An excisional biopsy may be performed in small, superficial lesions. The biopsy incision should be so located as not to compromise any definitive surgery to be performed later. Light microscopy may not be adequate in undifferentiated tumors. Immunohistochemistry and electron microscopy may be needed. Because of the variability of histology, the need for adequate tissue for immunologic studies, and the need to establish the histologic grade of a lesion, fine-needle aspiration cytology is not ideal in the majority of cases. It may be sufficient, however, to document a recurrence or confirm the metastatic nature of a lesion. In select instances, multiple core biopsies may provide adequate tissue for establishing the diagnosis.

Once the diagnosis of sarcoma is established, additional tests are required to stage the tumor and to plan appropriate treatment. CT scan of the primary site, CT of the chest and abdomen, angiography of the lesion, MRI of the tumor, and sometimes a bone scan are the tests most often needed. CT, MRI, and angiography help define the extent of the tumor and its relation to adjacent structures. Unless clinically indicated, there is no reason to obtain CT or MRI scans of the brain to rule out central nervous system metastases. If chemotherapy with agents such as doxorubicin is planned, determination of cardiac ejection fraction may be necessary. If Kaposi's sarcoma is diagnosed in an otherwise well individual, diagnostic tests for HIV infection and for immune competence should be performed.

Treatment plans should include evaluation for posttreatment rehabilitation of the patient, including the need for an appropriate prosthesis.

Recommended Approach

When the physician suspects soft tissue sarcoma, a prompt consultation with a surgical oncologist with special interest in sarcoma management is necessary. An incisional biopsy of the lesion is preferred. An excisional biopsy can be undertaken in small tumors. Immunohistochemistry may be needed to establish the nature of the malignancy. CT or MRI of the primary site will be needed to define the local extent of the tumor and its relation to the surrounding structures. CT of the chest will be necessary to rule out lung metastases. Routine MRI or CT scans of the brain are not indicated. A multidisciplinary approach is necessary in the management of many of the extremity sarcomas and these consultations should be obtained prior to any definitive treatment.

Therapeutic
Therapeutic Options

Surgery. Surgery is the principal method of treatment for soft tissue sarcomas. Radical surgery results in an approximately 85% local control rate. Radiation therapy is not a satisfactory primary treatment. In extremity sarcomas, conservative limb surgery followed by postoperative radiation (5000–6000 cGy) results in local control comparable to that achieved by radical amputation. Intraarterial chemotherapy, preoperative radiation, and a multimodal approach consisting of preoperative

chemotherapy, preoperative radiation, surgery, and postoperative radiation therapy are some examples of attempts at limb preservation in the treatment of sarcomas.

Complete reexcision of a locally recurrent tumor, in the absence of distant metastases, results in about 60% recurrence-free survival at 3 years. Isolated pulmonary metastases are best treated by resection, with an expected survival of 20 to 30% at 5 years.

Chemotherapy. Chemotherapy does not have a primary role in the management of sarcomas. Adjuvant chemotherapy, administered postoperatively in an attempt to eradicate microscopic disease, is still investigational. Available data do not support adjuvant chemotherapy in cases of nonextremity sarcomas. In cases of extremity sarcomas, data obtained so far from randomized studies do not indicate a clear-cut benefit.

Management of patients with metastatic sarcomas is unsatisfactory. Doxorubicin and ifosfamide are two drugs that have shown the most activity in sarcomas, each with approximately a 20% response rate. Because of the high incidence of hemorrhagic cystitis due to its metabolite acrolein, ifosfamide, an analog of cyclophosphamide, is administered with a uroprotective agent, MESNA (2-mercaptoethanesulfonate).

A 25 to 35% response rate, mostly partial, is seen when doxorubicin-containing regimens are used. Median survival for responding patients is about 50 weeks. The most widely used combination chemotherapy regimen at present is the MAID regimen developed at the Dana–Farber Cancer Institute by Elias et al., (1989). It consists of doxorubicin (20 mg/m^2 on days 1, 2, and 3), dacarbazine (300 mg/m^2 on days 1, 2, and 3), ifosfamide (2500 mg/m^2 on days 1, 2, and 3), and MESNA (2500 mg/m^2 on days 1, 2, 3, and 4). All the drugs are administered by continuous infusion. The schedule is repeated every 3 to 4 weeks. A response rate of 47% (10% complete and 37% partial responses) was obtained in a series of 105 patients. The overall median survival was 16 months.

The MAID regimen is potentially very toxic. In addition to the known side effects of chemotherapy such as nausea, vomiting, hair loss, and bone marrow suppression, doxorubicin administration is associated with the risk of tissue necrosis if there is extravasation and with the long-term risk of cardiomyopathy. The risk of clinical cardiomyopathy is less then 5% when the total dose does not exceed 500 mg/m^2. Continuous infusion of doxorubicin also appears to lessen the risk of cardiac toxicity. In addition to the risk of hemorrhagic cystitis, ifosfamide treatment may also result in central nervous system toxicity (somnolence, confusion, hallucinations, seizures) and renal and electrolyte abnormalities. In older individuals with metastatic sarcomas, single-agent chemotherapy may offer comparable palliation with much less toxicity. Single-agent doxorubicin (50–70 mg/m^2 IV every 3–4 weeks) or ifosfamide (5 g–7.5 g/m^2 in divided doses over 3–4 days along with MESNA) is a reasonable choice.

The treatment of AIDS-related Kaposi's sarcoma is evolving. So far, none of the available treatments has shown a beneficial impact on survival, although many of them do have a palliative effect. Patients with localized Kaposi's sarcoma may need only surgery or radiation therapy. When the lesions are more widespread (cutaneous or lymph node involvement), a combination of zidovudine (AZT) and interferon may be helpful. In aggressive Kaposi's sarcoma, combination chemotherapy may be tried in selected individuals. Doxorubicin, bleomycin, vincristine, vinblastine, and VP-16 (etoposide) are some of the agents with activity in this disease. Recently, liposomal doxorubicin was approved for use in this disease.

Recommended Approach

Multidisciplinary management of sarcomas has made the treatment complex but has increased the potential for cure. The primary physician should explain the diagnosis and management plans in a cautiously optimistic way. Although surgery is all that is needed for low-grade, localized lesions, high-grade and more advanced tumors may require the addition of radiation therapy and chemotherapy. Patients must be informed of the potential side effects of these modalities. Anxiety regarding the loss of limb and function must be handled delicately with a discussion concerning the potential for rehabilitation, including the use of a prosthesis.

In high-grade extremity sarcomas, decisions regarding preoperative or postoperative chemotherapy must be individualized. Where possible, patients should be encouraged to participate in prospective studies that address relative merits of multimodality therapies. When chemotherapy is considered, single-agent ifosfamide or doxorubicin or combination treatments such as the MAID regimen are to be evaluated on an individual basis.

Isolated local recurrences and isolated pulmonary metastases should be treated surgically. In cases of local recurrences, adjuvant radiation therapy can follow resection. It is not clear whether there is any additional benefit to postresection systemic chemotherapy.

FOLLOW-UP

Sarcomas can recur locally or with distant metastases, usually first in the lungs. High-grade sarcomas often recur within 1 to 2 years. Follow-up evaluation should, therefore, consist of a good history and physical examination, inspection of the original tumor site, SMA-12, and chest x-ray. Monthly visits may be necessary during the first year, with gradual change to 3- to 6-month visits thereafter. Weekly or biweekly follow-up is necessary during chemotherapy.

Patients should be instructed to consult the physician if the original symptoms recur, new ones appear, or the mass lesion returns. Fever, malaise, and bleeding during chemotherapy should be reported promptly. Physicians should be alert to long-term effects of chemotherapy such as doxorubicin-induced cardiomyopathy, radiation-induced fibrosis, myelodysplastic syndromes, and second malignancies.

DISCUSSION

Prevalence and Incidence

Soft tissue sarcomas are a complex group of neoplasms that have enough similarities in natural history, management, and prognosis to allow them to be considered together. Within this group, however, there is considerable diversity, and specialized knowledge is expected of physicians involved in the care of these patients.

With nearly 8000 cases occurring every year, these tumors account for less than 1% of new malignancies in the United States; however, in children under the age of 15, these are the fifth most common tumors. Nearly 60% of soft tissue sarcomas occur in extremities, most often around the knee. Retroperitoneal sarcomas are next in frequency.

Related Basic Science

Genetics and Altered Molecular Biology

Most of the sarcomas are without identifiable genetic predisposition. The risk of sarcomas in individuals with von Recklinghausen's disease has already been mentioned. Deletion of the *Rb* gene results in susceptibility to tumors.

Physiologic or Metabolic Derangements

Sarcomas, especially large retroperitoneal tumors, may give rise to hypoglycemia. The hypoglycemia may be due to several etiologic factors including the secretion of insulin-like growth factors, increased use of glucose by the tumors, or failure of the counterregulatory mechanisms in glucose homeostasis. Rapid response of a high-grade sarcoma to chemotherapy may result in tumor lysis syndrome.

Anatomic Derangement

Sarcomas lead to considerable distortion of the normal anatomy of the affected region. Retroperitoneal sarcomas can give rise to intestinal, vena caval, or urinary obstruction. Low-grade sarcomas can grow large before giving rise to any symptoms at all.

Natural History and Its Modification with Treatment

Soft tissue sarcomas exhibit varying degrees of malignancy, from the low-grade locally invasive liposarcomas to the highly anaplastic rhabdomyosarcomas. Although soft tissues can give rise to benign as well as malignant tumors, it is rare for a benign tumor to transform into a malignant one. Kaposi's sarcoma, often multicentric in origin, can be indolent or aggressive. The epidemic variant, associated with AIDS, tends to be aggressive.

The American Joint Committee staging system for soft tissue sarcomas is based on the size of the tumor (T), presence or absence of regional lymph node involvement (N), distant metastases (M), and the histologic grade of the tumor (G). Histologic grade of the tumor is the most important prognostic factor in the absence of distant metastases.

The advent of a multidisciplinary approach to the management of sarcomas has greatly reduced the use of radical surgery without decreasing the high (85–90%) local control rate. It is not yet possible to know whether neoadjuvant therapy is likely to improve 5-year survival rates. Data available from randomized studies of postoperative adjuvant chemotherapy have not shown a clear benefit from chemotherapy. Perioperative blood transfusions may have an adverse impact on the survival of sarcoma patients. The outcome of patients with AIDS-related Kaposi's sarcoma depends on the presence or absence of opportunistic infections. High-dose chemotherapy with autologous bone marrow or peripheral stem cell rescue is still experimental and is not of proven benefit.

Prevention

No preventive measures are available. Elimination of known risk factors such as asbestos exposure (mesothelioma) and HIV infection (Kaposi's sarcoma) is possible.

Cost Containment

The advent of CT and MRI has resulted in greater diagnostic accuracy and lessened the need for routine use of procedures such as angiography. Multimodality approaches have minimized the need for radical amputations, thereby improving the quality of life for patients. Routine use of adjuvant chemotherapy is not indicated outside of properly designed clinical trials. Use of high-dose chemotherapy with bone marrow reconstitution is still investigational and should not be recommended outside of clinical trials.

REFERENCES

Elias AD. Salvage therapy for soft tissue sarcomas. Semin Oncol 1994;21. (suppl. 7):76.

Elias A, Ryan L, Sulkes A, et al. Response to mensa, doxorubicin and decarbazine in 108 patients with metastatic or unresectable sarcoma and no prior chemotherapy. J Clin Oncol 1989;7:1208.

Kang H, Enzinger F, Breslin P, et al. Soft tissue sarcomas and military service in Vietnam: A case control study. J Natl Cancer Inst. 1987;79:693.

Martin RW, Hood AF, Farmer ER. Kaposi's sarcoma. Medicine 1993;72:245.

Sauter ER, Hoffman JP, Eisenberg BL. Diagnosis and surgical management of locally recurrent soft-tissue sarcomas of the extremity. Semin Oncol 1993;20:451.

Yang JC, Rosenberg SA, Glatstein EJ, Antman KH. Sarcomas of soft tissues. In: DeVita VT Jr, Hellman S, Rosenberg SA, eds. Cancer, principles and practice of oncology. 4th ed. Philadelphia: J. Lippincott, 1993:1436.

Cutaneous Malignant Melanoma

David H. Lawson, M.D.

DEFINITION

Malignant melanoma is an invasive cancer of transformed melanocytes. It usually arises in the skin, but it can originate in other sites where melanocytes are found, such as mucous membranes, the meninges, and other organs. Ocular melanomas are considered a separate entity.

ETIOLOGY

Sunlight, especially radiation in the ultraviolet B range, is probably the most important environmental factor in pathogenesis of melanoma. Ultraviolet B radiation may act by directly (or indirectly) transforming melanocytes, or it may act primarily by depressing cutaneous immunity. Episodic exposure, particularly that resulting in blistering sunburns, seems particularly harmful.

Host factors seem somewhat intertwined. Caucasians have 12 times the risk seen in blacks. Family history of melanoma increases risk two- to eightfold. Sun-sensitive skin is a risk factor, as is imunosuppression. The presence of atypical moles (also called dysplastic nevi) increases risk, although there continues to be disagreement about how to precisely define these. It has recently been demonstrated that patients with a larger-than-average number of benign melanocytic nevi are more prone to develop melanoma than others.

CRITERIA FOR DIAGNOSIS

Suggestive

The diagnosis is suggested by a cutaneous lesion with the characteristics described later under Physical Examination.

Definitive

The diagnosis is established by a full-thickness skin biopsy. When possible, the entire lesion should be removed, as melanoma may be present in only a portion of it. Shave biopsies are to be discouraged. Melanoma may present as nodal or visceral metastases without a known primary; diagnosis here may be established by excisional biopsy or by needle aspiration cytology. Immunohistochemical stains (HMB-45 and S-100) may be helpful in establishing the diagnosis. Borderline or difficult cases should be reviewed by an experienced dermatopathologist.

CLINICAL MANIFESTATIONS

Subjective

Patients may give a history of risk factors as outlined above, but many will not. For example, only 6 to 12% of patients with melanoma have a positive family history. Most patients with localized melanoma have no symptoms. The most common symptom is mild itching, burning, or tingling in the suspect lesion. Ulceration and bleeding of a pigmented lesion are usually late symptoms felt to indicate a worse prognosis. More frequently a patient simply reports a change in a mole or the appearance of a new lesion with no associated symptoms. Patients presenting with primary lesions in mucosal locations (mouth, rectum, female genitalia) may have symptoms referable to those sites, and those presenting with metastatic disease may have complaints related to the metastatic site.

Objective

Physical Examination

The American Academy of Dermatology has proposed "ABCD" criteria for recognizing suspicious pigmented lesions. "A" refers to asymmetry, meaning one half of a lesion is clearly different from the other. This may result from emergence of a papule or some other change in an existing mole. "B" refers to border irregularities, especially notching on the edges of a pigmented lesion, as compared with the smooth edges of benign nevi. "C" refers to color changes. Suspicious color characteristics include a change in color, development of a variety of colors in a previously homogeneous lesion, or appearance of red, white, or blue coloration in a nevus. "D" refers to diameter of the lesion. Many accept an upper limit of diameter of benign acquired nevi of 5 to 7 mm. Enlargement of a lesion or absolute size greater than 5 to 7 mm is cause for suspicion. Others have emphasized any change in a lesion, including the appearance of new pigmented lesions, as being the primary feature of a cutaneous melanoma. These criteria should be liberally applied; there are numerous examples of primary cutaneous melanomas that do not fit any of them. Nodular melanomas, which present as smooth, evenly pigmented nodules that may be less than 5 mm in diameter, are especially likely to be missed by too rigid application of these guidelines. Amelanotic melanomas are also deceptive. Melanomas presenting in subungual locations are easily overlooked. Any suspicious lesion should be referred to a dermatologist and/or biopsied, as the diagnosis can be established with minimum morbidity, and the consequences of failure to diagnose can be devastating.

There is increasing acceptance that there are variants of common acquired nevi that may be regarded as markers of increased risk for melanoma. These lesions were originally called dysplastic nevi. There is a great deal of controversy over the clinical and pathologic features of these lesions that might be regarded as diagnostic. Because of this, some have proposed renaming them atypical moles. Clinically, dysplastic nevi, or atypical moles, are frequently larger than common nevi. Their borders may be fuzzy and indistinct, giving them a mottled appearance. Typically they are macular, but many have a centrally elevated area that may or may not be palpable, which gives the lesion a "fried egg" appearance. Finding such a lesion in an unusual location (buttocks or female breast) heightens suspicion, but most dysplastic nevi/atypical moles will be in locations where nevi are commonly found. These lesions should also be reviewed by a dermatologist, and any biopsies should be reviewed by a dermatopathologist.

Once a lesion suspicious for melanoma is identified, the draining lymph nodes should be palpated and the skin between the lesion and the draining lymph nodes should be inspected for satellite lesions. There is increasing recognition that lymph node drainage, especially on the trunk and the head and neck region, is sometimes ambiguous. Because of this, all possible nodal drainage sites, including contralateral basins, should be examined. The patient should undergo an inspection of the entire skin, including the scalp and the genital areas, as this will not infrequently reveal other suspicious lesions. Finally the patient should be examined for metastases.

Routine Laboratory Abnormalities

There are none. Many physicians may choose to obtain baseline laboratory data at this point, but this can reasonably be deferred until after the diagnosis is made.

PLANS

Diagnostic

Differential Diagnosis

Ordinary nevi may cause concern but are usually characterized by even borders and even coloration. They rarely change or appear after adolescence except during pregnancy. Dysplastic nevi (atypical moles) frequently require biopsy or close follow-up by a dermatologist. The blue nevus is a blue-black nodule that may approach 1 cm in diameter; its border is smooth and well defined, and the patient usually states that it has been present for years without change. Seborrheic keratoses are usually tan to dark brown; they can be distinguished from melanoma by a waxy appearance and texture and by a "stuck-on" look. Lentigo simplex is a uniformly pigmented dark brown or black lesion, usually less than 5 mm, frequently with a spiculated appearance. Solar lentigines are frequently called liver spots; they are a uniform tan color and have no papular component. An occasional basal cell carcinoma will be pigmented and thus resemble a melanoma. Pyogenic granulomas are pinkish, friable lesions with a tendency for rapid growth; they may resemble amelanotic melanomas. Vascular lesions may also bear some resemblance to melanomas.

Diagnostic Options and Recommended Approach

There is no substitute for obtaining a biopsy, which should be done as quickly as possible.

Therapeutic

Therapeutic Options

Therapy of cutaneous malignant melanoma is based on stage of the lesion. Staging of the primary lesion is based on the extent of cutaneous invasion, which is expressed in reference to anatomic layers of the skin (Clark's levels) or as depth of the lesion at its thickest part as measured by a micrometer [Breslow's (1970) thickness]. Clark's levels (Clark et al., 1969) are as follows:

I   Involvement above the basal level only (also known as atypical melanocytic hyperplasia)
II   Invasion into the papillary dermis
III Extension of tumor to the papillary–reticular dermal interface without invasion of the reticular dermis
IV   Invasion of the reticular dermis
V   Invasion into the subcutaneous fat

Breslow's thickness is increasingly accepted as the superior factor; both are incorporated into the current American Joint Commission on Cancer staging system. Although other features, such as subtype, mitotic activity, and histologic regression, are important prognostically, therapeutic decisions are based on stage.

The treatment of primary cutaneous melanoma is surgical; the major area of controversy is width of margins, and ongoing clinical trials are rapidly providing a rational basis for these decisions. Clark's level I lesions can be treated with 0.5-cm margins of excision. Invasive melanomas up to 1 mm thick may be treated with 1-cm margins. Occasional local recurrences are seen when thicker melanomas are excised with 1-cm margins; therefore, most would recommend 2- to 3-cm margins for these lesions. Results from a current trial comparing 2-cm margins with 4-cm margins in melanomas 1 to 4 mm thick are expected soon.

A second controversial area is the appropriateness of elective lymph node dissection. It is generally accepted that node dissection should be performed for patients with clinically positive nodes and no evidence of distant metastases; however, no trials have yet demonstrated a benefit from elective lymph node dissection in patients with clinically negative nodes. It is generally accepted that lesions up to 1.0 mm thick rarely develop nodal or distant metastases; therefore, elective lymph node dissection does not appear to be justified. Lesions 4.0 mm or greater in depth develop distant metastases so frequently that elective node dissection seems unlikely to offer a survival benefit and therefore should not be offered. Pending the results of ongoing clinical trials, patients with lesions from 1.0 to 4.0 mm thick may be offered elective node dissection in selected instances based predominantly on other prognostic factors, for example, gender, location of lesion, mitotic rate.

As noted above, lymph node drainage of trunk and head and neck melanomas is frequently ambiguous, adding further uncertainty to decisions about elective node dissection. The recently described sentinel node concept may help in this regard. Dye or a radioisotopic compound is injected around the primary lesion site. The primary draining node (the "sentinel node"), identified by inspection for dye or by radioactivity, is removed. If this node is negative for melanoma, no further dissection is done. In experienced hands, the likelihood of finding a positive node if the sentinel node is negative is less than 1%. If the sentinel node is positive, a formal node dissection is done. This still leaves

unanswered the question of whether this whole approach confers a survival benefit.

There has been no accepted adjuvant therapy for melanoma. A large trial (recently completed) evaluates high-dose interferon versus low-dose interferon. Recently published results indicate that high doses of interferon improve 5-year survival by about 10%, but at the cost of considerable toxicity (Kirkwood, et al, 1996).

Treatment of metastatic melanoma is generally poor. There is growing acceptance of surgical resection of solitary metastases even if they involve lung, brain, or liver. Patients with a good performance status and with a long interval between resection of the original melanoma and recurrence are especially good candidates. Palliative resection of gastrointestinal metastases is also sometimes indicated.

External-beam radiation therapy may be considered for palliation of brain metastases, painful bone lesions, lesions causing spinal cord compression, or distressing soft tissue recurrences. Responses are seen in only 15 to 20% of patients, but these can be durable and useful to the patient. The role of radiation therapy in decreasing locoregional recurrences of high-risk lesions is currently being evaluated. Use of higher-than-usual radiation doses and decreased number of fractions is advocated by some.

Stereotactic radiosurgery (the "gamma knife") is gaining increasing acceptance for treatment of brain lesions, including metastases from melanoma. Control of the specific lesion treated for 2 years can be achieved in up to 60% of patients. The criteria for application of this technique are still being defined, but patients with smaller lesions (≤ 2 cm) and a small number of metastases (≤ 2–3) are preferred.

Melanomas sometimes present with extensive cutaneous involvement of an extremity and no visceral disease. This can result in extensive morbidity for the patient. Direct infusion of chemotherapy into the extremity (e.g., femoral artery) has been tried, but is no longer widely done. The more demanding technique of isolation perfusion, using melphalan with tumor necrosis factor or other agents, has shown promise in recent trials and should be considered in selected patients. Vascular compromise leading to amputation is an occasional complication.

Systemic chemotherapy remains disappointing. It is based on dacarbazine, which, as a single agent, gives 15 to 20% response rates, mostly partial. Whether addition of other agents to dacarbazine results in improved responses and, more importantly, improved survival and quality of life, is being tested in many centers. New agents are sorely needed; patient participation in ongoing trials is strongly encouraged.

Melanoma and renal cell carcinoma are the two cancers thought to be most likely amenable to a biological therapy approach, and there are numerous ongoing trials in this area. Alpha interferon induces responses in about 15% of patients; soft tissue and pulmonary sites are more likely to respond than others. Some of these responses can be long-lasting. The toxicity of interferon remains a concern. Interleukin-2 has been tested extensively in melanoma. Occasional responses to this agent are seen, but interleukin-2 (IL-2) did not win Food and Drug Administration approval for use in melanoma. Current research focuses on use of interleukin-2 and other cytokines, including novel delivery systems, and on the use of a variety of vaccines.

Recommended Approach

- *Atypical melanocytic hyperplasia* (Clark's level I): Excise with 0.5-cm margin.
- *Invasive melanoma 1.0 mm or thinner* (Breslow's thickness): Excise with 1-cm margin. Do not perform node dissection unless draining nodes are clinically positive.
- *Invasive melanoma from 1.0 to 4.0 mm:* Excise with 2- to 3-cm margins. Consider elective node dissection in higher-risk lesions, preferably in a center where the sentinel node technique can be used.
- *Invasive melanoma thicker than 4.0 mm:* Excise with 2- to 3-cm margins; no elective node dissection. Participate in trials evaluating adjuvant therapy, or receive high dose interferon.
- *Clinically positive lymph nodes:* Perform therapeutic node dissection, preferably in continuity with the primary lesion. Participate in adjuvant therapy trials, or receive high dose interferon.
- *Solitary metastasis in a patient with good performance status:* Re-

sect if possible. For brain metastasis, consider stereotactic radiosurgery.

- *Extensive limb (especially leg) involvement with no visceral metastases:* Perform isolation perfusion in a center experienced in this technique.
- *Metastatic disease:* Participate in ongoing chemotherapy and/or biotherapy trials. No treatment is an acceptable option for patients with indolent disease who do not want to experience the toxic effects of systemic therapy or for patients with poor performance status. For patients who want treatment outside a protocol, either single-agent dacarbazine or one of several combinations may be used, with interferon used at the time of progression.

FOLLOW-UP

For the patient who has undergone potentially curative resection, the most important aspect of follow-up is early detection of second primary melanomas, which will occur in 5% or more of these individuals. Full skin examination every 6 months is recommended.

There is no clearly established benefit from early detection of metastases becausee of lack of effective treatment; therefore, extensive use of imaging studies is discouraged. A reasonable plan would be history, physical examination, and routine laboratory tests every 3 months for the 2 years after diagnosis, and every 6 months thereafter. Annual chest x-rays are probably reasonable, but even this practice is supported more by tradition than by evidence of benefit.

Follow-up of patients with metastatic melanoma is dictated by demands of treatment. For those not receiving treatment, monthly visits are frequently required for symptom management and support; occasional patients with indolent disease may need less frequent follow-up. Hospice referrals are appropriate for patients in the last months of life.

DISCUSSION

Prevalence and Incidence

The incidence of melanoma is increasing faster than that of any other cancer. The reasons for this are not clear, but the increased incidence is not explained by changes in diagnostic criteria. It is estimated that by the year 2000, one in 90 Americans will develop melanoma. In 1991, there were 32,000 cases of melanoma and 6500 deaths.

Related Basic Science

Melanoma cells are used as models in many basic science studies because of the relative ease with which they can be harvested and grown in tissue culture. There is intense interest in defining genetic abnormalities important in melanoma pathogenesis and progression, and important progress is being made in this area.

For a variety of reasons, melanoma has been a favored target of immunotherapeutic approaches. One approach currently entering clinical trials is based on generating a humoral response to gangliosides, which are expressed in abundance on the surface of melanoma cells. There is also intense interest in defining melanoma antigens that may elicit a cy-totoxic T-cell response as opposed to a humoral response. Candidates include tyrosinase, a group of proteins collectively known as the MAGE family, and a factor known both as Melan-A and as MART-1. Attempts to vaccinate patients with immunogenic peptides derived from these proteins are just beginning. Another immunotherapeutic approach currently being evaluated relies on the tendency of lymphocytes harvested from melanoma lesions to home into melanoma even after they are manipulated ex vivo. This trait is being exploited in gene therapy trials.

Natural History and Its Modification with Treatment

Thin melanomas are almost always cured when properly excised. A variable proportion of thicker melanomas are also cured by surgery, as are some melanomas with nodal spread. Although surgical cure of metastatic lesions is doubtful, it is accepted that prolongation of life is possible in some instances. The impact of chemotherapy and immunotherapy on survival is minimal at best.

Most relapses from primary melanoma occur within 5 years, but patients remain at risk for at least 20 years. The interval between intial detection and relapse is longer for thinner lesions than for thicker lesions.

Prevention

On a societal level, prevention efforts should be directed toward preserving the ozone layer, educating the public and health care professionals on the dangers of sun exposure and on early detection of melanoma, and regulating tanning parlors. On the individual level, avoidance of excess sun exposure and frequent use of sunscreens (at least factor 15) are important. Although the theoretical appeal of screening for early melanoma is high, there are currently no clear screening guidelines for the general public. Individuals at increased risk should have full skin examinations once or twice a year.

Cost Containment

There are no effective cost containment strategies beyond avoidance of excessive testing during follow-up as outlined above.

REFERENCES

Balch CM, Houghton AN, Milton GW, et al. Cutaneous melanoma. Philadelphia: Lippincott, 1992.

Breslow A. Thickness, cross-sectional areas and depth of invasion in the prognosis of cutaneous melanoma. Ann Surg 1970;172:902.

Clark WH Jr., From L, Bernardino EA, Mihm MC. The histogenesis and biologic behavior of primary human malignant melanomas of the skin. *Cancer Res* 1969;29:705.

Friedman RJ, Rigel DS, Silverman MK, et al. Malignant melanoma in the 1990s: The continued importance of early detection and the role of physician examination and self-examination of the skin. CA 1991;41:201.

Kirkwood JM, Strawderman MH, Ernstoff MS, et al. Interferon alfa-2b adjuvant therapy of high-risk resected cutaneous melanoma: The Eastern Cooperative Oncology Group trial EST, nos. 1684. J Clin Oncol 1996;14:7.

Koh HK. Cutaneous melanoma. N Engl J Med 1991;325:171.

CHAPTER 3–28

Insulinoma (See Section 9, Chapter 33)

CHAPTER 3–29

Androgen- and Estrogen-Secreting Adrenal Tumors (See Section 9, Chapter 5)

CHAPTER 3–30
Thyroid Carcinoma (See Section 9, Chapter 14)

CHAPTER 3–31
Pituitary and Neighboring Tumors (See Section 9, Chapter 1)

CHAPTER 3–32
Multiple Endocrine Neoplasia Syndromes (See Section 9, Chapter 46)

CHAPTER 3–33
Malignant Tumors Involving Bone

Melvin R. Moore, M.D.

DEFINITION

Malignant tumors involving bone are classified into two broad categories: primary bone tumors, which are malignancies arising from the bone itself, and metastatic tumors, which involve bone by hematogenous dissemination or by direct extension.

ETIOLOGY

Primary tumors of bone may be associated with chromosomal changes. Sporadic osteogenic sarcomas often lack expression of the tumor suppressor gene *RBI* that is also associated with familial retinoblastoma. Children with familial retinoblastoma who are treated with radiation have a 7% risk of developing osteogenic sarcoma in the radiated field. A characteristic translocation between chromosomes 11 and 22 is found in Ewing's sarcoma. Abnormalities of chromosome 18 are seen in synovial sarcoma.

Sites of prior radiation therapy are at increased risk for osteogenic sarcoma as are sites involved by Paget's disease of bone.

The etiology of bone metastases is unclear. Malignancies often associated with spread to the skeleton include those of the lung, breast, kidney, prostate, and blood. Speculation regarding mechanisms for the tropism of some tumors to bone include genetic determinants of malignant potential, production of stimulatory or growth factors by the tumor or by bone and bone marrow elements, and local concentrations of calcium and many other logical but preliminary hypotheses remain unproven.

CRITERIA FOR DIAGNOSIS

Suggestive

Bone pain and pathologic fracture are the cardinal findings that suggest the diagnosis of malignancy involving the bone. The young patient with primary bone tumor also may have an associated soft tissue mass or, in the case of Ewing's sarcoma, systemic symptoms including fever, weight loss, and malaise. Metastatic bone tumors should be suspected in asymptomatic patients with newly diagnosed cancer that is likely to metastasize to bone. Multiple myeloma involves the bone in virtually all cases. Radiographic evidence of lytic or blastic bone destruction also raises the possibility of malignancy involving the bone. Asymptomatic patients with newly diagnosed cancer that is likely to metastasize to bone, in whom the presence of bone metastasis would change the primary management, should be evaluated by technetium-99*m* polyphosphate bone scan.

Definitive

Primary malignant tumors require a biopsy to confirm the diagnosis. Careful planning of the placement of the biopsy site and/or incision is critical for future attempts at limb salvage in sarcomas of the extremities. The major histologic categories of primary bone tumors include osteosarcoma, chondrosarcoma, giant cell tumor, Ewing's sarcoma, vascular tumors, connective tissue tumors, chordoma, and adamantinoma.

Radiographic and radionuclide evidence of bone metastasis is sufficient for a definitive diagnosis in the setting of active metastatic malignancy. Biopsy confirmation is required to confirm the diagnosis of metastatic bone tumor when bone x-ray films are equivocal and when there is no other known site of active systemic malignancy.

CLINICAL MANIFESTATIONS

Subjective

Patients at high risk for metastatic bone tumors include all patients with an established diagnosis of malignancy. Patients successfully treated for childhood retinoblastoma are at increased risk for osteogenic sarcoma.

Pain is the predominant complaint leading to a diagnosis of primary or metastatic malignancy involving the bone. Sudden onset of severe pain or worsening of existing pain suggests pathologic fracture. The pain is usually localized to the area of bone involved. A soft tissue mass or bony deformity which may be tender and painful is more commonly seen in primary bone tumors. Back pain in the setting of an abnormal x-ray film of the spine occurring in the setting of known or suspected malignancy has a high predictive value for spinal cord compression and should prompt magnetic resonance imaging of the spine on an emergency basis, even in the absence of any other neurologic finding. Cranial nerve palsy may be associated with bony involvement at the base of the skull in breast, prostate, and other malignancies.

Objective

Physical Examination

Physical findings include percussion tenderness over painful bony sites, deformity or ecchymoses secondary to pathologic fractures, and, less commonly, soft tissue mass.

Routine Laboratory Abnormalities

The most common routine laboratory value is an elevated serum alkaline phosphatase level. This finding may be absent in early bone metastasis or in purely lytic bone involvement (e.g., multiple myeloma). An elevated serum calcium may also be seen in patients with bone metastases. The extent of bony invasion is usually not well correlated with the occurrence or severity of hypercalcemia.

PLANS

Diagnostic

Differential Diagnosis

Benign conditions involving bone including Paget's disease of bone, developmental or congenital abnormalities, bone islands, venous lakes, bone infarcts, osteonecrosis, osteomyelitis, late effects of radiation, and benign tumors of bone must be considered and weighed in the context of all the aspects of the patient presentation when evaluating bony abnormalities. The presence of typical radiographic features of primary bone tumors (particularly Ewing's sarcoma and osteogenic sarcoma), multiple sites of skeletal involvement, recent onset of symptoms, and a known diagnosis of metastatic cancer are all suggestive of malignancy involving the bone. Biopsy confirmation is required for all primary bone tumors and for suspected metastatic lesions when the diagnosis is in doubt and the finding of bone metastasis would change clinical management.

Diagnostic Options

Evaluation of the presence and extent of bone involvement by malignant tumors uses the full range of imaging modalities and includes technetium-99m polyphosphate radionuclide bone scan, plain and tomographic x-ray films, computed tomography (CT) scan, and magnetic resonance imaging (MRI). Each of these modalities has a role to play in diagnosis and in management. Serum studies such as alkaline phosphatase, lactate dehydrogenase, and specific tumor markers (prostatic acid phosphatase, prostate specific antigen, carcinoembryonic antigen, CA 15-3) are neither sensitive nor specific enough for bone disease to be used in differential diagnosis, but may be of value in prognostication and follow-up. Biopsy procedures for primary bone neoplasms may range from fine-needle aspiration to incisional biopsy. As stated above, the placement of the biopsy incision may be critical in optimal future therapy. Metastatic tumor involving bone requires histologic confirmation of malignancy and tumor type from some site (not necessarily bone) and consideration of the total clinical picture.

Recommended Approach

All patients with suspected primary bone malignancy require a biopsy (see above). Imaging of the involved bone with plain x-ray and with CT or MRI and CT scan of the thorax is required as well. The approach to documenting and quantifying bone metastases depends on the primary tumor site and stage of the patient. A radionuclide scan is reasonably sensitive but not very specific as an initial strategy in staging patients in whom bone metastases are highly likely. The scan will be falsely negative in purely lytic disease like multiple myeloma. Plain x-ray films or special views of symptomatic skeletal areas are a recommended first step in evaluating patients for symptomatic bone metastasis. CT and MRI are usually reserved for cases in which clinical suspicion is high, less expensive imaging studies are not conclusive, and treatment options would be altered by the presence of bone metastases. Documentation of other metastatic sites and abnormal blood values may be helpful in concluding that symptoms or radiographic findings are due to metastatic malignancy.

Therapeutic

Therapeutic Options

Primary bone tumors are surgically resected whenever possible. The use of chemotherapy prior to and following surgical resection is considered standard in the management of osteosarcoma and Ewing's sarcoma. Radiation therapy is also an essential part of managing patients with Ewing's sarcoma (60 Gy to involved bones). Surgical options in the treatment of primary bone tumors of the extremities include amputation and limb salvage. Patients who are optimal candidates for limb salvage, which requires a more extensive and difficult surgical procedure and rehabilitation, are those who have upper extremity lesions and who are fully grown; however, limb salvage may be considered for any motivated patient with osteosarcoma of the extremity. Local control rates of osteosarcoma treated with limb salvage are well over 90%.

Patients with bone metastases are treated with palliative intent. The clinical problems that must be dealt with include bone pain, neurologic dysfunction (spinal cord compression), orthopaedic problems (impending or actual pathologic fracture), and hypercalcemia.

Options for adequate therapy of bone pain begin with treatment of the underlying cancer using chemotherapy, hormonal therapy, or external beam radiation therapy. Chemotherapy is especially effective in the palliation of bone pain associated with multiple myeloma, breast cancer, and small cell lung cancer. A trial of chemotherapy may also be indicated in tumor types that are not as sensitive to chemotherapy if the patient is otherwise stable. Hormonal therapy for breast cancer and prostate cancer may be very effective in the palliation of bone pain. According to the guidelines provided by the Agency for Health Care Policy and Research, the use of analgesics for the management of chronic pain will result in adequate pain control in well over 80% of patients with metastatic cancer involving bone. Nonsteroidal antiinflammatory agents given in full doses on a regular schedule are often quite effective. When opioids are used, regular dosing according to drug half-life and escalation of dose to achieve pain control are, along with adequate management of opioid side effects, the guiding principles for optimal pain control. External beam radiotherapy should be considered in all patients with local sites of pain that are poorly controlled with systemic therapy. Neurosurgical and neuroablative techniques as well as nonpharmacologic pain management strategies should be used according to the Agency for Health Care Policy and Research guidelines. Analgesia may also be achieved using targeted radiopharmaceuticals. Strontium-89 is currently available in the United States and is effective in achieving adequate analgesia in up to 80% of patients with bone metastases. Hematologic toxicity is usually tolerable and transient. Hemi-body radiation therapy is another alternative for treating intractable bone pain.

Management of spinal cord compression requires early diagnosis (before the onset of neurologic dysfunction) and rapid intervention using high doses of corticosteroids combined with radiation to the spine. Surgical management is required when neurologic function is deteriorating or radiation tolerance of the spinal cord would be exceeded due to prior radiation.

Impending or actual pathologic fracture is optimally treated with orthopaedic stabilization (often internal fixation) and external beam radiation therapy. The use of radiation with or without systemic anticancer therapy may be attempted if a fracture has not occurred.

Hypercalcemia is best managed with pamidronate in a dose of 90 mg given acutely over at least 4 hours. Effective antineoplastic chemotherapy or hormonal therapy is required for long-term control of hypercalcemia associated with malignancy. Patients with multiple myeloma- or lymphoma-associated hypercalcemia may also respond to corticosteroids.

Recommended Approach

Primary tumors of the bone require an experienced orthopaedic surgeon, medical oncologist, radiation oncologist, and radiologist for optimal treatment planning. Osteosarcoma should be managed with preoperative chemotherapy based on cisplatin and doxorubicin, limb salvage when possible or amputation, and postoperative multiagent chemotherapy based on the percentage necrosis (<90% versus >90%) in the primary tumor. This aggressive multimodality approach has improved disease-free survival from below 40% with surgery alone to greater than 60%. Initial chemotherapy and tumor resection are also indicated in patients with limited pulmonary spread of osteosarcoma. Ewing's sarcoma patients should receive chemotherapy (cyclophosphamide, vincristine, doxorubicin) before or during radiation with 60 Gy to the involved bone. Expendable bones should be resected. Cure rates have improved with the use of combined-modality therapy. Patients over age

16 still have a cure rate less than 50%. Other primary bone tumors are currently best treated with surgery and radiotherapy when total excision is not feasible.

Metastatic bone malignancy is managed according to the principles elucidated above (Therapeutic Options).

FOLLOW-UP

Osteogenic sarcoma patients in complete remission should be followed at 3-month intervals for the first 24 months following the completion of therapy. History, physical examination, alkaline phosphatase level, and chest x-ray should be obtained at each visit. CT scan of the chest should be performed at the completion of therapy and at 12 and 24 months. Frequency of evaluation may be decreased to every 6 months for years 3 and 4 and once a year thereafter with annual chest x-ray. Other diagnostic tests should be performed only when clinical signs or symptoms require evaluation. A similar follow-up schedule may be used for Ewing's sarcoma patients following treatment, with the addition of biochemical profiles to follow serum lactate dehydrogenase. Metastatic disease in osteogenic sarcoma may be approached with aggressive chemotherapy and surgery. Metastatic disease in Ewing's sarcoma may respond to additional chemotherapy including bone marrow-ablative doses with stem cell support.

Patients on systemic chemotherapy for metastatic disease require evaluation for response and toxicity prior to each cycle of treatment. Patients on hormonal regimens should be followed monthly until a stable response has been achieved and then every 3 months. Evaluation should include complete blood count, biochemical profile, and measurements of tumor response by physical examination or chest x-ray. More expensive or invasive tests of tumor response (bone imaging or CT scan) should be obtained every 3 months. The efficacy and toxicity of systemic analgesic therapy require frequent evaluations while doses are being titrated. These evaluations should include a quantitative pain assessment and careful history. Once stable and effective dosing is achieved, evaluations every 3 months should be sufficient.

DISCUSSION
Prevalence and Incidence

Primary bone malignancies are rare, constituting less than 1% of all malignancies and approximately 10% of malignancies diagnosed before age 20. Multiple myeloma and lymphoma account for up to 7% of adult malignancies. Precise estimates of the prevalence of metastatic disease involving bone vary with the primary tumor site. More than 70% of patients with metastatic cancer experience significant pain and a majority of these have pain related to bone metastases. Common malignancies associated with a high frequency of bone involvement include lung cancer, breast cancer, prostate cancer, renal cancer, and hematologic malignancies.

Related Basic Science

A genetic predisposition to osteosarcoma related to *RBI* inactivation and the association of t(11;22) with Ewing's sarcoma has been discussed under Etiology.

Our understanding of basic bone physiology and pathophysiology has improved in recent years. This information has opened the way to a better understanding of bone metastases and hypercalcemia. The cells involved in bone remodeling and maintenance are now understood to originate from bone marrow precursors. The osteoclast, or bone-resorbing cell, originates from the granulocyte–macrophage progenitor under the stimulation of interleukin-6 and interleukin-3. Interleukin-6 is produced in response to a variety of stimuli, including parathyroid hor-

mone, parathyroid hormone-related peptide, 1,25-dihydroxyvitamin D_3, tumor growth factors α and β, and tumor necrosis factor. The osteoblast that produces osteoid and, in quiescent form, lines quiescent bone surface originates from the marrow fibroblast colony-forming stem cell. In addition to laying down new bone the osteoblast plays an important role in osteoclast generation via the secretion of interleukin-11 and interleukin-6. Agents that are effective in the inhibition of osteoclast activity such as the bisphosphonates are effective in the therapy of hypercalcemia and are being evaluated in the prevention of bone metastases and therapy of bone pain. Antagonists to cytokines that stimulate bone resorption are being developed for trials in retarding bone loss in the setting of metastatic bone disease.

Natural History and Its Modification with Treatment

Multimodality therapy for primary tumors of bone has dramatically improved disease-free survival and cure for patients with osteosarcoma and Ewing's sarcoma. Improved imaging and surgical techniques have decreased the morbidity of therapy without compromising survival in primary bone tumors. Cure rates in excess of 60% are achieved in osteosarcoma and in excess of 40% in adults with Ewing's sarcoma. These patients require experienced multidisciplinary management from the time the diagnosis is suspected to achieve optimal results.

Metastatic disease in bone remains incurable, but is compatible with long survival in many clinical situations. Preventing complications of bone metastases such as pathologic fracture and spinal cord compression is an important and achievable goal of management. Treatment of the underlying malignancy determines the survival of most patients with metastatic bone disease. The appropriate use of analgesics in the management of bone pain should result in adequate pain relief with preservation of functional status in more than 80% of patients with bone metastases who have pain and should provide a major role for the primary physician.

Prevention

No preventive measures are currently available.

Cost Containment

The use of expensive imaging modalities should be limited to clinical situations where treatment decisions and/or outcome will be influenced by the results. In managing patients with metastatic malignancy involving bone, the prevention of neurologic sequelae of spinal cord compression will decrease the cost of patient care while improving the quality of life. Early intervention in managing potential orthopaedic problems, potential neurologic problems, and pain will lead to improved clinical outcomes.

REFERENCES

Ackery D, Yardley J. Radionuclide-targeted therapy for the management of metastatic bone pain. Semin Oncol 1993;20:27.

Fletcher JA, Kozakewich HP, Hoffer FA, et al. Diagnostic relevence of clonal chromosome aberrations in malignant soft-tissue tumors. N Engl J Med 1991;324:436.

Garrett RI. Bone destruction in cancer. Semin Oncol 1993;20:4.

Horowitz ME, Kinsella TJ, Wexler LH, et al. Total-body irradiation and autologous bone marrow transplant in the treatment of high-risk Ewing's sarcoma and rhabdomyosarcoma. J Clin Oncol 1993;11:1911.

Management of cancer pain. AHCPR Publication No. 94-0592. Washington, DC: U.S. Department of Health and Human Services. 1994.

Manolagas SC, Jilka RL. Bone marrow, cytokines, and bone remodeling: Emerging insights into the pathophysiology of osteoporosis. N Engl J Med 1995;332:305.

Meyers PA, Heller G, Healey JH, et al. Osteogenic sarcoma with clinically detectable metastasis at initial presentation. J Clin Oncol 1993;11:449.

Neoplasms of the Skin (See Section 3, Chapter 27 and Section 11, Chapters 15 and 16)

Brain Tumors (See Section 20, Chapter 10)

Brain Metastases

Randolph Martin York, M.D.

DEFINITION

A brain metastasis is the spread of a cancer in another part of the body to the brain parenchyma.

ETIOLOGY

The cancer cells separate from the primary cancer, gain access to the circulation, cross the blood–brain barrier, and grow in the brain substance.

CRITERIA FOR DIAGNOSIS

Suggestive

Any new neurologic symptom or sign in a patient with a history of a systemic cancer should suggest the diagnosis.

Definitive

A characteristic CT or MRI scan in a patient with an active, primary cancer that is known to spread to the brain can establish the diagnosis of brain metastases. If the patient has a cancer that infrequently metastasizes to brain and a positive CT or MRI scan, it is necessary to biopsy the lesion. Also, if a patient has had a cancer that frequently spreads to the central nervous system, has no evidence of systemic metastasis, and has a long disease-free interval from control of the primary cancer, biopsy is desirable for a definitive diagnosis. Occasionally, a brain metastasis may be the initial manifestation of a cancer of unknown primary site.

CLINICAL MANIFESTATIONS

Subjective

Patients with brain metastases frequently have altered mental status. This can range from subtle changes to obtundation. They frequently have a headache (it is the presenting symptom 50% of the time) that is characteristically worse on arising and may be associated with nausea and vomiting. Seizures, focal or major motor, are an initial symptom in 20% of patients, with an additional 10% occurrence rate later in the course of disease. As the metastases can be present in any area of the brain, a wide variety of neurologic symptoms can be seen. None are specific or characteristic for brain metastases. If there is sufficient cerebral edema to cause papilledema, the patient may have blurred vision.

Objective

Physical Examination

The neurologic examination can demonstrate a wide variety of abnormalities, depending on the location of the metastases. Papilledema can be seen on fundoscopic examination. Careful mental status examination can pick up subtle changes in memory or recent behavior in 75% of patients.

Routine Laboratory Abnormalities

There are no diagnostic routine laboratory abnormalities.

PLANS

Diagnosis

Differential Diagnosis

The differential diagnosis includes meningeal carcinomatosis, altered mental status from pain medications, hypercalcemia, infectious meningitis, psychiatric disorder, remote effect of cancer on the nervous system, and progressive multifocal leukoencephalopathy (see Chapter 3–40).

Diagnostic Options and Recommended Approach

A CT scan with contrast or an MRI scan is necessary to make a diagnosis. The CT scan characteristically shows a mass lesion with surrounding edema. The MRI scan, especially with the newer contrast agents, is more sensitive for smaller lesions than the CT scan. Multiple lesions are usually present. If only one lesion is present, consideration should be given to obtaining a biopsy (see Criteria for Diagnosis).

Therapeutic

Therapeutic Options

The immediate treatment for a patient with newly diagnosed brain metastases is *corticosteroids*. These drugs will decrease edema around the lesion(s) and result in symptomatic improvement in the large majority of patients. Steroids have no antitumor effect and do not affect survival. The preferred steroid is dexamethasone because of its low salt-retaining properties. The initial dose is 4 to 10 mg intravenously every 6 hours.

If the patient presents with seizures, *anticonvulsants* are necessary. Dilantin is the current drug of choice. Prophylactic dilantin in a patient who does not present with seizures has not been shown to decrease the incidence of subsequent seizures.

If the patient has a single metastasis and the systemic cancer is under reasonable control, *surgical removal* of the lesion is indicated. Eleven percent of single lesions are not malignant, and patients who do have a single metastasis resected have a better quality of life and live longer.

Radiation therapy is the mainstay of treatment for brain metastases. The response depends on the sensitivity to radiation of the metastasis. Lesions such as breast cancer and small cell lung cancer can respond well. Other histologies, such as melanoma and adenocarcinoma of the kidney, are relatively resistant to radiation. A newer technique for single metastases is stereotactic radiosurgery. This technique enables precise delivery of a high dose of radiation to a small intracranial target while sparing the surrounding normal brain. A recent review of 248 patients treated showed a median duration of survival of 9.4 months and local control rates at 1 year of 85% with very few side effects of treatment. Interestingly, radiation-resistant tumors did as well as radiosensitive ones. It is not clear yet if this approach is superior to surgery for single brain metastases.

Recommended Approach

The recommended approach is to start all patients on corticosteroids, resect single metastatic lesions, and use brain radiation for patients with more than one metastasis.

FOLLOW-UP

The patient should be seen at regular intervals to assess his or her status. The dose of dexamethasone should be tapered and discontinued if possible. Symptoms may require that it be restarted, however. Periodic CT or MRI scans can be done to assess response to radiation, and if symptoms recur.

DISCUSSION
Prevalence and Incidence

Spread of systemic cancer to the brain is a common occurrence, occurring in more than 250,000 patients per year in the United States.

Related Basic Science

Intracerebral metastases are the most common type of intracerebral cancer and are found in 12% of cancer patients at autopsy. Forty percent of these are single metastases. The most common cancers that cause brain metastases are breast cancer, lung cancer, and melanoma.

Symptoms are caused by the edema surrounding the lesion and the actual destruction of the brain by the metastasis. Corticosteroids act by decreasing the edema. The mechanism of control of cerebral edema by steroids is unknown.

Natural History and Its Modification with Treatment

Most patients with brain metastases will die from the systemic spread of the cancer, not directly from the brain metastases. As the brain metastases progress, however, the patient can suffer with increasingly severe headaches, altered mental status, and increasing neurologic abnormalities. Untreated patients live an average of 1 month. Patients treated with radiation have a median survival of 3 to 6 months.

Prevention

With the exception of small cell lung cancer, brain metastases are unpreventable. Prophylactic whole-brain radiation therapy can decrease significantly the subsequent development of brain metastases in patients with small cell lung cancer.

Cost Containment

Avoiding unnecessary studies such as electroencephalograms and skull films can decrease the cost of medical care. CT and MRI scans are very expensive and should be ordered only when they are clearly indicated and not on a "routine" basis.

REFERENCES

Alexander E III, Moriarity TM, Doris RB, et al. Stereotactic surgery for the definitive treatment of brain metastases. J Natl Cancer Inst 1995;87:34.
Laoffler JS, Kooy HM, Wen PY, et al. The treatment of recurrent brain metastases with stereotactic radiosurgery. J Clin Oncol 1990;8:576.
Patchell RA, Tibbs PA, Walsh JW, et al. A randomized trial of surgery in the treatment of single metastases to the brain. N Engl J Med 1990;322:494.
Pickren JW, Lopez G, Tzukada Y, et al. Brain metastases: An autopsy study. Cancer Treat Symp 1983;2:295.
Posner JB. Management of central nervous system metastases. Semin Oncol 1977;4:81.
Weissman DE. Glucocorticoid treatment for brain metastases and epidural spinal cord compression: A review. J Clin Oncol 1988;6:543.

CHAPTER 3–37

Pleural Effusion in Malignancy as Viewed by an Oncologist

P. Ravi Sarma, M.D.

DEFINITION

The presence of neoplastic cells in a pleural effusion defines it as a malignant pleural effusion.

ETIOLOGY

Pleural effusions are generally seen during the course of a known malignancy. Most often, effusions develop because of the spread of malignancy to the pleura. Sometimes an effusion develops as a result of other causes associated with malignancy: lymphatic obstruction from mediastinal adenopathy, postobstructive changes, opportunistic infections such as tuberculosis, hemorrhagic effusion caused by pulmonary emboli from the cancer-associated hypercoagulable state, as a drug reaction to chemotherapeutic agents like methotrexate, or polyserositis from cytokines such as granulocyte–macrophage colony-stimulating factor. Occasionally, pleural effusion may be the presenting manifestation of an occult primary lesion. Commonly this will be an adenocarcinoma. Pleural mesothelioma should be considered in this setting.

CRITERIA FOR DIAGNOSIS
Suggestive

Pleural effusions seen during the course of a malignancy are most often exudates. The possibility of a pleural effusion should be considered when a patient with known malignancy complains of shortness of breath, chest pain, or heaviness in the chest; has dullness on percussion; and has decreased breath sounds. A chest x-ray will confirm the presence of an effusion. Malignancy should always be considered in the evaluation of a patient with an exudative effusion and no known cancer.

Definitive

The diagnosis of malignant pleural effusion is established by a positive pleural fluid cytology or pleural biopsy. A presumptive diagnosis can be made if an exudative effusion is present in a person with known malignancy and no other cause for the effusion can be identified, even though pleural fluid cytology and pleural biopsy are negative.

CLINICAL MANIFESTATIONS

Subjective

See Chapters 13–6 and 13–7. There may be a recent or remote history of cancer or an unexplained effusion may be the first manifestation of a new cancer.

Objective

Physical Examination

See Chapters 13–6 and 13–7.

Routine Laboratory Abnormalities

A complete blood count may show anemia, leukocytosis, or thrombocytosis, nonspecific findings indicating an inflammatory process. If the effusion is part of a drug reaction, then eosinophilia may be noted. Routine chemistries (SMA-18) generally do not show any diagnostic abnormalities.

A chest x-ray will show the presence of pleural effusion. In cases where the effusion is minimal, there may only be "blunting" of the costal margin. In such instances, it will be necessary to obtain decubitus views to confirm the presence of fluid.

PLANS

Diagnostic

Differential Diagnosis

When a pleural effusion is noted during the course of a malignancy, it is important to establish the nature of the effusion. Transudative effusions are unlikely to be due to the malignancy. The differential diagnosis of exudative effusions involves both neoplastic and nonneoplastic causes. This was discussed above under Etiology and Criteria for Diagnosis.

Diagnostic Options

As a pleural effusion is often seen in conjunction with advancing mediastinal disease, it is important to look for coexisting complications such as pericardial effusion and superior vena caval obstruction.

A diagnostic thoracentesis should initiate the evaluation of a pleural effusion. When the effusion is small or does not layer out well on a lateral decubitus view of the chest, ultrasonic localization will be needed.

Pleural fluid should be sent for cytology, protein, and lactate dehydrogenase levels, and for appropriate cultures if the patient has fever or tuberculosis is suspected. The effusion should not be "tapped dry" at the time of initial thoracentesis. (If the initial studies are inconclusive, a pleural biopsy can be done at the second attempt, and this becomes difficult if the effusion has been completely drained.) About 50 to 100 mL of fluid is adequate for diagnostic studies.

In a study by Light and co-workers (1972), a pleural lactate dehydrogenase level greater than 200 IU, a pleural fluid:blood lactate dehydrogenase ratio greater than 0.6, and/or a pleural fluid:protein ratio greater than 0.5 indicated, with a predictive value of 99%, that the effusion was an exudate. When all the three tests were negative, there was a 98% certainty that the fluid was not an exudate. Other tests such as pleural fluid pH, glucose, and amylase are not helpful in diagnosing malignant effusions. These tests are helpful in excluding other conditions.

A positive pleural fluid cytology or positive pleural biopsy will be diagnostic of malignancy. It is important, however, to note that errors in interpretation of cytology or biopsy can lead to false-positive readings. The presence of reactive mesothelial cells or reactive lymphocytes and plasma cells can make it difficult to interpret a cytologic preparation or a biopsy specimen.

An exudative effusion can still be malignant even if both cytology and biopsy are negative. An exudative effusion in an individual with known malignancy and no other identifiable cause can be presumed malignant. Immunohistochemistry and flow cytometry can be used to distinguish reactive cells from neoplastic cells. When a pleural biopsy is planned, thoracoscopy will allow biopsy under direct visualization. The recent availability of video-assisted thoracoscopy has made this procedure even more useful. In cases of suspected mesothelioma, an open biopsy may be necessary before a definitive diagnosis can be made.

Recommended Approach

Pleural fluid cytology and, if necessary, pleural biopsy under direct visualization will establish the malignant nature of the effusion. It is important to remember that an exudative effusion can still be related to the malignancy, even in the absence of spread to the pleura.

Therapeutic

Therapeutic Options

The therapeutic options are summarized in Figure 3–37–1.

In general, where systemic treatment is available, no local treatment of the effusion is necessary in a stable patient. When local therapy is indicated, repeated thoracentesis should be avoided in rapidly reaccumulating effusions because of the likelihood of loculation. Where the effusion is due to mediastinal adenopathy causing lymphatic obstruction, mediastinal irradiation will control the effusion.

The best available local treatment consists of closed chest tube drainage and instillation of agents to obtain pleural sclerosis. The fluid should be completely drained to facilitate close approximation of both pleural surfaces. This is likely to be the case when the chest tube drainage is less than 100 to 150 mL in a 24-hour period. At that time, pleural sclerosis should be attempted.

Many agents were used in the past for pleural sclerosis. These included nitrogen mustard, thiotepa, quinacrine, talc, tetracycline, and bleomycin. When the manufacture of tetracycline was discontinued, doxycycline was used in its place. Currently, intrapleural doxycycline, bleomycin, and talc are the most widely used sclerosing agents. The antimalarial agent quinacrine is also an effective sclerosing agent. Although talc is very effective, its use requires insufflation under anesthesia using a thoracoscope. Talc slurry can be instilled through a chest tube, but experience with this technique is limited. A National Cancer Institute intergroup study is planned to compare intrapleural talc (5 g through a slurry), bleomycin (60 units), and doxycycline (500 mg) in the control of malignant pleural effusion.

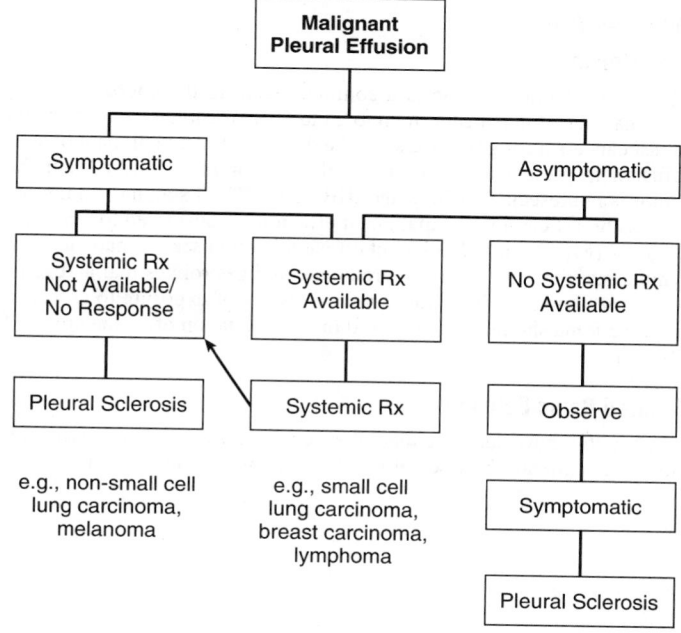

Figure 3–37–1. Approaches to the management of malignant pleural effusion.

The following steps are used to obtain pleural sclerosis:

- Place a closed chest tube to drain the fluid completely and allow full reexpansion of the lung. (It is important to know ahead of time that there is no loculation of the fluid.) Reaccumulation of fluid should be less than 100 to 150 mL in the 24 hours prior to instillation of the sclerosing agent.
- Premedicate with analgesics/narcotics, repeated as needed for pain control.
- Instill the sclerosing agent via the chest tube and clamp it.
- Turn the patient every 5 minutes for 15 to 30 minutes and every 15 minutes for another 90 minutes, to facilitate maximum contact of the sclerosing agent with the pleural surfaces. The chest tube may be left clamped for 2 to 6 hours.
- Unclamp and reconnect the tube to the water seal drainage system. The chest tube is removed when the lung has completely expanded (as noted on a follow-up x-ray) and pleural fluid no longer accumulates. This usually takes 24 to 48 hours. After the chest tube is removed, close the site with a suture.

Sometimes the procedure may have to be repeated two or three times to achieve pleural sclerosis. This is more likely to be the case when doxycycline is used as the sclerosing agent. As bleomycin is absorbed into the systemic circulation, intrapleural bleomycin should not be repeated unless careful consideration is given to the possibility of pulmonary toxicity from this drug.

In patients who are debilitated and who may have a very short life expectancy, the physician may perform an occasional thoracentesis for relief of symptoms and not attempt pleural sclerosis.

Surgical procedures such as pleurectomy and pleuroperitoneal shunt are rarely needed and should be considered only in patients who are otherwise in good general condition. These procedures may not be very effective.

Recommended Approach

The recommended approach is outlined in Figure 3–37–1.

FOLLOW-UP

Initially, biweekly to monthly follow-up visits may be necessary. Effusions tend to recur within 30 to 90 days, even after sclerosis. In such instances, if the patient's general condition remains good, a second attempt at sclerosis can be made.

DISCUSSION

Prevalence

Malignant pleural effusion is a common event in the course of many malignancies. It may occur in up to 25 to 50% of patients with lung and breast cancers during the course of the disease. When malignant pleural effusion is present at the initial evaluation of lung cancer, then the tumor is nonresectable (T4, stage IIIB, in the TNM staging). In tumors such as breast carcinoma, malignant effusion is considered to represent stage IV (M_1) disease. Malignant effusion is often seen in patients with lymphoma, sarcoma, ovarian carcinoma, and gastrointestinal and genitourinary tumors. In individuals with a history of exposure to asbestos, mesothelioma should be considered in the evaluation of an unexplained effusion.

Related Basic Science

In a healthy individual, the pleural space is only a potential space. Between the parietal and visceral layers of the pleura, only about 5 mL of fluid is present, just enough to lubricate the two surfaces. The fluid is formed on the parietal pleural surface and is primarily (80%) absorbed by the visceral pleural capillaries. Pleural lymphatics account for the absorption of the remaining 20% of the fluid. This whole process is very active, with nearly 5 to 10 L of fluid being formed each day. In the majority of patients with cancer, pleural effusion develops as a result of increased capillary permeability owing to tumor implants on the pleural surface or to lymphatic obstruction.

The presence of pleural effusion is a contraindication for the use of methotrexate. The effusion will serve as a reservoir for continuous release of the drug into the bloodstream, resulting in excessive and sometimes fatal toxicity. Calcium leucovorin will reverse or limit methotrexate toxicity. If there is severe leukopenia, use of a cytokine such as granulocyte colony-stimulating factor may also be required.

Natural History and Its Modification with Treatment

The course of a malignant effusion follows that of the underlying malignancy. Prognosis is good in patients with responsive tumors such as lymphomas and hormone-responsive breast cancer or prostate carcinoma. It is poor in non-small cell lung carcinoma, melanoma, and other tumors for which no effective systemic therapy is available. Pleural sclerosis controls the effusion and offers symptom relief in 50 to 60% of patients for several weeks. Eventually, with progression of the disease, the fluid reaccumulates.

Prevention

Effective treatment of the primary malignancy prevents the occurrence of pleural effusions. Preventive measures are directed toward preventing the various malignancies.

Cost Containment

Extensive evaluation of a pleural effusion is not necessary in patients with progressive systemic malignancy and should be avoided. Pleural fluid lactate dehydrogenase and protein determinations are sufficient to distinguish exudates from transudates. Other tests are not routinely indicated.

In individuals with advancing malignancy and limited life span, it may be possible to offer symptom palliation with an occasional thoracentesis and not have to perform thoracostomy tube drainage and pleural sclerosis.

When a sclerosing agent is used, the overall costs include the cost of the sclerosing agent as well as the costs associated with hospitalization and the need for repeat sclerosis. Not enough information is available to make a recommendation of one agent over the other based on cost alone.

REFERENCES

Light RN, MacGregor MI, Luchsinger PC, et al. Pleural effusions: The diagnostic separation of transudates and exudates. Ann Int Med 1972;77:507.

Pass HI. Treatment of malignant pleural and pericardial effusions. In: DeVita VT Jr, Hellman S, Rosenberg SA, (eds). Cancer, principles and practice of oncology. 4th ed. Philadelphia: Lippincott, 1993:2246.

Ruckdeschel JC. Controversy over sclerotherapy for malignant pleural effusions (letter). Ann Intern Med 1994;121:150.

Walker-Renard PB, Vaughn LM, Sahn SA. Chemical pleurodesis for malignant pleural effusions (review). Ann Intern Med 1994;120:56.

Spinal Cord Compression

Melvin R. Moore, M.D.

DEFINITION

Spinal cord compression due to malignancy is compression of the cord within its bony compartment by direct tumor growth or by vertebral body collapse caused by tumor growth within the spine (dura), contiguous with the spinal cord.

ETIOLOGY

Extradural invasion by tumor is found in more than 5% of patients with metastatic malignancy at autopsy. Underlying primary malignancies of the lung, breast, prostate, and kidney, multiple myeloma, lymphoma, and sarcomas are particular likely to be associated with spinal cord compression. Approximately three quarters of patients with a confirmed diagnosis of spinal cord compression due to malignancy have soft tissue masses and one quarter have bony collapse.

CRITERIA FOR DIAGNOSIS

Suggestive

In the setting of known cancer, back pain is suggestive of the diagnosis of spinal cord compression. The likelihood of the diagnosis is increased by radiographic or bone scan evidence of spinal metastases. Radicular pain is particularly indicative of the diagnosis of spinal cord compression. Sensory findings, motor weakness, and bladder and bowel dysfunction have great predictive value, but are late manifestations.

Definitive

The diagnosis of spinal cord compression is established by magnetic resonance imaging (MRI) of the spine or by contrast myelography.

CLINICAL MANIFESTATIONS

Subjective

Back pain, either local or radicular, is the initial symptom of spinal cord compression in more than 95% of patients. The onset of pain may precede additional neurologic symptoms or signs by many months. Radicular pain is more frequent in cervical cord compressions (over 80%) than in thoracic or lumbar compressions (about 50%). Radicular pain is usually bilateral and localizes the lesion to within one or two vertebral segments; however, high cervical lesions may present with lower radicular syndromes. Nonradicular pain may be poorly localized or associated with spinal tenderness. Pain often increases with lying down.

Although weakness is rarely an initial symptom, a majority of patients complain of leg weakness by the time of diagnosis. The weakness may be subtle, and unless the physician has a high index of suspicion, the symptom may not be elicited. As the results of therapy depend on the pretreatment neurologic status, every attempt should be made to evaluate any subjective complaint of leg weakness in patients with metastatic malignancy.

Loss of sensation in a spinal distribution below the level of compression usually lags behind pain and motor weakness. Numbness and paresthesias are the most common complaints, and they occur in almost 50% of patients by the time of diagnosis. Overflow urinary incontinence and obstipation due to autonomic compromise may occur early in the course of lower thoracic spinal cord compression.

Objective

Physical Examination

During physical examination, spinal tenderness to percussion is often present. Neck flexion and straight leg raising should be used to attempt to elicit radicular pain. Leg weakness is usually symmetric. Sensory loss includes pinprick, vibration, and position. The level of sensory loss is of great localizing value. Poor rectal sphincter tone and bladder distention are signs of autonomic dysfunction. Deep tendon reflexes may be lost acutely with neutral plantar responses and later may become hyperactive with extensor plantar responses.

Routine Laboratory Abnormalities

Routine blood work may demonstrate an elevated alkaline phosphatase level, anemia, or other nonspecific findings associated with systemic malignancy. The chest x-ray film may reveal loss of vertebral pedicle, blastic or lytic changes in vertebral bodies, or collapse of vertebral bodies.

PLANS
Diagnostic
Differential Diagnosis

Differential diagnosis of back pain includes the myriad disorders that cause back pain in patients without malignancy. Neurologic signs and symptoms may be caused by brain metastasis, chemotherapy side effects (vinca alkaloid- and cisplatin-induced neuropathy), or paraneoplastic syndromes. Benign causes of spinal cord compression and of neurologic signs and symptoms must be kept in mind.

Diagnostic Options

Diagnostic options include MRI, contrast computed tomography-guided myelography and conventional myelography. Among these options MRI is least morbid and equals computed tomography-guided myelography in sensitivity and specificity.

Recommended Approach

Back pain in a patient with known malignancy should be promptly evaluated by bone radiography and/or bone scan. The presence of an abnormality of the bone in this setting should prompt an emergency MRI scan of the spine. This workup should proceed in the absence of other neurologic signs or symptoms. The positive predictive value of a bone abnormality on x-ray film or scan in the evaluation of back pain in the setting of metastatic cancer is almost 60% in the absence of other neurologic findings.

Therapeutic

Radiation therapy to the spine and high-dose corticosteroid therapy constitute the recommended approach to spinal cord compression in the vast majority of cases. Radiation is usually begun on an emergency basis. High initial dose fractionation (e.g., 500 cGy) may be used for the first day or two of treatment in the presence of neurologic signs. Otherwise, a dose of 200 cGy/d for a total dose of 3500 to 4000 cGy is considered adequate and approaches the radiation tolerance of the spinal cord. Dexamethasone is initiated at a dose of 100 mg intravenously followed by 100 mg orally every day for the first week of treatment and is then rapidly tapered over a period of 2 weeks. Surgical decompression via laminectomy, or more optimally via an anterior approach, should be undertaken in the following situations: no known primary malignant diagnosis established; maximal radiation to the cord already given; neurologic deterioration while receiving maximal radiation therapy and dexamethasone. Treatment may not be indicated in patients with extremely advanced metastatic cancer whose life expectancy is less than a few weeks. Postoperative radiation therapy may begin on the fifth postoperative day. Patients with prostate and breast cancer should receive hormonal therapy if it has not already been tried. Patients with tumors that are responsive to systemic chemotherapy should begin treatment immediately following the completion of radiation therapy.

FOLLOW-UP

Careful daily neurologic evaluations are required during therapy, so that steroid dosages can be increased or surgery can be performed when indicated. After therapy is complete, follow-up visits and tests depend on the primary tumor diagnosis and on the course of systemic therapy.

DISCUSSION
Prevalence and Incidence

Between 5 and 10% of patients with metastatic malignancy experience spinal cord compression.

Related Basic Science

Invasion and compression of the spinal cord usually begin with involvement of the vertebral body or paravertebral nodes anterior to the spinal cord. The level of compression is thoracic in almost 70% of patients, lumbar in about 20%, and cervical in about 10%. High thoracic lesions have a worse prognosis because of the tenuous blood supply to the cord in the T1–4 area.

Natural History and Its Modification with Treatment

Neurologic function prior to therapy is the most significant prognostic variable. When therapy is initiated prior to the development of signs of myelopathy or radiculopathy in the patient presenting with pain, normal neurologic function following radiotherapy is virtually ensured. The situation is bleak, however, in patients presenting with neurologic dysfunction. Following radiation, slightly less than 80% of patients who were ambulatory before therapy are able to walk and less than 50% who had major motor weakness become ambulatory with therapy. Patients with lymphoma and multiple myeloma are most likely to regain

function (over 50%), followed closely by patients with breast carcinoma and prostate carcinoma (approximately 30%). The outlook for return of function is less favorable for all other tumor types. Patients who have slowly evolving neurologic dysfunction over weeks or months respond more favorably to therapy than those who have had a sudden onset of paralysis. Cord compressions caused by vertebral collapse are less likely to respond to radiation therapy than lesions caused by epidural mass.

Prevention

Earlier use of radiation therapy for painful areas of bone involvement in breast carcinoma, myeloma, prostatic carcinoma, and lung cancer may prevent the occurrence of spinal cord compression.

Cost Containment

Cost containment can be achieved by the rapid and appropriate diagnosis and therapy of patients with malignancy and back pain who are at risk for spinal cord compression. All too often, patients with metastatic malignancy and back pain are not evaluated for spinal cord compression until major neurologic deficits are present, resulting in the added morbidity and costs of caring for a patient who is paraparetic.

REFERENCES

Gilbert RW, Kim J, Posner JB. Epidural spinal cord compression from metastatic tumor: Diagnosis and treatment. Ann Neurol 1978;3:40.
Grant R, Papadopoulos SM, Sandler HM, Greenberg HS. Metastatic epidural spinal cord compression: Current concepts and treatment. J Neurooncol 1994;19(1):79.
Helweg-Larsen S, Sorensen PS. Symptoms and signs in metastatic spinal cord compression: A study of progression from first symptom until diagnosis in 153 patients. Eur J Cancer 1994;30A(3):396.
Rodichok LD, Harper GP, Ruckdeschel JC, et al. Early diagnosis of spinal epidural metastases. Am J Med 1981;70:1181.
Sorensen S, Helweg-Larsen S, Mouridsen H, Hansen HH. Effect of high-dose dexamethasone in carcinomatous metastatic spinal cord compression treated with radiotherapy: A randomised trial. Eur J Cancer. 1994;30A(1):22.

CHAPTER 3–39
Superior Vena Caval Syndrome (See Section 13, Chapter 40)

CHAPTER 3–40
Carcinomatous Meningitis
Randolph Martin York, M.D.

DEFINITION

Carcinomatous meningitis is the spread of cancer cells from a primary cancer in another part of the body to the meninges.

ETIOLOGY

The cancer cells separate from the primary cancer or its systemic metastases and spread via the systemic circulation to the meninges.

CRITERIA FOR DIAGNOSIS
Suggestive

The diagnosis is suggested when a patient with a history of a systemic malignancy develops neurologic signs and/or symptoms.

Definitive

The presence of malignant cells in the cerebrospinal fluid of a patient with a malignant neoplasm confirms the diagnosis of carcinomatous meningitis. The diagnosis may also be established in a patient with signs and symptoms of meningitis, negative cerebrospinal cytologic findings, but with some or all of the following cerebrospinal fluid abnormalities: elevated cerebrospinal fluid protein level, elevated opening pressure, low cerebrospinal fluid glucose level, and/or pleocytosis.

CLINICAL MANIFESTATIONS
Subjective

It is rare for a patient's initial symptoms of carcinoma to be those of carcinomatous meningitis. Most patients have breast carcinoma, lung carcinoma, malignant melanoma, diffuse non-Hodgkin's lymphoma, acute myelocytic leukemia, acute lymphocytic leukemia, the blast phase of chronic myelocytic leukemia, Burkitt's lymphoma, or T-cell lymphomas. Rarer causes include gastrointestinal tract adenocarcinomas and carcinomas of the ovary.

Headache frequently is an initial symptom; it occurs in 30 to 60% of patients. The headache may be quite severe and usually is not localized; the pain may be worse in the morning or have no temporal characteristics. A change in mental status, ranging from mild confusion, to memory loss, to lethargy, is also a frequent initial symptom. Symptoms of cranial nerve dysfunction often occur and are usually multiple and in different areas. Diplopia is the most common of these, followed by asymmetric facial paresis or paralysis, vestibular symptoms, unilateral or bilateral hearing loss, difficulty with swallowing, and, rarely, blindness. Spinal nerve root symptoms are seen about as frequently as the cranial nerve symptoms and may also occur at different parts of the spinal axis. Low back pain is the most common symptom, although pain in the legs may also occur. Asymmetric leg weakness often occurs, with symptoms in the arms seen less frequently. Sensory loss or paresthesias occurring in a dermatome distribution or "stocking–glove" pattern are also seen. Other occasional presenting symptoms are seizures, fecal or urinary incontinence, and nausea. None of these symptoms is specific for carcinomatous meningitis, but the diversity of symptoms in a given patient should strongly suggest the diagnosis. It is very unusual for the patient with carcinomatous meningitis to be without symptoms.

Objective

Physical Examination

The neurologic examination, like the symptoms, usually reveals abnormalities in several, often widely separated, areas of the craniospinal axis. A careful examination almost always demonstrates more objective signs than are suggested by the patient's symptoms. A detailed mental status examination is abnormal in approximately half of these patients on initial examination. Cranial nerve signs are found 30 to 70% of the time. Any cranial nerve may be involved, but the most frequent are the third, fourth, sixth, seventh, and fifth. Signs of spinal nerve root involvement include leg or arm weakness (usually asymmetric), sensory loss in a dermatome, and absent or asymmetric tendon reflexes. Nuchal rigidity and a positive straight-leg raising test are seen less often.

Routine Laboratory Abnormalities

There are no diagnostic routine laboratory abnormalities.

PLANS
Diagnostic
Differential Diagnosis

Diagnosis	Diagnostic Test or Observation
Excessive narcotic/ analgesic reaction	History and neurologic drug examination
	Discontinue medications
Metabolic abnormality	Focal findings unusual on examination
	Serum electrolytes, calcium, creatinine, glutamic–oxalacetic acid transaminase, bilirubin, alkaline phosphatase determinations
Parenchymal brain metastases	CT or brain scan positive
Infectious meningitis	Fever usually present
	Focal findings less frequent than with carcinomatous meningitis
	Positive culture, Gram stain, or antigen in cerebrospinal fluid
Psychiatric disorder	Neurologic examination normal
	Cerebrospinal fluid normal
	Positive history
Remote effect of carcinoma on the nervous system	Neurologic examination normal
	Negative cytologic findings

Diagnosis	Diagnostic Test or Observation
Progressive multifocal leukoencephalopathy	Negative cerebrospinal fluid cytologic examination
	CT scan positive

Diagnostic Options

The patient with a previous diagnosis of carcinoma who develops neurologic signs and symptoms may have any of a number of problems. Occasionally more than one problem exists, for example, hypercalcemia and carcinomatous meningitis. A careful history and neurologic examination can strongly suggest the diagnosis of carcinomatous meningitis if there are signs and symptoms of disease in different areas of the neuraxis. An MRI scan can strongly suggest the diagnosis if there is meningeal enhancement present.

Recommended Approach

The definitive diagnosis is made by examination of the cerebrospinal fluid. A CT or MRI scan should be done prior to the lumbar puncture to be sure that no parenchymal masses are present. The cerebrospinal fluid is almost never completely normal in carcinomatous meningitis, although it is often necessary to repeat the lumbar puncture several times before malignant cells can be demonstrated. The abnormalities found are listed in Table 3–40–1.

Therapeutic

Treatment should begin promptly and consists of the injection of drugs directly into the cerebrospinal fluid, with or without radiation therapy. The three drugs currently used most often are methotrexate, cytosine arabinoside, and thiotepa. Cytosine arabinoside is used primarily for hematologic malignancies. There is no advantage to using more than one drug. Initial treatment is the injection of either methotrexate or thiotepa by lumbar puncture twice a week until the cerebrospinal fluid is normal. If the cerebrospinal fluid is not markedly improved after four injections, a change to a different drug should be made. Once the cerebrospinal fluid is normal, the injections are decreased to once a week for two injections, and then maintained at monthly injections indefinitely.

An alternative to the use of repeated lumbar puncture for drug administration is the Ommaya reservoir. This subcutaneous reservoir is placed under the scalp with an attached catheter that is inserted, through a burr hole, into the lateral ventricle of the frontal lobe of the nondominant hemisphere. Once the reservoir is in place, the drug can be injected directly into the reservoir with much less discomfort and inconvenience to the patient. The Ommaya device also affords a better distribution of the drug in the cerebrospinal fluid than the lumbar puncture technique. Its disadvantages are that it requires a minor neurosurgical procedure and it is associated with problems in 10 to 15% of patients. These include infected catheter tip (which may or may not require its removal), misplaced catheter tip, occluded tip, and growth of tumor cells around the tip. If, however, the reservoir is placed in position by an experienced neurosurgeon using fluoroscopic control, and aseptic technique is used in injecting the drugs, complications should be minimal.

The exact role of radiation therapy in the treatment of carcinomatous meningitis is not well defined. It is frequently used along with intrathecal chemotherapy in pediatric patients with acute lymphoblastic leukemia. It is particularly useful when there are focal cranial or spinal nerve deficits that can be specifically irradiated, or if discrete masses are present.

TABLE 3–40–1. CEREBROSPINAL FLUID IN CARCINOMATOUS MENINGITIS

Test	Abnormality	Percent
Cytology	Positive	65–100
Protein	>50 mg/100mL	60–90
Glucose	<50 mg/100mL	50–80
Cell count	>4 cells	60–80
Opening pressure	>180 cm H_2O	70

Treatment is effective in the great majority of patients with leukemia and lymphoma. The symptoms of headache, nausea, and meningismus can be relieved in most patients, and the cerebrospinal fluid is expected to return to normal in the majority of patients. Cranial nerve deficits may persist, however, even in the presence of normal cerebrospinal fluid. Autopsy studies demonstrate that it is occasionally possible to eradicate lymphoma or leukemia cells from the leptomeninges; however, the development of carcinomatous meningitis in patients with leukemias and lymphomas is almost always associated with widespread systemic disease. Treatment for carcinomatous meningitis associated with solid tumors is less effective. Only 40 to 60% of patients achieve subjective improvement, and focal neurologic signs persist in the majority.

FOLLOW-UP

Follow-up visits after hospital discharge are necessary for further injections of the drugs into the cerebrospinal fluid. Periodic neurologic examinations and cerebrospinal fluid analysis for cell count, cytologic findings, and protein should be done to look for progressive disease.

DISCUSSION

Prevalence and Incidence

Five to eight percent of patients with solid tumors develop carcinomatous meningitis. The majority have breast cancer, small cell lung cancer, or malignant melanoma. Less frequent causes are gastric cancer, ovarian cancer, and non-small cell lung cancers. Meningeal carcinomatosis usually occurs in conjunction with systemic relapse of the disease.

Carcinomatous meningitis is more frequent in certain hematologic malignancies. In acute lymphocytic leukemia (without prophylactic central nervous system treatment), 50 to 70% of patients develop meningeal leukemia. In patients with acute myelocytic leukemia, carcinomatous meningitis occurs in approximately 5% of patients, usually in association with a bone marrow relapse. In chronic myelocytic leukemia, carcinomatous meningitis is rare in the chronic phase, but is seen in 5 to 10% of patients in blast crisis. The development of meningeal spread in patients with lymphoma depends largely on the histology. Nodular lymphomas rarely spread to the meninges, but diffuse lymphomas develop meningeal involvement 20 to 30% of the time. If the patient has bone marrow or testicular involvement or extranodal disease, the incidence is further increased.

Related Basic Science

Anatomic Considerations

On gross pathologic examination, a diffuse infiltration of the leptomeninges with malignant cells is seen. All the leptomeninges are usually involved, but the disease may occasionally be limited to the spinal cord or basal cisterns. Histologic examination reveals a thin layer of cells with a tendency to concentrate around the blood vessels and nerve roots. The tumor may ensheathe the meningeal arteries and veins and continue as cuffs or nodules in the perivascular space into the brain substance at the capillary level. Tumor cells also frequently encase the perineurium of the nerve roots or infiltrate the nerve sheath and extend along the course of the nerve.

The exact route by which tumor cells get to the meninges is unknown. The following routes are suspected: direct invasion through the choroid plexus, along the perivascular space of the meningeal vessels; secondary invasion from parenchymal tumor masses, via Batson's plexus; and retrograde extension from systemic lymph nodes in the perineural lymphatics.

Pathophysiology

The pathophysiology of the clinical manifestations of carcinomatous meningitis is not always clear. Symptoms and signs of nerve root irrita-

tion are caused frequently by direct invasion of the nerve parenchyma. Demyelination is also seen in the nerve roots and peripheral nerves. The location of the abnormality does not always correlate, however, with the location of the clinical signs and symptoms. The "cerebral symptoms"—headache and nausea—are thought to be due to increased cerebrospinal fluid pressure resulting from a block in the subarachnoid space by tumor cells; however, these symptoms can be seen without evidence of a subarachnoid block at autopsy.

The reason for the finding of a low glucose level in the cerebrospinal fluid is also obscure. Metabolism of glucose by the malignant cells and a defect in the transport of glucose into the cerebrospinal fluid are two postulated but unproven theories.

Natural History and Its Modification With Treatment

The natural history of untreated carcinomatous meningitis is steady progression of the neurologic signs and symptoms with the development of new ones in different areas of the neuroaxis. Death occurs within weeks in most patients.

As noted under Plans, Therapeutic, the response of the signs and symptoms to treatment varies with the underlying disease. Unfortunately, carcinomatous meningitis usually occurs in the setting of widespread systemic disease, and approximately 40 to 70% of these patients die of systemic disease while the meningeal disease is under control. It is possible to control carcinomatous meningitis for prolonged periods with treatment. Patients who have had their signs and symptoms controlled from 1 to 2 years have been reported.

Prevention

Prophylactic treatment to the central nervous system in acute lymphocytic leukemia in children has decreased the incidence of meningeal leukemia from 50 to 70% to 5%. This is the only disease in which preventive treatment is of proven value in decreasing the incidence of carcinomatous meningitis. The suggestion has been made to use prophylactic treatment in the blast phase of chronic myelocytic leukemia in a complete remission or in diffuse lymphomas with bone marrow involvement, but the success of this approach has not been shown.

Cost Containment

A careful history and neurologic examination suggest the diagnosis and preclude the use of a "shotgun" battery of neurologic tests. Electroencephalogram, electromyogram, skull series, and myelogram are rarely, if ever, indicated. It is not necessary to order a variety of tests on every sample of cerebrospinal fluid obtained.

REFERENCES

Bleyer WA, Byrne TN. Leptomeningeal cancer in leukemia and solid tumors. Curr Prob Cancer 1988;12(4):183.

Brereton HD, O'Donnell JF, Kent CH, et al. Spinal meningeal carcinomatosis in small-cell and squamous-cell carcinoma of the lung. Ann Intern Med 1978;88:517.

Grossman SA, Finkelstein DM, Ruckdeschel JC, et al. Randomized prospective comparison of intraventricular methotrexate and thiotepa in patients with previously untreated neoplastic meningitis. J Clin Oncol 1993;11:561.

Kokkoris CP. Leptomeningeal carcinomatosis: How does cancer reach the piarachnoid? Cancer 1983;51:154.

Little JR, Dale AJ, Okazaki H. Meningeal carcinomatosis. Arch Neurol 1974;30:138.

Olson ME, Chernik NL, Posner J. Infiltration of the leptomeninges by systemic cancer. Arch Neurol 1974;30:122.

Shapiro WR, Posner JN, Ushio Y, et al. Treatment of meningeal neoplasms. Cancer Treat Rep 1977;61:733.

Young RC, Howser DM, Anderson T, et al. Central nervous system complications of non-Hodgkin's lymphoma: The potential role for prophylactic therapy. Am J Med 1979;66:435.

Cancer-Associated Hypercalcemia

Randolph Martin York, M.D.

DEFINITION

An elevated serum calcium level in a patient with cancer who does not have another (benign) cause for hypercalcemia establishes the diagnosis.

ETIOLOGY

Hypercalcemia in cancer patients is most often caused by the secretion of a parathyroid hormone-related protein by the tumor. The tumor can also produce calcitriol. A third mechanism is osteolysis mediated by the local release of osteolytic factors, that is, tumor necrosis factor B and others.

CRITERIA FOR DIAGNOSIS

Suggestive

Altered mental status, especially excess drowsiness, in a patient with an active cancer should suggest the diagnosis.

Definitive

An elevated serum calcium level in a patient with an active cancer usually is sufficient for the diagnosis. Parathyroid hormone levels are almost always decreased in cancer-associated hypercalcemia.

CLINICAL MANIFESTATIONS

Subjective

Hypercalcemia may be seen on a routine laboratory test; the patient may have no symptoms. The most common symptom is altered mental status. This can vary from a mild confusion to coma. The patients often are constipated. Nausea and anorexia are also frequent. If the hypercalcemia is of long duration, polyuria is seen.

Objective

Physical Examination

Hypercalcemia causes no objective physical findings other than the abnormal mental status examination.

Routine Laboratory Abnormalities

Laboratory studies show elevated serum calcium levels. If bone metastases are present, the serum alkaline phosphatase level may be increased. If nephrocalcinosis is present, the blood urea nitrogen and creatinine will be increased. Cancer patients often have depressed serum albumin levels, and the serum calcium level should be appropriately corrected for the level of albumin.

Electrocardiograms will show a shortened QT interval.

PLANS

Diagnostic

Differential Diagnosis

Benign causes of hypercalcemia should be considered and ruled out as the clinical situation dictates (e.g., a patient with breast cancer with hypercalcemia and a negative bone scan).

Diagnostic Options and Recommended Approach

An elevated serum calcium level in a patient with an active cancer strongly suggests the diagnosis.

The bone scan or skeletal x-rays may show evidence of bony metastases. X-rays and scans will show evidence of the primary cancer (renal mass, etc.) and evidence of metastases.

Therapeutic

The initial treatment for hypercalcemia is intravenous saline. These patients are often dehydrated so that it may be necessary to use large volumes of fluid. At least 3 L per day should be given, paying careful attention to urine output and electrolyte balance. Some physicians prefer to add a loop diuretic such as furosemide (Lasix). It is not clear that this is necessary in the majority of the patients. Intravenous saline alone will result in a normal serum calcium level in 80% of patients.

Mithramycin is an effective calcium-lowering agent. The drug can be given only intravenously. The dose is 25 µg/kg. Mithramycin blocks calcium resorption from bone. Calcium levels decrease, often to normal levels, within 48 hours. It is generally necessary to repeat mithramycin every 4 to 5 days. Calcium levels are checked every day, and the next dose is given when the level begins to increase. Once a particular patient's pattern is established, mithramycin can easily be used on an outpatient basis. Few side or toxic effects are seen at this dose of mithramycin, which is considerably less than the antineoplastic dose.

The *biphosphonates* are an effective group of compounds in lowering serum calcium levels. These are potent inhibitors of osteoclastic bone resorption. Two biphosphonates are available in the United States: etidronate and pamidronate. Etidronate is given intravenously at a dose of 7.5 mg/kg mixed in 250 mL of saline over a 2- to 4-hour period daily for 3 to 7 days. If the response is rapid, that is, if the calcium level drops 2 to 3 mg after the first two or three doses, etidronate should be discontinued. Pamidronate is given as a slow intravenous infusion of 15 to 45 mg per day for up to 6 days. It may also be given as a single 24-hour infusion at a dose of 90 mg. Pamidronate can be given orally at a dose of 1200 mg daily for up to 5 days, but the intravenous route is preferred. Both biphosphonates can achieve normocalcemia in 60 to 100% of patients.

Calcitonin is another alternative for the treatment of cancer-associated hypercalcemia. Calcitonin is given intramuscularly or subcutaneously at a dose of 4 U/kg every 12 hours. The calcium-lowering effect of calcitonin is usually incomplete. Another disadvantage is the short duration of action, usually only 3 to 5 days. The concomitant use of corticosteroids can help delay this "escape phenomenon," but the short duration of action and the need for continuous injections every 12 hours limit the usefulness of calcitonin.

Yet another choice for lowering the calcium level in patients with cancer-associated hypercalcemia is *gallium nitrate*. It appears to act by inhibiting bone resorption. Gallium nitrate is administered as a constant intravenous infusion for 5 days at a daily dose of 200 mg/m^2 of body surface area. Gallium nitrate is nephrotoxic and should not be given to patients with renal insufficiency.

Corticosteroids may occasionally be useful in hypercalcemia associated with lymphoma or multiple myeloma. These compounds are not useful for solid tumor-associated hypercalcemia.

Oral *neutral phosphates* can help maintain calcium in the normal range. The dosage is 1 to 3 g/d in divided doses. Diarrhea is the dose-limiting side effect; however, it can often be controlled by diluting the phosphates in large volumes of water. There is no role for intravenous phosphates in the treatment of cancer-associated hypercalcemia.

FOLLOW-UP

Initially, patients need to be seen at least twice a week for serum calcium levels and treatment, if necessary.

DISCUSSION
Prevalence and Incidence

Hypercalcemia occurs in 10 to 20% of cancer patients and is the most frequent serious metabolic disorder associated with cancer. The vast majority of cancer-associated hypercalcemia is seen in association with breast cancer, non-small cell lung cancer, renal cell cancer, head and neck cancer, multiple myeloma, and lymphomas.

Related Basic Science

The pathogenesis of hypercalcemia in cancer patients has been the focus of a great deal of research in the past few years, with a great deal of new information being discovered. In the past it was thought that cancer caused hypercalcemia directly by local destruction of bone and, less often, by the production of "ectopic" parathyroid hormone.

In the early 1940s, it was suggested that the hypercalcemia in these patients was caused by a humoral product of the cancer. Later it was thought that this product was simply ectopic production of parathyroid hormone, and the term *pseudohyperparathyroidism* was used for this entity. More recently, this "humoral factor" was found to increase nephrogenous cyclic GMP production, indicating interaction with parathyroid hormone receptors in the proximal renal tubule; however, these patients also exhibited several phenomena that were opposite from those seen with classic hyperparathyroidism: marked increase in fractional calcium excretion, a striking reduction in 1,25-dihydroxyvitamin D levels, and normal or decreased parathyroid hormone levels. Subsequent work has identified a parathyroid hormone-related protein. It is homologous to parathyroid hormone in only 8 of the first 13 amino acids at the amino-terminal portion. Parathyroid hormone-related protein is elevated in approximately 80% of patients with cancer-related hypercalcemia, with and without bone metastases, and is thought to be the cause of the large majority of hypercalcemia in these patients.

In patients with multiple myeloma, local production of osteoclast-activating factors is responsible for hypercalcemia. These local activating factors are thought to be cytokines, the most prominent being transforming growth factor B. In patients with lymphoma and Hodgkin's disease, calcitriol levels are elevated, presumably as a result of direct production of calcitriol by the tumor cells, and thought to be the cause of the hypercalcemia.

Natural History and Its Modification With Treatment

If the underlying cancer can be successfully treated, the hypercalcemia will resolve. If there is no effective treatment for the cancer and the patient elects to take treatment for the hypercalcemia, it is often possible to control the calcium level and symptoms for several weeks to months. If the hypercalcemia is left untreated, the calcium levels rise and the patient becomes increasingly sleepy. Finally, the patient falls into a coma and dies. The process takes from a few days to a few weeks.

Prevention

There is no effective way to prevent cancer-associated hypercalcemia.

Cost Containment

It is not necessary to perform additional laboratory studies other than a calcium level in patients with hypercalcemia associated with cancer once the diagnosis is established and the treatment program is underway.

REFERENCES

Bajarunas DR. Clinical manifestations of cancer-related hypercalcemia. Semin Oncol 1990;17:16.

Bilezikian JP. Management of acute hypercalcemia. N Engl J Med 1992;326:1196.

Broadus AE, Mangin M, Ikeda K, et al. Humoral hypercalcemia of cancer: Identification of a novel parathyroid hormone-like peptide. N Engl J Med 1988;319:556.

Burtis WJ, Brady TG, Orloff JJ, et al. Immunochemical characterizations of circulating parathyroid hormone-related protein in patients with humoral hypercalcemia of cancer. N Engl J Med 1990;322:1106.

Seymour JF, Gagel RF, Hagemeister FB. Calcitriol production in hypercalcemic normocalcemic patients with non-Hodgkin's lymphoma. Ann Intern Med 1994;121:633.

Stewart AF, Horst R, Deftos LJ, et al. Biochemical evaluation of patients with cancer-associated hypercalcemia: Evidence for humoral and non-humoral groups. N Engl J Med 1980;303:1377.

CHAPTER 3–42

Ectopic Hormone Syndromes (See Section 9, Chapter 47)

Nutritional Disorders
Roland L. Weinsier, M.D., Dr.P.H.

CHAPTER 4–1

Unhealthy Eating Habits
Sarah L. Morgan, M.D., M.S., R.D.

DEFINITION

Nutritional status is the health and functional capacity of an individual in relation to intake, absorption, utilization, and excretion of nutrients. Optimal nutritional status is best maintained by consuming adequate amounts of energy, proteins (essential amino acids), fats (essential fatty acids), fluids, electrolytes, vitamins, and minerals. An imbalance, lack, or excess of food components causes undesirable nutritional status. The food consumption patterns that cause such deficiencies, excesses, or imbalances are called *unhealthy eating habits.*

ETIOLOGY

Unhealthy eating habits may occur in many clinical settings. Growing individuals (infants, adolescents, pregnant and lactating women), as well as individuals with the stress of disease states causing altered nutrient absorption, utilization, losses, or excretion are at risk for nutrient deficiencies, imbalances, or excesses. Specific socioeconomic factors such as limited income, inability to prepare food (i.e., limited mobility or arthritis), and specific target groups, for example, alcoholic individuals, frequently have unhealthy eating habits. Healthy individuals undergoing everyday stresses of modern life (family, work, exercise) do not have increased caloric needs out of proportion to caloric intake; however, such stresses may significantly alter patterns of food selection. Factors such as low fruit and vegetable intake, skipped meals, limited ability to prepare food, and frequent fast food and snack food consumption (intake of foods with high calorie and low nutrient density) are clues to the diagnosis of unhealthy eating habits.

CRITERIA FOR DIAGNOSIS

The diagnosis of unhealthy eating habits is best made by a synthesis of historical, clinical, anthropometric, and biochemical data as defined below. In addition, the presence of coexisting diseases (Table 4–1–1) is a clue to unhealthy eating habits.

CLINICAL MANIFESTATIONS
Subjective

Historically, efforts in nutritional therapeutics have centered around the detection and correction of states of nutrient deficiency. Diagnoses of nutrient deficiencies are still made when there is prolonged nutrient imbalance, in cases of hospital-associated malnutrition, and in undeveloped areas of the worlds; however, excesses of some nutrients are very common in the United States and often result in chronic disease states. The presence of diseases of overconsumption are a historical clue to excess of specific nutrients.

To make a diagnosis of unhealthy eating habits, a thorough nutrition history is essential. This includes questions about height, usual and recent weight, recent loss or gain of body weight, activity level, recent taste change, swallowing problems, nausea, vomiting, diarrhea, and constipation. The integrity of organs functionally related to the gastrointestinal tract including salivary glands, pancreas, liver, and bile ducts should be determined. Social factors such as income available for purchasing food and who does food purchasing and preparation often have an impact on nutritional status. The use of chewing tobacco, snuff, laxatives, alcoholic beverages, pica (the eating of nonfood substances), and vitamin/mineral supplements also affect the nutrition state.

Usual food intake should be assessed by taking a dietary history. Patients may be asked to describe usual food intake either prospectively or retrospectively. A recall of the past 24-hour intake, including amounts and methods of preparation, is frequently used. An open-ended question such as "Tell me what you had to eat yesterday?" can be used. Patients may also be asked to fill out a food frequency questionnaire, which is a list of foods and frequency options to specify how

TABLE 4-1-1. DISEASE STATES RELATED TO NUTRIENT EXCESS

Disease State	Nutrient Excess
Hypertension	Excess sodium, excess calories (obesity)
Atherosclerosis	Excess total fat, saturated fat, cholesterol, excess total calories (obesity)
Obesity	Excess caloric intake
Dental disease	Excess fermentable carbohydrate intake
Osteoporosis	High protein and caffeine intakes
Diabetes mellitus	Excess calories and carbohydrate intake
Cancers	Excess alcohol and total fat intake

often a food is consumed over an extended period. A brief food frequency history, asking how often fruits, vegetables, grain products, meat, fish, poultry, eggs, and milk products are consumed in an average day serves as a good check on the 24-hour recall. Prospectively, patients may keep at least a 3-day diary in which they record all food and snacks. In general, average usual food intakes will be more accurately estimated when done for several days with prospective methods. More specific information, including computerized nutrient intakes, can be obtained with the help of a registered/licensed dietitian.

Objective

Physical Examination

The objective of the nutritional physical examination is to estimate body composition and detect signs of nutrient deficiency or excess. Physical findings such as hypertension, arcus lipoides, tendon xanthomas, bruits, gingivitis, dental caries, kyphosis, and osteoarthritis can be clues to the diagnosis of overconsumption (see Table 4-1-1). The size of the adipose and muscle stores should particularly be assessed. Figure 4-1-1 shows body composition for an "ideal" 70-kg man. Body composition can be broken down into nutrients and tissues. The body composition of a normal woman is slightly different than that of an average man. Reference ideal adiposity is 13 to 17% for a male and 20 to 24% for a female.

Height and weight are two parameters that tell of body composition. The 1983 Metropolitan Life Insurance Tables of Desirable Weight for Men and Women can be used as guidelines. These guidelines have limitations including (1) the data may not be applicable to all ethnic and socioeconomic groups; (2) no information on body fat distribution is included; (3) no correction is made for aging; and (4) concurrent risk factors such as smoking are not taken into account. Overweight is defined as a weight greater than 20% of standard, and underweight is defined as a weight more than 20% below standard. As a rule of thumb, ideal weight for men can be estimated by allowing 106 pounds for the first 5 feet and another 6 pounds for each additional inch. For women, 100 pounds is allowed for the first 5 feet, with 5 pounds for each additional inch. The calculated value is within ± 10% of the ideal body weight. Overweight from excessive muscle mass must be distinguished from excessive adiposity.

The size of fat stores can be estimated by a variety of calculated and anthropometric measurements. The size as well as the distribution of adipose tissue is important, as intraabdominal fat deposition constitutes a greater cardiovascular risk than obesity alone. The body mass index, an indicator of adiposity, is the weight in kilograms divided by the height in meters squared. A body mass index greater than 26.4 for men and 25.8 for women corresponds to greater than 20% above desirable weight for height (obesity). There is an increase in mortality at a body mass index of 30 or greater. Because approximately 50% of body fat is subcutaneous, a variety of skinfold measurements made with skinfold calipers can be used to estimate body adiposity. Tables are available to evaluate the adequacy of various skinfolds.

The midarm muscle circumference can be used as an estimation of somatic (skeletal) muscle mass. The midarm muscle circumference is calculated by the following equation: circumference of nondominant arm taken halfway between the acromion and olecranon process − (3.14 × triceps skinfold in centimeters). The value obtained can be compared with published tables of standards to gauge adequacy.

Routine Laboratory Abnormalities

Many common laboratory tests can be evaluated from a nutritional perspective. A 24-hour urine collection of creatinine is often used to determine creatinine clearance. A creatinine-height index compares an individual's 24-hour urinary creatinine excretion with creatinine excretion expected for a person of the same sex and height. Such a collection is another measure of skeletal muscle mass, as the amount of creatinine formed from creatine phosphate is dependent on the mass of skeletal muscle. As an estimate, men excrete approximately 23 mg/kg of ideal body weight and women excrete approximately 18 mg/kg of ideal body weight. Values below this may be indicative of diminished skeletal muscle mass. A 24-hour urine for urea nitrogen can be used to calculate nitrogen balance.

The visceral muscle compartment of the body contains carrier proteins and immunoglobulins. The degree of catabolic stress and the size of the visceral muscle compartment can be estimated by the level of normalcy of proteins such as albumin, prealbumin, transferrin, and retinol-binding protein.

The hemoglobin and hematocrit should be evaluated. A differential diagnosis of a microcytic anemia is iron, copper, and pyridoxine deficiency. A differential diagnosis of a macrocytic anemia is folate and vitamin B_{12} deficiency. It must, however, be realized that anemia is a late finding of nutritional deficiencies.

Vitamin and mineral levels can also be assayed in a variety of tissues such as plasma, serum, red blood cells, white blood cells, and urine. Blood vitamin levels that are frequently assayed include vitamin A, thiamin, riboflavin, pyridoxine, vitamin C, plasma folate, red blood cell folate, vitamin B_{12}, vitamin D, and vitamin E.

PLANS
Diagnostic
Differential Diagnosis

As warranted on the basis of the physical examination, specialized tests may be used to further define body consumption and verify suspicions of nutrient deficiency or excess.

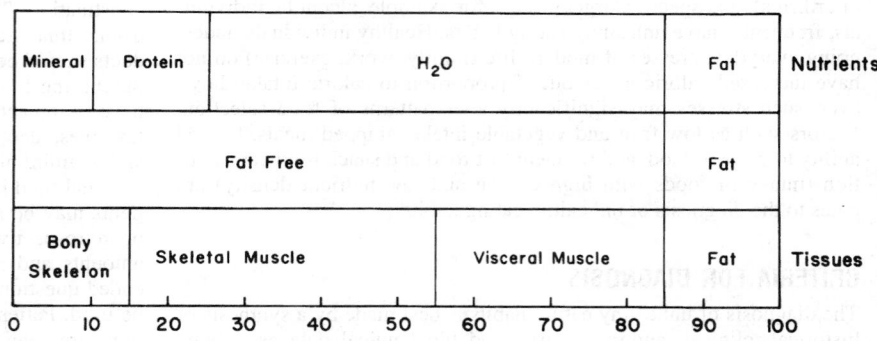

Figure 4-1-1. Body composition of a reference 70-kg man.

Recommended Approach

Table 4–1–2 lists additional tests to determine body composition; however, many of these are currently useful on a research basis. The history, physical examination, anthropometrics, and laboratory tests outlined previously constitute the recommended approach to making a diagnosis of unhealthy eating habits and nutrient deficiency or excess.

Therapeutic

The treatment of unhealthy eating habits is *dietary counseling* (nutrition education). Such counseling is most expertly done by a registered/licensed dietitian or a physician trained in clinical nutrition, but should be reinforced by the physician. Referral patterns should be established for expert dietary counseling in office practice.

Guidelines for a prudent diet have been recommended by the U.S. Department of Agriculture, the U.S. Department of Health and Human Services, the National Research Committee on Diet and Health, the American Heart Association, the Surgeon General of the United States, and the American Cancer Society. The Food Guide Pyramid is the visual representation of these guidelines (Figure 4–1–2). The majority of foods in the diet should include breads, cereal, rice, pasta, fruits, and vegetables. Protein foods chosen should be lean (i.e., 93% fat-free, skin removed) and dairy products should be low-fat. Paying attention to labels can help with prescription of healthy and therapeutic diets.

Eat a Variety of Foods. As no one food supplies all essential nutrients, several servings from the bread, cereal, rice, and pasta group; fruit group; vegetable group; milk, yogurt, and cheese group; and meat, poultry, fish, dry beans, eggs, and nuts group should be selected every day. The number of servings selected depends on age, sex, and life cycle period (e.g., pregnancy and lactation).

Vegetarianism. Alternative meal patterns such as vegetarianism are also conducive to good health. Vegetarianism refers to a consumption pattern omitting animal products, especially meat. Eggs and poultry products, milk products, and fish may or may not be included in the meal plan. Vegetarian diets tend to be lower in sodium, total and saturated fat, and iron, and higher in fiber and complex carbohydrates than the general American diet. Vitamin B_{12} deficiency may occur in strict vegetarians, who consume no animal products (vegans). While balancing of complementary plant proteins to ensure adequate essential amino acid intake was of concern in the past, it is now believed that an adequate quantity and quality of protein will be consumed if a wide variety of vegetables, legumes, nuts, and whole-grain bread and cereal products are consumed every day.

Vitamin Supplements. Approximately 35 to 40% of Americans consume vitamin/mineral supplements. Vitamin/mineral supplements are not necessary for the entire population of the United States. Vitamin supplements are indicated for the following persons: (1) women who are pregnant or breastfeeding; (2) newborns are commonly given a single dose of vitamin K to prevent bleeding; (3) infants who are given iron-fortified cereals starting at approximately 3 to 4 months of age to prevent iron deficiency; (4) some vegetarians who may not be receiving adequate calcium, iron, zinc, and vitamin B_{12} and may require supplementation; (5) individuals on very low calorie diets (<1000–1200 kcal/d), who may not meet their needs for all nutrients; (6) some individuals with high-risk lifestyles such as persons of low socioeconomic status, anorexics, and pregnant teenagers who may not have adequate vitamin and mineral intakes; (7) individuals with disease states causing altered nutrient absorption, utilization, or excretion; and (8) women in the periconceptual period, for whom folic acid supplements have been found to be useful in the prevention of neural tube defects. Taking a dietary history to determine usual food patterns is the best way to gauge if vitamin/minerals are necessary for a particular patient.

Because vitamin preparations are regulated as foods by the U.S. Food and Drug Administration, vitamin/mineral supplements are at the present not tightly regulated; however, there are regulations that prevent unproven claims to be placed on supplements. There are no regulations covering the bioavailability of vitamin/mineral supplements, and the formulation of vitamin supplements can change without notice. Vitamins with the designation USP (United States Pharmacopeia) can be relied on to contain vitamins in amounts specified by the Pharmacopeia of the United States; however, vitamin pill bottles now show information in the food labeling format. Some generalizations about the composition of multiple vitamin pills can be made:

- Most fat-soluble vitamins will not be present in more than 200% of the Recommended Dietary Allowance to avoid vitamin toxicity syndromes.
- Vitamins containing 400 μg of folate are not available without a prescription because of the possibility of exacerbating the neurologic sequelae of coexisting undiagnosed B_{12} deficiency with folate therapy.
- Vitamin K is generally not present in multiple vitamins because of the possibility of interaction in patients on coumadin therapy.

Vitamin/mineral supplements can be classified into two general categories: replacement-type and therapeutic-type vitamins. Replacement vitamin/mineral supplements generally contain vitamins and minerals in amounts of 50 to 150% of the daily value. Such vitamins are correctly prescribed as nutrient supplements to food intake. Therapeutic vitamins supplements contain vitamins and minerals in the range of 200 to 1000% of the daily value. Such vitamins are best used to treat vitamin and mineral deficiency states; medical illness with problems in nutrient absorption, utilization, or excretion; or inborn errors of metabolism. Whenever possible, single vitamin preparations should be used to replace specific documented nutrient deficiencies. Physicians should be aware of the specific content of vitamins before they are prescribed.

Maintain a Healthy Weight. Both obesity and the state of underweight carry increased morbidity and mortality. Obesity is associated with degenerative joint disease; cancers of the endometrium, breast, and gallbladder; coronary artery disease; diabetes (insulin resistance); hepatobiliary disease; hyperlipidemia; and hypertension. Avoidance of foods with high-fat content, foods with high concentrations of simple sugars (e.g., low-nutrient-density foods), and moderate exercise are important in the maintenance of ideal body weight.

Choose a Diet Low in Fat, Saturated Fat, and Cholesterol. Elevated cholesterol levels (total cholesterol > 200 mg/dL, low-density lipoprotein level > 130 mg/dL) have been found to be independent risk factors for coronary artery disease. A diet that restricts total fat, saturated fat, and cholesterol will help achieve the goals of less than 300 mg cholesterol per day and less than 30% of calories as fat. Fat intake can be reduced by limiting animal protein servings to 4 to 6 ounces per day (6 ounces is equal to the size of two decks of cards); limiting egg yolks to 3 to 4 per week; using low-fat dairy products; limiting added fats such as oils, margarine, and salad dressing; and using low-fat cooking methods (baking, grilling, roasting, boiling, broiling). The use of fats that are more liquid at room temperature will increase the intake of monounsaturated and polyunsaturated fats and decrease the intake of saturated fats.

TABLE 4–1–2. METHODS OF MEASURING BODY COMPOSITION

Method	Body Parameter Measured
Isotope dilution (deuterium or tritium)	Total body water
Total body K-40 counting	Fat-free mass
Urinary creatinine excretion	Fat-free mass and muscle mass
Anthropometrics	
Skinfolds	Fat mass
Midarm muscle circumference	Muscle mass
Neutron activation analysis	Absolute content of calcium, sodium, chloride, phosphorus, and nitrogen in the body
Urinary 3-methylhistidine	Skeletal muscle mass
Single- and dual-photon absorptiometry	Bone mineral content
Bioelectrical impedance and conductivity	Fat-free mass
Computed tomography	Organ size, fat, fat-free, and bone mass
Magnetic resonance imaging	Total body water

A Guide to Daily Food Choices

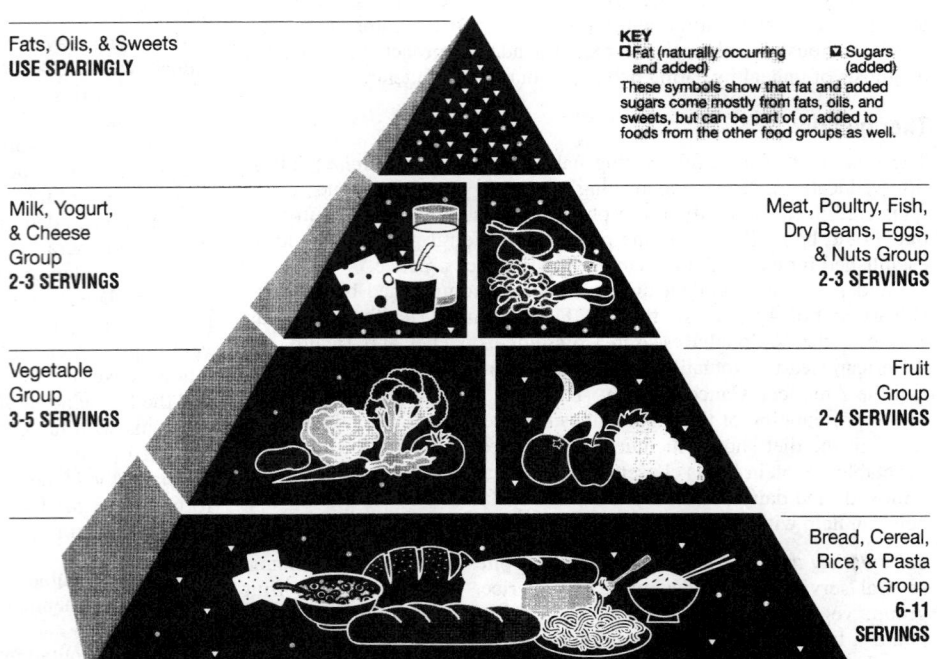

Fats, Oils, & Sweets
USE SPARINGLY

KEY
□ Fat (naturally occurring   ☑ Sugars
   and added)   (added)
These symbols show that fat and added sugars come mostly from fats, oils, and sweets, but can be part of or added to foods from the other food groups as well.

Milk, Yogurt, & Cheese Group
2-3 SERVINGS

Meat, Poultry, Fish, Dry Beans, Eggs, & Nuts Group
2-3 SERVINGS

Vegetable Group
3-5 SERVINGS

Fruit Group
2-4 SERVINGS

Bread, Cereal, Rice, & Pasta Group
6-11 SERVINGS

Figure 4–1–2. The food guide pyramid. *(Source: U.S. Department of Agriculture/U.S. Department of Health and Human Services).*

Choose a Diet with Plenty of Vegetables, Fruits, and Grain Products. Foods such as whole-grain breads and cereals, dried beans and peas, fruits, and vegetables are high in fiber and complex carbohydrates and low in calories. An intake of 20 to 35 g of fiber is suggested every day. To achieve such a fiber intake it is necessary to eat a serving of whole-grain bread or cereal and several servings of high-fiber fruits and vegetables each day. High-fiber food items are useful in the treatment of hyperlipidemia, impaired glucose tolerance, obesity, and constipation.

Use Sugar Only in Moderation. Foods containing simple sugars such as white and brown sugar, honey, and syrups (such as candies, cookies, cakes, and soft drinks) are high in calories and low in nutrients. Such foods are implicated in the causation of dental caries and obesity. Substitution of lower-sugar products such as fresh fruits and use of spices and flavorings instead of sugar are preferable.

Use Salt and Sodium Only in Moderation. Approximately 25% of Americans have hypertension and approximately 30% of the hypertensive population is sensitive to excessive sodium intake. The National Research Council has suggested an intake of 1100 to 3300 mg of sodium per day. For comparison purposes, this is approximately the amount of total sodium contained in one-half to one teaspoon of table salt (1150–2300 mg Na^+). Such a guideline requires removing the salt shaker from the table, using herbs instead of sodium salts, omitting foods containing sodium such as chips and pretzels, limiting foods such as vegetables canned with salt, and moderating use of condiments such as soy sauce and seasoned salts. Such recommendations will generally not be deleterious for non-sodium-sensitive individuals; however, some groups such as the elderly may risk dehydration by unnecessarily restricting sodium.

If You Drink Alcoholic Beverages, Do So in Moderation. Alcohol is a toxin to almost every tissue in the body. Excessive intake is related to cirrhosis of the liver. Smoking and alcohol act synergistically to increase the risk for cancers of the mouth, larynx, and esophagus. In addition, elevations in blood pressure are related to alcohol consumption of more than two drinks per day. Moderation is defined as no more than two drinks per day, and any alcohol consumption during pregnancy is considered excessive. One drink is defined as a 12-ounce glass of beer, a 5-ounce glass of wine, or 1.5 fluid ounces of distilled spirits.

Education about specific desired eating habits is critical to the treatment of unhealthy eating habits. It is important to teach patients which foods are optimal choices rather than spending too much time teaching which foods are poor choices. Such education must be done in terms of foods rather than specifying milligrams of nutrients or caloric levels to patients. Registered dietitians are uniquely qualified to translate dietary prescriptions into food patterns. The use of printed educational materials and food models is preferable during dietary instructions. Maintenance of food intake logs is useful in determining whether desired food consumption patterns have been reinforced and changed.

FOLLOW-UP

Follow-up for unhealthy dietary habits should be done at the same time of follow-up for other medical problems such as hypertension. Follow-up within 1 to 2 weeks of an initial dietary counseling session is necessary to ensure understanding of the desired new behaviors. For weight loss, weekly follow-up visits have been demonstrated to be beneficial. Referral to a registered/licensed dietitian is also effective.

DISCUSSION
Prevalence and Incidence

Of the ten leading causes of death in the United States in 1987, five were associated with dietary patterns (coronary heart disease, cancer, stroke, diabetes mellitus, chronic liver disease, and atherosclerosis). It is estimated that 1.5 million of the 2.1 million total deaths in 1987 were related to dietary causes.

Related Basic Science

The recommended dietary allowances (RDAs) have been set as nutrient requirements that exceed the nutrient needs of almost all individuals. Tables 4–1–3 and 4–1–4 display the 1989 RDAs and estimates of safe and adequate daily intakes for biotin, pantothenic acid, copper, manganese, fluoride, chromium, and molybdenum. In contrast to the RDAs for other nutrients, the RDA for energy is not a recommendation that exceeds the requirements of most individuals; rather, energy intake is expressed as an average requirement. Because free-living subjects have

TABLE 4-1-3. RECOMMENDED DIETARY ALLOWANCES,[a] REVISED 1989, FOOD AND NUTRITION BOARD, NATIONAL ACADEMY OF SCIENCES–NATIONAL RESEARCH COUNCIL (Designed for the Maintenance of Good Nutrition of Practically All Healthy People in the United States)

Category	Age (years) or Condition	Weight[b] (kg)	Weight[b] (lb)	Height[b] (cm)	Height[b] (in.)	Protein (g)	Vita-min A (μg RE)[c]	Vita-min D (μg)[d]	Vita-min E (mg α-TE)[e]	Vita-min K (μg)	Vita-min C (mg)	Thia-min (mg)	Ribo-flavin (mg)	Niacin (mg NE)[f]	Vita-min B6 (mg)	Fo-late (μg)	Vitamin B12 (μg)	Cal-cium (mg)	Phos-phorus (mg)	Mag-nesium (mg)	Iron (mg)	Zinc (mg)	Iodine (μg)	Sele-nium (μg)
Infants	0.0–0.5	6	13	60	24	13	375	7.5	3	5	30	0.3	0.4	5	0.3	25	0.3	400	300	40	6	5	40	10
	0.5–1.0	9	20	71	28	14	375	10	4	10	35	0.4	0.5	6	0.5	35	0.5	600	500	60	10	5	50	15
Children	1–3	13	29	90	35	16	400	10	6	15	40	0.7	0.8	9	1.0	50	0.7	800	800	80	10	10	70	20
	4–6	20	44	112	44	24	500	10	7	20	45	0.9	1.1	12	1.1	75	1.0	800	800	120	10	10	90	20
	7–10	28	62	132	52	28	700	10	7	30	45	1.0	1.2	13	1.4	100	1.4	800	800	170	10	10	120	30
Males	11–14	45	99	157	62	45	1000	10	10	45	50	1.3	1.5	17	1.7	150	2.0	1200	1200	270	12	15	150	40
	15–18	66	145	176	69	59	1000	10	10	65	60	1.5	1.8	20	2.0	200	2.0	1200	1200	400	12	15	150	50
	19–24	72	160	177	70	58	1000	10	10	70	60	1.5	1.7	19	2.0	200	2.0	1200	1200	350	10	15	150	70
	25–50	79	174	176	70	63	1000	5	10	80	60	1.5	1.7	19	2.0	200	2.0	800	800	350	10	15	150	70
	51+	77	170	173	68	63	1000	5	10	80	60	1.2	1.4	15	2.0	200	2.0	800	800	350	10	15	150	70
Females	11–14	46	101	157	62	46	800	10	8	45	50	1.1	1.3	15	1.4	150	2.0	1200	1200	280	15	12	150	45
	15–18	55	120	163	64	44	800	10	8	55	60	1.1	1.3	15	1.5	180	2.0	1200	1200	300	15	12	150	50
	19–24	58	128	164	65	46	800	10	8	60	60	1.1	1.3	15	1.6	180	2.0	1200	1200	280	15	12	150	55
	25–50	63	138	163	64	50	800	5	8	65	60	1.1	1.3	15	1.6	180	2.0	800	800	280	15	12	150	55
	51+	65	143	160	63	50	800	5	8	65	60	1.0	1.2	13	1.6	180	2.0	800	800	280	10	12	150	55
Pregnant						60	800	10	10	65	70	1.5	1.6	17	2.2	400	2.2	1200	1200	320	30	15	175	65
Lactating	1st 6 months					65	1300	10	12	65	95	1.6	1.8	20	2.1	280	2.6	1200	1200	355	15	19	200	75
	2nd 6 months					62	1200	10	11	65	90	1.6	1.7	20	2.1	260	2.6	1200	1200	340	15	16	200	75

[a]The allowances, expressed as average daily intakes over time, are intended to provide for individual variations among most normal persons as they live in the United States under usual environmental stresses. Diets should be based on a variety of common foods in order to provide other nutrients for which human requirements have been less well defined.

[b]Weights and heights of Reference Adults are actual medians for the U.S. population of the designated age, as reported by NHANES II. The median weights and heights of those under 19 years of age were taken from Hamill et al. (1979, see pp. 16–17). The use of these figures does not imply that the height-to-weight ratios are ideal.

[c]Retinol equivalents: 1 retinol equivalent = 1 μg retinol or 6 μg β-carotene. See text for calculation of vitamin A activity of diets as retinol equivalents.

[d]As cholecalciferol. 10 μg cholecalciferol = 400 IU of vitamin D.

[e]α-Tocopherol equivalents: 1 mg d-α tocopherol = 1 α-TE. See text for variation in allowances and calculation of vitamin E activity of the diet as α-tocopherol equivalents.

[f]1 NE (niacin equivalent) is equal to 1 mg of niacin or 60 mg of dietary tryptophan.

Source: Recommended dietary allowances. 10th ed. Copyright 1989 by the National Academy of Sciences. Courtesy of the National Academy Press, Washington, DC. Reproduced with permission.

TABLE 4–1–4. ESTIMATED SAFE AND ADEQUATE DAILY DIETARY INTAKES OF SELECTED VITAMINS AND MINERALS[a]

| | | | Trace Elements[b] | | | | | |
Category	Age (years)	Biotin (μg)	Pantothenic Acid (mg)	Copper (mg)	Manganese (mg)	Fluoride (mg)	Chromium (μg)	Molybdenum (μg)
Infants	0–0.5	10	2	0.4–0.6	0.3–0.6	0.1–0.5	10–40	15–30
	0.5–1	15	3	0.6–0.7	0.6–1.0	0.2–1.0	20–60	20–40
Children and adolescents	1–3	20	3	0.7–1.0	1.0–1.5	0.5–1.5	20–80	25–50
	4–6	25	3–4	1.0–1.5	1.5–2.0	1.0–2.5	30–120	30–75
	7–10	30	4–5	1.0–2.0	2.0–3.0	1.5–2.5	50–200	50–150
	11+	30–100	4–7	1.5–2.5	2.0–5.0	1.5–2.5	50–200	75–250
Adults		30–100	4–7	1.5–3.0	2.0–5.0	1.5–4.0	50–200	75–250

[a]Because there is less information on which to base allowances, these figures are not given in the main table of RDAs and are provided here in the form of ranges of recommended intakes.
[b]Because the toxic levels for many trace elements may be only several times usual intakes, the upper levels for the trace elements given in this table should not be habitually exceeded.
Source: Recommended Dietary Allowances. 10th ed. Copyright 1989 by the National Academy of Sciences. Courtesy of the National Academy Press, Washington, DC. Reproduced with permission.

free access to food and unrestricted energy expenditure, a balance must be reached for each individual in terms of energy intake and output. At present, the RDAs establish nutrient intakes for optimum metabolic and physiologic function, but do not necessarily address the issue of intake levels for disease prevention. For example, optimal ascorbate intake for prevention of vitamin C deficiency is likely different than levels recommended for the prevention of cancer.

Natural History and Its Modification with Treatment

Unhealthy eating habits may lead to states of deficiency or to chronic diseases of overconsumption. Epidemiologic, animal, and human trials have established the relationships between nutrients and disease. Modification of dietary patterns can have a significant impact on leading causes of death in industrialized societies.

Prevention

The best prevention of both overconsumption and underconsumption of nutrients is dietary counseling and education.

Cost Containment

Unhealthy eating habits can generally be diagnosed by a careful nutrition-related history and physical examination. More sophisticated laboratory and body composition tests should be requested only when there will be a difference in therapy based on their results. The selection of a healthy eating pattern has the possibility of saving millions of health care dollars.

REFERENCES

Committee on Diet and Health, Food and Nutrition Board, Commission on Life Sciences, National Research Council. Diet and health implications for reducing chronic disease risk. Washington, DC: Academy Press, 1989.
Frisancho AR. Anthropometric standards for the assessment of growth and nutritional status. Ann Arbor, University of Michigan Press, 1990.
National Research Council. Recommended dietary allowances. Washington, DC: National Academy Press, 1989.
Nutrition and your health: Dietary guidelines for Americans. 3rd ed. Washington, DC: USDA and USDHHS, 1990 (Home and Garden Bulletin No. 232); Food Guide Pyramid, Washington, DC: USDA and USDHHS, 1990
Shils ME, Olson JA, Shike M, eds. Modern nutrition in health and disease. 8th ed. Philadelphia: Lea & Febiger, 1994

CHAPTER 4–2

Hospital-Associated Malnutrition

Douglas C. Heimburger, M.D., M.S., Roland L. Weinsier, M.D., Dr.P.H.

DEFINITION

Hospital-associated malnutrition encompasses the range of nutrient deficiencies that appear as a result of inadequate nutritional support of patients with increased requirements or losses from illness.

ETIOLOGY

By far, the most common form of malnutrition in the hospital setting is that of protein–calorie malnutrition, manifesting as marasmus and kwashiorkor. Marasmus, or severe cachexia, is end-stage calorie deficiency; kwashiorkor is a maladaptive state developing during catabolic stress with protein deficiency.

CRITERIA FOR DIAGNOSIS

A high level of suspicion for the presence of protein–calorie malnutrition should occur when an acutely ill patient has been hospitalized for 2 or more weeks without aggressive nutritional support or when a patient presents to the hospital with a chronic wasting illness. Typical features

and laboratory findings in patients with marasmus and kwashiorkor are listed in Table 4–2–1.

When kwashiorkor is suspected, the diagnosis is usually confirmed by a serum albumin level less than 2.8 g/dL and at least one of the following: (1) poor wound healing, decubitus ulcers, skin breakdown; (2) easy hair pluckability (three or more hairs at a time removed easily and painlessly from the top of the head); (3) edema.

The diagnosis of marasmus is made on the basis of severe cachexia supported by anthropometric measurements revealing a triceps skinfold thickness (TSF) less than 3 mm and a midarm muscle circumference (MAMC) less than 15 cm (MAMC = arm circumference in cm − 3.14 × TSF in cm). The 24-hour urinary creatinine excretion is markedly reduced as compared with standards based on height (creatinine–height index).

CLINICAL MANIFESTATIONS
Subjective

Although multiple nutrient deficiencies may develop as a result of illness, kwashiorkor typically occurs in an acutely ill hospitalized patient

TABLE 4–2–1. COMPARISON OF MARASMUS AND KWASHIORKOR

	Marasmus	Kwashiorkor
Clinical setting	Decreased calorie intake	Decreased protein intake during stress state
Time course to develop	Months or years	Weeks
Clinical features	Starved appearance	Well-nourished appearance
	Weight <80% standard for height	Easy hair pluckability
	Triceps skinfold <3 mm	Edema
	Midarm muscle circumference <15 cm	
Laboratory findings	Creatinine–height index <60% standard	Serum albumin <2.8 g/dL
		Total iron binding capacity <200 µg/dL
		Lymphocytes< 1500/µL
		Anergy
Clinical course	Reasonably preserved responsiveness to short-term stress	Infections
		Poor wound healing, decubitus ulcers, skin breakdown
Mortality	Low, unless related to underlying disease	High

Source: Weinsier RL, Heimburger DC, Butterworth CE Jr. Handbook of clinical nutrition. 2nd ed. St. Louis: Mosby, 1989: 133. Reproduced with permission from the publisher and author.

who has suffered from multiple trauma, burns, or severe infection but who has not received adequate protein intake.

Marasmus develops more slowly over months or years as energy reserves slowly become depleted from failure to receive adequate calorie support. The typical time course for development is shown in Figure 4–2–1. Combined marasmus–kwashiorkor may develop when acute catabolic stress is superimposed on the semistarved cachectic individual.

Objective

Physical Examination

Patients with kwashiorkor usually present a well-nourished appearance, but tend to have evidence of poor wound healing with tendency to develop pressure sores, easy hair pluckability, and edema.

Marasmus is characterized by a starved appearance, including diminished skinfold thickness (triceps skinfold often less than 3 mm) and temporal and interosseous muscle wastage.

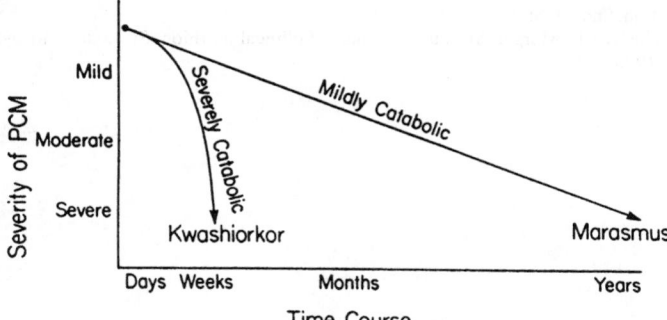

Figure 4–2–1 Time course of protein-calorie malnutrition (PCM). *Source: Weinsier RL, Heimburger DC, Butterworth CE Jr. Handbook of clinical nutrition. 2nd ed. St. Louis: Mosby, 1989. Reproduced with permission from the publisher and author.*

Routine Laboratory Abnormalities

Laboratory findings in kwashiorkor include reduced circulating proteins (serum albumin generally less than 2.8 g/dL, and total iron binding capacity generally less than 200 µg/dL); lymphocyte count is often reduced (less than 1500/µl); and anergy is generally present on routine skin testing.

Laboratory tests are often remarkably normal in marasmus, except perhaps for slight reductions in hematocrit and serum albumin. The latter tends to remain greater than 2.8 g/dL in the absence of acute stress or kwashiorkor.

PLANS
Diagnostic

It is important that the findings used to diagnose kwashiorkor not be caused by other coexisting conditions. Reduced serum albumin, although characteristic of the kwashiorkor state, may be a result of infection, trauma, liver failure, or protein-wasting disorders such as nephrotic syndrome. As well, a normal value may exist even in the presence of kwashiorkor if the patient is receiving albumin or plasma infusions. Although a low serum albumin level associated with physiologic stress (e.g., sepsis and trauma) does not necessarily indicate insufficient nutritional support, failure of the albumin level to rise after the stress subsides suggests that nutritional support is inadequate.

Because marasmus is an anthropometric diagnosis, it is not confounded by other conditions. If all body fat stores have been exhausted and muscle mass is depleted, marasmus is present by definition.

Therapeutic

The therapeutic approach to protein–calorie malnutrition is discussed in Chapter 4–3. The presence of kwashiorkor is associated with a high risk of medical and surgical complications and a high mortality rate. Consequently, nutritional support should be provided immediately, with the aim of meeting the patient's calorie and protein needs as quickly as possible. As marasmus is a chronic, fairly well-adapted form of starvation, rather than an acute illness, it should be treated cautiously. Although nutritional support is necessary, overly aggressive repletion can result in severe, even life-threatening metabolic imbalances such as hypophosphatemia and cardiorespiratory failure.

FOLLOW-UP

Patients with kwashiorkor are generally both acutely and severely ill and at great risk of medical and surgical complications. Hence, assessment and follow-up need to be done almost daily until there is a clear indication of a rise in albumin and appropriate responsiveness to surgical and/or medical interventions. Patients with the more chronic cachexia and marasmus can be followed as outpatients, monitoring weight, dietary pattern, and laboratory values as needed to document steady improvement in nutritional status. These are dealt with in more detail in Chapter 4–3.

DISCUSSION
Prevalence and Incidence

Persons with apparent adequate nutrient intake can become malnourished as a result of acute or chronic diseases that alter nutrient intake or metabolism (secondary malnutrition). This can occur in any context, but the acute care hospital setting dramatically illustrates the intricate relationship between nutrition and illness and the vital role nutritional support plays in influencing the outcome of the disease process. Protein–calorie malnutrition affects approximately one half of patients hospitalized for 2 or more weeks on general medical or surgical wards in U.S. hospitals. Patients with evidence of malnutrition have significantly longer average hospital stays and higher mortality rates and a greater frequency of surgical complications. Kwashiorkor in the United States occurs mainly in connection with acute, life-threatening illnesses such as trauma and sepsis or nearly any other illness seen in an intensive care unit.

Related Basic Science

In the presence of severe physiologic stress, protein and calorie requirements are increased at a time when intake is often reduced. Levels of both insulin and the counterregulatory hormones glucagon, cortisol, and catecholamines are increased. Cytokines such as tumor necrosis factor and interleukins are also elevated, and mediate the stress response. This results in increased energy expenditure in spite of starvation, proteolysis, and gluconeogenesis to provide energy-yielding glucose, markedly increased ureagenesis and urinary urea nitrogen excretion, and increased fatty acid utilization. This metabolic response reflects marked maladaptation to starvation (Table 4–2–2). The classic setting for the development of kwashiorkor is the acutely ill individual receiving routine intravenous solutions of 5% dextrose who is found to have poor responsiveness to antibiotics or delayed wound healing over the course of the subsequent few weeks. Although the etiologic mechanisms are not clear, it appears that the adaptive response of protein sparing normally seen in starvation is blocked by the physiologic stress and by carbohydrate infusion.

Marasmus represents the most severe or "end-stage" form of cachexia in which essentially all fat stores have been depleted as a result of starvation. Illnesses producing marasmus in the United States are chronic and indolent, such as cancer, malabsorption, and chronic pulmonary, cardiac, and renal diseases. In the absence of acute stress, marasmus represents a relatively well-adapted state of semistarvation in which the resting metabolic rate falls between 10 and 30%, slowing the rate of weight loss. Circulating insulin, counterregulatory hormone, and cytokine levels tend to be reduced, fatty acid utilization is increased, and the rate of endogenous protein breakdown is relatively slow. After about 10 days with total starvation, the unstressed individual's protein losses will amount to only 12 to 18 g/d, in contrast to losses of 100 g or more in patients with severe sepsis, trauma, or burns.

Natural History and Its Modification with Treatment

As shown in Figure 4–2–1, kwashiorkor can develop in as few as 10 days. The presence of full-blown kwashiorkor is an ominous sign. In this setting surgical wounds often dehisce, pressure sores develop, gastroparesis and diarrhea may occur with enteral feeding, the risk of gastrointestinal bleeding from stress ulceration is increased, and death from overwhelming infection frequently occurs despite antibiotic therapy. The contribution of kwashiorkor to mortality, independently from that of the underlying illness, is uncertain, but is probably quite significant. Recovery from marasmus, if uncomplicated by acute stress, is successful in almost every case if nutritional support is provided judiciously. Mortality from marasmus is related more to the underlying disease process than to the semistarved state per se.

Prevention

Malnutrition is more easily prevented than treated. The nutritionally "high-risk" patient tends to have one or more of the following characteristics:

- Gross underweight
- Recent loss of more than 10% of usual body weight
- Alcoholism

TABLE 4–2–2. PHYSIOLOGIC CHARACTERISTICS OF HYPO- AND HYPERMETABOLIC STATES

Metabolic Parameter	Hypometabolic, Nonstressed (Cachectic, Marasmic)	Hypermetabolic, Stressed (Kwashiorkor Risk)
Catecholamines, glucagon, cortisol, insulin	↓	↑
Metabolic rate	↓	↑
Proteolysis, gluconeogenesis	↓	↑
Urea excretion	↓	↑
Fat catabolism, fatty acid utilization	↑	↑
Adaptation to starvation	Normal	Abnormal

↓, decreased; ↑, increased.

Source: *Weinsier RL, Heimburger DC, Butterworth CE Jr. Handbook of clinical nutrition. 2nd ed. St. Louis: Mosby, 1989: 138. Reproduced with permission from the publisher and author.*

- NPO status for more than about 5 days while on simple intravenous solutions
- Protracted nutrient losses, such as from malabsorption, fistulas, draining abscesses, or renal dialysis
- Increased metabolic demands, such as from trauma, burns, or sepsis
- Use of medications with antinutrient or catabolic properties, such as steroids, immunosuppressants, and antitumor agents

The presence of any of these characteristics is a warning that the patient may be at increased risk for malnutrition and that efforts should be taken to monitor needs and provide support as indicated.

Cost Containment

The complications associated with kwashiorkor can be very costly. Prevention and adequate therapy are the keys to cost containment.

The laboratory tests required for the diagnosis of protein–calorie malnutrition are easily and inexpensively obtained. In most cases of hospital-associated malnutrition, support can be provided by oral intake or by enteral tube feeding. The more expensive parenteral route should be reserved for patients who have high nutrient requirements and cannot tolerate enteral feeding or need to avoid using the intestinal tract for therapeutic reasons.

REFERENCES

Blackburn GL, Bistrian BR, Maini BS, et al. Nutritional and metabolic assessment of the hospitalized patient. J Parenter Enter Nutr 1977;1:11.

Coats KG, Morgan SL, Bartolucci AA, Weinsier RL. Hospital-associated malnutrition: A re-evaluation 12 years later. J Am Diet Assoc 1993;93:27.

McMahon MM, Bistrian BR. The physiology of nutritional assessment and therapy in protein-calorie malnutrition. Dis Month 1990;36:378.

Weinsier RL, Heimburger DC, Butterworth CE Jr. Handbook of clinical nutrition. 2nd ed. St. Louis: Mosby, 1989.

Weinsier RL, Morgan SL. Fundamentals of clinical nutrition. St. Louis: Mosby, 1993.

CHAPTER 4–3
Inadequate Nutritional Support
Douglas C. Heimburger, M.D., M.S., and John L. Rombeau, M.D.

DEFINITION

The term *nutritional support* comprises the means through which essential nutrients, including calories, protein, essential fatty acids, vitamins, minerals, and trace elements, are provided to patients. It often implies involuntary means such as enteral and parenteral nutrition, but can include methods of increasing the adequacy of oral nutrient intake.

ETIOLOGY

Inadequate nutritional support occurs in two major clinical settings in the United States: acute and chronic illnesses. Acute illnesses, particularly catastrophic ones, cause substantial increases in nutrient requirements, particularly for calories, protein, and water-soluble vitamins, yet often result in complete cessation of nutrient intake. Chronic illnesses are sometimes associated with mild or moderate increases in the requirements for calories and protein, and may or may not be attended by reductions in intake.

CRITERIA FOR DIAGNOSIS
Suggestive

Inadequate nutritional support exists when a patient's nutritional intake is said to be inadequate for more than 5 days.

Definitive

There is no definitive means of diagnosing inadequate nutritional support.

CLINICAL MANIFESTATIONS
Subjective

The major cause of nutrient imbalance in ill persons is the underlying illness, which increases nutrient requirements and/or decreases intake. Nutrient intake is further compromised by limited income in some outpatients, but insufficient food supply is not the major cause of malnutrition in the U.S. patient population.

Outpatients with chronic illnesses sometimes complain of anorexia and weight loss. There are no symptoms of inadequate nutrient intake in acutely ill inpatients. They rarely complain of hunger, are generally unaware of weight loss, and rarely know when their complications are related to malnutrition.

Objective

The characteristic physical findings and laboratory test results in malnourished patients are discussed in Chapter 4–2. There are no physical findings or laboratory tests that alone indicate adequate or inadequate nutritional support. For example, although it may signify malnutrition, a low or decreasing serum albumin level does not necessarily reflect inadequate nutritional support. Rather, the adequacy of nutritional support is determined by a comparison of nutrient requirements with nutrient intake (i.e., nutrient balance). For example, energy expenditure, which is synonymous with calorie requirements, is most accurately estimated by measuring oxygen consumption (indirect calorimetry). In the absence of this capability, basal energy expenditure (BEE), expressed as kilocalories per day, can be estimated from height, weight, age, and gender using the Harris–Benedict equations:

$$\text{Women: BEE} = 655.10 + 9.56W + 1.85H - 4.68A$$

$$\text{Men: BEE} = 66.47 + 13.75W + 5.00H - 6.76A$$

where W = weight in kilograms, H = height in centimeters and A = age in years. Actual calorie requirements are estimated by adjusting the BEE by a factor that accounts for the stress of illness. With few exceptions, hospitalized patients have actual energy expenditures between 120 and 150% of basal, so multiplying the BEE by 1.2 to 1.5 yields a range that estimates the energy expenditure of most individuals. The lower value is used for patients without evidence of significant physiologic stress; the upper value is used for patients with marked stress, such as from sepsis or trauma.

As urea is a major by-product of protein catabolism, the amount of urinary urea nitrogen (UUN) excreted each day can be used to estimate the rate of protein catabolism (requirement) and to determine whether protein intake is adequate. Total protein loss can be calculated from the UUN as follows:

$$\text{protein loss (g)} = (\text{24-hour UUN} + 4) \times 6.25$$

The UUN must be expressed in grams per 24 hours. The 4 added to it represents a liberal estimate of the unmeasured nitrogen lost in the urine (e.g., creatinine and uric acid) and in sweat, hair, skin, and stool. The factor 6.25 (g protein/g nitrogen) converts from nitrogen to dietary protein.

In hospitalized patients, oral nutrient intake is calculated by dietitians, generally after noting which foods are absent from food trays returned to the dietary department. This is subject to a number of inaccuracies, particularly from the assumption that the patient has consumed whatever is removed from the tray. Calculation of intake of enteral and parenteral nutritional solutions is more likely to be accurate, but is still not precise. The nutrient intake of outpatients can be estimated by 24-hour dietary recalls or 1- to 4-day food records. The precision of these methods can be enhanced somewhat by using a computerized nutrient analysis program.

Other routine laboratory tests can provide additional information on the adequacy of current nutritional support. Although useful mainly for detecting malnutrition, as discussed in Chapter 4–2, a rise in an abnormally low serum albumin, transferrin, or iron binding capacity level may confirm that nutritional support is adequate. An increase or decrease in the blood urea nitrogen level, if not caused by gastrointestinal bleeding or by obvious changes in renal function or hydration, may indicate adequate or inadequate protein intake, respectively. Because these tests are obtained routinely in clinical medicine and do not entail additional costs, clinicians need only be familiar with their nutritional implications to obtain pertinent information on their patients' nutritional status.

PLANS
Diagnostic

The diagnostic tests used in monitoring nutritional support are discussed above.

Therapeutic
Therapeutic Options

Multidisciplinary nutrition support teams are available in many hospitals to assist in managing nutritional support appropriately. These teams provide the highest-quality nutritional care, and their presence may reduce both costs and complication rates, depending on local institutional variables.

Nutrient intake can be enhanced by using combinations of four access routes: two enteral (oral and tube feeding) and two parenteral (peripheral and central).

Recommended Approach

The clinician's objective should always be to use the safest, least costly, and most physiologic route available. This is obviously the oral route. The possibility that oral intake is impaired only by a problem with mastication should not be overlooked. Extraction of diseased teeth and provision of proper dentures may be all that is needed. The nutrient content of foods can be enhanced by supplementation with commercially available carbohydrate and protein powders. Nutritionally complete milkshakes can be prepared in the hospital or home, and a wide variety of commercial oral nutritional supplements are also available. These should be used whenever possible, to avoid the use of more invasive access techniques.

When oral supplementation does not increase intake sufficiently, the next route of choice is enteral feeding by tube. In the least invasive method, a soft, pliable, small-bore nasogastric feeding tube is used to infuse commercial nutritionally complete feeding formulas. The infusion is most often continuous, using a feeding pump, but for home or nursing home use, bolus feeding five or six times per day is usually preferable. Many of the commercial oral supplements are used in tube feeding, but many additional formulas are marketed specifically for tube feeding, without flavoring (Table 4–3–1). The most important features of these formulas are their energy density (1, 1.5, or 2 kcal/mL), protein content (<17%, 17–20%, or >20% of kcal), possible route of administration (tube/oral vs tube only), and cost ($/1000 kcal). Other features such as osmolality and the complexity of the protein component (whole proteins vs small peptides or free amino acids) are of much less importance in determining the adequacy of nutritional support or patient tolerance. Whenever possible, the formula used should meet, and not exceed, the patient's requirements for both calories and protein by being infused at a reasonable rate (≤125 mL/h). This is nearly always possible with the commercial formulas, but on occasion modular supplements such as powdered protein may be needed to fortify the content.

The most common adverse symptom associated with enteral feeding is diarrhea. Although it has been blamed on various factors such as hyperosmolar formulas, leading many to dilute feeding formulas and prolong inadequate nutrient intake, there is no documentation for this. The major factors producing diarrhea in tube-fed patients are probably unrelated to the feeding itself, and particularly include medications frequently used in critically ill patients, such as magnesium antacids and broad-spectrum antibiotics. A major cause of diarrhea that is often not recognized is the sorbitol present in elixirs of many medications used in tube-fed patients. Many of these elixirs, including acetaminophen, theophylline, phenobarbital, and cimetidine, often contain substantial amounts of sorbitol, but the quantity is most often not listed because the manufacturer considers it "inactive." When severe diarrhea occurs with enteral feeding, all magnesium antacids and elixir medications should be stopped or administered by another route, and other potential causes should be carefully sought. If there is no improvement after these steps

TABLE 4–3–1. NUTRITIONALLY COMPLETE, LACTOSE-FREE ENTERAL FEEDING FORMULAS

Category and Product	Manufacturer*	kcal/mL	mOsm/kg H₂O	Protein g/L	Protein % of kcal
1 kcal/mL					
Standard (<17% of kcal) or intermediate protein (17–20% of kcal)					
Tube/oral					
Ensure	Ross	1.06	470	37	14
Ensure HN	Ross	1.06	470	44	17
Resource	Sandoz	1.06	430	37	14
Tube only					
Osmolite	Ross	1.06	300	37	14
Isocal	Mead Johnson	1.06	270	34	13
Osmolite HN	Ross	1.06	300	44	17
Isocal HN	Mead Johnson	1.06	270	44	17
Fiber-containing					
Enrich	Ross	1.1	480	40	15
Sustacal with Fiber	Mead Johnson	1.06	480	46	17
Ultracal	Mead Johnson	1.06	310	44	17
Specialized needs					
Glucerna (glucose intolerance)	Ross	1	375	42	17
Lipisorb (malabsorption)	Mead Johnson	1.35	630	57	17
High protein (>20% of kcal)					
Sustacal	Mead Johnson	1	650	61	24
Promote	Ross	1	350	62	25
Replete	Clintec	1	350	63	25
1.5 kcal/mL					
Standard or intermediate protein					
Ensure Plus	Ross	1.5	690	55	15
Sustacal HC	Mead Johnson	1.5	670	61	16
Specialized needs					
Pulmocare (ventilatory failure)	Ross	1.5	520	63	17
High protein					
Traumacal	Mead Johnson	1.5	490	83	22
2 kcal/mL					
Standard or intermediate protein					
Magnacal	Sherwood	2	590	70	14
Isocal HCN	Mead Johnson	2	640	75	15
Two Cal HN	Ross	2	690	84	17
Specialized needs					
Nepro (renal failure)	Ross	2	635	70	14

*Mead Johnson & Co., Evansville, IN; Ross Laboratories, Columbus, OH: Sandoz Nutrition, Minneapolis, MN; Sherwood Medical, St. Louis, MO: Clintec Nutrition Co., Deerfield, IL.

are taken, the tube feeding should be stopped for 24 to 48 hours to determine whether it is responsible. The use of fiber-containing, isotonic, or peptide-based formulas does not improve the diarrhea in most instances. If no other measures are successful, kaolin–pectin preparations may be used.

The most serious complication of enteral feeding is pulmonary aspiration of retained gastric feeding. This occurs most often in neurologically impaired patients. Enteral feeding in these and other patients who are at increased risk for aspiration should be administered through a nasoenteric tube or surgical enterostomy placed in the small bowel, and the patient's head should be elevated during feeding. Periodic aspiration of stomach contents to measure gastric residual may be helpful, but is unreliable when small-bore feeding tubes are used.

Parenteral nutrition is required when the gastrointestinal tract is either nonfunctional or unsafe to use, such as after major abdominal surgery; in instances of intestinal ileus, obstruction, or resection resulting in short bowel syndrome; and in severe motility disorders. Parenteral nutrition is also indicated when it is desirable to rest the gastrointestinal tract for therapeutic reasons, such as in the treatment of severe regional enteritis, enteric fistulas, or prolonged pancreatitis.

Parenteral nutrition can be administered as the sole nutritional intake in a peripheral vein for several days, or longer as a supplement for inadequate enteral intake; however, it is difficult to meet nutritional needs using this route because the solution must be diluted to reduce the risk of phlebitis. Central venous nutrition is needed to meet nutritional requirements for more than a few days.

Dextrose and lipid emulsion supply the nonprotein calories in parenteral nutrition, and protein is given as crystalline amino acids. These three components are commonly admixed together in a 2-to 3-L bag in quantities sufficient for 24 hours ("3-in-1" solution or "total nutrient admixture"). Alternatively, the dextrose and amino acids are admixed and lipid is infused separately ("2-in-1" solution). Sample mixtures allowing varied intakes of carbohydrate, fat, and protein are listed in Table 4–3–2.

The complications of parenteral nutrition are chiefly septic and metabolic. Because the central venous line provides a portal of entry for organisms, rigorous aseptic technique in care of the catheter is extremely important in reducing the risk of sepsis. One of the most serious metabolic complications is cardiopulmonary failure induced by rapid refeeding of cachectic and marasmic patients. This risk can be minimized by increasing the feeding gradually over several days to allow these patients to adapt, and by providing a portion of the calories as fat, the energy source to which they are metabolically adapted. Hypophosphatemia, which frequently occurs during the first few days of feeding, exacerbates the refeeding heart failure and can be life-threatening by itself. Thus, ample phosphorus must be provided, and the serum phosphorus level carefully monitored, especially during the first few days.

Prolonged enteral feeding is often required in patients with permanent neurologic impairment or altered gastrointestinal anatomy. Long-term home parenteral nutrition can be life-saving for patients with short bowel syndrome after surgical resection for ischemic infarction or regional enteritis and for patients with prolonged intestinal obstruction or dysmotility. Both methods require surgical placement of a feeding catheter. The current procedure of choice for placing long-term enteral feeding tubes is the percutaneous endoscopic gastrostomy. It is less invasive and safer than operative gastrostomies, and does not require general anesthesia. These gastrostomies can be converted to jejunostomies by advancing the feeding tube through the pylorus. A laparoscopic technique for placing feeding gastrostomies and jejunostomies is also available. For long-term parenteral nutrition, Silastic central venous catheters are introduced through the subclavian vein and tunneled subcutaneously. With proper care, both percutaneous endoscopic gastrostomy tubes and Silastic central venous catheters can be maintained indefinitely. The major risks of both types of feeding are catheter-related sepsis and metabolic complications such as dehydration and electrolyte imbalance.

FOLLOW-UP

Because the patient and/or his or her family are solely responsible for adequate nutritional support in the home setting, they must monitor and record the level of intake and relevant symptoms such as diarrhea, vomiting, constipation, and weight changes. The persistence of these symptoms should prompt an office visit. A clinical dietitian can be very

TABLE 4–3–2. EXAMPLES OF PARENTERAL NUTRITION FORMULAS

Amino acids (% mL)*	Dextrose (% mL)*	IV lipid (% mL/d)†	Calorie density (kcal/mL)‡	Total volume mL/2000 kcal§
2-in-1, separate daily lipid, standard protein (12–14% protein, 59–61% CHO,‖ 27% fat)				
8.5–10% 500	50% 500	10% 500	1.02–1.05	1950
2-in-1, separate twice-weekly lipid, standard protein (17%, protein, 83% CHO)				
8.5% 500	50% 500	—	1.02	2000
2-in-1, separate daily lipid, high protein (22% protein, 51% CHO, 27% fat)				
10% 650	50% 350	10% 500	0.85	2200
2-in-1, separate twice-weekly lipid, high protein (20% protein, 80% CHO)				
10% 600	70% 400	—	1.2	1667
3-in-1, standard protein (15% protein, 60% CHO, 25% fat)				
10% 750	70% 500	20% 250	1.3	1500
3-in-1, high protein (20% protein, 60% CHO, 20% fat)				
10% 1000	70% 500	20% 200	1.2	1700
Peripheral, 2-in-1, separate daily lipid (24% protein, 48% CHO, 28% fat)				
8.5% 500	20% 500	10% 500	0.51	3340
Peripheral, 3-in-1 (16% protein, 32% CHO, 52% fat)				
8.5% 950	20% 940	10% 950	0.7	2840

*For 2-in-1 solutions, mL per 1-L container; for 3-in-1 solutions, mL/d. For these illustrations, it is assumed that 2-in-1 solutions are contained in 1-L bottles or bags, and 3-in-1 solutions in 2- or 3-L bags.
†In 3-in-1 solutions, lipid is admixed with the dextrose and amino acids. In 2-in-1 solutions, lipid is "piggybacked" into the total parenteral nutrition or infused in a separate IV line. When lipid is used twice weekly, the amount is not listed in this table.
‡For 2-in-1 solutions, calorie density is given only for the dextrose–amino acid mixture; 10% lipid emulsions yield 1.1 kcal/mL, and 20% lipid emulsions, 2.0 kcal/mL.
§For 2-in-1 solutions with separate daily lipid, includes 500 mL 10% IV lipid.
‖Carbohydrate.
Source: Weinsier RL, Heimburger DC, Butterworth CE Jr. Handbook of clinical nutrition. 2nd ed. St. Louis: Mosby, 1989. Reproduced with permission from the publisher and author.

helpful in quantifying dietary intake and proposing methods for improving it.

Nutritional support in hospitalized patients requires follow-up at least three times weekly to ensure adequate nutrient intake and avoid complications. In addition to monitoring for early complications such as congestive heart failure, the main features to be followed are laboratory values. Serum electrolyte, glucose, and phosphorus levels should initially be measured at least daily; once they are stable, they may be measured two to three times weekly. Liver enzymes (which may become elevated, but usually transiently) and serum albumin, calcium, magnesium, blood urea nitrogen, and creatinine levels should be measured once or twice weekly. Catheter dressings should be changed according to hospital protocols, and signs of inflammation or fever attended to promptly.

DISCUSSION
Prevalence and Incidence and Related Basic Science

The incidence and prevalence of malnutrition and the associated alterations in anatomy, physiology, and chemistry are discussed in Chapter 4–2.

Natural History and Its Modification with Treatment

The morbidity and mortality associated with malnutrition are covered in Chapter 4–2. There is no question that parenteral nutrition is life-saving and, therefore, cost-effective in patients with prolonged bowel obstruction or severe short bowel syndrome. Randomized, controlled trials of nutritional support in a number of patient groups, however, have not clearly documented reductions in morbidity and mortality rates. For example, parenteral nutrition may improve short-term wound healing and infection rates and, perhaps, mortality rates in severely malnourished preoperative and postoperative patients, but the same therapy may actually harm patients undergoing chemotherapy for cancer. Parenteral nutrition should be used in cancer patients who would die prematurely because of inoperable bowel obstruction or massive intestinal resection, but it should be used cautiously in other cancer patients.

Prevention

Because definite features of malnutrition may not manifest for weeks or months, and because physically evident malnutrition is often difficult to reverse, clinicians must include an assessment of nutritional intake in the daily care of their patients. Body weight and serum albumin levels are the best measures to use in outpatients. A dietitian's daily estimate of calorie and protein intake, along with periodic serum albumin levels, indicates when aggressive nutritional support should be instituted in hospitalized patients. Early use of enteral and parenteral support often prevents malnutrition.

Cost Containment

Because of the high cost of nutritional support, cost containment is a very important issue. Appropriate patient selection and choice of nutritional modalities are mandatory. Because of the considerable cost differences between parenteral and enteral nutrition, and between tube feeding and oral feeding, the more invasive methods should be used only when necessary. Specialized formulas such as those containing altered protein or amino acid profiles, which always entail greater cost, are seldom indicated. In managing parenteral nutrition, laboratory tests should be obtained daily for the first few days, but once the patient is stable the frequency of testing should decrease to reduce costs.

REFERENCES

Edes TE, Walk BE, Austin JL. Diarrhea in tube-fed patients: Feeding formula not necessarily the cause. Am J Med 1990;88:91.

Rombeau JL, Caldwell MD, eds. Clinical nutrition. Vol. 1: Enteral and tube feeding. 2nd ed. Philadelphia: Saunders, 1990.

Rombeau JL, Caldwell MD, eds. Clinical nutrition. Vol. 2: Parenteral nutrition. 2nd ed. Philadelphia: Saunders, 1993.

Rombeau JL, Rolandelli RH, Wilmore DW. Nutritional support. In: American College of Surgeons. Care of the surgical patient. Scientific American, 1994;II(10):1.

Weinsier RL, Heimburger DC, Butterworth CE Jr. Handbook of clinical nutrition. 2nd ed. St. Louis: Mosby, 1989.

CHAPTER 4–4

Vitamin Deficiencies and Excesses

Howerde E. Sauberlich, Ph.D.

Vitamin A (Retinol) Deficiency and Excess

DEFINITION

Vitamin A (retinol) is necessary for visual excitation, body growth, and the integrity of the immune system. It is needed for the synthesis of glycoproteins. Vitamin A is involved in the function of genes. Several carotenoids, especially β-carotene, may serve as a precursor to vitamin A. β-carotene is absorbed from the intestinal tract and converted into retinol, which is stored in the liver.

Vitamin A deficiency is expressed commonly as night blindness and keratomalacia.

Excessive intake of retinol is toxic.

ETIOLOGY

Vitamin A deficiency is usually the result of consumption of diets low in the fat-soluble vitamin retinol or low in retinol precursor carotenoids, such as β-carotene.

Diets are generally low in yellow and green vegetables and fruits. A deficiency of vitamin A is usually associated with poverty and nutritional ignorance. Vitamin A deficiency may occur with fat malabsorption.

Excess intakes of retinol may occur in children as well as in adults because of overzealous prophylactic vitamin therapy, extended self-medication, or food fads.

CRITERIA FOR DIAGNOSIS

See Clinical Manifestations. The normal serum plasma level of vitamin A is 30 to 90 µg/dL. A plasma level less than 20 µg/dL indicates vitamin A deficiency. Levels above 100 µg/dL indicate toxic levels.

CLINICAL MANIFESTATIONS

A deficiency of vitamin A produces xerophthalmia (ocular changes ranging from night blindness and conjunctival xerosis to corneal xerosis and ulceration); keratomalacia, an associated partial or total blindness; hyperkeratosis; anorexia; and susceptibility to infection.

Excessive intakes of retinol are toxic. Intakes of 50,000 IU (15 mg retinol) by adults and pregnant women and of 6000 IU by infants and children may produce toxic effects (vomiting, headache, alopecia, desquamation, dry and itching skin, bone abnormalities, liver damage). Excessive intakes of carotenoids are not toxic, but may produce yellow coloring of the skin.

PLANS

Diagnostic

When a deficiency state is suspected, the serum/plasma level of vitamin A should be determined. A deficiency state can be diagnosed when the serum/plasma level is less than 20 µg/dL.

Toxic effects of the vitamin may be noted when the plasma level is greater than 100 µg/dL.

Therapeutic

A severe deficiency should be treated (in both adults and children) with the intramuscular administration of 50,000 to 100,000 IU of vitamin A daily for several days. This regimen should be followed with oral intake of 5000 IU daily for several days, with diet modification.

Toxic effects related to excessive intake are managed by discontinuing the drug and using appropriate supportive therapy.

FOLLOW-UP

The therapeutic regimen described above usually prevents further ocular changes and reverses, in most instances, the clinical manifestations of the deficiency. Modifications of dietary habits will prevent both vitamin A deficiency and toxic manifestations.

DISCUSSION

Prevalence and Incidence

Deficiency may be observed in children less than 5 years of age as the result of inadequate dietary intake. The condition is rare in the United States, but is seen in some nonindustrialized countries.

Related Basic Science

Vitamin A (retinol) is essential for vision, cellular differentiation and proliferation, growth, reproduction, and proper function of the immune system. The vitamin is transported in blood as a complex with retinol-binding protein. Certain carotenoids, especially β-carotene, are converted to retinol.

Natural History and Its Modification With Treatment

Untreated, vitamin A deficiency will cause advanced stages of the conditions discussed under Clinical Manifestations. Appropriate treatment will correct the abnormalities if it is instituted early in the course of the illness.

The toxic effects resulting from excessive intake of vitamin A are relieved when the drug is stopped.

Prevention

Vitamin A deficiency can be prevented by appropriate intake of the vitamin. Men require 1000 µg of vitamin A daily, and women require 800 µg daily. Children require 400 to 700 µg daily (1 µg retinol = 3.3 IU, or 6 µg β-carotene = 10 IU).

The daily requirement of vitamin A may be obtained from yellow and green fruits and vegetables (e.g., carrots, spinach, cantaloupes, sweet potatoes, peaches), fortified milk, fish, eggs, and liver.

Cost Containment

Modest dietary changes, involving little expense, will provide the necessary intake of vitamin A to prevent its deficiency.

Vitamin D (Calciferol) Deficiency and Excess

DEFINITION

Vitamin D occurs in two forms: vitamin D_2 (ergocalciferol) and vitamin D_3 cholecalciferol). Both appear equally active in the human. Vitamin D_2 is formed by ultraviolet irradiation of ergosterol, a plant sterol. Vitamin D_3 is produced by the action of sunlight on the 7-dehydrocho-

lesterol present in the skin. Dietary sources of vitamin D are limited (eggs, liver, fortified milk, butter, margarine, and fatty fish).

Vitamin D is involved with the metabolism of calcium and the development of normal bones (see Chapters 9–36, 9–38, 9–39, 9–40).

Vitamin D deficiency results in rickets in infants and children and in osteomalacia in adults.

Excess vitamin D administration may produce headache, hypercalcemia, poor renal function, decalcification of bones, and retarded growth in children.

ETIOLOGY

Although rickets is rare in the United States, vitamin D deficiency may occur in infants who are breastfed and not supplemented with vitamin D nor exposed to sunlight, and in patients with vitamin D malabsorption. A deficiency state also can result from the inability to convert vitamin D to active forms, as may occur with kidney failure. Patients receiving anticonvulsant drugs (e.g., phenytoin or phenobarbital) for extended periods may develop rickets or osteomalacia.

Vitamin D should not be given in excess of recommended allowances.

CRITERIA FOR DIAGNOSIS

Evidence of osteomalacia or rickets may be detected in an x-ray of the skeleton. There are decreases in serum phosphate, calcium, 25-hydroxyvitamin D (normal, 25–40 ng/mL), and 1,25-dihydroxyvitamin D (normal, 15–60 pg/mL) levels, and increases in alkaline phosphatase, urinary hydroxyproline, and parathyroid hormone levels.

As little as 1800 IU (45 µg) of vitamin D_3 (cholecalciferol) may produce toxic effects in children.

CLINICAL MANIFESTATIONS

Vitamin D deficiency is characterized by inadequate mineralization of the bone. Severe deficiency in children results in deformation of the skeleton and is termed *rickets*. Tetany may occur. Radiologic examination of the bones reveals signs of rickets or osteomalacia.

PLANS

Diagnostic

Where there is evidence of osteomalacia or rickets, the x-ray of the skeleton permits an easy diagnosis. As stated above, there are decreases in serum phosphate, calcium, 25-hydroxyvitamin D, and 1,25-dihydroxyvitamin D levels and increases in alkaline phosphatase, urinary hydroxyproline, and parathyroid hormone levels.

Therapeutic

Rickets should be treated with 1000 IU daily of vitamin D_3 given orally. Vitamin D-resistant rickets may require increased supplementation. Osteomalacia should be treated with 50,000 IU of vitamin D_3 daily or 50 µg of calcidiol (25-hydroxyvitamin D_3) daily.

Toxic effects of excessive vitamin D intake include headache, weakness, hypercalcemia, impaired renal function, and retarded growth.

FOLLOW-UP

The major uses of vitamin D are to prevent and cure nutritional rickets, to treat hypoparathyroidism, and to treat metabolic rickets and osteomalacia.

Large doses of vitamin D may cause bone decalcification. Hence, because of its potential toxicity, vitamin D should not be given in excess of the recommended dietary allowance (10 µg vitamin D per day, which is equal to 400 IU, for both children and adults).

DISCUSSION

Prevalence and Incidence

Both rickets and osteomalacia are not commonly observed in the United States. Infants and children have the greatest need for vitamin

D. Elderly individuals not exposed to sunlight may require supplements of vitamin D.

Related Basic Science

Vitamin D is essential for normal calcium absorption and utilization in skeleton formation and for mineral homeostasis. Exposure of the skin to sunlight converts 7-dehydrocholesterol present to vitamin D_3, which is hydroxylated in the liver to 25-hydroxyvitamin D_3 and in the kidney to 1, 25-dihydroxyvitamin D_3.

Natural History and Its Modification With Treatment

Vitamin D deficiency occurs most frequently as a result of limited exposure to sunlight. Vitamin D supplements, increased exposure to sunlight, and diet modifications can prevent and treat vitamin D deficiency.

Prevention

In areas where sunlight is limited seasonally, dietary sources of vitamin D should be increased. Vitamin D supplements may be necessary, particularly for infants and children.

Vitamin D should not be given in excess of recommended allowances.

Cost Containment

Increased exposure to sunlight and modest dietary changes should prevent vitamin D deficiency with little expense.

Vitamin E (Tocopherols) Deficiency

DEFINITION

Vitamin E is the term given to the family of tocopherols with antioxidant properties. α-tocopherol has the highest biological activity.

A deficiency of vitamin E may occur in certain circumstances (see Criteria for Diagnosis).

Vitamin E excess causes no illness.

ETIOLOGY

Usually, diets readily provide adequate amounts of vitamin E. Vitamin E deficiency may occur in premature infants and in patients with fat malabsorption syndromes, such as uncontrolled celiac disease, chronic cholestasis, and pancreatic insufficiency.

CRITERIA FOR DIAGNOSIS

See Clinical Manifestations.

Vitamin E deficiency may occur in patients with cystic fibrosis, hepatic cholestatic disorders, and gastrointestinal dysfunction of fat absorption.

A low plasma level of tocopherol (<0.5 mg/dL) indicates a deficiency (see Plans). High plasma levels (>1.5 mg/dL) indicate excessive intake.

CLINICAL MANIFESTATIONS

A deficiency of vitamin E may result in erythrocyte hemolysis and creatinuria. Severe depletion produces neuromuscular disorders such as muscular dystrophy and spinocerebellar degeneration.

PLANS

Diagnostic

When the clinical settings described under Criteria for Diagnosis or the conditions described under Clinical Manifestations are present, it is proper to measure the plasma level of vitamin E. A plasma tocopherol level less than 0.15 mg/dL signifies vitamin E deficiency in premature infants.

Therapeutic

Vitamin E deficiency can be readily reversed with tocopherol therapy. Patients with malabsorption require maintenance therapy with vitamin E. Adults should be treated with 10 to 30 mg/d of vitamin E depending on their diet and ability to absorb fat. Premature infants may require oral supplements of 17 mg/d of vitamin E up to 3 months of age.

FOLLOW-UP

One International Unit of vitamin E is equivalent to 1 mg of α-tocopherol acetate. Oral intakes of the vitamin up to 800 IU per day have been taken without side effects. Plasma tocopherol levels will reflect the efficacy of vitamin E supplements or of dietary modifications.

DISCUSSION

Prevalence and Incidence

Pure dietary vitamin E deficiency is rare. The deficiency is usually associated with premature and low-birth-weight infants and individuals with cholestasis and other fat malabsorption syndromes.

Related Basic Science

Genetics

Patients with glucose-6-phosphate dehydrogenase deficiency, thalassemia major, glutathione peroxidase deficiency, and glutathione synthesis deficiency may respond to vitamin E; abetalipoproteinemia impairs transport of vitamin E.

Physiologic or Metabolic Derangement

The specific functions of vitamin E are not well defined. The vitamin appears to function in biological oxidations to protect intracellular membranes from lipid preoxidation damage. The vitamin is transported with lipoproteins and is stored in adipose tissue.

Natural History and Its Modification With Treatment

Large doses of vitamin E may be used prophylactically in premature infants to protect against retinopathy, hemolytic anemia, and bronchopulmonary dysplasia. Fat malabsorption syndromes may be corrected with oral intakes of 0.2 to 2 g of vitamin E.

Prevention

Vitamin E is provided by vegetable oils, margarine, butter, eggs, whole-grain cereals, meats, and fruits. Vegetables provide only small amounts of vitamin E. Diets high in polyunsaturated fatty acids increase vitamin E needs.

Vitamin E is nontoxic.

Cost Containment

Except for premature infants or patients with a fat malabsorption condition, diets should be able to provide adequate amounts of vitamin E.

Vitamin E is currently being hailed as one of the antioxidants that might help prevent atherosclerosis. More data are needed before the truth is known. At present, it is wiser and cheaper to rely on a proper diet.

Vitamin K Deficiency

DEFINITION

Vitamin K is a fat-soluble vitamin that occurs in two forms: vitamin K_1 (phylloquinone) is present in green plants, and vitamin K_2 (menaquinone) is produced by microorganisms in the intestinal tract.

The vitamin functions in the gamma carboxylation of proteins involved in blood clotting and of proteins found in other tissue.

Vitamin K deficiency usually manifests as an abnormally prolonged prothrombin time and its complications.

ETIOLOGY

Uncomplicated cases of dietary vitamin K deficiency rarely occur.

An increase in prothrombin time as a result of vitamin K deficiency occurs in persons with malabsorption problems (Crohn's disease, sprue, biliary obstruction, ulcerative colitis) or liver disease, in the hospitalized elderly, and in newborn infants. Intravenous feeding may result in vitamin K deficiency unless the vitamin is supplemented. The prolonged oral use of antibiotics, vitamin K antagonists (coumarin, warfarin), and other medications (e.g., quinine, quinidine, salicylates) may lead to a decrease in vitamin K levels.

CRITERIA FOR DIAGNOSIS

The diagnosis of vitamin K deficiency can be made when the prothrombin time is prolonged. As a rule, a prolonged prothrombin time is discovered in a patient who is bleeding or in a patient receiving warfarin whose prothrombin time is being monitored.

CLINICAL MANIFESTATIONS

Vitamin K deficiency should be considered when bleeding occurs and one of the conditions listed under Criteria for Diagnosis is present.

PLANS
Diagnostic

When vitamin K deficiency is suspected, the plasma prothrombin time should be measured. The normal prothrombin time is 2 seconds or less beyond the control level. Measurements of plasma vitamin K levels or of specific clotting factors are usually not available. Tests are available to separate the hypoprothrombinemia due to liver disease from that due to vitamin K deficiency.

Therapeutic

An abnormally prolonged prothrombin time may be normalized with the use of fresh-frozen plasma. A prolonged prothrombin time may be corrected in 12 to 24 hours with parenterally administered vitamin K. Vitamin K deficiency in newborn infants may be treated with a single dose of 0.5 to 1.0 mg intramuscularly.

A mild overdosage of anticoagulants (e.g., warfarin) may be treated with a single parenteral dose of 2.5 to 10 mg of vitamin K_1 (phytonadione, phylloquinone). Although vitamin K_1 is relatively nontoxic, rapid intravenous injections of the vitamin may produce flushing of the face, chest pain, cyanosis, and acute peripheral vascular failure. Parenteral administration of vitamin K is preferred.

FOLLOW-UP

The status of vitamin K needs to be regularly monitored. The standard one-step prothrombin time measurement is used.

DISCUSSION
Prevalence and Incidence

Dietary deficiency of vitamin K is seldom encountered, but it may be associated with malabsorption problems and the prolonged use of antibiotics, vitamin K antagonists, and certain medications (see Criteria for Diagnosis).

Related Basic Science

Vitamin K functions in gamma carboxylation of proteins involved in blood clotting and other proteins found in bone, kidney, plasma, and other tissues. In the absence of vitamin K or in the presence of vitamin K antagonists (e.g., warfarin, coumarin), vitamin K-dependent post-translational glutamyl carboxylase is inhibited, which results in the formation of abnormal forms of prothrombin that are inactive in blood coagulation.

Natural History and Its Modification With Treatment

Vitamin K deficiency occurs most often in newborns who normally have low tissue stores of vitamins at birth. A deficiency may occur in fat malabsorption syndromes. Overdosage of the anticoagulant warfarin may result in excessive bleeding. Each of the preceding conditions can be corrected with the administration of vitamin K.

Prevention

Vitamin K can be obtained readily from the diet (green leafy vegetables, meat, dairy products) and from intestinal bacterial synthesis. Adults require 70 to 140 μg/d vitamin K. A vitamin K deficiency in the normal adult is rare.

Cost Containment

If a vitamin K deficiency is suspected to exist, a prothrombin time measurement should be promptly performed and vitamin K administered. Additional monitoring may be necessary. Uncomplicated cases of vitamin K deficiency should require only dietary modifications. The average diet is believed to provide 300 to 500 μg of vitamin K daily.

Vitamin C (Ascorbic Acid) Deficiency and Excess

DEFINITION

Vitamin C is a water-soluble vitamin that exists in two forms, ascorbic acid and dehydroascorbic acid. Most of the vitamin C present in the diet is in the ascorbic acid form. The vitamin is labile in solution and readily destroyed by heat, oxidation, and alkali. The vitamin participates in many oxidation processes and is necessary for the synthesis of collagen.

Vitamin C deficiency may produce classic scurvy, a bleeding disorder, poor wound healing, and anemia.

Ingestion of 1 to 10 g may produce diarrhea and may interfere with the anticoagulant effects of warfarin.

ETIOLOGY

Vitamin C deficiency may occur in infants who are fed exclusively cow's milk and in elderly patients who eat a poor diet. Diets that are deficient in fruits, particularly citrus fruits, tomatoes, and various vegetables (broccoli, green peppers, cabbage, cauliflower), are inadequate in vitamin C and may lead to scurvy.

CRITERIA FOR DIAGNOSIS

The patient may present with a bleeding disorder, impaired wound healing, extensive burns, or anemia.

The diagnosis is made when the ascorbic acid plasma/serum level is found to be lower than normal (see Plans).

CLINICAL MANIFESTATIONS

Severe vitamin C deficiency causes scurvy. There may be evidence of bleeding gums, petechia, easy bruising, poor wound healing, and anemia. Infants may show impaired bone growth and subperiosteal hemorrhage; touching the arms and legs may be painful.

PLANS
Diagnostic

When there is evidence of poor nutrition and when the abnormalities discussed under Clinical Manifestations are present, the plasma/serum level of ascorbic acid should be measured. The diagnosis is made when the ascorbic acid plasma/serum level is found to be less than 0.2 mg/dL (normal, 0.3–1.5 mg/dL).

Therapeutic

The therapeutic dosage of ascorbic acid is 300 mg daily for 2 weeks or longer. Nutrition counseling should be given to correct the dietary inadequacies. The therapeutic dose for infants is 35 mg daily.

An excess of vitamin C may be treated by discontinuing the ingestion of excessive amounts of the vitamin.

FOLLOW-UP

Oral administration of ascorbic acid will promptly correct a vitamin C deficiency. Dietary modifications will prevent recurrence of a deficiency. Effectiveness of vitamin C supplementation and dietary modifications may be monitored by measurement of the plasma ascorbic acid level.

DISCUSSION
Prevalence and Incidence

Scurvy is seldom observed in the United States. When it does occur, it is usually associated with poor diets low in or devoid of sources of ascorbic acid.

Related Basic Science

Vitamin C participates in collagen formation, oxidation–reduction systems, and adrenal cortical function. Patients with extensive burns may require 200 to 500 mg daily to enhance healing. Smoking increases vitamin C requirements. Excess vitamin C is readily excreted in the urine.

Natural History and Its Modification With Treatment

Vitamin C deficiency as expressed by scurvy occurs as a result of diets devoid of fruits and other sources of ascorbic acid. Appropriate doses of vitamin C will reverse the illness. Simple diet modifications can prevent a vitamin C deficiency.

Prevention

Adult men and women require 60 mg per day of ascorbic acid. This amount can be readily obtained from a proper diet that includes citrus fruits, berries, tomatoes, cauliflower, broccoli, and fruit juices.

Cost Containment

Modest dietary changes to include sources of vitamin C will prevent a deficiency. Such changes involve little expense.

Evidence for the use of vitamin C to prevent colds is unconvincing.

Thiamin (Vitamin B₁) Deficiency

DEFINITION

Thiamin, also called vitamin B_1 is a B-complex vitamin. Thiamin pyrophosphate is the coenzyme form of the vitamin.

A deficiency of thiamin results in beriberi. The deficiency is associated with abnormalities of carbohydrate metabolism.

Thiamin toxicity from the excess of ingestion of thiamin has not been reported.

ETIOLOGY

Historically, thiamin deficiency was associated with populations who consumed polished rice as the main carbohydrate in the diet. With the fortification of polished rice with thiamin, the occurrence of beriberi is now rare.

Thiamin deficiency may be observed among alcoholics who have an increased requirement for the vitamin and commonly eat a poor diet. Thiamin deficiency is rarely caused by an inborn error of metabolism.

CRITERIA FOR DIAGNOSIS

The signs of thiamin deficiency are listed under Clinical Manifestations.

Thiamin deficiency is usually seen in patients who are alcoholics, patients whose nutritional status is poor, patients on long-term renal dialysis, and patients with chronic febrile illnesses. It may be seen in other patients when nutrition is inadequate.

Erythrocyte transketolase activity should be measured before and after the in vitro addition of thiamin pyrophosphate (see Plans).

The patient is either malnourished or is an alcoholic.

CLINICAL MANIFESTATIONS

Deficiency occurs as wet beriberi (tachycardia, cardiomegaly, high cardiac output, edema); dry beriberi (hypoesthesia, peripheral polyneuropathy with paresthesias, anesthesia); alcoholic polyneuropathy (anorexia, myelopathy, cerebellar signs, hypothermia); and Wernicke–Korsakoff syndrome (disorientation, fabulation, ataxia, nystagmus).

PLANS
Diagnostic

The deficiency should be suspected when the clinical setting and findings are those that are described.

Erythrocyte transketolase activity should be measured both before and after in vitro addition of thiamin pyrophosphate. Stimulation of 15 to 20% or higher is diagnostic of thiamin deficiency. The measurement of urinary levels of thiamin is useful but is generally not available.

Therapeutic

Thiamin deficiency should be treated with 5 to 10 mg of thiamin three times daily. Thiamin deficiency usually responds rapidly to thiamin therapy; dry beriberi responds more slowly.

FOLLOW-UP

The therapeutic regimen described above will promptly correct an uncomplicated thiamin deficiency. Avoidance of alcohol and the consumption of a proper diet will avoid the recurrence of a thiamin deficiency.

DISCUSSION
Prevalence and Incidence

Except for alcoholic patients, thiamin deficiency is seldom seen in the United States.

Related Basic Science
Genetics

Several rare thiamin-responsive inborn errors of metabolism have been reported. These include Wernicke–Korsakoff syndrome, branched-chain keto-acid decarboxylase deficiency (maple syrup urine disease), pyruvate dehydrogenase deficiency, and megaloblastic anemia associated with diabetes mellitus.

Physiologic or Metabolic Derangement

Thiamin pyrophosphate functions as a coenzyme for oxidative decarboxylation of α-keto acids and for activation of transketolase enzyme in the pentose phosphate pathway.

Natural History and Its Modification With Treatment

With the fortification of flour, rice, and other cereals with thiamin, uncomplicated deficiencies of the vitamin are rare. When encountered, the deficiency responds quickly to thiamin supplements.

Prevention

Thiamin fortification of flours and cereals has virtually eliminated deficiencies. Thiamin is also provided from liver, kidney, lean pork, legumes, and nuts.

Cost Containment

Diets usually provide ample amounts of thiamin. Only with alcoholic patients and thiamin genetic disorders are thiamin supplements required.

Riboflavin (Vitamin B₂) Deficiency

DEFINITION

Riboflavin, sometimes referred to as vitamin B_2, is a yellow water-soluble B-complex vitamin. The coenzyme forms of riboflavin (flavin mononucleotide [FMN] and flavin adenine dinucleotide {FAD] are associated with the activation of numerous enzymes.

Riboflavin deficiency occurs in patients who eat a poor diet and have certain clinical abnormalities (see Clinical Manifestations).

Riboflavin excess has not been reported to be toxic in human beings.

ETIOLOGY

Riboflavin deficiency may be seen in individuals whose diets are lacking in dairy products, especially milk, and other animal products. Patients who require hemodialysis or peritoneal dialysis may require more riboflavin than those who do not require such procedures.

CRITERIA FOR DIAGNOSIS

Riboflavin deficiency is more common in persons who regularly consume diets low in dairy products and animal protein foods. These persons may exhibit glossitis, visual impairment, and photophobia.

Erythrocyte glutathione reductase activity should be measured before and after the in vitro addition of flavin adenine dinucleotide (see Plans).

CLINICAL MANIFESTATIONS

The symptoms of riboflavin deficiency include visual impairment, photophobia, pruritus, and burning of the eyes. The patient may have glossitis, cheilosis, seborrheic dermatitis (face and scrotum), corneal vascularization, and normocytic and normochromic anemia.

PLANS
Diagnostic

Erythrocyte glutathione reductase activity should be measured before and after the in vitro addition of flavin adenine dinucleotide. A stimulation effect greater than 40% indicates a deficiency state; a stimulation effect of 20 to 40% indicates a marginally deficient state.

Therapeutic

Treatment is 5 to 10 mg daily of riboflavin orally for 1 week.

FOLLOW-UP

Riboflavin deficiency responds promptly to the oral administration of the vitamin. Erythrocyte glutathione reductase activity returns to normal with this treatment.

DISCUSSION
Prevalence and Incidence

Uncomplicated riboflavin deficiency is rare, although a subclinical deficiency may exist as evidenced by the occurrence of abnormal erythrocyte glutathione reductase activity.

Related Basic Science

Riboflavin is a component of flavin mononucleotide and flavin adenine dinucleotide, which serve as coenzymes of the flavoproteins that are involved in tissue oxidation and respiration processes. Rare genetic conditions may respond to therapeutic doses of riboflavin (e.g., acyl-coenzyme A dehydrogenase deficiency, ethyl-adipic aciduria).

Natural History and Its Modification With Treatment

Riboflavin deficiency usually occurs in association with other vitamin B-complex deficiency states. The patient should be taught the dietary items that are rich in riboflavin. The deficiency responds quickly to dietary modifications and to riboflavin supplements.

Prevention

Riboflavin deficiency may be prevented by the inclusion of milk and dairy products in the diet. Some greens, asparagus, broccoli, oranges, and whole-grain foods may also serve as sources of riboflavin.

Cost Containment

Simple dietary modifications with little, if any, added costs will prevent the occurrence of a riboflavin deficiency.

Vitamin B₆ (Pyridoxine) Deficiency and Excess

DEFINITION

Vitamin B_6 comprises the compounds pyridoxine, pyridoxal, and pyridoxamine, which are interconverted in the body. Vitamin B_6 in the phosphorylated form serves as the coenzyme for numerous enzyme reactions mostly associated with protein metabolism.

Overt vitamin B_6 deficiency is rare (see Etiology and Clinical Manifestations).

The toxicity of vitamin B_6 is low; the excess is excreted intact or as 4-pyridoxic acid. Extended intakes of 100 to 300 mg of vitamin B_6 were without side effects, but prolonged intakes of 500 mg daily may produce nerve damage.

ETIOLOGY

Pyridoxine deficiency may be due to an inborn error of metabolism. Although a dietary deficiency of vitamin B_6 may occur, deficiency is more often associated with prolonged use of certain drugs, alcoholics who eat poorly, and oral contraceptive users.

CRITERIA FOR DIAGNOSIS

The diagnosis should be suspected when the clinical manifestations are present (see Clinical Manifestations) in a patient who abuses alcohol or takes certain drugs.

A blood test is available (see Plans).

CLINICAL MANIFESTATIONS

Vitamin B_6 deficiency is characterized by nervous irritability, abnormal electroencephalograms, convulsive seizures, microcytic hypochromic anemia, depression, seborrheic dermatitis, and cheilosis. Deficiency occurs in alcoholics, oral contraceptive users, persons taking certain medications (e.g., isoniazid, penicillamine, hydralazine, anticonvulsants), and patients with inborn errors of metabolism, such as homocystinuria and xanthurenic aciduria.

Sensory nerve damage may develop in patients taking 500 mg of pyridoxine daily.

PLANS
Diagnostic

Erythrocyte asparate transaminase activity should be measured before and after the in vitro addition of pyridoxal phosphate. A stimulation effect greater than 80% indicates a vitamin B_6 deficiency. Plasma vitamin B_6 or urinary excretion of xanthurenic acid after a 5-g tryptophan load may also be measured.

Therapeutic

Vitamin B_6 deficiency is usually corrected with 10 to 25 mg of pyridoxine hydrochloride given daily. Persons with certain genetic disorders and patients taking isoniazid may require 20 to 300 mg daily.

The drug should be discontinued or the dose should be decreased when sensory nerve damage occurs.

FOLLOW-UP

The therapeutic regimen described usually promptly reverses the clinical manifestations of a deficiency. Efficacy may be determined with follow-up laboratory measurements.

DISCUSSION
Prevalence and Incidence

Vitamin B_6 requirements increase with increased protein consumption. But overt vitamin B_6 deficiency is rare. The neurologic side effects sometimes encountered with the use of isoniazid, penicillamine, cycloserine, and hydralazine may be reduced with vitamin B_6 supplements.

Related Basic Science

Vitamin B_6 as pyridoxal 5-phosphate functions as the coenzyme for numerous transaminases, decarboxylases, deaminases associated with amino acid metabolism, phosphorylase, the enzyme that converts glycogen to glucose 1-phosphate.

Natural History and Its Modification With Treatment

Vitamin B_6 deficiency is rarely encountered, but increased requirements for the vitamin may occur with the use of certain medications (see Clinical Manifestations). For example, isoniazid combines with pyridoxal or pyridoxal phosphate to inactivate vitamin B_6. Supplements of pyridoxine may be necessary to compensate for this inactivation.

Prevention

The patient should be taught that liver, meat, fish, and poultry are high in vitamin B_6; cereals and legumes are also sources of the vitamin. Vitamin B_6 supplements should be avoided by patients receiving levodopa for the treatment of Parkinson's disease.

Excessive intakes of pyridoxine should be avoided because of potential sensory nerve damage.

Cost Containment

Except for patients on the medications listed above, a proper diet will provide the requirements for vitamin B_6.

Niacin (Nicotinic Acid, Nicotinamide) Deficiency and Excess

DEFINITION

Niacin is a component of nicotinamide adenine dinucleotide (NAD) and nicotinamide adenine dinucleotide phosphate (NADP), which function as coenzymes in many metabolic processes.

Niacin deficiency is said to be present when the signs of pellagra occur in persons who eat an inadequate diet or have a disease, such as carcinoid tumor, in which pellagra is known to occur.

Niacin excess may produce liver disease. This may be seen in patients who take nicotinic acid for lipid disorders.

ETIOLOGY

Niacin is a water-soluble vitamin. The term applies to nicotinic acid and nicotinamide, with both forms capable of providing the niacin requirements of humans. Corn and cereal products may contain niacin in bound forms (niacytin) that are not biologically available to humans.

A deficiency in niacin results in pellagra. From 1900 to the 1930s, pellagra was widespread in the South and resulted in thousands of deaths. Inadequate sources of niacin due to poor diets that were high in corn products and low in meats appeared to have been the primary cause of pellagra. Today, niacin deficiency in the United States is almost limited to patients who chronically use excessive amounts of alcohol. The deficiency can also be seen rarely in patients with the carcinoid syndrome.

Nicotinic acid excess is seen in patients who take large doses of nicotinic acid for lipid abnormalities.

CRITERIA FOR DIAGNOSIS

Niacin deficiency may produce pellagra. It may be seen in patients who are alcoholics and in patients with malabsorption syndromes, thyrotoxicosis, diabetes mellitus, carcinoid syndrome, and Hartnup's disease.

A laboratory test is not generally available (see Plans).

Nicotinic acid excess occurs in patients who take the drug in an attempt to alter an abnormal blood lipid profile.

CLINICAL MANIFESTATIONS

A deficiency of niacin causes pellagra (diarrhea, dermatitis, dementia, death). Early symptoms and signs include anorexia, weakness, irritability, glossitis, insomnia, abdominal pain, forgetfulness, smelly diarrheal stools, and bright red mucous membranes. Bilateral symmetric dermal lesions may appear. They resemble severe sunburn, especially in areas exposed to sunlight. Dementia may occur as an advanced state of niacin deficiency.

Nicotinic acid excess may cause liver damage, gastrointestinal problems, and cardiac arrhythmias.

PLANS
Diagnostic

Laboratory tests for niacin deficiency are limited. Urinary levels of 2-pyridone and N'-methylnicotinamide are useful, but measurement is seldom available in clinical laboratories. A 2-pyridone/N'-methylnicotinamide ratio less than 1.0 is indicative of deficiency.

Liver tests should be ordered in any patient taking large amounts of nicotinic acid.

Therapeutic

Niacin deficiency should be treated with 150 to 500 mg of nicotinamide (niacinamide) per day orally in divided doses for 2 or 3 days, followed by 100 mg daily until symptoms resolve.

Large doses of nicotinic acid are used to treat hyperlipidemia (types II–V). Intakes of more than 1 g per day can produce liver damage, gastrointestinal problems, and cardiac arrhythmias. The toxic effects of nicotinic acid excess are treated simply by discontinuing the drug. Unpleasant flushing is produced by nicotinic acid, not nicotinamide. Flushing is not a harmful toxic effect and can be diminished by decreasing the dose and by taking aspirin.

FOLLOW-UP

Treatment of niacin deficiency with either nicotinic acid or nicotinamide produces a prompt response. Longer periods are required to clear up the dermal lesions.

Liver tests should be repeated a few weeks after the large doses of nicotinic acid have been discontinued.

DISCUSSION

Prevalence and Incidence

Classic pellagra is now seldom seen in the United States. Niacin deficiency is occasionally encountered in alcoholics who have subsisted on poor diets. It is also seen rarely in patients with other diseases (see also Criteria for Diagnosis).

Related Basic Science

Niacin is a component of the coenzymes nicotinamide adenine dinucleotide and nicotinamide adenine dinucleotide phosphate, which function in many metabolic processes, such as fatty acid metabolism, glycolysis, and tissue respiration. Adults require 15 mg of niacin daily. Dietary tryptophan may be converted to niacin (60 mg tryptophan is converted to 1 mg niacin).

Natural History and Its Modification With Treatment

Niacin deficiency as encountered in the United States is primarily the result of a poor diet and severe alcoholism. Correction of these two problems will prevent the recurrence of niacin deficiency. Patients with malabsorption syndromes and with certain other syndromes, such as Hartnup's disease, may require continuous niacin supplementation.

Prevention

Consumption of healthy diets will prevent niacin deficiency in the normal individual. Fish, poultry, and red meats are excellent sources of niacin or its precursor, tryptophan; cereals, legumes, and seeds are important but less reliable sources. Corn products and flours are generally fortified with niacin.

Cost Containment

Niacin is quite inexpensive and a deficiency responds promptly to relatively small amounts of the vitamin.

Thereafter, only a healthy diet is required to prevent its recurrence.

Folate (Folic Acid, Folacin) Deficiency

DEFINITION

Folate is a term applied to a group of compounds that contain a pteridine ring, *para*-aminobenzoic acid, and glutamic acid and possess biological activity. Folic acid (pteroylglutamic acid) is a synthetic form used in the treatment and prevention of a folate deficiency.

Folate deficiency produces a number of specific and nonspecific medical problems (see Clinical Manifestations).

No adverse effects have been noted with the oral intake of 10 mg of folate daily for 4 months.

ETIOLOGY

Folate deficiency is frequently encountered in subjects consuming poor diets, particularly diets low in fresh green vegetables. Folate deficiency may be observed in pregnancy and lactation as a result of increased demands for the vitamin. Folate deficiency may result from excessive alcohol consumption, malabsorption (e.g., tropical sprue), and certain medications (oral contraceptive agents, anticonvulsants). Inborn errors of folate metabolism occur infrequently.

CRITERIA FOR DIAGNOSIS

Low intakes of folate are relatively common in the United States, particularly in young women and the elderly.

In addition to the clinical conditions listed under Clinical Manifestations, the patient who is suspected of having folate deficiency should have serum folate and erythrocyte folate levels measured. The level of serum B_{12} must also be measured (see Plans).

CLINICAL MANIFESTATIONS

Folate deficiency is characterized by megaloblastic anemia, fatigue, weakness, pallor, sleeplessness, occasional forgetfulness, glossitis, and anorexia.

PLANS

Diagnostic

Megaloblastic anemia may result from a deficiency of either folate or vitamin B_{12}. Accordingly, the status of both nutrients is needed to make a correct diagnosis.

The serum folate level (normal, >3.0 ng/mL) and erythrocyte folate level (normal, >300 ng/mL) should be determined. Less than normal levels are diagnostic of folate deficiency. Serum vitamin B_{12} levels aid in the correct diagnosis. Formiminoglutamic acid excretion following a loading dose of 15 g of histidine may also be measured. Elevated serum levels of homocysteine (>12 µmol/L) may indicate a folate deficiency.

Therapeutic

After determining that a vitamin B_{12} deficiency does not coexist, the patient should be given oral doses of 1.0 mg of folic acid daily for 3 to 4 weeks. Persons with malabsorption syndromes may require 2 to 5 mg daily. Folic acid supplements (0.4 mg/d) during the periconceptional period may reduce the risk of a pregnancy affected by neural tube defects.

It is important to remember that folate replacement may correct certain aspects of megaloblastic anemia, but will not correct the neurologic abnormality known as subacute degeneration of the cord; vitamin B_{12} is needed for treatment of the latter.

FOLLOW-UP

The appropriate hematologic studies should be performed during the follow-up period (see Chapter 12–3).

DISCUSSION

Prevalence and Incidence

Folate deficiency may be observed during pregnancy. Deficiencies are encountered with sprue or intestinal malabsorption. Megaloblastic anemia caused by a dietary folate deficiency is occasionally observed in children.

Related Basic Science

Folate functions as a coenzyme for the transport of single carbon groups; in thymidine and purine synthesis; in formate, choline, and glycine formation; in histidine metabolism; and in methionine formation from homocysteine. Both vitamin B_{12} and folate are required for deoxyribonucleic acid synthesis and cell division.

Natural History and Its Modification With Treatment

A dietary deficiency of folate is usually correctable with diet modifications to include more fresh green vegetables and fruits (e.g., oranges) and folate supplements.

Prevention

The patient should be taught that rich sources of folate are green vegetables, greens, fruits, nuts, and grain products. It should be noted that as much as 50 to 95% of the folate present in foods may be lost during home cooking and food processing.

Folate supplements of 0.4 mg daily generally prevent folate deficiency during pregnancy.

Cost Containment

Normally, selection of a proper diet should meet the requirements for folate. The use of supplements during the periconceptional period and pregnancy has been recommended. Such supplements are relatively inexpensive.

Vitamin B$_{12}$ (Cobalamin) Deficiency

DEFINITION

Vitamin B$_{12}$ is a generic term for the two cobalamins that are active in the human. 5'-Deoxyadenosylcobalamin and methycobalamin function as vitamin B$_{12}$ coenzymes.

A deficiency of vitamin B$_{12}$ is said to be present when certain clinical abnormalities are discovered and objective hematologic evidence is documented (see Etiology and Clinical Manifestations).

Vitamin B$_{12}$ excess does not occur.

ETIOLOGY

A dietary deficiency of vitamin B$_{12}$ rarely occurs; it has only been reported in strict vegans who eat no food from animal sources. The deficiency is usually due to impaired absorption of vitamin B$_{12}$ as a result of inadequate production of the gastric intrinsic factor essential for absorption of the vitamin. Only rarely has a congenital defect in vitamin B$_{12}$ been reported (e.g., vitamin B$_{12}$-responsive methylmalonic acidemia). Inherited deficiency of transcobalamin II may cause megaloblastic anemia as a result of impaired transport of vitamin B$_{12}$ to the tissues.

CRITERIA FOR DIAGNOSIS
Suggestive

This deficiency state is difficult to diagnose on the basis of clinical signs or symptoms. Patients may have glossitis, stomatitis, pallor, peripheral neuropathy, macrocytic anemia (usually pernicious anemia), and megaloblastic bone marrow. Neuropsychiatric manifestations of vitamin B$_{12}$ deficiency may occur in the absence of anemia.

Predisposition to vitamin B$_{12}$ deficiency may result from achlorhydria, gastrectomy, ileal disease or resection, gluten enteropathy, tropical sprue, pancreatic insufficiency, or blind loop syndrome.

Definitive

The definitive diagnosis is made when the serum level of vitamin B$_{12}$ is found to be less than 200 pg/mL. The cause of the deficiency can be determined by additional testing (see Plans).

CLINICAL MANIFESTATIONS
Subjective

See Criteria for Diagnosis.

Objective
Physical Examination

See Criteria for Diagnosis.

Routine Laboratory Abnormalities

Macrocytic anemia is often present.

PLANS
Diagnostic
Differential Diagnosis

Vitamin B$_{12}$ deficiency must be separated from folic acid deficiency.

Recommended Approach

The serum level of vitamin B$_{12}$ should be measured (normal, 300–700 pg/mL). A deficiency of vitamin B$_{12}$ exists when the serum level is less than 200 pg/mL.

A Schilling test also should be performed. This radioisotopic vitamin B$_{12}$ absorption test permits a determination as to whether the vitamin B$_{12}$ deficiency is the result of a lack of intrinsic factor (pernicious anemia), is due to other forms of malabsorption, or is the result of a nutritional deficiency of the vitamin. Elevated serum levels of methylmalonic acid may serve as a specific and sensitive indicator of a vitamin B$_{12}$ or folate deficiency, which may result in elevated serum levels of homocysteine (>12 μmol/L).

Therapeutic

The patient should be given 100 μg of vitamin B$_{12}$ intramuscularly for 1 week; the maintenance dose is 100 μg per month intramuscularly. Patients at risk of developing a vitamin B$_{12}$ deficiency require long-term follow-up at regular intervals. Vegetarians who consume no animal products should take oral supplements.

Vitamin B$_{12}$ has very low toxicity.

FOLLOW-UP

Because of their close metabolic interrelationship, deficiency of either vitamin B$_{12}$ or folate may result in macrocytic anemia and megaloblastic bone marrow. As a follow-up, serum levels of both vitamin B$_{12}$ and folate should be measured periodically. Initially they should be measured every month for a few months and then every 6 to 12 months.

DISCUSSION
Prevalence and Incidence

Vitamin B$_{12}$ deficiency resulting from impaired absorption is the most common cause of pernicious anemia. The incidence is higher in older populations, in women, and in persons of northern European extraction.

Related Basic Science

Vitamin B$_{12}$ is essential for DNA synthesis in the maturation of erythrocytes; the removal of methyl groups from folate in the methionine transmethylation reaction; the functioning of folate; and odd-chain-length fatty acid metabolism.

Natural History and Its Modification With Treatment

Vitamin B$_{12}$ deficiency in the vegan can be quickly corrected with minor changes in the diet or with vitamin B$_{12}$ supplements. Patients with a megaloblastic anemia resulting from malabsorption of vitamin B$_{12}$ require regular injections of vitamin B$_{12}$ or large oral intakes of the vitamin to provide a successful treatment.

Prevention

The patient with a dietary deficiency of vitamin B$_{12}$ should be taught that animal products and vitamin B$_{12}$-fortified cereals are the main sources of vitamin B$_{12}$. Plants are devoid of vitamin B$_{12}$. For the patient with pernicious anemia, see Plans, Therapeutic.

Cost Containment

The patient with a vitamin B$_{12}$ deficiency resulting from inadequate absorption of the vitamin requires monthly injections or high oral doses of vitamin B$_{12}$. Routine injections are perhaps more reliable than oral supplements. Early diagnosis and appropriate treatment save money.

Pantothenic Acid Deficiency

DEFINITION

Panthothenic acid is a B-complex vitamin and serves as the precursor to coenzyme A and 4'-phosphopantetheine, the acyl carrier protein of fatty acid synthetase.

Panthothenic acid deficiency may be present whenever multiple B-complex vitamin deficiency occurs. Pantothenic acid excess has not been reported.

ETIOLOGY

Pantothenic acid is widespread in the diet; hence, an uncomplicated deficiency of the vitamin has not been observed. A deficiency may occur in patients who are malnourished and in alcoholic patients who eat improperly.

CRITERIA FOR DIAGNOSIS

Uncomplicated clinical cases of pantothenic acid have not been described.

The burning-feet syndrome described on rare occasions is associated with a multiple B-complex vitamin deficiency state that includes a deficiency of pantothenic acid.

Low blood and urine levels of pantothenic acid have been measured in chronically malnourished patients and poorly nourished alcoholic patients.

CLINICAL MANIFESTATIONS

The clinical manifestations of pantothenic acid deficiency are difficult to identify because the clinical manifestations of multiple vitamin B-complex deficiency may dominate the clinical picture.

PLANS
Diagnostic

A deficiency of pantothenic acid should be suspected in the clinical setting of malnutrition or in an alcoholic who eats poorly when there are no other clinical signs of multiple B-complex deficiency.

There is no satisfactory laboratory procedure. The diagnosis is usually based on clinical findings, although low whole blood (normal, 374 ± 113 ng/mL) and urine (4.0 ± 0.2 mg/d) levels of pantothenic acid are suggestive of a deficiency.

Therapeutic

The vitamin is not used alone but is included in multivitamin preparations. The oral dose is 10 to 100 mg per day.

FOLLOW-UP

As pantothenic deficiency has been associated with a multiple B-complex deficiency state, use of a multiple-vitamin preparation should provide correction.

DISCUSSION
Prevalence and Incidence

Isolated pantothenic acid deficiency is extremely rare. It accompanies multiple B-complex deficiency.

Related Basic Science

Pantothenic acid is a component of coenzyme A and acyl carrier protein. More than 70 enzymes are known to require coenzyme A or acyl carrier protein. Pantothenic acid is important in the oxidation of fatty acids; in the use of acetate derived from glucose, amino acids, and fatty acids; and in cholesterol and steroid hormone synthesis.

Natural History and Its Modification With Treatment

Although an uncomplicated dietary deficiency of pantothenic acid has not been observed, pantothenic acid is included regularly in multivitamin preparations. There is little risk of toxicity from ingestion of pantothenic acid. Except for occasional diarrhea, no toxic effects were observed with the consumption of 10 to 20 g of calcium pantothenate daily for 6 weeks.

Prevention

Pantothenic acid is widely distributed in foods. Large quantities of the vitamin are found in organ meats, legumes, and whole-grain cereals. The usual intake is 4 to 7 mg daily.

Cost Containment

Although there is little clinical evidence of a dietary deficiency of pantothenic acid, the vitamin is routinely added to multivitamin preparations. Pantothenic acid is safe and inexpensive.

Biotin Deficiency

DEFINITION

Biotin is a sulfur-containing vitamin of the vitamin B complex. Biotin is present in a wide variety of foods and is synthesized extensively by microorganisms in the lower gastrointestinal tract.

Biotin deficiency can produce nonspecific clinical abnormalities, but it is rare (see Etiology and Clinical Manifestations).

Biotin excess has not been reported.

ETIOLOGY

An inborn error of biotin metabolism (biotinidase deficiency) occurs, but is rare.

Biotin deficiency resulting from a poor dietary intake is rare. Avidin, present only in raw egg white, can bind biotin and prevent its absorption; however, only a few cases have been reported of a biotin deficiency caused by consumption of raw eggs.

Unfortified total parenteral nutrition and anticonvulsant drugs (e.g., phenytoin, primidone, phenobarbital) may induce a deficiency.

CRITERIA FOR DIAGNOSIS

Biotin deficiency should be suspected when the clinical features of the condition are present (see Clinical Manifestations) in persons who are receiving unfortified total parenteral nutrition; who are taking drugs such as phenytoin, primidone, and phenobarbital; or who eat uncooked egg whites.

The urinary excretion of biotin can be determined and the plasma level of biotin can be measured.

Finally, the clinical syndrome may be resolved with adequate doses of biotin.

CLINICAL MANIFESTATIONS

Deficiency of biotin may result in nausea, anorexia, vomiting, glossitis, depression, conjunctivitis, alopecia, perioral dermatitis, ataxia and other neurologic abnormalities, hypercholesterolemia, and a delay in development in children. Dietary deficiency with seborrheic dermatitis may occur in infants less than 6 months of age.

PLANS
Diagnostic

Microbiologic asays for plasma biotin levels (normal, 330–722 ng/L; abnormal, <250 ng/L) can be performed and the urinary excretion of biotin can be determined. Patients with inborn errors of biotin metabolism require special diagnostic procedures (e.g., fibroblast culture, measurement of urinary metabolites).

A therapeutic response to 100 µg of biotin daily may also be useful in making a diagnosis.

Therapeutic

The normal requirement for biotin ranges from 30 to 100 µg daily. Patients with inborn errors of biotin metabolism may respond to large doses of biotin (10–40 mg/d). Intestinal flora may provide a significant amount of biotin in human beings. The richest sources of biotin are liver, egg yolks, and cooked cereals.

FOLLOW-UP

Continuous, long-term, large doses of biotin are required to treat biotin deficiency resulting from an inborn error of metabolism. A proper diet should correct biotin deficiency caused by the excessive intake of egg whites. Long-term biotin supplementation may be needed by patients with malabsorption. The use of alternative drugs may be necessary when the deficiency is due to a drug.

No toxic effects have been reported with high levels of intake.

DISCUSSION
Prevalence and Incidence

Biotin deficiency is very rare and biotin excess does not occur.

Related Basic Science
Genetics

Inborn errors of biotin metabolism include biotinidase deficiency, holoenzyme synthetase deficiency, and carboxylase deficiency.

Physiologic or Metabolic Derangement

Biotin serves as a coenzyme for propionyl carboxylase, pyruvate carboxylase, acetylcoenzyme A carboxylase, and methylcrotonyl carboxylase. Biotin is effectively conserved by the recycling enabled by biotinidase. Absence of this enzyme markedly increases biotin requirements.

Natural History and Its Modification With Treatment

Inborn errors of biotin metabolism often respond to continuous treatment with high doses of biotin. Sometimes, as much as 10 mg per day

is used. Doses as high as 60 mg per day have been used to treat children without adverse effects for more than 6 months.

Prevention

Intestinal flora may provide a significant amount of biotin in human beings. The richest sources of biotin are liver, egg yolks, and cooked cereals.

Cost Containment

Except for the rare person with an inborn error of biotin metabolism, biotin supplements are not required.

REFERENCES

Combs GF Jr. The vitamins. New York: Academic Press, 1992.
Gilman AG, Goodman LS, Rall TW, Murad F, eds. Goodman and Gilman's the pharmacological basis of therapeutics. 7th ed. New York: Macmillan, 1985.
Minister of National Health and Welfare Canada. Nutrition recommendations. Ottawa: Canadian Government Publishing Centre, 1990.
National Research Council. Recommended dietary allowances. 10th ed. Washington, DC: National Academy Press, 1989.
Sauberlich HE, Dowdy RP, Skala JH. Laboratory tests for the assessment of nutritional status. Boca Raton, FL: CRC Press, 1974.
Shils ME, Olson JA, Shike M, eds. Modern nutrition in health and disease. 8th ed. Philadelphia: Lea & Febiger, 1993.

CHAPTER 4–5

Trace Element Deficiencies and Nutritional Excesses

Harold H. Sandstead, M.D.

DEFINITION

Trace elements are those elements present in tissues in microgram/gram or smaller amounts. Sixteen (iron, zinc, copper, selenium, iodine, fluorine, chromium, manganese, molybdenum, cobalt, boron, nickel, arsenic, silicon, vanadium, and lithium) are essential for mammals. The first 10 clearly affect human health. Iron and cobalt are discussed elsewhere (Chapters 12–2 and 12–3). Zinc, copper, selenium, iodine, fluorine, chromium, manganese, and molybdenum are reviewed here.

ETIOLOGY

Deficiencies occur when retention and utilization are insufficient for needs. Low dietary content, substances that interfere with utilization, or diseases may be the cause. Excesses occur when amounts retained exceed mechanisms of excretion. Food, water, and over-the-counter supplements are the main sources.

Zinc (Zn)

CRITERIA FOR DIAGNOSIS
Suggestive

A history of low consumption of red meat or shellfish such as oysters and high intake of unrefined cereals, legumes, and dairy products, with clinical signs, suggests deficiency. Excess is suggested by consumption of over-the-counter supplements or signs consistent with copper deficiency (see below).

Definitive

Correction of abnormalities by zinc repletion under conditions that control for other limiting nutrients indicates deficiency. High concentrations of zinc in plasma, urine, and hair, associated with impaired copper status, are evidence of excess.

CLINICAL MANIFESTATIONS
Subjective

Mild deficiency causes no complaints. Severe deficiency causes anorexia, dysgeusia and dysosmia, nyctalopia, stunting, recurrent infections, dermatitis, poor healing, hypogonadism, impotence, low fertility, abortion, teratology, newborn respiratory distress, ataxia, confusion, and impaired cognition. Mild excess causes no complaints. Severe excess causes arrythmias, dyspnea, metallic taste, headache, nausea, and vomiting.

Habitual diets low in red meat and high in unrefined cereals and dairy products; use of iron, calcium, or folate supplements; excess drinking of ethanol; intestinal malabsorption; hemolytic anemias; nephrotic syndrome; and recurrent catabolism increase the likelihood of deficiency. Zinc supplements that provide more than the recommended dietary allowance (RDA) are a cause of excess. Less frequent are food and water stored in galvanized containers.

Deficiency or excess among family members might indicate similar conditions or behaviors affecting the patient.

Objective
Physical Examination

No signs occur in mild deficiency or excess. Signs of severe deficiency include stunting, infected dermatitis, poorly healing bed sores, leg ulcers, wound dehiscence, pluckable hair and hair loss, bilateral angular oral fissures, atrophic glossitis, testicular atrophy, breast atrophy, and peripheral neuropathy. Severe excess causes signs of copper deficiency (see below).

Routine Laboratory Abnormalities

There are no diagnostic routine laboratory abnormalities.

PLANS
Diagnostic
Differential Diagnosis

Zinc deficiency must be distinguished from other causes of stunting, hypogonadism, low immunity, dermatitis, dysgeusia and dysosmia, nyctalopia, angular oral fissures, teratology, abortion, fetal distress, pregnancy complications, peripheral neuropathy, and impaired cognition. Excess must be distinguished from primary copper deficiency, thiomolybdate excess, and other metal intoxications.

Diagnostic Options and Recommended approach

For deficiency, first assess dietary and medical history and physical status. If consistent, proceed with laboratory studies. Measure serum ferritin. It is an indirect index of zinc status because bioavailable iron and zinc are obtained from the same foods. Measure plasma zinc. Though insensitive the most likely cause of low plasma zinc is zinc deficiency. Measure leukocyte zinc and lymphocyte nucleoside phosphorylase. These indicators are more sensitive and specific than plasma zinc. Measure hair zinc. Levels are often low in chronic deficiency, but may increase in severe deficiency because of slow hair growth. Conduct a controlled therapeutic trial after repleting other potentially deficient nutrients. Measure physical and functional signs before and after treatment. In some instances, function is impaired before plasma or leukocyte zinc or nucleoside phosphorylase are decreased.

For excess, assess the dietary and supplement history. Determine if foods have been stored in galvanized containers. Measure indices of copper status. Erythrocyte superoxide dismutase activity is highly sensitive to low copper status. Less sensitive are plasma copper and ceruloplasmin activity. Measure plasma, urine, and hair zinc.

Therapeutic

For mild deficiency, modify the diet to include good sources of zinc and supplement with 1 RDA. If deficiency is symptomatic give 2 to 3 RDAs of zinc. Deficiency caused by intestinal malabsorption or high urinary excretion may require larger amounts of zinc. When more than 2 RDAs of zinc are given for more than 30 days, monitor copper nutriture. For excess, stop the cause. Treat acute signs symptomatically. Give 2 to 3 mg copper daily for modest excess. If cardiac abnormalities are evident replete copper nutriture promptly with 5 to 10 mg/d.

FOLLOW-UP

Educate as to the cause of deficiency or excess. Modify the diet to prevent recurrence. Ascertain residual injuries and treat symptomatically.

DISCUSSION
Prevalence

Surveys of zinc intakes suggest mild deficiency is more prevalent than generally appreciated. The RDAs for children, women, and men is 10, 12, and 15 mg, respectively. Because the RDA is about 30% above requirement, risk of deficiency is about 50% when intakes are 70% or less of the RDA. The third National Health and Nutrition and Examination Survey (NHANES-III) found median zinc intakes for children 1 to 11 years old, and women 20 to 80 years old, of 6–8.6 and 6.6–8.6 mg, respectively. Thus, nearly half of U.S. children and women are at risk. Intakes of African-Americans and Mexican-Americans are usually lower than those of whites. About 70% of zinc in U.S. diets is provided by meat. Risk of deficiency is increased when diets provide little red meat, liver, or bivalve shellfish. Wheat bran, unrefined cereals, legumes, and dairy products lower zinc retention. Cereals and legumes

are rich in 5- and 6-phosphate inositols (phytate), the major dietary inhibitor of zinc absorption. NHANES-II found that the 25th percentile for serum ferritin of premenopausal U.S. women is 14 µg/dL. Zinc turnover is increased when serum ferritin is 20 µg/mL or lower, indicating low body stores. Other substances that impair zinc retention include products of Maillard browning, casein phosphopeptides, ferrous iron, calcium, folic acid supplements, clay, mineral oil, and cholestyramine. Intestinal malabsorption, inflammatory bowel diseases, hemolytic anemias, alcoholism, liver cirrhosis, nephrotic syndrome, catabolism, and inadequate zinc in total parenteral nutrition fluids cause conditioned zinc deficiency.

The prevalence of zinc excess is unknown. Over-the-counter supplements are likely sources. At least 20% of Americans consume nutritional supplements.

Related Basic Science
Genetics

Acrodermatitis enteropathica, a rare autosomal-recessive partial block in intestinal zinc absorption, causes severe deficiency. Illness becomes evident after breastfeeding stops. Signs include stunting, dermatitis, infections, and diarrhea. Death often occurs in infancy. Incomplete treatment of women with the illness resulted in neural tube defects in offspring.

Chemistry and Physiology

Zinc is essential for more than 200 enzymes representing all categories of the International Classification. Examples are carbonic anhydrase, alkaline phosphatase, alcohol dehydrogenase, deoxythymidine kinase, nucleoside phosphorylase, RNA polymerase, aminoacyl-tRNA synthetase, protein kinase C, and copper–zinc superoxide dismutase. Zinc affects the structure of many proteins including nucleoproteins, finger proteins, and thymulin. Zinc bound to ATP affects the sodium/potassium pump. Zinc status also affects the membrane SH:S-S ratio and calcium channels. Zinc induces synthesis of metallothionein, a cysteine-rich protein that binds zinc, copper, cadmium, and other metals.

Adults contain about 1.5 to 2.0 g of zinc, or about 30 µg/g fat-free tissue. About 60% is in muscle, 10% in viscera and brain, and 2.5% in skin. Most of the remainder is sequestered in bone. Parathyroid hormone increases turnover of bone zinc. About 80% of plasma zinc is loosely bound to albumin. Large amounts of zinc are secreted in pancreatic and intestinal enzymes and then reabsorbed. Zinc is excreted primarily in feces. Catabolism and exercise increase plasma zinc and urinary loss. Interleukin-1 and adrenocorticotropic hormone cause liver uptake of zinc.

A deficiency of zinc arrests cell division and protein synthesis. Membrane SH:S-S ratio, calcium influx, and sodium pump activity decrease. Peroxidation increases and cell-mediated immunity decreases. Anorexia, dysgeusia, dysosmia, nyctalopia, abortion, teratology, pregnancy dystocia, impaired clotting, increased red blood cell osmotic fragility, impaired cognition, and clinical signs, noted above, become evident.

An excess of zinc antagonizes copper absorption by inducing metallothionein synthesis in intestinal mucosal cells. Metallothionein binds copper, limits its passage into the body, and causes copper deficiency.

Natural History and Its Modification with Treatment

Deficiency from insufficient intake is usually gradual and unappreciated. Most abnormalities are rapidly cured by zinc repletion. Developmental and growth defects may be poorly reversible.

With the exception of acute poisoning, excess is usually gradual in onset. Recovery is facilitated by copper repletion. Injury to the cardiovascular system may be poorly reversible.

Prevention

Access to foods rich in bioavailable zinc is essential. Education plays an important role. Enrichment of commonly consumed foods with zinc is an unproved approach. Patients with diseases that interfere with zinc metabolism and the elderly can benefit from supplements. Supplementation is most effective when other nutrients are adequate. Excess can be prevented through education and regulation of access to pharmacologic supplements.

Copper (Cu)

CRITERIA FOR DIAGNOSIS
Suggestive

Diets low in unrefined cereals, legumes, seeds, nuts, and liver and use of zinc supplements suggest deficiency. Nutritional excess is suggested by use of over-the-counter copper supplements.

Definitive

For deficiency, cure of abnormalities by copper repletion is definitive. High concentrations of copper in blood, urine, and hair are evidence of excess.

CLINICAL MANIFESTATIONS
Subjective

Mild deficiency causes no complaints. Severe deficiency causes arrhythmias, dyspnea, weakness, pallor, and chest and bone pain. Mild excess causes no complaints. Excess, as occurs from ingestion of food and beverages contaminated with copper, causes metallic taste, headache, epigastric pain, nausea, vomiting, diarrhea, and collapse.

A diet low in unrefined cereals, legumes, seeds, nuts, and liver, with or without zinc, iron, and calcium supplements, suggests deficiency. Risk is increased by fat malabsorption, mineral oil, cholestyramine, and nephrotic syndrome. Thiomolybdates complex with copper and increase fecal and urinary losses. Parenteral nutrition fluids devoid of copper cause deficiency. Copper supplements or food and drink stored in copper containers increase the risk of excess.

Copper deficiency among other family members suggests their diets are inadequate or that zinc supplements have been used. Consumption of copper supplements or illness associated with food and drink stored in copper containers suggests excess.

Objective
Physical Examination

No signs occur in mild deficiency. Severe deficiency causes arrythmias, heart failure, hair dyspigmentation and fragility, hypochromic microcytic anemia, fractures, peripheral neuropathy, ataxia, mental retardation, and seizures. No abnormalities occur in mild excess. Severe excess can cause jaundice and collapse.

Routine Laboratory Abnormalities

In mild deficiency, serum low density lipoprotein cholesterol may increase and high density lipoprotein cholesterol may decrease. Leukopenia and microcytic anemia may occur with copper deficiency.

PLANS
Diagnostic
Differential Diagnosis

Copper deficiency must be distinguished from other causes of hypercholesterolemia, arrythmias, heart failure, fractures, neuropathy, ataxia, seizures and mental retardation, hair dyspigmentation, hypochromic microcytic anemia, and leukopenia. Copper excess must be distinguished from exposure to other toxic metals.

Diagnostic Options

For deficiency, options include the determination of erythrocyte superoxide dismutase and platelet cytochrome C oxidase activity, serum copper, ceruloplasmin activity, ceruloplasmin protein:ceruloplasmin enzyme ratio, serum high-density and low-density lipoprotein cholesterol,

activity of lipoprotein lipase and lecithin–cholesterol acyltransferase enzymes, leu- and met-enkephalin concentrations, leukocyte number, hemoglobin, and electrocardiogram.

Order X-ray films of the chest, abdomen, and bones. Perform a controlled therapeutic trial of copper. For excess, options include the measurement of copper in the blood, urine, and hair.

Recommended Approach

Assess dietary and medical history and physical status. Measure erythrocyte superoxide dismutase and platelet cytochrome C oxidase activities. These are sensitive indicators of copper status. If either of these indices is low, measure less sensitive indices to determine the severity of deficiency. Measure changes in function after a controlled therapeutic trial of copper. Assess excess by history and determine the amount of copper in the blood, urine, and hair.

Therapeutic
Therapeutic Options

For deficiency, options include copper repletion and diet modification. For excess, options include symptomatic care, stopping excess, and treatment with zinc sulfate and/or ammonium thiomolybdate, and/or penicillamine.

Recommended Approach

Treat mild deficiency with a short-term copper supplement of 3 mg/d and modify the diet to include good sources of copper. When deficiency is caused by a condition that impairs copper utilization, a 5 mg/d supplement is indicated. For severe deficiency, expedite repletion with 5 to 10 mg copper daily by mouth; then give 3 mg/d maintenance. In patients receiving parenteral nutrition, twice the absolute requirement is adequate unless drainage or catabolic losses are large.

Treat excess symptomatically and stop exposure. For severe excess, traditional treatment is penicillamine. Newer highly effective treatment is ammonium thiomolybdate. Its efficacy has been shown in other species and patients with Wilson's disease. Zinc sulfate, 50 to 100 mg three times daily, has been efficacious for maintenance in patients with Wilson's disease.

FOLLOW-UP

Follow-up is essential for treatment success and the education of patients. Whereas the signs of mild deficiency may disappear with treatment, the neurologic, cardiovascular, and bone effects of severe deficiency may not.

DISCUSSION
Prevalence

Severe copper deficiency is rare. Infants exclusively fed cow's milk and patients treated with excess zinc are examples. The prevalence of mild deficiency is uncertain. Copper content of commonly consumed diets and findings from metabolic studies suggest mild deficiency is more frequent than currently recognized. The National Academy of Sciences' estimated safe and adequate daily dietary intake (ESADDI) for copper in adults is 1.5 to 3.0 mg. NHANES-III found median intakes in men and women, aged 20 to 80, of 1.10–1.55 and 0.87–1.05 mg, respectively. Thus, nearly half of the U.S. adult population eats less copper than recommended. The amount of dietary copper needed increases as dietary zinc increases. Symptomatic copper deficiency has occurred in adults fed 0.9 mg of copper and 12 to 24 mg of zinc (Zn:Cu molar ratio > 16). Thus, zinc supplements increase the risk of copper deficiency. The prevalence of dietary copper excess is unknown.

Related Basic Science
Genetics

Wilson's disease and Menkes' syndrome are errors of copper metabolism. A defect in copper binding to ceruloplasmin also occurs. Menkes' syndrome is a rare X chromosome-linked defect of copper utilization by certain tissues. Features include kinky dyspigmented hair, arterial aneurysms, optic atrophy, osteopenia, fractures, demyelinization, neuropathy, and mental retardation. Death usually occurs in infancy. The defect in copper binding to ceruloplasmin has some features of Menkes' syndrome, but patients live to adolescence.

Chemistry and Physiology

Enzymes requiring copper include ceruloplasmin, cytochrome C oxidase, cytoplasmic copper–zinc and mitochondrial copper–manganese superoxide dismutase, tyrosinase, lysyl oxidase, and dopamine-β-hydroxylase.

Adults contain about 100 mg copper, or 2 µg/g fat-free tissue. About 30% is in viscera and brain. About 90% of plasma copper is bound to ceruloplasmin, which transports copper to tissues. In intestinal mucosal cells, liver, and other organs, copper complexes with metallothionein and other proteins. Copper excretion is primarily biliary, and most is not reabsorbed. Estrogens, cirrhosis, and Wilson's disease increase liver copper. Estrogens, interleukin-1, and the acute-phase response increase plasma ceruloplasmin.

Zinc is the principal dietary factor affecting copper status. Metallothionein induced by zinc binds copper in intestinal cells and blocks absorption. Ascorbic acid and fructose impair copper utilization. Thiomolybdates bind copper and increase excretion.

Mild deficiency causes low copper–zinc erythrocyte superoxide dismutase and platelet cytochrome C oxidase activities. Increased liver 3-hydroxy-3-methylglutaryl coenzyme A reductase activity increases synthesis of cholesterol. More severe deficiency impairs tyrosinase and causes hair dyspigmentation. Decreased crosslinking of keratin causes loss of hair tensile strength and curl. Decreased lysl oxidase activity and desmosine synthesis result in decreased crosslinking of collagen and elastin, resulting in aneurysms, osteopenia, and fractures. Low cytochrome C oxidase and dopamine-β-hydroxylase activities appear to contribute to poor myelination, ataxia, optic atrophy, and mental retardation. Decreases in the delta subunit of ATP synthase, nuclear-encoded cytochrome C oxidase subunits IV and V, copper–zinc superoxide dismutase, and the α_2 isoform of sodium/potassium ATPase are believed to contribute to myocardial injury. Increased clotting causes thrombi in cardiac atria and ventricles. Low iron utilization causes hypochromic microcytic anemia.

Copper overload of Wilson's disease is discussed elsewhere (see Chapter 19–83). Injury from nutritional excess is not well characterized in humans.

Natural History and Its Modification with Treatment

Selection of a diet low in bioavailable copper and relatively rich in zinc can lead to a marginal copper status. In this circumstance, limitations of copper retention by zinc supplements can cause severe deficiency. Diet modification, discontinuation of zinc supplements, and consumption of copper supplements restore copper homeostasis. Injuries to arterial walls, myocardium, bones, and the nervous system are in part irreversible. Nutritional copper excess is unlikely except in individuals who self-medicate. Stopping such supplements will prevent injury.

Prevention

Copper deficiency and excess can be prevented through nutrition education and regulation of supplements.

Selenium (Se)

CRITERIA FOR DIAGNOSIS
Suggestive

Residence in a region of low soil selenium content and subsistence on locally grown foods suggest deficiency. Deficiency of selenium may occur in patients receiving parenteral nutrition. Consumption of over-the-counter selenium supplements suggests excess.

Definitive

Low erythrocyte glutathione peroxidase activity, low plasma selenium level, and resolution of signs after selenium repletion indicate deficiency. High selenium levels in hair and nails indicate excess.

CLINICAL MANIFESTATIONS
Subjective

Mild deficiency causes no discomfort. Severe deficiency causes muscle weakness and pain, arrhythmias, and dyspnea. Mild excess causes no discomfort. Severe excess can cause fatigue, irritability, hair loss, abnormal nails, lameness, nausea, vomiting, diarrhea, paresthesias, and jaundice.

Residence in a region of low soil selenium content and subsistence on locally grown foods suggest deficiency. Selenium supplements and foods grown on soil of high selenium content suggest excess.

Deficiency or excess in family members who live with the respondent suggests similar findings.

Objective
Physical Examination

Mild deficiency causes no signs. Severe deficiency causes tender muscles, arrythmias, and signs of cardiomyopathy and heart failure. Mild excess causes no signs. Garlic breath, alopecia, nail deformities, dermatitis, edema, jaundice, ataxia, and peripheral neuropathy can occur in severe excess.

Routine Laboratory Abnormalities

There are no routine laboratory abnormalities.

PLANS
Diagnostic
Differential Diagnosis

A deficiency of selenium must be distinguished from other causes of skeletal and cardiac myopathy.

An excess of selenium must be distinguished from other causes of alopecia, nail deformities, dermatitis, edema, jaundice, ataxia, and peripheral neuropathy.

Diagnostic Options

For deficiency, options include the measurement of erythrocyte glutathione peroxidase and plasma and erythrocyte selenium, and controlled repletion of Se. For excess, options include the measurement of selenium in hair, nails, and urine.

Recommended Approach

For deficiency, ascertain the region of residence and analyze dietary and medical history. Measure erythrocyte glutathione peroxidase activity and/or plasma and erythrocyte selenium. For excess, determine use of selenium supplements and intake of foods grown on selenium-rich soil. Measure selenium in hair, nails, and urine.

Therapeutic

Treat mild deficiency with diet modification and a supplement that provides 1 RDA of selenium as selenomethionine. Treat severe deficiency expeditiously to prevent sudden death. Give 5 to 10 mg of selenium as selenomethionine daily by mouth until signs improve.

Treat excess symptomatically and stop intake. If severe, consider treatment with medications used in other species, including sodium arsenite and arsinate, copper sulfate, silver nitrate, sulfate, and bromobenzene.

FOLLOW-UP

Patient education and prevention of recurrence are achieved through follow-up.

DISCUSSION

Prevalence

In the United States, selenium deficiency is limited to patients receiving total parenteral nutrition. Clinical endemic selenium deficiency is limited to a geographic region extending from northern Thailand to Siberia. Rural populations that subsist on locally grown foods are affected. Several million people are at risk of death from cardiomyopathy (Keshan disease, named for a region of China). A usually nonpathogenic Coxsackie virus is implicated as a cofactor. Studies in mice have shown mutations of the virus that occur as a consequence of its passage through the selenium deficient host.

Dietary selenosis is described from the Great Plains of North America, Venezuela, and China. Unsupervised consumption of selenium also causes selenosis.

Related Basic Science

Selenium is essential for the activity of two enzymes: glutathione peroxidase and iodothyronine deiodinase. Glutathione peroxidase catalyzes transformation of hydrogen peroxide to water. Iodothyronine deiodinase removes iodine from thyroxine and triiodothyronine. Toxicity of selenite is related to its peroxidant properties. The cytotoxic effects of selenium and findings in rodents suggest that selenium might be a useful chemopreventive agent for cancer.

Total body selenium levels of North Americans averages about 15 mg. In contrast, New Zealanders contain about 5 mg. The selenium RDAs are 70 and 55 mg for men and women. Selenium-rich foods include seafood, visceral organs, meat, and cereals grown on selenium-rich soil. About 80 to 90% of dietary selenium is absorbed. Selenite utilization is less than organic selenium utilization. About 60% of plasma selenium is present in a selenocysteine protein of uncertain function. Urinary selenium reflects intake, accounting for 50 to 60% of excretion.

The major manifestation of deficiency is myopathy of skeletal and cardiac muscle. Low glutathione peroxidase activity allows peroxidation of lipids, thiols, and other susceptible molecules.

The chemical mechanism by which selenium toxicity causes alopecia, nail deformities and loss, dermatitis, edema, jaundice, and peripheral neuropathy is unclear.

Natural History and Its Modification with Treatment

Diets limited to foods low in selenium predispose for Keshan disease. Timely treatment prevents sudden death. Addition of selenium to table salt prevents deficiency.

Excess can occur when diets are based primarily on foods grown on high-selenium soil or when selenium supplementation is unsupervised. Stopping exposure results in gradual subsidence of symptoms. Presumably, medications used in other species will be efficacious in humans.

Prevention

In regions where food selenium content is low, enrichment of salt is an effective preventive method. Selenosis is prevented by dilution of foods rich in selenium with other foods low in selenium and by control of availability of selenium supplements.

Iodine (I)

CRITERIA FOR DIAGNOSIS

Suggestive

Goiter is consistent with deficiency. Goiter associated with seaweed consumption or thyrotoxicosis in the context of preexisting nontoxic goiter suggests excess.

Definitive

Low urinary iodine indicates deficiency. High urinary iodine indicates excess.

CLINICAL MANIFESTATIONS

Subjective

Swelling of the neck in the region of the thyroid gland is the most common symptom of deficiency. Swelling in the region of the thyroid, nervousness, and tremor, associated with previous goiter, are symptoms of excess.

Residence far from the sea and lack of foods containing iodine are typical of deficiency. Habitual consumption of seaweed or contaminated food or use of iodine supplements is typical of excess.

Goiter among family members suggests deficiency or excess.

Objective

Physical Examination

Goiter is the most common finding in deficiency. Others include hypothyroidism, cognitive deficits, spastic diplegia, deafness, stunting, delayed development, and epiphyseal dysgenesis.

Routine Laboratory Abnormalities

There are no diagnostic routine laboratory abnormalities.

PLANS

Diagnostic

Differential Diagnosis

Deficiency must be distinguished from other causes of goiter and mental retardation. Excess must be distinguished from other causes of goiter and thyrotoxicosis.

Diagnostic Options and Recommended Approach

Ascertain the demographic, dietary, and medical history. Measure serum and urine inorganic iodine.

Therapeutic

Therapeutic Options

For deficiency, treat with iodine. For excess, stop consumption of iodine-rich foods and supplements. Treat hypothyroidism with thyroxine, and thyrotoxicosis with antithyroid drugs and/or radioiodine (see Chapters 9–19 and 9–17).

Recommended Approach

For mild deficiency (urinary iodine excretion 50–100 µg/24 h), add iodized table salt to the diet. For moderate deficiency (urinary iodine excretion 25–50 µg/24 h), give iodized oil in a timely manner and add iodized table salt to the diet. For severe deficiency (urinary iodine < 25 µg/24 h), administration of iodine is urgent. Give iodized oil and ensure continued consumption of iodine-containing foods. Excess consumption of iodine is best treated by prevention. Treat thyrotoxicosis with antithyroid drugs and/or radioiodine.

FOLLOW-UP

Follow up to ensure that diets include iodine-containing foods, or that iodized oil is administered periodically in a timely manner.

DISCUSSION

Prevalence

Deficiency is nearly nonexistent in the United States and other countries where table salt is iodized and bread and milk are contaminated with iodine from processing. Intakes at or above the adult RDA of 150 µg daily are common. In contrast, nearly one billion people in less developed countries are at risk of iodine deficiency disorders. They live in mountainous and plains regions far from the sea where soil and water iodine levels are less than 2 µg/L. In these regions the prevalence of mild iodine deficiency disorders is about 5 to 20%; moderate disorders, up to 30%; severe disorders, 30% or more; and cretinism, 1 to 10%. Goitrogens in food and water increase the prevalence.

In the United States, some individuals consume more than 2000 µg/d from iodophor antiseptics in milk and iodate conditioners in bread. Thyrotoxicosis may occur in individuals who consume large amounts of iodine in the presence of preexisting goiter. Intakes of 50,000 to 80,000 µg/d from seaweed cause goiter.

Related Basic Science
Genetics

Errors of thyroid metabolism are discussed elsewhere (see Chapters 9–17 and 9–19).

Chemistry and Physiology

Water and food iodine is primarily inorganic. Like chloride, iodine penetrates all tissues. Its excretion is unregulated and reflects intake. The adult requirement is 1 to 2 µg/kg/d. Intakes of 50 to 1000 µg are considered safe. Adults contain 15 to 20 mg, mostly bound to tyrosine, of which 8 to 12 mg is in the thyroid gland. Peroxidase enzymes bind iodine to tyrosine residues of thyroglobulin protein in the colloid, to form diiodotyrosine and monoiodotyrosine, which are coupled to form 3,5,3'-triiodothyronine (T_3) and 3,5,3',5'-tetraiodothyronine (thyroxine, T_4). In the thyroid, selenium-dependent deiodinase enzymes remove iodine from T_4 and T_3. In tissues, outer-ring and inner-ring monodeiodinases form active 3,5,3'-T_3 and inactive 3,3'5'-T_3 (reverse T_3), respectively, from T_4. T_3 binds to a specific nuclear binding protein that mediates gene expression and to mitochondrial and other cell membranes. Outer-ring monodeiodinase predominates in brain. Inner-ring monodeiodinase predominates in liver and kidney.

Iodine concentrations are about 50 to 250 µg/L in human colostrum and 40 to 80 µg/L in milk. Common cow's milk contains similar amounts. Iodophores for treatment of mastitis and sterilization of milking equipment increase iodine concentrations substantially.

Deficiency impairs the function of all systems. Together the abnormalities are termed iodine deficiency disorders. When the thyroid iodine level is below 0.1%, low plasma thyroxine causes pituitary release of thyroid-stimulating hormone, which stimulates hyperplasia, increases iodine uptake by follicular cells, and eventually causes goiter.

Maternal iodine deficiency disorder caused by intakes less than 20 µg/d results in teratology, abortion, perinatal death, neurologic cretinism (severe mental retardation, spastic diplegia, and deafness, without hypothyroidism), and less common myxedematous cretinism (mental retardation, stunting, hypothyroidism, epiphyseal dysgenesis). Mixed forms occur. Neonatal iodine deficiency disorder causes goiter, hypothyroidism, and mental retardation. In children and adolescents, hypothyroidism, goiter, stunting, delayed development, mental retardation, and myxedematous cretinism occur. Adults display goiter, hypothyroidism, and impaired mental function.

Goitrogenic substances in food and water impair iodine metabolism. Goitrin (L-5-vinyl-2-thiooxalidone) from plants of the genus *Brassica* causes marked inhibition of thyroid metabolism. In usual circumstances, these foods are consumed in insufficient amounts to cause goiter. Cyanogenic glycosides from foods common to less developed countries (e.g., cassava, maize, sweet potato, bamboo, millet, and lima beans) are highly goitrogenic. Except for cassava, they are present in small amounts in edible portions and thus are not a problem. Cassava is a staple food of more than 250 million people in Africa and other tropical regions. When iodine intakes are below a critical threshold, thiocyanate causes goiter and cretinism by interfering with the binding of iodine to tyrosine and the formation of T_3 and T_4. Bacterial substances in water, high concentrations of certain minerals, and sulfur-bearing organic compounds have also been implicated in goiter.

Excess from habitual consumption of seaweed causes goiter. Hyperthyroidism is associated with consumption of large amounts of iodine by women with preexisting nontoxic goiter. Adverse effects on pregnancy are described in other species.

Natural History and Its Modification with Treatment

Iodine deficiency disorder occurs when intakes are insufficient relative to dietary goitrogens. Administration of iodized oil is efficacious.

Iodized table salt is effective maintenance therapy. Neurologic effects of cretinism and goiter are poorly reversible. Nutritional excess is limited to consumers of large amounts of seaweed or large amounts of iodine-contaminated bread and dairy products. Excess gradually subsides when exposure stops. Thyrotoxicosis responds to specific therapy.

Prevention

Iodine deficiency disorder is prevented by use of iodized table salt. Where iodized salt is not available, timely administration of iodized oil is effective. Education as to the hazards of excess iodine can reduce occurrence and morbidity.

Fluoride (F)

CRITERIA FOR DIAGNOSIS
Suggestive

Carious teeth suggest past low intakes of fluoride. Tooth mottling suggests past excess intakes of fluoride.

Definitive

Concentrations of fluoride in serum and urine indicate low and high intakes.

CLINICAL MANIFESTATIONS
Subjective

Tooth decay is associated with past low intakes. Tooth mottling occurs in past excess.

Residence in cities with surface water supplies that are not fluoridated is associated with low intakes. Residence in communities with well water may be associated with high intakes.

Tooth decay or mottling among family members suggests past low or high intake, respectively.

Objective
Physical Examination

Deficiency causes carious and missing teeth. Mild excess causes mottled enamel. Severe excess causes muscle weakness, genu valgum, genu varum, sabre tibea, and other bone deformities.

Routine Laboratory Abnormalities

There are no routine laboratory abnormalities.

PLANS
Diagnostic
Differential Diagnosis

Effects of deficiency and excess are characteristic. Exclude other causes of tooth decay, mottled and pitted enamel, muscle weakness, genu valgum, genu varum, sabre tibea, and arthritis.

Diagnostic Options

Options include the measurement of fluoride in the serum and urine.

Recommended Approach

Determine fluoride content of drinking water, diet, supplements, and dentifrice. Measure serum and urine fluoride levels.

Therapeutic

For deficiency, options include fluoride supplements and topical application of fluoride. For excess, options include bottled water for drinking and cooking and symptomatic care.

FOLLOW-UP

Follow-up allows education, periodic repair of teeth, and plaque removal.

DISCUSSION
Prevalence

Several million persons in the United States have carious or missing teeth from fluoride deficiency. Lifetime consumption of fluoride in water at a concentration of 0.7 to 1.2 mg/L is associated with a 50 to 65% lower prevalence of tooth decay than intakes less than 0.3 mg/L. Average fluoride intake of 6-month-old U.S. infants is within the ESADDI of 0.1 to 0.5 mg. In contrast, 2-year-old children and 15- to 19-year-old young men do not have adequate intakes (0.5–1.5 and 1.5–2.5 mg, respectively) unless water supplies contain more than 0.7 mg/L. For adults, the ESADDI is 1.5 to 4.0 mg. Food provides adults about 0.4 mg and water about 0.4 to 1.5 mg. Thus, individuals living in communities that do not fluoridate their drinking water are likely to be fluoride deficient. Tooth mottling occurs when water contains more than 2 mg/L. Recent data suggest a mild increase in this condition is increasing in cities both with and without fluoridated water. Sources might include fluoride-containing dentifrices.

Related Basic Science

About 75% of fluoride is absorbed. In the stomach, acid pH facilitates passive uptake of hydrogen fluoride. Fluoride crosses membranes by passive diffusion of hydrogen fluoride from low-pH to high-pH environments, where ionic fluoride dissociates. Intestinal absorption is not pH dependent. In osseous tissues, fluoride replaces hydroxyl ions in the appatite crystals, increasing their resistance to acid solubilization. In bone, concentrations tend to increase until about the fifth and sixth decades.

Deficiency of fluoride causes increased susceptibility to tooth decay. Epidemiologic evidence suggests that low fluoride levels contribute to osteoporosis; however, the relationship is uncertain.

Severe toxicity is unusual in the United States. Persons living in regions where well water fluoride is high and intakes are greater than 0.10 mg/kg/d display mottled and pitted tooth enamel. Severe skeletal fluorosis is caused by 10- to 20-year intakes of 10 to 25 mg/d. Manifestations include arthralgia, joint stiffness, lameness, bone pain, genu valgum, genu varum, sabre tibea and other bone deformities. Serum parathyroid hormone, alkaline phosphatase, and urine hydroxyproline are increased.

Natural History and Its Modification with Treatment

Deficiency during tooth formation results in poor resistance to decay. Effects of low fluoride levels on bone and susceptibility to osteoporosis are unclear. Fluoride supplements during tooth formation improve decay resistance. Later in life, fluoride enhances enamel remineralization and decreases plaque.

Tooth mottling occurs during formation. Skeletal fluorosis occurs over many years. Prevention is the only effective treatment.

Prevention

The American Dental Association recommends fluoride supplements of 0.25 mg/d for children under 2 years if drinking water contains less than 0.3 mg/L. From 2 to 3 years, daily supplements of 0.5 or 0.25 mg are recommended if drinking water supplies provide less than 0.3 or 0.3 to 0.7 mg/L, respectively. From 3 to 16 years, recommended supplements for these areas are 1.0 and 0.5 mg. No supplement is recommended if water contains more than 0.7 mg/L. Plaque is decreased by use of fluoride-containing dentifrice and mouth wash. When the fluoride level in water is more than 2 mg/L, bottled water should be used to prevent excess.

Chromium (Cr)

CRITERIA FOR DIAGNOSIS
Suggestive

Postprandial hypoglycemia, glucose intolerance, hypertriglyceridemia, and hypercholesterolemia are consistent with deficiency. Uncontrolled consumption of chromium supplements is consistent with excess.

Definitive

Relief of postprandial hypoglycemia, glucose intolerance, hypertriglyceridemia, or hypercholesterolemia after a controlled therapeutic trial of trivalent chromium (Cr^{3+}) is evidence of prior deficiency. Trivalent chromium excess is undescribed.

CLINICAL MANIFESTATIONS
Subjective

Postprandial weakness, polyurea, polydypsia, and hunger may occur in deficiency.

Habitual consumption of highly refined foods is consistent with deficiency. Type II diabetes mellitus among family members might indicate chromium deficiency.

Objective
Physical Examination

There are no signs of mild deficiency. Severe deficiency causes signs consistent with diabetes mellitus.

Routine Laboratory Abnormalities

Abnormalities include postprandial hypoglycemia, glucose intolerance, and elevated serum triglyceride and cholesterol levels.

PLANS
Diagnostic
Differential Diagnosis

Exclude other causes of postprandial hypoglycemia, glucose intolerance, hypertriglyceridemia, and hypercholesterolemia.

Diagnostic Options and Recommended Approach

Measure glucose tolerance, serum triglycerides, and serum cholesterol before and after 30 to 90 days of trivalent chromium supplementation with 400 μg/d.

Therapeutic

Increase the dietary intake of unrefined carbohydrates, meat, and liver. Treat with 400 μg trivalent chromium daily. Maintain status with a 100-μg supplement.

FOLLOW-UP

Follow-up is necessary for patient education and to confirm that chromium supplementation is efficacious.

DISCUSSION
Prevalence

The prevalence of deficiency is unknown. Results of controlled intervention trials in adults with abnormal glucose and lipid metabolism suggest that chromium deficiency is a problem in some patients.

Related Basic Science

Chromium is a transition element with four common oxidation states: 0, 2^+, 3^+, and 6^+. CR^{3+} is the most stable. Soft tissue chromium decreases with age. Catabolism, pregnancy, and glucosuria increase losses. Highly refined diets are low in bioavailable chromium. Low levels of chromium in water contribute to deficiency. Liver, wheat germ, brewer's yeast, seeds, and nuts are relatively rich in chromium. U.S. and Canadian diets usually provide less than 60 μg/d. The ESADDI for adults is 50 to 200 μg. About 1 to 2% is absorbed from diets. In vivo and in some foods, Cr^{3+} is organically bound. This complex (glucose tolerance factor) is believed to be the form that facilitates the action of insulin.

A deficiency of chromium may cause postprandial hypoglycemia, glucose intolerance, hypertriglyceridemia, impaired protein synthesis, and peripheral neuropathy. Patients receiving long-term total parenteral nutrition and infants with severe protein energy malnutrition have been shown to be chromium deficient.

Nutritional Cr^{3+} excess is unknown.

Natural History and Its Modification with Treatment

Deficiency usually occurs over many years. Chromium repletion improves the action of insulin and decreases symptoms and signs.

Prevention

Diets that include unrefined foods, meat, and visceral meats provide chromium.

Manganese (Mn)

CRITERIA FOR DIAGNOSIS
Suggestive

Human manganese deficiency is uncharacterized. Findings similar to those in other species might indicate deficiency. Consumption of well water and supplements is consistent with excess.

Definitive

Restoration of function after a controlled therapeutic trial of manganese provides evidence of deficiency. High concentrations of manganese in hair, blood, and urine indicate excess.

CLINICAL MANIFESTATIONS
Subjective

Symptoms of deficiency include bruising, fractures, polydypsia and polyuria, hair dyspigmentation, ataxia, and seizures. Weakness, pallor, and ataxia suggest excess.

Avoidance of unrefined cereals, seeds and nuts, and tea and coffee increase the risk of deficiency. Habitual intake of manganese-rich well water and supplements suggests excess.

Illnesses in siblings might indicate deficiency or excess.

Objective
Physical Examination

Signs of deficiency include dyspigmented hair, bruising, chondrodystrophy, fractures, gonadal atrophy, and ataxia. Excess causes pallor and ataxia.

Routine Laboratory Abnormalities

Deficiency in one human caused hypocholesterolemia and hypoprothrombinemia. Glucose intolerance occurs in other species. Excess causes low serum iron and anemia.

PLANS
Diagnostic
Differential Diagnosis

For deficiency, exclude other causes of chondrodysplasia, glucose intolerance, low prothrombin, and osteoporosis. For excess, exclude other causes of iron deficiency and anemia.

Diagnostic Options and Recommended Approach

Ascertain the manganese intake. Measure manganese in plasma and hair. In deficiency, measure response to manganese repletion.

Therapeutic

For deficiency, supplement with 3 to 5 mg/d and modify diet to include good sources of manganese. For excess, stop intake and replete iron nutriture.

FOLLOW-UP

Follow-up is important for patient education and to prevent recurrence.

DISCUSSION
Prevalence

Manganese deficiency has not been described in noninstitutionalized humans. Excess from consumption of well water or supplements and dialysis is rare.

Related Basic Science

Adults contain 10 to 20 mg of manganese. The ESADDI for adults is 2.0 to 5.0 mg. Bone, liver, kidney, pancreas, mitochondria, and melanin-containing tissues are rich in manganese. About 3% of dietary manganese is absorbed. Manganese absorption is inhibited by iron and calcium. Availability from human milk is higher than that from cow milk. Ethanol and estrogens increase retention. Unrefined cereals, legumes, seeds, nuts, and tea are rich in manganese. Retention from meat and fish is higher than that from legumes.

Mitochondrial superoxide dismutase, pyruvate carboxylase, and arginase are manganese metalloenzymes. Manganese is a specific cofactor for glycosyltransferases, phosphoenolypyruvate carboxykinase, and xylosyltransferase. Thus, manganese is essential for detoxification of superoxide, gluconeogenesis, urea metabolism, and mucopolysaccharide synthesis.

Manganese is one of the least toxic of the trace elements. It competes with iron for absorption. The chemistry of severe poisoning is uncertain. Effects of deficiency in other species suggest effects in humans. Decreases in manganese superoxide dismutase allow peroxidation of mitochondrial membranes, fatty liver, and impaired metabolism of ethanol. Synthesis of cholesterol precursors is decreased, causing low serum cholesterol. Prenatal deficiency affects beta cells of the pancreas, causing low insulin production and glucose intolerance. Low activities of pyruvate carboxylase and phosphoenolpyruvate carboxykinase impair gluconeogenesis. Low glycosyltransferase activity impairs mucopolysaccharide synthesis, causing low endochondral osteogenesis, bone deformities, fractures, and impaired otolith development. The last causes ataxia and abnormal posture. Testicular degeneration, defective ovulation, teratology, and fetal death impair reproduction. Impaired myelination is associated with ataxia and seizures.

An excess of manganese inhibits iron absorption and causes anemia. Gluconeogenesis is increased. Exposure from dialysis fluids has been associated with pancreatitis in one patient. Poisoning through inhalation causes a schizophrenic-like illness and parkinsonism. Similar illness has not been associated with oral excess.

Natural History and Its Modification with Treatment

Diets limited to dairy products, beer, and refined carbohydrates are low in manganese. Because the body does not have a store of manganese, such diets might cause manganese deficiency. Repletion of manganese status will correct chemical abnormalities. Morphologic abnormalities are likely to be poorly reversible. Oral manganese excess might occur through uncontrolled intake of supplements or by consumption of well water. Symptoms and signs should resolve when exposure stops and iron nutriture is repleted.

Prevention

Prevention is achieved through patient education.

Molybdenum (Mo)

CRITERIA FOR DIAGNOSIS
Suggestive

Diets devoid of nuts, seeds, and liver, low blood molybdenum concentrations, and renal stones suggest deficiency. Habitual consumption of supplements and/or food and water high in molybdenum and gout suggest excess.

Definitive

The concentrations of molybdenum in blood and urine provide evidence of deficiency or excess. Response to molybdenum repletion provides evidence of deficiency.

CLINICAL MANIFESTATIONS
Subjective

Deficient patients might complain of renal stones. Patients with excess might complain of gout, cardiac arrythmias, and pallor.

A diet low in molybdenum and self-medication with copper or tungsten are consistent with deficiency. Risk of excess is increased by self-medication with molybdenum and consumption of food and water high in molybdenum.

Xanthene renal stones among family members might indicate a deficiency. Gout and signs of copper deficiency might indicate an excess.

Objective
Physical Examination

Mild molybdenum deficiency has no signs. Severe deficiency can cause tachycardia, irritability, confusion, and coma. Signs of excess include gouty arthritis and signs of copper deficiency.

Routine Laboratory Abnormalities

In deficiency, the serum uric acid level is low. In excess, the serum uric acid level is increased and signs of copper deficiency are present.

PLANS
Diagnostic
Differential Diagnosis

For deficiency, exclude other causes of hyperxanthenuria and renal stones. For excess, exclude other causes of arthritis, renal stones, and copper deficiency.

Diagnostic Options and Recommended Approach

For deficiency, ascertain the diet history and use of copper and tungsten supplements. Measure molybdenum in blood and urine and xanthene in plasma and urine. For excess, determine molybdenum levels in soil, water, and foods from the area, the dietary history, and the use of molybdenum supplements. Measure molybdenum in blood and urine, serum and urine uric acid, and indices of copper status.

Therapeutic

For mild deficiency, replete molybdenum nutriture by diet. For more severe illness, give 500 µg molybdenum daily until illness subsides.

For excess, stop intake. If the patient is symptomatic, give 3 to 10 mg copper daily as copper sulfate and increase the dietary animal protein. Treat gout symptomatically.

FOLLOW-UP

Follow-up is essential for patient education and prevention of relapse.

DISCUSSION
Prevalence

Human dietary deficiency of molybdenum is unknown. Excess from water and diets has been described from Russia.

Related Basic Science
Genetics

At least two errors of molybdenum metabolism are known. An error in sulfite oxidase activity causes mental retardation, dislocation of ocular lenses, and high urinary levels of S-sulfo-L-cysteine, sulfite, and thiosulfite. An error in xanthene oxidase activity causes xanthenuria and renal calculi.

Chemistry and Physiology

Molybdenum coordinates with an alkyl phosphate-substituted pterin to form molybdopterin, which is a cofactor for xanthene oxidase, aldehyde oxidase, and sulfite oxidase. Purines, pyrimidines, pterins, and some aldehydes are oxidized by xanthene oxidase. Sulfite oxidase transforms sulfite from sulfur amino acids to sulfate. Molybdenum hydroxylase enzymes appear to function as microsomal monoxygenases in the metabolism of xenobiotics. Soil molybdenum content influences levels in foods. Foods relatively rich in molybdenum include legumes, unrefined cereals, nuts, dairy products, and liver. Tungsten and copper inhibit molybdenum utilization, and sulfate inhibits absorption and increases urinary excretion. U.S. adult intakes range from 40 to 460 µg/d. The ESADDI for adults is 75 to 250 mg. Dietary molybdenum is 20 to 80% absorbed.

Although dietary deficiency is unknown in humans, excess copper and tungsten antagonize molybdenum and cause maternal and fetal mortality in other species. One human became deficient while receiving total parenteral nutrition. He displayed confusion and coma; low plasma and urine uric acid; increased plasma xanthene, methionine, and sulfite; and increased urine xanthene and thiosulfate. Renal xanthene calculi occur in xanthene oxidase deficiency.

Excess molybdenum in other species decreases activities of glucose-6-phosphatase, succinic dehydrogenase, and acetylcholinesterase and synthesis of "active" sulfate. Molybdenum and sulfide form thiomolybdates that complex copper and cause its excretion. This phenomenon has been used for acute treatment of Wilson's disease. Molybdenum toxicity impairs thyroxine secretion. Other findings include stunting, subperiosteal hemorrhages, bone exostosis, defective endochondral ossification, osteopenia, fractures, and testicular atrophy. When copper nutriture is adequate, sulfur amino acids lower molybdenum toxicity. In contrast, when copper status is low, the resulting low sulfide oxidase activity allows small amounts of sulfide from sulfur amino acids to increase molybdenum toxicity. Humans who chronically consume 10 to 15 mg molybdenum daily in drinking water or diets that provide more than 1.5 mg/d display hyperuricemia, gout, and increased urine copper.

Natural History and Its Modification with Treatment

Dietary molybdenum deficiency is unknown in humans. In contrast, excess occurs when individuals are chronically exposed to high levels of molybdenum in water and food. Stopping exposure and repleting copper nutriture should relieve many symptoms.

Prevention

Prevention is achieved through appropriate diets and, where water levels of molybdenum are high, use of bottled water.

COST CONTAINMENT: TRACE ELEMENTS

To decrease the cost of evaluation, dietary, or supplement practices, the diseases that increase the risk of deficiency should be present before one proceeds with expensive laboratory tests. Prevention of deficiency or excess through education and appropriate dietary practices reduces the cost.

REFERENCES

Brown ML, ed. Present knowledge in nutrition. Washington, DC: International Life Sciences Institute, 1990.

Mertz W, ed. Trace elements in human and animal nutrition, vols. 1 and 2. 5th ed. Orlando, FL: Academic Press, 1986.

National Research Council. Recommended dietary allowances. 10th ed. Washington, DC: National Academy of Sciences, 1989.

Shils M, ed. Trace elements in parenteral nutrition. Bull NY Acad Med 1984;60:132.

CHAPTER 4–6

Underweight and Abnormal Weight Loss

Roland L. Weinsier, M.D., Dr.P.H.

DEFINITION

For the purposes of this discussion, *underweight* is defined as a weight-for-height that is below the reference standard range for individuals of the same gender and age, and *abnormal weight loss* is defined as involuntary weight loss that persists for at least 3 weeks.

ETIOLOGY

In general terms, weight loss reflects an imbalance of energy intake and expenditure. For a specific individual, the etiology may be either (1) increased energy requirements or losses, despite normal or even increased energy intake; or (2) reduced energy intake in the presence of normal or increased energy demands or losses.

CRITERIA FOR DIAGNOSIS

Suggestive

Loose-fitting clothes, ill-fitting dentures, or concern expressed by friends and relatives may well be the first clues to the occurrence of abnormal weight loss. Involuntary, continuous weight loss is cause for further evaluation despite the fact that weight loss per se tends to be a nonspecific manifestation of many disease processes.

Definitive

A body weight of less than 80% of reference standard (Figure 4–6–1) indicates an abnormal state in almost every instance. A lifelong history of being thin and otherwise in good health mitigates against the presence of an underlying disorder, although a lifelong weight below 80% of reference standard is unusual.

CLINICAL MANIFESTATIONS

Subjective

The body weight history in terms of total and rate of weight loss should be reviewed. This should include evaluation of the presence of normal or increased appetite versus anorexia. A diet history obtained as a 24-hour recall or a 3-day written intake record is valuable in identifying the underlying disease process. Weight loss associated with normal or increased dietary intake frequently points toward illnesses associated with hypermetabolic states or malabsorption syndromes. On the other hand, the presence of anorexia and/or decreased energy intake raises the possibility of psychiatric disorders and a variety of systemic diseases.

Objective

The presence of severe cachexia and a body weight below 80% of reference standard is generally associated with the clinical findings of generalized loss of subcutaneous fat, temporal and interosseous muscle wasting, and exaggerated bony prominences. It is important, however, to be aware that involuntary weight loss in a person who is of normal or above-normal body weight warrants further evaluation.

Although no tests are specifically abnormal in conditions of weight loss or underweight, anemia and decreased serum albumin levels are often present in the malnourished patient and may be indicative of underlying disease.

PLANS

Diagnostic

There is no differential diagnosis when the criteria for diagnosis are met. The differential diagnosis applies to the cause of the weight loss or underweight state.

Laboratory tests are selected as appropriate to rule out suspected underlying diseases. Any serious illness can cause weight loss; however, the more common causes and those that may be unrecognized at initial evaluation are outlined in Table 4–6–1. The presence or absence of a normal appetite and normal food intake is useful in differential diagnosis. It is noteworthy that a number of illnesses as well as injury may be associated with both decreased energy intake and increased energy requirements. In the absence of major signs and symptoms of disease, occult malignancy is probably the most common cause of involuntary weight loss, with the gastrointestinal tract being the most common site of origin.

Therapeutic

Even in the presence of severe underlying disease, weight loss is not obligatory and can be reversed with vigorous nutritional support. Various methods of providing enteral and parenteral nutrition are described in Chapter 4–3.

For individuals who are otherwise healthy but tend to remain unusually thin, weight gain is often difficult to achieve and, except for cosmetic reasons, is usually unnecessary. It may be helpful to use energy-dense, nutritional snacks such as combinations of nuts, seeds, oats, and dried fruits. The addition of body-building exercises is often useful to add muscle mass.

FOLLOW-UP

In most instances, gradual weight gain is well tolerated by the patient, and the frequency of follow-up is determined by the underlying illness; however, special attention is required for the severely cachectic patient in whom nutritional repletion is provided by parenteral nutrition. The chronically starved patient receiving high concentrations of intravenous glucose is at increased risk of severe refeeding complications, including hypophosphatemia and repletion heart failure. These patients should be

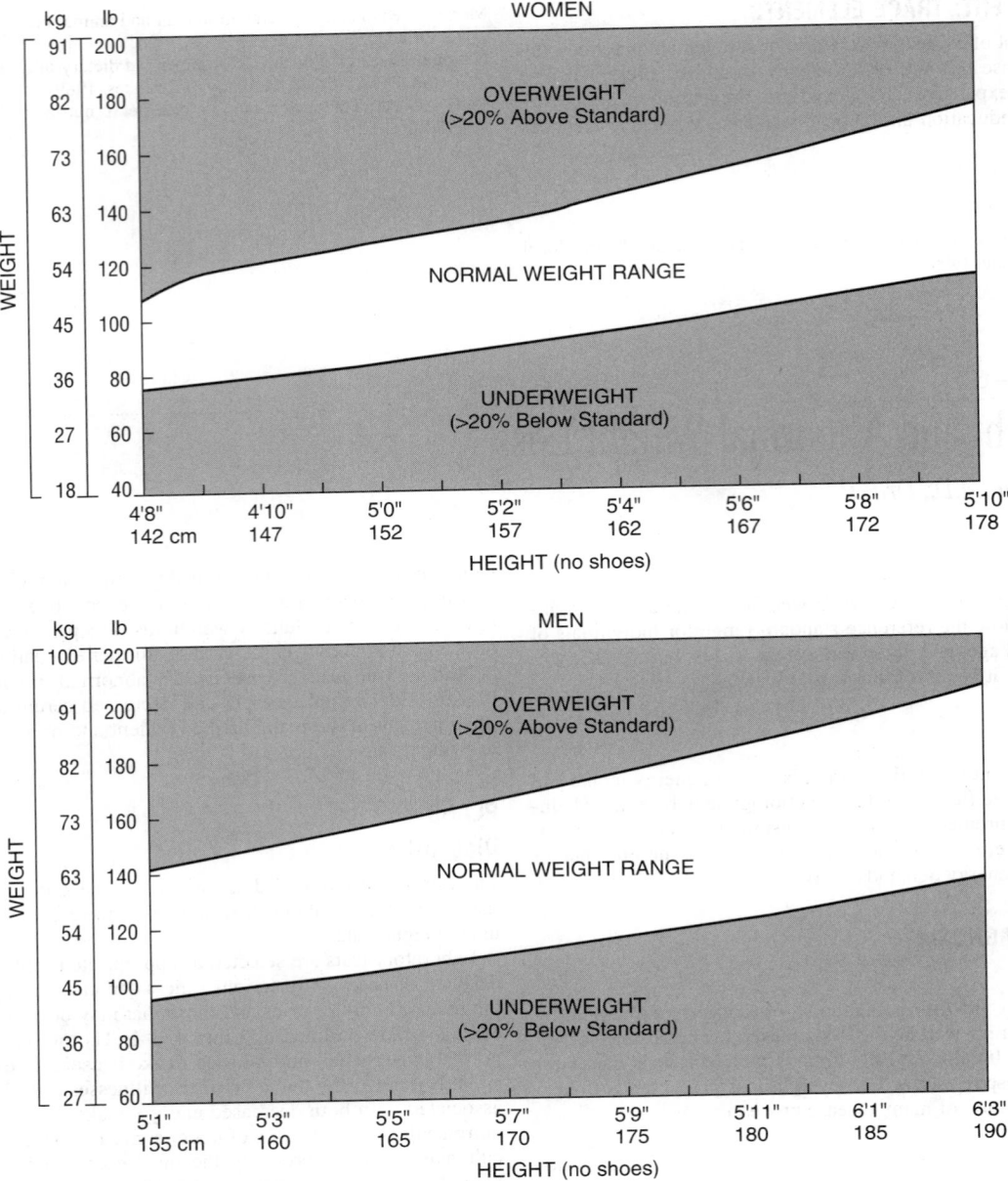

Figure 4–6–1. Weight–height reference graphs (adults). (*Source: Data adapted from Metropolitan Life Insurance Company: Build and Blood Pressure Study, 1959. From Weinsier RL, Heimburger DC, Butterworth CE Jr. Handbook of clinical nutrition. 2nd ed. St. Louis: Mosby, 1989. Reproduced with permission from the publisher and author, and the Metropolitan Life Insurance Company.*)

seen and their electrolytes and serum phosphorus levels checked daily during the first several days of intravenous repletion.

DISCUSSION
Prevalence

The prevalence rates of underweight status in the U.S. population are approximately 5% among adult men and 10% among adult women, when underweight is defined as at or below 90% of median weight-for-height.

Related Basic Science
Physiologic or Metabolic Derangement

The normal adaptation process of the semistarved but otherwise unstressed patient includes a reduction in resting metabolic rate, reduced secretion of insulin, decreased extrathyroidal conversion of triiodothyronine (T_3) from thyroxine, and a fall in the serum T_3:reverse T_3 ratio.

Generally, the rate of weight loss is a function of the energy deficit; however, obese individuals tend to have greater rates of weight loss than nonobese individuals. On the other hand, the fractional rate of weight loss (i.e., percentage of body weight lost per day) tends to be lower in the obese individual. Significant weight loss causes reductions of both lean body mass and fat mass. Again, the obese individual seems to have the advantage during semistarvation in using a smaller portion of body nitrogen per kilogram of weight lost.

Anatomic Derangement

The relative contributions of the lean and fat body compartments depend on (1) initial body fat mass and (2) the magnitude of the energy deficit. For example, a modest energy reduction (to about 1000 – 1500 kcal/d) in persons with little fat reserves may produce losses of one half or more of body weight as lean body mass; the same reduced energy intake in persons with greater fat mass tends to cause losses of less than one third of body weight as lean body mass. For the same level of fat

TABLE 4–6–1. POTENTIAL CAUSES OF WEIGHT LOSS ACCORDING TO CHANGES IN FOOD INTAKE

Intake Normal or Increased	Intake Decreased

Increased energy requirements
   Hyperthyroidism
   Pheochromocytoma
Decreased energy utilization
   Diabetes mellitus, uncontrolled
   Fat malabsorption syndromes
   Intestinal parasites
	Psychiatric disorders
	   Anorexia nervosa
	   Depression
	Systemic diseases
	   Adrenal insufficiency
	   Cardiac cachexia
	   Chronic inflammatory disease
	   Hepatobiliary disease
	   Leukemia, Hodgkin's disease
	   Occult malignancy
	   Pulmonary cachexia
	   Uremia
	Poisoning
	Injury
	Vomiting

mass, the lower the energy intake, the greater the percentage loss of lean body mass. As an example, a normal-weight individual who reduces daily energy intake from the range 1600 to 1900 kcal down to the range 450 to 900 kcal may experience an increased loss of lean body mass from approximately one fifth to as much as one half of the total weight loss.

Natural History and Its Modification with Treatment

Although the natural history of the weight loss depends on its etiology, rapid loss of 40 to 50% of usual body weight (equivalent to about one fourth to one third of body protein mass) may be fatal.

Prevention

The prevention of weight loss depends on its etiology and early recognition.

Cost Containment

In general, the preferred method for refeeding the semistarved individual is with oral supplements or the use of nasogastric or enterostomy feeding, in contrast to parenteral alimentation. The former approaches are not only more physiologic but more cost-effective.

REFERENCES

Forbes GB. Body composition: Influence of nutrition, disease, growth, and aging. In: Shils ME, Olson JA, Shike M, eds. Modern nutrition in health and disease. 8th ed. Philadelphia: Lea & Febiger, 1994.

Heymsfield SB, Tighe A, Wang Z-M. Nutritional assessment by anthropometric and biochemical methods. In: Shils ME, Olson JA, Shike M, eds. Modern nutrition in health and disease. 8th ed. Philadelphia: Lea & Febiger, 1994.

Keys A, Brozek J. Heuschel A, et al. The biology of human starvation. Minneapolis: University of Minnesota, 1950.

Moore FD, Olesin KH, McMurray JD, et al. The body cell mass and its supporting environment. Philadelphia: Saunders, 1963.

CHAPTER 4–7

Obesity (See Section 9, Chapter 34)

Immunologic and Allergic Disorders

James T. C. Li, M.D., Ph.D.

CHAPTER 5–1

Asthma (Chronic, Stable) as Viewed by an Allergist

Charles E. Reed, M.D.

DEFINITION (also see Section 13, Chapter 20)

A recent consensus states that "Asthma is a chronic inflammatory disorder of the airways in which many cells play a role, including mast cells and eosinophils. In susceptible individuals this inflammation causes symptoms which are usually associated with widespread but variable airflow obstruction that is often reversible either spontaneously or with treatment, and causes an increased airway responsiveness to a variety of stimuli" (National Education Program, 1991). Clinically, asthma is intermittent airway obstruction with dyspnea and wheezing; pathologically, asthma is chronic desquamating eosinophilic bronchitis; and physiologically, asthma is hyperreactive airway disease. *Chronic, stable asthma* implies that there is evidence of chronic dyspnea with wheezing, but the symptoms and signs are far less than they are during an acute episode. The National Heart, Lung and Blood Institute of the National Institutes of Health has sponsored the development of a National Asthma Education Program that is based on a wide international consensus of physicians from many disciplines, nurses, and educators. This chapter draws heavily on that program and deals mainly with chronic, stable asthma. See Table 5–1–1 for classification of asthma.

Etiology

The etiology of asthma is unknown. Indeed, it is not certain whether asthma is a complex disease with a single etiology, like AIDS, or whether it is several diseases with similar manifestations like hypertension. Two broad types of asthma are recognized: *extrinsic*, or *allergic*, and *intrinsic* or *nonallergic*. The following are three arguments in favor of a common underlying etiology for all cases of asthma: (1) Many patients with allergic asthma have chronic illness that persists after aller-

TABLE 5–1–1. CLASSIFICATION OF ASTHMA SEVERITY*

Asthma Severity	Clinical Features Before Treatment	Lung Function	Regular Medication Usually Required to Maintain Control
Mild	• Intermittent, brief symptoms < 1–2 times a week • Nocturnal asthma symptoms < 2 times a month • Asymptomatic between exacerbations	PEF >80% predicted at baseline PEF variability <20% PEF normal after bronchodilator	Intermittent inhaled short-acting β₂-agonist (taken as needed) only
Moderate	• Exacerbations > 1–2 times a week • Nocturnal asthma symptoms > 2 times a month • Symptoms requiring inhaled β₂-agonist almost daily	PEF 60-80% predicted at baseline PEF variability 20-30% PEF normal after bronchodilator	Daily inhaled antiinflammatory agent Possibly a daily long-acting bronchodilator, especially for nocturnal symptoms
Severe	• Frequent exacerbations • Continuous symptoms • Frequent nocturnal asthma symptoms • Physical activities limited by asthma • Hospitalization for asthma in previous year† • Previous life-threatening exacerbation†	PEF <60% predicted at baseline PEF variability >30% PEF below normal despite optimal therapy	Daily inhaled antiinflammatory agent at high doses Daily long-acting bronchodilator, especially for nocturnal symptoms Frequent use of systemic corticosteroids

*Note: The characteristics noted in this table are general, and the characteristics may overlap because asthma is highly variable. Furthermore, an individual's classification may change over time. One or more features may be present to be assigned a grade of severity. An individual should usually be assigned to the most severe grade in which any feature occurs. Once the minimum medication required to maintain control of asthma has been identified, then this medication requirement reflects the overall severity of the condition. PEF, peak expiratory flow rate.

†The potential severity—related to a patient's past history (e.g., a previous life-threatening exacerbation or a hospitalization for asthma in the previous year) as well as present status—should be considered at all times.

Source: From the National Heart, Lung and Blood Institute. International consensus report on diagnosis and treatment of asthma. Publication No. 92-3091. Bethesda, MD: U.S. Department of Health and Human Services, 1992.

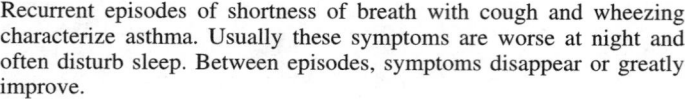

gen exposure is no longer present or have episodes provoked by respiratory infections or exposure to irritants. (2) The physiologic and histopathologic abnormalities are the same. (3) All patients respond similarly to pharmacologic management. As a practical matter it is more useful to identify the specific environmental events that precipitate symptoms in each individual patient than it is to worry about underlying etiology.

CRITERIA FOR DIAGNOSIS

Suggestive

Recurrent episodes of shortness of breath with cough and wheezing characterize asthma. Usually these symptoms are worse at night and often disturb sleep. Between episodes, symptoms disappear or greatly improve.

Definitive

Objective demonstration of reversible airway obstruction by spirometry is required for a definitive diagnosis of asthma and, equally importantly, for determining its severity. Spirometry should include measurement of reversibility after aerosol beta-adrenergic bronchodilator. In mild cases where the history is suggestive but the spirogram is normal, objective confirmation of reversible airway obstruction can be obtained with a methacholine provocative test or by providing the patient with a peak flowmeter to use at home or work when symptoms occur.

CLINICAL MANIFESTATIONS

Subjective

Symptoms

Episodic dyspnea, wheezing, and cough usually are so typical that the diagnosis is evident to both patient and physician. As the episode subsides, the cough produces thick mucoid sputum. These symptoms are often worse at night about 4:00 AM and wake the patient from sleep. Also characteristic are cough and dyspnea *after* (rather than during) exercise. Such exercise-induced asthma is more common in younger asthmatics simply because they are more likely to exercise vigorously. Exercise in cold air is an especially potent stimulus. Airborne irritants

such as dust, tobacco smoke, organic solvents, and air pollution (including ozone, sulfur and nitric oxides, and respirable particulates) also can provoke symptoms. These nonspecific stimuli are more likely to cause symptoms in the more severe cases who have a greater degree of airway hyperresponsiveness.

Viral respiratory infections often initiate a rather severe episode lasting days or weeks. Asthmatic patients frequently remark that they catch every cold that comes along. Many, but not all, allergic patients are well aware of some of the allergens that provoke their episodes. Cats, of course, are notorious. Changing the bed, vacuuming, or cleaning the basement cause symptoms in mite-allergic asthmatics. Seasonal or occupational symptoms can provide valuable clues. Although the allergic reaction of asthma is classified as *immediate hypersensitivity,* the reaction does not always occur immediately; it may be delayed several hours only to wake the patient at night. And it often persists several days.

Occasionally the symptoms are not typical. Cough without dyspnea but with eosinophilia has been called *cough-variant asthma,* but most cases of chronic cough have other causes.

Past History

Allergic patients with asthma often have other atopic diseases such as hay fever, atopic dermatitis, and anaphylaxis. Nasal polyps and sinusitis are also common, particularly in patients without allergy who are sensitive to aspirin. Medication history is especially relevant. Asthmatic reactions provoked by aspirin or other nonsteroidal antiinflammatory drugs may be fatal. Beta-adrenergic blocking drugs, even eyedrops for glaucoma, aggravate asthma. Cigarette smoking, either by the patient or by others in the household, needs consideration. Children born prematurely, particularly those with bronchopulmonary dysplasia, are at risk for asthma as they grow up. Because numerous concurrent illnesses influence the choice of treatment, the past history needs to be complete.

Family History

Children born of allergic parents are at increased risk of developing asthma, but a specific genetic basis for the disease has not yet been defined, and environmental risk factors seem more important in the pathogenesis of asthma. Genetics is not the only consideration in the family history. The social structure is far more important. Asthma is more severe and more difficult to manage in patients from lower socioeconomic groups or from dysfunctional families.

Objective

Physical Examination

Musical wheezes are the typical abnormality. This musical sound comes from an oboelike vibration of an airway that is almost completely closed, and indicates that the disease is moderately severe. Wheezing is often absent in mild asthma. The physical finding of mild diffuse airway obstruction is increased intensity of the sound of quiet breathing heard with the stethoscope held in from of the open mouth. At the other extreme of severity, when there is not sufficient air exchange to move air through severely obstructed airways, the chest may also be silent.

The skin may show the lesions of atopic dermatitis. The nasal mucosa often is pale and swollen, and nasal polyps may be present.

Routine Laboratory Abnormalities

Eosinophilia of more than 0.3×10^9/L is usually present, and offers a clue that obstructive airway disease is asthma and will respond to treatment. Eosinophilia is not, however, a sufficiently sensitive test to be definitive, particularly in mild cases. Chest x-ray is of little value in chronic stable asthma. It serves chiefly to exclude other diseases or complications.

PLANS

Diagnostic

Differential Diagnosis

Other types of obstructive lung diseases are the most common consideration. Although typical cases are easily distinguished by their history and reversibility of the obstruction, some patients with severe chronic asthma develop an element of irreversible disease, and some patients with chronic obstructive pulmonary disease respond very well to bronchodilators. Differential diagnosis in these overlap cases becomes rather pedantic, as treatment is similar. Interstitial fibrosis and pulmonary hypertension need to be considered, but are characterized by a restrictive rather than obstructive abnormality in the pulmonary function tests. Heart failure occasionally can be mistaken for asthma. And asthmatic patients with dependent edema from venous or lymphatic disease may be misdiagnosed with heart failure. Of course, a patient may have both asthma and heart disease. Hyperventilation syndrome needs to be considered in mild cases. Laryngeal dysfunction syndrome is often difficult to distinguish from asthma. This condition should be considered in young adults have had frequent courses of oral steroids, but whose spirometry is normal. The distinction is made by examining the larynx and performing spirometry during the episode.

Diagnostic Options and Recommended Approach

The history of episodes of cough and dyspnea that often wake the patient at night, the physical findings of musical wheezes (which may be absent in mild cases), the blood count with eosinophilia, and spirometry showing reversible obstruction usually provide the information needed for diagnosing moderately severe cases. Measurement of peak expiratory flow rate is commonly used as a substitute for the spirogram in following cases of asthma, but the more informative spirogram is invaluable in establishing the benchmark in each case for future interpretation of peak expiratory flow rate values. Mild cases may be free of obstruction at the time of the office visit. In such cases home peak flow monitoring or a bronchoprovocation test may be needed to establish occurrence of intermittent obstruction.

Diagnosis does not end with the determination that the patient has asthma. Its severity and the factors that provoke episodes must also be determined. The severity is determined by three parameters: (1) clinical features before treatment, (2) lung function, (3) medication required to maintain control (Table 5–1–1). Severity ranges from trivial episodes once or twice a year through mild daily symptoms to severe chronic

disease. Occasionally it is fatal. Clinical severity is determined not only by the frequency of the exacerbations, but also by the disruption the disease causes in the patient's life and in the family. Obviously, the physician will match the stringency of the management to the severity of the problem. Many of the recommendations discussed below are not appropriate for patients with very mild disease.

Allergy is an important etiologic factor in at least three quarters of all asthmatic patients in the community. Fortunately, the list of important airborne allergens is reasonably short (Table 5–1–2). Skin prick tests for the 10 or 20 allergens prevalent in each community should be performed at least once during the course of this chronic disease. Positive tests are valuable in planning management and negative tests in protecting the patient from useless intrusive interventions. Like all laboratory tests, allergy skin tests for specific immunoglobulin E antibody should be performed in a standardized manner using standardized reagents. They must be interpreted in the context of the patient's exposure. Communitywide outdoor allergens differ with the climate and vary with the season. Indoor allergens vary with the location and with the construction and furnishing of the home. Because the physician needs to know the details of these exposures, the performance and interpretation of skin tests is often best performed by a specialist. Serologic tests for immunoglobulin E antibody to airborne allergens may be indicated in patients who have severe skin disease or who have taken medications, such as long-acting antihistamines, that compromise the reliability of the skin test.

Asthma beginning in adult life suggests the possibility of an occupational allergen. Almost any airborne protein-containing mist or dust generated at the workplace can cause occupational allergy (Bernstein et al., 1993).

The role of gastroesophageal reflux in perpetuating asthma is controversial. Most patients with reflux do not have asthma and most patients with asthma do not have reflux. If reflux symptoms are present, an upper gastrointestinal series is a reasonable way to begin the investigation. Many patients with asthma have sinusitis. Acute sinusitis is often infectious. Chronic sinusitis is usually a manifestation of the same lymphocytic–eosinophilic inflammation in the sinuses that exists in the bronchi.

TABLE 5–1–2. ALLERGENS THAT CAUSE ASTHMA

Outdoor, communitywide
  Pollens
    Trees in the spring
    Grasses in the early summer and fall
    Weeds in the late summer and fall, especially the Compositae (ragweed and Russian thistle)
  Molds
    Alternaria and *Cladosporium* in warm humid weather all summer
Dwellings
  Domestic mites
    Dermatophagoides sp., *Blomia* sp.
  Pets
    Cats
    Dogs
    Other mammals
    Birds
  Cockroaches
  Molds
Occupational
  Chemicals
    Diisocyanates in plastics and paints
    Phthalic anhydride
    Ethylenediamine
    Platinum salts
  Organic dusts
    Barn and grain dust
    Wood dust
    Proteases in detergent and food processing plants
    Laboratory animals
    Powder from latex gloves
    Countless other dusts and mists

Therapeutic

In as much as asthma is highly variable, both between different patients and at different times in the same patient, management must be carefully individualized to achieve the objectives of controlling this chronic disease. Management is outcome oriented. The process by which the outcome is achieved is secondary. Ideally, treatment has the goals listed in Table 5–1–3.

In severe cases it is commonly necessary to compromise between some of these goals, because some are not always possible. For example, in severe asthma it may be necessary to accept the side effects of corticosteroids to avoid restricting activities unacceptably or to prevent severe exacerbations. Unfortunately, it is not yet certain that in the slow severe asthma the following program will prevent development of irreversible airway obstruction.

Management plans to achieve these goals can be considered in six parts (Table 5–1–4).

The aim of patient education is to provide the patient and family with the knowledge and skills needed to maintain asthma control. The emphasis must be on developing a partnership between the patient, family, and physician. The responsibility for the education (which is so complex it requires several sessions) lies with the physician, but it may be shared with other professionals. Respiratory technicians can instruct in inhaler technique. Pharmacists can teach about drugs. And many asthma clinics have a nurse-educator. Both verbal and written instructions are important, and the patient must have the opportunity to ask questions and participate in decisions. Excellent printed material is available from the National Asthma Education Program, PO Box 30104, Bethesda, MD 20824–0105. Some communities have asthma support groups to assist patients and families in understanding the disease. The educational program must be individualized to meet each patient's medical, social, and psychological needs. Furthermore, the knowledge and skills that the patient has acquired must be evaluated and expanded periodically.

Education should include the following components:

- Information about the diagnosis and the nature and natural history of the disease
- Information about the general principles of the management plan and the goals listed above
- Information about the drugs used for treatment: their action, duration, and specific purpose
- Coaching in how to use a metered-dose inhaler effectively and, when indicated, how to use a peak flowmeter at home

Difficulty using a metered-dose inhaler is the main reason for poor therapeutic response to medications. The recommended method is to exhale comfortably to the end of normal exhalation, place the inhaler an inch or two in front of the open mouth, and start to inhale slowly. Just after the start of inhalation, depress the canister and continue inhaling slowly to full lung inflation. Rest and repeat for the prescribed number of doses. It is necessary to watch the patient perform this maneuver on each visit. Half of them, at least, will not be inhaling effectively.

Objective Measurement of Lung Function. Symptoms and physical findings are unreliable measures of the severity of the obstruction. At the time of the initial visit, spirometry determines the severity and the immediate response to bronchodilator, and serves as a benchmark for interpreting

TABLE 5–1–3. GOALS: ASTHMA CONTROL OBJECTIVES

- Freedom from symptoms, day and night
- Preventing asthma exacerbations
- Maintaining pulmonary function as close to normal as possible
- No restriction of activities, including sports
- Avoiding adverse effects from asthma medications
- Preventing development of irreversible airway obstruction
- Preventing asthma mortality

TABLE 5–1–4. SIX-PART ASTHMA MANAGEMENT PROGRAM

1. Educate patients to develop a partnership in asthma management.
2. Assess and monitor asthma severity with objective monitoring of lung function.
3. Avoid or control exposure to important airborne allergens or irritants.
4. Establish medication plans for chronic treatment.
5. Establish plans for managing exacerbations.
6. Provide regular follow-up care.

peak expiratory flow rate (PEFR). Early in the course of chronic management it is important to determine the patient's best achievable value of forced expiratory volume in 1 second (FEV_1) or PEFR to use as a goal of control. For patients with moderate or severe asthma this determination may require treatment with oral corticosteroid for 2 weeks to achieve complete control. In many moderate and in all severe cases, home PEFR monitoring is needed to allow the patient to alter the medication regime and recognize increasing severity before it becomes an emergency. Because of the characteristic diurnal swings in severity of asthma, special attention is placed on the difference between the high evening and the low morning PEFR. Home PEFR monitoring in asthma is analogous to blood glucose monitoring in insulin-dependent diabetes and is equally important (and equally difficult to convince patients to perform).

Avoidance or Control of Exposure to Allergens and Other Triggers of Airway Inflammation. The best evidence confirming the therapeutic importance of avoiding allergens comes from follow-up studies of workers with occupational asthma after the occupational exposure ceases. If the exposure has been brief and the asthma mild, then recovery is good. But if exposure continues after asthma has become chronic, the recovery is frequently incomplete, and irreversible airway obstruction is quite common. Thus, early identification of allergens and control of exposure is important to reduce the severity and impairment from the disease. Discussion of the details of identifying and controlling exposure to allergens is beyond the scope of this chapter. The important indoor agents are mites, pets, and cockroaches in the home and many occupational causes of asthma in the workplace. Indoor humidity is the chief factor promoting mite growth. As a result, in climates of high humidity, mite allergy seems to be the most important environmental cause of asthma. And even in temperate or cold climates they are important. High desert and high plains climates formerly were free of domestic mites, and despite the popularity of swamp coolers significant infestation is still rare. The following reasonable measures can be used to reduce mite exposure: Encase the mattress and pillow in a cover nonpermeable to allergens. Wash the bedding weekly in hot water with an oxidizing containing bleach. Avoid sleeping or lying on upholstered furniture. Remove carpets laid on concrete slabs and any carpets from the bedroom. Avoid bedrooms that are below grade. Ideally, the bedroom should be on an upper floor. Keep indoor humidity less than 50% and dry up ecological niches where humidity is greater than 80%. To some extent, keeping humidity at 50% can be accomplished by reducing the generation of indoor humidity by proper venting of bathrooms and kitchens. Repair water leaks. Do not treat asthma exacerbations with humidifiers.

Exposure to outdoor allergens can be reduced by closing windows and using air conditioning. But reduced ventilation in tight energy-efficient houses often increases indoor humidity that promotes mite and mold growth. For patients allergic to pets, the only truly effective means of avoiding the allergen is to remove the animal from the house. Results are not immediate because cat allergen persists in the home many weeks after the animal is gone. Foods rarely cause asthma in adults, and when they do asthma is usually only part of a generalized anaphylactic reaction. The importance of food additives is controversial, and in individual cases only carefully performed double-blind challenges can identify such a trigger.

Immunotherapy is occasionally indicated to treat patients allergic to allergens such as pollens, molds, and mites that are abundant and cannot be effectively avoided.

Children born into homes where adults smoke have increased frequency of asthma and other respiratory illnesses. And asthma can reasonably be suspected of predisposing to chronic obstructive pulmonary disease in smokers. Regular exposure to second-hand smoke should be avoided, but symptoms developing after casual exposure to smoke, perfumes, or other irritants means that the asthma is inadequately controlled. The medication program should be advanced a step (Figure 5–1–1).

Viral respiratory infections are frequent triggers. Although influenza virus accounts for only a minority of these infections, it is the only pre-ventable one. Therefore, annual influenza immunization is recommended. Elderly patients with asthma are vulnerable to pneumococcus infection so at least one injection of Pneumovax is recommended also.

Establishment of Medication Plans for Chronic Management. The rich menu of asthma medications is organized in courses suitable for varying degrees of severity. Selection is based on symptoms, results of spirometry or peak expiratory flow rate, and response to previous treatment. A

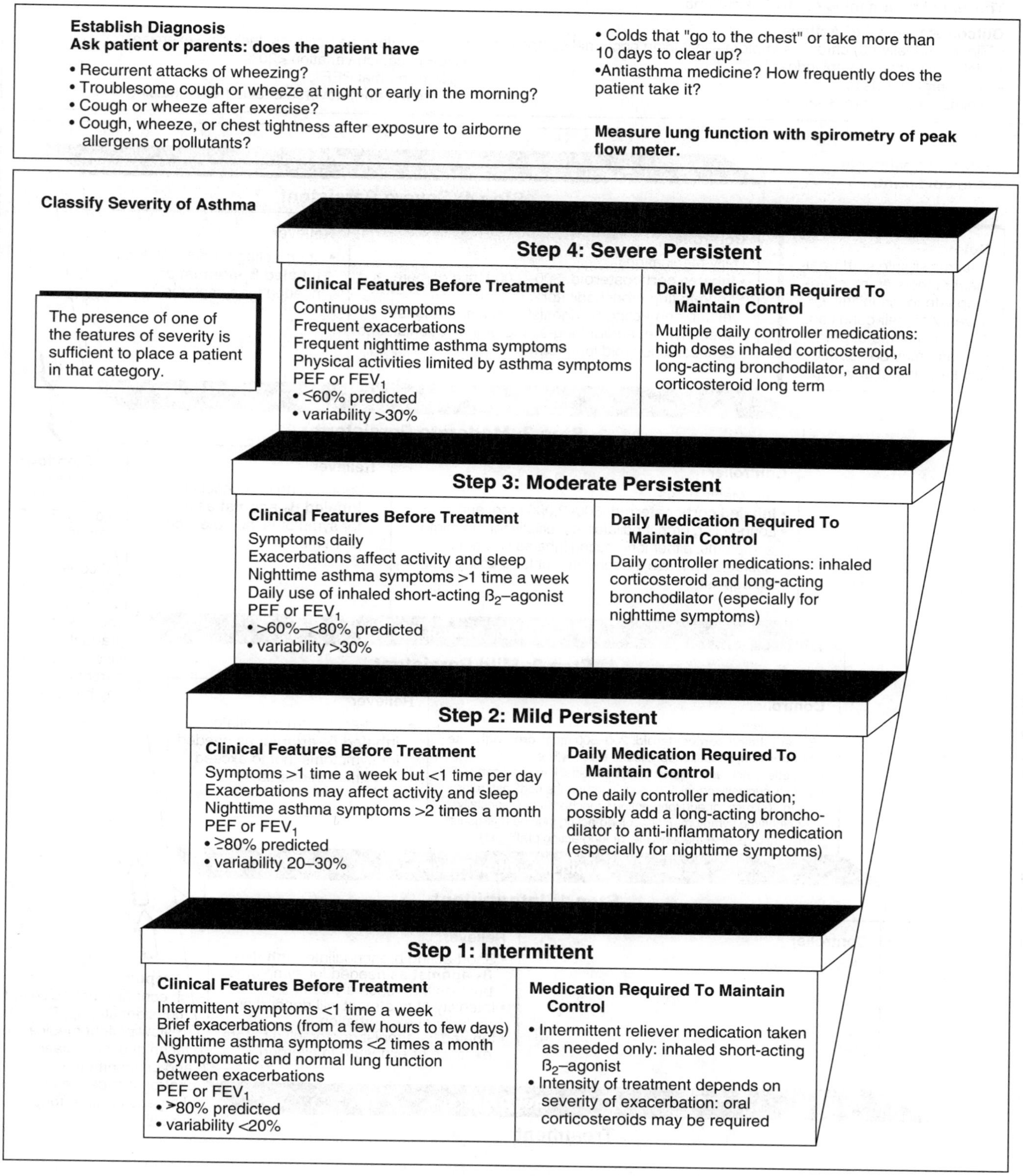

Establish Diagnosis
Ask patient or parents: does the patient have

- Recurrent attacks of wheezing?
- Troublesome cough or wheeze at night or early in the morning?
- Cough or wheeze after exercise?
- Cough, wheeze, or chest tightness after exposure to airborne allergens or pollutants?

- Colds that "go to the chest" or take more than 10 days to clear up?
- Antiasthma medicine? How frequently does the patient take it?

Measure lung function with spirometry of peak flow meter.

Classify Severity of Asthma

The presence of one of the features of severity is sufficient to place a patient in that category.

Step 4: Severe Persistent

Clinical Features Before Treatment
Continuous symptoms
Frequent exacerbations
Frequent nighttime asthma symptoms
Physical activities limited by asthma symptoms
PEF or FEV_1
- ≤60% predicted
- variability >30%

Daily Medication Required To Maintain Control
Multiple daily controller medications: high doses inhaled corticosteroid, long-acting bronchodilator, and oral corticosteroid long term

Step 3: Moderate Persistent

Clinical Features Before Treatment
Symptoms daily
Exacerbations affect activity and sleep
Nighttime asthma symptoms >1 time a week
Daily use of inhaled short-acting $β_2$–agonist
PEF or FEV_1
- >60%–<80% predicted
- variability >30%

Daily Medication Required To Maintain Control
Daily controller medications: inhaled corticosteroid and long-acting bronchodilator (especially for nighttime symptoms)

Step 2: Mild Persistent

Clinical Features Before Treatment
Symptoms >1 time a week but <1 time per day
Exacerbations may affect activity and sleep
Nighttime asthma symptoms >2 times a month
PEF or FEV_1
- ≥80% predicted
- variability 20–30%

Daily Medication Required To Maintain Control
One daily controller medication; possibly add a long-acting bronchodilator to anti-inflammatory medication (especially for nighttime symptoms)

Step 1: Intermittent

Clinical Features Before Treatment
Intermittent symptoms <1 time a week
Brief exacerbations (from a few hours to few days)
Nighttime asthma symptoms <2 times a month
Asymptomatic and normal lung function between exacerbations
PEF or FEV_1
- >80% predicted
- variability <20%

Medication Required To Maintain Control
- Intermittent reliever medication taken as needed only: inhaled short-acting $β_2$–agonist
- Intensity of treatment depends on severity of exacerbation: oral corticosteroids may be required

Figure 5–1–1. The long-term management of asthma: Diagnose and classify severity. (*Source: Global Initiative for Asthma. National Heart, Lung and Blood Institute; National Institutes of Health; Bethesda, MD 20892. Publication No. 95-3659, January, 1995. To order telephone 301-251-1222.*)

written program for each individual should include criteria for the patient to use in deciding when to change medication or to call the physician. The program is most conveniently considered a stepwise approach (Figure 5–1–2). Step 1 is a short-acting aerosol beta-adrenergic agonist at the time of acute symptoms or before activities that will provoke symptoms, such as exercise and exposure to an allergen. If such treatment is needed more that once or twice a day, proceed to step 2. Step 2 is an aerosol corticosteroid. The dose varies. The usual starting dose is two puffs four times a day, decreasing as tolerated to twice a day, or even once a day. Treatment is more effective four times a day, but compliance is better when the dosing is less frequent. Most patients prefer four puffs twice a day to two puffs four times a day. Metered-dose

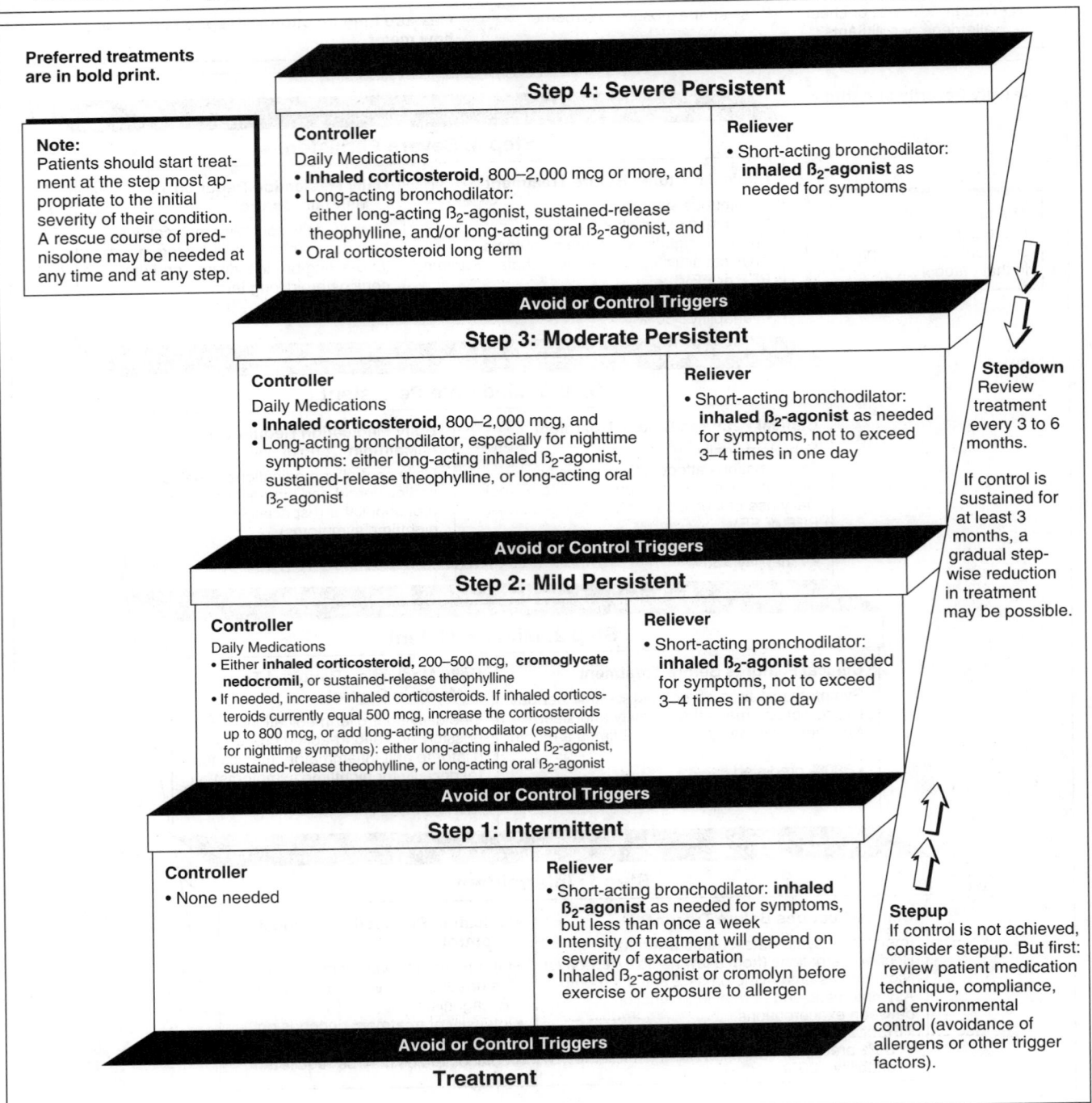

The aim of treatment is control of asthma

Outcome: Control of Asthma
- Minimal (ideally no) chronic symptoms, including nocturnal symptoms
- Minimal (infrequent) episodes
- No emergency visits
- Minimal need for prn β_2-agonist
- No limitations on activities, including exercise
- PEF circadian variation <20%
- (Near) normal PEF
- Minimal (or no) adverse effects from medicine

Preferred treatments are in bold print.

Note:
Patients should start treatment at the step most appropriate to the initial severity of their condition. A rescue course of prednisolone may be needed at any time and at any step.

Step 4: Severe Persistent

Controller
Daily Medications
- **Inhaled corticosteroid, 800–2,000 mcg or more,** and
- Long-acting bronchodilator: either long-acting β_2-agonist, sustained-release theophylline, and/or long-acting oral β_2-agonist, and
- Oral corticosteroid long term

Reliever
- Short-acting bronchodilator: **inhaled β_2-agonist** as needed for symptoms

Avoid or Control Triggers

Step 3: Moderate Persistent

Controller
Daily Medications
- **Inhaled corticosteroid, 800–2,000 mcg,** and
- Long-acting bronchodilator, especially for nighttime symptoms: either long-acting inhaled β_2-agonist, sustained-release theophylline, or long-acting oral β_2-agonist

Reliever
- Short-acting bronchodilator: **inhaled β_2-agonist** as needed for symptoms, not to exceed 3–4 times in one day

Avoid or Control Triggers

Step 2: Mild Persistent

Controller
Daily Medications
- Either **inhaled corticosteroid,** 200–500 mcg, **cromoglycate nedocromil,** or sustained-release theophylline
- If needed, increase inhaled corticosteroids. If inhaled corticosteroids currently equal 500 mcg, increase the corticosteroids up to 800 mcg, or add long-acting bronchodilator (especially for nighttime symptoms): either long-acting inhaled β_2-agonist, sustained-release theophylline, or long-acting oral β_2-agonist

Reliever
- Short-acting pronchodilator: **inhaled β_2-agonist** as needed for symptoms, not to exceed 3–4 times in one day

Avoid or Control Triggers

Step 1: Intermittent

Controller
- None needed

Reliever
- Short-acting bronchodilator: **inhaled β_2-agonist** as needed for symptoms, but less than once a week
- Intensity of treatment will depend on severity of exacerbation
- Inhaled β_2-agonist or cromolyn before exercise or exposure to allergen

Avoid or Control Triggers

Treatment

Stepdown
Review treatment every 3 to 6 months.

If control is sustained for at least 3 months, a gradual stepwise reduction in treatment may be possible.

Stepup
If control is not achieved, consider stepup. But first: review patient medication technique, compliance, and environmental control (avoidance of allergens or other trigger factors).

Figure 5–1–2. The long-term management of asthma: Treatments in the stepwise approach. (*Source: Global Initiative for Asthma. National Heart, Lung and Blood Institute; National Institutes of Health; Bethesda, MD 20892. Publication No. 95-3659, January, 1995. To order telephone 301-251-1222.*)

aerosol corticosteroids should always be inhaled through a spacer to reduce oropharyngeal deposition that causes local side effects and systemic absorption. There are two types of spacers: a simple reverse Venturi tube and a reservoir device. Azmacort Oral Inhaler (triamcinolone acetonide) is packaged with its own tube spacer. Reservoir spacers that can be used with metered-dose inhalers include the Aerochamber and Inspirease. Pulmocort (budesonide) will be marketed in a dry powder device that does not need a spacer. The most important reason for poor response to treatment is improper aerosol inhalation technique. At each follow-up visit, the patient should demonstrate mastery of this skill. If the short-acting beta-adrenergic agonist is needed as often as four times a day, a long-acting beta-adrenergic agonist (salmeterol) used twice a day provides smoother control. *Salmeterol is not suitable for acute symptoms. When acute symptoms occur, the short-acting beta adrenergic agonist should be inhaled as usual.* There are increasing reports of arrhythmias and fatalities when increasing doses of salmeterol have been wrongly inhaled instead of a short acting drug such as albuterol. Step 3 is to increase the aerosol glucocorticoids to three or four puffs four times a day. Larger doses are customary in Europe and Canada, but the more concentrated preparations that make larger doses practical are not available in the United States. Step 3 also includes salmeterol or sustained-release theophylline in a dose to achieve theophylline blood levels of 8 to 10 μg/mL. (not the level of 10–20 μg/mL required for optimum bronchodilitation). Again, short-acting beta-adrenergic agonists are to be used for acute symptoms. Step 4 is to add oral glucocorticoids. The usual program is prednisone 20 mg twice a day until control is achieved. Then the dose is reduced to the lowest dose that maintains control. If the dose required to achieve control is larger than 40 mg/d, the patient is considered "steroid resistant." One of the points the patient needs to know is that if the medication is discontinued after control has been achieved with aerosol or oral corticosteroids, the symptoms usually recur within about 3 weeks. If the steroid has been given for a brief flare from a viral infection, the medication program can return to the previous schedule that controlled the disease. But if the symptoms are chronic, reduction in dose should be gradual over several months. Patients with adrenal suppression from long-term oral corticosteroids may have fatal asthma if the medication is reduced abruptly.

Alternative choices can be considered in special cases. Some patients, especially elderly ones, cannot learn how to use metered-dose inhalers. For these patients, electric-powered jet nebulizers require less coordination to deliver beta-adrenergic agonists. Breath-actuated devices (e.g., the Autohaler delivering pirbuterol) are another alternative. Beta-adrenergic agonist tablets have few, if any, indications. The side effects and lesser efficacy of systemic beta-adrenergic agonists limit their value. Ipratropium, an anticholinergic aerosol, offers a substitute for some patients when tremor or cardiac effects complicate beta-adrenergic aerosols. Its onset is slower, and some patients do not respond to it, so it should be shown to be effective by objective tests.

Concern over safety has limited acceptance of aerosol corticosteroids. Their safety record for more than 20 years has been excellent, however. International consensus now considers that the benefits of controlled asthma far outweigh potential side effects and has recommended them as first choice in all but the mildest cases. The most frequent side effects are dysphonia and oropharyngeal candidiasis. These drugs are absorbed into the systemic circulation, and systemic corticosteroid effects are detectable with doses above six to eight puffs a day. Reduced cortisol excretion is evident, but clinically significant suppression of the hypophyseal–pituitary–adrenal axis is rare unless the dose is more than 2000 μg/d. Growth suppression in children has been studied intensively, but controversy continues as to whether aerosol corticosteroids truly suppress growth or merely delay the adolescent growth spurt. Many pediatricians, therefore, choose cromolyn or nedocromil for step 2, reserving corticosteroids for step 3. Although cromolyn and nedocromil are less effective than corticosteroids, they are almost devoid of serious side effects. In adults, similar caution is reasonable for insulin-dependent diabetics or elderly patients with severe osteoporosis. When systemic corticosteroids are required, the only advantage of the parenteral over the oral route is the assurance the dose is delivered and patient compliance is not a consideration. There is rarely an advantage of other more expensive preparations over prednisone. In very exceptional patients who are impossible to identify prospectively, the

pharmacokinetics of methylprednisolone may provide better control of asthma than prednisone.

Theophylline is less effective as a bronchodilator than beta-adrenergic agonists and does not add additional bronchodilation to optimal doses of aerosol beta-adrenergic agonists. Therefore, it is no longer advised as part of the emergency management of severe exacerbations. Doses required for maximal bronchodilation are associated with significant adverse effects and require careful monitoring of blood levels to avoid serious toxicity. At lower blood levels, theophylline is effective in reducing symptoms and improving peak expiratory flow rate in chronic mild to moderate asthma, and there is some evidence that the severity of the inflammation is reduced. A valuable practical advantage is that theophylline is an oral agent. Sustained-release formulations given only once or twice a day, being sure that one dose is taken at bedtime, often control mild cases, particularly those with prominent nocturnal symptoms. Thus, low-dose theophylline is an acceptable alternative to aerosol glucocorticoids in step 2 (Fig. 5–1–2).

Plans for Managing Exacerbations. The above program of written directions for the patient to follow when asthma becomes more severe will prevent or greatly reduce the severity of most exacerbations. Viral respiratory infections commonly provoke severe exacerbations that require a short course of oral steroids. And other severe exacerbations may occur for unknown reasons. Therefore, the patient should have a written plan for managing exacerbations at home. This plan should be individualized according to the patient's medical and social characteristics. These instructions should include the name and telephone number of the physician to call if there are questions or if the asthma is not responding. Patients with previous hospital or emergency treatment are more likely to need emergency care again. Figure 5–1–3 outlines the approach to this problem.

The characteristics of a fatality-prone asthmatic are shown in Table 5–1–5. A written crisis plan is especially important for the rare patient who is at risk of a fatal episode of asthma. This plan should include the warning signals, instructions for taking additional aerosol bronchodilator (but not relying on it to the exclusion of other medications), an extra dose of prednisone, prompt removal to the nearest emergency service, and directions for the emergency team, who may not know the patient and might not appreciate the urgency of the situation.

FOLLOW-UP

The initiation of a complex educational and management program for patients with moderate to severe disease usually requires several visits. After the plan is in place, regular follow-up visits are important to provide supervision, praise, and encouragement and to deal with problems that may lead to poor adherence of inadequate control. The following factors may need attention:

- Too complicated or awkward medication regimens. Consider changing to twice-a-day or once-a-day schedules. Long-acting medications are best taken late in the day to achieve a peak effect in the early morning hours when the disease is at its worst.
- Problems with inhaler devices. At each visit, ask the patient to demonstrate using the device to be certain that the medication is reaching the lung. More than half the time the technique will not be optimal. Some patients inadvertently continue to use an empty canister. Empty canisters float on their sides like a dead fish.
- Complacency, forgetfulness, or misunderstanding.
- Real or imagined side effects.
- Dislike of medications or fear of corticosteroids.
- Overreliance on bronchodilators.
- Underestimation of the severity of the disease.
- Cost of medications or health care.
- Stigmatization or other cultural factors.
- Anger/rebellion.

DISCUSSION
Prevalence

Incidence, prevalence, and mortality have been increasing throughout the Western world. Asthma is now a leading cause of illness and hospi-

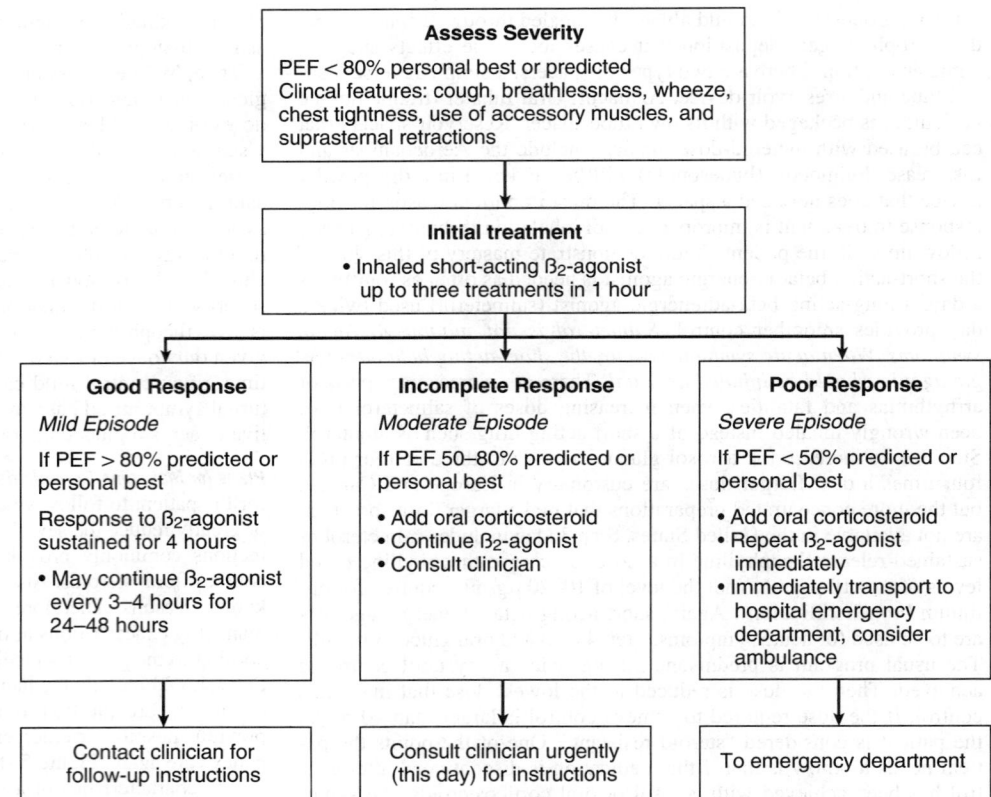

Figure 5–1–3. Management of exacerbation of asthma at home. *(Source: National Heart, Lung and Blood Institute. International consensus report on diagnosis and treatment of asthma. Publication No. 92-3091. Bethesda, MD: U.S. Department of Health and Human Services, 1992.)*

talization in children and young adults. In the past 20 years the incidence in some populations has doubled. The reasons for the increase are poorly understood but presumably are multifactorial and stem from as yet unidentified changes in both indoor and outdoor environment. Population differences offer clues. Prevalence is greater in New Zealand, Australia, and the United Kingdom than in the United States and Canada. Prevalence is greater in West Germany than in East Germany, although industrial pollution has been worse in the East. In the United States the incidence in infancy is about 1000/100,000. With increasing age, the incidence drops to about 100/100,000 at age 20, and then continues about the same throughout adult life. The prevalence of asthma is about 4% in adults. Prevalence and severity are both greater in African-Americans, especially in the inner cities.

Related Basic Science

Pathology

The typical changes of asthma are obstruction of the lumen by mucus and an inflammatory exudate containing activated lymphocytes and eosinophils; fragility and desquamation of the ciliated epithelium with areas of regeneration; deposition of collagen beneath the basement membrane; hyperemia and edema of the submucosa with infiltration by

TABLE 5–1–5. CHARACTERISTICS OF FATALITY-PRONE ASTHMATICS

- Previous life-threatening episodes
- Admission to the hospital within the past year
- Inadequate medical management
- Psychiatric, psychological, and social problems
- Age over 65
- African-American
- Lack of access to medical care

activated lymphocytes and eosinophils (neutrophils are conspicuously absent in most, but not all cases); increase in the number of mast cells in the wall; increase in goblet cells and submucosal mucus glands, similar to chronic bronchitis; and hypertrophy of smooth muscle in medium-sized airways. The fibrosis beneath the basement membrane in small airways is likely to be an important factor contributing to the development of permanent obstruction. Bronchial biopsies have not only confirmed that the abnormalities described in fatal asthma are present in milder cases but have provided the data that lead to the concepts of the pathogenesis of the allergic inflammation discussed below.

Physiologic Derangement

The primary physiologic characteristic of asthma is airway hyperresponsiveness (bronchospasm) to a wide variety of stimuli that operate through vagal reflex pathways or, in the case of neurotransmitters and mediators of inflammation, act directly on airway smooth muscle. Several different mechanisms operate to bring about this hyperresponsiveness. First, hereditary factors are apparent. Approximately half of healthy first-degree relatives of asthmatics have hyperresponsiveness. Second, geometric factors are important. The swelling of the airway mucosa reduces the lumen so that a small contraction of the smooth muscle has a greatly amplified effect on airway caliber and, thereby, on airflow resistance. Third, the bronchoconstrictive effects of the mediators of inflammation such as histamine, leukotrienes, and neuropeptides are synergistic with reflex bronchoconstriction. Finally, the major basic protein of the eosinophil granule inactivates M2 receptors in the vagal synapse. Normal M2 receptors inhibit neuromuscular transmission and reduce reflex bronchoconstriction.

The two chief physiologic consequences of airway obstruction are: (1) increased intrathoracic pressure and decreased venous return that reduces cardiac filling and cardiac output; and (2) hypoxemia and respiratory alkalosis that results from the fact that the airway obstruction is not uniform. Obstruction is complete in some airways and minimal in others. As a result, perfusion of underventilated areas of the lung causes mixing of nonoxygenated blood and arterial hypoxemia. Compensatory hyperventilation of the well-aerated part of the lung does not correct the ventilation–perfusion inequality, but does reduce the $PaCO_2$ and produces mild respiratory alkalosis. Acidosis occurs only when the obstruction is so severe that the FEV_1 is below 10 to 20%. One of the effects of hyperventilation in some patients is to set up a vicious cycle of increasing bronchoconstriction.

Immunologic Abnormalities

The past decade has seen intense cellular and molecular biological research into the immunologic mechanisms of asthma that has greatly expanded understanding of allergic inflammation. The acute asthmatic reaction to an allergen follows binding of allergenic protein to immunoglobulin E antibody attached to mast cells. This binding stimulates mast cells to release their granules that contain histamine, tryptase, and other molecules. In addition, important synthetic processes are stimulated to produce early-acting eicosanoids (prostaglandin D_2, leukotrienes) and late-acting cytokines that activate and localize eosinophils at the site of the late phase of the acute reaction. It is clear that many additional cells, particularly helper lymphocytes, are involved in initiating and perpetuating allergic inflammation. A particular variety of helper (CD4$^+$) lymphocytes (TH2-like) are abundant in the inflamed airways of asthma and are activated to produce a set of cytokines that promote synthesis of immunoglobulin E and secretory immunoglobulin A; growth, activation, and recruitment of eosinophils, neutrophils, and basophils; and growth of mast cells. These cytokines also stimulate epithelial cells and endothelial cells to produce adhesion molecules that localize the inflammatory cells in the airways. One of these adhesion molecules is ICAM-1, which is the receptor for rhinoviruses, a common initiator of asthmatic episodes. Eosinophils degranulate in the airway mucosa, where their toxic granule proteins kill ciliated epithelial cells and have other adverse effects, including increasing airway hyperresponsiveness. This exceedingly active field of research has clarified the action of corticosteroids to some extent. These compounds inhibit production of the eicosanoid mediators, inhibit production of cytokines by lymphocytes, and inhibit the action of cytokines on other cells including eosinophils.

Genetics

Asthma, at least allergic asthma, clusters in families, but inheritance cannot be explained by any single-gene model. Therefore, current genetics research interest centers on the relationship between particular genes and production of specific molecules of importance in allergic inflammation or airway hyperresponsiveness such as immunoglobulin E, various cytokokines, and beta-adrenergic and muscarinic receptors. In understanding the genetic basis for asthma, it is of considerable interest that after lung transplantation, occurrence of asthma resides in the transplanted lung, not in the recipient. That is, asthma develops in a normal person who received a transplant from an asthmatic person, and the lung transplanted from a normal person to an asthmatic does not become affected by the disease.

Natural History and Its Modification with Treatment

The course of asthma is variable. The profound truism that over time asthma will either improve, stay the same, or get worse is of little use to patients or their families who want a reasonably accurate prognosis, or to physicians who want to plan a realistic individualized management program that is not unnecessarily burdensome.

Asthma begins most often in early childhood, more commonly in boys than girls. Many infants with one or two episodes of wheezy bronchitis never develop chronic asthma. But many infants do. Several factors are associated with continued asthma throughout the childhood years. Perhaps the most important one is the capacity to develop immunoglobulin E antibody to allergens in the environment. Development of asthma and allergy to housedust mites correlates with the

amount of mite allergen in the home. Furthermore, persistence of asthma with episodes severe enough to require urgent treatment is associated with exposure to mites, pets, and cockroaches in the home and to maternal cigarette smoking.

The prognosis of children with asthma as they mature to adulthood is quite good. About a quarter become free of symptoms and have normal pulmonary function tests in early adult life. Half have occasional mild wheezing with exercise or respiratory infections. Only about 20% persist with frequent or persistent wheezing or reduced FEV_1. But by middle age, a third of those who were free of symptoms at age 21 have relapsed. Thus, about half of children with asthma have active disease as adults. Factors that predict persistence are onset before age 3, development of immunoglobulin E antibody to environmental allergens and continued exposure to them, infantile eczema, severe disease, and female sex. Measurement of airway hyperresponsiveness does not predict outcome sufficiently accurately to be a useful indicator of prognosis.

Prospective population-based studies of the natural history of asthma in adults are few and, like the studies in children, are limited by difficulties in defining the disease. Most of the patients whose asthma persists from childhood have allergy to various aeroallergens, but the new-onset asthmatics are rarely allergic unless they have developed occupational asthma. The following factors are associated with persistence of disease and decline in lung function:

- Severe disease with fixed airway obstruction
- Onset after age 40 and negative skin tests to common allergens
- Continued exposure to allergens (particularly occupational agents) after asthma has developed
- Cigarette smoking

The death rate and the age of death for adults with asthma are not statistically different from those of the population at large, but underlying asthma is often the cause of death from chronic respiratory failure after age 65. Although the asthma management plan described in this chapter reduces morbidity, it is not yet known whether treatment influences the long-term decline in lung function with development of irreversible obstruction.

Prevention

Parents can receive education about preventing asthma in their offspring. Cigarette smoking, damp houses, and indoor furry pets are avoidable risk factors. The child's bedroom ideally should be on an upper floor to reduce exposure to mites. The role of breastfeeding and diet remains controversial. Exposure of young children to respiratory viral infections in daycare centers is probably another risk factor. Asthmatic children exposed to rhinoviruses in the home are almost twice as likely to become infected as their nonasthmatic siblings. Little is known about preventing asthma in adults other than reducing occupational exposures.

Cost Containment

The chief opportunity for cost containment lies in preventing emergency room visits and hospital admissions by following the management plan described in this chapter.

REFERENCES

Bernstein IL, Chan-Yeung M, Malo J-L, Bernstein DI, eds. Asthma in the workplace. New York: Marcel Dekker, 1993.

Middleton E Jr, Reed CE, Ellis EF, et al., eds. Allergy principles and practice. 4th ed. St Louis: Mosby, 1993.

National Education Program. Guidelines for the diagnosis and management of asthma: Expert panel report. Publication No. 91-3042. Bethesda, MD: U.S. Department of Health and Human Services, 1991.

National Heart, Lung and Blood Institute. International consensus report on diagnosis and treatment of asthma. Publication No. 92-3091. Bethesda, MD: U.S. Department of Health and Human Services, 1992.

Asthma (Acute) as Viewed by an Allergist

Evangelos Frigas, M.D., Joel S. Klein, M.D., and Daniel E. Maddox, M.D.

DEFINITION

Acute asthma is a *rapid* decrease in bronchial airflow resulting from an abnormal narrowing in the caliber of the airways by an inflammatory process affecting the bronchi and bronchioles (see also Section 13, Chapter 20).

ETIOLOGY

The cause of asthma remains unknown. There are several precipitating and/or aggravating factors such as viral respiratory infections, exposure to environmental allergens (i.e., pollens, molds, house dust mites, animal proteins), exposure to occupational chemicals or allergens (i.e., isocyanates, enzyme detergents, flour), medications (such as aspirin and beta blockers), food additives (sulfites), exposure to cold air, exercise, and air pollution. The airborne allergens are the most important asthma triggers for patients with allergic type of asthma, whereas viral respiratory infections are the most common causes of acute exacerbations for patients with nonallergic or intrinsic type of asthma.

CRITERIA FOR DIAGNOSIS

Suggestive

A careful history and physical examination of the upper and lower respiratory tract, as well as the heart, are the essential steps in the diagnosis of asthma. Whenever possible, a few laboratory tests should be done, such as examination of the sputum for eosinophils or eosinophil by-products, pulmonary function tests, and a chest x-ray. By history, it is essential to establish the episodic nature and reversibility of airway obstruction. Usually there is a positive family history of asthma.

Definitive

The diagnosis of asthma is easily made when a patient presents with acute onset of wheezing, has a previous history of episodic wheezing, has a normal chest x-ray, has a decreased forced expiratory volume in 1 second (FEV_1) or peak expiratory flow rate, has evidence of blood or sputum eosinophilia, and responds promptly to anti-asthmatic therapy.

CLINICAL MANIFESTATIONS

Subjective

The symptoms of acute asthma are wheezing, cough, chest tightness, shortness of breath, and sputum production. All these symptoms may coexist; but an occasion, cough or chest tightness may be the only symptom of acute asthma. The sputum is thick and tenacious, may contain mucous plugs, and is usually clear unless there is secondary viral or bacterial infection. The wheezing is related to the degree of bronchial obstruction and movement of air. Usually the wheezing is a sound generated during expiration, but it may be heard also on inspiration as the severity of bronchial obstruction increases. When the bronchial obstruction is so severe that there is very limited movement of air, the wheezing may be absent.

Objective

Physical Examination

Wheezing, diminished movement of air, and prolonged expiration all can be best appreciated by the examining physician when, on chest auscultation, the stethoscope in the palm of one hand is placed on the sternum and the other palm on the posterior aspect of the patient's chest.

Routing Laboratory Abnormalities

There are no diagnostic routine laboratory abnormalities for *acute* asthma. Eosinophilia may be present, but this does not indicate an acute attack.

PLANS

Diagnostic

Differential Diagnosis

The differentiation of acute asthma from other acute respiratory diseases usually is not difficult. The main differential diagnoses are acute respiratory failure in a patient with a history of chronic obstructive pulmonary disease (emphysema), acute pulmonary edema, pneumonia, pulmonary embolism, anaphylaxis, pneumothorax, and upper airway obstruction by either tumor or laryngeal edema. The findings of moist bibasilar rales, S_3 gallop, distended neck veins, and increased vascularity on chest x-ray with cardiomegaly are suggestive of acute left ventricular failure (cardiac asthma). In acute pneumonia, the history, localized auscultatory findings, chest x-ray, and sputum Gram stain lead to the diagnosis. Acute respiratory failure in patients with emphysema is diagnosed on the basis of the history, and the chest x-ray shows hyperinflation with hyperlucency of both lung fields and flattening of the diaphragms. The patient with laryngeal obstruction presents with stridor. Harsh respiratory sounds are localized in the neck area, while wheezing throughout the lung fields is usually absent. Indirect laryngoscopy most of the time confirms this diagnosis. Pruritic pain is a tip-off for pneumothorax and pulmonary embolism. The diagnosis of pneumothorax is easily made with a chest x-ray. The chest x-ray is also quite useful in the diagnosis of massive pulmonary embolism; however, small recurrent pulmonary emboli may be very difficult to differentiate from asthma. The chest x-ray in these cases is usually normal, and the ventilation/perfusion lung scan may not be diagnostic. In these cases, pulmonary angiography may be necessary to establish the correct diagnosis. Finally, for the diagnosis of acute asthma, the history of periodic episodes of wheezing along with orthopnea and nocturnal awakening because of wheezing and dyspnea are almost pathognomonic for bronchial asthma. In fact, if there is no history of orthopnea or nocturnal symptoms of asthma, one should seriously doubt this diagnosis. In addition, there is usually valuable contributory evidence such as history of allergic rhinitis and eczema or a personal or family history of asthma or allergic diseases. A therapeutic response to bronchodilator therapy with or without systemic glucocorticoids represents the final confirmatory evidence for the diagnosis of asthma.

Diagnostic Options and Recommended Approach

The initial assessment of a patient presenting with acute asthma should include measurement of bronchial airflow (FEV_1 or peak expiratory flow rate). This parameter also serves as a reference point in assessing the patient's improvement during this acute phase of therapy. Either the peak flow rate or the FEV_1 is decreased during an acute attack of asthma.

The bronchial obstruction measured by the FEV_1 correlates with the peripheral total blood eosinophil count; i.e., the higher the total blood eosinophil count, the lower the FEV_1 measurement. The arterial blood gases continue to be overused and are rarely needed unless the patient with acute asthma is in extreme distress, appears tired, and is about to lapse into acute respiratory failure necessitating intubation and assisted ventilation. Whenever possible, pulse oximetry is a painless way of assessing the adequacy of arterial oxygenation and identifying those hypoxemic patients who require therapy with oxygen. When arterial blood gases are done, the most common derangement in patients presenting to the emergency room with acute asthma is hypocapnia with mild respiratory alkalosis from alveolar hyperventilation and mild to moderate hypoxemia. As bronchial obstruction to the airflow worsens and alveolar ventilation decreases, the hypocapnia increases toward normal with a pCO_2 around 40 mm Hg, which is an ominous sign indicative of impending acute respiratory failure.

Therapeutic

Whether in the emergency room or in the office, a physician treating a patient with acute asthma must have a clear understanding of the pathophysiology and specific goals of what therapy and the patient must achieve. The immediate goal of therapy is prompt relief of the respiratory symptoms by rapidly reversing the bronchial obstruction to the airflow. A second, and even more important, goal is the aggressive reversal of the bronchial inflammation with antiinflammatory medications to be continued long enough to allow the desquamated bronchial epithelium to regenerate. Once the patient has been stabilized and is free of symptoms, any precipitating or aggravating factors should be identified to prevent recurrences of acute episodes of asthma.

Therapeutic Options

To rapidly reverse the airflow obstruction in acute asthma, repetitive administration of sympathomimetics represents the best choice. The inhalation route of delivery, by means of either a metered-dose inhaler or a nebulization apparatus, is preferred. Concerns about delivering enough medication by inhalation into the lungs of severely obstructed patients have been resolved using sequential inhalations or continuous nebulization of these medications. The nebulization does not require the coordination on the part of the patient needed when metered-dose inhalers are used. Inhaled beta agonists, as well as subcutaneous epinephrine, are all well tolerated hemodynamically; however, in geriatric patients or in patients with coronary artery disease and cardiac arrhythmia, there is the constant threat of worsening of their heart condition. The most common side effects of the β_2-agonist bronchodilators are tremor, palpitations, and increased nervousness. Up to the present time, there is no evidence that one type of selective β_2 bronchodilator is any better than another in treating acute asthma.

The combination of aminophylline intravenously and a sympathomimetic bronchodilator by inhalation, which was one of the favorite modalities in the past, has not proven to be any better than the sequential use of β_2 bronchodilator in an emergency setting. Furthermore, the avoidance of combining intravenous aminophylline and the β_2 inhaled bronchodilator has caused fewer side effects. Currently, there is no indication for intravenous administration of aminophylline in the emergency room treatment of acute asthma, although intravenous aminophylline may be useful as the inpatient treatment of adult patients with an asthma exacerbation.

Although the sympathomimetics, parasympatholytics, and theophylline provide symptomatic relief in acute asthma, they do not reduce the bronchial inflammation and are toxic when overused. That is why treatment with glucocorticoids is essential for the reversal of the bronchial inflammation in acute asthma. There is not doubt that the beneficial effect of the glucocorticoids will require several days to be fully established. Nevertheless, therapy with glucocorticoids should not be delayed because this will cause an unnecessary prolongation of the healing process of the inflamed bronchi in asthma. The fears of incapacitating side effects from the use of systemic glucocorticoids are unfounded when close monitoring of the patient and intensive educational instructions are provided, coupled with the ability of the patient to quickly reach the attending physician or nurse practitioner by telephone. In a well-supervised health care delivery system with integrated services for emergency and ambulatory care of patients with acute asthma, the systemic glucocorticoids can be administered to every patient with acute asthma when they are initially evaluated either in the office or in the emergency room. The initial dose of systemic glucocorticoids continues to be a subject of debate among authorities and certainly is a matter of judgment on the part of the treating physician. The mistake most commonly made is not the initial dose of systemic glucocorticoids, but the failure to closely monitor the activity of this inflammatory process and accordingly adjust the glucocorticoid therapy. Today, the average treatment recommendation at the time a patient is

seen for an acute episode of asthma is 40 to 60 mg of prednisone daily in divided doses to be tapered to zero over the next 10 to 14 days, with reassessment of the patient by the attending physician 3, 7, and 14 days later.

Recommended Approach

After the patient is quickly assessed by history and physical examination, a measurement of the obstruction to the airflow is done for a pretreatment baseline. Then a β_2 agonist bronchodilator is administered sequentially by a metered-dose inhaler or compressor-driven nebulizer. The patient is reassessed every 15 to 30 minutes clinically, and the frequency of treatment is adjusted according to the severity of airflow obstruction, improvement of the overall clinical picture, and severity of side effects from therapy. After the first hour of treatment and if steady improvement has been documented, the dosing interval between treatments should be gradually increased. In those patients in whom improvement appears to be slow, treatment with anticholinergic medications may be added in the hope of providing additive bronchodilation, although the benefit, if any, is generally small. At times, changing the route of administration of the sympathomimetic medication from inhalation to subcutaneous injection may provide benefit in cases slow to improve. When significant airflow obstruction persists, the patient should be admitted to the hospital to guarantee an appropriate treatment schedule and to closely monitor the respiratory function. On the other hand, those patients who have improved their pretreatment baseline peak expiratory flow rate or FEV_1 to 70 to 80% of their predicted normal or their personal best may be treated on an ambulatory basis. Prior to dismissal, these patients should be checked 1 and 2 hours after the last bronchodilator treatment to make sure this improvement is stable and to identify those with highly labile asthma. Furthermore, these patients should be instructed in the proper technique of inhaler use, be taught how to monitor their decreased airflow by means of Wright peak flowmeter, and have specific instructions on therapy. This approach provides the patient with a crisis plan, knowing exactly what to do in any given situation.

FOLLOW-UP

For those patients who after emergency therapy fail to significantly improve as previously described, one should be cautious. If the decision is made not to hospitalize the patient, systemic glucocorticoids should be added to the previously mentioned treatment in the range between 40 and 60 mg of prednisone in divided doses. There are no optimal, widely accepted tapering schedules for prednisone bursts. Mistakes in dosage and undesirable side effects can be minimized by frequent reassessments of the patient's clinical picture. The bronchial inflammation that led to an acute episode of asthma is almost never resolved after this initial emergency treatment. If not hospitalized, a patient should be reexamine 3, 7, and 14 days from the acute attack of asthma to appropriately tailor the treatment to what is needed to prevent relapses and guarantee a favorable outcome with minimal side effects. These additional visits also serve to foster the patient's education in understanding the disease, to explain the goals of treatment, to look for the side effects of the medications used, to optimize the self-monitoring of asthma, and to review the crisis plan.

Overall, 2 hours in an office environment and 4 hours in an emergency room should be enough for an experienced physician to administer appropriate therapy to a patient with an acute attack of asthma and direct the patient to either the hospital or ambulatory care.

DISCUSSION

Prevalence and Incidence and Related Basic Science

In recent years, increasing morbidity and death from acute asthma, particularly among the African-American population of the inner cities, has received wide public attention. Significant research advances have been made in elucidating the nature of this inflammatory process over the last decade but, unfortunately, without any significant practical therapeutic application since the discovery of glucocorticoids. Aerosolized or parenteral glucocorticoids remain the main form of treatment directed at interrupting the bronchial inflammation in asthma. This inflammatory process, if left unchecked, accelerates the age-related loss in FEV_1, and the obstruction to the bronchial airflow may become irreversible (*asthme invétéré*). Acute asthma continues to be one of the most common emergencies in the practice of medicine in our time, with morbidity and mortality on the rise (Sheffer, 1991). Death usually occurs suddenly after a severe exacerbation of the disease, and the death rate is slightly more than 1 per 100,000 population.

Anatomic Derangement

Any of the previously mentioned (under etiology) precipitating or aggravating factors, alone or in combination, in susceptible individuals, may lead to an acute episode of asthma. The pathology hallmarks are eosinophilic bronchitis with desquamation and destruction of the bronchial mucosa, Charcot–Leyden crystals, and Creola bodies, which are easily detectable in freshly expectorated sputum (Figures 5–2–1 and

5–2–2). In the bronchi, areas of bronchial mucosa are completely stripped of epithelium that has shed in the bronchial lumen, leaving behind a denuded surface of exposed bronchial submucosa. Below the lamina propria there is amorphous tissue thickening made of components of collagen, complement, and immunoglobulins. Underneath this thickened area, the submucosa appears edematous and inflamed by a cellular infiltrate of mononuclear cells and lymphocytes in which, strikingly, the eosinophils predominate (Figure 5–2–1). In the expectorated sputum, in the bronchial lumen, and within the necrotic-appearing areas of the bronchi, deposits of the eosinophil-derived granule major basic protein (MPB) are found.

Altered Molecular Biology

Our current understanding of the sequence of events that brings on this unique eosinophilic desquamative bronchitis of asthma may be summarized as follows. Virus- or allergen-induced activation of TH_2 lymphocytes, macrophages, and bronchial epithelial cells leads to secretion of

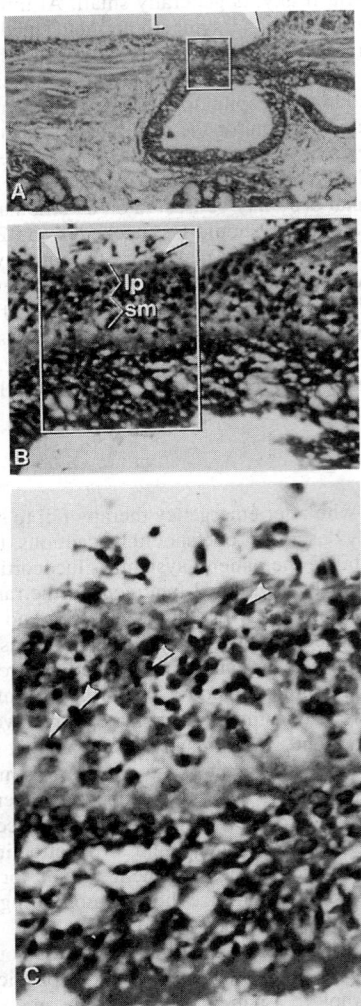

Figure 5–2–1. Bronchial mucosa abnormalities in acute asthma. **A.** A small bronchus, denuded of epithelium (arrowhead), exposing the lamina propria and bronchial lumen (L). **B.** Higher magnification of A, demonstrating exfoliated cells from the bronchial epithelium free in the lumen; a few reserve or basal cells are still attached on the lamina propria (arrowheads). The denuded lamina propria (lp) and submucosa (sm) are filled with a leukocytic infiltrate. **C.** Higher magnification of B, demonstrating the leukocytic infiltrate in the lamina propria and submucosal layer. At this magnification, these leukocytes are easily identified as eosinophils (arrowheads) because of their large refractile granules and the bilobed nucleus. Hematoxylin and eosin. Original magnification: A, × 100; B, × 400; C, × 1000. *(Source: Frigas E, Gleich GJ, et al. The eosinophil and the pathophysiology of asthma. J Allergy Clin Immunol 1986;77:527. Reproduced with permission from the publisher and author.)*

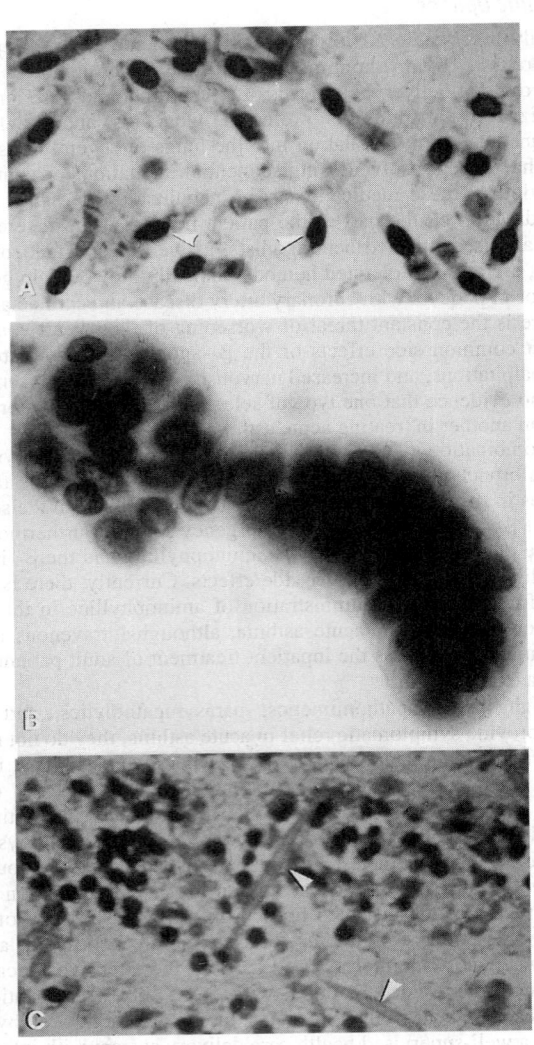

Figure 5–2–2. Sputum samples from patients with acute asthma. **A.** Elongated ciliated cells (arrowheads) desquamated from bronchial epithelium. When cells are viewed in a wet preparation, the cilia frequently are extremely motile, propelling themselves in a circular path. Papanicolaou stain. Original magnification:× 300. **B.** Creola body, a compact cluster of epithelial cells shed from the bronchial epithelium. Papanicolaou stain (× 400). **C.** Charcot–Leyden crystals (arrowheads) and eosinophils identified by their large refractile granules and bilobed nuclei. Hematoxylin and eosin. Original magnification: × 400. *(Source: Frigas E, Gleich GJ, et al. The eosinophil and the pathophysiology of asthma. J Allergy Clin Immunol 1986;77:527. Reproduced with permission from the publisher and author.)*

several interleukins, which attract in the bronchi large numbers of eosinophils. In this network of immunoregulatory interleukins, interleukin-4 and interleukin-5 appear to be particularly important. Interleukin-4 is needed to produce immunoglobulin E in response to allergenic stimuli, whereas interleukin-5 leads to the accumulation and activation of eosinophils in the bronchi. In addition, powerful eosinophilotactic mediators such as the platelet aggregating factor from activated eosinophils and macrophages, the 15-lipoxygenase products from eosinophils and the bronchial epithelium, and eosinophilotactic factors from activation of basophils and mast cells are all amplification mechanisms by which more eosinophils are attracted to the asthmatic bronchi, establishing a self-perpetuating vicious cycle. It is estimated that during an episode of acute asthma, more than half a billion eosinophils accumulate in the lungs. Regardless of which chemotactic mechanisms are ultimately responsible for the accumulation of eosinophils in the asthmatic bronchi, we have now recognized that the eosinophil is the main effector cell for the damage of the bronchial mucosa in asthma (Frigas et al., 1991). Specifically, we now know that the eosinophil, through its toxic granule proteins—major basic protein, eosinophil peroxidase, and eosinophilic cationic protein—injures the bronchial mucosa, causing ciliostatis, desquamation, and destruction of the mucosal cells (Frigas et al., 1991). At the molecular level, the major basic protein, because of its cationic charge, may be attracted to the negatively charged cell surface of a target, whereon apolar residues insert into and perturb the lipid milieu. The formation of transmembrane pores by eosinophilic cationic protein has been suggested as a possible mechanism for target cell damage. Major basic protein-, eosinophil peroxidase-, and eosinophilic cationic protein-mediated destruction of the mucociliary apparatus leads to exposure of nerve endings and inability to clear the bronchial sections. In addition to the destruction of the bronchial mucosa by the cationic proteins of the eosinophil, both eosinophils and mast cells secrete powerful bronchoconstrictors, such as leukotriene C4, that also contribute to the bronchial obstruction in asthma. In severe episodes of acute asthma, bronchial secretions may collect in such large quantities that the patient may die from asphyxiation.

Genetics

The genetics of the chronic bronchial inflammation in asthma are unknown. More than likely, we are dealing with a polygenic disease with variable clinical expression, depending on exposure to environmental factors.

Natural History and Its Modification with Treatment

In severe asthma this bronchial obstruction becomes refractory to therapy. More than half a century ago, the European scholars used the term *asthme invétéré* to describe this end stage in progression of asthma. This refractoriness seems to be directly related to the degree and duration of bronchial eosinophilia. The nature, either functional or anatomic, of this refractoriness to therapy remains unknown.

Prevention

At present asthma is not a preventable disease. Nevertheless, several well-known aggravating or precipitating factors such as aeroallergens (i.e., housedust mite allergen, mold allergens), viral respiratory infections, certain occupational agents, certain medications, air pollution, and cigarette smoking (even exposure to second-hand smoking) should be either appropriately addressed or strictly avoided. Vaccination with influenza and Pneumovax vaccines is logical and should be encouraged.

Cost Containment

With the escalation of prices of medications for asthma, therapy has now become prohibitive, especially among Medicare patients on fixed incomes. Aggressive, early administration of glucocorticoids in both the acute and the chronic care setting with compulsive monitoring of lung function with pulmonary function tests prevents costly hospitalizations. The most common omissions in the treatment of asthma leading to spiraling of medical costs are failure to address specific allergic and occupational factors; failure to start or adjust the dose of parenteral or aerosolized glucocorticoids according to the fluctuating needs of this disease; failure to closely monitor lung function by means of pulmonary function tests; and failure to educate asthmatic patients on the nature, treatment, and self-monitoring of their asthma. A meticulous investigation of the patient's environmental exposure at home and at work along with comprehensive testing with a battery of allergy skin tests is by far the more sensible, cost-effective way to treat asthma patients. Once the allergy and environmental triggers have been addressed and treatment is underway, all patients with asthma should be instructed in self-monitoring their treatment by means of a peak flowmeter and keeping a calendar of these measurements to be periodically brought to the attention of the physician who treats their asthma.

REFERENCES

Adams F. The extant works of ARETÆUS, the Cappadocian, Chapter IX on Asthma. London: Printed for the Sydenham Society, 1856:316.

Carryer HM, Koelsche GA, Prickman LE, et al. Effects of cortisone on bronchial asthma and hay fever occurring in subjects sensitive to ragweed pollen. Proc Staff Meet Mayo Clin 1950;25:482.

Frigas E, Loegering DA, Solley GO, et al. Elevated levels of the eosinophil granule major basic protein in the sputum of patients with bronchial asthma. Mayo Clin Proc 1981;56:345.

Frigas E, Motojima S, Gleich, GJ. The eosinophilic injury to the mucosa of the airways in the pathogenesis of bronchial asthma. Eur Respiratory J 1991;4(suppl. 13):123s.

Huber HL, Koessler KK. The pathology of bronchial asthma. Arch Intern Med 1922;30:689.

Sheffer AL. National Heart, Lung, and Blood Institute, National Asthma Education Program, Expert Panel Report. Guidelines for the diagnosis and management of asthma. J Allergy Clin Immunol 1991;88:427.

CHAPTER 5–3

Allergic Bronchopulmonary Aspergillosis

David A. Khan, M.D., and James T. C. Li, M.D., Ph.D.

DEFINITION

Allergic bronchopulmonary aspergillosis (ABPA) is a lung disease caused by an immunologic response to noninvasive *Aspergillus* fungi. Most cases of ABPA occur in patients with asthma but it is also relatively common in cystic fibrosis (also see Section 13, Chapter 19).

ETIOLOGY

Aspergillus species are ubiquitous and can become trapped in the thick mucus secretions of asthmatics, leading to colonization. Patients may then develop an antibody response directed at the *Aspergillus* species, resulting in elevated total immunoglobulin (Ig) E and specific IgE and

IgG levels. Interaction of fungal antigens and antibodies leads to a cascade of inflammatory cells and their mediators, resulting in eosinophilic inflammation and eventually bronchiectasis.

CRITERIA FOR DIAGNOSIS
Suggestive

Patients with asthma who have a history of recurrent infiltrates on chest radiographs, eosinophilia, and elevated total IgE levels (> 1000 ng/mL) should be suspected of having ABPA. Increasingly severe asthma requiring frequent systemic glucocorticoids is another indication to search for ABPA. A history of expectoration of brown mucus plugs may also suggest this diagnosis. Although not specific for ABPA, a positive skin test to *Aspergillus* is seen in virtually all patients and, in the context of the aforementioned features, warrants investigation. Finally, the presence of central bronchiectasis, in the absence of cystic fibrosis, is diagnostic of ABPA.

Definitive

Several clinical and laboratory features have been established as diagnostic criteria for ABPA (Table 5–3–1). As pulmonary infiltrates are transient and may not be present, especially if the patient is on prednisone, this is not an absolute criterion. Similarly, peripheral blood eosinophilia is usually present but may be masked by systemic glucocorticoids. A patient who meets all of the first seven diagnostic criteria in Table 5–3–1, regardless of the presence of central bronchiectasis, has ABPA.

CLINICAL MANIFESTATIONS
Subjective

Allergic bronchopulmonary aspergillosis may appear in any age group from infants to geriatric patients. Symptoms include cough, wheezing, dyspnea, sputum production, hemoptysis, fever, malaise, and chest pain, which is usually pleuritic. Most of these symptoms are intermittent and often indistinguishable from asthma. Sputum production may be continuous and varies from scanty to one-half cup per day. It may be mucoid, purulent, or blood streaked and can contain plugs. These mucus plugs consist of bronchial casts, are firm and cylindrical or pelletlike in shape, and vary in color from green to beige. Although exacerbations of ABPA can occur at any time, many patients have a seasonal rise in symptoms that correlates with total mold spore counts in their region.

Most patients have a past history of other allergic diseases, most commonly allergic rhinitis and atopic dermatitis, but urticaria, anaphylaxis, and drug and food allergy have also been reported in ABPA patients. Patients with ABPA and adult-onset asthma after age 30 often do not have other coexistent atopic diseases. Familial cases of ABPA have occurred, but these are rare.

Objective
Physical Examination

Findings on physical examination are dependent on the stage of disease. There are five stages of disease activity in ABPA: I (acute), II (remission), III (exacerbation), IV (corticosteroid-dependent asthma), and V (fibrotic). Patients in stages I (acute) or III (exacerbation) usually have

TABLE 5–3–1. DIAGNOSTIC CRITERIA

Asthma
Chest x-ray infiltrate (predominantly upper lobes)
Elevated total serum IgE
Peripheral blood eosinophilia
Positive *Aspergillus* skin test
Precipitating antibodies to *Aspergillus*
Elevated *Aspergillus*-specific IgE and IgG
Central bronchiectasis

rhonchi and wheezing and may have localized rales, or signs of consolidation such as egophony, dullness to percussion, or bronchial breath sounds. Stage II (remission) patients often have normal lung examinations. Patients in Stage IV (corticosteroid-dependent asthma) may have a normal chest examination or demonstrate wheezing, but should not have rales or signs of consolidation. Finally, stage V (fibrotic) patients have coarse rales localized to affected areas. These patients may progress to end-stage fibrotic lung disease with physical findings of tachypnea, cyanosis, clubbing, and cor pulmonale.

Routine Laboratory Abnormalities

These include leukocytosis, peripheral blood eosinophilia, elevated sedimentation rate, and various abnormalities on chest roentgenograms. Almost all patients have peripheral blood eosinophilia, most with total eosinophil counts greater than 1000 cells/mm^3. A multitude of radiographic abnormalities occur in ABPA including infiltrates, massive consolidation, and a variety of shadows such as tramline, parallel line, ring, toothpaste, and gloved finger shadows, which represent forms of dilated bronchi and secretions.

PLANS
Diagnostic
Differential Diagnosis

The differential diagnosis of ABPA includes disorders associated with bronchospasm, blood eosinophilia, elevated IgE levels, and infiltrates on chest radiographs. Eosinophilic lung diseases such as Churg–Strauss vasculitis, parasitic lung diseases (Loffler's syndrome, tropical pulmonary eosinophilia), drug reactions, and acute and chronic eosinophilic pneumonia may also present with some of these features. *Aspergillus* skin testing, *Aspergillus* serologies, and other clinical features can usually distinguish these disorders from ABPA. Mold-sensitive asthmatics are the most difficult group to distinguish from patients with ABPA. Approximately 25% of asthmatics demonstrate positive skin tests to *Aspergillus* and 10% have serum precipitating antibodies. *Aspergillus*-specific IgE and IgG antibody levels, however, are twofold higher in patients with ABPA than in mold-sensitive asthmatics. Finally, several other fungi are capable of causing allergic bronchopulmonary mycosis, such as *Curvularia*, *Candida*, *Helminthosporium*, and *Pseudallescheria*. Skin testing and serology specific for *Aspergillus* are negative, but sputum culture or precipitins to the putative fungus may be positive.

Diagnostic Options

Demonstration of immediate cutaneous reactivity to *Aspergillus* by prick and or intradermal testing is essential in diagnosing ABPA, as almost all patients will have strongly positive reactions. Total serum IgE is typically strikingly elevated (> 1000 ng/mL) in most patients, although it may be suppressed by glucocorticoid therapy. Serum *Aspergillus*-specific IgE and IgG levels are elevated and serum precipitins to *Aspergillus* are usually present in ABPA, but these may also be suppressed by steroids. Sputum culture is positive for *Aspergillus fumigatus* in most patients and fungal stains can demonstrate mycelia, especially in mucus plugs. Chest roentgenograms can demonstrate multiple abnormalities (see Clinical Manifestations, Objective), but may not reveal bronchiectasis; therefore, hilar tomography, high-resolution chest computed tomography scans, or bronchography may be required. Finally, early and late responses to intracutaneous skin tests or inhalational challenge with *Aspergillus* support the diagnosis of ABPA.

Recommended Approach

Past and current chest radiographs should always be evaluated for infiltrates, especially of the upper lobe, shadows (parallel line, ring, gloved finger, etc.), or honeycomb fibrosis. A leukocyte differential and total serum IgE are essential, because in the absence of systemic glucocorticoids, almost all patients will have peripheral eosinophilia greater than 500 cells/mm^3 and total serum IgE level greater than 1000 ng/mL. Patients with eosinophilia and elevated IgE levels in the context of an appropriate history should be referred to an allergist for *Aspergillus* skin testing. If prick and intradermal skin testing is negative, ABPA is unlikely, although other allergic bronchopulmonary mycoses should be considered. Precipitating antibodies to *Aspergillus* and *Aspergillus*-specific IgE and IgG help confirm the diagnosis, but only the latter may distinguish the mold-sensitive asthmatic from one with ABPA. Finally, in cases where preceding data cannot discriminate between mold-sensitive asthma and ABPA, high-resolution chest computed tomography is the method of choice for detecting central bronchiectasis, which is a hallmark of ABPA.

Therapeutic

Therapeutic Options

The primary treatment of ABPA is oral corticosteroids, which improves symptoms, resolves pulmonary infiltrates, and reduces total IgE level and peripheral eosinophilia. Antifungal medications have no role in ABPA. Inhaled corticosteroids have been used with mixed results in ABPA. High-dose inhaled beclomethasone (> 1500 µg/d) has been used successfully in a few patients with ABPA, but larger controlled studies are lacking. Environmental avoidance of sources of excessive mold spores, such as moldy hay or compost, may be prudent but a causal link between high mold exposure and the development of ABPA has not been established. Immunotherapy (allergy injections) has also been attempted without much success because of complications of local reactions at the injection site, asthma exacerbations, and development of pulmonary shadows. Furthermore, the theoretical risk of immune complex formation with immunotherapy makes it an inadvisable form of treatment. Inhaled and oral bronchodilators alleviate the bronchospasm of ABPA.

Recommended Approach

For patients with stage I (acute) or stage III (exacerbation) disease, prednisone should be initiated at 0.5 mg/kg/d given in the morning for 2 weeks (Table 5–3–2). Thereafter, the prednisone may be converted to alternate-day therapy at the same dose and continued for 2 to 3 months. Then the prednisone may be tapered and eventually discontinued if symptoms are controlled. The total IgE level should decline by at least 35% within 2 months of this therapy, but usually never reaches normal. Therefore, the goals of therapy should be to control symptoms and to resolve acute pulmonary infiltrates, but not to reduce total IgE to the lowest possible level. Exacerbations of wheezing without elevations in IgE or pulmonary infiltrates should not be considered ABPA exacerbations and can be treated as asthma. Inhaled corticosteroids should be used to control underlying asthma if required, but should not be relied on to manage ABPA. Inhaled beta agonists should be prescribed for control of bronchospasm (with or without theophylline). Most patients with ABPA should keep a peak expiratory flow rate diary.

FOLLOW-UP

Initial follow-up of patients with acute ABPA (stage I) should include a repeat chest radiograph after 2 months of therapy to document resolution of the acute infiltrate and close monitoring of total IgE levels, eosinophilia, and pulmonary function for 1 year. If the patient is in remission (stage II) and the total IgE , eosinophilia, and pulmonary function have reached stable levels, follow-up visits every 3 months for 1 year, then every 6 to 12 months thereafter, are recommended. Any

flare-up of symptoms suggestive of ABPA warrants repeat measurements of total IgE, eosinophilia, and pulmonary function.

DISCUSSION
Prevalence and Incidence

The actual prevalence and incidence of ABPA are unknown. Prospective studies of patients with asthma seen at various allergy clinics have yielded prevalence rates ranging from 6 to 28%, however, these studies may reflect referral bias and probably overestimate the prevalence seen in nonspecialty medical practices.

Related Basic Science

The pathophysiology of ABPA is not well understood. Early serologic and antigen challenge studies postulated type I (IgE mediated) and type III (immune complex) Gell and Coombs reactions playing a role in the pathogenesis. More recently, it has been hypothesized that ABPA is similar to the late-phase reaction in asthma, characterized by a variety of inflammatory cells and mediators, with the eosinophil and its tissue toxic proteins being prominent. Bronchoalveolar lavage studies have demonstrated elevated levels of *Aspergillus*-specific IgE, IgA, and IgG antibodies, with marked local production of specific IgE and IgA. This local antibody production does not, however account for the elevated total IgE. Recently, studies with peripheral blood and bronchoalveolar lavage have demonstrated that T lymphocytes in ABPA appear to be of the TH2 variety, capable of producing the cytokines interleukin-4 and interleukin-5, which are crucial in IgE production as well as activation and growth of eosinophils. These TH2 cells are also found in asthmatics and thought to play a critical role in the pathogenesis of asthma.

Natural History and Its Modification with Treatment

The course of ABPA is quite variable in a given patient. Most have episodic exacerbations of their disease followed by remission. End-stage fibrotic lung disease (stage V) is thought to be the result of repeated exacerbations of ABPA. Small groups of corticosteroid-dependent (stage IV) patients have been followed for several years with no evidence of deterioration of pulmonary function or development of pulmonary fibrosis. This suggests that prednisone therapy for exacerbations of ABPA may prevent the progression to the fibrotic stage; however, this remains to be established with certainty.

Prevention

Currently there are no known methods of preventing ABPA.

Cost Containment

The most cost-effective strategy for managing ABPA is to treat exacerbations early and prevent fibrotic lung disease. Aggressive management with prednisone and routine follow-up including total IgE levels and pulmonary function tests when indicated are fairly inexpensive. This relatively small cost is substantially less than the cost of hospitalizations for ABPA and the cost associated with the morbidity of end-stage lung disease, including loss of productivity of the patient.

REFERENCES

Greenberger PA, Patterson R. Diagnosis and management of allergic bronchopulmonary aspergillosis. Ann Allergy 1986;56:444.

Greenberger PA, Smith LJ, Hsu CCS, et al. Analysis of bronchoalveolar lavage in allergic bronchopulmonary aspergillosis: Divergent responses of antigen-specific antibodies and total IgE. J Allergy Clin Immunol 1988;82:164.

McCarthy DS, Pepys J. Allergic broncho-pulmonary aspergillosis: Clinical immunology: (1) Clinical features. Clin Allergy 1971;1:261.

Neeld DA, Goodman LR, Gurney JW, et al. Computerized tomography in the evaluation of allergic bronchopulmonary aspergillosis. Am Rev Respir Dis 1990;142:1200.

Schwartz HJ, Greenberger PA. The prevalence of allergic bronchopulmonary aspergillosis in patients with asthma, determined by serologic and radiologic criteria in patients at risk. J Lab Clin Med 1991;117:138.

Walker C, Bauer W, Braun RK, Menz G, et al. Activated T cells and cytokines in bronchoalveolar lavages from patients with various diseases associated with eosinophilia. Am J Respir Crit Care Med 1994;150:1038.

TABLE 5–3–2. MANAGEMENT

Acute/exacerbation
Prednisone 0.5 mg/kg/d × 2 weeks
Convert dose to alternate day × 2–3 months
Taper based on symptoms/chest x-ray
Follow-up
Serial total IgE, eosinophil count, and spirometry
and as needed with symptom flare-up

Allergic Rhinitis

David A. Khan, M.D., and James T. C. Li, M.D., Ph.D.

DEFINITION

Allergic rhinitis is a nasal disease caused by allergens that trigger a local hypersensitivity response. Although commonly known as hay fever, allergic rhinitis is not caused by hay nor does it produce fever.

ETIOLOGY

Allergic individuals produce specific immunoglobulin (Ig) E antibodies against a variety of allergens. These IgE antibodies attach to circulating basophils or mast cells located in mucosal and connective tissues, thus causing sensitization of these cells. Allergens that bind two IgE molecules cause crosslinking, which triggers the cell to degranulate. Mast cell degranulation is the initial event leading to a cascade of inflammatory cells and mediators which results in symptoms of allergic rhinitis.

CRITERIA FOR DIAGNOSIS

Suggestive

Allergic rhinitis may be seasonal or year round (perennial). Seasonal allergic rhinitis can often be diagnosed by history. A patient with symptoms of itchy, watery eyes, sneezing, rhinorrhea, and nasopharyngeal pruritus that occurs for weeks to months at the same time each year most likely has allergic rhinitis. Patients with perennial symptoms and others with less typical seasonal rhinitis may be more difficult to diagnose by history alone.

Definitive

The gold standard for the diagnosis of allergic rhinitis is the demonstration of specific IgE. This can be accomplished by allergen skin testing or blood tests that measure specific IgE to various allergens. The presence of specific IgE must correlate with the patient's symptoms for a valid diagnosis of allergic rhinitis.

CLINICAL MANIFESTATIONS

Subjective

Paroxysmal sneezing, watery rhinorrhea, and pruritus involving the eyes, nose, and throat are the most classic allergic symptoms. Symptoms of nasal congestion, postnasal drip, sore throat, and headache may also occur but are much less specific for allergic rhinitis. The vast majority of patients will have bilateral symptoms. Unilateral nasal symptoms may indicate a structural abnormality inside the nose (e.g., nasal polyps, deviated septum). Although fatigue may certainly be present in individuals with severe nasal obstruction (often as a result of impaired sleep), fatigue as a primary complaint is usually not caused by allergic rhinitis.

The time of year symptoms occur should be defined according to specific months (rather than "spring, summer, fall, or winter"), as these seasons occur at different times of the year depending on the individual. Some aeroallergens are unique to certain geographic areas or are present at different times of the year in different locales. Therefore, attention should be paid to a patient's symptoms with travel. Many patients with pollen allergy will note improvement when staying indoors in an air-conditioned environment. Triggers of symptoms should also be sought such as fresh-cut grass, animals, dust, and raking leaves, which are common triggers for many allergic rhinitis patients.

An environmental history is critical in the evaluation of patients. The presence of indoor pets and symptoms that occur when near the animals is of paramount importance, especially in perennial rhinitis. Feather pillows, down comforters, old mattresses, and bedroom carpeting make a nice haven for dust mites, the most common source of indoor allergens.

Although not an allergen, smoke (tobacco, wood) can certainly be an irritant which may aggravate any form of rhinitis. Indoor mold growth in bathrooms, basements, or dehumidifiers is another source of indoor allergens.

The family history in allergic rhinitis pertains to the presence of atopy. A family history of asthma, allergic rhinitis, or atopic dermatitis suggests an atopic background and, therefore, increases the risk of developing allergic rhinitis.

Objective

Physical Examination

Physical examination should be focused on the eyes, ears, and upper airway. Ocular findings of allergic conjunctivitis include scleral injection, cobblestoning of the conjunctiva, and "allergic shiners" (periorbital cyanosis), which represents venous congestion secondary to nasal obstruction of any cause. Serous otitis is a common complication and can be easily diagnosed using an otoscope. A thorough examination of the nose is helpful both in diagnosing allergic disease and in detecting other etiologies of rhinitis. Nasal turbinates are typically pale and boggy; however, this is not entirely specific for allergic disease. Secretions should be thin, clear, and occasionally white. Thickened yellow or green nasal mucus suggests sinus infection. The nasal septum should be examined for deviations, spurs, ulcers, or perforations. Nasal polyps appear as pale translucent masses often near the middle meatus and may cause rhinitis symptoms independent of allergies. Finally, the oropharynx should be examined for drainage and cobblestoning of the posterior pharynx.

Routine Laboratory Abnormalities

Routine laboratory studies are usually not indicated. A complete blood count with differential may show eosinophilia.

PLANS

Diagnostic

Differential Diagnosis

There are a multitude of causes of rhinitis (Table 5–4–1). Vasomotor rhinitis is the second most common cause after allergic rhinitis. It is characterized by perennial symptoms of nasal obstruction, rhinorrhea, and postnasal drip with little pruritus. These symptoms are exacerbated by irritants (strong odors, fumes), weather changes, and emotion. Nonallergic rhinitis with eosinophilia syndrome (NARES) is characterized by paroxysmal sneezing, rhinorrhea, nasal pruritus, and eosinophils on nasal smear. Rhinitis medicamentosa is due to prolonged use (more

TABLE 5–4–1. DIFFERENTIAL DIAGNOSIS

Allergic	Endocrine/Hormonal
Seasonal	Pregnancy
Perennial	Hypothyroidism
Nonallergic	Uncommon causes
Vasomotor	Atrophic rhinitis
Nonallergic rhinitis with eosinophilia syndrome	Granulomatous diseases
Nasal polyposis	Cerebrospinal fluid leak
	Tumors
Medication related (rhinitis medicamentosa)	
Estrogens	
Antihypertensives	
Topical decongestant sprays	

than 4 days) of topical decongestant sprays, which lead to rebound nasal congestion and tachyphylaxis. Other systemic medications that can cause rhinitis are oral contraceptives, conjugated estrogens, and antihypertensive agents, including reserpine, methyldopa, prazosin, and beta-blockers. One third of pregnant women develop rhinitis, which starts in the first trimester and does not resolve until delivery.

Diagnostic Options

There are basically two ways to demonstrate specific IgE: skin testing and in vitro methods. Skin testing is the most sensitive and specific method. It provides information within minutes and is much more cost-effective than in vitro methods. In vitro tests that detect specific IgE are usually performed only when skin testing cannot be done. Patients with dermographism or dermatitis or those taking medicines that interfere with skin testing (such as antihistamines, anticholinergics, and tricyclic antidepressants) and are unable to stop them may benefit from in vitro tests. Nasal smears are sometimes helpful in differentiating various forms of rhinitis, but they can be nonspecific. Eosinophils on nasal cytology tend to represent a steroid-responsive rhinitis such as allergic rhinitis or nonallergic rhinitis with eosinophilia syndrome.

Recommended Approach

A diagnosis of seasonal allergic rhinitis is usually suggested by history alone. Perennial allergic rhinitis, however, is more difficult to differentiate from other nonallergic entities on the basis of history and physical examination only. Demonstration of specific IgE in the context of an appropriate history is the definitive method of diagnosing allergy, and allergen skin testing is the preferred method. Allergic rhinitis and vasomotor rhinitis constitute the vast majority of rhinitis, and both may respond to similar medications. Therefore, if a patient responds to conventional treatment, it may not be necessary to perform testing for specific IgE.

Therapeutic

Therapeutic Options

Avoidance of allergens is the ideal form of therapy for allergic rhinitis. Unfortunately this is very difficult for most outdoor aeroallergens. Air conditioners are excellent pollen and mold filters and should be used whenever possible. Patients should be instructed to keep their car windows shut while driving during their allergy season. Indoor allergens, the source for most perennial symptoms, may also be reduced or eliminated. Dust mites live in warm, humid environments such as pillows, mattresses, carpets, and upholstered furniture. Covering pillows, mattresses, and box springs in plastic encasements, as well as washing bedding at least every other week in the hot cycle (> 130°F) is essential in the dust-allergic patient. Removing carpet from the bedroom is very effective in reducing mite allergen load, but should be done only when convenient for the patient or if there is a high degree of certainty that mites are a major cause of the patients' symptoms. Pet-allergic patients ideally should find a new home for their pets, but the majority of patients refuse this suggestion. A practical alternative is to keep the pet out of the bedroom.

Pharmacotherapy is indicated when avoidance measures are ineffective or impractical. Antihistamines are often used as first-line agents for allergic rhinitis. They are effective in reducing symptoms of sneezing, itching, and rhinorrhea but have little effect on nasal congestion. The use of the older antihistamines is often limited by their anticholinergic and sedative side effects. Second-generation antihistamines also have the advantage of longer duration, 12 hours for terfenadine (Seldane) and 24 hours for astemizole (Hismanal) and loratidine (Claritin), and are nonsedating. As both terfenadine and astemizole are metabolized by the cytochrome P450 liver enzymes, drugs that slow P450 metabolism (ketoconazole, erythromycin, cimetidine, etc.) should not be administered concomitantly because of the risk of fatal arrhythmias (Torsade de pointes). Similarly, these antihistamines should not be prescribed in dosages exceeding the manufacturers' guidelines.

Decongestants such as pseudoephedrine, phenylpropanolamine, and phenylephrine are helpful for nasal plugging and serous otitis media, a complication of rhinitis. These drugs may cause nervousness,

headache, insomnia, and diminished urinary flow. They are contraindicated in patients with glaucoma and those on monoamine oxidase inhibitors, and caution should be used in hypertensive patients. In general, patients with well-controlled mild hypertension are able to tolerate oral decongestants. Topical decongestant sprays should not be used chronically because of the risk of rhinitis medicamentosa, but are useful for acute situations such as airline trips to minimize the effects of pressure changes.

Anticholinergic medications are helpful for rhinorrhea, but because of their systemic anticholinergic effects, they may not be well tolerated, especially by the elderly. Intranasal ipratropium bromide is useful in this regard because it lacks systemic side effects.

Antiinflammatory agents are very effective in allergic rhinitis. Intranasal cromolyn sodium (Nasalcrom) is helpful in allergic rhinitis but must be used three or four times daily. It is extremely safe, with local irritation being the only significant side effect. Intranasal corticosteroids are effective in reducing all symptoms of rhinitis, although improvement may be delayed for up to 2 weeks. Intranasal corticosteroids are available as aqueous preparations (Vancenase AQ, Beconase AQ, Flonase, Nasalide) or freon-propelled formulations (Vancenase, Beconase, Nasacort, Rhinocort). Aqueous and freon-propelled preparations are equally efficacious but some patients prefer one type over another. Daily intranasal corticosteroids can be used safely for years. Local irritation is the most common side effect; this is most often seen with flunisolide. There are case reports of nasal septal perforation caused by intranasal corticosteroids, but these are rare and no causal relationship has been established. Like cromolyn sodium, intranasal corticosteroids are most effective when started 3 to 4 weeks prior to the allergy season and continued throughout the season.

Systemic corticosteroids should be avoided for the treatment of chronic allergic rhinitis because of the risk of severe adverse effects; however, in severe cases when other treatment modalities have failed, a short burst of systemic corticosteroids (e.g., prednisone 20–40 mg/day for 7 days) will provide prompt relief. In some patients, a burst of systemic steroids reduces nasal mucosal swelling, allowing penetration of an intranasal corticosteroid, which can then be used to control symptoms.

Allergic conjunctivitis may be refractory to treatment with oral or intranasal medications, and in these cases topical ocular therapy is indicated. Artificial tears are the most inexpensive therapy and can be tried first. Vasoconstrictor/antihistamine preparations (Vasocon-A, Naphcon-A) and the newer antihistamine levocobastine (Livostin) are also effective for ocular pruritus. Antiinflammatory agents such as the nonsteroidal antiinflammatory drug ketorolac (Acular) and the "mast cell stabilizers" cromolyn sodium (Crolom) and lodoxamide (Alomide) are also available, although the latter has not been proven effective in allergic conjunctivitis.

Immunotherapy (allergy injections) using high-potency extracts has been shown in double-blind placebo-controlled studies to be effective in the treatment of allergic rhinitis. It is the only form of therapy that alters the immune response to allergens. Immunotherapy is usually administered initially as weekly injections, with a progressive increase in dose of allergen. Once the "maintenance" dose has been achieved, the injection interval may be lengthened gradually to monthly injections. Immunotherapy is usually administered for at least 3 to 5 years, at which time a trial off immunotherapy may be considered. Because of the risk of a systemic allergic reaction (1–4%), which usually occurs within the first 30 minutes of an injection, immunotherapy should always be administered in a physician's office with appropriate resuscitative equipment available.

Recommended Approach

Allergic rhinitis is usually managed using a tiered approach (Table 5–4–2). Avoidance measures should always be employed; however, this is rarely effective as monotherapy for outdoor allergens. Pharmacotherapy should be used next, starting with antihistamines and decongestants if nasal plugging is significant. Intranasal therapy is indicated when the latter measures are not completely effective. Cromolyn sodium may be tried initially, especially in children, and if significant improvement is not achieved, intranasal corticosteroids should be pre-

TABLE 5-4-2. MANAGEMENT OF ALLERGIC RHINITIS

Avoidance of allergens	
Air conditioning	
Dust avoidance measures	
Pet washing/removal	
Pharmacotherapy	
Mild	Antihistamines
	Decongestants
	Artificial tears
Moderate	Nonsedating antihistamines
	Cromolyn sodium
	Intranasal glucocorticoids
	Ocular medications
Severe	Medications listed above
	Systemic glucocorticoids as needed
Immunotherapy	

scribed. Most patients can achieve control of their allergic rhinitis using an intiinflammatory spray and an antihistamine. Immunotherapy is indicated if the above measures do not provide satisfactory control.

FOLLOW-UP

For patients with seasonal rhinitis, it is important initially for them to return 1 month prior to the start of their next season to review avoidance measures and, if indicated, to start them on their intranasal corticosteroid early. This early follow-up is especially important for patients who have required systemic corticosteroids in the past. For patients with perennial rhinitis, reevaluation at 3 to 6 months to assess the impact of environmental controls such as dust and pet avoidance, as well as pharmacotherapy, is helpful. Once patients have been educated and are well controlled, follow-up at yearly intervals is reasonable.

DISCUSSION

Prevalence and Incidence

The total prevalence rate of allergic rhinitis for the United States is estimated at 20%, and is even higher in adolescence and decreases with advancing age. Most patients develop symptoms by age 20 and usually require at least 2 years of exposure to the offending allergen. The incidence of developing hay fever in college students has been shown to be 1%.

Related Basic Science

Genetics

Although no gene has yet been identified as a marker for allergic rhinitis, there appears to be a genetic predisposition in many patients. Most patients have a first-degree relative with hay fever. The risk of developing allergic rhinitis is estimated to be 50% if one parent has allergies and 66% if both are affected.

Immunology

Rhinitis is caused by the deposition of allergen in the nasal cavity, where it interacts with mast cells or basophils bearing specific IgE directed against a particular antigen. Crosslinking of two IgE molecules initiates a cascade of intracellular signals ultimately leading to degranulation of these cells. To elucidate the pathophysiology of allergic rhinitis, an experimental nasal challenge model has been developed where allergens are locally applied to the nose followed by serial nasal lavages to measure inflammatory cells and their mediators. Within 15 to 20 minutes of allergen challenge, symptoms of itching, sneezing, rhinorrhea, and congestion occur. This "early phase" is the result of release of mast cells and basophil mediators, including histamine, kinins, prostaglandin D_2, leukotrienes B_4, C_4, D_4, and E_4, and TAME-esterase. A "late-phase" reaction occurs 4 to 6 hours later characterized by similar mediator release (except prostaglandin D_2) and a cellular influx of eosinophils, neutrophils, and basophils. T lymphocytes also play a role in the late phase as a source of cytokines such as interleukin-5, which acts as an eosinophil activation and growth factor. Finally, adhesion molecules such as ICAM-1 and VCAM-1, which are upregulated on endothelial cells of patients with perennial allergic rhinitis, are involved in directing the migration of inflammatory cells to the tissues. This late-phase reaction is thought to be representative of chronic rhinitis and may explain why antiinflammatory agents are effective in this disease.

Natural History and Its Modification with Treatment

Allergic rhinitis usually appears during middle childhood or adolescence and stabilizes for several decades. During childhood, 20% of patients have a resolution of symptoms. Rhinitis typically improves by middle age and is rarely a problem in the elderly.

The natural history of rhinitis is only affected by allergen avoidance and immunotherapy, pharmacotherapy merely provides symptom control. Strict allergen avoidance will cause a resolution of allergic rhinitis: however, this is usually possible only for indoor allergens (especially pet dander) and occasionally for outdoor allergens by moving to an area without the specific allergen in the environment. Immunotherapy occasionally will result in complete desensitization, but normally its effect is to allow a tolerance of greater amounts of allergen. The beneficial effects of immunotherapy may even persist years after it is discontinued.

Prevention

Infants exposed to larger amounts of dust mite and pet dander have higher rates of developing specific IgE to these allergens. Furthermore, parental smoking is associated with an earlier onset of allergic rhinitis, higher IgE levels, and possibly increased specific IgE to pollens. Therefore, in infants with a high risk of developing allergic rhinitis, avoidance of dust mites, pets, and tobacco smoke may help prevent or at least delay the onset of allergic rhinitis.

Cost Containment

When possible, avoidance of allergens is the most effective and inexpensive form of therapy. Generic antihistamines and decongestants may also be tried; however, side effects may be limiting. Once symptoms are well controlled, medications should be weaned down to the least amount necessary for control of symptoms.

REFERENCES

Hogan MB, Grammer LC, Patterson R. Rhinitis. Ann Allergy 1994;72:293.

Montefort S, Feather IH, Wilson SJ, et al. The expression of leukocyte-endothelial adhesion molecules is increased in perennial allergic rhinitis. Am J Respir Cell Mol Biol 1992;7:393.

Naclerio RM. Allergic rhinitis. N Engl J Med 1991;325:860.

Ohman JL. Allergen immunotherapy. Med Clin North Am 1992;76:977.

Walden SM, Proud D, Bascom R, et al. Experimentally induced nasal responses. J Allergy Clin Immunol 1988;81:940.

Ying S, Durham SR, Barkans J, et al. T cells are the principal source of interleukin-5 mRNA in allergen-induced rhinitis. Am J Respir Cell Mol Biol 1993;9:356.

Urticaria and Angioedema
Harry A. Swedlund, M.D.

DEFINITION

Urticaria and angioedema are considered together because they both consist of edema of various layers of the skin and may coexist or occur separately. *Urticaria,* or hives, is a reaction of the skin marked by edematous lesions of the superficial portion of the dermis that appear as single or multiple blanching areas, usually raised with surrounding erythema, are pruritic, and generally last 24 to 72 hours. Angioedema is a fluid collection in the deeper layers of the skin without clear margins and sometimes without the characteristic itching. Any portion of the body may be affected by urticaria. Angioedema most commonly occurs in the lips, eyelids, and genitals, but may involve any skin or mucosal surface. Episodes of urticaria/angioedema are defined as acute if they last less than 6 weeks and chronic when they last more than 6 weeks.

ETIOLOGY

Acute cases of urticaria/angioedema may be due to immediate hypersensitivity reactions. Drugs, particularly penicillin and related drugs, are a common cause of acute lesions. Aspirin, nonsteroidal antiinflammatory drugs, sulfonamides, and many other drugs have been implicated in the cause of urticaria/angioedema. Another category of drugs associated with angioedema are the angiotensin converting enzyme inhibitors, which may cause angioedema soon after starting the drug but sometimes only after long periods of daily use. Radiologic contrast agents commonly cause acute urticaria. Blood products may cause urticaria/angioedema. Some patients develop urticaria or angioedema after eating foods such as shellfish, nuts, fresh fruits, chocolate, and tomatoes. These patients often are well aware of the food causing the symptoms and ordinarily do not consult a physician in this regard. Pollens and fungi may cause urticaria/angioedema with contact. Of special concern in recent years have been reactions to contact or inhalation of latex in medical workers, patients who have had several operations, and others who have had repeated exposure to latex articles, with symptoms ranging from contact urticaria to systemic anaphylaxis. Intestinal parasites may cause urticaria/angioedema. This is an uncommon problem in the United States, but should be considered in travelers to less developed countries. Serum sickness is frequently associated with urticaria/angioedema. Illnesses less commonly associated include malignant tumors, various collagen diseases, and infectious diseases such as hepatitis. Hereditary angioedema is an inherited complement-related disorder and is considered separately in Chapter 5–6. Mast cell infiltrates in the skin cause urticaria pigmentosa with characteristic reddish-brown macules and papules that urticate as a result of trauma. Various organs are infiltrated in systemic mastocytosis, and this is discussed in another chapter. Many physical factors cause urticaria/angioedema. Dermographism is diagnosed by the appearance of a wheal following a firm stroking of the skin. Pressure at any site of the body may cause urticaria/angioedema. Cold exposure may cause urticaria at the exposed site, and in some cases this is mediated by immunoglobulin E and passive transfer by serum has been demonstrated. Patients with cold urticaria may experience collapse and sometimes death from swimming in cool or cold water. Cholinergic urticaria is associated with small, itchy hives (1–2 mm) surrounded by erythema and often associated with hot baths, exercise, or any increase in body temperature. Solar urticaria is due to light exposure involving various portions of the light spectrum. Occupational exposure to vibration may cause vibratory angioedema. Exercise-induced anaphylaxis causes urticaria/angioedema as well as wheezing, hypotension, and pruritus. Urticaria on exposure to heat and aquagenic urticaria from contact with water are less common. Urticaria has been described as due to cutaneous vasculitis in certain patients. Urticaria/angioedema often occurs for no apparent reason and the cause may never be found.

CRITERIA FOR DIAGNOSIS
Suggestive

The appearance of hives and/or angioedema is often quite characteristic. Urticarial lesions occur in crops, usually in varying stages of development and disappearance. Angioedema is usually asymmetric and tends to involve areas of loose skin. Individual lesions generally last less than 48 hours.

Definitive

In some patients who appear to have urticaria/angioedema skin biopsies are done, but this is primarily to diagnose urticarial vasculitis or some other underlying condition.

CLINICAL MANIFESTATIONS
Subjective

Symptoms include intense itching and visible hives over any part of the body and/or evident angioedema, especially in eyelids, lips, and genitals. Angioedema may involve mucosal surfaces as well as the skin; in some patients, the mouth and tongue may be swollen. The airway may be compromised in patients with hereditary angioedema and less commonly in other types of angioedema, and this is at times life threatening. Patients with these conditions often have a personal and/or family atopic history including nasal allergy, asthma, and/or eczema, and many have had prior episodes of urticaria/angioedema.

Objective
Physical Examination

Urticaria presents a characteristic appearance of blanched wheals and surrounding erythema and is easily recognized by the physician as well as the patient. Angioedema presents as unexplained, nonpitting, asymmetric, sometimes brawny edema and usually is not well demarcated. The remainder of the physical examination is usually negative.

Routine Laboratory Abnormalities

No routine laboratory abnormalities are found in most patients with urticaria/angioedema.

PLANS
Diagnostic
Differential Diagnosis

The diagnosis of urticaria/angioedema is often evident in the patient who has a characteristic history and typical symptoms and findings on physical examination. As there may be various underlying factors in urticaria/angioedema, these should be considered in the history and physical examination. As discussed under Etiology, many causes are possible. Urticaria may appear, perhaps incidentally, in certain patients having hereditary angioedema, so the presence of urticaria does not rule out this diagnosis.

Diagnostic Options

Patients often relate the onset of acute urticaria/angioedema to a drug they have taken, a food eaten, or some event in their life. It is often difficult to prove or disprove these possibilities, but history and continuing observation are helpful, and cautious challenge to foods in question may be considered if reactions have been mild. Skin sensitization tests using the scratch or prick method have usually been unrewarding and are not recommended other than to test a specific agent, such as a penicillin derivative or a food implicated by history in selected cases. These tests should not be done if a reaction has been severe as the test may be dangerous. Elimination diets are often tried, but these are difficult to interpret as urticaria/angioedema tends to be intermittent. Double-blind, placebo-controlled food challenges may be informative, but these are difficult, time consuming, and generally done in a research setting. Stools for ova and parasites should be examined if the patient has traveled in a less developed country. The erythrocyte sedimentation rate may be helpful in detecting an underlying illness. Hepatitis tests should be done if there is a question of liver disease. Autoimmune diseases may be suggested by antinuclear antibody, C3, C4, CH_{50}, and rheumatoid factor testing. Malignancies are an uncommon cause of urticaria/angioedema, and search for these is unrewarding without suggestive symptoms. Stinging insects may cause urticaria/angioedema and venom skin testing is available when indicated. For cold urticaria, application of an ice cube to the forearm or other area will cause a definite large wheal. Cholinergic urticaria is exacerbated by warm baths and exercise. Solar urticaria may be demonstrated by light exposures. Pressure urticaria is made manifest by application of pressure, such as weights or a sandbag, to the skin. Vibratory urticaria diagnosis depends on demonstration of the lesions due to vibration. Water compresses cause aquagenic urticaria. Complement C4 and C1-esterase inhibitor studies are done if hereditary angioedema is a consideration. Sensitivity to latex should be suspected in medical workers and others exposed to latex articles, and a history of urticaria/angioedema on latex exposure should be sought. Skin tests and in vitro tests for latex allergy are available through allergy specialists. Challenge testing with latex gloves or other articles may be attempted with caution, but reactions are sometimes severe.

Recommended Approach

A careful history and physical examination are the keystones to diagnosis and treatment. In many patients, no cause can be detected. Patients with acute urticaria/angioedema may need no laboratory studies. Those patients with severe or chronic urticaria/angioedema should have laboratory studies depending on the clues presented in the history and physical examination in regard to underlying disease.

Therapeutic
Therapeutic Options

If a cause can be detected, it should be avoided and underlying illnesses treated. Urticaria/angioedema is usually treated with an H_1 antihistamine for symptomatic relief. Hydroxyzine (Atarax, Vistaril), 25 or 50 mg four times daily; diphenhydramine (Benadryl), 25 or 50 mg four times daily; chlorpheniramine (Chlor-Trimeton), 12 mg every 12 hours; and tripelennamine (PBZ), 25 or 50 mg four times daily, are time-honored drugs. (Cyproheptadine (Periactin), 4 mg three or four times daily, has been reported to be particularly effective for cold urticaria. Unfortunately, these drugs commonly cause drowsiness and many patients cannot tolerate this sedation, although sedation may decrease with continuing usage. Other side effects include irritability, insomnia, blurred vision, central nervous system stimulation, and anticholinergic effects such as drying of the mucous membranes and urinary retention. Second-generation H_1 antihistamines are much less likely to cause sedation. These include astemizole (Hismanal), 10 mg daily taken on an empty stomach; terfenadine (Seldane), 60 mg every 12 hours; and loratidine (Claritin), 10 mg daily. Serum levels of astemizole or terfenadine may be raised in patients with known or potential hepatic dysfunction due to alcohol abuse, occupational exposure to hepatotoxins, and pharmacologic hepatotoxins. Drugs that must be avoided in patients taking astemizole or terfenadine include the macrolide antibiotics (erythromycin, troleandomycin, and clarithromycin), the antidepressants nefazodone and fluzoxamine, and the oral antifungal agents (ketoconazole, itraconazole, fluconazole, and miconazole), as serious cardiac arrhythmias have been reported. A few patients taking H_1 antihistamines are helped by adding drugs blocking histamine H_2 receptors, and these include cimetidine (Tagamet), 300 mg two to four times daily, or ranitidine (Zantac), 150 mg twice daily. If these treatments fail, doxepin, 10 mg per day, should be given. Doxepin is a potent antihistamine and may cause unacceptable sedation. Patients with severe urticaria/angioedema unresponsive to antihistamines may be given a short course

of systemic glucocorticoids such as prednisone, 40 mg per day for 5 days, decreasing by 5 mg per day until cessation. Continued use of glucocorticoids causes many undesirable side effects and should be avoided if at all possible. Subcutaneous epinephrine 0.3 mL may be given for life-threatening angioedema of the airway.

Recommended Approach

First-generation H_1 antihistamines such as hydroxyzine, diphenydramine, tripelennamine, chlorpheniramine, cyproheptadine, and doxepin may be given. If sedation is a problem, the second generation H_1 antihistamines should be tried, and H_2 antihistamines may be added if helpful. Systemic glucocorticoids should be reserved for severe, intractable symptoms.

FOLLOW-UP

Long-term observation is necessary to determine the role of various possible causative factors and the effects of treatment, particularly in chronic urticaria/angioedema.

DISCUSSION
Prevalence

Urticaria is fairly common, especially in children, with up to 25% affected at some time. Urticaria/angioedema may occur at any age but is probably less common in adults. Fifteen to twenty percent of college students report urticaria/angioedema symptoms at some time.

Related Basic Science
Genetics

Individuals with a personal or family history of atopic diseases are more likely to suffer from urticaria/angioedema than the general population. Immunoglobulin E-mediated immediate hypersensitivity mechanisms have been demonstrated in specific reactions to penicillin and related drugs, inhalants, ingestants, venom, parasites, and, in certain situations, physical causes. Some patients with cold urticaria have been found to have an immunoglobulin E factor as shown by Prausnitz–Küstner passive transfer reaction. Some forms of urticaria/angioedema are hereditary. These include familial cold urticaria, hereditary vibratory angioedema, and familial urticaria, which includes the combination of amyloidosis, nerve deafness, and limb pain. Hereditary angioedema is described in Chapter 5–6. A rare hereditary disease involves C3b inactivator deficiency. Urticaria/angioedema due to aspirin, nonsteroidal antiinflammatory agents, and most other drugs appears to have no genetic basis.

Altered Molecular Biology

Mediators of urticaria/angioedema include histamine; prostaglandins; leukotrienes C, D, and E; platelet activating factor; complement factors; and bradykinin. Some of these factors are released by mast cells and this involves antigen–immunoglobulin E antibody interaction at the cell surface. These mediators are capable of causing the vasodilation, collection of edema fluid, and erythema typical of urticaria/angioedema.

Anatomic Derangement

Biopsy of acute urticaria shows edema with dilation of capillaries and venules in the superficial layers of the dermis. Angioedema shows similar changes in the deep areas of the skin and subcutaneous tissue. Necrotizing vasculitis is sometimes seen involving the small venules, and deposits of immunoglobulins, complement, and major basic protein of eosinophils have been demonstrated.

Natural History and its Modification with Treatment

Acute urticaria/angioedema is often self-limited and is responsive to antihistamine treatment. Chronic urticaria/angioedema tends to be a continuing and recurring problem. Some patients have urticaria/angioedema lasting years, and these patients pose a difficult diagnostic and therapeutic problem for the clinician as often no cause can be found.

Prevention

Avoidance of substances, contactants, or activities causing urticaria/angioedema is the prime method of prevention.

Cost Containment

Sometimes an extensive physical examination and laboratory testing are needed. In most patients, however, this is not necessary and treatment may be given for relief of symptoms. Several first-generation H_1 antihistamines are available without a prescription and are generally less expensive than the presciption-required second-generation H_1 antihistamines. As sedation is a problem with the first-generation H_1 anti-

histamines, second-generation H_1 antihistamines have become very popular due to avoidance of sedation.

REFERENCES

Bubak ME, Reed CE, Fransway AF, et al. Allergic reactions to latex among health-care workers. Mayo Clin Proc 1992;67:1075.

Kaplan AP. Urticaria and angioedema. In: Middleton E Jr, Reed CE, Ellis EF, et al. Allergy: Principles and practice. 4th ed. St. Louis: Mosby, 1993:1553.

Leiferman KM. A current perspective on the role of eosinophils in dermatologic diseases. J Am Acad Dermatol 1991;15:1101.

Slater EE, Merrill DD, Guess HA, et al. Clinical profile of angioedema associated with angiotensin converting-enzyme inhibition. JAMA 1988;260:967.

Woosley RL, Chen Y, Freiman JP, et al. Mechanism of the cardiotoxic actions of terfenadine. JAMA 1993;269:1532.

CHAPTER 5–6

Hereditary and Acquired Angioedema Caused by C1 Inhibitor Deficiency

Richard G. Van Dellen, M.D.

DEFINITION

Hereditary and acquired angioedema are attacks of angioedema caused by deficiency of the inhibitor of the first component of complement (C1 inhibitor [C1 INH]).

ETIOLOGY

Deficiency of C1 INH with angioedema can be hereditary or acquired. Acquired angioedema can be caused by other associated diseases, primarily lymphoproliferative B-cell malignancies, or by autoantibodies directed against the C1 INH.

Acquired angioedema has been reported in association with multiple myeloma, B-cell lymphoma, lymphosarcoma, chronic lymphocytic leukemia, myelofibrosis, Waldenström's macroglobulinemia, monoclonal gammopathy of undetermined significance, cold urticaria, autoimmune hemolytic anemia, systemic lupus erythematosus, Churg–Strauss vasculitis, adenocarcinoma of the stomach and rectum, cancer of the breast, and hydatid cysts of the liver.

CRITERIA FOR DIAGNOSIS

Suggestive

All patients who have attacks of angioedema with or without urticaria, particularly if the angioedema involves the larynx or is associated with abdominal pain, should have tests to rule out C1 INH deficiency. A family history of angioedema suggests the diagnosis of hereditary angioedema.

Definitive

For the diagnosis to be established, typical complement abnormalities must be documented: a low C4 or C2 value and a low C1 INH value, either quantitative or functional.

CLINICAL MANIFESTATIONS

Subjective

Deficiency of C1 INH results in attacks of nonpitting and nonpruritic angioedema involving various parts of the body. The angioedema is asymmetric, develops over hours, and usually lasts 2 to 4 days, resolving spontaneously and completely. Involvement of the throat, larynx, and gastrointestinal tract is common. Gastrointestinal involvement can cause nausea and vomiting, abdominal pain, diarrhea, small bowel obstruction, and hypotension from fluid sequestration. Urticaria, although

uncommon, may be present. The frequency and severity of attacks vary widely, as does involvement of the gastrointestinal tract and larynx.

In patients with hereditary angioedema, angioedema develops before age 10 years in 50% and before age 20 in 85%. Trauma, stress, and estrogens can precipitate attacks. Thirty to sixty-five percent of patients have involvement of the throat and larynx; deaths can occur from laryngeal edema. It is common for these patients to have had operations for abdominal pain, the diagnosis of multiple drug allergies, or the diagnosis of other gastrointestinal diseases, including regional enteritis. At the time of operation, the finding is marked bowel edema. Patients with the hereditary form usually have a positive family history of a similar illness, although this is absent in 20% of patients.

Hereditary angioedema is associated with systemic lupus erythematosus, polycystic ovaries, and immunoglobulin A nephropathy. The clinical presentation is similar in acquired angioedema, although a family history is absent and the disease usually starts later in life.

Objective

Physical Examination

During an attack, patients have asymmetric angioedema with or without urticaria. They can have findings of an acute abdomen, and differentiation between gastrointestinal angioedema and other causes of acute abdomen is often difficult. If the larynx is involved, hoarseness and respiratory distress might be present. Patients with acquired angioedema and malignancy might have physical findings of the underlying malignancy.

Routine Laboratory Abnormalities

Routine laboratory studies are normal in hereditary angioedema, and if abnormal in acquired angioedema, the abnormalities reflect the underlying malignancy.

PLANS

Diagnostic

Differential Diagnosis

Angioedema and urticaria are both very common; at times they are of unknown cause, but they are also associated with allergic reactions to foods and drugs, with infections, and with many other causes. Angioedema due to C1 inhibitor deficiency must be considered in patients with recurrent abdominal pain. These patients have been given other diagnoses including multiple drug allergies and regional enteritis.

Diagnostic Options and Recommended Approach

The diagnosis of hereditary or acquired angioedema is based on the finding of a low C1 INH value, either a quantitative inhibitor protein deficiency or a functional deficiency. About 15% of families with hereditary angioedema have a normal amount of the C1 INH protein, but it is functionally inactive. All patients have a low C4 or C2 value during attacks and usually between the attacks. The acquired form has a low C1q value, which is usually normal in the hereditary form (Table 5–6–1). The C3 value is normal. If the results of complement studies are normal between attacks, the studies should be repeated during an attack. Angioedema, C1 INH deficiency, a low C1q value, and no family history of angioedema are typical of acquired angioedema, and appropriate evaluation for malignancy should be done. The angioedema in the acquired form may precede the malignancy by as long as 7 years. If a small bowel radiograph is obtained during an attack with bowel involvement, the characteristic finding of mucosal edema called "thumbprinting" may be seen.

Therapeutic

Therapeutic Options and Recommended Approach

Prevention of attacks has centered on the use of androgens and antifibrinolytic agents (ε-aminocaproic acid or tranexamic acid). Not all patients need therapy to prevent attacks. Some patients' attacks are infrequent and mild, and no treatment should be given except for surgery, which is a time of increased risk. Androgens increase the production of C1 INH, and if large enough doses are given, the values of C1 INH, C4, and C2 return to normal. Methyltestosterone, 10 mg daily, can be used in males. For females, the impeded androgens danazol and stanozol are most commonly used. Oxymetholone and fluoxymesterone have also been used. Most of the studies on hereditary angioedema have centered on danazol and stanozolol. These drugs should not be used in children and adolescents before they have reached their full height, and they are contraindicated in pregnancy. Stanozolol should be started at a dose of 2 mg daily and adjusted depending on the need for control of the attacks. Ninety percent of patients require 2 mg daily or less to control the frequency of attacks substantially. Danazol should be started at a dose of 200 mg daily, and this also should be adjusted. In 82% of patients, the disease is controlled with 200 mg of danazol per day or less, and in some with as little as 50 mg a day. The dose of stanozolol and danazol should be reduced to the lowest possible dose that controls symptoms. The complement abnormalities do not need to be normal to prevent attacks. The side effects and complications from androgen and impeded androgen therapy include virilization and menstrual abnormalities in women, weight gain, hepatic dysfunction, liver tumors (adenomas and angiosarcoma), peliosis hepatica, microhematuria, myalgias, anxiety, tremulousness, and dizziness.

ε-Aminocaproic acid is used in doses of 8 to 16 g a day. Attacks recur if the dose is below 8 g a day and side effects are more frequent if the does is more than 20 g a day. Potential problems with ε-aminocaproic acid include muscle necrosis, myalgias, and thrombotic complications. The creatine kinase level should be monitored periodically, and use of ε-aminocaproic acid should be stopped before major surgery. Tranexamic acid is not available in the United States.

ε-Aminocaproic acid at 3 g per day in children younger than 11 years and at 6 g per day in children older than 11 has been reported to be effective, but control of symptoms was incomplete in some patients but without side effects.

Trauma, particularly dental work and other surgery involving trauma to the upper airway, can precipitate serious attacks of angioedema, although many patients have tolerated surgery without difficulty and without any preoperative preventive treatment. ε-Aminocaproic acid, fresh-frozen plasma (2 units 8 hours before the procedure), androgen therapy, and C1 INH concentrate have all been used with claimed success to prevent attacks of angioedema before dental work and other surgery in patients with hereditary angioedema, although no controlled studies have been done. C1 INH concentrate is not available in the United States. With our current knowledge, short-term therapy with stanozolol or danazol preoperatively is preferred. Three regimens have been advocated: (1) stanozolol, 4 mg every 6 hours for 5 days preoperatively; (2) danazol, 600 mg daily for 6 days preoperatively and 3 days postoperatively; (3) stanozolol, 6 mg a day for 6 days preoperatively and 3 days postoperatively.

Prevention of acquired angioedema has been more difficult. If an underlying disease is present, treatment of that disease has resulted in less frequent attacks or cure of the angioedema. Both androgens and antifibrinolytic agents have been used in acquired angioedema with variable success. Some patients improve with androgens, and others not at all. Antifibrinolytic agents may be more successful in preventing attacks in these patients.

Acute attacks should be managed expectantly with observation, with preparations for a tracheostomy if respiratory involvement threatens breathing and for fluids if the patient is dehydrated or hypovolemic. Symptomatic treatment may be needed for abdominal symptoms. Administration of C1 INH concentrate can shorten attacks, but it is not available in the United States. Fresh-frozen plasma should not be given during acute attacks of angioedema because it can prolong the duration of the attack. Antihistamines have not been shown to be effective. There are some anecdotal reports that epinephrine and systemic glucocorticosteroids reduce the duration of attacks of angioedema. Their efficacy has not been well documented. Epinephrine could be tried with laryngeal edema and should be safe in young patients. Although stanozolol, 4 mg every 6 hours, and tranexamic acid, 1 g every 3 to 4 hours over 12 to 15 hours, have been recommended for use early in acute attacks, there is no documentation of their efficacy. Because tranexamic acid is not available in the United States, ε-aminocaproic acid, 2 to 4 g every 4 hours for a maximum of 12 g, could be tried.

FOLLOW-UP

Patients with hereditary angioedema who have infrequent mild attacks and are not receiving treatment need no follow-up. They may need treatment before surgery. Those taking androgens or ε-aminocaproic acid for prevention need periodic monitoring of their progress, with attempts to reduce the dose of androgen when possible, and monitoring for side effects. These patients should have periodic creatine kinase determinations, and those taking androgens should have liver function tests and periodic imaging of the liver. Patients with acquired angioedema caused by a lymphoproliferative malignancy or other disease need appropriate follow-up for that particular disease. In acquired angioedema, the appearance of malignancy may be delayed years (7 years in one instance); thus, appropriate periodic evaluation is indicated.

DISCUSSION

Prevalence and Incidence

The estimated prevalence of hereditary angioedema in the general population is 1:50,000. Among those who have lymphoproliferative B-cell malignancies, the incidence of acquired angioedema is 0.5% or less.

Related Basic Science

Genetics

Hereditary angioedema is transmitted as an autosomal dominant trait. Hereditary angioedema is due to mutations within the C1 inhibitor

TABLE 5–6–1. ANGIOEDEMA CAUSED BY C1 INHIBITOR DEFICIENCY: COMPLEMENT ABNORMALITIES

	Hereditary Angioedema		Acquired Angioedema	
	Type I	Type II	Autoantibodies	Other diseases
C1 inhibitor				
Quantitative	Low	Normal	Low	Low
Functional	Low*	Low	Low*	Low*
C1q	Normal†	Normal†	Low†	Low†
C4 or C2	Low‡	Low‡	Low‡	Low‡

*The functional assay is not needed if the result of the quantitative assay is low.
†The C1q value is usually normal in hereditary angioedema, but it can be low. One patient with acquired angioedema has had a normal C1q value.
‡The C4 and C2 values are usually low, even between attacks, but they can be normal between attacks and low during attacks.

gene, which has been identified and cloned and is located on chromosome 11. The sites of the mutations span the entire gene. Among patients with hereditary angioedema, 85% of families have type 1, in which the C1 INH is low in both quantity and function, and 15% have type 2, in which the C1 INH is present in normal amounts but is dysfunctional (Table 5–6–1). In 15 to 20% of affected families, the disorder is due to new mutations. Patients with hereditary angioedema should receive genetic counseling.

Altered Molecular Biology

C1 INH prevents activation of the esterase component of the first component of complement (C1s). C1s cleaves its natural substrates, C4 and C2. C1 INH is a neuroaminoglycoprotein with a molecular weight of around 90,000. The exact molecular cause of episodes of angioedema in these patients remains unknown. A small polypeptide fragment derived from C2 has kininlike activity, which can cause angioedema. C1 INH also regulates activation of the coagulation, kinin, and fibrinolytic systems. During acute attacks, plasmin is generated along with a high-molecular-weight kininogen, both of which may contribute to the angioedema. Bradykinin has been implicated. Why patients have intermittent attacks remains unknown.

In acquired angioedema associated with B-cell lymphoproliferative disease, antibodies directed against the monoclonal protein of the malignancy have been demonstrated with resultant consumption of the C1 INH. In the other form of acquired angioedema, autoantibodies are directed against the C1 INH.

Natural History and Its Modification with Treatment

The natural history of acquired angioedema is unknown and is partly dependent on the underlying cause. The natural history of hereditary angioedema is variable, although before treatment 30% of affected patients are reported to have died from laryngeal edema. Prevention of attacks with medication and increased proficiency in treating airway compromise in emergency rooms have probably considerably decreased the incidence of death from laryngeal edema.

Prevention

The prevention of attacks with medication has been discussed fully (see Plans, Therapeutic). Estrogens have been shown to exacerbate attacks and should be avoided if possible. Angiotensin converting enzyme inhibitors are contraindicated in patients with C1 INH deficiency.

Cost Containment

Prevention of serious attacks with bowel and laryngeal edema should decrease the need for hospitalization and thus decrease costs associated with the disorder. Stanozolol is cheaper than the other drugs used. Once the diagnosis is confirmed, there is no need to repeat the complement laboratory studies frequently.

REFERENCES

Agostoni A, Cicardi M. Hereditary and acquired C1-inhibitor deficiency: Biological and clinical characteristics in 235 patients. Medicine 1992;71:206.
Cicardi M, Bisiani G, Cugno M, et al. Autoimmune C1 inhibitor deficiency: Report of eight patients. Am J Med 1993;95:169.
Frank MM, Gelfand JA, Atkinson JP. Hereditary angioedema: The clinical syndrome and its management. Ann Intern Med 1976;84:580.
Sheffer AL, Austen KF, Rosen FS, Fearon DT. Acquired deficiency of the inhibitor of the first component of complement: Report of five additional cases with commentary on the syndrome. J Allergy Clin Immunol 1985;75:640.
Sheffer AL, Fearon DT, Austen KF. Hereditary angioedema: A decade of management with stanozolol. J Allergy Clin Immunol 1987;80:855.

CHAPTER 5–7

Anaphylaxis

Michael W. Yocum, M.D.

DEFINITION

Anaphylaxis is a general term originally coined to describe the situation in which a reexposure to a toxin results not in the development of immunity or prophylaxis but in the opposite of protection, or anaphylaxis. This phenomenon was described in 1902 by Charles Richet, M.D.

ETIOLOGY

Anaphylaxis can result from a second exposure to a sensitizing antigen, such as foods, medications, insect stings and bites, xenogenic or heterologous proteins, and enzymes such as streptokinase. Anaphylaxis can also occur on first exposure to agents that cause direct release of mediators from mast cells, such as radiocontrast agents or narcotics, or by the activation of serum complement.

CRITERIA FOR DIAGNOSIS
Suggestive

Anaphylaxis is an acute, unexpected, allergic reaction occurring within minutes of the administration of an agent, usually parenterally, but sometimes orally. It may be life threatening and is considered a medical emergency. The administered agent is most frequently an antibiotic, but may be a radiocontrast agent or a Hymenoptera sting. Traditionally, anaphylaxis implied an immunoglobulin (Ig) E-triggered release, and anaphylactoid implied a non-IgE-triggered release of massive amounts of mediators from mast cells and basophils.

Definitive

The clue to the diagnosis is that the adverse allergic reaction occurs within seconds to minutes of a parenteral injection or within 1 hour of oral administration. Generally, the more rapid the onset of symptoms, the more severe the subsequent anaphylactic episode. A typical sequence of symptoms might include general pruritis, urticaria, anxiety, hypotension, tachycardia, fullness in the throat, wheezing, and abdominal cramps. The immediate onset of these allergic symptoms in the above-described clinical settings establishes the diagnosis of anaphylaxis.

CLINICAL MANIFESTATIONS
Subjective

Subjective symptoms include paresthesias of the face, lips, and tongue, an abnormal taste sensation, anxiety, and a prescient sense of impending doom. A frequent subjective symptom, which may presage laryngeal edema, is a sense of fullness in the throat. This symptom, however, could also represent esophageal angioedema. Dyspnea and chest discomfort result from decreased pulmonary compliance, air trapping, and acute alveolar emphysema.

Objective
Physical Examination

The major signs and symptoms of anaphylaxis involve four major organ systems (Table 5–7–1). Most anaphylactic episodes involve

TABLE 5–7–1. SYMPTOMS AND SIGNS OF ANAPHYLAXIS

A. Cutaneous 　　1. Flushing 　　2. Acral or general pruritis 　　3. Urticaria 　　4. Angioedema 　　5. Diaphoresis B. Respiratory 　　1. Conjunctivitis 　　2. Rhinitis 　　3. Oral pruritis 　　4. Brassy cough 　　5. Hoarseness 　　6. Aphonia 　　7. Tight throat 　　8. Dypsnea 　　9. Wheezing 　　10. Intraoral angioedema (buccal mucosa, tongue, palate) 　　11. Oropharyngeal, hypopharyngeal, or laryngeal edema 　　12. Cyanosis	C. Cardiovascular 　　1. Headache 　　2. Chest pain 　　3. Arrhythmia 　　4. Hypotension 　　5. Presyncope 　　6. Syncope 　　7. Tachycardia 　　8. Bradycardia 　　9. Orthostatic hypertension 　　10. Seizures 　　11. Shock D. Gastrointestinal 　　1. Nausea 　　2. Emesis 　　3. Dysphagia 　　4. Abdominal cramps 　　5. Diarrhea

symptoms from at least two organ systems, but they can consist of a single isolated symptom, such as syncope or laryngeal edema. Autopsies on victims of anaphylaxis reveal acute laryngeal edema, acute pulmonary emphysema, and increased eosinophilic infiltration of splenic and liver sinusoids, pulmonary capillaries, and the vessels and lamina propria of the upper respiratory tract. In persons who die of anaphylaxis, it is estimated that 70% die of respiratory causes and 24% die of cardiovascular causes. Fulminant pulmonary edema and adult respiratory distress syndrome may be anaphylactic presentations. Anaphylaxis causes acute cardiac dysfunction with arrhythmias, coronary vasoconstriction, and contractile failure.

Routine Laboratory Abnormalities

Occasionally, laboratory findings such as hemoconcentration with an elevated hemoglobin concentration and eosinophilia may be observed.

PLANS
Diagnostic
Differential Diagnosis

A few disorders mimic anaphylaxis and may cause some confusion. Vasovagal syncope is distinguished by pale, clammy skin, bradycardia, nausea, and the absence of cyanosis. Patients with pheochromocytoma do not flush; rather, they pale and experience headache, diaphoresis, palpitations, anxiety, nausea, tremors, and chest pains. Patients who have carcinoid syndrome experience flushing, salivation, tearing, bronchospasm, diarrhea, and valvular heart disease. Systemic mastocytosis, which itself causes anaphylaxis, also presents with bone pain and dermographism, and there may be lesions of urticaria pigmentosa.

Diagnostic Options

Laboratory investigations to rule out the diseases mentioned above include measurement of urine histamine value, radioactive bone scanning, and marrow biopsy for systemic mastocytosis; determination of urine free catecholamines for pheochromocytoma; and measurement of urine 5-hydroxyindoleacetic acid for carcinoid syndrome.

Serum complement activation with decreases of C3 and C4 and coagulation activation with decreases in factors V, VIII, fibrinogen, and high-molecular-weight kininogen are found in cases of severe anaphylaxis. Serum histamine and tryptase values are transiently elevated for approximately 30 and 90 minutes, respectively, after an anaphylactic episode.

Recommended Approach

Anaphylaxis, once diagnosed, must be investigated to identify or prove causation. Table 5–7–2 lists various causes of anaphylaxis and whether they are IgE-mediated, complement-mediated, or arachidonic acid-

mediated or due to direct release of mediators from mast cells. A careful history must be obtained, including medications, foods, pills, or ingestants taken before the anaphylactic episode. The IgE-mediated mechanisms can be verified by allergy skin tests. A referral to an allergist is clearly indicated for further evaluation of anaphylactic episodes.

Therapeutic
Therapeutic Options

The therapeutic agents, indications, dosages, and goals of anaphylaxis treatment are listed in Table 5–7–3. Therapy is broken down into initial and secondary treatment for pulmonary or cutaneous reactions and for cardiovascular reactions. Additional simple measures might include subcutaneous or intramuscular injection of epinephrine (1:1000), 0.3 mL directly into the site of an allergy shot, an injection for medication, or a Hymenoptera sting. For intramuscular or subcutaneous injections of a medication that triggers anaphylaxis, apply a tourniquet proximally to the site for 3 minutes and release for 1 minute cyclically and also apply ice to the injection site. For laryngospasm or uvular, hypopharyngeal, or laryngeal edema, an inhalation of three breaths from a metered-dose Medihaler-Epi inhaler (3M Pharmaceuticals, St. Paul, MN) is efficacious. Severe hypotension is due to distributive shock in which up to 40% of total plasma volume (1.2 L) may be lost to the extravascular space within 10 minutes, and up to 6 liters of intravenously administered fluids may be needed over 24 hours. Thus, intravenous fluid replacement is crucial and can be augmented by a hand pump to deliver a replacement rate of 200 mL per minute. Anaphylaxis can recur 6 to 12 hours after the event, and the administration of corticosteroids during the initial episode of anaphylaxis is thought to prevent this recurrence. All patients who suffer a severe anaphylactic episode should be hospitalized for at least 12 hours.

Recommended Approach

The greatest service to the patient after a cause of anaphylaxis has been detected is avoidance through education; in the case of a child, the parents must also be educated. Medical alert identification or jewelry should be carried or worn, and the patient should also be instructed in the use of self-administered epinephrine, e.g., EpiPen (Center Laboratories, Port Washington, NY). It should be emphasized that if adrenaline is self-administered for a reaction, the patient must still go immediately to a medical facility for emergency care. Anyone experiencing anaphylaxis or receiving immunotherapy should avoid the use of beta-adrenergic blocking drugs and angiotensin converting enzyme-inhibiting drugs. The patient should be advised to receive medications orally rather than parenterally on their first exposure, if possible. Patients with exercise-induced anaphylaxis should carry an EpiPen during exercise and only begin exercise at least 2 hours after a meal and with a partner. Patients suffering anaphylaxis to foods should be encouraged to pre-

TABLE 5–7–2. CAUSES OF ANAPHYLAXIS

A. IgE-mediated
  1. Antibiotics
     a. Penicillin, cephalosporins
     b. Sulfonamides
     c. Ciprofloxacin
     d. Amphotericin
     e. Others
  2. Other medications
     a. Ethylene oxide in dialysis tubing
     b. Muscle relaxants: hexamethonium, gallamine, pancuronium
     c. Pancreatic extracts
     d. Asparaginase
     e. Cisplatin
  3. Xenogenic or human proteins
     a. Horse antivenoms
     b. Murine antisera
     c. Murine monoclonal antibodies
     d. Factor VIII
     e. Fresh-frozen plasma
     f. Cryoprecipitates
     g. Vaccines with egg proteins
     h. Hymenoptera stings
     i. Triatoma bites
     j. Hydatid cyst fluid
     k. Seminal fluid glycoprotein
  4. Macromolecules
     a. Insulin
     b. Protamine sulfate
     c. Adrenocorticotropic hormone
     d. Enzymes: chymopapain, streptokinase, trypsin, allergy extracts
     e. Latex rubber
  5. Foods
     a. Tree nuts
     b. Peanuts
     c. Shrimp
     d. Buckwheat
     e. Codfish
     f. Cottonseed
     g. Flaxseed
     h. Egg
     i. Legumes
     j. Horseradish
     k. Mustard
     l. Chili pepper
     m. Dill seed
     n. Artichoke
     o. Corn
     p. Sunflower seed
     q. Cumin seed
     r. Salmon
     s. Kiwi fruit
     t. Others
  6. Urticarial syndromes
     a. Cold-induced urticaria
     b. Systemic cholinergic urticaria
B. Complement-mediated
  1. Human blood products: red cells, leukocytes, platelets
  2. IgA-deficient recipients of blood products (may also be IgE-mediated)
  3. Gamma globulin preparations
  4. Heparin–protamine complexes
  5. Dialysis membrane: cuprophane
  6. Antilymphocyte antibodies
C. Direct mast cell activation
  1. Opiates
  2. Tubocurarine
  3. Dextran and polysaccharides
  4. Radiocontrast agents
  5. Polymyxin B
  6. Induction agents: propanidid, thiopentone
  7. Systemic mastocytosis
D. Arachidonic acid modulators
  1. Aspirin
  2. Indomethacin
  3. Ibuprofen
  4. Naproxen
  5. Piroxicam
  6. Sulindac
  7. Tolmetin
  8. Others
E. Mechanism unknown
  1. Sulfites
  2. Exercise-induced anaphylaxis
  3. Progesterone-induced anaphylaxis
  4. Idiopathic anaphylaxis

pare their own meals, read labels carefully, and avoid food prepared by others, including that in restaurants.

FOLLOW-UP

Successful avoidance or control of future anaphylactic episodes, as well as documentation of cause, depends on follow-up visits. All patients who experience anaphylaxis should be evaluated and followed by a certified allergist. The patient should be seen 1, 3, and 6 months after an anaphylactic reaction. Follow-up visits enable the physician to test the patient's knowledge of what to avoid and ability to self-administer epinephrine. Patients who experience anaphylaxis from allergy immunotherapy injections should be reevaluated by their allergist before any further allergy shots are administered. All patients suffering Hymenoptera anaphylaxis should be evaluated by an allergist for venom desensitization. The tentative causes of anaphylaxis found during a 3-year period in 179 patients are listed in Table 5–7–4.

DISCUSSION
Prevalence and Incidence

The prevalence of severe and fatal anaphylaxis has been estimated for several inciting agents. Anaphylaxis occurs in 1% of patients who receive chymopapain injections, and this therapy for protruded interspinal disks is no longer routinely used. Anaphylaxis occurs in 1 of 5000 patients who receive general anesthetic and 1 of 2700 hospitalized patients. The latter patients typically react to either a drug or a diagnostic procedure. Anaphylaxis occurs in 0.7 to 0.8% of patients who receive penicillin injections or Hymenoptera stings, and the period incidence of visits for anaphylaxis to a community's emergency room has been found to be 0.09%. Anaphylaxis from allergen immunotherapy is, however, rare: the frequency is approximately 0.06%. Anaphylaxis occurs in 1 of 1500 patients given radiocontrast injections and in 0.45% of patients receiving hemodialysis. It is estimated that 1200 deaths a year occur from anaphylaxis, chiefly as a result of administration of drugs and radiocontrast media. Anaphylaxis is both more severe in its clinical expression and more frequent in patients with atopy.

Related Basic Science
Physiologic or Metabolic Derangement

The signs and symptoms of anaphylaxis are due to acute massive release of mediators, chiefly from mast cells. In systemic mastocytosis, mediator release causes flushing, hypotension, headache, and abdominal cramping. Mediators released from the mast cell include histamine, tryptase, prostaglandin D_2, platelet-activating factor, leukotriene C_4, and eosinophilic chemotactic factor of anaphylaxis. The plasma histamine value correlates with the severity and duration of the cardiopulmonary changes in anaphylactic shock. The mediators cause distributive shock, resulting in peripheral vasoconstriction, increased circulation time, and decreased skin perfusion. Histamine increases cardiac automaticity and contractility and the sinoatrial rate and causes coronary vasodilation via H_2 receptors, but it also causes decreased cardiac contractility, decreased atrio-ventricular conduction, and coronary vasoconstriction via H_1 receptors. Thus, H_1 and H_2 antihistamines offer the best protection against the cardiovascular effects of histamine, as proved by intravenous histamine challenge. Tryptase, a neutral protease, activates serum complement generating C3a, C4a, and C5a, cleaves high-molecular-weight kininogen to generate bradykinin, and cleaves fibrinogen. The complement components C3a, C4a, and C5a cause the direct release of mediators from mast cells. Chymase activates Hageman factor to initiate coagulation and activates angiotensinogen to generate angiotensin II. Platelet-activating factor decreases cardiac contractility, increases atrio-ventricular conduction, and is the most potent chemotaxin known for eosinophils. Eosinophilic chemotactic factor of anaphylaxis also is chemotactic for eosinophils and also stimulates them to produce platelet-activating factor. Leukotriene C_4 causes peripheral airway constriction, resulting in alveolar emphysema.

Cuprophane membranes used in hemodialysis activate serum complement via the alternate pathway, and polyacrylonitrile membranes activate the contact phase of coagulation and generate bradykinin. Bradykinin constricts bronchial smooth muscle and increases vascular permeability. Angiotensin converting enzyme also inactivates bradykinin and substance P, the latter a tachykinin that causes vasodilation and gastrointestinal muscle contraction.

TABLE 5–7–3. TREATMENT OF SYSTEMIC ANAPHYLAXIS IN ADULTS[a]

Reaction	Agents	Indications	Dosage	Goals
A. Pulmonary, cutaneous				
1. Initial therapy	Epinephrine	Wheezing Laryngeal edema Hives Angioedema	0.3–0.5 mL of 1:1000 SC every 10–20 min	Maintain airway patency Reverse vasodilation Reverse wheezing
	Oxygen	Hypoxemia, cyanosis	40–100%	Maintain $Po_2 > 60$ mm Hg
	Albuterol	Wheezing	0.3 mL (5% solution) in 2.5 mL saline nebulized	Reverse wheezing
2. Secondary therapy	Aminophylline	Wheezing	Loading dose (6 mg/kg IV over 30 min); 0.3–0.9 mg/kg/h IV as maintenance	Reverse wheezing
	Corticosteroids	Wheezing, laryngeal edema	Methylprednisolone 50 mg IV every 6 h	Reverse wheezing Reverse edema Prevent late-phase reaction
	Antihistamines	Hives, angioedema, arrhythmias	Diphenhydramine, 25–50 mg, IV, IM, or PO every 6–8 h	Reverse hives and angioedema, reverse H_1 effects of histamine
		Arrhythmias, vasodilation	Cimetidine 300 mg (diluted in 10 mL saline) IV or PO every 6 h	Reverse H_2 effects of histamine
B. Cardiovascular				
1. Initial therapy	Intravenous fluids	Hypotension	Saline or colloid 1 L every 20–30 min	Maintain systolic blood pressure > 80–100 mm Hg
	Epinephrine	Hypotension	1 mL of 1:1000 in 500 mL of D5W IV at 0.5–5 μg or 0.25–2.5 mL per minute	Maintain systolic blood pressure > 80–100 mm Hg
2. Secondary therapy	Military antishock trousers (MAST)	Hypotension	Apply to hips and legs	Maintain systolic blood pressure > 80–100 mm Hg
	Atropine	Bradycardia	1 mg IV push every 5 minutes × 3	Increase pulse
	Dopamine	Hypotension	1 mL of 40 mg in 100 mL D5W IV at 4–20 μg/kg/min (0.5–2 mL) per min	Increase pulse
	Norepinephrine	Hypotension	4 mg in 1 L D5W IV at 2–12 μg (0.5–3 mL) per min	Increase pulse
	Antihistamines	Hypotension	Same as above	Antagonize the H_1 and H_2 cardiac and vascular effects of histamine
	Glucagon	Hypotension	1 mg in 1 L D5W IV at 5–15 μg (5–15 mL) per min	Increase cardiac output

[a]Dosages, choice of specific agents, efficacy, and safety must be individualized.
Source: Bochner BS, Lichtenstein LM. Anaphylaxis. N Engl J Med 1991;324:1788. *Reproduced by permission of the* New England Journal of Medicine *and the author.*

Natural History and Its Modification with Treatment

Anaphylaxis may continue to recur unless its cause is found and avoided. Idiopathic anaphylaxis, which by definition has no cause, is an exception, and patients with this disorder may improve with the passage of time. There is evidence that careful avoidance of penicillin and

TABLE 5–7–4. TENTATIVE CAUSES OF ANAPHYLAXIS IN 179 MAYO CLINIC PATIENTS

Cause	Number (%) of Patients	
Food	59	(33)
Idiopathic	34	(19)
Hymenoptera sting	25	(14)
Medication*	23	(13)
False-positive diagnoses[†]	18	(10)
Exercise	12	(7)
Immunotherapy	5	(3)
Human plasma	1	(<1)
Latex	1	(<1)
Aeroallergen	1	(<1)

*Penicillin, amoxicillin, ampicillin, nonsteroidal antiinflammatory agents, sulfonamide, erythromycin, radioiodinated contrast agent, or ergotamine.
[†]Hives in 9, panic attacks in 3, asthma in 3, and serum sickness, macular rash, and angioedema in 1 each.
Source: Yocum MW, Khan DA. Assessment of patients who have experienced anaphylaxis: A 3-year survey. Mayo Clin Proc *1994;69:16. Reproduced by permission of Mayo Foundation.*

Hymenoptera stings can result in the loss of IgE antibody to these allergens. Severe food allergies such as those to tree nuts, peanuts, shrimp, and legumes are rarely outgrown and thus are lifelong. Persons with atopy have a higher risk of anaphylaxis, and patients anaphylactically sensitive to one medication have a higher risk of sensitivity to other medications. The prognosis of an anaphylactic episode is chiefly dependent on how quickly treatment, especially epinephrine, is administered.

Prevention

Avoidance of the provocative agent of anaphylaxis is effective prevention. Allergy evaluation is thus critical to determine the cause of ana-

TABLE 5–7–5. NONCONTRIBUTORY INVESTIGATIONS IN MAYO CLINIC PATIENTS WHO UNDERWENT ASSESSMENT FOR ANAPHYLAXIS

Test	Number of Patients	Result
C1 esterase inhibitor	33	Normal
Urinary histamine	18	Normal
5-Hydroxyindoleacetic acid	15	Normal
Metabisulfite challenge	15	Negative
Methylimidazoleacetic acid	11	Normal
Dye and preservative challenge	10	Negative
Serum tryptase	10	Normal
Serum complement	7	Normal
Serum cryoglobulin	7	Normal
Aspirin challenge	4	Negative

phylaxis. A careful drug history should be obtained, and medications, especially penicillin and its derivatives, should generally be given orally rather than parenterally if at all possible. Patients should be observed for 30 minutes after all injections given in the office. If allergy desensitization shots are given, the patient should first be queried regarding local reaction to previous allergy injections before receiving the scheduled injection. Patients allergic to Hymenoptera can be desensitized by allergy injections for maximal protection against stings. Patients who react to radiocontrast media can be premedicated with 50 mg of prednisone given orally 13 hours, 7 hours, and 1 hour before the administration of the contrast agent and with 50 mg of diphenhydramine and 50 mg of ephedrine orally 1 hour before administration. Alternatively, methylprednisolone, 32 mg given at 12 hours and 2 hours before the injection of radiocontrast material, has proved just as effective. Patients should be educated in the avoidance of foods they react to, taught how to read labels and understand what they read, and informed that oils from allergenic foods generally do no harm. Patients who experience exercise-induced anaphylaxis should avoid eating or using nonsteroidal antiinflammatory drugs for 2 to 4 hours before exercise, and they should exercise only with a partner. All patients with anaphylaxis should be provided with and instructed in the use of an EpiPen autoinjector and should wear a Medic-Alert bracelet or necklace.

Cost Containment

The most effective way to treat patients with anaphylaxis is to identify a cause, if possible, and institute education and avoidance. This approach prevents future visits to an emergency room and hospital admissions. Early referral to an allergist to investigate cause is invaluable. Several tests that are often ordered for the evaluation of patients with anaphylaxis are not helpful or cost-effective (Table 5–7–5).

REFERENCES

Bochner BS. Systemic anaphylaxis. Curr Ther Allergy Immunol Rheumatol 1992;4:146
Bush WH, Swanson DP. Acute reactions to intravascular contrast media: Type, risk factors, recognition and specific treatment. AJR 1991;157:1153.
Levy JH, Levi R. Diagnosis and treatment of anaphylactic/anaphylactoid reactions. Monogr Allergy 1992;30:130.
Richet C. Anaphylaxis. London: University Press, Constable, 1913.
Yocum MW, Khan DA. Assessment of patients who have experienced anaphylaxis: A 3-year survey. Mayo Clin Proc 1994;69:16.
Yunginger JW. Anaphylaxis. Curr Probl Pediatr 1992;22:130.

CHAPTER 5–8

Food Allergy

Susan Rudd Wynn, M.D.

DEFINITION

Food allergy is an immunoglobulin (Ig) E-mediated (type I hypersensitivity) reaction to antigens contained in food. For the purposes of this chapter, the term *food* includes all ingredients involved in the preparation of foods and beverages, including dyes and preservatives.

ETIOLOGY

Patients of any age may develop specific IgE antibodies to allergens contained in foods to which they have been previously exposed. When these specific IgE molecules interact with the food allergen in question, mast cell degranulation occurs and chemical mediators including histamine are released that cause the clinical manifestations of food allergy. Although there may be a positive family history of food allergy, the etiology of the development of specific IgE to foods is not known.

CRITERIA FOR DIAGNOSIS
Suggestive

Food allergy should be considered when patients develop allergic manifestations within 1 hour of eating or drinking. Symptoms should develop every time the allergen in question is eaten, even in minute quantities. Symptoms that develop hours or days after food ingestion make the diagnosis of food allergy much less likely. Ingestion of foods that are commonly associated with food allergy makes the diagnosis more likely; these include shellfish, peanuts, soybeans, fish, tree nuts, wheat, milk, and eggs.

Definitive

The diagnosis of food allergy can be made when a history of allergic symptoms on ingestion of a food is confirmed by the reproduction of the allergic response in the skin by epicutaneous testing or by demonstration of specific IgE antibodies by in vitro assays. Occasionally, a clear history of repeated reactions to the same food is sufficient to make the diagnosis. The "gold standard" for the diagnosis is a double-blind, placebo-controlled food challenge administered in a controlled clinical setting, but this unfortunately is seldom practical.

CLINICAL MANIFESTATIONS
Subjective

The symptoms of food allergy generally develop within minutes or ingestion. Oropharyngeal pruritus is often the first manifestation, followed by a generalized sensation of pruritus and warmth. An urticarial or maculopapular rash may develop; angioedema may involve pharyngeal structures and be life threatening. Dysphagia, hoarseness, and tightness in the throat are indicative of laryngeal edema; chest tightness, wheezing, and cough may also be present. There may be acute nausea, vomiting, abdominal cramping, and diarrhea. Lightheadedness or syncope may occur. Anaphylaxis occurs when there is involvement of multiple organ systems; this is the most devastating form of food allergy, and can be fatal. A small subset of patients with food anaphylaxis exhibit symptoms only if they exercise vigorously after eating the offending food. In patients who are highly sensitized, allergic symptoms may develop with mere inhalation or cutaneous contact with the food in question.

Significant food allergies developed in childhood may persist into adulthood. If an allergic reaction to food occurs anew in an adult, careful questioning may reveal a similar but less severe reaction on exposure to that food in the past. Other allergic syndromes are often present, including allergic rhinitis, asthma, atopic dermatitis, and urticaria/angioedema. There may be a positive family history of reactions to foods, occasionally but not necessarily to the same food.

Objective

Physical Examination

The physical examination of the patient having an acute reaction to food will have findings concentrated in the respiratory, cutaneous, and gastrointestinal systems.

Respiratory. There may be watery rhinorrhea, paroxysmal sneezing, inspiratory stridor, cough, or wheezing.

Cutaneous. Generalized flushing may be present, along with urticaria or a maculopapular rash. There may be angioedema, especially of the lips and tongue.

Gastrointestinal. The patient may have vomiting or diarrhea. The abdomen may be diffusely tender but no peritoneal signs should be present. Bowel sounds may be increased.

Other. Hypotension and tachycardia may be present. Cardiac arrhythmias, as well as loss of consciousness, can be observed in severe reactions.

Chronic manifestations of food allergy are usually cutaneous, and may be characterized by urticaria or atopic dermatitis.

Routine Laboratory Abnormalities

The role of the clinical laboratory in the management of food allergy is limited. Peripheral blood eosinophilia is not likely to be present except as a general indicator of ongoing allergic disease.

PLANS
Diagnostic
Differential Diagnosis

Table 5–8–1 summarizes the adverse reactions to food in adults, which can be broadly categorized into immunologic and nonimmunologic reactions.

Diagnostic Options

The diagnosis of food allergy may be obvious in a patient with recurring reactions to the same food, such as the patient who develops urticaria every time he eats shrimp. If, however, the ingredient responsible for the reaction is not readily apparent or if the reactions are severe, referral to an allergist is indicated for further diagnosis.

Allergy skin testing by the epicutaneous method (prick or puncture) is the diagnostic procedure of choice in determining the food responsible for a patient's allergic reaction. Commercially available aqueous solutions of food extracts are introduced into the upper layers of the epidermis; if specific IgE antibodies to that food extract are present, a wheal-and-flare response will occur within 20 minutes. Patients undergoing skin testing should not have taken H_1 or H_2 antihistamines within 72 hours of skin testing; the exception to this is astemizole, which must be eliminated 6 to 12 weeks or longer prior to skin testing. A negative skin test to a food makes significant allergic sensitization quite unlikely; however, there are many false-positive skin test reactions to foods. Positive food skin tests should then be evaluated along with the patient's history, at which time the diagnosis may be apparent. If multiple positive reactions are present, multiple foods may need to be eliminated from the diet for 2 weeks, then reintroduced one every 3 or 4

days under close medical supervision. Patients with a history of anaphylaxis should not reintroduce foods implicated in their reactions except in a controlled clinical setting where anaphylaxis can be treated.

In vitro tests for specific IgE testing yield a higher rate of false-negative and a lower rate of false-positive results than skin testing. In general, these tests should be performed only when skin testing is impossible or unsafe, that is, if antihistamines cannot be discontinued, in the presence of diffuse skin involvement, or if the allergic reaction is so severe that cutaneous contact with small amounts of allergen is judged to place the patient at risk for anaphylaxis.

Recommended Approach

With a clear history of typical symptoms and a highly suspected food allergen, diagnostic testing is not mandatory. If, however, there is suspicion regarding the nature of the reaction or the identity of the allergen, referral to an allergist for skin testing is the preferred diagnostic approach. While a definite diagnosis is pending, the patient must avoid any contact with foods implicated in the allergic reaction.

Therapeutic

The treatment of food allergy is the strict avoidance of the offending food. Prophylactic pharmacologic treatment with antihistamines or oral cromolyn sodium to allow the patient to eat the food in question is not recommended; this may place the patient at risk for anaphylaxis by masking its early symptoms.

Although IgE sensitization may rarely wane spontaneously, this should never be assumed and the patient should be prepared for the possibility of allergic reactions to persist indefinitely.

Patients with food allergy should have antihistamines readily available at all times. Diphenhydramine 25 to 50 mg should be taken by mouth immediately at the onset of symptoms. Other H_1 antihistamines can be substituted. Aqueous epinephrine 1:1000 (0.01 mL/kg up to 0.5 mL) should be available for self-administration in patients with systemic symptoms, and should be given along with antihistamines at the onset of symptoms in patients with a history of anaphylaxis. Several different epinephrine products are commercially available, but patients generally prefer an autoinjector because of its portability and ease of use.

After self-administration of epinephrine, the patient should undergo an immediate medical evaluation. A single injection of epinephrine may be insufficient to completely reverse the reaction, and additional therapy may be needed. The symptoms of anaphylaxis may fade but recur several hours later (biphasic anaphylaxis).

FOLLOW-UP

The patient with anaphylaxis to foods should be reevaluated within 1 month of the initial reaction to make sure that the foods in question are being properly avoided, the treatment plan for reactions is well understood, and epinephrine and antihistamines are close at hand.

DISCUSSION
Prevalence

Up to a quarter of the adult population will report some type of adverse reaction to foods, but the true prevalence as documented by double-blind, placebo-controlled food challenge has been estimated to be between 0.8 and 2.4%.

Related Basic Science

The specific immunologic defect in food allergy is the presence of specific IgE antibodies to food allergens; it is possible for normal patients to have small amounts of IgA, IgG, and IgM to foods. IgE molecules bind high-affinity receptors on mast cells and basophils, and when food antigen binds in a fashion whereby two IgE molecules are crosslinked, mast cell degranulation occurs. Preformed mediators such as histamine are related, causing pruritus and vasodilation, which are classic features of the allergic response. Other mediators such as prostaglandins and leukotrienes contribute to allergy symptoms. Chemotactic agents which are also contained in mast cell and basophil granules recruit inflamma-

TABLE 5–8–1. ADVERSE REACTIONS TO FOODS

I. Immunologic
  A. IgE-mediated
    1. Cutaneous: urticaria, angioedema, atopic dermatitis
    2. Respiratory: asthma, rhinitis, conjunctivitis
    3. Gastrointestinal: nausea, vomiting, diarrhea
    4. Systemic anaphylaxis
    5. Exercise-induced anaphylaxis
    6. Eosinophilic gastroenteritis
  B. Non-IgE-mediated
    1. Celiac disease, dermatitis herpetiformis
    2. Food-induced enteropathy
II. Nonimmunologic
  A. Primary gastrointestinal disease exacerbated by food
    1. Gastroesophageal reflux
    2. Peptic ulcer disease
    3. Gallbladder disease
    4. Lactose, disaccharidase deficiency
  B. Pharmacologic agents naturally occurring in food, such as caffeine, tyramine, theobromine, and histamine
  C. Infectious toxins, such as botulinum and aflatoxins
  D. Reactions to additives or preservatives, such as sulfiting agents and dyes
  E. Gustatory reflex rhinorrhea
  F. Idiosyncratic reactions

tory cells such as eosinophils and neutrophils to the site of the reaction. These cells release mediators of their own which are responsible for the late or biphasic reaction that can occur 8 to 12 hours after the initial antigen–antibody interaction.

As mast cells are concentrated in the skin, respiratory tract, and gut, the signs and symptoms of food allergy are concentrated in these areas. This helps with the differential diagnosis when a patient relates food-related symptoms in an area of the body that does not have high mast cell numbers, such as the central nervous system. It is not clear why some patients have unique constellations of symptoms with an allergic reaction to food; one patient with peanut allergy may merely exhibit oropharyngeal symptoms, whereas another will have systemic anaphylaxis. A large quantity of ingested food may be more likely to cause widespread mast cell degranulation, high histamine levels, and systemic symptoms, but tiny quantities of food allergen can cause anaphylaxis in extremely sensitive individuals. Children and adolescents with food allergy and concomitant asthma have been shown to be at risk for life-threatening anaphylaxis, but it is not known if a similar relationship exists in adults.

Natural History and Its Modification with Treatment

Immunoglobulin E-mediated food allergy may persist throughout a patient's life, although reactivity may lessen as exposure to pertinent food allergens is avoided over time. The severity of future reactions cannot be predicted, and every patient must be considered at risk for anaphylaxis.

Prevention

The development of specific IgE to food allergens cannot be prevented unless exposure to that antigen never occurs. Once sensitization occurs, the prevention of future reactions can be achieved only by strict avoidance of the food in question. Food anaphylaxis may occur even with minute amounts of ingested, touched, or inhaled food, and patients must be counseled to maintain a high index of suspicion when eating any food whose preparation has not been witnessed.

Food labels must be carefully studied before eating, even if the allergen in question is not readily suspected. Common food allergens such as peanut and soy are inexpensive and plentiful, and may be used to add protein or texture to anything from chili to candy bars. Patients must also be taught to recognize specific proteins that indicate the presence of food allergen, such as casein for milk or albumin for egg. If the label is not sufficiently detailed (e.g., merely listing "nuts" instead of peanuts), the presence of the food allergen in question should be assumed and the food avoided.

Cost Containment

The proper diagnosis and treatment of food allergy are inherently cost effective, for the prevention of severe reactions will reduce the need for emergency medical care.

Careful medication selection can also reduce costs. Generic diphenhydramine is readily available without a prescription. The most cost-effective way to prescribe epinephrine is to use ampules or multidose vials and tuberculin syringes, although patient acceptance of preparing and self-administering a conventional syringe is poor. Preprepared epinephrine syringes and autoinjectors generally cost less than $40.00.

REFERENCES

Metcalfe DD, Sampson HA, Simon RA, eds. Food allergy. Cambridge: Blackwell Scientific, 1991.

Sampson HA. Adverse reactions to foods. In: Middleton E, Reed CE, Ellis EF, et al., eds. *Allergy: Principles and practice.* 4th ed. St. Louis: Mosby, 1993:1661.

Sampson HA, Mendelson L, Rosen JP. Fatal and near-fatal anaphylaxis to food in children and adolescents. N Engl J Med 1992;327:380.

Yunginger JW, Sweeney KG, Sturner WQ, et al. Fatal food-induced anaphylaxis. JAMA 1988;260:1450.

CHAPTER 5–9

Stinging Insect Allergy

John W. Yunginger, M.D.

DEFINITION

Insect sting reactions are conveniently divided into *immediate* (<4 hours) and *delayed* (>4 hours), according to the time elapsed between sting and development of symptoms. Immediate reactions are in turn separated into local, large local, systemic, and toxic reactions. *Local reactions* are normal and involve transient pain, erythema, and swelling at the sting site. In *large local reactions,* the erythema and swelling are more extensive but still contiguous with the sting site. *Systemic reactions* involve signs and symptoms in areas remote from the sting site, and it is these reactions that warrant a diagnosis of stinging insect allergy. Toxic reactions are nonimmunologic and occur when a person receives multiple (>10) stings over a short period. Delayed reactions may present as glomerulonephritis, transverse myelitis, myocarditis, or serum sickness. The pathogenesis of delayed reactions is unclear; immune mechanisms may or may not be involved.

ETIOLOGY

Stinging insects are members of the Hymenoptera order and include bees (honey bees, bumble bees, sweat bees), vespids (wasps, hornets, yellow jackets), and fire ants. Domestic honey bees are generally mild mannered and do not sting without provocation. Their stingers are barbed and usually remain embedded in the victim, along with the attached venom sac. African honey bees are more defensive and hostile; their migration into the southwestern United States has resulted in increased numbers of sting reactions. Yellow jackets are ground-nesting predators that scavenge for food in trash cans; they are ill-tempered and often sting without provocation. Yellow hornets and white-faced hornets build aerial nests that resemble Japanese lanterns. Wasps build nests resembling honeycombs on roof overhangs or outbuildings. The coloration of wasps varies greatly in different geographic areas. Fire ants are widespread throughout the southeastern United States, where they build large subterranean nests. When stinging, the ant anchors itself by its mandibles and delivers multiple stings in a semicircular pattern; a sterile pustule usually forms at each sting site.

CRITERIA FOR DIAGNOSIS
Suggestive

The victim relates the story of being stung by an insect and describes the lesion that developed.

Definitive

The definitive diagnosis requires a historical description of a systemic reaction, as discussed under Definition, following one or two stings, plus a positive skin test to venom from the culprit insect (honey bee, wasp, yellow jacket, or hornet) or to an extract of crushed insect bodies (fire ant only).

CLINICAL MANIFESTATIONS

Subjective

Subjective symptoms may include generalized pruritus; hives; itching of the ear canals, palate, or throat; dyspnea, or constriction of the throat or chest; dysphagia; nausea; dizziness; and visual blurring.

Objective

Physical Examination

Physical examination may reveal generalized urticaria; angioedema of the lips, eyelids, face, hands, or feet; vomiting or diarrhea; or wheezing. Dizziness, hypotension, and loss of consciousness are encountered more commonly in adults than in children.

Routine Laboratory Abnormalities

Although systemic reactions are accompanied by elevations in plasma histamine and mast cell tryptase levels, these laboratory tests are not required to diagnose systemic reactions.

PLANS

Diagnostic

The diagnosis of insect sting allergy is usually apparent from the clinical history, but must always be confirmed by demonstrating the presence of venom-specific immunoglobulin (Ig) E antibodies. Conditions that simulate anaphylaxis, such as neurocardiogenic syncope and vocal cord dysfunction reactions, are occasionally triggered by insect stings. For adults who experience loss of consciousness following unwitnessed stings, the differential diagnosis also includes cardiac arrhythmia, myocardial infarction, and seizure disorder.

Venom-specific IgE antibodies are best demonstrated by intradermal skin testing with honey bee, wasp, yellow jacket, yellow hornet, and white-faced hornet venoms at concentrations ranging from 1 ng/mL to 1 μg/mL in a diluent containing human serum albumin as a stabilizer. Fire ant venom is not available commercially; patients suspected of being allergic to fire ant stings must be tested with a fire ant whole-body extract. Negative and positive control tests with diluent alone and histamine, respectively, should be placed along with the venom tests. Venom skin tests may be falsely negative for several days following a sting reaction, so testing is best performed 4 to 6 weeks after the reaction. The degree of skin test reactivity does not necessarily correlate with the severity of the sting reaction. Only persons who experience systemic reactions should be tested for venom-specific IgE antibodies.

Measurements of venom-specific IgE antibodies by immunoassay are offered by reference laboratories, but these assays are more expensive and less sensitive than skin testing.

Venom-specific IgE antibodies may be transiently elevated after uneventful stings, but usually return to normal levels over several weeks or months. In persons with insect sting allergy, loss of venom sensitivity can occur spontaneously over time.

Therapeutic

The acute sting reaction is treated symptomatically. Large local reactions are treated with ice packs; although antihistamines are universally recommended for these reactions, their efficacy has never been demonstrated by controlled trials. Systemic reactions should be treated with epinephrine 1:1000, 0.3 mL subcutaneously, repeated in 10 minutes if necessary. Supplemental treatment with oxygen, antihistamines, pressor agents, and glucocorticoids may be used if indicated. Anaphylaxis may be prolonged or recurrent, and the patient should be observed for several hours after initial therapy.

Long-term management of moderate to severe sting reactions should include venom immunotherapy. In such persons, the risk of a subsequent systemic reaction to a single sting is reduced to 1–2% from 25–60% by venom immunotherapy. Those venoms producing positive skin tests should be administered at weekly intervals, beginning with submicrogram doses and increasing to a maintenance dose of 100 μg for each venom. At that point, the interval between injections should be lengthened first to 4 weeks, then to 6 weeks. In vespid-sensitive persons with histories of mild to moderate sting reactions, usually 3 years of immunotherapy is sufficient; persons with histories of severe reactions, or who are honey bee sting sensitive, or who experience difficulty tolerating venom injections should receive 5 years of immunotherapy.

FOLLOW-UP

Persons experiencing systemic reactions to stings should be provided with epinephrine-containing kits for emergency use after any subsequent stings. Persons who experience repeated systemic reactions usually have stereotyped responses and thus become familiar with their own "early warning" symptoms. Sting-sensitive persons should receive education regarding insect identification, insect behavior, and nesting habits. Skin testing is indicated for those individuals who have experienced moderate or severe sting reactions.

For persons receiving venom immunotherapy, some experts advocate measurement of venom-specific IgG antibodies (blocking antibodies), but in our experience these measurements have not correlated with an individual's clinical response to deliberate insect sting challenges. Persons whose venom skin tests are negative following 3 years of venom immunotherapy can discontinue immunotherapy with minimal (<5%) risk of recurrence of sting sensitivity; however venom skin tests remain positive in most immunotherapy-treated patients.

DISCUSSION

Prevalence and Incidence

Allergic reactions to insect stings are reported by about 1% of adults. Cross-sectional surveys have reported a slightly greater prevalence of systemic reactions. About one quarter of patients are sensitive to insect venoms, as measured by skin test or immunoassay. About 40 deaths annually are attributed to Hymenoptera stings in the United States; most involve adults over age 45. Interestingly, in the majority of sting-induced fatalities, there is no history of a prior, nonfatal systemic reaction to an insect sting.

Related Basic Science

Insect venoms contain proinflammatory amines and peptides that cause the transient normal redness and swelling at the sting site. Systemic reactions are mediated by histamine and other mediators of anaphylaxis that are released from basophils and mast cells following the interaction of venom proteins with venom-specific IgE antibodies on the surface of these cells. Venom immunotherapy is effective through multiple mechanisms, including the induction of venom-specific IgG antibodies, inhibition of mast cell mediator release, and suppression of the IgE antibody response.

Natural History and Its Modification with Treatment

The risk of systemic sting reactions is less than 1% in persons without histories of systemic reactions and negative venom skin tests. About half of the adults with positive venom skin tests and a history of systemic reactions are at risk for systemic sting reaction. In persons with systemic reactions to stings who do not receive venom immunotherapy, the risk of repeat systemic reactions is higher among honey bee sting-sensitive persons than among vespid-sensitive persons. Only 5% of persons with large local reactions to stings will go on to develop systemic reactions with future stings.

Prevention

Long-term management of insect sting-sensitive persons involves education regarding insect avoidance, prompt self-treatment of anaphylaxis, and prophylactic venom immunotherapy. Spring-loaded automatic injection devices are available for epinephrine administration and should be prescribed by physicians who treat acute sting reactions. These kits are not a substitute for medical attention; symptoms may recur after the effect of the epinephrine wears off. Persons who are receiving venom immunotherapy should continue to carry epinephrine, in the unlikely event that multiple stings are received.

Cost Containment

Cost containment is accomplished by offering venom immunotherapy only to those persons who require it, thus reducing later costs of medical treatment of anaphylaxis and lost time from school or work. Costs can also be lowered by discontinuing venom immunotherapy after 5 years; preliminary evidence suggests that the recurrence rate of sting sensitivity in persons who stop injections at that point is about 5%.

REFERENCES

Keating MU, Kagey-Sobotka A, Hamilton RG, Yunginger JW. Clinical and immunologic follow-up of patients who discontinue venom immunotherapy. J Allergy Clin Immunol 1991;88:339.

Levine MI, Lockey RF, eds. Monograph on insect allergy. 2nd ed. Pittsburgh: American Academy of Allergy and Immunology, 1986.

Reisman RE. Stinging insect allergy. Med Clin North Am 1992;76:883.

Valentine MD. Anaphylaxis and stinging insect hypersensitivity. JAMA 1992;268:2830.

Van der Linden P-WG, Hack CE, Struyvenberg A, van der Zwan JK. Insect-sting challenge in 324 subjects with a previous anaphylactic reaction: Current criteria for insect-venom hypersensitivity do not predict the occurrence and the severity of anaphylaxis. J Allergy Clin Immunol 1994;94:151.

Yunginger JW. Insect allergy. In: Middleton E, Reed CE, Ellis EF, et al., eds. Allergy: Principles and practice. 4th ed. St. Louis: Mosby, 1993;1511.

CHAPTER 5–10

Latex Allergy

Loren W. Hunt, M.D.

DEFINITION

Allergy to latex is an apparently new allergic syndrome that is the result of immunoglobulin (Ig) E-mediated sensitivity to one or more components of latex found in raw latex sap or finished latex products. Although the terms *rubber, latex,* and *latex rubber* are often used interchangeably, to avoid confusion, the term *latex* is used in this chapter to refer to all products synthesized from latex sap.

ETIOLOGY

Latex allergy, for reasons yet to be understood, was not clinically recognized until 1979. Since that time, latex allergy has been reported in increasing frequency in individuals who are frequently exposed to latex products, such as gloves, condoms, and balloons. Following subsequent contact with these or other rubber products, affected individuals develop immediate symptoms of urticaria, rhinitis, asthma, angioedema, and anaphylaxis.

CRITERIA FOR DIAGNOSIS

Suggestive

Persons with IgE-mediated sensitivity to latex usually report localized urticarial lesions at points of skin contact with latex products, but can have flushing, generalized urticaria, wheezing, laryngeal edema, and hypotension following exposure of skin or mucosal surfaces to latex. Airborne latex particles can also cause conjunctivitis, rhinitis, asthma, or laryngeal edema in sensitized subjects. Often, the patient can relate symptoms temporally to contact with latex products, but at times, the causality of latex exposure is difficult to establish, particularly during surgical procedures, when other medications are being given, or when the latex exposure is airborne.

Definitive

Immunoglobulin E-mediated sensitivity to latex can be established by skin testing with latex extract or by demonstration of serum latex-specific IgE antibodies. Skin testing has caused systemic allergic reactions in very sensitive individuals and has therefore raised the question of safety as a diagnostic procedure in lieu of in vitro testing. Serum testing, however, has not been demonstrated to be as sensitive, being positive in only 55 to 85% of those with positive skin tests, depending on the group being tested, with the highest positive percentage occurring in those patients with spina bifida, who represent a high-risk group for severe reactions.

CLINICAL MANIFESTATIONS

Subjective

Although it is always unusual to discover a new type of allergy, it is particularly unusual to discover one that appears to be nearly isolated to the health care profession, both among health care workers and among patients. Individuals who have developed IgE-mediated sensitivity to latex commonly report that they have experienced other allergic problems in the past such as drug allergy, seasonal or perennial rhinitis, and asthma. In addition, many health care workers report that they have had a scaly contact-type hand dermatitis in the past prior to the development of more immediate symptoms of urticarial lesions at areas of contact with latex products, usually disposable latex gloves. Very frequent use of rubber products, particularly rubber gloves, also is reported by latex-allergic health care workers. Other latex-allergic individuals are patients, usually with urogenital abnormalities such as those associated with spina bifida, who have required frequent surgical procedures, catheterizations, or fecal disimpactions as part of their care. Once allergic sensitization has taken place, sensitized individuals can develop acute urticarial lesions at points of skin contact with latex products. These individuals can also experience more severe reactions such as generalized urticaria or anaphylaxis, or symptoms of rhinitis, conjunctivitis, asthma, or laryngeal edema from aeroallergen exposure. Systemic allergic reactions to latex can be severe and death has occurred.

Objective

Physical Examination

Allergic reactions to latex are similar to other allergic reactions in that they are of variable location, type, and severity. Areas of the skin in immediate contact with latex can develop raised, erythematous, urticarial lesions and angioedema can be present. Aeroallergen exposure can cause eye reddening, pruritus, and watering, and nasal pruritus and rhinorrhea with sneezing. Chest tightness, audible wheezing, and cough can also occur. More severe reactions often manifest as generalized urticaria, flushing, hypotension, and loss of consciousness.

Routine Laboratory Abnormalities

Laboratory findings compatible with hemoconcentration can be seen with anaphylaxis.

PLANS

Diagnostic

Latex allergy is relatively easily diagnosed by a positive skin test or latex-specific IgE antibody measurement in association with symptoms of immediate urticaria, rhinitis, asthma, or anaphylaxis occurring with an obvious exposure. Spirometric measurement or peak flow readings can document bronchospasm. The diagnosis can be difficult when the history is unavailable, such as for young pediatric patients, during surgical procedures, or when work-related symptoms in health care workers do not necessarily implicate latex exposure (e.g., when aeroallergen exposure is occurring). This occurs more frequently in high-glove-use areas where several health care workers are frequently changing gloves throughout the work shift. These instances require a high index of suspicion on the part of the physician confronting a patient with undiagnosed allergic symptoms in these settings.

Health care workers with suspected latex-induced asthma can be managed as any other patient with suspected occupationally induced asthma, with frequent peak flow measurements throughout the work day and during the waking hours after leaving work for several days in a row (usually 14). If skin testing is not available, serum samples for latex-specific IgE antibodies should be sought. In addition, a health care worker can stay away from the work environment for a period to see if symptoms improve. Although presently a research tool, latex aeroallergen levels have been measured and quantitatively appear to correlate with areas of the highest glove use, such as urologic suites, phlebotomy areas, operating rooms, and outpatient procedure areas.

Because prick skin testing has occasionally caused systemic reactions in very sensitive patients, the safety of skin testing all suspected latex-allergic patients has been a concern. If a patient has sustained an anaphylactic episode from latex exposure, serum IgE measurement would be prudent in an attempt to establish a definitive diagnosis, especially in pediatric patients with spina bifida. Because many allergic individuals are health care workers who can progress from relatively mild reactions to more severe reactions with subsequent exposures, skin testing is probably of less risk than failing to diagnose latex allergy in this population of individuals who will most likely continue to be exposed both from skin contact and from aerosolized allergen. Skin testing for latex, as with any allergen, should be performed by those experienced with the procedure, and resuscitative equipment should be available. Several laboratories can perform latex-specific IgE measurement on mailed serum samples from suspected patients, but unfortunately, there is no Food and Drug Administration-approved, commercially available skin testing extract for general use in the United States at this time.

Patients with perioperative anaphylaxis are quite challenging. At or near the time of surgical procedures, they are exposed to a variety of agents and medications that can produce systemic allergic reactions, such as blood products, contrast media, intravenous anesthetic agents and paralytics, antibiotics, and volume expanders, in addition to latex products. At times, if the diagnosis is in question, the patient will need allergic evaluation with respect to several of these items to establish the exact cause of the anaphylactic episode. All undiagnosed episodes of perioperative anaphylaxis should be evaluated for latex allergy, as these patients are at serious risk for anaphylaxis during any subsequent procedures.

Therapeutic

Allergic reactions to latex should be treated as any other allergic reactions. Urticaria, rhinitis, and conjunctivitis generally respond to oral antihistamines, and if urticaria is generalized, subcutaneous epinephrine should be administered. Bronchospasm can be treated with bronchodilators, and if flushing, laryngeal edema, or hypotension occurs, immediate administration of subcutaneous epinephrine is indicated, with supplemental intravenous fluids and oxygen if necessary.

Latex-allergic patients should avoid contact with latex products, particularly those formed over molds such as gloves, balloons, condoms, and latex toys. Patients should be given lists of obvious household latex products to avoid, and if they have sustained severe reactions, they should carry epinephrine. These patients should also have an identification bracelet or card stating "latex allergy" so that if they are rendered unconscious, fire or emergency medical service personnel will not wear latex gloves while examining them or rendering treatment.

Health care workers should also avoid obvious latex-containing medical equipment and should be given lists of these products. They also should avoid personal use of and exposure to latex gloves. If they have sustained symptoms from aeroallergen exposure, converting their entire work area over to nonlatex gloves is necessary. Relocation to a different work area may be needed if exposure cannot be reduced.

Patients with spina bifida should be maintained in a latex-free environment from the very beginning of their medical care because the prevalence of latex allergy is so high in this group. This means that they need to be maintained in a latex-free environment even if they have not acquired sensitivity. All patients who have latex allergy need to undergo personal physical and dental examinations, outpatient surgical or radiologic procedures, or operative procedures in a latex-free environment. Prepping prior to surgery with glucocorticoids, diphenhydramine, and ephedrine in a manner similar to that used for individuals with contrast medium hypersensitivity has been helpful, but has not prevented anaphylactic episodes in all patients, particularly those with spina bifida.

FOLLOW-UP

Health care workers with latex allergy should be instructed to call whenever problems should arise that may be the result of latex allergy. Those patients with spina bifida or other patients with latex allergy requiring frequent surgical procedures should be followed regularly by their allergist, and the allergist should be notified prior to any procedures so that the allergist, surgeon, anesthesiologist, and operating room team can work cooperatively to provide a latex-free surgical environment.

DISCUSSION

Prevalence and Incidence

The prevalence and incidence of latex allergy vary with the population being observed. Frequent use of rubber gloves, prior allergic disease, prior hand dermatitis, spina bifida with urogenital abnormalities, and possibly frequent surgical procedures all appear to be important risk factors for latex allergy. In health care workers who frequently use gloves, such as floor nurses and operating room personnel, the sensitivity rate may be as high as 10 to 15%, and in groups of physicians such as surgeons, radiologists, and cardiologists who perform a large number of procedures, the sensitivity rate may also be in a similar range. For those health care workers who do not or infrequently use latex gloves, the sensitivity may be around 1 to 5%. Patients with spina bifida may have sensitivity rates as high as 45%.

Related Basic Science

Disposable rubber gloves have been in use within the medical profession for more than 100 years, but prior to 1979, only contact dermatitis was reported with variable frequency. Why IgE-mediated latex sensitivity has so abruptly occurred since this time and has so extensively involved health care workers has been a source of debate. The Centers for Disease Control recommendation for universal precautions to protect against HIV and hepatitis virus exposure in 1987 increased the worldwide demand for gloves dramatically thereafter. Not only have health care workers used more gloves, thus increasing their exposure to latex allergen, but the gloves themselves may have changed. To meet the demand for gloves, the manufacturing processes may have been cut short with shorter duration or altered glove soaking to remove protein. In addition, many glove manufacturing companies have moved their operations closer to the source materials in Asia; thus, latex sap may be stored for shorter periods and may also contain less ammonia, a preservative that may reduce the antigenicity of the raw sap. Whether other manufacturing changes have taken place is still unknown.

Immunotransblotting procedures using serum from latex-allergic individuals have identified a number of molecular weight antigens between 2 and 100 kilodaltons that appear to be relevant as important proteins from latex that may be involved in the allergic syndrome. Patients with latex allergy can also develop cross-reactivity to a number of foods such as bananas, avocados, chestnuts, and other fruits. These food allergies are of interest and probably involve IgE-dependent reactivity to antigens in these plant foods that are similar to those found in latex. Glove powder, a crosslinked cornstarch, although rarely an allergen in these individuals, has been shown to bind latex allergen and probably facilitates the aerosolization of the latex allergen. It is of interest that patients with spina bifida may react to different proteins than do other latex-allergic patients. Health care workers may also react to different proteins than do other latex–allergic patients. Whether this risk group has a genetic predisposition to latex allergy is of interest.

Natural History and Its Modification with Treatment

Latex allergy represents a serious health hazard in sensitized patients. Nearly 15% of latex-allergic health care workers at some time sustain a systemic reaction prior to diagnosis and vigorous attempts at latex avoidance. Allergic reactions can be life threatening and even fatal. The amount of latex allergen an individual can come in contact with is probably quite variable, depending on exposure route, duration of contact with the latex product, and amount of latex allergen in the product. This most likely explains the variability in type and degree of severity of symptoms in those who have had multiple exposure symptoms. Many individuals sustaining systemic reactions have experienced several previous milder reactions to similar contacts with latex products that were not particularly bothersome, suggesting that at least in some individuals, the sensitivity can accelerate with the occurrence of more severe symptoms on subsequent exposure.

Methods have been developed to quantitate latex allergen content both in the air and in various latex products. Aeroallergen measurement should provide a vital tool to determine if environmental manipulation of work areas is successful in reducing exposure. In addition, now that allergen levels can be measured in rubber products, manufacturers can be assisted in producing less allergenic gloves, and health care facilities can purchase those gloves with lowest allergen content. This not only should help reduce symptoms in those sensitized to latex, but, it is hoped, should also reduce sensitization of new individuals.

Prevention

Latex avoidance is the only treatment currently available for those sensitized individuals who have had symptoms from latex exposure. Providing the latex-allergic patient with a list of household and medical items that contain latex is quite helpful, as is labeling of all medical products that contain latex. Establishing a latex-free environment for procedures in individuals who have latex allergy is necessary, and before medical procedures, patients with prior episodes of anaphylaxis caused by latex exposure can be prepped similarly to those with contrast medium hypersensitivity. All patients should inform their dentist and family doctor of their latex allergy so that latex gloves will not be used during their examinations. All patients with spina bifida should be maintained in a latex-free environment for their medical care, whether or not they have acquired sensitivity to latex. A trial of immunotherapy to latex allergen has not been attempted, as Food and Drug Administration-approved materials are not available, and there is considerable debate as to potential safety.

Cost Containment

It is of interest that there is no correlation between the expense of medical disposable latex gloves and their allergen content. Switching from latex gloves with high allergen content to those with low or undetectable latex allergen content has not increased the cost of providing suitable gloves for health care workers. In addition, although the establishment of latex-free operating and procedure rooms to accommodate latex-allergic patients is somewhat time consuming for the team involved, it does not increase operating room expense or material expense. Treatment of allergic episodes, by contrast, can be quite expensive if extended emergency room care or intensive care is needed. Health care facilities should pay particular attention to latex allergy as a risk management issue in that the individuals affected, especially health care workers and patients with spina bifida, should be questioned regarding possible latex allergy before procedures. If present, this allergy should be listed under medication allergies in the chart and a sign stating "latex allergy" should be posted above the patient's hospital bed.

REFERENCES

Hunt LW, Fransway AF, Reed CE, et al. An epidemic of occupational allergy to latex involving health care workers. J Occup and Environ Med, 1995;37:1204.

Nutter AF. Contact urticaria to rubber. Br J Dermatol 1979;101:597.

Slater JE, Chhabra SK. Latex antigens. J Allergy Clin Immunol, 1992;89:673.

Swanson MC, Bubak ME, Hunt LW, et al. Quantification of occupational latex aeroallergens in a medical center. J Allergy Clin Immunol 1994;94:445.

Yuninger JW, Jones RT, Fransway, AF, et al. Extractable latex allergens and proteins in disposable medical gloves and other rubber products. J Allergy Clin Immunol 1994;93:836.

CHAPTER 5–11

Penicillin and Other Beta-Lactam Drug Allergy

Richard G. Van Dellen, M.D.

DEFINITION

A drug-allergic reaction is an immunologically mediated reaction. The beta-lactam antibiotics include penicillin G, the semisynthetic penicillins, the cephalosporins, the monobactams, and the carbapenems.

ETIOLOGY

The cause is a hypersensitivity reaction to the drug being administered.

CRITERIA FOR DIAGNOSIS
Suggestive

The diagnosis of drug allergy is suspected when one of the known allergic reactions occurs during or after administration of an antibiotic (Table 5–11–1). If the allergic reaction stops after the drug is stopped, that is further suggestive evidence that the drug is the cause.

Definitive

There are no definitive diagnostic criteria for drug allergy. The diagnosis is made mostly on clinical grounds and cessation of the symptoms and findings when the drug is stopped. If the allergic reaction is mediated by immunoglobulin (Ig) E (e.g., anaphylaxis or urticaria), demonstration of IgE-specific antibodies by radioallergosorbent test or allergen-specific IgE antibody or skin tests is helpful if present, but not as helpful when absent. Skin tests to penicillin, when available, can be used for the diagnosis of penicillin allergy but are not advisable to confirm the diagnosis in most situations.

CLINICAL MANIFESTATIONS
Subjective

The symptoms depend on the type of allergic reaction that occurs but often involve the skin (Table 5–11–1). A past history of allergic reac-

TABLE 5–11–1. TYPES OF ALLERGIC REACTIONS TO BETA-LACTAM DRUGS

Immediate: within 1 hour	Anaphylaxis
	Urticaria
Accelerated: from 1 to 72 hours	Urticaria
	Exanthem, a macular or morbilliform rash
Late: after 72 hours	Exanthem, a macular or morbilliform rash
	Urticaria
	Serum sickness
	Hemolytic anemia
	Hepatitis
	Interstitial nephritis
	Neutropenia and thrombocytopenia
	Eosinophilia
	Drug fever
	Other skin reactions
	Stevens–Johnson syndrome
	Exfoliative dermatitis
	Toxic epidermal necrolysis
	Fixed drug eruptions (at sites of previous tinea infections)
	Contact dermatitis

tions to a beta-lactam drug, if present, might be helpful. In general, the family history is of no help. A rash or urticaria can occur late in a course of therapy or even a few days after the drug is stopped. The reaction can persist for weeks after stopping the drug.

Objective

Physical Examination

The physical findings depend on the type of reaction. The patient might have findings of anaphylaxis, fever, hives, or a skin rash. Patients with cytopenia or nephritis might have few findings, and the abnormalities would be discovered only by laboratory tests.

Routine Laboratory Abnormalities

Eosinophilia is helpful if present. Patients with cytopenias would have neutropenia or thrombocytopenia, and those with nephritis may have elevated urea, an abnormal urinalysis, and an elevated serum creatinine.

PLANS

Diagnostic

Differential Diagnosis

The differential diagnosis is limited when one drug is administered and a clear-cut allergic reaction occurs during the administration of the drug. The diagnosis may be complicated if multiple drugs are being administered or if the patient has some other intercurrent illness, which can cause findings similar to those of a drug reaction.

Diagnostic Options and Recommended Approach

The suspected antibiotic should be stopped. If the antibiotic is absolutely necessary, this presents a serious dilemma. Usually alternative antibiotics can be used. For the majority of drug-allergic reactions, no additional diagnostic tests are recommended. Skin tests to penicillin should not be done routinely.

Therapeutic

The antibiotic should be stopped. For acute anaphylaxis, epinephrine remains the drug of choice. If laryngeal edema is present, an airway may need to be established. For hypotension, fluids should be administered, and vasopressors may be required. Antihistamines should be given for urticaria and itching. Most drug-allergic reactions are self-limited, and stopping the drug with symptomatic treatment of the skin reaction with antihistamines is all that is needed. For cytopenias and nephritis, the severity of the reaction would determine whether addi-

tional therapy is needed. For severe allergic reactions, as short course of systemic glucocorticosteroids may be needed.

The patient should be instructed not to take the antibiotic that caused the reaction and to carry or wear medical alert information.

The problem a clinician often faces is the patient who has had a previous reaction to a penicillin drug and now needs a beta-lactam antibiotic. The following information may be helpful in guiding the approach to therapy in situations where penicillin or a beta-lactam antibiotic is needed despite a history of penicillin allergy

- Some patients are exquisitely sensitive to penicillin. Systemic reactions and death may occur from exposure to minute amounts of penicillin in these rare individuals with extreme sensitivity. These individuals need to avoid penicillin. Giving even minute amounts is life threatening.
- Of those patients with histories of penicillin allergy who are skin tested with major and minor determinant reagents, 80 to 90% can have negative immediate allergy skin tests. In these patients with negative allergy skin tests to penicillin who are then treated with penicillin, reactions occur in from 1 to 10%. IgE-mediated reactions occur in 4% or less. Those patients with histories of penicillin allergy and negative allergy skin test to penicillin can also take cephalosporins with similar low incidence of reactions.
- Those patients with histories of penicillin allergy and positive skin tests to penicillin have a high incidence of reactions to penicillin when penicillin is given, although the numbers so treated have been small.
- Patients with a history of penicillin allergy have a higher incidence of reaction to cephalosporin drugs (4–14.6%) than those without a history of penicillin allergy (1–2.5%) (Lin, 1992). For a third-generation cephalosporin (ceftazidine), the relative risk comparing patients with histories of penicillin allergy to those without a history of penicillin allergy was less than the risk with first- and second-generation cephalosporins (Lin, 1992). Thus, the risk of reaction to third-generation cephalosporins may be less than that to first- and second-generation cephalosporins in patients with histories of penicillin allergy.
- Patients with histories of penicillin allergy have developed serious anaphylactic reactions to the first administration of a cephalosporin drug.
- Patients with histories of allergic reactions to penicillins and positive skin tests to penicillin have been treated safely or challenged with cephalosporin drugs without reactions. Thus far, the number reported in the literature treated in this setting is small (around 100), but the incidence of reactions to cephalosporins is low (around 3%), though some reactions were severe.
- The monobactam aztreonam does not usually cross-react with penicillin.
- The carbapenem imipenem shows extensive cross-reactivity in in vitro studies with penicillin and should be avoided in penicillin-allergic patients.
- Patients with histories of penicillin allergy and positive penicillin skin tests have been successfully desensitized to penicillin. Some of those patients have experienced delayed immunologic reactions other than IgE-mediated reactions; some can be serious.

In those patients who need beta-lactam antibiotics for a serious infection and for whom alternative antibiotics are not possible, one approach would be:

- Do skin tests to penicillin if they are available. In this setting, where possible, patients with suspected allergy to penicillin should be referred to an allergy specialist for penicillin skin testing. If the skin tests to major and minor determinant reagents are negative, the risk of a reaction to penicillin or one of the cephalosporins is low. Give a small test dose first, observe the patient for 30 to 60 minutes, and then proceed with a full dose. Observe for another 60 minutes. Those patients who give a history of penicillin allergy and have negative penicillin skin tests may be resensitized during successful treatment with penicillin. The incidence of resensitization in this setting is low in children but higher in adults.

- If skin tests are not available and if the reaction to penicillin was mild and happened years ago, using a cephalosporin drug, if indicated, would be of low risk. To lessen the risk, give a small dose first under medical supervision, and then if no reaction occurs after 45 minutes, proceed with a full dose. There is a small risk of reaction in this setting. The risk may be less with third-generation cephalosporins.
- If the patients have positive skin tests to penicillin or if the patients have a history of a reaction to penicillin and skin tests are not available, desensitization could be considered. Suggested protocols for oral and intravenous desensitization to beta-lactam drugs are found in Tables 5–11–2, 5–11–3, and 5–11–4. In patients receiving desensitization, the physician should be prepared to treat an acute anaphylactic reaction and have appropriate equipment available should this occur. Delayed reactions do occur. The patients should be informed of the risk and benefits before proceeding.

Successful desensitization may result in resensitization, and these patients may again have an allergic reaction when reexposed.

FOLLOW-UP

In general, follow-up would depend on the severity of the allergic reaction. For most self-limited reactions, no follow-up is needed. Obviously, for cytopenias and nephritis, appropriate blood counts and renal function tests should be monitored.

DISCUSSION

Prevalence and Incidence

Anaphylaxis to penicillin occurs in from 0.02 to 0.1% of people and, in some series, even less frequently. Fatalities from penicillin have been reported at 0.002%. In one series there was 1 death among 94,605 patients who received penicillin (Lin, 1992; Weiss and Adkinson, 1988). Urticaria occurs in between 3 and 4.5% of patients. Ampicillin causes a morbilliform rash in from 7 to 9.5% of patients (Weiss and Adkinson, 1988). Ampicillin given with allopurinol results in an increased incidence of rash. Those patients with infectious mononucleosis who were given ampicillin had a high incidence of this morbilliform rash (69–100%) (Weiss and Adkinson, 1988). The reported overall incidence of reactions to penicillin of all kinds is as high as 10%.

Related Basic Science

Antibody response to penicillin occurs in all patients who receive the drug. IgG antibodies are found in all patients who have received penicillin. For the most part, these antibodies cause no problem. If IgG antibodies are present in high titer and high doses of penicillin are given, IgG antibodies could result in a hemolytic anemia or serum sickness. Possibly IgM immune complexes contribute to the exanthem in some patients.

Immunoglobulin E antibodies mediate urticarial reactions and anaphylaxis. Antibodies to different antigenic determinants of penicillin in the IgE class have been demonstrated. These have been called major and minor antigenic determinants. Skin test reagents have been developed to both the major (benzylpenicilloyl polylysine) and the minor determinants (benzylpenicillin, benzylpenicilloate, benzylpenilloate, and benzylpenicilloyl-n-propylamine).

Skin tests to penicillin are not for routine use. The only reagent commercially available is the benzylpenicilloyl polylysine. No reagents are available commercially for the minor determinants or for the semisynthetic penicillins, cephalosporins, monobactams, or carbapenems.

There is some risk to doing skin tests to penicillin. Although rare, systemic allergic reactions can occur in those highly allergic to penicillin, and deaths have been reported from skin testing to penicillin.

Natural History and Its Modification with Treatment

- Many patients lose their IgE-mediated allergy to penicillin. Positive allergy skin tests to penicillin can become negative over time. We

TABLE 5–11–2. PROTOCOL FOR DESENSITIZATION WITH BETA-LACTAM DRUGS

Be prepared to treat an anaphylactic reaction.

Patient should have an intravenous line in place.

Pharmacy could prepare the doses.

Give the drug orally or intravenously, the same way you plan to treat the patient.

Give doses every 15 minutes.

If the patient has a history of exquisite sensitivity, start with a thousandfold weaker dilution.

Following the last dose, observe for 30 minutes, then proceed with therapeutic doses.

TABLE 5–11–3. ORAL SCHEDULE

Step	Concentration (mg/mL)	Amount (mL)	Dose (mg)	Cumulative Dose (mg)
1	0.05	0.1	0.005	0.005
2	0.05	0.2	0.01	0.015
3	0.05	0.4	0.02	0.035
4	0.05	1.0	0.05	0.085
5	0.5	0.2	0.10	0.185
6	0.5	0.4	0.20	0.385
7	0.5	0.8	0.40	0.785
8	0.5	1.6	0.80	1.585
9	0.5	3.0	1.5	3
10	0.5	6.0	3.0	6
11	0.5	10.0	5.0	11
12	0.5	20.0	10.0	21
13	0.5	40.0	20.0	41
14	50	1	50.0	91
15	50	2	100.0	191
16	50	4	200.0	391
17	50	8	400.0	791

Source: Adapted from Sullivan TJ. Drug allergy. In: Middleton E Jr, Reed CE, Ellis EF, et al, eds. Allergy: Principles and practice. 4th ed. St. Louis: Mosby, 1993:1738. Reproduced with permission from the publisher and author.

TABLE 5–11–4. INTRAVENOUS SCHEDULE

Step	Concentration (mg/mL)	Amount (mL)	Dose (mg)	Cumulative Dose (mg)
1	0.01	0.1	0.001	0.001
2	0.01	0.2	0.002	0.003
3	0.01	0.4	0.004	0.007
4	0.01	0.8	0.008	0.015
5	0.01	1.6	0.016	0.031
6	0.01	3.2	0.032	0.063
7	0.01	6.4	0.064	0.127
8	0.01	12.8	0.128	0.255
9	0.01	25.0	0.250	0.505
10	1	0.5	0.50	1
11	1	1.0	1.00	2
12	1	2.0	2.00	4
13	1	4.0	4.00	8
14	1	8.0	8.00	16
15	1	16.0	16.00	32
16	100	0.30	30	62
17	100	0.60	60	122
18	100	1.2	120	242
19	100	2.5	250	492
20	100	5.0	500	992

Source: Adapted from Sullivan TJ. Drug allergy. In: Middleton E Jr, Reed CE, Ellis EF, et al, eds. Allergy: Principles and practice. 4th ed. St. Louis: Mosby, 1993:1738. Reproduced with permission from the publisher and author.

now know that some patients who have clear-cut allergic reactions to penicillin can subsequently take penicillin and cephalosporin drugs safely. The challenge is how to identify those patients.

- Cross-reacting antibodies have been demonstrated between penicillin and cephalosporins, but the clinical significance of these is not always known.
- Cephalosporins and other beta-lactam antibiotics can cause allergic reactions by themselves, unrelated to cross-reacting antibodies to penicillin.
- Some patients are allergic to only one of the penicillins and demonstrate no allergy either by skin testing or by challenge with other semisynthetic penicillins. Some patients demonstrate allergy to multiple beta-lactam antibiotics, by history, challenge, and skin tests. Currently there is no practical way to evaluate this variable specificity in individual patients.
- Patients with a history of allergic reactions to penicillin, versus those without a history of penicillin allergy, have a higher incidence of reactions to unrelated antibiotics.

Prevention

Patients who have allergic reactions to one of the penicillin drugs should avoid penicillin and other beta-lactam antibiotics. In retrospective studies of patients who died from penicillin administration, one fourth to one third of the patients had a history of allergy to penicillin. Avoidance poses little problem for most patients. Alternative antibiotics are available and should be used in those with histories of penicillin allergy.

Cost Containment

Penicillin G and some of the other semisynthetic penicillins are considerably cheaper and less toxic than alternatives. Considerable cost savings would occur if we could use penicillin drugs instead of more costly alternatives in those patients who give a history of penicillin allergy. Penicillin skin tests, should they become commercially available for general use, may help identify those patients who are not at risk for reactions and may enable us to use less costly and less toxic antibiotics.

REFERENCES

Lin RY. A perspective on penicillin allergy. Arch Intern Med 1992;152:930.
Saxon A, Beall GN, Rohr AS, Adelman DC. Immediate hypersensitivity reactions to beta-lactam antibiotics. Ann Intern Med 1987;107:207.
Weiss ME, Adkinson NF. Immediate hypersensitivity reactions to penicillin and related antibiotics. Clin Allergy 1988;18:515.

CHAPTER 5–12

Radiocontrast Medium Sensitivity

Joel S. Klein, M.D., Evangelos Frigas, M.D., and Daniel E. Maddox, M.D.

DEFINITION

Contrast media have been used routinely since the mid-1950s for excretory urography, angiography, and, more recently, computed tomography. Although they are relatively safe compounds, adverse reactions can still occur. The degree of severity can be designated as mild, moderate, or life threatening (Bush and Swanson, 1991). Mild, minor, or minimal reactions include nausea, metallic taste, vomiting (limited), urticaria (limited), tingling in the face or extremities, pruritus, and diaphoresis. Moderate reactions consist of faintness, severe vomiting, diffuse urticaria, facial edema, laryngeal edema, and mild bronchospasm. Severe reactions include hypotensive shock, pulmonary edema, convulsions, and respiratory and/or cardiac arrest.

ETIOLOGY

The etiology of adverse reactions to radiocontrast media can be classified into two categories: (1) immediate generalized reactions and (2) chemotoxic reactions (Bush and Swanson, 1991). Immediate generalized, or anaphylactoid (anaphylaxis-like), reactions occur independently of the dose or concentration of the agent above a certain threshold level. Although they resemble immediate hypersensitivity reactions, the exact cause remains unclear. These tend to occur within 20 minutes of intravascular exposure to radiocontrast media (Greenberger and Patterson, 1988) or within several hours of oral or nonintravascular administration.

Chemotoxic reactions consist of electrocardiographic, electrophysiologic, hemodynamic, or renal alterations that are directly dependent on the dose and concentration of the radiocontrast agent. These are due to specific physiochemical effects of the injected agent on the organs perfused by the agent. Their time of onset can overlap with that of immediate generalized reactions and may be clinically indistinguishable; however, the nephrotoxic effects appear later.

CRITERIA FOR DIAGNOSIS

Suggestive

The presence of radiocontrast medium sensitivity is considered when a cardiopulmonary, renal, gastrointestinal, mucocutaneous, or neurologic sign or symptom occurs within several hours of administration. The suspicion is increased if the patient has a certain preexisting condition, such as a history of asthma or cardiovascular disease, that has been associated with a greater risk of an adverse reaction.

Definitive

There are no laboratory or skin tests that reliably predict or diagnose radiocontrast medium sensitivity. Consequently, radiocontrast medium sensitivity is established by the history and clinical picture. The diagnosis is reasonably certain if the adverse reaction, except for renal failure, occurs within 20 minutes of administration in the absence of exposure to other agents.

CLINICAL MANIFESTATIONS

Subjective

Reactions to systemically administered contrast media vary widely. Clinically insignificant responses include nausea without retching or vomiting, metallic taste, tingling in the face or extremities, or a hot-flash sensation. More severe symptoms can include faintness, severe vomiting, headaches, rigors, dyspnea, wheezing, chest pain, and abdominal pain. A reliable personal history of a previous reaction to a conventional contrast agent without pretreatment may require access and review of the appropriate medical records.

Major risk factors associated with adverse reactions to contrast media include debilitating or severe illness, cardiovascular disease, and a history of asthma. People with allergic or atopic tendencies are considered to be at a higher risk for an adverse reaction than nonallergic individuals, even though immediate generalized reactions do not result from an antigen–antibody interaction. A family history of radiocontrast medium sensitivity has not been shown to predispose an individual to such reactions. Beta-blocker exposure has been shown to at least suggest a trend toward an increased incidence of reactions (Greenberger and Patterson, 1988). There is no firm evidence to support the notion that people with an adverse reaction to shellfish or to topical iodides (e.g., Betadine) are more likely to have a radiocontrast medium sensitivity. Other risk factors for radiocontrast medium sensitivity include renal insufficiency, diabetes mellitus, dehydration, blood dyscrasia, dysproteinemia, and anxiety.

Objective

Physical Examination

Most anaphylactoid reactions to radiocontrast media consist of urticaria, erythema, or angioedema. Other physical findings include tachypnea, wheezing, tachycardia, arrythmias, hypotension, facial edema, rigors, seizures, and loss of consciousness. Bradycardia, defined as a heart rate of 40 or fewer beats per minute, occurs in a minority of patients. In a series of 112,003 intravascular procedures, urticaria occurred in 1.45% of patients and dyspnea was reported in 0.25% of patients (Greenberger and Patterson, 1988). Severe reactions, defined as collapse, loss of consciousness, pulmonary edema, cardiac arrest, and arrythmias, have been reported to occur in 1 in 1000 to 1 in 769 procedures (Greenberger and Patterson, 1988).

Routine Laboratory Abnormalities

No routine laboratory abnormalities are diagnostic or predictive of radiocontrast medium sensitivity. Increases in plasma and 24-hour urinary histamine, decreases in total hemolytic complement values, increases in fibrin split products, and decreases in C1 esterase inhibitor have been reported. However, the degree of changes in these measurements does not correlate with the presence or absence of observable reactions.

PLANS

Diagnostic

Differential Diagnosis

Adverse reactions from administration of radiocontrast media should be differentiated from complications that may occur as a result of the patient's underlying disease, such as exacerbation of congestive heart failure, or examination-related maneuvers, such as catheter placement.

Diagnostic Options and Recommended Approach

The onset of signs and symptoms within 20 minutes or up to several hours after administration of a radiocontrast agent establishes the diagnosis of radiocontrast medium sensitivity. The sensitivity can be designated as an immediate generalized, or anaphylactoid, reaction if one or more of the following occur within approximately 20 minutes of exposure to radiocontrast media: urticaria, angioedema, bronchospasm, generalized pruritus, hypotension, and shock (Greenberger and Patterson, 1988). Chemotoxic reactions, however, can occur concomitantly with signs and symptoms suggestive of an immediate generalized reaction.

Plasma and 24-hour urinary histamine measurements are not routinely used to establish the diagnosis of radiocontrast medium sensitivity. Moreover, immunoglobulin E antibodies to radiocontrast medium have not been identified. Consequently, puncture or intradermal skin tests, radioallergosorbent tests, or radioallergosorbent inhibition methods cannot identify patients at risk for an immediate generalized reaction. In addition, intravenous pretesting has been reported to be insensitive in predicting serious or fatal reactions (Greenberger and Patterson, 1988).

Therapeutic

Treatment of a reaction to contrast medium entails adequate preparation. A specific protocol for dealing with specific reactions should be developed for rapid implementation. Access to additional assistance,

emergency drugs, and equipment should be immediate. Intravenous access should be maintained throughout the examination and until the potential for acute reactions has passed, reported to be within 15 minutes of injection of the agent (Bush and Swanson, 1991). Training in cardiopulmonary resuscitation is necessary and training in advanced cardiac life support is recommended. Simple measures such as elevating the patient's legs to improve central vascular volume should not be forgotten. Conventional treatments for specific signs and symptoms include the following (Bush and Swanson, 1991): (1) prochlorperazine for severe protracted vomiting; (2) injectable antihistamines for scattered protracted hives or diffuse severe hives; (3) subcutaneous epinephrine for mild to moderate bronchospasm; (4) intravenous epinephrine and albuterol inhalation for severe bronchospasm; (5) intravenous fluids for hypotension and tachycardia; (6) intravenous fluids and atropine for hypotension and bradycardia; and (7) diazepam for seizures.

FOLLOW-UP

Patients and/or family members should be educated about the risk of a recurrent adverse reaction to radiocontrast media. They should be reassured that premedication prophylaxis and/or low-osmolality contrast media can reduce the risk of a recurrence and that emergency therapy, if necessary, would be immediately available. The nature of the adverse reaction should be explained carefully to the patient and should be documented legibly in the medical record. Wearing a medical identification bracelet that indicates adverse reaction to radiocontrast media should be encouraged.

DISCUSSION

Incidence and Prevalence

For conventional radiocontrast media, the incidence of adverse side effects of all types has been approximately 5 to 8%. Moderate reactions, defined as those requiring therapy without hospitalization, have occurred in approximately 1.5% of infusions. Severe reactions, defined as those necessitating hospitalization for treatment, have occurred in 0.03 to 0.1% of infusions. The death rate with use of conventional contrast media has been reported to range from 1:10,931 to 1:75,000 or even 1:117,000 (Greenberger and Patterson, 1991).

Alternatively, the use of lower-osmolality contrast agents has been associated with a lower incidence of adverse reactions. Overall, the incidence has been reported to be 2.1%. Moderate reactions have occurred in 0.9% of infusions and severe reactions have occurred in 0.01% of infusions. The death rate with use of lower-osmolality contrast media has been reported to range from zero to 1:168,363 to 1:2,000,000 (Greenberger and Patterson, 1991).

The overall prevalence of reactions is greater for intravenous administration of radiocontrast media than for intraarterial infusion; however, intraarterial injections have been associated with a higher percentage of severe reactions. Bolus intravenous injections produce fewer reactions than drip intravenous infusions.

Related Basic Science

All radiographic contrast agents that are administered intravascularly incorporate iodine to generate a radiopaque image. Sodium iodide solution was the first one used in 1923 by Osborne and his colleagues, but was highly toxic. The conventional ionic radiocontrast media, diatrizoates and iothalamate, were developed in the 1950s (Figure 5–12–1). They are negatively charged in solution; either sodium, methylglucamine, or a mixture is used as a balancing cation. Consequently, conventional radiocontrast media are hypertonic to blood, with an osmolality ranging up to 1200 mOsm/kg (blood = 300 mOsm/kg).

Low-osmolality contrast agents (Figure 5–12–2) provide a 50% or greater reduction in osmolality. One of these, ioxaglate, is an ionic dimer that has six iodine atoms and a single negative charge balanced by a cation. The other three (iohexol, iopamidol, and ioversol) are nonionic monomers that consist of three iodine atoms attached to a fully substituted uncharged benzene ring. Although these four contrast medium agents have markedly lower osmolality, they also have slightly higher viscosities and can be inconvenient to infuse.

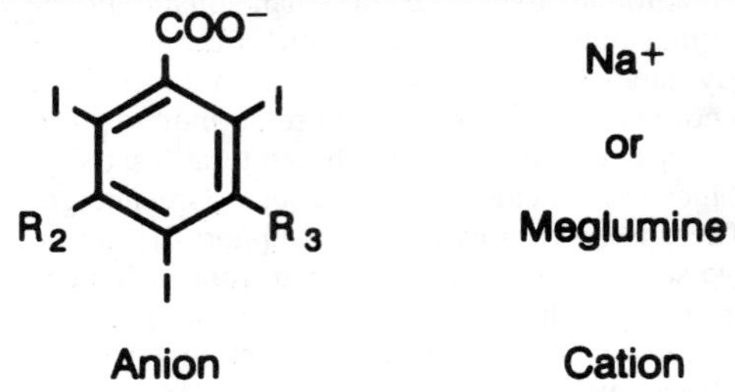

Figure 5–12–1. Chemical structures of the conventional ionic high-osmolality contrast media. *Source: King BF, Hartman GW, Williamson B Jr, et al. Low-osmolality contrast media: A current perspective. Mayo Clin Proc 1989;64:976. Reproduced with permission from the author and the publisher.*

	R_2	R_3	Proper name	Commercial name
	CH_2CONH	$NHCOCH_3$	Diatrizoate	Renografin, Hypaque, Angiovist
	CH_2CONH	$CONHCH_3$	Iothalamate	Conray, Renovue

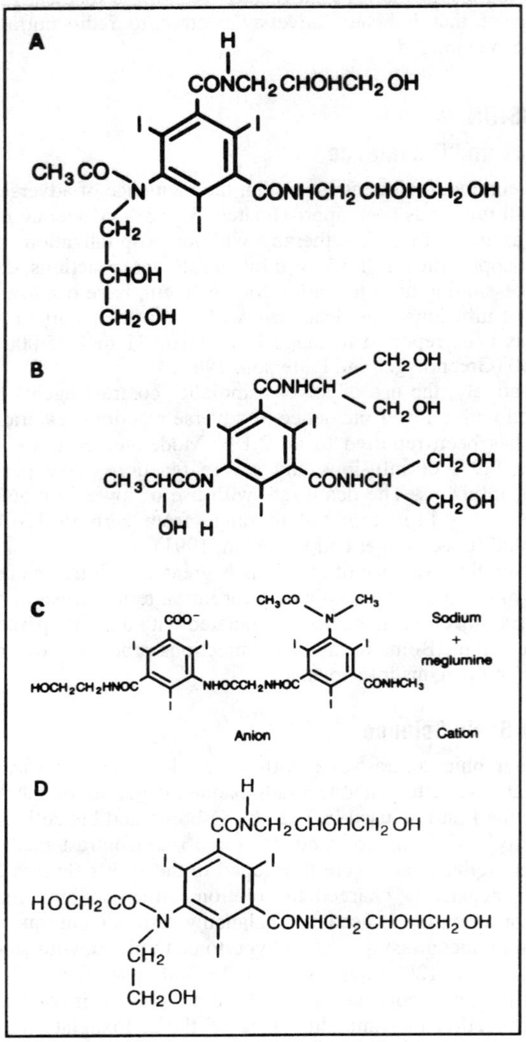

Figure 5–12–2. Chemical structures of the low-osmolality contrast media. **A.** Iohexol (nonionic monomer). **B.** Iopamidol (nonionic monomer). **C.** Ioxaglate (ionic dimer). **D.** Ioversol (nonionic monomer). *Source: King BF, Hartman GW, Williamson B Jr, et al. Low-osmolality contrast media: A current perspective. Mayo Clin Proc 1989;64:976. Reproduced with permission from the author and the publisher.*

The pathogenesis of immediate generalized reactions following administration of radiocontrast media remains unclear. Immediate generalized reactions mimic the effects of histamine and radiocontrast media can cause the direct release of histamine from mast cells and basophils; however, radiocontrast media do not react with tissue proteins to form a complete immunogen (hapten–protein conjugate) and immunoglobulin E antibodies to radiocontrast media have not been identified. Thus, an immunoglobulin E-mediated mechanism is unlikely. Although abnormalities of the complement cascade, fibrinolytic pathway, and kinin–kallikrein system have been described following infusion of radiocontrast media, they have not correlated closely with the presence of immediate generalized reactions.

Chemotoxic reactions are considered to be due to hyperosmolality, potential for calcium binding, viscosity, nature and concentration of its cations, alteration of red blood cells, and damage of vascular endothelium. Acute renal insufficiency is believed to be due to medullary ischemia from decreased renal blood flow and inadequate vasodilatory factors. Although low-osmolality contrast media are associated with less of these chemotoxic effects, they are associated with more coagulation and platelet aggregation in comparison with high-osmolality contrast media. This relative increase of coagulation and platelet aggregation seems to be less pronounced with the ionic dimer ioxaglate than with the nonionic monomers iohexol and iopamidol (King et al., 1989).

Natural History and Its Modification with Treatment

The prevalence of any adverse reaction to conventional radiocontrast media without pretreatment in patients with a prior reaction to a conventional agent is reported to be 17 to 35%, or three to eight times greater than the risk of the general population (Bush and Swanson, 1991). Data suggest that recurrence of a major life-threatening reaction is not always certain for an individual patient; however, the frequency of major life-threatening events remains higher compared with the incidence in the general population (Greenberger and Patterson, 1988).

Adverse reactions to intravascular contrast media appear to be most common for people 20 to 50 years old (Bush and Swanson, 1991). The incidence of minor reactions has been reported to range from 10.2% in the third decade of life to 4.3% in the eighth decade of life (Greenberger and Patterson, 1988); however, adverse reactions may be most severe in elderly people because they are frequently debilitated and have less ability to withstand a severe systemic reaction (Bush and Swanson, 1991). Fortunately, death is rare when treatment is prompt and adequate.

Prevention

In patients with a substantiated history of allergy or serious reaction (other than pain, nausea, or vasovagal reaction) after previous administration of a contrast agent, several options are available. Initially, alternative imaging studies (e.g., ultrasonography or magnetic resonance imaging) that do not use iodinated contrast material could be used. Reactions to gadopentetate dimeglumine, an ionic paramagnetic contrast agent for magnetic resonance imaging are uncommon (<1%), but a systemic anaphylactoid reaction can occur (Bush and Swanson, 1991).

If an iodinated contrast agent is absolutely required, the options are various regimens of pharmacologic prophylaxis or use of low-osmolality contrast media. The pretreatment regimen that is most commonly used follows (Greenberger and Patterson, 1988):

- Prednisone 50 mg orally 13, 7, and 1 hour before the procedure.
- Diphenhydramine 50 mg orally 1 hour before the procedure.
- Ephedrine 25 mg orally 1 hour before the procedure (to be withheld if unstable angina, arrhythmia, hypertension, possible aortic aneurysm, or other cardiovascular contraindication exists).

In patients unable to ingest tablets, hydrocortisone 200 mg intravenously can be substituted for prednisone and diphenhydramine can be administered intravenously. If an emergency radiographic contrast medium study is required in patients with a substantiated history of allergy or serious reaction: (1) hydrocortisone 200 mg intravenously should be given immediately and every 4 hours until the procedure begins; and (2) diphenhydramine 50 mg intravenously or intramuscularly should be given 1 hour before the procedure.

Other pharmacologic prophylaxis regimens used (Greenberger and Patterson, 1988) include (1) prednisone–diphenhydramine; (2) a two-dose methylprednisolone regimen; and (3) prednisone–diphenhydramine–ephedrine–cimetidine. Pretreatment of patients with prednisone–diphenhydramine–ephedrine has been reported to result in a statistically significant reduction in immediate generalized reactions compared with use of prednisone–diphenhydramine. Addition of cimetidine has been reported to increase the incidence of repeated reactions and is thus not recommended.

Low-osmolality radiocontrast media cause fewer minor adverse reactions, such as injection-site pain, nausea, and vomiting and fewer severe reactions. One approach to the choice between conventional radiocontrast media with preprocedural pharmacologic prophylaxis and low-osmolality radiocontrast media is to use low-osmolality radiocontrast media according to the guidelines of the American College of Radiology (Table 5–12–1). These have been updated to include sickle cell disease, risk of aspiration, and inability to determine the presence or absence of risk factors from the patient. Low-osmolality radiocontrast media may also be used for emergency procedures in those with a prior history of an immediate generalized reaction. The addition of prednisone–diphenhydramine or prednisone–diphenhydramine–ephedrine to low-osmolality radiocontrast media has also been advocated (Greenberger and Patterson, 1991).

Patients with prior symptoms not consistent with an immediate generalized reaction (e.g., pain, nausea, or vomiting) may be markedly anxious because they might have been instructed never to receive radiocontrast media again. Such patients may need pharmacologic prophylaxis with conventional radiocontrast media, or even low-osmolality radiocontrast media, to be reassured even though they are not at increased risk compared with the general population. The issue of using pharmacologic prophylaxis in all patients who are to receive conventional radiocontrast media is unresolved; however, Lasser et al. reported that pretreatment with a two-dose corticosteroid regimen lowered the severe reaction rate compared with pretreatment with placebo (Greenberger and Patterson, 1988).

Data are insufficient to favor the use of preprocedural pharmacologic prophylaxis with high-osmolality radiocontrast media over the use of low-osmolality radiocontrast media with or without preprocedural pharmacologic treatment. Although corticosteroid–antihistamine pretreatment with or without ephedrine reduces the occurrence of immediate generalized reactions, it has been suggested that it may not have a substantial effect on chemotoxic reactions. The decision to use a particular preventive regimen will require consideration of all the risk factors in each individual case.

Cost Containment

Although low-osmolality contrast media reduce the chances of a serious adverse reaction and of adverse reactions overall, they are 10 to 15 times more expensive than high-osmolality contrast agents. It has been calculated that the annual expense for high-osmolality contrast agents would be $21,000 for a typical cardiac catheterization laboratory that performs 2500 angiographic procedures per year. Alternatively, the annual expense would be $540,000 for the same laboratory if only low-osmolality contrast agents were used (Hirshfeld, 1992). On a national level, it has been estimated that the annual U.S. expenditure for contrast agents would be $80 million if only high-osmolality were used and $1.5 billion if low-osmolality contrast agents were universally used (Hirshfeld, 1992).

Studies do not appear to support the universal use of low-osmolality contrast agents because of the sizable majority of patients who are at low risk for an adverse reaction. Moreover, low-osmolality agents would not necessarily reduce the expenditures required to treat adverse reactions because they do not completely eliminate the occurrence of severe reactions, which are expensive to treat. Low-osmolality contrast media have been reported to be cost-effective when used in cardiac angiography for patients who were older than 60 or with unstable angina (Steinberg et al., 1992). The use of low-osmolality contrast media in cardiac angiography has also been suggested to be more cost-effective than their use in intravenous procedures, such as contrast-enhanced computed tomography of the body or intravenous pyelography (Steinberg et al., 1992). Further cost-analysis research is needed to identify any additional groups of high-risk patients whose safety would be enhanced by the use of low-osmolality contrast media in relation to the incremental cost. In the interim, decisions will still require clinical judgment.

TABLE 5–12–1. SITUATIONS THAT MAY WARRANT USE OF LOW-OSMOLALITY CONTRAST MEDIA

- Previous severe adverse reaction to contrast material, strongly allergic history, or asthma
- Cardiac dysfunction, including severe arrythmias, unstable angina pectoris, recent myocardial infarction, pulmonary hypertension, and congestive failure
- Generalized severe debilitation
- Potentially painful examination such as peripheral arteriography, external carotid arteriography, and lower limb phlebography
- Examinations such as digital angiography in which inadvertent motion must be minimized for optimal image quality

Source: King BF, Hartman GW, Williamson B Jr, et al. Low-osmolality contrast media: A current perspective. Mayo Clin Proc 1989;64:976. Reproduced with permission from the author and the publisher.

REFERENCES

Bush WH, Swanson DP. Acute reactions to intravascular contrast media: Types, risk factors, recognition and specific treatments. AJR 1991;157:1153.

Greenberger PA, Patterson R. Adverse reactions to radiocontrast media. Prog Cardiovasc Dis 1988;31(3):239.

Greenberger PA, Patterson R. The prevention of immediate generalized reactions to radiocontrast media in high-risk patients. JACI 1991;87:867.

Hirshfeld JW Jr. Low-osmolality contrast agents—Who needs them? N Engl J Med 1992;326(7):483.

King BF, Hartman GW, Williamson B Jr et al. Low-osmolality contrast media: A current perspective. Mayo Clin Proc 1989;64:976.

Steinberg EP, Moore RD, Powe NR, et al. Safety and cost effectiveness of high-osmolality as compared with low-osmolality contrast material in patients undergoing cardiac angiography. N Engl J Med 1992;326:425.

CHAPTER 5–13

Aspirin Sensitivity

Loren W. Hunt, M.D.

DEFINITION

The term *aspirin sensitivity* is commonly used to refer to an unwanted reaction immediately to 1 hour after aspirin ingestion.

ETIOLOGY

The respiratory reaction occurs in patients with chronic severe rhinitis, nasal polyposis, sinusitis, and severe asthma that is often recalcitrant to treatment and glucocorticoid dependent. These reactions do not occur in all patients with asthma, appear to be idiosyncratic, and can be precipitated by other nonsteroidal antiinflammatory drugs (NSAIDs) as well. To avoid confusion, this group of patients with aspirin sensitivity is described as having *aspirin-sensitive asthma*. Other types of aspirin sensitivity exist, however, and are probably caused by different mechanisms. Patients with chronic urticaria can experience worsening of their symptoms following ingestion of aspirin or other NSAIDs. A few patients appear to have a true aspirin allergy in that they experience urticaria, angioedema, or anaphylaxis immediately following aspirin ingestion and do not react to other drugs classified as NSAIDs. Immunoglobulin E antibodies against aspirin are occasionally found. These patients are otherwise healthy individuals who usually do not have other allergic diseases.

CRITERIA FOR DIAGNOSIS

Aspirin sensitivity is usually diagnosed by history alone of reactions that occur immediately after to within 1 hour of aspirin ingestion and manifest as acute urticaria, flushing, angioedema, intense wheezing, or anaphylaxis. In a few patients, the reactions occur only with aspirin and not other NSAIDs. There is usually prior evidence of aspirin ingestion. In patients with aspirin-induced asthma, a history of rapid (immediate to within 1 hour) onset of facial flushing, dyspnea, and intense wheezing following aspirin ingestion usually suggests the diagnosis. The diagnosis of aspirin sensitivity in this group can also be made by aspirin challenge combined with spirometry. Aspirin challenge can be performed with orally administered aspirin or with inhaled aspirin–lysine conjugates. When specific protocols for aspirin challenge are followed, about one fifth of patients with asthma can be found to be aspirin sensitive.

CLINICAL MANIFESTATIONS

Subjective

In the typical patient with aspirin-induced asthma, onset of severe perennial rhinitis with nasal polyposis, most often with accompanying sinusitis, occurs in the second or third decade of life. The asthma that follows is quite recalcitrant to treatment and often glucocorticoid dependent. The asthma is nonseasonal, and no allergic exposure history is evident. When these patients ingest aspirin, they develop acute wheezing, facial and neck flushing, and rhinorrhea. Symptoms can be catastrophic and immediate or can occur up to 60 minutes later, with rare patients developing wheezing 2 or more hours later. The reactions are of variable severity and death can occur. The reaction is not inhibited by antihistamines or sodium cromolyn, although cromolyn can retard the onset. Glucocorticoids, if given for several days, can produce some attenuation of wheezing, although single doses do not appear to be preventive. Aspirin avoidance has no effect on the underlying asthma or rhinosinusitis. Once aspirin sensitivity is present, other NSAIDs, even on first exposure, can evoke similar severe symptoms. Children with aspirin-sensitive asthma are less likely to have nasal polyps and more likely to have associated urticaria, but their reactions following aspirin ingestion are otherwise the same. Attempts to establish a genetic link among patients with aspirin-sensitive asthma have been unrewarding,

even in twin studies, and most aspirin-sensitive asthmatics do not have a family history of aspirin sensitivity.

In patients with preexisting chronic urticaria, aspirin ingestion can cause a worsening of skin eruption and pruritus, either immediately or within several hours. Although aspirin-induced exacerbations are prevented by avoidance, the course of the underlying urticaria is not affected.

Objective

Aspirin and NSAIDs are the most common causes of drug-induced asthmatic reactions, accounting for more than two thirds of reported cases. Physical examination reveals typical wheezing. Aspirin alone causes about one half of these. Aspirin-induced asthma does not appear to be mediated by immunoglobulin E and antiaspirin antibodies are not found. Skin tests to common allergens are no more frequently positive than in the general population. Aspirin and other NSAIDs often have vastly different molecular structures, which mitigates against an immunologic cause of the cross-sensitivity. What these agents have in common is the ability to exert biochemical inhibition of the molecule cyclooxygenase, a potent enzyme involved in arachidonic acid biotransformation. Their ability to induce severe bronchospasm appears to be directly related to their potency as cyclooxygenase inhibitors. Drugs structurally similar to aspirin, but with weak cyclooxygenase-inhibiting potential, usually do not produce bronchospasm with normally prescribed doses. Cross-sensitivity with tartrazine (FD&C No. 5) was once thought to occur, but this potential has not been confirmed by closely observed challenge studies.

No routine skin testing materials are available to distinguish the group of patients who have isolated sensitivity to aspirin resulting in urticaria or anaphylaxis. Those patients with chronic urticaria whose condition exacerbates with aspirin ingestion have no features distinguishing them from other patients with urticaria, and skin biopsies show findings consistent with urticaria.

PLANS

Diagnostic

History alone is used to diagnose most cases of isolated aspirin sensitivity. The clinical history is also quite helpful in patients with aspirin-sensitive asthma and aspirin-aggravated chronic urticaria. Challenge procedures, however, increase the sensitivity of discovering many other patients with chronic asthma or chronic urticaria whose symptoms are exacerbated on ingestion of aspirin or other NSAIDs.

The waxing and waning of symptoms in aspirin-sensitive patients with chronic urticaria make interpretation of aspirin challenge difficult. The patients are usually given traditional doses of aspirin, either 325 or 650 mg, and observed for several hours for visible signs of worsening urticaria, such as increased numbers of urticarial lesions, flushing, or areas of angioedema. Aspirin challenges are potentially hazardous and should be conducted under close expert supervision and where resuscitation equipment is readily available. Some investigators have shown increased levels of serum neutrophil chemotactic activity following aspirin challenge in these patients, but this in vitro tool is helpful for research purposes only and is not applicable to routine office practice.

In vitro diagnostic testing methods for aspirin-sensitive asthma are also not available to the practicing physician. Patients with this syndrome can be found to have increased urinary leukotriene E_4 levels following aspirin ingestion, increased nasal fluid leukotriene C_4 and histamine levels following nasal aspirin–lysine challenge, and increased bronchoalveolar lavage fluid leukotriene concentrations and decreased prostaglandin formation following aspirin–lysine inhalation challenge, and some investigators have found abnormal platelet sensitivity to aspirin in patients with aspirin-sensitive asthma. These procedures, although useful in research to elucidate possible mechanisms of aspirin-induced bronchospasm, are available only to research investigators.

Oral aspirin challenge remains the standard diagnostic test for patients with aspirin-sensitive asthma in whom the history is not obvious. As these patients can at times develop severe and even life-threatening bronchospasm following aspirin challenge, *the procedure should be performed only by pulmonologists or allergists experienced in these challenge methods.* The procedure for aspirin challenge has been well standardized by Stevenson (1984) and involves the oral administration of small doses of aspirin (3–30 mg) followed by incremental increases at 3-hour intervals while measuring spirometry. A 20% or greater drop in the forced expiratory volume in 1 second (FEV_1) is considered diagnostic.

Therapeutic

Aspirin-induced urticarial or anaphylactic reactions should be treated similarly to severe allergic reactions of other causes with the use of subcutaneous epinephrine, antihistamines, and intravenous fluids when needed to restore plasma volume and maintain blood pressure. Aspirin-aggravated urticaria can be treated with antihistamines as needed and topical glucocorticoids for localized recalcitrant lesions.

Patients with acute attacks of asthma precipitated by aspirin or other NSAIDs should be managed with bronchodilators, oxygen, intensive care monitoring and mechanical ventilation if needed, and glucocorticoids for several days following the reaction. In the absence of accidental aspirin or NSAID ingestion, the underlying rhinosinusitis or asthma should be managed with the goal of reducing mucosal inflammation to the lowest degree possible with topical and systemic glucocorticoids, antibiotics for purulent secretions, bronchodilators, and antihistamines if symptoms develop from contact with aeroallergens to which the patient might be sensitive. Nasal polyps can often be reduced with topical or systemic glucocorticoids, but frequently require surgical removal along with adequate sinus drainage.

Avoidance of aspirin is the principal management strategy for patients with isolated aspirin sensitivity or aspirin-aggravated chronic urticaria. These patients should be aware that a multitude of prescribed and over-the-counter medications contain aspirin and should examine labels of cold preparations, analgesics, or antiarthritic medications carefully. If they are uncertain as to whether or not a medication contains aspirin, they should consult their physician or pharmacist at once before using the medication.

Patients with aspirin-sensitive asthma should also pursue strict avoidance of aspirin and aspirin-containing products and should avoid other NSAIDs as well. At times, patients who have had symptoms related to severe atherosclerosis or arterial microembolization require daily antiplatelet therapy in the form of aspirin or related compounds that alter platelet adhesiveness. These patients can often be successfully desensitized to aspirin by being administered very small, subthreshold doses of aspirin followed by graduated increases over 24 to 48 hours. Desensitization is maintained with daily ingestion of 326 to 650 mg of aspirin and quickly reverses within 2 to 7 days of stopping the aspirin.

Within the past decade, aspirin desensitization has been viewed as a possible therapeutic modality for treatment of underlying rhinosinusitis and asthma. Patients with aspirin-sensitive asthma and rhinosinusitis can be desensitized under proper supervision and maintained long term on daily aspirin at a dose of 650 mg if tolerated. Some of these patients, after several months to years, have shown improvement in their symptoms of rhinitis with less nasal polyp formation and reduced asthma symptoms, and have required smaller doses of glucocorticoids for maintenance therapy. The decision to use aspirin desensitization to treat underlying severe rhinosinusitis and asthma is dependent on the response of these entities to other forms of therapy, the ability to desensitize the patient under proper supervision, and the compliance of the patient in taking a daily medication long term without skipping doses.

FOLLOW-UP

No regular follow-up is required for the occasional patient with isolated aspirin sensitivity if they always avoid aspirin and are careful to avoid aspirin-containing cold and pain preparations, particularly those that can be purchased over the counter. Patients with chronic urticaria and aspirin-sensitive asthma should be followed regularly to monitor medication compliance and disease activity. This is especially true for the patients with asthma that may be severe, with more frequent flares and more frequent or daily requirement for glucocorticoids. Patients with asthma should regularly monitor their airflow with peak flowmeters and develop a crisis plan with their local physician and emergency room if they have had attacks severe enough to warrant intensive care unit admission. Although most patients with aspirin-sensitive asthma do not have prominent sensitivity to aeroallergens, or at least are no more frequently positive to these skin tests than the general population, skin testing can occasionally be helpful to elucidate sensitivity to dust mites, molds, or cats, which may be an exacerbating factor in a small percentage of these patients.

DISCUSSION

Prevalence and Incidence

About 5 to 10% of patients with asthma will volunteer a history of aspirin and NSAID sensitivity. When aspirin challenge is used to assist in the diagnosis, the percentage with sensitivity rises to between 18 and 20%. If one is observing a population of patients with asthma whose disease is more severe, for example, having required frequent hospitalizations or use of glucocorticoids for control, the percentage with aspirin sensitivity is even higher. The prevalence of aspirin sensitivity is probably similar in patients with chronic urticaria. Isolated sensitivity to aspirin is much less common, probably less than 1% of the general population.

Related Basic Science

Aspirin-sensitive urticaria and aspirin-sensitive asthma appear to be biochemically mediated events that are significantly linked to the immunologic inflammation seen in these allergic diseases. Aspirin-sensitive asthma has been more extensively studied than aspirin-aggravated urticaria, but the events that precipitate the reactions are probably similar. The ability of aspirin and NSAIDs to block cyclooxygenase appears to be a critical factor in inducing the symptom exacerbations. Drugs that are structurally similar to aspirin, but weak cyclooxygenase inhibitors, rarely cause bronchospasm in usual therapeutic doses. Other NSAIDs, on the other hand, can induce reactions identical to those caused by aspirin in patients with asthma who have acquired aspirin sensitivity, and their potency in causing bronchospasm parallels their potency as cyclooxygenase-inhibiting agents. With cyclooxygenase blockade, products of cell membrane alteration and arachidonic acid formation are shunted toward the 5-lipoxygenase pathway, with resultant leukotriene production. This scenario could cause severe bronchospasm through a decrease in potentially beneficial cyclooxygenase products, such as prostaglandin$_2$, or through the formation of potent leukotrienes which are potent bronchoconstrictors and can alter vascular permeability leading to mucosal edema. Although there is ample experimental evidence that this metabolic shift indeed occurs, it does not explain why all patients with asthma do not experience bronchospasm on ingestion of aspirin or other NSAIDs. The uniqueness of patients with aspirin-sensitive asthma may stem from the fact that these patients have higher rates of basal leukotriene formation and higher levels of leukotrienes following aspirin ingestion than asthmatic patients without aspirin sensitivity. In addition, these patients appear to have an increased sensitivity to leukotrienes, when nebulized into their airway, that is much less following aspirin desensitization or than observed in asthmatics who are not aspirin sensitive. Also, the number of beta receptors on lymphocytes from patients with aspirin-sensitive asthma decreases when these cells are incubated with aspirin. This downregulation of the beta receptor, if also occurring in the airway, could disrupt the ability of endogenous catecholamines to promote airway tone and have an effect similar to that of acute beta blockade in patients who are aspirin sensitive. This effect, like increased leukotriene sensitivity, does not appear to occur in non-aspirin-sensitive asthmatics or normal control subjects.

Although difficult to define by skin testing or specific immunoglobulin E antibody measurement, isolated aspirin sensitivity resembles an immunoglobulin E-mediated process, in that the sensitivity is consistent over time and is not cross-reactive with other pharmacologic agents. Some success has been achieved with skin testing materials composed of aspirin–lysine or aspirin–polylysine conjugates in other countries, but these agents are not currently available in the United States.

Natural History and Its Modification with Treatment

Patients with isolated aspirin sensitivity rarely have problems with cautious aspirin avoidance and do not require regular follow-up. Patients with aspirin-sensitive urticaria and asthma usually need regular follow-up because of the severity of their underlying disease. Exacerbations of chronic urticaria can cause severe pruritus with scattered urticarial lesions, with or without associated angioedema. Angioedema and large urticarial lesions have significant morbidity and can cause temporary cosmetic disfigurement when occurring in facial areas; in addition, swelling of the tongue or upper airway can be life threatening if not treated promptly with epinephrine. At times, these patients require large doses of oral glucocorticoids for control and often require daily antihistamines for symptom management. Aspirin-sensitive asthma usually is quite severe, requiring daily use of bronchodilators, and is often glucocorticoid dependent. Long-term management requires maintenance of a functional daily existence, without excessive dyspnea or bouts of wheezing, and management of long-term complications of glucocorticoid side effects, such as osteoporosis, early cataract formation, glucose intolerance, hypertension, and weight gain. Patients who have experienced life-threatening asthmatic attacks require a crisis plan and close daily observance of their peak flow measurements combined with frequent office visits.

Research is required to determine whether aspirin desensitization as a method of altering the natural history of chronic morbidity from symptoms of rhinosinusitis or asthma is successful in altering the long-term outcome of patients with aspirin-sensitive asthma.

Prevention

The cause of aspirin-sensitive urticaria and aspirin-sensitive asthma remains unknown; therefore, no methods are available to prevent sensitivity from developing in select patients with chronic urticaria or asthma. Studies have been inconsistent as to evidence of a genetic predisposition. Avoidance of aspirin is vital to all three groups of patients with aspirin sensitivity.

Aspirin desensitization may prevent attacks caused by usual therapeutic doses of aspirin in those with aspirin-sensitive asthma, and, when they become available, drugs that inhibit the 5-lipoxygenase enzyme or leukotriene receptor may also offer effective prevention of drug-induced attacks as well as asthma management.

Cost Containment

Management of the long-term morbidity of the underlying diseases is the principal method of cost containment in the treatment of patients with aspirin-sensitive asthma or urticaria. Availability of less expensive daily bronchodilators and reduction of hospitalization and loss of productive work days will be crucial in decreasing the long-term cost of these diseases.

REFERENCES

Christie PE, Schmitz-Schumann M, Spur BW, et al. Airway responsiveness to leukotriene C$_4$ (LTC$_4$), leukotriene E$_4$ (LTE$_4$) and histamine in aspirin-sensitive asthmatic subjects. Eur Resp J 1993;6:1468.

Grzeleska-Rzymowska I, Szmidt M, Rozniecki J, et al. Aspirin-induced neutrophil chemotactic activity (NCA) in patients with aspirin-sensitive urticaria after desensitization to the drug. J Invest Allerg Clin Immunol 1994;4(1):28.

Krzysztof S, Dworski R, Soja J, et al. Eicosanoids in bronchoalveolar lavage fluid of aspirin-intolerant patients with asthma after aspirin challenge. Am J Respir Crit Care Med 1994;149:940.

Nasser SM, Bell GS, Foster S, et al. Effect of the 5-lipoxygenase inhibitor ZD2138 on aspirin-induced asthma. Thorax 1994;49:749.

Stevenson DD. Diagnosis, prevention and treatment of adverse reactions to aspirin and nonsteroidal anti-inflammatory drugs. J Allergy Clin Immunol 1984;74:617.

CHAPTER 5–14

Systemic Mast Cell Disease

Michael W. Yocum, M.D.

DEFINITION

Systemic mast cell disease is an abnormal proliferation of mast cells that infiltrate the bone marrow, spleen, liver, lymph nodes, gastrointestinal tract, and skin. It is most likely a true myeloproliferative disorder, because the mast cells are frequently atypical with lobulated nuclei.

ETIOLOGY

The cause of mastocytosis is unknown, but the disease is most likely due to whatever causes myeloproliferative disorders in general. Systemic mastocytosis may be associated with a dysmyelopoietic syndrome, a myeloproliferative disorder, acute nonlymphocytic leukemia, malignant lymphoma, chronic neutropenia, or mast cell leukemia. Rare cases of familial urticaria pigmentosa have been reported.

CRITERIA FOR DIAGNOSIS
Suggestive

A history of flushing episodes, described as a feeling of warmth, especially if accompanied by light-headedness or syncope, is very suggestive of systemic mast cell disease. These paroxysmal episodes of mediator release are usually followed by profound lethargy and prostration for days and then a period of recovery and an improved sense of well-being, which may last for a variable period. Patients may also present with a past medical history of recurrent anaphylaxis, peptic ulcer disease, chronic diarrhea, osteoporosis, or headaches. The family history is usually not helpful, except for the rare case of familial urticaria pigmentosa.

Definitive

A definitive diagnosis of systemic mast cell disease requires histologic evidence of mast cell proliferation, demonstrable by skin or bone marrow biopsy. If urticaria pigmentosa is found, biopsy of the lesions should be performed. Indiscriminate nonlesional skin biopsies are rarely helpful. Bone marrow aspiration and a trephine core biopsy should be done in all patients with suspected systemic mast cell disease to document systemic involvement, and these tests usually reveal nests of frequently atypical spindle-shaped mast cells. Evidence of mast cell mediator release is usually obtainable after a flushing episode. This evidence might include elevated serum tryptase (a mast cell granule protein) and urine methylimidazoleacetic acid (a histamine metabolite) levels.

CLINICAL MANIFESTATIONS
Subjective

In addition to the episodic flushing spells, constitutional symptoms of fever, night sweats, fatigue, and weight loss may be present. The patient may have bone pain, pathologic fractures, a history of osteoporosis, or symptoms of nausea, emesis, peptic ulcer, diarrhea, or malabsorption. Symptoms are rarely produced by the physical effects of mast cell proliferation, such as hepatosplenomegaly and lymphadenopathy, but more frequently are due to episodes of massive mast cell mediator release. Mast cell degranulation may be triggered by the ingestion of nonsteroidal antiinflammatory drugs, narcotic analgesics, or alcohol; physical exertion; mental stress; infection; high environmental temperature; the premenstrual state; Hymenoptera stings; or administration of radiographic contrast medium. The duration of a mediator release flushing episode may be only minutes or up to 2 hours; mild reactions are brief.

Objective
Physical Examination

The physical examination may reveal skin lesions of urticaria pigmentosa, dermatographism, telangiectasia macularis eruptiva perstans, nodular or bullous lesions, or a solitary mastocytoma. If lesions of urticaria pigmentosa are stroked, they urticate, a phenomenon called Darier's sign. It must be emphasized that up to 50% of patients with systemic mast cell disease do not have urticaria pigmentosa. Hepatosplenomegaly and lymphadenopathy may be detected on physical examination. If a flushing episode is observed, a bright, diffuse erythema may develop, chiefly over the head, neck, and upper trunk areas.

Routine Laboratory Abnormalities

Routine laboratory abnormalities are rarely found; however, anemia may be present, especially if peptic ulcer disease exists, and leukopenia, thrombocytopenia, or eosinophilia may be found. Results of liver function tests are usually normal, except for occasional elevations of the alkaline phosphatase level. Rarely, the peripheral blood smear may show mast cells in the circulation. The chest radiograph may demonstrate bone lesions in the ribs or spine, such as osteosporosis, osteosclerosis, and vertebral fractures.

PLANS
Diagnostic
Differential Diagnosis

Systemic mast cell disease may mimic several diseases that one must consider, such as carcinoid syndrome, recurrent anaphylaxis, multiple myeloma, metastatic carcinoma, osteoporosis, and Zollinger–Ellison syndrome. The entity of inappropriate mast cell activation syndrome is characterized by identical spells of massive mediator release, but it is not associated with an abnormal proliferation of mast cells.

Diagnostic Options

The diagnosis of systemic mast cell disease is based on the histologic findings, supported by clinical, biochemical, and radiographic data. Options include skin biopsy of urticaria pigmentosa or mastocytoma lesions; bone marrow aspiration and biopsy; determination of blood histamine, tryptase, calcitonin, and calcitonin gene-related peptide levels; and assays for urine histamine, methylimidazoleacetic acid, and prostaglandin D_2 metabolites. Radiographs of the upper gastrointestinal tract and small bowel can show peptic ulcers, gastric fold and bowel wall abnormalities, or mucosal changes. A radioisotopic bone scan, as well as plain bone radiographs of the skull, proximal long bones, ribs, and pelvis, may be helpful. A normal 5-hydroxyindoleacetic acid urine level should be determined to rule out the carcinoid syndrome.

Recommended Approach

Useful tests in the evaluation of systemic mast cell disease include radioisotopic bone scanning and determination of 24-hour urine methylimidazoleacetic acid and prostaglandin D_2 metabolite levels and serum calcitonin, tryptase, histamine, and calcitonin gene-related peptide levels. The urine methylimidazoleacetic acid level should be determined while the patient is on a histamine- and histidine-restricted diet. Upper gastrointestinal and small bowel follow-through radiographs may reveal peptic ulcer disease.

Skin and bone marrow are the two most useful sites for biopsy. All patients with suspected systemic mast cell disease should undergo biopsy, usually of the bone marrow. Patients with suspected cutaneous mastocytosis should have biopsy of skin lesions. Tissue specimens must be handled carefully, by plastic embedding in glycol methacrylate, and bone marrow specimens must not be decalcified. Special stains should include a metachromatic stain, such as Giemsa or toluidine blue, and an enzymatic stain, such as chloracetate esterase or aminocaproate esterase, as well as immunologic stains for tryptase. Nests of spindle-shaped mast cells, often with atypical features, are found mixed with eosinophils, lymphocytes, plasma cells, histiocytes, and fibroblasts.

Therapeutic
Therapeutic Options

There is no chemotherapeutic or radiotherapeutic protocol for cure of systemic mast cell disease, so therapy is symptomatic. Experimental use of interferon-α shows promise in inhibiting the abnormal mast cell proliferation, but this therapy is not yet approved. Treatment of any associated hematologic disorder is indicated. Symptomatic treatment consists of H_1 and H_2 antihistamines, oral cromolyn sodium for gastrointestinal symptoms, and parenteral epinephrine for flushing episodes. All patients should be instructed carefully in the use of and provided with injectable epinephrine for self-administration, 1;1000 dilution, 0.3 mL. Patients with systemic mast cell disease should avoid β_2-adrenergic blocking drugs and angiotensin converting enzyme inhibitor drugs.

Recommended Approach

All patients with systemic mast cell disease should take an antihistamine H_1 blocker to alleviate the diarrhea and pruritus and an antihistamine H_2 blocker to relieve symptoms of excessive gastric acid production and prevent gastric irritation from aspirin. Chlorpheniramine, 16 to 24 mg a day, plus ranitidine, 300 mg a day, are recommended. Oral cromolyn sodium, 100 mg before meals and 200 mg at bedtime, has been used successfully to control the abdominal cramping and diarrhea. Another alternative is aspirin, 3.9 to 5.2 g per day, to achieve a serum salicylate level of 20 to 30 mg/dL 4 hours after a dose. This therapy has been shown to decrease the frequency and intensity of flushing episodes, which if severe may be fatal; however, about 5 to 10% of patients with systemic mast cell disease are sensitive to aspirin and respond to as little as 20 mg with a massive mast cell mediator release reaction. If at all possible, these patients should be carefully desensitized to aspirin in an intensive care unit and slowly built up to tolerate therapeutic doses of aspirin.

If a mediator release episode accompanied by severe hypotension occurs, the best treatment is intravenously administered epinephrine, rather than other vasopressors. The infusion is begun at 4 μg per minute and titrated upward to 10 μg per minute if needed to sustain blood pressure. Weaning is performed by decreasing the rate by 1 μg per minute every 30 minutes until the patient is off the infusion.

FOLLOW-UP

Patients who are stable with fairly good control of symptoms should be followed at 4- to 6-month intervals during the first 3 years after diagnosis. During this interval, the prognosis can usually be ascertained because most of the early deaths occur during this period.

DISCUSSION
Prevalence and Incidence

Systemic mast cell disease is rare: approximately two patients a year have been seen at a tertiary referral center over a 31-year period. Almost all reported cases have been in whites. Among adult patients thought to have only urticaria pigmentosa, however, 50% have been found to have systemic involvement.

Related Basic Science

Mast cells are thought to originate from a pluripotent, bone marrow, hematopoietic stem cell. Early differentiation of the mast cell is dependent on interleukin-3 and is inhibited by granulocyte–macrophage colony-stimulating factor. Mast cells distribute to endothelial and epithelial basement membrane sites, along nerves, and about glandular structures rich in laminin, especially in cutaneous, pulmonary, and gastrointestinal tissues. Final differentiation of the mast cell into mucosal or connective tissue subtypes is determined by local growth factors produced by fibroblasts and stromal cells. Mast cells can release preformed and newly synthesized mediators by immunoglobulin E-dependent mechanisms or by non-immunoglobulin E stimuli. These mast cell mediators include histamine; heparin; tryptase; chymotryptase; leukotrienes C_4, D_4, and E_4; prostaglandin D_2; platelet-activating factor; interleukin-3; interleukin-5; tumor growth factor β; and tumor necrosis factor α. Several of these mediators have been implicated in disease manifestations. Histamine can cause flushing and diarrhea, prostaglandin D_2 and heparin can cause osteoporosis, and histamine and particularly calcitonin gene-related peptide can cause hypotension. Although intravenously administered prostaglandin D_2 causes hypotension in animals, it does not in humans. Tryptase may activate other mediators such as bradykinin.

During flushing attacks there is a substantial release of endogenous epinephrine, which not only works as a vasopressor but also directly inhibits mast cell mediator release.

Natural History and Its Modification with Treatment

Because mast cell disease has many forms, it is best to divide it into subtypes so as to predict disease modification with treatment as well as to predict prognosis in individual patients (Table 5–14–1). For pediatric patients who have only urticaria pigmentosa as a manifestation, 50% will have remission and be free of disease, but adults with urticaria pigmentosa do not have remission, and up to 50% have systemic disease. Patients with localized disease have a better prognosis than those with systemic disease. Indolent mastocytosis has a good prognosis and can be managed for decades with symptomatic treatment. Aggressive mastocytosis has a poor prognosis; the rapid expansion of mast cell numbers makes it difficult to manage, and death can occur during the first 3 years of disease. The prognosis of patients with systemic mast cell disease associated with a hematologic disorder is determined chiefly by the prognosis of the associated disorder and its response to therapy. Mast cell leukemia has the worst prognosis: the mean survival is less than 6 months, and it is resistant to all current forms of chemotherapy and radiation therapy.

Mast cell leukemia is diagnosed by finding that 10% or more of the circulating leukocytes consist of atypical mast cells. Further, poor prog-

TABLE 5–14–1. MAST CELL DISEASES

Localized
- Cutaneous: without visible lesions
- Cutaneous: with erythematous, acneiform papules, telangiectasia macularis eruptiva perstans, nodular or bullous lesions
- Cutaneous: urticaria pigmentosa
- Cutaneous: localized mastocytoma

Systemic
- Chronic, indolent mastocytosis with multiple organ involvement
- Aggressive, progressive mastocytosis
- Mastocytosis with an associated hematologic disorder: dysmyelopoietic syndrome, myeloproliferative disorder, acute nonlymphocytic leukemia, malignant lymphoma, chronic neutropenia, or thrombocytopenia
- Mast cell leukemia

nosis factors that have been determined to be significant in systemic mast cell disease are age of 65 years or older at diagnosis, male sex, low hemoglobin value, current or previous malignancy, and lobulated mast cell nuclei. It must, however, be reemphasized that any patient with systemic mast cell disease may die of shock when a massive mediator release reaction occurs. Thus, teaching the patient to self-administer subcutaneous epinephrine adequately has a significant immediate life-saving impact in this disease.

Prevention

There is no known way to prevent this disease.

Cost Containment

A careful history, along with the physician considering mastocytosis, is the best way to diagnose this disease. A selective laboratory evaluation, as suggested in the recommended diagnostic approach, is the most cost-effective. Patients have usually seen numerous physicians and undergone a myriad of expensive diagnostic tests for years before the correct diagnosis is made. Therefore, the biggest cost-containment effort should be toward an early, correct diagnosis.

REFERENCES

Butterfield JH, Kao PC, Klee, GG, Yocum MW. Aspirin idiosyncrasy in systemic mast cell disease: A new look at mediator release during aspirin desensitization. Mayo Clin Proc 1995;70:481.

Roberts LJ II, Oates JA. Disorders of vasodilator hormones: The carcinoid syndrome and mastocytosis. In: Wilson JD, Foster DW (editors). Williams Textbook of Endocrinology. 8th ed. Philadelphia: W.B. Saunders 1992:1619.

Roberts LJ II, Sweetman BJ, Lewis RA, et al. Increased production of prostaglandin O_2 in patients with systemic mastocytosis. N Engl J Med 1980;303:1400.

Travis WD, Li C-Y, Bergstrahl EJ, et al. Systemic mast cell disease: Analysis of 50 cases and literature review. Medicine 1988;67:345.

CHAPTER 5–15

Hypogammaglobulinemia

Quinton C. Callies, M.D.

DEFINITION

Immunoglobulins play a key role in host defense for protecting against microbial, viral, and fungal invasion. Immunoglobulin deficiency can present as a spectrum of antibody deficiency disorders involving various stages of B-cell maturational arrest as well as functional impairment. Specific syndromes can be categorized by finding low or absent levels of one or more immunoglobulin classes, or loss of their functional capacity, the entire spectrum leading to clinical symptoms of recurrent respiratory or gastrointestinal illness.

ETIOLOGY

Antibody deficiencies more commonly occur as a result of abnormalities in the primary DNA sequence or in the expression of individual immunoglobulin genes. In many instances, as shown by cloned C_H gene probes and Southern blotting, immunoglobulin (Ig) subclass deficiencies (IgG, IgG2, IgG4, and IgA/IgE) occur as a result of deletions of segments of the γ heavy-chain locus on chromosome 14. X-linked agammaglobulinemia recently has been linked to a specific defect in the B lymphocyte in that there is an abnormality in V_H to DJ_H immunoglobulin gene recombination (Figure 5–15–1). Single-point mutations in a structural gene with lack of an intradomain disulfide bond in some κ light-chain immunodeficiencies have resulted in loss of function of an antibody molecule. Up to 3% of healthy individuals may be heterozygous for multiple heavy-chain deletions as well as crossover of mispaired homologous regions.

CRITERIA FOR DIAGNOSIS

Suggestive

Recurrent bacterial or viral infections of the respiratory or gastrointestinal tract should alert the clinician that the infection may be a direct result of a deficiency in B-cell function, specifically IgG, IgA, or IgM.

Definitive

Serum levels should be measured only by quantitative techniques (radial immunodiffusion or nephelometry). The finding of diminished concentration of one or a combination of immunoglobulins (including IgG subclasses) leads to a diagnosis of humoral immunodeficiency. A less frequent, but nevertheless equally important, finding is subclass IgG deficiency, a functional inability to respond adequately to an antigen challenge in the presence of normal or near-normal immunoglobulin levels. Table 5–15–1 outlines an approach to the inclusion of specific syndromes that are associated with antibody deficiencies.

CLINICAL MANIFESTATIONS

Subjective

X-Linked Infantile Agammaglobulinemia

Patients first manifest with recurring infections with high-grade pyogenic bacterial organisms beginning at age 6 months to 2 years, when maternally transferred immunoglobulins are no longer present. Encapsulated organisms including streptococci, meningococci, and gram-negative organisms (ie, *Hemophilus*) are commonly found, presenting with otitis media, pharyngitis, bronchitis, sinusitis, and pneumonia. They may also present with septicemia, septic arthritis, and bacterial meningitis with repetitive bacterial insults over the years. They may also present with bronchiectasis, chronic sinusitis, and respiratory failure. Patients with an absence of B cells also have a propensity for development of infections due to echovirus with widespread tissue involvement. Arthritis is known to develop in 20 to 40% of patients,

TABLE 5–15–1. SYNDROMES ASSOCIATED WITH ANTIBODY DEFICIENCIES

Syndrome	Serum Immunoglobulins
X-linked infantile agammaglobulinemia	Panhypogammaglobulinemia
Common variable immunodeficiency	Panhypogammaglobulinemia
Selective IgA deficiency	IgA deficiency with or without IgG2 deficiency
Dysgammaglobulinemia	Reduced IgG, increased IgM
IgG subclass deficiency	Total IgG often normal with selective decrease of a specific IgG subclass
Severe combined immunodeficiency	Panhypogammaglobulinemia
Wiskott–Aldrich syndrome	
Ataxia telangiectasia	

Source: Schwartz S. Clinical use of immune serum globulin as replacement therapy in patients with primary immunodeficiency syndromes. In: Ballow M, ed. IVIG therapy today. Totowa, NJ: Humana Press, 1992:1. Reproduced with permission from the publisher and author.

usually with sterile effusions. Diarrhea and malabsorption have been associated with *Giardia* or *Campylobacter* infections in some patients.

Common Variable Immunodeficiency

The spectrum of clinical presentation in this immunodeficiency parallels that of infections in X-linked agammaglobulinemia. In contrast, both males and females are affected because common variable immunodeficiency has an autosomal recessive inheritance pattern. This heterogeneous immunodeficiency syndrome can occur at any time in life, although it occurs more commonly in adults. Some believe this immunodeficiency follows a viral infection. Opportunistic infections with *mycobacteria*, various fungi, and *Pneumocystis carinii* are due to clinically important abnormalities of the cell-mediated system as well as to humoral immunity. Most patients tolerate viral infections, although herpes zoster occurs in up to 20% of individuals with common variable immunodeficiency. As in X-linked agammaglobulinemia, an unusual enteroviral infection occurs, most commonly echovirus beginning as a meningoencephalitis that becomes chronic and progressive, associated with rashes, fever, edema, and hepatitis. Patients with this disorder frequently may run a course of chronic diarrhea with clinically significant malabsorption and weight loss due to *Giardia, Salmonella, Shigella,*

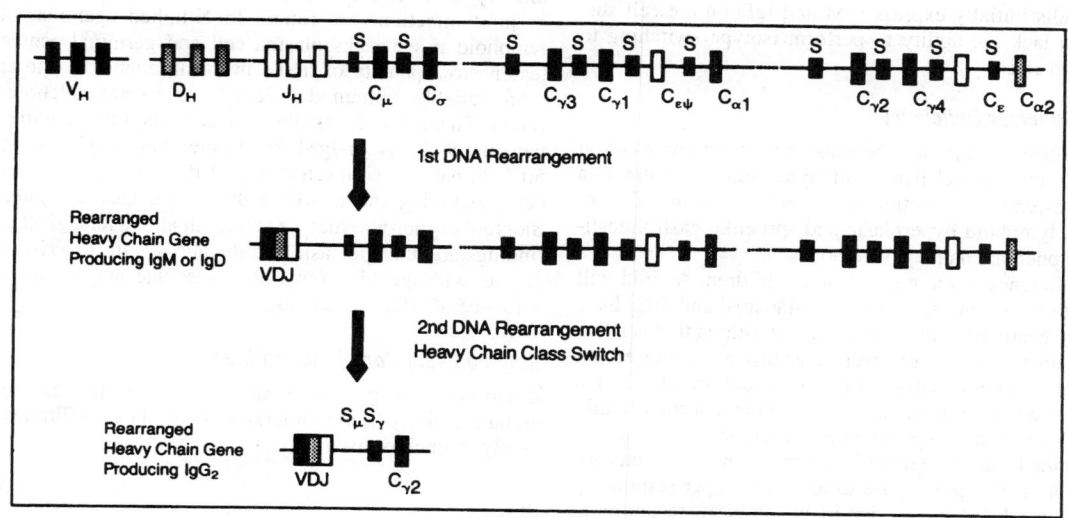

Figure 5–15–1. Schematic representation of the human gene line heavy-chain locus. The first DNA rearrangement assembles three regions—variable (V_H), diversity (D_H), and joining (J_H)—to complete the variable portion of the molecule. Later, a second DNA rearrangement may occur involving the homologous switch sites (S) that precede each constant (C_H) region. This results in a more distal constant region, such as $C_\gamma2$ moving next to the rearranged VDJ as in an immunoglobulin G2-producing cell. *(Source: Geha RS. IgG subclass deficiencies. In: Middleton E Jr, Reed CE, Ellis EF, et al, eds. Allergy: Principles and practice. 3rd ed., Update 1, St. Louis: Mosby, 1991:1. Reproduced with permission from the publisher and author.)*

and *Campylobacter* species. Inflammatory bowel disease indistinguishable from Crohn's disease or ulcerative colitis has been found.

Twenty percent of patients with common variable immunodeficiency develop autoimmune disorders such as Coombs-positive hemolytic anemia and idiopathic thrombocytopenic purpura. Although these patients are unable to develop a sufficient antibody response to infecting organisms, they are able to produce autoantibodies against red cells, platelets, and granulocytes. Pernicious anemia occurs in approximately 10% of patients with common variable immunodeficiency, but at an earlier age (third or fourth decade of life). In 30% of patients, splenomegaly and widespread lymphadenopathy develop. In many patients with common variable immunodeficiency, an asymmetric arthritis involving one set of joints develops, primarily knees and ankles, but this arthritis rarely leads to joint destruction.

Selective Immunoglobulin A Deficiency

Although IgA constitutes only 10 to 15% of total serum immunoglobulin, it is the major immunoglobulin in external secretions. IgA is monomeric in serum, whereas it exists as a dimer with secretory piece in secretions. The secretory IgA has certain biological features that potentiate its antiviral and antibacterial functions. In selective IgA deficiency, levels of serum IgA are less than 5 mg/dL, and serum levels of IgG, IgM, and IgE are entirely normal. Many patients are totally asymptomatic, as noted in blood donor pools with this immunodeficiency. Many patients do have increased sinopulmonary infections, and chronic diarrhea and autoimmunity occur. The frequency of atopy is high (up to 55%) in patients with IgA deficiency. Up to 40% of patients with selective IgA deficiency have anti-IgA antibodies and anaphylactic reactions, including fatal reactions that may occur on receiving whole blood, plasma, or other IgA-containing infusions. IgA deficiency with associated IgG2 and IgG4 deficiencies has been reported, and such patients may have increased susceptibility to bacterial organisms as well as destructive lung disease. A few of these patients have an asthmatic state and a more severe reactive airway picture with associated sinopulmonary infection.

Dysgammaglobulinemia (Hyper-IgM Syndrome)

This syndrome was originally described as an X-linked pattern; however, there now are autosomal recessive forms of this disorder. Affected patients have a high incidence of pyogenic sinopulmonary infection; some also manifest neutropenia, thrombocytopenia, and autoimmune disorders. They may also have significant hepatosplenomegaly and present with autoimmune hemolytic anemia. An increased serum IgM level develops with markedly decreased IgG and IgA levels. The B cells initially express IgM and IgD on the cell surface. They appear to lack the ability to perform isotype switching to other immunoglobulin classes.

Immunoglobulin G Subclass Deficiency

Selective IgG1 deficiency is rare, and because the largest contribution to total IgG is IgG1, the clinical pattern of hypogammaglobulinemia ranges from mild respiratory infection to severe disseminated bacteremia. In addition, lymphoid hyperplasia and spruelike gastrointestinal and autoimmune phenomena may develop.

Selective IgG2 deficiency is more common in children. A child will typically present with recurrent otitis media or sinusitis, and 40% have recurrent pneumonia. Many present with infectious asthma that is resistant to therapy. In some children, recurrent diarrhea is the presenting symptom. A large proportion of children improve such that by 7 or 8 years of age they become asymptomatic. Other members of their family (siblings, cousins) also may have IgG subclass deficiency.

IgG3 deficiency may be associated with recurrent sinopulmonary infections. This deficiency may predispose to recurrent upper respiratory tract infections because IgG3 is the dominant antibody response to *Branhamella catarrhalis* and the M component of *Streptococcus pyogenes*. These organisms commonly can be found in the upper airway and are commonly associated with bacterial sinusitis. Likewise, patients deficient in IgG3 may be increasingly sensitive to upper respiratory tract viral infections, which may precede acute sinusitis.

IgG4 deficiency with levels less than 1 mg/mL is often found in association with IgG2 deficiency. The deficiency is difficult to define because 15% of the population at large lack measurable IgG4.

Severe Combined Immunodeficiency

Patients with severe combined immunodeficiency usually die within the first 2 years of life of a severe defect in both the B-cell and T-cell immune systems. Immunoglobulin levels are very low for all isotypes except in Nezelof's syndrome, in which immunoglobulin levels may be normal or elevated.

Wiskott–Aldrich Syndrome

Wiskott–Aldrich syndrome is an X-linked disease that usually presents with a constellation of findings, including eczema, thrombocytopenia, and recurrent infection with a wide variety of bacterial, viral, and fungal organisms. The immunologic defects affect both humoral and cellular function. Autoimmune disorders are common in the form of vasculitis and hemolytic anemia. Twenty percent of patients have a susceptibility to lymphoreticular malignancy, including leukemia or Hodgkin's disease. There is a progressive decline in T-lymphocyte function, such that delayed hypersensitivity and allograft rejection no longer occur. Few patients if any reach adult life, depending on the degree of immunodeficiency expression.

Ataxia Telangiectasia

Ataxia telangiectasia is a disorder characterized by sinopulmonary infections, oculocutaneous telangiectasia, progressive cerebellar ataxia, and a relatively high incidence of epithelial carcinomas and lymphomas. Telangiectasia of dilated venules begins to appear between ages 2 and 8 years, involving bulbar conjunctiva, nose, and antecubital and popliteal spaces. Other skin abnormalities such as premature graying of hair, vitiligo, and atrophy of the skin occur. There usually is growth retardation. Endocrine abnormalities present in the form of testicular hypoplasia, ovarian absence or hypoplasia, and delayed or absent menstruation with lack of secondary sexual characteristics. Both cellular and humoral immunity are involved. Seventy percent of patients have an absence or extreme deficiency of serum and secretory IgA, 80% develop IgE deficiency, and most manifest reduced IgG2 and IgG4 subclasses.

Objective
Physical Examination

Physical findings are characteristically related to findings of sinus, pulmonary, or enteric infections. Less frequently, meningeal signs or skin or joint infections are found. In X-linked agammaglobulinemia, the lymphoid tissue lacks plasma cell and germinal center development, leading to a paucity of tissue in tonsil, adenoids, and spleen. In common variable immunodeficiency, significant splenomegaly may be found. There may be findings of arthritis with or without effusion. In patients with hyper-IgM syndrome, hepatosplenomegaly occurs in 50%. In patients with selective IgA deficiency, connective tissue disorders, including rheumatoid arthritis, changes of systemic lupus, and Sjögren's syndrome may be found. In ataxia telangiectasia, the obvious findings are telangiectasia and the ataxic gait. In Wiskott–Aldrich syndrome, widespread eczema and petechiae may be evident along with evidence of arthritis and vasculitis.

Routine Laboratory Abnormalities

Blood counts may show lymphopenia in some cases of hypogammaglobulinemia. Chest radiographs may show infiltrates or, less commonly, bronchiectasis.

PLANS
Diagnostic

The evaluation of a patient with recurrent infection requires a detailed history and physical examination with particular attention to findings that may help distinguish markers for a patient's basic defect. The skin may be observed for petechiae, telangiectasia, eczema, vitiligo, and monilial infection. Neurologic findings may reveal ataxia or infection of the central nervous system. Hypoplasia of the tonsils is an important finding in immunodeficiency disorders.

For evaluation of B-cell immune function, quantitation of serum immunoglobulins and isohemagglutinin titers is necessary. Results of radial diffusion studies that are two standard deviations below normal (95% confidence limits) for age- and race-matched controls can be considered indicative of hypogammaglobulinemia. In X-linked agammaglobulinemia, levels of all three major classes of immunoglobulins (IgG, IgA, IgM) are extremely low, whereas in common variable immunodeficiency, the levels are generally slightly higher. In selective IgA deficiency, only the level of IgA is extremely low or absent. In selective IgM deficiency, only extremely low levels of IgM are found. In X-linked hyper-IgM syndrome, the IgM value is normal or elevated and IgG and IgA levels are markedly decreased. With increasing identification of patients with subclass IgG deficiency (IgG1, IgG2, IgG3, and IgG4), levels two standard deviations below normal in one or more subclasses must be suspected to indicate functional immunodeficiency. Biological activity and antibody specificities for the various IgG subclasses are detailed in Tables 5–15–2 and 5–15–3, respectively. Antibody responses with selected antigens may evoke specific IgG subclass response; protein antigens preferentially elicit IgG1 subclass antibodies, and carbohydrate antigens evoke IgG2 subclass antibodies. Measurements of IgG subclasses must be interpreted cautiously. Normal healthy individuals can sometimes have clinically significant abnormalities of IgG subclasses.

To corroborate the functional abnormality of a specific IgG subclass, whether present in low or normal amounts in the proper clinical setting in patients with recurrent infections, pre- and postimmunization antibody titers to defined protein or carbohydrate antigens represent a definitive means of evaluating the integrity of the humoral immune system. Measurements of antibody levels to tetanus toxoid and *Hemophilus influenzae* type B vaccine may be obtained through various laboratories.

Differential Diagnosis

Rhinitides. To best evaluate IgE-mediated disease, allergy skin testing, examination of nasal secretions for eosinophils, and total eosinophil count with or without measurement of total serum IgE should help determine whether a patient has significant atopic disease. Chronic vasomotor rhinitis with polypoid hyperplasia or nasal polyps may lead to significant obstruction of the paranasal sinuses with repeated secondary infection. A careful otolaryngologic examination with computed tomography of the paranasal sinuses should be performed before diagnosing this condition. In addition, significant nasal septal deviation, concha bullosa defects, and sinus integrity from maxillofacial injuries can also be evaluated.

Ciliary Dysfunction. Ciliary dysfunction disorders are associated with recurrent sinusitis and bronchiectasis. In Kartegener's syndrome, sinusitis and bronchiectasis are associated with situs inversus. The diagnosis becomes evident when the cardiac shadow is in the right hemithorax. In immotile cilia syndrome, in which there is also a loss of dynein arms and poor mucociliary activity resulting in sinusitis and bronchiectasis, a nasal biopsy for electron microscopy will reveal the abnormality.

Cystic Fibrosis. Cystic fibrosis is associated with overproduction of sinus and bronchial secretions. The overproduction of thick, tenacious

TABLE 5–15–2. BIOLOGIC ACTIVITY OF IMMUNOGLOBULIN G SUBCLASSES

	IgG1	IgG2	IgG3	IgG4
Biological half-life (days)	25	23	9	25
Complement fixation	+	+	+	−
Placental transfer	+	±	+	+
Reactivity with staphylococcal protein A	+	+	+	+
Binding to FcR on monocytes	+	+	−	+
Binding to FcR on neutrophils	+	−	+	+

FcR, Fc receptor.

TABLE 5–15–3. ANTIBODY SPECIFICITIES OF HUMAN IMMUNOGLOBULIN G SUBCLASSES

	IgG1	IgG2	IgG3	IgG4
Rh (incomplete)	++++	0	+++	+
Treponema pallidum	++++	0	0	0
Teichoic acid (*Staphylococcus*)	++	++++	+	0
Bacterial polysaccharide (*Hemophilus influenzae,* pneumococcus organisms, meningococcus organisms)	0	++++	0	0
Tetanus toxoid	++++	+	+	+
DNA (lupus nephritis)	++++	+	+++	+

secretions overwhelms the ability of cilia to remove these secretions. The precise defect in cystic fibrosis is unknown, although a cystic fibrosis gene defect recently has been identified. Sweat sodium studies using iontophoresis are used to confirm this clinical disorder.

Other. Complement deficiencies (particularly terminal complement deficiencies, C5–8) and neutrophil disorders are uncommon immunologic causes of increased susceptibility to infection.

Therapeutic

The goal of treatment is to halt the end-organ damage that occurs with repeated infections. A mainstay of therapy has been the appropriate use of antibiotics, both therapeutically and prophylactically. Therapy may include ancillary antihistamines, decongestants, and intranasal steroids. In 1952, immune serum globulin was first used successfully in a young boy with agammaglobulinemia. The initial therapy was given intramuscularly, but intravenous immune globulin (IVIG) is now considered the treatment of choice for primary immunodeficiency diseases. The kinetics of IVIG are complex, and over the years there has been progressive refinement to allow the supply of greater amounts of monomeric IgG with less loss of effector function. Although IVIG contains a broad spectrum of antibodies against organisms, they are free of transmissible infectious agents, including human immunodeficiency virus. There are four commercially available preparations in the United States. The recommended dose of IVIG is 350 to 500 mg/kg per month. High-dose (500 mg/kg) IVIG therapy is indicated for acute echovirus infections. If antibodies to IgA are demonstrated, plasma from IgA-deficient donors may be secured through blood bank facilities. Systemic reactions, including dyspnea and back and flank pain with or without hypotension, occur in approximately 10% of patients. Delayed reactions, including rashes, fever, and severe anaphylactoid reactions, are much less frequent with intravenous than intramuscular administration of gamma globulin. (Gamma globulin replacement is not indicated for selective IgA deficiency.)

FOLLOW-UP

Many physicians administer 200 mg/kg IVIG every 4 weeks with antibiotics as minimal therapy. With this dosage, pulmonary function improves and irreversible pulmonary complications do not appear. Each patient should be individually studied, and initially monthly trough levels should be determined because there is variability in IgG production and catabolism. Serum IgG levels of 400 mg/dL or higher should be sought. Because most adverse reactions are relatively brief and may be associated with flow of infusion, the administration of IVIG is generally regarded to be relatively safe. Once a stable infusion procedure has been established, more and more patients receive administrations of their intravenous infusions at home through local or national home care organizations.

DISCUSSION

Prevalence and Incidence

Immunodeficiency diseases remain relatively uncommon, with a prevalence of 1 per 10,000 general population. Selective IgA deficiency occurs in 1 of 500 to 700 persons. Data regarding incidence otherwise are lacking.

Related Basic Science

Antibody-producing cells are derived from pluripotential hematopoietic stem cells in fetal life and in the bone marrow after birth. Along the course of differentiation, these hematopoietic cells eventually give rise to heavy chains on their surface. These pre-B cells eventually acquire the capacity to synthesize light chains to form IgM molecules, at which point they are then termed immature B cells with both IgM and IgD molecules on their surface. These B cells may undergo a class switch to IgG, IgA, or IgE on their membrane and eventually develop plasma cells with specific isotype secretion. In addition, there are multiple expressions of membrane-bound molecules along the B-cell maturation. Antibodies are immunoglobulin molecules with two primary functions: to bind specifically with antigen and to mediate the biological effects with antigen handling such as complement fixation and mast cell interaction for histamine release. The immunoglobulin molecules share a four-polypeptide structure. The heavy chains are encoded by genes on chromosome 14 and light-chain genes on chromosome 2. Five classes of heavy chains occur in humans. The immunoglobulin heavy-chain and light-chain genes do not encode as a continuous stretch of DNA but by gene segments. At some point in development to an immunoglobulin-producing plasma cell, a DNA rearrangement occurs.

In X-linked agammaglobulinemia, the defect lies in the inability to move from the pre-B cell to mature B cell, although the exact defect is not known. Chromosome map location of the defect is Xq21.33–22. In common variable immunodeficiency, there may be heterogeneity to the immunodeficiency: (1) intrinsic defect of the B cell to differentiate into an immunoglobulin-secreting cell in response to various stimuli; (2) after antigenic stimulation, interleukin-2 and interferon-γ mRNA expression are dramatically reduced; and (3) interleukin-2 is an important growth factor mainly produced by the activated T cell and may contribute to B-cell abnormality. In X-linked immunodeficiency with hyper-IgM syndrome, the genetic chromosome map has been localized to Xq24–27. The exact molecular mechanism responsible for hyper-IgM syndrome is not known, although a defect in the regulation of switch recombination has been implied.

In Wiskott–Aldrich syndrome, the biochemical basis for the immune and other cellular abnormalities remains unknown. An aberrant glycoprotein CD43 is found on the surface of T cells. Antigen-dependent T-cell activation is blocked, but this does not explain elevation of serum IgE or IgA or cutaneous anergy. Chromosome map location of the defect is Xp11.22–11.3.

Cytogenetic studies of ataxia telangiectasia reveal a very specific chromosome instability with multiple chromosome 7 or 14 rearrangements. The defect in this condition has been mapped to chromosome 11q22,23. Patients have an increased sensitivity to ionizing radiation. The DNA breaks involved in the production of immunoglobulin and T-cell receptor genes may explain the defect in the T-cell and B-cell immune response.

Natural History and Its Modification with Treatment

Morbidity and mortality in patients with immunoglobulin deficiencies were extremely high before the use of gamma globulin. Colonel Ogden Bruton, in 1952, described the first case of an X-linked infantile agammaglobulinemia successfully treated with gamma globulin intramuscularly. After that, the mainstay of treatment of hypogammaglobinemia was intramuscular injections of gamma globulin or fresh or frozen plasma. Then, in 1981, intravenous immunoglobulin became available. With the advent of IVIG, improved compliance and more consistent therapeutic levels could be maintained. Higher doses could be administered with fewer serious side effects. Increasing therapeutic use of IVIG

has allowed treatment of more subtle immunoglobulin functional deficiencies in which impaired antigen-specific IgG responses are demonstrated.

With replacement therapy, most patients with panhypogammaglobulinemia continue to have sinusitis, otitis, and pneumonitis, influenced in great part by past chronic infectious changes and bronchiectatic pulmonary involvement. Nevertheless, most patients report a substantially decreased number of infections and an overall improved sense of well-being. There may be an improvement in arthritis-associated and gastrointestinal-related symptoms in both agammaglobulinemia and common variable immunodeficiency. The severe echovirus-disseminated infection may be successfully ameliorated with prolonged use of high-dose IVIG (500 mg/kg). Mortality remains due to respiratory failure and cor pulmonale. Malignancy with lymphoreticular involvement is present in a small percentage of patients. Patients with Wiskott–Aldrich syndrome may benefit from IVIG if antibody synthesis is found to be defective and thrombocytopenia is present. Nevertheless, the treatment of choice is bone marrow transplantation. In ataxia telangiectasia, viral and bacterial infections may be influenced favorably by replacement IVIG because antibody response to viral and bacterial antigen is frequently abnormal.

Patients with X-linked agammaglobulinemia have survived into the third decade of life. Those with common variable immunodeficiency survive longer because their defect often begins in midlife. Those with selective IgA deficiency may have a normal life span. Patients with other selective immunodeficiencies have been insufficiently studied to determine their clinical course.

Prevention

There is no known prevention for B-cell disorders. Genetic counseling of "at-risk" females in X-linked immune deficiency disorders for carrier detection has been useful.

Cost Containment

The cost of IVIG, estimated to be $20,000 to $30,000 yearly, must be offset by use of a reduced amount of antibiotic, and the increased productive days at work or school must be considered when calculating the cost–benefit analysis. Furthermore, long-term reduction in the frequency of infections and their sequelae may lead to enhanced cost containment. Additionally, enhancement of the quality of life must be critically assessed.

It is important that patients presenting for evaluation of recurrent infections be carefully and thoughtfully investigated. IVIG is recommended only for patients with a clear history of recurrent bacterial infections and documented immunoglobulin deficiency, usually hypogammaglobulinemia.

REFERENCES

Ballow M, O'Neil KM. Approach to the patient with recurrent infections. In: Middleton E Jr, Reed CE, Ellis EF, et al, eds. *Allergy: Principles and practice.* 4th ed. St. Louis: Mosby, 1993:1027.

Fischer A, Gelfand EW, eds. Humoral immune deficiencies: X-linked agammaglobulinemia, common variable hypogammaglobulinemia, antibody deficiencies including IgA and IgG-subclasses, B-cell dysregulation, immunoglobulin substitution. *Immunodeficiency* 1993;4(1–4).

Geha RS. IgG subclass deficiencies. In: Middleton E Jr, Reed CE, Ellis EF, et al., eds. *Allergy: Principles and practice.* 3rd ed., Update 1. St. Louis: Mosby, 1991:1.

Kavanaugh AF, Huston DP. Immunoglobulin G subclass deficiency. *Insights Allergy* 1989;4(4).

Waldmann TA, Nelson DL. Inherited immunodeficiencies. In: Frank MM, Austen KF, Claman HN, Unanue ER, eds. *Samter's immunological diseases.* 5th ed. Boston: Little, Brown, 1995:387.

Serum Sickness

John A. Lust, M.D., Ph.D.

DEFINITION

Serum sickness is an immune complex-mediated hypersensitivity reaction characterized by fever, rash, edema, arthritis, and lymphadenopathy after exposure to a drug, venom, or foreign protein.

ETIOLOGY

Drug reactions are the most common cause of serum sickness today, and penicillin has become the most frequent etiologic agent. Penicillin is not ordinarily antigenic; however, it is capable of reacting chemically with body proteins to produce highly antigenic conjugates. Besides penicillins, other medications are procainamide, salicylates, streptomycin, cephalosporins, sulfonamides, barbiturates, and quinidine. Horse antithymocyte globulin, used as therapy for aplastic anemia, can cause serum sickness in humans that closely parallels the immunologic findings in animal models of serum sickness. In addition, heterologous antiserum against botulinum and *Clostridium welchii* (gas gangrene) toxins, black widow spiders, and snakes may also be etiologic agents. Hymenoptera venoms in bee stings can also cause serum sickness. More recently, serum sickness complicating streptokinase therapy for acute myocardial infarction has been observed in several patients.

CRITERIA FOR DIAGNOSIS
Suggestive

The onset of symptoms including fever, malaise, a cutaneous eruption, most often urticaria, arthralgias, lymphadenopathies, peripheral neuropathy, glomerulonephritis, or multiorgan vasculitis should make the physician consider the diagnosis of serum sickness.

Definitive

The onset of the above symptoms 7 to 14 days after exposure to heterologous serum or a drug, in association with high levels of circulating immune complexes and decreased serum C3 and C4 levels, is diagnostic of serum sickness.

CLINICAL MANIFESTATIONS
Subjective

From 1 to 3 weeks after injection of a foreign serum or exposure to an offending drug such as penicillin, there is abrupt onset of fever, arthralgia, muscle pain, nausea, and vomiting. More unusual but serious manifestations may include chest pain secondary to pericarditis, visual complaints from an optic neuritis, hypertension and lower-extremity edema secondary to nephritis, and weakness of an extremity from a unilateral mononeuritis. Serum sickness usually peaks within a few days and then subsides somewhat less rapidly over the next 1 to 2 weeks; however, clinical manifestations may develop within 12 to 36 hours on subsequent administration of the same foreign antigen. Subsequent reactions are often more severe and infrequently may even be fatal.

Objective
Physical Examination

The patient may demonstrate fever and urticarial or maculopapular skin eruptions. Urticaria may be accompanied or followed by purpura or erythema multiforme. Lymphadenopathy is first detected in the area draining the site of injection of the foreign protein, but subsequently becomes generalized. A friction rub may be audible in patients with pericarditis, and physical signs of congestive heart failure may be present. Arthritis mainly of the large joints can be observed. Neurological examination, if abnormal, most commonly reveals a unilateral mononeuritis; however, additional findings may include a Guillain–Barré syndrome, meningoencephalitis, or optic neuritis.

Routine Laboratory Abnormalities

The erythrocyte sedimentation rate is usually markedly elevated. There may be leukocytosis or leukopenia. Urinalysis may show hematuria and albuminuria. The serum creatinine may be elevated, but renal failure is rare.

PLANS
Diagnostic
Differential Diagnosis

When there is a history of exposure to a foreign protein by injection or venom, the diagnosis of serum sickness is apparent. If a vasculitis is suspected, the differential diagnosis should include other hypersensitivity, vasculitis syndromes such as Henoch–Schonlein; cryoglobulinemia; systemic lupus erythematosus; rheumatoid arthritis; Sjogren's syndrome; vasculitis associated with certain malignancies such as hairy cell leukemia; and a leukocytoclastic vasculitis associated with other underlying diseases, such as chronic active hepatitis, ulcerative colitis, infectious endocarditis, and primary biliary cirrhosis.

Diagnostic Options

Although tests that detect the presence of circulating immune complexes may not be readily available in all medical centers, several assays have been developed for clinical use. The C1q (first component of complement) binding assay will bind to immune complexes that contain immunoglobulin (Ig) G or M. Raji cell assay uses cells with a cell surface receptor for complement and is based on the fact that circulating immune complexes often contain complement components. There are also several radioimmunoassays for the detection of circulating immune complexes that contain IgG, IgM, or IgA.

Recommended Approach

A thorough history and physical examination will often allow one to identify a cause-and-effect relationship between the inciting antigen and subsequent serum sickness syndrome. Serum complement levels should be determined and may be markedly decreased. If available, circulating immune complexes measured by techniques such as the C1q binding assay and Raji cell assay should be performed and are diagnostic.

Therapeutic

Because serum sickness is a self-limited disorder, treatment is usually conservative and is directed toward making the patient comfortable until symptoms resolve. Salicylates will relieve fever and arthralgias, and antihistamines or topical steroids will control itching and dermatitis. Corticosteroid therapy is rarely necessary; however, prednisone may be required in more severe cases involving the kidneys or the central nervous system. A dose of approximately 1 to 2 mg/kg/d is appropriate, followed by a rapid taper after symptoms subside. Epinephrine is used in selected cases to control severe angioedema involving the upper airway.

FOLLOW-UP

Patients should be encouraged to avoid the etiologic drug or protein and do no require additional follow-up.

DISCUSSION
Prevalence and Incidence

The prevalence and incidence of serum sickness are unknown.

Related Basic Science

Serum sickness is the classic example of an immune complex-mediated type III hypersensitivity reaction. In the serum sickness model, the injection of antigen is followed by a slow progressive decline in the antigen level in the circulation over the first 8 days. Following this, there is a sudden acceleration in the clearance of antigen, representing the development of an immune response in the host. This results in the formation of antigen–antibody complexes (immune complexes) circulating in antigen excess and a decrease in serum complement levels. These immune complexes formed in antigen excess are most pathogenic because they are able to stimulate the complement cascade and induce the release of chemical mediators, such as vasoactive amines. At about days 12 to 14, the antigen disappears completely and free antibody is detectable. Pathologic lesions rapidly regress, and the host returns to normal over the next 1 to 2 weeks.

Natural History and Its Modification with Treatment

Serum sickness is a self-limited disorder, which typically resolves in 7 to 14 days after removal of the inciting antigen.

Prevention

Serum sickness can be prevented by avoiding those etiologic agents known to cause it. This is extremely important because the patient retains immunologic memory to have the same reactions on subsequent exposure to the same antigen. These reactions are often more severe.

Cost Containment

Medical costs are most easily minimized by prevention.

REFERENCES

Lawley TJ, Bielory L, Gascon P, et al. A prospective clinical and immunologic analysis of patients with serum sickness. N Engl J Med 1984;311:1407.

Patel A, Prussick R, Buchanan WW, Sauder DN. Serum sickness-like illness and leukocytoclastic vasculitis after intravenous streptokinase. J Am Acad Dermatol 1991;2:652.

CHAPTER 5–17

Cryoglobulinemia

John A. Lust, M.D., Ph.D.

DEFINITION

Cryoglobulinemia is a hypersensitivity vasculitis characterized by palpable purpura, usually of the lower extremities; glomerulonephritis; polyarthralgias; and peripheral neuropathy, caused by a cryoglobulin.

ETIOLOGY

Cryoglobulins are proteins that precipitate when cooled and dissolve when heated. Cryoglobulins may be classified as follows: (1) monoclonal (immunoglobulin [Ig] G, M, or A, or rarely monoclonal light chains); (2) mixed (two or more immunoglobulins, one of which is monoclonal); (3) polyclonal (no monoclonal immunoglobulin). Type II and III cryoglobulins are more common in patients with a vasculitis. Type I cryoglobulin is more typical of lymphoproliferative disease associated with a hyperviscosity syndrome, that is, Waldenström's macroglobulinemia.

CRITERIA FOR DIAGNOSIS
Suggestive

Cryoglobulinemia should be considered in any patient suspected of having a vasculitis syndrome. Purpuric lesions, often palpable, are strongly suggestive of cryoglobulinemia.

Definitive

A compatible clinical picture, a skin biopsy demonstrating a leukocytoclastic vasculitis, and a positive serum test for cryoglobulins is diagnostic.

CLINICAL MANIFESTATIONS
Subjective

Patients with cryoglobulinemia frequently complain of cutaneous lesions. Purpura usually occurs on the lower extremities and is typically raised. It can extend to the thighs, abdomen, and occasionally to the arms, but rarely to the face and trunk. The purpura may be precipitated by exposure to the cold. Raynaud's phenomenon and necrosis of the skin may occur. Involvement of the joints is symmetric and not migra-

tory. Patients may present with a peripheral neuropathy most commonly manifested by paresthesias.

Objective
Physical Examination

Purpuric lesions that are usually palpable and nonpruritic are the most common clinical finding. The purpuric lesions and cutaneous ulcers, if present, are usually found on the lower extremities. Involvement of the joints is symmetric and not migratory. Chronic deformities rarely develop. Raynaud's phenomenon can occur in the distal parts of the extremities and can lead to gangrene. Raynaud's phenomenon in the ears or nose should alert the physician to the diagnosis of cryoglobulinemia. Hepatomegaly and splenomegaly may be found in the majority of patients. Lower-extremity edema in association with hypertension may suggest an underlying glomerulonephritis. Clinical signs of a peripheral neuropathy and, rarely, a cerebrovascular accident may be present.

Routine Laboratory Abnormalities

The examination of the blood can show anemia, leukopenia or leukocytosis, thrombocytopenia, or thrombocytosis. The blood chemistry may show an elevated creatinine, an increased total protein and decreased albumin, and elevated liver function tests. The sedimentation rate is commonly elevated. Urinalysis may show hematuria and proteinuria.

PLANS
Diagnostic
Differential Diagnosis

The differential diagnosis should include other hypersensitivity vasculitic syndromes (see Differential Diagnosis for serum sickness in Chapter 5–16).

Diagnostic Options and Recommended Approach

Determination of cryoglobulins is done by obtaining 5 mL of fresh centrifuged serum, kept at 37°C, and then incubating it in an ice bath in a cold room for 24 hours. If no precipitate occurs in 24 hours, the specimen is kept at 0°C for 7 days. If a precipitate or gel is observed, the tube is centrifuged and the "cryocrit" level is read. The precipitate is washed in cold saline and is then placed in a 37°C water bath. Subsequently, immunoelectrophoresis is performed on the resuspended cryoprecipitate with monospecific antisera to IgG, IgA, IgM, kappa, and lambda. Based on this information, the cryoglobulin may be classified as type I (monoclonal), type 2 (mixed, monoclonal plus polyclonal), or type 3 (polyclonal).

Biopsy of a skin lesion or the kidney (if renal insufficiency is present) should be performed. The skin biopsy will demonstrate a leukocytoclastic vasculitis. Immunofluorescence studies may show immunoglobulin and complement in vasculitic lesions of the kidney and skin. In nearly 80% of renal biopsies, glomerular damage can be classified as diffuse proliferative glomerulonephritis with thickening of the glomerular basement membrane. Renal insufficiency, nephrotic syndrome, and end-stage renal failure may be seen. Hepatitis serologies should be obtained. Although the cause of mixed cryoglobulinemia is unknown, the majority of patients appear to have evidence of hepatitis C infection.

Therapeutic

The temperature at which the cryoglobulin precipitates is much more important than the amount of monoclonal protein. Several patients who have had 4 to 5 g/dL of a monoclonal IgG or IgM cryoglobulin that precipitated at 4°C had no symptoms whatever on exposure to cold; however, patients in whom the protein precipitated at 26°C experienced serious manifestations of cryoglobulinemia.

Patients should be instructed to avoid the cold. With progressive or recurrent disease, they may present with new purpuric lesions, an elevated creatinine, a low complement, and an increase in the urine total protein. Oral corticosteroids are the most common therapeutic agents. If there is no response, addition of cyclophosphamide, chlorambucil, or azathioprine may be helpful. Plasmapheresis has been effective in some instances for severe or rapidly progressive disease.

FOLLOW-UP

Follow-up is determined by the type of cryoglobulinemia and the severity of clinical disease. Cutaneous ulcerations require close follow-up with local and systemic care. Patients with a monoclonal protein and clinical disease with renal insufficiency and proteinuria necessitating chemotherapy require periodic monitoring of blood counts, serum creatinine, cryocrit, and urine total protein every 4 to 6 weeks. Patients with stable disease off treatment may be followed less frequently.

DISCUSSION
Prevalence and Incidence

This condition is rare.

Related Basic Science

Type I cryoglobulins are monoclonal proteins, most commonly IgM, and may be idiopathic or associated with Waldenström's macroglobulinemia or other lymphoproliferative disorders. Less frequently, patients with multiple myeloma may produce IgG or IgA cryoglobulins. Type I cryoglobulins usually do not have rheumatoid factor activity. Mixed cryoglobulins (type II), consist of a monoclonal protein, usually IgM, plus polyclonal immunoglobulins and often have rheumatoid factor activity. Type II cryoglobulinemia is associated with chronic lymphocytic leukemia and other lymphoproliferative disorders, rheumatoid arthritis and other autoimmune disorders, and infections. More than 95% of the monoclonal IgM in type II cryoglobulins has kappa light chains. In one report, 42% of patients with type II cryoglobulinemia had antibodies to hepatitis C and 84% had hepatitis C RNA. Type III or polyclonal cryoglobulinemia may also be found in association with infections such as hepatitis and connective tissue disorders. Type III cryoglobulins may demonstrate rheumatoid factor activity as well.

In cryoglobulinemia, pathologic abnormalities may result from cold exposure or from circulating immune complexes similar to that seen with serum sickness. Patients with modest amounts of monoclonal cryoglobulins, in the range 1 to 2 g/dL, may have pain, purpura, Raynaud's phenomenon, cyanosis, and ulceration on exposure to the cold from precipitation of the cryoglobulin. In addition, these immunoglobulins can combine with antigen and activate complement, leading to a cascade of inflammatory changes resulting in vasculitis. The vasculitis is responsible for most of the cutaneous, renal, rheumatologic, neurologic, and other manifestations of this disease.

Natural History and Its Modification with Treatment

The natural history depends on the type of cryoglobulin and the underlying illness. Clinical manifestations can wax and wane and spontaneous remissions may occur. Many patients with clinical disease including renal insufficiency in association with a monoclonal cryoglobulin may be effectively controlled with an alkylating agent and prednisone.

Prevention

Patients should avoid the cold. The clinical disease associated with immune complex deposition is probably not preventable.

Cost Containment

Plasma exchange should be reserved for severe cryoglobulinemia associated with vasculitis.

REFERENCES

Agnello V, Chung RT, Kaplan LM. A role for hepatitis C virus infection in type II cryoglobulinemia. N Engl J Med 1992;327:1490.
Kyle RA, Lust JA. The monoclonal gammopathies (paraproteins). In: Spiegel HE, ed. Advances in clinical chemistry. San Diego: Academic Press, 1990;28:145.

CHAPTER 5–18

AIDS (See Section 8, Chapter 76; Section 13, Chapter 44; and Section 22, Chapter 14)

CHAPTER 5–19

Antibiotic Allergy (See Section 5, Chapter 11 and Section 8, Chapter 78)

Joint and Muscle Disorders

Stephen B. Miller, M.D.

CHAPTER 6–1

Rheumatoid Arthritis

Stephen B. Miller, M.D., and Kathy Lynn, M.D.

DEFINITION

Rheumatoid arthritis is an inflammatory disorder characterized by a chronic symmetric polyarthritis, multisystemic extraarticular manifestations, and spontaneous exacerbations and remissions of disease activity.

ETIOLOGY

The etiology appears to be multifactorial with a strong immunogenetic association.

CRITERIA FOR DIAGNOSIS

Suggestive

Symmetric inflammatory involvement of the small joints of the hands and feet is a very typical early presentation. A unilateral or migratory pattern may be the predominant initial symptom. Fatigue and prolonged morning stiffness are often very prominent features. Other systemic symptoms include weakness, anorexia, malaise, weight loss, and fever.

Definitive

See Table 6–1–1.

TABLE 6–1–1. AMERICAN RHEUMATISM ASSOCIATION: 1987 REVISED CRITERIA FOR THE CLASSIFICATION OF RHEUMATOID ARTHRITIS

1. Morning stiffness lasting at least 1 hour
2. Arthritis of three or more joint areas simultaneously and observed by a physician
3. Arthritis of hand joints
4. Symmetric arthritis
5. Rheumatoid nodules
6. Serum rheumatoid factor
7. Radiographic changes typical of rheumatoid arthritis on posteroanterior hand and wrist radiographs, which must include erosions or unequivocal bony decalcification localized in or adjacent to the involved joint

For classification purposes, a patient shall be said to have rheumatoid arthritis if he or she has satisfied at least four of these criteria. Criteria 1 through 4 must have been present for at least 6 weeks.
Source: 1987 revised criteria for RA. Arthritis Rheum 1988;31:319. Reproduced from Arthritis & Rheumatism Journal, copyright 1988. Used by permission of the American College of Rheumatology.

CLINICAL MANIFESTATIONS

Subjective

The patient is often a woman in the age range 20 to 50, with the onset of pain and swelling in the small joints of the hands, wrists, and feet. There may be a family history of arthritis or an immunologic disorder. The presentation is usually insidious, often accompanied by prolonged morning stiffness, generalized fatigue, and insomnia. A common feature of the stiffness is articular gelling, which is a worsening of the stiffness with rest that improves with activity and correlates well with the activity of the illness. After limbering up in the morning with heat or exercise, the patient usually feels better as the day progresses.

Objective

Physical Examination

The most common and obvious findings are tenderness, swelling, and warmth of the involved joints. Joint effusions and painful decreased range of motion occur frequently. As the disease progresses, loss of mobility with development of fixed deformities and subluxations occurs. Accompanying this relentless inflammation is a variable loss of normal locomotor function and mobility.

Subcutaneous nodules commonly develop in areas of recurrent pressure such as the elbows. They often herald a more severe course and are associated with the development of extraarticular manifestations. The primary systems affected are the ocular, cardiopulmonary, neurologic, and vascular systems.

Ocular. Benign limited conjunctivitis or episcleritis is quite common and usually not serious; however, deeper involvement of the eye can occur with scleritis and, potentially, globe rupture and visual loss. Chronic dryness (keratoconjunctivitis sicca) often is a major contributor to the inflammatory eye problems and can itself cause loss of corneal integrity (corneal melt). When accompanied by xerostomia and parotid gland enlargement, this complex is known as Sjogren's syndrome.

Cardiopulmonary. Pleuropulmonary disease, particularly pleural effusions and interstitial fibrosis, is common. Solitary or multiple rheumatoid nodules may develop and be indistinguishable from malignancy except by biopsy. Pericarditis, although quite common, is rarely clinically significant. Myocardial and valvular involvement is also rarely of practical importance.

Neurologic. Peripheral entrapment neuropathies, especially of the median nerve (carpal tunnel syndrome), are common. Atlantoaxial subluxations causing cervical myelopathy or cord compression are potentially dreaded complications of severe aggressive chronic disease.

Vascular Rheumatoid vasculitis as manifested by small vessel arterial involvement is seen in the skin and potentially in any organ. Cutaneous lesions include nonspecific skin rashes and urticaria, digital arteritis, palpable purpura, and pyoderma gangrenosum. More serious and widespread vasculitis includes inflammation of the vasonervorum, giving rise to a potentially severe sensorimotor neuropathy that can evolve to quadriplegia. Fortunately, only a small subgroup of these patients develop a periarteritis nodosa-like picture with involvement of the mesenteric, renal, cerebral, and coronary arteries.

Routine Laboratory Abnormalities

Abnormalities in basic laboratory testing reflect the degree of active inflammation present at that time. Anemia is usually normocytic and normochromic unless complicated by blood loss with iron deficiency (normocytic hypochromic). As in other "anemias of chronic disease," defects in transfer and release of iron from the reticuloendothelial system are likely to be responsible for the chronic low-grade anemia. Leukocytes and platelets are normal, but mild to moderate thrombocytosis is often associated with very active disease. The routine chemical profile is normal except in very debilitated patients with a low total protein and albumin. Urinalysis is usually normal.

PLANS

Diagnostic

Differential Diagnosis

The insidious and variable presentations of rheumatoid arthritis allow for many diagnostic considerations. It is very important that physicians refrain from prematurely diagnosing rheumatoid arthritis. Adequate time must be given to observe the evolution of the disease process so that a definitive diagnosis and strong foundation for management can be established. The major entities strongly considered in the differential diagnosis include:

- Other connective tissue diseases (systemic lupus, scleroderma, polymyositis, and mixed connective tissue disease)
- Seronegative spondyloarthropathy (ankylosing spondylitis, psoriatic arthritis, Reiter's disease, enteropathic arthritis)
- Infectious arthritis (reactive arthritis, parvovirus, rubella, rheumatic fever, hepatitis-associated arthritis)
- Gout and pseudogout
- Polymyalgia rheumatica
- Fibrositis
- Miscellaneous (sarcoidosis, malignancy-associated arthritis, hand–shoulder syndrome)

Diagnostic Options

Although not a "diagnosis of exclusion," there is no one definitive laboratory test or procedure that conclusively identifies or excludes patients with rheumatoid arthritis. Ultimately the diagnosis is based on a comprehensive painstaking history, a meticulous physical examination with emphasis on the musculoskeletal system, and, most importantly, a period of observation of the clinical symptomatology as it evolves over the first year of disease.

The extensive diagnostic options include the following:

- Laboratory tests (sedimentation rate, rheumatoid factor, antinuclear antibody/anti-DNA, extractable nuclear antigens (RNP,SM), HLA-B27, antistreptolysin-O titer, angiotensin converting enzyme
- Synovial fluid analysis
- X-rays of affected joints
- Bone scan
- Synovial biopsy of affected joint

Recommended Approach

As previously emphasized, time is the critical factor in ultimately making a correct diagnosis of rheumatoid arthritis. Many of the diagnostic entities that are considered in the differential diagnosis can be quickly eliminated using time as an initial foundation. The other essential aspect of the diagnosis of rheumatoid arthritis is the objective evidence of chronic synovial proliferation.

A classic presentation of bilateral small joint objective inflammation of the hands, wrists, and feet observed over at least 3 to 6 months should strongly suggest the diagnosis. Prolonged morning stiffness, fatigue, an elevated sedimentation rate, and positive rheumatoid factor are also helpful. Synovial fluid analysis may show an uninfected inflammatory fluid but x-rays, bone scanning, and synovial biopsy are not likely to be of value in the early phases of diagnosis.

Chronicity and the development of synovial proliferation are basic to eliminating a number of acute and subacute disorders. These include septic arthritis (joint aspiration and culture), acute and subacute episodes of gout and pseudogout (crystal analysis of the synovial fluid), and acute rheumatic fever (positive strep culture, elevated antistreptolysin-O titer, etc.).

Diseases characterized primarily by soft tissue subjective symptoms, namely, polymyalgia rheumatica and fibrositis, can likewise be eliminated. The elderly patient with proximal soft tissue pain and a high sedimentation rate most likely has polymyalgia rheumatica, whereas the young or middle-aged woman with nonspecific soft tissue trigger points most likely has fibrositis.

Characteristic findings of specific connective tissue diseases should become increasingly obvious as the duration of observation increases. Young women with systemic features including rash, arthralgia, fever, anemia and leukopenia, and serologic evidence of a positive antinuclear antibody and anti-DNA most likely have active systemic lupus. Progressive skin tightness, Raynaud's phenomenon, and dysphagia should suggest a diagnosis of scleroderma. Proximal muscle weakness and elevated muscle enzymes with a myopathic electromyogram and positive muscle biopsy confirm the diagnosis of inflammatory muscle disease. Mixed connective tissue disease requires a positive RNP-extractable nuclear antigen for this classification of disease.

The seronegative spondyloarthropathies, in addition to classic ankylosing spondylitis, have characteristic multisystem involvement which establishes the diagnosis. The HLA-B27 antigen is helpful diagnostically in these disorders. The clinical picture of sarcoidosis is quite characteristic and an elevated angiotensin converting enzyme level should confirm this diagnosis. Hand–shoulder syndrome is a clinical diagnosis of progressive restriction unilaterally or bilaterally in the shoulder and hand that can follow a myocardial infarction or be idiopathic. No specialized testing is required to make the diagnosis. Finally, a host of nonspecific, self-limited, viral illnesses will be eliminated after resolution of symptoms in a few weeks.

In summary, the best approach to making a correct diagnosis of rheumatoid arthritis is to observe the patient closely over at least 3 to 6 months and often as long as a year. Indiscriminate and esoteric testing and procedures add considerable confusion and misdirection in the process of unraveling the correct diagnosis of this inflammatory arthropathy.

Therapeutic

Therapeutic Options

The therapeutic options include general measures, physical and occupational therapy, nonsteroidal antiinflammatory drugs, disease-modifying drugs, corticosteroids, and surgery.

Recommended Approach

A multidisciplinary approach to managing rheumatoid arthritis is absolutely necessary to provide the rheumatoid patient pain relief and maintenance of as normal daily functioning as possible. This "team concept" frequently will require the expertise of an orthopaedic surgeon, podiatrist, physical and occupational therapist, pharmacist, specialized nurse, and social worker.

Unlike many other rheumatic diseases, which are often of short duration and self-limited, the chronic inflammatory activity of rheumatoid arthritis is relentless, thereby requiring daily suppressive antiinflammatory long-term treatment. Therapeutic regimens should be aimed at producing the most benefit with the least toxicity and should be individualized for each patient. Initial priorities should emphasize patient and family education and the establishment of a strong doctor–patient relationship built on mutual respect and trust. Relief of pain, stiffness, and fatigue is an achievable early goal, whereas maintenance and quality of life are the major long-term objectives.

Once a comprehensive foundation of daily range-of-motion exercises, proper nutrition, and planned rest periods has been established,

an evaluation of additive pharmacologic therapy is indicated. Major factors to consider include age, gastrointestinal history, comorbidity, and duration and aggressiveness of disease.

The nonsteroidal antiinflammatory drugs (NSAIDs) represent the usual initial pharmacologic agents for day-to-day symptomatic suppression of pain, stiffness, and objective signs of joint inflammation. Unfortunately, available evidence demonstrates that NSAIDs, including salicylates, do not alter the natural disease process; however, they are very useful long-term medications with mild to moderate antiinflammatory activity. They also have analgesic and antipyretic properties such that significant pain and fever can sometimes be masked.

For most of the hundred years since its discovery, salicylates (aspirin) have been the standard NSAID. In the last two decades, however, numerous NSAIDs have been marketed worldwide, and many of the disadvantages of chronic salicylates have been overcome. The major practical problem is the very high round-the-clock dosing necessary to achieve equivalent adequate inflammatory suppression. Coupled with a much higher incidence of significant symptomatic gastritis and gastrointestinal bleeding, the advantage of very low cost is offset.

Adverse effects common to all NSAIDs include rashes, headaches, and peripheral edema. Reversible renal insufficiency occurs primarily in the elderly with preexisting renal disease. These untoward reactions are likely to be due to inhibition of normal physiologic functioning mediated by prostaglandins. Concurrent use of NSAIDs with coumadin may raise the prothrombin time and is an absolute contraindication with salicylates. Lithium and digoxin levels must be closely monitored when using NSAIDs.

There are many types of salicylate preparations, including enteric-coated, nonacetylated, and timed-release preparations. The same opportunity for individuality exists in the nonsalicylate NSAID market, including generics and short- or long-acting products. A nonrheumatologist cannot be expected to become very familiar with each new NSAID and its specific toxicity. Rather, the physician should become familiar with a few NSAIDs with different half-lives and learn when and how to use them most efficiently. Monitoring of complete blood count, platelets, and renal function is especially important at initiation of therapy and at 3- to 6-month intervals.

Commonly used short-half-life NSAIDs include ibuprofen (Motrin), flurbiprofen (Ansaid), ketoprofen (Orudis), indomethacin (Indocin), diclofenac (Voltaren), etodolac (Lodine), and tolmetin (Tolectin).

Commonly used long-half-life NSAIDs include naprosyn (Naproxen), piroxicam (Feldene), sulindac (Clinoril), nabumetone (Relafen), and oxaprozin (Daypro) (See Table 6–9–1).

Recent reevaluation of the long-term success of accepted traditional treatment regimens has unfortunately revealed a very gloomy picture. The disconcerting findings demonstrate that many patients are not aggressively treated early enough in the disease. Stronger medications that are more likely to induce remission are therefore given too late to modify the devastating consequences of unsuppressed chronic inflammation. The conventional wisdom has been to manage the rheumatoid patient by using a standard treatment pyramid of moving up the therapeutic ladder with increasingly more potent and more toxic medications necessary to combat the aggressive course of the disease. The major problem appears to be that taking these steps sequentially has delayed effective use of more potent single or combinations of medications much earlier in the course of the disease.

The "when" to initiate early aggressive treatment and "to whom" are critical and often difficult physician decisions. To induce a long-term remission, these disease-modifying drugs ideally should be used before radiographic evidence of erosive disease has occurred. Identifying patients early in the course of their disease that demonstrate poor prognostic indicators helps to support the use of more aggressive early treatment. Poor prognostic indicators include the presence of high-titer rheumatoid factor, extraarticular manifestations, and rapid functional disability. Other cofactors for more aggressive disease include lack of formal education, low socioeconomic status, men with onset of disease at a young age, and patients with many joints involved early in the disease.

A few words of caution are necessary. Although as a group, disease-modifying drugs are "considered" remittive, when critically analyzed the data are not available to verify strongly the conclusion that the long-term natural history of the disease is favorably affected. Another caveat is that all the disease-modifying drugs have much more potential for serious toxicity.

In summary, the "window of opportunity" is early in the disease (6–24 months), when failure to respond to a maximum conservative program has been established, and there is radiographic evidence of erosive disease or the development of serious systemic extraarticular manifestations.

Hydroxychloroquine (Plaquenil) and sulfasalazine (Azulfidine) are considered less potent disease-modifying drugs, and often one of these will be added to the nonsteroidal program. The choice of which of these to initiate is empiric and depends largely on the training, personal experience, and choice of the physician.

Hydroxychloroquine is an antimalarial drug whose mechanism of action is unknown. Initial dosage is 400 mg per day for 4 to 6 weeks, followed by 200 mg per day maintenance. Improvement may take 3 to 6 months, but response is usually favorable in 6 to 8 weeks. The major concern is retinopathy in the form of macula degeneration, which is very rare if the daily dose is below 400 mg and is rare even at 400 mg a day. Routine ophthalmology visits, usually at 6 to 12-month intervals, are instituted. Skin rashes and photosensitivity are common, but more serious toxic effects are rare.

Sulfasalazine is a drug that has been used for many years for the treatment of inflammatory bowel disease. Its mechanism of action in the treatment of rheumatoid arthritis remains unknown. The main side effects are gastrointestinal, including nausea, vomiting, and abdominal pain, but usually if there are any symptoms, they are quite low grade. Dosage is usually begun at 500 mg twice a day and increased by 500 mg per day over the next 2 to 4 weeks as tolerated to a therapeutic response. Usually, 2 to 3 g a day is required for a good clinical remission. Baseline complete blood count, chemical profile, and urinalysis should be done when using either of these drugs and about 1 month later. Monitoring can be at 3-month intervals, as marrow suppression with either hydroxychloroquine or sulfasalazine is rare.

Continuing evidence of aggressive active disease requires consideration of the potentially most potent immunosuppressive drugs. In the last 5 years, methotrexate has assumed a position of increasing prominence in the therapeutic armamentarium. It has become the disease-modifying drug of choice, largely replacing gold therapy (chrysotherapy), which had been the foundation of the therapeutic pyramid for 40 years. Although methotrexate is an antifolate, its mechanism of action is still unclear. Advantages over traditional chrysotherapy include oral versus parenteral administration, a much quicker response often in 4 to 6 weeks, and considerably less potential for side effects and serious toxic effects. Studies evaluating outcome measures such as radiographic erosive disease and functional class are suggesting a true disease modification. As worldwide experience grows, the true long-term value of methotrexate will become clear.

Methotrexate is usually given weekly, beginning with 7.5 mg taken over a 24-hour period 1 day per week and escalated if necessary to 15 to 20 mg per week. Many patients do very well taking 7.5 mg per week. Side effects are usually quite minimal, and serious toxic effects are rare. Patients may experience some low-grade nausea or anorexia for about a day after the weekly dosage. Monitoring of blood counts for cytopenias and transaminase elevations is usually done at 1 to 2-month intervals after baseline values are established.

The issue of hepatic toxicity with the potential development of cirrhosis has received widespread attention over the last 20 to 30 years. Prior to the last 5 years, a baseline liver biopsy was required and periodic biopsies were done after accumulation of total drug over 3 to 4 years. Recent meticulous review of the U.S. experience has shown that significant liver toxicity requiring cessation of methotrexate is extremely rare. Hepatic enzymes may not truly reflect the toxicity, but at this time persistent elevations of two to three times normal usually require temporary or sometimes permanent cessation of drug. Liver disease is a contraindication to methotrexate use and abstinence from alcohol is required. Diabetes and morbid obesity may be relative contraindications because of the potential for a steatotic liver.

Chrysotherapy as discussed above is increasingly being replaced by methotrexate as the disease-modifying drug of choice for early aggressive rheumatoid disease. Despite a recent pessimistic viewpoint as to the effectiveness of long-term gold use, however, many patients have been taking gold injections for decades and have actually done well. These patients should therefore not automatically be switched to methotrexate.

Heavy metals have a tradition of valuable therapeutic uses in modern medicine, but as with so many medications the actual mechanism of action is unknown. Gold must be laboriously accumulated by weekly injections, beginning with a test dose of 10 mg that within 2 weeks is increased up to a fixed dose of 50 mg per week. Clinical improvement usually cannot be anticipated until a total dose of 600 to 800 mg has been accumulated. If the response is good, the dosage frequency is reduced so that after 3 to 6 additional months, a patient often will be on a monthly maintenance of 50 mg intramuscularly. Orally administered gold (Ridaura) has been available for a number of years, but its therapeutic effectiveness has been disappointing compared with the injectable forms. Gold can be quite toxic, especially early in the treatment course, and weekly complete blood count and urinalysis monitoring for bone marrow suppression and proteinuria is mandatory. Minor sun-sensitive rashes and stomatitis are common, but reduction or holding of drug may be indicated to guard against potentially very serious generalized desquamation. Once these reactions have subsided, the drug can be reinstituted at its previous dosage.

Penicillamine is a chelating agent; however, its mechanism of action in rheumatoid arthritis is unknown. It was used extensively in the late seventies and early eighties, but toxicity and increasingly positive results with methotrexate have dramatically curtailed its use. The initial dosage scheduled was empirically defined and clearly was too toxic. Ultimately a "go very low, go very slow" regimen has evolved, which begins with 250 mg and adjusts upward in increments of 125 mg about every 2 months to a total of 750 to 1000 mg daily. Benefit usually is not appreciated before a few months. Monitoring monthly after stabilization of dose is mandatory. This includes complete blood count, urinalysis, and chemical profile. Penicillamine is a strange drug in that it may be associated with the induction of immune syndromes including Goodpasture's, systemic lupus, polymyositis, and myasthenia gravis. A common (20%) side effect usually occurring at about 6 to 8 weeks is a loss of taste. This is very disturbing to the patient, but consistently is reversible even without discontinuation of drug. Many patients, however, are so uncomfortable that they elect to discontinue the drug. Penicillamine should only be taken on an empty stomach and usually is not given in combination with another disease-modifying drug.

Cyclophosphamide (Cytoxan) and azathioprine (Imuran) are two immunosuppressive drugs that have been used with favorable outcomes in critical clinical situations. The most serious of these is life-threatening vasculitis, with involvement of multiple organ systems or progressive motor neuropathy leading to quadriplegia. Intravenous cyclophosphamide has shown favorable results in very high "pulse" doses over a few days, followed by monthly maintenance pulses. Unfortunately, the potential price paid for its use may be an increased incidence of malignancy, gonadal fibrosis, and severe hemorrhagic cystitis.

Azathioprine is less toxic and far less potent than cyclophosphamide. Its use is usually at the methotrexate level, but response rates and outcome measures are not as consistently impressive.

No discussion of the treatment of rheumatoid arthritis could be complete without discussing the use of corticosteroids. As is well known, corticosteroids are useful and commonly prescribed in two main situations:

- When disease activity is incapacitating during an induction period of a new disease-modifying drug (bridge therapy)
- In an acute, high-dosage, short tapering course for a persistent joint or systemic flare-up

The most serious long-term problems are accelerated osteopenia, avascular necrosis, cataracts, and diabetes. There remains no evidence that steroids favorably alter the natural history of the disease. In addition, many patients become dependent on low-dose prednisone and can never be weaned off it. Joint injections, if done sparingly every 3 to 6 months, may be very helpful.

Soft tissue surgery early in the disease, as well as reconstructive, total joint replacement and cervical spine surgery later in the disease, are very important positive steps in maintaining a comfortable functional patient.

FOLLOW-UP

Follow-up of the rheumatoid patient can be divided in two phases: an early diagnostic phase, and a long-term monitoring of disease activity and medications.

The initial presentation and symptom complex is often vague and the establishment of the diagnosis of rheumatoid arthritis can be time consuming and frustrating. Close observation with frequent office visits looking for additional clues to the diagnosis is often necessary. Physical examinations should be done very carefully and fluctuating laboratory tests suggestive of active inflammation (complete blood count and sedimentation rate) should be monitored. Repeat rheumatoid factor need not be done and baseline yearly x-rays are adequate.

Once the diagnosis has been established and a plan of treatment initiated, the patient's clinical and laboratory parameters should be routinely followed. The physician needs always to be vigilant in recognizing new areas of disease that may mandate a change in the basic treatment program. Disease-modifying drugs have their own specific schedules for safe monitoring as discussed previously. Finally, the patient should be encouraged to alert the physician if new concerns or questions arise. A phone call may suffice or an unscheduled office visit may be required. It must be remembered that the combination of the immunologic defects inherent in rheumatoid arthritis and the chronic use of potent immunosuppressive medications make the rheumatoid patient particularly susceptible to superimposed, often disguised comorbidity, for example, infection.

DISCUSSION
Prevalence

Rheumatoid arthritis occurs in about 1 to 3% of the general population. Female-to-male predominance is approximately 2:1 to 3:1, and the prevalence of the disease increases in both sexes with age. Onset is common between the ages of 20 and 45 years. It is worldwide in distribution and has been found in every ethnic or racial group that has been studied.

Related Basic Science
Immunogenetics

Rheumatoid arthritis is probably more than one disease and actually represents a group of conditions in which aberrant immunologic activity is likely to be involved. This "autoimmune" disease has a complex multifactoral cause that is both genetic and nongenetic. Host immune responses and their triggering by unknown target antigen(s) is a major schema that needs to be unraveled. Considerable progress has already been made in uncovering some of the genetic factors associated with rheumatoid arthritis.

Strong associations have positively associated susceptibility to rheumatoid arthritis with the major histocompatibility complex, human leukocyte antigen (HLA). The genes map to the class II region of the short arm of chromosome 6. HLA-DR4 is typically associated with a fourfold risk in caucasians. A second haplotype confirming susceptibility is HLA-DR1. The association with DR1 is clearly less strong than with DR4, but in certain populations DR4 may not be associated and DR1 may be associated. Further research has shown that there is a differential association of rheumatoid arthritis with different subtypes of DR4. This has been explained by the finding of differences in the amino acid sequences of the DR4 subtypes that are positively associated with the disease compared with those that are not. Differences between these subtypes are entirely confined to the third allelic hypervariable region of the DR β_1 chain. As little as a single amino acid substitution can abolish susceptibility, while change in a subtype may not change the susceptibility at all. Current research and genetic mapping techniques are underway to determine which HLA-DR allelic combinations confer not only increased susceptibility to rheumatoid arthritis but also severity of the disease. At this time, the available evidence strongly supports the DR4 association as a marker for disease severity, including particularly extraarticular manifestations.

Nongenetic Considerations

Despite this increasing evidence of immunogenetic influence, the great unknown remains the nongenetic component of susceptibility toward rheumatoid arthritis. Infectious agents have long been suspected of being antigenic triggers for rheumatoid arthritis, yet no organism has been cultured. Any component of a virus or bacteria can illicit an inflammatory antigenic response. Epstein–Barr virus, parvovirus, cytomegalovirus, and rubella have been extensively studied, but a convincing relationship has been unrewarding.

Heat-shock proteins have also been studied as possible etiologic agents but the evidence for association with rheumatoid arthritis is also circumstantial.

Once the genetically susceptible host has developed clinical evidence of rheumatoid arthritis, a massive inflammatory and immune response ensues. The normal synovial membrane is the initial site of the histologic pathology in rheumatoid arthritis. Normally, the synovium is a thin membrane that is one or two cells thick. Once the disease process is triggered, the synovium is infiltrated by lymphocytes, plasma cells, and polymorphonuclear leukocytes. This noninvasive structure is transformed into a hypertrophic, hypervascular invasive structure (pannus) capable of destroying articular cartilage and, ultimately, bone. This chronic synovial proliferation is the hallmark of rheumatoid arthritis.

The lymphocytes and plasma cells packed into the invading pannus synthesize large amounts of immunoglobulins. B-cell subsets become activated and committed to production of an immunoglobulin (Ig) M antibody specifically directed against the Fc portion of IgG. This IgM is so-called classic rheumatoid factor, but IgG and IgA rheumatoid factors, although of less importance, can also be formed. Rheumatoid factors form complexes with IgG in both the joint and the circulation. The extensive production and distribution of these immune complexes is critical in the development of severe inflammation locally and systemically. The complexes activate complement, initiating chemotaxis and the subsequent inflammatory cascade. Within the joint, polymorphonuclear leukocytes ingest these complexes, releasing lysosomal enzymes into the joint fluid, which, accompanied by further autolytic release as cell death occurs, markedly accelerates the inflammatory response. The circulating immune complexes may precipitate in vessel walls, giving rise to an inflammatory response in the form of a vasculitic syndrome with specific manifestations related to the organ system involved.

Natural History and Its Modification with Treatment

The onset of disease and pattern of presentation are extremely variable, but some generalizations can be made. Gradual onset is most common, usually representing more than 70% of patients. A much smaller group of about 15% of cases present with acute articular symptoms. Unfortunately, only a small subgroup presents with an initial flare and a prolonged remission.

The large majority of patients demonstrate a polycyclic pattern with a prolonged destructive course characterized by periods of remission and exacerbation. These patients usually remain functional with some joint deformity and decreased function. Extraarticular manifestations do occur, but are usually not disabling or life threatening. The other subset of patients have a progressive disease pattern characterized by relentless destruction and deformities of joints. These patients may experience life-threatening extraarticular complications, as well as severe toxic effects from long-term aggressive treatment with corticosteroids.

The mortality in rheumatoid arthritis has received considerable scrutiny and attention recently. Patients with uncomplicated disease have a significantly increased mortality compared with a matched population. Patients with more severe disease and particularly with associated extraarticular features may have a mortality comparable to that of some malignant diseases or coronary artery disease. Therefore, advanced rheumatoid arthritis should be viewed as a potentially lethal disease. Identifying high-risk patients early in their disease and instituting aggressive therapy are the keys to improving the long-term functional outcome and quality of life of rheumatoid patients.

Prevention

At this time, rheumatoid arthritis cannot be prevented.

Cost Containment

The cost of caring for the rheumatoid patient is high and potentially devastating. The chronicity and severity of the disease often result in loss of livelihood and subsequent, very costly disability. Requirements for frequent office visits and laboratory monitoring as well as huge monthly pharmaceutical bills further compound the severe financial drain. Frequent and specialized immunologic testing and x-rays are of little practical help and should be avoided. Recurrent arthrocentesis fluid need not be sent for full laboratory analysis unless there is concern for superimposed infection.

Hospital costs, which continue to spiral upward at an alarming pace, can be kept down with careful scrutiny of the potential benefits versus risks of hospitalization. Depression of acute flare-ups can often be handled as an outpatient, as can most arthroscopic procedures. When hospitalization is indicated, such as for disabling flare-ups or total joint replacements, a coordinated team approach is likely to attain uncompromising excellence in the shortest length of stay.

Finally, patients well educated in their disease can be very helpful in controlling cost. They should understand the importance of keeping themselves as healthy as possible by maintaining a nutritionally sound diet, following the recommended exercise and rest program, and complying faithfully with their medications. For example they should be alert to certain key signs of possible toxicity, such as a dark stool secondary to gastrointestinal bleeding, and report them to the physician so they can be handled earlier and costly and potentially fatal complications can be avoided.

REFERENCES

Brooks PM, Day RO. Nonsteroidal antiinflammatory drugs: Differences and similarities. N Engl J Med 1991;324:1716.

Kremer JM, Lee KJ. The safety and efficacy of the use of methotrexate in long-term therapy for rheumatoid arthritis. Arthritis Rheum 1986;29:822.

Pincus T, Callahan LF. Predictive value of quantitative physical and questionnaire measures of functional status for 9-year morbidity in rheumatoid arthritis. J Rheumatol 1992;19:1051.

Spector TD. Rheumatoid arthritis. In: Hochberg MC, ed. Epidemiology of rheumatic diseases. Rheum Dis Clin North Am 1990;16:513.

Wordsworth BP, Bell JI. The immunogenetics of rheumatoid arthritis. In: McDevitt HO, ed. Seminars in immunopathology. Berlin: Springer, 1992;14:59.

CHAPTER 6–2

Rheumatoid Lung Disease (See Section 13, Chapter 31)

CHAPTER 6–3

Ankylosing Spondylitis

Stephen B. Miller, M.D.

DEFINITION

Ankylosing spondylitis is a chronic inflammatory disorder characterized by spinal arthropathy and often associated with peripheral articular and extraarticular systemic involvement.

ETIOLOGY

A specific cause for ankylosing spondylitis has not as yet been elucidated. Increasing investigative evidence, however, strongly suggests an immunogenic mechanism (HLA-B27) is directly involved in a significant subset of patients with ankylosing spondylitis.

CRITERIA FOR DIAGNOSIS

Suggestive

Atraumatic, poorly localizable low back pain that begins insidiously in a young person suggests the diagnosis. The pain characteristically increases at rest, improves with activity, and has been present longer than 3 months.

Definitive

Radiographic evidence of bilateral sacroiliitis with or without spondylitis confirms the diagnosis.

CLINICAL MANIFESTATIONS

Subjective

The patient is usually younger than 40 and is more commonly male than female. Most often the onset of disease is axial with nonspecific low back aching. Low back injury or radiation into the legs is denied, and the pain often has been present for a few months. Bilateral hip and/or shoulder involvement is quite common. Onset of disease with asymmetric peripheral large joint inflammation or chest wall or anterolateral rib pain is sometimes encountered. A systemic presentation with primarily extraarticular features is infrequent, but may occur particularly with inflammatory eye symptoms. There may be a history of a family member, particularly a father or brother, with ankylosing spondylitis or some type of "spine arthritis."

Objective

Physical Examination

The findings on physical examination depend largely on the duration and aggressiveness of disease activity. Important clues to the diagnosis can be found by carefully examining the sacroiliac joints and lumbar spine.

Early in the disease, tenderness overlying the sacroiliac joints is often present; but this is quite variable. This is best appreciated by having the patient stand erect and bend forward while direct pressure is applied bilaterally with the thumbs to the sacroiliac regions. Various additional maneuvers have been described to elicit sacroiliac pain, however, with variable success. As the disease advances, sacroiliac tenderness becomes increasingly difficult to demonstrate.

Lumbar spine evaluation includes noting paravertebral muscle tenderness secondary to spasm, which is often present. Consistent abnormalities can be documented by assessing lumbar spinal mobility. Forward flexion with the knees locked demonstrates inability to touch the floor with the fingertips. Confirmation can be quantified by measuring a reduction in flexion by the Shober test. This well-accepted maneuver is done with the patient standing erect and the examiner marking the skin over the spinous process of the fifth lumbar vertebra and 10 cm above. Maximal forward flexion is attempted and normally should extend to 15 cm. A baseline of spinal restriction can then be recorded. Lateral bending and hyperextension will also be compromised.

An additional early physical sign of ankylosing spondylitis reflects the inflammatory involvement of the costochondral and costovertebral articulations. Chest expansion measured at the nipple line is less than normal, which is 5 cm or greater. Other nonaxial inflammatory interfaces (entheses) between tendon and bone include the tendinous insertions at the Achilles–calcaneal insertion and the plantar fascia insertion at the calcaneal tuberosity.

As the disease advances beyond the early inflammatory stage, characteristic structural changes are increasingly apparent. A characteristic posture develops as the lumbar spine becomes less flexible and involvement extends up the spine. Thoracic kyphosis gradually advances with flattening of the anterior chest, forward carriage of the head (measured by an increased distance between the occiput and wall on standing erect), and protuberant abdomen. In a practical sense, the only reasonable likelihood of seeing an extraarticular manifestation on physical examination would usually be a unilateral inflamed eye.

Routine Laboratory Abnormalities

Routine laboratory testing is quite unimpressive. Anemia usually is not present and, if so, is low grade and functionally insignificant. Chemical profiles and urinalysis are normal and a sedimentation rate and other acute-phase reactants are either normal or mildly elevated and correlate poorly with disease activity.

PLANS
Diagnostic
Differential Diagnosis

Low back pain may have nonspondylitic causes (see Chapter 6–21); may be due to spondylarthropathies (see Chapters 6–4 to 6–6); or may be caused by other disorders, such as ankylosing hyperostosis (Forestier's disease) and osteitis condensans ilii.

Diagnostic Options

Laboratory testing comprises a complete blood count, chemical profile, urinalysis, and HLA-B27 typing (optional). X-ray studies include films of the sacroiliac joints and lumbosacral spine (cervical and/or thoracic spine if clinically indicated) and arthrocentesis (if clinically indicated).

Recommended Approach

In the clinical setting of a patient younger than 40 with the insidious onset of atraumatic low back pain persisting beyond a few months, the diagnosis is often not difficult. The major differential issue is to eliminate mechanical back pain from suspected inflammatory pain; in particular, improvement with rest and worsening with exercise are strong differential points in favor of the former. Clinical suspicion can usually be confirmed by physical findings and radiographic evidence of sacroiliitis. Extensive additional laboratory and radiologic testing such as bone scans, computed axial tomography scans, and magnetic resonance imaging is extraneous and not indicated. As indicated above, testing for HLA-B27 antigen is optional, but may be indicated in circumstances where the patient may want more specific information related to possible genetic susceptibility and counseling. As sacroiliitis alone or associated with spondylitis often occurs in the setting of a "secondary" disease in the spondylarthropathy group, evidence should be sought historically and on physical examination for psoriasis, Reiter's syndrome, or inflammatory bowel disease (see Chapters 6–4 to 6–6). Additional specific diagnostic testing, for example, skin biopsy and upper gastrointestinal tract series, would then be carried out if indicated.

Therapeutic
Therapeutic Options

Therapeutic options include education; pharmacotherapy, for example, nonsteroidal antiinflammatory drugs, sulfasalazine (second-line therapy), and immunosuppressive agents (third-line therapy); physical ther-

apy; and surgery (cervical spine [fusion for C1–2 subluxation], wedge osteotomy [correction of severe kyphosis], disk space fusion [discitis], and total hip replacement).

Recommended Approach

At the time the diagnosis is established, the nature of the disease, its natural history, and possible genetic and familial implications should be discussed in depth. Emphasis should be clearly placed on the importance and central role of compliance with an intensive daily physical therapy program, which should begin daily and continue as an everyday part of the patient's life. The objectives of the therapeutic approach to ankylosing spondylitis include both early goals and long-term goals. Initially, the main emphasis should be placed on reduction of pain and stiffness so as to allow compliance with the prescribed exercise program. The long-term goals, in addition to maintaining symptomatic relief, are maintaining posture and as normal mobility as possible and keeping the patient gainfully employed.

If after a reasonable period of physical therapy, pain and stiffness persist and limit exercise compliance, a daily nonsteroidal antiinflammatory drug (NSAID) should be instituted. For many years, the favored medication in this group was phenylbutazone. Unfortunately, although quite rare, concern over the hematologic toxicity of phenylbutazone has greatly limited its use to only the most resistant cases. Indomethacin has also been used for many years with considerable symptomatic success, and once a stable exercise program is well underway, patients may reduce the dosage and frequency and use the sustained-release form at bedtime at a dose of 75 mg. Naproxyn sodium has a longer half-life and is also valuable for one-time dosing at bedtime. As gastrointestinal side effects are the major concern with the NSAIDs, caution should be used, particularly if the patient has a history of intolerance to this type of medication or some history of gastritis or possibly an ulcer. Many of these patients require an H_2 blocker that they take with NSAID on a full stomach. After establishment of a steady state, a trial of slowly tapering the NSAID should commence. The purpose is to find the lowest dose necessary to reduce or eliminate pain and stiffness so that the full effectiveness of the daily physical therapy program can be appreciated.

In cases where persistent inflammation continues despite maximal physical therapy and NSAIDs, sulfasalazine may be indicated. Sulfasalazine may be very helpful if begun early in the disease, after which it is usually titrated up to 1.5 to 2 g twice a day. Limited trials of immunosuppressive agents that were somewhat successful in the treatment of rheumatoid arthritis have been discouraging. In a small subset of patients a smoldering downhill course ensues with increasing disability and functional loss. Spinal surgery may be indicated to try and salvage a more erect posture so that the patient's line of sight is raised. The most common disease-related surgery is total hip replacement, which often is quite successful.

FOLLOW-UP

The need for medical observation is quite variable and depends on the severity and overall activity of the disease, as well as the need to monitor medication. Stable patients on NSAIDs should probably have routine laboratory work done about twice a year and see the physician concurrently.

DISCUSSION
Prevalence and Incidence

The prevalence of ankylosing spondylitis is estimated to be 0.50 to 1.00% of the adult Caucasian population. The annual incidence rate in the same population is 6.6 cases per 100,000. Although many more men than women are diagnosed with ankylosing spondylitis, the disease is actually not heavily weighted to males.

Related Basic Science
Genetics

HLA-B27 positivity is the likely common immunogenic link in the spondylarthropathies. How the HLA-B27 molecule is itself pathogenic is the central question, which as yet has not been answered. A number of hypotheses, however, have been advanced as the most likely mechanisms of disease:

- Infection with a microorganism triggers an immune response by CD8+ T cells.
- "Molecular mimicry" occurs between microorganisms presenting HLA-B27, such that an immune response is generated that cross-reacts with host connective tissue.
- HLA-B27, rather than the more direct associations just outlined, might program the thymus to select out certain T-cell receptors expressed on CD8+ T cells which would be clonally selective for certain microbial antigens producing an aberrant pathologic response.

Anatomic Derangement

The basic pathologic process characteristic of and unique to ankylosing spondylitis as the prototype disease in the spondyarthropathy group is known as enthesopathy. An enthesis is the site of insertion of a soft tissue structure into bone, namely, a tendon, ligament, or capsule at its anatomic connection. These changes are seen both clinically and radiographically. Clinically, pain and swelling and sometimes erythema are noted at the insertion of the Achilles tendon into the superior portion of the posterior calcaneous and the anteromedial quadrant of the calcaneous on the plantar surface corresponding to the insertion of the plantar fascia of the foot. Other symptomatic areas include the ischial tuberosities, anterior iliac crest, femoral trochanters, and spinous processes of the vertebrae. Radiographically, early changes include fuzzy proliferative findings such as spur formation; as the disease progresses, erosive changes develop. The characteristic lumbar spine abnormalities of squaring of the vertebrae are due to enthesitis at the superior and inferior corners of the vertebrae, which look fuzzy initially and clearly eroded later, giving rise ultimately to the classic bamboo spine.

Natural History and Its Modification with Treatment

Fortunately, most patients do quite well without aggressive treatment. Favorable factors include early diagnosis, practical education, and compliance with a comprehensive physical therapy program. Exacerbations and remissions punctuating low-grade inflammatory symptoms are commonly seen early in the disease. Time often stabilizes the pattern of involvement, with most patients maintaining their personal and professional independence. The great majority of patients carry out a daily exercise program and require either no drug therapy or an NSAID as needed. Unfortunately, a small subgroup of patients suffer unrelenting inflammation requiring maximal antiinflammatory medication and reconstructive surgery on the spine, hips, or both. An uncommon complication of ankylosing spondylitis is spinal fracture with relatively mild or no obvious trauma. An unexplained increase in pain, particularly in the cervical spine region, should alert the physician to consider an occult cervical fracture. Significant morbidity from extraarticular manifestations is fortunately rare, but occasionally severe aortitis with aortic regurgitation may require valve replacement.

Prevention

Ankylosing spondylitis cannot be prevented.

Cost Containment

Familiarity with the disease and a careful history and physical examination are essential to diagnosis. X-ray evidence of sacroiliitis and institution of a compulsory daily physical therapy program sometimes assisted by NSAIDs are the basis of evaluation and treatment. Expensive, relatively esoteric further testing and treatment are not indicated.

REFERENCES

Ahearn JM, Hochberg MC. Epidemiology and genetics of ankylosing spondylitis. J Rheumatol 1988;15(suppl 16):22.

Calin A, ed. Spondylarthropathies. Orlando, FL: Grune & Stratton, 1984.

Khan MA, ed. Spondyloarthropathies. Rheum Dis Clin North Am 1992;18:1.

Khan MA, van der Linden SM. A wider spectrum of spondyloarthropathies. Semin Arthritis Rheum 1990;20:107.

Resnick D, Niwayama G. Ankylosing spondylitis. In: Resnick D, Niwayama G, eds. Diagnosis of bone and joint disorders. Philadelphia: Saunders, 1981:1040.

CHAPTER 6–4

Arthritis Associated with Inflammatory Bowel Disease

Peter T. Singleton, M.D.

DEFINITION

Enteropathic arthritis may be defined as any or several arthritic symptoms occurring in the setting of inflammatory bowel disease. Though descriptions of inflammatory joint changes have been best studied in ulcerative colitis and Crohn's disease, similar musculoskeletal manifestations have been described in postenteritic reactive arthritis, Whipple's disease, Behçet's syndrome, bypass arthritis–dermatitis syndrome, and gluten-sensitive enteropathy. The inflammatory arthritis associated with a defined intestinal disease may be expressed as either or all of the following:

- Type I: peripheral synovitis of active inflammatory bowel disease
- Type II: ankylosing spondylitis
- Type III: peripheral synovitis of ankylosing spondylitis
- Type IV: sacroileitis alone
- Type V: septic sacroileitis/monarticular arthritis

The peripheral synovitis occurring in consonance with active inflammatory bowel disease will most frequently be found to be self-limited and nondeforming in contrast to the peripheral synovitis of ankylosing spondylitis, which typically manifests as a chronic form marked by erosive destruction and/or ankylosis of joints. Ankylosing spondylitis is a chronic inflammatory arthritis affecting principally the axial skeleton and occurs at a substantially increased frequency in HLA-B27 carriers with inflammatory bowel disease. Sacroileitis alone in inflammatory bowel disease may or may not be related to the presence of HLA-B27 and appears to be observed equally among males and females.

ETIOLOGY

Disease-related autoimmune dysfunction has been studied both in the inflammatory bowel model as well as the musculoskeletal manifestations so frequently observed in inflammatory bowel disease. Antibodies specific for mucopolysaccharides in colon epithelial cells and antibodies to *Escherichia coli* polysaccharides that cross-react to colon antigens have been well described in ulcerative colitis. Lymphotoxic antibodies and circulating antibodies to synthetic double-stranded RNA are seen in Crohn's disease. Increased numbers of mucosal B lymphocytes bearing surface immunoglobulin G are seen in both ulcerative colitis and Crohn's disease. Cross-reactive antibodies for the *Klebsiella* organisms in B27-positive individuals have been strongly associated with ankylosing spondylitis. A long list of organisms have been associated with reactive arthritis, including *Yersinia enterocolitica* 3 and 9,

Yersinia pseudotuberculosis, Giardia lamblia, Shigella dysenteriae, Salmonella enteritidis, and a host of others associated with the postenteritic form of arthritis. Of significance, *Yersinia*-associated immune complexes containing secretory immunoglobulin A have been detected both in the circulation and in the synovial fluid of patients with postenteritic arthritis.

CRITERIA FOR DIAGNOSIS

The diagnosis is made by establishing the relationship between joint disease and inflammatory bowel disease. See Clinical Manifestations.

CLINICAL MANIFESTATIONS
Subjective

The peripheral synovitis of Crohn's disease and ulcerative colitis share the cardinal features of painful swelling in one or more joints (usually fewer than four joints are involved) occurring with active inflammatory bowel disease. Often, symptoms begin in a single joint and evolve asymmetrically as a pauciarticular arthritis. There is no sex predilection, and the frequency of peripheral synovitis in inflammatory bowel disease has been reported to be between 10 and 20%, the higher frequency being seen in Crohn's disease. The knee, ankle, elbow, proximal interphalangeal joint of the finger, wrist, shoulder, and metacarpophalangeal joint are involved in descending order of frequency. Most often, articular symptoms begin after the onset of inflammatory bowel disease. Spontaneous abatement of joint symptoms within 2 weeks to 2 months is the rule in greater than 75% of the cases.

The tendency for peripheral synovitis to flare up with exacerbations of ulcerative colitis has been well documented; this observation has not been as clearly documented in Crohn's disease. Likewise, peripheral synovitis usually abates abruptly with surgical bowel resection in ulcerative colitis, whereas postoperative flare-ups in articular symptoms may be seen in Crohn's disease. In further contradistinction to Crohn's disease, ulcerative colitis is more frequently associated with peripheral arthritis in the presence of other major extraintestinal complications, for example, psuedomembranous polyposis and perianal disease. Peripheral synovitis of ulcerative colitis and Crohn's disease most often resolves completely with no residual joint damage or functional impairment.

The spondylitis of enteropathic arthritis presents as pain and stiffness in the lower back persisting for months, often worsened by rest, and partially relieved by physical activity. The clinical manifestations and physical signs of spondylitis in inflammatory bowel disease are indistinguishable from those of classic ankylosing spondylitis. Not infrequently, the onset of spondylitis precedes the onset of inflammatory bowel disease by several years, and the course of the spinal disease remains independent of the course and/or activity of the bowel disease in ulcerative colitis and in regional enteritis. The prevalence of ankylosing spondylitis in inflammatory bowel disease has been variously estimated between 2 and 25%, the higher frequency quoted for ulcerative colitis with slight male predominance. Although less than in ankylosing spondylitis alone, spondylitis in inflammatory bowel disease is strongly associated with the HLA-B27 antigen (50–72%). Although colitic spinal disease is usually independent of the activity in the bowel inflammation, spondylitis does correlate strongly with the presence of anterior uveitis.

Objective
Type I: Peripheral Synovitis of Active Inflammatory Bowel Disease

Physical Examination. Mild to moderate erythema, heat, and swelling may be noted in one or more joints. Often, symptoms of joint pain may be out of proportion to the findings on physical examination.

Routine Laboratory Abnormalities. When effusions are noted in involved joints, synovial fluid analysis reveals mild to moderate inflammatory changes. Typically, radiographic evidence of significant juxta-articular osteoporosis and erosive changes are not seen. Protean manifestations of malaise and easy fatigability frequently reflect activity of the bowel disease as well as fever and anemia. The erythrocyte sedimentation rate is elevated, and the rheumatoid factor test is negative.

Type II: Ankylosing Spondylitis

Physical Examination. Findings are typical of sacroileitis/spondylitis. Lower back pain complaints are accompanied by clinical evidence of sacroiliac tenderness and restricted motion in the lumbosacral spine.

Routine Laboratory Abnormalities. X-ray changes revealing symmetric sacroileitis with or without marginal syndesmophytes may be seen even prior to the development of inflammatory bowel disease. Plantar spurs of the calcaneus and periosteal changes at the ischial tuberosities and at the Achilles tendon insertion (enthesopathy) are often seen in advanced disease.

Type III: Peripheral Synovitis of Ankylosing Spondylitis

Physical Examination. There is often severe inflammatory joint disease with marked soft tissue swelling and inflammatory effusions in the involved joints (especially the hip). Dactylitis of the digits in the feet may be seen; there may be shoulder involvement and, rarely, involvement of the sternoclavicular and temporomandibular joints.

Routine Laboratory Abnormalities. In advanced disease, radiographic evidence of erosive changes and ankylosis of structures may be seen. In both type II and type III enteropathic arthritis, a strong correlation is seen with the HLA-B27 antigen. The rheumatoid factor, however, is not found.

Type IV: Sacroileitis Alone

Patients with inflammatory bowel disease may show radiographic and clinical evidence of sacroileitis but it is often asymptomatic. Sacroileitis without radiographic evidence of ankylosing spondylitis is two to three times more common than ankylosing spondylitis and is not dependent on association with HLA-B27 positivity in all cases.

Type V: Septic Sacroileitis/Monoarticular Arthritis

This rare complication has been described in Crohn's disease variously with resection of distal ileum, granulomatous involvement of the urinary bladder, and septic arthritis of the hip related to direct invasion of fecal organisms.

PLANS
Diagnostic
Differential Diagnosis

The differential diagnosis of enteropathic arthritis involves chiefly the development of arthritic symptoms in a patient with inflammatory bowel disease, as well as a critical, stepwise approach to exclusion of other etiologic possibilities.

Diagnostic tests used to confirm the diagnosis and evaluate disease activity are as follows:

- *Complete blood count:* Hypochromic, microtic anemia with moderate leukocytosis is typically seen during activity of the inflammatory bowel disease (with or without arthritis).
- *Erythrocyte sedimentation rate:* This rate is elevated during disease activity.
- *Synovial fluid analysis:* This should include cell count and differential, protein, glucose, crystallography, and appropriate cultures.
- *X-ray films:* X-rays of the sacroiliac joints and anteroposterior view of the pelvis frequently show bilateral changes with "rosary bead" erosions and pseudowidening of the joint; sclerosis and ankylotic changes may be observed in late disease. Periosteal changes at the ischial tuberosities and crest of the ilium may be present. X-ray of the lumbar spine on anteroposterior and lateral views may reveal squaring of vertebral bodies early and symmetric syndesmophytes in more advanced disease. X-ray of the peripheral joints in the presence of spondylitis may reveal changes ranging from soft tissue swelling to erosion and ankylosis of joint structures.
- *Upper gastrointestinal series with views of the small bowel:* This should be done to diagnose Crohn's disease.
- *Barium enema:* The barium enema is used to diagnose ulcerative colitis.

- *Endoscopy with biopsy:* This establishes the histologic diagnosis of inflammatory bowel disease as well as the activity and extent of disease.
- *Slit-lamp ocular examination:* This should be done to diagnose anterior uveitis in the presence of eye symptoms.
- *HLA typing:* Enteropathic arthritis is a clinical diagnosis in all of its forms. Routine typing for HLA-B27 antigen is often unnecessary and may not be helpful considering the large number of B27-negative individuals with enteropathic arthritis.

Differential diagnosis of crystal-induced arthropathy (especially calcium pyrophosphate dihydrate deposition disease) and infectious arthritis is accomplished best by performing a complete synovial fluid analysis, including crystal examination and culture of the fluid specimen.

Diagnostic Options

Diagnostic options are few in approaching enteropathic arthritis. It is important to remember that a careful clinical history and thorough physical examination combined with appropriate laboratory aids are absolutely necessary to establish a firm diagnosis of arthritis associated with inflammatory bowel disease.

Recommended Approach

It is recommended that each of the elements under Differential Diagnosis be followed carefully as outlined.

Therapeutic

The management of enteropathic arthritis revolves principally around conservative measures. In the peripheral synovitis of active inflammatory bowel disease, local measures (heat, splinting, and passive range-of-motion exercises) may be helpful. Occasionally, nonsteroidal antiinflammatory agents are necessary, but caution with respect to gastrointestinal blood loss in active inflammatory bowel disease is advisable. Control of the activity of ulcerative colitis and/or Crohn's disease is the major objective in definitive management of type I enteropathic arthritis.

Enteropathic arthritis types II and III represent a more significant therapeutic challenge. Management of type II is the same as that for ankylosing spondylitis not associated with bowel disease. Type III may require joint aspiration and local injection of corticosteroids in the absence of infection, in addition to following the conservative principles outlined previously. Because of the tendency for type III to cause severe joint contractures (especially in the hip and shoulder girdles), emphasis on (range-of motion) exercises is strongly recommended so that patients with spondylarthritis can maintain good muscle tone and endurance as well as range of motion in involved joints.

Patient education is a cardinal feature of managing any acute or chronic illness. With enteropathic arthritis, it is essential that the patient be reassured that the transient synovitis related to active inflammatory bowel disease is self-linked and not associated with long-term sequelae. If spondylarthropathy is found, the patient should be counseled concerning the nature of the disease, the specific medical therapy that may be required, and the critical importance of maintaining long-term follow-up under the close supervision of a physician.

FOLLOW-UP

In all forms of enteropathic arthritis, follow-up is often dictated by the status of the bowel disease as well as the arthritis. This is especially relevant to Type I. For patients with types II and III, follow-up should be determined on the basis of patient symptoms and/or the need for additional medical and physical therapy. Generally, visits at 4- to 6-week intervals are required in early, active disease. In further advanced spondylarthropathy under successful symptomatic control, office visits may be spaced 4 to 6 months apart.

DISCUSSION
Prevalence and Incidence

European studies have shown that 50 to 100 per 100,000 individuals develop ulcerative colitis, with similar figures for Crohn's disease. Both North American and European incidence figures have risen sharply in recent years with respect to Crohn's disease. Arthritis of peripheral joints is the single most common extracolonic manifestation in inflammatory bowel disease, ranging from 10 to 20% of cases. Isolated sacroiliitis is seen in approximately 15% of individuals with inflammatory bowel disease and ankylosing spondylitis in 6%, with an equal sex distribution. In adult disease, arthritis is more frequent in inflammatory bowel disease complicated by uveitis, aphthous stomatitis, pyoderma gangrenosum, erythema nodosum, and peritoneal abscess formation.

Related Basic Science

The peripheral synovitis of active inflammatory bowel disease is characteristically associated with active bowel disease and is seen in more than 20% of patients. Histopathologic confirmation of the synovitis has been described, as has the appearance of synovial-based granulomas in Crohn's disease. Recent evidence of transmissible ineffective agents in Crohn's disease and abnormalities in cell-mediated immunity, lymphocyte cytotoxicity, and the presence of circulating immune complexes has shed new light on the underlying pathogenesis of enteropathic arthritis. Although involvement of the lower extremity joints is most frequent, any joint may be affected by the synovitis of inflammatory bowel disease. Typical of type I is self-remission within weeks to months, with no evidence of erosive joint destruction. Consistent with the tendency for peripheral synovitis to adhere temporarily to the activity of inflammatory bowel disease, surgical resection of the bowel leads to complete remission of joint symptoms in ulcerative colitis, although less predictably in Crohn's disease. Perianal abscess formation and septic arthritis may be seen (especially in Crohn's disease). Arthropathy is generally more prevalent in patients who exhibit extraintestinal manifestations, for example, mucosal ulcerations, erythema nodosum, and uveitis, as well as the local complications of perianal disease, massive hemorrhage, and colonic pseudopolyps. Peripheral synovitis of inflammatory bowel disease is negatively associated with the HLA-B27 antigen and enteropathy; Rheumatoid factor activity in the serum and joint fluid is absent. Ankylosing spondylitis with or without peripheral synovitis tends to be a more chronic, progressive arthropathy, maintaining an independent association with the activity of the inflammatory bowel disease. The onset of spondylitis frequently antedates the development of enterocolitis, and the sex ratio (male:female) has been variously estimated as 1:7 to 3:1.

Peripheral synovitis of ankylosing spondylitis is noteworthy for its predilection for large joints of the lower extremities (especially hip) and the shoulder. Similar patterns of spondylitis and peripheral synovitis may be seen in Whipple's disease, Behçet's syndrome, reactive arthritis, and small intestinal bypass syndrome. If radiographic evidence of sacroiliitis is used as the sole criterion for spondylarthropathy, the prevalence of spinal disease in Crohn's disease may approach 16.4%, with a 10 to 20% frequency of peripheral arthropathy. There are no clinicopathologic or radiographic features distinguishing enteropathic spondylitis and idiopathic ankylosing spondylitis. Surgical resection of the diseased bowel in inflammatory bowel disease has no ameliorating effects on the course or activity of sacroiliitis/spondylitis, nor on the intimate association of the spondylitis with anterior uveitis. HLA-B27 antigen shows a strong correlation with colitis-associated spondylitis (66.7%) and Crohn's associated spondylitis (52.6%). Rheumatoid factor activity is generally absent in all forms of enteropathic spondylarthropathy.

Isolated sacroiliitis is observed much more frequently than ankylosing spondylitis. Radiographically, it may appear as mild symmetric disease with no evidence of ankylosis.

Septic sacroiliitis is fortunately a rare complication, as is septic arthritis of the hip. Each calls for immediate diagnosis and specific antibiotic therapy to prevent permanent joint destruction.

Natural History and Its Modification with Treatment

The typical course of peripheral synovitis of active inflammatory bowel disease is one of fluctuating activity dependent on the activity of the underlying bowel disease. The tendency for the peripheral synovitis to self-remit with no functional sequelae is characteristic.

Ankylosing spondylitis of inflammatory bowel disease and peripheral synovitis of ankylosing spondylitis generally show a more progressive course marked by remissions and exacerbations independent of the activity of the bowel disease. Complications of enteropathic spondylarthropathy, for example, uveitis, enthesopathy, osteoporosis–osteomalacia, cauda equina syndrome, aortic incompetence, and amyloidosis may dominate clinical concerns in long-term follow-up of patients.

Though types II and III present major challenges with respect to therapy, a comprehensive approach as previously discussed and emphasis on regular physical therapy provide for significant reductions in patients' symptoms. Isolated sacroileitis frequently requires no therapy and does not lead to permanent disabilities. Septic sacroileitis/monarticular arthritis represents a curable form when diagnosis is prompt and antibiotic therapy is appropriate.

Prevention

Currently, no proven method exists to prevent inflammatory bowel disease or its associated arthropathies.

Cost Containment

Emphasis should be placed on early diagnosis of enteropathic arthritis. A stepwise approach to sound management and follow-up principles is mandatory throughout the natural history of this illness.

REFERENCES

Calin A. Seronegative spondyloarthropathies. Scientific American Medicine 1993;3(15):1.
De Vries DD, Dekker-Saeys AJ, Gyodi E, et al. Absence of autoantibodies to peptides shared by HLA-B27.5 and *Klebsiella pneumoniae* nitrogenase in serum samples from HLA-B27 positive patients with ankylosing spondylitis and Reiter's syndrome. Ann Rheum Dis 1992;51:783.
Granfors K, Jalkanen D, Lindberg AA, et al. *Salmonella* lipopolysaccharide in synovial cells from patients with reactive arthritis. Lancet 1990;335:685.
Inman TD, Johnston EA, Hodge M, et al. Postdysenteric reactive arthritis: A clinical and immunogenetic study following an outbreak of salmonellosis. Arthritis Rheum 1988;31:1377.
Jacoby RK, Newell RLM, Hickling P. Ankylosing spondylitis and trauma: The medicolegal implications: A comparative study of patients with non-specific back pain. Ann Rheum Dis 1985;44:307.

CHAPTER 6–5

Psoriatic Arthritis

Steven A. Lauter, M.D.

DEFINITION

Psoriatic arthritis is a seronegative inflammatory arthropathy involving the peripheral joints and the spine that occurs in a patient with psoriasis.

ETIOLOGY

The etiology of psoriatic arthritis is felt to be multifactorial, involving a complex interplay of genetic, immune, and environmental factors such as infectious agents and physical trauma. Genetic factors are suggested by familial aggregation. HLA-B13, -B17, and -CW6 are increased in patients with psoriasis. Most studies have demonstrated an increased incidence of HLA-B27, -B38, -B39, and -DR7 in those patients with peripheral arthritis and HLA-B27 in those with spondylitis. Increased immunity and cross-reactivity to streptococcal antigens, decreased suppressor-T-cell function, and the presence of immune complexes may also play a role.

CRITERIA FOR DIAGNOSIS
Suggestive

About 80% of the time, the arthritis develops in a patient with known psoriasis, although the skin disease may be mild and sometimes well hidden. In another 10 to 20%, arthritis and psoriasis occur simultaneously. In about 10% of patients, the arthritis occurs before the psoriasis. The onset of psoriatic arthritis is most commonly in the third or fourth decade of life (similar to rheumatoid arthritis). Unlike rheumatoid arthritis, in which women predominate, the sex ratio is nearly equal.

The onset is subacute in two of three patients and acute in the other third.

The features of psoriatic arthritis are similar to those of Reiter's syndrome, ankylosing spondylitis, and the arthritis of inflammatory bowel disease; it is therefore classified as a seronegative (rheumatoid factor-negative) spondyloarthropathy. As with the other ailments, there are clues to suspect the diagnosis:

- Asymmetric arthropathy of mostly small joints in a patient with psoriasis

- Sausagelike digits and enthesopathy (inflammation of ligaments and tendons)
- Pitting of nails in a patient with psoriasis and arthritis
- X-ray findings of bony erosions, periostitis, and osteolysis of terminal phalanges

Definitive

The diagnosis of psoriatic arthritis may be made in the presence of psoriasis with a peripheral or spinal seronegative arthritis. The arthritis may be monoarticular or polyarticular, asymmetric or symmetric, and may also produce a sausagelike swelling of a digit (dactylitis) or even a destructive arthritis known as arthritis mutilans.

CLINICAL MANIFESTATIONS
Subjective

Both psoriasis and psoriatic arthritis are more common in first-degree relatives of patients with psoriatic arthritis than in the general population; however, it is likely that environmental factors may affect the clinical expression. Among these factors are local trauma and bacterial growth on the skin.

The articular symptoms of psoriatic arthritis may appear gradually in two of three patients and have a rather abrupt onset in the other third. At times, involvement of a toe or knee has resembled an acute flare of gout. Pain, swelling, and morning stiffness are common complaints. A previous history of documented psoriasis will be obtained in most, but in some the skin findings can be subtle and often overlooked or neglected by the patient. Back pain with significant stiffness usually indicates spinal involvement.

Objective
Physical Examination

Five patterns of arthritis are seen:

- *Asymmetric oligoarticular disease:* This is the most common form, involving 70% of those with psoriatic arthritis. One or several joints of the hands or feet are involved, typically the distal interphalangeal or proximal interphalangeal joints, usually patchy in distribution. Involvement of a tendon sheath may give rise to a sausage-type digit (dactylitis).

- *Distal interphalangeal joint involvement:* This so-called classic form is seen most often related to adjacent nail disease. Although sometimes considered the most typical, the true incidence is only 5 to 10%.
- *Symmetric polyarthritis:* Findings mimic those of rheumatoid arthritis. Most patients are seronegative and those who have a positive rheumatoid factor may have coexistent rheumatoid arthritis and psoriasis.
- *Psoriatic spondylitis:* The back findings may resemble those of idiopathic ankylosing spondylitis except for subtle radiologic features. True spondylitis occurs in 5 to 10% of the patients, although sacroiliitis is reported in 30% of psoriatic arthritis.
- *Arthritis mutilans:* In 5% or less of the patients a severely deforming type of arthritis appears with widespread destruction of joints, as well as osteolysis of the shafts of the digits. This may occur earlier in life and may be associated with severe psoriasis and sacroiliitis.

Psoriatic skin lesions are macular or papular with characteristic scaling and usually occur over the extensor surfaces. The skin findings vary from severe and extensive to very mild and may only be found in areas such as the umbilicus, rectal crease, or scalp. Nail changes such as pitting, onycholysis, and subungal hyperkeratosis are related to adjacent distal interphalangeal joint disease.

The extraarticular features are similar to those seen in ankylosing spondylitis and Reiter's syndrome. Eye involvement is observed in 30% of patients. This includes conjunctivitis in 20% and iritis in about 10%. Iritis does not correlate with disease severity. Other rare manifestations include aortic insufficiency, myopathy, and amyloidosis. Subcutaneous nodules, pleuritis, pericarditis, and vasculitis are not seen.

Routine Laboratory Abnormalities

The laboratory findings are nonspecific. They include a mild anemia, elevated sedimentation rate and often hyperuricemia.

The radiologic features include erosions of the distal interphalangeal joints along with tapering of the distal phalanges leading to the so-called "pencil-in-cup" deformity. Other findings include marginal erosions similar to those of rheumatoid arthritis, periostitis, sacroiliitis, and spondylitis.

PLANS
Diagnostic
Differential Diagnosis

The chief conditions to be differentiated include Reiter's syndrome and rheumatoid arthritis. Reiter's and psoriatic arthritis may exhibit some overlap. Keratodermia blennorrhagica is morphologically similar to psoriasis, and heel and spine involvement may be seen in both conditions; however, the mouth ulcers and urethritis of Reiter's syndrome are not seen in psoriatic arthritis and the typical x-ray findings of psoriatic arthritis are not found in Reiter's syndrome. Gout and pseudogout can be diagnosed by finding birefringent crystals on examination of synovial fluid. Rheumatoid arthritis is easily distinguished by a positive rheumatoid factor, but classic rheumatoid arthritis and psoriasis may occur together. The separation of these conditions should not require further testing.

Diagnostic Options

The diagnosis of psoriatic arthritis is based on the history and physical examination. As mentioned, the laboratory findings are nonspecific. Radiologic studies may reveal some characteristic findings such as the "pencil-in-cup" deformity secondary to whittling of the distal end of the phalanges, erosions, periostitis, ankylosis, and spinal involvement with sacroiliitis and ankylosing spondylitis.

Should a joint effusion be aspirated, it will show a white blood cell count of 2000 to 20,000/µL. Most of the cells will be neutrophils.

Recommended Approach

Psoriatic arthritis can be diagnosed usually in the setting of psoriasis and/or psoriatic nail disease along with a seronegative inflammatory arthritis. Special attention is paid to the clues described under the Criteria for Diagnosis. Further testing is usually not very helpful except in atypical cases.

Therapeutic
Therapeutic Options

There is no specific cure for the disease. The patient should be educated about the nature of the disease and its generally good prognosis. A good exercise program emphasizing the maintenance of range of motion of major joints should be outlined. Nonsteroidal antiinflammatory agents remain the mainstay of treatment. Indomethacin (Indocin), 25 to 50 mg four times daily, has often been used. Other commonly used drugs include naproxen (Naprosyn), 250 to 500 mg twice daily; diclofenac (Voltaren), 75 mg twice daily; sulindac (Clinoril), 200 mg twice daily; piroxicam (Feldene), 20 mg daily; ibuprofen (Motrin), 600 mg three or four times daily; and meclofenamate (Meclomen), 100 mg three or four times daily. The other available nonsteroidal drugs may also be employed. The most common side effects include gastrointestinal effects (dyspepsia or ulcer), headaches, rashes, fluid retention, and possible renal insufficiency.

The second-line or so called "remittive" drugs used in rheumatoid arthritis, namely, gold, antimalarial agents, d-penicillamine, and sulfasalazine, have also been used in psoriatic patients with some success. The psoriasis has occasionally flared from the use of the antimalarial agents. Of the immunosuppressive drugs, low-dose methotrexate is the most effective. It is given in doses of 7.5 to 15 mg per week as either a single dose or three doses over a 24-hour period. Both the skin and joints generally respond within 4 to 8 weeks. The main side effects include nausea and vomiting, stomatitis, potential bone marrow suppression, pneumonitis, hepatic dysfunction, and even cirrhosis. Because of the risk of teratogenesis and gonadal suppression, methotrexate should not be given to women who are pregnant and perhaps not at all to men and women in the childbearing years. Corticosteroids are occasionally given in low doses by mouth, but are most often administered via the intraarticular route. Psoriasis has occasionally flared on tapering of the steroids. It is also important to treat the skin effectively. Treatment programs include topical steroids and coal tars and photochemotherapy with 8-methoxypsoralens along with ultraviolet light (PUVA). In some patients, improving the skin seems to benefit the arthritis.

The indications for surgery are similar to those in rheumatoid arthritis. They include progressive deformity despite optimal medical treatment, unrelenting pain, and interference with the activities of normal daily living. Procedures performed include arthroplasty, arthrodesis, and occasionally synovectomy. There is a slightly increased risk of postoperative infection in those patients with extensive psoriasis near the involved joint.

Recommended Approach

Nonsteroidal antiinflammatory drugs are the initial agents I use. Most patients are also referred to a physical therapist to help maintain range of motion and prevent muscle atrophy. For more resistant disease, consideration is given to the use of methotrexate, gold salts, or sulfasalazine. Intraarticular corticosteroids and, less often, systemic corticosteroids may be considered. I recommend optimal control of the psoriasis.

FOLLOW-UP

After the initial visit the patient should be seen about 2 weeks later to review all tests and evaluate initial therapy. After that the patient should be seen at intervals of perhaps 4 to 12 weeks, depending on the severity of the arthritis and the types of medications given.

DISCUSSION
Prevalence and Incidence

The prevalence of psoriasis in the Caucasian population has been estimated at 1 to 2%. The frequency of inflammatory arthritis among patients with psoriasis varies according to study, but is probably in the range 5 to 7%. There is a relationship between incidence and severity of arthritis, the incidence increasing to about 40% in hospitalized patients with severe psoriasis. The disease occurs almost equally among men and women.

Related Basic Science

Genetics

Psoriasis is associated with HLA-B13, HLA-B17, and HLA-CW6, and genetic markers for psoriatic arthritis include HLA-B27, HLA-B38, HLA-B39, and HLA-DR7. HLA-B27 is reported in 20% of patients with peripheral arthritis and about 50% of patients with psoriatic spondylitis.

Anatomic Derangement

Light and electron microscopic studies of the synovium reveal vascular changes consisting of inflammatory cell infiltration, swelling of endothelial cells, and thickening of the blood vessels. Prominent subsynovial fibrosis is also noted. The etiology of psoriatic arthritis is unknown, and how these microvascular changes are related to the osteolytic resorption of phalanges is unclear.

Altered Molecular Biology

Recent studies have focused on a possible infectious etiology. Persons with psoriasis are more prone to local bacterial invasion of plaques with streptococcal or staphylococcal organisms. Elevated levels of bacterial cell wall antipeptidoglycan antibodies have been found in patients with psoriatic arthritis and other seronegative spondyloarthopathies. In addition, psoriatic arthritis has now been reported in patients with AIDS, and these patients have shown a tendency for severe skin lesions and destructive joint disease.

Psoriatic keratinocytes carrying HLA-DR molecules have been found with increased frequency in psoriatic arthritis. This may suggest that these cells present antigen to T cells, thus promoting the release of mediators resulting in an inflammatory response. Perhaps, *Streptococcus* is the responsible antigen. Local trauma is also documented as a trigger for adjacent osteolysis.

Natural History and Its Modification with Treatment

Most patients with psoriatic arthritis have a relatively good prognosis. Treatment with physical therapy and antiinflammatory drugs can be expected to reduce symptoms and help keep the patient functional. The exception is the 5% of patients with arthritis mutilans who are doomed to progressive joint deformity and destruction. In general, there is less disability and loss of work productivity than in rheumatoid arthritis. Severe complications, including aortic regurgitation, amyloidosis, and inflammatory eye disease, are rare. Mortality is usually related to gastrointestinal hemorrhage secondary to drug therapy or superimposed pneumonia related to immobilization from severe arthritis.

Prevention

There are no effective preventive measures. Some believe that optimal control of the skin may limit the joint disease and avoidance of trauma may also limit acute exacerbations.

Cost Containment

Limiting the use of extensive laboratory tests or x-rays will contain costs. HLA studies are not needed for making the diagnosis or establishing a prognosis. The patient's history and clinical assessment are the most useful indicators of the response to medical therapy.

REFERENCES

Espinoza LR, Aguilar JL, Berman A, et al. Rheumatic manifestations associated with human immunodeficiency virus infection. Arthritis Rheum 1989;32:1615.

Gerber LH, Espinoza LR. Psoriatic arthritis. San Diego: Harcourt Brace Jovanovich, 1985.

Gladman D. Toward unraveling the mystery of psoriatic arthritis. Arthritis Rheum 1993;36:881.

Michet CJ. Psoriatic arthritis. In: Kelly WN, Harris ED, Ruddy S, Sledge C, eds. Textbook of rheumatology. Philadelphia: Saunders, 1993;4:974.

Moll JMH, Wright V. Psoriatic arthritis. Semin Arthritis Rheum 1973;3:55.

CHAPTER 6–6

Reiter's Syndrome and Reactive Arthritis

Steven A. Lauter, M.D.

DEFINITION

Reiter's syndrome is a seronegative arthritis involving predominantly peripheral joints and occurring after an episode of urethritis or diarrhea. Reactive arthritis can be defined as any inflammatory arthropathy following an infection in which no viable microorganism is found in the synovial fluid. Although Reiter's syndrome may be narrowly defined as a subset of the reactive arthritides, most would equate the two conditions, especially because the etiology of Reiter's is not clearly known.

ETIOLOGY

The cause of Reiter's syndrome is felt to be a microbial agent that triggers the disease in a genetically susceptible host. The organisms implicated most often are *Shigella, Salmonella, Yersinia,* and *Campylobacter* in the gastrointestinal tract and *Chlamydia trachomatis* in the genitourinary tract.

CRITERIA FOR DIAGNOSIS

Suggestive

The diagnosis of Reiter's may be considered in a young person with a seronegative asymmetric arthropathy of the lower extremities. Other clues to the diagnosis include the following:

- Urethritis and/or cervicitis
- Recent diarrhea
- Conjunctivitis or iritis
- Circinate balanitis of the penis
- Keratodermia blennorrhagica
- Enthesopathy (inflammation of ligaments and tendons)
- Sausagelike digits
- Low back pain
- Painless oral ulcerations

Earlier literature on Reiter's syndrome described the typical triad of urethritis, conjunctivitis, and arthritis as being necessary for the diagnosis. It is now clear that many patients do not manifest the full triad.

Definitive

Present criteria for diagnosis include a patient with a seronegative lower-extremity arthropathy who has one or more of the clues listed above. Exclusions include classic ankylosing spondylitis and psoriatic arthritis, as well as other inflammatory disorders, such as rheumatoid arthritis, gout, and pseudogout, along with infectious diseases, such as HIV and gonococcal disease.

CLINICAL MANIFESTATIONS

Subjective

The most prominent symptom is the arthritis, with typically one to five joints involved. The arthritis is asymmetric, with a predilection for the lower extremities, especially the feet, ankles, and knees. Patients often complain of painful walking, owing to involvement of the metatarsal phalangeal joints. Other areas of discomfort include the plantar fascia, low back, and chest wall.

The next most common symptoms are urethritis in men and cervicitis in women. In some cases, it is mild enough that it is overlooked. The urethritis may occur postdysentery or may be the primary inciting event. Cervicitis in a woman is often asymptomatic and difficult to diagnose. It may be responsible for the chronic inflammation found in Pap smears.

The conjunctivitis, part of the original triad, is often very mild and fleeting and may be overlooked by the patient. Blurred vision, eye pain, and photophobia may indicate uveitis, often a later feature.

The mucocutaneous lesions of Reiter's syndrome are usually painless.

Many patients also have constitutional symptoms such as fatigue, weight loss, night sweats, and fever.

Objective

Physical Examination

The physical examination will often reveal an inflammatory synovitis of weight-bearing joints, especially the feet, ankles, knees, and lower spine. Large effusions may be noted with overlying erythema, tenderness, and decreased range of motion. A sausage-type digit may be found in the feet or hands secondary to enthesopathy or inflammation of ligaments or tendons. The Achilles tendon may also be inflamed, and there may be an associated plantar fasciitis. Tenderness of the sacroiliac joint and limitation of movement of the low back may signal spinal involvement.

Inspection of the genitalia may reveal the circinate balanitis of the penis. In men prostatitis or epididymoorchitis may be found. A mild staining of the underwear may be the only physical finding to suggest a nongonococcal urethritis. In women, a pelvic exam may reveal cervicitis.

The conjunctivitis is often so mild and fleeting that it goes unnoticed. There may be a mild "pink eye" with a sterile discharge. Uveitis, a later feature, is less common. A slit-lamp examination by an opthalmologist is helpful in making the diagnosis.

The shallow ulcerations of the palate and tongue are typically painless and must be looked for. Keratodermia blennorrhagica is more pathognomonic and involves small macules that develop into vesicles that are yellowish to yellowish red and found on the soles of the feet, especially under the metatarsals. They may become hyperkeratotic. The lesions are indistinguishable from pustular psoriasis.

Sacroiliitis occurs in about 50% of patients with Reiter's syndrome, most of whom are HLA B27 positive. The usual findings are tenderness over the sacroiliac joint and limitation of spinal movement. Occasionally, the spinal findings are indistinguishable from those of classic ankylosing spondylitis.

Cardiac involvement may present with aortic insufficiency similar to that of ankylosing spondylitis. Other manifestations seen rarely are heart block, arrhythmias, myocarditis, and pericarditis.

Routine Laboratory Abnormalities

The laboratory findings are nonspecific and nondiagnostic. The sedimentation rate is often elevated, but it may not correlate with disease activity. The white blood count may be elevated, but patients are usually not anemic in the early stages. The synovial fluid reveals an elevation of the leukocyte count, usually in the range 1000 to 30,000/mm. The glucose and protein are usually normal and the total hemolytic complement may be elevated. Synovial fluid analysis is most helpful in excluding other conditions such as gout and septic arthritis. HIV testing should also be done in those patients at risk.

PLANS

Diagnostic

Differential Diagnosis

Diseases to be considered in the differential diagnosis include septic arthritis, especially gonococcal arthritis, ankylosing spondylitis, psoriatic arthritis, the arthritis associated with inflammatory bowel disease, and rheumatoid arthritis. HIV infection should also be considered, as there are reports that Reiter's syndrome is more common in HIV-positive patients, who may themselves have a unique arthropathy.

Diagnostic Options

The laboratory findings in Reiter's syndrome are indicative of an inflammatory process. In addition to an elevated sedimentation rate, other markers include elevation of the C-reactive protein, hypoproliferative anemia, thrombocytosis, and leukocytosis. HLA-B27 is not required for the diagnosis, but may be helpful in atypical or so called "incomplete" cases.

Cultures of urethral fluid are most helpful in excluding gonorrhea, but could demonstrate *Chlamydia*.

Radiographs are generally normal early in the disease, but ill-defined erosions or reactive new bone formation may be seen in more chronic states. An asymmetric sacroiliitis may occur; if it is suspected but not seen on routine x-rays, a bone scan may be helpful.

Computed tomography and magnetic resonance imaging are only occasionally helpful in adding other information.

Recommended Approach

Reiter's syndrome is best diagnosed in the office or at the bedside on the basis of the history and physical examination. When a joint effusion is present, it is essential to obtain fluid to exclude infection or crystal disease such as gout.

The synovial fluid of patients with Reiter's syndrome reveals an elevation of the leukocyte count, usually in the range of 1000 to 30,000/mm.

Serum should be obtained for determination of the rheumatoid factor and occasionally the antistreptolysin-0 titer and HLA-B27. HIV testing should also be considered.

Therapeutic

Therapeutic Options

Most patients are symptomatic enough to require pharmacologic treatment in addition to rest and physical therapy. Acute and chronic flares are managed initially with a nonsteroidal antiinflammatory agent. Indomethacin (Indocin) 25 to 50 mg three to four times daily or 75 mg twice daily, is usually effective. Other commonly used drugs are diclofenac (Voltaren), 25 to 50 mg four times daily or 75 mg twice daily, and naproxen (Naprosyn), 375 to 500 mg twice daily. Frequent side effects of these agents include dyspepsia from either gastritis or ulcers, renal disease with edema or azotemia, and, less often, rashes, headaches, and dizziness.

Conjunctivitis usually does not require treatment. Recent evidence suggests that tetracycline may shorten the course of arthritis in those patients with chlamydial urethral infection.

Corticosteroids are used most often intraarticularly for treating one to three resistant joints or in the management of the plantar fasciitis or Achilles tendinitis. The technique and dosage employed are discussed elsewhere. Only rarely will large doses of oral corticosteroids (prednisone 40–80 mg) be needed. For the minority of patients who have progressive disease unresponsive to the above measures, consideration should be given to the use of immunosuppressive agents such as methotrexate (Rheumatrex) and azothiopine (Imuran).

Methotrexate in a dose of 7.5 to 15 mg per week has also been proven effective in treating keratodermia blennorrhagica. Side effects are described in Chapter 6–5. Azathioprine is slower acting than methotrexate and is usually given in a dose of 1 to 2 mg/kg body weight. Side effects include bone marrow suppression, nausea, gonadal depression, increased risk of infection, and a potential risk of future malignancy. Use of the latter two agents requires a special note of caution. Fulminant cases of AIDS have occurred in patients with Reiter's who were HIV positive and treated with immunosuppressive agents.

Recommended Approach

I usually begin treatment with indomethacin or one of the other non-steroidal antiinflammatory agents in the dosages described above. Current evidence suggests that urethritis be treated empirically with antibiotics such as tetracycline, unless cultures are done and are negative for *Chlamydia*. Corticosteroids are generally limited to intraarticular use except for the occasional oral use in severe flares. For chronic disease unresponsive to the above agents, I would consider the use of methotrexate or azathioprine.

FOLLOW-UP

The interval for follow-up visits depends on the severity of the arthritis as well as the extraarticular manifestations. Patients who have active disease are generally seen in 4 to 6 weeks to monitor response to medication and physical therapy. Those who are stable may be seen every 3 to 6 months, again depending on severity. Inactive patients probably need be seen only one time per year. The use of corticosteroids or immunosuppressive therapy will necessitate more frequent visits to monitor for toxicity.

DISCUSSION

Prevalence and Incidence

Reiter's syndrome is thought to be the most common form of acute arthritis in the young adult population. The true incidence is not well known, but studies have shown that 1 to 3% of individuals infected during an epidemic of bacterial diarrhea may develop Reiter's. There is a strong male prevalence in the venereal-onset Reiter's, but in the post-dysentery form the sex ratio is nearly equal.

Related Basic Science

Genetics

HLA-B27 is present in only 10% of the Caucasian population, and its strong association with Reiter's syndrome (80%) implies that genetic factors play a major role in the cause and expression of the disease. Recent studies have further elucidated the role of both genetic and infective agents in the pathogenesis of Reiter's syndrome. Reiter's syndrome may develop in 20% of HLA-B27-positive men with nongonococcal urethritis and in 20% of HLA-B27-positive patients with a previous diarrheal illness. The presence of HLA-B27 is associated with a 40 to 50% increased risk of developing arthritis. Two major theories have been postulated: (1) HLA-B27 is linked to a gene responsible for expression of the disease; (2) there is a cross-relationship between HLA-B27 and selected bacteria (molecular mimicry).

Anatomic Derangement

Pathologic studies of the synovium in Reiter's syndrome reveal nonspecific changes. Early on there are edema, vascular congestion, and mostly polymorphonuclear cells. Later there is more proliferation of fibroblasts and lymphocytes and the synovium may resemble that in rheumatoid arthritis. Further evidence for infective agents has recently been disclosed and it is felt that the deposition and persistence of bacterial antigens in the joint constitute an important feature of reactive arthritis. This suggests that the bacterial product may play a role in triggering a reactive arthritis in an HLA-B27-positive individual. Other studies have suggested direct involvement by an infective agent. *Chlamydia* agents have been found in the synovium of patients with Reiter's and *Yersinia* antigens have been found in the neutrophils and macrophages in the synovial fluid of patients with reactive arthritis.

Natural History And Its Modification With Treatment

In general, treatment has helped ameliorate the symptoms of Reiter's syndrome and reactive arthritis, without affecting the natural history. Almost 60% of patients have chronic relapses of peripheral arthritis when followed over a longer period, and nearly 35% of patients become disabled. Fifty percent of patients have back pain and evidence of sacroiliitis. The flares may recur spontaneously or follow a repeated genitourinary infection or a bout of diarrhea. No clinical features are especially helpful in establishing a prognosis. Those carrying HLA-B27 are more likely to have back pain, but not necessarily more severe or frequent relapses.

There is no increased mortality in Reiter's syndrome. The most serious complications such as aortic regurgitation and cardiac arrhythmias are fortunately rare.

Prevention

Uncontrolled observations suggest that the use of a condom prevents postvenereal flare-ups and may even prevent the initial attack. Likewise, it may prevent infection with HIV, which has been reported to coexist in some patients with Reiter's syndrome.

Cost Containment

Elimination of routine x-rays of involved joints early in the disease is important and avoiding the routine ordering of HLA-B27 typing may curtail costs. Early physical therapy may assist the patient in remaining employable.

REFERENCES

Calin A, Fries JF. An "experimental" epidemic of Reiter's syndrome revisited: Follow-up evidence on genetic and environmental factors. Ann Intern Med 1976;84:564

Fan PT, Yu DT. Reiter's syndrome. In: Kelly WN, Harris ED, Ruddy S, Sledge C, eds. Textbook of rheumatology. Philadelphia: Saunders, 1993;4:961.

Montgomery MM, Poske RM, Barton EM, et al. The mucocutaneous lesions of Reiter's syndrome. Ann Intern Med 1959;51:99.

Rahman MU, Cheema MA, Schumacher HR, Hudson AP. Molecular evidence for the presence of *Chlamydia* in the synovium of patients with Reiter's syndrome. Arthritis Rheum 1992;35:521.

Winchester R, Bernstein DH, Fischer HD, et al. The co-occurrence of Reiter's syndrome and acquired immunodeficiency. Ann Intern Med 1987;106:19.

CHAPTER 6–7

Gout

Carlos A. Agudelo, M.D.

DEFINITION

Gout or monosodium urate (MSU) deposition disease is a clinical syndrome characterized by chronic hyperuricemia, MSU deposits in or around joints, and recurrent attacks of acute self-limited arthritis favoring lower extremity joints. Untreated, the disease may progress to a polyarticular destructive process. In about 20% of patients, uric acid urolithiasis or urate nephropathy may occur.

ETIOLOGY

Chronically elevated levels of plasma urate are considered necessary for the development of gout. In some patients, the chronic hyperuricemia may lead to crystallization and formation of urate deposits in or around joints with subsequent bouts of acute arthritis. There are multiple causes of hyperuricemia.

CRITERIA FOR DIAGNOSIS
Suggestive

The American College of Rheumatology has developed highly suggestive criteria for classifying a patient as having gout (Table 6–7–1).

Definitive

The demonstration of intracellular MSU crystals in the joint fluid by polarizing light microscopy is considered a sine qua non in the diagnosis of gout. In the absence of this, a similar demonstration of MSU crystals in material aspirated from a subcutaneous tophaceous deposit is considered diagnostic.

CLINICAL MANIFESTATIONS
Subjective

Chronic hyperuricemia is a biochemical abnormality that may persist for many years or the life of the individual without clinical manifestations. In some patients, however, this asymptomatic period may end either by the sudden onset of the first gouty attack, the development of urolithiasis, or, occasionally, the appearance of subcutaneous visible tophaceous deposits in the absence of arthritis. The acute attack is quite characteristic. The usual patient is a man in the fourth or fifth decade who may be experiencing the very first attack, which is sudden in onset: the patient may be awakened in the early morning hours by excruciating pain at the first metatarsophalangeal (MTP) joint. This is followed by other signs of inflammation. Constitutional symptoms such as fever or stiffness are unusual in the early stages of the disease. Gout is a very treatable condition and if proper measures are taken early in the disease course no other attacks may occur. Uncontrolled, however, the disease may evolve into a chronic stage and subcutaneous deposits may appear. The acute episodes may become frequent and polyarticular, with subsequent damage of the joints and even the presence of chronic persistent inflammation that may mimic rheumatoid arthritis. In this stage, the disease may be accompanied by constitutional symptoms such as fever, stiffness, polyarthralgias, and myalgias.

In some patients a previous history of urolithiasis or a family history of gout will be elicited.

Objective

Physical Examination

During the early stages of the disease the physical examination may be completely normal except for the joint findings. The patient may be obese, hypertensive, and on diuretics. Trauma, surgery, and alcohol may be precipitating events. Most initial attacks are monoarticular and involve lower extremity joints, with more than 60% at the first MTP joint. Although *podagra* means pain in the foot and obviously has

TABLE 6–7–1. HIGHLY SUGGESTIVE CRITERIA FOR THE DIAGNOSIS OF GOUT

- More than one attack of acute arthritis
- Maximum inflammation developed within 1 day
- Monoarticular attack
- Redness observed over joint(s)
- Unilateral first metatarsophalangeal joint attack
- First metatarsophalangeal joint pain or swelling
- Unilateral tarsal joint attack
- Hyperuricemia
- Asymmetric swelling within a joint by roentgenogram
- Subcortical cysts without erosions by roentgenogram
- Suspected tophus
- Negative culture of joint fluid during attack

The presence of 6 of these 12 clinical, laboratory, and x-ray criteria are highly suggestive of gout.

Source: Wallace SL, Robinson H, Masi AT, et al. Preliminary criteria for the classification of the acute arthritis of primary gout. Arthritis Rheum 1977;20:895. Reproduced with permission from the American College of Rheumatology.

many causes, this term has been used to describe the acute gouty toe. Occasionally, and primarily in older patients, early attacks may be polyarticular, usually asymmetric in distribution, and may involve small joints of the hands. A careful search for subcutaneous deposits should be routine. These tophaceous deposits usually occur at the extensor surfaces of the elbows, over joints, finger pads, and ears. They may become quite large and have a firm consistency, but may be difficult to differentiate from rheumatoid nodules. In areas subject to repeated trauma, they may ulcerate, draining a white chalky material consisting of MSU crystals. Ulcerated tophaceous deposits may become infected. The involved joint(s) will be swollen, warm, erythematous, and very tender with functional impairment. Periarticular tissues such as bursas may be involved. Late in the attack, as it subsides, local desquamation may occur.

Routine Laboratory Abnormalities

Except for hyperuricemia, most routine laboratory tests are normal during the first years of the disease. Up to 20 to 30% of patients may have normal serum urate levels during the acute attack. A mild leukocytosis and slight elevation of the sedimentation rate may be present. Some degree of renal dysfunction is common in the older patient with gout, particularly women. Microscopic hematuria may be expected in those with urolithiasis. Hypercholesterolemia and hypertriglyceridemia may coexist.

PLANS
Diagnostic
Differential Diagnosis

The main diagnostic considerations in the patient with acute monoarthritis include infectious arthritis, including gonococcal arthritis; other crystal-induced arthropathies, such as calcium pyrophosphate deposition disease or pseudogout, hydroxyapatite deposition disease, and, rarely, microcrystalline corticosteroid-induced arthropathy (post-injection flare, iatrogenic); and trauma.

Diagnostic considerations in the patient with acute asymmetric polyarthritis include infectious arthritis, including gonococcal arthritis; crystal-induced arthropathies, as discussed before; Reiter's syndrome; Lyme arthritis; and palindromic rheumatism.

Diagnostic Options

Additional laboratory examination may include the following tests.

Measurement of 24-hour urinary uric acid excretion can be helpful in management, particularly in the young patient with gout and/or a history of urolithiasis. Excretion of more than 750 to 800 mg on a normal diet is considered overexcretion with an increase in urolithiasis, whereas excretion of less than 500 to 600 mg is considered underexcretion, probably reflecting a tubular defect. Most patients with primary gout are underexcretors.

Radiologic studies during the early attacks either are normal or show only soft tissue swelling. As the disease progresses if uncontrolled, joint damage may occur leading to a destructive type of arthritis with tophaceous deposits in joints, bone, and surrounding tissues. Radiologically these lesions may appear as punch-out defects, most often in the subchondral bone at the base of heads of phalanges. Their edges show a thin shell-like configuration or the so-called "overhanging margin." Deposits may occur at the distal interphalangeal joints of the hands and may be confused with or coincide with degenerative (Heberden's) nodules.

Positive rheumatoid factors have been described in patients with polyarticular gout and a significant history of alcohol ingestion.

The diagnosis of gout is established by the clinical presentation and the demonstration of intracellular MSU crystals under polarized light microscopy.

Joint aspiration and careful examination of the synovial fluid are necessary steps in the management of the patient with acute arthritis. A drop of the fluid should be immediately examined by an experienced observer under regular light and polarized light microscopy. The presence of intracellular, strongly negative birefringent crystals is diagnostic. As acute gout and infection may coincide in the same joint, a Gram smear and appropriate cultures should be obtained, particularly in the febrile, sick-appearing patient and in those with risk factors or comorbid conditions such as diabetes mellitus, renal insufficiency, alcoholism, and severe tophaceous gout. White blood cell count and differential of the fluid should show evidence of the inflammatory process, with most fluids having counts between 5000 and 30,000 white blood cells/mm^3. Other synovial fluid studies such as determination of protein, uric acid, and complement levels are unnecessary and costly. In the period between attacks the diagnosis may be confirmed by needle aspiration of subcutaneous tophaceous deposits demonstrating MSU crystals under polarized light or by aspiration of an asymptomatic but previously involved joint.

Recommended Approach

The diagnosis and management of the patient with acute arthritis are considered medical emergencies. Therefore, after a careful history and physical examination and after explanation of the procedure to the patient, under strict aseptic technique, joint aspiration with a complete synovial fluid examination including a careful search for crystals under polarized light microscopy as previously outlined should be done. In a few patients, MSU crystals may coincide with calcium pyrophosphate dihydrate crystals. The treating physician must remember that infection is always a diagnostic possibility in the patient with acute arthritis and that infectious arthritis may occasionally coincide with other arthropathies including acute gout. A complete blood count, platelet count, renal and liver function studies, serum uric acid levels, and roentgenogram of the involved joint(s) should be obtained.

Therapeutic

Therapeutic Options

Once the diagnosis of acute gout has been established, therapeutic options to control the acute inflammatory reaction include the following:

- Exclusion of concomitant infection
- Rest of inflamed joint(s)
- Nonsteroidal antiinflammatory drugs (NSAIDs)
- Intraarticular microcrystalline corticosteroid injection
- Intramuscular corticosteroid injection
- Adrenocorticotropic hormone
- Oral corticosteroid
- Colchicine
- Analgesics

After the attack has subsided and the joint returns to apparent normalcy, the physician must decide on prophylactic measures to avoid repeated attacks and whether medications to control the hyperuricemia are necessary. These measures and medications include lifestyle modifications, including diet, weight loss, restriction of alcohol consumption, and avoidance of medications such as diuretics if possible; colchicine or NSAIDs as prophylaxis; uricosuric agents; and xanthine oxidase inhibitors such as allopurinol.

Recommended Approach

Gout is a very treatable condition. Therapeutic options include those used to control the acute inflammatory reaction as previously listed. Once the attack has subsided, the physician must decide whether long term antiinflammatory prophylaxis and medication to control the hyperuricemia are necessary. Goals of therapy are to control the inflammatory process, to prevent further attacks and joint damage, to arrest or reverse tophaceous deposits, and to prevent urolithiasis or urate nephropathy. The clinical response to therapy is best achieved when antiinflammatory medications are used early during the attack. Uricosuric agents and allopurinol are not antiinflammatory agents and should not be used during the acute inflammatory process.

In the absence of aggravating factors or comorbid conditions such as renal insufficiency and peptic ulcer disease, or during the immediate postoperative period, NSAIDs are the first choice. Indomethacin in doses of 150 to 200 mg/d during the first 24 to 48 hours is quite effective. The dose should gradually be decreased to a maintenance dose of about 75 to 100

mg/d. Unfortunately, many patients, particularly the elderly, are unable to tolerate such high doses, developing significant side effects, including problems with mentation or those common to prostaglandin inhibition (reduced renal function, fluid retention, etc.). Other toxic effects common to use of NSAIDs are rashes, headaches, and drug–drug interactions with coumadin, digoxin, and lithium. It is best to avoid their concomitant use. Other NSAIDs useful during the attack include sulindac 200 mg twice daily, ibuprofen 800 mg three times daily, and naproxen 500 mg two or three times daily. Salicylates or aspirin at the doses needed for antiinflammatory action are uricosuric and are usually avoided.

For larger joints, an intraarticular microcrystalline corticosteroid injection is very effective (such as 40–80 mg of methylprednisolone acetate). Smaller doses may be used in smaller joints. Possible, although unusual, complications include infection, tendon rupture, local skin atrophy and hypopigmentation, and postinjection flare. As these are microcrystalline preparations, they may occasionally induce an acute self-limited synovitis, lasting a few hours. Similarly, intramuscular injections may effectively control the acute attack. Occasionally, short courses of oral or parenteral corticosteroids have been used. Several studies have shown adrenocorticotropic hormone injections of 40 units to be quite effective. These injections may be repeated at 8 to 12 hours if needed during the first 24 hours of therapy; except in patients treated with NSAIDs and kept on lower maintenance doses, we add colchicine at doses of 0.6 to 1.2 mg/d to the other previously mentioned measures as prophylaxis and to prevent rebound of the attack.

Colchicine was for many years the drug of choice in acute gout. Its effectiveness in this setting served diagnostic purposes. Because of its significant toxicity at the doses required to control the acute attack and because many other options are presently available as previously discussed, use of colchicine in acute gout has decreased. In selected patients, however, who have no contraindications to its use, colchicine can be quite safe and effective. Risk factors for toxicity include sepsis, bone marrow depression, renal insufficiency, liver disease or biliary obstruction, prior maintenance colchicine, and perhaps the older patient with acute gout. Medications such as cimetidine and tolbutamide may increase its toxicity.

Colchicine is well absorbed after oral administration. Its mechanism of action is not well understood, but it appears to interfere with the inflammatory reaction mediated by neutrophils. Orally, colchicine is given in doses ranging from 0.6 to 1.2 mg (1–2 tablets) every 1 to 2 hours, respectively, until 8 to 12 tablets are given, relief is obtained, or toxic effects develop (usually severe nausea, diarrhea, and vomiting). Unfortunately, at full doses, more than 50% of patients develop side effects. Once the attack is under good control, the medication may be continued at doses of 0.6 to 1.2 mg/d as prophylaxis to prevent further attacks and/or rebound of the attack. Colchicine may be administered intravenously, through an established intravenous line, as the medication may cause tissue damage if extravasated. One to two milligrams diluted in about 20 mL of normal saline is given slowly. The total dose should not exceed 4 mg for acute attacks, and the patient should not receive more colchicine by any route for at least 7 days. (See risk factors for cochicine use previously discussed.)

The long term goals of management of the patient with gout are control of hyperuricemia, thus preventing further attacks; reversal of tophaceous deposits; and avoidance or arrest of joint damage. The patient who has had one or only a few attacks, has normal renal function, no history of urolithiasis, a normal or decreased urinary uric acid level, and no tophaceous deposits may be managed conservatively with lifestyle modifications, weight control, increase fluid intake, and avoidance of alcohol and diuretics. Occasionally, 1 or 2 colchicine tablets as prophylaxis may prevent further attacks while the serum urate level normalizes with the above measures.

Should the approach described fail and the patient experience more attacks, definitive therapy with either uricosuric agents or allopurinol should be instituted. In those patients with renal insufficiency, a history of urolithiasis or severe tophaceous deposits or in overexcretors, allopurinol should be the drug of choice. Allopurinol, however, metabolizes to oxipurinol; both inhibit xanthine oxidase. The plasma half-life of oxipurinol is quite prolonged and increases significantly as renal function decreases, with the potential for significant toxicity, the so-called "allopurinol hypersensitivity syndrome" with severe dermatitis, fever, hepatitis, decrease in renal function, and a mortality that may approach 25%. For this reason, the physician must use caution in starting allopurinol, measure renal function, and reduce the dose accordingly. In those patients with a creatinine clearance less than 40 mL/min, 50 mg/d allopurinol should be the starting dose with careful follow-up. Patients with normal renal function are usually placed on 100 to 300 mg/d, and the dose may be increased gradually if necessary. Azathioprine requires xanthine oxidase for its metabolism and should not be combined with regular doses of allopurinol.

Measurement of urinary uric acid excretion is helpful primarily in the young patient with gout or urolithiasis who may be an overexcretor. Urinary excretion of more than 750 to 800 mg/24 h on a regular diet usually reflects overproduction and excretion, indicating a need for further studies to detect possible genetic enzymatic defects or myeloproliferative diseases. These patients require allopurinol.

Those patients with normal renal function, no history of urolithiasis, and normal or decreased excretion of urinary uric acid may be managed with uricosuric agents such as probenecid in doses of 500 to 1500 mg/d or sulfinpyrazone in doses of 200 to 600 mg/d. Both medications inhibit uric acid reabsorption, thus leading to uricosuria. Aspirin and nicotinic acid interfere with this uricosuric effect and the combination should be avoided.

FOLLOW-UP

The aim of long-term therapy is to gradually control the hyperuricemia to levels below 6.0 mg/dL. The patient should be educated regarding the disease process, alcohol ingestion, medications, possible side effects, and the need for follow-up. He or she is kept on maintenance NSAIDs or low doses of colchicine to prevent recurrences. Two to four weeks later, baseline studies are repeated, primarily to check possible renal, hepatic, or bone marrow effects of medications. If indicated, the results of 24-hour urinary uric acid excretion would now be available and definitive therapy with uricosuric agents or allopurinol should be instituted. We prefer to see the patient a month later, to check routine laboratory tests, compliance with medication(s), possible side effects, diet, alcohol ingestion, and so on. From then on, the patient may be seen at 3- to 6-month intervals depending on risk factors, need to check renal function, and other factors.

DISCUSSION

Prevalence and Incidence

The incidence of gout varies from 0.2 to 0.3 per 1000, with a prevalence of 2 to 2.6 per 1000. The prevalence increases with increasing age and increasing serum urate levels.

Related Basic Science

Metabolic Derangement

In humans and some primates, uric acid is the final product of purine metabolism. Other animals have uricase, which splits uric acid into allantoin and carbon dioxide. Human thus have a propensity to develop a relative hyperuricemia as compared with other animals. Small amounts of uricase are present in human erythrocytes, suggesting that we have higher levels of uric acid as a protective mechanism, as uric acid behaves as a powerful antioxidant in in vitro studies. Hyperuricemia is a common biochemical abnormality defined solely by serum urate level. Hyperuricemia alone is not a disease and as such should not be treated except to prevent the tumor lysis syndrome. About 13% of hospitalized men in the United States have hyperuricemia, and only a few of these men will ever develop gout. At 37°C, the saturation value of urate in plasma is about 7.0 mg/dL. Hyperuricemia is defined as a serum urate level above 7.0 mg/dL by the uricase method or 7.5 to 8.0 mg/dL by automated analysis. Adult levels are reached at puberty, with males averaging 1 mg/dL higher than females; the difference is thought to be due to an estrogen renal effect. After the menopause, female levels increase by about 1 mg/dL, thus approaching male levels.

There are multiple causes of hyperuricemia. The main mechanisms are an increase in uric acid production, such as that occurring in enzyme defects and in myeloproliferative disorders; a decrease in uric acid excretion; or a combination of these.

Genetics

The complete absence of the enzyme hypoxanthine–guanine phosphoribosyl transferase, or Lesch–Nyhan syndrome, occurs as a rare X-linked inborn error of metabolism leading to uric acid overproduction. These children develop choreoathetosis, mental retardation, and automutilation. A partial enzyme deficiency, X-linked as well, induces gout in males at an early age. Another enzyme defect is that associated with a variant of phosphoribosylpyrophosphate amidinotransferase, where the enzyme has an increased avidity for the substrate phosphoribosylpyrophosphate, leading to uric acid overproduction. Increased cell turnover or destruction leads to an increase in the final product of purine metabolism, uric acid.

Plasma urate is almost 100% filtered at the glomerulus. Subsequent reabsorption–secretion–reabsorption–excretion steps occur at the tubules until a final product of about 400 to 600 mg is excreted in the 24-hour urine under a purine-free diet. In some patients with chronic hyperuricemia, urate may precipitate as MSU crystals in or around joints. Low pH and low temperature favor precipitation. Although chronic hyperuricemia is required for urate precipitation and higher levels of uric acid correlate with an increased incidence of gout, not all individuals with chronic hyperuricemia are at the same risk for the development of gout. The precise mechanism(s) involved in urate precipitation is not well understood.

Some of the conditions or factors associated with hyperuricemia are primary gout; enzyme deficiencies; myeloproliferative disorders; psoriasis; sarcoidosis; renal insufficiency; lead exposure; ketoacidosis; obesity; hypertension; toxemia of pregnancy; and ingestion of drugs (alcohol, low-dose salicylates, diuretics, cytotoxic agents, cyclosporine, pyrazinamide, nicotinic acid).

Natural History and Its Modification with Treatment

As previously discussed, chronic hyperuricemia may, in some patients, lead to urolithiasis and urate precipitation in or around joints, eventually leading to attacks of arthritis. If uncontrolled, the disease may progress to a chronic destructive articular process and subcutaneous tophaceous deposits and renal dysfunction. These deposits may cause bone and joint damage. Normalization of urate levels is the goal of therapy, arresting or decreasing joint damage and decreasing the chances of urolithiasis as well as avoiding further inflammatory attacks.

Prevention

No preventive measures are presently available to avoid hyperuricemia in many patients or to avoid the process or processes leading to urate precipitation and the acute gouty attack. As there are many causes of hyperuricemia, however, some of these are preventable, such as avoiding diuretics whenever possible, primarily in those patients developing hyperuricemia and educating patients regarding weight control and alcohol ingestion.

Cost Containment

Asymptomatic hyperuricemia should not be treated. Educating the patient about the disease process, medications, compliance, and the role of possible precipitating factors is very important in controlling costs. Early diagnosis, with crystal identification, and the education of the physician regarding the multiple therapies available, possible contraindications, and side effects will decrease medical costs, especially when long-term therapy is needed.

REFERENCES

Agudelo CA. Crystal deposition diseases. In: Weisman M, Weinblatt M, eds. Treatment of rheumatic diseases. Philadelphia: Saunders, 1995:271.

Kelley WN. Hyperuricemia. In: Kelley WN, Harris ED, Ruddy S, Sledge CB, eds. Textbook of rheumatology. 4th ed. Philadelphia: Saunders, 1993;1:498.

Kelley WN, Schumacher HR. Gout. In: Kelley WN, Harris ED, Ruddy S, Sledge CB, eds. Textbook of rheumatology. 4th ed. Philadelphia: Saunders, 1993;2:1291.

Wallace SL, Robinson H, Masi AT, et al. Preliminary criteria for the classification of the acute arthritis of primary gout. Arthritis Rheum 1977;20:895.

Chondrocalcinosis (Pseudogout)

Carlos A. Agudelo, M.D.

DEFINITION

Pseudogout, or calcium pyrophosphate dihydrate (CPPD) deposition disease, is a form of arthropathy characterized by a variety of clinical presentations and CPPD deposits in joints. *Chondrocalcinosis* is the radiologic term used to describe such calcific deposits in hyaline cartilage and fibrocartilage.

ETIOLOGY

Different crystals including CPPD may induce an inflammatory articular reaction. As may monosodium urate crystals in gout, CPPD crystal deposits may be asymptomatic (chondrocalcinosis) or they may induce an acute or chronic, at times destructive, form of arthropathy. Factors leading to crystal deposition are not well understood.

CRITERIA FOR DIAGNOSIS
Suggestive

The presence of self-limited episodes of acute arthritis or of a chronic arthropathy with roentgenologic evidence of chondrocalcinosis is highly suggestive of CPPD deposition disease or pseudogout.

Definitive

As in other crystal-induced arthropathies, the definitive diagnosis of pseudogout requires careful examination of the synovial fluid with the demonstration of intracellular pleomorphic, weakly positively birefringent crystals by compensated polarized light microscopy. Occasionally, CPPD crystals may coexist with monosodium urate crystals in the same joint and/or an infectious process.

CLINICAL MANIFESTATIONS
Subjective

Several clinical presentations may be seen in association with CPPD crystals. Some individuals may be asymptomatic and chondrocalcinosis is only an incidental radiologic finding.

Some patients may present with bouts of acute self-limited arthritis as seen in gout. In others, however, the clinical presentation may resemble that of degenerative joint disease or osteoarthritis or a polyarticular form mimicking rheumatoid arthritis. Hereditary forms of the condition have been described.

Objective
Physical Examination

Calcium pyrophosphate dihydrate deposition disease is unusual in young individuals except for rare familial cases. Most patients are older, over 40 years of age, and the frequency increases with age. About 5% of the adult population have CPPD crystals in their knee joints at the time of death. The disease affects primarily larger joints, and the knee joint is to pseudogout what the first metatarsal phalangeal joint is to gout. Other frequently involved joints are the wrist, shoulder, and hip. During acute spells the joint will be swollen, warm, tender, and functionally impaired. Fever and problems with mentation have been described in the older patient with acute pseudogout. The disease may coincide with osteoarthritis of the same or other joints, and occasionally it may resemble other rheumatic diseases, including infectious arthritis, rheumatoid arthritis, osteoarthritis, traumatic arthritis, and neuropathic joint disease. Associated metabolic disorders, including hyperparathyroidism, ochronosis, hemochromatosis, and hypomagnesemia, have been described in about 5 to 10% of patients. Involvement of small joints of the hands may closely resemble rheumatoid arthritis

and involvement of metacarpophalangeal joints, primarily second and third joints, with chondrocalcinosis radiologically is suggestive of hemochromatosis.

Routine Laboratory Abnormalities

Most routine laboratory tests will be normal in the great majority of patients. The white count and sedimentation rate may be slightly elevated. Hypercalcemia and hypophosphatemia may be evident in the patient with concomitant hyperparathyroidism.

The chest x-ray film is normal.

PLANS
Diagnostic
Differential Diagnosis

Depending on the clinical presentation, the differential diagnosis of CPPD deposition disease may include infectious arthritis, other crystal-induced arthropathies such as gout and hydroxyapatite-induced arthropathy, osteoarthritis, rheumatoid arthritis, neuropathic joint disease, and, occasionally when there is spinal involvement, ankylosing spondylitis.

Diagnostic Options

The diagnosis of pseudogout or CPPD deposition disease is established by the clinical presentation, the radiologic evidence of chondrocalcinosis, and the demonstration of CPPD crystals by compensated polarized microscopy. Therefore, synovial fluid aspiration and a careful search for crystals and exclusion of an infectious nature are mandatory steps in the evaluation and management of the patient with acute arthritis.

Recommended Approach

After a thorough history and physical examination and explanation of the procedure to the patient, the acutely inflamed joint should be aspirated and a drop of fluid immediately examined by an experienced observer under polarized light microscopy. Gram smear and cultures should be performed whenever indicated. Routine studies should include a complete blood count; studies of renal and liver function; determinations of calcium, phosphorus, and serum iron levels; and roentgenogram of the involved joint(s).

Therapeutic
Therapeutic Options

For acute attacks, an approach similar to that described for gout is suggested (see Chapter 6–7). In patients with no comorbid conditions (chronic renal failure, peptic ulcer disease, etc), options include nonsteroidal antiinflammatory drugs, intrarticular microcrystalline corticosteroid injection, and adrenocorticotropic hormone (see Chapter 6–7). At times, adequate aspiration of the joint may be sufficient to alleviate the pain. Currently, no medications are available to prevent attacks; however, low-dose colchicine, as in gout, or a nonsteroidal antiinflammatory drug may be helpful in those patients with chronic forms of the disease.

Recommended Approach

Most attacks readily respond to the above-mentioned therapeutic measures. Analgesics may be useful in the complicated patient in whom there exist relative or absolute contraindications to the use of nonsteroidal antiinflammatory drugs, corticosteroids, or colchicine. We do not use colchicine in the management of acute attacks, as the increased doses required are often associated with significant side effects (see

Chapter 6–7). As previously outlined, however, colchicine may be useful at low doses, 0.6 to 1.2 mg/d, as prophylaxis.

FOLLOW-UP

The patient is usually seen within 1 to 4 weeks of the acute attack, to check on probable associated conditions. At that time, laboratory studies should be reviewed, to exclude possible abnormalities of calcium or iron metabolism, and, if the patient has been on nonsteroidal antiinflammatory drugs, to check possible renal dysfunction. The long-term management of the patient is dictated by comorbid conditions or medications.

DISCUSSION
Prevalence

Pseudogout is a relatively common condition. More than 20% of individuals in geriatric units may have radiologic evidence of chondrocalcinosis, and the prevalence increases with advancing age.

Related Basic Science

A familial form of the disease has been described in different populations. The mode of inheritance appears to be autosomal dominant. CPPD deposition disease has been associated with a number of metabolic conditions including hyperparathyroidism, hypophosphatasia, hemochromatosis, hypomagnesemia, and aging. The possible mechanisms involved in CPPD deposition are not understood. In some patients, the disease may progress to significant destruction of involved joint(s) Bony ankylosis may occur.

Natural History and Its Modification with Treatment

There is no way to predict the course of the disease in a particular patient. In some, recurrent acute attacks may be the norm, with apparent normalcy between attacks. Other patients, particularly those with polyarticular forms of the disease, may progress and develop significant damage with impairment of function. Occasionally, colchicine at low doses or nonsteroidal antiinflammatory drugs appear to be of some value in some patients. No medication presently available is capable of dissolving calcific deposits or arresting the progress of the disease.

Prevention

As the exact cause of the disease is unknown, no preventive measures are currently available.

Cost Containment

Awareness by the physician of the different forms of CPPD deposition disease or pseudogout, its diagnosis and management, as well as its possible associations will help to contain costs, as unnecessary medications or tests will be avoided.

REFERENCE

Howell DS. Diseases due to deposition of calcium pyrophosphate and hydroxiapatite. In: Kelley WN, Harris ED, Ruddy S, Sledge CB, eds. Textbook of rheumatology. Philadelphia: Saunders, 1981:1438.

CHAPTER 6–9

Osteoarthritis

Roland W. Moskowitz, M.D.

DEFINITION

Osteoarthritis is a disease of joints, characterized pathologically by erosive cartilage breakdown and proliferative osteophytic spurs and clinically by slow development of joint pain, stiffness, and limitation of motion.

ETIOLOGY

Osteoarthritis may be primary or secondary. Primary factors of importance include biomechanical abnormalities, gene mutations affecting cartilage matrix components, cytokines and degradative metalloproteases, and impaired chondrocyte synthetic responses. Examples of secondary underlying etiologic factors include posttraumatic injury, metabolic abnormalities such as hemochromatosis and chondrocalcinosis, postinflammatory arthritis, and biomechanical derangements such as tears of knee menisci or the anterior cruciate ligament.

CRITERIA FOR DIAGNOSIS
Suggestive

Suggestive criteria include joint pain, age over 50, joint crepitus (a crackling of the joint with movement), bony tenderness, bony enlargement, and absence of synovitis.

Definitive

Definitive evidence of osteoarthritis comprises radiographic evidence of osteophyte formation and cartilage loss (joint space narrowing). There are at present no specific diagnostic biochemical or immunologic studies.

CLINICAL MANIFESTATIONS
Subjective

Men and women are equally affected by osteoarthritis; prevalence, however, is greater in women than in men after age 55. Differences in the prevalence of osteoarthritis in blacks and whites have been noted, particularly when patterns of joint involvement are analyzed. Differences in occupation, lifestyle, and predisposing genetic factors may play a role. A hereditary component of the disease is seen in patients with involvement of the distal interphalangeal joints of the hands (Heberden's nodes) and in precocious primary generalized osteoarthritis. The role of obesity in the etiology of osteoarthritis remains controversial. The most consistent relationship appears to be with osteoarthritis of the knee in women. Physical stresses related to occupation or sports activities may lead to secondary osteoarthritis, such as is seen in manual laborers. Retrospective studies of the incidence of osteoarthritis of the knee in long-time runners reveal little or no increase in clinical or roentgenographic osteoarthritis findings; similar studies in long-distance runners, however, reveal an increased evidence of degenerative hip disease.

Symptoms of osteoarthritis are localized to the affected joints. The primary symptom is pain, seen initially after joint use; later it is present even at rest. Stiffness on awakening in the morning or after periods of inactivity is limited and usually less than 15 to 30 minutes in duration. Gelling, characterized by stiffness after inactivity, is common, particularly in lower-extremity joints of elderly patients. Acute inflammation is uncommon; when present, it suggests the presence of a coincidental arthritis such as pseudogout (calcium pyrophosphate dihydrate crystal deposition disease) or rheumatoid arthritis.

Objective

Physical Examination

Characteristic physical findings include localized tenderness and pain on passive motion. Crepitus, in which there is a crackling sound of the joint when it is moved, is common. It results from cartilage loss and irregularity of the joint surfaces. Joint swelling is usually bony, but there may be associated mild synovitis, particularly in later stages of the disease. Osteophyte spurs can at times be palpated along the margins of the affected joint. Progressive severe disease is characterized by gross joint deformity and subluxation.

Routine Laboratory Abnormalities

There are no specific diagnostic routine laboratory abnormalities indicative of primary osteoarthritis. Roentgenographic findings of osteophytes and loss of cartilage joint space are confirmatory. Other forms of arthritis are excluded by studies of the erythrocyte sedimentation rate, routine blood counts, and serum rheumatoid factor. Synovial fluid analysis, indicated in the presence of effusion, reveals "noninflammatory" findings. On gross appearance the synovial fluid is generally clear with good viscosity; microscopic analysis reveals a white blood cell count less than 2000/mm^3 and less than 25% polymorphonuclear leukocytes. Other forms of joint imaging, such as magnetic resonance imaging are generally not used except to exclude other diagnostic entities such as joint internal derangement.

PLANS

Diagnostic

Differential Diagnosis

Differential diagnosis varies depending on whether the presentation of osteoarthritis is monoarticular or polyarticular. In the presence of chronic monoarthritis, differential diagnoses to be considered are mechanical internal derangement, avascular necrosis, pigmented villonodular synovitis, and rheumatoid arthritis. In patients with polyarticular disease, entities that might be confused with generalized osteoarthritis include rheumatoid arthritis, psoriatic arthritis, Reiter's syndrome, sarcoid arthritis, hypertrophic osteoarthropathy, pseudogout (calcium pyrophosphate dihydrate crystal deposition disease), and chronic tophaceous gout.

Diagnostic Options

See Routine Laboratory Abnormalities.

Recommended Approach

In the presence of monoarticular disease, clinical examination is followed by x-ray examination of the involved joint. In the presence of synovial effusion, arthrocentesis with synovial fluid analysis is helpful to exclude other diagnostic entities. In the presence of more generalized osteoarthritis, laboratory studies to include an erythrocyte sedimentation rate and rheumatoid latex fixation test should be considered.

Therapeutic

Therapeutic Options

Treatment of osteoarthritis in its early stages is usually medical. Orthopaedic surgical considerations may be considered in the presence of severe biomechanical derangements, but are usually used later in the course of the disease process.

Recommended Approach

Management needs to be individualized depending on symptomatology and extent of disease. It is essential that the disease be neither undertreated nor overtreated. Protection of joints from overuse should be advised, especially if weight-bearing joints are involved. The stresses across weight-bearing joints such as the knee are increased three- to fivefold when walking as compared with standing! Overuse of involved joints such as in jogging or use of exercycles with high stress loads should be avoided. Fast walking is often tolerated, and swimming,

when feasible, is an excellent exercise. Weight reduction is often difficult because of decreased ability to maintain general activity; nevertheless, it should be recommended in patients with significant obesity. Physical therapy is directed toward maintaining and improving range of motion and use of heat for relief of pain and stiffness.

Many patients do well with analgesic agents alone, such as acetaminophen and propoxyphene. For many patients, however, use of an antiinflammatory/analgesic agent is necessary. Although aspirin, particularly in enteric-coated form, is tolerated by a number of patients, the newer nonsteroidal antiinflammatory drugs are generally associated with decreased toxicity and increased compliance in use (see Table 6–9–1). Side reactions common to a number of these agents include rash, gastrointestinal upset, peptic ulceration, edema, and hepatic abnormalities. Intraarticular injections of corticosteroids are helpful, particularly when associated with acute flares of inflammation; they should be used infrequently in weight-bearing joints. Avoidance of joint overuse for a period of days to weeks following injection is advisable. Injection into small joints of the hands is often long-lasting and particularly rewarding. Oral or parenteral therapy with adrenal corticosteroids is not recommended.

Orthopaedic surgical procedures including osteotomy, arthroplasty, fusion, and partial or total prosthetic replacements may be considered at various points in the disease process, depending on which joint is involved. Arthroscopic debridement and irrigation may provide variable periods of symptomatic relief.

FOLLOW-UP

It is advisable to see the patient several times in follow-up at 2- to 3-month intervals so as to complete diagnostic studies and to evaluate patient compliance and understanding of the therapeutic program. At these evaluations, complete blood count and differential, serum creatinine, and urinalysis should be performed if the patient is on nonsteroidal antiinflammatory agents so as to exclude presence of occult toxicity. Subsequent visits at 6-month intervals are satisfactory for assessing disease progress and patient response.

TABLE 6–9–1. CLINICAL RECOMMENDATIONS FOR USE OF NONSTEROIDAL ANTIINFLAMMATORY DRUGS

Nonsteroidal Anti-inflammatory Drug	Frequency of Administration	Usual Daily Dose Range (mg/d)	Maximum Recommended Dose (mg/d)
Propionic acids			
Fenoprofen (Nalfon)	tid or qid	800–2400	3200
Flurbiprofen (Ansaid)	bid or qid	200–300	300
Ibuprofen (Motrin)	tid to qid	600–2400	3200
Naproxen (Naprosyn)	bid	500–1000	1500
Ketoprofen (Orudis)	tid or qid	150–300	300
Ketoprofen (Oruvail)	qd	200	200
Oxaprozin (Daypro)	qd	1200	1800
Indole-/Indeneacetic Acids			
Indomethacin (Indocin)	tid or qid	75–200	200
Sulindac (Clinoril)	bid	300–400	400
Etodolac (Lodine)	tid or qid	600–1200	1200
Heteroarylacetic acids:			
Tolmetin (Tolectin)	tid or qid	600–1800	1800
Arylacetic acids			
Diclofenac (Voltaren)	bid or tid	100–150	200
Fenamic acids			
Meclofenamate (Meclomen)	tid or qid	200–400	400
Oxicams			
Piroxicam (Feldene)	qd	10–20	20
Fluorophenyl salicylate			
Diflunisal (Dolobid)	bid	500–1000	1500
Naphthylalkanone			
Nabumetone (Relafen)	qd or bid	1000–2000	2000

DISCUSSION
Prevalence

Osteoarthritis is the most common form of joint disease. Some degenerative changes in weight-bearing joints may be seen in almost all individuals by age 40; by age 75, the disease is almost universal. Men and women are similarly afflicted, although the prevalence is greater in men under age 45 and in women over age 55.

Related Basic Science
Biochemistry of Cartilage

Normal hyaline cartilage comprises four major constituents: chondrocytes, proteoglycans, collagens, and water. Chondrocytes, which make up only approximately 5% of the volume of normal human cartilage, are metabolically active and the source of matrix synthesis. Cartilage water interacting with proteoglycans gives cartilage its compressibility; collagen, on the other hand, is responsible for cartilage tensile strength. The major collagen of cartilage is type II collagen. Recent studies suggest the importance of so-called minor collagens, which make up 10 to 15% of cartilage collagens. The interplay of proteoglycan and collagen is important to cartilage structural integrity.

Pathology

Pathologic responses in osteoarthritis are characterized by two major processes: erosive ulcerative breakdown, and a proliferative response manifested by development of osteochondrophyte spurs. Histopathologic studies reveal that cartilage attempts to repair with increased chondrocyte proliferation and increased synthesis of proteoglycans and collagen. When synthesis is unable to keep up with degradative breakdown, osteoarthritis ensues.

Role of Inflammation

Synovial inflammation is frequently seen as a secondary component of the disease. Inflammation may be associated with calcium crystal deposition disease; a role for deposition of immune complexes has also been suggested. Proteolytic enzymes, including proteinases and collagenases, are important in cartilage degradation. Interleukin-1, derived from activated monocytes in synovium, can induce living cartilage to release/activate proteoglycanases and collagenases and to inhibit proteoglycan synthesis. This, and similar cytokines, may be involved in initiation or augmentation of the osteoarthritic process. Balancing the effect of these degradative enzymes and cytokines are growth peptides such as insulin-like growth factor 1 that are capable of stimulating matrix synthesis and chondrocyte proliferation.

Schema of Etiopathogenesis

Current data suggest a schema of pathogenesis whereby some unknown primary insult(s) may lead to release of proteolytic and collagenolytic enzymes, which degrade cartilage matrix. Cartilage repair characterized by increased matrix synthesis and cellular proliferation eventually fails, leading to osteoarthritis. Defects in the type II collagen gene with synthesis of a mutant type II collagen play a role in some previously considered idiopathic forms of the disease.

Natural History and Its Modification with Treatment

Few studies have defined with precision the prognostic outlook for patients with primary osteoarthritis. Disability relates to which specific joints are involved and is more commonly associated with disease of weight-bearing joints, such the knees and hips. Studies of disease progression suggest that not all cases of osteoarthritis inevitably deteriorate. Nevertheless, in most patients, the disease is progressive, with unpredictable variability in the rate of deterioration. Patients should be reassured that, in general, the outlook is favorable and disability uncommon; this contrasts with the poorer prognosis for patients with generalized inflammatory joint diseases such as rheumatoid arthritis. Studies suggest that appropriate exercises and weight reduction may be associated with decreased symptomatology; the role of weight reduction in ameliorating the basic disease process is as yet uncertain.

Prevention

The pace of the disease may be lessened by avoiding joint overuse and by reducing weight. Appropriate exercises to strengthen and to stabilize joints are beneficial. Osteoarthritis changes related to chronic sports injury, certain occupations such as mining, or repetitive overuse of joints should be assessed, and precautions taken to lessen joint loads.

Cost Containment

Cost of disease management can be decreased by using medications that are available in generic form. In addition, not all patients need be treated continuously for long periods; many will do satisfactorily with short courses of therapy used during exacerbations when the disease is more symptomatic. The use of analgesic agents that are nonirritating to the gastrointestinal tract are associated with fewer toxic side reactions; they accordingly require less coadministration of medications such as antacids and H_2 blockers. X-rays need not be repeated unless there is a marked and unexpected deterioration in joint function over time.

REFERENCES

Bradley JD, Brandt KD, Katz BP, et al. Comparison of an antiinflammatory dose of ibuprofen, an analgesic dose of ibuprofen, and acetaminophen in the treatment of patients with osteoarthritis of the knee. N Engl J Med 1991;325:87.

Felson DT. The course of osteoarthritis and factors that affect it. In: Moskowitz RW, editor-in-chief. Osteoarthritis, rheumatic disease clinics of North America. Philadelphia: Saunders, 1993:607.

Lane NE, Michel B, Bjorkengren A, et al. The risk of osteoarthritis with running and aging: A five year longitudinal study. J Rheumatol 1993;20:461.

Marti B, Knoblock M, Tschopp A, et al. Is excessive running predictive of degenerative hip disease? Controlled study of former elite athletes. Br Med J 1989;229:91.

Moskowitz RW. Clinical and laboratory findings in osteoarthritis. In: McCarty DJ, Koopman WJ, ed. Arthritis and allied conditions. 12th ed. Philadelphia: Lea & Febiger, 1993:1735.

Pun YL, Moskowitz RW, Lie S, et al. Clinical correlations of osteoarthritis associated with a single base mutation (arginine[519]-to-cysteine) in type II procollagen gene (COL2A1), a newly defined etiopathogenesis. Arthritis Rhem 1994;37:264.

CHAPTER 6–10

Nongonococcal Septic Arthritis

Harold P. Katner, M.D., and Stephen B. Miller, M.D.

DEFINITION

Septic arthritis is a joint space inflammatory response to bacterial invasion.

ETIOLOGY

Nongonococcal septic arthritis can be caused by hematogenous spread, direct extension, and/or iatrogenic or accidental introduction of bacteria into the synovial space. *Staphylococcus aureus, Streptococcus* species, and facultative or aerobic Gram-negative rods are the causative agents in the bulk of these infections; such agents as anaerobes, *Moraxella* species, *Hemophilus* species, and others have been reported. Relative frequencies of these organisms are age, host, and mode of acquisition dependent.

CRITERIA FOR DIAGNOSIS

Suggestive

Nongonococcal septic arthritis is suggested by a positive Gram and/or methylene blue stain of the synovial fluid demonstrating the bacterial pathogen(s).

Definitive

Diagnosis is definitive once the bacterial pathogen(s) is cultured and identified.

CLINICAL MANIFESTATIONS

Subjective

Nongonococcal bacterial septic arthritis presents with fever in approximately two thirds of cases and with only one joint involved in 90% of cases. The onset of symptoms is usually abrupt. Large joints (knees, hips, shoulder, wrist, and ankle) are most commonly affected and are usually painful, hot, and swollen. A history suggesting a primary source of the infection such as bronchopulmonary symptoms, genitourinary symptoms, or cutaneous lesions (cellulitis, rashes, or trauma) may be elicited. Trauma or intraarticular injections are predisposing factors. Patients with a history of rheumatoid arthritis, osteoarthritis, crystal-induced synovitis, diabetes mellitus, malignancies, AIDS, or injection drug abuse and those on immunosuppressive agents are all at increased risk of developing infectious arthritis. These patients, however, may present atypically. Fever may be low grade or absent. If the patient has preexisting painful joints from an underlying rheumatic condition, worsening of that pain by an infection may not initially be recognized.

Objective

Physical Examination

Typical Presentation. Mild elevation of the temperature is common, with less than 50% having temperatures higher than 39°C. The involved joint is impressively swollen, often with a large effusion. Extreme tenderness, heat, redness, and resistance to motion are common.

Atypical Presentation. Swelling, effusion, tenderness, heat, and redness of the suspected joint are often less severe than in the typical presentation. Early diagnosis of bacterial arthritis of the hip, shoulder, and sternoclavicular and sacroiliac joints may be difficult, as it is harder to demonstrate an effusion or elicit tenderness and other signs of inflammation at these sites.

Routine Laboratory Abnormalities

Routine laboratory studies usually reveal systemic infection, an elevated leukocyte count with a left shift, and an elevated erythrocyte sedimentation rate. Immunocompromised and at times normal hosts may present with a normal or only minimally elevated leukocyte count.

PLANS

Diagnosis

Differential Diagnosis

Gout, pseudogout, seronegative spondyloarthropathies, trauma, rheumatic fever, rheumatoid arthritis, inflammatory osteoarthritis, palindromic rheumatism, Lyme disease, viral-associated arthritis, tuberculosis, *Neisseria gonorrhoeae,* and Reiter's syndrome should be considered in the differential.

Diagnostic Options

Joint aspiration should be done for examination and culture of the fluid. Aseptic technique is essential to avoid inadvertent introduction of bacteria into the joint. Entry should never be through infected skin or subcutaneous tissue. Gross examination of the joint fluid reveals a yellow-reddish color, marked turbidity, reduced viscosity, and friable mucin clots. Microscopic examination reveals 10,000 to greater than 100,000 white blood cells per microliter, predominantly neutrophils (greater than 90%), and identifiable pyogenic organisms on Gram stain and culture. Laboratory studies reveal a synovial fluid-to-blood glucose ratio of less than 0.5 and a high lactic acid concentration. If the culture is negative and infection is strongly suspected, a synovial biopsy should be performed and appropriate cultures done. Blood cultures and cultures from other appropriate sites, such as sputum and urine, should be obtained if signs or symptoms indicate a primary source of infection. X-ray investigation of joint should be done with follow-up in 14 days to rule out bone and cartilage destruction.

Radionuclide scans may be of help in diagnosing sacroiliac, sternoclavicular, and early hip and shoulder infections. Magnetic resonance imaging and computed tomography are useful in detecting joint effusions and pathology that may suggest an infectious process.

Recommended Approach

Joint aspiration for appropriate culture and stains is essential. If sufficient fluid is obtained, a cell count and differential are very helpful in supporting an infectious etiology. The chemical analysis of the joint fluid is the least specific.

In patients at high risk for septic arthritis and systemic signs of infection, but no obvious localizing joint involvement, a three-phase radionuclide bone and joint scan is most helpful.

Therapeutic

Therapeutic Options

Once joint fluid analysis confirms or strongly suggests infection, therapy should begin immediately. If the Gram stain demonstrates an organism, initial therapy can be tailored to cover the most likely pathogens.

Gram-positive cocci (*S. aureus, Streptococcus pneumoniae,* viridans [α-hemolytic] group streptococci, group A and B [β-hemolytic] streptococci, and *Streptococcus intermedius* group) are responsible for more than 75% of nongonococcal infectious arthritis cases. Under ideal conditions, differentiation of staphylococcal and streptococcal (grapelike clusters versus chains or lancet-shaped diplococci as with *S. pneumoniae*) on Gram stain may be possible, but should not be used to decide on empiric treatment. Treatment can be adjusted once cultures and sensitivities are available.

Staphylococcus aureus

- Nafcillin 6 to 12 g/d in six doses
- Vancomycin 2 g/d in two to four doses and adjust once levels return

- Cefazolin 3 to 6 g/d in three doses
- Clindamycin 2.7 g/d in three doses

Streptococcus Species
- Penicillin G 10 to 24 million units/d in six divided doses
- Vancomycin, cefazolin, and clindamycin as above

Addition of an aminoglycoside may be necessary if the isolated streptococcus reveals penicillin tolerance

Enterococcus Species
- Ampicillin 6 to 12 g/d in six doses + gentamicin (dosage to be based on ideal body weight, renal function, and subsequent levels)
- Vancomycin 2 g/d in two to four divided doses (to be adjusted once levels available) + gentamicin (see above)

Gram-negative bacilli constitute less than 20% of the causative agents in nongonococcal septic arthritis. Enterobacteriaceae and *Pseudomonas aeruginosa* represent the majority of these organisms, with *Hemophilus influenzae* (pleomorphic) anaerobic Gram-negative rods being much less common.

Enterobacteriaceae (*Escherichia, Klebsiella, Enterobacter, Serratia, Proteus, etc.*)
Community Acquired
- Cefotaxime or ceftriaxone; consider addition of aminoglycoside
- Quinolones (ciprofloxacin, ofloxacin)
- Aztreonam

Nosocomially Acquired (hospital, nursing home)
- Ceftazidine + aminoglycoside

Pseudomonas aeruginosa
- Anti-pseudomonal penicillin (piperacillin, ticarcillin/clavulanate, piperacillin/tazobactam) or ceftazidime + aminoglycoside
- Imipenem/cilastin

Hemophilus influenzae
- Cefotaxime or ceftriaxone
- Ampicillin/sulbactam 3 mg IV every 6 hours

Anaerobes (*Fusobacterium, Bacteroides, etc.*)
- Metronidazole 15 mg/kg load, then 7.5 mg/kg every 6 hours
- Ampicillin/sulbactam 3 g IV every 6 hours

If the Gram stain is negative or difficult to interpret, initiating therapy for both *S. aureus* and Gram-negative organisms is indicated. In a sexually active patient, *N. gonorrhoeae* must be covered as well (see Chapter 6–11). Once a specific organism is isolated and sensitivities are known, the spectrum of therapy can be narrowed.

Daily aspirations of the joint are required to follow the effectiveness of the therapeutic regimen and reduce the products of inflammation and bacterial residue, which helps the response. A flow sheet is useful to follow the changes in gross characteristics of the fluid, cell counts, glucose levels, and repeated cultures. Progressive eradication of the joint infection can be measured by a gradual decrease in the leukocyte count and persistently normal culture. Another helpful indicator is decreasing lactic acid concentration.

General supportive measures include rest of the involved joint during the acute phase of the illness. Splinting helps to provide immobilization, which reduces pain and inflammation. Gradual range-of-motion and muscle-strengthening exercises are passively and then actively carried out. Weight bearing should be avoided until all signs of inflammation have subsided.

Radiologic abnormalities usually take several weeks to be detected and, therefore, are most useful in following the course of the infection rather than as an early diagnostic aid. The earliest change is usually osteoporosis, followed by juxtaarticular bone erosion and joint space narrowing due to destruction of articular cartilage. X-ray studies should be done initially, 2 weeks later, and then at 6- to 8-week intervals.

As soon as possible, the initial choice of antibiotic should be reevaluated in light of the culture result, and a decision made regarding joint drainage based on the daily aspirations and chemical analysis. If microbiologic identification reveals an organism that was not previously suspected, the appropriate antibiotic should be instituted.

After 5 to 8 days, the efficacy of the antibiotic treatment and joint drainage should be reassessed. The closely monitored improving flow sheet, decreased inflammation in the joint, and subsidence of systemic signs of infection indicate that therapy should be maintained without change until the joint has been totally restored to normal.

Surgical drainage should be considered in two situations: when the infection persists or is minimally improved, and when the joint is inaccessible to aspiration. The exact timing of the surgical drainage is variable, but generally by the end of the first week of definitive therapy, the decision should be obvious. If the organism is recovered early and sensitivity to the antibiotic is established, needle drainage is the preferred approach; this avoids converting a closed-space infection into an open draining wound. If, however, there is a delay in diagnosis and the organism is a *Staphylococcus* or a Gram-negative rod, open drainage is indicated. If a hip infection emanates from a contiguous extension such as a pelvic abscess, open drainage is preferred. Finally, when no positive bacteriologic culture has been obtained by the end of the first week and the clinical response is poor, open drainage and synovial biopsy are mandatory.

Direction of treatment in the face of adequate initial response is currently defined by the infecting organism. If streptococci or *H. influenzae* is the causative agent, 2 weeks of therapy is recommended. For staphylococci or Gram-negative bacilli, 3 weeks of therapy is recommended. Longer therapy may be required if juxtaarticular osteomyelitis develops or if response to treatment is inadequate within the above time frames. There are currently no recommendations for the use of intraarticular injections of antibiotics or the use of antibiotics in solution to irrigate joint spaces.

Recommended Approach

When Gram-positive cocci are found on Gram stain of synovial fluid, we recommend initiating vancomycin. Reports of methicillin-resistant *Staphylococcus aureus* and penicillin-resistant *Streptococcus pneumoniae* in community-acquired infections are increasing. As vancomycin resistance is still quite rare, this would provide adequate coverage until sensitivities have returned.

If Gram-negative bacilli are seen on Gram stain, we favor ceftazidime plus tobramycin. This would provide adequate antipseudomonal coverage until identification and sensitivities of the organism are known. If there is suspicion that the Gram-negative rod could be an anaerobe, ticarcillin/clavulanate or piperacillin/tazobactam plus tobramycin would provide both reasonable anaerobic and antipseudomonal coverage until culture and sensitivity test results were returned.

When no organisms are evident, but a bacterial etiology is strongly suspected, adding vancomycin to the above Gram-negative coverage should be adequate. Vancomycin plus imipenem/cilastin would also provide broad Gram-negative and Gram-positive coverage pending cultures.

FOLLOW-UP

At the time of discharge, patients should be instructed to notify their physician if increased swelling, heat, or pain occurs. Repeat synovial fluid cultures and studies should be carried out if signs of inflammation recur or do not resolve. If the patient is discharged on home intravenous antibiotics, appropriate studies should be drawn to monitor for complications of the antibiotics. The patient is always instructed to report any new fever, rashes, shortness of breath, generalized swelling, or ulcerations or lesions of the mouth. Complications of prolonged broad-spectrum antibiotic therapy include line sepsis and fungal superinfection. Once parenteral antibiotics have been completed, further treatment with oral antibiotics will depend on the organism, clinical course, evidence of underlying preexisting disease, and degree of infection resolution.

Radiologic comparison with the initial x-ray should be done at this time. Usually, extensive joint damage is not seen in the promptly treated case. Osteomyelitis may be present, suggesting the need for future debridement of the involved bone and prolongation of antibiotic treatment.

DISCUSSION

Prevalence and Incidence

The prevalence of septic arthritis is low in the general population. Since the mid-1960s, however, the percentage of septic arthritis patients who are elderly has risen considerably. Factors associated with this increase include the higher prevalence of underlying joint disease, systemic illness such as diabetes mellitus, neoplastic disease, chronic renal failure, as well as the decline in the immune system with aging.

Related Basic Science

Genetics

Genetic factors predisposing individuals to the systemic disorders noted above have the most influence on the prevalence of septic arthritis. Less frequently, underlying genetic factors influence the susceptibility of affected individuals to certain pathogens. *Ureaplasma urealyticum* is seen in patients with hypogammaglobulinemia, *Salmonella* in sickle cell patients, and *Neisseria meningitidis* in patients with complement deficiencies.

Physiologic and Anatomic Derangements

The series of events occurring in the infected joint represents an extremely complex interrelationship of metabolic, enzymatic, and immunologic processes woven together in response to the specific microbiologic invader. The presence of this foreign substance sets into motion an acute inflammatory mechanism in defense of the integrity of the joint cavity. This reaction has four phases: recognition of foreign material, generation of mediators of inflammation, local accumulation of polymorphonuclear leukocytes, and modulation of their function at the inflammatory locus. Engorgement and dilation of the synovial microvasculature lead to subsynovial tissue edema and marked increase in synovial fluid. Immunoglobulins and complement accumulate intrasynovially at levels similar to those found in plasma. The microorganism or its antigenic fragments form immune complexes within the joint cavity that are capable of inducing complement-mediated events such as histamine release, chemotaxis, and phagocytosis.

A critical issue in the physiologic approach to the infected joint is the concept of closed-space infection. Unlike cellulitis, for example, in which contact between the interstitial fluid and capillaries is almost direct, the substances in synovial fluid must reach subsynovial vessels first before gaining access to the general circulation. The egress of purulent exudate, therefore, is relatively decreased and fosters an adverse physiologic environment that allows dormant bacteria to survive in the joint milieu despite adequate concentrations of intrasynovial antibiotics. This phenomenon is the basis for the strong commitment to frequent joint drainage of pus.

Previous damage by trauma or arthritis predisposes the patient to infection. Impairment of host resistance by prior disease or treatment with corticosteroids or immunosuppressive agents increases the likelihood of joint infection. Uncontrolled infection leads to cartilage destruction secondary to multiple factors, including increased intrasynovial pressure, poor cartilage nutrition, and the effects of lytic enzymes released from inflammatory synovial tissue.

Natural History and Its Modification with Treatment

If septic arthritis is not treated, cartilage loss and erosion of subchondral bone occurs within 7 to 10 days. A secondary osteomyelitis and/or extension into contiguous soft tissue may occur. In certain settings a relatively high mortality is associated with septic arthritis. In the elderly, even with appropriate treatment, one fourth of all patients die while on treatment in the hospital. Underlying rheumatoid arthritis, delays in diagnosis, and Gram-negative bacillary infection are some of the problems associated with high mortality. By diagnosing the infection early and initiating appropriate therapy, mortality and morbidity are reduced.

Prevention

Although joint infection is not truly preventable, alertness to the predisposing conditions and various types of clinical presentation can result in prompt diagnosis and treatment before irreversible joint damage occurs. Prompt attention to penetrating wounds and traumatic injury to joints and the use of sterile technique during joint aspirations will minimize infection. The use of frequent corticosteroid intraarticular injections should be discouraged. Indications for long-term corticosteroids require very careful scrutiny. Educating drug abusers and others at high risk for septic arthritis (rheumatic diseases, immunosuppression, etc.) about typical and atypical presentations may help them in presenting earlier for evaluation and treatment.

Cost Containment

Early recognition and prompt institution of appropriate therapy reduce cost. Once response to initial therapy has been documented and no further drainage is required, intravenous antibiotics can be administered in an outpatient setting. With the availability of long-term peripheral and central intravenous catheters, patients and families can easily be taught to administer the antibiotics with home health care guidance.

REFERENCES

Goldenberg DK. Infectious arthritis complicating rheumatoid arthritis and other chronic rheumatic disorders. Arthritis Rheum 1989;32:496.

Ho G Jr, Bacterial arthritis. In: McCarty DJ, Koopman WJ, eds. Arthritis and allied conditions/a textbook of rheumatology, 12th ed. Malvern, PA: Lea & Febiger, 1993:116.

Schmid FR. Principles of diagnosis and treatment of bone and joint infections. In: McCarty DJ, Koopman WJ, eds. Arthritis and allied conditions/a textbook of rheumatology, 12th ed. Malvern, PA: Lea & Febiger, 1993:1975.

Shmerling RH, Delbanco TL, Tosteson AN, Trentham DE. Synovial fluid tests: What should be ordered? JAMA 1990;264:1009.

Smith JW, Piercy EA. Infectious arthritis. In: Mandell GL, Bennett JE, Dolin R, eds. Principles and practice of infectious diseases. 4th ed. New York: Churchill Livingstone, 1995:84.

CHAPTER 6–11

Gonococcal Arthritis

Jeffrey L. Stephens, M.D.

DEFINITION

Gonococcal arthritis is a bacterial arthritis caused by dissemination of gonococcal bacteria from mucosal surfaces.

ETIOLOGY

Gonococcal arthritis is caused by *Neisseria gonorrhoeae,* a small Gram-negative diplococcus in the family Neisseriaceae.

CRITERIA FOR DIAGNOSIS

Suggestive

In a patient who presents with an acute inflammatory arthritis, the diagnosis of gonococcal arthritis is suggested by isolation of the organism from the conjunctiva, pharynx, rectum, or urogenital area. The diagnosis is also possible if a therapeutic trial relieves the usual symptoms and signs (tenosynovitis, arthritis, dermatitis) or if the sexual partner of a patient with a typical presentation has a positive gonococcal culture.

Definitive

The diagnosis of gonococcal arthritis is definite when the organism is cultured (or shown by other means) from a nonmucosal site (skin, joint fluid, blood) in a patient with monoarticular or polyarticular arthritis and one or more of the usual manifestations, which include fever, tenosynovitis, and a typical rash.

CLINICAL MANIFESTATIONS

Subjective

Patients with disseminated gonococcal infection often present with complaints of fever and chills of 5 to 7 days' duration. Also, they note joint pain and swelling, and a rash is present in half the cases.

This disease generally affects young people who are sexually active, which is the group with the greatest risk of gonococcal disease in general. Women have this process more commonly than men, and there is increased risk of gonococcal dissemination in women who are pregnant or menstruating, probably because of the increased availability of iron. Also, patients with deficiencies in the late complement components (C5–C8) as well as those lacking serum bactericidal activity are at increased risk of dissemination.

Both men and women have local infection with gonorrhea in the great majority of cases. This varies from cervicitis and pharyngitis, which are usually asymptomatic, to urethritis, which may be symptomatic in half the cases. A personal or family history of rheumatic disease may obscure the diagnosis of disseminated gonococcal infection and delay appropriate therapy because of similar clinical signs and symptoms. Unusual visceral complications of disseminated gonococcal infection include osteomyelitis, myocarditis, pericarditis, endocarditis, perihepatitis (a hematogenous Fitzhugh–Curtis syndrome), and, rarely, meningitis.

Objective

Physical Examination

In a patient with disseminated gonococcal infection, the major findings on physical examination are the classic triad of tenosynovitis, arthritis, and dermatitis. The skin lesions vary widely. They probably represent septic emboli to the skin and often appear on the extremities, initially as macules or petechiae. They can progress to papules or pustules and occasionally form bullae or necrotic ulcers. More common findings are tenosynovitis and septic arthritis. These begin as diffuse arthralgias and a tenosynovitis that "migrates" from joint to joint. The tenosynovitis generally localizes in one or more joints, most often the knee. Other joints involved, in decreasing frequency, are the elbow, ankle, wrist, and small joints of the hand and feet, as well as others. The arthritis involves one joint about a third of the time and multiple joints around two thirds of the time. There is great variability in joint findings. There can be a true septic arthritis, with effusions and positive joint cultures (and usually negative blood cultures); this contrasts with the "arthritis–dermatitis complex," in which joint effusions are small or absent, and joint cultures are negative, but blood cultures are often positive. These two presentations represent the extremes of a spectrum of disease; individual patients may have findings of both.

Routine Laboratory Abnormalities

A complete blood count usually shows a leukocytosis, often with neutrophil predominance, though this may be absent in some cases. The sedimentation rate is normal or elevated. Urinalysis often shows pyuria, probably representing asymptomatic infection. The electrocardiogram may be abnormal, reflecting visceral involvement.

PLANS

Diagnostic

Differential Diagnosis

The signs and symptoms of disseminated gonococcal infection resemble those of many other disease states. The differential includes pyogenic arthritis, crystal-induced arthropathy, Reiter's syndrome, rheumatoid arthritis and other rheumatic diseases, secondary syphilis, and subacute bacterial endocarditis.

Diagnostic Options and Recommended Approach

Any patient felt to have disseminated gonococcal infection should have a careful history (including a sexual history) taken and a complete physical examination performed. Cultures of the blood, skin, synovial fluid, and mucosal sites such as the endocervix, urethra, anus, and pharynx should be obtained. The usual culture medium is Thayer-Martin or its modified version. Nonmucosal sites may have cultures placed on more standard media. Molecular probes, based on the polymerase chain reaction or ligase chain reaction and performed on urine specimens, show promise as alternatives to traditional culturing with similar sensitivity. Diagnostic arthrocentesis of involved joints should be done.

Joint fluid obtained during the arthritis–dermatitis complex is usually sterile and has cell counts of 20,000 leukocytes/mm^3 or less. True septic arthritis has joint fluid with cell counts in the range of 30,000 to 80,000 leukocytes/mm^3, and the ratio of glucose in the synovial fluid to that in serum is low.

Based on the initial evaluation of an ordered differential diagnosis, further laboratory studies may be warranted. These could include rheumatic studies such as antinuclear antibodies, rheumatoid factor, HLA-B27 determination, circulating immune complexes, and cryoglobulins. In addition, serum chemistries to evaluate uric acid levels and serum proteins, a sedimentation rate, antistreptolysin-O titer, and a hepatitis profile may be of interest. Lastly, radiography of the hands, chest, or sacroiliac joints may be indicated in certain instances, as is an electrocardiogram.

Therapeutic

Therapeutic Options

The mainstay of therapy is the use of specific antibacterial agents. With the worldwide spread of antibiotic resistance in the gonococcus (now including quinolones), the recommendation is to first use third-generation cephalosporins. Ceftriaxone (Rocephin), 1 g intravenously or intramuscularly every 24 hours, is the drug of choice. Ceftizoxime (Cefizox), 1 g intravenously every 8 hours, or cefotaxime (Claforan), 1 g intravenously every 8 hours, should also be effective. Those patients allergic to beta-lactams may be treated with spectinomycin (Trobicin), 2 g intramuscularly twice a day. Parenteral therapy should be continued until symptoms and signs have disappeared. At that point, usually 72 to 96 hours after institution of therapy, the patient may be switched to oral therapy with either ciprofloxacin (Cipro), 500 mg orally twice a day; cefixime (Suprax), 400 mg orally twice a day; cefuroxime, 250 mg orally four times a day; or several others to complete 7 to 10 days of therapy. Pregnant women should receive erythromycin base, 500 mg four times a day as an oral agent. Truly septic joints may require parenteral therapy for the entire course. If feasible, home intravenous therapy may be an option.

Because of frequent coinfection with *Chlamydia*, patients with gonococcal arthritis should also receive concomitant or follow-up treatment with doxycycline, 100 mg orally twice a day for 7 days (unless pregnant, in which case erythromycin base, 500 mg orally four times a day, is used).

Recommended Approach

Patients suspected of having gonococcal arthritis should be hospitalized to allow for proper cultures and other diagnostic tests to be obtained. As treatment is almost universally effective, hospitalization prevents visceral complications and ensures proper joint management. Joints with large or purulent effusions may benefit from repeated arthrocenteses. Joint pain may be improved by splinting and other conservative measures. Surgical joint drainage is generally not needed.

Patients should be told that they have an infectious disease that is sexually acquired and can be transmitted to others. They should be counseled that this disease is reportable from a public health standpoint and that recent sexual contacts should be identified so that referral and treatment may be offered. Moreover, they should also be offered voluntary screening for presence of antibodies to HIV after informed consent is obtained. Lastly, it should be stressed that although appropriate therapy almost always cures infection and prevents visceral complications, there is no immunity to repeat infection if again exposed.

FOLLOW-UP

The patient should be instructed to return for clinical evaluation 7 to 14 days after completion of antibiotics. During that visit, overall effectiveness of treatment should be assessed, as should the status of joints originally involved in the infection. Some patients may have persistent joint effusions for weeks after treatment. These effusions are generally benign and represent sterile inflammation. Any patient with a positive gonococcal culture (from any mucosal surface) should have a culture from that site repeated to document clearance. Lastly, condom promotion and other means of prevention should be reviewed and arrangements made for a repeat nontreponemal syphilis test about 4 weeks later.

DISCUSSION
Prevalence and Incidence

During the past 20 years, the incidence of gonococcal infection in the United States has decreased from more than 1 million cases per year to 500,000 per year. This rate of decline may be slowing. Also, there may be as many cases that go unreported as those reported. More troubling is the concentration of disease into two groups, the young and those at high risk for sexually transmitted diseases, a so-called core group of "repeaters." These groups provide a pool from which the disease could again increase in incidence. Groups at increased risk include sex workers, male homosexuals, and those in urban areas, especially the economically disadvantaged and African-Americans. Assuming gonococcal infection disseminates in no more than 5% of cases, there would be about 30,000 cases each year that could lead to gonococcal arthritis. The true prevalence of gonococcal infection is unknown.

Related Basic Science
Altered Molecular Biology

Gonorrhea is a disease that has been recognized since antiquity; however, the differentiation between gonococcal arthritis and other clinical syndromes (like Reiter's) was not possible until Neisser's identification of the gonococcus in the late nineteenth century. This was soon followed by its isolation from joint fluid and identification of its putative relationship with genitourinary disease. The gonococcus is a fastidious organism that grows best in a 5% carbon dioxide environment on special media at 37°C. The bacteria also produces oxidase and is found both intra- and extracellularly.

Even though our understanding of the pathobiology of the gonococcus has expanded considerably, the exact means whereby disseminated gonococcal infection leads to either the arthritis–dermatitis complex of symptoms or septic arthritis is unknown. Direct inoculation of the skin and joint after bacteremia is probably the predominant mechanism of infection; however, in animal studies, injections of killed organisms or gonococcal lipopolysaccharide also have caused arthritis, implicating immune-mediated or hypersensitivity phenomena in at least some cases.

After the gonococcus binds, often via its pili, to a mucosal surface, less than 5% of infections lead to dissemination. Classically, penicillin-sensitive strains, strains resistant to killing by nonimmune human serum, and other specific serotypes have shown increased frequency of dissemination. These strains appear to be decreasing at present, and dissemination is occurring from other strains. Recently, similar clinical syndromes have been noted with disseminated *Neisseria meningitidis* infections, and these may be increasing in incidence. Deficiencies of the terminal complement pathway (C5–C8) also increase the risk of dissemination in both meningococcal and gonococcal disease. About 10% of patients with disseminated gonococcal infections have a complement deficiency, and anyone who has repeated disseminated neisserial infections should have an assay to determine total hemolytic complement function (CH50).

Physiologic Derangement

Overall, the interaction between the human host and the gonococcus is complex. Both host defense and organism virulence factors play a part in whether infection occurs. The main host defenses include polymorphonuclear leukocyte function, mucosal factors, secretory immunoglobulins, and serum complement. Gonococcal envelope components such as pili, outer membrane proteins (porin, opacity proteins, reduction-modifiable protein), lipopolysaccharide, and peptidoglycan have all been associated with alterations of organism binding, killing, phagocytosis, and the like. As there is no immunity to reinfection, there has been interest in developing a vaccine, perhaps to pilus antigens. Unfortunately, a single gonococcal organism can produce pili that have different antigenic determinants. Resistance to antibiotics is both chromosomal and plasmid mediated. Lastly, genetic variation in gonoccocci is facilitated by DNA transformation, allowing direct transfer of DNA between organisms.

Natural History and Its Modification with Treatment

Prior to the introduction of antibiotics, it was common for purulent gonococcal arthritis to progress to frank destruction of articular cartilage or even bony ankylosis. With the early addition of specific antibacterial therapy, in the standard doses, there is little or no likelihood of subsequent joint damage. Complete resolution is the expected response when therapy is continued for the usual length of time.

Prevention

Prevention of gonococcal infections in general, and gonococcal arthritis in particular, lies mainly in improved public awareness and education regarding sexually transmitted diseases. This education should include recognition of symptoms and the need to seek treatment early. Promotion of abstinence and "safer sex" practices, including barrier methods for contraception (latex condoms for men, and, now probably, women) along with the use of spermicides like nonoxynol-9, provides the best means available for interrupting transmission of microorganisms spread by sexual contact. Because adolescents and young adults have had a disproportionate increase in the incidence of gonorrhea, prevention strategies should be tailored to these age groups. Finally, patients with known deficiencies in the terminal complement pathway should be advised as to their increased risk of disseminated neisserial infections and possible candidacy for gonococcal vaccination if this were developed.

Cost Containment

A high index of suspicion based on the clinical presentation, especially in the usual age groups, should lead to appropriate cultures being obtained. This should be followed by the early addition of specific antimicrobial therapy. This approach should minimize the need for lengthy hospital stays or multiple diagnostic tests.

REFERENCES

Goldenberg DL, Reed JI. Bacterial arthritis. N Engl J Med 1985;312:764.

Handsfield HH, Spurling PF. *Neisseria gonorrhoeae.* In: Mandell GL, Bennet JE, Dolin R, editors-in-chief. Principles and practice of infectious diseases. 4th ed. New York: Churchill Livingstone, 1995:1909.

Holmes KK, Counts GW, Beatty HN. Disseminated gonococcal infection. Ann Intern Med 1971;74:979.

Mahowald ML. Infectious arthritis. In: Schumacher HR, ed. Primer on the rheumatic diseases. 10th ed. Atlanta: Arthritis Foundation, 1993:192.

O'Brien JP, Goldenberg DL, Rioz PA. Disseminated gonococcal infection: A prospective analysis of 49 patients and a review of pathophysiology and immune mechanisms. Medicine 1983;62:395.

Panush RS, Kisch AL. Gonococcal arthritis. In: Hurst JW: editor-in-chief. Medicine for the practicing physician. 3rd ed. Boston: Butterworth-Heineman, 1992:216.

CHAPTER 6–12

Skeletal Tuberculosis

Stephen B. Miller, M.D.

DEFINITION

Skeletal tuberculosis is defined as bone and/or joint involvement secondary to infection with *Mycobacterium tuberculosis.*

ETIOLOGY

The condition is caused by the organism *M. tuberculosis.*

CRITERIA FOR DIAGNOSIS

Suggestive

The physician should suspect tuberculous arthritis in a patient who has a persistent inflammatory monoarticular arthritis, localized back pain, or localized tendinitis. Ancillary findings of value to strongly support the diagnosis include a positive intermediate-strength stabilized purified protein derivative (PPD-S), although advanced disease or old age may produce anergy, and/or evidence of tuberculosis elsewhere in the body in association with the characteristic clinical picture described above.

Definitive

Confirmation of the diagnosis requires demonstration of the organism. This can be accomplished by histologic evidence (caseating granulomata and acid-fast bacilli) or culture of synovial tissue in more than 90% of cases, and/or synovial fluid smear, culture, or guinea pig inoculation in approximately 80% of cases.

CLINICAL MANIFESTATIONS

Subjective

Articular tuberculosis is insidious in onset and may be present for years before the patient seeks medical help. Pain and swelling in a monoarticular weight-bearing joint are the usual presentation. Constitutional symptoms, with the exception of weight loss, are often minimal.

Spinal tuberculosis is initially characterized clinically by back pain. Sensory and/or motor deficits eventually occur in many patients.

There is often a family history of tuberculosis. Possible predisposing conditions include trauma, narcotic and alcohol dependency, HIV disease, diabetes mellitus, and other chronic debilitating diseases. Intraarticular steroids may sometimes be implicated in the recent history.

Objective

Physical Examination

Peripheral joint involvement is usually associated with marked swelling, although local heat may or may not be noted. Tenderness to palpation and stiffness are common features. The synovium is markedly thickened, giving a doughy consistency on palpation. The adjacent musculature is frequently disproportionately wasted. Usually there is significant limitation of motion, and lower-extremity involvement is accompanied by a limp. Tenosynovitis may be present in close proximity to the affected joint.

Examination of the tuberculous spine reveals varying degrees of muscle spasm, localized tenderness, kyphosis, and referred pain from root compression. Diminished sensation below the lesion level and cord compression are potentially serious complications.

Routine Laboratory Abnormalities

The complete blood count, routine chemical profile, and urinalysis are not usually helpful.

PLANS

Diagnostic

Differential Diagnosis

The differential diagnosis includes septic arthritis (usually monoarticular), infectious spondylitis, and metastatic malignancy to the spine.

Diagnostic Options

The diagnostic options include a skin test, x-ray of the affected part and chest, synovial fluid analysis, and biopsy of synovium (joint) or tissue (spinal lesions).

Recommended Approach

A skin test with intermediate-strength purified protein derivative (PPD-S) should be positive unless the patient is anergic because of advanced disease, old age, or immunosuppressive therapy. Depending on the duration of disease, x-ray films of the involved joint or area of spine may show suggestive destructive changes of bone, cartilage, or intervertebral disk often with associated abscess.

Examination of the joint fluid may reveal a white blood cell count of 10,000 to 20,000 / μL, depending on the stage and activity of the disease. The cells may be predominantly mononuclear. The mycobacterium may be shown by acid-fast stain. Guinea pig inoculation may help isolate the mycobacterium.

Biopsy of the synovium may show typical caseating granulomata on histologic examination. Culture of synovial tissue or spinal tissue usually confirms the diagnosis.

Therapeutic

Therapeutic Options

Therapeutic options include multidrug chemotherapy and surgery (special situations).

Recommended Approach

The treatment of skeletal tuberculosis is multidrug chemotherapy. The use of more than one drug makes the development of organism resistance less likely than if the drugs are used alone. Initially, the recommended combination is isoniazid (INH, Nydrozide), 5 to 10 mg/kg body weight up to 300 mg orally in a single daily dose, and rifampin (Rifadin, Rimactane), 10 to 20 mg/kg body weight in a single daily oral dose. Streptomycin, 20 mg/kg body weight up to 1 g intramuscularly daily, or pyrazinamide, 15 to 30 mg/kg up to 2 g daily, may be added for the first 2 months. A minimum of 2 years of drug therapy is usually recommended, although shorter treatment protocols are showing equal cure rates.

A surgical approach as an adjunctive measure to drug therapy is strongly considered in certain special situations. Evidence of extensive bone involvement beyond the articulating surfaces, especially in children with hip disease, is best treated with synovectomy and debridement. Severe destruction in weight-bearing joints requires arthrodesis. Most patients with spinal tuberculosis heal without surgical intervention. The exceptions are those with paraplegia or paraparesis, who often benefit from surgery.

FOLLOW-UP

Once appropriate chemotherapy is underway and progression is arrested, follow-up visits can be kept at intervals of 2 to 3 months until 2 years of chemotherapy is completed. Thereafter, the patient should be seen at yearly intervals to be sure the process has not reactivated.

DISCUSSION

Prevalence

Musculoskeletal tuberculosis usually occurs in patients 20 to 50 years old. Nonwhites are more commonly affected than whites and males more than females. It accounts for 10% of cases of extrapulmonary tuberculosis, or approximately 2% of all new cases of tuberculosis.

Related Basic Science

In the nonimmune patient, primary tuberculosis begins in the lungs and rapidly disseminates throughout the blood and lymphatics. The tubercle bacilli spread to all regions of the body, but resolution usually occurs with development of delayed hypersensitivity and cellular immunity. A few patients, however, develop widespread disease, sometimes involving one or two organ systems.

Tuberculosis in the immune individual shows an accelerated tissue response with local necrosis but relative containment of the process. A bronchus or blood vessel must be breached for dissemination to occur. Tuberculosis of bone can develop in three ways: by hematogenous spread; via lymphatics from chronic pleural, renal, or lymph node foci; or by reactivation of latent infection seeded in the primary invasion. Articular tuberculosis may occur from bloodstream seeding or from a contiguous osteomyelitic process. Synovitis is followed by the formation of caseating granulation tissue characterized by the presence of Langhans giant cells. This tissue spreads slowly over the cartilage surface as pannus, extending from the periphery and producing damage by pressure necrosis. Spontaneous resolution is rare, and ultimately, severe bone destruction, cold abscesses, sinus tract formation, and sometimes ankylosis result.

Natural History and Its Modification With Treatment

Untreated, the infection continues to progress slowly, with destruction of the articular cartilage and development of osteomyelitis and soft tissue abscesses in the adjacent area. The eventual outcome is total destruction of the joint or vertebra. The response to chemotherapy is good, with the eventual outcome depending on the amount of prior damage before therapy is begun.

Prevention

The prevention of tuberculous arthritis depends on the establishment of epidemiologic principles for eradication of the tuberculosis itself. Aggressive treatment of underlying or predisposing conditions, prophylactic antituberculosis therapy for patients with positive skin tests, and close household contact surveillance are the major preventive measures for this problem.

Cost Containment

Early diagnosis and treatment reduce the potential for long-term disability and the need for extensive medical care.

REFERENCES

Berney S, Golden M, Bishko F. Clinical and diagnostic features of tuberculous arthritis. Am J Med 1972;53:36.

Bocanegra TS. Mycobacterial, fungal and parasitic arthritides. In: Klippel JH, Dieppe PA, eds. Rheumatology. London: Mosby, 1994:4.5.1.

Garrido G, Gomez-Reino JJ, Fernandez-Dapica P, et al. A review of peripheral tuberculous arthritis. Semin Arthritis Rheum 1988;18:142.

Mehta JB, Dutt A, Harvil L, Mathews KM. Epidemiology of extrapulmonary tuberculosis: A comparative analysis with pre-AIDS era. Chest 1991;99:1134.

Snider DE, Salinas L, Kelly GD. Tuberculosis: An increasing problem among minorities in the United States. Public Health 1989;104:646.

CHAPTER 6–13

Rubella Arthritis

Stephen B. Miller, M.D.

DEFINITION

Rubella arthritis is a polyarticular, self-limited, nondeforming arthritis secondary to natural infection with rubella virus or vaccine-induced.

ETIOLOGY

This type of arthritis is, by definition, caused by the rubella virus.

CRITERIA FOR DIAGNOSIS

Suggestive

The patient is more likely to be female than male. The onset of acutely painful and stiff small joints of the hands, wrists, and knees is closely associated with clinical evidence of rubella occurring either naturally or after vaccination. Historically, evidence of rubella usually takes the form of varying degrees of malaise, fatigue, headache, and a recent or ongoing sore throat, cough, coryza, and rash (see Chapter 8–66).

Definitive

Definitive criteria for diagnosis are direct viral isolation and elevated titers of acute and convalescent rubella antibody.

CLINICAL MANIFESTATIONS

Subjective

Pain and stiffness of involved joints are the major symptoms. Except for fatigue, constitutional symptoms are absent.

Objective

Physical Examination

Joint examination may demonstrate pain on palpation or on motion of the involved joints. Swelling and erythema are sometimes appreciated. Carpal tunnel syndrome and tenosynovitis may be present. Helpful clues linking the arthritis with rubella are the characteristic morbilliform exanthem and posterior cervical lymphadenopathy.

Routine Laboratory Abnormalities

Laboratory data are generally inconsistent and nonspecific. Peripheral blood leukocytosis may occur, but normal counts are found in most patients. Moderate elevation of the sedimentation rate sometimes occurs.

PLANS

Diagnostic

Differential Diagnosis

The differential diagnosis includes other viral arthritides, rheumatoid arthritis, and Lyme disease.

Diagnostic Options

The diagnostic options include the following:

- Acute and convalescent serum for rubella antibody titers.
- Sedimentation rate: may be moderately elevated.
- Rheumatoid factor: may be elevated in 10 to 20% of cases.
- Synovial analysis: reveals a mild to moderate inflammatory fluid with either a mononuclear or polymorphonuclear predominance. Histologically, the synovium shows evidence of a nonspecific synovitis characterized by hypervascularity, synoviocyte hyperplasia, and varying degrees of round cell infiltrates and fibrinopurulent exudates.
- Direct viral isolation.

Recommended Approach

The determination of acute and convalescent antibody titers is usually all that is needed.

Therapeutic

Therapeutic Options

The therapeutic options include no specific treatment, nonsteroidal antiinflammatory drugs, and corticosteroids.

Recommended Approach

Specific treatment is usually not necessary. If nonsteroidal drugs are required, salicylates usually suffice. Corticosteroids are rarely used and only for very severe symptomatic cases.

FOLLOW-UP

The patient should be seen as often as necessary at the outset to establish the diagnosis and to ensure his or her comfort. The patient should be seen again in 6 to 8 weeks to check on the resolution of the arthritis.

DISCUSSION

Prevalence and Incidence

Up to 50% of infected adult women and up to 6% of adult men experience arthralgia and arthritis related to rubella. Vaccine-induced rubella has been reported in up to 15% of women.

Related Basic Science

The basic mechanisms responsible for the joint involvement in patients with rubella have not been studied extensively. The condition is most likely caused by an immunologic mechanism.

Natural History and Its Modification with Treatment

Arthritis caused by natural infection differs in a few ways from vaccine-induced arthritis. In the natural infection, the joint symptoms usually begin a few days after the onset of the rash, whereas the postvaccination arthritis occurs 2 to 4 weeks later. Rash is distinctly more common in natural infection, whereas isolated knee involvement and carpal tunnel syndrome are seen more frequently in the vaccine-induced arthritis.

Progression to permanent joint damage has not been documented. Treatment does not alter the disease process.

Prevention

The arthritis secondary to the natural infection would theoretically be preventable if everyone were to be vaccinated; however, as there is at least a 5 to 10% incidence of joint symptoms with the present vaccine strains, total prevention at this time is not possible.

Cost Containment

Knowledge of the association between arthritis and rubella and an understanding that the joint symptoms are self-limited should eliminate the need for extensive diagnostic testing and limit care to outpatient treatment only.

REFERENCES

Cusi MG, Metelli R, Valensin PE. Immune responses to rubella viruses after rubella vaccination. Arch Virol 1989;106:63.

Fraser JR, Cunningham AL, Hayes K, et al. Rubella arthritis in adults: Isolation of virus, cytology, and other aspects of the synovial reaction. Clin Exp Rheumatol 1983;1:287.

Smith CA, Petty RE, Tingle AJ. Rubella virus and arthritis. Rheum Dis Clin North Am 1987;13:265.

Tingle AJ, Allen M, Petty RE, et al. Rubella-associated arthritis: I. Comparative study of joint manifestations associated with natural rubella infection and RA 27/3 rubella immunization. Ann Rheum Dis 1986;45:110.

Tingle AJ, Pot KH, Yong FP, et al. Kinetics of isotype specific humoral immunity in rubella vaccine-associated arthropathy. Clin Immunol Immunopathol 1989;53:99.

CHAPTER 6–14

Lyme Arthritis (See Section 8, Chapter 48)

CHAPTER 6–15

Arthritis Associated with Hepatitis

Stephen B. Miller, M.D.

DEFINITION

The condition can be defined as arthralgia or arthritis occurring during the prodrome of hepatitis B virus infection.

ETIOLOGY

The condition is caused by the immunologic response to hepatitis B virus (HBV).

CRITERIA FOR DIAGNOSIS

Suggestive

Arthralgia or arthritis may occur in the prodrome of hepatitis B. It is usually symmetric and polyarticular and may be accompanied by urticaria or other skin eruptions.

Definitive

The hepatitis B surface antigen (HBsAG) is usually present in both blood and synovial fluid. There is often hypocomplementemia.

CLINICAL MANIFESTATIONS

Subjective

The patient is often young (third decade especially). The presentation can be extremely variable. The most typical onset is a sudden symmetric involvement of the small joints of the hands, particularly the distal and proximal interphalangeal joints. Large joints are also affected and include, in decreasing order, the knee, shoulder, ankle, elbow, and wrist. The arthritis usually lasts a few weeks, but may disappear in days or persist for months.

Accompanying the joint symptoms is likely to be a pruritic rash. Most often the arthritis and rash disappear prior to or at the time of the development of the jaundice. Systemic manifestations may include malaise, anorexia, nausea, vomiting, chills, and myalgias.

Objective

Physical Examination

Examination may reveal a wide spectrum of findings from severely tender, swollen, hot, and red joints to no objective signs of inflammation. The eruption is most often urticarial, but may be macular, papular, or petechial. The nonurticarial rashes are minimally erythematous and often found on the legs and, less frequently, the forearms. Most patients do not become clinically jaundiced.

Routine Laboratory Abnormalities

The serum transaminase level is often elevated. Otherwise, complete blood count, other routine blood chemistries, and urinalysis are not abnormal.

PLANS

Diagnostic

Differential Diagnosis

The differential diagnosis includes other viral arthritides, rheumatoid arthritis, and Lyme disease.

Diagnostic Options

Diagnostic options include determinations of levels of hepatitis B virus, hepatitis B surface, and hepatitis B e antigens; transaminases; CH50, C3, and C4; and cryoglobulins. Also, findings from synovial fluid analysis are variable and can range from a totally noninflammatory fluid (white blood cell count less than 1000 / μL with mostly mononuclear cells) to an infected-appearing fluid (white blood cell count of 100,000 μL with predominantly polymorphonuclear leukocytes). Total protein is usually elevated and glucose levels are normal.

Recommended Approach

The best approach seems to be to determine levels of hepatitis B virus, hepatitis B surface, and hepatitis B e antigens; transaminases; and CH50, C3, and C4.

Therapeutic

Therapeutic Options

The therapeutic options include no specific treatment and nonsteroidal antiinflammatory drugs.

Recommended Approach

No specific treatment is needed.

FOLLOW-UP

The need for follow-up for this condition is determined mainly by the primary disease, hepatitis (see Chapters 19–75 and 19–78). A repeat test for circulating hepatitis B surface antigen should be done 6 weeks after onset to ensure that it has disappeared from the circulation.

DISCUSSION

Incidence

Hepatitis B virus infection in its prodromal stage is associated with a transient polyarthritis in approximately one third of patients. There is no sexual preference.

Related Basic Science

This condition is felt to represent an immune complex disease; that is, circulating immune complexes may play a pathogenetic role in the arthritis associated with hepatitis B infection. These complexes contain hepatitis B surface antigen and anti-hepatitis B antibody, other immunoglobulins, and complement components. During the preicteric period, the complexes are in excess when active skin and joint symptoms are ongoing. As antibody excess ensues, the complexes disappear and the arthritis and rash resolve. This series of events is very similar to that observed in experimental serum sickness.

Natural History and Its Modification With Treatment

The arthritis and rash are short-lived and self-limited. Residual joint damage and chronic liver disease do not occur.

Prevention

As this form of arthritis is directly associated with the development of the hepatitis B infection, prevention of its occurrence depends on eradication of hepatitis B infection.

Cost Containment

Knowledge of the association of arthritis with hepatitis and its benign and self-limited course should minimize overall treatment costs.

REFERENCES

Alpert E, Isselbacher KJ, Schur PH. The pathogenesis of arthritis associated with viral hepatitis. N Engl J Med 1971;285:185.

Alpert E, Schur PH, Isselbacher KJ. Sequential changes of serum complement in HLA-related arthritis. N Engl J Med 1972;287:103.

Kalden JR. Viral arthritis. In: Klippel JH, Dieppe PA, eds. Rheumatology. London: Mosby, 1994:4.6.3.

Petty RE, Tingle AJ. Arthritis and viral infections. J Pediatr 1988;113(Suppl):948.

Sergent JS. Extrahepatic manifestations of hepatitis B infection. Bull Rheum Dis 1983;33(6):1.

CHAPTER 6-16

Polymyalgia Rheumatica

Emilio B. Gonzalez, M.D.

DEFINITION

Polymyalgia rheumatica, is a systemic rheumatic disorder that affects primarily individuals more than 50 years of age.

ETIOLOGY

The etiology is unknown.

CRITERIA FOR DIAGNOSIS

Suggestive

The syndrome is characterized by aching, tenderness, and morning stiffness involving the proximal extremities, mainly the shoulder and pelvic girdles. The patient is almost always older than 60. The duration of symptoms should be longer than 6 weeks, and the onset may be abrupt or insidious. A Westergren erythrocyte sedimentation rate is usually significantly elevated; however, patients with polymyalgia rheumatica and relatively normal sedimentation rates have been described. This appears to be the exception rather than the rule, and the typical patient with polymyalgia rheumatica would have an elevation of the sedimentation rate reflecting the systemic nature of the inflammatory process. Similarly, the pattern on a serum protein electrophoresis would reflect the presence of systemic inflammation. Mild anemia may be present, and systemic complaints such as anorexia, fatigue, weight loss, apathy, and low-grade fever may be present as well.

Definitive

Given the symptomatology described above, an excellent clinical response in 24 to 48 hours to treatment with low-dose steroids (prednisone 10–20 mg/d) is considered by some authors as a good criterion for a diagnosis of polymyalgia rheumatica.

It should be emphasized that polymyalgia rheumatica is mainly a diagnosis of exclusion in an elderly patient. Accordingly, no clinical or laboratory evidence for a connective tissue disease, malignancy, or occult infection must be present. It is for this reason that a duration of 6 weeks or longer is required as one of the criteria for diagnosis.

CLINICAL MANIFESTATIONS

Subjective

The patients are usually elderly women with a mean age of onset of 70 years. They complain of achiness, fatigue, stiffness, and shoulder, upper arm, hip, thigh, or groin pain. Most of the symptomatology is present in the shoulder and pelvic girdles. Knee pains with effusion has been described. Involvement of the shoulders is usually symmetric. On occasions, neck pain is present along with the shoulder girdle discomfort. Often, on questioning, these patients report difficulty combing their hair or getting up from a sitting position, such as from a chair, reflecting the involvement of the proximal extremities. Difficulty in ambulation may be present. The stiffness may improve with activity only to return later in the day. Poor appetite, malaise, apathy, poor sleep, and weight loss with resulting depression may ensue. Because of the malaise, stiffness, and fatigue, the patient's physical endurance is significantly compromised. Infrequently, only unilateral shoulder pain is present, which may be confused with bursitis or tendinitis.

Often, the onset of symptoms is sudden and abrupt; not infrequently, these patients remember the day and time when they started feeling ill. No precipitating factors have been identified. An insidious onset is not uncommon. Fever, usually of low grade, may be present.

If, in addition to polymyalgia rheumatica, symptoms and signs such as amaurosis fugax (visual transient ischemic attacks), headaches, limb or jaw claudication, and scalp or facial tenderness are present, alone or in combination, underlying giant cell arteritis should be suspected (see Chapter 7–11).

Objective

Physical Examination

Typically, little will be found on physical examination of patients with polymyalgia rheumatica. The shoulders, upper arms, and thighs may be somewhat tender to palpation or squeezing. The patients do not look sick; however, they appear stiff and deliberate in their movements. The limitation of active joint range of motion is likely owing to pain in the proximal musculature. Yet, gentle passive motion of proximal joints in polymyalgia rheumatica is nearly always normal.

The small joints in the hands and grip strength are normal. In a minority of patients (about 10%), however, knee effusions are present, as is involvement with synovitis of the small joints of the hands, including the wrists, suggesting an overlap syndrome with the presence of a rheumatoid arthritis-like condition.

On occasions, shoulder bursitis, bicipital tendinitis, and trochanteric bursitis are present. A "frozen shoulder" complication has been reported in patients with chronic shoulder tendinitis and resulting muscle atrophy.

Again, if in addition to polymyalgia rheumatica, signs such as scalp or facial tenderness and swollen, nodular, tender, and tortuous temporal arteries are present, giant cell arteritis should be suspected and managed appropriately (see Chapter 7–11).

Routine Laboratory Abnormalities

Pertinent routine laboratory findings include an elevation of the Westergren erythrocyte sedimentation rate and, on occasion, an inflammatory response pattern on serum protein electrophoresis. Thrombocytosis, mild normochromic, normocytic anemia, and mild elevation of hepatic enzymes may be found.

PLANS

Diagnostic

Differential Diagnosis

It is important to emphasize that polymyalgia rheumatica should be a diagnosis of exclusion. Attempts should be made to exclude the presence of a connective tissue disease, an underlying neoplasia, or occult infection, such as subacute bacterial endocarditis.

Numerous other disorders may mimic polymyalgia rheumatica. Rheumatoid arthritis may involve large proximal joints; however, there is nearly always small joint synovitis in the hands and wrists as well. A small minority of patients will have an overlap clinical syndrome with features of both polymyalgia rheumatica and rheumatoid arthritis. Polymyositis and dermatomyositis are inflammatory diseases of muscle with serum elevation of muscle enzymes (creatine phosphokinase) and typical electromyographic as well as muscle biopsy findings. These are all absent in polymyalgia rheumatica.

Similarly, there is no confirmed association between polymyalgia rheumatica and cancer; therefore, an exhaustive search for an underlying tumor is not warranted.

In patients with a clinical presentation suggestive of polymyalgia rheumatica but with a normal erythrocyte sedimentation rate, thyroid disorders, typically hypothyroidism, as well as fibrositis or fibromyalgia, need to be excluded. Fibromyalgia tends to affect a much younger population as compared with polymyalgia rheumatica.

Diagnostic Options and Recommended Approach

The diagnosis of polymyalgia rheumatica is based on the clinical findings described in an elderly patient who has an elevated Westergren erythrocyte sedimentation rate. The sedimentation rate may be greater than 100 mm in the first hour. Other laboratory findings would be consistent with the presence of systemic inflammation; however, they do not appreciably add to a specific diagnosis.

Approximately 10 to 15% of patients with polymyalgia rheumatica have concomitant giant cell arteritis, as suggested by signs and symptoms of this latter disorder: headaches, jaw claudication, visual blurring, sudden blindness, facial tenderness. Unfortunately, however, silent or "occult" giant cell arteritis may be present in seemingly pure polymyalgia rheumatica. Approximately 6 to 10% or 1 in 10 patients with pure polymyalgia rheumatica will have a positive temporal artery biopsy for giant cell arteritis.

Therapeutic

Therapeutic Options

Typically, patients with polymyalgia rheumatica derive an excellent response to low-dose prednisone, 10 to 20 mg a day, in a short period, usually 2 to 3 days. Some patients (about 20%) do well with nonsteroidal antiinflammatory agents without the addition of corticosteroids. This is important if the patient in question is a diabetic or has significant osteoporosis, relative contraindications to the use of steroids. Eventually, however, nearly all patients with polymyalgia rheumatica require treatment with low-dose prednisone.

Recommended Approach

A useful therapeutic strategy is to begin treatment with a nonsteroidal antiinflammatory agent for about 2 weeks before starting steroids. If the patient is still significantly symptomatic at the end of the 2 weeks of nonsteroidal antiinflammatory treatment, low-dose prednisone, 10 to 20 mg a day, is then started. On occasion, in patients who are steroid dependent, the addition of a nonsteroidal antiinflammatory agent may allow a more rapid reduction of the prednisone dose to 5 mg a day or lower and facilitate early steroid withdrawal. This may be useful, especially when treating a patient in whom prolonged steroid therapy is undesirable.

If giant cell arteritis is present, treatment with high-dose prednisone, 40 to 60 mg a day, is needed to suppress the arteritis and prevent potential blindness. It should be remembered that occult arteritis may be present in polymyalgia rheumatica and that low-dose prednisone, although appropriate to relieve the symptoms of polymyalgia, will not control the arteritis. In fact, blindness has been reported in patients with polymyalgia rheumatica (and occult giant cell arteritis) treated seemingly appropriately with low-dose prednisone. Most rheumatologists believe that the majority of patients with clinically "pure" polymyalgia rheumatica do not need a biopsy of the temporal artery, if no signs or symptoms suggestive of arteritis are present.

If the patient does not clinically improve promptly while on treatment with low-dose prednisone, or if headaches or new visual symptoms develop, an increase in the dose of prednisone and a temporal artery biopsy should be implemented as soon as possible. Further discussion of giant cell arteritis is offered in Chapter 7–11.

The duration of treatment with low-dose prednisone in polymyalgia rheumatica varies. Some patients do well and no longer require prednisone therapy after 6 months or so. Some patients have a recurrence of their polymyalgia rheumatica and require additional treatment with prednisone, perhaps for another year or two. A few patients become steroid dependent for the rest of their lives.

FOLLOW-UP

On the basis of available data, there is a small 1 to 2% theoretical risk of blindness (from occult giant cell arteritis) in patients with polymyalgia rheumatica while receiving treatment with low-dose prednisone. This risk is small enough for the physician to be reassuring; at the same time, he or she should educate the patient on issues relating to a temporal artery biopsy, including benefits against potential risks of low- versus high-dose prednisone therapy.

Because of the close association between polymyalgia rheumatica and giant cell arteritis, the patient should be alerted to notify the physician promptly if headaches, visual impairment, or other signs or symptoms suggestive of giant cell arteritis develop.

An occasional patient may demand that a temporal artery biopsy be done so as to make absolutely sure that there is no underlying silent giant cell arteritis. Such requests should not be ignored, particularly considering the present medicolegal climate in the United States. Even in classic cases of giant cell arteritis, however, a positive yield from a unilateral temporal artery biopsy is 70% at best (see Chapter 7–11).

Whether or not to biopsy remains a controversial issue in rheumatology, and the best decision is probably arrived at on an individual patient basis.

A patient with typical polymyalgia rheumatica will experience significant, often dramatic improvement in 2 to 3 days of treatment with low-dose prednisone. This welcome relief of symptoms may be reported back to the physician in the form of a telephone call. Indeed, in the practice of rheumatology, no other experience offers more professional gratification than the treatment of polymyalgia rheumatica with low-dose prednisone. If no improvement is noted in a few days, the diagnosis may need revision. Appropriate follow-up consists of office visits every 2 to 4 weeks, for the first 2 months. Thereafter, visits at intervals of 6 to 8 weeks should be adequate in most situations. If low-dose prednisone is required, it usually takes about 6 months before this can be totally discontinued. A gradual taper of the prednisone dose is usually undertaken, sometimes with the addition of a nonsteroidal antiinflammatory agent. Relapses may occur in a subset of patients. Laboratory parameters of systemic inflammation such as the sedimentation rate are usually normal by the end of the first month.

DISCUSSION
Prevalence and Incidence

The prevalence and incidence of polymyalgia rheumatica vary according to the patient population surveyed. Apparently, elderly white women of Northern European extraction appear to be particularly vulnerable. Clinical experience and new data suggest that polymyalgia rheumatica occurs in other ethnic groups as well, for example, African-Americans (Gonzalez et al., 1989). The average annual prevalence in Olmstead County, Minnesota, was 54 per 100,000 persons 50 years of age and older per year. In Goteborg, Sweden, the prevalence was 20 per 100,000 in a similar patient population.

The ratio of women to men is about 2:1, and the prevalence of this condition in older persons remains unexplained. In the United States and Europe, approximately 6 to 10% of patients with polymyalgia rheumatica have associated giant cell (cranial, temporal) arteritis. Not surprisingly, about 50% of patients with giant cell arteritis have polymyalgia rheumatica. In Scandinavian countries, the prevalence of underlying giant cell arteritis in patients with polymyalgia rheumatica is much greater and may reach 35 to 45%.

Related Basic Science

Pathologically, specimens from muscle biopsies have been normal; however, synovitis may be present in joints such as the knees. The presence of large joint synovitis in polymyalgia rheumatica has been documented by synovial biopsy, joint scanning procedures, radiographs, and arthroscopy. As previously mentioned, about 6 to 10% of patients with polymyalgia rheumatica may have underlying silent giant cell arteritis. Whether an associated vasculitis explains some of the clinical or laboratory features of the disease, such as transient transaminase elevation, remains uncertain. The association of giant cell arteritis with the presence of the major histocompatibility complex class II molecule HLA-DR4 has been reported. Interestingly, HLA-DR4 is also seen in patients with classic rheumatoid arthritis. T cells from patients with polymyalgia rheumatica and giant cell arteritis produce predominantly interleukin-2 and interferon gamma. In patients with only polymyalgia rheumatica, interferon gamma production is not seen, suggesting that this specific cytokine may be involved in the progression to giant cell arteritis. Increased production of interleukin-6, but not tumor necrosis factor α, has been observed in patients with giant cell arteritis and polymyalgia rheumatica.

Natural History and Its Modification with Treatment

Polymyalgia rheumatica is usually a benign disorder that responds well to low-dose prednisone therapy and, on occasion, even to nonsteroidal antiinflammatory agents; however, polymyalgia rheumatica becomes clinically important because of its common association with giant cell arteritis. This latter disorder may cause total blindness that is sometimes bilateral and irreversible if not treated early. Appropriate therapy for giant cell arteritis requires a regimen of high-dose prednisone, which is not usually necessary to treat polymyalgia rheumatica in its pure form.

Unfortunately, however, "occult" or silent giant cell arteritis may be present in seemingly pure polymyalgia rheumatica. The causes of these disorders remain unknown, and the exact nature of their relationship is still unclear.

The onset of polymyalgia rheumatica may be sudden or insidious. Often, when sudden, the patients may be able to recall the exact date and time when the symptoms developed. The duration of the illness may range from a few months to a few years. A few patients will have an overlap syndrome with small joint synovitis resembling rheumatoid arthritis. A majority of patients receiving appropriate treatment recover within 2 years and do not experience a relapse. A few patients become steroid dependent and suffer a relapse when prednisone is either decreased in dose or discontinued. When giant cell arteritis is present in addition to polymyalgia rheumatica, high-dose prednisone must be instituted to suppress the arteritis and prevent complications such as blindness.

Prevention

No preventive measures are currently available.

Cost Containment

The evaluation and treatment of patients with polymyalgia rheumatica are usually undertaken on an ambulatory basis. Patients with symptoms suggestive of underlying giant cell arteritis, such as headaches and visual disturbance, require a temporal or occipital artery biopsy for pathologic confirmation of arteritis.

An occasional well-informed patient may demand a temporal artery biopsy to more readily exclude underlying temporal arteritis. These cases are best handled on an individual patient basis. When a biopsy is not initially done, the patient should be alerted to any unexpected changes in the course of illness, such as new visual symptoms, headaches, or failure to adequately respond to low-dose prednisone. These should be reported back to the treating physician promptly.

REFERENCES

Chuang T-Y, Hunder GG, Ilstrup DM, Kurland LT. Polymyalgia rheumatica: A 10-year epidemiologic and clinical study. Ann Intern Med 1982;97:672.

Gonzalez EB, Varner WT, Lisse JR, et al. Giant-cell arteritis in the southern United States: An 11-year retrospective study from the Texas Gulf Coast. Arch Intern Med 1989;149:1561.

Hall S, Persellin S, Lie JT, et al. The therapeutic impact of temporal artery biopsy. Lancet 1983;2:1217.

Healey LA. Long-term follow-up of polymyalgia rheumatica: Evidence of synovitis. Semin Arthritis Rheum 1984;13:222.

Weyand CM, Hicok KC, Hunder GG, Goronzy JJ. Tissue cytokine patterns with polymyalgia rheumatica and giant cell arteritis. Ann Intern Med 1994;121:484.

CHAPTER 6–17

Fibromyalgia

Harvey Moldofsky, M.D.

DEFINITION

Fibromyalgia is a syndrome characterized by chronic diffuse musculoskeletal pain, multiple areas of tenderness in specific anatomic regions, chronic fatigue, nonrestorative sleep, and psychological distress.

ETIOLOGY

The etiology of fibromyalgia is unknown, but current information suggests that disordered central nervous system functions are linked to the peripheral muscle pain, fatigue, and psychological disturbances. One theory suggests that the disorder is the result of altered biological rhythms involving diurnal physiologic functions that are affected by seasonal or environmental influences and social or behavioral disturbances. This chronobiologic theory permits the study and treatment of the factors that influence and govern the recurrent patterns of the disordered sleeping–waking brain, bodily pain, and fatigue over time.

CRITERIA FOR DIAGNOSIS

The American College of Rheumatology 1990 criteria (Wolfe et al., 1990) for the classification of fibromyalgia are a history of widespread musculoskeletal pain for at least 3 months, and pain in 11 or more of the 18 tender point sites on digital palpation (Figure 6–17–1).

CLINICAL MANIFESTATIONS

Subjective

The symptoms may arise for no apparent reason or may follow identified emotionally distressing or noxious events. For example, the disorder may become evident following a nonphysically injurious automobile or work-related accident. Some patients develop the symptoms after a febrile illness and exhibit the features of chronic fatigue syndrome or myalgic encephalomyelitis. Indeed, there is considerable overlap between the symptoms of these latter diagnostic designations and those of fibromyalgia. The constellation of symptoms may accompany or complicate confirmed rheumatic or connective tissue disease, such as rheumatoid arthritis, osteoarthritis, ankylosing spondylitis, or systemic lupus erythematosus. Other comorbid illnesses include major depressive disorder, irritable bowel syndrome, migraine, and temporomandibular joint disorder.

The symptoms are exacerbated by humidity, dampness, cold, weather change, winter in northern climates, unaccustomed physical exertion, stationary posture for an extended time, and emotional distress. Temporary improvement may occur following applications of heat (e.g., heating pad, hot bath, or shower), a massage, acupuncture, stretching or mild exercise, relief of emotional distress or depression, and restful sleep. Personality features characterized by sensitivity, vigilance and perfectionism, as well as emotions such as worry, anxiety, and depression, enhance bodily preoccupations and may serve to per-

FIGURE 6–17–1. Tender point locations for the 1990 classification criteria for fibromyalgia (*The Three Graces,* after Baron Jean-Baptiste Regnault, 1793, Louvre Museum, Paris). (*Source: Wolf F, Smythe HA, Yunus MB, et al. Arthritis and Rheumatism 1990;3:160. Reproduced by permission of the American College of Rheumatology and the author.*)

petuate fibromyalgia symptoms. Ongoing insurance claims, litigation, or their resolutions have no effects on the pain, fatigue, and disordered sleep.

The musculoskeletal pain is considered widespread when the following sites are affected: pain in the left and right sides of the body, above and below the waist, and involvement of the axial skeleton; that is, cervical spine or anterior chest or thoracic spine or low back. The pain varies in intensity and distribution, and tends to be chronic. Patients often complain of recurrent headache. During acute flares the patient is intolerant to tight clothing or pressure applied to the affected regions.

The unrefreshing sleep is followed by generalized morning aching, stiffness, and exhaustion. The symptoms abate as the morning progresses so that the best time of day is between approximately 10 AM and 2 or 3 PM. In the late afternoon and evening, the symptoms increase. The symptoms of nonrestorative sleep occur in more than 75% of patients. The sleep is typically light or restless. Sometimes the patient or bedpartner reports involuntary kicking or movements of the lower limbs. Especially in men, there may be reported loud snoring and interruptions to breathing that suggest the possibility of sleep apnea, which disrupts sleep and contributes to the daytime complaints.

The patient often tires easily with minimal physical exertion or complains of problems with concentration and memory. Common domestic responsibilities, work requirements, and social or recreational activities may become burdensome and frustrating.

Between 20 and 70% of individuals with fibromyalgia have depression or have a family history of depression. Some patients describe phobic or anxiety symptoms.

Other symptoms of somatic and environmental sensitivities that occur variably include paresthesia or subjective swelling of the limbs, urinary frequency as the result of an irritable bladder, and intolerance to various foods, drugs, chemicals, environmental substances, and noise.

Objective

Physical Examination

The patient is likely to be a woman ranging in age from 20 to 50 years, but the syndrome also occurs in men, juveniles, and the elderly.

The patient relaxes poorly during the physical examination. There is no clinical evidence for joint pathology. Despite the complaint of pain and weakness, a full range of motor activity is demonstrable with gentle assistance. There is exquisite sensitivity to moderate pressure with

about 4 kg force of the examiner's thumb at 11 or more of the 18 tender point sites, which include the following:

- *Occiput:* bilateral, at the suboccipital muscle insertions
- *Low cervical:* bilateral, at the anterior aspects of the intertransverse spaces at C5 to C7
- *Trapezius:* bilateral, at the midpoint of the upper border
- *Supraspinatus:* bilateral, at origins, above the scapula spine near the medial border
- *Second rib:* bilateral, at the second costochondral junctions, just lateral to the junctions on the upper surfaces
- *Lateral epicondyle:* bilateral, 2 cm distal to the epicondyles
- *Gluteal:* bilateral, in the upper quadrants of buttocks in the anterior fold of muscle
- *Greater trochanter:* bilateral, posterior to the trochanteric prominence
- *Knee:* bilateral, at the medial fat pad proximal to the joint line

The patient may flinch or withdraw ("jump sign"). Often the patient acknowledges points of tenderness that are remote from the regions of concern. Gently rolling the skin and subcutaneous tissue overlying the upper part of the scapula between the thumb and the index fingers elicits skinfold tenderness and reactive hyperaemia. Grip strength is reduced, variable, or poorly sustained. Mental status examination shows no evidence of major depressive disorder.

Routine Laboratory Abnormalities

There are no routine laboratory abnormalities.

PLANS
Diagnostic
Differential Diagnosis

Myofascial Pain Disorder. The pain and stiffness are regional, rather than diffuse, with tenderness or trigger point(s) restricted to taut bands of skeletal muscle. Fatigue is absent. Localized anesthetic injections or stretching and topical anesthetic spray may relieve symptoms.

Chronic Fatigue Syndrome. The primary feature of chronic fatigue syndrome, (myalgic encephalomyelitis), emphasizes persistent or relapsing fatiguability for at least 6 months' duration that does not resolve with bed rest. The fatigue is so severe that the daily activities are reduced by more than 50%, and there is no evidence for any medical disease or primary major mental illness. Despite differing research criteria for chronic fatigue syndrome, the disorder carries many of the same clinical features as fibromyalgia so that the syndromes may be indistinguishable.

Rheumatoid Arthritis. The erythrocyte sedimentation rate should be within normal limits in fibromyalgia and elevated in rheumatoid arthritis. The hemogram is normal in fibromyalgia, whereas a normochromic normocytic anemia is often present in chronic rheumatoid arthritis. Rheumatoid factor is negative in fibromyalgia and is positive in 85% of patients with rheumatoid arthritis. There is no evidence for joint pathology in fibromyalgia, but clinical and radiologic evidence for joint disease is evident in rheumatoid arthritis. Sometimes, patients with rheumatoid arthritis may have "fibromyalgia syndrome" without active joint disease.

Osteoarthritis Radiologic examination shows narrowing of the joint spaces with osteoarthritis. For example, in osteoarthritis of the spine, there is narrowing of the intervertebral disk spaces, narrowing of the apophyseal joints with increased bone density, and margin spurring of the vertebral bodies. Patients with primary osteoarthritis of the distal joints of the hands and feet who have fibromyalgia symptoms of morning aching, stiffness, and nonrestorative sleep show sleep-related periodic involuntary limb movements (nocturnal myoclonus) in the sleep laboratory.

Systemic Lupus Erythematosus. The American Rheumatism Association criteria for systemic lupus erythematosus do not include muscle pain, stiffness, or fatigue. Antinuclear antibody is usually negative in fibromyalgia, but in about 8% of patients this test is positive in low titer (1:80 or less). Antibodies to native DNA are found in systemic lupus erythematosus. Some fibromyalgia patients show low serum complement, C3 and C4.

Diffuse Idiopathic Skeletal Hyperostosis (DISH, "Forestier's Disease"). Radiologic examination of the spine of patients with diffuse idiopathic skeletal hyperostosis shows ossification of ligamentous attachments with a distinct band of ossification of several contiguous thoracic vertebrae.

Hypothyroidism. Elevated thyroid-stimulating hormone levels and low triiodothyronine and tetraiodothyronine levels are found in hypothyroidism. Thyroid indices are normal in fibromyalgia.

Polymyalgia Rheumatica. An elevated erythrocyte sedimentation rate and a response to steroid drugs differentiate polymyalgia rheumatica from fibromyalgia.

Major Depressive Disorder. Dysphoric mood with loss of interest and pleasure, poor appetite, weight loss, psychomotor agitation or retardation, feelings of worthlessness, and recurrent suicidal ideation are features of major depressive disorder. Pains, not depressive symptoms, are prominent in fibromyalgia. Sleep laboratory studies show an abbreviated onset to rapid-eye-movement sleep in major depressive disorders. Rapid-eye-movement sleep is normal in fibromyalgia patients.

Diagnostic Options and Recommended Approach

Polysomnographic evaluation in the clinical sleep laboratory shows an alpha (7.5–11 Hz) electroencephalographic non–rapid-eye-movement sleep anomaly. Older patients, aged 45 to 65 years, are more likely to show sleep-related periodic (20- to 60-second intervals) involuntary leg movements and abbreviated, fragmented electroencephalographic sleep. Some patients may show sleep fragmentation as the result of sleep apnea. The Multiple Sleep Latency Test, which consists of a series of daytime naps at two-hourly intervals, does not show daytime electroencephalographic measures of irresistible sleepiness, and distinguishes tiredness as physical or psychological fatigue from subjective sleepiness.

Therapeutic

The physician should not dismiss the patient with information that no clinical or routine laboratory evidence for a disease can be found. Rather, the physician should indicate understanding of the disorder and that there is no evidence for crippling joint disease or chronic invalidism. The patient should be reassured that every effort will be made to control the symptoms even though there is no cure for the disorder.

Cognitive–behavioral therapy together with relaxation exercises and gentle aerobic fitness have proven helpful in overcoming the negative perceptions, the subjective weakness, and limited range of activities that often afflict patients with fibromyalgia.

Applications of heat, for example, a heating pad at night and/or a hot shower on awakening in the morning, together with simple analgesics such as acetylsalicylic acid or acetaminophen, provide some temporary relief. Narcotic analgesics may dull pain perception, but they are to be avoided because of their addictive potential. Nonsteroidal antiinflammatory drugs provide little lasting benefit. Tricyclic antidepressant medications improve the restorative quality of sleep and relieve pain and fatigue. Small doses of these drugs before bedtime, for example, amitriptyline (Elavil) 10 to 50 mg or cyclobenzaprine (Flexeril) 10 to 30 mg, may be helpful. Side effects may include drowsiness, dry mouth, and constipation. Patients with severe nocturnal restlessness who show sleep-related periodic limb movements may profit from clonazepam (Clonopin, Rivotril) 0.5 to 1.0 mg or nitrazepam (Mogadon) 5 to 10 mg before bedtime. These patients should avoid alcohol and caffeinated beverages that disturb sleep. For those patients with sleep apnea, nocturnal continuous positive air pressure, delivered by a nasal mask, may facilitate sleep and improve daytime symptoms. Zolpidem (Ambien) 10 to 15 mg and zopiclone (Imovane) 7.5 mg have been shown to improve sleep and energy without influencing the pain.

Physical therapy with massage or acupuncture may also provide transient relief. A graded, aerobic physical fitness program that favors swimming, cycling, or brisk walking may provide lasting improvement to sleep, energy, and tolerance to pain in patients who are able to engage in such a regular exercise scheme.

FOLLOW-UP

At the outset, the patient should be seen at frequent intervals (at least every 2–3 weeks) to supervise medications, assess therapeutic response, and provide reassurance, education, and encouragement. Should cognitive therapy be advisable to overcome depressive symptoms, specialized care will involve more frequent attendance with a psychotherapist. If the patient has achieved a satisfactory remission, an effort should be made to gradually wean the patient from the tricylic drug. Depending on the response, the patient can be seen less frequently (4–6 months) for clinical evaluation and reinforcement.

DISCUSSION
Prevalence

Surveys in various countries indicate a prevalence of about 1 to 3% in the adult population. More than 90% are women. In primary care practices, the frequency is between 2 and 6% of medical patients.

Related Basic Science

Derangement in sleep physiology and accompanying neuroendocrine and neurotransmitter functions have been demonstrated in studies of patients with fibromyalgia. Moldofsky (1975) proposed that the altered sleep physiology is a biological correlate to the subjective experience of light and or restless, unrefreshing sleep; morning diffuse musculoskeletal pain; tenderness in specific sites; and chronic fatigue. He has described an alpha (7.5–11 Hz) electroencephalographic non–rapid-eye-movement sleep anomaly, an arousal disorder during sleep, coincident with the myalgia, fatigue, and mood symptoms that afflict such patients. Noise disruption of slow-wave (deep) sleep has been found to be associated with the emergence of myalgia and fatigue in sedentary normal subjects, but not in physically fit subjects. Recent studies have shown a reduction in somatomedin-C, a product of liver metabolism of growth hormone, most of which is secreted during slow-wave sleep. Elevated levels of substance P have been found in the cerebrospinal fluid. Together with evidence for alteration in central nervous system serotonin metabolism and impairment in the hypothalamic–pituitary–adrenal axis, these neurotransmitters and endocrine functions are thought to influence pain, fatigue, and mood symptoms. Although disturbances in muscle metabolism have been suggested in studies, no conclusive or confirmed evidence for peripheral muscle dysfunction has been demonstrated.

Natural History and Its Modification with Treatment

The syndrome may be chronic, with episodes of exacerbation and remission of symptoms. Symptom control is possible, but there is no known cure. People who suffer from the condition continue to be productive as long as they are motivated. Once their productivity is interrupted, however, attempts at rehabilitation are rarely successful.

Prevention

At present, there is no proven method for the prevention of fibromyalgia.

Cost Containment

Cost containment is achieved through accurate diagnosis and the avoidance of unnecessary and expensive laboratory investigations and inappropriate medical or surgical interventions. Consistent support and judicious use of medications can prevent further physician shopping or vulnerability of patients to unproven therapies or quackery.

REFERENCES

Goldenberg DL. Fibromyalgia syndrome and its overlap with chronic fatigue syndrome. In: Dawson DM, Sabin TD, eds. Chronic fatigue syndrome. Boston: Little, Brown, 1993:75.

McCain GA. Treatment of the fibromyalgia syndrome, J Musculoskeletal Pain 1994;2:93.

Moldofsky H. Musculoskeletal symptoms and non-REM sleep disturbance in patients with "fibrositis syndrome" and healthy subjects. Psychosom Med 1975;37;341.

Moldofsky H. Chronobiological influences on fibromyalgia syndrome: Theoretical and therapeutic implications. Masi AT, ed. In: Baillière's clinical rheumatology. London: Baillière Tindall, 1994;8:801.

Russell IN, Orr MD, Littman B, et al. Elevated cerebrospinal fluid levels of substance P in patients with fibromyalgia syndrome. Arthritis Rheum 1994; 37;1593.

Wolfe F, Smythe HA, Yunus MB, et al. The American College of Rheumatology 1990 criteria for the classification of fibromyalgia. Report of the Multicenter Criteria Committee. Arthritis Rheum 1990;33:160.

CHAPTER 6–18

Bursitis

William P. Maier, M.D.

DEFINITION

A bursal structure is a closed saclike structure that lies in proximity to a joint capsule, tendons, ligaments, or overlying skin. It has a thin lining layer composed of synovial-like cells with an underlying layer of fibrovascular tissue. The bursa normally produces a small amount of fluid, which acts as lubricant enabling the two bursal surfaces to glide easily over one another, thereby minimizing friction between contiguous musculoskeletal structures. Bursitis is inflammation of a bursa by one of many possible causes, including infection, trauma, crystal-induced inflammation, and autoimmune inflammation. Common bursitis syndromes include olecranon bursitis, prepatellar bursitis, subacromial bursitis, infrapatellar bursitis, trochanteric bursitis, anserine bursitis, and retrocalcanea bursitis. Less common syndromes include semimembranosus bursitis (Baker's cyst), iliopsoas bursitis, and gluteal bursitis.

ETIOLOGY

The inflammatory process may be caused by trauma (overuse), infection, autoimmune disease (rheumatoid arthritis), or gout.

CRITERIA FOR DIAGNOSIS
Suggestive

The presenting symptoms of the bursitis syndromes usually are pain and sometimes swelling overlying the known location of the bursal sacs. Pain may be referred to other musculoskeletal structures contiguous to the bursa; therefore, careful physical examination is necessary to identify the source of the pain. When subcutaneous bursal sacs (olecranon and prepatellar) are inflamed by systemic illnesses such as rheumatoid arthritis, gout, or infection, additional clues to diagnosis may include fever, chills, and arthralgias. The prepatellar and olecranon bursas frequently present with local redness, swelling, and warmth that must be distinguished from septic arthritis.

Definitive

Definitive diagnosis of bursitis is made by detailed physical examination demonstrating the source of pain, swelling, and redness to be overlying a known bursa. It is imperative to demonstrate normal function of contiguous joints by passive range of motion, as well as to exclude abnormalities in regional tendons, muscles, and nerves.

CLINICAL MANIFESTATIONS
Subjective

Patients who develop subcutaneous bursitis may occasionally have a family history of articular problems when rheumatoid arthritis or gout is the underlying etiology. More important, an occupational history may provide a clue to the diagnosis. Occupational associations with bursitis include weaver's bottom (ischial–gluteal bursitis), miner's elbow (olecranon bursitis), and housemaid's knee (prepatellar bursitis).

Symptoms of subcutaneous bursitis are pain, swelling, and warmth over the involved bursa. If an infection is present, then fever and chills may be reported. Bursitis of a deep bursa is manifested by pain over the bursa with activity or with direct pressure. The pain may radiate some distance, as in the case of gluteal bursitis, in which the patient may complain of pain in a sciatic distribution.

Objective
Physical Examination

Physical findings of subcutaneous bursitis include induration, erythema, and effusion over the olecranon and prepatellar bursae. Gross distension of the bursal sac may be apparent. Marked soft tissue swelling surrounding the bursa may suggest a cellulitis-like process. Range of motion of the elbow and knee, respectively, should be normal. If there is significant limitation or pain on flexion, then a coincident arthritis must be suspected. Tophi or rheumatoid nodules should be sought during examination. A pustule or wound over the inflamed bursa may suggest infection.

Physical findings of deep bursal involvement are fewer and require prior knowledge of the anatomy of these deep structures. The examination is often normal except for pain on palpation of the bursa as well as pain elicited on active range of motion. Owing to the proximity of many deep bursae to tendons, it may not be possible to distinguish clearly between tendonitis and bursitis (e.g., between subacromial bursitis and supraspinous tendonitis). Compounding this difficulty is the common occurrence of a calcific tendonitis causing inflammation of a contiguous bursa.

Routine Laboratory Abnormalities

Laboratory findings will often be normal unless a systemic, nonmechanical cause is present. The Westergren sedimentation rate may be elevated by gout, rheumatoid arthritis, or infection. If gout is the underlying condition, then an elevated uric acid level may be noted on routine chemistry. An infectious bursitis may be manifested by leukocytosis.

PLANS
Diagnostic
Differential Diagnosis

The differential diagnosis of bursitis includes arthritis of contiguous joints, cervical or lumbar radiculopathy, tendonitis, local muscle dysfunction (myofascial pain or muscle rupture), as well as diseases of underlying bone, including tumor and stress fractures. Other less common conditions, for example, referred pain from abdominal organs or phlebitis, must also be considered.

Diagnostic Options

Diagnosis of bursal syndromes is primarily one of careful physical examination of the musculoskeletal system. Radiologic exam may exclude alternative diagnostic considerations, including calcific tendonitis or articular and bony pathology. Aspiration of subcutaneous bursae such as the olecranon and prepatellar bursae may be necessary to exclude gout or infection.

Recommended Approach

Careful and complete physical examination is adequate for diagnosis of most bursal syndromes, except when examination suggests the presence of soft tissue swelling and fluctuance of a known subcutaneous bursa, most commonly the olecranon or prepatellar bursa. Then needle aspiration for acquisition of diagnostic material is imperative. If bursal fluid is acquired, then gout must be excluded by polarized microscopic exam, which may reveal monosodium urate (negatively birefringent) crystals. Gram stain and culture of the bursal fluid may lead to the diagnosis of septic bursitis. Cell counts of inflammatory bursal fluids are usually lower than those of articular fluid but may be helpful in following the response of an infected bursa to antibiotic therapy.

Therapeutic

Therapeutic Options

Deep bursitis is managed with local heat, graded range-of-motion exercises, and oral nonsteroidal antiinflammatory agents such as aspirin (650–875 mg every 4 hours as needed). If symptoms are refractory or lead to loss of function (e.g., a frozen shoulder), then local instillation of a long-acting corticosteroid suspension such as prednisolone tebutate (Hydeltra-T.B.A.) or triamcinolone hexacetomide (Aristospan) may become necessary. One milliliter of suspension mixed with 1 to 2 ml of lidocaine (Xylocaine) is injected so as to infiltrate the area of maximal pain. Care must be taken to avoid injection into vessels, nerves, or tendons.

Treatment of subcutaneous bursitis requires prior diagnosis, including aspiration. If the process is noninfectious, then treatment of inflammation with percutaneous needle drainage and nonsteroidal antiinflammatory agents will be effective. If infection is demonstrated, then treatment is based on Gram stain and culture results. The majority of bursal infections are due to *Staphylococcus aureus* and will respond to oral or intravenous agents such as dicloxacillin (Diclox) and oxacillin. If systemic symptoms are prominent, then hospitalization may be necessary for parenteral antibiotics. Repeated aspiration of reaccumulated bursal fluid may be necessary to maximize response to antibiotics.

Surgery is seldom required for treatment of bursitis. Occasionally, a severe infection of the olecranon bursa may not respond to conventional treatment and may therefore require bursectomy with debridement of necrotic tissue.

Recommended Approach

Most bursal syndromes will respond to avoidance of exacerbating activities, local heat, and the strengthening of local muscles through conditioning. Nonsteroidal antiinflammatory agents may be of short-term use when these measures fail, but extended use of more than 2 or 3 weeks should be avoided when possible. Instillation of a local long-acting corticosteroid is often effective when the preceding measures fail. Surgery is a last resort and seldom is indicated.

FOLLOW-UP

Follow-up is determined by the response to therapeutic interventions. If symptoms of bursitis do not remit as expected, more extensive workup is indicated to identify other sources of referred pain, such as radiculopathy, or another explanation for persistent pain, such as fibrositis or undiagnosed systemic inflammatory disease.

DISCUSSION

Prevalence and Incidence

The true incidence of bursitis is unknown, but it is very common. It is undoubtedly a universal experience for anyone over 40 years of age and is one of the most common reasons for ambulatory visits to physicians. Clearly, the incidence is directly related to increasing age. The incidence of bursitis of the lower extremities is definitely increased by obesity.

Related Basic Science

Bursitis is a common musculoskeletal problem that results from an inflammatory process in or around one of the multitude of bursal sacs throughout the body. Bursae are small sacs lined by a synovial membrane located in strategic areas of the body to minimize friction between various components of the dynamic musculoskeletal system, including tendons, bones, and ligaments. There are two general categories of bursal sacs, with distinct diagnostic and therapeutic characteristics. The subcutaneous bursae include the olecranon and prepatellar bursae. These are often involved by systemic processes such as rheumatoid arthritis, gout, and infection. Deep bursae, however, which are more numerous, become clinically significant following mechanical stress or overuse.

Trauma is probably the most common cause of bursitis, precipitating inflammation following small tears in the involved bursae. Aging connective tissues are at higher risk for such microtears, and this is consistent with the fact that bursitis is more commonly seen in the elderly.

Natural History and Its Modification with Treatment

Bursitis may be an isolated injury that resolves over a period of weeks without recurrence. More frequently, bursitis is associated with conditions that predispose to recurrence, such as obesity, poor physical condition, and osteoarthritis.

Prevention

The best prevention for bursitis is to avoid excessive physical stress or any trauma that may cause bursitis. To condition the patient to withstand moderate stresses without resultant bursitis, the physician must encourage good range-of-motion maintenance in all joints adjacent to bursae that are prone to inflammation.

Cost Containment

Familiarity with the common forms of bursitis prevents excessive diagnostic workups by allowing rapid diagnosis and treatment by the physician.

REFERENCES

Bywaters EGL. The bursae of the body. Ann Rheum Dis 1965;24:215.

Bywaters EGL. Lesions of the bursae, tendons and tendon sheaths. Clin Rheum Dis 1979;5:883.

Canoso JJ. Idiopathic or traumatic olecranon bursitis. Arthritis Rheum 1981;24:905.

Ho G, Su EY. Antibiotic therapy of septic bursitis. Arthritis Rheum 1981;24:905.

Reilly JP, Nicholas JA. The chronically inflamed bursa. Clin Sports Med 1987;6;345.

Tenosynovitis

William P. Maier, M.D.

DEFINITION

Tenosynovitis describes numerous musculoskeletal syndromes where inflammation from various causes involves tendons or the synovial sheaths surrounding the tendons. Common tenosynovitis syndromes include superspinatus tendonitis, bicipital tendonitis, de Quervain's tenosynovitis (tendonitis of the abductor pollicis longus and extensor pollicis brevis), trigger finger (stenosing flexor tenosynovitis), patellar tendonitis, and Achilles tendonitis.

ETIOLOGY

The etiology of the inflammation in the tenosynovitis syndromes most commonly is overuse or trauma, but may also be gout, infection, or autoimmune diseases, including rheumatoid arthritis and systemic lupus erythematosus.

CRITERIA FOR DIAGNOSIS

Suggestive

Suggestive findings in the tendonitis syndromes are complaints of pain over known tendon structures and the aggravation of the pain by active range of motion of the joints crossed by the involved tendon.

DEFINITIVE

Definitive diagnosis of tenosynovitis requires careful musculoskeletal examination, confirming the tendon source of the symptoms and excluding pathology from other contiguous musculoskeletal structures, including joints, bursae, and nerves.

CLINICAL MANIFESTATIONS

Subjective

The patient usually complains of pain in the region of the involved tendon. Frequently there is a history of an abrupt onset of pain, although the onset may be gradual. A history of unusual physical effort preceding pain may be present. The pain is most often aching in quality and of variable severity. The pain is usually worse at night and with use of the involved tendon. If tenosynovitis is associated with a systemic disease (soft tissue infection or gout), then systemic symptoms such as fever and malaise may be present. An increased incidence of de Quervain's tenosynovitis is noted during pregnancy.

Objective

Physical Examination

There is localized tenderness over the involved tendon, and pain is provoked when the patient is asked to move the tendon against resistance (e.g., supination of the hand in bicipital tendonitis). If an inflammatory disease is present, then redness, warmth, and soft tissue swelling may be apparent. Inflammatory processes of the tendon sheaths most often involve the dorsum of the hands, feet, and ankle and may cause marked soft tissue swelling. The range of motion of contiguous joints may be limited by pain.

Routine Laboratory Abnormalities

Most often the examination will be normal in the overuse types of tendonitis. In inflammatory causes of tenosynovitis, there may be an associated anemia or elevation of the Westergren sedimentation rate.

PLANS

Diagnostic

Differential Diagnosis

The differential diagnosis of the tendonitis syndromes is wide and includes arthritis, bursitis, and referred pain from bony, intrathoracic, or intraabdominal sources. Other disease processes that must be considered include radiculopathy, carpal tunnel syndrome, and other compressive neuropathies. Complete tendon rupture of the supraspinatus (rotator cuff tear) and Achilles tendons must be diagnosed in a timely fashion.

Diagnostic Options

Diagnostic options include careful physical examination, history, and radiologic examination to assess contiguous joint integrity and to exclude calcific tendonitis. Arthrography or ultrasound may help in excluding rotator cuff tears or adhesive capsulitis. Laboratory investigation is helpful when an underlying inflammatory disease is suspected. Serologic studies may help confirm the presence of rheumatoid arthritis, systemic lupus erythematosus, or acute rheumatic fever. Studies on synovial fluid acquired by aspiration include crystal examination by polarized microscopy, as well as cultures and Gram stain.

Recommended Approach

Diagnosis is made by history and physical examination in most cases of overuse tenosynovitis. Calcific tendonitis requires radiologic examination of the soft tissues and documentation of calcium deposits in the tendon.

An inflammatory tenosynovitis of the dorsum of the hand or foot may require aspiration from synovial fluid, examination, and culture. Polarizing microscopic examination should be performed on any fluid so acquired.

Therapeutic

Therapeutic Options

Options for therapy include immobilization, avoidance of inciting activity, and application of ice or local heat. Physical therapy modalities such as iontophoresis and phonophoresis are often used in sport-associated tendonitis syndromes. Pharmacologic interventions include nonsteroidal antiinflammatory agents and analgesics, as well as the introduction of local long-acting corticosteroid preparations by direct injection of the tendon sheath. Surgery is reserved for complete tendon tears, refractory trigger finger, or de Quervain's tenosynovitis.

Recommended Approach

Immobilization of the painful extremity will usually significantly alleviate pain. Likewise, local application of heat often provides relief. Acetylsalicylic acid (aspirin), 650 to 875 mg every 4 hours as needed, or other antiinflammatory drugs not only help relieve pain, but also suppress inflammation. If symptoms are refractory, then injection of a local anesthetic mixed with a long-acting synthetic corticosteroid preparation, for example, 0.5 ml of 2% lidocaine hydrochloride (Xylocaine) mixed in a syringe with 10 to 20 mg of prednisolone tebutate (Hydeltra-T.B.A.), should be tried. As soon as the pain permits, the patient should begin active assisted range-of-motion exercises to prevent contracture.

FOLLOW-UP

Appropriate follow-up is necessary to ensure that loss of function has not occurred and to confirm response to therapy. The patients should be instructed to return if symptoms do not remit in 2 to 4 weeks.

DISCUSSION

Prevalence and Incidence

The tendonitis syndromes are very frequent maladies both for the athlete—but even more so for the middle-aged athlete—and the elderly. The true prevalence and incidence are impossible to calculate because of the frequency of subclinical disease.

Related Basic Science

The tendon glides through a sheath that is lined with synovial cells similar to those found lining the joint capsule. This synovial lining may become inflamed by any systemic illness that causes synovitis (Table 6–19–1).

The most commonly encountered cause of tenosynovitis, however, is trauma, specifically, forceful stretching. It is hypothesized that such forceful stretching produces microtears, which then initiate the inflammatory process.

The tendency to develop such overuse conditions increases with age. As degenerative changes develop within the connective tissues and the vasculature supplying these tissues, the elasticity of the tissues is reduced. The supraspinatus and the bicipital tendons are two sites in which these changes can be seen most clearly with aging; therefore, these sites are at high risk for tendonitis. In addition, calcification frequently occurs in these sites in association with inflammation.

Natural History and Its Modification with Treatment

Episodes of tenosynovitis are usually self-limiting, resolving over a period of weeks or months. The incidence of recurrence, however, is high. If appropriate physical therapy and treatment are not undertaken, then the possibility of contracture (frozen shoulder) exists.

TABLE 6–19–1. CAUSES OF INFLAMMATORY TENOSYNOVITIS

Acute rheumatic fever
Reiter's syndrome
Gout
Rheumatoid arthritis
Disseminated gonococcal infection
Soft tissue infection

Prevention

Avoidance of activities that produce unaccustomed forceful stretching of the tendon may prevent tendonitis. Appropriate warmup exercises and gradual toning programs will help avoid many episodes of overuse tendonitis.

Cost Containment

Tenosynovitis is often a self-limited, local problem that should be treated as such without extensive investigation unless otherwise indicated. Appropriate physical therapy may abort a chronic problem that may lead to absenteeism or loss of employment.

REFERENCES

Bywaters EGL. Lesions of bursae, tendons, and tendon sheaths. Clin Rheum Dis 1979;5:883.

Cofield RH. Rotator cuff disease of the shoulder. J Bone Joint Surg 1985;67A:974.

Leadbetter WB. Cell-matrix responses in tendon injury. Clin Sports Med 1992;11:533.

Schumacher HR, Dorwart BB, Korzenski OM. Occurrence of de Quervain's tendonitis during pregnancy. Arch Intern Med 1985;145:2083.

Uhholf HK, Sarkar K, Maynard JA. Calcific tendonitis. Clin Orthop 1976;118:164.

CHAPTER 6–20

Carpal Tunnel Syndrome

John R. Meadows, M.D.

DEFINITION

Carpal tunnel syndrome is an entrapment mononeuropathy of the median nerve at the wrist causing numbness, tingling, and weakness in the hand and sometimes pain in the entire upper extremity.

ETIOLOGY

This disorder results from compression of the median nerve in the carpal tunnel secondary to either an anatomically small canal or an increase in size of the contents within the canal. Some cases are related to underlying and perhaps treatable medical or surgical entities.

CRITERIA FOR DIAGNOSIS

Suggestive

Carpal tunnel syndrome should be considered in patients with complaints of numbness and paresthesias in the median innervation of the hand with pain possibly involving the entire upper extremity and shoulder. Weakness and loss of dexterity of the hand should also prompt consideration of the syndrome.

Definitive

The diagnosis is established by the median nerve location of symptoms and sensory deficit sometimes reproducible on provocative testing. Weakness and atrophy of thenar musculature are seen in later phases. Electrodiagnostic testing is confirmatory in all but 5 to 10% of early, mild cases.

CLINICAL MANIFESTATIONS

Subjective

The typical patient is usually a middle-aged woman with numbness and paresthesias in the median distribution of the hand. Symptoms may initially awaken the patient from sleep, and relief is attempted by shaking the hand or placing it in a dependent position. A dull ache may occur that can radiate proximally as far as the shoulder. Onset is gradual, and early on, symptoms are intermittent and may be exacerbated by increased use of the hand. Later, symptoms may be sustained with loss of dexterity and grip strength. Involvement is usually of the dominant hand, but bilaterality is not uncommon. A thorough history is essential in the identification of an underlying cause (see Related Basic Science).

Objective

Physical Examination

Examination may be normal in early stages. Loss of sensation is found in the median nerve distribution: the palmar aspect of digits 1 through 3, including the radial half of the ring finger. Should two-point discrimination be intact, more sensitive testing with light touch monofilaments is suggested. Weakness or atrophy of the thenar musculature is found in advanced cases.

Several provocative tests are helpful. Tinel's sign is positive if paresthesias in the median distribution are produced by tapping over the median nerve on the volar aspect of the wrist. Phalen's test is performed by maximally flexing the wrist for 60 seconds and is positive if paresthesias result. It should be noted that 20% of normal subjects will have Tinel's sign or a positive Phalen's test and neither is 100% sensitive. Features of acromegaly and rheumatoid arthritis should be sought. Gouty tophi, edema, and goiter should be noted as well.

Routine Laboratory Abnormalities

Complete blood count, chemical profile, and urinalysis are normal in patients with carpal tunnel syndrome unless related to an underlying medical problem. Abnormalities characteristic of those disorders will be seen such as an elevated blood sugar in diabetes mellitus or hyperuricemia in gout.

PLANS

Diagnostic

Differential Diagnosis

Considerations are limited to neurologic or vascular disease involving the upper extremity. Central lesions such as transient cortical ischemia produce sensory or motor abnormalities but no pain. Neck pain on range of motion, loss of deep tendon reflexes, and exacerbation of symptoms with cough are markers for cervical nerve root compression. Neuritis of the brachial plexus has an abrupt onset, early motor signs, and pain over the plexus. Thoracic outlet syndromes produce paresthesias and aching discomfort of the extremity, but usually no demonstrable sensory or motor deficits. Vasomotor symptoms, joint stiffness, and skin changes with antecedent injury or myocardial infarction raise the possibility of reflex sympathetic dystrophy. The median nerve may be compressed in the proximal forearm (pronator teres syndrome), causing more proximal palm numbness, with exacerbation of symptoms on resisted pronation and supination of the forearm. Measuring blood pressures in both arms and performing the Allen's test should exclude vascular occlusive disease. Raynaud's phenomenon is suspected in the setting of cold exposure followed by characteristic skin color changes of the hand. The hand–arm vibration syndrome, of vascular pathophysiology, produces symptoms very similar to those of carpal tunnel syndrome but not limited to the median territory.

Diagnostic Options

Anteroposterior and lateral radiography including carpal tunnel views is performed if there was preceding trauma or if examination reveals either an anatomic or functional abnormality of the wrist. Specialized imaging is not required. Electrodiagnostic testing is confirmatory in 90 to 95% of cases. In addition to defining the severity, it is useful in excluding other neuropathologic entities that are either coexisting with or mimicking carpal tunnel syndrome. False-negative results are obtained in early, mild presentations. Alleviation of symptoms on injection of a steroid and lidocaine combination is considered by some to be of diagnostic value when electrodiagnostic test results are equivocal.

If signs and symptoms suggest an underlying cause, further laboratory testing is indicated. A thyroid-stimulating hormone level is used to exclude thyroid hypofunction, and serum and urine electrophoreses are done to exclude paraproteinemias. Suspicion of connective tissue disease warrants determination of erythrocyte sedimentation rate and antinuclear antibody and rheumatoid factor titers. Tests for amyloidosis should be done if there are other clues to this condition.

Recommended Approach

Diagnostic efforts should localize compression of the median nerve to the wrist and identify any underlying cause. In a classic presentation, history and physical examination are sufficient for diagnostic near certainty. An atypical presentation may warrant a trial of conservative measures or performance of electrodiagnostic studies, particularly if clinical clues suggest other neuropathologic disease.

Once carpal tunnel syndrome is definite, consideration must be given to an additional, more proximal compression, as well as the presence of underlying medical or surgical illnesses in which treatment may result in the amelioration of the median neuropathy. Examples of such are levothyroxine and blood sugar control in hypothyroidism and diabetes mellitus, respectively, and surgical correction of anatomic abnormalities.

Therapeutic

Therapeutic Options

Conservative. Modification of causative activities, such as wrist support, keyboard lowering, adjustment of seat back and height, and alteration of work/rest cycles, or termination of the causal activity is the first step. Splinting of the wrist in neutral position either nocturnally or continuously is the mainstay of conservative management. As joint stiffness may occur, patients must be instructed to do periodic range of motion while splinted. Nonsteroidal antiinflammatory drugs provide some relief.

Interventional. Injection of dexamethasone, 4 mg with 2 mL of lidocaine (without epinephrine) via a 25-gauge needle positioned 1 cm proximal to the distal wrist crease on the ulnar side of the palmaris longus tendon with the needle at a 30° angle to the skin, is a diagnostic as well as therapeutic maneuver. Care must be taken not to inject a tendon or nerve directly, so if considerable resistance to injection is encountered or the patient experiences paresthesias, the needle must be repositioned. This may be repeated twice more at 3- to 6-week intervals. Relief is usually temporary, with symptom recurrence in 3 to 4 months. Complications include increased nerve deficit, infection, tendon rupture, and reflex sympathetic dystrophy.

Open surgical release by division of the transverse carpal ligament is the definitive interventional modality and results are usually good. The patient may return to light office work in 1 week, but may be unable for up to 6 months if the job involves high-intensity hand usage. Complications are infrequent and include incomplete decompression, cutaneous nerve severance with resultant dysesthesia, and incision hypersensitivity. Also seen are severance of the motor branch to the thenar musculature, hematoma, causalgia, tendon bow stringing, and, rarely, wound infection. Recently, endoscopic techniques have been introduced that result in less incisional pain and faster return to work; however, the technique is associated with more injury to neurovascular structures.

Recommended Approach

Once treatment of underlying conditions has been initiated, severe sensory or motor dysfunction mandates surgery. If symptoms are sensory and mild or electrodiagnostic studies indicate mild to moderate involvement, activities are modified and the wrist is splinted in neutral position. Nocturnal splinting may be all that is necessary if symptoms are limited to that time frame. A nonsteroidal antiinflammatory drug of choice (naproxen 500 mg bid) may be added. Improvement should be noted in 2 weeks and treatment is continued for 6 months. Of those with mild disease, 90% are expected to return to full activity. If a pregnant patient can be managed conservatively through delivery, most recover within 6 weeks. If the patient remains symptomatic, there are two options. Local steroids may be used pending resolution of a reversible condition, or one may proceed to surgery. During conservative management, any time weakness or atrophy is noted or if deficit progression is documented on electrodiagnostic testing, conservative measures should be abandoned.

FOLLOW-UP

With conservative treatment, visits at 1 and 6 months with a phone update in the interim are advised. Predictors of failure with conservative management are pretreatment symptom duration longer than 10 months, constant paresthesias, Phalen's test positive at less than 30 seconds, coexisting stenosing tenosynovitis, and age over 30. Those in whom a series of three steroid injections are employed should be seen at 6, 12, and 18 months. More than 90% of failures occur within 18 months.

Postoperatively, patients should perform range-of-motion exercises of the metacarpophalangeal joints. Further follow-up is at the discretion of the surgeon, but is usually at 2- to 6-week intervals. Early surgical failure is indicative of an incorrect diagnosis or incomplete release. Late failure, which occurs on average at the 11/2-year point, is due mostly to scar or tenosynovial hypertrophy. Reexploration produces excellent results in half and improvement in another third. Workers compensation cases have slower recovery and poorer results.

DISCUSSION
Prevalence
Population studies indicate that the prevalence of this condition varies widely from 50 to 125 cases per 100,000. The syndrome occurs twice as often in women. Controversy surrounds the occupational relatedness of carpal tunnel syndrome. Some feel that activity involving repetitive motions, awkward wrist positions, or high grip force is a predisposition; however, resolution of this issue is difficult in that controlled investigations have been thwarted by the difficulty of quantification of ergonomic exposure.

Related Basic Science
The carpal canal is bounded posteriorly by the carpal bones and their ligaments and, anteriorly, by the transverse carpal ligament. The median nerve and nine flexor tendons are contained within this space, which is only 10 mm in diameter at its narrowest point. Ischemia causes the early, intermittent symptoms. Prolonged compression leads to a persistent, demyelinating neuropathy. Any process that decreases canal size or increases the size of canal contents may lead to compression of the vulnerable nerve. Nonspecific tenosynovitis is the most common, with pregnancy, hypothyroidism, rheumatoid arthritis, and other connective tissue diseases not infrequently seen. Estrogen use, trauma, neoplastic lesions, osteoarthritis, acromegaly, and gout are causally related. Approximately 10% of long-term hemodialysis patients develop the syndrome secondary to amyloid deposition. Rare cases have been related to mycobacterial and fungal infections in the canal. Some embrace the concept that a "sick nerve," as seen in neuro-

pathic conditions such as diabetes mellitus, is more susceptible to compression. A nerve that is compressed in a second, more proximal location may also be more prone to distal pathology—the "double-crush" phenomenon.

Natural History and Its Modification with Treatment
Median nerve compression at the wrist may be asymptomatic or may produce symptoms that spontaneously resolve. Others proceed from sensory symptoms, to sensory deficit, and finally to weakness and atrophy. Full return to function is the rule with early intervention; however, in advanced clinical stages, treatment may allow only partial return of function.

Prevention
Workers in high-risk settings should be educated with regard to cumulative trauma disorders and instructed to report symptoms early. Physicians caring for patients with illnesses associated with carpal tunnel syndrome should periodically investigate this possibility. In most cases, advanced disability will be prevented by initiation of treatment at a reversible point in the disease.

Cost Containment
Conservative management and steroid injections are relatively inexpensive. Continued conservative treatment in a patient with obvious surgical indications is wasteful. Although some feel that plain radiographs and electrodiagnostic studies are prerequisites to surgery, others argue that an absolutely classic presentation obviates their need. Savings are realized if removal of an exacerbating factor brings about improvement to the point that surgery is not necessary. A laboratory search for underlying etiologies should be directed by history and physical examination.

REFERENCES
American Academy of Neurology. Practice parameter for carpal tunnel syndrome. Neurology 1993;43:2406.
Gelberman RH, Eaton R, Urbaniak J. Peripheral nerve compression. J Bone Joint Surg 1993;75A:1854.
Hunt TR, Osterman AL. Complications of the treatment of carpal tunnel syndrome. Hand Clin 1994;10:63.
Katz RT. Carpal tunnel syndrome: A practical review. Am Fam Physician 1994;49:1371.
Moore JS. Carpal tunnel syndrome. Occup Med 1992;7:741.
Rosenbaum RB. The role of imaging in the diagnosis of carpal tunnel syndrome. Invest Radiol 1993;28:1059.

CHAPTER 6–21
Low Back Pain
Stephen B. Miller, M.D., and David E. Mathis, M.D.

DEFINITION
Low back pain is defined as discomfort in the lumbosacral portion of the back with or without painful radiation into the hips, buttocks, or legs.

ETIOLOGY
The causes of low back pain are myriad, and a specific etiology often is not identified. With only a small percentage of cases secondary to serious medical diseases, the vast majority are attributed to regional mechanical disorders.

CRITERIA FOR DIAGNOSIS
Suggestive
The diagnosis of low back pain is subjectively made when the patient complains of an uncomfortable sensation in the lower region of the back.

Definitive
The definitive diagnosis of low back pain is made primarily from subjective complaints. Pain referred to the low back but not related to true back pathology must be considered, especially in atypical cases.

CLINICAL MANIFESTATIONS

Subjective

The complaint of low back pain is often nonspecific and chronic. Less frequently, the event that initiated the pain may be extracted from the history. A very detailed and carefully performed history is necessary. The physician must investigate the chronology of events leading up to the development of the back pain and the characteristics of the pain.

Analysis of the temporal evolution of pain should include the following:

- When and in what circumstances did the pain begin, and was it clearly associated with any injury? If the pain is injury related, did the injury occur at work?
- Has the pain progressed, regressed, or been stable since it was felt initially?
- Has the location of the pain changed? Has the pain become more extensive (radiation to contiguous regions), or are there new areas of involvement? Is the pain intermittent or continuous, and what factors seem to aggrative or improve the symptoms? What types of treatment, including medications, surgery, supports such as lumbosacral corsets, and various modes of physical therapy, have been tried and with what results?

The following characteristics of pain should be identified:

- *Intensity:* This factor is very difficult to quantitate, but some clues are absence from work and sleep disturbances.
- *Quality:* Quality is also very subjective and is complicated by many factors. Some helpful descriptions are "burning" in nerve root pain, "lightning" pain in a herniated disk or tumor, and a deeper or "boring" pain in intrinsic bone disorders.
- *Reproducibility:* Can the pain be duplicated by the action of either the patient or the examiner?

The systems review should also include any changes in bladder or bowel function. A search for historical clues to the presence of systemic illness is also mandatory, with special attention given to the presence of fever, weight loss, or night sweats. A past medical history of any prior immune-mediated/inflammatory disease, sickle cell disease, or malignancy, especially cancer of the breast or prostate, is important to elicit. Demographic features, especially the patient's work history and personal habits, are often revealing.

Objective

Physical Examination

The way the patient moves while walking, undressing, and getting onto the examining table may provide some clue about the severity of the pain.

Abnormal skin findings may indicate an occult spinal abnormality; for example, a café-au-lait spot could signify an underlying neurofibroma.

The entire spine and both buttocks should be examined, noting the level of the iliac crests, whether or not the spine is straight or curved, and whether there is a list to one side or the other. Nonlevel iliac crests (pelvic tilt) may be caused by muscle spasm, a shortened leg, or scoliosis. Scoliosis is defined as an abnormal lateral curvature of the spine. The curvature can be compensated if a plumb line dropped from the first thoracic vertebra is centered over the sacrum. An uncompensated spine is indicated by a list of the plumb line to either the left or the right of the sacrum (gluteal cleft). Structural scoliosis, which is due to intrinsic vertebral and thoracic rib abnormalities, can be differentiated from a functional scoliosis caused by leg-length discrepancy or pain by forward flexing of the spine.

Viewed laterally, the patient normally shows a slight lumbar lordosis and thoracic kyphosis. These curves are usually in balance such that an increase in one is compensated by a similar increase in the other. If an exaggerated thoracic kyphosis is not compensated by the lumbar lordosis, the patient leans backward in a posterior overcarriage. This is analogous to a list seen when viewing the patient posteriorly.

Spinal motions should be evaluated next. Flexion is evaluated by having the patient bend forward. Normally, the spine will show an even contour when viewed laterally. An accentuation of the thoracic curve is abnormal, as is a persistence of the angular lordotic curve, which indicates loss of flexibility of the lumbar spine. When viewed posteriorly, the forward bending may reveal rib deformity or a hump characteristic of scoliosis. In addition to these visual assessments, palpation of the lumbar spine may reveal increased paraspinal muscle spasm or less than the normal 1-in. spread between the second and fifth lumbar vertebrae; this indicates decreased lumbar spine mobility.

Backward bending is normally accompanied by an increase in the lumbar lordosis. If the lumbar lordosis is not accentuated, the motion is limited. Lateral flexion is evaluated by judging the degree of deviation from the upright midline position to both sides. Normally, this should be equal at about 30°. Rotation is measured by firmly holding the patient's pelvis and asking the patient to twist to either side.

Next, measurements should be made of the thigh and calves at similar levels and of the leg lengths from the anterosuperior iliac spine to the medical malleolus.

Hip motion is examined in abduction, adduction, internal rotation, and external rotation. Possible flexion contracture is evaluated by having the patient flex the contralateral hip maximally to flatten the lumbar lordosis; the angle between the horizontal and the maximally extended examined leg is then measured.

Palpation for areas of tenderness should include the vertebral bodies, pelvic prominences, sacrum, apophyseal joints, sarcoiliac joints, paravertebral and gluteal muscles, adjacent structures.

Percussion should be performed with the patient in a prone position or bending over the examining table, with a pillow under the abdomen, to accentuate the spinous processes. Percussion over the disk spaces may produce severe pain in the case of a herniated disk.

A rectal examination should be included, as should a bimanual vaginal examination, when indicated.

A thorough neurologic examination is required with particular emphasis on the straight-leg raising test. When performed properly, this is one of the most valuable maneuvers in the analysis of low back pain. With the patient lying supine and relaxed, the leg is elevated gradually to 90° or until the point of pain is reached. Some patients experience a tightness behind the thigh and knee, but this is not abnormal. Sciatica produces severe pain in the back, in the sciatic distribution of the affected leg, or both.

Routine Laboratory Abnormalities

Few if any laboratory tests are abnormal in the acute setting in patients with a negative history and minimal physical findings. The chemistry profile and blood count are generally unremarkable. Attention should be payed to serum calcium, alkaline phosphatase, and creatinine phosphokinase levels as possible markers for systemic disease.

A urine examination should be normal unless the pain is referred from a urinary infection or stone.

PLANS

Diagnostic

Differential Diagnosis and Diagnostic Options

See Table 6–21–1.

Recommended Approach

When faced acutely with a patient with a classic history and physical findings consistent with mechanical dysfunction, no further testing is needed. This will be the majority of cases. If, however, appropriate treatment fails, pain is chronic or atypical, the patient has a systemic illness or has had prior surgery or other manipulation, or reproducible new neurologic deficits are found, then testing with chemistry profiles, complete blood counts, plain x-ray and/or computed tomography scanning is needed. Depending on those results, consultation with a rheumatologist, orthopaedic surgeon, or neurosurgeon may be indicated prior to more invasive and expensive testing.

TABLE 6–21–1. LOW BACK PAIN: DIFFERENTIAL DIAGNOSIS AND DIAGNOSTIC OPTIONS

Differential Diagnosis	Diagnostic Options
Mechanical disorders	
Lumbosacral strain/sprain	A history of injury, sometimes minor, and tenderness and spasm of paravertebral muscles with limitation of motion of the lower back and normal x-ray films is diagnostic. If prolonged or atypical, computed tomography or magnetic resonance imaging may be indicated.
Degenerative disk disease, lumbar spondylosis	Generalized changes in the x-ray film of the lumbar spine almost always involve L3–4, L4–5, and L5–S1 interspaces. Often there are coexisting osteoarthritic changes, including sclerosis, apophyseal joint narrowing, and hypertrophic spurs.
Disk herniation	There is severe pain with radiation down the leg with specific neurologic abnormalities confirmed by computed tomography scan.
Spondylolisthesis	Slippage of L5 or S1 is confirmed radiographically.
Spinal stenosis	Symptoms may mimic root pain or claudication. Diagnosis is confirmed by myelography or transaxial tomography.
Fracture	Diagnosis is confirmed by radiography.
Infection	
Pyogenic or tuberulous vertebral osteomyelitis	In early stages, a positive culture from peripheral source, blood, or aspirated disk is diagnostic. Later, characteristic x-ray signs of disk space narrowing and destruction of contiguous vertebral margins confirm the diagnosis.
Inflammation	
Ankylosing spondylitis	Classic features in the x-ray film include bilateral sacroiliac involvement, squared verebrae, and typical "bamboo" spine. A positive HLA-B27 is helpful.
Spondylitis associated with psoriatic arthritis, inflammatory bowel disease, Reiter's syndrome	Sacroiliitis may be unilateral, or asymmetric. Lower incidence of positive HLA-B27 in addition to the specific features of each disease, i.e., psoriatic skin and nail lesions; bowel inflammation; and the triad of conjunctivitis, nongonococcal urethritis, and arthritis, respectively, suggest the diagnosis.
Visceral disorders	
Pyelonephritis, nephrolithiasis, pancreatitis, carcinoma of the pancreas, abdominal aortic aneurysm, retroperitoneal neoplasm	Referred pain to the back is an important part of the clinical presentation and helps to suspect the diagnosis. Please refer to the appropriate sections.

Therapeutic

Therapeutic Options

As there are a great number of causes of low back pain, treatment options abound. Conservative measures such as bed rest, antiinflammatory agents, analgesics, muscle relaxants, and back braces are all frequently used. Transcutaneous electrical nerve stimulation (TENS) units and acupuncture have been heralded by some. Spinal manipulative therapy and sacral base leveling are now available in many communities and may alleviate discomfort in select patient groups. Physical, spa, and massage therapy may help the physical and emotional well-being of many, and chronic pain centers offer hope for others. When pain is disabling or neurologic deficits occur, surgery is an option.

Recommended Approach

The principal means of acute management is rest. This is best achieved by forced bed rest for a period of time sufficient to allow the muscle spasm to subside and the root pressure to diminish. The value of traction is questionable; however, it may be useful in enforcing bed rest. Salicylates and other nonsteroidal antiinflammatory agents, muscle relaxants, and analgesics may be helpful initially. An exercise program carefully tailored to the specific needs of the patient is suggested in the early stages of recovery to help relieve spasm and, subsequently, to increase the strength of the abdominal and lumbar muscles. As the patient becomes more ambulatory, the use of a corset or back brace for a limited time may be of value in supporting the spine and decreasing the likelihood of reinjury. When the patient has the more common mechanical types of problems, the educational aspects of treatment are extremely important. Attention must be given to proper bending, sleeping position, lifting, driving a car, and other daily activities. Emphasis must be placed on a continuing exercise program to maintain good muscle tone and flexibility.

A surgical approach to mechanical back problems should be used with care. Results are predictably poor when surgery is exploratory, when evidence of disease is only subjective rather than objective, or when surgery is performed poorly. When surgery is performed on patients with objective findings who have failed to improve on a conservative regimen, the results are usually good.

FOLLOW-UP

The frequency of follow-up and the parameters to be followed in a follow-up program depend on the underlying cause of the back pain.

Mechanical etiologies may require simple rest and alteration in daily activities or more aggressive and prolonged treatment, including a comprehensive physical therapy program.

Consultation with orthopaedic surgeons, neurologists, or neurosurgeons may be required.

Infection demands establishing the causative agent, its source, and appropriate specific antimicrobial treatment.

Rheumatic disorders often require consultation with a rheumatologist, who should outline a treatment plan and work closely with the primary physician for long-term follow-up.

DISCUSSION

Prevalence and Incidence

Pain in the lower back remains one of the major causes of long-term disability and loss of earnings in all civilized societies. The direct cost of low back pain in the United States is $30 billion dollars. It ranks second only to upper respiratory tract infections as a source of loss of work. The prevalence of low back pain in the adult population is estimated to be about 80%, with an annual incidence of about 5%.

Related Basic Science

The human vertebral column is composed of two parts: the anterior segment, which contains two vertebral bodies separated by a disk, and the posterior segment, which consists of two articulations. Support, weight bearing, and absorbing shock are the functions of the anterior segment, whereas the posterior segment is responsible primarily for directional guidance and serves no weight-bearing function.

The lumbar region is the spine's major supporting segment, with transmission of the load to the lower extremities via the sacroiliac joints. It is composed of five functional units, the structure and function of which are dependent primarily on the status of the intervertebral disk. The wall of the disk or annulus is an intertwining fibroelastic mesh that surrounds and encapsulates the central cartilaginous matrix, the nucleus pulposus. The upper and lower plates of the disk are made of articular cartilage that composes the endplates of the adjacent vertebrae, keeping them separated. Shifts of fluid allow the vertebrae to move while maintaining a constant disk pressure.

The posterior portion of the functional unit is composed of two vertebral arches, two transverse processes, a central posterior spinous process, and inferior and superior articulations called facets. The paravertebral muscles attach to the processes of the posterior arch and the transverse and the posterior spinous processes. The facets are arthrodial joints that articulate in a gliding manner and direct movement between two adjacent vertebrae. The primary movements of the lumbar spine are flexion and extension, with little lateral bending and rotation. This is a consequence of the facet planes that lie in a vertical, sagittal direction.

The muscles of the back can be divided into two groups: short muscles, which include only one functional unit (i.e., they extend from one vertebra to an adjacent vertebra), and long muscles, which cross a number of functional units. The short muscles and the ligaments stabilize individual segments of the spine by binding together adjoining vertebrae, enabling long muscles to move a number of segments as a group.

The pathogenesis of low back pain is dependent on the relationship of the vertebrae to the neural structures. Termination of the spinal cord in the conus medullaris at the level of the L2 vertebral body is a critical anatomic point. Most pain results from irritation, compression, or injury of the cauda equina as it exits from the narrow foramina. The one well-accepted theory is that irritation, displacement, or compression of a nerve root in the canal or fibroosseous foraminal tunnel produces both local and radicular pain, with the latter component more prominent and often associated with a neurologic deficit.

Natural History and Its Modification with Treatment

The natural history and long-term prognosis for low back pain depend on many factors. Defining a precise underlying cause is often difficult and frustrating. Unfortunately, this encourages multiple physician exposure, which further compounds the problem. Periods of naturally occurring improvement and flare-ups are the rule, regardless of the etiology. This is especially true in lumbar disk disease and lumbosacral strain and sprain, which represent most causes of low back pain. Finally, probably the most significant factor in the outcome of low back pain is the duration of persistent symptoms. Less than 50% of patients who experience low back pain for more than 6 months ever return to gainful employment.

Prevention

Low back pain secondary to or associated with an infectious, inflammatory, metabolic, neoplastic, or visceral etiology cannot be viewed as preventable; however, in patients with mechanical back pain, particularly lumbosacral strain or sprain, the recurrences of pain can be reduced and chronic disability can be prevented by use of a properly supervised exercise program. The major goal is to preserve or restore proper mechanics to the low back by flattening the lumbar lordosis. The basic exercise to accomplish this is the pelvic tilt. This particular position will serve as the building block on which the major additional exercises are added. These include isometrically strengthening extensor muscles of the back, strengthening abdominal muscles, eliminating contractures of hip flexors, and stretching tight hamstring muscles. This basic program should be meticulously demonstrated and rigidly supervised to ensure proper execution.

Cost Containment

Treatment of chronic pain can be an enormous financial drain. Frequent loss of work time often compounded by flare-ups requiring prolonged hospitalizations creates major medical expenditures that are difficult to avoid. If costs are to be contained, the potentially preventive measures outlined above must be emphasized.

REFERENCES

Beaumont B, Paice E. Back pain. Occas Pap R Coll Gen Pract 1992;58:36.

Borenstein DG. Low back pain. In: Klippel JH, Dieppe PA, eds. Rheumatology. London: Mosby-Year Book Europe Limited, 1994:5.4.1.

Brown MD, Bjorn RL. Causes and cure of low back pain and sciatica. Orthop Clin North Am 1991;22(2).

Margo K. Diagnosis, treatment, and prognosis in patients with low back pain. Am Fam Physician 1994;49:171.

North RB. Acute back pain and disc herniation: Empting–Koschorke L. Chronic low back pain and failed back syndrome. In: Kassirer JP, ed. Current therapy in internal medicine. 3rd ed. Philadelphia: Decker, 1991:1632.

CHAPTER 6–22

Paget's Disease

Stephen B. Miller, M.D.

DEFINITION

Paget's disease is a localized disorder of bone remodeling characterized by bone resorption with compensatory new bone formation, resulting in disorganized bone at affected sites.

ETIOLOGY

The etiology is unknown.

CRITERIA FOR DIAGNOSIS
Suggestive

The patient with Paget's disease may present with pain in the area of involved bone, but more frequently, the disease is discovered incidentally on an x-ray film made for a different reason.

Definitive

The diagnosis of Paget's disease requires x-ray evidence of an area of typically mottled increase in bone density containing coarse trabeculation and the documentation of an elevated alkaline phosphatase level in the presence of normal serum calcium and phosphorus levels.

CLINICAL MANIFESTATIONS
Subjective

Most patients have either mild symptoms or none at all. The history may reveal that the disease was discovered inadvertently by x-ray or in the workup of an elevated alkaline phosphatase level. A parent or sibling may have the disease. When present, the pain is described as being deeply situated and aggravated by weight bearing; the pain is especially prominent in the pelvis, sacrum, and long bones. Persistent headache, dizziness, and reduced auditory acuity may be present. Rarely, symptoms of cord compression may occur; these include muscle weakness, incoordination, and respiratory difficulty.

Objective
Physical Examination

The physical signs may be extremely varied. The skeletal deformities are characterized by a kyphotic forward posture, with the chin resting on the upper chest and prominent clavicular enlargement. The skull is enlarged, especially frontally. Bowing of the femur and tibia, and less commonly of the proximal humerus, can be anticipated. Dental problems in the form of thickened cementum and partial root destruction, impaired hearing, prominent and tortuous temporal arteries, and angioid streaks around the optic disks complete the basic clinical picture. "Bone" pain may also occur in the hip and shoulder regions; the pain is accentuated when the patient demonstrates range of motion.

Routine Laboratory Abnormalities

The serum alkaline phosphatase level is the most valuable and reliable index of active Paget's disease. The heat-labile fraction is often elevated to extremely high levels and correlates well with bone turnover. The uric acid level may be elevated but not consistently. Serum calcium and phosphorus levels are normal.

PLANS
Diagnostic
Differential Diagnosis

The differential diagnosis includes osteoblastic metastases, particularly to the prostate; primary bone tumors; and hyperparathyroidism.

Diagnostic Options

The diagnostic options are x-rays of the bones, a bone scan, laboratory testing, and bone biopsy.

Recommended Approach

Establishing the diagnosis and presence of disease activity often requires a multidisciplinary approach.

The x-ray features vary depending on the relative amount of destruction and reconstruction, but these findings are the most definitive means of assessing bone involvement in Paget's disease. A characteristic sign is the so-called "tufts of cotton wool" appearance of the skull, with thickening and indistinctness of the external surface. The pelvis demonstrates the "brim sign," in which the coarse trabecular patterns help to differentiate the changes caused by Paget's disease from a metastatic neoplasm. The vertebral picture also shows sclerosis in the form of an "ivory vertebra," which is also extremely suggestive of Paget's disease. Incomplete fractures are seen on the convex surfaces of long bones as small transverse radiolucent lines. The most characteristic radiologic findings are a mottled increase in bone density, coarse trabeculation, incomplete fractures, "tufts of cotton wool" changes in the skull, and the "brim sign" in the pelvis.

The bone scan may show "hot spots" (increased uptake) of bone-seeking isotopes, demonstrating the extent and location of pagetic lesions. In localized involvement, the scan may be the only evidence of disease activity. Bone pain may be present without radiographic correlation. Increased uptake in a "normal" area with typical pagetic lesions in other sites is highly suggestive of involvement. A normal scan in association with a radiographic abnormality suggests inactivity at the specific site.

Laboratory testing in Paget's disease will demonstrate, in addition to an often markedly elevated alkaline phosphatase level, normal calcium and phosphorus levels. The other generally consistent abnormality is the 24-hour urinary hydroxyproline level, which is high in patients with active bone turnover secondary to Paget's disease.

Bone biopsy may be the only conclusive method to diagnose the rare complication of malignant degeneration.

Therapeutic
Therapeutic Options

The therapeutic options include no specific treatment, general measures, calcitonin, second-generation biphosphonates, and surgery.

Recommended Approach

Most patients with Paget's disease do not require specific treatment. Treatment is reserved for complications, including localized or diffuse bone pain, increasingly painful gait with postural disturbances, secondary osteoarthritis, hypercalcemia or hypercalciuria, and high-output cardiac failure.

A high fluid intake should be maintained when immobilization due to fracture or other illness occurs. This confinement to bed leads to rapid calcium mobilization with the potential development of serious hypercalcemia, hypercalciuria, and renal stones. Salicylates can be of considerable value in reducing bone pain as well as in suppressing disease activity, as evidenced by a reduction in alkaline phosphatase and urinary hydroxyproline levels.

A number of specialized drugs have been used with variable results. Calcitonin is available as salmon calcitonin (Calcimar) for treatment of bone pain. It reduces osteoclast-mediated bone resorption and, therefore, serum calcium levels. Relief of pain usually occurs within 2 to 6 weeks of treatment. Other observed benefits include reduction of neurologic deficits and disability, improvement of auditory acuity, decrease in cardiac output, and healing of osteolytic bone lesions. Chemical improvement can be monitored by noting the decrease in alkline phosphatase and urinary hydroxyproline levels. Salmon calcitonin is given subcutaneously or intramuscularly in a dose of 50 to 100 MRC units daily or three times a week until a satisfactory clinical or biochemical response is obtained. The maintenance dose is 50 MRC units three times a week. There are several drawbacks to the use of calcitonin; these include the need for parenteral administration, the possible development of neutralizing antibodies, the variable responsiveness, the induction of secondary hyperparathyroidism, and its expense. The most limiting is the plateau effect. Antibodies develop in more than 50% of patients, and a substantial number with higher titers become hormone resistant.

The second-generation biphosphonates are the newest compounds used in the treatment of Paget's disease. Most studies have been done using the drug pamidronate, either orally or intravenously. They act primarily on bone and can modify the crystal growth of hydroxyapatite by binding onto the crystal surface. Depending on concentration, the drugs may inhibit either crystal resorption or crystal growth. Significant lowering of serum alkaline phosphatase and urinary hydroxyproline levels can be anticipated and should be monitored closely. The greatest advantage of these compounds over calcitonin is the duration of remission, which can extend for years.

The recommended dose of pamidronate is 600 mg/d orally in a single daily dose for an average of 8 to 12 months. Re-treatment should be undertaken only after a drug-free period of at least 3 months and after it is evident that reactivation of the disease has occurred. Higher doses may be associated with the development of osteomalacia and an increased incidence of fractures.

FOLLOW-UP

The course of the disease can be followed objectively by repeating the alkaline phosphatase and urinary hydroxyproline determinations. High levels of both indicate rapid bone turnover, which correlates closely with active disease. These tests can therefore serve as an index of the efficacy of the treatment program.

DISCUSSION
Prevalence and Incidence

The exact prevalence of Paget's disease is difficult to ascertain because of wide differences between countries. About 3.5 to 5.5% of the population is affected up to age 50. The incidence doubles each decade thereafter to reach a maximum of 10% in the ninth decade. The patient is usually more than 40 years of age and more likely to be a man. There is a tenfold increased risk of developing the disease if parents or siblings have Paget's disease.

Related Basic Science

This disease can be viewed in three histologic stages: (1) osteoclastic, (2) osteoblastic, and (3) sclerotic and coarse trabecular.

The basic process in the early phase is one of extensive osteoclastic destruction accompanied by increased vascularity and fibrosis. Trabecular thinning, haversian canal enlargement, and cortical new bone formation lead to a fibrous bone that is soft and yields easily to weight bearing.

Next, the repair stage begins. Large numbers of osteoblasts lay down thick, coarse trabeculae of new bone, replacing the old cortical trabeculae. Repair and destruction occur simultaneously in a disorganized manner. The new trabeculae are distorted in shape and orientation and are joined by deeply staining cement lines arranged in a bizarre "mosaic pattern." In contrast to the soft fibrous bone, dense mosaic bone is brittle and easily fractured. Affected areas are well demarcated from normal areas, a feature that differentiates Paget's disease from metabolic bone disturbances. As bone repair is stimulated by activity, bones that are subjected to pressures of weight bearing and stresses of muscular activity show early and intense new bone formation. Thus, the long bones of the lower extremities and the vertebrae exhibit the dense bone of an active reparative process keeping pace with the destructive process, whereas in the skull, where these stresses are minimal, repair lags behind in the early stages, with destructive changes predominating. The condition may be confined to a portion of one bone initially, but gradually spreads to the remainder of the bones and almost invariably to other bones. Many areas escape involvement, and the distribution is asymmetric. Blood flow is excessive at the sites of lesions, as reflected pathologically by increased capillaries and venous "lakes."

Natural History and Its Modification with Treatment

The disease is usually slowly progressive over years. As bone involvement becomes more extensive, more widespread symptoms and deformities appear. The major complications are fractures and malignant degeneration.

Fractures are the most common complications, especially of the weight-bearing long bones. Fractures seem to occur more frequently in the early soft stage and tend to be incomplete fractures seen as radiolucencies on the convex surface of long bones. These fractures tend to heal rapidly, in contrast to late-stage dense bone fractures in which union is delayed. Fractures do not appear to predispose the patient to malignancy.

The most ominous complication of Paget's disease is the development of malignant degeneration. The elderly patient, especially a man with widespread disease, is most prone to this conversion. Fortunately, the overall incidence is well less than 1%. Osteogenic sarcoma is the usual type of tumor, but fibrosarcoma or round cell sarcoma can occur. An increase in pain and rapid increase in size of the bone herald the development of sarcoma. It is often multicentric and highly malignant, and appears as lytic changes in a medullary location. The humerus and skull are the most frequent sites of sarcomatous involvement.

The outlook for patients with symptomatic Paget's disease is much improved since the widespread use of second-generation biphosphonates. Symptomatic patients in their fifth decade should be treated aggressively, as should all patients in their eighth decade. It is as yet unclear whether therapy will reduce or eliminate the emergence of sarcoma.

The major potential benefits of treatment include relief of bone pain, treatment or prevention of hypercalcemia, prevention of neurologic deficits, and preparation for orthopaedic surgery when necessary. Total hip replacement for severe degenerative joint disease will often result in pain-free ambulation. Neurosurgery may occasionally be necessary for relief of nerve compression due to vertebral involvement.

Prevention

At present there is no proven method for the prevention of Paget's disease.

Cost Containment

Unlike many other conditions in which early diagnosis may achieve reduced costs, it is doubtful that this would be particularly helpful in Paget's disease. The area of greatest promise is in avoidance of overzealous, expensive drug regimens for relatively localized and mildly symptomatic disease.

REFERENCES

Adamson BB, Gallacher SJ, Byars J, et al. Pamidronate treatment of Paget's disease. Bone Miner 1992;17(suppl 1):S578.

Altman RD. Paget's disease of bone (osteitis deformans). Bull Rheum Dis 1984;34(3):8.

Krane SM. Skeletal metabolism in Paget's disease of bone. Arthritis Rheum 1980;23:1087.

Maldague B, Malghem J. Dynamic radiologic patterns of Paget's disease of bone. Clin Orthop 1987;217:126.

Nagant de Deuxchaisnes C. Paget's disease of bone: Medical management. In: De Groot LJ, ed. Endocrinology. 2nd ed. Philadelphia: Saunders, 1989:1211.

Connective Tissue Disease and the Vasculitides

Stephen B. Miller, M.D.

CHAPTER 7–1
··

Systemic Lupus Erythematosus

Jonathan Waltuck, M.D.

DEFINITION

Systemic lupus erythematosus (SLE) is a chronic, usually idiopathic, inflammatory disorder associated with autoimmunity, affecting multiple different organ systems with a severity that varies between patients and, over time, within the same patient.

ETIOLOGY

Despite decades of study the cause of SLE remains unknown. Autoimmunity is a hallmark of the disease, and satisfying explanations of etiology and pathogenesis may await a better understanding of the functioning of the cell-mediated and humoral immune systems. The clinical syndrome known as SLE may be an end result of several different pathologic processes and, thus, there may be no single etiology.

CRITERIA FOR DIAGNOSIS
Suggestive

The clinical manifestations of SLE are extremely variable, and most of the laboratory abnormalities found in patients with SLE are not specific to the disease. For these reasons, other diagnoses must be carefully con-

sidered before the diagnosis is accepted. Nevertheless, in multisystem diseases, especially those involving the skin and joints of young women, the diagnosis of SLE must be considered.

Definitive

In 1982 the American Rheumatism Association (now the American College of Rheumatology) set forth a list of 11 criteria, at least 4 of which should be present, not necessarily at the same time, to make a diagnosis of SLE (Table 7–1–1). It is likely that some patients in whom fewer than 4 criteria can be found have a similar or identical process.

If testing is properly performed, positive lupus erythematosus preparations, antibody to native DNA, and antibody to the Sm nuclear antigen are almost always associated with SLE.

CLINICAL MANIFESTATIONS
Subjective

Patients suffering from SLE can present with a wide variety of complaints involving many organ systems and frequently occurring simultaneously. Nevertheless, certain manifestations are far more common than others.

TABLE 7–1–1. THE 1982 REVISED CRITERIA FOR CLASSIFICATION OF SYSTEMIC LUPUS ERYTHEMATOSUS*

Criterion	Definition
1. Malar rash	Fixed erythema, flat or raised, over the malar eminences, tending to spare the nasolabial folds
2. Discoid rash	Erythematous raised patches with adherent keratotic scaling and follicular plugging; atrophic scarring may occur in older lesions
3. Photosensitivity	Skin rash as a result of unusual reaction to sunlight, by patient history or physician observation
4. Oral ulcers	Oral or nasopharyngeal ulceration, usually painless, observed by a physician
5. Arthritis	Nonerosive arthritis involving two or more peripheral joints, characterized by tenderness, swelling, or effusion
6. Serositis	a. Pleuritis: convincing history of pleuritic pain or rub heard by a physician or evidence of pleural effusion OR b. Pericarditis: documented by electrocardiogram or rub or evidence of pericardial effusion
7. Renal disorder	a. Persistent proteinuria greater than 0.5 g per day or greater than 3+ if quantitation not performed OR b. Cellular casts: may be red cell, hemoglobin, granular, tubular, or mixed
8. Neurologic disorder	a. Seizures: in the absence of offending drugs or known metabolic derangements, e.g., uremia, ketoacidosis, or electrolyte imbalance OR b. Psychosis: in the absence of offending drugs or known metabolic derangements, e.g., uremia, ketoacidosis, or electrolyte imbalance
9. Hematologic disorder	a. Hemolytic anemia: with reticulocytosis OR b. Leukopenia: less than $4000/mm^3$ total on two or more occasions OR c. Lymphopenia: less than $1500/mm^3$ on two or more occasions OR d. Thrombocytopenia: less than $100,000/mm^3$ in the absence of offending drugs
10. Immunologic disorder	a. Positive lupus erythematosus cell preparation OR b. Anti-DNA: antibody to native DNA in abnormal titer OR c. Anti-Sm; presence of antibody to Sm nuclear antigen OR d. False-positive serologic test for syphilis known to be positive for at least 6 months and confirmed by *Treponema pallidum* immobolization or fluorescent treponemal antibody absorption test
11. Antinuclear antibody	An abnormal titer of antinuclear antibody by immunofluorescence or an equivalent assay at any point in time and in the absence of drugs known to be associated with "drug-induced lupus" syndrome

*The proposed classfication is based on 11 criteria. For the purpose of identifying patients in clinical studies, a person shall be said to have systemic lupus erythematosus if any 4 or more of the 11 criteria are present, serially or simultaneously, during any interval of observation.
Source: Tan E, et al. Revised criteria for the classification of systemic lupus erythematosus. *Arthritis Rheum* 1982;25(11):274. Reproduced from Arthritis & Rheumatism Journal, *copyright 1982. Used by permission of the American College of Rheumatology.*

The skin will be involved at one time or another in most SLE patients. Often, rashes occur after exposure to sunlight and such exposure may lead to major flares involving other organ systems as well. Photosensitivity is described by about half of patients with SLE, more commonly in those with light skin and fair coloring. Alopecia, which may be diffuse or more localized to the frontal or temporal areas of the head, is common during periods of disease activity.

Musculoskeletal complaints are also quite common, occurring in a majority of patients. Arthralgias are most frequent, but frank arthritis occurs as well. The most commonly affected joints are those of the hands, especially the proximal interphalangeal joints and the wrists. Occasionally, early in the disease, the joints will be affected out of proportion to other organs and a diagnosis of rheumatoid arthritis may be difficult to exclude.

The patient may notice ankle edema. This is usually due to hypoalbuminemia from nephrotic syndrome, but may rarely be secondary to congestive heart failure. Unilateral leg swelling and pain may be caused by deep venous thrombosis, as many patients with SLE are hypercoagulable. Hypercoagulability may be related to the presence of antibodies directed against phospholipids, the so-called *antiphospholipid syndrome*. Second-trimester fetal losses are also associated with these antibodies.

Raynaud's syndrome, in which the fingers undergo a triphasic color change on exposure to cold or during periods of stress, is quite common. Classically, the fingers turn white followed by a bluish cyanotic hue, finally replaced by a red flush as vasodilation occurs. Frequently, the full three-color change does not occur, but patients complain of excessive hand sensitivity to the cold. Chest pain, cough, and dyspnea occur frequently and may be due to a variety of processes involving the lungs, pleura, diaphragm, costochondral joints, pericardium, and myocardium. Perhaps most common is pleuritic chest pain caused by inflammation of the pleura. This is commonly accompanied by pericarditis, and chest discomfort may be worsened by lying down. Hemoptysis is fortunately rare as it is often related to pulmonary hemorrhage, which carries a substantial mortality.

The nervous system is often affected. Psychiatric difficulties such as anxiety and depression are very common and are usually due to the stress and uncertainty inherent in having a chronic, potentially serious disease. Seizures occur in more than 10% of patients. Cerebrovascular accidents leading to focal neurologic abnormalities occur with a similar frequency. Severe abnormalities such as coma, psychosis, and paraparesis due to transverse myelitis occur occasionally and require therapy on an emergent basis. Headaches are very common and may be of the muscle tension or migraine type.

Constitutional symptoms including fever, fatigue, and weight loss may be prominent during periods of disease activity. Abdominal pain may occur and may be due to sterile peritonitis or, much more rarely, to mesenteric ischemia caused by thrombosis or vasculitis of mesenteric vessels. Pancreatitis is a rare complication of SLE.

Patients using certain medications, most commonly hydralazine and procainamide, may develop a syndrome similar to idiopathic SLE. Symptoms are generally milder, however, and often are limited to arthritis and pleuropericarditis. Idiopathic SLE in the elderly may be similar to this drug-induced syndrome.

Occasionally, patients give a history of autoimmune thrombocytopenia or hemolytic anemia prior to other manifestations of SLE. Patients with drug-induced lupus give a history of the illness for which the offending medication was prescribed.

Occasionally, other family members have SLE or other connective tissue disorders. First-degree relatives of people with SLE are at substantially increased risk of developing the disease and may, though asymptomatic, produce autoantibodies.

Objective

Physical Examination

Hypertension is often a sign of significant renal disease, and fever and tachycardia are common during exacerbations.

The skin examination may be quite helpful in establishing the diagnosis; in fact, SLE was originally recognized by its characteristic dermatologic manifestations and the skin is one of the most commonly involved organs. The classic types of skin involvement are classified as acute, subacute, and chronic. The most common acute rash is the malar or "butterfly" facial eruption, but other more dramatic acute eruptions occur. These rashes are usually associated with active systemic disease and occur mostly in sun-exposed areas (the nasolabial folds are usually spared). The rash is erythematous and slightly edematous, occasionally with some scale. Healing usually occurs without scarring. Subacute cutaneous lupus erythematosus lesions occur in about 10% of those with systemic disease. The lesions may be papulosquamous (psoriasiform) or may occur in multiple rings (annular polycyclic). Lesions may be on the chest, upper back, and extensor surfaces of the arms; the face is usually spared. Scarring is rare. Most patients with subacute cutaneous lupus erythematosus have in their serum antibodies to a particular nuclear protein known as Ro or SSA. Discoid lupus erythematosus lesions are chronic and occur in about a quarter of patients with SLE, but also occur without systemic disease. They are well-circumscribed annular plaques with adherent scales commonly occurring on the face, external ears, ear canals, scalp, and arms. Healing often occurs with scarring, atrophy, and hypopigmentation.

Cutaneous SLE lesions typically spare the knuckles. Oral ulcers may be found, especially on the hard palate. Ulcers also occur on the nasal septum.

The musculoskeletal examination may reveal synovitis, usually most prominent in the hands. Severe joint damage with loss of motion is distinctly atypical, and deformities are usually reducible. Avascular necrosis, most often involving the femoral heads, is a common complication in those patients treated with steroids.

Cerebrovascular accidents resulting from hypercoagulability or embolic events may lead to focal abnormalities on neurologic examination. In addition, diffuse central nervous system problems such as psychosis and altered levels of consciousness, including coma, may occur. As mentioned above, depression and anxiety are common. Transverse myelitis presenting as paraparesis is a rare devastating complication. Peripheral neuropathies, usually sensory, occur in 10 to 15% of patients.

Cardiovascular examination may reveal a pericardial rub or, much more rarely, signs of cardiac tamponade, such as distended neck veins and pulsus paradoxus. Aortic regurgitation may develop. Dullness at lung bases caused by the accumulation of pleural fluid is common.

Bacterial pnemonias occur as well, especially in patients using immunosuppressive medications.

Diffuse abdominal tenderness is most often due to sterile peritonitis. Peripheral edema and hypertension are the most common physical examination correlates of renal disease.

Moderate diffuse lymphadenopathy is noted at some point in about half of patients.

Routine Laboratory Abnormalities

Anemia is usually present during active disease and may be caused by a variety of problems including chronic inflammation, renal disease with decreased erythropoietin levels, and hemolysis. Leukopenia and especially lymphopenia may occur. Antiplatelet antibodies may lead to autoimmune thrombocytopenia.

Blood chemistry tests may demonstrate elevations of urea nitrogen or creatinine as a result of renal involvement. Routine urinalysis often reveals proteinuria and, occasionally, an active urine sediment with red cells and white cells. Cellular casts may be present with more severe (proliferative) renal lesions.

Erythrocyte sedimentation rate is usually high during active disease, but is not felt to correlate very well with disease activity.

PLANS
Diagnostic
Differential Diagnosis

A variety of infections including syphilis, Epstein–Barr virus, cytomegalovirus, HIV, Lyme borreliosis, tuberculosis, and subacute bacterial endocarditis may mimic some or all of the manifestations of SLE. The early stages of other connective tissue diseases such as scleroderma and rheumatoid arthritis may be confused with SLE. Occasionally, malignancies such as lymphoma are considered in the differential diagnosis. Patients with the fibromyalgia syndrome may present with a wide variety of complaints, which may superficially suggest SLE.

Diagnostic Options

Antinuclear antibodies are present in the serum of nearly everyone with SLE. They may also be found in other connective tissue diseases. Most people with antinuclear antibodies, however, have no condition related to these antibodies. Anti-Sm and anti-DNA antibodies have a much higher diagnostic specificity. Active SLE is usually associated with consumption of components of the complement cascade, which may be reflected by low levels of C3, C4, and CH50.

Recommended Approach

By keeping in mind the clinical and laboratory manifestations of SLE listed in Table 7–1–1, one may reasonably approach the patient suspected of having the disease. Laboratory tests may be used as an adjunct to the history and physical examination, but cannot supplant clinical judgment. Although delay in diagnosing SLE may prolong the period before proper treatment is provided, an incorrect diagnosis of SLE can also lead to needless problems, especially for the patient with fibromyalgia. Such patients may latch onto the diagnosis and be loathe to relinquish it.

Once the diagnosis has been established, organ involvement should be assessed. This is particularly important with regard to renal disease, which may often be asymptomatic but may greatly influence prognosis. Referral to a rheumatologist is probably indicated, if only for more definitive diagnosis and general guidelines for therapy.

Therapeutic
Therapeutic Options

Therapy for SLE ranges from observation and emotional support to cytotoxic agents and experimental procedures such as plasmapheresis. Overtreatment can be as damaging as undertreatment.

Recommended Approach

Skin manifestations of SLE can usually be treated with topical steroids and, if more severe or resistant, with antimalarial agents, such as hydroxychloroquine. This drug is usually started at a dose of 400 mg/d, but can often be tapered within a year to 200 mg/d. Ophthalmologic examinations should be performed every 6 months during therapy with hydroxychloroquine to detect incipient retinal damage. Arthritis can often be managed with nonsteroidal antiinflammatory drugs and/or antimalarial agents, though occasionally low doses of corticosteroids, for example, 10 mg/d prednisone, may be required. Severe constitutional symptoms, such as sustained high fevers, often must be treated with higher doses of corticosteroids, such as 1 mg/kg prednisone per day. In such cases, superimposed infections must be carefully excluded. Patients with SLE are quite prone to infectious complications because of complement consumption, occupation of Fc receptors in the reticuloendothelial system, and the effect of immunosuppressive drugs. Pneumococcal and salmonella infections must be ruled out.

Involvement of organs such as the heart, lungs, and central nervous system usually requires treatment with corticosteroids. The need for renal biopsies to assess SLE kidney involvement has been and remains controversial. In many cases, routine clinical and laboratory data permit the development of a treatment plan; in other cases, the extra information available through a biopsy is needed.

Systemic lupus erythematosus renal disease has been divided into five categories based on light microscopic characteristics (World Health Organization classes I–V). Class I is an essentially normal biopsy except for, perhaps, some mesangial immune complex deposits. Class II is mesangial nephritis involving cellular infiltration into the mesangium associated with immune complex deposition. This is felt by some to be a background lesion in SLE and clinical abnormalities are mild. Class III is focal proliferative nephritis involving cellular proliferation of segments of less than half of the glomeruli sampled. This more severe lesion may be associated with an active urinary sediment, hypertension, and progression to renal insufficiency. Class IV lupus nephritis or diffuse proliferative glomerulonephritis represents a very severe lesion involving marked glomerular cellular proliferation, often with significant glomerular damage such as crescent formation. Without aggressive therapy, progression to renal failure is common. Class V or membranous lupus glomerulonephritis involves thickening of the glomerular basement membrane without much cellular proliferation. The major manifestation is nephrotic syndrome. Assessment of the interstitium along with electron microscopic appearance and immunofluorescence may provide additional valuable information.

Proliferative renal lesions are often treated with intravenous pulse cyclophosphamide. A dose of 1 g/m^2 of body surface area is infused monthly while nadir white blood cell counts are carefully followed. Later, intervals between treatments may be prolonged to 3 months. Studies performed at the National Institutes of Health and elsewhere seem to indicate that cytotoxic agents are more effective than corticosteroids alone in treating severe renal involvement.

As SLE is an episodic disease, it is extremely important to withdraw therapy slowly when an exacerbation has quieted down, to spare the patient unnecessary drug toxicity. If prednisone has been started at 60 mg/d, it may be tapered at 5 mg/d at weekly intervals as long as the disease remains quiescent until a dose of 20 mg/d is reached, at which point the taper should be slowed.

Drug-induced lupus usually requires only withdrawal of the offending agent, with perhaps a short course of nonsteroidal antiinflammatory agents or steroids.

FOLLOW-UP

Patients with SLE should be evaluated at least once every 3 to 6 months, even if the disease is inactive. Careful physical examination and routine laboratory tests including urinalysis should be obtained each visit. Obviously, patients with active disease must be assessed much more frequently. Some advocate testing for complement and anti-DNA levels routinely, as decreasing complements or increasing anti-DNA levels may be associated with disease exacerbations. Other antibody levels are not associated with disease activity and should not be routinely assessed during follow-up.

DISCUSSION
Prevalence

The prevalence of SLE is approximately one in 10,000 people, but different demographic groups are at markedly different risks of developing the disease. Black and Asian women in the United States appear to be at increased risk. In adults, women are 10 times as likely to develop SLE as are men. The ratio is less dramatic in children and the elderly, and there is no sex predominance in drug-induced lupus.

Related Basic Science
Genetics

As mentioned above, relatives of patients with SLE are at increased risk of developing the disease. Identical twins are more often concordant in disease development than are fraternal twins. Certain human leukocyte antigens confer increased risk, specifically HLA-B8, HLA-DR2, and HLA-DR3. Congenital deficiencies of early complement

components, most commonly C4, also are associated with a higher incidence of SLE.

The above-noted racial associations also imply a genetic influence on disease expression.

Altered Molecular Biology

Current theories of the etiology of SLE involve viral infections and abnormalities in clearance of immune complexes or in programmed cell death. Any explanations must account for the female predominance and known genetic influences on the risk of disease development.

Much research has been performed on several strains of mice that demonstrate clinical and laboratory abnormalities similar to those of human SLE. Different strains manifest distinct T- and B-cell dysfunctions. Whether the demonstrated immune abnormalities are causative of the clinical syndrome remains unclear.

Physiologic or Metabolic Derangement

The hallmark of SLE is autoimmunity; in fact, SLE is considered the prototypical autoimmune disease. Possible explanations for the occurrence of autoantibodies include polyclonal B-cell activation, abnormalities of suppressor T cells, overactivity of helper T cells, alteration of host molecules so that they are perceived as antigenic, and cross-reactivity of antibodies directed against foreign molecules with the host tissues. Evidence exists supporting all of these hypotheses.

Antibodies directed against red cells and platelets may lead to the destruction of these blood elements. Anti-DNA antibodies are found in increased concentrations relative to serum in renal tissue, and severe renal disease is rare in patients without anti-DNA antibodies. In other cases, the pathogenicity of autoantibodies is less clear.

Antibodies directed against phospholipids are associated with a hypercoagulable state in SLE. Immune complexes are presumed to be involved in many of the clinical manifestations of SLE, though proof of this hypothesis is lacking. Immune complexes formed in the serum could deposit in different tissues, fix complement, and set up an inflammatory insult. Alternatively, complexes could form in situ when circulating antibodies attach to tissue antigens. More recently, it has been proposed that intravascular neutrophil aggregation due to complement activation plays a pathogenic role in many of the manifestations of SLE.

Natural History and Its Modification with Treatment

The outlook for patients with SLE has improved dramatically over the past few decades. At one time, most cases of SLE were diagnosed at autopsy, whereas today 10-year survival is 80 to 90%. Many factors have led to this improved prognosis. The disease is more accurately diagnosed today and thus many patients with milder disease are recognized. Faster and more effective treatment of severe manifestations has clearly had an effect. This is especially true of the use of cytotoxic agents in severe renal disease. Also important is the routine availability of dialysis for treatment failures and of more effective antibiotics to treat infectious complications.

Prevention

No specific measures are available to prevent the development of SLE. In photosensitive patients with SLE, sun exposure should be minimized. Patients with a history of drug-induced lupus should avoid the offending agent. In general, physicians do not (and should not) dissuade patients from pregnancy as they have in the past. Patients with active disease, however, specifically active renal disease, should postpone childbearing. Patients should be made aware of the possibility of flare during pregnancy. Issues regarding possible termination of pregnancy if severe complications occur should be thought through and discussed prior to conception.

Cost Containment

Complete history taking and careful physical examinations can often obviate the need for expensive diagnostic tests. Early therapy of disease flares may avoid costly hospitalizations.

REFERENCES

Baldwin DS, Lowenstein J, Rothfield N, et al. The clinical course of the proliferative and membranous forms of lupus nephritis. Ann Intern Med 1970;73:929.

Schur PH. Clinical features of SLE: In: Kelley WN, Harris ED, Ruddy S, Sledge CB, eds. Textbook of rheumatology. 4th ed. Philadelphia: Saunders, 1993:1017.

Steinberg AD, Raveche ES, Laskin CA, et al. Systemic lupus erythematosus: Insights from animal models. Ann Intern Med 1984;100:714.

Steinberg AD, Steinberg SC. Long term preservation of renal function in patients with lupus nephritis receiving treatment that includes cyclophosphamide versus those treated with prednisone only. Arthritis Rheum 1991;34:945.

West S. Neuropsychiatric lupus. Rheum Dis Clin North Am 1994;20:129.

CHAPTER 7–2

Lung Disease Due to Systemic Lupus Erythematosus (See Section 13, Chapter 32)

CHAPTER 7–3

Dermatomyositis and Polymyositis

Stephen B. Miller, M.D.

DEFINITION

Dermatomyositis and polymyositis are disorders of connective tissue characterized by chronic inflammation of striated muscle (polymyositis) and sometimes the skin (dermatomyositis).

ETIOLOGY

The etiology remains unknown.

CRITERIA FOR DIAGNOSIS

Suggestive

Symmetric painless proximal muscle weakness of limb girdles and anterior neck flexors with or without skin rash; elevation of serum enzymes, especially creatine kinase and aldolase; and electromyographic findings typical of an inflammatory myopathy are suggestive.

Definitive

Muscle biopsy confirming the diagnosis of an inflammatory myopathy is definitive.

CLINICAL MANIFESTATIONS

Subjective

The patient is usually in the fifth to sixth decade of life and may present with acute, subacute, or chronic symptoms, with weakness being the major complaint. In many cases, the patient may have noted a specific stimulus prior to the onset of the weakness, such as a febrile illness, a rash, or a benign infection or trauma. The weakness is usually noted first in the legs and later in the arms. Dysphagia is a common early complaint. The patient may note some difficulty in breathing relatively early in the course of the disease. In the very acute presentation, the patient may note severe muscle pain, which seems to override the weakness. Arthralgias are common, but a history of swelling, heat, or erythema in the joints is quite unusual.

Objective

Physical Examination

The most common presentation is moderate proximal muscle weakness, which is easily demonstrable in both the upper and lower extremities and particularly in the anterior neck flexors. Occasionally, the muscles may be markedly tender and indurated. The degree of weakness is quite variable.

There are a number of classic dermatologic features. Some patients demonstrate a lilac discoloration over the eyelids (heliotrope) with periorbital edema. The most distinctive and characteristic eruption is a scaly erythematous dermatitis overlying the dorsum of the hands (especially the metacarpophalangeal and proximal interphalangeal joints), known as Gottron's sign. This rash also may appear on the knees, elbows, medial malleoli, face, neck, and upper anterior torso. Hyperemia of the base, sides, and ends of the nails and fingers is also common. Less frequently, sclerodermatous-like thickening of the hands and arms may occur with telangiectasia and pigmentary changes. Much less commonly, there may be pulmonary abnormalities in the form of diffuse crackles or signs of congestive heart failure, arrhythmias, or heart block.

Routine Laboratory Abnormalities

Complete blood count, urinalysis, sedimentation rate, and chemical profiles are usually normal, with the exception of elevated transaminase levels reflecting muscle inflammation.

PLANS

Diagnostic

Differential Diagnosis

The following conditions should be considered:

- Myositis associated with other connective tissue diseases (scleroderma, systemic lupus erythematosus, and rheumatoid arthritis)
- Myositis associated with malignancy
- Myositis associated with infectious agents (influenza, coxsackievirus, HIV)
- Inclusion body myositis
- Drug- and toxin-induced myositis (penicillamine, eosinophilia–myalgia syndrome)
- Hypothyroidism
- Polymyalgia rheumatica

Diagnostic Options

The diagnostic options include determination of muscle enzyme levels, electromyogram, muscle biopsy, and skin biopsy.

Recommended Approach

The muscle enzyme levels should be abnormal. All muscle enzymes, that is, creatine kinase, aldolase, serum glutamic–oxaloacetic transaminase, and serum lactate dehydrogenase, will be elevated. The creatine kinase level is clearly the most reliable and most useful as an index of disease activity. Anemia is rare unless the disability is prolonged and severe or unless an associated malignancy is present. Antinuclear and anti-DNA antibodies are generally normal unless there are overlapping features of other connective tissue diseases.

The electromyogram should be done and is characterized by (1) polyphasic, short, small motor unit potentials; (2) fibrillation, positive sharp waves, increased insertional activity, and irritability; and (3) bizarre, high-frequency, repetitive discharges.

In selecting a muscle for biopsy, the quadriceps or deltoid muscle is usually preferred. It is important not to choose a severely weak muscle, as the changes may be primarily atrophic, or a muscle with normal strength. It is important to determine whether an electromyogram has been done prior to the biopsy, as artifactual abnormalities may occur if the biopsy is done in the area where the electromyograph needle was placed. The major microscopic changes include necrosis of type I and II fibers, phagocytosis, regeneration with basophilia, large vesicular sarcolemma nuclei and prominent nucleoli, atrophy in a perivascular distribution, variation in fiber size, and a perivascular inflammatory exudate.

The electromyogram plus evidence of inflammatory myositis provided by examination of a biopsy performed on a muscle with bilateral muscle weakness, elevation in enzymes, and sometimes the dermatologic features complete the essential observations needed to support the diagnosis.

Therapeutic

Therapeutic Options

The therapeutic options include corticosteroids; immunosuppressive agents such as methotrexate and azathioprine; and physical therapy.

Recommended Approach

Corticosteroids are the treatment of choice, usually starting with prednisone 60 mg/d or its equivalent, in divided doses. It often takes 3 to 4 months for a full response to occur. It is not uncommon for the patient to experience varying degrees of resistance, from a partial return of strength to a total lack of improvement. When resistance is clear-cut, the possible need for a second drug arises. This drug should provide a suppressive antiinflammatory effect and allow a reduction in corticosteroids without the loss of any improvement in muscle strength already obtained.

Methotrexate given orally in doses of 5 to 15 mg weekly or intravenously in doses of 0.5 to 0.8 mg/kg at weekly intervals has been found to be of value in 75% of refractory cases. Other immunosuppressive drugs—azathioprine (Imuran) and cyclophosphamide (Cytoxan)—have been tried and reported to be of benefit.

FOLLOW-UP

While the patient is on corticosteroids, the frequency of follow-up visits depends on individual circumstances. Generally in the early phases of the disease, the visits should be made as frequently as every 1 to 2 weeks. As the disease is better controlled and the prednisone is tapered, the frequency of the visits may be decreased to every 6 to 8 weeks. The tapering of prednisone should begin once the disease has stabilized and strength is much improved; however, the reduction in enzymes often lags far behind the clinical response. Reduction in steroids should be guided primarily by clinical parameters, namely, muscle strength, rather than by enzyme levels. If the enzyme levels rise in conjunction with obvious progression in muscle and skin inflammatory activity, then interruption of tapering and appropriate increases in steroids are indicated.

DISCUSSION

Prevalence and Incidence

Most cases occur in the fifth and sixth decades of life, with women predominating more than 2:1. The incidence depends on various populations, but is usually in the range of 2 to 10 new cases per million persons at risk.

Related Basic Science

Increasing evidence at the basic research level implicates both the cellular and humoral immune systems in the pathogenesis of inflammatory myopathy.

Direct examination of biopsy material illustrates the role of the cellular system in muscle damage. Different lymphocytes accumulate in different regions of the muscle in idiopathic inflammatory myopathy. In dermatomyositis, B and CD4+ T cells are relatively abundant, especially in the perimysial regions. By contrast, in polymyositis, endomysial CD8+ T cells predominate and B cells are sparse.

A significant number of cellular events have been found to differ between patients with active myositis and control populations. These include many phenotypic abnormalities of circulating lymphocytes, for example, decreased CD8 expression, increased major histocompatibility complex class II antigens (DR), and interleukin-2 expression, as well as homing to muscle as demonstrated by radiolabeled reinfusion scanning. Despite this growing body of compelling evidence that lymphocytes are critically involved in the causation of inflammatory myositis, their specific pathogenic role remains unknown.

A family of autoantibodies was recently discovered that occur almost exclusively in myositis patients (myositis-specific autoantibodies). This new information has led to a greater emphasis on investigating the humoral autoantibody system in myositis.

Myositis-specific autoantibodies are characterized by several important features:

- They are directed at proteins and ribonucleoproteins, which are present in every cell.
- They are targeted at intracellular molecules, usually intracytoplasmic molecules.
- Autoantigens (target molecules) are part of the protein synthetic machinery.

Myositis specific autoantibodies are usually present during active disease at the initial visit to the physician. Most are not "antinuclear" antibodies, as they are directed at intracytoplasmic components. Immunodiffusion using lines of identity with well-characterized antisera is required to further identify specific target antigens (ribonucleoproteins). Each autoantibody appears to be associated with a distinct clinical syndrome that has a group of common clinical findings, a predominant HLA-A type, and probably a selective response to therapy.

The clearest relationship between antibody and clinical pattern is that between anti-Jo-1 and polymyositis. The Jo-1 antibody system is found in 20 to 30% of patients with polymyositis, but much less frequently in dermatomyositis. A strong association exists between the presence of Jo-1 antibody and interstitial lung disease. These patients usually have fever, arthritis, Raynaud's phenomenon, and roughened lateral and palmar surfaces on index fingers, termed *machinist* or *mechanic's hands*. Almost all patients have the HLA-DRW52 alloantigen. Their clinical course is aggressive, often requiring immunosuppressive drugs in addition to corticosteroids.

Another group of patients demonstrate antibodies to a less well characterized antigen, Mi-2. They almost all have dermatomyositis, their HLA type is often DR7, and the disease is quite responsive to therapy. There are a number of associations of autoantibodies to other cytoplasmic proteins, but the illness and specific autoantigens have as yet not been well defined. In summary, the discovery of myositis-specific autoantibodies and some strong correlations with specific clinical and immunogenic groups suggest that these may be separate diseases that result from different environmental or genetic influences.

Natural History and Its Modification with Treatment

Early treatment as outlined above can often successfully control these diseases, allowing the individual to function normally. As previously mentioned the incidence of malignancies is increased in patients with dermatomyositis and polymyositis, especially with the former. Men and women over the age of 40 are usually affected equally. Suspicion should be especially high in the older patient with the acute florid onset of dermatomyositis. These neoplasms are usually carcinomas, generally found in proportions similar to those found in the nonmyositic population, that is, lung, prostate, and colon carcinomas in men, and breast, ovarian, and uterine carcinomas in women. In addition, the older the patient is at the onset of the disease, the higher is the mortality rate. Actually, after age 50, the incidence of malignancy determines the overall mortality rate.

Prevention

At present there is no proven method for the prevention of dermatomyositis or polymyositis.

Cost Containment

The strong likelihood of the development of a malignancy with dermatomyositis or polymyositis requires the physician to monitor these patients frequently with physical examinations, laboratory tests, diagnostic x-ray examinations, computed tomography scans, and other tests, when indicated. Attempts at cost containment would best be directed at decreasing long hospitalizations by substituting intensive outpatient surveillance and treatment.

REFERENCES

Bohan A, Peter JB. Polymyositis and dermatomyositis. N Engl J Med 1975;292:344.

Bohan A, Peter JB, Bowman RL, et al. A computer-assisted analysis of 153 patients with polymyositis and dermatomyositis. Medicine 1977;56:255.

Love LA, Leff RL, Fraser DD, et al. A new approach to the classification of idiopathic inflammatory myopathy: Myositis-specific autoantibodies define useful homogeneous patient groups. Medicine 1991;70:360.

Plotz PH. Current concepts in the idiopathic inflammatory myopathies: Polymyositis, dermatomyositis, and related disorders. Ann Intern Med 1989;111(2):143.

Plotz PH, Miller FW. Inflammatory muscle disease (etiology and pathogenesis). In: Klippel JH, Dieppe PA, eds. Rheumatology. London: Mosby, 1994:6.13.1

CHAPTER 7–4

Systemic Sclerosis (Scleroderma)

E. Carwile LeRoy, M.D.

DEFINITION

Systemic sclerosis, the generalized form of scleroderma, is an autoimmune disorder characterized by immune/inflammatory, vascular/microvascular, and fibrotic lesions of the skin, lungs, heart, kidneys, and gastrointestinal tract, leading eventually to atrophy and vascular insufficiency of these target organs.

ETIOLOGY

The etiology of systemic sclerosis is unknown. In the immunogenetically susceptible individual (usually female), certain triggers (viral, chemical, mechanical, temperature) initiate microvascular endothelial injury associated with distinctive autoantibody formation and fibroblast activation, leading to cell proliferation and matrix deposition resulting in perivascular and interstitial fibrosis.

CRITERIA FOR DIAGNOSIS
Suggestive

The typical patient is a woman between 25 and 50 years of age who has noted episodic and persistent swelling (edema) and tautness of the skin of the hands, face, or distal aspects of the extremities associated with tingling and numbness.

Definitive

A history of pallor and cyanosis of the fingers or toes associated with pain (Raynaud's phenomenon) can be elicited in almost all patients destined to develop systemic sclerosis; other features, such as difficulty swallowing and exertional dyspnea, should increase the suspicion. If examination of the skin proximal to the metacarpophalangeal joints demonstrates hidebound thickening, the diagnosis is definite; the presence of sclerodactyly or pitting of the distal phalanges (microinfarcts) adds support for the diagnosis, but neither is definitive (Table 7–4–1).

Two subsets of systemic sclerosis that differ in the rate at which internal organ involvement appears are diffuse cutaneous systemic sclerosis and limited cutaneous systemic sclerosis or CREST (calcinosis, Raynaud's phenomenon, esophageal dysmotility, sclerodactyly, and telangiectasia) (Table 7–4–2). There is considerable overlap in the different manifestations of the two types; for example, almost all patients with diffuse systemic sclerosis have most of the features of limited systemic sclerosis. At present, taut skin restricted and distal to the elbows, knees, and neck is a criterion for limited systemic sclerosis. More proximal or truncal involvement is diagnostic of diffuse systemic sclerosis, in whom the risk of internal organ involvement is high. Patients with limited cutaneous systemic sclerosis can also develop life-threatening internal organ involvement, which is usually isolated to the lungs and is chronic in onset (10–20 years after onset of Raynaud's phenomenon). Patients with limited systemic sclerosis also develop early esophageal disease, but cardiac or renal involvement is rare.

Disorders that can mimic systemic sclerosis but do so rarely are amyloidosis and sarcoidosis with cutaneous involvement; skin biopsy with special stains is definitive in identifying these possibilities.

CLINICAL MANIFESTATIONS
Subjective

Systemic sclerosis usually evolves in a group of patients who complain of episodic vasospasm (pallor, cyanosis on exposure to cold or stress).

TABLE 7–4–1. CRITERIA FOR DIAGNOSIS OF SYSTEMIC SCLEROSIS (SCLERODERMA)

A person may be said to have systemic sclerosis (scleroderma) if one major or two or more minor criteria listed below are present. Generalized forms of scleroderma, eosinophilic fasciitis, and the various forms of pseudoscleroderma are excluded from these criteria.

Major Criterion

Proximal scleroderma: symmetric thickening, tightening, and induration of the skin of the fingers and/or the skin proximal to the metacarpophalangeal or metatarsophalangeal joints. The changes may affect the entire extremity, face, neck, and trunk (thorax and abdomen).

Minor Criteria

Sclerodactyly: skin changes limited to the fingers.

Digital pitting scars or loss of substance from the finger pad: depressed areas at tips of fingers or loss of digital pad tissue as a result of ischemia.

Bibasilar pulmonary fibrosis: bilateral reticular pattern of linear or reticulonodular densities most pronounced in basilar portions of the lungs on standard chest roentgenogram; may assume appearance of diffuse mottling or "honeycomb lung." These changes should not be attributable to another lung disease.

Source: *Modified from Masi AT, Rodnan GP, Medsger TA Jr, et al. Preliminary criteria for the classification of systemic sclerosis (scleroderma).* Arthritis Rheum 1980;23:581. *Reproduced from* Arthritis & Rheumatism Journal, *copyright 1980. Used by permission of the American College of Rheumatology.*

TABLE 7–4–2. TWO SUBSETS OF GENERALIZED SCLERODERMA

Limited Cutaneous Systemic Sclerosis
Long prodrome of Raynaud's phenomenon only (months to years)
Skin changes distal to elbows and knees; can include face and neck
Nailfold capillary dilation; no capillary obliteration
Anticentromere antibodies (Hep-2 substrate)
Slightly increased risk if positive for HLA-DR1
Visceral involvement

Diffuse cutaneous systemic sclerosis
Onset of Raynaud's phenomenon and of puffy skin within 6 months of one another
Taut skin on arms, thighs, thorax, or abdomen
Nailfold capillary dilation and obliteration
Scl-70 autoantibodies (anti-topoisomerase I)
Slight genetic susceptibility (HLA-DQB$_1$)
Visceral involvement common in first 5 years (kidneys, lungs, gut, heart)
Skin may soften after 5 to 10 years

Source: From LeRoy EC, Krieg T, Black C, et al. Scleroderma (systemic sclerosis): Classification subsets and pathogenesis. J Rheum 1988;15:202. Reproduced with permission of the publisher and author.

From 5 to 20% of the adult population complain of Raynaud's, more so women in their hormonally active years and men occupationally exposed to chemicals or vibration. Those patients with Raynaud's destined to develop systemic sclerosis can be detected by a distinctive pattern of the capillaries in the nailfold skin observed under low-power microscopy and consisting of dilation of capillary loops and avascular areas. This test should be combined with autoimmune antibody testing and a complete history and physical examination.

The most common symptom of systemic sclerosis, Raynaud's phenomenon, can occur years before limited cutaneous disease; in diffuse involvement, it usually occurs at the onset of the skin disease or soon thereafter. Esophageal symptoms secondary to decreased peristalsis occur in three fourths of patients, most of whom complain of swallowing difficulty, regurgitation, and "heartburn." Symmetric arthralgia with joint swelling, tenderness, and stiffness may occur in a significant number of patients, at first difficult to distinguish from patients with systemic lupus erythematosus or rheumatoid arthritis. Approximately 50% of patients complain of dyspnea; up to 75% of patients have abnormalities on pulmonary function tests. Abdominal complaints such as bloating, cramping, episodic diarrhea, and constipation occur in 10 to 20 percent of patients, although radiographic and motility studies demonstrate a much higher frequency of intestinal involvement. Abnormal peristalsis and saccular dilations lead to intestinal overgrowth of microorganisms, increasing the abdominal complaints. Muscle weakness occurs in 10% of patients who may have typical myositis by evaluation of muscle enzymes, electromyography, and muscle biopsy. Myositis and myocarditis can coexist in these patients. Entrapment neuropathies occur in a minority of patients, with most complaints referable to the median nerve (carpal tunnel syndrome) and the trigeminal nerve (neuralgia).

Familial occurrence, reported among siblings, parent and child, and second-degree relatives, has been infrequent; an increased frequency of certain HLA antigens (DR1, DR3, and DR5) has been reported and confirmed when larger numbers of patients are studied. Recently, HLA associations with autoantibodies present have been stronger than those with disease subset. The increased prevalence of systemic sclerosis in mine workers exposed to silica dust has been recognized, with an approximate 25-fold increase in those with silicosis and an approximate 10-fold increase among those exposed to silica dust. Another well-documented occupational association is in workers exposed to monomers of vinyl chloride in the production of polyvinyl chloride (plastics). Several drugs have been implicated in the development of sclerodermatous manifestations. Pulmonary fibrosis and scleroderma are toxic effects of bleomycin and cisplatin, including diffuse skin thickening similar to diffuse scleroderma. Dermal fibrosis has been noted following the use of pentazocine, a nonnarcotic analgesic. Environmental exposure, such as the recently described scleroderma-like syndrome epidemic in Spain after ingestion of denatured rapeseed oil, has expanded the search for a common etiologic factor.

A recent epidemic associated with the ingestion of the essential amino acid L-tryptophan and called the eosinophilia–myalgia syndrome has emphasized that a distinctive subset of the spectrum of scleroderma-like illness, represented by the entities diffuse fasciitis with eosinophilia (also called eosinophilic fasciitis), toxic oil syndrome of Spain, and eosinophilia–myalgia syndrome can be recognized by the (1) absence of Raynaud's phenomenon, (2) presence of a normal nailfold capillary pattern, (3) sparing of the digits (i.e., absence of sclerodactyly), and (4) presence of eosinophilia. It is important to recognize this Raynaud's phenomenon-negative, capillary-negative, spared-digits subset because these patients usually have an environmental trigger that can be eliminated and they are more responsive than patients with idiopathic systemic sclerosis to glucocorticoid therapy.

The typical patient with eosinophilia–myalgia syndrome is female, is aged 40 to 70, and may be taking benzodiazepines for an affective disorder and 1 to 5 g of L-tryptophan for insomnia and/or anxiety when she notes the sudden onset of total body myalgia, edema of the extremities, and erythematous blotches on the trunk or extremities, which may be pruritic and initially resemble erythema nodosum. Eosinophilia is usually impressive, significant weight gain can often be documented, and the skin blotches rapidly become confluent, indurated, and puckered (peau d'orange effect). Table 7–4–3 lists the major complaints in 20 patients presenting to a multispecialty referral clinic; prompt relief of most, if not all, symptoms follows discontinuation of benzodiazepines and L-tryptophan and institution of 30 to 60 mg prednisone in divided daily doses. The pathogenesis of eosinophilia–myalgia syndrome and the mechanism of eosinophilia remain obscure. Severe peripheral neuropathy and eosinophilic pneumonitis, features also seen in persons who have ingested toxic oil, may lead to irreversible organ insufficiency. These distinctive syndromes can be grouped together under the concept of an environmental scleroderma spectrum (Smith and LeRoy, 1994).

TABLE 7–4–3. CLINICAL FEATURES OF 20 PATIENTS WITH THE EOSINOPHILIA–MYALGIA SYNDROME

Clinical Feature	Number of Patients
Symptoms	
Myalgia	20
Fatigue	20
Edema	
Extremities	10
Facial	10
Dysesthesias	6
Dyspnea on exertion	5
Weight loss	5
Low-grade fever	5
Paresthesias	4
Hair loss	4
Muscle cramping	4
Palpitations	3
Dysuria	3
Muscle weakness	3
Arthralgias	3
Signs	
Muscle tenderness	11
Skin rashes	10
Edema	
Extremities	10
Periorbital	4
Basilar rales	5
Muscle atrophy	2
Muscle weakness	2
Decreased vibratory perception	2
Cognitive deficit	1
Cranial nerve deficit	1

Source: From Martin RW, Duffy J, Engel AG, et al. The clinical spectrum of the eosinophilic myalgia syndrome associated with L-tryptophan ingestion. Clinical features in 20 patients and aspects of pathophysiology. Ann Intern Med 1990;113:124. Reproduced with permission from the publisher and author.

Objective

Physical Examination

The physical examination should include an extensive evaluation of the skin, especially of the hands, face, and digits, for evidence of edematous or taut skin. The presence of digital pitting, calcium deposits, and telangiectasia should be recorded, and ulcers should be evaluated for the presence of cellulitis or purulent drainage, signifying infection. Enlarged capillaries can often be seen grossly at the nailbed; they are better seen with a magnifying lens or low-power microscope. The facial area may show early skin changes, with drawing of the mouth (*mauskopf*) and loss of normal skin folds and wrinkles. Examination of the lungs may reveal coarse rales, friction rubs, or decreased expansion signifying pulmonary fibrosis or pleuritis. Examination of the heart should include assessment of heart size, murmurs, gallops, or rubs which might signify congestive heart failure or pericarditis. Ominous findings are accentuation of the second heart sound, tricuspid insufficiency, an abnormal A_2–P_2 split, or a pulmonary flow murmur, all of which correlate with pulmonary hypertension. The presence of systemic hypertension should alert the physician to possible renal involvement. The joints should be examined for the presence of synovitis, contractures, and tendon friction rubs. Pulses should be examined using Allen's test and Adson's test to assess for large vessel arterial disease as a cause for Raynaud's phenomenon. The neurologic examination should concentrate on possible nerve entrapment, with special attention to the wrist, to include tests for Tinel's and Phalen's signs for carpal tunnel syndrome (Table 7–4–4). The examination should include a search for muscle weakness, alopecia, skin rash, and oral ulcers, as lupus and dermatomyositis tend to overlap occasionally with systemic sclerosis.

Routine Laboratory Abnormalities

Laboratory evaluation should include a chest x-ray to demonstrate lung fibrosis (usually reticular pattern, but occasionally diffuse mottling or "honeycombing"), present in approximately 25% of patients; x-ray is not as sensitive as pulmonary function tests for detecting early lung disease. A prefibrotic inflammation termed *alveolitis* may require bronchoalveolar lavage or high-resolution chest computed tomography to identify.

An abnormal urinalysis, with hematuria and/or protein, may be the first indication of renal involvement, especially if associated with hypertension.

The complete blood count is usually normal, with a mild normochromic anemia occurring occasionally later in the disease; a microangiopathic hemolytic process can occur with renal disease.

Blood chemistries are usually normal unless renal involvement with elevations of blood urea nitrogen and creatinine levels has occurred or unless primary biliary cirrhosis described in association with limited cutaneous disease and elevation of liver function tests occurs.

Electrocardiographic monitoring (Holter) and echocardiogram (with Doppler) are indicators of cardiac involvement, with the more common abnormalities being nonspecific ST–T wave changes, left anterior fascicular block, septal infarction pattern, first-degree heart block, and QRS voltage abnormalities, in decreasing order of frequency, and peri-

cardial effusion, pulmonary hypertension, and wall motion abnormalities, respectively.

PLANS
Diagnostic
Differential Diagnosis

The diagnosis of systemic sclerosis is clinical, as demonstrated by the criteria in Table 7–4–1. In the patient who presents with Raynaud's phenomenon only, with sclerodactyly only, or with features more typical of other collagen–vascular diseases, such as myositis, hypocomplementemia, and hematologic abnormalities suggestive of systemic lupus in association with sclerodermatous skin changes, the diagnosis can be confusing.

Diagnostic Options and Recommended Approach

Nailfold capillaroscopy is useful in those patients who present with Raynaud's phenomenon only and with undifferentiated connective tissue disease. Precise calculation of both sensitivity and specificity of nailfold capillary microscopy depends heavily on the sample of the population chosen for predicting connective tissue disease in Raynaud's-only patients and undifferentiated connective tissue disease patients (Maricq, 1992). Thus, the absence of typical scleroderma nailfold capillaries (dropout and avascular areas) improves the prognosis (with a high confidence level) for Raynaud's-only patients and undifferentiated connective tissue disease patients. Another helpful test is the antinuclear antibody test, which should be done on a tissue culture substrate such as the Hep-2 cell line. This has increased the sensitivity of antinuclear antibody tests in scleroderma to 90% or greater, mainly because of detection of antinucleolar and anticentromere antibodies. It is difficult to give predictive values to these tests, as considerable variability occurs in different laboratories, but one large study including patients with various connective tissue disorders found a positive predictive value of the presence of anticentromere antibodies for diagnosing systemic sclerosis at approximately 90%, being positive mainly in Caucasian patients with limited systemic sclerosis. The anti-Scl-70 antibody (also called anti-topoisomerase I) has a high positive predictive value (80–90%), but lacks sensitivity. The presence of anticentromere antibodies is helpful as an aid in distinguishing limited cutaneous disease with a positive predictive value of 85 to 90%; it occurs in approximately 50% of patients with limited systemic sclerosis (Table 7–4–2). African-American, Mediterranean, and Japanese patients have a low relative prevalence of anticentromere antibodies and a higher prevalence of anti-topoisomerase I and newer antibodies, such as anti-RNA polymerases I and III, whose sensitivity and specificity are yet to be determined.

Therapeutic

Various drugs have been proposed as effective in and capable of changing the natural course of systemic sclerosis, but no controlled prospective trials have shown any drug to be definitely effective. Retrospective studies are difficult to analyze because of the variable natural course of the disease, including spontaneous improvement after several years. D-Penicillamine (Depen, Cuprimine), shown in retrospective studies to possibly improve skin disease, has serious adverse side effects, including bone marrow toxicity (leukopenia, thrombocytopenia, and aplastic anemia), renal toxicity (nephrotic syndrome), skin rash, fever, ageusia, and the occurrence of Goodpasture's syndrome and myasthenia gravis. The medication is given orally in dosages ranging from 250 to 1500 mg daily. Routine blood analysis, platelet counts, and urinalysis should be done monthly. Patients should be told of these side effects and the uncertain efficacy of the drug. Colchicine has been reported to improve skin disease at a dose of 0.5 to 2.0 mg daily and has relatively mild side effects, the more common being nausea, vomiting, and diarrhea; rarely, skin rash, renal toxicity, and bone marrow toxicity have been reported. The antiplatelet agents dipyridamole and aspirin have been used with subjective benefit; a recent prospective trial showed no significant objective benefit, although a different dosing scheme was used in this trial than in previous recommendations. The angiotensin converting enzyme

TABLE 7–4–4. SPECIAL SIGNS OF NERVE AND ARTERIAL INVOLVEMENT

Tinel's sign	Paresthesia in median nerve distribution produced by percussion over median nerve at wrist.
Phalen's sign	Paresthesia, numbness, or pain radiating into the median nerve distribution produced by forced flexion of wrist
Adson's test (modified)	Loss of pulse or appearance of axillary bruit with paresthesia produced by arm elevation or Valsalva maneuver with turning of neck
Allen's test	Simultaneous compression of radial and ulnar arteries with vigorous opening and closing of fist until hand and fingers blanch; a positive test is the absence of selective radial or ulnar filing when pressure is released

inhibitor captopril (Capoten), as well as other converting enzyme inhibitors, is the drug of choice for hypertension that occurs in association with systemic sclerosis, especially if evidence of renal insufficiency is present, because renal function has been shown to improve if the drug is started early in the course of renal involvement. Skin rash, neutropenia, and proteinuria are uncommon side effects and occur infrequently if the dosage is adjusted for renal function. Several agents have been shown to be effective in Raynaud's phenomenon: the calcium channel blocking agents nifedipine (Procardia) and diltiazem (Cardizem), alone or in combination with such alpha-adrenergic blocking agents as prazocin (Minipress). Esophageal reflux and dysphagia usually respond to head-of-bed elevation, avoidance of late meals, frequent small meals, and antacids. Histamine (H_2) blocking drugs, such as cimetidine (Tagamet) and ranitidine (Zantac), may be needed. Sucralfate (Carafate) has also recently been shown to be effective for the symptoms of dysphagia and reflux. Omeprazole, a newer agent that blocks the proton pump mechanism, is also promising in reflux esophagitis; more experience is needed in assessing its long-term side effects. A promotility agent (cisapride [Propulsid]) is also promising in early open trials.

There are very few indications for surgery, two potential ones being release of flexion contractures of the digits after the disease has reached a stable stage for at least 1 year and removal of calcium deposits that serve as a nidus of infection or that develop over pressure points, such as the buttocks, and cause pain. The results of these procedures are not always satisfactory, and unfortunately, any surgical procedure can disrupt precariously balanced renal or pulmonary function in patients with diffuse systemic sclerosis (Table 7–4–5).

Once taut skin has developed proximal to the digits, there is little doubt of the diagnosis. Most physicians and patients who read about systemic sclerosis are pessimistic about the prognosis, which often leads to patient despair and depression. Usually, systemic sclerosis does not progress to complete disability or disfigurement, and the outlook for patients is improving as newer agents are introduced, such as

TABLE 7–4–5. THERAPIES FOR SYSTEMIC SCLEROSIS

Skin	D-Penicillamine
	Moisturizing lotions
	Colchicine
Peripheral vascular, cutaneous ulcers, and digital necrosis	Calcium channel blockers (nifedipine, diltiazem, others)
	Local nitroglycerine
	Sympathetic blockade (epidural, digital, ganglion, pharmacologic)
Renal	Angiotensin converting enzyme inhibitors (captopril, enalopril, others)
	Dipyridamole and aspirin
Gastrointestinal	Omeprazole (Prilosec), for reflux esophagitis
	Cisapride (Propulsid)
	Elevate head of bed 6 in.
	Avoid meals for 4 hours before lying down
	Antacids
	H_2 blockers
Lung	
Pulmonary hypertension	Calcium channel blockers
	Parenteral prostacyclin
	Angiotensin converting enzyme inhibitors
Interstitial lung disease	Low-dose prednisone acutely
	Immunosuppressive agents (especially cyclophosphamide [Cytoxan])
Heart	
Pericardial effusion	Pericardial window
	Diuretics cautiously
	Prednisone if acute (with friction rub) and inflammatory
Myocarditis with microvascular insufficiency	Glucocorticoids
	Immunosuppressive agents
	Calcium channel blockers

captopril for renal involvement. The disease is not relentlessly progressive, as most patients reach a plateau stage and remain stable for many years, and eventually, skin softening usually does occur. Avoidance of cold weather exposure and contact of cold objects with the hands, in addition to proper clothing and gloves, is an important preventive measure for Raynaud's phenomenon. Advise patients to dress warmly over the trunk to induce peripheral vasodilation. Skin care with avoidance of trauma and the use of moisturizing creams is important. Occupational adjustments in those with exposure to chemicals or vibration is logical if financial risks can be minimized.

FOLLOW-UP

The frequency of follow-up depends on the clinical severity, the degree and type of organ involvement (Fig. 7–4–1), and the treatment plan, as the use of penicillamine requires frequent laboratory monitoring for toxicity. The periodic physical examination should include skin examination for ulcers, infection, or developing contractures. Careful auscultation of the lungs is important; development or worsening of rales (dry or Velcro) could mean progressing lung fibrosis. Recent evidence has shown that short-term intervention with steroid therapy during acute phases of pulmonary involvement with active inflammation may slow progression. We perform pulmonary function tests every 6 to 12 months or whenever the patient notes a change in respiratory status. Diagnostic techniques to uncover acute inflammatory changes in the lungs, such as bronchoalveolar lavage and high-resolution computed tomography, are useful for diagnosis and management. It is important to diagnose the prefibrotic state of alveolitis as early as possible (using lavage, computed tomography, or both) and to treat it aggressively with glucocorticoids and/or immunosuppressive agents to prevent irreversible pulmonary fibrosis. Stabilization of pulmonary function rather than actual improvement is the goal of therapy. Renal involvement should be detected early, with frequent self-administered systemic blood pressure determinations and creatinine clearances every 6 months in patients with diffuse systemic sclerosis. If dysphagia worsens, or if it is associated with weight loss, a barium swallow may detect an esophageal stricture. Periodic weighing helps to detect occult malabsorption or anorexia, of which patients do not always complain.

Patients should be aware of the more serious features of the disease, because early treatment could change the outcome. Symptoms of dyspnea, chest pain, severe headaches, and orthopnea or paroxysmal nocturnal dyspnea should prompt immediate contact with the physician. Other symptoms such as progressive dysphagia, worsening Raynaud's phenomenon, and progression of skin disease should be noted by the patient, but they do not require immediate attention. The patient should observe the skin for breakdown or ulcers and avoid contamination of these areas; if evidence of infection occurs, physician contact should be made for antibiotic therapy. Blood pressure monitoring is important, and patients should be instructed in this simple technique or have it performed monthly if stable, and daily to weekly if progressive and edematous. Elevated readings should be reported immediately to the physician.

DISCUSSION

Prevalence and Incidence

Various studies concerning the epidemiology of systemic sclerosis have estimated the annual incidence to be between 3 and 10 new cases per million of population, with a prevalence of approximately 60 to 200 per million population. These studies have also shown an increased female incidence of approximately 3:1, which is more pronounced (15:1) in the childbearing years; African-American women have a slightly greater risk than Caucasian women. Geographic factors are not significant except for an increased frequency of disease where mining is prevalent.

Related Basic Science

Anatomy

The skin is the most evident area of involvement; microscopically, subcutaneous fibrosis occurs with increased deposition of collagen, proteoglycan, and other extracellular matrix that may extend to surround ten-

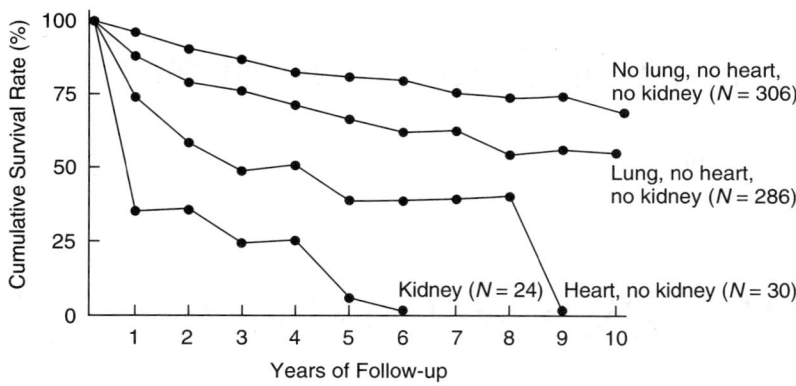

Figure 7–4–1. Cumulative survival rate in 915 patients with systemic sclerosis with and without clinical evidence of kidney, heart, or lung involvement at the time of evaluation at the University of Pittsburgh from 1972 to 1986. *(Modified from Medsger TA Jr. Systemic sclerosis (scleroderma), localized scleroderma, eosinophilic fasciitis, and calcinosis. In: McCarty DJ, ed. Arthritis and allied conditions. 11th ed. Philadelphia: Lea & Febiger, 1989:1118. Reproduced with permission from the publisher and author.)*

dons, muscle bundles, and joint capsules. Early in the disease, perivascular mononuclear cell infiltrates are present, and recently, increased mast cells have been noted. Whether these cells are primary initiators or secondary intensifiers is still a subject of inquiry. This same fibrosis occurs in internal organs, with obliterative small arterial lesions characterized by intimal proliferation, medial thinning, and adventitial fibrosis associated with ischemia and necrosis of tissue (Cannon et al., 1974). The skin fold of the fingernail is an area where capillary changes can be seen grossly or with low magnification. Endothelial injury in which both platelets and monocytes may participate may be a prerequisite for fibroblast and smooth muscle cell activation leading to fibrosis (LeRoy et al., 1989). Using DNA-based typing techniques, distinctive autoantibodies have been associated with certain HLA-DR and -DQ alleles with variable dependence on ethnic background (Arnett, et al., 1995).

Immunology

Selective autoimmunity is distinctive in systemic sclerosis and includes immune responses to centromere, topoisomerase I, RNA polymerases I and III, U1-ribonucleoprotein nucleolar components including fibrillarin (U3-ribonucleoprotein), type IV collagen, and laminin. A helper-T-cell component to fibrosis, possibly by cytokine activation of fibroblast matrix synthesis and proliferation, is suggested by the finding of elevated levels of soluble interleukin-2 and interleukin-2 receptors in plasma of patients with very active systemic sclerosis (Clements et al., 1994).

Natural History and Its Modification with Treatment

The morbidity of systemic sclerosis is variable, and it is difficult to predict to what degree each individual will develop internal organ involvement. The disease tends to occur in three stages: early, classic, and late or atrophic. The early phase is characterized by nonpitting puffiness of the hands or feet with a sensation of fullness on examination. This progresses to the classic stage, in which edematous skin is replaced by tight, hidebound skin. It is during this stage that the major morbidity and mortality of systemic sclerosis occur. Rapidly fulminant lung, cardiac, or kidney disease may develop in the diffuse variety, and this is more commonly associated with truncal skin involvement. Patients with limited cutaneous systemic sclerosis (CREST) tend not to go through a fulminant stage and rarely develop cardiac or renal involvement, but they do develop lung involvement (especially pulmonary hypertension), although at a slower rate. After 3 to 10 years, a stable phase of diffuse cutaneous disease is reached, where progression of skin disease has ended and the patient is left with whatever organ damage has occurred, contractures of the extremities (especially of the

hands), hidebound skin, subcutaneous calcifications, poor blood supply, ulcerations, necrosis of digits, and soft tissue infection. This represents the atrophic or late stage of the disease (which begins from 3 to 15 years after the onset of the illness), in which areas of the skin begin to soften. Contractures of the hands and pigmentary changes usually do not resolve to a significant degree. The mortality of systemic sclerosis is determined by internal organ involvement (Figure 7–4–1). Note the large proportion of patients with lung involvement, the most lethal organ involvement of the mid-1990s.

Prevention

No preventive measures are currently available, except the avoidance of known environmental triggers, discussed above.

Cost Containment

Several aspects of systemic sclerosis (such as Raynaud's phenomenon and esophageal dysmotility problems) can be treated with conservative measures. The patient should be instructed in these measures, which were discussed earlier in this chapter, before medication is prescribed. Several agents already mentioned, such as D-penicillamine and colchicine, which may alter the course of the disease, can be given an adequate trial; when the disease has been stable for 6 to 12 months, they should be discontinued. It is doubtful that any present medication reverses fibrosis once it occurs. Patients with limited cutaneous systemic sclerosis do not need follow-up as frequently as do patients with diffuse systemic sclerosis, nor do they require expensive screening procedures such as lung computed tomography as frequently.

REFERENCES

Arnett FC. HLA and autoimmunity in scleroderma (systemic sclerosis). In: Korn JH, LeRoy EC, eds. The immunopathogenesis of systemic sclerosis. Inter Rev Immunol, 1995;12:107.

Cannon PJ, Hassar M, Case DB, et al. The relationship of hypertension and renal failure in scleroderma (progressive systemic sclerosis) to structural and functional abnormalities of the renal cortical circulation. Medicine 1974;53:1.

Clements PJ, Silman AJ, White B, et al. Raynaud's phenomenon, scleroderma, overlap syndromes, and other fibrosing syndromes. Curr Opin Rheumatol, 1994;6:603.

LeRoy EC, Smith EA, Kahaleh MB, et al. A strategy for scleroderma (systemic sclerosis): Is transforming growth factor beta the answer? Arthritis Rheum 1989;32:817.

Maricq HR. Capillaroscopy in Raynaud's syndrome. Vasc Med Rev 1992;3:3.

Smith EA, LeRoy EC. Systemic sclerosis: Etiology and pathogenesis. In Klippel JH, Dieppe PA, eds. Rheumatology. London: Mosby-Year Book Europe, 1994:6-9.1–9.10.

CHAPTER 7–5
....
Pulmonary Disease Due to Progressive Systemic Sclerosis (Scleroderma)

(See Section 13, Chapter 33)

CHAPTER 7–6
....
Undifferentiated, Overlapping, and Mixed Connective Tissue Disorders

Joe G. Hardin, M.D.

DEFINITION

These disorders can be defined as connective tissue diseases that are insufficiently clinically developed to meet criteria for any one specific disease, *or* as connective tissue diseases with simultaneous or sequential clinical features typical of two or more individual diseases.

ETIOLOGY

Although genetics and hormonal factors play important etiologic roles in the connective tissue diseases, their ultimate cause(s) remains unknown.

CRITERIA FOR DIAGNOSIS
Suggestive

An understanding of the concepts of undifferentiated, overlapping, and mixed connective tissue disorders requires an understanding of the clinical and laboratory features of the well-differentiated and distinctive connective tissue diseases. These diseases are rheumatoid arthritis, systemic lupus erythematosus, progressive systemic sclerosis, dermatomyositis/polymyositis, and Sjogren's syndrome. There are no standard definitions or formal criteria for these three designations, and they are sometimes used interchangeably, although the practice is widely considered inappropriate. The term *undifferentiated* is usually employed when there are signs and symptoms suggestive of a connective tissue disease but the clinical picture is not distinctive enough to permit a precise diagnosis. The usual implication is that it is too early in the course of the disease to make a diagnosis and the passage of time will allow one to be made later. An "overlap," however, implies that more than one distinctive connective tissue disease may be diagnosed in one patient either at one point in time or sequentially. The usual implication of this diagnosis is that the patient has met the established or formal criteria for two or more different connective tissue diseases; however, the coexistence of one of these diseases and Sjogren's syndrome is usually not designated an overlap. Mixed connective tissue disease is regarded as a distinctive entity by some authorities because of its association with an antinuclear antibody—antinuclear ribonucleoprotein. Other authorities consider it to be a variant of systemic lupus erythematosus or a nonspecific overlap. It is usually defined as an undifferentiated or overlapping connective tissue disorder accompanied by high titers of circulating ribonucleoprotein antibodies and none of the other antinuclear antibodies considered to be characteristic of systemic lupus erythematosus.

All the connective tissue diseases—distinctive, undifferentiated, or overlapping—tend to be disorders of young or middle-aged women. Mixed connective tissue disease is eight times more common in women than in men, and it usually begins in the second or third decade. Unlike lupus, mixed connective tissue disease does not seem to have a predilection for certain ethnic or racial groups. It has not been induced by drugs, and its familial tendencies seem to be less than those of lupus and rheumatoid arthritis.

The undifferentiated, overlapping, and mixed connective tissue disorders are usually suggested by a combination of nonspecific systemic symptomatology (malaise, fatigability, myalgias, fever, anorexia, weight loss) and one or more of the more specific connective tissue disease sympoms, such as arthralgias/arthritis, Raynaud's phenomenon, and "lupoid" rashes. The diagnostic suspicion is usually heightened when there is a positive test for rheumatoid factors or antinuclear antibodies, especially the latter. An overlapping syndrome is suggested when a patient with one of the distinctive connective tissue diseases begins to exhibit features considered characteristic of another.

Definitive

As there are no formal criteria for these less well defined connective tissue disorders, there are no absolute requirements for their diagnoses, with one exception: most authorities would require the presence of circulating antiribonucleoprotein before diagnosing mixed connective tissue disease.

CLINICAL MANIFESTATIONS
Subjective

Except for the history of an occasional relative with connective tissue disease symptomatology, the family and background history of the patient with suspected connective tissue disease will generally be unrewarding. Patients with an undifferentiated syndrome or mixed connective tissue disease most commonly complain of malaise and fatigability, arthralgias, myalgias, fever, cold-induced digital vasospasm (Raynaud's phenomenon), and various mucocutaneous lesions. Common cutaneous symptoms, in additional to Raynaud's phenomenon, include puffy fingers and hands (often considered characteristic of mixed connective tissue disease), alopecia, sclerodactyly, malar rash, other maculopapular rashes, dyspigmentation, and photosensitivity. Other symptoms that frequently occur during the course of these disorders are pleuritic chest pain, dyspnea, muscle weakness, headache, symptoms of trigeminal neuropathy, a deforming arthritis, proximal scleroderma, and symptoms of eosphageal reflux.

Objective
Physical Examination

The two most common findings on physical examination of patients with undifferentiated or mixed syndromes relate to the joint and skin involvement, which occurs in the great majority. Most patients will have the physical findings of articular synovitis, frequently with a distribution typical of rheumatoid arthritis. Deformities suggestive of rheumatoid arthritis might be apparent in patients with mixed connective tissue disease or certain other overlap syndromes. In patients with mixed and undifferentiated disease, nonspecific maculopapular rashes, discoid lupus erythematosus, the consequences of Raynaud's phenomenon, sclerodactyly, diffuse hand and finger puffiness, malar rashes, changes in skin pigmentation, telangiectasia, palpable purpura, oral ulcers, or alopecia may be found. Other physical findings include generalized lymphadenopathy, muscle tenderness and weakness, pleural or pericardial friction rubs (or other signs of pleural effusions), evidence of a peripheral neuropathy (especially trigeminal), signs suggestive of

Sjögren's syndrome (dry eyes and mouth and parotid enlargement), and signs indicative of heart failure in patients with myocarditis.

Routine Laboratory Abnormalities

Routine laboratory abnormalities occur commonly in patients with connective tissue diseases. Considering primarily those with mixed connective tissue disease, the anemia of chronic disease occurs in about 75%, with leukopenia and thrombocytopenia being less frequent. Severe renal involvement is uncommon in mixed connective tissue disease, but 25% of patients have abnormal urinalyses from time to time, typically with proteinuria, cells, and casts. Myositis, often subclinical, is rather common in mixed connective tissue disease and may cause elevations in levels of serum glutamic–oxaloacetic transaminase and lactate dehydrogenase.

Most patients with mixed connective tissue disease have hypergammaglobulinemia, and about 10% have a false-positive serologic test for syphilis, suggesting the presence of an antiphospholipid antibody, which will be detectable in greater than 10% of these patients.

Routine chest x-ray films may disclose a pleural effusion, evidence of a pericardial effusion or dilated heart, pulmonary fibrosis, or evidence of pulmonary hypertension.

Electrocardiography may suggest pericarditis or myocarditis, or it may reflect the effects of mixed connective tissue disease on the lung.

PLANS
Diagnostic
Differential Diagnosis

Considering an undifferentiated or overlapping connective tissue disease diagnosis is itself an exercise in differential diagnosis: Which one, if any, of the basic connective tissue diseases seems most likely? If the question cannot be answered, an undifferentiated or overlapping diagnosis seems most appropriate.

Diagnostic Options and Recommended Approach

When faced with a patient with signs, symptoms, or routine laboratory abnormalities suggestive of a connective tissue disease, it is appropriate to obtain rheumatoid factor and antinuclear antibody tests. If both are negative and the clinical syndrome lacks distinguishing features, it will probably have to be considered undifferentiated. If only the rheumatoid factor test is positive, rheumatoid arthritis is suggested. If the antinuclear antibody test is positive, with or without a positive rheumatoid factor, it should be further investigated unless the clinical picture is distinctive. This further investigation involves testing for the specific antinuclear antibodies: anti-native DNA, anti-Sm, and antiribonucleoprotein. If all three are negative, an ill-defined syndrome will probably remain undifferentiated. If the anti-native DNA or anti-Sm test is positive, the diagnosis of systemic lupus erythematosus is strongly suggested. If these tests are negative and the antiribonucleoprotein test is significantly positive, mixed connective tissue disease becomes a likely diagnosis. Up to 75% of patients with this antinuclear antibody profile follow a clinical course compatible with mixed connective tissue disease. If diagnostic uncertainty persists after all of these tests are done, antibodies to SSA (Ro) and SSB (La) might be requested. If they (either or both) are positive, primary Sjögren's syndrome or systemic lupus erythematosus is suggested.

Recently, new antibody markers for mixed connective tissue disease have been proposed. Very high levels of an antibody reacting with the constitutive bovine 73-kDa heat shock protein may be specific for this diagnosis. Advances have been made in characterizing distinct autoantibodies against individual U1-RNA-associated proteins, so that it may be possible in the future to refine the specificity of the ribonucleoprotein antibody test and better characterize the overlapping syndromes.

Therapeutic
Therapeutic Options

Therapeutic options vary from none, which might be the best approach when the syndrome is undifferentiated and symptoms are minor, to aggressive therapy with cytotoxic–immunosuppressive drugs when there is a life- or organ-threatening manifestation of an overlap syndrome or mixed connective tissue disease. Experiences with drugs such as cyclophosphamide are tentative, however.

Recommended Approach

Treatment of the connective tissue diseases is directed toward specific manifestations, not specific diagnoses. Consequently, the therapy of the undifferentiated, overlapping, and mixed disorders differs little from the therapy of the individual distinctive diseases.

Adequate doses of nonsteroidal antiinflammatory drugs are used for the arthralgias and myalgias, and this may be the only drug treatment required.

Nifedipine (Procardia), in doses of 30 to 90 mg/d, has been shown to be effective in Raynaud's phenomenon.

Many patients require corticosteroids for the recalcitrant or severe manifestations of their disease. When benign manifestations such as arthralgias are being treated with corticosteroids, the lowest effective dose should be used for the shortest possible time. One of the characteristics of mixed connective tissue disease is its overall relative benignity and the responsiveness of its manifestations to moderate corticosteroid dosages. Whatever the manifestation being treated, patients with mixed connective tissue disease tend to require lower doses and shorter courses of corticosteroids than do patients with lupus or polymyositis.

At times, slow-acting or "remittive" drugs such as the gold salts may be indicated when rheumatoid arthritis is a dominant feature. Methotrexate might be effective for corticosteroid-resistant polymyositis, and high-dose pulse intravenous cyclophosphamide is beginning to be investigated as therapy for serious or life-threatening manifestations. Antimalarial agents (predominantly hydroxychloroquine) will benefit most connective tissue disease skin manifestations, and may prevent flares in mixed connective tissue disease as these drugs have been shown to do in systemic lupus.

FOLLOW-UP

As the undifferentiated, overlapping, and mixed connective tissue disorders tend to follow highly variable courses, the frequency of follow-up is typically determined by the patients' individual manifestations. For those with few or minor symptoms, visits at 3- to 6-month intervals should suffice. Periodic blood pressure determinations, blood counts, and careful urinalyses should be performed even when the patient is asymptomatic. Sometimes, erythrocyte sedimentation rates are helpful in determining disease activity, but the symptoms previously discussed will be the major clue to waxing disease activity in most patients.

Patients seldom require directions to report painful or unpleasant symptoms such as arthralgias, painful Raynaud's phenomenon, and myalgias, but they may be less concerned over rashes, fatigue, fever, weakness, weight loss, dysphagia, or mild dyspnea, and they should be instructed to report these symptoms. In general, it is wise for any patient with any connective tissue disease to call about any new symptom or a significant worsening of an old one.

DISCUSSION
Prevalence and Incidence

Probably most connective tissue diseases begin with an undifferentiated phase, and this phase may persist for months or years in some patients. No data are available on what the number might be. With the exception of the coexistence of Sjögren's syndrome and other individual connective tissue diseases, and with the exception of mixed connective tissue disease, true overlaps are considered uncommon. The coexistence of rheumatoid arthritis and lupus ("rhupus") and of progressive systemic sclerosis and polymyositis ("sclerodermatomyositis") has been reported, however. Mixed connective tissue disease seems to be slightly less common than lupus but more prevalent than polymyositis or progressive systemic sclerosis; precise incidence and prevalence data are not available.

Related Basic Science

The etiology and pathogenesis of the connective tissue diseases are under intensive investigation. The immunoregulatory disturbance of mixed connective tissue disease is similar to that of systemic lupus erythematosus; in both diseases there is diminished suppressor cell function associated with decreased circulating suppressor T cells. Subtle differences between the two diseases have been noted, however, and are being investigated. Both lupus and mixed connective tissue disease are associated with autoantibodies and circulating immune complexes. The ribonucleoprotein antibody, considered necessary for the diagnosis of mixed connective tissue disease, is directed against small nuclear ribonucleoproteins and may exert a favorable disease-modifying effect, perhaps partially accounting for the relative benignity of the disease. The pathology of mixed connective tissue disease is similar to that of lupus with three important exceptions: central nervous system and renal involvement occurs less frequently in mixed connective tissue disease and the arthritis of that disease may be more destructive than that of lupus. The 10 to 25% of patients with mixed connective tissue disease who have renal disease most often have a membranous glomerulonephritis, but an overt nephrotic syndrome or renal insufficiency is rather uncommon. Unlike in lupus, the arthropathy of mixed connective tissue disease may be erosive (a feature characteristic of rheumatoid arthritis).

Natural History and Its Modification with Treatment

A prospective collaborative study was begun a few years ago to help establish the natural history of undifferentiated connective tissue disease. Of 410 patients enrolled, 213 were considered to have early undifferentiated connective tissue disease. So far follow-up of this cohort has failed to disclose any trend in terms of disease evolution. Some interesting observations have been made, however; antinuclear antibodies are highly nonspecific, and Raynaud's phenomenon often occurs without arthralgias, for example.

Few data are available on the natural history of mixed connective tissue disease. Of the original 25 patients reported in 1972 (Sharp et al., 1972), 8 had died by 1980, but about one third of the deaths in this and other series were unrelated to the underlying disease. Rapidly progressive pulmonary hypertension has been a frequent cause of death in mixed connective tissue disease, but this event occurs rarely in lupus. Opportunistic infections are common causes of death in both diseases and underline the need for judicious steroid usage. Long-term survivors of mixed connective tissue disease frequently evolve a clinical picture characteristic of rheumatoid arthritis or progressive systemic sclerosis, whereas others experience a remission or continue to have sequential overlapping phenomena. There are too few observations to permit a more definite statement concerning the long-term course and prognosis of mixed connective tissue disease.

Prevention

No preventive measures are at present available.

Cost Containment

The undifferentiated, overlapping, and mixed connective tissue diseases generate two major avoidable expenses: confused patients seeking multiple medical opinions and the morbidity of unnecessary corticosteroid therapy. The laboratory studies necessary for a proper diagnosis are limited in number and, for the most part, need to be done only once. For most of the patients with these disorders, the follow-up care is based on symptoms, physical signs, and a few very basic laboratory tests such as routine blood counts and urinalyses.

REFERENCES

Alarcon GS, Williams GV, Singer JZ, et al. Early undifferentiated connective tissue disease: I. Early clinical manifestation in a large cohort of patients with undifferentiated connective tissue diseases compared with cohorts of well established connective tissue disease. J Rheumatol 1991;18:1332.
Alarcon-Segovia D, Cardiel MH. Comparison between three diagnostic criteria for mixed connective tissue disease: Study of 593 patients. J Rheumatol 1989;16:328.
Bulpitt KJ, Clements PH, Lachenbruch PA, et al. Early undifferentiated connective tissue disease: III. Outcome and prognostic indicators in early scleroderma (systemic sclerosis). Ann Intern Med 1993;118:602.
Clegg DO, Williams HJ, Singer JZ. Early undifferentiated connective tissue disease: II. Frequency of circulating antinuclear antibodies in patients with early rheumatic diseases. J Rheumatol 1991;18:1340.
Hoffman RW, Cassidy JT, Takeda Y, et al. U1-70-kd autoantibody-positive mixed connective tissue disease in children. Arthritis Rheum 1993;36:1599.
Kallenberg CGM. Overlapping syndromes, undifferentiated connective tissue disease, and other fibrosing conditions. Curr Opin Rheumatol 1993;5:809.
Mairesse N, Kahn MF, Appelboom T. Antibodies to the constitutive 73-kd-heat shock protein: A new marker of mixed connective tissue disease? Am J Med 1993;95:595.
Nimelstein SH, Brody S, McShane D, et al. Mixed connective tissue disease: A subsequent evaluation of the original 25 patients. Medicine 1980;59:239.
Sharp GC, Irvin WS, Tan EM, et al. Mixed connective tissue disease: An apparently distinct rheumatic disease syndrome associated with a specific antibody to an extractable nuclear antigen (ENA). Am J Med 1972;52:148.

CHAPTER 7–7

Sjögren's Syndrome

William P. Maier, M.D.

DEFINITION

Sjögren's syndrome is a T-cell-mediated autoimmune process affecting the exocrine glands and, at times, other organ systems, including the skin, lungs, central nervous system, and kidneys. It occurs in a primary form, unassociated with other systemic autoimmune diseases, or in a secondary form, associated with other disease, including systemic lupus erythematosus, rheumatoid arthritis, polymyositis, and systemic sclerosis.

ETIOLOGY

Sjögren's syndrome is an autoimmune disease in which inflammatory cells infiltrate and destroy exocrine glands, including salivary glands, tear glands, and the parotid gland.

CRITERIA FOR DIAGNOSIS
Suggestive

Sjögren's syndrome typically presents with dryness of the mouth and eyes, but also may present with extraglandular involvement such as arthritis, cutaneous vasculitis, and interstitial nephritis. Occasionally, an abnormal laboratory test such as anemia, elevation of the Westergren sedimentation rate, a positive antinuclear antibody, or rheumatoid factor may prompt investigation.

Definitive

No single laboratory test or physical finding can be used to diagnose Sjögren's syndrome. The most widely accepted criteria for diagnosing primary Sjögren's are those proposed by Fox and Saito (1994). The presence of four of these criteria suggests definite Sjögren's; the presence of three criteria suggests possible Sjögren's. Exclusions to diagnosis include preexisting lymphoma, graft-versus-host disease, acquired immunodeficiency syndrome, and sarcoidosis.

Keratoconjunctivitis sicca
- Decreased tear flow rate, using Schirmer's test (<9 mm of wetting in 5 minutes), and
- Increased staining with rose bengal or fluorescein dye

Xerostomia
- Symptomatic xerostomia, and
- Decreased basal and stimulated salivary flow rate

Extensive lymphocytic infiltrate on minor salivary flow gland biopsy (focus score of at least $2/4mm^2$, using the Greenspan scale) obtained through normal buccal mucosa

Laboratory evidence of a systemic autoimmune disease
- Positive rheumatoid factor
- Positive antinuclear antibody
- Positive SSA or SSB antibody

CLINICAL MANIFESTATIONS

Subjective

The most common complaints in patients with Sjögren's syndrome are dry mouth, dry eyes, a gritty sensation in the eyes, and enlargement of the parotid and salivary glands. If extraglandular involvement is present, patients may complain of skin rashes (cutaneous vasculitis), shortness of breath and cough (alveolitis), recurrent kidney stones (renal tubular acidosis), or joint pain and swelling.

Objective

Physical examination

Physical findings may be subtle, such as dry mucous membranes and decreased salivary pooling in the floor of the mouth. If severe eye dryness has caused corneal damage, examination may reveal injected conjunctival vessels. Slit-lamp examination of the eyes will frequently demonstrate corneal tears or punctate keratitis. Examination of the parotid glands and salivary glands may demonstrate enlargement.

Extraglandular complications would include the finding of palpable purpura on examination of the extremities, dry crackles on pulmonary examination, and symmetric articular swelling and pain on palpation of joints.

Routine Laboratory Abnormalities

Laboratory abnormalities might include evidence of interstitial pulmonary infiltration on chest x-ray films, evidence of systemic inflammation with anemia of chronic disease, and elevation of the erythrocyte sedimentation rate. Renal insufficiency may be present as may pyuria and hematuria if there is active interstitial nephritis or severe nephrolithiasis.

PLANS

Diagnosis

Differential Diagnosis

Conditions that may mimic Sjögren's syndrome are other inflammatory and infiltrative diseases involving the tear and salivary glands. One needs to consider lymphoma, sarcoidosis, viral infection (mumps, Epstein–Barr virus, coxsackie A), HIV infection, and graft-versus-host disease. Iodides can cause acute swelling of the salivary glands, as can alcoholism. The other systemic autoimmune diseases noted above also must be considered as possible overlap syndromes.

Diagnostic Options

Diagnosis of Sjögren's syndrome depends on acquiring the history of dry eyes and dry mouth, documenting the presence of decreased tear and salivary flow and presence of lymphocytic infiltrate in the minor salivary glands by histologic examination, as well as identifying evidence of autoantibodies, including antinuclear, RF, SSA, and SSB anti-

bodies. Immunogenetic studies demonstrate an increased incidence of the type II major histocompatibility markers DR2 and DR3 in these patients. Documenting decreased tear production has been accomplished by Schirmer's test and by fluorescein and rose bengal dyes that demonstrate corneal changes caused by decreased tear flow. Quantifying salivary flow is more difficult and may not be available outside research centers where cannulation of Stensen's duct is done. Diminished salivary flow can be detected on physical examination by the absence of the normal saliva pool under the tongue or the adherence of a wooden tongue blade to the buccal mucosa. Diagnostic pitfalls include the presence of medications that decrease saliva flow, such as tricyclic antidepressants, diuretics, and antihistamines.

Recommended Approach

The correct diagnosis of Sjögren's syndrome may be made on careful history, physical examination, and serologic testing. More often, definite diagnosis requires a multispecialty approach, with an opthalmologist providing information about tear production and a otolaryngologist providing a good sample of minor salivary gland tissue for histologic examination.

Therapeutic

Therapeutic Options

There is no known effective therapy for exocrine inflammatory component of Sjögren's syndrome, although a recent trial of interferon-alfa suggested a beneficial effect of saliva production. Immunosuppressants, including cyclosporin A, have shown little benefit in careful studies. Symptomatic therapy of dry mouth and dry eyes includes aggressive use of artificial tears and saliva. Maneuvers such as chewing gum and sucking hard sugarless candy may stimulate saliva production.

Extraglandular complications of Sjögren's syndrome may require specific intervention. Joint pain may require regular use of nonsteroidal antiinflammatory agents. If renal tubular acidosis is present, then alkalinization of the urine may be necessary to avoid recurrent nephrolithiasis. The presence of vasculitis, central nervous system involvement, interstitial nephritis, or alveolitis may require the use of corticosteroids or other immunosuppressants.

The only indication for surgery in Sjögren's syndrome is corneal irritation severe enough to warrant occlusion of the nasolacrimal ducts by temporary occlusion or permanently by electrocoagulation.

Recommended Approach

If the patient has no major extraglandular complications, then symptomatic therapy with artificial tears and saliva is indicated. If corneal irritation is severe, then ophthalmologic intervention with tear conservation efforts, including punctal occlusion, is imperative.

FOLLOW-UP

Frequency of follow-up is determined by the severity of the eye disease and the activity and presence of extraglandular or renal disease.

DISCUSSION

Prevalence and Incidence

The incidence and prevalence of primary and secondary Sjögren's syndrome are unknown. The estimated incidence of primary Sjögren's is 1% of the general population. The disease is most common in adult women but can occur in all age groups, including children. The incidence of secondary Sjögren's in patients with rheumatoid arthritis is 15%.

Related Basic Science

Genetics

Immunogenetic studies demonstrate an increased incidence of the type II major histocompatibility complex marker DR3 (especially the HLA B8 DR3 DRw52 phenotype) in patients of northern European ancestry with primary Sjögren's syndrome, but not in other populations. This immunogenetic association occurs in less than 50% of Caucasian patients with primary Sjögren's and, therefore, is not adequate explanation for the immunologic abnormalities in the disease.

Recent description of "autogenes" like *bcl-2* that cause a delay in apoptosis (programmed cell death) of B and T lymphocytes may be a breakthrough in identifying the cause of the systemic autoimmune diseases, including Sjögren's syndrome.

Molecular Biology

The molecular biology of Sjögren's syndrome has revealed that the inflammatory cells infiltrating the exocrine glands are primarily CD4-positive cytotoxic T cells. There is evidence that certain viral agents, including Epstein–Barr virus, hepatitis C virus, and human T-lymphotropic virus type I, initiate this CD4-mediated process by causing the expression of abnormal membrane antigens (viral or host) on glandular epithelial cells in immunogenetically susceptible individuals.

In addition to the glandular inflammation, hypergammaglobulinemia, high titers of rheumatoid factor, antinuclear lupus antibodies, and autoantibodies to the SSA and SSB ribonucleoproteins (anti-SSA, anti-SSB) suggest a loss of suppression of autoimmune B-cell clones. This may be promoted by the excessive CD4 helper response or by the expression of so-called autogenes that delay programmed cell death of these autoantibody-producing B-cell clones. It is hoped a unifying explanation of the cellular and humoral autoimmune abnormalities in Sjögren's syndrome will soon be available.

Natural History and its Modification with Treatment

Sjögren's syndrome is a chronic disease without cure that in the absence of major organ involvement such as vasculitis, pulmonary fibrosis, or central nervous system involvement should not shorten life. Life-threatening complications can occur, including systemic vasculitis, central nervous system vasculitis, and lymphoma. The incidence of lymphoma is estimated to be 40-fold increased over that expected in the normal population. Other than diagnosis and treatment of the above complications, no treatment has clearly altered the natural history of this disease.

Prevention

Preventive measures, such as the use of moisturizing tears and careful dental follow-ups, are clearly helpful in preventing the complications of dry eyes and dry mouth.

Cost Containment

Cost containment measures in the management of Sjögren's syndrome include the selective use of serologic data and expeditious salivary gland biopsy to establish a diagnosis with certainty.

REFERENCES

Block KJ, Buchanan WW, Wohl MJ, Bunim JJ. Sjögren's syndrome: A clinical pathological and serological study of sixty-two cases. Medicine 1965;44:187.

Foster H, Stephenson A, Walker D, et al. Linkage studies of HLA and primary Sjögren's syndrome in multicase families. Arthritis Rheum 1993;36:473.

Fox RI, Saito I. Criteria for diagnosis of Sjögren's syndrome. *Rheum Dis Clin North Am* 1994;20:391.

Moutsopoulos HM, Chused TM, Mann DL, et al. Sjögren's syndrome (sicca syndrome): Current issues. Ann Intern Medicine 1980;92:212.

Saito I, Serrenius B, Compton TK, Fox RI. Detection of Epstein–Barr virus DNA by polymerase chain reaction in blood and tissue biopsies from patients with Sjögren's syndrome. J Exp Med 1989;169:2191.

Talal N. Oncogenes, autogenes, and rheumatic diseases. Arthritis Rheum 1994;37:1421.

CHAPTER 7–8

Polyarteritis Nodosa

Paul Katz, M.D.

DEFINITION

Polyarteritis nodosa is the term applied to the group of systemic necrotizing vasculitides characterized by small- and medium-sized arterial vasculitis in many organ systems.

ETIOLOGY

In most instances, no inciting cause can be identified, although exposure to antigen(s) and the subsequent development of immune complexes is likely operative in most instances. The illness has been associated with hepatitis B and C, serous otitis media, allergy hyposensitization, hairy cell leukemia, and collagen–vascular diseases, usually systemic lupus erythematosus and rheumatoid arthritis.

CRITERIA FOR DIAGNOSIS

Suggestive

This syndrome should be suspected in individuals presenting with symptoms indicative of multiple organ system involvement; early, constitutional complaints may predominate, which may greatly delay the diagnosis. Given the myriad and diversity of signs and symptoms in these disorders, histologic proof or angiograpic evidence of vasculitis in the proper clinical setting is mandatory to establish the presence of the polyarteritis nodosa group of systemic necrotizing vasculitides.

Definitive

The term *polyarteritis nodosa* is perhaps best reserved for that disease first described by Kussmaul and Meier in 1866. It is now apparent that there are several disorders with histologies similar to that of "classic" polyarteritis nodosa; it is therefore preferable to refer to these disorders collectively as the polyarteritis nodosa group of systemic necrotizing vasculitides. Included in this category are three syndromes: classic polyarteritis nodosa, allergic angiitis and granulomatosis (Churg–Strauss syndrome), and the polyangiitis group of systemic necrotizing vasculitides, hereafter called the "overlap" syndrome.

CLINICAL MANIFESTATIONS
Subjective

As noted above, the early symptoms of polyarteritis nodosa may be extremely nonspecific, and up to 75% of affected subjects may complain of malaise, fatigue, weight loss, headache, abdominal pain, and myalgias; this nonspecificity may result in unwanted delays in diagnosis. In this regard, the degree of such symptoms may in no way reflect the extent or severity of the underlying process. Only when the process becomes more advanced do patients begin to report complaints indicative of malignant hypertension, mononeuritis multiplex, catastrophic intraabdominal events, cerebrovascular accidents, and other such late events.

Objective
Physical Examination

The nature of the abnormal physical findings is dependent on which organs are involved in the vasculitic process. Hypertension secondary to renal vascular involvement is noted in approximately 30% of patients with polyarteritis nodosa. Cutaneous small vessel vasculitis most commonly manifests as palpable purpura, which may be restricted to the distal lower extremities but may be present as nodules or livedo reticularis. Nervous system involvement may appear as peripheral nerve abnormalities, such as mononeuritis multiplex and polyneuropathy, or as central nervous system disease with impairment of cerebral, cerebellar, or brain stem function. Typically, patients with classic polyarteritis nodosa lack pulmonary involvement; however, those with allergic angiitis and granulomatosis usually have a history of atopic disease, which most frequently manifests as asthma. Thus one should look for signs of bronchospasm as well as other evidence of lung disease. Cardiac disease in polyarteritis nodosa is generally a late finding and is apparent as coronary arteritis and insufficiency, pericarditis, or heart failure. Eye changes may be observable as retinal vasculitis, cytoid bodies, or hypertensive vascular changes. Objective joint findings are rarely present despite complaints of arthralgias in these patients.

Routine Laboratory Abnormalities

Although never diagnostic, routine laboratory tests are frequently abnormal in the polyarteritis nodosa group of systemic necrotizing vasculitides; these reflect the underlying inflammatory process as well as the end-organ result of the vasculitis. Virtually all patients will display elevations in the erythrocyte sedimentation rate, with levels frequently greater than 90 mm/h with the Westergren method. The complete blood count will often reveal a leukocytosis of greater than 10,000 cells/μL and hematocrit below 35%. Patients with allergic angiitis and granulomatosis usually have peripheral blood eosinophilia (> 1000 cells/μL). Similarly indicative of the inflammatory nature of these processes is thrombocytosis (> 400,000 platelets/μL), which is found in one half of subjects. Routine urinalysis is abnormal in 70% of patients with polyarteritis nodosa, with proteinuria, hematuria, or cellular casts usually detected. By definition, individuals with classic polyarteritis nodosa lack pulmonary involvement, and chest radiographs are normal; however, patients with allergic angiitis and granulomatosis ordinarily display such roentgenographic findings as fleeting infiltrates, consolidation, and/or nodules.

PLANS
Diagnostic
Differential Diagnosis

The differential diagnosis of polyarteritis nodosa is fairly broad, depending on the organ system(s) involved. Usually included in the differential are other forms of systemic necrotizing vasculitis and other "autoimmune" diseases.

Diagnostic Options

Diagnosis of the polyarteritis nodosa group of systemic necrotizing vasculitides is most reliably and rapidly made by the demonstration of necrotizing vasculitis of small- or medium-sized muscular arteries in a patient with the aforementioned clinical findings. Biopsy sites should be selected on the basis of the likelihood of detecting abnormalities and on the accessibility of the site. Thus, it is prudent to obtain tissue from clinically involved locales, such as muscle, peripheral nerve, and skin. Blind biopsies of asymptomatic sites are highly unlikely to yield diagnostic information. It is also possible to establish the diagnosis by angiographic techniques in many instances by the demonstration of "pseudoaneurysms," vessel beading, or vessel narrowing. These findings are usually detected in renal, hepatic, or abdominal visceral vessels in patients with objective clinical abnormalities in these areas. Thus, angiography will most frequently reveal vasculitic changes in individuals with hypertension, renal dysfunction, abnormal urinalysis, abdominal pain, or other signs of visceral involvement.

Recommended Approach

Recent studies have addressed the approach to these syndromes with regard to diagnostic yield. On the basis of a retrospective study of 18 patients, Albert et al. (1988a) determined that the choice of procedures should be based on symptoms. Thus, the usual initial invasive procedure was electromyography and nerve conduction velocity determina-

tions in symptomatic subjects to identify specific muscle and/or nerve involvement, followed by biopsy of these sites. If these procedures failed to yield a diagnosis, visceral angiography was the next diagnostic tool of choice. In the absence of symptomatic sites for biopsy, visceral angiography was recommended.

These procedures are necessary, as the diagnosis of the polyarteritis nodosa group of systemic necrotizing vasculitides cannot be established without these studies. Once the diagnosis is made, however, routine laboratory tests such as the erythrocyte sedimentation rate may be useful in monitoring disease activity. It has been demonstrated that early and correct treatment of these syndromes can produce a reversal of the angiographic abnormalities.

Therapeutic

In individuals without fulminant disease who do not appear to be in imminent danger of major end-organ failure, a trial of corticosteroids alone is warranted. This is generally initiated as prednisone (1 mg/kg body weight per day in three to four divided doses). As the disease process comes under control, the prednisone is consolidated to a single morning dose; if the patient's condition remains stable for 1 to 2 months, attempts should be made to convert this to an alternate-day regimen to minimize corticosteroid side effects. This schedule should be continued as long as suppression of the disease is required or until a dose of prednisone is reached below which the symptoms and signs of the process reappear.

In patients who fail to respond to the preceding regimen within 3 to 4 weeks or who display new and progressive signs of active disease while receiving corticosteroids, a more aggressive approach is necessary. In this regard, use of the cytotoxic agent cyclophosphamide (Cytoxan) according to the protocol originally employed in Wegener's granulomatosis has been successful (see Chapter 7–9). This drug is given orally as a single dose of 1 to 2 mg/kg body weight per day in concert with prednisone as prescribed above. The prednisone is used until a cyclophosphamide response is observed, which is generally within 2 weeks, and is then tapered to an alternate-day regimen, which is then employed for as long as is dictated by the course of the disease (usually 4–6 months). The initial dose of cyclophosphamide is adjusted to maintain the white blood cell count in the range 3000 to 4000 cells μ/L with an absolute granulocyte count of no less than 1500 cells/μL. It should be noted that the leukopenic effects of cyclophosphamide are delayed for 5 to 7 days following drug administration. Cyclophosphamide is given for 1 year after complete remission has been maintained by clinical and laboratory criteria and is then decreased in 25-mg decrements every 2 months until discontinued or until the disease process reappears.

There has been interest in the use of intermittent, high-dose intravenous "pulse" cyclosphosphamide, as has been used in lupus nephritis, to minimize the toxicity of this drug. Despite anecdotal reports of small numbers of patients who seemingly responded to this regimen, recent data from a prospective study performed at the National Institutes of Health (Hoffman et al., 1990) have shown that "pulse" treatment is less likely to induce sustained remissions than conventional, low-dose, daily oral cyclophosphamide in patients with related disease, Wegener's granulomatosis. Therefore, the latter protocol remains the treatment of choice.

The side effects of cyclophosphamide and prednisone are outlined in detail in Chapter 7–9. The major side effects of cyclophosphamide include leukopenia, hemorrhagic cystitis, sterility, alopecia, and the risk of neoplasia. The well-known effects of the hypercortisolism observed with prednisone need not be reiterated here.

FOLLOW-UP

Once the diagnosis of polyarteritis nodosa has been established and the patient has reached stable doses of cyclophosphamide and prednisone, the physician will need to see the individual initially on a weekly basis. This will be necessary to assess disease activity as well as to check the white blood cell count. The patient should be specifically questioned about symptoms that may herald a recrudescence or progression of the underlying disease; these are detailed above. A complete physical examination with special emphasis on organ systems at risk for the appearance of polyarteritis nodosa should be performed. In particular, the blood pressure, fundi, and neurologic and cutaneous systems warrant detailed consideration. Routine laboratory tests such as the complete blood count, urinalysis, and erythrocyte sedimentation rate should be monitored at each office visit. As dictated by the appearance of other signs or symptoms, other studies may be needed. Repeat angiography or rebiopsy is unnecessary unless there is a question of recurrence of polyarteritis nodosa.

Patients should be told that the reappearance of previously quiescent signs of the basic disease necessitates consultation with the physician. The occurrence of new complaints, regardless of their perceived triviality, should be reported. The development of symptoms suggestive of unexpected drug effects, such as the fever and infection associated with leukopenia or the hematuria associated with hemorrhagic cystitis, should be promptly reported, given the possible consequences of these adverse reactions.

DISCUSSION
Prevalence

The polyarteritis nodosa group of systemic necrotizing vasculitides comprises uncommon diseases, yet several cases are seen each year at most university medical centers. Patients usually present between the ages 40 and 50 years, yet these processes have been described in infants and the elderly. There is a slight male predominance.

Related Basic Science

Histologically, these diseases are characterized by necrotizing vasculitis involving small- and medium-sized muscular arteries; patients with allergic angiitis and granulomatosis and with the "overlap" syndrome also may manifest small vessel vasculitis. The inflammatory infiltrate is generally composed of acute inflammatory cells. Patients with allergic angiitis and granulomatosis also have eosinophils within vasculitic lesions. Granulomata are unusual in classic polyarteritis nodosa but may be found in allergic angiitis and granulomatosis within, adjacent to, and spatially removed from inflamed vessels. These diseases are noted for the multiplicity of organ system involvement, and virtually any system may be involved.

Natural History and Its Modification with Treatment

The short-term morbidity associated with the polyarteritis nodosa group of systemic necrotizing vasculitides is determined by the rapidity with which correct therapy is instituted and whether irreversible end-organ dysfunction or failure has occured. Thus, even patients successfully treated as described above may be left with some residue of the disease, usually as the remnants of peripheral nerve involvement or impairment in renal function. Many of these abnormalities can be reversed with prolonged treatment, and it is not unusual for peripheral nerve dysfunction to persist for months before function is restored. Therefore, the short-term and even long-term morbidity of these diseases can be largely avoided with early diagnosis and the initiation of the correct form of treatment. It also should be noted that some of the morbidity that develops may be secondary to the agents used in therapy, such as the infections resulting from cyclophosphamide-induced leukopenia.

In the absence of therapy, the 5-year survival for the polyarteritis nodosa group of systemic necrotizing vasculitides is approximately 5 to 10%; if one restricts this to include only patients with disseminated disease, the mortality without treatment approaches 100%. The use of cor-

ticosteroids improved this figure to 50%, although the survival was still significantly lower in those individuals with hypertension or renal disease. Results from the National Institutes of Health have shown that early treatment with combined cyclophosphamide and prednisone produced remissions in 14 of 17 patients treated with the protocol outlined above. In many cases it was possible to discontinue corticosteroids and use cyclophosphamide as the sole agent. These studies emphasize the need for rapid diagnosis and treatment to avoid morbidity and mortality and to induce long-lasting remissions.

Prevention

Given the unknown etiology and pathogenesis of the polyarteritis nodosa group of systemic necrotizing vasculitides, no prevention is possible. Because of the associations with exposure to certain known antigens (e.g., hepatitis B and C, allergy hyposensitization), individuals exposed to these potential immunogens may be at risk for the development of these diseases. As many patients with allergic angiitis and granulomatosis have underlying atopic disease, this too should be considered a predisposition, although no means of prevention in this group is possible.

Cost Containment

Key to the limitation of costs in these patients is the establishment of the diagnosis as quickly as possible with the procedure with the highest yield. Thus, biopsy of symptomatic or clinically abnormal sites is far more likely to demonstrate the typical histologic changes than biopsy of normal and seemingly uninvolved areas. Similarly, angiography is most frequently positive in patients with signs and symptoms referable to the organ system involved, such as hypertension, renal function abnormalities, or abdominal pain, for example.

A recent retrospective analysis has shown that a diagnostic evaluation of these patients based on the biopsy of symptomatic sites with visceral angiography if the biopsies are negative is the most cost-effective approach and is associated with lower morbidity than the performance of repeated, undirected testing.

There is little in the way of cost containment for drugs; cyclosphosphamide and prednisone are the agents of choice. More expensive corticosteroid preparations such as prednisolone are unnecessary.

REFERENCES

Albert DA, Rimon D, Silverstein MD. The diagnosis of polyarteritis nodosa: I. A literature-based decision analysis approach. Arthritis Rheum 1988a; 31:1117.

Albert DA, Silverstein MD, Paunicka K, et al. The diagnosis of polyarteritis nodosa: II. Empirical verification of a decision analysis model. Arthritis Rheum 1988b;31:1128.

Fauci AS, Haynes BF, Katz P. The spectrum of vasculitis: Clinical, pathologic, immunologic, and therapeutic considerations. Ann Intern Med 1978;89:660.

Fauci AS, Katz P, Haynes BF, Wolff SM. Cyclophosphamide therapy of severe systemic necrotizing vasculitis. N Engl J Med 1979;301:235.

Frohnert PP, Sheps SG. Long-term follow-up study of periarteritis nodosa. Am J Med 1967;43:8.

Hoffman GS, Leavitt RY, Fleisher TA, et al. Treatment of Wegener's granulomatosis with intermittent high-dose intravenous cyclophosphamide. Am J Med 1990;89:403.

Katz P, Fauci AS. Systemic vasculitis. In: Frank MM, Austen KF, Claman HN, Unanue ER, eds. Samter's immunological diseases. Boston: Little, Brown, 1995.

Rose GA, Spencer H. Polyarteritis nodosa. Q J Med 1957;26:43.

Zeck PM. Periarteritis nodosa and other forms of necrotizing angiitis. N Engl J Med 1953;248:764.

CHAPTER 7–9
Wegener's Granulomatosis
Paul Katz, M.D.

DEFINITION

Wegener's granulomatosis is a form of systemic necrotizing vasculitis characterized by the triad of necrotizing granulomatous vasculitis of the upper and lower respiratory tract, glomerulonephritis, and small vessel vasculitis.

ETIOLOGY

The etiology of Wegener's granulomatosis is unknown.

CRITERIA FOR DIAGNOSIS
Suggestive

The diagnosis is suggested by the clinical manifestations of upper airway disease (e.g., sinusitis), pulmonary findings (e.g., cough, hemoptysis, pulmonary nodules), and renal abnormalities (e.g., hematuria, red blood cell casts, impaired kidney function). Laboratory results that support, but do not conclusively confirm, the diagnosis include elevated erythrocyte sedimentation rate and positive serum antineutrophil cytoplasmic antibodies in a cytoplasmic pattern.

Definitive

The diagnosis is established by finding necrotizing granulomatous vasculitis on histologic examination of involved tissue. Lung biopsy is the procedure of choice, although the diagnosis can often be made by biopsy of sites of clinically apparent disease.

CLINICAL MANIFESTATIONS
Subjective

The onset of Wegener's granulomatosis is generally insidious, and presenting symptoms are usually nonspecific and rarely of help initially. Ordinarily, patients complain of malaise and fatigue and only later report signs and symptoms referable to the upper and lower airways. Upper airway manifestations include sinusitis, otitis media, rhinorrhea, and ulcerated lesions of the nasal mucosa. With time and in the absence of therapy, this inflammatory process may eventually result in the development of the characteristic saddle-nose deformity, which, although not pathognomonic, is helpful in suggesting the diagnosis.

Pulmonary complaints are unusual in the absence of upper airway disease. When present, these include cough, chest pain, and hemoptysis. It should, however, be remembered that chest disease may be entirely asymptomatic and apparent only radiographically. Despite the frequency of renal involvement in Wegener's granulomatosis, renal disease is rarely symptomatic at the time of presentation; as will be discussed, evidence of kidney disease may be documented by laboratory testing.

Less frequent presenting manifestations that may accompany the preceding include eye signs (conjunctivitis, episcleritis, proptosis), cutaneous lesions (ulcerations, nodules, papules), hearing loss, or headache. Of note, up to 50% of affected individuals may have a polyarticular, symmetric arthritis/arthralgia that may mimic rheumatoid arthritis clinically.

Objective
Physical Examination

Physical findings may be surprisingly absent at the time of presentation. Thus, subjective findings may greatly supersede objective abnormalities. When present, however, these are referable to those areas affected subjectively. In this regard, there may be evidence of sinusitis, nasal crusting, saddle-nose deformity, rhinorrhea, or middle ear involvement. Rarely, erosions through the overlying skin of the nose and sinuses may occur; nonetheless, such lesions should raise the index of suspicion for another process, such as midline granuloma or a neoplasm. Signs of ocular inflammation, as described above, also may be present, and a thorough ophthalmologic assessment should be performed. Chest signs are conspicuous by their absence, but localized rales, rhonchi, and wheezes may be demonstrable. A search for evidence of small vessel cutaneous vasculitis should be performed; these lesions are often localized to dependent areas. The aforementioned joint signs may involve particularly large joints such as the knee and ankle. Nervous system disease is rarely apparent at the time of presentation, but it may develop in up to 20% of subjects during the course of the illness. This may be present as mononeuritis multiplex or cranial nerve involvement, usually of nerve II, V, VII, VIII, IX, or XII. Even less frequent is heart disease, which may manifest as acute pericarditis, myocarditis, or congestive heart failure.

Routine Laboratory Abnormalities

Routine laboratory studies add little to the diagnosis of Wegener's granulomatosis. Reported abnormalities have included leukocytosis, anemia of chronic disease (normochromic, normocytic), and thrombocytosis; it is likely that these findings are related to the chronic, inflammatory nature of Wegener's granulomatosis. Equally nonspecific but invaluable in following the course of this illness is the erythrocyte sedimentation rate, which is uniformly elevated and which parallels the activity of Wegener's granulomatosis. Levels equal to or greater than 100 mm/h by the Westergren method are usual. In the absence of another underlying cause such as infection, elevations in the erythrocyte sedimentation rate should be construed as indicative of active Wegener's granulomatosis until proven otherwise. In many patients with disease seemingly under control and clinically quiescent, an abnormal erythrocyte sedimentation rate may be the only parameter suggesting disease persistence (see Plans, Therapeutic).

Serum antineutrophil cytoplasmic antibodies (ANCAs) displaying reactivity to proteinase 3 are detected by cytoplasmic staining (c-ANCA). This pattern is believed to be fairly specific for granulomatous vasculitis, especially Wegener's granulomatosis. Perinuclear staining (p-ANCA) may be seen in a variety of conditions including Wegener's granulomatosis, microscopic polyarteritis nodosa, Churg–Strauss vasculitis, Kawasaki disease, and systemic lupus erythematosus with necrotizing crescentic glomerulonephritis.

In patients with renal involvement, abnormalities of urinalysis such as proteinuria, hematuria (usually microscopic), and red cell casts may be noted.

Routine chest roentgenograms are abnormal in the majority of patients, even those lacking respiratory complaints. The radiographic findings are usually bilateral and are frequently mistaken for metastatic disease. Typically, one sees multiple nodular densities that have a tendency to cavitate. Twenty percent of radiographs demonstrate pleural effusions; hilar lymphadenopathy suggests diagnoses other than Wegener's granulomatosis.

PLANS
Diagnostic
Differential Diagnosis

The differential of Wegener's granulomatosis includes other pulmonary–renal syndromes such as Goodpasture's syndrome, Churg–Strauss vasculitis, polyangiitis overlap syndrome, and lupus. Non-"autoimmune" causes such as infection and malignancy need to be considered and underscore the necessity for histologic confirmation of the diagnosis.

Diagnostic Options

Interestingly, particularly in view of the articular symptoms in Wegener's granulomatosis, rheumatoid factor positivity may be apparent
in approximately one third of patients, with mean titers of 1:128; this
finding is secondary to hyperactivity of the immune system rather than
to rheumatoid arthritis specifically. In this regard, elevation of serum
immunoglobulins (Ig) A and M may be seen prior to treatment, and circulating immune complexes are detectable in 40% of patients.

Recent evidence has suggested the presence of an unusual autoantibody in patients with Wegener's granulomatosis. Antineutrophil cytoplasmic antibodies are IgG antibodies reactive to intracytoplasmic neutrophil antigens found in serum from patients with this disease, as well
as several other forms of systemic vasculitis, and from some patients
with systemic lupus erythematosus with nephritis. Antineutrophil
cytoplasmic antibodies display reactivity and specificity to a 29,000-
molecular-weight serine protease (proteinase 3) present in neutrophilic
azurophilic granules or to myeloperoxidase.

The diagnosis of Wegener's granulomatosis depends on the demonstration of typical histologic changes in the correct clinical setting.
Necrotizing granulomatous vasculitis is most frequently seen by open
lung biopsy, which is the procedure of choice. Transbronchial biopsy,
although easier and often less risky, is subject to sampling error and
may result in the loss of valuable time awaiting the processing of
pathology specimens that may be nondiagnostic. The chest surgeon
should be directed to areas that appear abnormal at the time of the procedure or that have been visualized as radiographically involved. It is
desirable for the surgeon to obtain large pieces of tissue, which should
be processed for microbiologic culture (routine, fungal, mycobacterial)
and stained for microorganisms and to exclude neoplasia. The availability of video-assisted thoracoscopic surgery may reduce the necessity for open lung biopsy.

The upper airways, despite the frequency of involvement and the
ease of access, are less desirable sites for biopsy because of sampling
error, the difficulty in obtaining adequate tissue, and the common finding of nonspecific inflammation. Similarly, percutaneous renal biopsy
is unlikely to demonstrate granulomatous vasculitis; typical histopathology ranges from focal and segmental glomerulonephritis to flagrant crescentic glomerulonephritis. Nonetheless, these findings in the
appropriate clinical setting would strongly support the diagnosis of
Wegener's granulomatosis. Despite the presence of the classic clinical
triad, tissue confirmation is mandatory in all cases, and physicians
should pursue this until the pathologic diagnosis of Wegener's granulomatosis is made.

As noted above, serum antineutrophil cytoplasmic antibodies may be
present in diseases other than Wegener's granulomatosis, thereby limiting their usefulness as a diagnostic tool. The presence of antineutrophil
cytoplasmic antibiodies should therefore not obscure the need for histologic confirmation of this diagnosis.

Recommended Approach

Tissue biopsy is mandatory. Lung biopsy is the procedure of choice, although other sites may be necessary and/or preferable depending on the
severity of the illness, the risks of surgery, and the organ system involved.

Therapeutic

Therapeutic Options

Currently, it is recommended that Wegener's granulomatosis be treated
with cytotoxic drugs; in this regard, cyclophosphamide (Cytoxan) has
been the agent of choice. Therapy is generally initiated with this drug at
a dose of 1 to 2 mg/kg body weight per day as a single dose. As cyclophosphamide is well absorbed orally, parenteral administration
should be reserved for patients unable to take oral medications or those
who develop nausea and vomiting with this route. A response to this
drug is generally observed within 2 weeks. The dose should be adjusted
to lower the peripheral white blood cell count to 3000 to 4000 cells/μL,
with an absolute granulocyte count of no less than 1000 to 1500
cells/μL. The reasons for this are twofold: first, a maximal therapeutic
response may not be observed until this degree of leukopenia is

achieved; second, it is extremely unlikely that any infectious complications will be noted with white counts no lower than these levels. It
should be remembered that there is delayed onset in the appearance of
cyclophosphamide-induced leukopenia; effects are generally not observed for 5 to 7 days following drug administration and one therefore
needs to appreciate the "slope" of decline in white cell number. Thus,
as the leukocyte count begins to drop, it may well be necessary to lower
the dose of cyclophosphamide concomitantly to avoid unacceptable
leukopenia. In patients with extremely fulminant and rapidly progressive disease, therapy may be started with cyclophosphamide 3 to 4
mg/kg per day for several days to hasten the therapeutic response. After
this interval, the dose is reduced to the standard 1 to 2 mg/kg per day.

Given the recent enthusiasm for using high-dose, intermittent
"pulse" cyclophosphamide in lupus nephritis to minimize drug toxicity
while maintaining effectiveness, similar protocols have been tried in
patients with Wegener's granulomatosis. Unfortunately, this regimen is
less efficacious in inducing and sustaining remissions in this disease
than is cyclophosphamide administered as described above.

Methotrexate, given weekly in low doses comparable to those used
in rheumatoid arthritis, has shown promise in this disease. This drug
may be particularly useful in patients with less aggressive or more limited disease or in those individuals unable to receive cyclophosphamide.

Simultaneously with cyclophosphamide, corticosteroids, usually as
prednisone, are started at a dose of 1 mg/kg body weight per day in
three to four divided doses. Following a response to cyclophosphamide,
this prednisone regimen is converted to a single morning dose and then
to an alternate-day regimen gradually over the next 1 to 2 months. Although not every patient with Wegener's granulomatosis will require
corticosteroids at the onset of treatment, most will, if for no other reason than to lessen disease activity until the onset of a cyclophosphamide response. Absolute indications for corticosteroids include
renal disease, eye involvement, severe lung disease, and significant
constitutional symptoms.

The most serious side effect of cyclophosphamide is leukopenia,
which is generally predictable and can be avoided if the white blood
cell count is routinely checked. Leukopenia, if severe and prolonged,
may result in the development of opportunistic infections. Generally,
withholding this drug for several days after the discovery of the
leukopenia will permit its easy reinstitution within a few days after the
leukocyte count has returned to an acceptable level. Other significant
adverse effects of this agent include hemorrhagic cystitis, which appears to result from the prolonged exposure of bladder epithelium to a
cyclophosphamide metabolite, acrolein. It is recommended that patients
with Wegener's granulomatosis consume 1 to 2 quarts of liquid per day
and empty the bladder frequently, including during the night. Patients
treated with cyclophosphamide for more than several months will invariably become sterile; however, it may be that the chronicity of this
disease and its inflammatory nature also contribute to the observed gonadal dysfunction. Hair loss may occur, but hair returns following discontinuation of the drug. Of theoretical and perhaps actual concern is
the possible development of tumors; this has been observed in patients
with other diseases treated with this drug.

The side effects of corticosteroids are well known to all physicians
and need not be reiterated here. Suffice it to say that every possible effort should be made to taper prednisone to as low a dose as possible,
preferable to an alternate-day schedule.

Anecdotal reports have suggested that trimethoprim–sulfamethoxazole might be effective in some patients. The use of this agent as the
sole treatment for Wegener's granulomatosis cannot be supported, particularly in patients with life-threatening disease.

Recommended Approach

Based on the above, low-dose daily cyclophosphamide and corticosteroids are the drugs of choice for most patients with Wegener's granulomatosis. Patients should be told that Wegener's granulomatosis is a
disease of unknown cause that attacks multiple organ systems; however, if treated early, aggressively, and prior to the onset of irreversible
end-organ dysfunction, long-lasting remissions and even cures can be
achieved. Affected individuals should realize that prolonged and per-

haps lifelong therapy with cyclophosphamide will be necessary. It is incumbent on the treating physician to inform the subject of the potential side effects of the medications to be used and the necessity for careful follow-up.

FOLLOW-UP

Early in the course of the disease, frequent follow-up is necessary. In general, most patients will be hospitalized for diagnosis and the institution of treatment. Following stabilization of the process in the hospital, the patient can be safely discharged and managed on an outpatient basis. Assuming that the subject has been released from the hospital with Wegener's granulomatosis under relatively good control and with acceptable and stable leukocyte counts, weekly physician visits should suffice. At each visit, the patient should be questioned about the presence or absence of constitutional, respiratory (upper and lower), renal (hematuria), and other complaints referable to previously involved organ systems. In addition, symptoms suggestive of drug side effects that are anticipated (alopecia, sterility) or unanticipated (fever, hemorrhagic cystitis, infection) should be sought. A complete physical examination should be performed at each visit, with particular attention given to the upper and lower airways. The complete blood count with leukocyte differential and the erythrocyte sedimentation rate should be obtained to assess the degree of drug-induced leukopenia and the level of disease activity, respectively. It should be noted that the erythrocyte sedimentation rate is the best indicator of active Wegener's granulomatosis. Other helpful studies include renal function tests, urinalysis, and chest radiographs. The frequency with which these are obtained is in large measure dictated by the activity of Wegener's granulomatosis as well as the presence of signs and symptoms referable to these systems.

Patients should be apprised of those symptoms that may herald a flare-up of Wegener's granulomatosis, such as nasal discharge, sinusitis, fever, pulmonary complaints, and new constitutional findings (increased fatigue, weight loss), as well as those that may indicate untoward drug effects (fever, hematuria, infection). In a disease such as Wegener's granulomatosis, which may rapidly and insidiously progress, the wise physician encourages frequent interactions with the patient.

DISCUSSION
Prevalence and Incidence

Although the incidence and prevalence of Wegener's granulomatosis are unknown, it is a rare disease, yet one that most internists will personally encounter at some time. Most patients present in middle age, but the disease has been described in the very young and the very old. Males are slightly more affected than females.

Related Basic Science

Wegener's granulomatosis is one of the granulomatous vasculitides, and its etiology is unknown. The involvement of the respiratory tract in most patients suggests that an as yet unidentified antigen(s) may be responsible. There are data that support an immune complex-mediated pathogenesis for this disease; immune complexes have been found in the sera of some patients, and immunoglobulin and complement may likewise be demonstrated in some pathologic specimens. The finding of an increased frequency of the HLA antigen B8 in Wegener's granulomatosis patients suggests a genetic predisposition to this disorder; of note, this haplotype is also increased in other "autoimmune" disorders, such as juvenile-onset diabetes, Sjögren's syndrome, and dermatitis herpetiformis.

Serum antineutrophil cytoplasmic antibodies detected by cytoplasmic staining (c-ANCAs) are directed against a 29-kDa serine proteinase in primary granules, termed proteinase 3. Following activation, neutrophils and monocytes may express proteinase 3. c-ANCAs can bind to this proteinase and induce degranulation and initiation of the respiratory burst, which can damage endothelial cells. p-ANCA staining occurs because of antibodies reactive to myeloid lysosomal enzymes, including myeloperoxidase and elastase.

Natural History and Its Modification with Treatment

Prior to the use of cytotoxic therapy, the prognosis for Wegener's granulomatosis was dismal, with most patients succumbing to renal failure within 6 months of the time of diagnosis. Since the advent of the combined cyclophosphamide and prednisone regimen described above, Wegener's granulomatosis should now be considered a treatable and often curable disease.

Data from long-term studies at the National Institutes of Health indicate that most patients with Wegener's granulomatosis can be put into remission if the disease is treated early and aggressively, prior to the development of irreversible end-organ dysfunction. The majority of patients require continuous therapy, although some individuals may be able to discontinue all medications.

Therapy with cyclophosphamide and prednisone is not without risk, however. Infectious complications secondary to leukopenia can usually be averted by close monitoring of white blood cell counts and adjustment of cyclophosphamide dosage. Regrettably, the development of herpes zoster may have no relationship to leukopenia.

Other complications of cyclophosphamide therapy include hemorrhagic cystitis, carcinoma of the bladder, and late secondary malignancies, which are usually hematopoietic.

Prevention

There is no known prevention or risk factor for Wegener's granulomatosis.

Cost Containment

The often nonspecific and insidious presentation of Wegener's granulomatosis may delay the diagnosis of this disease, thereby greatly increasing the cost. When the index of suspicion is raised, however, every attempt should be made to establish the diagnosis as quickly as possible to avoid both unnecessary delays in beginning the correct treatment and excessive costs. Therefore, accessible biopsy sites that are likely to yield the diagnosis are favored; open lung biopsy is preferable to transbronchial, upper airway, or renal biopsy in most instances.

Few cost containment therapeutic options are available, as cyclophosphamide and prednisone are the agents of choice. The use of more expensive corticosteroid preparations, such as prednisolone, should be discouraged.

REFERENCES

Fahey J, Leonard E, Churg J, Godman GC. Wegener's granulomatosis. Am J Med 1954;17:168.

Falk RJ, Terrell RS, Charles LA, Jeannette JC. Antineutrophil cytoplasmic autoantibodies induce neutrophils to degranulate and produce oxygen radicals in vitro. Proc Natl Acad Sci USA 1990;87:4115.

Fauci AS, Haynes BF, Katz P. The spectrum of vasculitis: Clinical, pathologic, immunologic, and therapeutic considerations. Ann Intern Med 1978;89:660.

Fauci AS, Haynes BF, Katz P, Wolff SM. Wegener's granulomatosis: Prospective clinical and therapeutic experience with 85 patients for 21 years. Ann Intern Med 1983;98:76.

Fauci AS, Wolff SM. Wegener's granulomatosis: Studies in eighteen patients and a review of the literature. Medicine 1973;52:535.

Godman GC, Churg J. Wegener's granulomatosis: Pathology and review of the literature. Arch Pathol 1954;58:533.

Goldschmeding R, van der Schoot CE, ten Bokkel Huinink D, et al. Wegener's granulomatosis autoantibodies identify a novel diisopropylfluorophosphate-binding protein in the lysosomes of normal human neutrophils. J Clin Invest 1989;84:1577.

Hoffman GS, Kerr GS, Leavitt RY, et al. Wegener's granulomatosis: An analysis of 158 patients. Ann Intern Med 1992;116:488.

Hoffman GS, Leavitt RY, Fleisher TA, et al. Treatment of Wegener's granulomatosis with intermittent high-dose intravenous cyclophosphamide. Am J Med 1990;89:403.

Hoffman GS, Leavitt RY, Kerr GS, et al. The treatment of Wegener's granulomatosis with glucocorticoids and methotrexate. Arthritis Rheum 1992;35:1322.

Katz P, Fauci AS. Systemic vasculitis. In: Frank MM, Austen KF, Claman HN, Unanue ER, eds. Samter's immunological diseases. Boston: Little, Brown, 1995.

CHAPTER 7–10

Hypersensitivity Vasculitis

Paul Katz, M.D.

DEFINITION

Hypersensitivity vasculitis is the term applied to inflammation of small blood vessels (arterioles, capillaries, postcapillary venules).

ETIOLOGY

Frequently, hypersensitivity vasculitis appears 7 to 10 days following antigen exposure; the antigen, when identifiable, may be a microorganisms, a drug, a heterologous protein, or an autologous antigen. Hypersensitivity vasculitis may occur as a primary entity or secondary to an underlying disease such as a malignancy or a connective tissue disease.

CRITERIA FOR DIAGNOSIS

The diagnosis of hypersensitivity vasculitis is made on the basis of histologic evidence of small vessel (arterioles, capillaries, postcapillary venules) vasculitis. Although any organ system can be involved, this process most commonly affects the skin.

Suggestive

Clues to the correct diagnosis include the presence of cutaneous, non-thrombocytopenic, palpable purpura in concert with previous antigen exposure; however, it should be realized that the presenting manifestations may be protean, and dermatologic abnormalities may not always be apparent. These lesions may have a tendency to recur, particularly when an offending antigen cannot be identified.

Definitive

As noted above, the definite diagnosis of hypersensitivity vasculitis requires the histologic evidence of small vessel inflammation with the typical finding of *leukocytoclasia,* a term that refers to the presence of nuclear debris from invading and now degenerated white blood cells.

CLINICAL MANIFESTATIONS

Subjective

Patients with hypersensitivity vasculitis usually present with cutaneous lesions that are often confined to the lower extremities and dependent areas. The most frequently encountered skin manifestation is palpable purpura, with lesions generally at the same stage of development. Hemorrhage, petechiae, vesicles, urticaria, nodules, and livedo reticularis rather than palpable purpura may be apparent. Although most commonly seen on the legs, these lesions also may appear on mucous membranes, conjunctivae, the face, and the ears. These lesions may be asymptomatic, but patients also may complain of edema, burning, stinging, pain, or pruritus. Constitutional complaints are unusual in the absence of an underlying disease but may include fever (20% of patients), fatigue, and malaise.

Palpable purpuric lesions may vary in size, ranging from a few millimeters to 10 cm. They are usually symmetrically distributed on the lower extremities. Systemic involvement in hypersensitivity vasculitis is again uncommon except in the setting of a primary disorder. Some 40% of patients will have articular disease as arthralgias or arthritis. Evidence of kidney involvement is noted in approximately 40% of patients, usually as asymptomatic and microscopic hematuria. Gastrointestinal abnormalities may be apparent in 15% of individuals as upper or lower tract bleeding. Peripheral neuropathy has been reported in 10% of patients.

Objective

Physical Examination

Again, the primary objective abnormalities are restricted to the skin; it should be noted that there are multiple causes of palpable purpura other than hypersensitivity vasculitis and these should be carefully considered. Physicians should note whether the lesions are in the same or differing stages of evolution: patients with hypersensitivity vasculitis usually have lesions of similar age. Signs of underlying diseases such as connective tissue diseases should be sought. Needless to say, a complete physical examination is mandatory in all patients in whom this diagnosis is considered.

Routine Laboratory Abnormalities

Routine laboratory tests may be normal and are rarely of help even when abnormal. Leukocytosis and elevations in the erythrocyte sedimentation rate may be present but are not necessary for diagnosis. Mild peripheral blood eosinophilia may be present. In patients with rheumatoid arthritis or systemic lupus erythematosus, the serologic hallmarks of these diseases may be present. As noted above, urinalysis may reveal hematuria in a minority of patients and routine chest radiographs may detect infiltrates or pleural effusions in 20% of patients.

PLANS

Diagnostic

Differential Diagnosis

The diagnostic differential depends on the appearance of cutaneous lesions. Therefore, those patients with palpable purpura may need evaluation for infection or coagulopathy. The possibility of "allergic" reactions should always be considered.

Diagnostic Options and Recommended Approach

The diagnosis of hypersensitivity vasculitis depends on the histologic demonstration of leukocytoclastic vasculitis involving small vessels, most notably the postcapillary venules. This can usually be demonstrated by a simple punch biopsy of the dermis, although excisional specimens may be needed in some instances if the typical changes are inapparent. Again, it should be remembered that not all palpable purpura is hypersensitivity vasculitis; histologic confirmation is mandatory. In any patient with biopsy-proven hypersensitivity vasculitis, a search for underlying disease should be undertaken.

Therapeutic

Therapeutic Options

In instances where an offending antigen can be identified, mere removal of this may be all that is needed; thus, discontinuation of a drug such as an antibiotic or treatment of an infection may be all that is required. In these circumstances, resolution of the skin lesions is usually apparent within 2 weeks. When an underlying condition such as rheumatoid arthritis, systemic lupus erythematosus, or a malignancy can be found, therapy should be directed at this condition rather than solely at the hypersensitivity vasculitis. Symptomatic relief of the skin lesions may be achieved through the use of antihistamines and antiinflammatory agents. A short course of corticosteroids, given as prednisone 40 to 60 mg per day with a quick taper, may shorten the time to resolution and may diminish subjective symptoms. The side effects of the preceding agents are well known and need not be repeated here.

The choice of therapy is somewhat more difficult in the patient who fails to respond to the above measures and who develops corticosteroid-induced side effects. Other options in such patients include colchicine, antimalarial drugs such as hydroxychloroquine (Plaquenil), and dapsone; furthermore, some individuals may respond to cytotoxic agents such as methotrexate, azathioprine (Imuran), or cyclophosphamide (Cytoxan).

Recommended Approach

The patient should be told that he or she has a condition that can usually be traced to an offending agent that has induced an abnormal reaction in the immune system. It should be emphasized that the illness is most frequently self-limiting, with resolution following removal of the offender. Symptoms can be reduced with the preceding treatments, which should be needed only for a short period. In individuals with an underlying disease related to the appearance of the hypersensitivity vasculitis, the patient should be informed that treatment will be directed at the primary condition. Complications of hypersensitivity vasculitis are unlikely, particularly when an offending antigen can be found. It should be emphasized that a brief course of one of the preceding medications is unlikely to produce any substantial side effects. In patients in whom no predisposing factor can be demonstrated, the possibility of recurrences of the illness should be raised.

FOLLOW-UP

In cases of hypersensitivity vasculitis where a casual agent can be ascertained, the frequency of follow-up should be dictated by the rapidity of resolution; thus, in patients whose skin lesions rapidly clear after removal of the offending antigen, no further steps need be taken. In patients whose lesions are more severe and may require treatment, return visits at 1-week intervals are appropriate until resolution. When an underlying disease is present, the timing of follow-up should be determined by the nature of the primary condition. Laboratory studies are rarely of help in following the course of hypersensitivity vasculitis.

Patients should be told to report any worsening in the skin lesions or the development of extracutaneous symptoms. Furthermore, the tendency of hypersensitivity vasculitis to recur, particularly when no initiating antigen can be determined, should be reemphasized.

DISCUSSION
Prevalence and Incidence

The exact incidence and prevalence of hypersensitivity vasculitis are uncertain; however, it is decidedly more common than most of the other vasculitic processes. Most internists will likely encounter several cases during their careers.

Related Basic Science

There appears to be a slight female predominance. In many, but not all, cases a possible precipitating antigen can be identified. Today, the most commonly identifiable antigens implicated are medications.

Hypersensitivity vasculitis is mediated via immune complex deposition within blood vessel walls, which elicits an inflammatory response through activation of the complement cascade. In this regard, immunoglobulin and/or complement are often demonstrable in biopsy specimens of affected vessels. In some instances it has been possible to identify the antigen in the complex, such as hepatitis B, streptococcal, staphylococcal, or mycobacterial antigens. Other offending microorganisms include cytomegalovirus and the human immunodeficiency virus.

Often, and perhaps in the majority of cases, it is impossible to determine the nature of the offending agent either clinically or by laboratory techniques. Hypersensitivity vasculitis often follows the time course of typical serum sickness: skin lesions appear 7 to 10 days following antigen exposure when immune complexes are present in the circulation in a state of relative antigen excess.

A number of clinically segregatable conditions may be characterized by hypersensitivity vasculitis. Included in this group are serum sickness, Henoch–Schönlein purpura, essential mixed cryoglobulinemia, connective tissue disease (rheumatoid arthritis, systemic lupus erythematosus), and malignancy (usually lymphoreticular). In these cases, the vasculitic process may be a major or minor component of the primary condition.

Natural History and its Modification with Treatment

As emphasized above, hypersensitivity vasculitis is usually a self-limited entity with little in the way of long-term morbidity. In individuals without an underlying condition, the disease may have a tendency to recur and may develop into a chronic process. The morbidity in patients with one of the aforementioned associated diseases is usually attributable to the primary illness. In some instances, the development of renal function impairment or chronic hepatitis (in association with hepatitis B infection) has been reported. Secondary infection of open skin lesions may be a problem in some cases.

Mortality secondary to hypersensitivity vasculitis is distinctly uncommon and is rarely seen in the absence of another disease; thus, patients may die with, rather than from, the vasculitis.

Prevention

There is no known prevention for hypersensitivity vasculitis. Individuals with documented reactions to known antigens should avoid exposure to these if possible.

Cost Containment

The costs in hypersensitivity vasculitis can be reduced in part by the avoidance of unnecessary procedures that are unlikely to yield significant diagnostic or prognostic data. Biopsies should be obtained in all patients, and a careful search for one of the preceding predisposing underlying conditions is mandatory. When symptomatic relief is needed, aspirin and antihistamines may be useful and are relatively inexpensive. If corticosteroid treatment is deemed necessary, the use of a relatively short-acting and inexpensive preparation such as prednisone is warranted.

REFERENCES

Braverman IM, Yen A. Demonstration of immune complexes in spontaneous histamine-induced lesions and in normal skin of patients with leukocytoclastic angiitis. J Invest Dermatol 1975;64:105.

Cream JJ. Clinical and immunologic aspects of cutaneous vasculitis. Q J Med 1976;45:255.

Fauci AS, Haynes BF, Katz P. The spectrum of vasculitis: Clinical, pathologic, immunologic, and therapeutic considerations. Ann Intern Med 1978;89:660.

Katz P, Fauci AS. Vasculitis. In: Gupta S, Talal N, eds. The immunology of rheumatic diseases. New York: Plenum Medical Book, 1985.

McCombs RP. Systemic "allergic" vasculitis: Clinical and pathological relationships. JAMA 1965;194:1059.

Winkelmann RK, Ditto WB. Cutaneous and visceral syndromes of necrotizing or "allergic" angiitis: A study of 38 cases. Medicine 1964;43:59.

CHAPTER 7–11

Giant Cell (Temporal, Cranial) Arteritis

Emilio B. Gonzalez, M.D.

DEFINITION

Giant cell arteritis, also called cranial or temporal arteritis, is a systemic granulomatous form of vasculitis with a predilection to affect the large extracranial arteries of the head and neck, especially the temporal artery.

ETIOLOGY

The etiology is unknown.

CRITERIA FOR DIAGNOSIS

Suggestive

The diagnosis is usually suggested by a constellation of symptoms and signs emanating from inflammation of the involved vessels, usually the temporal artery (see Clinical Manifestations). Uncommonly, fever of "unknown origin" or severe anemia may be the presenting sign. The disorder afflicts primarily persons older than 50 years of age, and the ratio of women to men is about 2:1.

Definitive

The diagnosis should be confirmed by a temporal or other large vessel biopsy demonstrating granulomatous arterial inflammation with or without giant cells.

CLINICAL MANIFESTATIONS

Subjective

The major symptoms of giant cell arteritis are headaches, polymyalgia rheumatica (see Chapter 6–16), arthralgias and myalgias, and jaw claudication. Often, constitutional symptoms are present and they include anorexia, malaise, and fatigue. Fever and weight loss may be present. Other typical symptoms are ophthalmologic–neurologic, such as blurred vision, vertigo, amaurosis fugax (or visual transient ischemic attacks), and diplopia. Less common findings include sore throat, cough, depression, psychosis, acute hearing loss, angina pectoris, strokes, and symptoms attributable to peripheral neuropathy.

The onset may be insidious or abrupt, and in most cases no underlying or precipitating disorder(s) is identified. Frequently, the symptoms of giant cell arteritis have been present for weeks or months before the diagnosis is made. Headache represents the most common complaint and is present in about two thirds of patients. Its location may be temporal, frontal, or occipital, or it may be felt throughout the scalp, and is typically severe. Scalp tenderness may be so intense that patients who previously wore hats or wigs may be obligated to stop this practice. The headaches may be persistent or intermittent, and may well be absent at the time of the medical evaluation.

Polymyalgia rheumatica may be present in up to half of patients with giant cell arteritis. This syndrome includes pain and stiffness of the shoulder and pelvic girdles and is discussed in Chapter 6–16.

Asymmetric joint swellings and ill-defined joint and muscle aches and pains may also be part of the musculoskeletal complaints in giant cell arteritis.

"Jaw claudication" takes the form of intermittent claudication of the chewing muscles, particularly during meat mastication. On occasion, intense facial tenderness to palpation is observed by the patient or examiner, presumably secondary to inflammatory involvement by the underlying arteritis of the masseteric muscles.

The jaw pain is usually bilateral and may be constant, perhaps due to muscle spasms. Pain and swelling of the tongue have been described.

Symptoms of claudication may also be present in the arms, legs, and muscles of deglutition while eating.

Visual symptoms, either blurred vision or amaurosis fugax, may develop transiently or be permanent in one or both eyes. If blindness occurs, this tends to be early during the course of illness, and fortunately is frequently unilateral. If, however, unilateral blindness develops, the second eye may promptly follow in a matter of days to weeks. Yet, it is somewhat reassuring that if blindness has not occurred early, it seems less probable to develop later, after symptoms of giant cell arteritis have been present for several months.

Objective

Physical Examination

Arterial inflammation is found most often in vessels that originate from the aortic arch; however, almost any artery in the body as well as some veins can be affected. The most prevalent severe involvement has been noted to occur in the superficial temporal arteries, vertebral arteries, and ophthalmic and posterior ciliary arteries. Less frequent involvement is seen in the internal carotid, external carotid, and central retinal arteries.

All peripheral arteries should be examined carefully, looking for signs of inflammation such as tenderness, nodularity, and the presence of bruits on auscultation. Intracranial arteries appear not to be commonly involved.

The major signs and physical findings in giant cell arteritis may be grouped as local, ophthalmologic, neurologic, musculoskeletal, and systemic. The local findings include tenderness of the artery, nodulations and tortuosity of the vessel, a pulseless artery, and a locally or diffusely tender scalp. The major ophthalmologic sign is blindness (10–20% of patients), and a fundoscopic examination may show changes of ischemic optic neuritis. It should, however, be remembered that blindness may be present with a normal fundoscopic evaluation, particularly if this is done immediately after the appearance of visual loss. Rarely, blindness may be central secondary to arteritic infarction of the visual center in the occipital cortex.

The main neurologic findings are strokes and peripheral neuropathies. Musculoskeletal signs may include synovitis and joint limitation of motion. Most of the joint and muscle aches and pains in giant cell arteritis can be attributed to associated polymyalgia rheumatica without frank arthritis.

Systemic signs are fever and weight loss. A clinical presentation with fever of "unknown origin" has been described in giant cell arteritis. The fever is usually of low grade, however; rarely, it may suggest sepsis because of a spiking pattern with chills. Deaths from giant cell arteritis have occurred as a result of strokes, aortitis with aneurysmal rupture, and myocardial infarction from coronary arteritis.

Routine Laboratory Abnormalities

Laboratory abnormalities reflect the systemic nature of the arteritic process. A Westergren erythrocyte sedimentation rate is usually markedly elevated, as are other acute-phase reactants. Disturbingly enough, however, biopsy-proven cases of giant cell arteritis have been well documented with normal or nearly normal erythrocyte sedimentation rates. The pattern on a serum protein electrophoresis may reflect systemic inflammation with mild polyclonal hypergammaglobulinemia. A complete blood count may demonstrate mild leukocytosis, mild to moderate and rarely severe normochromic normocytic anemia, and mild thrombocytosis. Hepatic transaminases may be elevated in 25% of patients. Frank hepatitis from giant cell arteritis is unusual.

PLANS

Diagnostic

Differential Diagnosis

The diagnosis of giant cell arteritis should be suspected in any elderly patient with headaches, visual symptoms, polymyalgia rheumatica, scalp or facial tenderness, jaw claudication, and pain in the temples with a tender, pulseless, prominent, and nodular temporal artery. If the erythrocyte sedimentation rate is significantly elevated in a patient with the above-described classic symptomatology, a diagnostic impression of giant cell arteritis should come rather easily on clinical grounds alone, and ideally, this should be confirmed with a biopsy of the temporal, occipital, or facial artery.

Unfortunately, however, clinical presentations, especially for this disorder, are not always typical, and often, a clinical diagnosis of giant cell arteritis becomes a difficult task for the clinician. For example, headaches represent a common complaint in the general population, bursitis and tendinitis in the shoulders are frequent in elderly patients, and prominent or even tortuous temporal arteries do not necessarily indicate the presence of underlying arteritis. Pain localized to the temples may simply be secondary to tension headaches with spastic scalp muscles. Strokes are not uncommon in the elderly, and fever is usually interpreted as an infectious process until proven otherwise.

Similarly, the right clinical interpretation for a number of visual complaints may be difficult, unless they are absolutely typical of amaurosis fugax. To complicate matters further, giant cell arteritis has been documented in patients with normal erythrocyte sedimentation rates.

Several studies have repeatedly demonstrated that a positive yield from a unilateral temporal artery biopsy is no greater than 60% at best. Often, a contralateral temporal artery biopsy or an occipital artery biopsy becomes necessary to document giant cell arteritis. The segmentary nature and "patchy" anatomic distribution of giant cell arteritis have long been recognized. Sampling inadequacies along with "skip" lesions may be some of the reasons for the negative biopsy findings in the presence of obvious giant cell arteritis. Obviously, the diagnostic dilemma is compounded if the clinical presentation is somewhat atypical.

Diagnostic Options

Because performing a temporal artery biopsy is not feasible or desirable in every patient, and because as many as 50% of unilateral biopsy specimens in patients with classic giant cell arteritis may be negative, clinical criteria have been developed and used over the years to diagnose giant cell arteritis without a biopsy or when results of a unilateral biopsy are negative. These clinical criteria are an elevated Westergren erythrocyte sedimentation rate and at least three of the following clinical findings: severe headaches; polymyalgia rheumatica; tender temporal arteries; jaw claudication; visual disturbances such as amaurosis fugax, blindness, or diplopia not attributable to other factors; no clinical or laboratory evidence of other connective tissue disease, such as rheumatoid arthritis or systemic lupus erythematosus; favorable response to corticosteroid therapy.

Recommended Approach

Because of the relatively low yield seen in temporal artery biopsies, a negative unilateral biopsy finding would still permit a diagnosis of probable giant cell arteritis, if the clinical presentation if otherwise typical. Yet, a biopsy confirmation of a diagnosis of giant cell arteritis is desirable and certainly indicated in the following circumstances: atypical clinical presentations such as fever of unknown origin; strokes with high erythrocyte sedimentation rates; presence of relative contraindications to steroid therapy, such as diabetes mellitus, osteoporosis, and compression fractures; polymyalgia rheumatica with headaches, visual symptoms, or both; clinical presentation in young patients (less than 50 years of age); "pure" polymyalgia rheumatica in patients of Scandinavian ancestry because of the high incidence of occult associated giant cell arteritis in that population.

When a biopsy is recommended, care should be taken to resect a large enough segment of artery of at least 5 cm to avoid missing the typical histopathologic changes because of the segmentary nature of the disease with the presence of "skip" lesions with normal vascular wall tissue inbetween.

Angiograms of large vessels such as the aorta may show the presence of aneurysmal dilatations arising from granulomatous aortitis.

Therapeutic

Therapeutic Options

Appropriate treatment for giant cell arteritis is high-dose corticosteroid therapy, for example, prednisone 40 to 60 mg administered preferably as a single dose every morning. Other corticosteroid equivalents may be used instead of prednisone. This treatment should be started as soon as the diagnosis is established or even strongly suspected so as to prevent blindness, the most feared complication.

A common practice is to start prednisone immediately if the diagnostic suspicion is clinically strong, and arrange for a temporal artery biopsy as soon as possible, ideally within a few days. It is believed that prednisone treatment would not appreciably alter the pathologic changes in the temporal artery, if the biopsy is done within the first 2 weeks following initiation of steroid therapy.

If the clinical presentation leaves doubts as to presence of giant cell arteritis, and the first biopsy is negative, biopsy of a contralateral temporal artery or an occipital artery should be performed in an effort to document histopathologic changes of giant cell arteritis.

Recommended Approach

A temporal artery biopsy is recommended whenever feasible. In equivocal and atypical presentations, a biopsy confirmation should be aggressively pursued before committing the patient to high-dose prednisone therapy, particularly if relative contraindications are present, as discussed under Plans, Diagnostic.

The initial 40 to 60 mg of prednisone should be continued daily until all reversible symptoms and signs have resolved and the erythrocyte sedimentation rate has reverted to normal. This usually occurs within a month of initiation of therapy; however, it may take longer. Thereafter, the dose of prednisone is gradually reduced over a period of several months. Most patients require a minimum of 6 months of daily prednisone therapy; some patients need at least a year or two of prednisone administration, usually at a low dose, and a few become corticosteroid dependent for the rest of their lives.

In the average patient who responds well to initial prednisone treatment, relapses may ensue. Spontaneous flare-ups may develop in an unpredictable fashion. Whenever these occur, a brief period of higher prednisone doses may be necessary. Usually, but not always, clinical recurrences are accompanied by a rise in the erythrocyte sedimentation rate, and the reverse may also be true: continuous elevation of the erythrocyte sedimentation rate in the face of complete clinical remissions. A great deal of clinical judgment is often required in the management of many patients with diagnosed giant cell arteritis during their follow-up visits. The decision as to whether an increase in the prednisone dose is warranted in a given clinical situation is probably best arrived at on an individual patient basis.

Obviously, the daily prednisone dose should be lowered and eventually discontinued as soon as the clinical picture permits this safely without risking a recurrence of giant cell arteritis.

Other immunosuppressive agents such as azathioprine (Imuran) and, particularly, methotrexate have been tried with variable success; adequate clinical trials attesting to their efficacy are needed. If, however, steroid therapy is undesirable or has caused severe side effects, this author recommends a trial of weekly methotrexate, 7.5 to 15 mg orally or intramuscularly. This should be done following an initial course of high-dose prednisone. Surgical resections of aortic aneurysms as well as vascular bypass procedures have been successfully performed in a number of patients.

FOLLOW-UP

Pertinent issues dealing with yields in unilateral temporal artery biopsies, the nature of the illness, and side effects of corticosteroids need to be discussed with the patient and family members at length. It may be reassuring to the patient to know that most cases of giant cell arteritis require steroid treatment for no longer than a year or two and that the response is usually excellent. The patient should be instructed to take the daily prednisone dose in the mornings and how to proceed with gradual tapering of the dose when this becomes necessary. Similarly, the addition of daily calcium supplementation may be welcome by most patients in an effort to minimize steroid-induced osteopenia.

Finally, all patients should be alerted as to the signs and symptoms signaling a potential relapse and asked to notify their physicians promptly.

Initial biweekly visits are followed by monthly and later every-2-month follow-up visits. Resolution of most symptoms and signs of the disease, as well as a return towards normal of the erythrocyte sedimentation rate, should be seen within the first month.

DISCUSSION

Prevalence and Incidence

The average annual incidence of giant cell arteritis in populations over age 50 in Olmsted County, Minnesota, was estimated to be 11.7 per 100,000 people (Huston et al., 1978). These figures are considerably higher in Scandinavian countries, approaching 28.6 per 100,000 in Sweden and 76.6 per 100,000 in Denmark (Boesen and Sorensen, 1987). Traditionally, giant cell arteritis has been considered a disease of elderly white women and to be possibly related solely to ethnic extraction; however, a number of reports, including an 11-year retrospective study in the southern United States (Gonzalez et al., 1989), have clearly documented the existence of this condition in black patients as well. Yet, giant cell arteritis appears underrepresented in the southern United States as compared with northern colder climates in this country. The etiology of the disorder is unknown; one wonders if the expression of temporal arteritis results from a complex interaction between ethnicity, climate, and environmental factors in a manner similar to that seen in multiple sclerosis? In Hispanics, temporal arteritis is rare, although Takayasu's disease, another type of giant cell granulomatous arteritis seen in younger persons, is rather common in Mexican mestizos.

Related Basic Science

Histopathology

Histologic specimens from biopsied temporal arteries have shown mononuclear cell infiltrations in the media, particularly in the region of the interna elastica lamina. The infiltrates can be extensive and extend into the adventitia, particularly in vessels that contain a lot of elastin. Intimal thickening can also be seen. Granulomas containing multinucleated giant cells, histiocytes, and lymphocytes are often present. Interestingly, giant cells need not be present in the granulomatous inflammation.

Most of the infiltrating lymphocytes appear to be CD4-positive or of the helper/inducer subset. Eosinophils can be present, but neutrophils are sparse.

Thrombosis may develop at sites of active inflammation with subsequent recanalization. In mild cases, inflammatory changes seem confined to the region of the internal or external elastica lamina or adventitia. With marked inflammation, all layers of the arterial wall are affected. Fibrinoid necrosis is present much less often than in other types of vasculitis.

Immunology

Immunoglobulin and complement deposition, intracellularly and adjacent to the internal elastica lamina in temporal artery biopsy samples, has been found in some involved arteries. Federici et al. (1984) corre-lated elevated levels of von Willebrand factor with ocular involvement in three patients with normal erythrocyte sedimentation rates, and these investigators suggested that this determination may be of help in the differential diagnosis of giant cell arteritis. It has been suggested that the presence of anticardiolipin antibodies correlates with more severe vascular involvement, for example, strokes, in patients with giant cell arteritis.

The association of giant cell arteritis with the presence of the major histocompatibility complex class II molecule HLA-DR4 has been reported. Interestingly, HLA-DR4 is also seen in patients with classic rheumatoid arthritis. Increased production of interleukin-6 but not tumor necrosis factor α has been found in patients with giant cell arteritis and polymyalgia rheumatica. T cells from vasculitic lesions in giant cell arteritis produce predominantly interleukin-2 and interferon gamma. Interestingly, in patients with polymyalgia rheumatica, interferon gamma production is not seen, suggesting that this specific cytokine may be involved in the progression to giant cell arteritis.

Natural History and Its Modification with Treatment

Most patients will have their disease controlled with corticosteroid therapy, and prednisone can usually be withdrawn in the first 2 years. Relapses can occur on occasion. Fortunately, most patients do not experience an associated increased mortality from giant cell arteritis. Deaths, of course, have been reported in patients with this disorder, and are believed to be secondary to strokes, ruptured aortic aneurysms, and myocardial infarctions.

Prevention

No preventive measures are currently available. In patients who present with pure polymyalgia rheumatica, however, the astute clinician will keep in mind the possibility of underlying silent or occult giant cell arteritis.

Cost Containment

The diagnosis and treatment of giant cell arteritis are usually undertaken in an ambulatory care setting. Temporal artery biopsy may be done as an outpatient procedure under local anesthesia. A biopsy usually requires a second office or hospital visit in a few days. Angiograms may be necessary in patients with claudication.

Understandably, when the presentation of giant cell arteritis is atypical—angina, strokes, fever of unknown origin, severe anemia—a prolonged hospitalization with multiple investigations may be unavoidable before a final diagnosis is made. Obviously, early recognition and treatment will reduce morbidity and mortality and contain associated medical costs incurred in such circumstances.

REFERENCES

Boesen P, Sorensen SF. Giant cell arteritis, temporal arteritis and polymyalgia rheumatica in a Danish county. Arthritis Rheum 1987;30:294.

Federici AB, Fox RI, Espinoza LR, et al. Elevation of von Willebrand factor is independent of erythrocyte sedimentation rate and persists after glucocorticoid treatment in giant cell arteritis. Arthritis Rheum 1984;27:1043.

Gonzalez EB, Varner WT, Lisse JR, et al. Giant-cell arteritis in the southern United States: An 11-year retrospective study from the Texas Gulf Coast. Arch Intern Med 1989;149:1561.

Healy LA, Wilske KR. Manifestations of giant cell arteritis. Med Clin North Am 1977;61:261.

Huston KA, Hunder GG, Lie JT, et al. Temporal arteritis: A 25-year epidemiologic, clinical, and pathological study. Ann Intern Med 1978;88:162.

Weyand CM, Hicok KC, Hunder GG, Goronzy JJ. Tissue cytokine patterns in patients with polymyalgia rheumatica and giant cell arteritis. Ann Intern Med 1994;121:484.

Infectious Diseases Problems

Jonas A. Shulman, M.D., David S. Stephens, M.D.

CHAPTER 8–1

The Acutely Ill Patient With Suspected Serious Bacterial Infection

Jonas A. Shulman, M.D., and W. Lee Hand, M.D.

DEFINITION

A physician may see patients who are acutely ill in whom the physician suspects, but cannot initially prove, that the condition is caused by a serious bacterial infection. The physician may also determine that he or she must begin therapy prior to establishing a definite diagnosis. This chapter describes the orderly diagnostic and therapeutic approach to the problem.

ETIOLOGY

See Table 8–1–1.

CRITERIA FOR DIAGNOSIS

Suggestive

This chapter discusses the approach to the acutely ill patient who has clinical findings that suggest a severe bacterial infection requiring the rapid onset of empiric antimicrobial therapy. Once the results of bacteriologic data become available 24 to 48 hours later, more specific and well-defined treatment regimens can be employed.

Definitive

The definitive diagnosis of pyogenic bacterial infection generally depends on the results of bacteriologic culture. Unfortunately, for most pyogenic infections, this information is not available for 24 to 48 hours. Therefore, when serious bacterial infection is suspected in an acutely ill patient, one must initiate antimicrobial therapy before the diagnosis is confirmed by the results of cultures.

CLINICAL MANIFESTATIONS

Subjective

A patient with a serious bacterial infection generally complains of fever, malaise, myalgias, chills (sometimes shaking), and headache. At times, gastrointestinal symptomatology also may be noted. In the elderly or in patients with chronic renal failure, fever may be absent and serious bacterial infection can present in an insidious fashion.

In addition to the general, nonspecific findings noted above, careful questioning may direct one's attention to a specific site of infection, such as the upper respiratory tract, lower respiratory tract, central nervous system, urinary tract, gastrointestinal tract, genital tract, heart, or skin. Also, if the patient complains of a skin rash or swollen glands in addition to fever, certain specific diagnostic possibilities should be considered (see Chapters 8–5 and 8–6).

A detailed epidemiologic history, including information about travel, animal contact, and tick bites, may prove useful in suggesting certain diagnostic entities (see Chapters 8–34, 8–36, and 8–37). Similarly, a history of exposure to other infected individuals or to contaminated food may be helpful.

Careful elicitation of a medical history is imperative. For example, if a febrile illness occurs in a patient with known prior valvular heart disease or with the problem of intravenous drug abuse, bacterial endocarditis must be considered. If a patient is immunocompromised due to either an underlying host defense abnormality or to immunosuppressive therapy, specific bacterial infections known to be frequent in these settings must be given careful consideration (Table 8–1–2).

Objective

Physical Examination

Fever, or at times, hypothermia, is a common physical finding in patients with severe bacterial infection. Marked sweating, shaking chills, and a flushed appearance may be noted. In certain forms of overwhelm-

ing bacterial infection, especially Gram-negative rod bacteremia, the patient may show evidence of shock, with hypotension, cool extremities, and peripheral cyanosis. Early findings may include tachypnea and/or altered mental status. In the appropriate setting, these findings should lead to rapid institution of both supportive and antimicrobial therapy, thereby possibly preventing progression of the bacteremic process to the full-fledged shock syndrome (see Chapter 8–2).

A careful and comprehensive examination should be performed with special attention to the following:

- Hyperthermia or hypothermia
- Presence of shock
- Skin rash, hemorrhages, skin or soft tissue infection (including decubiti)
- Stiff neck
- Focal neurologic findings
- Pharyngitis
- Regional or generalized adenopathy
- Infected eardrums
- Conjunctival or retinal lesions
- Swollen or bleeding gums and adequacy of dental care
- Pulmonary abnormalities such as localized wheezes, rales, or consolidation
- Cardiac examination with search for evidence of valvular abnormalities and the presence of heart failure
- Abdominal tenderness, rebound, masses, or absent bowel sounds
- Jaundice
- Joint or muscle tenderness or swelling
- Presence of pain over bone
- Urethral discharge
- Urinary tract findings such as flank tenderness
- Pelvic tenderness or discharge
- Rectal or prostatic tenderness
- Indwelling intravascular or urinary catheters
- Endotracheal tube or tracheostomy

Routine Laboratory Abnormalities

The routine laboratory abnormalities may be nonspecific but include leukocytosis, pyuria, and sepsis of pneumonitis on the chest x-ray film.

PLANS

Diagnostic

Each of the preceding findings may be very helpful in delineating the likely site of infection and the etiologic agents likely to be responsible for the systemic symptomatology. This, in turn, allows the clinician to collect the appropriate smears and cultures and then to devise a rational empiric antimicrobial regimen. In addition, the findings point to the need for various adjunctive therapies, such as treatment of shock, drainage of pus, and ventilatory therapy, as well as the possible need for relief of an obstructed lumen, such as a blocked ureter or obstructed biliary system.

A very ill patient suspected of having a serious bacterial infection should have the following laboratory data collected in addition to the routine laboratory tests: blood cultures (three sets); urine culture; arterial blood gas determination if shock or ventilatory problems are noted (see Chapter 8–2).

Depending on the site or sites of infection identified or suspected by the prior clinical manifestations, Gram stains of appropriately collected body secretions (e.g., sputum, spinal fluid, urethral discharge, joint fluid, urine, stool, pus from wounds or abscesses) or skin lesions should be evaluated immediately. If diarrhea is present, a search for and identification of leukocytes might point to an invasive diarrheal pathogen

TABLE 8–1–1. INITIAL EMPIRIC REGIMENS FOR SEVERAL COMMON BACTERIAL INFECTIONS IN SEVERELY ILL ADULTS WHILE AWAITING RESULTS OF MORE DEFINITIVE LABORATORY TESTS*†

Disease Process	Likely Pathogen(s)	Initial Therapy	
Meningitis (see/Chapter 8–9; Table 8–9–2; Table 8–9–3)			
Gall bladder infection	Enterobacteriaceae; *Bacteroides*; streptococci; *Clostridium*	Piperacillin-tazobactam or ampicillin-sulbactam	Or ceftizoxime or cefotaxime or ampicillin plus metronidazole plus an aminoglycoside
Pelvic infection	Gonococcus; anaerobes; *Chlamydia*; Enterobacteriaceae; streptococci	Ceftriaxone plus doxycycline plus clindamycin	Or ampicillin plus clindamycin plus aminoglycoside followed by doxycycline
Pyelonephritis	Enterobacteriaceae; occasionally enterococci	Ceftriaxone alone or piperacillin-tazobactam with or without an aminoglycoside	Or ampicillin plus an aminoglycoside
Prostatitis, acute >35 years of age	Enterobacteriaceae; streptococci	Trimethoprim-sulfamethoxazole	Or a fluroquinolone
Pneumonia (see Chapters 8–14 and 8–15; Table 8–14–2)			
Peritonitis, suspected bowel perforation	Enterobacteriaceae; anaerobes, including *Bacteroides fragilis*; enterococci; other streptococci, *Pseudomonas*	Imipenem-cilastin alone or piperacillin-tazobactam and an aminoglycoside	Or ampicillin-sulbactam plus an aminoglycoside or ceftriaxone plus metronidazole or clindamycin
Bacteremia† (without obvious site)			
Community-acquired† and noncompromised host	Enterobacteriaceae; *S. Aureus*‡ pneumococcus‖, streptococcus; rarely *Pseudomonas*	Ceftriaxone or piperacillin-tazobactam plus vanocomycin	Or Imipenem-cilastin alone or with vancomycin
Neutropenic host and/or hospital-acquired†	Above and *Pseudomonas*; *S. epidermidis*; *S. aureus*‡; enterococcus	Piperacillin-tazobactam plus aminoglycoside plus vancomycin or aztreonam plus aminoglycoside plus vancomycin	Or ceftazidime§ plus aminoglycoside plus or minus vancomycin

*If the Gram stain of the cerebrospinal fluid, peritoneal fluid, sputum, or other body fluid demonstrates a specific pathogen, the initial regimen should be appropriately simplified and directed primarily against that pathogen.

†Other initial choices are possible. Helpful guidelines are available in Abramowicz (1990). The choice of one aminoglycoside over another or one third-generation cephalosporin or antipseudomonal penicillin over another may depend on local factors, including likely pathogens in a given hospital environment of cost and/or toxicity factors.

‡Whenever methicillin–resistant staphylococci are a significant problem in a hospital and are likely pathogens, vancomycin must be included in the initial recommendation.

§Of the third-generation cephalosporins, ceftazidime is considered the most effective antipseudomonal agent.

‖Because of increased resistance of pneumococci to penicillin G, cefotaxime or ceftriaxone is indicated for initial therapy for serious pneumococcal infections, especially in meningitis. At times and in certain areas where pneumococci may be multiresistant even to third-generation cephalosporins, vancomycin should also be added until in vitro sensitivity studies clarify the susceptibility pattern of the pneumococcus.

such as *Campylobacter jejuni, Salmonella,* and *Shigella.* Cultures should be obtained from any of the above or other sites of suspected infection as dictated by clinical findings. When a collection of potentially infected closed-space fluid can be aspirated, such as from an abscess cavity, it should be collected in a syringe and the needle corked so that the specimen can be immediately taken to the laboratory for aerobic and anaerobic cultures.

If the site of infection cannot be located by history, physical examination, or initial laboratory tests, more detailed, directed studies such as additional x-rays, computed tomography scans, and ultrasonography may be required.

In some instances the clinical presentation may be so classic as to predict the specific etiology of infection with a high degree of probability. Examples of such a presentation include toxic shock syndrome, meningococcemia, and disseminated gonococcal infection. In other instances, if the site of infection can be identified, specific smears and cultures may be able to determine accurately the specific etiologic pathogen. Gram stains of appropriate body fluids may allow a very accurate prediction of the pathogenic organism(s). Once the specific site (or sites) of infection is identified, the likely pathogens can be predicted with considerable accuracy. After the suspected site of infection and the likely pathogens are determined, empiric antimicrobial therapy directed at the probable etiologic agents should be initiated. Thus, the patient

can be treated with an effective regimen long before the specific microorganism is isolated by culture.

Therapeutic

Refer to Table 8–1–1 for guidelines concerning the initial choice of antimicrobial regimens for treatment of serious bacterial infection. Note that when one is able to obtain additional information from smears or other rapid diagnostic studies, an even more specific regimen can be employed. The annual issue of *The Medical Letter* noted in the References can be very helpful in the selection of an appropriate empiric or directed regimen.

In addition to antibiotics, management of serious infectious diseases demands attention to the need for cardiovascular, pulmonary, and nutritional support. Loculated infections or infected foreign bodies may require surgical approaches for control.

The patient should be informed that a bacterial infection is suspected and that the site of infection has either been determined or is being searched for by appropriate studies. If indicated, it should be explained that initial antimicrobial therapy will be directed toward the likely pathogens and based on the clinical findings. The patient can be told that the antibacterial therapy may be revised when the laboratory studies are completed. Depending on the setting, the seriousness of the

TABLE 8–1–2. LIKELY BACTERIAL PATHOGENS RELATED TO SPECIFIC ENTITIES

Host Defense Problem	Likely Bacterial Pathogens
Splenectomy	Pneumococci, *Hemophilus influenzae*, meningococci
Neutropenia	Gram-negative aerobic bacilli, staphylococci (*Staphylococcus aureus* and *Staphylococcus epidermidis*)
AIDS	Recurrent *Salmonella* bacteremia with or without gastroenteritis; *S. aureus* bacteremia; disseminated mycobacterial infection (especially *Mycobacterium avium–intracellulare*); pneumococcal bacteremia and meningitis

problem should be reviewed and the patient appropriately assured of the availability and types of diagnostic studies, the use of effective antimicrobial and supportive therapy, and the need for surgical therapy when indicated.

FOLLOW-UP

Follow-up is dependent primarily on the specific bacterial infection. As a general guideline, if the patient fails to respond to what appears to be appropriate therapy, possible reasons for the failure should be considered. These include the following:

- Undrained pus
- Infected prosthetic material
- Inadequate dose or route of administration of the antibiotic
- Antagonism among the antimicrobial drugs being given
- Superinfection
- Wrong initial diagnosis
- New infections, such as intravenous catheter-associated septic phlebitis
- Underlying noninfectious process
- Changing resistance pattern of the original organism
- Development of drug fever or drug-induced disease

DISCUSSION
Prevalence and Incidence

This condition is generally uncommon, but is commonly seen in hospitalized patients.

Related Basic Science

Much of this chapter is concerned with the choice of an appropriate antimicrobial regimen in the initial treatment of a suspected bacterial infection. In addition to the specific therapy, it is imperative that one recognize the need for adjunctive, supportive care to treat the consequences of infection, Thus, immediate attention must be paid to maintaining adequate blood pressure, fluid balance, acid–base balance, ventilation, nutrition, and drainage or surgical debridement when required. Without consideration of these factors, antibiotics may prove to be ineffective for many infections.

The guidelines and principles for appropriate empiric choice of an antimicrobial should include consideration of the following points:

- Is a bacterial infection present?
- Can the probable site or sites of infection be identified?
- If appropriate, can a rapid smear of a body fluid be made or another rapid diagnostic test be done to identify the specific pathogen or pathogens?
- Have all appropriate cultures been obtained?
- How rapidly and by what route should antibiotics be administered if they are to be used?
- What antibiotic or antibiotics are likely to be effective against the pathogen(s) demonstrated by the rapid smears of appropriate material or by knowledge of the bacteria likely to produce infection at the suspected site?

- Is a bactericidal, as opposed to a bacteriostatic, antibiotic likely to be necessary? Four settings in which bactericidal antibiotics are indicated include bacterial endocarditis, bacterial meningitis, osteomyelitis, and bacterial infection in the setting of severe neutropenia (<500 neutrophils/μL).
- Of the possible antimicrobial agents that could be selected, which is the least expensive agent that has the narrowest spectrum to accomplish the therapeutic objective? The drug must be delivered adequately to the site of infection, preferably providing an antimicrobial concentration at least several times the concentration required to inhibit or kill the pathogen.
- Which of the possible antibiotics that meet the criteria listed above has the least toxicity?
- Are there host factors present that might influence the selection of antibiotic regimen? Examples include allergy, glucose-6-phosphate dehydrogenase deficiency, renal or hepatic disease, and pregnancy.
- After consideration of all these factors, an appropriate empiric regimen can be selected and instituted. A more appropriate and, perhaps, less toxic and less expensive regimen may be substituted if the results from the bacteriology laboratory suggest that such therapy would be just as effective.

These principles allow for the development of a rational approach to empiric antimicrobial selection and may prevent the needless use of toxic or very expensive agents as well as those with exceptionally broad spectra, which might lead to superinfection with other microorganisms (such as highly resistant bacteria and fungi). The guidelines stress the need to refine therapy once the results from the microbiology laboratory are available.

Natural History and Its Modification with Treatment

The natural history of bacterial infections and the outcome of therapy relate primarily to the specific type of infection and are covered in various chapters in this book. In all instances, however, the outcome of infection is dependent on the interaction of the bacterial pathogen (and its virulence factors and invasive capabilities) with the host's antibacterial defense mechanisms. Thus, when host defense mechanisms are intact, the outcome of some infections may be in the host's favor, even if the antimicrobial agent selected is not the most appropriate; however, appropriate antimicrobial therapy may be the only means of controlling infection when host factors are severely compromised, such as in severe neutropenia. In fact, at times in this setting, even optimal antimicrobial therapy may not be effective. In most serious infections, the combination of an appropriate antibiotic regimen and reasonably competent host defense mechanisms will control the illness and produce a favorable outcome. In general, the earlier one initiates adequate antibacterial therapy and appropriate adjunctive measures, such as treatment of shock or surgical drainage, the more successful is the outcome. If the infection can be controlled before the adverse consequences of the inflammatory response become rampant, the patient is likely to fare much better.

Prevention

Prevention of the individual infections caused by bacteria are covered in the specific chapters dealing with each infection. Good sanitation, careful handwashing, and adequate food and other hygienic practices are important in the reduction of some of these serious infections. Infections that can be prevented by antimicrobial agents are considered in Chapter 8–82, and those prevented by vaccines and antiserum are discussed in Chapter 8–83.

Whenever possible, the use of an appropriate agent with a narrow or well-directed spectrum is recommended to help reduce the chances for selecting resistant bacteria. This may prevent superinfection in the patient and avoid the development of more antibiotic-resistant bacteria in the animate and inanimate environments.

In addition, following the guidelines developed by the Centers for Disease Control to reduce hospital-associated infections will help prevent cross-infections and cut down on the serious problems of acquisition of infection in the hospital environment.

Cost Containment

Many different antibiotic regimens may be capable of successfully treating a given infection. Comparisons of cost per dose, number of doses per day, and methods of administration may lead to savings of hundreds of thousands of dollars for hospital pharmacies and to equally important savings for individual patients. Current trends toward the use of parenteral antibiotics with prolonged half-lives that allow for only one or two times per day dosing have been noted. These agents not only may make administration easier and less costly in the hospital, but also may allow parenteral therapy to be given more easily at home or in the outpatient setting. As the prices of antibiotics vary considerably from region to region and day to day, one must become familiar with the costs at the hospitals and pharmacies that are used in one's own practice to provide effective therapy as cheaply as possible. In some instances, oral agents such as ciprofloxacin may produce serum levels that are adequate to treat some serious Gram-negative infections, thereby avoiding more costly parenteral therapy.

REFERENCES

Abramowicz M, ed. The choice of antimicrobial drugs. Med Lett 1990;32:41.
Kim JH, Gallis HA. Observations on spiraling empiricism: Its causes, allure, and perils, with particular reference to antibiotic therapy. Am J Med 1989;87:201.
Moellering RC Jr, Kunz LJ, Poitras JW, et al. Microbiologic basis for the rational use of antibiotics. South Med J 1977;70(Suppl.):8.
Stumacher RJ, ed. Clinical infectious diseases. Philadelphia: Saunders, 1987:40.
Weinstein L. General considerations. In: Goodman LS, Gilman A, eds. The pharmacological basis of therapeutics. New York: Macmillan, 1970:1154.
Weinstein L, Dalton AC. Host determinants of response to antimicrobial agents. N Engl J Med 1968;279:467.
Young LS. Empiric antimicrobial therapy in the neutropenic host. N Engl J Med 1986;315:580.

CHAPTER 8–2

Bacteremia and Septic Shock

Molly E. Eaton, M.D., and James P. Steinberg, M.D.

DEFINITION

Bacteremia is invasion of the bloodstream by bacteria. Depending on the host and circumstances, bacteremia can be transient and clinically silent, can provoke fever or other systemic signs of infection, or can be life-threatening. Septic shock can be defined as infection-induced hypotension refractory to fluid resuscitation with evidence of tissue hypoperfusion. Septic shock is usually, but not always, accompanied by demonstrable bacteremia.

ETIOLOGY

Aerobic Gram-negative bacilli are the classic causes of septic shock, being found in 30 to 80% of cases; however, septic shock can also result from Gram-positive bacteremia (5–24%) and fungemia. On occasion, no etiologic agent can be identified.

CRITERIA FOR DIAGNOSIS

Suggestive

The presence of a significant infection is suggested by certain systemic signs, commonly called the systemic inflammatory response syndrome or SIRS (Table 8–2–1). In the appropriate hosts, including patients with severe underlying diseases or immunosuppressive conditions, patients with intravascular devices, and those with a local site of infection, these systemic signs along with hypotension should raise concern about a bacteremic infection and the potential for life-threatening septic shock.

Definitive

Definitive diagnosis of bacteremia requires laboratory isolation of a pathogen with a blood culture. For many bacteria, one positive blood culture is significant. For bacteria that are part of the normal skin flora, isolation in multiple cultures is necessary to exclude contamination. The definitive diagnosis of septic shock is made by fulfilling the criteria outlined in Table 8–2–1.

CLINICAL MANIFESTATIONS

Subjective

Fever, chills, malaise, apprehension, and shortness of breath are early but nonspecific consequences of bacteremia. Vomiting and/or diarrhea are seen in a few patients. These symptoms may be absent or unimpressive in elderly patients, who may present only with confusion. A local site of infection (lung, urinary tract, surgical wound, gastrointestinal tract, indwelling catheter, etc.), which serves as a source of bacteremia, may cause prominent symptoms. Serious preexisting medical diseases such as diabetes, cirrhosis, congestive heart failure, uremia, and HIV infection are risk factors for bacteremia.

Objective

Physical Examination

Fever and prostration, although nonspecific, are early manifestations of bacteremia. In the absence of overt pulmonary disease, hyperventilation with resultant respiratory alkalosis and arterial hypoxemia is a diagnostic clue. Mental confusion, altered consciousness, and hypothermia may be prominent, especially in the elderly. Skin manifestations of bacteremia include hemorrhagic lesions due to disseminated intravascular coagulation and specific lesions due to infection (e.g., ecthyma gangrenosum in *Pseudomonas aeruginosa* bacteremia). Circulatory shock (arterial hypotension with inadequate perfusion of vital organs) is a common complication of Gram-negative rod bacteremia. Perhaps 40% of Gram-negative rod bacteremic episodes provoke shock, which causes a marked increase in mortality (approximately 50%). Decreased consciousness, oliguria, and metabolic (lactic) acidosis reflect poor tissue perfusion. Warm extremities may be present during early septic shock, but vasoconstriction and cool extremities usually follow as shock progresses. The adult respiratory distress syndrome (ARDS), or "shock lung," is a major complication of Gram-negative rod bacteremia and is associated with high mortality. The recently described syndrome of multiple organ failure typically occurs in patients with refractory septic shock after the development of ARDS. Progressive dysfunction

TABLE 8–2–1. CONSENSUS CONFERENCE DEFINITIONS

Systemic inflammatory response syndrome (SIRS). Two or more of the following:
- Temperature >38°C or <36°C
- Heart rate >90 beats/min
- Respiratory rate >20 breaths/min
- White blood cell count >12.0 × 10^9/L, <4.0 × 10^9/L, or >0.10 immature forms (bands)

Sepsis. SIRS plus a documented infection (positive culture for organism).

Severe sepsis. Sepsis associated with organ dysfunction, hypoperfusion abnormalities, or hypotension. Hypoperfusion abnormalities include, but are not limited to, lactic acidosis, oliguria, and an acute alteration in mental status.

Septic shock. Sepsis-induced hypotension despite fluid resuscitation plus hypoperfusion abnormalities.

Source: Slightly modified from members of the ACCP/SCCM Consensus Conference Committee. American College of Chest Physicians/Society of Critical Care Medicine Consensus Conference: Definitions for sepsis and organ failure and guidelines for the use of innovative therapies in sepsis. Crit Care Med 1992;20(6):866. Reproduced with permission from the publisher. Copyright 1992 by Williams and Wilkins.

of other organs including the kidneys, liver, heart, and central nervous system ensues; prognosis is dismal.

Routine Laboratory Abnormalities

Leukopenia may be present early in Gram-negative rod bacteremia but is followed within a few hours by leukocytosis. Regardless of the total white blood cell count, neutrophilia with an increased percentage of band forms is usually present. The peripheral smear may show neutrophils with toxic granulations, cytoplasmic vacuoles, and Döhle bodies. The presence of red blood cell fragments suggests disseminated intravascular coagulation. Thrombocytopenia (or decreasing platelet counts) is observed in more than 50% of patients with bacteremia and does not usually indicate the presence of disseminated intravascular coagulation. Hyperbilirubinemia and elevated transaminase levels are also commonly found. Arterial blood gases reflect the respiratory and cardiovascular changes noted above; thus, early respiratory alkalosis secondary to hyperventilation may be followed by metabolic acidosis when circulatory shock develops. Hypoxemia may become severe and life-threatening if ARDS develops.

PLANS
Diagnostic
Differential Diagnosis

Septic shock is associated with bacteremia or fungemia in 50 to 90% of cases. SIRS, with similar organ dysfunction, can occur with other conditions, for example, severe hypovolemia, congestive heart failure, trauma, severe pancreatitis, and drug intoxications. Hemodynamic monitoring is sometimes required to differentiate these conditions.

Diagnostic Options and Recommended Approach

A local infection, when this is the source of bacteremia, provides material for examination and culture. Careful evaluation of Gram-stained smears and proper culture specimens from infected sites (sputum, pus, urine, aspirated material from site of soft tissue infection, etc.) should be performed. Two to three sets of blood cultures should be obtained before the initiation of antibiotic therapy. This number of cultures will detect more than 90% of true bacteremias in the previously untreated patient. In patients who are receiving antibiotics prior to the onset of clinical sepsis, additional sets of blood cultures may be required. The blood cultures often detect bacterial growth within 24 hours of processing; by 72 hours, more than 90% of ultimately positive blood cultures show bacterial growth. Clinical sepsis can occur without demonstrable bacteremia, especially if the patient has previously been receiving antibiotics. In patients with shock of undetermined etiology, measurement

of central venous or pulmonary artery pressures may be necessary to exclude hypovolemia as a cause of decreased systemic pressures. Adequate monitoring (central venous line, Swan–Ganz catheter) of therapeutic efforts is needed.

Therapeutic
Therapeutic Options

Antibiotics. Treatment with appropriate antibiotics (drugs to which the infecting organism is susceptible) reduces mortality in Gram-negative rod bacteremia, even after onset of shock. Initial therapy depends on the clinical setting and the presumed source of the bacteremia. Treatment with two antimicrobial agents (e.g., beta-lactam and aminoglycoside) is often initiated for "unknown" bacteremia in hospitalized patients. Vancomycin should be added to the regimen when methicillin-resistant *Staphylococcus aureus* or *epidermidis* infection is considered to be a reasonable possibility. Antimicrobial selection should be appropriately altered when the results of blood cultures are known. The role of combination antibiotic therapy for Gram-negative rod bacteremia is a matter of considerable debate. The administration of antibiotic combinations with demonstrated "synergy" against the infecting organism may improve survival in patients with neutropenia and "rapidly fatal" underlying disease (especially in those with *Pseudomonas aeruginosa* bacteremia).

Hemodynamic Measures. Vasodilation (in early Gram-negative shock), capillary leak, peripheral pooling of blood, fluid sequestration at sites of inflammation, and volume loss due to vomiting, diarrhea, bleeding, and fever all contribute to a decrease in effective circulating volume. Other than appropriate antibiotic therapy, *prompt expansion of intravascular volume* is the most important measure in the correction of shock due to bacteremia. For plasma volume expansion, colloid-containing substances and crystalloid solutions each have advocates. Fluid resuscitation should be aggressive until the pulmonary wedge pressure reaches 15 to 18 mm Hg. If ARDS is present, the pulmonary wedge pressure should be maintained at the lower end of the range to decrease extravasation of fluid into the lung.

Vasoactive drugs should be used if the preceding measures prove inadequate. Dopamine is considered by most authorities to be the sympathetic amine of choice and is used to increase blood pressure in patients who remain hypotensive despite aggressive fluid support. Dopamine supports the blood pressure by increasing myocardial contractility and heart rate and by reducing blood flow to skeletal muscle while producing vasodilation and increasing perfusion to the renal, coronary, mesenteric, and cerebral vessels. At low doses, increased urine flow is observed in most patients, although at higher doses renal blood flow may be reduced. Dopamine produces fewer ventricular arrhythmias than isoproterenol or norepinephrine. The initial infusion rate of dopamine is 2 to 5 µg/kg per minute but may be increased up to 20 µg/kg per minute, if necessary.

Corticosteroids. On the basis of encouraging data from animal models, high-dose corticosteroids were at one time widely used in the treatment of septic shock; however, several recent large clinical trials showed no benefit from high-dose steroids and a disturbing number of superinfections in the steroid-treated patients. Consequently, most experts feel that the only role of corticosteroids in the treatment of septic shock is in patients with suspected adrenal insufficiency.

Correction of Metabolic Acidosis. Temporary correction of the lactic acidosis accompanying septic shock may be achieved by intravenous administration of sodium bicarbonate. Improvement in tissue perfusion by the measures noted above often corrects the cellular hypoxia that produces lactic acidosis.

Heparin. Disseminated intravascular coagulation frequently occurs with bacteremic shock. Intravascular coagulation can be corrected by heparin, but this does not influence overall survival. Disseminated intravascular coagulation generally ceases when shock is corrected; consequently, heparin is not recommended in most instances. In patients with uncontrolled shock, disseminated intravascular coagulation, and subsequent bleeding, heparin, and replacement therapy (platelets, fresh-frozen plasma, and cryoprecipitate) may be necessary.

Treatment of Adult Respiratory Distress Syndrome.
Pulmonary endothelial damage in septic shock may lead to increased capillary permeability and result in interstitial and alveolar edema. Interference with oxygen exchange may lead to severe arterial hypoxemia. Appropriate therapy includes intubation and oxygen administration via mechanical ventilation with positive end-expiratory pressure. Pulmonary wedge pressure should be maintained in the low-to-normal range if possible, to minimize transduction of fluid into the pulmonary interstitium.

Immunotherapy and Other Experimental Therapy.
Endotoxin (lipopolysaccharide), a component of the Gram-negative bacterial cell wall, is sufficient to initiate the sepsis syndrome. The possibility that specific human immune globulin against conserved regions of lipopolysaccharide might improve survival in Gram-negative rod bacteremia was evaluated in several studies. Human polyclonal antibodies (J5) and two monoclonal antibodies (HA-1A and -E5) were tested. After initial trials were encouraging, subsequent trials failed to confirm any survival advantages from the anti-endotoxin antibodies.

At this time, it appears that the available antibodies to lipopolysaccharide do not have a role in treatment of sepsis, but several other antibodies to lipopolysaccharide have been described and may be tested in the future. Other strategies to block the effects of endotoxin are in developmental phases, including lipopolysaccharide-neutralizing proteins and lipid A analogs, which act as competitive endotoxin antagonists.

New therapies may also be targeted against secondary mediators of inflammation that are generated by the host immune system in response to bacteremia. These targets have the advantage of not being specific to Gram-negative sepsis. Monoclonal antibodies to tumor necrosis factor α are currently in clinical trials. Further studies are needed to confirm their efficacy. Other experimental approaches under investigation include inhibition of interleukin-1 by monoclonal antibodies or receptor antagonists, monoclonal antibodies to interferon gamma, and antagonism of other cytokines that increase the inflammatory response. There is, however, evidence that low levels of tumor necrosis factor α and interferon gamma are protective in endotoxin challenge by inducing tolerance. Therefore, designing new therapies for sepsis may be as complicated as understanding its pathophysiology.

Many other experimental approaches to the treatment of sepsis are under investigation, largely in animal models or early human trials. Opiate inhibitors (naloxone) were not effective in carefully controlled studies. Arachidonate metabolites seem to play a role in septic shock. Thromboxane A_2 and leukotrienes have deleterious effects, whereas prostaglandins may be beneficial. Nonsteroidal antiinflammatory agents inhibit the cyclooxygenase-mediated synthesis of prostaglandins and thromboxanes and are under investigation for their role in therapy; however, direct inhibition of thromboxane may be preferred to preserve prostaglandin synthesis. Ketoconazole is a thromboxane synthetase inhibitor that is currently being investigated. Inhibitors of bradykinin, platelet-activating factor, nitric oxide synthase, and superoxide generation are just a few of the many newer approaches to treatment of sepsis under early investigation. None of these therapies have been shown to have significant clinical benefit.

Recommended Approach

Although many new therapeutic options exist, empiric antibiotic therapy targeted toward the expected pathogens and correction of hemodynamic abnormalities remain the mainstays of therapy of septic shock. An aggressive search for the source of infection should be undertaken because signs of sepsis may be refractory to therapy until the underlying problem is corrected. When a particular pathogen is identified, antibiotic coverage should be narrowed based on the results of susceptibility testing.

FOLLOW-UP

Long-term follow-up is designed for observation and management of the patient's underlying disease(s). The risk of recurrent bacteremia is greater in patients with an intravascular device, undrained abscess, persistent neutropenia, or other serious underlying disease.

DISCUSSION
Prevalence and Incidence

Aerobic organisms that produce bacteremia and shock include Gram-positive cocci (*S. aureus, S. epidermidis,* and streptococci, especially pneumococci), Gram-negative cocci (*Neisseria meningitidis, Neisseria gonorrhoeae*), and Gram-negative bacilli. Strict anaerobic organisms may also cause bacteremia. Perhaps 10% of bacteremias are polymicrobial. Gram-negative rod bacteremia causes 70 to 80% of septic shock episodes. The Gram-negative bacilli that commonly cause bacteremia (in order of frequency) include *Escherichia coli,* the *Klebsiella–Enterobacter–Serratia* group, *Pseudomonas aeruginosa,* and *Proteus* species. Estimates vary, but 80,000 to 200,000 episodes of Gram-negative rod bacteremia with 20,000 to 50,000 deaths occur each year. Gram-negative rod bacteremias are usually secondary to infections at other sites such as surgical wounds, urinary tract infections, and intraabdominal infections. Gram-positive organisms are currently the most common causes of nosocomial bacteremias, in large part due to intravascular device-related infections.

Related Basic Science

Both microbial and host factors are of importance in the pathogenesis of Gram-negative rod infections. Gram-negative rod infections tend to be opportunistic in nature, and commonly occur in the compromised host. Many infections are nosocomial because of their occurrence in ill, aggressively treated, and hospitalized patients. The source of the infecting organisms is usually endogenous (from the patient's own flora), but it may be exogenous. Normal individuals are relatively resistant to these organisms, but changes in bacterial flora (as occur with antibiotics, illness, alcoholism, etc.), foreign bodies that bypass local host defenses, and immunosuppressive or cytotoxic therapy may lead to invasion and serious infection.

Gram-negative bacilli possess a variety of properties that contribute to their ability to cause serious infection, including septicemia. Important virulence factors include the abilities to adhere to mucosal surfaces (which often is a prerequisite for bloodstream invasion), to avoid complement-mediated lysis (serum resistance), and to avoid phagocytosis, often with the assistance of an antiphagocytic capsule. Survival in the bloodstream alone, however, does not explain the often fatal consequences of Gram-negative bacteremia. Some Gram-negative bacilli such as *P. aeruginosa* produce extracellular toxins or enzymes that damage tissue and contribute to virulence. In addition, two cell surface antigens found on Gram-negative bacilli are important: the capsular antigen (K antigen in *E. coli*) and the O antigen (or lipopolysaccharide). The capsular antigen has been postulated to increase virulence both by promoting adherence and by protecting the organism from phagocytosis.

The O (or somatic) antigen is a heat-stable lipopolysaccharide that has been studied extensively because of its immunologic importance and because the molecule possesses endotoxin activity. The lipopolysaccharide has three components: an O-specific polysaccharide of repeated units, a core polysaccharide, and lipid A. The O polysaccharide accounts for the antigenic specificity of the bacterial strain, whereas the core polysaccharide–lipid A complex shows little species-to-species variation. Lipid A is responsible for the endotoxin activity of the molecule, and several lines of evidence suggest that it plays a major role in the pathogenesis of Gram-negative bacteremia. In experimental animals, intact lipopolysaccharide or solubilized lipid A produces fever, hypotension, leukopenia followed by leukocytosis, disseminated intravascular coagulation, complement activation, and shock. When give to human volunteers, endotoxin produces hemodynamic changes similar to those seen with septic shock. In addition, high antibody titers to endotoxin, naturally occurring or produced by immunization with *E. coli* J5 mutants, appear to improve survival in Gram-negative septic shock. The above data suggest that endotoxins are important, but they are by no means the only factors responsible for the manifestations of septic shock. Other bacterial cell wall and cell membrane constituents are probably important, as are a variety of exotoxins, including *Pseudomonas* exotoxin A. As Gram-positive organisms do not contain endotoxin but are quite capable of causing bacteremic shock, factors other than endotoxin must be important. Staphylococcal enterotoxins, toxic shock syndrome toxin 1, and some streptococcal toxins can induce the same inflammatory mediators induced by endotoxin and are capable of producing many of the manifestations of septic shock. These toxins are superantigens and can stimulate the release of a variety of cytokines.

The effects of endotoxin appear to be mediated through the release of a variety of biologically active substances. Recent data suggest that the most important of these mediators may be tumor necrosis factor α or cachectin, which is a cytokine produced by macrophages and other mononuclear cells. In healthy volunteers, endotoxin infusion stimulates a brief but measurable rise in serum tumor necrosis factor α levels followed by the symptoms, fever, and tachycardia suggestive of Gram-negative bacteremia. These symptoms and signs can be produced by infusion of recombinant tumor necrosis factor α alone. In addition, antibody to tumor necrosis factor α given prior to endotoxin challenge prevents many of the expected consequences of endotoxin administration, suggesting that tumor necrosis factor α release is necessary to realize the biologic effects of endotoxin.

Endotoxin also is responsible for the activation of Hageman factor, which can activate the bradykinin system, coagulation cascade, and fibrinolytic system. Bradykinin release produces vasodilation and increased vascular permeability, which may contribute to the decreased vascular resistance and intravascular volume depletion seen with septic shock. Although decreased vascular resistance is initially associated with a hyperdynamic state and increased cardiac output, myocardial function later becomes depressed and cardiac output falls. The specific mediators that impair myocardial performance have not been identified, but a myocardial depressant factor is presumed. Activation of the coagulation and fibrinolytic systems is important in the evolution of the disseminated intravascular coagulation that often accompanies septic shock. Endotoxin can also activate the complement system with resultant increased leukocyte migration and generation of vasodilator substances (anaphylatoxins, especially C5a).

The development of ARDS as a complication of Gram-negative rod bacteremia greatly increases mortality. In this syndrome there is pulmonary microvascular and alveolar epithelial damage, causing increased capillary permeability and subsequent "high-protein" pulmonary edema. Complement activation during bacteremia leads to C5a-mediated aggregation of granulocytes in the pulmonary microvasculature. The ensuing endothelial and lung damage may be related to release of toxic oxygen products by granulocytes and to the action of arachidonate metabolites. Leukopenia, also observed at an early stage of Gram-negative rod bacteremia, presumably reflects the clumping and margination of leukocytes in various vascular sites, including the lung. Whether full-blown ARDS develops during bacteremia (either Gram-positive or Gram-negative) probably depends on the degree of alveolar capillary damage.

Thrombocytopenia is frequently present in Gram-positive and Gram-negative bacteremia. Endotoxin induces platelet aggregation which could contribute to thrombocytopenia in Gram-negative rod bacteremia. Most bacteremic patients with thrombocytopenia do not have evidence of disseminated intravascular coagulation; however, severe thrombocytopenia (<50,000/μL) is generally associated with disseminated intravascular coagulation. Overt disseminated intravascular coagulation is found largely in patients with shock. Endothelial damage, release of platelet factors, production of tumor necrosis factor/cachectin, and activation of the Hageman factor (factor XII) may all play a role in bacteremia-induced disseminated intravascular coagulation.

Activation of the complement system is another consequence of bacteremia. Both the alternative and classic pathways, but especially the former, may be activated in patients who will develop or have developed shock. Complement levels are usually normal in patients with uncomplicated bacteremia.

Natural History and Its Modification with Treatment

The overall mortality in patients with Gram-negative rod bacteremia is 25% and correlates with type and severity of underlying disease and with hemodynamic complications. Factors such as age, granulocytopenia, azotemia, congestive heart failure, diabetes mellitus, nosocomial infections, and prior therapy with antibiotics, corticosteroids, and antimetabolites increase mortality. Bacteremia due to some organisms (e.g., *P. aeruginosa*) is associated with poor prognosis; this in part reflects the propensity of these organisms to infect compromised patients. The presence of established shock with a low cardiac output carries a poor prognosis.

Failure of treatment is often due to the persistence of underlying factors that predispose the patient to bacteremic infection. These factors include foreign bodies (e.g., intravascular lines and devices), abscesses, and unresponsive acute leukemia. Many of the systemic and hemodynamic consequences of septic shock are due to endotoxin or other bacterial products; however, the inflammatory mediators triggered by these substances are produced by the host. Therefore, it is not surprising that the shock syndrome does not always respond to antibiotics alone. In fact, antibiotics sometimes precipitate early clinical deterioration by causing endotoxin release as they injure the microbe.

Prevention

Measures that may reduce the likelihood of nosocomial infections, including bacteremia, are aseptic technique for catheter insertion and other invasive procedures, avoidance of cross-contamination, and wise use of antimicrobial agents. Antibiotic prophylaxis in certain high-risk groups (especially neutropenic patients) continues to be a subject for study.

Cost Containment

The major effective means of cost containment are the efforts to decrease infection in hospitalized patients by the judicious use of antimicrobial agents, immunosuppressive therapy, invasive procedures, and compliance with infection control protocols. An unnecessary intravenous device left in place longer than required not only dramatically increases the cost of care, but also places the patient at risk for secondary infections or other complications that could also jeopardize outcome and require even more expensive hospitalization and therapy. If early manifestations of infection are recognized, rapid institution of treatment may prevent the development of septic shock.

REFERENCES

ACCP/SCCM Consensus Conference Committee. American College of Chest Physicians/Society of Critical Care Medicine Consensus Conference: Definitions for sepsis and organ failure and guidelines for the use of innovative therapies in sepsis. Crit Care Med 1992;20:864.

Bone R. Sepsis syndrome: New insights into its pathogenesis and treatment. Infect Dis Clin North Am 1991;5:793.

Lynn WA, Cohen J. Adjunctive therapy for septic shock: A review of experimental approaches. Clin Infect Dis 1995;20:143.

Parillo JA. Mechanisms of disease: Pathogenetic mechanisms of septic shock. N Engl J Med 1993;20:1471.

Weinstein MP, Teller LB, Murphy JR, et al. The clinical significance of positive blood cultures: A comprehensive analysis of 500 episodes of bacteremia and fungemia in adults. I. Laboratory and epidemiologic observations. Rev Infect Dis 1983;5:35.

Fever of Unknown Origin of Long Duration

Jonas A. Shulman, M.D.

DEFINITION

A temperature remaining about 38.3°C (101°F) for more than 2 weeks and unexplained after a week of thorough evaluation in a hospital is defined as a fever of unknown origin of long duration.

ETIOLOGY

Fever of unknown origin of long duration as defined above may be caused by an infectious process (bacterial or viral), neoplastic disease, connective tissue disease and arteritis, or drugs, or may be factitious in origin (Table 8–3–1).

CRITERIA FOR DIAGNOSIS

See Definition.

CLINICAL MANIFESTATIONS

Subjective

The patient may complain of feeling hot, sweating, malaise, headache, myalgias, and chills or chilly feelings. Other subjective manifestations are largely related to the specific cause of the fever. A discussion of these causes can be found under Plans, Diagnostic.

Objective

The temperature is above 38.3°C (101°F). The objective findings, including abnormalities in the routine laboratory examination, are determined by the cause of the fever (see below).

PLANS

Diagnostic

Differential Diagnosis

See Table 8–3–1.

Diagnostic Options and Recommended Approach

See Table 8–3–1. The following is a compendium of causes of fever of unknown origin. The rapidity and invasiveness of the workup depend on the clinical state of the patient, the amount of weight loss, and the clinical clues present. This list should be used to reiterate the common etiologies of fevers of unknown etiology and demonstrate the studies most likely to allow for diagnosis when that etiology is suspected. This list should be used only as a guide to remind the clinician of appropriate studies if the clinical data suggest that a given entity is a likely cause of the patient's problem. Each workup should be distinctly individualized.

In general, the diagnostic plans include history, physical examination, sigmoidoscopy, complete blood count, routine chemistries, rapid plasma reagin test, blood and urine cultures, and chest x-ray. If significant skin lesions or enlarged lymph nodes are seen, a biopsy may be indicated. Intravenous pyelography and a gallbladder study are relatively noninvasive techniques that might be done at this phase of the evaluation. If no diagnostic clues are forthcoming from the preceding studies, more sophisticated serologic or microbiologic studies may be ordered. Biopsies of the liver, bone marrow, and/or temporal artery may be appropriate. Various radiographic and/or nuclear medicine studies may be indicated, such as gallium and bone scanning, abdominal and pelvic ultrasonography, sinus x-rays, dental x-rays, gastrointestinal x-rays or endoscopy, and body computed scanning. If significant fever persists and a downhill course continues, laparoscopy and/or laparotomy may be required, although at times observation or specific therapeutic trials (e.g.,

for tuberculosis or amebiasis) may be justified. Careful consideration of possible factitious fever or iatrogenic fever is indicated in all phases of the workup, especially in health care workers.

Therapeutic

Treat the specific cause when found. Avoid nonspecific therapy, as this can delay the eventual diagnosis.

The patient must be instructed about the many etiologies to be considered and the difficult workup that may be needed to determine the etiology of the fever. The patient needs to have explained the necessity of making a specific diagnosis to allow for specific therapy. The length of time required to make a diagnosis and the large number of tests needed require the physician to be very supportive of the patients and his or her family, as there usually is a great deal of anxiety involved with all concerned.

FOLLOW-UP

Follow-up depends entirely on the determined etiology. If none can be found, then repeated reviews of history and physical examination leading to selected tests and, at times, therapeutic trials are required.

DISCUSSION

Prevalence and Incidence

Fever of unknown origin of long duration as defined here is relatively uncommon when compared with fever of unknown cause of short duration. This is true because fever of short duration is often caused by a self-limiting infection, viral or bacterial, even though the exact etiology is not proven.

Related Basic Science

Fever is a product of a complex neurovascular response regulated by the hypothalamus. Endotoxin, bacteria, viruses, 5α-H, 3β-OH steroids, antigen–antibody complexes, and delayed hypersensitivity are among the many triggers that can stimulate the release of endogenous mediators from monocytes and tissue macrophages. These endogenous pyrogens, including interleukin-1, tumor necrosis factor (cachectin), and certain interferons are low-molecular-weight proteins capable of stimulating the hypothalamic temperature regulatory center. They appear to act at least in part by causing increased prostaglandin E and F stimulation in the central nervous system. Thus, many infections and noninfectious stimuli may act through a single mechanism in causing a febrile response. Other stimulants of increased metabolic activity such as epinephrine release, seizure activity, exercise, and increased thyroid hormone can also cause an elevation in temperature. There are increasing data to suggest that fever may be beneficial to the host in the control of infection.

Natural History and Its Modification with Treatment

The natural history of the fever is determined by the cause of the problem. Ten to twenty percent of long-term fevers remain undiagnosed. Some of these resolve spontaneously. With long-term follow-up, others eventually are diagnosed as new symptoms or findings appear. Collagen diseases, factitious fevers, lymphomas, chronic granulomatous disease of the liver, and some chronic viral infections such as cytomegalovirus, Epstein–Barr virus, and HIV infection may become more obvious during follow-up evaluations. Of all the cases of fever of unknown origin that are eventually diagnosed, about one third are proven to be infectious, one third due to malignancy, and one third due to connective tissue diseases.

TABLE 8–3–1. DIFFERENTIAL DIAGNOSIS OF FEVER OF UNKNOWN ORIGIN

Diagnostic Possibility	Diagnostic Tests or Observations
Systemic infections	
Tuberculosis	PPD; chest x-ray; liver tests; bone marrow and liver biopsy with appropriate smears and cultures; if chest infiltrate is present, a transbronchial biopsy, lavage, or open lung biopsy may be helpful; urine cultures for tuberculosis. Note that in AIDS, atypical mycobacterial infection is especially common. See Chapter 13–41.
Infective endocarditis	Blood cultures × 3 for aerobes, anaerobes, and fungi; echocardiography; Q fever serology. See Chapter 8–12.
Bacterial infections	
Salmonellosis	Blood, stool, and urine cultures; *Salmonella typhi* serology
Brucellosis	Blood and bone marrow cultures; *Brucella* serology, including *B. canis*
Tularemia	Tularemia serology
Yersiniosis	Blood and stool cultures (notify laboratory before submitting); *Yersinia* serology
Borreliosis	Wright's strain of peripheral smear during febrile episode
Psittacosis	Psittacosis serology
Fungal infection	
Histoplasmosis, coccidioidomycosis, blastomycosis and cryptococcosis	Biopsy with smear and culture of skin lesions, bone marrow, liver; lumbar puncture with cerebrospinal fluid cultures and serology; serology for appropriate antibody and antigen; chest x-ray with sputum cultures; if an infiltrate is present, transbronchial or open lung biopsy; urine cultures for fungi
Parasitic infestation	
Amebiasis	Stool for ova and parasites; sigmoidoscopy with smears and biopsy if appropriate; liver tests; chest x-ray; liver scan; amebic serology. See Chapters 8–58, 8–60, and 8–64.
Malaria and *Borrelia recurrentis*	Thick and thin smears for malaria parasites; *B. recurrentis* serology. See Chapter 8–61.
Toxoplasmosis	Lymph node biopsy can be highly suggestive; *Toxoplasma* serology (IgG and IgM antibody). See Chapter 8–62.
Viral infections	
Cytomegalovirus	WBC may be decreased and differential may show increased lymphocytes and atypical lymphocytes; abnormal liver tests; culture of blood and urine for virus; liver biopsy and search for inclusions; CMV serology— IgG and IgM. See Chapter 8–71.
Epstein–Barr virus	Monospot test; WBC and differential showing increased lymphocytes and atypical lymphocytes; specific EBV serology; abnormal liver tests.
HIV-1, HIV-2	HIV-1 serology (ELISA and Western blot); WBC and especially lymphocytes may be decreased; helper T cells decreased; skin test anergy common. HIV-2 serology may be needed, especially in patients from Africa. Prolonged fever may be due not only to the virus itself but also to the multiple opportunistic infections such as toxoplasmosis, atypical tuberculosis, pneumocystis pneumonia, and other infections, and by tumors such as lymphomas that are frequently seen in these patients. See Chapter 8–76.
Localized infections	
Right upper quadrant infections (liver abscess, cholecystitis, or cholangitis; empyema of the gallbladder)	See Chapter 8–21.
Intraabdominal abscesses (pancreatic, subphrenic, subhepatic, appendiceal, rectal, diverticular, splenic, perirectal, tubo-ovarian)	See Chapter 8–21.
Genitourinary tract (perinephric or intrarenal abscess, prostatic abscess; ureteral obstruction with infection; pyelonephritis)	See Chapter 8–23.
Sinusitis	See Chapter 21–29.
Osteomyelitis	See Chapter 8–27.
Intravascular infection other than endocarditis	Search for aneurysms, prosthesis, or arteriovenous fistulas
Neoplasms	
Benign: atrial myxoma	Echocardiogram. See Chapter 15–59.
Malignant: Reticuloendothelial cell tumors; lymphomas; Hodgkin's disease	See Chapter 12–24.
Hematologic: acute leukemias	See Chapter 12–31.
Metastatic: any source, especially if liver metastasis present	
Solid localized tumors: liver, pancreas, stomach, kidney, lung with infection behind an obstructing lesion	See Section 3.
Connective tissue diseases	
Systemic lupus erythematosus	See Chapter 7–1.
Rheumatoid arthritis (especially juvenile variant)	
Polyarteritis nodosa	
Allergic vasculitis	
Polymyalgia rheumatica	
Giant cell arteritis	
Rheumatic fever	
Miscellaneous	
Factitious or autogenic fever	Look for pulse–temperature dissociation; absence of normal diurnal variation; normal temperature of a freshly voided urine specimen; high fever with no sweats or chills; frequent occurrence in health care personnel; unusual polymicrobial bacteremias without an obvious source
Familial Mediterranean fever	Obtain family history of Sephardic Jewish, Arab, or Armenian background; high sedimentation rate and fibrinogen with febrile episodes associated with bouts of polyserositis

(continued)

TABLE 8–3–1. (*Continued*)

Diagnostic Possibility	Diagnostic Tests or Observations
Alcoholic hepatitis	See Chapters 19–75 to 19–77.
Thyroiditis	See Chapter 9–15.
Addison's disease	See Chapter 9–11.
Drug fever	Check all medications.
Pelvic thrombophlebitis	See Chapter 15–70.
Multiple pulmonary emboli	See Chapter 15–57.
Whipple's disease	See Chapter 19–42.
Inflammatory bowel disease	See Chapters 20–73 and 20–74.
Regional enteritis	See Chapters 19–52 and 19–53.
Ulcerative colitis	See Chapter 19–53.
Sarcoidosis	See Chapter 13–37.
Wegener's granulomatosis	See Chapter 7–9. A new serologic test, the antineutrophilia cytoplasmic antibody test, may be helpful in making this diagnosis, along with appropriate sinus and chest x-rays, renal studies, and biopsy of involved tissues.

LP, lumbar puncture; CSF, cerebrospinal fluid; CMV, cytomegalovirus; WBC, white blood cell count; EBV, Epstein–Barr virus.

Prevention

The prevention of fever of unknown origin depends on the preventability of the specific disease causing the fever.

Cost Containment

Great care in the workup of a long-term fever of unknown origin is needed. One must establish a very careful data base and update it frequently so that a carefully tailored laboratory approach is developed for the patient rather than a nondirected approach that can lead to almost every laboratory study now available. For example, atypical lymphocytosis should lead initially to a workup for Epstein–Barr virus mononucleosis, cytomegalovirus infection, acute HIV infection, or toxoplasmosis and not to a computed axial tomography scan of the abdomen.

REFERENCES

Dinarello CA, Cannon JG, Wolff SM. New concepts on the pathogenesis of fever. Rev Infect Dis 1988;10:168.

Esposito AL, Gleckman RA. A diagnostic approach to the adult with fever of unknown origin. Arch Intern Med 1979;139:575.

Jacoby GA, Swartz MN. Fever of unexplained origin. N Engl J Med 1973;289:1407.

Larson EB, Featherstone HJ, Petersdorf RG. Prolonged fever of unknown origin: diagnosis and followup of 105 cases, 1970–1980. Medicine (Baltimore) 1982;61:269.

Mackowiak PA, LeMaistre CF. Drug fever: A critical appraisal of conventional concepts. Ann Intern Med 1987;106:728.

Petersdorf RG, Beeson RB. Fever of unexplained origin: Report on 100 cases. Medicine (Baltimore) 1961;40:1.

CHAPTER 8–4

Fever Appearing in a Hospitalized Patient

Rafael L. Jurado, M.D., and John E. McGowan, Jr., M.D.

DEFINITION

Fever appearing in a hospitalized patient is defined as a rectal temperature above 100.8°F (38.2°C) that develops on or after the second hospitalization day.

ETIOLOGY

The vast majority of fevers appearing in hospitalized patients are infectious in origin (nosocomial infections) (Table 8–4–1). Nonetheless, it is important to consider noninfectious etiologies (Table 8–4–2).

CRITERIA FOR DIAGNOSIS

Suggestive

The nonspecific signs and symptoms of a febrile process, added to the occasionally specific complaints and findings of the disorders outlined in Tables 8–4–1 and 8–4–2, may suggest the etiology of fever in the hospitalized patient.

Definitive

See tables 8–4–1 and 8–4–2.

CLINICAL MANIFESTATIONS

See Table 8–4–1.

PLANS

Diagnostic

Differential Diagnosis

There are several important noninfectious causes of fever. For diagnostic considerations of processes causing fever in a hospitalized patient, see Tables 8–4–1 and 8–4–2 and the specific chapters.

Diagnostic Options

The same general diagnostic considerations apply as for a patient who develops fever outside the hospital, but the distribution of the likelihood of specific entities is somewhat different. It is important to remember that some infectious processes can have incubation periods exceeding the arbitrary limit of 2 days as stated under Definition. Thus, some patients fitting the definition may be developing the clinical manifestations of an infectious process acquired prior to their hospitaliza-

TABLE 8–4–1. INFECTIOUS CAUSES OF FEVER IN THE HOSPITALIZED PATIENT

Likely Diagnostic Possibility	Diagnostic Tests or Observations
Intravascular therapy sepsis	Inspect cannula site. Remove and semiquantitatively culture cannula. Culture fluid if contamination is likely.
Infected prosthesis	If patient has had surgery, review the record and determine if a prosthesis has been placed. If fever fails to respond quickly to antibiotics, and infection is suspected, attention to a possible infected prosthesis is required. If an infected heart valve is suspected, echocardiography including transesophageal echocardiography may be helpful.
Nosocomial bacteriuria (especially if patient has been catheterized)	Examine and culture urine for bacteria and yeast.
Lower respiratory infection associated with ventilator therapy	Culture fluid containers on ventilatory equipment if more than one case. Discontinue ventilation therapy if possible.
Aspiration pneumonia	See Chapter 8–14.
Surgical wound infection	Inspect wound for erythema, pus, etc. Culture wound drainage if present. If need be, search for deep abscess with appropriate scans.
Postperfusion syndrome	See Chapters 8–71 and 8–73 (cytomegalovirus and Epstein–Barr virus).

TABLE 8–4–2. NONINFECTIOUS CAUSES OF FEVER IN THE HOSPITALIZED PATIENT

Likely Diagnostic Possibility	Diagnostic Tests or Observations
Drug reaction	Review drug list and discontinue all medications not absolutely necessary, especially those newly prescribed. Consider Jarisch–Herxheimer reaction in appropriate infections (see Chapter 8–79).
Noninfectious inflammatory diseases (arthritis, phlebitis, etc.)	See Section 6 and Chapter 15–70.
Ischemia (stroke, extremity)	See Chapters 15–69 and 20–19.
Anesthesia-induced fever (including malignant hyperthermia)	Review chart for operative record (if any).
Atelectasis following surgery	Examine chest. Review chest posteroanterior and lateral x-ray films.
Phlebitis due to intravascular therapy	Inspect site of intravascular catheters.
Transfusion reaction	Discontinue administration of blood product. Culture product if microbial contamination is suspected.
Pulmonary embolus	See Chapter 15–57.
Postcardiotomy syndrome	Examine chart for history of chest or cardiac surgery. Examine chest for pleural or pericardial rub, and electrocardiogram for evidence of pericarditis. See Chapter 15–54.
Neoplastic disease	Examine chart for presence and relationship to therapy. Fever is more likely in lymphoma and leukemia. Diagnosis is one of exclusion after evaluation for infection.

tion. Among infectious etiologies, the most frequent ones are those of the urinary and respiratory tract.

Recommended Approach

See Tables 8–4–1 and 8–4–2.

Therapeutic

Therapeutic Options

Specific therapy depends on the cause of the fever. If the patient develops hypotension or other manifestations of sepsis, empiric antimicrobial therapy may be required for suspected bacterial infection. In this situation, treatment with a combination of a β-lactam drug such as ticarcillin– clavulanic acid and an aminoglycoside would be appropriate, as the usual bacterial pathogens involved in nosocomial infection are *Staphylococcus aureus*, enterococci, or Gram-negative bacilli. Organisms causing nosocomial infection are frequently resistant to many commonly used antimicrobial agents. Vancomycin must be added to the empiric regimen when *S. aureus* or coagulase-negative staphylococcal strains resistant to methicillin and similar drugs are prevalent.

In leukopenic patients, empiric therapy with a β-lactam drug with antipseudomonal activity (piperacillin, ceftazidime, imipenem, etc.) plus an aminoglycoside is warranted, as *Pseudomonas aeruginosa* is a possible pathogen. Knowledge of the pattern of likely pathogens and their susceptibilities in a specific hospital is necessary to choose appropriate therapy.

Antipyretics are not routinely administered because they may obscure the fever pattern. Most important in therapy is removal of predisposing catheters and other devices (see Table 8–4–1).

Recommended Approach

Specific therapeutic options are strongly influenced by the highest diagnostic possibilities outlined in Tables 8–4–1 and 8–4–2. If the patient develops hypotension or other manifestations of sepsis, empiric antibiotics may be required, according to the suspected site of origin of sepsis. In selecting antibiotics for suspected nosocomial infections, strong consideration must be given to the sensitivity patterns for the suspected microorganisms in the particular hospital. Such records are usually available from the microbiology laboratory. Removal of suspected catheters and other predisposing devices is an important diagnostic (culture of the device may yield important etiologic information) and

therapeutic consideration. Antipyretics are not to be routinely administered because they may obscure the evolution of the fever and its response to the therapeutic interventions.

FOLLOW-UP

Follow-up depends on the specific entity involved.

DISCUSSION

Prevalence and Incidence

It is not possible to quote prevalence and incidence figures for the variety of disorders mentioned in Tables 8–4–1 and 8–4–2. Suffice it to say that nosocomial infections occur in approximately 2 million patients per year, with related costs of more than $2 billion.

Related Basic Science

For discussion of fever itself, see Chapters 8–3, 8–5, and 8–6.

Natural History and Its Modification with Treatment

It is dependent on the specific entity involved.

Prevention

Proper use of instruments and rigid adherence to procedures in the hospital are the best means of decreasing the likelihood of many of the entities listed in Table 8–4–1. In addition, only drugs that are absolutely necessary should be prescribed, as drug allergy is one of the major causes of fever in a hospitalized patient. Proper use of isolation precautions can also decrease the likelihood of cross-infections in the hospital.

Cost Containment

The prevention of infections in hospitalized patients is the only way to decrease the cost.

REFERENCES

Bur DH, Makadon HJ, Friedland G, et al. Fever in hospitalized mental patients: Characteristics and significance. J Gen Intern Med 1988;3:119.

Filice GA, Weiler MD, Hughes RA, Gerding DN. Nosocomial febrile illnesses in patients on an internal medicine service. Arch Intern Med 1989;149:319.

Garibaldi RA, Brodine S, Matsumiya S, Coleman M. Evidence for the noninfectious etiology of early postoperative fever. Infect Control 1985;6:273.

Leibovici L, Cohen O, Wysenbeek AJ. Occult bacterial infection in adults with unexplained fever: Validation of a diagnostic index. Arch Intern Med 1990;150:1270.

McGowan JE Jr, Rose RC, Jacobs NF, et al. Fever in hospitalized patients. Am J Med 1987;82:580.

Talbot GH, Provencher M, Cassileth PA. Persistent fever after recovery from granulocytopenia in acute leukemia. Arch Intern Med 1988;148:129.

CHAPTER 8–5

Fever and Rash

Nigel J. Raymond, M.D., David S. Stephens, M.D., and Thomas F. Sellers, Jr., M.D.

DEFINITION

This symptom–sign complex is defined as the simultaneous or related occurrence of fever reaching or exceeding 38°C and rash of unidentified cause. (Localized skin lesions such as furuncles or infected injuries with resultant fever are not considered in this chapter.)

ETIOLOGY

Rash with fever is a manifestation of many infectious diseases, some noninfectious systemic diseases, and a few primary dermatoses.

CLINICAL MANIFESTATIONS

Subjective

The patient may complain of the usual symptoms accompanying fever: feeling hot, sweating, chills or chilly feelings, headache, muscle aching, easy fatigability. The patient may or may not notice a rash or may complain of itching, stinging, or tenderness of the affected skin areas.

Objective

Most of the objective data are determined by the specific cause of the fever and rash. Although fever is usually confirmed by measurement of an elevated temperature and many skin rashes are immediately evident, there are rashes that may not be obvious at the time fever is noted. Frequent careful inspection may be necessary to detect them.

PLANS

Diagnostic

Early diagnosis of fever and rash may benefit the patient and prevent spread. Examples are infections requiring early treatment to reduce the high morbidity and mortality of untreated or late-treated cases (e.g., Rocky Mountain spotted fever and meningococcemia). There are also situations in which an early diagnosis may prevent or minimize the exposure of susceptible contacts to a contagious infection (e.g., varicella or rubella). It is important, therefore, to search for an early rash in patients with fever and to look for it in the anatomic areas where such lesions usually first occur.

Many rashes begin as erythematous macules, before the lesions take on a more characteristic form or distribution. At this early stage one must rely on other clinical features and epidemiologic circumstances for clues to their etiology. Later, the evolving stages of the rash may suggest a specific etiology as listed in Table 8–5–1.

The cause of the fever-rash illness may be suggested by other clinical features, such as the presence of rash in a particular anatomic location or by associated involvement of other organs, as shown in Table 8–5–2. Table 8–5–3 summarizes the most important considerations in evaluating fever and rashes and includes a brief outline of diagnostic plans. For more detail, refer to the chapters on specific diseases.

Therapeutic

The key to successful therapy is early correct diagnosis. Antibiotics may be required before the etiology is confirmed, but it should be possible to secure material for appropriate cultures and other diagnostic procedures before beginning treatment. For treatment, see the chapters on specific diseases.

If the disease suspected is communicable, the physician should inform the patient and his or her contacts of the risk and provide them with the measures necessary to prevent spread to others. When the cause of a fever and rash is determined to be a reportable disease, the cause should be reported to the local public health authorities.

FOLLOW-UP

See the specific chapters for the diseases listed in Table 8–5–1.

DISCUSSION

Prevalence and Incidence

Fever and rash are very common.

Related Basic Science

Exanthems may result from the presence of causative microorganisms in the skin or as manifestations of immune reactions to the pathogen. The former mechanism may afford practical diagnostic information through the identification of the organism in the skin lesions, as in cases of vesicular rash of herpes simplex and varicella–zoster viruses (by means of a Tzanck test), Rocky Mountain spotted fever (immunofluorescence in tissue from the skin lesions), and meningococcemia (Gram stain showing Gram-negative diplococci).

Exanthems secondary to immune mechanisms can be further classified according to the Coombs–Gell pattern of immune reactions as follows:

- *Type I* (immediate mitogen–antibody reaction mediated by immunoglobulin E). A prototype situation is the urticarial rash that may follow administration of an antibiotic (most commonly penicillin) to an already febrile patient.
- *Type III* (immune complex disease). A serum sickness reaction, either secondary to an infectious agent (hepatitis B virus, prodromal phase) or following administration of certain antimicrobial agents. Fever may be due to serum sickness itself or to a preexisting febrile illness for which the antibiotic was given.
- *Type IV* (cell-mediated immunity, delayed hypersensitivity). This type of reaction appears to be essential for the rash of vaccinia and other vesicular eruptions.

For details and references on specific diseases, please see the corresponding chapters.

TABLE 8–5–1. EVOLVING PATTERNS OF FEBRILE RASHES AND POSSIBLE ETIOLOGIES

Macular → Papular
Brucellosis
Colorado tick fever
Dengue
Drug allergy
Enterovirus infection
Erythema chronicum migrans
Erythema infectiosum
Gonococcemia
Gram-negative bacillemia
Herpes simplex
Herpes zoster
HIV infection
Infectious mononucleosis
Leptospirosis
Listeriosis
Measles, typical and "atypical"
Meningococcemia
Miliariasis
Rat bite fever *(Streptobacillus moniliformis)*
Rickettsialpox
Rocky Mountain spotted fever
Roseola infantum
Rubella
Sarcoid
Staphylococcal toxic shock (late)
Syphilis, secondary
Systemic lupus erythematosus
Toxoplasmosis
Typhoid
Typhus, murine and epidemic
Varicella

Macular → Papular → Vesicular (or Bullous)
Ecthyma grangrenosum
Erysipelas
Erythema multiforme
Gonococcemia
Hand, foot, and mouth disease (Coxsackie A)
Herpangina
Herpes simplex
Herpes zoster
Measles, "atypical"
Miliariasis
Rat bite fever *(Streptobacillus moniliformis)*
Rickettsialpox
Staphylococcus aureus bacteremia
Varicella
Vibrio vulnificus primary septicemia

Macular → Petechial
Colorado tick fever
Coxsackievirus infection (types A9, B2, B3, B4, B5)
Echovirus infection (types 3, 4, 9)
Gonococcemia
Gram-negative bacillemia
Hemorrhagic fever
Measles, typical (rare) and "atypical"
Meningococcemia
Relapsing fever
Respiratory syncytial virus infection
Rocky Mountain spotted fever
Scarlet fever
Staphylococcal toxic shock
Staphylococcus aureus bacteremia

Typhus, murine and epidemic
Viral hepatitis

Macular → Petechial → Purpuric
Brazilian purpuric fever *(hemophilus influenzae* infection)
Brucellosis
Dengue
Gram-negative rod bacillemia
Hemorrhagic fever (nondengue)
Measles, typical (rare) and "atypical"
Meningococcemia
Rocky Mountain spotted fever
Typhus, epidemic
Vasculitis
Wegener's granulomatosis

Diffuse Erythema → Macular
Drug allergy
HIV infection
Infectious mononucleosis
Kawasaki disease
Keratoconjunctivitis sicca
Necrolytic migratory erythema
Respiratory syncytial virus infection
Scarlet fever
Staphylococcal scalded-skin syndrome
Staphylococcal toxic shock
Still's disease

Localized Erythematous Patches
Acute febrile neutrophilic dermatosis
Dermatomyositis
Erysipelas
Erysipeloid
Erythema chronicum migrans (Lyme disease)
Erythema infectiosum
Familial Mediterranean fever
Kawasaki disease
Leptospirosis (Fort Bragg or pretibial fever)
Sarcoidosis

Erythema → Macular Petechial
Corynebacterium hemolyticum infection
Drug allergy
Infectious mononucleosis
Scarlet fever
Staphylococcal toxic shock

Erythema → Vesicular (or Bullous)
Acute febrile neutrophilic dermatosis
Erysipelas
Erythema multiforme
Graft-versus-host disease
Miliaria
Mycoplasma pneumoniae infection
Staphylococcal scalded-skin syndrome
Zinc deficiency

Erythematous Nodule
Acne fulminans
Erythema nodosum

Skin Necrosis
Brazilian hemorrhagic fever
Gram-negative sepsis
Meningococcemia
Rocky Mountain spotted fever

TABLE 8–5–2. FEVER AND RASH: ADDITIONAL FEATURES

Palm–Sole Involvement
Atypical measles (rubeola)
Drug reaction
Erythema multiforme
Hand, foot, and mouth disease (echovirus)
Kawasaki disease
Rocky Mountain spotted fever
Syphilis, secondary
Toxic shock syndrome

Rash Predominantly on Extremities
Allergic purpura
Brucellosis
Erythema nodosum
Gonococcemia
Parvovirus (reticular)
Pyoderma gangrenosum
Rocky Mountain spotted fever

Lymphadenopathy
Generalized
  Drug reaction (serum sickness)
  Infectious mononucleosis
  Sarcoidosis
  Syphilis, secondary
  Systemic lupus erythematosus
  Toxoplasmosis
Cervical
  Kawasaki disease
  Rubella
  Scarlet fever
Hilar
  Atypical measles (rubeola)
  Sarcoidosis
Local
  Cat scratch fever
  Tularemia

Desquamation
Arcanobacterium hemolyticum infection
Drug allergy
Graft-versus-host disease
Kawasaki disease
Measles
Necrolytic migratory erythema
Rocky Mountain spotted fever
Scarlet fever
Toxic shock syndrome

Mucosal Membrane Lesions (enanthems)
Herpes simplex
Infectious mononucleosis (palatal petechiae)

Kawasaki disease (strawberry tongue)
Measles (Koplik's spots)
Rubella (Forscheimer's spots)
Scarlet fever (strawberry tongue)
Toxic shock syndrome (strawberry tongue)

Ulcerative or Vesicular Stomatitis
Hand, foot, and mouth disease
Herpes simplex
Histoplasmosis
Inflammatory bowel disease
Syphilis, secondary
Systemic lupus erythematosus

Meningitis
Cryptococcosis
Enteroviral meningitis
HIV infection
Leptospirosis
Meningococcemia
Rocky Mountain spotted fever
Syphilis, secondary

Pulmonary Infiltrate
Adenovirus (types 7, 7a)
Atypical measles (rubeola)
Blastomycosis
Coccidioidomycosis
Cryptococcosis
Fat embolism
Herpes simplex virus 1
Histoplasmosis
Mycoplasma pneumoniae infection
Neisseria meningitidis
Psittacosis
Rocky Mountain spotted fever
Sarcoidosis
Varicella–zoster virus

Arthritis or Arthralgia
Allergic purpura
Disseminated gonococcal infection
Erythema chronicum migrans (Lyme disease)
Erythema marginatum (acute rheumatic fever)
Hepatitis B virus, prodromal phase
Parvovirus B19 (especially in adults)
Reiter's syndrome
Rubella
Still's disease
Systemic lupus erythematosus

Natural History and Its Modification with Treatment

See specific chapter on the disease listed in Table 8–5–1.

Prevention

See specific chapter on the disease listed in Table 8–5–1.

Cost Containment

See specific chapter on the disease listed in Table 8–5–1.

REFERENCES

Ariza J, Servitze O, Pallarés R, et al. Characteristic cutaneous lesions in patients with brucellosis. Arch Dermatol 1989;125:380.
Cherry JD. Contemporary infectious exanthems. Clin Infect Dis 1993;16:199.
Mawhorter SD, Effron D, Blinkhorn R, Spagnuolo PJ. Cutaneous manifestations of toxoplasmosis. Clin Infect Dis 1992;14:1084.
Seifert MH, Warin AP, Miller A. Articular and cutaneous manifestations of gonorrhoea: Review of sixteen cases. Ann Rheum Dis 1974;33:140.

TABLE 8–5–3. CAUSES OF FEVER AND RASH

	Type of Rash (→ indicates progression)	Where to Look Early	When Rash May First Appear after Fever Begins	Diagnostic Tests	Remarks
Treatable Causes of Fever and Rash When Early Diagnosis Is Important to the Patient					
Brazilian purpuric fever (*Hemophilus influenzae*, biogroup *aegyptius*)	Macular→purpuric→ necrotic	Face, extremities	2–3 d	Cultures (blood)	Often follows 2–3 d after acute conjunctivitis; disease seen only in tropics so far, but the organism occurs in the United States
Brucellosis	Erythema→papular→ purpuric or nodule	Trunk, legs; spares face	Variable	Cultures, serology	Especially with *Brucella melitensis;* rash with original presentation or relapse
(*Arcanobacterium*) *Corynebacterium hemolyticum* infection	Blanching erythema→ petechiae→ desquamation; erythema multiforme	Trunk, limbs	1–2 d	Cultures	Cause of acute pharyngitis in young adults; mimics scarlet fever
Erysipelas (*Streptococcus pyogenes*)	Spreading, raised, well-demarcated erythema, marked edema→central vesicular and crusting	Face (cheeks and nose), rare elsewhere	Hours	Clinical, response to antibiotic; culture from advancing border of skin lesions	Predominant intradermal localization; usually marked systemic toxicity
Erythema chronicum migrant (Lyme disease, *Borrelia burgdorferi*)	Single or several lesions; macules or papules→ spreading warm erythema with central clearing	Proximal extremities or trunk	Variable, but rash and fever usually simultaneous	Clinical; epidemiology, serology	Tick borne; in later stages arthritis common; nerve palsies, meningitis, cardiac conduction defects seen; relapses common
Gonococcemia (*Neisseria gonorrhoeae*)	Macular or purpuric spot →papular→vesicular→ grayish pustule; tender; hemorrhage common	Pressure points on elbows, knees, ankles, knuckles; occurs primarily on extremities	Varies, 2–7 d	Smears from skin lesions; cultures from pustules, blood, joints, urethra, rectum, throat	Single or multiple arthritis almost always present; occasional tenosynovitis; two thirds of cases are in women
Gram-negative bacteria a. Sepsis	Macular→papular or macular→petechial→ purpuric→necrotic	Isolated lesions anywhere, especially on trunk	Hours	Blood culture; urine or pus culture	Due to many species of Gram-negative bacteria from gastrointestinal, respiratory tracts, skin; often compromised host
b. Ecthyma gangrenosum	Macular→indurated nodule→large hemorrhagic vesicle→central necrosis→ulcer	Anogenital region, axillae, groin	1–2 d	Blood culture, biopsy	Usually compromised host; due to *Pseudomonas aeruginosa;* sometimes other Gram-negative bacteria
Leptospira spp. a. Leptosporosis	Macules→maculopapular	Head, neck, trunk, arms	3–4 d	Serology; cultures of blood, urine, CSF; muscle biopsy in first week	Rash uncommon; conjunctivitis common; aseptic meningitis may develop
b. Fort Bragg fever ("pretibial fever")	Symmetrical raised, erythematous	Pretibial areas	3–4 d	Serology; cultures of blood, urine, CSF	Due to *Leptospira autumnalis;* splenomegaly in 90% of cases
Listeria "granulomatosis infantiseptica" (*Listeria monocytogenes*)	Maculopapular (infants) ulcers and tiny cutaneous granulomas	Trunk, extremities, pharynx	Variable; rash may precede fever	Cultures of skin, blood, CSF; Gram stain of meconium, skin lesions, or eyes	Transplacental infections; disseminated abscesses or granulomas; early treatment imperative
Meningococcemia (*Neisseria meningitidis*)	Macular/maculopapular→ petechial→purpuric→ sometimes gangrene	Isolated lesions anywhere	1–2 h	CSF Gram stain latex; cultures of CSF, blood	Meningitis, arthralgia common; rash progresses rapidly; rarely chronic relapsing or illness
Mycoplasma pneumoniae infection	Multiple rash forms described; some macular→papular→ vesicular; may be associated with erythema multiforme, major or minor	General; extremities, trunk, face	Variable, up to 14 d	Serology; culture of respiratory tract	Other rashes described include erythema, scaling, pityriasis, rosacea-like lesions, urticaria, and erythema nodosum; majority have no rash
Psittacosis–ornithosis (*Chlamydia psittaci*)	Pale macules (blanching), "Horder's spots"	Upper abdomen, thorax, lower midback	Second week	Serology	Rash similar to typical "rose spots"; associated with pneumonitis; exposure to birds

(continued)

TABLE 8–5–3. *(Continued)*

	Type of Rash (→ indicates progression)	Where to Look Early	When Rash May First Appear after Fever Begins	Diagnostic Tests	Remarks
Rat bite fever a. Due to *Spirillum minus*	Reddish brown macules, resembling rose spots of typhoid or "blotchy violaceous"	Spreading from site of rat bite→trunk→ extremities	Variable	Clinical; dark field; animal inoculation	When fever relapses, rash returns and become generalized, bite site heals and then becomes inflamed; regional lymphangitis (more common in Asia)
b. Due to *Streptobacillus moniliformis*	Macular→maculopapular →vesicular, petechial	Extremities, including palms and soles, especially periarticular	Varies, 1–10 d	Blood culture	Arthritis and leukocytosis characteristic; bite not inflamed; rat-contaminated foods are alternate source
Relapsing fever (*Borrelia recurrentis*)	Macular→petechial	Shoulders, sides of trunk, inner arms and thighs	2–3 d, at end of primary fever episode	Blood smears	Rash unusual; louseborne or tickborne; febrile relapses lack rash; due to *Borrelia* spp.
Rickettsialpox (*Rickettsia akari*)	Generalized papular→ 1–2 cm vesicles→ crusting	Usually covered, hairy areas	Range, 0–9 d after fever (average, 2–3 d)	Serology (CF or IFA)	Papule ulcerates with eschar formation at site of mouse bite; urban disease usually
Rocky Mountain spotted fever (*Rickettsia rickettsii*)	Macular→maculopapular →petechial→purpuric →acral necrosis	Inside surfaces of wrists and ankles; later palms and soles; spreads to trunk; rarely centrifugal	2–5 d; half by day 3	Biopsy skin lesion with FA stains, if available; serology (late)	10–15% rash delayed or absent; faint early rash may be brought out by application of heat to wrists or ankles; must begin appropriate antibiotics on suspicion of Rocky Mountain spotted fever
Scarlet fever (*Streptococcus pyogenes*)	Blanching erythema→ punctate→petechiae→ desquamation	Neck, upper chest; spares palms, soles and face; circumoral pallor, strawberry tongue	1–2 d	Throat culture for group A streptococcus	Pharyngitis common; nausea, vomiting, abdominal pain common; rarely wound infected with group A streptococcus
Staphylococcus aureus a. Bacteremia	Petechial→pustular→ purpuric (rare)	Generalized	Hours	Cultures of blood, lesions; smears	Often associated with endocarditis and infected pulmonary emboli; may activate complement, causing findings resembling meningococcemia
b. Toxic shock (similar syndrome also occurs with *Streptococcus pyogenes*)	Diffuse erythema, conjunctival hyperemia →petechial→sometimes maculopapular late→ desquamation (usually hands and feet)	Palms and soles, pubis, axillae	1–2 d	Clinical; cultures of staphylococcal colonization sites, purulent lesions	Due to toxic shock toxin; 95% of cases are in women; may be associated wtih *S. aureus* vaginal colonization; usually occurs during menses; incidence higher in tampon users; shock, high fever, vomiting, diarrhea; may recur; mortality 10–15%
c. Staphylococcal scalded-skin syndrome (SSSS)	Diffuse erythema→ bullae, diffuse exfoliation	Face and trunk; extremities less frequent	Hours	Cultures of staphylococcal colonization sites, purulent lesions; skin biopsy	Group II phage 71 strains; positive Nikolsky sign; most common in newborns and children; due to staphylococcal epidermolytic toxin
Syphilis, secondary (*Treponema pallidum*)	Skin: macular, maculopapular, pustular–papulo squamous; mouth and genital region: no vesicles, mucous patches; intertriginous regions(condylomata latum):painless, raised moist areas with erythematous border	Trunk and proximal limbs; skin: hairline; mucous patches of mouth, anogenital region; condylomata latum in intertriginous areas; palms and soles classic	Varies, usually 4–6 w after primary infection	Dark field (if no antibiotics); serology	Fever usually mild or absent; lesions, especially mucous patches, are teeming with spirochetes; often general lymph node enlargement; may exacerbate with antibiotic treatment (Jarisch–Herxheimer reaction)
Toxoplasmosis (*Toxoplasma gondii*)	Macular→maculopapular	Trunk; generally spares palms, soles, and scalp	Variable, 1–14 d	Serology; muscle or node biopsy	Rash rare; lymphadenopathy usually not present when rash presents

TABLE 8–5–3. *(Continued)*

	Type of Rash (→ indicates progression)	Where to Look Early	When Rash May First Appear after Fever Begins	Diagnostic Tests	Remarks
Typhoid (*Salmonella typhi*)	Macules (blanching), "rose spots"	Upper abdomen, thorax, lower midback	Second week	Cultures of blood, skin lesion; serology (poor)	Difficult to see rash on dark skin
Typhus, epidemic (*Rickettsia prowazekii*)	Macular→maculopapular →petechial→purpuric	Axillae; trunk, generalized	4–5 d	Skin biopsy; serology (e.g., IFA, CF)	Transmission by body louse; humans principal reservoir; indigenous cases in United States related to flying squirrels
Typhus, murine (*Rickettsia typhi*)	Macular→maculopapular →petechial	Axillae, trunk	4–5 d	Serology	Milder than Rocky Mountain spotted fever or epidemic typhus
Vibrio vulnificus infection					
a. Primary septicemia	Vesicles→bullae→ ulcers, cellulitis	Extremities	36 h	Clinical; cultures of blood, stool	Predilection for patients with hepatic cirrhosis; ingestion of raw seafood, especially oysters; 16-h incubation period
b. Wound infection	Rapidly spreading cellulitis	Extremities	Skin lesion precedes fever	Clinical; culture of blood, lesion	Exposure of wound to seawater; 12-h incubation period

Diseases for Which Specific Treatment May Not Be Required, but for Which the Spread to Other Persons Is a Major Concern of Early Diagnosis

	Type of Rash (→ indicates progression)	Where to Look Early	When Rash May First Appear after Fever Begins	Diagnostic Tests	Remarks
Enterovirus					
a. Coxsackie A and B, echovirus	Macular→maculopapular; rarely vesicular	Head, neck, trunk	Variable: some at onset of fever, others at end	Stool or throat culture for virus; serology	Especially young children; may resemble rubella or roseola; aseptic meningitis common
b. Hand, foot, and mouth disease	Macular→maculopapular →vesicular; ulcers in mouth	Mouth, hands and feet, buttocks	1–2 d	Stool or throat culture for virus; serology	Due to several Coxsackie A types, especially A-16; generally mild
c. Herpangina	Vesicular with red edges	Pharynx	Hours	Stool and throat culture for virus; serologic	Coxsackie A
Erythema infectiosum ("fifth disease," parvovirus B19)	Malar erythema→ maculopapular; often reticulated	Slapped cheek appearance; reticular rash on extremities	1–2 d	Clinical; serology	Usually affects children; recurrent and evanescent; brought out by sunlight, exercise, etc.; fever rare except in adults who also may have arthralgia
Herpes simplex (1 and 2)	Macular→maculopapular →vesicular→pustular; painful	Mouth, pharynx, perianal, genitals, fingers; rarely generalized	1–3 d	Biopsy; culture; direct FA on scraped lesion; serology	Recurrent disease prominent; usually febrile with initial infection, less so with recurrences, frequent in immunosuppressed patients
Herpes zoster	Macular→papular-vesicular→scab→	Any dermatome, especially intercostal, trigeminal; may disseminate	4–5 d	Clinical; culture; direct FA; EM of vesicle fluid	Local hyperesthesia of skin or itching precedes rash; pain in dermatome often after lesions clear; same virus as varicella
HIV-1					
a. Acute seroconversion	Maculopapular	Trunk	Variable	Serology; clinical; biopsy of lesions for histology and culture	Seen in ~50%
b. Secondary dermatologic	Includes seborrheic dermatitis, extensive folliculitis, ichthyosis	—	Variable	Same as above	Eosinophilic folliculitis may respond to UV light
c. Opportunistic, neoplastic, allergic	—	—	Variable	Same as above	Includes Kaposi's sarcoma; drug eruptions common
Measles					
a. Typical	Macular→maculopapular →later desquamation; rarely petechial or purpuric	Face→trunk→ extremities; Koplik's spots: blue-gray specks on a red base on the buccal mucosa	2–3 d	Clinical and epidemiologic; serologic	Often respiratory symptoms, cough, pharyngitis, conjunctivitis; signs may be mild or absent in individuals with partial immunity
b. Atypical	Macular→ maculopapular→ vesicular or petechial→ purpuric	Rash may start on extremities; progresses upward; peripheral edema	2–3 d	Clinical; epidemiology; serology	Received killed (live) rubeola virus years earlier; often with pneumonia; usually young adults; illness tends to be severe

(continued)

TABLE 8–5–3. (*Continued*)

	Type of Rash (→ indicates progression)	Where to Look Early	When Rash May First Appear after Fever Begins	Diagnostic Tests	Remarks
Respiratory syncytial virus infection	Erythema→macular→petechial	Face, shoulders, trunk	Early, 1–3 d	Culture for virus; serology	Primarily childen; uncommon
Roseola, exanthem subitum (HHvb)	Macular→papular	Abdomen, neck, behind ears	3–5 days; often as fever resolves	Clinical; epidemiology	Sudden onset; child (<3 y); high fever; excellent prognosis
Rubella*	Macular→maculopapular	Face and neck, trunk	1–7 d, usualy 3 d	Clinical; epidemiology; serology	Often posterior cervical lymph node enlargement; arthralgia and arthritis common in adults
Varicella	Macular→maculopapular→vesicular→umbilicated pustule→scab crops of varying stages	Face and trunk	1–2 d	Clinicial; epidemiology; electron microscopic or IFA exam of cells at base of vesicle; serologic	Often itching; sometimes single initial pustule; pneumonia in adults occasionally
Viral hepatitis (hepatitis A, B)	Erythema→maculopetechial or urticarial	Extremities, generalized	Early	Hepatic function; serologic antigen and antibody tests	Transient rash occurs in preicteric phase, often with arthralgia

Other Infectious Causes of Fever and Rash

	Type of Rash (→ indicates progression)	Where to Look Early	When Rash May First Appear after Fever Begins	Diagnostic Tests	Remarks
Blastomycosis (*Blastomyces hominis*)	Localized granulomas: papulopustular→crusted verrucous or ulcerative	Face, extremities	Variable	Culture; serology; skin biopsy	Often with pulmonary infection; dogs frequent hosts; probable soil organism
Coccidioidomycosis (*Coccidioides immitis*)	a. Diffuse erythema→macular b. Erythema multiforme/nodosum c. Localized papule→granuloma	Face, extremities	Variable	Culture; serologic; biopsy	Souce in soil of arid valleys of southwest United States; associated with pulmonary/meningeal infection
Colorado tick fever	Macular→maculopapular; rare petechial	Extremities, generalized	1–2 d	Serology; FA stain of erythrocytes	Rash uncommon; fever often diphasic ("saddleback"); 50% have tick bite history; Rocky Mountain area and northwest United States
Cryptococcosis (*Cryptococcus neoformans*)	Localized papules→pustules→abscesses or crusted granuloma	Face, extremities	Variable	Culture; cryptococcal antigen; skin biopsy; India ink exam of CSF	Source in soil; often with meningitis/pulmonary infection, especially immunocompromised host
Dengue	Transient diffuse erythema or macular→maculopapular	Thorax, inner arms	3–4 d	Serology; clinical; epidemiology	Myalgia severe; saddleback fever; mosquito-borne
Erysipeloid (*Erysipelothrix rhusiopathiae*)	Erythema→spreading with central clearing	Usually fingers; hands, wrists, forearms	Variable	Clinical; culture of advancing edge of lesion	Occupation infection: handlers of fish, veterinarians, farmers, meat packers, food handlers (meat); no suppuration; fever in 10%
Hemorrhagic fevers (arenaviruses; arboviruses; also see Dengue)	a. Erythema b. Maculopapular c. Petechial, ecchymosis	Face, neck, thorax Trunk Palate, conjunctivae, axillae, peripheral	3–7 d	Serology; geographic location	Transmission: mosquitos, ticks, some from rodents; common features: thrombocytopenia, hemorrhage, capillary leak syndromes, shock
Histoplasmosis (*Histoplasma capsulatum*)	a. Localized granuloma→ulcers	Mouth, tongue	Variable	Culture; biopsy; serology	Source in soil, especially Ohio–Mississippi Valley; often associated with acute or chronic pulmonary infection
Infectious mononucleosis	Petechial, erythematous, or macular; maculopapular	Trunk, proximal extremities; usually spares face	4–5 d	Serology; clinical; blood smear	Due to Epstein–Barr virus or cytomegalovirus; rash may be precipitated or aggravated by ampicillin
Kawasaki disease (mucocutaneous lymph node syndrome)	Erythematous→macular→polymorphous; edema	Trunk	3–5 d	Clinical; exclusion of other similar diseases	Possible infectious etiology; conjunctivitis; pharyngitis; cheilitis; strawberry tongue; cervical lymphadenopathy; cardiac abnormality in many

TABLE 8–5–3. (*Continued*)

Noninfectious Presentations of Fever and Rash

	Type of Rash (→ indicates progression)	Where to Look Early	When Rash May First Appear after Fever Begins	Diagnostic Tests	Remarks
Acne fulminans	Inflammatory nodules with ulceration	Chest, back	Variable but may have explosive onset	Clinicial; biopsy	Especially in teenage males, usually with leukocytosis
Acute febrile neutrophilic dermatosis (Sweet's disease; hypersensitivity vasculitis and Henoch–Schonlein purpura)	Raised erythematous plaques; some have raised margins with central ulceration	Face, extremities	Variable	Clinical; skin biopsy	May have post-streptococcal, drug or food allergy cause; associated with arthritis, renal disease, abdominal pain
Dermatomyositis	Erythema (heliotrope) of upper eyelids; malar ("butterfly") rash; flat-topped papules over dorsal interphalangeal joints (Gottron's papules)	Face, neck, upper arms	Variable	Serum antibodies, enzymes; electromyelography	Associated muscle disease; patient usually aged 40–60 y
Drug allergy	Highly variable; often morbilliform, urticarial, maculopapular, or petechial	Variable, usually more on face and trunk than extremities	Variable	Clinical; exclusion	Most rashes occur within 1–2 w of commencing drug (about half of penicillin reactions occur later); as a rule, patients are not "toxic" with drug reactions
Erythema marginatum	Varying and evanescent; erythematous, curvilinear lesions	Trunk, extremities	Variable	Clinical (manifestation of acute rheumatic fever); antistreptococcal antibodies	Major sign of acute rheumatic fever
Erythema multiforme	Erythematous plaque with central violaceous depression (iris lesions),bullae	Hands and feet; mouth and anogenital region; trunk	Variable	Clinical; biopsy; fungal, mycoplasma, and herpes serology	Due to drugs, systemic fungus infection, mycoplasma, herpes simplex, or unknown cause
Erythema nodosum	Painful, deep subcutaneous nodules, with overlying dusky redness	Extensor surfaces, usually shins	Variable	Clinical; biopsy; fungal and streptococcal serology; PPD	Discomfort worse at night; arthralgia; due to streptococcal infection, drugs, tuberculosis, systemic fungus infection, etc.
Familial Mediterranean fever	Erythematous patches or swellings; transient	Lower extremities	Variable	Clinical	Etiology unknown; occurs in persons of Mediterranean origin; inherited
Fat embolism	Petechial	Root of neck; axillae, upper trunk, conjunctivae	1–3 d after injury	Decreased arterial oxygen tension; fat stain of blood clot; kidney, skin biopsy	Associated with long-bone fracture; other findings: acute pulmonary distress, hypoxemia, fever, altered mental state
Graft-versus-host disease	Erythema→maculo-papular→bullous; may desquamate	Face, palms, soles, extremities	10–40 d after transplant	Clinical	In recipients of bone marrow transplants or immunosuppressed patients receiving nonirradiated blood transfusions
Inflammatory bowel disease (pyoderma gangrenosum)	Hemorrhagic bullae or nodules→ulceration	Lower extremities, abdomen	Variable	Clinical; biopsy	1% of Crohn's disease or ulcerative colitis; stomatitis also present
Keratoconjunctivitis sicca	Erythema	Variable	Variable	Biopsy, serology	Manifestation of Sjögren's syndrome
Miliaria (heat rash)	Watery vesicles, with or without erythematous or papular bases	Intertriginous or covered areas	Hours	Clinical, exclusion	Consequence of sweating; with fever may mimic specific fever–rash process
Necrolytic migratory erythema	Erythematous plaques→ desquamation→ erosion	Intertriginous and periorificial areas	Variable	Blood glucose, plasma glucagon, clinical picture	Associated with glucagonoma
Reiter's syndrome	Vesicles→scaly hyperkeratotic	Feet, hands	Variable, chronic	Tissue type HLA-B27; clinical	Rash is keratoderma blennorrhagicum; disease triggered by *Shigella* infection; associated with arthritis

(*continued*)

TABLE 8–5–3. (Continued)

	Type of Rash (→ indicates progression)	Where to Look Early	When Rash May First Appear after Fever Begins	Diagnostic Tests	Remarks
Sarcoid	Maculopapular, erythematous plaques; violaceous ulcer (lupus pernio)	Face, neck	Variable	Biopsy; clinical	About one third of patients have skin lesions
Still's disease (juvenile rheumatoid arthritis)	Erythema→macular, salmon-colored	Face, trunk, extremities	Early, may precede arthritis	Serology	Usually in children, occasionaly adults
Systemic lupus erythematosus	Scaly erythematous or maculopapular	Malar area and areas exposed to sunlight	Variable	Clinical; biopsy; antinuclear antibody; double-stranded DNA; and Sm antibodies	Usually other objective findings of systemic lupus erythematosus
Vasculitis	Palpable purpura	Variable	Variable	Biopsy	Sometimes associated with streptococcal or hepatitis B infection or drug reaction
Zinc deficiency	Pustulobullous	Extremities, mouth, anal and genital areas	Variable	Zinc levels	Associated with malabsorption, especially in infants

CSF, cerebrospinal fluid; CF, complement fixation; EM, electronmicroscopy; FA, fluorescent antibody; IFA, indirect fluorescent antibody.

CHAPTER 8–6

Fever and Adenopathy Caused by Infections

Jonas A. Shulman, M.D.

DEFINITION

When a patient has fever plus localized or generalized adenopathy, it is referred to initially as fever and adenopathy. When an infectious cause is identified, the condition is referred to as fever and adenopathy caused by an infection.

ETIOLOGY

The specific etiologies of fever and adenopathy caused by infection are listed in Table 8–6–1. Fever and adenopathy caused by neoplastic processes is not discussed.

CRITERIA FOR DIAGNOSIS

Suggestive

The presence of a combination of either regional or generalized lymphadenopathy and fever should suggest the possibility of an infectious etiology. Although this combination of findings may be caused by noninfectious etiologies, such as lymphoma and phenytoin hypersensitivity, a variety of infectious lymphadenopathies must be considered, as many may be treatable with specifically selected antimicrobial agents.

Definitive

To fully meet the requirement for specifically diagnosing an infectious lymphadenopathy, the pathology and cultures of the lymph node or the cultures or smears obtained from other involved sites must demonstrate the etiologic agent or its effects. Epidemiologic history, clinical manifestations, blood cultures, and appropriate serologic methods demonstrating fourfold rises in antibody titers are also helpful in proving some specific infectious etiologies. Lymphadenopathy syndromes caused by or associated with HIV infection are discussed in detail in Chapters 8–31 and 8–76.

CLINICAL MANIFESTATIONS

Subjective and objective manifestations of some of the more important causes of regional and generalized adenopathy are described in Table 8–6–1.

PLANS

Diagnostic

Differential Diagnosis

See Table 8–6–1. As it is helpful to consider the differential diagnosis of fever and regional adenopathy separately from that of fever and generalized adenopathy in evaluating a patient for infectious causes, these syndromes are considered separately in this chapter. This classification is similar to that used by Shulman and Schlossberg (1980).

Diagnostic Options and Recommended Approach

Depending on the clinical manifestations and on the location of the adenopathy, specific laboratory studies are required. Biopsies with special stains and cultures may be helpful but are often not necessary. Serologic studies are useful in the diagnosis of many of these diseases. Appropriate studies are outlined in Table 8–6–2 for each suspected diagnosis.

Therapeutic

Specific therapy demands strong suspicion or proof of a specific etiology. Table 8–6–2 presents the antimicrobial agents of choice for each diagnostic possibility.

Patients should be informed that the lymph node inflammation is an effort of the body's defense mechanism to limit infection by a foreign agent. Many of the infectious causes of lymphadenopathy are self-limited or can be treated with appropriate specific antimicrobial agents. The patient therefore must understand the importance of doing the specific diagnostic studies to identify the likely pathogen. Proper education for the patient depends on the specific disease process encountered and is discussed in the chapter devoted to that entity.

TABLE 8–6–1. CLINICAL MANIFESTATIONS OF REGIONAL AND GENERALIZED ADENOPATHY

Disease	Clinical Manifestations	Disease	Clinical Manifestations
A. Localized lymphadenopathy 1. Cervical adenopathy a. Viral (nonspecific)	Short-lived illness with sore throat, fever, and tender adenopathy. Difficult to differentiate from streptococcal pharyngitis clinically. Vesicular lesions in the pharynx are present in some viral infections.	b. Cat scratch disease	1–3 weeks after cat contact, lesion appears at scratch site, followed by regional node enlargement (usually axillary). Nodes may become fluctuant. Occasional patients have constitutional signs.
b. Infectious mononucleosis	Most cases occur in adolescents and young adults who present with fever, sore throat, and cervical lymphadenopathy. Palatal petechiae, splenomegaly, supraorbital edema, and maculopapular rash also may be seen. A pseudomembrane similar to that found in diphtheria may be noted in the pharynx. Adenopathy may be generalized (See Chapter 8–72).	c. Tularemia	Ulceroglandular tularemia: slightly painful papule that ulcerates, causing inflammation of regional nodes; these become tender, hot, and enlarged; accompanied by fever, myalgia, headache. Handling carcasses usually causes lesions on the hand with epitrochlear and axillary adenopathy. Arthropods may produce inoculation in different sites and resultant adenopathy may be cervical, inguinal, etc. Disease also has typhoidal or pulmonary forms, and in these forms adenopathy may be generalized.
c. Group A streptococcal	Sore throat, fever, and tender adenopathy; at times, marked difficulty swallowing. Exudative pharyngitis is frequently seen with streptococcal infection, but may be caused by many viruses, including Epstein–Barr virus.	d. Plague	Fever and tender regional bubo, usually inguinal; can suppurate and drain spontaneously. If untreated, may progress to septicemia, meningitis, and pneumonia. Bleeding tendency may produce ecchymoses. Disease of wild and domestic rodents transmitted to humans by rat flea. In United States, endemic in the Southwest.
d. Diphtheria	Severe cases seen only in unimmunized individuals. Pharyngeal gray pseudomembrane. Minimal pharyngeal discomfort. Enlargement of cervical nodes and edema of the anterior neck and submandibular areas (bull neck) may be seen. Laryngeal involvement may occur. Complications include myocarditis and peripheral or cranial nerve palsies.	e. Rat bite fever (*Spirillum minus*)	Incubation period 1–4 weeks, then rat bite flares when systemic illness begins. Regional nodes swell, become tender and matted. May be accompanied by fever, rash, polyarthritis, or arthralgia.
e. Mucocutaneous lymph node syndrome (Kawasaki's disease)	Fever not responsive to antibiotics. Conjunctival infection, "strawberry" tongue, erythematous rash, cervical adenopathy, and desquamation around the fingertips are common findings. Usually self-limited, but mortality (from coronary arteritis) is 1 to 2%. Most cases are in children.	f. Sporotrichosis	Primary lesion: ulcerating nodule on extremities causing intermittent hard, red, suppurating nodules along lymph channels, with regional adenopathy. No pain, fever, or other constitutional symptoms. Organism lives on vegetation and in soil. Infection seen in people who work on farms or with plants or who are exposed to contaminated vegetation.
f. Tuberculous adenitis	Nodes may be painless or painful and may become fluctuant, causing draining sinuses. Both atypical mycobacterial disease and that caused by *Mycobacterium tuberculosis* are being seen with increased frequency in patients infected with HIV. *M. tuberculosis:* multiple groups of nodes involved, frequently bilaterally. May see evidence of tuberculosis elsewhere. Atypical mycobacteria: usually in children; nodes are typically unilateral, usually one group is enlarged. Usually no evidence of disease elsewhere. Negative contact history.	g. Herpes zoster infections	Clustered vesicles in unilateral segmental distribution. Paresthesias, severe neuralgia, and fever may accompany or precede rash by several days. May be associated with states of immunosuppression. Regional adenitis is not very tender.
		h. Herpetic whitlow	Swollen tender vesicular lesions on the pulp of the fingers; painful and tender regional adenopathy. Especially prevalent in nurses and dental personnel.
2. Occipital adenopathy a. Nonspecific scalp infection (bacterial)	Local signs of inflammation	4. Inguinal adenopathy a. Primary syphilis	Painless genital chancre. Inguinal adenopathy that is painless, firm, freely movable, and nonsuppurating. Nodes may remain for months even though chancre heals in 2–6 weeks. Male homosexuals are at high risk for genital, anorectal, and oral chancres.
b. Rubella	Fever and faint pink macular rash. Adenopathy: back of neck, especially in the posterior chain and in suboccipital region. Adenopathy may be generalized. Nodes are small and only rarely tender; they may precede the rash.	b. Lymphogranuloma venereum	Primary painless genital papule/vesicle. Nodes: bilateral or unilateral inguinal adenopathy. Nodes may become matted, multilocular, and suppurative, leading to multiple fistulas. Nodes tend to enlarge both above and below inguinal ligament. May produce rectal disease with diarrhea in females and homosexual males. Also seen at times are constitutional signs, including arthralgia and myalgias.
3. Peripheral adenopathy (location varies with inoculation site) a. Bacterial adenitis (associated with skin infection caused by group A streptococci or other pyogens)	Streptococcal nodes are enlarged, tender, painful. Sometimes no source apparent for lymphangitis. May have overlying cellulitis. May progress to lymphedema with repeated attacks.	c. Chancroid	Genital chancres, often multiple, painful, tender, and not indurated. Inguinal adenopathy painful and tender. Unilateral in two thirds. Untreated nodes may become matted and form a unilocular suppurative bubo. May rupture, causing a large single ulcer.

(continued)

TABLE 8–6–1. (*Continued*)

Disease	Clinical Manifestations	Disease	Clinical Manifestations
d. Genital herpes infection (herpes virus hominis, type II)	Painful vesicles on penis or in vagina and cervical area. Rectal and perineal lesion sites are common, especially in homosexual men. May recur. Regional tender nodes are not uncommon.		smooth, and may be painful and tender. They rarely suppurate. Rash may be present. May present as fever of unknown origin, myocarditis, pericarditis, encephalitis, pneumonitis, or hepatitis.
B. Generalized lymphadenopathy		7. Tularemia	See (A) Localized Lymphadenopathy
1. Infectious mononucleosis	See (A) Localized Lymphadenopathy	8. Tuberculosis	Usually evidence of tuberculous infection elsewhere, particularly in the lungs. At times, presents with normal chest x-ray.
2. Rubella	See (A) Localized Lymphadenopathy		
3. Cytomegalovirus (CMV)	This agent causes a variety of clinical manifestations and frequently produces asymptomatic illness. Adenopathy may be seen in both congenital and acquired disease and, at times, is prominent in adult patients who present with an infectious mononucleosis-like syndrome. Fever and hepatitis are common.	9. Histoplasmosis	In disseminated histoplasmosis, may see generalized lymphadenopathy along with the hepatosplenomegaly and, at times, oral ulcerations.
		10. Secondary syphilis	Fever, diffuse rash, often including palms and soles, and localized lymphadenopathy, which is nontender, often including preauricular and post-auricular, occipital, and epitrochlear nodes. These may remain palpable for months after other signs of secondary syphilis have disappeared.
4. Measles	Fever, coryza, cough, Koplik's spots, red splotchy rash on face, then on trunk. Lymphadenopathy may be generalized or predominate in occipital, mastoid, or posterior cervical region.		
5. Dengue	"Breakbone fever," with severe back and bone pain. Prodromal coryza, headache, myalgias, rash, arthralgias, ocular soreness, scleral infection. Adenopathy is present in posterior cervical, epitrochlear, and inguinal chains and is usually nontender. Illness is diphasic.	11. HIV infection, AIDS, and AIDS-related complex (ARC)	Seen especially in male homosexuals, hemophiliacs, IV drug abusers, and rarely in other groups. Can be transmitted by blood transfusions or sexual activity (homosexual or heterosexual). Can be associated with Kaposi's sarcoma or opportunistic infections. Mortality rate very high. An infectious mononucleosis-like illness has been reported following initial exposure to HIV infection. See Chapter 8–76.
6. Toxoplasmosis	Infectious mononucleosis-like illness, with fever, generalized lymphadenopathy, especially in cervical region. Nodes are firm, discreet,		

Source: Modified from Shulman JA, Schlossberg D. Handbook for differential diagnosis of infectious diseases. Vol 212. New York: Appleton-Century-Crofts, 1980. Reproduced with permission from publisher and author.

FOLLOW-UP

The tremendous diversity of infectious diseases in which lymphadenopathy is prominent precludes any simple statements concerning follow-up. Each patient must be followed clinically until resolution occurs or until the exact diagnosis is known and the course can be predicted. See the specific chapter relating to the disease entity suspected for further assistance in planning follow-up.

DISCUSSION

Prevalence and Incidence

Fever and adenopathy caused by infection is a common condition, especially during childhood.

Related Basic Science

The lymph nodes in the human number more than 600 and are important as filters of microbial organisms, producers of antibodies, and processors of lymphocytes. They represent one of the major components in the body's defense against infection. In a local infection the regional nodes are involved, but if this barrier is overcome, the infection may spread to the blood and to more distant nodes.

When lymph nodes are acutely involved, there is evidence of a cellular infiltration with neutrophils and lymphocytes, an increase in macrophages, and edema. In certain illnesses, such as staphylococcal adenitis or plague, fluctuance may be present. Even infections not classically due to pyogenic organisms such as lymphogranuloma venereum and cat scratch fever may produce fluctuance.

More chronic inflammation of the lymph nodes produces a mononuclear cell inflammation. Usually this inflammatory response is not very specific, but in certain illnesses, such as toxoplasmosis, the architectural findings may in fact be almost pathognomonic. The presence of caseous necrosis, giant cells, and epithelioid granulomas, although not diagnostic, may point to certain diagnostic possibilities, such as tuberculosis, atypical tuberculosis, fungal infections, tularemia, cat scratch disease, lymphogranuloma venereum, and noninfectious processes such as sar-

coidosis. Specific stains such as acid-fast, Gomori's silver, Wharthin's silver, and periodic acid–Schiff may help identify the etiologic agent.

Natural History and Its Modification with Treatment

Each of the causes of lymphadenopathy produces an illness with a different natural history and therefore different approaches toward prevention. The reader should refer to the specific chapter dealing with the appropriate disease entity under consideration for further information.

Prevention

See Natural History and Its Modification with Treatment

Cost Containment

Careful planning of appropriate laboratory studies may help in obtaining a diagnosis and instituting specific treatment quickly, thereby decreasing costs. Knowledge of the site of the adenopathy and the clinical clues outlined should assist in streamlining diagnostic techniques. Some of the illnesses, such as rubeola and rubella, are nearly totally preventable.

REFERENCES

Elliot DL, Tolle SW, Goldberg L, et al. Pet-associated illness. N Engl J Med 1985;313:985.

McCabe RE, Brooks RG, Dorfman RF, et al. Clinical spectrum in 107 cases of toxoplasmic lymphadenopathy. Rev Infect Dis 1987;9:754.

Shulman JA, Schlossberg D, eds. Localized and generalized lymphadenopathy. In: Handbook for differential diagnosis of infectious diseases. Vol. 212. New York: Appleton-Century-Crofts, 1980:25.

Spark, RP, Fried ML, Bean CK, et al. Nontuberculous mycobacterial adenitis of childhood: The ten-year experience at a community hospital. Am J Dis Child 1988;142:106.

Tindall B, Barker S, Donovan B, et al. Characterization of the acute clinical illness associated with the human immunodeficiency virus infection. Arch Intern Med 1988;149:945.

Young LS, Bicknell DS, Archer BG, et al. Tularemia epidemic: Vermont 1968. Forty-seven cases linked to contact with muskrats. N Engl J Med 1969;280:1253.

TABLE 8–6–2. APPROACH TO THE DIAGNOSIS AND THERAPY OF REGIONAL AND GENERALIZED LYMPHADENOPATHY CAUSED BY INFECTIONS

Disease	Diagnostic Clues	Initial Treatment
A. Localized lymphadenopathy		
1. Cervical adenopathy		
a. Viral (nonspecific)	Exclusion of streptococcal pharyngitis by culture. May do viral culture and serologic studies in selected instances.	Supportive.
b. Infectious	Lymphocytosis with many atypical cells seen in peripheral smear. Serology very helpful ("mono spot" or "heterophile" test). If preceding serology is negative, do serology for toxoplasmosis, CMV, HIV, as well as specific EBV serology.	Supportive in most cases. Corticosteroids are helpful for laryngeal obstruction, extreme toxicity, hematologic, and neurologic complications.
c. Group A streptococcal	Throat culture.	Penicillin G. 10 days of adequate chemotherapy required.
d. Diphtheria	Culture on Loeffler's medium. A smear of the exudative lesion stained with fluorescence-labeled diphtheria antitoxin is very helpful.	Antitoxin as soon as diagnosis is strongly suspected. Erythromycin is indicated to eliminate carriage of organism.
e. Mucocutaneous lymph node syndrome	Clinical presentation; failure to prove another specific etiology, particularly streptococcal scarlet fever, Rocky Mountain spotted fever, and toxic shock syndrome.	High-dose aspirin and intravenous gamma globulin.
f. Tuberculous adenitis	Chest x-ray. Skin test. Smear and culture of sputum and of gastric washings: node biopsy shows wide spectrum: giant cells, tubercles, caseous necrosis, fibrosis, calcification. Node must be cultured, as organisms may be difficult to visualize with acid-fast bacillus stains. In disease due to *Mycobacterium tuberculosis,* the PPD is almost always positive unless patient is immunocompromised.	*M. tuberculosis:* Isoniazid, rifampin, and ethambutol; surgery needed only for diagnosis and for occasional drainage of cold abscess. Atypical mycobacteria: excision is usually curative. If antibacterial agents are used, sensitivities should be known, as resistance is common. If associated with severe systemic disease, some advise rifampin, ethambutol, clofazimine, ciprofloxacin, and amikacin.
2. Occipital adenopathy		
a. Nonspecific scalp infection	Clinical presentation. Culture and Gram stain of infected site.	Antibiotics as per Gram stain, culture and sensitivity tests, or per likely pathogens at that site.
b. Rubella	Serology helpful. Virus may be isolated from pharynx.	Supportive.
3. Peripheral adenopathy (location varies with inoculation site)		
a. Bacterial adenitis (associated with skin infection caused by group A streptococci or other pyrogens)	Can aspirate node and smear and culture if etiologic diagnosis is in doubt. Usually clinical characteristics are sufficient and the node does not require aspiration. Local cellulitis or skin lesions present should be aspirated, Gram stained, and cultured.	If streptococcal, use penicillin G. Some prefer antistaphylococcal penicillin to treat both staphylococci and streptococci. If other pyogens suspected, choose antibiotic on basis of predicted sensitivities.
b. Cat scratch disease	Intradermal skin test (nonstandardized and not generally available). Biopsy of node will show epithelioid granulomas, microabscesses, caseous necrosis, and giant cells, but rarely is a biopsy indicated. Special silver stains may demonstrate the bacterium now thought to be the cause of this disease. Epidemiologic history and clinical course usually suffice.	If node purulent, may aspirate; however, almost never needs excision. Will heal without specific therapy, but some suggest that ciprofloxacin or trimethoprim–sulfamethoxazole may be helpful in severe cases.
c. Tularemia	Serology is helpful, but becomes positive only after 10 days. Culture (on cystine-containing medium) of blood, sputum, exudates, and gastric washings. Biopsy of node rarely needed, but if done, should be cultured and may show granulomas, microabscesses, caseous necrosis, and giant cells.	Streptomycin or gentamicin.
d. Plague	Smear and culture blood, aspirate of bubo, and sputum; Giemsa stain better than Gram stain for visualization of Gram-negative safety-pin-shaped organisms. Direct fluorescent antiserum stain very useful. Serology helpful, but not positive until second week.	Streptomycin and tetracycline or chloramphenicol, but antibiotic sensitivity patterns are important to obtain and may dictate a different approach. Contacts of pneumonia cases should be treated with tetracycline, and patients with pneumonia require strictest respiratory isolation.
e. Rat bite fever *(Spirillum minus)*	Dark field of bite, rash, or node aspirate will show organism; VDRL frequently positive. Specific serology indicated.	Penicillin G or tetracycline.
f. Sporotrichosis	Difficult to see organisms on smear, but can grow on Sabouraud's agar if nodule is aspirated.	Oral iodides for local disease. Amphotericin B for systemic disease.
g. Herpes zoster infection	Usually, diagnosis can be made on basis of clinical findings alone. Scrapings from the base of a vesicle, when stained with Wright's or Giemsa stain, may demonstrate multinucleated giant cells and intranuclear inclusions. These findings are characteristic, but not pathognomonic for varicella–zoster virus. Electron microscopy or fluorescent antibody applied to smears from the base of the vesicle can be helpful. Serology.	Supportive, unless disseminated or in an immunocompromised host. High-dose acyclovir is useful in these latter settings.
h. Herpetic whitlow	Vesicle can be unroofed, Gram stained, cultured for bacteria and virus, and also stained for viral inclusions. Direct fluorescent antibody also helpful in rapid diagnosis. Viral cultures are usually positive in 24–72 hours. Area of pulp inflammation should not be incised.	Symptomatic.
4. Usually inguinal		
a. Primary syphilis	Dark field of primary lesion. Serology helpful, but in primary disease may not become positive until 6 weeks after infection acquired. See Chapter 8–46.	Benzathine penicillin G.

(continued)

TABLE 8–6–2. (*Continued*)

Disease	Diagnostic Clues	Initial Treatment
b. Lymphogranuloma venereum	Organism may be isolated from pus in tissue culture, but this technique is not generally available. Frei skin test: positive for life, false negative in 40%. Serology helpful. Biopsy characteristic: granulomas, microabscesses, caseous necrosis, and giant cells	Doxycycline.
c. Chancroid	Smear and culture of node aspirate (specialized media).	Aspirate node if tense, to prevent spontaneous rupture. Erythromycin or ceftriaxone.
d. Genital herpes infection (herpesvirus hominis, type II)	Clinical appearance. May recur. Cervical smear shows atypical cells. Viral inclusions and multinucleated giant cells can be seen if lesion scraped and stained. Viral cultures should be positive for herpes within 24–72 hours. Direct fluorescent antibody is a helpful rapid test.	Acyclovir may be useful especially in primary attacks or in very severe episodes. In some instances it is used to prevent recurrences.
B. Generalized lymphadenopathy 1. Infectious mononucleosis	See (A) Localized Adenopathy.	Supportive in most cases. Corticosteroids are helpful for laryngeal obstruction, extreme toxicity, and hematologic and neurologic complications.
2. Rubella	See (A) Localized Lymphadenopathy.	Supportive.
3. Cytomegalovirus	Culture urine, throat, and blood for CMV. Examine urine for inclusion bodies (rarely positive in acquired infections). A new simple test for rapid electron microscopy on urine and other fluids for CMV is available. It is especially helpful in newborns. Abnormal liver function test. Peripheral smear: increased number of lymphocytes and many atypical cells, suggestive of infectious mononucleosis. Negative mono spot test, heterophile, and EBV serology. CMV-IgG and CMV-IgM serology helpful.	No specific therapy indicated in most cases of actue CMV infection. With serious CMV infections in immunocompromised patients (e.g., retinitis or colitis in AIDS patients), ganciclovir is beneficial.
4. Measles	Usually, diagnosis is obvious clinically and laboratory studies need not be performed. Slight decrease in peripheral WBC. Warthin–Finkleday cells in stained sputum and urine. Isolation of virus from urine and sputum. Serology helpful. Nodes show increased germinal follicles and multinucleated giant cells; same changes are seen in other organs.	After known exposure, gamma globulin is helpful in modifying illness if given early in incubation period. Prevention is ideally carried out long before exposure by appropriate administration of live measles vaccine. See Chapter 8–67.
5. Dengue	Frequently WBC is very low. History of travel to an endemic area. Virus isolation from blood. Serology helpful.	Symptomatic only.
6. Toxoplasmosis	Serology is helpful (see Chapter 8–62). Lymph node biopsy findings are helpful even if no organisms are seen, but are not pathognomonic and sometimes resemble lymphoma. Agent may be isolated by inoculation of infectious tissue in mice. Wright's or Giemsa stains of muscle, node, or cerebrospinal fluid may demonstrate trophozoites or cysts. Electron microscopy is helpful in brain biopsies in central nervous system infection.	Pyrimethamine and sulfadiazine for severe cases (give folinic acid as well). (Most cases in the immunocompetent host are self-limited and do not require therapy.)
7. Tularemia	See (A) Localized Adenopathy.	See (A) Localized Lymphadenopathy.
8. Tuberculosis	Chest x-ray, skin test. Smear and culture of sputum, culture of gastric washings. Node biopsy may show giant cells, tubercles, caseous necrosis, fibrosis, calcification; lesion identical to those seen in other organs. Node must be cultured, as organisms are difficult to visualize. Bone marrow, lung, and liver biopsies and culture are helpful diagnostic studies if node is not diagnostic.	*M. tuberculosis:* Isoniazid plus rifampin plus ethambutol (corticosteroids useful for extreme toxicity). Atypical tuberculosis: see (A) Localized Lymphadenopathy.
9. Histoplasmosis	Culture marrow, blood, sputum, and/or lymph nodes on specialized media. Lung and liver biopsy may be helpful as well. Smear of these specimens to look for organisms in macrophages. Serology helpful. See Chapter 8–55.	Amphotericin B if disease is progressive or severe. Ketoconazole is an effective alternative in many cases.
10. Secondary syphilis	Dark field of moist areas of rash; VDRL is as sensitive as FTA-ABS in secondary syphilis, but is not as specific, so both tests should be done. See Chapter 8–46.	Benzathine penicillin G. (Higher doses of penicillin or longer courses recommended by some experts for patients also infected with HIV.)
11. HIV infection	Serology for HIV; lymphopenia; depressed helper T cell (CD4) count. Presence of opportunistic infections such as *Pneumocystis* and *Candida* seen with HIV-related immunosuppression. Cases seen with acute seroconversion (e.g., acute HIV mononucleosis syndrome) require repeat HIV antibody testing in about 6 weeks to 3–6 months for diagnosis; polymerase chain reaction or p24 antigen detection of viral particles may be diagnostic before antibody can be detected. Lymph node enlargement in HIV-positive individuals may also be caused by lymphoma, other tumors, and opportunistic infections.	HIV lympadenopathy in itself does not require specific therapy; however, if the CD4 count is below 500 cells/μL, azidothymidine (AZT) therapy is started and maintained for life if possible. When the CD4 count drops below 200 cells/μL, prophylactic treatment for *Pneumocystis carinii* infection is also begun (see Chapter 8–63). Opportunistic infection and tumors are managed on the basis of the specific etiology.

CMV, cytomegalovirus; EBV, Epstein–Barr virus; PPD, purified protein derivative; VDRL, Venereal Disease Research Laboratory test; WBC, white blood cell count; FTA-ABS, fluorescent treponemal antibody absorption.
Source: Modified from Shulman JA, Schlossberg D. *Handbook for differential diagnosis of infectious diseases.* Vol. 212. New York: Appleton-Century-Crofts, 1980. Reproduced with permission from the publisher and author.

CHAPTER 8–7

Infection and the Presence of Cerebrospinal Fluid White Cell Pleocytosis

Jonas A. Shulman, M.D., and David Rimland, M.D.

DEFINITION

Pleocytosis is defined as the finding of more than five white cells or one polymorphonuclear leukocyte (PMN) per microliter in cerebrospinal fluid (CSF) in the absence of a traumatic lumbar puncture.

ETIOLOGY

Cerebrospinal fluid pleocytosis may be caused by noninfectious agents, but this chapter emphasizes the infectious etiologies as noted in the tables.

CRITERIA FOR DIAGNOSIS

In the absence of a traumatic lumbar puncture, a finding of more than five white cells per microliter or of even one PMN in the CSF constitutes a pleocytosis, and infection must be considered as a potential etiology. Proof of infection requires either a culture or visualization of a pathogen or appropriate serologic studies.

CLINICAL MANIFESTATIONS
Subjective

Most patients undergo lumbar punctures because of headache, fever, and/or stiff neck, but many other symptoms of central nervous system illness such as confusion, delirium, coma, seizures, paralysis, and other focal disturbances may suggest the need for spinal fluid examination. Findings suggestive of neurologic disease in an individual who is at high risk for HIV infection should especially prompt a need for cerebrospinal fluid evaluation. These patients are at significant risk for a variety of infections, such as cryptococcal meningitis, toxoplasma brain abscess, and HIV encephalopathy.

Objective

Physical Examination

A stiff neck is a common but not always present sign of meningeal inflammation. Evidence of altered mental status, seizure activity, paralysis, or other focal findings may be present. Evidence suggestive of increased intracranial pressure or a mass lesion may preclude a lumbar puncture until a brain scan, computed tomography scan, or magnetic resonance imaging scan is performed and no mass lesion is detected. Even in this setting, however, if bacterial meningitis is strongly suspected a lumbar puncture should not be withheld because the etiologic agent must be identified.

We thank Drs. Richard Prokesch and Samuel Webster for their contribution to this chapter in the previous editions of this book.

TABLE 8–7–1. CEREBROSPINAL FLUID: ROUTINE LABORATORY STUDIES

Tube 1	Red and white cell count and differential
Tube 2	Protein, glucose (simultaneous blood glucose)
Tube 3	Gram stains, acid-fast bacillus smears and cultures (bacteriologic, fungal, tuberculin—as clinically indicated)
Tube 4	Repeat red and white cell count and differential (as in tube 1 if the lumbar puncture is bloody initially)
Tube 5	Miscellaneous tests as appropriate (India ink, VDRL, cryptococcal antigen, other fungal serologies, lactic acid, viral cultures, etc.)

Source: Modified from Shulman JA, Schlossberg D, eds. Cerebrospinal fluid pleocytosis. In: Handbook of differential diagnosis of infectious diseases. New York: Appleton-Century-Crofts, 1980:30. Reproduced with permission from the publisher and author.
VDRL, Veneral Disease Research Laboratory test.

Routine Laboratory Abnormalities

See Table 8–7–1.

PLANS
Diagnostic

Once spinal fluid is obtained it should be sent immediately to the laboratory for the studies noted in Table 8–7–1. This group of studies allows one to determine which of the CSF profiles noted in Table 8–7–2 is present and should assist in initial differentiation of the likely etiologic possibilities. These possibilities are shown in Table 8–7–3.

The possible diagnoses and helpful studies when a purulent profile (Table 8–7–2) is obtained are outlined in Chapter 8–9. Some specific observations are also included in Table 8–7–4.

Therapeutic

The specific cause, when found, must be treated. If a bacterial or rickettsial process is suspected, the patient must be treated immediately. Viral infections, except for herpes type I encephalitis, occasional herpes type II, cytomegalovirus, and herpes zoster central nervous system infection, are not usually treatable with specific agents. Some central nervous system infections caused by HIV can be treated with azidothymidine (AZT). The therapy of choice for some of the more common treatable causes of infectious CSF pleocytosis is summarized in Table 8–7–5. If pyogenic meningitis is suspected, see Chapter 8–9 for details of therapy. If specific organisms are not identified, empiric therapy should be administered for the most likely etiologic possibilities.

FOLLOW-UP

Follow-up depends entirely on the specific etiology. If no etiology is found, then repeated reviews of the history and physical examination,

TABLE 8–7–2. CEREBROSPINAL FLUID PROFILES

Type	White Blood Cells (No./μL)	Predominant Cell	Glucose (mg/dL)	Protein (mg/dL)	Lactate (mg/dL)
Normal	<5	Mononuclear	≥40% or more simultaneous blood glucose	<50	<35
Purulent	500–20,000	90% PMNs	Low	100–700	>35
Lymphocytic					
Low glucose	25–500	Mononuclear (PMNs early)	Low or normal	50–500	>35
Normal glucose	5–100	Mononuclear (PMNs early)	Normal, occasionally low	<100	<35

PMNs, polymorphonuclear leukocytes.
Source: Modified from Shulman JA, Schlossberg D, eds. Cerebrospinal fluid pleocytosis. In: Handbook of differential diagnosis of infectious diseases. New York: Appleton-Century-Crofts, 1980:26. Reproduced with permission from the publisher and author.

TABLE 8–7–3. MAJOR CEREBROSPINAL FLUID PROFILES AND THEIR DIFFERENTIAL DIAGNOSIS

Purulent Profile
Infectious causes
  Common
    Bacterial meningitis
  Uncommon
    Viral meningitis (early phase only)
    Parameningeal infections, especially with rupture into the subarachnoid space
    Naeglerial (amebic) meningitis
    Bacterial endocarditis with septic emboli or vasculitis
Noninfectious causes
  Rare
    Chemical meningitis (contrast media, medications, etc.)
    Hypersensitivity meningitis
    Unusual diseases (Behçet's, Molleret's)

Lymphocytic: Low-Glucose Profile
Common
  Tuberculous meningitis
  Fungal meningitis
Uncommon
  Bacterial meningitis (rarely in partially treated meningitis)
  Viral meningitis (mumps, lymphocytic choriomeningitis, at times others)
Noninfectious causes
  Carcinomatous meningitis
  Sarcoidosis

Lymphocytic: Normal-Glucose Profile
Common
  Viral meningoencephalitis
  Postinfectious encephalomyelitis
Less common
  Parameningeal infections
  Granulomatous (fungal/tuberculin) meningitis (early)
  Bacterial endocarditis with septic emboli or vasculitis
Uncommon
  Bacterial meningitis (partially treated, listerial, syphilis, leptospirosis)
  Parasitic diseases (trichinosis, toxoplasmosis, trypanosomiasis)
  Rickettsial diseases
Noninfectious cause
  Central nervous system vasculitis

Source: Modified from Shulman JA, Schlossberg D, eds. Cerebrospinal fluid pleocytosis. In: Handbook of differential diagnosis of infectious diseases. New York: Appleton-Century-Crofts, 1980:26. Reproduced with permission from the publisher and author.

as well as repeated CSF studies, are indicated to help suggest additional evaluation.

DISCUSSION

Prevalence and Incidence

The prevalence and incidence are not known.

Related Basic Science

See Chapter 8–9 for a detailed discussion of normal and pathogenic CSF mechanisms. A cellular response in the spinal fluid may be triggered by numerous microbial pathogens, as well as tumors, subarachnoid hemorrhages, vasculitides, demyelinating processes, toxins, chemicals, and diseases of unknown etiology such as sarcoid and Behçet's syndrome. The illnesses discussed in this chapter are the more common and/or the more treatable. The profiles described (see Table 8–7–2) relate to whether the response is primarily neutrophilic or monocytic and whether or not a low CSF sugar is produced. The mechanism of the low CSF sugar is thought to relate primarily to a decrease in active transport of glucose into the CSF from the blood, although CSF cells, bacteria, and phagocytosis may contribute to the low sugar in certain instances.

Natural History and Its Modification with Treatment

The natural history depends entirely on the specific cause of the CSF pleocytosis and is therefore covered in the specific chapters.

Prevention

See other chapters relating to the specific etiologies of CSF pleocytosis.

One method of prevention of bacterial central nervous system infections is rapid and appropriate treatment of the primary source of the infection, such as the preceding pneumonia or otitis media, before it extends to involve the central nervous system. HIV infection can be avoided by not participating in known high-risk activities. A number of viral infections such as polio, measles, and mumps can be prevented by vaccination. Similarly, *Hemophilus influenzae*, meningococcal, and pneumococcal vaccines can reduce the incidence of bacterial meningitis.

Cost Containment

Preventive measures such as specific vaccines, prophylactic medications, and avoidance of certain activities can certainly reduce the cost of

TABLE 8–7–4. POSSIBLE DIAGNOSES AND CORRESPONDING TESTS AND OBSERVATIONS

Diagnostic Possibility	Diagnostic Tests or Observations
Purulent profile	
Bacterial meningitis	Gram stain is positive in 80% of cases. Culture is positive in 90–95% of cases. If Gram stain is negative, do methylene blue stain in an attempt to demonstrate the bacteria. In addition to cerebrospinal fluid, blood cultures, Gram stains of petechiae, counterimmunoelectrophoresis and other methods of antigen detection, and limulus tests may be helpful. If anaerobic organisms grow, suspect a ruptured brain abscess.
Naeglerial meningitis	Gram stain and cultures are normal, but wet mounts and cresyl fast stains may be positive. Discuss culture techniques with laboratories. Diving in freshwater lakes is an important epidemiologic clue.
Parameningeal infections	Gram stain and culture are negative unless rupture into the subarachnoid space has occurred. Frequent clues include focal findings, history or findings of ear, nose, and throat infections, lung abscess, or right-to-left shunts in congenital heart disease.
Bacterial endocarditis	Gram stains and/or cultures may or may not be positive. Blood cultures are positive in over 90% of cases. Other stigmata of endocarditis may be present (see Chapter 8–12).
Chemical meningitis	Gram stain and culture are negative. Keratin may be noted under polarized light if a dermoid cyst is present. Prior use of intrathecal drugs such as methotrexate or myelography dye may be a clue.
Behçet's syndrome	Gram stains and culture are negative. Involvement of eye, mucous membranes, gastrointestinal tract, and other organs may provide a clue.
Lymphocytic, low-glucose cerebrospinal fluid	
Tuberculous meningitis	Mononuclear cells predominate, although in early phases PMNs may predominate. Acid-fast smear is positive in only about 10% of cases, but mycobacterial cultures are positive in about 80% of cases. If a pellicle is present, it should be stained to increase yield. Tuberculostearate may be detected in CSF. Chest x-ray and PPD should be checked and may give supportive data. A liver, lung, or bone marrow biopsy and culture may prove helpful.
Fungal meningitis	Mononuclear cells predominate except early in the disease process. In HIV-infected patients, no WBCs may be detected, and the only indicator of cryptococcal meningitis may be a positive cryptococcal antigen, India ink preparation, and/or culture. Sugar may be normal in early phases. Cryptococcal meningitis has a positive India ink preparation about 50% of the time and positive antigen test about 95% of the time. In HIV-infectd patients, serum cryptococcal antigens are very likely to be positive. Cultures of CSF, urine, blood, and skin lesions should also be obtained for cryptococci. Sputum smears and cultures should be obtained if the chest x-ray is abnormal. Cryptococcal meningitis

TABLE 8–7–4. (Continued)

Diagnostic Possibility	Diagnostic Tests or Observations
	should be strongly considered in patients at risk for AIDS (see Chapter 8–76). For histoplasmosis and coccidioidomycosis, complement fixation tests and cultures of CSF and sera are helpful. For blastomycosis, CSF cultures are needed. Obviously, a search for fungus in other tissues such as lung or marrow may be helpful.
Carcinomatous meningitis	Mononuclear and/or tumor cells are present. The sugar may be decreased or normal. Cytologic examination of CSF may prove the diagnosis.
Sarcoid meningitis	Chest x-ray, liver tests, lymph node and liver biopsies may be helpful as well as a Kveim skin test or a high level of angiotensin-converting enzyme in serum.
Bacterial meningitis	See above (Bacterial Meningitis). Rarely, this profile is seen in partially treated infections and in *Listeria* meningitis.
Viral meningitis	See below (Viral Meningoencephalitis). Rarely, low sugar levels are seen, especially in mumps, herpes, and lymphocytic choriomeningitis.
Lymphocytic, normal-glucose cerebrospinal fluid	
Viral meningoencephalitis	Mononuclear cells predominate, although in early phases PMNs may dominate. Protein is usually less than 100 mg/dL. Gram stain and bacterial cultures are negative, but CSF viral cultures may be positive. In addition, viral cultures should be performed on pharyngeal and rectal swabs. Viral serologic studies are indicated.
	Vaccination history is important in consideration of polio, mumps, and postvaccinal encephalitis.
	History of risk for HIV infection may suggest possible HIV meningoencephalitis and need for studies to detect antibody or viral antigens.
	Herpes hominis type I encephalitis is especially suspect with focal temporal lobe signs. Nonspecific aids include CT scan, EEG, brain scan, and angiography. A normal EEG argues against this diagnosis. Diagnosis is definitively made by brain biopsy with stains and viral cultures (see Chapter 8–11). In a highly suspect case many times patients are treated with acyclovir without biopsy.
Parameningeal infections (these include brain abscess, subdural empyema, epidural abscess, cerebral thrombophlebitis, and cranial osteomyelitis)	CSF reveals negative Gram stain and culture. Prior sites of infection, especially ear, nose, throat and lung, and right-to-left shunts in patients with congenital heart disease are predisposing factors. Blood cultures should be done. Brain scan, EEG, CT scan, and/or angiography are helpful. Skull, sinus, and mastoid films are also needed. If spinal epidural abscess is suspected, spine x-rays are indicated, and myelography and/or a directed CT scan may be needed. MRI is sometimes useful.
Granulomatous meningitis	See above (Tuberculous Meningitis and Fungal Meningitis)
Bacterial meningitis (partially treated)	See above (Bacterial Meningitis)
Syphilis	VDRL on CSF (see Chapter 8–46). VDRL and FTA-ABS on serum.
Leptospirosis	Culture blood, urine, and CSF on special media (discuss with laboratory). Acute and convalescent serology. Negative Gram stain and routine cultures of CSF. Suspect especially in patients with severe muscle aches, high creatine kinase levels, peripheral neutrophilia, hepatic and renal dysfunction.
Lyme disease	Especially suspected in patients who give a history of a skin rash suggestive of erythema chronicum migrans. Diagnosis is based on clinical findings and positive Lyme serology. Serology at times not positive until 6 months after infection. Newer tests being developed including polymerase chain reaction (PCR) for detection of components of the organism and more refined serology for the serum and CSF.
Parasitic diseases	
Toxoplasmosis	Serology, acute and convalescent. Wright's or Giemsa stain of CSF. Brain biopsy with specific stains may be required. If adenopathy present, biopsy may be highly characteristic. Toxoplasmosis should be strongly considered in patients at risk for AIDS (see Chapter 8–76).
Trichinosis	May see eosinophils in the CSF as well as peripheral blood. Serology and muscle biopsy helpful.
Malaria	Peripheral blood smears, thick and thin.
Rickettsial diseases	Minimal increase in cells— lymphocytes and/or PMNs with slight increase in protein.
	Specific acute and convalescent serologies are diagnostic in most cases. Proteux OX serology is very nonspecific. If a rash is present, as it almost always is, biopsy and staining with specific fluorescent antibody may make the diagnosis more rapidly. Usually diagnosis is made on clinical grounds. In United States, Rocky Mountain spotted fever is a likely rickettsial infection, and the tick bite history, rash, clinical course, and time of year (April–September) may be highly suggestive (see Chapters 8–49 and 8–50).
Central nervous system vasculitis	See Chapters 7–1 and 7–11.

PMN, polymorphonuclear leukocytes; PPD, purified protein derivative; WBCs, white blood cells; EEG, electroencephalography; FTA-ABS, fluorescent treponemal antibody, absorption; CT, computed tomography; MRI, magnetic resonance imaging.

TABLE 8–7–5. THERAPY OF MORE COMMON TREATABLE CAUSES OF INFECTIOUS CEREBROSPINAL FLUID PLEOCYTOSIS

Specific Agent	Therapy of Choice
Bacterial meningitis	See Chapter 8–9
Naeglerial meningitis	Amphotericin B and rifampin
Parameningeal infections	See Chapter 8–10
Bacterial endocarditis	Acute: Either nafcillin or vancomycin and gentamicin
	Subacute: Either ampicillin or vancomycin and gentamicin
Tuberculous meningitis	Isoniazid, rifampin, and ethambutol or pyrizinamide
Fungal meningitis	Amphotericin B. If cryptococcus is suspected or found, add 5-flucytosine (see Chapter 8–9). Oral fluconazole can be given after an initial course of amphotericin B.
Herpesvirus hominis type I encephalitis and occasional cases of herpesvirus hominis type II infection or herpes zoster encephalitis	Intravenous acyclovir
HIV infection	In selected cases azidothymidine (AZT) is used (see Chapter 8–76).
Syphilitic meningitis	Penicillin G
Leptospirosis	Penicillin G
Lyme disease	Ceftriaxone or penicillin G
Toxoplasmosis	Pyrimethamine and sulfadiazine (add folinic acid)

(continued)

TABLE 8–7–5. (*Continued*)

Specific Agent	Therapy of Choice
Trichinosis	Corticosteroids and thiabendazole
Malaria	See Chapter 8–61.
Rickettsial meningitis	Chloramphenicol or tetracycline.

managing these serious central nervous system infections. Once meningitis occurs, rapid diagnosis and efficient planning of diagnostic studies are superb ways to contain cost. For example, if syphilis is not considered and a simple CSF Venereal Disease Research Laboratory test is not obtained, a prolonged illness and many unnecessary tests may ensue.

REFERENCES

Conly JM, Ronald AR. Cerebrospinal fluid as a diagnostic body fluid. Am J Med 1983;75(1B):102.

Gray LD, Fedorko DP. Laboratory diagnosis of bacterial meningitis. Clin Microbiol Rev 1992;5:130.

Karandanis D, Shulman JA. Recent survey of infectious meningitis in adults: A review of laboratory findings in bacterial, tuberculous, and aseptic meningitis. South J Med 1976;69:449.

Martin WJ. Rapid and reliable techniques for the laboratory detection of bacterial meningitis. Am J Med 1983;75(1B):119.

Shulman JA, Schlossberg D, eds. Cerebrospinal fluid pleocytosis. In: Handbook for differential diagnosis of infectious diseases. New York: Appleton-Century-Crofts, 1980:25.

Swartz MN, Dodge PR. Bacterial meningitis: Review of selected aspects. N Engl J Med 1965;272:725.

CHAPTER 8–8

Tuberculosis (Including Chemoprophylaxis and Atypical Mycobacteria)

(See Section 13, Chapter 41)

CHAPTER 8–9

Meningitis

Rafael A. Caputi, M.D., Monica M. Farley, M.D., and David Rimland, M.D.

DEFINITION

Meningitis is an inflammatory process affecting the leptomeninges and the intervening cerebrospinal fluid (CSF), manifested by pleocytosis in almost all cases.

ETIOLOGY

Until recently, *Hemophilus influenzae* was the most commonly identified etiology overall (45%), followed by *Streptococcus pneumoniae* (18%) and *Neisseria meningitidis* (14%). Although incidence rates vary somewhat by race, season, and region, the incidence of specific pathogens and case fatality rates are most influenced by age. For example, in neonates (infants <1 month of age), group B streptococcus is the most common causative organism, whereas *H. influenzae* predominates in those aged 1 month to 4 years, *N. meningitidis* is most common in older children and young adults (ages 5–29 years), and *S. pneumoniae* predominates in those over age 30.

Most recently, however, it has become clear that the epidemiology of bacterial meningitis is rapidly changing, particularly in the United States. Since the introduction of *H. influenzae* type b (Hib) polysaccharide–protein conjugate vaccine, the incidence in children of invasive Hib disease, including meningitis, has been dramatically reduced. The Centers for Disease Control and Prevention recently reported an 82% decrease in the incidence of Hib meningitis between 1985 and 1991 in children less than 5 years old, a decrease that coincided with increased distribution of Hib vaccine. In addition, many institutions, particularly large teaching hospitals, have noted an increase in nosocomial meningitis, due mainly to Gram-negative bacilli (other than *H. influenzae*).

Table 8–9–1 lists the etiologic agents of meningitis and includes the associated epidemiologic features and laboratory findings.

CRITERIA FOR DIAGNOSIS

Suggestive

A clinical presentation that includes fever, stiff neck, and altered mental status is suggestive of acute meningitis. Photophobia and vomiting may also occur; however, symptoms are often less specific in neonates, infants, and the elderly. CSF pleocytosis or abnormal CSF protein or glucose levels may also suggest the diagnosis.

Definitive

A positive CSF culture (bacterial, viral, fungal, etc.) establishes the diagnosis; however, the etiology may be established clinically by correlating results of the CSF examination (see Chapter 8–7) with other serologic, bacteriologic, and clinical data.

CLINICAL MANIFESTATIONS

Subjective

Severe headache, fever, and stiff neck are common complaints of patients with meningitis. Although the symptoms of viral meningitis tend

We thank Dr. Richard Prokesch for his contribution to this chapter in the previous editions of this book.

TABLE 8–9–1. CLINICAL CLUES TO ETIOLOGY OF MENINGITIS

Organism	Clinical Setting	Helpful Adjunctive* Laboratory Data
Bacterial Infection		
Group B streptococcus	Neonates; less commonly in elderly and immunocompromised adults	Blood cultures, cultures of maternal vagina and cervix
Pneumococcus	Sickle cell disease; alcoholism; multiple myeloma; HIV infection; hypogammaglobulinemia; splenectomy; head trauma; recurrent meningitis; pneumonia; endocarditis; otitis; sinusitis; mastoiditis	Latex antigen test, blood cultures, sinus films, mastoid films, chest x-ray
Meningococcus	Epidemic meningitis; military recruits; characteristic rash; healthy adults and children; winter and spring	Blood cultures, Gram stain from petechial scrapings, Gram stain of buffy coat
Staphylococcus (aureus or epidermidis)	Malignancy; trauma; neurosurgical procedures; endocarditis; infected ventricular shunts	Blood cultures, ventricular fluid culture
Hemophilus influenzae	2 months to 3 years old; pharyngitis; sinusitis; otitis media; epiglottitis	Latex test, blood cultures
Listeria monocytogenes	Malignancy, especially lymphoma; alcoholism; diabetes mellitus; neonates; immunologic defects (especially T cell); foodborne outbreak association	Blood cultures, "tumbling motility"
Gram-negative bacteria (other than Neisseria meningitidis and H. Influenzae)	Neonates; trauma; neurosurgical procedures; carcinoma; hospital-acquired disease	Blood cultures
Borreliaburgdorferi	Lyme disease; may occur in secondary or tertiary stage; history of tick bite or erythema chronicum migrans not always present; may be associated with cranial nerve palsies or radiculopathy	Serology (in a laboratory with special expertise), PCR testing also helpful
Leptospira	Water contaminated with infected animal urine; conjunctivitis; hepatitis; renal involvement	Blood cultures, acute/convalescent serology
Treponema pallidum	Syphilis; may occur in secondary, latent or tertiary phase	Blood and CSF nontreponemal studies are helpful, but occasionally CSF VDRL can be negative. A positive FTA-ABS in peripheral blood is nearly always positive
Mycobacterium tuberculosis	Pulmonary or miliary tuberculosis; tuberculosis exposure	Chest x-ray, skin test
Parasitic Disease		
Naegleria (amebic)	Diving into freshwater lakes (especially southeastern United States)	Wet prep or cresyl violet stain of CSF
Fungal Infection		
Cryptococcus	Most frequently seen in patients with HIV infection and at times in other immunocompromised patients (renal failure, malignancy, diabetes mellitus, immunosuppressive drugs)	India ink; cryptococcal antigen on CSF and blood; cultures of urine, blood, and bone marrow for Cryptococcus
Viral Infection		
HIV	May occur with acute seroconversion or a later stage; may be associated with radiculopathy, myelitis, or encephalitis	Acute and convalescent serology. In early disease, PCR or p24 antigen testing may be helpful.
Mumps	Late spring–winter; parotitis; orchitis; pancreatitis	Acute/convalescent serology
Enteroviruses (echovirus, Coxsackie virus)	Late summer–early fall; pleurodynia; herpangina; myopericarditis; maculopapular or petechial rash	Viral cultures of CSF and stool, acute/convalescent serology
Enteroviruses (poliovirus)	Rare now; may be associated with vaccination or contact with recently vaccinated individual; paralysis may be present	Viral cultures of stool, acute/convalescent serology
Arbovirus	Summer–fall; encephalitis symptoms may be prominent; usually in epidemics	Acute/convalescent serology
Lymphocytic choriomeningitis	Mice or hamsters	Acute/convalescent serology
Herpesvirus hominis type 2	Not seasonal; local genital lesion may be present	Viral cultures, acute/convalescent serology
Epstein–Barr virus	Not seasonal; mononucleosis syndrome	Complete blood count with differential, atypical lymphocytes, mono spot, acute/convalescent serology
Influenza	Winter, known influenza epidemic; pneumonia	Acute/convalescent serology
Herpesvirus hominis type I	Not seasonal; frequently local encephalitis findings, especially temporoparietal lobes; local mucous membrane lesions rare	EEG, computed tomography scan, brain biopsy with cultures, spinal fluid PCR needed for diagnosis

CSF, cerebrospinal fluid; VDRL, Venereal Disease Research Laboratory test; FTA-ABS, fluorescent treponemal antibody absorption; PCR, polymerase chain reaction; EEG, electroencephalogram.

*In addition to CSF studies (i.e., cell counts, protein, glucose, Gram stain, bacterial cultures, cryptococcal antigen, and, when appropriate, India ink preparations, acid-fast bacillus smears, and fungal, tuberculosis, and viral cultures.

to be milder and less fulminant than those of bacterial meningitis, there is a great deal of overlap.

Clinical clues in the history can suggest a specific etiologic agent (see Table 8–9–1). In community-acquired bacterial meningitis, antecedent upper respiratory tract infection is common (40%). Between 25 and 75% of patients with bacterial meningitis have a rapid onset (within 24 hours) of headache, lethargy, fever, and nuchal rigidity. Photophobia is more often associated with viral meningitis.

The infectious agents that cause meningitis are distinctly related to the patient's age, and symptoms vary markedly in the various age groups. Many of the usual meningeal symptoms such as stiff neck and fever are absent in young children and in the elderly. In infants, irritability, poor feeding, and vomiting may be the only symptoms noted by parents. Fever, headache, stiff neck, and altered mental status (confusion, lethargy, etc.) are the most frequent presenting complaints in the other age groups.

Objective

Physical Examination

Fever is present in more than 80% of patients with bacterial, viral, and granulomatous meningitis. Some patients present with convulsions, altered mental status, or focal neurologic findings. Although focal neurologic signs are seen with meningitis (10%), they should lead the clinician to initiate a careful search for a localized cerebral process (e.g., cerebral abscess, venous sinus thrombosis). Papilledema is rare and suggests another diagnosis.

Nuchal rigidity is a classic physical finding reflecting meningeal irritation. Kernig's sign (pain in the hamstrings and back on extension of the knee with patient supine and the thigh perpendicular to the trunk) and Brudzinski's sign (neck flexion producing knee and hip flexion) are present in only 50% of patients but are helpful findings when detected. Most patients with meningitis have an altered sensorium (approximately 80%). Vomiting and seizures occur in approximately one third of patients. Bulging fontanelles are commonly noted in neonates and young infants with meningitis. Petechiae are useful clues if present, but are found in only 50% of patients with meningococcemia. The mastoids or sinuses may be tender, and signs of otitis, pharyngitis, and pheumonia are found in up to 30% of patients, depending on the implicated pathogen.

In the elderly or debilitated patient, a change in mental status, ranging from confusion or lethargy to coma, may be the only indication of meningitis. Meningeal signs and fever may be entirely absent, so that the signs are, at times, mistakenly attributed to a noninfectious cerebrovascular event or dementia.

Routine Laboratory Abnormalities

Routine laboratory test results are not very helpful in diagnosis. The peripheral white blood cell count is greater then 10,000/μL in nearly 75% of patients with bacterial meningitis, but is less frequently elevated in patients with viral (about 15%) or tuberculous meningitis.

PLANS

Diagnostic

Differential Diagnosis

A wide variety of microbial pathogens are associated with infectious meningitis (Table 8–9–1). The differential diagnosis of meningitis includes other central nervous system infections such as brain abscess, subdural empyema, and epidural abscess; encephalitis, including that due to herpes simplex virus; neurosyphilis; amebic meningoencephalitis; and central nervous system manifestations of acute endocarditis. Noninfectious diagnoses to be considered include sarcoidosis, neoplasms, drug-induced meningitis due to nonsteroidal antiinflammatory agents and trimethoprim–sulfamethoxazole, and vasculitis of the central nervous system.

Diagnostic Options

A diagnosis of meningitis can be suspected on the basis of clinical clues, but must be confirmed and rests on examination of the CSF. The typical findings of bacterial meningitis (e.g., increased opening pressure, raised protein and leukocyte concentrations with hypoglycorrhachia) are generally found, but any specific finding may be absent in an individual patient. Although at times patients with viral meningitis may show white counts in the spinal fluid of greater than 1000/μL, in most cases counts in this range suggest bacterial meningitis. A markedly elevated CSF protein level (greater than 150 mg/dL) and a depressed glucose level (less than 50% of the blood glucose), although common in bacterial, tuberculous, and fungal meningitis, are unusual in viral meningitis.

Although not conclusively established, elevations of CSF lactate may facilitate differentiation of partially treated bacterial meningitis from a viral syndrome. Various enzymes, for example, lactate dehydrogenase and creatine phosphokinase, are increased in the CSF during bacterial meningitis, but the specificity of these findings is poor and delineation of enzyme concentrations has not proved useful in the clinical situation.

The CSF culture remains the gold standard for diagnosis but is positive in only 70 to 80% of patients. Most initial decisions are based on the appearance of the CSF Gram stain; the sensitivity of this test correlates with the bacterial concentration within CSF and is therefore influenced by previous antimicrobial therapy. Latex agglutination has become an important tool for the rapid diagnosis of bacterial meningitis, even in settings where the CSF culture is negative. The sensitivity of this test is highly dependent on the pathogen and the experience within the clinical microbiology laboratory. Antigen detection in the spinal fluid is useful in the rapid diagnosis of cryptococcal meningitis, especially in patients with HIV infection. The CSF limulus lysate assay is nearly 100% sensitive in detecting endotoxin within the cerebrospinal fluid; however, this assay is not widely available and seldom alters the initial therapeutic approach.

Blood cultures are very helpful in the diagnosis of bacterial meningitis, because they are positive in 40 to 70% of such patients. Stains of petechiae or of a buffy coat smear of peripheral blood are particularly useful in suspected meningococcemia. Detection of meningococcal and mycobacterial DNA in cerebrospinal fluid by polymerase chain reaction appears promising and may not be influenced by prior antimicrobial therapy. Despite a plethora of new tests, the diagnosis of meningitis most often still rests on proper interpretations of traditional CSF parameters.

Recommended Approach

The physician should perform a lumbar puncture when meningitis is suspected. The initial approach to a patient requires rapid assessment and evaluation. The only absolute contraindication to a lumbar puncture is infection overlying the area to be punctured. Increased intracranial pressure suggestive of an intracranial mass, a bleeding diathesis, and spinal cord tumors are relative contraindications. In the setting of focal neurologic signs or papilledema, a computed tomography scan should be done prior to the lumbar puncture. If suspicion remains high for purulent meningitis, a lumbar puncture may still be performed using a small-gauge needle and withdrawing only a small amount of fluid for Gram stain and culture.

Therapeutic

The general approach to a patient with bacterial meningitis requires recognition of the problem, early identification of the pathogen, and rapid initiation of antimicrobial therapy. The initial therapy of bacterial meningitis is empiric unless the organism can be definitely identified on Gram stain. Appropriate empiric therapy depends on the patient's history and age, epidemiology, and existence of an underlying disease (Table 8–9–2). Of course, once the etiology is clear, therapy should be modified and made as specific as possible (Tables 8–9–3 and 8–9–4). Only antibiotics known to penetrate the CSF effectively should be used to treat bacterial meningitis. Therapy for cryptococcal meningitis is detailed in Chapter 8–54.

The dosing regimens (intermittent versus continuous infusion of drugs) have been studied principally for penicillin G and appear to have comparable efficacy. The duration of therapy, like many other regimens for serious infections, remains largely empiric, but is generally 10 to 14 days for most patients. The time from the initial evaluation to antimicrobial administration should not exceed 30 minutes. If a computed tomography scan is ordered but meningitis remains a likely consideration, antimicrobial therapy should be instituted during the procedure after blood cultures are obtained. Although this practice may render the CSF culture negative, the profile will still suggest a bacterial process in the vast majority of cases of bacterial meningitis treated empirically during the computed tomography scan.

Adjunctive therapy with dexamethasone (0.15 mg/kg every 6 hours for 4 days) is currently recommended for children with bacterial meningitis, based on recent data showing a decrease in sensorineural hearing loss. Although the majority of children in these trials had *H. influenzae* meningitis, it seems reasonable the benefits of steroids will extend to children infected with other pathogens. The benefits of adjunctive corticosteroids in other age groups (e.g., neonates and adults) is less clear, but treatment may be considered in adults with bacterial meningitis who present in coma or with focal neurologic findings.

TABLE 8–9–2. EMPIRIC THERAPY OF PURULENT MENINGITIS

Age	Suspected Organisms	Standard Therapy	IV dosage/24 h	Alternatives
0–3 wk	Group B streptococci Gram-negative enterics *Listeria monocytogenes*	Ampicillin plus cefotaxime	150–200 mg/kg 100–150 mg/kg	Ampicillin plus aminoglycoside
4–12 wk	Group B streptococci Gram-negative enterics *L. monocytogenes* *Hemophilus influenzae* *Streptococcus pneumonia*	Ampicillin plus cefotaxime	200–250 mg/kg 200 mg/kg	Ampicillin plus aminoglycoside (gentamicin 5 mg/kg)
3 mo–18 y	*H. influenzae* *S. pneumoniae*[†] *N. meningitidis*	Third-generation* cephalosporins (cefotaxime or ceftriaxone)	Cefotaxime 200 mg/kg or ceftriaxone 100 mg/kg (max 4 g)	Ampicillin plus chloramphenicol (100 mg/kg)
18–60 y	*S. pneumoniae*[†] *N. meningitidis*	Third-generation* cephalosporins[‡]	Ceftriaxone 2–4 g or cefotaxime 12 g or ampicillin 12 g	Penicillin G (24 million U) or chloramphenicol (4–6 g)
>60 y	*S. pneumoniae*[†] *N. meningitidis* *L. monocytogenes*	Third-generation* cephalosporins plus ampicillin	Ceftriaxone 2–4 g or cefotaxime 12 g or ampicillin 12 g	Ampicillin plus aminoglycoside, trimethoprim–sulfamethoxazole (10–20 mg/kg)

*Third-generation cephalosporins, cefotaxime and ceftriaxone, have been studied most intensively. Ceftriaxone is avoided in neonates due to concerns of bilirubin displacement because of the high protein binding of this compound. Ceftizoxime has also been employed successfully.
[†]In areas with multiresistant pneumococci, vancomycin should be added; also add rifampin if on steroids, until in vitro susceptibility studies are done.
[‡]Add ampicillin if *L. monocytogenes* is suspected.

In patients who have had neurosurgical procedures or who have carcinoma, *Staphylococcus aureus* and coagulase-negative *Staphylococcus* are quite likely and vancomycin should be added; Gram-negative meningitis should also be considered. If *Pseudomonas aeruginosa* is suspected, ceftazidime and an aminoglycoside should be used.

TABLE 8–9–3. ANTIBIOTIC TREATMENT FOR BACTERIAL MENINGITIS OF KNOWN ETIOLOGY IN ADULTS

Organism	Preferred Antibiotic	IV dosage/24 h	Alternative Antibiotic	IV dosage/24 h
Streptococcus pneumoniae				
Penicillin-susceptible	Pencillin G or ampicillin	24 million U 12 g	Ceftriaxone Cefotaxime	2–4 g 12 g
Penicillin-resistant, cephalosporin-susceptible	Ceftriaxone	2–4 g	Chloramphenicol Cefotaxime	4–6 g 12 g
Penicillin- and cephalosporin-resistant)	Vancomycin (± rifampin)	2–4 g	Vancomycin —	2–4 g
Neisseria meningitidis	Penicillin G or ampicillin	24 million U 12 g	Ceftriaxone Cefotaxime Chloramphenicol	2–4 g 12 g 4–6 g
Hemophilus influenzae				
β-lactamase-negative	Ampicillin	12 g	Ceftriaxone Cefotaxime Chloramphenicol	2–4 g 12 g 4–6 g
β-lactamase-positive, 30–40%	Ceftriaxone Cefotaxime	2–4 g 12 g	Chloramphenicol	4–6 g
Group B streptococci	Penicillin G or ampicillin (± gentamicin)	24 million U 12 g 3–5 mg/kg	Cefotaxime Ceftriaxone Vancomycin Chloramphenicol	12 g 2–4 g 2–4 g 4–6 g
Listeria monocytogenes	Penicillin G or ampicillin (± gentamicin)	24 million U 12 g 3–5 mg/kg	Trimethoprim–Sulfamethoxazole	10–20 mg/kg
Staphylococcus aureus				
Methicillin-susceptible	Nafcillin or oxacillin ± rifampin	12 g 600 mg PO	Vancomycin	2–4 g
Methicillin-resistant	Vancomycin ± rifampin	2–4 g 600 mg PO	Trimethoprim–sulfamethoxazole plus rifampin	10–20 mg/kg 600 mg PO
Staphylococcus (coagulase-negative)	Vancomycin ± rifampin	2–4 g 600 mg PO	Consider teicoplanin	Consult specialist
Enterobacteriaceae*	Ceftriaxone or cefotaxime	2–4 g 12 g	Piperacillin[†] plus aminoglycosides	18–24 g 5 mg/kg
*Pseudomonas aeruginosa**	Ceftazidime plus gentamicin or tobramycin	6–12 g 5 mg/kg	Piperacillin[†] plus gentamicin or tobramycin Consider intrathecal gentamicin	18–24 g 5 mg/kg

*Antibiotic choice contingent on known susceptibility.
[†]Carboxypenicillins may also be used. Aztreonam, imipenem, and quinolones (e.g., ciprofloxacin or ofloxacin) are also possible alternatives, but their effectiveness in bacterial meningitis has not been as clearly established. Of the quinolones, ofloxacin may give higher cerebrospinal fluid levels than ciprofloxacin.

TABLE 8–9–4.   CEREBROSPINAL FLUID PENETRATION OF ANTIBIOTICS USED TO TREAT MENINGITIS

Antibiotic	Penetration	Use in Meningitis
Penicillins	Poor in absence of meningeal inflammation; good if inflammation present	Mainstay of therapy of susceptible organisms
Aminoglycosides	Poor	Synergy in vitro for group B streptococci and *Listeria monocytogenes;* whether addition provides added efficacy in vivo is unknown; also used for Enterococcus and *Pseudomonas* meningitis
Chloramphenicol	Excellent (30–50% plasma levels)	Excellent drug where clinically appropriate (although bacteriologic failures in some cases of Enterobacteriaceae meningitis have occurred even when the organisms are sensitive); transient bone marrow suppression common; aplastic anemia rare
Cephalosporins (first- and second-generation)	Poor (except for cefuroxime)	None; even cefuroxime should not be used, as it has been associated with treatment failures
Cephalosporins (third-generation: cefotaxime, ceftriaxone, ceftizoxime, ceftazidime)	Fair but more than adequate for therapy	Drug of choice for empiric therapy of purulent meningitis
Vancomycin	Poor to fair	Reports of successful treatment of *Staphylococcus aureus* and coagulase-negative *Staphylococcus,* as well as for *Streptococcus pneumoniae* and *Neisseria meningitidis* highly resistant to penicillin
Tetracyclines	Fair	Rarely, if ever indicated
Erythromycin	Fair to poor	Rarely used for penicillin-allergic patients
Sulfonamides	Excellent	For infection due to susceptible meningococci and *Nocardia*
Rifampin	Excellent	Useful in tuberculosis; also for combination in staphylococcal meningitis and resistant pneumococcal meningitis
Isoniazid	Excellent	For tuberculous meningitis
Metronidazole	Good	For anaerobic infections due to *Bacteroides* or *Fusobacterium*
Trimethoprim	Excellent	Useful in combination with sulfonamides for *Listeria* and *Enterobacter* meningitis
Aztreonam	Good	Clinical efficacy not established
Imipenem	Good	Clinical efficacy not established

Other supportive measures such as ventilatory assistance, antiseizure medications, and appropriate intravenous fluids may be necessary. In addition, close observation and treatment of any complication such as shock, disseminated intravascular coagulation, or the syndrome of inappropriate antidiuresis are mandatory.

FOLLOW-UP

If the patient has shown a good clinical response, especially in proven bacterial meningitis, it is not necessary to repeat the lumbar puncture. If the clinical response is not striking after 3 to 4 days of appropriate therapy, or if the patient's condition worsens, careful reevaluation should be done with another lumbar puncture. If significant fever persists after the first 5 days, a more thorough evaluation for complications specific to meningitis (e.g., subdural effusions, parameningeal foci, venous sinus or arterial thrombosis, or cerebral abscess formation) is indicated. In children with bacterial meningitis, follow-up to detect hearing defects or subtle chronic neurologic injury is indicated.

Nonneurologic findings, associated especially with pneumococcal meningitis, include endocarditis, pneumonia, and arthritis. A nonsuppurative arthritis and pericarditis can be seen during convalescence from meningococcal disease and are thought to be an immunologic phenomenon. If viral meningitis is suspected, CSF and rectal swab specimens should be obtained for viral isolation at the time of the illness, as should acute sera. Convalescent sera should be drawn approximately 1 month after the acute illness to help specifically identify the viral etiology. Patients with AIDS and cryptococcal infection need continued close observation for both potential relapse and possible toxicity of the lifelong antifungal therapy.

DISCUSSION
Prevalence and Incidence

The incidence of bacterial meningitis in the United States has been estimated to be 20,000 to 30,000 cases annually. A substantial decline

(82%) in invasive *H. influenzae* disease has been observed in the United States since the introduction of new vaccines in the mid-1980s (Quagliarello and Scheld, 1993). At the same time, many institutions have noted an increase in nosocomial meningitis cases.

Related Basic Science

Most cases of bacterial meningitis appear to be hematogenous in origin. The process generally requires a series of steps including bacterial attachment to and invasion of the epithelial surface, followed by bloodstream and subarachnoid space invasion. The initial steps have been studied most extensively in *Neisseria meningitidis* and *H. influenzae*. Both organisms colonize the nasopharyngeal epithelium, attaching to nonciliated epithelial cells. The organisms may then either penetrate directly into epithelial cells (as is the case for meningococcus) or invade between adjacent epithelial cells (*H. influenzae*). Following successful colonization and invasion, the organisms produce a bacteremia that may lead to meningitis.

Meningitis may also arise through spread from a contiguous focus of infection (e.g., sinusitis, otitis, or mastoiditis) or by direct entry into the central nervous system (e.g., head trauma, neurosurgery, or following lumbar puncture).

Pathogenesis and tissue injury result from a complex interaction of bacterial virulence factors, inflammatory mediators such as cytokines and granulocytes, and their products. The pathologic hallmark of meningitis is an inflammatory exudate within the subarachnoid space. Specifically, subcapsular bacterial surface components (e.g., cell wall components of *S. pneumoniae* and lipopolysaccharide of *H. influenzae, N. meningitidis,* and *Escherichia coli*) induce the local production and secretion of inflammatory cytokines within the CSF, particularly interleukin-1, interleukin-6, and tumor necrosis factor. In bacterial meningitis, the neutrophil count increases and the CSF glucose level drops (likely secondary to a decrease in glucose transport). If the infection is viral, fungal, tuberculous, or spirochetal, the neutrophil count increases early but is then replaced by monocytic leukocytes.

Natural History and Its Modification with Treatment

Several factors are helpful in predicting prognosis in meningitis. Increased morbidity and mortality occur in neonates as well as in the elderly. The most important predictor is the initial severity of the illness; gravely ill patients presenting with serious focal neurologic signs or in coma do poorly. Underlying conditions such as immunosuppressant medications, malignancy, HIV infection, and alcoholism worsen the prognosis.

Prognosis also depends on the causative organism. Pneumococcal meningitis has a particularly bad prognosis, with a mortality of 30 to 50% and significant residual neurologic defects in the survivors. In meningococcal meningitis, appearance of a rash within 12 hours of presentation, shock, a normal or decreased peripheral white count, and minimal CSF pleocytosis are associated with a poor outcome.

Prevention

Few diseases ignite the fear that develops when bacterial meningitis strikes a community. Its potential for communicability and fatality frightens families and health care workers alike. Prevention of meningitis with routine vaccination programs is very cost effective, as noted by the decline in the number of meningitis cases caused by polio and *H. influenzae* type b.

Meningococcal meningitis may produce large or small epidemics of disease, and prophylaxis in certain groups of close contacts is known to be effective. Rifampin (5 mg/kg in children <1 year old, 10 mg/kg in older children, or 600 mg in adults, given every 12 hours for a total of four doses) is the prophylactic antibiotic of choice. Ciprofloxacin is also effective; a single dose of 500 or 750 mg is more than 90% effective in eradicating pharyngeal carriage. Minocycline has been almost as effective as rifampin in eliminating *N. meningitidis* from nasopharyngeal carriers, but it is not commonly used because of reports of vestibular side effects. Rifampin chemoprophylaxis is also effective in preventing *H. influenzae* meningitis in close contacts, eliminating nasopharyngeal carriage.

Chemoprophylaxis is recommended only for close contacts (e.g., household members and others with prolonged intimate contact with the patient) or for anyone who has had exposure to the patient's oral secretions (e.g., mouth-to-mouth resuscitation). Routine vaccination with meningococcal vaccine is not warranted because the risk of infection is low in the United States, because a vaccine against serogroup B (responsible for approximately 50% of meningococcal disease in this country) is not yet available, and because the meningococcal vaccine is poorly immunogenic for children younger than 2 years.

Cost Containment

Early diagnosis and identification of the etiologic agents responsible (i.e., early lumbar puncture with appropriate studies) allow the quickest specific therapy and prevent complications that can add to the length of the hospitalization and to the number of tests, procedures, and medications, as well as to the morbidity. Appropriate antibiotic prophylaxis and use of the available vaccines will reduce cases of meningitis and in this way significantly contain costs.

REFERENCES

Durand ML, Calderwood SB, et al. Acute bacterial meningitis in adults. N Engl J Med 1993;328:21.

Quagliarello VJ, Scheld WM. Bacterial meningitis: Pathogenesis, pathophysiology, and progress. N Engl J Med 1992;327:864.

Quagliarello VJ, Scheld WM. New perspectives on bacterial meningitis. Clin Infect Dis 1993;17:603.

Simpson, DM, Tagliati M. Neurologic manifestations of HIV infection. Ann Intern Med 1994;121:769.

Stephens DS, Farley MM. Pathogenic events during infection of the human nasopharynx with *Neisseria meningitidis* and *Haemophilus influenzae*. Rev Infect Dis 1991;13:22.

Townsend GC, Scheld WM. Adjunctive therapy for bacterial meningitis: Rationale for use, current status, and prospects for the future. Clin Infect Dis1993;17 (suppl. 2):S537.

Wenger JD. Impact of *Haemophilus influenzae* type b vaccines on the epidemiology of bacterial meningitis. Infect Agents Dis 1993;2:324.

CHAPTER 8–10

Parameningeal Infections

Juliette Morgan, M.D., David Rimland, M.D., and Jonas A. Shulman, M.D.

DEFINITION

The parameningeal infections are a group of localized pyogenic infections adjacent to the meninges; they include brain abscess, subdural empyema, cerebral epidural abscess, spinal epidural abscess, and suppurative phlebitis of the intracranial veins.

ETIOLOGY

Clinical studies have shown that these infections usually occur in the setting of contiguous infection in the paranasal sinuses, middle ear, or skull or following neurologic surgeries. Less frequently, distant infections with metastatic spread also can cause any of these processes. They are usually caused by pyogenic organisms, although in the immunocompromised host, abscesses caused by *Toxoplasma*, *Nocardia*, fungi, spirochetes, or mycobacteria can occur.

CRITERIA FOR DIAGNOSIS
Suggestive

All these localized infections can produce meningeal signs and cerebrospinal fluid abnormalities (see Chapter 8–7). Focal neurologic findings are frequently present and suggest the presence of a brain abscess, subdural or epidural empyema, or suppurative intracranial phlebitis, especially when signs of infection are present.

Objective

The specific cluster of clinical abnormalities required to make a definitive diagnosis depends on the particular entity involved. Regardless of the localization of the process, the identification of pus or phlegmon (granulation tissue) at the site of infection is diagnostic.

CLINICAL MANIFESTATIONS
Subjective

The symptoms for these localized infections vary depending on the particular disease process (Table 8–10–1). The progression of symptoms may be indolent or fulminant, but duration before presentation is usually less than 2 weeks.

Objective
Physical Examination

The physical findings relate in part to the underlying source of infection (e.g., sinusitis, otitis media) and vary with the type and the localization of the specific infection (see Table 8–10–1).

TABLE 8–10–1. CLINICAL MANIFESTATIONS OF PARAMENINGEAL INFECTIONS

Infection	Symptoms	Physical Findings*
Brain abscess	Headache, fever, inability to think clearly, nausea, vomiting, stiff neck	Fever, altered mental status, focal neurologic findings, seizures, nuchal rigidity, papilledema
Subdural empyema	Fever, focal headache, vomiting	Fever, meningismus, altered mental status, rapid appearance of focal neurologic signs
Cerebral epidural abscess	Focal pain becoming a generalized headache	Focal neurologic signs, seizures, cranial nerve palsies, papilledema
Spinal epidural abscess	Localized back pain, paresthesias, paralysis	Nuchal rigidity, local spinal tenderness, sensory and motor deficits
Suppurative intracranial phlebitis	Eye swelling, double vision, headache, facial pain	Orbital edema, chemosis, ocular palsies; others depend on venous system involved

*In addition to those related to underlying problem (e.g., sinusitis, otitis media).

Routine Laboratory Abnormalities

Routine laboratory studies are rarely helpful in making a specific diagnosis. Many patients have a moderate leukocytosis, but up to 40% may have normal leukocyte counts. The erythrocyte sedimentation rate is usually moderately elevated (45–50 mm/h). The serum sodium level is sometimes low secondary to inappropriate secretion of antidiuretic hormone.

PLANS
Diagnostic
Differential Diagnosis

Symptoms of the previous predisposing illness associated with new neurologic findings, new meningeal findings, or localized edema should raise the clinical suspicion of an intracranial process. Differentiating the various possible entities is made easier when the localizing nature of the new manifestations are taken into account (see Table 8–10–1).

Diagnostic Options

For all the parameningeal infections, skull and sinus x-rays are useful to discover an extracerebral focus of infection. A radionuclide brain scan or computed tomography (CT) scan will make the diagnosis of a brain abscess and/or epidural empyema in at least 95% of cases, but nondiagnostic CT scans in subdural empyemas have, not infrequently, been noted. This may cause delay in the treatment and therefore is associated with poorer outcome. Magnetic resonance imaging (MRI) is helpful in these cases and may be the procedure of choice. When a spinal epidural abscess is suspected, myelography with CT scanning has been the procedure of choice, with MRI rapidly replacing it because of its excellent diagnostic capability and avoidance of contrast agents. The diagnosis of suppurative intracranial phlebitis is made by angiography, with special emphasis on the venous phase.

Lumbar punctures are dangerous to perform in patients with parameningeal infections because of the risk of herniation. If cerebrospinal fluid is examined, it usually demonstrates increased opening pressure, mild leukocytic pleocytosis, normal glucose level, and moderately elevated protein level (see Chapter 8–7). It has been suggested that if normal cerebrospinal fluid is present, this almost completely excludes the possibility of a subdural empyema. The cerebrospinal fluid Gram stain will be negative unless there has been rupture into the ventricles.

Blood cultures should always be obtained, as they may help define the microbiology of the pyogenic process in some central nervous system infections.

Recommended Approach

In the face of a rapidly progressing decline in the mental status of a patient with a known pyogenic process, such as sinusitis or otitis media,

MRI scanning to determine the presence of a subdural empyema would be the optimal option. Angiography must be considered in those cases where phlebitis is highly suspected. CT scan is the recommended alternative in the other entities, where progression of symptoms is less prominent and delay of diagnosis is not with such significant impact on the outcome.

Therapeutic

The therapy of parameningeal infections usually includes a combination of antimicrobial agents and surgical or CT-guided drainage. The choice of antibiotics depends in part on the knowledge of the ability of the agent to penetrate brain tissue or abscesses and the in vitro activity against the microbial pathogens usually responsible for each type of parameningeal process. Because the bacterial etiology of the parameningeal infection varies somewhat with the specific pyogenic process (see below), the recommended empiric regimens also differ (Table 8–10–2). If a specific etiology can be defined, therapy can be directed more specifically. The duration of therapy is not well defined, but it is usually at least 8 weeks for brain abscesses and at least 3 weeks for spinal and epidural empyemas.

The value of steroids in the treatment of brain abscesses is controversial and cannot be routinely suggested. On the other hand, they are not clearly contraindicated and are frequently used if there is a marked increase in intracranial pressure. Similarly, the benefit of anticoagulant use in the therapy of suppurative intracranial thrombophlebitis is not well defined.

Surgical or CT-directed drainage is essentially mandatory for all localized parameningeal infection, although at times medical therapy alone may cure some brain abscesses. The type of drainage is controversial, with some favoring aspiration alone and others favoring excision of the encapsulating abscess. Recent studies have shown excellent responses to antimicrobial agents alone in nonencapsulated, multiple brain abscesses. This approach should be attempted only if the patient can be followed carefully with sequential CT or MRI scans.

In patients with HIV infection empiric therapy for suspected *Toxoplasma* brain abscess with pyrimethamine and sulfadiazine is reasonable. If repeat CT scan does not show improvement after 2 weeks, surgical aspiration or biopsy is indicated to attempt to make a definitive diagnosis, as a variety of other infectious processes or tumors may mimic central nervous system toxoplasmosis in the HIV-infected patient.

The patient should be told about the specific parameningeal infection, with an explanation of the seriousness of the disease and emphasis on the significant morbidity and mortality. The importance of appropriate drainage also must be emphasized. In addition, the patient should understand the need for prolonged antibiotic therapy and the potential complications of the specific pyogenic infection. Patients with *Toxoplasma* brain abscesses and HIV infection need to understand that, if

TABLE 8–10–2. EMPIRIC ANTIBIOTIC REGIMENS FOR PARAMENINGEAL INFECTIONS

Parameningeal Infection	Antibiotic	Dosage/24 h (for adults with normal renal function)
Brain abscess	Penicillin* plus chloramphenicol† or metronidazole	20 million U 4–6 g 2 g
Subdural abscess or epidural empyema	Nafcillin plus chloramphenicol or metronidazole	12 g 4–6 g 2 g
Spinal epidural abscess	Nafcillin plus gentamicin	12 g 5 mg/kg/d
Cerebral thrombophlebitis	Nafcillin plus chloramphenicol or metronidazole	12 g 4–6 g 2 g

*If staphylococci are suspected, nafcillin may be substituted for penicillin G.
†If aerobic Gram-negative bacilli are strongly suspected, a third-generation cephalosporin (not cefoperazone) may be indicated.

they improve, they will require anti-*Toxoplasma* therapy for life to prevent relapse.

FOLLOW-UP

After beginning empiric or directed antibiotic therapy, patients with brain abscesses must be followed carefully, especially if surgery has not been performed. Weekly CT scans are helpful in deciding the need for surgery (e.g., if encapsulation occurs), and prophylactic antiseizure medications are often given. The duration of intravenous antibiotic therapy may be 4 to 6 weeks and may be followed by an additional 2 to 6 months of antibiotic therapy by the oral route. The patient should be seen every 2 to 4 weeks for several months after the completion of therapy to ensure resolution of the process, and long-term follow-up may be necessary for months.

The patient should be warned about the recurrence of symptoms, especially fever, headaches, and focal neurologic findings.

DISCUSSION
Prevalence and Incidence

The incidence of brain abscess has been estimated to be 1 in 10,000 general hospital admissions per year, with an equal male:female ratio and a median patient age of 30 to 40 years. Subdural empyema is a less common disease, but it accounts for 20% of all localized parameningeal infections. The complications of sinusitis are seen mainly in a younger population, second and third decades of life, and with a significant association with the male sex (the male:female ratio is nearly 4:1). The incidence of epidural and subdural empyemas as complications of intracranial procedures ranges from 0.43 to 4.3%. The postoperative intracranial infections are more likely to occur in older patients, 50 to 60 years old, with an equal distribution in males and females. Spinal epidural abscesses are uncommon and there are no good data on the incidence.

Related Basic Science

Brain abscesses result from direct extension of a contiguous infection in the head or along the valveless diploic veins, which provide the anatomic bridge between the sinuses, meninges, and brain parenchyma. They can also arise from a hematogenous source. Abscesses arising from the sinuses or middle ear are usually located in the frontal or temporal lobes, and are solitary. Hematogenous brain abscesses are usually multiple and result from metastatic seeding from the pulmonary infections, infective endocarditis, congenital heart disease with right-to-left shunts, or other forms of sepsis. The course of abscess formation includes diffuse cerebritis with edema and influx of leukocytes, liquefaction, and finally encapsulation. It is after this last stage that the expanding mass lesion may result in uncal or brainstem herniation or ventricular rupture. The bacteriology of brain abscesses depends on the source of infection. Patients with postoperative processes have a high incidence of Gram-negative aerobic bacteria, whereas the predominant

organisms seen in patients with sinusitis are streptococci, both anaerobic and aerobic. *Bacteroides* and staphylococci can also be seen.

The brain is surrounded by two layers of meninges, the dura and the arachnoid, which enclose a potential subdural space crossed by numerous small emissary veins. Natural anatomic barriers separate the subdural space into compartments that limit the spread of infection; however, these can rapidly become space-occupying lesions. Subdural empyema usually has a polymicrobial etiology, with common involvement of anaerobes, aerobic streptococci, and staphylococci.

Natural History and Its Modification with Treatment

The morbidity and mortality of brain abscesses depend in part on the time delay until diagnosis. An adverse prognosis is also associated with poor localization, multiple deep abscesses, ventricular rupture, coma, fungal etiology, and inappropriate antimicrobial therapy. The mass effect may produce irreversible brain injury resulting in serious neurologic sequelae. Seizures complicate brain abscesses in nearly 35% of cases. Overall, there is a 15 to 20% mortality.

For subdural empyema, prompt treatment results in a good recovery, but seizures may complicate 42% of cases. The overall mortality is 14 to 18%. Spinal epidural abscesses have a good prognosis if surgery is performed before the development of radicular symptoms; most series report a mortality of 10 to 20%. Suppurative intracranial phlebitis has a poor prognosis, with an overall mortality of 34%; the prognosis is worse if the patient presents with coma or generalized seizures.

Prevention

The prevention of all the parameningeal infections and associated complications centers on the early and aggressive treatment of the predisposing conditions such as sinusitis and otitis media.

Cost Containment

Prevention, early diagnosis, and therapy of parameningeal infections result in cost savings if serious complications do not develop. Successful treatment of early brain abscesses without surgery reduces costs even further.

REFERENCES

Chun CH, Johnson JD, Hofsetter M, et al. Brain abscess: A review of recent experience. Ann Intern Med 1975;82:571.
Clayman GL, Adams GL, Paugh DR, Koopmann CF. Intracranial complications of paranasal sinusitis: A combined institutional review. Laryngoscope 1991;101:234.
Hlavin ML, Kaminski HJ, Fenstermaker RA, White RJ. Intracranial suppuration: A modern decade of postoperative subdural empyema and epidural abscess. Neurosurgery 1994;34:974.
Rosenfeld EA, Rowley AH. Infectious intracranial complications of sinusitis, other than meningitis in children: 12 year review. Clin Infect Dis 1994;18:750.
Silverberg AL, DiNubile MJ. Subdural empyema and cranial epidural abscess. Med Clin North Am 1985;69:361.

CHAPTER 8–11

Encephalitis

Rafael A. Caputi, M.D., David Rimland, M.D., and David S. Stephens, M.D.

DEFINITION

The term *encephalitis* is used when there is clinical or pathologic evidence of involvement of the cerebral hemispheres, brain stem, or cerebellum by an infectious agent or by a postinfectious or parainfectious demyelinating process causing inflammation.

ETIOLOGY

The etiologies of acute encephalitis are quite extensive. Many viral pathogens have been associated with encephalitis; the two endemic causes of encephalitis in the United States are herpes simplex virus and rabies virus. Interestingly, herpes simplex virus type 2, which is the most common cause of genital herpes and a frequent cause of viral meningitis, only rarely results in encephalitis. Rabies virus is more common in developing countries. Arboviruses, arthropod-borne viruses, are a common cause of sporadic and epidemic encephalitis in the United States. HIV encephalopathy will probably become the most common cause of viral infection of the central nervous system worldwide.

Nonviral causes of acute encephalitis are bacterial infections (e.g., tuberculosis, Lyme disease, syphilis, brain abscess, rickettsial diseases), fungal infections (*Cryptococcus*), parasites (*Plasmodium falciparum*), and noninfectious etiologies such as toxic encephalopathy, vascular disease, and sarcoidosis (Table 8–11–1).

CRITERIA FOR DIAGNOSIS
Suggestive

The cluster of an altered level of consciousness (ranging from confusion to coma), signs of cerebral parenchymal involvement, an acute onset of febrile illness, and cerebrospinal fluid pleocytosis strongly suggests the diagnosis.

The disease occurs as a primary infection when the encephalitis is the presenting form of the disease and is due to direct invasion and replication of virus within the central nervous system. Encephalitis can also occur as a secondary complication 2 to 12 days after an acute process such as measles or mumps or in association with administration of certain vaccines. An associated meningitis may occur, leading to the term *meningoencephalitis*.

Definitive

A brain biopsy can confirm a diagnosis of viral encephalitis and exclude other treatable diseases. Acute and convalescent sera are essential to diagnosis of many of the viral encephalitides, especially those caused by arboviruses. Polymerase chain reaction (to amplify DNA from cerebrospinal fluid for herpes simplex infection is very sensitive and specific (80–90%). This test is also useful for diagnosing arboviral encephalopathies.

TABLE 8–11–1. COMMON CAUSES OF ENCEPHALITIS

Viral		Nonviral
Direct Invasion	Postinfection	
Herpes simplex	Rubella	Tuberculosis
Herpes zoster	Mumps	Brucellosis
Polio	Measles	Mycoplasma
Togaviruses	Epstein–Barr	Rocky Mountain spotted fever
Eastern, Western, and	Influenza	Lyme disease
Venezuelan equine	Varicella zoster	Leptospirosis
encephalitis, St. Louis	Vaccine related	*Ehrlichia*
encephalitis		Listeriosis
Mumps		Q fever
Measles		Syphilis
Lymphocytic choriomeningitis		*Plasmodium falciparum*
Colorado tick fever		*Toxoplasma*
Rabies		*Cryptococcus*
Epstein–Barr virus		Coccidioidomycosis
Cytomegalovirus		Infective endocarditis
HIV		Whipples's disease
Herpes B virus		Brain abscess
Progressive multifocal encephalopathy		*Naegleria, Acanthamoeba*
		Vascular disease
		Sarcoidosis
		Toxic encephalopathy
		Typhus
		Prion-associated encephalopathies (e.g., Creutzfeldt–Jakob)

CLINICAL MANIFESTATIONS
Subjective

Clinical complaints common to most of the encephalitides include headache, fever, an altered level of consciousness, disorientation, behavioral and speech disturbances, and neurologic symptoms. These are sometimes focal but generally diffuse, such as hemiparesis and seizures. Most of the diseases discussed here have a relatively rapid onset, over a period of days. Hallucinations are uncommon except in herpes encephalitis. These clinical findings distinguish a patient with encephalitis from one with viral meningitis, who usually has only nuchal rigidity, headache, fever, and photophobia.

Seasonal and geographic variations are important in suggesting specific etiologic agents. Insect vectors abound in the spring and summer and are important in the transmission of some of the etiologic agents (e.g., mosquitoes for arboviruses, ticks for *Rickettsia*). Enteroviral infections occur in late summer and early fall.

A history of an animal bite is obviously important in making a diagnosis of rabies. The predisposition of herpes simplex to infect the temporal lobe leads to clinical findings of aphasia, anosmia, temporal lobe seizures, and focal neurologic deficits.

Patients should be questioned about risk factors for HIV infection, as HIV can cause a subacute encephalitis.

Objective
Physical Examination

Most patients present with fever, alterations in consciousness (lethargy, confusion, stupor, coma), and meningismus. Other findings include focal neurologic signs (cranial nerve palsies, paresis, nystagmus), tremors (especially in western equine and St. Louis encephalitis), and papilledema.

In patients with acute viral encephalitis, the distinction between generalized and focal neurologic findings is essential. The most common cause of focal encephalopathic findings is herpes simplex virus, and findings of bizarre behavior and aphasia should suggest herpes encephalitis involving the temporal lobe. Specific rashes should suggest Rocky Mountain spotted fever, typhus, Lyme disease, or herpes zoster encephalitis.

Routine Laboratory Abnormalities

Routine laboratory tests are not helpful in making a diagnosis. The peripheral white blood cell count may be normal, elevated, or decreased; atypical lymphocytes could suggest Epstein–Barr virus infection, cytomegalovirus infection, or acute toxoplasmosis. The serum sodium level may be decreased because of the inappropriate secretion of antidiuretic hormone. The serum amylase level may be increased in mumps.

The routine chest x-ray film is usually normal, but it may show pulmonary infiltrates if the encephalitis is associated with *Mycoplasma*, typhus, or lymphocytic choriomeningitis.

PLANS
Diagnostic
Differential Diagnosis

The differential diagnosis in a patient presenting with an altered level of consciousness and neurologic signs of cerebral parenchymal involvement includes acute meningitis, usually associated with severe headache, fever, nuchal rigidity, and visual disturbances (photophobia). Papilledema and/or focal neurologic deficits in a patient with meningeal symptoms suggest the possibility of a cerebral abscess. Common underlying conditions in patients with brain abscess and other parameningeal foci include endocarditis, lung abscess, sinusitis, middle ear infection, and antecedent head trauma or neurosurgery. If central nervous system imaging reveals a mass lesion, a neurologic and/or neurosurgical evaluation should be considered. Brain biopsy may be indicated, depending on the clinical circumstances.

Diagnostic Options

Examination of cerebrospinal fluid is essential in diagnosing encephalitis, unless its collection is contraindicated because of an increase in the intracranial pressure. A moderate pleocytosis (10–1000 cells/µL), predominantly mononuclear, is usually present. Polymorphonuclear leukocytes may predominate in amoebic meningoencephalitis, and erythrocytes are common in herpes and *Naegleria* encephalitis and in acute necrotizing hemorrhagic leukoencephalitis.

The cerebrospinal fluid protein level is usually only moderately elevated (< 100–150 mg/dL), but the glucose level is usually normal, except in mumps, amoebic, and fungal encephalitis (hypoglycorrhachia). A small percentage of patients (approximately 3–5%) with severe viral infection of the central nervous system, such as herpes simplex encephalitis, have completely normal cerebrospinal fluid. Specific cerebrospinal fluid antibody concentrations may be helpful in making certain diagnoses, especially if compared with the serum antibody levels (e.g., syphilis, measles, rubella). An antigen test for cryptococcal disease is helpful for its diagnosis. Direct examination of the cerebrospinal fluid may be helpful in making a diagnosis of cryptococcal disease (India ink preparation) and *Naegleria* encephalitis (wet preparation). Cultures of the cerebrospinal fluid are useful in diagnosing some of the nonviral causes of encephalitis (see Table 8–11–1) and certain viral causes (e.g., Venezuelan equine encephalitis).

Neurodiagnostic techniques, including electroencephalography, computed tomography, and magnetic resonance imaging, can provide useful information in the investigation of patients with altered mental status. Electroencephalography is useful for diagnosing herpes simplex encephalitis, in which a characteristic periodic high-voltage spike wave activity originates from the temporal lobe, and slow wave complexes (intervals of 2 or 3 seconds) are highly suggestive of herpes simplex virus infection in the brain. A brain biopsy is usually necessary to confirm a diagnosis of herpes encephalitis and to exclude other treatable diseases.

Brain biopsy is generally safe when performed by an experienced neurosurgeon. Unique histopathologic features include Cowdry type A inclusion bodies and Negri bodies, associated with herpesvirus infections and rabies, respectively. The diagnosis of rabies can sometimes be made by immunofluorescence staining of corneal smears.

Acute and convalescent sera are essential to diagnosis of many of the viral causes of encephalitis, especially arboviruses. As HIV infection and Lyme disease become increasingly common, serologic studies to detect these diseases are also indicated. An enzyme-linked immunosorbent assay that detects immunoglobulin M antibodies in the cerebrospinal fluid of patients with presumed Japanese B encephalitis is sensitive and specific. A polymerase chain reaction test on cerebrospinal fluid has good sensitivity and specificity for herpes simplex virus in the diagnosis of herpes simplex virus encephalitis as well as other infectious causes of encephalitis.

Recommended Approach

As herpes simplex virus encephalitis and many of the other causes of encephalitis are treatable diseases, a thorough and aggressive investigation should be performed in patients with encephalitis. Lumbar puncture is important in diagnosis. Cerebrospinal fluid serology may be helpful in making certain diagnoses (e.g., syphilis). Cultures of spinal fluid are useful in diagnosing bacterial infection, fungal infection, and tuberculosis. Neurodiagnostic imaging should always be obtained. Electroencephalography is useful in diagnosing herpes simplex virus encephalitis. HIV disease should also be investigated. If the patient does not improve and the etiology is still unclear, brain biopsy is recommended.

THERAPEUTICS

Many of the nonviral causes of encephalitis (Table 8–11–1) are treatable, and an aggressive search for these diseases is necessary. The specific treatment is addressed in the appropriate chapters. The only two viral encephalitides that are clearly treatable are herpes encephalitis and HIV encephalitis. Treatment with acyclovir (12.5–15 mg/kg every 8 hours for 10 days) can reduce both morbidity and mortality from herpes encephalitis. Zidovudine (AZT) in total doses of 600 to 1200 mg/d may reverse some neurologic problems associated with HIV encephalopathy.

Vigorous supportive treatment is important in patients with encephalitis, as they may be ill for weeks. Complications from ventilators and catheters must be minimized. Cerebral edema may be controlled with mannitol or corticosteroids. Extreme hyperthermia should be minimized with antipyretics. Dilantin should be considered to prevent seizures.

FOLLOW-UP

The prolonged course of most of these illnesses mandates careful follow-up of nutrition, fluid and electrolyte balance, and potential nosocomial problems. Avoidance of pressure sores, ventilator and catheter complications, and thrombophlebitis is obviously important. Deep venous thrombosis prophylaxis with anticoagulation should be considered.

Reassessment of the neurologic status of the patient is required, with the interval of follow-up dependent on the patient's clinical course.

DISCUSSION

Prevalence and Incidence

The many causes of encephalitis make it difficult to define the incidence or demographic features of these disease processes. According to the Centers for Disease Control and Prevention, approximately 2000 cases of encephalitis occur in the United States each year, most of them mild.

Herpes simplex virus causes 10 to 20% of all cases of encephalitis in the United States, with an estimated frequency of 1 in 250,000 to 1 in 500,000 persons per year. Japanese B encephalitis is a major medical problem in China, Southeast Asia, and India; as many as 20,000 cases per year have been reported in these areas.

Related Basic Science

Encephalitis is usually caused by direct invasion by the etiologic agent. The brain is reached by the bloodstream, peripheral nerves (e.g., rabies), or olfactory nerves (e.g., free-living amoeba).

Neuronal infection leads to focal or generalized seizures, involvement of oligodendroglia results in demyelination, and cortical parenchymal swelling results in the altered state of consciousness. The acute demyelinating diseases following viral exanthems or respiratory infections are probably due to sensitization to central myelin. A late demyelination syndrome has also been reported after herpes simplex virus infections of the central nervous system.

Natural History and Its Modification with Treatment

Morbidity from encephalitis is related to both the acute disease and the complications that arise during convalescence (e.g., nosocomial infections, pulmonary emboli). Overall, 10% of patients with encephalitis die, but the mortality is much higher in herpes encephalitis (70–80% if untreated) and Eastern equine encephalitis (50–70%). Severe neurologic sequelae are common, especially with the latter two etiologies.

Prevention

Most aspects of prevention are directed toward the cases of encephalitis caused by arboviruses. Surveillance for cases and outbreaks is very important, so that reports to the local health department can be made. The resulting attempts at vector control (e.g., spraying for mosquitoes) are critical in limiting outbreaks. Health education and personal protection against tick bites are the best preventive measures, especially in high-risk areas for tickborne causes of disease.

The control of poliomyelitis through vaccination has greatly decreased the incidence of poliovirus infections of the central nervous system. Herpes B virus has been reported to have caused several cases of severe or fatal encephalitis. This virus is transmitted by monkey bite, and the disease is preventable if proper animal handling is employed.

Vaccination of horses has also been useful in preventing outbreaks of the equine-related encephalitides. Vaccination of dogs and cats is obviously important in limiting the potential for exposure to rabies. Prevention of rabies infection by administration of vaccine and antiserum after exposure, particularly in persons bitten by an animal that had not been provoked, is critical. Vaccines should be administered to animal handlers at risk.

Early treatment of Lyme disease may prevent the neurologic sequelae. In addition, efforts directed at the prevention of spread of HIV infection in the community will decrease the incidence of HIV encephalopathy.

Cost Containment

The prevention of certain causes of encephalitis is the most important aspect of cost containment. Appropriate use of diagnostic tests and specific treatment for the treatable diseases are also critical. The prolonged recovery stage of these diseases requires the appropriate use of hospital versus home care. During hospitalization, attention to infection control procedures may decrease the cost of complicating nosocomial infections.

REFERENCES

Arbovirus disease, United States, 1993. MMWR 1994;43:395.
Fishman RA. Cerebrospinal fluid in diseases of the nervous system. 2nd ed. Philadelphia: Saunders, 1992:277.
Ho DD, Hirsh MS. Acute viral encephalitis. Med Clin North Am 1985;69:415.
Simpson DM, Tagliati M. Neurologic manifestations of HIV infection. Ann Intern Med 1994;121:769.
Summary of notifiable diseases, United States, 1987. MMWR 1987;36:4.
Whitley RJ. Herpes simplex virus infections of the central nervous system: A review. Am J Med 1988;85 (suppl. 2):61.
Whitley RJ. Viral encephalitis. N Engl J Med 1990;323:242.

CHAPTER 8–12

Infective Endocarditis

Christine A. Zurawski, M.D., and David Rimland, M.D.

DEFINITION

Infective endocarditis is defined as microbial infection of a platelet–fibrin vegetation on the endothelial surface of the heart.

ETIOLOGY

Infective endocarditis develops as the result of bacterial or fungal infection involving the lesions of congenital or valvular heart disease. It may occur when there is no evidence of valvular or congenital heart disease.

CRITERIA FOR DIAGNOSIS

Suggestive

Unexplained fever in a patient with valvular or congenital heart disease should alert the clinician to the possible diagnosis of infective endocarditis.

Fever due to endocarditis can occur when there is no evidence of valvular or congenital heart disease.

Definitive

The diagnosis of infective endocarditis is usually made by positive blood cultures for bacteria or fungi in a patient with clinical evidence of cardiac valve disease or congenital heart disease.

CLINICAL MANIFESTATION

Subjective

Recent studies indicate that only about 50% of patients with infective endocarditis have underlying valvular disease and up to 25% of cases are nosocomial (Watanakunakorn and Burkert, 1993). Given this information, a number of risk groups have been identified. Information should be sought about underlying heart disease, especially rheumatic or congenital (including mitral valve prolapse and asymmetric septal hypertrophy). A history of intravenous drug abuse, the presence of prosthetic valves, as well as recent invasive procedures or hospitalization in which intravenous catheters were used, are also extremely important information to obtain.

Most patients present with non-specific findings such as fever (80–90%), chills (40%), weakness (38%), sweats (24%), anorexia or weight loss (25%), and malaise (25%). Symptoms suggestive of heart failure (dyspnea, 36%; cough, 24%) or embolic phenomena (skin lesions, 20%; stroke, 18%) are common. Musculoskeletal symptoms such as arthralgias, myalgias, and arthritis are also common complaints.

Objective

Physical Examination

Because of earlier diagnosis and changes in the microbiological profile of infective endocarditis, many patients do not present with what were previously "classic" findings of endocarditis. Fever and a heart murmur (80–90%) are still the most common abnormalities on physical examination. Embolic phenomena (to the brain, spleen, and kidney) and skin manifestations (petechiae, splinter hemorrhages, Osler's nodes, or Janeway lesions) are found in less than 50% of patients. Signs of congestive heart failure may be seen in up to two thirds of patients. Less common findings include splenomegaly (20–30%), septic complications (pneumonia or meningitis, 20%), mycotic aneurysms (20%), clubbing (10–20%), renal failure (10–20%), and retinal lesions/Roth's spots (5–10%).

Routine Laboratory Abnormalities

The complete blood count is usually abnormal, with anemia (70–90%), leukocytosis (20–30%) or leukopenia (5–15%), and thrombocytopenia (5–15%). Abnormalities of renal function that occur frequently include proteinuria (50–65%), microscopic hematuria (30–50%), elevated creatinine (5–15%), and red cell casts (12%).

PLANS

Diagnostic

Differential Diagnosis

In forming the differential diagnosis, considerations should include bacteremia or fungemia without endocarditis; thrombotic noninfective (marantic) endocarditis; atrial myxoma; and septic emboli from a noncardiac source.

Diagnostic Options and Recommended Approach

In the appropriate clinical setting and with the objective data previously mentioned, positive blood cultures confirm the diagnosis of infective endocarditis. Three sets of blood cultures identify 99% of the cases. When cultures are negative, additional diagnostic tests may be indicated. Special cultures (on selective or supplemental media), serologic tests, or teichoic acid antibodies may identify specific organisms. Cultures obtained by arterial or cardiac catheterization are occasionally positive when peripheral venous blood cultures are not.

Other nonspecific markers for inflammation and immune hyperreactivity that are commonly seen are elevated sedimentation rate (90–100%), circulating immune complexes (nearly 100%), rheumatoid factor (40–50%), mixed cryoglobulins (85–95%), hyperglobulinemia (20–30%), and hypocomplementemia (5–15%).

The use of the echocardiogram has received a significant amount of attention recently as a diagnostic tool. The transthoracic echocardiogram is the least sensitive, identifying vegetations in only 30 to 60% percent of confirmed cases, and the transesophageal echocardiogram has a sensitivity of approximately 90%; however, there is a significant false-negative rate with both tests (20%), and the sensitivity is markedly decreased when prosthetic valves are involved. The echocardiogram should be used in the proper clinical setting along with other historical, objective, and laboratory findings to assist in making the diagnosis. The echocardiogram should not be used to "rule in" or "rule out" the diagnosis of infective endocarditis.

Therapeutic

Therapeutic Options and Recommended Approach

High-dose parenteral antibiotics with bactericidal activity must be given for prolonged periods (4–6 weeks) to treat infective endocarditis effectively. The specific antibiotic selected for treatment should be determined by antimicrobial susceptibility tests. Treatment can be monitored with serum bactericidal activity, but these tests are not standardized and may not correlate with clinical response. The specific antimicrobial regimens for the most common bacteria are listed in Table 8–12–1.

Approximately 20 to 60% of infective endocarditis is caused by staphylococcal species. Empiric antibiotic therapy, when endocarditis is suspected, should include an antimicrobial agent with antistaphylococcal activity, such as a penicillinase-resistant penicillin or vancomycin.

Special Therapeutic Situations. Endocarditis caused by aerobic Gram-negative bacilli has a very high mortality rate. Therapy should be guided by measurement of serum bactericidal activity and often requires combinations of drugs (penicillins or cephalosporins and aminoglycosides). Fungal endocarditis is also highly fatal and almost always requires surgical excision of the valve in addition to parenteral antifungal therapy with amphotericin B. Patients with negative blood cultures who are being treated for infective endocarditis pose a difficult problem. A regimen to cover enterococcus (ampicillin plus aminoglycoside) is usually chosen, but some would add a penicillinase-resistant penicillin to better cover *Staphylococcus*.

Antimicrobial choices for the treatment of infective endocarditis on a prosthetic valve are based on the same criteria noted above. Treatment in this group should be extended to 8 weeks and early surgical intervention is often indicated.

Surgical Therapy. The important adjunctive role of valve replacement for infective endocarditis has recently been emphasized. As most patients with this disease die of heart failure, early aggressive surgical intervention has become critical. The current indications for surgery include refractory congestive heart failure; major systemic embolic events (more than one); uncontrolled infection; ineffective antimicrobial therapy (fungal endocarditis, prosthetic valve, resistant microorganisms); and major myocardial involvement (e.g., valve ring abscess).

The patient should be told about the seriousness of an infection involving the heart valves. The patient should understand that high-dose intravenous antibiotics must be used for a prolonged period, and that he or she must be followed closely for the development of complications. Emphasize that the patient must be given prophylactic antibiotics before undergoing any invasive procedure.

FOLLOW-UP

During therapy patients must be observed daily for the development of congestive heart failure, embolic phenomena, and mycotic aneurysms. The occurrence of fever during therapy not only requires a search for a nosocomial source, but also necessitates evaluation for occult abscesses, development of resistance, and drug fever.

After completion of therapy, the patient should be observed for a few days to ensure the absence of fever and should then be followed every few weeks for several months so that late complications (e.g., congestive heart failure) can be promptly treated. Again, the patient should clearly understand the need for antimicrobial prophylaxis before undergoing any invasive procedures.

DISCUSSION
Prevalence and Incidence

The incidence of infective endocarditis varies considerably among different risk groups. A recent population-based study defined an incidence of approximately 4 cases per 100,000 person-years.

Related Basic Science

The development of infective endocarditis, especially the subacute variety (see below), requires the interaction of several factors. Valvular endothelium must first be altered to make it attractive for bacterial or fungal deposition; this alteration may result from hemodynamic turbu-

TABLE 8–12–1. ANTIMICROBIAL REGIMENS FOR INFECTIVE ENDOCARDITIS

Organism	Antimicrobial Agent	Dose/24 h*	Alternative Antimicrobial Agent (severe drug allergy)	Dose/24h*	Total weeks of therapy
Penicillin-sensitive streptococci† (viridans streptococci, nonenterococcal group D streptococci)	Penicillin G	10–20 million U	Cephalothin or vancomycin	12 g 2 g	4
Penicillin-resistant streptococci (enterococcus)	Penicillin G and gentamicin	20 million U 3 mg/kg	Vancomycin and gentamicin‡	2 g 3 mg/kg	4–6
Staphylococcus aureus†	Penicillianse-resistant penicillin (oxacillin or nafcillin) or cephalosporin (cephalothin, cefazolin)	12 g 12 g 6–8 g	Vancomycin	2 g	4–6
Staphylococcus epidermidis	Vancomycin and rifampin and gentamicin	2 gm 600 mg (PO) 3 mg/kg			6 6 1–2

*Doses may require modification in renal failure.
†The need for an aminoglycoside as an additional drug has been suggested. For penicillin-sensitive streptococci, the addition of streptomycin or gentamicin allows reduction to a 2-week course for uncomplicated disease.
‡Or other aminoglycoside if the enterococcus is resistant to gentamicin.

lence, trauma, or other unrecognized forces. Platelet–fibrin deposition on the altered endothelium produces a sterile thrombus—the so-called nonbacterial thrombotic endocarditis. Bacteria or fungi that reach this site (see below) can then adhere and colonize the thrombus. After colonization, the microorganisms multiply and produce further platelet and fibrin deposition, which results in the formation of a mature vegetation. In acute endocarditis, caused by *Staphylococcus aureus, Streptococcus pneumoniae,* or other organisms, there is apparently no need for underlying valvular abnormality; these organisms may directly invade normal valves.

The source of bacteremia in the development of infective endocarditis can be quite variable, but it is clear that transient bacteremia is a common occurrence in normal people. This bacteremia occurs whenever a mucosal membrane heavily colonized with bacteria is traumatized. Typical sources of this bacteremia include dental manipulation and gastrointestinal or genitourinary procedures. The particular bacteria causing infective endocarditis vary, but the source of bacteremia and characteristics of bacterial adherence are probably critical.

The distribution of organisms causing infective endocarditis in a recent series is shown in Table 8–12–2. The valves involved vary, but most studies indicate a distribution of mitral (28–45%), aortic (5–36%), aortic plus mitral (5–36%), tricuspid (0–6%), and pulmonary (<1%). In specific groups (see below) this distribution may be quite different (Watanakunakorn and Burkert, 1993).

The clinical consequences of infective endocarditis depend on four results of the infection: local invasion, bacteremia, emboli, and immunologic phenomena. Local invasion of the valve may result in perforation of the valve leaflet, development of a valve ring abscess or aneurysm, or rupture of the chordae tendineae, papillary muscles, or interventricular septum. These structural abnormalities produce the signs noted above (cardiac conduction disturbances, cardiac murmurs, or congestive heart failure). Myocarditis, pericarditis, coronary emboli resulting in infarction, and myocardial abscesses are also commonly found at autopsy. The bacteremia seen in infective endocarditis is usually low grade but probably produces the findings of fever, chills, weakness, sweats, and malaise.

Emboli are commonly found at autopsy (in kidneys, spleen, and brain) but may also produce serious complications during life. Metastatic infections (abscesses, meningitis, etc.) are especially common with acute endocarditis. The recently elucidated immunologic phenomena seen in infective endocarditis probably produce many of the clinical manifestations previously ascribed to emboli. Deposition of circulating immune complexes in skin, blood vessels, and kidneys produces the cutaneous lesions, renal disease (glomerulonephritis), and many of the musculoskeletal manifestations of the disease.

Two special aspects of infective endocarditis deserve emphasis: the disease as seen in drug addicts and in patients with prosthetic valves. Intravenous drug abusers have a high risk of developing infective endocarditis, and *S. aureus,* aerobic Gram-negative bacilli, and fungi are especially common in this group. Signs and symptoms may be subtle, especially as most of the cases in addicts produce isolated tricuspid valve involvement, often with septic pulmonary emboli. Perhaps because of

this valve involvement and the patient's otherwise good health, infective endocarditis in addicts has a very low mortality.

Infective endocarditis involving a prosthetic valve may occur early (within 60 days of valve placement) or late (after 60 days). The overall incidence is 1 to 4% in the first year and 1% yearly thereafter. Although the late-onset disease resembles natural valve endocarditis, with a similar bacteriologic profile and mortality, the early-onset disease is often due to staphylococci and aerobic Gram-negative bacilli and is associated with a high mortality. The late-onset disease requires longer-duration therapy (8 weeks) and often necessitates surgical intervention.

Natural History and Its Modification with Treatment

Untreated infective endocarditis is almost universally fatal; even in the antibiotic era, overall mortality may still approach 35%. Mortality varies widely depending on a number of prognostic factors including infecting organism, age, underlying heart disease, site of infection, delay in starting effective treatment, prior cardiovascular surgery, drug addiction, and other underlying disease.

At present, congestive heart failure accounts for 70 to 90% of deaths due to infective endocarditis, although other cardiac complications such as myocardial abscesses, myocardial infarction, and arrhythmias account for a small percentage. Complications of septic emboli to the central nervous system and rupture of a mycotic aneurysm are unusual causes of death. Uncontrolled infection is rarely a cause of death except in undiagnosed cases.

The classification of infective endocarditis into acute and subacute forms is no longer emphasized but may still be useful in predicting death in days to a few weeks (acute) versus death in 6 weeks to months (subacute) for untreated disease. This classification may be helpful in deciding on the urgency of therapy in suspected cases.

Prevention

Transient bacteremia is a common occurrence. Persons with valvular disease should be encouraged to maintain good dental hygiene and promptly see a physician for the care of any illness with the potential of producing bacteremia. The treatment of such patients who are to undergo procedures is more difficult. Even in patients with known underlying valvular disease, invasive procedures associated with bacteremia rarely produce infective endocarditis. Decisions about the use of prophylactic antibiotics before these procedures are empiric and supported by no clinical studies. Prophylaxis is directed against organisms that are likely to cause endocarditis after procedures involving areas suitable for colonization: viridans streptococci in dental or upper respiratory tract procedures and enterococci in genitourinary or gastrointestinal tract surgery or instrumentation. The specific indications for prophylaxis are listed in Table 8–12–3, and the current antibiotic regimens recommended by the American Heart Association are listed in Table 8–12–4.

Cost Containment

As in most other diseases, prevention is the most effective method of containing costs. Once the disease is established, intelligent use of the laboratory for diagnosis and follow-up and the choice of the best and least expensive antibiotic regimen limit costs. Recent reports attempting to limit hospitalization time for endocarditis by using short-course (e.g., 2 weeks) therapy or orally administered antibiotics must be viewed with caution; only when appropriate serum bactericidal studies are available and careful follow-up is possible should such regimens be attempted.

TABLE 8–12–2. BACTERIOLOGY OF INFECTIVE ENDOCARDITIS

Organism	Percent of Cases
Streptococci	30–50
Viridans	15–20
Enterococci	5–15
Other	3–25
Staphylococcus	20–60
aureus	10–30
epidermidis	1–6
Aerobic Gram-negative bacilli	5–13
Fungi	2–6
Miscellaneous	5
Mixed	1–3
Culture negative	5

TABLE 8–12–3. PROCEDURES FOR WHICH PROPHYLAXIS IS INDICATED

- All dental procedures likely to induce gingival bleeding
- Tonsillectomy and/or adenoidectomy
- Surgical procedures or biopsy involving respiratory mucosa
- Bronchoscopy, especially with a rigid bronchoscope
- Incision and drainage of infected tissue
- Selected genitourinary and gastrointestinal procedures

TABLE 8–12–4. PROPHYLAXIS OF INFECTIVE ENDOCARDITIS: SPECIFIC REGIMENS IN ADULTS

	Dental/Respiratory Tract Procedures	Gastrointestinal/Genitourinary Procedures
Standard regimen	*Oral:* amoxicillin 3 g 1 h before procedure; then 1.5 g 6 h after *Parenteral:* ampicillin 2 g IV 30–60 min before procedure and 1 g IV 6 h after	Ampicillin 2.0 g IM or IV plus gentamicin 1.5 mg/kg IM or IV given 30–60 min before procedure; one follow-up dose of each may be given 8 h later *or* amoxicillin 1.5 g PO 6 h after initial dose
Special regimens		
For maximal protection (e.g., patients with prosthetic valves)	Ampicillin 1.0 to 2.0 g IM or IV *plus* gentamicin 1.5 mg/kg IM or IV 30 min before procedure, followed by 1.0 g oral penicillin V 6 h later; alternatively the parenteral regimen may be repeated once 8 h later	
For penicillin-allergic patients	*Oral:* Erythromycin 1.0 g 1 h before and 500 mg 6 h later *Parenteral:* Vancomycin 1.0 g IV slowly over 1 h, starting 1 h before	*Parenteral:* vancomycin 1.0 g IV slowly over 1 h plus gentamicin 1.5 mg/kg IM or IV given 1 h before procedure; may be repeated once 8–12 h later
For minor or repetitive procedures in low-risk patients		Amoxicillin 3.0 g orally 1 h before procedure and 1.5 g 6 h later

REFERENCES

Bayer AS. Infective endocarditis. Clin Infect Dis 1993;17:313.

Bisno AL, Dismukes WE, Durack DT, et al. Antimicrobial treatment of infective endocarditis due to viridans streptococci, enterococci, and staphylococci. JAMA 1989;261:1471.

Durak DT. Prevention of infective endocarditis. N Engl J Med 1995;332:38.

Lukes AS, Bright DK, Durack DT. Diagnosis of infective endocarditis. Infect Dis Clin North Am 1993;7(1):1.

Scheld WM, Sande MA. Endocarditis and intravascular infections. In: Mandell GL, Bennett JE, Douglas RG, eds. Principles and practice of infectious diseases. New York: Churchill Livingstone, 1995.

Watanakunakorn C, Burkert T. Infective endocarditis at a large community hospital, 1980–1990 (a review of 210 cases). Medicine 1993;72(2):90.

Weinstein L, Schlesinger J. Pathoanatomic, pathophysiologic, and clinical correlations in endocarditis. N Engl J Med 1974;291:832.

CHAPTER 8–13

Infections of the Upper Respiratory Tract

Nigel J. Raymond, M.D., Phyllis E. Kozarsky, M.D., and David S. Stephens, M.D.

DEFINITION

Infections of the upper respiratory tract include those of the nasopharynx, paranasal sinuses, middle ear, epiglottis, and larynx.

ETIOLOGY

Various bacteria and viruses are responsible for infections of the upper respiratory tract (see Table 8–13–1).

CRITERIA FOR DIAGNOSIS

Suggestive

Infections of the upper respiratory tract represent the leading reason for visits to a physician in the United States. These infections include the common cold and influenza, sinusitis, otitis media, pharyngitis, epiglottitis, laryngitis, and bronchitis. Diagnosis is usually made on clinical grounds.

Definitive

Most of these infections are bacterial or viral in etiology. A specific diagnosis may be confirmed by isolation of the infecting microorganism (e.g., group A streptococcal pharyngitis) or by serologic studies, but for uncomplicated infections, this may not always be appropriate or cost-effective. Many of the illnesses included in this chapter are discussed in greater detail in the chapters dealing with individual infections.

CLINICAL MANIFESTATIONS

See Table 8–13–1.

PLANS

See Table 8–13–1.

FOLLOW-UP

Some of these infections (e.g., common cold) can be managed on an outpatient basis and may not require follow-up unless complications develop. Others may require limited follow-up (e.g., otitis media) to ensure success of therapy. Still others are life threatening (e.g., bacterial epiglottitis) and require immediate hospitalization and frequent contact to assess response to therapy. Follow-up laboratory tests usually are not needed for most of these infections unless symptoms such as fever, pain, and cough persist or new symptoms develop. For example, patients who have cough beyond the acute illness may require further diagnostic studies such as chest x-ray, sputum cytology, sputum culture, and bronchoscopy to exclude pneumonitis, tumor, or foreign body.

DISCUSSION

Prevalence and Incidence and Related Basic Science

Common cold

The **common cold** is a mild illness of the upper respiratory tract. Many viruses cause the syndrome, notably rhinoviruses, coronaviruses, adenoviruses, influenza viruses, parainfluenza viruses, and respiratory syncytial virus. Rhinoviruses and adenoviruses in particular have many strains, resulting in a large number of possible causes.

The cold is indeed common. During the winter months in the United States, the prevalence reaches about 15% of persons per week and accounts for a large number of absences from school and work. It does not seem to be the cold weather itself that accounts for the increased ill-

TABLE 8–13–1. UPPER RESPIRATORY INFECTIONS: CLINICAL MANIFESTATIONS AND DIAGNOSTIC AND THERAPEUTIC APPROACHES

Infection	Subjective	Objective	Diagnostic	Therapeutic
Common cold	Runny nose, nasal congestion, stuffiness, low-grade fever, malaise	Edematous boggy nasal turbinates, mucoid discharge, low-grade fever	Clinical	Self-limited, rest, fluids, mild analgesia, decongestants
Influenza	Abrupt onset, fever, chills, headache, myalgias; followed by cough, nasal discharge; usually winter months, epidemic outbreaks	High fever, face flushed, eyes red and watery, clear nasal discharge, lassitude	Clinical; occasionally, viral culture or serology may be indicated for confirmation of diagnosis	As for common cold, and monitoring for development of pneumonia or other complications
Sinusitis	Fever, pain over infected sinus, purulent nasal discharge; follows common cold or influenza: cough; maxillary toothache; poor response to decongestants	Tenderness and swelling over infected sinus; purulence from middle meatus; opacity on transillumination of frontal or maxillary sinus; objective findings may be minimal	Clinical; x-ray or computed tomography of sinuses (most sensitive); *Streptococcus pneumoniae*, nontypable *Hemophilus influenzae*, and *Moraxella catarrhalis* cause most acute sinusitis	Antibiotics as for acute otitis media; nasal decongestants may be helpful but antihistamines usually are not; surgical drainage may be required if medical therapy fails or symptoms recur
Otitis media	Otalgia, hearing loss, fever, irritability, ear drainage (perforation of tympanic membrane)	Bulging of tympanic membrane, loss of normal tympanic membrane landmarks and motion, rupture of tympanic membrane	Pneumatic otoscopy or tympanometry to document fluid in the middle ear, together with a consistent clinical illness; *Streptococcus pneumoniae*, nontypable *Hemophilus influenzae*, and *Moraxella catarrhalis* cause most acute otitis; tympanocentesis cultures if initial antibiotic regimen fails	Simple analgesics; initial antibiotic regimen can usually be amoxicillin; trimethoprim–sulfamethoxazole, amoxicillin–clavulanic acid, cefuroxime–axetil, or erythromycin–sulfisoxazole may be useful in some cases if no response to amoxicillin
Pharyngitis	Sore throat, fever, cervical node tenderness; concomitant symptoms of common viral causes of pharyngitis	Erythematous, edematous pharynx; tonsillar enlargement, exudate, fever, and anterior cervical adenopathy (streptococcal); generalized adenopathy, splenomegaly (infectious mononucleosis); conjunctivitis (adenovirus); discrete vesicles on erythematous base (herpangina or primary herpes pharyngitis); diffuse muscosal white exudate (oral thrush)	Clinical; throat culture (group A streptococci); rapid streptococcal antigen detection kits (good specificity, sometimes poor sensitivity), when negative do confirmatory throat culture; Monospot (infectious mononucleosis); potassium hydroxide preparation (oral thrush); diphtheria, gonococcal: culture on suitable medium	Depends on etiology: 10 d of penicillin V or erythromycin for group A streptococci; supportive care for infectious mononucleosis; nystatin, clotrimazole gargles, or, if severe, oral ketoconazole or fluconazole for oral thrush
Epiglottitis	Child 2–6 y; occasionally seen in adults:abrupt-onset fever, dysphagia, sore throat, respiratory distress, hoarseness	Respiratory stridor, toxic appearance; leukocytosis	Clinical; laryngoscopic visualization of edematous "cherry red" epiglottis; lateral neck film showing enlarged epiglottis; cultures of blood, epiglottis	Maintainance of airway, insertion of endotracheal tube or tracheostomy at time of visualization of epiglottis; intravenous cefuroxime, ceftriaxone, trimethoprim–sulfamethoxazole, or chloramphenicol
Laryngitis	Lowered pitch of voice, cough; concurrent or preceding cold or influenza	Hoarseness	Clinical; throat culture to rule out group A streptococci	Most are self-limited; rest voice; penicillin or erythromycin for group A streptococcal infections
Laryngotracheitis	Hoarseness, cough, stridor; preceding common cold	Usually child 3 mo–3 years; characteristic cough, inspiratory stridor, rhonchi, wheezing, fever	Clinical; distinguish from epiglottitis, foreign body aspiration; neck x-rays (may be unreliable)	Close observation, may require intensive supportive care including oxygen, sometimes intubation (? nebulized racemic epinephrine)

ness, but perhaps it is the exposure to more individuals in enclosed surroundings that increases the likelihood of infection.

Cold viruses are transmitted by droplet spread (by small and large particles) and by hand contact. It has been shown that virus can be picked up not only by direct contact with those infected, but also from dry surfaces on which the virus resides. After inoculation, virus multiplies in the upper respiratory mucosa, causing inflammation and exudation. The incubation period is usually 3 to 5 days, after which the individual becomes symptomatic. Influenza may present as a common cold or be characterized by high fever and myalgia (Table 8–13–1). The pathogenesis of influenza is discussed in Chapter 8-66.

Sinusitis

Sinusitis is an infection of any of the paranasal sinuses, which include the maxillary, frontal, ethmoid, and sphenoid sinuses. Sinusitis is more common during the colder months of the year and is found more often in adults than in children. Viral colds, anatomic nasal abnormalities such as nasal septal deviation, allergic rhinitis, or an immunodeficiency may predispose to acute bacterial sinusitis. Acute bacterial sinusitis is most commonly due to *Streptococcus pneumoniae*, unencapsulated *Hemophilis influenzae*, and *Moraxella catarrhalis*. Maxillary sinusitis due to anaerobes is associated with dental infection. Nosocomial sinusitis may be due to Gram-negative bacilli. A variety of fungi may cause acute sinusitis in immunosuppressed hosts or chronic sinusitis in normal hosts. Bacterial invasion of the sinuses leads to mucosal inflammation with exudate formation, which may cause the characteristic air–fluid level seen on sinus radiographs. Patients may have multiple episodes of sinusitis leading to destruction of the ciliated columnar lining of the sinuses and predisposing to chronic sinusitis. *Staphylococcus,* viridans streptococci, and anaerobes are also isolated in chronic sinusitis; in this setting sinus irrigation, surgical drainage procedures, and antibiotics for acute exacerbations may be appropriate.

Otitis Media

Otitis media is infection in the middle ear. It is one of the most common infections in children, particularly those less than 5 years of age, and its incidence decreases with age. Infection is more common in the winter months and occurs more often in males than in females. The major causes of otitis media are *Streptococcus pneumoniae,* nontypable *Hemophilus influenzae,* and *Moraxella catarrhalis. Mycoplasma pneumoniae* has been associated with bullous myringitis, which may accompany the atypical pneumonia caused by this organism. The primary defect responsible for fluid accumulation in the middle ear in otitis media is inflammation of the eustachian tube, which normally drains secretions into the nasopharynx. This inflammation may often be due to viral infections, such as influenza and respiratory syncytial virus, which have sometimes also been cultured from middle ear fluid. Sometimes the eustachian tubes remain obstructed for long periods, predisposing to recurrent and chronic infection.

Pharyngitis

Pharyngitis is a broad term referring to inflammation of the pharynx. It may be caused by a number of viral and bacterial pathogens, and its epidemiology is dependent on the particular organism responsible. Pharyngitis is very common, and in general, it occurs with greatest frequency in the colder months.

Adenoviruses are the most common cause of viral pharyngitis. In addition, Coxsackie virus A, influenza viruses A and B, parainfluenza viruses, respiratory syncytial virus, Epstein–Barr virus, HIV, and cytomegalovirus can cause pharyngitis. The latter three are often associated with mononucleosis syndromes. The pharyngitis in Epstein–Barr mononucleosis usually occurs early in the disease and may be exudative. It is accompanied by fever and cervical lymphadenopathy. Generalized adenopathy and splenomegaly may be present. Mononucleosis caused by cytomegalovirus infection usually does not cause an exudative pharyngitis. Pharyngitis may occur during acute HIV infection. Herpangina caused by Coxsackie virus is characterized by a pharyngitis with small localized vesicular lesions, high fever, and constitutional symptoms, particularly in children. Primary herpes infection may cause pharyngitis. Often this accompanies gingivostomatitis and is quite debilitating, with fever and tender cervical lymphadenopathy. Vesicles or superficial ulcerations on the palate are characteristic if present. Pharyngoconjunctival fever is caused by adenovirus and is quite severe. Many of these patients have associated follicular conjunctivitis. This illness is common in military recruits, and unlike other illnesses causing pharyngitis, it occurs often during the summer.

Group A hemolytic streptococcal infections account for about 15% of all cases of pharyngitis. It occurs more often in school-aged children, with one infection on average every 3 to 5 years. Often there are high fever, tonsillar enlargement, an exudate, and tender cervical lymphadenopathy, although people also may be asymptomatic carriers. Group A streptococcal infections are spread by direct contact from person to person. It is common for infection to spread within a household or a classroom. M protein found on the surface of group A streptococci is a major virulence factor. Patients develop type-specific antibody to M-protein, which is protective against reinfection with group A streptococci of the same M-protein type but not other types. Extracellular products elaborated by the streptococci, such as hyaluronidase, streptokinase, and DNAases, probably account for the spread through tissues, the inflammation, and the exudate formation. Group C and G streptococci may cause pharyngitis in older children and in foodborne outbreaks, but rarely if ever cause glomerulonephritis or rheumatic fever. *Arcanobacterium (Corynebacterium) hemolyticum* may cause pharyngitis that mimics *Streptococcus pyogenes.* A scarlatiniform rash may be seen associated with *A. hemolyticum* pharyngitis.

Pharyngitis due to **gonococci** may also occur, although in many patients symptoms may be minimal. When gonococcal urethritis, cervicitis, or proctitis is suspected, a pharyngeal culture on appropriate medium should also be done. All patients with suspected disseminated gonorrhea infection should have a pharyngeal culture.

A more recently recognized cause of pharyngitis, as well as sinusitis, bronchitis, and pneumonia, is *Chlamydia pneumoniae.* There is usually little fever, but cough and hoarseness are common. Like *Mycoplasma pneumoniae, Chlamydia pneumoniae* affects mostly older children and young adults. Mixed anaerobic infection of the pharynx (**Vincent's angina**) occasionally occurs. The organism *Fusobacterium necrophorum* is associated with these infections, and it causes a foul odor and a severe exudative pharyngitis.

Diphtheria

Diphtheria rarely occurs in this country because of immunization; however, in other countries and in low socioeconomic areas of the United States, it is still seen. *Corynebacterium diphtheriae* is a Gram-positive pleomorphic bacillus that grows on special media under anaerobic conditions. Transmission is mainly by droplet spread, and exotoxin is responsible for the local and systemic effects, which may be severe. In the pharynx, inflammation occurs with exudation and formation of a membrane adherent to the mucosa. This membrane may extend down the respiratory tree and cause obstruction.

Oropharyngeal Candida Infection

Oropharyngeal *Candida* infections are seen most often in patients who have cellular immune dysfunction. Patients who are infected with HIV or who have AIDS often present with oropharyngeal thrush. In addition, patients undergoing chemotherapy or who are on high-dose steroids are also predisposed. The whitish coat can cover the tongue, the buccal mucosa, and the pharynx and cause sore throat. Esophageal involvement may cause severe dysphagia.

Epiglottitis

Acute **epiglottitis** is a life-threatening illness. Fortunately, it is rare. The most common responsible pathogen is *Hemophilus influenzae* type b, although other *Hemophilus* species, pneumococci, other streptococci, and staphylococci also may be responsible. The infection is seen in young children and may rapidly progress from a mild upper respiratory illness to obstruction. Bacteremia is common with epiglottitis.

Acute Laryngitis

Acute laryngitis is a common ailment. Acute **laryngitis** in adults is usually viral, commonly rhinovirus, influenza virus, and adenovirus, for which antibiotics are not indicated. *Streptococcus pneumoniae* and *Moraxella catarrhalis* (and *Corynebacterium diphtheriae*) may cause laryngitis, and can be isolated using nasopharyngeal cultures.

Laryngotracheitis

Acute **laryngotracheitis** (croup), a syndrome characterized by laryngeal edema and stridor, is common in children, particularly those of preschool age. Viruses associated with the syndrome include parainfluenza viruses 1, 2, and 3 and influenza viruses A and B. *Mycoplasma pneumoniae* occasionally causes croup, mostly in older children. Characteristic of croup are inflammation and secretion of large amounts of exudate into the respiratory tree, causing narrowing at the subglottic level and resulting in the signs and symptoms of obstruction. Parainfluenza virus type 1 has been the predominant cause of the peak incidence of croup during fall. Hypoxemia, airway obstruction, and viral pneumonia are complications for which close observation and supportive measures are required.

Bronchitis

Bronchitis is discussed in Chapters 13–14 and 13–15.

Natural History and Its Modification with Treatment

Although morbidity with upper respiratory infection is quite high, mortality is low. The common cold is a self-limited illness. Sinusitis usually responds to decongestants and antibiotics, although sometimes drainage of the infected sinus is required. Rarely, there is extension of infection that may lead to osteomyelitis or brain abscess.

Acute otitis media may resolve spontaneously in approximately 80% of children, and may be followed by an effusion, which resolves over several weeks. Recurrent acute otitis is more common in children whose first episode occurs at an early age, who are not breastfed, and who attend daycare. Some chronic effusions lasting months ("glue ear") may cause hearing deficit and learning delay; acute infectious exacerbations may occur. Spread of infection from the middle ear may lead to mastoiditis, meningitis, or brain abscess.

Complications of Group A streptococcal pharyngitis can be categorized as suppurative, toxic, and nonsuppurative. Patients with peritonsillar abscess may complain of increasingly sore throat and dysphagia. On examination, the soft palate on the involved side may be edematous or even fluctuant, the uvula is pushed away from the midline, and the tonsillar area is quite swollen. There are enlarged, tender cervical nodes. Very rarely, the infection can invade into the neck and jugular vein to cause thrombophlebitis. Other suppurative infections include retropharyngeal abscess, sinusitis, acute otitis media, and mastoiditis.

Toxic complications include scarlet fever and the streptococcal toxic shock syndrome. Acute rheumatic fever and acute glomerulonephritis occur; outbreaks of rheumatic fever still occur in the United States.

The major complication of epiglottitis is respiratory tract obstruction, which may develop rapidly. Some patients require tracheostomy.

Prevention

Prevention of upper respiratory infections is difficult for several reasons. First, the number of persons infected is large. Second, transmission of the viruses and bacteria often occurs during the incubation period of the illness. And finally, many individuals may be asymptomatic carriers; however, simple measures, such as washing one's hands, often may prevent transmission. Also, it is common sense to carefully dispose of one's mucus secretions during an illness. There is some evidence that increased humidification indoors during the winter months helps prevent the acquisition of infection.

Prevention of rheumatic fever requires prompt treatment of group A streptococcal pharyngitis. A 10-day course of penicillin V has been shown to be more effective than 5 days in this regard. In patients who have a history of rheumatic fever, prevention of recurrence of group A streptococcal pharyngitis requires the continuous administration of daily sulfonamides or penicillin or monthly benzathine penicillin G.

Reduction in acute otitis media frequency may be achieved with breastfeeding during the first year, elimination of household tobacco smoke, and use of small rather than large daycare arrangements for in-

fants and toddlers. Antimicrobial prophylaxis with amoxicillin or sulfisoxazole has been shown to reduce acute otitis media frequency in children with a history of recurrent acute otitis media. Potential problems with this approach include emergence of resistant bacteria, drug reactions, and suppression of symptoms without affecting the disease process.

Perhaps one of the best ways of decreasing the severity or chronicity of respiratory infections in patients who smoke is to encourage them to stop. In addition, there is mounting evidence that even "passive" smoking and air pollution have a deleterious effect on the lungs and increase respiratory infections.

Pneumococcal and influenza vaccines are recommended for the prevention of these illnesses in high-risk populations; however, current polysaccharide pneumococcal vaccines are insufficiently immunogenic to be used for routine prevention of acute otitis media in young children. Conjugate *Hemophilus influenzae* (HiB) vaccines are effective for infants and children. The introduction of routine childhood HiB vaccination beginning at 2 months has been associated with a dramatic reduction in the prevalence of HiB disease.

Cost Containment

The medical expense of the common cold is enormous if one thinks in terms of days lost from work and school as well as physician visits. In fact, upper respiratory infections account for about 90% of general medical practice during the winter.

Increasing antibiotic resistance, particularly by *Streptococcus pneumoniae*, threatens to reverse progress in preventing complications of bacterial upper respiratory tract infections. Alternatives to current first-line antibiotics are often more expensive or have more side effects. The widespread use of antibiotics for upper respiratory infections is an important factor contributing to the emergence of resistant strains. Practical clinical approaches are needed that improve diagnostic accuracy and that limit antibiotic use more specifically to those infections where the natural history will be altered. Overall, the best method of cost containment is prevention.

REFERENCES

Canafax DM, Giebink GS. Antimicrobial treatment of acute otitis media. Ann Otol Rhinol Laryngol 1994; suppl. 163:11.

Cressman WR, Myer CM. Diagnosis and management of croup and epiglottitis. Pediat Clin North Am 1994;41:265.

Mandell GL, Bennett JE, Dolin R, eds. Principles and practice of infectious diseases. 4th ed. New York: Churchill Livingstone, 1995.

Round table on current issues in pediatric ear, nose and throat infections. Pediat Infect Dis J 1994;13 (suppl.1):S5.

Smith MBH, Feldman W. Over-the-counter cold medications: A critical review of clinical trials between 1950 and 1991. JAMA 1993; 269:2258.

Williams JW, Simel DL. Does this patient have sinusitis? Diagnosing acute sinusitis by history and physical examination. JAMA 1993;270:1242.

CHAPTER 8–14

Pneumonia Caused by Pyogenic Bacteria

Jay C. Butler, M.D., and Carl A. Perlino, M.D.

DEFINITION

Pneumonia is an inflammation of the lung due to an infectious agent. This chapter discusses pneumonias associated with pyogenic bacteria (e.g., *Streptococcus pneumoniae*, *Hemophilus influenzae*); succeeding chapters address the clinical aspects of the so-called "atypical pneumonias" due to infection with *Mycoplasma pneumoniae*, *Chlamydia pneumoniae*, and *Legionella* species (Chapter 8–15) and chronic pneumonia syndrome, including disease caused by *Mycobacterium tuberculosis* and fungal pathogens (Chapter 13–14 and 8–18). It should, however, be noted that the clinical, routine laboratory, and radiographic findings of

pyogenic and "atypical" pneumonia overlap widely, and it is often not possible to reliably distinguish between pneumonias of various etiologies without specific diagnostic testing.

ETIOLOGY

The etiology of pneumonia is diverse. *Streptococcus pneumoniae* (pneumococcus) is the most common cause of community-acquired pneumonia in adults. Even in prospective etiologic studies with extensive diagnostic testing, however, the etiology remains unknown for as many as 40% of patients with pneumonia.

CRITERIA FOR DIAGNOSIS

Suggestive

A febrile illness with cough, dyspnea, or chest pain together with new infiltrates demonstrated by chest x-ray is highly suggestive of pneumonia. Numerous polymorphonuclear leukocytes and a predominance of a single organism in a Gram-stained sputum specimen may indicate pneumonia caused by pyogenic bacteria.

Definitive

The definitive etiologic diagnosis of pneumonia depends on the agent involved. The definitive diagnosis of pneumonia due to pyogenic bacteria, which often colonize the oropharynx and contaminate expectorated sputum collected for culture, can be difficult unless the organism is recovered from a normally sterile site (e.g., blood, pleural fluid). The majority of pneumonia cases are managed either empirically or on the basis of culture of expectorated sputum without a definitive etiologic diagnosis.

CLINICAL MANIFESTATIONS

Subjective

Symptoms suggestive of bacterial pneumonia include fever, chills, cough (which may be productive or nonproductive), pleuritic chest pain, and dyspnea. Respiratory symptoms may be absent in elderly or immunocompromised patients with pneumonia.

Although the etiology of pneumonia cannot be reliably determined on the basis of the clinical findings alone, a complete history with particular attention to underlying medical conditions and history of travel, occupation, exposure to animals, and recent hospitalization can be very helpful in identifying the likely etiologic agent.

Pneumococcal pneumonia frequently occurs in persons who are otherwise healthy, but is especially common among the elderly and those with underlying illness (see Prevention). Epidemic pneumococcal pneumonia may occur among otherwise healthy young adults in special situations such as military camps and prisons. Pneumonia due to *Hemophilus influenzae* and *Moraxella catarrhalis* develops predominantly in patients with chronic obstructive pulmonary disease. Staphylococcal pneumonia may complicate influenza or may be a cause of nosocomial infection in hospitalized patients. *Klebsiella pneumoniae* is occasionally a cause of pneumonia in alcoholic or malnourished patients or in patients with chronic obstructive pulmonary disease. *K. pneumoniae* and other Gram-negative aerobic bacilli such as *Escherichia coli, Proteus, Enterobacter, Pseudomonas, Serratia,* and *Acinetobacter* are important causes of nosocomial pneumonia. Nosocomial pneumonias due to pneumococcal infection do occur but less commonly than those due to Gram-negative bacilli and *Staphylococcus aureus.* Anaerobic infections are a likely cause of infection in patients who aspirate large amounts of infected material from the oropharynx, for example, patients with pyorrhea and those who aspirate because of seizures, abnormal swallowing mechanisms, poor cough reflex, or decreased consciousness. *Neisseria meningitidis* is a rare cause of pneumonia but can occasionally cause epidemic disease.

Objective

Physical Examination

Fever is present in most patients with pneumonia, but elderly, alcoholic, severely malnourished, and renal dialysis-dependent patients may not mount a febrile response. Some patients may in fact present with hypothermia (core temperature <35°C). Tachypnea may be present. Intercostal or sternal retraction, the use of accessory respiratory muscles, nasal flaring, and cyanosis occur in patients with significant respiratory compromise. Splinting, decreased motion of one side of the chest on inspiration, may suggest bronchial obstruction or significant pleural inflammation causing pain on chest motion.

Auscultation of the chest of patients with lobar pneumonia often reveals egophony ("e to a" changes), whispered pectoriloquy, bronchial breath sounds, and rales. The chest wall overlying the consolidated lobe may be dull to percussion. A pleural rub indicates an area of pleural inflammation, and associated pleural fluid may produce dullness to percussion and diminished breath sounds. Extrapulmonary manifestation may be significant. Altered mental status may indicate significant hypoxemia, systemic toxicity, associated abnormalities of serum electrolytes, or complicating meningitis. Metastatic foci of infection may rarely occur, and signs of endocarditis or septic arthritis may be detected.

Routine Laboratory Abnormalities

The chest radiograph is the single most important test used in the evaluation of patients with suspected pneumonia. Radiographic manifestations of pneumonia are diverse and may include alveolar or interstitial infiltrates, nodules, cavitation, effusion, and hilar lymphadenopathy. Early in the course of infection, and in elderly patients who may be volume depleted, the radiographic changes may be minimal and even appear to worsen with administration of intravenous fluid and antibiotics. Although several studies have demonstrated that radiologists are unable to differentiate pyogenic from "atypical pneumonia" on the basis of the chest x-ray film, some findings are very suggestive of certain organisms. *Staphylococcus aureus* may cause multiple thin-walled cavities. A localized infiltrate with an air–fluid level, particularly in the lower lobes, suggests an anaerobic lung abscess.

In bacterial pneumonia, the leukocyte count is often elevated with an increased proportion of immature neutrophils. A leukocyte count above 15,000 cells/cm^3 usually indicates pyogenic bacterial infection, but lower counts do not exclude the diagnosis. Leukopenia may occur in patients with overwhelming infection or in alcoholic patients. Anemia may be present due to underlying illness, a chronic pulmonary infection such as tuberculosis or anaerobic lung abscess, or, rarely, hemolysis with pneumococcal sepsis. Arterial blood gas analysis and transcutaneous arterial saturation measurement may show varying degrees of hypoxemia. Blood gases often show respiratory alkalosis, but may demonstrate acidosis and elevated carbon dioxide levels indicating impending respiratory failure.

PLANS

Diagnostic

Differential Diagnosis

Bacterial pneumonia must be distinguished from noninfectious causes of fever and pulmonary infiltrates. A list of conditions included in the differential diagnosis of bacterial pneumonia and approaches that may aid in their diagnosis is found in Table 8–14–1.

Diagnostic Options and Recommended Approach

All patients hospitalized with pneumonia should have blood drawn for culture, and if a specimen can be obtained, sputum should be collected for Gram stain and culture. Examination of a Gram-stained sputum specimen may be useful in guiding initial therapy. Specimens of expectorated sputum submitted for Gram stain and culture for pyogenic bacteria should contain fewer than 5 to 10 squamous epithelial cells and

TABLE 8–14–1. CONDITIONS INCLUDED IN THE DIFFERENTIAL DIAGNOSIS OF BACTERIAL PNEUMONIA AND METHODS OF EVALUATION

Condition	Diagnostic Test or Observation
Pulmonary infarction	Ventilation–perfusion scan; pulmonary arteriography
Pulmonary contusion	History of trauma
Intrapulmonary hemorrhage	Concomitant bleeding diathesis
Atelectasis	Resolution with chest physiotherapy; ventilation–perfusion scan
Chemical pneumonitis	History or exposure
Acute hypersensitivity pneumonitis	History of symptoms following occupational or environmental exposure; serum precipitins; lung biopsy
Immune complex pneumonia	Involvement of skin and other organs; antinuclear antibodies; cryoglobulins; complement levels; circulating immune complexes; lung biopsy

more than 25 leukocytes per low-power (100×) field. The specimen must be adequately stained and decolorized (the nuclei of leukocytes should be pink). The sputum Gram stain is most useful for guiding therapy when there is a predominance of a single organism. Unfortunately, approximately one half of patients hospitalized with pneumonia are unable to produce an adequate sputum specimen, many pneumonias are due to agents that cannot be detected by Gram stain (*Chlamydia pneumoniae, Legionella* species, *Mycoplasma pneumoniae*), and the appearance of organisms on Gram stain may be altered by prior antibiotic therapy. Cultures of expectorated sputum from patients with pneumonia may yield organisms simply colonizing the oropharynx in addition to those playing an etiologic role. Therefore, sputum culture results must be interpreted in light of the results of an adequate sputum Gram stain. Antibiotic susceptibility testing of organisms isolated from sputum can provide useful information for guiding therapy when results of Gram stain and culture are concordant. Respiratory secretions obtained by nasotracheal suction and routine bronchoscopy may be useful but should be interpreted with the same caution as expectorated sputum. The sensitivity and specificity of bronchoscopy are improved by use of a protected brush catheter to obtain specimens. Transtracheal aspiration was used in the past to obtain respiratory secretions, but this method may not totally eliminate contamination by oropharyngeal organisms and should be performed only by those experienced with the procedure. Culture of specimens obtained by transthoracic lung aspiration may obviate oropharyngeal contamination but carries the risk of pneumothorax and bleeding.

Because pneumonia caused by agents other than pyogenic bacteria cannot be diagnosed by routine bacteriologic techniques, additional diagnostic testing may be indicated. Approaches that aid in evaluating for these agents are outlined in Chapter 8–15.

If pleural fluid is present, a diagnostic thoracentesis should be performed. Gram stain and culture of aspirated fluid may identify the pathogen. Fluid should also be obtained for white blood cell with differential cell count and determination of pH, and protein, lactate dehydrogenase, and glucose concentrations in order to evaluate for pleural empyema. Although up to 40% of bacterial pneumonias are associated with radiographically detectable pleural fluid, empyema develops in only a small proportion of cases. Unfortunately, empyema cannot be distinguished from uncomplicated parapneumonic effusion on the basis of clinical or radiographic findings. If bacteria are visualized or recovered from purulent pleural fluid, the diagnosis of empyema is straightforward; however, Gram stain of pleural fluid may not reveal organisms, even in frank empyema. Other laboratory studies of pleural fluid that suggest empyema include low pH (particularly if below 7.10), glucose concentration less than 40 mg/mL, lactate dehydrogenase concentration greater than 1000 IU/L, and leukocyte count greater than 25,000 cells/mL with a predominance of polymorphonuclear leukocytes.

In selected cases, additional imaging may be indicated. Ultrasonography can be useful to localize loculated pleural fluid for aspiration. High-resolution computed tomography may be indicated to identify cavitation within an infiltrate, lung nodules, hilar adenopathy, lymph nodes or tumor causing bronchial obstruction, or unsuspected collections of pleural fluid.

The decision to collect specimens for serologic tests or special stains, to obtain respiratory secretions by invasive procedures, or to perform additional imaging must be individualized. Additional testing is most likely to provide useful information about patients with (1) history of travel or animal exposure suggesting a specific etiologic agent, (2) compromised immunity due to medication or underlying illness, (3) illness that is not responding to antimicrobial therapy, (4) respiratory illness epidemiologically associated with a pneumonia outbreak of unknown etiology, or (5) suspected pulmonary infection with agents requiring immediate public health intervention to prevent further transmission (e.g., *Mycobacterium tuberculosis, Yersinia pestis*.)

Therapeutic

Because of the nonspecificity of clinical and radiographic findings in determining a specific etiology and the time required to obtain results of specific diagnostic tests, initial therapy for pneumonia is empiric. The choice of initial therapy for bacterial pneumonia should be based on the (1) the severity of illness, (2) whether infection is nosocomial or community-acquired, (3) the findings on a Gram-stained sputum specimen, if available, (4) local antibiotic susceptibility patterns, and (5) underlying medical condition of the patient (Table 8–14–2). The physician must first decide whether or not outpatient therapy is appropriate. Outpatient therapy for pneumonia should be limited to young, otherwise healthy persons who are not severely ill. Elderly patients, those with underlying medical conditions, and patients with evidence of severe illness or complications should be hospitalized (Table 8–14–3). For outpatient therapy of community-acquired pneumonia in young, otherwise healthy patients, a macrolide antibiotic or a tetracycline provides the convenience of oral therapy and activity against *Mycoplasma* and *Chlamydia pneumoniae*. For community-acquired pneumonia re-

TABLE 8–14–2. SUGGESTED INITIAL EMPIRIC THERAPY FOR BACTERIAL PNEUMONIA

Setting	Predominant Organism on Sputum Gram Stain	Antibiotics
Young, otherwise healthy patient not requiring, hospitalization	Not available or no predominant organism	Macrolide,* tetracycline, or doxycycline
Community-acquired, requiring hospitalization	Not available or no predominant organism	Cefuroxime, ceftriaxone, or cefotaxime *plus* macrolide*
Community-acquired, requiring hospitalization	Gram-positive diplococci	Cefuroxime, ceftriaxone, or cefotaxime in areas where strains with penicillin resistance are common
Community-acquired	Gram-negative cocci or coccobacilli	Cefuroxime, ceftriaxone, or cefotaxime
Community-acquired	Gram-positive cocci in clusters	Oxacillin, nafcillin, or cefazolin **or** Vancomycin in areas where methicillin-resistant strains are common
Community-acquired, suspected aspiration	Not available or no predominant organism	Clindamycin and ceftriaxone
Hospital-acquired†	Not available, no predominant organism, or Gram-negative bacilli	Piperacillin (±tazobactam) or ciprofloxacin aminoglycoside or aztreonam **or** Imipenem–cilastatin
Hospital-acquired	Gram-positive cocci in clusters	Vancomycin

*Erythromycin, azithromycin, clarithromycin.
†Selection of an antibiotic for empiric therapy of nosocomial pneumonia caused by pyogenic bacteria must be guided by local susceptibility patterns. Consider macrolide if *Legionella* suspected as a pathogen.

TABLE 8–14–3. SUGGESTED INDICATIONS FOR HOSPITALIZATION OF ADULTS WITH BACTERIAL PNEUMONIA

- Hypoxemia (<60 mm Hg) or hypercapnia
- Significant dyspnea or tachypnea (≥30 breaths/min)
- Hypotension or other evidence of sepsis
- Leukopenia or marked leukocytosis (>25,000 cells/cm^3)
- Age ≥65 years
- Significant underlying disease (including asplenia, sickle cell disease, chronic obstructive pulmonary disease, bronchiectasis, cystic fibrosis, diabetes mellitus, chronic renal failure, chronic liver disease, congestive heart failure)
- Chest x-ray findings of pleural fluid or alveolar infiltrates involving more than one lobe, or cavitation
- Depressed level of consciousness
- Inability to comply with oral therapy

quiring hospitalization in patients unable to produce an adequate sputum specimen, the combination of an extended-spectrum cephalosporin with activity against *Streptococcus pneumoniae* in combination with a macrolide agent provides broad coverage for the vast majority of possible etiologic agents. The finding of a large number of Gram-positive diplococci in an adequately collected and stained sputum specimen suggests pneumococcal pneumonia. Penicillin G is the drug of choice for pneumococcal infections and is likely adequate even for pneumonia caused by strains with intermediate-level penicillin resistance (minimal inhibitory concentration [MIC] 0.1–1.0 μg/mL). For seriously ill patients with suspected pneumococcal infection possibly due to a penicillin-resistant strain, an extended-spectrum cephalosporin may be preferable until the results of susceptibility testing are available. Little information is currently available on the best treatment for pneumonia caused by pneumococcal strains with high-level resistance to penicillin (MIC>1 μg/L), but vancomycin therapy should probably be reserved for patients with evidence of metastatic infection (e.g., meningitis). Gram-negative diplococci or coccobacilli may indicate *Hemophilus influenzae* or *Moraxella catarrhalis* infection, and an extended-spectrum cephalosporin or trimethoprim–sulfamethoxazole may be used initially. If Gram-positive cocci in clusters suggestive of *Staphylococcus aureus* are predominant in a specimen, a penicillinase-resistant penicillin (e.g., oxacillin, nafcillin) or cefazolin should be given. Vancomycin is preferable until antibiotic susceptibilities are known for suspected staphylococcal pneumonia in areas where methicillin-resistant strains are common or if infection is hospital-acquired. Other regimens are indicated in special circumstances: an agent with activity against *Pseudomonas aeruginosa* is required for hospital-acquired infection and for patients with bronchiectasis or cystic fibrosis. Coverage against anaerobic bacteria may be necessary following aspiration. Initial antibiotic therapy should be modified according to results of cultures, sensitivity testing, and response to therapy. The least expensive and least toxic antibiotic to which the organism is susceptible should be selected.

Pleural fluid should be drained for diagnostic purposes, for relief of respiratory compromise, and for evaluation for empyema. If empyema is present, early placement of a thoracostomy tube will speed resolution of symptoms and help prevent loculation of the fluid. Loculated collections of empyema fluid often require open thoracostomy for adequate drainage.

Few data are available on the appropriate time to switch patients from intravenous antibiotics to oral therapy or on the optimal duration of antimicrobial therapy for bacterial pneumonia. Use of oral antibiotics requires a medically compliant patient with a functioning gastrointestinal tract who has improved on parenteral therapy and the availability of an oral agent with activity against the suspected or confirmed etiologic agent. In general, the duration of therapy should be based on etiology and the response to treatment. Uncomplicated, pneumococcal pneumonia may be treated for 3 or 4 days after resolution of symptoms, generally 7 to 10 days. Ten days of treatment is probably adequate for most pneumonias not requiring hospitalization and treated with oral agents. Persons with pneumonia due to *H. influenzae* and *M. catarrhalis* may require treatment for 10 to 14 days. Those with disease caused by staphylococci, Gram-negative bacilli, and anaerobes should be treated for 14 to 21 days, whereas lung abscess generally requires a longer course of treatment.

FOLLOW-UP

With appropriate antimicrobial therapy, clinical improvement should occur within 48 to 72 hours. Fever may continue for 2 to 4 days, with defervescence occurring most rapidly in pneumococcal pneumonia and more slowly for other etiologic agents. Rales may be audible for more than a week after initiation of adequate therapy. The chest x-ray film may show progression of infiltrates or development of a pleural effusion soon after therapy is started. This is not an indication for change of therapy, if an otherwise good clinical response to treatment is observed with improvement in fever and dyspnea. Complete resolution of radiographic abnormalities may require 1 to 2 months. For patients with evidence of bacterial pneumonia who have persistent fever and/or clinical and radiographic deterioration while receiving antibiotics, a number of possible explanations must be considered, including infection with a drug-resistant organism; infection with an unsuspected organism that is not being adequately treated; undiagnosed underlying illness (e.g., bronchogenic carcinoma, HIV infection); noninfectious etiology; or metastatic infection such as empyema, meningitis, endocarditis, or septic arthritis.

DISCUSSION

Prevalence and Incidence

Pneumonia is the sixth leading cause of death and the leading cause of death due to an acute infectious disease in the United States. Because pneumonia is not a reportable disease, estimates of the prevalence and incidence are based on hospital- and community-based studies. From these studies, it can be estimated that 2 to 4 million cases of community-acquired pneumonia occur in the United States annually, resulting in 500,000 to 1 million hospitalizations. Attack rates are highest among young children, the elderly, those who are immunosuppressed by underlying illness or medications, and persons with underlying pulmonary illness. Incidence rates may also be higher among certain racial groups, particularly American Indians and Alaskan natives. Nosocomial pneumonia develops in 4 to 8 per 1000 hospitalized patients and accounts for 15% of all hospital-associated infections.

Related Basic Science

Normal host defenses against microorganisms invading the respiratory tract include impaction of large (>10 μm in diameter) airborne particles in the upper airway, an intact gag reflex, the ability to cough, the ciliary and secretory functions of the respiratory epithelium, the phagocytic and secretory action of alveolar macrophages, and systemic humoral and cellular immune responses. Compromise of any of these defense mechanisms increases the chance that bacteria may reach the lung and pneumonia may occur. Organisms reach the lung through the bloodstream, following inhalation of infectious aerosols, or by aspiration of material from the oropharynx. For pyogenic bacteria, aspiration is the most common mechanism. Potential pathogens are often present in the oropharynx before they cause pulmonary infection. Anaerobic bacteria predominate in the normal indigenous flora of the oropharynx. Alpha-hemolytic streptococci are the most common aerobic bacteria, but a number of other potential pathogenic organisms may be recovered from the oropharynx of healthy persons, including pneumococci, *Hemophilus* species, staphylococci, *Moraxella catarrhalis, Neisseria* species, and *Corynebacterium* species. Aerobic Gram-negative bacilli are also often present, but in very low numbers. Antibiotic therapy and poorly defined factors that accompany serious illness allow for overgrowth of Gram-negative bacilli, accounting for the important etiologic role that these organisms play in hospital-acquired pneumonia.

Some degree of aspiration occurs in all individuals, especially during sleep. Bacteria that are caught in bronchial secretions are removed by the ciliary action of bronchial epithelial cells, which continuously move the organisms toward the pharynx. Organisms that reach the alveolar space are normally phagocytized and killed by alveolar macrophages. A number of pathogenic organisms have special characteristics that allow them either to escape phagocytosis or to reproduce within macrophages. For example, a polysaccharide capsule enables pneumococci to resist phagocytosis by alveolar macrophages and neutrophils and to multiply rapidly in the alveolar space; however, when type-specific anticapsular antibody is present in response to vaccination or prior infection, phagocytosis is enhanced, and the bacteria are destroyed.

Normal pulmonary defense mechanisms may be interrupted by several clinically recognizable conditions. Large numbers of bacteria may be aspirated by a patient with pyorrhea or during periods of depressed consciousness, and the normal capacity of the lung to clear these organisms may be overwhelmed. Normal ciliary function may be disrupted by cigarette smoke or a preceding *Mycoplasma* infection. Macrophage function is affected by chronic ethanol consumption, diabetic ketoacidosis, or antecedent influenza infection. Defects in the alternate complement system associated with sickle cell disease make phagocytosis of encapsulated organisms less efficient.

The growth of bacteria in the alveolar space attracts polymorphonuclear leukocytes and causes the production of cytokines, leading to accumulation of fluid and inflammatory cells in the alveolar space. Fluid in the alveolar space interferes with gas exchange. Appropriate antibiotics usually stop bacterial multiplication and allow clearance of the bacteria and subsequent healing. Pneumococci usually do not cause destruction of lung tissue, and in most cases, the normal architecture is restored when the infection clears; however, staphylococci, anaerobic bacteria, and Gram-negative bacilli may destroy normal lung architecture.

Natural History and Its Modification with Treatment

Before the advent of antibiotics, the mortality rate for pneumococcal pneumonia approached 30% in young healthy adults and was higher among the elderly and debilitated. Despite the use of antibiotics and intensive care support, approximately 25% of community-acquired pneumonia cases requiring hospitalization are fatal, and mortality attributable to pneumonia actually increased during the 1980s. Factors contributing to these findings are not completely understood but include the increasing proportion of the population that is elderly or immunocompromised and the emergence of Gram-negative bacilli as a major cause of hospital-acquired pneumonia.

Prevention

Pneumococcal polysaccharide vaccine provides protection against 23 pneumococcal serotypes associated with 85 to 90% of invasive infections. A single dose of pneumococcal vaccine should be administered to persons at increased risk of serious infection including those with splenic dysfunction or anatomic asplenia, chronic cardiovascular or pulmonary diseases, diabetes mellitus, alcoholism, cirrhosis, hematologic malignancy, chronic renal insufficiency, nephrotic syndrome, organ transplantation, or HIV infection, and all persons age 65 years or older. Pneumococcal vaccine is efficacious for prevention of pneumococcal bacteremia caused by the serotypes included in the vaccine for patients in many of these risk groups, but its efficacy for prevention of pneumococcal pneumonia without bacteremia is debated. For most patients, revaccination is not routinely recommended; however, revaccination may be prudent 6 or more years after previous doses for persons at highest risk of fatal pneumococcal infection (such as asplenic persons) or for those likely to have a rapid decline in pneumococcal antibody levels, such as patients with nephrotic syndrome, renal insufficiency, or organ transplantation. Prevention of pneumococcal infection by vaccination has become more crucial as strains resistant to multiple drugs have become more prevalent.

Influenza vaccine can decrease incidence of influenza infection and thus reduce the risk of subsequent bacterial pneumonia. Persons at increased risk for influenza-related complications include all persons age 65 years and older, residents of nursing homes and other long-term care facilities, persons with chronic disorders of the pulmonary or cardiovascular system and patients with chronic metabolic diseases (including diabetes mellitus), renal dysfunction, hemoglobinopathies, or immunosuppression. Influenza vaccine should be given annually during the fall. Influenza and pneumococcal vaccine may be administered concurrently at different sites. Although not a substitute for vaccination, postexposure chemoprophylaxis with the antiviral agent amantadine or rimantadine may prevent complications caused by type A influenza.

Measures to prevent nosocomial pneumonia caused by pyogenic bacteria include elevating the head of the bed and other steps to decrease aspiration, appropriate disinfection of respiratory therapy equipment, and infection control practices to prevent cross-contamination via hands of personnel. Prophylactic antibiotics have no role in the prevention of bacterial pneumonia in adults. Injudicious use of antibiotics appears to play an important role in the development of drug resistance by bacteria.

In view of the association between cigarette smoking and a number of chronic pulmonary diseases and the effect of smoke on ciliary function, smoking cessation probably plays a critical role in the prevention of pneumonia.

Cost Containment

Effective cost containment is currently limited to the prevention of pneumonia by the use of the vaccines noted above and by decreasing exposure to cigarette smoke. Improved laboratory tests that allow rapid identification of the infecting agent may become available in the future and will reduce the need for empiric therapy with more costly broad-spectrum agents and multiple-drug regimens.

REFERENCES

Bartlett JG. Current concepts: Community-acquired pneumonia. N Engl J Med 1995;333:1618.

Bartlett JG, O'Keefe P, Tally FP, et al. Bacteriology of hospital-acquired pneumonia. Arch Intern Med 1986;146:868.

Fang GD, Fine M, Orloff J, et al. New and emerging etiologies for community-acquired pneumonia with implications for therapy: A prospective multicenter study of 359 cases. Medicine 1990;69:307.

Friedland IR, McCracken GH. Management of infections caused by antibiotic-resistant *Streptococcus pneumoniae*. N Engl J Med 1994;331:377.

LaForce FM. Antibacterial therapy for lower respiratory tract infections in adults: a review. Clin Infect Dis 1992; 14(suppl. 2):S233.

Mandell LA. Antibiotics for pneumonia therapy. Med Clin North Am 1994;78:997.

Marrie TJ. Community-acquired pneumonia. Clin Infect Dis 1994;18:501.

Strange C, Sahn SA. Management of parapneumonic pleural effusions and empyema. Infect Dis Clin North Am 1991; 5:539.

"Atypical Pneumonias" or Pneumonia Caused by Other than Classic Pyogenic Bacteria

Barbara J. Marston, M.D., and Jonas A. Shulman, M.D.

DEFINITION

The term *atypical pneumonia* has traditionally been used to describe pneumonia in which the production of purulent sputum is minimal or absent.

ETIOLOGY

Organisms regarded as causes of this syndrome include *Mycoplasma pneumoniae, Legionella* species, *Chlamydia pneumoniae* (TWAR), viruses, *Chlamydia trachomatis, Chlamydia psittaci, Coxiella burnetii,* and uncommon bacterial pathogens such as *Francisella tularensis;* these organisms are discussed in this chapter. Bacteria associated with classic pyogenic pneumonia, such as *Streptococcus pneumoniae, Hemophilus influenzae,* aerobic Gram-negative rods, mixed mouth flora organisms, other streptococci, and staphylococci are discussed in Chapter 8–14. *Pneumocystis carinii,* a common cause of pneumonitis in persons infected with human immunodeficiency virus (HIV), is discussed in Chapter 8–76.

CRITERIA FOR DIAGNOSIS

Suggestive

Importantly, neither the absence of sputum production nor the presence of other symptoms or signs is pathognomonic for infection with the "atypical" organisms listed above; risk factors and epidemiologic features may be more reliable predictors of a specific etiologic agent. Findings from large epidemiologic studies may allow development of algorithms that facilitate prediction of etiologic agent based on a combination of clinical and laboratory features.

An abnormal chest x-ray film, systemic symptoms of inflammation such as fever and malaise, and respiratory tract complaints such as cough and/or dyspnea are very suggestive of pneumonia.

Definitive

A definitive etiologic agent is identified in a minority of patients with pneumonia, even when extensive diagnostic testing is conducted in a study setting. Available diagnostic tests include culture of lung tissue or respiratory tract secretions, detection of nucleic acids, detection of microbial antigens in respiratory secretions or urine, and serologic studies. Proper interpretation requires an understanding of the sensitivity and specificity of these tests. For example, *Chlamydia pneumoniae* can be cultured from the sputum of persons without symptoms, whereas the presence of *Legionella* organisms in respiratory secretions is almost always associated with disease.

CLINICAL MANIFESTATIONS

Subjective

Symptoms of the "atypical" pneumonias may vary depending on the pathogen but no one symptom is diagnostic of a specific etiologic agent. Symptoms frequently seen in all of these infections include fever, malaise, cough, headache, and dyspnea.

Infection with *Mycoplasma pneumoniae* may be asymptomatic, or may result in myringitis or other upper respiratory symptoms. A minority of patients develop pneumonia. Sputum production varies from

scant to thick and blood streaked; pharyngitis and headache are common features.

In the first recognized *Legionella pneumophila* outbreak, clinical illness was characterized by malaise, myalgias, cough, fever, and slight headache. Nonproductive cough, pleuritic chest pain, dyspnea, abdominal symptoms, and delirium or obtundation were also common.

Pharyngitis and laryngitis have been common findings in persons infected with *Chlamydia pneumoniae* and may precede the onset of bronchitis and/or pneumonia by 2 to 3 weeks.

Pneumonia due to *Coxiella burnetii* is characterized by fatigue, malaise, chills, and sweats. Cough is a relatively uncommon complaint.

Demographic characteristics of the patient may be more helpful than clinical presentation in predicting pneumonia etiology. For example, atypical pneumonia in the first few months of life is usually caused by *Chlamydia trachomatis* or by herpes simplex, respiratory syncytial, or parainfluenza viruses. In the older child or young adult, the most common agents of atypical pneumonia are *M. pneumoniae, Chl. pneumoniae,* and, during epidemics, influenza. Occasionally, other viruses, such as parainfluenza, adenovirus, respiratory syncytial virus, and, less frequently, varicella, rubeola, and herpes simplex may cause this syndrome. In the older age group, *Legionella, Chl. pneumoniae,* and *Mycoplasma* are all important considerations, and again influenza and parainfluenza viruses also must be considered, especially in an outbreak setting.

Other epidemiologic history may also be quite helpful. *Mycoplasma* pneumonia is often introduced into the family by small children. The incubation period is 2 to 3 weeks and the attack rate in families is high. Both endemic and epidemic Legionnaires' disease occur. In epidemic settings, it may be possible to identify a common exposure to a source of infected aerosols such as contaminated cooling tower or potable water system. *Chlamydia pneumoniae* appears to spread by person-to-person transmission; no bird or animal reservoir has been identified.

Detailed questions concerning living habits, travel, diet, and pets may point toward unusual diagnostic considerations. Examples include *C. burnetii* (Q fever) in slaughterhouse workers or persons exposed to parturient animals, *Chl. psittaci* (psittacosis) in patients exposed to birds, *F. tularensis* (tularemia) in rabbit hunters, or plague or hantavirus pulmonary syndrome in campers in the southwestern United States. Patients at risk for HIV infection, such as homosexual males, injection drug users, hemophiliacs, and blood transfusion recipients, are at risk for pneumonia caused by *Pneumocystis carinii* and cytomegalovirus (see Chapters 8–63 and 8–71). Patients who are immunocompromised by illnesses or immunosuppressive medications may develop pulmonary infection with a variety of opportunistic pathogens. These agents are discussed in Chapter 8–31.

Family history is not generally helpful in establishing either the diagnosis of atypical pneumonia or a specific etiologic agent.

Objective

Physical Examination

In many patients with atypical pneumonias, the physical examination is normal or only mildly abnormal, and evidence of frank consolidation is absent. On the other hand, the chest x-ray film may be markedly abnormal. Although certain physical examination findings are classically associated with specific agents, efforts to predict microbial etiology based on these findings are generally unsuccessful.

Patients with *Mycoplasma* infection may have bullous myringitis. Unilateral pneumonitis is most common in outpatients, whereas lobar consolidation is more frequent among hospitalized patients. Patients with *Chl. pneumoniae* may have fever, rhonchi, and rales; consolida-

We thank Dr. David S. Stephens for his contribution to this chapter in the third edition of this book.

tion is infrequent. In viral pneumonia, physical examination findings may be normal. Physical findings in pneumonia due to *C. burnetti* are generally not distinguishing.

Routine Laboratory Abnormalities

Patients with *Mycoplasma* develop a broad range of radiographic changes; the most common chest radiographic picture is one of lower unilobar pneumonitis. In Legionnaires' disease, the chest x-ray film frequently shows progressive multilobar involvement. In viral pneumonias, the peripheral white blood cell count ranges from low or normal to minimally elevated. An elevated hematocrit may be due to hemoconcentration in hantavirus pulmonary syndrome (Sin Nombre Virus infection). For most viral pneumonias, the most common chest x-ray film appearance is a patchy, segmental consolidation limited to one lower lobe; pleural involvement is rare and cavitation does not occur. Diffuse interstitial/alveolar infiltrates have been characteristic in patients with hantavirus pulmonary syndrome. Patients with Q fever may have laboratory evidence of hepatitis. The radiographic picture in Q fever is variable, although the classic changes are multiple rounded opacities.

The value of sputum Gram stain and culture in the evaluation of pneumonia patients has been widely debated. Because of poor specificity and sensitivity, these studies are often not reliable determinants of pneumonia etiology. An important reason to obtain sputum cultures is to recover bacterial pathogens for antimicrobial susceptibility testing. As clinical features have not yet been shown to allow accurate distinction between "typical" and "atypical" agents, these studies are reasonable in any patient with pneumonia.

PLANS
Diagnostic

In many settings, effective antibiotic therapy can be chosen in the absence of an established etiology. The routine use of extensive serologic evaluation or other diagnostic tests is not mandatory; however, a search for a specific etiologic agent is critical in the setting of an epidemic (so that appropriate control measures can be instituted) or if infection with unusual organisms such as *C. burnetii* or *F. tularensis* is likely. Patients in whom antibiotic-resistant organisms are likely, those with very severe pneumonia, and those who fail to respond to initial therapy also warrant more extensive diagnostic evaluation.

Available diagnostic tests are described in Table 8–15–1, listed in approximate order of utility.

Therapeutic

Risk factors for pneumonia-related mortality include underlying illness, age, the presence of significant tachypnea, tachycardia, or hypotension, hypoxia, and multilobe involvement. Pleuritic chest pain is associated with better outcome. These features are the most important considerations in determining the need for hospitalization.

All patients with pneumonia require attention to oxygenation, fluid balance, and electrolyte concentrations. Complications such as pleural effusion and empyema should also be anticipated.

If an etiologic organism is identified, specific antimicrobial therapy can be instituted. Optimal antimicrobial agents for pneumonia caused by specific etiologic agents are listed in Table 8–15–2.

TABLE 8–15–1. DIAGNOSTIC TESTS FOR SPECIFIC ETIOLOGIC AGENTS OF PNEUMONIA

Diagnostic Consideration	Diagnostic Tests and Observations
Mycoplasma pneumoniae	Specific pharyngeal or sputum cultures are helpful if available. *M. pneumoniae* has been recovered from healthy persons; therefore, recovery of *Mycoplasma* by culture is not 100% specific for infection.
	Cold agglutinins are not specific, but a titer of ≥1:64 or a positive bedside test is suggestive of *M. pneumoniae* infection. Cold agglutinins are present in >50% of cases of severe pneumonitis.
	A fourfold rise in antibodies to *M. pneumoniae* can be detected in most persons with infection. Assays for complement fixing antibodies have been evaluated extensively. Newer ELISA-based assays for IgG and IgM are promising; however, the anti-*Mycoplasma* IgG antibodies detected by ELISA are persistent, and may be detected in the absence of acute infection. IgM assays may be insensitive early in infection.
	Specific DNA probes have been recently introduced and may prove useful in diagnosis of *M. pneumoniae* infection.
Legionella infections (*L. pneumophila*, *L. micdadei*, other *Legionella*)	Isolation of *Legionella* organisms from culture of respiratory tract secretions on specialized media (buffered charcoal yeast extract [BCYE]) is specific for *Legionella* infection.
	Detection of urinary antigen is a rapid, sensitive (> 80%), and specific (> 95%) test for *Legionella pneumophila* serogroup 1 (LP1); more broad-spectrum tests are in development and may be available soon.
	A fourfold rise in reciprocal titer of anti-LP1 antibody to ≥ 1:64 by indirect immunofluorescence is also a specific and sensitive means of retrospective diagnosis. Although cross-reactivity between LP1 and other species and serogroups has been documented, antibody detection using antigens from species other than LP1 has not been well standardized. ELISA tests are being developed.
	Although a single reciprocal antibody titer ≥ 1:256 (by indirect immunofluorescence) is used to define cases of Legionnaires' disease in outbreak settings, this criterion is not reliable in sporadically occurring pneumonia.
	The accuracy of direct fluorescent antibody tests in detecting *Legionella* antigen varies depending on the criteria used to define a positive test (when higher cutoffs are used to define a positive test, specificity is good, but the test becomes insensitive).
Chlamydia pneumoniae	A positive complement fixation test (fourfold rise in antibody titers) establishes the presence of infection with a chlamydial organism but does not distinguish among species. Species identification requires microimmunofluorescence testing, which is not widely available. For these tests, a fourfold rise in IgG or IgM antibody to *Chl. pneumoniae* and reciprocal titers of IgM antibody of ≥ 1:16 have been interpreted as evidence of primary infection.
	Recovery of *Chl. pneumoniae* in cultures suggests infection, but is not 100% specific, as the organism can be recovered from nasopharyngeal secretions of approximately 5% of healthy persons.
	Polymerase chain reaction has been used to detect *Chl. pneumoniae* in respiratory secretions.
Viruses	Viral cultures of sputum or throat swabs can be performed. Acute and convalescent serology for influenza, parainfluenza, adenovirus, respiratory syncytial, and other viruses are also available.
	Hantavirus pulmonary syndrome can be diagnosed on the basis of serologic and polymerase chain reaction-based tests available from the Centers for Disease Control and Prevention, Atlanta, Georgia.
Coxiella burnetii	Diagnosis is usually made by demonstrating a fourfold rise in antibody titers. See also Chapter 8–50.
Chlamydia psittaci	Methods of diagnosis are similar to those for *Chl. pneumoniae*.
Chlamydia trachomatis (in infant pneumonia)	Methods of diagnosis are similar to those for *Chl. pneumoniae*. Accurate culture and antigen detection tests are also available.
Francisella tularensis	Serologic testing is available. Because tularemia can be transmitted to laboratory personnel, laboratories must be informed of the suspicion of tularemia if culture is requested.

ELISA, enzyme-linked immunosorbent assay; Ig, immunoglobulin.

TABLE 8–15–2. OPTIMAL ANTIBIOTIC THERAPY FOR SPECIFIC ETIOLOGIC AGENTS OF PNEUMONIA

Organism Suspected	Antimicrobial Agent	Alternative
Mycoplasma pneumoniae	Erythromycin, tetracycline	Clarithromycin, azithromycin
Legionella pneumophilia	Erythromycin ± rifampin	Ciprofloxacin ± rifampin **or** clarithromycin ± rifampin **or** azithromycin ± rifampin
Chlamydia pneumoniae	Tetracycline	Erythromycin **or** clarithromycin
Virus	Available agents include amantadine and rimantadine for influenza A and acyclovir for herpes simplex. Gancyclovir (± immune globulin) may be indicated in some patients with cytomegalovirus. Ribavirin may be indicated for some patients with severe respiratory syncytial virus infection. No specific therapy has been established for hantavirus pulmonary syndrome. Antimicrobial treatment is not indicated for other viral pneumonias.	
Coxiella burnetii	Tetracycline	Chloramphenicol **or** fluoroquinolone
Chlamydia psittaci	Tetracycline	Chloramphenicol
Chlamydia trachomatis (infant)	Erythromycin	Sulfonamide
Yersinia pestis	Streptomycin	Tetracycline **or** chloramphenicol **or** gentamicin

When a specific etiologic agent has not been established, empiric therapy for pneumonia should be selected based on severity of illness, age of the patient, and epidemiologic setting. By taking these factors into account, antimicrobial therapy for the most likely etiologies can be chosen. Recommended therapies for specific circumstances are given in Chapter 8–14.

Few studies have examined the appropriate duration of antibiotic therapy and optimal time to change from intravenous to oral therapy. General recommendations are that intravenous antibiotics be continued until fever and respiratory symptoms are well controlled. Total duration of therapy for most pneumonias is 10 to 14 days; however, symptoms of pneumonias caused by *Mycoplasma, Legionella,* and *Chl. pneumoniae* may persist and longer duration of therapy may be required. Because azithromycin persists in tissues, the duration of adequate tissue levels of this drug extends beyond the duration of pill intake (e.g., a 5-day treatment course results in therapeutic tissue levels for more than 10 days).

FOLLOW-UP

The frequency of chest x-rays is determined by the clinical course. Repeated chest x-rays are warranted daily or every other day if fever, dyspnea, or oxygenation worsen. If the patient improves, the chest x-ray need not be repeated except at discharge, and then monthly until resolution. Six weeks or longer may be required for pulmonary infiltrates to clear.

Outpatients with atypical pneumonia should be evaluated at least every 3 to 4 days to assess progress and possible need for hospitalization. For stable or improving patients, repeat x-rays should be done at 1 week and then monthly until the infiltrate has cleared.

In patients with persistent x-ray findings after 2 or 3 months, consultation with an infectious diseases or pulmonary specialist is indicated.

DISCUSSION

This discussion focuses on the four major causes of "atypical" pneumonia: *Mycoplasma, Legionella, Chlamydia,* and viruses.

Prevalence and Incidence

Although the peak incidence of *M. pneumoniae* infections is between the ages of 5 and 19 years, it is important to remember that this pathogen causes illness in all age groups. *Mycoplasma* pneumonias occur throughout the year. The incubation period may be as long as 31 days; infection frequently is introduced into the family by a child, spreading slowly to other family members by the respiratory route. Antibody appears protective, although rare second attacks have occurred. *Mycoplasma* is responsible for approximately 4% of pneumonias among patients who are admitted to the hospital and a greater proportion of pneumonias among outpatients.

Since the description of *Legionella* infection in 1976, a great deal has been learned about the responsible pathogens and the epidemiology of *Legionella* infections. Illness occurs both sporadically and in epidemics. Most outbreaks have occurred during the summer months. Infection results from inhalation of aerosols of water containing the bacteria. A variety of aerosol sources have been implicated in *Legionella* outbreaks, including cooling towers, evaporative condensers, showers, hot tubs and whirlpool spas, and respiratory therapy equipment. Air conditioning systems in large buildings may play a role in disease transmission if the air intake is near a source of a contaminated aerosol. The attack rate for Legionnaires' disease is highest in older individuals, males, smokers, and persons with underlying lung disease, malignancy, renal dysfunction, or immunodeficiency. Although persons infected with HIV are at increased risk for Legionnaires' disease, *Legionella* infection remains uncommon in HIV-infected persons. Person-to-person transmission has not been seen. In the United States, the incidence of Legionnaires' disease varies geographically, with higher rates in the Northeast and northern Midwest. *Legionella* infection accounts for 2 to 6% of pneumonias among patients requiring hospital admission.

Chlamydia pneumoniae has been identified as a cause of both pneumonia and upper respiratory tract infection. Among college students, *Chl. pneumoniae* accounts for as many as 13% of clinically diagnosed pneumonias. Epidemiologic data provide evidence for a link between *Chl. pneumoniae* infection and subsequent reactive airway disease and atherosclerosis.

An impressive number of viruses may cause pneumonia, but a few viruses are responsible for the majority of cases of viral pneumonia. Etiologies vary with age, environment, and the presence of underlying disease. In adults, the leading cause of viral pneumonia is influenza. Epidemic influenza A strains are most important, but pneumonia is also seen in association with influenza B infection. Respiratory syncytial virus may be an underrecognized cause of pneumonia in adults.

Related Basic Science

Mycoplasma organisms are the smallest known free-living organisms. Unlike classic bacteria, these organisms lack a rigid cell wall. They are capable of growing on agar media containing yeast extract and 20% horse serum, in tissue cultures, or in chorioallantoic membranes of chick embryos. Growth in culture requires from 1 to 2 weeks. *Mycoplasma* organisms are not vulnerable to cell wall-active antibiotics such as penicillin and cephalosporins, but are susceptible to erythromycin and tetracycline. *Mycoplasma* organisms attach to the luminal surface of ciliated respiratory epithelial cells, where they multiply and release cytotoxins. These toxins have an inhibitory effect on respiratory cilia and damage other respiratory tissues. Histologic examination of lung tissue from persons with *Mycoplasma* infection reveals an interstitial pneumonitis with a mononuclear-type alveolar exudate. The organisms can be cultured for approximately 4 weeks after the onset of the clinical illness, even in the presence of circulating antibody.

Legionella pneumophila is a fastidious Gram-negative bacillus that inhabits a variety of natural or manmade aquatic environments. *Legionella* grows best on buffered-charcoal yeast (BCYE) agar in the presence of 5% CO_2. More than 30 species have been described.

Legionella organisms can be isolated from the lungs or sputum of infected patients and, more rarely, from the pleural space or blood. They can be found extracellularly and within alveolar macrophages using silver stains or direct fluorescent antibody techniques.

By molecular and immunologic techniques, *Chl. pneumoniae* is distinct from *Chl. trachomatis* and *Chl. psittaci*. All *Chlamydia* species are obligate intracellular parasites and are dependent on host cells as a source of energy. Neither the pathogenesis of pneumonia caused by *Chl. pneumoniae* nor the links to chronic disease are completely understood.

Influenza predisposes to bacterial pneumonia by compromising normal clearance mechanisms in the lower respiratory tract (mucociliary and alveolar macrophage function).

Natural History and Its Modification with Treatment

In *Mycoplasma* pneumonia, mortality is rare and most symptoms clear within 2 to 3 weeks, even without treatment. Cough may persist. Treatment of *Mycoplasma* pneumonia alters the natural history of the disease by reducing the duration of fever and malaise, the length of hospitalization, and the duration of radiologic abnormalities. Treatment does not eradicate the organisms or prevent continued shedding (shedding may persist for as long as 8 weeks in some patients). Abnormal radiologic findings may persist longer than clinical symptoms. Overall mortality is less than 1%.

A variety of uncommon complications may occur during the course of *Mycoplasma* infections. Among the most severe are the development of Guillain–Barré syndrome, cold agglutinin-induced hemolytic anemia, Stevens–Johnson syndrome, myopericarditis, and meningitis. In patients with sickle cell disease, *Mycoplasma* pneumonia may be especially severe.

After an incubation period of 2 to 10 days, Legionnaires' disease usually presents acutely. In patients who recover, defervescence occurs on about the eighth day of illness. Radiographic improvement follows several days later, although in some patients this may take 2 to 3 months. Pulmonary fibrosis occurs in some survivors. Prognosis is worst for patients who are immunocompromised. Erythromycin treatment appears to be of benefit in decreasing mortality and morbidity. If the erythromycin is discontinued too early, a relapse may occur. The mortality rate for persons hospitalized with Legionnaires' disease is approximately 15%.

Pneumonia due to *Chl. pneumoniae* is usually mild in young adults. Some patients have a biphasic illness with initial sore throat and fever followed in 2 or 3 weeks by bronchitis and pneumonia.

Approximately 5% of influenza cases are associated with severe lower respiratory tract infection, which is characterized by a necrotizing hemorrhagic tracheobronchitis and alveolitis with rapid progression. This may be especially severe in patients with high pulmonary venous pressures. Other complications include bacterial pneumonia, viral myocarditis, myositis with myoglobinuria, encephalitis, postinfluenzal asthenia, Guillain–Barré syndrome, and Reye's syndrome. In children with influenza, the use of aspirin may increase the risk of Reye's syndrome. Superimposed bacterial pneumonia (specifically with pneumococci, staphylococci, and *Hemophilus influenzae*) usually occurs 5 to 7 days after the initial onset of influenza. This is manifest as recrudescence of fever and chills and development of purulent sputum and new or increasing pulmonary infiltrates. Both influenza and complicating bacterial pneumonia occur most often in the elderly and in individuals with underlying illnesses such as heart disease, obstructive pulmonary disease, alcoholism, diabetes mellitus, and immune suppression.

Prevention

Measures to prevent *Mycoplasma* and *Chl. pneumoniae* pneumonia have not been established. Prevention of *Legionella* pneumonia depends on identification and elimination of the environmental source of contaminated aerosols. Prevention of influenza is covered in Chapter 8–66. Psittacosis is now rare because stringent public health laws control the breeding and sale of psittacine birds. Patients with psittacosis should be isolated (respiratory), as severe secondary cases have occurred in medical personnel exposed to untreated patients. The use of gloves in handling of animal carcasses may help prevent the spread of tularemia and Q fever, and avoidance of activities that result in contact with rodent urine may reduce the risk of hantavirus pulmonary syndrome.

Cost Containment

The preventive measures described above provide the most effective means of cost containment. The use of influenza vaccine and amantadine or rimantadine in the appropriate populations is especially helpful. A detailed history may help to select appropriate diagnostic studies and antimicrobial regimens.

REFERENCES:

Fang G, Fine M, Orloff J, et al. New and emerging etiologies for community-acquired pneumonia with implications for therapy. Medicine 1990;69:307.

Farr BM, Kaise DL, Harrison BDW, Connolly CK. Prediction of microbial aetiology at admission to hospital for pneumonia from the presenting clinical features. Thorax 1989;44:1031.

Fine MJ, Orloff JJ, Arisumi D, et al. Prognosis of patients hospitalized with community-acquired pneumonia. Am J Med 1990;88:5-1N–5-8N.

Grayston JT, Campbell LA, Kuo CC, et al. A new respiratory tract pathogen: *Chlamydia pneumoniae* strain TWAR. J Infect Dis 1990;161:618.

Hoge CW, Breiman RF. Advances in the epidemiology and control of *Legionella* infections. Epidemiol Rev 1991;13:329.

Marston BJ, Lipman HB, Breiman RF. Surveillance for Legionnaires' disease: Risk factors for morbidity and mortality. Arch Intern Med 1994;154:2417.

Niederman MS, Bass JB, Campbell GD, et al. Guidelines for the initial management of adults with community-acquired pneumonia: Diagnosis, assessment of severity, and initial antimicrobial therapy. Am Rev Respir Dis 1993;148:1418.

Ortqvist A, Hedlund J, Grillnew L, et al. Aetiology, outcome and prognostic factors in community-acquired pneumonia requiring hospitalization. Eur Respir J 1990;3:1105.

Suravleff JJ, Yu VL, Shonnard JW, et al. Diagnosis of Legionnaires' disease: An update of laboratory methods with new emphasis on isolation by culture. JAMA 1983;250:1981.

The choice of antibacterial drugs. Med Lett 1994;36:53.

Chronic Pneumonia Syndrome

Barbara J. Marston, M.D., and Jay C. Butler, M.D.

DEFINITION

Chronic pneumonia syndrome is a pulmonary parenchymal process that has been present for weeks or months rather than days. Illness manifests as persistent or progressive pulmonary symptoms associated with an abnormal chest roentgenogram.

ETIOLOGY

The chronic pneumonia syndrome may be due to a vast array of infectious and noninfectious causes (Table 8–16–1).

CRITERIA FOR DIAGNOSIS

Suggestive

A diagnosis of chronic pneumonia syndrome may be made in a patient with persistent pulmonary symptoms and an abnormal chest roentgenogram with no established etiology.

Definitive

In some patients with chronic pneumonia syndrome no definitive etiology is ever established; when an etiology is confirmed, it is often on the basis of culture or histopathologic examination of tissues obtained with invasive procedures such as transbronchial or open lung biopsies.

CLINICAL MANIFESTATIONS

Subjective

No single symptom complex is common to all patients. Pulmonary symptoms vary widely, but may include a new or persistent cough, sputum production with or without hemoptysis, chest pain (which may be pleuritic), and dyspnea. Constitutional symptoms including fever, chills, and malaise may be present regardless of etiology. Occasionally, extrapulmonary symptoms are present and may include skin lesions, arthritis, arthralgias, headache, focal neurologic complaints, and genitourinary symptoms. It is important to obtain information about underlying diseases, travel, exposures to drugs or chemicals, and exposures to animals or other environmental sources of infectious or toxic agents. Older persons are at relatively high risk for chronic bacterial pneumonia, whereas African-Americans, Native Americans, and Filipinos are at increased risk for severe disease due to *Coccidioides immitis* and other systemic fungal infections.

Patients with preexisting chronic obstructive pulmonary disease are at risk for superimposed pulmonary histoplasmosis or atypical mycobacteriosis and those with diabetes are at higher risk for chronic pneumonia due to mycobacteria or persistent bacterial infection. Patients with impaired levels of consciousness due to alcoholism, seizure disorders, or strokes may develop chronic pneumonia resulting from recurrent aspiration. Similarly, structural abnormalities, such as an endobronchial lesion, may result in chronic bacterial pneumonia. Certain infectious diseases are associated with travel to endemic areas, such as coccidioidomycosis (southwestern United States), histoplasmosis (south and north-central United States), melioidosis (Southeast Asia), echinococcosis (Middle East), and paragonimiasis (Far East). Sandblasters (silicosis), shipyard workers (asbestosis), farmers (coccidioidomycosis), spelunkers (histoplasmosis), woodsmen (blastomycosis), and sheep herders (echinococcosis) are persons at risk for chronic pneumonia caused by occupational or environmental exposures. Exposure to irritant gases or thermophilic actinomycetes may also result in chronic pneumonia.

A family history of tuberculosis or certain other infections suggests the possibility of exposure to these organisms. Some causes of the chronic pneumonia syndrome such as connective tissue disorders may have a hereditary component.

Objective

Physical Examination

Physical examination of the chest is generally not helpful in differentiating specific causes of chronic pneumonia. The presence of tachycardia, cardiomegaly, peripheral edema, or a gallop rhythm suggests that the pulmonary disease may have a cardiac cause. Signs of multisystem disease, such as skin ulcers and nodules, jaundice, hepatosplenomegaly, adenopathy, and ascites, may suggest specific etiologies.

Routine Laboratory Abnormalities

Routine laboratory studies may provide clues to specific diagnoses. For example, pancytopenia suggests bone marrow involvement as a complication of miliary tuberculosis, disseminated histoplasmosis, or metastatic tumor. Leukopenia should raise the possibility of systemic lupus erythematosus, sarcoidosis, tuberculosis, or histoplasmosis, whereas isolated lymphopenia should suggest AIDS and its associated opportunistic pulmonary infectious diseases.

Of the routine tests, the most valuable is the chest roentgenogram. In general, disorders that cause chronic pneumonia can be grouped into three major classes of radiographic abnormality: (1) bronchopneumonia, lobar consolidation, or diffuse patchy infiltrates; (2) cavitary lung disease, with or without pulmonary nodules; (3) diffuse interstitial pneumonitis and fibrosis. Although these radiologic patterns may be helpful in suggesting possible causes, there is no radiographic picture that is clearly diagnostic of any specific disorder.

PLANS

Diagnostic

Differential Diagnosis

The differential diagnosis in chronic pneumonia syndrome is broad (Table 8–16–1). In addition to infection with bacteria, fungi, helminths, or protozoa, chronic pneumonia may be caused by noninfectious processes such as neoplastic pulmonary infiltration, vasculitis, drug reaction, chemical inhalation, exposure to radiation, pulmonary infarction, pneumoconiosis, chronic hypersensitivity pneumonitis, and idiopathic lung disease.

Diagnostic Options and Recommended Approach

Studies of the sputum should include Gram stain for routine bacteria and *Actinomyces* species, acid-fast or fluorochrome stains for *Nocardia* and *Mycobacterium* species, wet mounts and special stains for fungi, and cytologic preparations for neoplastic cells and eosinophils. Sputum, along with other body fluids, such as blood, urine, pleural and synovial fluids (when present), and cerebrospinal fluid (in patients with central nervous system disease), should be cultured on appropriate media. New techniques such as DNA amplification using polymerase chain reaction are being developed for many infectious agents and may be useful if cultures are negative. Tuberculin skin testing is indicated for most patients. Unless there is a history of travel to an endemic area, skin testing for *Histoplasma capsulatum* and *Coccidioides immitis* is of limited value because positive tests are common in adults living in endemic areas, and skin test reactivity may be unrelated to the etiology of

We thank Dr. Michael S. Saag and Dr. William E. Dismukes for their contribution to this chapter in the previous editions of this book.

TABLE 8–16–1. CAUSES OF CHRONIC PNEUMONIA

Infectious agents that typically cause chronic pneumonia
- Bacteria and actinomycetes
  - Mixed aerobic–anaerobic bacteria
  - *Nocardia* spp.
  - *Rhodococcus equi*
  - *Actinomyces* spp.
  - *Pseudomonas pseudomallei*
- Mycobacteria
  - *Mycobacterium tuberculosis*
  - *Mycobacterium kansasii*
  - *Mycobacterium avium–intracellulare* complex
- Fungi
  - *Coccidioides immitis*
  - *Histoplasma capsulatum*
  - *Cryptococcus neoformans*
  - *Blastomyces dermatitidis*
  - *Sporothrix schenckii*
  - *Paracoccidioides brasiliensis*
- Worms
  - *Echinococcus granulosus*
  - *Schistosoma hematobium*
  - *Schistosoma japonicum*
  - *Schistosoma mansoni*
  - *Paragonimus westermani*
- Protozoa
  - *Entamoeba histolytica*

Noninfectious causes
- Neoplasia
  - Carcinoma (primary or metastatic)
  - Kaposi's sarcoma
  - Lymphoma
- Lymphomatoid granulomatosis
- Sarcoidosis
- Vasculitis
  - Systemic lupus erythematosus
  - Polyarteritis nodosa
  - Allergic angiitis and granulomatosis (Churg–Strauss syndrome)
  - Rheumatoid arthritis
  - Mixed connective tissue syndrome
  - Wegener's granulomatosis
- Drugs
  - Acetylsalicylic acid
  - Amiodarone
  - Azathioprine
  - Bleomycin
  - Bromocriptine
  - Busulfan
  - Chlordiazepoxide
  - Cocaine
  - Cyclophosphamide
  - Cytarabine
  - Gold salts
  - Interleukin-2
  - Melphalan
  - 6-Mercaptopurine
  - Methotrexate
  - Methysergide
  - Mitomycin
  - Narcotic analgesics
  - Nitrofurantoin
  - Nitrosoureas
  - Nonsteroidal antiinflammatory drugs
  - Phenytoin
  - Procarbazine
  - Sulfonamides
  - Tocainide
  - Vinblastine
  - Vindesine
- Chemicals or inhalants
- Radiation
- Recurrent pulmonary infarction
- Pulmonary infiltration with eosinophilia syndrome
  - Loeffler's syndrome (usually transient)
  - Tropical eosinophilia
  - Pneumonia plus asthma (e.g., allergic bronchopulmonary aspergillosis)
  - Vasculitis
  - Eosinophilic pneumonia (chronic)
- Pneumoconiosis
- Chronic form of hypersensitivity pneumonitis (extrinsic allergic alveolitis)
- Other lung disease (unknown cause)
  - Bronchiolitis obliterans organizing pneumonia
  - Interstitial pneumonia
    - Usual interstitial pneumonia
    - Desquamative interstitial pneumonia
    - Lymphoid interstitial pneumonia
    - Giant cell interstitial pneumonia
- Eosinophilic granuloma
- Goodpasture's syndrome
- Pulmonary alveolar proteinosis (phospholipidosis)
- Pulmonary alveolar microlithiasis
- Idiopathic pulmonary hemosiderosis

Source: Adapted from Dismukes WE. Chronic pneumonia. In: Mandell GL, Douglas RG, Bennett JE, eds. Principles and practice of infectious diseases. 3rd ed. New York: Churchill Livingstone, 1990:565. Reproduced with permission of the author and publisher.

the chronic pneumonia syndrome. Moreover, patients with systemic fungal infections may not exhibit delayed hypersensitivity to the corresponding skin test antigens. Serologic tests may be helpful in confirming the presence of vasculitides such as Wegener's granulomatosis (antineutrophil cytoplasmic antibody [ANCA]) or connective tissue diseases (double-stranded DNA in lupus erythematosus or rheumatoid factor in rheumatoid arthritis).

Pulmonary function testing with arterial blood gas analysis may suggest a particular etiology, such as occupational lung disease, if a restrictive pattern is seen, and is important in assessment of need for treatment with oxygen.

High-resolution computed tomography can help to identify cavities, lung nodules, hilar adenopathy, lymph nodes or tumor causing bronchial obstruction, or unsuspected collections of pleural fluid and to localize optimal sites for biopsy.

Biopsy of extrapulmonary disease sites such as skin, mucous membranes, bone marrow, liver, and lymph nodes for culture and histopathology may yield the diagnosis and obviate the need for an invasive pulmonary procedure; however, invasive pulmonary procedures are often needed to establish the definitive diagnosis. Bronchoscopy with transbronchial biopsy and bronchoalveolar lavage is an effective means of obtaining material from the lung parenchyma and airway for culture and histopathologic examination. Open lung biopsy is the most invasive procedure and requires general anesthesia, yet it is the test with the highest diagnostic yield, especially when tissue is cultured and examined with appropriate histopathologic stains.

Therapeutic

As the causes of chronic pneumonia are so diverse, accurate diagnosis is critical to the institution of appropriate therapy (see specific chapters in this book). Frequently, the patient's condition is stable enough to allow a thorough diagnostic workup prior to the institution of therapy. In the rare situation of serious, life-threatening illness, empiric therapy based on the clinical and radiographic presentation is warranted; however, efforts to determine the specific etiology of the illness should be aggressively continued even after therapy has been initiated, and the treatment should be appropriately adjusted once a specific diagnosis is made. The decision to treat empirically, observe without therapy, or repeat the evaluation should be individualized based on available clinical and epidemiologic data. Patients who smoke should be encouraged to stop, regardless of the etiology of the pulmonary disease. In all patients, supportive measures should be instituted, such as correction of hypoxemia, if present. Rarely, lobectomy or pneumonectomy may be necessary as a lifesaving therapeutic maneuver in patients with progressive destructive pneumonia and nonfunction of the involved lung.

FOLLOW-UP

Follow-up should be individualized based on the specific cause of the chronic pneumonia. Long-term follow-up with serial chest x-rays to detect evidence of disease progression or stabilization is appropriate for most patients with chronic pneumonia syndrome.

DISCUSSION

Prevalence and Incidence

Of the specific etiologies of chronic pneumonia listed in Table 8–16–1, tuberculosis is the condition for which the most epidemiologic information is available. In developed countries, the incidence of tuberculosis declined during the second half of the 20th century. In the United States, however, the number of tuberculosis cases occurring annually has increased since 1985. Attack rates have increased most dramatically among persons 25 to 44 years old. Factors contributing to the recent resurgence of tuberculosis include immigration of persons from countries with a high prevalence of tuberculosis, the increased risk of tuberculosis disease for persons coinfected with HIV, transmission within institutional settings such as prisons and shelters for the homeless, and a general decline in public health services. Coincident with the increasing incidence of tuberculosis in many areas has been the increasing prevalence of multiple drug-resistant *Mycobacterium tuberculosis* (MDRTB) strains.

The incidence of disease due to mycobacteria other than *M. tuberculosis* also appears to be increasing to the United States. The high prevalence of *Mycobacterium avium* complex (MAC) infection among persons with AIDS is a major contributing factor.

Related Basic Science

Mycobacterium tuberculosis is primarily transmitted person to person within airborne droplet nuclei generated during coughing, sneezing, or speaking by persons with active pulmonary or laryngeal tuberculosis. Droplet nuclei 1 to 5 µm in diameter may pass through the upper airway and the tracheobronchial tree to reach the alveoli, where they are ingested by alveolar macrophages, and neutrophils. Tuberculosis bacilli survive within phagocytic cells and are carried via the pulmonary lymphatics to the hilar nodes. The bacilli may continue to multiply and eventually enter the bloodstream and disseminate widely. The lungs can be reinoculated by hematogenous spread, often in the posterior apical segment of an upper lobe. Delayed-type hypersensitivity develops over the next several days to weeks, resulting in the death of infected phagocytes and surrounding cells and producing a lesion characterized by an area of central caseous necrosis surrounded by inflammatory cells. Cellular destruction may progress, resulting in clinical disease and even death, but in most immunocompetent hosts, multiplication of the organisms is suppressed by cell-mediated immunity, and the lesion eventually heals with residual scarring. The infected patient may be asymptomatic at this point and the only evidence of infection is a positive tuberculin skin test or a residual pulmonary nodule with hilar node enlargement (Ghon complex) visible by chest x-ray. Following primary infection, host immunity generally keeps the bacilli in check. In some instances, however, multiplication and spread of the organisms recur and tuberculosis disease develops. Disease will develop during the first year following infection in approximately 5% of infected persons, and another 5% will develop disease sometime later in life. Certain conditions are associated with an increased risk of developing tuberculosis disease including diabetes mellitus, silicosis, end-stage renal disease, and immunosuppression. Persons with HIV infection who are infected with *M. tuberculosis* have approximately an 8% *annual* risk of developing active tuberculosis.

Natural History and Its Modification with Treatment

Prior to the availability of effective chemotherapeutic agents, mortality from tuberculosis disease was 50 to 60%. Results from recent studies of therapy for pulmonary infections caused by mycobacteria other than *M. tuberculosis* and disseminated *M. avium* complex infections among patients with AIDS are encouraging, but few data are available regarding long-term survival following treatment of these infections.

Prevention

Prompt diagnosis, appropriate isolation, and administration of effective chemotherapy for persons with tuberculosis disease reduce the risk of further transmission. Additionally, identification of persons recently infected (i.e., with new tuberculin skin test reactivity) and administration of chemoprophylaxis markedly reduce the progression of infection to disease. Therefore, prompt reporting of tuberculosis cases to public health authorities and investigation to identify additional persons needing chemotherapy or chemoprophylaxis form the foundation of tuberculosis prevention. Vaccination with bacille Calmette–Guérin (BCG) is used to prevent tuberculosis disease in many parts of the world, but in the United States, bacille Calmette–Guérin is recommended only for selected situations with an extremely high risk of disease. Effective means to prevent other infectious causes of chronic pneumonia are generally not available.

Prevention of occupational lung disease, such as the pneumoconioses and hypersensitivity pneumonitis, requires recognition of the hazard to institute environmental controls and use of appropriate respiratory protection devices.

Cost Containment

Evaluation of patients with chronic pneumonia can often be performed on an outpatient basis to avoid the expense of hospitalization. For patients requiring hospital admission, careful planning and scheduling of diagnostic procedures should reduce the length of stay. Treatment of most causes of chronic pneumonia can be initiated either without hospitalization or following discharge.

REFERENCES

Barnes PF, Barrows SA. Tuberculosis in the 1990s. Ann Intern Med 1993;119:400.

Crystal RG, Gadek JE, Ferans VJ, et al. Interstitial lung disease: Current concepts of pathogenesis, staging and therapy. Am J Med 1981;70:542.

Goodwin RA Jr, Owens FT, Snell JD, et al. Chronic pulmonary histoplasmosis. Medicine 1976;55:413.

Leavitt RY, Fauci AS. Pulmonary vasculitis. Am Rev Respir Dis 1986;134:513.

Orens JB, Sitrin RG, Lynch JP III. The approach to nonresolving pneumonia. Med Clin North Am 1994;78:1143.

Wolinsky E. Mycobacterial diseases other than tuberculosis. Clin Infect Dis 1992;15:1.

CHAPTER 8–17

Infectious Gastroenteritis

Christine A. Wanke, M.D., and Richard L. Guerrant, M.D.

DEFINITION

Infectious gastroenteritis is a commonly used term for enteric infections of the small bowel or colon. Although there are infectious causes of gastritis such as *Helicobacter pylori,* this agent and gastritis in general are not dealt with in this chapter. Although the term *enteritis* implies an inflammatory process, the inflammatory diarrheal diseases are only a subset of the overall group of infectious diarrheal illnesses. The term *infectious diarrhea* encompasses a group of diseases that are defined by a change in the frequency or consistency of stools and are caused by an infectious agent.

ETIOLOGY

The infectious pathogens that cause diarrhea may be bacterial, viral, or parasitic (Table 8–17–1). On rare occasions, fungal infections of the gastrointestinal tract may cause diarrheal disease.

CRITERIA FOR DIAGNOSIS

Suggestive

The clues to a diagnosis of infectious gastroenteritis usually include diarrhea, nausea and/or vomiting, abdominal pain, and anorexia, especially in an epidemiologic setting that would suggest a higher risk for acquisition of this syndrome. Weight loss may also occur. Fever, bloody diarrhea, rectal pain with defecation are additional important clues in the differential diagnosis, as these symptoms suggest that an invasive organism is likely the cause.

Definitive

The definitive diagnosis of infectious diarrhea is dependent on the identification of the causative agent in the stool or bowel, in the setting of acute or subacute diarrhea or abdominal pain, anorexia, nausea, or vomiting. Often, however, the isolation of a particular pathogen is not cost-effective or feasible and the diagnosis rests on the clinical and epidemiologic setting and on the exclusion of anatomic, functional, or medication-related causes, such as intussusception, malignancy, laxatives, and tube feedings.

CLINICAL MANIFESTATIONS

Subjective

There are several clinical settings in the United States in which infectious diarrhea might be anticipated. The dry or winter season is the period of high risk in temperate climates. Infectious diarrhea is often seen in clusters; as such, it commonly occurs in families with small children as they have not acquired immunity to these pathogens. Additional groups known to be at risk for infectious diarrhea include persons with exposure to children in daycare centers or exposure in institutions where sanitation is not optimal, homosexual males, travelers returning from tropical or developing areas, those who eat raw seafood, and those with a history of antibiotic use. Hospitalized patients and immunocompromised patients are also at increased risk for infectious diarrhea. Therefore, pertinent exposure history to obtain from a patient with a diarrheal illness includes the presence of children or pets in the home, a history of recent antibiotic use, and the regular use of H_2 blockers. The patient's sexual history may be pertinent. It is also important to determine the source of drinking water available to the patient, as the consumption of well or creek water has been associated with an increased incidence of disease; it is important to determine the dietary habits of patients, including whether they cook for themselves, eat raw meat or seafood or unpasteurized dairy products, or frequently eat in fast food restaurants. Persons spending time in crowded conditions (institutions or daycare centers), on Native American reservations, in a crowded inner city, or in the poorer areas of the southern United States may also be at increased risk for infectious diarrhea. A complete history of recent travel should also be obtained, as outbreaks occur not only in travelers to the less developed world but on cruise ships, on airplanes, and in mountainous outdoor areas. Highly publicized outbreaks of diarrheal disease such as that which occurred when the city water supply in Milwaukee, Wisconsin, was contaminated with *Cryptosporidium* emphasize the need to obtain a complete travel history. A medical history should also be obtained, as medications and underlying illnesses may predispose to infectious diarrhea as well.

The symptoms of infectious gastroenteritis most commonly include diarrhea, nausea, vomiting, abdominal cramping or pain, and anorexia. A physician should also ascertain the number of stools per day and the duration of the illness, as well as the character of the stool and other symptoms. It is important to determine whether a patient has complaints compatible with dehydration, such as lightheadedness and decreased urination. Bloody diarrhea, fever, and tenesmus (pain on defecation) are important historic clues to inflammatory enteritis or more systemic disease.

Objective

Physical Examination

The physical findings are nonspecific. Bowel sounds may be hyperactive and abdominal tenderness may be present. Frank peritoneal signs should raise the concern of some additional problem, although a severe inflammatory colitis such as that caused by *Clostridium difficile* may present with some peritoneal signs. Tenderness on rectal examination suggests an infectious proctitis. Every patient must be assessed carefully for signs of dehydration, including orthostatic blood pressure and pulse determinations, dry mucus membranes, sunken eyes, and decreased skin turgor. Lethargy may occur with severe dehydration and in infants the fontanel may be sunken. Temperature elevations may suggest an inflammatory or systemic process.

Routine Laboratory Abnormalities

In infectious diarrhea the single most important test is gross examination of the stool. If the stool is liquid or contains blood or mucus, mi-

TABLE 8–17–1. PATHOGENS IN INFECTIOUS DIARRHEA

Pathogen	Small Bowel (Noninflammatory)	Colon (Inflammatory)
Bacteria	Enterotoxigenic *Escherichia coli*	*Shigella**
	Enteropathogenic *E. coli*	*Campylobacter**
	Vibrio cholerae	*Salmonella**
	Staphylococcus aureus food poisoning	*Yersinia**
	Bacillus Cereus food poisoning	*Vibrio parahemolyticus**
	Clostridium perfringens food poisoning	Enteroinvasive *E. coli**
		Clostridium difficile
Virus	Rotavirus	
	Norwalk and related agents	
Parasite	*Giardia*	*Entamoeba histolytica*
	Cryptosporidium	*Balantidium coli*
	Isospora	
	Microsporidia[†]	
	Cyclospora	

*May present early with watery, small bowel-like diarrhea, but is classically associated with an inflammatory diarrheal presentation.

[†]To date, only one case reported in a non-HIV-infected traveler; may well occur more frequently.

croscopic examination should be done promptly to look for leukocytes and/or ova and parasites. A single stool examination may not reveal parasites even when they are present because of the sporadic nature of shedding or a dilutional effect if the diarrhea is voluminous. Three fresh, separate stools should be obtained when blood or mucus is present. A positive Hemoccult test may suggest an inflammatory process although it may also become positive with irritation from frequent stooling if the diarrhea is severe. Other laboratory tests are nonspecific. The white blood count may be elevated in invasive bacterial diarrheas and decreased with viral pathogens. Eosinophilia is rarely seen with infectious diarrhea, except on occasion with strongyloidiasis or *Dientamoeba fragilis*. Hemoconcentration may be present with dehydration. Electrolyte determination may confirm the presence of dehydration with increased blood urea nitrogen or creatinine levels. On rare occasions, bloody diarrhea (caused by *Escherichia coli* 0157:H7 or *Shigella dysenteriae* among other pathogens) may be followed by an episode of hemolytic uremic syndrome, in which case hemolytic anemia would be present as well as decreased renal function. Total body or serum potassium may be low if diarrhea has been of long duration or is particularly severe. In this particular case, the electrocardiographic changes of hypokalemia and flattened T or U waves may be seen. Urinalysis may show elevated specific gravity with dehydration.

PLANS
Diagnostic
Differential Diagnosis

The major differential in infectious diarrheal disease is the need to separate the inflammatory and invasive diarrheas from the noninvasive, secretory diarrheas (Table 8–17–1). The diagnosis of inflammatory bowel disease must be considered in the patient who presents for evaluation with bloody diarrhea and fever; history of travel, medications, ingestions, stool examination, and duration of disease assist in distinguishing infectious from noninfectious diarrheal illness. Similarly,

an elderly patient with abdominal pain and bloody diarrhea may have ischemic colitis rather than an infectious etiology for their presentation.

Diagnostic Options and Recommended Approach

The diagnostic plan should first include stool examination to look for leukocytes, ova, and parasites, as these tests can help select patients requiring further evaluation (Figure 8–17–1). If leukocytes are present in stool, *Shigella, Salmonella, Campylobacter, Yersinia*, invasive *E. coli*, and *C. difficile* should be considered as potential pathogens and stool cultures are indicated. Specific media or methods may be needed to isolate pathogens such as *Yersinia*, enterohemorrhagic *E. coli* (associated with bloody, noninflammatory diarrhea), or *Campylobacter jejuni*. If leukocytes are seen and history includes recent antibiotic use, one should send stool for *C. difficile* cytotoxin assay as well as culture. If there is seafood or seacoast exposure, cultures should be obtained for *Vibrio* species that may cause inflammatory or noninflammatory diarrhea. If fever is present in a patient with fecal leukocytes, blood cultures for *Salmonella* are indicated, especially in older adults, patients with intravascular foreign material, and any immunocompromised patient.

If fecal leukocytes are not seen, the suspected etiologic agents include the performed toxins most often associated with food poisoning, viral agents and toxigenic bacteria, in which case routine stool culture would be unrewarding. Specific toxin testing requires specialized laboratory facilities and is rarely warranted in individual sporadic cases. Enzyme-linked immunosorbent assay for rotavirus may be performed on stool, but is not generally warranted. Depending on the level of clinical suspicion, the search for ova and parasites should be continued. When nausea and bloating are the predominant symptoms with prolonged, noninflammatory diarrhea, *Giardia lamblia* or *Cryptosporidium* should be strongly suspected. A small bowel aspirate or string test (Hedeco, Palo Alto, CA) may be necessary to document *Giardia* trophozoites or cysts if they are not found in stool. New fluorescent antibody stains to detect both *Crytosporidium* and *Giardia* are very sensitive, however. In

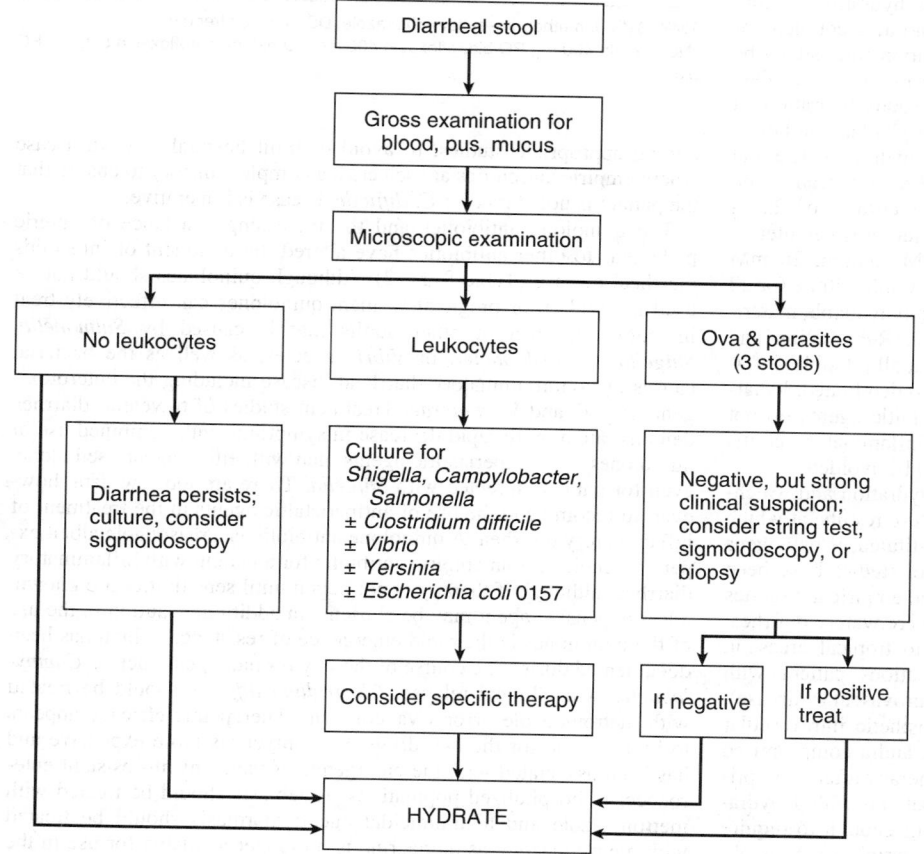

Figure 8–17–1. Laboratory evaluation of diarrhea.

a patient with day-care, animal, or travel exposure, cryptosporidiosis must also be considered. In a patient with a recent history of travel and a prolonged episode of noninflammatory diarrhea, the stool should also be examined with a modified acid-fast stain for *Cyclospora cayatenensis*. A careful search for parasites should be conducted in patients with homosexual exposure, contact with animals, consumption of unpasteurized milk, or a history of recent travel.

In a homosexual patient with bloody or mucoid diarrhea, amebiasis should be suspected along with *Shigella, Campylobacter,* or *Chlamydia* infection. If multiple stool examinations do not document the amebae, amebic serology may be helpful or the patient could be considered for sigmoidoscopy. Immunocompromised patients including patients infected with HIV may present with severe and/or prolonged diarrhea and weight loss and be infected with *Cryptosporidium, Microsporidium, Isospora belli, Mycobacterium avium–intracellulare,* or cytomegalovirus. These pathogens may require special stool stains (*Cryptosporidium* and *Microsporidium*), small bowel biopsy with electron microscopic examination (*Microsporidium*), or small bowel or colonic biopsy with special stains and culture (*M. avium–intracellulare* or cytomegalovirus) for documentation. Immunocompromised patients may also present with systemic, prolonged or complicated *Salmonella, Shigella,* and *Campylobacter* infections.

Radiologic studies are of little assistance; upright and supine abdominal films help rule out complications such as obstruction, free air from a perforated viscus, and toxic megacolon. Barium studies should not be done initially because barium interferes with the evaluation of stool specimens.

When a patient is suspected of having inflammatory bowel disease sigmoidoscopy with mucosal biopsy and culture should be considered to exclude *C. difficile, Campylobacter,* and *Entamoeba histolytica* infections. Sigmoidoscopy should be performed promptly in a sexually active homosexual male without HIV who complains of tenesmus, rectal pain, and frequent defecation as proctitis may be of gonococcal, herpetic, chlamydial, or syphilitic etiology.

Therapeutic

The most important therapy in diarrheal illness is hydration (Figure 8–17–1, Table 8–17–2). Because glucose and amino acid-coupled absorption remains largely intact with diarrhea, hydration can usually be achieved and maintained by an oral glucose (or sucrose) and electrolyte solution. This has several advantages over intravenous hydration. It stimulates recovery of mucosal enzymes, is safer, is available at home, and is considerably less expensive than intravenous hydration. The oral rehydration solution recommended by the World Health Organization is composed of 3.5 g of NaCl, 2.9 g trisodium citrate (or 2.5 g NaHCO$_3$), 1.5 g KCl, and 20 g glucose (or 40 g sucrose) per liter of water. The composition of this solution is 90 mM sodium, 20 mM potassium, 80 mM chloride, 111 mM glucose, and 10 mM citrate (or 20 mM bicarbonate) per liter. Alternative remedies from available materials are appropriate for adults with mild diarrhea. Rehydration and maintenance of hydration should be done orally if at all possible; intravenous hydration should be reserved for patients too debilitated, lethargic, or nauseated to tolerate oral fluids. Antiperistaltic agents do not prevent sufficient fluid loss and may worsen an inflammatory colitis such as shigellosis or *C. difficile* disease and should be avoided.

Patients may be managed conservatively with hydration and watchful observation pending stool examination and culture results, at which point antibiotics or antiparasitic agents may be instituted, if pathogens are recovered. Alternatively, after appropriate stool studies have been obtained, patients may be treated with hydration and empiric antibiotics if the clinical condition warrants. Patients with severe watery diarrhea, especially those with a history of recent travel to tropical areas, in whom dehydration could cause significant complications (patients with severe heart disease, the elderly, patients with neurovascular disease); patients with inflammatory diarrhea and any prosthetic intravascular material; and patients with inflammatory diarrhea and a compromised immune system might be considered for empiric therapy after appropriate stool studies have been obtained. In addition, patients with dehydration or inflammatory diarrhea who appear to be ill enough to require hospitalization might be treated empirically with antibiotics after ob-

TABLE 8–17–2. TREATMENT OF DIARRHEA

Agent	Modality	Comment
Any agent	Hydration	Oral rehydration solution is preferable.
Shigella, Campylobacter, Yersinia, Salmonella	Oral quinolone* bid for 3–5 d	Check sensitivities; use TMP–SMX if *Shigella* or *Salmonella* sensitive. Macrolides (erythro, azithro, clarithro) may be used for *Campylobacter*.
Clostridium difficile	Metronidazole 250 mg PO q6h for 7–10 d	Stop antibiotics, if possible. Vancomycin should be reserved for patients who cannot tolerate metronidazole. Relapses after therapy are common.
Amebiasis	Metronidazole 750 mg PO tid for 10 d, followed by iodo-quinol 650 mg PO tid for 20 d	Alternative luminicidal agents include paromomycin 500 mg PO tid for 7 d. Relapses may occur.
Giardiasis	Metronidazole 250 mg PO tid for 10 d	Relapses may occur.
Cryptosporidia	Paromomycin 500 mg PO qid (duration unclear)	Treatment other than hydration may not be necessary in noncompromised patients. Therapy may not be effective in compromised (especially HIV-infected) patients. Azithromycin and hyperimmune bovine colostrum may have some effect in HIV-infected patients.
Isospora	TMP–SMX 1 DS PO qid for 10 d, then bid for 3 wk	
Cyclospora	TMP–SMX 1 DS PO bid for 3 d	

TMP–SMX, trimethoprim–sulfamethoxazole; DS, double strength.
*Norfloxacin 400 mg PO bid, ofloxacin 400 mg PO bid, or ciprofloxacin 500 mg PO bid.

taining appropriate studies, to avoid or limit hospital stay. In a case where empiric antibiotics are selected, a complete history to ensure that the patient is not at risk for *C. difficile* disease is imperative.

The quinolone antibiotics and the increasing resistance of enteric pathogens to other antibiotics have altered the treatment of infectious diarrheal disease (Table 8–17–2). Although quinolones should not be used in children or pregnant women, quinolones can effectively treat infectious diarrhea in other adults that is caused by *Salmonella, Shigella, Campylobacter,* or *Vibrio* species, as well as the bacterial causes of noninflammatory diarrheal disease including the enterotoxigenic *E. coli* and *V. cholerae*. Treatment studies of travelers' diarrhea demonstrate a more rapid decrease in symptoms with combined use of quinolones and antiperistaltic agents than with either agent used alone, even for patients infected with *Shigella*. There are too few data, however, to recommend the use of antiperistaltic agents in the treatment of inflammatory diarrhea. A quinolone antibiotic is a reasonable albeit expensive choice for an empiric antibiotic for a patient with inflammatory diarrhea, although if therapy is not begun until sensitivities are known, a less expensive agent may be chosen. An additional caution in the use of the quinolones is the rapid emergence of resistance, which has been documented during the course of therapy for pathogens such as *Campylobacter* with clinical relapse. *Clostridium difficile* should be treated with metronidazole or oral vancomycin. Therapeutic efficacy appears to be the same for the two drugs; vancomycin is more expensive and has been associated with the emergence of vancomycin-resistant enterococci in hospitalized populations. Amebiasis should be treated with metronidazole and a luminicidal agent; giardiasis should be treated with metronidazole, as quinacrine is no longer available for use in the

United States. *Cryptosporidium* may be treated with paromomycin, a nonabsorbed antibiotic; however, cryptosporidiosis is a self-limited disease in patients with intact immune function and may not reliably respond to therapy in patients with compromised immune function. *Microsporidium* may respond to treatment with albendazole, which is not routinely available in the United States, and *Cyclospora* and *Isospora* may respond to treatment with trimethoprim–sulfamethoxazole.

Infectious diarrheal syndromes caused by agents such as rotavirus and the Norwalk-like agents should be treated with hydration. The food poisoning syndromes caused by *Staphylococcus, Bacillus cereus,* or *Clostridium perfringens* should also be managed with hydration; antibiotics would be of no benefit in either case. Returned travelers with a watery diarrheal syndrome may respond to antibiotics such as trimethoprim–sulfamethoxazole, if organisms are sensitive, or to a quinolone antibiotic, but these are generally self-limited illnesses as well.

Patients should be educated about the importance of hydration with ongoing diarrheal illness, and made aware that they can roughly gauge their hydration status by ensuring that they are urinating normal amounts. Education to prevent diarrheal disease may be useful, particularly in travelers, who can reduce their risk for diarrheal disease by drinking only bottled water and hot tea or coffee and avoiding ice, unpeeled, uncooked foods, or foods that have been cooked and then allowed to stand for a prolonged period (i.e., steam table buffets).

FOLLOW-UP

Follow-up and further evaluation should be considered if diarrhea persists longer than 7 to 10 days, especially if peritoneal signs, high fever, or gross blood in the stool develops or if the diarrhea is accompanied by significant weight loss. Close contact between patient and physician about symptoms and progress should be encouraged. Diarrhea that recurs after therapy or spontaneous clinical improvement should also be reevaluated. Persistent unresponsive diarrhea with weight loss or fever should suggest evaluation for inflammatory bowel disease or consideration of underlying medical illness such as HIV infection. Patients with a history of frequent, severe diarrheal illnesses of any etiology could be evaluated for immunoglobulin A deficiency.

DISCUSSION
Prevalence and Incidence

Infectious diarrheal disease is an extremely common problem worldwide and in the developing world is one of the most frequent causes of morbidity and mortality. In the United States, infectious diarrheal illnesses occur frequently but are usually self-limited and, if hydration is maintained, not life threatening. Outbreaks of infectious diarrheal illness do occur in the United States and may be caused by food or water supplies contaminated by a variety of pathogens, such as one of the Norwalk-like agents, *Salmonella, Cryptosporidium, Giardia, Shigella,* and *E. coli* 0157:H7, among others. These outbreaks may be extensive and a recent cryptosporidiosis outbreak related to a public water supply in Wisconsin involved several thousand individuals. Infectious diarrheal illnesses may be more significant in compromised hosts, who include individuals at the extremes of age, as well as patients who are malnourished or immunocompromised by disease or therapy.

Related Basic Science

The pathophysiology of diarrheal illness depends on the pathogen involved. The infectious agent is usually acquired by ingestion; the fecal–oral route is most common. The number of organisms required to establish infection varies with the virulence of the organism and the defenses of the host. Infection with *Shigella* or *Campylobacter* may be established with very few organisms (fewer than 10^2); inocula of *Salmonella* or *E. coli* need to be much higher (10^6–10^8) to establish disease. A patient with reduced gastric acid, whether from antacids, histamine blockers, or prior surgery, is more susceptible to pathogens that might otherwise be killed in the stomach before they reach the small bowel. The presence of the normal bacterial flora in the upper small bowel is

also important is reducing the ease with which a pathogen can establish itself; the recent use of antibiotics may also predispose an individual to the acquisition of a pathogen.

Attachment of organisms to the small bowel is usually the initiating step in the production of disease. Bacteria that produce toxins but do not attach to small bowel do not produce diarrheal disease in volunteers. Attachment is important for both bacterial and parasitic pathogens, including *E. coli, Shigella, Salmonella,* and, presumably, *Giardia* and *Cryptosporidium.* After attachment, a pathogen may produce a disease by elaboration of toxins that cause fluid secretion or are toxic to cells. Various groups of *E. coli,* including the enteropathogenic *E. coli,* may produce disease by the process of attachment, which may initiate a series of secretory signal transduction pathways within the small bowel enterocyte. The viral pathogens produce disease by the invasion of the small bowel mucosa with dysfunction of mucosal brush border enzymes and disruption of normal mucosal architecture and absorptive processes. Dysfunction of the brush border enzymes may cause transient malabsorption of disaccharides, which may contribute osmotically to diarrhea.

Invasive agents produce dysenteric diarrheal disease in the colon. These invasive organisms may also produce toxins, which can cause systemic symptoms as well as local tissue damage. Examples include toxins presumed to cause seizures in shigellosis and the association of hemolytic uremic syndrome with both *Shigella* and *E. coli* 0157:H7. *Entamoeba histolytica* also invades the colon.

Natural History and Its Modification with Treatment

The self-limited infectious gastrointestinal illnesses such as food poisoning and illnesses caused by viral agents usually last no longer than 3 to 7 days. The diarrheal illnesses caused by the bacterial agents should also be self-limited in the normal host and should persist no longer than 7 to 10 days. If diarrhea persists longer than 10 days, further evaluation, as described above, looking for parasites, other treatable pathogens, or noninfectious causes, should be considered. The course of the bacterial diarrheal illnesses may be shortened with the use of antibiotic therapy.

Prevention

Preventive measures should stress personal hygiene with good hand washing. Food preparation issues such as the adequate cooking of beef to prevent *E. coli* 0157:H7; the care with which poultry is handled; the avoidance of consuming inadequately cooked or raw intact shell eggs, which may transmit *Salmonella;* and avoiding raw meat, shellfish, or unpasteurized dairy products may also be discussed. Although there is exciting progress in the development of vaccines for enteric illnesses, the multiplicity of organisms that cause this syndrome limit the possibilities of preventing all diarrheal disease with vaccination. Currently, typhoid and cholera vaccines are available, which are moderately effective for limited periods. Travelers to areas of high risk can be educated about the prevention and management of diarrheal illness. Most experts do not recommend the routine use of prophylactic antibiotics for travelers.

Cost Containment

A cost-effective approach to the evaluation and management of infectious diarrheal disease includes careful history and consideration prior to obtaining stool cultures. Indications for stool cultures include the presence of blood or fecal leukocytes, fever, persistent diarrhea, or systemic illness. Stool cultures are not generally warranted in a patient with watery diarrhea who develops diarrhea after 3 days or more of hospitalization. The use of early, aggressive oral rehydration can avoid the necessity for intravenous hydration. Radiologic studies can generally be avoided as they add little to the management of uncomplicated diarrheal disease. Antimicrobial therapy should be reserved for specific indications such as documented or suspected *Shigella; Campylobacter, Yersinia,* or *Vibrio* infection; severe or invasive disease caused by *E. coli*; and the compromised patient or a patient who is being considered for hospitalization.

REFERENCES

Avery ME, Snyder JD. Oral therapy for acute diarrhea. N Eng J Med 1990;323:891.

Blacklow NR, Greenberg HB. Viral gastroenteritis. N Engl J Med 1991;325:252.

Guerrant RL. Lessons from diarrheal disease. J Infect Dis 1994;169:1206.

Guerrant RL, Bobak DA. Bacterial and protozoal gastroenteritis. N Engl J Med 1991;325:327.

Mayer HB, Wanke CA. Diagnostic strategies in HIV-infected patients with diarrhea. AIDS 1994;8:1639.

CHAPTER 8–18

Foodborne Diseases

James M. Hughes, M.D., and Frederick J. Angulo, D.V.M., Ph.D.

DEFINITION

Foodborne diseases are acute illnesses caused by the ingestion of contaminated food and usually characterized by gastrointestinal, and, in some instances, neurologic signs and symptoms.

ETIOLOGY

Foodborne diseases may result from ingestion by a susceptible individual of food contaminated by microorganisms, toxins elaborated by microorganisms, or a variety of chemicals.

CRITERIA FOR DIAGNOSIS

Suggestive

Generally, illness is characterized by an incubation period of 1 week or less and symptoms and signs related to the gastrointestinal tract or nervous system. A number of other infections that can be transmitted by foods (e.g., hepatitis A, trichinosis, listeriosis, group A streptococcal pharyngitis) are not addressed in this chapter because these infections typically have longer incubation periods and/or involve other organ systems. Foodborne diseases most often occur in the community setting, but outbreaks involving patients in hospitals, extended-care facilities, prisons, and other institutional settings have been reported. Foodborne diseases affect both children and adults. Affected individuals are most often otherwise healthy, although infants, the elderly, and individuals with impaired gastric acid secretion are most susceptible to many foodborne diseases and suffer the most severe consequences when illness occurs. The major clue to the diagnosis is the temporal association of similar illnesses involving the gastrointestinal tract or neurologic system in two or more individuals who have recently shared a common meal. Clinical and epidemiologic features of the illness provide clues to the specific etiologic agent (Table 8–18–1).

Definitive

Diagnosis of the syndrome may be confirmed by identification of the etiologic agent or toxin in specimens from ill individuals or in the implicated food. In some instances, a serologic antibody response may be diagnostic.

CLINICAL MANIFESTATIONS

Subjective

Although any individual may develop a foodborne disease, risk factors for the syndrome are infancy, advanced age, immunosuppressive therapy, and conditions characterized by hypochlorhydria or achlorhydria. Symptoms reflect involvement of the gastrointestinal tract and nervous system. Symptoms related to gastrointestinal tract involvement may include fever, chills, abdominal cramps, nausea, vomiting, diarrhea, and tenesmus. Neurologic symptoms typically reflect involvement of the peripheral nervous system and may include numbness, tingling, reversal of hot and cold temperature sensation, and, in severe cases, weakness, blurred vision, diplopia, dysphonia, dysphagia, and generalized weakness.

Objective

Physical Examination

Physical examination of patients with illnesses involving primarily the gastrointestinal tract may reveal fever, tachycardia, and abdominal tenderness. In patients with illness involving the nervous system, physical examination may reveal signs of cranial nerve dysfunction and muscle weakness.

Routine Laboratory Abnormalities

Routine laboratory tests are generally not helpful in making the diagnosis. Severely dehydrated individuals may have evidence of hemoconcentration. Patients with an illness caused by invasive pathogens may have leukocytosis. Severely ill individuals may manifest hypokalemia and elevations of blood urea nitrogen and creatinine.

PLANS

Diagnostic

Differential Diagnosis

See Table 8–18–1.

Diagnostic Options

The diagnostic approach must be based on the differential diagnosis formulated after careful evaluation of information obtained from the clinical and epidemiologic history and physical examination.

Recommended Approach

Examination of stool specimens from patients with illnesses involving primarily the gastrointestinal tract may reveal blood or mucus. The presence of polymorphonuclear leukocytes in fresh stool specimens stained with methylene blue suggests that an invasive enteric pathogen (e.g., *Shigella*, *Campylobacter jejuni*) is responsible.

A stool culture is appropriate for any individual with an acute diarrheal illness in an effort to identify *Salmonella*, *Shigella*, *Campylobacter*, *Bacillus cereus*, enterohemorrhagic *Escherichia coli* (i.e., *E. coli* 0157:H7), enterotoxigenic *E. coli*, *Clostridium perfringens* (>10^6/g), *Vibrio*, and *Yersinia*. When illness is characterized primarily by nausea and vomiting, vomitus may be cultured for evidence of *Staphylococcus aureus* and stool may be cultured for *Bacillus cereus*. If heavy metal intoxication is suspected, vomitus may be analyzed for the chemical or chemicals suspected. When the neurologic system is involved and botulism is suspected, serum and stool specimens from the patient should be obtained for analysis for botulinum toxin and the stool should be cultured for evidence of *Clostridium botulinum*. These tests can be arranged by contacting the state health department. If the neurologic symptoms and signs and the epidemiologic history suggest the possibility of fish or shellfish poisoning, laboratory studies on specimens from patients are not likely to provide useful information. Studies of the suspect or implicated food item may provide useful confirmatory diagnostic evidence. Foods may be cultured for bacterial pathogens or assayed for the presence of botulinum toxin, or ciguatoxin, or for histamine content in the case of suspected scombroid fish poisoning. In the case

TABLE 8–18–1. CLINICAL AND EPIDEMIOLOGIC CLUES TO SELECTED ETIOLOGIC AGENTS OF FOOD POISONING

Agent	Gastrointestinal Manifestations		Neurologic Manifestations		Fever	Feces		Incubation Period (h)	Common Foods	Seasonality
	Vomiting	Diarrhea	Sensory	Motor		Blood	Polymorpho-nuclear Leukocytes			
Bacteria										
Bacillus cereus										
Short incubation type	+	±	–	–	–	–	–	1–6	Fried rice	None
Long incubation type	–	+	–	–	–	–	–	8–24	Meats, vegetables,	None
Campylobacter jejuni	±	+	–	–	+	+	+	48–240	Raw milk, poultry, beef	Spring, summer
Clostridium botulinum	±	±	–	±	–	–	–	18–36	Vegetables, fish, fruits	Summer, fall
Clostridium perfringens	–	+	–	–	–	–	–	6–24	Beef, poultry, gravy	Fall, spring, winter
Escherichia coli										
Enterotoxigenic	±	+	–	–	–	–	–	6–48	Cheese, Mexican food, vegetables	None
Enteroinvasive	±	+	–	–	+	+	+	16–48	Cheese	None
Enterohemorrhagic	±	+	–	–	–	+	±	72–120	Hamburger	None
Salmonella	±	+	–	–	+	±	+	6–48	Animal and dairy products, eggs	Summer
Shigella	±	+	–	–	+	+	+	48–96	Egg salads	Summer
Staphylococcus aureus	+	±	–	–	–	–	–	2–4	Ham, egg salads, pastries	Summer
Vibrio cholerae 01	±	+	–	–	–	–	–	24–120	Shellfish	Variable
Vibrio cholerae non-01	±	+	–	–	–	–	–	24–120	Shellfish	Unknown
Vibrio parahaemolyticus	±	+	–	–	+	±	±	4–30	Crabs	Spring, fall, summer
Yersinia enterocolitica	–	±	–	–	+	–	±	96–144	Milk, tofu	None
Viruses										
Norwalk-like agents	+	+	–	–	±	–	–	16–72	Shellfish, salads	None
Astroviruses	+	+	–	–	+	–	–	24–36	Shellfish	Unknown
Caliciviruses	+	+	–	–	±	–	–	24–72	Shellfish	Unknown
Parasites										
Cryptosporidium parvum	+	+	–	–	+	–	–	48–288	Apple cider	Summer
Chemicals										
Scombroid	+	+	+	–	–	–	–	≤1	Fish	None
Ciguatoxin	+	+	+	±	–	–	–	2–8	Fish	Spring, summer
Paralytic shellfish poisoning	±	±	+	±	–	–	–	< 1–4	Shellfish	Summer, fall
Heavy metals	+	+	–	–	–	–	–	< 1 h	Acidic beverages	None
Mushrooms containing anatoxins	–	+	–	–	–	–	–	1–24	Mushrooms	Spring, fall
Monosodium glutamate	–	–	+	–	–	–	–	< 1 h	Chinese food	None

+, commonly present; ±, occasionally present; –, rarely present.
Source: Bean NH, Goulding JS, Loa C, Angulo FJ. Foodborne disease outbreaks, 1988–91. MMWR (in press).

of mushroom poisoning, the mushrooms can be identified by an experienced mycologist or the toxin can be identified in gastric contents, blood, urine, or fecal specimens.

When submitting specimens to the clinical laboratory, the laboratory should be alerted that a foodborne illness or an outbreak of food poisoning is suspected, so that the need to use specific media or culture conditions and other diagnostic procedures can be evaluated. For example, laboratories should be informed if an *E. coli* 0157:H7 infection is suspected, as many laboratories only use the appropriate medium to detect *E. coli* 0157:H7 (sorbitol–MacConkey) on physician requests. If the organism or toxin is identified from specimens of two or more ill persons who ingested a common food, an outbreak is confirmed. Most clinical laboratories do not perform tests for viral agents. If a viral gastroenteritis outbreak is suspected, the health department should be notified and sera and stool may be collected for analysis at a reference laboratory.

Therapeutic

Therapy for the patient with a foodborne disease is primarily supportive. In the case of the patient with severe, acute gastrointestinal fluid loss, fluids and electrolytes may be replaced by the intravenous route.

In milder cases, treatment with glucose-containing oral electrolyte solutions suffices. Antimicrobial agents may be useful in the treatment of foodborne diseases caused by *Shigella* and *Campylobacter jejuni*. Specific agents, doses, routes of administration, and side effects are detailed in Chapter 8–17. Antiperistaltic agents such as diphenoxylate (Lomotil) and loperamide (Imodium) may be given for severe abdominal cramps; however, these drugs should not be used if fever or fecal leukocytes are present, because use of these agents may exacerbate illnesses caused by invasive pathogens. Antiperistaltic agents should not be given to children.

The therapy of botulism consists of the administration of intravenous botulinum antitoxin and supportive measures, with careful attention to ventilatory assistance and prevention of complications such as decubitus ulcers and nosocomial infections.

Therapy for the severe form of mushroom poisoning caused by species of mushrooms containing anatoxins includes use of cathartics and enemas in an effort to remove unabsorbed toxin, intravenous administration of glucose to counteract the hypoglycemia that may occur, and possibly administration of thioctic acid (thioctacid). Therapy for heavy metal intoxications and fish and shellfish poisoning is supportive; mannitol has been used for ciguatoxin intoxication.

The patient should be told that the disease is usually self-limiting and that full recovery can be anticipated. Patients with bacterial foodborne disease should be told whether an antimicrobial agent is indicated and, if so, how long it should be taken. All patients with an infectious cause of foodborne disease should be reminded of the need to observe strict standards of personal hygiene during the illness. Those with salmonellosis should be counseled that an asymptomatic, convalescent carrier state may exist for several weeks and occasionally a few months after full recovery and should be told whether or not follow-up cultures are indicated. Patients with any type of foodborne disease should be told how they most likely acquired the illness and should be advised regarding appropriate steps to prevent acquisition of a similar illness in the future.

FOLLOW-UP

As foodborne diseases are generally self-limiting, prolonged follow-up of patients is usually not required. Patients who are health care, daycare center, or food service workers should not work during their illness. In addition, patients in the health care or food service profession who have E. coli 0157:H7, Salmonella, or shigella infection should be restricted in their activities until convalescent carriage resolves and should be advised to return for follow-up cultures until two or three cultures taken at least 24 hours apart in the absence of antimicrobial therapy are negative.

DISCUSSION
Prevalence and Incidence

From 1972 through 1991, between 300 and 650 outbreaks of foodborne diseases affecting 10,000 to 31,000 people were reported annually to the Centers for Disease Control and Prevention. In more than half of

the outbreaks, the etiologic agent was not identified. The numbers of outbreaks and cases caused by different specific etiologic agents reported from 1988 through 1991 are listed in Table 8–18–2. These figures certainly underestimate the true magnitude of the problem of foodborne diseases, but they do provide an indication of the relative frequency of the commonly recognized etiologic agents.

Related Basic Science

Agents responsible for bacterial foodborne diseases cause illness either by production of preformed enterotoxin in food (S. aureus, some strains of Bacillus cereus); production of enterotoxin in vivo (Clostridium perfringens; enterotoxigenic E. coli, Vibrio cholerae 01; invasion of the intestinal mucosa (e.g., Shigella, Campylobacter jejuni); production of cytotoxin (enterohemorrhagic E. coli); or penetration of the gastrointestinal mucosa with proliferation in regional lymphatic tissue and occasional systemic dissemination (e.g., Salmonella, Yersinia enterocolitica). The 27-nm Norwalk and Norwalk-like agents proliferate in and destroy mucosal epithelial cells. Botulinum toxin inhibits the release of acetylcholine at nerve endings. The mechanism of action of many of the toxins responsible for chemical foodborne diseases, including heavy metal and fish and shellfish poisoning, is not well understood.

Natural History and Its Modification with Treatment

Complications of foodborne diseases are rare in the normal host, with the exception of patients affected with botulism or mushroom poisoning caused by species of mushrooms containing anatoxins. Several severe chronic sequelae have been associated with foodborne diseases, however, including Guillain-Barré syndrome (Campylobacter infection), reactive arthritis (several foodborne infections), and hemolytic–uremic syndrome (E. coli 0157:H7). Infants, the elderly, and those

TABLE 8–18–2. NUMBER OF FOODBORNE DISEASE OUTBREAKS AND CASES OF KNOWN ETIOLOGY REPORTED TO THE CENTERS FOR DISEASE CONTROL AND PREVENTION, BY ETIOLOGIC AGENT, 1988–1991

Agent	Number of outbreaks	Percentage of total	Number of cases	Percentage of total
Bacteria			18,343	57.6
Salmonella	469	54.8	120	0.4
Clostridium botulinum	56	6.5	1,963	6.2
Staphylococcus aureus	44	5.1	2,889	9.1
Clostridium perfringens	28	3.3	4,784	15.0
Shigella	24	2.8	594	1.9
Campylobacter	21	2.4	491	1.5
Bacillus cereus	18	2.1	225	0.7
Escherichia coli	8	0.9	21	0.1
Vibrio parahemolyticus	4	0.5	135	0.4
Streptococcus, group A	2	0.2	6	—
Vibrio cholerae	2	0.2	2	—
Vibrio vulnificus	1	0.1	2	—
Listeria monocyogenes	1	0.1		
Subtotal	678	79.0	29,575	92.9
Chemicals				
Scombrotoxin	61	7.1	379	1.2
Ciguatoxin	41	4.8	168	0.5
Shellfish poisoning	5	0.6	65	0.2
Mushroom poisoning	5	0.6	18	0.1
Heavy metals	3	0.3	26	0.1
Other chemicals	9	1.0	65	0.2
Subtotal	124	14.4	721	2.3
Parasites				
Trichinella spiralis	10	1.2	195	0.6
Giardia	6	0.7	182	0.6
Subtotal	16	1.9	377	1.2
Viruses				
Hepatitis A	35	4.1	1,690	5.3
Norwalk	1	0.1	42	0.1
Subtotal	36	4.2	1,732	5.4
Total	854	99.5	32,405	101.8

Source: Bean NH, Goulding JS, Loa C, Angulo FJ. Foodborne disease outbreaks, 1988–91. MMWR (unpublished data, CDC).

with underlying diseases with altered immune status are most likely to experience complications.

With the exceptions of botulism and mushroom poisoning, mortality caused by foodborne diseases is rare; however, epidemiologic evidence suggests that foodborne diseases are associated with as many as 9000 deaths each year. Deaths in outbreaks of foodborne disease most often occur in elderly patients in extended-care facilities.

Prevention

Prevention of foodborne diseases caused by infectious agents depends on proper food handling techniques, with emphasis on strict personal hygiene, adequate cooking, careful attention to avoidance of cross-contamination of raw and cooked food, and holding of food at appropriate temperatures (i.e., below 40°F for refrigerated items and above 140°F for hot items).

Prevention of heavy metal poisoning requires adequate maintenance of vending machines and avoidance of storage of acidic beverages in metallic containers. Prevention of fish poisoning requires avoidance of large tropical fish in the case of ciguatera and compliance with seasonal or emergency quarantines of shellfish harvesting areas in the case of shellfish poisoning. Prevention of mushroom poisoning requires refraining from eating wild mushrooms.

When an outbreak of foodborne disease is suspected, it is imperative that local health authorities be notified so that an investigation can be promptly conducted. This course of action is required to prevent additional cases due to subsequent ingestion of contaminated food and prompt recognition and control when the outbreak involves a contaminated commercial food.

Prevention of foodborne diseases also involves avoidance of ingestion of certain high-risk food items (listed in Table 8–18–1) such as raw or undercooked milk, eggs, poultry, meat, and seafood (including raw oysters and clams).

Cost Containment

In general, diagnostic evaluation of the patient with suspected food poisoning should include a limited number of laboratory tests. For individuals with diarrhea, an examination of a fresh stool specimen stained with methylene blue should be performed. If fecal leukocytes are seen, the patient is moderately or severely ill, or fever is present, a stool culture is appropriate. A stool culture, including sorbitol–MacConkey medium, should also be conducted for individuals with bloody diarrhea. For those with severe vomiting or diarrhea, serum electrolytes, blood urea nitrogen, and creatinine levels should be determined, and if fever is present, blood cultures may be indicated. Hospitalization is generally not necessary, except in the very young, the elderly, the debilitated, and persons in whom the diagnosis of botulism, shellfish poisoning, or mushroom poisoning caused by species containing anatoxins is suspected.

Repeat stool cultures and additional laboratory tests should generally be avoided. In an outbreak setting in which a large number of people are known to be ill and the etiologic agent is known from initial patients, initial stool cultures on subsequent patients may be unnecessary once the cause of the outbreak is recognized. Follow-up stool cultures are necessary only for individuals with *E. coli* 0157:H7, *Salmonella,* or *Shigella* infections, who work in a setting such as a hospital, daycare center, or food service establishment, where the risk of transmission is increased.

Routine preemployment or periodic follow-up examinations of asymptomatic food service workers for enteric pathogens are not cost-effective and should not be performed.

REFERENCES

Ames, IA: Foodborne pathogens: Risks and consequences. Task force report No. 122. ISSN 01944088. Council for Agricultural Science and Technology, September 1994.

Angulo FJ, Swerdlow DL. Bacterial enteric infections in persons with human immunodeficiency virus. Clin Infect Dis 1995;21 (suppl 1):584.

Bean NH, Goulding JS, Loa C, Angulo FJ. Foodborne disease outbreaks, 1988–91. MMWR, in press.

Bean NH, Griffin PM. Foodborne disease outbreaks in the United States, 1973–1987: Pathogens, vehicles, and trends. J Food Protect 1990;53:804.

Hedberg CW, MacDonald KL, Osterholm MT. Changing epidemiology of foodborne disease: A Minnesota perspective. Clin Infect Dis 1994;18:671.

CHAPTER 8–19

Peritonitis

Richard L. Hengel, M.D., and Carl A. Perlino, M.D.

DEFINITION

Peritonitis is an acute or chronic inflammation of the peritoneal surface.

ETIOLOGY

Inflammation usually occurs due to the presence of infectious agents, bacteria, fungi, or mycobacteria, but occasionally is due to chemical irritation from pancreatic enzymes, bile, or exogenous foreign material. This chapter considers the infectious causes of acute peritonitis.

CRITERIA FOR DIAGNOSIS
Suggestive

The gastrointestinal tract is normally colonized with a variety of aerobic and anaerobic bacteria and yeast, the largest numbers being found in the distal small intestine and large intestine of the normal host. The stomach and duodenum are relatively free of organisms unless an abnormality in peristalsis or intestinal obstruction is present, in which case the number of organisms increases. Peritonitis occurs most often because of the introduction of microbial contents of the intestine into the peritoneal cavity due to intestinal perforation or to inflammation of an adjacent structure, such as occurs in cholecystitis. Peritonitis also can occur due to introduction of bacteria or yeast by an indwelling peritoneal catheter in patients receiving peritoneal dialysis. These are examples of secondary peritonitis.

Alternatively, peritonitis may occur in patients with cirrhosis and ascites without any obvious intraabdominal source of infection, so-called primary or spontaneous bacterial peritonitis (SBP).

The diagnosis of peritonitis is suggested by the presence of systemic evidence of infection such as fever, local symptoms of abdominal pain, and signs of peritoneal irritation.

Definitive

The diagnosis of peritonitis can be confirmed by surgical exploration or diagnostic paracentesis, which demonstrate an inflammatory reaction. Appropriate cultures may reveal the infectious etiology.

CLINICAL MANIFESTATIONS
Subjective

Peritonitis may occur acutely and unexpectedly because of spontaneous rupture or leakage from a diseased intestine, after abdominal trauma, after a surgical procedure, as a complication of local intestinal obstruction, or as a complication of local inflammation associated with acute appendicitis, diverticulitis, or cholecystitis.

The earliest symptom is usually localized abdominal pain appropriate to the site of initial involvement. Frequently, host defenses are unable to localize or wall off the infection, and in short order the pain becomes diffuse and may be exacerbated by movement of the patient. Complaints of anorexia may precede the onset of pain, and nausea is common following the onset of pain. Increased thirst may indicate dry oral mucosa due to rapid, shallow respirations or a decreased effective intravascular volume. Vomiting may occur, but diarrhea is an uncommon complaint. Tenesmus may occur with lower abdominal sources of infection such as with appendicitis or diverticulitis. Most patients complain of fever or chills.

Abdominal pain, gastrointestinal upset, and fever frequently accompany peritonitis in patients on peritoneal dialysis and in the cirrhotic with ascites and SBP. Additionally, the patient on dialysis may notice that the dialysate has turned cloudy, and the patient with cirrhosis may have a change in mental status due to hepatic encephalopathy or the onset of other complications of liver failure such as variceal bleeding and hepatorenal syndrome.

Objective

Physical Examination

The patient with peritonitis is generally febrile with tachycardia. Pallor, a weak thready pulse, and a postural change in blood pressure or hypotension all reflect intravascular volume depletion and sepsis syndrome heralding septic shock. Tachypnea may result from diaphragmatic splinting or compensation for metabolic acidosis.

The patient avoids movement or jarring. Abdominal guarding and tenderness are present, maximal over the site of involvement. Similarly, rebound tenderness may suggest the site of involvement directly or indirectly. Rectal and pelvic examinations may provide vital clues to localization of infection in peritonitis. Signs of ileus may be present with absent bowel sounds, distention, and hyperresonance to percussion.

Local findings in patients undergoing peritoneal dialysis may be less dramatic, and as mentioned the dialysate fluid may be cloudy. Similarly, the patient with SBP may have minimal local abdominal findings but may present with altered mental status and signs of hepatic encephalopathy. Finally, as with many diseases, presentation in the elderly may be subtle: signs and symptoms may be minimal.

Routine Laboratory Abnormalities

The leukocyte count may be normal, but it is most often elevated, with a predominance of polymorphonuclear leukocytes and an increased number of band forms. The hematocrit and the blood urea nitrogen and serum creatinine levels are often elevated, indicating hemoconcentration, decreased intravascular volume, and decreased renal plasma flow. Urinalysis and urine culture help to define a urinary source of infection.

PLANS

Diagnostic

Differential Diagnosis

The differential diagnosis of abdominal pain that might mimic peritonitis is wide. Intrathoracic pathology such as myocardial infarction, pericardial disease, pleural disease, aortic disease, and esophageal disease can present with abdominal pain. Intraabdominal sources of pain include gastroenteritis, inflammatory bowel disease, intestinal obstruction (including volvulus, intussusception, and strangulated hernias), pancreatitis, cholecystitis, peptic ulcer disease, renal colic, pyelonephritis, bladder outlet obstruction, diverticulitis, severe constipation, colitis, and mesenteric adenitis. Other causes of abdominal pain include mesenteric vascular events, collagen–vascular disorders with serositis, metabolic derangements such as porphyria, and genetic diseases such as familial Mediterranean fever. Pelvic inflammatory disease is a major cause of abdominal pain in women presenting to the emergency department. Sickle cell crisis often presents with abdominal pain.

Diagnostic Options

The presence of peritonitis is strongly suggested by the patient's history and physical examination, but further evaluation should be done to confirm the diagnosis. A chest roentgenogram must be obtained to ensure that the abdominal symptoms are not secondary to a lower lobe pneumonia. Flat and upright abdominal films confirm some of the physical findings. The large and small intestines may be distended; air–fluid levels may be present in the intestines. Intestinal perforation may lead to air under the diaphragm detected on the upright films. Fluid in the abdominal cavity can obliterate the psoas shadows. In addition to routine laboratory investigations listed above, blood cultures should be obtained prior to any therapy.

In most instances, the diagnosis of peritonitis and the source of the infection are confirmed by abdominal exploration. Cultures obtained at that time aid in the subsequent antibiotic management.

In special circumstances diagnostic paracentesis plays an important role. It is the cornerstone of diagnosis in SBP and peritonitis complicating peritoneal dialysis. Ascitic fluid is sent for cell count and differential Gram stain, culture, and, in the case of suspected SBP, albumin (with paired serum albumin). A wide albumin gradient (serum albumin − ascites albumin concentration of >1.1 g/dL) would support the diagnosis of portal hypertension and cirrhosis and, therefore, SBP; a narrow albumin gradient (<1.1 g/dL) would lead one to question the diagnosis of SBP. An ascitic fluid absolute cell count of polymorphonuclear cells (PMNs) of more than 250/mm^3 is consistent with the diagnosis of SBP in the patient with ascites due to cirrhosis. In the patient undergoing peritoneal dialysis, the diagnosis of peritonitis is suggested by an absolute white cell count in dialysate fluid of more than 100 cells/mm^3 (with >50% being PMNs).

Some authorities believe an increased yield in the microbiology laboratory may be obtained by directly inoculating 10 mL of ascitic fluid or peritoneal dialysate fluid into a routine blood culture bottle at the bedside. Similarly, Gram stain becomes more sensitive when 10 to 20 mL of either fluid is centrifuged, and the sediment submitted for stain.

Recommended Approach

Peritonitis is usually a surgical disease apart from SBP and peritonitis complicating peritoneal dialysis. Following simultaneous diagnostic and therapeutic measures in the emergency department, it should become obvious from history, physical examination, and initial investigations which patients can be treated medically and which should be evaluated surgically.

Therapeutic

Therapeutic Options

All cases of suspected peritonitis should be treated as medical or surgical emergencies. Oxygenation, ventilation, circulatory volume, and renal perfusion need to be addressed first to ensure the patient is adequately resuscitated. Early diagnosis and, in the case of an intraabdominal source, prompt surgical intervention are essential. With surgical disease antibiotics play an important but subordinate role. Nevertheless, once appropriate cultures have been taken, appropriate antibiotics should be administered promptly.

Various antibiotics can be used alone or in combination as long as the spectrum of activity includes the predominant bacteria found in the gut. Clindamycin plus gentamicin, with or without the addition of ampicillin to add activity against enterococci, has been the standard antimicrobial regimen in the recent past. Other regimens are equally effective and are especially indicated when there is a concern over the possible toxicity of aminoglycosides. Cefoxitin, cefotetan, ceftizoxime, ampicillin–sulbactam, ticarcillin–clavulinic acid, pipercillin–tazobactam, and imipenem–cilastin have activity against *Bacteroides fragilis* and aerobic Gram-negative bacilli, such as *Escherichia coli,* and may be effective as single agents. Initial antimicrobial therapy should be modified depending on the results of cultures obtained at surgery.

Peritonitis complicating peritoneal dialysis is usually treated with medical therapy. Because bacteria are introduced through the peritoneal catheter or from the skin through the incision made to introduce the catheter, surgical intervention usually is not necessary. In this situation,

Gram-positive organisms, including coagulase-negative staphylococci and *Staphylococcus aureus,* are the most common cause; infections due to aerobic Gram-negative bacilli also occur. Initial empiric antibiotic therapy can be varied and will subsequently depend on the results of cultures and the local patterns of microbial resistance. The increasing incidence of methicillin resistance in coagulase-negative and positive staphylococci has made the empiric choice of vancomycin common. It is usually used with an aminoglycoside for coverage of aerobic Gram-negative organisms, although ototoxicity is a theoretical concern. The use of either systemic or intraperitoneal antibiotics, or both, has been successful. Surgical removal of the intraperitoneal catheter is indicated if the patient shows no response to appropriate antibiotic therapy. This maneuver is usually necessary in patients with fungal peritonitis.

Patients with SBP are also treated appropriately with antibiotics alone unless there is clinical evidence of the illness being secondary to an abdominal source. *Escherichia coli,* other aerobic Gram-negative bacilli, or enterococci are the most common causes of SBP. Traditionally, duration of therapy has been 10 to 14 days, but it appears as though 5 days may be just as effective. Use of a third-generation cephalosporin such as cefotaxime has been effective. Alternatives include extended-spectrum penicillins, imipenem–cilastin, or beta-lactam–beta-lactamase inhibitor combinations. Aminoglycosides should be avoided because of the risk of nephrotoxicity in patients with hepatic failure. Empiric therapy can be modified pending initial cultures and follow-up studies.

Recommended Approach

Prompt surgical evaluation and treatment are paramount in patients with surgical peritoneal disease. After appropriate cultures are obtained, antibiotics should be administered as soon as possible.

In the case of SBP, monotherapy with a third-generation cephalosporin such as cefotaxime for a total of 5 days is recommended, providing follow-up paracentesis demonstrates resolving peritonitis, or initial peritoneal cultures do not suggest an alternative diagnosis to SBP, such as intraabdominal abscess.

Peritonitis due to susceptible Gram-positive bacteria complicating peritoneal dialysis can be treated effectively with 1 g of intraperitoneal vancomycin, roughly once weekly when the trough level falls below 10 mg/dL. Many clinicians also treat empirically with a 3 mg/kg loading dose of gentamicin until cultures disprove a Gram-negative pathogen. The duration of therapy is usually 10 to 14 days.

FOLLOW-UP

The patient with secondary peritonitis is appropriately treated in hospital, and follow-up is indicated by the clinical course. The physician should be alert to the continued presence of fever and an elevated leukocyte count as indications of continued abdominal infection and abscess formation. Eventual evaluation for an abscess, when necessary, is best performed using a computed tomographic scan of the abdomen.

Patients with peritonitis associated with peritoneal dialysis can be followed as outpatients to ensure resolution of symptoms, clearing of dialysate, and laboratory confirmation of resolving inflammation. Reinforcement of sterile technique should be emphasized to help prevent a recurrence.

Following empiric therapy for SBP, a follow-up paracentesis should be done at 48 hours to determine adequacy of therapy. Absolute PMN count should be less than 250 cells/mm^3 and cultures negative. If these criteria are fulfilled, then a 5-day course of antibiotics is appropriate. If there is no resolution of symptoms and the peritoneal cell count is not improving, the diagnosis should be questioned and an alternative explanation such as the possibility of secondary peritonitis or a resistant or uncommon organism causing disease should be entertained.

DISCUSSION
Prevalence and Incidence

Infection in peritoneal dialysis occurs at a rate of roughly one episode per year. One half of patients will have had an episode of peritonitis

within the first 6 months of initiating dialysis. Recurrent infections are a problem for one quarter of patients.

Between 5 and 10% of patients with alcoholic cirrhosis develop SBP. Recurrent infection is not uncommon.

Related Basic Science

Peritonitis occurs in all age groups. Most often peritoneal infection occurs secondary to perforation of a hollow viscus. Thus, peritonitis is a likely complication of a penetrating gastric or duodenal ulcer, cholecystitis, appendicitis, diverticulitis, or leakage from a colonic carcinoma or a surgical anastomosis. Blunt or penetrating abdominal trauma or the presence of a chronic peritoneal catheter also may lead to this entity. Patients with ascites due to liver failure are a special group at risk for peritonitis. In these patients, peritonitis occurs as a primary infection without documented contamination of the peritoneum by intestinal contents. Transient bacteremia and transhepatic seeding of ascitic fluid deficient in proteins normally protective against infection appear to be the pathogenesis of SBP rather than transmural migration of microbes from the intestinal lumen as was previously thought.

Soiling of the peritoneum with bacteria leads to an acute inflammatory response and the exudation of significant amounts of fluid into the peritoneal cavity, resulting in decreased intravascular volume and possibly overt shock. Renal failure due to acute tubular necrosis as well as hypoxia and pulmonary infiltrates may appear as complications. The patient becomes acutely catabolic, necessitating attention to the patient's nutritional requirements.

Peritonitis due to intestinal perforation is polymicrobial, reflecting the flora of the gastrointestinal tract. Usually, aerobic enteric bacteria and anaerobic bacteria can be cultured from the peritoneal cavity. Blood cultures, however, may be positive for only one organism.

Natural History and Its Modification with Treatment

The local inflammatory response in the abdominal cavity often leads to walling off of areas of infection or abscess formation. Hepatic abscess also may occur because of drainage of bacteria in the portal venous system. Surgical intervention prevents these complications in the majority of circumstances through adequate debridement and drainage.

The mortality associated with peritonitis depends on a number of host factors and the severity of disease. Peritonitis associated with peritoneal dialysis usually responds to antibiotic therapy, whereas peritonitis occurring in the patient with cirrhosis and ascites may be associated with a high mortality rate.

Prevention

Most causes of secondary peritonitis are difficult to prevent other than those associated with complications of surgical procedures, in which case careful technique and antibiotic prophylaxis, when indicated, limit complications.

Peritonitis complicating peritoneal dialysis can be prevented by education and meticulous attention to aseptic technique. In the case of SBP, cessation of alcohol or any other hepatic toxins and compliance with medical therapy may help to limit subsequent infection. The role of antibiotic prophylaxis in this patient population is not yet clear.

Cost Containment

Prompt evaluation and treatment of patients presenting with any form of peritonitis help minimize morbidity and therefore, costs. Timing and use of investigations having the greatest diagnostic yield help the clinician avoid circumstances where no diagnosis has been made, the patient is on therapy, and further investigations are ordered to try to establish the diagnosis. Every effort should be made to obtain cultures prior to administering antibiotics, but not delaying their administration.

REFERENCES

Ahrenholz DH, Simmons RL. Peritonitis and other intraabdominal infections. In: Simmons RL, Howard RJ, eds. Surgical infectious diseases. New York: Appleton-Century-Crofts, 1982:795.
Bartlett JF, Louie TJ, Gorbach SL, Omderan K. Therapeutic efficacy of 29 an-

timicrobial regimens in experimental intraabdominal sepsis. Rev Infect Dis 1981;3:535

Bhura M, Ganger D, Jensen D. Spontaneous bacterial peritonitis: An update on evaluation, management, and prevention. Am J Med 1994;97:169.

Eisenberb ES, Leviton I, Soeiro R. Fungal peritonitis in patients receiving peritoneal dialysis: Experience with 11 patients and review for the literature. Rev Infect Dis 1986;8:309.

Feingold SM, Wexler HM. Therapeutic implications of bacteriologic findings in

mixed aerobid–anaerobic infections. Antimicrob Agents Chemother 1988;32:611.

Peterson PK, Matzke GR, Keane WF. Current concepts in the management of peritonitis in continuous ambulatory peritoneal dialysis patients. Rev Infect Dis 1987;9:604.

Saklayen MG. CAPD peritonitis: Incidence, pathogens, diagnosis, and management. Med Clin North Am 1990;74:997

CHAPTER 8–20

Spontaneous Bacterial Peritonitis (See Section 19, Chapter 86)

CHAPTER 8–21

Abdominal Pyogenic Abscess

Clifford J. Gunthel, M.D., and Carl A. Perlino, M.D.

DEFINITION

An abdominal abscess is a localized collection of purulent material found within the peritoneal cavity adjacent to the intraabdominal viscera or within the abdominal organs themselves.

ETIOLOGY

Abdominal abscesses may arise following contamination of the peritoneum with contents of the gastrointestinal or biliary tract. This commonly occurs following perforation which may be due to abdominal surgical procedures, abdominal trauma, or acute pyogenic infections involving abdominal viscera (such as appendicitis, diverticulitis, and cholecystitis). Additionally, hematogenous or lymphatic spread from an extraabdominal site of infection (such as endocarditis) may give rise to abscess formation in such organs as the liver and spleen.

CRITERIA FOR DIAGNOSIS

Suggestive

The diagnosis of an abdominal abscess is frequently suggested in the appropriate epidemiologic and clinical setting by the presence of fever, localized abdominal tenderness, and leukocytosis. The persistence of fever, leukocytosis, or abdominal symptoms despite treatment with appropriate antibiotics may indicate an abscess formation which is characteristically inaccessible to antimicrobial agents and normal host defenses.

Definitive

The definitive diagnosis of intraabdominal abscesses is usually obtained through specialized radiologic imagery techniques. Computed tomography (CT) scan and ultrasonography are reliable and reasonably accurate diagnostic procedures. At times an abdominal abscess can be diagnosed correctly only by surgical exploration, aspiration, or autopsy examination.

CLINICAL MANIFESTATIONS

Subjective

Most patients have a history of one or more factors that predispose to an increased risk for the development of localized intraabdominal infections (Table 8–21–1). A travel history may lead to consideration of an amebic abscess or an echinoceal cyst in the liver.

The frequency and duration of symptoms in patients with an abdominal abscess are variable. Fever, chills, and abdominal pain are common.

The abdominal pain is often localized to a specific area, but it may be generalized. Depending on the location of the abscess, the patient also may complain of nausea, vomiting, dyspnea, pleuritic pain, hiccups, or shoulder pain. At times, an occult abscess appears insidiously in the setting of a fever of unknown origin. A paucity of symptoms should not dissuade the clinician from searching for an abscess, especially if an unexplained fever occurs in the appropriate clinical setting.

Objective

Physical Examination

Fever is almost universal in patients with abdominal abscesses. Tenderness elicited on abdominal or rectal examination often localizes the approximate site of the infection. Many patients have abdominal tenderness localized to the costal margins with a subphrenic abscess; the upper abdominal quadrants with hepatic, splenic, or pancreatic abscesses; or the lower abdominal quadrants with periappendiceal or peridiverticular abscesses. At times, the tenderness is more generalized, suggesting diffuse peritoneal irritation. Findings of a pleural effusion on physical examination may be present in conjunction with a subphrenic abscess. Jaundice may be present.

Routine Laboratory Abnormalities

Leukocytosis, with or without an increase in immature polymorphonuclear leukocytes, is common. Anemia may be present in patients with a

TABLE 8–21–1. INTRAABDOMINAL PYOGENIC ABSCESSES: CAUSATIVE FACTORS

Location	Causative Factors
Intraperitoneal	
Perihepatic, subphrenic, and subhepatic	Peritonitis, surgery (stomach, biliary, colon), localized infection (appendicitis), trauma (penetrating and blunt)
Lower abdomen	Peritonitis, surgery (pelvic, colon), localized infection (appendicitis, diverticulitis), trauma
Pelvic	Postpartum, after cesarean section, surgery (hysterectomy), pelvic inflammatory disease
Visceral	
Pancreatic	Pancreatitis (acute, chronic, postoperative)
Hepatic	Biliary infection (cholangitis), portal spread (pyelophlebitis), contiguous infection (gallbladder), hematogenous spread, trauma, amebiasis
Splenic	Trauma, sickle cell disease, bacteremia (endocarditis, salmonellosis)

chronic course. Elevation of liver tests, primarily alkaline phosphatase and at times bilirubin, occurs with intrahepatic abscesses or with an extrahepatic abscess that compromises biliary drainage. Similarly, the serum amylase level is elevated in approximately half of patients with a pancreatic abscess. Blood cultures are variably positive.

Abnormalities found on chest roentgenogram that suggest an abscess adjacent to the diaphragm include an elevated or immobile diaphragm, basilar atelectasis, lower lobe pulmonary infiltrates, and pleural effusion.

PLANS
Diagnostic
Differential Diagnosis

The diagnosis of abdominal abscesses is challenging; the differential diagnosis is broad and includes most causes of intraabdominal infection or inflammation. Peritonitis, hepatitis, cholecystitis, cholangitis, pancreatitis, appendicitis, diverticulitis, splenic infarction, pyelonephritis, and pelvic inflammatory disease are among the more common illnesses that may present similarly to intraabdominal abscesses.

Diagnostic Options

Radiographic and nuclear medicine techniques are helpful in confirming the clinical impression of localized intraabdominal infection. Abdominal flat and upright radiographs should be performed and may suggest a mass lesion by displacement of normal gas patterns in the area of an abscess.

A more specific and helpful approach to the detection of intraabdominal abscesses is the use of ultrasonography or CT. Each technique is able to detect cystic lesions in the abdomen suggestive of fluid-filled abscess cavities. Ultrasound evaluation of the abdomen may be hampered by excessive gas in the intestine in the case of an ileus, but it is accurate in evaluation of the liver and adjacent structures and the pelvis. Ultrasound is especially helpful in evaluating the gallbladder and the pelvis in female patients. In general, however, CT examination of the abdomen is the most helpful technique presently available for detecting an abscess. A definitive diagnosis can sometimes be made by percutaneous needle aspiration of the abscess directed by CT. By use of the CT scan, the presence of an abdominal abscess can be correctly determined in more than 90% of cases.

Other radioisotope scanning techniques such as liver scans, liver lung scans, hepato-iminodiacetic acid scans, endoscopic retrograde cholangiopancreatography, radiolabeled leukocyte indium scans, and gallium scans have been used to detect and localize intraabdominal abscesses, but the sensitivity and specificity of these techniques are less than those of ultrasonography and CT scanning. They are useful only occasionally. Contrast studies, including upper gastrointestinal series, barium enema, and intravenous pyelography, may demonstrate displacement of visceral structures from their normal positions or an intraluminal mass effect from an adjacent abscess. The results obtained by CT scanning and ultrasonography are usually more reliable than the results obtained by contract studies, and the use of the CT scan or ultrasound is preferred in most circumstances; however, contract studies may occasionally give helpful information not available from the other procedures. Consultation with a surgeon and radiologist is important to determine the most appropriate diagnostic approach. When evaluating the patient for biliary obstruction or pancreatic disease, hepato-iminodiacetic acid scans and/or endoscopic retrograde cholangiopancreatography are additional useful techniques.

Recommended Approach

If an abdominal abscess is suspected, a CT scan of the abdomen would be the preferred method of establishing the diagnosis.

Therapeutic
Therapeutic Options

As a general rule, all abdominal abscesses require proper drainage to achieve a cure. An exception to this rule is the hepatic abscess caused by *Entamoeba histolytica*. In the past, drainage has been achieved using direct surgical techniques, but more recently, a CT-directed percutaneous aspiration and catheter drainage have been useful in many cases, thereby obviating surgery. The type of drainage procedure should be decided in consultation with a radiologist and surgeon and depends on the location and type of abscess. Occasionally, as in the case of multiple small liver abscesses, adequate drainage is not practical, and appropriate, long-term, parenteral antibiotic therapy has been successful. Antibiotic therapy of abdominal abscesses also is important to attempt to prevent extension of the infection and to lessen the chance of abscess recurrence.

The empiric choice of antibiotic therapy should reflect the probable antibiotic susceptibility of the normal flora of the intestinal tract. As the majority of abdominal abscesses are polymicrobial, containing both aerobic and anaerobic bacteria (see Related Basic Science), initial antibiotic therapy appropriately consists of a drug or drugs effective against both anaerobic bacteria and enteric Gram-negative bacilli. Various regimens can be used. Clindamycin plus an aminoglycoside, such as gentamicin, in appropriate doses, gives broad empiric coverage. The choice of aminoglycoside should be based on whether the infection is hospital or community acquired and the overall likelihood of the presence of gentamicin-resistant enteric organisms in a hospital-acquired infection. Often, hospitalized patients have a greater likelihood of being colonized in the gastrointestinal tract with more resistant organisms than are patients who have not been in the hospital. In some instances, an aminoglycoside such as amikacin, which is less likely to be inactivated by hospital-acquired Gram-negative bacilli, may be appropriate. Other regimens may include metronidazole (an antibiotic effective against anaerobic organisms) plus an aminoglycoside or single-agent regimens using parenteral cefoxitin (Mefoxin), ceftizoxime (Cefizox), or imipenem–cilastin (Primaxin). Also effective are the combination beta-lactamase and beta-lactam agents such as ampicillin–sulbactam (Unasyn), ticarcillin–clavulanate (Timentin), and piperacillin–tazobactam (Zosyn). When multiple abscesses in a visceral organ are present, hematogenous spread from an extraabdominal source and infection with *Staphylococcus aureus* are likely, and a beta-lactamase-resistant penicillin (such as nafcillin) or a narrow-spectrum cephalosporin (such as cefazolin) may be used until culture results are obtained. For treatment of amebic abscess, see Chapter 8–58.

Recommended Approach

Because the cornerstone of the management of abscesses involves drainage, consultation with a surgeon and a radiologist is recommended to determine the most appropriate procedure for achieving adequate drainage. As discussed above, a number of empiric antimicrobial regimens are appropriate in the management of abdominal abscesses. Clindamycin 900 mg every 8 hours plus gentamicin 1.7 mg/kg administered every 8 hours, adjusted for renal function, provides adequate broad empiric coverage.

FOLLOW-UP

Because these infections are associated with a high degree of morbidity, close inpatient and, eventually, outpatient follow-up is necessary. One should be especially aware of the possibility of recurrence, often signaled by signs and symptoms similar to those of the original infection.

DISCUSSION
Prevalence and Incidence

As previously discussed, there are a myriad of potential etiologies of abdominal abscesses. Population-based studies investigating the overall incidence of abdominal abscesses have not been performed. Appendicitis is one of the more common antecedent medical conditions to abscess formation. Using this as an example, a California population-based study estimated the incidence rates for abscesses complicating appendicitis to be in the range 5 to 7 per 100,000 (Luckmann, 1989).

Related Basic Science

Abdominal abscesses, which can be solitary or multiple, can be divided into intraperitoneal and visceral infections. The route of spread and localization of infection for intraperitoneal abscesses is dependent on the normal anatomic relationships of the peritoneal folds and mesenteric attachments. Common areas of localization in the peritoneum are the perihepatic spaces, lumbar gutters, intramesenteric folds, and pelvic recesses. The subphrenic and subhepatic spaces, which can be divided into the right subphrenic space (anterior and posterior compartments), the right subhepatic space (superior and inferior compartments), the left subphrenic space, and the lesser sac, are particularly common sites for abscess formation. Localized lower quadrant abscesses may occur secondary to appendicitis or diverticulitis. Periappendiceal or peridiverticular abscesses are in general the most common intraabdominal abscesses because of the prevalence of appendicitis and diverticulitis in the population.

Visceral abscesses can localize in the liver, spleen, or pancreas. Intrahepatic or perihepatic abscesses are commonly associated with gallbladder infection or appendicitis, pancreatic abscesses are likely complications of a pancreatic pseudocyst, and splenic abscesses, although uncommon, may be found as a secondary, hematogenous extension of infection associated with bacterial endocarditis.

The bacteriology of intraabdominal abscesses varies with the source of infection. Most abscesses are polymicrobial and contain both aerobic and anaerobic organisms. The enteric Gram-negative bacilli, including *Escherichia coli* and the other Enterobacteriaceae, frequently have been implicated. In recent years, with improved anaerobic culture techniques, anaerobes have been found in as many as 80% of abdominal abscesses. *Bacteroides fragilis,* other *Bacteroides* species, clostridia, fusobacteria, and anaerobic Gram-positive cocci can be found regularly. At times, *Candida* species may be found, especially in abscesses related to the upper gastrointestinal tract.

In certain types of abscesses, especially those in the liver or spleen, aerobic and anaerobic streptococci and *Staphylococcus aureus* may be the offending organisms. *Entamoeba histolytica* is an important cause of liver abscess, especially in patients who have traveled to an endemic area such as Mexico.

It is necessary to obtain adequate specimens of pus for aerobic and anaerobic cultures and Gram stain at the time of drainage of an abdominal abscess so that, if necessary, empiric antibiotic therapy can be appropriately changed on the basis of the culture results. Obtaining a swab of pus only is inadequate, and it is best to obtain pus in a capped syringe or in anaerobic transport medium to send to the laboratory for culture. If amebic disease is a possibility, appropriate stains of abscess aspirates should be performed. In addition, an amebic serologic test will likely be a very helpful diagnostic tool.

Natural History and Its Modification with Treatment

A number of antecedent causative factors can be implicated in the development of an abdominal abscess (see Table 8–21–1). With intraperitoneal abscesses, prior surgery and penetrating abdominal trauma are major sources of the infection from which the abscess arises. Visceral abscesses may be secondary to hematogenous seeding (e.g., bacterial

endocarditis), spread from a contiguous infection such as cholecystitis, or spread from a more remote site in the abdomen. Numerous complications may arise, including local hemorrhage from erosion into blood vessels, intraabdominal spread with subsequent peritonitis and bacteremia, gastrointestinal bleeding, and often, a long, debilitating illness.

The mortality of abdominal abscesses without proper drainage is generally said to approach 100%. With prompt recognition and drainage, the mortality is still significant and may be as high as 25 to 60% depending on the type and location of the abscess and the overall condition of the patient. Some recent data suggest that in certain circumstances some hepatic abscesses may respond to medical therapy alone, without surgical drainage. Patients with amebic abscesses of the liver nearly always do well with appropriate medical therapy alone, if the condition is diagnosed early.

Prevention

The major steps in prevention of abdominal abscesses in recent years have been in the area of surgical technique and antibiotic prophylaxis during surgery. Early detection and drainage of the abscess may prevent death.

Cost Containment

Since the possibility of an intraabdominal abscess invariably leads to many diagnostic studies, drainage, and prolonged hospitalization, any measures that would decrease its incidence would be extremely cost effective. Appropriate antimicrobial prophylaxis for abdominal surgery is an important means of preventing postoperative infectious complications. Excellent surgical technique is even more important.

Once an intraabdominal abscess is suspected, carefully selecting the diagnostic procedures that are most likely to give an answer rather than blindly ordering many diagnostic studies may markedly reduce the cost.

REFERENCES

Altemeir WA, Culbertson WR, Fullen WD, et al. Intra-abdominal abscesses. Am J Surg 1973;25:70.
Gazelle GS, Mueller PR. Abdominal abscess: Imaging and intervention. Rad Clin North Am 1994;32:913.
Levison MA. Percutaneous versus operative drainage of intra-abdominal abscesses. Infect Dis Clin North Am 1992;6:525.
Lorber B, Swenson RM. The bacteriology of intra-abdominal infections. Surg Clin North Am 1975;55:1349.
Luckmann R. Incidence and case fatality rates for acute appendicitis in California: A population-based study of the effects of age. Am J Epidemiol 1989;129:905.
Nichols RL. Intra-abdominal infection: An overview. Rev Infect Dis 1985; 7(Suppl. 4):S709.
Sawyer MD, Dunn DL. Antimicrobial therapy of intraabdominal sepsis. Infect Dis Clin North Am 1992;6:545.

CHAPTER 8–22

Appendicitis

Clifford J. Gunthel, M.D., and Carl A. Perlino, M.D.

DEFINITION

Appendicitis is acute inflammation of the appendix giving rise to the clinical syndrome of abdominal pain and tenderness. Peritonitis, the extension of the inflammatory process into the general abdominal cavity, may ensue following the rupture of the inflamed appendix.

ETIOLOGY

Obstruction of the appendiceal lumen is the usual initial event in the development of appendicitis. This is commonly caused by a concretion or fecalith. Other etiologies include adhesions, strictures, parasites, lymphoid hyperplasia, and tumors.

CRITERIA FOR DIAGNOSIS
Suggestive

Appendicitis is an illness most appropriately cared for by a surgeon. Because the patient may first seek attention from his or her primary care provider, it is necessary for all clinicians to be aware of this disease and the problems of diagnosis and therapy.

Appendicitis can occur in any age group, but it is most common in the second and third decades of life. It affects previously healthy individuals, and apparently is not associated with other major predisposing factors. The diagnosis should be considered in any patient presenting with symptoms of anorexia, nausea or vomiting, and abdominal pain.

Definitive

The definitive diagnosis can be made only by surgical removal and pathologic examination of the appendix.

CLINICAL MANIFESTATIONS
Subjective

The patient commonly complains of the acute onset of diffuse abdominal pain, localized to the epigastric or periumbilical area of the abdomen. The pain is usually constant. Associated symptoms of anorexia and nausea are almost universal and most often occur with the onset of pain. Vomiting is a less common complaint, and many doctors feel that if vomiting antedates the onset of abdominal pain, a diagnosis other than appendicitis should be considered. Diarrhea or crampy abdominal pain, although occasionally seen with appendicitis, also should raise the suspicion of another disorder, such as infectious gastroenteritis.

Over a period of a few hours the pain of appendicitis migrates to the right lower quadrant, and the patient is often able to indicate a specific area to localize the pain (McBurney's point).

A history of increased intensity of pain in the right lower quadrant by jarring movements may be elicited. Occasional patients, those with a retrocecal appendix, may complain of right-sided flank pain rather than anterior abdominal pain. Painful micturition, due to ureteral irritation, may also accompany pelvic or retrocecal appendicitis.

Objective
Physical Examination

Tenderness on palpation and involuntary guarding in the right lower quadrant of the abdomen are the most common clinical signs of acute appendicitis. Localized rebound tenderness also can be demonstrated in individuals with local peritoneal inflammation. Diffuse abdominal tenderness with rebound should suggest the complication of generalized peritonitis secondary to perforation or gangrene of the appendix. Occasionally, a mass effect in the right lower quadrant can be demonstrated by palpation of the abdomen in patients with local abscess formation.

Rectal and, in women, pelvic examinations demonstrate localization of tenderness to the right side of the pelvis. Bowel sounds are heard in most patients with acute, nonperforating appendicitis, and the absence of bowel sounds indicates diffuse peritonitis.

Fever is common, but the presence or severity of fever does not correlate with the presence or absence of appendicitis. A high body temperature (>39°C) accompanied by true rigors is uncommon in appendicitis unless diffuse peritonitis has occurred.

The pulse rate may be elevated. This finding is nonspecific and reflects patient agitation, dehydration, and fever, as well as appendicitis. The rate may be greater than 100 in patients with peritonitis, but it is not a particularly helpful finding unless accompanied by other signs of this complication.

Routine Laboratory Abnormalities

The white blood count is usually elevated in patients with appendicitis, most commonly to 13,000 to 15,000/µL. Higher counts may be indicative of a ruptured appendix with diffuse peritonitis. The range of white blood counts is wide, however, and the count may be normal.

A urinalysis may show greater than five leukocytes per high-power microscope field in patients with documented appendicitis, but this is not particularly helpful in establishing the diagnosis. Pyuria and hematuria due to ureteral irritation may be clues to pelvic or retrocecal appendicitis. An abnormal urinalysis may, however, indicate an infection of the urinary tract as a cause of the abdominal pain and should lead to appropriate evaluation.

The chest radiograph is important to determine whether lower lobe pneumonia may be the cause of the presenting abdominal symptoms.

PLANS
Diagnostic
Differential Diagnosis

The differential diagnosis of appendicitis includes pancreatitis, cholecystitis, salpingitis, infectious gastroenteritis, inflammatory bowel disease, and mesenteric adenitis. The diagnosis of appendicitis is made primarily using the history and physical examination. If the initial evaluation of the patient is uncertain, or if the history suggests another of these diagnoses, obtaining a serum amylase level or an abdominal ultrasound with attention to the area of the gallbladder may be helpful. A pelvic examination also is indicated to evaluate the possibility of pelvic inflammatory disease. Occasionally, computed tomography scanning may be extremely helpful in the detection of a retroperitoneal appendicitis.

Diagnostic Options

When appendicitis is suspected, the patient should be referred to a surgeon as soon as possible for evaluation and treatment. Occasionally, abdominal flat and upright radiographs may aid in the diagnosis and should be obtained. Findings suggestive of appendicitis include psoas obliteration, scoliosis to the right, a fecalith in the area of the appendix, and air–fluid levels localized to the right lower quadrant. In some studies, lower abdominal and/or pelvic ultrasound has helped in the diagnosis.

A short period of observation may be recommended by the surgeon to help differentiate between appendicitis and other possible diagnoses if the diagnosis is uncertain. The patient is given intravenous fluids, nothing by mouth, and repeat blood leukocyte counts and physical examinations are performed. An increasing leukocyte count or worsening of symptoms would be an indication for surgery. Following this approach, occasional patients show resolution of symptoms and signs of the abdominal problem, thus avoiding unnecessary surgery.

Therapeutic
Therapeutic Options

The treatment of choice for appendicitis is surgical removal of the appendix. Newer surgical techniques such as laproscopic appendectomy appear to be of benefit, resulting in less postoperative discomfort and decreased time of hospitalization.

If perforation or rupture of the appendix is suspected, such as in elderly patients (where this complication is common) or in patients with clinical signs of peritonitis, concomitant antibiotic therapy should be given. Antibiotics effective against the likely bacterial flora of the normal large intestine, such as cefoxitin (Mefoxin), a combination such as cefazolin (Ancef, Kefzol) plus metronidazole (Flagyl), or a combination β-lactam and β-lactamase agent such as ampicillin–sulbactam (Unasyn), are appropriate.

The use of antibiotics for patients with acute appendicitis in which perforation is not suspected is somewhat controversial. In this case, the surgical procedure is considered curative and antibiotic therapy unnecessary; however, some authors have shown a decrease in surgical wound infections in patients undergoing appendectomy for nonperforated appendicitis with the use of preoperative antibiotics. Also, the diagnosis of perforated appendicitis cannot be made clinically with absolute accuracy, and it is reasonable to give antibiotics immediately prior to surgery in all patients and continue them postoperatively only if perforation and peritonitis are found at surgery.

Intravenous fluids are a necessary adjunct to the surgical therapy of appendicitis.

Recommended Approach

If acute appendicitis is suspected, a prompt surgical consultation should be obtained. Once the decision to intervene surgically has been made, the medical management preoperatively includes the administration of antibiotics immediately prior to surgery. Reasonable regimens include cefoxitin 1 g intravenously or cefazolin 1 g plus metronidazole 900 mg intravenously. Postoperatively, these antibiotics should be continued only if perforation and peritonitis are discovered during surgery.

FOLLOW-UP

Depending on the progress of the patient after surgery and the need for parenteral antibiotics, the hospital stay of the patient may range from a few days to 1 to 2 weeks. During this time, the presence of fever, complaints of abdominal pain, the appearance and duration of ileus and abdominal distention, abdominal tenderness, and the appearance of the surgical wound should be assessed. Recovery is heralded by the disappearance of fever and abdominal pain and the return of the blood leukocyte count to normal. A desire to eat and the return of normal bowel function are expected early in the uncomplicated convalescence.

On discharge, the patient should be instructed to observe the wound for erythema, swelling, tenderness, or discharge and to seek medical care if fever or abdominal pain recurs. A postoperative visit should be scheduled after discharge, and subsequent evaluation will depend on the progress of the patient.

DISCUSSION
Prevalence and Incidence

Acute appendicitis is the most common cause of the acute, nontraumatic, surgical abdomen. The overall incidence of appendicitis is approximately 1.1 per 1000 population. Appendicitis occurs in any age group, but the highest incidence rates are observed in persons in their teens and early twenties. In this age group, acute appendicitis is more prevalent in men than in women. Conversely, the disease is more likely to occur in women in older, adult-aged groups. Appendectomy is one of the most frequently performed surgical procedures in the United States. Interestingly, declining rates of appendicitis have been reported from industrialized countries in recent years. The reason for this is uncertain, but may be related to changes in diet and increased use of antibiotics.

Related Basic Science

Appendicitis usually occurs because of obstruction of the appendiceal lumen with a hard, dried collection of stool, or fecalith, which becomes calcified and can be demonstrated occasionally by abdominal radiographs. The obstruction causes collection of mucus in the appendiceal lumen, swelling of the appendix, edema due to venous and lymphatic obstruction, and, finally, necrosis due to arteriolar obstruction. Invasion of the appendiceal wall by normal bowel organisms then occurs. Rupture may follow with subsequent local peritoneal inflammation or diffuse peritonitis. The most common bacteria involved are *Bacteroides fragilis*, *Escherichia coli*, and other intestinal coliforms.

Natural History and Its Modification with Treatment

Perforation of the appendix with subsequent local or diffuse peritoneal inflammation occurs in approximately 20% of patients with acute appendicitis and is more commonly found in elderly patients and in those who seek medical attention later in the course of their disease. Patients with perforated appendicitis are more likely to incur complications of therapy, such as postoperative wound infection and formation of abdominal abscesses.

Mortality in acute appendicitis is less than 1% and is more likely to occur in patients who have perforation and in those over 60 years of age.

Prevention

No preventive measures are apparently available. Epidemiologic population studies do suggest that a lifelong increased intake of dietary fiber may decrease the incidence of this disease.

Cost Containment

The use of appropriate antibiotics beginning immediately prior to surgery may well decrease the incidence of subsequent postoperative complications.

REFERENCES

Addiss DG, Shaffer N, Fowler BS, et al. The epidemiology of appendicitis and appendectomy in the United States. Am J Epidemiol 1990;132:910.
Lewis FR, Holcroft JW, Boey J, et al. Appendicitis: A critical review of diagnosis and treatment in 1000 cases. Arch Surg 1975;110:677.
Sherman R. Abdominal pain. In: Walker KE, Hall D, Hurst JW, eds. Clinical methods: The history, physical, and laboratory examination. 3rd ed. Reading, MA: Butterworths, 1986.
Silen W. Appendicitis. In Silen W, ed. Copes' early diagnosis of the acute abdomen. 18th ed. New York: Oxford University Press, 1991:67.
Silen ML, Tracy TR Jr. The right lower quadrant "revisited." Pediat Clin North Am 1993;40:1201
Williamson WA, Bush RD, Williams LF Jr. Retrocecal appendicitis. Am J Surg 1981;141:507.

CHAPTER 8–23
Urinary Tract Infections

James W. Smith, M.D.

DEFINITION

Urinary tract infection is defined as a combination of clinical symptoms along with a significant number of viable microorganisms in urine obtained in an aseptic manner. Patients with urinary tract infections constitute a wide clinical spectrum, from lower tract symptoms with dysuria and frequency or cloudy urine to invasive infection of the kidney with a septic picture.

ETIOLOGY

Urinary tract infections in women at any decade of life and in men over the age of 50 are generally caused by *Escherichia coli*. Patients who have indwelling catheters, however, are at risk of acquiring very resistant Gram-negative organisms, including *Pseudomonas aeruginosa*.

Gram-positive organisms rarely cause infection, although *Staphylococcus saprophyticus* and *Enterococcus* may occur alone or *Enterococcus* may be associated with Gram-negative organisms. Infection with *Candida* species follows in the wake of treatment of standard pathogens.

CRITERIA FOR DIAGNOSIS
Suggestive

The factors responsible for significant morbidity are listed in Table 8–23–1. Both women and men with burning on urination (dysuria) and urinary frequency would be suspected of having urinary tract infection, but many other conditions, such as sexually transmitted diseases and nonspecific vaginitis in women and urethritis and prostatitis in men, may present with the same symptoms.

TABLE 8–23–1. FACTORS RESPONSIBLE FOR SIGNIFICANT MORBIDITY WITH URINARY TRACT INFECTION

Congenital urinary tract anomalies
Infants younger than 6 with severe reflux
Analgesic nephropathy
Obstruction with indwelling catheters
Struvite stone formation with urea-splitting bacteria
Pregnancy

Definitive

The presence of clinical symptoms including fever and urinary dysfunction along with significant pyuria (see Chapter 16–6) and bacteriuria is required for a definitive diagnosis.

CLINICAL MANIFESTATIONS
Subjective

Urinary tract infections are among the most frequent symptomatic infections in women and a secondary event in persons with indwelling catheters who are admitted to hospitals. Certain individuals are also predisposed on the basis of genetic defects; these are particularly devastating in young males born with genetic abnormalities of the urinary tract, who frequently die secondary to progressive urinary tract infection in the first year of life. History of previous occurrences is frequently obtained.

Symptomatic urinary tract infections are notably associated with dysuria (pain on voiding) and frequency of voiding. The urine is frequently cloudy and rarely may be dark with blood plainly visible. Other symptoms include temperature elevations above 38°C, lower back pain, and unilateral or bilateral costovertebral pain, representing referred pain from inflammation of the kidney. Patients, particularly those at the extremes of life, also may present with gastrointestinal symptoms, including nausea, vomiting, and diarrhea. In a small proportion, urinary output may be decreased in patients who are septic or in those who have an obstructed indwelling catheter.

Objective
Physical Examination

The physical examination may be entirely normal in some, approximately one half will have suprapubic tenderness, and a smaller proportion will have pain in the costovertebral angle with fist percussion. Patients who have perinephric abscesses may present with a bulging flank due to enlargement of the kidney, particularly when symptoms have been present for weeks.

Routine Laboratory Abnormalities

The major laboratory clue is the presence of pyuria and bacteriuria. A positive urine leukocyte esterase (dipstick) test or urine slide examination showing more than 20 white blood cells per high-power field is sufficiently predictive of infection to institute therapy. Urinary tract infection can also be suspected if the urine nitrite test is positive or unstained sediment or urine shows 10 organisms per high-power field. This correlates with the presence of 10^5 or more bacteria per milliliter of urine. The peripheral white blood cell count also may be elevated with left shift, but this is an inconstant finding.

PLANS
Diagnostic
Differential Diagnosis

Women who present with dysuria and frequency should be examined for possibility of vaginitis; if vaginal discharge is present with pyuria, gonococcal or chlamydial infection must be considered. Men with prostatitis may present with pyuria and frequency, so evaluation of prostate is needed with culture of terminal portion of the urine.

Diagnostic Options and Recommended Approach

If the patient has no vaginal discharge and has internal dysuria (felt to be inside the body), then a urinalysis should be obtained and therapy prescribed if pyuria is present. A small proportion of women with pyuria will have a low count in the urine ($10^2 - 10^3$ bacteria/mL), so therapy can be offered without culture. If the patient is febrile, a clean voided midstream urine and blood cultures should be obtained, as a positive culture will provide meaningful information on duration and type of therapy. Further diagnostic studies, such as intravenous pyelogram, are not indicated for the usual patient with urinary tract infection. If, however, the patient continues to be febrile after therapy is administered for 3 days or longer, then ultrasonographic examination of the kidney for possible perinephric or intrarenal abscess should be performed. If this is abnormal but not diagnostic, then computed tomography can be used.

Therapeutic

If the person is only mildly symptomatic with absent or low-grade fever, then a 3-day course of two tablets of trimethoprim–sulfamethoxazole twice daily is effective in treating most women. The efficacy of trimethoprim–sulfamethoxazole exceeds that of ampicillin and oral cephalosporins. Only a select number of patients need a longer 7-day course of therapy, including women with diabetes, those with recurrent infection, and those who are elderly. Pregnant women can be treated with ampicillin or nitrofurantoin. If the patients are allergic to sulfonamides or have a resistant organism, then a quinolone such as ciprofloxacin 500 mg twice daily, ofloxacin 400 mg twice daily, or lomofloxacin 400 mg daily can be given. As men more frequently have a relapse of their upper urinary tract infections, a 2- to 3-week course with an effective oral agent is indicated with close follow-up. Symptomatic patients with significant temperature elevation and difficulty retaining fluids should be admitted to the hospital and administered parenteral antibiotics. The preferred initial treatment for women with significant infection is trimethoprim (160 mg/kg)–sulfamethoxazole (800 mg/kg) every 8 hours combined with an aminoglycoside such as gentamicin (3.0 mg/kg every 24 hours, adjusted for renal function abnormalities). This combination, generally effective against *E. coli,* is more effective in eradicating the organism from the kidney. Alternative therapy is with ceftriaxone 2 g daily or intravenous ciprofloxacin 400 mg every 12 hours. Parenteral antibiotics should be administered until patients have been afebrile for 24 to 48 hours. Then they can be switched to an oral agent such as trimethoprim–sulfamethoxazole or a quinolone given for the remainder of a 14-day treatment course. For patients who relapse within 1 month of treatment, a 2-week course with an oral agent is indicated. Patients who have a recurrent infection more than 1 month after therapy are treated as described above.

The rare patient who has persistence of fever after 3 days of therapy and is shown to have a perinephric abscess should have drainage either by a needle-directed aspiration using computed tomography or with an operative procedure. Occasionally, an intrarenal process, termed *nephronia,* can be demonstrated by ultrasonography in patients who continue to be febrile. This condition responds to combination therapy with an appropriate antibiotic and an aminoglycoside, which is continued 2 to 4 weeks parenterally after clinical response.

FOLLOW-UP

If the patient is treated as an outpatient, it is not necessary to see the patient after therapy is instituted if he or she responds satisfactorily. If patients relapse, urine culture can be obtained and therapy adjusted to an appropriate agent. For hospitalized patients, it is preferable to repeat a urine culture after 2 or 3 days of therapy, if symptoms persist. A post-treatment follow-up culture can be obtained at 2 weeks.

DISCUSSION
Prevalence

The exact prevalence of urinary tract infection is higher in women at all ages, particularly from twenty to forty years with up to one-third of all women having a urinary tract infection at some time; after forty, men have an increasing rate of urinary infection but at one-tenth the rate of women.

Related Basic Science

Women with a propensity for frequent urinary tract infections have been shown to have organisms adherent to vaginal epithelial cells that enter the bladder following transient obstruction, as with sexual intercourse, especially with use of a diaphragm. The increased risk for men relates to the decrease in ability to empty the bladder completely because of mild or moderate prostatic obstruction. Urinary tract organisms causing lower tract infections tend to have a P Fimbial genotype, a hemolysin phenotype, and an adhesion determinant, which promote the binding of *E. coli* to urinary epithelium cells. The organisms found responsible for upper tract infection belong to particular O and K serotypes, which adhere to uroepithelium and kidney cells. A significant host response with production of local antibody occurs with kidney infection. This antibody attaches to bacteria in urinary sediment (positive antibody-coated bacteria) and may be responsible for a decrease in clinical symptomatology noted with recurrent infections. Hence, patients with chronic upper urinary tract infections may have minimal symptoms, whereas individuals with their first-time infection will have significant signs of inflammation.

Natural History and Its Modification with Treatment

The factors responsible for the morbidity of urinary tract infection are listed in Table 8–23–1. Most individuals with urinary tract infections respond promptly to appropriate antimicrobial therapy. Very few of these individuals develop progressive renal failure or die, save those who develop septic shock, such as with severe obstructive disease or a perinephric abscess that is not recognized. Recurrent urinary tract infection occurs in up to one third of women and a majority of men. Some develop high blood pressure, but few will have any evidence of renal function abnormality. Even bacteriuria in the elderly residents of nursing facilities is not associated with increased mortality. Recurrent infections in association with urea-forming organisms such as *Proteus mirabilis* can lead to kidney stones, so these persons should be followed closely and given long-term suppressive therapy. Progressive renal failure or death due to complications of an infection occurred in association with interstitial nephritis following ingestion of phenacetin.

Prevention

Patients who have recurrent infections (two or more every 6 months) or those patients who relapse within 1 month of therapy should receive either nitrofurantoin (50 mg) or trimethoprim–sulfamethoxazole ($\frac{1}{2}$ tablet) every other day for a period. If infections recur after discontinuing the drug, this therapy can be given indefinitely. Alternatively, therapy with any of the two above-mentioned drugs on the morning after sexual intercourse has been highly effective in preventing recurrences in women. Pregnant women with bacteriuria can be given nitrofurantoin daily until the termination of pregnancy to prevent infections, which might lead to prematurity or low birth weight. Postmenopausal women not on estrogen will have reduced frequency of urinary tract infection if

given intravaginal estrogens. Cranberry juice also may prevent urinary tract infection as it prevents bacteria from adhering to epithelial cells. Men with recurrent symptomatic urinary tract infections need to be treated continuously, alternating daily administration of the above two drugs every 6 months, which will prevent significant side effects.

There is no indication for urethral dilation or surgical manipulation. Recurrent urologic procedures may place the patient at risk of introducing resistant bacteria, which may be extremely difficult to eradicate. Urinary surgery is indicated only for individuals with severe anatomic defects, such as male children under 1 year of age. In the adult, the presence of reflux does not correlate with clinical course of urinary tract infections, so diversionary procedures are not indicated.

No preventive therapy is indicated for patients with indwelling urinary catheterization. It is preferable to train patients to do in-and-out catheterization, as these patients have a lower likelihood of symptomatic urinary tract infections. Patients who have indwelling catheters should maintain adequate urine flow through oral intake of fluids. Catheter changes are required only when sediment increases in quantity. Although urinary tract infection frequently recurs in those who have ileal diversion procedures, there is no benefit that accrues with preventive therapy in these individuals. Hence, for both these situations, treatment of the symptomatic infection only is indicated.

Cost Containment

The most cost-effective treatment, trimethoprim–sulfamethoxazole, is also useful as an antimicrobial prophylactic agent when episodes are more frequent than twice yearly. Oral quinolones can be given if the person is allergic to sulfonamides and if the organism is resistant to the first-line agent, as they are less expensive than parenteral agents. Any number of parenteral drugs are effective, but the lease expensive and most efficacious therapy is a combination of trimethoprim–sulfamethoxazole and gentamicin. More expensive drugs, such as amikacin and imipenem, would be used only in patients with indwelling catheters or recurrent infections who acquire gentamicin-resistant organisms in the hospital. Home instruction or nursing home instruction of patients to use in-and-out catheterization rather than indwelling catheters is highly cost-effective and will prevent severe clinical occurrences.

REFERENCES

Nicolle LE, Henderson E, Bjornson J, et al. The association of bacteriuria with resident characteristics and survival in elderly institutionalized men. Ann Intern Med 1987;106:682.
Ronald AR. Current concepts in the management of urinary tract infections in adults. Med Clin North Am 1984;68:335.
Smith JW. Southwestern internal medicine conference: Prognosis in pyelonephritis: Promise or progress? Am J Med Sci 1989;296:53.
Stamm WE, Hooton TM. Management of urinary tract infection in adults. N Engl J Med 1993;329:1328.
Stapleton M, Moseley S, Stamm WE. Urovirulence determinants in *Escherichia coli* isolates causing first-episode and recurrent cystitis in women. J Infect Dis 1991;163:773.

CHAPTER 8–24

Urethritis

Kimberly A. Workowski, M.D., Thomas M. Hooton, M.D., and Walter E. Stamm, M.D.

DEFINITION

Urethritis, or inflammation of the urethra, is almost always caused by a sexually transmitted pathogen. The diagnosis of urethritis in a male is suggested by a urethral discharge and manifested by urethral leukocytosis on microscopy or pyuria in a first-voided urinary sediment. Urethritis in a woman is manifested by pyuria and a urine culture negative for uropathogens.

ETIOLOGY

Urethritis can be divided into gonococcal and nongonococcal urethritis. Gonococcal urethritis is diagnosed when *Neisseria gonorrhoeae* is identified in culture. Nongonococcal urethritis (NGU) is diagnosed when urethritis is present without detection of the gonococcus. *Chlamydia trachomatis* and *Ureaplasma urealyticum* are the most frequent pathogens isolated in nongonococcal urethritis. Additional organisms associated with NGU include *Mycoplasma genitalium, Trichomonas vaginalis,* and herpes simplex virus. In approximately one third of the NGU cases, no recognized pathogens are identified. In homosexual men who practice insertive rectal intercourse, and in some heterosexual men, coliform bacteria may cause urethritis and cystitis.

CRITERIA FOR DIAGNOSIS
Suggestive

A careful sexual history often reveals recent unprotected sexual exposure. Urethritis should be considered when urethral discharge, dysuria, or meatal pruritus is evident. Perineal pain, urinary frequency and urgency, hematuria, and chills or fever are infrequent. Gonococcal urethritis is usually purulent and develops 2 to 6 days after sexual exposure. NGU tends to manifest as a mucoid discharge or meatal crusting, and has a longer incubation period of 2 to 3 weeks. Inguinal adenopathy and constitutional symptoms suggest herpes simplex infection. Additionally, asymptomatic infections should be considered in the male partners of women with cervicitis and pelvic inflammatory disease and in female partners of men with urethritis.

Definitive

The diagnosis of urethritis is established by a urethral discharge or dysuria and objective evidence of urethritis (urethral leukocytosis in urethral Gram stain or first-voided urine specimen).

CLINICAL MANIFESTATIONS
Subjective

Most men with urethritis complain of urethral discharge, dysuria, or meatal pruritus. Men with NGU may have vague symptomatology of long duration and a thin mucoid discharge that may not be noticeable after the first morning urination; however, these clinical features cannot be relied on to distinguish between gonococcal and nongonococcal urethritis. Additionally, urethritis is often asymptomatic in men, especially in sexual contacts. Symptoms in women are often indistinguishable from those associated with simple cystitis including dysuria but not hematuria or suprapubic pain. These symptoms are often milder and of longer duration than in cystitis. Patients of either sex often give a history of recent sexual contact with a new partner.

Objective
Physical Examination

Urethral discharge and leukocytosis are typically more obvious in the early morning before first urination, especially with NGU, and this is often the best time to make a diagnosis. Recent urination may result in a falsely negative examination for discharge and urethral leukocytosis, but this has little effect on culture results. Discharge may be apparent only after stripping of the penis from the base to the meatus several times. A urethral specimen is obtained by insertion of a thin urogenital swab into the urethral meatus. The swab is rolled over a glass slide which is Gram stained and examined for leukocytosis. Women with urethritis rarely exhibit any spontaneous or expressible urethral discharge. Urethritis associated with herpes simplex infection is usually accompanied by external genital lesions. Urethritis due to *Trichomonas* should be considered in men with urethral symptoms with minimal urethral discharge.

Routine Laboratory Abnormalities

Leukocytes may be found in the spun urine specimen. Hematuria is usually absent. The urethral swab is very valuable and is discussed in Diagnostic Options.

PLANS
Diagnostic
Differential Diagnosis

The majority of cases of urethritis are secondary to a sexually transmitted disease; however, urethritis can occur in association with prostatitis,

urinary tract infection, urethral stricture, urinary catheterization, chemical irritation, Reiter's syndrome, cervicitis, or Stevens–Johnson syndrome.

Diagnostic Options

Urethral leukocytosis is defined as the presence of an average of five or more polymorphonuclear cells (PMNs) among three to five 1000× fields in a Gram-stained urethral swab specimen or 15 or more PMNs in any of five randomly selected 400× fields in the spun sediment of a 5- to 10-mL first-voided urine specimen. Men with urethritis also can be identified on the basis of a positive leukocyte esterase test on first-voided urine. Urethral leukocytosis without evidence of intracellular Gram-negative diplococci is consistent with NGU. Objective findings of urethritis in women include 10 or more PMNs per 1000× field on a Gram stained urethral smear or the presence of sterile pyuria.

The distinction between a gonococcal and nongonococcal etiology can usually be made accurately in symptomatic men by examination of the urethral Gram stain for evidence of typical intracellular Gram-negative diplococci. The presence of such organisms is highly specific and sufficient to diagnose gonorrhea, whereas their absence allows one to exclude gonorrhea reliably. Urethral cultures for *N. gonorrhoeae* are necessary when organisms have atypical morphology, when typically appearing organisms are found only extracellularly, and when the patient is asymptomatic (Gram stain sensitivity, 60%). A chlamydial etiology of urethritis can be established by culture, direct antigen tests, genetic probes, or by an automated polymerase chain reaction. Recent documentation of the excellent sensitivity and specificity of polymerase chain reaction enhances our ability to detect *C. trachomatis*. It is not warranted to culture routinely for *U. urealyticum,* as this organism is highly prevalent in normal males and culture results in the individual patient are not meaningful. A cell culture for herpes simplex virus should be obtained in individuals who have severe dysuria, regional adenopathy, genital ulcers or vesicles, and constitutional symptoms. Mild urethral leukocytosis in the absence of symptoms and discharge may warrant an early-morning reevaluation within a few days. Cystitis must be considered in a man with dysuria and pyuria that is not associated with urethral discharge or urethral leukocytosis. A culture of midstream urine is indicated in such cases.

Diagnostic criteria are less well established in a woman with urethritis. Urethral discharge is specific but not sensitive. Although it has been reported that 10 or more PMNs per 1000× field in a Gram-stained urethral specimen is diagnostic, the sensitivity and specificity of this test are unknown. As such, a urethral Gram stain is not generally recommended as a routine procedure in the evaluation for urethritis in women. The diagnosis is usually made in sexually active women who present with dysuria and sterile pyuria in whom *N. gonorrhoeae* or *C. trachomatis* is isolated from the urethra and/or cervix. The presence of coexistent sexually transmitted infections such as bartholinitis, mucopurulent cervicitis, and proctitis, and the absence of hematuria and suprapubic tenderness favor a diagnosis of urethritis.

It is important to recognize that patients of either sex may have urethral infection with *N. gonorrhoeae* or *C. trachomatis* in the absence of symptoms or objective evidence of urethritis. This situation often applies when contacts of infected persons are examined. Urethritis due to these pathogens is often accompanied by infection at other exposed sites, such as the cervix or rectum, and culture of such sites may be indicated.

Recommended Approach

The presence of urethritis is established by an observable urethral discharge and Gram stain or first-voided urine leukocytosis. Urethral swabs are inserted 2 to 4 cm into the urethral meatus for *C. trachomatis* and *N. gonorrhoeae* cultures. The urethral Gram stain is examined for evidence of *N. gonorrhoeae*. Culture for the gonococcus is indicated even if the organism is identified on the Gram stain so that antibiotic susceptibility testing can be performed. If the patient is symptomatic and the urethral Gram stain is equivocal, a first-voided urine specimen should be obtained to look for leukocytosis. As gonorrhea and chlamydial infections may be present without direct evidence of urethral inflammation, cultures are indicated in individuals at high risk of infection. If gonococcal infection is detected by Gram stain, treatment for gonorrhea as well as chlamydia is warranted due to the possibility of dual infection. If there is no evidence of gonococcal infection on Gram stain, therapy for NGU is initiated. An integral part of the management is to ensure that partners are also evaluated and treated.

Therapeutic

Therapeutic Options

Penicillin is no longer recommended for empiric treatment of gonorrhea because of the spread of infections caused by penicillin-resistant strains. Recommended gonococcal regimens include single-dose therapy with either ceftriaxone, cefixime, ciprofloxacin, or ofloxacin. There has been emergence of tetracycline resistance in the United States and other countries; therefore, tetracycline alone is not a recommended regimen. Erythromycin also is less effective than other regimens for the treatment of gonorrhea and should not be used alone in this condition. *Chlamydia trachomatis* can be isolated from the urethra in 20 to 30% of men with urethral gonorrhea and often results in postgonococcal urethritis if therapy does not include an effective antichlamydial regimen. Doxycycline, azithromycin, or ofloxacin are acceptable therapeutic regimens for *C. trachomatis* infections. Both *C. trachomatis* and *U. urealyticum* usually respond well to the tetracycline and erythromycin classes of antibiotics; however, tetracycline-resistant *Ureaplasma* strains have increased in occurrence and require treatment with erythromycin.

Recommended Approach for Gonococcal Urethritis

General. Treatment comprises the use of ceftriaxone (125–250 mg intramuscularly), plus one of the following chlamydial regimens—doxycycline (100 mg orally twice daily for 7 days), or azithromycin (1 g orally once), erythromycin base (500 mg orally four times daily for 7 days), or erythromycin ethylsuccinate (800 mg orally four times daily for 7 days).

Alternative Regimens. Ciprofloxacin 500 mg orally once, ofloxacin 400 mg orally once, cefixime 400 mg orally once, ceftizoxime 500 mg intramuscularly once, and spectinomycin 2.0 g intramuscularly are alternative regimens. All of these regimens should be followed with an antichlamydial regimen.

Adolescents. Quinolones such as ciprofloxacin and ofloxacin should not be used in patients less than 16 years of age.

Pregnancy. Ciprofloxacin and ofloxacin are contraindicated and erythromycin ethylsuccinate or base rather than a tetracycline should be used as the antichlamydial regimen.

Penicillin-allergic Patients. Spectinomycin (2.0 g intramuscularly) or a quinolone, such as ciprofloxacin (500 mg orally once) or ofloxacin (400 mg orally once), is followed by an antichlamydial regimen.

Treatment of Sex Partners. All sexual contacts within the last 30 days of heterosexual persons with gonococcal urethritis should be examined, cultured at all exposed sites *(N. gonorrhoeae, C. trachomatis),* and treated with one of the regimens effective against both *N. gonorrhoeae* and *C. trachomatis*. Contacts of homosexual men should be examined, cultured, and treated with an antigonococcal regimen.

Treatment Failure. Individuals who fail on treatment should be given ceftriaxone (125–250 mg intramuscularly), followed by an antichlamydial regimen. Many "treatment failures" are actually reinfections and indicate a need for improved sex partner referral and patient education.

Special Considerations. All patients with gonorrhea should have a serologic test for syphilis and be offered HIV testing.

Recommended Approach for Nongonococcal Urethritis

Treatment consists of doxycycline (100 mg orally twice daily for 7 days), azithromycin (1 g orally once), erythromycin base or erythromycin stearate (500 mg orally four times daily for 7 days), or erythromycin ethylsuccinate (800 mg orally four times daily for 7 days). If high-dose erythromycin schedules are not tolerated, any of the erythromycin regimens listed at half the dosage orally four times daily for 14 days is recommended.

Pregnancy. Either erythromycin base or erythromycin ethylsuccinate is recommended.

Treatment of Sex Partners. All sexual contacts within the last 30 days should be examined, cultured at all exposed sites *(N. gonorrhoeae, C. trachomatis),* and treated with an antichlamydial regimen.

Treatment Failure. As many as 50% of men with NGU from whom neither *C. trachomatis* nor *U. urealyticum* is isolated will have persistent or recurrent urethritis within 6 weeks of initial treatment. If *C. trachomatis* is initially isolated, approximately one fifth of men will not be cured at 6 weeks. If posttreatment urethritis is documented, and if reinfection or poor compliance in taking medications appears to be the reason for treatment failure, the patient should be retreated with doxycycline. If there is no apparent explanation for the treatment failure, one of the listed erythromycin regimens or azithromycin should be tried, as tetracycline-resistant *U. urealyticum* is known to cause some of these infections.

Persistent urethritis after re-treatment necessitates a thorough workup to determine whether less common etiologic pathogens, such as *Trichomonas vaginalis* and herpes simplex are present. In such patients, cultures for *C. trachomatis* are almost always negative and those for *U. urealyticum* are only occasionally positive. The penis should be carefully palpated for foreign bodies or other urethral abnormalities. The role of evaluation of the prostate in men with persistent urethritis has not been established. The majority of these men with persistent urethritis have prostatic fluid leukocytosis, but it is uncertain whether the two conditions are causally associated or whether the presence of prostatitis affects therapeutic outcome. Likewise, the role of urethroscopy is unclear, and has no proven benefit in patient management. Although supportive data are lacking, patients with persistent urethritis are often given therapeutic trials of doxycycline, erythromycin, or trimethoprim–sulfamethoxazole for several weeks. A 3-week regimen of erythromycin, compared with placebo, appears to result in objective improvement, at least in men with prostatic inflammation. Most patients' symptoms and signs resolve over a period of weeks or months, although they occasionally recur months later. Examination of steady sex partners who have been appropriately treated as contacts is usually unrewarding, and re-treatment is not indicated unless cultures warrant. It is unclear whether a comparable syndrome develops in women treated for urethritis. Patients should be told that their infection is sexually transmitted and that their partner or partners have a high likelihood of harboring the causative agent, often as an asymptomatic infection. Gonorrhea can be found in 80% of female sexual partners and chlamydial infection in 45 to 75% of female sex partners of men with gonococcal or chlamydial urethritis. Likewise, male contacts of women with genital gonococcal or chlamydial infection harbor urethral gonococci or chlamydia in approximately 75 and 50% of cases, respectively. Female patients should be warned of the significant risk of developing pelvic inflammatory disease and its long-term sequelae of infertility, ectopic pregnancy, and chronic pelvic pain if they are not appropriately treated.

All sexual contacts should be advised to visit their health care provider for an examination, have gonorrhea and chlamydia cultures obtained of all exposed sites, and be provided a therapeutic regimen comparable to that used in the patient. The patient should abstain from sex until the patient's and partner's treatment regimens and follow-up have been completed. If it is not possible or practical to abstain, condoms are probably protective if used properly.

FOLLOW-UP

Failure of treatment of gonococcal urethritis following a regimen of ceftriaxone and doxycycline is rare; therefore, a test of cure is not essential. Patients with persistent symptoms following treatment should return for examination. Patients with gonococcal urethritis who have not been treated with a recommended therapeutic regimen should return for a test of cure 4 to 7 days after the last dose of antimicrobial agents, whether or not symptoms persist. All previously infected sites should be cultured. All such women should have rectal cultures for *N.*

gonorrhoeae obtained at follow-up, as up to 30% of treatment failures in women are found only at that site, whether or not the rectum was culture positive before treatment. Patients treated with spectinomycin or a quinolone should have a serologic test for syphilis 1 month after treatment. All posttreatment isolates should be evaluated for antimicrobial susceptibility and subsequent re-treatment strategies must take such data into account. Patients treated for NGU, regardless of whether chlamydia was isolated, do not require follow-up evaluation unless symptoms persist or recur.

DISCUSSION
Incidence and Prevalence
Urethritis is the most common sexually transmitted syndrome among men in the United States. Approximately 1 million cases of gonococcal urethritis and 3 million cases of NGU occur each year. The actual incidence of gonococcal urethritis is more precise due to governmental requirements for health department reportability, whereas NGU cases are not uniformly reported. Additionally, 30% of men with NGU have recurrent or persistent urethritis after therapeutic intervention.

Related Basic Science
Neisseria gonorrhoeae
Neisseria gonorrhoeae is a strictly aerobic Gram-negative diplococcus that grows best at 35 to 37°C in an atmosphere of 3 to 4% carbon dioxide. Identification is based on colony morphology, Gram stain appearance, oxidase reaction, carbohydrate utilization, and fluorescent antibody staining. This species can be distinguished from other *Neisseria* species by its ability to use glucose but not maltose, sucrose, or lactose and with immunofluorescence tests.

Pili cover the external surface of the gonococcus and are thought to enhance virulence by mediating attachment to nonciliated epithelial cells and by impeding phagocytosis. Antibodies to pili inhibit attachment and promote phagocytosis. Specific proteins identified in the outer membrane appear to be responsible for attachment to epithelial cells and phagocytic cells and for initiating endocytosis into the epithelial cell. The lipopolysaccharide, through endotoxin activity, contributes to local cytotoxicity, inflammation, fever, and systemic toxicity.

Penicillin has been the standard therapeutic agent for gonorrhea since the drug was developed in the 1940s. Over the years, however, the organism has developed increasing resistance to penicillin by one of two methods: chromosomal mutations that decrease the binding or permeability of penicillin (also tetracycline and spectinomycin) to the gonococcus, and plasmid-mediated production of penicillinase, which renders the antibiotic ineffective. Isolates manifesting one or both of these resistance mechanisms are increasingly common in the United States. Spectinomycin resistance appears to be increasing but presently is uncommon, so it remains a useful agent. Periodic assessment of resistance prevalence is recommended in communities to determine optimal empiric treatment regimens.

Chlamydia trachomatis
Chlamydiae are obligatory intracellular parasites that possess cell walls and membranes with some similarities to those of Gram-negative bacteria but with a unique growth cycle. Chlamydiae cannot be grown on artificial media, thus requiring cell culture for in vitro growth. In vivo, the organisms attach to and penetrate (induced phagocytosis) squamocolumnar cells and inhibit phagolysosomal fusion, thereby preventing their destruction. The infective particle is called an elementary body, which undergoes subsequent intracellular transformation to its dividing form, the reticulate body. New elementary bodies are produced every 48 to 72 hours, causing cell rupture and death and the release of infective particles.

Ureaplasma urealyticum
Ureaplasma urealyticum is a genital *Mycoplasma* species that has been implicated as a cause of NGU in men; however, because it can be isolated from the urethra of more than half of healthy sexually active men,

its role in urethritis has been difficult to establish. It is generally believed that it accounts for approximately 20% of cases of NGU in men. Specific serotypes may be more pathogenic. Because of its high prevalence in normal men, routine cultures are not indicated in the evaluation of urethritis. Its role in urethritis in women is unknown.

Other Organisms
A multitude of organisms have been proposed as possible etiologic agents in patients with NGU in whom *C. trachomatis* or *U. urealyticum* cannot be isolated. *Trichomonas vaginalis* has been isolated from both men and women with urethritis. Yeast infections do not appear to be important agents in this condition. Herpes simplex virus infections are frequently associated with urethritis, but urethral infections without external lesions account for only a small proportion of cases of NGU. *Mycoplasma genitalium* has recently been associated with acute *Chlamydia*-negative NGU, but more information is needed for confirmation and to establish a causal link. Many species of aerobic and anaerobic bacteria have been evaluated, but none has been established as an important pathogen in this condition.

Natural History and Its Modification with Treatment
Although acute urethritis is generally a self-limited disorder even without treatment, complications were common in the preantibiotic era. Thus, the major impact of treatment may be prevention of sequelae. In some patients, untreated gonococcal urethritis may remain symptomatic for many months, and untreated chlamydial infections may persist for years as low-grade infections. Appropriate treatment usually causes eradication of the infecting organism and resolution of symptoms within a few days.

Complications of gonococcal urethritis in men include acute epididymoorchitis, disseminated gonococcal infection, penile lymphangitis, periurethral abscess, prostatitis, seminal vesiculitis, and inflammatory urethral stricture. These complications are now rare in the United States, with the exception of epididymoorchitis and disseminated infection.

Acute epididymoorchitis complicates NGU in a minority of patients. Reiter's syndrome, manifested by urethritis, conjunctivitis, arthritis, and dermatitis, occurs in an occasional patient following chlamydial urethritis. Stricture formation appears to be uncommon and it is difficult to prove a causal relationship, even in men with persistent urethritis lasting months or years. There are no data that demonstrate that infertility results from persistent urethritis. It is controversial whether urethritis can be caused by *Chlamydia* or *Ureaplasma*, but recent data support an association between urethritis and prostatitis.

The natural history of untreated gonococcal or chlamydial urethritis in women is unknown; however, it is likely that ascending infection occurs in many women. These organisms can cause mucopurulent cervicitis, then endometritis, and subsequently salpingitis. The exact timing of these sequelae and their preventability by antimicrobial agents are unknown.

Prevention
Education of all sexually active persons is necessary for optimal prevention. Urethritis is preventable by the appropriate treatment of patients and all sexual contacts, sexual abstinence, or conscientious use of condoms until treatment and appropriate follow-up are completed. Asymptomatic cases should be sought by routine culture screening for gonorrhea and chlamydia in high-risk individuals and clinics.

Cost Containment
The Gram-stained urethral smear provides information with high sensitivity and specificity as to the presence of gonorrhea in a man with symptomatic urethritis. Confirmatory cultures are not necessary except in situations previously defined. Men with NGU do not need chlamydial cultures if they are to receive one of the recommended antichlamydial regimens. Likewise, men treated for NGU need no follow-up evaluation if symptoms resolve. Direct antigen assays or the polymerase chain reaction for *N. gonorrhoeae* and *C. trachomatis* may eventually obviate the need for cultures and result in cost-effective evaluation of

patients. Routine screening for gonorrhea and chlamydia in asymptomatic men and women attending sexually transmitted disease clinics, family planning clinics, and other clinics with high-risk clients is an effective means of identifying and treating transmitters. Testing first-voided urine from asymptomatic men using the leukocyte esterase test is an inexpensive but insensitive means of screening for urethritis. Routine urethral cultures for *U. urealyticum* and the less common pathogens believed to cause urethritis are not indicated. Likewise, routine prostatic localization tests are not indicated for acute urethritis, and their usefulness in persistent urethritis has not been demonstrated. Urethroscopy is an expensive and invasive procedure with unestablished value in men with persistent urethritis; it should probably be reserved for patients in whom there is high suspicion of urethral abnormalities or in whom there is objective evidence of urethritis over many months.

REFERENCES

Bowie WR. Urethritis in males. In: Holmes KK, Mardh P-A, Sparling PF, Wiesner PJ, eds. Sexually transmitted diseases. New York: McGraw-Hill, 1990:627.

Centers for Disease Control and Prevention. Sexually transmitted diseases treatment guidelines. MMWR 1993;42:1

Holmes KK, Handsfield HH, Wang SP, et al. Etiology of nongonococcal urethritis. N Engl J Med 1975;292:1199.

Hooton TM, Wong ES, Barnes RC, et al. Erythromycin for persistent or recurrent nongonococcal urethritis: A randomized, placebo-controlled trial. Ann Intern Med 1990;113:21.

Horner JP, Gilroy CD, Thomas BJ, et al. *Mycoplasma genitalium* and nongonococcal urethritis. Lancet 1994;343:790.

Latham RH, Stamm WE. Urethral syndrome in women. Urol Clin North Am 1984;11:95.

Martin DH, Mroczkowski TF, Daly ZA, et al. A controlled trial of a single dose of azithromycin for the treatment of *Chlamydia* urethritis and cervicitis. N Engl J Med 1992;327:921.

Stamm WE, Koutsky LA, Benedetti JK et al. *Chlamydia trachomatis* urethral infections in men: Prevalence, risk factors, and clinical manifestations. Ann Intern Med 1984;100:47.

CHAPTER 8–25

Vaginitis

Melody Pratt Palmore, M.D., and Amy A. Swartz, M.D.

DEFINITION

Vaginitis is an inflammation of the vagina that causes a vaginal discharge containing the offending microorganisms as well as polymorphonuclear leukocytes, inflammatory changes of the vaginal canal, the epithelialized ectocervix, and frequently the perivulvar area. Vaginal infections in adult women are among the most common gynecologic complaints both in public health clinics and in private physicians' offices. In general, these are infections of postpubertal women.

ETIOLOGY

A frequent cause of vaginitis is *Trichomonas vaginalis,* seen in an estimated 3 million women in the United States each year. One of several *Candida* species accounts for approximately one third of all vaginitis cases seen in private physicians' offices. What was previously termed *Hemophilus vaginalis* or *Gardnerella*-associated vaginitis is now termed bacterial vaginosis because an inflammatory reaction of the epithelium is not part of the syndrome. This entity is classified with the other vaginitides because coinfection with more than one agent is common. These three types of infection account for more than 95% of all vaginitis in the United States. Other organisms, such as *Chlamydia trachomatis, Neisseria gonorrhoeae,* group A β-hemolytic streptococci, and *Shigella* species, may be causes of vulvovaginitis in infants and young girls.

CRITERIA FOR DIAGNOSIS
Suggestive

The major symptoms that bring women with vaginitis to medical attention are persistent vaginal discharge, vulvar pruritus, and/or tenderness or offensive vaginal odor.

Definitive

All three diseases may be diagnosed and distinguished by examining a wet mount and Gram-stained preparation of vaginal secretions taken at the time of pelvic examination. The diagnosis of trichomoniasis requires the demonstration of motile trophozoites in vaginal secretions or in urine by either light microscopy or culture. The diagnosis of yeast infections requires first that *Trichomonas* be ruled out as the cause of vaginitis, and then the demonstration of the yeasts on direct examination of vaginal secretions by light microscopy or culture. Bacterial vaginosis may be diagnosed by the exclusion of the other two entities plus the findings on direct examination of vaginal material by both wet mount and Gram stain, which is characterized by the absence of an inflammatory reaction, the absence of the normal lactobacilli, the presence of "clue cells," and the presence of a strong fishy odor to the vaginal secretions after the addition of a drop of 10% potassium hydroxide.

CLINICAL MANIFESTATIONS
Subjective

The symptoms of trichomoniasis and candidiasis overlap so much that one cannot use them to clinically distinguish between the two conditions. Women experience the acute onset of increased vaginal discharge, which may be a variety of colors. It may be quite profuse in *Trichomonas* and occasionally frothy (less than 10% of patients), whereas it tends to be thicker and more curdy in candidiasis (up to 25% of patients). Initially, vulvar pruritus is the major complaint, but vulvar soreness because of inflammation and excoriation is also common. Women with bacterial vaginosis rarely have copious vaginal discharge or pruritus. Here the major complaint is a scant, offensively malodorous discharge that does not respond to douching.

Trichomoniasis is primarily a sexually transmitted infection, whereas candidiasis is not transmitted sexually in the majority of patients. There is still controversy regarding the sexual transmissibility of bacterial vaginosis. Some sources promote the idea by suggesting that therapeutic cures may require simultaneous treatment of the partner. Arguments against sexual transmission are supported by the detection of bacterial vaginosis in virginal women.

Objective

In trichomoniasis and candidiasis, a vaginal discharge may be seen in the vaginal canal, and in the posterior fornix, that is often adherent to the cervix and vaginal walls in all symptomatic women. The discharge may be copious, filling the vaginal canal and spilling onto the vulva, or scant, thinly coating the vaginal wall. Color may vary from white to

We thank Dr. Sumner E. Thompson III for his contribution to this chapter in the previous editions of this book.

yellow to green or even brown. The odor of the discharge may vary from odorless to foul. Infection of the cervix and vaginal walls is common, and less often there is reddening and excoriations of the vulva. The perianal area also may appear inflamed. The clinical picture is quite different in bacterial vaginosis: the vaginal discharge is thin and scanty. It is uniform grayish white in color and adherent to the vaginal walls. Infection of the cervix and vaginal walls is absent, and infection and excoriation of the vulva are absent. The discharge almost always has a strong, disagreeable odor.

Routine Laboratory Abnormalities

The urinalysis is frequently abnormal in women with vaginitis. Motile trichomonads and polymorphonuclear leukocytes may be seen in freshly voided urine. Bacteriuria, most often with Gram-negative rods, is associated with bacterial vaginosis (Table 8–25–1).

PLANS
Diagnostic
Differential Diagnosis

Infection or inflammation of other sites in the female genitourinary tract may present with symptoms similar to those of vaginitis. Other causes of inflammation including foreign body vaginitis, sexually transmitted diseases, neoplasms, and atrophic vaginitis need to be considered in the differential.

Diagnostic Options

Trichomoniasis. A wet mount of freshly obtained vaginal material is the most rapid and convenient means of diagnosis. A wet mount is prepared by swirling a swab containing material taken from the posterior vaginal pool in a test tube containing 1 mL normal saline, placing a drop of this suspension on a glass slide, coverslipping the drop, and immediately examining it under high dry magnification with the condenser racked down for maximum contrast. The wet mount is diagnostic if even one motile trichomonad is seen. A negative wet mount does not rule out trichomoniasis in a symptomatic patient. The organism can produce an exotoxin that can cause an inflammatory reaction out of proportion to the number of organisms involved. Large numbers of polymorphonuclear leukocytes are also commonly found. The sensitivity of this procedure compared with culture is only slightly greater than 50%, but the specificity approaches 100%. Douching within 24 hours of examination reduces wet mount, but not culture, sensitivity. The culture has a sensitivity of 85 to 95% and is considered the "gold standard"; however, routine diagnostic culture is not readily available in the United States. Other disadvantages include the cost and the delay in confirming diagnosis. Other diagnostic methods include the Gram, Giemsa, and Papanicolaou stains. A new serologic test, the direct enzyme immunoassay (EIA), has the potential of becoming an in-office procedure in the near future. It has a sensitivity greater than that of the wet mount but less than that of culture, and may eventually replace the wet mount as the recommended diagnostic procedure.

Currently, the wet mount is still the recommended approach. Its advantages are its cost and convenience.

Candidiasis. Both the wet mount and Gram stain of vaginal secretions may be used. After first examining the wet mount for trichomonads and deciding it is negative, a drop of 10% potassium hydroxide solution should be allowed to flow under the coverslip by capillary action and the preparation examined after 10 or 15 seconds. The potassium hydroxide will lyse the ubiquitous cornified epithelial cells, making the

translucent yeast forms much more visible. On Gram stain, yeasts appear as large, budding oval bodies and filamentous forms that are intensely Gram-positive. Polymorphonuclear leukocytes are usually present in abundance. Care must be taken to not overinterpret these tests, because yeasts are normal inhabitants of the female genital tract. One is justified in assuming yeast is a pathogen only after trichomoniasis has been excluded and if there are numerous yeast forms in conjunction with polymorphonuclear leukocytes.

Bacterial Vaginosis. Examination of a wet mount and a Gram-stained smear of vaginal secretions is the simplest method of establishing the diagnosis. The characteristic findings on wet mount are a paucity or absence of the normal bacterial flora, that is, lactobacilli (which are large Gram-variable rods on Gram stain) and the presence of "clue cells" (epithelial cells with a granular appearance on wet mount that are covered with closely adherent bacteria that on Gram stain are Gram-negative coccobacilli). An additional rapid confirmatory test is the "sniff test," which is performed by adding a drop of 10% potassium hydroxide to the wet mount and noting the appearance of an unpleasant fishy odor due to the liberation of volatile amines, products of anaerobic metabolism. The vaginal pH is always greater than 5.0 in this condition (the normal pH is <4.5).

Therapeutic

Trichomoniasis. Metronidazole (Flagyl), either 2 g given orally as a single dose or 500 mg twice daily orally for 7 days, is 90% effective. Single-dose intravaginal metronidazole has been shown to be inferior to single-dose oral metronidazole. In the past several years there have been reports of high-level metronidazole resistance worldwide, and the incidence appears to be increasing. High-level resistance is difficult to treat and generally requires higher doses of metronidazole and longer courses of treatment, which can be complicated by severe neurologic side effects. Case reports have suggested that combination of oral and vaginal metronidazole may be a therapeutic option. Tinidazole, which is not available in the United States, may be effective in curing refractory cases. As trichomoniasis is a multisite infection, acidifying douches are rarely curative. Sex partners should also receive simultaneous treatment with 2 g metronidazole (although this dose may have a lower efficacy in men). At this dose level, the most serious side effect is a disulfiram (Antabuse)-like reaction if alcohol is taken. Patients should be warned not to consume alcohol for 2 days following therapy. Metronidazole is contraindicated in early pregnancy. Vinegar douches can decrease the parasite load and markedly decrease symptoms during this time. Metronidazole may be given safely during the last trimester of pregnancy, but should be reserved for severely symptomatic women who do not respond to topical therapy such as povidine–iodine (Betadine) or clotrimazole. Topical therapy provides symptomatic relief but not definitive cure. Nonoxynol-9 shows in vitro efficacy and appears to provide symptomatic relief but rarely definitive cure.

Currently, oral single-dose metronidazole is recommended; however, there are several options available and treatment must be tailored to the individual patient.

Candidiasis. The imidazoles, clotrimazole (Lotrimin, Gyne-Lotrimin) and miconazole (Mycostat), are superior to the polyenes, nystatin (Mycostatin) and candicidin, for treatment. Both vaginal tablets and creams produce equal cure rates. Standard therapy had consisted of 100 mg of the imidazole drugs intravaginally nightly for 7 nights. More recently, regimens consisting of 3 nights of therapy have produced cure rates of around 90%. Fluconazole (Diflucan), a new triazole, is also highly effective. Several trials using a single dose of fluconazole 150 mg showed cure rates between 81 and 93%. Many women expressed a strong preference for the shorter course of oral therapy. Even with single-dose therapy, approximately 15% of patients have some type of gastrointestinal toxicity.

The current recommendation for treatment of uncomplicated candidal vaginitis is single-dose fluconazole. The drug's safety in pregnancy and breastfeeding is unknown.

Bacterial Vaginosis. Metronidazole (Flagyl), 500 mg orally twice daily for 7 days, has emerged as the treatment of choice. Single dose-metronidazole, 2-g oral dose, may be as effective as the 7-day course, with

TABLE 8–25–1. SYMPTOMS ASSOCIATED WITH VAGINITIS

Vaginitis Type	Discharge (%)	Itching (%)	Odor (%)
Normal findings	25	20	10
Trichomoniasis	80	80	20
Yeast infection	60	50	19
Bacterial vaginosis	40	17	65

cure rates of 80 to 90%. Clindamycin 300 mg orally twice daily for 7 days is an alternative regimen. More recent studies indicate that intravaginal clindamycin 2% (1 applicatorful = 5 g), used once daily for 7 days, produced cure rates similar to those of the standard oral metronidazole regimen. Candidal vaginitis did, however, occur in approximately 10% of patients who received intravaginal clindamycin. There are no data on the use of intravaginal clindamycin in pregnancy. Another alternative treatment is intravaginal metronidazole 0.75% cream (1 applicatorful = 5 g) applied twice daily for 5 days. This regimen was also shown to be as effective as oral metronidazole for 7 days. Overall, the incidence of side effects with topical therapy was less because of the minimal systemic absorption. Treatment of sexual partners is not indicated at this time.

Many regimens are available for the treatment of bacterial vaginosis; however, metronidazole 500 mg twice daily for 7 days continues to be the "gold standard." Patients who are intolerant to metronidazole may require alternative therapy.

FOLLOW-UP

Follow-up visits after completion of therapy are not routinely indicated. Recurrence of discharge, malodor, or vaginal itching or burning after therapy is complete should prompt a return visit. In women who have chronic recurrent candidiasis, once the pattern is established, patients can be instructed to begin treatment at home at the first signs of infection and to come to the physician only if symptoms persist after starting treatment. It should be stressed that douching rarely cures vaginitis and may make it worse in some cases. The disease is also common and often severe, with recurrences being common in women infected with HIV. Women with difficult-to-control, recurrent candidiasis should be evaluated for diabetes. Women with a tendency for recurrent candidiasis also should be warned that taking broad-spectrum antibiotics such as tetracycline and ampicillin can cause an attack. They may wish to treat themselves with an antifungal agent while they are taking these antibiotics. Sex partners should be examined if vaginitis recurs more than three times in a 6-month period.

DISCUSSION

Prevalence and Incidence

Bacterial vaginosis is currently the most common cause of vaginitis among women of childbearing years. Approximately one half of all women with bacterial vaginosis are asymptomatic. *Trichomonas vaginalis* accounts for approximately 3 million cases of vaginitis in the United States each year. Vaginitis caused by *Candida* develops in approximately one fourth of women in their childbearing years.

Related Basic Science

Trichomoniasis. Trichomonads are flagellated protozoans with a wide host range. Human beings harbor at least four species: *Trichomonas tenax* and *T. oralis* in the oral cavity, *Pentatrichomonas hominis* intestinally, and *T. vaginalis* in the genital tract. Only *T. vaginalis* is thought to be pathogenic. The epidemiology of trichomoniasis is not completely understood. Although the disease is unquestionably sexually transmitted, it is possible that it also may be transmitted through fomites, on washcloths and towels. Women may be infected for years without symptoms. The cause of overt disease years after asymptomatic infection is not known. Changes in vaginal pH affect the parasite load markedly: trichomonads prefer an alkaline pH (up to 5.5 or greater) for proliferation. This may explain the onset of symptoms at the time of the menses, as blood is an excellent buffer. Postmenopausal women may develop symptomatic infections coincident with the rise in vaginal pH as estrogen levels fall.

Trichomonas attaches to mucous membranes. Although in experimental infections the organism destroys the epithelial cells it contacts, the mechanism by which it produces disease is not known. Because of its ability to cause erosive disease, trichomoniasis may increase the risk of HIV transmission. Virulence factors have not been clearly identified. Repeated trichomonal infections are common. Although antibodies and cellular immune responses can be documented, they do not appear to be protective. Trichomonads are actively phagocytized, usually by groups of polymorphonuclear neutrophils (PMNs), which are capable of

killing the parasite by oxidative mechanisms. How much this contributes to limiting the infection is not known.

Candidiasis. A variety of *Candida* species are capable of causing vaginitis and cannot be distinguished from each other clinically. *Candida* species normally inhabit the vagina and perirectal area in up to 30% of women. It is likely that this colonization is also the source of infection and that vaginal candidiasis is not primarily a sexually transmitted disease. This is borne out by the observation that *candidal* vaginitis is not found more frequently in women with other sexually transmitted infections; however, penile candidiasis in men is usually acquired sexually.

Candida albicans adheres more readily to epithelial cells than many other related yeast species, which may account in part for its being the most common yeast causing vaginitis. The second most frequent isolate is *C. glabrata,* seen in approximately 10 to 15% of cases. *Candida krusei* accounted for up to 7.5% of cases of yeast vaginitis in one series. Both organisms may be more difficult to eradicate with standard therapies. Little else is known about *Candida* toxins or enzymes as virulence factors. The pathogenetic factors that convert an asymptomatic saprophyte into a pathogen are not known.

Vulvovaginal candidiasis appears to be more common or more severe in women infected with HIV, although there are no data at this time to use this infection as a marker. There does not appear to be a need to change treatment only because a patient is infected with HIV.

Bacterial Vaginosis. The epidemiology of this infection is not well understood. It now seems likely that the syndrome has a polymicrobial etiology characterized by a massive bacterial overgrowth involving certain anaerobic bacteria, facultative Gram-negative rods, and mycoplasmas. Some studies have found that the disease is sexually transmitted, whereas other have not been able to demonstrate this.

Gardnerella vaginalis has been traditionally associated with the infection, but has not proven to be the sole cause of bacterial vaginosis. Anaerobic bacteria have also been associated with this disease, and some investigators have concluded that a combination of *Gardnerella* and certain anaerobes were needed to produce this syndrome. The exact microorganisms required are not known, but several anaerobes are potentially involved. A new genus, *Mobiluncus,* appears to be a component of the mixture of bacteria most likely to cause disease. Genital mycoplasmas, especially *Mycoplasma hominis,* also appear to be implicated. Current thinking suggests that the major pathogenic event appears to relate to a shift in the ecology of the multitude of various microorganisms that normally reside in the vaginal tract. The cause of this shift in vaginal flora is not known, but it is likely due to pH changes.

The hallmark of vaginitis is the presence of an inflammatory exudate in the vaginal canal with inflammatory changes in the vaginal epithelium often extending to the vaginal cervix, vulva, and perirectal skin. In bacterial vaginosis, however, the inflammation is not present. Other common features of these conditions are a change in the vaginal pH toward alkalinity and a decrease in the normal vaginal flora. It is not clear whether the vaginal pH changes come first, allowing secondary growth of pathogens, or whether the primary change is a loss of lactobacilli and metabolism of glycogen to lactate, which keeps the premenopausal vagina normally acid.

Natural History and Its Modification with Treatment

In general, the three vaginal infections described above are not associated with complications, although their recurrent nature takes its toll in psychologic trauma. Recently, there has been some information to suggest that bacterial vaginosis, because of the massive overgrowth of a variety of bacteria, may be associated with increased risk of urinary tract infection, chorioamnionitis, premature labor and delivery, and maternal postpartum infectious complications. It has also been postulated that bacterial vaginosis, particularly in women with intrauterine devices, may predispose to pelvic inflammatory disease.

Prevention

No well-grounded preventive measures for any of these infections have been found. The treatment of sexual partners of women with trichomoniasis is important to prevent reinfection. Identification and modification of risk factors for recurrent candidiasis, such as diabetes mellitus, corticosteroid and other immunosuppressive therapy, broad-spectrum antibiotic use, and oral contraceptive therapy, may help decrease the number of episodes. One study showed daily ingestion of yogurt containing *Lactobacillus acidophilus* decreased both candidal colonization and infection. The role of barrier contraceptives, which have utility in preventing a variety of sexually transmitted infections, has not been well studied in the prevention of the major forms of vaginal infection.

Cost Containment

A simple wet mount or Gram stain can be used to diagnose the majority of cases of vaginitis at the time of the initial examination. The majority of patients can be managed with a single visit. Cultures, which are much more expensive, also usually require reevaluation of the patient at a second visit. They should be reserved for the few patients who are diagnostic puzzles. The short treatment course for trichomoniasis (2 g metronidazole) should always be tried first because the drug is expensive. Similarly, single-dose fluconazole treatment for candidal vaginitis should be tried in women with first or infrequent infections. The one-time dose is not only less expensive than multiple doses of intravaginal creams, but also serves to increase compliance. The cost of topical metronidazole and clindamycin is considerably higher than that of oral metronidazole and should be taken into account when choosing a treatment regimen for bacterial vaginosis.

REFERENCES

Dhar J, Arya OP, Timmins DJ, et al. Treatment of bacterial vaginosis with a three day course of 2% clindamycin vaginal cream: A pilot study. Genitourin Med 1994;70:121.

Hilton E, Isenberg H, Alperstein P, et al. Ingestion of yogurt containing *Lactobacillus acidophilus* as prophylaxis for candidal vaginitis. Ann Intern Med 1992;116:353.

Holst E. Bacterial vaginosis: Microbiology and clinical findings. Eur J Clin Bacteriol 1987;6:536.

Lossick JG, Kent HL. Vulvovaginitis: Causes and therapies: Trichomoniasis: Trends in diagnosis and management. Am J Obstet Gynecol 1991;165:1217.

Oral fluconazole for vaginal candidiasis. Med Lett 1994;36:81.

Rein MF. Vulvovaginitis and cervicitis. In: Mandell GL, Bennett JE, Dolin R, eds. Mandell, Douglas and Bennett's principles and practice of infectious diseases. 4th ed. New York: Churchill Livingstone, 1995:1.

Sweet RL. New approaches for the treatment of bacterial vaginosis. Am J Obstet Gynecol 1993;169:479.

Thomason JL, Gelbart SM, Scaglione NJ. Bacterial vaginosis: Current review with indications for asymptomatic therapy. Am J Obstet Gynecol 1991;165:1210.

Tidwell BH, Lushbaugh WB, Laughlin MD. A double-blind placebo-controlled trial of single-dose intravaginal versus single-dose oral metronidazole in the treatment of trichomonal vaginitis. J Infect Dis 1994;170:242.

CHAPTER 8–26

Pelvic Inflammatory Disease (Salpingitis–Peritonitis)

Kimberly A. Workowski, M.D.

DEFINITION

Pelvic inflammatory disease is a clinical syndrome associated with an ascending spread of microorganisms from the vaginal canal or endocervix to the endometrium, fallopian tubes, and contiguous structures.

ETIOLOGY

Acute pelvic inflammatory disease (PID) is caused by the sexually transmitted organisms *Neisseria gonorrhoeae* and *Chlamydia trachomatis* and organisms that constitute the endogenous flora of the lower genital tract. Most older studies of the microbial etiology of PID are based on rates of isolation from the cervix and not from the upper genital tract. Recent studies using fallopian tube and endometrial sampling have demonstrated discrepancies between microbial isolates from the lower and upper genital tract. The isolation of *N. gonorrhoeae* from the upper genital tract is inversely related to the duration of symptoms, whereas *C. trachomatis* has been isolated from the upper genital tract of women with chronic PID. Additionally, women with concomitant cervical and tubal infection have chlamydia isolated at a higher rate than gonorrhea; however, isolation of more than one species of sexually transmitted pathogens is common in women with acute PID. One role of these pathogens is to break down host defenses in the endocervix and allow passage of pathogenic bacteria. Alterations in the vaginal flora, including anaerobic streptococci, *Escherichia coli*, *Gardnerella vaginalis*, *Bacteroides* species, and peptostreptococci, probably play a role in ascending infection. It is believed that gonococci and chlamydiae are instrumental in the initial infection of the upper genital tract, and as the infection progresses, anaerobes and facultative aerobes become more prominent. About 20% of women with a laparoscopic diagnosis of PID have no pathogen identified.

CRITERIA FOR DIAGNOSIS
Suggestive

Initially, mild or transient symptoms from the lower genital and urinary tracts may go unrecognized. The onset of pelvic or lower abdominal pain is usually regarded as the first manifestation of ascending infection. Complaints of lower abdominal pain, particularly when coupled with recent menstrual irregularities and increased vaginal discharge in women who are sexually active, should make one consider the diagnosis of PID. A thorough sexual history may reveal certain epidemiologic variables that influence the risk of PID, including multiple sexual partners, young age, past history of PID, recent use of an intrauterine device for contraception, onset during menses, and a partner with a sexually transmitted disease or urethritis. The use of oral contraceptives is associated with a decreased risk that a lower genital tract infection will ascend to the upper genital tract, probably due to alteration in cervical mucus and endometrial tissue.

Pelvic inflammatory disease may also be seen in older women who have had instrumentation of the uterine cavity, hysterosalpingography, abortion, or dilation and curettage.

Definitive

The variable presentation of PID represents a challenge for clinicians, and thus clinical criteria for the diagnosis have been proposed but not validated. These diagnostic criteria include lower abdominal pain with cervical motion/adnexal tenderness plus one or more of the following: temperature higher than 38°C, leukocytosis, purulent culdocentesis, inflammatory mass on pelvic examination or ultrasound, erythrocyte sedimentation rate greater than 15 mm/h, or evidence of *N. gonorrhoeae* and/or *C. trachomatis* in the endocervix. Strict reliance on these clinical criteria, however, may result in misdiagnosis, resulting in progression of infection and potential serious sequelae. Routine laparoscopy for the diagnosis of salpingitis has revealed that clinical criteria for the diagnosis of PID are correct only two thirds of the time. It is clear that even strict clinical criteria do not have a high degree of accuracy when com-

We thank Dr. Sumner E. Thompson III for his contribution to this chapter in the previous editions of this book.

pared with laparoscopic diagnosis (Table 8–26–1), but the use of laparoscopy for diagnosis must be weighted against the expense and risk of the procedure.

An unequivocal diagnosis can be established only by visual inspection of the salpinges at laparoscopy or laparotomy by the demonstration of an inflammatory exudate within the tubal lumen, and is recommended when the diagnosis is unclear. A presumptive diagnosis may be made by the demonstration of purulent material in the pelvic cul-de-sac, needle aspiration in conjunction with other physical findings, or endometrial biopsy with demonstration of endometritis.

CLINICAL MANIFESTATIONS
Subjective

There is no pathognomonic presentation of salpingitis. The most common complaint is crampy, dull and constant lower abdominal pain that is often mistaken for mittelschmerz or menstrual cramps because the onset of symptoms frequently coincides with the menses. Abnormal menstrual cycles characterized by increased flow, postcoital bleeding, or spotting between menstrual periods are common. Patients may notice fever, but night sweats and chills are uncommon. An abnormal vaginal discharge may be present in about half of the women. In cases complicated by pelvic peritonitis, the patient may present with severe abdominal pain, vomiting, loose stools, and dyspareunia. Dysuria is present in up to 20% of patients. Right upper quadrant discomfort may suggest concomitant perihepatitis.

Objective
Physical Examination

A bimanual pelvic examination reveals unilateral or bilateral adnexal tenderness in most patients. Most women also exhibit pain on side-to-side traction of the cervix because this stretches inflamed pelvic ligaments. A palpable swelling of one or both adnexa is found in about half of the women with PID. A purulent vaginal or endocervical discharge is found in the majority of women. Fever is present in one third of women and tends to be more common in those patients with gonococcal or severe polymicrobial infection. In early or mild PID, tenderness confined to the uterine cervix is common. This probably due to an endometritis preceding the onset of tubal extension. In the earliest stages of the disease, when infection is confined to the endosalpinx alone, no abdominal tenderness may be elicited. In disease that has extended beyond the tubes, swellings may be palpated near tubal structures, the ovary, or the cul-de-sac. In long-standing disease, especially with repeated bouts of infection, the tubes may be fixed, hard, and convoluted. Rebound tenderness and decreased bowel sounds in the lower abdominal quadrants may be present if there is pelvic peritonitis. There may be inflammation of the liver capsule producing tenderness to palpation in the right upper quadrant (Fitz-Hugh-Curtis syndrome).

Routine Laboratory Abnormalities

There is a peripheral leukocytosis.

PLANS
Diagnostic
Differential Diagnosis

Although the differential diagnosis (Table 8–26–2) can be quite inclusive, the two main diagnoses to consider are appendicitis and ectopic pregnancy. In acute appendicitis, the duration of abdominal pain is shorter, gastrointestinal pain is prominent, and diffuse abdominal pain often shifts to the right lower quadrant. Laparoscopy should be used when this differentiation is ambiguous. In many instances it is impossible to distinguish between early ectopic pregnancy and mild PID using clinical criteria. As such, it is important to exclude pregnancy before diagnosing pelvic inflammatory disease.

Diagnostic Options and Recommended Approach

No clinical findings are absolutely diagnostic of bacterial salpingitis, and many cases are mild. As a lower genital tract infection often precedes most cases of PID, direct microscopy of vaginal contents and cervical mucus is recommended. Examination of endocervical discharge for the presence of 30 or more polymorphonuclear leukocytes per oil immersion field has been advocated to document mucopurulent cervicitis. Cervical cultures should be performed for *N. gonorrhoeae* and *C. trachomatis*; however, cervical cultures do not give conclusive information on the etiology of the tubal infection. In addition to lower abdominal pain and tenderness, an elevated erythrocyte sedimentation rate, sustained fever, and presence of an adnexal mass are highly suggestive. A pelvic ultrasound may be useful by delineating an adnexal inflammatory mass or abscess or demonstrating dilated or thickened fallopian tubes. Occasionally, a laparoscopy may be needed for diagnosis, but even laparoscopic examination may be normal in the early phases of this infection if inflammation is confined to the endothelium. To establish the etiology of tubal infection, specimens should be obtained from the tubal mucosa. For the detection of etiologic agents in endometrial, tubal, and cul-de-sac specimens, the polymerase chain reaction for chlamydial detection and gonococcal cultures may be used.

TABLE 8–26–1. FREQUENCY OF VARIOUS SYMPTOMS AND SIGNS AMONG WOMEN SUBJECTED TO LAPAROSCOPY BECAUSE OF ASSUMED SALPINGITIS*

| Symptom or Sign | Findings at Laparoscopy | |
	Acute Salpingitis (% [n = 623])	Normal Fallopian Tubes[†] (% [n = 184])
Low abdominal pain	100	100
Metrorrhagia	35.5	42.9
Urethritis symptoms	18.6	20.1
Lower genital tract infection		
Purulent vaginal contents on microscopy	100	100
Symptom of discharge	54.6	56.5
Vomiting or nausea	10.3	9.2
Proctitis symptoms	6.9	2.7
Febrile illness (>38.0°C) at admission	32.9	14.1
Palpable adnexal swelling	49.4	24.5

*Diagnosed on the basis of minimum criteria of low abdominal pain, pain on pelvic examination, and objective signs of a genital infection.
[†]Lower genital tract infection only.
Source: Westrom L, Mardh P-A. Pelvic inflammatory disease: I. Epidemiology, diagnosis, clinical manifestations and sequelae. In: Holmes KK, Mardh P-A, eds. International perspectives on sexually transmitted diseases: Impact on venereology, fertility, and maternal and infant morbidity. New York: McGraw-Hill, 1982. Reproduced with permission from the author and the publisher.

TABLE 8–26–2. DIFFERENTIAL DIAGNOSIS OF PELVIC INFLAMMATORY DISEASE

Diagnostic Possibility	Diagnostic Tests or Observations
Tuberculosis	Rare in the United States; purified protein derivative skin test; chest x-ray; endometrial or tubal biopsy for histology and culture
Actinomycosis	Usually associated with intrauterine devices; endometrial biopsy for histology and culture; crush preparation for sulfur granules; culture intrauterine device
Appendicitis	Culdocentesis, however, a ruptured appendiceal abscess may also be associated with free pus in the cul-de-sac; laparoscopy; surgical intervention
Ruptured ectopic pregnancy	Culdocentesis to demonstrate free blood within the peritoneal cavity; pelvic ultrasound; laparoscopy; surgical intervention
Twisted ovarian cyst; ovarian carcinoma necrosis; ruptured graafian follicle	Cyst may be palpable on pelvic examination; laparoscopy; cell count; usually foul-smelling cervical discharge
Septic abortion	Dilation and curettage for products of conception

Therapeutic

Therapeutic Options

Antimicrobial regimens must provide broad-spectrum coverage of likely pathogens including *N. gonorrhoeae*, *C. trachomatis*, anaerobes, and facultative aerobes. Several antimicrobial regimens have proven effectiveness in both clinical and microbiologic cure rates, but few studies have been performed to assess the elimination of endometrial and tubal infection or the incidence of tubal infertility and ectopic pregnancy. The results of cultures obtained from the lower and upper genital tract before treatment must be considered and may eventually guide a revision in therapy. No single regimen has been established for the treatment of PID. Many experts recommend that women with severe infection and those with an unclear diagnosis be hospitalized for observation until a diagnosis is established or there is clinical improvement. Additionally, hospitalization is recommended in the following situations: when pelvic abscess is suspected, pregnancy, adolescent patient, concomitant HIV infection, inability to tolerate oral medications, failure to respond to an outpatient regimen, lack of reliable follow-up.

Recommended Approach

Outpatient Management. (1) Cefoxitin 2.0 g intramuscularly plus probenecid 1 g orally in a single dose or ceftriaxone 250 mg intramuscularly or other parenteral third-generation cephalosporins (ceftizoxime or cefotaxime) plus doxycycline 100 mg orally twice a day for 10 to 14 days. (2) Ofloxacin 400 mg orally twice daily for 14 days plus either clindamycin 450 mg orally four times a day or metronidazole 500 mg orally twice daily for 14 days. Follow-up examination should be performed within 72 hours. Patients who do not respond to these regimens within 48 to 72 hours should be hospitalized to confirm the diagnosis and for parenteral treatment. The sexual partners of women with PID should be evaluated for sexually transmitted diseases and treated with regimens effective for *N. gonorrhoeae* and *C. trachomatis*.

Inpatient Management. (1) Cefoxitin 2.0 g intravenously every 6 hours or cefotetan 2 g intravenously every 12 hours plus doxycycline 100 mg intravenously or orally every 12 hours should be administered. This regimen is continued for 48 hours after the patient begins to improve, after which oral doxycycline is continued for a total of 10 to 14 days. (2) Clindamycin 900 mg intravenously every 8 hours plus gentamicin in an initial dose of 2.0 mg/kg body weight, and thereafter a maintenance dose of 1.5 mg/kg intravenously every 8 hours. This regimen is continued for 48 hours after the patient begins to improve; then doxycycline 100 mg orally twice daily is continued for 10 to 14 days. Limited data support the use of other inpatient regimens; however ampicillin/sulbactam plus doxycycline appears effective in small clinical trials.

Hospitalized patients should show marked improvement (defervescence, reduction in abdominal and uterine/adnexal tenderness) within 3 to 5 days of therapeutic intervention. Patients who do not demonstrate improvement usually require further diagnostic tests or surgical intervention. Surgical intervention should be done on an emergent basis if a ruptured or leaking abscess is suspected. Repeat pelvic examination during therapy is important, as abscesses not palpable because of abdominal guarding may be felt as peritoneal signs abate. In addition to patients with a ruptured tuboovarian abscess, some patients with a large pelvic abscess may need surgical drainage or transabdominal needle aspiration with imaging guidance. The presence of an intrauterine device may delay improvement, and it should be removed as soon as possible after starting antibiotic therapy.

FOLLOW-UP

Even with adequate diagnosis and prompt, accurate treatment, relapse or recurrence occurs in 5 to 10% of patients. Re-treatment of outpatients may be initiated with any of the outpatient regimens described above, particularly if reinfection (as opposed to relapse) is suspected. Follow-up visits with complete pelvic examination should occur 48 to 72 hours after beginning therapy in outpatients and at 1 and 3 to 4 weeks. Women who experience return of abdominal pain or recurrence of menstrual abnormalities or vaginal discharge should be encouraged

to return for evaluation. Patients should have a bimanual pelvic examination at each visit, with assessment of changes in tenderness of the uterine fundus, the fallopian tubes, or other adnexal structures. Changes in the size of the tubes and changes in the size of abscess should be documented. Persistence of tenderness or failure of an abscess to decrease in size should prompt hospitalization. An abscess that decreases in size but does not disappear may eventually require surgery.

The sexual partners of women with gonococcal or chlamydial pelvic inflammatory disease should be examined and treated to prevent reinfection of the patient. Sex partners should be treated empirically with regimens effective against both *N. gonorrhoeae* and *C. trachomatis* regardless of the apparent etiology of PID or pathogens isolated from the infected woman.

A sketch of the uterus and tubes is helpful in explaining the location of the infection and how it developed. If the infection is gonococcal or chlamydial, the sexual mode of transmission should be explained, stressing the need for examination and treatment of the sex partner before returning to sexual activity.

If the patient was using an intrauterine device, explain why it is important not to use one again, and explore alternative methods of contraception. Stress the use of condoms, especially those impregnated with nonoxynol-9, and spermicidal foams because of their sexually transmitted disease-preventive aspects. Women with one sexually transmitted disease are at high risk for acquiring others; therefore, a rapid plasma reagin test and HIV testing are recommended.

DISCUSSION

Prevalence and Incidence

About 1 million women a year are treated for acute PID at an annual cost of more than $4 billion. Although pelvic inflammatory disease may occur without apparent sequelae, resultant complications such as ectopic pregnancy, tubal infertility, and chronic pelvic pain may be evident years later. The highest annual incidence appears to be in nulliparous women below the age of 25.

Related Basic Science

Acute salpingitis is primarily a consequence of sexually transmitted organisms, usually the gonococcus and chlamydia, and other bacteria normally resident in the genital tract such as anaerobic streptococci, *Bacteroides* species, *Escherichia coli,* and *Mycoplasma* species. *Chlamydia trachomatis* and *Neisseria gonorrhoeae* are the primary pathogens of the endocervical canal that enable other vaginal flora to ascend into the endometrium. Age-related changes in cervical ectopy and hormonal changes that occur during menses may enhance spread of infection into the upper genital tract.

The pathogenesis of chronic chlamydial infection of the upper genital tract does not appear to result from a direct effect of organism replication, but by the host response to the infection. Repeated inoculations of *C. trachomatis* into the fallopian tubes of animal models reveal a mononuclear cell infiltrate with resultant tubal scarring and peritubal adhesions. Recent reports have implicated a genus-specific 57-kDa protein in this pathogenic response, and some studies have shown demonstrable antibody responses in women with PID or ectopic pregnancy.

Human fallopian tube cultures have revealed that gonococci are capable of invading epithelial cells and producing extracellular products that are damaging to host cells. Tissue damage may be due to lipooligosaccharides and peptidoglycan, substances found on the gonococcal surface. Molecules of lipooligosaccharides from different gonococci may vary in their ability to activate complement in the presence of immunoglobulins and, thus, in the generation of complement-derived neutrophil chemoattractant C5a. This may be important in the pathogenic potential of a gonococcal infection at mucosal sites, particularly in the upper genital tract.

Natural History and Its Modification with Treatment

Epidemiologic studies have shown that women begin experiencing their first episodes of salpingitis after becoming sexually active. In this setting, it is likely that sexually transmitted agents are the principal pathogens. In populations at high risk for acquiring sexually transmitted diseases, repeated exposure to these agents results in repeated bouts of salpingitis and, presumably, increasing tubal epithelial dysfunction. With each episode of salpingitis there is an increased chance that the women will be infertile. Later, sexually transmitted organisms are less important than the patient's normal vaginal flora in producing repeated infections; tubal architecture may become obliterated, and tuboovarian or pelvic abscess are then important contributors to morbidity and mortality.

Most women with PID recover completely, but some are left with postinfection damage to the reproductive structures. Such damage constitutes the basis for late sequelae of PID, including chronic pelvic pain, infertility, and ectopic pregnancy. Chronic pelvic pain, commonly associated with pelvic adhesions, is correlated with the number of episodes of PID and is more common in infertile women. Various studies have documented pregnancy rates of 25 to 80% after acute episodes of PID; however, the postinfection fertility rate is significantly lower with each successive episode of PID. There is also increasing evidence of asymptomatic tubal disease, but sparse information exists on the pathophysiology and the magnitude of this entity. Additionally, based on a large number of clinical and seroepidemiologic studies, women who have had PID have a 7- to 10-fold increased risk for ectopic pregnancy.

Prevention

The establishment of a diagnosis of a first episode of salpingitis identifies a woman at high risk for developing the chronic sequelae. Efforts should be made to ensure long-term follow-up (6–12 months) after therapy is complete. Intrauterine devices must be removed and reliable alternative methods of birth control substituted if fertility is to be preserved. The use of condoms should be encouraged. Every effort should be made to examine all sexual partners and treat them appropriately.

Education is extremely important in the control of PID-producing sexually transmitted diseases. Women at risk for sexually transmitted diseases should be screened for cervical infection regardless of physical findings or symptomatology. This is particularly relevant to women with chlamydial infection, as the majority of lower genital tract infections are asymptomatic.

Cost Containment

The economic burden of PID to the U.S. economy has been estimated to be in excess of $4 billion annually. The bulk of this cost is not only for diagnosis and treatment of the acute episode, but hospitalization for repeat episodes, days missed from work and treatment of the chronic sequelae including chronic abdominal pain, infertility, and ectopic pregnancy. Although there are some experts who espouse this view, not all women require hospitalization. In patients presenting with most of the symptoms and signs described above, laparoscopy should be reserved for those in whom the diagnosis is uncertain or who are not clinically responding. Cultures to detect the gonococcus should be routinely done on all women suspected of having PID. The most common methods available for evaluation of chlamydial infection currently include direct antigen testing and DNA probes, which have approximate sensitivities of 80 to 85% in symptomatic women. Chlamydial cultures are labor intensive and expensive and may be available only in university settings; as such they may not be cost-effective in the management of patients with PID. Additionally, early identification of chlamydial infection in screening of high-risk asymptomatic women may allow for earlier treatment and a reduced incidence of ascending infection into the upper genital tract. The use of the polymerase chain reaction for the detection of *C. trachomatis* in screening high-risk individuals using urine specimens may ultimately prove cost-effective due to its enhanced sensitivity and specificity over culture and in its ability to identify early infections. Azithromycin, recently approved for the treatment of uncomplicated chlamydial cervicitis and urethritis, has been shown to be a cost-effective therapeutic regimen compared with doxycycline, as compliance is ensured with the former single-dose therapy.

REFERENCES

Dodson MG. Antibiotic regimens for treating acute pelvic inflammatory disease. J Reprod Med 1994;39:285.

Kahn JG, Walker CK, Washington AE, et al. Diagnosing pelvic inflammatory disease. JAMA 1991;266:2594.

McCormack WM. Pelvic inflammatory disease. N Engl J Med 1994;330:115.

Paavonen J, Kiviat NB, Brunham H, et al. Prevalence and manifestations of endometritis among women with cervicitis. Am J Obstet Gynecol 1986;152:280.

Washington AE, Aral SO, Wolner-Hanssen P, et al. Assessing risk for pelvic inflammatory disease and its sequelae. JAMA 1991;266:2581.

Wasserheit JN, Bell TA, Kiviat NB. Microbial causes of proven PID and efficacy of clindamycin and tobramycin. Ann Intern Med 1986;104:187.

Westrom L, Mardh P-A, Acute pelvic inflammatory disease. In: Holmes KK, Mardh P-A, Sparling PF, et al., eds. Sexually transmitted diseases. New York: McGraw-Hill, 1990:593.

CHAPTER 8–27

Infections of Bone (Osteomyelitis)

Monica M. Farley, M.D.

DEFINITION

Osteomyelitis is defined as microbial invasion and destruction of bone. The disease occurs in a wide variety of clinical settings in both children and adults and can follow an acute or chronic course.

ETIOLOGY

Osteomyelitis is typically a bacterial infection; *Staphylococcus aureus* is most commonly isolated but a variety of Gram-positive, Gram-negative, aerobic, and anaerobic pathogens have been reported. Fungi and mycobacteria are important but less frequent causes of osteomyelitis.

CRITERIA FOR DIAGNOSIS
Suggestive

The diagnosis should be considered in an otherwise healthy child who develops painful swelling of an extremity in association with fever and chills. Osteomyelitis in adults occurs most often in the elderly and is frequently related to specific predisposing factors such as open trauma, surgery, chronic vascular disease, and peripheral neuropathy. Clinical findings that suggest the diagnosis in adults include local signs of inflammation, bone pain, and wound or sinus tract drainage. Typical radiographic changes may become evident 7 to 10 days after the onset of infection.

Definitive

Definitive diagnosis of osteomyelitis is dependent on isolation of the pathogen from the bone lesion or from blood cultures when there is radiographic or radionucleotide evidence of osteomyelitis.

CLINICAL MANIFESTATIONS
Subjective

The pertinent history and symptomatology are distinctly related to the clinical type of osteomyelitis (Table 8–27–1). In children with

TABLE 8–27–1. TYPES OF OSTEOMYELITIS

Clinical Category	Bones Involved	Bacteriology	Clinical Features
Childhood hematogenous	Long bones of lower extremities; occasionally upper extremities	*Staphylococcus aureus* in 50% of cases	Blood cultures positive in 50–60% of cases; abrupt onset of symptoms; systemic toxicity
Neonates			
Healthy	Single bone	Group B streptococcus	Spread to adjacent joint common
High risk	Multiple sites	*S. aureus, Escherichia coli*	Symptoms may be vague
Adult hematogenous	Predilection for vertebrae	*S. aureus* most common; increasing incidence of Gram-negative bacilli	Age > 50; fewer systemic symptoms; local symptoms predominate; sedimentation rate increased; sources: urinary tract, skin, respiratory tract; spinal epidural abscess a serious complication
Spread from adjacent sites	Long bones of lower extremities, mandible, skull	*S. aureus* most common; frequently mixed, including anaerobes; *Pseudomonas* common with puncture wounds; *Pasteurella* with animal bites	Associated with postoperative infection; posttraumatic; adjacent soft tissue infection, i.e., sinuses, teeth, puncture wounds, animal bites
Vascular insufficiency	Small bones, feet, toes	Mixed Gram-positive and Gram-negative, including anaerobes	Strong association with diabetes mellitus and peripheral vascular disease; elderly age group (50–70); difficult to cure; frequently requires amputation
Sickle cell disease	Possibly multiple simultaneous sites	Frequently Gram-negative; *Salmonella* common	Difficult to distinguish from bone infarct
Intravenous drug abuse	Vertebral, sternoclavicular, pelvis	Gram-negative, particularly *Pseudomonas aeruginosa* and *Serratia; S. aureus*	Generally indolent course; frequently requires debridement procedure
Hemodialysis	Ribs, thoracic spine	*S. aureus*	X-ray changes resemble renal osteodystrophy; presumed hematogenous source
Tuberculosis*			

*See Chapter 13–41.

hematogenous infection, there is frequently a history of prior blunt trauma to the affected area. Patients with osteomyelitis that has spread from an adjacent site may have a history of open trauma, orthopaedic surgery, puncture wound, animal bites, or chronically infected teeth or sinuses. Diabetes mellitus and atherosclerotic peripheral vascular disease are associated with infection of the small bones of the feet. Sickle cell anemia, intravenous drug abuse, and hemodialysis are all predisposing factors in specific clinical types of osteomyelitis.

Children with hematogenous osteomyelitis usually experience abrupt onset of high fever and prominent systemic toxicity. Local pain and altered range of motion are generally limited to a single bone. In contrast, adults experience very few systemic symptoms. The most common complaints are local pain and swelling. Fever is variable and may be low grade or transient. If chronic infection develops, intermittent drainage from an overlying sinus tract may occur.

Objective

Physical Examination

Common physical findings include local tenderness, edema, and erythema overlying the affected bone. The presence of a fluctuant mass in children should suggest a subperiosteal abscess. Neonatal osteomyelitis frequently spreads to the adjacent joint and should be suspected when a joint effusion is detected. Sinus tracts, with or without drainage, are frequently seen with chronic osteomyelitis. Careful neurologic examination for signs of cord compression is critical in patients with vertebral osteomyelitis.

Routine Laboratory Abnormalities

Routine laboratory evaluation does not specifically contribute to the diagnosis. The white blood cell count may be elevated, especially in children with hematogenous osteomyelitis. Although nonspecific, the erythrocyte sedimentation rate is elevated in the majority of patients. Blood chemistry values including calcium and alkaline phosphatase levels are usually within normal limits.

PLANS

Diagnostic

Differential Diagnosis

Primary or metastatic bone tumors must be considered in patients presenting with bone pain and destructive bone lesions. Extensive soft tissue infections, bone infarcts in sickle cell patients, and, occasionally, osteoarthritis may be difficult to distinguish from osteomyelitis, particularly in the setting of a positive radionucleotide scan.

Diagnostic Options

In view of the need for prolonged antimicrobial therapy and the risk of progression to chronic disease if improperly treated, specific bacteriologic diagnosis is essential. Blood cultures are positive in 50 to 60% of patients with hematogenous osteomyelitis. In the remaining patients, aspiration or biopsy of the involved bone remains the diagnostic procedure of choice. This is particularly important in chronic infection, in which there is poor correlation between sinus tract cultures and the underlying bone pathogen. Biopsy specimens should be routinely cultured for aerobic and anaerobic bacteria, mycobacteria, and fungi.

Radiographic changes associated with infection include lytic lesions, periosteal elevation, cortical irregularity, and demineralization. These changes may not be evident for 7 to 10 days after the onset of infection. Later in the course of infection, segments of necrotic, devascularized bone can become separated to form sequestra. Rapid growth of the periosteum (involucrum) and pathologic fractures can be seen radiographically in chronic osteomyelitis. Computed tomography (CT) has been useful in defining small areas of cortical destruction, early periosteal proliferation, and soft tissue extension when plain films are not helpful. CT scanning is of particular value in the evaluation of vertebral osteomyelitis, in which identification of local soft tissue extension is essential. CT scans are also useful in directing percutaneous needle biopsies for microbiologic diagnosis. Magnetic resonance imaging (MRI) may be useful in differentiating between soft tissue and bone infections and evaluating complicated chronic osteomyelitis; however, the MRI image may be significantly distorted in areas of metal implants, and neoplastic bone lesions may be difficult to differentiate from infected bone. For these reasons and because of the substantial cost, MRI imaging should not be part of routine evaluation of suspected osteomyelitis.

Radionucleotide imaging provides a valuable additional diagnostic option for detection and localization of osseous infection in patients with suggestive clinical findings but nondiagnostic roentgenographic results. Technetium-99m (^{99m}Tc), gallium-67 (^{67}Ga) citrate, and indium-111 (^{111}In) chloride scans may be suggestive of acute osteomyelitis as early as 3 days into infection and well before the appearance of radiographic abnormalities. Technetium-99m is concentrated in areas of increased blood flow and reactive new bone formation, providing a sharp bone image; however, false-negative scans may occur when blood flow is significantly impaired. Gallium and indium concentrate in areas of inflammation, including collections of polymorphonuclear leukocytes, macrophages, and malignant tumors. The bone image is less distinct, and differentiating between soft tissue and bone infection may be difficult. Sequential technetium–gallium imaging may improve specificity for osteomyelitis.

Recommended Approach

Identification of a specific bacteriologic agent is the highest priority in the diagnosis of osteomyelitis. Culture of bone aspirate or biopsy material for aerobic and anaerobic bacteria, fungi, and mycobacteria is essential in most cases. Blood cultures should be obtained in all patients with suspected acute osteomyelitis. Plain radiographs of symptomatic areas should be routinely obtained. Radionucleotide imaging should be used as an adjunct to radiography when plain films are negative or inconclusive and in infants and young children who have poor localization of symptoms. CT scanning and MRI should be reserved for complicated cases to distinguish between soft tissue and bone infection, to direct biopsy procedures, or to evaluate suspected soft tissue extension of bone infections such as an epidural abscess complicating vertebral osteomyelitis.

Therapeutic

Appropriate antimicrobial therapy for acute osteomyelitis must be given for prolonged periods (4–6 weeks) to ensure effective treatment. A 19% failure rate in children with acute infection treated for less than 3 weeks has been reported. The optimal antibiotic regimen for treatment of chronic infection has not been firmly established. Four to six weeks of parenteral therapy followed by prolonged oral antibiotics is a common approach. Selection of a specific antibiotic(s) is determined by antimicrobial susceptibility testing of organisms isolated from blood or bone cultures.

Studies of treatment of acute osteomyelitis in children have shown an approximately 95% cure rate with brief initial parenteral antibiotic therapy (approximately 7–14 days) followed by oral drug administration to complete 3 to 6 weeks of therapy (Tetzlaff et al., 1978). These studies have carefully monitored compliance and documented adequate serum bactericidal levels on oral therapy. Therefore, this therapeutic approach has become standard in children whose infection is diagnosed and treated early, who show a good clinical response to initial treatment and can be appropriately monitored. Home administration of parenteral antibiotics after clinical stabilization has been used in adults to eliminate the need for prolonged hospitalization. Experience with the new fluoroquinolones shows oral ciprofloxacin to be a well-tolerated and effective alternative to parenteral antibiotics in the treatment of Gram-negative osteomyelitis in adults. It is not, however, recommended as single-drug therapy for infections caused by Gram-positive organisms (particularly S. aureus) or, anaerobes (Waldvogel, 1989) or for treatment of osteomyelitis in children.

When diagnosed and treated early, most cases of acute osteomyelitis can be managed effectively with antibiotics alone. Surgical intervention becomes an essential component of therapy when significant bone necrosis has occurred. Drainage of abscesses, removal of sequestra, and resection of all necrotic bone are critical for long-term cure of chronic osteomyelitis. Recent surgical advances have provided new techniques to deal with the large defects of soft tissue and bone resulting from debridement procedures (Cierny, 1990). Thorough surgical debridement, use of bone grafts with or without local tissue flaps or free flaps, and

specific antimicrobial therapy have become the standard approach to the management of chronic osteomyelitis. Antibiotic-impregnated polymethyl methacrylate beads can be used temporarily to fill bony defects resulting from debridement procedures and as adjuvant therapy; beads are removed several weeks later and often replaced with a bone graft.

FOLLOW-UP

The patient should be followed closely during the course of antibiotic therapy for evidence of adequate clinical response. If initially present, elevation of temperature and white blood cell count should normalize during treatment. Follow-up radiographic examinations may be necessary for months or years after treatment to assess accurately the final outcome of bone healing. Patients should be informed that recurrences do occur and that they should report symptoms of pain and swelling or the development of a draining sinus tract immediately.

DISCUSSION
Prevalence and Incidence

The incidence of osteomyelitis has a biphasic pattern, occurring most often in children under 10 years of age and adults over age 50. Children are usually healthy and have a single long bone involved, and the initial source of their infection is often not apparent. Hematogenous osteomyelitis in adults has a predilection for the spine. Infection of the long bones in adults may occur following open reduction of traumatic fractures. Elderly patients with long-standing diabetes are particularly susceptible to osteomyelitis of the feet related to vascular insufficiency and peripheral neuropathy. Infection in intravenous drug abusers frequently involves such unusual sites as the sternoclavicular area and pelvic girdle in addition to the spine.

Related Basic Science

Bacterial pathogens account for the majority of etiologic agents, and S. aureus is responsible for more than 50% of cases; however, the incidence of Gram-negative osteomyelitis has increased in recent years. Examples include Gram-negative enteric organisms associated with hematogenous vertebral osteomyelitis, Pseudomonas aeruginosa frequently isolated from infection associated with puncture wounds and in intravenous drug abusers, and Salmonella strains commonly responsible for infection in sickle cell patients. Mycobacterium tuberculosis of the spine remains an important clinical entity, particularly in developing countries, and is discussed elsewhere in this book (see Chapter 13–41). Occasionally, fungi are found to be the causative agents in bone infection.

In children, infection most often occurs in the metaphysis of rapidly growing long bones. As outlined in Table 8–27–1, adult osteomyelitis involves a variety of locations dependent on the clinical type of infection. Pathogenic mechanisms require a combination of factors, including compromised vascularity and accumulation of inflammatory products, in addition to the microbial agent. This process results in bone necrosis and demineralization. Formation of segments of devascularized bone called sequestra creates a potential focus for residual bacteria. Resorption of necrotic bone is followed by periosteal activation and new bone formation. In neonates, metaphyseal capillaries penetrate the growth plate, allowing spread of infection to the epiphysis and adjacent joint space. Infection in older children is contained by the growth plate, but lateral spread occurs, breaking through the cortex and lifting the loose periosteum, potentiating subperiosteal abscess formation. As the growth plate is reabsorbed in adults, the threat of subarticular spread of osteomyelitis returns.

Natural History and Its Modification with Treatment

Prompt diagnosis and treatment of acute hematogenous infection are usually associated with excellent outcome and little or no chronic morbidity. Osteomyelitis resulting from vascular insufficiency is poorly responsive to therapy and often requires amputation for cure. Chronic bone infection may be quite refractory to long-term cure and has been known to recur as long as 40 years after initial diagnosis.

Prevention

There are no well-defined measures to prevent acute osteomyelitis other than rapid and appropriate treatment of a primary source of infection when identified; however, it is well established that progression from acute to chronic osteomyelitis can best be prevented by prompt diagnosis, selection of the optimal antimicrobial agent and length of therapy, and adequate surgical drainage.

Cost Containment

The refractory nature of chronic osteomyelitis, frequently requiring months and sometimes years of therapy, can result in enormous medical costs. Therefore, as discussed above, measures that reduce the risk of progression to chronic infection can result in significant cost containment. Hospitalization costs can be reduced by the use of home intravenous therapy teams or oral antimicrobial agents. Well-monitored outpatient therapy represents a cost-effective management option in appropriately selected patients.

REFERENCES

Cierny G III. Chronic osteomyelitis: Results of treatment. Instruct Course Lect 1990;39:495.

Green NE. The use of bone scans for the detection of osteomyelitis. Instruct Course Lect 1983;39:40.

Sapico F, Montgomerie J. Pyogenic vertebral osteomyelitis: Report of nine cases and review of the literature. Rev Infect Dis 1979;1:754.

Tetzlaff TR, McCracken GH, Nelson JD. Oral antibiotic therapy for skeletal infections of children. J Pediatr 1978;92:485.

Waldvogel FA. Use of quinolones for the treatment of osteomyelitis and septic arthritis. Rev Infect Dis 1989;2(suppl 5):S1259.

Waldvogel FA, Vasey H. Ostomyelitis: The past decade. N Engl J Med 1989;303:360.

CHAPTER 8–28

Pyogenic Eye Infections

Phyllis E. Kozarsky, M.D., and Alan M. Kozarsky, M.D.

DEFINITION

Pyogenic eye infections refer to bacterial or, occasionally, fungal infections of the eye and its adnexa.

ETIOLOGY

Uncontrolled replication of pathogenic bacteria or fungi invading the eye, eyelids, and orbit causes pyogenic infections.

CRITERIA FOR DIAGNOSIS

Suggestive

Examination of the eye and its adnexa usually suggests ocular inflammation.

Definitive

Eye infections included in this discussion are hordeolum (stye), conjunctivitis, corneal ulcer, endophthalmitis, preseptal cellulitis, and orbital cellulitis. A diagnosis is made when the symptoms and signs readily fit specific patterns of inflammation or when infection is proven by culture.

CLINICAL MANIFESTATIONS

Subjective

Patients with a hordeolum (stye) often complain of localized discomfort or pressure under the eyelid. They also may have a foreign-body sensation.

Symptoms of acute bacterial conjunctivitis are burning, irritation, itching, and sticking together of the eyelids on awakening. Usually patients say the symptoms began in one eye and, several days later, became bilateral. Unilateral bacterial conjunctivitis is more unusual. Patients with viral conjunctivitis often have a similar clinical presentation, but they may in addition have associated upper respiratory symptoms. The predominance of itching, especially in an atopic patient or in one with hayfever, may suggest an allergic rather than an infectious etiology for the conjunctivitis. Patients with chronic conjunctivitis often present with the same symptoms as acute infection. By definition, however, the illness will have lasted several weeks despite treatment for usual bacteria. The etiology of chronic conjunctivitis is more likely viral or chlamydial. A careful history regarding contacts is important, as acute bacterial or viral conjunctivitis can be rapidly transmitted within the family unit and these organisms can cause epidemics. In addition, a sexual history in adolescents and young adults may be important, as both gonococci and *Chlamydia* are causes of conjunctivitis and infected patients may have genitourinary symptoms such as dysuria and discharge.

Persons with recent eye trauma, those who wear contact lenses, and comatose patients with exposure keratitis are all predisposed to corneal ulcers. Symptoms include pain, discharge, photophobia, and blurred vision.

Most endophthalmitis (or infection within the globe) occurs after interocular surgery; however, penetrating eye trauma or a corneal ulcer also may lead to endophthalmitis. The general practitioner or internist is most likely to see bacterial endophthalmitis in its metastatic form. Patients who are bacteremic, particularly those with endocarditis, may develop endophthalmitis from hematogenous spread. The most common cause of hematogenously spread endophthalmitis is *Candida* species. This is seen in the patient with neutropenia on broad-spectrum antibiotics who develops fungemia. These patients may complain of red eyes, decreasing vision, and pain.

Patients with preseptal (eyelid) cellulitis often complain of swelling of the lids, redness, and warmth. Because the infection remains localized and anterior to the orbital septum, orbital structures are not involved. In contrast, patients with orbital cellulitis frequently have proptosis, limitation of extraocular motility, and decreased visual acuity. They also may have associated symptoms of sinusitis. In addition, they complain of high fever, chills (from concomitant bacteremia), and general malaise.

Objective

Physical Examination

A hordeolum (stye) can be seen as a small pustule on examination of the eyelid margin where the patient complains of discomfort.

Signs of acute conjunctivitis are discharge and diffuse conjunctival hyperemia. These signs may be confused with those of other diseases causing a red eye. It is quite important to distinguish conjunctivitis from these other, more severe conditions because some can lead to permanent loss of vision (i.e., acute narrow-angle glaucoma, recurrent herpes simplex keratitis) (Table 8–28–1).

Occasionally, the inferior tarsal conjunctivae will have a cobblestone appearance. These lesions represent large conjunctival lymphoid follicles. Preauricular lymphadenopathy also may be appreciated in some patients with conjunctivitis. Lymphadenopathy and conjunctival follicles are more characteristic of viral and chlamydial infection. Usually in the patient with acute conjunctivitis, no other abnormal physical

TABLE 8–28–1. COMMON CAUSES OF A RED EYE

	Acute Conjunctivitis	Herpes Simplex Keratitis	Iritis (Uveitis)	Acute Narrow-angle Glaucoma
Cornea	Clear	May be partially opacified	Clear	Steamy
Discharge	Yes	No	No	No
Pupil	Normal	Usually normal	Miotic	Midfixed
Preexisting or concomitant viral illness	Sometimes	No	No	No
Injection	Peripheral	Perilimbal	Perilimbal	Perilimbal
Visual acuity	Minimally affected	Variably affected	Variably affected	Decreased

findings will be found. Exceptions are gonococcal or chlamydial conjunctivitis, where a careful genitourinary examination may yield pelvic tenderness or discharge in a woman or penile discharge in a man. Patients with acute conjunctivitis will not be febrile, nor will routine laboratory tests be abnormal.

Patients with a bacterial corneal ulcer have a white, gray, or yellow infiltrate on their cornea, marked conjunctival hyperemia, mucopurulent discharge, possible hypopyon (pus in the anterior chamber), and severe pain.

Patients who develop endophthalmitis often exhibit severe conjunctival hyperemia, chemosis (conjunctival edema), marked lid edema, and severe pain. An anterior chamber hypopyon that is visible as a white fluid level may also develop. Visual acuity is decreased.

The patient with preseptal cellulitis has extensive edema and erythema of the involved area (often the face and the forehead), including the lid. The inflamed, swollen eyelids cannot be easily opened, but when visualized, the globe is normal with a full range of motion. There is no afferent pupillary defect (Marcus Gunn pupil), and visual acuity is unaffected.

Patients with orbital cellulitis also have lid edema and pain. In addition, they exhibit proptosis, afferent pupillary defect, diminished visual acuity, and decreased or absent extraocular movements. They also may have sinus tenderness if the orbital infection represents spread from a paranasal sinus. The patients appear acutely ill. Their temperature is often greater than 101°F.

Routine Laboratory Abnormalities

The white blood cell count is significantly elevated with a left shift in patients with orbital cellulitis.

PLANS
Diagnostic
Differential Diagnosis

Examination of the patient with a hordeolum is sufficient to make the diagnosis. Sometimes it is difficult to differentiate this from a chalazion, which is a nidus of chronic granulomatous inflammation in an obstructed eyelid sebaceous gland.

Diagnostic Options and Recommended Approach

The diagnosis of conjunctivitis is made by history and physical examination, as well as by using the information in Table 8–28–1. The more difficult task is differentiating bacterial from viral and allergic causes. The character of the discharge may be slightly varied—more watery in viral or allergic and more purulent in bacterial conjunctivitis. Patients with viral conjunctivitis often have preauricular and submandibular adenopathy. The presence of follicles of the tarsal conjunctivae suggest viral or chlamydial infection. Many ophthalmologists feel that it is expensive and unnecessary in most instances to differentiate between the causes of acute conjunctivitis because the usual bacterial agents are easily treated by most topical antibiotics, and viral conjunctivitis is typically self-limited. Therefore in typical cases, conjunctival cultures are not recommended.

There are several situations in which it is important to perform tests to determine the specific etiology. First, neonates with virulent-appearing conjunctivitis require evaluation by a specialist who can culture the conjunctivae for bacterial pathogens as well as scrape for *Chlamydia* staining and culture. Second, in cases of severe mucopurulent conjunctivitis, a Gram stain of the discharge should be performed. It may reveal Gram-negative diplococci in polymorphonuclear leukocytes, characteristic of gonococcal infection. Patients with suspected gonococcal conjunctivitis should also have blood cultures, as well as cultures of their pharynx, rectum, urethra, and cervix. They should be referred immediately to an ophthalmologist, as unlike other forms of conjunctivitis, this may permanently damage vision and requires a specific therapeutic regimen. Third, a patient who develops purulent conjunctivitis in the hospital may require a Gram stain and culture of the drainage, as these infections may be caused by aerobic, Gram-negative organisms. Finally, patients with conjunctivitis who have had signs and symptoms for over 2 weeks require evaluation by a ophthalmologist.

The diagnosis of corneal ulcer and endophthalmitis may be suspected by the nonophthalmologist on clinical grounds. For evaluation and proper therapy, these patients should be referred to an opthalmologist.

Both preseptal cellulitis and orbital cellulitis may be identified by examination. Blood cultures can be helpful, as these patients are often bacteremic. In orbital cellulitis, x-ray films of the sinuses may suggest contiguous spread from adjacent sinusitis. Computed tomography or magnetic resonance imaging scans of the head and sinuses have been used to document sinus involvement or intraorbital abscess. If a collection of fluid is drained, the material should be sent for culture because it may give a clue to the agent(s) responsible. Phycomycosis (*Rhizopus* and *Mucor*) is a cause of acute necrotizing sinus and/or orbital inflammation that is often lethal. These organisms should be suspected in the immunosuppressed host or in the diabetic patient in ketoacidosis with orbital cellulitis.

Therapeutic

A hordeolum may be treated with warm compresses to the eye for 15 minutes several times per day until the pustule opens and drains. Topical antibiotics are not required, but they may be given in the form of polymyxin B and bacitracin ointment (Polysporin).

Topical antibiotics are the mainstay of treatment for acute conjunctivitis. Sulfacetamide drops 10% (1 drop four times daily to the involved eye) are given for 1 week to 10 days. Sulfa drops are efficacious and inexpensive and cover the usual causes of bacterial conjunctivitis. Sulfa drops rarely cause local sensitization, but patients who are allergic to sulfas should not receive them. Drops containing a combination of polymyxin B and trimethoprim are available and may be more desirable than those containing sulfa. Polymyxin B and bacitracin ointment (applied twice daily) also constitute excellent treatment. Some patients, however, are uncomfortable with ointment on their eyes. Some ophthalmologists use aminoglycoside drops (i.e., gentamicin). In most uncomplicated cases of conjunctivitis, aminoglycosides are not necessary, but for hospital-acquired Gram-negative bacterial conjunctivitis they may be indicated. Aminoglycoside drops used frequently and for an extended period can cause an irritative keratoconjunctivitis that may cause an eye to be persistently red. Physicians should avoid preparations containing neomycin because about 10% of individuals will have a hypersensitivity reaction to it. Quinolone-containing eyedrops are now available commercially and are effective against the majority of bacterial pathogens causing conjunctivitis; however, their expense as well as the development of bacterial resistance mitigates against their routine use. Also, drops containing steroids should be avoided. Sometimes the eye of a patient with herpes simplex keratitis will mimic conjunctivitis, and if these eyes are treated with preparations containing steroids, the cornea may be permanently damaged. Although chloramphenicol eyedrops are still widely used, they should be avoided, unless alternative drugs are not available, because they have been implicated in cases of aplastic anemia.

The etiologic diagnosis of conjunctivitis in the neonate dictates the specific therapy. A specialist should be consulted for an appropriate regimen.

Any patient who fails to respond to treatment within several days, deteriorates on therapy, or has decreased visual acuity should be immediately referred to an ophthalmologist. Corneal ulcers and endophthalmitis are treated by the ophthalmologist.

Because the causative organisms of preseptal cellulitis are skin organisms such as streptococci and staphylococci, a semisynthetic penicillin (oxacillin or nafcillin) or a first-generation cephalosporin (cefazolin or cephalothin) may be used. The dose given is often dependent on the extent of the cellulitis and whether the patient is bacteremic. In general, for oxacillin, nafcillin, or cephalothin, 1 g intravenously every 6 hours to 2 g intravenously every 4 hours, is used. For cefazolin (Ancef), 1 or 2 g intravenously every 8 hours is used. Occasionally, when the cellulitis is minimal, oral dicloxacillin or an oral cephalosporin may be used at a dose of 500 mg orally four times daily. Therapy should be continued until all signs and symptoms have subsided.

Orbital cellulitis is a more serious infection. The antibiotics listed above for preseptal cellulitis are used in higher doses for orbital cellulitis. Sometimes when a patient has accompanying sinusitis, *Hemophilus influenzae* may be isolated from aspirated material, and therefore, a second- or third-generation cephalosporin may be used (cefuroxime or ceftriaxone). Anaerobes and Gram-negative rods are unusual causes of orbital cellulitis, but if they are isolated from drainage or from the blood, appropriate antimicrobial agents should be selected to cover these. If the computed tomography scan suggests abscess or sinus fluid, surgical drainage may be required for cure. In patients with AIDS, *Pseudomonas aeruginosa* causes sinusitis more frequently than in the normal host and, therefore, needs to be considered as a cause of orbital infection.

FOLLOW-UP

A hordeolum or simple conjunctivitis is self-limited and usually needs no follow-up. If the infection persists, referral should be made to an ophthalmologist. Corneal ulcers and endophthalmitis are followed by an eye specialist. Preseptal cellulitis and orbital cellulitis are followed carefully in the hospital until they have subsided.

DISCUSSION

Prevalence and Incidence

Although hordeolum and conjunctivitis are common afflictions, corneal ulceration, orbital cellulitis, and endophthalmitis are notably infrequent.

Related Basic Science

The eye has several natural defenses against infection: blinking, a tear film containing immunoglobulins, a lower than body temperature, and an epithelial covering. Bacterial flora normally occur on the eye and its adnexa. The most common organisms are staphylococci, streptococci, diphtheroids, and, sometimes, anaerobes and Gram-negative rods. In the case of an eye infection, if the eye or conjunctiva is swabbed and cultured, organisms of the normal flora may grow and may or may not reveal the etiology of the infection (i.e., a viral conjunctivitis, if cultured, may grow *Staphylococcus epidermidis*). On the other hand, many infections of the eye are caused by normal flora that have managed to overcome the eye's defenses.

A hordeolum is a common, localized staphylococcal infection of the eyelash follicles. There may be inflammation of the superficial meibomian glands or the glands of Zeis and Moll.

Conjunctivitis is inflammation of the tarsal and bulbar conjunctivae. Local vessel dilation promotes leakage of fluid and inflammatory cells. As mentioned previously, conjunctivitis may be caused by bacteria, viruses (such as adenovirus, influenza, and measles), *Chlamydia*, allergy, or toxins. Rarely, in other parts of the world, parasites may cause conjunctivitis. The major bacteria causing conjunctivitis are staphylococcal and streptococcal species. In children, *Hemophilus* species are more important, and in young, sexually active adults, gonococci and *Chlamydia* must be considered. Ophthalmia neonatorum may be caused by gonococci, other bacteria, or *Chlamydia*.

Chronic corneal disease or trauma may lead to a defect in the corneal epithelium enabling organisms to enter. Inflammatory cells then follow and elaborate proteolytic enzymes leading to a stromal abscess. Individuals using contact lenses, particularly soft lenses, which require effective disinfection, are predisposed to these infections. Organisms that are part of the normal flora are the most common causes of corneal ulcers, although hospitalized patients are more likely to develop Gram-negative ulcers.

Endophthalmitis is rare and occurs most commonly after intraocular surgery, with an incidence of approximately 0.001% following cataract extraction. Endophthalmitis following perforation of an ulcer or following hematogenous spread in a septic patient is also quite rare.

Preseptal cellulitis is a common form of cellulitis caused by direct inoculation of skin flora into the superficial layers of the periocular area. Orbital cellulitis may occur by the same mechanism and may be caused by the same organisms. Often, however, orbital cellulitis is caused by contiguous spread from adjacent sinusitis.

Natural History and Its Modification with Treatment

Hordeola and conjunctivitis are self-limited infections that cause little morbidity, even if not treated. *Chlamydia* of certain immunotypes cause trachoma and may eventually cause corneal scarring if not treated. Chronic trachoma is the most common cause of irreversible blindness in the world, although it is seen rarely in the United States in immigrants and American Indians. Rarely, a hyperacute conjunctivitis (e.g., gonococcal) will cause a corneal ulcer. Corneal ulcers, if untreated, may perforate and cause endophthalmitis. Even when aggressively treated some corneal ulcers will cause permanent scarring or perforation of the globe. And finally, even in the best of circumstances, at least 50% of patients with endophthalmitis lose useful vision.

When treated early, preseptal cellulitis resolves quickly. When the orbit is involved, aggressive treatment is necessary. Extension of preseptal cellulitis to the orbit and cavernous sinus thrombosis is rare unless a patient remains untreated or unless infection is caused by a particularly invasive organism such as *Mucor*.

Prevention

Prevention of hordeola involves treating skin conditions such as rosacea and attending to lid hygiene, thus preventing blepharitis.

Conjunctivitis can be prevented by washing hands often, especially before touching the face or eyes, and by preventing contact with items used by others who have conjunctivitis, such as towels, wash cloths, and makeup.

Prophylactic topical silver nitrate solution, antibiotic eyedrops, or a commercially available povidone–iodine solution is given to all infants to try to prevent ophthalmia neonatorum due to gonococci and other bacteria. If, however, neonatal conjunctivitis does occur, parents also must be treated for the offending organism. In cases of gonococcal or chlamydial conjunctivitis in the adult, sexual contacts must be fully evaluated and treated if appropriate.

Corneal ulcers can be prevented by adhering strictly to recommendations for disinfecting contact lenses, especially soft lenses. Because there is an increased incidence of corneal ulcers in individuals using extended-wear lenses, some physicians feel that no one should wear lenses while sleeping. This, however, remains controversial among ophthalmologists.

Modern ophthalmic surgical technique and prophylactic antibiotics have decreased the incidence of postoperative endophthalmitis. Prompt evaluation and treatment of suspected bacteremias may prevent hematogenous endophthalmitis. Prevention of eye trauma and treatment of sinusitis may help prevent preseptal cellulitis and orbital cellulitis.

Cost Containment

The best way of curtailing the costs due to eye infection is prevention. With bacterial conjunctivitis occurring so frequently, sulfa, sulfa–polymyxin, and gentamicin eyedrops are effective and less expensive than quinolone preparations.

REFERENCES

Albert DM, Jakobiec FA, eds. Principles and practice of ophthalmology. Phildelphia: Saunders, 1994.

Duane TD, Jager EA, eds. Clinical ophthalmology, vols. 2,4,5. Philadelphia: Harper & Row, 1994.

Leibowitz HM, Pratt MV, Flagstad U, et al. Human conjunctivitis: I. Diagnostic evaluation. Arch Ophthalmol 1976a;94:1747.

Leibowitz HM, Pratt MV, Flagstad U, et al. Human conjunctivitis: II. Treatment. Arch Ophthalmol 1976b:94:1752.

Newell FW. Ophthalmology principles and concepts. Chicago: Mosby Year Book, 1992.

Ronnerstam R, Persson K, Hansson H, Renmarker K. Prevalence of chlamydial eye infection in patients attending an eye clinic, a VD clinic, and in healthy persons. Br J Ophthalmol 1985;69:385.

Schein OD, Glynn RJ, Poggio EC, et al. Microbial Keratitis Study Group. The relative risk of ulcerative keratitis among users of daily-wear and extended-wear soft contact lenses: A case–control study. N Engl J Med 1989;321:773.

CHAPTER 8–29

Infections of the Skin and Soft Tissue

Kathryn E. Arnold, M.D., David S. Stephens, M.D., and David Schlossberg, M.D.

DEFINITION

The skin, normally a barrier to infection, may itself become infected either superficially or with deeper extension into the dermis or subcutaneous tissue. Predisposing factors include compromised skin integrity, altered host defenses, impaired circulation, and compromised sebaceous or lymphatic drainage.

ETIOLOGY

Infections of the skin and soft tissue are caused by a wide range of bacteria, viruses, fungi, and parasites.

CRITERIA FOR DIAGNOSIS

Suggestive

Diagnosis is often suspected by the clinical presentation and appearance of the lesion.

Definitive

Microbiologic cultures, Gram or other special stains of material from the lesion, lesional biopsy, and serologic studies may be needed to establish or confirm the diagnosis.

CLINICAL MANIFESTATIONS

Subjective

A brief summary of common clinical manifestations of dermatologic infections may be found in Table 8–29–1. In addition to determining symptoms and rapidity of onset, epidemiologic history (e.g., occupation, activities, exposures) may be important in suggesting a diagnosis. For example, a history of handling saltwater fish or shellfish or of exposure to saltwater in a patient with cellulitis may suggest infection with *Vibrio* or *Erysipelothrix* species.

Objective

The distribution and morphologic appearance of skin lesions are extremely important in the evaluation of possible etiologies. Lesions may be widespread or distributed only over exposed areas; they may be pustular, vesicular, bullous, papular, maculopapular, ulcerative, or plaque-like, suggesting differing pathologies. Color and appearance of the lesion and the nature of material obtained from the lesion are also important. For example, bacterial infections of the skin, such as those caused by *Staphylococcus aureus* or *Streptococcus pyogenes*, are usually associated with signs of inflammation (e.g., redness, pain, heat, swelling, and purulent drainage), whereas many fungal infections of the skin are chronic and show little evidence of acute inflammation. Table 8–29–2 includes descriptions of the skin lesions that may be seen with systemic infections in normal hosts (see also Chapter 8–5). Table 8–29–3 describes skin lesions caused by infectious agents in AIDS patients.

PLANS

Diagnostic

Differential Diagnosis

Infections of the skin and soft tissues must be distinguished from noninfectious causes of similar skin lesions, such as pyoderma gangrenosum and (in some cases) cutaneous neoplasia (Table 8–29–4). Skin lesions caused by noninfectious processes may also become secondarily infected.

Diagnostic Options and Recommended Approach

Microbiologic culture of the infected site and demonstration of the microorganisms on stains or biopsy are the preferred tests for diagnosis.

Therapeutic

Choice of antimicrobial therapy depends on the site of infection, the etiologic agent, the sensitivity of the organism to antimicrobial agents, and patient factors. Surgical debridement in certain infections may be as critical as the selection of the most appropriate antimicrobial agent. Tables 8–29–1 through 8–29–3 and 8–29–5 and 8–29–6 list some of the therapeutic measures and antimicrobial agents used for treatment of specific infections of skin and soft tissue.

FOLLOW-UP

Most skin infections may be followed clinically for signs of improvement. When margins are visible in an area of cellulitis, marking the edge of the lesion allows one to assess the lesion for extension or regression. Linear erythema extending proximally from the lesion suggests lymphangitic spread of the infection. Development of deep bullous lesions, necrosis, crepitus, or anesthesia is an indication for surgical evaluation. Deeper infections may require surgical exploration and repeated debridement to ensure viability of remaining tissue.

DISCUSSION

Prevalence and Incidence

Skin and soft tissue infections are extremely common throughout the world, particularly among persons living under conditions of poor hygiene and those predisposed to infection through chronic illness, immunosuppression, or compromised anatomy.

Related Basic Science

Trauma, ischemia, foreign bodies, and edema are major factors predisposing to local infections of skin and soft tissues. The common primary pyodermas caused by Gram-positive cocci (*Staphylococcus aureus* and

TABLE 8–29–1. PRIMARY PYODERMAS

Infection	Clinical Manifestations		Common Etiologic Agents	Plans	
	Subjective	*Objective*		*Diagnostic*	*Therapeutic*
Impetigo	Crusted lesions usually on extremities, local pruritus, seen most often in young children, spread by contact	Vesicular lesions progress rapidly to pustules covered with thick yellow crust, regional lymphadenitis	*Streptococcus pyogenes, Staphylococcus aureus* (increased prevalence in recent studies)	Clinical, wound culture (remove crust), Gram stain; increased anti-DNase B titer in 90% of group A streptococcal impetigo, weak antistreptolysin O titer	Local care, penicillin G or antistaphylococcal penicillin; alternatives: erythromycin, mupirocin ointment; highly communicable
Bullous impetigo		Vesicles progress to thin-walled flaccid bullae with clear yellow fluid; unroof to form pale brown "varnished" crust	*S. aureus*, phage group II		Antistaphylococcal penicillin (e.g., cloxacillin, dicloxacillin), erythromycin
Scalded skin	Abrupt-onset fever, skin tenderness, erythroderma, large flaccid bullae	Widespread, large flaccid bullae with Nikolsky sign (separation at dermal–epidermal border); unroof to expose bright red, tender dermis	*S. aureus* producing exfoliative exotoxin	Clinical, wound or mucous membrane culture; toxin-mediated organism usually absent in skin lesions	Fluid replacement, saline compresses, IV nafcillin; corticosteroids contraindicated
Erysipelas	Fever, red painful enlarging lesion, often on face or on legs in setting of lymphedema	Superficial cellulitis with marked lymphatic involvement: advancing elevated erythematous borders sharply demarcated from normal skin	Group A streptococci	Clinical	Penicillin G or erythromycin; may require IV antibiotics
Cellulitis	History of trauma or skin lesion, pain, erythema, rapidly spreading; exposures (e.g., salt-water bathing, fish handling) may suggest etiologies other than *S. pyogenes* and *S. aureus*	Fever, swelling, tenderness, erythema, regional adenopathy; in contrast to erysipelas, borders less distinct and not elevated	*S. pyogenes, S. aureus* in immunocompetent, less commonly *Vibrio* spp., *Erysipelothrix* (erysipeloid); variety of pathogens in immunosuppressed, see Chapter 8–31); *Hemophilus influenzae* in young children; mixed Gram-positives, Gram-negatives, and anaerobes in diabetic foot infections	Clinical, blood, wound culture	Penicillin G or antistaphylococcal penicillin for usual pathogens; broader coverage for compromised host (e.g., diabetic foot)
Folliculitis	Red, painful (sometimes pruritic) papules at base of hairs, especially on face	Small erythematous nodules, pustules around hair follicles	*S. aureus* (*Pseudomonas aeruginosa* if acquired in whirlpool or swimming pool)	Clinical, wound culture	Local care, antistaphylococcal penicillin (quinolone for whirlpool folliculitis)
Furuncles, carbuncles, hidradenitis suppurativa	See Chapter 11–9		*S. aureus*	Clinical, wound culture, Gram stain	Incision and drainage except hidradenitis suppurativa; promote drainage with moist heat; antistaphylococcal penicillin
Paronychia	Swelling, pain, redness around nailbed	Palpation provokes exquisite pain	*S. aureus*, group A streptococci, *Candida*, *Pseudomonas aeruginosa*	Clinical, Gram stain, KOH preparation	Local care, appropriate antibiotic or topical antifungal agent

Streptococcus pyogenes) frequently occur following skin trauma. As reviewed in Chapters 8–38 and 8–39, these organisms possess specific virulence factors that include surface components (e.g., teichoic acid, M-protein) and the production of extracellular toxins. Bacterial infections of the skin and soft tissues are usually associated with classic signs of acute inflammation (redness, pain, warmth, and swelling).

The pathogenesis of cutaneous manifestations of systemic infection is varied. Presence of the infectious agent in the skin, microemboli, vasculitis, disseminated intravascular coagulation, and immune complex deposition may contribute to the specific cutaneous lesions seen in systemic infection.

Bacterial infections of subcutaneous tissues and muscle result from contamination during traumatic injury, spread from a contiguous site of infection, or, less commonly, spread by a hematogenous route. The nature of the infecting organism and the extent of ischemic tissue damage are responsible for differences in clinical presentation. For example, gas gangrene is caused by anaerobic Gram-positive bacilli of the genus *Clostridium* (predominantly *C. perfringens*). Gas gangrene usually follows severe traumatic injury to muscle during which soil or foreign material contaminated with *Clostridium* endospores has been introduced. The presence of devitalized tissue creates an anaerobic environment, which is critical for growth of this organism. Devitalized tissue result-

TABLE 8–29–2. CUTANEOUS INVOLVEMENT BY SYSTEMIC INFECTIONS

Infection	Clinical Manifestations		Common Etiologic Agents	Plans	
	Subjective	*Objective*		*Diagnostic*	*Therapeutic*
Endocarditis	Fever, malaise	Fever, heart murmur, petechiae, Osler's nodes, splinter hemorrhage, Janeway's lesions, Roth spots	See Chapter 8–12	Blood cultures, echocardiogram	See Chapter 8–12
Gonococcemia	See Chapter 8–42	Few scattered purpuric pustules on distal extremities, tenosynovitis, arthritis	*Neisseria gonorrhoeae*	Gram stain of pustule; culture of blood, skin lesion, urethra, cervix, pharynx, rectum, joint fluid	Ceftriaxone
Meningococcemia	Acutely ill, fever, rash, ± headache	Macules, petechiae, purpura, purpura fulminans, distal symmetric gangrene	*Neisseria meningitidis*	Blood or cerebrospinal fluid culture	High-dose IV penicillin, prophylaxis for close contacts
Pseudomonas aeruginosa sepsis and occasionally sepsis due to other Gram-negative bacilli	Immunocompromised, often neutropenic patient; fever; acutely ill	Painful red maculopapular lesions, become purpura, ecthyma gangrenosum (gray-black eschar on lower trunk, extremities)	*Pseudomonas aeruginosa*, other Gram-negative bacilli	Gram stain and culture of lesion, blood cultures	Aminoglycoside *plus* antipseudomonal penicillin or ceftazidime
Enteric fever	See Chapter 8–17	Rose spots: crops of small pink papules on chest, back, abdomen appear after 7–10 d of fever	Salmonella typhi	Blood, urine, stool cultures	Ampicillin, trimethoprim–sulfamethoxazole, chloramphenicol
Toxic erythemas Scarlet fever	See chapter 8–39	Diffuse erythroderma sparing circumoral area, strawberry tongue, pastia's lines; desquamation on convalescence	*Streptococcus pyogenes*	See Chapter 8–39	See Chapter 8–39
Toxic shock syndrome	See Chapters 8–38 and 8–39	Scarlet fever-like erythroderma	*Staphylococcus aureus, S. pyogenes*	See Chapters 8–38 and 8–39	See Chapters 8–38 and 8–39
Mucocutaneous lymph node syndrome (Kawasaki syndrome)	Prolonged fever, erythroderma, conjunctival injection	Fever, conjunctival suffusion, generalized erythroderma lymphadenopathy, desquamation on convalesence	Unknown	Clinical	Aspirin, gamma globulin
Erythema infectiosum (fifth disease)	See Chapter 11–11; in children, facial rash "slapped cheek" appearance; in adults, variable "lacelike" rash, arthralgias	Erythematous rash, arthropathy in adults, transient maturation arrest of erythrocytes, aplastic crisis in congenital hemolytic anemia	Human parvovirus B19	Anti-human parvovirus B19 immunoglobulin M antibody (in active phase of illness)	Usually self-limited; transfusion, as needed, intravenous immunoglobulin in some patients

TABLE 8–29–3. AIDS-ASSOCIATED SKIN INFECTIONS

Infection	Clinical Manifestations		Etiologic Agents	Plans	
	Subjective	*Objective*		*Diagnostic*	*Therapeutic*
Bacillary angiomatosis	Skin nodules	Erythematous, friable nodules and plaques	*Bartonella (Rochalimaea)* spp.	Biopsy, polymerase chain reaction, serology	Prolonged erythromycin or doxycycline
Molluscum contagiosum	Painless papules on face, trunk, genitals	Small, firm papules with pearly white surface, may be umbilicated	Cutaneous poxvirus, similar lesions in disseminated *cryptococcosis*	Clinical, biopsy, crush preparation	Local ablation (e.g., liquid nitrogen)
Kaposi's sarcoma	Nodules, often on lower extremities, in mouth	Red-purple nodules, plaques	Neoplasia secondary to probable herpesvirus	Biopsy, clinical	Interferon-alfa, chemotherapy for severe disease
Oral hairy leukoplakia	Asymptomatic	Raised, white lesion of epithelial cells of oral mucosa	Epstein–Barr virus	Clinical	None
Candidiasis	Rash, mouth pain/acid sensitivity	Salmon pink papules with "satellite" lesions; oral:	*Candida* spp.	Gram stain or KOH preparation of lesion	Topical miconazole, systemic ketoconazole, fluconazole; refractory: amphotericin B

TABLE 8–29–3. (*Continued*)

Infection	Clinical Manifestations		Etiologic Agents	Plans	
	Subjective	*Objective*		*Diagnostic*	*Therapeutic*
Herpes zoster (shingles)	Pain, itching, rash	hyperplastic or atrophic changes with white plaques; Dermatomal distribution; painful crops of vesicles evolving to pustules, shallow crusted ulcers	Varicella zoster virus	Clinical, Tzanck smear	Acyclovir
Condylomata	Usually asymptomatic	Flesh-colored papules	Human papillomavirus	Clinical; Biopsy if persistent; may be carcinoma in situ	Local ablation
Syphilis	See Chapter 8–46	Primary: chancre; secondary: maculopapular rash; tertiary: gumma	*Treponema pallidum*	Dark-field exam, serology	See Centers for Disease Control and Prevention Sexually Transmitted Diseases Treatment Guidelines (Chapter 8–46)
Disseminated opportunistic infections: cryptococcosis, histoplasmosis, coccidioidomycosis, toxoplasmosis	See individual chapters (8–54, 8–55, 8–57, 8–62)	See individual chapters		See individual chapters	See individual chapters

TABLE 8–29–4. INFECTIOUS CAUSES OF SPECIFIC SKIN LESIONS

Infection	Clinical Manifestations		Etiologic Agents
	Subjective	*Objective*	
Acute ulcer or pustule	Symptoms vary with etiologic agent	Ulcerative or pustular lesion; specific signs depend on etiologic agent	Genital ulcers (primary syphilis, genital herpes, chancroid lymphogranuloma venereum, granuloma inguinale) anthrax, cutaneous diphtheria, tularemia, ecthyma contagiosum (Orf), Milker's nodes
Vesicles (localized)	Localized vesicular rash, usually painful	Grouped vesicles on erythematous base, progress to superficial ulcers	Herpes simplex virus (HSV)-1, HSV-2: herpes labialis, genital herpes, herpetic whitlow; Varicella–zoster virus: herpes zoster (shingles); *vibrio* spp.
Vesicles (generalized)	Painful or sometimes pruritic vesicular lesions	Generalized vesicular eruption	Hand, foot, and mouth disease, varicella, disseminated herpes zoster, eczema herpeticum, rickettsial pox
Verrucae (wartlike)	Chronic lesions on genital area skin and mucus membranes	Cauliflower-surfaced keratotic papules	Condyloma acuminatum, common warts
Chronic ulcers/nodular lesions	Chronic draining ulcer	Varies with specific etiologic agent	Actinomycosis, nocardiosis, blastomycosis, chromomycosis, sporotrichosis, coccidioidomycosis, histoplasmosis, cutaneous tuberculosis, atypical mycobacterial infection, leprosy, leishmaniasis, syphilis
Maculopapular rashes	Generalized red rash	Generalized erythematous maculopapular eruption; may or may not be confluent depending on infection	Enteric fever, scarlet fever, toxic shock syndrome, measles, atypical measles, Kawasaki's syndrome, erythema infectiosum (fifth disease), rat bite fever, syphilis, typhus, leptospirosis
Urticaria	Generalized pruritic rash, appears quickly and leaves without scar or pigment	Pink plaques, wheals	Hepatitis B, infectious mononucleosis, *Mycoplasma pneumoniae*, cercarial dermatitis, other parasitic infestations
Petechiae, purpura, ecchymosis	Generalized rash	Macular lesions, petechiae, purpura	Endocarditis, gonococcemia, meningococcemia, sepsis, Rocky Mountain spotted fever, dengue, hemorrhagic fever viruses, plague, typhus
Erythema nodosum	Painful, tender nodule on lower extremities	Erythematous, warm nodules over anterior tibia	Tuberculosis, leprosy, coccidioidomycosis, histoplasmosis, psittacosis, among a number of infectious agents
Erythema chronicum migrans	Large red plaque; onset summer and fall in endemic areas, fever, malaise, associated joint pain; occasionally tick bite is remembered	Spreading, indurated erythematous areas surrounding pale center; often on thigh, buttocks, or near axilla	Lyme disease
Cutaneous larva migrans	"Creeping eruption" occurs in persons in southern United States, children, farmers, those walking barefoot on beaches	Advancing linear or serpiginous plaque usually on hands, feet	Larvae of nematodes
Erythema marginatum	Acute rheumatic fever	Focal evanescent circinate erythema, usually on trunk or proximal extremities	Follows infection with *Streptococcus pyogenes*; see Chapter 8–38

TABLE 8-29-5. INFECTIONS OF SUBCUTANEOUS TISSUE

Infection	Clinical Manifestations		Common Etiologic Agents	Plans	
	Subjective	*Objective*		*Diagnostic*	*Therapeutic*
Infectious gangrene (progressive bacterial synergistic gangrene, necrotizing cellulitis/fasciitis, streptococcal gangrene, Fournier's gangrene)	Rapidly progressive, painful, exudative lesion; fever; predisposing factors: surgery, trauma, vascular insufficiency, diabetes mellitus	Specific objective findings vary depending on specific syndrome and etiologic agent; all are characterized by necrosis and often crepitus	Progressive bacterial synergistic gangrene (microaerophilic streptococci, *Staphylococcus aureus*, Gram-negative bacilli); necrotizing cellulitis/fasciitis (anaerobic streptococci plus *E. coli*, *Enterobacter*, *Klebsiella*, or *Proteus*); streptococcal gangrene (group A streptococci); clostridial cellulitis (*Clostridium perfringens*); Fournier's gangrene (mixed aerobic-anaerobic fasciitis around male genitals)	Clinical, Gram stain, culture of exudate; soft tissue x-rays may reveal gas	Surgical exploration and debridement essential; antibiotics appropriate for specific etiologic agents, and including anaerobic coverage
Subcutaneous abscesses	Painful, swollen areas usually seen with symptoms of other infection	Tender, warm, fluctuant lesions	Occur secondary to infections in contiguous foci or as complication of bacteremia (e.g., *S. aureus*)	Clinical, aspiration and Gram stain, culture	Appropriate antimicrobial agent, surgical drainage
Bites	Human or animal bite	See Chapter 8-36	See Chapter 8-36	Clinical	See Chapter 8-36
Acute lymphangitis	Red streak, rapid onset	Linear erythematous streak extending proximally from infected lesion	Usually group A streptococci, rarely *S. aureus*, *Pasteurella* spp.	Clinical	IV penicillin or nafcillin, cefazolin
Chronic lymphangitis	Red streak, may show "beading", subacute onset	As above	Rare; pathogens include sporotrichosis among gardeners, *Mycobacterium marinum* among fish fanciers, filariasis in persons from endemic areas	Clinical	Appropriate antimicrobial agent dependent on specific etiology
Acute suppurative lymphadenitis	Pain, fever, "swollen glands"	Tender, swollen regional lymph nodes	Common: group A streptococci, *S. aureus*; Less common: *Mycobacterium tuberculosis*, nontuberculous mycobacteria, tularemia, Kawasaki's disease, *Histoplasma*, *Coccoidioides*, *Bartonella* (cat-scratch disease), *Toxoplasma* spp.; Inguinal nodes; consider lymphogranuloma venereum, chancroid, *Yersinia pestis* (plague)	Clinical; strep associated with sore throat, staph with nearby skin lesion, *Bartonella henselae* with cat scratch, tuberculosis with prior exposure, etc.	Varies with suspected pathogen; empiric therapy often begins with penicillin, dicloxacillin; if bubonic plague suspected, treat early with streptomycin, tetracycline
Decubitus ulcers	Bedridden patients with chronic debilitating illnesses, immobility, altered sensation in affected area	Ulcer in areas of chronic irritation, especially sacral area, extremities	Anaerobes, enterococci, Gram-negative bacilli	Clinical	Antimicrobial agents as needed, local care; relieve source of irritation/pressure

ing from arterial insufficiency is also a major factor in the pathogenesis of necrotizing fasciitis and myositis caused by a mixture of anaerobic and aerobic bacteria (Tables 8-29-4 and 8-29-5).

Infections of the lower extremity in diabetic patients warrant special mention because of their frequent occurrence. Because of impaired sensation, diabetics are predisposed to trauma and secondary infection of distal extremities. Healing is impaired by compromised microvascular circulation. In addition to coverage for staphylococci and streptococci, diabetic foot infections may require coverage for anaerobes and Enterobacteriaciae unless the etiology can be established with certainty.

Natural History and Its Modification with Treatment

Morbidity and mortality are determined by the site of infection, the etiologic agent responsible for the infection, and the presence of complicating diseases. For example, primary pyodermas due to certain

TABLE 8–29–6. MYOSITIS (INFECTION OF SKELETAL MUSCLE)

Infection	Clinical Manifestations		Common Etiologic Agents	Plans	
	Subjective	*Objective*		*Diagnostic*	*Therapeutic*
Clostridial gas gangrene	Severe pain, prostration, incubation period 6 h to 4 d, follows muscle injury and contamination (e.g., traumatic wound, bowel or biliary tract surgery) ± arterial insufficiency of extremities	Tachycardia, hypotension, temperature less than 101°F, edema, local tenderness, serosanguineous discharge, positive Gram stain (Gram-positive bacilli, few polys), crepitus, leukocytosis; surrounding skin edematous, white, or yellow; blebs may develop	*Clostridium perfringens* and other clostridial species	Clinical appearance, culture, Gram stain of pus; x-rays show gas in feathery linear pattern	Emergency surgical debridement; high-dose penicillin G and clindamycin (chloramphenicol or imipenem alternatives); possibly hyperbaric O$_2$
Nonclostridial fasciitis/myositis	Pain, fever, usually occurs on lower extremities or perineum, history of traumatic lesion that may be minimal; often seen in patients with diabetes mellitus or vascular insufficiency	Erythematous, swollen area, initially painful and exquisitely tender, but may progress to anesthesia; ± bullae; fever, tachycardia, systemic toxicity, leukocytosis, foul-smelling pus, crepitus	Mixture of anaerobes (anaerobic streptococci, *Bacteroides* spp.) and facultative Gram-negative bacilli (*Escherichia coli, Klebsiella*)	Clinical: Gram stain (mixed Gram-positive and Gram-negative organisms), culture of lesion ± positive blood cultures	Surgical debridement, antibiotics such as aminoglycoside and clindamycin
Pyomyositis (primary muscle abscess)	Subacute-onset localized muscle pain, approximately 20% give history of recent trauma to area, fever; occurs predominantly in tropics	Swelling, local erythema, leukocytosis; heat and tenderness may be minimal	*Staphylococcus aureus*	Aspiration of pus, Gram stain, culture	Antistaphylococcal penicillin, surgical drainage
Psoas abscess	Fever, lower abdominal and back pain; pain extends to knee or hip	Limping, inability to extend at hip, psoas sign ± tender mass in groin; may be a complication of vertebral osteomyelitis, intraabdominal infection, perinephric abscess	Varied; *S. aureus*, bowel flora, *Mycobacterium tuberculosis*	Computed tomography scan, culture, Gram stain, AFB smear	Drainage, antibiotics depending on etiology, origin of infection
Myalgias	Muscle aches	Muscle tenderness	Influenza, dengue, Rocky Mountain spotted fever, toxoplasmosis	CPK, serology, cultures	Depends on etiology
Trichinosis	Fever, muscle aches, weakness, history of eating undercooked pork or bear meat	Periorbital edema, eosinophilia	*Trichinella*	Clinical presentation, serology, muscle biopsy	Bedrest, salicylates
Acute rhabdomyolysis	Diffuse muscle pain	Muscle tenderness, myoglobinuria, elevated creatinine, blood urea nitrogen	Influenza and other viruses (Coxsackie, echovirus, Epstein–Barr, adenovirus, HIV), Legionnaires' disease, leptospirosis, rickettsial infection, sepsis, many noninfectious causes	Elevated CPK myoglobinuria	Hydration, monitor renal function, antibiotics for specific bacterial infections

AFB, acid-fast bacillus; CPK, creatine phosphokinase.

"nephritogenic strains" of *Streptococcus pyogenes* may lead to post-streptococcal glomerulonephritis in children, and pyoderma due to *Staphylococcus aureus* may produce bacteremia and endocarditis, especially in patients with underlying illness such as diabetes mellitus. Secondary thrombophlebitis is a common complication of cellulitis involving the lower extremities.

Prevention

Some infections of the skin and soft tissues are preventable. For a diabetic patient who is susceptible to cuts and abrasions on the feet because of impaired sensation, it is important to wear shoes that fit properly, to avoid trauma, and to examine the extremities regularly for cuts or abrasions. Frequently, such lesions go unnoticed by the patient.

Another preventable cause of cellulitis is recurrent cellulitis of the legs associated with tinea pedis. This is particularly common at the site of previous saphenous vein removal for use in coronary artery bypass graft surgery. Eradication of the tinea pedis usually prevents recurrent cellulitis in such patients.

Cost Containment

Careful cleansing and debridement of cutaneous lesions, coupled with early antimicrobial treatment, may limit the extent of a soft tissue infection. Aspiration of an area of cellulitis for Gram stain and culture is a low-yield procedure and should probably be undertaken only if an unusual pathogen is suspected.

REFERENCES

CDC. Sexually Transmitted Diseases Treatment Guidelines. MMWR 1993;42(Suppl):RR14.

Dover JS, Johnson RA. Cutaneous manifestations of human immunodeficiency virus infection, parts I and II. Arch Dermatol 1991;127:1383, 1549.

Lewis RT. Necrotizing soft tissue infections. Infect Dis Clin North Am 1992;6:693.

Swartz MN. Cellulitis and subcutaneous tissue infections. In: Mandell GL, Bennett JE, Dolin R, eds. Principles and practice of infectious diseases. 4th ed. New York: Churchill Livingstone, 1995: 909.

Swartz MN. Myositis. In: Mandell GL, Bennett JE, Dolin R, eds. Principles and practice of infectious diseases. 4th ed. New York: Churchill Livingstone, 1995:929.

Swartz MN. Lymphadenitis and lymphangitis. In: Mandell GL, Bennett JE, Dolin R, eds. Principles and practice of infectious diseases. 4th ed. New York: Churchill Livingstone, 1995:936.

CHAPTER 8–30

Infection in the Elderly

Stephen W. Schwarzmann, M.D., and Jonas A. Shulman, M.D.

DEFINITION

The Social Security Administration has defined the elderly as those individuals who are 65 years of age or older and the very elderly as those individuals who are greater than 85 years of age. An infection in individuals 65 years or older is categorized as infection in the elderly.

ETIOLOGY

The age-related problems of decreasing function of cell-mediated immunity and local defense as well as underlying chronic disease contribute to the increased problem of infection in this population.

CRITERIA FOR DIAGNOSIS
Suggestive

The diagnosis of infection frequently presents atypically. The most commonly seen infections are pneumonia, urinary tract infections, and infections of skin and soft tissue. These and other infectious processes not infrequently present with general malaise, confusion, or as a worsening of preexisting symptoms such as a deterioration of a preexistent hemiparesis. The most important clue to infection in the elderly is an unexplained change in the patient. It has been suggested that the clinical features of infection in the elderly are similar to those of a younger patient who is taking corticosteroids.

Definitive

A definitive diagnosis of infection in the elderly can be made when objective evidence of infection is discovered. Such evidence may be an abnormal chest x-ray film, positive blood cultures, white cells in the urine, an abnormal computed axial tomography scan of the abdomen, and so on. See Plans, Diagnostic.

CLINICAL MANIFESTATIONS
Subjective

Infection in this population frequently occurs in the setting of preexistent disability or at least some dependency on others. The patient may often be living independently but may require help in general housekeeping or shopping. Other medical problems such as chronic obstructive lung disease. atherosclerotic coronary heart disease, chronic neurologic disease such as hemiparesis from stroke, diabetes, arthritis, or malignancy may itself be causing symptoms, an exaggeration of which is attributed to the preexistent illness and not to a superimposed infection. The patient with chronic arthritis who develops increasing pain and swelling in a joint may write it off to "I'm supposed to hurt because I have arthritis" and fail to report the worsening of symptoms to his or her physician. Frequently the patient is unable to give a history and the caregivers should then be consulted. A history of decreasing activity (i.e., patient does not want to get out of bed), increasing confusion, or increasing falls or incontinence may often be the only presenting clues to underlying infection.

Objective
Physical Examination

The physical findings of infection in the elderly may be quite varied. A typical presentation may be seen such as fever, cough, rales, and purulent sputum production in pneumonia or fever and flank pain in acute pyelonephritis. Alternatively, the physical signs usually relied on to identify an infection or focus of infection may frequently be absent. The patient may be hypothermic and, rather than localize the infection with findings of rales or flank tenderness, may present with increasing confusion, immobility, increased falling, incontinence of urine or stool, or fecal impaction. These nonspecific symptoms have been called the "geriatric giants" of infection and may be the only clue to infection. It is also important to be aware of false positives. A stiff neck in an elderly person can be the result of dementia, Parkinson's disease, cervical arthritis, or cerebrovascular disease. Abdominal tenderness with rebound may be a result of fecal impaction and not a perforated viscus, which itself may be silent in this age group. As mentioned before, the ability to mount a febrile response is often lost in the elderly and hypothermia may be noted. Checking body temperature every 4 to 6 hours might avoid missing a fever, and in the patient who is dehydrated or mouth breathing, a rectal temperature more accurately reflects body temperature.

Routine Laboratory Abnormalities

The ability to mount a leukocytosis seems to be maintained in the elderly, and elevation of the white blood cell count to 11,000 or more will be seen in two thirds of the patients. In those patients who fail to do this, a shift to the left in the white cell differential with appearance of bandemia will usually occur and provide some support for the diagnosis of an infection. Although not diagnostic, a sedimentation rate of 50 or greater is usually seen in significant infection and may offer additional laboratory support for the presence of infection. The chest x-ray film may be negative at the time of presentation of a patient with pneumonia and should be repeated in 12 to 24 hours if the source of the patient's infection has not yet been identified. The cause for the delay in development of an infiltrate has been attributed to dehydration with appearance of an infiltrate on rehydration, but proof for this is still lacking. A urinalysis usually shows pyuria in the setting of a urinary tract infection, though exceptions to this are not infrequent and a urine culture as well as blood cultures should be a routine part of the laboratory evaluation of any possible infection.

PLANS

Diagnostic

A nonspecific decline in patient performance is the single most important clue to the possible presence of infection. The most frequently seen examples of nonspecific decline, a history frequently taken from the caregiver, and thorough physical examination and support from the white blood cell count, differential, and erythrocyte sedimentation rate should help increase the suspicion for infection. If these findings are positive, then a search to localize the infection should be made, recognizing that lung, kidney, and skin are the most frequent sites of infection. Pneumonia and intraabdominal infection are the most commonly missed infections and close attention should be given to these areas if the site of infection remains enigmatic. Follow up chest x-ray or computed tomography scan of abdomen and pelvis may offer additional diagnostic help. If the patient presents with a more typical presentation of infection (i.e., fever, flank pain, and dysuria), studies appropriate to the affected area are indicated.

Therapeutic

Treatment of infections in the elderly follows the same principles as that in younger patients. Drainage of pus, relief of obstruction, and selection of an antibiotic regimen based on the microbiology of the infection, defined either by culture or by "statistically most likely," are required. Major differences in the selection and dosing of an antibiotic in the elderly relate to physiologic changes of aging with resultant changes in pharmacokinetics and the concomitant use of other drugs for treatment of other underlying illness that might interfere with the antibiotic (i.e., calcium and tetracycline). Because of changes in aging in the gastrointestinal tract, including decreased motility, decreased gastric acid, decreased splanchnic blood flow, and decreased motility, alterations in dissolution of the drug and rate of absorption may be significantly less. In general, however, the ultimate extent of absorption is not altered. More importantly, renal function as defined by creatinine clearance declines with age, even though the serum creatinine may remain normal. A serum creatinine of 1 in a 25-year-old patient may equate with a creatinine clearance of 100 mL/min, whereas a similar serum creatinine in an 85-year-old may reflect a creatinine clearance half that in the younger patient. This apparent discrepancy between serum creatinine and creatinine clearance relates to decreased production of endogenous creatinine due to decreased muscle mass, decreased protein intake, and decreased exercise. Nowhere is the recognition of this fact more important than in the dosing of aminoglycosides. In this setting it is frequently desirable to increase the interval between doses, thereby allowing maintenance of therapeutic peak levels yet avoiding toxic trough levels. Appropriate monitoring of aminoglycoside blood levels is very important in this age group. Volume of distribution is altered with age. Increased fat, reduced lean body mass, and reduced total intracellular water reduce the volume of distribution of water-soluble antibiotics and increase that of the fat-soluble drugs. The decrease in serum albumin that normally occurs in aging reduces the number of binding sites to which highly protein-bound antibiotics adhere, allowing for higher levels of free antibiotic. This may have some pertinence with the methylthiotetrazole-containing cephalosporins cefamandole (Mandol), cefotetan (Cefotan), and cefoperazone (Cefobid), in which higher levels of free antibiotic might allow a greater adverse effect of methylthiotetrazole on the prothrombin time.

Hepatic metabolism and biliary excretion are also reduced in the aging process and, although not as well defined as in the case of renal excretion, may prolong the half-life of antibiotics that are eliminated primarily by the hepatic route (i.e., cefoperazone, ceftriaxone [Rocephin]). As both these antibiotics have dual excretion (kidney and hepatic), a potential reduction in frequency of dosing would relate to declines in both renal and hepatic elimination.

In general, the β-lactam antibiotics represent a good choice of antibiotic class for treatment of infections in the elderly. They have a varied spectrum of bactericidal activity, a high therapeutic ratio, and a good safety profile. Alternative antibiotic therapy, particularly in urinary tract infections and bacterial diarrhea, would include trimethoprim–sulfamethoxazole (Bactrim, Septra) and the fluoroquinolones (Cipro, Noroxin). In mixed infections in which both aerobic and anaerobic bacteria are active (i.e., aspiration pneumonia, intraabdominal infection due to fecal contamination or soft tissue infections such as a diabetic foot infection or decubitus ulcer with cellulitis), the penicillinase-inhibiting antibiotics, such as clavulanic acid–amoxicillin (Augmentin), sulbactam–ampicillin (Unasyn), and claviulanic acid–ticarcillin (Timentin), offer excellent coverage and efficacy. In addition to the well-defined nephrotoxicity and ototoxicity of the aminoglycosides, this class of antibiotic also functions under the handicap of a marked loss of potency in low-pH environments and the need for oxygen, which is required by the active metabolic process that gives the aminoglycoside access to the interior of the bacterial cell. When one considers that the average pH of an abscess is 5.7 and that of infected bronchial mucus is 6.48, and that mixed infections occur in a low-oxygen-tension environment, it is not surprising that this class of antibiotics does not perform well in pulmonary and mixed infections. These drugs are most frequently used for their synergistic activity with β-lactam antibiotics and vancomycin and for the prevention of development of resistance by Gram-negative bacteria.

Both the patient and his or her caregivers at home should recognize that the typical manifestations of infection as they occur in the general population may be masked in the elderly. Recognizing one of the "geriatric giants" (i.e., confusion or delirium, falling and postural instability, immobility, incontinence of urine, and incontinence or impaction of stool) as a possible first sign of infection can result in earlier diagnosis and better prognosis. In addition, it is important to recognize that the response to therapy in the elderly is significantly slower than that in younger people. A liberal dose of patience is required. Slowness of the rate of improvement need not be of concern so long as the direction is toward improvement.

FOLLOW-UP

Because infection in the elderly is often predisposed by an underlying condition, for example, chronic obstructive pulmonary disease predisposing to pneumonia, appropriate follow-up includes monitoring and reassessment of the underlying condition in convalescence. Improvement of the infection itself requires monitoring of the presenting symptoms as well as return to normal of the white blood cell count, differential, and erythrocyte sedimentation rate, though the latter may require several weeks to normalize. Failure of a positive response to therapy might suggest inappropriate antibiotic selection, development of a superinfection, or failure to surgically intervene in the drainage of pus or relief of obstruction. As with infection in any age group, it is important to separate colonizing infection from invasive infection. A follow-up sputum culture in a patient receiving antibiotic therapy for a microbiologically defined pneumonia may show the presence of a new organism, often a Gram-negative aerobe such as an Enterobacteriaceae. If the patient is clinically improving, showing a decrease in sputum production, remission of fever, and a more normal white blood cell count and differential, the diagnosis of colonization should be made and no new antibiotic treatment given. Conversely, if the patient experiences relapse of cough, fever, an increase in purulent sputum, and an increasing white blood cell count with bandemia, invasive infection (a superinfection) is properly diagnosed and antibiotics appropriate to the newly isolated organism should be started.

DISCUSSION

Prevalence and Incidence

Indeed, in the elderly there is an increased incidence of both community-acquired and nosocomial infections, an increased susceptibility to infections, and differences in the clinical presentation that infections may take.

With the aging of our population, a much greater proportion of physicians' time will be spent in dealing with problems of the elderly.

As a result of multiple factors, including a decline in cell-mediated immunity and chronic disease that reduces local resistance factors, infection occurs with greater frequency and higher mortality in the elderly.

Related Basic Science

Cell-mediated immunity appears to be the arm of the immune system that normally declines most in old age. This predisposes to infections such as herpes zoster (shingles) and to aggressive tuberculosis, which is often associated with a loss of skin test sensitivity. Polymorph function appears to remain normal, and humoral antibody, if previously acquired (i.e., animistic), likewise remains near normal. Response to a new antigen, such as a pneumococcal vaccine, may be blunted and ineffective.

Changes in local defense mechanisms generally relate to underlying chronic disease. Immobility may lead to bed sores, incontinence to urinary tract infections, and stroke to blunted cough reflex and aspiration.

Long-term care facilities have become a fact of life for more than a million elderly. As a result of a combination of a greater degree of chronic debilitating disease and close contact with other patients and personnel, the nursing home tends to be associated with an increased risk of lower respiratory tract, urinary tract, and skin infections, any one of which can be associated with bacteremia. The microbiology of these infections more closely parallels that of hospital-acquired infections which are due to methicillin-resistant *Staphylococcus* and multiple-antibiotic-resistant Gram-negative bacilli. In contrast to community-acquired pneumonia which is due predominantly to *Streptococcus pneumoniae* and *Hemophilus influenzae*, nursing home-acquired pneumonia more frequently is caused by a mixed infection including Gram-negative bacilli and anaerobes. Urinary tract infections acquired in the nursing home more likely relate to chronic Foley catheter use, are caused more often by antibiotic-resistant organisms, and often are complicated by bacteremia, which may not uncommonly become fatal. Prophylactic antibiotics in the setting of chronic Foley catheter drainage are not useful and promote development of resistance. The major preventive effort revolves about limiting the use of catheters and increasing the use of diapers. When a Foley must be used, maintenance of a high urine output can reduce the incidence of bacteremia. On the other hand, asymptomatic bacteremia in an otherwise well elderly patient usually clears spontaneously and does not require antibiotic therapy.

Skin and soft tissue infections are likewise seen with greater frequency because of immobility predisposing to decubitus ulcers and long-standing diabetes and peripheral vascular disease predisposing to chronic foot infections. In both these instances, the microbiology is commonly mixed and includes Gram-positive cocci, Gram-negative bacilli, and anaerobes. Thinning of the skin as a result of aging and years of solar injury, as well as chronic edema as a result of congestive heart failure, varicose veins, or postsurgical events, predisposes to acute cellulitis and lymphangitis frequently due to *Streptococcus* groups A, B, C, G. The skin may also be the site of entry of a *Staphylococcus* that may then cause endocarditis on a calcific aortic valve.

Natural History and Its Modification with Treatment

As the body ages, the built-in reserve that organ systems started with is gradually lost and normal function may require operating at full capac-

ity with no reserve to be called on at a time of stress such as infection. In the patient with chronic cerebrovascular disease or heart disease, the stress of an infection may present as a failure of that organ system rather than more typically as a febrile illness with the associated typical symptoms of the infection. As a result, one of the "geriatric giants: such as confusion or immobility becomes the presentation of the infection. From this point, the patient is at increased risk of failure of other organ systems and greater risk of morbidity and mortality.

Prevention

Unfortunately, old age is a natural phenomenon that cannot be prevented. The incidence of infection can be reduced by a number of measures.

Pneumonia can be reduced by prophylactic measures against influenza. Regular use of the appropriate influenza vaccine and drugs such as amantadine can reduce one of the major predispositions to pneumonia. The polyvalent pneumococcal vaccine should be given before old age is reached, perhaps in the decade before age 65 or sooner in patients with chronic lung disease. When given to the elderly, the efficacy of the vaccine appears to be reduced. In the nursing home, constant vigilance for tuberculosis is necessary. Infection introduced by a new patient can spread rapidly to other patients.

Limiting the use of Foley catheters in favor of diapers or intermittent catheterization may reduce the incidence of urinary tract infections.

Routine examination of the feet of diabetic patients to identify local injury or other predisposition to infection may avert a prolonged illness if not amputation.

Those patients who are confined to a bed or wheelchair are at greatest risk of the development of decubitus ulcers. Maintenance of good nutrition (serum albumin ≥ 3.5) and avoidance of constant pressure on dependent areas of skin by frequent turning or use of specialized air mattresses may reduce the incidence of this complication.

Cost Containment

As much of the infection that occurs in the elderly is nosocomial, prevention is a major factor in cost containment. In dealing with established infection, early recognition of one of the "geriatric giants" as a sign of infection that increases morbidity and mortality may lead to earlier diagnosis and treatment and, thus, lower costs.

REFERENCES

Adler WH. Immune function in the elderly. Geriatrics 1989;44(suppl. A)7.

Fox RA. Atypical presentation of geriatric infections. Geriatrics 1988;43:58.

Greenblatt DJ, Sellers EM, Shader RI. Drug disposition in old age. N Engl J Med 1982;84:1081.

Saviteer SM, Samsa GI, Ratala WA. Nosocomial infections in the elderly. Am J Med 1988;84:661.

Schneider EL. Infectious disease in the elderly. Ann Intern Med 1983;98:395.

Verghese A, Berk SL. Bacterial pneumonia in the elderly. Medicine 1983;62:271.

CHAPTER 8–31

Infections in the Compromised Host

James P. Steinberg, M.D., and W. Lee Hand, M.D.

DEFINITION

A wide variety of diseases or conditions impair the host defenses and predispose to infection (Table 8–31–1). This chapter outlines the array of defects in host defenses, lists the major causes of these defects, and discusses the infections that result from the impaired immunity.

ETIOLOGY

Many of the microorganisms that cause infection in the compromised host are of low virulence and seldom produce illness in the normal host. More virulent organisms, however, can cause life-threatening or recurrent infections in the immunocompromised population.

TABLE 8–31–1. DEFECTS IN HOST DEFENSE MECHANISMS AND ASSOCIATED INFECTIONS

Defect	Infecting Organisms	Clinical Manifestations
I. Impaired skin and mucous membrane barriers		
A. Compromised physical barriers		
1. Cystic fibrosis, immotile cilia		Pneumonia—see Chapters 8–14 and 8–15
2. Tracheostomy, tracheal intubation	Aerobic Gram-negative bacilli including	
3. Urinary tract obstructive lesions, bladder catheters	*Pseudomonas aeruginosa*	
4. Intravascular access devices	Skin organisms (especially staphylococci) enterococci	Urinary tract infection—see Chapter 8–23
5. Surgical procedures, burns	Other members of "normal flora"	Bacteremia—see Chapter 8–2
6. Other mucosal disruption (tumor, ulceration, etc.)	*Candida*	Soft tissue infections—see Chapter 8–29
B. Loss of chemical factors	*Salmonella*	Enteritis— see Chapter 8–17
1. Achlorhydria	*Mycobacterium tuberculosis*	Tuberculosis—see Chapter 13–41
C. Alteration of normal microbial flora		
1. Antibiotics	Aerobic, Gram-negative bacilli	
2. Alcoholism	Enterococci	
3. Severe illness	*Staphylococcus aureus*	Pneumonia—see Chapter 8–14, 8–15
4. Insulin-dependent diabetes mellitus	*Candida*	
5. Renal dialysis	*Clostridium difficile*	Bacteremia—see Chapter 8–2
		Pseudomembranous colitis—see Chapter 19–60
II. Abnormal humoral immunity (B-cell defects)		
A. Primary deficiency		
1. Congenital, X-linked agammaglobulinemia	Pyogenic bacteria	Pneumonia, bacteremia (systemic complications), sinusitis, bronchiectasis—see above and Chapter 8–12
	Enteroviruses	Chronic viral central nervous system infection
2. Selective immunoglobulin (Ig) deficiency		
IgA	IgA—variable; often free of infection	Sinopulmonary infection—see above
IgG (including subclass deficiency)	IgG, IgM— pyogenic bacteria	Pneumonia, sinusitis, bacteremia—see above
IgM		
3. Ig deficiency with increased IgM	Pyogenic bacteria	Pneumonia, bacteremia—see above
4. Common variable immunodeficiency ("acquired" hypogammaglobulinemia)	Pyogenia bacteria	Pneumonia, sinusitis, bacteremia, bronchiectasis— see above
	Giardia lamblia	Giardiasis—see Chapter 19–36
B. Secondary deficiency		
1. Multiple myeloma	Biphasic: early—*Streptococcus pneumoniae, Hemophilus influenzae, Neisseria meningtides;* late—Gram-negative rods, *S. aureus*	Pneumonia, bacteremia (systemic complications)— see above
2. Protein loss (intestinal, renal)	Pyogenic bacteria	
III. Defective cell-mediated immunity (T-cell defects)		
A. Primary deficiency	Intracellular organisms (viruses, fungi, mycobacteria)	
1. Thymic hypoplasia		
B. Secondary deficiency		
1. Hodgkin's disease		
2. Sarcoidosis	Intracellular organisms, pyogenic bacteria	
3. Systemic intracellular infections	*Nocardia*	See above and Chapters 8–51, 8–53, 8–57, 8–62,
4. Malnutrition	*Cryptococcus neoformans*	8–63, 8–70, 8–71, 8–74
5. Corticosteroids, cytotoxic drugs	Herpesviruses	
6. Renal failure	Other	
7. Radiation therapy		
8. Autoimmune disease		
9. AIDS	*Pneumocystis carinii, Cryptococcus, Toxoplasma,* cytomegalovirus, Mycobacteria	See above and Chapter 8–76
IV. Combined deficiency of humoral and cell-mediated immunity		
A. Primary deficiency		
1. Severe combined immunodeficiency	All types of organisms	See appropriate chapters listed above
2. Wiskott–Aldrich syndrome	All types (especially pyogenic)	Pneumonia, bacteremia—see above
3. Immunodeficiency with ataxia telangiectasia		
B. Secondary deficiency		
1. Chronic lymphocytic leukemia	*S. pneumoniae*, encapsulated organisms, *Escherichia coli*	See appropriate chapters listed above
2. Immunosuppression, cytotoxic drugs	Various organisms	
V. Phagocyte dysfunction (abnormalities of polymorphonuclear and/or mononuclear phagocytes)		
A. Primary defects		
1. Congenital neutropenia	Many types of bacteria, catalase-positive organisms	
2. Chronic granulomatous disease (CGD)	*S. aureus*, Gram-negative bacilli and opportunistic fungi (*Candida, Aspergillus*)	See Chapters 8–38, 8–39, 8–51, 8–52
3. Chediak–Higashi syndrome	*S. aureus* and pyogenic bacteria	See Chapter 8–38

(continued)

TABLE 8–31–1. (*Continued*)

Defect	Infecting Organisms	Clinical Manifestations
4. Myeloperoxidase deficiency 5. Glucose-6-phosphate dehydrogenase deficiency (homozygous)	?*Candida albicans* (usually without infection) Similar to CGD	See Chapter 8–51
B. Secondary defects 1. Neutropenia secondary to bone marrow suppression or peripheral destruction	Gram-negative bacilli, staphylococci, streptococci, *Candida*, *Aspergillus*, *Mucor*, herpesvirus, plus many unusual organisms	See Chapters 8–38, 8–39, 8–42, 8–51, 8–52, 8–70
2. Disorders of chemotaxis and opsonization (antibody and complement deficiencies)	Various bacteria (especially pyogenic)	See chapters on abnormal humoral immunity and complement system abnormalities
3. Inhibitors of chemotactic factors (alcoholic liver disease, Hodgkin's disease)	?	
4. Phagocyte dysfunction associated with thermal injury, irradiation, acute leukemia, etc.	Various bacteria	
5. Decreased leukocyte movement or function due to drugs (corticosteroids, ethanol, parenteral hyperalimentation)	Various bacteria	
C. Specific defects in tissue macrophage function 1. "Reticuloendothelial system" dysfunction (splenectomy, sickle cell anemia, cirrhosis)	Pyogenic bacteria, enteric organisms	Bacteremia, pneumonia, and meningitis (see above)
2. Decreased alveolar macrophage function (ethanol, hyperoxia, hypoxia, alveolar fluid, corticosteroids, viral respiratory infections, etc.)	Various bacteria	Pneumonia— see above
VI. Complement system abnormalities A. Primary defects 1. C1, C2, C4 deficiency	*S. pneumoniae*, encapsulated bacteria	Sinopulmonary infections
2. C3 deficiency	Encapsulated bacteria (more severe)	
3. C5, C6, C7, C8 deficiency	*Neisseria*	Meningitis—see above
B. Secondary deficiency 1. Decreased C3 (cirrhosis, systemic lupus erythematosus)	Pyogenic and enteric organisms	
2. Alternative complement pathway abnormality (sickle cell disease)	*S. pneumoniae, Salmonella*	Bacteremia, pneumonia, and meningitis—see above

CRITERIA FOR DIAGNOSIS

Suggestive

Although the underlying disease is usually established at the time of a complicating infection, an unusual, recurrent, or severe infection may be the initial clue to an underlying disease process that impairs one or more host defenses. Fever may be the only manifestation of an infection. Because the consequences of delayed recognition of an infection may be catastrophic, therapy often must be initiated before a definitive diagnosis is made. At the time of presentation with an acute illness, it may be impossible to distinguish infection from complications related to the underlying disease.

Definitive

The definitive diagnosis of an infection in a compromised host is usually established microbiologically; however, some of the pathogens can be difficult to isolate in culture, and at times, the diagnosis hinges on obtaining the appropriate histopathologic specimens. For an increasing number of pathogens, the polymerase chain reaction and other newer technologies allow for rapid diagnoses. In certain immunosuppressive illnesses including AIDS, the ability to generate specific antibody is impaired, preventing serologic confirmation of an infection.

CLINICAL MANIFESTATIONS

Details of the clinical manifestations of many of the infections that occur in compromised hosts are addressed in the chapters pertaining to the specific clinical syndromes or the particular pathogens (Table 8–31–1).

Subjective

Although the pertinent history and symptoms vary depending on the underlying diseases and infections, a few general comments can be made regarding the compromised host. A careful history of the underlying medical illness, including past and present treatment of that illness, is essential to assess the risk of infection and the likely potential pathogens. For example, the history of a splenectomy performed during the initial staging of Hodgkin's disease would increase suspicion of pneumococcal disease in the acutely ill patient. Knowledge of the dose and duration of immunosuppressive therapy is also very important; corticosteroids administered in doses higher than 10 mg of prednisone per day for several weeks or longer should be considered immunosuppressive. Many patients with immunodeficiency states receive antibiotic therapy, either for treatment of recurrent infection or for prophylaxis. A history of antibiotic administration increases the likelihood of infection with an antibiotic-resistant pathogen.

In the patient with frequent or severe infections, a detailed history of the sites and causative organisms of past infections may suggest a problem with one or more arms of the host defenses. Clues can also be garnered from the family history, as many immunodeficiencies are inherited. For example, patients (and close family members of patients) with *Neisseria meningitidis* or disseminated gonococcal infections should be evaluated for terminal complement component deficiency.

Objective

Physical Examination

The specific findings depend on the underlying illnesses and infections outlined in Table 8–31–1. It must be remembered that the underlying defect in host defenses may alter the typical manifestations of infection. For example, staphylococcal infections in the neutropenic patient may not suppurate, and signs of cellulitis may be unimpressive even with extensive tissue involvement. Corticosteroid therapy can mask fever or other signs of inflammation. A careful search should be made for skin lesions, not only because cutaneous manifestations are relatively common in the compromised host, but also because tissue specimens are often necessary to make a rapid and specific diagnosis when routine cultures are not helpful.

Routine Laboratory Abnormalities

The complete blood count and differential cell counts provide essential information, especially in the patient with known hematologic malignancy or who has received cytotoxic therapy. The risk of bacterial infection increases dramatically when the absolute neutrophil count decreases below 500 cells/μL. Examination of the peripheral smear may reveal abnormalities (e.g., blast forms, rouleaux, neutrophils with abnormal lysosomes in Chediak–Higashi syndrome) that suggest or are diagnostic of an immunosuppressive illness. Because immunoglobulins make up a large portion of the globulin fraction of serum proteins, a decreased globulin fraction may be a clue to hypogammaglobulinemia, whereas an elevated total protein level may suggest a paraproteinemia or multiple myeloma.

PLANS
Diagnostic
Differential Diagnosis

The major pathogens that cause infection in the various immunodeficiency states are listed in Table 8–31–1. At times, it may be difficult to differentiate infection from manifestations of the underlying immunosuppressive illness or from the untoward effects of therapy. For example, pulmonary infiltrates in patients with malignancy may result from infection, the underlying neoplasm, or drug-induced pneumonitis.

Diagnostic Options

Evaluation of underlying defects in host defenses may be simple or quite complex. Section 5 describes the diagnostic procedures of value in patients with suspected primary defects in specific immune mechanisms. A general approach to the evaluation of patients with an abnormality in host defenses is outlined in Table 8–31–2.

In addition to routine stains and cultures, a variety of special studies may be appropriate depending on the clinical setting and the suspected pathogens. In addition to serologic testing, cytologic examination, and viral cultures, newer technologies such as polymerase chain reaction are available to assist with the diagnosis of certain viral infections including cytomegalovirus. For pathogens such as *Legionella*, several diagnostic options are available, including indirect and direct fluorescent antibody staining, culture on special media, and urinary antigen detection. Not infrequently, the diagnosis hinges on obtaining adequate tissue specimens for histopathologic examination.

Recommended Approach

The range of pathogens that infect immunocompromised patients is diverse and many of the pathogens cannot be identified by routine laboratory measures. In addition, untreated infection can progress rapidly in this population. Consequently, an aggressive diagnostic approach is often warranted, especially when severe immunosuppression is present and when the signs of infection progress rapidly. When evidence of focal infection is present, biopsy of skin lesions, mucosal lesions, or other involved structures should be performed promptly in the acutely ill patient. The development of pulmonary infiltrates is a common occurrence in the compromised host (Table 8–31–3). Pulmonary disease is frequently superimposed on a background of hematologic malignancy, intensive cytotoxic or immunosuppressive drug therapy, and/or radiation therapy. To make an accurate diagnosis, fiberoptic bronchoscopy with bronchial brushing, bronchoalveolar lavage, and sometimes transbronchial biopsy is often necessary. In some cases, an open surgical biopsy or percutaneous needle biopsy is required. The preferred diagnostic approach must be individualized and is dependent on factors such as the rapidity of onset and severity of pulmonary disease, presence of a coagulopathy, and nature of the pulmonary disease (location, diffuse versus focal disease).

TABLE 8–31–2. DEFECTS IN HOST DEFENSE MECHANISMS: EVALUATION AND THERAPEUTIC MEASURES

Defect	Methods of Evaluation	Therapeutic Measures
Impaired skin and mucous membrane barriers	Physical examination Radiographic studies Endoscopic procedures	Removal of foreign bodies Drainage and other appropriate surgical procedures Discontinuation of inappropriate drugs (antibiotics, ethanol)

Abnormal humoral immunity	Serum protein electrophoresis
	Immunoglobulin quantitation including IgG subclasses
	Specific antibody levels
	In vitro lymphocyte studies
	  B- and T-cell counts (surface markers)
	  B-cell mitogenic and antigenic response
		Immune serum globulin (intramuscular and intravenous preparations); fresh plasma in some circumstances

Defective cell-mediated immunity	Skin testing (delayed hypersensitivity)
	In vitro lymphocyte tests
	  T-cell subsets (surface markers)
	  T-cell mitogenic and antigenic response
	  Cytokine production
		Reversal of malnutrition
		Reduction of immunosuppressive drugs (especially corticosteroids)
		Treatment of underlying disorder
		Other therapy is experimental (lymphokines, etc.)

Phagocyte dysfunction	Leukocyte counts
	Skin window techniques
	In vitro techniques (polymorphonuclear and mononuclear phagocytes)
	  Adherence (nylon wool columns)
	  Chemotaxis (chambers)
	  Phagocytosis (nitroblue tetrazolium test, bacteria, zymosan, etc.)
	  Microbicidal function (bacteria, fungi)
		Colony-stimulating factor for neutropenia, especially when secondary to cytotoxic therapy

Complement system abnormalities	Total hemolytic complement assay (tests classic activation pathway and terminal components) Assay of individual components (immunoquantitation of C3 and C4 readily available) Biological activity (chemotaxis, opsonization)	Fresh plasma to replace deficient factor Vaccination (meningococcal, pneumococcal)

TABLE 8–31–3. ETIOLOGY OF PULMONARY DISEASE IN THE COMPROMISED HOST

Infectious
    Viruses (Herpesviruses especially CMV, RSV, influenza virus)
    Bacteria (typical bacteria, *Legionella, Mycobacteria, Nocardia*)
    Fungi (*Cryptococcus, Aspergillus,* mucormycosis)
    Protozoa (*Pneumocystis carinii, Toxoplasma*)
    Helminths (strongyloides hyperinfection)
Non-infectious
    Underlying disease (neoplasm)
    Drug induced
    Radiation
    Hemorrhage
    Edema
    Emboli

Therapeutic

Therapeutic Options

Treatment of the infections that occur in the compromised host is discussed in the chapters considering those specific infections. Therapeutic measures currently used to correct deficient host defenses in adults are outlined in Table 8–31–2.

Recommended Approach

Although the principles of antimicrobial therapy in the compromised host are similar to those in the normal host, a few comments should be made. Empiric antibiotic therapy should be instituted promptly in the febrile neutropenic patient because signs of sepsis can develop rapidly before culture results are available. In the neutropenic host, bactericidal rather than bacteriostatic agents should be used; with documented Gram-negative bacteremia, survival may be improved when two bactericidal agents are administered. In certain situations, it may be advantageous to lengthen the duration of antimicrobial therapy in this population. Chronic suppressive therapy may be necessary in certain situations.

FOLLOW-UP

The frequency and character of follow-up are determined by both the infectious process and the type of underlying disease. Some of the illnesses that predispose to infection are transient, requiring only short-term follow-up; others are lifelong problems, often with escalating infectious complications which can ultimately lead to death.

DISCUSSION

Prevalence and Incidence

The prevalence and incidence of the various immunodeficiency states vary widely. Some of the inherited deficiencies are very rare. For example, with many of the complement deficiency states, fewer than 50 persons with the specific defects have been reported, and the prevalence of chronic granulomatous disease is 1 per 1 million persons. Other immunodeficiency states such as AIDS are, unfortunately, common. Many of the most common compromising conditions such as corticosteroid therapy, other immunosuppressive therapy, and use of devices that compromise physical barriers are iatrogenic.

Related Basic Science

Both nonspecific and immunologically specific host defenses are crucial in protection against infection. Immunologically nonspecific host defenses are especially important in protection against invasion by organisms from the indigenous flora. These defenses include skin and mucous membrane barriers, phagocytic cells, and certain humoral factors. The skin and mucous membrane barriers consist of physical barriers, chemical factors (e.g., gastric acid, skin fatty acids), and microbial antagonism in the intestinal tract (competition for nutrients, creation of inhibitory environment). Polymorphonuclear leukocytes are essential for protection against pyogenic bacteria, whereas mononuclear phagocytes are required for protection against intracellular parasites (my-

cobacteria, some other bacteria, many fungi, and viruses). One of the most important nonspecific humoral protective mechanisms is the complement system. Activation of the complement system by the alternative pathway, which can be initiated by organisms in the absence of specific antibody, is an effective "natural" protective mechanism. Types of complement antibacterial function include bactericidal (lytic) activity against susceptible Gram-negative bacilli and opsonization (via activated C3), which may be necessary to promote phagocytosis.

Immunologically specific host defenses against infection are the result of contact with the infecting organisms or with an appropriate vaccine. Immunologic responses are classically divided into those mediated by antibodies (humoral immunity) and those mediated by cells (delayed hypersensitivity, cell-mediated immunity). Both depend on the activity of lymphocytes, the immunologically specific cells that interact with antigen to initiate the immune response. There are two distinct systems of these lymphoid cells; one is dependent on the presence of the thymus (T lymphocytes) and the other (B lymphocytes) is independent of the thymus. After antigen stimulation, B cells proliferate into lymphocytes and plasma cells that synthesize antibody. Sensitized T lymphocytes mediate the functions of cell-mediated immunity. T cells cooperate during the immune response to most antigens by interacting with (stimulating or suppressing) B-lymphoid cells during antibody production.

Immunoglobulins G, M, and A (especially secretory immunoglobulin IgA) antibodies against bacteria, fungi, and viruses are known. In general, circulating antibody is important in preventing the spread of microorganisms to distant sites. Antibody in secretions may prevent invasion of mucous membranes. The following are antibody-mediated antibacterial mechanisms of action:

- Antitoxin function (IgG and secretory IgA antitoxins described)
- Bactericidal activity (certain Gram-negative bacilli require antibody and complement)
- Opsonization (IgG but not IgM is directly opsonic, i.e., there are phagocyte receptors for the Fc portion of IgG but not for the IgM molecule); IgM participates in the opsonization process by activation of the complement system)
- Interference with bacterial adherence (especially secretory IgA in the respiratory and intestinal tracts)

Antiviral functions of antibody are similar to antibacterial mechanisms:

- Viral neutralization (induced defect in viral uncoating, blocking cellular infection)
- Viral lysis (antibody plus complement)
- Opsonization
- Antibody-mediated cytotoxicity (destruction of virus-infected cells by antibody, in association with complement and/or cytotoxic lymphocytes)

Antimicrobial functions of the complement system are much more efficient in the presence of specific antibody which activates the classic (as well as the alternative) pathway. Under these conditions, complement-mediated cell membrane attack (bactericidal activity or viral lysis) and opsonization are generally more effective.

Acquired resistance to intracellular organisms is a function of cell-mediated immunity and is mediated largely by activated macrophages. Actively sensitized lymphocytes are the immunologically specific cells that trigger this response. When these T lymphocytes are stimulated by antigen, biologically active substances (cytokines) are released. Cytokines, especially interferon gamma, are responsible for the phenomenon of macrophage activation, whereby these phagocytes develop an enhanced capacity for ingesting and killing a variety of organisms. Thus, the cell-mediated immune function of acquired microbial resistance is specific in initiation (antigen stimulation of T lymphocyte, the immunologically specific cell), but is nonspecifically expressed by activated macrophages (the immunologically nonspecific effector cell).

Cell-mediated immunity can play a role in protection against viral infections in ways other than by activation of macrophages. The immunologically specific cell, the T lymphocyte, can act on virus directly (cytotoxicity against infected cells) or indirectly by the release of chemical mediators such as interferon. Production of interferon by sensitized lymphocytes during the cell-mediated immune response leads to very high local concentrations. This immune-specific interferon response may be an important means of limiting viral infection.

Interference with these protective mechanisms often leads to invasion by organisms against which the altered host defense is required for protection. As an oversimplification, resistance to infection with certain bacterial, viral, and fungal pathogens can be summarized as follows.

Bacteria. Antibody, complement, polymorphonuclear leukocyte function, and reticuloendothelial system function are important in protection against extracellular, pyogenic bacteria. For example, hypogammaglobulinemia predisposes to serous pneumococcal infections; terminal complement factor (C5–C8) deficiency is associated with systemic neisserial infection; granulocyte abnormalities often lead to bacteremia and other infections due to Gram-negative bacilli or staphylococci. On the other hand, cell-mediated immunity is required for resistance to facultative intracellular bacteria (especially *Mycobacteria* and *Legionella,* but including *Brucella, Listeria,* and certain *Salmonella*).

Viruses. Current clinical and experimental data suggest that cell-mediated immunity is of particular importance in infections with varicella–zoster virus, herpes simplex virus, cytomegalovirus, and measles virus. On the other hand, humoral immunity is crucial in protection against influenza virus, arbovirus, and enterovirus infection. X-linked agammaglobulinemia may be associated with chronic enterovirus central nervous system infection.

Fungi. The cell-mediated immune response is thought to be the major host defense against most of the agents that can produce systemic mycotic infections in normal humans. In the United States, such infections are caused by *Cryptococcus neoformans, Histoplasma capsulatum, Blastomyces dermatitidis,* or *Cocciodioides immitis.* Opportunistic behavior may be exhibited by these fungi (with the possible exception of *Blastomyces*), so that progressive disease is especially likely in the debilitated and compromised host with defective cell-mediated immunity. Impaired cell-mediated immunity also predisposes to mucosal and superficial candidal infections. Granulocyte function appears to be important in protection against invasive and systemic infection with so-called opportunistic fungi, which rarely (if ever) produce systemic infection in healthy persons. These fungi (mostly species of *Candida, Aspergillus, Torulopsis, Rhizopus,* and *Mucor*) can cause serious illness in the compromised host with abnormal granulocyte function (and often defective skin and mucous membrane barriers).

Parasites. Cell-mediated immunity is the major protective mechanism against infection due to *Pneumocystis carinii, Toxoplasma gondii,* and disseminated strongyloidiasis. For example, *Pneumocystis* pneumonia is the most common presenting infection in patients with AIDS. Humoral immunity is apparently crucial in protection against *Giardia* infection, which is a common complication of hypogammaglobulinemia. Reticuloendothelial function is important in controlling infections

TABLE 8–31–4. PREVENTION OF INFECTION IN THE COMPROMISED HOST

Measures to reduce the risk on nosocomial infection
   No unnecessary invasive procedures
   Aseptic technique for intravenous lines, urinary catheters, etc.
   Avoidance of cross-contamination
   Prevention of enteric colonization (neutropenic patients)
Immunoprophylaxis
   Active vaccination
     Influenza, pneumococcal and other vaccinations in appropriate patients
      Pseudomonas aeruginosa vaccine in burn patients (investigational)
   Passive vaccination
     Pooled and specific immunoglobulins
     Antiserum to enterobacterial lipopolysaccharide core antigen (investigational)
   Colony stimulating factors
Antimicrobial prophylaxis (options now exist for antiviral, antibacterial, antifungal, and antiprotozoal prophylaxis)

caused by *Babesia* or *Plasmodia* (malaria). These infections are especially severe following a splenectomy.

Natural History and Its Modification with Treatment

See the appropriate chapters on underlying illnesses and complicating infections. For many of the diseases listed in Table 8–31–1, from primary immunodeficiencies to malignancies to autoimmune diseases such as systemic lupus erythematosus, infection is a leading cause of death.

Prevention

See Table 8–31–4 and Chapters 8–2, 8–80, and 8–81. It should be remembered that patients with impaired host defenses, with rare exception, should not receive live virus vaccines.

Cost Containment

The appropriate chapters on both the underlying illness and the complicating infection should be consulted. Before embarking on an evaluation for a possible immunodeficiency state, the clinician should be cognizant of the prevalence of a particular immunodeficiency and the availability of a specific therapy should a defect in immune function be confirmed.

REFERENCES

Anaisser E, Bodey GP, Kantarjian H, et al. New spectrum of fungal infections in patients with cancer. Rev Infect Dis 1989;11:369.
Berkman SA, Lee ML, Gale RP. Clinical uses of intravenous immunoglobulins. Ann Intern Med 1990;112:278.
Buckley RH. Immunodeficiency diseases. JAMA 1992;268:2797.
Kaufmann SHE. Immunity to intracellular bacteria. Annu Rev Immunol 1993;11:129.
Sneller MC, Strober W, Eisenstein E, et al. New insights into common variable immunodeficiency. Ann Intern Med 1993;118:720.

CHAPTER 8–32

Infection in the Organ Transplant Recipient

Christine A. Zurawski, M.D., Clifford J. Gunthel, M.D., and Carl A. Perlino, M.D.

DEFINITION

Infection in the organ transplant recipient is defined as any illness caused by an infectious agent following organ transplantation.

ETIOLOGY

The recipient of a transplanted organ is at special risk for infection and disease from a broad range of microorganisms. Specifically, nosocomial infections associated with surgery and prolonged postoperative care in an intensive care unit setting are common. Also, transplant recipients are usually significantly immunosuppressed due to a prolonged debilitating illness and chronic organ failure prior to the transplant. Posttransplant, the patient routinely receives immunosuppressive drugs to prevent or treat organ rejection. These drugs have a primary effect on cell-mediated immune function and predispose to reactivation of preexisting, latent, cell-associated viral infections and to infections with intracellular bacteria and fungi. Environmental exposure to microorganisms of low virulence, which are unlikely to cause disease in healthy individuals, may also lead to significant disease in the transplant recipient.

CRITERIA FOR DIAGNOSIS

Suggestive

Nearly any sign or symptom, especially constitutional symptoms such as fever, in a transplant recipient may suggest possible infection.

Definitive

A definitive diagnosis of infection in an organ transplant recipient requires demonstration of infectious organisms on histologic examination of tissue or a positive culture in the correct clinical setting.

CLINICAL MANIFESTATIONS

Subjective

Infectious complications in patients with solid organ transplants can be divided into two categories: early and late infections. The epidemiology of the infection as well as the time in which it occurs can help to predict the likely pathogens. The infections are likely to be either primary (exogenous) in origin or reactivation (endogenous) of latent infection in the host.

Early infections are defined as those occurring less than 3 months after transplantation. Seventy to eighty percent of all serious infections occur during this time. Within the first month, most infections are nosocomial and involve bacterial pathogens. Prolonged periods of intubation, stay in the intensive care unit, and invasive monitoring devices all increase the risk for nosocomial infection. Donor-related infections also occur between months 1 and 3. The most common infections that occur early after transplantation are listed in Table 8–32–1.

Donor-related infections occur via the transplant from a previously infected donor to a recipient who has not been previously exposed. They often occur within the first few months of transplantation, when immunosuppression is highest. These infections are often screened for in the donor and recipient prior to transplantation to help assess the risk for future infection in the recipient. Primary cytomegalovirus infection and toxoplasmosis are the most common infections in this category. Recurrent invasive cytomegalovirus infection is likely to occur in patients who have received OKT3, a murine monoclonal antibody for treatment of rejection or for prophylaxis of early rejection.

Late infections are defined as those occurring more than 3 months after transplantation. Late infections affect an estimated 20% of patients per year. As the period from transplantation lengthens, community-acquired infections also become more common. Late and subacute infections in the transplant recipient are listed in Table 8–32–2.

Epstein–Barr virus, along with the use of cyclosporine or OKT3 as an immunosuppressive agent, is associated with the occurrence of lymphoproliferative disease, including B-cell lymphomas. The incidence of this disorder is highest between the third and sixth month after transplantation, but may occur at any time during immunosuppression.

The presentation of infection in the organ transplant recipient depends on the infecting organism and the organ system involved. Fever, although not always present, is often the first clinical finding that suggests the possibility of infection. Any new sign or symptom in a transplant patient, however, should alert the physician that an infection may be developing.

All patients being evaluated for an organ transplant should have purified protein derivative (PPD) skin test and serologic evaluation for prior cytomegalovirus, hepatitis B and C, and HIV. The results of these tests as well as those performed on the donor are of utmost importance in helping to establish the etiology of a suspected infection in these patients.

A complete history including the possibility of environmental exposures (past or present) and previous infections is particularly helpful in the diagnosis of infections in the transplant recipient. For example, it is important to know the geographic area and type of environment (inner city or rural) in which the patient has lived (Table 8–32–3). Histoplasmosis may occur in patients living in the Ohio River Valley. In the same manner, a history of pulmonary tuberculosis in a close family member is important to obtain. Possible exposures within the hospital are also important considerations with regard to infections with organisms such as *Pseudomonas, Legionella,* and *Aspergillus* species.

The medication profile can also aid in predicting the types of infections a transplant recipient may develop. The type and dose of all immunosuppressive agents should be noted. It is also important to inquire about whether patients are taking prophylactic medications such as trimethoprim–sulfamethoxazole to prevent *Pneumocystis* pneumonia, acyclovir for herpes, or isoniazid for tuberculosis.

Objective

Physical Examination

A complete physical examination should be performed on all individuals with transplanted organs when they present with symptoms suggestive of infection. The presence of lymphadenopathy should be of particular concern. Specific emphasis should be placed on the organ system involved, as this is the most likely site of infection. For instance, 80% of all infections in lung transplant patients involve the lungs, mediastinum, or pleural spaces. The same reasoning holds true for cardiac, liver, and renal transplants.

Routine Laboratory Abnormalities

Routine laboratory tests such as urinalysis, complete blood count, electrolytes, and hepatic profile can often provide clues as to the location of possible infection; however, immunosuppressive agents may alter pa-

TABLE 8–32–1. EARLY PRIMARY INFECTIONS IN THE TRANSPLANT RECIPIENT

Organ System Involved	Likely Pathogen	Clinical Manifestations
Lung (pneumonia)	Enterobacteriaceae	See Chapter 8–14
	Pseudomonas	
	Staphylococcus	See Chapter 8–38
	Candida	See Chapter 8–51
	Cytomegalovirus	See Chapter 8–71
Bloodstream infection	Enterobacteriaceae	See Chapter 8–2
	Pseudomonas	
	Staphylococcus	See Chapter 8–38
	Candida	See Chapter 8–51
Urinary tract infection	Enterobacteriaceae	See Chapter 8–23
	Pseudomonas	
	Enterococcus	
	Candida	
Local infection associated with surgical wounds, mediastinitis, peritonitis, abdominal abscess	Various bacteria and yeasts	See Chapters 8–21, 8–29, and 19–86

TABLE 8–32–2. REACTIVATION INFECTIONS AND SUBACUTE INFECTIONS IN THE TRANSPLANT RECIPIENT

Organ System Involved	Likely Pathogen	Clinical Manifestations
Lung	*Mycobacterium tuberculosis*	See Chapter 13–41
	Cytomegalovirus	See Chapter 8–71
	Herpes simplex virus	See Chapter 8–70
	Pneumocystis carinii	See Chapter 8–63
Liver (hepatitis)	Cytomegalovirus	See Chapter 8–71
	Hepatitis B, C (non-A, non-B)	See Chapter 19–75
Urinary tract infections	Herpes simplex virus	See Chapter 8–70
Systemic infections	Cytomegalovirus	See Chapter 8–71
	Epstein–Barr virus	See Chapter 8–72
Skin	Herpes simplex	See Chapter 8–70
	Varicella–zoster	See Chapters 8–70 and 8–74

TABLE 8–32–3. INFECTIONS FROM ENVIRONMENTAL SOURCES AND LATE INFECTIONS IN THE TRANSPLANT RECIPIENT

Organ System Involved	Likely Pathogen	Clinical Manifestations
Lung (pneumonia)	*Aspergillus*	See Chapter 8–52
	Nocardia	
	Nontuberculous mycobacteria	See Chapter 13–41
	Pneumocystis	See Chapter 8–63
Meningitis	*Cryptococcus*	See Chapter 8–54

tients' ability to respond appropriately to infection and their laboratory results may be misleading. For instance, patients who are taking azathioprine, prednisone, or cyclosporine may not have a leukocytosis, even in the face of a serious bacterial infection. As with all laboratory tests, clinical correlation is necessary.

PLANS

Diagnostic

Differential Diagnosis

Establishing the cause of an infection in an organ transplant recipient is necessary so that specific therapy can be instituted. Similar to the problems encountered in the immune suppressed individual, the specific etiology of the infection may be difficult to obtain. Evaluation of any suspected infection should be approached as outlined in Chapter 8–1.

Diagnostic Options and Recommended Approach

Imaging studies such as computed tomography and invasive procedures such as bronchoscopy and lymph node biopsy should be employed aggressively when results of initial screening tests fail to reveal an etiology for the patient's symptoms or physical findings. This allows for rapid diagnosis and institution of appropriate therapy, which is critical in this patient population.

Prior to performance of the transplant, the patient and the patient's family should be informed of the risk of infection that may come with the transplant surgery and the subsequent immunosuppression. The concepts of primary infection that may accompany the surgery and of reactivation infection should be discussed so that the patient and family have some knowledge of the potential problems. They should be informed of the possible serious nature of complications but should know that most are treatable if diagnosed.

FOLLOW-UP

Follow-up depends on the infection; reference to the appropriate chapter should be made.

DISCUSSION

Prevalence and Incidence

The incidence of infectious complications in this patient population depends largely on the organ transplanted and the type of infection. In all transplant patients, the incidence of infection is highest during the first few months after transplantation. The incidence of specific infections is discussed under Clinical Manifestations.

Related Basic Science

Infection remains a major factor in posttransplant morbidity and death. With the introduction of cyclosporine as an immunosuppressive agent, the number of infections has decreased as compared with infections occurring in patients receiving prednisone and azathioprine as primary immunosuppressive agents. All organ transplant recipients remain at risk for infection, however. Liver transplants carry the highest risk and renal transplants the lowest risk of infection. This difference is probably due to the more complex surgery involved in liver transplantation.

Organ transplantation is possible because of the use of immunosuppressive agents to help control rejection of the transplanted organ. Azathioprine (Imuran), corticosteroids, and cyclosporine (Sandimmune) are the usual agents used for this purpose. Azathioprine affects cell-mediated immune responses and also affects antibody production. The major side effect of this drug is bone marrow suppression manifested by dose-related leukopenia. Prednisone affects primarily cell-mediated immunity by preventing T-cell activation. The side effects of prednisone are well known and include upper gastrointestinal bleeding, hyperglycemia, and sodium and water retention. Cyclosporine has been used as the main agent for the prevention of organ rejection since it was introduced in 1981. Cyclosporine acts by inhibiting T lymphocytes, especially helper T cells. Unlike azathioprine, cyclosporine has little effect on neutrophils. Hypertension and dose-related nephrotoxicity are common side effects of cyclosporine.

Additional agents can be used to prevent or treat graft rejection. These include high-dose oral or intravenous corticosteroids, polyclonal antilymphocyte or antithymocyte globulin, and murine monoclonal antibody against the T3 antigen of the lymphocyte cell wall. The polyclonal globulins and the monoclonal antibody have been used to prevent early organ rejection after transplantation and are also used to treat acute rejection.

Clinical experience has shown that the long-term use of high-dose corticosteroids or use of high pulse doses of intravenous corticosteroids definitely increases the risk of infection in the transplant recipient, especially those infections that are usually controlled by cell-mediated immunity. Use of the polyclonal antilymphocyte globulin, murine monoclonal antibody particularly, increases the risk of invasive disease due to cytomegalovirus, especially when these agents are used as part of the initial immunosuppressive regimen during the posttransplant period.

Natural History and Its Modification with Treatment

A number of different infections can complicate organ transplantation. The appropriate chapters concerning each of these should be consulted.

Prevention

Preoperative screening of organ donors for possible latent infection is critical. This should include purified protein derivative and serology for cytomegalovirus, hepatitis B and C, and HIV infection. The administration of pneumococcal vaccine prior to the transplant seems appropriate to help prevent pneumococcal infection. Influenza vaccine should be given yearly (see Chapter 8–81). Excellent surgical technique and attention to infection control will help decrease the incidence of infection. Prophylactic antibiotics are given prior to surgery and in the immediate postoperative period in an attempt to decrease surgical infections. All infection control procedures should be faithfully carried out to avoid nosocomial infection.

Cost Containment

The overall cost of organ transplantation remains high. By paying attention to prevention of infection, costly hospitalizations and therapy can be avoided.

REFERENCES

Dummer S, Kusne S. Liver transplantation and related infections (review). Semin Respir Infect 1993;8:191.

Hibberd PL, Rubin RH. Renal transplantation and related infections (review). Semin Respir Infect 1993;8:216.

Paradis IL, Williams P. Infection after lung transplantation (review). Semin Respir Infect 1993;8:207.

Petri WA Jr. Infections in heart transplant recipients (review). Clin Infect Dis 1994;18:141, Quiz 147.

Cardiac Transplantation • Complications (See Section 15, Chapter 62)

Infections in Travelers

Susan L. F. McLellan, M.D., and Phyllis E. Kozarsky, M.D.

DEFINITION

Infections in returning travelers range from common problems such as viral respiratory illness and superficial tinea to more exotic diseases such as dengue fever and brucellosis. Upper respiratory infections, tuberculosis, skin and wound infections, and viral illnesses such as those responsible for mononucleosis and the typical "childhood diseases" are not discussed here. Similarly, numerous sexually transmitted diseases are found in returning travelers, and there is understandable concern about the transmission of HIV in this setting. Details on these problems can be found in the respective chapters. This chapter focuses on the more notable infectious diseases and syndromes acquired by travelers journeying to the developing world.

ETIOLOGY

Many of the diseases acquired by travelers are due to parasites that may require specific vectors or conditions existing primarily in the developing world. A number of bacterial and viral diseases, as well as many parasites, are spread via unsafe water or contaminated food and maintained in areas where poor sanitation systems exist. It is important to note that short-term travelers who visit the developing world and the tropics but who stay in luxury hotels and confine themselves to tourist destinations are much less likely to encounter unusual pathogens.

CRITERIA FOR DIAGNOSIS

Suggestive

Diarrhea occurs in about 40% of persons traveling to high-risk areas from industrialized regions. The most frequent causes are summarized in Table 8–34–1. Traveler's diarrhea usually begins abruptly, and patients often complain of other associated symptoms such as fever, nausea, vomiting, cramps, tenesmus, and dysentery (blood and mucus in stools). Some parasites also cause abdominal complaints but may be asymptomatic. Rash, fever, respiratory complaints, and myalgia are also common symptoms of a variety of illnesses in travelers. Eosinophilia, defined as an absolute eosinophil count greater than 400 to 500 cells/μL, is a finding suggestive of parasitic disease, even in the asymptomatic patient. The degree of eosinophilia is based on the extent of tissue invasion by the parasite. Protozoan infections such as malaria, amebiasis, and giardiasis are not generally associated with eosinophilia. Table 8–34–2 summarizes some of the parasitic infections that cause a high eosinophil count.

Definitive

Important diagnostic tests that may yield a definitive diagnosis include blood cultures; stool examinations, including preparations for ova and parasites, acid-fast stains, culture, and certain specific antibody techniques; thick and thin blood smears; and serologic assays. Occasionally, tissue biopsies are required.

We thank Herbert L. Dupont, M.D., for his contribution to this chapter in the previous edition of this book.

CLINICAL MANIFESTATIONS

Subjective

The most frequent symptoms prompting investigation for travel-related illness are diarrhea and fever, followed by rash, jaundice, adenopathy, and pulmonary complaints. Tables 8–34–2 and 8–34–3 list some of the subjective manifestations of travel-related infections. The most important information to gather from the traveler is a complete travel history; this includes a detailed itinerary, length of stay, season, and information regarding food, water, housing, and exposure to insects and animals. In addition, any preventive or prophylactic measures should be recounted.

Objective

Physical Examination

Many patients have a normal physical examination. Some illnesses manifest with adenopathy, hepatosplenomegaly, rash, or fever. Tables 8–34–2 and 8–34–3 list some of the physical findings found in the more common causes of travelers' infections.

TABLE 8–34–1. COMMON CAUSES OF TRAVELER'S DIARRHEA

Etiology	Laboratory Evaluation
Bacteria	
Escherichia coli (various types)	Stool culture followed by special assays for toxin production; serotyping; invasion; adherence
Shigella sp.	Stool culture
Salmonella sp.	Stool culture and serotyping
Campylobacter sp.	Stool culture using specialized media; increased carbon dioxide environment and incubator temperature 42° C
Vibrio sp.	Stool culture using thiosulfate citrate bile salt sucrose agar
Yersinia enterocolitica	Stool culture using Cefsulodin–Irgasan–Novobiocin agar if suspected; cold enrichment may be helpful
Aeromonas hydrophilia	Stool culture; trypticase soy agar with sheep blood and ampicillin
Plesiomonas shigelloides	Stool culture, bile–peptone broth or trypticase soy agar with ampicillin
Clostridium difficile	History of previous antibiotic use; *C. difficile* toxin assay and *C. difficile* culture; endoscopy to demonstrate pseudomembranes
Viruses	
Rotaviruses	Rapid viral antigen detection tests
Norwalk-like agents	Laboratory confirmation available as research technique
Protozoans	
Giardia lamblia	Stool O&P × 3, "string test," small bowel drainage, duodenal biopsy
Entamoeba histolytica	Stool O&P × 3, rectal/colon biopsy, serology
Cryptosporidium	Stool O&P × 3, modified acid-fast stain, detection with specific monoclonal antibody techniques
Isospora belli	Stool O&P × 3
Cyclospora cayetanensis	Stool for acid-fast bacilli

O&P, ova and parasites.

TABLE 8–34–2. CAUSES OF EOSINOPHILIA IN THE RETURNING TRAVELER

Cause	Common Signs and Symptoms	Environmental Exposure	Diagnostic Procedures
Trichinella spiralis	Fever, myalgias, periorbital edema	Eating inadequately processed pork; worldwide	Muscle biopsy, serology
Toxocara canis	Fever, abdominal pain, hepatomegaly	Exposure to dogs; worldwide	Serology; larvae in tissues, liver
Strongyloides stercoralis	Abdominal pain, diarrhea, skin lesions; autoinfection may cause overwhelming systemic disease in immunocompromised hosts	Transmitted by skin contact with soil contaminated by larvae, autoinfection; tropics, subtropics	Stool examinations, small bowel aspirate or biopsy, tissue biopsy, serology
Ascaris lumbricoides	Asymptomatic, steatorrhea, intestinal obstruction, transient pneumonitis	Hand-to-mouth transmission; worldwide	Stool examination, small bowel aspirate
Ancyclostom duodenalis, Necator americanis	Asymptomatic rash at site of larval penetration, transient pneumonitis, abdominal discomfort	Transmission by contact with contaminated soil and skin penetration; worldwide	Stool examination
Schistosoma sp.	Acute: fever, serum sickness-like illness Chronic: Abdominal discomfort, hepatosplenomegaly (*S. hematosium* hematuria)	Exposure to fresh water in endemic areas; Africa, South America, Caribbean, Asia, Southeast Asia, Middle East	Stool and urine examinations, rectal biopsy, serology
Echinococcus granulosus	Abdominal mass (hydatid cysts) in liver, or lung cysts	Exposure to dog feces; found in sheep- and cattle-raising areas of world	Chest x-ray, CT scan, serology
Wuchereria bancrofti, Brugia malayi, Brugia timori	Asymptomatic, lymphangitis, lymphadenitis, lymphedema, hydrocele	Transmitted by mosquitoes; requires prolonged exposure; tropics and subtropics	Day and night blood smears, examination of hydrocele fluid, chylous urine, serology
Loa loa	Transient subcutaneous swellings, pruritis, subconjunctival migration of worm	Transmitted by flies; West and Central Africa	Day blood smears, identification of adult in the eye
Onchocerca volvulus	Fibrous nodules in skin, keratitis	Transmitted by black flies; Africa, Central and South America	Microfilariae in skin snips or in cornea or anterior chamber on slit-lamp examination; adults found in skin nodules; Mazzotti test, serology
Mansonella sp.	Asymptomatic, dermatitis	Transmitted by midges and black flies; Central and South America, Africa.	Blood smears, skin snips; adults occasionally found in fatty tissues
Filaria sp. causing tropical pulmonary eosinophilia	Recurrent paroxysmal dry cough, wheezing, dyspnea, malaise, hepatosplenomegaly, lymphadenopathy	Exposure to animal and/or human filaria; tropics	Reticulonodular infiltrates on chest x-ray, serology, clinical diagnosis
Fasciola hepatica	Acute: fever, right upper quadrant pain Chronic: asymptomatic, biliary obstruction	Transmitted by ingestion of infective metacercariae; sheep-raising areas of world	Stool or biliary examinations
Fasciola buski	Asymptomatic, diarrhea, abdominal pain	Ingestion of infected plants; Far East, Southeast Asia	Stool examination
Paragonimus westermani	Asymptomatic, cough, hemoptysis, bronchitis	Consumption of freshwater crustaceans; West Africa, Far East, Indian subcontinent, Central and South America	Stool or sputum examination, serology

CT, computed tomography.

Routine Laboratory Abnormalities

Anemia and thrombocytopenia may be seen in malaria, particularly that caused by *Plasmodium falciparum*. With most travel-related illnesses such as uncomplicated diarrhea and respiratory infection, there will be no laboratory abnormalities. Eosinophilia is seen in some parasitic diseases. Patients with hepatitis have abnormalities of their liver enzymes. Refer to Tables 8–34–2 and 8–34–3 for specific findings in different diseases.

PLANS
Diagnostic
Differential Diagnosis

The differential diagnosis depends on the presenting symptoms and signs and the patient's travel history. It is important to remember that not all illnesses occurring in travelers are related to travel, and chronic diseases, neoplasms, and autoimmune disease must be considered as well.

Diagnostic Options

Some illnesses, such as many cases of traveler's diarrhea, can be diagnosed and treated on the basis of history and symptoms alone. Others require more diagnostic effort. The types of diagnostic procedures appropriate to various illnesses are given in Tables 8–34–1, 8–34–2, and 8–34–3.

Recommended Approach

In some cases the initial evaluation (after history and physical examination) includes a complete blood count and differential, a chemistry panel including liver enzymes, urinalysis, tuberculin skin test, and stool examination for culture and parasite examination. If there are pulmonary signs or symptoms, a chest x-ray film should be obtained. Other procedures, such as blood smears, biopsies, computed tomography scans, or specialized serologies may be appropriate depending on the presentation and the suspected pathogens. Refer to Tables 8–34–1, 8–34–2, and 8–34–3 for specific recommendations.

Therapeutic
Therapeutic Options

Most cases of traveler's diarrhea are self-limited and resolve without antibiotic therapy. If the illness is mild, the patient can be managed with hydration and antidiarrheal medications alone. It is usually preferable to use an antibiotic along with loperamide for the treatment of moderate to severe acute diarrhea.

TABLE 8–34–3. COMMON SYSTEMIC INFECTIONS IN RETURNING TRAVELERS

Disease	Epidemiologic History	Clinical Manifestations and Laboratory Examination	Treatment*
Malaria	Travel to endemic area; rarely blood or IV transmitted	Fever, headache, chills, splenomegaly, anemia, thrombocytopenia; blood smear diagnostic.	See Chapter 8–61
Amebiasis (extraintestinal)	Ingestion of contaminated food, water; worldwide	Fever; often causes abscess in right lobe of liver; elevated right hemidiaphragm; CT scan and aspiration; serology	See Chapter 8–58 Metronidazole plus iodoquinol, or dehydroemetine and chloroquine plus iodoquinol
Typhoid fever	Ingestion of contaminated food; usually in the developing world	Fever, headache, myalgia, constipation; blood culture, stool culture, bone marrow culture	Ciprofloxacin, TMP–SMX, chloramphenicol, ampicillin, third-generation cephalosporin†
Hepatitis A	Fecal–oral transmission; worldwide, more common in developing countries.	Incubation period 1 mo; fever, RUQ tenderness, jaundice, anorexia, fatigue; serology	Supportive
Hepatitis B	Transmitted by contaminated needles, blood, sexual contact; worldwide	Incubation period 2–3 mo; fever, RUQ tenderness, jaundice, anorexia, fatigue, may become chronic and progressive; serology	Acute: supportive Chronic: steroids, azothioprine, interferon in selected patients
Hepatitis E	Transmitted by contaminated food and water; outbreaks in India, Pakistan, Russia, China, Africa, Peru, Mexico	Incubation period approximately 1 mo; fever, RUQ tenderness; clinical diagnosis; alkaline phosphatase often higher than seen in other causes of viral hepatitis; serology available through CDC	Supportive
Dengue fever	Exposure to *Aedes* sp. mosquitoes; many tropical/subtropical areas; hemorrhagic variety usually from Southeast Asia and Caribbean	Fever, headache, back pain, arthralgias, rash; serology	Supportive
Leptospirosis	Contact with infected urine of animals, especially rats; worldwide	Fever, chills, headache, myalgia, conjunctivitis, adenopathy, rash; biphasic illness: jaundice later; cultures of blood, cerebrospinal fluid, urine; serology	Penicillin
Schistosomiasis (acute)	Flukes penetrate skin during contact with fresh water; endemic in Caribbean, South America, Africa, Middle East, Southeast Asia	Usually occurs 4–8 w after infection; fever, chills, headache, cough, hepatosplenomegaly; clinical diagnosis early; later, stool for ova and parasites, rectal biopsy, serology	Praziquantel
Rickettsioses	History of tick/mite bite or louse exposure; worldwide.	Fever, rash, headache, myalgias; specific serology.	Tetracycline, chloramphenicol
Filariasis	Transmitted by infected mosquitoes in tropics/subtropics; need extended exposure for infection; Africa, Latin America, Indian subcontinent	Fever, lymphedema, hydrocele; blood and/or skin examination for microfilariae; serology	Diethylcarbamazine, or mebendazole plus ivermectin (investigational)
Tuberculosis	History of close and prolonged contact with infected individuals; worldwide	Fever, chills, weight loss, cough, adenopathy; sputum for acid-fast bacilli, lymph node biopsy	Isoniazid, rifampin, ethambutal, pyrazinamide; other drugs available for multidrug-resistant strains

TMP–SMX, trimethoprim–sulfamethoxazole; RUQ, right upper quadrant; CT, computed tomography; CDC, Centers for Disease Control and Prevention.
*Specific therapeutic recommendations, including doses, may be found in chapters that specifically cover the disease or in a textbook of tropical medicine. As new information becomes available, recommended treatment regimens periodically change.
†Be aware that *S. typhi* infections acquired in various parts of the world show different antibiotic sensitivities.

Appropriate therapy of other infections depends on a suspected diagnosis. Recommended options can be found in Table 8–34–3 and in the referenced issue of *The Medical Letter*. If the problem is complicated or the patient has underlying conditions, consultation should be requested. The Centers for Disease Control and Prevention has a 24-hour telephone number, (404) 332–4559, through which specialists can be consulted. Also, a number of travel clinics operate in the United States, and these are a good resource for the physician seeking assistance with the management of travel-related illness.

Recommended Approach

For diarrhea, the most common complaint of travelers, the mainstay of therapy is rehydration, whether or not specific therapy is employed. Except in extreme cases, this can be accomplished orally, either with prepackaged rehydration solutions or with commonly available clear liquids such as juices, broths and soft drinks. For mild to moderate illness, the use of either bismuth subsalicylate or loperamide is extremely helpful (the latter should be avoided in children). If symptoms are primarily lower gastrointestinal and empiric antibiotic treatment is chosen, a quinolone given for 3 to 5 days will usually be effective. Trimetho-

prim–sulfamethoxazole is also an option, but many organisms causing traveler's diarrhea have become resistant to this combination. More chronic diarrhea, with symptoms of nausea and bloating, suggests *Giardia lamblia*. This organism can be difficult to isolate, and if suspected, an empiric trial of metronidazole is in order. When a causative organism is identified, the therapy can be tailored. Specific therapy for bacterial causes of diarrhea can be found in other chapters in this text.

Recommendations for the treatment of systemic infections found in travelers are given in Table 8–34–3. Specific treatment for parasitic agents can be found in *The Medical Letter* issue devoted to drugs for parasitic infections (1993, Volume 35, Issue 911). Occasionally, the cause for problems such as asymptomatic eosinophilia will remain unclear, and in some of these cases, empiric broad-spectrum antiparasitic therapy is indicated. In these cases, a physician specialist in clinical tropical medicine should be consulted.

FOLLOW-UP

For minor infections, especially in the short-term traveler, no follow-up is needed unless the patient's symptoms do not resolve. Recommendations for follow-up in other circumstances depend on the illness being treated. Patients treated for systemic illnesses often require repeat blood smears (malaria, filariasis), convalescent serology (rickettsiosis, leptospirosis), or monitoring of liver function (hepatitis). Those treated for intestinal parasite infections require follow-up to monitor clearing. It should be kept in mind that eosinophilia resolves over months after the offending infection has been treated.

Examination of the returning long-term traveler is important even if he or she feels well. Many infections acquired in the developing areas of the world have long latent periods; screening these returning travelers helps uncover problems that may be asymptomatic. A physical examination and basic laboratory tests should be done: complete blood count and differential, liver function tests, tuberculin skin test, and at least three stool examinations for ova and parasites. A chest x-ray film and serologies for hepatitis, schistosomiasis, and/or HIV may also be recommended.

Some returning travelers present with fever of unknown origin, and time and patience are required when explaining the necessity for what may be a protracted period of evaluation. Most of these illnesses have low communicability, and the patient, family, and health care provider should not use special isolation practices. Occasionally, diseases such as malaria and typhoid fever relapse, and individuals treated for these infections need to be aware of this possibility. If the patient has been treated for parasites on the basis of eosinophilia without isolation of an organism, follow-up is required. As some infections remain latent for months to years after exposure, the traveler should be reminded to inform his or her future health care professionals of previous travel.

DISCUSSION
Prevalence and Incidence

Between 50 and 75% of short-term travelers to the tropics or subtropics develop some health impairment. Only 5% require medical attention, and less than 1% require hospitalization; however, these impairments may be costly to the traveler in terms of lost time and disruption of travel. Table 8–34–4 categorizes travel–related illness by risk of acquisition.

The incidence of traveler's diarrhea depends on the destination. In general, the highest-risk destinations include most of the developing countries of Latin America, Africa, the Middle East, and Asia. Intermediate-risk destinations include most of southern Europe and a few Caribbean islands (e.g., Haiti). Low-risk destinations include the United States, Canada, northern Europe, Australia, New Zealand, and most of the Caribbean islands. The risk of acquiring diarrhea is also based on the number of dietary "mistakes," the number of offending organisms ingested, and the gastric pH.

Related Basic Science

The reader is referred to the appropriate chapters in this book or to a tropical medicine text for information on the basic science of specific infections.

Natural History and Its Modification with Treatment

Most travel-related infections are self-limited or easily treated, and patients may be reassured to that effect. A small number of patients have serious systemic illnesses that require hospitalization. The outcome in these cases is determined by the diagnosis and the underlying health of the individual.

Prevention

In few other situations is preventive medicine more important than in the reduction of infections among travelers to disease-endemic areas. Nearly all the serious infectious diseases encountered in the developing world can be reduced in frequency by adequate pretravel planning. The first key to prevention is to be aware of the special infections endemic to the area being visited. Second, it is important to determine the precautions needed to reduce the chance of exposure to the agents found in an area or to increase host resistance to infectious microorganisms if they are encountered. In addition, travelers with underlying chronic illnesses need to check with their doctors to be sure that they will not need additional medical care while abroad. Pregnant or nursing moth-

TABLE 8–34–4. TRAVELER'S RISK OF ACQUISITION OF CERTAIN INFECTIOUS DISEASES IN DEVELOPING COUNTRIES

High Risk	Moderate Risk	Low Risk	Very Low Risk
Diarrhea	Nonspecific	Amebiasis	AIDS
Upper respiratory	gastroenteritis	Ascariasis	Echinococcosis
infection	Giardiasis	Childhood viral	Filariasis
	Hepatitis A	infections	Hookworm
	Malaria (without	Hepatitis B	Paragonimiasis
	appropriate	Hepatitis C	Schistosomiasis
	prophylaxis)	(epidemic)	Toxocariasis
	Salmonellosis	Leptospirosis	Trichinosis
	Cryptosporidiosis	Strongyloidiasis	Trypanosomiasis
	Sexually	Tuberculosis	Typhus
	transmitted	Typhoid fever	Brucellosis
	diseases		Cholera
	(gonorrhea,		
	chlamydia, herpes		
	simplex)		
	Shigellosis		
	Superficial		
	fungal		
	infection		
	Dengue fever		

Source: Adapted from Halstead SB, Warren KS, eds. Diseases of travelers and immigrants. Kalamazoo, MI: Upjohn, 1988:20. Reproduced with permission from the publisher.

ers, adults traveling with small children, and the elderly need specialized counseling and may be advised to avoid certain high-risk destinations.

Prevention of the major infections can be divided into three broad categories: prevention by immunization, by avoiding insect bites, and by exercising good principles of food and beverage selection. Table 8–34–5 lists immunizations used for travelers and gives indications for their use. Routine immunizations such as polio, diphtheria/tetanus, measles/mumps/rubella (MMR), influenza, and pneumococcal vaccines should also be updated when necessary. Prevention of insect-borne diseases such as malaria and dengue fever requires the use of insect repellents such as those containing the chemical DEET. Permethrin-containing products may also be used on clothing and on bed nets. Long sleeves, long pants, shoes, and socks should be worn when outdoors between dusk and dawn. Those visiting areas endemic for schistosomiasis should avoid swimming or bathing in freshwater lakes, streams, rivers, or irrigation channels.

The frequency of traveler's diarrhea, typhoid, hepatitis A, and many parasites may be reduced substantially by eating and drinking safe items. Anything served steaming hot, fruits that are self-peeled, breads, rice, and bottled beverages, particularly if carbonated, are usually safe. Items that should be avoided include foods remaining at room temperature buffet-style, hot sauces on the table, salads, desserts, tap water (including ice), and milk. Travelers need to exercise caution even when eating food served on commercial airlines originating from the developing world. Iodine and chlorine tablets, as well as a variety of portable, inexpensive water purifiers that contain effective iodination are available from camping stores.

Preventive medications reduce the frequency of diarrhea and are useful for certain travelers. Bismuth subsalicylate (Pepto-Bismol) reduces the risk of diarrhea by 66%. The drug is taken in a dosage of 2 tablets four times per day. The major side effects are blackening of the stool and tongue and constipation. Tinnitus may occur, especially if this drug is taken with other salicylate-containing drugs. It should not be used for more than 3 weeks. Some antimicrobial agents may be more effective but are associated with more side effects. An oral quinolone daily (or, in Mexico, trimethoprim–sulfamethoxazole) may be taken by travelers embarking on short trips who must remain free of diarrhea and who understand completely the risks of the medication (resistant flora, skin rashes, and more serious side effects).

For health information regarding travel, the Centers for Disease Control and Prevention (CDC) has a 24-hour telephone number, (404) 332–4559, offering menu options, including food and water precau-

TABLE 8-34-5. IMMUNIZATIONS USED IN TRAVELERS*

Immunization	Indications
Yellow fever	For travel to rural areas in endemic zones in tropical South America and Africa; some countries in Africa require certificate of immunization
Cholera	Limited efficacy; some countries require documentation of immunization within 6 months of entry
Diphtheria/tetanus	Booster every 10 y
Polio	Booster of oral polio vaccine (OPV) or inactivated polio vaccine (IPV) for travelers to developing countries
Immune globulin	For protection against hepatitis A in persons traveling to areas of poor hygiene; effective for 3–6 mo
Hepatitis B	For health care workers in developing world or those planning a long-term stay in highly endemic areas
Measles	For individuals born after 1956 who have not had documented measles or have not been reimmunized since 1980 (cannot be given at the same time as immune globulin)
Meningococcal meningitis	For travelers to areas where epidemics are occurring, particularly sub-Saharan Africa from December to June
Typhoid	For those with intense exposure to contaminated food and water; vaccines available are about 70% effective
Rabies	For travelers who will be handling animals and for long-term travelers who will be living in endemic areas
Plague	Rarely used; for travelers to endemic areas who will be in contact with animals
Japanese encephalitis	For travelers, particularly long-term, who will be living in rural rice-growing areas of Asia with exposure to mosquitoes; now available in United States; available through U.S. embassies in Asia

*Assumption is made that all individuals have completed a primary series of protective immunizations. If not, the traveler should receive a primary series. Special recommendations may apply for young children, pregnant women, and immunocompromised individuals.

tions, malaria prevention, and immunizations. *Health Information for International Travel* is a CDC publication updated yearly that contains a large body of information on disease prevention. Travel clinics are growing in number in the United States and are a good resource for persons planning to visit the developing world. A current list of North American Clinical Consultants in Tropical Medicine and Travel Clinics can be obtained from the American Society of Tropical Medicine and Hygiene.

Cost Containment

In infections of travelers, the key to cost containment is prevention. The cost of immunization and prophylactic medications is far less than treatment of illness. Not all preventive measures used are cost-effective; the inactivated cholera vaccine is an example of a preventive measure where cost (both financial and side effects) does not justify the limited efficacy; however, most other preventive strategies are quite cost-effective. Once a patient is ill, an evaluation that is conducted in a logical sequence, starting with the more general and less expensive screening tests, will reduce the expense of diagnosis. Most travel-related illnesses can be treated in an outpatient setting.

REFERENCES

Abramowicz M, ed. Drugs for parasitic infections. Med Lett 1993;35:111.
DuPont HL, Ericsson CD. Prevention and treatment of traveler's diarrhea. N Engl J Med 1993;328:1821.
Gardner P, ed. Health issues of international travelers. Infect Dis Clin North Am 1992;6(2).
Halstead SB, Warren KS, eds. Diseases of travelers and immigrants. Kalamazoo, MI: Upjohn, 1988:20.
Philpott J, Keystone JS. Eosinophilia: An approach to the problem in the returning traveler. Travel Med Int 1987:51.
Wolfe MS, ed. Travel medicine. Med Clin North Am 1992;76(6).

CHAPTER 8-35

Infections in Intravenous Drug Abusers

James P. Steinberg, M.D.

DEFINITION

Infections in intravenous drug abusers include any infection linked directly or indirectly to the injection of illicit drugs.

ETIOLOGY

Many infections are a direct consequence of inoculating one of a variety of microorganisms into the bloodstream or soft tissues. Other associated infections are more indirectly related, such as a sexually transmitted disease acquired from a sex-for-drugs exchange, tuberculosis occurring in a malnourished drug abuser living in crowded conditions, an aspiration pneumonia following a drug-induced stupor, or an opportunistic infection in a patient with AIDS who acquired HIV infection from intravenous drug use.

CRITERIA FOR DIAGNOSIS
Suggestive

Fever in an intravenous drug abuser potentially represents serious infection, and there are frequently no or few clues at the time of presentation to suggest a specific diagnosis. On the other hand, certain infections (including tricuspid valve *Staphylococcus aureus* endocarditis and sternoclavicular septic arthritis) are characteristic of intravenous drug abuse and should alert the clinician to this possibility even when the history of drug abuse is lacking.

Definitive

Because of the diversity of pathogens that cause infection in intravenous drug abusers, the specific diagnosis usually is dependent on the results of cultures or serologic testing. Unfortunately, concomitant antibiotic abuse is common and cultures may be negative, thus precluding a specific diagnosis.

CLINICAL MANIFESTATIONS
Subjective

A history of parenteral drug use can usually be elicited by direct questioning of the patient, at which time the pattern of drug use and time of the most recent injection should be documented. All drug abusers should be considered at possible risk for HIV infection, regardless of an admitted history of needle sharing. It is also important to determine which drugs have been used parenterally, because some bacterial infections are clearly associated with certain types of drug use. Antibiotic abuse is also common among drug users, and a history of such abuse increases the likelihood of infection caused by methicillin-resistant *Staphylococcus aureus* (MRSA) or other antibiotic-resistant bacteria. Abuse of other substances (nonparenteral drugs, alcohol, tobacco) is common and can cause host defense disturbances that further predispose the intravenous drug abuser to infection.

Fever and/or chills are common presenting manifestations of infection associated with drug abuse and often occur in the absence of localizing symptoms. Cough, pleuritic chest pain, and shortness of breath may be due to pneumonia or septic pulmonary emboli. A prolonged history of respiratory symptoms, fever, and weight loss should suggest HIV infection, tuberculosis, or anaerobic lung abscess. Soft tissue infections usually present with pain and swelling at the site of drug injection; fever or constitutional symptoms may be absent. Localized pain and swelling are also common symptoms in septic arthritis and osteomyelitis. Patients with spinal epidural infections may give a history of back pain of several months' duration prior to the onset of leg weakness.

Table 8–35–1 lists infections commonly associated with parenteral drug abuse. The clinical presentation for many of these infections can be found in the chapters devoted to the specific infections.

Objective
Physical Examination

The parenteral drug abuser may be thin and wasted because of malnutrition, alcoholism, or chronic infection. Telltale scars from repeated needle punctures, or "tracks," are often present. Some drug abusers use groin, axillary, or other vessels that are not as conspicuous as the arm veins. The larger or deeper vessels are often used when arm and leg veins become sclerosed. The presence of generalized lymphadenopathy or thrush suggests possible HIV infection.

The most common infections on parenteral drug abusers are abscesses, cellulitis, and other soft tissue infections at the injection site. Severe pain, marked induration, rapid progression with or without necrosis or crepitus, and accompanying systemic toxicity suggest a severe process such as necrotizing fasciitis. Ulcerations at the site of "skin popping" may become secondarily infected. Septic phlebitis produces induration or fluctuance over a vein. An enlarging or pulsatile mass, especially in the groin, suggests a mycotic aneurysm or arteriovenous fistula.

Fever is often the only sign of serious infection in drug abusers. Tricuspid valve endocarditis, which accounts for 50 to 75% of endocarditis in this population, rarely presents with peripheral signs such as splinter hemorrhages, Osler's nodes, and Janeway lesions. In addition, a murmur is absent in one third of patients with tricuspid valve endocarditis. When audible, the holosystolic murmur of tricuspid regurgitation is typically louder during inspiration. More commonly, fever in a drug abuser is due to pulmonary infection ranging from lobar pneumonia to tuberculosis to anaerobic aspiration pneumonia. In addition, respiratory symptoms and signs may predominate with tricuspid endocarditis because of associated septic pulmonary emboli and pneumonia.

Signs of metastatic infection include point tenderness over the spine in hematogenous osteomyelitis and focal swelling and tenderness over the sternoclavicular, sacroiliac, symphysis pubis, knee, or, less commonly, other joints in septic arthritis. Signs of spinal cord compression

TABLE 8–35–1. INFECTIONS IN INTRAVENOUS DRUG ABUSERS (UNRELATED TO HIV-INDUCED IMMUNOSUPPRESSION)

Syndrome	Predominant Organisms

Soft tissue infections
  Cellulitis
  Subcutaneous abscesses
  Necrotizing fasciitis
  Gas gangrene
  Pyomyositis
	Staphylococcus aureus, streptococci (β-hemolytic and others), enterococci, coagulase-negative staphylococci, *Pseudomonas aeruginosa* and other Gram-negative bacilli, *Clostridium* and other anaerobes, *Candida* sp.

Bacteremia	Dependent on principal infection

Endocarditis
  Right-sided
  Left-sided and mixed
	S. aureus
	S. aureus, streptococci, *Pseudomonas*, and others

Peripheral vascular infections
  Septic thrombophlebitis
  Arteriovenous fistula
  Mycotic aneurysm
	S. aureus, other Gram-positive organisms, *Pseudomonas*, other Gram-negative bacilli, fungi

Pneumonia*
 	
  Aspiration
  Pulmonary emboli
	Streptococcus pneumoniae, *Mycobacterium tuberculosis*
	Mixed aerobic and anaerobic
	S. aureus

Central nervous system infections*
  Meningitis
  Brain abscess
  Spinal epidural abscesses
	
	S. aureus (with endocarditis), others
	Pyogenic bacteria, *Nocardia*, fungi
	S. aureus, *M. tuberculosis*

Endophthalmitis	*Candida* sp., *Aspergillus* sp., *S. aureus*, *Bacillus* sp., others
Osteomyelitis, septic arthritis	*S. aureus*, *Pseudomonas*, many others including fungi
Hepatitis	Hepatitis A, B, C, D, and E
Sexually transmitted diseases	*Treponema pallidum*, *Neisseria gonorrhoeae*, others
AIDS	HIV-1, rarely HIV-2 (also HTLV-1 and HTLV-2)
Other	*Clostridium tetani*, *Clostridium botulinum*, *Plasmodium* sp.

HTLV, human T-lymphotropic virus.
*HIV-related opportunistic infections can be difficult to differentiate from many of the above diseases and should be considered in patients with diffuse pneumonia, meningitis, and focal central nervous system lesions.

may be seen with epidural abscesses. Eye pain with loss of vision suggests bacterial or fungal endophthalmitis.

Routine Laboratory Abnormalities

Abnormalities on laboratory tests performed at the time of hospital admission can be caused by a variety of infections. The white blood cell count can be elevated, normal, or low. Leukopenia in the setting of an acutely ill patient could reflect a viral illness, malnutrition, alcohol-related bone marrow suppression, or HIV infection. Routine chemistry panels are helpful in the diagnosis of acute and chronic viral hepatitis. Polyclonal hypergammaglobulinemia may reflect chronic stimulation of the immune system from the injection of foreign antigens, chronic liver disease, or concomitant HIV infection.

The chest radiograph can be very helpful in the detection of pulmonary infections, which are frequent in this population. The diagnosis of right-sided endocarditis is suggested by multiple small peripheral cavitary infiltrates. It should be noted that septic phlebitis without endocarditis can also cause multiple septic pulmonary emboli.

PLANS
Diagnostic
Differential Diagnosis

Drug abusers can develop noninfectious processes that resemble many of the infections listed in Table 8–35–1. When evaluating a drug abuser who presents with neurologic signs and symptoms, the clinician must also consider drug overdose, anoxia, trauma, and withdrawal syndromes. Shortness of breath may reflect a noninfectious pulmonary complication such as heroin-induced pulmonary edema and talc granulomatosis. Cocaine-induced myocardial ischemia or infarction can cause cardiogenic shock or pulmonary edema and be confused with acute endocarditis.

Recommended Approach

Because the history and physical examination alone cannot reliably exclude serious infections such as endocarditis, blood cultures should be obtained from all intravenous drug abusers with fever. Up to 10 to 15% of febrile parenteral drug abusers presenting to a hospital emergency room have endocarditis. An even larger number are bacteremic without valvular infection; most have evidence of localized infection elsewhere. Echocardiography is 50 to 90% sensitive in detecting vegetations and may be very helpful diagnostically. Because endocarditis occurs frequently in drug abusers, a vegetation seen on echocardiogram at times may be a remnant from a previous infection, thus leading to the erroneous diagnosis of active endocarditis. Serial chest x-ray films can help detect the changing pulmonary infiltrates and the rapidly evolving cavitary densities seen with tricuspid endocarditis. Appropriate stains and cultures of expectorated sputum are helpful in the detection of pulmonary tuberculosis and in the etiologic diagnosis of bacterial pneumonia. *Staphylococcus aureus* is the likely pathogen in the setting of septic pulmonary emboli in these patients.

When focal infection is present, appropriate stains and cultures should be obtained. Fungal cultures may be helpful because fungi have been associated with bone and joint infections, central nervous system infections, endocarditis, endophthalmitis, and other infections in intravenous drug abusers. Fluctuance at the site of soft tissue infection or septic phlebitis should lead to aspiration. Synovial fluid should be obtained for cell count, stains, and cultures when septic arthritis is suspected. Blood cultures identify the pathogen in only a minority of patients with osteomyelitis. Consequently, cultures of bone (occasionally by open biopsy) or adjacent deep soft tissue infection may be needed to make a correct microbiologic diagnosis.

All parenteral drug abusers should be tested for antibodies to HIV. Knowledge that a febrile drug abuser is seronegative for HIV dramatically narrows the differential diagnosis and can avoid unnecessary diagnostic studies. In early HIV infection, however, antibody may not be detected and repeat serologic testing in 6 weeks to 3 months or other methods of diagnosis such as p24 antigen assay or polymerase chain reaction may be needed. Syphilis serology and hepatitis B serology should be part of the routine blood work. In the setting of acute viral hepatitis, testing for hepatitis A, B, and C, as well as hepatitis D (the delta agent), may be appropriate.

Therapeutic

Therapeutic Options

Although antibiotic therapy is sufficient for many of the bacterial infections occurring in drug abusers, surgical intervention is integral to the management of many infections, including severe soft tissue infections, visceral abscesses, osteomyelitis, endophthalmitis, and mycotic aneurysms. Cardiac valve replacement may be lifesaving in the short-term but, because of the high rate of continued drug use, does not confer a favorable long-term prognosis.

Recommended Approach

When an empiric antibiotic regimen is chosen for an intravenous drug abuser with a potentially serious bacterial infection, the presumed pathogen(s) and local resistance patterns must be considered. These patients are more likely to be infected with antibiotic-resistant bacteria, including methicillin-resistant *S. aureus*. Consequently, vancomycin (1 g intravenously every 12 hours with normal renal function) may be appropriate empiric antistaphylococcal therapy. The addition of an aminoglycoside provides adequate initial Gram-negative rod coverage. When a specific pathogen has been recovered and susceptibility testing performed, the antibiotic regimen can be simplified.

With few exceptions, antibiotic treatment of bacterial infections in the drug abuser is the same as in the normal host. A 2-week course of nafcillin and an aminoglycoside is usually curative for staphylococcal tricuspid endocarditis. Vancomycin does not sterilize the blood as rapidly as β-lactamase stable penicillins, and until clinical studies demonstrate efficacy, a 2-week regimen with vancomycin cannot be recommended.

FOLLOW-UP

Because of problems related to noncompliance and because of the appropriate reluctance of physicians to administer intravenous antibiotics to parenteral drug abusers on an outpatient basis, antibiotic therapy of serious bacterial infections often must be completed while the patient is hospitalized. Methadone clinics are convenient sites for outpatient follow-up of drug abusers. A supervised twice-weekly regimen may facilitate outpatient management of tuberculosis.

DISCUSSION

Prevalence and Incidence

No accurate statistics are available, but the number of intravenous drug abusers in the United States is probably between 500,000 and 1,200,000. Heroin is the prototype of parenterally used drugs, although many other drugs are injected intravenously, the type of which vary both regionally and from year to year.

Related Basic Science

The microorganisms that are inoculated during injection of the illicit drug can arise from several sources including the blood contaminating a shared needle or syringe, a contaminated drug, nonsterile water used to solubilize the drug, skin flora, and saliva. The type of drug injected may have some bearing on the organism causing infection. For example, heroin must be dissolved in boiling water, which probably affords some protection against waterborne Gram-negative bacilli or other organisms that could contaminate the drug paraphernalia. Other drugs such as cocaine and pentazocine with tripelennamine ("T's and Blues") are soluble in water at room temperature and are more likely to be contaminated with waterborne organisms such as *Pseudomonas aeruginosa*. On the other hand, most staphylococci causing infections in addicts emanate from the patient's flora, as demonstrated by studies that show identity between the blood isolate and the strain colonizing the nares.

Although subtle defects in the immune system of addicts were described before the HIV epidemic, most non-HIV-associated infections with unusual organisms of low virulence, including fungi, can probably be explained by the direct intravenous inoculation of microorganisms and are not due to a markedly impaired host response. Malnutrition and a variety of chronic illnesses can suppress the immune system of drug abusers.

Natural History and Its Modification with Treatment

The saying "there are no old drug addicts" is obviously not completely accurate, but does underscore the fact that a high mortality is associated with parenteral drug abuse. Many of the infections discussed above are associated with severe morbidity and death, which are at times compounded by delays in seeking medical care and by noncompliance with treatment. The 10-year survival following valve replacement for endocarditis is about 10%.

Within 2 to 3 years of initiating parenteral drug use, up to 90% of addicts develop serologic evidence of hepatitis B infection. In addition, 60 to 80% of parenteral drug abusers have antibody to hepatitis C. There are considerable regional variations in HIV seroprevalence in parenteral drug abusers, with prevalence rates ranging from less than 10% to more than 50% in the New York metropolitan area and in parts of Italy.

Prevention

Prevention of drug abuse is a formidable challenge. Drug use is intimately tied to many of our societal problems, including an economically disadvantaged underclass, disintegrating family units, and an underfunded educational system.

Preventing infections in parenteral drug abusers is also a problem because this population is not likely to change behavior patterns, even when the health benefit is clear. For example, adherence to "safer sex" practices is much lower in drug abusers than in other populations at risk of HIV transmission, and most drug abusers have multiple sex partners. Drug abusers are also less likely to complete the vaccination series for hepatitis B. Nonetheless, vaccinations of drug abusers should be encouraged, especially with pneumococcal, hepatitis B, and diphtheria/tetanus vaccines. Unfortunately, most parenteral drug abusers have already been infected with hepatitis B virus before they present for medical attention.

A minority of parenteral drug abusers use new injection equipment with each drug injection and less than 20% use bleach to sterilize the "works." The practice of dispensing sterile needles and syringes to addicts probably decreases HIV transmission; however, for a variety of reasons, needle dispensing programs have faced political and societal opposition.

Cost Containment

Treatment of the infectious complications of parenteral drug abuse is expensive and it is probably not feasible to shift a significant portion of

this treatment to outpatient facilities. The cost of the preventive measures discussed above is also large, but effective prevention would reduce not only the medical costs of drug abuse but also the enormous social costs.

REFERENCES

Cherubin CE, Sapira JD. The medical complications of drug addiction and the medical assessment of the intravenous drug user: 25 years later. Ann Intern Med 1993;119:1017.

Crane LR, Levine DP, Zervos MJ, Cummings G. Bacteremia in narcotic addicts at the Detroit Medical Center: I. Microbiology, risk factors, and empiric therapy. Rev Infect Dis 1986;8:364.

Haverkos HW, Lange WR. Serious infections other than human immunodeficiency virus among intravenous drug abusers. J Infect Dis 1990;161:894.

Marantz PR, Linzer M, Feiner CJ, et al. Inability to predict diagnosis in febrile intravenous drug abusers. Ann Intern Med 1987;106:823.

Weisse AB, Heller DR, Schimenti RJ, et al. The febrile parenteral drug user: A prospective study in 121 patients. Am J Med 1993;94:274.

CHAPTER 8–36

Infections Related to Animal Bites

Sue Anne Brenner, M.D., and Phyllis E. Kozarsky, M.D.

DEFINITION

Animal bites can lead to both local and systemic infections.

ETIOLOGY

Depending on the animal that caused the bite, many different organisms can infect bite wounds. Most common are α-hemolytic streptococci, *Staphylococcus* species, and *Pasteurella multocida*. Other aerobes such as *Streptococcus intermedius*, β-hemolytic streptococci, *Eikenella corrodens*, *Capnocytophaga canimorsus*, *Micrococcus* species, *Actinobacillus actinomycetemcomitans*, *Hemophilus aphrophilus* and other *Hemophilus* species, and, rarely, enteric Gram-negative bacilli may be isolated. Anaerobes include *Actinomyces* species, *Bacteroides* species, *Fusobacterium* species, *Peptostreptococcus* species, *Eubacterium* species, *Veillonella parvula*, and *Leptotrichia buccalus*. Mixed infections are common. In addition, *Bartonella henselae* may be isolated from cat scratch and bite wounds.

CRITERIA FOR DIAGNOSIS
Suggestive

The most common bites to become infected are puncture wounds caused by cats and hand bites by humans. The most common infections associated with animal bites are local infections, including cellulitis and lymphangitis, but sometimes systemic illnesses such as tularemia and rat bite fever may develop. Topics discussed in this chapter are local infections and common systemic syndromes following bites. Rabies is also discussed.

Most patients, except sometimes those who present with rabies, give a history of animal bite. Inspection of the injury site often reveals teeth marks, a skin tear, or puncture wound. Usually, the area immediately surrounding the bite is erythematous, swollen, and tender. Scratch marks may be seen along with the bite. Occasionally, particularly in children, multiple bite wounds may be seen on different parts of the body; therefore, if the patient cannot relate an adequate history, a careful and complete examination should be done to check for multiple bite sites.

Definitive

The above subjective findings plus isolation of organisms mentioned under Etiology confirm infection of a bite.

CLINICAL MANIFESTATIONS
Subjective

The most important information the patient can relay is the type of animal that bit him or her and in what circumstances the bite occurred. Included in this information are how long ago the incident occurred, where it occurred, whether the animal was known or a stray, and if the bite was provoked by attempted feeding or handling of the animal.

Symptoms of local infection include the development of redness, pain, and swelling around the wound. Drainage also may be noted. If the bite was on a hand, the fingers may begin to feel stiff.

If the patient becomes bacteremic, he or she may present with fever, chills, and other symptoms of diffuse organ system involvement (e.g., chest pain, cough, dizziness).

The incubation period for rabies is usually 2 to 10 weeks, although cases have been reported to occur many years after exposure. The prodrome of rabies is nonspecific. Burning may occur at the site of the wound. Patients complain of malaise, fever, headache, nausea, vomiting, and diarrhea. This flulike syndrome is followed by neurologic symptoms, such as anxiety and inability to control one's behavior.

Objective
Physical Examination

Signs of local animal bite wound infection include inflammation, swelling, and serosanguineous or purulent drainage. Cellulitis may involve just the wound area or may spread extensively. Cutaneous gangrene can develop in certain infections. Local adenopathy also may be appreciated. Distal pulses and motor and sensory function should be evaluated.

Puncture wounds of the hand may show only erythema at the site, but swelling of the dorsum of the hand may indicate deeper infection, and septic arthritis due to tooth penetration of joints may occur. Osteomyelitis, meningitis and abscess formation can also complicate bites.

Objective signs of bacteremia may be visible with fever and chills. In addition, the patient may have signs of pneumonia, meningitis, endocarditis, or septic shock.

The major finding in patients during the prodrome of rabies is a change in behavior, with hyperactivity and apprehension. This may last about 1 week and is followed by altered mental status with confusion, salivation, combativeness, tremors, seizures, paralysis, and coma. These signs may be aggravated by environmental stimuli, and spasms may be precipitated by air movement or by seeing or drinking water (hydrophobia).

Routine Laboratory Abnormalities

Routine laboratory data following bites are nonspecific. If the patient has cellulitis or is bacteremic, the white blood cell count may be elevated; in osteomyelitis and other chronic infections, the erythrocyte sedimentation rate may be elevated. If pneumonia has developed, the chest x-ray film will reveal an infiltrate.

PLANS
Diagnostic
Differential Diagnosis

Generally a history of a bite is given, and the differential diagnosis includes any of the organisms mentioned in the beginning of this chapter. In a rapidly developing cellulitis, the most common causative agent is *Pasteurella*.

Most patients who present after a bite give a history indicating this. Occasionally, patients are ashamed to tell the physician that they have sustained a human bite. Therefore, when seeing a patient with a laceration or puncture wound, physicians should ask specifically what caused it.

Diagnostic Options

Culture of wounds taken immediately after a bite shows the organisms present in the wound, but a culture does not help predict whether or not the wound will become infected. Certain factors, however, do increase the likelihood that a bite will become infected, and they include advanced age, diabetes, bite on an upper extremity, puncture wound (particularly of the hand), and a delay in seeking treatment.

If the wound is already infected, cultures should always be done and the laboratory should be informed that the material is from a bite wound so it can specifically look for organisms such as *Pasteurella* and anaerobes. Sometimes areas of cellulitis can be evaluated by aspirating material from the leading edge of the erythema and by sending that for Gram stain and culture. If an abscess has developed, it should be drained or aspirated and cultured. If the bite was deep or the patient delayed seeking treatment, an x-ray of the wound may be helpful in looking for osteomyelitis or gas in the soft tissues.

If the patient is febrile or appears toxic, blood cultures should be obtained. For septic patients, it is sometimes helpful to do a Gram stain of the buffy coat to try to determine the causative organism rapidly. This is especially true in asplenic patients who present in shock following a dog bite.

About 25% of patients who develop rabies give no animal exposure history, so rabies should be suspected in any patient who presents with encephalitis of unknown etiology. In many areas of the world rabies is endemic (e.g., Asia, Africa, Latin America), particularly in dogs, and therefore travelers who return from these areas and then develop changes in behavior or neurologic signs and symptoms should be highly suspect. Unfortunately, the diagnosis of rabies is often made postmortem. There are no tests to diagnose rabies during its long incu-

bation period. After the onset of illness, serologic tests on both the blood and the cerebrospinal fluid may be performed. A lumbar puncture should be done to rule out other causes of a change in mental status. The cerebrospinal fluid in rabies is nonspecific, often with normal protein and glucose levels. The cerebrospinal fluid white blood cell count may be slightly elevated. The standard serologic test at this time is the rapid fluorescent focus inhibition test, and positive titers may be detected 1 to 2 weeks after the onset of signs and symptoms. Some laboratories are able to isolate the virus from sputum, cerebrospinal fluid, or tissue. Earlier diagnosis can sometimes be made by sending a skin biopsy from the back of the patient's neck, a brain biopsy, or a corneal impression to the Centers for Disease Control and Prevention (CDC) or to the state health department for direct immunofluorescence antibody testing for rabies. The neck skin biopsy seems to be the most reliable. For specific recommendations and interpretation of tests results, the physician should contact the local health department or the CDC.

Recommended Approach

The patient should be carefully examined for signs of both local and systemic infection. The wound should be cultured as described in the previous section.

Therapeutic
Therapeutic Options

Because Gram-stained smears of specimens from infected bites may not always be predictive of culture results, empiric therapy is often necessary. For the initial treatment of infection due to animal bites that are mild enough to warrant outpatient care, antibiotics such as amoxicillin–clavulanic acid (Augmentin), penicillin VK, dicloxacillin (Dynapen), cephalosporins, and erythromycin may be used. Some authors believe that because *Pasteurella* species cause up to 50% of cat bite infections, dicloxacillin, oral cephalosporins, and erythromycin should not be used and, instead, recommend tetracycline. Interestingly, despite suboptimal in vitro response to some of these antibiotics, the clinical outcome using them has been good in infections due to *Pasteurella*, and, in general, tetracyclines are not the antibiotics of choice for potential cellulitis or soft tissue infections. Patients with human bite infections usually should be treated with penicillin; however, because some experts believe that human bites have a greater likelihood of becoming infected with *Staphylococcus aureus*, a semisynthetic penicillin such as amoxicillin–clavulanic acid or dicloxacillin should be used. Once culture results are available, the antibiotic regimen should be changed appropriately. Patients should be treated until the infection is healed, which may take several weeks. Prophylaxis of uninfected bite wounds from animals such as cats and dogs should continue for 3 to 5 days.

Admission to the hospital should be considered when a patient has signs of systemic infection; if cellulitis is severe, has crossed a joint, has spread rapidly, or has not responded to oral therapy; and when infections are known to involve a joint, bone, tendon, or nerve.

For hospitalized patients with serious bite wound infections, empiric antibiotic therapy should be broad until culture results are available. Often an agent or agents are used that cover Gram-positive, Gram-negative, and anaerobic organisms. Antibiotics such as ticarcillin–clavulanic acid (3.1 g intravenously every 4–6 hours, adjusted for renal insufficiency) or imipenem–cilastin (Primaxin, 500 mg intravenously every 6–8 hours, adjusted for severe renal insufficiency) may be used for initial treatment.

For the patient who has evidence of pneumonia, endocarditis, or meningitis following a dog or cat bite, high-dose intravenous penicillin G or ampicillin plus a third-generation cephalosporin are good choices until culture results are available.

The patient with osteomyelitis usually requires long-term intravenous therapy (6–8 weeks). The antibiotic(s) depends on culture results.

Treatment of rabies is unsatisfactory, and there are few well-documented cases of survival. When rabies is suspected, strict isolation should be instituted, as should aggressive supportive care, including the avoidance of feeding and stimulation and provision of adequate sedation, fluids, and early ventilatory support.

Recommended Approach

Infected animal bites should be cleaned, and devitalized tissue should be removed. All patients should receive tetanus prophylaxis (see Chapter 8–81 for specific instructions). Some require admission to the hospital, and affected limbs should be immobilized and elevated. Neither puncture wounds, nor those that are infected, nor those examined more than 24 hours after a bite should be closed with sutures.

Wound cultures can guide therapy (see previous section).

FOLLOW-UP

Patients with bite wounds should understand that the wound may become infected and that if pain, swelling, or erythema is noted, they should return to the physician. Patients with an infected wound should be told that the infection can spread to joints or bones, causing disability, and may rarely require amputation. Families of patients who are bacteremic need to know that mortality is high, particularly if the patient is asplenic, has an afunctional spleen (e.g., patients with sickle cell disease or cirrhosis), or is immunocompromised for other reasons.

Patients who have been bitten by a potentially rabid animal and who receive prophylaxis for rabies should be informed of the signs and symptoms of the illness. They should call their health department for advice concerning management or quarantine of the animal involved. The families of patients with rabies need to understand that the disease is almost universally fatal.

Patients with animal bites that are not infected need no follow-up after the initial visit unless signs and symptoms of infection occur. In patients with infected wounds, follow-up is dependent on the severity of the infection. Those with deep or extensive infections or with hand infections should be followed in the hospital.

DISCUSSION

Prevalence and Incidence

In the United States every year about 2 million people are bitten by animals or by another person. Of these, up to 50% of cat bites, 20% of human bites, and 5% of dog bites become infected.

Most bites in the United States occur in males under age 30 and are simple injuries. Most animals are known to their victims and are not strays. Animal and human bites account for roughly 1% to 2% of emergency room visits. Bites commonly occur on the extremities, but they are also found on the face and trunk.

Related Basic Science

Infection in bites is caused by exposure of subcutaneous tissue to skin flora and flora from the mouth and saliva of the animal. As more than 60 species of aerobic and anaerobic bacteria have been isolated from a dog's mouth alone, infection due to bite wounds may be caused by a variety of different organisms. Most dog and cat bite wound infections are polymicrobial. In some studies, up to 70% of cats and 65% of dogs harbor P. multocida in their mouths. This organism is responsible for about 80% of cat bite infections and about 50% of dog bite infections. P. multocida is a Gram-negative coccobacillus that exhibits bipolar staining. It grows on enriched media such as blood and is easily isolated. Infection caused by P. multocida usually manifests as a very painful and rapidly developing cellulitis within the first day of a bite. Serosanguineous drainage may be noted. Local adenopathy occurs in up to one third of these patients, and tenosynovitis or osteomyelitis may develop. Less than 15% of patients develop systemic illness with bacteremia and pneumonia. Endocarditis and meningitis rarely occur. P. multocida is also found in cattle, horses, swine, sheep, rats, hamsters, and other animals. Antibiotics that are effective against Pasteurella are penicillin, ampicillin, tetracycline, chloramphenicol, and cephalosporins, especially cefuroxime. Semisynthetic penicillins such as oxacillin and dicloxacillin (oral) are not as effective.

Capnocytophaga canimorsus (formerly CDC group DF-2) is a pleo-morphic, long, thin Gram-negative rod that grows slowly on chocolate agar. It is part of the oral flora in some dogs and can cause fulminant sepsis in asplenic patients, alcoholics, and, rarely, even normal, otherwise healthy persons. Meningitis, shock, disseminated intravascular coagulation, and death can follow. Patients with C. canimorsus bacteremia usually present with signs and symptoms 1 to 7 days after the bite. The bite wound often appears as a necrotizing eschar, and gangrene is not uncommon. Milder illness is usually seen in patients with normal spleens. Penicillin is the drug of choice for suspected C. canimorsus infection, although clindamycin, erythromycin, tetracycline, chloramphenicol, and first-generation cephalosporins all seem to have some activity. Other unclassified Gram-negative rod infections from dog bites can also cause similar syndromes (e.g., EF-4, II-J, II-R).

Other organisms that can cause infections in dog and cat bites are streptococci, staphylococci, corynebacteria, Enterobacter species, Hemophilus, Neisseria, Klebsiella species, and a variety of anaerobes (Bacteroides species, fusobacteria, and anaerobic streptococci). Mixed infections are common. Cat bites and scratches may transmit Bartonella henselae, a cause of cat scratch disease, and fever, hepatomegaly, and splenomegaly in immunocompromised patients. Human bites may be infected with the same bacteria as dog and cat bites except for Pasteurella and the alphanumeric Gram-negative rods. Some believe that Staphylococcus aureus, group A Streptococcus, and Eikenella corrodens are more likely to cause infections in human bites. E. corrodens is a small, straight, Gram-negative rod that grows well on blood agar in 3 to 10% CO_2. It may be detected in 25% of clenched-fist injuries. The organism is susceptible to penicillin, ampicillin, chloramphenicol, some cephalosporins, and tetracycline, but is resistant to clindamycin and aminoglycosides.

Rabies is an RNA virus that belongs to the family Rhabdoviridae. It causes disease in many animals throughout the world. In the United States, where domestic animal control programs have been active for more than 20 years, and where domestic animal rabies vaccination is widespread, rabies is more commonly found in wild animals. In fact, the number of cases of wild animal rabies in the United States has increased in the last several years and stands at about 4000 cases reported per year. Worldwide, however, dogs and cats are the major reservoirs for the disease. Indeed, about half the cases of human rabies reported in the past 5 years have occurred among individuals who had recently been to rabies-endemic areas outside the United States and who had exposure to presumed "domestic animals." Human rabies has decreased sharply in this county in the past 30 years, with 94 cases reported from 1946 through 1949 and fewer than 20 cases reported from 1982 through 1990.

Natural History and Its Modification with Treatment

Other more unusual infections caused by bites include actinomycosis, blastomycosis, tuberculosis, hepatitis B, and tetanus. There is also concern that HIV may be transmitted via a human bite. In addition, herpesvirus simiae (B virus) infections have occurred in animal handlers and laboratory workers in primate centers due to bites from cynomolgus monkeys.

In general, animal bite wounds tend to do better than human bite wounds for several reasons: animal bites are usually more superficial; the occlusive surfaces of the teeth in animals tear in a linear fashion; the injury is one of shearing and not of direct impact; patients seek help sooner with animal bites; and many human bites are caused by biting a clenched fist, where the metacarpophalangeal joint is easily entered during a blow. After a clenched-fist injury, the patient extends his or her fingers, allowing the dorsal expansion hood to seal off the wound and encourage growth of microorganisms and spread of infection into adjacent bursae, webbed spaces, and palmar and volar areas. And, finally, many human bites involve the genitals, where the outcome can be devastating.

Prevention

Prevention of animal bites involves supporting leash laws and animal control programs and not allowing children to be unattended with animals. Education of children in the proper handling of animals is also helpful, as children below the age of 10 are the most often injured.

Prevention of infection requires that those bitten see a physician shortly after the event, as a delay of 12 hours or longer markedly increases the complication rate.

To prevent infection, all wounds should be debrided if devitalized tissue is present. Wounds should be washed with soap and water immediately and then irrigated under high pressure (with at least 100 mL of normal saline pushed through a 19-gauge needle). If edema is present, the wound should be elevated.

Most physicians believe that simple lacerations may be sutured except if they are on the hand or if they are human bites. Puncture wounds should not be closed; the area should be splinted and elevated.

In an otherwise healthy individual, antibiotic prophylaxis of a simple dog bite may not be necessary. For any other bite wounds, data concerning antibiotic prophylaxis to prevent infection are controversial. Some physicians believe that antibiotics should be given to all patients with bite wounds except those who present more than 24 hours after the injury and who have no evidence of infection. Most physicians, however, agree that all patients with "high-risk" wounds (i.e., bites on the hand or puncture wounds, bites of the head and neck, and bites in elderly or immunocompromised patients) should receive prophylaxis. Prophylaxis consists of oral amoxicillin–clavulanic acid (500 mg three times daily for several days). Allergic patients may receive an oral cephalosporin or tetracycline.

For prevention of tetanus, the guidelines in Chapter 8–81 should be followed. Preexposure prophylaxis against rabies is advisable for veterinarians, certain animal handlers, spelunkers, and individuals living or traveling in areas of high endemicity for longer than 1 month. Some antimalarial agents (chloroquine, mefloquine), however, may blunt the antibody response to human diploid cell vaccine. Thus, if a traveler is taking chloroquine or mefloquine for malaria chemoprophylaxis, the series must be completed before initiation of antimalarial agents. If this is not possible, the intramuscular route can be used.

The need for postexposure rabies prophylaxis depends on the biting animal and the geographic region in which the incident occurred. Table 8–36–1 should be used as a guide to determine whether postexposure prophylaxis is recommended. Note that if postexposure prophylaxis is used, both the vaccine and immune globulin are necessary. If there is any doubt, a local or state health department or the Viral Division at the CDC should be contacted for advice. The CDC Information Hotline is (404) 332–4555.

The risk of transmission of rabies from a human patient to hospital personnel is extremely low. If rabies is suspected, however, the patient should be placed in isolation. Only contacts who have experienced contamination of mucous membranes or who have been in contact with open wounds with infectious material should receive prophylaxis.

Cost Containment

The combination of medical costs, lost income, and the cost of torn clothing add up to over $25 million spent annually because of animal and human bites. It is estimated that an emergency room visit for a small puncture wound may cost as much as $150 to $200. Other than encouraging victims to seek medical attention early, the best method of cost containment is prevention.

TABLE 8–36–1. RABIES POSTEXPOSURE PROPHYLAXIS GUIDE

Animal Species	Condition of Animal at Time of Attack	Treatment of Exposed Person
Domestic Dog and Cat	Healthy and available for 10 days of observation	None, unless animal develops rabies*
	Rabid or suspected rabid	RIG† and HDCV
	Unknown (escaped)	Consult public health officials if treatment is indicated, give RIG† and HDCV
Wild		
Skunk, bat, fox, coyote, raccoon, bobcat, and other carnivores	Regard as rabid unless proven negative by laboratory tests‡	RIG† and HDCV
Other		
Livestock, rodents, and lagomorphs (rabbits and hares)	Consider individually; local and state public health officials should be consulted on questions about the need for rabies prophylaxis; bites of squirrels, hamsters, guinea pigs, gerbils, chipmunks, rats, mice, other rodents, rabbits, and hares almost never call for antirabies prophylaxis	

RIG, rabies immune globulin; HDCV, human diploid cell vaccine.
*During the usual holding period of 10 days, begin treatment with RIG and HDCV at first sign of rabies in a dog or cat that has bitten someone. The symptomatic animal should be killed immediately and tested.
†If RIG is not available, use antirabies serum, equine (ARS). Do not use more than the recommended dosage.
‡The animal should be killed and tested as soon as possible. Holding for observation is not recommended.
Note: These recommendations are only a guide. In applying them, take into account the animal species involved, the circumstances of the bite or other exposure, the vaccination status of the animal, and the presence of rabies in the region. Local or state public health officials should be consulted if questions arise about the need for rabies prophylaxis.
Source: Centers for Disease Control and Prevention. Recommendation of the Immunization Practices Advisory Committee (ACIP). Rabies prevention, United States. MMWR 1991;40:3.

REFERENCES

Callaham M. Controversies in antibiotic choices for bite wounds. Ann Emerg Med 1988;17:1321.

Centers for Disease Control. Rabies prevention: Supplementary statement on the preexposure use of human diploid cell vaccine by the intradermal route. MMWR 1986;35:767.

Centers for Disease Control. Health information for international travel 1994. HHS Publication No. (CDC) 94-8280. Washington, DC: U.S. Government Printing Office, 1994:128

Goldstein EJC. Bite wounds and infection. Clin Infect Dis 1992;14:633.

Goldstein EJC, Citron DM. Comparative activities of ceturoxime, amoxicillin, clavulanic acid, ciprofloxacin, enoxacin, and ofloxacin against aerobic & anaerobic bacteria isolated from bite wounds. Antimicro Agents Chemo 1988;32(8):1143.

Kullberg BJ, Westerdorp BGJ, van't Wont JW, Meinders AE. Purpura fulminans and symmetrical gangrene caused by *Capnocytophaga canimorsus* septicemia: A complication of dog bite. Medicine 1991;70(5):287.

Macgregor RR. Infections caused by animal bites and scratches. In: Harrison's textbook of medicine. 12th ed. New York: McGraw-Hill, 1991:550.

CHAPTER 8–37

Infections Related to Insect (Arthropod) Bites

Susan L. F. McLellan, M.D., and Phyllis E. Kozarsky, M.D.

DEFINITION

This chapter focuses on systemic illnesses caused by bites of insect (arthropod) vectors in the United States. Many of these are covered in more depth in other chapters. Some illnesses that are not transmitted in the United States but are common in other parts of the world are mentioned briefly.

ETIOLOGY

Insects serve as vectors for the transmission of organisms such as rickettsiae, viruses, certain bacteria, and protozoa that cause disease. A number of different arthropods carry agents of disease, including ticks, mosquitoes, lice, fleas, and mites. These vectors may be widespread in the environment or within a specific geographic area, or they may be found only in association with specific animal carriers.

CRITERIA FOR DIAGNOSIS
Suggestive

The clinical history may suggest the diagnosis of a vectorborne disease. Routine laboratory examinations may or may not be normal depending on the illness; refer to Tables 8–37–1 and 8–37–2 for characteristics of specific illnesses.

Definitive

Some of these diseases can be diagnosed by blood cultures or direct visualization of the organism in tissue or blood. Many, however, require serology and the diagnosis may not be confirmed until after the patient has been treated and either improved or deteriorated. See Tables 8–37–1 and 8–37–2 for specific tests for each illness.

CLINICAL MANIFESTATIONS
Subjective

The clinical history of the patient's illness is very important, as diagnosis is often made on the basis of clinical suspicion. Symptoms vary depending on the disease. A patient may give a history of being bitten by an insect, but in many cases this history will not be obtained. Information about a patient's travel history, activities, hobbies, occupation, and housing is important and may give clues to the types of insects to which the patient may have been exposed. It should be asked if precautions were taken to avoid bites during suspected exposure to vectors.

Objective
Physical Examination

The physical findings in different diseases are listed in Tables 8–37–1 and 8–37–2. In the case of insect bites, often a small bite mark may be visible. It may turn into a papule or ulcer as in tularemia or an eschar as in rickettsialpox. A number of arthropodborne diseases display a characteristic rash. Fever and myalgia are common.

Routine Laboratory Abnormalities

See Tables 8–37–1 and 8–37–2.

PLANS
Diagnostic
Differential Diagnosis

As the primary symptoms of many of these illnesses are fever and malaise, the differential diagnosis will at first include a variety of problems including influenza and other viral illnesses, gastroenteritis, bacte-

rial sepsis, and bacterial or viral meningitis. Some of the persistent diseases such as Lyme disease and relapsing fever may mimic autoimmune disease or neoplasm.

Diagnostic Options

In the case of a mild illness, the diagnosis may often be made on clinical grounds. If making the specific diagnosis is important, routine laboratory examinations should be followed by specific serologies, blood smears, cultures, or direct visualization of the organism by antibody or other techniques. In patients with meningitic or encephalitic presentations, lumbar puncture is required and sometimes special assays can be performed on cerebrospinal fluid. It is frequently wise to collect samples of acute and convalescent sera and to save specimens of sera and cerebrospinal fluid for later analysis if the evolution of the illness suggests a new diagnosis.

Recommended Approach

The specific assays and diagnostic tests appropriate to different diseases are listed in Tables 8–37–1 and 8–37–2.

Therapeutic
Therapeutic Options

Many arthropodborne diseases are self-limited, and if the patient is already improving by the time diagnosis is made, no therapy may be necessary. In some cases there is no specific therapy and supportive care is all that can be offered. In severely ill patients it is wise to treat presumptively for the suspected diseases, as diagnosis may take a long time.

Recommended Approach

Specific therapies for various illnesses are listed in Table 8–37–2.

FOLLOW-UP

The otherwise healthy patient who has an illness such as murine typhus or babesiosis can be assured that he or she will improve; however, many patients with other illnesses in this group require hospitalization. While hospitalized, the patient can be further evaluated, specialized blood tests may be performed, and the patient's status can be very closely monitored. After improvement, the patient may require a follow-up visit to assess his or her status and, in some cases, to obtain a convalescent serology to confirm a diagnosis. Some of these illnesses may have different phases (e.g., Lyme disease, relapsing fever, malaria), and a patient experiencing additional symptoms should be reevaluated.

DISCUSSION
Prevalence and Incidence
See Table 8–37–1.

Related Basic Science

Except for tick paralysis, which is caused by a neurotoxin produced by the tick, all of the diseases discussed here are caused by organisms that are carried by arthropods and transmitted to humans. In many cases there is an animal reservoir for the pathogen, and the human is an incidental host. In others, humans are the primary hosts and the presence of a susceptible human population is necessary to perpetuate the life cycle of the disease-causing organism. For further details see Tables 8–37–1 and 8–37–2 or the references listed below.

TABLE 8–37–1. DISEASES CAUSED BY INSECT (ARTHROPOD) VECTORS

Insect or Arthropod Vector	Disease	Etiologic Agent	Clinical Manifestations	Geographic Areas of Exposure
Hard tick	Rocky Mountain spotted fever	*Rickettsia rickettsii*	Fever, gastrointestinal complaints, lethargy, headache; 3–5 d of fever, rash begins peripherally and spreads to trunk and may be evanescent (palms and soles involved); occasionally pneumonia, DIC, shock, and death	Forests of United States, particularly South Atlantic region
Hard tick	Colorado tick fever	Colorado tick fever virus (orbivirus)	Headache, backache, fever (frequently biphasic), leukopenia, sequence of 2–3 d of fever, then a symptom-free interval followed by return of fever	Western United States at elevations greater than 4000 ft
Hard tick	Lyme disease	*Borrelia burgdorferi*	Erythema chronicum migrans (annular expanding rash) followed in 1–30 d by fever, headache, myalgias (stage 1); may cause cardiac arrhythmias or heart block; aseptic meningitis may occur (stage 2); arthritis in large joints, (stage 3); asymptomatic, infection common	Most common in northeastern United States, although increasingly reported all over United States and Europe
Hard tick	Tick paralysis	Neurotoxin from tick	Anorexia; ataxia 4–6 d after attachment; leads to flaccid ascending paralysis; may include bulbar and respiratory paralysis	All tick-infested areas of the United States, Canada, southern Europe, South America, Australia
Hard tick	Babesiosis	*Babesia microti* (and other species)	Fever, chills, sweats, headache, myalgia, anorexia; fulminant in asplenic patients	Long Island Sound area, Nantucket, Martha's Vineyard, Wisconsin, Northern California, Mexico, Europe
Tick	Ehrlichiosis	*Ehrlichia chaffeensis*	Fever, pulse–temperature dissociation, headache, anorexia, leukopenia (lymphopenia), thrombocytopenia, sometimes elevated liver tests; rash occasionally present, not specific	Being recognized with increased frequency in south and south-central United States; also other areas as index of suspicion increases
Louse	Epidemic relapsing fever	*Borrelia recurrentis*	Usually fever lasts 3–4 d after a febrile period of about 1 w; followed by nausea, vomiting, diarrhea, myalgia, headache; rash in 30%	Forested mountainous areas of western United States; rodent hibernation areas
Soft tick	Endemic relapsing fever	*Borrelia hermsii turicatae B. parkeri*	Similar to epidemic form	Worldwide
Hard tick, deerfly, horsefly	Tularemia (rabbit fever)	*Francisella tularensis*	Fever, chills, malaise may appear in different forms: ulceroglandular (primary lesion and local lymphadenopathy [most common]), oculoglandular ("typhoidal") with prostration and weight loss (10%), pharyngeal; pneumonia may occur	Occurs in most areas of the northern hemisphere; may also become ill by exposure to infected rabbit or rarely by animal bite
Mosquito	Dengue fever	Dengue virus (flavivirus)	Incubation period about 1 w; fever, chills, headache, myalgia, prostration; days 3–5 diffuse rash begins on trunk → centrifugally; lymphadenopathy; leukopenia; hemoconcentration; may cause hemorrhagic fever, shock	Southern Texas in United States, Caribbean; occurs worldwide; endemic in tropics, on the increase in the Americas
Mosquito	Malaria	*Plasmodium falciparum, P. vivax, P. ovale, P. malariae*	Paroxysms of high fever, chills, malaise, headache, myalgia, fatigue	In United States, most often found in travelers to tropical endemic areas; also found in intravenous drug abusers and after blood transfusions
Mosquito and hard tick	Western equine, Eastern equine, St. Louis, California, Venezuelan encephalitis	St. Louis encephalitis virus (flavivirus); CE virus (bunyavirus); VEE, EEE, WEE viruses (alphaviruses)	Mild febrile illness → encephalitis; EEE more acute and rapidly progressive; SLE more severe in elderly; peaks in August and September; many subclinical cases, except EEE	*WEE:* southwestern and eastern United States; *EEE:* swamps eastern United States and western United States; *VEE:* southern United States, Central America, South America, Mexico; *SLE:* North America, Central and South America
Flea	Murine (endemic) typhus	*Rickettsia typhi*	Same as epidemic typhus, but milder; mild rash spreads from trunk peripherally in ∼50%; elevated aspartate aminotransferase	Rodent-infested areas where fleas' feces may contaminate broken skin; most cases in United States from Texas
Rodent flea	Plague	*Yersinia pestis*	Fever, lymphadenitis (bubo), pneumonia, septicemia (this form rapidly fatal)	Western United States, India, Vietnam, South America; outbreaks in Africa
Mouse mite	Rickettsialpox	*Rickettsia akari*	Incubation period 9–14 d; eschar at site of bite with local lymphadenopathy, chills, fever, headache, myalgia; generalized papular rash on days 2–3; leukopenia, rare complications	Crowded urban settings; rodent-infested areas of United States, South Africa, Korea, USSR.
Louse	Epidemic typhus	*Rickettsia prowazekii*	Fever, myalgia, headache; rash begins on trunk and spreads peripherally	Classic louse-borne disease does not occur in United States except in recrudescent form (Brill–Zinsser) in eastern European immigrants who had primary infection in 1940s; some cases in Eastern Coastal states carried by flying squirrels

DIC, disseminated intravascular coagulation; →, leading to CE, California encephalitis; VEE, Venezuelan encephalitis; EEE, Eastern equine encephalitis; WEE, Western equine encephalitis; SLE, St. Louis encephalitis.

TABLE 8–37–2. DIAGNOSIS AND TREATMENT OF DISEASES CAUSED BY INSECT (ARTHROPOD) VECTORS

Disease	Diagnosis	Therapy	Comments
Rocky Mountain spotted fever	Serology, fluorescent antibody stain of skin or tissue, clinical suspicion, PCR may be available soon	Tetracycline or doxycycline; chloramphenicol	Number of cases increasing in past several years; mortality still up to 10%
Colorado tick fever	Isolation of virus from blood or CSF; fluorescent antibody of blood; serology; if neurologic symptoms, CSF lymphocytosis often found	Supportive	Occurs in spring and early summer; usually self-limited disease; may be very severe in young children
Lyme disease	Clinical suspicion; serology; organism difficult to isolate by culture or on skin biopsy	Doxycycline or tetracycline; penicillin G; ceftriaxone (depending on stage); erythromycin if allergy present	Most commonly reported vectorborne disease in United States; only about one third give history of tick bite; higher incidence in summer; serology difficult to interpret; diagnosis often difficult when rash not present
Tick paralysis	Clinical picture	In U.S. species, removing tick is curative in 48 h; rare use of tick antitoxin	Mortality about 10% if undiagnosed; neurotoxin can sometimes be isolated from tick
Babesiosis	Microscopic examination of blood for intraerythrocytic parasites; clinical suspicion	Supportive; clindamycin and quinine; exchange transfusion; many antimalarial agents not effective	Must be differentiated from malaria; schizonts and gametocytes not produced
Ehrlichiosis	Serology, leukocyte inclusion bodies.	Tetracycline; chloramphenicol	Being recognized with increasing frequency in United States
Relapsing fever	Darkfield examination; peripheral smear (see organisms)	Tetracycline; chloramphenicol (erythromycin)	Mortality about 5%, but usually self-limited; treatment may cause Jarisch–Herxheimer reaction
Tularemia	Serology; rarely may be cultured; fluorescent antibody staining of tissue	Streptomycin (gentamicin, tetracycline, chloramphenicol may not be as efficacious)	Tickborne disease occurs in spring and summer; rabbit-exposure tularemia more common in winter; mortality about 1%; vaccine available for laboratory workers
Dengue fever ("break-bone fever")	Clinical picture, serology	Supportive	Epidemics occur when new serotypes are introduced into an area; pandemics occur in Caribbean; vaccines currently being evaluated
Malaria	Clinical suspicion; microscopic examination of blood for intraerythrocytic parasites	Chloroquine and primaquine for *Plasmodium vivax* and *P. ovale* (to eradicate extraerythrocytic phase); check for G6PD deficiency; regimens for *P. falciparum* include quinine; see Chapter 8–61	*P. falciparum* causes high parasitemia, "blackwater fever," shock, death; recommendations on prophylaxis change; see text
WEE, EEE, SLE, CE, VEE	Serology; rarely, isolation of virus; *EEE:* histochemical staining for antigen	Supportive	Peaks in August and September; these illnesses are caused by different families of RNA viruses; children seem more susceptible to neurologic sequelae; outbreaks often related to human manipulation of environment
Murine (endemic) typhus	Weil–Felix positive (OX-19 and often OX-2); specific serology	Tetracycline or doxycycline; chloramphenicol	Relapses may occur; incidence has decreased since 1940s; mortality very low
Plague	Blood cultures; sputum cultures; node aspiration	Streptomycin gentamicin, kanamycin; tetracycline; chloramphenicol for meningitis and ophthalmitis (trimethoprim–sulfamethoxazole)	Occurs more frequently in warm months; mortality about 15%; vaccine available for those at high risk; all patients with suspected plague should be placed in isolation for 2 d
Rickettsialpox	Serology (Weil–Felix test negative); clinical setting	Tetracycline	Symptoms resolve rapidly with treatment; outbreaks still occur in United States.
Epidemic typhus	Clinical suspicion; Weil–Felix reaction positive (but indistinguishable from murine typhus); specific serology; PCR may be available soon	Chloramphenicol; tetracycline or doxycycline	Mortality as high as 40% (particularly in elderly)

CSF, cerebrospinal fluid; G6PD, glucose-6-phosphate dehydrogenase; PCR, polymerase chain reaction; WEE, EEE, SLE, CE, VEE as in Table 8–37–1.

Natural History and Its Modification with Treatment

See Tables 8–37–1 and 8–37–2.

Prevention

Prevention is the best way of combating these illnesses. In general, people who spend considerable time outdoors are more apt to be bitten by insects. Those who plan to be outdoors in high-risk locations, especially in tropical areas, should use insect repellents. Repellents should be used over all exposed surfaces and should be applied again after swimming or perspiring. Repellent should also be applied to clothing. Long sleeves and pants are preferable, and should be closed at the waist, ankles, and wrists. If sleeping in areas that are not climate-controlled, mosquito netting should be used.

Individuals outdoors in areas where tickborne diseases occur should periodically check themselves for ticks, particularly in places where they would not be readily noticeable, such as skin creases and the scalp. Pets should also be checked for ticks, and care should be taken to remove them if discovered. Acetone or ether may be used on the tick to release it. A hot object such as a match may also be used, as may asphyxiating materials such as mineral oil and peanut better.

Many vectorborne diseases have been controlled by general improvement in sanitation and public health measures. The vector of rickettsialpox is usually found in substandard urban dwellings, and control of mice and improvement in housing conditions have curtailed transmission of this illness. Body lice are the vector of epidemic typhus. The increased social importance of personal cleanliness and improvements in the overall standard of living account for the decreased incidence of this form of typhus in the United States; however, there have been cases of serologically documented epidemic typhus in this country that are thought to be due to exposure to flying squirrels, transmitted perhaps via fleas.

The only disease discussed here for which there is reliable prophylaxis is malaria. Most individuals should take prophylactic doses of mefloquine or chloroquine when visiting malarious areas (see Chapter 8–61). If additional information is desired, it may be obtained from the Malaria Branch of the Centers for Disease Control and Prevention (CDC) in Atlanta, Georgia, or from the traveler's hotline at the CDC, (404) 332–4559. A rickettsial disease hotline is also available, (404) 332–4555. There is debate about the advisability of administering prophylaxis against Lyme disease after a tick bite in a Lyme-endemic area. In most circumstances, prophylaxis is not recommended.

Cost Containment

Prevention is the most effective method of cost containment for vectorborne diseases. Periodic surveillance of ticks in certain areas of the United States is done to check for the organisms they harbor, and mosquito control programs in this and many other countries help to reduce, though rarely eradicate, the transmission of disease. Individuals who enjoy the outdoors should be aware of vectorborne diseases and take steps to protect themselves. Research is ongoing on the production of vaccines against malaria as well as other illnesses such as dengue and Lyme disease, but at present they are not available. Unfortunately, very little can be done to curtail the cost of caring for patients once they have acquired these diseases.

REFERENCES

Buchstein SR, Gardner P. Lyme disease. Infect Dis Clin North Am 1991;5:103.

Doan-Wiggins L. Tick-borne diseases. Emerg Med Clinics North Am 1991;9:303.

Goldman DP, Artensein AW, Bolan CD. Human ehrlichiosis: A newly recognized tickborne disease. Am Fam Physician 1992;46:199.

Saah AJ. Rickettsia akari (rickettsialpox). In: Mandel GL, Bennett JE, Dolin R, eds. Principles and practice of infectious diseases. 4th ed. New York: Churchill Livingstone, 1995:1727.

Tsai TF. Arboviral infections in the United States. Infect Dis Clin North Am 1991;5:73.

CHAPTER 8–38

Staphylococcal Infections

Henry M. Blumberg, M.D.

DEFINITION

Staphylococci are Gram-positive bacteria; the term *Staphylococcus* is derived from the Greek name *staphyle* ("bunch of grapes") and was chosen by a Scottish surgeon, Sir Alexander Ogdson, because of the characteristic microscopic arrangement of clusters. *Staphylococcus aureus* is the most important human pathogen that colonizes the skin of most humans. Disruption of skin or mucous membranes by trauma or surgery can lead to localized skin and soft tissue infection; occasionally, organisms invade lymphatics and the blood, leading to bacteremia and metastatic infections. Coagulase-negative staphylococci (e.g., *Staphylococcus epidermidis*) are important nosocomial pathogens with a predilection for infecting vascular catheters and prosthetic devices.

ETIOLOGY

Staphylococci are Gram-positive cocci that produce catalase and have a strong tendency to form clusters. They are members of the family Micrococciae and are nonmotile, non-spore-forming, aerobic or facultative anaerobic organisms. Staphylococci are differentiated primarily by their ability to produce coagulase, an enzyme that congeals rabbit serum. All staphylococcal strains that produce coagulase are designated *Staphylococcus aureus*. Commercially available kits using specific antibodies linked to latex particles or beads can distinguish *S. aureus* from coagulase-negative staphylococci (e.g., *S. epidermidis*) by particle agglutination.

CRITERIA FOR DIAGNOSIS

Suggestive

Staphylococcus aureus cause a wide range of diseases, from skin and soft tissue infections to bacteremia, with metastatic complications such as endocarditis, arthritis, pneumonia, and deep-seated abscesses. *Staphylococcus aureus* can affect both immunocompetent patients (causing skin and soft tissue infections, for instance) and those with altered host defenses often related to surgery, burns, intravenous drug abuse, or medical devices including intravenous catheters. Methicillin-resistant *S. aureus* organisms are major nosocomial pathogens in many hospitals in the United States and worldwide. In the past the coagulase-negative staphylococci, *S. epidermidis* in particular, have been dismissed as skin contaminants, but in recent years have been recognized as important and common nosocomial pathogens. Patients with central venous catheters or prosthetic devices are most commonly afflicted. *Staphylococcus saprophyticus*, which can be differentiated from other coagulase-negative staphylococci on the basis of resistance to novobiocin, is a common (second after *Escherichia coli*) cause of urinary tract infections in young, sexually active women.

Definitive

The diagnosis of staphylococcal infections is made by Gram stain and microbiologic culture. Cultured material can include aspirated pus or tissue, blood, or other normally sterile body fluids.

CLINICAL MANIFESTATIONS

Subjective

See Table 8–38–1.

Objective

See Table 8–38–1. *Cutaneous infections* due to *S aureus* are the most common type of staphylococcal infection. Disruption of skin and mucous membranes by trauma or surgery can lead to local infections. Occasionally, multiplying bacteria can overcome local phagocytic mechanisms and gain access to lymphatic channels and the bloodstream. Staphylococcal septicemia causes systemic symptoms and can lead to metastatic infections such as endocarditis, pneumonia, osteomyelitis, septic arthritis, meningitis, and abscess formation. Toxin-mediated syndromes, staphylococcal bacteremia and septicemia, and infection of foreign devices are discussed in further detail below. A more detailed description of the clinical manifestations of specific infections can be found in other chapters dealing with each clinical syndrome (e.g., endocarditis, pneumonia).

Three toxins produced by *S. aureus* can result in three clinical syndromes: staphylococcal food poisoning, staphylococcal scalded-skin syndrome, and toxic shock syndrome. Staphylococcal food poisoning

TABLE 8–38–1. CLINICAL MANIFESTATIONS OF STAPHYLOCOCCAL INFECTIONS

Organism	Infection	Subjective	Objective
Staphylococcus aureus	Cutaneous infections (localized)		
	Folliculitis	Red, painful, but sometimes pruritic rash around hair follicles, especially on face of males	Minute erythematous nodules, pustules around hair follicles
	Furuncle	Localized painful nodule, red, swollen, hot, located predominantly on face, neck, buttocks	Deep-seated infection around hair follicles
	Carbuncle	Painful lesion, fever, malaise, usually on base of neck and back	Indurated large lesion, multiple drainage sites, leukocytosis, fever
	Bullous impetigo	Painful, fluid-filled lesion, occurs predominantly in children	Vesicular, bullous lesions, yellow cloudy fluid
	Hidradenitis suppurativa	Drainage, pain in axillary area, chronic, recurrent, occasionally can occur in genital area	Sinus tracts, furuncles in axilla
	Mastitis	Nursing mother, pain in breast, most commonly occurs 2–3 weeks puerperium	Tender erythematous lobule, abscess
	Wound infection	Recent traumatic or surgical wound, pain, swelling at site	Erythema, edema, fever, purulent drainage
	Other infections		
	IV catheter infection	Pain, swelling at site of catheter, often leads to bacteremia with associated symptoms (see below)	Erythema, tenderness, swelling, purulent drainage, at times no local findings noted
	Staphylococcal scalded-skin syndrome	Fever, skin tenderness, red rash, multiple fluid-filled lesions, usually occurs in young children, much less common in adults	Large, clear bullae, positive Nikolsky's sign, exfoliation
	Toxic shock syndrome	Abrupt onset, fever, generalized red rash, occurs predominantly in menstruating women	Hypotension, diffuse erythematous rash, leukocytosis, multiple organ dysfunction; desquamates in late stages; hair loss and nail injury may occur late in the illness (see Table 8–38–2)
	Septicemia and endocarditis	History of recent local staphylococcal infection, presence of vascular catheter, history of IV drug abuse, fever, rigors, arthralgias	Acutely ill, evidence of embolic phenomenon (e.g., petechiae, Roth spots, splinter hemorrhages), tachycardia, heart murmur (also see Chapter 8–12)
	Purulent pericarditis	Fever, chest pain, patient often immunosuppressed, results from hematogenous spread or direct trauma	Pericardial friction rub may be present
	Pneumonia	Cough, fever, results from hematogenous (e.g., right-sided endocarditis) or inhalational (e.g., following influenza or nosocomial aspiration), spread may be complicated by empyema	Infiltrate or multiple abscesses on chest x-ray film
	Pyomyositis (primary muscle abscess)	Localized muscle pain, fever, more common in tropical areas but recently increasingly reported in temperate climates in immunosuppressed patients (especially in AIDS)	Swelling, tenderness, woody texture on palpation, computed tomography scan demonstrates abscess formation within musculature
	Osteomyelitis	Fever, long bone pain (children), back pain (adults); hematogenous disease in children and occasionally elderly adults; disease secondary to contiguous focus of infection or due to vascular insufficiency in adults	Intense pain with percussion
	Septic arthritis and bursitis	Joint pain, fever	Hot, swollen, tender joint or bursa
	Staphylococcal food poisoning	Abrupt onset of nausea and vomiting followed by abdominal cramps and diarrhea	Dehydration, afebrile
Staphylococcus epidermidis	Infections of indwelling foreign devices	See text for list of devices commonly infected, may present as bacteremia	Signs of purulence or erythema may be minimal
	Osteomyelitis (sternal osteomyelitis, infection surrounding prosthetic joint)	Recent cardiac surgery, prosthetic joint, hemodialysis catheter	Fever, tenderness
	Bacteremia	Immunocompromised patient (e.g., neutropenia, presence of Hickman or other central IV catheter)	Fever, rigors, malaise, at times skin lesions (pustules, petechiae) or evidence of metastatic infection
	Endophthalmitis	Recent ocular surgery	See Chapter 8–28
	Urinary tract infections	Hospitalized patient, history of urinary tract complications (surgery, Foley catheter)	Pyuria, bacteriuria
Staphylococcus saprophyticus	Urinary tract infections	Sexually active women 16–35 years old, dysuria, frequency	Pyuria, bacteriuria

Source: *Stephens DS. Infections caused by gram-positive cocci. In: Hurst JW, ed. Medicine for the practicing physician. 2nd ed. Boston: Butterworths, 1988:348. Adapted with permission from the publisher and author.*

results from the ingestion of foods containing preformed heat-stable enterotoxin B. The toxin itself is not produced in the gastrointestinal tract. Two to 8 hours after ingestion, the patient has an onset of nausea, vomiting, and diarrhea. Typically patients remain afebrile, and the disease is self-limited.

Staphylococcal scalded-skin syndrome most commonly affects in-

fants and young children and is much less common in adults. The syndrome usually begins with perioral erythema and a sunburnlike tender rash that spreads over the entire body in 2 to 3 days. Bullae appear and then burst, leading to partial or total desquamation with denuded skin resembling a burn. Friction applied to apparently healthy skin will cause it to wrinkle and separate (Nikolsky's sign). The disease is caused by toxin (exfoliatin)-producing strains of *S. aureus* and begins with a localized cutaneous infection. Fever and leukocytosis are usually mild. Mortality is low, and recovery usually occurs.

Toxic shock syndrome is a multisystem disorder caused by toxin (usually toxic shock syndrome toxin 1)-producing strains of *S. aureus*. Patients with this disorder are usually not bacteremic. Subjective and objective manifestations, as well as diagnostic criteria, are listed in Table 8–38–2. The large majority of cases occur in menstruating women and are associated with tampon use and an increased growth of intravaginal *S. aureus* and enhanced toxin production. An epidemic of cases in 1980 to 1981 was associated with hyperabsorbent tampons, and their withdrawal from the market has been paralleled by a decreased prevalence of toxic shock syndrome. In up to 20% of cases, toxic shock syndrome occurs in nonmenstruating women, men, and children and has been linked to local *S. aureus* infection such as abscesses, osteomyelitis, postsurgical infection, and postinfluenza pneumonia. At times, the primary focus of infection can be inconspicuous despite yielding positive cultures for *S. aureus*.

Bacteremia due to *S. aureus* generally arises from local infections that gain access to the bloodstream (extracellular foci) or from intravascular foci such as intravenous catheters, dialysis access sites, and intravenous drug abuse. Up to one third of patients with bacteremia do not have an identifiable focus.

Staphylococcus aureus septicemia can produce clinical manifestations identical to those of Gram-negative septic shock (Chapter 8–2), with death occurring within 24 hours. More commonly, however, the disease progresses a bit more slowly. Some patients present with a flu-like illness. Most patients experience fever, chills, and occasionally arthralgias and myalgias, and less commonly pleuritic chest pain and back pain. Endocarditis (Chapter 8–12) is a major complication of *S. aureus* bacteremia. *Staphylococcus aureus* is the second most common cause of bacterial endocarditis overall and the most common cause of endocarditis in intravenous drug abusers. Intravenous drug abusers more commonly have right-sided cardiac lesions (e.g., tricuspid valve disease) often associated with septic pulmonary emboli. Mortality is less than 10% in this group, which is significantly lower than in those with *S. aureus* endocarditis due to left-sided (i.e., aortic and/or mitral valve) disease, where mortality may be as high as 40 to 70%. Both normal and abnormal cardiac valves can be affected, although patients who are older, frequently hospitalized, and with underlying disease are most commonly infected. The disease typically pursues an acute course with high fever, progressive anemia, frequent embolic and extracardiac septic complications, as well as valve ring and myocardial abscesses.

Staphylococci are the most common cause of infections associated with foreign devices such as intravenous catheters, prosthetic joints and heart valves, cerebrospinal fluid shunts, peritoneal and hemodialysis catheters, pacemaker wires and power packs, and vascular grafts. With the exception of hemodialysis catheters, which are more commonly infected with *S. aureus,* coagulase-negative staphylococci are the most frequently isolated etiologic agents in these settings.

Coagulase-negative staphylococci are the most common cause of nosocomial bacteremia, usually occurring in the presence of an indwelling central venous catheter. Some confusion can arise, as these organisms are also the most common blood culture contaminant. It is important, therefore, to obtain multiple blood cultures from separate venipuncture sites and to interpret the microbiologic data in the context of the clinical setting. In general, in patients with significant bacteremia, multiple blood cultures are positive. Many patients with bacteremia may have few symptoms or only fever. Immunosuppressed patients such as cancer patients with central venous catheters and those who are neutropenic appear to have increased morbidity and mortality.

Although coagulase-negative staphylococci only rarely cause native valve endocarditis, these organisms are the most common cause of prosthetic valve endocarditis. Most patients with prosthetic valves have complicated infections frequently necessitating valve replacement. Infection usually occurs within the first year following surgery and is thought to be related to inoculation of organism at the time of surgery. Valve dysfunction and fever may be the only findings associated with an infected prosthetic valve.

Similarly, coagulase-negative staphylococci cause the majority of prosthetic joint infections. Infections in this setting can occur more than 1 year after implantation and are often of an indolent nature, although they are quite devastating, as infected prostheses usually must be removed and successful reimplantation may be difficult. The diagnosis may be suggested by pain in the affected joint occasionally accompanied by swelling, erythema, joint dislocation or drainage, and low-grade fever.

Routine Laboratory Abnormalities

Patients with staphylococcal bacteremia or endocarditis usually have elevated white blood cell counts with a marked shift to the left; occasionally some patients may have a decreased white blood cell count. A mild anemia may be present. In addition, thrombocytopenia may be present in some patients and can be seen if disseminated intravascular coagulation is present. Not uncommonly, there may be mild renal insufficiency due to prerenal or intrinsic renal disease. Patients with *S. aureus* bacteremia or endocarditis can develop pyelonephritis, renal abscesses, or diffuse or focal glomerulonephritis. Urinalysis may therefore reveal white blood cells, red blood cells, and casts (granular, white and red blood cells). Routine laboratory abnormalities seen in patients with toxic shock syndrome are noted in Table 8–38–2.

PLANS
Diagnostic
Differential Diagnosis

Staphylococcus aureus causes a wide range of diseases as described under Criteria for Diagnosis and should be considered in the differential diagnosis of skin and soft tissue infections and nosocomial and community-acquired bacteremia which can be associated with metastatic abscesses. *Staphylococcus epidermidis* should be considered in the differential diagnosis of nosocomial bacteremias, especially among patients with central venous catheters and in patients with prosthetic device infections.

Diagnostic Options and Recommended Approach

Gram stain of purulent material from the infected site may be helpful in suggesting the diagnosis; microbiologic culture of the infected site is necessary for a definitive diagnosis. Obtaining several sets of blood cultures is important when bacteremia and/or endocarditis is suspected, and catheter-tip cultures are of use when bloodstream infections are possibly catheter related.

Echocardiography may help make a positive diagnosis of endocarditis, although it is important to emphasize that a negative test does not exclude the possibility of endocarditis. Echocardiography should be carried out in all cases of *S. aureus* bacteremia when a clearly defined

TABLE 8–38–2. CENTERS FOR DISEASE CONTROL AND PREVENTION CRITERIA FOR THE DIAGNOSIS OF TOXIC SHOCK SYNDROME

Temperature (>)38.9°C
Systolic blood pressure (<)90 mm Hg
Rash with subsequent desquamation, especially on palms and soles
Involvement of three or more of the following organ systems:
  Gastrointestinal: vomiting, profuse diarrhea
  Mascular: severe myalgias or greater than fivefold increase in creatinine
    phosphokinase
  Mucous membranes (vagina, conjunctivae, pharynx): frank hyperemia
  Renal insufficiency: blood urea nitrogen or creatinine at least twice upper limit of
    normal, with pyuria in absence of urinary tract infection
  Liver: hepatitis (bilirubin, serum aspartate and serum alanine aminotransferases at
    least twice upper limit of normal)
  Blood: thrombocytopenia <100,000 cells/μL
  Central nervous system: disorientation without focal neurologic signs
Negative results of the serologic tests for Rocky Mountain spotted fever, leptospirosis,
  and measles

Source: *From Waldvogel FA. Staphylococcus aureus (including toxic shock syndrome). In: Mandell GL, Douglass RG Jr, Bennett JE, eds. Principles and practice of infectious diseases. 3rd ed. New York: Churchill Livingstone 1990:1500. Reproduced with permission from the publisher and author.*

focus of infection is not known and when endocarditis is possible. Transesophageal echocardiography may be especially helpful in detecting vegetations and valve injury. Computed tomography can be useful in assessing deep-seated metastatic abscesses.

Therapeutic

Therapeutic Options

The dose, route, and length of antibiotic treatment depend on the site of infection and the pharmacokinetics of the antibiotic. General guidelines are listed below.

Recommended Approach

Susceptibility testing is important in ensuring that a patient is treated with the appropriate drug. More than 90% of S. aureus, both community-acquired and nosocomial isolates, are resistant to penicillin; therefore, penicillin should never be used for empiric treatment of staphylococcal infections. Penicillinase-resistant penicillins such as nafcillin and oxacillin are the drugs of choice for serious methicillin-susceptible staphylococcal infections. Nafcillin and oxacillin are used because they are less toxic than methicillin. The dose of nafcillin or oxacillin for adults with normal renal function with serious infections is 2 g every 4 hours intravenously (total of 12 g/d). A first-generation cephalosporin (e.g., cefazolin 1–2 g every 8 hours) is an alternative drug for infections outside the brain and can be used in patients with mild penicillin allergy. Beta-lactam drugs are the preferred agent to treat methicillin-susceptible S. aureus infections. Vancomycin is an alternative treatment for serious infections due to S. aureus in patients with severe beta-lactam allergies (e.g., anaphylaxis). Oral penicillinase-resistant penicillins such as cloxacillin and dicloxacillin are available for the treatment of minor staphylococcal infections. Erythromycin, clindamycin, first-generation cephalosporins (e.g., cephalexin), and trimethoprim–sulfamethoxozole are alternative oral drugs.

Parenteral vancomycin remains the drug of choice for methicillin-resistant S. aureus infections. Beta-lactamase drugs are not effective in the treatment of methicillin-resistant S. aureus infections. To date, no effective alternatives exist, and the initial enthusiasm for the potential uses of the quinolones (such as ciprofloxacin) has been tempered by the rapid development of resistance in S. aureus, especially methicillin-resistant S. aureus. In hospitals where the prevalence of methicillin-resistant S. aureus is high, vancomycin should be used as initial empiric therapy for nosocomial staphylococcal infections pending results of susceptibility testing.

Most S. epidermidis are methicillin resistant, and vancomycin is generally used in the treatment of such infections. Rifampin and gentamicin are also included in regimens for the treatment of prosthetic valve endocarditis due to coagulase-negative staphylococci.

Staphylococcus saprophyticus is susceptible to most antibiotics used to treat urinary tract infections including trimethoprim–sulfamethoxazole.

Patients with staphylococcal endocarditis require a minimum of 4 weeks of parenteral therapy. Those with prosthetic devices require a minimum of 6 weeks of therapy and usually require removal and replacement of the device. Patients with osteomyelitis or septic arthritis also generally require a minimum of 4 to 6 weeks of therapy. "Short-course" combination antibiotic therapy (parenteral semisynthetic penicillin such as nafcillin or oxacillin plus an aminoglycoside for 2 weeks' duration) for right-sided endocarditis due to methicillin-susceptible S. aureus in injection drug users is a consideration in highly selected patients. Such patients should have a clinical and microbiologic response within 96 hours, be hemodynamically stable, and have no evidence of embolic events or metastatic infections.

The duration of treatment in other types of patients with S. aureus bacteremia is somewhat controversial, as it can be difficult at times to differentiate bacteremia from endocarditis. Patients with a removable source of infection, without evidence of endocarditis, who are relatively young and without underlying chronic disease or cardiac valvular disease, may be considered for short course treatment consisting of a 2-week course of parenteral therapy. In all other patients it is prudent to treat for a full 4 weeks because of the propensity for S. aureus to cause metastatic infections and endocarditis. Patients with no clear source of

infection should be treated for a minimum of 4 weeks with parenteral therapy.

Those with nosocomial S. epidermidis bacteremia, usually occurring in the setting of a central intravenous catheter, are generally treated by removal of the line and 10 to 14 days of parenteral antibiotic therapy.

Effective therapy of staphylococcal infections also includes drainage and debridement of the primary focus of infection (e.g., soft tissue abscess or removal of venous catheter). Some patients with long-term catheters, such as the Hickman and Broviac types, can be treated successfully without removing the catheters. This occurs more commonly with infections caused by coagulase-negative staphylococci and rarely in patients with S. aureus infection. If the patient is critically ill, if there is no response to treatment in the first few days of therapy, or if there are persistently positive blood cultures despite appropriate therapy, the long-term catheter should be removed. Patients with infected prosthetic devices frequently require removal of the device in addition to antibiotic treatment.

FOLLOW-UP

Frequency of routine follow-up is determined by the site of infection, severity of infection, and patient factors such as underlying disease. Recurrence of symptoms (e.g., fever, swelling, erythema) or appearance or development of new symptoms (e.g., appearance of rash) should prompt immediate follow-up.

DISCUSSION
Prevalence and Incidence

Staphylococcus aureus remains a major human pathogen that colonizes and infects both hospitalized patients with altered host defenses and healthy, immunologically competent individuals in the community. Shortly after birth, many neonates are colonized (skin, gastrointestinal tract). In children and adults the anterior nasal vestibule is the most common reservoir, and at any given time 20 to 40% of adults are estimated to be carriers. Most children and adults will be intermittently colonized by harboring organisms in the nasopharynx, on skin, or rarely intravaginally. For unknown reasons, some healthy individuals are persistent carriers. Certain groups such as diabetics receiving insulin injections, patients on hemodialysis, intravenous drug abusers, and health care workers have higher carrier rates. From colonized sites, S. aureus can contaminate any location on the skin or mucous membranes or other subjects by interpersonal transfer. If local barriers are disrupted by trauma or surgery, S. aureus can gain access and cause skin or soft tissue infections, occasionally gaining access to the bloodstream and causing bacteremia, with the potential for metastatic infections.

Staphylococcus epidermidis and other coagulase-negative staphylococci are resident bacteria and natural inhabitants of human skin. In the past they have been dismissed as culture contaminants, but in recent years they have been recognized as important pathogens and are the most common cause of nosocomial bacteremia, accounting for up to 50% of such infections. Although coagulase-negative staphylococci are often thought to be of low virulence, they can be associated with significant morbidity and sometimes mortality and have been demonstrated to prolong hospital stays (by 7–19 days) and frequently necessitate removal of a catheter or prosthetic device. Hospital-associated S. epidermidis infections are usually multiply antibiotic resistant (including >80% resistance to methicillin and other beta-lactam antibiotics). Colonization of patients and hospital staff with such strains is thought to precede infections with these organisms.

Staphylococci (especially S. aureus) are the leading cause of community-acquired skin and soft tissue infections as well as posttraumatic infections. Excluding urinary tract infections, staphylococci (S. aureus and S. epidermidis) are the most common cause of nosocomial infections in U.S. hospitals. They are the most frequently isolated pathogen in primary and secondary nosocomial bacteremias and in surgical site infections. The prevalence of methicillin-resistant S. aureus has continued to increase over the past two decades and is now encountered in hospitals of all types and sizes. The prevalence of methicillin-resistant S. aureus varies widely between hospitals but accounts for between 30 and 65% of *S. aureus* isolates recovered from patients at some institutions.

Related Basic Science

Infection by staphylococci usually results from a combination of bacterial virulence factors and altered host defenses. *Staphylococcus aureus* is among the hardiest of the non-spore-forming bacteria and can survive under harsh conditions. Microbial factors include cell wall constituents (peptidoglycan, teichoic acid), important enzymes (catalase, beta-lactamase, hyaluronidase), and toxins. *Staphylococcus aureus* can elaborate a number of toxins, several of which result in toxin-mediated disease, as discussed above. In addition, many strains of *S. aureus* possess a polysaccharide capsule, which may play a role in pathogenesis. Other important virulence factors include those involved with adherence, the capacity of *S. aureus* to persist intracellularly in certain phagocytes, and the potential to acquire resistance to antimicrobial agents.

Altered host defenses, such as disruption of skin and mucous membranes or the presence of foreign devices, can lead to staphylococcal infections. Polymorphonuclear leukocyte chemotactic defects predispose to infection, as seen in patients with Job's syndrome (high IgE level, recurrent skin infections, and eczema), Chediak–Higashi syndrome (defined clinically by recurrent *S. aureus* infections and albinism), Wiscott–Aldrich syndrome (an X-linked disorder characterized by severe eczema, thrombocytopenia, and susceptibility to infection), and Down syndrome. Acquired chemotaxic defects in patients with diabetes mellitus, rheumatoid arthritis, and severe bacterial infections may also predispose these patients to staphylococcal infections. In addition, patients with chronic granulomatous disease have recurrent infections due to staphylococci, other catalase-positive bacteria, and fungi because of defective phagocytes that lack microbicidal oxidative activity. Finally qualitative and quantitative defects among phagocytes in HIV-infected individuals may predispose these patients to developing staphylococcal infections.

Multiple bacterial factors may be important in the pathogenesis of prosthetic device infections due to coagulase-negative staphylococci and these factors may differ with types of materials, devices, and organisms. Investigations into the pathogenesis of foreign body-related infections associated with *S. epidermidis* have examined the role of an exopolysaccharide ("slime"), which appears to be a complex mixture of several monosaccharides, proteins, and other poorly characterized constituents. Many investigators believe that exopolysaccharide plays an important role in (1) the later stages of adherence of these organisms to plastic surfaces, (2) their resistance to phagocytosis, and (3) failure of antimicrobial agents, through its action as a mechanical barrier. Some *S. epidermidis* also produce a toxin similar to the *S. aureus* delta toxin, which may play a role in the pathogenesis of neonatal necrotizing enterocolitis.

Natural History and Its Modification with Treatment

Morbidity and mortality are related to the site and severity of infection, the nature of the underlying illness, age, and, to some extent, the virulence of the organism. Clearly the introduction of effective antibiotics beginning about 50 years ago has dramatically changed the prognosis for patients with serious staphylococcal infections such as endocarditis which were almost universally fatal in the preantibiotic era.

Prevention

Careful and frequent hand washing by all health care personnel is of great importance in limiting staff-to-patient and patient-to-patient spread of staphylococci. A number of hospitals employ procedures to isolate patients, such as those with methicillin-resistant *S. aureus* infection or colonization, in an attempt to control nosocomial spread of organisms. Eradication of carriage of methicillin-resistant *S. aureus* has been attempted but has met with limited success. Intranasal 2% mupirocin appears to be the most effective topical agent for methicillin-resistant and -susceptible *S. aureus* although rapid development of mupirocin resistance has been noted. Eradication of *S. aureus* from the nares of hemodialysis patients has been shown to be effective in reducing shunt infections. Antibiotic prophylaxis of patients undergoing a variety of surgical procedures has proven useful in decreasing the incidence of postoperative wound infections. Finally, changing peripheral intravenous catheters at least every 72 hours and frequently changing (every 5–7 days) or removing central venous catheters when they are no longer required may help prevent staphylococcal infections.

Cost Containment

Preventing nosocomial staphylococcal infections is the most effective means of cost containment. A rapid and specific diagnosis is also beneficial. Use of proven antibiotics rather than newer and often more expensive agents is recommended.

Outpatient (home or office) intravenous therapy for patients who require long-term parenteral antibiotics but who are stable is a means by which costs can also be reduced.

REFERENCES

Boyce JM, Jackson MM, Pugliese G, et al. Methicillin-resistant *Staphylococcus aureus* (MRSA): A briefing for acute care hospitals and nursing facilities. Infect Control Hosp Epidemiol 1994;15:105.

DiNubile MJ. Short-course antibiotic therapy for right-sided endocarditis caused by *Staphylococcus aureus* in injection drug users. Ann Intern Med 1994;121:873.

Jernigan JA, Farr BM. Short course therapy of catheter-related *Staphylococcus aureus* bacteremia: A meta-analysis. Ann Intern Med 1993;119:304.

Mulligan ME, Murray-Leisure KA, Ribner BS, et al. Methicillin-resistant *Staphylococcus aureus:* A consensus review of the microbiology, pathogenesis, epidemiology with implications for prevention and management. Am J Med 1993;94:313.

Rupp ME, Archer GL. Coagulase-negative staphylococci: Pathogens associated with medical progress. Clin Infect Dis 1994;19:231.

Sheagren JN, Staphylococcus aureus: The persistent pathogen. N Engl J Med 1984;310:1368, 1437.

Waldvogel FA. *Staphylococcus aureus* (including toxic shock syndrome). In: Mandell GL, Douglass RG Jr, Bennett JE, eds. Principles and practice of infectious diseases. 4th ed. New York: Churchill Livingstone, 1995:1754.

CHAPTER 8–39

Infections Caused by Streptococci and Enterococci

Kathryn E. Arnold, M.D., Monica M. Farley, M.D., and David S. Stephens, M.D.

DEFINITION

These infections are caused by pathogenic bacteria of the genera *Streptococcus* and *Enterococcus*.

ETIOLOGY

The genus *Streptococcus* includes more than 30 species of bacteria, including the major human pathogens *S. pyogenes* (group A streptococci), *S. agalactiae* (group B streptococci), *S. pneumoniae* (pneumococci), and viridans streptococci. There are at least 12 species of the genus *Enterococcus,* but most human enterococcal infections are caused by *E. faecalis* or *E. faecium.*

CRITERIA FOR DIAGNOSIS

Suggestive

These bacteria frequently colonize human skin and mucous membranes, and cause a variety of common infections when these barriers are overcome (Table 8–39–1).

Definitive

Because asymptomatic carriage of these organisms is common, isolation of the organism in culture does not prove its pathogenicity, but is supportive of the presumptive diagnosis in the appropriate clinical setting.

Streptococci and enterococci are spherical or ovoid bacteria that form pairs or chains in microbiologic culture, and retain crystal violet during Gram staining (Gram-positive). When grown on blood agar, they may be subdivided by their ability to lyse red blood cells either completely (β-hemolysis), partially (α-hemolysis), or not at all (γ-hemolysis). They are further classified by cell wall carbohydrates into serogroups, with most human pathogens belonging to groups A, B, C, D, and G.

Streptococcus pyogenes are β-hemolytic streptococci that possess the group A cell wall carbohydrate. In the appropriate clinical setting, presumptive diagnosis of infection with *S. pyogenes* may be made by isolation of the organism in culture or by detection in clinical specimens of group A carbohydrate antigen by latex agglutination or enzyme immunoassay. Recent infection with *S. pyogenes* is suggested by increased serum antibody directed against streptococcal hemolysin (antistreptolysin O).

Streptococcus agalactiae possess the group B cell wall antigen and usually exhibit a smaller zone of β-hemolysis than group A streptococci. Detection of group B antigen using hyperimmune serum or monoclonal antibodies is possible by latex agglutination and several other methods. Production of cAMP factor, bacitracin sensitivity, and failure to hydrolyze bile esculin distinguish group B from other β-hemolytic streptococci.

Streptococcus pneumoniae break down hemoglobin, producing the green color characteristic of α-hemolysis. They are catalase negative, bile soluble, and (usually) optochin susceptible. In the appropriate clinical setting, infection with *S. pneumoniae* is suggested by the presence on Gram stain of abundant Gram-positive, lancet-shaped diplococci, growth of the organism from a good-quality clinical specimen, or (when the patient has received prior antibiotics) immunologic detection of capsular antigen.

Viridans streptococci are α-hemolytic or γ-hemolytic and have no recognizable group-specific antigen. They are distinguished from *S. pneumoniae* by optochin resistance and bile insolubility, and from enterococci by failure to grow in 6.5% NaCl.

Certain group D streptococci have recently been designated as the separate genus *Enterococcus* based on DNA studies. Presumptive laboratory identification of enterococci is made by growth in 6.5% NaCl and the ability to hydrolyze esculin in the presence of bile. Other laboratory tests are used to distinguish enterococci from other Gram-positive cocci (pediococci, leuconostocs, lactococci). Species identification and antibiotic susceptibility are important in determining therapeutic options.

CLINICAL MANIFESTATIONS

See Table 8–39–2. Streptococci cause a variety of common infections such as pharyngitis, otitis media, pneumonia, bacteremia, and cutaneous infections. On occasion, more serious infections such as meningitis, endocarditis, fasciitis, sepsis, and toxic shock syndrome occur. Nonsuppurative sequelae of *S. pyogenes* infections include glomerulonephritis and rheumatic fever. Enterococci are an important cause of endocarditis and a major cause of nosocomial infections (as a part of polymicrobial infection). Enterococci are the second leading cause

TABLE 8–39–1. MAJOR INFECTIONS CAUSED BY STREPTOCOCCI AND ENTEROCOCCI

Streptococcus pyogenes (group A streptococcus)
  Cutaneous infections: cellulitis, impetigo, erysipelas
  Soft tissue infections: myonecrosis, necrotizing fasciitis
  Pharyngitis, peritonsillar abscess, retropharyngeal abscess
  Scarlet fever
  Acute otitis media
  Acute sinusitis
  Pneumonia
  Streptococcal toxic shock syndrome
  Nonsuppurative sequelae: rheumatic fever, poststreptococcal glomerulonephritis
Streptococcus agalactiae (group B streptococcus)
  Neonatal sepsis and meningitis
  Postpartum infections: endometritis, wound infection associated with cesarean
    section
  Adult infections: often in compromised host (diabetes mellitus, cirrhosis, renal
    failure, etc.)
    Skin, soft tissue, and bone infections
    Bacteremia
    Urosepsis
    Pneumonia
    Meningitis
    Endocarditis
Streptococcus pneumoniae (pneumococcus)
  Pneumonia (complications: empyema, pericarditis)
  Bacteremia
  Otitis media
  Sinusitis
  Meningitis
  Arthritis
  Peritonitis (spontaneous bacterial)
Viridans streptococci
  Endocarditis
  Suppurative infections: intraabdominal abscess, brain abscess
    (especially *S. milleri*)
  Bacteremia and septic shock (chemotherapy patients with neutropenia)
Enterococcus faecalis, E. faecium, and nonenterococcal group D streptococci
  Endocarditis
  Urinary tract infections
  Intraabdominal abscess (usually associated with other organisms)
  Biliary tract infections
  Wound infections: diabetic foot, decubitus ulcers (usually in association with other
    organisms)
  Neonatal sepsis and meningitis

TABLE 8–39–2. CLINICAL MANIFESTATIONS OF STREPTOCOCCAL AND ENTEROCOCCAL INFECTIONS

Organism	Infection	Subjective	Objective
Streptococcus pyogenes (group A streptococcus)	Cutaneous and soft tissue infections: Cellulitis and lymphangitis	Pain, swelling, redness, tender regional lymph nodes, chills, fever	Erythema, linear streaks, swelling; often at site of impaired lymphatic drainage, tinea pedis, wound, or burn
	Impetigo (pyoderma)	Crusted lesions, often pruritic or painful, over exposed areas, especially lower extremities; typically child 2–5; tropical or summer weather	Pustules, honey-colored crust over erythematous base
	Erysipelas	Localized erythema; swelling, most often on face; fever; chills; systemic toxicity	Rapidly advancing, tender, edematous, erythematous, well-demarcated lesion ± peau d'orange appearance
	Myonecrosis, necrotizing fasciitis	Abrupt-onset pain, swelling, myalgia, high fever, systemic toxicity	Rapid evolution; edema, dusky or mottled skin (± bullae), relative anesthesia; fever, systemic toxicity; may be associated with toxic shock syndrome
	Pharyngitis	Sore throat, fever, headache, malaise	Erythematous posterior pharynx; gray–white tonsillar exudate; *tender* lymph node angle of jaw; fever; leukocytosis; may be complicated by peritonsillar or retropharyngeal abscess; clinical signs not diagnostic, culture recommended; 70–90% also have positive rapid "strep" test
	Scarlet fever	Erythematous macular "sandpaper" rash, usually associated with sore throat, caused by strains that produce erythrogenic toxin	Diffuse, blanching, fine-macular rash, sparing palms and soles; circumoral pallor, "strawberry" tongue; followed by desquamation
	Streptococcal toxic shock syndrome	Lethargy, confusion	Hypotension plus two or more of the following: hepatic or renal dysfunction, coagulopathy, respiratory distress, generalized erythroderma, soft tissue necrosis
	Pneumonia	Abrupt-onset fever, chills, cough, pleuritic chest pain	Bronchopneumonia; rapid accumulation of empyema fluid
	Nonsuppurative sequelae: Acute rheumatic fever	Polyarthralgia, fever, recent sore throat	Jones' criteria: carditis, polyarthritis, chorea, subcutaneous nodules, erythema marginatum, antistreptococcal antibodies
	Acute glomerulonephritis	Edema, tea-colored urine, malaise, weakness, recent sore throat or pyoderma	Periorbital edema, hypertension, severe proteinuria, hematuria, antistreptococcal antibodies
Streptococcus agalactiae (group B streptococcus)	Neonatal infections: "Early-onset" GBS	Infant <5 d old, mother ill; lethargy, poor feeding, jaundice, apnea, grunting respirations	Tachypnea, grunting, pallor, jaundice, apnea, bradycardia, bacteremia, pneumonia, meningitis, high mortality
	"Late-onset" GBS	Infant 7 d–3 mo old, mother not ill; lethargy, poor feeding, irritability, fever	Tachypnea, fever, lethargy, bacteremia, meningitis
	Adult infections: Postpartum endometritis, cesarean section wound infection	Fever, malaise	Uterine tenderness, abnormal lochia
	Bacteremia	Seen with increased frequency in patients with diabetes mellitus, alcoholic cirrhosis, neurologic impairment, malignancies, renal failure	Fever, rigors
	Endocarditis (see Chapter 8–12)	Fever	Fever, heart murmur, embolic phenomena, anemia
	Skin, soft tissue, and bone infections	Similar to group A infections; seen with increased frequency in patients with diabetes mellitus, especially those with foot ulcers	Surgical debridement may be necessary
Streptococcus pneumoniae (pneumococcus)	General risk factors	Age <2 y, elderly, sickle cell disease, splenectomy, diabetes, COPD, renal failure, congestive heart failure, hepatic cirrhosis, alcoholism, multiple myeloma, Hodgkin's disease, HIV, immunosuppressive medications, transplant recipients, cerebrospinal fluid leak, neurosurgery	
	Pneumonia	Cough, rigor, fever, purulent sputum, pleurisy	Rales, infiltrate on chest x-ray, leukocytosis, sputum Gram stain: many white blood cells, few squamous epithelial cells, abundant Gram-positive diplococci
	Bronchitis	Cough, purulent sputum, history of chronic obstructive pulmonary disease	Rhonchi, negative chest x-ray, sputum Gram Stain as above
	Otitis media (see Chapter 21–5)	Otalgia, fever	Erythema, loss of tympanic membrane landmarks
	Acute sinusitis	Pain, swelling over involved sinus, fever, headache	Sinus tenderness, air fluid level in sinus
	Bacteremia (asplenia)	History of sickle cell disease or splenectomy	Hypotension, disseminated intravascular coagulation
	Bacteremia (alcoholism) "ALPS"	History of alcohol abuse	Hypotension, leukopenia, adult respiratory distress syndrome
	Meningitis	Headache, photophobia, meningismus, fever	Meningismus, cerebrospinal fluid pleocytosis with elevated protein and low glucose, Gram-positive diplococci or positive latex agglutination

TABLE 8–39–2. (*Continued*)

Organism	Infection	Subjective	Objective
Enterococcus faecalis, E. faecium (Enterococcus)	Endocarditis (see Chapter 8–12)	Fever, rigors	Fever, heart murmur, embolic phenomena, anemia
Viridans streptococci	Urinary tract infections	Dysuria, frequency	Pyuria, bacteriuria
	Intraabdominal abscess	Fever, abdominal pain	Abdominal tenderness, leukocytosis
	Biliary tract infection	Fever, right upper quadrant pain	Right upper quadrant tenderness, jaundice
	Endocarditis (see Chapter 8–12)	Subacute presentation, fever, malaise	Poor dentition, heart murmur, embolic phenomena, anemia
	Bacteremia/sepsis	Recent chemotherapy, fever	Fever, hypotension, neutropenia, ± mucositis
	Intraabdominal abscess, brain abscess	Varies with clinical infection: *S. milleri* most common viridans species associated with suppurative infections	See specific chapters

GBS, group B streptococci; COPD, chronic obstructive pulmonary disease; ALPS, alcoholic leukopenic pneumococcal sepsis.

of wound infections and the third most frequent isolate from wounds and the bloodstream. They are often involved in intraabdominal abscesses where bowel integrity has been violated, cause biliary tract infections, and are found in infections of surgical wounds, diabetic foot infections, and decubitus ulcers. Specific clinical manifestations are outlined in Table 8–39–2.

PLANS
Diagnostic
Diagnostic Options

Microbiologic culture of the infected site is the preferred test for diagnosis of streptococcal and enterococcal infections; however, Gram stain of purulent material may be helpful when cultures are not revealing, as a rapid diagnostic tool, and in making decisions regarding initial antibiotic therapy. Rapid diagnosis of group A streptococcal pharyngitis

using latex agglutination or enzyme-linked immunoassay is a commonly used tool in the office practice setting. The specificity of currently available rapid "strep" tests is high enough to confidently initiate immediate antibiotic therapy in patients with a positive test. Exclusive use of rapid diagnostic tests, however, will miss some patients with positive throat cultures due to lower sensitivity (70–90%). Diagnosis of rheumatic fever or poststreptococcal glomerulonephritis includes documentation of previous infection with group A streptococcus; rheumatic fever rarely occurs without concurrent elevations of antistreptococcal antibodies (antistreptolysin O, anti-DNase B, antihyaluronidase). Although antistreptolysin O response may be weak in pyoderma-associated glomerulonephritis, anti-DNase B is usually present. A specific rapid enzyme immunoassay may detect the presence of group B streptococci in vaginal secretions during labor, but is only 20 to 60% sensitive when compared with culture. For this reason, screening cultures of vaginal and rectal secretions are recommended at 35 to 37 weeks of gestation (Table 8–39–3). Latex agglutination is sometimes used to de-

TABLE 8–39–3. PREVENTION OF STREPTOCOCCAL AND ENTEROCOCCAL INFECTIONS

Disease Prevented	Target Population	Method*
Acute rheumatic fever	Patients with group A streptococcal pharyngitis	Penicillin × 10 d, begun within 7–9 d of symptom onset

Secondary rheumatic fever	Patients with previous acute rheumatic fever: risk is lifelong, although declines with age.	Preferred: penicillin G benzathine 1.2 million units IM q4wk
		Alternatives:
		  Sulfadiazine 1 g PO qd
		  Penicillin V 250 mg PO bid
		  Erythromycin stearate 250 mg PO bid

Neonatal group B streptococcal (GBS) infection†	**Parturient women at risk for GBS:**
	A. Previous infant with GBS disease
	B. GBS bacteriuria during this pregnancy
	C. Intrapartum risk factor:
	  Preterm labor (<37 wk gestation)
	  Fever during labor (≥38°C)
	  Prolonged rupture of membranes (≥ 18 h)
	D. Women with anogenital GBS colonization at 35–37 weeks gestation
		Recommended intrapartum antibiotics:
		Penicillin G 5 million U IV load, then 2.5 million U IV q4h until delivery.
		Penicillin allergic: Clindamycin 900 mg IV q8h until delivery. Therapy should be initiated as soon as possible after onset of labor or rupture of membranes.

Endocarditis	Patients with underlying cardiac conditions undergoing dental or surgical procedure	Antibiotic prophylaxis (see Chapter 8–12)
Pneumococcal infections	Patients < 2 y old	Conjugate vaccines under development; no current effective vaccine; penicillin prophylaxis for those at high risk
	Patients 2 y and older with medical conditions that increase risk for pneumococcal infection: HIV infection, diabetes, chronic obstructive pulmonary disease, renal failure, congestive heart failure, cirrhosis, alcoholism, splenectomy, sickle cell disease, Hodgkin's disease, multiple myeloma, immunosuppressive medication, organ transplant, cerebrospinal fluid leak, neurosurgery; careful review of medical risk factors in adults ≥ age 50 is strongly advised; patients 65 and older regardless of medical conditions	23-valent pneumococcal polysaccharide vaccine given once; revaccination generally safe: therefore, if vaccination status is unknown, administer vaccine; for those at highest risk due to rapidly waning immunity (e.g., splenectomy, Hodgkin's disease, multiple myeloma, organ transplant), consider revaccination after 5–7 y; some authorities recommend routine revaccination at age 65 y provided previous vaccine was at least 6 y earlier
	Children 2 and older at very high risk (e.g., sickle cell disease, asplenia, nephrotic syndrome, renal failure, transplant)	Pneumococcal vaccine at 2 y; consider revaccination after 3–5 y; consider penicillin prophylaxis until adulthood
	Splenectomy	Pneumococcal vaccine given (when possible) at least 2 wk prior to surgery

*For details, see Group B Streptococcal Disease Prevention Guidelines, MMWR 1996 [In press].

tect the presence of pneumococcal antigen in specimens from normally sterile sites (e.g., cerebrospinal fluid) when negative cultures are anticipated, such as after antibiotics are given.

Recommended Approach

Whenever possible, microbiologic culture of the affected site should be obtained before administration of antibiotics. If signs of systemic toxicity are present, blood cultures should be drawn. Rapid strep tests may be used for the detection of group A streptococcal antigen in pharyngitis but, if negative, should be confirmed by throat culture.

Therapeutic

Therapeutic Options

See Table 8–39–4.

Recommended Approach

β-Lactam antibiotics, in particular the penicillins, have long been the drugs of choice for most infections caused by streptococci. *S pyogenes, S. agalactiae,* and viridans streptococci remain highly susceptible to penicillins; however, treatment failure with penicillin may occur in severe streptococcal infections (such as necrotizing fasciitis and streptococcal toxic shock syndrome) due to slower growth of the organism or ongoing toxin production. In these conditions, addition of clindamycin should be strongly considered. In addition, the rapidly increasing prevalence of drug-resistant *S. pneumoniae* now complicates treatment decisions when this pathogen is suspected. Pneumococcus that are resistant to penicillin are often resistant to macrolides, tetracycline, and trimethoprim–sulfamethoxazole, and may be resistant to extended-spectrum cephalosporins as well. Cephalosporin resistance is particularly problematic, as these drugs are often used empirically to treat seri-

TABLE 8–39–4. TREATMENT OF STREPTOCOCCAL AND ENTEROCOCCAL INFECTIONS

Organism/Infection	Antibiotics*	Indications for Surgery
Streptococcus pyogenes (group A streptococci) Cellulitis, lymphangitis, impetigo, erysipelas, pharyngitis, scarlet fever, otitis media, acute sinusitis	(Unless known to be caused by group A streptococci, therapy for cellulitis, impetigo, and lymphangitis should include agent active against staphylococci, e.g., cefazolin 1.5 g IV q6h, nafcillin 1–2 g IV q4h.) Streptococcal infections: Penicillin G benzathine 1.2 million units IM × 1 Penicillin V 250–500 mg PO q6h × 10 days Hospitalized patients: aqueous penicillin G, 1 million units IV q4h	Incision and drainage of abscess if present
Myonecrosis, necrotizing fasciitis, streptococcal toxic shock syndrome	High-dose penicillin G (20–24 million units qd), plus strongly consider clindamycin 900 mg IV q8h	Debridement essential if necrotic tissue present
Streptococcus agalactiae (group B streptococci) Bacteremia	Penicillin G, 12 million units qd × 10 d	
Meningitis	Penicillin G, 20–24 million units qd × 14 d	
Endocarditis	Penicillin G, 24 million units qd × 4 wk Penicillin G plus aminoglycoside × 4 wk	See Chapter 8–12
Viridans streptococci Endocarditis	Penicillin G alone or penicillin G plus aminoglycoside (see Chapter 8–12 for dosages)	See Chapter 8–12
Streptococcus pneumoniae (pneumococcus) Otitis media, sinusitis	First line: amoxicillin 500 mg PO q8h × 10–14 d Treatment failure: Trimethoprim–sulfamethoxazole 160/800 PO bid Clarithromycin 500 mg PO q12h Clindamycin 150–450 mg PO q6h ± rifampin 600 mg bid Refractory otitis media: ceftriaxone 1–2 g IM/IV qd × 3 d	Failure to respond to antibiotic therapy
Pneumonia, empyema, bacteremia, endocarditis, arthritis	Hospitalized, moderately ill patient: Penicillin G 10–18 million units qd Cefuroxime 1.5 g IV/IM q8h Cefotaxime 1 g IV q8h to 2 g IV q4h Ceftriaxone 1–2 g IV/IM q12–24h Failure to respond to above therapy or debilitated or critically ill patient: vancomycin 1 g IV q12h + cefotaxime/ceftriaxone until susceptibilities available	Drainage of empyema, joint effusion
Meningitis	First line: Cefotaxime 2 g IV q4H or Ceftriaxone 2 g IV q12h Plus (because of increasing concerns about multidrug-resistant pneumococci in communities) recommend empirically adding vancomycin 1 g IV q12h to above therapy until susceptibilities known, AND, if steroids used, consider adding rifampin 600 mg PO q12h	
Enterococcus faecalis, E. faecium (enterococcus) Urinary tract, wound, or soft tissue infection	Isolate β-lactam susceptible: (mildly ill) amoxicillin 500 mg PO q8h or ampicillin 1–2 g IV q4–6h Isolate β-lactam resistant: vancomycin 1 g IV q12h	Debridement of soft tissue infections in some cases
Endocarditis, meningitis, or bacteremia Vancomycin-resistant infection (any site)	Ampicillin or vancomycin plus gentamicin or streptomycin Optimal management not established: contact isolation, infectious disease consultation	

*Adult dosage in patients with normal renal and hepatic function. In penicillin-allergic patients, macrolides, certain cephalosporins, or vancomycin may be used depending on organism and susceptibility pattern, site of infection, and nature of allergy.

ous infections. Resistance to chloramphenicol, carbapenems, quinolones, and tetracyclines is also observed, and if these agents are to be used, susceptibility testing should be performed. Fortunately, resistance to vancomycin and teicoplanin has not been described. In many pneumococcal infections (e.g., otitis media, pneumonia, sinusitis) an isolate is not obtained for susceptibility testing, and empiric therapy is the rule. For these infections, if the patient is not seriously ill, β-lactams (amoxicillin, cefuroxime) are appropriate first-line agents. Because epidemiologic data suggest a significant and growing prevalence of drug-resistant pneumococci, for patients who are seriously ill with a suspected pneumococcal infection (e.g., meningitis, pneumonia requiring intensive care), vancomycin should be added to either cefotaxime or ceftriaxone until susceptibility of the isolate to β-lactams can be confirmed. If pneumococci are susceptible to β-lactams, these bactericidal antibiotics are preferred, particularly in meningitis, where maximal cerebrospinal fluid penetration is required.

Similarly, multiply drug-resistant enterococci have emerged as a major therapeutic problem in the treatment of serious enterococcal infections (e.g., endocarditis). Enterococci may be resistant to β-lactams, aminoglycosides, vancomycin, teicoplanin, and quinolones. For wound, soft tissue, and urinary tract infections caused by β-lactam-susceptible strains, ampicillin remains the drug of choice. For enterococci resistant to β-lactams, vancomycin may be the agent of choice. Ampicillin/sulbactam, amoxicillin/clavulanate, or imipenem can be used in settings where β-lactamase is the mechanism of the β-lactam resistance. For serious infections, ampicillin or vancomycin in combination with gentamicin or streptomycin is recommended for bactericidal synergy. In settings where multidrug resistance is present, choices are not well established. Combinations of penicillin plus vancomycin plus aminoglycosides or combinations including teicoplanin, rifampin, and ciprofloxacin may be used. Careful assessment of antimicrobial resistance of the enterococcal isolate is critical in these settings. Infectious disease consultation is recommended.

FOLLOW-UP

Patients with group A streptococcal pharyngitis do not require followup cultures unless symptoms persist. Rheumatic fever patients are followed regularly to monitor cardiac complications and administer prophylactic antibiotics. Patients with pneumococcal infections should be evaluated for pneumococcal vaccine using the criteria in Table 8–39–3. Follow-up of patients with group B streptococcal or enterococcal infections is generally dependent on other underlying diseases.

DISCUSSION
Prevalence and Incidence

Each year, *S. pneumoniae* causes an estimated 3000 cases of meningitis, 50,000 cases of bacteremia, and 500,000 cases of pneumonia, resulting in 40,000 deaths in the United States. In addition, this pathogen causes 30 to 50% of acute otitis media, resulting in 7.5 to 15 million office visits annually.

Related Basic Science

Streptococcus pyogenes is usually spread by respiratory droplet particles and infections are more common in the winter. Spread by fomites and epidemic foodborne outbreaks has also been described. Asymptomatic carriage is common; group A streptococci can be recovered from 10 to 20% of adults and 10 to 40% of children who are asymptomatic. Virulence factors such as M protein and extracellular toxins such as hemolysins, streptokinase, deoxyribonucleases, and streptococcal pyrogenic exotoxins (SPE A, SPE B, SPE C), as well as host factors, determine the severity of infection.

Streptococcus agalactiae frequently colonizes the female genital tract, as well as the oropharynx and lower gastrointestinal tract. Neonatal infection may occur when the organism is acquired during parturition.

Streptococcus pneumoniae frequently colonizes the nasopharynx, and is the most common cause of bacterial pneumonia and bacterial meningitis in adults. More than 80 different serotypes are recognized

based on differing polysaccharide capsules. Capsular polysaccharide is the major virulence factor, and type-specific humoral immunity is important for limiting infection. For this reason, pneumococcal infections are most common among the very young and the elderly. Increasing drug resistance is a serious problem. Resistance to β-lactam antibiotics occurs through changes in penicillin-binding proteins, not through β-lactamases. Prevention of some pneumococcal infections is possible with use of the pneumococcal polysaccharide vaccine. Newer-generation protein-conjugate pneumococcal vaccines are being developed.

Enterococcal infections are often acquired from the patient's own flora; however, recent epidemiologic studies indicate person-to-person transmission or transmission by medical equipment may also be important means of spread. A major problem with enterococci is resistance to multiple antimicrobial agents. Enterococci are intrinsically resistant to clindamycin, penicillinase-resistant penicillins, cephalosporins, and monobactams, and exhibit low-level resistance to aminoglycosides and the glycopeptides vancomycin and teicoplanin. Acquired resistance is due to the spread of multidrug-resistant plasmids and transposons among enterococci and between enterococci and other bacterial species.

Natural History and Its Modification with Treatment

A dramatic decline in the incidence of rheumatic fever and glomerulonephritis has been observed in the latter part of the 20th century, and because this trend began before the widespread availability of antimicrobial agents, it is thought to reflect improvements in living conditions and general health. Despite this, since the late 1980s, resurgences of rheumatic fever and severe group A streptococcal infections have been reported in the United States and worldwide.

Emergence of drug resistance among pneumococci and enterococci is a serious problem for practicing physicians, and is a direct result of evolutionary pressure selecting for microbes capable of surviving in the presence of these agents. Judicious antibiotic use (knowing the pathogen, targeting the pathogen with the appropriate antibiotic, in the appropriate dose, for the appropriate duration) is the best way to decrease selection of resistant microbes.

Prevention

Treatment of group A streptococcal pharyngitis within 7 to 9 days of onset with penicillin for 10 days prevents rheumatic fever. Secondary prevention of rheumatic fever consists of benzathine penicillin G, 1.2 million units intramuscularly every 4 weeks. Treatment of group A streptococcal infections does not uniformly prevent poststreptococcal glomerulonephritis. Prevention of neonatal group B streptococcal infections is possible by intrapartum chemoprophylaxis of group B streptococcal carriers, although it may be difficult to determine at the time of labor which patients are carriers. The most appropriate approach to chemoprophylaxis is an area of current study (see Table 8–39–3).

Patients with underlying cardiac conditions should receive antibiotic prophylaxis before dental procedures to prevent endocarditis due to viridans streptococci (see Chapter 8–12).

Despite the availability of a safe, cost-effective vaccine for prevention of pneumococcal infections in high-risk groups, this vaccine is greatly underutilized. Especially with the emergence of drug-resistant pneumococci, it is critically important that practicing physicians recognize opportunities to vaccinate patients at risk for pneumococcal infection (see Table 8–39–3). In addition, conservative use of antimicrobial agents may decrease the rapid proliferation of drug resistance among microbes.

Conservative use of antibiotics (e.g., vancomycin), hand washing, and isolation of patients with multidrug-resistant enterococci have been suggested to reduce the risk of dissemination.

Cost Containment

Although prevention of infections is optimal, a rapid, specific diagnosis is the most effective means of cost containment when infection occurs. With the emergence of drug-resistant pneumococcal and enterococcal infections, therapy has become increasingly expensive and complex. Eliminating unnecessary antimicrobial use may reduce the selective pressure favoring the spread of drug-resistant microbes.

REFERENCES

Arduino RC, Murray BE. Enterococcus: Antimicrobial resistance. In: Mandell GL, Bennett JE, Dolin R, eds. Mandell, Douglas, and Bennett's principles and practice of infectious diseases. 4th ed. New York: Churchill Livingstone, 1995;2(4).

CDC. Group B Streptococcal Prevention Guidelines. MMWR 1996 (in press).

Fedson DS, Shapiro ED, LaForce FM. Pneumococcal vaccine after 15 years of use: another view. *Arch Intern Med* 1994;154:2531.

Friedland ER, McCracken GH. Management of infections caused by antibiotic-resistant *Streptococcus pneumoniae*. *N Engl J Med* 1994;331:377.

Stevens DL. Invasive group A streptococcus infections. *Clin Infect Dis* 1992;14:2.

CHAPTER 8–40

Infections Caused by Meningococci

Bradley A. Perkins, M.D., Robert W. Pinner, M.D., and David S. Stephens, M.D.

DEFINITION

These infections are caused by the Gram-negative bacterial pathogen *Neisseria meningitidis*. *N. meningitidis* (the meningococcus) causes a spectrum of clinical syndromes but is most often associated with meningitis and a distinctive, severe sepsis called meningococcemia. *N. meningitidis* is unique among major bacterial causes of meningitis for its capacity to cause epidemic as well as endemic disease.

ETIOLOGY

Neisseria meningitidis is a Gram-negative diplococcus. It is a member of the family Neisseriaceae, and is found only in humans.

CRITERIA FOR DIAGNOSIS

Suggestive

Meningococcal meningitis usually presents with acute onset of fever, headache, and stiff neck, sometimes accompanied by altered mental status and signs of meningeal inflammation (e.g., Kernig's sign and Brudzinski's sign). Fever along with a petechial or purpuric rash heralds meningococcemia, which may be accompanied by shock, disseminated intravascular coagulation, and multiorgan system failure.

Definitive

Isolation of *N. meningitidis* from a normally sterile site such as cerebrospinal fluid, blood, and, less commonly, joint, pleural, or pericardial fluid, provides a definitive diagnosis of meningococcal disease. Detection of meningococcal antigen in these fluids provides strong evidence for the diagnosis, as does a Gram stain of cerebrospinal fluid showing Gram-negative diplococci.

CLINICAL MANIFESTATIONS

Subjective

Meningococcal infections can be categorized into three clinical presentations: (1) meningitis, (2) septicemia (meningococcemia), (3) local meningococcal infection. Subjective manifestations vary according to the specific presentation (Table 8–40–1). Headache, fever, and stiff neck are the most common symptoms in patients presenting with meningococcal meningitis. Alteration in mental status may also occur, and the patient may have a rash.

Fever, rash, and prostration of acute onset are the principal manifestations of meningococcemia. Rarely, patients with meningococcal bacteremia may present with prolonged intermittent fevers, rash, arthralgias, and headaches, a syndrome known as *chronic meningococcemia*. Subjective manifestations of focal meningococcal infection (e.g., peri-

TABLE 8–40–1. CLINICAL MANIFESTATIONS OF MENINGOCOCCAL DISEASE*

Syndrome	Subjective	Objective
Meningococcal meningitis	Headache, fever, occasional rash, stiff neck, alteration of mental status, vomiting	Meningismus and other signs of meningeal inflammation (e.g., Kernig's and Brudzinski's signs); occasional petechial or maculopapular rash; neutrophilic leucocytosis in CSF, low CSF glucose, elevated CSF protein; cranial nerve palsies, especially 4th, 6th, 7th, and 8th cranial nerves
Meningococcemia	Fever, rash	Petechial, purpuric, or maculopapular rash
Fulminant meningococcemia (purpura fulminans, Waterhouse–Friderichsen syndrome)	Fever, extensive rash, prostration	Extensive petechial purpuric rash, hypotension, circulatory collapse, disseminated intravascular coagulation
Focal infection[†]		
Septic arthritis	Fever, joint swelling, pain	Joint effusion, severe pain on motion
Pneumonia	Productive cough, fever	Fever, purulent sputum containing Gram-negative diplococci, rales, infiltrates on chest roentgenogram
Purulent pericarditis	Fever, chest pain	Pericardial friction rub, pericardial effusion
Conjunctivitis	Pain, eye discharge	Conjunctival erythema, purulent discharge
Urethritis	Dysuria, discharge	Purulent urethral discharge
Chronic meningococcemia	Persistent fever, rash, joint aches, headache, illness of 6–8 wk	Petechial rash or rash resembling gonococcemia

CSF, cerebrospinal fluid.
*Not all may be present in an individual patient.
†May present as a primary infection or as a late complication of meningococcemia.

carditis, arthritis, pneumonia) vary according to the site of infection (Table 8–40–1).

Objective

Physical Examination

The major objective manifestations of meningococcal infections are listed in Table 8–40–1. Fever is seen in most meningococcal infections. Petechial or purpuric rash is characteristic of bloodstream invasion by meningococci; however, some patients may have a maculopapular rash, and some may have no rash. Meningeal inflammation may manifest as Kernig's sign and/or Brudzinski's sign. Kernig's sign is resistance to passive extension of the leg when the hip is flexed while supine. Brudzinski's sign is spontaneous flexion of hips and knees with passive flexion of the neck. Signs of pericarditis or arthritis and neurologic signs such as seizures and cranial nerve palsies occasionally occur later in the illness. Not all objective manifestations may be present in an individual patient, especially in the very young or very old.

Routine Laboratory Abnormalities

Elevation of white blood count with a predominance of polymorphonuclear leukocytes on differential count is the most common abnormality on routine laboratory evaluation.

PLANS

Diagnostic

Differential Diagnosis

Other causes of bacterial meningitis, such as *Streptococcus pneumoniae* and *Hemophilus influenzae* type b, are the most likely considerations in the differential diagnosis of meningococcal meningitis. Tuberculous meningitis, cryptococcal or other fungal meningitis, and viral meningitis should also be considered. Diseases with rashes that may mimic meningococcemia include rickettsial diseases such as Rocky Mountain spotted fever and epidemic typhus; viral exanthems such as echovirus type 9; bacterial endocarditis; septicemia due to *H. influenzae* type b or the clone of *H. influenzae* biotype *aegyptius* responsible for Brazilian purpuric fever; infections due to *Streptobacillus moniliformis* and *Spirillum minus*; gonococcemia; and vasculitis syndromes.

Diagnostic Options

Blood cultures are often positive in patients with meningococcal disease.

Meningitis can be suspected on clinical grounds, but a lumbar puncture should be performed to obtain cerebrospinal fluid for culture, antigen detection, Gram stain, cell count with differential, protein, and glucose to confirm the diagnosis and identify the cause. Rarely, a lumbar puncture may be contraindicated, such as when a soft tissue infection overlies the lumbar puncture area, when a bleeding diathesis is present, or when an intracerebral mass lesion is suspected. Cerebrospinal fluid in patients with meningococcal meningitis generally shows abundant white blood cells ($1000-5000/mm^3$) with a differential of predominantly polymorphonuclear leukocytes ($\geq 80\%$), elevated protein (100–500 mg/dL), and decreased glucose (≤ 40 mg/dL); however, these findings may vary, particularly in patients with partially treated meningitis.

When a focal infection is suspected, appropriate specimens should be obtained for culture. In the case of septic arthritis, for example, fluid should be aspirated from the site of infection for culture, antigen detection, Gram stain, and cell count with differential.

A positive result in an antigen detection test, such as latex agglutination, can be used to confirm diagnosis; however, antigen detection tests are not sufficiently sensitive to exclude a diagnosis of meningococcal disease when they are negative. As *N. meningitidis* is somewhat fastidious in vitro and readily susceptible to antimicrobial agents, cultures will not always be positive in cases of meningococcal disease. A Gram stain of fluid from a normally sterile site (e.g., cerebrospinal fluid) showing characteristic Gram-negative diplococci also suggests meningococcal disease and can be obtained rapidly. Approximately 5 to 10% of humans may be nasopharyngeal carriers of *N. meningitidis*; therefore, isolation of *N. meningitidis* from the nose or throat of an asymptomatic person does not provide evidence of disease and does not require treatment.

Recommended Approach

For all patients with suspected meningitis or meningococcemia, blood cultures and cerebrospinal fluid should be obtained for culture. Cerebrospinal fluid should also be sent for antigen detection, Gram stain, cell count with differential, protein, and glucose. For patients with suspected focal infections, appropriate specimens should be sent for culture. As survival of patients with meningococcal disease depends on prompt recognition and appropriate treatment, antibiotics should be administered based on clinical suspicion. Appropriate diagnostic procedures should be performed, but treatment should not be delayed.

Therapeutic

Therapeutic Options

Penicillin and some of the newer intravenous cephalosporins, notably ceftriaxone (Rocephin), cefuroxime (Kefurox, Zinacef), and cefotaxime (Claforan), have been shown to penetrate the blood–brain barrier and to treat meningococcal meningitis successfully. High-level penicillin resistance due to β-lactamase production has been reported among strains from southern Africa. No such strains have been identified in the United States, although a few strains with relative resistance to penicillin have been detected. The clinical significance of relative resistance to penicillin is uncertain; however, continued surveillance will be needed to monitor trends in antimicrobial susceptibility of meningococci in the United States. Chloramphenicol (Chlorcetin) is an effective agent in patients who are allergic to β-lactam antibiotics.

Recent studies suggest that corticosteroids may be beneficial in bacterial meningitis in children, but this issue requires further study. The use of steroids in fulminant meningococcemia remains controversial.

Surgical therapy may be indicated for drainage in purulent pericarditis, in some cases of septic arthritis, and as treatment for necrotic tissue following purpura fulminans.

Recommended Approach

In the United States, high-dose intravenous penicillin, 20 to 24 million units per day in adults, remains the drug of choice for meningococcal meningitis, meningococcemia, septic arthritis, pneumonia, and chronic meningococcemia. Seven to ten days of treatment is usually sufficient.

The patient and family should be informed that meningococcal disease is a serious infection caused by a bacterium, but that effective antibiotics are available for treating this infection; however, the prognosis depends on the clinical syndrome and the severity of infection. Household members and other intimate contacts of the patient are at increased risk of contracting meningococcal disease and should receive antibiotic prophylaxis (see below).

FOLLOW-UP

Antimicrobial resistance should be considered when patients with documented meningococcal infections fail to respond to therapy or are slow in resolving their infections.

Long-term follow-up considerations depend on whether there are long-term sequelae such as limb necrosis, hearing impairment, mental retardation, and more subtle learning disabilities that require attention.

Patients with complement deficiencies are at increased risk for subsequent meningococcal infections. These infections may be prevented by administration of tetravalent meningococcal vaccine. Consideration should be given to screening all persons who have had meningococcal disease for hemolytic complement activity (CH^{50}) during recovery from illness or at the time of follow-up; if CH^{50} is abnormally low, meningococcal vaccine should be given. Complement deficiencies are most likely to be identified (1) among patients with a previous episode of meningococcal disease, or who have a family member with a history of meningococcal disease; (2) when disease is caused by meningococcal serogroups other than serogroup B; (3) when disease is endemic rather than epidemic; and (4) among older children and adults with meningococcal disease.

DISCUSSION
Prevalence and Incidence

The incidence of meningococcal disease in the United States is approximately 0.9 case per 100,000 population. Meningococcal disease is seasonal, with the highest attack rates occurring in mid- to late winter and the lowest in late summer. The highest age-specific incidence occurs in infants 3 to 5 months old, and approximately half the cases occur in children 2 years or younger. There is no significant difference in attack rates between males and females, but African-Americans and Latinos in this country have higher attack rates than whites.

In some developing countries, endemic rates may be as high as 10 to 25 per 100,000. During epidemics, particularly in the so-called "meningitis belt" of sub-Saharan Africa, attack rates may reach 100 to 500 per 100,000 or higher. In the "meningitis belt," epidemics occur during the dry season and end when the rainy season begins. Epidemics tend to shift the age distribution toward older individuals, although most cases still occur in children. Why large epidemics occur is not well understood and has been the subject of considerable epidemiologic research. A combination of factors, including virulence characteristics of epidemic strains, population susceptibility, socioeconomic factors, climate, and perhaps infectious cofactors, probably contribute to the occurrence of epidemics.

Although 13 serogroups of *N. meningitidis* have been defined by composition of the capsular polysaccharide, five of these, A, B, C, Y, and W135, account for nearly all disease. Subtyping schemes based on differences among strains in the outer membrane proteins or lipopolysaccharides have also been devised. Serogroups B and C, in nearly equal proportions, account for approximately 95% of meningococcal disease in this country. Virtually no serogroup A meningococcal disease has occurred in the United States in recent years; however, serogroup A is the most common group associated with epidemics. Sporadic disease is caused by a variety of different strains, whereas in epidemics, a single strain is generally responsible for nearly all disease.

Related Basic Science

The human nasopharynx is the natural habitat for the meningococcus. The organism is carried asymptomatically by 5 to 10% of the normal population during nonepidemic periods. Transmission occurs from individual to individual via large droplet nuclei and usually requires contact with secretions. Occasionally, meningococcal colonization of other mucosal surfaces (e.g., conjunctiva, urethra, rectal mucosa) results in symptomatic disease. Meningococci occasionally cause pneumonia, presumably owing to aspiration of nasopharyngeal secretions. In some individuals, exposure and nasopharyngeal colonization by meningococci are followed by invasion and multiplication in the bloodstream. Survival of meningococci in the bloodstream is facilitated by its polysaccharide capsule, by the absence of serum bactericidal antibodies, and by deficiencies in complement, particularly terminal complement components.

Meningococcal bacteremia results in meningococcemia, purpura fulminans, chronic meningococcemia, or meningitis, or leads to localized infections such as pericarditis and arthritis. Many of the clinical features of meningococcemia appear to be due to release of lipopolysaccharide (endotoxin). Tumor necrosis factor and other cytokines also appear to be involved in the pathogenesis of meningococcemia and meningococcal meningitis. Meningoencephalitis may also occur, although the mechanisms by which meningococci penetrate the blood–brain barrier to invade the subcranial space are not known.

Natural History and Its Modification with Treatment

Sensorineural hearing impairment, seizures, and mental retardation can result from meningococcal meningitis, although the precise incidence of these sequelae is not known. When limb necrosis complicates meningococcal sepsis, surgical debridement or amputation may be required.

Prior to the use of antibiotics, the case fatality rate for meningococcal meningitis was 50 to 80%. Overall case fatality rates in the United States range from 12 to 14%; the case fatality rates are nearly twice as high for meningococcemia as for meningitis.

Prevention

The risk of secondary disease in close contacts of patients with meningococcal disease is 500 to 1000 times the risk of the general population. Based on this increased risk, antibiotic prophylaxis is recommended for intimate contacts of patients, including household members, day-care center contacts, and anyone directly exposed to the patient's oral secretions. Casual contacts and hospital personnel providing routine care are not at increased risk and do not require prophylaxis. The drug of choice for antibiotic prophylaxis is rifampin (Rifadin), 600 mg every 12 hours for 2 days. The dose for children 1 month of age or older is 10 mg/kg every 12 hours, and for children under 1 month of age, it is 5 mg/kg every 12 hours. Rifampin prophylaxis is not recommended for pregnant women. Ciprofloxacin, given as a single 500-mg oral dose, is a reasonable alternative to the multidose rifampin regimen, although it is not recommended for use among persons less than 18 years of age or in pregnant or lactating women. Ceftriaxone can also be used as a single intramuscular injection (125 mg for children, 250 mg for adults) and may be considered for antibiotic prophylaxis of pregnant women.

In the United States, the currently licensed meningococcal vaccine provides protection against disease caused by *N. meningitidis* serogroups A, C, Y, and W135, but not serogroup B. Vaccination is the main public health tool available to control outbreaks. In the United States, for example, 21 outbreaks of serogroup C meningococcal disease occurred from 1980 through 1993, resulting in administration of approximately 214,000 doses of vaccine for outbreak control. Meningococcal vaccine is also recommended for asplenic persons and persons with complement deficiencies. Of note, HIV-infected individuals do not appear to be at an increased risk for meningococcal disease. Travelers to areas with high endemic rates or areas susceptible to epidemics may benefit from vaccination prior to travel.

Except for military personnel, meningococcal vaccine is not routinely recommended in the United States because about half the meningococcal disease is caused by serogroup B, for which no vaccine is currently available, and because more than half the cases occur in children under age 4, in whom the duration of protection conferred by available vaccines is limited. Improved meningococcal vaccines for protection against disease caused by serogroups A, C, Y, and W-135 are being developed.

Several serogroup B meningococcal vaccines have recently been shown to be effective among older children and adults in large clinical trials outside the United States. Additional studies are needed prior to more general use of these vaccines and licensure in the United States.

Cost Containment

Rapid diagnosis is critical and is accomplished by prompt recognition of the clinical features of the disease, Gram stain of purulent material, and growth of the meningococcus or detection of meningococcal antigen in blood, cerebrospinal fluid, or other sterile site. In the United States, penicillin remains the drug of choice for most meningococcal infections. As new vaccines become available in the United States, particularly ones providing durable protection in young children against disease caused by serogroup C and B meningococci, routine infant immunization against meningococcal disease is likely to provide a cost-effective means for prevention of disease.

REFERENCES

Apicella MA. *Neisseria meningitidis.* In: Mandell GL, Bennett JE, Dolin, R eds. Mandell, Douglas, and Bennett's principles and practice of infectious diseases. 4th ed. New York: Churchill Livingstone, 1995.

Goldschneider F, Gotschlich EC, Artenstein M. Human immunity to the meningococcus: I. The Role of humoral antibodies. J Exp Med 1969;129:1307.

Jackson LA, Wenger JD. Laboratory-based surveillance for meningococcal disease in selected areas, United States, 1989–1991. MMWR 1993;42:21.

Peltola H. Meningococcal disease: Still with us. Rev Infect Dis 1983;5:71.

Stephens DS, Farley MM. Mechanisms of pathogenesis of *Neisseria meningitidis* and *Haemophilus influenzae* at the human nasopharynx. Rev Infect Dis 1991;13:22.

Infections Caused by *Hemophilus Influenzae*
Monica M. Farley, M.D.

DEFINITION

Hemophilus influenzae is an exclusive human pathogen of worldwide clinical significance. Infections occur in both children and adults, frequently involve the upper or lower respiratory tract, and in some cases lead to serious invasive disease such as meningitis.

ETIOLOGY

H. influenzae is a pleomorphic Gram-negative rod that may be serologically classified by its polysaccharide capsule type (a–f) or by the lack of capsular material (nontypable). Until recently, capsular serotype b was the most common cause of bacterial meningitis in the United States and was responsible for more than 95% of invasive childhood *H. influenzae* disease. A variety of diseases caused by both typable and nontypable *H. influenzae* occur in adults. Table 8–41–1 lists the major infections caused by *H. influenzae*.

CRITERIA FOR DIAGNOSIS
Suggestive

H. influenzae should be suspected in patients with clinical syndromes associated with *H. influenzae* (Table 8–41–1), particularly those with identified epidemiologic associations (Table 8–41–2). In general, young children with invasive *H. influenzae* disease are otherwise healthy; however, for reasons not well understood, the frequency of disease is significantly higher among Alaskan Eskimo and American Indian children. Adults with *H. influenzae* disease frequently have underlying problems of host defenses. Respiratory infection often occurs in adults with chronic obstructive lung disease. Recent reports suggest an increased risk of *H. influenzae* pneumonia and bacteremia in patients infected with HIV. Adults with invasive *H. influenzae* disease usually have significant underlying conditions including lung disease, malignancy, alcoholism, diabetes, and collagen–vascular diseases.

Definitive

Culture of *H. influenzae* from a normally sterile site (e.g., blood, cerebrospinal fluid, synovial fluid) definitively identifies invasive *H. influenzae* disease.

TABLE 8–41–1. MAJOR INFECTIONS CAUSED BY HEMOPHILUS INFLUENZAE

Meningitis
Epiglottitis
Other respiratory tract infections
  Pneumonia
  Bronchitis
  Otitis media
  Sinusitis
Cellulitis (facial)
Genital infections
  Endometritis/chorioamnionitis
  Postpartum fever
  Pelvic inflammatory disease
  Tuboovarian abscess
Septic arthritis
H. influenzae biogroup *aegyptius* infections
  Acute contagious conjunctivitis
  Brazilian purpuric fever
Endocarditis (very rare, usually in patients with underlying valvular disease; other *Hemophilus* species more common cause of endocarditis)
Urinary tract infections (very rare, usually in patients with structural abnormalities)

Antigen detection (i.e., identification of *H. influenzae* capsular polysaccharide in the cerebrospinal or joint fluid) and characteristic Gram stains are also used as diagnostic tools but are not as definitive as culture. Diagnosis of local respiratory tract disease is dependent on examination of appropriately obtained clinical specimens for characteristic Gram stain.

CLINICAL MANIFESTATIONS

The patient's history, symptoms, physical findings, and laboratory abnormalities vary according to the specific infection and whether the patient is a child or an adult.

Subjective

See Table 8–41–2.

Objective

See Table 8–41–2.

PLANS
Diagnostic
Differential Diagnosis

The appropriate differential diagnosis varies depending on the clinical infection and the age of the patient. In the case of respiratory infections such as otitis media, sinusitis, bronchitis, and pneumonia, other respiratory pathogens such as *Streptococcus pneumoniae, Moraxella catarrhalis,* and a number of respiratory viruses should also be considered.

Diagnostic Options and Recommended Approach

The diagnosis of infection due to *H. influenzae* should be based on Gram stain and culture of appropriate clinical specimens. Isolation of the organism from normally sterile body fluids provides a definitive diagnosis; however, owing to the frequency of respiratory colonization, the diagnosis of pneumonia, bronchitis, or other respiratory tract infections must include other parameters (e.g., Gram stain showing predominance of the organism, lack of other pathogens isolated, and clinical setting). *H. influenzae* is a fastidious organism requiring two blood-derived factors (X factor: hemin or hematin; V factor: nicotinamide adenine dinucleotide [NAD]) for growth in the laboratory. These growth requirements serve as major criteria for identification of *H. influenzae* and allow separation of it from other *Hemophilus* species. Recovery of *H. influenzae* from specimens other than blood requires culture on media such as chocolate agar and Levinthal broth, which provide X and V factors. Incubation in carbon dioxide enhances growth. The presence of *H. influenzae* type b capsular antigen can be detected in clinical specimens by immunoelectrophoresis, latex agglutination, or enzyme-linked immunosorbent assay; these assays have been useful tools in evaluating children with partially treated meningitis.

Therapeutic
Therapeutic Options

Ampicillin-resistant *H. influenzae* type b strains were first reported in the mid-1970s. Since then, the rate of ampicillin resistance has risen steadily to current levels of 20 to 35% and higher. The majority of resistance results from plasmid-mediated β-lactamase production, but in a small percentage of cases, alterations in penicillin-binding proteins are responsible. The rate of ampicillin resistance in nontypable strains, although less than that in type b strains, is also increasing. Therefore, the use of ampicillin alone for empiric therapy of serious *H. influenzae*

TABLE 8–41–2. CLINICAL MANIFESTATIONS OF *HEMOPHILUS INFLUENZAE* INFECTIONS

Infection	Epidemiology/Background	Subjective	Objective
Meningitis	Children <2 y; American Indians, Alaskan Eskimos at increased risk; adults account for 3–20% of acute community-acquired bacterial meningitis	Fever, lethargy; adults may have past history of closed head trauma, sinusitis, otitis media, alcoholism	Altered mental status, nuchal rigidity (less often seen in children), neutrophilic cerebrospinal fluid pleocytosis, exclusively type b disease in children; adults type b or nontypable
Epiglottitis	Children 2–7 y most often affected; increased reports in adults in recent years	Sore throat, difficulty swallowing, fever	Rapidly progressive dysphagia, drooling stridor, complete airway obstruction may occur; lateral neck x-ray shows enlarged epiglottis (thumb sign); blood cultures often positive for type b strains
Pneumonia/tracheobronchitis	Uncommon in children; seen in adults with underlying lung disease or other immunocompromised states	Productive cough, shortness of breath, fever, pleuritic chest pain	Wheezes, rales, signs of consolidation, leukocytosis, hypoxia; chest x-ray film shows segmental, lobar, or interstitial infiltrates; often nontypable strains
Otitis media	Most often seen in children <2 y; also seen with increasing frequency in older children and adults	Fever, ear pain, impaired hearing	Tympanic membrane erythema, fluid in middle ear; usually nontypable strains
Sinusitis	Second leading cause of acute sinusitis in both children and adults (*Streptococcus pneumoniae* leading cause)	Facial pain, purulent nasal discharge, headache	Erythema and tenderness of involved sinus sometimes present; opacity of sinus on transillumination, sinus x-rays show opacity, air–fluid levels, or mucosal thickening; associated with nontypable strains
Cellulitis	Occurs in young children	Fever, facial tenderness	Raised, warm, tender, reddish-blue area involving facial or periorbital region associated with type b strains
Genital	Women of childbearing years, sexually active women	Lower quadrant pain, prolonged rupture of membranes, premature rupture of membranes, peripartum fever	Chorioamnionitis, mild peripartum febrile illness, pelvic inflammatory disease, tuboovarian abscess, usually nontypable strains, association of biotype IV strains with genital site of isolation
Septic arthritis	Children <2 y; responsible for 1–2% adult septic arthritis; typically occurs in older adults with predisposing conditions	Children; pain and decreased mobility of single joint, symptoms may be subtle; adults; fever, chills, multiple joints may be involved	*Children:* single large weight-bearing joint swelling, tenderness; *adults:* large joints most common; purulent synovial fluid, cultures usually positive for type b strains
Acute contagious conjunctivitis	*H. influenzae* biogroup *aegyptius* (formerly *H. aegyptius*, Koch–Weeks bacillus) usually seen in children	Crusting discharge, eye discomfort	Purulent conjunctivitis
Brazilian purpuric fever	Newly recognized pediatric disease caused by single clone *H. influenzae* biogroup *aegyptius;* most cases geographically limited to Brazil (2 cases reported from Australia not caused by Brazilian clone)	Fever, abdominal pain/vomiting; history of conjunctivitis within 30 d preceding onset of fever	Petechiae or purpura, shock; no evidence of meningitis; blood cultures positive for *H. influenzae* biogroup *aegyptius;* 50–70% mortality rate

infections is not currently recommended. Chloramphenicol resistance has been reported with variable frequency in Europe and less often in the United States (<1%). The combination of ampicillin (Amcill and others) and chloramphenicol (Chlorcetin and others) has been the recommended regimen for empiric treatment of *H. influenzae* meningitis in children (ampicillin, 200 to 300 mg/kg/d, divided into 6-hourly doses; and chloramphenicol, 75–100 mg/kg/d, divided into 6-hourly doses). Because of the common dose-related, reversible bone marrow toxicity and extremely rare, irreversible bone marrow aplasia associated with chloramphenicol, however, many physicians prefer third-generation cephalosporins for *H. influenzae* meningitis and other life-threatening forms of disease.

Several third-generation cephalosporins have proven effective against many serious *H. influenzae* diseases, including meningitis. These include cefotaxime (Claforan: children, 200 mg/kg/d in 6-hourly doses; adults, 2–4 g every 4–6 hours) and ceftriaxone (Rocephin: children, 75–100 mg/kg once daily or given in divided doses every 12 hours; adults, 2–4 g once daily or given in divided doses every 12 hours). Delayed cerebrospinal fluid sterilization, relapse, and treatment failures have been reported with the use of cefuroxime (Zinacef and others), a second-generation cephalosporin, for treatment of children with *H. influenzae* meningitis. This drug has, however, been used successfully in adults with *H. influenzae* lower respiratory tract infections requiring parenteral therapy. Most pediatric experts now recommend the use of corticosteroids in the treatment of *H. influenzae* meningitis in young children, as it appears to decrease the incidence of severe neurologic sequelae.

For less serious infections, a number of oral antibiotics are available. Ampicillin and amoxicillin are often effective against upper respiratory infections such as otitis media and sinusitis. Several alternatives are available when ampicillin resistance is suspected or proven including trimethoprim–sulfamethoxazole, amoxicillin–clavulanate, cefuroxime–axetil, and the newer macrolides (clarithromycin, azithromycin).

Recommended Approach

I recommend using a third-generation cephalosporin (either ceftriaxone or cefotaxime) for meningitis, epiglottitis, and other life-threatening *H. influenzae* infections. For lower respiratory tract infections requiring hospitalization, cefuroxime is a reasonable first choice. In choosing an oral antibiotic for less serious respiratory infections, the clinician should consider cost, side effects, and patient compliance issues.

FOLLOW-UP

Appropriate follow-up is determined by the severity of the specific *H. influenzae* infection, the patient's age, and the presence of underlying diseases. Recurrence of symptoms (fever, meningismus) or development of new symptoms should prompt immediate follow-up. Patients with *H. influenzae* pneumonia should have a repeat chest x-ray 2 to 3 months after treatment to document resolution of the infiltrate. Infants recovering from *H. influenzae* meningitis require careful follow-up to detect developmental delays and/or hearing impairment.

DISCUSSION
Prevalence and Incidence

A substantial decline in childhood *H. influenzae* type b disease has been noted in recent years related to the introduction of effective conjugate vaccines. In the United States, the annual incidence of type b disease among children less than 5 years of age decreased from 37/100,000 in 1989 to 11/100,000 in 1991 (Adams et al., 1993) and has continued to decline since that time.

The annual incidence of adult invasive *H. influenzae* disease is approximately 1.7/100,000 adults, representing over 4000 cases in the United States each year (Farley et al., 1992). Although exact figures are difficult to obtain, localized respiratory tract infections such as pneumonia, bronchitis, otitis media, and sinusitis are common and encountered significantly more often than invasive disease.

Related Basic Science

In 1892, Pfeiffer reported the isolation of a blood-loving bacterium that he believed to be the etiologic agent of influenza. Despite the subsequent identification of the influenza virus, the *H. influenzae* nomenclature refers to this original description. In 1931, Pittman reported the occurrence of both encapsulated and nonencapsulated (nontypable) strains. She described six antigenically distinct capsular serotypes (a–f). The type b polysaccharide capsule is composed of polyribose ribitol phosphate. Among encapsulated strains, type b has been the predominant pathogen responsible for most systemic disease; however, since the introduction of effective type b vaccines, the relative proportion of infections caused by other capsular serotypes, particularly serotype f, is growing. Nontypable (nonencapsulated) strains most often cause local respiratory tract infections; however, nontypable strains are responsible for at least one half of invasive *H. influenzae* infections in adults. Population genetic studies suggest that strains of *H. influenzae* type b worldwide are of restricted clonal origin, whereas nontypable strains are genetically distinct from type b strains and show a greater degree of heterogeneity.

Humans are the only known natural host for *H. influenzae*. Organisms initially gain entry to host tissue via the respiratory tract, which also serves as a reservoir for colonization. Nasopharyngeal carriage rates for nontypable strains may range from 50 to 80%. Type b carriage rates are 3 to 5% in the general population but may be considerably higher in certain populations (e.g., children in day-care centers).

Anticapsular antibody (anti-polyribose ribitol phosphate) is of major importance in the protection against clinical disease with *H. influenzae* type b. Protective maternal anti-polyribose ribitol phosphate antibody is generally present from birth to 2 months of age. Thereafter, anti-polyribose ribitol phosphate antibody is low or absent until 2 to 3 years of age, coinciding with the peak incidence of invasive *H. influenzae* type b disease. The ability to generate protective antibody to the type b polysaccharide capsule (a T cell-independent antigen) begins to develop at 18 to 24 months and persists in older children and adults who are at a relatively decreased risk for invasive type b disease. Because of the extensive heterogeneity among nontypable *H. influenzae* isolates, antisomatic antibodies offer little to no cross-protection, and recurrent nontypable infections are common.

Natural History and Its Modification with Treatment

The morbidity of *H. influenzae* infections is related to the site and severity of diseases. Permanent sequelae, including language delay, mental retardation, and hearing impairment, are reported in a significant number of children recovering from *H. influenzae* meningitis. Epiglottitis can result in abrupt airway obstruction, resulting in permanent neurologic deficits or death, particularly if diagnosis and treatment are delayed. Nontypable *H. influenzae* bronchitis and pneumonia have been associated with exacerbations of chronic obstructive lung disease.

The mortality of *H. influenzae* disease is also related to the site and severity of infection and to whether it occurs in children or adults. The mortality of *H. influenzae* meningitis in children is currently 5 or 6%. Fatal airway obstruction from epiglottitis occurs in approximately 7% of adults, but in less than 1% of the pediatric population, where early recognition and prophylactic airway management are common practice.

Invasive *H. influenzae* disease in adults (including bacteremic pneumonia) is associated with high mortality (20–30%), in part due to advanced age and associated underlying diseases.

Prevention

Secondary attack rates among young children who are household or day-care contacts of an index case of *H. influenzae* type b are estimated at between 1 and 4%. Rifampin given in a dosage of 20 mg/kg/d (maximum dose 600 mg/d) once daily for 4 days is effective in eradicating the nasopharyngeal carriage of *H. influenzae* type b. Chemoprophylaxis with rifampin (Rifadin) is currently recommended for all household contacts (including adults) of an index type b case when other susceptible children (<4 years) are in the home. Such chemoprophylaxis should also be strongly considered for nursery school and daycare contacts.

Nosocomial spread and outbreaks of nontypable and type b *H. influenzae* disease have been reported in the pediatric setting and in geriatric units. Rigorous infection control precautions and treatment of colonized or infected patients and staff have been initiated in attempts to control further spread. The incidence of nosocomial secondary cases and optimal measures of prevention remain to be determined.

The first *H. influenzae* type b vaccine composed of the polyribose ribitol phosphate polysaccharide was licensed for use in children in 1985. Unfortunately, this vaccine was poorly immunogenic in children under 18 months of age (who are at highest risk of disease) and less than optimally effective in preventing disease in older children. The second-generation *H. influenzae* type b vaccines use polyribose ribitol phosphate conjugated to various protein antigens to enhance immunogenicity. The conjugate vaccines are significantly more immunogenic and effective in disease prevention in children over 18 months than the polyribose ribitol phosphate vaccine. In addition, several of the conjugative vaccines are immunogenic and effective in infants when given in multiple doses and were licensed for use in infants in 1990.

The Immunization Practices Advisory Committee (ACIP) currently recommends that all children be given one of the *Hemophilus* type b conjugate vaccines as a vaccine series beginning at 2 months of age. The introduction of the conjugate vaccines has resulted in the near elimination of invasive *H. influenzae* disease in young children in the United States. Unexpectedly, the vaccine also appears to significantly reduce nasopharyngeal colonization with type b organisms. The effect of widespread childhood immunization against *H. influenzae* type b on long-term immunity and the spectrum of adult disease will require long-term follow-up studies. Currently, there are no effective measures for the prevention of nontypable disease (either invasive or local respiratory infection).

Cost Containment

Effective polyribose ribitol phosphate conjugate vaccines demonstrate the most effective preventive measure for type b disease in children. In the first few years since licensure, the conjugate vaccines have prevented an estimated 10,000 to 16,000 cases of type b disease in children per year. Such preventive measures offer the most effective means of cost containment. Appropriate chemoprophylaxis with rifampin is another modality and can decrease the incidence of serious secondary infection and treatment thereof. Rapid, specific diagnosis and selection of the least expensive effective antibiotic also help reduce health care costs.

REFERENCES

Adams WG, Deaver KA, Cochi SL, et al. Decline of childhood *Haemophilus influenzae* type b (Hib) disease in the Hib vaccine era. JAMA 1993;269:221.

Farley MM, Stephens DS, Brachman PS, et al. Invasive *H. influenzae* disease in adults. Ann Intern Med 1992;116:806.

Glode MP, Daum RS, Goldmann DA, et al. *H. influenzae* type b meningitis: A contagious disease of children. Br Med J 1980;280:899.

Murphy TF, Apicella MA. Nontypable *H. influenzae*: A review of clinical aspects, surface antigens, and the human immune response to infection. Rev Infect Dis 1987;9:1.

Pfeiffer R. Vorlaufige Mittheilungen uber die erreger der influenza. 1892;18:28.

Pittman M. Variation and type specificity in the bacterial species *H. influenzae*. J Exp Med 1931;53:471.

Quinones CA, Memon MA, Sarosi GA. Bacteremic *H. influenzae* pneumonia in the adult. Semin Respir Infect 1989;4:12.

Wenger JD, Ward JI, Broome CV. Prevention of *H. influenzae* type b disease: Vaccines and passive prophylaxis. Curr Clin Top Infect Dis 1989;10:306.

CHAPTER 8–42

Gonococcal Infections

Jeffrey L. Lennox, M.D., and David S. Stephens, M.D.

DEFINITION

Uncomplicated genital gonorrhea is a localized, superficial infection of the urethral mucosa of men and women and the uterine endocervical mucosa of women due to *Neisseria gonorrhoeae.*

ETIOLOGY

Gonorrhea is transmitted between heterosexual or homosexual partners by sexual contact. Therefore, the disease is seen most often in sexually active teenagers and young adults.

CRITERIA FOR DIAGNOSIS
Suggestive

The onset of dysuria and urethral discharge in men or an abnormal vaginal discharge in women, particularly in the setting of recent sexual activity with a new partner or partners with any of these symptoms, is characteristic but not pathognomonic of gonorrhea.

The infection is characterized by a polymorphonuclear leukocytic exudative reaction. Gonococcal infections may be presumptively diagnosed by finding kidney bean-shaped Gram-negative pairs of bacteria that appear to be within the cytoplasm of polymorphonuclear leukocytes in a Gram-stained smear of urethral exudates or urinary sediments from men or women or in endocervical smears from women.

Definitive

A definitive diagnosis requires culture confirmation of *N. gonorrhoeae.* Confirmation is important in cases of rape, child molestation, or isolation of organisms from nongenital sites in any patient.

CLINICAL MANIFESTATIONS
Subjective

A knowledge of recent sexual activity, the number of sexual partners, their sex, and the type of exposure are important because gonorrhea occurs only after sexual contact. Virtually any nonkeratinized mucosal surface is susceptible to infection. Thus, orogenital and rectal intercourse may spread infection to the pharynx and rectum.

Men

Most men with urethral gonorrhea, the most common syndrome in men, complain of the sudden onset of severe dysuria and notice a discharge that becomes thick, yellowish, and copious within days. All degrees of milder symptoms occur. Homosexual men frequently also have infections of the pharynx and rectum. Pharyngeal infections are usually asymptomatic. Rectal infections may be asymptomatic, but may be associated with rectal discharge, tenesmus, or painful bowel movements. Extension of the infection to the epididymis occurs in 0.5% of untreated urethral infections in the United States. Testicular pain and swelling in association with discharge are characteristic of gonococcal epididymitis.

Women

Fewer women than men have any specific complaints with gonorrhea. In the most common infection, gonococcal endocervicitis, there are often complaints of vaginal discharge. Dysuria and abnormal uterine bleeding are other frequent but nonspecific complaints. Although about half the women with endocervical infections also have rectal gonococcal colonization, rectal symptoms are uncommon.

Both Sexes

The most common systemic symptoms of gonococcemia are chills, fevers, and polyarthralgias, usually involving the distal extremities; however, any joint or combination of joints may be affected. Gonococcal meningitis and endocarditis, which are rare, may occasionally be suspected when the syndrome described above is combined with a clinical picture of meningitis or endocarditis.

Objective
Men

In the first day after onset of symptoms, the urethral discharge may be scant, clear, and mucoid. Usually the discharge rapidly becomes copious and purulent; often the underpants are stained with a yellowish or greenish discoloration. Edema and erythema of the urethral meatus are common. Extension of infection to contiguous sites is uncommon in the United States (Table 8–42–1). Significant inguinal adenopathy is unusual and is a nonspecific finding. Signs of proctitis in men with rectal gonorrhea include purulent discharge, erythema, and pain, which is usually severe enough to preclude an adequate digital examination.

TABLE 8–42–1. SPECTRUM OF GONOCOCCAL INFECTIONS

Type of Infection/Syndrome	Relative Frequency of Occurrence
Men	
Anterior urethritis	++++++
Proctitis (homosexuals)	+++
Pharyngeal (homosexuals)	+++
Epididymitis	++
Penile lymphangitis	+
Penile edema syndrome	+
Periurethral abscess	+
Tysonitis	+
Cowperitis	+
Prostatitis	?+
Women	
Endocervicitis	++++++
Rectal Infection	++++
Urethritis	+++
Bartholin abscess	+++
Salpingitis	+++
Perihepatitis	++
Pharyngeal	++
Both sexes	
Conjunctivitis (adult)	+
Tenosynovitis–dermatitis	++++++
Septic arthritis	++
Meningitis	+
Endocarditis/pericarditis	+

We thank Dr. Sumner E. Thompson III for his contribution to this chapter in the previous editions of this book.

Women

Mucopurulent discharge from the endocervix can be seen during the speculum examination in most women with gonococcal cervicitis. Mucopurulent cervicitis is now recognized as a clinical entity that is diagnostic of either gonococcal or chlamydial infection. It consists of an endocervical discharge that has polymorphonuclear leukocytes on Gram stain. This specimen is verified as originating from the endocervix (rather than representing a vaginal contaminant) by evidence of a yellowish exudate on a white cotton swab inserted into the endocervix under direct vision. The endocervical mucosa is also friable, and may bleed on manipulation. Compression of Skein's and Bartholin's glands may yield purulent material at the ductal opening. Gentle stripping of the urethra may occasionally express purulent material. The syndrome of perihepatitis may occur in women when the gonococcal infection spreads from the fallopian tubes to the hepatic capsule. The objective findings in salpingitis are discussed in Chapter 8–26. Anorectal infections are rarely associated with visible inflammatory changes.

Both Sexes

Pharyngeal Infections. The presence of an exudative tonsillitis or submandibular or cervical adenopathy does not correlate with the recovery of gonococci.

Disseminated Infections. Skin lesions are the primary signs of gonococcemia. They are usually small, discrete, palpable, few in number (3–20), and found on the hands, wrists, and feet. They are often tender and may be petechial, papular, pustular, hemorrhagic, or necrotic. Often more than one type is simultaneously present. Inflamed joints and periarticular soft tissues are usually extremely tender, swollen, and erythematous. This may be accompanied by redness and swelling along tendon sheaths, resembling lymphangitis, especially in the hands and wrists. A true septic monoarticular arthritis can occur with all the clinical features of a joint space infection. A myopericarditis may occur after gonococcemia and is characterized by pericardial friction rubs and electrocardiographic changes; there are no pathognomonic features. Endocarditis is usually associated with changing murmurs and emboli because it is associated with acute valve destruction.

PLANS
Diagnostic

Gram stain and culture on selective media are the cornerstone of diagnosis. The finding of typical Gram-negative diplococci within the cytoplasm of polymorphonuclear leukocytes from a purulent urethral exudate is 95% sensitive and specific for the diagnosis of gonorrhea in men. The predictive value of a positive test is about 95%, and for a negative test it is 96%. Culture confirmation, therefore, is rarely indicated if an experienced individual interprets the smear. Discharge may be scant or nondemonstrable, however, and in this setting, gonococci may be difficult to demonstrate on smear. In this case, culture on a selective medium is necessary to make the correct diagnosis. Smears from the rectum or pharynx are of no value because of confusion with other bacteria normally found in these locations. A meticulously performed Gram stain of material obtained directly from the endocervix is about 50% sensitive and 90% specific if only typical intracellular bacteria are counted as positive. The predictive value of a positive test is around 90%, but for a negative test it falls to about 50%. A positive smear in females must be confirmed by culture. Purulent material expressed from the ducts of Bartholin's glands or the female urethra also should be Gram stained for gonococci.

Blood cultures are positive in about half the patients with the arthralgia–tenosynovitis form of gonococcemia and in less than 10% of those presenting with septic arthritis. Synovial fluid cultures are positive in about half the patients with septic arthritis. Skin lesions rarely, if ever, yield *N. gonorrhoeae* on culture, but a Gram stain of material scraped from a lesion, particularly if it is pustular or contains fluid, may be positive. Meningococcemia can occasionally produce a similar syndrome; a Gram stain cannot distinguish between the two diseases. Blood cultures should be marked to alert the laboratory to use the special procedures required for the isolation of *N. gonorrhoeae*.

From 15 to 30% of men and women who have gonorrhea also have a simultaneous infection with *Chlamydia trachomatis* in the same location. This coexistent infection cannot be picked up by examination of a Gram-stained smear and requires special testing for detection.

Several tests have been developed to detect gonococcal antigens in urethral or cervical secretions. These tests vary in their sensitivity, but most are no better than a Gram stain. Such antigen detection tests may be useful in a situation in which an experienced Gram stain interpreter is not available.

Gonococcal resistance to penicillins and tetracyclines has increased dramatically over the past decade. Although some experts recommend antibiotic sensitivity testing of all gonococcal strains, the utility of such testing is in question given the present lack of resistance to modern therapies.

Therapeutic

National recommendations for the treatment of gonorrhea were updated by the Centers for Disease Control and Prevention in 1993.

Uncomplicated Urethral, Endocervical, or Rectal Infections in Men and Women

The major considerations in choosing therapy are single-dose efficacy (when possible) of the antibiotic used and simultaneous treatment of coexisting chlamydial infections, which may occur in 30% or more of persons with gonorrhea.

Recommended Regimens. Ceftriaxone 125 mg intramuscularly in a single dose, or cefixime 400 mg orally as a single dose, or ciprofloxacin 500 mg orally as a single dose, or ofloxacin 400 mg orally as a single dose is recommended. All of these regimens should also include either doxycycline 100 mg orally twice a day for 7 days or azithromycin 1 g orally as a single dose to treat for a possible co-infection with *C. trachomatis.*

Alternative Regimens. Spectinomycin (Trobicin) 2 g intramuscularly in a single dose plus doxycycline as above; either enoxacin (Penetrex) 400 mg or norfloxacin (Noroxin) 800 mg orally as a single dose, plus doxycycline as above; cefuroxime axetil (Ceftin) 1 g orally once plus probenecid (Benacin); cefotaxime (Claforan) 500 mg intramuscularly once; and ceftizoxime 500 mg intramuscularly once are followed by the doxycycline regimen described above. Doxycycline and tetracycline are no longer considered adequate therapy for gonococcal infection, but are added to treat coexisting chlamydial infection. For patients who cannot take a tetracycline (e.g., pregnant women), erythromycin base or stearate, 500 mg orally four times a day for 7 days, may be substituted.

Other Considerations. All patients with gonorrhea should have a serologic test for syphilis and should be offered confidential counseling and testing for HIV infection. Most patients with incubating syphilis (those who are seronegative and have no signs of disease) may be cured by regimens containing beta-lactams (e.g., ceftriaxone) or tetracyclines. Spectinomycin and the quinolones (i.e., ciprofloxacin and norfloxacin) have not been shown to be active against incubating syphilis, and these patients need further follow-up and repeat testing. Mixing 1% lidocaine (without epinephrine) with the ceftriaxone has been shown to reduce the pain of injection without altering ceftriaxone pharmacokinetics. Similar data are not available for the other cephalosporins. Partners exposed to the index case within the preceding 30 days should be examined, cultured, and treated presumptively.

Pharyngeal Infections

Ceftriaxone 250 mg intramuscularly once is recommended. An alternative regimen is ciprofloxacin 500 mg orally as a single dose.

Treatment During Pregnancy

Ceftriaxone 250 mg intramuscularly once plus an erythromycin 500 mg orally four times a day for 7 days is recommended. Those who are allergic to cephalosporins should be given spectinomycin 2 g intramuscularly. Quinolones should not be used during pregnancy due to the potential for fetal toxicity.

Disseminated Gonococcal Infections

Hospitalization is recommended for initial therapy, especially for patients who cannot reliably comply with treatment, have uncertain diagnoses, or have purulent synovial effusions or other complications. Patients should be examined for endocarditis and meningitis.

Ceftriaxone 1 g intramuscularly or intravenously every 24 hours, or ceftizoxime 1 g intravenously every 8 hours, or cefotaxime 1 g intravenously every 8 hours is recommended. Patients who are allergic to beta-lactams should be treated with spectinomycin 2 g intramuscularly every 12 hours. When the infecting strain is found to be penicillin-sensitive, parenteral treatment may be switched to ampicillin 1 g every 6 hours. Reliable patients with uncomplicated disease may be discharged 24 to 48 hours after symptoms resolve and therapy completed for a total of 1 week with an oral regimen: cefuroxime axetil 500 mg twice a day, or amoxicillin 500 mg/clavulanic acid 125 mg (Augmentin) three times a day, or, if not pregnant, ciprofloxacin 500 mg twice a day. Patients should be tested for chlamydial infection or, if that is not feasible, should be simultaneously treated with doxycycline for 7 days.

Meningitis and Endocarditis

High-dose intravenous therapy with an agent effective against the strain, such as ceftriaxone 1 to 2 g every 12 hours, is recommended. Meningitis is treated for 12 to 14 days and endocarditis for 4 weeks. Patients with these infections or recurrent disseminated gonococcal infection should be evaluated for complement deficiencies.

Salpingitis and Epididymitis

The outpatient treatment of acute gonococcal salpingitis is outlined in Chapter 8–26. Both the gonococcus and chlamydia may cause a similar syndrome; therefore, empiric therapy for both organisms should be used, for example, ceftriaxone 250 mg intramuscularly in one dose followed by doxycycline 100 mg twice a day for 10 days.

FOLLOW-UP

Treatment failures following combined ceftriaxone–doxycycline therapy are uncommon. A routine follow-up "test of cure" is no longer indicated. Those who have persistent symptoms should return for reevaluation. Cultures should be taken from the infected sites and from the anal canal of all women who have been treated for gonorrhea. The patient who is a treatment failure with any of the recommended regimens should either be treated with spectinomycin 2.0 g intramuscularly or re-treated with ceftriaxone 250 mg intramuscularly. Most infections after adequate therapy are reinfections and indicate the need for partner therapy and patient education. If following cultures are positive, the isolate should undergo sensitivity testing to determine if antibiotic resistance has developed. In the best of circumstances, 3 to 5% of patients will fail a single course of appropriately given and taken antibiotic therapy. Recurrence of symptoms is not a reliable means of assessing early treatment failure. Many patients will be entirely asymptomatic for longer than a week. Gram-stained smears are also generally not helpful, even in men, for confirming a treatment failure.

DISCUSSION
Prevalence and Incidence

The prevalence of gonorrhea in the world population is unknown. Estimates of the prevalence of gonorrhea in pregnant women in the developing world vary from 5 to 10%. In the United States, there were approximately 443,000 cases reported in 1993. The number of reported cases in the United States has declined each year since 1975. The highest incidence rates occurred in minorities in the age range from 15 to 24 years. In 1993 the male:female case ratio in the United States was 1:2. (Centers for Disease Control and Prevention; data on file).

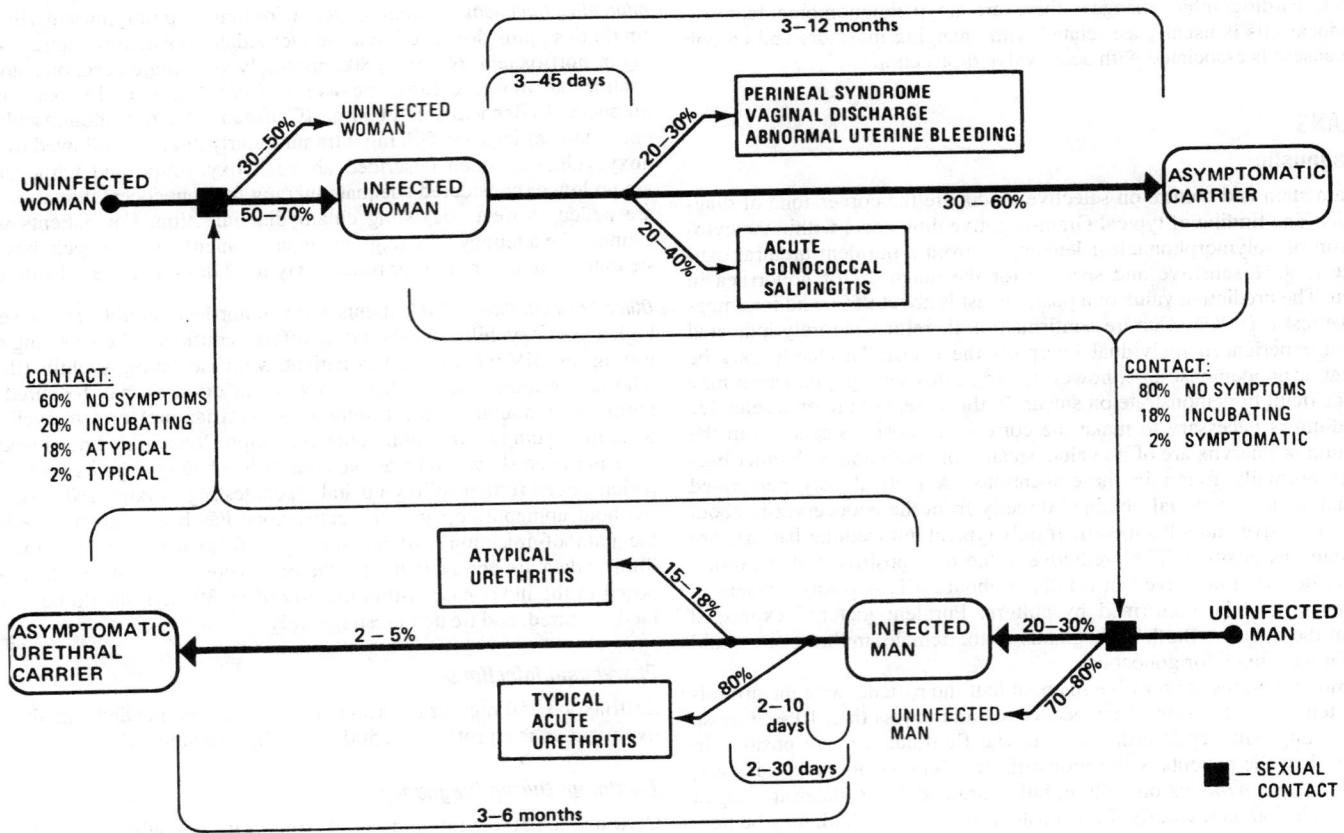

Figure 8–42–1. Simplified diagram of the heterosexual transmission of gonorrhea related to the disease status of an infected patient. *(Source: Wiesner PJ, Thompson SE III. Gonococcal diseases. In: Dowling HF, ed. DM 1980;26:5. Reproduced with permission from the publisher and author. © 1980. Year Book Medical Publishers, Inc. Chicago.)*

Related Basic Science

Close contact of the gonococcus with an epithelial surface is most important in initiating infection. Pili—thin, proteinaceous extensions of the gonococcal surface into the environment—appear to be partially responsible for this interaction. Pili also appear to be important in inhibiting phagocytosis. In experimental infections, gonococci rapidly invade and destroy epithelial cells. Natural infection is usually accompanied by an intense polymorphonuclear leukocyte response; however, for unknown reasons, gonococcal infections in the rectum and pharynx behave more like simple colonization and are not usually accompanied by an exudative response.

From the time antimicrobial agents were first used to treat gonorrhea, resistance has been a problem: first the sulfonamides, then the penicillins and erythromycin, and most recently the tetracyclines. Antimicrobial resistance consists of plasmid-mediated penicillin resistance, high-level plasmid-mediated tetracycline resistance, and chromosomally mediated resistance to a wide variety of antimicrobial agents. Since 1987, the Centers for Disease Control and Prevention has been conducting national surveys of gonococcal resistance patterns. In 1992, 10% of strains across the United States were penicillinase producing, 6% had high-level tetracycline resistance, and 19% had chromosomally mediated resistance to penicillin, tetracycline, or cefoxitin. Thus, 35% of all strains tested were resistant to one or more of the antibiotics formerly used most often for treatment.

Natural History and Its Modification with Treatment

See Figure 8–42–1. To read this figure, begin with the uninfected woman at the top left and work to the right; also begin with the uninfected man at the bottom right and work left. Interactions between the two are indicated with thin lines, and the outcomes are indicated by boxes. Men and women with asymptomatic infections may remain infected for prolonged periods, and because they do not seek treatment, they tend to accumulate in the high-risk population. They are probably major contributors to the spread and maintenance of this disease in the community.

Prevention

The factors that contribute to the spread of gonorrhea are complex and rooted in ingrained social behavioral patterns. As a vaccine is lacking, reliance must be placed on developing educational programs that effectively reach high-risk populations, upgrading clinical services to make effective, rapid therapy easily available to the patient, routinely screening high-risk groups at every opportunity, and providing contact tracing appropriate to the social environment. All health care providers can accomplish something in all four of these key areas during their contact with patients with gonorrhea.

Cost Containment

Uncomplicated gonorrhea is inexpensive to diagnose and treat. A Gram stain of urethral exudate in men can be done in minutes, and no culture is required in most cases. Culture is required at other sites in men and at all sites in women. Biochemical confirmation that the *Neisseria* species involved is *N. gonorrhoeae* is not required for urethral and cervical isolates, resulting in significant savings. Exceptions to this would be rape and child abuse cases, where confirmatory testing is always required. It is not cost effective to use a direct antigen detection method or serologic test, as these always require culture confirmation to establish the diagnosis; thus the cost is more than double that of culture alone. In uncomplicated gonorrhea, no other routine laboratory tests add to the diagnostic accuracy of the smear and culture.

REFERENCES

Barnes RC, Holmes KK. Epidemiology of gonorrhea. Epidemiol Rev 1984;6:1.

Centers for Disease Control and Prevention. 1993 STD treatment guidelines. MMWR 1993;42(RR 14):47.

Hook EW, Handsfield HH. Gonococcal infections in the adult. In: Holmes KK, Mardh P-A, Sparling PF, et al, eds. Sexually transmitted diseases. New York: McGraw-Hill, 1990:149.

Rice RJ, Thompson SE. Treatment of uncomplicated infections due to *Neisseria gonorrhoeae*: A review of clinical efficacy and *in vitro* susceptibility studies from 1982 to 1985. JAMA 1986;255:1739.

Stamm WE, Guinan ME, Johnson C, et al. Effect of treatment regimens for *Neisseria gonorrhoeae* on simultaneous infection with *Chlamydia trachomatis*. N Engl J Med 1984;310:545.

Wiesner PJ, Thompson SE. Gonococcal infections. In: Evans AS, Feldman HA, eds. Bacterial infections of humans: Epidemiology and control. New York: Plenum Medical Books, 1982:235.

CHAPTER 8–43

Nongonococcal Septic Arthritis (See Section 6, Chapter 10)

CHAPTER 8–44

Gonococcal Arthritis (See Section 6, Chapter 11)

CHAPTER 8–45

Skeletal Tuberculosis (See Section 6, Chapter 12)

CHAPTER 8–46

Acquired Infectious Syphilis

Rafael L. Jurado, M.D., Jeffrey L. Lennox, M.D., and Molly E. Eaton, M.D.

DEFINITION

Syphilis is a systemic contagious disease of lifelong chronicity, transmitted mainly through sexual contact and transplacentally.

ETIOLOGY

Syphilis is caused by *Treponema pallidum*, a member of the Treponematacea family.

CRITERIA FOR DIAGNOSIS

Suggestive

The diagnosis is based on the clues found in the history, physical examination, and laboratory tests. Syphilis is a sexually transmitted infection. Consequently, the majority of cases occur in the sexually active population. One should suspect the acute phase of the disease in sexually active individuals presenting with painless genital or mucous membrane ulcers (primary syphilis) or rash of almost any type and/or lymphadenopathy (secondary syphilis). Late syphilis (tertiary) is suggested by a combination of serologic tests (see below) and the presence of aortic insufficiency, any neuropsychiatric disorder, or musculoskeletal signs and symptoms compatible with gummatous disease (see below).

Definitive

There are no pathognomonic clinical criteria for the definite diagnosis of syphilis. The only absolute diagnostic test is the demonstration of typical motile spirochetes in chancres or in the moist skin lesions of secondary or congenital syphilis. A nontreponemal test (NTT) titer of 1:16 or greater and/or an unequivocally positive specific treponemal test (TT), even without clinical stigmata of syphilis, is virtually diagnostic of infection at any time in the past. An NTT titer of 1:64 or greater, with a confirmatory fluorescent treponemal antibody absorption test, is diagnostic of syphilis or other nonvenereal treponematoses caused by agents closely related to *Treponema pallidum* such as yaws and pinta. The laboratory tests are listed in Table 8–46–1.

CLINICAL MANIFESTATIONS

Subjective

Most patients are asymptomatic throughout much of the course of their disease. Other than the physical presence of the syphilitic chancre, primary syphilis is asymptomatic. If secondary infection of the ulcer occurs, it may become painful. During secondary syphilis, which usually occurs within 6 weeks of the onset of the chancre, the most common manifestation is a nonpruritic generalized skin rash that may be accompanied by flulike symptoms. Headache, hoarseness, and arthralgia may be prominent complaints. By definition, there are no symptoms during latency, the next phase of the disease. Latency may last for the life of the patient. Symptoms during late syphilis are generally referable to the central nervous, musculoskeletal, and cardiovascular systems.

Objective

Physical Examination

It is rather distinct, according to the particular stage of the disease.

Primary Syphilis. The chancre is the first objective sign of disease. Classically, it is painless, solitary, and indurated; it has sharp margins and is associated with prominent and nontender regional adenopathy. Note

two important caveats: Regarding location, the lesion may be found anywhere on the male or female genitalia, rectum, pharynx, or, more importantly, other cutaneous sites used for sexual activity such as the tongue, finger, or nipple. Second, the classic clinical characteristics apply to only about 60% of cases. Up to 40% of chancres may be atypical by being painful, nonindurated, or multiple.

Secondary Syphilis. See Table 8–46–2. This stage of syphilis can literally run the gamut of internal medicine manifestations. It was probably secondary syphilis to which Osler was referring when he said: "Know syphilis in all its manifestations and relations, and all Medicine will be given onto you." Approximately a quarter of patients have relapses of their secondary signs and symptoms, and almost all of these relapses occur within 2 years of the first episode of secondary syphilis. It is this 2-year period that divides syphilis into early (contagious) and late (noncontagious, with some exceptions for congenital syphilis).

Early latency defines asymptomatic cases before the end of the 2-year period. Late latency refers to those asymptomatic individuals after 2 years have elapsed.

Latent Syphilis. This is the period from the disappearance of symptoms and signs of secondary disease until the appearance of relapsing secondary syphilis or manifestations of tertiary disease. There are no objective signs of disease during latency.

Tertiary Syphilis. Symptomatic late syphilis is called tertiary; its clinical syndromes fit the acronym ABC for aortitis, benign (gummatous), and central nervous system (CNS).

Cardiovascular Syphilis. Changes in the cardiovascular system occur in about 75% of patients with late syphilis, but clinical manifestations are seen in less than 12% of patients (Table 8–46–3). Aortitis, with root dilation and root-related aortic insufficiency, is the main manifestation. Data from the Oslo study (Clark and Danbolt, 1964) suggest that less than 12% of untreated patients will develop this complication. The longer the patient goes without therapy, the higher the likelihood that aortic disease will disappear. *Treponema pallidum* has a unique tropism for the vasa vasorum of the ascending aorta. It is important to recognize

TABLE 8–46–1. SEROLOGIC TESTS FOR SYPHILIS

Nontreponemal tests (NTTs): Venereal Disease Research
  Laboratory (VDRL), rapid plasma reagin (RPR)
    Highly nonspecific and sensitive
    Technically nondemanding and inexpensive
    Titratable: used for activity follow-up
Treponemal tests (TTs): fluorescent treponemal antibody absorption (FTA-ABS),
  microhemagglutination *Treponema pallidum* (MHA-TP)
    Highly specific and sensitive
    Technically demanding and expensive
    Nontitratable and "immortal"; not useful for follow-up of disease activity.
Results of the commonly used NTTs (VDRL and RPR) may vary by one serial dilution on repeated testing. Thus, titer changes of less than two serial dilutions (fourfold change) are rarely meaningful.
When using NTTs to follow up on treatment, the same NTT must be used all the time as titers of VDRL and RPR may not necessarily be comparable.
In the past, treponemal tests were believed to be immortal (i.e., they were expected to remain positive for the duration of the patient's life). This myth has suffered two blows: HIV can change a positive TT to negative; this "seroregression" occurs as the immune system wanes, indicated by a decreasing CD4 count. It has been reported that the TT becomes negative following benzathine penicillin treatment for primary syphilis. The FTA-ABS became negative in 24% of cases and the MHA-TP, in 13% of cases.

We thank Dr. Sumner E. Thompson III for his contribution to this chapter in the previous editions of this book.

TABLE 8–46–2. SECONDARY SYPHILIS

Sign	Comments
Cutaneous	
Skin	May be faint or limited to certain parts of the body; all types of lesions, and often different types, can appear simultaneously or sequentially; rash on palms and/or soles is classic
Split papules	Occur in intertriginous areas; nasolabial, postauricular, and corners of lips; condyloma lata, wartlike excrescences, usually in moist genital regions, can be confused with classic genital warts.
Mucous patches	Erosive lesions of mucous membranes covered with a white-gray membrane; seen in oral cavity, cheeks, tongue especially, also in vagina
Alopecia	Classically described as "moth eaten" (i.e., patchy); thinning of outer third of eyebrows; loss of eye lashes and beard also occurs
Constitutional	
Flulike syndrome	Myalgias, malaise, headache, photophobia, arthralgias, usually mild
Lymphadenopathy	Generalized, usually more significant than shotty, nontender
Hepatitis	Hepatic enlargement with mild derangement of liver enzymes
Splenomegaly	Usually with hepatomegaly

that cardiovascular syphilis may be present with a "false-negative" Venereal Disease Research Laboratory (VDRL) test (by the "burnout" phenomenon). The inflammation may have subsided, accounting for the falsely negative NTT, but the constant normal hemodynamic stress may continue to distend the aortic root, weakened by the earlier treponemal invasion.

Benign (Gummatous) Syphilis. This is now a very rare condition in the United States. Carcinoma is usually the first diagnosis entertained. Gummatous syphilis is an inflammatory process with either proliferative or tissue-destructive features, occurring most often in the skin or bones; however, any tissue may be involved. Other organ systems that may be involved are the esophagus, stomach, liver, and much less often, the upper and lower respiratory tracts and the CNS. The term benign is appropriate in the majority of cases, as most gummas are located in the musculoskeletal system and the skin; however, they become malignant when located in the CNS or liver (hepar lobatum). The lesions are granulomatous, probably mediated by a hypersensitivity reaction to treponemes. It follows that the VDRL is reactive in the majority of cases.

Late (Tertiary) Neurosyphilis. See Table 8–46–4. Neurosyphilis can be either asymptomatic (positive plasma NTT and/or positive TT and abnormal cerebrospinal fluid in the absence of neuropsychiatric manifestations) or symptomatic, which by convention and convenience is staged into meningovascular (the earliest form, usually starting 5 years after the acquisition of syphilis), general paresis (appearing 10–20 years after the initial infection), and tabes dorsalis (appearing 15–35 years after primary syphilis).

It is important to emphasize that this clean-cut classification is more of a convenience than a reality, and the reader is well advised to remember that "patients don't read textbooks." In the antibiotic era, be-

TABLE 8–46–3. OBJECTIVE FINDINGS IN CARDIOVASCULAR SYPHILIS

Syndrome	Major Finding
Aortic aneurysm	Involves ascending aorta from valves of Valsalva to midthoracic region; auscultative findings of aortic insufficiency; aneurysm with "eggshell" calcifications
Coronary artery disease	Sudden death; late-onset angina; isolated right and left main coronary proximal narrowing
Aortic valvular disease	Pure aortic insufficiency without stenosis is hallmark; this is due to aortic ring dilation

TABLE 8–46–4. CLASSIFICATION OF OBJECTIVE FINDINGS IN NEUROSYPHILIS

Syndrome	Major Findings
Asymptomatic neurosyphilis	In CSF, lymphocytosis; (+) VDRL; increased protein; normal glucose; (−) Gram stain
Meningeal neurosyphilis	
Uncomplicated	Aseptic meningitis picture
Acute hydrocephalus	Signs of increased intracranial pressure; (+) Kernig's; papilledema
With cerebritis	Seizures, aphasia, hemiplegia
Cranial nerve palsies (basilar meningitis)	Multiple nerves involved, especially III, VI, VII, VIII (bilateral sensorineural hearing loss); blood RPR/VDRL (+) > 98%; CSF VDRL (+) > 98%; 100–2000 lymphocytes/μL; protein usually > 20 mg/dL; decreased glucose in 50%
Meningovascular syphilis	Signs of a CVA in young adult: seizures, aphasia, hemiparesis; Argyll–Robertson pupils in 10%; blood serology (+) in 99%; CSF VDRL also (+), 100–500 lymphocytes; protein 50–250 mg/dL; glucose usually within normal limits
Parenchymatous neurosyphilis	
General paresis	Argyll–Robertson pupils in 25%; other pupil abnormalities in 60%; slurred speech in 30%; tremor in 20%; altered reflexes in 50%; EEG abnormalities in most patients; plantars, normal blood serology (+) in only 50–60% of cases; FTA-ABS (+) in 100%; CSF: VDRL (+) in 75%; 8–100 lymphocytes; protein 50–100 mg/dL
Tabes dorsalis	Pupil abnormalities: Argyll–Robertson in 95%; (−) ankle jerks/knee jerks in 95%; (+) Romberg in 50%; impaired vibration/position sense in 50%; broad-based slapping gait in 75%; blood serology (+) in less than 50%; FTA-ABS (+) in 100%; CSF: VDRL variable; 4–100 lymphocytes; protein normal to 95 mg/dL

CSF, cerebrospinal fluid; CVA, cerebrovascular accident; VDRL, Venereal Disease Research Laboratory; FTA-ABS, fluorescent treponemal antibody absorption.

cause of the administration of antibiotics for other purposes, neurosyphilis presents more frequently as seizures or neuro-ophthalmology syndromes.

The same issue of false negative applies in connection with cardiovascular syphilis (e.g., the NTT may be falsely negative). This is even more important in neurosyphilis, where a negative NTT (the usual test requested in evaluating neurosyphilis) stops the workup from including a lumbar puncture which may in fact be needed to make a diagnosis.

Routine Laboratory Abnormalities

The serologic tests for syphilis are no longer performed routinely on patients in the United States. The routine laboratory tests are usually noncontributory in primary and secondary syphilis. The electrocardiogram may show left ventricular hypertrophy when there is aortic regurgitation, and the chest x-ray film may reveal a left ventricular enlargement and calcification of the aortic root or a thoracic aneurysm, when there is cardiovascular syphilis.

PLANS
Diagnostic

Differential Diagnosis

The differential diagnosis is dependent on the particular state of syphilis. For primary syphilis, entities to be considered include chancroid, granuloma inguinale, herpes simplex, and lymphogranuloma venereum. The diagnosis of primary syphilis rests on dark-field examination and appropriate use of syphilis serology. Appropriate diagnostic tests for the other entities mentioned are needed, as patients can simultaneously acquire more than one sexually transmitted disease. For secondary syphilis, the main differential diagnoses include papulosquamous disorders of the skin (see Chapter 11–6) and diseases associated with diffuse lymphadenopathy (see Chapter 8–6), but the reader must remember that the spectrum of manifestations of this stage of syphilis extends beyond those two main manifestations. The main diagnostic considerations for cardiovascular syphilis are those entities associated with aortic regurgitation (see Chapter 15–36). Neurosyphilis really expands the spectrum of neurologic disorders, such that no specific entities can be mentioned. In summary, syphilis needs to be considered in a wide array of clinical disorders, and frequently, thoughtful interpretation of clinical and serologic data is the recommended diagnostic approach.

Diagnostic Options

Syphilis should never be diagnosed on clinical grounds alone. A search for *T. pallidum* in the chancre or moist skin or mucous membrane lesions of secondary syphilis by dark-field microscopy is of primary importance. If this is not feasible due to lack of a dark-field microscope or lack of suitable lesions to test, the clinician must rely on serology (see Table 8–46–1). The interpretation of these tests is not always straightforward.

Recommended Approach

Two situations generate questions regarding syphilis serologies: (1) When faced with a patient in whom syphilis is a possible diagnosis, what test should be ordered? (2) If the tests were done before seeing the patient, how should the results be interpreted? We recommend following the possible combination of NTT and TT results outlined in Table 8–46–5 to obtain answers to these two diagnostic questions.

NTT+, TT+

- *Syphilis untreated:* At any stage (primary, secondary, or tertiary), this combination may be evidence of untreated syphilis. The percentage of both types of tests being positive in the different stages of the disease varies (Table 8–46–6).
- *Syphilis treated, "late."* The NTT's chance of reverting to negative after successful therapy varies with the stage of the disease. Following treatment of primary lues, the NTT returns to negative in almost all patients in 1 year. Following treatment of secondary lues, the serology returns to negative in 2 years for about 75% of patients. In the case of successfully treated tertiary syphilis (success being defined on clinical grounds and, when pertinent, cerebrospinal fluid analysis), the NTTs may decline very slowly and may never reach undetectable levels.
- *Infection with other members of the genus Treponema:* Yaws (*T. pallidum* subsp. *pertenue*), pinta (*T. carateum*), and bejel (*T. pallidum* subsp. *endemicum*) are impossible to differentiate serologically from syphilis. Here, the diagnosis hinges on clincoepidemiologic grounds. When in doubt, assume that it is syphilis and treat according to the clinical circumstances. Because members of the genus *Borrelia* share antigens with treponemes, immunologic cross-reactivity is expected to occur in the treponemal tests.

TABLE 8–46–5. DIFFERENT COMBINATIONS OF THE NONTREPONEMAL (NTT) AND TREPONEMAL (TT) TESTS

NTT+, TT+	Syphilis, untreated
	Syphilis treated "late"
	Nonvenereal treponematosis
	Any of the B subset plus a coincidental biological false positive
	Both NTT and TT false positive (systemic Lupus erythematosus)
NTT–, TT+	Syphilis treated successfully
	Late syphilis, untreated
	Primary syphilis, "early"
	Secondary syphilis, with prozone
	False-positive TT
	HIV, end stage
NTT+, TT–	Biologically false positives
NTT–, TT–	Primary syphilis, "very early"
	HIV: see references by Hass and Hicks
	Primary syphilis after treatment

TABLE 8–46–6. STAGES OF NONTREPONEMAL AND TREPONEMAL (TT) TESTS

Clinical Stage	Nontreponemal Tests	Treponemal Tests
Primary	75.0%	85.0%
Secondary	99.9%	100.0%
Tertiary	60–80%	95.0%

- *Successfully treated syphilis* with a coincidental biological false positive (see below).
- *Both NTT and TT false positive.* Systemic lupus erythematosus and other diseases with aberrant/exuberant antibody production occasionally result in both NTT and TT being false positive. This subset requires careful clinical analysis, and it may be the only reason to resort to the technically difficult *T. pallidum* immobilization.

NNT–, TT+

- *Primary syphilis:* Although the test of choice for primary syphilis is the dark-field microscopic examination of the suspect chancre, both the NTT and the TT may become positive in early primary syphilis.
- *Secondary syphilis with the prozone phenomenon:* For an agglutination reaction to be visibly positive, the antigen/antibody combination must be in an optimal ratio, defined by the zone of equivalence. An excess of antibody puts the ratio in the prozone, making the test false negative. Routinely, laboratories do not test for the prozone effect because it is very rare. When its presence is suspected, the physician needs to ask the laboratory to dilute the serum, which will bring the antibody back to the zone of equivalence, making the reaction positive (the titer will go from negative or weakly reactive to a greater than four fold higher titer).
- *Late syphilis untreated:* In the natural history of syphilis (e.g., untreated), the NTT may become spontaneously negative in 20 to 40%, usually after a long period. This creates the scenario for a very frequently missed diagnosis of neurosyphilis in elderly patients undergoing investigation for dementing diseases. If a NTT is ordered, it has a statistical chance of being false negative in up to 40% of patients who truly have syphilis. In this situation, TTs have a much higher sensitivity (95–98%).
- *Syphilis, successfully treated:* As described earlier, this combination is seen in variable stages of syphilis at the time of therapy.
- *False-positive TT:* As no test is perfect, so do TTs have very rare false positives. This may occur in pregnancy, drug addiction, and systemic lupus erythematosus. Other reported conditions associated with false-positive TTs include progressive systemic sclerosis, mixed collagen tissue disease, cirrhosis, lymphosarcoma, meningioma, carcinoma of the colon, autoimmune hemolytic anemia, and leprosy. Occasionally, false-positive fluorescent treponemal antibody absorption tests occur in healthy adults with negative NTTs; many such false positives revert to negative within 1 year.
- *HIV, end stage:* Patients with end-stage AIDS (with very low CD4 counts) have been reported to have secondary syphilis with very low NTT. Two biopsy-proven cases of secondary syphilis with a positive TT were seen at Walter Reed Medical Center with VDRL test scores of 1.2 (CD4 of 14) and 1.8 (CD4 of 56) (personal communication). The scenario is set for other such patients to present with active secondary syphilis (which usually has a very high titer NTT) with positive TT and negative NTT (in these patients, the prozone phenomenon was excluded, as was the Hicks phenomenon; see below).

NTT+, TT–

- *Biologic false positive:* The NTT is notoriously nonspecific (for each true-positive NTT in a general population, there are probably 20 false-positive NTTs). Thus, it must be confirmed with a TT. Usually, a false-positive NTT is of low titer (<1:8); occasionally, very high titers have been reported, usually with gammopathies. A practical approach to the false-positive NTT is to divide them into acute (<6 months' duration) and chronic (>6 months' duration). Acute biologic false positives are legion. Chronic biologic false positives can be committed to memory through the pneumonic AAA-M:

A1—autoimmune: Systemic lupus erythematosus will produce a false-positive NTT in 15 to 20% of cases.

A2—age: As seen with other serologies (e.g., antinuclear antibodies), the antibodies that mediate the nonsyphilitic NTT increase with age. By age 80, the prevalence of a false-positive NTT is 10%, another reason not to order a NTT in elderly patients being worked up for dementia. Such patients are more likely to have a false-positive than a true-positive NTT, the bottom line being that NTT+ individuals must be further investigated with a TT.

A3—addiction: In some reports, as many as 40% of intravenous drug abusers have a false-positive NTT. This is probably secondary to overstimulation of their immune system by the large amounts and diversity of the "foreign" antigens they inject.

M—*Miscellaneous:* pregnancy, leprosy, malignancy, macroglobulinemia, drugs.

NTT–, TT–

- *Primary, "very early" syphilis:* In primary syphilis, the TT is positive in 70 to 80%, whereas the NTT is positive in only 60 to 70% of cases. The diagnostic test of choice for primary syphilis is a dark-field examination. One quarter of dark-field positive patients are TT-, the same occurring for NTT in 30 to 40% of patients.
- *HIV:* There are two subsets of this cause of NTT and TT being negative in the presence of syphilis in the HIV-infected patient.

The Hass phenomenon: A recent report (Hass et al., 1990) on the influence of HIV immunosuppression of TT has changed the dogma that TT were "immortal." In the pre-AIDS era, the TT would remain positive for life, regardless of therapy or time. Hass et al. reported that the TT may spontaneously revert to negative in HIV-positive patients and that this association was seen in patients whose CD4 counts were under 200. They analyzed the serology of 109 homosexual males with a documented history of treated syphilis and compared the TT results with records of prior results and confirmed on stored serum samples. Although none of the HIV-negative patients lost TT reactivity, 7% of HIV-positive asymptomatic patients and 38% of HIV-positive symptomatic patients lost reactivity.

The Hicks phenomenon: Hicks et al. (1987) described an HIV-positive patient with a negative NTT (prozone was excluded) and positive TT in the face of clinical and biopsy-proven secondary syphilis. Once the diagnosis was established, both serologies became positive 3 weeks into therapy. The explanation for the Hicks phenomenon appears to be the so-called delayed seroconversion. In view of the immunologic aberrations seen in HIV-positive individuals, one should not abandon the diagnosis of secondary syphilis in an HIV-positive person on the basis of negative serologies (both NTT and TT) alone. If the index of suspicion is high enough, other tests must be done (dark-field, skin biopsy with treponemal, and fluorescent antibody direct stains). Furthermore, to exclude the possibility of a delayed seroconversion, both NTT and TT should be repeated several weeks later.

Primary syphilis, following therapy: Romanowski et al. (1991) reported that the TT became negative following benzathine penicillin treatment for primary syphilis. The fluorescent treponemal antibody absorption test became negative in about a quarter of cases, and the microhemagglutination *Treponema pallidum* test, in 13% of cases.

Therapeutic

Therapeutic Options

The latest Public Health Service Recommendations (Centers for Disease Control and Prevention, 1993) constitute the framework for treating syphilis.

Recommended Approach

Treatment should be instituted only after weighing all the diagnostic evidence, and then it should be administered in fully therapeutic doses as recommended by the U.S. Public Health Service. Patients with primary, secondary, or latent disease known to be of under 1-year duration should be treated with benzathine penicillin G 2.4 million units by intramuscular injection at a single session. For those allergic to penicillin, doxycycline (Vibramycin) 100 mg orally twice daily for 2 weeks or ceftriaxone (Rocephin) 250 mg intramuscularly once daily for 10 days should be used. Patients with syphilis longer than 1 year's duration (latent syphilis longer than 1 year or of unknown duration, cardiovascular syphilis, or gummatous syphilis) should be treated with benzathine penicillin G 2.4 million units intramuscularly weekly for 3 successive weeks. For those allergic to penicillin, doxycycline 100 mg orally twice a day for 2 weeks can be used.

For neurosyphilis, aqueous crystalline penicillin G 2 to 4 million units intravenously every 4 hours for 10 to 14 days is recommended because of the low cerebrospinal fluid levels found with benzathine penicillin or aqueous procaine penicillin G. No proven effective alternative is available for patients allergic to penicillin; desensitization to penicillin is recommended.

For infants with congenital syphilis and abnormal spinal fluid findings, treatment consists of aqueous crystalline penicillin G, 50,000 U/kg intramuscularly or intravenously daily for more than 10 to 14 days, or aqueous procaine penicillin G, 50,000 U/kg intramuscularly for more than 10 to 14 days. For infants with congenital syphilis and normal cerebrospinal fluid, benzathine penicillin G 50,000 U/kg intramuscularly in a single injection should be used.

Pregnant women should be treated with the same dosage of penicillin as nonpregnant patients. For pregnant women with syphilis and a reliable history of penicillin allergy, there are no acceptable antibiotic alternatives. Intravenous tetracyclines are contraindicated because of dental staining and hypoplasia in the fetus and the risk of hepatotoxicity in pregnant women. Erythromycin, although recommended by some, has a failure rate of 13 to 30%. Thus, pregnant women with a history of penicillin allergy should undergo skin testing and, if the results are positive, should be desensitized.

Although the efficacy of penicillin in treating syphilis is indisputable, there has never been a well-controlled study to determine optimal doses or length of treatment. The U.S. Public Health Service recommendations mentioned above are minimal effective schedules. Because some patients may relapse or become reinfected, follow-up with quantitative NTT titers every few months for at least 1 year is important. In early syphilis, the titer, if elevated, should begin to decline within 1 to 2 months and should become negative within 6 to 18 months. A high (1:16) stationary or rising titer should prompt retreatment. In late syphilis, a high titer should fall after adequate therapy, but it will do so unpredictably, and in a significant proportion of individuals it may remain positive at low titers for life.

Early "incubating" syphilis is probably aborted by the treatment of gonorrhea with ceftriazone 250 mg intramuscularly. Tetracycline is also probably effective in this setting. As there is a high risk of infection in sex partners exposed to infectious (early) syphilis within 3 months, these contacts should receive full therapeutic doses of antibiotics regardless of clinical or serologic findings (so-called epidemiologic treatment, see below).

Since the inception of therapy of syphilis with penicillin in the 1940s, there have been no confirmed cases of increasing penicillin resistance of *T. pallidum*.

A significant proportion of cases of early syphilis in the United States occur in homosexual men. As many of them do not realize that they are infected, because the primary chancre may not be visible or suspected because of its location in the rectum or oropharynx, they are recognized as having syphilis only if serology is obtained. There is also increasing anecdotal evidence to suggest that, when the lesions of secondary syphilis appear in immunosuppressed individuals, they may be atypical and thus not be appropriately diagnosed. The recommended penicillin doses probably represent minimal effective doses. The cellular immune system is undoubtedly as important as antibiotics in overcoming an active syphilitic infection. Therefore, in HIV-positive patients, there is a real concern that previous recommendations for treatment are inadequate, particularly for treating neurosyphilis. Anecdotal reports suggest that a single dose of benzathine penicillin may fail to cure early syphilis in HIV-positive patients. These patients may relapse and develop asymptomatic or symptomatic neurosyphilis; however, the most recent recommendations of the U.S. Public Health Service (Centers for Disease Control and Prevention, 1993) do not distinguish between HIV-positive and HIV-negative individuals, although many clinicians suggest more aggressive therapeutic regimens (higher dosage or longer course) in patients with underlying HIV infection.

FOLLOW-UP

The maximal fall in serologic titer is seen during the first year after adequate treatment; the decline is slower, the later the treatment is instituted. Patients should be examined and have repeat NTTs every 2 to 3 months after treatment until the serum NTT titer stabilizes. After this time, no specific follow-up visits need to be scheduled.

DISCUSSION

Prevalence and Incidence

Prevalence figures for syphilis showed a steady and significant decline (88% decrease from 1943 to 1977) but such favorable trends have stopped in recent times (Centers for Disease Control and Prevention, 1991). As a matter of fact, from 1986 through 1990, there was a 97% increase in the total number of cases reported annually. Incidence figures have paralleled the above data. Peak incidence of syphilis occurs in the 15- to 34-year-old group.

Related Basic Science

Understanding the pathogenesis of the disease and the host's reaction to it is fundamental in having a clear grasp of the global picture of syphilis. *Treponema pallidum* can penetrate intact mucous membrane and probably normal skin as well. Shortly thereafter, it rapidly enters local lymphatics and probably disseminates widely through the bloodstream. The organisms are slow to divide, probably accounting in part for the long incubation period before the chancre appears. Blood of individuals in this phase may be infectious. When the local tissue organisms reach a high titer, the chancre forms. Organisms are easy to demonstrate in these lesions. Spontaneous healing occurs in several weeks. The secondary or generalized form of the disease becomes evident after the chancre has healed, usually appearing 6 to 8 weeks after contact. Even if untreated, this phase wanes spontaneously and the patient enters the latent stage. In this phase, there are no symptoms or clinical manifestations. A diagnosis may be established by serology only. The patient may remain in this stage for life. Relapse to a secondary-like phase is most common during the first 2 years of latency. Late syphilis, which occurs in about 30% of untreated patients, usually involves the CNS or aorta. Gummata are rare.

Various classes of humoral antibody appear during the course of syphilis. The serologic tests available today have probably reached the zenith of perfection. Further significant advances are unlikely in our serodiagnostic capabilities in the near future. Antibodies to *T. pallidum*, which fortuitously cross-react with an artificial lipid antigen, are measured in the nontreponemal, nonspecific, or reaginic tests (reagin in this sense is not to be confused with the skin-fixing immunoglobulin E antibodies). These tests generally become positive during the first few weeks after infection. Occasionally, they may still be negative even after the chancre appears. They are virtually always positive late in primary and during secondary and early latent syphilis. Titers drop naturally over the years and may become undetectable, even in untreated syphilis. They respond to treatment (see above). Very early treatment of syphilis may abort a response altogether; in primary disease, titers become undetectable within a year, and in secondary disease, within 2 years. Immunity to reinfection has been demonstrated but is not absolute. Antibodies probably have some role in this partial immunity, but infection can be induced in the presence of circulating antibodies. Cell-mediated immunity is probably the most important mechanism. Resistance to infection can be transferred by T lymphocytes in rabbits. The degree of protection induced after treatment varies inversely with the duration of disease before therapy is initiated. Because immunity appears to play some role in resistance to infection, a vaccine may be possible.

Natural History and Its Modification with Treatment

Two studies have documented the natural course of untreated disease: the Oslo study (Clark and Danbolt, 1964) of more than 2000 patients with early syphilis in the preantibiotic era and the Tuskegee study (Rockwell et al., 1964) of more than 400 black men with seropositive late latent syphilis. In the Oslo study, 24% of patients developed a clinical relapse of disease within the first 2 years of latency. In patients developing tertiary disease, 16% developed gummatous syphilis, 12% had cardiovascular syphilis, and 6.5% had neurosyphilis. Of those autopsied, 35% of men and 22% of women had cardiovascular involvement. In the Tuskegee study, cardiovascular disease (including hypertension) was more common than neurologic complications, both clinically and in autopsies. Late complications seem to be more common in men than in women, CNS complications being more common in whites, and cardiovascular complications more common in blacks.

Prevention

Monogamous sex practiced cojointly by both partners is the most inexpensive and effective method of avoiding disease. Contact tracing and epidemiologic treatment of sexual contacts (treatment with full therapeutic doses of penicillin of individuals thought to be at high risk of having the disease but in whom the disease is not unequivocally established) constitute the most effective means of prevention of disease transmission. Condoms, properly used, reduce syphilis transmission, as does avoidance of casual sexual contact and sexual contact with prostitutes.

Cost Containment

Being a relatively easy condition to diagnose and treat early, cost containment of syphilis should be relatively straightforward. A high index of suspicion for syphilis and use of readily available simple laboratory tests allow for early diagnosis and treatment, thus preventing spread of the disease, late complications, and spread to others. This and contact tracing should reduce costly intravenous therapy recommended for treating neurosyphilis.

REFERENCES

Centers for Disease Control and Prevention. Sexually transmitted diseases treatment guideline. MMWR 1993;38:5.

Clark EG, Danbolt N. The Oslo study of the natural course of untreated syphilis. Med Clin North Am 1964;48:613.

Fiumara NJ. Treatment of primary and secondary syphilis: Serologic response. JAMA 1980;243:2500.

Hass JB, Bolan G, Larsen SA, et al. Sensitivity of treponemal tests for detecting prior treated syphilis during HIV infection. J Infect Dis 1990;162:862.

Hicks CB, Benson DM, Lupton GP, et al. Seronegative secondary syphilis in a patient with HIV with Kaposi sarcoma. Ann Intern Med 1987;107:492.

Musher DM, Hamill RJ, Baughn RE. Effect of human immune deficiency virus (HIV) infection on the course of syphilis and on the response to treatment. Ann Intern Med 1990;113:872.

Rockwell DH, Yobs AR, Moore MB Jr. The Tuskegee study of untreated syphilis: The 30th year of observation. Arch Intern Med 1964;114:792.

Romanowski B, Sutherland R, Fick GH, et al. Serologic response to treatment of infectious syphilis. Ann Intern Med 1991;114:1005.

Swartz MN. Neurosyphilis. In Holmes KK, et al., eds. Sexually transmitted diseases. 2nd ed. New York: McGraw-Hill, 1990:231.

Leptospirosis

Sue Anne Brenner, M.D., Jonas A. Shulman, M.D., and W. Edmund Farrar, M.D.

DEFINITION

Leptospirosis is an acute systemic infectious disease caused by spirochetes of the genus *Leptospira*.

ETIOLOGY

Leptospira organisms are finely coiled, motile spirochetes, approximately 0.1 μm wide by 6 μm to 20 μm long, with bent or hooked ends. There is only one species, *Leptospira interrogans*, but there are approximately 170 serotypes of pathogenic leptospires.

CRITERIA FOR DIAGNOSIS

Suggestive

The epidemiologic setting (occupational or recreational contact with animals or infected urine) or the clinical picture (severe febrile illness or aseptic meningitis, with or without jaundice and/or renal failure) may suggest an infection with *Leptospira*.

Definitive

Definitive diagnosis requires either isolation of the organism or demonstration of a specific serologic response.

CLINICAL MANIFESTATIONS

Subjective

A careful epidemiologic history is important. Many patients give a history of recent contact, either in their occupation or recreational activities, with animals or with water or soil contaminated with animal urine. Farmers, veterinarians, abattoir workers, campers, and swimmers are all at increased risk of infection with these organisms.

Asymptomatic infection is very common. Among patients who become ill, 90% have the milder anicteric form of the disease, and only 5 to 10% have severe leptospirosis with jaundice (Weil's disease).

Leptospirosis often follows a biphasic course. After an incubation period of 7 to 12 days (range, 2–20 days), the initial "septicemic" phase begins; it usually lasts 4 to 7 days. In anicteric leptospirosis, the septicemic phase is characterized by abrupt onset of fever, headache, severe muscle aches, malaise, prostration, and, occasionally, circulatory collapse. High remittent fever, chills, persistent headache, severe myalgias, abdominal pain, and nausea and vomiting persist for several days. The temperature may then return to normal, and the patient is afebrile for a day or two. Then the second, "immune," phase of the illness ensues. In anicteric patients the predominant symptom during the immune stage of the disease is headache, which is characteristically intense, unremitting, throbbing, and poorly controlled by analgesics. It is usually frontal or bitemporal and may be associated with retrobulbar pain. Occurrence of headache during the second phase of illness usually heralds the onset of clinical meningitis. Mild delirium is common; more severe mental changes such as hallucinations are rare. Myalgia most commonly involves muscles of the calf, paraspinal region, abdomen, and neck and may be very severe. Nausea, vomiting, and abdominal pain occur in some combination in up to 95% of patients. Fever is usually low grade or absent.

Objective

Physical Examination

The most common physical findings during the second phase of leptospirosis are fever, muscle tenderness and cramps, nuchal rigidity, conjunctival suffusion, adenopathy, and hepatosplenomegaly. Most patients have tachycardia, but bradycardia occurs occasionally. Ocular manifestations including suffusion of the bulbar conjunctiva, photophobia, ocular pain, and conjunctival hemorrhage are relatively common and may suggest the diagnosis. Less common are signs of pulmonary involvement (with infiltrates, cough, hemoptysis, and, rarely, adult respiratory distress syndrome), pharyngitis, rash, and cervical and generalized lymphadenopathy. Characteristic raised erythematous lesions 1 to 5 cm in diameter in the pretibial area have been described in *L. autumnalis* infections and are part of the syndrome called *Fort Bragg fever*. Uveitis, usually appearing several months after the acute illness, may have a prolonged chronic or recurrent course. In patients with severe leptospirosis (Weil's disease), jaundice is a characteristic feature, and renal failure, hemorrhages, vascular collapse, and severe alterations in consciousness may also occur.

Electrocardiographic abnormalities, including heart block and signs of pericardial effusion, may occur during the leptospiremic phase, and in severe cases congestive heart failure and cardiogenic shock may develop.

In pregnant women, spontaneous abortion is more likely to occur if leptospirosis occurs in the early months of pregnancy, although congenital leptospirosis is rare.

Routine Laboratory Abnormalities

In anicteric hepatitis the total white blood cell count is normal or slightly elevated and the erythrocyte sedimentation rate is increased. Serum creatine phosphokinase is often modestly elevated. In Weil's disease hyperbilirubinemia, elevated serum transaminases, azotemia, proteinuria, and thrombocytopenia may occur and, along with hyperamylasemia, indicate more severe disease.

PLANS

Diagnostic

Differential Diagnosis

Leptospirosis needs to be considered in the differential diagnosis of any "flulike" illness or fever of undetermined origin occurring in an epidemiologic setting conducive to exposure to leptospires. Leptospirosis must be distinguished from hantavirus infection. It should also be considered in patients with meningitis or meningoencephalitis, hepatitis, or acute renal failure, especially if the epidemiologic setting is suggestive or if any of the specific clinical features described above are present (see Differential Diagnosis in Chapter 8–49).

Diagnostic Options

The definitive diagnosis of leptospirosis depends on laboratory findings: isolation of the organism from a clinical specimen or a compatible clinical illness. Presumptive diagnosis may be based on finding either a microscopic agglutination titer of 1:100 or higher or a positive slide agglutination test in the presence of a compatible clinical illness. The test should be carried out, or at least confirmed, in a laboratory experienced in the diagnosis of leptospirosis.

Isolation of leptospires from body fluids or tissues requires special laboratory techniques and media but is otherwise not difficult. The organisms can be isolated from blood or cerebrospinal fluid only during the first 10 days of illness, but may be isolated from the urine throughout the second week. Fletcher, EMJH, and Tween 80–albumin media are semisolid media useful in primary isolation of leptospires. One to three drops of the specimen to be cultured should be added to 3 to 5 mL of culture medium. The cultures are incubated for 5 to 6 weeks at 28 to 30°C, in the dark. Leptospires grow in a concentrated ring 0.5 to 1 cm below the surface of the medium, usually appearing 6 to 14 days after inoculation. As the organisms remain viable in anticoagulated blood for up to 11 days, specimens can be mailed to a reference laboratory for culture. (Citrate should not be used as the anticoagulant.) A radiometric method using the BACTEC 460 system (Johnston Laboratories) allows detection of leptospires in human blood after only 2 to 5 days of incubation. Leptospires can sometimes be identified by dark-field examination of cerebrospinal fluid by experienced laboratory workers or in tissue specimens by silver impregnation techniques.

Examination of the cerebrospinal fluid reveals abnormalities characteristic of aseptic meningitis; pleocytosis, usually mononuclear; elevated protein concentration; and normal concentration of glucose.

The diagnosis is usually made by serologic tests. The macroscopic slide agglutination test using killed antigen is the most useful for screening, but the microscopic agglutination test using live antigen is more specific. In both tests antigen pools containing representatives of the most common serogroups are used. As there is much cross-reaction among serogroups, many patients exhibit a positive reaction even if they are infected with serogroups not represented in the pools, but a few patients remain seronegative. Agglutinins appear on the 6th to 12th day of illness, and the maximum titer is usually reached in the third or fourth week. Antibiotic therapy may suppress or delay development of an antibody response. If the convalescent serum, drawn at least 2 weeks after onset of illness, is negative, another test should be performed 2 weeks later. Highly specific and sensitive enzyme-linked immunosorbent assay and Dot-enzyme-linked immunosorbent assay techniques for detection of leptospiral immunoglobulin M antibodies have been developed recently.

Recommended Approach

An attempt should be made to isolate leptospires from patients prior to initiation of antibiotic therapy, because only when the organism is isolated can the infecting serotype be accurately identified. Identification of the specific serotype is important to determine which serotypes are likely causes of human and animal infection in a given locality and to detect an epidemiologic connection among infections acquired through exposure to a common source.

Therapeutic

Therapeutic Options

Leptospirosis is usually a mild illness and in these patients antimicrobial therapy may be unnecessary; most patients will have recovered by the time the diagnosis is made. Antibiotic therapy can be effective in severe leptospirosis even when treatment is delayed until relatively late in the course of the illness. A polymerase chain reaction (PCR) has been developed for detection of *Leptospira* but is not widely in use.

Recommended Approach

In severely ill patients treatment with either penicillin G (1.5 million U every 6 hours) or ampicillin (500–1000 mg every 6 hours) should be initiated by the intravenous route even if the patient has been ill for several days. If the patient is allergic to penicillin, doxycycline (100 mg twice daily intravenously) may be used. In less severe cases when the patient can tolerate oral therapy, doxycycline (Vibramycin) 100 mg twice daily; ampicillin 500 to 750 mg every 6 hours; or amoxicillin 500 mg every 6 hours may be used. Treatment should be continued for 5 to 7 days. Doxycycline and other tetracyclines should be avoided in pregnant women and in children under the age of 8.

Careful clinical observation and general supportive therapy are especially important in the management of severe leptospirosis to detect and treat such life-threatening complications as renal failure, hypotension, and hemorrhage. Hemodialysis may be necessary in cases of prolonged severe renal failure. In addition, Jarisch–Herxheimer reactions similar to those seen in syphilis are possible, with hypotension, tachycardia, fever, and death possible within hours of the first adequate dose of antibiotic.

FOLLOW-UP

The natural history and mode of transmission of leptospirosis should be explained to the patient. Education of the patient may allow modifications in the workplace or recreational activities that reduce exposure to leptospires.

Mild anicteric leptospirosis is usually an acute illness from which the patient recovers completely in a short time, and no lengthy follow-up is required. Even in severe Weil's disease, abnormalities in liver function and other manifestations of disease usually return to normal. Severe tubular necrosis, chronic or relapsing uveitis, and rare neurologic complications such as peripheral neuritis, myelitis, and Guillain–Barré syndrome may persist for many weeks or months and require long-term follow-up.

DISCUSSION

Prevalence and Incidence

For the past 20 years, only 50 to 100 cases of leptospirosis have been reported annually in the United States. As most cases are mild and the clinical picture is often nonspecific, the true incidence of leptospirosis is probably significantly higher than these figures indicate. Serologic evidence of prior infection is detected in approximately 15% of abattoir and packing-house workers and veterinarians.

Leptospirosis is a zoonosis of worldwide distribution, affecting many species of wild and domestic mammals. The incidence of human infection, in a particular time and place, is determined by the nature of contact, both direct and indirect, with infected animals. Human beings are usually dead-end hosts; person-to-person transmission is extremely rare. Indirect contact with infected animals, via water or soil contaminated with infected urine, is a more common cause of human infection than direct animal contact. Occupational exposure (farmers, veterinarians, abattoir workers) and recreational exposure (campers, swimmers) are not uncommon. Worldwide, rats are the most common source of human infection; in the United States the most important sources of infection are dogs and livestock. Wild animals represent an important reservoir for continually reinfecting populations of domestic animals.

Related Basic Science

Leptospirosis is primarily a disease of wild and domestic mammals; human beings are infected only incidentally through direct or indirect contact with animals.

After they penetrate the intact mucous membranes or abraded skin, leptospires enter the bloodstream and are rapidly carried to all parts of the body, including the cerebrospinal fluid and eyes. The jaundice that occurs in severe cases is due primarily to hepatocellular dysfunction, usually without necrosis. Renal failure is primarily a result of tubular damage, and leptospires are commonly seen in the tubular lumen. Whether the tubular lesion is due to hypoxemia, or to a direct toxic effect of the leptospires, or to an immunologic reaction is not known. Organisms have disappeared from the cerebrospinal fluid by the time signs of meningitis appear, and the meningitis may be the result of an immunologic reaction.

Natural History and Its Modification with Treatment

Anicteric leptospirosis is nearly always a mild disease, and serious complications of any kind are very uncommon. In jaundiced patients with Weil's disease, renal failure caused by acute tubular necrosis, major hemorrhage in various organs, cardiovascular collapse owing to hemorrhagic myocarditis, meningoencephalitis, and acute cholecystitis may occur.

At present, the case fatality rate in Weil's disease is approximately 5 to 10%; it is significantly higher in individuals older than 60.

Prevention

Prevention of human leptospirosis is very difficult because of the impossibility of eliminating the large animal reservoir of infection. Vaccination of domestic livestock and pets is widely practiced in the United States and has greatly reduced the incidence of infection in some species. Renal infection can still occur in vaccinated dogs, and human beings have become infected from dogs that have been adequately immunized. In some areas effective rat control, disinfection of contaminated work areas, and prohibition of swimming in contaminated waters have effectively reduced the incidence of the disease. Doxycycline 200 mg orally once a week prevents leptospiral infection and may be useful for individuals who anticipate intense exposure for a limited period.

Cost Containment

Early and accurate diagnosis of leptospirosis may obviate the performance of imaging studies and other expensive diagnostic procedures. Prompt and appropriate treatment may shorten the duration of hospitalization and morbidity and reduce the likelihood of serious complications.

REFERENCES

Farrar WE. *Leptospira* species (leptospirosis). In: Mandell GL, Douglas RG, Bennett JE, eds. Principles and practice of infectious disease. 4th ed. New York: Churchill Livingstone, 1995:2137.

Hindrichsen S, Medeiros de Andrade A, Clement J, et al. Hantavirus infection in Brazilian patients from Recife with suspected leptospirosis. Lancet 1993;341:50.

Sanford JP. Leptospirosis. In: Wilson JD, Braunwald E, Isselbacer KJ, et al (eds). Harrison's Principles of internal medicine. 12th ed. New York: McGraw-Hill, 1991:663.

Vaughan C, Cronin CC, Walsh EK, Whelton M. The Jarisch–Herxheimer reaction in leptospirosis. Postgrad Med J 1994;70:118.

Watt G, Padre LP, Tuazon M, Calubaquib C. Skeletal and cardiac muscle involvement in severe, late leptospirosis. J Infect Dis 1990;162:266.

CHAPTER 8–48

Lyme Disease

James P. Steinberg, M.D., and Jonas A. Shulman, M.D.

DEFINITION

Lyme disease, or Lyme borreliosis, is a multisystem vectorborne disease. Early Lyme disease is dominated by a distinctive rash, erythema migrans, whereas the later stages involve the joints, heart, and nervous system.

ETIOLOGY

Lyme disease is caused by the spirochete *Borrelia burgdorferi*. Ticks of the *Ixodes* genus serve as the vector for Lyme disease; the spring and summer feeding of the ticks and the distribution of the ticks and their hosts account for the seasonal and geographic clustering of cases of Lyme disease.

CRITERIA FOR DIAGNOSIS
Suggestive

The diagnosis of early (stage 1) Lyme disease is established clinically, based on the appearance of erythema migrans. The manifestations of early disseminated (stage 2) and late (stage 3) disease are less specific and the diagnosis is usually not made on clinical grounds alone.

Definitive

No supporting serologic or other laboratory data are needed to confirm the diagnosis of erythema migrans.

Diagnosis of the later stages of Lyme disease is usually made by the combination of a compatible clinical illness, exposure to an area where the disease is prevalent, serologic evidence of *B. burgdorferi* infection, and the exclusion of other diseases that can mimic Lyme disease. *Borrelia* cultures are not widely available and are not of sufficient sensitivity to be useful to the clinician.

Lyme disease can be difficult to diagnose. Many of the signs and symptoms are nonspecific, and the commercial serologic assays currently available are neither highly sensitive nor highly specific. In addition, media coverage of Lyme disease, which at times has been more sensational than accurate, has led many persons with a variety of clinical syndromes to seek medical treatment for what they believe to be Lyme disease. Use of the current serologic assays in this population with a low prevalence of disease has resulted in many incorrect diagnoses of Lyme disease.

CLINICAL MANIFESTATIONS
Subjective

Although most patients with Lyme disease reside in, or report travel to, a tick-infested area, only 30% recall a tick bite, probable because of the minute size of the *Ixodes* tick. Most patients with stage 1 Lyme disease complain of a rash that may be pruritic, burning, or occasionally painful. Days to weeks following the initial rash (which occurs at the site of the tick bite), about 50% of untreated patients complain of the development of additional lesions. The rash is often accompanied by constitutional symptoms including fatigue, fever, chills, intermittent myalgias and arthralgias, headaches, and mild neck stiffness.

Patients presenting months following acquisition of the disease may recall a rash (untreated) but usually have symptoms from involvement of the musculoskeletal system, nervous system, and/or heart. This has been called stage 2 or early disseminated infection. Joint pain occurs in more than 60% of patients and is the most common symptom of early disseminated Lyme disease. The arthralgias typically begin weeks to months after infection, are intermittent and migratory, and usually involve one or two joints at a time. The early arthralgias are often followed by more intense pains and swelling of the knees or other large joints. Lasting weeks to months, these episodes of arthritis may be followed by periods of complete remission; however, if left untreated these joint symptoms can wax and wane for years or, rarely, lead to persistent symptoms and disability.

The neurologic symptoms of early disseminated Lyme disease occur in 15 to 20% of patients. The headache that occurs in this stage is more constant than the headache accompanying the rash of early Lyme disease. Patients may also complain of stiff neck, unilateral or bilateral facial droop, paresthesias, pain, or weakness involving an extremity or the trunk. Symptoms of memory loss and mood swings are mild, if present.

Cardiac involvement occurs in 4 to 8% of patients with early disseminated disease, usually within a month of onset of illness. The major symptoms are syncope and dizziness from various degrees of heart block.

We thank Dr. Lincoln Miller for his contribution to this chapter in the third edition of this book.

Persistent infection or stage 3 Lyme disease can develop 1 or more years after initial infection and is dominated by arthritis and involvement of the nervous system. The joint pain that occurs in this stage also involves the large joints more frequently than small joints; unlike the arthritis of early Lyme disease, the pain is more persistent and frequently lasts more than 1 year without remission. Impaired memory, difficulty concentrating, and disordered sleep are common manifestations of the encephalopathy seen in stage 3 Lyme disease. Pain in the area of the spine accompanied by tingling or shooting pains in the extremities occurs with the axonal polyneuropathy of chronic Lyme disease. Some patients complain of a "pins and needles" stocking glove peripheral neuropathy. The entire spectrum of neurologic symptoms and signs of late Lyme disease remains to be defined.

Objective
Physical Examination

Sixty to eighty percent of patients with Lyme disease develop erythema migrans (also called erythema chronicum migrans). This erythematous annular rash develops a few days to 1 month (mean, 7 days) following inoculation of the spirochete. Beginning as a small red macule or papule at the site of the tick bite, the rash gradually expands, reaching a mean diameter of 15 cm, although the size is quite variable and can range from a few centimeters to more than 50 cm in diameter. There usually is some degree of central clearing, but the rash occasionally remains uniformly red or develops concentric rings (Figure 8–48–1). An indurated papule, vesicle, or small area of necrosis may be obvious at the site of the bite. Secondary annular lesions develop days to weeks following the primary erythema migrans lesion in about 50% of cases. These secondary lesions can be numerous, are generally smaller than the primary rash, and lack the central lesion at the site of the bite. Both primary and secondary rashes persist for weeks to several months and can recur. Rarely, patients develop a diffuse erythema, urticaria, malar rash, or conjunctivitis.

The neurologic findings of Lyme disease are diverse. Signs of meningeal irritation may accompany the headache of early disseminated disease. The most common focal finding is facial nerve palsy, which can be unilateral or bilateral. Less common findings include asymmetric motor or sensory radiculopathy, mononeuritis, and myelitis. Late neurologic involvement is characterized by encephalopathy (90%), with memory loss being the most frequent finding, polyradiculopathy (70%), often with diminished sensation on light touch and pinprick testing, and, rarely, leukoencephalitis with spastic paresis.

During the intermittent bouts of arthritis of early disseminated Lyme disease, joint effusions and periarticular swelling are common. The arthritis is usually asymmetric and intermittent, and the knee is the most frequently involved. Lyme disease usually is not confused with

classic septic arthritis, as warmth and erythema are usually much less intense. Only 10% of patients with the arthritis of Lyme disease develop chronic joint disease with progression to erosion of bone and cartilage and loss of joint motion.

The skin lesion acrodermatitis chronica atrophicans has been described primarily in the European literature. The lesion appears on an extremity and is characterized by bluish red plaques or nodules that eventually become atrophic. For unknown reasons, this very late manifestation of Lyme disease is rarely, if ever, seen in the United States.

Routine Laboratory Abnormalities

Routine laboratory tests are usually normal or mildly abnormal but are helpful in excluding other diseases that can mimic Lyme disease. The sedimentation rate is elevated in about 50% of cases. The electrocardiogram can show variable degrees of atrioventricular block including Wenkebach or third-degree heart block with cardiac involvement. Very rarely, an enlarged cardiac silhouette from pericarditis or pancarditis is seen on the chest radiograph. Bone radiographs may show erosive changes of periarticular bone in patients with chronic Lyme arthritis.

PLANS
Diagnostic
Differential Diagnosis

The appearance of erythema migrans is pathognomonic, and the classic rash is readily distinguished from other dermatologic conditions. An early lesion, when small, may have the appearance of a local reaction to an insect bite. The differential diagnosis of erythema migrans also includes erysipelas, contact dermatitis (especially from poison ivy), fixed drug eruption, tinea, and granuloma annulare. Acrodermatitis chronica atrophicans may have the appearance of localized scleroderma. Persistent Lyme disease is frequently confused with other entities whose symptoms are nonspecific, including the chronic fatigue syndrome and fibromyalgia. Unlike Lyme disease, the physical examination is usually normal with these two entities.

Diagnostic Options

The pitfalls in interpreting Lyme serology cannot be overemphasized. The serologic testing that is widely available from commercial laboratories by enzyme-linked immunosorbent assay or indirect fluorescent antibody is not standardized and there is considerable intralaboratory variation in test results. False-positive Lyme serology can occur in 2 to 5% of healthy persons, in patients with autoimmune diseases such as systemic lupus erythematosus and rheumatoid arthritis, and with other spirochetal diseases including syphilis. Lyme disease can in turn cause false-positive specific syphilis serology (FTA). The practice of ordering Lyme serology as part of the evaluation of patients with nonspecific symptoms such as fatigue and depression, especially in areas where Lyme disease is not endemic, has led to many inaccurate diagnoses of Lyme disease. Lyme serologic testing should be requested only to verify a diagnosis that has been suggested by epidemiologic and clinical evidence. Almost all patients with stage 2 or 3 disease have demonstrable antibody to *B. burgdorferi,* and a negative assay performed by a reputable laboratory should raise doubt about the diagnosis of Lyme disease. An exception to this statement is in patients who develop signs of late Lyme after early antibiotic treatment for erythema migrans in which the development of antibody has been aborted. In these patients, T-cell proliferative responses to *B. burgdorferi* can be demonstrated. The incidence of seronegative Lyme disease has not been determined but is probably less than 5%.

The Western blot for Lyme disease is more specific than either the enzyme-linked immunosorbent assay or the indirect fluorescent antibody test and, although not standardized, can be used to confirm indeterminate or positive screening tests. Serologic tests using recombinant spirochetal antigens will probably replace the current generation of tests.

Spirochetes have occasionally been seen and cultivated from a variety of tissues; however, these diagnostic measures are low yield and not routinely performed.

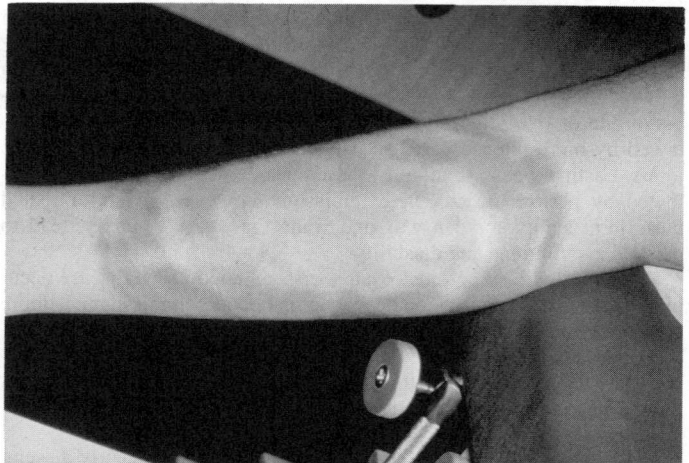

Figure 8–48–1. Annular rash of erythema migrans. *(From Centers for Disease Control and Prevention, Atlanta, GA, (public domain.)*

Recommended Approach

The diagnosis of erythema migrans is made by the characteristic appearance of the rash and a history of possible exposure to *B. burgdorferi*. In this setting, serologic confirmation of the diagnosis is not needed and, in fact, may not be possible. Only a minority of patients with erythema migrans have detectable antibody to *B. burgdorferi* at the time of presentation, and if prompt antibiotic therapy is administered, seroconversion may not occur.

Because of the problem of false-positive Lyme serology and because of a background seroprevalence of up to 10% in endemic areas, a positive serologic test for Lyme disease in a patient with neurologic or joint symptoms may not be sufficient evidence to establish the diagnosis of Lyme disease. In patients with meningitis during the early disseminated period, the cerebrospinal fluid may simulate the findings seen in viral meningitis, with a lymphocytic pleocytosis of 100 cells/mm^3, mildly elevated protein level, and normal glucose concentration. Objective evidence of neurologic impairment should be sought in patients with syndromes compatible with chronic neuroborreliosis. Patients with encephalopathy usually have objective evidence of memory impairment or abnormal cerebrospinal fluid studies. The majority of patients with polyradiculopathy have abnormal electrophysiologic evidence of axonal polyneuropathy or electromyographic evidence of denervation. Measurement of intrathecal production of antibody to *B. burgdorferi* in patients with suspected neuroborreliosis can be very useful diagnostically.

Synovial fluid in patients with arthritis has a variable white blood cell count that can range from 500 to more than 100,000/mm^3 with a neutrophilic predominance. Immune complexes are invariably present. Polymerase chain reaction can detect *B. burgdorferi* DNA from the synovial fluid of patients with Lyme arthritis. This test may prove useful to distinguish patients with active spirochetal infection from those whose joint symptoms are due to autoreactivity. An autoimmune process, perhaps stimulated by spirochetal antigens, may be the cause of the chronic arthritis that develops in about 10% of patients and may be refractory to antibiotic therapy. These patients are more likely to have HLA-DR4 and perhaps HLA-DR2.

Therapeutic

Therapeutic Options and Recommended Approach

Current antibiotic recommendations for the treatment of Lyme disease are listed in Table 8–48–1. No regimen is 100% effective and relapse

TABLE 8–48–1. TREATMENT REGIMENS FOR LYME DISEASE

A. Manifestations for Which Oral Therapy Is Usually Effective
Erythema migrans
Early disseminated disease
Arthritis
First-degree atrioventricular block with PR interval < 0.3 s
Facial palsy
Acrodermatitis

Oral Regimens*

Adults	Children
Doxycycline 100 mg bid	Amoxicillin 50 mg/kg/d divided tid
Amoxicillin 500 mg tid	Cefuroxime axetil 250 mg bid
Alternative: cefuroxime axetil 500 mg bid	Erythromycin 250 mg or 30 mg/kg/d in divided doses (for penicillin allergy)

B. Manifestations That Require Parenteral Therapy
Neurologic disease
Cardiac disease with high-grade atrioventricular block
On occasion, refractory arthritis

Parenteral Regimens†

Adults	Children
Ceftriaxone 2 g daily	Ceftriaxone 75–100 mg/kg/d
Cefotraxime 2 g three times a day	Penicillin G 300,000 U/kg/d
Penicillin G 20–24 million U daily	

*Erythema migrans is usually treated for 10 to 21 days. For other manifestations, the oral regimen is generally continued for 20 to 30 days.
†Parenteral therapy is usually given for 14 to 28 days.

can occur after treatment of any stage of illness; however, prompt therapy for erythema migrans is less likely to be associated with long-term morbidity than treatment of later stages. Doxycycline and amoxicillin are considered the first-line oral agents for adults. Neurologic disease is treated with parenteral agents, although some suggest that patients with isolated facial nerve palsy with normal cerebrospinal fluid can be treated with oral medication. In addition to the antimicrobial therapy administered for cardiac disease, a temporary cardiac pacemaker may be needed for severe heart block. Because the heart block is transient, a permanent pacemaker is rarely required. Patients with chronic arthritis refractory to antibiotic therapy may benefit from antiinflammatory agents or arthroscopic synovectomy. Major therapeutic questions that remain unanswered at this time include the following: When should parenteral agents be instituted to treat arthritis? When should patients with persistent neurologic or joint disease be re-treated? What is the optimal treatment during pregnancy? There are no well-controlled studies to support long-term (e.g., several months) parenteral therapy for chronic neurologic syndromes. This approach, which has vocal advocates, has been associated with line-related sepsis and ceftriaxone-induced biliary tract disease.

FOLLOW-UP

Patients with erythema migrans require follow-up if the diagnosis is uncertain, if the rash fails to respond as expected, or if additional manifestations of Lyme disease develop. With appropriate antibiotic therapy, the rash should begin to fade within a few days to 1 week. Because the symptoms and signs of disseminated disease can take weeks to months to respond to therapy and can recur despite therapy, patients with the later stages may require long-term follow-up. Antibodies to *B. burgdorferi* may decline following therapy, but the response is highly variable. Consequently, measurement of serial titers to assess response to therapy is not recommended.

DISCUSSION
Prevalence and Incidence

Lyme disease is the most common vectorborne disease in the United States. More than 50,000 cases have been reported to the Centers for Disease Control and Prevention since surveillance was initiated in 1982. After increasing dramatically during the 1980s, the number of reported cases reached a plateau in 1989; in 1993, about 8000 cases were reported. Whether this plateau represents an artifact of reporting or a true stabilization of the number of cases is unknown. Because of the problems of overdiagnosis, misclassification, and underreporting, the actual incidence of Lyme disease is unknown. Lyme disease has been reported from more than 40 states, but the vast majority of cases occur in three regions: a crescent from coastal Massachusetts to New Jersey, rural Wisconsin and Minnesota, and near the northern California–Oregon border. Lyme disease has also been reported from Europe, Great Britain, Russia, China, Japan, and Australia.

Related Basic Science

Several species of *Ixodes* ticks have been implicated in disease transmission including *I. scapularis* (*I. dammini*) in the Northeast and Midwest, *I. pacificus* in California and Oregon, and *I. ricinus* in Europe. In highly endemic areas on the East Coast, up to 50% of adult *Ixodes* ticks harbor *B. burgdorferi*. The size and range of the tick population in turn are dependent on the number of white-tailed deer, which is the preferred host for the adult tick. Although not important in determining the range of the tick population, the white-footed mouse, *peromyscus leucopus,* is important for disease transmission because the mouse can develop a chronic spirochetemia, which serves to transmit the spirochete from tick to tick. In Europe, the mammalian hosts for the *Ixodes* ticks are somewhat different and the transmission cycles are more complex.

During its 2-year lifespan, an *Ixodes* tick feeds once during each of the three developmental stages. The newly hatched larval tick feeds in late summer; if the blood meal is taken from a spirochetemic mouse, the spirochetes infect the tick and remain in the midgut. The following spring or early summer, the infected nymphal tick transmits the spirochete during its blood meal. At the time of feeding, the spirochetes migrate to the tick's salivary glands, prior to infecting the host. Because both the larval and nymphal stages frequently feed on the white-footed mouse, the spirochete can be transmitted from one generation of tick to the next (horizontal transmission). The adult tick feeds in autumn, typically on the white-tailed deer. All stages of the tick can feed on many hosts, but the nymph is more inclined to feed on humans and thus is the major vector for Lyme disease. The nymphal tick is minute, about the size of the head of a pin (Figure 8–48–2); consequently, most patients with Lyme disease do not recall a tick bite.

Laboratory models have shown that the tick must be attached to the host for at least 24 hours to allow transmission of the spirochete. Erythema migrans is initiated by local proliferation of the spirochete at the site of the tick bite. The organism has been visualized in and recovered from the skin lesion. When bacteremic spread of the organism occurs, the constitutional symptoms of disseminated disease and the manifestations of the musculoskeletal, nervous system, and cardiac systems appear. Chronic arthritis develops predominantly in individuals with particular major histocompatibility complex class II alleles, suggesting that some of the chronic signs of disease may be due to autoreactivity rather than spirochetal proliferation. This explanation could account for the persistence or recurrence of disease following antibiotic treatment. On the other hand, spirochetes have been seen isolated from joints, skin, and other organs years after disease onset, suggesting that at least some of the later manifestations are due to persistence of microbial infection.

Natural History and Its Modification with Treatment

The separation of clinical disease into stages is imperfect and is taken from similar classifications used with other spirochetal diseases such as syphilis. The stages may overlap clinically and temporally, and classification is not meant to imply a necessary progression from one stage to the next. For example, some patients have erythema migrans (stage 1 or early localized disease) and never develop a recognized disseminated disease (stage 2). Others may develop chronic arthritis or late neurologic disease (stage 3) without prior recognized Lyme disease. The presence of antibody to *B. burgdorferi* in asymptomatic residents of endemic areas suggests that subclinical disease may occur. Subclinical infection is more common in Europe. Other differences in European Lyme disease include a lower incidence of erythema migrans, late dermatologic manifestations such as acrodermatitis chronica atrophicans, an infrequency of joint findings, and a different spectrum of neurologic disease. These clinical distinctions are probable due to differences in the prevalent strains of *B. burgdorferi,* a concept supported by DNA relatedness studies.

Most patients who receive appropriate treatment for erythema migrans have no long-term sequelae; however, persons with a longer duration of infection prior to antibiotic therapy have more chronic joint symptoms and more memory impairment compared to those without a history of Lyme disease. Chronic arthritis and encephalitis may lead to significant long-term disability in a small number of cases. Fatal pancarditis has been reported, but deaths from Lyme disease are very rare. Transplacental transmission of *B. burgdorferi* can occur but is rare.

Prevention

Patients who reside in areas endemic for *B. burgdorferi* should cover their extremities and/or use insect repellents in the spring and summer

Figure 8–48–2. Larval, nymphal, and adult (smallest to largest) stages of *Borrelia burgdorferi. (From Centers for Disease Control and Prevention, Atlanta, GA, public domain.)*

when exposure to ticks can be anticipated. Nightly "tick checks" have been advocated. Prophylactic antibiotics following tick bite have not been recommended because the risk of disease following tick bite is under 2%, even in endemic areas. Informing patients that ticks must feed longer than 24 hours to transmit Lyme disease often reassures the anxious patient who has discovered a tick. In some areas, efforts have been made to control the resident deer population and/or to reduce the number of ticks.

Cost Containment

Judicious ordering of Lyme serology would minimize the number of false-positive diagnoses and thus reduce unnecessary treatment. Use of oral rather than parenteral regimens, when appropriate, dramatically reduces cost. Because ceftriaxone (Rocephin) can be administered once a day, parenteral treatment of Lyme disease, when indicated, can usually be accomplished on an outpatient basis, reducing the need for costly hospitalization. Long-term or chronic antibiotic administration for persistent symptoms is not warranted; oftentimes the persistent symptoms are caused by entities other than Lyme disease.

REFERENCES

Barbour AG, Fish D. The biologic and social phenomenon of Lyme disease. Science 1993;260:1610.

Logigian EL, Kaplan RF, Steere AC. Chronic neurologic manifestations of Lyme disease. N Engl J Med 1990;323:1438.

Nocton JJ, Dressler F, Rutledge BJ, et al. Detection of *Borrelia burgdorferi* DNA by polymerase chain reaction in synovial fluid from patients with Lyme disease. N Engl J Med 1994;330:229.

Rahn DW, Malawista SE. Lyme disease: Recommendations for diagnosis and treatment. Ann Intern Med 1991;114:472.

Steere AC. Lyme disease. N Engl J Med 1989;321:586.

CHAPTER 8–49
Rocky Mountain Spotted Fever
Jonas A. Shulman, M.D.

DEFINITION

Rocky Mountain spotted fever is a serious disease caused by *Rickettsia rickettsii.* The organism invades the vascular endothelium throughout the entire body. The disease is seen in individuals who live outside the Rocky Mountain area and is much more complicated than the name implies.

ETIOLOGY

Rocky Mountain spotted fever is caused by *R. rickettsii,* which, like other Rickettsiaceae, is an intracellular parasite that is usually maintained in an insect–animal reservoir (see Related Basic Science).

CRITERIA FOR DIAGNOSIS

In the appropriate clinical setting, a fourfold rise in specific antibodies to *R. rickettsii* (complement fixation, rickettsial microagglutination, or indirect fluorescent antibody) from acute to convalescent serum is a simple marker for the specific diagnosis of Rocky Mountain spotted fever. Diagnosis by this serologic test is helpful only retrospectively, however, as the specific antibody titer rises too late in the clinical course for adequate therapy to be initiated if fatalities are to be prevented.

Suggestive

Most clinicians would consider the sudden onset of fever, headache, and appropriate skin rash as grounds for treatment in the right epidemiologic setting, especially if a history of tick contact can be ascertained.

Definitive

An immunofluorescence technique for detecting the specific antigen of the *Rickettsia* in skin lesion biopsies or conjunctival biopsies is useful for rapid diagnosis. Cultures and animal inoculations are rarely performed in the clinical laboratory setting.

CLINICAL MANIFESTATIONS
Subjective

The patient usually complains of a sudden onset of fever, headache, and myalgias, followed in a few days by a rash (Table 8–49–1). The rash usually begins on the extremities, especially the wrists, ankles, feet, and hands (including palms and soles), and spreads to the trunk. The patient may come from any state, but the majority of cases are reported from the southeastern part of the United States and occur from May to September. The south-central states such as Oklahoma and Texas also report numerous cases. The history of a tick bite or of possible tick exposure 2 to 7 days before abrupt illness begins is frequently obtained. In severe cases, mental confusion may be noted.

TABLE 8–49–1. CLUES TO EARLY CLINICAL RECOGNITION OF ROCKY MOUNTAIN SPOTTED FEVER

- Sudden onset of fever in spring or summer
- Severe unrelenting headache
- Muscle aches and tenderness
- Early appearance of rash on wrists and ankles
- Rash on palms and soles
- Splenomegaly
- Periorbital nonpitting edema of face or extremities
- Shift toward immature polymorphonuclear lymphocytes

Objective
Physical Examination

The patient may appear confused or obtunded and may look very ill in severe cases. By the third to fifth day of the illness, a rash is noted in more than 90% of patients. Initially, the rash is macular and occurs about the wrists and ankles; it then spreads to the trunk and, at times, the face. The rash progresses, especially if treatment is delayed, to a maculopapular and eventually a petechial rash. The characteristic spread and the involvement of the palms and soles with a nontender rash are diagnostic features. In severe cases, purpura and necrotic lesions may appear. Enlargement of the spleen and, at times, the liver is noted in some patients. Rarely, findings of pneumonitis, myocarditis, renal failure, and vascular collapse are present.

Routine Laboratory Abnormalities

Laboratory findings include a variable leukocyte count with a frequent increase in polymorphonuclear leukocytes and/or bands. Thrombocytopenia is common, and disseminated intravascular clotting can occur. Hyponatremia is also common.

PLANS
Diagnostic
Differential Diagnosis

The differential diagnosis of fever and rash should be reviewed (see Chapter 8–5). Possibilities include febrile viral exanthems, measles, atypical measles, meningococcemia, infectious mononucleosis, toxic shock syndrome, relapsing fever, typhoid fever, and leptospirosis, as well as drug rash in the setting of another cause of fever. If thrombocytopenia is marked, vasculitis or idiopathic or thrombotic thrombocytopenia purpura may be suspected. Other rickettsial diseases such as murine or epidemic typhus may be considered but are distinctly less common, and the evolution of the rash is quite different. Epidemic typhus has been reported in the United States and must be differentiated on the basis of serologic tests. Before the rash appears, the illness is impossible to differentiate from other severe febrile illnesses, but the occurrence of fever, headache, and myalgias in an appropriate epidemiologic setting may be very suggestive and may require empiric treatment, especially if a history of tick exposure is obtained. Ehrlichiosis is a newly recognized disease that may resemble Rocky Mountain spotted fever, is tickborne, and in some areas of the country may be more common than the rickettsial diseases. Rash may occur but is not a common feature. If ehrlichiosis is suspected, specific serologic studies should be obtained (see Chapter 8–50).

Diagnostic Options and Recommended Approach

Specific serologic findings (as noted above) on both acute and convalescent sera are the most practical diagnostic tests. Isolation of the organism from blood, although very specific, is possible in embryonated chicken eggs or in guinea pigs; however, it is hazardous and is not a rapid technique. These procedures should be attempted only in research-oriented laboratories. The Weil–Felix reaction is not very sensitive or specific and should not be used unless specific serologic tests cannot be obtained. Remember that diagnostic titers in any of these serologic tests are not reached until the second week of illness, and the physician cannot wait for these confirmatory tests to begin treatment. If direct immunofluorescence tests are available to detect antigen in skin biopsies, a rapid laboratory diagnosis may be possible.

Because of the need for an early diagnosis, the clinical features noted above must be used to decide whether treatment should be started.

Therapy should never be delayed while awaiting laboratory confirmation.

Therapeutic

Tetracycline (2 g/d in an adult) or chloramphenicol (3–4 g/d in an adult) is very effective, especially if therapy is started early. Improvement is noted in 24 to 48 hours, although the fever may persist 3 to 4 days. Therapy is usually given for 10 days.

Complications that may require supportive therapy include myocarditis, congestive heart failure, azotemia, thrombocytopenia, disseminated intravascular coagulation, adult respiratory distress syndrome, and hypovolemia. Corticosteroids may prove helpful in severely ill individuals.

Inform the patient of the diagnosis and tell him or her that the outlook with appropriate therapy is very good. Other family members or friends should be seen by a physician if fever and headache occur, as they too may have been exposed to infected ticks in the same area.

Methods of tick removal should be taught to everyone exposed to the same environment.

Recovery is usually complete, although occasionally severe vasculitis may cause gangrene or the vasculitis may cause an injury that does not completely recover in any area of potential vascular damage such as the brain, lungs, and heart. One should follow patients until clinical and laboratory findings have returned to normal.

DISCUSSION

Prevalence and Incidence

Human beings are only occasionally infected, usually by the bite of a tick, but sometimes by aerosolization or mucous membrane contact in the laboratory. In the United States, the disease has been increasing in incidence and has been reported in almost all states. More than half the patients come from southeastern states, especially Virginia, Tennessee, North and South Carolina, Maryland, and Georgia. Less than 5% of patients currently come from the Rocky Mountain region. Recently, Oklahoma, Texas, and Arkansas have reported numerous cases. Focal "hot spots" of high attack rates within states are common. Most cases occur in spring and summer when ticks are active. Dogs may be important in transferring infected ticks from woody areas into the more immediate human environment.

Related Basic Science

The tick vectors include the dog tick, *Dermacentor variabilis;* the wood tick, *D. andersoni;* and the Lone Star tick. Once infected, these ticks are infected for life and may pass the infection to offspring by maternal transovarian transmission, or they may infect rodents or other mammals, including, on rare occasions, human beings.

Once the organisms are inoculated into a human being, a diffuse infection of the vascular endothelium occurs throughout the microvasculature after a 2- to 7-day incubation period. This vasculitis is the basic lesion of the disease and involves the skin, heart, brain, muscles, and lung. Thrombosis and microinfarction may occur. Fluid leaking into the extravascular space because of the vascular injury can occur and can

lead to hypoalbuminemia, renal failure, and/or shock. Depending on the degree of injury to the various organs, myocarditis, heart failure, coma, and renal failure can occur. Thrombocytopenia with or without disseminated intravascular clotting is also thought to be related at least in part to the vasculitis.

Natural History and Its Modification with Treatment

In untreated patients, this disease has a mortality of 10 to 50% depending on the age of the patient, incubation period, and probably strain variations in virulence. With treatment, the mortality is now about 5 to 10%, with more deaths occurring in the older age group. If patients receive appropriate treatment within the first 6 days of illness, the mortality can be reduced essentially to zero. Early clinical suspicion leading to specific therapy is the key. Some fatalities have occurred in patients for whom the illness was atypical, in whom the rash had been missed or was not present, when the clinician was awaiting laboratory confirmation before treatment was given, or when no exposure to ticks was noted.

Prevention

Avoidance of contact with areas infected with ticks, use of insect repellents and protective clothing, and body searches to remove attached ticks are the mainstays of prevention. When removing ticks, the use of tweezers to remove the whole tick and careful washing of the area are helpful. Infected ticks should not be pulled off by hand, as crushing the tick can contaminate the wound or cause finger abrasions. A killed vaccine of questionable merit has been used primarily for laboratory workers.

Cost Containment

The diagnosis and treatment are very inexpensive. Hospitalization may be required if the patient is very ill, and the expense, of course, varies with the complications. Early diagnosis and treatment markedly reduce the possibility of serious complications. Prevention of the disease by preventing prolonged tick attachment helps reduce the incidence and in this way reduces the cost of this infection.

REFERENCES

Centers for Disease Control and Prevention. Rocky Mountain spotted fever and human ehrlichiosis—United States, 1989. MMWR 1990;39:281.

Helmick CG, Bernard KW, D'Angelo LJ. Rocky Mountain spotted fever: Clinical, laboratory, and epidemiological features of 262 cases. J Infect Dis 1984;150:480.

Kirk JL, Fine DP, Sexton DJ, Muchmore HG. Rocky Mountain spotted fever: A clinical review based on 48 confirmed cases, 1943–1986. Medicine 1990;69:35.

Salgo MP, Telzak EE, Currie B, et al. A focus of Rocky Mountain spotted fever within New York City. N Engl J Med 1988;318:1345.

Sellers TF Jr. Rocky Mountain spotted fever. In: Spittell JA Jr, ed. Practice of medicine. Vol. 3. Hagerstown, MD: Harper & Row, 1975:1.

Walker DH, Cain BG, Olmstead PM. Laboratory diagnosis of Rocky Mountain spotted fever by immunofluorescent demonstration of *Rickettsia rickettsii* in cutaneous lesions. Am J Clin Pathol 1978;69:619.

CHAPTER 8–50

Other Rickettsial Diseases (Including Q Fever and Ehrlichiosis)

Sue Anne Brenner, M.D., and David Rimland, M.D.

DEFINITION

The rickettsiae are obligate intracellular Gram-negative coccobacilli that are transmitted by fleas, ticks, mites, and lice, causing a variety of febrile diseases. Q fever (Q for query) is a febrile illness, usually pneumonia, usually transmitted by animal contact. Ehrlichiosis is a febrile illness transmitted by ticks.

ETIOLOGY

Rickettsial diseases are caused by microorganisms of the family Rickettsiaceae. Q fever is caused by *Coxiella burnetti.* Ehrlichiosis is caused by *Ehrlichia chafeensis* and possibly by other related *Ehrlichia* species.

CRITERIA FOR DIAGNOSIS
Suggestive

The triad of fever, headache, and rash occurring during the appropriate season and epidemiologic setting should suggest a rickettsial disease. There may be myalgias, nausea, vomiting, diarrhea, chest pain, and cough. Q fever is generally not associated with a rash, and *E. chafeensis* and murine typhus infections are not associated with rashes in many cases. Even in Rocky Mountain spotted fever, a rash is not seen in 10% of cases.

Definitive

The diagnosis of these diseases is made serologically by a significant (fourfold) increase in titers as determined by specific serologic tests (complement fixation, direct or indirect immunofluorescence, or enzyme-linked immunosorbent assay). In Rocky Mountain spotted fever the organism may be found in the skin or conjunctival biopsy by immunofluorescent staining, and immunohistologic stains are available for detection of *Rickettsia typhi* (murine typhus) in affected tissues. Isolation of the organism is possible but is performed in only a few laboratories. Polymerase chain reaction methods are available for many of these illnesses in a few laboratories, but the clinical utility of these tests has not been well defined.

CLINICAL MANIFESTATIONS

The geographic distribution, epidemiologic setting, insect vector, animal reservoir, type of rash, and other symptomatology of each of the rickettsialike diseases are presented in Table 8–50–1. Rocky Mountain spotted fever is presented as a separate topic in Chapter 8–49.

In general, rickettsial diseases produce fever, headache, and myalgias followed within 2 to 5 days by rash. Brill–Zinsser disease, recrudescent *Rickettsia prowazekii,* may occur decades after the original infection. In Q fever, rash is rare. The patient may be asymptomatic or

present with an abrupt onset of an influenza-like illness with fever, headache, myalgias, severe malaise, mild nonproductive cough, sore throat, and profuse sweating. Rarely, jaundice may be present. The incubation period for Q fever is 2 to 6 weeks.

In ehrlichiosis, a macular rash is present in less than half the patients. Onset is usually abrupt. Frequently there is a history of a tick bite 1 to 3 weeks prior to illness onset.

Objective
Physical Examination

The rash is usually macular or maculopapular, progresses from the trunk to the extremities (unlike Rocky mountain spotted fever), and may become petechial. In contrast to the others, rickettsialpox is heralded by a single papule that enlarges, becomes an eschar, and is followed by a macular rash that becomes vesicular within a few days; local cutaneous reactions may also be seen with scrub typhus and boutonneuse fever. In louseborne typhus (*R. prowazekii*), the rash may become evident in the axillary folds. The spectrum of disease varies from a mild illness (e.g., rickettsialpox) to a severe life-threatening illness (e.g., epidemic typhus). Vascular events such as cerebral thrombosis and peripheral gangrene may occur.

In Q fever, physical examination is usually negative except for fever (101–105°F), occasional rales on chest examination, and infrequent hepatomegaly and splenomegaly. Rarely, signs of infective endocarditis (see Chapter 8–12) may be present in the chronic form of the disease, and there may be no fever. Most cases of Q fever endocarditis involve the aortic or mitral valve in patients with prosthetic valves or preexisting valvular disease. Cases have occurred as long as 20 years after *C. burnetti* exposure. Other complications of Q fever include encephalitis, pericarditis, myocarditis, osteomyelitis, bone marrow necrosis, vascular graft infection, palpable purpura, and hemolytic anemia.

In ehrlichiosis, lymphadenopathy, edema of the extremities, respiratory insufficiency (up to one in five patients require mechanical ventila-

TABLE 8–50–1. CLINICAL MANIFESTATIONS OF THE OTHER RICKETTSIAL DISEASES

Disease	Subjective				Objective	
	Geographic Exposure	Arthropod/ Animal Exposure	Epidemiologic Setting	Symptoms*	Signs†	Routine Laboratory Findings
Rickettsialpox	United States, former USSR, Korea, Africa	Mite bite/mouse	Poor urban settings	Chills, photophobia, sore throat, cough	Eschar at site of bite	Moderate leukopenia Elevated sedimentation rate
Epidemic typhus	South America, Africa, Asia, United States	Louse bite/human Flying squirrel in United States	Wintertime; extreme crowding	Severe prostration	Petechial component to rash	
Brill–Zinsser	Immigrants from any areas with epidemic typhus	None except for primary infection	Variable	Milder than epidemic typhus	Rash in only 60–80%	
Murine typhus	Worldwide	Flea bite/rodents	Summer and autumn; rat exposure, especially in southeastern United States	Milder than epidemic typhus	Truncal rash in many which may spread to extremities; pneumonitis not uncommon	
Scrub typhus	South Pacific, Asia, Australia	Mite bite (chigger)/ wild rodents	In United States only imported cases	Cough	Eschar (80%), adenopathy, splenomegaly, conjnctivitis, delirium followed by maculopapular rash	Leukopenia (40%), lymphocytosis, occasionally proteinuria, occasionally elevated liver enzymes
Q fever	Worldwide	No vector/sheep, cattle, goats	Animal exposure	Cough, sore throat, fever		Pulmonary infiltrates, elevated liver enzymes
Ehrlichiosis	Worldwide	Tick bite	Summer; rural and suburban	Nausea, cough	Rash in less than half	Leukopenia, thrombocytopenia, elevated transaminase levels

*All have myalgias, fever, and headache.
†Most have rash.

tion), hepatitis, renal insufficiency, central nervous system abnormalities, disseminated intravascular coagulation, and gastrointestinal hemorrhage can occur.

Routine Laboratory Abnormalities

In many rickettsial diseases, leukopenia occurs early during the disease, with leukocytosis later; there may be thrombocytopenia, anemia, and coagulopathy. Often hepatic transaminases are mildly elevated. Spinal fluid often shows a lymphocytic pleocytosis and elevated protein.

In Q fever, the white blood cell count may be normal or elevated. Anemia, hyperglobulinemia, elevated erythrocyte sedimentation rate, and elevation of liver enzymes (two to three times normal) are often present. In Q fever meningitis, spinal fluid may be normal or show a lymphocytic or, rarely, a neutrophilic pleocytosis; the protein is usually elevated.

Unlike Q fever, in ehrlichiosis, the white blood cell count may be reduced, with neutropenia, lymphopenia, or both. Thrombocytopenia and elevated serum transaminase levels are also seen. Spinal fluid usually shows a lymphocytic pleocytosis and elevated protein.

PLANS
Diagnostic
Differential Diagnosis

This group of rickettsial diseases must be differentiated from other illnesses that induce fever and a rash (see Chapter 8–5). The symptoms and signs of Q fever are very nonspecific and suggest a variety of diseases. These diseases should be considered in the differential diagnosis of several pneumonias (Mycoplasma, Legionnaire's disease, psittacosis, tularemia), hepatitis (especially granulomatous hepatitis), and culture-negative endocarditis. The differential diagnosis may also include infectious mononucleosis, varicella, measles, rubella, typhoid fever, toxic shock syndrome, brucellosis, Dengue fever, Colorado tick fever, babesiosis, Lyme disease, meningococcemia, gonococcemia, toxic shock syndrome, secondary syphilis, leptospirosis, hepatitis, enteroviral infection, typhoid fever, collagen–vascular diseases, and neoplasms. Simultaneous infection with more than one arthropod-borne disease can occur.

Diagnostic Options

Routine blood cultures are negative. The Weil–Felix reaction is available in many hospital laboratories, but is very nonspecific, becoming positive only after 2 to 3 weeks of illness. Group-specific and type-specific complement fixation tests are usually available only at state laboratories and, again, are usually not positive before 2 to 3 weeks. If Brill–Zinsser disease is a consideration, anti-R. prowazekii immunoglobulin G level will be high, with a low immunoglobulin M level. Indirect immunofluorescence assays are available for some rickettsial diseases, including Q fever and ehrlichiosis. Immunohistologic analysis of skin biopsies has recently been described for rickettsialpox and may become useful for other rickettsial diseases. The specific reactions for rickettsial diseases are listed in Table 8–50–2.

Chest x-ray films often show infiltrates, most frequently in the lower lobes in Q fever.

Recommended Approach

If the clinical picture suggests any of these diseases, the appropriate serology (see the above section) should be ordered. A fourfold rise in serologic titer between ill and convalescent sera (6–8 weeks after presentation) is confirmatory. Early antibiotic treatment, though recommended, may blunt the antibody response.

Therapeutic
Therapeutic Options

Because serology is usually not suggestive of infection until the second week of infection, usually, if a rickettsial disease is suspected, therapy should be started without waiting for a definitive diagnosis. For all these rickettsial diseases, the treatment is tetracycline (25 mg/kg/d),

TABLE 8–50–2. SPECIFIC SEROLOGIC REACTIONS FOR EACH RICKETTSIAL DISEASE

Disease	Agent	Weil–Felix Reactions*			Complement† Fixation
		OX-19	OX-2	OX-K	
Rocky Mountain spotted fever	Rickettsia rickettsii	+	+	−	+
Rickettsialpox	R. akari	−	−	−	+
Epidemic typhus	R. prowazekii	+	±	−	+ (IgM, IgG)
Brill–Zinsser disease	R. prowazekii	±	−	−	+ (IgG)
Murine typhus	R. typhi	+	±	−	+
Scrub typhus	R. tsutsugamushi	−	−	− (50%)	+ (with specific antigens)
Q fever	Coxiella burnetti	−	−	−	+
Ehrlichiosis	Ehrlichia chafeensis	−	−	−	Serologic test (IFA+)

Ig, immunoglobulin; IFA, indirect fluorescent antibody.
*Significant titers include a fourfold rise between acute and convalescent sera or a single titer ≥ 1/160.
†For the specific antigen.

doxycycline (100 mg orally twice daily), or chloramphenicol (50 mg/kg/d) given in four equal doses. Fluoroquinolones may also be effective. For scrub typhus, some data suggest that tetracycline produces a better response. The duration of therapy is not clear, but at least 3 to 5 days, including at least 2 days after response, seems reasonable.

Although most cases of Q fever are self-limited, there is no way to predict which patients will develop complications, so it is reasonable to treat all patients with active infection. Q fever hepatitis can be treated for 2 weeks. The chronic form of Q fever, subacute endocarditis, requires many months of therapy and often valve excision for cure. Tetracycline or doxycycline plus trimethoprim–sulfamethoxazole or rifampin have been used. In a recent study, doxycycline plus pefloxacin or ofloxacin led to a mortality rate lower than those resulting from other antibiotic regimens. Chloroquine plus doxycycline is currently being investigated and shows preliminary favorable results. Therapy for 3 years or until antibody titers fall is recommended; some authors recommend treatment indefinitely for endocarditis.

Doxycycline and chloramphenicol have been used to treat ehrlichiosis, but there are no definitive studies comparing the two regimens. Appropriate facilities for patients who require intensive care should be available.

Recommended Approach

Doxycycline or tetracycline for 6 to 10 days can be used to treat uncomplicated rickettsial diseases. Uncomplicated Q fever can be treated with doxycycline. For Q fever hepatitis, doxycycline should be continued for 2 weeks. For patients with Q fever endocarditis, treatment consisting of 2 years or more of doxycycline plus a fluoroquinolone (see above) may be the best regimen.

Doxycycline 100 mg twice daily or tetracycline 25 mg/kg/d in four doses should be continued for several days (total of 6–10 days) after defervescence for patients with ehrlichiosis.

FOLLOW-UP

With therapy, defervescence usually occurs within 72 hours. Patients showing rapid resolution of clinical findings with therapy do not need any specific follow-up except for an analysis of convalescent serum to confirm the diagnosis. Some patients may relapse if treated early in the course of the disease; these patients may need to be seen 1 to 2 weeks after treatment. Occasional relapses occur in Q fever, so the patient should be told to return if symptoms recur. Patients with chronic Q fever should have serum titers checked every 6 months while on therapy and every 3 months for the first 2 years after completion of therapy. Individuals with a history of infection or exposure to Q fever may remain seropositive for a long time.

DISCUSSION
Prevalence and Incidence

Rickettsial diseases can be seen where arthropod vectors are found. Louseborne typhus can occur in epidemics when people are placed in crowded conditions where bathing and changing of clothes occur infrequently (wars, disasters).

Q fever is endemic in many countries. The organism is ubiquitous and infects many animals; cattle, sheep, and goats are the primary reservoirs for humans. The disease in humans has a worldwide prevalence, although its incidence is unknown. It is usually an occupational disease (abattoir workers, farmers, veterinarians, goatherds). It is more common in spring and summer.

Ehrlichiosis is seen in areas where tick exposure is common, including rural, recreational, domestic, and occupational settings. In the United States, it has been found primarily in the southern, central, mid-Atlantic, and a few western states. *Ehrlichia sennetsu* infection is seen in Japan.

Related Basic Science

Rickettsia are obligate intracellular organisms producing a broad range of diseases. Other obligate intracellular bacteria include organisms in the genera *Coxiella* (Q fever) and *Ehrlichia* (ehrlichiosis). Except for louseborne epidemic typhus, human beings are an incidental host; the natural reservoirs are usually small mammals and insects. Numerous strains of *Rickettsia* have been described worldwide, but only a few of the rickettsial diseases are endemic in the United States: Rocky Mountain spotted fever, murine typhus, rickettsialpox, and Brill–Zinsser disease. Recently, epidemic typhus has been recognized as enzootic in flying squirrels in the United States, and human cases have been detected.

The pathogenesis of many of these rickettsial diseases is identical to that of Rocky Mountain spotted fever: infection of endothelial cells with a resultant vasculitis. All the clinical findings are secondary to this vasculitis. In Q fever and ehrlichiosis, however, there is generally no vasculitis.

Q fever is caused by *Coxiella burnetti,* a rod-shaped intracellular organism. It resembles the rickettsia but is classified separately because it does not require arthropod vectors, it is differentially filterable through certain filters, and it is resistant to both drying and many chemical agents to which rickettsiae are susceptible. Transmission to humans usually occurs by the inhalation of the organism found in the urine, feces, and placenta of infected animals. Occasionally, cases develop from the ingestion of unpasteurized milk or through laboratory exposure. Aerosolized organisms can travel long distances, and individuals not directly involved in research using sheep have been infected. Several outbreaks have been described that were related to parturient cats, and rarely Q fever can be transmitted by blood transfusion.

Human ehrlichiosis is caused by *Ehrlichia chafeenis* in the United States and by *Ehrlichia sennetsu* in Japan. The organisms are small (0.5 μm) Gram-negative bacteria that grow in host membrane-bound cytoplasmic vacuoles and are tropic for leukocytes and other hematopoietic cells. Canine ehrlichiosis has a worldwide distribution, but human disease related to the *Ehrlichia canis*-like agent has been described only since 1986. Transmission to humans is thought to be by tick bite, perhaps from *Amblyomma americanum.* Data suggest that in some areas of the United States, ehrlichiosis is more common than Rocky Mountain spotted fever and the other rickettsial diseases discussed here.

Natural History and Its Modification with Treatment

In untreated patients, these rickettsial diseases have a variable course. Rickettsialpox is a nonfatal disease, and fever lasts only 1 week. Fever may last 2 weeks in epidemic typhus, and it is followed by a prolonged convalescence (2–3 months); mortality may be as high as 60%. Murine typhus and scrub typhus produce fever for approximately 2 weeks. When patients are treated appropriately, they respond dramatically and the fever resolves within 24 to 48 hours. Relapses may occur if therapy is given early and for less than 5 days.

Untreated Q fever lasts 2 to 3 weeks and has a mortality rate of less than 1%. Relapses may occur, and rarely the chronic form of the disease with infective endocarditis develops. This latter form of illness may have a mortality rate of up to 60%.

Preliminary information suggests that untreated ehrlichiosis has a mortality of less than 5%, although convalescence from the disease may be prolonged. The full spectrum of disease caused by *E. chafeensis* is still not known.

Prevention

Rodent control and vector control are the most reasonable methods of preventing rickettsialpox and murine typhus. Scrub typhus may be controlled by these same measures and by using insect repellents. Epidemic typhus is best controlled by altering the conditions of crowding that encourage louse infestation. A vaccine is available only for epidemic typhus and should be given to laboratory personnel working with *Rickettsia prowazeki,* persons exposed to the vector in the field, and medical personnel in endemic areas caring for patients with typhus. Brill–Zinsser disease can be prevented only by preventing the primary infection with epidemic typhus. Prevention of human ehrlichiosis relies on avoidance of exposure to ticks and prompt removal of ticks (including mouth parts) from the body and cleansing of affected areas after tick removal.

The main thrust in preventing Q fever is to minimize exposure to the organism by pasteurizing milk from cattle, sheep, and goats in endemic areas and autoclaving the sputum and urine of clinical patients. It is difficult to identify and eradicate infection from animal herds, but vaccination may decrease the number of organisms shed by parturient animals. Isolation precautions in research facilities using sheep may limit exposure of both researchers and nearby residents. Several different types of vaccine (killed particulate, soluble antigen, and live attenuated) are available for high-risk groups, but all the vaccines suffer from a high incidence of local and systemic reactions.

Cost Containment

The diagnosis and therapy of these diseases are very inexpensive unless complications arise. Early recognition and therapy can prevent serious morbidity (such as renal failure or adult respiratory distress syndrome) and mortality.

REFERENCES

Font-Creus B, Buella-Cueto F, Espejo-Arenas E, et al. Mediterranean spotted fever: A cooperative study of 227 cases. Rev Infect Dis 1985;7:635.
Raoult D. Treatment of Q fever. Antimicrob Agents Chemother 1993;37:1733.
Reiner LG. Q fever. Clin Microbiol Rev 1993;6:193.
Sawyer LA, Fishbein DB, McDade JE. Q fever: Current concepts. Rev Infect Dis 1987;9:935.
Walker DH, Dumler JS. Ehrlichiosis. In: Mandell GL, Douglas RG, Bennett JE, eds. Principles and practice of infectious diseases. 4th ed. New York: Churchill Livingstone, 1995:1747.
Wong B, Singer C, Armstrong D, et al. Rickettsialpox: Case report and epidemiologic review. JAMA 1979;242:1998.
Woodward T. Rickettsial diseases. In: Harrison's textbook of medicine. 12th ed. New York: McGraw-Hill, 1991:753.

Candidiasis

Susan M. Ray, M.D., Stephen W. Schwarzmann, M.D., and Jonas A. Shulman, M.D.

DEFINITION

Candidiasis is infection caused by *Candida* species (Table 8–51–1). These infections can be superficial and localized to skin or mucous membranes or may become bloodborne and disseminated to a number of deeper organs. *Hematogenous candidiasis* is the term used to identify all infections involving the bloodstream and may be further characterized as candidemia, disseminated candidiasis, or both. *Candidemia* is defined as the isolation of any pathogenic species of *Candida* from at least one blood culture specimen and may or may not be catheter-associated. Disseminated candidiasis may be acute or chronic. Acute disseminated candidiasis describes patients who present with multiple noncontiguous organ infections due to *Candida* species acquired from hematogenous spread. Chronic disseminated candidiasis is also known as hepatosplenic candidiasis and refers to a syndrome of fever, abdominal pain, elevated liver function tests, characteristic findings on radiography of abdominal organs, and identification of *Candida* species on examination of infected organ tissue or blood.

ETIOLOGY

Candida organisms have been separated into more than 150 species. Only 10 of these species—*C. albicans, C. tropicalis, C. glabrata, C. pseudotropicalis, C. guilliermondi, C. parapsilosis, C. krusei, C. lusitaniae, C. rugosa,* and *C. stellatoidea* (now considered *C. albicans*)—are routinely recovered from human infection.

CRITERIA FOR DIAGNOSIS

Suggestive

Severe infection with *Candida* usually occurs as a result of immunosuppression, granulocytopenia, and/or iatrogenic factors such as antibiotic therapy. Clues to the diagnosis of superficial candidiasis include patient complaints of a pruritic or burning rash on the skin or mucocutaneous surfaces, dyspareunia and vaginal discharge, or dysphagia or odynophagia associated with thrush (a white, curdlike exudate on the mucosal surface of the mouth and tongue). Disseminated candidiasis is often suspected when fever or a septic state in an immunocompromised or postoperative host cannot be identified as having a bacterial origin, and the patient fails to respond to broad-spectrum antibacterial agents.

The rare condition of chronic mucocutaneous candidiasis is suggested by very severe chronic, recurrent *Candida* mucocutaneous infection. This generally appears in childhood or early adulthood and is associated with defective T-cell immunity and, at times, with endocrine abnormalities.

Definitive

The definitive diagnosis of superficial infection with this fungus depends on the visualization of budding yeast and pseudohyphae on microscopy, at times confirmed by culture of the involved skin or mucous membrane in the presence of characteristic clinical manifestations (e.g., thrush in the oropharynx). Candidemia or disseminated candidiasis is diagnosed by detection of the organism in blood cultures and/or in usually sterile body fluids (such as peritoneal fluid) or in biopsy material from deep tissues. When present, rather specific retinal findings strongly suggest the presence of disseminated *Candida* infection. Peritonitis, hepatosplenic disease, and intraabdominal abscesses due to *Candida* are diagnosed by the demonstration of the organisms in the stain or culture of the fluid or pus obtained by aspiration or surgical drainage.

CLINICAL MANIFESTATIONS

Subjective

Candida species are present in normal flora of the mouth, the entire gastrointestinal tract, and the vagina. The skin is not normally colonized by *Candida* organisms, but maceration or similar skin injury, especially in perioral or perineal areas, frequently results in colonization. It is only when normal host defense mechanisms break down that these usually harmless commensals become pathogenic and cause disease.

Symptoms caused by superficial infection with *Candida* are generally localized to the skin or the mucous membranes of the mouth, esophagus, vaginal tract, and glans penis. Involvement of the skin and mucocutaneous surfaces may produce itching or burning associated with obvious skin eruption, particularly in sites where skin surfaces are in close proximity, such as the crural folds, interdigital webs of fingers and toes, and submammary regions. The nails may become thickened and deformed. Involvement of the mucous membranes of the mouth may be present, with pain and a complaint of cottage cheese curdlike patches on the tongue or other mouth surfaces. In other patients, pain and fissuring at the angle of the mouth, or angular cheilitis, may be the major complaint. A patient with candidal infection of the esophagus may be asymptomatic or may present with dysphagia, odynophagia, and substernal or epigastric pain. Patients who present with findings suggestive of esophageal candidiasis, who are not receiving antibiotics or immunosuppressive agents, should be examined for the presence of an underlying HIV infection. Symptoms of vaginal candidiasis include itching or burning, dyspareunia, and a white cheeselike, odorless discharge. *Candida* balanitis may present as a pruritic and occasionally painful eruption on the glans penis. Contiguous infection with *Candida* species along an indwelling peritoneal catheter used for chronic dialysis can cause peritonitis with symptoms similar to those seen in bacterial peritonitis.

The subjective complaints of candidemia or disseminated candidiasis are not specific for this infection and frequently are masked by the symptoms of the underlying immunosuppressive state or dominated by the local symptoms of superficial *Candida* infection. The relatively

TABLE 8–51–1. CLINICAL SYNDROMES ASSOCIATED WITH CANDIDA INFECTION

Localized mucous membrane and cutaneous infections
  Thrush
  Esophagitis
  Other gastrointestinal mucosal candidiasis
  Vaginitis
  Cutaneous processes (e.g., folliculitis, generalized balanitis, intertrigo, paronychia, onychomycosis, diaper rash, perianal rash)
  Chronic mucocutaneous candidiasis
Hematogenous candidal infections
  Candidemia
  Disseminated candidiasis with or without candidemia (multiple organs are usually involved; eye and skin findings are helpful in recognizing this entity in some patients)
Deep organ involvement
  Central nervous system
  Lung
  Endocardium
  Urinary tract
  Joint, bone, muscle
  Peritoneum
  Pancreas, liver, spleen, gallbladder
  Intravascular devices
  Eye
  Others

abrupt onset of unilateral visual distortion is an important complaint that can be seen with *Candida* endopthalmitis and should suggest disseminated candidal infection in an immunocompromised host or in a patient receiving hyperalimentation postoperatively. Although involvement of kidney, liver, heart, brain, and spleen is common in disseminated infection, symptoms related to these sites are usually not evident unless far advanced disease is present. The syndrome of hepatosplenic candidiasis is seen in leukemic patients recovering from cytotoxic chemotherapy. Fever and upper quadrant abdominal pain occurring at the time of recovery from neutropenia suggest the diagnosis.

Objective

Physical Examination

The physical findings of localized *Candida* skin infection are manifested by vesiculopapular, erythematous, coalescing lesions that progress to maceration and fissuring and can occur at virtually any site at which skin surfaces are in close contact and therefore likely to rub. The regions most frequently involved include the axillae, groin, inframammary and perineal areas, interdigital webs, umbilicus, and intergluteal fold. Chronic paronychial infection may occur as a consequence of frequent immersion of the hands in water, causing erythema, swelling, pain, purulent drainage, and, ultimately, thickened, deformed nails and onycholysis. Cheilosis due to *Candida* presents with erythema and fissuring at the corners of the mouth.

Thrush may take on several forms but most commonly presents as a white, curdlike exudate that at times may leave a raw, bleeding, painful surface when removed. Left undisturbed, the lesions are usually painless and show little evidence of inflammation. The exudate is actually a pseudomembrane composed of actively multiplying *Candida* organisms, desquamated epithelial cells, leukocytes, and oral debris. Any region of the mouth may be involved.

Oral thrush also may appear as an atrophic lesion unassociated with any exudate. Acute atrophic candidiasis may occur de novo or after shedding of the fungal exudate. It presents as a painful atrophic erosion of the oral mucosa, especially of the tongue, and occurs after antibiotic-induced depression of the normal bacterial flora. Chronic atrophic candidiasis occurs as a complication of full upper denture placement and is also referred to as "denture sore mouth." It involves the part of the palate that makes contact with the denture and is characterized by chronic erythema and edema.

Involvement of the esophagus may represent an extension of the infection from the mouth, but it occurs equally often in the absence of thrush.

No specific features of the physical examination establish the diagnosis of disseminated candidiasis, although fundoscopic examination sometimes shows a characteristic cottonball-like lesion that originates on the retina and extends into the vitreous, ultimately obscuring the retina. Biopsy of the acneiform skin eruption, complete with "white pustules," that appears will demonstrate the organism. Other skin nodules, papules, or petechial lesions may be sites of disseminated candidiasis, and biopsy of these lesions may be the only way to prove the diagnosis. When one detects the presence of superficial *Candida* lesions in a severely immunocompromised or postoperative patient and there is evidence of unexplained fever and concern about sepsis, especially with negative blood cultures for bacteria, the clinician should be particularly attuned to the possibility of a disseminated infection. Lethargy or altered mental status, vague abdominal distress, and fever unresponsive to broad-spectrum antibiotic therapy in immunocompromised patients are features that always suggest the need to consider disseminated *Candida* infection.

Routine Laboratory Abnormalities

The presence of pseudomycelial forms of *Candida* in the urine on microscopic examination suggests the presence of active urinary tract infection but cannot determine whether the infection reached the urinary tract via the urethral or the hematogenous route. Involvement of the liver in disseminated candidiasis may be associated with elevated liver function tests, especially alkaline phosphatase.

PLANS

Diagnostic

Differential Diagnosis

Superficial or Mucocutaneous Candidiasis. Because *Candida* species may be present on skin and mucosal surfaces as colonizing agents, the most important differential diagnosis when *Candida* species are found on these surfaces is that of colonization versus infection. Physical findings and histopathology are used to make this determination (see appropriate sections for discussion).

Disseminated Candidiasis. This diagnosis may be suspected when an immunocompromised host presents with fever unresponsive to broad-spectrum antibiotics and widespread maculopapular skin lesions. Other infectious agents that may have a similar presentation in immunocompromised hosts include *Staphylococcus aureus, Pseudomonas aeruginosa, Mycobacterium hemophilum, Cryptococcus neoformans, Histoplasma capsulatum, Blastomyces dermatitidis, Coccidiodes immitis,* and *Fusarium* species. The specific etiology should be sought with blood cultures and biopsy and culture of skin lesions (see below).

Diagnostic Options and Recommended Approach

Establishing the diagnosis of a superficial *Candida* infection requires demonstration of actively multiplying invading organisms. Simple culture of a surface lesion does not separate normal colonization from active invasive infection, and microscopic examination showing pseudomycelial forms of *Candida* species is required. Tissue obtained at biopsy or scraping of a surface lesion examined on a glass slide using potassium hydroxide, periodic acid–Schiff, or Gram stain is usually adequate for assessment. Esophageal candidiasis can be detected only by esophagoscopy with appropriate biopsy studies, although barium swallows sometimes show a characteristic "cobblestone" appearance.

The diagnosis of disseminated candidiasis first requires a strong index of suspicion. Any combination of prolonged antibiotic therapy, multiple invasive procedures, insertion of prosthetic devices or other foreign material (e.g., intravenous catheters in place for prolonged parenteral hyperalimentation), severe granulocytopenia, or other evidence of an underlying immunocompromised state or immunosuppressive therapy should alert the clinician to the possibility of this diagnosis. Multiple positive blood cultures are diagnostic, but negative blood cultures do not eliminate the possibility, as disseminated *Candida* infection involving deep organs can occur without *Candida* species being detected in the blood. Isolator centrifugation culture methods have considerably enhanced the isolation of fungi in the blood and can be very helpful in the diagnosis of possible bloodstream infection with *Candida* species. The use of lysis centrifugation tubes for blood culture can increase the yield of fungal isolates and, in turn, assist in detecting disseminated fungal infection. Examination of an embolus removed from a major artery is another way in which specific candidal infection can be recognized despite negative blood cultures, and *Candida* endocarditis has been diagnosed in this manner.

Candiduria is present in most instances of disseminated *Candida* infection because the organism frequently invades the kidney and, in turn, is found in the urine. Most positive urine cultures do not indicate the presence of disseminated disease, however, but represent local bladder colonization. If an intravenous catheter is removed, culture of the catheter tip may reveal *Candida* and may support, but not prove, the presence of a disseminated fungal process. As soon as the diagnosis of disseminated candidiasis is suspected, skin biopsy of any suspicious lesions and blood and urine cultures should be performed to detect the presence of this organism. Despite multiple efforts to develop good tests to detect candidal antigens in the blood, thus far this procedure remains experimental.

Therapeutic

Choice of therapy for candidiasis is determined by the site and extent of disease and may also be influenced by underlying disease.

Superficial candidal infections of the skin or mucous membranes of the mouth or genital tract are best treated with a topical agent. The imidazole compound miconazole (Micatin, Monistat), available as a 2% dermatologic or intravaginal cream, and clotrimazole, available as a 1% dermatologic cream or lotion, a vaginal cream or tablet, or an oral 20-mg troche, represent the drugs of choice for the various superficial infections. For dermatologic indications, the cream or lotion is applied twice daily. In vaginal infections, a single application of cream or a vaginal tablet inserted once daily for 7 days is appropriate. Thrush is treated with the oral troche, which is dissolved and held in the mouth for several minutes before swallowing, five times daily. Nystatin is available as an oral tablet, oral suspension, dermatologic cream, and intravaginal tablet and is used in a manner similar to the imidazoles.

More severe superficial candidal infection may require systemic therapy. Ketoconazole (Nizoral) is an oral 200-mg tablet given once daily for superficial candidal infection. A low pH of the stomach is required for dissolution of the pill and release of the free drug for absorption. If the patient is taking antacids or H_2 blockers, care should be taken in the timing of the single ketoconazole dose to avoid the effect on the stomach pH. Liver injury induced by ketoconazole is seen in less than 1% of patients. The drug must be discontinued promptly if jaundice or other manifestations of possible hepatitis appear. Timely measurement of serum aspartate and alanine aminotransferases, with prompt discontinuation of ketoconazole if a major rise in these enzymes occurs, will prevent serious hepatic necrosis. Breast tenderness, gynecomastia, and diminished sexual potency can be seen with prolonged administration of the drug in men. These findings result from suppression of plasma testosterone and are reversible when the drug is discontinued. Some degree of adrenal insufficiency can be produced when high doses of the drug are given, but this rarely is clinically significant. Multiple drug interactions occur with ketoconazole administration and should be reviewed if the patient is being treated with other agents.

Fluconazole (Diflucan) is a triazole that acts much like ketoconazole by inhibiting fungal ergosterol synthesis, resulting in a fungistatic effect on *Candida*. It is an excellent drug for severe superficial candidiasis, especially when drug interactions or gastric pH problems make ketoconazole difficult to use or therapy with topical agents has been unsuccessful. The drug has superior pharmacologic properties in that it penetrates tissue and body fluids, including the cerebrospinal fluid, at concentrations approaching those in the serum. The skin and urine levels exceed those in the serum. Fluconazole is excreted essentially unmetabolized in the urine. The half-life of 30 hours in serum permits once-daily dosing with normal renal function. When the creatinine clearance is between 20 and 50 mL/min, the dose is given every other day, and when less than 20 mL/min, every 72 hours. Fluconazole does not require an acid medium for "activation," and is remarkably free of serious side effects such as the hepatitis seen with the other azoles. It likewise has not been associated with symptomatic changes in androgen or cholesterol metabolism. Concomitant administration of cyclosporin, phenytoin, or warfarin can increase plasma levels of these drugs, and this requires careful monitoring of the serum levels to prevent toxicity. In addition, fluconazole is quite expensive. Normally, the drug is given in a daily dose of 100 mg in superficial candidal infections.

Candidemia must be treated with a systemic antifungal agent. In patients with catheter-associated candidemia, removal of the implicated intravenous (or arterial) catheter is critical to the success of the therapy. The standard therapy for any hematogenous *Candida* infection is amphotericin B, but recent experience indicates that selected patients with uncomplicated candidemia may be treated with high-dose fluconazole (400 mg/d). Fluconazole for candidemia should be used only in patients who are not neutropenic and not severely immunocompromised and should not be used against *C. krusei* or *C. glabrata,* species that may not be susceptible to fluconazole. The fluconazole should be given intravenously to ensure adequate bioavailability. The optimal length of therapy for uncomplicated candidemia with fluconazole is uncertain, but a minimum of 2 weeks after the last positive blood culture is a reasonable choice. Evidence of an adequate response to therapy would include repeated negative blood cultures, defervescence, and resolution of leukocytosis. Patients who do not have an adequate response to fluconazole or who develop evidence of disseminated candidiasis should be treated with amphotericin B.

The treatment of candidemia in neutropenic patients and of disseminated candidiasis requires parenteral therapy with amphotericin B. Amphotericin B is given as a single daily infusion, with an increase in the daily dose to a level of 0.4 to 1.0 mg/kg/d. Renal function, potassium, magnesium, and hematologic parameters should be followed two to three times a week to prevent complications of this therapy. Once the desired daily dose has been reached and the infection has stabilized, the drug can be given at twice the concentration on alternate days (no more than 1 mg/kg/d) without significant loss of efficacy. No major reduction in dose is made in patients with hepatic or renal insufficiency or in those on dialysis. Side effects (most commonly fever, chills, nausea, and vomiting) occur in up to 70% of patients during administration and can be managed with a regimen of premedications which may include acetaminophen, diphenhydramine, corticosteroids, or heparin. The total dose of amphotericin B required for successful treatment of disseminated infection is not well established and therefore is determined by patient response and status of the underlying immunosuppressive state. A practical approach is to reassess the status of the infection after 250 to 500 mg of amphotericin B has been administered. Many recommend a total dose of 1 to 2 g for treating severe disseminated or deep candidal infections. If the patient has improved and the underlying immunosuppression or other host defense abnormality has been corrected (e.g., remission achieved in acute leukemia), the drug can sometimes be stopped before a total dose of 1 to 2 g is reached.

In disseminated infection, one may consider combined therapy of amphotericin and flucytosine (Ancobon), as evidence exists to suggest potential synergy. Flucytosine is available as an oral preparation only, and the daily total dose is 150 mg/kg administered in four equally divided doses in adults with normal renal function. The drug is well absorbed from the gastrointestinal tract and efficiently penetrates the cerebrospinal and other body fluids. Excretion is exclusively by the kidney, and the daily dose must be reduced proportionally as the creatinine clearance is reduced. Serum levels of flucytosine must be monitored closely, as serious bone marrow toxicity may ensue if the recommended levels are exceeded, especially in the presence of renal insufficiency. Toxicity due to flucytosine is more frequent when the drug is given in combination with amphotericin B. Because resistance develops rapidly, flucytosine should not be used as a single agent in the treatment of *Candida* infection.

Candiduria may reflect infection originating in the upper or lower urinary tract. If persistent infection is limited to the bladder, treatment with a continuous bladder irrigation of amphotericin B (50 µg/mL in 1 L sterile distilled water) at a rate of 1 L per 24 hours or more may be successful. Fluconazole has also proven useful in the treatment of urinary tract infections with *Candida* and may be preferred over amphotericin B bladder washes because of the ease of administration. A 3-day course of fluconazole should be adequate for an uncomplicated bladder infection. Catheter-induced candiduria reflecting simple colonization of the bladder usually clears spontaneously without antifungal treatment if the catheter can be removed.

FOLLOW-UP

The follow-up required in both superficial and deep candidiasis relates to both the severity of the infection and the degree of defective host resistance that allowed the organism to attain pathologic significance. In the case of superficial skin or mucosal disease, reinspection of the involved areas is usually all that is needed. In disseminated infection a major parameter of follow-up relates to the fever curve and the general clinical condition of the patient. Repeat blood cultures are important and should remain negative after therapy is terminated.

Long-term follow-up is required for patients with chronic mucocutaneous candidiasis. Because of the multiple areas involved and the complexity of this unusual problem, the expertise of the dermatologist, immunologist, gastroenterologist, gynecologist, pediatrician, and general internist or family doctor is frequently required.

DISCUSSION
Prevalence and Incidence

Although disease caused by *Candida* has been recognized for 150 years, the emergence of this organism as a major pathogen has occurred since the advent of the antibiotic era and has been catapulted into prominence with the development of immunosuppressive and cytotoxic agents, prosthetic devices, hyperalimentation, internal monitoring devices, surgical advances such as transplantation, and the AIDS epidemic. According to data from the National Nosocomial Infections Surveillance System, *Candida* species are the fifth most common primary bloodstream pathogen and the seventh most common pathogen to cause nosocomial infection.

Related Basic Science

Candida organisms are imperfect fungi that reproduce by budding and grow in routine blood culture bottles and agar media within 24 to 72 hours. Although some 80 strains of *Candida* have been identified, only 10 of them—*C. albicans, C. tropicalis, C. glabrata, C. pseudotropicalis, C. guilliermondi, C. parapsilosis, C. lusitaniae, C. rugosa, C. krusei,* and *C. stellatoidea* (now considered *C. albicans*)—are routinely recovered from human infection. These organisms form part of the normal flora in the gastrointestinal tract, the female genital tract, and on macerated skin, and it is from these sites that clinically significant infection originates. Transmission from person to person is uncommon but may occur during sexual contact or during birth, with resultant thrush in the newborn. *Candida tropicalis* has been recognized as a particularly aggressive organism in the setting of granulocytopenia, and its presence should increase the index of suspicion of serious disseminated infection.

A feature common to many of the predisposing causes of *Candida* infection is a loss of intact skin or mucous membrane barriers, although it has been shown experimentally that challenge of even the normal gastrointestinal tract with a very large inoculum of *Candida,* such as drinking a concentrated suspension of viable *Candida* organisms, will result in candidemia and candiduria. Thus, antibiotics may predispose to candidiasis by allowing unopposed overgrowth of the organism in its normal sites of colonization.

A variety of components of the host defense system are important in protecting against this organism. T cells appear to have a major role in suppressing growth of the organism on skin and mucous membrane surfaces, and a deficiency in T-cell function (cell-mediated immunity) such as occurs in HIV infection or chronic mucocutaneous candidiasis results in chronic surface infection but only rarely in disseminated disease. It is in the clinical setting of severely impaired granulocyte function that disseminated candidiasis is particularly likely to occur. Polymorphonuclear leukocytes have the ability to damage and ingest pseudohyphae and to kill blastospheres and may be assisted by eosinophils and monocytes. Although humoral factors may have an important adjunctive role with granulocytes, antibodies themselves are not candidacidal.

In gastrointestinal injury, especially in the upper tract such as a perforated duodenal ulcer or a postoperative anastomotic leak, *Candida* may escape from the gastrointestinal lumen and lead to a significant peritonitis or abscess. *Candida* are being recognized increasingly as important pathogens complicating bowel surgery, producing both local and systemic infections.

The pathologic changes that occur in parenchymal tissue invaded by *Candida* are characterized by microabscesses with intervening normal tissue. Polymorphonuclear leukocytes respond to the organism first and are soon followed by histiocytes and giant cells. In severely immunosuppressed patients, however, there is little inflammatory response, and the histologic findings are those of "abscess" made up of *Candida* organism and necrotic tissue. Deep infection involving the brain can be manifested by diffusely scattered microabscesses and clinical features that vary from no observable abnormalities to changes in mental alertness to coma. Involvement of the meninges is usually associated with features typical of meningeal irritation. Involvement of the myocardium may also be reflected clinically by nonspecific electrocardiographic changes or by more classic features of myocarditis. The pericardium and endocardium also may be the target of *Candida* organisms, with features similar to their bacterial counterparts. Liver involvement may cause liver test abnormalities and clinical jaundice. Large multiple liver abscesses may occur in some patients, and the or-

ganism may not be readily observed in the aspirate, sometimes making the diagnosis difficult.

Natural History and Its Modification with Treatment

The natural history of untreated *Candida* infection relates to the circumstances in which the infection developed. Most superficial candidal infections can be treated successfully and suppressed with chronic therapy if they recur repeatedly. In the most severe form of superficial infection in chronic mucocutaneous candidiasis, however, scarring and stricture of the skin and mucous membrane surfaces may lead to esophageal and vaginal stricture with its attendant complications, chronic paronychia, and skin deformity and disfigurement. The use of systemic antifungal therapy in patients with chronic mucocutaneous candidiasis results in remission of superficial infection which may be sustained if the underlying immune defect can be corrected (this has been possible with *Candida*-specific transfer factor).

Disseminated infection in the setting of a severe underlying disease such as acute leukemia can lead to death as a result of overwhelming sepsis, with hypotension, adult respiratory distress syndrome, disseminated intravascular coagulation, and/or multiple organ failure being present. Other patients with disseminated disease develop metastatic involvement of the kidney, brain, myocardium, liver, eye, skin, or lung (or any combination thereof) with resultant organ injury. *Candida* endophthalmitis can lead to loss of vision. Untreated severe *Candida* esophagitis can lead to severe pain, weight loss, and malnutrition. Therapy of uncomplicated candidemia may prevent the development of disseminated infection. Therapy for disseminated infection is most likely to be successful if the immunocompromising condition(s), such as neutropenia, can be reversed.

Prevention

As *Candida* organisms represent normal commensal flora, it is impossible to prevent the initial acquisition of the organism, although in some centers local antifungal agents are used to try to decrease colonization of the gastrointestinal tract. Disease occurs when the organism overgrows the normal flora and/or breaks through its normal barriers. Prevention, therefore, relates to the avoidance of unnecessary antibiotic therapy and invasive procedures. As a general rule, excessive and prolonged broad-spectrum antibiotic administration should be avoided unless there is a definite indication for their continued use. When certain procedures, such as insertion of indwelling intravenous catheters, are performed, meticulous care of the skin site using sterile technique and timely removal and changes of intravenous line sites will reduce the incidence of infection. Similarly, avoiding prolonged use of indwelling urinary catheters, when possible, will reduce the incidence of candiduria.

Oral anticandidal drugs have been advocated by some as a means of suppressing the overgrowth of *Candida* organisms in the gastrointestinal tract during periods of severe granulocytopenia, such as during chemotherapy in acute leukemia, and have met with variable success in the prevention of disseminated infection in these settings.

Because in many cases localized *Candida* infection is not preventable, attention to early detection of thrush and other localized *Candida* infections may lead the clinician to look aggressively for evidence of systemic candidiasis in the right clinical setting. If systemic candidiasis is strongly suspected, empiric therapy with amphotericin B should be started even if the blood cultures have not demonstrated the presence of this organism. This therapy, although potentially toxic, may prevent a fatal outcome.

Cost Containment

The diagnosis of superficial *Candida* infection can usually be readily made by clinical findings and microscopic examination of scrapings from the surface involved; therefore, it is an unnecessary expense to perform cultures. A meticulous physical examination, especially fundoscopic examination of the eye, and a search for typical skin lesions and other sites of *Candida* colonization will assist the clinician in earlier diagnosis of widespread *Candida* infection and may reduce the complications of fungal sepsis, thereby decreasing hospital costs. In the setting of suspected disseminated candidiasis, blood cultures taken in routine media may be adequate, but are not considered by many microbiologists to be as good at detecting fungemias as the more expensive lysis centrifugation methods. Because early detection of disseminated *Candida* infection may prevent multiorgan involvement and death, the enhanced cost of this special method for fungal isolation is considered by many to be worthwhile in settings where systemic *Candida* infection is likely, and in the long run it may reduce the cost of these difficult-to-treat infections.

REFERENCES

Anttila VJ, Ruutu P, Bondestam S, et al. Hepatosplenic yeast infection in patients with acute leukemia: A diagnostic problem. Clin Infect Dis 1994;18:979.

Bodey GP, ed. Candidiasis: Pathogenesis, diagnosis and treatment. 2nd ed. New York: Raven Press, 1993.

Como JA, Dismukes WE. Oral azole drugs as systemic antifungal therapy. N Engl J Med 1994;330:263.

Fisher JF, Newman CL, Sobel JD. Yeast in the urine: Solutions for a budding problem. Clin Infect Dis 1995;20:183.

Khoo SH, Bond J, Denning DW. Administering amphotericin B: A practical approach. J Antimicrob Chemother 1994;33:203.

Ng TTC, Denning DW. Fluconazole resistance in *Candida* in patients with AIDS: A therapeutic approach. J Infect 1993;26:117.

Rex JH, Bennett JE, Sugar AM, et al. A randomized trial comparing fluconazole with amphotericin B for the treatment of candidemia in patients without neutropenia. N Engl J Med 1994;331:1325.

CHAPTER 8–52

Aspergillosis

David Rimland, M.D.

DEFINITION

Aspergillosis is defined as any of several disease syndromes produced by the fungus *Aspergillus*.

ETIOLOGY

The syndromes discussed below are produced by several species of the fungus *Aspergillus*. The specific syndrome is related to a number of different immunologic responses of the host.

CRITERIA FOR DIAGNOSIS

Suggestive

The clinical clues suggesting a diagnosis of aspergillosis depend on the clinical syndrome. The underlying conditions, symptoms, and signs are outlined in Table 8–52–1.

Definitive

Invasive aspergillosis is definitively diagnosed by histologic evidence of tissue invasion and confirmed by culture. Appropriate serologic tests support the diagnosis of aspergilloma and allergic bronchopulmonary aspergillosis. In other forms of aspergillosis the appropriate clinical syndrome, supported by cultural or histologic data, confirms the diagnosis.

CLINICAL MANIFESTATIONS

Subjective and objective findings are quite variable, depending on the clinical syndrome, as noted in Table 8–52–1.

PLANS

Diagnostic

The specific diagnostic approach depends on the particular clinical syndrome present. For invasive disease, especially in the compromised host, the suspicion of aspergillosis warrants aggressive diagnostic procedures, including a biopsy of the involved organ (usually lung) (see Chapter 8–31). Fungal cultures are occasionally helpful, but it must be remembered that cultures alone, without the appropriate clinical syndrome, are often worthless (e.g., sputum, urine, stool, wound, cornea)

TABLE 8–52–1. SUBJECTIVE AND OBJECTIVE FINDINGS IN ASPERGILLOSIS

Syndrome	Subjective	Objective
Invasive aspergillosis	Underlying conditions: leukemia, immunosuppressive therapy, corticosteroids, organ and bone marrow transplants, AIDS Symptoms: variable and depend on organ system involved (e.g., lungs—cough, chest pain, hemoptysis)	Organ involvement: lungs, intestines, brain, kidney, liver; high fever; pulmonary consolidation
Chronic necrotizing pulmonary aspergillosis	Underlying conditions: pulmonary disease, steroids, diabetes, alcoholism, malnutrition Symptoms: fever, weight loss, cough	Pulmonary consolidation
Aspergilloma	Underlying conditions: tuberculosis, sarcoidosis, bronchogenic carcinoma, lung abscess Hemoptysis (50–80%), cough, chest pain	Upper lobe movable mass within cavity on chest x-ray; positive sputum culture; multiple precipitin bands
Allergic bronchopulmonary aspergillosis	History of atopy and asthma; recurrent cough, wheezing, fever Expectoration of brown plugs	Wheezing, asthma; transient pulmonary infiltrates; blood and sputum eosinophilia (more than 10%): serum precipitins; very elevated IgE: skin allergy to aspergillus: type I (immediate wheal and flare) and type 2 (2- to 6-h Arthus type): aspergillus in sputum (70–100%)
Hypersensitivity pneumonitis	Fever, dyspnea 24 h after exposure to spores (e.g., malt workers)	Miliary pattern on chest film; delayed type of skin test; serum precipitins
Sinusitis	Pain, fullness, nasal obstruction or discharge; in compromised host, proptosis, evidence of local or central nervous system invasion	Tenderness over nontransilluminating sinus (especially maxillary): sinus x-rays; opacification; in invasive disease, destruction of bony plates
Other local invasive disease: eye, ear, brain, endocarditis, intestine, bone	Underlying conditions: drug addiction, prosthetic valve, immunosuppression; variable symptoms	Variable, depends on site involved

and are usually negative in some syndromes (e.g., blood, bone marrow, cerebrospinal fluid). Serologic tests (e.g., immunoglobulin G precipitins) are not helpful for invasive disease but will support the diagnosis of aspergilloma or allergic bronchopulmonary aspergillosis. Other diagnostic tests, including specific x-ray studies, are dictated by the organ system involved.

Therapeutic

Specific treatment varies considerably depending on the clinical syndrome (Table 8–52–2).

FOLLOW-UP

For invasive disease, the duration of therapy is not well defined. Recurrences are possible, especially if immunosuppressive therapy is maintained, so patients must be carefully followed. Patients with allergic bronchopulmonary aspergillosis being treated with corticosteroids should be monitored for progression of their disease (i.e., development of chronic pulmonary changes or dissemination) and for complications of therapy.

DISCUSSION

Prevalence, Incidence, and Related Basic Science

Aspergillus is a ubiquitous fungus that grows well in decaying vegetation, compost, cereal grains, cotton, wool, and hay. Many species exist, but only a few (especially *A. fumigatus* and *A. flavus*) produce disease in humans. Speciation of the fungus is performed by analysis of colonial morphology and examination of the distinctive spores. In tissue the fungus can be identified by the septate, dichotomous branching, 2- to 4-μm-wide hyphae. Most of the clinical syndromes produced by *Aspergillus* follow inhalation of the spores from the environment. Host factors, including specific structural or immunologic defects, then determine the type of disease that evolves. The syndromes described above may follow tissue invasion, superficial colonization, or antigenic stimulation with resultant reactions mediated by immunoglobulin (Ig) E or IgG antibodies or sensitized lymphocytes. Invasive aspergillosis usually develops only in hosts with severe defects in cellular and humoral immunity. Chronic necrotizing pulmonary aspergillosis can occur in persons with underlying pulmonary disease, especially if they are mildly immunocompromised by low-dose corticosteroids, diabetes mellitus, alcoholism, or malnutrition. Aspergillomas require only a cavity in the lung as a background for growth and are not associated with any specific immunologic defect. Allergic bronchopulmonary aspergillosis is probably mediated by specific IgE and IgG antibodies; the latter are involved in immune complexes that contribute to the pathologic changes.

Natural History and Its Modification with Treatment

Invasive aspergillosis, especially disseminated disease, has a very poor prognosis, although early diagnosis may allow therapy at a time when it can be useful. Aspergillomas may produce no serious disease or may even resolve without therapy. Untreated, allergic bronchopulmonary aspergillosis often progresses to produce lobar contractions, honeycombing, and proximal bronchiectasis. Treatment with corticosteroids probably prevents these late complications and reduces the frequency of acute relapses.

TABLE 8–52–2. TREATMENT REGIMENS FOR ASPERGILLOSIS

Syndrome	Therapy
Invasive aspergillosis	Amphotericin B (0.5–0.6 mg/kg/d) for total of 2–3 g May add rifampin (600 mg/d) Itraconazole (400 mg/d) may be useful in milder disease
Chronic necrotizing pulmonary aspergillosis	Amphotericin B (see above) Surgical resection, if necessary
Aspergilloma	Controversial choices include observation, surgical excision (especially with massive hemoptysis), and intracavitary amphotericin B
Allergic bronchopulmonary aspergillosis	Oral corticosteroids (prednisone, 10 mg/d) or beclomethasone
Hypersensitivity pneumonitis	Avoid exposure to antigen Corticosteroids of questionable use
Sinusitis	Drainage and curettage; invasive disease in compromised host probably requires amphotericin B
Other local invasive disease	Excision of involved area (e.g., valve in endocarditis) usually is necessary

Prevention

Invasive aspergillosis is rarely preventable, as the fungus is ubiquitous and the compromised hosts in which it develops will continue to be present. Occasional outbreaks of invasive aspergillosis related to hospital construction or renovation suggest that disease could be prevented by reducing the risk of transmission of airborne fungi to immunocompromised patients. If major reconstruction is underway, these types of patients may need to be cared for elsewhere in the hospital system. As noted above, relapses of allergic bronchopulmonary aspergillosis can probably be reduced with appropriate therapy. Some nosocomial outbreaks have been reported to be related to the contamination of air (e.g., on burn units).

Cost Containment

Prevention of common-source outbreaks of *Aspergillus* infections will clearly reduce some costs. This includes reduction of contamination of air in high-risk areas (e.g., burn or transplant units). In the individual patient, rapid etiologic diagnosis may help early therapy and prevent inappropriate therapy for other illnesses that are simulated by aspergillosis.

REFERENCES

Barnes AJ, Denning DW. Aspergillus: Significance as a pathogen. Rev Med Microbiol 1993;4:176.
Denning DW, Stevens DA. Antifungal and surgical treatment of invasive aspergillosis: Review of 2,121 published cases. Rev Infect Dis 1990;12:1147.
Levitz SM. Aspergillosis. Infect Dis Clin North Am 1989;3:1.
Walsh TJ. Invasive pulmonary aspergillosis in patients with neoplastic diseases. Semin Respir Infect 1990;5:11.
Young RC, Bennett JE, Vogel CL, et al. Aspergillosis: The spectrum of disease in 98 patients. Medicine 1970;49:147.

Mucormycosis (Zygomycosis, Phycomycosis)

John A. Jernigan, M.D.

DEFINITION

Mucormycosis is the name given to a group of diseases caused by fungi of the order Mucorales, in the class Zygomycetes. These invasive infections often involve the respiratory tract and central nervous system, but many other organ systems can be involved. The clinical course is aggressive and often results in death. Pathologic hallmarks include invasion of blood vessels, tissue infarction, and necrosis. The terms *phycomycosis* and *zygomycosis* have also been applied to these infections.

ETIOLOGY

A number of different fungi within the class Zygomycetes can cause mucormycosis, and the clinical course cannot be distinguished based on the genus and species of the isolate. The organisms most often isolated from patients with mucormycosis belong to the genera *Rhizopus, Rhizomucor,* and *Absidia.* Other genera causing mucormycosis include *Mucor, Cunninghamella, Mortierella, Saksenaea,* and *Apophysomyces.* These fungi are ubiquitous, soil-dwelling organisms that grow in the environment and in tissue as hyphae and, therefore, are considered molds. They grow at a wide range of temperatures and can usually be isolated from culture after 2 to 5 days of incubation. Although exposure to these organisms is probably universal, mucormycosis is seen almost exclusively among those with some underlying immune predisposition.

CRITERIA FOR DIAGNOSIS

Suggestive

Mucormycosis is usually seen in patients with diabetes mellitus, severe immunosuppression, or trauma. The hallmarks of the illness are signs of vascular invasion and tissue necrosis in a febrile patient. Black eschars and black discharges, especially on the nasal mucosa and palate, should alert the clinician to the diagnosis. Other clinical clues, especially among patients with diabetic ketoacidosis, include facial pain, orbital cellulitis with or without cranial nerve dysfunction, sinusitis with radiographic evidence of bony erosion, and decreased level of consciousness that persists after metabolic derangements of diabetic ketoacidosis are corrected. Physicians should be alerted to the diagnosis if suggestive findings occur in patients receiving deferoxamine chelation therapy (usually in the setting of renal failure and hemodialysis), a recently recognized risk factor associated with mucormycosis. Mucormycosis should also be included in the differential diagnosis for neutropenic patients with aggressive pneumonitis.

Definitive

The definitive diagnosis is made by demonstrating fungi of the order Mucorales in the tissue of a biopsy specimen, either by isolating the organism from culture or by visualizing characteristic hyphae by histologic examination.

CLINICAL MANIFESTATIONS

The clinical manifestations of mucormycosis are generally divided into distinct syndromes based on clinical presentation and the body site involved. These include rhinocerebral, pulmonary, central nervous system, cutaneous, gastrointestinal, and disseminated mucormycosis. The clinical manifestations of the various syndromes including usual clinical setting and objective and subjective findings are listed in Table 8–53–1. There are sporadic reports of mucormycosis involving bone,

kidney, bladder, heart, mediastinum, or other sites that do not fit well into one of the above categories.

Routine Laboratory Abnormalities

Routine laboratory abnormalities are not helpful in the diagnosis of mucormycosis, but may reflect the associated underlying disease process such as diabetic ketoacidosis or hematologic malignancy.

PLANS

Diagnostic

Differential Diagnosis

Diseases that can resemble rhinocerebral mucormycosis include aspergillosis of the sinuses, ocular tumors (usually much more indolent than mucormycosis), and cavernous sinus thrombosis complicating other craniofacial infections. Pulmonary aspergillosis can mimic pulmonary mucormycosis. Rarely, cutaneous mucormycosis can resemble ecthyma gangrenosum, a lesion more commonly associated with bacterial pathogens, most commonly *Pseudomonas aeruginosa.* Disseminated mucormycosis manifested by fever and necrotic skin lesions may be mistaken for a systemic vasculitis.

Diagnostic Options and Recommended Approach

Suggestive evidence of rhinocerebral disease can often be seen with radiographic examination of the sinuses. Plain sinus films may show sinusoidal mucosal thickening, air–fluid levels, or complete opacification. Bony erosion of sinus walls or the orbit may be seen. Computed tomography and magnetic resonance imaging are more sensitive than plain films for showing orbital involvement, and in central nervous system disease, brain abscesses can usually be seen. Cerebrospinal fluid results are nonspecific, and lumbar puncture is rarely indicated. A leukocytosis is seen in about 50% of patients with central nervous system mucormycosis; cerebrospinal fluid protein is variable, and hypoglycorrhachia is extremely uncommon.

The diagnosis depends on demonstrating the organism in tissue biopsy specimens. A high index of suspicion, aggressive evaluation, and early diagnosis are necessary to limit the mortality of mucormycosis. Careful physical examination should be performed to identify any black eschars or discharges, especially on the nasal mucosa or soft palate. Suspicious lesions should be biopsied and submitted for culture and histopathologic examination. Organisms can sometimes be identified by potassium hydroxide examination of touch preparations of the fresh biopsy specimen. These fungi can readily be seen on permanent tissue sections with hematoxylin and eosin, periodic acid–Schiff (PAS), and Gomori methenamine silver stains. The organisms typically appear as broad (10–20 µm), nonseptate (or rarely septate) hyphae with branches occurring at right angles. This is in contrast to *Aspergillus, Fusarium,* and *Pseudallescheria,* which are thinner, are septate, and branch at more acute angles.

It should be noted that positive cultures from swabs of affected tissues are not diagnostic of mucormycosis, as such cultures may merely represent colonization. Blood cultures are rarely positive.

Therapeutic

In most cases, the successful management of mucormycosis involves three major components: antifungal chemotherapy, aggressive surgical debridement (if possible), and address of the underlying predisposition.

The only known effective antifungal agent is amphotericin B. It should be given initially in high doses, between 1 and 1.5 mg/kg/d. Once the infection is under control, a lower dose or alternate-day dosing can be considered. The total duration of treatment depends on the response to therapy and the severity of the underlying immune defect.

This chapter represents an update of a chapter written by Dr. John Holman in the third edition. Previous material is used with his written permission.

TABLE 8–53–1. CLINICAL MANIFESTATIONS OF MUCORMYCOSIS IN DIFFERENT SITES OF INFECTION

Clinical Syndrome	Clinical Setting	Subjective	Objective
Rhinocerebral	Diabetes mellitus, usually with acidosis; hematologic malignancy with prolonged neutropenia; deferoxamine therapy; corticosteroids	Facial pain, headache, fever, visual disturbance, ocular pain, facial numbness, confusion	Black discharge from nares or black eschar of the nose or palate, proptosis, decreased visual acuity, chemosis, ophthalmoplegia, altered level of consciousness, cranial nerve palsies
Pulmonary	Malignancy, particularly leukemia with neutropenia; transplant recipients; rarely seen in diabetes mellitus	Nonproductive cough, dyspnea, fever, chest pain	Hemoptysis (late); variable chest examination: chest x-ray demonstrates infiltrates, cavities; usually disease is unilateral early but can disseminate; respiratory failure
Central nervous system	Diabetes mellitus usually with acidosis; intravenous drug use; open head trauma	Headache, fever, lethargy, speech disturbance, unilateral weakness	May have same objective findings as in rhinocerebral disease, as most common cause of CNS mucormycosis is direct extension of fungus through paranasal sinuses into brain; cranial nerve involvement, hemiparesis, seizures, ataxia, coma
Cutaneous	Extensive burns; traumatic wounds with extensive tissue damage and soil contamination; elasticized adhesive (bandages); metastatic skin lesion in widely disseminated disease	Pain, rash, fever	Necrotic skin lesions, nonhealing wound, fistulas, vesicles, pustules, skin biopsy revealing nonseptate branched hyphae in tissue and blood vessel
Gastrointestinal	Extreme malnutrition; more common in developing countries	Abdominal pain, distention, nausea and vomiting, fever, bloody diarrhea	Ileus, necrotic ulcers and gangrene of any segment of intestine or stomach; stomach, ileum, and colon most frequent sites
Disseminated	Complication of pulmonary mucormycosis; burns or severe wounds that are grossly contaminated; intravenous drug use (rare); neutropenia; deferoxamine therapy	See Pulmonary and CNS mucormycosis	See Pulmonary and CNS mucormycosis; painful skin lesions with erythema and central necrosis may develop; these lesions are secondary to fungemia, and biopsy of tissue will demonstrate hyphae

CNS, central nervous system.

A total dose of 3 to 6 g may be necessary to cure the patient. Amphotericin B in the high doses mentioned above will frequently have side effects, including febrile reactions, reversible nephrotoxicity, hypokalemia, and hypomagnesemia.

Aggressive surgical debridement of necrotic tissue, when possible, is advised. In many cases necrotic tissue will continue to appear following debridement, necessitating repeated surgical procedures. Patients with rhinocerebral disease are commonly left with residual disfigurement, and may require major reconstructive surgery if they survive.

An attempt should be made to address underlying conditions predisposing to mucormycosis. Aggressive correction of the metabolic consequences of diabetic ketoacidosis should be pursued, and immunosuppressive drugs should be minimized or discontinued if possible.

FOLLOW-UP

Patients with mucormycosis need careful monitoring by their physician until the disease is cured. Meticulous ophthalmologic, neurologic, and neurosurgical examination is necessary. Repeated radiographic examination may be required to assess response to therapy. Frequent monitoring of renal function and electrolytes is necessary to monitor for complications of amphotericin B. Chronic infection and late sequelae following completion of apparently successful therapy have been reported. All survivors should therefore be carefully monitored for signs of indolent or residual infection even after completion of therapy.

DISCUSSION

Prevalence and Incidence

Although exposure to the Mucorales is probably universal, mucormycosis is a rare disease. Precise estimates of prevalence and incidence are not known, but the disease is more common among those with underlying immune predisposition (see Table 8–53–1). Several cases have been reported in patients with AIDS, but unlike its role in the dramatic increase in incidence of some other opportunistic infections, the AIDS epidemic has not had major impact on the number of reported cases of mucormycosis. The group most recently recognized as at risk for mucormycosis comprises patients receiving deferoxamine chelation therapy, usually in the setting of chronic hemodialysis. These cases, however, are still relatively rare.

Related Basic Science

The fungus usually enters the body via the respiratory tract. Rarely, primary cutaneous mucormycosis can occur as a result of direct inoculation. The precise mechanisms of host defense are not well understood. Both macrophages and neutrophils seem to be important in controlling infection. Neither antibody nor complement is responsible for inhibition of growth of the Mucorales. Once the spores are deposited on respiratory mucosal surfaces, germination must occur if the organism is to grow. In normal hosts, macrophages inhibit germination and therefore prevent infection. In mouse and rabbit models, macrophages from steroid-treated or diabetic animals do not possess the normal ability to inhibit spore germination. The reasons for this defect are not known; it cannot be fully accounted for solely by hyperglycemia and ketoacidosis. The association of deferoxamine with mucormycosis has raised interest in a theory that interactions between transferrin, iron molecules, and the fungal spores may be important. Such interactions have been observed, though they are poorly understood.

Once the organism establishes growth, the hyphae invade tissue. They have an affinity for invading blood vessels, resulting in vasculitis, thrombosis, hemorrhage, and tissue necrosis, the histopathologic hallmarks of mucormycosis.

Natural History and Its Modification with Treatment

Mucormycosis is characterized by a very aggressive clinical course. Without treatment, mortality approaches 100%. In rhinocerebral disease, the hyphae spread by direct extension from the upper respiratory tract into the brain, resulting in coma and death. Other forms of mucormycosis can disseminate to distant sites with resultant tissue destruction, thrombosis, and death.

Even with appropriate therapy, the overall mortality remains as high as 50%. Mortality is highest among those with pulmonary, central nervous system, or disseminated disease. With early diagnosis and aggressive therapy, mortality as low as 15 to 30% has been reported in some studies of rhinocerebral disease.

Prevention

There are no well-documented methods of preventing mucormycosis. In neutropenic hospitalized patients such as those being treated for hematologic malignancy, rooms equipped with high-efficiency particulate air (HEPA) filters may reduce the risk, but the cost-effectiveness of this approach is probably low. Limiting the use of deferoxamine therapy among hemodialysis patients may prevent mucormycosis in this clinical setting.

Cost Containment

Early diagnosis and treatment may result in a more favorable clinical course and decreased need for hospital care, thereby reducing costs.

REFERENCES

Boelaert JR. Mucormycosis (zygomycosis): Is there news for the clinician? J Infect 1994;28(suppl. 1):1.
Sugar AM. Mucormycosis. Clin Infect Dis 1992;14(suppl):1:S126.
Sugar AM. Agents of mucormycosis and related species. In: Mandell GL, Bennett JE, Dolin R, eds. Mandell, Douglas, and Bennett's principles and practice of infectious diseases. 4th ed. New York: Churchill Livingstone, 1995:2311.
Tedder M, Spratt JA, Anstadt MP, et al. Pulmonary mucormycosis: Results of medical and surgical therapy. Ann Thorac Surg 1994;57:1044.

CHAPTER 8–54

Cryptococcosis

Robert W. Pinner, M.D., Michael S. Saag, M.D., Rana A. Hajjeh, M.D., and William E. Dismukes, M.D.

DEFINITION

Cryptococcosis is a systemic mycosis that affects principally persons with compromised cell-mediated immunity, particularly those with advanced HIV infection. Cryptococcosis most commonly involves the central nervous system and lower respiratory tract, but may also involve other tissues, such as skin, bone, eye, heart, kidney, prostate, and testis.

ETIOLOGY

Cryptococcosis is caused by the encapsulated yeast *Cryptococcus neoformans,* which resides mainly in the soil and is distributed worldwide.

CRITERIA FOR DIAGNOSIS
Suggestive

A presumptive diagnosis can be made by histopathologic visualization of the organism in body fluids or biopsied lesions. A positive test for cryptococcal antigen in the cerebrospinal fluid of patients with lymphocytic meningitis strongly supports a diagnosis of cryptococcal meningitis.

Definitive

Definitive diagnosis of cryptococcosis is established by culture of the organism from the involved site.

CLINICAL MANIFESTATIONS
Subjective

Table 8–54–1 presents information about clinical features, diagnosis, and management of the various clinical syndromes of cryptococcosis.

The most common clinical manifestation of cryptococcosis is meningoencephalitis. The onset may be acute or gradual over several weeks or even months. Headache and a history of fever are the most common symptoms. Central nervous system symptoms such as irritability, dizziness, and depressed consciousness may be reported, as may other nonspecific symptoms such as nausea and vomiting. Pulmonary cryptococcosis may or may not be accompanied by symptoms; fever, cough, and dyspnea generally characterize pulmonary cryptococcosis in AIDS patients.

As cryptococcosis affects primarily persons with compromised cellular immunity, the past medical history is essential.

Objective
Physical Examination

See Table 8–54–1. Nuchal rigidity and other classic findings of meningeal irritation are often absent in cryptococcal meningitis, particularly in patients with HIV infection.

Routine Laboratory Abnormalities

No abnormalities in routine laboratory results distinguish cryptococcosis.

PLANS
Diagnostic

See Table 8–54–1.

Differential Diagnosis

Central Nervous System Disease. The differential diagnosis of cryptococcosis includes other causes of chronic meningoencephalitis and aseptic meningitis: fungal meningitis caused by *Histoplasma capsulatum* or *Coccidioides immitis* when the patient has been exposed to areas where these diseases are endemic; tuberculosis; syphilis; HIV infection itself; unusual infections such as those caused by *Actinomyces, Nocardia, Brucella,* and *Sporothrix* species; and noninfectious causes (e.g., carcinomatous meningitis).

Pulmonary Disease. In patients with AIDS, pulmonary cryptococcosis typically manifests as fever, cough, pleuritic chest pain, and diffuse interstitial and intraalveolar infiltrates on chest x-ray, symptoms and signs that also characterize other causes of pneumonia in AIDS patients, such as *Pneumocystis carinii, Mycobacterium tuberculosis,* and other bacteria and fungi. Patients with pulmonary cryptococcosis without HIV infection may have one or more defined lesions seen on chest x-ray which may be mistaken for malignancy; cryptococci may also be found without associated symptoms in the respiratory tract of persons with chronic lung disease.

Skin Disease. Cryptococcal cutaneous lesions have a variety of appearances (e.g., papules, umbilicated papules, ulcers, abscesses, cellulitis) and should be distinguished from other lesions of molluscum contagiosum, herpesvirus infections, other cutaneous fungal infections, or even Kaposi's sarcoma.

Diagnostic Options and Recommended Approach

Central Nervous System Disease. Examination of cerebrospinal fluid (CSF) is necessary to make the diagnosis of cryptococcal meningitis, and repeated lumbar punctures may be necessary. Aside from a positive culture of the CSF, the latex agglutination test for detection of cryptococcal antigen in the CSF has the highest predictive value of disease. India ink preparations of CSF should also be performed. Two thirds of patients have positive India ink tests; however, this test must be performed by laboratory personnel who have experience identifying true budding yeasts, with their refractile cytoplasmic inclusions and thick capsules. The biochemistry and cellular examinations of the CSF usu-

TABLE 8–54–1. CRYPTOCOCCOSIS: CLINICAL MANIFESTATIONS, DIAGNOSIS, AND TREATMENT

Clinical syndrome	Clinical manifestations		Diagnosis	Treatment
	Subjective	*Objective*		
Central nervous system Meningitis	Headache, fever, nausea, vomiting, impairment of memory or judgment, blurred vision, dizziness, clumsiness, seizures	*PE:* Fever, nuchal rigidity; lethargy, stupor, or coma in 40%; papilledema, rarely cranial nerve palsies or other focal findings; meningeal signs often absent in HIV-infected patients *CXR:* May be abnormal if concomitant pulmonary cryptococcosis (see Pulmonary Disease)	*CSF:* Elevated intracranial pressure; lymphocytic pleocytosis; hypoglycorrhachia (less than 50% serum glucose); elevated protein (50–300 mg/dL); cryptococcal antigen, positive in 90%; India ink, positive in 50%; culture (most important test) *Evaluation for extrameningeal disease:* CXR and cultures of blood, urine, sputum *CT scan:* Patients with focal neurologic findings or refractory disease	AMB 0.5–1.0 mg/kg/d plus flucytosine 100 mg/kg/d in 4 divided doses for 4–6 wk; **or** AMB 0.3–0.5 mg/kg/d plus flucytosine 150 mg/kg/d in 4 divided doses for 4–6 wk; **or** AMB alone if flucytosine not tolerated *AIDS patients:* AMB with or without flucytosine; or fluconazole 400 mg/d for 10 wk; **or** AMB with flucytosine for 2 wk followed by fluconazole 400 mg/d for 8–10 wk; maintenance therapy required (fluconazole 200 mg/d); *Other immunocompromised hosts e.g., organ transplant:* minimum of 6 wk of AMB/flucytosine therapy; see text
Cryptococcoma	Hemiparesis, hemianopia, focal seizures, rarely symptoms of meningitis only	*PE:* See above; usually focal neurologic findings	*CT scan:* Look for contrast-enhancing single or multiple mass lesions *CSF:* See above; some patients will not have meningitis	Combination AMB/flucytosine as in meningitis; at least 6 wk of therapy; consider surgical excision of single accessible lesion
Pulmonary disease Asymptomatic	None	None	*Culture:* Sputum *CSF:* Essential; see text	*Normal host:* None *AIDS patients:* Fluconazole 200 mg/d
Acute pneumonia	Fever, malaise, night sweats, chest pain, dyspnea, cough, hemoptysis	*PE:* Usually normal *CXR:* Alveolar or interstitial infiltrates or multiple small, rounded opacities; cavities or pleural effusion uncommon	*Culture:* Sputum, pleural fluid (if present), bronchial washings, or lung tissue *Histopathology with special stains:* Lung tissue serology—test for serum cryptococcal antigen *CSF:* Essential; see text and see Meningitis	*Normal host:* With stable pulmonary disease and no extrapulmonary involvement, observation only *Normal host with advancing pulmonary disease or extrapulmonary non-CNS involvement:* Fluconazole for at least 6 mo *AIDS patients:* fluconazole *Other immunocompromised host or seriously ill patient or patient with concomitant CNS disease:* AMB 0.5–0.7 mg/kg/d plus flucytosine 100–150 mg/kg/d in 4 divided doses; total dose AMB 15–20 mg/kg or fluconazole 400 mg/d for at least 6 mo
Chronic pneumonia (nodules or masses)	Often asymptomatic; cough, hemoptysis (rarely)	*CXR:* Solitary nodule or mass often mistaken for neoplasm	*Culture and histopathology with special stains:* Lung tissue *Evaluation for extrapulmonary disease:* CSF, blood, urine, skin	See Acute pneumonia
Skin Usually immuno-compromised patients	Often associated with pulmonary or CNS disease, symptoms variable, depending on other sites of involvement	*PE:* Vesicles, ulcers, nodules, pustules, papules, plaques, subcutaneous abscesses, or cellulitis	*Culture and histopathology:* Skin *Evaluation for extracutaneous sites of involvement*	AMB 0.3–0.5 mg/kg/d or fluconazole 400 mg/d; depends on host; see Pulmonary disease

PE, physical examination; CXR, chest x-ray; CNS, central nervous system; CSF, cerebrospinal fluid; CT, computed tomography; AMB, amphotericin B.

ally reveal abnormalities, such as elevated protein, low glucose, and lymphocytic pleocytosis, but these abnormalities may not be pronounced. As elevated CSF pressure is associated with poor prognosis in non-AIDS patients and probably in AIDS patients as well, measurement of opening pressure should be a routine part of the lumbar puncture in patients suspected of having cryptococcal meningitis. Computed tomography of the head is indicated primarily in patients with papilledema, altered sensorium, or focal neurologic signs, or in those whose illness fails to respond to therapy.

Extraneural dissemination occurs frequently, warranting blood cultures, which are often positive.

Pulmonary Disease. Pulmonary cryptococcosis can be diagnosed by isolation of the organism from respiratory secretions or biopsy material from pulmonary lesions. *Cryptococcus neoformans* may colonize the respiratory tract without causing disease. Nevertheless, a positive sputum culture in a normal or immunocompromised patient, with or without other signs or symptoms of cryptococcal disease, should prompt an evaluation for extrapulmonary disease, including blood cultures and a lumbar puncture.

THERAPEUTIC

Therapeutic Options and Recommended Approach

Central Nervous System Disease. Therapy, particularly for AIDS patients, should be tailored to the severity of disease and the urgency of providing therapy as an outpatient rather than in the hospital. The standard primary therapy for cryptococcal meningoencephalitis, developed from clinical trials conducted before the HIV epidemic, includes amphotericin B 0.5–1.0 mg/kg/d intravenously plus flucytosine 100 mg/kg orally (in four divided doses) daily. Combinations including lower doses of amphotericin B and higher doses of flucytosine are also effective. Amphotericin B alone may be used, particularly in patients who cannot tolerate flucytosine. Recent clinical experience using the triazole drugs (fluconazole and, to a lesser extent, itraconazole) with AIDS patients has shown that these agents have an important role in the management of cryptococcal meningitis. Fluconazole (400 mg/d) is comparably effective to amphotericin B for patients who present with milder syndromes, although most experts prefer to initiate treatment with amphotericin B for at least 2 weeks before changing to fluconazole (400 mg/d) for an additional 8 to 10 weeks.

Some patients with AIDS and cryptococcal meningitis develop elevated intracranial pressure, with or without evidence of hydrocephalus on computed tomography scan. Because this complication may result in the development of serious neurologic sequelae or death, patients with AIDS should be evaluated at least weekly during the first 4 weeks of therapy for any change in clinical status. If deterioration occurs, serial lumbar punctures or temporary ventricular drainage with intracranial pressure monitoring via a ventriculostomy is indicated. The use of corticosteroids in this setting remains controversial. Patients with persistently elevated intracranial pressure require a permanent ventricular shunting procedure.

As cryptococcosis in AIDS patients is rarely if ever cured, initial therapy must be followed by lifelong maintenance treatment. Fluconazole 200 mg/d orally is the optimal current choice for maintenance therapy after therapy for acute cryptococcal meningitis in patients with AIDS.

Pulmonary Disease. In the normal host, pulmonary cryptococcosis often resolves without specific antifungal therapy, although these patients require careful follow-up; however, recent availability of oral antifungal agents has led some to recommend therapy in all cases of pulmonary cryptococcosis, regardless of underlying immune status. In immunocompromised patients, pulmonary cryptococcosis generally results in dissemination in the absence of therapy and requires therapy comparable to treatment of cryptococcal meningitis.

Other Sites. Any patient with skin, bone, or other form of extraneural cryptococcosis should be assumed to have disseminated disease and should receive chemotherapy with an azole or combination amphotericin B and flucytosine, depending on the host immune status and site of disease.

Pharmacologic Treatment

Amphotericin B. Intravenous infusion of amphotericin B (Fungizone) may be associated with fever, shaking chills, nausea, vomiting, phlebitis, and, rarely, anaphylactic reactions. Antipyretics, analgesics, antiemetics, heparin, and/or hydrocortisone are often administered concomitantly with amphotericin B to prevent or ameliorate adverse effects. Long-term amphotericin B therapy is frequently associated with anemia, mild to moderate azotemia, hypokalemia, and, occasionally, renal tubular acidosis. Less commonly, leukopenia, thrombocytopenia, hypomagnesemia, and hepatic dysfunction are noted.

Flucytosine. Flucytosine should not be used alone because of the high likelihood of the emergence of resistant cryptococci during therapy. Serious side effects associated with flucytosine include leukopenia, thrombocytopenia, nausea, vomiting, diarrhea, and hepatitis, any of which may require reduction in dosage or discontinuation of therapy. As flucytosine is excreted primarily in the urine, the dosage should be reduced by 50% when creatinine clearance is between 25 and 50 mL per minute and by 75% when clearance is between 10 and 25 mL per minute. For patients with severe renal insufficiency or renal failure requiring dialysis, the dosage should be based on serum levels of flucytosine (usual therapeutic range, 50–100 µg/mL). Because of concerns about toxicity, some authorities would reserve use of flucytosine in AIDS patients for situations in which plasma levels can be monitored.

Triazoles. The availability of triazole drugs has greatly widened options for managing cryptococcal meningitis. Fluconazole has excellent oral bioavailability and penetration into the CSF (70–80% of serum levels) and has been approved as an alternative to amphotericin B in selected patients with AIDS and cryptococcal meningitis. Fluconazole is generally well tolerated; occasional adverse effects include nausea, vomiting, elevated transaminase levels, and skin rash. To date, there are no reports of fluconazole-induced adrenal insufficiency or suppression of testosterone synthesis, a concern with imidazole agents. Itraconazole, another triazole antifungal agent, may also be effective despite its low

concentrations in the CSF, though the role of this agent in the management of cryptococcal meningitis is not clearly established. Adverse effects are also unusual with itraconazole; they include nausea and vomiting, pruritus and rash, asymptomatic elevation of transaminase levels, headache, and dizziness, as well as drug-induced hypokalemia and peripheral edema, which are peculiar to itraconazole. Ketoconazole, an imidazole, should not be used in the treatment of cryptococcal meningitis. All of the azole antifungal agents, including ketoconazole, fluconazole, and itraconazole, have the potential to interact with various drugs, including cyclosporine, phenytoin, rifampin, rifabutin, warfarin, certain antihistamine drugs, and digoxin.

FOLLOW-UP

During therapy, patients receiving amphotericin B should be evaluated weekly for evidence of deteriorating renal function, hypokalemia, hypomagnesemia, and anemia. Similarly, patients taking flucytosine should be monitored weekly for abnormalities in liver, kidney, and bone marrow function, and patients taking fluconazole or itraconazole should be monitored monthly for evidence of liver dysfunction.

After therapy is stopped, all patients, regardless of type of disease, should be evaluated for recurrence at quarterly intervals for up to 1 year. As relapse of cryptococcal meningitis occurs in about 20% of non-AIDS patients, CSF should be obtained for culture and determination of cryptococcal antigen titers at the end of therapy and 1, 6, and 12 months after therapy. The CSF must be sterile at the end of therapy. After therapy, if cultures become positive or cryptococcal antigen titers show a significant increase, re-treatment is indicated. Patients treated for extraneural disease alone should immediately report any new symptoms of central nervous system disease to their physician.

AIDS patients with cryptococcosis require ongoing suppressive therapy (see above).

DISCUSSION
Prevalence and Incidence

Precise estimates of the incidence of cryptococcosis are not available because there has not been surveillance for this disease; however, beginning in the early 1980s, cryptococcosis increased tremendously as AIDS became the major predisposing factor to this infection. Extrapulmonary cryptococcosis has been reported in approximately 17,000 or 6.2% of the reported cases of AIDS in the United States (Centers for Disease Control and Prevention [CDC] AIDS surveillance data through September 1993); however, this number underestimates the occurrence of cryptococcosis in persons with AIDS, as cryptococcosis occurring after the diagnosis of AIDS may not be reported to the CDC AIDS surveillance system. Cryptococcosis may be less frequent in pediatric AIDS cases.

Related Basic Science

Advanced HIV infection is now by far the most common predisposing condition for cryptococcosis, although persons with lymphoreticular malignancies and persons receiving immunosuppressive therapy, especially prolonged corticosteroid therapy, have a substantially increased risk. Among HIV-infected persons, the highest rates of cryptococcosis occur in those with low CD4 T-lymphocyte counts, almost always below 100 cells/mm^3. Cryptococcosis has been reported to occur with increased frequency among AIDS patients who are black, male, or injection drug users, but the explanations for these observations remain unclear; however, cryptococcosis also occurs in persons without apparent predisposing factors.

Antigenic differences in the outer capsule of the organism define two varieties of *C. neoformans*: *C. neoformans* var. *neoformans* and *C. neoformans* var. *gattii*. *C. neoformans* var. *neoformans* is responsible for the majority of cases of cryptococcosis; *C. neoformans* var. *gattii* is distributed predominantly in Australia, Asia, and Southern California and appears to be unusual as a cause of cryptococcosis in AIDS patients, even where it is endemic.

Cryptococcus neoformans var. *neoformans* is widely distributed in soil throughout the world. Areas contaminated with pigeon droppings are a particularly rich source of the organism. Some reports link exposures to pigeon feces with human cryptococcosis, but proof that avian excreta is the primary source of environmental exposure for most persons is lacking.

Infections with *C. neoformans* generally begin with an asymptomatic pulmonary focus following inhalation of the organism. Most cases probably result from new infection, although some may result from reactivation of a latent focus, as can occur with coccidioidomycosis, histoplasmosis, and tuberculosis. Person-to-person transmission is not believed to occur.

Following initial infection, there is hematogenous dissemination to various organs. The absence of complement and a soluble anticryptococcal factor in the CSF, as well as a decrease or absent inflammatory response to cryptococci in brain tissue, may explain the preferential involvement of the central nervous system. Basilar arachnoiditis is most prominent, but is often accompanied by inflammation throughout the cerebral cortex and basal ganglia. Tissue damage is caused by multiplying foci of organisms; however, organ dysfunction is uncommon.

Natural History and Its Modification with Treatment

In normal hosts, disease localized to the lungs may spontaneously regress without therapy. In contrast, untreated meningeal or disseminated cryptococcal disease is uniformly fatal. The mortality in treated patients is highly dependent on underlying disease and the patient's status at the time of diagnosis. For example, among patients with cryptococcal meningitis, an immunocompromised organ transplant recipient who presents in coma has a much poorer prognosis than a "normal host" with only headache and normal findings on neurologic examination. Similarly, because of the refractoriness to therapy for cryptococcosis in patients with AIDS, lifetime maintenance therapy is indicated.

Prevention

No particular behaviors have been shown to be effective in lowering the risk of developing cryptococcosis, although avoiding sites likely to be heavily contaminated with *C. neoformans* might reduce the risk of exposure to the organism. Some evidence suggests that prophylactic use of triazole antifungal agents may reduce the occurrence of cryptococcosis in those at risk; however, this practice has not been demonstrated to prolong survival and its cost-effectiveness has not been well evaluated. The role of antifungal prophylaxis for cryptococcosis, therefore, remains unclear. Close medical supervision of high-risk patients generally allows early diagnosis of disease and may be the best strategy to improve outcomes of therapy for cryptococcosis.

Cost Containment

Early diagnosis and treatment are the most effective means to reduce complications, minimize the likelihood of relapse, and thereby cut the cost of therapy. Combination therapy with amphotericin B and flucytosine shortens the duration of therapy and, when given in an outpatient setting to selected patients, further reduces hospital costs. Oral fluconazole therapy in an ambulatory setting for selected patients is less expensive than combination amphotericin B and flucytosine administered to hospitalized patients. Although some physicians may wish to consider prophylactic use of triazoles to prevent cryptococcosis in HIV-infected patients with CD4 lymphocyte counts below 50 cells/mm^3, this is an expensive approach; indications for considering prophylaxis for cryptococcosis remain unresolved at this time. Routine screening of HIV-infected patients for cryptococcal antigen is not warranted.

REFERENCES

Como JA, Dismukes WE. Oral azole drugs as systemic antifungal therapy. N Engl J Med 1994;330:263.

Diamond RD. *Cryptococcus neoformans.* In: Mandell GL, Bennett JE, Dolin R, eds. Mandell, Douglas, and Bennett's principles and practice of infectious diseases. 4th ed. New York: Churchill Livingstone, 1995.

Dismukes WE. Management of cryptococcosis. Clin Infect Dis 1993;17(suppl. 2):S507.

Kwon-Chung KJ, Bennett JE. Cryptococcosis. In: Medical mycology. Philadelphia/London: Lea & Febiger, 1992:397.

Powderly WG. Cryptococcal meningitis and AIDS. Clin Infect Dis 1993;17:837.

White MH, Armstrong D. Cryptococcosis. In: Management of infection in HIV disease. Infect Dis Clin North Am 1994;8:383.

CHAPTER 8–55

Histoplasmosis

Rana A. Hajjeh, M.D., Michael S. Saag, M.D., Robert W. Pinner, M.D., and William E. Dismukes, M.D.

DEFINITION

Histoplasmosis is a systemic disease caused by infection with the fungus *Histoplasma capsulatum.*

ETIOLOGY

Histoplasma capsulatum is a dimorphic fungus that exists in the mycelial stage in the environment and in laboratory cultures, but transforms into a budding yeast in host tissues.

CRITERIA FOR DIAGNOSIS

Histoplasmosis includes a wide spectrum of clinical syndromes, the most common of which is an asymptomatic or a self-limited upper respiratory tract infection. Less frequently, histoplasmosis may present as chronic cavitary pulmonary disease, as progressive disseminated multiorgan disease, or as an immune-mediated disease of the mediastinum or eye. Disseminated histoplasmosis has been recognized as an opportunistic infection in immunocompromised patients, such as patients with HIV infection, in whom it is considered to be an AIDS-defining illness.

Suggestive

Histoplasmosis should be suspected in previously healthy persons who live or have traveled to disease-endemic areas with findings suggestive of atypical pneumonia, patients with chronic obstructive pulmonary disease who develop upper lobe fibrocavitary disease, or immunocompromised persons with unexplained fever. Disseminated histoplasmosis should also be suspected in HIV-infected persons who present with septic shock.

Definitive

Definitive diagnosis is established by isolation of the organism; however, a more rapid presumptive diagnosis can be made by visualization of the yeast form of the fungus with special stains on histopathologic sections of biopsied lesions.

CLINICAL MANIFESTATIONS

In addition to the various clinical manifestations mentioned above, histoplasmosis has been reported to manifest as a syndrome resembling septicemia in 5 to 10% of patients with AIDS. These patients present with shock, respiratory insufficiency, hepatic and renal failure, and rhabdomyolysis, and have a high mortality.

Subjective and objective clinical manifestations are summarized in Table 8–55–1.

PLANS
Diagnostic
Differential Diagnosis

Acute pulmonary histoplasmosis can resemble a variety of upper respiratory illnesses or community-acquired pneumonias, especially atypical pneumonias. Chronic cavitary histoplasmosis should be differentiated from pulmonary tuberculosis. The differential diagnosis of disseminated histoplasmosis includes tuberculosis and other systemic mycoses, such as disseminated coccidioidomycosis and blastomycosis. In persons with HIV infection with septic shock-like presentation (see Clinical Manifestations), bacteremia should be ruled out.

Diagnostic Options

Serologic tests are important adjuncts in the diagnosis of histoplasmosis. The most commonly used serologic methods are complement fixation and immunodiffusion assays to detect antibodies to *H. capsulatum*. A sensitive and specific radioimmunoassay for the detection of *H. capsulatum* polysaccharide antigen in body fluids has been developed; the urine antigen test is very helpful in the diagnosis and follow-up of disseminated histoplasmosis in patients with AIDS.

Recommended Approach

See Table 8–55–1.

Therapeutic
Therapeutic Options

The therapeutic options for histoplasmosis have broadened considerably since the introduction of the oral azole drugs. Amphotericin B is still the treatment of choice for life-threatening disease and for infections that do not respond to azole drugs.

Recommended Approach

See Table 8–55–1.

FOLLOW-UP

Patients with asymptomatic or acute pulmonary histoplasmosis rarely require long-term follow-up; however, patients with chronic cavitary histoplasmosis should be followed with serial monthly chest x-rays to document resolution of the pneumonitis and change in the cavity wall thickness. Underlying chronic obstructive pulmonary disease should be managed appropriately. Disseminated histoplasmosis requires close observation for new lesions, evidence of extension, and complications of drug therapy. Patients receiving ketoconazole or itraconazole should have monthly tests of liver enzymes. Ketoconazole or itraconazole should be stopped and amphotericin B therapy instituted if liver enzyme levels become significantly abnormal or if disease progression is noted.

After therapy is stopped, patients should be evaluated for evidence of recurrent disease initially at monthly intervals and then every 6 months for 2 to 3 years. Patients with AIDS should continue to receive suppressive therapy with itraconazole (200 mg/d) for life. Because of the potential for the development of adrenal insufficiency or recurrent disease after therapy has been completed, regular follow-up evaluations are mandatory. Patients should promptly report any suspicious symptoms or signs such as progressive shortness of breath, hemoptysis, recurrent fever, oral ulcers, and progressive malaise.

DISCUSSION
Prevalence and Incidence

Histoplasmosis is endemic in the south-central and midcentral United States, mostly in the areas surrounding the Mississippi and Ohio river valleys. It is also endemic in most of Latin America; a few cases have been reported from Southeast Asia and Europe.

More than 80% of persons living in disease-endemic areas are infected before the age of 18. Although disseminated histoplasmosis is reported as the AIDS-defining illness for only 1% of AIDS patients reported to the Centers for Disease Control and Prevention (CDC) AIDS surveillance, it occurs in about 5% of AIDS patients who reside in histoplasmosis-endemic areas and in up to 27% of AIDS patients in Indianapolis. Person-to-person spread is not believed to be important in disease transmission.

Related Basic Science

Small aerosolized spores of *H. capsulatum* are first inhaled and then deposited in the nonciliated regions of the lung, including the alveoli. The organisms induce a local inflammatory response consisting primarily of monocytes and macrophages, which in turn ingest the yeasts. Initially, in nonimmune persons, the macrophages are unable to kill the yeasts and the organisms multiply intracellularly. Infected macrophages seed reticuloendothelial tissues, such as the regional lymph nodes and spleen, setting up microfoci of infection. In the normal host, once antigen-specific cell-mediated immunity becomes established, the infection is contained. Vasculitis, thrombosis, and necrosis in infected areas are often present at this stage, resulting in enlargement of regional lymph nodes. The lymphadenopathy usually resolves over the ensuing 2 to 4 months with fibrosis and, ultimately, calcification. In contrast, the reticuloendothelial system in individuals with impaired cellular immunity is unable to contain the infection, and viable *H. capsulatum* organisms disseminate throughout the body.

Bird and bat guano provide an excellent growth medium for *H. capsulatum*. Consequently, soil containing heavy accumulations of chicken, pigeon, blackbird, or starling droppings and areas frequented by bats, such as caves, hollow trees, attics, and old buildings, are common environmental sources of the fungus.

Natural History and Its Modification with Treatment

Acute pulmonary histoplasmosis is generally self-limited and requires no therapy. The course of chronic pulmonary disease depends on the degree of progression of the pulmonary lesions and the underlying condition of the patient's lungs. If cavitation is not present, persistent active disease is unlikely. When there is progressive infection and persistent cavitation, spontaneous resolution occurs in fewer than 20% of patients. Untreated disseminated histoplasmosis will progress from mild disease to more severe disease and, ultimately, death, especially in immunocompromised patients. HIV-infected persons with disseminated histoplasmosis who present with septic shock have high mortality despite treatment. The long-term prognosis for patients with mediastinal granulomas is excellent; however, patients with mediastinal fibrosis are much more likely to develop complications such as superior vena cava syndrome, progressive pulmonary hypertension, cor pulmonale, and esophageal obstruction. Visual loss in persons with presumed ocular histoplasmosis syndrome usually can be stabilized, but not reversed, with therapy.

Prevention

Exposure to airborne spores of *H. capsulatum* in areas of endemic disease is unavoidable. In these areas, when there is ongoing mechanical disturbance of accumulations of bird or bat droppings, or of soil known to be heavily infested with these droppings, precautions should be taken to minimize exposure to aerosolized dust. These precautions may include thoroughly wetting the area that will be disturbed and wearing masks. The role of prophylactic antifungal therapy for persons with HIV infection is not yet defined, but is currently under study.

Cost Containment

As the majority of patients with histoplasmosis require no therapy, accurate early diagnosis with appropriate patient reassurance is the most effective means of reducing costs. Outpatient therapy with oral ketoconazole or itraconazole or, if necessary, intravenous amphotericin B on an alternate-day schedule should be instituted when feasible. Ag-

TABLE 8–55–1. HISTOPLASMOSIS: CLINICAL MANIFESTATIONS, DIAGNOSIS, AND TREATMENT

Clinical Syndrome	Clinical Manifestations		Diagnosis	Treatment
	Subjective	*Objective*		
Pulmonary disease **Acute** Asymptomatic	None	None or patchy pneumonitis on CXR	*Epidemiology:* Common-source outbreak *Serology:* Complement fixation (fourfold rise in convalescent titer, or single titer ≥ 1:32) Histoplasmin skin test conversion	None
Symptomatic	Fever, chills, nonproductive cough, dull substernal chest pain, malaise, headache, myalgias	*PE:* Fever, chest exam usually normal, occasionally rales; rarely pericarditis, *Erythema nodosum* or *E. multiforme* *CXR:* Single or multiple areas patchy pneumonitis; later hilar adenopathy, calcified nodules	*Serology:* as above	None (usually spontaneous recovery over 2 to 4 wk) If severe or prolonged pulmonary disease or immunocompromised host: AMB 0.3–0.5 mg/kg/d for 2–4 wk, or ketoconazole 400 mg or itraconazole 200 mg PO for 2–6 mo
Chronic (cavitary): usually underlying chronic obstructive pulmonary disease	Indolent course; cough, moderate weight loss (commonly), fever, night sweats, malaise; aching chest pain (25%); hemoptysis (infrequent); asymptomatic (20%)	*PE:* Findings consistent with chronic obstructive pulmonary disease *CXR:* Early—apical interstitial infiltrate; late—dense pneumonitis adjacent to preexisting cavities or bullae, fibronodular scarring, progressive cavitary enlargement	*Serology and skin tests:* Of limited value in endemic areas *Cultures:* Sputum (positive 20–40%), bronchial washings *Culture and histopathology with special stains:* Lung tissue	*Pneumonitis without cavity:* No antifungal therapy *Cavity wall thickness < 2 mm:* Conservative management *Cavity wall thickness >2 mm:* Ketoconazole 400 mg or itraconazole 200 mg bid for at least 6 mo, or AMB total dose 30–35 mg/kg *Surgery for intractable hemoptysis:* Only if pulmonary function allows (rarely feasible)
Progressive disseminated disease Multiorgan disease: usually immuno-compromised host; if normal host, infants or elderly	High fever, malaise, cough, dyspnea, weight loss, oral lesions	*PE:* Fever, hepatosplenomegaly, lymphadenopathy, inspiratory rales, mucosal ulcerations; *Patient with AIDS:* 5–10% present with septic shock picture *LAB:* Anemia, leukopenia, thrombocytopenia; abnormal liver function tests *CXR:* Patchy infiltrates, hilar adenopathy, or interstitial pneumonitis	*Serology:* CF titer ≥ 1:32; immunodiffusion positive for M or H bands *Cultures and histopathology with special strains:* Peripheral blood (organisms in leukocytes), or tissue from oropharyngeal ulcer, bone marrow, liver, lung, CNS, or other involved site *Patients with AIDS:* RIA for polysaccharide antigen useful for diagnosis and follow-up	*Normal hosts:* Non-life threatening disease—ketoconazole 400 mg or itraconazole 200 mg bid for at least 6 mo; disease progression, life-threatening disease, or CNS disease—AMB, total dose 30–35 mg/kg *Immunocompromised hosts:* AMB, total dose 30–35 mg/kg *Patients with AIDS:* AMB as for immunocompromised hosts for severe disease: itraconazole 200 mg bid for 12 wk, itraconazole 200 mg qd as maintenance therapy for life
Local disease	Constitutional symptoms including weight loss, low-grade fever, malaise; other symptoms variable, depending on site, abdominal tenderness, meningismus, focal neurologic signs	*PE:* Fever heptasplenomegaly (30–50%), oropharyngeal ulcers, signs of Addison's disease, heme-positive stools and hypoglycorrhachia	Same as for Multiorgan disease. *CSF:* Abnormal in CNS disease with lymphocytic pleocytosis, protein elevation	See Multiorgan disease
Immune-mediated disease Mediastinal granuloma/fibrosis	Cough, dyspnea, chest pain, hemoptysis, dysphagia, odynophagia, hematemesis, weight loss, fever, symptoms of SVC syndrome	*PE:* Nonspecific (except in patients with SVC syndrome) *LAB:* Usually normal *CXR:* Mediastinal widening; right paratracheal or hilar mass	*Serology:* CF titer ≥ 1:32; may be normal *Chest CT scan:* Define mass, location *Barium swallow, endoscopy:* Evaluate erosive disease *Mediastinal biopsy:* Required for definitive tissue diagnosis; may not be necessary in children with middle mediastinal mass and CF titer ≥ 1:32	*Conservative management:* Mediastinal fibrosis, SVC syndrome, asymptomatic or mildly symptomatic disease *Surgical:* Enucleation or partial resection effective for some patients with granuloma *Antifungal therapy for patients with erosive complications:* Ketoconazole 400 mg or itraconazole 200 mg bid for 6 mo
Presumed ocular histoplasmosis syndrome	Painless loss of visual acuity, scotomata, blindness; rarely asymptomatic	*Examination of retina:* Scattered, yellow, punched-out, atrophic lesions; macular choroiditis; circumpapillary scarring	*Ophthalmologic examination:* Highly characteristic	Laser photocoagulation or corticosteroids

CXR, chest x-ray; PE, physical examination; AMB, amphotericin B; LAB, laboratory tests; CF, complement fixation; CNS, central nervous system; SVC, superior vena cava; RIA, radioimmunoassay; CT, computed tomography.

gressive therapy for the underlying chronic obstructive pulmonary disease in patients with noncavitary chronic pulmonary histoplasmosis may help prevent cavitation, thereby circumventing the need for the expense of antifungal therapy.

REFERENCES

Dismukes WE, Kauffman CA, Chapman SW, et al. Itraconazole therapy for blastomycosis and histoplasmosis. Am J Med 1992;93:489.
Goodwin RA, Des Prez RM. State of the art: Histoplasmosis. Am Rev Respir Dis 1978;117:929.
National Institute of Allergy and Infectious Disease Mycoses Study Group (Dismukes WE, Cloud G, et al.). Treatment of blastomycosis and histoplasmosis with ketoconazole: Results of a prospective randomized clinical trial. Ann Intern Med 1985;103:861.
Wheat J. Histoplasmosis and coccidioidomycosis in individuals with AIDS. Infect Dis Clin North Am 1994;8:467.
Wheat LJ, Connolly-Stringfield PA, Baker RL, et al. Disseminated histoplasmosis in the acquired immunodeficiency syndrome: Clinical findings, diagnosis, and treatment, and review of the literature. Medicine 1990;69:261.
Wheat LJ, Connolly-Stringfield P, Kohler RB, et al. *Histoplasma capsulatum* polysaccharide antigen detection in diagnosis and management of disseminated histoplasmosis in patients with acquired immunodeficiency syndrome. Am J Med 1989;87:396.

CHAPTER 8–56

Blastomycosis

Michael S. Saag, M.D., and William E. Dismukes, M.D.

DEFINITION

Blastomycosis is a disease caused by the fungus *Blastomyces dermatitidis.*

ETIOLOGY

Blastomycosis, a disease caused by the dimorphic fungus *B. dermatitidis,* infects primarily the lungs, commonly disseminates to skin, bone, and the genitourinary tract, and rarely involves the liver, spleen, thyroid, gastrointestinal tract, pericardium, adrenal glands, or central nervous system.

CRITERIA FOR DIAGNOSIS

Suggestive

Although originally reported in North America, the disease occurs worldwide and should be suspected in persons with chronic pneumonia, especially those with concomitant skin, bone, or genitourinary system disease.

Definitive

Cultural isolation or histopathologic demonstration of the typical broad-based budding yeast form of *B. dermatitidis* in body tissues, sputum, or body fluids is required for definitive diagnosis.

CLINICAL MANIFESTATIONS

See Table 8–56–1.

PLANS

Diagnostic

Differential Diagnosis

Pulmonary Disease. Most commonly, pulmonary blastomycosis is associated with a chronic pneumonia syndrome, manifested by chronic productive cough, pleuritic chest pain, weight loss, and low-grade fever. Chest radiographs typically show lobar consolidation, one or more fibromodular infiltrates, or mass lesions, with or without cavitation. Disorders that often mimic pulmonary blastomycosis include other fungal diseases such as cryptococcosis, histoplasmosis, coccidioidomycosis; granulomatous diseases such as tuberculosis and sarcoidosis; nocardiosis; and noninfectious diseases, for example, carcinoma, Wegener's granulomatosis, and bronchiolitis obliterans organizing pneumonia.

Cutaneous Disease. The skin lesions of blastomycosis, which are of two general types, verrucous and ulcerative, tend to occur more commonly on exposed parts, such as the face and extremities. Cutaneous blastomycosis must be distinguished from cutaneous disease associated with sporotrichosis, coccidioidomycosis, phaeohyphomycoses (caused by dematiacious fungi), nocardiosis, and malignancies. Other skin conditions that should be excluded are pyoderma granulosum, ecthyma gangrenosum, and factitial ulceration.

Diagnostic Options and Recommended Approach

See Table 8–56–1. Blastomycin, a crude antigenic mixture prepared from filtrates of *B. dermatitidis* cultures, is unreliable as a skin test preparation and therefore is not helpful in the diagnosis of blastomycosis. There is no other reliable skin test antigen. Serologic tests for blastomycosis are equally unhelpful. Many patients with proven blastomycosis have negative complement fixation tests. A positive immunodiffusion test for antibody against the A antigen may indicate recent or current infection with blastomycosis; however, a positive test is not diagnostic and should be used only to stimulate a more thorough search for the disease.

Therapeutic

See Table 8–56–1. For a detailed description of antifungal agents and their adverse effects, please refer to Chapter 8–54. Until the past few years, amphotericin B was considered the mainstay of therapy for all forms of blastomycosis. Recent studies have shown that oral antifungal azole agents, ketoconazole and itraconazole, are highly effective in blastomycosis and far less toxic than amphotericin B. In addition, these drugs offer the advantage of chronic or maintenance therapy in an outpatient setting. Itraconazole appears to be as effective as ketoconazole and is better tolerated.

Fluconazole at comparable doses is less effective than either ketoconazole or itraconazole.

Based on current data, amphotericin B should be reserved for seriously ill patients, those with central nervous system disease, and those with progressive disease while on oral azoles.

The patient with acute pulmonary disease should be informed that the illness is often self-limited and only close observation without therapy is required. Patients with chronic pulmonary or disseminated disease should be told that therapy is necessary and is usually effective. Those who require therapy but do not receive it for whatever reason usually develop progressive disease, which may be fatal. Compliance with medical therapy, therefore, should be stressed. Inform the patient and family that blastomycosis is not believed to be contagious. Any adverse effects attributed to the medication or symptoms of progression of disease should be reported to the physician immediately.

FOLLOW-UP

Patients receiving an oral antifungal azole should be seen at 2 weeks, 4 weeks, and then monthly while on therapy. At each visit signs of progressive disseminated disease should be sought and tests of liver function obtained. Patients receiving amphotericin B should have weekly evaluations of renal and bone marrow function and measurements of

TABLE 8–56–1. BLASTOMYCOSIS: CLINICAL MANIFESTATIONS, DIAGNOSIS, AND TREATMENT

Clinical Syndrome	Clinical Manifestations		Diagnosis	Treatment
	Subjective	*Objective*		
Pulmonary disease **Acute** Asymptomatic	None	None	*Epidemiology:* common-source outbreak *Culture:* sputum, rarely positive	None
Symptomatic	Usually abrupt onset; cough, chest pain, dyspnea, fever, chills, headache, myalgias, arthralgias, fatigue	*PE:* fever *CXR:* airspace disease, infiltrates, nodular densities, pleural effusion (occasionally), miliary pattern (rarely), hilar enlargement (rarely)	*Wet preparation with 10% potassium hydroxide* *Blastomycin skin test:* unreliable (see text) *Serology:* unreliable (see text) Examination for evidence of dissemination	*Normal host:* observation; usually self-limited disease; treat only if evidence of progression of disease or dissemination; see Chronic Pulmonary Disease *Immunocompromised host* (*uncommon*): AMB 0.3–0.5 mg/kg/d or total dose approx 30 mg/kg
Chronic	Malaise, weight loss, fever, night sweats, cough, hemoptysis, chest pain, dyspnea, hoarseness; often accompanying skin lesions	*PE:* Fever; rales, rhonchi, rub (uncommonly); skin lesions (25–35%) *CXR:* Airspace disease, bronchopneumonia most common; nodules or mass; reticulonodular pattern or pleural disease; rarely cavitation	*Wet preparation and culture:* sputum *Culture and histopathology with special stains:* bronchial washings, lung tissue, pleural fluid *Wet preparation and culture:* skin lesions, if present	*Normal host:* ketoconazole 400 mg/d or itraconazole 200–400 mg/d for at least 6 mo; if failure, increase dose or AMB, total dose approx 30 mg/kg *Immunocompromised host:* AMB, total dose approx 30 mg/kg
Disseminated disease* Skin	Often the chief complaint; sharply demarcated pustules, nodules, or ulcers, occasionally pruritic	*PE:* multiple papules or pustules, progressing to verrucous or ulcerative lesions, on hands, wrists, lower legs, and/or face; rarely subcutaneous nodules or oropharyngeal and nasopharyngeal lesions	*Wet preparation and culture:* pus or skin tissue *Histopathology with special stains:* skin	See Chronic Pulmonary Disease (also see Chapter 8–16)
Bone and joint	Soft tissue abscess, draining sinus, swollen painful joint, bone pain	*PE:* tenderness of involved site (vertebra, skull, ribs, epiphysis of long bones most frequently); joint effusion, warmth, erythema *X-rays:* lytic, well-delineated, "punched-out" lesion	*Wet preparation, culture, and histopathology with special stains:* Bone tissue, joint fluid, synovium, and tissue from another site, e.g., skin	See Chronic Pulmonary Disease (also see Chapter 8–16)
Genitourinary	Fever, dysuria, frequency, scrotal pain	*PE:* tender, enlarged, nodular prostate; tender or swollen testicle, epididymis *U/A:* hematuria, pyuria	*Wet preparation and culture:* early morning urine and prostatic fluid after massage *Culture and histopathology with special stains:* prostate, epididymal, or testicular tissue	See Chronic Pulmonary Disease (also see Chapter 8–16)
Central nervous system	Fever, nausea, vomiting, headache, stiff neck, back pain, confusion, lethargy: focal neurologic deficits	*PE:* abnormal mental status, focal neurologic findings, signs of epidural abscess (back tenderness, loss of spinal cord function), or signs of chronic meningitis	*Examination of CSF:* lymphocytic pleocytosis, low glucose, elevated protein, Gram stain, culture (low yield), CF test *CT scan:* look for intracerebral mass or hydrocephalus *Myelogram (if signs of epidural abscess):* CSF "block"	AMB, total dose 30–40 mg/kg

PE, physical examination; CXR, chest x-ray; AMB, amphotericin B; U/A, urinalysis; CSF, cerebrospinal fluid; CF, complement fixation; CT, computed tomography.
*Most patients with disseminated disease typically have pulmonary and/or skin involvement.

serum potassium. After therapy has been completed, patients should be screened for evidence of recurrent disease at 1, 3, and 6 months and annually thereafter for several years.

Patients should understand the chronic nature of the disease, the possibility of late recurrence, and the need for extended follow-up with the physician. Any symptoms of recurrent disease, such as cough, fatigue, weight loss, and skin lesions, should be reported promptly.

DISCUSSION
Prevalence and Incidence

Blastomycosis has been reported worldwide but appears to be endemic in the south-central and north-central states in the Mississippi and Ohio River valleys, the states and provinces that border the Great Lakes, and along the shores of the St. Lawrence River. Epidemiologic studies are limited, however, by the unavailability of reliable skin tests and serologic markers. Recent studies indicate that *B. dermatitidis* resides in warm, moist soil enriched by organic debris. Persons with occupational or avocational exposure to soil and the outdoors appear to be at highest risk of acquiring infection. Animals, including dogs and horses, are also susceptible.

Related Basic Science

Blastomycosis begins as a pulmonary disease as a consequence of inhalation of aerosolized *B. dermatitidis* spores into the alveoli. The initial inflammatory response is characterized by clusters of polymorphonuclear leukocytes, which readily ingest the organisms; however, intracellular killing of the organisms by the leukocytes is poor. The early neutrophilic inflammatory response is followed by a cellular immune response, characterized by the appearance of epithelioid cells and giant cells and subsequently noncaseating granulomas. The primary infection may remain confined to the lung or may disseminate to other sites in the body such as skin, bone, and genitourinary tract. Once disseminated, a local chronic inflammatory response similar to that in the lung is established, often with microabscesses and, occasionally, sinus tract formation.

Natural History and Its Modification with Treatment

Acute symptomatic pulmonary disease seems to be a self-limited process that resolves without specific therapy in normal hosts; however, miliary disease may develop acutely in some untreated patients or more chronic forms of disseminated disease may present later. Approximately 40% of patients with more advanced or chronic blastomycosis present with lung disease only; another 20% present with evidence of pulmonary disease and disease in at least one other site; and 40% present with disease in an extrapulmonary site, usually the skin, without any evidence of pulmonary involvement. Of the patients who require therapy and are normal hosts, about 80 to 90% are cured by oral azole therapy. The cure rate for immunocompromised patients and those who fail an oral azole is strongly dependent on the nature and severity of the underlying disease or predisposing condition. Patients with central nervous system involvement have the worst prognosis with the highest mortality rate. Blastomycosis, in contrast to coccidioidomycosis and histoplasmosis, rarely occurs in persons infected with HIV.

Prevention

There is no definitive way to prevent blastomycosis.

Cost Containment

Emphasis should be placed on early recognition of disease and rapid institution of therapy when required. Outpatient therapy with an oral drug such as ketoconazole or itraconazole is preferable and helps minimize costs. Money should not be spent on skin tests or serologic studies.

REFERENCES

Bradsher RW. Blastomycosis. Infect Dis Clin North Am 1992;14:582.
Klein BS, Vergeront JM, Davis JP. Epidemiologic aspects of blastomycosis, the enigmatic systemic mycosis. Semin Respir Infect 1986;1:29.
Pappas PG, Pottage JC, Powderly WG, et al. Blastomycosis in patients with the acquired immunodeficiency syndrome. Ann Intern Med 1992;116:847.
Pappas PG, Threlkeld MG, Bedsole GD, et al. Blastomycosis in immunocompromised patients. Medicine 1993;72:311.
Sarosi GA, Davies SF, Phillips JR. Self-limited blastomycosis: A report of 39 cases. Semin Respir Infect 1986;1:40.

CHAPTER 8–57

Coccidioidomycosis

Rana A. Hajjeh, M.D., Michael S. Saag, M.D., Robert W. Pinner, M.D., and William E. Dismukes, M.D.

DEFINITION

Coccidioidomycosis is a systemic disease caused by infection with the fungus *Coccidioides immitis.*

ETIOLOGY

Coccidioides immitis is a dimorphic fungus that resides in the soil in certain parts of the southwestern United States, northern Mexico, and certain regions of Central and South America.

CRITERIA FOR DIAGNOSIS

Suggestive

Coccidioidomycosis should be suspected in persons with acute or chronic pulmonary disease or syndromes that could represent disseminated coccidioidomycosis, who live in or have recently traveled through an area where *C. immitis* is endemic.

Definitive

The diagnosis is established by culture of the organism or demonstration of the typical spherules of *C. immitis* in body fluids or in histopathologic sections of biopsied lesions.

CLINICAL MANIFESTATIONS

Approximately 60% of persons infected with *C. immitis* remain asymptomatic. Symptomatic coccidioidomycosis has a wide clinical spectrum, ranging from mild influenza-like illness to serious pneumonia to widespread dissemination. Dissemination outside the lungs occurs in less than 1% of infections. Dissemination most commonly occurs to the skin, bone, joints, and central nervous system. Coccidioidal meningitis is a particularly serious manifestation of disseminated disease. With the advent of the AIDS epidemic, disseminated coccidioidomycosis has emerged as an important opportunistic infection, and in persons infected with HIV, it is considered an AIDS-defining illness. Persons with AIDS can have severe and often fatal illness, especially pneumonitis. Coccidioidal disease in HIV-infected persons is usually associated with a CD4 count below 250/μl.

Subjective and objective clinical manifestations are summarized in Table 8–57–1.

PLANS

Diagnostic

Differential Diagnosis

Acute coccidioidomycosis can resemble a variety of upper respiratory illnesses, community-acquired pneumonias, or connective tissue diseases. The differential diagnosis for disseminated coccidioidomycosis includes tuberculosis and other systemic mycoses, such as histoplasmosis and blastomycosis. Coccidioidal meningitis can resemble a variety of chronic meningitides due to tuberculosis, cryptococcosis, and disseminated histoplasmosis.

Diagnostic Options

Unlike those for other systemic fungal diseases, the serologic and immunologic tests for *C. immitis* infection are well established and helpful. Among persons living in a disease-endemic area, a positive skin test indicates prior exposure. Skin tests performed with either coccidioidin or spherulin antigens are positive in more than 95% of patients with primary coccidioidomycosis. Of the two antigenic mixtures, spherulin is more sensitive. Absence of skin test reactivity in a person with demonstrated coccidioidal infection may signal dissemination.

A positive tube precipitin test, which detects primarily immunoglobulin M antibody, is indicative of current or recent infection. Precipitin antibodies rarely persist. In contrast, complement-fixing antibodies appear later and persist longer. The complement fixation test, which detects immunoglobulin G antibodies, is diagnostic of recent infection (conversion from negative to positive). In persons with HIV infection, coccidioidal serologic tests, especially the tube precipitin test, are less

TABLE 8–57–1. COCCIDIOIDOMYCOSIS: CLINICAL MANIFESTATIONS, DIAGNOSIS, AND TREATMENT

Clinical Syndrome	Clinical Manifestations		Diagnosis	Treatment
	Subjective	*Objective*		
Pulmonary diseases **Primary infection** Asymptomatic (60%)	None	None or patchy pneumonitis on CXR	*Epidemiology:* Live in or visited endemic area *Coccidioidin or spherulin skin test:* Conversion *Serology:* Often negative in asymptomatic persons	None
Symptomatic (acute) (40%)	Fever, cough, chest pain, dyspnea, chills, malaise, myalgias, night sweats, rash	*PE:* Fever; occasional rales; toxic erythema, erythema nodosum, or erythema multiforme; arthralgias, arthritis *LAB:* Eosinophilia (commonly) *CXR:* Single or multiple patchy infiltrates, hilar adenopathy, plural effusion (occasionally); HIV-infected persons—miliary pattern (40%)	*Coccidioidin or spherulin skin test:* Conversion *Serology:* IgM precipitin (Ab) positive within weeks of infection; CF Ab appears later, more sustained, correlates with prognosis *Wet preparation and cultures:* Sputum	None: self-limited in 95%; 5% progress to chronic persistent or progressive pneumonia; 0.5% develop disseminated disease; if severe disease or patient in high-risk group, AMB, itraconazole, or fluconazole therapy indicated
Chronic pneumonia (persistent or progressive)	Fever, prostration, chest pain, productive cough, hemoptysis, weight loss; asymptomatic (cavitary or nodular disease)	*CXR:* Persistent—infiltrates clear very slowly, occasionally nodules (midlung field) or cavities (usually single in upper lung fields); progressive—biapical fibronodular lesions with multiple cavities	As in primary symptomatic infection: negative skin test or CF Ab titer ≥ 1:32 implies worse prognosis *Culture and histopathology with special strains:* Lung tissue	See text *AMB:* Total dose dependent on severity of disease *Fluconazole, ketoconazole, itraconazole:* 400 mg qd for months to years for less severe disease *Surgery:* For severe hemoptysis, enlarging cavity, bronchopleural fistula, pyopneumothorax
Disseminated disease* Skin†	May be chief complaint	*PE:* Verrucous granulomas, especially at nasolabial folds: nodules, ulcers, subcutaneous abscesses with or without sinus tracts	*Skin test:* Negative reaction implies worse prognosis *Serology:* CF Ab titer ≥ 1:32 implies worse prognosis *Culture and histopathology with special stains:* Skin	See text *AMB:* Total dose 15–35 mg/kg, depending on severity of disease *Fluconazole, itraconazole:* Long-term suppressive therapy
Bone and joint	Local pain, swelling, warmth; symptoms of primary disease often present	*PE:* Fever, local tenderness; virtually any bone may be involved, especially at sites of ligament or tendon insertion; most commonly vertebra, tibia, skull, metatarsals, and metacarpals *X-ray:* Rarefaction, periosteal proliferation, soft tissue swelling; occasionally lytic lesions	*Arthrocentesis for synovial fluid:* No diagnostic pattern; cultures rarely positive; CF Ab may be present *Culture and histopathology with special strains:* Synovium, bone	See text *AMB:* Total dose dependent on severity of disease *Fluconazole, itraconazole:* Long-term suppressive therapy
Meningitis	Headache, fever, weakness confusion, lethargy, vomiting, seizures, abnormal behavior, diplopia, ataxia, focal neurologic deficits	*PE:* Often nonspecific nuchal rigidity (occasionally), cranial nerve and focal neurologic deficits (variable); often signs of extrameningeal disease	*CSF:* Lymphocytic pleocytosis (occasionally esoinophils); elevated protein; hypoglycorrhachia; CF Ab titer in 75–90%; culture positive in 20–40%; rarely spherules seen on wet preparation *CT scan:* Look for hydrocephalus (common) or mass lesion (rare)	See Text *Fluconazole:* 400–800 mg, if patient is conscious *AMB* (IV): Total dose, 15–30 mg/kg *AMB* (intrathecal): Given via lumbar, cisternal, cervical, or ventricular route; frequency and duration dependent on patient improvement and CF Ab titer response *Surgery:* Ventricular shunt for hydrocephalus

CXR, chest x-ray; PE, physical examination; Ab, antibody; CF, complement-fixing; AMB, amphotericin B; CSF, cerebrospinal fluid; LAB, laboratory tests; CT, computed tomography.
*Dissemination usually occurs early in disease
†Erythema nodosum, erythema multiforme, and toxic erythema are not considered manifestations of disseminated disease.

sensitive in detecting active coccidioidal disease. Serial measurements of complement-fixing antibodies can be used as an indicator of disease activity; a complement fixation titer of 1:32 or higher usually indicates progression of the disease or dissemination. A positive complement fixation test on the cerebrospinal fluid is diagnostic of coccidioidal meningitis, and complement-fixing antibodies can be present in up to 95% of patients with this form of disease. Owing to the highly infectious nature of *C. immitis,* clinical laboratories should take appropriate precautions when this organism is suspected.

Recommended Approach

See Table 8–57–1.

Therapeutic

Therapeutic Options

Although most patients with primary disease recover without antifungal therapy, patients with severe or progressive disease and those at high risk of dissemination (see Natural History and Its Modification with Treatment) should be treated.

Amphotericin B is the conventional mode of therapy for coccidioidomycosis, and is still considered to be the first line for life-threatening illness. The dose of amphotericin B is variable (range: 15–35 mg/kg, or a total dose of 2–3 g), and is highly dependent on clinical and radiographic response, site(s) of disease, skin test status, and change in complement-fixing antibody titer. For patients with coccidioidal meningitis who are treated with amphotericin B, intrathecal administration is needed in addition to a systemic course. Intrathecal amphotericin B may be given via the lumbar, cisternal, ventricular, or cervical route, and the dosage must be based on the individual patient's tolerance. Adverse effects vary with the site of injection but generally include headache, nausea, vomiting, radicular pain, paresthesias, nerve palsies, disequilibrium, and gait disturbances. Intrathecal amphotericin B generally is initiated at a dose of 0.025 mg and increased in a stepwise fashion to a dose of 0.5 to 1.0 mg given one to four times per week. As coccidioidal meningitis is rarely seen, especially in non-disease-endemic areas, physicians treating patients with this condition are advised to consult with physicians who have more experience in the management of this form of the disease and intrathecal therapy. Therapy for central nervous system disease is often lifelong. Early placement of a cerebrospinal fluid shunt may prevent irreversible brain damage in patients who develop hydrocephalus.

Oral azole antifungal agents have become increasingly important in the management of coccidioidomycosis, and studies are underway to better define the role of these agents. Although ketoconazole was found to be relatively effective for the treatment of nonmeningeal disseminated coccidioidal disease, the required doses were so large that intolerable side effects were produced; ketoconazole should not be used for the treatment of coccidioidal meningitis. Fluconazole at doses of 400 to 800 mg/d was found to be effective for treatment of coccidioidal meningitis; however, high relapse rates mandate that the drug be administered over prolonged periods, and in persons with HIV infection, for life. As fluconazole has minimal side effects, this option continues to be attractive when compared with intrathecal amphotericin B. Itraconazole also appears to be effective for nonmeningeal coccidioidal disease.

Recommended Approach

See Table 8–57–1.

Either fluconazole or itraconazole at doses of 400 mg/d can be used as first-line therapy for extrapulmonary nonmeningeal coccidioidal disease; however, it should be noted that neither fluconazole nor any other azole drug is currently approved by the Food and Drug Administration to treat coccidioidal disease. Fluconazole is also a reasonable alternative to amphotericin B for treatment of coccidioidal meningitis. Amphotericin B should be used for patients for whom azole therapy has been unsuccessful. Amphotericin B should also be used to treat HIV-infected persons who present with evidence of diffuse bilateral reticulonodular infiltrates (miliary pattern) on chest radiography.

FOLLOW-UP

Patients with acute, symptomatic pulmonary disease should be closely monitored for evidence of extrapulmonary disease and followed with serial serologic tests and chest radiographs until pulmonary infiltrates clear or stabilize. High-risk patients require especially close follow-up to assess disease progression. All patients with central nervous system disease should be evaluated frequently for the development of hydrocephalus. After the initial period of hospitalization, patients with coccidioidal meningitis who are treated with amphotericin B may need to return to the physician's office several times per week, weekly, or monthly for intrathecal amphotericin B. In addition, all patients who require therapy with amphotericin B should be evaluated weekly for hypokalemia and renal and bone marrow dysfunction. Patients who receive an azole drug should have monthly tests of liver enzymes. Physicians should carefully instruct patients concerning the need for extended medical follow-up with the physician because of the high relapse rate of the disease. Any symptom of recurrent or disseminated disease should be reported promptly.

DISCUSSION
Prevalence and Incidence

In disease-endemic areas, prevalence rates of infection with *C. immitis,* as measured by skin test reactivity, may be as high as 68% by early adulthood. Coccidioidomycosis has been reported in up to 6% of HIV-infected persons in disease-endemic areas. The actual incidence of the disease is not known. Incidence may vary from year to year depending on the weather conditions; in Southern California, most primary infections develop in the latter part of the summer. During 1992 and 1993, more than 4000 cases of coccidioidomycosis were reported annually in California, which was 10 times the annual average of cases reported during 1981–1990. Most new cases occur in persons who move into a disease-endemic area or have recently traveled through such an area.

Related Basic Science

Infection with *C. immitis* is caused by inhalation of airborne arthrospores. Following inhalation, these spores are deposited in the alveoli, where they progressively enlarge and develop a thick wall. The resultant spherule contains hundreds of endospores that, on release, may seed the lung parenchyma or spread hematogenously to distant organs. Whereas polymorphonuclear leukocytes and macrophages are able to ingest but not readily kill endospores, macrophages stimulated by specific lymphokines that promote phagolysosomal fusion are more easily able to kill ingested endospores. Cell-mediated immunity, therefore, is critical to host defense against *C. immitis.*

Natural History and Its Modification with Treatment

Within regions where *C. immitis* is endemic, infection can occur without any specific predisposition. Among persons who become infected, blacks, Filipinos and other Asians, Hispanics, women who acquire the infection in the third trimester of pregnancy, and persons with AIDS or other immunosuppressive conditions are all at increased risk of developing disseminated coccidioidomycosis. There is no person-to-person transmission of the infection. Infected individuals whose skin test is nonreactive or who develop a very high or rapidly rising complement-fixing antibody titer are more likely to have severe extrapulmonary disease, which may be progressive and fatal. Conversion of skin test reactivity from negative to positive or a complement-fixing antibody titer that declines during therapy is associated with a more favorable prognosis.

Coccidioidomycosis tends to disseminate early; however, disseminated disease involving a single extrapulmonary focus, with the exception of the central nervous system, generally indicates a favorable prognosis. Approximately 50% of patients with nonmeningeal dissemination and 100% of patients with meningeal dissemination die if not treated. The effectiveness of therapy in preventing morbidity and mortality is difficult to assess because of spontaneous exacerbations and remissions of nonmeningeal disease.

Prevention

Persons at high risk for disseminated disease who live in or travel to disease-endemic areas should avoid activities likely to expose them to large amounts of contaminated dust. Also, during soil excavation in disease-endemic regions, measures to control dust should be emphasized and workers should wear masks on the job site.

Cost Containment

There are no effective preventive measures that would reduce costs. When a patient has a form of coccidioidal disease that requires therapy, outpatient treatment with an oral azole antifungal or alternate-day amphotericin B is preferable from a cost perspective.

REFERENCES

Ampel NM, Dols CL, Galgiani JN. Coccidioidomycosis during human immunodeficiency virus infection: Results of a prospective study in a coccidioidal endemic area. Am J Med 1993;94:235.

Drutz DJ, Catanzaro A. Coccidioidomycosis (parts 1 and 2): State of the art. Am Rev Respir Dis 1978;117:559, 727.

Galgiani JN. Coccidioidomycosis. West J Med 1993;159:153.

Galgiani JN, Cantazaro A, Cloud GA, et al. Fluconazole therapy for coccidioidal meningitis. Ann Intern Med 1993;119:28.

Graybill JR. Treatment of coccidioidomycosis. Curr Top Med Mycol 1993;5:151.

Pappagianis D, Zimmer BL. Serology of coccidioidomycosis. Clin Microbiol Rev 1990;3:247.

CHAPTER 8–58

Amebiasis

Juliette Morgan, M.D., and Carlos del Rio, M.D.

DEFINITION

Amebiasis is the presence of cysts or trophozoites of the protozoa *Entamoeba histolytica* in the gut or other organs.

ETIOLOGY

Entamoeba histolytica, a pseudopod-forming protozoan, is responsible for human amebiasis. The morphologically indistinguishable pathogenic and nonpathogenic strains were previously classified as the same species, but with the introduction of DNA and RNA probes, these organisms have been reclassified and renamed. The nonpathogenic amebas are now referred to as *E. dispar.*

The cysts of *E. histolytica* (infectious stage) are excreted by asymptomatic or minimally symptomatic individuals. They may remain viable for prolonged periods and, through contaminated food or drink, eventually are ingested. In the colon they can excyst and transform into trophozoites, the form responsible for invasive disease.

CRITERIA FOR DIAGNOSIS
Suggestive

Immigrants from or travelers to *E. histolytica*-endemic areas with gastrointestinal symptoms that range from chronic mild complaints to acute fulminant colitis may have amebiasis. It is also found commonly in asymptomatic households or sexual contacts of persons returning from endemic areas, and especially in promiscuous male homosexuals.

Definitive

Finding cysts or trophozoites in stool or rectal biopsy or trophozoites in other organs (i.e., liver) establishes the diagnosis of amebiasis. Serology in patients with extraintestinal amebiasis is 95% sensitive. In the intestinal forms of amebiasis the serologic assay is much less sensitive and, therefore, more helpful in the patient who is not from an endemic area. In a traveler with a compatible clinical presentation, positive serology is significant. The serologic response to ameba may remain positive for many years, thus not distinguishing present from past exposure.

CLINICAL MANIFESTATIONS

The presentations can be categorized into intestinal and extraintestinal amebiasis, of which amebic liver abscess is the most common form.

We thank Dr. Richard Prokesch for his contribution to this chapter in the previous editions of this book.

Subjective
Intestinal Amebiasis

As many as 90% of those infected are asymptomatic. Most of these individuals never develop any illness and spontaneously clear their infection within weeks or months. The symptomatic patients with a noninvasive disease (only cysts are present) may exhibit nonspecific gastrointestinal symptoms, including abdominal pain and increased frequency of bowel movements, that may be intermittent and alternating with constipation. When the disease becomes "invasive," only trophozoites are seen. Symptoms are gradual and nonspecific with abdominal pain, watery diarrhea, and blood and mucus in stool (amebic dysentery). Fever is rare and usually suggests a complication. In this presentation, as opposed to the invasive bacterial diarrheas, the constitutional symptoms are relatively minor and appetite is usually retained. When colitis is present, segmental ulceration can occur. These may coalesce and become superinfected with bacteria and infrequently cause toxic megacolon. The ulcerations can perforate and result in peritonitis or persist and become fibrotic, eventually forming an "ameboma."

Extraintestinal Amebiasis (Amebic Liver Abscess)

Extraintestinal amebiasis results from previous intestinal infection, and can occur concurrently with colitis (only about 15%); however, usually there is no history of intestinal amebiasis and stool examination is negative. Liver abscess frequently has an acute onset with abdominal pain localized to the right upper quadrant, epigastrium, or right shoulder and usually dull in quality. About 90% of patients have fever, malaise, and anorexia. Less often the onset is more gradual with weight loss and other constitutional symptoms. If the abscess is located in the left liver lobe, the pain can radiate to the left shoulder.

Objective
Intestinal Amebiasis

Physical Examination. In the nonill patient, findings are nonspecific, with occasional lower quadrant pain to palpation, mild hepatic tenderness, and hepatomegaly even in the absence of an abscess. The more severely ill patient may have a toxic appearance with dehydration, diffuse abdominal pain, and occasionally a palpable mass (ameboma) or evidence of colonic distention (toxic megacolon).

Routine Laboratory Abnormalities. Routine laboratory tests may be normal, but most patients have heme-positive stools.

Extraintestinal Amebiasis (Amebic Liver Abscess)

Physical Examination. Liver enlargement associated with pain on palpation, often with point tenderness, is the most important sign. If the abscess is located high under the diaphragm, decreased breath sounds, intercostal tenderness, and dullness to percussion over the right lower chest will be apparent, even without a palpable enlarged liver. High fevers, frequently over 39°C, are common. Jaundice is rare and is usually associated with a secondarily infected pyogenic abscess.

Routine Laboratory Abnormalities. More than half of the patients are anemic and have leukocytosis with a left shift. Eosinophilia, however, is absent. Abnormalities of liver tests are mild and are not distinctive. The chest x-ray film may show an elevated hemidiaphragm, right pleural effusion, or atelectasis.

PLANS
Diagnostic
Intestinal Amebiasis

Differential Diagnosis. The differential diagnosis includes other infectious and noninfectious causes of diarrhea and gastrointestinal disease in travelers to or immigrants from endemic areas.

Diagnostic Options and Recommended Approach. Routine laboratory tests are not helpful. Stool examination is the key to diagnosis, but is one of the most difficult tests to perform correctly in the clinical laboratory; false-positive and false-negative results are common. False-negative results are due to use of antimicrobial agents, agents that lyse trophozoites (soap and tap water enemas), and particulate matter (barium or bismuth) that obscures the organisms. Causes of false-positive results include the presence of leukocytes that are misread as amebas and the presence of other amebas that are confused with *E. histolytica*. Having one negative stool examination by no means rules out the diagnosis. If a proper specimen is obtained from an ill patient, there is an 80% probability of finding the organism in three samples and a 90% probability if six samples are available. Stool should be examined within the hour of passage, but if delays are unavoidable, the specimen should be refrigerated at 4°C or preserved in formalin and polyvinyl alcohol. Samples can be directly mounted on a slide in saline, to look for motile erythrocyte-containing trophozoites, or a Wheatley's trichrome-stained slide can be prepared, which can be sent to a reference laboratory for confirmation. Stool is usually positive for occult blood, but the presence of "a lot" of fecal leukocytes makes the diagnosis of amebiasis less likely, because of the lysis of neutrophils by *E. histolytica* (the organism lives up to its name: "lytica"), differentiating amebiasis from invasive bacterial diarrheal diseases such as shigellosis. The indirect hemagglutination test has a 70% sensitivity in the active intestinal form. In the asymptomatic cyst carrier, it is 10% sensitive and should not be used for diagnosis.

Extraintestinal Amebiasis (Amebic Liver Abscess)

Differential Diagnosis. The differential diagnosis includes pyogenic abscess, equinococcal cyst, and metastatic or primary tumor, including hemangioma. Amebic abscesses are usually single and in the right lobe, whereas pyogenic abscesses are multiple and frequently found in the setting of biliary tract disease or other intraabdominal pathology.

Diagnostic Options and Recommended Approach. Serology is helpful, particularly if the patient is not from an endemic area. Typically the diagnosis is made based on the epidemiologic setting and the radiographic findings, along with a positive serology. Radioisotope liver scans, ultrasonography, computed tomography, and magnetic resonance imaging will locate the lesion, but ultrasonography is the most cost-effective imaging technique to make the diagnosis and it is only slightly less sensitive than the other techniques. The capsule has a thin wall and the fluid in the abscess, if aspirated, has the typical appearance of "anchovy paste" and is odorless. The aspirate should be examined for amebas, under wet mount and with a stained preparation. The trophozoites are usually not seen, as they are located in the wall of the abscess rather than in the liquefied central area of the abscess. *Aspiration of the abscess is usually not required for diagnosis.* Occasionally, a patient with an amebic liver abscess who has an acute presentation will have a negative amebic serology, which, when repeated approximately 1 week later, becomes positive. The most sensitive of the serologic studies is

indirect hemagglutination (95% sensitive in extraintestinal disease), which remains positive for years; therefore, it does not differentiate present from past infections. Counterimmunoelectrophoresis and gel diffusion tests are less sensitive but universally available; they become negative 2 to 3 months after cure and thus can be helpful if a patient is from an endemic area.

Therapeutic

Symptomatic persons with intestinal or extraintestinal disease should be treated first with a nitroimidazole and then with a luminal agent. Asymptomatic persons (i.e, asymptomatic cyst passers) who are not at high risk for reinfection should be treated with a luminal agent.

Intestinal Amebiasis

The use of an effective drug regimen and supportive care, if dehydration and electrolyte losses have occurred from diarrhea, constitute the therapy of intestinal amebiasis. In therapeutic trials of amebic dysentery, metronidazole (the only nitroimidazole available in the United States) followed by iodoquinol is the preferred regimen. A dose of 750 mg of metronidazole three times a day for 10 days cured the vast majority of symptomatic adult patients. Although not universally successful in curing amebic dysentery, metronidazole has proven so effective that if symptoms are not relieved within 24 hours of initiation therapy, the diagnosis should be doubted. The luminal agents are added to eradicate intestinal carriage. They do not treat the cysts per se but rather the trophozoites that are in the lumen of the gut and have not invaded the gut wall. Stool examination in asymptomatic cyst passers may not reveal any trophozoites because these are converted to cysts as they pass through the gut. Iodoquinol is given after the metronidazole in symptomatic patients and as a single agent to cyst passers, for a 20-day course. Other agents available include paromomycin and diloxanide furoate, these being available through the Centers for Disease Control and Prevention (404–639–3267) in cases of continuous cyst passage despite appropriate treatment or intolerance to the previous drugs mentioned. The dose of metronidazole indicated for amebiasis is higher than the recommended dose for giardiasis and is frequently associated with side effects, mainly nausea and vomiting. Emetine and dehydroemetine should be reserved for the serious complications of intestinal amebiasis or for patients failing to respond to metronidazole, as their toxicity is so great.

Extraintestinal Amebiasis (Amebic Liver Abscess)

Metronidazole is the drug of choice. A dosage of 750 mg three times a day for 10 days is highly effective. Emetine (1 mg/kg/d, maximum 60 mg, given intramuscularly for 3–5 days) is also effective. Of note, it is rarely necessary to combine metronidazole with emetine or dehydroemetime and these last two drugs can be quite toxic. Chloroquine can be combined with metronidazole or with dehydroemetine, but this also is rarely necessary. As mentioned above, a course of iodoquinol should follow the metronidazole to eradicate the intestinal cyst carriage.

Smaller and moderate-sized lesions usually do not need any drainage and should be left to be reabsorbed. Larger lesions or those that are difficult to diagnose can be aspirated, keeping in mind that the trophozoites are located in the walls, rather than the liquefied area.

FOLLOW-UP
Intestinal Amebiasis

Stool should be examined after therapy is completed and again approximately 1 month after treatment, as relapses can occur even in those apparently cured. Patients should be instructed to report recurrent symptoms to their physician.

Extraintestinal Amebiasis (Amebic Liver Abscess)

Healing of a successfully treated abscess requires 2 to 10 months. Repeat radiologic studies such as liver scans can be used to demonstrate resolution of the abscess. The abscess cavity may take months to resolve, and at times persistent cystic lesions occur.

DISCUSSION
Prevalence and Incidence

Entamoeba histolytica is very common worldwide, especially in developing countries, where is it an important cause of death from acute diarrhea. It is estimated that up to 20% of the population is infected with this protozoan. The prevalence in the United States is less than 5%, with higher rates reported in custodial institutions and on Indian reservations.

Related Basic Science
Intestinal Amebiasis

Entamoeba histolytica usually resides as a harmless commensal in the lumen of the human bowel. Two forms are found in the stool: the cyst (1–10 μm in diameter), which is found predominantly in formed specimens, and the motile trophozoite (10–50 μm in diameter), which is found in bloody and mucoid stool. As the cysts are resistant to gastric acid, to lysis in water, and to chlorine in concentrations found in most water purification systems, it is the form of the ameba that is most infectious to other persons. Virulence factors for *E. histolytica* have begun to be understood, but invasive amebiasis usually occurs when sanitary conditions are poor.

The recognition of nonpathogenic strains and differentiating them from ones capable of causing serious invasive disease are the focus of many researchers. The use of monoclonal antibodies in enzyme-linked immunosorbent assays on stool specimens has produced very encouraging clinical trial results. The monoclonal antibodies are directed against antigens that are present on pathogenic strains only and in this way can differentiate them from the more predominant forms of *Entamoeba* (especially in developed countries), which are nonpathogenic and therefore do not require treatment.

The pathogenesis of *E. histolytica* infection is under intense study. Pathogenic *E. histolytica* organisms are clearly different from nonpathogenic strains (*E. dispar*) and are capable of adhering to colonic cells and human polymorphonuclear leukocytes via the presence of specific lectins enabling them to produce their cytotoxic and lytic effect on tissues. Colonic epithelium can be directly invaded. Inflammatory cells are found only at the edges of the amebic lesions, a finding consistent with the observation that trophozoites have the capacity to destroy leukocytes when they make direct contact. In fact, with the lysis of neutrophils by *E. histolytica*, a variety of toxic neutrophilic metabolic products are released that play a part in the destruction of certain host tissues, especially the liver. *E. histolytica* contains multiple proteolytic enzymes, proteinases, and glucosaminidases and neuraminidases that may also injure tissues. An enterotoxin is also present that may have a role in the production of diarrhea.

Immunity to amebiasis is complex and still not well understood. Both serum antibody and coproantibody increase after invasive disease. Some investigators suggest that antibody to the 170-kDa adherence lectin subunit may be protective among those who have experienced invasive disease. Cell-mediated immunity probably also has a role, especially in limiting the invasiveness of *E. histolytica* and in preventing recurrence. Depression of T-cell numbers and, in turn, of cell-mediated immunity is associated with reports of more severe and at times fulminant amebic disease in some situations (e.g., corticosteroid administration). On the other hand, patients with HIV infection have not been shown to have an increased incidence of severe invasive amebiasis, a finding that suggests that the initial invasion of the intestinal mucosa does not involve cell-mediated immunity. Amebiasis, however, is a treatable cause of diarrhea in persons with HIV infection.

Extraintestinal Amebiasis (Amebic Liver Abscess)

See discussion under Intestinal Amebiasis. It should be pointed out that nonspecific hepatomegaly frequently occurs with moderate to severe intestinal amebiasis. The enlargement is likely to be a toxic reaction (liver scan is normal) that resolves with appropriate antiamebic therapy.

Natural History and Its Modification with Treatment
Intestinal Amebiasis

The most common complication of intestinal amebiasis is hepatic amebic abscess (see below). The most dangerous complication (case fatality rate increases from less than 1% to approximately 40%) is peritonitis. Less common complications include amebic strictures (anus, rectum, or sigmoid); amebic granuloma (ameboma), which is most commonly found in the cecum; acute hemorrhage; cutaneous involvement in the perianal area; and a self-limited syndrome clinically akin to ulcerative colitis, "ulcerative postdysenteric colitis." As steroid or immunosuppressive therapy can cause severe exacerbation of quiescent amebic intestinal disease, clinicians should carefully rule out amebiasis before these medications are employed to treat other syndromes with similar symptoms and signs (e.g., ulcerative colitis or idiopathic granulomatous colitis or ileitis).

Amebic Liver Abscess

Without prompt therapy, rupture may occur, with extension into contiguous areas. The thorax is most commonly affected. Pleural effusion, right lower lobe atelectasis, consolidation, empyema, lung abscess, and bronchopleural fistulas may result. Peritonitis occurring from rupture of a hepatic abscess is a serious complication, but it has a better prognosis than that arising from amebic dysentery. The most serious complication of an amebic abscess is amebic pericarditis, which may occur if the rare left liver lobe abscess ruptures.

Prevention

No prophylactic regimen has proven completely effective for intestinal amebiasis or amebic liver abscess. Upgrading sanitary and living conditions and appropriate water treatment would decrease infection and disease. Travelers may protect themselves by drinking only boiled or iodinated water. Vegetables and fruits should be washed with strong detergents and rinsed with an acid such as acetic acid or vinegar for 10 to 15 minutes to remove amebic cysts. The early detection and treatment of intestinal amebiasis (both symptomatic and asymptomatic) will decrease the incidence of hepatic amebiasis and its complications.

Cost Containment

Early diagnosis and treatment prevent the complications that are responsible for increasing the cost of medical care for these diseases.

REFERENCES

Adams EB, McLeod IN. Invasive amebiasis: I. Amebic dysentery and its complications. Medicine 1977;56:315.
Adams EB, McLeod IN. Invasive amebiasis: II. Amebic liver abscess and its complications. Medicine 1977;56:325.
Greenstein AJ, Sachar DB. Pyogenic and amebic abscesses of the liver. Semin Liver Dis 1988;8:210.
Haque R, Kress K, Wood S, et al. Diagnosis of pathogenic *Entamoeba histolytica* infection using a stool ELISA based on monoclonal antibodies to the galactose-specific adhesin. J Infect Dis 1993;167:247.
Katzenstein D, Rickerson V, Braude A. New concepts of amebic liver abscess derived from hepatic imaging, serodiagnosis, and hepatic enzymes in 67 consecutive cases in San Diego. Medicine (Baltimore) 1982;61:237.
Petri WA, Mann BJ. Molecular mechanisms of invasion by *Entamoeba histolytica*. Semin Cell Biol 1993;4:305.
Ravdin JI. Pathogenesis of disease with *Entamoeba histolytica*: Studies of adherence toxins and contact-dependent cytolysis. Rev Infect Dis 1986;8:247.
Ravdin JI, ed. Amebiasis: Human infection by *Entamoeba histolytica*. New York: Churchill Livingstone, 1988:1.
Reed SL. Amebiasis: An update. Clin Infect Dis 1992;14:385.

CHAPTER 8–59

Cryptosporidiosis and Microsporidiosis

John A. Jernigan, M.D., and David S. Stephens, M.D.

DEFINITION

Cryptosporidiosis is the name given to disease caused by the protozoan parasite *Cryptosporidium*. The major manifestation of cryptosporidiosis is diarrheal illness. *Cryptosporidium* can affect both normal and immunocompromised hosts, but its major impact has been among patients with AIDS, in whom it can cause severe diarrhea, biliary tract disease, and, possibly, respiratory disease.

Microsporidiosis is caused by infection with protozoa belonging to the phylum Microspora. Microspora infections have been implicated as a cause of diarrheal illness and biliary tract disease among immunocompromised patients that is clinically indistinguishable from cryptosporidiosis. In immunocompromised patients, the infection can disseminate to involve the eyes, lungs, muscles, bladder, kidneys, liver, and peritoneum. Myositis, keratoconjunctivitis, and pulmonary disease in the absence of concomitant enteric illness have also been described. Microsporidiosis has only rarely been reported in immunocompetent hosts, most commonly manifested as keratoconjunctivitis. The role of microsporidia in diarrhea in normal individuals is unknown.

ETIOLOGY

Cryptosporidium is a protozoan parasite belonging to the phylum Apicomplexa. It is grouped with the coccidia, and is related to *Toxoplasma, Isospora, Babesia,* and *Plasmodium.* The organism was discovered around the turn of the century, but was first recognized as a human pathogen about 20 years ago, and only in the last decade has it been recognized as a major cause of diarrhea worldwide. The name given to the species causing human disease is *Cryptosporidium parvum.*

Protozoa belonging to the order Microsporida of the phylum Microspora are commonly referred to as microsporidia. They are obligately intracellular, spore-producing protozoa with a wide host range among vertebrates and invertebrates. Microsporidia belonging to five genera have been identified in human infections: *Encephalitozoon (E. cuniculi, E. hellem), Pleistophora* (species unidentified), *Nosema (N. connori, N. corneum, N. ocularum), Enterocytozoon (E. bieneusi),* and *Septata (S. intestinalis).*

CRITERIA FOR DIAGNOSIS

Suggestive

Cryptosporidiosis and/or microsporidiosis should be suspected in individuals with AIDS who present with chronic persistent or intermittent diarrhea, malabsorption, and weight loss in the absence of other identifiable causes. In addition, cryptosporidiosis and microsporidiosis should be suspected in AIDS patients presenting with signs and symptoms of cholangitis. Microsporidiosis is most commonly seen in AIDS patients with an absolute CD4 T-lymphocyte count less than $100/mm^3$.

Cryptosporidiosis should also be included in the differential diagnosis of persistent diarrhea among immunocompetent persons residing in developing countries, among travelers returning from such areas, and among patients having extensive farm animal contact.

Cryptosporidiosis is being increasingly recognized in the United States as an important cause of diarrhea outbreaks due to contaminated water and of daycare-associated diarrhea in the United States. Physicians caring for persons with diarrhea in these epidemiologic settings should consider cryptosporidiosis as a possible etiology.

Definitive

The definitive diagnosis is made by identifying *Cryptosporidium* oocysts or microsporidial spores in stool, bile, or duodenal aspirates, or by identifying these and other developmental stages in tissue biopsies.

CLINICAL MANIFESTATIONS

Subjective

The presentation of cryptosporidiosis is dependent on the underlying immune state. In immunocompetent persons, the illness begins after an incubation period of about 2 weeks. The spectrum of illness ranges from vague epigastric pain, dyspepsia, and mild, watery, nonbloody diarrhea to severe cholera-like diarrhea associated with crampy abdominal pain, vomiting, low-grade fever, weight loss, anorexia, malaise, and flatulence. In these patients the illness is self-limited, usually resolving in less than 2 weeks, although it may persist for up to 4 weeks. Asymptomatic infection can occur. In immunocompromised patients, particularly those with AIDS, cryptosporidial infection typically begins with mild diarrhea and progresses to voluminous watery diarrhea with malabsorption. Patients are usually afebrile. The diarrhea is often exacerbated by food intake. Unlike immunocompetent patients, patients with severe immunodeficiency such as AIDS may not clear the organism, and infection can often persist for the remainder of the patient's life.

Cryptosporidium parvum has been identified in respiratory specimens from a number of immunocompromised patients with respiratory illness. Its etiologic role in pulmonary disease, however, remains uncertain.

Microsporidial infection has been implicated as a cause of diarrheal illness in immunocompromised patients that is clinically indistinguishable from cryptosporidiosis. Its importance in normal hosts, however, remains uncertain. An acute, self-limiting diarrheal illness in an immunocompetent individual with intestinal *Enterocytozoon* infection has recently been reported, suggesting that microsporidia may be more common in immunocompetent individuals than previously suspected.

Both microsporidial and cryptosporidial infections have been implicated as a cause of AIDS-related cholangitis and acalculous cholecystitis. Symptoms include epigastric or right upper quadrant pain, weight loss, and fever, often in the setting of unexplained chronic diarrhea. Jaundice is an uncommon manifestation of biliary disease due to *Cryptosporidium* or microsporidia.

Patients with keratoconjunctivitis due to microsporidia may complain of dry eyes, ocular pain, excessive tearing, or foreign body sensation.

Objective

Physical Examination

The physical findings in patients with cryptosporidiosis or microsporidiosis are nonspecific. AIDS patients with these infections often have evidence of significant weight loss and wasting. In those with biliary involvement, there may be right upper quadrant pain and fever.

In keratoconjunctivitis, conjunctival hyperemia is common. A superficial, punctate keratopathy is often present on slit-lamp examination.

Routine Laboratory Abnormalities

Routine laboratory findings are also relatively nonspecific. With both infections, there may be mild elevations in hepatic transaminase levels. Alkaline phosphatase is commonly elevated, especially in patients with cholangitis. Fecal leukocytes and occult blood are absent on stool examination.

PLANS

Diagnostic

Differential Diagnosis

Other diagnoses to consider in immunocompromised patients with chronic diarrhea include bacterial enteric pathogens (i.e., *Salmonella,*

Shigella, Campylobacter, Clostridium difficile); other protozoa (i.e., *Giardia, Entamoeba histolytica, Cyclospora, Isospora*); cytomegalovirus; *Mycobacterium avium* complex; bacterial overgrowth; and idiopathic HIV enteropathy.

Diagnostic Options

The diagnosis of cryptosporidiosis is usually based on the identification of oocysts in stool, duodenal, or bile specimens by modified acid-fast staining or immunofluorescence techniques. With modified acid-fast stains the oocysts appear as red, oval or crescent-shaped organisms 4 to 6 μm in diameter. Concentration techniques may aid in the diagnosis when small numbers of organisms are present. Highly sensitive and specific immunofluorescence tests are now available that use monoclonal antibodies directed at the oocyst wall or enzyme-linked immunosorbent assay antigen capture methods. In AIDS patients with microsporidiosis, the CD4 lymphocyte count is usually less than 100/mm^3. There is usually evidence of malabsorption if fecal fat and D-xylose testing is performed.

In tissue, *Cryptosporidium* can be readily identified using routine hematoxylin and eosin stain, although the organism tends to undergo rapid autolysis. Tissue specimens should therefore be processed rapidly to increase diagnostic yield. *Cryptosporidium* can also easily be identified using electron microscopy of intestinal biopsies, but this technique is usually not necessary for diagnosis. Serologic tests specific for *Cryptosporidium* are available, but are usually not used for diagnosis in the clinical setting.

The diagnosis of microsporidiosis is difficult because of the organism's small size (1–2 μm), its location deep in epithelial cell cytoplasm, and its poor staining qualities with most routine stains. The most reliable method of diagnosis remains electron microscopic examination of intestinal biopsies. Several methods for detecting the organism in tissue specimens by light microscopy have been used successfully, including Giemsa-stained touch preparations of intestinal biopsy specimens, Brown–Hopps stain of paraffin-embedded sections, and methylene blue–azure II–basic fuchsin stain of plastic-embedded sections. There are an increasing number of techniques used to identify microsporidial spores in stool, including Weber's modified trichrome stain and Chromotrope 2R, which stain spores pinkish red. Several tests are available that use fluorescence microscopy, and indirect immunofluorescence assays using polyclonal or monoclonal antibodies have also been used. The precise clinical role of many of these tests remains undetermined.

For diagnosis of biliary involvement endoscopic retrograde cholangiopancreatography is the most sensitive diagnostic approach. Radiographic findings may include intra- and/or extrahepatic biliary duct changes, often resembling idiopathic sclerosing cholangitis and often associated with papillary stenosis. Aspirates from the biliary tree help to establish a microbiologic diagnosis.

Recommended Approach

Immunocompromised patients with chronic diarrhea suggestive of small bowel pathology and evidence of malabsorption and wasting should have at least three separate stools submitted for ova and parasite examination, including modified acid-fast stain and Weber's modified trichrome stain. Culture for routine enteric bacterial pathogens and assay for *Clostridium difficile* toxin should also be performed on at least one stool specimen. If no diagnosis is made after the above, the patient should undergo upper gastrointestinal endoscopy with duodenal aspirate and small bowel biopsy. The biopsy should be stained with hematoxylin and eosin, Brown–Hopps stain, and modified acid-fast stain, as well as with Giemsa stain of a touch preparation of the specimen. Submitting the biopsy for electron microscopy may be considered if the diagnosis is not made by other methods. The duodenal aspirate should be stained with modified acid-fast stain as well as trichrome stain.

Therapeutic

Therapeutic Options

The optimal treatment for cryptosporidiosis has yet to be defined. Although many drugs have been tested, recent interest has focused on paromomycin, a poorly absorbed aminoglycoside. In a recent randomized trial, paromomycin was found to produce modest improvement in clinical and parasitologic parameters in AIDS patients with cryptosporidiosis. Azithromycin 900 to 1200 mg/d has shown efficacy in uncontrolled trials, but its precise role awaits confirmation in controlled trials. A small number of patients have been successfully treated with hyperimmune bovine colostrum and bovine transfer factor (an extract of lymph nodes from calves with cryptosporidiosis). Although it is hypothesized that immunoglobulins G and A may be the active components for these experimental modalities, the mechanism of action is unknown.

There is no proven effective therapy for microsporidiosis. Albendazole 400 mg twice daily given for 3 to 4 weeks for diarrheal illness has shown some success in small numbers of patients, but relapse appears to be common. Metronidazole (500 mg 3 times daily) has been reported to give transient responses in some patients. Preliminary data suggest that atovaquone may also be effective. For ocular disease, there are anecdotal reports of success with fumagillin, an agent used to control microsporidiosis in honeybees, and propamidine isethionate drops (0.1%) four times daily.

Nonspecific symptomatic treatment modalities have been of great use in the treatment of cryptosporidial and microsporidial diarrhea. Octreotide, a somatostatin analog that inhibits secretion of gastrointestinal hormones, was thought to provide some benefit in cryptosporidiosis based on initial studies. A prospective multicenter trial, however, showed that it had only modest effect. Its use in microsporidiosis has produced variable results. Antidiarrheal agents, such as loperamide, diphenoxylate, kaolin and pectin, bismuth subsalicylate, and opiates are often used to control symptoms. Introducing low-fat diets and reducing complex carbohydrate intake in patients with documented malabsorption may provide significant relief of symptoms.

Recommended Approach

Patients with documented cryptosporidiosis should be treated with paromomycin 500 mg orally every 6 hours for 2 weeks. If this fails, a trial of azithromycin 1000 mg daily should be given.

In patients with documented microsporidiosis, albendazole 400 mg twice daily for 3 to 4 weeks can be given. Unfortunately, the drug is not currently marketed in the United States and must be obtained from the manufacturer. If the drug is not available or is ineffective, a trial of metronidazole is warranted.

For patients with cryptosporidiosis or microsporidiosis who fail to respond to antimicrobial therapy, octreotide 100 to 500 μg subcutaneously three times daily can be attempted. If response is still insufficient, patients must be managed with dietary modification (low fat, low complex carbohydrates) and nonspecific antidiarrheal agents (loperamide, etc.)

FOLLOW-UP

Patients with cryptosporidiosis or microsporidiosis do not require specific laboratory or clinical testing for follow-up. Close clinical monitoring of symptoms is sufficient.

DISCUSSION

Prevalence

Cryptosporidiosis has been reported on six continents and is most prevalent in less developed regions. Stool surveys among patients with diarrhea in North America and the United Kingdom have shown prevalence rates of less than 5%. In contrast, reported prevalence rates in Africa, Asia, and Central and South America are as high as 20%, and in many studies *Cryptosporidium* has been found to be the most significant enteropathogen causing diarrheal illness. In AIDS patients with diarrhea, a prevalence of about 15% is seen in the United States, whereas rates up to 40% are seen in developing regions. Seroprevalence studies show that infection with *Cryptosporidium* may be even more common than predicted in stool surveys. In the United States and United Kingdom, seroprevalence is around 30%, whereas in developing countries as many as two thirds of residents have antibodies to *Cryptosporidium*.

Little is known about the prevalence of microsporidiosis. Prevalence studies using small bowel biopsies suggest that one third to one half of American and European AIDS patients with chronic diarrhea may be infected with microsporidia.

Related Basic Science

The pathophysiologic mechanisms of diarrhea associated with *Cryptosporidium* and microsporidia are poorly understood. The histopathologic features of both infections are similar. The organisms are usually found close to the microvillous border of small bowel epithelial cells, where the developmental cycle takes place. There are blunting and loss of villi, lengthening of crypts, and infiltration of the lamina propria with lymphocytes, polymorphonuclear leukocytes, and plasma cells. It has been hypothesized that such damage may lead to malabsorption and impaired digestion, resulting in a change in osmotic pressure across the gut wall and influx of fluid into the lumen of the intestine. The often secretory, "cholera-like" diarrhea seen with these infections raises the possibility of toxin-mediated hypersecretion into the gut, but no such toxin has been identified.

Natural History and Its Modification with Treatment

In immunocompetent individuals, cryptosporidiosis is self-limited, usually resolving in less than 2 weeks, although it may persist for up to 4 weeks. Treatment of immunocompetent patients with cryptosporidiosis has not been widely studied, though there are anecdotal reports of responses to paromomycin therapy. The role of microsporidia in disease among immunocompetent hosts is unknown.

Unlike immunocompetent patients, patients with AIDS apparently cannot clear infection with *Cryptosporidium* or microsporidia, and disease often persists for the remainder of the patient's life. As discussed above, responses to therapy have been inconsistent.

Prevention

Cryptosporidium is spread by two main mechanisms, waterborne and person-to-person. Prevention involves avoiding contaminated water and minimizing fecal–oral contact among close contacts of known cases via the usual enteric precautions. Unfortunately, *Cryptosporidium* is highly resistant to chlorination and is not eliminated by standard water treatment measures. It has been found in about two thirds of water samples tested throughout the United States. The organism can be inactivated by bringing it to a rolling boil for at least 1 minute. Boiled or bottled drinking water should be considered for patients with AIDS. In addition, these patients should avoid exposure to farm animals.

The epidemiology of microsporidial infection is not well understood. Many investigators feel that fecal–oral spread is likely. It therefore seems prudent to pay attention to hand washing and appropriate personal hygiene, especially when in contact with known cases.

Cost Containment

Costs can be minimized by judicious management of the diagnostic workup in AIDS patients with chronic diarrhea. Repeated stool specimen examination is unlikely to be helpful after three separate stool examinations have failed to yield an etiology. At this point endoscopy should be performed to optimize diagnostic yield. The clinician should carefully consider which portion of the gastrointestinal tract to examine first; differentiating small bowel pathology from large bowel pathology in patients with diarrhea is often possible by clinical history, enabling the clinician to avoid an unnecessary endoscopic procedure.

Although electron microscopy is the gold standard diagnostic test for microsporidiosis, its routine use in diagnosis may not be the most cost-effective approach, especially because therapeutic options are limited.

REFERENCES

Asmuth DM, DeGirolami PC, Federman M, et al. Clinical features of microsporidiosis in patients with AIDS. Clin Infect Dis 1994;18:819.

Bryan RT. Microsporidia. In: Mandell GL, Bennett JE, Dolin R, eds. Mandell, Douglas, and Bennett's principles and practice of infectious diseases. 4th ed. New York: Churchill Livingstone, 1995:2512.

MacKenzie WR, Hoxie NJ, Proctor ME. A massive outbreak in Milwaukee of *Cryptosporidium* infection transmitted through public water supply. *N Eng J Med* 1994;331:161.

Mannheimer SB, Soave R. Protozoal infections in patients with AIDS: Cryptosporidiosis, isosporiasis, cyclosporiasis, and microsporidiosis. *Infect Dis Clin North Am* 1994;8:483.

Ungar BLP. *Cryptosporidium*. In: Mandell GL, Bennett JE, Dolin R, eds. Mandell, Douglas, and Bennett's principles and practice of infectious diseases. 4th ed. New York: Churchill Livingstone, 1995:2500.

CHAPTER 8–60

Strongyloidiasis

Henry M. Blumberg, M.D., and Jonas A. Shulman, M.D.

DEFINITION

Strongyloidiasis is one of the major human intestinal nematode infections and is usually caused by *Strongyloides stercoralis*, which is widely distributed in the tropics and subtropics. Occasionally, strongyloidiasis is caused by *Strongyloides fuelleborni*.

ETIOLOGY

Strongyloides stercoralis can exist in either parasitic or free-living form. The complex life cycle of this organism is shown in Figure 8–60–1. Filariform larvae penetrate the skin and pass via the bloodstream to the lungs, where they penetrate into alveoli. After ascending the tracheobronchial tree, they are swallowed and reach the small intestine, where the larvae mature into adults and fertilization occurs. Adult females burrow into the mucosa and deposit eggs, which rapidly hatch in the intestinal lumen and generate rhabditiform larvae that are excreted in the stool. During the free-living period, which occurs in topsoil in warm climates, adult female worms produce eggs that develop into rhabditiform larvae before maturing into invasive filariform larvae.

Strongyloides stercoralis is unique among helminths in that it can also complete its life cycle within the host. This occurs when rhabditiform larvae spontaneously transform within the colon into invasive filariform larvae that can directly penetrate colonic or cutaneous tissue to reinfect the host and perpetuate infection. This autoinfection cycle provides a mechanism by which *S. stercoralis* may persist for years after infection in the absence of exogenous reinfection. In addition, an accelerated autoinfection cycle, which can occur in immunocompromised hosts, leads to extremely heavy parasite burdens, giving rise to the hyperinfection syndrome and disseminated disease.

We thank Dr. Richard Prokesch for his contribution to this chapter in the previous editions of this book.

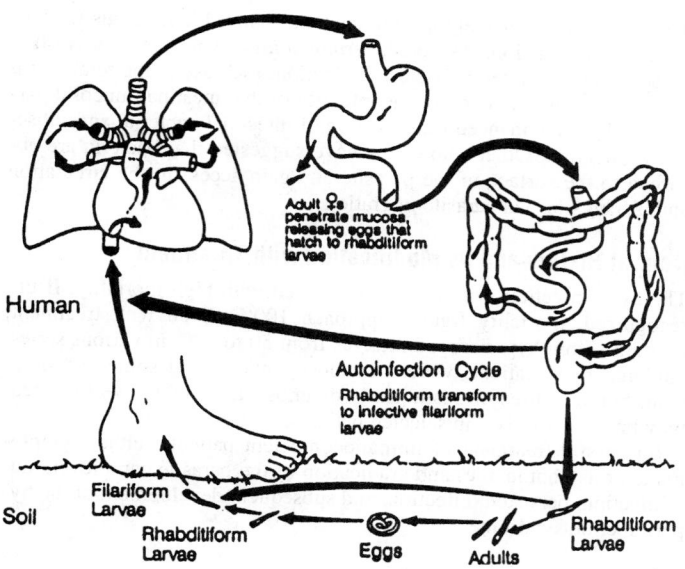

Figure 8–60–1. Life cycle of the nematode *Strongyloides stercoralis*. (Source: Modified from Longworth DL, Weller PF. Hyperinfection with strongyloidiasis. In: Remington JS, Swartz MN, eds. Current clinical topics in infectious diseases. New York: McGraw-Hill, 1986:1. Reproduced with permission from the publisher and author.)

CRITERIA FOR DIAGNOSIS
Suggestive

Strongyloidiasis should be suspected in patients with abdominal pain, diarrhea, or urticaria, particularly if they have lived in an endemic area. A skin rash (larva currens) may occasionally be present. Sudden deterioration in an immunosuppressed patient suggests the possibility of disseminated strongyloidiasis. Immunosuppression predisposes infected individuals to overwhelming disseminated *S. stercoralis* infection, which can be accompanied by bacterial superinfection, sepsis, and even death.

Definitive

A definite diagnosis of this disease can be made by finding *S. stercoralis* larvae in the feces, duodenal fluid, sputum, or lung.

CLINICAL MANIFESTATIONS
Subjective

Worldwide, most infected individuals have uncomplicated disease. In fact, up to one half of patients infected with the nematode *S. stercoralis* are asymptomatic or have only vague abdominal complaints. The symptoms of strongyloidiasis generally correspond to the three stages of infection: invasion of the skin, migration of larvae, and penetration of the intestinal mucosa by adult worms (Figure 8–60–1). A pruritic, papular erythematous rash may develop at the site of penetration of the filariform larvae. A times, a Loeffler-like syndrome with eosinophilia occurs as larvae migrate through the lungs; it is characterized by cough, shortness of breath, fever, hemoptysis, and wheezing. The most common symptoms are related to the gastrointestinal tract, and complaints of abdominal pain (often burning and epigastric in location), diarrhea, and occasionally nausea and vomiting occur when adult worms invade the intestinal mucosa. Weight loss (with evidence of malabsorption or a protein-losing enteropathy), anorexia, malaise, and fever are other reported symptoms.

The hallmark of symptomatic chronic strongyloidiasis is cutaneous involvement manifested by maculopapular or nonspecific urticarial eruptions that can be recurrent. A migratory urticarial rash called larva currens ("running larva") or creeping eruption is said to be pathognomonic. This transient rash, lasting hours to days, appears most commonly on the perineum, buttocks, and thighs, as penetration of autoin-

fecting filariform larvae from the stool is most likely to occur at these sites.

Autoinfection may lead to an overwhelming hyperinfection syndrome. Patients with the hyperinfection syndrome are usually immunocompromised because of administration of corticosteroids or other immunosuppressive drugs, renal transplantation and systemic lupus erythematosus (usually in the presence of corticosteroid administration), malignancies (especially lymphoma and leukemia), lepromatous leprosy, malnutrition, or other debilitating diseases. Patients with HIV infection are also at risk for hyperinfection.

Onset of the hyperinfection syndrome may be insidious or acute. Gastrointestinal and pulmonary symptoms are characteristic, although typically more severe than in uncomplicated disease. If hyperinfection is not recognized early, severe abdominal pain with intestinal obstruction, massive gastrointestinal bleeding, severe malabsorption, or diffuse peritonitis can ensue. Symptoms of shock, pneumonitis, respiratory insufficiency, fever, and neurologic symptoms such as stupor and coma are also frequently present.

Objective
Physical Examination

Physical examination of the patient with strongyloidiasis may reveal an erythematous papular rash or urticaria. Pulmonary examination, especially in the patient with the hyperinfection syndrome, may be significant for dyspnea, bronchospasm, respiratory insufficiency, and evidence of pneumonitis. Mild generalized discomfort may be elicited on palpation of the abdomen in patients with uncomplicated disease and early hyperinfection; however, as the hyperinfection syndrome progresses, physical findings may suggest an acute surgical abdomen.

In severely immunocompromised patients, the hyperinfection syndrome has been complicated by widespread dissemination of filariform larvae to organs not normally involved in the life cycle of the parasite (e.g., central nervous system, liver). Clinically evident hepatic disease with jaundice and hepatomegaly on physical examination has been noted. Granulomatous hepatitis secondary to parenchymal invasion by filariform larvae may also occur. Manifestations of neurologic involvement in the hyperinfection syndrome include altered mental status, parasitic meningitis, and brain abscess.

Routine Laboratory Abnormalities

Laboratory examination frequently reveals eosinophilia in immunocompetent patients with uncomplicated disease, although this can be an intermittent finding. Patients with the hyperinfection syndrome usually do not have eosinophilia, as immunosuppressive therapy (e.g. corticosteroids) or a concomitant pyogenic infection can suppress eosinophilia. *Strongyloides* hyperinfection and dissemination are frequently associated with systemic bacterial infection, most commonly bacteremia due to Gram-negative enteric organisms or enterococci. Associated bacterial pneumonia and meningitis, as well as other infections, have also been reported.

Liver function tests may be abnormal in patients with hepatic involvement.

In the hyperinfection syndrome, chest x-ray studies may reveal alveolar infiltrates, often progressing to a pattern resembling the adult respiratory distress syndrome.

PLANS
Diagnostic
Differential Diagnosis

Consideration of strongyloidiasis in the differential diagnosis is obviously important in making the diagnosis as early as possible. A thorough demographic and travel history should be obtained.

Diagnostic Options and Recommended Approach

Definitive diagnosis depends on demonstrating the presence of *S. stercoralis* larvae in biological specimens such as stool, duodenal fluid, and sputum. Stool examination is generally performed initially. Examination of fresh feces or stool that has been immediately fixed with formalin or polyvinyl alcohol is essential, as rapid disintegration of larvae can occur in refrigerated stool. A stool-concentrating technique greatly increases the diagnostic yield. Examination of the proximal small bowel contents may establish the diagnosis and should be performed if stool examination is negative and strongyloidiasis is suspected. This can be accomplished easily by use of the highly sensitive string test (Enterotest, Hedeco, Palo Alto, CA). With this test, a gelatin capsule and 140 cm of white nylon line are swallowed, withdrawn after 4 hours, and examined for parasites. Sputum examination may reveal larvae in patients with hyperinfection and pulmonary involvement. Serology employing a *Strongyloides* larval antigen enzyme-linked immunosorbent assay is thought to be a sensitive diagnostic test in the immunocompetent patient.

Therapeutic

Thiabendazole is considered the drug of choice for the treatment of patients with strongyloidiasis, but is associated with some toxicity and is not uniformly effective. In immunocompetent patients, the dosage is 25 mg/kg twice a day for 2 days (maximum dose of 3g/d). A minimum of a 5- to 7-day course of therapy is recommended for patients with the hyperinfection syndrome/disseminated disease, although a more prolonged course of therapy (14 days) may be required in some patients with hyperinfection to eradicate the parasite. Major adverse effects of thiabendazole therapy include anorexia, nausea, vomiting, diarrhea, abdominal discomfort, confusion, dizziness, rash, leukopenia, and transient elevation in aspartate aminotransferase level.

Alternative treatments (which are not approved by the Food and Drug Administration and thus not readily available in the United States) include albendazole, which is felt by some authorities to be superior to thiabendazole. Albendazole is available on a compassionate basis from the manufacturer (Smith Kline Beecham Pharmaceuticals). Ivermectin is another alternative drug that appears to be as efficacious as thiabendazole or albendazole. It is available from the Centers for Disease Control and Prevention.

When all agents fail to eradicate infection in immunosuppressed patients, a practical approach is to minimize the worm burden by giving short course of thiabendazole each month (e.g., 25 mg/kg twice daily for 1 day each month).

FOLLOW-UP

Daily sputum and stool examinations for filariform larvae of *Strongyloides* should be performed to aid in individualizing the duration of therapy in immunocompromised patients with hyperinfection. In addition, a final duodenal aspirate may be indicated prior to discontinuation of thiabendazole therapy in such patients. As reactivation of reinfection of patients living in endemic areas can occur, close follow-up with periodic stool or duodenal aspirate examination is recommended.

Immunocompetent patients should have a follow-up stool examination (or duodenal aspirate) after therapy to document eradication.

DISCUSSION
Prevalence and Incidence

Strongyloidiasis is endemic throughout the tropics and subtropical areas; more than 100,000 million people worldwide are believed to be infected with *S. stercoralis*. In some tropical areas the prevalence of infection may exceed 25%. Strongyloidiasis is also endemic to warm and humid southeastern states, where prevalence rates have been reported to be up to 4%. Most cases diagnosed in the United States have occurred in immigrants from endemic areas and overseas travelers.

Related Basic Science

The host–parasite interaction and factors determining host susceptibility and resistance to *S. stercoralis* infection are poorly understood. Intact cell-mediated immunity appears to be important in preventing hyperinfection and disseminated disease, as systemic strongyloidiasis

occurs almost exclusively in immunocompromised individuals with altered T-cell function. As noted, *Strongyloides* hyperinfection is often associated with systemic bacterial infection. Increase in the total worm burden is thought to damage the integrity of the intestinal mucosal barrier, leading to enhanced translocation of intestinal bacterial and subsequent infection. Others, however, have suggested that bacteria are absorbed to the surface of the parasite and gain access to the circulation and distant sites via parasite migration.

Natural History and Its Modification with Treatment

The hyperinfection syndrome is associated with high mortality. If unrecognized, mortality figures approach 100%. Even with treatment, mortality from hyperinfection ranges from 50 to 70% in various series, although most patients were immunosuppressed and some had other contributing causes of death. Early diagnosis and aggressive treatment may improve survival in selected patients.

Successful treatment of immunocompetent patients (either symptomatic or asymptomatic) and eradication of the parasite can prevent autoinfection, persistent infection, and subsequent development of the hyperinfection syndrome.

Prevention

A thorough medical and geographic history should be obtained prior to the administration of immunosuppressive therapy (e.g., corticosteroids, cytotoxic chemotherapy). All patients who are to be placed on immunosuppressive therapy and who have lived in or traveled to an endemic area should be screened for the presence of *S. stercoralis*. This should include stool and duodenal aspirate samples. If *S. stercoralis* is detected, treatment should be given and parasitologic cure documented prior to the initiation of immunosuppressive therapy.

As a number of immunosuppressed patients who survived hyperinfection after successful treatment with thiabendazole reacquired infection when they returned to their residence in an endemic area, some authors have recommended monthly prophylactic treatment (thiabendazole 25 mg/kg twice daily for 1–2 days each month) for these patients if they remain chronically immunosuppressed.

Infection is acquired most commonly when infective larvae in the soil where human feces have been deposited come in contact with the skin. As transmission of *S. stercoralis* is facilitated by poor personal and public hygiene, worldwide control of strongyloidiasis is dependent on improved standards of living and installation of effective waste disposal facilities.

Cost Containment

Prevention of the hyperinfection syndrome in patients who are to undergo immunosuppressive therapy and use of the string test to sample duodenal contents (thus avoiding endoscopy) are two examples of ways costs can be contained.

REFERENCES

Berk SL, Berghese A, Alvarez S, et al. Clinical and epidemiologic features of strongyloidiasis: A prospective study in rural Tennessee. Arch Intern Med 1987;147:1257.

Celedon JC, Mathur-Wagh U, Fox J, et al. Systemic strongyloidiasis in patients infected with the human immunodeficiency virus: A report of three cases and review of the literature. Medicine 1994;73:256.

Grove DI. Strongyloidiasis. In: Warren KS, Mahmoud AAF, eds. Tropical and geographical medicine. New York: McGraw-Hill, 1990:393.

Grove DI. Strongyloidiasis: A conundrum for gastroenterologists. Gut 1994;35:437.

Liu LX, Weller PF. Strongyloidiasis and other intestinal nematode infections. Infect Dis Clin North Am 1993;7:655.

Purvis RS, Beightler EL, Diven DG, et al. *Strongyloides stercoralis* hyperinfection. Int J Dermatol 1992;31:160.

Wehner JH, Kirsch CM, Kagawa FT, et al. The prevalence and response to therapy of *Strongyloides stercoralis* in patients with asthma from endemic areas. Chest 1994;106:762.

CHAPTER 8–61

Malaria and Babesiosis

Susan L.F. McLellan, M.D., and Phyllis E. Kozarsky, M.D.

DEFINITION

Malaria and babesiosis are febrile infections caused by protozoa of the class Sporozoa, genuses *Plasmodium* and *Babesia,* which parasitize human erythrocytes.

ETIOLOGY

Malaria is transmitted by the bite of the female anopheline mosquito, and is widely distributed in Asia, Africa, Latin America, and the Caribbean Basin (Figure 8–61–1). Four species cause human disease: *P. falciparum, P. vivax, P. ovale,* and *P. malariae.* Babesiosis is a zoonosis that is occasionally transmitted to humans by ticks (*Ixodes* spp.). In Europe the responsible species is *B. divergens,* a parasite of cattle. In the United States the primary species causing human disease is *B. microti,* a parasite of rodents, which is found primarily in the Northeast. An as yet unnamed species of *Babesia* has also been discovered in Washington State and California.

CRITERIA FOR DIAGNOSIS
Suggestive

Malaria should be considered as a cause of fever or flulike symptoms in any individual returning from travel in, or native to, a malarious area of the world. That the individual has taken malaria prophylaxis during his or her time abroad does not rule out the disease. The geographic area the patient has visited may suggest which species is most likely. Babesiosis should be considered in any patient with fever and a history of a tick bite, particularly if the person has recently visited the coastal areas and islands of New England.

Definitive

Both malaria and babesiosis may be definitively diagnosed by finding the characteristic intraerythrocytic parasites in thick or thin blood smears stained with Giemsa or similar stain. Serologic assays also exist for both parasites but are useful primarily in epidemiologic studies and not for diagnosis of acute disease.

CLINICAL MANIFESTATIONS
Subjective
Malaria

There is often a mild "viral"-like prodrome with headache and myalgia, which occurs a day or two before the onset of the paroxysmal phase of the disease. The classic paroxysm consists of three phases: a cold phase, during which the patient complains of chills; the hot phase, with high fever, headache, nausea, vomiting, and delirium; and defervescence, with profuse sweating followed by sleep. The entire cycle takes 6 to 10 hours; however, not all patients follow the classic pattern, and an irregular pattern of fever should not reduce suspicion for the diagnosis. Malaria should be considered in any traveler with a flulike illness who is returning from an endemic area.

Babesiosis

Babesiosis is usually a mild illness in the immunocompetent host, and often goes unrecognized; however, it can be a fatal illness in the asplenic or immunocompromised patient. Patients complain of fever, chills, myalgia, fatigue, headaches, anorexia, generalized weakness, and sweats, which may occur during the day or night. Symptoms tend to wax and wane over several weeks before the patient seeks care.

Objective
Acute Malaria

Physical Examination. The physical examination is often normal if the patient is examined between paroxysms. During the paroxysm, fever is invariably present, often as high as 106°F. Fever may be sustained or irregular, however, and the pattern of fever is not a reliable indicator of the type of malaria. Orthostatic hypotension is often present in falciparum malaria. Splenomegaly with or without hepatomegaly is seen in about one third of acute cases. Faint scleral icterus is often seen. Various neurologic complications occasionally occur in falciparum malaria, and include seizures, hallucinations, and meningismus.

Routine Laboratory Abnormalities. A mild normochromic normocytic anemia is usually present. In falciparum malaria, the anemia may be severe, and schistocytes may be present on blood smear. The total white blood cell count and differential are usually normal. Thrombocytopenia is often found in falciparum malaria. Aspartate aminotransferase, lactate dehydrogenase, alkaline phosphatase, and bilirubin levels may be mildly elevated. Examination of the cerebrospinal fluid is usually normal, even in patients with neurologic manifestations.

Chest radiograph, electrocardiogram, and urinalysis are usually normal except in falciparum malaria, where one may see signs of congestive heart failure, arrhythmias, hemoglobinuria, and myoglobinuria (blackwater fever). Large quantities of albumin may be found in the urine during fever or if the patient develops nephrotic syndrome.

Babesiosis

Physical Examination. Most infections with *B. microti* appear to be subclinical. Fever (usually not above 102°F) and hepatosplenomegaly are the most common findings. Rash and lymphadenopathy are not seen.

Routine Laboratory Abnormalities. There may be a normocytic normochromic anemia and schistocytes. Hemolytic anemia, which may be mild to severe, is a characteristic of the infection and is characterized by a decreased serum haptoglobin level and an elevated reticulocyte count. The percentage of parasitized red blood cells is nearly always less than 10% in immunocompetent patients. Thrombocytopenia is common; the total white blood cell count and differential are usually normal. Direct Coombs' test may be positive. There are often modest elevations of aspartate aminotransferase, lactate dehydrogenase, and alkaline phosphatase levels and total and indirect portions of the bilirubin. During active infection there is often a decrease in total complement levels and a polyclonal gammopathy.

PLANS
Diagnostic
Differential Diagnosis

The differential diagnosis of malaria is broad and includes common illnesses found in the United States as well as other diseases endemic to the areas where the patient has traveled. Malaria may mimic influenza, especially at the outset. Other febrile illnesses to include in the differential are leishmaniasis, gastroenteritis, hepatitis, amebic liver abscess, relapsing fever, yellow fever, typhoid fever, tuberculosis, brucellosis, endocarditis, pyelonephritis, trypanosomiasis, poliomyelitis, and numerous viral illnesses.

The differential diagnosis of babesiosis also includes influenza, as well as Lyme disease, gastroenteritis, many viral syndromes, hepatitis, tuberculosis, and noninfectious conditions such as collagen–vascular disease and blood disorders.

We thank Dr. Sumner E. Thompson III for his contribution to this chapter in the previous editions of this book.

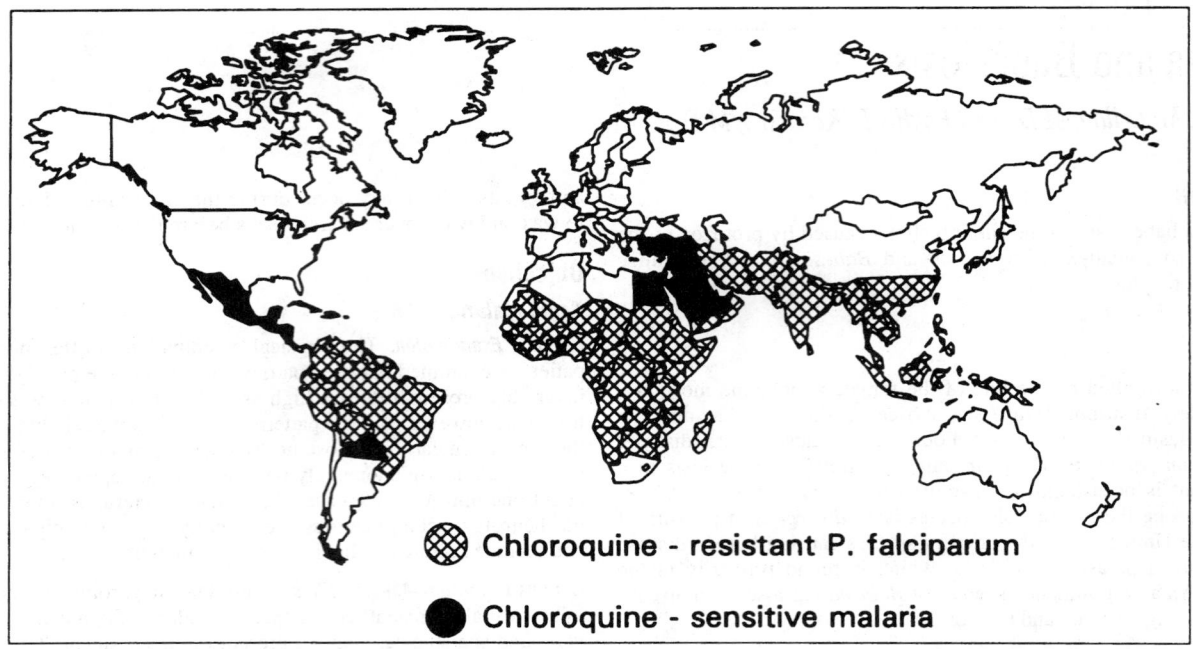

⊗ **Chloroquine - resistant P. falciparum**

● **Chloroquine - sensitive malaria**

Figure 8–61–1. Distribution of malaria and chloroquine-resistant *Plasmodium falciparum*, 1994 *(Provided by the Centers for Disease Control and Prevention.)*

Diagnostic Options

For both diseases, the diagnosis should be confirmed by examination of a blood film stained with Giemsa or a similar stain. *Babesia* are often confused with *P. falciparum* on smear. The "Maltese cross" tetrad of intraerythrocytic merozoites is a diagnostic but uncommon finding for *Babesia*. Schizonts, gametocytes, and pigment may be seen with malaria but are absent in babesiosis. Smears should be positive 2 to 4 weeks after infection.

Serologic tests are available for both diseases and can be obtained through the Centers for Disease Control and Prevention. The serologic assays for malaria are not always helpful as they do not differentiate between past and present infection. The indirect fluorescent antibody (IFA) test for babesiosis may be helpful in detecting clinical infection. Serum titers may rise to greater than 1:1024, within a few weeks of infection (> 1:256 is considered indicative of recent infection). *Babesia microti* infection can be confirmed by intraperitoneal inoculation of a patient's blood into golden hamsters.

Recommended Approach

Thick and thin blood smears provide the definitive diagnosis for both diseases, and they are rapidly and widely available. If malaria is suspected, thick smears should be examined if the thin smears are negative or questionable, as they are in 20 to 25% of cases. If the first smears are not diagnostic, examination of smears should be repeated at intervals during the next several days. The number of smears examined is much more critical than the timing of the smears.

In the diagnosis of malaria it is critical to determine if the patient has falciparum malaria or not, as it is the only form that, because of the high rate of erythrocyte parasitization, may end fatally if not treated properly. In falciparum malaria it is essential to monitor actual parasite counts (parasites per cubic millimeter or percentage of erythrocytes parasitized) closely (every 8 hours) during the first 2 to 3 days of therapy.

Therapeutic

Malaria

Therapeutic Options. Treatment of malaria is becoming more difficult due to the spread of drug-resistant strains of *P. falciparum*. Chloroquine resistance has been recognized since 1961 and is widespread (see

Figure 8–61–1). Multidrug-resistant strains of *P. falciparum* also exist. Resistance to Fansidar is common in parts of Southeast Asia and the Amazon basin, and mefloquine resistance is reported from Thailand and Cambodia. The other species of malaria have historically been sensitive to chloroquine, but recently chloroquine-resistant strains of *P. vivax* have been reported from Indonesia and New Guinea. The particular therapeutic regimen used is dependent on the infecting species, the geographic area in which the illness was acquired, and the percentage of erythrocytes infected.

Recommended Approach. See Tables 8–61–1 and 8–61–2 for specific recommendations and dosages of antimalarial medications. In addition to the administration of specific antimalarial agents, attention should be given to supportive measures for prevention and treatment of complications such as electrolyte and fluid abnormalities, respiratory distress syndrome, renal insufficiency, and cerebral involvement. For patients with high levels of parasites (usually > 10%), exchange transfusion is also recommended.

Treatment of malaria in children and in pregnant women is not specifically addressed in these guidelines. It is wise in these circumstances and in the case of severe disease to obtain assistance from the physicians at the malaria branch of the Centers for Disease Control and Prevention (770–488–4046) or from others who have experience with these categories of patients.

Babesiosis

Therapeutic Options. No universally effective therapeutic regimens are currently available. In patients with severe disease (usually asplenic individuals, but also the elderly or immunocompromised), treatment should be attempted. The mainstay of therapy is the combination of clindamycin and quinine, and there is evidence that azithromycin may be substituted for clindamycin in the regimen. Chloroquine, often given when the parasite is confused with malaria on smear, is not effective. Exchange transfusion may be helpful in severely ill individuals with high-grade parasitemia (> 10%). Steroids may be useful in the patient with severe Coombs'-positive hemolytic anemia.

Recommended Approach. Clindamycin 600 mg intravenously or orally every 6 to 8 hours and quinine 650 mg orally every 6 to 8 hours should be administered for 7 to 10 days. If azithromycin is substituted for the clindamycin, the dose is 500 to 1000 mg per day.

TABLE 8–61–1. TREATMENT OF CHLOROQUINE-SENSITIVE MALARIA *PLASMODIUM VIVAX,* * *P. OVALE,* * *P. MALARIAE,* AND CHLOROQUINE-SENSITIVE *P. FALCIPARUM*

Drug	Adult Dose	Side Effects
Oral		
Chloroquine phosphate	600 mg base (1 g salt), then 300 mg base (500 mg salt) 6 h later, followed by 300 mg base (500 mg salt) at 24 and 48 h	Dizziness, nausea, headache
Parenteral†		
Quinidine gluconate‡	10 mg/kg loading dose (max 600 mg) in normal saline IV slowly over 1 h followed by IV infusion of 0.02 mg/kg/min (for 3 d maximum)	Cinchonism, i.e., tinnitus, vertigo, nausea, dysphoria, headache; arrhythmias; several rare severe idiosyncratic reactions; hypoglycemia
Alternatives		
Quinine dihydrochloride§	20 mg salt/kg (max 1200 mg) loading dose, in 10 mL/kg 5% dextrose over 4 h, followed by 10 mg salt/kg (max 600 mg) over 2–4 h q8h (max 1800 mg/d) until oral treatment is started 200 mg base (250 mg salt) IM q6h	Same as for quinine

*For prevention of relapses in *P. vivax* or *P. ovale,* primaquine phosphate should be used after a normal level of glucose-6-phosphate dehydrogenase has been documented: 15 mg base daily × 2 weeks or 45 mg base per week × 8 weeks.
†Vital signs and electrocardiogram should be monitored. Oral therapy should start as soon as tolerated.
‡Although felt by many experts to be more effective than quinine, this regimen is still considered investigational by the Food and Drug Administration.
§Available in United States only from the Centers for Disease Control and Prevention (770–488–4046, 404–639–2888).

FOLLOW-UP

Malaria

In mild cases of malaria due to *P. vivax, P. ovale,* or *P. malariae,* the patient may be treated as an outpatient. Those with falciparum malaria should be treated in the hospital to allow close observation and to follow parasite counts. Individuals treated as outpatients usually need only two follow-up visits. The first visit should be 3 days after beginning chloroquine therapy. During that visit, thick and thin blood smears should be taken and examined for parasites. The liver and spleen should be palpated and their size and tenderness noted. A 14-day course of primaquine should be started for patients who acquired their infection in areas endemic for *P. vivax* or *P. ovale,* after testing for glucose-6-phosphate dehydrogenase deficiency. Three weeks later, at the second follow-up visit, spleen and liver size and tenderness should again be noted and thick and thin blood smears taken. In patients with uncomplicated falciparum malaria, only one visit a few days after discharge is necessary. In those with complications, follow-up must be individualized based on the organ system involved and the recovery or progressive nature of the impairment, such as the sequelae of acute renal failure or respiratory distress syndrome.

Patients should be alerted to the possibility of relapse with any type of malaria, but especially with *P. vivax* or *P. ovale,* in which reseeding of the bloodstream from the liver can occur. In suspected chloroquine-resistant falciparum malaria, eradication from the bloodstream might not be complete. Patients should be urged to return immediately if they again begin to experience fever or any of the symptoms they experienced during the illness.

Babesiosis

Patients with functioning spleens and mild to moderate illness require no specific follow-up after treatment. They should be told that therapy may not completely eradicate the infection, but that the immune system of the body eventually will. Once they are over the clinical illness, they will not relapse, even though parasites are still present in the blood; however, complete recovery may be prolonged. Patients with no or nonfunctioning spleens or those who experienced severe illness should

TABLE 8–61–2. TREATMENT OF CHLOROQUINE-RESISTANT *PLASMODIUM FALCIPARUM* MALARIA

Drug	Adult Dose	Side Effects
Quinine sulfate	650 mg tid × 3 d (× 7 d if acquired in Thailand)	Cinchonism
plus		
Pyrimethamine–sulfadoxine	3 tablets at once, each containing 25 mg pyrimethamine and 500 mg sulfadoxine	Rash, bone marrow toxicity, hepatitis, Stevens–Johnson syndrome
or		
Tetracycline	250 mg qid × 7 d	Increased sun sensitivity, nausea, yeast infections
or		
Doxycycline	100 mg qd × 7 d	Same as for tetracycline
Alternatives		
Mefloquine	1250 mg once	Nausea, vomiting, diarrhea, dizziness, psychosis, seizures
Halofantrine*	500 mg q6h × 3 doses, repeat in 1 w	Gastrointestinal disturbance, prolongation of QTc + PR intervals; electrocardiogram must be checked before and after therapy
Parenteral†		
Quinidine gluconate	As in Table 8–61–1	Cinchonism, predisposition to hypoglycemia and "blackwater fever" (hemolytic anemia, hemoglobinuria, jaundice)
or		
Quinine dihydrochloride	As in Table 8–61–1	Same as for quinidine gluconate

*Parenteral regimens should be changed to oral as soon as patient's condition permits.
†Halofantrine is not available in the United States.
Source: Adapted from Abramowicz CE, ed. Drugs for parasitic infection. Med Lett 1993;35(911):116. Reproduced with permission from the publisher and editor.

probably be followed on a biweekly basis for the first 2 months after recovery. Thick and thin blood smears should be examined, and a second course of therapy as an outpatient should be considered if parasites persist. If fever returns, the patient should be urged to return immediately for blood smear examination.

DISCUSSION

Malaria

Prevalence and Incidence. Malaria is the most important of the parasitic infections. The number of new cases each year is estimated at 120 million, and the annual number of deaths is greater than 1 million. There has been an increase in the number of cases in endemic areas, and correspondingly over the past 10 years the incidence of imported cases of *P. falciparum* in the United states has risen more than 10-fold. This increase has been due to failure of mosquito eradication programs and to increasing resistance of *P. falciparum* to traditional antimalarial agents. Because more and more Americans are traveling to malaria-endemic areas, it is important that we reacquaint ourselves with this illness. Most cases of malaria in the United States occur in travelers, although occasionally the disease occurs in transfusion recipients or in intravenous drug users.

Related Basic Science. Four species of the genus *Plasmodium* infect human beings: *vivax, falciparum, malariae,* and *ovale.* Anopheline mosquitoes are the only arthropod vector. Transmission varies directly with the ambient temperature and does not proceed below 60°F or above 100°F. The incubation period in humans also varies with the ambient temperature, and is at least 8 to 10 days.

In humans, there are two phases of the disease: the hepatic phase and the erythrocytic phase. The hepatic phase, which occurs first, is not associated with clinical disease. All signs and symptoms are due to the subsequent parasitization and rupture of the red blood cells, which are the most important aspects of malarial infection. In *P. vivax* and *P. ovale* infections, only the young (polychromatic) red cells can be infected, limiting total parasite counts to less than 10% of red blood cells. Falciparum malaria differs from the other three types in two major ways. First, red blood cells in all stages of development may be parasitized, allowing very high levels of parasitemia to be rapidly attained. This density of parasitemia in part accounts for the higher mortality associated with falciparum malaria than with the other types. Second, once parasites have left the liver to invade red blood cells, the hepatic phase ends; as no parasites remain in the liver, latent infections do not occur. This is also true of malaria due to *P. malariae;* however, in the latter, relapses can occur years after infection due to persistence of the parasite in the microcirculation. Such relapses are termed *recrudescence.*

Natural History and Its Modification with Treatment. Morbidity can be significant in nonfalciparum malaria infections. Because of the lengthy incubation or latent periods sometimes seen, patients and physicians alike occasionally fail to make the connection between a febrile illness and previous travel, which results in a delay of diagnosis.

Infection of nonimmune persons by *P. falciparum* should be considered a medical emergency, as death may occur within several hours. If more than 20% of a person's red blood cells are parasitized, mortality reaches 50%. Extensive parasitization may lead to a rapidly progressive hemolytic anemia and splenic sequestration of erythrocytes. There is also some evidence for an immune hemolytic anemia. The sudden release of large amounts of intravascular hemoglobin may cause hemoglobinuria and renal failure (blackwater fever). Vasodilation occurs with fever and causes rapid and massive fluid shifts resulting in orthostasis, hyponatremia, and cerebral and pulmonary edema. Red blood cells parasitized by *P. falciparum* are less deformable and "stickier" than normal cells, facilitating sludging in capillaries and widespread microthrombus formation. A polyclonal gammopathy is usually present, as are a number of other aberrant immunologic findings: false-positive syphilis serology, macroglobulinemia, rheumatoid factor, and cold agglutinins. Immune complex disease in the kidneys is seen primarily in children with chronic *P. malariae* infections. These children develop a nephrotic syndrome that is unresponsive to steroids or antimetabolites. Hypersplenism, seen in highly endemic areas, may lead to anemia, neutropenia, and thrombocytopenia.

Rapid diagnosis and treatment can prevent or reduce many of the manifestations of malaria, although patients who present with cerebral malaria may follow a fulminant course. In less serious disease response to therapy is usually rapid. Patients infected with *P. ovale* or *P. vivax,* even after cure of their acute infection, must take a course of primaquine to eradicate extraerythrocytic forms of the parasite.

Most of the deaths due to malaria in Americans occur after the traveler has returned to the United States. The most important factors contributing to fatal outcomes are failure to take prophylaxis, delay in seeking medical attention, misdiagnosis, and advanced age.

Prevention. Table 8–61–3 summarizes the recommended chemoprophylactic regimens for adult U.S. travelers to malaria-endemic areas. Some of these medications are not safe for children or for pregnant women, and prophylaxis in these individuals should be considered separately. In addition, despite these general guidelines, the prescribing of any antimalarial agent is not without potential side effects. For this reason, not only should the physician consider the geographic area being visited by the traveler but also the traveler's medical history, allergies, other medications being taken, and activities during travel. For example, mefloquine, which became available in the United States in 1990, is the agent of choice for the prevention of chloroquine-resistant falciparum malaria, but is contraindicated in persons with certain psychiatric illnesses and seizure disorders and for those who are dependent on fine motor skills (such as rock climbers and flight crews). Physicians and travelers may make use of the International Travelers' Hotline at the Centers for Disease Control and Prevention (404–332–4559) for specific information about transmission risks in various geographic areas. Specialized travel clinics are also available to the public, and travelers should consider visiting one of these facilities for more specific information tailored to their needs.

Because no antimalarial medication ensures complete protection, it is imperative that travelers protect themselves against mosquito bites be-

TABLE 8–61–3. MALARIA CHEMOPROPHYLAXIS FOR ADULTS

Geographical Area	Regimen of Choice	Alternatives
Areas of chloroquine-sensitive *P falciparum* (Mexico, Central America, Caribbean, Middle East)	Chloroquine phosphate: 500 mg (300 mg base) once/wk beginning 1 wk before and continuing for 4 wk after last exposure	Proguanil: 200 mg daily while in malarious region and continuing for 4 wk after last exposure*
Areas of chloroquine-resistant *P. falciparum* (South America, Amazon, Asia, Africa, Southeast Asia, Oceania)	Mefloquine: 250 mg once/wk beginning 1 wk before and continuing for 4 wk after last exposure	1. Daily doxycycline[†] 2. Chloroquine plus daily proguanil (in Africa south of the Sahara) 3. Chloroquine phosphate as above plus pyrimethamine–sulfadoxine[‡] standby

*Efficacy is questionable; not generally recommended. Not available in the United States.
[†]100 mg daily starting 2 days before and continuing for 4 weeks after last exposure.
[‡]Three tablets taken at once for presumptive treatment.
Source: Adapted from Abramowicz CE, ed. Drugs for parasitic infections. Med Lett 1993;35(911):116. Reproduced with permission from the publisher and editor.

tween dusk and dawn. Wearing closely woven protective clothing that covers the arms and legs and using insect repellent on exposed skin aid the traveler in preventing bites. Sleeping in screened areas with mosquito netting is also important when not in a climate-controlled environment.

Patients who have had malaria are asked not to be blood donors, even after treatment.

Cost Containment. Prophylaxis is extremely cost effective for malaria. The thick and thin blood smears used for diagnosis are very inexpensive, are the definitive diagnostic modality, and should be obtained liberally early in the evaluation of undiagnosed fever. Not all patients with malaria need hospitalization for therapy, and outpatient treatment for nonfalciparum malaria is frequently an option.

Babesiosis

Prevalence and Incidence. Babesiosis due to *B. microti* has been recognized most frequently in New England in the summer months when individuals are likely to come in contact with infected ticks. Sporadic cases have occurred in other areas of the country, and there is evidence for at least two other species causing human disease in the United States.

Related Basic Science. There are more than 75 species of *Babesia* worldwide. The rodent strain, *B. microti,* and the cattle strains, *B. divergens* and *B. bovis,* are the ones that most frequently cause human disease. *Ixodes scapularis,* the same tick that transmits Lyme disease, transmits babesiosis to humans from rodent via the deer, the natural reservoir of the organism. Like malaria, the disease is transmitted by the bite of the infected arthropod; but in addition, the organism is transmitted transovarially, so the tick is also a reservoir. The incubation period is usually 1 to 3 weeks but may be up to 6 weeks. As the nymph is the main biter of humans and is quite small, most patients do not recall a tick bite. Transfusion-associated babesiosis has occurred from both platelet and frozen erythrocyte preparations. Transplacental transmission has also been described.

Organisms enter red blood cells directly after the bite, and subsequently mature and divide. Unlike malaria, there is no hepatic phase. Infected erythrocytes eventually rupture, and other erythrocytes are invaded. An intact spleen is an important line of defense against babesiosis.

Natural History and Its Modification with Treatment. Most *Babesia* infections are probably asymptomatic or mild in the normal, healthy host.

Prolonged parasitemia may occur with a functional spleen, but this is also usually asymptomatic. Severe, fulminant infections with hemolytic anemia, hemoglobinuria, and renal failure may occur in splenectomized individuals. Immunosuppressive therapy, advanced age, and other intercurrent infections are associated with exacerbations of clinical disease. *Babesia* infections are rarely fatal in the normal host, although the course of the disease is occasionally protracted and parasitemia may last for months. Fatalities are usually confined to individuals with either no spleen or an afunctional spleen.

Therapy for babesiosis may reduce the level and shorten the duration of parasitemia; however, none of the regimens is completely effective and response to therapy may be slow.

Prevention. There is no chemoprophylaxis for babesiosis. In endemic areas recommendations include wearing long-sleeved shirts, long pants, and socks and tucking pants legs into socks or boots during the summer. Diethyltoluamide (DEET) should be applied to skin or clothes. Permethrin can be applied to clothing. Pets should be inspected regularly for the presence of ticks. Asplenic patients and patients possibly infected with HIV should take special precautions and, when possible, should avoid highly endemic areas from May to September. Persons who have had the disease are not infectious to others but should be cautioned against becoming blood donors.

Cost Containment. As with malaria, the value of the blood smear as an inexpensive diagnostic tool cannot be overemphasized. Most patients with babesiosis can be treated as outpatients. Only those who are extremely ill require hospitalization.

REFERENCES

Abramowitz CE, ed. Drugs for parasitic infections. Med Lett 1993;35(911):115.
Hoffman, SL. Diagnosis, treatment, and prevention of malaria. Med Clin North Am 1992;76:1327.
Meldrum SC, Birkhead GS, White DJ, et al. Human babesiosis in New York State: An epidemiological description of 136 cases. Clin Infect Dis 1992;15:1019.
Quick RE, Herwaldt BL, Thomford JW, et al. Babesiosis in Washington State: A new species of *Babesia?* Ann Intern Med 1993;119:284.
Zucker R, Campbell C. Malaria: Principles of prevention and treatment. Infect Dis Clin North Am 1993;7:547.

CHAPTER 8–62

Toxoplasmosis

Rafael A. Caputi, M.D., and Phyllis E. Kozarsky, M.D.

DEFINITION

The term *toxoplasmosis* has been used to refer to both infection and disease caused by *Toxoplasma gondii*. The distinction between infection and disease is important clinically and epidemiologically. *Toxoplasma* infection refers to the presence of the protozoan in persons regardless of whether they have clinical manifestations; *toxoplasmosis* refers to the disease caused by the organism.

ETIOLOGY

Toxoplasmosis is the disease caused by *Toxoplasma gondii*. This organism is an obligate intracellular parasite that is found worldwide.

CRITERIA FOR DIAGNOSIS

Suggestive

Toxoplasmosis may occur in the otherwise healthy individual presenting with lymphadenopathy and a mononucleosis-like syndrome with fever, malaise, headaches but significant disease occurs most often in the immunocompromised host (patients with cellular immune dysfunction, transplants, AIDS, and those taking immunosuppressive drugs) and can present with symptoms of disseminated disease. More than 50% of these patients have central nervous system involvement. Congenital toxoplasmosis should be suspected in neonates of mothers who acquire infection at any time during pregnancy. Ocular toxoplasmosis needs to be considered in patients with chorioretinitis and visual disturbances.

Definitive

The definitive diagnosis of acute infection with *Toxoplasma* is made by demonstration of tachyzoites in sections or preparations of tissues and body fluids, of cysts in the placenta or tissues of a fetus or newborn, and of characteristic lymph node histology.

CLINICAL MANIFESTATIONS

The clinical picture in toxoplasmosis ranges from asymptomatic infection to disseminated, rapidly fatal disease depending on the host involved. It is helpful, therefore, to divide the syndromes into categories: (1) congenital infection, (2) infection in the normal host, (3) infection in the immunocompromised patient, (4) ocular infection.

Subjective

Symptoms of congenital transmission may occur at birth or years thereafter. Most infected newborns have no symptoms at birth but may later develop signs of infection. In the neonate, seizures, feeding problems, respiratory distress, and diarrhea are common.

Most acquired *Toxoplasma* infections are clinically silent in the normal host. Between 20 and 70% of American adults have immunoglobulin G antibodies to *Toxoplasma*, indicating previous infection; these numbers are higher elsewhere in the world. The most common clinical manifestation of acute infection in the normal host is lymphadenopathy. Patients may present with a mononucleosis-like syndrome characterized by fever, fatigue, myalgia, headache, and sore throat; a maculopapular rash sparing the palms and soles may also occur.

The immunocompromised host may present with symptoms of disseminated disease, and more than 50% of these individuals have signs and symptoms referable to the central nervous system. In the United States, toxoplasmic encephalitis develops in 3 to 10% of patients with AIDS. In Europe and Africa, where the overall seroprevalence of *Toxoplasma* is higher, it is estimated that toxoplasmic encephalitis ultimately develops in 25 to 50% of patients with AIDS. Other patients with cellular immune dysfunction are also predisposed to disseminated infection. Common symptoms include cough, shortness of breath, chest pain, abdominal pain, focal weakness, seizures, psychosis, and cognitive impairment.

Ocular toxoplasmosis is for the most part congenital and leaves the patient with an asymptomatic latent chorioretinal scar. If eye infection is acquired or reactivates, visual disturbances occur. *Toxoplasma* has been estimated to cause approximately 35% of cases of chorioretinitis in the United States and in Central and Western Europe.

Objective

Physical Examination

Objective evidence of congenital infection in the neonate consists of fever, hepatosplenomegaly, rash, jaundice, hydrocephaly, microcephaly, retinochoroiditis, thrombocytopenia, and anemia. It must be remembered that these signs are all nonspecific and must be distinguished from other illnesses causing the TORCH syndrome (toxoplasmosis, rubella, cytomegalovirus, herpes simplex virus). Some children with subclinical infection at birth may develop blindness, chorioretinitis, seizures, hearing loss, or psychomotor retardation.

The most frequent physical finding in normal adolescents or adults with acquired toxoplasmosis is cervical lymphadenopathy. The cervical nodes (either a single posterior one or multiple nodes) are most frequently involved, and discovery of their involvement is often incidental. Suboccipital, supraclavicular, axillary, and inguinal nodes may also be involved. Nodes are discrete, nontender, nonsuppurative, and usually localized. It is estimated that up to 15% of unexplained adenopathy is due to toxoplasmosis.

Other findings in acquired toxoplasmosis are fever, maculopapular rash, hepatosplenomegaly, hepatitis, and muscle tenderness. In these patients with a mononucleosis-like syndrome, atypical lymphocytosis also may be detected on routine examination of peripheral blood. The

lymphadenopathic form of toxoplasmosis is self-limited, but lymphadenopathy or malaise may persist or recur for months. Rarely, complications such as myocarditis, pericarditis, pericardial effusion, polymyositis, pneumonitis, and meningoencephalitis may occur in the immunocompetent host.

In the immunocompromised patient one looks for interstitial pneumonia, myocarditis, and, particularly, evidence of neurologic disease, such as altered mental status, focal findings, seizures, and cranial nerve abnormalities. These patients also may manifest signs of diffuse organ involvement.

Ocular toxoplasmosis in the latent form can be appreciated as a chorioretinal scar, a hyperpigmented lesion with whitish gray plaques; older lesions are atrophic. Acute lesions are yellowish white, cottony patches. With reactivation there is an indistinct view of the retina on direct ophthalmoscopy typically called a "headlight in the fog" because of the vitreal inflammation. Iritis may occasionally occur.

Routine Laboratory Abnormalities

Routine laboratory data may show abnormalities related to specific organ involvement (i.e., hepatitis), and a chest x-ray film may show evidence of interstitial pneumonia or an enlarged mediastinum when a pericardial effusion is present. The electrocardiogram may suggest pericarditis.

PLANS

Diagnostic

Differential Diagnosis

The differential diagnosis of lymphadenopathy in the immunocompetent patient is quite extensive and includes (1) infectious processes such as mononucleosis, syphilis, cytomegalovirus, acute HIV infection, as well as other viral, parasitic, fungal, or chlamydial infections; (2) drug reactions (due to phenytoin or serum sickness); (3) malignancy such as lymphomas, other hematologic malignancies, and carcinoma of the breast or gastrointestinal tract; and (4) miscellaneous conditions such as sarcoidosis and systemic lupus erythematosus.

Up to 70% of mass lesions of the brain in patients with AIDS are due to toxoplasmosis. Other causes include primary central nervous system lymphoma (20–30%), progressive multifocal leukoencephalopathy (10–20%), and, less frequently, Kaposi's sarcoma, fungal and tuberculous abscesses, and herpes encephalitis. In the neonate with fever, rash, hepatosplenomegaly, and anemia, toxoplasmosis must be distinguished from other illnesses causing the TORCH syndrome.

Diagnostic Options

Definitive diagnosis of acute toxoplasmosis is made by histologic demonstration of tachyzoites or trophozoites in tissues or body fluids.

The finding of cysts in tissue reflects past infection and cannot generally be used to diagnose acute illness. Also, lymph nodes that are involved have a characteristic histology. Lymph node biopsy, however, is usually not necessary because lymphadenopathy is seen most often in the lymphadenopathic variety of toxoplasmosis, which is self-limited. When lymphadenopathy is persistent, biopsy can be helpful.

Serology remains the primary method of diagnosis and often requires results from more than one serologic test. The titers in such tests may vary when performed by different laboratories or with different commercial kits. The Sabin–Feldman dye test, indirect fluorescent antibody (IFA) test, indirect hemagglutination test, and enzyme-linked immunosorbent assay are the methods most widely used for diagnosis of toxoplasmosis.

The Sabin–Feldman dye test is a sensitive and specific test principally for detection of IgG antibodies to *T. gondii* and remains the reference test against which others are evaluated. There are no known cross-reactions or false positives. Because it requires live organisms, however, it is not readily available. The IFA test is the most widely available and measures the same antibodies as the dye test. Dye test and IFA test antibodies usually appear 1 to 2 weeks after infection, reach high titers in 6 to 8 weeks, and then gradually decline over months to years; low titers commonly persist for life.

The hemagglutination test should not be used to measure IgM antibodies nor for the diagnosis of congenital infection. "Natural" IgM antibodies frequently cause nonspecific agglutination in serum that is negative by the dye and IFA tests. Antibodies measured by indirect hemagglutination appear later than IFA antibodies.

The IgM indirect fluorescent antibody (IgM-IFA) test is useful for the diagnosis of acute infection because IgM antibodies appear faster (as early as 5 days after infection) and disappear sooner than IgG antibodies. Rheumatoid factor and antinuclear antibodies may cause false positive reactions.

Detection of IgM antibodies by the double-sandwich enzyme-linked immunosorbent assay is more sensitive and specific than the IgM-IFA test. Rheumatoid factor and antinuclear antibodies do not cause false-positive test results. The double-sandwich IgM enzyme-linked immunosorbent assay detects approximately 75% of infants with proven congenital infection, whereas the IgM-IFA detects only 25% of such cases. The IgM immunosorbent agglutination assay (IgM-ISAGA) or agglutination test is also valuable for detecting IgM antibodies.

Specific IgA antibodies may be detected by enzyme-linked immunosorbent assay and IgM immunosorbent agglutination assay in the sera of acutely infected adults and congenitally infected infants. This method is recommended for all newborns and fetal serum samples, as the detection of IgA antibodies appears to be most sensitive for the diagnosis of congenital *Toxoplasma* infection.

Polymerase chain reaction can be used to amplify DNA of *T. gondii*. This appears to be a promising technique to detect parasitic DNA in cerebrospinal fluid and amniotic fluid. The diagnosis of active ocular toxoplasmosis is difficult and should be made by an ophthalmologist. Low serologic titers are frequently seen in ocular disease.

Recommended Approach

In general, IgM antibodies appear early in the illness and become negative within a few months, though they may persist for more than 1 year at low titers. The greatest value in detecting IgM antibodies is in determining whether a pregnant woman has recently been infected. A negative test virtually rules out recently acquired infection, unless sera are tested so early that an antibody response has not yet developed. The presence of IgM antibodies without IgG antibodies is seen with acute infection, but a false-positive IgM needs to be ruled out by repeating the test in 2 weeks. If IgM antibodies are still detected and no IgG antibodies are present, a false-positive test should be suspected. IgG antibodies should develop if there is true infection.

Immunoglobulin G antibodies increase to a peak by the fourth week of illness and usually remain elevated at a lower titer for the remainder of the patient's life. Therefore, to make a diagnosis of acute toxoplasmosis, a fourfold rise in *Toxoplasma*-specific IgG antibodies or detection of IgM antibodies is required. In addition, a single very high IgG tier is also compatible with acute infection.

Serologic testing in immunocompromised patients is not as reliable. It has been noted that patients with AIDS and central nervous system toxoplasmosis rarely have an elevated IgM antibody titer to toxoplasmosis, but IgG antibodies are detectable in virtually all patients before the development of encephalitis. It is therefore important to determine the status of antibody to *T. gondii* in all HIV-positive patients. To diagnose toxoplasmic encephalitis in patients with AIDS, a computed tomography scan with contrast or a magnetic resonance imaging scan, which is more sensitive, should be obtained. Cerebrospinal fluid findings in toxoplasmosis are nonspecific, with mild mononuclear pleocytosis, an elevated protein, and normal glucose. If mass lesions are seen on brain scan, a therapeutic trial is administered. Lesions usually regress and patients improve clinically within 2 to 3 weeks of initiation of therapy. If there is no improvement, a biopsy is then indicated.

Therapeutic

The combination of sulfadiazine (or triple sulfas) and pyrimethamine is the major treatment for toxoplasmosis. In adults with severe disease or immunocompromised patients, a sulfadiazine loading dose of 75 mg/kg (up to 4 g) is given followed by 75 to 100 mg/kg per day (up to 8 g per day) in four divided doses. Also, a pyrimethamine loading dose of 100 to 200 mg is often given, followed by 50 to 100 mg every day for at least 6 weeks. Patients with AIDS are treated indefinitely with a maintenance regimen. Common side effects of sulfonamides include rash, leukopenia, and hepatitis. Pyrimethamine may cause gastrointestinal distress, headache, and bone marrow suppression. Folinic acid (10 mg/d orally) is added to the regimen to counteract anemia.

An alternative regimen for toxoplasmic encephalitis in AIDS is clindamycin (900 mg) intravenously or orally every 8 hours and pyrimethamine (and folinic acid). Also, atovaquone and azithromycin have been used for patients who fail or who are intolerant of standard treatment. Their efficacy has not yet been established.

If a pregnant woman acquires infection and is treated, the risk of congenital infection is decreased but not eliminated. The administration of spiramycin (3 g/d) reportedly reduces the frequency of maternal transmission of *T. gondii* by 60%. In the United States, spiramycin can be obtained from the U.S. Food and Drug Administration, (301) 443–4280. Because of experimental data suggesting that, once infected, the placenta remains infected for the duration of the pregnancy, it is recommended that treatment with spiramycin be continued throughout pregnancy. If spiramycin is not available, treatment with sulfadiazine alone (4 g/d) is effective; pyrimethamine is teratogenic during the first trimester of pregnancy.

Patients with active chorioretinitis should be treated with pyrimethamine and sulfadiazine for 6 weeks, after which a good clinical response is seen in 60 to 70% of cases. Photocoagulation has been used to treat active lesions.

Indications for treatment of toxoplasmosis include severe acute toxoplasmosis, toxoplasmosis in the immunocompromised host, congenital disease, acute ocular disease, and acute illness in certain pregnant patients.

FOLLOW-UP

The normal host should understand that he or she has a parasitic infection that usually causes very little problem and will resolve on its own. If the patient is pregnant, consultation should be obtained to discuss possible fetal complications and modes of treatment. Patients with AIDS and central nervous system toxoplasmosis must understand that they will require lifelong suppressive therapy, without which relapse is very likely. Immunocompromised patients (particularly those with AIDS) should be followed by a specialist who can assess the signs and symptoms of neurologic disease. Hematologic studies are required to assess the bone marrow toxicity commonly seen with pyrimethamine.

Patients with ocular toxoplasmosis should be followed by an ophthalmologist.

DISCUSSION
Prevalence and Incidence

The prevalence of *Toxoplasma* seropositivity appears to have decreased, in at least some populations, over the past two to three decades. For example, the seroprevalence rates for pregnant women in Palo Alto, California, were 27% in 1964 and 10% in 1987. The cause is not apparent but might include improved hygiene. The seroconversion rate among women of childbearing age in the United States is approximately 0.8% per year.

Related Basic Science

Toxoplasma gondii is a ubiquitous obligate intracellular protozoa that infects most mammalian species. The organism exists in three forms: (1) the tachyzoite or invasive form, which is responsible for acute infection; (2) the cyst form (latent organism), which is found in tissues of mammals for the life of animal and may contain thousands of organisms; and (3) the oocyst, which is formed by the sexual cycle of the organism in the definitive hosts, members of the cat family. Only members of the cat family have been reported to excrete oocysts. Cats become infected by eating prey or raw meat, after which they asymptomatically excrete oocysts for approximately 2 weeks. The oocysts become infectious for humans after maturation (sporulation), which occurs only after the oocysts have been excreted. Transmission to humans occurs by one of several routes: ingestion of food or material contaminated by oocysts from cat feces; ingestion of cysts in undercooked food; transplacental transmission from an acutely infected mother; or, rarely, from blood or leukocyte transfusions or organ transplantation.

Toxoplasma gondii infects humans or other animals when organisms are released from ingested cysts or oocysts and intestinal proteolytic enzymes and acid liberate tachyzoites in the human intestinal tract. The tachyzoites invade the intestinal epithelium and spread hematogenously or via lymphatics to tissues where they form cysts. The cysts may remain latent for the life of the host, but may reactivate if the individual becomes immunosuppressed.

Natural History and Its Modification with Treatment

Because the overall prevalence of *Toxoplasma* seropositivity in humans is so high, it is assumed that most individuals acquire asymptomatic infection or mild nonspecific illness from this parasite. In the immunocompromised host the clinical illness usually represents reactivation of a latent focus of infection rather than recently acquired infection. These patients are predisposed to fatal dissemination.

Prevention

Prevention of infection by *T. gondii* is most important for immunodeficient patients and seronegative pregnant women. Recommendations include the following:

- Avoid raw or undercooked meat. Cook meat to 66° C; smoking or freezing will decrease the number of viable organisms but may not kill all of them. Cook eggs and do not drink unpasteurized milk.
- Wash hands after handling raw meat and before eating.
- Wash hands after handling cats.
- Wash fruits and vegetables before consumption.
- Avoid contact with mucous membranes of mouth and eyes while handling raw meat.
- Wear gloves while working in soil.
- Cover children's sand boxes when not in use.

- Feed cats only with dried, canned, or cooked meat.
- Change cat litter box daily. Pregnant women should avoid contact with the litter box.
- Control flies and roaches, which may be vectors of cysts.

Primary prophylaxis with trimethoprim–sulfamethoxazole (1 DS/d) or dapsone (100 mg/d) plus pyrimethamine, 50 mg/week, (and folinic acid) is necessary in patients with AIDS and serologic evidence of latent *T. gondii* infection.

Cost Containment

Cost containment is not a major issue with toxoplasmosis, as it is often an asymptomatic or mild disease. Avoidance of congenital toxoplasmosis is important. Secondary prevention with serologic screening of pregnant women is important. All pregnant women must be tested as early as possible, preferably no later than at 10 to 12 weeks of gestation. Toxoplasmosis in immunodeficiency is potentially costly in terms of diagnosis, follow-up, and long-term treatment.

REFERENCES

Boyer KM, McAuley JB. Congenital toxoplasmosis. Semin Pediat Infect Dis 1994;5:42.
Carter AO, Gelmon SB, Wells GA, Toepell AP. The effectiveness of a prenatal education programme for the prevention of congenital toxoplasmosis. Epidemiol Infect 1989;103:539.
Israelski DM, Remington JS. Toxoplasmosis in patients with cancer. Clin Infect Dis 1993;17(suppl. 2):S423.
Luft BJ, Remington JS. Toxoplasmic encephalitis in AIDS. Clin Infect Dis 1992;15:211.
McCabe R, Remington JS. Toxoplasmosis: The time has come. N Engl J Med 1988;318:313.
Wong SY, Remington JS. Toxoplasmosis in pregnancy. Clin Infect Dis 1994;18:853.

CHAPTER 8–63

Pneumocystis carinii Infection

John A. Jernigan, M.D., and Carl A. Perlino, M.D.

DEFINITION

Pneumocystis carinii is a major cause of pneumonia in patients who have significant impairment of cellular immune function. Pneumonia due to *Pneumocystis carinii* is most commonly seen in patients with AIDS, but also occurs in patients immunosuppressed because of medication (e.g., organ transplant patients), hematologic malignancy (most commonly lymphoma), or hypogammaglobulinemia and in infants with severe protein-calorie malnutrition.

ETIOLOGY

Pneumocystis carinii is an opportunistic pathogen found in the lungs of humans and various animals, existing as both trophozoite and cyst stages. Its taxonomic classification has been a matter of some controversy. Originally classified as a protozoa based on its morphology, lack of growth on fungal media, and susceptibility to antiprotozoal agents, molecular genetic analysis now suggests that *Pneumocystis* may be more closely related to fungi. The natural habitat of the organism is unknown.

CRITERIA FOR DIAGNOSIS
Suggestive

Pneumocystis carinii pneumonia (PCP) should be suspected in patients with conditions associated with defective cell-mediated immunity

(most commonly AIDS) who present with fever, dyspnea, minimally or nonproductive cough, and bilateral interstitial infiltrates on chest radiograph.

Definitive

Definitive diagnosis of infection due to *P. carinii* can be made by histopathologic demonstration of *P. carinii* cysts or trophozoites in lung tissue, respiratory secretions, or, occasionally, tissue obtained from other organs. Currently, no method of isolating the organism in culture is available.

CLINICAL MANIFESTATIONS
Subjective

The most common symptoms associated with PCP are fever, dyspnea, and a cough productive of little, if any, sputum. For patients with predisposing conditions other than AIDS, the presentation is acute, with symptoms usually occurring over 1 to 2 weeks, frequently following tapering of immunosuppressive drugs such as steroids. Patients with AIDS, however, are likely to complain of symptoms of fever, cough, and subtle changes in respiratory function over a more prolonged period of weeks to months before presenting to the physician. Chills may be a presenting complaint in up to half the patients with PCP. Chest pain occurs less commonly and is unlikely to be truly pleuritic in nature. Other symptoms such as nausea, vomiting, and diarrhea are not commonly seen with PCP, and the presence of these symptoms should raise suspicion of other causes of pneumonia, such as *Legionella*, or conditions related to the underlying disease of the patient.

Objective

Physical Examination

Fever is almost a universal finding in patients with PCP. Tachypnea is present, and in more advanced disease, other signs compatible with air hunger, such as nasal flaring and cyanosis, may be detected. Splinting, as seen in patients with bacterial pneumonia and associated pleural inflammation, is rarely encountered. The physical examination of the chest is nonspecific, but PCP may be suggested in a patient with severe tachypnea and an essentially normal lung examination. Bilateral rales, however, may be found in approximately a third of patients. Signs of consolidation should make one suspicious of a diagnosis other than PCP. Signs attributable to organ systems other than the lung are not usually found in PCP.

Routine Laboratory Abnormalities

Abnormalities in the arterial blood gas determination are characteristic, but early in the disease changes may be mild. Hypoxia, hypocarbia, and alkalosis are the most common findings. The alveolar–arteriolar oxygen gradient is characteristically increased. Occasionally, patients with AIDS and PCP may have adequate oxygen saturation at rest, but become hypoxemic only with exertion. The absence of a decline in oxygen saturation with exercise argues strongly against the diagnosis.

Other routine laboratory abnormalities are nonspecific. Serum lactate dehydrogenase levels may be elevated with acute disease and decrease with therapy, but a similar pattern can be seen with other diseases.

The chest roentgenogram can be highly suggestive of PCP. Most commonly, it will demonstrate bilateral infiltrates with increased densities in the perihilar lung fields. Late in the disease, bilateral interstitial–alveolar infiltrates may completely involve both lung fields. Less common radiographic manifestations include localized infiltrates involving only one lung, pneumatocoeles, nodules, cavities, and pneumothorax. Also, as many as 10 to 15% of HIV-infected patients with documented PCP will have a normal chest roentgenogram when the diagnosis is made. Patients who have been receiving aerosolized pentamidine for prophylaxis of PCP may present with infiltrates limited to the upper lobes due to the primary distribution of the aerosolized pentamidine to the lower lobes.

PLANS

Diagnostic

Differential Diagnosis

The differential diagnosis of pneumonia in immunodeficient patients, especially those with AIDS, is broad. Infectious processes to be considered include pyogenic and atypical bacterial pathogens (including *Legionella*, *Nocardia*, and *Rhodococcus equi*); mycobacteria (*Mycobacterium tuberculosis* and nontuberculous mycobacteria); fungi (including *Cryptococcus, Histoplasma, Coccidioides*); protozoa (*Toxoplasma*, microsporidia, and possibly *Cryptosporidium*); and viruses (cytomegalovirus). Noninfectious causes include Kaposi's sarcoma, lymphoma, and lymphoid interstitial pneumonitis.

Diagnostic Options

The diagnosis of PCP is usually made by demonstrating cysts or trophozoites of the organism in respiratory specimens. The least invasive method of collecting a diagnostic specimen is by induction of sputum via inhalation of nebulized hypertonic saline. The sensitivity of this method among AIDS patients with PCP varies widely among centers (from less than 50% to 90%), and seems dependent on the level of interest and experience in performing the procedure.

A more reliable method of obtaining a diagnostic specimen is fiberoptic bronchoscopy. This procedure provides the diagnosis in greater than 90% of patients with PCP. Bronchoalveolar lavage is usually adequate to make the diagnosis, especially if more than one lobe is sampled. Transbronchial biopsy may be diagnostic in patients for

whom the bronchoalveolar lavage was negative, but there is increased risk of complications such as pneumothorax and bleeding with this procedure.

The most invasive approach to the diagnosis of PCP is open lung biopsy. This may be considered in patients for whom bronchoscopy has failed to yield a diagnosis, the diagnosis remains unclear, and there is inadequate response to empiric therapy.

The organism can readily be demonstrated in respiratory specimens with the use of histologic stains such as methenamine silver and Wright–Giemsa. Calcofluor white, a chemofluorescent agent that binds to polymers of fungi and *Pneumocystis*, can also be used. Immunofluorescence methods that use monoclonal antibodies directed against *Pneumocystis* antigens have been widely employed and have been shown to be more sensitive than histologic stains in detecting *Pneumocystis*. Polymerase chain reaction-based methods may prove to be the most sensitive mode of detection available, but these techniques must be considered experimental at present.

Recommended Approach

For AIDS patients and other persons at risk who present with signs and symptoms consistent with PCP, we recommend obtaining one or more samples of induced sputum to be examined with histopathologic stains (i.e., methenamine silver or Wright–Giemsa) and/or immunofluorescence techniques. If the specimen is negative, proceed with fiberoptic bronchoscopy with bronchoalveolar lavage, and examine the bronchoalveolar lavage sample in the same manner as the induced sputum. If there is still no definitive diagnosis nor response to empiric therapy, obtain a transbronchial biopsy. If negative, the physician can consider open lung biopsy, though the risks and benefits of proceeding with this invasive procedure versus those of empiric therapy must be carefully weighed.

Therapeutic

Therapeutic Options

Trimethoprim–sulfamethoxazole (Bactrim, Septra) is the antimicrobial agent of choice in the treatment of PCP. The drug is given in an amount based on a trimethoprim dose of 15 to 20 mg/kg body weight per day divided into four equal doses. Parenteral therapy should be used for patients who are very ill or for those who cannot tolerate oral therapy. Non-AIDS patients with PCP responding to therapy with trimethoprim–sulfamethoxazole usually show signs of improvement within 3 to 4 days of beginning therapy. The therapeutic response of patients with AIDS may be more delayed, taking up to 5 to 7 days before any improvement is seen. When a patient with PCP shows no evidence of improvement after 5 to 7 days of appropriate therapy with trimethoprim–sulfamethoxazole, therapeutic failure is a possibility and a change in therapy should be considered, although a good clinical response may require up to 14 days after beginning therapy. Reactions to trimethoprim–sulfamethoxazole, including rash, fever, leukopenia, thrombocytopenia, and hepatitis, may occur during therapy. Side effects are especially common in AIDS patients, occurring in up to 80% of patients treated with this drug. Mild adverse reactions such as skin rash are not necessarily indications for discontinuing the drug. Conservative measures such as the use of antihistamines may allow uneventful completion of therapy; however, about half of those who experience an adverse effect require withdrawal of the drug.

For patients requiring parenteral therapy and for whom trimethoprim–sulfamethoxazole cannot be used, pentamidine isethionate in a dose of 4 mg/kg/d in a single daily dose is an effective alternative choice. Pentamidine therapy may be associated with numerous toxic effects, including renal and liver dysfunction, cardiac arrhythmias, pancreatitis, hypotension with rapid intravenous administration, hypoglycemia, and hyperglycemia.

Other alternative regimens include the combination of trimethoprim (15 mg/kg/d in four oral doses) and dapsone (100 mg orally per day); the combination of clindamycin (300–450 mg orally four times daily or 600 mg intravenously every 6 hours) and primaquine (15 mg base orally every day); and, for mild to moderate disease only, atovaquone (750 mg orally three times daily). Adverse effects to dapsone include methemoglobinemia, rash, fever, nausea, vomiting, and, hemolysis in patients with glucose-6-phosphate dehydrogenase (G6PD) deficiency. Primaquine can also cause hemolysis in glucose-6-phosphate dehydrogenase-deficient patients, and therefore patients should be screened for this deficiency prior to being treated with these drugs. Atovaquone has poor bioavailability; taking the drug with food enhances absorption and results in higher serum levels.

Trimetrexate, a lipid-soluble derivative of methotrexate, has activity against *P. carinii* and has shown some success in the treatment of PCP when given at a dose of 45 mg/m^2 body surface area intravenously every day. It is usually reserved for cases in which other regimens have failed or are contraindicated. Its major toxic effect is bone marrow suppression, which can be ameliorated by the concomitant administration of leucovorin (20 mg/m^2 four times daily).

Patients with PCP may show temporary clinical deterioration with the initiation of anti-*Pneumocystis* therapy, presumably due to the host inflammatory response to antigens released from dying organisms. For this reason, the adjunctive use of steroids in treating PCP has been studied. Steroids administered within the first 72 hours of therapy have been shown to lessen the decline in oxygenation and improve survival in severe PCP. Although the optimal dose and duration are still undetermined, an expert panel has recommended that the following regimen be initiated in all adults with moderate to severe pneumocystosis (as defined by arterial oxygen pressure < 70 mm Hg or an alveolar–arterial oxygen gradient of > 35 mm Hg): prednisone 40 mg twice daily for 5 days, followed by 40 mg once daily for 5 days, then 20 mg once daily for an additional 10 days.

Recommended Approach

The agent of choice in treating PCP is trimethoprim–sulfamethoxazole (15–20 mg/kg/d trimethoprim divided into four doses per day for 21 days). For severe cases the drug should be given parenterally, but for mild to moderate cases, oral therapy may be used.

The second-line choice for severe disease is pentamidine isethionate (4 mg/kg/d in a single daily dose for 21 days).

Second-line choices for mild to moderate disease include the combination of trimethoprim (15/mg/kg/d in four oral doses) and dapsone (100 mg orally per day) for 21 days; the combination of clindamycin (300–450 mg orally four times daily or 600 mg intravenously every 6 hours) and primaquine (15 mg base orally every day) for 21 days; and atovaquone (750 mg orally three times daily) for 21 days.

All patients presenting with an arterial oxygen pressure below 70 mm Hg or an alveolar–arterial oxygen gradient greater than 35 mm Hg should be treated with adjunctive steroids (see doses above).

FOLLOW-UP

Follow-up is determined by the response to therapy. Some cases require hospitalization for the full course of therapy with careful checks of oxygen saturation and other clinical parameters, whereas others can be changed to oral therapy and followed as outpatients. Because any patient with a history of PCP is at extremely high risk for relapse, prophylactic therapy is indicated in all recovered PCP patients (see below).

DISCUSSION

Prevalence and Incidence

Prior to the 1980s, PCP was rare. In the past 10 years, however, the emergence of AIDS has produced a dramatic increase in the incidence of pneumocystosis; it occurs in approximately 80% of patients with AIDS in the absence of prophylaxis. As prophylactic regimens have increased in use, the incidence of this infection has started to decrease. Pneumocystosis, however, remains one of the most important opportunistic infections among patients with AIDS, representing about 50% of the initial AIDS-defining diagnosis.

Despite the dramatic increase in incidence, little is known about the epidemiology of *Pneumocystis* infections. Although clinical disease occurs almost exclusively among immunosuppressed individuals, serologic studies suggest that asymptomatic *P. carinii* infection is almost universal and usually occurs before the age of 3. Exposure is presumed to result from inhalation of infectious particles, but the environmental reservoir is unknown.

Related Basic Science

The mode of entry is presumably inhalation into the lungs, where it is thought that infection is initiated by attachment of the organism to alveolar type I cells. It is not known whether exposed persons remain latently infected for long periods or if infection is transient. The nature of the immune defects that allow the organism to cause clinical disease is incompletely understood, but in addition to inadequate cell-mediated immune response, impairment in humoral immunity may be important. In the setting of immune defects that fail to control the organism, *P. carinii* proliferates, gradually filling the alveolar spaces and causing a decrease in the alveolar–arterial oxygen gradient, decreased diffusion capacity, decreased lung compliance, and decreased lung volumes.

Natural History and Its Modification with Treatment

If left untreated, patients with PCP usually develop progressive worsening of oxygenation, respiratory failure, and death. The prognosis for treated patients correlates with the degree of hypoxemia at the time of presentation. Survival rates greater than 90% can be expected in those with initial arterial oxygen pressures higher than 70 mm Hg, but the risk of death increases in patients with lower presenting arterial oxygen pressures. The overall survival rate for patients with PCP who develop respiratory failure is 30 to 40%.

Prevention

Prophylactic anti-*Pneumocystis* regimens have proven to be very effective at preventing disease among those who are at risk. Several prophylactic regimens are listed in Table 8–63–1.

For patients with HIV infection, prophylaxis is recommended for those with a CD4 lymphocyte count less than 200/mm^3; those with thrush or unexplained fever for longer than 2 weeks, regardless of CD4 count; any patient with a previous history of PCP.

Recommendations for patients without HIV infection are not as well

TABLE 8–63–1. RECOMMENDATIONS FOR PNEUMOCYSTIS PNEUMONIA PROPHYLAXIS IN PATIENTS INFECTED WITH HIV

	Drug	Dose	Comments
Preferred	Trimethoprim–sulfamethoxazole (TMP–SMZ)	1 double-strength tablet (160 mg TMP/ 800 mg SMZ) daily or 3 d weekly	*Advantages:* effective, well studied, more effective than pentamidine, inexpensive *Disadvantages:* side effects common
Alternatives	Aerosolized pentamidine	300 mg monthly by Respirgard II nebulizer (requires compressed air source) *or* 60 mg every 2 wk by Fisoneb nebulizer (hand held and portable)	*Advantages:* effective, well studied *Disadvantages:* not as effective as TMP–SMZ, expensive, risk of spread of pulmonary pathogens during therapy, increased risk of extrapulmonary pneumocystosis, less effective if underlying bullous or obstructive lung disease, increased risk of pneumothorax
	Dapsone	50–100 mg PO daily	*Advantage:* less expensive than pentamidine *Disadvantages:* efficacy less well studied, though appears to be at least as effective as pentamidine, side effects common, contraindicated in glucose-6-phosphate dehydrogenase-deficient patients

established. Most would agree that patients with previous history of PCP should receive prophylaxis. Other patients in whom prophylaxis should be considered include those with primary immunodeficiencies (particularly severe combined immunodeficiency), lymphoreticular malignancies, and organ transplantation.

Cost Containment

Prevention of disease through the use of prophylactic medication is the single most effective way to contain costs. Because PCP in patients with AIDS tends to be subacute in onset, those patients who are diagnosed when their disease is still mild can safely be treated as outpatients, provided response to therapy can be monitored closely. A high index of suspicion and early diagnosis help to minimize the number of patients requiring hospitalization. In addition, patients who initially require hospitalization can have anti-*Pneumocystis* therapy changed from parenteral to oral administration when clinically stable, allowing completion of therapy as an outpatient.

REFERENCES

National Institutes of Health–University of California Expert Panel for Corticosteroids as Adjunctive Therapy for *Pneumocystis* Pneumonia. Consensus statement on the use of corticosteroids as adjunctive therapy for *Pneumocystis* pneumonia in the acquired immunodeficiency syndrome. N Engl J Med 1990;323:1500.

Phair J, Munoz A, Detels R, et al. The risk of *Pneumocystis carinii* pneumonia among men infected with human immunodeficiency virus type 1. N Engl J Med 1990;322:161.

U.S. Public Health Task Force on Anti-*Pneumocystis* Prophylaxis in Individuals Infected with HIV. Recommendations for prophylaxis against *Pneumocystis* pneumonia for adults and adolescents infected with human immunodeficiency virus. MMWR 1992;41(RR-4):1.

Walzer PD. *Pneumocystic carinii*. In: Mandell GL, Bennett JE, Dolin R, eds: Principles and practice of infectious diseases. 4th ed. New York: Churchill Livingstone, 1995.

CHAPTER 8–64

Some Important Protozoal and Helminthic Infections

Juliette Morgan, M.D., and Jonas A. Shulman, M.D.

DEFINITION

The disease(s) can be defined as clinical manifestations caused by the presence of helminthic or protozoal parasites in any human organ or tissue.

ETIOLOGY

The list of organisms within the classification of Protozoa and Helminths capable of causing human disease is extensive. We have divided these infections into those that are commonly acquired in "Western" societies, although still more prevalent in developing countries, and those that are found only in individuals who have traveled to or are originally from endemic areas and are referred to as *tropical diseases*. Table 8–64–1 lists the parasites commonly seen in the United States and other developed nations, and Table 8–64–2 lists the parasites found in travelers and immigrants almost exclusively.

CRITERIA FOR DIAGNOSIS

Suggestive

For most of these parasitic diseases the epidemiologic data, such as country or area of origin, travel history, food and drinking water sources and handling, and fresh water exposure are the important clues for diagnosis. The symptoms are diverse and relate to the organ(s) involved in each illness.

Definitive

Usually definitive diagnosis relies on the identification of the parasite itself, in one of its stages of development. The typical situation is the passage of a worm or cysts in stool or the finding of, for example, amastigotes in a skin biopsy. Also, the human immunologic response to the infection can be used as a diagnostic tool, that is, determination of antibody titers in chronic Chagas' disease or schistosomiasis. A common dilemma seen in patients that are born in areas endemic for a particular disease is the clinical significance of a positive serologic assay for that disease, if a patient presents with symptoms compatible with this particular illness, given that even with prior treatment the antibody response is likely to remain present and therefore these immunodiagnostic assays do not differentiate past, treated or not, and present infection. See Table 8–64–1 and 8–64–2 for criteria for diagnosis of each infection.

CLINICAL MANIFESTATIONS

See Table 8–64–1. The clinical presentations of the "tropical diseases" are described briefly in Table 8–64–2.

PLANS

Diagnostic

The appropriate specimen related to the clinical illness should be sent for diagnostic studies. The laboratory should be informed what parasitic infection is in the differential diagnosis and what special studies are needed. Serologic studies are frequently difficult to obtain from nonspecialized laboratories, but the Centers for Disease Control and Prevention (CDC) can frequently perform diagnostic serologic assays that are not routinely available and encourage practicing physicians with diagnostic dilemmas to request information and diagnostic procedures.

Therapeutic

The treatment of the various diseases depends on the etiologic agent (see Tables 8–64–1 and 8–64–2).

FOLLOW-UP

The original specimens sent for diagnosis are frequently reexamined to determine efficacy of treatment or possible reinfection.

DISCUSSION

Some of the common "tropical diseases" and other parasitic illnesses are briefly discussed here.

Prevalence and Incidence, Related Basic Science, and Natural History and Its Modification with Treatment

Trichuris trichiura, a nematode or roundworm, is one of the most prevalent worm infections in the world. In the United States alone, it is estimated that more than 2 million people are infected, especially in the southeastern rural regions. Humans are the principal host, and they are

We thank Dr. John Maloney for his contribution to this chapter in the third edition of this book.

TABLE 8–64–1. HELMINTHIC AND PROTOZOAL INFECTIONS COMMONLY FOUND WORLDWIDE

Common Name/Parasite	Criteria for Diagnosis: Suggestive and Definitive	Clinical Manifestations	Treatment
Pinworm: *Enterobius vermicularis*	Children are mostly affected, as are their caretakers, through spread of eggs by sheets, underclothing, and hands. Worldwide distribution, most common helminthiasis in United States. Pressing cellophane tape to the perianal area early in the morning and examining the tape microscopically for the presence of eggs. Three examinations will detect close to 100% of pinworm infections.	Most are asymptomatic or mild abdominal pain. Anal pruritus, worse at night, is classic presentation. Complications occur outside of normal parasite habitat: appendicitis, vulvovaginitis, and increased incidence of urinary infections in girls who are infested.	Pyrantel pamoate 11 mg/kg once (max 1 g), repeat after 2 wk. Alternative: mebendazole.
Whipworm: *Trichuris trichiura*	Identification of characteristic eggs in stool. Transmission favors conditions found in the tropics (Caribbean islands particularly), but > 2 million cases were estimated in United States (contamination of poorly washed foods). Diagnosis is usually incidental, because infection is Westernized countries is usually asymptomatic. Intensity of infection and morbidity is much higher in children.	Classic dysentery syndrome associated in intense infection with diarrhea, mucus and blood, rectal prolapse, and anemia. Chronic infection can cause growth stunting, chronic loose stools, and malnutrition. Parasite load varies greatly between individuals, even in highly endemic areas. Infections usually asymptomatic in Westernized countries	Mebendazole 100 mg bid for 3 d. Alternative: albendazole.
Hookworm: *Ancylostoma duodenale* and *Necator americanus*	Identification of characteristic eggs in stool. Found in rural tropics, where fecal contamination of soil, suitable environment, and skin–soil contact determine prevalence. White race more susceptible than black for prevalence and intensity of infection (as seen in southern states in United States). Peak age is in adult life.	"Ground itch," with skin eruptions, associated with penetration of worms. With migration of worms throughout the lungs, cough, bronchospasm, hemoptysis, fleeting infiltrates, and eosinophilia can be seen (Loeffler's syndrome). Adult worms can cause a variety of nonspecific gastrointestinal complaints, but anemia and hypoalbuminemia are the prominent features accompanied by mental apathy, lassitude, pallor, and end-organ damage with symptoms related to this (cardiac insufficiency, etc). The degree of blood loss, the patient's state of nutrition, and worm burden are what determine the degree of severity of illness. Generally an asymptomatic infection with mild eosiniphilia in developed nations.	Mebendazole 100 mg bid for 3 d. Alternatives: pyrantel pamoate, albendazole.
Roundworm: *Ascaris lumbricoides*	Identification of characteristic eggs in stool. Found in epidemic proportions in southeast United States. Usually asymptomatic and found incidentally on stool examination or by passage of worm in stool.	May be asymptomatic in healthy host with low burden. Vague abdominal complaints are prevailing presentation associated wtih pallor, headache, and occasionally malnutrition. Heavy infestations can cause intestinal or even biliary obstruction. The migration of worms through the lungs can also cause Loeffler's syndrome.	Mebendazole 100 mg bid for 3 d. Alternatives: albendazole, pyrantel pamoate.
Trichinosis: *Trichinella spiralis*	Most of the subclinical cases go undiagnosed. Routine stool examination rarely detects worms; muscle biopsy is most accurate although seldom employed. Immunodiagnostic tests are being developed. Infection through oral route. Humans who eat undercooked wild animal meat are exposed to the sylvatic trichinosis. Urban trichinosis involves mainly infected pork (especially sausage). Slow worldwide decline in incidence for unclear reasons has been noted.	Penetration of the worms into the intestinal mucosa can cause nausea, vomiting, and diarrhea. The migration can cause vasculitis with localized edema, particularly of face and hands. Wandering worms can cause a variety of presentations according to the localization (myocarditis, encephalitis, pleuritis, etc.). Penetration into muscular tissue is associated with pain and swelling at the site and peripheral eosinophilia.	Severe cases may require corticosteroids plus mebendazole 200–400 mg tid for 3 d, then 400–500 mg tid for 10 d. Thiabendazole, if given early, may be effective. No satisfactory regimen is available.
Beef Tapeworm: *Taenia saginatus*	Identification of characteristic gravid proglottids in stool. Eggs are best found using the cellophane tape method. Infections occur worldwide, but no reliable statistics available. Commonly found in United States, Europe, South America, and Africa. Undercooked beef has the infective *Cystericercus bovis*.	Most frequent complaint is discharge of proglottids per rectum. Some "irritative effect" of the intestinal mucosa with abdominal pain, nausea, changes in appetite, headache, hyperexcitability, and increased levels of immunoglobulin E.	Praziquantel 5–10 mg/kg once (not Food and Drug Administration approved for this indication in United States). Alternative: niclosamide.
Threadworm *Strongyloides stercoralis*	See Chapter 8–60		
Toxoplasmosis *Toxoplasma gondii*	See Chapter 8–62		
Giardiasis *Giardia intestinalis*	See Chapter 19–36		

TABLE 8–64–2. HELMINTHIC AND PROTOZOAL INFECTIONS SEEN ALMOST EXCLUSIVELY IN TRAVELERS AND TO IMMIGRANTS FROM ENDEMIC AREAS

Parasite/ Common name	Criteria for Diagnosis: Suggestive (based on geographic site of endemnicity)	Definitive	Clinical Manifestations/ Major Illness	Treatment
Helminths **Nematodes**				
Onchocerca volvulus / river blindness	Africa, Central and South America	Skin snip: identification of microfilariae	Blindness, subcutaneous nodules	Ivermectin
Wuchereria bancrofti / filiariasis	Tropics and subtropics	Thick film of blood best results when obtained at night: identification of microfilariae; serologies for patients with obstructive disease	Elephantiasis, tropical pulmonary eosinophilia, lymphadenitis	Diethylcarbamazine
Trematodes				
Clonorchis sinensis	Far East, especially China, Hong Kong, Korea, Thailand, and Vietnam	Identification of eggs in stool	Biliary obstruction, possibly cholangiocarcinoma	Praziquantel
Paragonimus westermani / lung fluke	Far East, Indian subcontinent	Identification of adult worm from resected tissue	Cough, hemoptysis, or mass effect in ectopic sites	Praziquantel (not FDA approved for this indication in United States); alternative: bithionol
Fasciola hepatica / liver fluke	Latin America, Europe, Asia, Africa, and West Africa (worldwide where sheep are raised)	Identification of eggs in stool; ELISA also available	Hepatomegaly/obstructive hepatic injury	Bithionol
Fasciolopsis buski / intestinal fluke	Far East and Southeast Asia	Identification of eggs in stool	Diarrhea	Praziquantel: alternative: niclosamide (neither approved by FDA for this indication in United States)
Schistosomia spp./bilharzia		Identificatin of eggs in stool, urine, or tissue biopsy; ELISA and Western blot also available		Praziquantel
Schistosoma hematobium	Middle East and Africa		Hematuria, obstructive urinary symptoms	
Schistosoma japonicum	Japan, Phillipines, and China		Abdominal pain, diarrhea, hepato-splenomegaly, and failure	
Schistosoma mekongi			Same as above	
Schistosoma mansonii	South Asia, Carribbean, South American, and Africa		Same as above	
Cestodes				
Diphyllobothrium latum / fish tapeworm	Countries or areas where raw fish is commonly eaten, such as Scandinavia, the Baltics, Japan, and Alaska	Identification of eggs or proglottids in stool	Macrocytic anemia	Praziquantel (not approved by FDA for this indication in United States); alternative; niclosamide
Taenia saginatus / beef tapeworm	Worldwide, but especially in Yugoslavia, Ethiopia, Kenya, and Moslem countries	Identification of scolex or a gravid proglottid	Abdominal pain, eosinophilia	Praziquantel; alternative: niclosamide
Taenia solium / pork tapeworm	Worldwide, but especially in Mexico, Central and South America, Africa, Eastern Europe, China, Pakistan, and India	Identification of scolex or a gravid proglottid; rarely, identification of cysticerci in resected tissue; ELISA	Abdominal pain, cystercercosis neurocystercercosis	Praziquantel
Equinococcus granulosis / hydatid cyst	Common in sheep and cattle-raising areas, especially New Zealand, Australia, Argentina, parts of Africa, Greece, Lebanon, and Eastern Europe	Identification of hydatids in resected tissue; ELISA and immunoblot	Liver, lung, and splenic systs	Albendazole, surgical resection
Protozoa				
Naegleria fowleri / "free-living amebas"	Southern United States, Czechoslovakia, Australia, England, New Zealand, and Mexico	Identification of organism in CSF	Primary amebic meningoencephalitis	Amphotericin? (not approved by FDA for this indication in United States)
Acanthamoeba spp. / "free-living ameba"	Seen in United States, Australia, distribution is probably similar to that of Naegleria	Identification of organism in CSF	Encephalitis (especially in immunocompromised host)	Unknown

(continued)

TABLE 8–64–2. (*Continued*)

Parasite/ Common name	Criteria for Diagnosis		Clinical Manifestations/ Major Illness	Treatment
	Suggestive (based on geographic site of endemnicity)	Definitive		
Leishmania donovani / kalaazar (visceral)	India, Pakistan, China, East Africa, and Mediterranean	Identification of the parasite from splenic or bone marrow aspirate, liver or lymph node biopsy; serologies available	Disseminated disease with bone marrow involvement and hepatosplenomegaly	Sodium stibogluconate, meglumine antimonate
Leishmania spp. / mucosal cutaneous leishmaniasis	Latin America, Middle East, India, Pakistan, and Africa	Identification of parasite from lesion scrapings or biopsy; serologies less reliable	Cutaneous and/or mucosal lesions	Sodium stibogluconate, meglumine antimonate
Trypanosoma brucei / African sleeping sickness	East Africa	Identification of parasite from induration site or peripheral blood smear, thick and thin	Meningoencephalitis	Suramin
Trypanosoma cruzii / Chagas' disease	Latin America	Identification of parasites from peripheral smear or culture; xenodiagnosis; serologies available	Myocarditis, esophageal or colonic abnormalities	Nifurtimox, benznidazole

ELISA, enzyme-linked immunosorbent assay; FDA, Food and Drug Administration; CSF, cerebrospinal fluid

infected by ingesting embryonated ova in contaminated food or drink. Soil pollution by human and some animal feces is important in the life cycle of this parasite, as it is here that the ova persist until ingested by humans. After ingestion, the eggs develop into adult worms, which take up residence in the cecum and ascending colon, embedding their heads in the intestinal mucosa. If not treated, *Trichuris* can cause chronic diarrhea with growth stunting because of malnutrition and chronic abdominal discomfort.

Enterobiasis is the most common of all helminthic infestions in the United States, especially among children. *Enterobius vermicularis*, the organism responsible for pinworm infection, is a white, threadlike structure about 1 cm in length that inhabits the cecum. The gravid females migrate during the night to the perianal region to lay their eggs. These eggs readily embryonate in about 6 hours and contaminate the bed, sheets, nightclothes, and household dust. Because of the intense perianal itching produced, patients frequently contaminate their nails and hands and may spread the infection to others as well as reinfect themselves. Complications can occur if the infection is not diagnosed and are related to the parasite being out of its normal habitat: appendicitis, vulvovaginitis, and an increased incidence of urinary infections in girls who are infested.

Ascaris is probably the most common helminthic infection worldwide. These 15- to 35-cm adult worms inhabit the lumen of the gastrointestinal tract. Each female worm produces about 200,000 ova per day. These ova can live in the soil for years under very adverse conditions and infect human beings. When ingested by humans, these ova hatch, then penetrate the wall of the small bowel and enter the venous bloodstream, proceeding to the pulmonary arteries. In the lung they break through the pulmonary capillaries and enter the alveoli, and this can produce small hemorrhages that cause local edema and congestion, clinically known as Loefflers's pneumonia. The larvae are swallowed and return to the intestine to develop into mature worms. Clinical symptoms correlate, as with most parasitic diseases, with the life cycle of this parasite. Malnutrition, intestinal obstructions, and even biliary obstructions can occur in heavily infected children who go untreated.

Hookworm is no longer common in the United States; it is an extremely common helminthic infection elsewhere in the world, especially in tropical and subtropical regions. About 25% of the world's population is infected. Adult worms inhabit the upper part of the small bowel and attach to the mucosa by their buccal capsule. The host's daily blood loss through this mechanism is about 0.2 mL per worm for *Ancylostoma* duodenale and less for *Necator americanus*. To produce serious disease, a heavy infection is required. Multiple eggs are laid daily and are excreted by humans, contaminating the soil. Under appropriate conditions, these ova hatch into infective larvae, which can penetrate the skin of humans. The larvae enter the lungs, invade the alveoli and bronchi, and during this phase produce pulmonary symptoms. The larvae are then swallowed and take up residence in the small bowel,

where they develop into adult worms. In areas where soil is heavily contaminated by feces containing hookworm ova, infection is common, especially if humans walk barefoot. Only a heavy burden of worms is likely to result in serious iron deficiency anemia, and many hookworm infections are, in fact, asymptomatic. Anemia and hypoalbuminemia are the prominent features of prolonged heavy infections in children, accompanied by mental apathy, lassitude, pallor, and symptoms related to organ damage (cardiac insufficiency, etc.).

Schistosoma are widespread in Africa, Latin America, and Asia, infecting more than 200 million people. The infection cannot be acquired in the United States, as the snails that are required as an intermediate host are not found in this country. The three major clinical syndromes seen in schistosomiasis have been described (see Table 8–64–2), and each relates to the three different stages of the development of the parasite in the human, namely, the cercariae, the mature worms, and the eggs. Thus, swimmer's itch is related to skin penetration of the cercariae and is thought to be caused in part by sensitization as a result of a prior exposure to this parasite. The syndrome of Katayama fever, which occurs about 1 to 2 months after the initial exposure to the parasite, appears to be an immune complex disease related to a massive challenge of egg deposition when the worms mature. The third stage, that of chronic infection, is related to the deposition of a large number of eggs in either the mesenteric plexus (*Schistosoma mansoni*, *S. mekongi*, or *S. japonicum*) or the bladder venous plexus (*S. hematobium*). The host responds to the egg deposition with granuloma formation and an eosinophilic infiltration, which eventually may involve the liver and intestine or, in the case of *S. hematobium*, the bladder. The pathologic process resembles a delayed hypersensitivity reaction. The injury produced by the egg-induced granuloma that goes without appropriate treatment may result later in significant fibrous tissue deposition. This can lead to problems related to obstruction of the blood flow to the liver or the lungs or obstruction of the urine flow.

Trichinosis is distributed widely throughout the world. The larvae of *Trichinella spiralis* are found in the muscles of many carnivorous animals. Humans are infected by the ingestion of raw or inadequately cooked meat, especially pork. In the United States, only about 200 cases are reported annually, although studies suggest that many cases are asymptomatic, undiagnosed, or not reported. Occasional epidemics due to common-source exposure occur. The life cycle of *T. spiralis* is important to the understanding of the disease. Viable infective larvae encysted in poorly cooked meat are ingested by humans, and adult worms develop in the small intestine. The fertilized female worm releases multiple larvae that invade the bloodstream and reach the skeletal muscle and at times other organs, such as the heart and brain. Inflammatory lesions and eosinophils are seen at these sites. In the muscles, the larvae may become encysted, and although clinical symptoms occur for only 2 to 6 weeks, the larvae can remain viable for several years and the cysts may calcify. The illness is usually self-limited, although rarely complications secondary to myocarditis or encephalitis are fatal despite appropriate therapy.

Neurocysticercosis is one of the most common causes of epilepsy in endemic areas, and immigration to the United States has drastically increased the prevalence of this disease. Neurocysticercosis should be considered in any immigrant from a developing country with neurologic signs or symptoms. In the normal life cycle of *Taenia solium*, the cestode responsible for cysticercosis, humans are the definitive host. Adult worms live in the human intestine and excrete vast quantities of eggs. Pigs are intermediate hosts and become infected by ingesting food contaminated by human feces. Embryos are released and migrate to the muscle, brain, and other organs, where cysticerci then develop. Humans are reinfected by eating poorly cooked pork. Humans develop neurocysticercosis by ingesting food contaminated by human feces containing tapeworm eggs, becoming inadvertent intermediate hosts. Embryos travel to the brain and other organs, where cysticerci develop after several weeks. Thus, unlike most other tapeworm infections, humans can serve as both definitive and intermediate host to *T. solium*. Depending on the location of the cysticerci and the intensity of the host's immune response, clinical symptoms may then develop. Neurocysticercosis may remain asymptomatic. The number of cysticerci, their location, and the intensity of the host response are factors dictating the patient's prognosis. Long-term complications also include hydrocephalus.

The population infected with *Trypanosoma cruzi* in Latin America is estimated to be around 16 to 18 million, according to the World Health Organization. This hemoflagellate protozoa is transmitted by triatomine insects, which are prevalent in rural areas of several Latin American countries. As with leishmanial parasites, infection via blood transfusion is also possible, as are congenital infections. The parasite is acquired by the vector as it ingests a blood meal from a parasitemic host. *Trypanosoma cruzi* then replicates the gut of the triatome, and is passed on to the next host, through the feces deposited as the insect is ingesting its blood meal. The different manifestations of Chagas' disease are thought to be related to both variations in the parasite and immune-mediated host responses. If the acute infection is not diagnosed and treated, as more often occurs, the disease becomes "clinically latent" and, after about three decades, has cardiac and/or digestive manifestations. Treatment in the chronic phase has yet to be proven of any efficacy.

Prevention

Prevention of pinworms is difficult, but careful washing of bed clothing, good hand washing, and treatment of all close household contacts who are infected may prevent or halt infection. *Ascaris* infections can be prevented by improved sanitation, good hand washing, careful food preparation and storage, and good sewage disposal. Hookworm infections can be prevented by better sewage disposal and the wearing of shoes in areas where hookworm is prevalent, such as most subtropical and tropical parts of the world. Prevention of trichuriasis is dependent on improved sanitation and sewage disposal, good food preparation, and good hand washing.

Trichinosis occurring from pork has been reasonably limited in the United States. In general, swine are now grain-fed, but occasional pigs are still fed garbage that may include bits of uncooked infected meat, or a pig can also become infected by eating a rat that has trichinella. If meat is properly cooked to a temperature of 55°C, the pathogen is readily destroyed. One should be particularly careful that sausage is properly cooked.

Neurocysticercosis can be prevented by the sanitary disposal of human feces. Thorough cooking of pork will prevent humans from acquiring an intestinal infection with adult *T. solium*.

Prevention of the spread of schistosmiasis is not a problem in the United States, because the appropriate species of snails required in the life cycle of this parasite does not exist here. In many other parts of the world, where the proper intermediate snail host is present, prevention of this disease is a major public health priority. Efforts include rapid treatment of identified cases with careful follow-up for laboratory cure, attempts to selectively destroy the intermediate host (snails), and avoidance by humans of fresh water exposure in regions where infective cercariae are known to be present and where new cases of schistosomiasis are appearing.

Trypanosoma cruzi infection is strongly linked to rural dwellings where the vector is likely to inhabit. Eradicating the vector and avoiding exposure are the only effective measures. If exposure cannot be avoided, using bed nets may be helpful. The possibility of transfusion-acquired infection could be reduced if routine screening were performed in all areas of endemicity. Immigrants from endemic areas that donate blood in countries that do not screen for *T. cruzi* carry a small but real risk.

As with as other vectorborne parasitic diseases, *Leishmania* can be prevented on an individual level with measures aimed at decreasing the contact with the vector of *Leishmania*, the sand fly. Repellents like DEET (*N, N*-diethylmethylbenzamide) can be applied to exposed skin and bed nets and clothing; impregnation with permethrin can also help.

Cost Containment

If early diagnosis is made in any of the infections noted, there are significant benefits for reduction in costs and elaborate workup for other possible disease processes. Early diagnosis of schistosomiasis, Chagas' disease, and cysticercosis is especially important, as later serious and costly complications can potentially be avoided.

REFERENCES

Bia FJ, Barry M. Parasitic infections of the central nervous system. Neurol Clin 1986;4:171.

Del Brutto OH, Sotelo J. Neurocysticercosis: An update. Rev Infect Dis 1988;10:1075.

Drugs for parasitic infections. Med Lett Drugs Ther 1993;35:111.

Mahmoud AAF. Schistosomiasis. In: Warren KS, Mahmoud AAF, eds. Tropical and geographical medicine. New York: McGraw-Hill, 1984;443.

Schmidt GD, Roberts LS, eds. Foundations of parasitology, 4th ed. St. Louis, Missouri: Times Mirror/Mosby College Publishing, 1989

Symposium on parasitic infections. Pediatr Clin North Am 1985;4:32.

CHAPTER 8–65

Common Cold

Robert B. Couch, M.D.

DEFINITION

A common cold is an acute, self-limited, infectious disorder characterized by nasal obstruction and/or discharge and frequently accompanied by sneezing, sore throat, and nonproductive cough.

ETIOLOGY

It is well established that viruses cause most, and possibly all, infectious colds. More than 200 distinct viruses can produce colds; these viruses and their relative significance as causes of colds among adults are summarized in Table 8–65–1.

CRITERIA FOR DIAGNOSIS
Suggestive

A constellation of acute upper respiratory symptoms with a predominance of sneezing, nasal obstruction, and discharge suggests a diagnosis of common cold.

TABLE 8–65–1. VIRUSES THAT CAUSE COMMON COLDS AMONG ADULTS

Family and Genus	Relative Significance
Picornaviridae	
Rhinoviruses	++++
Enteroviruses	+
Coronaviridae (coronaviruses)	++
Paramyxoviridae	
Parainfluenza viruses	+
Respiratory syncytial viruses	+
Orthomyxoviridae (influenze viruses)	+
Adenoviridae (adenoviruses)	+

+, infrequent; ++++, very frequent

Definitive

For decisions on clinical care, presence of the common cold syndrome and absence of a history of hayfever or exposure to noxious substances may be considered as providing a definitive diagnosis. Although not necessary for optimal care, isolation of one of the causative viruses from a person with the common cold syndrome would solidify the diagnosis.

CLINICAL MANIFESTATIONS
Subjective

The common cold usually begins with a sensation of "dry" throat that the subject may recognize as located in the posterior nasopharynx. This is followed in 24 hours or less by the appearance of sneezing, nasal obstruction, and thin, watery nasal discharge. A mild, generalized headache and "hacking," nonproductive cough are usually present; a great variety of other symptoms such as eye irritation, chest pain, chilliness, malaise, myalgias, anorexia, abdominal pain, vomiting, and diarrhea also may be reported.

Objective
Physical Examination

Nasal obstruction and/or nasal discharge are readily apparent on examination, and the nasal mucosa is hyperemic or pale and edematous. Minimal erythema of the pharynx and tender anterior cervical nodes may be present, but abnormal physical findings are otherwise not detected. About 10 to 20% of patients exhibit fever, usually less than 101°F.

Routine Laboratory Abnormalities

An elevation in total white blood cell and neutrophil counts and a reduction in lymphocyte counts in peripheral blood may be seen on the first day of illness, but counts return to normal in 1 or 2 days. Erythrocyte sedimentation rates are commonly elevated, but other clinical laboratory tests are within normal limits.

PLANS
Diagnostic
Differential Diagnosis

The common cold syndrome may follow infection with a causative virus and may be simulated by exposure to an allergen among patients with hayfever and exposure to airborne noxious substances.

Diagnostic Options and Recommended Approach

Obtaining a description of acute onset of disease with a constellation of signs and symptoms described above is sufficient for a diagnosis of common cold. Absence of other possible causes such as hayfever and exposure to noxious substances and evidence for community exposure such as presence of other cases in the family confirm the infectious nature of the illness.

Infectious common colds are assumed to be caused by one of a great number of viruses that cause the acute respiratory diseases. Although demonstration of the presence of the infection with one of these viruses would provide a definitive diagnosis, methods for such a demonstration are not generally available to the practicing physician and are not necessary at present for optimal patient care. When sore throat is a major complaint, it is important to rule out streptococcal pharyngitis by testing for presence of group A streptococci.

Therapeutic
Therapeutic Options

There is no specific antiviral therapy available for infectious colds. Therapy is directed toward alleviation of symptoms. For this purpose, a great variety of single and combinations of drugs are available.

Recommended Approach

Therapy for colds should be directed at alleviation of the most distressing symptoms only. Activity should be curtailed in keeping with the extent of symptoms. Adequate diet should be maintained and oral fluids encouraged. Fever greater than 101°F and significant headache may be treated with analgesics such as aspirin and acetaminophen in doses of 0.6 g or ibuprofen in doses of 200 mg every 4 to 6 hours as needed. Use of aspirin and acetaminophen was associated with decreased antibody response and longer duration of viral shedding in one study, but the overall effect would be minimal for a healthy adult. Nasal obstruction may be relieved by decongestants such as pseudoephedrine (Sudafed) in doses of 30 to 60 mg three to four times daily or by topical use of nasal decongestants such as 0.25% phenylephrine (Neo-Synephrine), 0.1% xylometazoline (Otrivin), or 0.05% oxymetazoline (Afrin) by nasal spray or intranasal drops. Phenylephrine may be used three to four times daily, whereas the latter two topical medications are used every 12 hours. Decongestants either should not be used or should be used sparingly in persons with cardiovascular disease because of possible increases in blood pressure or heart rate. In addition, persons should be cautioned to use a topical preparation no more often than recommended and for no longer than 4 or 5 days so as to avoid medication-induced nasal congestion.

Antihistamines exert a drying effect on secretions and, when used alone, do not relieve nasal congestion. Any desire to use these for reduction of rhinorrhea must take into account the drowsiness and impaired work performance that may follow use of many preparations. Sore throat may be relieved by frequent use of warm salt water gargles (a half teaspoonful of salt to 4 oz of water), and both sore throat and hoarseness may be relieved by periods of breathing humidified air. Cough does not usually require therapy, but troublesome cough may be treated with cough suppressants. Many preparations are available that contain dextromethorphan (the preferred suppressant) and decongestants, but therapy for cough alone should employ a preparation containing dextromethorphan only as the active ingredient. It may be given in doses of 10 to 30 mg every 4 to 6 hours.

FOLLOW-UP

No follow-up is indicated for common cold illnesses, but physicians may desire reassurance of recovery among patients with severe underlying disease such as diabetes and chronic airways disease. A telephone report usually suffices for this purpose.

The basis for any follow-up of persons with colds should be the occurrence of a complication. Patients should be advised of the possible complications and asked to return if indications of their occurrence appear. The most common complications of colds are otitis media and sinusitis, although bacterial pneumonia also may follow colds, particularly among persons with chronic lung disease. Ear pain, stuffiness, or impaired hearing should prompt a repeat visit for ear examination. This complication is common among small children but is uncommon among adults. Anterior facial (sinus) headache or persistent nasal symptoms beyond 10 to 14 days should prompt a return visit because of the possible presence of a complicating sinusitis. Occurrence of a new episode of chest pain or increase in cough or sputum production also should prompt a return visit. Finally, a general warning to initiate a physician contact with occurrence of new symptoms not present at the time of the initial contact or increase in severity of symptoms should suffice for detection of uncommon complications.

DISCUSSION
Prevalence and Incidence

More than half of all acute illnesses occurring annually in the United States are respiratory, and about half of these are designated as common colds. Estimates from National Health Survey data indicate that about one in every two adults in the United States develops a "disabling" cold each year; including minor colds brings the estimate closer to an average of one for every adult. The incidence of colds is similar in all geographic areas of the United States and in both sexes; it is twofold to threefold greater in winter than in summer and twofold to threefold greater among children than among adults.

Related Basic Science

In civilian populations, the infecting agent is usually introduced into a family by a school-aged child who acquired the infection from a classmate or playmate. Under these conditions, 20 to 50% of other family members will develop colds. Using rhinovirus as a model for common colds has indicated that infection is transferred by close contact: a susceptible family member either inoculates his or her nose or eye with virus on fingers that were virus-contaminated or inhales a virus-containing aerosol produced by an infected person. These studies also indicated that persons with severe colds were most likely to effect this contamination.

Rhinoviruses are estimated to cause 30 to 50% of colds among adults; in combination with coronaviruses, they cause over half of adult colds. Both virus groups are prevalent throughout the world; in temperate climates, rhinoviruses are prevalent in fall and early spring and coronaviruses in winter. More than 100 distinct rhinovirus serotypes have been identified, and surveillance of populations usually indicates the presence of several serotypes during the same period. Although reinfection with the same rhinovirus serotype can occur, both epidemiologic and volunteer challenge studies indicate that immunity develops after infection and this immunity can prevent reinfection. The mediator of this protection appears to be specific antibody in nasal secretions that is primarily immunoglobulin A and derived from local lymphoid tissues. The vasoactive peptides, including bradykinin, are elevated in rhinovirus colds and may have a role in the pathogenesis of symptoms.

Natural History and Its Modification with Treatment

The incubation period of colds varies between 1 and 14 days depending on the causative virus. In most cases, illness begins with a sensation of nasopharyngeal irritation that is soon followed by sneezing, nasal obstruction, and rhinorrhea. The duration of maximal illness is 2 to 4 days, but the average overall duration is about 8 days; complete recovery is the rule. Medication to ameliorate the major symptoms does not alter the duration of illness.

About 1 in 200 adults develops a complicating acute bacterial sinusitis, usually ethmoid or maxillary; however, "cloudy" sinuses on x-ray films in association with persistent nasal symptoms are more common. A complicating otitis media is common in children but uncommon in adults. Patients with pneumococcal and other bacterial pneumonias frequently relate a history of prior upper respiratory disease. Although prospective studies have not documented a predisposition from colds, it is prudent to consider the complication as possible and to counsel patients appropriately. Other complications reported to follow upper respiratory illness, such as the Guillain–Barré syndrome, Reye's syndrome, and acute encephalomyelitis, are very low frequency complications.

Prevention

There is no established method for the prevention of colds. Because of the incidence of colds, quarantine of patients is not appropriate, as such a procedure would be disruptive to society. The risk of transmission associated with occurrence of a severe cold, however, indicates the desirability of a recommendation for avoidance of societal contacts for the 1- to 3-day duration of maximal symptoms. Persons with colds should practice liberal use of facial tissues to minimize hand and environmental contamination, and persons with colds and those exposed to such persons should frequently wash their hands so as to minimize the transfer of virus to nose or eye. Studies of interferon compounds for prevention of rhinovirus colds have provided evidence of effectiveness, but precise guidelines for their use have not been developed. Development of vaccines against cold viruses has been stymied by the large number of serotypes that can cause infection; however, a discovery of a molecule (ICAM-1) similar to the human cell receptor used by the majority of rhinovirus serotypes for cell infection and of chemicals capable of blocking the receptor site is one example of new data suggesting that it may someday be possible to provide effective chemotherapy.

Cost Containment

A significant containment of the "cost" of colds can result only from implementation of the suggested effective preventive measures. The major contribution of physicians in this area at present consists of patient and family education and minimal use of unnecessary diagnostic tests and therapeutic medicines. Ordinary colds do not require the use of diagnostic laboratory tests (see Plans, Diagnostic), and the most frequent complication (sinusitis) requires no more than sinus x-rays and a possible bacteriologic culture. Antibiotics are not effective against viruses and should not be used for treatment of uncomplicated colds; symptomatic therapy should be minimal and directed only at the most troublesome symptoms. Antibiotic therapy is sometimes required if bacterial complications such as sinusitis, otitis, or pneumonia complicate a prior viral infection.

REFERENCES

Couch RB. The common cold: Control? J Infect Dis 1984;150:167.

Curley FJ, Irwin RS, Pratter MR, et al. Cough and the common cold. Am Rev Respir Dis 1988;138:305.

Farr BM, Gwaltney JM Jr, Hendley JO, et al. A randomized controlled trial of glucocorticoid prophylaxis against experimental rhinovirus infection. J Infect Dis 1990;162:1173.

Gwaltney JM Jr, Phillips CD, Miller RD, Riker DK. Computed tomographic study of the common cold. N Engl J Med 1994;330:25.

Perlman PE, Ginn DR. Respiratory infections in ambulatory adults: Choosing the best treatment. Postgrad Med 1990;87:175.

Sperber SJ, Hayden FB. Mini-review: Chemotherapy of rhinovirus colds. Antimicrob Agents Chemother 1988;32:409.

Influenza

Robert B. Couch, M.D.

DEFINITION

Influenza is an acute infectious disorder characterized by abrupt onset of fever, headache, nonproductive cough, and myalgias. It is accompanied by a variety of other symptoms indicating disease of the upper and lower respiratory tracts that is producing a significant systemic reaction

ETIOLOGY

The influenza syndrome among adults is most commonly caused by one of the influenza viruses, although other respiratory viruses, *Mycoplasma pneumoniae* and *Chlamydia pneumoniae*, may produce the same syndrome. When findings of pneumonia (see Chapter 8–15) are present, the latter agents as well as a number of other diagnostic possibilities must be considered. When sore throat is prominent, streptococcal pharyngitis may be causing the symptoms.

CRITERIA FOR DIAGNOSIS

Suggestive

Presence of the syndrome described under Definition is sufficient for a diagnosis of influenza. Occurrence during a community epidemic of febrile respiratory disease involving all age groups is important evidence that a given case of influenza is probably attributable to infection with one of the influenza viruses.

Definitive

A definitive diagnosis of influenza requires demonstration of infection with an influenza virus or one of the infectious agents that can cause the influenza syndrome in a person exhibiting the typical illness.

CLINICAL MANIFESTATIONS

Subjective

The influenza syndrome is sudden in onset and characterized initially by fever and systemic symptoms. The systemic symptoms include myalgias, malaise, headache, fever, chilliness, anorexia, and general prostration. Initially or within 24 hours, sore throat, runny nose, and nonproductive cough that frequently occurs in paroxysms and is accompanied by substernal discomfort appear. Patients also may report photophobia, sneezing, nasal obstruction, hoarseness, nausea, vomiting, diarrhea, and abdominal pain, but these symptoms are less frequent than those noted above.

Objective

Physical Examination

Patients appear acutely ill and are coughing. Fever of 101 to 104°F is usually seen. Minimal to moderate nasal obstruction and thin nasal discharge may be present. Despite complaints of sore throat, minimal inflammation is usually seen on examination. Tender anterior cervical nodes may be present, and tenderness may be reported on lateral movement of the trachea. A breath through the mouth will provoke cough that is nonproductive or productive of only small amounts of mucoid or slightly purulent sputum. Examination of the chest is usually negative, but may reveal wheezing or an occasional rale. Muscles may be tender on palpation, but the remainder of the examination is negative.

We thank Dr. John E. McGowan, Jr., for this contribution to this chapter in the third edition of this book.

Routine Laboratory Abnormalities

An elevation in total white blood cell and neutrophil counts and a reduction in lymphocytes are frequently seen during the first day of illness. Normal counts or leukopenia owing to a reduction in neutrophils and lymphocytes is seen on later days. Erythrocyte sedimentation rates are usually elevated. Minimal proteinuria attributable to fever may be present, but other clinical laboratory tests are within normal limits.

PLANS

Diagnostic

Differential Diagnosis

Guidance for diagnostic approaches is provided by a careful history of the acute illness. The presence of upper and/or lower respiratory tract symptoms is necessary for a diagnosis of influenza, as fever and systemic symptoms may be seen as the early or major manifestations of a large number of other febrile diseases. If the patient has had recent exposure to other similar cases in the family or elsewhere, the diagnosis is supported. Febrile respiratory disease with minimal systemic symptoms is caused by the same agents that can cause influenza with its prominent systemic symptoms. If the patient is seen during a community epidemic of acute febrile respiratory disease including influenza in the winter, infection with an influenza virus is likely.

Diagnostic Options

A definitive diagnosis of influenza requires demonstration of infection with one of the respiratory viruses by identification of the infecting agent or demonstration of a rise in specific serum antibody (see Chapter 8–15 for the diagnosis and treatment of *M. pneumoniae* and *C. pneumoniae* infections). As most of these illnesses are self-limited and facilities for providing a specific etiologic diagnosis are not generally available, it is frequently unnecessary to determine the specific etiology to provide proper patient care. The exception to this is illness caused by a type A influenza virus, for which specific treatment is available. This infection may be assumed to be present when persons with the influenza syndrome are seen during a community epidemic known to be caused by type A influenza viruses. Cases seen at other times may be caused by any one of the acute respiratory disease agents, including type A influenza viruses.

Recommended Approach

If the influenzal illness is considered of sufficient severity to recommend hospitalization, a specific diagnosis should be sought. Obtaining specific virologic diagnosis provides a prognosis as well as guidance for therapy. The number of diagnostic laboratories capable of proving infection with a respiratory virus is increasing. For such testing, a combined nasal wash (with normal saline) and throat swab specimen is obtained for virus detection, but a combined nose and throat swab specimen is a useful alternative. Methods for obtaining a rapid specific virologic diagnosis in a few hours are available, but sensitivity varies greatly among methods.

If the patient with influenza is presumed to be infected with an influenza A virus and is in a category that could benefit from treatment with specific antiviral therapy (see later), one of the rapid diagnostic methods should be employed to prove the diagnosis, although it is reasonable to employ this therapy even if obtaining a specific diagnosis is not possible.

Therapeutic

Therapy for cases of influenza occurring outside of type A influenza virus epidemics should be directed at alleviation of the most distressing symptoms only. Activity should be curtailed during the 2- to 5-day period of severe illness; adequate diet should be maintained and oral fluids encouraged. Fever greater than 101°F, headache, and myalgias may be treated with aspirin or acetaminophen in doses of 0.6 g every 3 to 6 hours as needed. Acetaminophen is preferred for young adults because of the association of influenza and aspirin use with the occurrence of Reye's syndrome. Propoxyphene (Darvon) in doses of 65 mg is acceptable if only an analgesic effect is desired. Nasal obstruction may be treated with oral or tropical decongestants as described for common cold therapy (see Chapter 8–65). As noted for colds, it is preferable not to use antihistamines and to use salt water gargles, humidified air, and/or analgesics for sore throat and hoarseness. In contrast to colds, cough is usually severe enough to require some suppressive therapy. A preparation containing dextromethorphan alone is preferred; it may be given in doses of 10 to 30 mg every 4 to 6 hours. If this therapy is not sufficient and no contraindication exists, codeine in doses of 30 to 65 mg every 6 hours may be used.

If the case of influenza is probably caused by a type A influenza virus (see Plans, Diagnostic) and the patient has been ill for less than 48 hours, amantadine hydrochloride (Symmetrel) or rimantadine hydrochloride (Flumadine) should be given as a 200-mg single dose to begin and 100 mg twice daily thereafter for a period of 3 to 5 days. These antiviral agents are ineffective for influenza B virus infections.

Amantadine may produce a variety of side effects, but central nervous system symptoms predominate and include drowsiness, insomnia, nervousness, and tremulousness. Amantadine is excreted unchanged through the kidney; for this reason, persons over age 65 and those with seizure disorders or other altered mental or behavioral conditions should be treated with only 100 mg daily. Published schedules of dosages should be consulted for persons with underlying renal disease. Persons with high blood levels, such as may occur with overdosage in elderly persons or those with renal disease, may exhibit hallucinations and seizures. Central nervous system side effects are dose related and abate with withdrawal of drug.

Rimantadine produces fewer side effects than amantadine but central nervous system symptoms may be seen. In contrast to amantadine, rimantadine is metabolized by the liver and then excreted by the kidney. Although side effect information is somewhat incomplete, a reduction in daily dosage of rimantadine to 100 mg per day is recommended for elderly nursing home residents and persons with severe hepatic or renal dysfunction. As with amantadine, side effects abate with withdrawal of drug.

Antiviral agent-resistant virus will emerge in a large proportion of persons treated for illness with amantadine or rimantadine. Such persons benefit from therapy but may represent a source of resistant virus for other persons, including those with underlying disease who could benefit from antiviral prophylaxis or therapy. For this reason, treatment of acutely ill but otherwise healthy persons residing in households containing persons with underlying disease is discouraged.

FOLLOW-UP

No follow-up of persons with influenza is indicated, but physicians may desire reassurance of recovery among patients with severe underlying disease such as diabetes and chronic airways disease. A telephone report usually suffices for this purpose.

Patients should be advised of possible complications and asked to return if indications of their occurrence appear. The most common complications of influenza are sinusitis, otitis media, and pneumonia. Otitis media is uncommon among adults, whereas sinusitis is relatively common. Patients should be advised that symptoms referable to the ear or sinuses, as outlined for the common cold (see Chapter 8–65), should prompt physician contact; similarly, a general warning to initiate contact with occurrence of new symptoms, recurrence of fever or symptoms after a well interval, and increase in severity of symptoms should suffice for detection of uncommon complications. Because of its frequency, special comment on pneumonia is indicated, particularly for elderly persons and those with chronic underlying disease. Patients should be alerted to return if a new fever, shaking chills, dyspnea, chest pain, or sputum production should occur. Although the virus causing the influenza also may produce pneumonia, most cases represent secondary bacterial pneumonia (see Chapter 8–15 for diagnosis and treatment).

Persons being treated with amantadine or rimantadine should be warned of the side effects. If an otherwise healthy person is being treated, they may be advised to continue therapy until completed unless they find the symptoms distressing, in which case the medication may be stopped. If the person possesses an underlying disease, the patient should be instructed to contact the physician for side effect symptoms. If the complaints could be attributable to the antiviral agent, it is advisable to discontinue the drug and follow the patient until return to the baseline state.

DISCUSSION

Prevalence and Incidence

About one of every two adults in the United States develops a "disabling" case of influenza each year. Variation in this frequency may occur and is determined by the frequency that year of influenza caused by infection with one of the influenza viruses. The disease occurs in all geographic areas, in both sexes equally, in greater numbers in winter than in summer, and in greater numbers of children than adults. Infection with an influenza virus (type A or B) occurs in about one in every six adults each year, and about half of them seek health care because of illness. Death occurs annually in about 1 in 1500 persons with an underlying disease.

Related Basic Science

Influenza tends to occur in outbreaks among persons congregating indoors during the winter and is presumed to be transmitted by means of small-particle aerosols produced by coughing. The clearest examples of such outbreaks are those caused by adenoviruses in military recruits (prior to the widespread use of vaccine) and those caused by influenza viruses in civilian populations. Type A or B influenza virus is responsible for an epidemic annually in the United States and causes considerable disease in the period before and after the epidemic. In the initial phases, infection and illness occur predominantly in schoolchildren, and this is reflected in school absenteeism, physician visits, and pediatric hospital admissions. These children then bring the virus into the home, where preschool children and adults acquire infection. Infection and illness among adults are then reflected in industrial absenteeism, adult hospital admissions, and an increase in influenza–pneumonia mortality among elderly and chronically ill persons.

As indicated earlier, most cases of influenza are caused by viruses, but some nonviral agents may produce the same syndrome. All respiratory viruses (see Table 8–65–1) are capable of causing influenza; however, among civilian adults, the influenza viruses are most prominent. These viruses exhibit antigenic variation, and this variation accounts for the recurring epidemics seen in human populations. Only type A viruses exhibit the major antigenic variation that causes pandemics such as those in 1918 and 1957. These viruses are designated as subtypes, and the major surface antigens hemagglutinin and neuraminidase are used for classification. Three human virus subtypes are described: A/H1N1, which appeared in 1918; A/H2N2 (Asian), which appeared in 1957; and A/H3N2 (Hong Kong), which appeared in 1968. When new subtypes appear, the entire population is usually susceptible. Minor antigenic variation is exhibited by both type A and B viruses and accounts for the annual epidemic. As the surface antigens change, immunity becomes progressively less cross-reactive, so that susceptibility is renewed and a repeat infection and illness occur. These viruses are classified based on similarity to a prototype virus; A/Johannesburg/33/94 (H3N2) is an example of a prototype virus.

Natural History and Its Modification with Treatment

The incubation period for influenza varies between 1 and 14 to 21 days depending on the causative agent. The incubation period for influenza virus infections is 1 to 5 days. Although cases may be insidious in onset, most persons have sudden onset of fever, chilliness, headache, and myalgias. Sore throat, cough that is nonproductive or productive of only small amounts of sputum, and rhinorrhea soon occur. Paroxysmal coughing accompanied by substernal pain indicates tracheobronchitis, the usual major disease site. Maximal illness lasts for 1 to 5 days, but symptoms persist for an additional 1 to 3 weeks. Full and complete recovery is to be expected, although physicians and patients should be alert for complications. Sinusitis and otitis media and rare central nervous system complications may occur as described for the common cold (see Chapter 8–65). Of particular interest, however, are the patterns of pneumonia that may complicate influenza virus infections.

A case assumed to be influenza but with an area of localized wheezing or rales on chest examination may exhibit a segmental infiltrate on x-ray. Such a case represents severe influenza, but complete recovery is expected. On rare occasions, a case of influenza progresses to exhibit dyspnea, tachypnea, and hypoxemia owing to the occurrence of bilateral interstitial pneumonia; among patients with underlying heart disease, an alveolar pneumonia with copious amounts of pink, frothy sputum may ensue. These severe manifestations of influenza (viral) pneumonia carry a high mortality rate. Occasional patients will exhibit the complication of a combined viral–bacterial pneumonia, in whom the findings of a bacterial pneumonia are superimposed on those of influenza, but the most common pneumonia pattern is for bacterial pneumonia (see Chapter 8–14) to occur a few days after improvement in the influenza symptoms. Persons most likely to develop bacterial pneumonia are elderly persons and those with chronic underlying diseases, particularly those with cardiovascular and pulmonary disease.

Patients with influenza A virus infection who are treated with amantadine or rimantadine experience a more rapid resolution of fever and associated symptoms. Prevention of complications because of treatment of an influenza A infection with an antiviral agent has not been demonstrated nor has benefit in treatment of influenza A virus pneumonia.

Prevention

Because of the high incidence of influenza, quarantine of patients is not appropriate; however, persons who are acutely ill and coughing should avoid societal contacts. Infection of military recruits with adenovirus is avoided in that population by ingestion of an enteric-coated capsule containing live virus vaccine.

Infection with one of the influenza viruses may be prevented by the use of inactivated influenza virus vaccine or amantadine or rimantadine. The vaccine and recommendations for its use are outlined in Table 8–66–1. Immunosuppressed patients, including those with HIV infection, are less likely to have an antibody response develop, even if given a booster dose of vaccine. Chemoprophylaxis with amantadine or rimantadine is an alternative to vaccine for type A influenza and may be used for outbreak control when influenza A virus spread is occurring in institutions housing high-risk persons, as short-term prophylaxis during the period in which an antibody response is developing in recently immunized persons, when vaccine is unavailable, for individuals in whom vaccination is contraindicated, for immunocompromised persons (e.g., patients with AIDS, or chronic renal disease) who may not produce antibody in response to the vaccine, and for unimmunized health care workers who care for high-risk individuals during an outbreak. When amantadine or rimantadine is used, type A influenza virus must be known to be causing the epidemic. The standard prophylactic dose for persons 14 years of age and older is 200 mg orally daily. The dosage of amantadine should be reduced to 100 mg daily for persons over 65 years of age, for those with seizure disorders or other altered mental or behavioral conditions, and for those with renal disease; the

TABLE 8–66–1. INFLUENZA VIRUS VACCINE

Vaccine
"Whole-virus": formalin-inactivated partially purified virus grown in chicken embryos
"Split-virus": chemically treated virus to reduce potential for reactogenicity
Contains current type A and B viruses
Dose is 0.5 mL intramuscularly for adults; special dosing schedule for children under 9 years
Contraindicated if patient is allergic to eggs
Local reactions in up to 33%; 1 to 5% systemic reactions
70 to 80% effective in years when epidemic strain is included in vaccine

Recommended for
Those with chronic cardiovascular or pulmonary disorders, including asthma
Residents of nursing homes and other chronic care facilities
Those over 64 years of age
Those with chronic metabolic disease (including diabetes mellitus), kidney disease, hemoglobinopathies, and immunosuppression
Children and teenagers receiving long-term aspirin therapy
Persons who have extensive contact with the above groups

May be used for
Persons rendering essential community services
Any person who wishes to prevent influenza

dose of rimantadine should be reduced to 100 mg daily for elderly persons in nursing homes and those with severe hepatic or renal disease (see Therapeutic). The antiviral agent should be continued for the duration of the epidemic period, usually 4 to 6 weeks. Patients should be warned of drug side effects (as outlined under Follow-up).

Cost Containment

The most significant cost containment procedure available is the use of influenza vaccine or amantadine or rimantadine for prevention of influenza. Estimates are that less than half of the risk population is vaccinated annually in the United States, whereas institutions with a vaccination program may vaccinate 60 to 90% of such persons annually. Minimal use of diagnostic tests (which are unnecessary unless a complication is suspected), restriction of medications prescribed to those for the most distressing symptoms, and use of amantadine or rimantadine for type A influenza virus infection will provide cost control for care of ill patients.

REFERENCES

Centers for Disease Control and Prevention. Prevention and control of influenza: Recommendations of the Immunization Practices Advisory Committee (ACIP). Part I: Vaccines. MMWR 5;44(RR-3).

Couch RB, Kasel JA, Glezen WP, et al. Influenza and its control in person and populations. J Infect Dis 1986;153:431.

Douglas RG Jr. Prophylaxis and treatment of influenza. N Engl J Med 1990;322:443.

Kilbourne ED. Influenza. New York: Plenum, 1987.

Margolis KL, Nichol KL, Poland GA, Pluhar RE. Frequency of adverse reactions to influenza vaccine in the elderly: A randomized, placebo-controlled trial. JAMA 1990;264:1139.

Nichol LK, Margolis KL, Wuorenma J, Von Sternberg T. The efficacy and cost effectiveness of vaccination against influenza among elderly persons living in the community. N Engl J Med 1994;331:778.

Measles, Rubella, and Other Viral Exanthems

John E. McGowan, Jr., M.D., Lincoln P. Miller, M.D., and Carl A. Perlino, M.D.

DEFINITION

Viral exanthems are systemic diseases caused by viruses in which presence of skin rash is a prominent feature. Considered here are those due to measles, rubella, and viral agents that are not considered in other chapters of this section.

ETIOLOGY

Measles is caused by rubeola virus, a paramyxovirus, and rubella by rubella virus, a member of the togaviruses. Both are RNA-containing viruses, but otherwise are quite dissimilar. Several other viruses also cause exanthematous diseases; these are discussed in other chapters or listed in Table 8–67–1.

CRITERIA FOR DIAGNOSIS
Suggestive

Presence of the characteristic prodrome and skin rash is satisfactory for clinical diagnosis of measles and satisfactory as well for diagnosis of rubella, but less frequently present. Measles is an acute febrile illness characterized by a prodrome (usually malaise, headache, conjunctivitis, cough productive of sputum, and coryza), followed by the appearance of a characteristic enanthem and a maculopapular rash on the face that subsequently extends to the trunk and extremities. Atypical measles is a variant of measles that occurs in individuals who previously have been immunized with the killed measles virus vaccine. It is characterized by a febrile prodrome followed by a rash that first appears on the distal extremities and then proceeds to the trunk and face. Rubella is suggested by typical clinical history and appearance of the rash plus a clear history of exposure.

Definitive

Measles diagnosis is confirmed by documenting a fourfold increase of measles antibody in convalescent serum when compared with acute serum. An extremely high measles antibody titer early in the illness is confirmatory of atypical measles syndrome.

Rubella is confirmed by fourfold rise or fall in the titer of antibody by hemagglutination inhibition or equivalent methods (enzyme immunoassay, etc.) or by an elevated titer of rubella-specific immunoglobulin M antibody.

Diagnosis of other viral exanthems can be made in the presence of rash and positive culture or serologic evidence of infection with one of a variety of viruses. The clinical picture alone is only infrequently diagnostic. Some of the possible entities are dealt with in other chapters (See Chapters 8–69 [mumps], 8–70 [herpes infections], 8–74 [varicella–zoster infections], and 8–75 [paravovirus B19]). Others are listed in Table 8–67–1.

CLINICAL MANIFESTATIONS
Subjective

In measles, a history of contact with another individual ill with measles is often elicited. A usual incubation period of 10 to 14 days is followed by complaints of fever, malaise, anorexia, sore throat, photophobia, nausea, and headache. Coryza and cough usually are present; vomiting and diarrhea are less often observed. Shortness of breath demands consideration of primary measles pneumonia or a complicating bacterial pulmonary infection. Symptoms of confusion, somnolence, or seizures may occur at any stage of the illness and suggest the possibility of measles encephalitis.

The prodromal symptoms of atypical measles may be similar to the early symptoms of measles infection listed above; alternatively, fever

and/or rash alone may be the initial manifestations. A history of arthralgias is more common in atypical measles than in the typical syndrome. Dyspnea, reflecting pulmonary involvement, is also a common complaint.

Often, children with rubella have no symptoms. In adults and some children, fever, malaise, and anorexia may exist for some days before a rash appears.

Symptoms of the other viral exanthems vary according to the agent involved (see Table 8–67–1). Fever and malaise prior to the onset of rash are common to many.

The patient must be questioned about prior occurrence of febrile illnesses with rash, because these may bear on the likelihood that the current episode represents measles, rubella, and so on. Atypical measles occurs only in persons immunized with the killed measles vaccine.

Objective
Physical Examination

In measles, fever above 38.5°C (101°F) is common. Also frequent are conjunctivitis and Koplik's spots, which are discrete gray-white papules on an erythematous base that are observed on the buccal mucosa opposite the first or second molar. These often occur immediately prior to the onset of rash. Less commonly, lesions are present on the palate and inner lips. The exanthem usually persists for several days. About 2 to 3 days after the onset of prodromal symptoms (see above), an erythematous maculopapular rash appears, usually beginning on the face and spreading to the trunk and extremities. It persists for about 5 days, and involved areas may become confluent and then desquamate as the rash clears. Lymphadenopathy and abdominal pain, especially in the right upper quadrant, are common as well in hospitalized adults.

In atypical measles, the prodromal symptoms are followed by a polymorphic rash (macules, papules, vesicles, urticaria, petechia, or purpura) beginning on the palms and soles and extending to the trunk. Alternatively, high fever and rash may appear concurrently, or the rash may be absent. The rash occasionally is pruritic. Conjunctival or palatal petechiae may be present; Koplik's spots are absent.

Rash and adenopathy are the main physical findings of rubella. The maculopapular rash often begins on the face and neck, progresses to the body and limbs, and then desquamates or disappears after 3 to 6 days. Adenopathy usually involves posterior auricular, posterior cervical, and suboccipital nodes, may last for weeks, and on occasion is accompanied by splenomegaly. Upper respiratory signs, fever, and conjunctivitis often accompany the rash.

Other viral exanthems have rashes of a variety of forms and distributions (Table 8–67–1). They may or may not be pruritic.

Routine Laboratory Abnormalities

In measles, leukopenia is common in uncomplicated disease, especially after the rash appears. Thrombocytopenia may occur occasionally. In young adults, mild increases in serum transaminase levels and lactic dehydrogenase levels may be seen, but hyperbilirubinemia is rare.

In atypical measles, eosinophilia is not uncommon and serum transaminase levels often are elevated. Coagulation tests may reveal results typical of disseminated intravascular coagulation, a rare complication of atypical measles.

Thrombocytopenia occasionally is seen with rubella infection.

PLANS
Diagnostic
Differential Diagnosis

The skin rash associated with measles can resemble that of rubella or other exanthems (see Table 8–67–1).

TABLE 8–67–1. SELECTED VIRAL EXANTHEMS OTHER THAN MEASLES OR RUBELLA

Viral Agent	Illness	Rash Form	Rash Distribution	Rash Duration	Associated Features	Diagnosis	Natural History
Dengue virus types 1 to 4 (flaviviruses)	Dengue fever	Maculopapular (occasionally petechial)	Chest, then spreads outward	3–4 d	Fever, chills, headache, backache, myalgia, arthralgia, adenopathy, leukopenia, jaundice (rare)	Culture of serum or serologic testing	Usually self-limited; hemorrhage or shock can develop
Smallpox virus	Smallpox	Maculopapular; evolves to vesicles over 24–48 h; then to pustules, which form scabs	Face and scalp; then arms and legs; less on trunk, but chest and back affected	14–21 d	High fever, myalgia, often backache, abdominal pain; lack of upper respiratory symptoms helps distinguish from measles	Culture of blood, throat, urine, conjunctiva, and skin vesicles; electron microscopy or direct fluorescent antibody on skin lesion most rapid	Encephalitis or hemorrhage can develop
Vaccinia virus	Vaccinia (cowpox)	Necrosis at vaccination site; vesicles	At vaccination site; vesicles all over body; at atopic dermatitis sites	3–6 d	Fever, malaise	Culture of virus from lesions	Usually benign: encephalitis, myocarditis, or bleeding may develop
Orf virus (bovine pustular stomatitis virus)	Pustular dermatitis	Papule, then nodule, then papilloma	Usually one lesion, on finger	21–35d	Fever, adenopathy, adenitis	Lesion progression plus history of contact with sheep or goats	Self-limited
Milkers' node virus	Milkers' nodules	Papule, then nodule	Site of contact with cattle	30–60 d	None	Lesion progression and contact history	Self-limited; nodule is painless
Presumed poxvirus (leporipox)	Molluscum contagiosum	Firm, umbilicated papules	Entire body, mucous membranes; most common on trunk and genitals	45–75 d	None	Appearance; no culture or serology available	Self-limited
Herpes simplex virus type 6	Roseola (exanthem subitum)	Maculopapular	Trunk and neck; appears as fever lyses	12–48 h	Fever, coryza, pharyngitis, cervical and posterior auricular adenopathy	Appearance of rash as fever ends; occurs primarily in infants	Self-limited
Possible virus	Kawasaki disease (mucocutaneous lymph node syndrome)	Morbilliform rash, erythema multiforme, or rash like scarlet fever	Trunk, may spread to face or extremities	5–15 d	Fever, adenopathy, conjunctivitis, fissured lips, dried red oral mucosa, "strawberry tongue," red palms and soles, desquamation	Clinical picture; no culture or serology available; must rule out toxic shock syndrome, scarlet fever, leptospirosis, Rocky Mountain spotted fever	Some type of cardiac involvement in 20% of cases; cardiac damage may result from coronary artery vasculitis
Enterovirus (echovirus and Coxsackie virus)	Variable exanthematous diseases	Discrete macules/papules, occasionally petechial	Face and chest primarily	1–6 d; usually appears as fever ends	Fever, pharyngitis, occasionally meningitis or pleurisy	Clinical picture and serology; culture stool and/or throat	Usually self-limited; encephalitis can follow, and mental deficiency can follow infection in infancy; persisting infection more likely in children with host defense abnormality
	Hand, foot, and mouth disease (vesicular stomatitis)	Clear gray vesicles occasional papules	Tongue, lips, buccal mucosa; palms, soles, hands, feet	7–10 d	Fever, malaise, abdominal pain, sore mouth or throat	Clinical picture, serology, culture of vesicles; must rule out herpes simplex and varicella	
	Herpangina	Gray-white papules or vesicles	Tonsils, uvula, soft palate	4–7 d	Fever, back pain, headache, sore throat, conjunctivitis	Clinical picture plus culture of lesions	

The clinical presentation of atypical measles may be similar to that seen in other infections, such as Rocky Mountain spotted fever, secondary syphilis, varicella, meningococcemia, disseminated gonococcal infection, and enteroviral infection.

It is difficult to differentiate the rash of rubella from other infections such as mononucleosis, measles, scarlet fever, erythema infectiosum, roseola, and enteroviral infections. When adenopathy is the prominent manifestation, toxoplasmosis may be considered as well.

Diagnostic Options

Culture of measles virus is technically difficult and not widely available. The hemagglutination inhibition and enzyme immunoassay (EIA) methods are the most commonly used serologic techniques for detecting measles antibody. Antibodies appear 2 to 3 days after the onset of rash.

The hemagglutination inhibition method remains the standard for diagnosis of rubella, but enzyme immunoassay and latex agglutination tests for immunoglobulin (Ig) G or M antibodies have replaced the older method in many laboratories. A new radioimmunoassay for IgM antibody in saliva may make screening easier. In a newly pregnant woman, the demonstration of a rubella-specific IgG in one serum sample, by one of these assays, is evidence of immunity to rubella. Acute rubella infection can be diagnosed either by the demonstration of rubella-specific IgM in one serum sample or by the fourfold or greater increase in rubella antibody titer in acute and convalescent specimens tested in the same assay system. For neonates suspected of having congenital rubella, the presence of rubella-specific IgM indicates that transplacental infection has occurred. If no rubella-specific IgM is present in the neonate's blood, serial testing of the infant's serum is required to detect whether the titer of the IgG antibody is rising (indicating acute infection of the child) or falling (indicating passively acquired maternal antibody). Rubella virus also can be cultured from nasal specimens of adults and from throat swabs, blood, and urine of infants with congenial infection.

Radiologic investigation of the chest may be useful. An interstitial pneumonia may occur in persons with measles, especially adults. The diagnosis of primary measles pneumonia may be confirmed, in the absence of other causes, by the demonstration of multinucleated giant cells on cytologic examination of sputum, bronchoalveolar lavage specimens, or transbronchial biopsy. In atypical measles, the chest roentgenogram is often abnormal; bilateral bronchopneumonia, lobar infiltrates, or pleural effusion may be present. Blood gas determination reveals hypoxia and hypocarbia. Cardiomegaly with electrocardiographic abnormalities may indicate pericarditis occurring as a complication.

Measles encephalitis is characterized by lymphocytes in the spinal fluid, while protein and glucose are normal or mildly increased.

Recommended Approach

When an outbreak of measles is occurring in the community, when classic signs and symptoms are present, or when contact with a case of suspected measles antedates symptoms and signs of illness, a clinical diagnosis of measles may often be made with reasonable assurance. Otherwise, serologic testing is needed. Complications, particularly that of measles pneumonia, require constant vigilance in patient evaluation and diagnostic techniques described above when their presence is suspected. Specific serologic diagnosis of atypical measles is made by demonstrating a high antibody titer early in the illness.

Facilities for isolation of rubella virus are not readily available, so serologic testing is the method usually used. One must determine whether a woman of childbearing age with rubella is pregnant, because severe consequences can occur to a fetus infected transplacentally during early pregnancy. The methods discussed above are germane.

Diagnosis of other viral exanthems is difficult; no test is available for some agents (see Table 8–67–1). For others, causation may be difficult to establish by serologic testing.

Therapeutic

Therapeutic Options

No specific antiviral therapy is available for either typical or atypical measles; ribavarin has activity in the laboratory against measles virus,

but clinical studies to support its use are lacking. Vitamin A, 200,000 IU/d per day orally for 2 to 3 days, is suggested for children with severe measles. It is not as clear whether this is helpful for adults; however, vitamin A therapy is a major advance in reducing mortality and morbidity in severe measles. Rest and fluids are appropriate in uncomplicated cases; antibiotics are not indicated unless bacterial infection is documented. Supportive therapy also includes antipyretic agents.

Therapy for rubella is directed toward relieving symptoms of fever or arthralgia. No specific antiviral therapy is available. Immune serum globulin may be administered to a woman exposed to rubella during pregnancy who is found susceptible to the disease and who could not consider abortion. The immune globulin suppresses symptoms but does not prevent viremia, so fetal infection can still occur.

No specific therapy is available for most of the exanthems listed in Table 8–67–1.

Recommended Approach

As no specific therapies are available for these agents, attention focuses on supportive symptomatic treatment and counseling.

FOLLOW-UP

Most cases of uncomplicated measles probably are not seen by a physician. When a case is encountered, telephone follow-up is suggested because of the possibility of a secondary bacterial infection (otitis media, pneumonia, etc.) or of measles encephalitis.

No follow-up for rubella is needed unless persisting arthritis or arthralgia requires further visits for symptomatic treatment or unless the infected patient is pregnant, as considered above.

DISCUSSION

Prevalence and Incidence

Before measles virus vaccine was available in the United States, more than 400,000 cases were reported each year. Since vaccine licensure in 1963, vigorous vaccination programs resulted in a marked reduction in the reported incidence of measles to an all-time low of about 1500 cases in 1983. The number of cases then rose again, with almost 28,000 reported cases in 1990. Data on recent cases analyzed by the Centers for Disease Control and Prevention (CDC) showed that the rise resulted from failure to implement current vaccine strategy, resulting in large numbers of unvaccinated persons, particularly in the preschool population, and from vaccine failure, apparent as cases among school-aged children and young adults who had previously been vaccinated. In January through August of 1994, 814 cases of measles were reported, a substantial increase from 1993. Almost half of the cases occurred in unimmunized individuals, usually those with religious or philosophic objection to vaccination.

Atypical measles is less frequent today, as the population who received killed measles vaccine and are exposed to wild measles virus is becoming smaller with each year since that vaccine was used in the 1960s.

Rubella occurs infrequently in the United States today. The last major epidemic was in 1964, and cases of both rubella and congenital rubella syndrome have been infrequent in the past decade. There were 1401 reported rubella cases in 1991; annual case counts then declined to fewer than 200 in 1992 and 1993. In the interval January to August 1994, 204 cases of rubella and 2 cases of congenital rubella syndrome were reported for the United States.

Related Basic Science

Genetics

Manifestations of congenital rubella are determined in part by the time in pregnancy when the mother is infected. When infection occurs in the first trimester, about half of the infants will be affected; the risk decreases as infection occurs later in pregnancy. The most common manifestations—deafness, cataract, glaucoma, and cardiac anatomic defects—are associated with infection early in pregnancy.

Altered Molecular Biology

The syndrome of atypical measles presumably represents hypersensitivity in a host who is partially immune. The mechanisms involved are not clear; measles virus has not been isolated.

Anatomic Derangement

Congenital rubella syndrome produces infants who shed large amounts of virus for months. The virus persists in the lymphoreticular cells of the blood and synovium of adults and children with chronic rheumatic disease.

Natural History and Its Modification with Treatment

Most individuals with measles have a self-limited illness that lasts 7 to 10 days. Measles pneumonia may arise as part of the viral infection itself or from bacterial superinfection. Measles encephalitis occurs in about 1 in 1000 cases. Encephalitis risk is greater in adults, and the disease may be quite severe, resulting in permanent neurologic deficits. In addition, subacute sclerosing panencephalitis is thought to be a rare late complication (onset years after acute measles).

The disease associated with atypical measles is usually somewhat more prolonged than classic measles. Persistence of nodular lesions on chest roentgenogram has been documented in some of these extended cases.

Symptoms of acute rubella usually resolve within a week. In about 30% of adult women, arthritis (or arthralgia) of wrists, fingers, and knees may appear with onset of the rash, and continue for up to 6 weeks. The major hazard of rubella is concomitant infection of the fetus, leading to cataract or glaucoma, mental retardation, congenital heart disease, and impaired hearing. These complications are more likely to result if the primary infection occurred during the first 2 months of pregnancy (approximately 50% chance of congenital rubella syndrome or spontaneous abortion). Rubella onset in the neonatal period also can lead to death. Rubella occurs primarily in the spring and now occurs frequently in young adults and adolescents as well as in children. College, prison, workplace, and hospital outbreaks account for the recent increase in occurrence. Humans constitute the only reservoir, and the disease is spread in droplets from the respiratory tract. The incubation period ranges from 10 to 23 days, averaging 17 days. Although patients may shed virus from the nasopharynx from 10 days before rash until 15 days afterward, they are most contagious while the rash is present. Children with congenital rubella syndrome can excrete virus in nasopharyngeal secretions and in urine for weeks to months after birth.

The natural history of other exanthems is quite variable (see Table 8–67–1).

Prevention

Measles

In 1963, both a formalin-killed and a live attenuated (Edmonston B) vaccine were licensed. After recognition of the syndrome of atypical measles in those who received the killed vaccine, its use was discontinued in 1968. Newer attenuated live products are currently used in the United States. Because of the rise in the number of cases of measles in the late 1980s, the CDC made new recommendations for measles immunization. Now recommended are two doses of measles vaccine, given in the trivalent combination of measles/mumps/rubella (MMR) vaccines. The first dose should be given at age 15 months (at 12 months in areas at high risk for measles), and the second at 4 to 6 years of age. Serologic response is demonstrated in about 95% of those vaccinated. Colleges and similar institutions that require matriculating students to provide documentation of two doses of measles vaccine after their first birthday (or other evidence of measles immunity) have had fewer outbreaks than those that do not. The CDC also recommends that all health care workers beginning employment or training should be required to provide documentation similar to that for colleges. About 10% of those immunized with live attenuated measles vaccine develop fever about 1 week after immunization, and occasionally a patient will develop a transient rash. Mild, transient gait disturbance may occur after MMR vaccine. Active immunization with live attenuated measles vaccine is contraindicated for persons who have deficient cell-mediated immunity, for those allergic to egg protein, and for pregnant women. Vaccinating asymptomatic children infected with HIV is recommended. Even immunizing symptomatic children with HIV infection who live in areas with known measles transmission also should be considered, as measles illness in these children can be quite severe. Measles immunity persists even as HIV-related immunodeficiency increases. Limited data indicate that MMR side effects in children with HIV infection are no worse than for children without this infection. After exposure to measles, the disease can be prevented in susceptible individuals by the administration of vaccine (if within 72 hours of exposure) or by giving immune serum globulin (if within 6 days of exposure).

Rubella

Immunization with live attenuated rubella virus vaccine (RA 27/3 strain) provides lasting immunity. The CDC recommends one dose of rubella vaccine as a component of MMR vaccine administered at age 15 months and a second dose at school entry. Pregnancy is a contraindication to rubella vaccine because of the small risk of congenital rubella syndrome. Reasonable precautions should be taken to prevent vaccination of pregnant women, including asking women if they are pregnant or may become pregnant within the next 3 months. Those answering yes should be excluded from vaccination. If vaccination does occur within 3 months before or after conception, the risk of congenital rubella syndrome still is negligible; the CDC states that this should not be a sole reason to consider interruption of pregnancy. Persons without evidence of rubella immunity (especially susceptible women of childbearing age) who travel abroad should be vaccinated, because rates of rubella are higher in many countries than they are in the United States. The vaccine virus does not appear to be transmissible, even to household contacts. Arthralgia and/or arthritis after immunization are more common in adults than in children; these findings occur about 1 to 3 weeks after vaccination and persist for an average of 3 days.

Persons with measles or rubella who are hospitalized require respiratory isolation, as well as blood and body fluid precautions, because of the possibility of airborne spread of their virus. Infants with congenital rubella may transmit virus for about 1 year after birth and present particular dangers to nonimmune health care workers.

Cost Containment

Effective immunization programs and more effective vaccines could lower costs for treating patients with acute measles or rubella. More important, they could eliminate the great expense associated with care for patients with congenital defects caused by rubella or for those with complications of measles. The cost-effectiveness of such preventive programs has been demonstrated by several studies.

REFERENCES

Boyd AS. Laboratory testing in patients with morbilliform viral eruptions. Dermatol Clin 1994;12:69.

Centers for Disease Control and Prevention. Update: Childhood vaccine-preventable diseases—United States, 1994. JAMA 1994;272:1318.

Gellin BG, Katz SL. Measles: State of the art and future directions. J Infect Dis 1994;170(supply. 1):S2.

Mulholland K. Measles and pertussis in developing countries with good vaccine coverage. Lancet 1995;345:305.

Poland GA, Jacobson RM. Failure to reach the goal of measles elimination: Apparent paradox of measles infections in immunized persons. Arch Intern Med 1994;154:1815.

Wong RD, Goetz MB, Mathisen G, Henry D. Clinical and laboratory features of measles in hospitalized adults. Am J Med 1993;95:377.

Rubella Arthritis (See Section 6, Chapter 13)

CHAPTER 8–69
Mumps

Dominique M. Anwar-Bruni, M.D., and Carl A. Perlino, M.D.

DEFINITION

Mumps is a viral infection causing painful swelling of the salivary glands, usually the parotid, in a nonimmune individual previously exposed to an active case.

ETIOLOGY

Mumps belong to the Paramyxoviridae family. The virus is spread by airborne droplets, direct contact, or respiratory fomites.

CRITERIA FOR DIAGNOSIS
Suggestive

Painful swelling of the parotid glands or other salivary glands is strongly suggestive, especially in nonimmune individuals. There may be a short prodromal period with low-grade fever and general malaise. Thirty to forty percent of infections are subclinical.

Definitive

The diagnosis of parotitis due to mumps virus is most often made on clinical grounds only. Mumps virus may be isolated from saliva or throat washings and also from cerebrospinal fluid in cases of mumps meningitis. A fourfold rise in complement-fixing antibodies in paired sera is also diagnostic. Mumps immunoglobulin M may help diagnose acute infection.

CLINICAL MANIFESTATIONS
Subjective

A history of exposure to an active case of mumps in family members or school contacts is often elicited. The period between exposure and onset of symptoms is variable, but it is usually between 2 and 3 weeks. Subjective complaints depend on the organ system involved, most likely the parotid and other salivary glands. In this case, a brief, mild, prodromal illness of general malaise, anorexia, and fever occurs followed by pain, tenderness, and progressive swelling of a single parotid gland. Symptoms involving the other gland may then be observed. The patient may complain of difficulty in mastication because of local pain and swelling. A sharp increase in pain while eating and drinking citrus fruit juices, suggesting partial obstruction of ductal tissue, is common. The constitutional symptoms seen early in the disease usually regress after the adenitis reaches its peak intensity.

Infection with mumps virus also occasionally may produce symptoms of aseptic meningitis, encephalitis, epididymoorchitis, pancreatitis, and, less commonly, a migratory polyarthritis, oophoritis, or thyroiditis.

Mumps infection of the central nervous system is most often asymptomatic. Symptoms of headache and pain on neck flexion suggest clinical aseptic meningitis and may occur in direct temporal relation to or in the absence of symptoms of parotitis. The illness is clinically indistinguishable from aseptic meningitis due to other causes.

Epididymoorchitis may occur in as many as 25% of postpubertal males with mumps, but it is uncommon in children. The onset of symptoms is usually abrupt, occurring within 1 week of the onset of parotitis, but similar to other extrasalivary gland involvement, it can precede,

coincide with, or occur in the absence of parotitis. Swelling and pain of one testicle are usually observed. Bilateral involvement occurs occasionally.

Objective
Physical Examination

Parotid enlargement and tenderness are the most frequent manifestations of mumps, but any combination of salivary gland swelling may be seen. In more than two thirds of patients, both parotid glands are involved; contralateral involvement usually appears within 1 to 5 days of the initial parotitis. Great variability in the degree of parotid swelling may occur; minor enlargement can be detected more easily by examining the patient from behind, looking for the loss of the normal regional contour at the angle of the mandible. Salivary glands other than the parotids are involved clinically in up to 10% of patients, usually occurring in association with parotitis. Erythema and local warmth are usually not apparent in mumps; if they are present, they suggest bacterial parotitis.

Meningismus may be detected clinically in some patients. The presence of confusion or alteration of consciousness suggests the presence of encephalitis and may occur in association with parotitis due to direct central nervous system invasion of the virus or, later in the disease, as a postinfectious encephalitis probably due to immune complex formation and local demyelinization. An elevated serum amylase level should suggest mumps as the etiology of the central nervous system findings, even in the absence of clinical parotitis.

Routine Laboratory Abnormalities

The white blood cell and differential counts are normal, or there may be a mild leukopenia with relative lymphocytosis. In the case of orchitis, pancreatitis, or aseptic meningitis, there may be a leukocytosis with a greater percentage of neutrophilia. Serum amylase is commonly elevated with or without pancreatitis, and may remain elevated for 2 to 3 weeks.

PLANS
Diagnostic
Differential Diagnosis

Other noninfectious causes of bilateral parotid enlargement include diabetes mellitus, malnutrition, cirrhosis, hyperlipidemia, Sjögren's syndrome, and sarcoidosis. This enlargement may also be a drug-related illness (ingestion of iodides, phenylbutazone, phenothiazines, bromides, or thiouracil). Tumors, cysts, or ductal obstruction may cause chronic and painless unilateral parotid enlargement.

Among infectious causes, *Staphylococcus aureus* may cause suppurative parotitis in dehydrated, chronically ill, or postoperative patients or in persons with poor oral intake and inadequate oral hygiene. Diagnosis is made by the presence of a local erythematous skin overlying the gland, with pus expressed from Stensen's duct, and of a marked leukocytosis.

Less common viral parotitis etiologies are parainfluenza, Coxsackie virus, and influenza A virus.

Diagnostic Options

Mumps virus may be isolated from saliva, throat washings, and urine during the clinical illness (from 1 day before to 4 to 5 days after the onset of disease). Cultivation may be made on a variety of cell line cultures. Hemabsorption and indirect immunofluorescence are rather sensitive. Serologic tests have variable sensitivity and specificity mainly because of cross-reactivity with other paramyxovirus antigens.

Current laboratory methods include measurement of the serum immunoglobulin G component using an enzyme-linked immunosorbent assay in both acute and convalescent phase samples. Highly specific and sensitive results are obtained by the antibody-capture enzyme immunoassay.

In case of suspicion of mumps meningitis, the spinal fluid will demonstrate lymphocytic pleocytosis, a mildly elevated protein level, and sometimes hypoglycorrhachia. Mumps virus may also be isolated from the spinal fluid in the early phases of the central nervous system infection.

Recommended Approach

Usually, the diagnosis can be made on the basis of characteristic symptoms and signs. The above-mentioned diagnostic options should be considered when complications are apparent and the diagnosis is unclear.

Therapeutic

Therapeutic Option

No specific therapy is available, and only symptomatic relief can be offered. Acetaminophen or salicylates are useful for reducing fever and pain. In patients with orchitis, analgesics (especially narcotics if there is no suspicion of pancreatitis) and immobilization are useful. Application of cold packs may relieve the symptoms. Steroids have never been shown to be effective in this situation. Pancreatitis should be treated depending on the symptoms.

Recommended Approach and Follow-Up

In patients who seek medical attention for parotitis or extraglandular illness, a short-term follow-up is necessary as the illness is self-limited. The benign nature of mumps parotitis should be explained, specifying that no antimicrobial therapy is available. In the case of orchitis, reassurance concerning the fears of impotence and sterility is important. The patient and relatives have to be advised that aseptic meningitis (incidence, 10%) or encephalitis (incidence, 1/6000) may occur, even if sequelae are rare. Patients should be attentive to the appearance of symptoms suggesting pancreatitis, pericarditis, arthritis, or renal dysfunction.

DISCUSSION

Prevalence and Incidence

Since the introduction of the live vaccine in 1967, there has been more than a 95% decline in the incidence of mumps among children in the United States. This disease remains a problem worldwide, however. Mumps afflicts primarily young school-aged children. Afflicted adults often present with a more severe disease involving extraglandular sites. Parotitis is the usual presentation of mumps in 60 to 70% of cases. Epididymoorchitis has an incidence of 20% in postpubertal males.

Related Basic Science

Mumps is an RNA virus, member of the Paramyxoviridae family and *Paramyxovirus* genus. Viral infection is limited to human beings, occurring after direct contact with either a symptomatic or an asymptomatic infected person. The respiratory infection occurs first, followed by the secondary viremia and the infection of other organs.

Natural History and Its Modification with Treatment

Mumps is usually a benign disease running its course in 7 to 10 days without sequelae. Transient deafness may occur during acute illness in up to 4% of patients. Permanent deafness is usually unilateral and rare, attributed to endolymphatic labyrinthitis. Mumps orchitis, though a serious complication, is generally unilateral and is not often associated with impotence or sterility. Fatalities in relation to mumps are extremely rare and are the consequence of encephalitis, myocarditis, or nephritis.

Prevention

Patients with clinical mumps should be isolated until the parotid swelling has resolved, since as the virus is present in the saliva several days before the development of clinical parotitis, the spread of infection may be difficult to control. All susceptible medical personnel should obtain an adequate immunization. Some recommend that susceptible hospital personnel exposed to a case of mumps should not work from the 12th to the 26th day after exposure to avoid possible transmission. All college students should be checked for their mumps immunity (history of vaccination).

Since 1967, an effective live attenuated vaccine produced in chick embryo cell culture has been available, either as a monovalent vaccine or a trivalent measles/mumps/rubella (MMR) vaccine. The trivalent vaccine is given to children over the age of 15 months; the monovalent vaccine should be administered to susceptible adults. Persons born before 1957 are likely to have had natural infection, but as an increased percentage of cases occur among adults, vaccine may be offered to older adults without a history of clinical mumps.

The vaccine, given as a single subcutaneous dose, produces a subclinical and noncontagious infection. Very few side effects have been observed; occasionally, however, mild parotitis may occur. Ninety to ninety-five percent of susceptible recipients have a lifelong protective antibody formation when the vaccine is given in normal circumstances. In outbreak-based studies, the vaccine efficacy may be lower, however, ranging from 75 to 91% if vaccine is given in association with the outbreak. As there is at least 5% of vaccine failure and 5% secondary failure (loss of antibodies over time), some recommend revaccination of all teenagers.

Persons with history of anaphylactic reaction to eggs or neomycin should not be vaccinated. As the vaccine is a live attenuate virus, it should not be administered to pregnant women, patients receiving immunosuppressive therapy, persons with congenital or acquired immunodeficiencies, or patients with malignancies. It is, however, current clinical practice to use the measles/mumps/rubella vaccine in patients with HIV or AIDS infection.

The efficacy of immune serum globulin or mumps immune globulin in preventing the disease after exposure had not been established.

Cost Containment

Vaccination is the most effective means to prevent mumps immune. Testing for susceptibility before vaccination is not necessary, and often is not reliable or cost-effective. Also see Prevention.

REFERENCES

Briss P, Fehrs L, Parker R, et al. Sustained transmission of mumps in a highly vaccinated population: Assessment of primary vaccine failure and waning vaccine-induced immunity. J Infect Dis 1994;169:77.

Carter H, Campbell H. Rational use of measles, mumps and rubella (MMR) vaccine. Drugs 1993;45:677.

Childhood vaccine-preventable diseases—United States. MMWR 1994;43(39): 718.

Malengreau M. Reappearance of post-vaccination infection of measles, rubella and mumps. Should adolescents be revaccinated? Pediatrie 1992;47(9):597.

Pomeroy C, Colin Jordan M. Mumps. In: Hoeprich PD, Jordan MC, Ronald AR (eds). Infectious diseases. 5th ed. Philadelphia: Lippincott, 1994:829.

Herpes Infections • Herpes Simplex and Human Herpes Viruses 6 and 7

Richard L. Hengel, M.D.

DEFINITION

Herpes infection is defined as infection with members of the viral family Herpesviridae: herpes simplex virus 1 or 2 (HSV 1 or HSV 2) and human herpesvirus 6 or 7 (HHV 6 or HHV 7).

ETIOLOGY

Herpes simplex virus 1 is the usual cause of orolabial herpes and the most common cause of sporadic aseptic meningitis. HSV 2 is the usual cause of genital herpes and occasionally disseminated herpetic disease in the neonate. HHV 6 is the etiology of exanthem subitum (roseola infantum) in children. HHV 7 has not yet been associated with disease.

CRITERIA FOR DIAGNOSIS
Suggestive

Herpes simplex virus 1 is commonly acquired in childhood, presumably through shared oral secretions. Most of the infections are asymptomatic, but one should consider the diagnosis of primary infection in children who present with gingivostomatitis or pharyngitis and subsequent vesiculation of the oral mucosa. If a patient escapes primary infection in childhood they may manifest their primary infection as an adult with tonsillitis or pharyngitis. The manifestation of recurrent disease is usually painful grouped vesicles or ulcerations in the nasolabial region. HSV 1 should be the leading consideration in any patient with the findings of aseptic meningitis. Similarly, patients presenting with unilateral conjunctivitis, especially with dendritic keratitis or blepharitis with vesiculation should prompt the physician to consider HSV 1 as the cause.

In adolescents and adults, HSV 2 causes the vast majority of genital herpes, although HSV 1 can also cause disease, presumably because of orogenital sexual practices. The difference between primary and recurrent genital herpes is one of degree: primary infection is more severe, but otherwise resembles recurrent disease. As with HSV 1, most infections with HSV 2 are asymptomatic. Occasionally, HSV 2 may be acquired perinatally when disease is associated with a primary infection in the mother. In contrast to children and adults, disseminated HSV 2 infection would be a major consideration in neonatal aseptic meningitis.

Following primary infection, recurrent painful grouped vesicles or ulcerations occurring in the nasolabial region or the genital regions are common for HSV 1 and 2. These last a few days to weeks and resolve spontaneously only to recur in the same areas, and are classic, making an accurate clinical diagnosis possible. Many patients experience a characteristic prodrome of tingling, itching, numbness, or burning. This may begin minutes to hours before the lesions erupt; the prodrome is pathognomonic for herpes viruses and helps in diagnosis.

Human herpesvirus 6 causes exanthem subitum, a disease of childhood. A sudden onset of high fever for 2 to 3 days followed by a morbilliform rash when the fever subsides is typical. Occasionally, a patient who escapes primary infection in childhood develops a mononucleosis-like illness in adolescence or adulthood as a manifestation of the primary illness. Some have suggested a role for HHV-6 in AIDS and in chronic fatigue syndrome, but this is highly controversial. The roles HHV 6 and HHV 7 play in other disease processes remain the subject of ongoing research.

Definitive

The gold standard for documentation of HSV infection is tissue culture and immunologic typing. Serology also provides the opportunity to di-

We thank Dr. Sumner E. Thompson III for his contribution to this chapter in the previous editions of this book.

agnose illness. Finally, making a diagnosis rapidly at the bedside is possible by making a Giemsa-stained smear (Tzanck preparation) from the base of a recently developed lesion. Typical multinucleated giant cells with Cowdry type A intranuclear inclusions would be consistent with either HSV 1, HSV 2, or varicella–zoster virus (VZV) infection.

As for HHV 6 or HHV 7, serology is available in the research laboratory, but has not yet found clinical utility.

CLINICAL MANIFESTATIONS
Subjective
Primary Infections

Primary infection with HHV 6 is a pediatric disease as discussed above. There is little understanding of its role in adult disease. Primary infections with HSV 1 or HSV 2 occur in patients with no preexisting antibody. Disease caused by the herpes simplex viruses is the focus of the remainder of this chapter.

Oral. Ninety-five percent or more of primary HSV infections in children are asymptomatic. Most infections occur in children under 5 years of age after an incubation period of 2 to 12 days. Gingivostomatitis and pharyngitis are the two most common clinical syndromes, accompanied by high fever, malaise, and even dehydration. In young adults, primary infection often presents as posterior pharyngitis or tonsillitis. The first infection in most adults generally presents as painful clustered sores on the lip margin, with mild fever and malaise. It too may present as gingivostomatitis with pharyngitis, however.

Ocular. Herpes eye infections are nearly always due to HSV 1 and are characterized by the sudden onset of unilateral light sensitivity, redness, tearing, pain, and swelling of the eyelid. Blurring and diminution of vision occur when the cornea is involved (dendritic keratitis). Herpes eye infections are the most common cause of corneal blindness in the United States.

Genital. Herpes simplex virus 2 causes primary infection seen in adolescents and young adults 70 to 95% of the time. The incubation period is 2 to 7 days. In men, crops of vesicular lesions on erythematous bases appear on the glans penis or the penile shaft. About 25% of men have concurrent symptoms of urethritis characterized by dysuria out of proportion to the amount of urethral discharge. Rectal involvement with herpetic lesions is common in homosexual men. Women may notice similar crops of vesicles that may ulcerate and often become covered by a grayish-white exudate on the vulva, perineum, buttocks, or thighs. Women frequently notice an increase in vaginal discharge and experience severe dysuria or even urinary retention. A prodrome is unusual; however, fever, malaise, and tender inguinal adenopathy frequently accompany the vesicles. Headache and neck stiffness, the symptoms of aseptic meningitis, occur in 6 to 10% of primary HSV 2 infections. The herpetic sacral radioculomyelitis that accompanies genital infection and that may lead to urinary retention and severe constipation may also cause neuralgia. Pain radiating down the legs or into the thighs or buttocks is its usual manifestation.

Meningoencephalitis. Although herpes simplex encephalitis is a rare complication of herpetic infection, it is the most common acute sporadic viral disease of the brain recognized in the United States. HSV 1 can cause an encephalitis in any age group, in either sex, and during any time of the year. Early in the encephalitis the patient may notice headache, nausea, vomiting, fever, chills, and muscle aches. Later, there may be olfactory hallucinations, episodes of irrational behavior, speech difficulties, and focal seizures. The course in untreated patients is rapidly progressive, leading to coma and death in several days in about 70% of patients. HSV 2 genital infection is commonly associated with aseptic meningitis, but the involvement is minimal and does not impact on therapy. Lumbar puncture in the setting of routine genital herpes is not recommended.

Other. Infection at any skin site may occur. Intense pain or itching followed by the emergence of deep vesicles, which often coalesce and ulcerate, characterizes primary distal finger infection—herpetic whitlow. Commonly, there are associated fever, tender axillary adenopathy, and neuralgia characterized as shooting pains up the hand and arm. HSV 1 causes most lesions among medical and dental personnel (e.g., herpetic whitlow). In the general community they are more commonly due to HSV 2. Perirectal and rectal HSV 2 infections are common in male homosexuals. Severe rectal pain (especially during defecation), itching, rectal discharge, and constipation, are common complaints. Fever, chills, malaise, headache, urinary retention, and sacral neuralgias manifesting as pain radiating down the legs or onto the buttocks or thighs are also associated with primary rectal infections.

Recurrent Infections

Oral. Tingling, burning, or itching at the site minutes to hours before lesions appear constitute the hallmark of infection and occur in about 65% of patients. This prodrome usually heralds each new crop of lesions. Pain is most severe in the first 2 or 3 days, while lesions are appearing. Systemic complaints are rare.

Ocular. Recurrences are common and are similar to the initial infection. Progressive, permanent loss of visual acuity may occur with recurrence.

Genital. Recurrences are common and are similar to the initial infection. The severity of symptoms is generally less for recurrences than for primary episodes. About half these patients experience paresthesias at the site of recurrence just before lesions occur. Aseptic meningitis may occur with genital recurrences.

Objective

Physical Examination

Oral. Primary infection usually occurs in childhood. Asymptomatic infection is common. Early lesions are vesicular eruptions that occur on the posterior palate, fauces (throat), buccal mucosa, tongue, sublingual mucosa, or lips. By the time of examination the vesicles have usually advanced to ulcers. New crops of lesions may occur. Fever is typically present. The breath is fetid. Often the child is drooling and has bilateral cervical adenopathy; however, the mucosal lesions last 10 to 14 days with no sequelae. Rarely, the cervical adenopathy may persist for weeks.

Recurrent oral herpes in children, adolescents, and adults usually occurs as grouped vesicles at the vermilion border of the lips or, less frequently, the chin or the border of the nares. Lesions heal within 8 to 10 days. Local adenopathy also may occur.

Ocular. A unilateral, follicular conjunctivitis with marked chemosis is classic. There is often associated blepharitis with vesicles on the lid margin. Dendritic ulcers on the corneal surface are pathognomonic, but they are present in less than one third of the patients. Even when these ulcers are present, they may be difficult to detect without a slit-lamp examination. Healing of the conjunctivitis usually occurs in 2 to 3 weeks.

Genital. The finding of painful vesicular lesions on an erythematous base is characteristic, especially when associated with fever and tender inguinal adenopathy; however, the lesions often have ulcerated or crusted over when first seen by the physician. The appearance of crops of lesions in different stages of evolution is helpful. Ulcers are usually shallow with sharp, erythematous margins and are exquisitely tender. In most areas, especially in women, the ulcers rapidly become covered with a grayish-white exudate. Painful linear ulcerations extending from the posterior fourchette toward the rectum are sometimes noted. About 75% of women with primary HSV 2 infections develop cervicitis, often an erosive process. Often the virus can be isolated from the endocervix even if the cervix appears normal on visual inspection. Both men and women develop inguinal adenopathy, frequently bilaterally. Rectal ex-

amination may show loss of anal tone. The bulbocavernosus reflex may be diminished in men.

Meningoencephalitis. Mild meningeal signs are seen in meningitis associated with HSV 2 and in the early stages of encephalitis associated with HSV 1 infections. In the later stages of encephalitis, speech disorders, focal seizures, and mental status deterioration with progression to coma are all possibilities.

Other. Rectal lesions are typically ulcerative and may extend from the perineal skin to the rectal crypts. Anoscopy or flexible sigmoidoscopy may show these lesions. The vesicles of herpetic whitlow are usually deep and periungual. When ulcerated and crusted they may be difficult to distinguish from bacterial paronychia. HIV disease predisposes the patient to extensive skin involvement.

Routine Laboratory Abnormalities

There are few clues to the diagnosis of orolabial or genital herpes with routine laboratory methods. Occasionally, routine methods aid in the diagnosis of disseminated herpetic diseases in special circumstances such as the neonate or the immunocompromised host, when the chest roentgenogram identifies pulmonary involvement or routine blood tests detect coagulopathies or hepatic derangements.

PLANS

Diagnostic

Differential Diagnosis

Herpes zoster may cause vesicular lesions of the face. With pharyngeal or tonsillar involvement other possible etiologies include streptococcal pharyngitis or diphtheria, aphthous stomatitis, and Stevens–Johnson syndrome. Ocular involvement may be confused with other viral and bacterial pathogens, trauma, chemical conjunctivitis, or autoimmune involvement. In genital disease the differential diagnosis of ulcerative lesions includes syphilis, varicella–zoster, chancroid, donovonsosis, lymphogranuloma venereum, cutaneous fungal infections, Behçet's syndrome, and carcinoma. Finally, herpes encephalitis or meningitis may have presentations similar to those of other sporadic or epidemic forms of viral encephalitis. Tuberculous or fungal meningitis, brain abscess, autoimmune diseases, cerebral vascular accidents, toxic metabolic states, and congenital enzyme deficiencies are other possibilities.

Diagnostic Options

The Tzanck test may provide a rapid confirmatory bedside test to narrow the differential diagnosis to HSV 1, HSV 2, and VZV. Sensitivity of the test is greatest within the first 24 to 48 hours, possibly as high as 90%. This drops rapidly below 50% in the ulcerative stage, and lower still if taken from a crusted lesion.

Viral tissue culture shows cytopathic effects characteristic of herpes simplex virus within 24 to 48 hours. As with the Tzanck test, it is important to culture vesicles as soon as possible as the highest viral titers are found in them. The viral inoculum is an important determinant in the success of culture. The virus is fragile ex vivo, so rapid transport and processing should be done. Holding the specimen at 4°C for up to 2 hours is acceptable. The viral strains are identified using immunologic methods. An appropriate specimen for culture includes samples from vesicles, ulcers, and cornea, and occasionally biopsy material from invasive procedures such as brain biopsy or from tissue obtained at endoscopy or bronchoscopy. Cerebrospinal fluid produces a poor culture yield.

Serology for HSV 1 and HSV 2 plays a limited role in clinical practice because of the prevalence of antibodies in the general population. The presence of immunoglobulin M antibodies and fourfold rises in titers is not particularly helpful. Currently available commercial enzyme assays that claim strain specificity between HSV 1 and HSV 2 are inaccurate by more reliable methods such as immunodot or Western immunoblot assays. These latter tests are not generally available in the clinical setting.

In cases of suspected herpes encephalitis, examination of the cerebrospinal fluid in both HSV 1 and HSV 2 infections usually shows a mononuclear pleocytosis. Occasionally one sees a picture with mixed mononuclear and neutrophilic leukocytes. The cell count may reach up to 1000 leukocytes/μL, but counts of 200 to 600 are much more common. Red cells are occasionally seen because the HSV 1 encephalitis is a necrotizing hemorrhagic process. Elevated protein levels are usual in both processes. Hypoglycorrhachia occasionally occurs, but glucose is most often normal. Viral cultures of the cerebrospinal fluid are frequently positive in the aseptic meningitis associated with HSV 2 infection. Cerebrospinal fluid cultures almost never show virus in cases of encephalitis associated with HSV 1. Other investigations may demonstrate the temporal lobe involvement typical of herpes encephalitis. These include magnetic resonance imaging (MRI) and computed tomography (CT) imaging of the brain and electroencephalography. Brain biopsy with histology and culture remains the gold standard. A cerebrospinal fluid diagnosis using reliable polymerase chain reaction or gene probe technology would supplant the role of biopsy.

Recommended Approach

Making the definitive diagnosis of orolabial herpes should probably occur only when culture results will affect subsequent management. This is the case in severe gingivostomatitis where therapeutic options depend on knowing the diagnosis. Otherwise, presumptive diagnosis is sufficient if encountering a typical clinical presentation.

Genital herpes, on the other hand, is associated with significant psychosocial stressors and definitive diagnosis is recommended if possible. Alternatively, in the appropriate setting many clinicians would consider a positive Tzanck test adequate evidence of disease.

All patients with symptoms of meningitis or encephalitis need examination of the cerebrospinal fluid. If the picture is one of aseptic meningitis, then empiric treatment of herpes encephalitis is in order while awaiting further imaging studies or electroencephalography.

Serology is probably best used as a screening tool in the transplant population to decide who is a candidate for prophylaxis.

Therapeutic

Therapeutic Options

Acyclovir. Acyclovir is a drug converted in the cell to an inhibitor of HSV DNA polymerase. Acyclovir is available topically, orally, and intravenously. The topical preparation has efficacy, but less than systemic preparations.

Oral acyclovir is used for many herpetic infections, particularly genital herpes. The primary infection responds to acyclovir by decreasing the duration of illness, decreasing the symptoms, and decreasing the amount of viral shedding. The recommended dose is 200 mg five times daily for 10 days. One might use a similar dose regimen for a primary oral infection, but most adult patients will have already seroconverted in childhood. Recurrent infections do not respond as well to acyclovir, and I do not recommend its use for this indication.

Patients who suffer frequent genital recurrences (more than six per year), or whose recurrences are associated with complications (such as erythema multiforme, aseptic meningitis, or eczema herpeticum) may benefit from suppressive therapy with acyclovir 200 mg four times daily for 3 months, then 200 mg three times daily or 400 mg once daily if symptoms allow. Breakthrough symptoms occur, but there is generally a reduction in the number and severity of episodes.

Immunocompromised patients may similarly benefit from suppressive therapy. Dosages may vary from 200 to 400 mg two to five times daily. Also, treatment doses (versus suppressive doses) are higher, 400 mg five times daily for 7 days. Viral resistance is becoming a problem, however.

More serious infections require intravenous acyclovir. Treatment of severe mucocutaneous disease is 5 mg/kg intravenously every 8 hours for 7 days. Treatment of disseminated infections including encephalitis is with 10 mg/kg intravenously every 8 hours for 10 days.

Trifluridine. In the treatment of herpes keratitis, trifluridine appears more effective than vidarabine. The dosage is one drop of a 1% solution every 2 hours while awake. These patients should be under the supervision of an ophthalmologist because of the risk of blindness.

Vidarabine. Vidarabine has displayed efficacy in the treatment of herpes infections, but it is less versatile and more toxic that acyclovir. Uses of vidarabine include topical application in herpes keratitis and intravenous administration in neonatal herpes infections and adult encephalitis. For the latter indication it is a drug of second choice. Its side effects are tremor, paresthesias, ataxia, and occasionally seizures.

Recommended Approach

Antiviral medications have most benefit in primary mucocutaneous disease. I do not recommend their use for recurrent disease except as suppressive therapy as outlined above. Topical therapy is expensive and is less effective than systemic therapy. If treatment is indicated then we recommend oral rather than topical therapy.

FOLLOW-UP

No specific follow-up for uncomplicated oral or genital herpes is necessary once an accurate diagnosis is established. For severe primary infections not requiring hospitalization, patients should be seen every 3 days. The advancement or regression of lesions and change in local adenopathy should be noted. In women, the cervix should be visualized and lesions noted on each visit.

DISCUSSION

Prevalence and Incidence

The herpesvirus family is one that has remarkable distribution through human populations. Infection by at least one of the family is likely by adulthood. Spread is probably through infected secretions.

The seroprevalence of HSV 1 varies by geography and socioeconomic class and ranges from 50 to 100% in adult populations (Peterslund, 1991). Almost all children from lower socioeconomic classes are seropositive by puberty. There is some evidence to suggest that seropositivity to HSV 1 may mitigate primary infection with HSV 2.

Seroprevalence of HSV 2 has greater variability and depends on age, race, geography, and socioeconomic class, but primarily sexual activity. Thus seroprevalence rates range from 5 to 90% with 30% as a rough mean (Mertz, 1993; Peterslund, 1991).

Twenty to 40% of the population suffers from recurrent labial herpes. For HSV 2, 60 to 90% of those who actually experienced a first episode of genital herpes suffer recurrences. Recall, however, that infection is asymptomatic in most patients, anywhere from 50 to 90% (Mertz, 1993).

Other herpes infections are uncommon. Roughly 5% of patients attending eye clinics have herpes keratitis. Of these, 25 to 50% have recurrences within 1 year. Neonatal herpes occurs in one in 2000 to 10,000 live births. Herpes encephalitis occurs in between one in 250,000 and 500,000 persons per year (Hirsch, 1995).

Human herpesvirus 6 is even more prevalent than the herpes simplex viruses. One hundred percent of children are seropositive by the age of 3. This number drops to 60% by adulthood presumably because of waning antibody (Rathmore, 1993; Oren, 1992).

Related Basic Science

The major mode of spread is by direct contact with lesions shedding virus or with virus-containing secretions. At least half of those infected have subclinical illness, yet will shed virus that can infect others.

The herpes simplex viruses themselves have three common characteristics. First, after initial infection of superficial tissues, they travel through peripheral sensory nerves and enter sensory or autonomic root ganglia. Second, once in the ganglia, they establish latency by integrating into host DNA, with cessation of expression of functional proteins. Third, after stimuli or spontaneously, the virus may reactivate, begin replication, and produce clinical recrudescence.

Factors known to trigger reactivation include physical stimuli such as sunlight, cold, febrile illnesses, intercourse, menses, and emotional stresses. Often, however, no stimuli for reactivation can be identified. Exogenous reinfection likely occurs.

Natural History and Its Modification with Treatment

Herpes infections are most often asymptomatic. Latency is another of their characteristics. For otherwise healthy patients who do experience illness, it is usually a self-limited illness with an average duration of 10 to 14 days. Recurrences are generally less severe than primary infections. Treatment with acyclovir shortens the duration of illness, decrease symptoms, and decreases viral shedding.

Prevention

The avoidance of kissing or touching oral lesions or of sexual activity when genital lesions are present is the simplest and most effective preventive measure. In the absence of lesions, routine condom use during vaginal or anal incourse should be encouraged. Medical and dental personnel should wear gloves when touching potentially infectious lesions. Hospitalized patients with widespread infections should be isolated. Nursery personnel with active oral or hand infections should take special precautions when handling infants. Those with active genital lesions should practice rigorous handwashing.

The prevention of herpesvirus infection in the newborn is controversial. A prudent course at this time is to recommend cesarean section for women with genital lesions at delivery if the fetal membranes are intact. If the membranes are ruptured there are no convincing data that cesarean section is superior to vaginal delivery in preventing infection.

Cost Containment

Viral cultures are expensive. Their use in the diagnosis of herpesvirus infections should be limited to the following: patients with primary infections or atypical presentations; pregnant women suspected of having herpetic infections, particularly in the third trimester; infants with suspicious lesions born to these women; patients with suspected ocular infections; immunocompromised patients with suspected disseminated disease; and patients with encephalitis from whom biopsy material has been obtained. Serologic tests are rarely helpful in the diagnosis of herpesvirus infection, and their use as a screening tool should not occur outside the transplant setting.

REFERENCES

Corey L. Genital herpes. In: Holmes KK, Mardh PA, Sparling PF, eds. Sexually transmitted diseases. 2nd ed. New York: McGraw-Hill, 1990:391.

Hirsch MS. Herpes simplex virus. In: Mandell GL, Bennett JE, Dolin R, eds. Principles and practice of infectious diseases. 4th ed. New York: Churchill Livingstone, 1995.

Lafferty WE. Recurrences after oral and genital herpes simplex virus infections: Influence of anatomic site and viral type. N Engl J Med 1987;316:1444.

Mertz GJ. Epidemiology of genital herpes infections. Infect Dis Clin North Am 1993;7:825.

Peterslund N. Herpes virus infections: An overview of the clinical manifestations. Scand J Infect 1991 (suppl. 78):15.

Rathmore M. Human herpes virus 6. South Med J 1993;86:1187.

Oren D. Sobel J. Human herpesvirus 6: Review. Clin Dermatol 1992;14:741.

Straus SE, Takiff HE, Seidlin M, et al. Suppression of frequently recurring genital herpes: A placebo-controlled trial of oral acyclovir. N Engl J Med 1984;310:1545.

CHAPTER 8–71

Cytomegalovirus Infection

Richard L. Hengel, M.D., and Carl A. Perlino, M.D.

DEFINITION

Cytomegalovirus infection is defined as infection with cytomegalovirus, a member of the herpesvirus family.

ETIOLOGY

Cytomegalovirus is a ubiquitous viral organism with widespread distribution in humans. It causes disease in only a minority of normal hosts, but is an important pathogen in immunocompromised individuals.

CRITERIA FOR DIAGNOSIS

Suggestive

In the majority of individuals, infection with cytomegalovirus is asymptomatic and remains undiagnosed during the lifetime of the patient. Most primary infections occur in utero, in the neonate, during early childhood, or during early adulthood concomitant with the onset of sexual activity. Like other members of the herpesvirus group, cytomegalovirus leads to an asymptomatic chronic infection. In certain situations, however, such as multiple blood transfusions, organ transplantation, AIDS, other immunosuppressive states, or occasionally in the normal host, an initial cytomegalovirus infection or reactivation of latent virus may lead to clinical illness.

In the normal host, a mononucleosis illness with a negative heterophil antibody should make one think of cytomegalovirus disease. In the immunocompromised patient, the virus can result in a wide variety of signs and symptoms, and the reader is referred to Clinical Manifestations for diagnostic clues.

Definitive

The diagnosis of cytomegalovirus infection can be made serologically, by demonstrating virus in culture, or indirectly from cytologic changes. The presence of antibody or positive viral cultures, however, may be seen in the absence of overt disease. In the appropriate clinical setting involving an ill patient, disease due to primary infection is suggested by a fourfold rise in titer of specific antibody or by finding typical intranuclear inclusions in tissue obtained by biopsy or at autopsy. Additionally, monoclonal antibodies to specific cytomegalovirus antigens have proven to be a useful adjunct to diagnosis, particularly in histologic diagnosis from involved organ sites such as lung or gastrointestinal tract biopsy material. It is important to remember that infection does not necessarily imply disease, but does result in seroconversion.

CLINICAL MANIFESTATIONS

The clinical manifestations of cytomegalovirus infection vary widely from inapparent infection to widespread disease involving all tissues. It is helpful to group the various clinical syndromes according to the epidemiology associated with the illness: infections occurring congenitally, in neonates, and in children; infections in normal adolescents and adults; and infections in the immunocompromised patient. This chapter addresses primarily the latter two groups.

Subjective

The most common illness caused by cytomegalovirus in normal teenagers and young adults is cytomegalovirus mononucleosis. There is rarely a history, but sexual contact is presumably the major mode of transmission in this age group. Occasionally, a history of recent blood transfusions may be present, indicating infection may have been transmitted by this route.

Fever is the most common complaint and may be protracted in some individuals. Fever also may be the only complaint. General malaise, anorexia, weight loss, chills, and myalgias are common. Less often, symptoms of sore throat, adenopathy, cough, or severe, cramping abdominal pain occur. Rarely, the Guillain–Barré syndrome or encephalitis with symptoms of headache, confusion, and seizures may be seen in the normal adult.

Immunocompromised patients such as organ or bone marrow transplant recipients and patients with AIDS are at risk for disease due to cytomegalovirus infection. In these patients, a febrile illness may occur that is similar to cytomegalovirus mononucleosis in the normal host; however, symptoms of specific organ system involvement are more likely to occur in the immunocompromised patient. Cytomegalovirus pneumonia, occurring alone or in conjunction with pneumonia due to *Pneumocystis carinii,* is a particularly common problem in these patients, although it is more of a problem in the transplant patient than the AIDS patient. Dyspnea and a nonproductive, hacking cough indicate pulmonary involvement. Cytomegalovirus retinitis leading to a painless, progressive loss of vision is particularly a problem in the late stages of AIDS. Also seen in these patients is cytomegalovirus involving the gastrointestinal tract, which presents with variable symptoms depending on the specific location of the lesions, ranging from odynophagia, to severe abdominal pain with nausea or vomiting, to gastrointestinal bleeding, to symptoms of colitis with diarrhea with or without bleeding. Symptoms of Addison's disease (orthostatic dizziness, nausea, vomiting, lethargy, and fever) indicating cytomegalovirus adrenalitis may occur.

Objective

Physical Examination

Fever is the most common physical finding in the immunocompetent patient with cytomegalovirus infection, and the patient may appear otherwise normal. In contrast to patients with the mononucleosis syndrome due to Epstein–Barr virus, patients with cytomegalovirus mononucleosis are less likely to have purulent pharyngitis, although slight pharyngeal erythema may be present. Lymphadenopathy, detected primarily in the cervical region, and splenomegaly may be present. Hepatomegaly is uncommon, even in patients with abnormal liver enzyme levels.

Routine Laboratory Abnormalities

Patients with cytomegalovirus mononucleosis often lack atypical lymphocytosis early in the illness, but usually develop an absolute lymphocytosis with atypical lymphocytes after the second week of illness. Hepatic enzyme levels are abnormal in most patients. Heterophile antibodies are not detected, but spuriously abnormal cold agglutinins or cryoglobulins may be present.

Occasionally, roentgenographic evidence of an interstitial pneumonia may develop in patients with cytomegalovirus mononucleosis. Laboratory abnormalities compatible with a granulomatous hepatitis, a myocarditis with abnormalities in the electrocardiogram, a hemolytic anemia, or thrombocytopenia may occur with cytomegalovirus mononucleosis or may be the only laboratory abnormality indicative of cytomegalovirus infection.

The spinal fluid in patients with clinical signs of encephalitis is characterized by a normal or elevated leukocyte count composed mostly of mononuclear cells. A mildly elevated protein level and, occasionally, hypoglycorrhachia are present. The electroencephalogram is diffusely abnormal or shows temporal lobe localization.

Although most patients with acquired adult cytomegalovirus infection have limited signs of infection, immunocompromised patients often have evidence of transplant rejection. In addition, hypoxemia, an abnormal chest roentgenogram, anemia, leukopenia, thrombocytopenia, abnormal liver enzyme levels, gastrointestinal ulcerations, adrenal involvement, and jaundice are seen in the more severe cases. Retinitis may be present, and exudative changes with hemorrhage are quite characteristic, primarily in patients with AIDS.

PLANS

Diagnostic

Differential Diagnosis

In the normal host, cytomegalovirus infection is usually asymptomatic. When symptomatic, it manifests as mononucleosis and is difficult to distinguish from Epstein–Barr virus mononucleosis. Acute HIV infection is another possibility. Although other acute viral syndromes may share features of mononucleosis, their spectrum of clinical manifesta-

tions should be sufficiently different as to distinguish them. Specifically, severe pharyngitis and abrupt onset of toxic symptoms favor the diagnosis of mononucleosis syndrome. Nonviral causes of a similar illness include streptococcal pharyngitis and acute toxoplasmosis.

In the immunocompromised individual the differential diagnosis depends on the specific organ system involved and the epidemiology of that specific patient group.

Diagnostic Options

Various serologic tests are available for the diagnosis of cytomegalovirus infection in patients with acquired infection: indirect hemagglutination, latex agglutination, complement fixation, indirect fluorescent antibody, anticomplement immunofluorescent antibody, radioimmunoassay, and enzyme-linked immunosorbent assay have all been used. A fourfold rise in the immunoglobulin (Ig) G antibody titer measured by these tests is indicative of infection. A high titer of IgM antibody is helpful in the diagnosis of acute infection, except perhaps in the case of homosexual men who may have persistent elevations of IgM.

The diagnosis of disease in the immunocompromised patient may be more difficult, as levels of antibody in patients chronically infected may vary spontaneously and may not correlate with disease or positive cultures. The issue is confused further by the fact that certain patients, such as renal transplant recipients, may excrete virus in the urine with a frequency approaching 90%. Viremia also may be detected without evidence of disease. Homosexual men with AIDS in particular seem to shed the virus with great frequency without necessarily any evidence of disease. Although not 100% specific, the diagnosis of invasive cytomegalic disease in immunocompromised patients is best made by cytologic examination of tissue in conjunction with either serologic, culture, or antigenic evidence of cytomegalovirus. Monoclonal antibodies have improved the sensitivity and specificity of tissue diagnosis.

Recommended Approach

For the normal adult a heterophile-negative mononucleosis illness is usually resolved or resolving by the time a paired serum sample for cytomegalovirus IgG would be available to confirm a fourfold rise in antibody titer. IgM titers may be helpful in these circumstances but may be nonspecific in certain patient groups. In the case of AIDS patients, a presumptive diagnosis is usually made in the case of typical findings of cytomegalovirus retinitis. Similarly, evidence of adrenal suppression and cytomegalovirus viremia would be sufficient to establish the presumptive diagnosis of adrenalitis. The diagnosis of cytomegalovirus pneumonia in AIDS patients requires histologic confirmation from tissue. On the other hand, in the case of transplant patients, typical cytology from bronchoalveolar lavage fluid suffices. Finally, in cases of suspected gastrointestinal involvement, biopsy is of primary importance in distinguishing cytomegalovirus from other pathologic entities.

Therapeutic

Therapeutic Options

Ganciclovir and foscarnet are the two agents recognized to be most efficacious in the treatment of cytomegalovirus-related disease. Ganciclovir is generally begun at a dose of 5 mg/kg twice daily for a period of 14 days. In AIDS patients with cytomegalovirus retinitis, this is followed by maintenance of 6 mg/kg daily for 5 days per week. The major side effects to watch for are bone marrow toxicity (especially neutropenia and thrombocytopenia in patients with diminished reserves or on other agents with similar toxicity), nausea, vomiting, and, less commonly, phlebitis, disorientation, psychosis, and hepatitis.

Foscarnet is administered at a dose of 60 mg/kg every 8 hours for a period of 14 days followed by maintenance of 120 mg/kg daily when indicated. The main toxic effects of foscarnet are renal: azotemia and electrolyte disturbances are most prominent, and may be prevented, at least in part, by adequate saline infusion prior to administration. Other possible toxic effects include anemia, phlebitis, nausea, and tremors.

Recommended Approach

No intervention is advocated for the normal host with limited symptomatic disease. Therapy is usually initiated for immunocompromised individuals and depends on the epidemiologic group and organ system involved.

In the case of cytomegalovirus retinitis in AIDS, treatment is life-long. The approach for other organ systems and other patient populations is not as clear-cut, and consultation with an infectious disease specialist is recommended. For example, there is probably a role for therapy in cytomegalovirus disease of the gastrointestinal tract, but life-long treatment is probably not warranted. Pneumonia is less responsive to antiviral agents alone, but combination therapy with cytomegalovirus hyperimmune globulin is beneficial, especially in the transplant population. Again, a finite period of therapy such as 2 weeks is probably indicated, but vigilance must be maintained to rule out recrudescent disease.

FOLLOW-UP

Patients with cytomegalovirus mononucleosis are usually cared for in an office setting. Like heterophile-positive Epstein–Barr virus mononucleosis, cytomegalovirus mononucleosis may have a protracted course, with symptoms lasting weeks to months. The acute symptoms and laboratory abnormalities, such as abnormal liver enzyme levels, may resolve, only to be followed by a period of nonspecific malaise and asthenia. How often a patient is seen is determined by the possible need for acute intervention to asses the course of new symptoms and to document clearing of abnormal findings.

The follow-up of immunocompromised patients depends on their underlying disease and prognosis. Most patients remain at risk for either ongoing or recurrent disease for the period they are immunocompromised, and follow-up should be planned accordingly. Patients receiving treatment for retinitis need frequent eye examinations by an ophthalmologist to ensure the disease is not progressing despite therapy.

DISCUSSION
Prevalence and Incidence

Seroprevalence of antibody to cytomegalovirus varies from 40 to 100% depending on geography, socioeconomic class, and other variables such as number of sexual partners.

As many as 2% of all newborn infants may have serologic evidence of intrauterine infection, whereas only 10% of newborn infants have clinically apparent disease.

Related Basic Science

The cytomegalovirus is a ubiquitous agent that can cause primary infection at any time of life, but most commonly in childhood or young adulthood. Infection with this agent is not synonymous with illness, however. Furthermore, because the virus persists subclinically in leukocytes and other tissues and is controlled by adequate host immunity, interruption of normal immunity by concomitant illness or therapy may lead to subsequent virologic and clinical evidence of viral replication and tissue invasion.

Several sources of infection and methods of transmission have been defined. Transplacental transfer during intrauterine gestation or at delivery from an infected mother shedding virus from the uterine cervix is a common source. Primary maternal infection leading to congenital infection results in more severe disease than does congenital infection from a mother with evidence of prior infection with cytomegalovirus. The same is true of perinatal infection, although in both cases the neonate seems to be affected less than the fetus. Transfer of maternal antibody presumably has a protective effect on both the fetus and neonate. Other sources of virus early in life appear to be breast milk and, possibly, shared secretions among children, as may happen at day-care centers. Adults do not appear, to any significant degree, to spread cytomegalovirus to children in this manner.

Seroconversion may follow blood transfusion, indicating primary infection by this route, and leads to the clinical syndrome of posttransfu-

sion mononucleosis in some patients. The risk of infection is greater when larger volumes of blood are transfused. Venereal transmission of cytomegalovirus is thought to occur by infection or colonization and subsequent shedding at the uterine cervix and in semen.

Despite the fact that severe disease due to cytomegalovirus is more likely to occur in individuals with severe primary or secondary defects in immunity, the role of specific host defenses in controlling infection is not clear. Evidence for ongoing infection, such as renal excretion of the virus, continues despite apparently high levels of antibody. It appears that factors affecting cell-mediated immunity play a central role in predisposing patients to severe infection and illness.

Natural History and Its Modification with Treatment

Asymptomatic infection is most common. When symptomatic, normal adults infected with cytomegalovirus most often experience a self-limited disease with excellent prospects of full recovery. Infections such as cytomegalovirus mononucleosis may run a protracted course, however. In contrast to infections in normal patients, infections in immunocompromised patients often may be progressive, even leading to death. Alternatively, the patient may die of unrelated causes with ongoing evidence of chronic cytomegalovirus disease.

The effectiveness of treatment depends on the organ system involved. For example, the course of cytomegalovirus retinitis is only slowed with treatment, and progression still occurs. The response of gastrointestinal and pulmonary infections is more variable, and may depend more on underlying host factors.

Prevention

Despite its ubiquity and the high degree of seropositivity in most populations, there may be opportunities for prevention or prophylaxis. Prophylaxis of at-risk populations remains the topic of ongoing research, and vaccines or passive immunotherapy may prove to be effective methods of prevention.

The transplantation of organs from a donor with serologic evidence of prior cytomegalovirus infection to a seronegative recipient, or transfusion of blood from a cytomegalovirus-positive donor to a cytomegalovirus-negative recipient may lead to primary infection in the recipient. Screening of donors for serologic evidence of prior cytomegalovirus infection is appropriate.

High-dose acyclovir has been shown to prevent symptomatic cytomegalovirus infection in kidney and bone marrow transplant recipients. As acyclovir has poor in vitro activity against cytomegalovirus, this finding is not explained. Similarly, ganciclovir prophylaxis has been shown to be beneficial in the solid organ and bone marrow transplant setting. There appears to be benefit from prophylaxis with cytomegalovirus hyperimmune globulin in transplant patients.

Cost Containment

Knowledge of the limitations of investigations help eliminate unnecessary costs. The lack of specificity of serology in most circumstances is an example. Comfort with making a clinical diagnosis, such as in the case of cytomegalovirus retinitis, also saves money by eliminating unnecessary investigations.

REFERENCES

Balfour HH Jr. Management of cytomegalovirus disease with antiviral drugs. Rev Infect Dis 1990;12(suppl. 7): S849.
Drew WL. Cytomegalovirus infection in patients with AIDS. Clin Infect Dis 1992;14:608.
Ho M. Epidemiology of cytomegalovirus infections. Rev Infect Dis 1990;12(suppl. 7):S701.
Osborn JE. Cytomegalovirus: Pathogenicity, immunology and vaccine initiatives. J Infect Dis 1981;143:618.
Smith MA, Brennessel DJ. Cytomegalovirus. Infect Dis Clin North Am 1994;8:427.

CHAPTER 8–72

Infectious Mononucleosis

Carlos del Rio, M.D., Stephen W. Schwarzmann, M.D., and Charles M. Huguley, Jr., M.D.

DEFINITION

Infectious mononucleosis is a febrile illness associated with malaise, sore throat, and lymphadenopathy due, in most cases, to primary infection with Epstein–Barr virus (EBV).

ETIOLOGY

Epstein–Barr virus is the etiologic agent of heterophile-positive infectious mononucleosis; however, EBV may also be the cause of heterophile-negative infectious mononucleosis. In addition, cytomegalovirus, *Toxoplasma gondii,* and acute HIV infection need to be considered.

CRITERIA FOR DIAGNOSIS

Suggestive

The classic clinical form of infectious mononucleosis usually occurs in adolescence or early adulthood. In this age group the onset of illness may be gradual, with a 1- to 2-week prodrome of malaise, fatigue, and lymphadenopathy. The clinical triad of sore throat, fever, and lymphadenopathy in an otherwise healthy young adult should make the physician suspect the diagnosis. In younger children, infectious mononucleosis may present as it does in adolescence, but mild or asymptomatic infection is more common.

Skin rashes, failure to thrive, periorbital and palpebral edema, otitis media, significant airway obstruction, pneumonia, and neurologic manifestations including seizures and meningoencephalitis are seen rarely in childhood infection. In adults, particularly those over age 40, lymphadenopathy and sore throat are less frequent, with fever and malaise as the major presenting complaints. Patients with infectious mononucleosis who receive ampicillin frequently develop a pruritic rash, which should make the physician suspect the diagnosis.

The expanded spectrum of EBV infection is just now being recognized; many persons with primary EBV infection, especially children, are asymptomatic or only mildly symptomatic. In others, the disease can be severe, associated with major complications or even death. Overwhelming EBV infection has been described in patients with the X-linked combined variable immunodeficiency (Duncan's disease).

Definitive

In the adolescent, the combination of malaise, fever, exudative pharyngitis, and lymphadenopathy associated with an absolute lymphocytosis (more than 50% lymphocytes, many of which are atypical [10% or more of the total lymphocytes are atypical]) plus a positive "mono-spot" test establishes the diagnosis of infectious mononucleosis. Not all of these findings are present in a significant number of patients, however, and the diagnosis of infectious mononucleosis can be made only by serologic means, by detection of specific antibodies against EBV (Table 8–72–1).

CLINICAL MANIFESTATIONS

Subjective

Infection is spread by intimate contact, usually salivary. The disease often begins with a prodrome of malaise, fatigue, and anorexia that may last 1 to 2 weeks. This is followed by fever, which may be quite high and associated with chills, and a sore throat that can preclude swallowing. Some patients complain of headache, myalgias, nausea, and abdominal discomfort; others may have symptoms of cardiac or neurologic disease, signifying EBV infection at these sites. In some cases, the initial manifestation of infectious mononucleosis is a complication of the disease such as hemolytic anemia, encephalitis, or another neurologic manifestation.

Objective

Physical Examination

The patient with infectious mononucleosis typically appears ill. Malaise and fatigue are obvious. Fever may be higher than 40°C, with an accordingly rapid pulse rate. A fine, generalized, maculopapular erythematous rash is seen in 3 to 10% of patients, and, although uncommon, jaundice may be present (Hoagland, 1952). Petechiae at the junction of the hard and soft palate is a helpful clue. More importantly, the throat shows lymphoid hyperplasia, with the tonsils occasionally enlarging to the point of touching. There is marked erythema with exudate, not unlike that seen with an acute streptococcal pharyngitis.

Rarely, a pseudomembrane can result in respiratory distress. Lymphadenopathy occurs in 95% of patients but may be absent in those over 40 years of age (Hoagland, 1952). The lymph nodes in the anterior and posterior cervical chains are most often involved, but generalized lymphadenopathy is also common. The nodes are firm, discrete, not matted, commonly tender, and usually movable. Splenomegaly is seen in half of these patients. The spleen is characteristically soft and difficult to palpate; however, aggressive palpation of the spleen must be avoided for fear of rupture. Although liver enzyme levels are elevated in more than 90% of patients, the liver is enlarged in only about 10% of patients (Hoagland, 1952). Jaundice is uncommon and may be seen in 5 to 10% of patients, and may result from liver involvement and/or acute hemolysis (Hoagland, 1952). Among the relatively rare complications of this exceedingly common illness are Guillain–Barré syndrome, encephalitis, splenic rupture (0.2–0.5%), thrombocytopenia, and an autoimmune hemolytic anemia (3%) (Hoagland, 1952).

Hematologic features suggestive of the diagnosis are present in most cases. In classic cases, the white cell count shows more than 50% lymphocytes and monocytes, with more than 10% "atypical" lymphocytes present in more than 20% of patients. When a hematologist uses the term *atypical lymphocyte,* it most likely indicates the abnormal cells of infectious mononucleosis or cells resembling them. These abnormal lymphocytes are atypical in a characteristic manner: they are large; the

TABLE 8–72–1. EPSTEIN–BARR VIRUS SEROLOGY AND DETECTION OF PATIENT SUSCEPTIBILITY, PRIOR INFECTION, AND CHANGES IN ACUTE RECENT INFECTION

Serology	Susceptibility	Acute Infection	Prior Infection
VCA-IgM	Negative	Positive*	Negative
VCA-IgG	Negative	Positive†	Positive
EA-D	Negative	Variable‡	Variable
EA-R	Negative	Rarely positive§	Variable
EBNA	Negative	Negative‖	Positive
Heterophile or "mono-spot" test	Negative	Positive ¶	Negative

VCA, viral capsid antigen; Ig, immunoglobulin; EA-D, diffuse component of early antigen; EA-R, restricted component of early antigen; EBNA, Epstein–Barr virus determined nuclear antibody.

*VCA-IgM becomes positive 1 to 3 weeks after infection and lasts only 4 to 8 weeks.

†VCA-IgG becomes positive 1 to 3 weeks after infection and lasts for life.

‡EA-D appears in many patients usually 3 to 4 weeks after infection and lasts 3 to 6 months and may reappear intermittently.

§EA-R appears in a small number of patients, generally weeks to months after infection, and may last months or years.

‖EBNA is usually not present early in the illness; it appears 4 to 8 weeks after acute infection and lasts for life. An EBNA that goes from negative to positive is very strong evidence that the patient had an infection in the prior few months.

¶Heterophile or "mono-spot" test is seen with acute infection after 1 to 2 weeks in about 90% of cases. It may be elevated for 3 to 6 months and occasionally longer.

nuclei are large, often lobulated, indented, or cleaved, and frequently contain nucleoli; the cytoplasm may be basophilic and is characteristically vacuolated or foamy. These cells are derived from the T-cell line and are therefore not infected with EBV, which infects B cells.

Routine Laboratory Abnormalities

During the first week of illness the white blood cell count is usually normal, but leukopenia may occasionally be present. After the first week, significant leukocytosis is common (10,000–25,000 cells/μL). Platelet and red blood cell counts are usually normal. These are reassuring findings in a disease that may at times mimic an acute leukemia.

Abnormalities in serum liver enzymes, especially the transaminases, occur in more than 90% of patients; in fact, one should doubt the diagnosis of EBV infectious mononucleosis if the patient has normal transaminase levels. Bilirubin is mildly elevated in about 10% of cases but is very rarely above 8 mg/dL.

PLANS
Diagnostic
Differential Diagnosis

The presence of jaundice may lead one to confuse infectious mononucleosis with infectious hepatitis. The typical mononuclear cells (atypical lymphocytes) may occur in infectious hepatitis, but they are less consistently seen and are usually less than 10% of the differential. Rubella virus, adenovirus, and other viral infections may also cause the presence of a few "atypical" lymphocytes in the peripheral blood smear. Appropriate serologic testing can help identify each of these illnesses.

Diagnostic Options and Recommended Approach

The diagnosis of infectious mononucleosis rests on serologic testing. The heterophile antibody is present in more than 90% of clinically typical patients if they are followed long enough. The heterophile antibody is usually present at the end of the first week of illness, peaks at 2 to 3 weeks, and persists for 4 to 8 weeks, although it may be detected for 18 months or longer. The heterophile antibody or "mono-spot" test is seen in acute infection after 1 to 2 weeks in about 90% of cases. It may be elevated for 3 to 6 months and occasionally longer. The heterophile antibody test is an assay for nonspecific immunoglobulin (Ig) M agglutinins, which react with sheep, horse, or beef red cells but not with guinea pig kidney cells. Somewhat similar antibodies may also be present in serum sickness. In infectious mononucleosis, the titer does not drop after absorption with guinea pig kidney (usually no more than one tube), whereas in serum sickness or normal serum, the antibodies are completely absorbed. The infectious mononucleosis sheep cell agglutinins are completely absorbed by beef red cells. A more specific and more sensitive test that does not require absorption uses beef red cells. A titer of 1:40 or greater in either test is diagnostic. A rapid, sensitive, and reliable procedure in general use is the "mono-spot" test, which uses agglutination of horse red cells and absorption with fine suspensions of guinea pig kidney and beef red cell stroma. In addition to the heterophile antibody, infection results in antibodies detected by indirect immunofluorescence against antigenic components of EBV. Thus, antibody developing against the viral capsid antigen; the early antigen which is divided into the diffuse component and the restricted component; and the EBV-determined nuclear antigen offers additional information relating to the diagnosis of infectious mononucleosis which can be useful for the diagnosis of heterophile-negative or atypical cases (Table 8–72–1). In acute infectious mononucleosis the heterophile antibody test becomes positive first, usually by the time of initial presentation. The viral capsid antigen IgM, quickly followed by diffuse early antigen, occurs next, with viral capsid antigen IgG appearing very slightly later. The presence of IgM viral capsid antigen antibodies is diagnostic of acute EBV infection. Appearance of EBV-determined nuclear antigen occurs last, possibly as a result of the later release of EBV nuclear antigen by T cell-mediated cytolysis; it represents a successful immune response and the advent of convalescence. IgG viral capsid antigen and anti-EBV-determined nuclear antigen antibodies remain

positive for life. Antibody to the diffuse component of the early antigen appears transiently during the acute phase of infectious mononucleosis and is correlated with severe disease. Persistence of this antibody may be seen in patients with nasopharyngeal carcinoma. Antibodies against the restricted component of the early antigen are rarely seen in infectious mononucleosis and appear more frequently in pediatric primary infection, in epidemic Burkitt's lymphoma, and in some immunodeficiency syndromes such as AIDS.

If hemolytic anemia occurs, it is often due to a cold hemolysin with anti-"i" specificity. Other antibodies may also be found, especially antiplatelet antibody, leading to immune thrombocytopenia. A throat culture should be obtained not only to complete the differential diagnosis, but also because *Streptococcus pyogenes* is often concomitantly present with infectious mononucleosis. Because of the complications associated with group A streptococcal throat infection, this infection should be treated promptly, but not with a penicillin antibiotic, because the addition of a penicillin, especially ampicillin, carries a 60 to 80% risk of a diffuse skin rash, usually appearing approximately 1 week after the first dose of the antibiotic. This does not appear to be a true allergic reaction, and penicillins can be used if clearly needed in the future.

The most frequent cause of heterophile-negative infectious mononucleosis is acute cytomegalovirus infection. Following a blood transfusion, a heterophile-negative infectious mononucleosis may be due to cytomegalovirus or to HIV, as well as to EBV. Sore throat and generalized lymphadenopathy may be absent in some of these cases. The diagnosis of cytomegalovirus or HIV mononucleosis is usually made by serologic testing, virus isolation, or antigen detection. Toxoplasmosis rarely resembles mononucleosis, and serologic tests will allow diagnosis, especially if *Toxoplasma* IgM antibody is elevated.

Therapeutic

There is no specific therapy for infectious mononucleosis and care is largely supportive. Because of the patient's malaise and fatigue, activity should be limited to what the patient can tolerate comfortably; however, contact sports should be avoided, especially if splenomegaly is present, to prevent the possibility of splenic rupture. Corticosteroid administration may lead to symptomatic improvement, but it should be recommended only in the presence of respiratory obstruction, severe central nervous system involvement, marked thrombocytopenia, or hemolytic anemia. In these situations, prednisone is given in doses of 40 to 60 mg daily for a limited period. Prednisone is also used, at a dose of 40 mg daily, to reduce the toxicity that can be seen in some very severe cases, but the routine use of corticosteroids for mononucleosis is definitely not warranted. The use of acyclovir (Zovirax) in the treatment of infectious mononucleosis has been studied in several clinical trials. The findings showed that acyclovir did inhibit oropharyngeal shedding of EBV, but had only minimal effect on the course of the disease; thus, acyclovir is not recommended in cases of infectious mononucleosis. In nearly all instances, the patient shows an uncomplicated improvement and needs mainly rest, antipyretics, and adequate fluids until the disease remits.

Infectious mononucleosis is common and generally self-limited. The patient must be alerted to the likely possibility of a relatively prolonged period of asthenia after recovery from the acute phase of the illness. This may continue for weeks, if not months. Contact sports in which potential injury to the spleen may occur should be avoided well into convalescence, at least until the spleen is no longer palpable. Some authorities suggest that participation in contact sports be excluded for 2 to 3 months. No specific isolation precautions are required except for mouth-to-mouth contact, which should be avoided during acute infection. The virus is transmitted by saliva and may be found in saliva 18 months after acute infection. It can also be isolated from throat washings in 10 to 20% of healthy adults and in up to 50% of severely immunocompromised hosts. It is so prevalent that nearly everyone will be infected with EBV at some time during their lives.

FOLLOW-UP

The need for follow-up relates to complications of the infection and to the host in which the infection occurs. In the previously healthy adolescent or young adult who has recovered, no long-term follow-up is required.

DISCUSSION

Prevalence and Incidence

Infection with EBV is almost universal, and by adulthood, close to 100% of the population has serologic evidence of past infection. Primary EBV infection occurs at an earlier age in developing countries and among lower socioeconomic groups. Children living in developing nations are usually infected with EBV by age 5, but in the United States primary infection is often delayed until adolescence. The incidence of infectious mononucleosis in the United States is about 50 cases per 100,000 per year. The peak incidence is among those who are 15 to 24 years old.

Related Basic Science

Epstein-Barr virus has been established as the cause of heterophile-positive infectious mononucleosis. EBV is a herpesvirus originally isolated from a cell line derived from Burkitt's lymphoma. The organism infects B lymphocytes, which, once infected, grow continuously in vitro, an event that has been called *immortalization* or *transformation*. The EBV receptor has been identified as the receptor for the d region of the third component of complement (C3d), which is also known as CD21. Once EBV infects B lymphocytes in vivo, the virus may establish a latent infection in which small numbers of nonproductive, circular, episomal viral genomes are present, or, in other cells, the virus reproduces in the cell, releasing mature virions. There is a polyclonal T-cell response to the infected B cell. The "infectious mononucleosis cells" in the blood are T cells. The severe pharyngitis results from the attack of infected B cells by cytotoxic T cells in tonsillar tissue. Transmission of the virus is primarily through saliva, although some cases have been transmitted by blood transfusion. In underdeveloped countries, the majority of the population is seropositive by age 4 to 5. In the United States, infection is not uncommonly delayed to adolescence and adulthood. The infection in children may be quite mild, but in adolescence about two thirds of recently infected patients are symptomatic. Once infection has been acquired, the virus remains in the host for life. Shedding of the virus in throat washings may recur intermittently, with about 10 to 20% of the normal, previously infected population being positive at any given time. For this reason, culture of throat washings for EBV does not establish a diagnosis of acute EBV mononucleosis. The incubation period is estimated to be 4 to 7 weeks.

Infection in immunocompromised patients, particularly in patients with AIDS and those who have had organ transplants, has been associated with an increase in the frequency of EBV-associated diseases. Infection with EBV in hereditary X-linked lymphoproliferative syndrome in males has been associated with severe or fatal infectious mononucleosis. It has been suggested that the underlying disease allows unregulated cytotoxic lymphocytic responses to EBV syndrome. Furthermore, T-cell suppression of B cells in these hosts may result in acquired hypogammaglobulinemia and a sustained polyclonal B-cell lymphoma. Lymphoproliferative disorders have also been associated with EBV in organ transplant recipients and in patients with severe immunosuppression such as AIDS. In HIV infection EBV has been associated with an interstitial lymphoid pneumonia that may occur rarely in the lungs of some children; oral hairy leukoplakia is also associated with EBV in HIV infection. The EBV genome has also been found in Reed–Sternberg cells of some patients with Hodgkin's disease and in the bone marrow of some patients with aplastic anemia. The virus has been shown to be the cause of Burkitt's lymphoma in Africa. Cofactors, for example, malaria, may be important in the ability of EBV to cause this lymphoma. In Southeast Asia, EBV appears to have a role in the development of nasopharyngeal carcinoma in middle-aged and elderly men. In this setting, there appear to be increased levels of IgA antibodies against viral capsid antigen and diffuse early antigen. Thus, environmental and/or genetic factors may play a role in the pathogenesis of EBV-associated neoplasias.

Many of the complications of infectious mononucleosis in normal hosts appear to be related to autoimmune factors. Thus, the neutropenia, thrombocytopenia, aplastic anemia, erythrophagocytic syndromes, arthritis, and neurologic disorders that occur either during acute illness or as a postinfectious complication may be a reflection of virus-induced activation of immunologically "silent" B-cell clones or of the later appearance of antibodies to antigenic epitopes shared both by virus and host proteins.

Natural History and Its Modification with Treatment

The essential clinical features of infectious mononucleosis have been described. The prognosis is excellent, and death, except in the rare genetically susceptible individual, is exceedingly rare. The acute phase of the disease generally lasts 2 to 4 weeks. The pharyngitis and fever subside in 2 to 3 weeks and the lymphadenopathy and splenomegaly in 4 to 6 weeks. It is not unusual for the fatigue and malaise to persist for months.

There are a number of published reports based primarily on anecdotal information of patients who have experienced chronic or recurrent infectious mononucleosis, with symptoms of disabling fatigue. With the advent of EBV-specific serologic tests, such patients with otherwise unexplained chronic fatigue have been studied, and some investigators attributed this syndrome to a "chronic form of infectious mononucleosis." It is now clear that EBV is not the cause of chronic fatigue (see Chapter 8–73).

Prevention

Considering the mode of spread and ubiquity of this infection, the only means of prevention would appear to be the development of a vaccine. Several candidate vaccines are under development but none is yet available for clinical use.

Cost Containment

It is important to make an accurate diagnosis of infectious mononucleosis in the proper setting to avoid unnecessary tests. Most patients do not require specific EBV serologic tests, and the use of the "mono-spot" test together with the typical clinical syndrome and leukocyte differential are all that is necessary to establish the diagnosis. On the other hand, in complex cases of unexplained fever or in some of the rare neurologic and other unusual syndromes caused by EBV, when the "mono-spot" test is negative, EBV serology may be crucial and may provide the diagnosis, at times allowing the clinician to avoid more tests and invasive procedures such as lymph node or liver biopsies.

REFERENCES

Ballerini P, Gaidano G, Gong J, et al. Molecular pathogenesis of HIV-associated lymphoma. AIDS Res Hum Retroviruses 1992;8:731–735.

Brandfonbrener A, Epstein A, Wu S, Phair J. Corticosteroid therapy in Epstein–Barr virus infection. Arch Intern Med 1986;146:337.

Dorsky DI, Crumpacker CS. Drugs five years: Acyclovir. Ann Intern Med 1987;107:859.

Heath CW Jr, Brodsky AL, Potolsky AI. Infectious mononucleosis in a general population. Am J Epidemiol 1972;95:46.

Hoagland RJ. Infectious mononucleosis. Am J Med 1952;13:158.

Horwitz CA, Henle W, Henle G, et al. Clinical and laboratory evaluation of elderly patients with heterophile antibody positive infectious mononucleosis: Report of seven patients ages 40 to 78. Am J Med 1976;61:333.

Horwitz CA, Henle W, Henle G, et al. Heterophile negative infectious mononucleosis and mononucleosis-like illness: Laboratory confirmation of 43 cases. Am J Med 1977;63:947.

Lopez-Navidad A, Domingo P, Cadafalch J, et al. Acute appendicitis complicating infectious mononucleosis: Case report and review. Rev Infect Dis 1990;12:297.

Schlossberg D, ed. Infectious mononucleosis. 2nd ed New York: Springer-Verlag, 1989.

Stites DP, Leikola J. Infectious mononucleosis. Semin Hematol 1971;8:243.

Straus SE, Cohen JI, Tosato G, et al. Epstein–Barr virus infections: Biology, pathogenesis and management. Ann Intern Med 1992;118:45.

Chronic Fatigue Syndrome

Carlos del Rio, M.D., and Jonas A. Shulman, M.D.

DEFINITION

Chronic fatigue syndrome is a clinically defined condition characterized by severe debilitating and disabling fatigue and a combination of symptoms, which may include malaise, fever, sore throat, painful swollen lymph nodes, headaches, myalgias, arthralgias, confusion, and a decreased ability to concentrate.

ETIOLOGY

No specific etiology has been found for what we know as "chronic fatigue syndrome" even though multiple infectious agents, mostly viruses, have been postulated as possible etiologies. Every one of the possible etiologic agents has been passed in and out of favor over time. Other suggested etiologies include underlying immune defects and, most recently, neurally mediated hypotension. Those etiologic factors remain unproven.

CRITERIA FOR DIAGNOSIS

Suggestive

Chronic fatigue syndrome has been a poorly understood disorder that has as its central feature severe fatigue. Because of the difficulties in diagnosing chronic fatigue syndrome, the Centers for Disease Control and Prevention convened an expert panel in 1988 and developed a case definition for this syndrome (Table 8–73–1). The diagnosis depends on the presence of a combination of these complaints plus the inability to diagnose a number of other illnesses that may present with similar findings. Unfortunately, these criteria, while helpful in epidemiologic investigations, are less helpful to the clinician in individual cases.

Definitive

Besides the current "working case definition" no pathognomonic signs, symptoms, or laboratory tests for this condition have been established.

CLINICAL MANIFESTATIONS

Subjective

The range of symptoms reported by patients with chronic fatigue syndrome is extensive. The cardinal complaints are fatigue that fails to resolve with bed rest and that is severe enough to reduce daily activity by more than 50% and cognitive dysfunction. Other symptoms include depression, pharyngitis, headaches, myalgias or arthralgia, painful lymph nodes, and sleep disturbances. The fatigue may vary in intensity from day to day, and there may be periods of apparent remission. Approximately 70% of patients with chronic fatigue syndrome are women in the fourth or fifth decade of life who are of middle and upper middle class. Frequently, there is a history of a flulike illness preceding the process. Many patients also have a prior history of atopy or allergic illness.

Objective

Physical Examination

The physical examination is usually normal. On occasion one may document a low-grade fever (37.6–38.6°C orally), nonexudative pharyngitis, and tender anterior or posterior cervical or axillary nodes. These findings are not present throughout the duration of the disease, however, and may be caused simply by intercurrent illness unrelated to the chronic fatigue syndrome.

Routine Laboratory Abnormalities

Routine laboratory examination including an erythrocyte sedimentation rate is usually normal.

PLANS

Diagnostic

Differential Diagnosis

Disorders causing similar complaints have been described variously in the literature as chronic brucellosis, sporadic postinfectious neurasthenia, benign myalgic encephalomyelitis, chronic candidiasis, postviral fatigue syndrome, chronic Epstein–Barr virus (EBV) syndrome, or chronic mononucleosis-like syndrome and candidiasis hypersensitivity syndrome. They may all represent the same or similar illnesses. Similarly, fibrositis or fibromyalgia is an illness that resembles chronic fatigue syndrome in many respects.

The differential diagnosis of chronic fatigue syndrome is extensive, as any chronic illness can produce the same or a similar constellation of nonspecific manifestations.

Diagnostic Options and Recommended Approach

Because of the difficulties in diagnosing chronic fatigue syndrome and with the hope of unifying diagnostic criteria among clinicians and researchers, a working case definition has been proposed (see Table 8–73–1). The definition requires the presence of two major criteria: (1) persistent or relapsing fatigue of new onset that does not resolve with bed rest and that is severe enough to reduce or impair average daily activity below 50% of the premorbid level of activity; and (2) the persistence of symptoms for a period of at least 6 months, with the exclusion

---

TABLE 8–73–1. WORKING CASE DEFINITION OF CHRONIC FATIGUE SYNDROME

To be considered as having chronic fatigue syndrome, the patient must fulfill both major criteria and either 6 or more of the 11 symptom criteria and 2 or more of the 3 physical criteria or 8 or more of the 11 symptom criteria.

Major Criteria
1. New onset of persistent or relapsing severe fatigue
2. Exclusion of any systemic condition that causes similar symptoms

Minor Criteria
Symptom or Historical Criteria
(symptoms must begin on or after the onset of increased fatigue and must persist or recur over a period of at least 6 months.)
1. Mild fever or chills
2. Sore throat
3. Painful lymph nodes (anterior or posterior cervical or auxillary)
4. Unexplained generalized weakness
5. Myalgia
6. Prolonged (>24 hours) generalized fatigue following previously tolerable levels of exercise
7. Generalized headaches
8. Migratory arthralgias
9. Neuropsychological symptoms
10. Sleep disturbance
11. Patient's description of initial onset of symptoms as acute or subacute

Physical Criteria
Physical criteria must be documented by a physician on at least two occasions at least 1 month apart.
1. Low-grade fever (36.6–38.6°C orally)
2. Nonexudative pharyngitis
3. Palpable or tender anterior or posterior cervical or axillary nodes (<2 cm in diameter)

Source: Slightly modified and reproduced, with permission, from Holmes GP, Kaplan JE, Gantz NM, et al. Chronic fatigue syndrome: A working case definition. Ann Intern Med 1988;108:387.

by thorough history, physical examination, and appropriate laboratory studies of other clinical illnesses that may cause similar symptoms. The extent of the laboratory investigation necessary to exclude other illnesses is not well defined; however a complete blood count, erythrocyte sedimentation rate, and blood urea nitrogen, serum creatinine, glucose, transaminase, and thyroid-stimulating hormone levels are probably all that are needed in the initial evaluation of the patient who presents with the chief complaint of fatigue. Other testing may be indicated, however, depending on the clinical and epidemiologic history and the findings on physical examination. Additionally, in any patient being evaluated for fatigue today, a special effort should be made to look for evidence of HIV infection. An HIV antibody test may be necessary to exclude this possibility.

So-called minor criteria include 11 symptoms and three physical findings. To fulfill the definition of chronic fatigue syndrome, the patient must exhibit both major criteria and either 6 or more of the minor symptoms together with 2 or more of the physical criteria, or 8 or more of the minor symptoms. The validity, sensitivity, and specificity of this case definition have yet to be tested.

With the first descriptions of chronic fatigue syndrome, it was suggested that there were elevated antibodies present against the diffuse and/or restricted components of the early antigen of EBV and against the viral capsid antigen. This prompted several laboratories to advertise specific EBV serologic studies as a useful diagnostic tool for this syndrome, which some believed was due to a "chronic Epstein–Barr infection." Unfortunately, EBV infection is almost universal and, like other herpesvirus infections, is also invariably chronic; elevated titers of antibody to the early antigen are found in a wide variety of clinical conditions and are in no way specific for the chronic fatigue syndrome. For this reason, serologic testing for EBV antibodies has not proven to be useful in the diagnosis of patients with suspected chronic fatigue syndrome.

Some patients with chronic fatigue syndrome, however, have been found to have a deficiency of an immunoglobulin class or subclass. There have been reports of a variety of subtle immunologic abnormalities detected in patients with this syndrome. Performing these tests should currently be reserved for research purposes as they have not been proven to be useful for diagnostic purposes.

Therapeutic

Currently, there is no specific treatment for patients suffering with chronic fatigue syndrome. Once other diagnoses have been excluded, the management is largely supportive. Acyclovir was found to be of no value in a placebo-controlled trial. Similarly, nystatin was shown to be of no benefit in a placebo-controlled trial. Other therapies such as cimetidine (Tagamet), nifedipine (Procardia), corticosteroids, intramuscular immunoglobulin, immunomodulators, and vitamins have been tried in uncontrolled trials and reported to be of some value in anecdotal reports, but none has been proven to be of benefit.

Three trials have been conducted using intravenous immunoglobulin therapy in patients with chronic fatigue syndrome. The rationale for immunoglobulin therapy is based on the finding that a deficiency of immunoglobulin classes and subclasses has been demonstrated in some patients with this syndrome. Although one trial suggested benefits, two have failed to show a similar benefit, and at present, there is not enough evidence to recommend that intravenous immunoglobulin be given to patients with chronic fatigue syndrome. Similarly, transfer factor combined with cognitive–behavioral therapy was found to be ineffective in a well-conducted clinical trial.

The symptoms of depression may be ameliorated by tricyclic antidepressants given in low dosages. No randomized trials have been conducted to see whether they are effective in the long-term management of chronic fatigue syndrome, but a study in somewhat similar patients with fibromyalgia suggests that antidepressants in low doses (e.g., amitriptyline 25–50 mg at bedtime) combined at times with nonsteroidal antiinflammatory drugs are more effective than placebo in improving symptoms of fatigue, myalgias, and sleep impairment.

The patient must understand that the illness, although debilitating, is not fatal and that remission is likely. It is important to reassure the patient that no other serious illness is present, even though at times it is impossible to be absolutely certain of the accuracy of the diagnosis of chronic fatigue syndrome (as no specific diagnostic test is available). The extent of the workup depends on the patient's exact symptoms and signs, and the need for various tests should be explained. It is important to reassure the patient that the fatigue and other symptoms that the patient is experiencing are real and that, in most cases, the syndrome gradually subsides. Instructing the patient on the importance of a balanced diet, moderate exercise, sufficient rest, and stress control is probably the best advice the clinician can offer the patient with chronic fatigue syndrome. At times the depression may be severe, and the need for psychological counseling, if required, must be explained.

FOLLOW-UP

One of the difficulties in managing the patient with chronic fatigue syndrome is that the types of symptoms, together with the reported remissions and exacerbations, require repeated evaluation and consideration of a variety of other disease processes. A weight change of more than 10% of baseline in the absence of dieting should make the clinician consider an alternative diagnosis and further evaluation. Follow-up visits at specific intervals, with supportive psychotherapy and counseling, are sometimes very beneficial in the care of patients with chronic fatigue syndrome. The frequency of these follow-up intervals must be individualized.

DISCUSSION
Prevalence and Incidence

In the United States it is estimated that about a quarter of the general adult population has fatigue lasting 2 weeks or longer. Because the diagnosis of chronic fatigue syndrome requires that the fatigue last more than 6 months, only a fraction of those with prolonged fatigue actually fulfill the diagnostic criteria for chronic fatigue syndrome. The prevalence of chronic fatigue syndrome has been estimated to be about 20 cases per 100,000 persons. The incidence is unknown.

Related Basic Science

The pathogenesis of chronic fatigue syndrome is unknown. Several studies have suggested that the cause is likely to be a persistent viral infection, and much work to identify a viral cause for this syndrome has ensued. Among the viral candidates that have been proposed are the Epstein–Barr virus, human herpesvirus 6 (HHV-6), Coxsackie B viruses, and most recently the human retroviruses. Unfortunately, at this time it appears unlikely that any of these viruses are responsible for more than a small fraction of cases of chronic fatigue syndrome. Recent studies suggest that immunologic abnormalities (such as immunoglobulins and various lymphocytes involved in cell-mediated immunity) are of little importance in the development of this syndrome. Many suspect that chronic fatigue syndrome may represent not one disease, but rather the end result of several different disease processes. Recently Bou-Holaigah and others (1995) have suggested a relationship between neurally mediated hypotension and chronic fatigue syndrome.

Natural History and Its Modification with Treatment

Apparent epidemics or outbreaks of chronic fatigue syndrome have been reported, but there is little evidence to suggest that chronic fatigue syndrome is readily, if at all, communicable. The natural history of chronic fatigue syndrome is also not established. The prognosis varies from patient to patient, but it appears that remissions are not uncommon over a period of 1 to 2 years.

Prevention

Little is known about the causes of chronic fatigue syndrome, and thus no specific preventive measures can be offered.

Cost Containment

It is important not to embark on repeated costly workups in patients suffering from this syndrome. Generally, a thorough history and physical examination followed by a reasonable selective battery of laboratory tests are all that is needed to exclude other illnesses that may be confused with chronic fatigue syndrome. Repeat EBV serologies are expensive, appear to be of little to no value, and are difficult or impossible to interpret.

REFERENCES

Blondell-Hill E, Shafran SD. Treatment of the chronic fatigue syndrome: A review and practical guide. Drugs 1993;46:639.

Bou-Holaigah I, Rowe PC, Kan J, Calkins H. The relationship between neurally mediated hypotension and the chronic fatigue syndrome. JAMA 1995;274:961.

Chronic fatigue syndrome: Current concepts. Conference Proceedings, Albany, NY, October 3–4, 1992. Clin Infect Dis 1994;18 (suppl. 1):S1.

Fukuda K, Strauss SE, Hickie I, et al. The chronic fatigue syndrome: A comprehensive approach to its definition and study. Ann Intern Med 1994;121:953.

Holmes GP, Kaplan JE, Gants NM, et al. Chronic fatigue syndrome: A working case definition. Ann Intern Med 1988;108:387.

Khan AS, Heneine WM, Chapman LE, et al. Assessment of a retrovirus sequence and other possible risk factors for the chronic fatigue syndrome in adults. Ann Intern Med 1993;118:241.

Klonoff DC. Chronic fatigue syndrome. Clin Infect Dis 1992;15:812.

Lane TJ, Matthews DA, Manu P. The low yield of physical examination and laboratory investigations of patients with chronic fatigue. Am J Med Sci 1990;299:313.

Lloyd AR, Hickie I, Brockman A, et al. Immunologic and psychologic therapy for patients with chronic fatigue syndrome: A double-blind, placebo-controlled trial. Am J Med 1993;94:197.

Lloyd A, Hickie I, Wakefield D, et al. A double-blind, placebo-controlled trial of intravenous immunoglobulin therapy in patients with chronic fatigue syndrome. Am J Med 1990;89:561.

Wilson A, Hickie I, Lloyd A, Wakefield D. The treatment of chronic fatigue syndrome: Science and speculation. Am J Med 1994;96:544.

CHAPTER 8–74

Varicella–Zoster Infections (Chickenpox and Shingles)

John E. McGowan, Jr., M.D., Rafael L. Jurado, M.D., and Jonas A. Shulman, M.D.

DEFINITION

Varicella–zoster infections are defined as systemic diseases due to infection with varicella–zoster virus, with different manifestations for the first episode (the clinical syndrome of chickenpox) and for recurrence (a clinical syndrome called zoster or shingles).

ETIOLOGY

The infection is caused by varicella–zoster virus (VZV), one of the herpes family of viruses.

CRITERIA FOR DIAGNOSIS

Suggestive

Presence of the characteristic history and skin rash is satisfactory for clinical diagnosis of either primary infection (chickenpox) or recurrent infection (shingles or zoster).

Definitive

Antibody to VZV can be measured by a number of different methods today. Presence of a high standing titer of antibody or a fourfold rise or fall in antibody titer is diagnostic of prior VZV infection. Such laboratory testing is rarely required in patients with characteristic clinical pictures. It is useful when the rash illness is difficult to characterize. Viral culture is a definitive method of diagnosis, but not available as widely as is testing for antibody.

CLINICAL MANIFESTATIONS

Subjective

Fever, chills, myalgia, malaise, and arthralgia frequently precede the varicella rash, which usually is pruritic. In zoster, pain often develops in the affected area several days before the onset of the rash, especially in the elderly. At times this is very confusing to the clinician before the rash appears. Malaise and fatigue often are present as well.

A careful history should be taken from all patients who present with zoster to be certain no underlying immunosuppressive diseases, such as lymphoma or other malignancies or AIDS are present, and that no immunosuppressive treatment is being given.

Other family members who have had recent illnesses including rash should be identified, as the appearance of a patient's symptoms after a characteristic incubation period after that contact (approximately 13–15 days) helps to identify atypical exanthems as varicella.

Objective

Physical Examination

Varicella infection is associated with a generalized vesicular rash and a mild temperature elevation, which may occur prior to the appearance of the rash. The rash usually begins on the head or trunk, spreading centrifugally to limbs and mucous membranes (enanthem). The earliest lesions are red macules, which then vesiculate, become pustular, and crust over. Lesions in one body area are at different stages ("crops") from those in another area. The number of lesions may vary from 10 to several hundred. In immunocompromised patients, especially those with AIDS, and in leukemic children, lesions may continue to form for weeks, may be more numerous, may have a hemorrhagic base, and may take longer than the usual 1 to 2 weeks to heal.

Zoster infection is associated with varicella-like eruptions involving one to three dermatomes, most often on the chest or back. Lesions may continue to appear over a period of several days. On occasion, typical pain occurs without skin lesions. Dissemination to other parts of the body may occur in patients with depressed cellular immunity.

Routine Laboratory Abnormalities

There are no routine laboratory abnormalities relevant to diagnosis of this entity.

PLANS

Diagnostic

Differential Diagnosis

The skin rash associated with varicella–zoster infection can be confused with smallpox (now eradicated except for the possibility of laboratory accident); disseminated vaccinia infection (no longer occurs with ending of vaccination against smallpox); other herpesvirus infections such as generalized herpes simplex (see Chapter 8–70); and infections with enteroviruses such as Coxsackie virus. Varicella can be confused with impetigo (see Chapter 8–29).

Diagnostic Options

A Tzanck preparation (Wright or Giemsa stain of vesicle fluid scrapings) may be used to demonstrate large, multinucleated epithelial giant cells in VZV infection, but the test is neither sensitive nor specific. The virus can be isolated from vesicles during the first 4 days of rash, but this is rarely necessary. Recent infection can be documented by complement fixation test, but the antibody becomes undetectable within 1 year. For more distant infection, a fluorescent antibody to membrane antigen (FAMA) test, immunofluorescence, latex agglutination test, or enzyme immunoassay (EIA) should be used.

Recommended Approach

Laboratory testing is rarely required. Diagnosis of both chickenpox and zoster is usually based on the characteristic history and physical examination. In patients who present with herpes zoster, further physical examination is indicated to look for evidence of diseases associated with depressed T-cell function, especially lymphoma, other malignancy, or HIV infection. If this examination fails to reveal any reason to suspect underlying disease, no further diagnostic evaluation for such problems is necessary. If, however, any underlying immunosuppressive disease is suggested, appropriate laboratory and roentgenographic procedures should be done. Zoster cases in persons with apparently intact immunity usually occur in persons over age 50 years; when zoster occurs in a younger individual, he or she must be evaluated for possible immunosuppressive conditions.

Therapeutic

Therapeutic Options

Uncomplicated varicella is managed primarily with drying lotions (e.g., calamine lotion) and/or antihistamine drugs to decrease itching, as well as with measures to reduce the likelihood of a secondary bacterial infection. Aspirin should be avoided in varicella infection, as Reye's syndrome may be more likely in this illness if aspirin is used. Patients with zoster infection require analgesics for pain.

Uncomplicated varicella in patients with normal host defenses may respond somewhat faster when treated with oral acyclovir, *if it is begun within 24 hours after the rash first appears.* It is not clear at present that this benefit outweighs the cost of the drug, but groups like the American Academy of Pediatrics recommend this use for varicella in adolescents and adults with normal host defenses. If treatment is given, a dose of 800 mg orally five times per day for 5 to 7 days is appropriate. Dosage must be adjusted in renal failure. This oral acyclovir therapy may also be appropriate for pregnant women, in whom varicella pneumonia may be more severe when it occurs. Better documented is the benefit of acyclovir in varicella when the patient is immunocompromised and thus at risk for developing severe disease (e.g., in patients with reticuloendothelial malignancies, organ transplant, or AIDS). Intravenous acyclovir in a dose of 10 mg/kg (which will require dose adjustments in renal failure), infused over a 1-hour period, is given every 8 hours for 7 to 10 days.

For herpes zoster in adults (especially those older than 50) with normal host defenses or in immunocompromised hosts with mild disease, 800 mg of oral acyclovir five times daily for 7 to 10 days, *if begun within 48 to 72 hours of onset,* may accelerate healing and decrease acute pain. In severe localized zoster (that involving more than one dermatome or the trigeminal nerve) or in disseminated zoster, parenteral acyclovir in the regimen described above for varicella is appropriate. Treatment of acute herpes zoster with acyclovir for 21 days or addition of prednisolone to acyclovir therapy confers only slight benefits compared with the standard 7-day treatment course with acyclovir alone. None of these regimens reduces the frequency of postherpetic neuralgia.

In one clinical trial, treatment of acute uncomplicated zoster infection in adults with famciclovir, 500 mg orally three times daily for 7 days, reduced the median duration of postherpetic neuralgia in comparison with placebo. The effect was most pronounced when therapy was begun within the first 48 hours of rash onset and in patients 50 years or older. In another trial, however, no difference in duration of postherpetic neuralgia was noted in comparison with that in patients given the acyclovir regimen described above.

Recommended Approach

Acyclovir should be used in the situations of higher risk outlined above. Use of steroids does not appear beneficial. Famciclovir may prove useful for postherpetic pain, but further data are needed on safety and efficacy before its role becomes clear.

FOLLOW-UP

Ordinarily no follow-up is necessary in varicella–zoster infections after the infection resolves. The major exception is patients with postherpetic neuralgia, who may require extensive further care to deal with their pain.

DISCUSSION
Prevalence and Incidence

Varicella–zoster infection is ubiquitous; incidence rates approach that of the birth rate in a given country. Nearly all persons (90%) will have contracted the disease before the age of 10 years. Zoster infections occur in about half a million persons per year in the United States, and prevalence is especially high in the elderly. Varicella occurs most frequently during the winter and spring months, and has an incubation period of 10 to 21 days. Transmission is usually by respiratory spread, and direct contact with vesicular or pustular lesions also may result in the disease. The most contagious period stretches from 1 to 2 days before the onset of rash until about 4 days after the rash appears. Once crusting occurs, the virus is no longer easily isolated. The syndrome produced by varicella–zoster virus is highly contagious; the other herpesviruses require more prolonged contact.

Related Basic Science
Genetics

Congenital varicella syndrome occasionally results when the mother acquires varicella–zoster virus infection during early pregnancy, especially in weeks 13 to 20, whereas no illness usually develops in those infants whose mother is infected later in pregnancy. Occasional women with antibodies to varicella–zoster virus prior to pregnancy have developed varicella but no fetal complications developed.

Altered Molecular Biology

Most patients 50 years or older who present with zoster are not known to be immunosuppressed and will not be found to have serious underlying illness such as malignancy or AIDS. Occasionally, however, zoster may be a harbinger of these or other diseases with severe underlying defects in T-cell function.

Physiologic or Metabolic Derangement

Children with compromised host defenses may have "progressive varicella," with high fever and new skin lesions appearing for up to 2 weeks. Pneumonia, hepatitis, meningitis, or encephalitis also may occur.

Anatomic Derangement

Skin vesicles involve degenerative changes in epithelial cells with appearance of multinucleated giant cells and eosinophilic intranuclear inclusions. The fluid in the vesicle becomes cloudy because of the influx of white cells and debris associated with the inflammatory response. Rupture of the vesicle is most likely; some gradually resolve, most often without scarring. Varicella–zoster virus shares with the other herpesviruses (herpes simplex, Epstein–Barr, and cytomegalovirus) a tendency to latency and reactivation later in life. Multiple dorsal root ganglia are the site for this persistence.

Natural History and Its Modification with Treatment

In varicella infection, the appearance of new skin lesions usually subsides after 4 to 7 days. Crusting and drying up of individual lesions occur about 4 days after their onset; failure of crusting to occur may indicate an inadequate host defense response. Complications of varicella include pneumonitis (almost exclusively seen in adults), myocarditis, pericarditis, hepatitis, and encephalitis. Acute cerebellar ataxia is rare and usually resolves completely. Mortality rates in adults approach 30 per 100,000. Reye's syndrome sometimes follows chickenpox, as do secondary bacterial infections of the skin or respiratory tract, but this occurs more often in children than in adults.

In zoster, crusting often begins in the second week and usually is completed by the end of week 3. Complications of zoster infection include acute cerebellar ataxia (frequency 1 in 4000 patients under 15 years of age) and a focal granulomatous angiitis in the anterior cerebral circulation, leading to acute contralateral hemiplegia, which follows ophthalmic involvement. A continuing severe pain ("postherpetic neuralgia") may persist after the crusted lesions have dried up, especially in the elderly and in the immunosuppressed. It persists in 10% of patients over 40 years of age and in 20 to 50% of patients over 60 years of age.

The disseminated forms (progressive varicella or disseminated zoster infection) can affect many organs, can persist for weeks, and, on occasion, can lead to death in a susceptible immunocompromised patient.

Prevention

Varicella infection is ordinarily mild in children. In nonimmune adults and children at risk of severe infection (immunosuppressed and leukemic patients, newborns whose mothers had chickenpox around the time of delivery, etc.) and in pregnant women known to be seronegative who have clearly been exposed, passive immunization with varicella–zoster immune globulin (VZIG) within 72 hours of exposure may ameliorate the illness.

Clinical trials have shown a live attenuated vaccine to be effective in preventing disease. It is now licensed for use in the United States. Even this attenuated vaccine can cause severe disease in some severely immunocompromised patients.

Cost Containment

Screening health care workers for antibodies to varicella–zoster virus before episodes of nosocomial exposure occur has been recommended as a cost-saving measure; this has been implemented infrequently because cost savings are not clear in comparison to performing this screening at time of exposure. Likewise, the cost-effectiveness of the use of varicella vaccine is not yet clear.

REFERENCES

Balfour HH Jr. Current management of varicella zoster virus infections. J Med Virol 1993;suppl. 1:74.

Enders G, Miller E, Cradock-Watson J, et al. Consequences of varicella and herpes zoster in pregnancy: Prospective study of 1739 cases. Lancet 1994;343:1547.

Lieu TA, Cochi SL, Black SB, et al. Cost-effectiveness of a routine varicella vaccination program for US children. JAMA 1994;271:375.

Plotkin SA. Vaccines for varicella–zoster virus and cytomegalovirus: Recent progress. Science 1994;265:1383.

Weller TH. Varicella and herpes zoster: A perspective and overview. J Infect Dis 1992; 166(suppl. 1):S1.

Wood MJ, Johnson RW, McKendrick MW, et al. A randomized trial of acyclovir for 7 days or 21 days with and without prednisolone for treatment of acute herpes zoster. N Engl J Med 1994;330:896.

CHAPTER 8–75

Human Parvovirus B19 Infections

Susan M. Ray, M.D., and Jonas A. Shulman, M.D.

DEFINITION

Several clinical syndromes have been recognized as being caused by human parvovirus B19.

Erythema infectiosum is a common childhood illness characterized by a "slapped cheek" rash. It is also known as "fifth disease."

Acute peripheral symmetric polyarthropathy occurs in the convalescent phase of B19 infection in adults and is recognized more commonly in women than men.

Parvovirus B19 is identified as the cause of more than 80% of cases of *transient aplastic crisis* in patients with chronic hemolytic anemias.

Nonimmune hydrops fetalis is an uncommon adverse outcome when a susceptible woman is infected with parvovirus during pregnancy.

Chronic parvovirus B19 aplastic anemia is an infrequent result of B19 infection in patients with congenital or acquired (usually HIV-infected or leukemic patients) immunodeficiency.

ETIOLOGY

Human parvovirus B19 is a small, nonenveloped, single-stranded DNA virus in the genus *Parvovirus* of the family Parvoviridae. The genus *Parvovirus* includes species-specific viruses such as canine parvovirus and feline panleukopenia virus. Parvovirus B19 is the only parvovirus known to infect humans.

CRITERIA FOR DIAGNOSIS

Suggestive

In the pediatric age group, the diagnosis of erythema infectiosum (fifth disease) is usually based primarily on the presence of the characteristic clinical syndrome of the "slapped cheek" appearance and the reticular "lacelike" rash, which are preceded by manifestations of a mild systemic infectious illness with fever, malaise, and myalgias. Definitive diagnosis of this syndrome by serology is usually unnecessary.

Acute infection with parvovirus B19 is almost certain in patients with sickle cell disease (or other chronic hemolytic anemias) who present with transient aplastic crisis characterized by a drop in the baseline hematocrit and absence (or very low level) of reticulocytosis. Other syndromes associated with parvovirus B19 infection are not specific enough to allow for diagnosis based on clinical criteria alone.

Definitive

Diagnosis of human parvovirus B19 infection in adults or of atypical cases in children must be confirmed by detection of the specific anti-human parvovirus B19 immunoglobulin (Ig) M antibody, which usually appears in the serum shortly after the onset of clinical manifestations and persists for 1 to 2 months. The presence of anti-human parvovirus B19 IgG antibody alone in the absence of an IgM response indicates only that prior human parvovirus B19 infection has occurred; it does not indicate acute infection.

The diagnosis of human parvovirus B19-induced transient aplastic crisis in patients with hemolytic anemias can be confirmed by the presence of anti-human parvovirus B19 IgM antibody, which is frequently first detected about 3 days after the onset of the recovering reticulocytosis.

We thank Dr. Robert Yancey for his contribution to this chapter in the third edition of this book.

The diagnosis of chronic aplastic anemia owing to human parvovirus B19 requires bone marrow examination, which may be supplemented with electron microscopy or detection of viral DNA or viral proteins by the use of molecular technology. The bone marrow in these patients, as in those with the transient aplastic crisis syndrome, usually demonstrates the pathognomonic giant pronormoblasts. As most of the patients with human parvovirus B19-related chronic aplastic anemia are immunocompromised, anti-human parvovirus B19 IgM antibody is usually not detected.

There are no established serologic methods to diagnose in utero infection with human parvovirus B19. Maternal anti-human parvovirus B19 IgM will be present for 1 to 2 months in an infected mother, but the detection of this antibody in maternal serum does not necessarily indicate that transplacental infection has occurred. Transplacental infection appears to occur in about 25 to 33% of cases in which the mother is infected during pregnancy, but the risk of fetal loss or adverse effect is less than 10%. Prenatal diagnosis of intrauterine infection is possible by detecting fetal IgM response (present in up to 45% of infected fetuses) or by using nucleic acid hybridization or polymerase chain reaction technology to examine fetal blood or amniotic fluid for the presence of viral DNA. Postmortem confirmation of fetal infection can be accomplished by electron microscopic demonstration of viral particles in fetal tissue or fluids or detection of viral DNA as described above. Hydrops fetalis from any etiology may be suspected by abnormalities seen with fetal ultrasound and by elevation in α-fetoprotein.

CLINICAL MANIFESTATIONS
Subjective

Approximately 20% of patients acutely infected with human parvovirus B19 are asymptomatic. Symptoms of human parvovirus B19 infection vary with the age of the patient and with the presence of certain underlying illnesses. Symptoms are usually milder in children than in adults. As noted above, pediatric patients characteristically have a short period of nonspecific symptoms such as fever, malaise, and myalgias preceding the onset of a rather typical rash, which is occasionally pruritic. When the rash appears, the child usually begins to feel well. Arthralgias are present in only a minority of pediatric cases (Table 8–75–1).

Adults with symptomatic B19 infection may present with an erythema infectiosum syndrome as described above, but in about 50% of adults, the presentation is an acute polyarthropathy, with fewer than half of these patients reporting a prior rash illness. This polyarthropathy is more common in women than in men. Arthralgias of multiple joints are common and most often involve the hands (metacarpophalangeal

and proximal interphalangeal joints), knees, wrists, and ankles. They are generally symmetric and of acute onset, are rarely persistent or recurrent, and may be the predominant and at times the only symptom of human parvovirus B19 infection. Severe arthralgias usually last only 1 to 2 weeks, but in 20% of women, joint symptoms may wax and wane for months or occasionally even years. Another common and unique feature of human parvovirus B19 infection in adults is the occurrence of paresthesias of the hands and feet that may last several days and can be painful.

Patients with transient aplastic crisis have pallor, weakness, and lethargy following a nonspecific prodromal illness that lasts from 1 to 7 days. Skin rash is uncommon. Some patients may complain of severe bone pain at the time of presentation. These patients usually have a previously documented history of sickle cell disease or some other chronic hemoglobinopathy.

Subjective symptoms of the human parvovirus B19-associated chronic aplastic anemia are nonspecific and are similar to those of a chronic anemia due to any cause.

Objective
Physical Examination

In the child with human parvovirus B19 infection, the "slapped cheek" facial erythema is characteristic. The rash is usually "lacelike" in appearance but may be morbilliform, vesicular, or occasionally purpuric. It is generally present for only a few days, but in some patients may recur with bathing, emotional stress, or sunlight exposure. In healthy adults infected with human parvovirus B19, the rash is detected in only about half the cases and may have a highly variable appearance. Cases mimicking cutaneous vasculitis have been described.

Arthropathy in these patients is usually polyarticular, acute in onset, and generally symmetric. Redness and mild swelling of the joints may be noted.

Patients with transient aplastic crisis present with signs of acute, severe anemia. Fever at the time of presentation is not uncommon and splenomegaly has been documented in a few cases. As noted above, skin rash is noted infrequently.

Infection with human parvovirus B19 during pregnancy presents with clinical manifestations similar to those seen in other normal adults. There are frequently no objective findings to indicate that transplacental infection has occurred; however, hydrops fetalis has been described in association with in-utero infection in some pregnancies and may be detected by ultrasound and elevated α-fetoprotein levels.

The patient with chronic B19 aplastic anemia presents with signs of chronic anemia. Fever is variable. Rash and joint symptoms in these patients are unusual.

Routine Laboratory Abnormalities

Leukopenia, thrombocytopenia, and a transient minimal decline in hemoglobin level may be observed, but in healthy immunocompetent patients, the slight abnormality normalizes quickly and is usually of no clinical significance.

The patient with transient aplastic crisis presents with sudden drop in hematocrit and reticulocytopenia. The resultant anemia is often severe enough to require transfusion. Transient thrombocytopenia and neutropenia are reported commonly. Bone marrow function usually returns to normal within days.

The persistent human parvovirus B19 infection that occurs in immunodeficient patients such as patients with HIV infection presents with a severe anemia (often transfusion-requiring) and absence of reticulocytosis.

PLANS
Diagnostic
Differential Diagnosis

The differential diagnosis of the rash of erythema infectiosum includes erysipelas, scarlet fever, rubella, roseola infantum (caused by human herpesvirus 6), infectious mononucleosis, echovirus, and Coxsackie

TABLE 8–75–1. CLINICAL MANIFESTATIONS OF PARVOVIRUS B19 INFECTION

Disease	Characteristics
Erythema infectiosum (fifth disease)	A common childhood illness. "Slapped cheek" is evident in 80%, arthralgias rarely occur. Disease is nearly always mild and self-limited.
Acute parvovirus B19 infection in healthy adults	Flulike upper respiratory symptoms, sometimes with faint rash. Manifestations of joint inflammation are reported in 80%; it often mimics sudden-onset rheumatoid arthritis. Infection is usually self-limited, but some patients with arthritis may have symptoms for months.
Hydrops fetalis, fetal loss	B19 infections in pregnancy (in which the mother may be symptomatic or asymptomatic) can cause adverse consequences for the fetus in fewer than 10% of cases.
Transient aplastic crisis	In patients with chronic hemolytic anemias such as sickle cell anemia, a moderate to severe increase in anemia may be seen owing to a marked decrease in erythropoiesis. The reticulocyte count is severely depressed. Pallor and lethargy are common symptoms.
Chronic parvovirus B19 aplastic anemia	Seen in patients with various types of immunodeficiency (inherited or acquired), such as HIV-infected patients, leukemic patients undergoing chemotherapy, and, rarely, in patients with other types of immunodeficiency.

virus infections. A "slapped cheek" rash is characteristic only of human parvovirus B19.

The adult patient often presents with a polyarthropathy with or without a rash. The differential diagnosis may be quite long, and the diagnosis of human parvovirus B19 may not be considered. Adults presenting with acute symmetric polyarthropathy may have a transient reactive inflammatory arthritis, early rheumatoid arthritis, or adult-onset Still's disease. The most commonly identified viral causes of symmetric polyarthritis are human parvovirus B19 and rubella (after natural infection and after vaccination with live attenuated virus). In some human parvovirus B19 infections, confusion due to a transient false-positive test for rubella IgM or for rheumatoid factor may occur. Other common viral infections to be considered, but that cause arthritis less frequently, include hepatitis B, mumps, enteroviruses, Epstein–Barr virus, herpes simplex, varicella zoster, and adenoviruses. In addition to rheumatoid arthritis, adult-onset Still's disease, and viral infections, other diseases that can be confused with human parvovirus B19 arthropathy include rheumatic fever, systemic lupus erythematosus, subacute bacterial endocarditis, and disseminated gonococcal infections.

Transient aplastic crisis in patients with hemolytic anemias is almost uniformly caused by infection with parvovirus B19. Other viral infections such as cytomegalovirus and Epstein–Barr virus have been associated with transient aplastic crisis in a few reported cases.

Nonimmune hydrops fetalis has been associated with a variety of disorders, though in as many as 50% of cases, the cause is unknown. Cardiovascular and chromosomal abnormalities account for most of the identified etiologies. Parvovirus B19 probably accounts for about 10% of all cases of nonimmune hydrops. Other infectious causes of nonimmune hydrops include syphilis, cytomegalovirus, toxoplasmosis, herpes simplex, and rubella.

A patient with chronic aplastic anemia and immunodeficiency may have multiple reasons for bone marrow suppression. The most commonly identified causes of red cell aplasia in patients with HIV infection are "chronic disease" (adequate iron stores but ineffective erythropoiesis with normocytic, normochromic cells), medications (such as zidovudine or dapsone), nutritional deficiencies, and infiltrative disease (infectious or neoplastic).

Diagnostic Options

If laboratory confirmation of infection is necessary (in adults, atypical cases, suspected fetal or chronic infection), there are several tests that can be performed to detect antiviral antibodies, viral antigen, or viral DNA. Human B19 antibody (IgM or IgG) can be detected using radioimmunoassay or enzyme immunoassay in commercially available kits. Recombinant cell lines that express B19 capsid proteins have been developed and provide a renewable source of antigen suitable for commercial kits. Tests for detection of viral antigen using monoclonal antibody to B19 are not very sensitive but may be used in histologic examinations. The most sensitive tests for B19 are nucleic acid hybridization and polymerase chain reaction for the detection of viral DNA. These techniques can be applied to most clinical specimens including serum, fetal blood, amniotic fluid, respiratory secretions, fresh tissues, and paraffin-embedded tissues, but are not widely available outside of the research setting.

Examination of bone marrow with light microscopy reveals characteristic giant pronormoblasts. Electron microscopy of bone marrow, fetal tissue, and serum may reveal virus particles.

Recommended Approach

The pediatric patient with the typical syndrome of human parvovirus B19 infection requires no diagnostic laboratory tests. The clinical presentation is usually diagnostic, although an epidemiologic history of other similar cases may provide additional help in confirming the clinical impression.

A history that an adult presenting with polyarthritis has recently been exposed to a child with classic fifth disease should alert the clinician to the possibility of human parvovirus B19 infection. In most adult infections, laboratory evaluation is necessary to prove infection. As rubella or rubella vaccination in adults may at times produce a similar clinical constellation of findings, a history of recent rubella vaccination should be sought, and in some cases acute and convalescent rubella serology

may be indicated to rule out rubella infection. Anti-human parvovirus B19 IgM assays performed during the proper period are generally diagnostic. The IgM antibody response to this infection remains positive for only 30 to 60 days; therefore, this serology should be obtained as soon as the diagnosis is suspected. A false-negative result sometimes occurs if the serology is obtained too early (in the first few days of the infection) or if it is not obtained until 4 to 8 weeks later. Human parvovirus B19 IgM antibody is fairly consistently positive by the third day after the onset of rash or arthralgias. A clear-cut rise (fourfold or greater) in human parvovirus B19-IgG antibody may also be used for diagnosis in some cases.

In HIV-positive patients with pure red cell aplasia owing to human parvovirus B19 infection, anti-human parvovirus B19 IgM (and IgG) antibodies may not be detectable. These patients may have characteristic giant pronormoblasts in the bone marrow that are highly suggestive of infection. Viral infection in these patients can be detected by assay of serum, peripheral blood, and bone marrow using polymerase chain reaction or nucleic acid hybridization to look for the presence of viral DNA.

Diagnostic tests to detect fetal human parvovirus B19 infection before birth should include serial α-fetoprotein assays and ultrasonography, as these tests may demonstrate the early development of hydrops fetalis. The detection of maternal IgM antibody suggests the diagnosis in many cases, though IgM may no longer be detectable by the time fetal disease is recognized. The detection of fetal IgM in fetal blood or amniotic fluid can make the diagnosis pre- or postnatally, but these antibody tests are insensitive, especially when the mother is IgM negative at the time of the test. Specific tests to determine the presence of virus or viral components in the fetus at or before birth can be performed in a few laboratories. Polymerase chain reaction assay for B19 DNA performed on fetal blood or amniotic fluid is a more sensitive test than fetal IgM for the diagnosis of intrauterine infection.

Therapeutic

No specific therapy is required for human parvovirus B19 infection in healthy adults or children. Symptomatic treatment of arthropathy with antiinflammatory drugs, physical therapy, rest, and reassurance that this disease is nearly always self-limited are usually all that is necessary.

Patients with transient aplastic crisis and chronic B19 infection should receive transfusions of packed red blood cells as necessary. No specific treatment is effective or necessary for transient aplastic crisis.

Patients who are chronically infected with human parvovirus B19 owing to an immunodeficiency such as HIV infection or some other underlying immune deficiency may achieve remission or even cure with intravenous immunoglobulin. Once the diagnosis of chronic B19 infection is established, the patient should be treated with a 5- to 10-day course of daily infusion of a commercial immunoglobulin preparation. Some patients are cured after a single course, but those who relapse are likely to respond to repeated courses.

Intrauterine B19 infection has been managed in a research setting with high-risk intrauterine transfusion, but controlled clinical trials are needed to define the type and timing of optimal treatment for the B19-infected fetus.

FOLLOW-UP

Only patients with chronic parvovirus B19 infections require regular follow-up, as these patients may fail to respond to therapy or have a relapse of viral activity after treatment with immunoglobulin. Response to therapy can be correlated with a rise in reticulocyte count and a decrease in or disappearance of viral DNA in serum, if this is measured. Repeated measurement of hematocrit and reticulocyte count at monthly intervals should be sufficient to detect changes suggesting a relapse. As stated previously, patients who relapse may respond to repeated courses of immunoglobulin.

DISCUSSION
Prevalence and Incidence

Parvovirus B19 is a common infection in humans worldwide. Infection generally occurs between the ages of 5 and 10 years, and by the age of

15 years, 50% of children have detectable IgG. Most people become infected during their lifetime, with more than 90% of the elderly having detectable antibody. The prevalence of chronic parvovirus infection in AIDS patients with anemia was less than 5% in one study. The incidence of B19 infection in women of childbearing age has been measured at 1.5% seroconversion per year.

Related Basic Science

Human parvovirus B19 was first discovered in 1975 in the blood of an asymptomatic donor. For some 6 years it enjoyed the unusual distinction of being an identified human virus without a disease. In 1981, human parvovirus B19 was recognized as the cause of the transient aplastic crisis syndrome, and soon thereafter it was identified as the cause of erythema infectiosum.

Human parvovirus B19 is a small DNA nonenveloped virus, the genome of which contains a single linear strand of DNA coding for two capsid (structural) proteins, VP-1 and VP-2, and a nonstructural protein (NS1). The bone marrow early erythrocyte precursors (pronormoblasts and normoblasts) are the preferred sites of viral infection and replication. The viral receptor has been shown to be the erythrocyte blood group P antigen. Giant pronormoblasts are produced. Productive B19 infection is cytotoxic and induces red cell aplasia. In vitro replication of the virus has been achieved in specialized bone marrow cultures, but there is no system for the isolation of B19 from clinical specimens.

Neutralizing antibody to capsid protein is important in control of B19 infection, and the pattern of parvovirus disease is strongly influenced by the immune response. In immunocompetent individuals the infection is terminated by the specific antibodies produced, which appear to neutralize the ability of the virus to infect erythrocyte progenitor cells. The accompanying rash and arthropathy are most likely caused by immune complexes. In individuals who do not develop an appropriate immune response, infection may produce aplastic anemia. Similarly, in patients with a need for increased red cell production, such as those with hemolytic anemia, the temporary interruption of red cell marrow production may lead to a transient aplastic anemia. Although there is no evidence that the virus can replicate in cells other than erythroid progenitors, the virus can affect the growth of other cells (such as megakaryocytes) in culture. This effect may explain the thrombocytopenia and neutropenia that are occasionally observed.

Natural History and Its Modification with Treatment

Transmission of human parvovirus B19 is by respiratory droplets and also probably via fomites. The incubation period is usually 4 to 14 days but may be up to 20 days. Transfusion-acquired infection has been documented in hemophiliacs. Viremia generally occurs from 7 to 12 days after exposure and resolves with the appearance of the rash or arthralgias, at which point the patient is no longer considered infectious. These latter findings are thought to be related to antigen–antibody complexes. Generally, the illness is self-limited, although in some patients the arthropathy may persist or recur for several months.

Human parvovirus B19 infection during pregnancy usually results in the delivery of a healthy newborn; however, there is an association with an increased risk of fetal death and nonimmune hydrops. Fetal death appears to be more likely if human parvovirus B19 infection is acquired before 20 weeks' gestation. Hydrops fetalis is an uncommon but dreaded complication and is probably caused by fetal bone marrow suppression and direct viral effects on the fetal myocardium. Two prospective studies of pregnant women with serologic evidence of recent B19 infection estimated the risk of adverse outcome at less than 10% overall. Liveborn infants have shown no malformations or developmental problems attributable to intrauterine B19 infection. Recent studies have shown that fetal hydrops may resolve spontaneously in some cases. More data are needed for a clear understanding of the risks of a human parvovirus B19 infection during pregnancy.

Chronic red cell aplasia caused by persistent human parvovirus B19 infection has been described in patients undergoing chemotherapy for leukemia and other lymphoproliferative disorders and is being recognized with increasing frequency in patients with AIDS. It may also be seen in patients with immunoglobulin deficiency. A chronic human parvovirus B19-induced red cell aplasia syndrome has been described

in several patients who are capable of generating anti-human parvovirus B19 IgM but who cannot "switch" to production of anti-human parvovirus B19 IgG. Thus, it appears that T cells and immunoglobulins are important in preventing the persistence of human parvovirus B19 infection. The common defect in the patients with chronic parvovirus B19 infection is the inability to produce sufficient neutralizing anticapsid antibody. These patients improve when they recover their ability to produce antibody (i.e., after recovery from chemotherapy) or when they are treated with intravenous immunoglobulin. As outlined under Plans, Therapeutic, such treatments may have to be repeated.

The transient aplastic crisis has been described most commonly in association with sickle cell anemia, but also occurs in other hemolytic anemias such as pyruvate kinase deficiency and hereditary spherocytosis.

Prevention

Prevention of human parvovirus B19 infection in the community is probably impossible. Nonimmune pregnant women or those who do not know their immune status should take efforts to avoid respiratory or fomite contact if fifth disease cases are occurring in the community. It is recommended that hospitalized patients with transient aplastic crisis and patients with human parvovirus B19-associated chronic aplastic anemia be placed in combined contact and respiratory isolation (as for respiratory syncytial virus), as they may remain infectious during these illnesses. In fact, nosocomial human parvovirus B19 transmission has been documented in association with the transient aplastic crisis syndrome and is a matter of concern for both pregnant hospital personnel and susceptible immunocompromised patients. Infection control protocols to decrease nosocomial spread will likely be developed in the near future as a better understanding of the likelihood of the risk of serious consequences is evolved. The ability of prophylactic immune globulin administered to a susceptible individual after exposure to human parvovirus B19 to prevent complications of infection is not known. No vaccine is available yet, but human trials of a vaccine composed of empty parvovirus capsids are expected in the near future.

As yet, there is no evidence to support routine screening of all female hospital employees or of all pregnant patients for human parvovirus B19 immunity.

Cost Containment

Children with typical fifth disease can be readily diagnosed on the basis of clinical manifestations, eliminating the expense of serologic testing. The rapid recognition of human parvovirus B19 infection in most adult cases by use of appropriate human parvovirus B19 serology does not commit the patient to expensive tests and treatments. Rather, this specific serology identifies the diagnosis and prevents unnecessary expense in searching for or treating other diseases, such as seronegative rheumatoid arthritis or systemic lupus erythematosus. The utility of routine testing for human parvovirus B19 in all patients with transient aplastic crisis remains to be established. The rare immunodeficient patient who develops pure red cell aplasia due to human parvovirus B19 may require fewer hospitalizations and transfusions if diagnosed appropriately and treated with immune sera, thereby decreasing the overall costs of the illness. Nosocomial spread from these infected patients may also be decreased, reducing costs even further.

REFERENCES

Brown KE, Young NS, Johnson ML. Molecular, cellular and clinical aspects of parvovirus B19 infection. Crit Rev Oncol Hematol 1994;16:1.
Centers for Disease Control. Risks associated with human parvovirus B19 infection. MMWR 1989;38:80.
Frickhofen N, Abkowitz JL, Safford M, et al. Persistent B19 parvovirus infection in patients infected with human immunodeficiency virus type 1 (HIV-1): A treatable cause of anemia in AIDS. Ann Intern Med 1990;113:926.
Naides SW. Infection control measures for human parvovirus B19 in the hospital setting. Infect Control Hosp Epidemiol 1989;10:326.
Public Health Laboratory Service Working Party on Fifth Disease. Prospective study of human parvovirus (B19) infection in pregnancy. Br Med J 1990;300:1166.
Torok TJ. Parvovirus B19 and human disease. Adv Intern Med 1992;37:431.

CHAPTER 8–76

Human Immunodeficiency Virus Infection and the Acquired Immunodeficiency Syndrome

Thomas J. Spira, M.D.

DEFINITION

Human immunodeficiency virus (HIV) infection causes a progressive immunodeficiency which can develop over the course of a decade. Acute infection may be relatively nonspecific in its manifestations (a mononucleosis-like syndrome) or, in rare cases, may be associated with opportunistic infections. A long so-called "latent" period may be relatively asymptomatic. With the development of severe immunodeficiency and opportunistic infections or malignancies, the disease is known as the acquired immunodeficiency syndrome (AIDS).

ETIOLOGY

Human immunodeficiency virus infection and AIDS are caused by species-specific human RNA viruses in the lentivirus subfamily of retroviruses, namely, HIV-1 and HIV-2. Both cause severe immunodeficiency and neurologic disease. Related viruses cause similar disease in monkeys and cats.

CRITERIA FOR DIAGNOSIS

Suggestive

Human immunodeficiency virus infection should be suspected in any patient exhibiting manifestations of immunodeficiency without an apparent etiology. Even in the absence of clinical signs of immunodeficiency, suspicion should be high in those in exposure categories with the highest numbers of cases of infection, namely, homosexual men; injecting drug users; individuals with hemophilia; recipients of blood transfusions, blood components, or tissues; and heterosexual contacts of the preceding groups. Sexual contacts of individuals without known exposure to HIV but with multiple sexual partners are also at higher risk. Individuals with tuberculosis, especially those with atypical presentations, may also have concurrent HIV infection. Those with sexually transmitted diseases and pregnant women in areas of high prevalence are also at higher risk for HIV infection.

Definitive

The diagnosis of HIV infection is made by the detection of serum antibodies to HIV. Most commonly, this is done using an enzyme-linked immunosorbent assay to screen for antibodies against viral proteins. If positive, the assay is repeated and, if still positive, is confirmed with another test such as the Western blot assay or immunofluorescence assay.

Current recommendations are that anyone at risk for HIV infection be tested for HIV antibodies and, if positive, have quantitation of their CD4+ T cells (helper/inducer T) to determine their place in the spectrum of infection.

CLINICAL MANIFESTATIONS

Subjective

Human immunodeficiency virus infection may initially be asymptomatic or manifest itself as an acute mononucleosis-like syndrome with fever, fatigue, malaise, myalgia, arthralgia, sweats, anorexia, weight loss, photophobia, sore throat, nausea, vomiting, diarrhea, headache, transient maculopapular rash, and/or lymphadenopathy. Neurologic abnormalities including encephalitis, meningitis, peripheral neuropathy, and/or cognitive or affective changes may also occur. This acute disease usually occurs 2 to 4 weeks after exposure and may last several weeks with complete resolution. The infected individual may then be asymptomatic for several years. During this period, some of the neurologic abnormalities may recur or newly develop, and the patient may describe problems with short-term memory or with the ability to do simple tasks. The patient's mood or personality may be affected, more commonly with a change toward apathy or depression, although agitation or mania can also develop. Neuropathies, such as acute demyelinating polyneuropathy (Guillain–Barré syndrome), chronic inflammatory demyelinating neuropathy, and a multiple sclerosis-like illness, can also occur.

The initial manifestation of AIDS varies from individual to individual and even from risk group to risk group. Overall, the disease that occurs most frequently is *Pneumocystis carinii* pneumonia (PCP). A variety of other opportunistic infections and opportunistic malignancies can also occur; these are listed in Table 8–76–1. Among homosexual or bisexual men, Kaposi's sarcoma is the next most frequently occurring opportunistic disease that would suggest the diagnosis of AIDS. Among the other risk groups, Kaposi's sarcoma occurs relatively infrequently. These infections or malignancies may occur in a previously asymptomatic individual or they may occur in a setting of less severe infections or constitutional symptoms such as chronic fatigue or malaise, low-grade fevers, night sweats, weight loss, and diarrhea.

TABLE 8–76–1. OPPORTUNISTIC DISEASES IN AIDS

Protozoal Infections
Pneumocystis carinii pneumonia
Toxoplasma gondii encephalitis or disseminated infection
Cryptosporidium enteritis, lasting longer than 1 month
Isospora belli enteritis, lasting longer than 1 month

Fungal Infections
Candida esophagitis or disseminated infection
Cryptococcus neoformans meningitis or disseminated infection
Histoplasma capsulatum disseminated infection

Bacterial Infections
Mycobacterium avium–intracellulare disseminated infection
Mycobacterium tuberculosis disseminated infection
Mycobacterium kansasi disseminated infection
Salmonella bacteremia
Listeria monocytogenes bacteremia
Rhodococcus equi pneumonia

Viral Infections
Cytomegalovirus retinitis and disseminated infection
Herpes simplex esophagitis and mucocutaneous lesions lasting longer than 1 month
Varicella–zoster disseminated infection
Papovavirus-associated progressive multifocal leukoencephalopathy

Helminthic Infections
Strongyloides stercoralis disseminated infection

Tumors
Kaposi's sarcoma
Primary brain lymphoma
Diffuse undifferentiated non-Hodgkin's lymphoma or Burkitt's-like lymphoma
Hodgkin's disease

Other
Lymphocytic interstitial pneumonitis (associated with Epstein-Barr virus)

Note: This listing does not include every infection or tumor found in individuals with AIDS.

Objective

Physical Examination

Physical findings with acute HIV infection include fever, sweats, weight loss, diarrhea, a maculopapular rash, sore throat, and disseminated lymphadenopathy. These usually resolve in several weeks, although the lymphadenopathy may persist.

During the so-called "latent" period of the infection, physical findings are usually absent. Some individuals may begin having minor opportunistic infections such as varicella–zoster infection (shingles), papillomavirus infection (warts), disseminated molluscum contagiosum, bacterial folliculitis, and dermatophyte infection. Seborrheic dermatitis and psoriasis may also appear. Increasing immunodeficiency may exacerbate some of these conditions. Other conditions such as oral candidiasis (thrush) and oral hairy leukoplakia may develop. Oral candidiasis may present in the classic pseudomembranous form with white plaques on mucosal surfaces or as erythematous patches, hyperkeratotic white lesions, or angular cheilitis. Oral hairy leukoplakia was initially described only in individuals with HIV infection, but has subsequently been observed with other causes of immunodeficiency such as bone marrow transplantation. A condition resembling oral hairy leukoplakia in normal individuals has also been described. Oral hairy leukoplakia appears as painless, filiform white lesions on the lateral aspects of the tongue. Other oral findings associated with HIV infection include gingivitis and periodontitis, herpes simplex virus infection, cytomegalovirus infection with oral ulceration, recurrent aphthous ulcers, papillomavirus infection, and Kaposi's sarcoma lesions. Parotid enlargement, although more common in children, can be seen in adults, sometimes accompanied by xerostomia.

Lymphadenopathy or splenomegaly may be found, although these do not correlate with disease progression.

The physical findings of the opportunistic infections associated with AIDS are presented in their appropriate sections in the text. These are not substantially different in this setting than in other situations of immunodeficiency. Kaposi's sarcoma may first appear as a cutaneous lesion on the extremities, trunk, or head. It may be a violaceous macule or plaque or a brown or red papule. These lesions are neither pruritic nor painful. In addition to the skin, lesions may occur throughout the gastrointestinal tract, where they are usually silent. They are readily visible in the oral cavity, where they occur most frequently on the hard and soft palate and gums as areas of red to violet discoloration. In addition, Kaposi's sarcoma may involve lymph nodes in a minority of individuals who have chronic generalized lymphadenopathy as a manifestation of infection with HIV. This may precede cutaneous or gastrointestinal tract involvement. Tuberculosis may present typically early in the course of HIV infection, but will present more atypically with increasing immunodeficiency. Then it tends to be more disseminated with mediastinal or hilar lymphadenopathy and a negative PPD skin test. Radiographic manifestations are also atypical, with lower lobe infiltrates, absence of cavities, or miliary pattern.

Routine Laboratory Abnormalities

Routine laboratory examination may reveal anemia, leukopenia, or thrombocytopenia. Anemia, which can increase over the course of the disease, has been associated with clinical progression. This is usually normocytic. Leukopenia may be present late in the disease, often due to lymphopenia. Neutropenia can also contribute to the leukopenia, especially in late disease. Thrombocytopenia also occurs, most frequently in late disease, and is most commonly due to HIV-associated idiopathic thrombocytopenic purpura. Rarely, thrombotic thrombocytopenic purpura can occur.

Serum chemistry tests can show a decreased albumin and elevate gamma globulin, resulting in a decreased albumin/gamma globulin ratio. Liver function test abnormalities may relate to the increased incidence of hepatitis, both B and C in some individuals at high risk for HIV infection. Cholesterol levels can decrease early in HIV infection and remain low into late infection. Triglceride levels tend to increase. Some patients with higher levels are at risk for triglceride-induced pancreatitis.

PLANS

Diagnostic

Differential Diagnosis

As noted under Criteria for Diagnosis, the diagnosis of HIV infection is made by finding antibodies to HIV antigens. Enzyme-linked immunosorbent assay is the most commonly used method for screening. An initially reactive test must be repeated on the same specimen in duplicate and, if still reactive, must be confirmed by Western blot or immunofluorescence assay. Only if both the screening and confirmatory tests are positive should the result be reported to the patient. In some cases, especially in populations with a low prevalence rate, the screening test may be reactive but the confirmatory test is usually nonreactive. Consensus criteria, such as those of the Association of State and Territorial Public Health Laboratory Directors, have been established for determining what are positive, indeterminate, and negative Western blots (Centers for Disease Control and Prevention, 1989). A positive test must reveal antibodies to two of the major viral proteins: p24, gp41, and gp160/120. An indeterminate pattern, one with other band patterns, may represent cross-reacting antibodies or antibodies to non-viral cellular proteins contaminating the antigen preparation or an early or late stage of HIV infection. Those with indeterminate Western blot tests should have them repeated after 3 to 6 months. It may also be useful to obtain a second specimen from individuals who have a weakly reactive enzyme-linked immunosorbent assay and are negative or indeterminate by immunofluorescence assay or Western blot.

Human immunodeficiency virus can also be detected directly. The p24 core protein of the virus can be detected in the serum of about 20 to 30% of patients using an antigen-capture enzyme-linked immunosorbent assay. The sensitivity of this assay has been improved by acidification of the serum to dissociate the antigen from antigen–antibody complexes. The virus can also be detected in infected cells or plasma by coculture with suitable recipient cells, either stimulated normal peripheral blood lymphocytes or continuously cultured cell lines. Proviral DNA can be detected using the polymerase chain reaction to specifically amplify portions of proviral DNA, followed by use of specific probes to detect the DNA, or viral RNA can be directly detected using RNA-specific probes or by first reverse-transcribing the RNA to DNA followed by polymerase chain reaction and specific probes to detect the DNA. Viral load in plasma can be determined using either a branched-chain DNA amplification technique or a quantitative competitive polymerase chain reaction technique. The clinical usefulness of such testing is currently being evaluated.

The diagnosis of AIDS can often be made on clinical grounds alone. The first goal is the diagnosis of the opportunistic infection or malignancy. Some of these opportunistic diseases are listed in Table 8–76–1. The procedures for diagnosing these diseases are discussed in their appropriate chapters. Some infections that may also occur in the normal host are considered to be indicative of AIDS if found in conjunction with a positive test for HIV. The diagnosis of Kaposi's sarcoma is made by biopsy and histologic examination of a suspected lesion. It must be emphasized that not all skin lesions in persons at risk for the disease will necessarily prove to be Kaposi's sarcoma. A newly recognized opportunistic infection, bacillary angiomatosis (epithelioid angiomatosis), caused by *Rochalimaea henselae* or *Rochalimaea quintana,* causes a proliferation of small blood vessels in the skin and visceral organs and is sometimes mistaken for Kaposi's sarcoma. With the diagnosis of an appropriate opportunistic infection or malignancy in an individual without any other identifiable cause for cell-mediated immunodeficiency and who is HIV positive, the diagnosis of AIDS is made. Rare individuals may have opportunistic disease, be HIV negative by all tests, and have low CD4+ T-lymphocyte counts. This entity has been call idiopathic CD4+ T lymphocytopenia and has a better prognosis than does HIV infection. Currently, in 96% of instances, the individual who has AIDS will be a member of one of the groups at high risk for developing the disease. Although not necessary for diagnosis, immunologic testing is often done both for confirmation and to determine the time to initiate treatment (i.e., zidovudine, *P. carinii* pneumonia prophylaxis). This testing usually reveals abnormally low numbers of helper inducer T cells and impaired mitogen and antigen responsiveness.

In 1993, the Centers for Disease Control and Prevention expanded the definition of AIDS used for national surveillance purposes to include pulmonary tuberculosis, recurrent pneumonia, and invasive cervical cancer in the presence of HIV infection. Also included were all HIV-infected persons who have fewer than 200 CD4+ T lymphocytes/μL, or a CD4+ T-lymphocyte percentage of total lymphocytes of less than 14. This definition is used by all states for AIDS case reporting. Diagnosis is therefore made either by the diagnosis of an AIDS-defining condition as noted above or by meeting the CD+4 T-lymphocyte level criterion.

Diagnostic Options and Recommended Approach

A newly diagnosed patient with HIV infection should have a baseline history and physical examination. A Pap smear should be included in women because of the increased incidence of cervical dysplasia and invasive cervical carcinoma. Laboratory screening should include beside routine complete blood count with differential and chemistries; testing for syphilis (VDRL or RPR) with confirmation (FTA-ABS, TPHA, ELISA), toxoplasmosis (IgG), tuberculosis (PPD), and cryptococcal antigen; and a hepatitis screen (HBV sAg, sAb, cAb and HCV Ab if indicated). A chest x-ray should also be done. A CD4+ T-lymphocyte count and percentage should be obtained to determine the patient's stage of disease. Counseling regarding the disease and methods to prevent transmission should also be provided.

Therapeutic

The current recommended initial treatment for HIV is zidovudine (azidothymidine, AZT). This drug suppresses viral replication by inhibiting the viral reverse transcriptase. High levels can be achieved in the cerebrospinal fluid, which is necessary for the treatment of central nervous system disease caused by HIV. Zidovudine is currently recommended at a dosage of 500 to 600 mg/d (100 mg every 4 hours while awake or 200 mg every 8 hours orally). Toxic effects that may occur during the first several weeks of therapy include headache, malaise, nausea, vomiting, rash, fever, insomnia, abdominal discomfort, and diarrhea. Often these resolve with continued therapy. Occasionally, these effects may persist or be sufficiently severe to require either reduction in dosage or cessation of therapy. Dosage reduction below 300 mg/d is probably not effective. Zidovudine can cause bone marrow suppression, most commonly with the development of anemia or neutropenia. Thrombocytopenia is less common. Red cell macrocytosis is common. Severe anemia may be treated with dosage reduction, periodic blood transfusion, or, in those with low erythropoietin levels, recombinant human erythropoietin. Severe neutropenia can similarly be treated with dosage reduction and/or granulocyte colony-stimulating factor therapy. The effect on the bone marrow is reversible on cessation of therapy, and in some patients a switch to an alternative antiretroviral agent that lacks this toxicity should be considered. Other long-term toxic effects include myopathy with proximal muscle weakness, usually in the lower extremities, and elevation in serum creatine kinase. Nail pigmentation also may occur.

Based on the results of several clinical trials, there is some controversy on when therapy should be initiated. An NIAID State-of-the-Art conference has recommended no therapy for those who are asymptomatic with a CD4+ T-lymphocyte count higher than 500/μL. These patients should continue to be observed with clinical and immunologic monitoring (CD4+ T-cell count) every 6 months. For those who are asymptomatic but have a CD4+ T-cell count of 200 to 500/μL, there is an option: either to initiate zidovudine therapy or to continue to be observed with clinical and immunologic monitoring for disease progression without the initiation of antiretroviral therapy. The subsequent development of HIV-related symptoms or laboratory evidence of disease progression, such as a rapid decline in CD4+ T-cell counts, would support the initiation of zidovudine therapy. Symptomatic patients, other than those with acute HIV infection, with CD4+ T-cell counts of 200 to 500/μL and no prior antiretroviral therapy should initiate zidovudine therapy. Asymptomatic or symptomatic patients with CD4+ T-cell

counts below 200/μL and no prior antiretroviral therapy should also initiate zidovudine therapy.

There is also a lack of consensus on when to initiate modifications in therapy. The State-of-the-Art conference recommended that for patients tolerating zidovudine who are clinically stable (CD4+ T-cell count greater than 300/μL with no recent trend toward decline in CD4+ T-cell count), zidovudine therapy should be continued. For patients tolerating zidovudine who are clinically stable but who have evidence of further immunodeficiency (CD4+ T-cell count less than 300/μL, either zidovudine may be continued or a switch can be made to didanosine. Symptomatic patients with CD4+ T-cell counts between 50 and 500/μL who experience therapeutic failure on zidovudine or who become intolerant of zidovudine should initiate an alternative antiretroviral therapy. Similarly, those with CD4+ T-cell counts less than 50/μL who experience a therapeutic failure on zidovudine should initiate an alternative antiretroviral therapy (didanosine or zalcitabine). For asymptomatic patients with CD4+ T-cell counts greater than 500/μL who are intolerant of initial therapy with zidovudine, antiretroviral therapy should be discontinued and the patient should be observed with clinical and laboratory monitoring every 6 months. Asymptomatic patients with a CD4+ T-cell count between 50 and 500/uL who are intolerant of initial therapy with zidovudine should initiate alternative antiretroviral monotherapy. Patients with a CD4+ T-cell count less than 50/μL who are intolerant of initial therapy with zidovudine should initiate alternative antiretroviral therapy or consider the option of discontinuing all antiretroviral therapy.

In addition to zidovudine, three other antiretroviral agents, all nucleoside analogs like zidovudine, are Food and Drug Administration approved for use in HIV infection. Didanosine (dideoxyinosine, ddI), zalcitabine (dideoxycitidine, ddC), and stavudine (deoxydidehydrothymine, d4T) all have shown evidence of viral suppression in vitro and in vivo, and their toxicities differ from that of zidovudine. They are indicated as second-line drugs as noted above. All are free of significant bone marrow toxicity but have their own spectrum of toxicities. Didanosine preparations are buffered, as the drug is rapidly degraded at an acid pH. Didanosine is available as a chewable, dispersible buffered tablet and as a buffered powder for oral solution. The dosages are adjusted to the patient's weight and are administered twice daily (≥60 kg, 200-mg chewable tablet or 250 mg buffered powder; <60 kg, 125-mg chewable tablet or 167 mg of buffered powder). Absorption is better if taken on an empty stomach. Drugs that require an acid pH should be taken 0.5 hour before or 1 to 2 hours after didanosine. Toxic effects of didanosine include peripheral neuropathy, pancreatitis, hyperamylasemia, hyperuricemia, abdominal pain, and skin rash. Toxic effects associated with the citrate buffer include dry mouth, altered taste, nausea (more with the chewable tablets), and diarrhea (more with the buffered powder). Didanosine should be avoided or used with caution in those with a previous history of pancreatitis, in alcoholics, or in those taking other medications that are toxic to the pancreas. Zalcitabine is used at 0.75 mg orally every 8 hours. Toxic effects include peripheral neuropathy, pancreatitis (rare), skin rash, oral ulcers, dysphagia, abdominal pain, headache, and myalgia. Half-dosages have been used in patients who have had mild neuropathy, which resolved after discontinuing therapy. Stavudine is used at doses of 30 mg for those less than 60 kg and 40 mg for those 60 kg, or heavier, orally, twice daily. Toxic effects include peripheral neuropathy, pancreatitis (rare), nausea, vomiting, abdominal pain, diarrhea, skin rash, headache, sleep disorders and mania. In vitro, there is evidence of antagonism with zidovudine so that these agents are not used together.

Other approaches to treatment using other classes of drugs are currently under evaluation. Nevirapine and other nonnucleoside viral reverse transcriptase inhibitors, saquinavir and other viral protease inhibitors, and additional nucleoside analog reverse transcriptase inhibitors such as lamivudine (3-thiacytidine, 3TC) are being tested in combination with approved antiretroviral agents. As viral resistance develops relatively rapidly with monotherapy with agents like nevirapine and saquinavir, combination therapy is being compared with the existing monotherapy approach.

In addition, recombinant interferon alfa has been licensed for the treatment of AIDS-related Kaposi's sarcoma. Thirty to fifty percent of patients had a major objective response accompanied by longer survival.

FOLLOW-UP

The extent of follow-up for patients with HIV infection is determined by their stage of infection. Those in an early stage of infection with few or no signs or symptoms may be followed as infrequently as every 6 months. As noted above, as CD4+ T-cell counts approach the levels where treatment decisions are made (i.e., 500/µL and 200/µL), visits every 3 months are recommended. At any CD4+ T-cell level, if other medical problems or HIV-related problems occur, more frequent visits may be necessary. Also, when treatment such as zidovudine is begun, visits may need to be more frequent initially.

Patients with early Kaposi's sarcoma who are otherwise in good health can be followed as infrequently as once every 3 months. During these visits, clinical progression of the disease is evaluated, looking for evidence of the development of lesions that may require treatment. These include lesions on the feet, which may cause pain on walking, or lesions on the face or other readily visible areas, which are sometimes treated for cosmetic reasons. The number of lesions and the rate of development of new lesions tend to correlate with the level of immunodeficiency. Severe cutaneous or internal organ involvement often prompts therapeutic intervention. Patients with opportunistic infections are usually followed more frequently, often monthly. Some opportunistic infections such as cryptococcal disease, *Salmonella* enteritis, and severe mucous membrane candidiasis require prolonged treatment. More frequent visits for monitoring for response to treatment and for possible toxic effects of treatment are often necessary.

As previously stated, because of the wide range of manifestations of the various opportunistic infections seen in AIDS, it is difficult to inform the patient of all the possible symptoms that may occur. Prolonged fever, increase in night sweats, chronic diarrhea, severe headaches or other neurologic changes, and progressive shortness of breath should all prompt a follow-up visit to the physician. Any unusual symptom should at least prompt a call to the physician to determine if follow-up is required.

DISCUSSION
Prevalence and Incidence

Acquired immunodeficiency syndrome is the severe end of the spectrum of disease caused by HIV. Since the first patients were diagnosed in 1978 and 1979, more than 400,000 individuals in the United States have developed the disease. The epidemic curves for the disease by risk group for men and women are shown in Figure 8–76–1. It has been estimated that about 750,000 people in the United States may be HIV infected. The cases of AIDS tend to occur in certain major metropolitan areas: 16% occurring in New York City; 4.9% in San Francisco; 3% in Los Angeles; and between 2 and 3% each in Miami, Washington, DC, Chicago, Houston, Newark, Philadelphia, and San Juan, Puerto Rico (Centers for Disease Control surveillance data, unpublished, 1995).

Although more prevalent in urban areas (85%), the disease in the United States has spread in recent years to smaller towns (9.5%) and rural areas (5%). Maps showing the incidence of reported cases of AIDS per 100,000 population in men and women in the United States during 1994 are shown in Figure 8–76–2. AIDS is the leading cause of death among men 25 to 44 years of age in the United States and the fourth among women 25 to 44 years of age (Centers for Disease Control surveillance data, unpublished, 1992). Cases among homosexual or bisexual men are the most widely distributed, whereas cases among injecting drug users are concentrated in the Northeast and in Puerto Rico. Cases among persons with hemophilia are also broadly distributed. Transfusion-associated cases tend to come from those areas with cases in the other risk groups. Pediatric cases are either transfusion-associated or in infants born to parents in risk groups, predominantly injecting drug users or persons who have had sex with an injecting drug user. Cases among heterosexual sex partners of those in risk groups occur

primarily among partners of injecting drug users or of HIV-infected persons where the risk was not specified.

Related Basic Science

Human immunodeficiency virus, the etiologic agent of AIDS, is a retrovirus of the lentivirus group, which includes such animal viruses as feline immunodeficiency virus, visna virus of sheep, and equine infectious anemia virus. Currently, at least two strains of HIV have been identified. HIV-1 causes the majority of AIDS cases occurring in central Africa, the Americas, Europe, and other parts of the world. HIV-2 has been isolated from individuals with AIDS in West Africa and is still relatively restricted to that region.

The virus consists of RNA and the enzyme reverse transcriptase (RNA-dependent DNA polymerase) surrounded by a cylindrical core made up of core proteins. This, in turn, is surrounded by a glycoprotein envelope. The viral genome of HIV-1 codes for three groups of proteins common to all retroviruses. The *gag* gene codes for the p55 precursor of the p15 and p24 core proteins and the p17 matrix protein, which appears to be located inside the viral envelope bilayer. The *env* gene codes for the gp160 precursor of the gp120 outer surface membrane glycoprotein and the gp41 transmembrane glycoprotein. The *pol* gene codes for the p65/p51 reverse transcriptase, which transcribes the viral RNA into proviral DNA, the p31 endonuclease (integrase), and the p22 protease. In addition to the above structural genes, the virus has a variety of regulatory genes such as *tat,* which controls the synthesis of all viral proteins, *rev,* which regulates the synthesis of structural proteins, and *nef,* which downregulates virus replication.

The virus has been isolated from blood, plasma, semen, saliva, tears, urine, cerebrospinal fluid, cervical secretions, and breast milk, as well as tissues such as bone marrow, lymph nodes, and brain. It is transmitted primarily by homosexual or heterosexual contact, parenteral inoculation of infected blood or blood products, transplantation of infected tissues, artificial insemination with infected semen, or from infected mother to newborn child (i.e., in utero infection, perinatally, or through infected breast milk). There is no evidence to support transmission by casual contact or by insect vectors. There is evidence suggesting that individuals either undergoing acute HIV infection or those at later stages of the infection, when viral load is increased, are more likely to transmit the infection than those in the so-called "latent" stage of the infection.

The virus binds with high affinity to helper/inducer T cells by way of the CD4 antigen on the cell's surface. This binding involves the gp120 outer surface membrane glycoprotein of the virus. On infection of the cell, the viral genome is transcribed into proviral cDNA, which is then integrated into the cell's native DNA in the nucleus. The incorporated proviral DNA may remain latent within the cell for an extended period and then may reactivate. This leads to replication, formation of messenger RNA coding for viral proteins, translation into viral proteins, viral assembly, and budding from the cell surface. Syncytium formation may follow through the binding of gp120 on infected cells with CD4 on uninfected cells. The precise mechanism of the death of the helper/inducer T cell is unknown. As the helper/inducer T cell has major effects on other cells of the immune system, this destruction results in a variety of cell-mediated immune defects which lead to opportunistic diseases. The helper/inducer T cell is required for optimal development of suppressor/cytotoxic T (CD8+) cells and natural killer cells, which are of importance in immune surveillance. The helper/inducer T cell also "helps" autologous B cells to proliferate and differentiate into immunoglobulin-producing cells. It also is involved in the production of a variety of lymphokines such as interleukin-2, interferon gamma, tumor necrosis factor B, interleukin-4, interleukin-5, interleukin-6, tumor necrosis factor, and granulocyte–macrophage colony-stimulating factor. Quantitation of CD4+ T lymphocytes (helper/inducer T cells) in the peripheral blood of patients with HIV infection is the most commonly used laboratory method for assessing the stage of the infection. CD4+ T-lymphocyte percentage and numbers tend to decrease over time, although the rate of decrease is subject to individual variation. The CD4+ T-lymphocyte count is inversely related to the risk of developing AIDS over a given period. In patients with opportunistic infections the counts

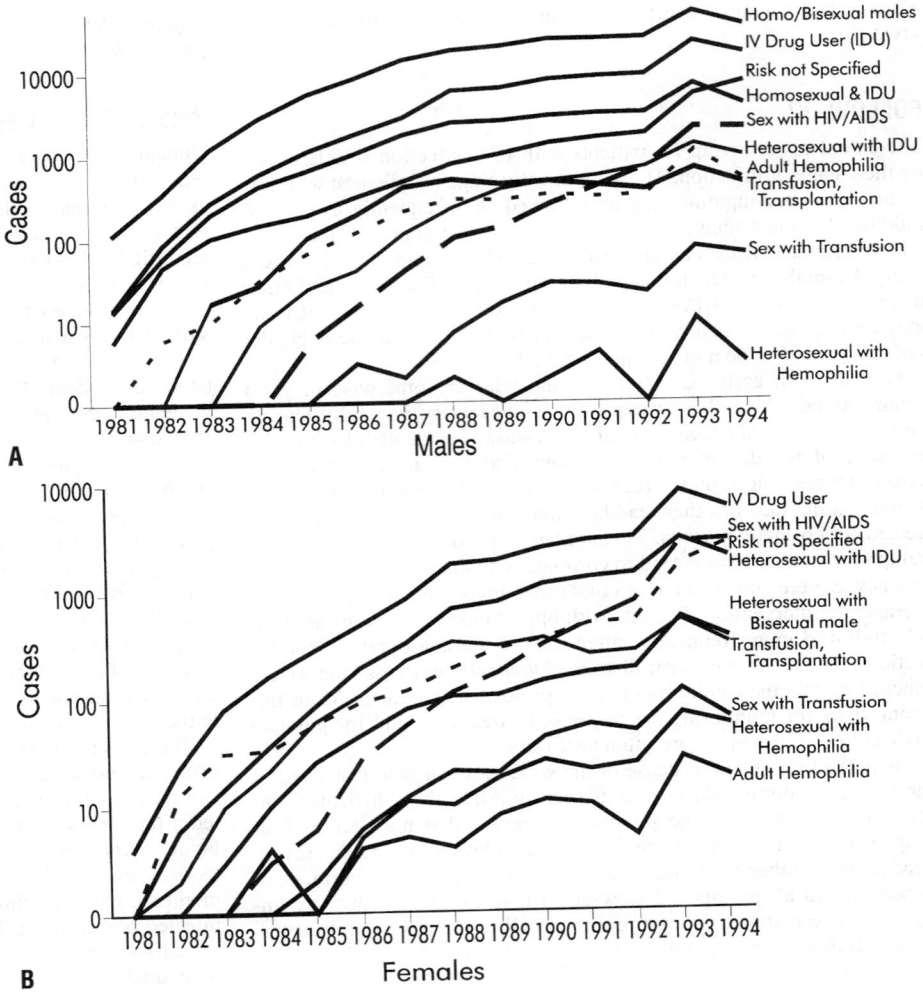

Figure 8–76–1. Reported AIDS cases, United States, by risk group. **A.** Males. **B.** Females. *(Source: Centers for Disease Control and Prevention, Atlanta, GA, unpublished data.)*

are usually below 200/μL and often below 100/μL (normal, >400/μL). Suppressor/cytotoxic T (CD8+) cells may be high, normal, or low, depending on the stage of the disease. They increase early in acute infection and may go down only late in the infection.

Human immunodeficiency virus also can infect other cells that have less CD4 on their surfaces than do CD4+ T lymphocytes. These include a subset of monocytes and macrophages, which may form a reservoir for the virus and may be a vehicle for central nervous system infection. Some neurons and glial cells can also be infected and may cause the neurologic disease associated with the virus. Bone marrow myeloid precursor cells can also be infected and may also form a reservoir for the virus.

A variety of other abnormalities occur, some of which have prognostic importance. There is often polyclonal B-cell activation with hypergammaglobulinemia, in adults usually of IgA and/or IgG, while in children of IgG, IgA, and IgM. Natural killer cell activity and T-cell capacity to lyse virally infected cells are diminished. The production of lymphokines such as interleukin-2 and interferon gamma is defective. Immune complexes are usually elevated as are levels of an acid-labile interferon alfa. Some of the nonspecific abnormalities, such as elevated levels of neopterin, B_2-microglobulin, and soluble interleukin-2 receptor, are markers of mononuclear cell activation and are among the best studied of the nonspecific markers of prognosis.

Natural History and Its Modification with Treatment

Studies of the natural history of HIV infection are incomplete and changing secondary to developments in the treatment of the infection. The interval between infection with HIV and the development of AIDS is estimated to be between 7 and 10 years based on data derived from

studies of individuals for whom the time of infection is known. These include studies of persons who have developed transfusion-associated AIDS, studies of a number of cohorts of homosexual men, and studies of persons with hemophilia. These studies are based primarily on data collected prior to the institution of zidovudine treatment for non-AIDS patients.

Antiretroviral therapy delays disease progression with a greater delay in those who start therapy at higher CD4+ T-lymphocyte levels. Delaying the start of zidovudine therapy until the development of AIDS or symptomatic HIV infection and a CD4+ T-lymphocyte count less than 200/μL did not result in a delay in the time to disease progression or death in one large trial. This lack of a delay may have been affected by the study design, which later allowed open-label therapy for those with CD4+ T-lymphocyte counts of <500/μL.

The clinical course of infection varies among individuals. In some, an acute illness develops consisting of an acute febrile illness with pharyngitis, lymphadenopathy, arthralgia, myalgia, and an erythematous maculopapular rash. This may be accompanied by headache, anorexia, malaise, and weight loss. Some patients may have neurologic involvement with peripheral neuropathy, meningoencephalitis, or radiculopathy. Minor opportunistic infections such as thrush can occur, and rarely, AIDS-defining opportunistic infections such as *Candida* esophagitis or *P. carinii* pneumonia can be seen. During this period there is viremia and a drop in CD4+ T lymphocytes. As antibodies to the virus develop over several weeks, the viremia and clinical illness usually subside, although some patients may have persistence of fatigue or lymphadenopathy.

Following the acute primary infection, an asymptomatic phase develops that may last several years. It was thought that viral activity was absent or at very low levels during this period, but recent examination of

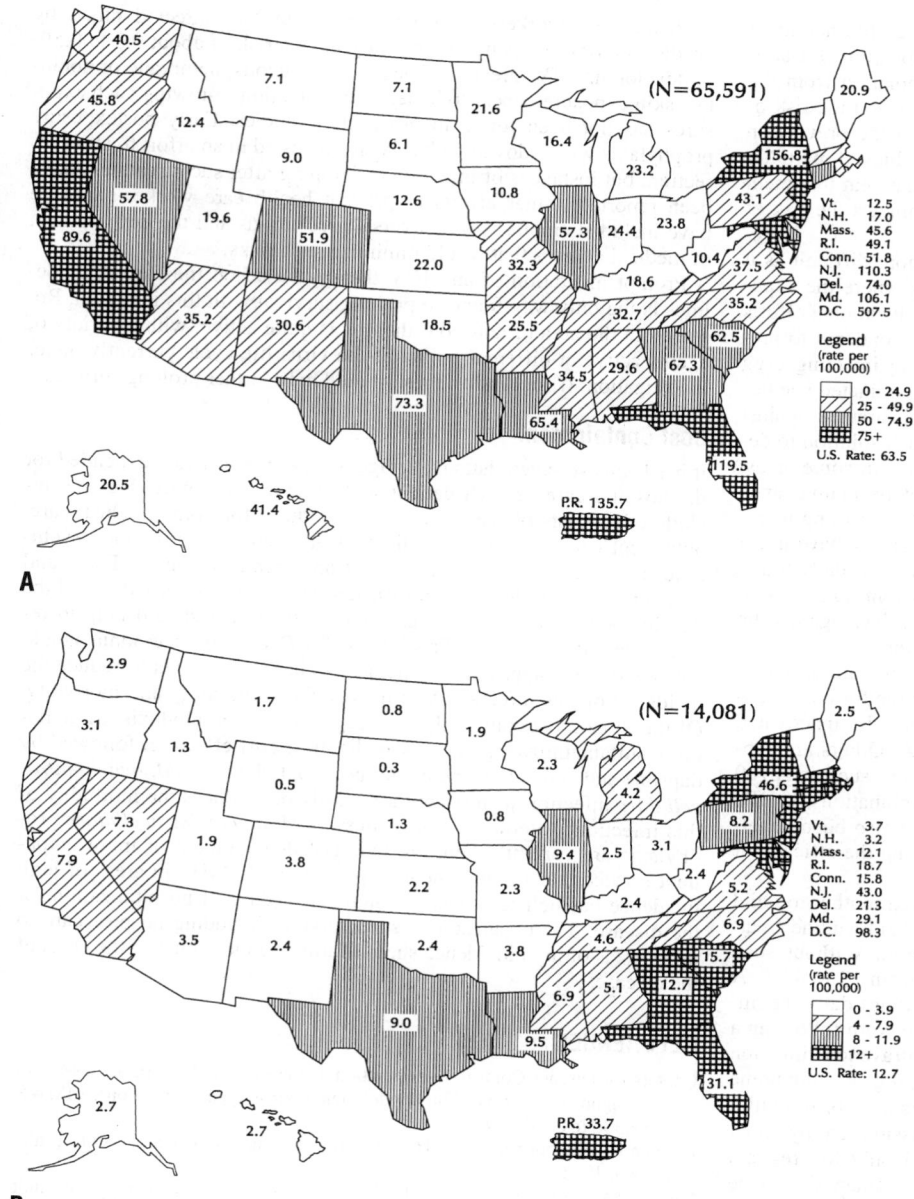

Figure 8–76–2. Adult/adolescent AIDS annual rates per 100,000 population, for cases reported in 1994 United States. **A.** Males. **B.** Females. *(Source: Centers for Disease Control and Prevention, Atlanta, GA, unpublished data.)*

lymphoid organs such as lymph nodes has revealed high rates of viral replication and viral load, even during the so-called "latent" period. Although, in peripheral blood, only about 1 in 10,000 CD4+ T lymphocytes may be infected, 1 in 10 to 100 may be infected in lymphoid organs. Virus replication can be interrupted using antiretroviral agents, with plasma HIV levels dropping in half every 2 days. Concomitantly, CD4+ T-lymphocyte levels in the peripheral blood double every 15 days. These data reveal that the virus is constantly being produced by infected cells and then rapidly cleared. This finding has suggested to some clinicians that antiretroviral therapy should be initiated early in the clinical course, even when the peripheral blood viral load may be low, to prevent destruction of the CD4+ T lymphocytes and consequent immunodeficiency. The decline in CD4+ T lymphocytes is usually associated with an increase in viral load. It may be either acute or gradual over the course of many years. It is still unclear what precipitates an acute decline or what prevents such a decline in those with a more gradual decline. Antiretroviral therapy results in a drop in viral load and an increase in CD4+ T-lymphocyte counts. With zidovudine, counts will again begin to drop after a variable time interval. This interval is longer for those starting zidovudine with higher CD4+ T-lymphocyte counts and shorter for those with lower counts. HIV becomes resistant to zidovudine through a series of mutations in the viral reverse transcriptase gene. Resistant strains can begin to be seen as early as 6 months after the initiation of therapy.

The therapeutic intervention that has had the greatest influence on prolonging survival in HIV infection is the use of prophylaxis for *P. carinii* pneumonia. Pneumocystosis is rarely seen in compliant patients. As this continues to be one of the most common and earliest major opportunistic infections in HIV infection, patients who meet the criteria for prophylaxis should be started on such treatment. Trimethoprim–sulfamethoxazole for *P. carinii* pneumonia prophylaxis has the additional benefit of preventing toxoplasmosis. Also recommended for prophylaxis of *Mycobacterium avium–intracellulare* infections is rifabutin (300 mg orally daily). This treatment reduces the risk of *M. avium–intracellulare* infection by about two thirds and should be considered for patients with a CD4+ T-lymphocyte count below 100/μL. There should be awareness that this drug interacts with a variety of other drugs used in this patient population.

Prevention

Although prevention of HIV-related disease can be achieved only through avoidance of exposure to HIV, progress has been made in two areas. The first is in the prevention of transfusion-related AIDS by the screening of donors on the basis of history, with the elimination of those with high risk factors, and screening of blood donations for antibodies to the virus (begun in April 1985), with elimination from the blood supply of those that are positive. This has minimized the risk of new cases developing in the future. The second is in the prevention among persons with hemophilia. This has been achieved partially through screening blood donations but also through the heat treatment of factor VIII preparations, which kills HIV and eliminates the risk of transmission by this product.

Preventing HIV infection in other risk groups is more difficult as it requires significant changes in lifestyle. In situations where the exposure to the virus is primarily through sexual contact, educational efforts have been directed toward abstinence and the use of condoms to prevent exposure to possibly infected secretions. Among injecting drug users, in whom exposure is thought to be through contaminated needles or other paraphernalia, educational efforts have been directed against sharing of needles and other equipment, to using bleach solution to decontaminate needles, and to needle exchange programs in some areas. Enrollment into treatment programs, such as methadone maintenance programs, has also been recommended as a means of preventing infection in this population. Although these efforts at prevention have had a modicum of success, as evidenced by declining rates of sexually transmitted diseases in some areas, they are unlikely to prevent transmission completely. This will require the development of vaccines against the virus and/or an effective treatment to eliminate the virus.

A number of vaccines to prevent HIV infection are at various stages of development and testing. Some use whole virus in the form of attenuated live virus with stable deletion mutants, formalin-inactivated whole virus, or pseudovirions, which lack viral RNA. Others are subunit vaccines using recombinant viral structural proteins, such as gp160 and gp120, or peptides from structural proteins. Combinations of HIV subunits and live virus vectors such as vaccinia have also been developed. Many questions remain to be answered regarding the efficacy of such vaccines.

Reduction of the transmission of HIV from infected mother to child perinatally has been achieved through a regimen of zidovudine treatment of the pregnant woman and the newborn child. Without such treatment, perinatal transmission rates have ranged from 13 to 40%. A regimen of 100 mg of zidovudine taken orally five times daily, beginning between 14 and 34 weeks of gestation, and 1 mg/kg/h following a 2 mg/k loading dose over an hour as a continuous intravenous infusion during labor for the mother, accompanied by 2 mg/kg of zidovudine syrup orally four times daily beginning 8 to 12 hours after birth until 6 weeks of age for the infant, has reduced the transmission rate by about two thirds. Because such treatment can be offered only to pregnant women who are known to be HIV infected, such women should be counseled and encouraged to be tested for HIV. Current Public Health Service recommendations are for voluntary testing. HIV-infected women in the United States are also advised not to breastfeed. For pregnant women who also have tuberculosis, teratogenic medications (e.g., streptomycin, pyrazinamide) are discouraged. Counseling regarding reproductive options should also be provided.

Health care workers who are exposed to HIV-infected blood by needlestick or other penetrating injury have a risk of about 0.3 to 0.5% of developing HIV infection. The risks of mucous membrane or nonintact skin exposure appear to be less, and infection following such exposures has not been found in prospective studies. Early postexposure prophylaxis with zidovudine has been suggested in an effort to abort infection, but instances of infection developing after such treatment have been reported. Other efforts to prevent health care worker exposure have included emphasis on universal precautions and the development of medical devices that would minimize such risks.

Prompt institution of anti-HIV therapy based on the current guidelines is the only way found to prolong survival with this infection. Research in the area of anti-HIV therapy is quite active, with a variety of agents active at different points of the virus life cycle currently under investigation. If successful, these should help further prolong survival.

Cost Containment

It has been estimated that an average of $147,000 is being expended for the hospital care of each patient with AIDS. This figure does not include other costs of the disease such as those for home medical care, outpatient care, outpatient medication, laboratory testing, and psychiatric counseling, as well as losses from premature death. Early and rapid diagnosis of the opportunistic diseases occurring in AIDS and the development of effective drugs for their treatment should help to reduce some of these costs. Prophylaxis for *P. carinii* pneumonia should be started at the appropriate time, as this has been shown to reduce the incidence of this infection with its associated mortality and morbidity. Of the three most commonly used regimens for prophylaxis, trimethoprim–sulfamethoxazole therapy is the most cost-effective, followed by dapsone and aerosolized pentamidine. Prophylaxis for *M. avium–intracellulare* infection with rifabutin is costly but reduces the morbidity of this infection. Alternative antibiotics for *M. avium–intracellulare* prophylaxis are currently being tested. The development of more outpatient services for the treatment of patients with AIDS in areas of high incidence has helped reduce the number of days of hospitalization for the disease. The expansion of such services including hospice care to other areas of high incidence should further reduce some of the costs of the disease.

REFERENCES

Centers for Disease Control. Interpretation and use of the Western blot assay for serodiagnosis of human immunodeficiency virus type 1 infections. MMWR 1989;38(Nos. 5–7):89.

Libman H, Witzburg RA, eds. HIV infection: A clinical manual. Boston: Little, Brown, 1993.

Sande MA, Carpenter CCJ, Cobbs CG, et al. Antiretroviral therapy for adult HIV-infected patients. JAMA 1993;270:2583.

Sande MA, Volberding PA, eds. The medical management of AIDS. Philadelphia: Saunders, 1995.

Wormser GP, ed. AIDS and other manifestations of HIV infection. New York: Raven Press, 1992.

CHAPTER 8–77

Human T-Cell Lymphotrophic Virus Type I Infections

Clifford J. Gunthel, M.D., and Carlos del Rio, M.D.

DEFINITION

Human T-cell lymphotrophic virus type I (HTLV-I) is a type C RNA retrovirus of the family Retroviridae, subfamily Oncovirinae. As a RNA retrovirus, HTLV-I is capable of infecting human hosts and integrating itself into the host's genome as proviral DNA. Although the majority of individuals infected with this retrovirus remain asymptomatic throughout life, HTLV-I infections can induce specific human diseases. Adult T-cell leukemia–lymphoma and tropical spastic paraparesis/HTLV-I-associated myelopathy are two diseased definitely associated with HTLV-I infections.

ETIOLOGY

Four retroviruses are known to cause disease in humans: human T-cell lymphotrophic viruses type I (HTLV-I) and type II (HTLV-II), and human immunodeficiency viruses type I (HIV-I) and type 2 (HIV-2). Each of these retroviruses infects the T lymphocytes, but the diseases with which they are associated are quite diverse. HTLV-I usually is not associated with symptomatic disease; however, in 3 to 7% of infected patients, it can cause adult T-cell leukemia–lymphoma or tropical spastic parapareses/HTLV-I-associated myelopathy. HTLV-II has been isolated from two patients with a T-cell variant of hairy cell leukemia; however, no clear associations have been established between HTLV-II infections and lymphoproliferative illnesses. Many patients may have antibodies present to these viruses but may be asymptomatic. This chapter discusses only the disorders associated with HTLV-I.

CRITERIA FOR DIAGNOSIS
Suggestive

Adult T-cell leukemia–lymphoma is characterized by a malignant aggressive proliferation of HTLV-I-infected T lymphocytes; it is seen in southwestern Japan, the Caribbean, central Africa, and the southeastern United States. Often patients present with constitutional symptoms such as fever, weakness, anorexia, and weight loss. Skin lesions, hypercalcemia, and the characteristic lymphocytes in the peripheral blood showing indentation of the nucleus should alert the clinician to the diagnosis. The proportion of atypical lymphocytes in the blood is generally 0.5 to 10%.

Tropical spastic paraparesis, or HTLV-I-associated myelopathy, is a slowly progressive encephalomyelopathy that affects adults from areas endemic for HTLV-I. It is characterized by symmetric weakness and spastic paraparesis or paraplegia, spasticity of the upper extremities, and bladder dysfunction. The diagnosis should be considered in patients with spastic paraparesis or paraplegia with pyramidal signs that is chronic and slowly progressive, and for which no spinal cord compression can be found by myelography or magnetic resonance imaging.

Other disease associated with HTLV-I infection include cases of inflammatory arthropathy, polymyositis, and uveitis. A syndrome of infectious dermatitis has been reported in children infected with HTLV-I.

A history of prior blood transfusion or of parental drug abuse may heighten the awareness that an HTLV-I infection may be present.

Definitive

In patients with the aforementioned clinical findings, the diagnosis is confirmed by establishing infection with HTLV-I. This is generally achieved by demonstrating specific antibodies to HTLV-I in the serum and/or cerebrospinal fluid. The most specific evidence of infection with HTLV-I is the presence of virus in the blood as demonstrated by growth in tissue cultures. Additionally, the presence of virus, viral products, or components of the virus' genetic sequence can be detected using polymerase chain reaction techniques.

The presence of HTLV-I antibody in the serum is diagnostic of prior infection, and most patients who are seropositive remain asymptomatic.

CLINICAL MANIFESTATIONS
Subjective

Patients with adult T-cell leukemia–lymphoma have lived in areas that are endemic for HTLV-I. Patients from the southeastern United States and the Caribbean typically present younger (median age, midforties) than those from Japan (median age, midsixties). Initially, patients present with an acute illness characterized by constitutional symptoms such as fever, night sweats, fatigue, and weight loss. These patients often present with complaints of symptoms related to the rapid development of diffuse peripheral lymphadenopathy, extensive skin lesions, recurrent superficial fungal infections, and/or symptoms of hypercalcemia such as confusion, somnolence, anorexia, nausea, constipation, polydipsia, and polyuria. The interval between the onset of symptoms and the diagnosis is usually brief, with a median of 2 months, but the interval between clinical disease and initial HTLV-I infections is generally many years.

Patients with HTLV-I-associated myelopathy are usually female (4:1 female-to-male ratio) and present with symptoms in the fifth decade of life. They complain of the gradual onset of bilateral weakness and stiff-

ness of the lower extremities, disturbances of gait, ataxia, and back pain, as well as numbness of dysesthesias. Impotence or diminished libido is common. Urinary symptoms such as incontinence or frequency and constipation are also frequent complaints.

Objective

The most important findings on physical examination of patients with adult T-cell leukemia–lymphoma include skin lesions, lymphadenopathy, hepatomegaly, and splenomegaly. The cutaneous manifestations are varied and include localized or diffuse infiltration, nodules, papules, erythema, plaques, and, at times, a generalized erythrodermic dermatitis, which may be similar to the erythrodermic rash seen in mycosis fungoides (a cutaneous T-cell lymphoma not caused by HTLV-I).

The leukocyte count is markedly elevated in most patients, with counts up to 100,000 cell/μL. There is a lymphocytosis, with some of the circulating lymphocytes having a characteristic indented, multilobed, and frequently clover leaf-shaped nucleus. In some patients the irregularities of the lymphocytes may resemble the abnormal cells seen in the Sézary syndrome. Some patients may present with a lymphomatous form of adult T-cell leukemia–lymphoma, and in these cases the leukocyte count may be normal with only a few abnormal lymphocytes. The infected/abnormal lymphocytes are of the helper–inducer T-cell type (CD4+ cells). The serum lactate dehydrogenase level is elevated, and a commonly increased serum calcium level is difficult to control without chemotherapy. Hypercalcemia is associated with elevated alkaline phosphatase levels. Diffuse lytic lesions can be seen on roentgenograms in patients with hypercalcemia and an elevated alkaline phosphatase. A radionucleotide bone scan, or "superscan," may show abnormalities suggestive of metabolic bone disease. Biopsies of these lytic bone areas reveal activated osteoclasts without tumor involvement. The chest x-ray may show interstitial pulmonary infiltrates, as well as mediastinal adenopathy. Evidence of opportunistic infection such as fever and chills with disseminated *Mycobacterium avium–intracellulare* may be seen.

Patients presenting with HTLV-I-associated myelopathy have spastic paraparesis, hyperreflexia, proximal muscle weakness in the lower extremities, and only mild sensory changes. Rectal tone may be decreased. Cognitive function is normal. The cerebrospinal fluid may be normal or may show a slight pleocytosis, elevated protein levels, and oligoclonal bands. On occasion, atypical cells have been seen in the cerebrospinal fluid. Myelography, computed tomography, and magnetic resonance imaging are usually normal in patients with this disease or show evidence of white matter lesions in the thoracic region of the spinal cord.

Patients with HTLV-I polymyositis have characteristic findings of proximal and symmetric muscle wasting, raising serum muscle enzyme levels, myopathic features on electromyography, and muscle changes of inflammation, necrosis, and degeneration.

PLANS
Diagnostic
Differential Diagnosis

Characteristically, adult T-cell leukemia–lymphoma progresses with a fulminant, rapid clinical course, resulting in ultimate mortality. Variations from this clinical picture have been recognized, prompting the classification of adult T-cell leukemia–lymphoma into four subtypes: smoldering, chronic, lymphomatous, and acute. Smoldering adult T-cell leukemia–lymphoma is characterized by skin lesions with normal leukocyte counts and no evidence of visceral involvement. Duration in the smoldering subtype may be quite prolonged (5–10 years) before proceeding to more aggressive stages. Clinically the chronic type of adult T-cell leukemia–lymphoma is similar to the smoldering form; however, there is an absolute lymphocytosis. Lymphadenopathy and visceral involvement may be present. The lymphomatous and acute types are the more characteristic forms of adult T-cell leukemia–lymphoma with skin, lymphatic, and visceral involvement, hypercalcemia, and immunodeficiency. The progression is rapid and survival is short. Given this clinical presentation, adult T-cell leukemia–lymphoma is difficult to distinguish from other types of cutaneous T-cell lymphomas.

Mycosis fungoides and Sézary syndrome may resemble adult T-cell leukemia–lymphoma both clinically and histologically. Demonstration of HTLV-I infection is needed to make the diagnosis of adult T-cell leukemia–lymphoma.

The clinical features of HTLV-I-associated myelopathy may be confused with multiple sclerosis. Absence of optic neuritis and eye movement disorders in HTLV-I-associated myelopathy may help to distinguish this illness from multiple sclerosis. The clinical course in HTLV-I-associated myelopathy is chronic and progressive. Periods of spontaneous remission, characteristic of multiple sclerosis, are rare in HTLV-I-associated myelopathy.

Diagnostic Options and Recommended Approach

The diagnosis of adult T-cell leukemia–lymphoma can be made by skin biopsy, lymph node biopsy, or examination of a peripheral blood smear in the appropriate clinical setting. Biopsies of involved skin or lymph nodes reveal diffuse infiltration by lymphoma, with abnormal pleomorphic lymphocytes that are of the mature helper–inducer T-cell phenotype (CD4+, CD8-, TdT-, TAC antigen+) . The serum of these patients shows the presence of antibodies to HTLV-I, and the malignant cells can be demonstrated to have proviral DNA integrated into their genome.

The diagnosis of HTLV-I-associated myelopathy can be suspected on the basis of the clinical epidemiologic features but requires laboratory confirmation. The serum and cerebrospinal fluid of these patients frequently contain antibodies against HTLV-I; however, only about 70 to 85% of patients with clinical disease are seropositive. Thus, a negative serology for HTLV-I antibodies does not exclude the diagnosis, but makes it difficult to implicate HTLV-I as the etiology of the illness unless the virus or its products can be demonstrated.

Currently, several serologic assays are commercially available with excellent sensitivity and specificity to detect the presence of antibodies against HTLV-I using the enzyme-linked immunosorbent assay. Antibody detected in this matter must be confirmed by Western immunoblotting or radioimmunoprecipitation assay.

Therapeutic

Therapeutic Options

In adult T-cell leukemia–lymphoma, intensive combination chemotherapy may produce remission, but the duration of benefit is usually brief. This disease is similarly refractory to bone marrow transplantation. Preliminary work has demonstrated a response to combination interferon-alfa and antiretroviral (zidovudine/ddI) therapy. The median survival for patients with acute presentations of adult T-cell leukemia–lymphoma is only 6 months. Salvage-type chemotherapy is usually not useful once the patient has a relapse. The disease should be treated by an expert in oncology when possible.

In tropical spastic paraparesis there is evidence that corticosteroids may improve some of the neurologic symptoms, although the response is usually transient. Some improvement has been reported with interferon-alfa, intravenous gamma globulin, and plasmapheresis. Zidovudine therapy has not proven to be of any benefit in HTLV-I-associated myelopathy.

Recommended Approach

For the acute form of adult T-cell leukemia–lymphoma, combination chemotherapy such as CHOP-like regimens should be administered under the supervision of an oncologist.

In HTLV-I-associated myelopathy, spasticity may improve with prednisone 60 mg orally daily.

Patients must be made aware of the modes of spread of HTLV-I infection and should avoid blood donation, breastfeeding, unprotected sex, or sharing of contaminated needles. Several studies have documented familial clustering (which suggests that there may have been spread by intimate nonsexual contact), sexual, and possibly perinatal transmission. Viral transmission via blood transfusion has been documented, and this is of considerable concern, especially in endemic regions. As the seroprevalence is high in intravenous drug users, transmission by contaminated needles is also considered to be important. Thus, although all the factors involved in the transmission of HTLV-I are not known, the same public health measures that are used for HIV or hepatitis B infection should be useful in preventing spread of this infection. Concern about the possible transmission of HTLV-I via transfusion has led many authorities to conclude that blood or tissue donors should be screened for evidence of antibodies against HTLV-I.

Patients and their families should be aware of the dismal prognosis of adult T-cell leukemia–lymphoma and of the gradual but continued progression of the neuromuscular findings in HTLV-I-associated myelopathy or polymyositis. Asymptomatic but potentially infectious HTLV-I-infected individuals must understand that, although they are capable of transmitting infection to others and therefore should use precautions similar to those recommended for HIV-infected patients, they themselves have a very low risk of developing an HTLV-I-related disease. In fact, it appears that asymptomatic HTLV-I infection is much less likely than HIV infection to progress to serious clinical illness and death.

FOLLOW-UP

Opportunistic infections similar to those seen in patients with AIDS occur in patients with adult T-cell leukemia–lymphoma but are less common than in HIV-infected patients. Patients must be followed carefully so that these infections are recognized and treated early. In patients with adult T-cell leukemia–lymphoma, follow-up depends partially on the types of chemotherapy and on the degree of hypercalcemia. In patients with HTLV-I-associated myelopathy the disease evolves more slowly, with progressive neurologic impairment occurring over several years.

DISCUSSION
Prevalence and Incidence

Infection with HTLV-I is endemic in areas of southwestern Japan, the Caribbean, northern South America, and the southeastern United States, occurring especially in African-American persons. There is a gradual age-dependent increase in seropositivity, with a peak incidence occurring between ages 40 and 60. It is estimated that in southwestern Japan, 20% of the population is seropositive; however, fewer than 1% of seropositive individuals go on to develop adult T-cell leukemia–lymphoma. HTLV-I is rare in the general population of the United States. A large serologic study of nearly 40,000 blood donors found 0.025% to be positive for antibodies against HTLV-I (Williams et al., 1988). In certain populations of intravenous drug users, however, a seroprevalence rate as high as 40% has been found.

Related Basic Science

Human T-cell lymphotrophic virus type I is a type C lymphotrophic retrovirus that was first isolated by Poiesz and colleagues in 1978 from a patient with a T-cell lymphoma (Poiesz et al., 1980). HTLV-I and HTLV-II are members of the family Retroviridae, subfamily Oncovirinae. They are single-stranded RNA viruses that have a unique enzyme: reverse transcriptase. This enzyme is a virally encoded RNA-dependent DNA polymerase that transfers the virus' genetic information from RNA to double-stranded DNA (provirus), which is integrated into the host cell genome to enable viral replication.

The genome of HTLV-I encodes four major genes, none of which are oncogenes. Following incorporation of HTLV-I proviral DNA into the host CD4+ cell genome, the product of the transactivating gene ("tax" gene) may be found in the nucleus of infected cells and appears to have a crucial role in T-cell transformation. When this "tax" gene is induced by various metabolic triggers, it can stimulate further viral replication in an autostimulating fashion. The "tax" protein also stimulates enhanced production of interleukin-2 and interleukin-2 receptors. This disturbance of the normal T-cell growth-regulating system likely is responsible for T-cell transformation and subsequent malignant changes.

Natural History and Its Modification with Treatment

Despite the relatively high seroprevalence rates in endemic populations, the clinical diseases associated with HTLV-I are rare. Little is known why only a small percentage of seropositive individuals progress to clinical illness. Evidence suggests that there is a relationship between HLA haplotypes and the development of HTLV-I-associated diseases. Why some patients go on to develop adult T-cell leukemia–lymphoma and others HTLV-I-associated myelopathy is also unclear. Few patients have been reported who have both HTLV-I-associated diseases.

Concurrent infection with HTLV-I and HIV has been documented, which is not surprising as the routes of transmission are somewhat similar. The consequences of dual infection are unclear at this time, however.

The natural routes of transmission of HTLV-I are not totally known but appear to involve passage of infected cells; however, familial clustering of seropositivity and clinical disease suggests that intimate contact may facilitate spread of the virus. Transmission can occur via blood transfusion, sexual contact (most frequently from male to female), from mother to infant through breast milk, and possibly in utero. Approximately half of the children born to antibody-positive mothers become seropositive in the first 24 months of life. Interestingly, HTLV-I infection appears to be much less common than HIV infection in the homosexual male population.

For those individuals who do develop adult T-cell leukemia–lymphoma or HTLV-I-associated myelopathy, therapy has very little impact on the clinical course. In either syndrome, if remission is induced with therapy, the effect is usually short-lived.

Prevention

The observed patterns of HTLV-I infection indicate that the virus is not highly contagious and that, unlike HIV, transmission of HTLV-I requires the transfer of infected cells and cannot be transmitted through cell-free body fluids. Using autologous blood transfusion when possible and limiting the number of units of blood that are transfused until HTLV-I serologic testing is universally available should decrease the number of seroconversions following transfusion of blood products. To decrease the risk of infection, patients should be instructed to use condoms, to avoid promiscuous sexual behavior, and not to share needles. The control of intravenous drug abuse will be an important means to stem the spread of HTLV-I infection in the United States. Nosocomial spread should be preventable by strict adherence to routine blood and body fluid precautions. In addition, women who test positive for HTLV-I infection should be encouraged not to breastfeed. An HTLV-I vaccine is currently not available; however, experimental vaccines using the envelope antigen have proven successful in animal models.

Cost Containment

In areas where HTLV-I infection is prevalent, it may prove beneficial to test blood for the presence of prior HTLV-I infection before transfusion as a way of reducing the incidence of infection. The tests may be expensive for many developing nations, and at this point HTLV-I testing is not being used widely. In the United States, blood banks are now routinely screening donors for HTLV-I seropositivity.

REFERENCES

Davey FR, Hutchinson RE. Pathology and immunology of adult T cell leukemia/lymphoma. Curr Opin Oncol 1991;3:13.

Gessain A, Gout O. Chronic myelopathy associated with human T-lymphotrophic virus type I (HTLV-I). Ann Intern Med 192;117:933.

Höllsberg P, Hafler DA. Pathogenesis of diseases induced by human lymphotropic virus type I infection. N Engl J Med 1993;328:1173.

Khabbaz RF, Onorato IM, Cannon RO, et al. Seroprevalence of HTLV-I and HTLV-II among intravenous drug users and persons in clinics for sexually transmitted diseases. N Engl J Med 1992;326:375.

Poiesz BJ, Ruscetti FW, Gazdar AF, et al. Detection and isolation of type C retrovirus particles from fresh and cultured lymphocytes of a patient with cutaneous T-Cell lymphoma. Proc Natl Acad Sci USA 1980;77:7415.

Williams AE, Fang CT, Slamon DJ, et al. Seroprevalence and epidemiological correlates of HTLV-I infection in U.S. blood donors. Science 1988;240:643.

Yamaguchi K, Takatsuki K. Adult T cell leukemia-lymphoma. Baillieres Clin Haematol 1993;6:899.

CHAPTER 8–78

Antibiotic Allergy

David Rimland, M.D.

DEFINITION

Allergy to an antibiotic is defined by the appearance of various subjective and objective findings after exposure to the drug. These findings are not pathognomonic but only suggestive, and defined by previous well-characterized responses to antigens.

ETIOLOGY

Allergic reactions are the result of an immune response involving specific antibody or sensitized lymphocytes.

CRITERIA FOR DIAGNOSIS
Suggestive

Although none of the following criteria are pathognomonic, a combination of these findings should suggest an allergic reaction: no resemblance to the pharmacologic action of the drug; elicited by minute amounts of drug after an initial induction period of 5 to 7 days; reappearance promptly on readministration of the drug; including symptoms classic for allergic reactions to macromolecular antigens; and cross-reactivity with drugs of similar structure.

Definitive

There are no definitive methods to diagnose an allergic reaction to an antibiotic, but the combination of the criteria mentioned above, sometimes supported by the specific laboratory tests noted below, are strongly suggestive.

CLINICAL MANIFESTATIONS
Subjective and Objective

The subjective and objective findings in a patient with an allergic reaction to an antibiotic vary considerably depending on the type of reaction. These reactions can be classified by the time of onset after administration of the drug and by the organ systems involved (Table 8–78–1).

Routine Laboratory Abnormalities

There are no routine laboratory abnormalities in patients with antibiotic allergy. Peripheral blood eosinophilia is seen occasionally, especially if a cutaneous eruption occurs. Anemia, leukopenia, or thrombocytopenia may occur if a specific hematologic reaction develops. Urine abnormalities such as hematuria, albuminuria, and eosinophils in the urine may develop if interstitial nephritis is the allergic phenomenon.

TABLE 8–78–1. SUBJECTIVE AND OBJECTIVE FINDINGS IN A PATIENT WITH ANTIBIOTIC ALLERGY

Type of Reaction	Subjective	Objective
Immediate (2–30 min)		
Anaphylaxis	Extreme anxiety	
	Dizziness, unconsciousness	Hypotension, shock
	Wheezing	Wheezing
	Hoarseness, choking	Laryngeal edema
	Shortness of breath	Tachypnea, hypoxia
	Rash with intense itching	Urticaria, edema, flushing
	Diarrhea	
Any components of anaphylaxis occurring independently (e.g., urticaria, asthma)	See above	See above
Accelerated (1–72 h)		
Urticaria	See above	
Laryngeal edema	See above	
Late (more than 3 d)		
Serum sickness	Pruritic rash	Urticaria
	Fever	Fever
	Joint swelling	Arthritis
	Adenopathy	Adenopathy
		Transient glomerulonephritis
Skin eruptions	Rash (description depends on type)	Rash of several types: morbilliform, maculopapular, urticaria, erythema multiforme, erythema nodosum, photosensitivity
Drug fever	Fever without other symptoms, beginning 5 to 8 d after drug	Intermittent or continuous fever, occasional eosinophilia
Other unusual reactions		
Hemolytic anemia	Weakness, shortness of breath	Anemia with evidence of hemolysis, positive Coombs' test
Thrombocytopenia	Cutaneous bleeding or hematuria, melena	Petechiae, purpura, hematuria, positive stool guaiac, thrombocytopenia
Neutropenia	Symptoms of infection (e.g., fever, chills, cough)	Leukopenia, findings of specific infection
Interstitial nephritis	Oliguria, hematuria; associated rash	Hematuria, albuminuria, oliguria, azotemia, eosinophilia, rash (at times), eosinophilia in the urine
Cholestatic jaundice	Nausea, abdominal pain, jaundice	Hepatomegaly, jaundice, elevated alkaline phosphatase and bilirubin levels, cholestasis by liver biopsy
Vasculitis	Variable, depending on organ systems involved	Variable (e.g., cutaneous lesions, glomerulonephritis)

PLANS
Diagnostic
Differential Diagnosis

As no diagnostic criteria are pathognomonic for an allergic reaction, a combination of the findings outlined under Criteria for Diagnosis must be used. Other types of drug reactions that are not allergic must be differentiated. Intolerance, defined as a normal qualitative but quantitatively increased pharmacologic effect of the drug, may occasionally be difficult to differentiate. Idiosyncrasy, a qualitatively abnormal response to a drug, is not based on an immunologic reaction but is often mediated by an isolated enzymatic defect. The hemolytic anemia produced by several antibiotics in patients with glucose-6-phosphate dehydrogenase-deficient red blood cells is a fairly common example of an idiosyncratic reaction.

Diagnostic Options and Recommended Approach

An extreme, but not usually warranted, method to diagnose an allergic reaction is to rechallenge the patient with the suspected antibiotic. The accelerated production of the original reaction would be very suggestive of an allergic reaction.

The laboratory is of limited usefulness in diagnosing allergic reactions to antibiotics. Although several research procedures (e.g., basophil degranulation test, histamine release, and lymphocyte transformation) have been described, only two types of tests are routinely available to confirm the presence of specific IgE antibodies to the implicated agent. Skin tests (scratch and intracutaneous) are presently well defined to investigate only penicillin allergy. The appearance of a wheal-and-flare reaction within 15 minutes of infection of either benzylpenicilloyl polylysine (major determinant mixture commercially available as Pre-Pen from Schwarz Pharma, Milwaukee, WI) or minor determinant mixture (prepared from standard penicillin G) is a good predictor of an immediate or accelerated allergic reaction. If both skin

tests are negative, the chances of developing a serious reaction to penicillin are very small. The radioallergosorbent test for specific penicillin IgE antibodies is also a reliable in vitro test to predict penicillin allergy.

Therapeutic

The first and most important step in treating an allergic reaction to an antibiotic is to discontinue the drug, if possible. Most of the allergic reactions noted in Table 8–78–1 will resolve with this measure alone. For immediate, severe allergic reactions (e.g., anaphylaxis or laryngeal edema), the treatment of choice is epinephrine, 0.5 to 1.0 mL of 1:1000 aqueous solution given subcutaneously; respiratory support with oxygen and hemodynamic support with vasoconstrictors may occasionally be necessary. Antihistamines and corticosteroids have no proven role in these severe reactions, but these drugs may be beneficial in the treatment of some of the delayed or unusual types of allergic reactions.

FOLLOW-UP

For most allergic reactions to antibiotics, no follow-up is required after manifestations of the reaction have resolved. If some of the unusual manifestations of drug allergy, such as hemolytic anemia and thrombocytopenia, have occurred, blood counts should be repeated to ensure that these complications have resolved.

When a patient is labeled as allergic to a drug, a careful description of the allergic response should be given in the patient's record, as other physicians may wish to determine at a future time the accuracy of the diagnosis of drug allergy.

DISCUSSION
Prevalence and Incidence

Reliable data concerning the frequency of antibiotic allergy are not available, as most of the well-designed studies do not differentiate between adverse and allergic reactions. A few studies have suggested that 1 to 3% of all hospitalized patients develop a cutaneous reaction to an antibiotic, but the incidence of other allergic reactions is not defined. The risk of a fatal allergic reaction has been estimated at 1 in 50,000.

Related Basic Science

An allergic reaction to an antibiotic occurs only after the drug has elicited an immune response leading to the production of specific antibody or sensitized lymphocytes. Most antibiotics are too small to elicit an immune response by themselves and must complex to a protein to become an immunogen. The factors that determine the type of antibody response or whether any response occurs are not known, although both drug factors (e.g., chemical structure and mode of administration) and host factors (e.g., age and underlying diseases) seem to be important. Although many allergic reactions probably have complex pathogenetic mechanisms, the Gell–Coombs classification of immunologic responses offers a useful framework to analyze some known reactions (Table 8–78–2).

For type I responses, the antigen (antibiotic) interacts with immunoglobulin E antibody attached to mast cells or basophils, releasing a number of vasoactive substances that produce the clinical symptoms. In type II reactions, antibodies may be directed to a number of different cell types, producing lysis or injury of the cell. Type III reactions are mediated by circulating complexes of antigen and antibody; the clinical syndrome produced depends on the site of deposition of the complex (e.g., renal glomerulus, skin) and the subsequent activation of complement, attraction of phagocytic cells, and inflammatory response. Type IV reactions are mediated by sensitized lymphocytes that subsequently release a number of substances (lymphokines) that attract cells to the area and produce a specific type of inflammatory response.

Unfortunately, the immunologic mechanisms mediating most types of allergic reactions (e.g., morbilliform or maculopapular eruptions) are not known.

Natural History and Its Modification with Treatment

Most of the common allergic reactions (e.g., rash or drug fever) resolve within a few days of discontinuing the drug. Serum sickness and some of the hematopoietic reactions may take several weeks to resolve, but no relapses occur unless the patient is reexposed to the offending antibiotic. The same type of allergic reaction usually recurs on reexposure to the antibiotic.

Prevention

A careful drug allergy history should be obtained and recorded on every patient. For patients with a well-documented history of antibiotic

TABLE 8–78–2. GELL–COOMBS CLASSIFICATION OF IMMUNOLOGIC RESPONSES

Type of Response	Mediator of Response	Clinical Example
I. Anaphylactic	IgE	Anaphylaxis
II. Cytotoxic	IgG or IgM with or without complement	Penicillin-induced hemolytic anemia
III. Antigen–antibody complex	IgG with antigen and complement	Serum sickness
IV. Delayed hypersensitivity	Sensitized lymphocyte	Contact dermatitis

Ig, immunoglobulin.

allergy, the best method to prevent a recurrence obviously is to avoid exposure to the antibiotic. Skin testing or the radioallergosorbent test may be useful, although not routinely performed, for patients needing antibiotic therapy. If a specific antibiotic must be given to a patient with a serious allergic history to that drug, a desensitization procedure should be performed. Any patient given a parenteral drug with allergic potential should probably be observed for 30 minutes before being dismissed, so that any immediate allergic reaction can be promptly treated.

Cost Containment

The prevention of an allergic reaction is the most efficient way to reduce the cost of the disease. Antibiotics should not be given indiscriminately and should certainly not be given to a person with a history of allergy to the particular drug or closely related compound.

REFERENCES

Lin RY. A perspective on penicillin allergy. Arch Int Med 1992;152:930.
Parker CW. Drug allergy. N Engl J Med 1975;292:511.
Roujeau JC, Stern RS. Severe adverse cutaneous reactions to drugs. N Engl J Med 1994;331:1272.
Saxon A, Beall GN, Rohr AS, et al. Immediate hypersensitivity reactions to beta-lactam antibiotics. Ann Intern Med 1987;107:204.
Sogn DD. Prevention of allergic reactions to penicillin. J Allergy Clin Immunol 1987;78:1051.
Wendel GD Jr, Stark BJ, Jamison RB, et al. Penicillin allergy and desensitization in serious infections during pregnancy. N Engl J Med 1985;312:1229.

CHAPTER 8–79

Adverse Effects of Antimicrobial Therapy

Rafael L. Jurado, M.D., and John E. McGowan, Jr., M.D.

DEFINITION

An adverse effect of antimicrobial therapy is any unwanted manifestation that occurs in temporal association with the administration of one or more antimicrobial agent(s). Many organ systems may be affected by these reactions. It follows that, at times, it may be difficult to decide whether a sign and symptom complex is due to the patient's underlying disorder, to the antimicrobial agent(s), or to other therapeutic interventions.

ETIOLOGY

The etiopathogenetic mechanisms implicated in the wide spectrum of adverse effects to antimicrobial agents are numerous and in many cases unknown. The majority of adverse effects to antimicrobial agents are mediated by the different pathogenic mechanisms of allergic reactions described in the Gell-Coombs classification. Some adverse effects are mediated by the changes in the endogenous microflora that the antibiotics cause.

CRITERIA FOR DIAGNOSIS
Suggestive

The temporal association between starting an antimicrobial agent and the appearance of an adverse effect, together with the cessation of the

We thank Dr. Richard Prokesch for his contribution to this chapter in the previous editions of this book.

TABLE 8–79–1. ADVERSE EFFECTS OF ANTIMICROBIAL THERAPY: CLINICAL MANIFESTATIONS AND PLANS

Diagnosis	Subjective/Objective	Most Common Offending Agents	Risk Factor/Therapy/Comment
Systemic Manifestations			
Type 1 immediate hyper-sensitivity reaction (anaphylaxis)	Hypotension, bronchospasm, urticaria, laryngeal edema; elevated IgE; positive intradermal reaction to skin test with major and minor determinants (penicillins)	Penicillins, cephalosporins, tetracyclines, sulfonamides, streptomycin, nitrofurantoin, chloramphenicol	Cross-reactivity between penicillins, cephalosporins, and imipenem/cilastatin (4-fold increase in anaphylaxis in patients with past history of penicillin reaction; overall, cephalosporin reaction in 5–10% of penicillin-allergic patients). Aztreonam seems much less likely to cross-react with other β-lactams
Type 3 immune complex-mediated reaction (serum sickness)	Fever, urticarial rash, adenopathy, arthralgias, nephritis	Penicillins, cephalosporins, sulfonamides, tetracyclines, streptomycin, rifampin; trimethoprim–sulfamethoxazole especially likely in AIDS	Circulating immune complexes responsible; intermittent therapy with rifampin can produce fever, chills, interstitial nephritis, and is thought to be a type 3 reaction
Drug fever	Fever may reach any height and show any pattern of temporal variation. Duration of fever after discontinuation of offending agent depends on half-life of causative drug or metabolite	Penicillins, cephalosporins, sulfonamides, streptomycin, nitrofurantoin, polymixins, INH	Diagnosis made more difficult when patient is also receiving other therapeutic agents. This is a diagnosis of exclusion
Jarisch–Herxheimer reaction	1–2 h after first dose of antibiotic—fever, malaise, hypotension, rash (with syphilis); lasts 12–18 h	Penicillin (especially), erythromycin, tetracycline, chloramphenicol	Occurs in therapy of syphilis (especially secondary), Lyme disease, relapsing fever; release of products from dying spirochetes probable source; a "pseudoallergic" reaction
Monoamine oxidase inhibition	Flushing, chills, headache	INH	After ingestion of certain foods rich in tyramine (Swiss cheese, red wine)
"Gray syndrome"	Abdominal distention, vomiting, cyanosis, lethargy, vasomotor collapse, death	Chloramphenicol	Results from toxic levels of drug overdose or in neonates and adults with liver failure in whom glucuronyl transferase is deficient and drug is not conjugated for excretion
Dermatologic Manifestations			
Rash	May have any appearance: macular, papular, vesicular, urticarial, petechial, and purpuric most common	Penicillins (especially ampicillin), cephalosporins, aminoglycosides, erythromycin, nitrofurantoin, rifampin, vancomycin, trimethoprim, quinolones, 5-cytosine, vidarabine, ribavirin	Patients with mononucleosis or chronic lymphocytic leukemia have a high incidence of rash after ampicillin; patients with AIDS have high incidence of rash after trimethoprim–sulfamethoxazole
Erythema multiforme	Target lesions, mucous membrane involvement, systemic symptoms with Stevens–Johnson syndrome; skin biopsy diagnostic	Penicillins, sulfonamides, tetracyclines	Systemic steroids helpful in severe reactions
Exfoliative dermatitis	Generalized erythema, exfoliation; skin biopsy diagnostic	Sulfonamides, trimethoprim, penicillins, INH	Systemic steroids helpful; supportive therapy with fluids important
Toxic epidermal necrolysis	Erythema, epidermal detachment; skin biopsy diagnostic	Sulfonamides, penicillins, tetracyclines	Treatment as for exfoliative dermatitis
Hypersensitivity angiitis	Palpable purpura; may have other organ system involvement (renal, muscle, gastrointestinal tract, etc.); skin biopsy reveals vasculitis	Sulfonamides, penicillins	Treatment as for exfoliative dermatitis
Photosensitivity	Increased sunburn response with blistering; discoloration of nails + oncholysis	Tetracyclines (especially democlocyline); sulfonamides, penicillins, INH, quinolones	Sunscreens or avoidance of sun exposure helpful
Pellagra	Associated peripheral neuropathy and anemia	INH	Treat with daily pyridoxine
Nail hyperpigmentation	Progressive darkening	AZT	Prominent in black persons
Pulmonary Manifestations			
Pulmonary infiltrates with eosinophilia	Fever, chills, cough, dyspnea, pulmonary infiltrates, pleural effusions, peripheral eosinophilia common	Nitrofurantoin, penicillins, sulfonamides	Resolves quickly after stopping drug; more common in the elderly
Pulmonary fibrosis	As above, except for absence of fever, pleural effusions, and eosinophilia	Nitrofurantoin	Slowly progressive with chronic use (>6 mo); reversible if drug stopped early
Drug-induced lupus	Fever, pneumonitis, pleural effusions, pericarditis, positive antinuclear antibody to single-stranded DNA	INH, penicillins, tetracyclines, streptomycin	Anti-double-stranded nuclear antibody negative
Hypersensitivity angiitis	See Dermatologic Manifestations	Penicillin, sulfonamides	See Dermatologic Manifestations

TABLE 8–79–1. (*Continued*)

Diagnosis	Subjective/Objective	Most Common Offending Agents	Risk Factor/Therapy/Comment
Gastrointestinal and Hepatic Manifestations			
Mouth discoloration (so-called black tongue)	None	Penicillin	—
Taste	Dysgeusia, metallic taste	ddI, metronidazole, clindamycin, ethionamide, pentamidine, carbenicillin	—
Aphthous ulcers, stomatitis	Pain	ddC, ddI, foscarnet, proguanil, penicillins	—
Esophageal ulcers	Dysphagia, odinophagia	Doxycycline, ddC, foscarnet, AZT	—
Abdominal pain	Severe pain, normal exam	Clofazimine	Has led to laparotomy
Intestinal intolerance	Diarrhea, nausea, abdominal pain; occasionally vomiting	Many antimicrobial agents, especially erythromycin, tetracycline, metronidazole, sulfonamides, trimethoprim, quinolones, nitrofurantoin, 5-flucytosine, ketoconazole, vidarabine, acyclovir	Often dose-related; discontinue offending drug
Clostridium difficile-associated diarrhea and pseudomembranous colitis	Diarrhea, fever, abdominal cramps; pseudomembranes on endoscopy; positive stool for *C. difficile* toxin in severe cases	Any antimicrobial agent, most frequent after clindamycin	Must stop offending drug; oral metronidazole or vancomycin often effective therapy; relapse in about 20%
Hepatocellular necrosis	Symptoms and signs and laboratory findings as in viral hepatitis (see Chapter 19–75)	INH, rifampin (<1%), oxacillin, nafcillin, carbenicillin, nitrofurantoin, ketoconazole (rare)	INH: hepatitis seen in ∼1%, rare in those <35 y of age and ∼2.5% in those >50 y. Rifampin: liver disease less common than with INH; slow acetylators at higher risk. Penicillins: damage mild with semisynthetic penicillins and dose-related; severe damage (not dose-related) with fever, rash, and eosinophilia; high-dose carbenicillin can result in mild hepatocellular injury. Nitrofurantoin: nitrofurantoin can cause injury with fever, rash, and eosinophilia; not dose-related. Tetracycline: injury from tetracycline can mimic Reye's syndrome; dose-related toxic mechanism; risk increased with renal failure or if administered during third trimester of pregnancy
Enzyme abnormality	Elevated transaminase determinations in absence of clinical evidence of damage	INH (seen in ∼15% of patients); oxacillin, carbenicillin (see above); imipenem (2–4%); rifampin (1–2%); erythromycin estolate; clindamycin; trimethoprim; ketoconazole (2–5%)	In some cases, probably represents a direct interference of drug with laboratory determination of enzyme level (e.g., erythromycin estolate leads to false elevation of SGOT [test])
Cholestatic jaundice	Signs and symptoms of hypersensitivity frequent	Erythromycin estolate and erythromycin ethylsuccinate	Rarer in children than in adults
Mixed cytotoxic and cholestatic injury	Signs of hypersensitivity nearly always present	Sulfonamides	—
Chronic active hepatitis	See Chapter 19–78	INH, sulfonamides, nitrofurantoin	—
Abnormal bilirubin metabolism	Jaundice	Flavaspidic acid	Competes with bilirubin for binding to a ligand; may cause unconjugated hyperbilirubinemia
Neonatal jaundice	Jaundice	Novobiocin, chloramphenicol	Inhibition of glucuronyl transferase
Pancreatitis	Severe abdominal pain, nausea, vomiting, elevated serum amylase	Pentamidine, ddC, ddI, erythromycin, tetracycline, sulfonamides, metronidazole, nitrofurantoin	—
Biliary sludging-stone formation	Syndrome mimicking acute cholecystitis	Ceftriaxone	Dose-dependent
Renal Manifestations			
Prerenal azotemia	Increased blood urea nitrogen out of proportion to creatinine	Tetrcycline, amphotericin B	Antianabolic effect may aggravate uremia, acidosis, and hyperphosphatemia in patients with preexisting renal disease
Glomerulonephritis	See Chapters 16–18 and 16–19; vascular skin lesions almost always seen	Penicillins, sulfonamides	Often part of a systemic hypersensitivity syndrome (see above)

(*continued*)

TABLE 8–79–1. (*Continued*)

Diagnosis	Subjective/Objective	Most Common Offending Agents	Risk Factor/Therapy/Comment
Proximal tubular dysfunction; acute tubular necrosis	See Chapter 16–17; for aminoglycosides, reduced glomerular filtration rate may be only manifestation; urine sediment usually benign; occasionally proteinuria, granular casts, or oliguria will be seen; for other agents, especially polymixin, proteinuria, and abnormal urine sediment are quite common—2% of patients develop acute tubular necrosis	Aminoglycosides; polymixins; vancomycin (rare); cephaloridine; foscarnet	Streptomycin in antituberculous doses not nephrotoxic, parenteral neomycin highly nephrotoxic, other aminoglyosides inbetween; risk factors include older age, preexisting renal disease, prior aminoglycoside use, concomitant liver disease; hypotension, concurrent ethacrynic acid or amphotericin B; usually reversible when associated with aminoglycosides; reversal less likely with other drugs
Fanconi's syndrome	Renal tubular acidosis, aminoaciduria, hypokalemia, hypouricemia	Outdated tetracyclines (rare with recent formulations)	Recovery usually ensues when drug discontinued, but may occur slowly
Renal tubular acidosis (distal)	Hypokalemia, hypomagnesemia	Amphotericin B	Some dysfunction reversible after drug stops
Interstitial nephritis	Acute renal failure, may be oliguric; fever—90%; rash—25%; urinalysis: hematuria, proteinuria, pyruvia—95%; no casts; eosinophiluria common; eosinophilia in ~80%	Methicillin (most common), other penicillins, cephalosporins; rarely, sulfonamides, rifampin, nitrofurantoin	Corticosteroids may be helpful; seen in intermittent rifampin therapy
Obstructive uropathy	Hematuria, crystalluria, renal colic, oliguric or anuric renal failure	Older sulfonamides (sulfapyridine, sulfadiazine); acyclovir	Increased risk with dehydration and acid urine; infuse acyclovir slowly to reduce risk of this complication
Sodium and potassium overload	Worsening heart failure, hypokalemic alkalosis	Penicillins (especially carbenicillin and ticarcillin), some cephalosporins	From increased load of nonreabsorbable anion in distal tubule; sodium penicillin G contains 1.7 mEq Na^+, carbenicillin and ticarcillin contain 4.7 mEq/g, and potassium penicillin contains 1.7 mEq K^+ per million units
Nephrogenic diabetes insipidus	See Chapter 9–42	Demeclocycline; foscarnet	Drug inhibits effect of antidiuretic hormone on renal tubule; this effect is used to treat syndrome of inappropriate diuresis (see Chapter 9–43)
Hematologic Manifestations			
Aplastic anemia	Pancytopenia, hypocellular bone marrow during or after therapy	Chloramphenicol (occurs in ~1:30,000 patients)	Not dose-related, an idiosyncratic reaction; irreversible
Bone marrow suppression	Increased serum iron and total iron-binding capacity; decreased reticulocyte count and hematocrit; vacuolated precursor cells	Chloramphenicol (occurs in most patients treated with the drug)	Dose-related; correlates with levels >25 µg/mL; preexisting liver disease is risk factor; reversible when drop is stopped
	Granulocytopenia, anemia (but platelet count often increased, not decreased)	AZT	More frequent in patients with pretherapy CD4 cell count <200/µL; transfusion, erythropoietin therapy, or zidovudine dose reduction often required to manage severe anemia
	Normochromic, normocytic anemia	Ribavirin	—
	Granulocytopenia, thrombocytopenia; anemia less frequent	Ganciclovir	Dose-related; usually reversible when drug stops
	Megaloblastic anemia	High-dose trimethoprim–sulfamethoxazole or trimethoprim alone	Patients with decreased folic acid stores at risk; therapy; folinic acid
Agranulocytosis, neutropenia, or leukopenia	Fever, chills, severe neutropenia	Sulfonamides, high-dose semisynthetic penicillins	Immunologic mechanism (not dose-related)
	No systemic signs; neutropenia	Penicillins, cephalosporins, imipenem, nitrofurantoin, 5-flucytosine	Dose-related, direct marrow suppression
Hemolytic anemia	Positive nongamma Coombs' test	Sulfonamides, INH, rifampin	Not dose-related; drug plus antidrug immune complex activates complement, resulting in hemolysis
	Positive gamma Coombs' test	Penicillins, occasionally cephalosporins	Occurs with prolonged high-dose therapy; drug or metabolite coupled to red cell surface forming antigenic complex; complement not involved
	Glucose-6-phosphate dehydrogenase deficiency	Chloramphenicol, nitrofurantoin, dapsone, primaquine	Only Mediterranean-type glucose-6-phosphatase dehydrogenase affected by chloramphenicol
Atypical lymphocytosis		Tetracyclines	
Acute hemolysis		Chloramphenicol, sulfonamides, nitrofurantoin, nalidixic acid	Occurs in some patients with glucose-6-phosphate dehydrogenase deficiency
Thrombocytopenia		Penicillins, cephalosporins, sulfonamides, trimethoprim, INH, rifampin, 5-flucytosine	Immunologic mechanisms most frequent

(continued)

TABLE 8–79–1. (*Continued*)

Diagnosis	Subjective/Objective	Most Common Offending Agents	Risk Factor/Therapy/Comment
Bleeding	Absence of adequate diet, increased prothrombin time; bleeding or ooze from venipunctures, other wounds	Broad-spectrum antimicrobial agents	Vitamin K deficiency because of change in intestinal flora
	Increased bleeding time determination	Carbenicillin, tricarcillin; moxalactam, cefoperazone	Bind to ADP receptor site on platelets and prevent normal contraction of platelet; moxalactam can interfere with hemostasis by hypoprothrombinemia, platelet dysfunction, or immune-mediated thrombocytopenia
Neurologic Manifestations			
Encephalopathy	Decreased level of consciousness, hyperreflexia, myoclonus, seizures, headache, etc.	Penicillins and cephalosporins, imipenem (seizures), metronidazole, INH, acyclovir, zidovudine, ganciclovir, foscarnet	Occurs with very high doses of the β-lactam drugs; renal impairment and preexisting neurologic disease increase risk
	Lethargy, confusion, impaired recent memory, asterixis, etc.	Chloramphenicol; colistin; amantadine, rimantadine (rare, dose-related); vidarabine, acyclovir	With chloramphenicol, occurs with doses of 4–8 g/d; hard to distinguish from hepatic encephalopathy
	Acute confusional state psychosis	INH, cycloserine, amantadine	Problem accurs when amantadine combined with anticholinergics or levodopa
Glucuronyl transferase deficiency	Kernicterus	Sulfonamides	Displace unconjugated bilirubin from albumin, freeing it to diffuse into cerebrospinal fluid
Pseudotumor cerebri	Headaches, vomiting, blurred vision, blurring of optic disks, elevated cerebrospinal fluid opening pressure	Tetracyclines; occasionally nitrofurantoin, nalidixic acid	Occurs primarily in infants, who present with bulging fontanelles; must differentiate from cerebrospinal fluid block, tumor infection
Allergic meningitis	Meningismus, cerebrospinal fluid findings like bacterial meningitis	Sulfonamides, trimethoprim, metronidazole, INH	Extremely rare
Ototoxicity			
Auditory	Tinnitus, high-frequency hearing loss	Aminoglycosides, erythromycin (high doses); vancomycin	In aminoglycoside ototoxicity, preexisting renal failure, older age, prior aminoglycosides, high serum levels are risk factors; not always reversible
Vestibular	Nausea, vomiting, vertigo, nystagmus	Aminoglycosides, minocycline	
Optic neuritis	Impaired vision; decreased perception of the color green (ethambutol)	Ethambutol, chloramphenicol, INH (rare)	More likely with ethambutol when given dose of 25/mg/kg/d or more; more likely with chloramphenicol when given for extended periods
Peripheral neuropathy	Distal mixed sensorimotor neuropathy (see Chapter 20–1)	INH, nitrofurantoin, colistin, metronidazole, ddC, ddI, AZT, dapsone, ethionamide, chloramphenicol	For INH, patients with decreased pyridoxine stores (e.g., chronic alcoholics), prior neuropathy (e.g., diabetics), and slow acetylators are at increased risk; for nitrofurantoin, preexisting renal disease is risk factor
Neuromuscular blockade	Prolonged postanesthetic respiratory depression; aggravation of usual symptoms in myasthenia; apnea	Aminoglycosides, polymyxins, lincomycin	Aminoglycosides block presynaptic cell by affecting calcium ion flux—effect reversed by calcium infusion; aminoglycosides and other drugs listed block postsynaptic acetylcholine receptor site; problem enhanced by succinylcholine, curare-like drugs, magnesium, and especially by rapid infusion of drugs—prevent by giving these drugs slowly in diluted solution
Procaine reaction	Acute, intense neuropsychiatric reaction occurring within minutes of administration—sense of impending doom, audiovisual hallucinations, tinnitus, vertigo	Procaine penicillin	Due to inadvertent entry of procaine into bloodstream; clears within minutes as procaine metabolizes; often mistaken for allergic reaction
Cardiovascular Manifestations			
Torsade de pointes syndrome	Serious ventricular arrhythmia, which can lead to ventricular fibrillation	Erythromycin, ketoconazole, itroconazole, clarythromycin	Especially when used in combination with astemizole or terfenadine
Endocrinologic Manifestations			
Adrenal insufficiency	Decreased response to infection	Ketoconazole	Interferes with steroidogenesis; must consider in HIV-infected individuals receiving drug, as more likely to have other causes of adrenal insufficiency (cytomegalovirus, histoplasmosis, cryptococcosis)
Gynecomastia	Breast enlargement in males, sometimes accompanied by decreased serum testosterone levels and/or impotence	Ketoconazole	Dose-dependent
Hypocalcemia	Tetany	Foscarnet	Concomitant use of pentamidine increases risk
Aktered glucose metabolism	Symptomatic hypoglycemia or chronic hyperglycemia	Pentamidine	Hypoglycemia frequent during infusion; cumulative effect on pancreatic beta cells may lead to chronic hyperglycemia

INH, isoniazid; ddI, didanosine; ddC, zalcitabine (dideoxycytidine); AZT, azidothymidine (zidovudine); SGOT, serum glutamic–oxaloacetic acid transaminase.

side effect with discontinuation of the medication, is the strongest suggestive criterion. Other factors that can have the weight of suggestive criteria include the reported incidence of the specific side effect and the nature of the reaction.

Definitive

Rechallenging the patient with the same antimicrobial agent, with reproduction of the same side effect, is the only definitive criterion. Many times, such rechallenge may not be advisable, depending on the severity of the adverse effect.

CLINICAL MANIFESTATIONS

See Table 8–79–1.

PLANS

See Table 8–79–1.

FOLLOW-UP

All patients receiving antimicrobial agents need to be followed to evaluate both the beneficial effects of the medications as well as any early clinical manifestations of their potential side effects.

To establish with a high degree of certainty that these clinical or laboratory manifestations were indeed an antimicrobial-related side effect, one has to discontinue the use of the implicated drug and observe for the improvement or disappearance of the manifestions referred to above. If such clearance occurs in a timely fashion following discontinuation of the suspected medication, no further follow-up is required for this particular problem. A description of the nature and manifestations of the side effect should be entered into the patient's medical record. Such entry and careful explanation of the side effect to the patient and/or family should prevent future exposure of the patient to the same antimicrobial agent when the nature and severity of the side effect dictate so.

DISCUSSION

Prevalence and Incidence

As some of these adverse effects to antimicrobial agents are dose dependent, while others are idiosyncratic, it is not possible to quote incidence and prevalence figures. Even with those dose-dependent side effects, incidence and prevalence vary widely, depending on multiple factors (gender, race, age, underlying disease, coadministration of other medications).

Related Basic Science

Immune responses to drug determinants occur in only a small percentage of exposed patients, and clinical expression of drug allergy occurs in only a fraction of responding patients. Several factors have been identified that influence the expression of immune responses and clinical reactions to drugs. Sustained immune responses to drugs are more likely in adults with specific HLA phenotypes and drug metabolism propensities, more likely when the drug or drug metabolites are highly reactive with proteins, more likely with high doses and long durations of exposure, and more likely after topical rather than parenteral therapy, which is in turn more sensitizing than oral therapy. The purity and chemical state of a drug can influence the likelihood of a response. Responses to different classes of drugs appear to be influenced to different degrees by these factors.

Natural History and Its Modification with Treatment

Most adverse effects to antimicrobial agents are expected to cease with the discontinuation of the medication. The exact time to clearance depends on the particular antimicrobial agent involved, the severity of the side effect, the mechanisms of the adverse reaction, and the metabolic and excretory pathways of the antimicrobial agent and/or its metabolites. Some adverse reactions are reversible and clear rapidly (in a matter of days), whereas others (i.e., chloramphenicol-induced bone marrow aplasia) are irreversible and need specific therapies (i.e., bone marrow transplantation).

Prevention

Obtaining a history of prior reactions from the patient or his or her medical record is the crucial preventive step. As with any other medication, judicious use of antimicrobial agents is paramount in avoiding unnecessary side effects. One needs to carefully consider the individual patient in trying to predict the statistical possibility of adverse reactions to a given antimicrobial agent. A good example is the effect of age on the incidence of isoniazid hepatitis.

Cost Containment

Prevention of drug reaction by the measures listed above would decrease expenditures for diagnostic and therapeutic measures needed after the reaction occurs.

REFERENCES

Caldwell GR, Cluff LE. Adverse reaction to antimicrobial agents. JAMA 1974;230:77.
Gilbert DN, Bennett WM. Use of antimicrobial drugs in renal failure. Infect Dis Clin North Am 1989;3:517.
Neuman M. Relationships between chemical structure and adverse effects of antibacterial and antifungal agents. Chemioterapia 1987;6:299.
Norrby SR. Problems in evaluation of adverse reactions to beta-lactam antibiotics. Rev Infect Dis 1986;S358.
Sattler FR, Weitekamp MR, Sayegh A, Ballard JO. Impaired hemostasis caused by beta-lactam antibiotics. Am J Surg 1988;155(5A):30.
Saxon A. Antibiotic choices for the penicillin-allergic patient. Postgrad Med 1988;83:135.

CHAPTER 8–80

Prevention of Infection by the Use of Antimicrobial Agents

James P. Steinberg, M.D.

DEFINITION

This chapter discusses the prophylactic use of antimicrobial agents for a variety of situations including prevention of bacterial endocarditis (Table 8–80–1), prevention of infection following a variety of exposures or in patients with certain underlying disease processes (Table 8–80–2), and perioperative prophylaxis for selected surgical procedures (Table 8–80–3). Malaria prophylaxis is discussed in Chapter 8–61.

ETIOLOGY

Many of the infections for which antimicrobial prophylaxis is recommended are caused by bacteria that are part of the normal human flora and pose a risk to the host following a violation of a defense barrier, such as the skin or intestinal mucosa. Some potentially preventable infections occur in hosts with increased susceptibility to infection due to

We thank Dr. Adam J. Leaderman and Dr. Jonas A. Shulman for their contribution to this chapter in the previous edition of this book.

TABLE 8–80–1. PREVENTION OF BACTERIAL ENDOCARDITIS

A. Common cardiac conditions* for which endocarditis prophylaxis *is* indicated
   1. Prosthetic cardiac valves
   2. Most congenital cardiac malformations
   3. Surgically constructed systemic pulmonary shunts
   4. Rheumatic and other acquired valvular dysfunction
   5. Idiopathic hypertrophic subaortic stenosis
   6. Previous history of bacterial endocarditis
   7. Mitral valve prolapse with insufficiency

B. Common cardiac conditions for which endocarditis prophylaxis is *not* indicated
   1. Isolated secundum atrial septal defect
   2. Secundum atrial septal defect more than 6 mo following repair without residual defect
   3. Patent ductus arteriosus more than 6 mo following repair
   4. Ventricular septal defect more than 6 mo following repair without residual defect
   5. Postoperative coronary artery bypass graft
   6. Pacemaker or implantable defibrillator

C. Procedures for which endocarditis prophylaxis is indicated[†]
   1. All dental procedures likely to induce gingival bleeding
   2. Tonsillectomy and/or adenoidectomy
   3. Surgical procedures or biopsies involving respiratory mucosa
   4. Rigid bronchoscopy
   5. Incision and drainage of infected tissue
   6. Genitourinary procedures (see Part E)
      a. Cystoscopy
      b. Prostatic surgery
      c. Urethral catheterization for patient with significant bacteriuria
      d. Urinary tract surgery
      e. Vaginal hysterectomy
      f. Other gynecologic procedures, including vaginal delivery, if infection is suspected
   7. Gastrointestinal procedures (see Part E)
      a. Gallbladder surgery
      b. Colonic surgery
      c. Esophageal dilation
      d. Sclerotherapy of esophageal varices
      e. Colonoscopy
      f. Proctosigmoidoscopy with biopsy

D. Recommended regimens for endocarditis prophylaxis for dental and respiratory tract procedures
   1. Standard regimens
      a. Dental procedures that cause gingival bleeding — Amoxicillin 3.0 g PO 1 h before, then 1.5 g 6 h later; if unable to take PO, then ampicillin 2 g IM/IV 30–60 min before and 1 g 6 h later
      b. Oral and/or respiratory tract surgery
   2. Special regimens
      a. Parenteral regimen for use when maximal protection is desired (e.g., prosthetic valves or past endocarditis) (AHA now recommends using its standard regimen for high-risk patients, even those with prosthetic valves; some clinicians may prefer to use the parenteral regimen.) — Ampicillin 2 g IM/IV plus gentamicin 1.5 mg/kg IM/IV 30 min before procedure, then amoxicillin 1.5 g PO 6 h later
      Alternative: Parenteral regimen may be repeated once 8 h later. (If allergic to penicillin, give gentamicin as above, and vancomycin 1 g IV given over 1 h, starting 1h before surgery.)
   3. Penicillin-allergic patients
      a. Oral regimens — Erythromycin ethylsuccinate 800 mg or erythromycin stearate 1.0 g PO 2 h before, then 500 mg 6 h later
      or
      Clindamycin 300 mg PO 1 h before and 150 mg PO 6 h later
      b. Parenteral regimen — Vancomycin 1 g IV slowly over 1 h, starting 1 h before procedure; no repeat dose needed

E. Endocarditis prophylaxis for gastrointestinal/genitourinary procedures
   1. Gastrointestinal/genitourinary procedures (see Part C) — Ampicillin 2 g IM/IV plus gentamicin 1.5 mg/kg IM/IV given $\frac{1}{2}$–1 h before procedure, followed by amoxicillin 1.5 g PO 6 h later; alternatively, each may be given 8 h later in patients with normal renal function
   2. Oral regimens for minor or repetitive procedures in low-risk patients — Amoxicillin 3 g PO 1 h before procedure and 1.5 g PO 6 h later
   3. Penicillin-allergic patients — Vancomycin 1 g IV slowly over 1 h plus gentamicin 1.5 mg/kg IM/IV given 1 h before procedure; may be repeated once 8 h later in patients with normal renal function

*Common conditions listed; not meant to be all-inclusive.
†Prophylaxis indicated only for patients with cardiac lesions that increase their risk of endocarditis (see Part A). For patients at high risk of endocarditis, such as those with prosthetic valves or who have had previous endocarditis, physicians may consider prophylactic antibiotics for low risk procedures involving the gastrointestinal, genitourinary, or lower respiratory tracts.

Source: Adapted from Dajani S, Bisno AL, Chung KJ, et al. Prevention of bacterial endocarditis: Recommendations by the American Heart Association. JAMA 1990;264:2919. © American Medical Association. Reproduced with permission from the American Medical Association and the author.

TABLE 8–80–2. PROPHYLAXIS WITH ANTIMICROBIAL AGENTS

Disease/Condition	Causative Agent(s)	Treatment*	Comments
Hemophilus influenzae exposure	*H. influenzae*	Rifampin 20 mg/kg qd × 4 d (maximum 600 mg qd)	Recommended for all household contacts (children and adults) where there are children less than 4 y old. Close contacts in nursery and daycare centers should receive rifampin. Index case also should be treated with rifampin.
Meningococcal exposure	*Neisseria meningitidis*	Rifampin 10 mg/kg q12h × 4 doses (maximum = 600 mg q12h)	Only for close contacts—family, day care, or nursery. Not necessary for medical personnel unless exceptionally close contact occurs, such as mouth-to-mouth resuscitation. Ciprofloxacin may be a useful alternative in adults in a dose of 500 mg bid for 5 d. Single dose of ceftriaxone 250 mg IM may be effective.
Pertussis exposure	*Bordetella pertussis*	Erythromycin 50 mg/kg/d divided in 4 doses for 14 d (maximum = 500 mg qid)	For close contacts who are not immunized, especially those less than 1 y old.
Postsplenectomy (including children with sickle cell disease)	Encapsulated organisms, especially pneumococcus	Benzathine penicillin G 1.2 million units IM every month for 2 y after surgery or penicillin V 250 mg bid	Consider ampicillin instead of penicillin G for children less than 4 y of age because of increased risk of *Hemophilus* infection in that age group. Patients should always have penicillin or ampicillin available so that if they are not near a physician and become febrile, they can begin treatment while arranging to see a physician. Should receive pneumococcal and meningococcal vaccine before splenectomy when possible and after surgery if not. The increasing problem of penicillin-resistant pneumococcus complicates the strategy and increases the importance of vaccination.
Rheumatic fever (secondary prophylaxis)	Group A streptococci	Benzathine penicillin G 1.2 million units IM every month; may change to oral regimen as adult	As alternatives to parenteral regimen, sulfadiazine 1 g/d PO or penicillin V 250 mg PO bid.
Rape victim	Sexually transmitted agents	Ceftriaxone 250 mg IM, plus doxycycline 100 mg bid × 7 d	Perform wet preparation for *Trichomonas.* Culture for gonorrhea. Collect serology for syphilis acutely and repeat in 6–8 wk. Consider saving an acute and 6- to 8-wk serum for possible HIV and hepatitis B serologies.
Sexual contacts	*Neisseria gonorrhoeae* or *Chlamydia trachomatis*	Ceftriaxone 250 mg IM plus doxycycline, 100 mg bid × 7 d	Metronidazole (Flagyl) has Antabuse-like effect; no alcohol should be taken when receiving this agent. Regimen for gonorrhea and chlamydia is probably effective against incubating syphilis.
	Trichomonas vaginalis	Metronidazole, 2 g PO, 1 dose	
	Treponema pallidum	Benzathine penicillin G 2.4 million units IM	
Travelers' diarrhea, "turista"	*Escherichia coli,* enterotoxigenic	If prescribed, bismuth subsalicylate 2 tabs qid or a fluoroquinolone (ciprofloxacin 500 mg, norfloxacin 400 mg, ofloxacin 300 mg qd)	Not routinely recommended by most experts; recommended only for those who could not tolerate "turista" for either medical or social reasons. Prompt treatment of diarrhea with antimotility agents and a 3-d course of a fluoroquinolone for moderate to severe diarrhea is probably a superior strategy
Tuberculosis	*Mycobacterium tuberculosis*	Isoniazid (INH), 10 mg/kg/d (max 300 mg/d) for 6 mo– 1 y (HIV-seropositive patients should receive at least 1 y)	Recommended (1) for recent converters from a negative to positive PPD (PPD should be intermediate strength) in previous 2 y; (2) for PPD+ persons (presumed recent converters) who are in close contact with a person with active disease; (3) for PPD+ persons less than 35 years of age; (4) for PPD+ persons whose chest x-ray is consistent with past tuberculosis and who have not received INH previously (optional); (5) for PPD+ persons (a) who are receiving immunosuppressive drugs, (b) who have lymphoproliferative malignancy, (c) who have silicosis, (d) after gastrectomy, (e) patients who are HIV-seropositive; (6) for PPD– child less than 5 y of age, who is in close contact with active case. These children should get INH for 3 mo and then have PPD repeated; if PPD still negative, may stop INH. For PPD converters following exposure to drug-resistant tuberculosis, no clear prophylactic guidelines have been established. Consider a multidrug regimen based on the susceptibility pattern of the resistant strain, if known.
Recurrent urinary tract infections	Usually Gram-negative bacilli	Trimethoprim–sulfameth-oxazole ½ single-strength tab qd, trimethoprim 100 mg qd, or nitrofurantoin 50 mg qd × 6 mo	Indicated in some persons with three or more recurrent urinary tract infections per year; also indicated in persons with frequent infections who are at risk for renal damage with each infection (children with significant vesicoureteral reflux and adults with obstructive uropathy). If infections recur after prophylaxis is stopped, may need to reinstitute prophylaxis.
Chronic bronchitis and bronchiectasis	Pneumococcus, *H. influenzae*	Tetracycline, 500 mg qid amoxicillin 500 mg tid erythromycin 250 mg qid or 333 mg tid trimethoprim–sulfamethoxa-zole 1 DS bid	Only indicated for those with frequent recurrent infections (≥4 per year); many schedules have been employed; some physicians elect to give patients antibiotics to be taken at the first sign of infection.
Bites 　Animal	*Pasteurella multocida,* α-hemolytic streptococci, *Staphylococcus aureus*	Penicillin VK, 500 mg qid; amoxicillin–clavulanic acid, 250 mg tid; tetracycline 500 mg qid (for patients with penicillin allergy)	Cat bites clearly require prophylactic antibiotics because of the high incidence of *Pasteurella* infection. Many would treat all patients with dog bites presenting in the emergency room, but the infection rate is lower than with cat bites. Patients without spleens should definitely receive prophylaxis following dog bites because of the potential for overwhelming infection caused by *capnocytophaga canimorsus* (formerly DF-2).

TABLE 8–80–2. (*Continued*)

Disease/Condition	Causative Agent(s)	Treatment*	Comments
Bites (*continued*)			
Human	*Streptococcus viridans*, mouth anaerobes, *Eikenella, S. aureus*	Amoxicillin–clavulanic acid 250 mg tid; penicillin 500 mg qid; clindamycin 150 mg qid	*Eikenella* is resistant to clindamycin. Bites from hospitalized patients may cause infection with nosocomial Gram-negative bacilli.
Influenza	Type A influenza	Amantadine or rimantadine 100 mg PO bid for duration of risk; give for 2 wk if vaccine is administered at same time	70–90% efficacious—usually given to persons who were not adequately vaccinated, but may be given to vaccinated individuals for increased protection. In elderly, may use 100 mg amantadine qd. See Chapter 8–81. Rimantadine has fewer side effects.

PPD, purified protein derivative
*Treatment doses, unless specifically stated, are for adults with normal renal function and no history of allergy.

altered immunity or predisposing conditions such as abnormal heart valves. Other infections are caused by virulent organisms, the exposure to which can produce disease in normal hosts.

CRITERIA FOR DIAGNOSIS

Antimicrobial agents are frequently used in an attempt to prevent infection, but they are of proven prophylactic benefit in only a few situations. The criteria for appropriate antimicrobial prophylaxis include the ability to reduce serious and significant infection while maintaining relatively low toxicity and cost and avoiding a high incidence of superinfection.

CLINICAL MANIFESTATIONS
Subjective

As part of a comprehensive evaluation of any patient, information on underlying problems that require antimicrobial prophylaxis should be sought. A history of significant murmur, congenital heart disease, a prior bout of endocarditis, or rheumatic fever should be explored. A history of a hemoglobinopathy, such as sickle cell anemia, or of significant trauma should alert the clinician to the possible absence of a spleen. A detailed surgical history should be obtained paying particular attention to a previous splenectomy or implantation of a prosthetic cardiac valve or graft. Recurrent respiratory tract, urinary tract, or cutaneous infections may indicate an underlying immunologic or anatomic abnormality. In addition to determining the cause of recurrent infections, the clinician should delineate the frequency, severity, and morbidity associated with these infections to assess the need for prophylactic antibiotics. Antibiotic allergies should be characterized; many patients interpret any untoward reaction to an antibiotic, including nausea and diarrhea, as an "allergy." In the setting of a possible exposure to communicable infections such as meningococcal or *Hemophilus influenzae* meningitis, the details of the possible exposure are key to determining the need for prophylactic antibiotics.

TABLE 8–80–3. RECOMMENDED ANTIBIOTICS FOR SURGICAL PROPHYLAXIS

Procedure	Prophylactic Regimen*	Initial Dose	Comments
Appendectomy	Cefoxitin	1 g IV	For perforated appendix, continue antibiotics for 3–5 d.
Cholecystectomy (high-risk patients)	Cefazolin	1 g IV	Factors favoring bacteria in bile are (1) age > 70 y, (2) recent attack of cholecystitis, (3) jaundice, (4) previous biliary tract surgery, (5) emergent surgery needed, (6) recent fever/chills.
Colon resection	Neomycin plus erythromycin **or** cefoxitin IV alone (optional)	1 g PO/1 g PO 1 g IV	Mode of oral preparation for colon surgery: After adequate catharsis, give neomycin, 1 g PO at 1 PM, 2 PM, 11 PM; erythromycin 1 g PO at 1 PM, 2 PM, 11 PM
Gastric resection (high-risk patients)	Cefazolin	1 g IV	High-risk patients are those who undergo surgery for bleeding or obstructing duodenal or gastric ulcer or malignancy; also gastric bypass or cutaneous endoscopic gastrostostomy. Patients with perforations should be treated with therapeutic regimen as opposed to prophylactic regimen.
Clean surgery (cardiac, vascular, orthopaedic, craniotomy)	Cefazolin **or** vancomycin (if significant problems with methicillin-resistant staphylococci are present in your hospital)	1 g IV 1 g IV	Prophylaxis is indicated for most cardiac procedures; orthopaedic procedures including joint replacement and open reduction–internal fixation of fractures; vascular procedures including insertion of a vascular prosthesis, abdominal aortic surgery, peripheral vascular surgery, and limb amputations for ischemia. For many neurosurgical procedures (other than craniotomy), prophylactic antibiotics are of no proven benefit.
Head and neck surgery (when respiratory or alimentary tract is entered)	Clindamycin plus Gentamicin or Cefazolin (alone)	900 mg IV 1.5 mg/kg IV 1 g IV	
Hysterectomy, urgent caesarean section	Cefazolin	1 g IV	Indicated for both vaginal and abdominal hysterectomy. For cesarean section, the antibiotic should be given after the umbilical cord is clamped.
Prostatectomy	Agent should be based on sensitivities of organism in urine or prostatic secretions		No clear indication if urine is sterile.

*First dose of antibiotics is given 30 min to 1 h before surgery. Single-dose prophylaxis is appropriate for most procedures. For long operations, depending on the half-life of the antimicrobial used, a second dose may be required to keep the tissue level adequate. Prophylactic antibiotics should not be continued for more than 24 h following the procedure.

Objective

A careful cardiac examination is important to characterize the significance of a murmur. In the absence of a regurgitant murmur, most authorities do not recommend endocarditis prophylaxis with mitral valve prolapse. Abdominal scars should prompt questioning about past surgical procedures.

Routine Laboratory Abnormalities

A peripheral blood smear may reveal evidence of Howell–Jolly bodies or the presence of sickle or other abnormal cells. Findings such as these suggest a hemoglobinopathy and/or the possibility of functional asplenia. Chest radiograph abnormalities may suggest inactive tuberculosis.

PLANS

Diagnostic

With few exceptions, no specific diagnostic plans are required for the use of antimicrobial prophylaxis other than documentation of a specific underlying disease process that necessitates prophylaxis or recognition of the need for a surgical procedure for which prophylaxis will be beneficial. Testing for delayed hypersensitivity to purified protein derivative is important to assess the need for prophylactic isoniazid following exposure to active tuberculosis. In certain individuals, liver enzymes should be obtained before beginning isoniazid prophylaxis.

For patients embarking on foreign travel, a reference booklet entitled *Health Information for International Travel* (HHS Publication CDC 94-8280—the "94" reflecting the most recent year of publication) is published yearly and is available through the U.S. Department of Health and Human Services. A call to the Advice for Travelers desk at the Centers for Disease Control and Prevention in Atlanta, Georgia, 404–332–4559, also may be helpful in planning appropriate prophylactic measures for travelers. In many cities, sophisticated international travel medicine clinics have been established to provide updated assistance in this ever-changing field (see Chapter 8–34).

Therapeutic

This chapter does not deal specifically with the therapy of any of the diseases discussed, only with prevention. Conditions for which prophylaxis is recommended and the antimicrobial regimens are listed in Tables 8–80–1, 8–80–2, and 8–80–3.

FOLLOW-UP

As no prophylactic regimen is completely effective, the patient treated with prophylactic antibiotics should be advised to report promptly to the physician the occurrence of any illness. In addition, the patient should report any side effects immediately. For example, patients receiving isoniazid prophylaxis should be followed periodically, as severe hepatic toxicity can occur and is potentially fatal if the medication is not discontinued. Isoniazid hepatitis usually develops within the first 3 months of therapy; the risk of hepatitis increases with age. Monthly measurements of serum transaminase levels are often recommended to minimize risk of hepatotoxicity. When prophylaxis is required for years, as in rheumatic fever, compliance may wane with time. Periodic follow-up can help reinforce the importance of continued prophylaxis.

DISCUSSION

Prevalence and Incidence

The occurrence of endocarditis in patients with valvular heart disease is low, even following procedures that induce bacteremia. Because of this low incidence, a study designed to demonstrate a beneficial effect of antibiotic prophylaxis would require a very large number of subjects. For this reason, studies attempting to validate the endocarditis prophylaxis recommendations listed in this chapter have not and probably will not be done. The incidence of postoperative infections depends on the type of surgery, duration of surgery, and host risk factors.

Related Basic Science

The occurrence of infection is related to the interaction between the microorganism and the host defense system. Humans have a vast array of defense mechanisms including the cellular and the humoral immune systems. In many instances the most important host defenses are the inherent protective barriers, such as unbroken skin and mucous membranes, and the normal microflora that inhabit these areas. Infection can occur when the natural defenses are compromised or when the microorganisms are so virulent that they overcome a normal set of host defenses. In either situation, prophylactic antibiotics can shift the balance in favor of the host.

Prophylactic antibiotics are most effective when they are directed at a single microorganism and when the risk of infection is high. Most of their proven benefit in disease prevention has occurred with certain surgical procedures, meningococcal and *H. influenzae* infections, malaria (see Chapter 8–61), recurrences of rheumatic fever, and tuberculosis. As previously stated, prophylactic antibiotics have not been shown to be of definite benefit in the prevention of bacterial endocarditis. In this situation, the recommendations for prophylaxis are based on the likely benefit and very low risk of adverse effects of antibiotics, as well as data on endocarditis in some experimental animal models.

Regarding perioperative antimicrobial prophylaxis, important considerations include determining which procedures require prophylaxis, the choice of antimicrobial agents, and the optimal timing and duration of antibiotic use. Antibiotics are most clearly beneficial when the risk of infection is high (e.g., surgery of the colon or female genital tract) or when infection would produce disastrous consequences (e.g., implantation of a microorganism on a prosthetic heart valve or in a prosthetic hip). For surgeries with relatively low rates of infection, the decision to use antibiotic prophylaxis should be based on the results of carefully conducted clinical trials. For many types of clean surgical procedures, such as inguinal hernia repair, the risk of antimicrobial prophylaxis is greater than the possible benefits; when good surgical technique is used in these situations, the wound infection rate should be so low that antibiotic prophylaxis is not warranted.

Choice of an appropriate antibiotic for prophylaxis is based on awareness of the organisms likely to cause postoperative infections after the specific surgical procedure, as well as on knowledge of the indigenous microflora present in the environment to be manipulated. In situations such as gastrointestinal and gynecologic surgery, it is impossible to develop a regimen active against the entire microbial flora present at the site. Fortunately, this is not necessary, as evidenced by studies showing that cefazolin is effective in many gynecologic procedures despite its lack of inhibition of some organisms that are part of the normal vaginal flora. Thus, in general, antibiotic prophylaxis is effective when significant numbers of the flora, including the pathogens most likely to be encountered, can be inhibited. Whether the antibiotics are effective by reducing the total microbial load, by changing the balance of the microbial flora, or by removing microbes that are especially virulent is not completely known.

Animal studies in the 1960s and, more recently, clinical studies have shown that parenteral antibiotics are most effective when they are started just prior to surgery so that high concentrations of the antibiotic are achieved when the skin is incised and persist throughout the surgical procedure. If antibiotics are started after surgery is begun, the prophylactic effect is markedly diminished. In general, single-dose prophylaxis is sufficient and probably optimal. During long procedures, a second dose can be given 3 to 4 hours after the initial dose to ensure that high concentrations of the agent are present for the duration of the procedure. Prophylactic antibiotics should not be continued for more than 24 hours after the procedure. Unfortunately, prophylactic antibiotics frequently are given postoperatively for 72 hours or longer, a practice that has no added benefit, clearly increases the cost and risk of toxicity, and probably increases the rate of serious superinfections.

Natural History and Its Modification with Treatment

The natural history of the specific disease for which prevention is used is quite variable and is discussed in the specific chapters dealing with each of the disease processes. Although the intent of antimicrobial prophylaxis is to prevent infection, sometimes the disease is modified but not prevented. For example, influenza following amantadine prophylaxis is likely to be milder than if no prophylaxis was administered. Prophylaxis can also alter the microbiology of infections, particularly postoperative infections.

Prevention

It is important to note that in addition to antimicrobial agents, other factors are important in the prevention of illness. Vaccination as a prophylactic procedure is discussed in Chapter 8–81. In the setting of travel to lesser developed areas of the world, simple measures, such as the avoidance of poorly cooked meats and vegetables, unpeeled fruits, and inadequately purified water and milk, is important in the prevention of enteric illnesses. In patients with cardiac valvular disease or implanted prosthetic devices, attention should be directed toward the maintenance of good oral hygiene and the care of any local infection of the skin or mucous membranes. Similarly, the prevention of surgical wound infections is influenced more by excellent surgical technique and appropriate antiseptic practices than by the use of antimicrobial agents.

Cost Containment

In addition to decreasing morbidity and mortality, one of the primary potential benefits of prophylactic antibiotics is cost containment. By preventing secondary cases of diseases such as meningococcal infection and tuberculosis, prolonged hospitalizations and expensive antimicrobial and supportive regimens may be avoided. When serious infectious complications of surgery can be prevented, considerable cost savings are possible, a fact that has been well documented in the recent literature. To maximize this economic benefit, however, prophylactic parenteral antibiotics should be given only during the period of maximal benefit, namely, just prior to the initial surgical incision and no longer than 24 hours after surgery in most situations. Use of the more expensive antibiotics, including third-generation cephalosporins, dramatically increases the cost of antibiotic prophylaxis for surgical procedures without any documented decrease in the infection rate, and these agents are less active against *Staphylococcus aureus*, a major pathogen causing postoperative wound infections. In addition, selective pressure from broad spectrum antibiotic use may contribute to the development of antibiotic-resistant bacteria. Antibiotic resistance threatens to negate some of our prophylactic strategies and necessitate changes to more costly and possibly more toxic agents.

The 1990 American Heart Association recommendations for bacterial endocarditis prophylaxis take cost (and practicality) into consideration by shortening the course of prophylactic antibiotics, advocating oral regimens for many patients at high risk for endocarditis, and not recommending prophylaxis for patients at low risk of developing endocarditis, including patients with mitral valve prolapse without regurgitation. Nonetheless, because the risk of endocarditis following invasive procedures for most patients with valvular disease is very low, it is unlikely that endocarditis prophylaxis is a cost-effective strategy.

REFERENCES

Antimicrobial prophylaxis in surgery. Med Lett 1993;35:91.
Dajani AS, Bisno AL, Chung KJ, et al. Prevention of bacterial endocarditis: Recommendations by the American Heart Association. JAMA 1990;264:2919.
Durack DT. Drug therapy: Prevention of infective endocarditis. N Engl J Med 1995;332:38.
Wenzel RP. Preoperative antibiotic prophylaxis. N Engl J Med 1992;326:337.

CHAPTER 8–81

The Need for Immunization

Naomi Bock, M.D., and David Rimland, M.D.

DEFINITION

Immunization is the act of artificially inducing immunity or providing protection from disease.

ETIOLOGY

Immunizing agents are vaccines, toxoids, and immunoglobulins.

CRITERIA FOR DIAGNOSIS

Immunization may be required in three different circumstances: before disease exposure, after exposure but before the onset of disease, and after the onset of disease. Immunization of adults, before exposure, for vaccine-preventable diseases should be a routine practice of physicians. An immunization history should be obtained from each new patient and updated periodically. The Task Force on Adult Immunization recommends that age 50 be established as a time for review of preventive health measures, evaluating the need for pneumococcal vaccine, annual influenza immunization, and tetanus/diphtheria primary or booster immunization. Table 8–81–1 lists the five vaccines most often used for routine adult immunization.

The need for immunization after exposure but before disease onset and that after onset of disease differ, but include lack of a documented history of the disease or immunization, requirement for a booster dose of vaccine, and need for therapy with an antitoxin.

CLINICAL MANIFESTATIONS
Subjective

Some of the diseases for which immunizing agents are available produce typical manifestations that can be clinically diagnosed. A history obtained from the patient relating physician-documented mumps or measles is adequate to assume protection. For other diseases, such as rubella, clinical diagnosis is inexact, and only serologic proof of protection should be accepted. A well-documented history of having received an appropriate vaccine at an appropriate age also precludes the need for immunization with that agent. A patient's profession, plans for travel, residence, exposure to a disease, or symptoms of a particular disease requiring antitoxin therapy may also dictate the need for immunization.

TABLE 8–81–1. ROUTINE IMMUNIZATION OF ADULTS

Vaccine	Recommendations
Pneumococcal	All adults age ≥65 y; all younger adults with risk factors. Reimmunization is recommended at age 65 if 6 or more years have passed since first pneumococcal immunization
Influenza	Yearly for all adults age ≥65 y; all younger adults with risk factors. Offer to other healthy younger adults
Hepatitis B	Sexually active young adults; high-risk groups. Assess serologic response in persons age ≥30
Measles/mumps/rubella (MMR)	Adults born after 1956 without proof of immunity or documentation of previous immunization; two doses for special risk groups
Tetanus/diphtheria (Td)	Completion of primary (three-dose) immunization schedule followed by either Td boosters every 10 years, or a single midlife (at age 50) booster for persons who have completed the full pediatric series, including the teenage/young adult booster

Source: Reproduced with permission from American College of Physicians Task Force on Adult Immunization and Infectious Diseases Society of America, Guide for Adult Immunization, 3rd ed. American College of Physicians: Philadelphia; 1994.

TABLE 8–81–2. MISCONCEPTIONS CONCERNING CONTRAINDICATIONS TO ADULT IMMUNIZATION

The following are *not* contraindications to vaccination:

1. Reaction to a previous vaccination consisting only of mild to moderate local tenderness, redness and/or swelling, or fever less than 40.5°C
2. Mild acute illness with or without low-grade fever
3. Current antimicrobial therapy or convalescence from a recent illness
4. Household contact with a pregnant woman
5. Recent exposure to an infectious disease
6. Breastfeeding
7. Personal history of "allergies," including allergy to penicillin or other antibiotics, excluding anaphylactic reactions to neomycin (e.g., combined measles/mumps/rubella vaccine) or streptomycin (e.g., oral polio vaccine)
8. Family history of "allergies," adverse reactions to vaccination, or seizures

Source: Reproduced with permission from American College of Physicians Task Force on Adult Immunization and Infectious Diseases Society of America, Guide for Adult Immunization, 3rd ed. American College of Physicians: Philadelphia; 1994.

Objective

The physical examination is not applicable except when the patient needs antitoxin therapy for botulism, diphtheria, or tetanus. In these situations, the physical examination shows signs of the specific disease entity.

The need for immunization for a particular disease may be proven by serologic testing. Although serologic determinations can be performed for many diseases, the only tests that are routinely available are those for antibody to rubella, mumps, hepatitis A (immunoglobulin G), and hepatitis B surface and core antibody.

PLANS

Diagnostic

For diseases requiring immunization before disease exposure, documentation of a history of disease or immunization for the disease is important. Information from physicians, school or military service records, and health department records may be very useful. Diseases for which routine serologic testing is available should be evaluated by submitting appropriate sera to hospital or state laboratories. In every situation in which vaccines are being administered, a thorough search for contraindications to immunization should be made. The live agent vaccines (e.g., rubella, mumps, poliomyelitis, yellow fever, vaccinia, oral typhoid, and bacille Calmette–Guérin) should not be given to pregnant women or patients who are immunocompromised because of underlying disease or chemotherapy for such diseases. The most common allergic component of vaccines is egg protein found in vaccines pre-

pared in chicken embryonal cultures or emryonated chicken eggs (e.g., influenza, measles, mumps, and yellow fever vaccines). People who eat eggs or egg-containing products can receive these vaccines. Misconceptions concerning contraindications are common and lead to unnecessary avoidance of immunization. Table 8–81–2 lists some common misconceptions. When immunizations are being given after disease exposure or after the onset of disease, appropriate diagnostic tests to confirm the diagnosis should be performed.

Therapeutic

The five vaccines listed in Table 8–81–3 are those used most often for routine adult immunization. Missed opportunities for administering these vaccines during acute care or routine physician visits are well documented. Only one third of high-risk persons receive influenza vaccine each year and fewer than 20% have ever received pneumococcal vaccine. Physicians caring for adult patients need to develop strategies for providing routine immunizations.

Specific information about the diseases for which immunization should be given after exposure but before the onset of symptoms (diphtheria, tetanus, rabies, viral hepatitis, measles, poliomyelitis, varicella, rubella) or after the onset of symptoms of disease (diphtheria, tetanus, botulism) should be sought in the appropriate chapters.

For travelers to foreign countries, requirements depend on the area of travel and change frequently. Detailed information is available in *Health Information for International Travel*, published annually by the U.S. Public Health Service, and available from the Centers for Disease Control and Prevention (CDC), Division of Quarantine, Atlanta, GA 30333, or from the Superintendent of Documents, U.S. Government Printing Office, Washington, DC 20402. Up-to-date automated information is available from the CDC by telephone, (404) 332–4559, or fax, (404) 332–4565.

FOLLOW-UP

Several of the immunizing agents require booster doses or annual vaccinations. An office- or clinic-based strategy for providing appropriate follow-up is necessary. Occasionally, preexposure prophylaxis (e.g., rabies) requires verification of the production of antibody, and appropriate serologic tests must be performed. For two diseases, tetanus and diphtheria, antitoxin therapy of the clinical diseases must be followed up by active immunization.

DISCUSSION

Prevalence and Incidence

In the United States each year between 50,000 to 70,000 deaths from pneumococcal pneumonia, influenza, or hepatitis B, vaccine-preventable diseases, occur in adults (Table 8–81–3). The poor record of

TABLE 8–81–3. ESTIMATES OF THE EFFECT OF FULL USE OF THE VACCINES NOW ADVOCATED FOR ADULTS

Diseases	Estimated Number of Annual Deaths Among Adults	Estimated Vaccine Efficacy* (%)	Current Vaccine Use† (%)	Number of Additional Preventable Deaths/Years‡
Influenza	20,000§	70	30	9,800
Pneumococcal infection	40,000	60	14	20,640
Hepatitis B	5,000	90	10‖	4,050
Tetanus/diphtheria	<25	99	40¶	<15
Traveler's diseases (cholera, typhoid, Japanese encephalitis, yellow fever, poliomyelitis, rabies)	<10	—	—	<10
Measles/mumps/rubella	<30	95	Varying	<30

*These composite estimates indicate efficacy in immunocompetent adults. In the elderly and immunocompromised, efficacy estimates are lower.
†Percentage of targeted groups that are in compliance with current recommendations. Rates vary among different targeted groups.
‡(Potential additional vaccine use) × (estimated vaccine efficacy) × (estimated annual deaths).
§Varying (range, 0–40,000).
‖Varies widely (1–60%) among different target groups.
¶Estimate based on seroprevalence data.
Source: Gardner P, Schaffner W. Immunization of adults. N Engl J Med 1993;328:1252. Copyright 1993, Massachusetts Medical Society, all rights reserved.

immunization among adults has been attributed to doubts about the efficacy and safety of vaccines on the part of the public and of physicians; uncertainty about specific recommendations; misconceptions about contraindications; issues of liability; lack of systematic strategies for immunizing adults; and inadequate reimbursement to providers.

Related Basic Science

Active induction of immunity stimulates the production of antibody in the recipient and is especially useful against diseases that are caused by a single or a small number of agents. Active immunization is attainable with vaccines containing live attenuated agents (e.g., measles, mumps, or rubella viruses), inactivated agents (e.g., influenza and rabies viruses, injectable typhoid and cholera bacilli), or toxoids (e.g., tetanus and diphtheria). In general, these immunizing agents produce long-lasting immunity, but some period is required between administration of the agent and the onset of its effect.

Passive immunization involves the administration of preformed antibody obtained from a human or animal. These agents may be useful for postexposure prophylaxis (e.g., viral hepatitis) or for therapy of disease (e.g., diphtheria, tetanus, or botulism antitoxins). Although the onset of effect is rapid after administration, the duration of immunity is short-lived.

Natural History and Its Modification with Treatment

The need for immunization constantly changes as persons age, develop chronic illnesses, or are exposed to new environments, and as new immunizing agents become available. Physicians must remain alert to these changes and provide information and immunization as needed.

Prevention

The goal of immunization is the prevention of disease.

Cost Containment

The cost of immunizing agents is obviously much less than the cost of treating the diseases against which they are directed. Using routine or acute care patient visits as an opportunity to provide immunization is cost-effective.

REFERENCES

Centers for Disease Control and Prevention. Recommendations of the Immunization Practices Advisory Committee (ACIP): General recommendations on immunization. MMWR 1994;43(RR-1).

Gardner P, Schaffner W. Immunization of adults. N Engl J Med 1993;328:1252.

Guide for adult immunization. 3rd ed. Philadelphia: American College of Physicians, 1994.

Rimland D, McGowan JE, Shulman JA. Immunization for the internist. Ann Intern Med 1976;85:622.

CHAPTER 8–82

Bacterial and Viral Infections of the Nervous System

Darwin R. Boor, M.D., and Donal A. Costigan, M.B., B. Ch., B.A.O.

DEFINITION

Infections of the nervous system cover a broad spectrum of clinical manifestations that overlap with other noninfectious disorders (Table 8–82–1). Infections of muscle (myositis, Table 8–82–2), nerve (Neuritis, Table 8–82–3), the meninges (meningitis, Tables 8–82–4 and 8–82–5), the meninges and brain (meningoencephalitis, Table 8–82–6), and the parameningeal spaces (e.g., epidural abscesses, Table 8–82–7) usually present with signs and symptoms of inflammation of the affected structure and are often associated with evidence of systemic toxicity.

ETIOLOGY

See Tables 8–82–2 through 8–82–7.

CRITERIA FOR DIAGNOSIS

Suggestive

Although a wide variety of organisms are involved in each of these infectious processes, in each case the history and condition of the patient prior to and during the infection tend to point to likely agents. Acute serologic tests, microscopic screening (e.g., Gram stains), and preliminary culture results often suggest specific causes.

Definitive

A definitive diagnosis is usually reached by growing and identifying the specific organism in culture or by definitively identifying the organism on microscopic examination. New organism-specific antibody tests allow earlier diagnosis. They also increase the yield and specificity of initial microscopic examinations. Screening for traces of organism-specific genetic markers from infected material may someday play a major role in the rapid diagnosis of life-threatening infections.

CLINICAL MANIFESTATIONS

Subjective

Clinical signs and symptoms usually point to the site of infection and often suggest potential etiologies (see Table 8–82–1 to 8–82–7). Travel to endemic regions or history of recent exposure to individuals with similar or related symptoms may also point to specific etiologies. Reports of organism-specific reactions may lead to a tentative organism-specific diagnosis.

Objective

Physical Examination

Physical examination should be oriented toward identifying the overall health of the patient, localizing the likely site or sites of infection, and screening for organism-specific features such as characteristic rashes or, in the case of multiple abscesses, potential embolic sources.

Routine Laboratory Abnormalities

Laboratory findings vary greatly based on the site of infection and the agent involved. Screening tests such as complete blood counts, erythrocyte sedimentation rates, acute serologies, and microscopic examination of infected materials may add evidence to suggest a potential etiologic agent (e.g., systemic eosinophilia with parasitic infections) or may lead to a tentative diagnosis when organisms are identified with an organism-specific stain or serology. Significantly elevated white blood cell counts, especially when associated with increases in granulocytes,

TABLE 8–82–1. INFECTIONS OF THE NERVOUS SYSTEM: AN OVERVIEW

Infection	Criteria for Diagnosis	Clinical Manifestations	
		Subjective	*Objective*
Myositis (Table 8–82–2)	Inflammation of muscle tissue (especially voluntary muscles). May be due to infection, parasitic infestations, or systemic diseases.	Muscle pain. May be accompanied by swelling and/or weakness.	Muscle tenderness, swelling, and/or weakness. Creatine kinase and aldolase frequently elevated. May have myopathic changes on electromyography.
Neuritis (Table 8–82–3)	Inflammation of a nerve (or nerves). Most frequently associated with degenerative processes, systemic disease, or local trauma, but may be due to direct infection, parainfectious inflammatory response, or toxin exposure.	Numbness, paresthesia, and weakness.	Alterations in sensation and/or motor function most frequently suggesting a multifocal or generalized process. Nerve conduction studies may be abnormal.
Meningitis (Tables 8–82–4 and 8–82–5) and meningoencephalitis (Table 8–82–6)	Inflammatory disorders of the meninges alone or the meninges and brain. *Hemophilus influenzae, Neisseria meningitidis,* and *Streptococcus pneumoniae* account for 75% of all cases of bacterial meningitis. *Listeria monocytogenes* is the next most common bacterial cause. Encephalitis may be produced either by direct invasion of the brain by an infectious agent or by a parainfectious process and is usually associated with meningitis (i.e., meningoencephalitis). The enteroviruses account for the majority of cases of meningoencephalitis and carry a relatively benign prognosis.	Headache, fever, and stiff neck are common presenting complaints but may be extremely mild in cases of viral meningitis. Other symptoms include nausea, vomiting, and photophobia. At times convulsions, altered consciousness, and/or focal neurologic findings. Patients may have had antecedent respiratory tract, sinus, ear, or pharyngeal symptoms. Geographic and seasonal variations may suggest potential etiologies.	Signs may be minimal in the very young and the very old. Signs of upper or lower respiratory tract infection should increase one's level of suspicion. Examination frequently demonstrates fever and meningismus. Altered consciousness, altered behavior, seizures, or significant central neurologic deficits point to an encephalitis component. Rashes, if present, may suggest a specific etiology (e.g., herpes zoster, Lyme disease, meningococcal meningitis, Rocky mountain spotted fever, syphilis). Routine laboratory results may point to the type of process. The peripheral white blood cell count and erythrocyte sedimentation rate are often elevated with bacterial infections and may be normal or reduced with viral infections. Blood and other peripheral cultures, and chest, sinus, and mastoid x-rays may be of benefit.
Parameningeal infections (Table 8–82–7)	Parameningeal infections are localized processes adjacent to the meninges and include brain and epidural abscesses, sinusitis, mastoiditis, and suppurative phlebitis. Focal neurologic deficits and/or aseptic meningitis frequently lead to neuroimaging and to a preliminary diagnosis.	Symptoms from these infections depend on the particular entity and location. Progression of symptoms may be indolent or fulminant. Differential diagnosis includes aseptic meningitis.	Physical findings are related to the location of the infection. Routine laboratory tests are seldom helpful, although the erythrocyte sedimentation rate is often elevated.

TABLE 8–82–2. MYOSITIS

Infection	Clinical Manifestations		Etiologic Agent
	Subjective	*Objective*	
Gas gangrene	Follows penetrating wounds, presents as severe pain.	Fever, local swelling, tenderness, crepitations, leukocytosis, Gram-positive bacilli on Gram stain.	Clostridial species, most frequently *Clostridium perfringens*
Pyomyositis (primary abscess)	Subacute onset. May follow local trauma (including injections).	Fever, local swelling, erythema, heat, tenderness, leukocytosis, various organisms on Gram stain.	*Staphylococcus aureus* Anaerobes Facultative Gram-negative bacilli
Trichinosis	Gastroenteritis followed by fever, myalgias, and weakness following consumption of undercooked pork.	Periorbital edema, eosinophilia, positive serology or muscle biopsy	*Trichinella*
Periinfectious myositis	Myalgia and recent or current infection.	Muscle tenderness, elevated creatine kinase, positive serology or culture.	Numerous bacterial and viral agents, including *Babesia* sp. (babesiosis), *Borrelia burgdorferi* (Lyme disease), *Hemophilus influenzae, Mycoplasma pneumoniae, Rickettsia* sp. (Rocky Mountain spotted fever, Q fever, typhus, etc.), toxoplasmosis, and Dengue virus (breakbone fever)
Rhabdomyolysis	Myalgias and possible secondary renal failure.	Muscle tenderness, elevated creatine kinase, myoglobinuria, evidence of secondary renal failure (if present).	Influenza and other viruses Legionnaire's disease Sepsis Medications Other causes

TABLE 8–82–3. NEURITIS

Infection	Clinical Manifestations		Etiologic Agent
	Subjective	*Objective*	
Periinfectious polyneuritis	Multifocal or generalized neuropathic symptoms. May be associated with fever, headache, and stiff neck.	Multifocal or generalized neuropathy. Possible fever and meningismus	*Borrelia burgdorferi* *Corynebacterium diphtheriae* Epstein–Barr virus Hepatitis viruses HIV *Mycoplasma* Herpes zoster
Herpes zoster	Dermatomal zone of altered sensation with or withour motor changes followed by the appearance of a rash respecting the same dermatome. Most frequently seen in immuno-compromised hosts.	Dermatomal vesicular eruption with variable sensory and motor alterations. Cornea involvement may occur with involvement of the ophthalmic division of the trigeminal nerve. Culture positive.	
Leprosy	Lepromatous form characterized by insidious onset and progression of symmetric nerve involvement with sensory loss and secondary joint and skin injuries. Tubercular form characterized by relatively abrupt onset and self-limited course with asymmetric nerve involvement. Usually there is a clear history of living in an area endemic for leprosy during childhood.	Characteristic pale anesthetic macular skin lesions and superficial nerve thickening-associated sensory changes frequently limited to cooler body tissues. Acid-fast bacilli in skin lesions or nasal or pinna scrapings, which grow on transfer to mouse footpads or armadillos.	*Mycobacterium leprae*

TABLE 8–82–4. BACTERIAL MENINGITIS

Infection	Clinical Manifestations	
	Subjective	*Objective*
Bacterial meningitis	Headache, fever, and stiff neck are common presenting complaints. Other symptoms include nausea, vomiting, and photophobia. At times convulsions, altered consciousness, and/or focal neurologic findings. Patients may have had anticedent respiratory tract, sinus, ear, or pharyngeal symptoms.	CSF pleocytosis (white blood cells, 5–100,000/mm^3) with low glucose and elevated protein. Gram or methylene blue stain and cultures usually positive. Newer techniques such as counterimmunoelectrophoresis provide rapid specific diagnoses for limited number of organisms. Gram stains and cultures from other sites may be helpful.
Gram-negative bacteria (except *Hemophilus influenzae* and *Neisseria meningitidis*)	Neonates, trauma, hospital acquired.	Blood cultures may be positive.
Group B streptococcus	Neonates.	Cultures of blood and maternal vagina and cervix may be positive.
Hemophilus influenzae	Children and older adults. Associated upper respiratory tract infection.	Blood cultures or CSF antigen test may be positive.
Legionella pneumophilia	Meningoencephalitis.	CSF and computed tomography of the brain are often normal. Serology usually positive.
Leptospira	Onset following exposure to contaminated water. *Initial phase:* severe muscle aches, conjunctivitis, hepatitis, and renal involvement. *Late phase:* "aseptic" meningitis.	*Initial phase:* Elevated creatine kinase, peripheral neutrophilia, hepatic or renal dysfunction. Positive blood, CSF, and urine cultures. Gram stain negative. Serology may be positive. *Late ("immune") phase:* lymphocytic meningitis (may be sterile). Serology usually positive.
Listeria monocytogenes	Meningoencephalitis in an immunocompromised or debilitated host (especially T-cell disorders).	Blood cultures often positive. Characteristic "tumbling motility."
Mycobacterium tuberculosis	Gradually evolving stiff neck and fever. Incidence appears to follow that of tuberculosis in the community.	CSF mononuclear cell predominance (polys early) with a low glucose. CSF acid-fast bacillus smear is typically negative. CSF cultures are frequently positive but may require weeks of incubation. Positive chest radiograph or purified protein derivative support diagnosis. Consider liver, lung, bone, or kidney biopsy and culture.
Neisseria meningitidis	Rapidly evolving epidemic bacterial meningitis in healthy young adults during the winter and spring months associated with characteristic (petechial/purpuric/ecchymotic) skin rash.	Blood cultures and Gram stains are often positive.

(continued)

TABLE 8–82–4. (*Continued*)

	Clinical Manifestations	
Infection	*Subjective*	*Objective*
Streptococcus pneumoniae (pneumococcus)	Meningitis in young children and old adults frequently preceded by pneumonia, sinusitis, otitis, or mastoiditis. Recurrent attacks may reflect CSF fistulas (cribriform plate, sinuses) due to trauma, tumor, congenital anomaly, etc. Also seen with disorders such as alcoholism, sickle cell disease, multiple myeloma.	Sinus, mastoid, or pulmonary infection may be present on radiograph. CSF antigen tests and blood cultures often positive.
Staphylococcus (*aureus* or *epidermidis*)	Malignancy, trauma, neurosurgical procedures, infected ventricular shunt, or endocarditis.	Blood cultures often positive.
Syphilis	Meningitis in 25% of cases. Evidence of cerebrovascular infarctions in meningovascular form of the disease. Development of neurosyphilis over months to years with initial asymptomatic stage.	Abnormal CSF with positive rapid plasma reagin and VDRL or fluorescent treponeal antibody absorption test.

CSF, cerebrospinal fluid.

tend to suggest nonviral etiologies. Changes in serum chemistry are often related to systemic effects of the infection.

PLANS
Diagnostic
Differential Diagnosis

Because of the serious and potentially life-threatening nature of most nervous system infections, infection should be in the initial differential diagnosis for most neurologic disorders. Its place on the differential diagnosis should increase if the patient is seriously or acutely ill or if there are local or systemic signs of inflammation or infection. Some inflammatory disorders of the nervous system are not the result of infectious agents (e.g., neurologic complications of connective tissue disease, sarcoidosis, and certain toxic exposures). These noninfectious disorders should remain in the differential diagnosis of potential nervous system infections, if appropriate for the site and nature of the suspected infection, until a specific infectious etiology is identified. With infections of the nervous system, the differential diagnosis for the etiologic organism will vary according to the site of the infection, according to host-related factors such as health and immunity, and according to non-host-related factors such as the season of the year and modes of transmission.

Diagnostic Options and Recommended Approach

The diagnostic evaluation of suspected nervous system infections varies according to the type of infection. Lumbar puncture (LP) should

TABLE 8–82–5. VIRAL ("ASEPTIC") MENINGITIS

	Clinical Manifestations	
Infection	*Subjective*	*Objective*
Viral "aseptic" meningitis	Headache, fever, and stiff neck are common presenting complaints but may be extremely mild. Other symptoms include nausea, vomiting, and photophobia. At times convulsions, altered consciousness, and/or focal neurologic findings. Patients may have had antecedent respiratory tract, sinus, ear, or pharyngeal symptoms. Geographic and seasonal variations may suggest potential etiologies.	Monocytic or lymphocytic "nonpurulent" CSF. CSF glucose and protein usually normal. Stains and cultures are often negative. New techniques such as enzyme-linked immunosorbent assay allow rapid detection of a limited number of cases.
Arboviruses	Summer and fall. May be associated with encephalitis. Occasionally epidemic.	Serology.
Enteroviruses (Echo, Coxsackie)	Late summer and early fall; pleurodynia, herpangina, myopericarditis, maculopapular or petechial rash.	CSF and stool cultures. Serology.
Enteroviruses (polio)	Epidemic progressive aseptic meningoencephalitis. Progressive paralysis. Most often associated with vaccination or contact with recently vaccinated individuals. Paralytic form often progressive over 48 hours.	Viral cultures and serology may be positive.
Epstein–Barr virus	Mononucleosis syndrome with meningismus. Meningo-encephalitis often associated with mononucleosis.	Positive monospot or other serology.
Herpes (simplex) hominis type 1	Rapidly progressive meningoencephalitis.	Focal meningoencephalitis (temporal and inferior frontal regions most frequently affected). Brain biopsy with rapid fluorescent antibody determination and subsequent culture. Serology.
Herpes (simplex) hominis Type 2	Meningoencephalitis.	Genital lesions may be present. Cultures and serology often positive.
HIV	Headache, fever, and neck stiffness in an individual at risk for HIV infection.	Fever and meningismus. Serology and antigen detection. Viral cultures. May recur with a cyclic pattern.
Influenza	Winter epidemics at times associated with pneumonia.	Meningitis. Positive serology.
Lymphocytic choriomeningitis	Late fall and winter. Exposure to infected mice or hamsters.	Severe progressive meningoencephalitis. Serology.
Mumps	Late spring and winter. Parotitis, pancreatitis, orchitis, oophoritis. Males more often affected than females.	Meningoencephalitis. Serology.

CSF, cerebrospinal fluid.

TABLE 8–82–6. MENINGOENCEPHALITIS

Viral Causes	Nonviral Causes
Epidemic and sporadic encephalitis, arthropodborne (arboviruses)	Actnomycosis
Bunyaviridae	
California group encephalitis	Gram-negative bacilli
Flaviviridae	Brucellosis
Brazilian, Japanese B, and St. Louis encephalitis and others	Gram-positive bacilli
Reoviridae	Listeria: *Listeria monocytogenes*
Colorado tick fever	
Togaviridae	Mycobacteria
Alphaviruses: Eastern, Western, and Venezuelan equine encephalitis and others	Tuberculosis
	Mycoplasma
	Mycoses
Epidemic and sporadic encephalitis, animalborne	
Rhabdoviridae	*Cryptococcus*
Rabies	
	Histoplasma
Epidemic encephalitis, humanborne	*Nocardia*
Picornaviridae	Protozoa
Enterovirus: polioviruses, Coxsackievirus, Echovirus	*Nagleria*
	Acanthamoeba
Retroviridae	
Lentiviruses: HIV, human T-cell leukemia virus type I	Toxoplasmosis: *Toxoplasma gondii*
	Malaria: *Plasmodium falciparum*
Sporadic encephalitis, humanborne	
Adenoviridae	Trypanosomiasis and Chagas' disease
Adenovirus	*Rickettsia*
Arenaviridae	Rocky Mountain and other spotted fevers
Lymphocytic choriomeningitis	Typhus
Herpetoviridae	*Ehrlichia canis*
Herpesviruses: herpes simplex types 1 and 2 and varicella–zoster	Spirochetes
	Syphilis (meningovascular): *Treponema pallidum*
Epstein–Barr	
Cytomegalovirus	Relapsing fever: *Borrelia*
Paramyxoviridae	Lyme disease: *Borrelia burgdorferi*
Morbillivirus: measles	Leptospirosis
Paramyxovirus: mumps	Other bacteria
Postinfection encephalitis	Cat-scratch disease
Herpetoviridae	Possible infectious etiology
Herpesviruses: varicella–zoster	Whipple's disease
Epstein–Barr	Behçet's disease
Myxoviridae	
Influenzavirus: Influenza A and B	
Paramyxoviridae	
Morbillivirus: measles	
Paramyxovirus: mumps	
Poxviridae	
Orthopoxvirus: Vaccinia	
Togaviridae	
Rubivirus: Rubella	

be considered whenever a central nervous system infection is suspected. With parameningeal infections (including brain abscesses), LP is seldom diagnostic, even if it reveals a pleocytosis. The only absolute contraindication to LP is infection at the planned puncture site. Mass lesions, increased intracranial pressure, bleeding diathesis, spinal cord tumors, and spinal vascular malformations are all relative contraindications. LP should be approached with extreme caution if one or more of these conditions is present. Computed tomography or magnetic resonance imaging with contrast will identify most intracranial mass lesions and may establish the primary source for some bacterial and fungal infections. Images should include the sinuses. Magnetic resonance imaging is preferable. With extracranial infections, preliminary localized bone and soft tissue x-rays may point to a specific diagnosis and often help to guide subsequent computed tomography and magnetic resonance imaging of these sites. Radionuclide scans (including labeled

white blood cell studies), myelograms, and angiograms may provide valuable information under carefully selected conditions. Blood cultures frequently identify the organism responsible for pyogenic processes.

Cerebrospinal fluid analysis should include cell counts, protein, glucose, Gram stain, and bacterial cultures. Other studies (i.e., India ink, cryptococcal antigen, fungal culture, acid-fast bacillus smears, tuberculosis culture, and viral culture) should be obtained if indicated. Special tests to detect foreign antigens, endotoxins, and other organism specific by-products in the spinal fluid or blood may be of benefit in the rapid detection of Gram-negative enterobacterial, *Hemophilus influenzae* meningococcal, pneumococcal, and group B streptococcal infections. These tests employ several different techniques including counterimmunoelectrophoresis, enzyme-linked immunosorbent assay, latex particle agglutination, radioimmunoassay, and special gas–liquid chromatography. New tests are constantly being developed and a brief conversation with the microbiology staff or infectious disease consultants usually reveals which procedures are available locally. If the patient's initial cerebrospinal fluid analysis is not diagnostic or the patient fails to respond to appropriate therapy, a repeat LP should be considered.

Therapeutic

A potentially treatable etiology should be assumed whenever an infection of the nervous system is suspected. If empiric therapy is indicated, it should be initiated as soon as the appropriate diagnostic studies have been performed (Table 8–82–8). Initial therapy is usually based on the patient's age and underlying disease(s). More specific treatment is provided as precise diagnostic information (including antibiotic sensitivities) becomes available (Table 8–82–9). Only antibiotics that are known to be effective in the treatment of nervous system infections should be used. Treatment of focal abscesses usually includes surgical drainage because antibiotic therapy alone often fails to maintain microbicidal concentrations within many abscess cavities. Extended therapy is generally required and maintenance therapy may be indicated for opportunistic infections in immunocompromised hosts. Long-term management should also include nutritional support, maintenance of fluid and electrolyte balance, prevention of nosocomial infections and complications (e.g., pressure sores, catheter injuries, thrombophlebitis), and rehabilitation.

Patients and their families should be informed of the serious nature of these illnesses. They may be offered hope that with appropriate treatment the infection can usually be controlled and frequently eliminated. Extra time is often necessary to discuss LP and surgical procedures (e.g., brain biopsy). Fear of these procedures is often based on misinformation. Updated information concerning the course of treatment and the potential for recovery of function should be provided on a regular basis. Patients should be forewarned that relapses do occasionally occur after what is felt to be adequate therapy and they should be advised to watch for signs of recurrent infection.

FOLLOW-UP

If the patient fails to respond to therapy or if symptoms suggestive of a relapse occur, a careful reevaluation should be conducted. Routine imaging to follow the course of localized infections is warranted.

DISCUSSION
Prevalence and Incidence

The prevalence and incidence of viral and bacterial infections of the nervous system vary widely depending on the location of the patient, the time of year, and where the patient is being evaluated.

Related Basic Science

Most portions of the nervous system are protected from direct contact with the remainder of the body by the blood–brain and blood–nerve barriers. The cells constituting these barriers are closely joined by tight junctions, which help to prevent the passage of many substances and infectious agents. Pyogenic infections of the nervous system appear to

TABLE 8–82–7. PARAMENINGEAL INFECTIONS AND BRAIN ABSCESSES

Infection	Clinical Manifestations		Etiologic Agent
	Subjective	*Objective*	
Brain abscess	Headache, fever, confusion, nausea, vomiting, stiff neck; possible history of a primary infection (sinuses, ear, or mastoids in 40% of cases).	Fever, altered mental status, focal neurologic deficits, seizures, nuchal rigidity, papilledema. Possible evidence of primary infection site. Skull and sinus films to look for primary source. Increased intracranial pressure.	Streptococci (anaerobic or microaerophilic) often with other anaerobes. *Staphylococcus aureus* *Bacteroides* *Enterobacter* Actinomycoses *Candida* *Cryptococcus* *Nocardia* Toxoplasmosis Cysticercosis Schistosomiasis
Subdural empyema	Fever, headache (possibly focal), nausea, and vomiting.	Fever, meningismus, altered mental status, rapid evolution of focal signs.	Aerobic streptococci *Streptococcus pneumoniae* *Hemophilus influenzae* Gram-negative bacteria Anaerobes *Bacteroides*
Cerebral epidural abscess	Fever, headache (possibly focal), nausea, and vomiting.	Fever, altered mental status, focal neurologic signs including seizures. Possible cranial neuropathies.	Streptococci (aerobic and anaerobic) *S. aureus*
Spinal epidural abscess	Localized back pain, possible paresthesia and paralysis. Acute and chronic cases occur.	Nuchal rigidity, local spinal tenderness, possible sensory and/or motor deficits.	*S. aureus* streptococci (aerobic and anaerobic) *Escherichia coli* *Pseudomonas aeruginosa* Tuberculosis
Suppurative intracranial phlebitis	Focal pain becoming a generalized headache. Fever and malaise. Chronic sinus or mastoid infection. Eye swelling, diplopia, headache, soft tissue pain.	Focal neurologic signs, seizures, cranial nerve palsies, papilledema on x-rays of sinuses and mastoids. Various cranial nerve palsies and other focal neurologic deficits depending on affected vessel(s).	*S. aureus* *Staphylococcus epidermidis,* Streptococci (aerobic and anaerobic) Gram-negative bacilli

occur primarily by hematogenous spread or by extension from adjacent structures. It is notable that direct injection of virulent bacteria into animal brains seldom results in abscess formation.

Clinical manifestations vary according to the location and the organism involved. Acute meningitis is often associated with delirium and other signs of encephalopathy which may correlate with the nonspecific

TABLE 8–82–8. EMPIRIC ANTIBIOTIC THERAPY IN CENTRAL NERVOUS SYSTEM INFECTIONS IN ADULTS

Suspected Source	Empiric Therapy
Unknown meningitis	Ampicillin or penicillin G*
Unknown central nervous system	Nafcillin† + chloramphenicol or metronidazole + cefotaxime or ceftriaxone‡§
Right-to-left cardiac shunt or pulmonary infection	Penicillin G* + chloramphenicol or metronidazole ± cefotaxime or ceftriaxone‡
Encocarditis	Nafcillin†
Oral cavity	Penicillin G* + chloramphenicol or metronidazole
Penetrating trauma or cerebrospinal fluid fistula	Nafcillin† + cefotaxime or ceftriaxone‡
Sinusitis	Nafcillin† + chloramphenicol or metronidazole + cefotaxime or ceftriaxone‡

*Alter selection if specific agent (especially *Staphylococcus aureus* or Gram-negative bacilli) or penicillin resistance is suspected.
†Consider vancomycin if penicillin allergic or if nafcillin resistance is suspected.
‡The ability of third-generation cephalosporins to penetrate central nervous system abscesses has not been conclusively established. Adding an aminoglycoside should be considered.
§With brain and spinal cord abscess(es), if immunosuppression is suspected, consider adding sulfadiazine and pryrimethamine to cover *Toxoplasma gondii.*

glial reaction seen in the superficial layers of the cerebral cortex. Secondary necrosis may occur in response to arteritis or phlebitis and is particularly prominent and often hemorrhagic in the case of herpetic encephalitis. Involvement of cortical neurons in meningoencephalitis can produce a progressive encephalopathy with behavioral changes, hallucinations, and/or focal neurologic deficits and may lead to focal or generalized seizures. Loss of oligodendroglia results in central demyelination and secondary blockade of neuronal conduction. Loss of Schwann cells peripherally produces a similar condition. Secondary edema may produce sufficient mass effect to produce circulatory compromise or tissue compression. Chronic meningitis is often complicated by impaired cerebrospinal fluid circulation (i.e., communicating hydrocephalus) and secondary entrapment of individual nerves and nerve roots.

Natural History and Its Modification with Treatment

The organism involved and the initial severity of the infection are the two major factors determining the eventual outcome in infections of the nervous system. The presence of underlying medical conditions that compromise immunologic function also contributes to the production of more severe infections. Although many of the more common nervous system infections are not fatal, the mortality figures for some infections are significant. Up to 15% of cases of *Hemophilus influenzae* meningitis and 30% of cases of pneumococcal meningitis are fatal. The fatality rate is above 50% for eastern equine encephalitis, and for untreated herpes encephalitis, it may be as high as 80%.

Prevention

A significant number of the most serious infections of the nervous system are preventable. Vaccinations have nearly eliminated polio in the United States. They have been shown to be effective in preventing the neurologic complications of measles, mumps, and rabies. They appear to reduce the frequency of neurologic infection due to *Hemophilus in-*

TABLE 8–82–9. ANTIBIOTICS COMMONLY USED TO TREAT CENTRAL NERVOUS SYSTEM INFECTIONS

Antibiotic	Dose Schedule*	Organisms
Penicillin G	24 MU/24 h IV (q4h)	Gm+ and GM–, *Clostridium*, *Escherichia coli*, *Hemophilus influenzae*, *Neisseria meningitidis*, group A, B, and D streptococcis, *Proteus mirabilis*, and *Streptococcus pneumoniae*
Ampicillin	4–12 g/24 h IV (q4h)	Gm+ and Gm– (resistance), *Bacteroides*, *H. influenzae* (some strains), *Listeria monocytogenes*, *N. meningitidis*, Group A, B, and D, streptococcis, and *S. pneumoniae*
Nafcillin	12 g/24 h IV (q4h)	Gm+ (*Staphylococcus aureus*)
Oxacillin	12 g/24 h IV (q4h)	Gm+ (*S. aureus*)
Cefotaxime	6 g/24 h IV (q4h)	Many Gm+ Gm– and anaerobes, Gm-bacilli, *H. influenzae*, *N. meningitidis*, *S. pneumoniae*
Ceftaxidime	6 g/24 h IV (q8h)	Many Gm+ Gm– and anaerobes, Gm-bacilli, *H. influenzae*, *Pseudomonas aeruginosa*
Ceftriaxone	4 g/24 h IV (q12h)	Many Gm+ Gm– and anaerobes, Gm-bacilli, *H. influenzae*, *N. meningitidis*, *S. pneumoniae*
Rifampin	1.2 g/24 h PO (q12h)	*N. meningitidis* prophylaxis (48 h only)
Sulfadiazine	4 g/24 h IV (q6h)	*Toxoplasma gondii* (with pyrimethamine)
Tetracycline	1 g/24 h IV (q12h)	Gm+, Gm–, *Rickettsia*
Vancomycin	2–3 g/24 h IV(q6h)	*S. aureus*, *S. epidermidis*, *S. pneumoniae*
Zidovudine	0.5–1 g/24 h PO (q4h)	HIV
Pyrimethamine	75 mg/24 h IV (q8h)	*T. gondii* (with sulfadiazine)
Chloramphenicol	50 mg/kg/24 h IV (q4h)	Anaerobes, *H. influenzae*, *S. pneumoniae*, *N. meningitidis*, *Rickettsia*
Gentamicin	5 mg/kg/24 h IV (q8h)	Gm– bacilli, *P. aeruginosa* (if sensitive)
Metronidazole	15 mg/kg/load IV; 30 mg/kg/24 h IV (q6h)	Anaerobes
Tobramycin	5 mg/kg/24 h IV (q8h)	Gm– bacilli, *P. aeruginosa* (if sensitive)
Carbenicillin	0.3 g/kg/24 h IV (q4h)	*P. aeruginosa* (with aminoglycoside)
Ticarcillin	0.2–0.6 g/kg/24 h IV (q4h)	*P. aeruginosa* (with aminoglycoside)

MU, million units; Gm+, Gram positive; Gm-, Gram negative.
*Above doses are approximations for otherwise normal adults. Antibiotic selection and final dosage should be tailored to each patient.

fluenzae and possibly due to pneumococcus in susceptible hosts. Many infections still occur in epidemic proportions, and appropriate isolation and prophylaxis of exposed individuals may help to limit the outbreaks. Epidemics due to arboviruses may be limited by vector control. Vaccination of horses, dogs, and cats limits the potential for human exposure to certain infectious agents. More recently, screening of blood products and appropriate sterilization or disposal of medical and surgical equipment along with the use of "safe" sexual techniques have been shown to reduce the risk of transmission of a number of bloodborne and/or sexually transmitted infections.

Cost Containment

Early diagnosis, empiric therapy, and selection of etiology-specific treatment once the responsible agent has been identified will minimize morbidity and may reduce hospitalization. Institution of appropriate public health measures may lead to either diagnosis and treatment of secondary cases and may result in lower transmission rates.

REFERENCES

Baker A, Ojemann R, Swartz M, et al. Spinal epidural abscess. N Engl J Med 1975;293:463.
Bolan G, Barza M. Acute bacterial meningitis in children and adults. Med Clin North Am 1985;69:231.
Brewer N, MacCarty C, Wellman W. Brain abscess: A review of recent experience. Ann Intern Med 1975;82:571.
Carpenter R, Petersdorf R. The clinical spectrum of bacterial meningitis. Am J Med 1962;33:262.
Davidson M, Steiner R. Magnetic resonance imaging in infections of the central nervous system. AJNR 1985;6:499.
Feldman H. Meningococcal infections. Adv Intern Med 1972;18:117.
Garvey G. Current concepts of bacterial infections of the central nervous system: Bacterial meningitis and bacterial brain abscess. J Neurosurg 1983;59:735.
Ho D, Hirsh M. Acute viral encephalitis. Med Clin North Am 1985;69:415.
Hooper D, Pruit A, Rubin R. Central nervous system infection in the chronically immunosuppressed. Medicine 1982;61:166.
Johnson R. Viral infections of the nervous system. New York: Raven Press, 1982.
Kaplan K. Brain abscess. Med Clin North Am 1985;69:345.
Karandanis D, Shulman J. Recent survey of infectious meningitis in adults: A review of laboratory findings in bacterial, tuberculous, and aseptic meningitis. South Med J 1976;69:449.
Kaufman D, Miller M, Steigbigel N. Subdural empyema: An analysis of 17 recent cases and review of the literature. Medicine 1975;54:485.
Mandell G, Douglas R, Bennett J, eds. Principles and practices of infectious diseases. 3rd ed. New York: Churchill Livingstone, 1990.
Martin W. Rapid and reliable techniques for the laboratory detection of bacterial meningitis. Am J Med 1983;75(1B):119.
Salaki J, Louria D, Chmel H. Fungal and yeast infections of the central nervous system: A clinical review. Medicine (Baltimore) 1984;63:108.
Schlech W, Ward J, Band J, et al. Bacterial meningitis in the United States 1978–1981. JAMA 1985;253:1749.
Silverberg A, DiNubile M. Subdural empyema and cranial epidural abscess. Med Clin North Am 1985;69:361.
Southwick F, Richardson E, Swartz M. Septic thrombosis of the dural venous sinuses. Medicine 1986;65:82.
Swartz M, Dodge P. Bacterial meningitis: A review of selected aspects. N Engl J Med 1965;272:725.
Sze G, Simmons B, Krol G, et al. Dural sinus thrombosis: Verification with spin-echo techniques. AJNR 1988;9:679.
Underman A, Overturg G, Leedom J. Bacterial meningitis—1978. DM 1978;24(5):1.
Weiner L, Fleming J. Viral infections of the nervous system. J Neurosurg 1984;61:207.
Weisberg L. Clinical–CT correlations in intracranial suppurative (bacterial) disease. Neurology (NY) 1984;34:509.
Wilhelm C, Elner J. Chronic meningitis. Neurol Clin 1986;4:115.

Endocrine and Metabolic Disorders

Nelson B. Watts, M.D., Suzanne S. P. Gebhart, M.D.

CHAPTER 9–1

Pituitary and Neighboring Tumors

C. Michael Cawley, M.D., and George T. Tindall, M.D.

DEFINITION

The pituitary gland, along with the hypothalamus, provides central control over many endocrinologic functions of the human body. The gland lies in the bony *sella turcica* formed by the medial aspects of the sphenoid bones in the midline. The sella is flanked on either side by the cavernous sinuses, the contents of which include the carotid arteries and cranial nerves III, IV, V1, V2, and VI. Above the sella lies the intercavernous sinus, the pituitary stalk, the hypothalamus, and the optic nerves and chiasm. These are the structures at risk from a space-occupying lesion in the region of the sella. The pituitary gland is composed of two lobes: the anterior lobe or adenohypophysis, and the posterior lobe or neurohypophysis. The adenohypophysis is formed from an extension of the primitive stomodeum called *Rathke's pouch*; the neurohypophysis is formed by a downpouching of the diencephalon in the floor of the third ventricle.

A host of lesions may arise from the pituitary gland or its neighboring structures. These lesions may be neoplastic or nonneoplastic. In either case, they manifest clinically by either hyper- or hyposecretion of one or more of the pituitary gland's products, or by compression of nearby anatomic structures causing specific neurologic deficits. Adenohypophyseal tumors are the most common of all lesions. These tumors are almost always benign, and are composed of collections of secretory or nonsecretory cells arising from the anterior lobe of the pituitary gland. These lesions, termed *adenomas*, are classified as microadenomas if they are 1 cm or less in diameter; if greater than 1 cm in diameter, they are termed *macroadenomas*.

ETIOLOGY

As noted above, true adenomas of the adenohypophysis are by far the most common lesions found in the region of the sella. Adenomas account for approximately 36% of sellar and juxtasellar lesions in large series. These are benign tumors, the genesis of which is not well delineated. Some of these tumors are associated with the syndrome of multiple endocrine neoplasia type I, but most are not. Other neoplastic lesions arising from the pituitary include craniopharyngiomas (9% in adults, 50% in children), pituitary carcinomas, and sarcomas. Neighboring tumors not of pituitary origin include hypothalamic and optic apparatus gliomas (11%), meningiomas (10%), chordomas (1%), germ cell tumors (1%), lymphomas (1%), neuromas (1%), lipomas, hemangioblastomas, neuroblastomas, plasmacytomas, dermoids, and epidermoid tumors. Nonneoplastic lesions that affect pituitary structure and function include aneurysms (most often of the anterior communicating or internal carotid arteries [7%]), arachnoid cysts (2%), Rathke's cleft cysts (2%), hamartomas (2%), and the special case of the *empty sella syndrome* (3%). Adenohypophyseal hyperplasia not associated with

neoplasia is also described. Inflammatory disorders such as pituitary granulomas, sarcoidosis, histiocytosis X, lymphocytic hypophysitis, and bacterial and parasitic infections may affect the pituitary.

CRITERIA FOR DIAGNOSIS
Suggestive

Pituitary tumors may be found in both symptomatic or asymptomatic patients. Symptoms most often encountered relate to derangement of pituitary function or compression of adjacent anatomic structures. Clinical pictures consistent with pituitary dysfunction include acromegaly, Cushing's disease, amenorrhea–galactorrhea syndrome, hypogonadism, hypothyroidism, hypoadrenalism, and diabetes insipidus. Compromise of neural structures caused by an expanding mass lesion most often manifests as a bitemporal visual field defect, ophthalmoplegia, headaches, or partial or complete hypopituitarism.

Definitive

When the clinical clues are consistent with the diagnosis of a pituitary tumor, evaluation of the pituitary axes with laboratory tests is indicated. These, together with formal neurophthalmologic testing including visual fields, and radiographic investigation, will reliably detect a space-occupying lesion of the pituitary gland.

CLINICAL MANIFESTATIONS
Subjective

Family history is of little importance in patients suspected of harboring pituitary tumors, with the exception of those families suffering multiple endocrine neoplasia syndrome type I. Neither occupational nor environmental factors appear to play an important role in the pathogenesis of pituitary tumors. A history of previous irradiation to the region of the sella may suggest a radiation-induced tumor. The clinical signs and symptoms of pituitary adenomas reflect the functional status of the tumor, its size, and any extrasellar extension. The patient may be asymptomatic or complain of one or more of the following symptoms:

- Headache (usually constant in duration, but variable in location)
- Decreased vision
- Decreased libido, impotence (males)
- Amenorrhea or oligomenorrhea (females)
- Infertility
- Decreased breast size (in females)
- Increased breast size (in males)
- Galactorrhea

- Cold intolerance
- Weight loss or gain
- Easy fatigability
- Lethargy
- Memory loss
- Anorexia
- Postural dizziness or faintness
- Decreased body hair
- Polyuria
- Polydipsia

Patients with hypersecreting tumors may have any or none of the preceding symptoms, as well as specific syndromes related to one of three major categories: (1) prolactin secretion (galactorrhea–amenorrhea); (2) growth hormone secretion (acromegaly in the adult, gigantism in the prepubertal child); (3) adrenocorticotropic hormone (ACTH) secretion (Cushing's disease). Excess secretion of thyrotropin (thyroid-stimulating hormone) and gonadotropins also occurs.

Objective

Physical Examination

Physical findings range from obvious features of acromegaly to completely asymptomatic. They vary according to both the secretory state and mass effects of the tumor. Both secretory and nonsecretory tumors may manifest with any or all of the following symptoms, which are related solely to mass effects: decreased visual acuity; bitemporal visual field defects (early—upper or lower quadrantanopia, late—hemianopia, rarely blindness); papilledema; optic disk pallor; ophthalmoplegia (most often a third nerve palsy); secondary hypogonadism (decreased body hair, puffy sallow skin, facial wrinkling, atrophic testes in males, decreased breast size in females); secondary hypothyroidism (slow mentation, prolonged relaxation of deep tendon reflexes); secondary hypoadrenocorticism (general or postural hypotension and decreased skin pigmentation).

Patients with hypersecreting tumors may have none or all of the preceding manifestations. They most often exhibit signs and symptoms referable to the particular pituitary hormone that is being produced excessively: prolactin (galactorrhea in females, rarely in males, and/or gynecomastia); growth hormone (signs of acromegaly); ACTH (signs of Cushing's disease).

Routine Laboratory Abnormalities

No diagnostic abnormalities are found in the results of routine laboratory examination.

PLANS
Diagnostic

Differential Diagnosis

The differential diagnosis of a patient presenting with the preceding signs and symptoms is extensive; however, once a careful history and physical examination have been completed, a constellation of symptoms and signs will suggest that a malfunction of the pituitary and/or its neighboring structures is likely. Once suspicion has been focused on lesions of the pituitary, the differential diagnosis is narrowed to include the possible lesions listed earlier in this chapter. As the different types of pituitary region tumors may present with varying combinations of signs and symptoms, every suspected case should undergo the same three-part evaluation outlined below.

Diagnostic Options and Recommended Approach

Along each of these diagnostic avenues, many different studies may be used to diagnose pituitary or neighboring tumors, but the goal should be to obtain the minimal data necessary by the least invasive techniques in the shortest time possible to arrive at a diagnosis.

Endocrinologic Studies. The two goals in the evaluation of the endocrinologic axes are the detection of hormone deficiencies (and assessment of pituitary reserve), and the recognition of hypersecretion by hormone-producing tumors. The anterior and posterior pituitary lobes produce several hormones, and laboratory assays are available for their determination as well as for a quantification of the hormones produced by target organs.

Deficiencies of cortisol, thyroxine, and gonadal hormone should be ascertained, as replacement therapy may be indicated even though only subtle clinical changes may be apparent. Determination of low prolactin levels and growth hormone reserves is not necessary, as deficiencies of these hormones pose no significant clinical problems in the adult patient. Antidiuretic hormone produced by the posterior pituitary needs no quantification, as deficiency of this hormone is usually clinically apparent and can be detected indirectly by simple screening tests. If more in-depth tests of pituitary reserves are indicated, the entire hypothalamic–pituitary–target organ axis should be considered for each hormone. Table 9–1–1 lists a simple battery of tests routinely performed at Emory University Hospital in evaluating these patients before surgery.

HYPOTHALAMIC–PITUITARY–ADRENAL AXIS. A fasting morning serum cortisol level is usually an adequate indicator of an intact axis if it is within the normal range. If clinical suspicion of adrenal insufficiency exists, or if the serum cortisol measurements are equivocal, a cosyntropin test is indicated. A potent synthetic analog of ACTH, cosyntropin should result in a significant rise in serum cortisol if the adrenal response is intact. Serum ACTH measurement and a challenge with corticotropin-releasing hormone are more definitive tests of pituitary ACTH reserve. If hypercortisolemia is documented, determination of the cause is essential (see Chapter 9–6).

Inferior petrosal sinus sampling is an invasive test used to document a pituitary source of hypercortisolemia and to lateralize the source of the secretion of excess ACTH to one side of the pituitary in cases with unequivocal pituitary hypercortisolemia. Care must always be taken to exclude a source of ectopic ACTH such as may occur with other tumors (e.g., small cell lung cancer).

HYPOTHALAMIC–PITUITARY–THYROID AXIS. The basic screening test is the free thyroxine level. If clinical or laboratory evidence suggests an abnormal axis, a more complete assessment can be made with thyrotropin-releasing hormone stimulation and determination of triiodothyronine levels.

HYPOTHALAMIC–PITUITARY–GONADAL AXIS. Sex hormone determinations (estradiol in women and testosterone in men) are usually adequate. If abnormalities exist, stimulation tests of pituitary function using gonadotropin-releasing hormone may be used.

PROLACTIN. Prolactin levels should be measured in all patients. They may be elevated secondary to tumor hypersecretion or compression of the normal prolactin-secreting gland (the "stalk effect"). This stalk effect is due to loss of the normal dopaminergic inhibition of prolactin secretion. Provocative tests are not necessary.

GROWTH HORMONE. Routine screening for growth hormone deficiency is unnecessary in the adult patient. In cases of suspected acromegaly, evaluation should be performed as outlined in Chapter 9–3.

TABLE 9–1–1. METHODS OF ASSESSMENT OF PITUITARY RESERVE

Before surgery
   Prolactin measurement in all patients
   Adrenals: morning serum cortisol level or cosyntropin stimulation test
   Thyroid: free thyroxine level
   Gonads: sex hormone determinations
   Antidiuretic hormone: serum sodium level, urine output

2–4 days after surgery
   Adrenals: morning serum cortisol level (24 hours after last dose of hydrocortisone)
   Thyroid: deferred
   Gonads: deferred
   Antidiuretic hormone: serum sodium level, urine output

1 month after surgery
   Adrenals: cosyntropin stimulation test
   Thyroid: free thyroxine level
   Gonads: sex hormone determinations
   Antidiuretic hormone: serum sodium level, urine output

Visual Field Testing. Formal visual field testing should be performed in any patient who has subjective loss of vision, visual field defects by confrontation, or radiographic evidence of tumor compressing any portion of the visual pathways. Automated testing is preferred as it allows for more reliable repeat examinations. Bitemporal defects are most often found.

Neuroradiographic Imaging. Magnetic resonance imaging has become the study of choice in the evaluation of sellar lesions in the past 10 years. Plain films, angiography, pneumoencephalography, metrizamide cisternography, and even computed tomography have been almost completely replaced by the exquisite images afforded by magnetic resonance imaging. The tumors may be imaged in any plane, although the most useful are the sagittal and coronal, and these images allow definition of the extension of the tumor into the anterior, middle, and posterior fossae. The images graphically depict any compression of nearby anatomic structures such as the optic apparatus and any invasion into the cavernous sinus. Gadolinium enhancement adds to the examination and is much less dangerous than contrast-enhanced computed tomography. Magnetic resonance imaging also reliably alerts the neurosurgeon to the possibility of an aneurysm masquerading as a tumor and thus may help prevent intraoperative disaster.

No distinctive imaging abnormalities are associated with nonfunctioning tumors that can differentiate them from hyperfunctioning tumors. Recent research into the use of pituitary positron emission tomography scanning has yielded equivocal results. Thus, although laboratory tests and surgical pathology will continue to define the exact nature of the lesion, magnetic resonance imaging will remain the most sensitive and clinically useful tool in surgical planning and in constructing a differential diagnosis for sellar and juxtasellar masses.

Therapeutic

Pharmacologic Treatment. Over the past 15 years, medical therapy of certain pituitary region lesions has diminished the role of surgery. Most prolactin-secreting adenomas can be treated with dopamine agonists such as bromocriptine and pergolide. Growth hormone-secreting tumors may also respond to dopamide agonists; however, more recently the somatostatin analog octreotide has been used with greater success in both nonsurgical and presurgical treatment. Ketoconazole, an antifungal agent, is now being used with limited success in the treatment of certain cases of Cushing's disease. Surgery, however, remains the mainstay of therapy for acromegaly, Cushing's disease, and many prolactin-secreting tumors. Patients with nonfunctional tumors of the sellar or juxtasellar region have only two effective therapeutic options: surgery or irradiation.

Surgery. If the lesion is deemed surgically resectable and the patient is a good surgical risk, an operative approach is planned to best access the lesion with the least harm to normal structures. Transcranial approaches are indicated only for lesions with significant and unusual extension above the sella. In the majority of cases, the transsphenoidal approach is appropriate. First described by Schloffer in 1907, the transsphenoidal approach to tumors of the sella is a proven and safe method of treating the great majority of pituitary tumors. The procedure is performed on an elective basis, except in the circumstance of pituitary apoplexy (rapid evacuation of the offending hematoma in these cases is mandatory if vision is to be saved). General anesthesia is required, as is a small abdominal incision for the harvesting of a fat graft. Entrance to the nasal septum and sphenoid sinus is achieved by either a small sublabial or a nasal incision. The operative microscope, and in some cases fluoroscopy, is used to assist the surgeon. The procedure is generally well tolerated. The mortality for transsphenoidal surgery is less than 0.5% in large series. Complications include postoperative cerebrospinal fluid leak, diabetes insipidus, meningitis, and sinusitis. These occur in approximately 2% of cases. The duration of hospitalization is typically 4 to 5 days, barring serious complications.

Pituitary surgery requires proper corticosteroid coverage during and after the procedure. Hydrocortisone should be given in divided doses of 300 mg on the day of surgery and gradually reduced by 50 to 100 mg each day thereafter until it can be discontinued. If the patient had adrenal insufficiency prior to surgery, the steroids should be continued in physiologic doses of 20 to 30 mg daily after the fifth postoperative day. The need for reinstitution of hydrocortisone manifests as the acute onset of anorexia, nausea, weakness, postural dizziness, and postural hypotension. Discontinuation of maintenance steroid therapy should follow documentation of a recovered hypothalamic–pituitary–adrenal axis. A morning serum cortisol measurement (24 hours after the postoperative hydrocortisone is discontinued) greater than 10 µg/dL is highly indicative of a normal axis.

Transient diabetes insipidus occurs in about 25% of patients undergoing surgery. In less than 2%, it may persist several months or permanently. It is suspected when a patient's urinary output exceeds fluid intake by 300 mL per hour, and is substantiated by the finding of a urine:serum osmolality ratio less than 1, a serum sodium greater than 145 mEq/L, and a urine specific gravity less than 1.005. In the acute postoperative period, diabetes insipidus is best managed using aqueous vasopressin 5 units subcutaneously every 4 to 8 hours as needed until normal urinary concentrating ability returns. Should longer treatment be needed, intranasal desmopressin acetate 0.1 mL at bedtime usually suffices.

Ten days after surgery, the protocol of pituitary function tests is repeated to determine the correction of old or the creation of new deficits. In more than 90% of patients, function that was normal prior to surgery is preserved afterward, and in about 10 to 15% of patients with previously existing deficits, normal function is restored. The effectiveness of surgical treatment of nonfunctioning tumors is evaluated largely by symptomatic relief and/or cure of the disease. Visual field defects and visual acuity often improve postoperatively if the deficits have not been long-standing, though the primary goal of surgical decompression is always to halt any progression in neurologic symptoms. As noted above, a small but significant percentage of patients rebound from hypopituitarism secondary to mass effects of a sellar tumor.

Recurrence is the true indicator of the surgical cure rate. Depending on the extension of the tumor and the aggressiveness of the surgical excision, recurrence rates are usually in the 5 to 15% range. Often these recurrences are asymptomatic and no further therapy is required. Henderson's review (1939) of Dr. Harvey Cushing's series indicated that if there were a symptomatic recurrence, the symptoms appeared within 3 years in 70% and within 5 years in 95% of patients. No recurrences were reported later than 8 years.

Radiotherapy. Irradiation may also be effective in treating pituitary tumors in certain cases. Currently, it is used primarily as an adjunct to surgical therapy. Although some authorities recommend routine postoperative irradiation in patients with large, nonfunctional adenomas following surgery, we believe irradiation should be reserved for those patients in whom surgery fails to achieve a cure or in whom the tumor recurs after a period of apparent cure. In the case of a recurrence, only those patients with new clinical findings who are poor candidates for repeat surgical or medical intervention should undergo radiation therapy. In these situations, conventional external-beam therapy is delivered in fractionated doses totaling approximately 4000 to 4500 rad. Focused radiation therapy may be of use in certain cases; however, this modality is appropriate only for lesions less than 2.5 cm in diameter. Furthermore, the close proximity of the hypothalamus, optic nerves, and optic chiasm to any sellar lesion places these structures at significant risk for radiation injury.

FOLLOW-UP

After discharge from the hospital, the patient should be seen again at 1 month and at 3- and 6-month intervals thereafter. Serial determinations of any hormone levels found to be excessive prior to surgery are obtained every 3 to 6 months. Appropriate replacement therapy is provided for persistent pituitary–target organ deficiencies. Follow-up magnetic resonance imaging studies with gadolinium enhancement are done only as clinically indicated (new symptoms or progression of previously existing symptoms) or if there is evidence of recurrent pituitary hypersecretion. If visual field defects were present before surgery, periodic visual field testing should be continued afterward.

Patients who experience headaches, visual disturbances, or symptoms of endocrine dysfunction that were not present previously should return for follow-up evaluation.

DISCUSSION

Prevalence and Incidence

Pituitary tumors account for 5 to 15% of intracranial tumors, with an incidence of 0.1 to 0.2% per year. As noted above, adenomas constitute approximately one third of all sellar region tumors. An additional third comprises gliomas, meningiomas, and craniopharyngiomas in roughly equal proportions. The less common sellar masses make up the final third. There is a slight female preponderance in most series of pituitary adenomas and certainly of meningiomas. Fully half of the sellar masses encountered in children prove to be craniopharyngiomas.

Related Basic Science

Pathobiology

Cushing was the first to describe and categorize pituitary tumors in detail. From his time until very recently, these tumors have been classified according to their tinctorial characteristics in hematoxylin and eosin histologic preparations. Thus, the terms *chromophobic, eosinophilic,* and *basophilic* were given to pituitary adenomas. Although certain hypersecretory tumors show fairly consistent staining patterns (e.g., acromegaly, eosinophilic adenoma; Cushing's disease, basophilic adenoma), many do not, and a surprising number of secreting tumors are chromophobic. Because of these nonuniform staining characteristics, it is now considered more appropriate to classify these tumors according to their secretory activity. The dominant hypersecretory hormone may be easily assayed with peripheral blood samples, and most neuropathologic laboratories can now perform routine immunohistochemistry to determine the secretory product of the tumor cell population. As noted above, adenomas are also classified according to size. Microadenomas are being found with increasing frequency as a result of refinements in diagnostic and microsurgical techniques and now outnumber the larger tumors by more than 3 to 1.

Six types of functioning adenomas have been identified based on their secretory characteristics. In each type, immunocytochemical–ultrastructural studies using immunoperoxidase antiserum techniques and electron microscopy have identified specific peptide-secreting granules in the cytoplasm of each of these respective hypersecretory tumor cells:

- Prolactin-secreting adenomas (accounting for up to 60% of functional adenomas)
- Growth hormone-secreting adenomas (accounting for 25% of functional adenomas)
- ACTH/melanocyte-stimulating hormone-secreting adenomas (accounting for 10% of functional adenomas)
- Growth hormone/prolactin-secreting adenomas
- Thyroid-stimulating hormone-secreting adenomas (very rare)
- Follicle-stimulating/luteinizing hormone-secreting adenomas

Nonfunctioning adenomas, also known as "null cell adenomas," account for approximately 15 to 20% of all pituitary tumors. In early stages of growth they do not appreciably derange pituitary function, but as they grow larger they affect the trophic hormones in a characteristic pattern. Growth hormone is usually the first to become deficient, followed by follicle-stimulating hormone, luteinizing hormone, thyroid-stimulating hormone, and ACTH. Compromise of the lactotrophic cells may at any time lead to hypoprolactinemia. Conversely, compromise of the dopaminergic outflow from the hypothalamus disinhibits the lactotrophs, resulting in hyperprolactinemia and pseudoprolactinoma. The serum prolactin level in this situation is usually below 100 to 150 ng/mL and may be ascribed to the stalk effect rather than to true tumor hypersecretory activity.

Mass effects may be exerted by both functional and nonfunctional tumors, although patients with the former more often present with signs of endocrinopathy as their chief complaint. The anatomic structures at risk from an enlarging mass lesion have been described. Visual field defects occur in 20 to 40% of patients, are due to pressure on the optic chiasm superior to the sella turcica, and are classically bitemporal. Headaches are nonspecific, although in some patients they are bitemporal and are present in 80% of cases. In the absence of increased intracranial pressure (which would be caused only by a large tumor extending to the ventricular system), the common headache is likely due to irritation of the pain-sensitive dura.

The pathogenesis of pituitary tumors remains obscure. Recent advances in tumor genetics have yet to be applied widely to these largely benign tumors. Some recent work suggests that a certain oncogene, c-*myc*, is overexpressed in a subgroup of pituitary tumors, and this subgroup is not limited to any particular immunohistochemical type. There are also indications that second messenger alterations may play a role in the growth of pituitary tumors as they do in other human tumors.

The question is frequently raised whether hypothalamic dysfunction may initiate or abet the growth of adenomas. Although there is little direct evidence to support such a hypothesis, it has been noted that in approximately 20% of patients with acromegaly, growth hormone secretion can be suppressed by an oral glucose load and stimulated by hypoglycemia. The mechanism of these effects intimately involves the hypothalamic–pituitary axis. Likewise, ACTH-secreting tumors in Cushing's disease also exhibit at least a partial dependence on hypothalamic control. Some authorities have also suggested that prolactin-secreting adenomas may be the result of chronic hyposecretion of dopamine by the hypothalamus.

Natural History and Its Modification with Treatment

Sellar region tumors other than pituitary tumors follow very different natural courses. The meningiomas are very slow growing and rarely threaten life, but tumors in this area of the intracranial cavity can produce devastating neurologic deficits. Gliomas in this region are usually low grade and are often followed conservatively until vision is threatened. Craniopharyngiomas may enlarge to produce global mass effects and should be treated promptly with surgery or radiation.

Pituitary adenomas, whether large or small, secretory or nonsecretory, have a variable course that may range from long periods of indolence to aggressive behavior with rapid growth, total destruction of normal pituitary function, chiasmal compression, and encroachment on the cranial nerves. Most lie between these extremes. The ultimate behavior of an individual tumor is unpredictable, and for this reason appropriate therapy should be offered to the patient as soon as the diagnosis is made.

Although rare, one distressing development can be that of pituitary apoplexy, or spontaneous hemorrhagic infarction, which is signaled by the onset of severe headaches, diminished visual acuity, hypotension or shock, alterations of consciousness, and, in some cases, death. A few patients recover spontaneously without surgical intervention, although appropriate replacement therapy is usually needed. Interestingly, some patients with Cushing's disease and acromegaly have undergone spontaneous remission following an episode of pituitary apoplexy.

Prevention

No preventive measures are currently available as no behavioral, toxic, or environmental links have been made with the incidence of pituitary tumors.

Cost Containment

The costs encountered with the initial diagnostic and therapeutic procedures can be minimized by confining the initial investigation to the collection of the data needed to arrive at a diagnosis. Follow-up costs are reasonable and are related primarily to the need for postoperative visits at 3- to 6-month intervals and periodic hormone determinations as indicated by individual circumstances. The time between follow-up visits may be lengthened, eventually to a biyearly basis if no evidence of recurrence is noted within the first 2 to 4 years.

REFERENCES

Bakay I. The results of 300 pituitary operations (Professor Herbert Olivecrona's series). J Neurosurg 1950;7:240.

Black PMcL, Hsu DW, Klibanski A, et al. Hormone production in clinically nonfunctioning pituitary adenomas. Clin Res 1987;34:642A.

Black PMcL, Zervas NT, Candia GL. Incidence and management of complications of transsphenoidal operation for pituitary tumors. Neurosurgery 1987;20(6):920.

Daughaday WH. The anterior pituitary. In: Wilson JD, Foster DW, eds. Williams' textbook of endocrinology. Philadelphia: Saunders, 1985:568.

Henderson WR. The pituitary adenomata: A follow-up study of surgical results in 338 cases (Dr. Harvey Cushing's series). Br J Surg 1939;26:811.

Osborn AG. Handbook of neuroradiology. St. Louis: Mosby-Year Book, 1991:331.

Tindall GT, Barrow DL. Tumors of the sellar and parasellar area in adults. In: Youmans JR, ed. Neurological surgery. Philadelphia: Saunders, 1990:3447.

Tindall GT, Cawley CM. Pituitary tumors: Recent advances in diagnosis and predicting surgical outcome. Crit Rev Neurosurg 1994;4:164.

Wilson CB. A decade of pituitary microsurgery. J Neurosurg 1984;61:814.

Woloschak M, Roberts JL, Post K. c-*myc*, c-*fos*, and c-*myb* gene expression in human pituitary adenomas. J Clin Endocrinol Metab 1994;79(1):253.

Zervas NT. Surgical results in pituitary adenomas: Results of an international survey. In: Black PMcL, Zervas NT, Ridgeway EG Jr, Martin JB, eds. Secretory tumors of the pituitary gland. New York: Raven Press, 1984:377.

CHAPTER 9–2

Hypopituitarism

Lewis S. Blevins, Jr., M.D.

DEFINITION

Hypopituitarism is defined as the cessation of normal anterior pituitary function.

ETIOLOGY

Pituitary diseases interfering with the synthesis or secretion of anterior pituitary hormones (or both) can cause hypopituitarism. Disorders of the hypothalamus and pituitary stalk can impair the secretion and transport of hypothalamic hormones and lead to decreased hormone production and release by the pituitary gland.

CRITERIA FOR DIAGNOSIS

Suggestive

Clinical features of partial or complete deficiencies of two or more of the glands regulated by the anterior pituitary are suggestive of hypopituitarism. Type 1 polyglandular autoimmune syndrome (Schmidt's syndrome) is also suggested by coexisting hypothyroidism and adrenal insufficiency. Hyperprolactinemia and diabetes insipidus suggest specific disorders that often cause hypopituitarism.

Definitive

Biochemical evidence of deficiencies of one or more anterior pituitary and corresponding target gland hormones establishes a diagnosis of hypopituitarism. A diagnosis of Schmidt's syndrome is established by deficiencies of cortisol and thyroid hormone and elevations in the corresponding anterior pituitary hormones adrenocorticotropic hormone (ACTH) and thyroid-stimulating hormone (TSH), respectively.

CLINICAL MANIFESTATIONS

The manifestations of hypopituitarism vary depending on the extent, degree, and rate of occurrence of pituitary hormonal deficiencies. The symptoms and signs also depend on the underlying cause and whether the disorder is insidious or acute in onset.

Subjective

Adrenocorticotropic hormone deficiency, or central adrenocortical insufficiency, results in symptoms attributed to hypocortisolemia. Malaise, fatigue, anorexia, and weight loss are common. Nausea, vomiting, and orthostatic dizziness are infrequent. Dramatic symptoms, often accompanied by hypoglycemia, can occur in patients with partial ACTH deficiency in response to acute illnesses or stressors, and in those taking medications that accelerate the metabolism (phenytoin, ri-

fampin, phenobarbital) or impair the biosynthesis (ketoconazole, aminoglutethemide) of cortisol. A similar presentation can occur following pituitary surgery or withdrawal of glucocorticoid therapy.

Thyroid-stimulating hormone deficiency results in central hypothyroidism. Symptoms are due to hypothyroxinemia, but are rarely as severe as in primary hypothyroidism. Common complaints include fatigue, weakness, weight gain, cold intolerance, muscle cramps, impaired mentation, constipation, periorbital swelling, and dry skin and hair.

Gonadotropin (luteinizing hormone [LH] and follicle-stimulating hormone [FSH]) deficiency leads to sex steroid hormone deficiency and is often referred to as either central, or hypogonadotropic, hypogonadism. The spectrum of menstrual disorders includes oligomenorrhea, anovulatory menses, and amenorrhea. Women may also complain of vaginal dryness, dyspareunia, a diminished libido, atrophy of the breasts, and infertility. Men occasionally present with weakness, fatigue, a diminished libido, and either impotence or erectile dysfunction. Hot flashes can occur in women and men. Gonadotropin deficiency prior to the completion of sexual maturation results in pubertal arrest.

Parents of growth hormone-deficient children or adolescents often express concerns regarding their child's decreased growth rate or height compared with children of the same age. Symptoms of growth hormone deficiency in adults are nonspecific and include decreased exercise tolerance, fatigue, decreased strength, and impaired social functioning.

The major complaint related to prolactin deficiency is failure to secrete an adequate quantity of breast milk in the puerperium.

Patients with vasopressin deficiency (neurogenic diabetes insipidus) complain of polyuria, polydipsia, nocturia, and thirst. Some patients indicate a preference for iced liquids.

Pituitary and hypothalamic tumors and diseases can cause headaches, visual abnormalities, rhinorrhea, epistaxis, and other symptoms due to the mass. A careful assessment of past medical history and review of systems may reveal the underlying cause of hypopituitarism.

Objective

Physical Examination

The hyperpigmentation associated with primary adrenal insufficiency is not seen in patients with central adrenocortical insufficiency. In fact, most patients have pallor and a sallow complexion. Adrenal androgen deficiency can result in decreased or absent axillary and pubic hair, especially when hypogonadism is also present. Postural hypotension is rare.

Signs of hypothyroidism include bradycardia, diastolic hypertension, hypothermia, delay in the relaxation phase of the deep tendon reflexes, periorbital edema, nonpitting edema of the lower extremities, pallor, pericardial and pleural effusions, and slowed mental functions. Goiter is not a feature of hypothyroidism due to TSH deficiency.

Patients with hypogonadotropic hypogonadism often have fine wrin-

See Appendix 2, Dynamic Tests of Pituitary Function, by Lewis S. Blevins, Jr., M.D.

kling of the skin about the face. Men may also have gynecomastia, soft or small testes, and diminished facial and body hair. Common findings in women include atrophy of the vaginal mucosa, diminished axillary and pubic hair, and atrophy of the breasts. Delayed maturation of the breasts, genitalia, and pubic hair identifies adolescents with arrested puberty.

Children with growth hormone deficiency usually have short stature. In adults, growth hormone deficiency probably results in diminished strength and increased body fat content.

Signs of diabetes insipidus include postural hypotension, dry oral mucous membranes, poor skin turgor, and other features of dehydration.

Optic disk pallor, papilledema, abnormal visual fields by confrontation, cerebrospinal fluid rhinorrhea, and extraocular muscle palsies may be present in patients with large pituitary or hypothalamic tumors. Physical features of a syndrome of anterior pituitary hormonal hypersecretion (acromegaly, cushingoid habitus, galactorrhea) may be apparent in patients with large functioning pituitary tumors. Other physical findings depend on the etiology of the hypopituitarism.

Routine Laboratory Abnormalities

Mild hyponatremia is common in patients with adrenocortical insufficiency. Serum potassium is usually normal in patients with ACTH deficiency. Laboratory findings in patients with diabetes insipidus include hypernatremia and decreased urine specific gravity. Normochromic normocytic anemia is relatively common in hypopituitarism and may be due to either cortisol, thyroid, or sex steroid hormone deficiency. Hypercholesterolemia, increased alkaline phosphatase, and elevated serum transaminase levels often accompany hypothyroidism. Growth hormone deficiency and adrenocortical insufficiency can cause hypoglycemia.

PLANS
Diagnostic
Differential Diagnosis

The differential diagnosis of hypopituitarism is listed in Table 9–2–1.

Nearly one third of patients with pituitary macroadenomas have one or more anterior pituitary hormone deficiencies at presentation. Hypopituitarism in the setting of a pituitary tumor can be due to interruption of the pituitary stalk, compression of the normal pituitary gland, or ischemic pituitary necrosis from compression of nutrient blood vessels. Anterior pituitary hormonal deficits occasionally reverse following resection of the tumor. Approximately 25% of patients with pituitary tumors develop hypopituitarism following injury during transsphenoidal

TABLE 9–2–1. CAUSES OF HYPOPITUITARISM

Pituitary tumor
Pituitary apoplexy or infarction
Transsphenoidal pituitary surgery
Empty sella syndrome
Lymphocytic hypophysitis
Hemochromatosis
Granulomatous diseases
Hypothalamic tumors
Metastases
Sellar and suprasellar cysts
Irradiation
Head trauma
Congenital defects
Isolated and functional disorders
  Adrenocorticocotropic hormone deficiency
  Thyroid-stimulating hormone deficiency
  Gonadotropin deficiency
  Growth hormone deficiency

pituitary surgery. Postsurgical diabetes insipidus is usually apparent within 12 to 24 hours.

Pituitary infarction or hemorrhage can occur in patients with pituitary adenomas, diabetes mellitus, sickle cell disease, and coagulopathies, and following obstetric catastrophe that results in shock (Sheehan's syndrome). Acute ACTH deficiency, severe headache, diplopia, meningismus, and altered sensorium are characteristic features of pituitary tumor apoplexy.

In patients with primary empty sella syndrome, an incomplete diaphragma sellae allows arachnoid membranes to herniate into the sella turcica. Intracranial pressure flattens the pituitary against the walls of the sella and cerebrospinal fluid fills the void, giving the appearance of an "empty" sella. In most patients, anterior pituitary function is normal. In some patients, however, an empty sella is associated with hyperprolactinemia and partial hypopituitarism. Hypopituitarism is more common in patients with an empty sella due to pituitary surgery or irradiation, pituitary apoplexy, and sarcoidosis. Lymphocytic (autoimmune) hypophysitis is characterized by a lymphocytic and plasmacytic infiltration of the pituitary gland. Symptomatic patients usually present with a sellar mass and one or more anterior pituitary hormonal deficiencies. A majority of reported cases have occurred in association with pregnancy, but the disorder has affected women who are not of childbearing age and men.

Patients with hemochromatosis and other iron overload disorders (i.e., thalassemics treated with blood transfusions) can develop anterior pituitary failure. Hypogonadism is common and, in some patients, may be due to iron-induced hypothalamic or testicular dysfunction.

Granulomatous disorders affecting the hypothalamus and pituitary stalk often cause hypopituitarism, diabetes insipidus, and hyperprolactinemia. Other features of neurosarcoidosis include cranial nerve palsies, leptomeningitis, and hydrocephalus. Many patients have symptoms and signs of systemic sarcoidosis. Patients with tuberculous meningitis and tuberculomas usually have other clinical features of pulmonary or disseminated tuberculosis. Langerhans cell histiocytosis (histiocytosis X) is more common in children and young adults. Syphilis, toxoplasmosis, cryptococcosis and other fungal disorders, and giant cell granulomatous hypophysitis can also cause hypopituitarism.

Hypothalamic tumors can result in hormonal deficiencies, hyperprolactinemia, diabetes insipidus, and other features of hypothalamic dysregulation (somnolence, hyperphagia, obesity, poikilothermia). Craniopharyngiomas, the most commonly encountered tumors, probably arise from remnant cells of Rathke's pouch. Meningioma, glioma, hamartoma, lymphoma, and germinoma are uncommon.

Metastases (breast, lung) to the hypothalamus and pituitary stalk can cause diabetes insipidus and varying degrees of pituitary hypofunction. Symptoms and signs of hypopituitarism are often attributed to the underlying malignancy. Invasive neighboring tumors (chordoma, nasopharyngeal carcinoma) can also cause hypopituitarism.

Cystic lesions, including Rathke's cleft cysts, craniopharyngiomas, epidermoid cysts, and arachnoid cysts, are rare causes of hypopituitarism. Carotid artery aneurysms can mimic cysts and parasellar tumors.

Adjunctive or primary radiotherapy for pituitary tumors, nasopharyngeal carcinomas, acute lymphocytic leukemia, and other intracranial neoplasms can result in hypopituitarism. Approximately one half of pituitary tumor patients treated with radiotherapy develop one or more anterior pituitary hormone deficiencies. Hypopituitarism associated with cranial irradiation is usually due to hypothalamic injury.

Hypopituitarism following head trauma is usually due to hypothalamic or pituitary stalk injury. Diabetes insipidus is common. Affected patients usually have a fracture of the base of the skull, cranial nerve palsies, and a history of unconsciousness following the inciting event.

Congenital hypopituitarism is often associated with neurophthalmologic and craniofacial abnormalities or birth trauma; some cases are idiopathic. Hypoglycemic seizures in the neonatal period and small genitalia are often the first clues to the diagnosis. Occasional patients present with short stature and hypothyroidism but have normal adrenal and gonadal function.

The most common cause of isolated ACTH deficiency is withdrawal of supraphysiologic doses of glucocorticoids used to treat various inflammatory disorders. Functional suppression of the hypothalamic—

pituitary–adrenal axis is more common in patients treated chronically with high doses of glucocorticoids administered more than once daily. Isolated ACTH deficiency has been reported in patients with benign intracranial hypertension, lymphocytic hypophysitis, and following head trauma. Isolated TSH deficiency is rare and may be inherited or due to other causes of hypopituitarism. (Undetectable TSH and decreased free thyroxine levels can occur in patients with Grave's disease rendered hypothyroid by treatment with antithyroid drugs and iodine-131 and in patients entering the hypothyroid phase of subacute and lymphocytic (painless) thyroiditis. Recovery of the "suppressed" hypothalamus and pituitary usually occurs 4 to 12 weeks following the development of thyroid hormone deficiency.) Isolated growth hormone deficiency is a common cause of short stature. Children with chronic illnesses, malnutrition, and significant psychosocial stressors often have functional growth hormone deficiency. Kallman's syndrome, a disorder characterized by deficient gonadotropin-releasing hormone secretion by the hypothalamus, is associated with anosmia or hyposmia and other midline neurologic abnormalities. Hyperprolactinemia is a common cause of isolated hypogonadotropic hypogonadism. Functional gonadotropin deficiency is common in athletes, professional dancers, and patients with eating disorders, significant physical (chronic illness), and psychosocial stressors. Supraphysiologic doses of anabolic steroids suppress the gonadotropins. Sex steroid hormone concentrations are usually low unless the administered drug is testosterone. Isolated neurogenic diabetes insipidus is rare and is usually familial or idiopathic.

Diagnostic Options

The diagnostic evaluation of suspected hypopituitarism begins with a history and physical examination to search for an etiology and to assess pituitary function. Diagnostic tests and imaging studies should be based on findings that suggest a specific cause of hypopituitarism. With only a few exceptions, laboratory tests should include measurement of pituitary and corresponding target gland hormones. Dynamic tests of hypothalamic and pituitary function are occasionally required (see Appendix 2).

Recommended Approach

Magnetic resonance imaging of the hypothalamus and pituitary should be performed when the cause of hypopituitarism is not obvious. Primary and metastatic tumors, cysts, infiltrative disorders, and other anatomic abnormalities are readily identified. Resection or stereotactic biopsy of an obvious mass may be necessary to establish a specific diagnosis. When indicated, appropriate tests should be performed to confirm other diagnostic possibilities (*i.e.,* iron studies and ferritin in suspected hemochromatosis, purified protein derivative [PPD] and chest x-rays in suspected tuberculosis, rapid plasma reagin or fluorescent treponemal antibody absorption test in suspected neurosyphilis, angiotensin-converting enzyme level in suspected sarcoidosis, formal testing of olfaction is suspected Kallman's syndrome).

Random measurements of plasma ACTH are reliable in the evaluation of primary adrenal insufficiency but are not recommended in the evaluation of patients with suspected ACTH deficiency. Acceptable screening tests for central adrenocortical insufficiency include measurement of the morning serum cortisol and the standard ACTH stimulation test. Both tests provide indirect assessments of the integrity of the hypothalamic–pituitary unit and are most reliable in patients with long-standing (>1 month) ACTH deficiency. Patients with acute hypopituitarism (*i.e.,* following pituitary surgery) often have normal adrenocortical responses to exogenous ACTH. Deficient trophic hormone stimulation ultimately leads to atrophy of the adrenal cortex and impaired cortisol production. Morning cortisols less than 3 μg/dL in patients with hypothalamic and pituitary disease are diagnostic of adrenocortical insufficiency, and in most instances, confirmatory studies are not required. An ACTH-stimulated cortisol less than 20 μg/dL identifies patients with adrenal insufficiency. Dynamic tests for ACTH deficiency include the insulin-induced hypoglycemia and metyrapone tests. Insulin-induced hypoglycemia permits assessment of hypothalamic–pituitary–adrenal responsiveness to stress. The overnight metyrapone test provides an assessment of hypothalamic and pituitary negative feedback responses. Administration of metyrapone, an inhibitor of the corti-

sol biosynthetic enzyme 11β-hydroxylase, induces adrenal insufficiency. In normal individuals, cortisol deficiency provokes ACTH secretion and results in stimulation of the adrenal cortex and increased serum levels of 11-deoxycortisol, a substrate of 11β-hydroxylase. A subnormal metyrapone-stimulated 11-deoxycortisol level is a fairly reliable indicator of adrenal insufficiency.

A low or "low-normal" free thyroxine (T_4) concentration or free thyroxine index (total thyroxine multiplied by the triiodothyronine [T_3] resin uptake) identifies most patients with hypothyroidism. The serum TSH concentration is either low or inappropriately "normal" in patients with hypothyroidism due to TSH deficiency. In contrast, patients with primary hypothyroidism have a high serum TSH. The thyrotropin-releasing hormone stimulation test is of little value in the routine diagnostic evaluation of patients with suspected TSH deficiency.

Cyclical menses occurring on a monthly basis exclude gonadotropin deficiency. Low serum estradiol concentrations and low or inappropriately normal FSH concentrations in amenorrheic and postmenopausal women indicate gonadotropin deficiency. Low serum testosterone levels and low or inappropriately "normal" LH concentrations are characteristic of gonadotropin deficiency in men. The gonadotropin-releasing hormone stimulation test is not recommended in the routine evaluation of patients with suspected gonadotropin deficiency.

Measurement of the serum prolactin concentration is an integral part of the evaluation of patients with suspected hypopituitarism. Hyperprolactinemia is a clue to the presence of either a prolactin-secreting macroadenoma, acromegaly, or a disorder of the pituitary stalk or hypothalamus. Intrinsic pituitary disease is suggested by a normal or low serum prolactin in conjunction with other anterior pituitary hormonal deficiencies.

Tests for growth hormone deficiency should be reserved for children with short stature. A gender- and age-specific height under the third percentile and a growth velocity less than 4 cm in 1 year are suggestive of, but not specific for, growth hormone deficiency. Bone age, as determined by standardized radiographs of the wrist and hand, is frequently delayed. Although random serum growth hormone measurements cannot distinguish children with intact growth hormone from those with growth hormone deficiency, plasma levels of insulin-like growth factor 1, a marker of integrated growth hormone secretion, are usually low. Provocative tests of growth hormone reserve include the insulin-induced hypoglycemia test and the levodopa, arginine, and clonidine stimulation tests. Subnormal growth hormone responses in at least two of these tests are required to establish a diagnosis of growth hormone deficiency.

The polyuria due to vasopressin deficiency is characterized by a 24-hour urine volume greater than 30 mL/kg body weight, urine osmolarity less than 300 mOsm/kg H_2O, and urine specific gravity less than 1.010. The serum sodium is usually greater than 145 mEq/L and the serum osmolarity approaches 295 mOsm/kg H_2O. A formal water deprivation test may be required to establish a diagnosis of partial diabetes insipidus, but should not be attempted in hypernatremic patients.

Therapeutic

Therapeutic Options

The therapeutic plan for patients with hypopituitarism should include treatment of the underlying disorder, hormone replacement therapy, and patient education. Initial therapy depends on the specific disorder causing the hypopituitarism. The goals of replacement therapy include reversal of the features attributed to hormone deficiencies and normalization of target gland hormone concentrations. Replacement therapy involves administration of deficient target gland hormones. In some instances, however, treatment with hypothalamic and pituitary hormones is necessary.

Recommended Approach

There is considerable debate regarding the most appropriate glucocorticoid replacement regimen for central adrenocortical insufficiency. In most adults, hydrocortisone (cortisol) provides sufficient glucocorticoid effect. Administration of 20 mg orally in the morning and 10 mg orally in the late afternoon approximates the normal diurnal variation in cortisol production. Prednisone 5 mg orally in the morning and 2.5 mg orally in the late afternoon is an acceptable alternative to hydrocortisone. Occasional patients require either more or less than the recommended doses. Resolution of symptoms and signs of adrenal insufficiency and avoidance of cortisol excess (iatrogenic Cushing's syndrome) are the goals of therapy. The adequacy of glucocorticoid replacement cannot be reliably assessed by standard laboratory tests. Cortisol levels are usually high following a dose and low just prior to a subsequent dose. Collection of a 24-hour urine specimen for free cortisol is probably the most useful test for identification of patients on excessive glucocorticoid replacement. Every patient should be educated regarding glucocorticoid dose adjustments during intercurrent illnesses and significant stressors (see Chapter 11). Patients with concomitant thyroxine and cortisol deficiencies should be treated with glucocorticoids prior to the institution of thyroid hormone replacement. Otherwise, increases in the circulating thyroxine concentration can accelerate the metabolism of cortisol in patients with partial ACTH deficiency and precipitate acute adrenal insufficiency. In contrast to patients with primary adrenal insufficiency, mineralocorticoid replacement is not required because aldosterone secretion is regulated by the renin–angiotensin system and is unaffected by anterior pituitary dysfunction.

Levothyroxine sodium is the drug of choice for the treatment of central hypothyroidism. Adults require approximately 1.6 µg levothyroxine per kilogram body weight administered as a single daily dose. The average daily replacement dose ranges from 75 to 150. Dose requirements are somewhat lower in elderly patients. In the elderly and patients with known or suspected atherosclerotic coronary artery disease, replacement therapy should be initiated with 25 µg daily and increased as tolerated by 12.5- or 25-µg increments at 2- to 4-week intervals until a replacement dose is achieved. Adequate replacement therapy results in restoration of clinical and biochemical euthyroidism and avoidance of hyperthyroidism. Patients should be evaluated 6 to 8 weeks following dose adjustments. A sufficient dose of levothyroxine restores the serum free thyroxine concentration and free thyroxine index to the mid- or upper portion of the normal range. The serum TSH concentration is not a reliable measure of levothyroxine dose adequacy in patients with central hypothyroidism.

Treatment of hypogonadism restores adequate sexual function, decreases the risk of osteoporotic fractures, and results in improvement in the patient's sense of well-being. An effective treatment regimen for hypogonadal men is testosterone enanthate 200 mg intramuscularly on the 1st and 15th days of each month. The clinical response is the most important indicator of the adequacy of therapy. Men with less than satisfactory responses to standard replacement therapy should be evaluated for other causes of impotence and sexual dysfunction. Measurement of the serum testosterone concentration midway between consecutive injections and just prior to an injection can be used to identify patients receiving subtherapeutic or excessive doses of testosterone. Dose adjustments by 50 mg are usually sufficient to correct errors in dosage administration. Transdermal (scrotal) testosterone patches are available in 4- and 6-mg daily doses. Serum testosterone levels usually normalize and approximate the normal diurnal variation.

Sex hormone replacement in hypogonadal women can be accomplished by several effective regimens. Conjugated estrogens, 0.625 to 1.25 mg daily on days 1 through 25 of each calendar month, are sufficient to preserve bone mineral density, control vasomotor symptoms, and reverse complaints due to atrophic vaginitis. Medroxyprogesterone 5 to 10 mg on days 15 through 25 of each calendar month should be administered to women who have a uterus. This regimen will induce periodic sloughing of the estrogen-stimulated endometrium and decrease the risk of endometrial hyperplasia and cancer. Formulations containing esterified estrogens (0.625–1.25 mg) and methyltestosterone (1.25–2.5 mg) are effective alternatives to estrogens in women who also complain of decreased libido. Oral contraceptives containing ethinyl estradiol (35 µg) are effective in treating hypogonadism and are favored by women of reproductive age. Most patients tolerate any of these regimens well. Dosage reduction is required in patients complaining of weight gain, fluid retention, and depression. Treatment with LH, FSH, human menopausal gonadotropins, human chorionic gonadotropin, and gonadotropin-releasing hormone successfully restores fertility in a significant proportion of hypogonadal men and women. The specifics of therapy with these agents are beyond the scope of this chapter.

The efficacy of growth hormone replacement in growth hormone-deficient adults is not yet established. Growth hormone replacement therapy is indicated in children with short stature who have documented growth hormone deficiency. Treatment should be initiated and supervised by an endocrinologist.

Indications for treatment of neurogenic diabetes insipidus include polyuria that disrupts the patient's daily acitivities, urine output in excess of 4 to 6 L daily, and clinical or laboratory evidence of associated dehydration. Intranasal desamino-D-arginine vasopressin (dDAVP) 5 to 10 µg at bedtime will alleviate nocturia and provide relief from daytime polyuria in many patients. Occasional patients require 20 to 30 µg daily in divided doses. Patients should be permitted to adjust the dosage and timing of drug administration depending on their daily schedule. Measurements of oral fluid intake, urine output, body weight, urine and plasma osmolarities, and serum sodium concentration permit an assessment of the adequacy of therapy. The most feared complication of treatment is volume expansion and hyponatremia with attendant central nervous system signs.

FOLLOW-UP

Initial follow-up visits at 1- to 3-month interrals permit initiation and monitoring of therapy. Patients with treated hypopituitarism require follow-up at 6- to 12-month intervals. Visits should include clinical assessments of disease activity and the effectiveness of therapy directed against the primary disease process. Magnetic resonance imaging of the pituitary and hypothalamus should be performed to assess the response to initial therapy and when clinical features suggest recurrent disease (*i.e.,* mass effects due to pituitary tumor). Problem-oriented history, physical, and laboratory examinations permit an assessment of the efficacy and complications of hormone replacement therapy. Follow-up visits should include continuing patient education about hypopituitarism and replacement therapy. Patients should be instructed regarding the consequences of noncompliance with therapy. Glucocorticoid dosage adjustments during acute illnesses or severe stresses should be reemphasized. Patients should be instructed to obtain identification cards and jewelry (Medic-Alert bracelets or tags) indicating their diagnosis and dependency on specific hormone replacement drugs.

DISCUSSION

Prevalence and Incidence

The actual prevalence and incidence of hypopituitarism are unknown.

Related Basic Science

Anterior pituitary function is largely influenced by circulating pituitary target gland hormone concentrations (feedback regulation) and by hypothalamic regulatory hormones, which are synthesized by hypothalamic neurons, secreted into the blood, and transported to the anterior pituitary by the hypothalamic–pituitary portal blood vessels (Tables 9–2–2 and 9–2–3). Arginine vasopressin is synthesized in the hypothalamus, then transported to the posterior pituitary for storage. Plasma hyperosmolarity, hypotension, and nausea provoke release of vasopressin into the circulation. Vasopressin acts on the distal and collecting tubules in the kidney to promote resorption of water from urine. Hypopituitarism can result from any disorder that disrupts the normal anatomy or physiology of the hypothalamic–pituitary unit (see Differential Diagnosis). Insufficient hypothalamic-releasing hormone stimulation results in secretion of anterior pituitary hormones of reduced bioactivity. Anterior pituitary peptide hormones are measured by radioimmunoassay, which does not provide any information regarding the activity of the hormone. These observations explain the occurrence of target gland deficiencies despite "normal" anterior pituitary hormone concentrations.

Genetics and Altered Molecular Biology

Kallman's syndrome is characterized by isolated hypogonadotropic hypogonadism and anosmia or hyposmia due to abnormal development of the olfactory system. Gonadotropin-releasing hormone-producing neurons originate in the olfactory placode and migrate into the hypothala-

TABLE 9–2–2. TARGET GLAND FEEDBACK REGULATION OF ANTERIOR PITUITARY HORMONE SECRETION

Anterior Pituitary Hormone	Target Gland Hormone	Effect on Pituitary Hormone
Adrenocorticotropic hormone	Cortisol	Negative
Thyroid-stimulating hormone	T_4, T_3	Negative*
Follicle-stimulating hormone FSH (women)	Estradiol	Negative/positive†
Luteinizing hormone		
Women	Progesterone	Negative/positive‡
Men	Testosterone	Negative§
Growth hormone	Insulin-like growth factor 1	Negative
Prolactin	?	?

T_4, thyroxine; T_3, triiodothyronine.
*Feedback is mediated by conversion of T_4 to T_3.
†Estradiol stimulates the preovulatory surge in luteinizing hormone.
‡Progesterone stimulates the midcycle surge in follicle-stimulating hormone
§Feedback is mediated by conversion of testosterone to estradiol.

TABLE 9–2–3. HYPOTHALAMIC REGULATION OF ANTERIOR PITUITARY HORMONE SECRETION

Anterior Pituitary Hormone	Hypothalamic Hormone	Effect on Pituitary Hormone
Adrenocorticotropic hormone	Corticotropin-releasing hormone	Positive
Thyroid-stimulating hormone	Thyrotropin-releasing hormone	Positive
Follicle-stimulating and luteinizing hormones	Gonadotropin-releasing hormone	Positive
Growth hormone	Growth hormone-releasing hormone	Positive
	Somatostatin	Negative
Prolactin	Dopamine	Negative
	Vasoactive intestinal peptide	Positive
	Thyrotropin-releasing hormone	Positive

mus during embryologic development. A candidate gene for the X-linked form of Kallman's syndrome has been identified and localized to the short arm of the X chromosome. The predicted protein product has sequence homology with axonal path-finding molecules. These observations suggest that the unique association of anosmia and hypogonadism can be explained by a mutation in the X-linked Kallman's gene which probably results in abnormal migration of neurons originating in the olfactory placode.

Pit-1 is a transcription factor involved in the control of growth hormone, prolactin, and TSH-β subunit gene transcription and, therefore, regulates production of these hormones. Mutations in the gene encoding Pit-1 have been described in individuals with combined pituitary hormone deficiencies.

Natural History and Its Modification with Treatment

The natural history of hypopituitarism depends on the underlying disease process. Anterior pituitary hormonal deficiencies may reverse or improve in patients who are successfully treated for their underlying disorder (i.e., following pituitary surgery, glucocorticoid treatment of sarcoidosis). In many patients, however, anterior pituitary hormonal deficiencies are permanent. Additional hormone deficiencies may develop in patients with partial hypopituitarism (i.e., following cranial irradiation). Mortality is largely dependent on the underlying illness. An increased incidence of cardiovascular events has been reported in patients with hypopituitarism.

Prevention

Therapy directed at the disorder responsible for hypopituitarism may prevent or delay the onset of hormonal deficiencies. In many cases, however, the hypopituitarism is established at the time of presentation. Complications of target gland hormonal deficiencies can be prevented by adequate hormone replacement.

Cost Containment

Judicious use and interpretation of screening and dynamic endocrine tests can minimize the expense of evaluating patients with suspected hypopituitarism. For example, patients with historical and physical features suggestive of Kallman's syndrome or functional gonadotropin deficiency need not undergo extensive testing of anterior pituitary function. Interpretation of laboratory test results in conjunction with clinical findings can obviate the need for expensive and time-consuming dynamic tests. Follow-up laboratory tests to assess the adequacy of hormone replacement should be performed only on an annual basis or also when hormone over- or underreplacement is suspected. Magnetic resonance imaging of the pituitary and hypothalamus should be performed only when it is necessary to assess the response to primary therapy and search for recurrent disease.

REFERENCES

Dufour DR, Gaskin JH, Jubiz WA. Dynamic procedures in endocrinology. In: Becker KL, ed. Principles and practice of endocrinology and metabolism. Philadelphia: Lippincott, 1990:1762.

Legouis R, Hardelin J-P, Levilliers J, et al. The candidate gene for the X-linked Kallan syndrome encodes a protein related to adhesion molecules. Cell 1991;67:423.

Paffle RW, DiMattia GE, Parks JS, et al., Mutation of the POU-specific domain of pit-1 and hypopituitarism without pituitary hypoplasia. Science 1992;257:1118.

Pinchera A, Martino E, Faglia G, Central hypothyroidism. In: Braverman LE, Utiger RD, eds. The thyroid. 6th ed. Philadelphia: Lippincott, 1991:968.

Vance ML. Hypopituitarism. N Engl J Med 1994;330:1651.

Acromegaly

Nelson B. Watts, M.D., and George T. Tindall, M.D.

DEFINITION

Acromegaly is the syndrome resulting from chronic hypersecretion of growth hormone (GH). In children, chronic hypersecretion of GH also causes increased linear growth and is called pituitary gigantism. Pituitary gigantism is discussed further in Chapter 9–45.

ETIOLOGY

Most patients with acromegaly or pituitary gigantism have GH-secreting pituitary tumors. The majority of these tumors (70–75%) are large enough to be seen by computed tomography or magnetic resonance imaging of the pituitary gland. The character of these tumors is variable. Typically, secretory granules that contain GH by immunoperoxidase staining are seen on electron microscopy. On light microscopy with hematoxylin and eosin stain, the granules usually appear eosinophilic (or acidophilic), but sometimes do not stain (chromophobic). Up to one third of GH-secreting tumors also secrete prolactin. In some of these mixed tumors, prolactin is secreted by the same cell type as GH; in others, prolactin-secreting cells are intermixed in the tumor with GH-secreting cells.

It is not known whether GH-secreting tumors arise as the result of a primary disorder in the pituitary gland or from a defect in the hypothalamus, such as an excess of GH-releasing hormone, that leads secondarily to the pituitary tumor. There is evidence for and against both possibilities; most evidence favors a primary disorder in the pituitary gland.

Rare causes of acromegaly include excessive production of GH-releasing hormone (either ectopic, produced by pancreatic islet cell tumors or carcinoid tumors of the lung or intestine, or from a central nervous system source such as a hamartoma in the hypothalamus). At least one case of ectopic production of GH by a pancreatic neoplasm has been described.

CRITERIA FOR DIAGNOSIS

Suggestive

The symptoms of acromegaly depend on the stage of the disease. Because the onset is often insidious, a high degree of clinical suspicion is needed to make an early diagnosis. Changing facial features and increasing shoe, ring, or hat size would warrant further consideration, and the diagnosis should be entertained in any patient with unexplained neuropathy or puzzling rheumatic symptoms. Pituitary gigantism is rare, but should be suspected in children who show unusually rapid growth.

Definitive

The classic diagnostic test is the measurement of serum GH 60 minutes after administration of 100 g oral glucose solution; failure of the GH level to be suppressed to less than 2 ng/mL is diagnostic for acromegaly. An elevated level of insulin-like growth factor I (also known as somatomedin C) is usually found.

CLINICAL MANIFESTATIONS

Subjective

Common presenting complaints are related to peripheral neuropathy (paresthesias, weakness of muscle groups), particularly carpal tunnel syndrome; headache, which is seen in 55 to 65% of patients and is probably related to mass effect from a pituitary tumor; malocclusion of the teeth; and increased, malodorous sweating. Joint pain and stiffness are common.

Family history is usually not contributory in patients with acromegaly; however, acromegaly is sometimes seen as part of multi-ple endocrine neoplasia type I, which also includes hyperparathyroidism and islet cell tumors of the pancreas (see Chapter 9–46).

Objective

Physical Examination

In advanced cases, bony and soft tissue overgrowth is striking (Figure 9–3–1). Serial photographs can be useful to demonstrate the coarsening of facial features that accompanies this disorder; most patients can readily produce a driver's license photograph, but sometimes a look at the family photo album is necessary. The lips are large and the tongue may appear too large for the mouth. The lower jaw is prominent, often with an overbite and wide-spaced teeth. Increased frontal bossing is common. Feet are large and hands are broad and "spadelike." Most patients with acromegaly are aware of these changes, but usually do not volunteer the information, which must be elicited by specific questioning. Elongation of the ribs leads to a "barrel chest." Degenerative joint disease may be present, sometimes with neuropathic joint destruction. The skin is thick and doughy, often with many skin tags. There may be an increase in body hair. Increased sweating is often apparent on examination; the sweat has an oily feel and a bad odor. Signs of peripheral neuropathy may be present, including motor or sensory deficits, diminished or absent deep tendon reflexes, and evidence of neural compression syndromes such as carpal tunnel syndrome. Goiter is often present. Arterial pressure may be elevated. Cardiac enlargement may be noted. Galactorrhea is found in 20% of women with acromegaly. Signs of hypopituitarism, visual field defects, and, rarely, cranial nerve impairment, may herald a large pituitary tumor.

Routine Laboratory Examination

Abnormalities in routine laboratory studies can include glucose intolerance or fasting hyperglycemia, glycosuria, and elevated serum phosphorus. Although urinary calcium excretion is frequently increased, serum calcium levels are usually normal. Evidence of cardiomegaly may be seen on chest x-ray films or electrocardiogram.

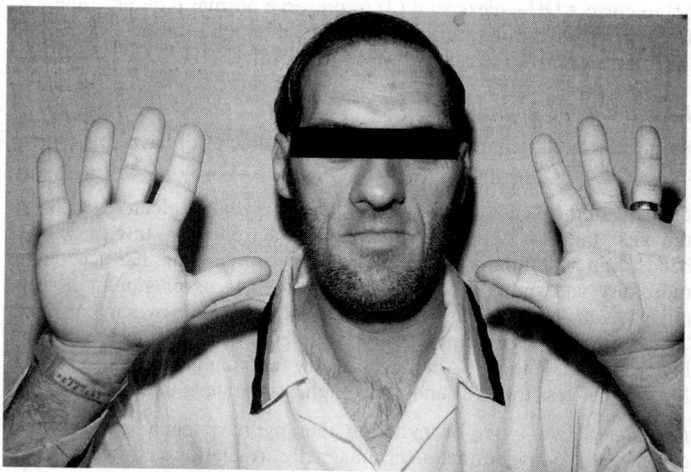

Figure 9–3–1. Typical facial features of a patient with acromegaly. *(Source: Tindall GT, Barrow DL. Disorders of the pituitary. St. Louis, MO: Mosby, 1986. Reproduced with permission from the publisher.)*

PLANS

Diagnostic

Differential Diagnosis

Acromegaly may resemble hypothyroidism. The two can be differentiated by measurement of serum levels of thyroid-stimulating hormone and thyroxine. Once acromegaly has been diagnosed, the cause should be identified. In more than 90% of cases, a pituitary adenoma is the cause. Excessive secretion of GH-releasing hormone is the next most likely cause, usually ectopic (from an abdominal tumor), but sometimes from central nervous system sites. Ectopic secretion of GH occurs rarely. The location of the source of excessive GH secretion can usually be identified by magnetic resonance imaging of the pituitary or by computed tomography of the chest or abdomen. In unusual cases, selective venous sampling for GH measurement may be necessary. Levels of GH-releasing hormone can be measured in peripheral blood, but this test is usually not helpful.

Diagnostic Options

Hypersecretion of GH can be demonstrated by measuring GH on random samples, after glucose suppression, or after stimulation with thyrotropin-releasing hormone or gonadotropin-releasing hormone. Hypersecretion is reflected in the serum level of insulin-like growth factor I.

Recommended Approach

The most straightforward approach to diagnosis is measurement of the serum level of insulin-like growth factor I. This determination can be done without prior patient preparation and without regard for time of day or previous food intake. Elevated values are consistent with acromegaly. The classic diagnostic test for acromegaly is measurement of serum GH 1 hour after oral administration of 100 g of glucose solution. A clearly elevated GH level (>10 ng/mL) after oral glucose administration, combined with the clinical picture, makes the diagnosis of acromegaly secure, whereas a normal level of GH after oral glucose (<2 ng/mL) essentially rules out the diagnosis. Only a small percentage of subjects being investigated for acromegaly will have a post-glucose GH level that is intermediate (2–10 ng/mL). Often, endocrinologists use both of these tests (GH and insulin-like growth factor I measurement) for confirmation of the diagnosis.

Computed tomography or magnetic resonance imaging will often show a tumor in patients with acromegaly; however, these studies should be deferred until biochemical evidence of GH excess has been established.

Therapeutic

Therapeutic Options

The goals of treatment is acromegaly are (1) to eliminate mass effects, (2) to correct GH excess, and (3) to preserve normal pituitary function. Depending on the duration and severity of manifestations, signs and symptoms of GH excess may or may not resolve.

Recommended Approach

Surgery, irradiation, and pharmacologic treatment all have roles in the treatment of acromegaly.

Surgery. In most cases, transsphenoidal surgery with selective tumor removal is the best option for treatment of acromegaly. In experienced hands, this operation offers the best chance for cure and has acceptable morbidity and mortality. The cure rate with transsphenoidal surgery ranges from 44 to 90% among reported series, with an average of about 70 to 75%; success is more likely in patients with smaller tumors and lower initial GH levels. Anterior pituitary function is usually preserved. Mortality is less than 1% and the complication rate is under 4%.

Irradiation. Two types of radiation therapy have been used to treat acromegaly: conventional electromagnetic irradiation and heavy particle irradiation. Conventional electromagnetic irradiation (e.g., cobalt) has been shown to be effective for pituitary tumors causing acromegaly, leading to a reduction in GH levels and clinical improvement in 70% to 80% of patients. The beneficial effects of radiation are slow to appear (often 2 to 4 years), however, and there are serious potential delayed risks of radiation, including hypopituitarism and radiation necrosis. Conventional radiation should be reserved for treatment of patients with surgically incurable or recurrent tumors or when surgery cannot be performed because of poor health. Heavy particle irradiation (e.g., proton beam therapy) can provide good control of acromegaly with an acceptable incidence of side effects. The use of this therapeutic modality has declined in the last 15 to 20 years because of increasing use of transsphenoidal surgery and concerns over the long-term effects of high doses of irradiation. Also, heavy particle therapy requires specialized equipment that is available in only two centers in the United States.

Pharmacologic Treatment. Over the years, a number of drugs have been used to treat acromegaly. These include chlorpromazine (Thorazine), estrogens, antiserotonin agents (cyproheptadine [Periactin]), dopamine agonists, and the somatostatin analog octreotide. Dopamine agonists such as bromocriptine (Parlodel) are effective in lowering serum GH levels in up to 75% of patients, but in only 20% are the levels reduced to normal; patients with acromegaly in whom prolactin is also elevated are more likely to have a favorable response to bromocriptine. The dosage of bromocriptine required in acromegaly ranges from 15 to 50 mg/d. Withdrawal of bromocriptine is associated with a prompt return of elevated serum GH levels. In contrast to prolactinomas, GH-secreting tumors do not usually shrink with bromocriptine. For these reasons, bromocriptine is not satisfactory as primary treatment for acromegaly.

Octreotide (Sandostatin), when administered by subcutaneous injection, causes a suppression of GH secretion in normal subjects and in 90% of patients with acromegaly, with normalization of GH levels and long-term control in approximately 40% of cases. A dose of 100 to 200 µg every 8 hours is usually required to inhibit GH secretion for 24 hours. Good responses to octreotide are most likely if the initial GH level is below 20 ng/mL. Tumor size decreases in about half of the patients treated with octreotide, but regrowth occurs after withdrawal of the drug. Side effects are related to suppression of gastrointestinal motility (loose stools, abdominal discomfort, nausea, flatulence). Cholelithiasis is a frequent complication of octreotide treatment and must be looked for with periodic gallbladder ultrasonography. Longer-acting forms of somatostatin are being studied in clinical trials and appear to be promising. Patients who fail to have a satisfactory response to octreotide alone may respond to a combination of octreotide and bromocriptine.

Pharmacologic treatment is rarely used as primary therapy for acromegaly. It may be chosen for patients who are not candidates for surgery and for control of hypersecretion of GH while waiting for the beneficial effects of radiation. There is evidence that surgical cure is enhanced when patients with GH-secreting macroadenomas are treated with octreotide for several months prior to surgery.

FOLLOW-UP

Periodic reassessment of GH production after surgery is advisable. Criteria for "cure" are a normal basal GH level and normal GH dynamic responses. If the basal GH is less than 2 ng/mL, normal dynamics can be assumed; if the basal GH is greater than 10 ng/mL, abnormal dynamics are almost certain. Patients with intermediate GH levels should be tested further with oral glucose suppression or with stimulation tests using thyrotropin-releasing hormone, gonadotropin-releasing hormone, or both. Some authorities believe that insulin-like growth factor I levels correlate better with clinical activity than GH levels and recommend this test in addition to GH measurement. Patients should be carefully followed for enlargement or recurrence of a pituitary mass lesion (including magnetic resonance imaging of the sella and visual field determinations). Neurologic examination should be performed and cardiac status assessed. If hormone deficiencies are present, replacement therapy must be instituted and monitored.

Lifelong follow-up of patients with acromegaly is advisable. If the patient has had surgical treatment, GH measurement and any other indicated hormone tests, such as evaluation of pituitary hormone reserve, should be done 1 month following surgery. If tests are normal, the patient is asked to return in 6 months and at least yearly thereafter. Because of the increased incidence of colon polyps and colon malignancies, periodic colonoscopy is advisable.

DISCUSSION

Prevalence and Incidence

The prevalence of acromegaly is 50 to 70 cases per million population. The incidence is approximately 3 cases per million. Pituitary gigantism is rare. GH-secreting adenomas account for approximately 10% of all pituitary tumors. They usually occur in the middle decades for life, though they can occur at any age. Acromegaly affects both sexes equally.

Related Basic Science

Genetics and Altered Molecular Biology

Studies using X chromosome inactivation indicate that most if not all GH-secreting tumors are monoclonal, evidence favoring a primary pituitary disorder as the cause of these tumors. In 35 to 40% of cases, the alpha subunit of the guanine nucleotide binding protein (Gs) contains a common point mutation at one of two sites that is crucial for its regulatory activity, resulting in a constitutive activation of adenylate cyclic and enhanced adenosine monophosphate (AMP) production. AMP could serve as a mitogen or a stimulus to GH production and release, or both. Tumors with this mutation contain dense secretory granules and tend to be smaller than those without the mutation.

Physiologic or Metabolic Derangement and Anatomic Derangement

In normal subjects, GH release from the pituitary gland is regulated primarily by a stimulatory peptide from the hypothalamus, GH-releasing hormone. There is also an inhibitory hypothalamic factor, somatostatin, sometimes known as somatotropin release-inhibiting factor. Other hypothalamic factors, such as thyrotropin-releasing and gonadotropin-releasing hormones, do not affect GH release in normal subjects.

Normal secretion of GH is episodic, with several peaks during a 24-hour period, particularly after stress or exercise and an hour or so after the onset of deep sleep. Increases in plasma glucose levels normally cause a decrease in GH levels, and hypoglycemia stimulates a rise in GH.

Many aspects of GH dynamics are abnormal in acromegaly. GH secretion is sustained in some patients but episodic in others, sometimes with wide fluctuations. Even when GH is only slightly elevated, oral glucose has no suppressive effect; this lack of GH suppression after oral glucose is the basis for the classic diagnostic approach. Many patients with acromegaly show a decrease in GH level after administra-

tion of the dopamine agonist bromocriptine, which does not affect GH secretion in normal subjects. Approximately 50% of patients with acromegaly show an increase in GH levels after administration of thyrotropin-releasing hormone, and 50% respond to gonadotropin-releasing hormone with an increase in GH levels. Demonstration of these abnormal dynamic responses is useful in the patient whose postglucose GH level is not diagnostically elevated. From the perspective of clinical research, investigating these abnormal responses should provide further knowledge regarding etiology, pathophysiology, and response to treatment.

Most of the effects of GH on cartilage and other tissues occur through another group of hormones, the somatomedins. These hormones are produced by the liver in response to GH. The most important of these compounds is insulin-like growth factor I, formerly known as somatomedin C. Somatomedins stimulate uptake of sulfate by cartilage and were first called *sulfation factors*. Their actions are more general, however, and include increased synthesis of collagen and proteoglycans, inhibition of lipolysis, and other metabolic effects including positive balances of nitrogen, phosphorus, potassium, magnesium, and calcium and an increase in protein synthesis. GH has divergent effects on carbohydrate metabolism; initially, an injection of GH causes a fall in blood glucose; chronic GH excess inhibits glucose entry into cells, antagonistic to the action of insulin. This leads to glucose intolerance and, in some cases, overt diabetes.

Chronic hypersecretion of GH, through increased production of insulin-like growth factor I, leads to the recognizable increases in growth of soft tissues, cartilage, and bone that are characteristic of acromegaly. Thickening of the skin is due to interstitial edema, deposits of hyaluronates, and increased connective tissue. The metabolic changes of acromegaly result from the actions of GH on fuel and mineral metabolism.

Natural History and Its Modification with Treatment

Morbidity from acromegaly occurs primarily from peripheral neuropathy (foot drop, muscle atrophy, Charcot joints), cardiovascular problems (hypertension, cardiomegaly, sometimes with fulminant congestive heart failure), and mass effects from the pituitary tumor (visual field defects or blindness, cranial nerve involvement, and hypopituitarism). Although some patients with acromegaly have a benign course and occasional spontaneous remissions occur, the overall life expectancy of patients with untreated acromegaly is reduced. By the fifth decade, the death rate of patients with acromegaly is twice that of the general population. Several studies have shown an increase in deaths from vascular, malignant, and respiratory disorders that is partly reduced with treatment. Patients with acromegaly have a predisposition

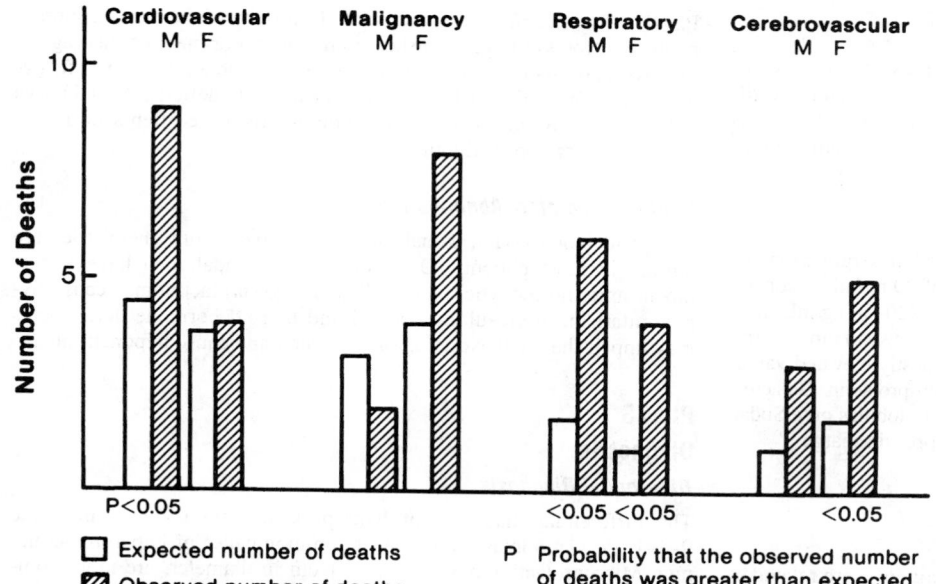

Figure 9–3–2. Common causes of death in acromegaly. □, Expected number of deaths; ▨ observed number of deaths; P, probability that the observed number of deaths was greater than expected. Source: Wright AD, Hill DM, Lowy C, et al. Mortality in Acromegaly. J Med 1970;39:1. Reproduced by permission of Oxford University Press.

toward colonic polyps and carcinoma of the colon, as well as other malignancies. Figure 9–3–2 compares the most common causes of death in patients with acromegaly with expected death rates.

Prevention

No prevention measures are currently available. More research is needed in this field.

Cost Containment

When acromegaly is suspected, diagnostic tests should be ordered in a systematic and stepwise fashion. Because most patients with acromegaly will have the diagnosis established by an elevated level of insulin-like growth factor I or an elevated GH concentration after oral glucose administration, additional tests are usually unnecessary. Other studies, such as pituitary magnetic resonance imaging, should be deferred until the diagnosis of acromegaly has been documented with biochemical data.

Because many of the consequences of acromegaly cannot be reversed once the disease is well established, early detection and treatment of acromegaly are desirable. This requires a high degree of clinical suspicion.

REFERENCES

Chang-DeMoranville, BM, Jackson IMD. Diagnosis and endocrine testing in acromegaly. Endocrinol Metab Clin North Am 1992;21:649.
Frohman LA. Therapeutic options in acromegaly. J Clin Endocrinol Metab 1991;72:1175.
Lieberman SA, Hoffman AR. Sequelae to acromegaly: Reversibility with treatment for the primary disease. Horm Metab Res 1990;22:313.
Melmed S. Acromegaly. N Engl J Med 1990;322:966.
Tindall GT, Oyesiku NM, Watts NB, et al. Transphenoidal adenomectomy for growth-hormone secreting pituitary adenomas in acromegaly: Outcome analysis and determinants of failure. J Neurosurg 1993;78:205.

CHAPTER 9–4

Hyperprolactinemia and Galactorrhea

Lewis S. Blevins, Jr., M.D.

DEFINITION

Hyperprolactinemia is defined as a persistently elevated serum prolactin concentration. Galactorrhea is a persistent milky discharge from the breast in a man or a nonpuerperal woman.

ETIOLOGY

Prolactin is synthesized and secreted by the lactotrophes (cells) of the anterior pituitary gland. Hyperprolactinemia can be caused by any drug or disease process that stimulates prolactin secretion and by a neoplastic (prolactinoma) or nonneoplastic (hyperplasia), proliferation of lactotropes. Galactorrhea can result from any of the causes of hyperprolactinemia. Nearly one half of patients with galactorrhea have a normal prolactin level. In these patients, galactorrhea is usually ascribed to residual postpartum lactation, prior use of oral contraceptives, or fibrocystic breast disease.

CRITERIA FOR DIAGNOSIS

Suggestive

Hyperprolactinemia is suspected when a patient presents with symptoms or signs of gonadal dysfunction, such as amenorrhea and infertility in women or impotence and loss of libido in men. Galactorrhea is suggested by a yellowish, whitish, or clear oily discharge from the nipple of the breast.

Definitive

Hyperprolactinemia is confirmed by measuring a random serum prolactin. In most radioimmunoassays, a prolactin in excess of 20 ng/mL is considered abnormal. Modest elevations in serum prolactin (20–50 ng/mL) may reflect the stress of venipuncture or a physiologic response to nipple stimulation during a breast examination. Therefore, modestly elevated values should be confirmed by measuring the fasting serum prolactin. Galactorrhea can be firmly established by the presence of fat globules on a Sudan black-stained microscope slide preparation of the nipple discharge.

CLINICAL MANIFESTATIONS

Subjective

The main complaints associated with hyperprolactinemia are related to gonadal dysfunction. In women, menstrual abnormalities may include

variation in the cycle length, oligomenorrhea, and amenorrhea. Infertility is common. Vaginal dryness, dyspareunia, hot flashes, and loss of libido can also occur. In men, common complaints include loss of libido, erectile dysfunction, and, rarely, breast tenderness. Headache, visual disturbances, and symptoms of hypopituitarism may occur in patients with large prolactinomas. Hyperprolactinemia during adolescence can arrest puberty or cause primary amenorrhea.

Review of the patient's past medical history and current medications may identify diseases and drugs that cause hyperprolactinemia.

Rare patients with prolactinomas have the syndrome known as multiple endocrine neoplasia type I. This autosomal dominant disorder is characterized by parathyroid hyperplasia and hypercalcemia, pituitary tumors, and pancreatic islet cell tumors (Zollinger–Ellison syndrome, insulinoma). A careful review of the family and past medical history will identify most patients with this uncommon disorder.

Objective

Physical Examination

Physical findings in women may include atrophy of the breasts, spontaneous or expressible galactorrhea, thinning and dryness of the vaginal mucosa, and hirsutism. In men, the testes may be atrophic or soft; gynecomastia and galactorrhea are rare. Visual field deficits, cranial nerve palsies, and physical features of hypopituitarism are often seen in patients with large prolactinomas.

Routine Laboratory Abnormalities

Complete blood count, urinalysis, and routine serum chemistries are normal in most patients. Occasional hypogonadal men have a normochromic, normocytic anemia. When large prolactinomas cause hypopituitarism, the resulting cortisol and thyroid hormone deficiencies may impair the renal excretion of free water and cause hyponatremia.

PLANS

Diagnostic

Differential Diagnosis

The differential diagnosis of hyperprolactinemia is listed in Table 9–4–1. Prolactinomas are the most common cause of hyperprolactinemia. Microprolactinomas, less than 1 cm in diameter, are more common in women, and are associated with modest elevations in the serum

TABLE 9–4–1. DIFFERENTIAL DIAGNOSIS OF HYPERPROLACTINEMIA

Prolactinoma
   Microadenoma
   Macroadenoma
Acromegaly (one third of patients)
Interruption of the pituitary stalk
   Pseudoprolactinoma (nonsecreting pituitary macroadenoma)
   Metastasis (breast cancer, lung cancer, lymphoma)
   Granulomatous disease (sarcoidosis, tuberculosis, histiocytosis)
   Pituitary surgery
Hypothalamic tumors (craniopharyngioma)
Pregnancy
Drugs
   Phenothiazine
   Metoclopramide
   Tricyclic antidepressants
   Reserpine
   α-Methyldopa
   Verapamil
   Estrogens
Medical disorders
   Hypothyroidism
   Cirrhosis
   Chronic renal failure
Neurogenic disorders
   Spinal cord tumors
   Chest wall disease (injury, herpes zoster)
Idiopathic

prolactin concentration. Macroprolactinomas, greater than 1 cm in diameter, are more common in men, and in most instances, the serum prolactin concentration exceeds 200 ng/mL and is often more than 1000 ng/mL. Hypothalamic tumors and disease processes can interrupt the pituitary stalk and cause moderate elevations in the serum prolactin (< 200 ng/mL). Large pituitary tumors that do not secrete prolactin (pseudoprolactinomas) can also interrupt the pituitary stalk and cause prolactin levels as high as 200 ng/mL. In drug-induced hyperprolactinemia, the serum prolactin rarely exceeds 150 ng/mL. A 10- to 15-fold rise in the serum prolactin concentration occurs during pregnancy. Hyperprolactinemia can occur in patients with severe primary hypothyroidism; associated hyperplasia of the thyroid-stimulating hormone-producing cells of the anterior pituitary can mimic a pituitary tumor and result in an erroneous diagnosis of prolactinoma. A diagnosis of idiopathic hyperprolactinemia is rendered when obvious causes of hyperprolactinemia have been excluded.

Diagnostic Options

Magnetic resonance imaging with gadolinium-DPTA enhancement provides greater resolution of tissue planes than does computed tomography and, therefore, is the preferred imaging modality in the evaluation of diseases of the hypothalamus and the pituitary gland.

Recommended Approach

A careful history should be taken and physical examination and routine laboratory studies performed in all patients to identify the underlying cause of hyperprolactinemia. The serum concentration of thyroid-stimulating hormone should be measured. A qualitative serum determination of the beta subunit of human chorionic gonadotropin is indicated in women of childbearing age. Magnetic resonance imaging of the sella turcica is indicated when an obvious cause of hyperprolactinemia cannot be found and when disorders of the pituitary and hypothalamus are suspected. Approximately three fourths of microprolactinomas are visualized as either a hypo- or hyperdense region within the pituitary gland. Pituitary asymmetry and deviation of the infundibulum to the contralateral side of the pituitary may also be observed. Because of their size, macroprolactinomas are always visualized. In some patients, extension into the suprasellar cistern, compression of the optic chiasm,

or invasion of the cavernous sinuses may be apparent. Hypothalamic tumors are usually large and occupy the region above the sella turcica. Metastases and granulomatous disorders often result in diffuse or nodular enlargement of the pituitary stalk.

Specific tests for anterior pituitary and target gland hormone deficiencies should be performed when hyperprolactinemia is attributed to either hypothalamic or pituitary disease. The gonadal dysfunction caused by hyperprolactinemia is characterized and confirmed by low serum concentrations of the sex hormones (estradiol, testosterone) and either normal or low follicle-stimulating hormone and luteinizing hormone levels. In patients with long-standing hyperprolactinemia and hypogonadism, dual-energy x-ray absorptiometry bone scans should be performed to evaluate for decreased bone mineral density, which is a risk factor for osteoporotic fractures of the spine, hip, and wrist. X-ray examination of the thoracic and lumbar spine is indicated when there are historical or physical features (back pain, kyphosis, decrease in height) that suggest osteoporotic compression fractures.

Therapeutic

The main therapeutic objectives in patients with hyperprolactinemia are to (1) restore gonadal function, (2) abolish galactorrhea, (3) reverse visual field deficits and other mass effects of a macroprolactinoma, and (4) normalize the serum prolactin concentration.

Therapeutic Options

Therapeutic options for treating patients with prolactinomas include (1) observation, (2) pharmacologic treatment, (3) surgery, and (4) irradiation.

Observation. Reliable patients with either microprolactinomas or idiopathic hyperprolactinemia and normal gonadal function do not necessarily require therapy and can be followed at regular intervals. The risk of clinically significant growth of untreated microadenomas is less than 5%. Idiopathic hyperprolactinemia will spontaneously resolve in more than one-third of patients.

Pharmacologic Treatment. Bromocriptine, a dopamine agonist, is the only drug approved by the U.S. Food and Drug Administration for the treatment of hyperprolactinemia. In women with microprolactinomas, ovulatory menses and fertility are restored within 6 to 8 weeks of the initiation of therapy. Galactorrhea either resolves or diminishes in intensity in nearly all patients. Erectile function and libido improve in men who do not have concomitant hypopituitarism. Normalization of the serum prolactin concentration is accomplished in many patients, and the level achieved is less than 10% of the pretreatment value in most. Clinically significant, often dramatic, tumor shrinkage is achieved in three quarters of patients within 6 to 12 weeks. In some patients with invasive macroprolactinomas, however, 12 months of therapy may be required to achieve maximal diminution in tumor size. Unfortunately, tumor regresstion is due only to involution of the neoplastic lactotropes and not to actual cell death. Therefore, tumor reexpansion can occur when treatment with bromocriptine is interrupted.

Side effects of bromocriptine include nausea, headache, orthostatic dizziness, and nasal congestion. Cerebrospinal fluid rhinorrhea may complicate therapy of macroprolactinomas. In these instances, it is presumed that inferior growth of the prolactinoma causes a defect in the floor of the sella turcica, and superior growth violates the arachnoid membranes. Bromocriptine-induced shrinkage of the tumor permits flow of cerebrospinal fluid through the communication between the subarachnoid space and the nasal cavities. Acute bacterial meningitis is a feared complication of cerebrospinal rhinorrhea. The rhinorrhea may resolve spontaneously or require neurosurgical correction.

Surgery. Transsphenoidal microsurgery is preferred over other surgical approaches to pituitary adenomas. The likelihood of cure following transsphenoidal surgery is dependent on the size and invasiveness of the prolactinoma, the preoperative prolactin concentration, and the skill and experience of the neurosurgeon. Early cure rates range from 70 to 85% for microprolactinomas, and from 30 to 40% for macroprolactinomas and in patients with a serum prolactin greater than 200 ng/mL. Hyperprolactinemia recurs in 16 to 80% of patients within 5 to 10 years of transsphenoidal surgery. Surgery is associated with an increased risk of subsequent partial or complete hypopituitarism.

Irradiation. Conventional supravoltage irradiation is not effective primary therapy in patients with prolactinomas because the serum prolactin concentration is only rarely normalized. Furthermore, the maximum lowering of the serum prolactin concentration is not achieved for several years. Approximately one half of patients develop one or more anterior pituitary hormone deficiencies within 10 years of irradiation.

Recommended Approach

Primary therapy should always be directed at the disorder responsible for the hyperprolactinemia. For example, levothyroxine replacement therapy is the preferred treatment for patients with hyperprolactinemia caused by hypothyroidism. Patients with hyperprolactinemia due to sarcoidosis affecting the hypothalamus and pituitary stalk respond to high-dose glucocorticoids. Patients with hypothalamic tumors should undergo surgery and patients with metastases to the pituitary stalk should be treated for their underlying malignancy. In patients with drug-induced hyperprolactinemia, discontinuance of the offending agent usually results in normalization of the serum prolactin. In some patients, however, it is not prudent to discontinue medication (i.e., phenothiazine-treated patients with schizophrenia), and in others, the underlying cause of hyperprolactinemia may not be treatable. In these circumstances, patients with nonneoplastic disorders and clinical and biochemical evidence of normal gonadal function do not require specific therapy for hyperprolactinemia. Bromocriptine is, however, indicated to lower the serum prolactin when hypogonadism is present. Sex hormone replacement therapy should be considered if hypogonadism persists following an adequate trial of bromocriptine.

Bromocriptine is the preferred initial treatment in nearly all patients with prolactinomas. Treatment should be initiated with 1.25 mg orally at bedtime and escalated every 3 to 4 days, initially to 2.5 mg at bedtime, then 2.5 mg twice daily, and then 2.5 mg three times daily. The smallest effective dose can be identified by measuring the serum prolactin during dose escalation. If a dosage of 2.5 mg three times daily is achieved, the serum prolactin should be measured 3 to 4 weeks later to determine if further increases in the dose are necessary. Occasional patients require 15 to 20 mg bromocriptine daily. A more aggressive approach to dose escalation should be taken in patients with macroprolactinomas and visual field deficits.

Side effects of bromocriptine usually resolve within the first week or two of therapy. The incidence and severity of side effects can be reduced by initiating therapy at bedtime, escalating the dose slowly, and instructing the patient to take the drug with food. Nasal congestion responds to treatment with sympathomimetic agents.

Women of reproductive age should be instructed to use a barrier method of contraception for 3 to 6 months following the initiation of treatment with bromocriptine. This practice permits the physician and the patient to determine whether menses have returned to normal and to establish the average menstrual cycle length. Then, if fertility is desired, the contraceptive method can be discontinued. The patient should be instructed to notify the treating physician and report for serum quantitative human chorionic gonadotropin determination if menses are delayed by 3 to 5 days. Bromocriptine should be discontinued if the serum human chorionic gonadotropin test is positive, even though there is no conclusive proof of an increased incidence of adverse maternal or fetal effects when bromocriptine is taken during pregnancy. Clinically significant tumor expansion during pregnancy occurs in only 15% of patients with macroprolactinomas and in 2% of patients with microprolactinomas. In most cases, tumor expansion manifests as intractable headaches or visual field deficits, and therapy with bromocriptine should be resumed. Alternatively, transsphenoidal surgery can be performed during the second trimester of pregnancy.

Attempts at transsphenoidal resection of prolactinomas are indicated when patients fail to respond to or are intolerant of bromocriptine. Other indications include sudden or marked visual field deficits, pituitary tumor apoplexy, persistent cerebrospinal fluid rhinorrhea or epistaxis that requires surgical correction, and patient preference. Patients should be informed regarding the likelihood or cure prior to surgical intervention.

Irradiation is occasionally useful as adjunctive therapy in patients with recurrent or residual disease following transsphenoidal surgery. Further increases in tumor size are rare following successful treatment. Treatment with bromocriptine is usually required while awaiting the beneficial effects of irradiation.

FOLLOW-UP

Patients with hyperprolactinemia should have regular follow-up visits at 3- to 6-month intervals during the first year following definitive therapy, and at 6- to 12-month intervals thereafter, to maintain control of the hyperprolactinemia and to detect recurrent disease in patients cured by initial therapy. Patients undergoing observation in lieu of definitive therapy should be followed at 3-month intervals. Follow-up visits should include assessments of gonadal function and the activity and complications of the disorder responsible for hyperprolactinemia. Compliance with and effectiveness of therapy can be assessed by measuring the serum prolactin. Magnetic resonance imaging is indicated to assess for tumor shrinkage in response to bromocriptine. Most bromocriptine-responsive prolactinomas decrease in size within 6 to 12 weeks. Tumors that fail to regress are either bromocriptine-resistant prolactinomas or pseudoprolactinomas and should be resected. Clinical, biochemical, or radiologic evidence of either an insufficient response to primary therapy or recurrent disease should prompt immediate reevaluation and appropriate revision of the therapeutic plan.

DISCUSSION

Prevalence and Incidence

Hyperprolactinemia is present in approximately one sixth of women with amenorrhea and more than one half of those with galactorrhea. Less than one tenth of men with impotence have hyperprolactinemia. Prolactinomas account for 30 to 40% of all pituitary tumors encountered in clinical practice.

Related Basic Science

Physiologic or Metabolic Derangement

Prolactin, a polypeptide hormone, is secreted in an episodic fashion by the lactotropes of the anterior pituitary gland. Dopamine, a neurotransmitter produced by the tuberoinfundibular neurons in the hypothalamus, is transported to the anterior pituitary by the hypothalamic–pituitary portal veins. Dopamine binds to the D_2 dopamine receptor on the lactotropes of the anterior pituitary and exerts a tonic inhibitory influence on prolactin synthesis and secretion. Drugs or disease processes that interfere with the synthesis, release, transport, or action of dopamine can cause hyperprolactinemia. There is no conclusive evidence that treatment with neuroleptic medications causes prolactinomas. Hypothalamic thyrotropin-releasing hormone is a putative prolactin-releasing factor. Hyperprolactinemia in patients with primary hypothyroidism is probably due to increases in portal vein thyrotropin-releasing hormone levels in response to thyroid hormone deficiency.

Renal failure results in impaired degradation and delayed clearance of prolactin from the blood. Increased concentrations of plasma estrogens (drugs, pregnancy, cirrhosis) cause lactotrope hyperplasia and hyperprolactinemia. Estrogens do not cause prolactinomas in humans. Neurogenic disorders stimulate the reflex arcs that are responsible for the physiologic increase in prolactin following nipple stimulation.

Hyperprolactinemia causes hypogonadism primarily by interfering with the pulsatile secretion of gonadotropin-releasing hormone from the hypothalamus. As a result, follicle-stimulating hormone and luteinizing hormone are not synthesized or secreted in the pattern necessary to stimulate adequate hormone production by the gonads. Hyperprolactinemia may also interfere with gonadotropin production by the pituitary gland and directly interfere with the synthesis of testosterone, estradiol, and progesterone.

Altered Molecular Biology

Prolactinomas are monoclonal tumors and probably arise de novo. The exact role and mechanisms of hypothalamic dysfunction, growth factors, transcriptional activating factors, and oncogenes in the pathogenesis of these tumors have not been defined.

Natural History and Its Modification with Treatment

Untreated hyperprolactinemia can cause persistent hypogonadism and complications associated with sex steroid hormone deficiency (i.e., osteoporosis, anemia). Prolactinomas may increase in size and cause hypopituitarism or invasion and destruction of structures in close proximity to the sella turcica. In most patients, therapy can reverse and prevent these complications.

Prevention

Prolactinomas cannot be prevented. Hyperprolactinemia can be prevented in some instances by early recognition and treatment of the underlying cause (i.e., treatment of hypothyroidism).

Cost Containment

A thorough history and physical examination obviate the need for expensive biochemical and radiologic tests in many patients. Magnetic resonance imaging of the pituitary and hypothalamus should be reserved for patients in whom other causes of hyperprolactinemia have not been identified.

REFERENCES

Bevan JS, Webster J, Burke CW, Scanlon MF. Dopamine agonists in pituitary tumor shrinkage. Endocr Rev 1992;3:220.

Faria MA Jr, Tindall GT. Transsphenoidal microsurgery for prolactin secreting pituitary adenomas. J Neurosurg 1982;56:33.

Molitch ME. Management of prolactinomas. Annu Rev Med 1989;40:225.

Molitch ME, Elton RL, Blackwell RE, et al. Bromocriptine as primary therapy for prolactin secreting macroadenomas: Results of a prospective multicenter study. J Clin Endocrinol Metab 1985;60:698.

Thorner MO, Vance ML, Horvath E, Kovacs K. The anterior pituitary. In: Wilson JD, Foster DW, eds. *Williams Textbook of Endocrinology.* 8th ed. Philadelphia: Saunders, 1992;221.

Vance ML, Evans WS, Thorner MO. Bromocriptine. Ann Intern Med 1984;100:78.

CHAPTER 9–5

Adrenal Nodules and Tumors

David E. Schteingart, M.D.

DEFINITION

Adrenal nodules and tumors are irregular enlargements of the adrenal glands and can be unilateral or bilateral. These lesions are discovered in the course of an investigation for abdominal complaints with computed tomographic (CT) scanning or as a result of investigation of the etiology of clinical syndromes of adrenocortical hormone excess.

ETIOLOGY

These lesions may represent primary adrenocortical or medullary tumors, tumors from other organs that are metastatic to the adrenal, and adrenal cysts and hematomas. Adrenal hematomas can be large and, if present unilaterally, they may be confused with a large adrenal tumor. Bilateral adrenal hematomas have been found in association with the onset of primary adrenal cortical insufficiency in patients who have been on anticoagulants and have experienced severe physical stress. Some nonfunctioning incidentally found adrenal masses, especially on the left side, may not be of adrenal origin. Lesions in the upper pole of the kidney, liver, gallbladder, pancreas, stomach, and colon, retroperitoneal lesions, and retroperitoneal lymphadenopathy have occasionally been imaged in the area of the adrenals and confused for an adrenal tumor. Patients with a family history of multiple endocrine neoplasia are at risk for developing bilateral nodular hyperplasia. No specific environmental factors have been associated with the development of adrenal tumors.

CRITERIA FOR DIAGNOSIS

Suggestive

Adrenal masses are first suspected by the finding on abdominal CT or magnetic resonance imaging of adrenal enlargement.

Definitive

A definitive diagnosis of an adrenal cortical tumor requires, in addition to the imaging procedures, a definition of their functional activity by measurement of catecholamines and catecholamine metabolites, as well as cortisol, aldosterone, androgens, and estrogens, at baseline and following dynamic testing. Radionuclide scanning combined with CT scanning of the adrenal glands helps determine if the adrenal tumor is benign or malignant, and functioning or nonfunctioning. Solid adrenal masses greater than 4 cm in diameter are highly suspicious of representing an adrenocortical carcinoma.

Adrenocortical masses can be easily detected by CT scanning. Scintigraphy with iodocholesterol provides not only an image reflective of the structure of the adrenal gland, but also information about its function. Patients with cortisol-secreting adrenal cortical adenomas suppress pituitary adrenocorticotropic hormone (ACTH) secretion and the function of the contralateral gland and demonstrate unilateral concentration of the tracer. Patients with Cushing's syndrome secondary to an adrenal cortical carcinoma usually fail to show tracer uptake in either side, as carcinomas have relatively low functional activity per gram of tissue and fail to concentrate iodocholesterol in quantities sufficient to produce an image. Cases have been described, however, in which patients with adrenal cortical carcinoma show a positive image with iodocholesterol. Patients with primary micronodular hyperplasia show asymmetric uptake with greater activity on the side of the predominant nodules. This finding is important in determining the presence of bilateral adrenocortical disease, as a CT scan of the adrenal glands may show a mass on one side and surgical resection of that mass may not result in remission if the contralateral gland is also abnormal.

Adrenal medullary tumors, pheochromocytomas or paragangliomas, are confirmed with the demonstration of elevated plasma and urinary catecholamine levels and a positive radionuclide scan with meta-iodobenzylguanidine.

CLINICAL MANIFESTATIONS

Subjective

Nonfunctioning adrenal tumors or nodules are discovered in patients who are being investigated for abdominal symptoms. The symptoms may not be related to the presence of the adrenal mass. In contrast, functioning adrenal masses or bilateral adrenocortical nodular hyperplasia that secrete excessive amounts of adrenocortical hormones are recognized by the clinical presentation and hormonal profile. Patients may present with Cushing's syndrome, primary aldosteronism, and syndromes of virilization or feminization. Patients with adrenal medullary lesions (pheochromocytomas) may present with clinical and biochemical manifestations of catecholamine excess. Symptoms of Cushing's syndrome include weight gain with a truncal distribution, muscle atrophy in the upper and lower extremities with proximal muscle weakness, atrophy of the skin, purple striae, facial rounding and plethora, hirsutism, acne, irritability, and insomnia. Patients with primary aldosteronism complain of weakness, headaches, muscle cramps, polydipsia, polyuria, and nocturia. Women with a virilizing syndrome complain of amenorrhea, acne and hirsutism, balding, deepening of the voice, and clitoromegaly. Men with feminization complain of gynecomastia and impotence. Manifestations of pheochromocytoma include headaches, palpitations, tremulousness, sweating, and pallor during periods of active catecholamine secretion.

Objective

Physical Examination

Patients with a nonfunctioning adrenocortical carcinoma in whom the tumor has achieved a large size may demonstrate a palpable abdominal mass. In functioning adrenal masses, the findings are related to the hormonal syndrome present. Patients with Cushing's syndrome exhibit truncal obesity with fullness of the face and neck, including preauricular areas, upper lip, supraclavicular fossa, and cervicodorsal area. The abdomen is protruberant, whereas the upper and lower extremities are thin as a result of the truncal distribution of adiposity and skeletal muscle atrophy. The skin is thin, especially over the dorsum of the hands, flexor surface of the forearm, and anterior aspect of the legs, and wide purple striae are present over the abdomen, axillary areas, and upper thighs. Hirsutism is both lanugal and coarse depending on whether cortisol or androgens prevail as the inciting stimulus for hair growth. Keratosis pillaris is observed with cortisol excess and acne with androgen excess. Verrucous vulgaris lesions of the skin are seen frequently in patients with cortisol excess. Muscle strength testing reveals weakness of the proximal musculature, which is best demonstrated by asking patients to squat and rise unassisted or to rise from a chair without support. Edema of the lower extremities may be present. There is systolic and diastolic hypertension and men may demonstrate gynecomastia. The most significant objective finding in patients with primary aldosteronism is hypertension, but they may also demonstrate hyporeflexia if severely hypokalemic. Women with a virilizing syndrome show acne and hirsutism over the face, chest, abdomen, and extremities. There may be bitemporal recession of the hairline and vertex balding. Examination of the genitalia reveals clitoromegaly. A virilizing syndrome is difficult to elicit in men. A feminizing syndrome in men is characterized by bilateral gynecomastia, which is usually tender, and if the excess estrogen secretion has been present for some time, mild testicular atrophy may be observed. Although pure syndromes are observed in benign adrenocortical adenomas, mixed syndromes of cortisol and androgen secretion are seen with adrenocortical carcinoma. Patients with a pheochromocytoma are found to be hypertensive and may occasionally exhibit orthostatic hypotension.

Routine Laboratory Abnormalities

The abnormalities in routine laboratory studies depend on the hormonal syndrome produced by the tumor. Patients with Cushing's syndrome may exhibit fasting or postprandial hyperglycemia and electrolyte abnormalities with hypernatremia, hypokalemia, and metabolic acidosis. The electrolyte findings are usually associated with very high cortisol secretion. The hematologic survey may show leukocytosis with neutrophilia. Patients with aldosterone-secreting tumors show electrolyte abnormalities with serum potassium levels, often below 3.0 mEq/L, hypernatremia (sodium usually > 145 mEq/L), and metabolic alkalosis. The degree of abnormality of serum bicarbonate is inversely proportional to the severity of the hypokalemia. Occasionally, patients may present with elevated fasting and postprandial glucose levels. Patients with adrenal carcinoma with hepatic metastases may show elevated levels of hepatic enzymes, particularly lactate dehydrogenase and alkaline phosphatase. Patients with pheochromocytomas may exhibit intermittently elevated serum glucose levels or an abnormal glucose tolerance test.

PLANS

Diagnostic

Differential Diagnosis

The differential diagnosis includes primary adrenal abnormalities (adrenal adenomas, carcinomas, pheochromocytomas, myelolipomas,

cysts) and secondary causes of nodularity (metastatic carcinoma, granulomatous disease, hemorrhage). Once an adrenal nodule is discovered, its functional state must be determined.

Diagnostic Options and Recommended Approach

Specific hormonal measurements should be obtained at baseline and during challenge testing. Although some patients with nonfunctioning adrenal masses may have completely normal steroid hormone secretion, other patients may have normal baseline steroid hormone secretion but fail to respond to dynamic testing, indicating autonomous secretion of hormones by the tumor. Although no specific signs of Cushing's syndrome are noted in these patients, they frequently exhibit hypertension, generalized obesity, and non-insulin-dependent diabetes mellitus, which improve after surgical resection. Normal hypothalamic–pituitary–adrenal function is characterized by normal baseline ACTH and cortisol levels, a normal circadian rhythm of ACTH and cortisol, and normal ACTH and cortisol response to the negative feedback effect of dexamethasone. These characteristics of normal pituitary–adrenal function may be absent in patients with functioning adrenal masses, even when the baseline hormone levels appear to be normal. In these circumstances, baseline urinary 17-hydroxycorticoid and free cortisol levels are normal. Serum cortisol levels at 8:00 AM may be normal while ACTH levels are low. The cortisol levels do not change when levels are measured at different times of the day or night. An overnight dexamethasone suppression test with 1 (low dose) or 8 (high dose) mg fails to show suppression of the "normal" baseline cortisol level. Patients with Cushing's syndrome secondary to either a unilateral adrenal mass or bilateral nodular hyperplasia exhibit elevated baseline urinary 17-hydroxycorticoid and free cortisol levels, elevated 8:00 AM serum cortisol levels, and suppressed corresponding ACTH levels. The cortisol levels do not change following administration of a high dose of dexamethasone. Aldosterone-secreting tumors are associated with high serum aldosterone and low (suppressed) plasma renin levels. In patients with a virilizing syndrome, serum dehydroepiandrosterone, androstenedione, and testosterone levels should be obtained at baseline. Serum dehydroepiandrosterone sulfate levels are usually above 10,000 ng/mL and serum testosterone levels are greater than 2 ng/mL. With feminizing syndromes, serum estradiol levels are found to be high. In the presence of an adrenal mass, it is seldom necessary to use stimulating or suppressive tests to establish the diagnosis of a hormone-secreting adrenal tumor. Catecholamine secretion by pheochromocytomas may be intermittent, and plasma and urinary catecholamine levels may be found elevated only at the time of increased activity of the tumor. Repeated measurement of plasma and urine catecholamine levels, particularly the initiation of collection of samples at the time of symptoms, may improve the probability of finding such tumors.

Additional imaging of the adrenal masses may be helpful in determining their origin. Homogeneous, slightly negative CT attenuation is likely to be associated with adrenocortical adenomas, whereas nonhomogeneous lesions or lesions that contain calcifications are most likely to be malignant. Fat content in benign tumors is usually higher than in malignant lesions. Using chemical shift magnetic resonance imaging, which highlights the presence of fat, for masses between 3 and 6 cm, it is possible to distinguish between adenomas and nonadenoma lesions with 100% specificity and 83% sensitivity. Adrenal scintigraphy with 6β-[131I]iodomethyl-19-norcholesterol can provide additional evidence of whether the tumor is benign or malignant, especially in tumors less than 2 cm in diameter. The findings on adrenal scintigraphy are compared with those on CT. Concordant lesions in which uptake is coincidental with the mass observed on CT scanning are most likely benign, whereas discordant lesions in which the uptake is contralateral to the CT found mass have a high probability of being malignant. Selective venous catheterization and sampling can provide confirmation about the secretory activity of the mass. Higher levels of steroid hormones and catecholamines may be observed on the side of the adrenal mass as compared with the contralateral side. Tumor size is another important consideration in the assessment of whether a mass is benign or malignant. Small masses are usually benign, whereas larger lesions are more likely to be malignant. There is disagreement, however, as to what specific tumor size helps distinguish benign from malignant lesions. Lesions that are less than 4 cm in diameter are most likely benign, but occasionally a mass less than 4 cm has been found to increase in size over time and turn out to be malignant. Lesions larger than 4 cm have a greater probability of being malignant, but still close to 75% of these masses are benign.

Therapeutic

The algorithm shown in Figure 9–5–1 could help in the management of an incidentally found adrenal mass.

It is first important to determine if the lesion is solid or cystic. If a mass is cystic, it is recommended that it be aspirated under CT or ultrasound guidance. If the aspirate is clear, the probability is high that it is a benign cyst and it should be observed. A hemorrhagic aspirate, on the other hand, may be associated with adrenal carcinoma and the mass should be excised. A solid mass should be evaluated on the basis of size and function. A nonfunctioning lesion smaller than 4 cm should be observed, whereas functioning masses, even with low levels of activity, should be removed. Solid masses greater than 4 cm in diameter should be surgically excised. Adrenal tumors causing Cushing's syndrome should be surgically removed. As the contralateral gland is usually suppressed, patients should receive coverage with hydrocortisone during the surgery and in the immediate postoperative period. Furthermore, replacement with hydrocortisone in physiologic amounts may need to be continued 6 to 12 months postoperatively, until there is recovery of normal pituitary–adrenal function and patients no longer depend on exogenous steroids for maintenance of physiologic glucocorticoid levels. Aldosterone, androgen, or estrogen-secreting tumors should also be surgically excised.

Fine-needle biopsy under ultrasound or CT guidance may be helpful in determining the nature of an adrenal mass. When performed by an experienced radiologist, these biopsies may confirm the presence of metastatic disease, myelolipomas, adrenal carcinomas, or adenomas. Morbidity associated with postbiopsy hemorrhage has been described in 10% of cases and a hypertensive crisis can be provoked during the procedure in patients with a pheochromocytoma.

Patients with functioning adrenal tumors or primary nodular hyperplasia should be informed that these lesions are the cause of many of the clinical symptoms that they present. The use of adrenal inhibitors, although they may temporarily diminish excessive hormone production by the adrenal lesion, do not provide permanent cure of the condition. Surgical resection of the adrenal tumor or bilateral adrenalectomy in the case of primary bilateral nodular hyperplasia is the best definitive treatment for these conditions. In cases of cortisol-producing adrenal lesions, patients should be told of the need to continue with cortisol replacement therapy until there is full recovery of their own pituitary–adrenal function.

FOLLOW-UP

After the initial diagnosis, patients with a unilateral solid adrenal mass less than 4 cm in diameter should be followed up with repeat adrenal CT scanning at 3, 9, and 18 months; once a year for the next 2 years; and less often thereafter. This follow-up is necessary to determine if the tumor mass has increased in size, in which case it should be removed. Functioning adrenal masses should be removed and patients subsequently seen every 2 months for the first year to determine the timing of discontinuation of hydrocortisone replacement therapy.

DISCUSSION
Prevalence and Incidence

Adrenocortical tumors and primary nodular hyperplasia are relatively rare. Adrenal masses larger than 8 mm can be found in about 10% of autopsies and unsuspected masses in about 5% of abdominal CT scans. These masses are uncommon under the age of 30 and their prevalence increases with age. Thus, an incidentally discovered adrenal mass in a young person should be followed more closely and for a longer period to rule out malignancy. Silent, nonfunctioning adrenal masses are discovered more commonly among African-Americans and in patients with diabetes mellitus, obesity, and hypertension.

Related Basic Science
Physiologic or Metabolic Derangement

Functioning tumors usually present with the clinical manifestations of hormone excess. If they produce cortisol, they result in Cushing's syndrome; if they secrete aldosterone, they result in primary aldosteronism; and if they secrete androgens, they result in virilizing syndromes. Cortisol-secreting tumors are found in 30% of patients presenting with Cushing's syndrome and aldosterone-secreting lesions in 2 to 3% of patients with essential hypertension. Androgen- and estrogen-secreting tumors are very rare. Benign functioning adrenal adenomas are usually monosecreting lesions. In contrast, functioning adrenocortical carcinomas are likely to produce more than one hormone and produce a mixed hormone syndrome. Patients with cortisol-secreting adrenal carcinomas frequently have excessive androgen production and clinically present with a mixed Cushing's and virilizing syndrome.

Anatomic Derangement

Adrenal adenomas are usually well encapsulated and do not metastasize, whereas adrenal carcinomas are large and have invasive characteristics. Primary bilateral micronodular hyperplasia is characterized by the presence in the adrenal cortex of one or more yellow nodules visible to the naked eye and often 2 to 3 cm in diameter. Its pathogenesis is

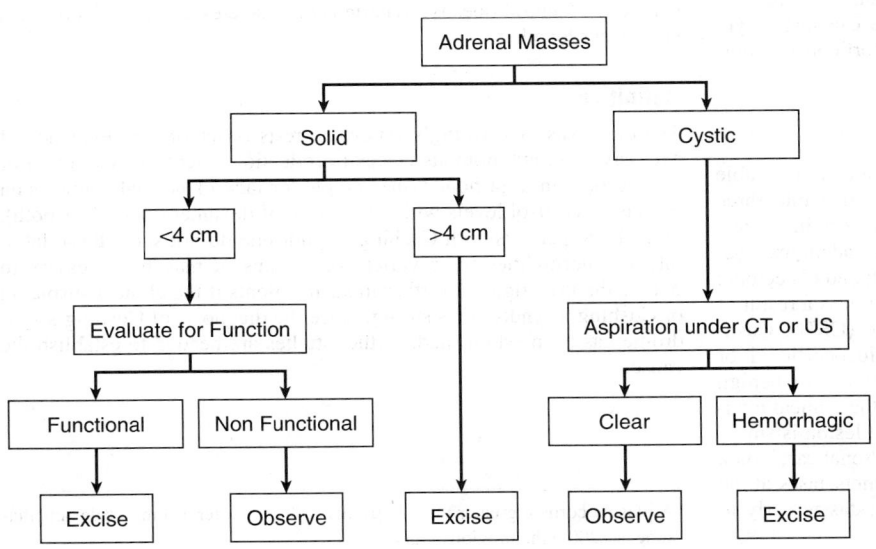

Figure 9–5–1. Algorithm for the management of an incidentally found adrenal mass. CT, computed tomography; US, ultrasound.

unknown. It is not clear if this type of hyperplasia is primary adrenal in origin or the result of a combined mechanism in which the pituitary predominates initially while the adrenal becomes eventually autonomous. Histologically, the micronodules consist of clear cells arranged in acini and cords, which are occasionally encapsulated and surrounded by simpler micronodular cortical hyperplasia. Frequency of mitotic figures is low. In addition, there is a form of ACTH-independent micronodular adrenal disease in which there are darkly pigmented micronodules in the presence of atrophy of the perinodular adrenal tissue and disorganization of normal zonation of the cortex. Microscopically, the nodules are composed predominantly of large globular cortical cells with granular eosinophilic cytoplasm that often contains lipofuscin. There may be familial aggregation of some of these patients with coexistence of microlentigo and blue nevi, cutaneous myxomas, single or multiple atrial or ventricular myxomas, and large cell fibroadenomas. The affected siblings have the human leukocyte antigen (HLA) type A-1, B-8, and DR-3 haplotypes, which are common to many autoimmune diseases. It has been reported that the hypercortisolism in this condition may be due to circulating immunoglobulins of the immunoglobulin G type.

Natural History and Its Modification with Treatment

Nonfunctioning small adrenal masses less than 4 cm in diameter usually remain stable for many years. Malignant lesions, however, may initially be small and slowly enlarge over the subsequent years. In contrast, functioning adrenal tumors or primary nodular hyperplasia is associated with significant morbidity, which depends on the metabolic effects of the hormones produced in excess. Adrenal carcinomas are generally aggressive lesions with a tendency to show early local recurrence and distant metastases. Life expectancy once the tumor has metastasized is less than 2 years, although chemotherapy instituted early can significantly prolong survival.

Prevention

The etiology of most adrenal masses is unknown and no specific measures are recognized that can prevent the development of these lesions.

Cost Containment

The major cost of evaluating adrenal tumors or nodules is the initial imaging procedure and the hormonal evaluation required to determine the functioning character of the lesion. Much of this evaluation can be carried out on an outpatient basis, although hospitalization for some aspects of the evaluation, such as assessing the presence or absence of normal circadian rhythm, may be required. For nonfunctioning lesions, the major cost is the repeat CT scanning of the adrenals to determine if they increase in size.

REFERENCES

Abecassis M, McLoughlin MJ, Langer B, Kudlow JE. Serendipitous adrenal masses: Prevalence, significance and management. Am J Surg 1985;149:783.

Gabrardi F, Carlone M, Bozzola A, Galli L. Adrenal incidentalomas: What is the role of fine needle biopsy. Int Urol Nephrol 1991;23:197.

Reincke M, Nieke J, Krestin GP, et al. Preclinical Cushing's syndrome in adrenal "incidentalomas": Comparison with Cushing's syndrome. J Clin Endocrinol Metab 1992;75:826.

Siren JE, Haapiainen RK, Huikuri KT, Siuula AH. Incidentalomas of the adrenal gland: 36 operated patients and review of the literature. World J Surg 1993;17:634.

Thompson NW, Cheung PSY. Diagnosis and treatment of functioning and nonfunctioning adrenocortical neoplasms including incidentalomas. Surg Clin North Am 1987;67:423.

CHAPTER 9–6

Cushing's Syndrome

Nelson B. Watts, M.D.

DEFINITION

Cushing's syndrome comprises the signs and symptoms resulting from levels of glucocorticoids that are excessive because of either sustained production of cortisol by the adrenal glands or ingestion of glucocorticoids. Cushing's disease is the term used to describe Cushing's syndrome resulting from excessive production of adrenocorticotropic hormone (ACTH) by a pituitary tumor.

ETIOLOGY

The disorders that cause Cushing's syndrome are shown in Table 9–6–1. The causes of Cushing's syndrome can be divided into three general categories: (1) Cushing's syndrome of pituitary origin (excessive production of ACTH, usually by a pituitary microadenoma); (2) cortisol-producing adrenal tumors, benign or malignant; and (3) ectopic production of ACTH. Rarely, Cushing's syndrome occurs as a result of ectopic production of corticotropin-releasing hormone (CRH). Cushing's syndrome may also result from exogenous glucocorticoid or ACTH treatment. Patients with Cushing's syndrome due to benign adrenal tumors are usually diagnosed early because of the clinical manifestations of cortisol excess at a time when the adrenal lesion is small. In contrast, patients with Cushing's syndrome due to adrenal carcinoma have large bulky tumors, often with local invasion or metastases at the time of presentation. Adrenal carcinomas tend to metastasize early to liver, lungs, and lymph nodes.

CRITERIA FOR DIAGNOSIS

Suggestive

The diagnosis should be considered when several of the usual signs and symptoms (central obesity, hypertension, diabetes mellitus, depression, etc.) occur together.

Definitive

The diagnosis of Cushing's syndrome rests on laboratory evidence of excessive and autonomous cortisol production (increased excretion of free cortisol in a 24-hour urine sample, or lack of normal suppression of plasma cortisol levels with a low dose of dexamethasone,* or both). Occasional patients with Cushing's syndrome do not show these laboratory abnormalities for a variety of reasons; it may be necessary to pursue the investigation further in such patients if the clinical suspicion of Cushing's syndrome is strong. Once the diagnosis of Cushing's syndrome has been established, further studies are needed to establish the cause.

---

*A plasma cortisol greater than 10 μg/dL at 0800 h after 1.0 mg of dexamethasone at 2200 h the previous night.

TABLE 9–6–1. NATURALLY OCCURRING CUSHING'S SYNDROME

Cause	Relative Prevalence (%)
ACTH-secreting pituitary tumor (Cushing's disease)	60–70
Adrenal adenoma	10–15
Adrenal carcinoma	5–10
Ectopic production of ACTH	5
Ectopic production of CRH	rare

ACTH, adrenocorticotropic hormone; CRH, corticotropin-releasing hormone.

CLINICAL MANIFESTATIONS

Subjective

Patients with Cushing's syndrome usually experience weight gain and a change in appearance. Frequent complaints include easy fatigue, muscle weakness (especially proximal muscle groups), easy bruising, poor wound healing, thinning of scalp hair, increased face and body hair in women, and alteration in reproductive function (in women, oligomenorrhea or amenorrhea; in men, decreased libido, impotence, or both). Depression and emotional lability are common. Rarely, hyperpigmentation or weight loss may occur, depending on the underlying cause of Cushing's syndrome (most likely with ectopic production of ACTH).

Family history is not usually contributory, except that Cushing's syndrome may be part of multiple endocrine neoplasia syndrome type I (see Chapter 9–46).

Objective

Physical Examination

Physical findings of Cushing's syndrome may be subtle but are often quite striking. The face is round and plethoric ("moon face") and fat pads are increased in the supraclavicular areas and over the upper thoracic spine ("buffalo hump"). Obesity is generalized in 50% of cases; in the remaining 50%, central obesity stands out in striking contrast to relatively slender extremities. The skin is atrophic, sometimes tissue paper thin, with broad, purple striae over the flanks, breasts, and lower abdomen. Often, there are ecchymoses and purpura. Scalp hair is usually sparse and fine, but there may be increased hair on the face and trunk; acne is often present. Systemic arterial hypertension is common. Generalized muscle wasting may be present, with pronounced weakness in proximal muscle groups.

When Cushing's syndrome results from ectopic production of ACTH by a malignancy (ectopic ACTH syndrome), the usual signs may be overshadowed by cachexia caused by the malignancy. Hyperpigmentation of the skin and mucous membranes may be seen with the ectopic ACTH syndrome and, less commonly, with ACTH excess due to a pituitary adenoma.

Routine Laboratory Abnormalities

Routine laboratory findings include leukocytosis (often with absent eosinophils), glucose intolerance (sometimes with fasting hyperglycemia or overt diabetes), and hypokalemia, which is usually mild. In the ectopic ACTH syndrome, hyperglycemia and hypokalemia may be pronounced, frequently with a metabolic alkalosis. Electrocardiogram and chest x-ray films often show changes of left ventricular hypertrophy. Osteoporosis may be apparent on lateral chest x-ray films, sometimes with spinal compression fractures.

PLANS

Two levels of testing are necessary when evaluating a patient for Cushing's syndrome: first, to establish or rule out the presence of hypercortisolism, and second, if hypercortisolism is present, to establish the etiology.

Diagnostic: Ruling in/out Hypercortisolism

Differential Diagnosis

To distinguish Cushing's syndrome from "pseudo-Cushing's" states, a simple approach is recommended. Obesity, hypertension, diabetes, and many of the other clinical manifestations of Cushing's syndrome are not specific to Cushing's syndrome and are frequently seen in the absence of hypercortisolism. Because Cushing's syndrome is an uncommon condition, most patients in whom the possibility of Cushing's syndrome is considered will not have the disorder. It is desirable to have a simple but sensitive test to rule out Cushing's syndrome when it is not present and to identify essentially all patients who have the condition.

Diagnostic Options

Cortisol can be measured in blood or urine.

Recommended Approach

The best test to determine the presence or absence of Cushing's syndrome is measurement of 24-hour urine free cortisol excretion, which is almost 100% sensitive and specific in unstressed patients; false-negative tests are rare, except in stress or in chronic alcoholism. Another satisfactory approach is the overnight dexamethasone suppression test, where 1.0 mg of dexamethasone (a potent glucocorticoid) is given orally at 2200 h and the plasma cortisol level is measured at 0800 h the next day. With this test, the plasma cortisol level is greater than 10 µg/dL in patients with Cushing's syndrome and less than 2 µg/dL in most normal subjects. False-positive results are seen more commonly with the overnight dexamethasone suppression test than with urinary free cortisol measurement and may be due to stress (which overrides the negative feedback of dexamethasone), anticonvulsant treatment (which accelerates the metabolism of dexamethasone), estrogen treatment (which increases cortisol-binding globulin), and unipolar depression (which alters the hypothalamic–pituitary–adrenal axis). If a single test is done to rule out Cushing's syndrome, 24-hour urinary free cortisol measurement is preferred when it is possible to obtain a 24-hour urine sample and the overnight 1-mg dexamethasone suppression test is done when blood sampling is more convenient.

Other common approaches to the diagnosis of Cushing's syndrome include measurement of plasma cortisol levels on morning and evening blood samples to see if a normal diurnal variation in plasma cortisol occurs and determination of 24-hour urine 17-hydroxycorticosteroids (known as 17-OHCS or 17-OHS). These strategies are not recommended because they lack sensitivity (i.e., many patients with Cushing's syndrome have normal results) and specificity (i.e., many patients without Cushing's syndrome have abnormal results).

In rare patients with Cushing's syndrome, hypercortisolism is mild or intermittent. In these patients, establishing the diagnosis is difficult when the disorder is strongly suspected on clinical grounds but laboratory tests are normal or equivocal. Conversely, it may be difficult to disprove the diagnosis of Cushing's syndrome when laboratory tests are abnormal but clinical suspicion is low. The classic low-dose dexamethasone suppression test described by Liddle et al. (1960) will usually resolve this question, though rare patients with Cushing's syndrome show a normal response. The low-dose Liddle test consists of 24-hour urine 17-OHCS measurements daily for 2 baseline days, followed by 2 days with the patient taking dexamethasone 0.5 mg orally every 6 hours. Normal subjects show a fall in urinary 17-OHCS levels to less than 4.0 mg/g of creatinine. It may be useful to measure urinary free cortisol during the low-dose dexamethasone suppression test; however, reference ranges are not available.

An alternate approach to measuring urine 17-OHCS during the low-dose dexamethasone suppression test, though less well established, is to measure the plasma cortisol level at 1600 h on day 2 of low-dose dexamethasone administration; a normal response is suppression of plasma cortisol levels to less than 2 µg/dL.

Diagnostic: Establishing Etiology of Hypercortisolism

Differential Diagnosis

Once the diagnosis of Cushing's syndrome has been confirmed (elevated 24-hour urine free cortisol excretion, abnormal overnight 1-mg dexamethasone suppression test, or both), additional studies are needed to establish the etiology.

Diagnostic Options

Because treatment of Cushing's syndrome usually involves a major surgical procedure, it is important to have a high degree of certainty regarding the etiology. This requires a comprehensive study of each patient, because no single test can be relied on in all cases. Unless all the initial data strongly suggest a cause, it is advisable to proceed with confirmatory testing.

The classic approach to the differential diagnosis of Cushing's syndrome begins with biochemical testing (Table 9–6–2A) and is supplemented by anatomic tests (Table 9–6–2B). The low-dose dexamethasone suppression test (0.5 mg q6h) may be deleted from this scheme if the diagnosis of Cushing's syndrome is clear-cut, but this test provides a final chance to substantiate the diagnosis.

The pattern of biochemical test results generally indicates the source of Cushing's syndrome. Plasma ACTH levels are low in Cushing's syndrome due to adrenal tumors, markedly elevated in Cushing's syndrome due to ectopic production of ACTH, and slightly increased or "normal" (inappropriately high for the elevated level of cortisol) in Cushing's syndrome of pituitary origin. Suppression of urinary 17-hydroxycorticosteroids of at least 64% of baseline and urinary free cortisol of at least 90% of baseline with the high-dose dexamethasone suppression test is 100% specific for an ACTH-secreting pituitary tumor (Cushing's disease); lesser degrees of suppression are compatible with Cushing's disease but may also be seen with ectopic secretion of ACTH. Stimulation studies with metyrapone or CRH usually elicit a response in patients with Cushing's syndrome of pituitary origin but not in patients with other forms. Anomalous results occur in the presence of episodic or cyclic glucocorticoid excess or if the metabolic clearance of dexamethasone is accelerated or prolonged.

Recommended Approach

The classic scheme for differential diagnosis of Cushing's syndrome requires a lengthy hospitalization. It is possible to arrive at an appropri-

TABLE 9–6–2. COMPLETE LABORATORY EVALUATION FOR CUSHING'S SYNDROME

A. Biochemical parameters

Day	Tests	Conditions
1	24-h urine 17-OHCS and free cortisol 0800 Plasma cortisol and ACTH 2200 Plasma cortisol and ACTH	Baseline
2	24-h urine 17-OHCS and free cortisol	Baseline
3	24-h urine 17-OHCS and free cortisol	Dexamethasone 0.5 mg PO q6h × 8 doses, begin at 0600 on day 3
4	24-h urine 17-OHCS and free cortisol 2200 Plasma cortisol and ACTH	
5	24-h urine 17-OHCS and free cortisol	Dexamethasone 2.0 mg PO q6h × 8 doses, begin at 0600 on day 5
6	24-h urine 17-OHCS and free cortisol 2200 Plasma cortisol and ACTH	
7	24-h urine 17-OHCS	Metyrapone 750 mg PO q4h × 6 doses, begin at 0600 on day 7
8	24-h urine 17-OHCS	

B. Anatomic Tests

Computed tomography of the adrenal glands (all patients)

Magnetic resonance imaging of the pituitary

Chest x-ray or computed tomography

C. Supplementary Studies

Simultaneous adrenal vein sampling for cortisol measurement

Selective venous sampling for ACTH measurement
  Central versus peripheral to determine ectopic versus pituitary source
  Petrosal sinus samples for lateralization of pituitary source
    (with or without corticotropin-releasing hormone stimulation)

ACTH, adrenocorticotropic hormone; 17-OHCS, 17-hydroxycorticosteroids.

ate diagnosis in most patients with a simpler, outpatient approach (Figure 9–6–1). Plasma ACTH measurement identifies patients whose Cushing's syndrome is ACTH dependent (pituitary tumor or ectopic ACTH secretion) or ACTH independent (adrenal tumor). Computed tomographic adrenal imaging will confirm an adrenal tumor in ACTH-independent cases and will show bilateral adrenal enlargement (or no definite adrenal abnormality) in ACTH-dependent cases. To differentiate between a pituitary source and ectopic ACTH secretion, an 8-mg overnight dexamethasone suppression test can be used in place of the 2-day high-dose dexamethasone suppression test; suppression of plasma cortisol to below 10 μg/dL indicates a pituitary source, whereas failure of plasma cortisol to fall below 10 mg/dL indicates ectopic ACTH. The CRH stimulation test may be a satisfactory substitute for the 8-mg overnight dexamethasone suppression test; patients with (pituitary) Cushing's disease show exaggerated increases in plasma ACTH and cortisol levels after CRH, whereas patients with ectopic ACTH secretion show no change in plasma cortisol or ACTH levels.

Radiographic studies of the adrenal glands should be done in all patients with biochemically confirmed Cushing's syndrome. Adrenal tumors that cause Cushing's syndrome are usually large enough to be seen by computed tomography, but asymmetric adrenal hyperplasia may give the appearance of tumor. Computed tomography or magnetic resonance imaging of the pituitary should be performed only if Cushing's syndrome of pituitary origin is suggested by biochemical data; pituitary tumors that cause Cushing's syndrome are usually small, often less than 5 mm in diameter, and can be demonstrated radiographically only in approximately 50% of cases. Routine chest x-rays should be done in all patients, with computed tomography scans of the chest performed in patients suspected of having ectopic ACTH secretion.

Other useful diagnostic tests (Table 9–6–2C) when the differential diagnosis is in question include selective adrenal vein catheterization, to demonstrate a cortisol gradient from the side of the adrenal tumor, and iodocholesterol scanning, to identify hyperfunctioning adrenal tissue.

Selective venous sampling for ACTH measurement is useful to distinguish an ectopic from a pituitary source of ACTH production and, if pituitary ACTH excess is present, to identify the side of the tumor. The latter is done by bilateral simultaneous catheterization of the inferior petrosal venous sinuses, which drain blood from the pituitary gland. ACTH gradients from pituitary tumors become even more pronounced after CRH stimulation. Some experts believe that petrosal sinus sampling for ACTH levels should be done in all patients with ACTH-dependent Cushing's syndrome to distinguish patients who have occult ectopic ACTH secretion from those with ACTH-secreting pituitary tumors. This test requires an invasive radiologist with considerable expertise, is expensive, and may be complicated by permanent neurologic sequelae. It should be done in patients with ACTH-dependent Cushing's syndrome who fail to show diagnostic responses to high-dose dexamethasone suppression and who do not have a pituitary tumor detected with magnetic resonance imaging.

Therapeutic

Therapeutic Options

Ideal treatment for Cushing's syndrome would (1) correct the hypercortisolism by eliminating the underlying cause, (2) preserve other endocrine function, and (3) restore normal function of the hypothalamic–pituitary–adrenal axis. These goals are often not fully met by current modalities, which for Cushing's syndrome of pituitary origin (Cushing's disease) include pituitary surgery, bilateral adrenalectomy, pituitary irradiation, drugs that reduce pituitary ACTH release, and drugs that inhibit adrenal hormone synthesis.

Recommended Approach

Currently, transsphenoidal pituitary surgery by an experienced neurosurgeon is the treatment of choice for most patients with Cushing's syndrome of pituitary origin. A few patients with Cushing's syndrome have pituitary macroadenomas (greater than 1 cm in diameter); cure rates for these patients are not as good as results for those in whom a pituitary microadenoma (less than 1 cm in diameter) can be identified and selectively removed, resulting in a cure in approximately 85% of cases.

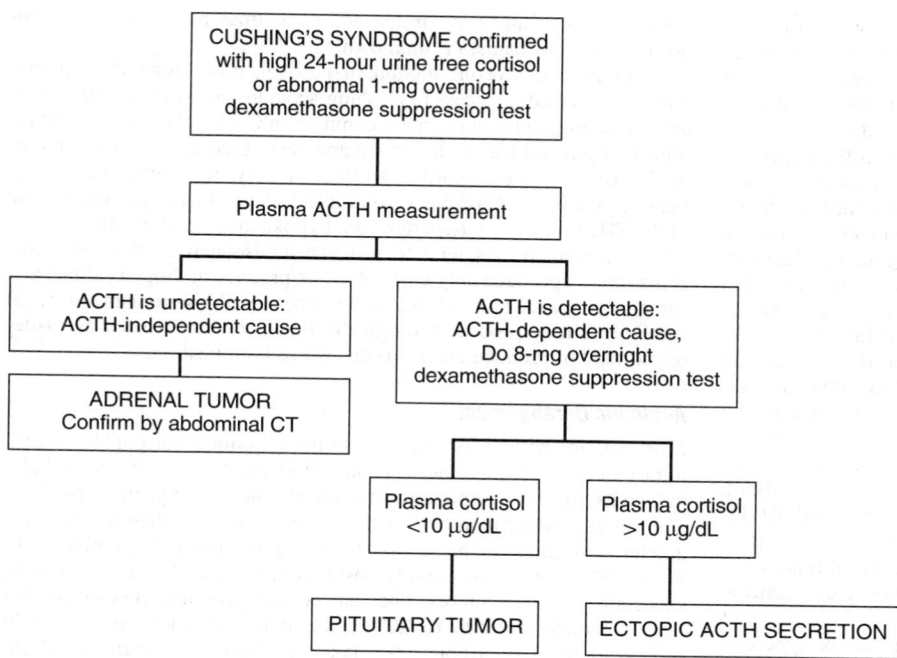

Figure 9–6–1. Outpatient evaluation for Cushing's syndrome. Patients whose results do not fit clearly within these categories should have the classic inpatient evaluation (Table 9–6–2). ACTH, adrenocorticotropic hormone; CT, computed tomography.

If preoperative petrosal sinus ACTH samples have shown a gradient of ACTH from one side and a tumor cannot be seen at surgery, a hemihypophysectomy may be done. If a microadenoma still cannot be found, subtotal hypophysectomy is advisable and usually corrects the hypercortisolism, but at the expense of hypopituitarism and the need for lifelong hormone replacement therapy. As the prolonged hypercortisolism of Cushing's disease suppresses the normal hypothalamic–pituitary–adrenal axis, glucocorticoid coverage is required during surgery and often for several months after selective tumor removal; in some patients, glucocorticoid treatment must be continued lifelong. Pituitary function is usually preserved when selective tumor removal is done. Morbidity (less than 10%) and mortality (less than 1%) are acceptably low.

Medical treatment is not usually recommended as primary therapy for Cushing's syndrome, but may be useful when surgical treatment has failed or is contraindicated, or as an adjunct to other forms of treatment (given preoperatively to improve the patient's state for surgery, or combined with pituitary irradiation to hasten clinical improvement). There are three main classes of drugs to consider: (1) drugs that act on the pituitary or hypothalamus (cyproheptadine), (2) adrenolytic agents (mitotane, also known as o,p'-DDD), and (3) blockers of adrenal steroid synthesis (metyrapone, aminoglutethimide, ketoconazole, and others). Cyproheptadine, a serotonin antagonist, has been reported to correct the abnormalites of Cushing's syndrome in a few patients with Cushing's syndrome of pituitary origin, presumably by reducing a stimulatory effect on the pituitary; response to cyproheptadine suggests that some cases of "pituitary" Cushing's are due to a hypothalamic disorder rather than a primary defect in the pituitary. Most patients with Cushing's syndrome of pituitary origin do not respond to this agent, however, and those who do respond often have side effects including severe lethargy or excessive appetite. The use of mitotane and the inhibitors of adrenal hormone synthesis is limited by toxic side effects, with the exception of ketoconazole, which is sometimes effective and generally well tolerated.

Conventional irradiation to the pituitary (4500–5000 rad) is effective in correcting hypercortisolism in 20 to 40% of patients with Cushing's syndrome of pituitary origin and causes some improvement in another 40%. Irradiation, however, may lead to deficiencies of other pituitary hormones and, rarely, to optic nerve damage, brain necrosis, or cranial neoplasms. Clinical improvement after pituitary irradiation may not be apparent for 1 to 2 years after treatment. Proton beam irradiation is limited to two centers in the United States because it requires specialized equipment; it gives a higher percentage of "cures" than conventional

radiation, up to 90 to 95%, and has a more rapid onset of effect, but results in a higher frequency of hypopituitarism. Proton beam irradiation cannot be used for tumors with extrasellar extension.

Bilateral total adrenalectomy is a more traumatic operation than transsphenoidal pituitary surgery and is frequently complicated by wound infections, poor healing, and thromboembolic events. Morbidity occurs in 15 to 20% of patients; mortality from adrenalectomy is probably less than 5%. Although adrenalectomy corrects the hypercortisolism of Cushing's syndrome of pituitary origin (unless an extraadrenal remnant is left behind), patients so treated are dependent on lifelong glucocorticoid and mineralocorticoid replacement therapy. Also, up to 30% of patients treated by adrenalectomy develop Nelson's syndrome, hyperpigmentation caused by an aggressive ACTH-secreting tumor that does not respond well to any treatment. The hyperpigmentation of Nelson's syndrome is the result of melanocyte-stimulating hormone-like effects of the high level of ACTH.

The treatment of choice for Cushing's syndrome caused by an adrenal tumor is surgical removal of the tumor. The contralateral adrenal gland should eventually regain normal function, though glucocorticoid treatment may be needed for 6 to 12 months, until the hypothalamic–pituitary–adrenal axis has recovered. For adrenal carcinoma with metastases, debulking the tumor mass with surgery is advisable. The adrenolytic agent mitotane (o,p'-DDD) usually reduces cortisol production and helps control the signs and symptoms of Cushing's syndrome; it may also cause some reduction in tumor size and, in a few cases, apparent "cures." Radiation and other cancer chemotherapeutic drugs have not proved effective, in part because adrenal cancer cells often express the multiple drug resistance gene, which pumps chemotherapy drugs out of the cells. Mitotane (and some other drugs) block this pump; preliminary experience using mitotane and combination chemotherapy is encouraging.

In Cushing's syndrome caused by ectopic production of ACTH, treatment should be directed at the underlying tumor. If signs or symptoms of hypercortisolism are severe, ketoconazole or another inhibitor of adrenal hormone synthesis can be useful.

FOLLOW-UP

The patient should be told the nature of the disease and the expected natural history without treatment. As none of the current options for Cushing's syndrome is ideal, the patient should be involved in selecting treatment, with the risks and benefits of all forms of treatment explained. The patient should be told of the likelihood of temporary glucocorticoid dependency and the possibility that glucocorticoid dependency may be permanent. If maintenance glucocorticoid therapy is required, the patient should be advised to increase the dose in stressful situations and to carry identification indicating glucocorticoid dependence. See Chapter 9–11 for guidelines on replacement therapy.

After treatment, the patient should be retested to see if the hypercortisolism has been corrected. Most patients require glucocorticoid replacement immediately and for several months after pituitary or adrenal surgery. For purposes of testing, glucocorticoid treatment should be changed temporarily to dexamethasone, a potent, long-acting glucocorticoid that does not interfere with cortisol determinations. It is useful to measure 24-hour urine free cortisol excretion as well as to perform a 1-mg overnight dexamethasone suppression test in the first few weeks after surgery. Patients receiving maintenance glucocorticoid treatment should be studied periodically to determine if normal hypothalamic–pituitary–adrenal function has been restored. This is done by measuring a morning plasma cortisol level 24 hours after the last hydrocortisone dose; a value less than 10 μg/dL indicates continued suppression of the hypothalamic–pituitary–adrenal axis; a level greater than 10 μg/dL shows some recovery of function. Additional testing (rapid ACTH stimulation test, insulin tolerance test, or metyrapone test) would be necessary to determine if recovery has been complete. Until function of the hypothalamic–pituitary–adrenal axis is restored, glucocorticoid therapy with hydrocortisone should be continued.

Additional monitoring should include any consequences of hypercortisolism that were present prior to treatment, such as hypertension, osteoporosis, and diabetes. The patient should also be tested for any adverse effects of treatment, such as hypopituitarism following pituitary surgery or irradiation. Patients with Cushing's syndrome of pituitary origin must be tested periodically with computed tomography or magnetic resonance imaging and visual field determinations for persistence or recurrence of their pituitary tumor.

DISCUSSION

Prevalence and Incidence

The prevalence of Cushing's syndrome is approximately 40 cases per million and the incidence is between 1 and 2 cases per million population. Cushing's syndrome of pituitary origin affects females nine times more commonly than males and may occur at any age, but is unusual in children. Ectopic ACTH syndrome affects males ten times more often than females. Cortisol-producing adrenal tumors do not show a sexual predominance. Adrenal carcinoma is most common in the fourth and fifth decades.

Related Basic Science

Physiologic or Metabolic Derangement

Normally, secretion of ACTH and cortisol is cyclic; there is a diurnal rhythm, with highest levels in the morning and low values in the evening and at night. Regardless of etiology, patients with all forms of Cushing's syndrome show a sustained increase in cortisol. In most patients with Cushing's syndrome, the normal diurnal rhythm is lost. Simply maintaining the morning level of cortisol throughout the night will lead to the clinical manifestations of Cushing's syndrome, which include decreased protein synthesis, nitrogen wasting, glucose intolerance (sometimes with fasting hyperglycemia), and changes in mineral metabolism (sodium retention and wasting of potassium and calcium). Although lean body mass is often reduced because of the decrease in protein synthesis, obesity occurs as a result of increased food intake and decreased turnover of fatty acids. Osteoporosis results from increased bone resorption and decreased bone formation. Vertebral compression fractures may occur and cause chronic back pain; the resulting spinal deformities may contribute to the overall appearance of central obesity. Muscle weakness results from diminished muscle protein synthesis as well as from hypokalemia. Thromboembolic disorders are seen as a result of increases in clotting factors II, V, and VIII. Compromise of the immune system can predispose to opportunistic infections. Secretion of luteinizing hormone is inhibited by excessive cortisol, resulting in menstrual irregularities in females and diminished libido and infertility in males. Emotional disturbances, particularly depression, are

common in Cushing's syndrome and sometimes reach psychotic proportions; the mechanism is unknown.

In addition to overproduction of cortisol, other adrenal hormones may be produced in excess in Cushing's syndrome. Modest increases in adrenal androgen production are common in Cushing's syndrome of pituitary origin and lead to hirsutism and acne. Increases in mineralocorticoids or the mineralocorticoid effect of very high levels of cortisol may be striking in Cushing's syndrome because of ectopic production of ACTH and result in hypertension, hypokalemia, and metabolic alkalosis. Adrenal tumors tend to produce an isolated class of steroids; some tumors produce only cortisol, some produce androgens alone, and some secrete only mineralocorticoids (primary aldosteronism). Adrenal carcinomas may produce biologically inactive steroids such as 11-deoxycortisol or produce estrogens and cause feminization.

Anatomic Derangement

Most patients with "Cushing's syndrome of pituitary origin" have a pituitary tumor; although there is some evidence to suggest a hypothalamic cause for these tumors, most evidence supports a primary pituitary abnormality. More than half of these tumors are less than 5 mm in diameter, too small to be demonstrated by current radiographic techniques. The tumors are usually basophilic, but may be chromophobic, especially the large tumors. The cells contain proopiomelanocortin, the large precursor molecule to ACTH, which also includes the amino acid sequences for β-lipotropin, α-melanocyte-stimulating hormone, β-endorphin, and met-enkephalin. Immunoperoxidase staining of these tumors is almost always positive for ACTH, with variable presence of other proopiomelanocortin-derived hormones. ACTH secretion from these tumors is resistant to the inhibitory effect of normal glucocorticoid levels, but usually can be suppressed by high doses of glucocorticoids. The ACTH response to an intravenous injection of CRH is exaggerated. Up to 10% of pituitary tumors causing Cushing's syndrome are large enough to exert some mass effect, including compromise of visual fields, involvement of cranial nerves, and hypopituitarism.

The adrenal glands of patients with Cushing's syndrome of pituitary origin usually show bilateral diffuse hyperplasia. In some cases, however, the adrenal hyperplasia is nodular. In these patients, it appears that excessive ACTH production from the pituitary initiates nodular hyperplasia of the adrenal glands, which then become autonomous, and may continue to cause hypercortisolism despite removal of the pituitary ACTH source.

Malignant tumors that produce ACTH are usually clinically obvious. The most common malignant tumors associated with ectopic ACTH secretion are small cell carcinoma of the lung, thymoma, carcinoid tumors, and medullary thyroid carcinoma. Patients with ectopic ACTH secretion by malignancies often lack the obesity and striae typical of other forms of Cushing's syndrome and present instead with weight loss, severe hypertension, hypokalemia, myopathy, diabetes, and hyperpigmentation. Their course is often rapidly fatal. Benign tumors (e.g., bronchial carcinoid) that cause ectopic ACTH syndrome may mimic Cushing's syndrome of pituitary origin on clinical grounds and must be differentiated on the basis of biochemical criteria (Figure 9–6–1) or selective venous sampling for ACTH determination.

Natural History and Its Modification with Treatment

The onset and progression of Cushing's syndrome can be gradual or fulminant. Mortality from untreated Cushing's syndrome of pituitary origin approaches 50% at 5 years. Morbidity and mortality result from diabetes and hypertension-associated vascular complications, osteoporosis with compression fractures, infection, thromboembolic phenomena, and emotional disturbances. Effective treatment reduces morbidity and mortality.

Prevention

No preventive measures are available; more research is needed in this area.

Cost Containment

Appropriate use of diagnostic tests is essential for cost containment. Once the presence of hypercortisolism has been confirmed by an elevated 24-hour urinary free cortisol excretion or abnormal 1-mg overnight dexamethasone suppression test, the patient should be referred to a medical center experienced in the diagnosis and treatment of Cushing's syndrome for further evaluation. It is generally advisable to have the evaluation performed at the institution where the surgery is to be done. A piecemeal approach to the differential diagnosis is rarely satisfactory and should be discouraged to avoid repetition in testing.

REFERENCES

Extabe J, Vasquez JA. Morbidity and mortality in Cushing's disease: An epidemiologic approach. Clin Endocrinol 1994;40:479.

Flack MR, Oldfield EH, Cutler GB Jr, et al. Urine free cortisol in the high-dose dexamethasone suppression test for the differential diagnosis of Cushing syndrome. Ann Intern Med 1992;116:211.

Kaye TB, Crapo L. The Cushing syndrome: An update on diagnostic tests. Ann Intern Med 1990;112:434.

Liddle GW. Tests of pituitary-adrenal suppressibility in the diagnosis of Cushing's syndrome. J Clin Endocrinol Metab 1960;20:1539.

Oldfield EH, Doppman JL, Nieman LK, et al. Petrosal sinus sampling with and without corticotropin-releasing hormone for the differential diagnosis of Cushing's syndrome. N Engl J Med 1991;325:897.

Tindall GT, Herring CJ, Clark RV, et al. Cushing's disease: Results of transsphenoidal microsurgery with emphasis on surgical failures. J Neurosurg 1990;72:363.

CHAPTER 9–7

Glucocorticoid Therapy Complications

Victoria C. Musey, M.D.

DEFINITION

Glucocorticoid therapy complications are clinical problems that develop as a result of treatment with glucocorticoid preparations (cortisone, prednisone, prednisolone, and dexamethasone) for medical conditions such as collagen–vascular disorders, bronchial asthma, blood dyscrasias, and graft-versus-host rejection following organ or tissue transplant. The complications are those of Cushing's syndrome (cushingoid features, muscle weakness and atrophy, osteoporosis, inhibition of skeletal growth rate, increased susceptibility to infection, impaired wound healing, psychiatric disorders, and papilledema) and suppression of function of the hypothalamic–pituitary–adrenal axis.

ETIOLOGY

The complications result from high-dose and prolonged treatment with glucocorticoids.

CRITERIA FOR DIAGNOSIS

Suggestive

A history of long-term treatment with glucocorticoids is indicative of the diagnosis.

Definitive

The presence of cushingoid features together with a history of long-term treatment with glucocorticoids is enough to establish the diagnosis of exogenous Cushing's syndrome.

CLINICAL MANIFESTATIONS

Subjective

Patients may complain of one or more of the following: weight gain, increased appetite, epigastic distress, insomnia, easy bruisability, and, occasionally, polyuria, polydipsia, difficulty in climbing stairs or rising from a chair, and decreasing vision. There may be a history of frequent bacterial and fungal infections and delayed wound healing. Parents of a child treated with glucocorticoids may note that the child is gaining weight rapidly but is not growing in height. There may be a history of pain in the hips, knees, and shoulders, back pain with or without trauma, and vertebral or rib fractures.

For several weeks or months following discontinuation of glucocorticoid therapy, patients may complain of a decreased sense of well-being, weakness, fatigue, nausea, depression, postural hypotension, and arthralgias.

Objective

Physical Examination

The physical findings may be any or all of those that occur with Cushing's syndrome. These include central obesity involving the face, neck, trunk, and abdomen; rounding of the face, resulting in the characteristic "moon face"; prominent fat pads in the supraclavicular and dorsocervical areas; and purplish striae in the abdominal, buttock, and thigh areas. There may be boils and furuncles of the skin, fungal infections of the nailbeds and vagina, decreased visual acuity due to a cataract, and evidence of proximal muscle weakness and wasting of the lower extremities.

Patients seen during the first 3 to 6 months following discontinuation of prolonged glucocorticoid therapy may have postural hypotension.

Routine Laboratory Abnormalities

The findings in routine blood counts, biochemical profiles, electrolytes, and urinalysis are similar to those of Cushing's syndrome.

PLANS

Diagnostic

Differential Diagnosis

Endogenous hypercortisolism due to pituitary tumor, adrenal tumor, and ectopic adrenocorticotropic hormone (ACTH) secretion must be considered in all patients with Cushing's syndrome; however, a history of high-dose prolonged glucocorticoid therapy in a patient with cushingoid features who does not have hirsutism, acne, and menstrual disorders helps to differentiate between endogenous and exogenous causes of Cushing's syndrome.

Usually there is little difficulty in determining whether glucocorticoid therapy is responsible for a given problem. A differential diagnosis for each complication must, however, be considered to rule out other causes or contributing factors.

Glucose intolerance occurs frequently during the period of glucocorticoid therapy. In patients with familial predisposition to diabetes, frank diabetes mellitus occurs and persists after glucocorticocoid therapy is stopped.

Proximal muscle wasting and weakness in the extremities may occur as a complication of glucocorticoid therapy, but may also occur as a result of muscle disease, endocrine disorder (hyperthyroidism, hyperparathyroidism), and metabolic disorders.

Osteoporosis is one of the complications of glucocorticoid therapy. It may also occur as a complication of primary hyperparathyroidism, hyperthyroidism, hypogonadism (estrogen and testosterone deficiency), hyperprolactinemia, and alcoholism.

Osteonecrosis may develop with glucocorticoid therapy and the humeral and femoral heads are most commonly involved. Other causes include trauma, hemoglobinopathies (e.g., sickle cell disease), and collagen–vascular disorders.

Glucocorticoid therapy inhibits skeletal growth rate in children, but the role of the underlying medical condition for which steroids are being used and/or malnutrition must be considered.

Increased susceptibility to infection is one of the feared complications of chronic glucocorticoid therapy. Although any type of infection may occur, those involving fungal and Gram-negative organisms are common and usually involve the skin and genitourinary tract. Reactivation of tuberculosis does not seem to occur with increased frequency in such patients.

Essential hypertension must be considered in a patient who develops hypertension during glucocorticoid therapy. Hypertension due solely to glucocorticoid therapy is usually reversible with discontinuation of therapy, but in some patients it persists, more likely representing latent essential hypertension that has been brought out by the steroid therapy.

Mental and emotional disorders are known to be associated with glucocorticoid therapy, but other reasons for these problems such as chronic illness and genetic or environmental predispositions to emotional disorders may play a role.

Papilledema may occur with glucocorticoid therapy as a result of elevated intracranial pressure (pseudotumor cerebri). Other causes of increased intracranial pressure include intracranial lesions (e.g., tumors, encephalitis, aneurysms), systemic arterial hypertension, acute glaucoma, orbital tumors, and medications such as oral contraceptives, tetracycline, nalidixic acid, and danazol.

Long-term glucocorticoid therapy can cause the development of a cataract on the posterior capsule of the lens (posterior subcapsular cataract). This type of cataract can also occur with diabetes mellitus and trauma to the eye.

Complications related to discontinuation of glucocorticoid therapy include the steroid withdrawal syndrome and suppression of the hypothalamic–pituitary–adrenal axis. The steroid withdrawal syndrome usually develops when the glucocorticoid dose is being reduced. Presenting symptoms are suggestive of adrenocortical insufficiency even though patients may be receiving supraphysiologic or physiologic doses of glucocorticoids.

Persistent suppression of the hypothalamic–pituitary–adrenal axis may last as long as 18 months. This constitutes secondary adrenal insufficiency.

Diagnostic Options

Diagnostic options are those for Cushing's syndrome and include plasma and urinary steroid levels to document elevated levels of cortisol. Other diagnostic options depend on the specific complication that has developed.

Evaluation of the integrity of the hypothalamic–pituitary–adrenal axis can be performed with ACTH, metyrapone, and insulin-induced hypoglycemia as discussed in Chapter 9–11.

Recommended Approach

Plasma and urinary steroid levels vary according to the glucocorticoid being used and, as a general rule, are not obtained while patients are taking glucocorticoids.

The rapid ACTH stimulation test is used to document persistent suppression of the hypothalamic–pituitary–adrenal axis. A subnormal response is indicative of persistent suppression of the axis; however, a normal response is not necessarily predictive of normal responsiveness of the axis during stress. Suppression of hypothalamic–pituitary–adrenal function is suspected in any patient who has been on pharmacologic doses of glucocorticoids for more than 3 weeks, and is assumed to be present in any patient with clinical features of Cushing's syndrome. Assessment of the axis is not necessary unless (1) glucocorticoid dosage has been reduced to physiologic levels for more than 2 months and complete withdrawal is contemplated; or (2) glucocorticoid therapy has been discontinued for several months and recovery of the axis is

being evaluated. The decision to withdraw physiologic doses of glucocorticoid can be made with a normal early morning plasma cortisol level drawn 24 hours after the last dose of hydrocortisone. Persistent suppression of the axis after patients have been off of a maintenance dose of hydrocortisone for more than 2 months can be determined with the rapid ACTH stimulation test.

Therapeutic

Therapeutic Options

Treatment of steroid complications depends on the particular problems involved. Most of the complications are reversible with discontinuation of the glucocorticoid, although the time for reversal may be a few days to several months. Therefore, in the management of patients with serious complications of glucocorticoid therapy, consideration should be given to discontinuation of the glucocorticoid or to alteration in dose and schedule of administration if this is permitted by the underlying medical condition for which the drug is being used.

Patients with suppression of the hypothalamic–pituitary–adrenal axis function should be treated as having secondary adrenal insufficiency (as discussed in Chapter 9–11).

Recommended Approach

In patients who have been on long-term glucocorticoid therapy, any attempt to discontinue glucocorticoids should be gradual by reducing the dose (e.g., 2.5- to 5-mg decrements in prednisone per week) toward physiologic levels over several weeks to avoid exacerbation of the primary medical condition and steroid withdrawal symptoms. If steroid withdrawal symptoms occur and are severe and persistent, reinstitution of glucocorticoid therapy in low doses or an increase in glucocorticoid dose to the former dosage level will provide relief of symptoms. Tapering of dosage can then proceed with much lower decrements.

Following discontinuation of glucocorticoid therapy, it may take several months for recovery of normal hypothalamic–pituitary–adrenal function. Thus, stress doses of glucocorticoids (see Chapter 9–11) should be given during periods of stress such as medical illness, surgery, and invasive procedures until it has been ascertained that normal pituitary–adrenal function has been reestablished.

FOLLOW-UP

The patient is followed at periodic intervals, the frequency of which is determined by the complication being treated and the anticipated period of recovery of normal pituitary–adrenal function.

DISCUSSION

Prevalence and Incidence

Iatrogenic Cushing's syndrome is the most common cause of Cushing's syndrome. Compared with endogenous Cushing's syndrome, osteonecrosis, benign intracranial hypertension (pseudotumor cerebri), and posterior subcapsular cataracts occur more frequently with glucocorticoid therapy. It is difficult to determine the incidence of the different complications, as not all cases are reported, but it appears that osteonecrosis occurs more commonly with glucocorticoid therapy than with any other condition, accounting for about 50% of all cases. Steroid-induced osteoporosis is the most common cause of secondary osteoporosis. About 25% of patients treated with glucocorticoids develop an increased intraocular pressure.

Related Basic Science

The complications of glucocorticoid therapy can best be understood by considering the effects of excess cortisol on various organ systems of the body. Physiologic amounts of cortisol are necessary for the proper function of certain life-supporting systems, but supraphysiologic levels over long periods cause undesirable, though predictable, effects on these and other body systems. This is true of all glucocorticoids, whether natural (cortisol, cortisone) or synthetic (prednisone, prednisolone, dexamethasone, etc.); all glucocorticoids, given in equivalent antiinflammatory doses, have the potential to produce the same undesirable effects. The dosage associated with these complications is generally greater than the equivalent of 30 mg cortisol per day for several weeks or longer.

When cortisol is given to a human subject who is on a maintenance diet, the result is increased body fat and change in the distribution of fat, but no increased body weight. Increased body weight occurs only if patients are allowed to eat ad libitum according to their appetites, which are indeed increased by cortisol excess. The increased body fat is probably the consequence of increased insulin secretion resulting from cortisol-induced insulin resistance.

Gluconeogenesis and peripheral inhibition of the action of insulin in fat and muscle probably account for the glucose intolerance that occurs during glucocorticoid therapy.

Corticosteroids cause breakdown of proteins to provide amino acids for gluconeogenesis. They also induce changes in the ribosomal and mitochondrial function of the muscles. These and other effects (antianabolic action) are most pronounced in large muscle groups, thus accounting for proximal muscle wasting and weakness.

Probably several effects of glucocorticoids are responsible for the development of osteoporosis. These include the inhibition of collagen synthesis and, thus, of protein matrix formation; a decrease in bone formation; mobilization of calcium from the skeleton with excessive calcium excretion in the urine; and decreased gut absorption of calcium.

Osteonecrosis occurs in some patients and is probably a variant manifestation of the effects of glucocorticoids on bone metabolism. It usually involves the femoral and humeral heads of bone. Osteonecrosis can occur even in patients who do not have symptoms of bone loss.

Delay of skeletal and general body maturation is explained on the basis of corticosteroid-induced protein catabolism, inhibition of collagen formation, inhibition of growth hormone secretion, and inhibition of the anabolic effects of adrenal and gonadal androgens.

Peptic ulcer disease is thought to be a complication of glucocorticoid therapy, but recent studies have not supported this belief. On the other hand, it is likely that corticosteroids, by virtue of their general proteolytic effect and ability to inhibit collagen formation, can cause breakdown or retard the healing of a previously existing ulcer and, in this way, may lead to the complication of perforation or hemorrhage.

Increased susceptibility to infection is due to the suppressive effect of excess glucocorticoids on the immunologic and inflammatory responses of the body, reactions that are necessary for controlling and warding off infections.

Impaired wound healing is related to the inhibitory effect of excessive glucocorticoid on collagen formation. The same effect also accounts for epidermal thinning, striae, and ecchymoses.

The exact mechanism for the development of hypertension during glucocorticoid administration is not known, but several theories have been proposed. These include sodium retention, increased plasma volume as a result of a shift of fluid from the intracellular compartment to the extracellular compartment, increased synthesis of angiotensinogen (which can raise angiotensin levels), and enhanced vascular responsiveness to catecholamines. The incidence of hypertension is not as high in patients receiving synthetic analogs of cortisol, probably because the analogs have less mineralocorticoid activity than cortisol. The difference in the incidence rates of hypertension between patients treated with glucorticoids and those with endogenous glucocorticoids has led some to pose that the hypertensive effects of the adrenal steroid hormones may not be related to the known classic effects of glucocorticoid and mineralocorticoid hormones.

Glucocorticoids affect certain cerebral enzyme systems, but it is not known how these systems relate to mental and emotional disorders associated with steroid therapy.

Although the mechanism of the steroid withdrawal syndrome is not known, it does not appear to be due to suppression of the hypothalamic–pituitary–adrenal axis, as the syndrome may develop in patients with documented normal function of the axis. As symptoms also develop during the period of reduction in glucocorticoid dosage, it is possible that the change from a high to a low dose of glucocorticoid is responsible.

Exogenous glucocorticoids like endogenous glucocorticoids exert a negative feedback effect on the hypothalamic–pituitary–adrenal axis to suppress hypothalamic production of corticotropin-releasing hormone and pituitary ACTH secretion. Lack of ACTH effect on the adrenal glands results in atrophy of adrenocortical tissue and loss of cortisol secretion. The degree of suppression of the axis depends on the dose and duration of glucocorticoid use. Administration of pharmacologic doses of glucocorticoids for more than 3 weeks is enough to suppress hypothalamic–pituitary–adrenal function.

Natural History and Its Modification with Treatment

The natural history depends on the particular complication, the feasibility of stopping the corticosteroid, and the reversibility of the complication after the steroid is discontinued. Fortunately, most of the complications, with the exception of osteoporotic fractures and osteonecrosis, are reversible after the steroid is stopped. Thus, within hours to days of discontinuation of glucocorticoid therapy, the metabolic and immunosuppressive effects reverse. The other manifestations of glucocorticoid excess, such as cushingoid appearance, fat distribution, and skin changes, take weeks to months to disappear.

Recovery of hypothalamic–pituitary–adrenal function may take several months, with recovery of corticotropin secretion preceding that of ACTH secretion, which also precedes recovery of cortisol secretion.

Prevention

None of the complications can be effectively prevented by any known therapeutic measure in a patient who requires high doses of glucocorticoid for a long period.* The incidence, frequency, and severity of complications may be reduced by giving the glucocorticoid as a single dose every other day if the underlying disease process permits this alteration. Symptoms of adrenal insufficiency can be prevented by slow withdrawal rather than abrupt withdrawal from long-term glucocorticoid therapy.

Cost Containment

Cost containment varies according to the particular complication involved and the time needed for follow-up during and after glucocorticoid withdrawal. Most laboratory tests can be kept to a minimum during this period.

REFERENCES

Axelrod L. Glucocorticoid therapy. Medicine 1976;55:39.

Bynny RL. Withdrawal from glucocorticoid therapy. N Engl J Med 1976;295:30.

Graber AL, Ney RL, Nicholson WE, et al. Natural history of pituitary adrenal recovery following long-term suppression with corticosteroids. J Clin Endocrinol Metab 1965;25:11.

Krakoff LR. Glucocorticoid excess syndromes causing hypertension. Cardiol Clin 1988;6(4):537.

Lukert BP, Raisz LG. Glucocorticoid-induced osteoporosis: Pathogenesis and management. Ann Intern Med 1990;112:352.

---

*Steroid-induced bone loss may be reduced or eliminated by increasing calcium intake, supplementing vitamin D, and adding sex steroids or bisphosphonates when appropriate.

Congenital Adrenal Hyperplasia

Nelson B. Watts, M.D.

DEFINITION

Congenital adrenal hyperplasia comprises several genetic disorders. In all of these, the production of cortisol (and sometimes other adrenal hormones) is impaired because of a deficiency of one of several enzymes in the synthetic pathways of adrenal hormone synthesis.

ETIOLOGY

These conditions are inherited in an autosomal recessive fashion.

CRITERIA FOR DIAGNOSIS
Suggestive

The clinical settings vary, and include (in different combinations, depending on the defect) abnormal external genitalia in newborns of both sexes (with females sometimes appearing as males with cryptorchidism); salt-wasting crisis in neonates; rapid early growth but eventual short stature in both sexes; early sexual maturation in males; hirsutism or virilization in females (often beginning in childhood but sometimes presenting at adolescence), and, in the rare varieties, failure to undergo puberty; and hypertension with hypokalemia.

Definitive

The diagnosis in all cases can be made by demonstrating excessive amounts of specific precursor steroids in blood or urine and showing that levels of these compounds can be suppressed by administration of glucocorticoids. In most instances, precursor steroids will be elevated in a basal sample; sometimes, stimulation with adrenocorticotropic hormone (ACTH) is necessary to demonstrate the chemical abnormality.

CLINICAL MANIFESTATIONS

Signs and symptoms of the different varieties of congenital adrenal hyperplasia vary with the specific enzyme that is deficient and with the completeness of the defect. Table 9–8–1 lists the enzyme abnormalities, specific steroid compounds that are produced in excess, and classes of adrenal hormones that are deficient or excessive.

TABLE 9–8–1. TYPES OF CONGENITAL ADRENAL HYPERPLASIA

Deficient Enzyme	Immediate Precursor	Deficiency	Excess
21-Hydroxylase	17-OH-progesterone	G	A
	Progesterone	M	
11-Hydroxylase M (aldosterone)	11-Deoxycortisol	G	M (DOC) A
3β-Hydroxysteroid dehydrogenase*	Pregnenolone	G	Weak androgens (DHEA)
	17-OH-Pregnenolone	M	
	DHEA	GS	
17-Hydroxylase	Progesterone	G	M (aldosterone)
	Pregnenolone	GS	
	DOC		
20,22-Desmolase*	Cholesterol	G, M, GS	None

A, androgens; G, glucocorticoids; M, mineralocorticoids; GS, gonadal steroids (testosterone and estrogen); DOC, deoxycorticosterone; DHEA, dehydroepiandrosterone.
*Also affects gonads.

Subjective

Symptoms of congenital adrenal hyperplasia include those related to mineralocorticoid deficiency (anorexia, nausea, vomiting, dehydration, circulatory collapse); androgen excess (rapid early growth in both sexes, increased body and facial hair in females and early sexual development in males, infertility in both sexes); and gonadal hormone (testosterone and estrogens) deficiency (failure of puberty to occur). There may be a family history of affected siblings or unexplained neonatal deaths.

Objective
Physical Examination

Abnormal physical findings can be explained by the types of steroid compounds that are deficient or increased and the severity of the enzyme defect.

- *In utero androgen excess:* Female pseudohermaphroditism is the result, with genital abnormalities that range from severe (the appearance of a cryptorchid male), to moderate (labioscrotal fusion, hypospadias, clitoromegaly), to mild (slight clitoral enlargement); there are no manifestations in males.
- *Postnatal androgen excess:* Both males and females show early rapid linear growth; however, excessive androgens lead to premature closure of the ephiphyses and reduced final stature. Males show signs of sexual maturation beginning at age 3 or 4 (pubic hair growth and enlargement of the penis, but the testes remain small). In females, continued androgen excess is manifest by signs of virilization such as increased face and body hair, oily skin, acne, deepening of the voice, and a male body habitus; menses may be irregular.
- *Intrauterine androgen deficiency:* Males show incomplete development of external genital structures, including bifid scrotum, micropenis, and varying degrees of hypospadias; there are no effects in females.
- *Deficient gonadal steroid production* (testosterone and estrogens): The child fails to undergo puberty or develop secondary sex characteristics.
- *Mineralocorticoid deficiency:* Hypotension, dehydration, and shock (salt-wasting crisis) usually manifest in the first few weeks after birth.
- *Mineralocorticoid excess:* Fluid retention and hypertension result.
- *Severe ACTH excess:* The skin and mucous membranes are hyperpigmented.

Routine Laboratory Abnormalities

The results of routine laboratory tests show the effects of excessive mineralocorticoid activity (hypokalemia and metabolic alkalosis, sometimes with mild hypernatremia) or mineralocorticoid deficiency (hyponatremia and hyperkalemia, sometimes with a metabolic acidosis); otherwise, routine laboratory tests are normal.

PLANS
Diagnostic
Differential Diagnosis

Infants with ambiguous genitalia must have a karyotype analysis to rule out sex chromosome abnormalities. Other diagnostic considerations in patients with ambiguous genitalia include intrauterine androgen exposure, partial androgen resistance, 5 α-reductase deficiency, or developmental genital abnormalities such as hypospadias and cryptorchidism. Demonstration of abnormal steroid production establishes the diagnosis of congenital adrenal hyperplasia, though levels may not be diagnostically increased until 2 to 3 weeks after birth.

If increased adrenal androgen levels are found in children or adults, congenital adrenal hyperplasia should be distinguished from hormone-producing adrenal neoplasms by demonstrating a reduction in the elevated hormone levels with glucocorticoid treatment; this often can be accomplished simply by instituting treatment with hydrocortisone (as outlined in Plans, Therapeutic) and repeating the abnormal tests after 3 or 4 weeks, or as a standard low-dose dexamethasone suppression test (see Chapter 9–6).

Neonatal salt-wasting crisis manifests as poor appetite, weight loss, and vomiting, progressing to shock and vascular collapse. This must be differentiated from such conditions as hypertrophic pyloric stenosis, gastroenteritis, and septic shock. Measurement of serum electrolytes and pH is useful, with metabolic acidosis seen in infants with salt-wasting crisis and hypokalemic metabolic alkalosis seen with gastrointestinal disorders.

The presentation of congenital adrenal hyperplasia may be delayed until childhood. Females with virilization must be evaluated for androgen-producing tumors of the ovaries or adrenals; males showing early signs of sexual maturation must be tested for tumors of the central nervous system and other causes of early pubertal development.

In adolescent females, "nonclassic" or "late-onset" congenital hyperplasia must be differentiated from virilizing adrenal or ovarian tumors, idiopathic hirsutism, and polycystic ovary syndrome (see Hirsutism, Chapter 9–26). Measurement of blood levels of testosterone and dehydroepiandrosterone before and after dexamethasone is useful, as are computed tomographic scans of the adrenal glands and ultrasound studies of the ovaries.

Diagnostic Options

Demonstrating abnormal levels of precursor steroids in plasma is the key to establishing the general diagnosis of congenital adrenal hyperplasia and identifying the specific defect.

Recommended Approach

In almost all varieties except 17-hydroxylase deficiency (which is rare), urinary 17-ketosteroid excretion is increased. Elevations of specific precursors of cortisol can be demonstrated in plasma: 17-hydroxyprogesterone in 21-hydroxylase deficiency, 11-deoxycortisol in 11-hydroxylase deficiency, 17-hydroxypregnenolone in 3β-steroid dehydrogenase deficiency. In classic cases, basal concentrations of these steroids are sufficiently elevated to establish the diagnosis. In mild cases or in heterozygotes, it is often necessary to measure the steroids after stimulation with ACTH to show the abnormality. Azziz et al. (1989) suggest that late-onset 21-hydroxylase deficiency should be tested for by measuring basal 17-hydroxyprogesterone concentration; patients with levels greater than 6 mmol/L (200 mg/dL) should have an ACTH stimulation test; a 17-hydroxyprogesterone level greater than 36.3 mmol/L (1200 mg/dL) after ACTH stimulation is diagnostic. New et al. (1983) have developed a useful nomogram for basal and ACTH-stimulated 17-hydroxyprogesterone measurement in 21-hydroxylase deficiency. Other hormone reference values are shown in Table 9–8–2.

Prenatal diagnosis can sometimes be made by hormone measurements in amniotic fluid and, in the case of 21-hydroxylase deficiency, by HLA typing and restriction length fragment polymorphysms from chorionic villi. HLA typing is also useful to identify heterozygote carriers of 21-hydroxylase deficiency. Neonatal screening for congenital adrenal hyperplasia is mandatory in several states.

Therapeutic

Therapeutic Options

Ideal treatment for congenital adrenal hyperplasia would be replacement of the defective gene. Until that treatment is available, glucocorticoid therapy (and treatment with mineralocorticoids and sex steroids, when indicated) will replace the deficient hormones and reduce the excessive secretion of ACTH, reducing the levels of precursor steroids.

TABLE 9–8–2. HORMONAL REFERENCE DATA FOR CONGENITAL ADRENAL HYPERPLASIA*

Compound	Age	Normal Range
Urine		
17-Ketosteroids	2 wk–2 y	0–1 mg/d
	2–6 y	0–2
	6–10 y	1–4
	10–12 y	1–6
	12–14 y	3–10
	14–16 y	5–12
	Adult man	9–22
	Adult woman	6–15
Pregnanetriol	2 wk–2 y	0.02–0.2 mg/d
	2–5 y	<0.5
	5–15 y	<1.5
	Adult	<2.0
Plasma		
Androstenedione	Males	
	1–3 mo	20–45 ng/dL
	3–5 mo	10–40
	Adult	75–125
	Females	
	1–3 mo	15–25
	3–5 mo	10–15
	Adult	110–190
Dehydroepiandrosterone	Child	1–3 ng/mL
	Adult man	1.7–4.2
	Adult woman	2.0–5.2
Deoxycorticosterone	Adult	40–150 pg/mL (approx)
11-Deoxycortisol	Adult	0.5–1.2 μg/dL
17-Hydroxypregnenolone	Adult	0.3–3.5 ng/mL
17-Hydroxyprogesterone	Male (child)	0.1–0.3 ng/mL
	Male (adult)	0.2–1.8
	Female (child)	0.2–0.5
	Female (follicular)	0.2–0.8
	Female (luteal)	0.8–3.0
	Post ACTH stimulation	<3.3

*Reference ranges for plasma aldosterone, estradiol, and testosterone should be readily available from most commercial laboratories.
Data from New MI, Lorenzen F, Lerner AJ, et al. Genotyping steroid 21-hydroxylase deficiency: Hormonal reference data. J Clin Endocrinol Metab 1983;57: 320. See also Lashansky G, Saenger P, Fishman K, et al. Normative data for adrenal steroidogenesis in a healthy pediatric population: Age- and sex-related changes after adrenocorticotropin stimulation. J Clin Endocrinol Metab 1991;73:674.

Recommended Approach

Lifelong glucocorticoid replacement therapy is essential in all cases of congenital adrenal hyperplasia. Glucocorticoids restore normal feedback inhibition to the pituitary gland, resulting in diminished ACTH secretion and reduced stimulation of the adrenal glands to make the undesirable steroid precursors. In infants, the usual regimen is cortisone acetate 12.5 mg/m^2/d given as an intramuscular injection of three times the daily dose every 3 days. After 2 years of age, the oral route of administration is preferred; because oral cortisone acetate or hydrocortisone is less active than the parenteral form, the usual oral dose of cortisone acetate is 25 mg/m^2/d (equivalent to hydrocortisone 20 mg/m^2/d). For adults, a typical schedule is hydrocortisone 10 mg three times a day. This differs from the recommended schedule for patients with adrenal insufficiency, for whom the usual dose is 20 mg in the morning and 10 mg in the afternoon or early evening; in congenital adrenal hyperplasia, giving a dose at night helps dampen the expected early-morning surge of ACTH. Glucocorticoid therapy must be monitored closely in these patients and the dose adjusted to meet individual needs. Excessive doses lead to growth retardation and features of Cushing's syndrome, whereas an insufficient dose will not suppress the undesired steroids. Growth rate, bone age, and steroid hormone production (either urine 17-ketosteroids or plasma levels of steroid precursors) should be checked at regular intervals.

Mineralocorticoid replacement may not be needed if salt wasting is mild; simply increasing dietary sodium may be sufficient. Medication for mineralocorticoid deficiency, when required, is usually provided as fludrocortisone (Florinef); the typical adult dose range is 0.1 to 0.3 mg daily. The salt-losing tendency may decrease by age 5 or so, allowing mineralocorticoid treatment to be reduced or discontinued. For mineralocorticoid excess, spironolactone (Aldactone), an inhibitor of aldosterone, is usually sufficient in a dose of 25 mg four times a day. Mineralocorticoid therapy can be monitored by measuring blood pressure, serum electrolytes, and, if necessary, plasma renin activity; spironolactone therapy can be assessed by following these same parameters. In patients with deficient gonadal steroid production, sex hormone replacement must be started at the time of puberty.

Many males with 21-hydroxylase deficiency experience precocious puberty, probably triggered by high adrenal androgen levels. Inhibitory analogs of gonadotropin-releasing hormone may be useful for treatment of precocious puberty.

Surgical correction of the genital abnormalities in females is usually quite successful. Division of fused labia and recession (*not* resection) of the enlarged clitoris should be done in the first year of life; vaginal plastic surgery is probably best deferred until puberty. Reconstructive surgery is not always satisfactory in chromosomal males with intrauterine androgen deficiency and incomplete development of male external genitalia. A decision on gender assignment should be made early. If male genital deformities are mild, surgery can be done to repair scrotal and penile abnormalities. If surgery cannot provide genitalia that will be sufficient for sexual performance as a male, the parents should be encouraged to consider having the gonadal tissue removed and rear the patient as a female.

Administration of dexamethasone to the mother during an affected pregnancy may eliminate or reduce the masculinization of the female fetus. To be effective, dexamethasone treatment must be instituted early, within 5 to 7 weeks of conception, often before the diagnosis can be confirmed by amniocentesis or chorionic villus sampling.

Acute treatment of the patient in crisis must include "stress doses" of glucocorticoids and volume resuscitation (see Chapter 9–11).

FOLLOW-UP

Until full skeletal growth is complete, patients with congenital adrenal hyperplasia should be seen frequently, about every 3 months. Linear growth and weight gain should be carefully plotted, periodic x-rays for bone age performed, and urine or blood steroid measurements done to assess the adequacy of suppressive therapy. Most authorities favor measurement of urinary 17-ketosteroids, with normal 24-hour 17-ketosteroid excretion values being the best indication of adequate suppression. In patients with mineralocorticoid abnormalities, blood pressure and serum electrolytes should be monitored as well. After growth and development are complete, visits once or twice a year should be adequate.

Genetic counseling is an important part of management. All varieties of congenital adrenal hyperplasia are inherited in an autosomal recessive pattern. Heterozygotes can be identified by ACTH testing or, in the case of 21-hydroxylase deficiency, by HLA typing (see Discussion). Parents (and eventually the patient) should be assured that sexual function can be normal despite abnormalities of external genitalia. Supportive counseling may be helpful for the parents of an affected child, as well as for the patient. Lifelong medication is mandatory. Patients should be advised to increase their dose of glucocorticoid in the event of stress or to take their glucocorticoid by injection if they are unable to take it orally. Patients should carry identification such as a wallet card and wear a bracelet or necklace indicating that they require steroids.

DISCUSSION
Prevalence and Incidence

Classic 21-hydroxylase deficiency is by far the most common form of congenital adrenal hyperplasia, occurring in approximately 1 of 15,000 Caucasian births, accounting for 90 to 95% of cases of congenital adrenal hyperplasia. "Nonclassic" 21-hydroxylase deficiency appears to affect between 1 and 2% of hirsute Caucasian women. 11-Hydroxylase deficiency occurs in about 1 in 200,000 live births in this country.

17-Hydroxylase deficiency, 3-hydroxysteroid dehydrogenase deficiency, and 20,22-desmolase deficiency are rare.

Related Basic Science
Genetics

The gene for 21-hydroxylase deficiency is located on the short arm of chromosome 6 and is closely linked to the HLA-B locus, associated with an increased frequency of Bw47 and a slight increase in Bw51, Bw52, Bw60, and Dr7. In affected kindreds, HLA typing is quite useful for the detection of heterozygote carriers and for prenatal diagnosis. The gene for 17-hydroxylase (which also has 17, 20-lyase activity) is located on chromosome 10. The genes for 11-hydroxylase deficiency and 3 β-hydroxysteroid dehydrogenase deficiency are not HLA linked.

Altered Molecular Biology

The genetic defect in congenital adrenal hyperplasia involves changes in a structural gene for the corresponding cytochrome P450 (for 21-hydroxylase deficiency, P405c21). Multiple mutations of the CYP21B gene that codes for 21-hydroxylase have been described that result in diminished or absent gene activity. Most of these involve single-point mutations or deletions.

Patients with 17-hydroxylase deficiency have a variety of molecular changes: nonsense mutations, deletions, duplications, and single-point mutations in cytochrome P450c17, all of which result in an inactive gene product.

Thus far, no patients with 11-hyroxylase deficiency have been found to have deletions or rearrangements of the OH11 gene.

Physiologic or Metabolic Derangement

Congenital adrenal hyperplasia is also known as "adrenogenital syndrome" because of the striking genital abnormalities seen in affected infants. All of these disorders are transmitted by autosomal recessive inheritance. Table 9–8–1 lists the various types of defects included under the heading congenital adrenal hyperplasia and Figure 9–8–1 shows the synthetic pathways and enzymes. This discussion provides, first, general information about these disorders and, then, specific details regarding each type.

The common feature of these disorders is a diminished capacity for cortisol production. Deficiency of cortisol leads to excessive production of ACTH by the pituitary gland, which causes hyperplasia of the adrenal glands and overproduction of precursor steroids. Some of these precursors have biological activity and some are shunted to other pathways (e.g., from the glucocorticoid pathway to the androgen pathway). Depending on the specific enzyme that is deficient, there may also be insufficient production of mineralocorticoids, adrenal androgens, or gonadal steroids (testosterone and estrogens). Biologically active precursors that may accumulate include androgens and mineralocorticoids. Clinical manifestations vary depending on hormone classes that are deficient, those that are excessive, and the degree of completeness of the enzyme deficiency.

The manifestations of adrenal hormone deficiencies are varied. Except in neonates and severely affected infants, glucocorticoid deficiency in patients with congenital adrenal hyperplasia is usually not severe enough to be apparent in the basal state, but the inability to increase cortisol production at times of stress can result in manifestations of adrenal insufficiency. The other features are listed in Table 9–8–1 and discussed under Clinical Manifestations.

21-Hydroxylase is necessary for conversion of 17-hydroxyprogesterone to 11-deoxycortisol and on to cortisol, and of progesterone to deoxycorticosterone and on to aldosterone (Fig. 9–8–1). The result of a complete deficiency of 21-hydroxylase is a rise in all compounds in the steroidogenic pathways that precede the enzyme: progesterone, 17-hydroxyprogesterone, and adrenal androgens (mainly androstenedione, which is converted to testosterone in peripheral tissues). Urinary excretion of 17-ketosteroids is increased, as is that of pregnanetriol, the most important metabolite of 17-hydroxyprogesterone.

In the most severe or salt-wasting form (type 2) of 21-hydroxylase deficiency, the defect involves the zona glomerulosa of the adrenal gland as well as the zona fasciculata, resulting in deficiency of both al-

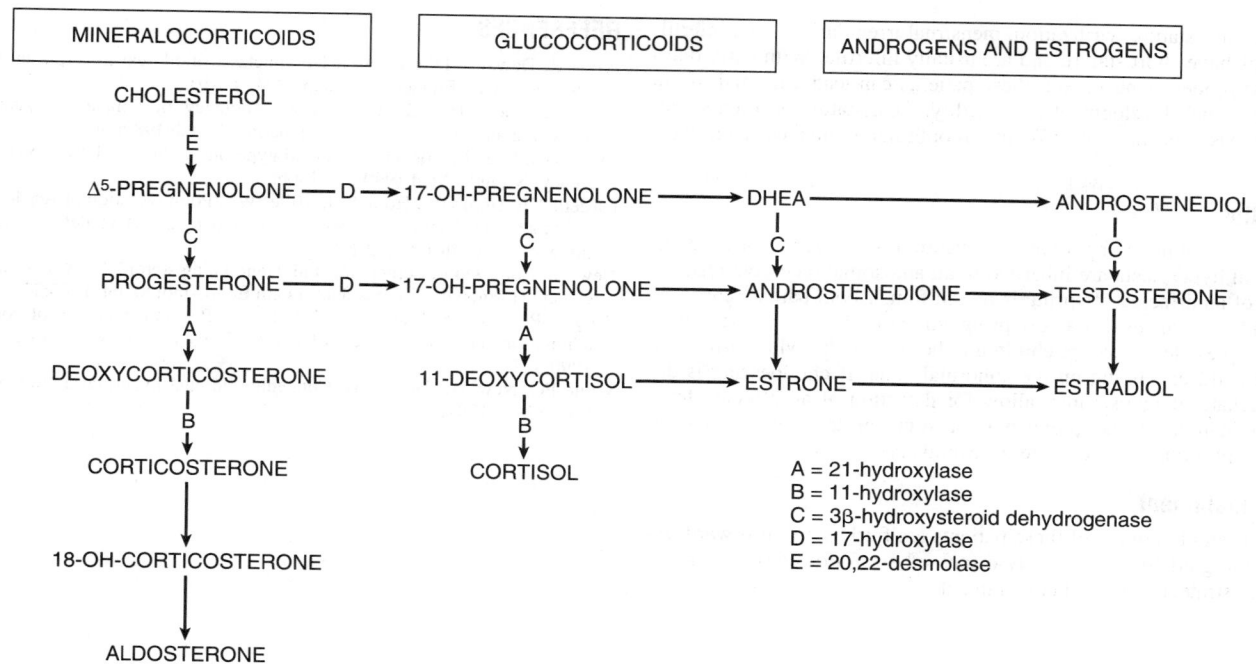

Figure 9–8–1. Pathways of adrenal hormone synthesis. 21-hydroxylase; 11-hydroxylase; 3β-hydroxysteroid dehydrogenase; 17-hydroxylase; 20,22-desmolase. DHEA, dehydroepiandrosterone.

dosterone and cortisol. In most infants so affected, a salt-wasting crisis occurs 6 to 14 days after birth, manifest by severe dehydration, hyponatremia, hyperkalemia, acidosis, and shock. In 21-hydroxylase deficiency type 1, salt wasting is mild or does not occur.

21-Hydroxylase deficiency may become apparent at puberty, where it is termed "nonclassic," "late onset," "attenuated," "cryptic," or "acquired." These terms are misnomers, as the enzyme deficiency is present at birth; however, the late-onset form is genetically different from the classic form. At the time of puberty, affected females develop hirsutism and oligomenorrhea, and may show the features of polycystic ovary syndrome, including polycystic ovaries (see Hirsutism, Chapter 9–26). Basal serum concentrations of 17-hydryxyprogesterone are elevated in some women with this condition, but not all. An exaggerated rise in serum 17-hydroxyprogesterone levels after ACTH stimulation serves as a useful diagnostic test; however, some women with the biochemical abnormalities of heterozygous 21-hydroxylase deficiency do not develop hirsutism, indicating that end-organ sensitivity plays a role in the phenotypic expression. As "late-onset" congenital adrenal hyperplasia does not appear to be a common cause of hirsutism, routine screening of hirsute women for 21-hydroxylase deficiency is not warranted.

The enzyme 11-hydroxylase promotes conversion of 11-deoxycortisol to cortisol and conversion of deoxycorticosterone to aldosterone. Even though deficiency of this enzyme leads to reduced aldosterone production, deoxycorticosterone accumulates and exerts sufficient mineralocorticoid activity to cause retention of sodium and water, arterial hypertension, and suppression of plasma renin activity. Sometimes, hypertension does not appear until adulthood. Hypokalemia is uncommon in these patients.

In 17-hydroxylase deficiency, affected subjects show hypertension and hypokalemic alkalosis.

Complete deficiency of 3β-hydroxysteroid dehydrogenase is incompatible with life. A partial defect results in deficient synthesis of glucocorticoids, mineralocorticoids, and gonadal steroids. Urinary 17-ketosteroid levels are increased, as are plasma levels of 17-hydroxypregnenolone and other precursor steroids. Salt wasting may be present.

In 17-hydroxylase deficiency, further conversion of progesterone and pregnenolone to cortisol or adrenal androgens is impaired and the production of gonadal steroids is reduced. There is excessive production of deoxycorticosterone, which exerts a pronounced mineralocorticoid effect and suppresses plasma renin activity and aldosterone production. 17-Ketosteroid excretion is low.

A deficiency of 20,22-desmolase is important in the early steps of steroid synthesis and a complete deficiency is incompatible with life. Even when given replacement glucocorticoid and mineralocorticoid therapy, all affected infants have died.

Anatomic Derangement

In both types of 21-hydroxylase deficiency, as a result of intrauterine exposure to excessive androgens, affected female infants have ambiguous external genitalia, sometimes even a male appearance when the defect is severe, though internal genitalia (uterus, tubes, and ovaries) are usually normal. In milder cases, the patient's genitalia may appear normal at birth, with signs of virilization beginning at age 3 or so. Affected males usually do not show any genital abnormalities at birth but begin to show signs of puberty, such as growth of pubic hair and enlargement of the penis (but not the testes), within a few years. Both males and females show rapid early growth, but final height is reduced because of premature closure of the epiphyses.

In cases of 11-hydroxylase deficiency, androgen excess leads to female pseudohermaphroditism at birth and postnatal virilization in both males and females. Mildly affected males may have only hypertension or gynecomastia as a result of conversion of androgens to estrogens.

Virilization occurs with 3β-hydroxysteroid dehydrogenase deficiency probably because of conversion of dehydroepiandrosterone to testosterone in the liver, where 3β-hydroxysteroid dehydrogenase is under separate genetic control. Affected males show varying degrees of pseudohermaphroditism. Affected females often show slight clitoral enlargement; virilization similar to that seen with polycystic ovary syndrome may appear in childhood or adolescence.

Females with 17-hydroxylase deficiency have sexual infantilism and males have varying degrees of pseudohermaphroditism. Pubic and axillary hair is scant. Adult patients may present as phenotypic females with primary amenorrhea and hypertension.

Natural History and Its Modification with Treatment

Severely affected infants will die if the disorder is not compensated or treated. In cases where the defect is mild or late to present, females experience short stature, virilization, menstrual irregularities, and infertility. Males have short stature and are usually infertile. With early diagnosis and proper management, these patients can lead a normal life in terms of sexual development and fertility; final stature is often somewhat decreased because of difficulty in optimizing glucocorticoid therapy.

Prevention

Genetic counseling is important in prevention. As all forms of congenital adrenal hyperplasia are inherited in an autosomal recessive fashion, the risk of an affected offspring is one in four if both parents carry the gene, and the chances that an offspring will carry the trait is one in two. Some couples elect to adopt children rather than risk giving birth to an affected child or passing on the abnormal gene. If childbearing is desired, prenatal diagnosis may allow for detection of an affected fetus and termination of the pregnancy or prenatal treatment. Neonatal screening programs now operate in several states.

Cost Containment

Diagnosis and treatment of these patients are fairly straightforward. As long as the guidelines previously discussed are followed, there are no particular strategies for cost containment.

REFERENCES

Azziz R, Dewailly D, Owerbach D. Nonclassical adrenal hyperplasia: Current concepts. J Clin Endocrinol Metab 1994;78:810.

Azziz R, Zacur HA. 21-hydroxylase deficiency in female hypergonadism: Screening and diagnosis. J Clin Endocrinol Metab 1989;69:577.

Cutler GB, Laue L. Congenital adrenal hyperplasia due to 21-hydroxylase deficiency. N Engl J Med 1990;323:1806.

Fardella CE, Hum DW, Homoki J, Miller WL. Point mutation of Arg440 to His in cytochrome P450c17 causes severe 17 α-hydroxylase deficiency. J Clin Endocrinol Metab 1994;79:160.

New MI, Lorenzen F, Lerner AJ, et al. Genotyping steroid 21-hydroxylase deficiency: Hormonal reference data. J Clin Endocrinol Metab 1983;57:320.

Pang S, Pollack MS, Marshall RN, Imken L. Prenatal treatment of congenital adrenal hyperplasia due to 21-hydroxylase deficiency. N Engl J Med 1990;322:111.

White PC, New MI, Dupont B. Congenital adrenal hyperplasia (two parts). N Engl J Med 1987;316:1519, 1580.

CHAPTER 9–9
Hyperaldosteronism (See Section 14, Chapter 6)

CHAPTER 9–10
Primary Aldosteronism (See Section 14, Chapter 6)

CHAPTER 9–11
Adrenal Failure

David E. Schteingart, M.D.

DEFINITION

Adrenal failure results from cessation of normal secretion of two major adrenocortical hormones, cortisol and aldosterone. It can develop as a consequence of destruction or suppression of the adrenal cortex (primary adrenocortical insufficiency) or as a result of failure of pituitary adrenocorticotropic hormone (ACTH) secretion (secondary adrenal insufficiency).

ETIOLOGY

Causes of primary adrenocortical insufficiency include autoimmune adrenalitis, whereby antigens in the adrenal cortex trigger the production of adrenal cell surface-reactive autoantibodies, which subsequently induce the inflammatory response leading to the destruction of the adrenal cortex. A variable asymptomatic period with subtle adrenal dysfunction may precede the onset of clinical manifestations. Autoimmune primary adrenocortical insufficiency is the most common form of adrenal insufficiency in the United States. Patients with autoimmune Addison's disease show familial prevalence of this condition and other associated autoimmune endocrinopathies, including Hashimoto's thyroiditis with primary hypothyroidism, Graves' disease, insulin-dependent diabetes mellitus, idiopathic hypoparathyroidism, pernicious anemia, primary gonadal failure, and pituitary insufficiency. These patients show a statistical association with HLA haplotypes, especially HLA-B8 and HLA-DW3.

Other frequent causes of primary adrenocortical insufficiency are infectious, including tuberculosis and fungal infections such as coccidioidomycosis, histoplasmosis, and blastomycosis. Bilateral adrenal hemorrhage with consequent adrenocortical insufficiency can occur with severe sepsis, pneumonia, recent abdominal surgery, heparin therapy, and coagulopathies. These patients usually present with clinical manifestations of adrenal insufficiency, and a computed tomography scan of the abdomen reveals the presence of bilateral adrenal masses which regress over a period of time and are consistent with bilateral adrenal hematomas.

Adrenal cortical involvement has been shown in patients with HIV infection. Autopsies of patients who died with AIDS have shown evidence of destruction of the adrenal cortex and clinically there is a decrease in cortisol response to synthetic ACTH. The adrenal insufficiency observed with HIV infection appears to be related to superimposed cytomegalovirus infection, which is found in 84% of autopsy cases of patients with AIDS.

Infiltrative diseases involving the adrenal glands can lead to adrenocortical insufficiency. These include lymphomas, primary amyloidosis, and metastatic neoplastic disease. In some cases, adrenal insufficiency is the first manifestation of lymphoma. The involvement of the adrenals by infiltrative diseases has to be severe and bilateral to induce clinical manifestations of adrenal insufficiency.

Congenital adrenocortical hypoplasia with familial glucocorticoid deficiency has recently been described in children who present with adrenocortical insufficiency.

Iatrogenic diseases lead to adrenal insufficiency including bilateral adrenalectomy, treatment with adrenalytic drugs such as mitotane, and administration of anticoagulants, which in the presence of severe stress may lead to bilateral adrenal hemorrhages.

Enzyme deficiencies are also associated with adrenal insufficiency. These may be congenital and involve 21-, 11-, and 17-hydroxylase or iatrogenically induced by the administration of adrenal inhibitors with selective suppression of hydroxylase, such as metyrapone, an 11β-hydroxylase inhibitor, ketoconazole, an inhibitor of 17- and 21-hydroxylase, and aminoglutethimide, an inhibitor of cholesterol side-chain cleavage and 11β-hydroxylase.

The most common cause of secondary adrenocortical insufficiency is chronic suppression of ACTH secretion by chronic glucocorticoid therapy.

Other causes include pituitary tumors, which destroy normal pituitary cells, pituitary infarction resulting from a cerebrovascular accident, or postpartum necrosis of the pituitary gland.

Surgical hypophysectomy for the treatment of pituitary disease also results in panhypopituitarism and secondary adrenal insufficiency. In these cases, renin and aldosterone secretion is usually preserved and patients present mainly with clinical manifestations of cortisol deficiency.

In patients with isolated renin deficiency, aldosteronopenia may be the presenting disorder. Renin deficiency is seen in patients who develop hyporeninemic hypoaldosteronism as a consequence of diabetic nephropathy, chronic renal failure, or the administration of indomethacin and angiotensin-converting enzyme inhibitors. The main clinical expression of this deficiency is hyperkalemia.

A rare familial variety of primary adrenal insufficiency is adrenoleukodystrophy, a condition in which general adrenocortical failure is present together with destruction of the cerebral white matter. This condition, which has an X-linked transmission, shows large areas of cerebral demyelination and accumulation of specific lipidlike material in the adrenocortical cells.

CRITERIA FOR DIAGNOSIS
Suggestive

The diagnosis of primary adrenal insufficiency is suspected in patients who present with anorexia, weight loss, nausea, vomiting, chronic fatigue, and increased pigmentation of the skin. Secondary adrenal insufficiency should be considered in patients who have received therapy with glucocorticoids for long periods, have pituitary tumors, or have undergone pituitary surgery.

Definitive

A definitive diagnosis of primary adrenal insufficiency depends on the demonstration of high ACTH and low cortisol levels and incomplete or absent adrenocortical response to the injection of corticotropin. The diagnosis of secondary adrenal insufficiency is based on the demonstration of low ACTH and cortisol levels and the lack of ACTH response to ACTH secretagogues such as insulin-induced hypoglycemia and corticotropin-releasing hormone.

CLINICAL MANIFESTATIONS
Subjective

Adrenal failure is usually found as a sporadic occurrence but certain forms of adrenal insufficiency can occur in families, especially those with an autoimmune etiology in which siblings and especially homozygotic twins may be affected. In these patients, other autoimmune diseases such as hypothyroidism, hypoparathyroidism, insulin-dependent diabetes mellitus, and pernicious anemia have been found. An infectious etiology is found in many patients with adrenal failure. People who live in environments where exposure to these infectious agents occurs are potentially at risk for developing adrenal failure. Included among these causes are tuberculosis, coccidioidomycosis, histoplasmosis, blastomycosis, and HIV-II infection.

The most frequent symptoms associated with primary adrenal failure are fatigue, pigmentation, anorexia, weight loss, and hypotension, which occur in more than 90% of all patients. The fatigue appears to be present constantly and is aggravated by physical activity. Patients describe a profound asthenia and have difficulty getting out of bed. The pigmentation is described by patients as a persistent tan over areas exposed to sunlight and darkening of areas not normally exposed, such as nipples, scars, and genitalia. Dark-skinned individuals relate increased depth of their natural skin pigmentation over the preceeding months or years. Occasionally, patients complain of vitiligo. Dizziness is most prominent when patients are upright and especially when they change from the recumbent to the standing position. Generalized muscle and joint pains and abdominal pain are also described. Patients with secondary adrenal insufficiency have similar symptoms, except for the absence of pigmentation and postural dizziness. In fact, patients may notice a decrease in skin pigmentation and ability to tan when exposed to sunlight. Associated with symptoms of adrenal insufficiency are symptoms related to the deficiency of other pituitary hormones, including amenorrhea in women, impotence in men, dry skin, cold intolerance, and increased lethargy.

Objective
Physical Examination

Patients with primary adrenal insufficiency exhibit hyperpigmentation of skin and mucous membranes. There is accentuation of skin pigmentation over the distal portions of both upper and lower extremities, particularly the dorsum of the hands and palmar creases. Elbows and knees are dark and there is increased pigmentation of scars and nipples. Patients may exhibit an increased number of pigmented nevi which acquire a jet-black color. Lips may appear irregularly pigmented, and there is increased pigmentation of the gingival margin, in addition to pigmented spots over the buccal mucosa and palate. The pigmentation in the buccal mucosa is less specific in dark-skinned individuals. Vitiligo may be seen over the face and extremities in about 10% of patients. Manifestations of intravascular volume depletion include low systolic and diastolic blood pressure and orthostatic hypotension. When patients assume the upright posture, there is a decrease in both systolic and diastolic blood pressure of greater than 20 mm Hg and an increase in heart rate of greater than 20 beats per minute which persists for more than 3 minutes. Women with primary adrenal insufficiency have a decrease in body hair.

Patients with secondary adrenal insufficiency appear pale, with decreased pigmentation of the skin. The presence of hypogonadism with decreased sexual hair and mammary gland atrophy in women and decreased testicular size in men may indicate concomitant failure of other pituitary tropic hormones.

Patients with primary adrenal insufficiency may have associated endocrine deficiencies caused by autoimmune pluriglandular failure. Thus, clinical findings of hypothyroidism and hypogonadism in patients with adrenal insufficiency do not necessarily indicate panhypopituitarism. In contrast to the hypopigmented patients with panhypopituitarism, those with autoimmune pluriglandular failure are usually hyperpigmented.

Routine Laboratory Abnormalities

Laboratory findings include manifestations of aldosterone and cortisol deficiency. Prominent manifestations of aldosterone deficiency are hyponatremia, hyperkalemia, metabolic acidosis, and urinary sodium excretion in excess of 20 mEq/L. Because of intravascular volume contraction, blood urea nitrogen and serum creatinine are increased. The most severe electrolyte and renal changes are observed in patients with chronic adrenal failure who have developed superimposed acute adrenal insufficiency as a consequence of stress with vomiting and diarrhea. Patients with secondary adrenal insufficiency who have normal aldosterone secretion may also develop hyponatremia as a result of impaired free water clearance. Cortisol deficiency is associated with hematologic changes, including normochromic normocytic anemia, leukopenia with relative lymphocytosis, and eosinophilia. Fasting hypoglycemia is seen in patients who have been eating poorly.

Radiographic examination reveals a small-sized heart.

PLANS

Diagnostic

Differential Diagnosis

Hormonal measurements reveal low serum and urine cortisol levels in all patients with adrenocortical insufficiency. Serum aldosterone levels are low in patients with primary adrenal insufficiency and normal or low in patients with secondary adrenal insufficiency. When aldosterone levels are low, plasma renin levels are usually high. In the presence of low cortisol levels, the level of plasma ACTH defines the type of adrenal insufficiency. Patients with primary adrenal insufficiency have high ACTH levels, whereas levels are low in patients with adrenal insufficiency secondary to hypopituitarism.

Diagnostic Options and Recommended Approach

Patients whose clinical presentation suggests adrenal insufficiency should have biochemical confirmation and a definitive diagnosis established prior to institution of long-term therapy.

Adrenal calcifications can be seen on a plain radiograph of the abdomen in patients in whom the etiology of the adrenal insufficiency is granulomatous disease. Abdominal computed tomographic scanning shows small adrenals in patients with autoimmune disease and enlarged adrenals or adrenal masses in patients with either granulomatous disease or adrenal hemorrhage.

As this biochemical confirmation may take some time before it is completed and severe adrenal insufficiency may develop while the patient is awaiting results, therapy should be initiated immediately and either continued or discontinued once a definitive diagnosis has been made. A diagnosis of primary adrenal insufficiency is based on the finding of low random cortisol and aldosterone levels together with high ACTH and renin levels. This combination of findings is unique for primary adrenocortical insufficiency. Other conditions that increase ACTH, such as stress, also increase cortisol levels, whereas those conditions that increase renin, such as low-sodium diets, correspondingly increase aldosterone levels. Conversely, low cortisol levels obtained in the late evening hours are associated with low ACTH levels, whereas low aldosterone levels in patients on high-sodium intake are associated with correspondingly low renin values. Immediately after obtaining a basal sample, patients should receive 250 µg of synthetic corticotropin intravenously. Blood samples for cortisol are obtained 30 and 60 minutes thereafter. An increment of greater than 10 µg/dL and peak values above 20 µg/dL usually rule out adrenal insufficiency.

Patients who have been on chronic glucocorticoid therapy have suppressed ACTH and cortisol levels and may develop secondary adrenal insufficiency when corticosteroid therapy is discontinued. A diagnosis of concomitant primary adrenocortical insufficiency in such patients is difficult and may require the demonstration of failure to respond to prolonged ACTH stimulation. In such cases, a prolonged corticotropin stimulation test should be performed by the administration of a solution containing 250 µg of synthetic corticotropin over a 12-hour period for 2 to 3 consecutive days. Patients with suppressed ACTH levels secondary to glucocorticoid therapy exhibit a gradually increasing cortisol response, whereas patients with primary adrenal insufficiency fail to respond.

Additional studies can be performed to evaluate the etiology of adrenal insufficiency. They include imaging of the adrenals by computed tomographic scanning, thyroid function tests, and determination of serum calcium and phosphorus levels to investigate for associated autoimmune endocrinopathies, and combined pituitary function tests in patients suspected of panhypopituitarism.

Therapeutic

Treatment of chronic adrenal insufficiency requires the administration of cortisol in physiologic replacement amounts. The most commonly used preparation is hydrocortisone, which is given in amounts of 20 to 30 mg daily in unequally divided doses to mimic the normal circadian rhythm of cortisol secretion. The largest dose of 10 to 15 mg is given on arising and the smallest dose, 5 mg, is given shortly before bedtime. Larger doses given at bedtime may cause insomnia. Cortisol is preferred to other synthetic glucocorticoid analogs with low sodium-retaining activity, as it helps to better maintain sodium balance. In addition to cortisol, patients with primary adrenal insufficiency require replacement with fludrocortisol, a preparation similar in mineralocorticoid activity to aldosterone. The usual dose is 0.05 to 0.2 mg daily, adjusted according to serum electrolyte and blood pressure response. The dose given should be sufficient to eliminate orthostatic hypotension or tachycardia but hypokalemia or hypertension should be avoided. Patients with essential hypertension may have an exaggerated sensitivity to mineralocorticoids and develop sodium retention and hypertension. In those patients, the dose of fludrocortisol should be reduced. Patients with associated endocrinopathies or hypopituitarism may require concomitant replacement with thyroxine and gonadal hormones.

Patients with secondary adrenal insufficiency usually require replacement therapy with cortisol alone. Occasionally, prolonged ACTH deficiency can cause marked adrenocortical atrophy and impaired aldosterone secretion. In those cases, replacement therapy with fludrocortisol is also indicated.

Acute adrenal failure is a medical emergency. It may develop as a result of progression of undiagnosed or untreated chronic adrenocortical insufficiency or in patients with chronic adrenal insufficiency who develop acute stress for which appropriate adjustments in cortisol therapy have not been made. Frequently, these patients have suffered intercurrent infection, trauma, or acute surgical stress. They present with nausea, vomiting, rapid weight loss, and hypotension. In those circumstances, the presence of pigmentation should raise suspicion of primary adrenal insufficiency.

After preliminary laboratory studies, including serum electrolytes, blood urea nitrogen, creatinine, blood survey, cortisol, aldosterone, ACTH, and renin, an intravenous line is established through which the patient should receive an infusion of a 5% dextrose in 0.9% sodium chloride solution at a rate sufficient to deliver 1 L over the next hour. Simultaneously, 250 µg of synthetic corticotropin should be injected as an intravenous bolus. Blood samples for cortisol are obtained 30 and 60 minutes thereafter. Once the samples have been obtained, the patient should receive hydrocortisone sodium succinate 100 mg intravenously, followed by an infusion of a solution containing hydrocortisone to be administered at a rate of 10 mg an hour for the next 5 hours. Patients may require additional intravenous fluids in an amount designed to restore intravascular volume and correct the abnormal electrolyte findings. Restoration of normal blood pressure and heart rate should be the goal of therapy.

Patients with more severe hyperkalemia (serum potassium levels, greater than 6 mEq/L) may require, in addition to hydrocortisone, the administration of glucose and insulin or potassium-binding resins to lower serum potassium.

Once patients have recovered from the acute manifestations of adrenocortical insufficiency, the dose of cortisol and fludrocortisol should be gradually reduced to the replacement doses described above.

Maintenance steroid therapy is to be altered under conditions of stress. Physical stress, such as fever-producing systemic infections, trauma, and major surgery with general anesthesia, requires an increase in the dose of cortisol. The dose and duration of this increment vary with the type of stress. Systemic infections causing fever require a doubling of the replacement amount of cortisol until the infectious process is brought under control and the patient is no longer febrile.

Patients undergoing surgery with general anesthesia should receive larger doses of cortisol as follows: 100 mg hydrocortisone is given intravenously on-call and followed by 50 mg every 8 hours for the first postoperative day. This dose of hydrocortisone is subsequently tapered back to replacement doses within the next 3 to 4 days if the patient is free of surgical complications. Sustained administration of large doses of cortisol should be avoided, as they may induce metabolic side effects and other undesirable effects during recovery from a surgical illness, including protein catabolism, delayed wound healing, immunosuppression, suppression of the inflammatory response, increased susceptibility to infection, sodium and water retention, hypertension, and hyperglycemia.

Psychological stress usually does not require increases in the maintenance dose of cortisol.

During hot, humid weather, patients with primary adrenal insufficiency may experience increased sweating with consequent increased sodium and water losses. The dose of fludrocortisol may need to be increased to maintain normal electrolytes and intravascular volume. Symptoms associated with mineralocorticoid deficiency are frequently similar to those caused by glucocorticoid deficiency. In these circumstances, it is important to determine precisely if an increase in fludrocortisol or cortisol is necessary. Observing the conditions under which the symptoms have appeared, such as general stress or increased sodium and water losses, usually helps make the correct choice.

Patients with adrenal insufficiency have, in most cases, an irreversible medical condition, and should be instructed on how to manage their disease in a variety of circumstances. They should be encouraged to lead a normal life and not fail to take the replacement therapy, because this therapy is essential for life. Written information concerning the nature of their disease and the physiologic effects of cortisol and aldosterone or their analogs should be given. The written information should contain instructions on how to vary the dose of cortisol and fludrocortisol as needed under stress conditions. Patients should be advised to avoid hot and humid environments and not to limit their sodium intake, because both sodium and fludrocortisol are necessary to maintain normal fluid and electrolyte balance. If they were to become ill with nausea and vomiting and unable to keep medications down, patients should be advised to consult a physician immediately or go to an emergency room where medications can be administered parenterally and they can receive intravenous hydration. Intercurrent conditions that are normally treated at home can, in patients with adrenal insufficiency, require inpatient care. Patients should be advised to wear either a necklace or bracelet with a tag that indicates they have adrenal insufficiency and they are cortisol dependent. This is particularly important for situations in which patients become unconscious and need to receive emergency care. The physician's knowledge of the patient's condition can obviate delays in cortisol replacement.

FOLLOW-UP

After the initial diagnosis and institution of therapy, patients should be seen every 2 months for the first 6 months to establish adequacy of steroid replacement therapy. They should also be seen during the summer months to ascertain the adequacy of replacement therapy in a warmer environment. After the first year, patients may be seen only once a year, at which time they should be checked not only for adequacy of replacement therapy but also for the development of manifestations of other endocrine gland failure. Patients should be instructed to consult with a physician immediately if an intercurrent illness develops that requires adjustment in therapy.

DISCUSSION
Prevalence and Incidence

Primary adrenal insufficiency is uncommon. Secondary adrenal insufficiency as a result of anatomic lesions of the pituitary or hypothalamus is uncommon as well. Secondary adrenal insufficiency is a common consequence of corticosteroid therapy; its incidence and prevalence thus depend on the frequency of therapeutic use of glucocorticoids and withdrawal from glucocorticoid therapy.

Related Basic Science
Physiologic or Metabolic Derangement

Adrenocortical insufficiency results from cessation of normal secretion of adrenocortical hormones. Cortisol insufficiency leads to depletion of gluconeogenic substrates and suppressed gluconeogenesis and hepatic glucose production. In addition, there is increased sensitivity of the liver and peripheral tissues to the action of insulin, which results in increased glucose transport. A clinical consequence of these changes is the development of fasting hypoglycemia with possible neuroglucopenia. Lack of cortisol also leads to decreased renin substrate production, decreased vascular sensitivity to the effect of angiotensin II and norepinephrine, and increased vasodilator prostaglandin E2 and kallikrein. These

changes lead to development of hypotension. A decrease in the feedback suppression of pro-opiomelanocortin synthesis by cortisol leads to high α and β melanocyte-stimulating hormone levels and the development of hyperpigmentation. In addition, major changes occur with aldosteronopenia, including natriuresis, isosmotic water loss, and increased potassium and hydrogen ion reabsorption. The clinical consequences of these changes are hyponatremia, development of extracellular fluid volume depletion and hypotension, hyperkalemia, metabolic acidosis, and cardiac arrhythmias. Volume depletion also leads to stimulation of renin release. The decrease in cortisol also leads to increased arginine vasopressin secretion and a decrease in free water clearance. While restoring volume, the water retention is likely to further depress sodium levels. Finally, a decrease in androgen production is particularly significant in women in whom there is a decrease in axillary and pubic hair growth.

In primary adrenal insufficiency (Addison's disease) there is destruction of the adrenal cortex with inability to synthesize and secrete all major adrenal cortical steroid hormones. This includes cortisol, aldosterone, and androgens. In contrast, secondary adrenal insufficiency develops as a result of either ACTH or renin deficiency, leading to isolated cortisol or aldosterone deficiency.

Natural History and Its Modification with Treatment

If left untreated, patients with adrenocortical insufficiency may develop progression of symptoms leading to acute adrenal failure, a condition that is fatal if not treated. Patients who are adequately treated with steroid replacement therapy can live a normal life and have normal life expectancy. In its early stages, patients may present with loss of adrenocortical reserve such that they are able to maintain normal cortisol levels in unstressed conditions; however, they fail to respond to stress, and may become acutely adrenal insufficient in the face of stressful events. If early stages of adrenal insufficiency are identified, patients should receive full therapy to prevent more severe manifestations of adrenal insufficiency. Patients with autoimmune disease may develop other endocrinopathies as a consequence of autoimmune involvement of other endocrine glands. The physician should check the patient periodically for such occurrences. In most cases, a medical history focused on these other endocrine conditions should determine the extent of laboratory testing. Patients with secondary adrenal insufficiency usually require replacement with other hormones to treat thyroid or gonadal failure. When panhypopituitarism is caused by a pituitary tumor, the prognosis of the adrenal insufficiency is determined by the clinical course of the pituitary disease.

Prevention

Although autoimmune adrenocortical insufficiency cannot be prevented at the present time, that which develops as a result of infection and particularly by granulomatous diseases can be avoided by early diagnosis and therapy of these conditions. Similarly, overzealous anticoagulant therapy in patients who are septic may prevent the development of adrenal hemorrhages, which can lead to adrenal insufficiency.

Cost Containment

The initial diagnosis of adrenocortical insufficiency can be performed on an outpatient basis and the cost limited only to the office visit and hormonal testing. The cost is clearly higher when patients need to be treated for acute adrenal insufficiency, as this may require admission to a critical care unit for intensive fluid, electrolyte, and steroid therapy, in addition to close cardiovascular and biochemical monitoring. Subsequent cost of treatment is related to the use of cortisol and fludrocortisol. At the time patients are seen for follow-up on a yearly basis, a general biochemical profile, including electrolytes and glucose, should be requested. Investigation for associated autoimmune endocrinopathies should be pursued only if suspicion of these conditions arises from a carefully obtained history and physical examination.

REFERENCES
Boscaro M, Betterle C, Somiko N, et al. Early adrenal hypofunction in patients with organ specific autoantibodies and no clinical adrenal insufficiency. J Clin Endocrinol Metab 1994;79:452.

Eisenbarth GS, Wilson PW, Ward F, et al. The pluriglandular failure syndrome: Disease inheritance, HLA type and immune function. Ann Intern Med 1979;91:528.

Sim SC, Kitzman DW, Sheedy PF II, Northcutt RC. Adrenal insufficiency for bilateral adrenal hemorrhage. Mayo Clin Proc 1990;65:664.

Tan SU, Burton M. Hyporeninemic hypoaldosteronism, an overlooked cause of hyperkalemia. Arch Intern Med 1981;141:30.

Werbel SS, Ober KK. Acute adrenal insufficiency. Endocrinol Metab Clin North Am 1993;22:303.

CHAPTER 9–12

Thyroid Enlargement

Ernest L. Mazzaferri, MD

DEFINITION

Focal or diffuse thyroid enlargement, usually termed *goiter*, is a non-specific physical finding that may be caused by a variety of thyroid disorders and nonthyroidal diseases. This chapter deals with diffuse and multinodular goiters. A diffuse goiter is a palpable enlargement of the thyroid gland that may or may not be symmetric. Its surface may be smooth or irregular and its consistency can range from very firm to soft but the gland contains no palpable nodules. A multinodular goiter is an enlarged thyroid gland that has one or more palpable nodules of various size. An isolated thyroid nodule is a palpable swelling in an otherwise normal thyroid gland. The latter is discussed in Chapter 9–13. The patient with a diffuse or multinodular goiter may have normal thyroid function or may be hypothyroid or thyrotoxic.

ETIOLOGY

In some instances, the thyroid gland is infiltrated with inflammatory cells, fibrous tissue, tumor, or other substances such as amyloid. In other instances, it is unable to synthesize thyroid hormone normally for a variety of reasons and enlarges due to a compensatory rise in pituitary thyroid-stimulating hormone secretion. In yet other instances, the gland enlarges in response to abnormal circulating thyroid stimulators, which occur in Graves' disease. Multinodular colloid goiter, perhaps the most common form of goiter in the United States, develops as the result of thyroid nodular hyperplasia that evolves for uncertain reasons and in response to an unknown stimulus. Dietary iodine deficiency is the most common cause of goiter worldwide but is rarely, if ever, encountered in the United States. In regions of the world where it still exists, however, large portions of the population develop diffuse goiters that typically evolve into multinodular goiters as the person ages. The disorders causing goiter are summarized in Table 9–12–1.

CRITERIA FOR DIAGNOSIS

Suggestive

It is difficult to set precise limits for the definition of thyroid enlargement because gland size varies with age and from one geographic area to another. Some criteria can be inferred from the size and location of the normal thyroid gland. The fully developed normal thyroid contains two lateral lobes connected by a medial band of thyroid tissue termed the *isthmus*. The lateral lobes are symmetric, although the right lobe is typically somewhat larger than the left. The pyramidal lobe is a remnant of the embryonic connection between the thyroid and pharynx that sometimes persists as an upward extension from the thyroid isthmus slightly to the left of the midline. It is palpable in about one third of normal persons, especially pubertal girls and women.

The normal thyroid weighs about 2 g at birth and reaches about 15 g at puberty, remaining between 10 and 15 g in most adults in geographic areas where dietary iodine is sufficient such as the United States. The thyroid is larger in areas of iodine deficiency. Symptoms that suggest thyroid enlargement or thyroid metabolic dysfunction or an examination that shows the gland to be slightly enlarged is often the first clue to a thyroid problem. Accurate imaging techniques can precisely identify thyroid gland enlargement and blood tests can distinguish early thyroid dysfunction.

Definitive

Each thyroid lobe normally measures about 4 cm from superior to inferior pole in the adult, is about 3 cm across at its widest dimension, and is about 1 cm thick, measurements that are easily made with ultrasonography. Most of the lateral lobes are seated behind the strap muscles, and the most posterior-lateral portions are deep in the neck next to the trachea, where they are difficult to palpate (Figure 9–12–1). The normal thyroid is barely discernible on examination and contains no palpable nodules. An enlarged gland may be easily seen or can be appreciated by palpation, and may be visualized with certain techniques such as radionuclide scans, ultrasonography, or computed tomography scans.

Diffuse or nodular goiters occur in patients who may have hyperthyroidism or hypothyroidism or who have normal thyroid function (euthyroid). In Table 9–12–1, goitrous thyroid diseases are classified according to their functional manifestations. Symptoms of thyrotoxicosis or hypothyroidism may cause the patient to seek medical attention, or pressure symptoms from the goiter may call attention to the problem.

Thyroid enlargement may be quite obvious on inspection or palpation of the neck, which is sufficient to identify a diffuse or nodular goiter. When a thyroid abnormality is suspected but is uncertain by physical examination, thyroid imaging techniques may provide further clues to its presence. The finding of a goiter is in itself insufficient information to diagnose the underlying thyroid disease.

CLINICAL MANIFESTATIONS

Subjective

Symptoms

The patient may develop symptoms due to thyroid dysfunction, either thyrotoxicosis or hypothyroidism, or may have discomfort caused by the goiter itself. Large, benign goiters are usually surprisingly asymptomatic and painless; however, benign goiters can cause symptomatic compression or displacement of surrounding structures, resulting in exertional dyspnea, dysphagia, hoarseness, dysphonia, positional wheezing, stridor, or cough. Spontaneous intranodular hemorrhage occurs in multinodular colloid goiter, sometimes causing pain in the nodule that may radiate to the ear. Some undergo rapid growth or are accompanied by pain or hemoptysis, symptoms of local invasion. If the goiter is substernal it may cause the superior vena cava syndrome. If the goiter is at the level of the narrow thoracic inlet, tracheal or esophageal compression is particularly likely. Thoracic inlet compression results in facial plethora, dysphonia, hoarseness, dizziness, and shortness of breath.

Past History

The principal environmental factor responsible for goiter, iodine deficiency, is now practically nonexistent in the United States. The most commonly recognized goitrogens in the United States are medications (Table 9–12–1).

Family History

Patients with goiters due to Graves' disease or Hashimoto's thyroiditis have a genetic predisposition to autoimmune thyroid disease, causing

TABLE 9–12–1. CAUSES OF THYROID ENLARGEMENT

Disorders Characterized by Euthyroid Goiter
Diffuse or multinodular sporadic goiter
  Unknown causes
  Congenital defects in hormone synthesis
  Chemical agents (e.g., iodide, lithium, amiodarone, sodium *para*-aminosalicylic acid)
  Dietary goitrogens
  Infiltration (amyloid or hemochromatosis)
  Malignancy (thyroid lymphoma or carcinoma)
  Autoimmune disease (Graves' and Hashimoto's diseases)
Endemic diffuse or multinodular goiter
  Iodine deficiency or excess
  Dietary goitrogens
Uninodular goiter
  Functional nodule
    Autonomously hyperfunctioning adenomas
    Thyroid-stimulating hormone-dependent thyroid tissue
  Nonfunctional nodule
    Tumors
    Benign adenomas, colloid nodules, etc.
    Malignancy, primary or metastatic
    Hemorrhage or infarct of nodule
    Thyroid cyst
Thyroiditis
  Suppurative (acute bacterial)
  Subacute (viral)
  Chronic lymphocytic (Hashimoto's thyroiditis)
  Chronic invasive fibrous (Riedel's struma)
  Chronic suppurative (e.g., tuberculosis)

Disorders Characterized by Hypothyroid Goiter
Diffuse or multinodular goiter
  Hashimoto's thyroiditis (autoimmune chronic lymphocytic)
  Endemic iodine deficiency
  Hereditary defects in hormonogenesis
  Goitrogens
    Iodine (in susceptible persons)*
    Antithyroid drugs (e.g., propylthiouracil)
    Lithium*
    Phenylbutazone, oxyphenbutazone
    Aminoglutethamide
    Sodium *para*-aminosalicyclic acid
    Resorcinol ointment
    Other
Infiltrative diseases
  Amyloidosis
  Sarcoidosis
  Lymphoma
  Cystinosis
  Malignancy (primary thyroidal)
  Other

Disorders Characterized by Thyrotoxic Goiter
Diffuse or multinodular goiter
  Unknown cause (multinodular toxic goiter)
  Graves' disease
    Thyroiditis
    Hashimoto's thyroiditis
    Subacute (viral)
    Silent (lymphocytic spontaneously resolving thyrotoxic)
Malignancy with circulating thyroid stimulators
  Choriocarcinoma, hydatidiform mole
  Embryonal cell carcinoma of the testes
Pituitary
  Thyroid-stimulating hormone-producing tumors
  Selective resistance to thyroid hormone
  Acromegaly
Exogenous iodine (Jod–Basedow)
Uninodular goiter due to
  Autonomously hyperfunctioning nodule
  Thyroiditis (same as above)

*May also cause thyrotoxicosis.

them to cluster within families, but these disorders do not display a specific pattern of inheritance. These disorders have a striking predilection for women. Congenital goiters are often familial with variable patterns of inheritance. Familial medullary thyroid carcinoma is inherited as an autosomal dominant trait.

Objective

Physical Examination

According to the World Health Organization definition, goiter may be barely palpable (grade I), palpably and visibly enlarged (grade II), or very large (grade III). Physical findings due to thyroid enlargement itself generally are few. Shining a light across the neck will highlight a small goiter, which may become readily visible when the patient swallows and the gland can be seen moving upward. The patient should be seated comfortably during the examination while the thyroid is palpated, with one hand from the front or with both hands from behind. The patient should be given a glass of water to sip to facilitate repeated swallowing while both lateral lobes, the isthmus, and the pyramidal lobe are palpated. The right lobe of a diffuse goiter is often larger than the left. Regardless of its cause, a goiter of several years' duration is generally firm and nontender and may have an irregular surface. After many years, diffuse colloid goiters almost invariably develop palpable nodularity. Patients with Hashimoto's or Graves' disease tend to have firm goiters. Hashimoto's goiters are often described as being bosselated (covered with small knobs). Large, nontender cervical lymph nodes suggest a thyroid malignancy, even in a diffusely enlarged gland. Auscultation of a diffuse toxic goiter may disclose a systolic bruit over the gland or a continuous venous hum in the lateral neck. Large benign goiters can produce a superior mediastinal syndrome with facial edema and plethora and venous distention in the neck and upper chest. A substernal goiter may cause choking and facial suffusion when the neck is flexed and the arms are raised above the head. This maneuver, which raises a retrosternal goiter into the thoracic inlet and aggravates the neck compression, is termed the *thyroid cork* or *Pemberton's sign*. Vocal cord paralysis, usually a sign of malignancy, may rarely occur with benign tumors.

Routine Laboratory Abnormalities

Routine tests are normal unless the patient has thyrotoxicosis or hypothyroidism, which can alter blood chemistries and the electrocardiogram.

Patients with a substernal goiter usually have an abnormal chest x-ray showing an anterior superior mediastinal mass that can extend to the level of the aortic arch. When the goiter is retrosternal, other tests may be necessary in the symptomatic patient.

PLANS
Diagnostic
Differential Diagnosis

First determine the patient's thyroid functional status. Is the patient thyrotoxic, hypothyroid, or euthyroid? Each has its own differential diagnosis, listed in Table 9–12–1. Next, determine the physical characteristics of the thyroid gland. Does the patient have a diffuse or nodular goiter? If the goiter is nodular, is there more than one nodule and is the gland generally enlarged? Does the goiter extend retrosternally? Answering these questions will point to the correct set of conditions listed in Table 9–12–1.

Diagnostic Options

The serum thyroid-stimulating hormone (TSH) should be measured in every patient with a goiter. If it is normal, no other thyroid function tests are necessary. If serum TSH is abnormal, one must measure the concentrations of circulating thyroid hormones, thyroxine (T_4) and triiodothyronine (T_3). Total serum thyroid hormone concentrations can be measured directly, but estimating free hormone levels is more important because they reflect the biologically active forms of thyroid hormone. Estimates of serum free T_4 or T_3 are made either by radioimunoassays designed to measure free hormone levels or by

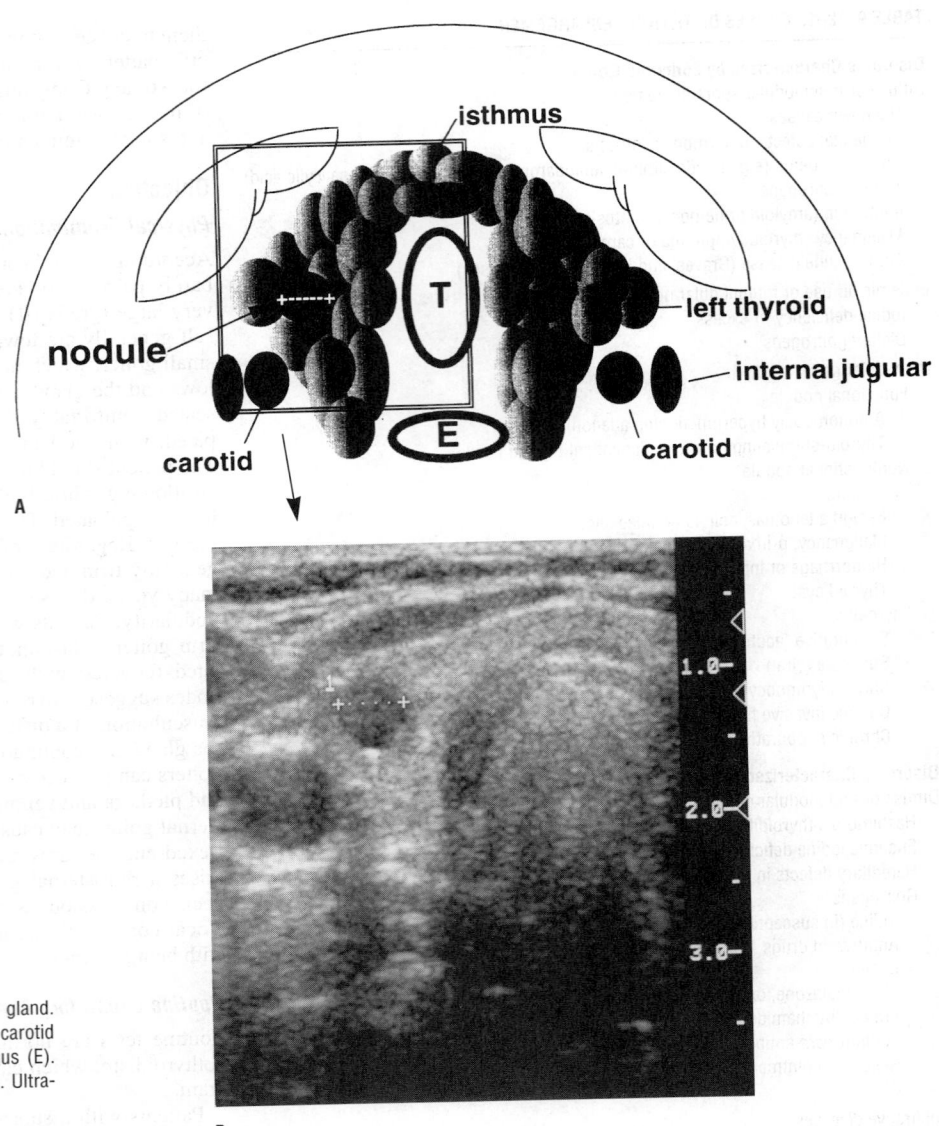

Figure 9–12–1. Ultrasonography of normal thyroid gland. **A.** Schematic of transverse view of neck showing thyroid, carotid arteries, internal jugular veins, trachea (T), and esophagus (E). **B.** The box represents the area shown on the ultrasound. Ultrasound showing a 0.5-cm nodule in the right thyroid lobe.

calculation from the total T_4 or T_3 and another test that measures the serum thyroid hormone-binding capacity (e.g., T_3 resin uptake test). Thyroid imaging can be done with radionuclide (^{123}I, which is preferred, or ^{99m}Tc) scans, thyroid ultrasonography, and computed tomography or magnetic resonance imaging. Antithyroid antibodies (antithyroglobulin and antimicrosomal) are obtained when there is clinical suspicion of Hashimoto's thyroiditis.

Pulmonary function tests may demonstrate upper airway obstruction with lowered peak flow rates and an altered flow-volume loop. Of the several tests available, the inspiratory–expiratory flow-volume loop is probably the most sensitive indicator of upper airway obstruction, particularly if the test is performed with the patient supine. Another test that can identify airway obstruction is computed tomography, which will delineate the extent of tracheal compression and will help differentiate a retrosternal goiter from an aneurysm. A barium swallow will show whether the esophagus is compressed, but is rarely necessary.

Recommended Approach

If serum TSH is high (>6 μU/mL), the patient may be hypothyroid and the free T_4 should be estimated. A normal or low free T_4 and a high TSH indicate hypothyroidism; measuring serum T_3 is not useful because many nonthyroidal disorders suppress its levels into the hypothyroid range. If serum TSH is below the detection limits of the assay

(≤0.04 μU/mL), the patient may be thyrotoxic and free T_4 should be measured; free T_3 is obtained if free T_4 is normal. Either or both are high in overt thyrotoxicosis, but both can be normal in subclinical thyrotoxicosis.

Thyroidal radioiodine (^{123}I) uptake and imaging studies are done routinely in thyrotoxic patients, but not others. Scans are rarely necessary in those with hypothyroidism or an isolated thyroid nodule. Multinodular toxic goiters or a single autonomously hyperfunctioning thyroid nodule shows increased radioiodine uptake in the palpable nodules, but little or no uptake in the surrounding tissues. Total radioiodine uptake may be within normal limits. In thyrotoxic Graves' disease, radioiodine uptake is increased and the scan shows homogeneous uptake.

It is important to understand that imaging studies do not rule in or exclude a diagnosis of thyrotoxicosis or hypothyroidism. This is done by blood tests. Nor do imaging studies define nodularity. This is done by palpation or ultrasonography. Imaging studies merely indicate the functional activity of one or more areas of the gland and may or may not correlate with the patient's thyroid functional status or the presence of thyroid nodules. For instance, a patient who is severely thyrotoxic from thyroid hormone ingestion will have a very low ^{123}I thyroidal uptake. Patients with Hashimoto's thyroiditis have an unpredictable and patchy thyroidal uptake of radionuclide. A hypothyroid patient with Hashimoto's thyroiditis may have a high ^{123}I uptake with low circulating serum thyroid hormone levels due to an intrathyroidal block in thyroid hormone synthesis. Moreover, areas of decreased radioiodine uptake (cold areas), which are common in patients with Hashimoto's thyroiditis, do not necessarily imply thyroid nodularity.

When a suspicious nodule exists within a goiter or when neoplastic disease is suspected in a rapidly growing, symptomatic thyroid with cervical lymphadenopathy, fine-needle aspiration biopsy is indicated as described in Chapter 9–13; however, most diffuse goiters do not require this procedure for diagnosis.

Therapeutic

Therapeutic Options

Treatment is employed to correct thyroid dysfunction or to alleviate symptoms caused by the goiter itself. The first should be identified by the physician, but the second should be determined by the patient. Some tolerate an enlarged gland very well, whereas others do not. Long-term thyroid hormone therapy that suppresses serum TSH to levels well below normal is not advised. Patients treated this way, especially those over age 50 years, may develop osteoporosis (especially postmenopausal women), left ventricular dysfunction, and atrial fibrillation.

Recommended Approach

For the patient with goitrous hypothyroidism, synthetic levothyroxine is the drug of choice because of its chemical stability, reliability, smooth action, and once-daily mode of administration. The goal is to reduce serum TSH into the normal range. The daily dose is approximately 1.6 μg/kg in adults between the ages of 18 and 60. Younger patients need larger doses and patients over age 60 require less. Serum TSH should be determined 2 months after the full estimated daily dose has been achieved. The dose is adjusted to maintain the TSH in the normal range. Patients under age 50 with mild hypothyroidism initially can be given at least half the total daily dose immediately, followed by the full daily replacement within a week. The most serious adverse side effects of thyroid hormone therapy are cardiovascular. Angina, cardiac arrhythmias, and congestive heart failure may occur in older patients, especially in those with full-blown myxedema of long duration, and in others with underlying heart conditions, or coronary artery disease. In patients who have these disorders or who might experience adverse reactions, the initial daily dose of levothyroxine should be about 12.5 to 25 μg, which should be increased in increments of 12.5 to 25 μg every 2 weeks until either the full maintenance dose is achieved or adverse effects begin to occur. There are occasionally other adverse side effects such as transient hand tremor or mental irritability and frank manic behavior.

Reactions to thyroid hormone replacement may occur within the first week of therapy. The most serious are angina, palpitations, and shortness of breath. There is usually a mild diuresis resulting in about a 5-pound weight loss. There also may be transient muscle cramps, tremor, and a vague sense of irritability or malaise lasting about a week. With full replacement therapy, the symptoms of hypothyroidism abate within a few months but the goiter may take many months to regress. The patient should be given instructions to enhance compliance and should be reminded not to take another medicine that interferes with thyroid hormone absorption such as sucralfate, aluminum hydroxide antacids, iron, or bile salt binders such as cholestyramine.

Treatment is less likely to benefit the patient with a long-standing euthyroid diffuse goiter with normal serum TSH concentrations. These goiters may not shrink when treated with levothyroxine, although some become smaller after prolonged therapy. It is difficult to predict which will enlarge further or become multinodular without therapy.

Multinodular euthyroid goiters, especially large ones, almost never regress with thyroid hormone therapy. Moreover, they may cause thyrotoxicosis because the nodules function independently of TSH. Late in their clinical course, multinodular goiters often cause thyrotoxicosis. Radioiodine is effective in treating multinodular goiters, even those not causing hyperthyroidism. Thyrotoxic Graves' disease may be treated with antithyroid drugs, propylthiouracil, or methimazole or with radioactive iodine or surgery. Treatment of thyrotoxicosis is discussed in detail in Chapter 9–17. Surgery is occasionally necessary to alleviate symptoms in patients with diffuse or nodular goiter. The main indica-

tions for surgery are obstructive or pressure symptoms caused by benign thyroid disease or a fine-needle aspiration biopsy diagnosis or strong suspicion of malignancy. The selection of thyroid nodules for surgery is discussed in Chapter 9–13.

FOLLOW-UP

Patients with goiter, regardless of their initial thyroid functional activity, should be seen at yearly intervals when signs and symptoms of thyrotoxicosis and hypothyroidism should be sought. The thyroid examination should focus on changes since the last examination, and a hand-drawn picture of the thyroid should be made in the office notes at each visit. If there is suspicion that the goiter is changing, ultrasonography should be done to document it. This is especially important with nodular thyroid disease. A TSH level is obtained in all patients. This is because the dose of thyroid hormone often requires adjustments and patients who are clinically euthyroid may develop subtle thyroid dysfunction not apparent on examination.

DISCUSSION

Prevalence and Incidence

The exact prevalence and incidence of nontoxic goiter in the United States are uncertain, but it is clearly the most common of all thyroid diseases, increasing with age and affecting many of the population over age 50. Thyroid disease is three- to eightfold more common in women, depending on its etiology. In adolescent females, mild thyroid enlargement occurs so often that it is considered a physiologic occurrence. The prevalence of most thyroid diseases increases with age. After age 60, about 4 to 5% develop thyroid nodules and another 1 to 2% have overt hypothyroidism. Graves' disease, the most common cause of thyrotoxicosis in the United States, occurs in up to 1% of the adult population and is seen particularly often in women in the third and fourth decades of life.

Related Basic Science

Graves' disease and Hashimoto's thyroiditis are autoimmune disorders in which the thyroid is the target organ of an abnormal immune response. In Graves' disease, abnormal circulating thyroid-stimulating immunoglobulins cause thyroid enlargement and increase its functional activity. Some patients with Graves' disease, however, develop goiter but remain euthyroid. In Hashimoto's thyroiditis, the autoimmune response results in lymphocytic infiltration with germinal centers, degeneration of the thyroid follicles, and diffuse fibrosis. Patients with Hashimoto's thyroiditis usually remain euthyroid or develop hypothyroidism, but some develop thyrotoxicosis that is clinically indistinguishable from Graves' disease. Both Graves' disease and Hashimoto's thyroiditis may be components of a multiple endocrine deficiency syndrome involving the adrenals, parathyroids, pancreas, and gonads.

The cause of nontoxic colloid goiter is less certain. In some it may develop in response to drugs that contain iodine or are intrinsically goitrogenic. In others it is the result of unrecognized familial dyshormonogenesis. In most, however, its cause remains uncertain even after intensive investigation, although it involves the evolution of cell clones that function autonomously. There seems to be a participatory role of TSH in the development and early maintenance of some euthyroid goiters, as suppressive doses of thyroid hormone cause some to shrink. TSH may be slightly elevated initially, but it is usually normal in those with long-standing goiter. In contrast, TSH tends to rise and remain elevated in those with chronic lymphocytic thyroiditis.

Natural History and Its Modification with Treatment

The natural history of goiter depends on the underlying pathology. Hashimoto's disease has an unpredictable course, but most remain euthyroid over several years' follow-up. In contrast, those with serum TSH levels greater than 20 μU/mL or very high antithyroid antibody titers develop overt hypothyroidism within a few years. Patients with simple colloid goiters over many years develop thyroid nodularity with evidence of functional autonomy and eventually many become thyrotoxic. Patients with goiter, regardless of its cause, are very sensitive to iodine and may develop either hypothyroidism or thyrotoxicosis when given pharmacologic doses. There is no reason to treat goiter with iodine, an old practice that has been long abandoned.

Prevention

A continuous supply of dietary iodine is necessary to prevent goiter and for thyroid hormone synthesis. In this country, the main sources are iodized salt, red meat, white bread, fish, and canned foods. More than adequate amounts of iodine are present in the American diet, but this is not true in some parts of the world. In euthyroid adults, net thyroidal uptake of iodine must be about 75 µg daily to prevent goiter. Although different among the various regions in the United States, there has been a gradual rise in our dietary intake of iodine. An American ingesting about 2800 calories has an average daily iodine intake of 700 µg. There are few other preventive measures except the avoidance of pharmacologic doses of iodine in patients with euthyroid goiters.

Cost Containment

Simple euthyroid colloid goiter can be readily recognized clinically and initially requires only a TSH measurement. Imaging studies, although commonly done in practice, are not required in the patient with a normal TSH. Radioiodine uptake and scans should be done in thyrotoxic patients. When thyroid hormone therapy is required, levothyroxine is the preparation of choice and can be given for only a few cents daily. Once the correct dose of levothyroxine has been found, patients can be followed with TSH measurements alone once a year. When the levothyroxine dose is adjusted, TSH should be measured 2 months later.

The major expense incurred in treating patients with euthyroid goiter is due to surgery. Only patients with intractable symptoms of obstruction or in whom the fine-needle aspiration biopsy reveals cancer or is indeterminate should undergo surgery (see Chapter 9–13). Many who are thyrotoxic can be treated with radioiodine. This is substantially less expensive than surgery, and it is very effective in reducing goiter size even in euthyroid patients, although ^{131}I therapy is not yet approved by the FDA for the treatment of euthyroid goiter. Many patients require no specific therapy and can be followed with simple surveillance and serum TSH measurement once yearly.

REFERENCES

Celani MF. Levothyroxine suppressive therapy in the medical management of nontoxic benign multinodular goiter. Exp Clin Endocrinol 1993;101:326.

Huysmans DA, Hermus AR, Corstens FH, Kloppenborg PW. Long-term results of two schedules of radioiodine treatment for toxic multinodular goitre. Eur J Nucl Med 1993;20:1056.

Jayme JJ, Ladenson PW. Subclinical thyroid dysfunction in the elderly. Trends Endocrinol Metab 1994;5:79.

Mandel SJ, Brent GA, Larsen PR. Levothyroxine therapy in patients with thyroid disease. Ann Intern Med 1993;119:492.

Nygaard B, Hegedus L, Gervil M, et al. Radioiodine treatment of multinodular non-toxic goitre. Br Med J 1993;307:828.

CHAPTER 9–13

Thyroid Nodules

Ernest L. Mazzaferri, MD

DEFINITION

A solitary nodule is a palpably discrete nodule within an otherwise apparently normal thyroid gland. It must be distinguished from one or more palpable nodules within a multinodular colloid goiter. Although this chapter deals with the palpably solitary thyroid nodule, this is not an entirely satisfactory designation because many clinically "solitary" nodules are multiple when examined by ultrasonography or at surgery. Moreover, a multinodular goiter may contain a suspicious nodule which should be regarded with the same concern as an isolated thyroid nodule.

ETIOLOGY

Thyroid nodularity is a nonspecific finding which may be caused by virtually any thyroid disorder and is occasionally due to nonthyroidal disease. Although the main concern is thyroid malignancy, most are benign lesions. Table 9–13–1 lists the causes of thyroid nodules.

Some patients have a genetic predisposition to thyroid carcinoma. Medullary thyroid carcinoma may be inherited as an autosomal dominant trait in the multiple endocrine neoplasia type IIa and IIb or familial medullary thyroid carcinoma syndromes (see Chapter 9–14). Papillary thyroid carcinoma rarely is clustered among members of one family, probably inherited as an autosomal dominant trait. It also is part of several familial syndromes (see Chapter 9–14).

The principal environmental factor involved in the pathogenesis of thyroid carcinoma is ionizing radiation. X-ray therapy was first introduced in 1914 as therapy for "status thymicolymphaticus," a condition now known as "sudden infant death syndrome." By 1920, it was considered good medical practice for the treatment of this and a number of other benign conditions, including enlarged tonsils and adenoids, deafness, cervical adenitis, mastoiditis, sinusitis, hemangiomas and keloids, tinea capitis, and acne. It was not until 1959 that the first association between childhood irradiation and thyroid carcinoma was made. By the early 1960s, this association was clearly documented and clarified. Its magnitude was underscored in the 1970s by reports that many children with thyroid carcinoma had undergone head or neck irradiation in infancy. A series of publications warned that this continued to occur in the 1980s, but recently the problem may have reached its peak in the United States; however, children exposed to fallout in the Chernobyl nuclear reactor accident have been developing thyroid neoplasms at a rapid rate. The risk is lower in adults exposed to radiation. In children, the risk of developing thyroid carcinoma is proportional to the dose and is linear between 10 and 2000 rad. At higher thyroid radiation doses,

TABLE 9–13–1. CAUSES OF ISOLATED THYROID NODULES

Adenomas	Infections
Follicular	Granulomas
Macrofollicular (simple colloid)	Abscess
Embryonal (fetal)	Graves' disease
Hürthle cell (oxyphil, oncocytic)	Developmental abnormalities
Atypical	Unilateral lobe agenesis
Others	Cystic hygroma
Autonomously hyperfunctioning	Dermoid tumors
Cysts	Teratoma
Pure cysts	Carcinoma
Mixed cystic–solid lesions	Primary thyroid
Thyroiditis	Papillary
Acute	Follicular
Subacute	Medullary
Chronic (Hashimoto's thyroiditis)	Anaplastic
Riedel's struma	Others
	Secondary (metastatic)
	Lymphoma of thyroid

the risk is substantially smaller. The latent period from radiation to detection ranges from about 3.5 years to an apparent peak about 35 years later. Although a few children treated with radiation at high doses for Hodgkin's disease have developed thyroid cancer, the thyroid usually is shielded during therapy. Radioiodine used diagnostically or to treat hyperthyroidism, even in children, has not been shown to cause thyroid carcinoma. The exact frequency of carcinoma following irradiation varies with the thyroid radiation dose. Following childhood head or neck irradiation, palpable thyroid nodules occur in about 30%; about one third of the nodules are malignant.

CRITERIA FOR DIAGNOSIS
Suggestive

A thyroid nodule may be suggested by symptoms of thyroid dysfunction (either hypothyroidism or thyrotoxicosis), a pressure sensation in the neck, dysphagia, unexplained hoarseness, chronic cough, positional cough or stridor, or a sensation of neck discomfort when supine. In most cases the diagnosis is suggested by an asymptomatic neck lump noticed by the patient or found on routine examination. Less often, a family history of thyroid cancer may suggest the diagnosis. A family history of thyroid cancer or of type II multiple endocrine neoplasia often prompts the patient to seek medical advice and should trigger further evaluation. Members of kindreds with multiple endocrine neoplasia type II or familial medullary thyroid carcinoma should be encouraged to participate in screening programs for medullary thyroid carcinoma.

Definitive

Thyroid nodules may be quite apparent on inspection or palpation of the neck, which is sufficient evidence for their diagnosis. When a thyroid nodule is suspected but not clearly identified by physical examination, ultrasonography may document its presence; however, this test discloses abnormalities in up to half the general population and must be interpreted in the light of clinical findings. Identifying a thyroid nodule by examination or ultrasonography does not distinguish its cause but is reason for further testing. The diagnostic possibilities for an isolated thyroid nodule are listed in Table 9–13–1. Although the majority are benign lesions, a few are malignant. The latter raises the most concern and is the main reason the pathology of a nodule must be identified. A definitive diagnosis requires biopsy in almost all cases.

CLINICAL MANIFESTATIONS
Subjective

Symptoms

Most thyroid nodules, regardless of their pathology, are asymptomatic. Symptoms are usually due to pressure on contiguous neck structures causing dysphagia and a choking or pressure sensation, complaints that occur with both benign and malignant lesions. Some symptoms, however, such as hoarseness due to vocal cord paralysis, severe dysphagia, and hemoptysis, are more ominous because they often indicate that a malignant tumor is invading neck tissues. Pain, tenderness, and rapid growth of the nodule may occur, or pain may be referred to the ear, which is usually the result of inflammation or hemorrhagic infarction. In younger patients these symptoms often accompany thyroiditis or hemorrhage into a benign nodule, but in older patients they suggest anaplastic thyroid carcinoma or thyroid lymphoma. A few patients have autonomously hyperfunctioning (hot) thyroid nodules, which may or may not cause thyrotoxicosis. Symptoms are typically mild and difficult to ascribe to thyroid dysfunction. Mild irritability, palpitations, and minor weight loss may be all the younger patient notices. Older thyrotoxic patients can experience atrial fibrillation and other serious cardiac arrhythmias, heart failure, apparent dementia of obscure cause, substantial weight loss, and muscle weakness.

Past History

A history of prior head and neck x-ray therapy for benign or malignant conditions should be carefully elicited. Patients often do not know if they were treated with x-rays as an infant, but this history may be obtained from a parent. A history of other radiation exposures should be elicited. For instance, some children who lived in Nevada and Utah in the 1950s and 1960s were exposed to fallout from above-ground nuclear weapons testing.

Family History

A family history of papillary thyroid cancer or of type II multiple endocrine neoplasia should be elicited.

Objective
Physical Examination

A thyroid nodule may be barely palpable or may be large enough to be visible. Other than this, physical findings due to the nodule itself are relatively few. Shining a light across the neck will highlight the nodule as it moves upward while the patient swallows. Thyroid nodules may range in character from soft, smooth, bulging, sharply outlined, discrete, and cystic lesions to firm or hard, irregular, and poorly defined masses; however, the physical characteristics of the nodule give little clue to the diagnosis. Benign nodules may be stony hard and irregular, whereas papillary carcinoma may be smooth, well circumscribed, and soft. Most thyroid nodules are nontender. A few are exquisitely tender. In younger patients this is a sign of thyroiditis or hemorrhage into a benign nodule, but in older persons it often indicates malignancy. Large, nontender cervical lymph nodes suggest a thyroid malignancy. A midline node just above and slightly to the left of the thyroid isthmus, termed a *Delphian node*, may be a signal of carcinoma. A thyroglossal duct cyst is found in the same location but is identified by its upward movement when the tongue is protruded.

Routine Laboratory Abnormalities

The routine laboratory test results are normal. Occasionally, the chest x-ray will reveal substernal extension of a goiter and, rarely, will show metastases of thyroid carcinoma.

PLANS
Diagnostic

Differential Diagnosis

The differential diagnosis of a solitary thyroid nodule is summarized in Table 9–13–1.

Diagnostic Options

No laboratory tests other than a TSH are usually required. TSH will be suppressed to undetectable levels (usually ≤0.04 μ/mL) in thyrotoxic patients and elevated above normal (≥6 μU/mL) in some with thyroiditis. The available options include imaging the nodule with ultrasonography, radioiodine (^{123}I), which is preferred, technetium (^{99m}Tc), computed tomography, or magnetic resonance imaging scans. The nodule's response to thyroid hormone suppression can be used as a diagnostic test, but is not recommended. None of these techniques reliably identifies malignant nodules. The most widely used and accurate means of identifying the pathology of a nodule is fine-needle aspiration biopsy.

Recommended Approach

Fine-needle aspiration biopsy (FNAB) can be done in the office with a 25-gauge needle attached to a 20-cc syringe that is best held in a specially designed syringe aspirator. The nodule is steadied with one hand and biopsied by inserting the needle into the mass and moving its tip about 30° several times to loosen the tissue before aspirating for 2 to 3 seconds. The negative pressure is relaxed and the needle is withdrawn from the nodule. A satisfactory specimen remains in the needle itself and is immediately transferred to a slide by removing the needle momentarily, drawing a few milliliters of air into the syringe, replacing the needle, and using the air to gently force the specimen onto the slide. Alcohol-fixed smears can be stained by the Papanicolaou method or with hematoxylin and eosin. An example of satisfactory specimen is depicted in Figure 9–13–1. There are virtually no serious complications

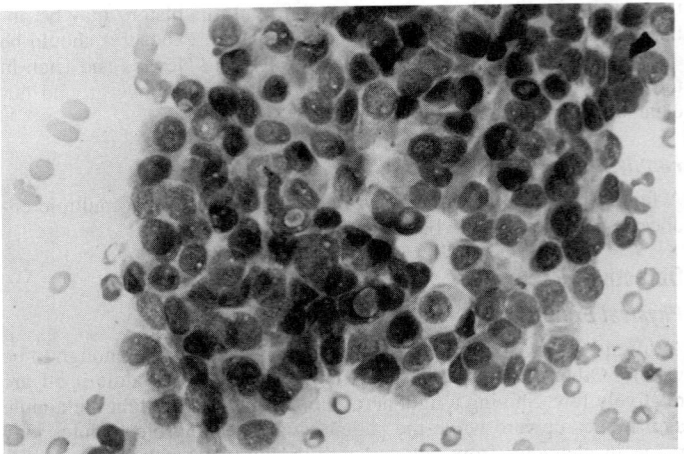

Figure 9–13–1. Photomicrograph of a specimen showing a fine-needle aspiration biopsy cytology specimen. This is a papillary cancer specimen showing crowded eccentric variable-sized nuclei, powdery chromatin, prominent nucleoli, intranuclear inclusions, nuclear grooves, and abundant cytoplasm without colloid (×375).

with FNAB, whereas larger needles may cause hemorrhage and recurrent laryngeal nerve damage. The main technical problem with FNAB is an inadequate specimen resulting from attempting to biopsy small (<1 cm) lesions, less accessible nodules (distal lateral lobe lesions), or nodules larger than 4 to 5 cm that are hemorrhagic. When an adequate specimen is obtained, an experienced cytologist will report one of three possibilities: benign, malignant, or indeterminate (Figure 9–13–2). Papillary carcinoma is usually recognized by its distinct cytologic features. Medullary and anaplastic thyroid carcinoma and thyroid lymphoma are easily identified as malignant by FNAB. Follicular carcinoma and adenoma, however, usually cannot be differentiated and are reported simply as a follicular tumor. This is an indeterminate cytology result, reported in about 20 to 30% of biopsies. Thyroiditis is a major cause of a false-positive cancer diagnosis.

Cystic lesions account for about 20% of the thyroid nodules biopsied. Purely cystic lesions are usually benign, but partly solid lesions may be malignant. The cytology of a cystic malignant lesion may be obscured by the necrotic hemorrhagic material in the specimen. Accordingly, after the cystic lesion has been aspirated, the residual nodule

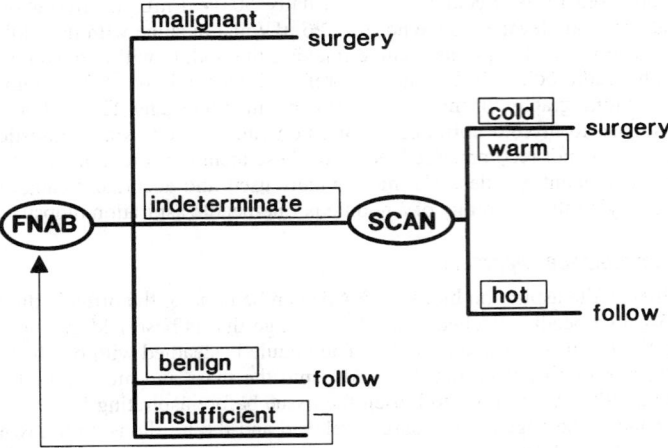

Figure 9–13–2. Sequence for the evaluation of patients with a thyroid nodule. The results of radionuclide scanning are expressed at "hot," "warm," or "cold," to indicate the function of the nodule in relation to the normal thyroid tissue in the patient. FNAB, fine-needle aspiration biopsy. (*Source: Mazzaferri EL. Management of a solitary thyroid nodule. N Engl J Med 1993;328:553. Reproduced with permission from the publisher and author.*)

should be aspirated. Papillary thyroid carcinoma frequently presents as a hemorrhagic cystic lesion. Cystic cancers are one of the main causes of false-negative thyroid aspiration cytology. Attempting to make a cytologic diagnosis on a scant specimen is a major cause of this problem.

If the cytology reveals malignancy, the nodule should be excised. If it shows a benign disorder, no further diagnostic studies are necessary. To be certain that the lesion is benign, the specimen should contain abundant colloid and normal follicular cells. Thyroiditis can also be identified, but the presence of atypical cells and Hürthle cells may suggest cancer. If the cytology shows sheets of follicular cells without colloid, this is an indeterminate specimen and a thyroid scintiscan should be done (Figure 9–13–2). Hot nodules are almost never malignant. A hot nodule causing thyrotoxicosis concentrates most or all of the ^{123}I compared with the normal surrounding thyroid parenchyma. Some do not cause clinically obvious thyrotoxicosis but suppress the serum TSH to the assay's detection limits (≤ 0.04 μU/mL), which indicates occult thyrotoxicosis. Others have normal thyroid function.

For many years, physicians used thyroid hormone suppression of TSH to differentiate benign and malignant nodules. This was based on the notion that malignant nodules would continue to grow, while benign lesions, because of their TSH dependency, would remain unchanged or shrink. This has proven unreliable. Nodules that initially appear to shrink or remain stable for years may be malignant. The only response that excludes malignancy is total disappearance of the nodule by examination and ultrasonography, which seldom occurs. Accordingly, this is not a test that should be used routinely in the diagnosis of thyroid nodules.

Therapeutic

Therapeutic Options

Many thyroid nodules require no therapy. Others can be treated with thyroid hormone alone and a few require surgical excision. Malignant nodules require more extensive treatment (see Chapter 9–14).

Recommended Approach

Therapy of thyroid nodules is dictated by the lesion's pathology. They can be divided into benign colloid nodules that do not disturb thyroid function, cystic thyroid nodules, benign hyperfunctional colloid nodules, nodules with indeterminate cytology, and those following head or neck irradiation and malignant nodules.

Benign colloid nodules that do not alter thyroid function usually require no therapy. These are usually a dominant nodule in an otherwise clinically imperceptible multinodular gland. They can be treated with thyroid hormone using a daily dose of 1.6 μg/kg levothyroxine in adults, but this practice has come under increasing criticism. This is because thyroid hormone suppression of TSH has been shown to be no better than placebo in prospective randomized studies in which patients have been treated for periods as long as several years. Proponents of thyroid hormone suppression argue that these are relatively short-term studies and that at least half the benign colloid nodules treated this way undergo a 50% reduction in size. Perhaps the most serious problems, however, relate to the long-term adverse effects of TSH suppression therapy. It can lead to loss of bone mineral content, particularly in postmenopausal women but also in children. In patients over 65, TSH suppression over a decade is associated with a rate of atrial fibrillation that is threefold that in euthyroid persons. Other more subtle cardiac abnormalities may occur. Patients with TSH chronically suppressed by thyroid hormone have more atrial premature beats than control subjects and their echocardiograms show modest enhancement of left ventricular contractile function. Of much more concern, patients without a history of heart disease may develop left ventricular hypertrophy demonstrable by echocardiography. These observations raise serious concern about the cardiac effects of long-term suppressive thyroid hormone therapy. Thus, older euthyroid adults and postmenopausal women with benign colloid nodules are best left untreated unless thyroid hormone is given for short periods under careful supervision. Even then, the TSH should be maintained in the low normal range. Treating younger patients with thyroid hormone may be safer, but is more effective with clinically obvious multinodular colloid goiter than with an isolated thyroid nodule.

The fluid from benign cystic lesions can be repeatedly evacuated by needle aspiration but about half persist. Some treat them with ethanol injection, a practice that has become popular in European clinics. Large hemorrhagic lesions usually require surgical excision.

Functional (hot) thyroid nodules not causing thyrotoxicosis can be left untreated, whereas those causing thyrotoxicosis are treated with either ^{131}I or surgery. The main benefits of surgery are the rapidity and certainty of cure, which must be balanced against its substantial cost. Radioiodine is usually effective in nodules smaller than 3 to 4 cm, where it will cure the thyrotoxicosis without destroying normal thyroid tissue, but the mass itself is likely to persist. The main advantages of ^{131}I are its low cost relative to surgery and the fact that the patient does not require hospitalization.

Patients with a history of head or neck x-ray treatments who have nodular thyroid disease require surgery if the FNAB is suspicious or shows malignant cells. This is a special problem because the surrounding thyroid tissue may eventually develop further disease and often contains occult malignancies. Thus it is best to perform near-total thyroidectomy in previously irradiated patients.

Nonfunctional benign thyroid adenomas (lesions with indeterminate cytology) should be surgically removed along with a small amount of surrounding thyroid tissue, leaving most of the thyroid intact until the final histologic sections of the nodule are studied. Malignant nodules pose special therapeutic problems that are discussed in detail in Chapter 9–14.

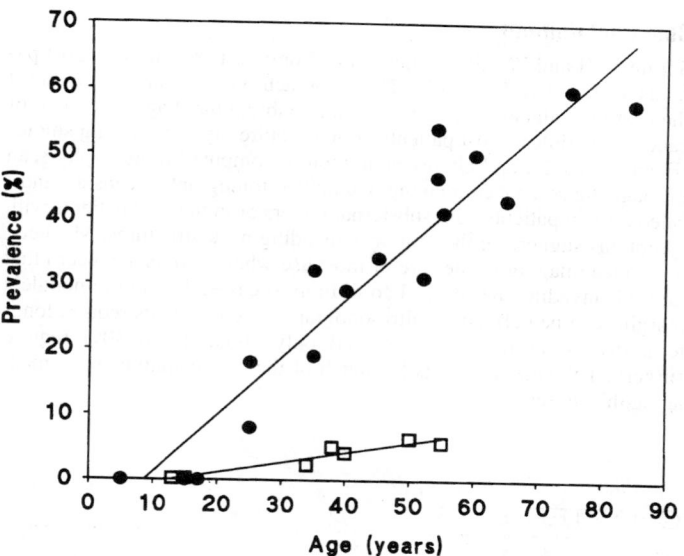

Figure 9–13–3. Prevalence of thyroid nodules detected at autopsy or by ultrasonography (•) or palpation (□). *(Source: Mazzaferri EL. Management of a solitary thyroid nodule. N Engl J Med 1993;328:553. Reproduced with permission from the publisher and author.)*

FOLLOW-UP

Patients must be assured that although most thyroid nodules are benign, the few malignant ones can be identified; but the identification process may take months to accomplish. About 3% of negative FNAB results are false-negative tests. When this occurs, the nodule's true character usually becomes apparent over about a year's follow-up. Over this time, malignant nodules show distinct growth as determined by ultrasonography. The patient should be assured that most thyroid carcinomas are very slow growing neoplasms which offer an excellent chance for cure. Accordingly, the odds are overwhelmingly in favor of a good response with accurate diagnosis and appropriate therapy. Patients require follow-up over several years, regardless of the diagnosis.

Euthyroid patients with thyroid nodules that have been accurately diagnosed should be followed at yearly intervals. For patients with benign thyroid lesions, the character and size of the nodule should be assessed by physical examination or ultrasonography and the patient's metabolic status should be evaluated by serum TSH measurement. Euthyroid patients with hot nodules should be warned of the symptoms of thyrotoxicosis and nodule infarction. The latter causes neck pain radiating to the ear and neck tenderness that ordinarily lasts only a few days and can be controlled with minor analgesics. When there is a sudden change in the size of the nodule or symptoms of nodule infarction occur, thyroid ultrasonography will identify intranodular hemorrhage and differentiate it from rapid nodular growth.

DISCUSSION
Prevalence

The prevalence of thyroid nodules increases steadily during life, beginning in the first several decades and extending through the later years (Figure 9–13–3). About 1% of nonirradiated children and about 6 to 7% of the older population have them. About 80% occur in women and the majority are benign. Only 1 person in about 28,000 in the general population develops clinically apparent thyroid carcinoma.

Related Basic Science

Except for the 5% of thyroid nodules that are hyperfunctional (hot), most do not alter thyroid function. Hot nodules, which may or may not cause thyrotoxicosis, occur with a five- to tenfold greater frequency in women than in men. Hot nodules are distributed about equally in patients older and younger than age 40. Histologically, hot nodules are follicular adenomas or adenomatoid (hyperplastic) nodules. When the lesion is small, the surrounding thyroid parenchyma functions nor-

mally. As it grows and secretes more thyroid hormone, TSH and the normal surrounding thyroid tissues become increasingly more suppressed. Eventually, the remainder of the thyroid gland may atrophy and show complete suppression of thyroid function. A hot nodule frequently shows central degeneration and may undergo frank hemorrhagic infarction, changing to a hypofunctional nodule. The origin of the hot nodule remains uncertain, but probably involves the replication of distinct cell clones that become functionally autonomous.

Natural History and Its Modification with Treatment

The natural history of most benign thyroid nodules is not well understood, partly because the cytologic designation *benign colloid nodule* may refer to either a hyperplastic colloid nodule or, less often, a simple follicular adenoma. The risk that a follicular adenoma will undergo malignant degeneration is unknown, but it is possible that some highly cellular or atypical adenomas do develop into cancers. Many authorities believe that monoclonal follicular adenomas undergo malignant degeneration. Follicular adenomas may have such atypical cellular appearance that some consider them carcinomas in situ. Multinodular colloid goiter almost never undergoes malignant degeneration unless it contains monoclonal nodules, as sometimes happens, that may give rise to follicular cancer.

It is not clear that suppressive therapy with thyroid hormone modifies the natural history of benign thyroid nodules. About half undergo at least a 50% reduction in size with thyroid hormone therapy; however, many studies indicate that nearly the same occurs without therapy. Of patients with colloid nodules followed prospectively without therapy, about one fourth show at least a 50% spontaneous reduction in size over 6 months to 3 years. In some studies, about 20% of nodules disappear completely, another 15% decrease in size, and 50% remain unchanged without thyroid hormone therapy; about 15% grow. Among patients with hot nodules, about 20% have thyrotoxicosis (mostly patients 40 years of age or older with a nodule 3 cm or more in diameter). A few undergo acute hemorrhagic infarction that causes transient thyrotoxicosis; however, thyrotoxicosis develops in less than 10% of euthyroid patients with hot nodules who are followed for up to 6 years.

The main preventive measure in the development of thyroid nodules is the avoidance of therapeutic x-rays to the head or neck. If x-ray therapy cannot be avoided, as in the treatment of Hodgkin's disease, the thyroid gland should be shielded.

Cost Containment

Serum TSH and FNAB are the first and only tests required in most patients with a thyroid nodule. This approach has substantially reduced the cost of evaluation while more than doubling the diagnostic yield of cancer in nodules. Most patients do not require thyroid imaging studies (Figure 9–13–2), and almost none require computed tomography scan or magnetic resonance imaging. Computed tomography scans are indicated only in patients with substernal goiters or in unusual patients with symptoms suggesting that tumor is invading neck structures. Magnetic resonance imaging studies are of most use when there is a concern that tumor is invading the cervical cord. In most cases, the thyroid nodule's margins can be defined by ultrasonography. Few patients require long-term thyroid hormone therapy and only about 20 to 30% require surgery. The latter accounts for much of the cost containment in managing this disease.

REFERENCES

Caruso D, Mazzaferri EL. Fine needle aspiration biopsy in the management of thyroid nodules. Endocrinologist 1991;1:194.
Ezzat S, Sarti DA, Cain DR, Braunstein GD. Thyroid incidentalomas: Prevalence by palpation and ultrasonography. Arch Intern Med 1994;154:1838.
Gharib H. Fine-needle aspiration biopsy of thyroid nodules: Advantages, limitations, and effect. Mayo Clin Proc 1994;69:44.
Gönczi J, Szabolcs I, Kovacs Z, et al. Ultrasonography of the thyroid gland in hospitalized, chronically ill geriatric patients: Thyroid volume, its relationship to age and disease, and the prevalence of diffuse and nodular goiter. J Clin Ultrasound 1994;22:257.
Hamburger JI. Extensive personal experience: Diagnosis of thyroid nodules by fine needle biopsy: Use and abuse. J Clin Endocrinol Metab 1994;79:335.
Mazzaferri EL. Management of a solitary thyroid nodule. N Engl J Med 1993;328:553.

CHAPTER 9–14

Thyroid Carcinoma

Ernest L. Mazzaferri, M.D.

DEFINITION

Thyroid carcinoma originates from thyroid follicular cells or calcitonin-secreting cells (C cells) and consists of a group of neoplasms with distinctly different histologic characteristics and strikingly different clinical behavior. There are four major types of thyroid carcinoma: papillary, follicular, medullary, and anaplastic (Table 9–14–1).

ETIOLOGY

The principal environmental factor involved in the pathogenesis of thyroid carcinoma is ionizing radiation. Dietary iodine has an effect on the development of thyroid cancer. In geographic regions where dietary iodine is low, the incidence of follicular cancer is greater than that of papillary cancer; the frequency of the two reverses when iodine is added to the diet.

Papillary thyroid carcinoma, which is rarely clustered in kindreds and is also part of several familial syndromes including Gardner's syndrome (familial adenomatous polyposis), Cowden's disease (hamartomas, multinodular goiters, and thyroid, breast, colon, and lung cancers), and familial chemodectomas, is the most common form of thyroid cancer in the United States. The prevalence of papillary thyroid cancer is increased 100-fold in patients with Gardner's syndrome. About 20% of medullary thyroid carcinomas (MTCs) are inherited as an autosomal dominant trait with a high degree of penetrance as one of four familial syndromes (Table 9–14–2). The responsible gene is the *RET* proto-oncogene located on chromosome 10, where point mutations lead to the familial disease. Multiple endocrine neoplasia (MEN) type IIa is the most common. MEN IIb may appear both as an inherited disorder and as *de novo* disease. The third, familial MTC, may occur without other components of MEN IIa. In the fourth and the rarest variant, MTC is associated with a pruritic skin lesion located over the upper back (cutaneous lichen amyloidosis). There is no known etiology for sporadic medullary thyroid carcinoma.

CRITERIA FOR DIAGNOSIS

Suggestive

The main clue to the diagnosis of well-differentiated thyroid carcinoma is usually an asymptomatic thyroid lump, which is either first noticed

TABLE 9–14–1. MALIGNANT THYROID TUMORS

Epithelial tumors
  Follicular carcinoma
    Hürthle cell variant*
    Minimally invasive
    Widely invasive*
  Papillary carcinoma
    Follicular variant†
    Microcarcinoma
    Tall cell variant*
    Columnar variant*
    Diffuse sclerosis variant*
    Encapsulated
  Medullary carcinoma
    Sporadic
    Familial (four syndromes)
  Undifferentiated (anaplastic) carcinoma
  Others
    Poorly differentiated insular carcinoma
Nonepithelial tumors
  Fibrosarcoma
  Malignant hemangioendothelioma
  Teratomas
  Malignant lymphoma
Tumors metastatic to thyroid

*Worse prognosis than the usual variants.
†Possibly worse prognosis than usual variants.

TABLE 9–14–2. MEDULLARY THYROID CARCINOMA

Sporadic form
  Unilateral thyroid tumors
  No somatic lesions
Familial endocrine neoplasia IIa
  Medullary thyroid carcinoma (bilateral)
  Pheochromocytoma (bilateral)
  Hyperparathyroidism
Familial multiple endocrine neoplasia IIb
  Medullary thyroid carcinoma (bilateral)
  Pheochromocytoma (bilateral)
  Abnormal phenotype
    Multiple mucosal neuromas
    Intestinal ganglioneuromas
    Skeletal abnormalities (marfanoid habitus)
    Ophthalmic abnormalities
Familial medullary thyroid carcinoma (only)
Familial medullary thyroid carcinoma
  Associated with cutaneous lichen amyloidosis

by the patient or found on routine examination. A history of prior head or neck irradiation, neck symptoms, or symptoms from distant metastases may suggest the diagnosis. MTC is often discovered in screening programs of members of affected kindreds.

Definitive

Papillary and follicular thyroid cancers arise from thyroid follicular cells. They are identified by fine-needle aspiration biopsy or on permanent histologic sections. MTC arises from thyroid calcitonin-secreting cells and often requires special tissue staining for calcitonin to differentiate it from anaplastic carcinoma. The other *in vivo* criterion for the identification of MTC is an abnormal plasma calcitonin concentration. Familial MTC can now be identified by genetic testing. Anaplastic carcinoma arises from follicular cells and may originate from well-differentiated tumors. Thyroid lymphoma is usually a B-cell neoplasm.

CLINICAL MANIFESTATIONS
Subjective

Patients with well-differentiated thyroid carcinoma are usually asymptomatic or nearly so. Tumor pressing on contiguous neck structures causes dysphagia, choking, or a pressure sensation. Larger tumors can invade neck structures, producing laryngeal nerve damage and vocal cord paralysis. Tracheal invasion leads to hemoptysis and underscores a tumor's aggressive behavior. Pain, tenderness, and rapid growth of a goiter may be symptoms of anaplastic carcinoma or lymphoma. Distant metastases causing bone pain, pathologic fracture, cord compression, neurologic deficits from brain metastases, or hemoptysis may be the initial manifestations of tumor, particularly follicular or Hürthle cell cancers.

Medullary thyroid carcinoma synthesizes calcitonin, serotonin, prostaglandins, adrenocorticotropic hormone, and other substances. About 10% of MTC patients have flushing episodes, possibly due to tumor release of prostaglandins and serotonin. The only recognized clinical manifestation of high circulating concentrations of calcitonin is a secretory diarrhea that occurs in about 30% of patients, usually with bulky tumors. Ectopic secretion of adrenocorticotropic hormone, because of the indolent course of MTC, may cause typical Cushing's syndrome.

Objective
Physical Examination

Most well-differentiated thyroid carcinomas present as an isolated thyroid nodule. More advanced tumors may appear as a diffusely enlarged or multinodular thyroid. There are no characteristics of the malignant nodule itself that are distinct enough to distinguish it from a benign thyroid lesion. Cervical lymph nodes, found in up to half the patients with papillary thyroid carcinoma, are sometimes the only palpable abnormality. There usually is no apparent thyroid lesion when familial MTC is discovered during routine calcitonin screening. MEN IIb patients can be identified by their marfanoid habitus and ganglioneuromas of the tarsal plates, lips, and tongue.

Routine Laboratory Abnormalities

Routine laboratory tests are usually normal, except for patients with the MEN IIa syndrome, who may have asymptomatic hypercalcemia.

The chest x-ray film may show metastases.

PLANS
Diagnostic
Differential Diagnosis

The differential diagnosis of a solitary thyroid nodule is summarized in Chapter 9–13. Large malignant tumors, regardless of their histology, are usually very invasive and symptomatic, displaying rapid growth with palpable cervical lymph nodes in many cases.

Diagnostic Options

The best means of identifying a nodule's pathology is fine-needle aspiration biopsy. Patients suspected of having MTC should have plasma calcitonin and carcinoembryonic antigen measurements and genetic testing. Serum thyroglobulin is elevated in patients with papillary and follicular thyroid carcinoma, but is used only for follow-up after therapy.

Recommended Approach

Except for follicular cancer, thyroid carcinoma can be diagnosed by fine-needle aspiration biopsy. Papillary thyroid cancer can be identified by its cytologic features in 95% of the cases. Fewer than half the follicular thyroid cancers can be recognized this way; most require careful histologic study of fixed specimens. MTC usually can be distinguished as malignant by fine-needle aspiration biopsy, although its medullary identity may not be immediately apparent. This diagnosis often requires special immunohistologic staining for calcitonin. Plasma calcitonin testing detects most cases of MTC and C-cell hyperplasia (the earliest histologically recognizable phase of the disease). This is not done routinely in patients with thyroid nodules unless there is reason to suspect MTC.

Screening family members of known or suspected MTC kindreds requires a different diagnostic approach. Until recently, calcitonin stimulation tests were the only way to detect the earliest phase of the disease, C-cell hyperplasia; however, this has changed dramatically with the identification of the responsible genetic mutations. The inherited defects associated with both MEN II syndromes and familial MTC have been mapped to the centromeric region of chromosome 10. Sequence analysis of germ-line DNA from these three syndromes has revealed missense point mutations in the *RET* proto-oncogene. Detection of these mutant alleles in kindred members is possible with a polymerase chain reaction test. This accurate, rapid, and reproducible test is the preferred method for screening MEN II and familial MTC kindreds. It provides a basis for preventive thyroidectomy. With a positive test, the resected thyroid gland shows C-cell hyperplasia with or without MTC. In family members who have inherited a *RET* mutation, after appropriate genetic counseling, total thyroidectomy is indicated regardless of the plasma calcitonin values. When direct DNA testing does not identify the mutation, linkage analysis and provocative calcitonin testing may be used to find affected members.

Therapeutic
Therapeutic Options

Primary therapy for thyroid cancer, regardless of its histologic type, is surgery whenever possible. The next most preferable therapy is radioiodine (^{131}I) if the tumor concentrates the isotope. External radiation is the next most effective treatment and chemotherapy is the last therapeutic option that is exercised. Therapy for papillary and follicular cancer is different than for MTC or anaplastic thyroid carcinoma or lymphoma.

Recommended Approach

Papillary and Follicular Thyroid Carcinoma. Most are treated with total or near-total thyroidectomy and ^{131}I. Small tumors (<1.5 cm diameter) confined to the thyroid can be treated with less extensive thyroidectomy without radioiodine, but this is not the preferred treatment for several reasons. First, occult intrathyroidal metastases often are not apparent until the gland has been studied by permanent sections. Second, neck metastases cannot be identified with ^{131}I scans if there is a large thyroid remnant. Third, follow-up with thyroglobulin is not accurate unless the thyroid has been totally ablated. We treat all papillary thyroid carcinomas larger than 1.5 cm in diameter, especially those that are multicentric, locally invasive, or metastatic, with total or near-total thyroidectomy followed by ^{131}I ablation and thyroid hormone suppression. Cervical lymph node metastases do not require radical neck dissection unless the tumor is extensively invading lateral neck structures. When completion thyroidectomy is performed routinely, about 30% of patients have tumor in the thyroid remnant.

Follicular carcinoma is treated with total or near-total thyroidectomy followed by ^{131}I and thyroid hormone unless it is minimally invasive, in which case subtotal thyroidectomy and thyroid hormone suppression alone may be adequate therapy. But similar to papillary cancer, the tumor's histologic characteristics often are not apparent until the final histologic sections have been studied. For the same reasons noted above for papillary cancer, we prefer total or near-total thyroidectomy for follicular cancer when the diagnosis is known preoperatively. We almost always recommend completion thyroidectomy when the diagnosis of follicular cancer first becomes apparent on study of a thyroid nodule's permanent sections and only lobectomy was performed.

The main risks of total thyroidectomy, hypoparathyroidism and recurrent laryngeal nerve damage, are substantially reduced by performing near-total thyroidectomy. This operation leaves enough thyroid tissue on the unaffected side to ensure that the parathyroids and recurrent nerve are not damaged. The rate of permanent hypoparathyroidism is in the range of 1% when the operation is done by experienced surgeons. Recurrent laryngeal nerve damage also occurs in fewer than 1% of patients. These complications occur more often with bulky invasive tumors that have a poor prognosis when they cannot be ablated with surgery and radioiodine.

Radioiodine (^{131}I) is given postoperatively to ablate residual normal thyroid tissue, termed *remnant ablation*, or to treat residual carcinoma. Small ^{131}I doses (30 mCi) obliterate thyroid bed radioiodine uptake in about 80% of patients only if the surgeon leaves less than a few grams of thyroid tissue. Small doses impart relatively little total-body radiation and dramatically reduce cost because patients do not require hospitalization. Treatment of residual or metastatic carcinoma requires high ^{131}I doses (100–200 mCi), which must be given in the hospital. Metastases that concentrate ^{131}I are usually treated every 6 to 12 months until they are ablated or fail to concentrate ^{131}I. The total cumulative dose of ^{131}I is kept below 500 mCi in children and below about 800 mCi in adults, unless the metastases are life-threatening and continue to concentrate ^{131}I. The main risks of large cumulative doses of ^{131}I are the induction of leukemia, damage to reproductive tissue causing infertility or genetic damage, and pulmonary fibrosis. When repeat doses are given at 6- to 12-month intervals and the total doses are kept below the limits noted, these risks are extremely low.

Thyroid hormone is given in doses sufficient to keep serum thyroid-stimulating hormone at low-normal levels. Thyroid hormone should not be prescribed in amounts that cause thyrotoxicosis. Long-term subclinical thyrotoxicosis has serious skeletal and cardiac side effects that can be avoided by keeping the serum thyroid-stimulating hormone in the low-normal range (see Chapter 9–17).

Medullary Thyroid Carcinoma. Surgery offers the only chance for cure of this tumor. It should be performed as early as possible after the disease is detected. Prior to thyroidectomy, pheochromocytoma must be rigorously excluded (see Chapter 14–8). Treatment is total thyroidectomy, because the disease is often multicentric, even in patients with a negative family history who may be unsuspected index cases of affected kindreds. Because cervical node metastases occur early and influence survival adversely, all patients with MTC should undergo routine dissection of lymph nodes in the central neck compartment. The lateral lymph nodes are excised when they contain tumor, but radical neck dissection is not recommended unless the jugular vein, accessory nerve, or sternocleidomastoid muscle is invaded by tumor. Inoperable disease can be palliatively treated with external radiation; however, some feel this has an adverse effect on tumor growth. Doxorubicin (Adriamycin) may be given to treat widespread, life-threatening disease.

Anaplastic Thyroid Carcinoma. This tumor may be treated with surgery followed by external radiation given at a dose of 4500 to 5000 rad. A good tumor response is seen in about half the patients, and an occasional individual experiences a complete remission. Chemotherapy is not standard, but most use doxorubicin alone or in combination with other drugs. Every reasonable attempt should be made to preserve the airway in patients with this disease, as it is often compromised by bulky invasive tumor. Median survival is in the range of 6 months.

Thyroid Lymphoma. Thyroid surgery should be limited to excising enough tissue to relieve any airway obstruction, which occurs commonly. Without evidence of spread beyond the neck, external radiation

alone may be sufficient, but we prefer combining external radiation and chemotherapy, which is highly effective in eradicating the disease.

FOLLOW-UP

Papillary and Follicular Thyroid Carcinoma. Serum thyroglobulin determinations and whole-body ^{131}I imaging together detect recurrent or residual disease in most patients, providing total thyroid ablation has been done. Thyroglobulin should be measured while the patient is off levothyroxine and is invalidated by circulating antithyroglobulin antibodies. Thyroglobulin should be measured while the patient takes thyroid hormone only after complete thyroid ablation has been achieved. Under thyroid-stimulating hormone stimulation, thyroglobulin has a higher sensitivity than whole-body ^{131}I scanning, but its false-positive rate also rises. Serum thyroglobulin levels measured in different assays vary considerably because neither a thyroglobulin standard nor a standard antibody has been adopted.

Patients are evaluated every 6 to 12 months depending on the severity of the disease. Whole-body ^{131}I scans are done after levothyroxine has been stopped or the dosage reduced to half for about 6 weeks to raise the serum thyroid-stimulating hormone level to at least 30 μU/mL. If levothyroxine is completely stopped, patients are given liothyronine sodium (T_3) for the first 4 of the 6 weeks to alleviate the symptoms of hypothyroidism. Human recombinant thyroid-stimulating hormone (Thyrogen) raises serum thyroid-stimulating hormone to levels comparable with those seen after thyroid hormone withdrawal. When released by the Food and Drug Administration for general use, it is likely to dramatically change the methods of follow-up. We follow our patients with both total-body ^{131}I scans and serum thyroglobulin determinations until the scan shows less than 1% uptake. Thereafter, follow-up with serum thyroglobulin alone is safe if the patient has been treated with near-total or total thyroidectomy and ^{131}I ablation. This can be done while the patient is taking thyroid hormone, providing serum thyroglobulin levels remain under 5 ng/mL. If serum thyroglobulin rises above 5 ng/mL while the patient is taking thyroid hormone, or if other indications of recurrent disease are present, imaging studies are necessary. Patients who have had only subtotal thyroidectomy are much more difficult to evaluate because whole-body ^{131}I scans and serum thyroglobulin measurements are less specific.

Medullary Thyroid Cancer. If a patient has a positive DNA test or bilateral MTCs, all first-degree relatives must be screened with genetic testing, regardless of a negative family history. Once a MTC kindred is identified, all family members should be tested and undergo appropriate counseling. Family members with MTC should have annual screening for hyperparathyroidism (MEN IIa) and pheochromocytoma (MEN IIa and IIb), with serum calcium levels and urinary catecholamines and metanephrine determinations. Follow-up for MTC should be done at 6- to 12-month intervals with basal serum calcitonin and carcinoembryonic antigen. When calcitonin or carcinoembryonic antigen is elevated, a chest x-ray should be done. Other options are imaging with computed tomography or magnetic resonance imaging, ^{99m}Tc-dimercaptosuccinic acid scintigraphy and somatostatin receptor imaging.

DISCUSSION
Prevalence and Incidence

New cases of thyroid cancer are relatively uncommon, affecting only about 1 in 28,000 persons annually in the United States. Papillary carcinoma constitutes about 80% of all thyroid carcinomas, follicular carcinoma accounts for less than 10%, and the remainder are medullary (5%) or anaplastic (<5%) thyroid carcinomas or lymphomas (<5%). About 1200 deaths are estimated to occur from the disease each year in this country. Most are due to highly invasive follicular, medullary, or anaplastic thyroid carcinomas.

Related Basic Science

Well-differentiated thyroid carcinomas arising from follicular cells are classified by the World Health Organization classification of thyroid tumors as papillary and follicular carcinomas (Table 9–14–1). There is some overlap among the four basic histologic patterns and certain important variants exist that alter tumor behavior. A tumor's histologic identity is based on a constellation of features, not all of which are regularly present.

Papillary Cancer. Papillary cancers are recognized by their unique cellular characteristics, particularly their distinctive nuclear features (see Figure 9–13–1) that may be present even in tumors with a predominantly follicular architecture. Tumors with mixed papillary and follicular features are classified as papillary cancers. This is the type of cancer most often caused by external-beam radiotherapy. Its incidence peaks in the third and fourth decades of life, declining slowly thereafter, and is threefold more common in women than men.

Follicular Carcinoma. In geographic areas with insufficient dietary iodide, 40% of thyroid cancers are follicular. Adding iodide to the diet decreases its frequency and increases that of papillary cancer. Follicular carcinoma is threefold more common in women and is diagnosed in patients about a decade older than those with papillary cancer. Nonetheless, many are under age 40 and have minimally invasive tumors. It is uncommon in children after therapeutic head and neck irradiation and seldom occurs as an incidental finding at autopsy.

Medullary Carcinoma. Medullary thyroid carcinoma is composed of round or spindle cells in a stoma rich in amyloid and is defined by C-cell differentiation. A subgroup of mixed tumors exists with morphologic features of medullary and follicular (or rarely papillary) carcinoma that contain both immunoreactive calcitonin and thyroglobulin. MTC accounts for 3 to 10% of all thyroid cancers, but in the general population the lower figure is probably more accurate. Most with sporadic MTC are adults who average about 50 years of age at diagnosis, but children can be affected. In MTC kindreds the age at diagnosis is younger than in the sporadic cases, averaging about 20 years. This will be reduced further with widespread use of genetic testing.

Anaplastic (Undifferentiated) Carcinoma. These highly malignant tumors are composed of undifferentiated cells and must be distinguished from other similar-appearing tumors that have a better prognosis. Almost all tumors formerly considered small cell carcinomas are now recognized as thyroid lymphomas. Other tumors that can be mistaken for anaplastic thyroid carcinoma include MTC, poorly differentiated insular carcinoma, and columnar-variant papillary carcinoma. Anaplastic thyroid carcinoma is primarily a disease of older persons. It affects both sexes about equally and occurs with greatest frequency in the seventh decade of life. Only about 5% of persons afflicted with this tumor are aged 40 or less, and it almost never is seen before the age of 20. Many anaplastic tumors appear to have dedifferentiated from well-differentiated tumors.

Thyroid Lymphoma. Primary thyroid lymphoma is an uncommon but life-threatening disorder that may pose major diagnostic and therapeutic difficulties. Most are B-cell lymphomas that have a predilection to involve the gastrointestinal tract. The mean age at diagnosis is about 60 years, and women outnumber men almost 3:1. Patients with Hashimoto's thyroiditis have about an 80-fold increased risk of developing thyroid lymphoma. Nonetheless, this neoplasm affects only about one in every 2 million persons in the United States.

Natural History and Its Modification with Treatment

In addition to the tumor's histologic characteristics, prognosis depends on two principal features: tumor stage and the patient's age at the time of diagnosis. Any thyroid cancer, regardless of its histology, diagnosed after age 60 has a higher mortality rate (Figure 9–14–1). Men with differentiated thyroid carcinoma tend to fare less well than women. Tumor stage is estimated from primary tumor size, tumor invasion into adjacent neck tissues, and metastases to lymph node and distant sites.

Ten-year survival rates are about 90% for papillary and about 80% for follicular cancer; however prognosis differs among subsets of patients. In our patients whose mean age was about 36 years at the time of diagnosis, the 30-year cancer-specific mortality rate was only 8% but the recurrence rate was 30% (Figure 9–14–2) (Mazzaferri and Jhiang, 1994). Two thirds of the recurrences were in the first decade after therapy; the others recurred years later. Tumor recurrence in the neck may be the first indication of a poor outcome that leads to death. From one third to half the patients who die have uncontrolled local disease. Compared with older patients, those below age 20 at the time of diagnosis have tumors that are larger and more invasive. Tumors in younger patients also recur more often after initial therapy than those in older patients (Figure 9–14–1). Nonetheless, few young patients die of disease. Other features that impart a very favorable prognosis are tumor size less than 1.5 cm and complete tumor encapsulation.

Prognosis is guarded with papillary cancers that are multicentric, large, locally invasive, or metastatic. Nodal metastases occur in about 35% of adults and about 80% of children with papillary cancer and in about 15% with follicular cancer. Patients with mediastinal and bilateral cervical node metastases have higher recurrence and mortality rates. The most aggressive tumors are those with cervical node metastases and local invasion in patients over age 45.

Follicular carcinoma is usually a solitary encapsulated thyroid tumor that is more aggressive than papillary cancer. Widely invasive follicular tumors are easily recognized as cancer. They invade blood vessels, the surrounding thyroid parenchyma, and neck structures. Highly invasive tumors have a poor prognosis: 80% develop metastases and about 20%

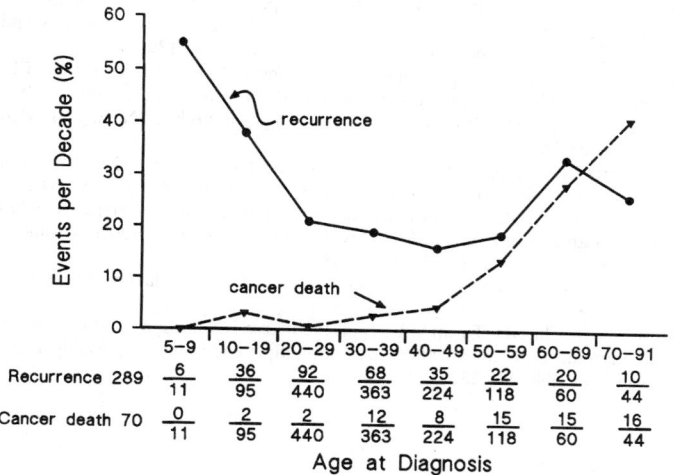

Figure 9–14–1. Tumor recurrence and cancer deaths according to age at the time of diagnosis. See legend to Figure 9–14–2. *(Source: Mazzaferri EL, Jhiang SM. Long-term impact of initial surgical and medical therapy on papillary and follicular thyroid cancer. Am J Med 1994;97:418. Reproduced with permission from the publisher.)*

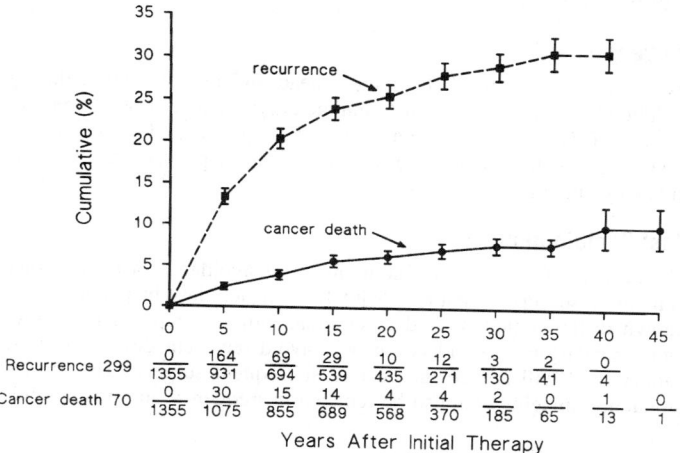

Figure 9–14–2. Tumor recurrence and cancer deaths. Vertical bars represent standard errors. Numerators are the number of events during, and denominators the number of patients at the end of, each time interval. Vertical bars are standard errors of the mean. *(Source: Mazzaferri EL, Jhiang SM. Long-term impact of initial surgical and medical therapy on papillary and follicular thyroid cancer. Am J Med 1994;97:418. Reproduced with permission from the publisher.)*

die of tumor. More often, however, follicular cancer is encapsulated and minimally invasive, closely resembling a follicular adenoma. Malignancy can be identified only on permanent histologic sections. The main diagnostic criteria are cancer cells penetrating the tumor capsule and blood vessels. The latter may have a worse prognosis than capsular invasion alone, but minimally invasive follicular tumors have a good prognosis and very few metastasize to distant sites. Survival rates with papillary and follicular tumors are similar in patients of comparable age and disease stage. Both have equally good prognoses if they are confined to the thyroid or are only minimally invasive, and both have poor outcomes if they are widely invasive or metastatic to distant sites.

Distant metastases occur in almost 10% with papillary and 25% with follicular cancer; about half are present at diagnosis. Papillary cancers metastasize via lymphatics to the lungs, typically manifesting diffuse bilateral pulmonary metastases. Follicular cancers metastasize by hematogenous routes to lung, and both tumors spread by this route to bone, central nervous system, and other sites. Distant metastases occur, in order of increasing frequency, with papillary (10%), follicular (25%), and Hürthle cell (35%) cancers. The most common site is lung (>50%) followed by bone and the central nervous system and other soft tissues. Outcome with distant metastases is influenced mainly by the patient's age and the following tumor features: metastatic site, ability to concentrate ^{131}I, and morphology on chest x-ray. Although some survive decades, especially younger patients with papillary cancer, about half the adults die within 5 years regardless of whether they have metastatic papillary or follicular cancer. Patients under age 20 have much higher survival rates. Prognosis is best with diffuse pulmonary metastases seen only on whole-body ^{131}I imaging and is worse when they do not concentrate ^{131}I or appear as large lung nodules. A few adults with distant metastases have survived 30 years or longer with very little therapy.

There is good evidence that tumor recurrence is prevented with low-dose ^{131}I remnant ablation. A large number of studies show that ^{131}I is effective therapy for differentiated thyroid carcinoma (Mazzaferri, 1993). We found 30-year recurrence rates were lowest (15%) after ^{131}I plus thyroid hormone therapy; they were 30% with thyroid hormone alone, 40% with no medical therapy, and 63% after external radiation plus thyroid hormone (P<.001 between and among the four) (Mazzaferri and Jhiang, 1994). At 30 years, cancer death rates were 3% in the ^{131}I group, 6% in those treated with thyroid hormone alone, and 12% following no medical therapy (P<.001 for all comparisons, but ^{131}I vs thyroid hormone alone, P=.3) (Mazzaferi and Jhiang, 1994). When only patients with tumors larger than 1.5 cm who did not have distant metastases at diagnosis were considered, those treated with ^{131}I had lower 30-year recurrence rates (16% vs 38%, P<.001) and cancer mortality rates (3% vs 9%, P=.03) (Figure 9–14–3) than those not treated with ^{131}I (n=802).

Prevention

Except for avoidance of therapeutic head and neck radiation during childhood and adolescence, differentiated thyroid cancer cannot be prevented. MTC can be prevented in members of affected kindreds who have prophylactic thyroidectomy as the result of positive genetic testing at a young age.

Cost Containment

The principal feature of cost containment is avoidance of unnecessary diagnostic surgery in patients with thyroid nodules. In patients with known differentiated thyroid carcinoma, initial therapy that employs total or near-total thyroidectomy will avoid recurrent disease in most patients and will reduce the cost of subsequent surgery. Thyroid radionuclide imaging can also be reduced in frequency and patients fol-

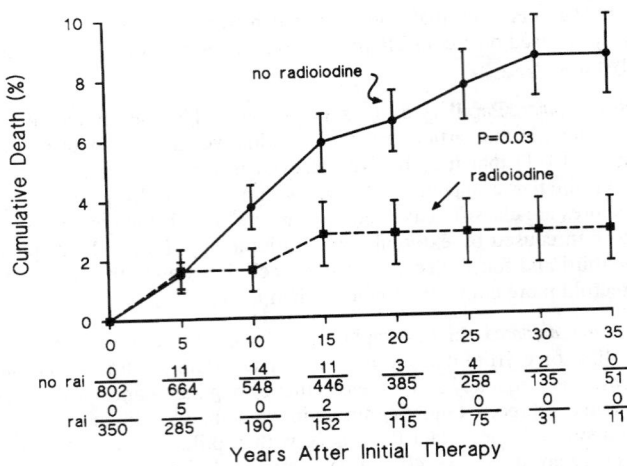

Figure 9–14–3. Cancer mortality in patients with stage II or III tumors treated either with (n= 305) or without (n=802) ^{131}I. Of those treated with ^{131}I, more were men (38% vs 30%, P=.02) and more had lymph node metastases (53% vs 45%, P<.05) and stage III tumors (23% vs 16%, P<.01). The two groups were comparable with respect to other risk factors. See legend to Figure 9–14–2. *(Source: Mazzaferri EL, Jhiang SM. Long-term impact of initial surgical and medical therapy on papillary and follicular thyroid cancer. Am J Med 1994;97:418. Reproduced with permission from the publisher.)*

lowed with serum thyroglobulin determinations alone after total thyroid ablation. Low-dose ^{131}I sharply reduces the cost of thyroid ablation because it avoids hospitalization.

REFERENCES

Blaugrund JE, Johns MM Jr, Eby YJ, et al. *RET* proto-oncogene mutations in inherited and sporadic medullary thyroid cancer. Hum Mol Genet 1994;3:1895.

Carlson KM, Dou S, Chi D, et al. Single missense mutation in the tyrosine kinase catalytic domain of the *RET* protooncogene is associated with multiple endocrine neoplasia type 2B. Proc Natl Acad Sci USA 1994;91:1579.

Lips CJM, Landsvater RM, Höppener JWM, et al. Clinical screening as compared with DNA analysis in families with multiple endocrine neoplasia type 2A. N Engl J Med 1994;331:828.

Mazzaferri EL. Treating differentiated thyroid carcinoma: Where do we draw the line? Mayo Clin Proc 1991a;66:105.

Mazzaferri EL. Carcinoma of follicular epithelium: Radioiodine and other treatments and outcomes. In: Braverman LE, Utiger RD, eds. The thyroid: A fundamental and clinical test. 6th ed. Philadelphia: Lippincott, 1991b;1138.

Mazzaferri EL. Thyroid cancer in thyroid nodules: Finding a needle in a haystack. Am J Med 1992a;93:359.

Mazzaferri EL. Management of intrathyroidal papillary thyroid carcinoma. In: Mazzaferri EL, Kreisberg RA, Bar RS, eds. Advances in endocrinology and metabolism, vol. 3. St. Louis: Mosby Year Book, 1992b;139.

Mazzaferri EL. Thyroid carcinoma: Papillary and follicular. In: Mazzaferri EL, Samaan N, eds. Endocrine tumors. Boston: Blackwell Scientific, 1993a;278.

Mazzaferri EL. Management of a solitary thyroid nodule. N Engl J Med 1993b;328:553.

Mazzaferri EL, Jhiang SM. Long-term impact of initial surgical and medical therapy on papillary and follicular thyroid cancer. Am J Med 1994;97:418.

Mazzaferri EL, Oertel YC. Primary malignant lymphoma and related lymphoproliferative disorders. In: Mazzaferri EL, Samaan N, eds. Endocrine tumors. Boston: Blackwell Scientific, 1993:348.

Mazzaferri EL, Samaan N, eds. Endocrine tumors. Boston: Blackwell Scientific, 1993:378.

Wells SA Jr, Chi DD, Toshima K, et al. Predictive DNA testing and prophylactic thyroidectomy in patients at risk for multiple endocrine neoplasia type 2A. Ann Surg 1994;220:237.

Thyroiditis

Robert Volpé, M.D.

DEFINITION

Thyroiditis is a term that encompasses a group of disorders manifesting inflammation or infiltration of the thyroid gland. A temporal classification would include acute (suppurative), subacute (painful or painless), and chronic thyroiditis. Postpartum thyroiditis may be considered a variant of painless thyroiditis, but is discussed separately here because of some unique features. Chronic thyroiditis is typified by autoimmune (Hashimoto's) thyroiditis; other rare forms of chronic thyroiditis (such as Riedel's struma) are not discussed.

ETIOLOGY

A classification based on etiology would include infective (including viral, the probable cause of subacute thyroiditis), autoimmune, radiation-induced, traumatic, and idiopathic (including Riedel's struma). Specific points of etiology relating to each of the entities are mentioned in relation to the individual disorder, under Criteria for Diagnosis.

CRITERIA FOR DIAGNOSIS

Acute Suppurative Thyroiditis

Suggestive. Acute suppurative thyroiditis represents a bacterial, fungal, or parasitic infection of the thyroid gland. It is rare, is sometimes preceded by pyogenic infection in the pharynx or upper airway, or may result from hematogenous spread from distant sites. Fever, leukocytosis, and a swollen, painful, tender thyroid mass are salient features.

Definitive. Aspiration of purulent material yielding positive specific microorganisms on culture confirms the diagnosis.

Painful Subacute Thyroiditis

Suggestive. Painful subacute (de Quervain's) thyroiditis, of probable viral origin, is characterized by a painful, tender thyroid enlargement and a systemic reaction. Leukocytosis is unusual. The clinical course usually includes a thyrotoxic phase, followed by euthyroid, hypothyroid, and recovery phases.

Definitive. A low radioactive iodine thyroidal uptake and a high erythrocyte sedimentation rate are cardinal features.

Painless Thyroiditis

Suggestive. Painless thyroiditis, which may be autoimmune in nature, also manifests a thyrotoxic phase, followed by a hypothyroid phase. There is only a minimal or absent systemic reaction, and the erythrocyte sedimentation rate is normal or slightly elevated. The thyroid gland may be normal or slightly enlarged, and is not tender. Clinical evidence of hyperthyroidism may be minimal. There is, as in de Quervain's thyroiditis, no evidence of ophthalmopathy.

Definitive. This condition is associated with a low radioactive iodine uptake.

Postpartum Thyroiditis

Suggestive. Postpartum thyroiditis is a form of autoimmune thyroiditis that occurs 3 to 9 months following pregnancy, and is usually transient. The features are similar to those noted above for painless thyroiditis.

Definitive. Antimicrosomal (antithyroperoxidase) antibodies are characteristic.

Hashimoto's Thyroiditis

Suggestive. Hashimoto's thyroiditis is a chronic autoimmune inflammatory disorder of the thyroid gland, in which destruction of thyroid parenchyma is mediated via an immune assault. Affected patients are usually female, typically present with an asymptomatic goiter, and may have clinical and laboratory features of hypothyroidism.

Definitive. High titers of thyroid autoantibodies (particularly antithyroperoxidase) are the rule.

CLINICAL MANIFESTATIONS

Acute Suppurative Thyroiditis

Subjective. Salient symptoms include pain, tenderness, dysphagia, local warmth, erythema, and feverishness.

Objective.

PHYSICAL EXAMINATION. The left lobe is more often involved than the right. An erythematous thyroid mass is palpable, with marked tenderness.

ROUTINE LABORATORY ABNORMALITIES. Leukocytosis occurs in three fourths of patients; its absence might signify anaerobic infection.

Painful Subacute Thyroiditis

Subjective. Initial symptoms may last 3 to 8 weeks and include pain in the thyroid region, radiating to the angle of the jaw or ear on the affected side, together with feverishness, sweating, heat intolerance, malaise, nervousness, and rapid heartbeat.

Objective.

PHYSICAL EXAMINATION. The thyroid gland is moderately enlarged, sometimes exquisitely tender, and firm. One or both lobes are affected, sometimes sequentially ("creeping thyroiditis"). Mild signs of hyperthyroidism are present, but there is no ophthalmopathy.

Routine Laboratory Abnormalities. The leukocyte count is normal or slightly elevated and the sed rate is usually very high. Thyroid hormones are elevated in the initial phase, coupled with a low radioactive iodine uptake. Thyroid hormone levels later fall.

Painless Thyroiditis

Subjective. The clinical course relates to the thyroid functional changes, which are as described for subacute thyroiditis. There is no neck pain and no systemic symptoms.

Objective.

PHYSICAL EXAMINATION. Physical examination may reveal thyroid enlargement (nontender), with clinical evidence of mild thyrotoxicosis. The thyroid is usually slightly to moderately enlarged, but may even be normal in size.

ROUTINE LABORATORY ABNORMALITIES. Thyroid function tests are similar to subacute thyroiditis. Sed rate is not elevated.

Postpartum Thyroiditis

Subjective. An initial thyrotoxic phase may be experienced, occurring 3 to 5 months postpartum, characterized by symptoms of malaise, fatigue, and weight loss, but usually more overt symptoms of hyperthyroidism are absent. Some patients are asymptomatic. More overt and persistent symptoms may signify postpartum Graves' disease.

Hypothyroidism (with or without preceding thyrotoxicosis) occurs in postpartum thyroiditis 3 to 9 months following delivery. Fatigue, lethargy, apathy, depression, and weight gain are common, but symptoms of overt hypothyroidism are usually absent. Spontaneous recovery occurs in most patients, frequently with persistence of a goiter and thyroid antibodies.

Objective.

PHYSICAL EXAMINATION. Examination reveals signs of mild thyrotoxicosis or hypothyroidism. A goiter is usually palpated, most prominently during the hypothyroid phase.

ROUTINE LABORATORY ABNORMALITIES. Routine laboratory examination reveals either elevated or subnormal thyroid function tests. Thyroid antibodies are demonstrable.

Hashimoto's (Autoimmune) Thyroiditis

Subjective. A family history of goiter or autoimmune thyroid disease is often elicited. An increased incidence of other organ-specific autoimmune diseases (e.g., insulin-dependent diabetes mellitus, vitiligo, pernicious anemia, Addison's disease) is encountered in the patients or their families. Patients should be alerted to this possibility.

Patients may have an asymptomatic goiter or present with symptoms of hypothyroidism. Occasionally, there is mild thyroidal discomfort or, rarely, pain.

Objective.

PHYSICAL EXAMINATION. The thyroid gland is generally diffusely enlarged, firm, and lobulated. Discrete nodules may be present but are uncommon. In some, the thyroid is completely atrophied. Signs of hypothyroidism, when present, include dry cool skin, puffy extremities and face, husky voice, and a delayed relaxation phase of the tendon reflexes.

ROUTINE LABORATORY ABNORMALITIES. Routine laboratory examination may reveal thyroid dysfunction, but thyroid antibodies are almost invariable.

PLANS
Diagnostic
Acute Suppurative Thyroiditis

It may be difficult to distinguish from painful subacute thyroiditis in its early stages. Unlike subacute thyroiditis, however, thyroid function is usually normal in suppurative thyroiditis, although occasionally the serum thyroxine (T_4) and triiodothyronine (T_3) levels may be elevated. Thyroid antibodies are generally negative. Early abscess formation may be demonstrable by ultrasonography. Needle biopsy for Gram stain and culture usually result in diagnosis and an identified microorganism.

Painful Subacute Thyroiditis

Thyroid function tests and thyroidal uptake of radioactive iodine show similar results in painful, painless, and postpartum thyroiditis. Initially, serum levels of T_4 and T_3 (and free T_4 and T_3) are elevated, whereas thyroid-stimulating hormone is suppressed. Plasma thyroglobulin is increased, distinguishing these conditions from surreptitious T_4 administration. The T_4 and T_3 levels subsequently fall either to normal or to hypothyroid levels (the latter accompanied by a rise in serum levels of thyroid-stimulating hormone). The initial 24-hour thyroidal uptake of radioactive iodine is very low (1–2%), in contrast to the high uptake in Graves' disease. The erythrocyte sedimentation rate is markedly elevated, often over 100 mm/h. Thyroid antibodies are detectable in a minority of patients and are transitory.

Painless Thyroiditis

Thyroid function tests parallel those for subacute thyroiditis, but the sedimentation rate is either normal or minimally elevated. Thyroid antibodies may be absent or present in low titer.

Postpartum Thyroiditis

Thyroid function tests may be elevated initially, but often there is no demonstrable hyperthyroid phase, and thyroid hormone levels may be low when first measured. Thyroid antibodies (particularly antithyroperoxidase) are usually present, and decline as thyroid function returns to normal. High titers in early pregnancy predict postpartum thyroiditis.

Hashimoto's Thyroiditis

Characteristically, thyroid autoantibodies (particularly antithyroperoxidase) are detectable in high titer. They may be found at similar levels in Graves' disease and in lesser amounts in other disorders. In patients who have overt hypothyroidism, concentrations of free T_4 and free T_3 are decreased, associated with elevated levels of thyroid-stimulating hormone. In "compensated hypothyroidism," levels of free T_4 and T_3 are normal, but the level of thyroid-stimulating hormone (the most sensitive index of impending thyroid failure) is elevated. Twenty-four-hour thyroid uptake of radioactive iodine is variable and, thus, not useful; likewise, thyroid scan shows nonspecific nonhomogeneity. Biopsies are generally not required to make a diagnosis.

Therapeutic
Acute Suppurative Thyroiditis

Antibiotics directed against the specific organism encountered (by smear, culture, and sensitivity) are generally administered by the intravenous route initially, followed by oral antibiotics for an additional 7 to 10 days. Incision and drainage are often required before the disease will settle. Occasionally, thyroid lobectomy is required for a stubborn infection.

Subacute Painful Thyroiditis

For mild cases, enteric-coated aspirin (650 mg orally four times daily) or nonsteroidal antiinflammatory drugs provide symptomatic relief. In more severe instances, prednisone in divided doses of 40 mg daily almost invariably provides relief within 24 to 48 hours; this dosage should be maintained for about 1 week, with gradual tapering and discontinuance over the next 6 weeks. If symptoms recur, a second course of prednisone may be necessary. Symptoms of thyrotoxicosis may require a beta-adrenergic blocker, for example, propranolol (Inderal), 10 to 20 mg four times daily. Antithyroid drug therapy is inappropriate, as the thyrotoxic phase is due to a destructive process rather than increased production of thyroid hormone. In the subsequent transient hypothyroid phase, thyroxine therapy (e.g., 0.1 mg daily) may be appropriate for a few months.

Painless Thyroiditis

The thyrotoxic phase may require treatment with propranolol (10–20 mg orally four times daily) for a few weeks for symptomatic control.

Postpartum Thyroiditis

If necessary, the thyrotoxic phase can be controlled symptomatically with propranolol as above. During the hypothyroid phase, treatment consists of daily thyroxine in doses adjusted to maintain serum level of thyroid-stimulating hormone in the low normal (or slightly below normal) range. The usual dosage of thyroxine is 1.5 μg/kg/d. Although postpartum thyroiditis is generally self-limiting, its very high recurrence rate makes it appropriate to continue thyroxine therapy for life; this prevents clinical recurrences and the later development of chronic thyroiditis.

Hashimoto's Thyroiditis

Patients with hypothyroidism should be treated with thyroxine as noted above. If a goiter is present, the objective should be to suppress the level of thyroid-stimulating hormone below normal so the goiter will regress; the dosage of thyroxine should be adjusted to accomplish this. The previous concern that this might cause osteoporosis has not been confirmed by recent studies. Elderly patients or those with coronary artery disease should be started at doses of thyroxine of 0.025 mg daily, to be increased monthly, reaching a maximum of ~0.075 mg daily. It is important to maintain such patients in a slightly hypothyroid status so as to reduce the work of the heart.

FOLLOW-UP
Acute Suppurative Thyroiditis

After antibiotics have been withdrawn, recurrence of manifestations call for reassessment and a further course of antibiotics, followed by either incision and drainage or lobectomy. Otherwise, patients should be reviewed 1 to 2 weeks after cessation of treatment and again at 6 and 12 months to ensure that the infection has been eradicated.

Painful Subacute Thyroiditis

The patient should be seen 1 week after initiation of therapy to ensure that a proper response to medication has occurred, and should return again after treatment has been withdrawn. The thyroid may remain enlarged and firm for several weeks after pain has subsided. Thyroid function tests should be performed about every 6 to 8 weeks so as to detect the changing status of thyroid function, from hyperthyroidism through euthyroidism to hypothyroidism, and then to recovery in most instances. Annual subsequent visits are appropriate.

Painless Thyroiditis

Follow-up should take place about every 6 weeks as patients go through similar changes in thyroid function as described above for subacute thyroiditis. As recurrences are common, patients should be advised to return if symptoms recur and at least should have an annual reassessment.

Postpartum Thyroiditis

If it is decided to discontinue thyroxine, this may be carried out 1 year after delivery, followed by reassessment 6 weeks later. Patients should then be reassessed annually as well as after subsequent pregnancies. If, on the other hand, they are maintained on permanent thyroxine therapy, an annual reassessment, plus postpartum assessments, would suffice.

Hashimoto's Thyroiditis

Patients taking thyroxine should have thyroid function tests performed 2 to 3 months after initiation of treatment and should then be routinely examined annually, with emphasis on goiter size and thyroid function tests. Untreated euthyroid patients should be followed annually, given the tendency for goiter enlargement and the development of hypothyroidism (then requiring thyroxine).

DISCUSSION

Acute Suppurative Thyroiditis

Prevalence and Incidence. This disorder is rare, with only about 200 cases having been reported.

Related Basic Science. The thyroid seems resistant to pyogenic infection because of its rich blood supply, lymphatic drainage, high iodide content, and protective capsule. Infection may be superimposed on a preceding goiter or congenital thyroid anomalies (e.g., thyroglossal duct cyst, or fistula between the left piriform sinus and the left thyroid lobe), or may result from a pyogenic infection in the upper respiratory tract or elsewhere by hematogenous spread. The usual microorganisms detected are *Staphylococcus* and *Streptococcus*; Gram-negative and anaerobic organisms are encountered less frequently. Fungal infections have also been reported, sometimes in immunocompromised hosts.

Painful Subacute Thyroiditis

Prevalence and Incidence. The prevalence of subacute thyroiditis varies considerably around the world. It seems more prevalent in temperate zones, particularly in northern North America. Even there, it is relatively uncommon, with a tendency to appear in spring and autumn. Females are afflicted about six times as often as males, generally in young adulthood.

Related Basic Science. An association with a variety of viral infections, the presence of viral antibodies, the finding of cytopathic viruses in thyroid tissue, and a course that simulates viral disease together suggest a viral etiology. Viral inclusion bodies, however, have not been observed in the affected thyroid tissue, and definitive proof of a viral causation is still not conclusive. A genetic factor is demonstrable through an increased frequency of HLA-B35, which is present in more than 70% of cases. The disease is characterized pathologically by destruction of the thyroid follicular lining with extravasation of colloid into the interstices, with infiltration of the follicles first by neutrophils and then by histiocytes; the latter surround the disrupted colloid both inside and outside the damaged follicles, resulting in a "pseudo-giant cell" or "pseudogranulomatous" appearance.

The disrupted colloid is broken down by enzymes released by the destroyed thyroid tissue, leading to the release of thyroid hormones (and thyroglobulin) into the circulation, resulting in thyrotoxicosis. The low thyroidal radioactive iodine uptake is due to the widespread disruption of the thyroid follicles. As the amount of preformed thyroid hormone is limited and the capacity to synthesize new hormone is impaired by the inflammatory process, the manifestations of thyrotoxicosis can last only about 6 to 8 weeks. The gland is then depleted, leading to a transient hypothyroid phase. With spontaneous recovery (which is almost invariable) the follicles regenerate and normal function is restored.

Painless Thyroiditis

Prevalence and Incidence. The incidence of painless thyroiditis is unknown, as symptoms may be mild or absent, and it is probable that many with this condition never seek medical attention. The detected disorder is relatively uncommon, although it seems to be encountered more often in northern North America and Japan than in Europe. Females predominate in a ratio of 1.5:1 to 2:1, with onset in the third to sixth decade.

Related Basic Science. In some instances, there has been a clustering of cases in summer and autumn, and in others, clustering has occurred within a common environment, suggesting a viral etiology. No viral antibodies appear, however, and there is no laboratory evidence to confirm a viral etiology. The pathology is that of a diffuse lymphoid infiltration; in some patients thyroid antibodies appear (~50%), and there is sometimes an association with nonthyroidal or thyroid autoimmune disease. Moreover, non-pregnancy-related painless thyroiditis bears a close resemblance to postpartum thyroiditis, which seems clearly to be autoimmune in nature. These elements have led investigators to the view that many cases of painless thyroiditis are also autoimmune in etiology. The condition may actually turn out to be heterogeneous in origin.

As with subacute thyroiditis, thyroid parenchymal destruction accounts for the thyrotoxic phase, and depletion for the subsequent hypothyroid phase. With recovery, thyroid histology is restored to normal.

Postpartum Thyroiditis

Prevalence and Incidence. The prevalence of postpartum thyroiditis is approximately 5 to 6% in prospective studies.

Related Basic Science. In those women with antithyroperoxidase (antimicrosomal) antibodies before or in pregnancy, the subsequent development of postpartum thyroiditis is almost certain. The disease results from immunologic alterations occurring during and after pregnancy superimposed on a genetic susceptibility; during pregnancy, there is amelioration of autoimmune processes (with a decline of all antibodies), followed by a rebound in the months after delivery. During these months, thyroid antibodies reach their peak, the goiter enlarges, and thyroid dysfunction occurs, characterized by a thyrotoxic followed by a hypothyroid phase, or a hypothyroid phase alone. Gradual recovery takes place thereafter, which may be incomplete. It is similar in pathology and pathophysiology to painless thyroiditis.

Hashimoto's Thyroiditis

Prevalence and Incidence. The prevalence of Hashimoto's thyroiditis is 3 to 4% of the population; it occurs preponderantly in females, is unusual before puberty, reaches a peak about the fourth to fifth decade, but continues to increase in elderly women. Some degree of lymphocytic infiltration of the thyroid can be detected in more than 20% of thyroids from elderly women at necropsy. It is the most common form of spontaneous hypothyroidism in North America.

Related Basic Science. Hashimoto's thyroiditis results from an autoimmune process whereby helper T lymphocytes become sensitized to thyroid cell antigens, thus initiating an immune assault that results in thyroid cell damage. This in turn may be due to a defect in specific antigen activation of suppressor (regulatory) T lymphocytes, as a result of a genetic abnormality in specific antigen presenting genes. These may relate to the HLA system, responsible for antigen presentation. In Caucasians, the goitrous form of Hashimoto's thyroiditis is associated with HLA-DR5, whereas the nongoitrous form is associated with HLA-B8 and HLA-DR3.

Pathology shows lymphocytic infiltration, lymphoid follicles with germinal centers, destruction of follicles, fibrosis, and the presence of eosinophilic Hürthle cells in the classic form. In some, however, only lymphoid infiltration is seen, whereas, conversely, in others, fibrosis predominates.

NATURAL HISTORY AND ITS MODIFICATION WITH TREATMENT

Acute Suppurative Thyroiditis

In children, recurrences are common, perhaps because of the frequent presence of congenital anomalies predisposing to infection. Complications are related to the nature of the underlying infection and the presence of abscess formation. Most acute pyogenic infections are eradicated at the time of first treatment and do not recur; however, some indolent organisms may be encountered where the infection goes on to become chronic.

Painful Subacute Thyroiditis

Patients generally present during the thyrotoxic phase, which lasts 6 to 8 weeks until the gland is depleted of hormone. Pain and systemic symptoms persist during this interval if untreated, but usually respond rapidly to treatment. A hypothyroid phase usually follows, lasting a few months before complete recovery occurs. Less than 1% go on to permanent hypothyroidism. Recurrences are unusual.

Painless Thyroiditis

The evolution (minus the pain and systemic symptoms) is similar to that seen in subacute thyroiditis. Clinical symptoms are usually alleviated by treatment. Recurrences are common.

Postpartum Thyroiditis

Symptoms of hypothyroidism may be severe but are ameliorated by thyroxine. Recurrences after future pregnancies are common, and many ultimately culminate with chronic thyroiditis. This can be prevented with long-term thyroxine therapy.

Hashimoto's Thyroiditis

The major complication is progressive hypothyroidism, readily controlled with thyroxine therapy. Goiters usually regress on treatment. Despite therapy, goiters rarely continue to enlarge; the possibility of lymphoma, a rare complication, should be considered if enlargement is seen. In addition, other autoimmune diseases such as Addison's disease and type I diabetes occasionally develop.

PREVENTION

There is no known prevention for any of the diseases described.

COST CONTAINMENT

A careful history and physical examination, with selective and judicious use of laboratory tests as suggested, should lead to early diagnosis and treatment of these entities, thus reducing health care costs. The guidelines for management and follow-up described, if followed, should avoid needless expense.

REFERENCES

Volpé R. Infective thyroiditis. In: Burrow GN, Oppenheimer JH, Volpé R, eds. Thyroid function and disease. Philadelphia: Saunders, 1989:175.
Volpé R. Subacute thyroiditis. In: Burrow GN, Oppenheimer JH, Volpé R, eds. Thyroid function and disease. Philadelphia: Saunders, 1989:179.
Volpé R. Immunology of the thyroid. In: Volpé R, ed. Autoimmune diseases of the endocrine system, Boca Raton, FL: CRC Press, 1990:73.
Volpé R. Autoimmune thyroiditis. In: Braverman LE, Utiger RD, eds. The thyroid, a fundamental and clinical text. 6th ed. Philadelphia: Lippincott, 1991:921.
Walfish PG, Badenhoop K. Postpartum thyroiditis: A variant of Hashimoto thyroiditis? In: Nagataki S. Mori T, Torizuka K, eds. Eighty years of Hashimoto disease. International Congress Series No. 1028. Amsterdam: Excerpta Medica/Elsevier, 1993:171.

CHAPTER 9–16

Tests of Thyroid Function

Ian D. Hay, M.B., Ph.D. and George G. Klee, M.D., Ph.D.

DEFINITION

Thyroid function tests are abnormal when the results are above or below the levels established for the normal range.

ETIOLOGY

Thyroid function tests are abnormal when the physician suspects hyper- or hypofunction of the thyroid gland.

CRITERIA FOR DIAGNOSIS

It is well recognized that after diabetes mellitus, thyroid disease represents the most common endocrine disorder. Not surprisingly, thyroid function tests are regularly requested by the practicing physician. The most popular tests used to confirm or refute a diagnosis of thyroid dysfunction in the past have been those that measure total or free serum thyroid hormone levels (Table 9–16–1). Now, however, almost all regional and hospital clinical chemistry laboratories are performing "sensitive" immunometric assays of serum thyrotropin, and many can also provide further tests that may occasionally be needed to establish or exclude a diagnosis of thyroid gland disease (Table 9–16–2). As the list of available thyroid function tests is so extensive, it behooves the practicing physician to appreciate the limitations of the individual tests and to be capable of developing a cost-effective approach to the laboratory diagnosis of the principal thyroid disorders.

CLINICAL MANIFESTATIONS

Tests of thyroid function are obviously only adjuncts to proper clinical assessment of patients. These tests should be obtained only after an accurate history and a careful physical examination, including an anterior neck examination, have been completed. The American Thyroid Association currently recommends that the *tests of thyroid function should not be part of multiphasic screening for patients who are not suspected to have thyroid disease, except in certain high-risk populations* (Surks et al., 1990).

Suspect populations include the newborn, for whom screening for

TABLE 9–16–1. COMMON LABORATORY TESTS OF THYROID SECRETORY FUNCTION

Name of Test	Abbreviation
Total thyroid hormone concentrations	
Thyroxine	T_4
Triiodothyronine	T_3
Free thyroid hormone concentrations	
Free T_4	FT_4
Free T_3	FT_3
Estimates of thyroid hormone binding	
Thyroid hormone binding ratio	THBR
Free thyroid hormone estimates	
Free T_4 index	FT_4I ($T_4 \times$ THBR)
Free T_3 index	FT_3I ($T_3 \times$ THBR)
Free T_4 estimate	FT_4E
Free T_3 estimate	FT_3E

TABLE 9–16–3. PRINCIPAL CAUSES OF INCREASED OR DECREASED T_4-BINDING GLOBULIN CONCENTRATION OR AFFINITY RESULTING IN MISLEADING SERUM T_4 VALUES

Increase	Decrease
Estrogens	Testosterone
Pregnancy	Corticosteroids
Infectious hepatitis	Chronic illness
Chronic hepatitis	Hepatic failure
Neonatal state	Protein malnutrition
Acute intermittent porphyria	Nephrotic syndrome
Inherited	Inherited

congenital hypothyroidism is mandatory; individuals with a strong family history of thyroid disease; postpartum women 4 to 8 weeks after delivery; women aged more than 50 years, especially with palpable thyroid enlargement; and patients with autoimmune diseases such as Addison's disease, pernicious anemia, myasthenia gravis, and type 1 diabetes mellitus.

PLANS

Diagnostic

Diagnostic Options

When thyroid dysfunction is suspected, the diagnostic investigation is typically started with a thyroid screening test. In the recent past, this laboratory tests has most frequently been a direct measure of thyroid secretory function, and over the past 20 years, serum thyroxine (T_4) measurement has probably been the most requested single test of thyroid function. Although triiodothyronine (T_3) measurements are useful in the diagnosis of thyrotoxicosis, they are often misleading in patients with hypothyroidism or nonthyroid illness, and have not therefore been recommended for primary thyroid testing. The major disadvantage of T_4 and T_3 measurements is that almost all the measured thyroid hormone is protein bound, whereas it is the tiny free component that determines the clinical status of the patient. Thus, in circumstances where thyroid hormone-binding protein concentrations are significantly altered, the total values may not represent the biologically active free components. Table 9–16–3 outlines the principal causes of increased or decreased concentrations of T_4-binding globulin, the principal thyroid hormone-binding protein.

Because of the dependence of the T_4 value on serum protein binding and the cumbersome nature of the techniques involved in direct measurement of free T_4, practicing physicians have long relied on indirect estimates of serum free T_4, such as the free T_4 index. The free T_4 index might be considered as an "adjusted" T_4 value because it represents a

TABLE 9–16–2. FURTHER LABORATORY TESTS USEFUL IN ESTABLISHING OR EXCLUDING THYROID GLAND DISEASE

Name of Test	Abbreviation
Tests for autoimmune thyroid disease	
Thyroid microsomal antibody	TMAb
Thyroglobulin antibody	TgAb
Thyroid-stimulating hormone receptor antibody	TRAb
Markers of abnormal thyroid hormone binding	
T_4-binding globulin	TBG
T_4-binding prealbumin	TBPA
Markers of differentiated thyroid function	
Thyroglobulin	Tg
Calcitonin	CT

value for T_4 concentration adjusted for the variations present in the patient's binding proteins. The factor that allows the adjustment is the thyroid hormone binding ratio, a ratio derived traditionally from a T_3 resin uptake test, which involves analysis of the distribution of radiolabeled T_3 in a diluted serum sample. The free T_4 index, derived from the product of the T_4 and the thyroid hormone binding ratio, has been the most popular method for estimating free T_4 levels. The values for free T_4 derived from most so-called "direct" assay kits, using either "one-step" or "two-step" techniques, should be considered no more than free T_4 estimates. Direct measurements of free T_4 in protein-free dialysate of serum are considered the "gold standard" for free T_4, but these measurements are not routinely used because of complexity and time delays.

Because of these technical problems with true free T_4 measurements, clinicians have been increasingly relying on the sensitive measurement of serum thyrotropin levels, which, because of the thyroid–pituitary feedback system, can be considered indirect measures of serum free T_4 levels in patients without hypothalamic–pituitary disease. The improved sensitivity of the newer thyrotropin immunometric assays has expanded the clinical utility of thyrotropin measurement from its traditional role of diagnosing primary hypothyroidism to include the distinction of euthyroidism from possible hyperthyroidism, and the substitution of accurate basal "sensitive" thyrotropin measurements for the now largely superseded thyrotropin-releasing hormone stimulation test, which formerly was the gold standard in most algorithms for the diagnosis of thyroid dysfunction.

The laboratory confirmation of a diagnosis of either hypo- or hyperthyroidism can generally be made with a combination of a sensitive thyrotropin measurement and a free T_4 estimate. As outlined in Chapters 9–12, 9–13, and 9–15, determining the exact etiology of thyroid disease may necessitate the use of fine-needle aspiration biopsy, radioiodine uptake tests, or thyroid scintiscanning; however, as the most common causes of thyroid dysfunction are organ-specific autoimmune disease, the thyroid autoantibody markers shown in Table 9–16–2 have a role to play in the diagnosis of either Hashimoto's or Graves' disease. Euthyroid hyperthyroxinemeia caused by inherited abnormalities of T_4-binding globulin or T_4-binding prealbumin, or familial dysalbuminemia, may require measurement of these carrier proteins by specific immunoassay or polyacrylamide electrophoresis.

Thyroglobulin and calcitonin may be considered markers of differentiated thyroid function and represent products of the thyroid follicular cells or C cells, respectively. As outlined in Chapter 9–14 and 9–17, serum thyroglobulin has a role to play in the monitoring of patients with thyroid cancer of follicular cell origin, and also in the diagnosis of thyrotoxicosis factitia. Basal and pentagastrin-stimulated calcitonin levels are essential for the early diagnosis of medullary (C-cell) thyroid carcinoma and in the monitoring of treatment efficiency in that condition, whether sporadic or familial.

Recommended Approach

To facilitate the rapid evaluation of thyroid dysfunction, while minimizing overall test utilization, we favor the concept of a "thyroid cascade" (Klee and Hay, 1994) for ordering biochemical thyroid tests. When this cascade is ordered, sensitive thyrotropin is initially measured; if it is normal, the testing is complete. If it is either elevated or decreased, free T$_4$ is automatically measured and reported. Microsomal antibodies are measured on all patients with elevated thyrotropin levels. With thyrotropin levels less than 0.1 mU/L, third/fourth-generation thyrotropin measurements are performed, and if free T$_4$ is normal, the T$_3$ or free T$_3$ is also measured. Details of the proposed, cascaded testing procedure are shown in Figure 9–16–1.

Therapeutic

The principal reason for ordering thyroid function tests is to diagnose or exclude hyper- or hypothyroidism. When thyroid dysfunction is confirmed, the definitive therapy of these conditions is as described in Chapters 9–17 and 9–18. The advent of sensitive thyrotropin measurements has enabled the accurate titration of T$_4$ treatment doses to permit the achievement of serum thyrotropin levels less than 0.1 mU/L in patients on T$_4$ suppressive therapy for goiter or differentiated thyroid cancer, and readily detectable levels (>0.3 mU/L) within the euthyroid range for patients taking T$_4$ replacement therapy for hypothyroidism.

As many of the classic signs and symptoms of myxedema and thyrotoxicosis take months to develop, the changes in thyroid function tests (which may occur within days to weeks during a subacute thyroiditis or after therapeutic intervention in thyrotoxicosis) can often provide information that may predict the likely outcome of disease or can signify a response to lack of response to treatment. Such information can be relayed to the patient in a timely fashion and, when indicated, T$_4$ replacement therapy can often be instituted before urgent symptoms develop.

In patients at risk of developing autoimmune thyroid disease or postpartum thyroid dysfunction, thyroid antibody measurements may permit a more accurate counseling of the patient. In patients with Hashimoto's disease and a positive thyroid microsomal antibody test, the measurement of serum thyrotropin may allow the diagnosis of hypothyroidism at an early (subclinical) stage. In patients with Graves' ophthalmopathy or patients with autonomously functioning nodular

disease, measurement of sensitive thyrotropin and T$_3$ or free T$_3$ estimate can often provide early warning to the patient of impending thyrotoxicosis. In patients on appropriate T$_4$ replacement therapy, the measurement of sensitive thyrotropin can confirm the adequacy of treatment in a compliant patient, but in the situation of noncompliance, the test value can also be used as an incentive for the patient to follow more closely the prescribed therapeutic regimen.

FOLLOW-UP

The need for subsequent thyroid function tests is dictated by the patient's thyroid disease and the therapeutic goals that have been established. It is generally accepted that sensitive thyrotropin measurements in patients on T$_4$ replacement should be checked 6 to 8 weeks after initiating or changing a T$_4$ dose to allow the hypothalamic–pituitary system a "full readout" response to the new circulating T$_4$ status. After achieving a serum thyrotropin within the euthyroid range, measurement of sensitive thyrotropin should be repeated at 12- or 18-month intervals, provided that the T$_4$ formulation does not change and patient compliance is maintained. The timing of testing after the different types of therapy for thyrotoxicosis is described in Chapter 9–17.

DISCUSSION
Prevalence and Incidence

There are no data regarding the prevalence and incidence of abnormal thyroid function tests.

Related Basic Science

Estimates of serum free T$_4$ provide a measure of thyroid gland secretory function, whereas sensitive thyrotropin measurements serve as sensitive and specific indicators of the biological effects of circulating

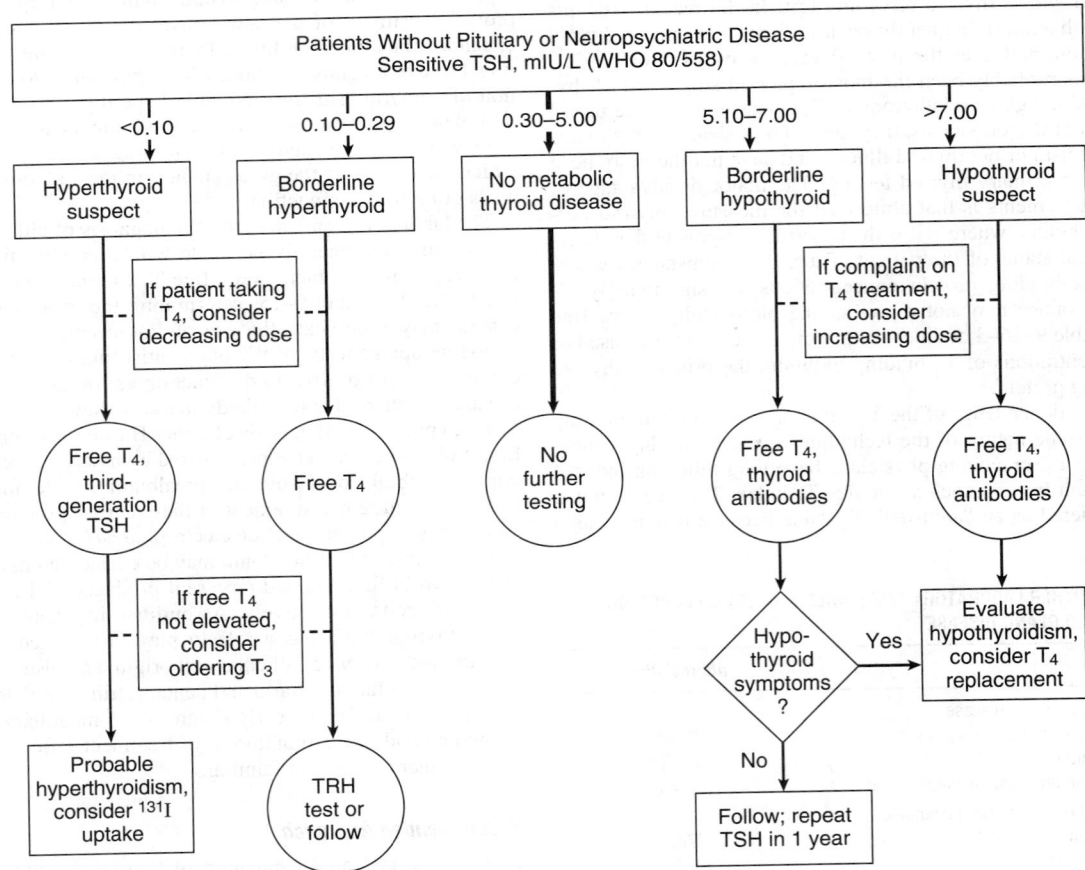

Figure 9–16–1. Proposed cascaded testing procedure for efficient evaluation of functional thyroid status. TSH, thyroid-stimulating hormone; TRH, thyrotropin-releasing hormone; T$_3$, triiodothyronine; T$_4$, thyroxine. (*Source: Klee GG, Hay ID. Biochemical thyroid function testing. Mayo Clin Proc 1994;69:469. Reproduced with permission from the publisher and author.*)

thyroid hormones. The two tests provide complementary information such that, if both free T_4 and sensitive thyrotropin are normal, the patient is almost certainly euthyroid. On the other hand, if free T_4 is low and sensitive thyrotropin elevated, or free T_4 is high and sensitive thyrotropin subnormal, the diagnosis is usually primary hypo- or hyperthyroidism, respectively.

When the two tests (free T_4 and sensitive thyrotropin) are compared, it is recognized that sensitive thyrotropin is the more responsive and accurate indicator of thyroid dysfunction. Recent careful studies of the free T_4–thyrotropin interaction have shown, first, that small changes in free T_4 levels will produce a manyfold greater response in sensitive thyrotropin levels and, second, that each patient appears to possess a unique thyrotropin setpoint relative to the free T_4 level. These observations help explain why sensitive thyrotropin measurement can detect early phases of thyroid dysfunction (e.g., subclinical hypo- or hyperthyroidism), and can be used to optimize individual T_4 replacement therapy.

The ability of sensitive thyrotropin measurements to assess thyroid status appropriately is, by definition, dependent on a healthy hypothalamic–pituitary–thyroid axis. In unusual cases of hypothalamic or pituitary disease, normal thyroid stimulating hormone levels may be seen in the face of substantially reduced free T_4 levels and clinical hypothyroidism. More commonly, disparities between sensitive thyrotropin and free T_4 levels are related to systemic illnesses, as in hospitalized sick adults, major psychiatric disturbance (especially manic psychosis), and pharmacologic use of hormones (e.g., glucocorticoids or dopamine, which may transiently inhibit thyrotropin secretion). The changes seen in thyroid function tests with nonendocrine chronic illnesses are considered in further detail in Chapter 9–49.

Natural History and Its Modification with Treatment

The natural history for all the diseases for which thyroid function tests are performed is discussed in specific chapters.

Prevention

The need for thyroid function testing is dictated by the presence of thyroid disease. With the exception of avoiding therapeutic head or neck irradiation in childhood or adolescence and not ingesting excessive or inadequate amounts of dietary iodine, no preventive measures for controlling thyroid disease are currently available.

Cost Containment

In general, the individual costs for the laboratory tests of thyroid function shown in Tables 9–16–1 and 9–16–2 are relatively low; however, the aggregate costs for thyroid testing can be substantial. Increasingly, the newer sensitive thyrotropin measurements are being used in a "first-line" capacity, and in patients with a high likelihood of primary thyroid disease, the sensitive thyrotropin and T_4 or free T_4 estimate are often being ordered simultaneously.

We believe that the use of a "thyroid cascade" scheme can result in significant cost savings. In a typical clinical practice, more than 80% of patients would have normal serum thyrotropin values and the cascade would eliminate the routine measurement of T_4 or free T_4 of these patients. Clearly, the cost of thyroid testing would be reduced even further if physicians confined their testing to patients at high risk of thyroid dysfunction and made their selection of tests with a specific thyroid diagnosis in mind.

REFERENCES

Caldwell G, Kellett HA, Gow SM, et al. A new strategy for thyroid function testing. Lancet 1985;1:1117.

Hay ID, Klee GG. Thyroid dysfunction. Endocrinol Metab Clin North Am 1988;17:473.

Klee GG, Hay ID. Biochemical thyroid function testing. Mayo Clin Proc 1994;69:469.

Nicoloff JT, Spencer CA. The use and misuse of the sensitive thyrotropin assays. J Clin Metab 1990;71:764.

Ross DS, Daniels GH, Gouveia D. The use of limitations of chemiluminescent thyrotropin assays as a single thyroid function test in an out-patient endocrine clinic. J Clin Endocrinol Metab 1990;71:764.

Surks MI, Chopra IJ, Mariash CN, et al. American Thyroid Association guidelines for use of laboratory tests in thyroid disorders. JAMA 1990;263:1529.

CHAPTER 9–17

Hyperthyroidism

David F. Gardner, M.D.

DEFINITION

Hyperthyroidism is a clinical syndrome of diverse etiologies that have in common an increase in circulating thyroid hormone concentrations. The clinical signs and symptoms reflect the effects of these excess thyroid hormone levels on various organ systems.

ETIOLOGY

The causes of hyperthyroidism, in their approximate order of frequency, are summarized in Table 9–17–1. Graves' disease is the most common cause of hyperthyroidism in the United States, and the first five causes listed in the table account for 98 to 99% of all patients with hyperthyroidism.

CRITERIA FOR DIAGNOSIS
Suggestive

The diagnosis of hyperthyroidism should be suspected in any patient with typical clinical manifestations, particularly nervousness, heat intolerance, unexplained weight loss, palpitations, and fatigue, in association with a goiter. Individual patients, however, may not manifest all the classic signs and symptoms of hyperthyroidism. This is particularly true in the elderly, in whom unexplained weight loss and cardiovascular disease are often the predominant clinical manifestations.

Definitive

In the majority of patients, the diagnosis is based on the demonstration of an elevated serum free thyroxine (T_4) concentration and suppressed

TABLE 9–17–1. CAUSES OF HYPERTHYROIDISM

Graves' disease

Toxic multinodular goiter

Solitary hyperfunctioning nodule

Subacute thyroiditis

Exogenous thyroid hormone (iatrogenic or factitious)

Pituitary tumor secreting thyroid-stimulating hormone

Trophoblastic tumors

Struma ovarii

Follicular thyroid carcinoma (metastatic)

Iodine-induced thyrotoxicosis

Selective pituitary resistance to thyroid hormone

serum thyrotropin (thyroid–stimulating hormone) concentration, in association with appropriate signs and symptoms (see below). An occasional patient with typical clinical manifestations of hyperthyroidism but a normal serum free T_4 concentration will require a serum triiodothyronine (T_3) determination to confirm the diagnosis.

CLINICAL MANIFESTATIONS
Subjective

Although the symptoms of hyperthyroidism vary from patient to patient, the following are most often reported: nervousness, increased sweating, heat intolerance, fatigue, dyspnea, palpitations, weakness, weight loss despite an increased appetite, eye symptoms, and hyperdefecation. Nervousness may manifest in a variety of ways, including irritability, restlessness, difficulty concentrating, emotional lability, and insomnia. Weakness may be generalized, but is most prominent in the proximal musculature. Dyspnea and palpitations are most frequent in older patients with underlying cardiovascular disease, but also occur in younger patients with no evidence of preexisting cardiopulmonary disease. Weight loss is common despite patient reports of increased caloric intake, although a small percentage of hyperthyroid patients may actually gain weight. Increased frequency of bowel movements is often reported, but frank diarrhea is uncommon. Less common complaints include a change in menstrual pattern, pruritis, excessive hair loss, and gynecomastia.

The eye disease of hyperthyroidism is divided into two categories: noninfiltrative and infiltrative. The former refers to ocular manifestations associated with thyroid hormone excess of any cause, and the latter refers to the specific ocular signs and symptoms of Graves' disease. The hyperthyroid patient without Graves' disease has few eye symptoms. Symptoms associated with the infiltrative ophthalmopathy of Graves' disease include persistent eye irritation, excessive lacrimation, photophobia, diplopia, and, rarely, a decrease in visual acuity.

The term *masked* or *apathetic hyperthyroidism* describes the atypical hyperthyroid patient who lacks many of the classic symptoms of this disorder. These patients are usually elderly and present with unexplained weight loss, muscle weakness, atrial fibrillation, and heart failure. The diagnosis is often overlooked because these patients lack more typical beta-adrenergic symptoms such as nervousness and heat intolerance.

Objective
Physical Examination

The patient's general appearance may be the first clue that thyroid hyperfunction is present. The typical patient is hyperactive and appears to have lost weight. Speech is often rapid and rambling, and facial features may reflect anxiety and apprehension.

Vital signs and cardiac examination reflect the hypermetabolic state. Most hyperthyroid patients have a resting tachycardia, and atrial fibrillation is common in older patients. The peripheral pulses are bounding, reflecting the widened pulse pressure associated with an increased cardiac output and decreased peripheral vascular resistance. Cardiac examination reveals a hyperdynamic apical impulse and often a systolic flow murmur.

The skin is warm, moist, and smooth with a velvety texture. Hair often becomes fine in texture and easily falls out, occasionally causing significant alopecia. The nails may become soft and distal margin separated from the nailbed (onycholysis).

Eye findings are classified into those associated with hyperthyroidism per se (noninfiltrative) and those specific for Graves' disease (infiltrative). Retraction of the upper lid is the most common noninfiltrative sign and results in a characteristic stare or bright-eyed look. Lid lag may be elicited by having the patient turn his or her gaze slowly downward; the upper lid "lags" behind the globe in its downward movement so that the sclera is visible above the iris. Lid retraction may result in the appearance of proptosis (exophthalmos), but true globe protrusion should be documented by exophthalmometry. The features of Graves' ophthalmopathy are discussed in Chapter 9–18. Both infiltrative and noninfiltrative eye findings may be asymmetric.

The thyroid gland is usually enlarged, although the absence of a goiter does not exclude the diagnosis. This is particularly true in the elderly, in whom clear-cut thyroid enlargement may be present in only two thirds of patients. A substernal thyroid also may be overlooked on routine physical examination. The characteristics of the goiter vary with the etiology of the hyperthyroidism. In Graves' disease, the thyroid is usually symmetrically enlarged, consistency may be soft or firm, and the surface is smooth. The gland may be slightly tender, and the markedly increased blood flow may result in a venous hum, bruit, or palpable thrill. Toxic multinodular goiters tend to be larger than those of Graves' disease, asymmetric, firm, and irregular, with two or more discrete modules. A solitary hyperfunctioning nodule will present as a single large nodule, usually greater than 3 cm in diameter, with the rest of the gland being nonpalpable. Subacute thyroiditis is associated with marked tenderness of a moderately enlarged and often asymmetric gland. The absence of a goiter in a hyperthyroid patient should suggest the possibility of struma ovarii or ingestion of exogenous thyroid hormone.

Neurologic examination is remarkable for a fine tremor of the tongue and outstretched hands. Deep tendon reflexes are hyperactive, with acceleration of both the contraction and relaxation phases. Muscle weakness is common and, in more severe cases, is associated with objective muscle wasting. The proximal musculature is generally affected more than distal groups.

Routine Laboratory Abnormalities

Routine laboratory studies show nonspecific abnormalities in uncomplicated hyperthyroidism. A mild normochromic normocytic anemia may be present, although severe anemia is unusual. Mild granulocytopenia with a relative lymphocytosis may also be present. Abnormalities in serum chemistries seen in some hyperthyroid patients include hypercalcemia, an elevated alkaline phosphatase level, and hypocholesterolemia.

The electrocardiogram reflects the cardiovascular changes—sinus tachycardia or atrial fibrillation.

PLANS
Diagnostic
Differential Diagnosis

In most patients, the constellation of clinical findings, summarized above, along with a goiter, provides strong evidence for a diagnosis of hyperthyroidism. Because of the variability of clinical findings in some patients, however, other disorders occasionally require consideration. These include psychiatric disorders such as anxiety, panic attacks, and bipolar states. Substance abuse, particularly with amphetamines and cocaine, may mimic some of the clinical features of hyperthyroidism, as do overdoses of some anticholinergic agents and beta-adrenergic agonists. The paroxysmal nervousness, tremulousness, sweating, and tachycardia associated with pheochromocytomas may suggest hyperthyroidism; however, a careful history documenting the episodic nature of these symptoms in pheochromocytoma patients should distinguish them from the persistent symptoms of hyperthyroidism. The combination of weight loss with a good appetite may suggest diabetes mellitus or a malabsorption syndrome.

Diagnostic Options

The diagnosis of hyperthyroidism ultimately rests on the demonstration of elevated concentrations of circulating thyroid hormones. Two different diagnostic approaches are now available for the evaluation of patients with suspected hyperthyroidism: one starting with a determination of the free thyroxine concentration, the other with the serum thyroid-stimulating hormone (TSH) concentration.

The availability of "sensitive" TSH immunoassays provides a highly effective approach to the diagnosis of hyperthyroidism. In the past, the clinical utility of serum TSH measurements in the diagnosis of hyperthyroidism was limited by the inadequate sensitivity of the assay. Newer TSH assays have sensitivities as low as 0.01 µU/mL and readily discriminate between the low values occasionally seen in normal persons, and the markedly depressed values seen in patients with hyperthyroidism. A strategy based on the use of the serum TSH concentration as the initial diagnostic study in a patient with suspected hyperthyroidism is outlined in Figure 9–17–1.

The algorithm in Figure 9–17–2 outlines an approach based on the determination of the free T_4 concentration. Measurement of the serum T4 concentration alone may result in an erroneous assessment of the patient's clinical status. Alterations in the concentration of serum thyroid hormone-binding proteins, particularly thyroxine-binding globulin, alter the total T_4 concentration without affecting the free T_4 concentration. As it is the free hormone that is metabolically active, initial studies should measure the free T_4 in serum. The free T_4 index (FTI), calculated from the total T_4 concentration and T_3-resin uptake, provides an excellent estimate of the free T_4 concentration. Studies have documented that the FTI correlates extremely well with more direct measurements of the free T_4 concentration.

An occasional patient with a suggestive clinical presentation will have a suppressed TSH level but a normal free T_4 concentration. This patient should be evaluated with a serum T_3 determination. The syndrome of hyperthyroidism with a normal serum free T_4 concentration and elevated serum T_3 concentration has been called T_3 hyperthyroidism or T_3 thyrotoxicosis and probably accounts for about 5% of all hyperthyroid patients. Patients with normal serum free T_4 and T_3 concentrations but suppressed TSH levels are said to have "subclinical hyperthyroidism."

Controversy remains as to which study, the free thyroxine index or serum TSH, should be ordered as the *initial* test in a patient with suspected hyperthyroidism. Either strategy should be effective if the algorithms outlined in the figures are followed.

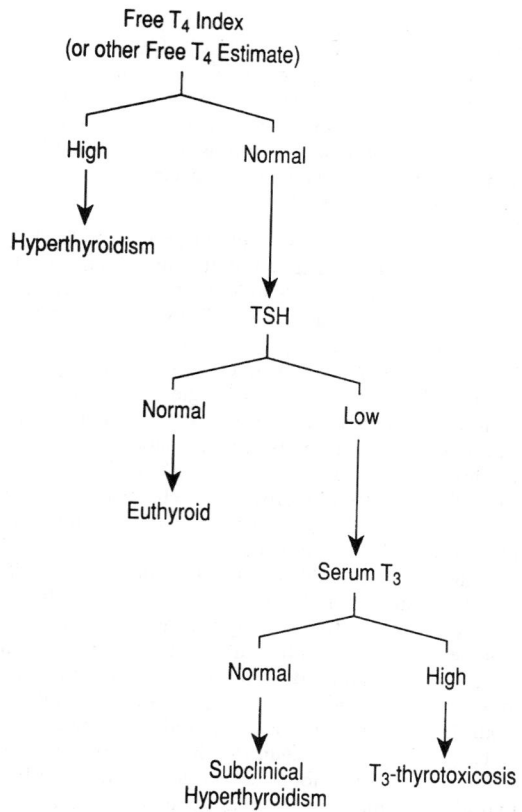

Figure 9–17–2. Algorithm for the diagnosis of hyperthyroidism using the serum free thyroxine as the initial diagnostic study. TSH, thyroid-stimulating hormone.

The sensitive TSH assay has replaced the thyrotropin-releasing hormone test in the evaluation of patients with suspected hyperthyroidism, who have borderline results on standard serum thyroid hormone measurements. In normal persons, the TSH concentration rises rapidly after intravenous injection of thyrotropin-releasing hormone, usually peaking between 15 and 30 minutes. In hyperthyroid patients, the TSH response is blunted or absent; a normal TSH response effectively excludes the diagnosis of hyperthyroidism. Several studies have now documented that a low basal serum TSH level is highly predictive of a blunted TSH response to thyrotropin-releasing hormone, so that the more cumbersome and costly thyrotropin-releasing hormone test can now be eliminated. The role of in vivo radioisotopic tests (24-hour radioactive iodine uptake and scan) in the diagnosis of hyperthyroidism is controversial. In the majority of patients, these studies should not be used to make a diagnosis of hyperthyroidism. They may, however, be useful in defining the etiology of the hyperthyroidism.

Recommended Approach

The serum TSH concentration is the ideal screening test for patients with suspected hyperthyroidism, as a normal result essentially excludes the diagnosis. The only exceptions to this rule are the extremely rare patients with TSH-secreting pituitary tumors and selective pituitary resistance to thyroid hormone. A low serum TSH, however, is not absolutely diagnostic of hyperthyroidism. A low TSH in the absence of hyperthyroidism is occasionally seen in the first trimester of pregnancy, in patients receiving glucocorticoid therapy, in patients with acute, severe nonthyroidal and psychiatric disorders, and even in normal elderly individuals.

Therapeutic

Therapeutic Options

Therapy varies with the cause of the hyperthyroidism. Exogenous hyperthyroidism responds to adjustment or cessation of thyroid hormone

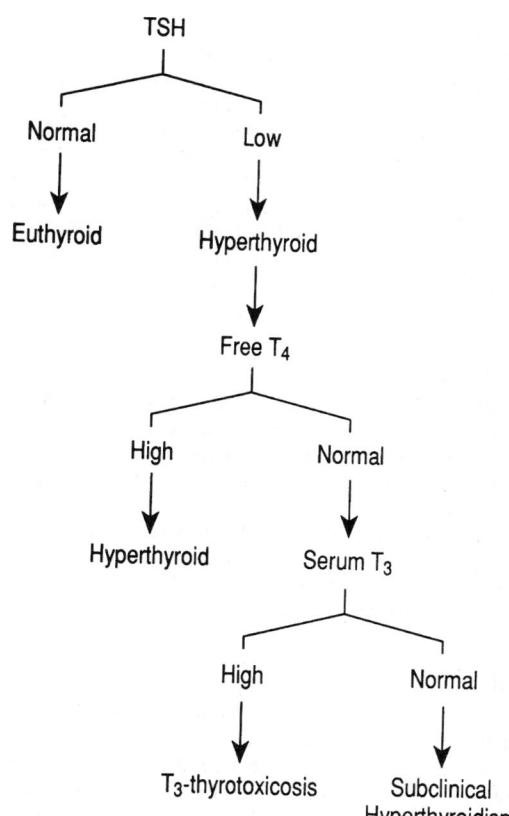

Figure 9–17–1. Algorithm for the diagnosis of hyperthyroidism using the sensitive thyroid-stimulating hormone (TSH) assay as the initial diagnostic study.

therapy. Patients with TSH-producing pituitary tumors, trophoblastic tumors, struma ovarii, or widespread thyroid follicular carcinoma require therapy directed at the primary neoplasm. Many of these patients, however, require correction of their hyperthyroidism with antithyroid drugs (see below) prior to definitive treatment of their tumor. Subacute thyroiditis is a self-limited disorder in most patients, usually requiring only symptomatic treatment. The unique aspects of therapy for Graves' disease are discussed in Chapter 9–18.

Pharmacologic Treatment. The drugs most often used to treat hyperthyroidism are the thiourea agents propylthiouracil and methimazole (Tapazole). Their major action is inhibition of thyroid hormone synthesis, although propylthiouracil also has inhibitory effects on the conversion of T_4 to T_3. The usual initial dose of propylthiouracil is 300 mg/d given in divided doses every 8 hours. The typical starting dose of methimazole is 30 mg/d, administered as a single morning dose. After 3 to 4 weeks of therapy, the doses of these drugs often require adjustment downward to prevent hypothyroidism. Some patients, however, require significantly higher doses to achieve the euthyroid state. The most common side effects of the thioureas are rash, fever, and arthralgias, which may occur in up to 5% of patients. The most serious toxic effect is agranulocytosis, with an estimated incidence of 0.1 to 0.4%. The onset of agranulocytosis is sudden, usually occurring within the first 3 months of therapy, and reversible with cessation of the drug. Patients must be educated to discontinue therapy if they develop a fever, sore throat, or other evidence of infection and contact their physician immediately. Other less common side effects include hepatic dysfunction (hepatitis or cholestatic jaundice) and a lupus-like syndrome.

Antithyroid drugs effectively lower thyroid hormone concentrations in all patients with hyperthyroidism if given in sufficient doses; however, as the thioureas have no long-term effects on the underlying cause of hyperthyroidism, some form of ablative therapy (radioactive iodine or surgery) is ultimately necessary. The only exception is the patient with Graves' disease who goes into spontaneous remission (see Chapter 9–18).

Iodine, in the form of sodium and potassium iodide, has important antithyroid actions and is occasionally used in the management of the acutely ill thyrotoxic patient. Its most significant effect clinically is acute inhibition of thyroid hormone release and, when used in conjunction with one of the thiourea agents, can result in rapid lowering of circulating thyroid hormone concentrations. Iodine is usually administered in the form of SSKI, which contains 38 mg iodide per drop; the usual dose is 5 drops three times daily. As most hyperthyroid patients "escape" from the antithyroid effects of iodine, it should be considered only as an adjunct to other forms of antithyroid therapy.

The beta-adrenergic blocking agents have assumed an important role in the clinical management of the hyperthyroid patient. Although these drugs have no direct effect on thyroid hormone secretion, they effectively reverse many of the signs and symptoms of hyperthyroidism. Patients report improvement in nervousness, palpitations, sweating, and tremor, as well as an improvement in their overall sense of well-being. Both cardioselective and nonselective beta blockers are effective in this regard. A reasonable starting dose for a cardioselective agent such as atenolol is 50 mg every morning and, for a nonselective agent such as propranolol, 20 mg every 6 hours. All beta blockers should be used with extreme caution in patients with congestive heart failure, although the negative chronotropic effects of these agents may improve left ventricular function in some patients with hyperthyroidism and a rapid ventricular response. Although some beta blockers have a modest inhibitory effect on T_4-to-T_3 conversion, they should not be considered a primary therapeutic modality. They do not reverse the negative nitrogen and calcium balance associated with hyperthyroidism, nor do they restore weight loss. Therefore, they are adjuncts to more specific therapies that lower serum thyroid hormone concentrations.

Radioactive Iodine. Radioactive iodine therapy is the treatment of choice for hyperthyroidism in adults in many centers because it is effective, safe, and convenient to administer. The accumulation of this isotope in the thyroid destroys thyroid follicular cells, in effect, a "medical" thyroidectomy. The effectiveness of therapy has been convincingly demonstrated, with 85 to 90% of patients cured by a single dose. Patients with toxic multinodular goiter may be more resistant to radioio-

dine therapy and, therefore, require higher doses of the isotope at the time of initial therapy. Acute complications are rare. The only proven long-term complication is hypothyroidism, although there has recently been concern that radioactive iodine may worsen ophthalmopathy in some patients with Graves' disease. The size of the initial dose of radioiodine determines the incidence of hypothyroidism in the first year after therapy, but an annual incidence rate of approximately 3% per year is observed even after low initial doses. Lowering the dose of radioactive iodine decreases the incidence of hypothyroidism in the first year, at the expense of a lower overall cure rate. A common concern is the possibility of radiation-induced carcinogenesis and teratogenesis. To date, however, there is no evidence of an increased incidence of carcinoma or genetic damage in patients receiving radioactive iodine at any age. On the basis of these data, it is now common practice to administer radioactive iodine to patients of all ages, including children and adolescents. This is still a controversial issue, however, and some clinicians limit radioiodine to patients beyond the childbearing years.

Surgery. The indications for surgery for hyperthyroidism are limited. Possible surgical candidates include children and adolescents, pregnant women not responding to or having an adverse reaction to antithyroid drugs, and patients refusing radioactive iodine therapy. The major complications of thyroid surgery include hypoparathyroidism, recurrent laryngeal nerve injury, and hypothyroidism. If the decision is made to operate, antithyroid drugs should be administered preoperatively until the patient is euthyroid. Traditionally, iodine is added to the regimen for 2 weeks prior to surgery to reduce the vascularity of the gland. It has been suggested that propranolol alone is adequate preoperative therapy, but this approach remains controversial.

Management of Thyroid Storm. Thyroid storm is an uncommon, life-threatening condition usually occurring in patients with previously unrecognized or inadequately treated hyperthyroidism. Precipitating factors include surgery, obstetrical delivery, infection, or any other stressful medical illness. Typical clinical features include fever, delirium, and exaggerated signs of thyrotoxicosis. Cardiovascular manifestations in the form of congestive heart failure and atrial fibrillation with a rapid ventricular response may dominate the clinical picture. An aggressive therapeutic approach is warranted because of the significant mortality associated with this disorder. Antithyroid therapy should include both propylthiouracil (300 mg every 6 hours) and iodides. The latter should be administered after propylthiouracil therapy has been initiated, either as SSKI (10 drops orally every 8 hours) or as sodium iodide (500 mg intravenously every 8 hours). Beta-adrenergic blocking agents should be added to specific antithyroid drug therapy. Conventional therapy also includes stress doses of glucocorticoids (100 mg hydrocortisone every 8 hours). Careful management of any underlying medical disorders and maintenance of adequate hydration are important in the overall management of these critically ill patients.

Recommended Approach

Definitive therapy for patients with hyperthyroidism due to toxic multinodular goiters and solitary hyperfunctioning nodules is radioactive iodine. Therapy for hyperthyroidism due to Graves' disease is discussed in the next chapter. All hyperthyroid patients may benefit from symptomatic therapy with beta-blocking agents. Finally, in patients with life-threatening complications of hyperthyroidism, rapid correction of the hyperthyroid state requires the use of antithyroid drugs, often in combination with iodides. Once stabilized, patients can then receive radioactive iodine therapy.

FOLLOW-UP

Follow-up depends on the form of therapy selected. Patients starting antithyroid drugs should be seen after 3 to 4 weeks for clinical and laboratory assessment. Dosage adjustments in the first several months necessitate frequent office visits, although intervals between visits can be extended once a stable regimen has been established. Patients are usually seen 4 to 6 weeks after radioactive iodine treatment and then every 2 months for the next 6 months unless symptoms of hypothyroidism appear earlier. All patients are at indefinite risk for developing hypothyroidism, and yearly office visits are recommended after the initial period of observation.

DISCUSSION
Prevalence and Incidence

Hyperthyroidism is a common disorder. A community survey in Great Britain in the 1970s estimated the incidence to be 1 to 2 cases per 1000 per year, with women affected 10 times more frequently than men. (Tunbridge et al. 1977)

Related Basic Science

The fundamental abnormality in hyperthyroidism of any cause is the unregulated or autonomous production of thyroid hormones. Normally, the thyroid gland secretes T_3 and T_4 under the stimulus of pituitary TSH, which in turn is under negative feedback control by these hormones. In the hyperthyroid patient, thyroid hormone secretion is not under feedback control, and it is the chronic exposure of body tissues to excessive levels of thyroid hormones that results in the typical signs and symptoms. The particular thyroid anatomy that is observed reflects the underlying pathophysiology: Diffuse thyroid enlargement is seen in Graves' disease, TSH-producing pituitary tumors, and trophoblastic tumors, as each is associated with a direct thyroid stimulator (thyrotropin receptor antibody, TSH, and human chorionic gonadotropin, respectively). Absence of a goiter is associated with exogenous thyroid hormone ingestion and struma ovarii, both of which suppress TSH secretion. Nodular thyroid enlargement is associated with the benign thyroid neoplasms of toxic multinodular goiter and solitary hyperfunctioning thyroid nodules. Thyroid tenderness with a goiter is the typical finding in patients with subacute thyroiditis, in whom inflammation and cellular injury result in the unregulated leakage of thyroid hormones into the circulation.

Natural History and Its Modification with Treatment

With the exception of Graves' disease and subacute thyroiditis, none of the known causes of hyperthyroidism is associated with spontaneous remission. Thus, therapeutic intervention is necessary to alter the natural history of the disease. The severity of complications varies with the duration of the hyperthyroidism and the presence of underlying disease. Older patients tolerate hyperthyroidism less well than younger patients, and this is most dramatic in the area of cardiovascular manifestations.

Meaningful mortality statistics are not currently available.

Prevention

The only known preventative measure is the avoidance of excessive iodine in patients at risk for iodine-induced thyrotoxicosis, that is, euthyroid patients with multinodular goiters and solitary hyperfunctioning nodules. Patients with a family history of Graves' disease should be aware of their predisposition to hyperthyroidism and seek early medical attention if suggestive symptoms appear.

Cost Containment

In the majority of patients, diagnosis and management can be carried out safely and efficiently in the ambulatory care setting. The algorithms outlined in Figures 9–17–1 and 9–17–2 will minimize the cost of diagnosis. The serum TSH concentration is the best screening test for the diagnosis of hyperthyroidism. Both antithyroid drugs and radioactive iodine, the mainstays of therapy for hyperthyroidism, are relatively inexpensive treatment modalities. In vivo radioisotopic tests should not be routinely used to diagnose hyperthyroidism, although they may prove useful in defining the etiology of the disorder.

REFERENCES

Franklyn JA. Drug therapy: The management of hyperthyroidism. N Engl J Med 1994;330:1731
Klein I, Becker DV, Levey GS. Treatment of hyperthyroid disease. Ann Intern Med 1994;121:281.
Loughney MH, Burman KD. Unusual forms of thyrotoxicosis. Adv Endocrinol Metab 1994;5:349
Tunbridge WMG, Evered DE, Hall R, et al. The spectrum of thyroid disease in a community: The Whickham survey. Clin Endocrinol 1977;7:481
Ventrella SM, Klein I. Beta-adrenergic receptor blocking drugs in the management of hyperthyroidism. Endocrinologist 1994;4:391.
Wilbur JF. Hyperthyroidism in the elderly. Adv Endocrinol Metab 1933;4:143.

CHAPTER 9–18
Graves' Disease
David F. Gardner, M.D.

DEFINITION

Graves' disease is a systemic autoimmune disorder characterized by hyperthyroidism, diffuse thyroid enlargement, and extrathyroidal manifestations involving the eyes, skin, and digits.

ETIOLOGY

There is considerable evidence supporting an immune basis for both the hyperthyroidism of Graves' disease and the extrathyroidal features of this disorder. The direct stimulus for thyroid hyperfunction is a circulating antibody with specificity for the thyroid-stimulating hormone (TSH) receptor. Binding of this antibody to the TSH receptor initiates the same series of intracellular events associated with TSH binding, resulting in the stimulation of thyroid hormone synthesis and secretion.

CRITERIA FOR DIAGNOSIS
Suggestive

The diagnosis of Graves' disease should be suspected in any patient with typical signs and symptoms of hyperthyroidism in association with a diffuse goiter, exophthalmos, infiltrative dermopathy, or thyroid acropachy. In hyperthyroid patients with diffuse thyroid enlargement, but without the extrathyroidal features of Graves' disease, the diagnosis is one of exclusion. An occasional patient will manifest one of the extrathyroidal features (usually ophthalmopathy) of Graves' disease without clinical or laboratory evidence of hyperthyroidism. This presentation is referred to as euthyroid Graves' disease.

Definitive

Definitive diagnosis requires the demonstration of elevated thyroid hormone and suppressed TSH concentrations, in association with a diffuse goiter and one of the extrathyroidal features described above. The diagnosis may also be confirmed by the demonstration of thyrotropin receptor antibody in the serum of a patient with hyperthyroidism or a euthyroid patient with one of the extrathyroidal manifestations.

CLINICAL MANIFESTATIONS
Subjective

The symptoms of hyperthyroidism have been summarized in Chapter 9–17, and only those specific for Graves' disease are discussed here. Infiltrative ophthalmopathy is associated primarily with symptoms of eye irritation. Patients often complain of a gritty or foreign-body sensation, excessive lacrimation, photophobia, and sensitivity to smoke and wind. When there is significant exophthalmos, the patient may complain of a feeling of pressure behind the eyes, and involvement of the extraocular muscles may result in symptoms of diplopia. In cases of severe ophthalmopathy, visual acuity may be affected secondary to corneal ulceration or optic neuropathy. The other extrathyroidal manifestations, infiltrative dermopathy and thyroid acropachy, are usually asymptomatic but may be cosmetically undesirable.

Objective

Physical Examination

The characteristic physical findings of hyperthyroidism are summarized in Chapter 9–17. The major signs of Graves' ophthalmopathy are exophthalmos (proptosis), conjunctival inflammation, and extraocular muscle dysfunction. Proptosis is probably the most common eye finding. It is usually bilateral, but asymmetry is common. As lid retraction may give the appearance of globe protrusion, the degree of proptosis should be documented with an exophthalmometer. Conjunctival involvement may result in chemosis, conjunctival injection, and periorbital puffiness. Extraocular muscle involvement most often results in restriction of upward gaze, although there may be limitation of eye movements in all directions. Decreased visual acuity may result from either direct compression or vascular compromise of the optic nerve. Corneal ulceration may result from the patient's inability to close the eyes because of severe proptosis.

Infiltrative dermopathy (localized or pretibial myxedema) is usually found over the pretibial area near the ankles, but may rarely involve the extensor surfaces of the hands and forearms. The lesions appear as raised, nontender, indurated plaques with a characteristic "orange peel" texture. They may be nodular or become confluent, covering much of the pretibial surface. The vast majority of patients with this lesion have preexisting opthalmopathy. Thyroid acropachy, the rarest extrathyroidal manifestation of Graves' disease, presents as clubbing of the digits of the hands and feet, with accompanying radiographic changes of periosteal involvement.

Routine Laboratory Abnormalities

Abnormalities of routine laboratory studies are similar to those seen in other forms of hyperthyroidism. In addition, there is an increased incidence of pernicious anemia in patients with Graves' disease. Occasionally, the thymus is enlarged, resulting in an anterior mediastinal mass on routine chest x-ray.

PLANS

Diagnostic

Differential Diagnosis

The differential diagnosis of hyperthyroidism is summarized in Chapter 9–17. The differential diagnosis of Graves' disease includes other disorders associated with proptosis. These are primary and metastatic orbital neoplasms, orbital pseudotumor, granulomatous disorders such as sarcoidosis and Wegener's granulomatosis, orbital infections, and vascular anomalies such as carotid-cavernous sinus fistulas. One form of subacute thyroiditis, "painless" thyroiditis, may be clinically indistinguishable from Graves' disease, when extrathyroidal features of Graves' disease are absent. "Painless" thyroiditis, however, is a spontaneously resolving disorder, with most patients returning to the euthyroid state within 6 to 8 weeks.

Diagnostic Options

The diagnosis of hyperthyroidism is outlined in detail in Chapter 9–17. The diagnosis of Graves' disease in most patients is based on the finding of hyperthyroidism in association with a diffuse goiter or one of the characteristic extrathyroidal manifestations. Although other forms of hyperthyroidism such as TSH-secreting pituitary tumors and trophoblastic tumors are associated with diffuse thyroid enlargement, these disorders are sufficiently rare that they should not be pursued unless there is some other supporting clinical evidence. Euthyroid Graves'

disease should be suspected in patients with characteristic Graves' ophthalmopathy but no clinical or biochemical evidence of hyperthyroidism. The diagnosis of euthyroid Graves' disease can be substantiated by orbital computed tomography, which demonstrates characteristic enlargement of the extraocular muscles. The diagnosis may also be confirmed by the detection of thyrotropin receptor antibody in the patient's serum.

Recommended Approach

Graves' disease should be diagnosed in the hyperthyroid patient with a diffuse goiter and one of the extrathyroidal manifestations, usually ophthalmopathy. In the absence of one of these latter findings, it is a diagnosis of exclusion. This is usually not difficult, as physical examination should readily distinguish patients with nodular goiter and subacute thyroiditis. The other causes of hyperthyroidism listed in Table 9–17–1 are sufficiently rare that they should be diagnosed only when there is other supporting evidence.

Therapeutic

Therapeutic Options

The treatment modalities outlined in Chapter 9–17 can be applied to the treatment of Graves' disease; however, the therapeutic approach to Graves' patients must take into account a unique characteristic of this disorder: the occurrence of spontaneous remissions. The exact incidence of remissions is controversial, with estimates usually ranging from 20 to 50%. It is the occurrence of these remissions that has led to the considerable controversy surrounding the "best" treatment for the disorder. Probably the single most important factor in deciding between radioactive iodine therapy and antithyroid drugs is the age of the patient. Most experienced clinicians favor a trial of antithyroid drugs in children and adolescents; radioactive iodine is the treatment of choice in patients beyond the reproductive years. Controversy thus surrounds the management of Graves' disease in young adults. The major advantage of antithyroid drugs is that they do not cause permanent hypothyroidism and can be discontinued if remission occurs. Radioactive iodine, however, is easy to administer, is almost uniformly effective in correcting hyperthyroidism, and is not associated with any major long-term adverse effects other than hypothyroidism. The decision to use drugs or ablative therapy must be made on an individual basis, with the patient's understanding of the alternatives and the physician's personal experience being the determining factors. With either form of therapy, indefinite follow-up is necessary to monitor for the recurrence of hyperthyroidism or the development of hypothyroidism.

The usual starting dose of propylthiouracil is 300 mg/d, and that of methimazole, 30 mg/d. The goal of therapy is to maintain thyroid function tests in the upper end of the normal range. This may require progressive reduction from the starting dose or upward titration of the dose. The ideal duration of therapy is controversial. Some studies suggest that the rate of remission is related to the duration of therapy, whereas others advocate cessation of therapy once the euthyroid state has been achieved. Although this issue remains unresolved, most experts agree that these agents should be administered for at least 1 year before considering the patient a treatment failure. A recent study from Japan has documented a remission rate greater than 95% in a small group of patients with Graves' disease in whom l-thyroxine was added to methimazole after euthyroidism was achieved with this antithyroid agent. If this observation can be confirmed, it may significantly alter the approach to therapy in patients of all ages.

The clinical course of the extrathyroidal manifestations of Graves' disease is extremely variable, often bearing no relation to the course of the hyperthyroidism. Symptomatic ophthalmopathy often responds to methylcellulose eyedrops, application of lubricating ointments at bedtime, and, if corneal exposure occurs, patching of the eyes. More severe ophthalmopathy may require the use of systemic corticosteroids, orbital irradiation, or surgical decompression of the orbit. Patients with advanced opthalmopathy require regular follow-up with an ophthalmologist for longitudinal assessment of visual acuity and corneal abrasions. Several recent papers have suggested that opthalmopathy may be exacerbated by radioactive iodine therapy, and alternative approaches should be used in patients with significant eye disease. This issue remains controversial, and at least one large retrospective study did not confirm this finding.

Infiltrative dermopathy, although primarily a cosmetic problem, may respond to occlusive steroid dressings or intralesional steroid injections.

Recommended Approach

Children and adolescents should be offered a trial of antithyroid drugs. As methimazole can be administered on a once-daily basis, it is preferred over propylthiouracil. In addition, agranulocytosis appears to be quite unusual if the dose of methimazole is less than 30 mg/d. Patients over the age of 40 are best treated with radioactive iodine. Individual patient and physician preferences determine therapy in patients between the ages of 20 and 40. Patients with hyperthyroidism due to Graves' disease may also benefit from symptomatic therapy with beta blockers. Graves' disease during pregnancy should be treated with propylthiouracil.

FOLLOW-UP

Follow-up for drug and radioactive iodine therapy has been discussed in Chapter 9–17. All patients with Graves' disease, including patients who have received drug therapy alone, are at risk for the development of hypothyroidism. Patients with moderate to severe ophthalmopathy should have regular follow-up with an opthalmologist for assessment of visual acuity and corneal injury.

DISCUSSION
Prevalence and Incidence

The annual incidence rate of Graves' disease in the United States has been estimated to range from 0.02 to 0.4%. Although the disorder has been reported in infants and the elderly, it occurs most commonly in women between the ages of 20 and 40.

Related Basic Science
Genetics

The role of genetic factors in Graves' disease has been confirmed in several studies. Numerous families have been described with multiple affected members. In addition, predisposition to Graves' disease has been associated with the inheritance of specific histocompatibility antigens, particularly HLA-DR3. Although emotional factors have been suggested as playing a role in the initiation of Graves' disease, there is little hard evidence to support this hypothesis.

Physiologic or Metabolic Derangement

There is considerable evidence supporting an autoimmune basis for Graves' disease. Numerous abnormalities in both humoral and cell-me-

diated immunity have been demonstrated. Like many autoimmune disorders, Graves' disease occurs with much greater frequency in women, and the clinical course is characterized by remissions and exacerbations. The most important immunologic abnormality is the presence of an immunoglobulin that binds to the TSH receptor on thyroid plasma membranes. This autoantibody stimulates thyroid hormone synthesis and secretion and is thus responsible for the hyperthyroidism associated with Graves' disease. The current terminology to describe this autoantibody is thyrotropin receptor antibody (TRAb) or thyroid-stimulating antibody (TSAb), although it is still perhaps best known by the older term, long-acting thyroid stimulator (LATS). There is also a considerable body of evidence supporting an autoimmune basis for the extrathyroidal manifestations of Graves' disease. Antibodies to eye muscle antigens have been documented in a significant number of patients with Graves' ophthalmopathy.

Natural History and Its Modification with Treatment

As previously discussed, the natural history of Graves' disease is characterized by spontaneous remissions. The clinical sequelae of hyperthyroidism are discussed in Chapter 9–17.

Prevention

No preventive measures are currently available.

Cost Containment

In the majority of patients, the diagnosis of Graves' disease is based on clinical signs and symptoms along with the relatively inexpensive studies needed to document the hyperthyroid state. Radioisotopic studies, thyrotropin-releasing hormone testing, and measurement of thyrotropin receptor antibody levels should be reserved for evaluation of patients with borderline results on routine studies or a confusing clinical presentation.

REFERENCES

Burch HB, Wartofsky L. Graves' ophthalmopathy: Current concepts regarding pathogenesis and management. Endocr Rev 1993;14:747.
Cooper DS. Antithyroid drugs and radioiodine therapy: A grain of (iodized) salt. Ann Intern Med 1994;121:612.
Hashizume K, Ichikawa K, Sakurai A, et al. Administration of thyroxine in treated Graves' disease: Effects on the level of antibodies to TSH receptors and on the risk of recurrence of hyperthyroidism. N Engl J Med 1991;324:947.
Roti E, Minelli R, Gardini E, Braverman LE. Controversies in the treatment of thyrotoxicosis. Adv Endocrinol Metab 1994;5:429.
Solomon B, Glinoer D, Lagasse R, Wartofsky L. Current trends in the management of Graves' disease. J Clin Endocrinol Metab 1990;70:1518.
Volpé R. Graves' disease. In: Braverman LE, Utiger RD, eds. The thyroid. 6th ed. Philadelphia: Lippincott, 1991:31.

CHAPTER 9–19

Hypothyroidism

John F. Wilber, M.D.

DEFINITION

Hypothyroidism, characterized by below-normal circulating concentrations of bioactive thyroid hormones (free thyroxine [T_4] and free tri-iodothyronine [T_3]), causes a constellation of systems marked by slowing down of physical and mental functions. The most important clinical features of hypothyroidism include reductions of mental, cardiovascular, and neuromuscular activities.

ETIOLOGY

Most forms of hypothyroidism are "primary" (failure of the thyroid per se).

CRITERIA FOR DIAGNOSIS
Suggestive

Slowing of physical or mental functions, or both, or unexplained weight gain is suggestive of thyroid failure.

Definitive

Because most forms of hypothyroidism are due to thyroid gland failure, plasma thyroid-stimulating hormone (TSH) concentrations are typically elevated, often more than 20 μU/L (normal is usually between 0.3 and 5.0 μU/L). Serum free thyroxine levels are usually reduced. Hypothyroidism caused by pituitary or hypothalamic disorders is characterized by a low concentration of serum free thyroxine and a TSH level that is "not elevated" (low either in absolute or relative terms).

CLINICAL MANIFESTATIONS
Subjective

In its severest form, classic myxedema is easy to recognize. More frequently, however, hypothyroidism is subtle and its recognition is difficult. Nevertheless, it is crucial to identify thyroid insufficiency because left untreated it can become a chronic, progressive, and potentially lethal process. The clinical spectrum embraces subclinical hypothyroidism to myxedema coma.

Common symptomatology includes slow and hoarse speech, lethargy, intolerance to cold, impaired memory, constipation, and slow movements. Symptoms tend to be insidious and often require months to years to evolve into a clear clinical picture. Mucopolysaccharides accumulate in the dermis, associated with complaints of coarse, dry skin and facial puffiness. Patients often note slowing of mentation with reductions in recent memory function, cognition, and somnolence. Fertility and libido are decreased, and exercise tolerance is diminished. Impotence is common and may not be reversed completely with thyroxine treatment. Altered gonadal function in women in marked by lower estradiol concentrations, irregular anovulatory cycles, and menorrhagia.

Objective
Physical Examination

Patients are characteristically hypothermic and bradycardic and commonly exhibit diastolic hypertension and weight gain. Examination of the skin reveals thickening, dryness, and coarsening of the dermis, with atrophy of the epidermis, associated with thickening and brittleness of the nails and hair. There may be nonpitting peripheral edema (myxedema) and periorbital edema. The skin may appear yellow due to carotene accumulation. The tongue is enlarged, and facial puffiness and thinning of the lateral eyebrows are common, with loss of expressiveness and lid drooping. The voice is often low-pitched and hoarse, and speech is slowed.

The thyroid gland may be enlarged, decreased in size, or even absent, depending on the underlying etiology.

Examination of the cardiovascular system often reveals bradycardia, decreased cardiac output, and cardiac enlargement (which can indicate either pericardial effusion or diastolic hypertension).

Alterations in capillary permeability can result in pleural, peritoneal, and synovial fluid accumulation.

Muscle strength is usually diminished. Joints may show capsular thickening.

The most important neurologic sign is delay in the contraction and relaxation phases of deep tendon reflexes, seen best when ankle jerks are elicited with the patient in the kneeling position on a chair. Nerve deafness can be present. Other neurologic abnormalities can include the carpal tunnel, polyneuropathy, and cerebellar ataxia syndromes.

Routine Laboratory Abnormalities

Fluid disturbances include decreased plasma volume and free water clearance, which can be accompanied by hyponatremia and a depressed sensorium. Nausea and vomiting can attend slowed gastrointestinal motility, which occasionally results in paralytic ileus and distention. Reduced energy expenditure causes lower heat production, weight gain, and cold intolerance.

Hepatic and renal clearances of pharmacologic agents are reduced. Thus, the actions of digoxin, opiates, dilantin may be prolonged. Prolactin secretion may be augmented, which can cause galactorrhea and amenorrhea.

Abnormal routine tests reveal mild anemia (normocytic or macrocytic) with hemoglobin concentrations as low as 8 to 9 g/dL. Minimal proteinuria may be present. Protein synthesis and catabolism are inhibited in most triiodothyronine-sensitive tissues. Thus, low-density lipoprotein cholesterol is elevated due to a new steady state because the delay in its clearance exceeds the lower low-density lipoprotein synthetic rate. Although resistance to parathyroid hormone actions develop in bone, bone density, calcium and phosphate concentrations remain normal.

PLANS
Diagnostic
Differential Diagnosis

It is important to distinguish between hypothyroidism and nonthyroidal illness, which may lower thyroid indices in otherwise clinically euthyroid patients. A useful distinction is that patients with nonthyroidal disease can have decreased serum thyroxine (T_4) levels, but normal serum free T_4 concentrations, excluding hypothyroidism. Ultrasensitive TSH assays have been applied to patients with nonthyroidal illness who show suppression of TSH values to between 0.3 and less than 0.005 mU/L. All these patients, however, exhibit elevations of TSH after stimulation by TRH, in contrast to most patients with central hypothyroidism. Finally, because the concentration of reverse T_3 (rT_3) is normal or elevated in NTI states, in contrast to decreased rT_3 concentrations in hypothyroidism, measurements of reverse T_3 also may be helpful in making this distinction.

Diagnostic Options and Recommended Approach

The cardinal laboratory feature of all forms of reduced thyroid function, excepting the syndrome of peripheral resistance to thyroid hormones, are lowered serum T_4 concentrations; however, as 99.9% of thyroxine is protein bound, reductions in serum T_4 concentrations can result from lowered serum binding proteins. Thus an assessment of the normalcy of serum thyroid hormone-binding proteins must always be performed in conjunction with serum total T_4 measurements, using the T_3-resin uptake or an equivalent test (to estimate free T_4). This test assesses thyroxine-binding globulin unsaturation, and is not a determination of circulating T_3 concentrations. In hypothyroidism, the lowered serum T_4 concentrations are associated with enhanced thyroxine-binding globulin unsaturation, so that T_3-resin values characteristically also are below normal. In general, when serum T_4 and T_3-resin uptake values depart from normal in the *opposite* direction, a binding protein disturbance and not hypothyroidism should be considered as the cause of the reduced serum T_4. Occasionally, T_4 values can be within the population normal range in patients with overt hypothyroidism. Therefore, measurements of TSH by radioimmunoassay are extremely valuable as concentrations are invariably elevated in overt hypothyroidism and are usually greater than 10 mU/L. Third- and fourth-generation immuno-chemiluminometric assays for human TSH have been developed that demonstrate extraordinary sensitivity, 10- to 100-fold greater than that of second-generation TSH assays. Thyrotropin-releasing hormone testing in the evaluation of thyroid status has now become obviated largely because of the development of these ultrasensitive TSH assays. Thus, two main tests, (1) T_4, T_3-resin test or free T_4 index and (2) basal TSH concentration, are used to determine whether or not hypothyroidism is present.

Measurement of circulating T_3 by radioimmunoassay, in contrast to T_4, is not recommended routinely because T_3 concentrations are normal in approximately 30% of hypothyroid patients, whereas low T_3 concentrations are nonspecific and often reflect nonthyroidal illnesses that impair peripheral T_4 5'-monodeiodination to T_3. Similarly, thyroidal uptakes with ^{131}I or $^{99}TcO_4$ are not used routinely, because normal and hypothyroid values frequently overlap.

Other indices have been developed to reflect metabolic state, such as sex hormone-binding globulin. In men, serum testosterone is lowered because sex hormone-binding globulin is reduced; however, free testosterone levels are normal. Because of their nonspecificity, other indices such as serum enzymes (glutamic-oxaloacetic acid transaminase creatinine phosphokinase), serum cholesterol, ß-carotene, and quantitation of the Achilles reflex relaxation time should not be used as primary diagnostic tools in hypothyroidism.

Therapeutic

The treatment of hypothyroidism with thyroid hormones is one of the most satisfying therapeutic experiences in all of internal medicine. The administration of a single, inexpensive, nontoxic, and nonallergic molecule can effect the complete restoration of normal physiology and complete reversal of symptomatology. A number of equivalent preparations of thyroid hormones are available. Therapy is accomplished best with administration of synthetic levothyroxine, which can achieve normal concentrations of both T_4 and T_3, 80% of which is generated peripherally from circulating T_4. Of the four commercially available preparations (Synthroid, Levoxyl, Levo T, and Levothroid), Levoxyl is somewhat less expensive. Triiodothyronine itself (Cytomel) should not be used in treatment, as its half-life is short and the resultant rapid excursions in serum T_3 concentrations above and below normal can predispose the typically elderly patient population to supraventricular tachyarrhythmias. In the elderly, therapy should be initiated with the smallest possible dosage of levothyroxine (12.5–25 μg orally daily), with progressive but very gradual increments at approximately 4- to 6-week intervals until full replacement is achieved, to a final dosage schedule range of 0.125 to 0.2 mg/d. Mean T_4 requirements in humans are 1.6 μg/kg/d. Attention should be focused on possible precipitation of angina pectoris, myocardial infarction, and congestive heart failure in the elderly, requiring immediate reduction in T_4 dosage. In contrast, in young otherwise healthy individuals, full replacement therapy can be begun immediately. Larger dosages of T_4 may be required in selected circumstances, including malabsorption states, cirrhosis, and children, where the usual maintenance requirements are somewhat higher.

In the elderly, recent evidence suggests that full replacement often can be achieved with lower dosages, approximately 0.1 mg of thyroxine per day in subjects over 40 years and occasionally in dosages as low as 0.050 mg/d in subjects over 60 years of age. Because of the large variance at any age, dosage predictions at specific age intervals are quite imprecise and must be individualized. Lower T_4 requirements in the elderly have been identified primarily in men.

Interactions with three medications warrant discussion. Oral anticoagulant effects may be enhanced, creating a hemorrhagic diathesis. Second, diabetics may have lower insulin or oral agent requirements. Finally, oral cholestyramine can bind T_4 in the gut and thereby raise requirements for T_4.

The most important criterion of optimal therapy is reestablishment of clinical well-being, in association with normalized serum total T_4 and serum TSH concentrations. In central hypothyroidism, T_4 dosages should be adjusted to achieve a midnormal *free* T_4 concentration.

FOLLOW-UP

The primary modalities to be assessed carefully during follow-up should emphasize clinical features, without excessive dependency on laboratory parameters. Most signs and symptoms (weight, pulse, reflexes, skin facies, patient's subjective state) disappear gradually over a 1- to 2-month interval, with slower resolution of some features (e.g., anemia) than of others (weight gain due to mucopolysaccharide retention, serum TSH and cholesterol concentrations), which normalize rapidly. Appropriate laboratory indices include serum T_4, T_3-resin uptake, serum TSH levels, as well as selective electrocardiograms in the elderly. Angina due to associated coronary atherosclerosis may be precipitated by replacement therapy. Because THS normalization may require a longer time interval in long-standing primary hypothyroidism with pituitary TSH cell hypertrophy, further elevations in T_4 dosage above the normal range should not be undertaken for the first 6 months.

DISCUSSION

Prevalence

Spontaneous hypothyroidism is infrequent, with a prevalence of 1 to 2% and occurs much more commonly in women (8- to 10-fold). It is more often detected in areas of environmental iodine deficiency.

Related Basic Science

Most hypothyroidism is a result of thyroid dysfunction itself (primary) (Table 9–19–1). In the United States, idiopathic atrophy is the leading cause, in which the thyroid gland becomes atrophic and fibrotic with a few residual follicles and infiltration with lymphocytes and plasma cells, suggesting the end state of chronic lymphocytic thyroiditis (Hashimoto's thyroiditis), the next most common entity. Hashimoto's thyroiditis occurs predominantly in women between the third and sixth decades. Painless and firm thyromegaly is associated with lymphocytic infiltration and high circulating antibody titers to thyroid microsomal antigen (antithyroid peroxidase) and thyroglobulin in more than 90% of patients. The impaired thyroid function in chronic autoimmune thyroiditis is thought to be due to both antibody- and cell-mediated events. In addition to antibodies to thyroid peroxidase and thyroglobulin, TSH binding-inhibitory or TSH-blocking antibodies may be present (40% of patients), which can lead to hypothyroidism by interfering with the normal thyroid stimulation by pituitary TSH. Such antibodies are stimulated by cytokines from CD4+ T cells sensitized by thyroid antigenic determinants. Thyrocytes are also injured by cell-mediated immunity, initiated by binding of thyroid antigens associated with HLA class I molecules to the surface of suppressor T cells. T cells are activated to secrete cytokines that stimulate natural killer cell formation from T cells. Women develop Hashimoto's thyroiditis 8 to 10 times more frequently than men, and up to one-half of offspring of patients with

TABLE 9–19–1. ETIOLOGY OF HYPOTHYROIDISM

	Primary Hypothyroidism (Thyroid Failure)	Secondary Hypothyroidism (Pituitary TSH Deficiency)	Tertiary Hypothyroidism (Hypothalamic TRH Deficiency)
Laboratory characteristics			
T_4 concentration	Low	Low	Low
TSH concentration	Elevated	Not elevated or below normal	Not elevated or below normal
TRH response	Exaggerated	Usually blunted	Usually intact but delayed
Causes	Idiopathic atrophy	Pituitary adenomas	Hypothalamic adenomas
	Chronic lymphocytic (Hashimoto's) thyroiditis	Pituitary ischemic necrosis	Infiltrative processes
	After thyroidectomy	Hypophysectomy	Granulomas
	After ^{131}I administration	Craniopharyngiomas	Cysts
	Iodine deficiency, antithyroid substances	Trauma	Trauma
	Il-2, LAK cell therapy of neoplasms (melanoma, colorectal cancer)	Hemochromatosis	
	Congenital hypothyroidism (dysgenesis, errors in hormonogenesis)	Hypophysitis	
	Transient hypothyroidism (painless thyroiditis after ^{131}I or surgical therapy or discontinuation of T_4 therapy)	Metastatic cancer	
	Generalized resistance to thyroid hormones		

T_4, thyroxine; TSH, thyroid-stimulating hormone; TRH, thyrotropin-releasing hormone; IL-2, interleukin-2; LAK, lymphokine-activated killer.

chronic thyroiditis have antithyroid antibodies. HLA haplotypes that increase in prevalence include HLA-DR3 and -DR5. Closely related to chronic lymphocytic thyroiditis is a transient form of autoimmune thyroiditis, most commonly occurring postpartum. This condition is associated with transient thyrotoxicosis, followed in about half of subjects by transient hypothyroidism. Hypothyroidism usually develops 1 to 8 months following parturition and lasts from a few weeks to a couple of months. Unlike Hashimoto's thyroiditis, thyroid injury is completely reversible.

Other causes of primary thyroid failure less frequently encountered include environmental and hereditary determinants. Dietary goitrogens, including antithyroid drugs (e.g., thioamides, lithium, resorcinol), excessive iodide intake in susceptible individuals, and foods in the Cruciferae family, such as cabbage, white turnips, and rutabaga, may elicit hypothyroidism in iodine-deficient subjects. Endemic goiter, due to iodine deficiency itself, is found most commonly throughout the Andes, Himalayas, the Alps, Greece, mountainous areas of China, and the New Guinea Highlands.

Primary hypothyroidism has been identified also after treatment of malignancies with interleukin-2 and lymphokine-activated killer cells. Seven of 34 treated patients with colorectal carcinoma, melanoma, or lymphoma developed laboratory evidence of hypothyroidism after being treated with this therapeutic regimen. Five of these seven symptomatic patients had elevated antimicrosome antibody titers after treatment, and two developed antibodies to thyroglobulin. These data demonstrate that treatment of advanced neoplasia with interleukin-2 and lymphokine-activated killer cells can produce hypothyroidism by exasercbating preexisting, subclinical autoimmune thyroiditis.

Genetically determined defects in the formation of thyroid hormones can also lead to thyroid deficiency with goiter in childhood. Abnormalities have been described in iodide transport, iodide organification, iodotyrosine coupling, thyroglobulin biosynthesis, iodide conservation (deshalogenase defect), and TSH resistance that have provided insights into normal human thyroid hormonogenesis.

Pituitary (secondary, second-degree) and hypothalamic (tertiary, third-degree) hypothyroidism are much rarer and are caused by pituitary tumors, pituitary necrosis, hypophysitis, hypothalamic tumors, granulomatous lesions, irradiation, or trauma. Dopamine, the somatostatin analog octeotride, and glucocorticoids can inhibit TSH secretion also, but rarely lead to overt hypothyroidism.

Hypothyroidism may also develop from hereditary pituitary or generalized resistance to the action of thyroid hormones. Such patients exhibit high circulating T_4 concentrations with normal if slightly elevated serum TSH values, thyrogomegaly, and little biological effect from administered thyroid hormones. Considerable knowledge has been gained concerning the molecular pathophysiology of this syndrome since the cloning and characterization of intracellular thyroid hormone receptors for T_3. Almost all patients with this syndrome appear to have a mutation in the ligand (T_3) binding domain of the thyroid receptor isoform TR-β1. As the DNA-binding and dimerization domains of the TR-β1 receptor remain intact, transcriptionally inactive dimers can form between mutant and TRs and wild-type RXRs that can interfere with T_3-mediated gene transcription. Most patients belong to the group with "generalized resistance to thyroid hormone." The less common variant of "pituitary resistance to thyroid hormone" exhibits manifestations of thyroid hormone excess at the level of the periphery due to resistance only to the action of T_3 at the pituitary level with resultant TSH elevations. Generalized resistance to thyroid hormone most commonly is inherited in an autosomal dominant mode, with equal sex frequency. The syndrome should be suspected in individuals with elevated serum T_4 levels, normal or elevated TSH levels, and thyroid gland enlargement. These patients need to be differentiated from patients receiving excessive L-thyroxine replacement, abnormalities of excess thyroxine-binding globulin, familial dysalbuminemic hyperthyroxinemia, and T_4 elevations due to T_4 antibodies. The first principle of therapy is to void any treatment that lowers serum hormone concentrations. If the patient has undergone inappropriate ^{131}I-ablative therapy, L-thyroxine replacement therapy should be given, as in adults treated with ^{131}I for Graves' disease. T_4 may be given judiciously also to patients who are poorly

compensated, but routine treatment with thyroid hormone remains controversial. Establishing the mode of inheritance in a particular family is imperative to provide proper genetic counseling. Prenatal diagnosis can be achieved by DNA analysis through amniocentesis. The logical approach to treating pituitary resistant forms of this syndrome is the application of drugs that suppress TSH secretion, including glucocorticoids, dopaminergic drugs, somatostatin analogs, or thyroid hormone analogs that can reduce T_3 metabolic actions. None of these drugs is ideal. Administration of physiologic amounts of thyroid hormone in a daily single dose has been found effective in suppressing TSH and ameliorating the hypermetabolic state in one family with the pituitary form of thyroid hormone resistance.

Natural History and Its Modification with Treatment

Untreated hypothyroidism can lead to progressive myxedema, somnolence and myxedema coma (0.1%), often precipitated by intercurrent illnesses or environmental cold exposure. Myxedema coma must be differentiated from secondary comas in the setting of hypothyroidism, often precipitated by excessive use of opiates or hypnotics, water intoxication, or carbon dioxide narcosis from ventilatory failure. Myxedema coma requires aggressive therapy with parenteral thyroxine therapy (200–500 μg intravenously), with additional supportive measures, including treatment of intercurrent infections.

When hypothyroidism is treated appropriately, complications are virtually unknown and morbidity and mortality are not encountered. Excessive T_4 replacement can lead to thyrotoxicosis factitia and attendant cardiac arrythmias, and predisposes also to osteoporosis.

Prevention

Environmental causes of hypothyroidism can be prevented by iodine prophylaxis (iodized salt) and avoidance of dietary goitrogens. Surgical and radioiodine causes of thyroid deficiency can be minimized by avoidance of excessive thyroidal ablation. At present, there are no known measures for prevention of Hashimoto's thyroiditis, a hereditary disease.

Hypothyroidism commonly recurs because patients spontaneously cease replacement therapy without medical instruction, so constant vigilance is required to ensure lifelong continuation of the treatment program. The untreated hypothyroid patient is particularly sensitive to a host of pharmacologic agents, including general anesthetics, opiates, barbiturates, and other mood-altering chemicals.

Cost Containment

Thyroid hormone replacement therapy is inexpensive, and the small cost savings from generic levothyroxine cannot justify its usage instead of commercial preparations, in which T_4 content is more rigorously standardized. Laboratory costs can be contained also by judicious use of serum T_4 and TSH measurements (once per year) in compliant patients.

REFERENCES

Carnell NE, Wilber JF. Primary hypothyroidism. In: Bardin CW, ed. Current therapy in endocrinology and metabolism. St. Louis: Mosby, 1994:82.

DeGroot LJ, Larson PR, Refetoff S, et al., eds. Adult hypothyroidism. In: Thyroid and its disease. 5th ed. New York: John Wiley & Sons, 1984:546.

Hull WW. On a cretinoid state supervening in adult life in women. Trans Clin Soc Lond 1974;7:180.

Ord WM. On mydodema, a term proposed to be applied to an essential condition in the cretinoid affection occasionally observed in middle-aged women. Medico-chir Trans 1971;64:185.

Refetoff S, Weiss RE, Usala SJ. The syndromes of resistance to thyroid hormone. Endocr Rev 1993;14:348.

Sakurai A, Takeda K, Ain K, et al. Generalized resistance to thyroid hormone associated with a mutation in the ligand-binding domain of the human thyroid hormone receptor β. Proc Natl Acad Sci USA 1989;86:8977.

Weeks I, Sturgess M, Siddle K, et al. A high sensitivity immunochemiluminometric assay for hTSH. Clin Endocrinol 1984;20:489.

Male Hypogonadism

Richard V. Clark, M.D., Ph.D.

DEFINITION

Male hypogonadism is defined as the failure of the testes either to produce adequate levels of testosterone for normal masculinization and sexual function or to produce adequate numbers of normal motile sperm for fertility.

ETIOLOGY

A variety of clinical conditions can be associated with hypogonadism, as damage to either the testes, the pituitary gland, or the hypothalamus can impair testicular function (Tables 9–20–1 and 9–20–2). Testicular injury can be caused by a variety of factors including mumps orchitis, heat or radiation exposure, chemotherapeutic agents (especially cyclophosphamide, chlorambucil, nitrosoureas, and procarbazine), toxins such as ethylene dibromide and dichloropropane, and testicular trauma or torsion. There are several genetic conditions associated with primary testicular failure. The most classic is Klinefelter's syndrome, 47,XXY, characterized by seminiferous tubule sclerosis and hyalinization with azoospermia and loss of androgen production. Several other genetic disorders can lead to impaired synthesis of testosterone or decreased target cell sensitivity. Moreover, normal gonadotropin stimulation of the testes can be disrupted by pituitary tumors, hyperprolactinemia, craniopharyngiomas, and hypothalamic lesions.

CRITERIA FOR DIAGNOSIS

Suggestive

The major features suggesting male hypogonadism are impotence or loss of libido, failure to pubesce by age 15, and infertility for more than 1 year.

TABLE 9–20–1. CAUSES OF PRIMARY TESTICULAR FAILURE, HYPERGONADOTROPIC HYPOGONADISM

Chromosomal disorders
  Klinefelter's syndrome: 47,XXY
  Klinefelter's mosaic: 46,XY/47,XXY
  Gonadal dysgenesis: 45,XO/46,XY
  XYY syndrome: 47,XYY
  True hermaphrodite: 46,XY/46,XX
Androgen biosynthetic defect
  5α-Reductase deficiency
  17,20-Desmolase deficiency
  17α-Hydroxylase deficiency
  17α-Ketosteroid reductase deficiency
  3β-Hydroxysteroid dehydrogenase deficiency
Androgen receptor defect
  Testicular feminization
  Partial androgen resistance (Reifenstein's syndrome)
Testicular injury
  Mumps orchitis
  Autoimmune orchitis
  Radiation
  Chemotherapy (cyclosphosphamide, procarbazine)
  Trauma
  Toxins (pesticides, alcohol)
  Chronic diseases
  Heat, fever
  Vascular insufficiency
  Hemochromatosis
Failure of testicular development
  Cryptorchidism
  Anorchia (vanishing testes)

Definitive

Hypogonadism is confirmed by a low testosterone level and/or an abnormally low sperm count on semen analysis. Primary testicular failure is characterized by a low testosterone level in the presence of elevated gonadotropin levels, whereas secondary testicular failure (pituitary lesion) and tertiary testicular failure (hypothalamic lesion) are characterized by low gonadotropin levels despite an abnormally low testosterone level. Although sperm production is dependent on normal hormonal stimulation of the seminiferous epithelium by testosterone and gonadotropins, inadequate sperm production can occur despite normal levels of testosterone, luteinizing hormone, and follicle-stimulating hormone.

CLINICAL MANIFESTATION

Subjective

The major complaints of previously virilized men who develop hypogonadism relate to loss of sexual function (impotence, decreased libido, or ejaculatory failure) and infertility. Young men are more likely to present with failure to initiate or complete puberty or with gynecomastia. Rarely do patients complain of loss of facial or body hair or decreased muscle mass. Progressive fatigue and loss of strength are vague symptoms and usually not perceived as possibly related to reduced androgen levels.

Patients should be carefully questioned about current medications, exposure to radiation, exposure of the testes to excessive heat, and excessive consumption of alcohol or marijuana. Certain drugs, particularly chemotherapeutic agents, antiandrogens (such as cimetidine and spironolactone), antidepressants, and centrally acting antihypertensive agents, can impair testicular function or induce impotence. Several causes of hypogonadism have an apparent genetic basis, including virtually all steroid synthetic defects and androgen-resistant syndromes. All patients should be questioned regarding other affected family members, with particular emphasis on history of cryptorchidism, failure to pubesce, or ambiguous sexual development.

TABLE 9–20–2. CAUSES OF SECONDARY TESTICULAR FAILURE, HYPOGONADOTROPIC HYPOGONADISM

Idiopathic hypogonadotropic hypogonadism
  Complete, usually with anosmia
  Partial, with incomplete virilization
  Selective follicle-stimulating hormone deficiency
  Selective luteinizing hormone deficiency
Hyperprolactinemia
  Prolactin-secreting pituitary adenoma
  Drugs (phenothiazines, antidepressants)
  Idiopathic
Pituitary or hypothalamic insufficiency
  Mass lesion of pituitary
  Mass lesion of hypothalamus
  Injury to pituitary stalk
  Granulomatous disease (sarcoid, histiocytosis)
  Hemochromatosis
Delayed puberty
Other endocrinopathies
  Thyroid dysfunction
  Cushing's syndrome
  Acromegaly

Objective

Physical Examination

Hypogonadism may develop in a male after normal puberty and full masculinization have occurred. In these cases, external genitalia are usually normal and pubic hair is present, although often the size of the testes (normal volume is greater than 20 mL or 4.5 × 2.7 cm) and the amount of facial and body hair may be reduced. Patients who have failed to enter or complete puberty show absent or minimal androgen-dependent differentiation, including lack of pubic or axillary hair, poor scrotal rugae, small testes (less than 15 mL in volume, 4.0 × 2.5 cm; prepubertal size is less than 4 mL in volume, 2.5 × 1.5 cm), and short penis (less than 3 cm in length), and they may have hypospadias or ambiguous genitalia. Small, firm testes suggest Klinefelter's syndrome. A eunuchoid habitus can be demonstrated by an arm span 2 in. greater than height, or lower body segment (heel to pubis) 2 in. longer than upper body segment (pubis to crown); patients should also be checked for female versus male distribution of fat and inadequate development of muscle. Gynecomastia is demonstrated by palpable glandular tissue extending beyond the margins of the nipple and areolar diameter greater than 2 cm. Patients with hypogonadotropic hypogonadism may have anosmia or midline defects such as harelip and cleft palate.

Routine Laboratory Abnormalities

Routine laboratory tests are typically normal.

PLANS

Diagnostic

Differential Diagnosis

Hypogonadism is established by demonstration of low total testosterone levels (usually <280 mg/dL) or an abnormal semen analysis, especially one showing azoospermia, or both. Gonadotropin levels should be checked to distinguish primary from secondary testicular failure. Prolactin and estradiol levels should be checked to rule out elevated levels, which could impair testicular function.

Primary testicular failure is associated with elevated luteinizing hormone and follicle-stimulating hormone levels, and secondary testicular failure is associated with low or normal luteinizing hormone and follicle-stimulating hormone levels. Causes of these conditions are listed in Tables 9–20–1 and 9–20–2.

Diagnostic Options

Specialized tests include a karyotype, which can be useful in the evaluation of unexplained primary testicular failure with small, firm testes (such as Klinefelter's syndrome). Testicular biopsies can be useful to rule out obstructive azoospermia or to demonstrate an inflammatory or infiltrative process, but a routine biopsy is of questionable value. Evaluation of steroid synthetic defects is discussed in Chapters 9–8 and 9–27.

Hypogonadotropic conditions usually require evaluation of pituitary function with a gonadotropin-releasing hormone (GnRH) stimulation test. This test involves injection of 100 μg of gonadotropin-releasing hormone intravenously, with samples for luteinizing hormone and follicle-stimulating hormone drawn at 0, 15, 30, 60, and 90 minutes. Normally, luteinizing hormone and follicle-stimulating hormone levels rise to a peak greater than 10 mIU/mL at 15 to 30 minutes. Intact pituitary not exposed to regular GnRH stimulation may respond only after five to seven daily injections of gonadotropin-releasing hormone for a "priming" effect. Such a pattern is characteristic of hypothalamic insufficiency. Morphologic evaluation to rule out a mass lesion is also important, particularly when there is a negative response to GnRH. Magnetic resonance imaging of the sella and hypothalamus using coronal sections is the preferred test to localize a lesion.

Delayed puberty can be difficult to demonstrate conclusively. Lack of testicular growth over a 4- to 6-month period in a boy 15 years or older is suggestive of impaired testicular stimulation rather than constitutional delay. GnRH stimulation test is usually negative in both situations, unless the defect is gonadal. A positive test suggests the onset of puberty and can be demonstrated by progressive testicular growth.

Recommended Approach

Initial laboratory studies should include a testosterone level. If this is low, follow-up studies would include luteinizing hormone, follicle-stimulating hormone, and estradiol levels to distinguish primary from secondary failure. In cases of unexpected secondary testicular failure (hypogonadotropic hypogonadism), a morphologic study (magnetic resonance imaging or computed tomography) of the pituitary should be considered based on the clinical picture. A semen analysis is useful as a measure of testicular function and is necessary in cases of infertility.

Therapeutic

Therapeutic Options

Treatment is based on resolving the underlying condition or providing hormonal replacement when the condition is irreversible. Goals of hormonal replacement can be induction or maintenance of virilization and sexual function or induction of sperm production and attainment of fertility. Virilization can be easily initiated and maintained using adequate dose of either testosterone enanthate (Delatestryl) or testosterone cypionate (Depotestosterone) at a dose of 200 mg intramuscularly every 2 weeks. Human chorionic gonadotropin (Pregnyl, Profasi) at a dose of 1500 to 2000 U intramuscularly three times a week can induce endogenous testosterone production by direct stimulation of Leydig cells, but it is useful only in cases of hypogonadotropic hypogonadism with intact testes. Treatment to induce sperm production is discussed in Chapter 9–21.

Side effects of testosterone enanthate include elevation of hematocrit (which may be great enough to cause hyperviscosity syndrome), sodium retention (which is usually minor unless there is an underlying heart disease or renal failure), and conversion of testosterone to estradiol by aromatization (which may induce gynecomastia, although this usually occurs only at higher than recommended doses). The prostate tends to regress in hypogonadal states, and risk of prostatic hypertrophy and carcinoma is returned to normal with replacement therapy. Therapy with human chorionic gonadotropin frequently induces elevated estradiol levels. This can induce transient gynecomastia, similar to pubertal gynecomastia, but this is rarely persistent. Minor sodium retention also can occur. Oral androgens are ineffective at standard doses for full virilization, and can induce liver injury with elevation of alkaline phosphatase and conjugated bilirubin levels. Rare but serious side effects of oral androgens at standard doses are the development of hepatomas, peliosis hepatitis (blood-filled cysts in the liver), and hepatic carcinoma.

Recommended Approach

Unless fertility is of immediate concern, treatment is begun with testosterone replacement. Patient education should be stressed because of the degree of personal identity associated with gonadal function. The patient should be advised that hypogonadism is treatable, but requires continuous therapy. Patients should also be told that this therapy will induce the usual criteria for manhood, virilization, and sexual potency, and that gonadal dysfunction is a treatable condition and not a reflection of their manhood or family background. Fertility is discussed in Chapter 9–21. For couples in whom the man has suffered a gradual onset of hypogonadism with subsequent loss of sexual intimacy, rapid replacement therapy can greatly increase the male's libido and potency, potentially disrupting the relationship. Such couples should be told to expect a period of transition, and it may be necessary to begin therapy at a reduced dose, such as 50 to 100 mg testosterone enanthate intramuscularly every 2 weeks.

FOLLOW-UP

Patients with hypogonadism require regular follow-up. This is partly determined by the underlying cause of the hypogonadism, but even those patients with a stable, irreversible condition who are on hormonal replacement should be seen at least annually. Such visits confirm compliance with prescribed dosage and allow monitoring for side effects, particularly checking hematocrit, liver function tests, and the prostate. Patients have a propensity to adjust the dosage of testosterone enanthate in both directions. Excess dosage should be strongly discouraged because it increases the risk of side effects and has little effect on potency, although it may increase libido.

DISCUSSION
Prevalence and Incidence

Most forms of hypogonadism are uncommon, though the incidence of erectile dysfunction increases significantly after age 50. Most of the genetic disorders of steroid synthesis or receptor abnormality are quite rare. Klinefelter's syndrome is usually estimated to have an incidence around 1 in 400 based on neonatal screening, but the prevalence in the adult population seems to be lower.

Related Basic Science

Male sexual differentiation and virilization are dependent on a variety of factors, including adequate stimulation of Leydig cells in fetal life, conversion of testosterone to the active metabolite dihydrotestosterone, and uptake in the cell nucleus of the steroid–cytoplasmic receptor complex to induce the cellular response via messenger RNA and protein synthesis in target tissues. In addition, the Y chromosome carries specific genetic information, the sex-determining region, that appears necessary for testicular differentiation. The fetal testes also must produce Müllerian inhibiting factor to suppress development of the oviducts, uterus, and upper vagina. After androgen-dependent differentiation of the sexual organs in the fetus, the next major phase of sexual development occurs at puberty. The onset is marked by the development of pubic and axillary hair, the formation of scrotal rugae, and growth of the penis and testes. Gonadotropins are secreted in nocturnal pulses in early puberty, causing testosterone levels to be elevated at night but low during the day.

Testosterone acts directly on the pituitary–hypothalamic axis for negative feedback, on the seminiferous epithelium for sperm production, and on formation of the wolffian ducts (vas deferens and epididymis). The 5α-reduced metabolite of testosterone, dihydrotestosterone, induces external virilization, development and function of the accessory sex glands (prostate and seminal vesicles), and development of male secondary sex characteristics during puberty, such as body and facial hair, muscle mass, and penile growth. Normal production of testosterone by the Leydig cells is dependent on pulsatile release of gonadotropin-releasing hormone by the hypothalamus and pulsatile secretion of luteinizing hormone and follicle-stimulating hormone by the pituitary gland. The normal number of such pulses is 12 to 15 per day, and a reduced frequency of pulses or inadequate levels of luteinizing hormone and follicle-stimulating hormone lead to inadequate testicular stimulation and secondary hypogonadism. In primary testicular failure, there is loss of negative feedback by testicular steroids on the hypothalamus and pituitary. This results in larger and more frequent pulses of gonadotropin-releasing hormone and increased sensitivity of the pituitary to gonadotropin-releasing hormone, causing elevated levels of both luteinizing hormone and follicle-stimulating hormone. Certain long-acting gonadotropin-releasing agonists and antagonists have been effective in suppressing testicular function by decreasing or blocking cellular receptors to gonadotropin-releasing hormone and inhibiting production of luteinizing hormone and follicle-stimulating hormone by the pituitary. This is useful in suppressing gonadal function as in treating hormonally sensitive cancer such as prostate, and may allow development of a male contraceptive by suppression of spermatogenesis.

Natural History and Its Modification with Treatment

The natural history of hypogonadism depends on the underlying process. Acute androgen deficiency produces a characteristic series of responses. Libido and potency are affected most rapidly, usually within 2 to 6 weeks, and are followed by loss of facial and body hair and a decrease in muscle mass, which occur over several weeks to several months. Bone density in men is partly androgen dependent, and hypogonadal men are at risk for osteoporosis. There is no known increase in mortality associated with hypogonadism.

Prevention

The major aspects of prevention are avoidance of substances known to impair testicular function such as radiation, excess heat as in prolonged baths, aromatic chemicals and fuels, certain pesticides, certain drugs as mentioned, and heavy alcohol consumption.

Cost Containment

Minimal evaluation for hypogonadism includes blood samples for testosterone, luteinizing hormone, follicle-stimulating hormone, and prolactin. Because of the pulsatile secretion of luteinizing hormone and follicle-stimulating hormone, single random samples may reflect pulse peaks or troughs. The drawing of three samples over 40 to 60 minutes gives representative levels: pooling the serum allows averaging by mixing, which is more cost effective than the arithmetic averaging of three separate samples. A gonadotropin-releasing hormone stimulation test and computed tomography scan or magnetic resonance imaging of the sella are indicated in hypogonadotropic conditions. The most cost-effective therapy is achieved with testosterone enanthate or cypionate especially when self-administered by the patient. For induction of spermatogenesis, human chorionic gonadotropin can be effective alone if testicular volume is greater than 4 to 6 mL (see Chapter 9–21).

REFERENCES

Clark RV. Clinical andrology: History and physical examination. Endocrinol Metab Clin North Amer. 1994; 23:699.

Griffin JE, Wilson JD. Disorders of the testes and male reproductive tract. In: Wilson JD, Foster DW, eds. Williams's textbook of endocrinology. 8th ed. Philadelphia: Saunders, 1992:799.

Paulsen CA, Gordon DL, Carpenter RW, et al. Klinefelter's syndrome and its variants: A hormonal and chromosomal study. Recent Prog Horm Res 1968;24:321.

Plymate SR, Tenover JS, Bremner WJ. Circadian variation in testosterone, sex-hormone-binding globulin, and calculated non-sex-hormone-binding globulin-bound testosterone in healthy young and elderly men. J Androl 1989;10:366.

Whitcomb RW, Crowley WF. Diagnosis and treatment of isolated gonadotropin-releasing hormone deficiency in men. J Clin Endocrinol Metab 1990;70:3.

CHAPTER 9–21

Male Infertility as Viewed by an Endocrinologist

Richard V. Clark, M.D., Ph.D.

DEFINITION

Male infertility is defined as the inability to induce a pregnancy during unprotected intercourse with a presumably fertile female partner for a minimum period of 1 year.

ETIOLOGY

Infertility involves a couple and therefore can be based on male factors, female factors, or both. A male factor is suspected when the female partner has a normal menstrual cycle with ovulation, adequate duration of the luteal phase, patency of the oviducts, and lack of pelvic pathology, especially endometriosis. Male factor causes secondary to conditions that affect sperm production or function are discussed in this chapter. Impaired spermatogenesis is frequently associated with testicular injury and variable effects on Leydig cell function and androgen production. Conditions that can cause androgen deficiency can also reduce sperm production, and typically, the seminiferous tubules are more sensitive than androgen-producing cells. Radiation, heat, chemotherapeutic agents, and certain chemicals and drugs are more likely to cause low sperm counts and infertility than low testosterone levels and hypogonadism. Certain conditions such as cryptorchidism and varicocele are often associated with poor sperm production, but show minimal effects on androgen production. Certain genetic disorders, such as protein carboxylmethylase deficiency (impaired metabolism) and Kartagener's syndrome (lack of dynein arms in sperm flagella), can have specific effects on sperm function without any impact on spermatogonia or Leydig cells. Conversely, Klinefelter's syndrome is associated with both loss of the germ cell component of the seminiferous tubules and impaired Leydig cell function, resulting in gynecomastia and delayed puberty. Conditions that impair hypothalamic–pituitary stimulation of the testes enough to cause overt androgen deficiency also cause reduced sperm production. For most infertile men, however, no causal factor is identified and the infertility is regarded as idiopathic.

CRITERIA FOR DIAGNOSIS
Suggestive

The diagnosis is suggested if a man has an abnormal semen analysis, either a low sperm count, poor motility, or abnormal morphology (Table 9–21–1), associated with infertility.

Definitive

As infertility involves a couple, subtle or unsuspected female factors can contribute to a couple's infertility. Selection of minimal semen characteristics for fertility has been infeasible except for azoospermia and nonmotile sperm (necrospermia). Instead, probability assessments are more useful (see Table 9–21–1). Generally, sperm concentrations less than 10×10^6/mL, motility less than 40%, or normal morphology less than 40% are associated with a poor probability of fertility. Long periods of unprotected intercourse, however, can lead to an occasional pregnancy by men with dismal sperm counts or poor motility. Practically, poor semen characteristics with a normal female partner and 1 to 2 years of unprotected intercourse without pregnancy indicate a male factor.

CLINICAL MANIFESTATIONS
Subjective

Family history should be elicited for familial disorders suggesting testicular failure, such as cryptorchidism, abnormal sexual development, and infertility. Patients should be questioned regarding exposure to

known testicular toxins either by occupation (such as exposure to radiation or pesticides) or through personal habits (such as excessive use of alcohol, marijuana, or hot baths). Certain drugs are directly toxic to the testes, especially antimetabolites, particularly cyclophosphamide and procarbazine, and antiandrogens such as spironolactone and cimetidiene. Coital habits should also be questioned regarding mechanics, frequency, and timing during the partner's menstrual cycle to confirm complete intromission during periods of likely ovulation. The patient should be questioned regarding in utero exposure to unusual compounds, particularly diethylstilbestrol, which can induce epididymal cysts and cryptorchidism. Men with hypogonadism caused by hormonal abnormalities frequently complain of impotence or loss of libido (see Chapter 9–20). The majority of infertile males, however, have normal testosterone levels and have no signs or symptoms of androgen deficiency, so-called euhormonal infertility.

Objective
Physical Examination

The physical examination should be directed toward determining whether normal sexual differentiation has occurred and the degree of virilization (see Chapter 9–20). Mild gynecomastia is a common finding in androgen deficiency, but rare with euhormonal infertility. The genitalia should be examined for specific features that can be associated with infertility: reduced testicular size (<15 mL in volume, 4.0×2.5 cm), soft testicular consistency (indicative of atrophy), presence of testicular masses or epididymal nodules (suggestive of blockage or cysts), and presence of varicocele (best determined with patient standing and performing a Valsalva maneuver). In addition, a prostatic examination should be done to evaluate for enlargement or tenderness suggestive of prostatitis.

Routine Laboratory Abnormalities

Routine laboratory tests are usually normal.

PLANS
Diagnostic
Differential Diagnosis

The common causes of male infertility are listed in Table 9–21–2. Although for the majority of infertile men no causal factor is identified, reversible causes should be sought, especially exposure to potential toxins, hypogonadotropic hypogonadism, presence of varicocele, and obstructive azoospermia.

Diagnostic Options

Unfortunately, there are no direct methods to assess a man's fertility potential, as exist in animal husbandry. Therefore, indirect measures are used, and the semen analysis is the most widely accepted approach. A semen sample should be collected after 1 to 2 days abstinence, as prolonged abstinence can factitiously elevate sperm count and decrease motility. Table 9–21–1 outlines the values for particular semen parameters associated with good, equivocal, or poor fertilization potential. Samples with poor characteristics should be repeated at least once for verification. Patients with azoospermia and testes of normal size and consistency should be considered for testicular biopsy to rule out obstructive azoospermia.

Recommended Approach

Patients with either abnormalities of the genital examination or marginal semen parameters should have a hormonal analysis (as outlined in Chapter 9–20), including blood samples for testosterone, estradiol, luteinizing hormone, follicle-stimulating hormone, and prolactin. Possible prostatic infection suggested by clinical examination or leukocytes in the semen should be evaluated by culture of a urine sample after prostatic massage. The female partner should be evaluated by an experienced reproductive gynecologist to rule out unappreciated female factors. Testicular biopsy has little clinical utility except to rule out obstructive azoospermia.

TABLE 9–21–1. CLASSIFICATION OF SEMEN CHARACTERISTICS BASED ON FERTILITY POTENTIAL

Semen Characteristic	Fertility Potential		
	Good	*Equivocal*	*Poor*
Total sperm	$> 60 \times 10^6$	$40–59 \times 10^6$	$< 40 \times 10^6$
Sperm density	$> 20 \times 10^6$/mL	$10–19 \times 10^6$/mL	$< 10 \times 10^6$/mL
Volume	> 2.0 mL	1.0–1.9 mL	< 1.0 mL
Motility	> 60%	40–59%	< 40%
Motility quality	> 3.0	2.5–2.9	< 2.5
Oval forms	> 60%	40–59%	< 40%

Source: Clark RV, Sherins RJ. Use of semen analysis in the evaluation of the infertile couple. In: Santen RJ, Swerdloff RS, eds. Male reproductive dysfunction. New York: Marcel Dekker, 1986;253. Reproduced with permission from the publisher and author.

TABLE 9–21–2. CAUSES OF MALE INFERTILITY

Irreversible
    Chromosomal abnormality
    Bilateral cryptorchidism
    Primary testicular injury (radiation, mumps, orchitis, etc.)
    Nonmotile sperm (necrospermia)
    Absent vas deferens
Potentially reversible
    Idiopathic oligospermia
    Hypogonadotropic hypogonadism
    Varicocele
    Drug or toxin
    Ductal obstruction
    Retrograde ejaculation
    Systemic illness
    Immunologic factors
Unrecognized female factor
    Abnormal coital habits
    Short luteal phase
    Anovulation
    Tubal obstruction
    Cervical factor

Therapeutic

Therapeutic Options

Treatment is based on the underlying disorder. The most common condition, idiopathic oligospermic infertility, has no medical therapy that has been shown to be useful in controlled clinical trials. Several treatments have been advocated based on limited series without benefit of proper controls or adequate data collection. In addition, documentation of paternity is rarely presented. The most common medical therapy is clomiphene at a dose of 25 to 50 mg per day for 3 to 6 months; however, rigorous documentation of efficacy is not available. Varicocele repair is effective in 10 to 30% of men with easily palpable varicocele, based on controlled studies. Ductal obstruction can be reversed (vasovasotomy, epididymostomy), but this procedure requires very skilled microsurgical technique.

Gamete manipulation provides the best opportunity for fertility in men with idiopathic oligospermic infertility. Techniques range from sperm washing to recover motile sperm for in utero insemination, to in vitro fertilization. Strategies to accomplish fertilization with very low sperm counts now include either placing sperm in close contact with the oocyte by insertion under the zona pellucida and directly inserting a single sperm into an oocyte. Suprisingly, though experience is limited, such techniques are efficacious with no apparent increase in fetal loss or birth defects.

Hypogonadotropic hypogonadism can be treated by replacement with gonadotropin injections to induce both endogenous testosterone production and spermatogenesis. Therapy is initiated with human chorionic gonadotropin (Pregnyl, Profasi) at a dose of 1500 to 2000 U given intramuscularly three times a week. This is continued for at least 24 months, with periodic measurement of testicular volume and serum testosterone levels to assess response to therapy. If sperm do not appear in the ejaculate by 12 to 18 months, then human menopausal gonadotropin (Pergonal) should be added at a dose of 37.5 to 75 U given intramuscularly three times a week. More than 50% of men with hypogonadotropic hypogonadism become sperm positive and fertile on this regimen over 12 to 36 months. Testicular volume is an important predictor, with a success rate greater than 75% in those men with initial testicular volumes greater than 4 to 6 mL.

Recommended Approach

Men with idiopathic oligospermic infertility should be considered for gamete manipulation with their own sperm or artificial insemination of their partner with donor sperm. Varicocele can be considered for repair, though this does not seem necessary for gamete manipulation. Adoption is a time-honored alternative that should always be considered. Statements that "fertility is impossible" should be avoided, as fertility

can occur except in cases of absolute azoospermia or nonmotile sperm. Empiric medical therapy is not recommended, though agents such as clomiphene seem to have little risk.

FOLLOW-UP

Patients with infertility should be followed during any therapy. There are no known sequelae associated with infertility that require routine follow-up in the absence of active treatment. While on treatment, patients should be assessed at periodic intervals (3–6 months) for testicular changes or any side effects of the therapy given. Semen samples also should be checked at 3- to 6-month intervals for response to therapy.

DISCUSSION
Prevalence and Incidence

The prevalence of infertility among couples is usually estimated between 20 and 30%, and 35 to 50% of these are considered male factor in cause. Adequate prospective studies are not available to give a valid estimate of incidence. Average sperm counts appear to have gradually declined over the past several decades, possibly because of increasing industrialization and environmental contamination. This hypothesis is controversial, and much of the early data on sperm counts and fertility is difficult to interpret.

Related Basic Science

Initiation of spermatogenesis by the seminiferous epithelium requires high intratesticular levels of testosterone as induced by luteinizing hormone stimulation of the Leydig cells. This induces germ cell maturation and divisions from spermatogonia and spermatocytes through the meiotic process in which diploid pachytene spermatocytes become haploid spermatids. Follicle-stimulating hormone is clearly necessary for the completion of the maturation of spermatids (spermiogenesis) and the release of mature spermatids. Sperm undergo further differentiation necessary for fertility during passage through the epididymis. This appears to involve predominantly alterations in cell surface receptors and nuclear chromatin; this process is androgen dependent. Impairment of spermatogenesis despite normal hormone levels may be due to subtle imbalances in hormone ratios (androgens to estrogens), subtle chromosomal abnormalities that impair sperm function, immunologic factors in the male or female reproductive tract, or alterations in the sperm, such as defects in cell surface receptor complexes for egg recognition and attachment, or abnormal flagellar motion. Causes of only a few of these conditions are well understood. An example is the absence of protein carboxylmethylase in the sperm of certain men with necrospermia.

The question of minimal semen characteristics necessary for fertility is difficult. Pregnancy routinely occurs in the female partners of men on therapy for hypogonadotropic hypogonadism who have sperm counts less than 10×10^6/mL. In addition, normal men given compounds to suppress spermatogenesis can still induce pregnancies with sperm counts less than 1×10^6/mL. These studies highlight that only a few good sperm are necessary to induce pregnancy, and suggest that other factors in addition to sperm count and motility impair the fertilizing capacity of sperm in men with oligospermic infertility.

Natural History and Its Modification with Treatment

The natural history of male infertility is poorly understood. In most cases of idiopathic oligospermia, there is little change in seminal characteristics if these are initially poor. In men with equivocal characteristics, there can be a wide range of variability, and an occasional specimen from a man with generally poor-quality semen will exhibit good sperm characteristics.

Prevention

The major aspect of prevention is avoidance of substances known to impair testicular function such as radiation, excess heat as in prolonged baths, aromatic chemicals and fuels, certain pesticides, certain drugs as mentioned, and moderation of alcohol consumption.

Cost Containment

Evaluation can be performed on infertile men on an outpatient basis. Laboratory data should be confined to semen analyses and hormonal determinations. Many additional tests are available, such as the hamster oocyte penetration assay, but these determinations presently do not provide information that substantially alters the clinical approach.

REFERENCES

Bostofte E, Bagger P, Michael A, et al. Fertility prognosis for infertile men: Results of follow-up study of semen analysis in infertile men from two populations. Fertil Steril 1990;54:1100.

Clark RV, Sherins RJ. Treatment of men with idiopathic oligospermic infertility using the aromatase inhibitor, testolactone: Results of a double blinded, randomized placebo controlled trial with crossover. J Androl 1989;10:240.

Laufer N, Simon A. Treatment of male infertility by gamete micromanipulation. Hum Reprod 1992;7(suppl 1):73.

Nagao RR, Plymate SR, Berger RE, et al. Comparison of gonadal function between fertile and infertile men with varicoceles. Fertil Steril 1986;46:930.

Overstreet JW, ed. Male infertility. Infert Reprod Med Clin North Am 1992;3:1.

CHAPTER 9–22

Gynecomastia

D. Lynn Loriaux, M.D., Ph.D.

DEFINITION

Gynecomastia is the descriptive term applied to female breast development in the male subject. The histologic demonstration of estrogen effect in breast tissue, that is, ductular hypertrophy in the subareolar tissue, is essential.

ETIOLOGY

Gynecomastia is an estrogen-mediated process; the etiology of true gynecomastia is always increased estrogen effect. In the adult man, this can be caused by increased exposure of breast tissue to estrogen or by decreased exposure to androgen, androgen acting as an antagonist to estrogen action (see Table 9–22–1).

CRITERIA FOR DIAGNOSIS

Suggestive

Gynecomastia is the most obvious clinical manifestation of feminization in men. It represents normal female breast development in an abnormal setting. Gynecomastia is a clinical sign that can be associated with normal development (e.g., puberty) or can be the harbinger of serious disease (e.g., feminizing adrenal carcinoma). The differential diagnosis of gynecomastia is presented in Table 9–22–1. Gynecomastia is estrogen mediated. Because breasts, once developed, rarely regress completely, the finding of gynecomastia does not necessarily indicate that the estrogen excess is current.

The normal male breast consists of an areola less than 2.5 cm in diameter separated from the chest wall by connective tissue. Estrogen induces subareolar glandular development that is followed by the deposition of a conical pad of fat and fibrous tissue. In the final stages of development, the subareolar pad of glandular tissue regresses.

Definitive

The presence of physical findings compatible with any of these developmental stages justifies the diagnosis of gynecomastia.

CLINICAL MANIFESTATIONS

Subjective

The most common symptoms of gynecomastia are anxiety about the possibility of breast carcinoma and concern over physical appearance. Some patients also complain of tenderness, burning, and itching of the areolas and nipples. Breast secretions are rare.

Objective

Physical Examination

Inspection can reveal a spectrum of findings ranging from the apparently normal male breast to the apparently normal female breast. Thus, palpation of the breast is critical in establishing the diagnosis. Glandular tissue usually has a granular consistency when compared with fat. Early in the evolution of the development of the breast, the glandular tissue is confined to the subareolar space. As development progresses, fat cells separated by connective tissue septae containing the ducts of the milk-producing cells of the breast appear. Ultimately, the subareolar disk of glandular tissue is resorbed. Findings other than these (e.g., nodules, skin fixation, discoloration, expressible secretions) suggest a process different from true gynecomastia, such as breast carcinoma.

Routine Laboratory Abnormalities

There are no diagnostic routine laboratory abnormalities.

TABLE 9–22–1. CAUSES OF GYNECOMASTIA

Increased estrogen effect
  Estrogen-secreting tumors: Leydig cell tumors, adrenal carcinoma
  Increased testicular estrogen secretion: human chorionic gonadotropin-secreting tumors
  Accelerated peripheral aromatization: cirrhosis, obesity, familial increase in aromatase activity
  Drugs and food contaminants: cardiac glycosides, diethylstilbestrol
  Increased sex hormone-binding globulin concentration: thyrotoxicosis

Decreased androgen effect
  Testicular failure: Klinefelter's syndrome, chemotherapy, etc.
  Testosterone biosynthetic enzyme defects
  Gonadal dysgenesis
  Androgen resistance
  Drugs: spironolactone, cimetidine (androgen receptor blockade), mitotane (o, p'-DDD) (Leydig cell injury)

Mechanisms in dispute
  Pubertal gynecomastia
  Refeeding gynecomastia

PLANS
Diagnostic
Differential Diagnosis
The differential diagnosis of gynecomastia is listed in Table 9–22–1.

Diagnostic Options and Recommended Approach
Adolescents with only a subareolar pad of glandular tissue of less than 3 years' duration can be excluded from further evaluation. In other subjects, an evaluation designed to identify serious underlying disease should be pursued. Liver function tests, thyroid function tests, and measurements of luteinizing hormone, follicle-stimulating hormone, estrone, and estradiol are indicated. Elevated luteinizing hormone and/or follicle-stimulating hormone levels suggest either primary gonadal failure or a human chorionic gonadotropin-secreting neoplasm. Normal levels of plasma human chorionic gonadotropin measured with a specific assay exclude a trophoblastic tumor; a karyotype identifies most patients with Klinefelter's syndrome. The presence of low gonadotropin levels associated with an elevated estrone level suggests liver disease. Low gonadotropin levels associated with an elevated estradiol level suggest an estrogen-secreting tumor, such as Leydig cell adenoma or a feminizing adrenal carcinoma. When all these tests are normal, which is the usual case, a diagnosis of idiopathic gynecomastia is made. This group of patients should be followed for at least 1 year, as outlined below, to exclude processes such as Leydig cell tumor that may not be detected on the initial examinations.

Therapeutic
The appropriate treatment of gynecomastia depends on the underlying cause and the extent of progression of the process. If breast development has not progressed to the stage of fat deposition, successful treatment of the underlying disorder can result in complete or nearly complete regression of the breast. If fat has been deposited, complete regression is unlikely. This situation is analogous to that which follows castration of women in the reproductive years; the breasts remain essentially unchanged even though the stimulus for their development has been removed. Thus, breast development of this magnitude requires corrective surgery. This should be performed by a plastic surgeon experienced with the procedure.

The patient should be told that gynecomastia is usually a benign condition and often a feature of normal male sexual development. He should understand that a medical evaluation is necessary to exclude the few serious disorders that can cause gynecomastia. It should be emphasized that most men will have transient gynecomastia at some time in their life. It should be pointed out that normal sexual function and fertility (assuming some underlying disorder does not preclude this) are not jeopardized by this condition. The fact that surgery is cosmetically curative and that the condition rarely recurs should be made clear. Pictures of patients with gynecomastia before and after surgery are useful in establishing realistic expectations.

FOLLOW-UP
The duration and frequency of follow-up visits to the physician should be dictated by the underlying illness. Patients with an initial diagnosis of idiopathic gynecomastia should be seen at 3-month intervals for 1 year. The patient should be carefully examined for signs of progression and, if they are found, the laboratory evaluation should be repeated. Testicular tumors, particularly Leydig cell adenomas, can have gynecomastia as the first clinical sign. Thus, the testes must be examined carefully for masses and changes in size and symmetry.

DISCUSSION
Prevalence and Incidence
Gynecomastia is a common condition. It occurs in about 70% of boys during puberty and is found in many men over the age of 65. Gynecomastia also can be a prominent clinical manifestation of a number of serious disorders. These are outlined in Table 9–22–1.

Related Basic Science
Gynecomastia is the result of increased estrogen effect. Several different mechanisms can cause this. Examples include neoplasms secreting estradiol directly into the circulation (e.g., feminizing adrenal carcinoma), accelerated aromatization of adrenal preestrogens (e.g., cirrhosis of the liver), increased plasma concentrations of sex hormone-binding globulin leading to enhanced estrogen bioactivity (thyrotoxicosis), reduced testicular androgen secretion (e.g., Klinefelter's syndrome), and reduced androgen action (e.g., syndromes of androgen resistance such as testicular feminization). Drugs also can cause gynecomastia; spironolactone and cimetidine are antiandrogens, digitoxin is an impeded estrogen, and mitotane (o, p'-DDD, Lysadren), a drug used for the treatment of adrenal carcinoma and Cushing's disease, seems to cause gynecomastia by impairing Leydig cell function. Alcohol causes gynecomastia by a combination of decreased testicular androgen section, increased hepatic aromatization of preestrogens, and increased levels of sex hormone-binding globulin. All these mechanisms result in increased estrogen action and stimulate the breast to develop along the normal female pattern.

Natural History and Its Modification with Treatment
Gynecomastia occurs in most boys during puberty. It rarely progresses far enough to require surgery, regressing completely in a period of 2 years or less in almost every instance. If the process progresses to the stage of fat deposition, however, complete resolution will not occur and cosmetic surgery will be required. It is not known if the incidence of breast carcinoma is increased in men with gynecomastia.

Prevention
In general, gynecomastia is not a preventable disorder. The one exception is the use of x-irradiation to prevent gynecomastia in men with metastatic prostate carcinoma in whom high-dose estrogen treatment is used. In this group, 900 rad to the breast area before initiation of estrogen treatment prevents the occurrence of gynecomastia. This is generally considered to be justified in men with metastatic carcinoma.

Cost Containment
The clinical examination is the key to cost containment. If gynecomastia has progressed to the point of unsightly fat deposition, a full evaluation is indicated, as is early surgical intervention. In the absence of fat deposition, adolescents need no evaluation beyond a careful history and physical examination unless progression occurs. Older men need a full evaluation, but with early intervention, they can recover without the need for costly surgery. Generally unnecessary are mammograms, skull films, and 17-ketosteroid and urinary estrogen determinations.

REFERENCES
Braunstein GD. Gynecomastia. N Engl J Med 1993;328:490.

Moore DC, Schlaepfer LV, Paunter L, Sizonenko P. Hormonal changes during puberty. V. Transient pubertal gynecomastia: abnormal androgen–estrogen ratios. J Clin Endocrinol Metab 1984;58:492.

Nutall FQ. Gynecomastia as a physical finding in normal men. J Clin Endocrinol Metab 1979;48:338.

Nydick M, Bustos J, Dale J, Rawson R. Gynecomastia in adolescent boys. JAMA 1961;178:449.

Wilson J, Aiman J, Macdonald P. The pathogenesis of gynecomastia. Adv Intern Med 1980;25:1.

Amenorrhea (See Section 10, Chapter 2)

Ovarian Failure and Turner's Syndrome

Nelson B. Watts, M.D.

DEFINITION

Ovarian failure is the cessation of hormone production and gametogenesis by the ovaries. This is usually a natural process, occurs at an average age of 50, and is termed the *menopause* (see Chapter 10–3). Cessation of ovarian function prior to age 40 is considered abnormal.

ETIOLOGY

Primary ovarian failure, characterized by elevations of pituitary gonadotropins (luteinizing hormone and follicle-stimulating hormone) in the face of low gonadal function, results from a variety of factors (Table 9–24–1). Autoimmune destruction of the ovaries occurs, often in association with other organ-specific autoimmune disorders such as insulin-dependent diabetes mellitus, Hashimoto's thyroiditis, and Addison's disease (see Chapter 9–48). The ovaries may be resistant to normal gonadotropin stimulation (the "resistant ovary" syndrome); in these cases, immature follicles are present on ovarian biopsy. The consequence of surgical removal of the ovaries is obvious; pelvic irradiation or cancer cytotoxic chemotherapeutic drugs such as cyclophosphamide are other causes of ovarian destruction. A few patients have been reported with evidence for secretion of gonadotropins with reduced biological activity. The hormonal patterns in these patients are the same as found in primary ovarian failure (low estrogens with elevated luteinizing hormone and follicle-stimulating hormone).

CRITERIA FOR DIAGNOSIS

Suggestive

The clinical picture of ovarian failure includes amenorrhea, often with signs and symptoms of estrogen deficiency such as hot flashes and vaginal atrophy. Failure to menstruate (amenorrhea) and failure to ovulate (anovulation) are features of ovarian failure, but both are seen in a variety of other conditions (see Chapter 10–2).

A specific form of ovarian failure, Turner's syndrome (gonadal dysgenesis), is due to the absence of one of the X chromosomes. Turner's syndrome manifests in phenotypic females as short stature, sexual infantilism, failure of puberty to occur (primary amenorrhea), and various other somatic manifestations. In variants of Turner's syndrome due to chromosomal mosaicism or other sex chromosome abnormalities, these findings may be less severe than in the classic form.

TABLE 9–24–1. CAUSES OF PRIMARY OVARIAN FAILURE

Failure of the ovaries to develop
    Gonadal dysgenesis (Turner's syndrome, others)
Failure of the ovaries to respond normally to gonadotropins
    Gonadotropin-resistant ovary syndrome
Ovarian destruction
    Autoimmune reaction
    Drugs (chemotherapeutic drugs such as cyclophosphamide)
    Irradiation
    Toxins
    Oophorectomy
Idiopathic premature menopause

Definitive

In the appropriate clinical setting, the diagnosis of ovarian failure can be made by observing target organs for a lack of estrogen effect or by demonstrating low levels of estradiol in serum or urine. Patients with ovarian failure should be investigated further to identify the cause. Primary ovarian failure results from abnormalities of the ovaries and is accompanied by an elevation of plasma gonadotropin levels; secondary ovarian failure results from disorders of the pituitary, hypothalamus, or higher centers, with deficient production of gonadotropins leading to failure of the ovaries. The terms *primary* and *secondary*, when applied to gonadal status, point to the involvement of peripheral or central glands; when applied to women with amenorrhea, *primary* means failure of menses ever to occur and *secondary* means that menses occurred for a time and then ceased.

The diagnosis of Turner's syndrome is made by chromosome analysis, with the classic karyotype being 45,X.

CLINICAL MANIFESTATIONS

Subjective

A characteristic manifestation of ovarian failure is the absence of menstrual periods (amenorrhea). In some women with ovarian failure, menses fail to occur at the expected time of puberty (primary amenorrhea). The onset of secondary amenorrhea may be abrupt, or may be preceded by weeks or months of irregular menses (oligomenorrhea). Symptoms of ovarian failure are due largely to estrogen deficiency and include vasomotor instability (hot flashes) and vaginal and urethral dryness as a result of atrophy of the mucous membranes of the genitourinary tract. Stress urinary incontinence may occur. Psychological difficulties (anxiety and depression) may occur and are sometimes quite severe. If ovarian failure has been present for many years without treatment, back pain may result from osteoporosis and vertebral compression fractures.

Patients with Turner's syndrome, in addition to having primary amenorrhea, often complain of swelling of the hands and feet, which is due to lymphedema.

Objective

Physical Examination

Abnormal physical findings in patients with ovarian failure are those of estrogen deficiency. The vaginal mucosa lacks its normal moist, rugated appearance and there is no endocervical mucus. Atrophy of breast tissue may occur. If the disorder was present before puberty, estrogen-dependent secondary sex characteristics (breast development and increased subcutaneous fat) will be absent or incomplete. Spinal compression fractures caused by osteoporosis can lead to kyphosis and loss of height.

Patients with Turner's syndrome are usually short, with a mean height of 4 ft 8 in.(142 cm, range 133–153 cm). Growth is slow, and by 5 years of age, patients are usually more than two standard deviations below expected height. Figure 9–24–1 shows a typical patient with Turner's syndrome. Distinctive features include a small jaw and fish–like mouth; epicanthal folds; ptosis; low-set, rotated, or deformed ears; a high-arched palate; webbing of the neck; a square and shield-like chest with small, wide-spaced nipples; and congenital lymphedema

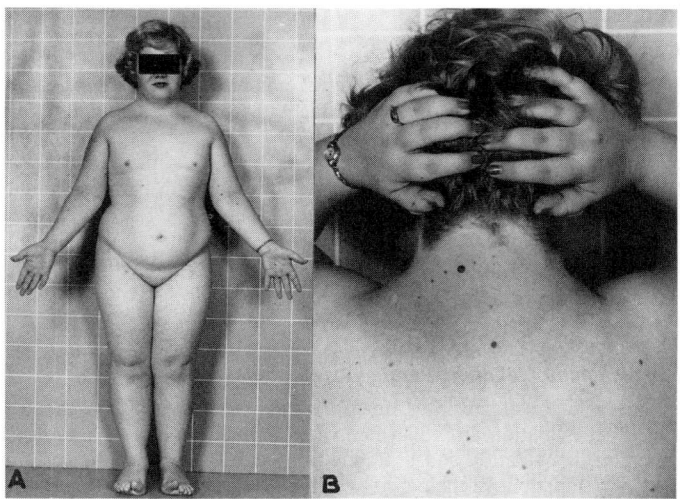

Figure 9–24–1 Patient with Turner's syndrome, illustrating many of the classic somatic features (see text). *(Source: Williams RH, ed Textbook of endocrinology. 3rd ed. Philadelphia: Saunders, 1962. Reproduced with permission from the publisher and author. Photograph courtesy of Judson J. Van Wyk, M.D.)*

of the hands and feet. Many patients have renal anomalies (i.e., rotation of the kidney, horseshoe kidney, duplication of the renal pelvis and ureter, hydronephrosis) and skeletal abnormalities (i.e., shortened fourth metacarpals or metatarsals, increased carrying angle of the arms [cubitus valgus], delayed bony maturation, osteoporosis). The genital ducts and external genitalia are phenotypically female but immature. If laparotomy or laparoscopy is done, long fibrous streaks of connective tissue without definite germ cell elements are found parallel to the fallopian tubes.

Associated disorders that occur with increased frequency in Turner's syndrome are Hashimoto's thyroiditis, rheumatoid arthritis, and inflammatory bowel disease. Evidence of these conditions may be present on physical examination.

Routine Laboratory Abnormalities

With the exception of osteoporosis, which may be seen on chest x-ray films, routine laboratory tests do not show any abnormalities as the result of ovarian failure. Patients with Turner's syndrome may have fasting or postprandial hyperglycemia and evidence of cardiac enlargement on electrocardiogram or chest x-ray film.

PLANS
Diagnostic
Differential Diagnosis

Primary ovarian failure must be distinguished from other causes of amenorrhea such as absence of the uterus, endometrial atrophy or destruction, and absence or obstruction of the vagina. Deficiency of gonadotropin-releasing hormone or pituitary gonadotropins results in secondary ovarian failure. Turner's syndrome must be distinguished from other causes of short stature.

Diagnostic Options

Ovarian failure can be distinguished from pituitary or hypothalamic disorders by measuring serum levels of estradiol and pituitary gonadotropins. Confirmation of the chromosomal pattern characteristic of Turner's syndrome can be done indirectly by buccal smear or by karyotype analysis.

Recommended Approach

Physical findings of estrogen deficiency, especially vaginal atrophy, are often striking and specific, and are usually more accurate indicators of estrogen status than laboratory estrogen determinations. Estradiol, the

major sex steroid produced by the ovaries, can be measured in blood or urine to confirm the clinical impression. Measurement of plasma gonadotropins (luteinizing hormone and follicle-stimulating hormone) provides the information needed to determine whether the problem lies in the ovaries or in higher centers such as the pituitary, hypothalamus, and central nervous system. Elevated gonadotropin levels (luteinizing hormone and follicle-stimulating hormone both ≥30 IU/L) are seen with ovarian failure, and low values, often <5 IU/L are seen with central etiologies of ovarian failure. If the patient desires fertility and tests indicate an ovarian problem, ovarian biopsy may be needed.

The definitive test for Turner's syndrome is karyotype analysis. This test provides information about chromosome deletion, isochromosomes, and mosaicism. The buccal smear for sex chromatin is not an adequate screening test, but, when properly performed, gives additional information. In normal females, 20 to 30% of buccal mucosa cells contain a sex chromatin body (Barr body). Patients with Turner's syndrome who have the classic 45,X chromosomal constitution have no sex chromatin bodies. In mosaic states, however, the number of sex chromatin bodies may be reduced, normal, or increased. If an X isochromosome is present, the size of the Barr body will reflect the size of the isochromosome. Fluorescent staining for Y chromosome material is useful. An intravenous pyelogram should be done to evaluate possible renal anomalies. Additional tests in patients with Turner's syndrome should include evaluation of cardiac status, hearing, thyroid function, glucose tolerance, and bone density.

Therapeutic
Therapeutic Options

Therapy of ovarian failure depends in part on the specific goals and desires of the patient. Options include ovarian hormone replacement therapy or measures directed at restoring fertility.

Recommended Approach

Even in asymptomatic women, estrogen therapy is generally advisable, at least until the expected age of the menopause (age 50), to minimize the rapid loss of bone that occurs in the hypoestrogenemic state and for its favorable effects on the cardiovascular system. Most of the troublesome signs and symptoms of ovarian failure (hot flashes and vaginal dryness) are relieved by estrogen treatment. If secondary sexual development has been incomplete, estrogen treatment will lead to breast development and feminization of body contours.

It is advisable to give estrogen in combination with cyclical progestin to avoid endometrial hyperplasia or endometrial carcinoma. A typical schedule is conjugated estrogens (Premarin), 0.625 or 1.25 mg orally every day, and medroxyprogesterone acetate (Provera), 10 mg orally days 1 through 12 monthly. Transdermal, intravaginal, or parenteral estrogens may also be used.

Estrogens are contraindicated in women with estrogen-dependent tumors such as carcinoma of the breast. Some women taking estrogens develop troublesome breast tenderness or worsening of fibrocystic breast disease. Estrogen treatment is associated with an increased risk of gallstones and, in some women, may cause or aggravate thromboembolic disorders, systemic arterial hypertension, edema, migraine headaches, hypertriglyceridemia, or glucose intolerance. For women who cannot take estrogens, some relief of hot flashes and other symptoms can be found with a variety of nonhormonal medications (Watts, 1989). More details on the risks and benefits of estrogen therapy can be found in Chapter 10–3.

In women with primary ovarian disease, fertility can be achieved only rarely, though occasional success has been reported with glucocorticoids in autoimmune ovarian failure or with estrogen or high-dose gonadotropin treatment in the gonadotropin-resistant ovary syndrome. If, however, the cause of ovarian failure lies in the pituitary, hypothalamus, or higher centers, ovulation and conception are realistic aims. In patients with pituitary or hypothalamic failure, ovulation can be induced with a combination of human menopausal gonadotropins (Pergonal) and human chorionic gonadotropin (A.P.L., Glukor, Profasi). This therapy is associated with an increased frequency of multiple births and can cause severe ovarian hyperstimulation; it should be limited to specialized centers. Women with hypothalamic disease can achieve ovulation with pulsatile administration of gonadotropin-releasing hormone. When amenorrhea is due to hyperprolactinemia, bromocriptine (Parlodel) usually restores normal reproductive function.

There are specific therapeutic considerations for patients with Turner's syndrome: short stature, failure to pubesce, and physical deformities. The reason for short stature in Turner's syndrome is unknown. Treatment for 1 or 2 years with growth hormone or an anabolic steroid such as oxandrolone (Anavar), 0.07 to 0.125 mg/kg/d, or fluoxymesterone (Android-F, Halotestin) may increase final height, though only by an inch or two. The use of anabolic steroids to increase growth may have undesirable androgenic effects, including hirsutism and acne. Estrogen therapy is necessary to promote development of secondary sex characteristics. Some authorities suggest postponing estrogen therapy until after age 15, fearing that earlier treatment will reduce final height. These fears do not appear to be well founded; it seems advisable to start estrogen therapy by age 13 to minimize the psychological problems associated with delayed sexual maturation. Conjugated estrogens are begun in a low dose, 0.3 mg daily, and gradually increased over 2 to 3 years to a full dose; then cyclical therapy with progestin is added. Hormone therapy may be discontinued at the expected time of the menopause, approximately age 50. Plastic surgery may be useful for improving the appearance of the webbed neck and external genital abnormalities. Because of the increased risk of neoplasia, all gonadal tissue should be removed early if any of the patient's cells contain a Y chromosome.

FOLLOW-UP

While taking estrogen and progestin therapy, patients should be followed at least yearly with blood pressure determinations and pelvic examinations. Papanicolaou smears and screening mammography should be performed according to the guidelines of the American Cancer Society. Plasma glucose should be measured periodically. Hormone measurements are usually not helpful in assessing the adequacy of estrogen replacement therapy, but determination of luteinizing hormone, follicle-stimulating hormone, and estradiol (or total estrogens) may be useful if the patient does not experience an adequate clinical response. Patients should be instructed to report any intermenstrual bleeding or missed menstrual periods.

Patients with Turner's syndrome should have regular physical examinations with emphasis on blood pressure and the cardiovascular system. Thyroid function and blood glucose determinations should be done. Known cardiac or genitourinary abnormalities should be followed. Supportive counseling is often necessary for the patient with her parents.

Fertility is most unlikely in primary ovarian failure, although there are occasional exceptions. This should be discussed frankly with the patient and her spouse. If the defect causing ovarian failure is central (pituitary or hypothalamic) and fertility is desired, treatment options for ovulation induction should be reviewed. The need for continuing estrogen therapy to prevent osteoporosis must be emphasized, as some women might choose to discontinue therapy or to take it erratically if they fail to appreciate this goal.

Education is important in the management of patients with Turner's syndrome. A frank discussion should be held with the parents of the patient at the time the diagnosis is made. At adolescence and again in adulthood, the diagnosis should be discussed with the patient, with particular emphasis on the lack of potential for reproduction. The parents and the patient should be assured that the subject is normal in all respects aside from ovarian function and that treatment will ensure that the patient leads a satisfactory life as a woman except for reproduction. A fulfilling marriage and sex life can be anticipated, and adoption of a child or children can permit a full family life.

DISCUSSION
Prevalence and Incidence

Classic Turner's syndrome, 45,X, occurs in 1 in 10,000 live births of phenotypic females; however, considerable loss of chromosomally abnormal embryos and fetuses occurs. It is estimated the 10% of all spontaneous abortions are of the 45,X chromosome constitution.

Related Basic Science
Genetics

The 45,X abnormality of Turner's syndrome results from the loss of an X chromosome, which can occur during gametogenesis in either parent or as an error in mitosis during the first cleavage of the zygote. The underlying cause is not known; there is no association with advanced maternal age. Chromosomal mosaicism is common, with patterns including 45,X/46,XX; 45,X/47,XXX; and 45,X/46,XX/47,XXX. Other chromosomal anomalies that may present as variants of Turner's syndrome include isochromosomes of the long or short arms of the X chromosome, ring chromosomes, and mosaics that include Y chromosomes, such as 45,X/46,XY; 45,X/47,XYY; and 45,X/46,XY/47,XYY.

Physiologic or Metabolic Derangement

Cessation of cyclic ovarian function leads to a decrease in the frequency of ovulation, irregular menstrual periods, and, eventually, total cessation of ovulation and hormone production. As the follicular and hormonal functions of the ovaries fail, levels of pituitary gonadotropins become elevated. Initially, follicle-stimulating hormone rises, and subsequently, luteinizing hormone increases; estradiol falls to low levels. Production of estrone, a less potent estrogen, is maintained through peripheral conversion of adrenal androgens, but is not sufficient to maintain normal estrogen effects. The mechanism of vasomotor instability is not clear, but seems related to central factors; vasomotor flushes are not seen in women with ovarian failure due to pituitary or hypothalamic disease or when ovarian function has never begun (e.g., Turner's syndrome).

When ovarian failure is due to pituitary or hypothalamic disease, levels of luteinizing hormone and follicle-stimulating hormone are low or inappropriately "normal" despite low levels of estrogen. This may result from tumors or infiltrative lesions that interfere with the production of gonadotropins or gonadotropin-releasing hormone, or from inhibition of normal gonadotrope function by excessive prolactin levels (see Chapter 9–4). Not uncommonly, no specific cause for central ovarian failure can be found and the case is termed *hypothalamic amenorrhea*. Factors that have been implicated in hypothalamic amenorrhea include psychological stress and weight loss (anorexia nervosa is a striking example of both), intensive physical training, and a variety of acute and chronic diseases. It was hoped that the gonadotropin-releasing hormone stimulation test would elucidate the nature of the lesion in these women, but the results have been disappointing.

Adrenal androgens increase normally at the time of puberty and some pubic and axillary hair appears. Hormone production by gonadal tissue may occur in Turner's syndrome and is more likely with mosaic variants. If menses occur, they usually cease at an early age. The occurrence of spontaneous breast development usually signals the presence of an estrogen-secreting gonadal neoplasm. In patients with the Y chromosome, even though the phenotype is female, virilization may occur at puberty.

Anatomic Derangement

Vaginal and urethral atrophy and osteoporosis occur because of the lack of normal estrogen effects on these target tissues; estrogen lack also leads to increased bone resorption. Patients with ovarian failure that begins before puberty (e.g., Turner's syndrome) present with failure to begin menstruation, failure to develop normal secondary sex characteristics, or both.

The phenotypes of Turner's syndrome variants can be quite diverse. Cardiovascular anomalies are four times more common with the 45,X constitution compared with variant forms. Coarctation of the aorta and congenital lymphedema occur almost exclusively with 45,X. Renal and skeletal abnormalities occur with equal frequency in classic Turner's syndrome and its variants. Mental retardation is rare in 45,X Turner's syndrome but is common in variants with isochromosomes. The character of the gonads depends on the ratio of normal to abnormal cells, ranging from streak gonads, hypoplastic or dysgenetic ovaries or testes, to relatively normal gonadal tissue. Some internal müllerian structures are usually found, regardless of chromosomal constitution. In patients who have a mosaic that contains a Y chromosome, the external genitalia may be either female or ambiguous, with two thirds of these patients being reared as females. Table 9–24–2 compares 45,X Turner's syndrome with variant forms.

An increased risk of gonadal neoplasia is associated with Y chromosome abnormalities, possibly because of prolonged stimulation of germ cells by high levels of luteinizing hormone and follicle-stimulating hormone. Early prophylactic removal of all gonadal tissue in Turner's variant patients with Y chromosomes is advisable unless there is histologically normal testicular tissue in the scrotum. Pelvic sonography or computed tomography can be used to visualize gonadal tissue. Evidence of hormonally active gonadal tissue can be obtained by measuring serum testosterone or estradiol after stimulation with human chorionic gonadotropin. Rare patients with true 45,X chromosome constitution have been reported to undergo menarche and experience pregnancy.

Natural History and Its Modification with Treatment

Accelerated bone loss follows spontaneous or surgical menopause; the end result depends on the age at which estrogen deficiency occurs. Spinal compression fractures can lead to considerable morbidity, and hip fractures cause significant morbidity and mortality. Estrogen deficiency is associated with an increased risk of cardiovascular disease; estrogen therapy significantly reduces this risk. Vasomotor flashes and psychological problems associated with estrogen deficiency may be mild and transient, but are sometimes severe. Vaginal dryness can be most distressing to a sexually active woman.

Patients with Turner's syndrome may have associated conditions that result in increased morbidity and mortality, including systemic arterial hypertension and cardiac and renal abnormalities.

Prevention

Menopause occurs earlier in women who smoke, perhaps because smoking accelerates the metabolism of estrogens. Discontinuation of cigarette use may be effective in prolonging reproductive function. No other preventive measures are currently available for Turner's syndrome or other causes of ovarian failure. More research is needed in this field.

Cost Containment

The major costs are the initial workup, continuing medication, and follow-up. Following the guidelines in this chapter should minimize unnecessary expenses.

Evaluation and management of patients with Turner's syndrome are fairly straightforward. Chromosome analysis is costly but essential to

TABLE 9–24–2 COMPARISON OF 45,X TURNER'S SYNDROME WITH VARIANT FORMS

	45,X	Mosaics, Other Variants
External genitalia	Female	Variable (female, ambiguous, male)
Internal genitalia		
Wolffian structures	Absent	Variable
Müllerian structures	Normal female	Variable
Gonads	Streak	Variable (streak, dysgenetic, or normal)
Habitus	Short stature, sexual infantilism, somatic stigmata	May be sexually infantile, virilized, or show breast growth; usually short
Hormone profile, after puberty	LH and FSH high, estradiol low	LH and FSH high, estradiol or testosterone may be high with neoplasm
Lymphedema	Common	Rare
Cardiac anomalies	Common, especially coarctation of aorta	Less common, coarctation rare
Renal anomalies	Common	Common
Skeletal anomalies	Common	Common
Mental retardation	Rare	Common

LH, luteinizing hormone; FSH, follicle-stimulating hormone.

the diagnosis, and baseline cardiac and renal evaluations are needed for completeness.

REFERENCES

Cohen I, Speroff L. Premature ovarian failure: Update. Obstet Gynecol Surv 1991;46:156.

Grumbach MM, Conte FA. Disorders of sex differentiation. In: Wilson JD, Foster DW, ed. Williams' textbook of endocrinology. 8th ed. Philadelphia: Saunders, 1992:853.

Grundy D, Rubin SM, Petitti DB, et al. Hormone therapy to prevent disease and prolong life in postmenopausal women. Ann Intern Med 1992;117:1016.

Holl RW, Kunze D, Etzrodt H, et al. Turner syndrome: Final height, glucose tolerance, bone density and psychosocial status in 25 adult patients. Eur J Pediatr 1994;153:11.

Saenger. The current status of diagnosis and therapeutic interventions in Turner's syndrome. J Clin Endocrinol Metab 1993;77:297.

Watts NB. Nonhormonal treatment of menopause. In: Notelovitz M, ed. Managing the menopause: An update. New York: McGraw-Hill, 1989:17.

CHAPTER 9–25

Menopause (See Section 10, Chapter 3)

CHAPTER 9–26

Hirsutism, Virilization, and Androgen Excess

Roger S. Rittmaster, M.D.

DEFINITION

Hirsutism is the presence of excess hair growth in women. *Hyperandrogenism* refers to the unwanted clinical manifestations of androgens (hirsutism, acne, male-pattern baldness, anovulation) or to the presence of elevated levels of androgens in the blood. Both hirsutism and hyperandrogenism are socially defined; they can exist in the absence of any underlying disorder. *Virilization* refers to extreme hyperandrogenism.

Except when used to describe masculinization of the external genitalia, it is a poorly defined term that has limited clinical utility.

ETIOLOGY

Hirsutism may be caused by either increased secretion of androgens from the ovaries and adrenal glands or increased sensitivity of the skin to androgens. Both problems coexist in many hirsute women. Skin sensitivity is controlled in part by the enzyme 5α-reductase, which converts testosterone to its active form in the skin, dihydrotestosterone. Hirsute women have higher levels of 5α-reductase in areas of the skin with excess hair growth than nonhirsute women.

CRITERIA FOR DIAGNOSIS
Suggestive

Hirsutism is generally defined by social norms and therefore depends on individual perceptions as well as ethnic background. Twenty-five to 35% of unselected young women have hair over the lower abdomen, around the areolae, or on the face (mainly the upper lip). Body hair growth in women increases with age at least up to the time of menopause, and facial hair growth increases even after menopause. Unfortunately, these normal hair patterns are unacceptable to many women. From a practical standpoint, it is reasonable to treat "excess" hair growth in any woman in whom it causes a significant psychological, social, or cosmetic problem.

Similarly, there is no good objective definition for hyperandrogenism. Women may have severe acne, hirsutism or even male-pattern baldness with normal female androgen levels.

Definitive

The more severe the cosmetic problem, the greater is the concern that a serious underlying medical problem exists. Although one can define hyperandrogenism as a serum level of testosterone, androstenedione, or dehydroepiandrosterone sulfate above the normal range, only levels high enough to suggest a neoplasm warrant a change in the diagnostic approach.

The most common cause of biochemical hyperandrogenism in women is polycystic ovary syndrome. This is a clinical diagnosis consisting of anovulation (causing menstrual irregularity or amenorrhea) and hyperandrogenism. Although the ovaries may be enlarged and polycystic, this is not necessary for the diagnosis. The hyperandrogenism often arises from both the adrenal glands and ovaries. Obese women with polycystic ovarian syndrome usually have insulin resistance.

CLINICAL MANIFESTATIONS
Subjective

Benign forms of hyperandrogenism usually begin around puberty, during a period of weight gain, or after a woman stops using an oral contraceptive. Hirsutism usually progresses slowly over time, although a rapid worsening of hair growth may occur during adolescence. Menstrual irregularity commonly begins shortly after menarche. In some women, infertility may be the presenting complaint. Hyperandrogenic women with a family history of male-pattern baldness often experience scalp hair thinning. Acne is dependent on androgens; however, many other factors contribute to its presence, and its severity correlates poorly with the degree of hyperandrogenism. Although marked deepening of the voice suggests severe androgen excess, slight changes in pitch can occur with mild hyperandrogenism. A family history of hirsutism or menstrual irregularity is common in women with benign forms of hyperandrogenism. Finally, hyperandrogenism can cause significant psychological distress, which may be out of proportion to the objective manifestations of androgen excess.

Hyperandrogenism caused by adrenal or ovarian neoplasms is rare and is usually characterized by the rapid progression of severe hirsutism, deepening of the voice, scalp hair thinning, and amenorrhea. The history is the most important clue to the diagnosis of an androgen-secreting tumor. The late-onset forms of congenital adrenal hyperplasia are clinically indistinguishable from other causes of hyperandrogenism and can be diagnosed only by appropriate laboratory evaluation (see below).

Objective
Physical Examination

In the hirsute woman, the physical examination is directed at confirming the androgen dependency of hirsutism and ruling out serious under-lying diseases. Excess hair growth that occurs primarily over the central abdomen, chest, upper lip, chin, lower back or shoulders indicates androgen-dependent hirsutism. Hirsutism characterized by diffuse, fine hair growth over the entire trunk and face suggests either drug-induced hirsutism or familial, androgen-independent hirsutism. Physicians often score the hirsutism on a scale of 0 to 4 in areas of androgen-dependent hair growth (upper and lower back, upper lip, chin, sideburns, chest, upper and lower abdomen, and thighs). Such a scoring system has high interobserver variability and is semiquantitative at best. Nevertheless, it provides a rapid method of recording the distribution and approximate severity of the hirsutism.

Androgen-secreting tumors are rare and are not generally palpable on physical examination. Hirsutism is rarely the presenting feature of Cushing's syndrome and other physical features coexist (hypertension, central obesity, bruising, striae, facial plethora, proximal muscle weakness). Occasionally, the obesity and hyperandrogenism of Cushing's syndrome masquerade as polycystic ovary syndrome, but usually the presence or absence of other features makes this distinction. Acanthosis nigricans (thickening and darkening of skin folds primarily on the back of the neck and in the axilla) occurs frequently in obese women with polycystic ovary syndrome and is a sign of hyperinsulinemia, not hyperandrogenism.

Routine Laboratory Abnormalities

Because hirsutism and hyperandrogenism are often defined clinically, affected women may have no routine laboratory abnormalities.

PLANS
Diagnostic
Differential Diagnosis

The differential diagnosis of hyperandrogenism includes ovarian and adrenal causes of androgen excess (Table 9-26-1). More than 95% of women with androgen-dependent hirsutism will have either no underlying abnormality ("idiopathic hirsutism") or polycystic ovary syndrome. About 1% of women have late-onset congenital adrenal hyperplasia (21-hydroxylase deficiency). Other androgenic forms of congenital adrenal hyperplasia (11-hydroxylase and 3β-hydroxysteroid dehydrogenase deficiencies) are sufficiently rare that screening for these enzyme defects is unnecessary. Cushing's syndrome is a rare cause of hirsutism and usually is suspected because of the clinical features of hypercortisolism. Adrenal and ovarian tumors are exceedingly rare and are often suspected based on a history of rapidly worsening hyperandrogenism and a physical examination indicating severe androgen excess. Exogenous androgen abuse is an uncommon cause of hirsutism, but some physicians prescribe supraphysiologic doses of androgens as part of postmenopausal hormone therapy.

Most hirsute women with ovulatory menstrual cycles have normal serum levels of testosterone (<80 ng/dL or 2.8 nmol/L). Women with polycystic ovary syndrome may have normal or elevated serum testosterone levels. Sex-hormone-binding globulin is frequently reduced in such women as a result of hyperinsulinemia, and hence the free testos-

TABLE 9–26–1. CAUSES OF HYPERANDROGENISM AND THEIR APPROXIMATE FREQUENCY

Adrenal	
Congenital adrenal hyperplasia	
21-Hydroxylase deficiency	1%
11-Hydroxylase deficiency	<<1%
3β-Hydroxysteroid dehydrogenase deficiency	<<1%
Cushing's syndrome	<1%
Androgen-secreting adrenal tumors	<<1%
Ovary	
Severe insulin resistance	1%
Androgen-secreting ovarian neoplasms	<<1%
Combined adrenal and ovary	95%
Polycystic ovary syndrome	
Idiopathic hirsutism (also includes increased skin sensitivity to androgens)	

terone is elevated more frequently than the total testosterone. With polycystic ovary syndrome and severe insulin resistance, serum testosterone levels may reach the normal male range (around 300 ng/dL or 11 nmol/L), raising concerns about an androgen-secreting tumor. Testosterone levels under 170 ng/dL (6 nmol/L) are uncommon in androgen-secreting tumors.

Dehydroepiandrosterone sulfate is an adrenal steroid that has been used as a marker of adrenal androgen secretion. Its level may be elevated in hirsute women, and it is commonly greater than twice the upper limit of normal in androgen-secreting adrenal tumors. On the other hand, dehydroepiandrosterone sulfate correlates only modestly with other measures of adrenal androgen secretion, is usually normal in women with late-onset congenital adrenal hyperplasia, and may be normal in some androgen-secreting adrenal adenomas.

Women with polycystic ovary syndrome often demonstrate other laboratory abnormalities including an elevated ratio of serum luteinizing hormone to follicle–stimulating hormone, hyperinsulinemia with or without glucose intolerance, and mildly elevated serum levels of prolactin and 17-hydroxyprogesterone. Hyperlipidemia and diabetes are common in family members, and such women are predisposed to develop these problems. Women with late-onset congenital adrenal hyperplasia have marked elevation of serum 17–hydroxyprogesterone, either basally or after adrenocorticotropic hormone stimulation.

Diagnostic Options and Recommended Approach

For women with mild to moderate hirsutism and ovulatory menses, usually no hormonal evaluation is necessary. Such women could have late-onset congenital adrenal hyperplasia, but the hirsutism responds better to standard treatment with antiandrogens than to adrenal suppression with glucocorticoids.

The laboratory evaluation in women who present with hyperandrogenism and irregular menses is directed at ruling out serious underlying disorders. A reasonable hormonal evaluation includes a serum testosterone, 17-hydroxyprogesterone, prolactin, and possibly luteinizing hormone and follicle-stimulating hormone. A serum total testosterone should be measured to screen for androgen-secreting tumors (see above). A 17-hydroxyprogesterone level should be drawn between 7 and 9 AM to screen for 21-hydroxylase deficiency. A level less than 200 ng/dL (6 nmol/L) rules out this diagnosis; a serum level over 1500 ng/dL (45 nmol/L) is diagnostic of homozygous 21-hydroxylase deficiency. Mildly elevated values (<1000 ng/dL [30 nmol/L]) may be seen in both heterozygous and homozygous 21-hydroxylase deficiency and in polycystic ovary syndrome. To distinguish between these conditions, 17-hydroxyprogesterone should be measured 30 to 60 minutes after the intravenous administration of 250 µg synthetic adrenocorticotropic hormone. Levels over 1500 ng/dL (45 nmol/L) are diagnostic of 21-hydroxylase deficiency. A serum prolactin level should be obtained to rule out a prolactinoma (which can cause amenorrhea). Serum follicle-stimulating hormone is elevated in women with ovarian failure and serum luteinizing hormone is elevated in many women with polycystic ovary syndrome. Pituitary stimulation tests and ovarian and adrenal suppression tests are unnecessary in the routine evaluation of hirsute women. Women with polycystic ovary syndrome should also be screened for hyperlipidemia and diabetes.

For women with a history of rapidly progressive hirsutism and a markedly elevated serum testosterone, ovarian ultrasound and adrenal computed tomography or magnetic resonance imaging should be done to search for an androgen-secreting tumor. All androgen-secreting adrenal neoplasms should be visible radiologically. If an ovarian tumor is still suspected after negative imaging studies, selective ovarian venous catheterization may be necessary, but such studies should be done and interpreted only by individuals with extensive experience using this technique. If Cushing's syndrome is suspected, a 24-hour urine collection for cortisol excretion is the best screening test.

Therapeutic

Therapeutic Options

General Comments. Common androgen-related problems include hirsutism, acne, male-pattern baldness, menstrual irregularity, and infertility. Associated problems in women with polycystic ovary syndrome in-

clude endometrial hyperplasia, obesity, glucose intolerance, dyslipidemia, and hypertension. Occasionally, a patient has an underlying problem allowing specific therapy, such as an androgen-secreting tumor, Cushing's syndrome, or congenital adrenal hyperplasia. More commonly, medical therapies are directed at the presenting complaint.

Acne is best treated with topical agents or, in severe cases, isotretinoin (Accutane). Oral contraceptives or antiandrogens may be used as adjunctive therapy to local dermatologic treatments. Male-pattern baldness responds to many of the same treatments as hirsutism (see below for details). Women with oligomenorrhea or amenorrhea should be treated with oral contraceptives or cyclic progesterone (e.g., medroxyprogesterone acetate, 5 mg daily for 12 to 14 days every 1 to 2 months) to prevent endometrial hyperplasia. Infertility due to anovulation is best treated with ovulation-inducing medications such as clomiphene citrate. Surgical approaches include ovarian wedge resection, laser vaporization of the ovarian capsule, and ovarian electrocautery.

Mechanical Treatment of Hirsutism. Mechanical treatments of hirsutism include shaving, bleaching, depilatory creams, plucking, waxing, and electrolysis. With the possible exception of electrolysis, mechanical treatments do not change the underlying natural history, but they can result in a marked cosmetic improvement. Shaving does not increase hair growth, although a stubble may result, because the fine leading end of the hair shaft is removed. Bleaching and depilatory creams work best for fine hair. With coarse hair, the greater duration of time needed for an adequate cosmetic result can lead to skin irritation. Plucking can control hirsutism, but it may lead to scarring in some women. Electrolysis can effectively control localized hirsutism, but it is not a permanent solution for many women. When electrolysis is combined with medical therapy, a more rapid improvement in the hirsutism can be expected.

Medical Treatments of Hirsutism. Although hirsutism is not a disease, the social and psychological consequences can be devastating. Therefore, the most important factor in deciding to use drugs is the patients's perception of the problem. Most hirsute women develop gradually more facial and body hair with time. Early treatment is especially important in adolescents and young women who have rapidly worsening hirsutism or a family history of severe hirsutism. Because drug treatment is not a cure, the medications need to be continued indefinitely. No drug is currently approved in the United States or Canada for treatment of hirsutism.

Drug treatments include suppressing ovarian androgen production with oral contraceptives or gonadotropin-releasing hormone agonists, suppressing adrenal androgen production with glucocorticoids, blocking androgen action with antiandrogens (androgen receptor blockers), and decreasing dihydrotestosterone production with 5α-reductase inhibitors (Table 9–26-2).

Oral contraceptives decrease ovarian androgen secretion by inhibiting pituitary luteinizing hormone secretion. Although the androgenicity of the progestin component varies, and much fanfare has been made over the newer nonandrogenic progestins (desogestrel, norgestimate, gestodene), there are no comparative clinical studies to indicate that the newer progestins are superior to older formulations for treating hirsutism. On a theoretical basis, oral contraceptives containing cyproterone acetate, an antiandrogenic progestin, would be best, but such a

TABLE 9–26-2. MEDICAL TREATMENTS OF HIRSUTISM

Ovarian suppression
  Oral contraceptives
  Cyproterone acetate
  Gonadotropin-releasing hormone agonists
Adrenal suppression
  Glucocorticoids
Androgen receptor blockers
  Spironolactone
  Cyproterone acetate
  Flutamide
5α-Reductase inhibitors
  Finasteride

pill is not available in the United States or Canada. In my experience, birth control pills alone are only modestly effective for the treatment of hirsutism. About 10% of women improve, 50% have stable hirsutism, and 40% continue to develop more hair growth on oral contraceptives.

Gonadotropin-releasing hormone agonists suppress gonadal function by decreasing secretion of follicle-stimulating hormone and luteinizing hormone. They are usually given by monthly intramuscular injections. Because both estrogens and androgens are suppressed, they are often given with oral contraceptives to prevent symptoms of estrogen deficiency. Gonadotropin-releasing hormone agonists work best for women with severe polycystic ovary syndrome. Their major disadvantage is their expense, and they should be used only by physicians experienced in their use.

Glucocorticoids (hydrocortisone, prednisone, dexamethasone) are the oldest treatment of hirsutism, but now are being replaced by more effective therapies. Although they may be useful in some women with adrenal hyperandrogenism, adequate doses often cause weight gain and nocturia (early symptoms of Cushing's syndrome), and about 10% of women develop a drug-induced hirsutism (increased vellus hair growth). Glucocorticoids are useful for the treatment of anovulation in women with late-onset congenital adrenal hyperplasia; however, the hirsutism in such women responds better to antiandrogens.

Antiandrogens (spironolactone, cyproterone acetate, flutamide) are the medical treatments of choice for hirsutism. They reduce the amount of hair growth in at least 70% of hirsute women and prevent worsening hirsutism in the remainder. *Spironolactone* is usually given in a starting dose of 50 mg twice daily, which may be doubled if no improvement is seen with 6 months of treatment. The most common side effect is increased frequency of menses, which occurs in about 20% of women. This can be treated by reducing the dose or adding an oral contraceptive. Spironolactone is contraindicated in women with renal insufficiency, in patients taking other potassium-retaining medications, and in pregnancy. *Cyproterone acetate* is a potent progestin and antiandrogen. It is often given as 25 to 50 mg daily for the first 10 days of a birth control pill cycle. As a progestin, it suppresses ovarian androgen secretion and works best in women with polycystic ovary syndrome. Side effects are usually only those attributable to the oral contraceptive, although it occasionally causes amenorrhea or an elevation of liver enzymes. It is available only outside the United States. *Flutamide* is given as 125 to 250 mg twice daily. Its efficacy is similar to that of spironolactone. Its most serious potential side effect is a drug-induced hepatitis. It is more expensive than other antiandrogens.

Finasteride, the only 5α-reductase inhibitor currently available, is approved for treatment of benign prostatic hyperplasia. Its use in women is limited, but early experience suggests that it may be as effective as spironolactone. It is available only as a 5-mg tablet, although doses as low as 1 mg daily are likely to be as effective. No clinically important side effects have been observed in women, but it would be expected to cause ambiguous genitalia in male offspring of women who use it during pregnancy.

Recommended Approach

Spironolactone, with or without an oral contraceptive, is the medical treatment of choice for hirsute women. Cyproterone acetate is an excellent alternative, especially in women with polycystic ovary syndrome. For women who do not tolerate spironolactone, flutamide is a reasonable choice but is expensive. Finasteride may also be a good alternative. Women with severe polycystic ovary syndrome respond best to gonadotropin-releasing hormone analogs or cyproterone acetate plus a birth control pill. In women using antiandrogens or 5α-reductase inhibitors, adequate contraception is essential.

FOLLOW-UP

It may take as long as 6 months for medical treatment of hirsutism to be effective, and changes in therapy before then should be made only when unacceptable side effects occur. Renal function and potassium should be monitored in women receiving spironolactone, and liver enzymes should be followed in women taking cyproterone acetate or flutamide.

DISCUSSION
Prevalence

Because hyperandrogenism is often defined by social values, its prevalence is uncertain. Up to 5% of reproductive-age women have polycystic ovary syndrome. At least 25% of women have terminal hairs over the lower abdomen, around the areola, or over the upper lip.

Related Basic Science

Adrenal androgens are a normal by-product of cortisol synthesis, and ovarian androgens are a normal by-product of estrogen synthesis. Hirsute women as a group have increased androgen production rates and increased skin 5α-reductase activity. In many women, hirsutism is simply one end of the normal spectrum of androgen production and skin sensitivity to androgens. About 1% of hirsute women inherit 21-hydroxylase deficiency, an autosomal recessive form of adrenal hyperandrogenism.

Polycystic ovary syndrome has multiple etiologies leading to a clinical picture of hyperandrogenic anovulation. Women with polycystic ovary syndrome tend to have insulin resistance, hypersecretion of luteinizing hormone, and increased ovarian and adrenal androgen production. Many such women inherit a tendency to insulin resistance, which is exacerbated by obesity. The obesity-induced hyperinsulinism causes, or is closely associated with the cause of, anovulation, in as much as weight loss can restore ovulatory menses and normal androgen levels.

Natural History and Its Modification with Treatment

Women tend to develop more facial and body hair with age. This is a function of duration of exposure to androgens. Medical treatment of hirsutism can prevent worsening in nearly all women and decrease hair growth in at least 70%. Nevertheless, medical treatment is not a cure and hair regrowth can be expected after medical treatment is stopped.

Women with polycystic ovary syndrome are at increased risk for developing endometrial hyperplasia and cancer, hypertension, hyperlipidemia, diabetes, and coronary artery disease.

Prevention

Disfiguring hirsutism can be prevented with the early institution of antiandrogen therapy. This is especially important for adolescent girls. The best prevention for polycystic ovary syndrome is avoidance of weight gain. Nevertheless, many women with polycystic ovary syndrome are not obese. The early institution of an oral contraceptive can help control the hirsutism, irregular menses, and predisposition to endometrial cancer.

Cost Containment

Medical therapy for hirsutism should not be expensive. Spironolactone is a generic medication and 50 mg twice daily should cost less than $30 per month. The cost can be reduced by using one half of a 100-mg tablet rather than two 25-mg tablets. The cost of cyproterone acetate is similar to that of spironolactone when it is given as 50 mg daily for 10 days each month, and 25 mg (half-tablet) is probably as effective for most women. Flutamide is much more expensive and, in my experience, no more effective than spironolactone. Finasteride, when given as 5 mg daily (the only tablet size available), costs about $60 per month. One milligram daily is probably as effective.

REFERENCES

Azziz R, Dewailly D, Owerbach D. Nonclassic adrenal hyperplasia: Current concepts. J Clin Endocrinol Metab 1994;78:810.

Dunaif A, Givens J, Merriam G, Haseltine F, eds. Current issues in endocrinology and metabolism: Polycystic ovary syndrome. Cambridge, MA: Blackwell Scientific, 1992.

Pasquali R, Francesco C. The impact of obesity on hyperandrogenism and polycystic ovary syndrome in premenopausal women. Clin Endocrinol (Oxf) 1993;39:1.

Rittmaster RS. Hyperandrogenism. In: Copeland LJ, ed. Textbook of gynecology. Philadelphia: Saunders, 1993:414.

CHAPTER 9–27
Ambiguous Genitalia
Gordon B. Cutler, Jr., M.D.

DEFINITION
The external genitalia are ambiguous when they have not differentiated fully along either the male or female pattern (Figure 9–27–1).

ETIOLOGY
Most children with ambiguous genitalia have single–gene defects that affect the production or action of androgens. Other causes include sex chromosome mosaicism (or other genetic defects) leading to abnormal gonadal differentiation, nonhormonal embryogenic defects associated with genital abnormalities, and intrauterine exposure to androgenic or antiandrogenic drugs.

CRITERIA FOR DIAGNOSIS
Suggestive
Ambiguous genitalia are ideally detected when the newborn is first examined. In practice, however, subtle degrees of ambiguity may not be detected at birth. Such patients, whether reared as male or female, may come to medical attention later because of salt-wasting crisis, short stature or another feature of Turner's syndrome, inguinal hernia, infertility, or gonadal tumor. Additionally, girls may present because of palpable masses in the labia or groin, clitoromegaly and virilization during childhood or adolescence, hypertension, or primary amenorrhea. Boys may be seen because of cryptorchidism, hypospadias, inadequate pubertal masculinization, cyclic hematuria, or gynecomastia.

Recognition that the genitalia are ambiguous is unavoidable when the physician is uncertain whether the newborn child is a boy or a girl. The possibility of an intersex disorder also should be evaluated, however, in the apparent boy who has cryptorchidism or hypospadias and in the apparent girl who has a labial or inguinal mass, enlarged clitoris, or posterior fusion of the labia.

Definitive
Ambiguous genitalia result from many different disorders that affect virtually every known step in the sequence of normal sexual differentiation (Figures 9–27–1, 9–27–2; Table 9–27–1). When ambiguous genitalia are recognized at birth, the physician's first obligation is to be aware that the child may have salt-wasting congenital adrenal hyperplasia, which is a life-threatening disorder. The second obligation is to

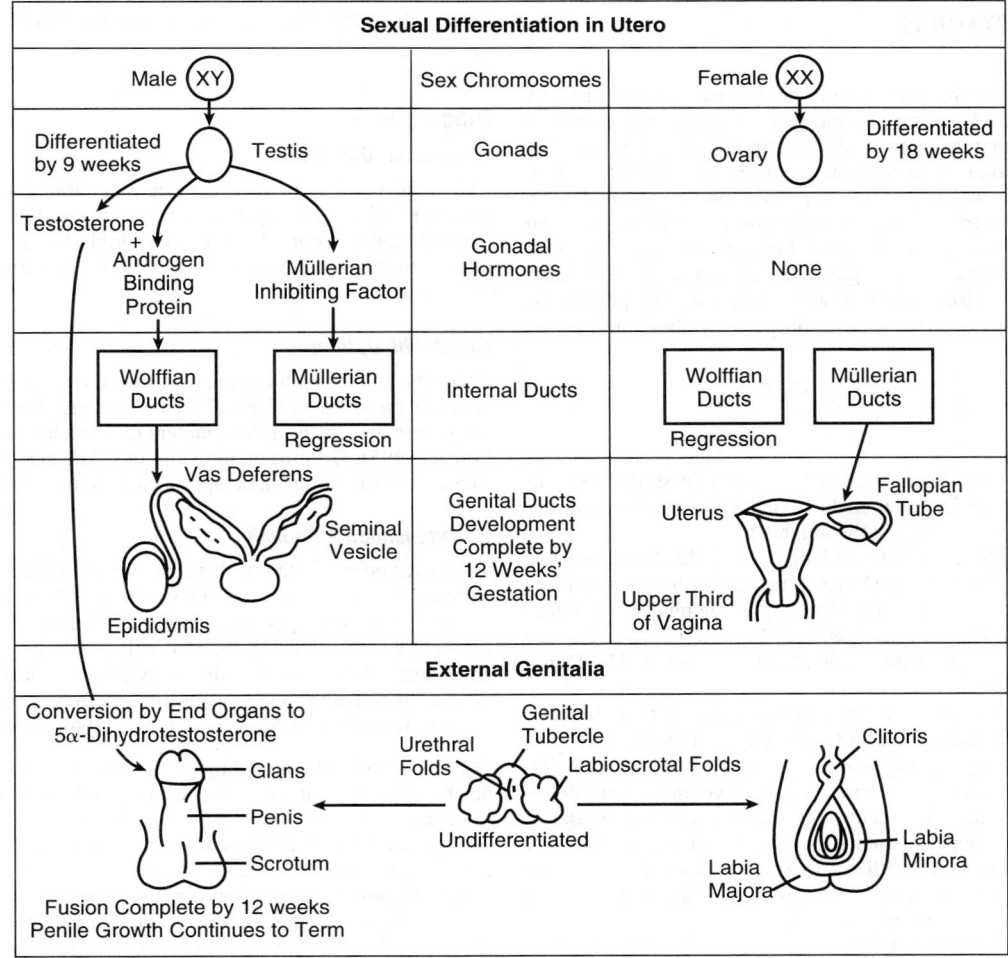

Figure 9–27–1. Normal sexual differentiation in utero (*Source: Parks JS. Intersex. In: Kaplan SA, ed. Clinical pediatric and adolescent endocrinology. Philadelphia: Saunders, 1985:328. Reproduced with permission from the publisher and author.*)

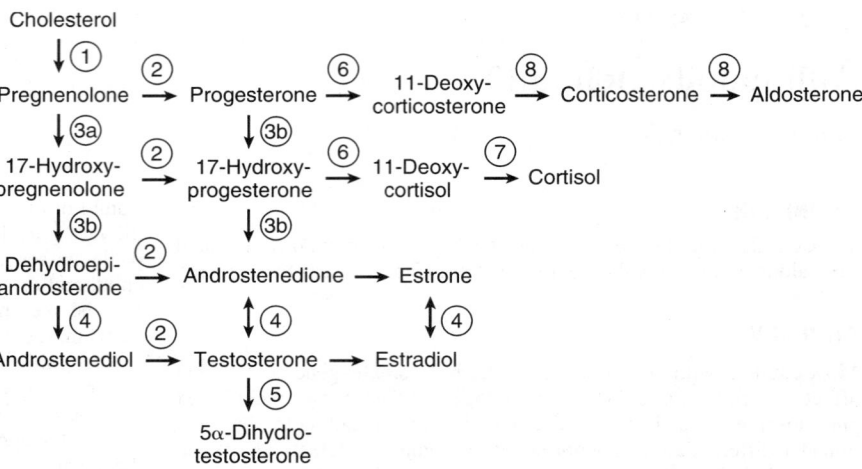

Figure 9-27-2. Steroid biosynthetic pathway. The enzymes shown are (1) 20,22-desmolase; (2) 3β-hydroxysteroid dehydrogenase/Δ^5, Δ^4-isomerase; (3a) 17-hydroxylase; (3b) 17,20-desmolase; (4) 17-ketosteroid reductase; (5) 5α-reductase; (6) 21-hydroxylase; (7) 11β-hydroxylase; (8) aldosterone synthetase. Enzymes 1, 2, and 3, which are essential for synthesis of both cortisol and sex steroid, are present in both adrenal gland and gonad. Enzymes 6, 7, and 8, which are unique to cortisol and aldosterone biosynthesis, are present in adrenal gland but not in gonad. Enzyme 5 carries out the peripheral conversion of testosterone to the more potent androgen dihydrotestosterone in androgen target cells. Defects in enzymes 1, 2, 6, 8, and occasionally 7 may cause life-threatening salt-wasting crises within 1 to 2 weeks of birth.

pursue expeditiously those diagnostic steps that are essential to allow an appropriate sex assignment for the child. Sex assignment frequently can and should be made before a definitive diagnosis is reached. Although sex assignment reduces the urgency for subsequent diagnostic efforts, definitive diagnosis should be sought to free the parents of unfounded suspicion about the cause, to help them evaluate the risk for future pregnancies, and to assist the physician in caring for the patient. Despite impressive advances in diagnosis, however, a significant proportion of cases remain idiopathic.

CLINICAL MANIFESTATIONS
Subjective

A complete pedigree of the child should be constructed, with inquiry about the occurrence of genital abnormalities, unexplained deaths of older siblings (who may have had salt-wasting congenital adrenal hyperplasia), and maternal aunts with amenorrhea and infertility (who may have androgen resistance). Androgen resistance is inherited as an X-linked recessive disorder. Congenital adrenal hyperplasia, testicular biosynthetic defects, and 5α-reductase deficiency all have autosomal recessive inheritance. Disorders of gonadal differentiation are usually sporadic. The history should address events during pregnancy, such as maternal illness and the use of androgens, synthetic progestins, and other drugs.

Objective

Physical Examination

The physical examination should address two issues. First, is the size of the phallus adequate for eventual male sexual function? Second, are there physical findings that suggest the diagnosis?

The average penile length (stretched length along the dorsum) of the term male infant is 3.5 ± 0.4 cm. Dimensions of length and width less than 2 × 0.9 cm raise concern of the adequacy of the phallus for future male sexual function. Dimensions less than 1.5 × 0.7 cm raise grave concern. Dimensions for premature male infants are provided by Donahoe and Crawford (1986).

Many of the abnormal physical findings associated with ambiguous genitalia are described under Criteria for Diagnosis. Findings that provide clues to the underlying diagnosis are given in Table 9-27-2. Patients with congenital adrenal hyperplasia may develop signs of dehydration, hypotension, and salt-wasting crisis during the first weeks of life. They may have hyperpigmentation due to elevated levels of adrenocorticotropic hormone. Virilized 46,XX females with congenital adrenal hyperplasia have symmetric external genitalia and gonads are not palpable in the scrotum or labioscrotal folds.

Patients with mixed gonadal dysgenesis have a palpable inguinal or scrotal gonad and asymmetric labioscrotal folds 50% of the time. Features of Turner's syndrome occur in two thirds of patients. Patients with true hermaphroditism have a palpable ovotestis, with a firm ovar-

ian end and a soft testicular end, 30% of the time. Gonadal asymmetry is frequent, with a unilaterally palpable gonad (ovotestis or testis) in 50%, bilaterally palpable gonads in 10%, and intraabdominal gonads in 40%.

Routine Laboratory Abnormalities

The routine laboratory studies are normal except in infants with salt-wasting congenital adrenal hyperplasia. These infants develop hyperkalemia, hyponatremia, and acidosis as they approach adrenal crisis. The electrocardiogram may reveal evidence of hyperkalemia in the acutely ill child before the blood chemistry results are available.

PLANS
Diagnostic
Differential Diagnosis

The large number of disorders causing ambiguous genitalia can be grouped into three categories: virilization of the 46,XX female (60%), undermasculinization of the 46, XY child (30%), and ambiguous genitalia with abnormal karyotype (45,X or sex chromosome mosaicism, 10%) (Table 9-27-1).

Diagnostic Options

The tests that are useful in the differential diagnosis of ambiguous genitalia are provided in Table 9-27-1. Several algorithms for the use of these tests are given in the chapters by Donahoe and Crawford (1986), Forest (1995), Grumbach and Conte (1992), and Migeon et al. (1994). The author's recommended approach is given below.

Recommended Approach

Whenever possible, the evaluation should be guided by physicians experienced in this condition. This will usually involve a pediatric endocrinologist and a pediatric urologist. The goals of evaluation are to arrive at a working diagnosis that will permit early sex assignment, to determine whether or not the individual has salt-wasting congenital adrenal hyperplasia, and to establish a definitive diagnosis in those patients in whom this is possible with available methods.

Sex Assignment. The most important single test is the karyotype. It cannot be obtained immediately, and thus a buccal smear and test for Y fluorescence are done for preliminary information. The buccal smear is used to determine the frequency of Barr chromatin bodies, which indicate the presence of a second X chromosome. Y fluorescence, if present, indicates that the patient carries a Y chromosome.

The patient with the normal female complement of chromatin bodies and no Y fluorescence will usually have a 46,XX karyotype. If such a patient lacks palpable gonads, the diagnosis will usually be 21-hydroxylase deficiency. A single palpable gonad, especially if firm at one pole and soft at the other, suggests true hermaphroditism. Regardless of the

TABLE 9–27–1. DIFFERENTIAL DIAGNOSIS OF DISORDERS CAUSING AMBIGUOUS GENITALIA

Disorder	Frequency (%)*	Test or Procedure	Preferred Sex Assignment
Virilization of 46,XX female	60	Karyotype	Female
Congenital adrenal hyperplasia	44	Urinary 17-ketosteroids	
21-Hydroxylase deficiency	40	Plasma 17-hydroxyprogesterone	
11-Hydroxylase deficiency	3	Plasma 11-deoxycortisol	
3β-HSD deficiency	1	Plasma 17-hydroxypregnenolone	
True hermaphroditism†	1	Urethrogram, ultrasound or MRI, gonadal biopsy	
Maternal virilizing disorder	Rare	Maternal plasma testosterone	
Maternal ingestion of androgens	15*	History	
Nonhormonal embryogenic defect	Rare		
Undermasculinization of 46,XY child	30	Karyotype	Depends on phallus size
Abnormal gonadal differentiation	20	hCG test	
Testicular regression syndrome‡	Rare		
Mixed gonadal dysgenesis§	5	Urethrogram, ultrasound or MRI, gonadal biopsy	Female
True hermaphroditism†	Rare	Urethrogram, ultrasound or MRI, gonadal biopsy	
Leydig cell agenesis	Rare	Gonadal biopsy	
Idiopathic	15		
Testosterone biosynthetic defect	3	hCG test	
20,22-Desmolase deficiency	Rare	Deficiency of all steroid hormones	
3β-HSD deficiency	1	Plasma 17-hydroxypregnenolone	
17-Hydroxylase deficiency	Rare	Plasma progesterone	
17,20-Desmolase deficiency	1	Plasma 17-hydroxyprogesterone	
17-Ketosteroid reductase deficiency	1	Plasma androstenedione	
Defective tissue metabolism of testosterone	1	hCG test, 5α-reductase assay in skin fibroblasts	
5α-Reductase deficiency			
Tissue resistance to androgen	5	Androgen receptor assay in fibroblasts; response to testosterone administration	Female
Severe (testicular feminization and its variant forms)			
Partial (Reifenstein's syndrome and its variants)			
Drug-induced interference with dihydrotestosterone synthesis or action‖	NA	History	
Deficient testicular stimulation due to hypopituitarism or isolated gonadotropin deficiency (microphallus)	NA	Tests of thyroid, adrenal, growth hormone (see text)	Male
Nonhormonal embryogenic defect	1		
Ambiguous genitalia and abnormal karyotype	10	Karyotype	
Mixed gonadal dysgenesis§	9	Urethrogram, ultrasound or MRI, gonadal biopsy	Female
True Hermaphroditism†	1	Urethrogram, ultrasound or MRI, gonadal biopsy	

3β-HSD, 3β-hydroxysteroid dehydrogenase Δ^5, Δ^4-isomerase; MRI, magnetic resonance imaging; hCG, human chorionic gonadotropin; NA, not available
*Data primarily from the series of Wilkins (1965) and of Forest et al. (1979). The current incidence of maternal ingestion of androgens is likely to be lower owing to increased recognition of the virilizing potential of synthetic progestins.
†The gonads in true hermaphroditism contain, by definition, both ovarian and testicular tissue, usually in an asymmetric distribution such as ovary and testis (30%), ovary and ovotestis (30%), or ovotestis and testis (10%). In addition to apparently normal 46,XX (57%) or 46,XY (12%) karyotypes, individuals with true hermaphroditism may have mosaic karyotypes (31%) such as 46,XX/46,XY; 46,XX/47,XXY; 46,XY/47,XXY; 45,X/46,XY; and 45,X/47,XXY.
‡Unexplained fetal disappearance of testicular tissue ("vanishing testis syndrome") after masculinization of the external genitalia has begun.
§The gonads in mixed gonadal dysgenesis usually develop asymmetrically as a dysgenetic testis and a streak gonad (70%). Either the streak or testis may be replaced by gonadoblastoma. Normal ovarian tissue is not present. Variants include bilateral dysgenetic testes or bilateral streak gonads containing clumps of Leydig cells. In addition to apparently normal 46,XY karyotype (30%), the karyotype may be 45,X (15%) or mosaic (55%), such as 45,X/46,XY; 45,X/47,XXY; or 45,X/46,XY/46,XX. The frequent presence of a 45,X cell line gives rise to features of Turner's syndrome in about two thirds of cases.
‖Drugs known or suspected of interfering with dihydrotestosterone synthesis or action include synthetic progestins (medroxyprogesterone, norethisterone, hydroxyprogesterone caproate); antiandrogens (spironolactone, cimetidine, cyproterone acetate, flutamide); steroid synthesis inhibitors (ketoconazole, aminoglutethimide, trilostane); and anticonvulsants (phenytoin).

appearance of the external genitalia, all 46,XX newborns should be reared as females because of their potential for normal female sexual function, including reproduction. A possible exception is the 46,XX true hermaphrodite with male external genitalia and bilateral scrotal gonads. The testes in true hermaphrodites, however, invariably have abnormalities of the seminiferous tubules, and fertility has been observed only in individuals reared as females.

The chromatin-negative newborn with ambiguous genitalia may have a 45,X; 46,XY; or mosaic karyotype. A unilateral palpable gonad with asymmetric labioscrotal folds suggests mixed gonadal dysgenesis or true hermaphroditism. Patients with either of these disorders usually have a palpable uterus on rectal examination, whereas undermasculinized 46,XY patients with other disorders usually lack müllerian duct derivatives. When the features of Turner's syndrome are present, the diagnosis is almost certain to be mixed gonadal dysgenesis. Such individuals should be reared as females regardless of the external genitalia

because the short stature often associated with this diagnosis will be relatively less severe in a female.

The chromatin-negative, Y-fluorescence-positive newborn with bilateral inguinal or scrotal gonads will usually have a 46,XY karyotype and a gonadal or target cell defect resulting in undermasculinization. Male sex assignment in such patients should be made only when it appears certain that the penis will be adequate for sexual intercourse. Many clinicians have commented that the most tragic outcome in the management of ambiguous genitalia is the individual reared as a male in whom construction of a functional penis proves impossible.

Many chromatin-negative newborns will have an inadequate phallus and should receive a female sex assignment. Some will have a phallus of normal male size with minimal hypospadias and should be assigned as males.

The greatest difficulty in early sex assignment arises in the newborn with the well-formed microphallus or a phallus of borderline size with

TABLE 9-27-2. ABNORMAL PHYSICAL FINDINGS OF POTENTIAL DIAGNOSTIC VALUE IN THE CHILD WITH AMBIGUOUS GENITALIA, GROUPED ACCORDING TO KARYOTYPE

Finding	Associated diagnosis
46,XX karyotype	
Symmetric male external genitalia with bilateral cryptorchidism	Congenital adrenal hyperplasia (usually 21-hydroxylase deficiency)
Dehydration, hypotensive crisis	Congenital adrenal hyperplasia
Hypermelanotic skin around nipples, genitalia, and midline abdominal raphe	Congenital adrenal hyperplasia
Asymmetric labioscrotal folds with palpable gonad or ovotestis*	True hermaphroditism
Gastrointestinal or urinary tract anomaly	Nonhormonal embryogenic defect
46,XY karyotype	
Palpable ovotestis*	True hermaphroditism
Asymmetric labioscrotal folds	Mixed gonadal dysgenesis or true hermaphroditism
Dehydration, salt-wasting crisis	3β-HSD deficiency or 20,22-desmolase deficiency
Gastrointestinal or urinary tract anomaly	Nonhormonal embryogenic defect
45,X/46,XY and other mosaic karyotypes	
Features of Turner's syndrome†	Mixed gonadal dysgenesis
Abdominal mass	Mixed gonadal dysgenesis with gonadoblastoma
Palpable ovotestis*	True hermaphroditism

3β-HSD, 3β-hydroxysteroid dehydrogenase/Δ^5, Δ^4-isomerase.

*A characteristic feature of approximately 80% of ovotestes is an end-to-end arrangement with a firm ovarian portion and a soft testicular portion.

†Short stature, congenital lymphedema of the dorsa of the hands and feet (Bonnevie–Ullrich syndrome), peculiar facies with mandibulofacial disproportion and underdevelopment of the chin, low-set ears, low hairline, webbing of the neck, shield-like chest with widely spaced nipples, pigmented nevi, cubitus valgus, shortening of the fourth metacarpal, and coarctation of the aorta.

TABLE 9-27-3. EXAMPLES OF NONHORMONAL EMBRYOGENIC DEFECTS ASSOCIATED WITH GENITAL ABNORMALITIES

Bifid penis with bladder extrophy
Penoscrotal transposition
Penile agenesis and imperforate anus
46,XY infants with Wilms' tumor, hypertension, and renal disease
46,XX infants with renal agenesis
46,XX infants with cryptophthalmos syndrome

significant hypospadias. Individuals who have these phenotypes because of androgen resistance are likely to do poorly as males, with feminization at puberty and inadequate growth of the phallus. Unfortunately, no rapid means to exclude androgen resistance is available, although research efforts to achieve this are underway. Thus, some physicians choose to recommend female assignment in such children, which ensures the potential for adult sexual function. Other physicians defer sex assignment until after evaluating the response to testosterone enanthate in oil (100mg/m^2 IM) monthly for three doses (normal increase in penile length, 2.0 ± 0.6 cm [SD]). Failure of the penis to lengthen significantly suggests that it lacks the capacity for normal growth and that a female sex assignment should be recommended.

A well-formed microphallus may result from inadequate stimulation of a normally differentiated testis owing to panhypopituitarism or isolated hypogonadotropic hypogonadism. This condition responds well to androgen administration during the first months of life. A male sex assignment should be made in such cases. Diagnosis of panhypopituitarism can be made by measuring the basal levels of total and free serum thyroxine, the cortisol level 60 minutes after intravenous or intramuscular administration of 0.25 mg/m^2 cosyntropin (Cortosyn)(normal, >18 μg/dL), and the growth hormone response to provocative stimuli such as levodopa or arginine-insulin infusion. The neonatal diagnosis of isolated hypogonadotropic hypogonadism (Kallmann's syndrome) cannot be established with certainty. In the setting of microphallus, however, the diagnosis is suggested by a positive family history, associated midline defects (such as cleft lip, cleft palate, and anosmia), or absence of the normal neonatal rise in gonadotropin and testosterone levels at 3 to 8 months of age.

Nonhormonal defects in embryogenesis may give rise to genital abnormalities (Table 9-27-3). Such defects are recognized by their associated anomalies or by a genital appearance inconsistent with partial virilization along the normal male pattern. Further information about these disorders can be found in the articles by Grumbach and Conte (1992), Migeon et al. (1994), and Forest (1995). As in other children with ambiguous genitalia, male sex assignment should be made only when it appears certain that the penis will be adequate for sexual intercourse.

Screening for Salt-Wasting Congenital Adrenal Hyperplasia. After a decision regarding the sex of rearing has been reached (or, in some cases, deferred), the physician should determine whether or not the patient has salt-wasting congenital adrenal hyperplasia. The child should be monitored for signs of dehydration, hypotension, and the electrolyte abnormalities of adrenal insufficiency (hyperkalemia, hyponatremia, and acidosis). A single urine specimen should be sent for urinary 17-ketosteroid and creatinine determinations, and the 24-hour 17-ketosteroid excretion should be calculated assuming a daily creatinine excretion of 12.5 mg/kg of body weight in the neonate. 17-Ketosteroid levels below 0.5 mg/d generally exclude congenital adrenal hyperplasia (except for the rare case of 20,22-desmolase deficiency), levels from 0.5 to 2.5 mg/d are indeterminate, and levels above 2.5 mg/d suggest the diagnosis. Plasma measurements are more definitive and should be obtained, but the results are likely to take longer (Table 9-27-1). If the child is first evaluated after hydrocortisone treatment has been started for adrenal crisis, the diagnosis can still be made within several days, without discontinuing treatment, by measuring the appropriate plasma steroids (Table 9-27-1, Figure 9-27-2) 60 minutes after administering cosyntropin, 0.25 mg/m^2 intramuscularly or intravenously.

Definitive Diagnosis. After addressing the issues of sex of rearing and the possibility of life-threatening adrenal insufficiency, the physician should pursue a definitive diagnosis. For the 46,XX patient, tests already outlined will usually indicate the diagnosis of 21-hydroxylase deficiency. If congenital adrenal hyperplasia is excluded, and if there is no evidence of maternal source of androgen or of a nonhormonal embryogenic defect, the diagnosis is likely to be true hermaphroditism. A urethrogram showing a unicornuate uterus would support the diagnosis, as a testis or ovotestis will usually cause regression of the adjacent müllerian duct. Similar information can be obtained noninvasively by magnetic resonance imaging. Final diagnosis requires the demonstration of both ovarian and testicular tissue by gonadal biopsy, which should be done at the time of correction of the external genitalia (see Plans, Therapeutic).

The undermasculinized 46,XY newborn should receive a human chorionic gonadotropin (Pregnyl) stimulation test with measurement of basal and stimulated levels of testosterone, dihydrotestosterone, and their precursors (Table 9-27-1, Figure 9-27-2). An absent response of testosterone and its precursors in the setting of low adrenal steroid levels and salt-wasting indicates 20,22-desmolase deficiency. An absent response of testosterone and its precursors with normal adrenal function suggests testicular regression syndrome or Leydig cell agenesis. A deficient testosterone response with a proportionate decrease in precursor responses suggests mixed gonadal dysgenesis (or its variant forms), Leydig cell hypoplasia, or true hermaphroditism (with a poorly developed testicular component). A normal or deficient testosterone response with an elevated precursor response suggests an enzymatic block immediately following the elevated precursor. An elevated testosterone:dihydrotestosterone ratio suggests 5α-reductase deficiency. A normal response of testosterone and its precursors is consistent with true hermaphroditism, androgen resistance, or idiopathic 46,XY undermasculinization.

Several different protocols for human chorionic gonadotropin testing are in use (Parks, 1982; Grumbach and Conte, 1992; Forest, 1995). To our knowledge, normal values for testosterone and precursor responses in newborns have not been established for any of the different tests. We prefer the protocol of Forest et al. (1979), for which normal values have been published for children aged 6 months to 16 years. Human chorionic gonadotropin, 1500 IU, is administered intramuscularly every 48 hours for seven doses, with a blood sample taken before the first injection and 24 hours after the last injection.

When access to research measurements of 5α-reductase activity or androgen receptors can be achieved, genital skin should be obtained for fibroblast culture by punch biopsy or during surgical correction of the genitalia. Androgen receptors can be assessed in terms of stability, concentration, affinity, and nuclear binding. A defect in any of these parameters provides evidence for androgen resistance. Several research laboratories can now also identify the precise mutation of the androgen receptor gene that causes the androgen resistance.

A sizable proportion of undermasculinized 46,XY children will have normal results in all the preceding tests. Some of these children have been found to have abnormal testicular biopsies with the Sertoli cell only or spermatogenic arrest pattern. It has been postulated that such children may have subtle abnormalities of gonadal differentiation that led to a delay in fetal testosterone secretion. Such a delay could produce failure to virilize the external genitalia normally during the critical time period (before 12 weeks of gestation) when full masculinization can be achieved. This could explain ambiguous genitalia despite apparently normal testosterone synthesis and action when tested in childhood.

Therapeutic

Therapeutic Options

Therapy usually requires both medical and surgical treatment, depending on the specific diagnosis. Although the details of treatment vary slightly at different centers, the approach outlined below reflects the major conceptual aspects of treatment for this complex disorder.

Recommended Approach

Treatment depends on the diagnosis. Drug treatment of children with intersex disorders has the objectives of correcting adrenal insufficiency and suppressing adrenal androgen secretion in congenital adrenal hyperplasia, enlarging small penises in children who are to be reared as males, and ensuring appropriate secondary sexual development at puberty. The medical treatment of congenital adrenal hyperplasia is described in Chapter 9–8. The emergency treatment of salt-wasting crisis in congenital adrenal hyperplasia is identical to the treatment of acute adrenal insufficiency of any cause (see Chapter 9–11).

To enlarge the phallus, testosterone enanthate in oil (Delatestryl), 100 mg/m^2, is administered intramuscularly every 3 to 4 weeks. Treatment for 3 to 6 months is usually sufficient, but treatment may be continued longer or readministered if necessary. Responsiveness of the penis to testosterone appears to be greatest early in life, and thus the greatest benefit from treatment is obtained with early use.

To induce feminization at puberty in girls who have undergone gonadectomy because of the risk of gonadal malignancy or to prevent pubertal virilization, we initially administer ethinyl estradiol (Estinyl), 5 µg orally daily, for 1 to 2 years beginning at about age 11. This causes a puberal growth spurt without undue bone age acceleration and thus helps to optimize height. This is particularly important in short girls with mixed gonadal dysgenesis. Subsequently, the dose of ethinyl estradiol is increased to 10 µg daily for 1 year, and then it is further increased by 10 µg/d until significant breakthrough bleeding occurs. At this point, cyclic withdrawal bleeding is induced by administering ethinyl estradiol for the first 25 days of each month and by adding medroxyprogesterone acetate (Provera), 10 mg orally daily, from days 16 to 25. One may also induce cyclic withdrawal bleeding by switching to a standard oral contraceptive preparation such as ethinyl estradiol/norethindrone (Ortho-Norvum 7/7/7 or 10/11).

To induce pubertal masculinization in boys, testosterone enanthate in oil (Delatestryl), 50 mg, is administered intramuscularly every 3 to 4 weeks for 6 months. The dose is then increased gradually to a full replacement level of 200 mg every 2 weeks.

The side effects of testosterone administration to induce penile growth in the newborn period include increased growth rate and bone age advancement, with a resultant decline in adult height. Approxi-

mately 1 in. of adult height will be lost for each year of treatment before the normal age of puberty. This is a secondary issue compared with achieving the potential for normal adult sexual function. Other unwanted potential effects at this age include acne, spontaneous erections, deepening of the voice, gynecomastia, and pubic, axillary, and facial hair growth. Long-term testosterone therapy in adults may have the adverse effect of urethral obstruction due to benign prostatic hypertrophy. The side effects of oral estrogen therapy are discussed in Chapters 9–24 and 10–3.

Surgical treatment of children with ambiguous genitalia is undertaken to correct the external genitalia along the male or female pattern, to establish definitively the diagnosis of true hermaphroditism or of mixed gonadal dysgenesis, and to remove Y-chromosome-containing intraabdominal gonads that have a high probability of malignant degeneration.

The procedure to reconstruct the external genitalia along female lines consists of clitoral recession, vaginoplasty, and labioscrotal reduction. The surgical approach is similar regardless of diagnosis. The reconstruction is usually done between 3 and 6 months of age. It can be done in the newborn period, however, when circumstances suggest that the child might otherwise be rejected. Depending on the position at which the vagina enters the urogenital sinus and the degree of vaginal development, vaginoplasty may have to be deferred until 2 years of age or until late adolescence. Reconstruction along male lines is also undertaken as early as possible, frequently after testosterone treatment to enlarge the penis.

Gonadal biopsy for diagnosis of true hermaphroditism or of mixed gonadal dysgenesis should be done at the time of repair of the external genitalia. True hermaphrodites to be reared as females should undergo removal of all testicular tissue, using frozen sections to monitor the removal of the testicular portion of ovotestes. All individuals bearing a Y-containing cell line and all 46,XX true hermaphrodites should undergo orchiopexy or removal of all intraabdominal gonads because of the risk of malignancy. Gonads brought into the scrotum should be followed carefully for malignancy. The optimum time for gonadectomy is probably infancy in all diagnostic groups. Some physicians, however, prefer to defer gonadectomy in patients with androgen resistance until after feminization at puberty. Donahoe and Crawford (1986) provide an excellent discussion of the surgical management of ambiguous genitalia.

All parents of the child with ambiguous genitalia should be told the following: Your child has a problem involving the sex organs. The formation of the sex organs is not yet finished. This is a situation that has happened to other children. Experience has shown that the formation of the sex organs can be completed and that your child will be able to have normal adult sexual function. The first step in this process will be to examine your child carefully and to obtain tests that will help us to understand why the sex organs are unfinished. These tests will permit us to determine in which direction, male or female, the sex organs should be finished. These tests often take about 2 weeks. During this time, it usually is easiest to delay announcement of the birth except to those close relatives in whom you can confide.

Recognition and communication of the problem will ordinarily be followed by expert consultation to guide the subsequent diagnostic evaluation and management. It is helpful to designate one experienced individual as the principal source of information for the parents. The parents will ordinarily need medical explanations, assisted by anatomic diagrams, that are suitable to their education and intellectual capacity. Until sufficient information for sex assignment is available, discussions should use neutral language such as sex organ (rather than penis or clitoris), genital folds (rather than scrotum or labia), and gonads. Such language is also important in explaining diagnostic results. Thus the 46,XY infant with androgen resistance, who is to be reared as a girl, should be described as having a gonad (not testis) that is not properly developed and that must be removed because of a risk of malignancy.

In conveying diagnostic information, we also avoid such terms as *true hermaphroditism* and *pseudohermaphroditism*. We would describe a girl with true hermaphroditism as having a form of abnormal gonadal formation (or gonadal dysgenesis) in which improperly developed portions of the ovary must be removed because of their tendency to cause virilization and to undergo malignant degeneration.

No single explanation, however, will prove satisfactory to all parents. Medically sophisticated parents may seek to know the full details of the chromosomal and other testing to assure themselves of the correctness of the decisions involving their child. In this situation it may be useful to emphasize that gender identity is entirely determined by the appearance of the external genitalia and the resultant sex of rearing. Concern may be expressed that the 46,XY individual has male chromosomes and that the true sex is male. We emphasize that the Y chromosome is only one element of male differentiation and that regardless of the chromosomes in a cell, the cell cannot be considered authentically male if it cannot function in the male fashion. Either the Y chromosome lacks essential male elements or their expression is blocked by the absence of other genes necessary for normal male development. In either case, the cell is not authentically male.

Parents should be informed that infertility is to be expected, except in 46,XX females and in rare true hermaphrodites. They will need considerable advice concerning whether to attempt to conceal the fact that there was a problem (usually inadvisable); what to tell siblings, other family members, friends, co-workers, and later the child; and how to handle the issue of others seeing the external genitalia prior to repair.

FOLLOW-UP

Follow-up for congenital adrenal hyperplasia should be every 2 to 3 months during the first 2 years of life and at least every 6 months until adult height is attained. Follow-up for the other diagnoses must be as frequent as is needed to complete the diagnostic evaluation, to assist the parents in resolving their many concerns, and to plan and follow the surgical correction. Once correction of the external genitalia has been completed, follow-up until subsequent surgery (vaginoplasty or further penoscrotal revision, if needed) should involve primarily the provision of accurate and appropriate information. The starting point in providing information to the child is to inquire. "What do you understand about your medical condition?" This may open the way to clearing up harmful misunderstandings for which both parent and child are at risk.

Parents of children receiving hydrocortisone treatment for 21-hydroxylase deficiency should consult the physician for signs of either inadequate or excessive hydrocortisone dose. Inadequate hydrocortisone leads to poor adrenal suppression, increased adrenal androgen, increased growth rate, and progressive virilization. Excessive hydrocortisone leads to weight gain, decreased growth rate, and other signs of Cushing's syndrome.

DISCUSSION
Prevalence and Incidence

The incidence of classic 21-hydroxylase deficiency is 1 in 14,000 Caucasian births.

The incidence of hypospadias in males has been estimated at 1 to 8 per 1000 male births. Approximately 90 percent of cases are coronal hypospadias. An endocrine cause can be found in 5 to 15% of cases. The remainder must currently be classified as nonhormonal embryogenic defects. (These cases have not been included in the frequency estimates of Table 9–27–1, however, because they far outnumber the more serious cases in which there are associated anomalies.)

The incidence of the severe form of androgen resistance (testicular feminization and its variants), which leads to a female sex of rearing, is estimated at 1 in 20,000 to 64,000 male births.

Related Basic Science
Genetics

The genetics of ambiguous genitalia depend on the underlying diagnosis. Congenital adrenal hyperplasia, defects of dihydrotestosterone synthesis, and Leydig cell hypoplasia are autosomal recessive disorders. The Denys–Drash syndrome (nephropathy, genital abnormalities, and Wilms' tumor), which is a nonhormonal embryogenic defect, results from autosomal dominant mutations of the Wilms' tumor gene. Androgen resistance is an X-linked disorder. Sex chromosome mosaicism leading to mixed gonadal dysgenesis or true hermaphroditism is sporadic.

Altered Molecular Biology

Several different molecular events give rise to adrenal 21-hydroxylase deficiency, including deletions, gene conversion events, and missense and nonsense point mutations. The frequency of defects involving the 21-hydroxylase gene results from a nearby pseudogene that arose through an ancestral gene duplication. Meiotic pairing and recombination between the gene and pseudogene can delete portions of the active gene or can incorporate mutations from the inactive pseudogene (gene conversion).

Leydig cell hypoplasia results from loss-of-function missense or nonsense mutations in the gene encoding the luteinizing hormone receptor.

Androgen resistance usually results from missense mutations, nonsense mutations, or deletions involving the androgen receptor. Depending on their location, mutations in the androgen receptor may impair ligand binding, nuclear localization, DNA binding, receptor dimerization, or transcriptional activation.

Most defects of dihydrotestosterone synthesis result from missense, nonsense, or splice site mutations in the respective gene. As with congenital adrenal hyperplasia, most patients are compound heterozygotes for different mutations, except when there is consanguinity within the family; however, patients with cholesterol 20,22-desmolase deficiency do not have a structural defect in this gene. Rather the defect appears to reside in steroidogenic acute regulatory protein, which delivers cholesterol to the enzyme by transporting it across the external mitochondrial membrane.

Physiologic Derangement

Classic 21-hydroxylase deficiency impairs aldosterone and cortisol synthesis, leading to increased adrenocorticotropin production and adrenal hyperplasia in an attempt to overcome the enzymatic defect. The accumulation of the 21-hydroxylase precursor, 17-hydroxyprogesterone, spills into the androgen pathway, causing virilization. Approximately two thirds of patients have a sufficiently severe block that they will develop clinically apparent salt wasting if not treated (21-hydroxylase activity less than 1% of normal). The remaining one third have a milder enzyme deficiency that causes virilization without clinically apparent salt wasting (21-hydroxylase activity approximately 2% of normal).

Cholesterol 20,22-desmolase deficiency and 3β-hydroxysteroid dehydrogenase deficiency also produce salt wasting and may lead to death from adrenal crisis. 11-Hydroxylase deficiency, by contrast, may produce salt wasting in infancy, when the infant is most vulnerable to salt loss, but hypertension later in childhood, due to accumulation of 11-deoxycorticosterone. 17-Hydroxylase deficiency also causes accumulation of 11-deoxycorticosterone, leading to hypertension.

3β-hydroxysteroid dehydrogenase deficiency has the unique feature of causing ambiguous genitalia in both sexes. Boys are undermasculinized as a result of impaired gonadal testosterone production at the critical time for male genital development. Girls are masculinized, however, because of hepatic and peripheral production of testosterone, by a distinct 3β-hydroxysteroid dehydrogenase gene, from the elevated circulating levels of the adrenal precursors dehydroepiandrosterone and androstenediol. The apparent paradox of masculinization of girls and undermasculinization of boys is explained by the fact that the same disorder can raise the testosterone levels of girls while lowering the testosterone level of boys. Additionally, the hepatic gene for 3β-hydroxysteroid dehydrogenase may be expressed later in fetal life than the adrenal and gonadal gene, so that its contribution to circulating androgen levels may occur after the critical period for full masculinization of the male fetus.

The altered anatomy of these disorders can be summarized as follows: First, 46,XX females become virilized when androgens from the fetal adrenal gland (congenital adrenal hyperplasia), an ovotestis or testis (true hermaphroditism), or the mother cause the external genitalia to differentiate along the male pattern (Figure 9–27–1, 9–27–2; Table 9–27–1). As müllerian regression in the male is under the control of a distinct testicular hormone (müllerian inhibiting factor), the internal genital ducts are those of a normal female (except for the true hermaphrodite, in whom there may be müllerian regression adjacent to the testis or ovotestis). Second, newborns with a 46,XY cell line may fail to masculinize normally because of interference with gonadal formation, dihydrotestosterone synthesis, or androgen action (Figures 9–27–1, 9–27–2; Table 9–27–1). Children with idiopathic 46,XY undermasculinization are currently thought to have experienced a delay in gonadal differentiation that led to inadequate testosterone synthesis during the critical period (less than 12 weeks' gestation) in which full masculinization of the external genitalia can be achieved. Third, children of either sex may develop ambiguous genitalia as a result of a nonhormonal embryogenic defect.

Natural History and Its Modification with Treatment

Properly managed, the morbidity of ambiguous genitalia should be limited to adult short stature in mixed gonadal dysgenesis and congenital adrenal hyperplasia and the surgical morbidity associated with correction of the genitalia. Improperly managed, morbidity may include multiple unsuccessful repairs of the external genitalia, confused gender identity, and low self-esteem. Over- or undertreatment of 21-hydroxylase deficiency may yield Cushing's syndrome on the one hand or progressive virilization and adrenal crisis on the other. Failure to perform timely removal of intraabdominal Y-chromosome-bearing gonads may lead to gonadal malignancy.

Mortality in children with ambiguous genitalia may result from salt-wasting crisis in congenital adrenal hyperplasia or from gonadoblastoma (which may be present at birth) and germinoma in disorders associated with intraabdominal Y-chromosome-bearing gonad. The deficiency of males in series of patients with congenital adrenal hyperplasia and the history of neonatal deaths consistent with salt-losing crisis in the older siblings of affected patients suggest that up to 20% of patients with salt-losing congenital adrenal hyperplasia die of undiagnosed adrenal insufficiency during the neonatal period. Newborn screening programs, such as those in Japan and the states of Alaska, Washington, Texas, and Illinois, can prevent such deaths.

Prevention

The major means of preventing ambiguous genitalia is avoidance of drugs during pregnancy, particularly at 8 to 12 weeks of gestation, when masculinization of the external genitalia normally occurs. Drugs to avoid, if possible, include synthetic progestins (medroxyprogesterone, norethisterone, hydroxyprogesterone caproate); androgenic or anabolic steroids (oxandrolone, fluoxymesterone, methyltestosterone); antiandrogens (cyproterone acetate, spironolactone, cimetidine, flutamide); steroid synthesis inhibitors (ketoconazole, aminoglutethimide, trilostane); and anticonvulsants (phenytoin).

Mothers who are at risk of having girls with ambiguous genitalia because of 21-hydroxylase deficiency can prevent virilization of female fetuses by taking dexamethasone (Decadron), 20 μg/kg body weight orally daily (in 3 doses) throughout pregnancy to suppress the fetal adrenal gland. Treatment must be started by 7 weeks of fetal life. Dexamethasone should be used in preference to other glucocorticoids because of its superior ability to cross the placenta. To be effective, treatment must be started before it can be known whether the child is a female (males are not at risk for ambiguous genitalia in 21-hydroxylase deficiency) and whether he or she has 21-hydroxylase deficiency. On the average, therefore, eight fetuses (four males and four females) would have to be exposed to dexamethasone to treat one female fetus with homozygous 21-hydroxylase deficiency (assuming both parents are heterozygous).

Cost Containment

We recommend an organized approach to diagnosis, as outlined herein, in which testing is guided by the karyotype and physical examination. We also advocate that the surgical procedures be done by a surgeon with recognized expertise in the correction of ambiguous genitalia. The cost of travel to obtain such expertise will be minor compared with the costs consequent to an initial poor result.

REFERENCES

Donahoe PK, Crawford JD. Ambiguous genitalia in the newborn. In: Welch KJ, Randolph JG. Ravitch MM, et al., eds. Pediatric surgery. 4th ed. Chicago: Year Book Medical, 1986:1363.

Forest MG. Diagnosis and treatment of disorders of sexual development. In: DeGroot LJ, editor-in-chief. Endocrinology. 3rd ed. Philadelphia: Saunders, 1995:1901.

Forest MG, De Peretti E, David M, et al. Dosage de la testosterone et de ses precurseurs avant et apres test de stimulation par l'hCG dans 52 cas de pseudohermaphroditisme masculin: Apport au diagnostic etiologique. Pediatrics 1979;34:519.

Grumbach MM, Conte FA. Disorders of sexual differentiation. In: Wilson JD, Foster DW, eds. Textbook of endocrinology. 8th ed. Philadelphia: W.B. Saunders, 1992:933.

Migeon CJ, Berkovitz GD, Brown TR. Sexual differentiation and ambiguity. In: Kappy MS, Blizzard RM, Migeon CJ, eds. The diagnosis and treatment of endocrine disorders in childhood and adolescence. 4th ed. Springfield, IL: Charles C Thomas, 1994:577.

Parks JS. Intersex. In: Kaplan SA, ed. Clinical pediatric and adolescent endocrinology. Philadelphia: Saunders, 1982:327.

Wilkins L. The diagnosis and treatment of endocrine disorders in childhood and adolescence. 3rd ed. Springfield, IL: Charles C Thomas, 1965:297.

CHAPTER 9–28

Precocious Puberty

Gordon B. Cutler, Jr., M.D.

DEFINITION

Puberty is precocious when it begins before the age of 8 years in girls and before the age of 9 years in boys. The earliest sign of precocious puberty may be breast budding, pubic hair, or menarche in girls or genital enlargement in boys.

ETIOLOGY

The etiologies of precocious puberty, in order of decreasing frequency, are idiopathic, neoplastic, genetic, and factitious.

CRITERIA FOR DIAGNOSIS

Suggestive

The girl under 3 years of age with isolated breast development without a growth spurt or bone age advancement usually has premature thelarche, not precocious puberty. Similarly, the boy or girl with isolated pubic hair development without a growth spurt or bone age advancement may have premature adrenarche rather than precocious puberty. Both premature thelarche and premature adrenarche are benign disorders that do not affect skeletal growth or the subsequent onset of the normal pubertal mechanism.

The early appearance of both breasts and pubic hair in a girl or genital enlargement and pubic hair in a boy generally indicates that the child has precocious puberty.

Definitive

The preceding findings in association with a pubertal growth spurt (an approximate doubling of the prepubertal growth rate) and an advanced bone age constitute definitive evidence of precocious puberty.

CLINICAL MANIFESTATIONS

Subjective

A family history of neurofibromatosis, congenital adrenal hyperplasia, or familial male precocious puberty (an autosomal dominant disorder expressed only in boys) may suggest the diagnosis. Potential exogenous sources of sex steroids should be sought, such as oral contraceptive pills, estrogen-containing hair creams, meat from animals illegally treated with estrogen at the time of slaughter, family members involved in the manufacture of estrogens, and anabolic steroids used for the treatment of short stature.

The child with precocious puberty usually develops an adult body odor, with an increase in the perceived need to bathe or to use deodorants. The skin and hair often become more oily, leading to blackheads, acne, and more frequent shampooing. The parents may observe that the child is outgrowing his or her clothes more rapidly. Girls may develop a mucus-containing vaginal discharge that stains the underwear, which often occurs far in advance of menarche. Behavior may be normal or may be marked by moodiness and a withdrawal from usual activities. Boys may experience spontaneous erections (leading to nocturnal emissions or masturbation), increased muscle strength, and deepening of the voice. They may become more aggressive and less responsive to parental authority.

Objective

Physical Examination

The abnormal physical findings can be divided into those that are attributable to the increased sex steroid levels (Table 9–28–1), which would be normal if they occurred at an appropriate age, and those that are attributable to the underlying cause of the precocious puberty (Table 9–28–2).

The stage of breast, pubic hair, and genital development should be determined as described by Grumbach and Styne (1992). Stage I is prepubertal, stage V is adult, and stages II, III, and IV are intermediate degrees of development. The stage of pubertal development may have diagnostic value. For example, the breast development of premature thelarche rarely progresses beyond stage III. The stage of pubertal development also helps to predict subsequent events. Menarche, for example, occurs on average during stage IV (breast and pubic hair) in children with central precocious puberty. The average time spent in each intermediate stage is 1 year, although this varies considerably from individual to individual.

The physician should ask: Is the puberty appropriate for the sex of the child (isosexual precocious puberty), or is it appropriate for the opposite sex (contrasexual)? Contrasexual precocious puberty (feminization [stage III or more breast development] in a boy, or clitoromegaly

TABLE 9–28–1. PHYSICAL FINDINGS ATTRIBUTABLE TO INCREASED SEX STEROID LEVELS IN PRECOCIOUS PUBERTY

Girls	Boys	Both Sexes
Breast development	Testicular enlargement*	Pubic and axillary hair
Estrogenized vaginal mucosa	Penile enlargement	Increased height and weight
Uterine and/or ovarian enlargement	Muscular development	Oily skin, comedones, acne
	Facial and body hair	
	Deep voice	

*Testicular length of 2.5 cm or greater or testicular volume of 4 mL or greater.

TABLE 9–28–2. ABNORMAL PHYSICAL FINDINGS THAT HAVE POTENTIAL DIAGNOSTIC USEFULNESS IN PRECOCIOUS PUBERTY

Finding	Associated Diagnosis
Hypertension*	11-Hydroxylase deficiency or adrenal tumor
Hyperpigmented skin spots	McCune–Albright syndrome[†] or neurofibromatosis[‡]
Adrenal mass	Adrenocortical carcinoma
Ovarian mass	Ovarian tumor or McCune–Albright syndrome[§]
Testicular mass	Testicular tumor or adrenal rest tumor of the testis
Bone deformity	McCune–Albright syndrome
Neurologic abnormality	Central nervous system lesion

*Blood pressure must be elevated for height age, not chronologic age (to allow for the expected increase due to increased body size).
[†]The McCune–Albright syndrome is the triad of hyperpigmented skin spots, polyostotic fibrous dysplasia, and precocious puberty. The skin spots have irregular borders ("coast of Maine").
[‡]The spots have smooth borders ("coast of California")
[§]Patients with McCune–Albright syndrome frequently have large unilateral ovarian cysts (up to 4 cm in diameter), which may raise unwarranted concern of an ovarian malignancy.

and other signs of virilization in a girl) implies a peripheral mechanism, such as congenital adrenal hyperplasia or adrenal or gonadal tumor. Isosexual precocious puberty may arise from either a central or a peripheral mechanism.

Routine Laboratory Abnormalities

The routine laboratory studies are almost invariably normal. Hypokalemia may occur as the result of excess mineralocorticoid secretion in 11-hydroxylase deficiency or adrenal tumor. Hypernatremia or hyponatremia may result from diabetes insipidus or inappropriate antidiuretic hormone secretion associated with central nervous system lesions. An elevated cholesterol level is usually present in precocious puberty secondary to severe hypothyroidism. Tests of liver function may be abnormal in the event of primary (e.g., human chorionic gonadotropin-secreting hepatoblastoma) or metastatic hepatic tumor.

PLANS

Diagnostic

Differential Diagnosis

The diagnosis of precocious puberty is established by the clinical features described above in association with an advanced bone age (except in hypothyroidism or in other coexisting disorders that retard the bone age). Laboratory and radiologic procedures, however, are usually essential for appropriate differential diagnosis (Table 9–28–3).

Diagnostic Options

Some of the forms of premature sexual development, such as premature thelarche and premature adrenarche, are benign and either nonprogressive or slowly progressive. Among girls with central precocious puberty, the most common etiology is idiopathic. Thus, there is room for clinical judgment regarding the pace and extent of the diagnostic evaluation, particularly when the presumptive diagnosis can be established by the clinical features.

Recommended Approach

If the clinical features are consistent with premature thelarche (isolated breast development in a young girl), and if there are no additional features suggesting central or peripheral precocious puberty, it is appropriate to follow the patient initially at intervals of 3 to 6 months. If the bone age becomes advanced during follow-up or if other signs of puberty develop, a more extensive evaluation must be undertaken.

In the case of isolated pubic hair development, the presumed adrenal source of androgen may be confirmed by measuring plasma dehydroepiandrosterone sulfate, which should be distinctly elevated for age but within the range observed during normal adrenarche. To exclude

TABLE 9–28–3. DIFFERENTIAL DIAGNOSIS OF PREMATURE SEXUAL DEVELOPMENT

Disorder	Test or Procedure
Premature thelarche	
Premature adrenarche	Plasma DHEAS
Central precocious puberty	Plasma luteinizing hormone, follicle-stimulating hormone*
Idiopathic	
Central nervous system lesion	Head CT or MRI scan
Secondary to peripheral precocious puberty	
Peripheral precocious puberty	
Adrenal	
21-Hydroxylase deficiency†	Plasma 17-hydroxyprogesterone
11-Hydroxylase deficiency‡	Plasma 11-deoxycortisol
Tumor	Sonogram or CT scan
Gonadal	
McCune–Albright syndrome	Skeletal survey or bone scan
Familial male	
Tumor	Sonogram
Ectopic human chorionic gonadotropin-secreting neoplasm	Plasma human chorionic gonadotropin
Hypothyroidism	Plasma thyroxine, thyroid-stimulating hormone
Massive extraglandular aromatization	Plasma estradiol, estrone
Primary cortisol resistance	Urine free cortisol
Factitious	

DHEAS, dehydroepiandrosterone sulfate; CT, computed tomography; MRI, magnetic resonance imaging.

*These should be measured basally and at 30, 60, and 90 minutes after administering luteinizing hormone-releasing hormone (100 μg IV).

†The most common form of congenital adrenal hyperplasia.

‡The second most common form of congenital adrenal hyperplasia.

definitively the diagnosis of nonclassic (or late-onset) 21-hydroxylase deficiency, which may also present clinically as isolated pubic hair development, one may measure the plasma 17-hydroxyprogesterone level 30 minutes after intravenous administration of 0.25 mg cosyntropin (α1–24-corticotropin [Cortrosyn], synthetic adrenocorticotropic hormone). A 17-hydroxyprogesterone level that exceeds the highest level observed in heterozygous carriers of 21-hydroxylase deficiency (>1500 ng/dL) strongly suggests the diagnosis of homozygous 21-hydroxylase deficiency. This diagnosis is confirmed when suppression of 17-hydroxyprogesterone by exogenous glucocorticoid excludes the possibility of adrenal or gonadal tumor.

The clinical value of establishing definitively whether a girl who appears to have premature adrenarche actually has nonclassic 21-hydroxylase deficiency is that those who have this diagnosis (approximately 5 to 10% of girls with isolated pubic hair development) are at increased risk for subsequent development of severe acne, hirsutism, menstrual irregularity, and infertility, whereas girls with premature adrenarche are not. The most cost-effective approach, however, would be to reserve this evaluation for those girls who develop additional signs of androgen excess.

If the child has more than just isolated breast or pubic hair development, the physician must consider the full differential diagnosis of central and peripheral precocious puberty. Certain disorders, such as neurofibromatosis, classic McCune–Albright syndrome, exogenous sex steroid exposure, and familial male precocious puberty, can usually be diagnosed by history and physical examination alone (see Table 9–28–2).

Other disorders need be considered only in restricted clinical settings. Precocious puberty associated with hypothyroidism, for example, is invariably accompanied by other signs of severe hypothyroidism, such as short stature and delayed bone age. Ectopic human chorionic gonadotropin-secreting tumors arising outside the gonads, such as dysgerminomas and hepatoblastomas, usually need be considered only in boys, as human chorionic gonadotropin, except at extraordinarily elevated levels, does not activate the ovary in the absence of follicle-stimulating hormone. Massive extraglandular aromatization is an extremely

rare disorder that need be considered only in children who become feminized at the time of adrenarche (age 7 or 8).

These and other considerations make it impractical to suggest an inflexible checklist of tests to be done on all children with precocious puberty. The approach outlined below is thus intended to be used flexibly as the clinical situation dictates.

If the diagnosis is not initially apparent on clinical grounds, the gonadotropin response to luteinizing hormone-releasing hormone, 100 μg intravenously, with blood samples at 30, 60, and 90 minutes, should be used to determine whether there is pubertal activation of the hypothalamic–pituitary unit. A peak luteinizing hormone level (measured in International Units per liter) that exceeds the peak follicle-stimulating hormone level indicates pubertal activation of the hypothalamus and pituitary. The converse indicates prepubertal function. Further information on the interpretation of this test is available from Oerter et al. (1990).

When a pubertal response to luteinizing hormone-releasing hormone is present (90% of girls and 77% of boys in the NIH experience [Pescovitz et al., 1986]; Table 9–28–4), a head computed tomography or magnetic resonance imaging scan should be performed to detect the cases of central precocious puberty that are due to a central nervous system lesion. Hypothalamic hamartoma is the most common lesion. It appears on computed tomography scans as a mass that projects downward from the anterior hypothalamus into the suprasellar cistern and does not enhance with iodinated contrast agent. Other central nervous system causes of precocious puberty include neurofibromatosis, arachnoid cyst, optic glioma, astrocytoma, neuroblastoma, myelomeningocele, dermoid teratoma, subdural hematoma, and congenital hydrocephalus. If the computed tomography scan is normal, the diagnosis is either idiopathic central precocious puberty or peripheral precocious puberty with secondary central activation (see Table 9–28–3).

The category of peripheral precocious puberty with secondary central activation accounted for 13% of the children in the NIH series who had pubertal gonadotropin responses to luteinizing hormone–releasing hormone (6% of girls and 39% of boys) (Pescovitz et al., 1986). Secondary central precocious puberty is postulated to arise when the mechanism controlling central puberty is activated by a critical level of somatic or skeletal maturity that has been achieved prematurely because of the underlying peripheral precocious puberty. Secondary central precocious puberty has been observed in both sexes and in nearly all forms of peripheral precocious puberty, including 21-hydroxylase and 11-hydroxylase deficiency, adrenal adenoma, McCune–Albright syndrome, familial male precocious puberty, and oxandrolone treatment. Thus the diagnosis of peripheral precocious puberty must be entertained in children with a pubertal gonadotropin response to luteinizing hormone-

TABLE 9–28–4. CAUSES OF PRECOCIOUS PUBERTY IN CHILDREN REFERRED TO THE NATIONAL INSTITUTES OF HEALTH BETWEEN 1979 AND 1983

Disorder	Number of Patients	
	Girls	Boys
Central precocious puberty		
Idiopathic	47	1
Central nervous system lesion		
Hypothalamic hamartoma	13	9
Other	21	6
Secondary to peripheral precocious puberty	(5)*	(10)*
Subtotal	81	16
Peripheral precocious puberty		
Adrenal		
Tumor	2	0
21-Hydroxylase deficiency	2	8
Gonadal		
McCune–Albright syndrome	9	0
Familial male		9
Factitious	1	1
Subtotal	14	18
Total	95	34

*Not included in the central precocious puberty subtotal because they are included below under peripheral precocious puberty.

releasing hormone and a normal computed tomography scan, as well as in children who have a prepubertal gonadotropin response to luteinizing hormone-releasing hormone.

When a prepubertal gonadotropin response to luteinizing hormone-releasing hormone indicates a peripheral cause of precocious puberty, the most likely diagnoses are 21-hydroxylase deficiency, the McCune–Albright syndrome, and familial male precocious puberty (Table 9–28–4). If the diagnosis cannot be made clinically, the principal tests are plasma 17-hydroxyprogesterone determination, plasma human chorionic gonadotropin determination (in boys), and adrenal and gonadal ultrasonography. Skeletal survey or bone scan may detect fibrous dysplasia in patients with variants of McCune–Albright syndrome who lack the characteristic skin lesions. Additional tests that may be useful in special circumstances are listed in Table 9–28–3.

Therapeutic

Therapeutic Options

The major therapeutic decision is whether or not to treat the child with central precocious puberty who is progressing slowly through puberty or who is near the normal age for pubertal onset. Puberty is a normal physiologic process, and thus the inconvenience, expense, and risks of treatment must be outweighed by the expected benefit. A second decision concerns the treatment of boys with familial male-limited precocious puberty, who appear to respond equally well to the testosterone synthesis inhibitor, ketoconazole and to the antiandrogen spironolactone, combined with the inhibitor of androgen-to-estrogen conversion, testolactone. Ketoconazole treatment is cheaper and more convenient, but it carries the risk of serious hepatotoxicity.

Recommended Approach

The treatment depends on the diagnosis. Premature thelarche and premature adrenarche are benign disorders that should not be treated. Children with these disorders should initially be seen at least every 6 months, however, because of the possibility that the diagnosis is in error and that other signs of puberty will emerge.

Children with isolated pubic hair development because of the non-classic form of 21-hydroxylase deficiency (also called the attenuated or late-onset form) do not require treatment unless other signs of androgen excess develop, such as a growth spurt, significant advancement of bone age (more than 2 standard deviations ahead of chronologic age), acne, or facial hair. Untreated children with this disorder nearly always have normal growth and adult height, whereas glucocorticoid treatment, if excessive, carries the risk of stunting growth and impairing adult height. If treatment is required, satisfactory clinical results can usually be achieved with hydrocortisone (e.g., Cortef) given as a single morning oral dose not exceeding 10 mg/m^2 of body surface area. The medical treatment of classic 21-hydroxylase deficiency is described in Chapter 9–8.

Children with central precocious puberty respond dramatically to treatment with long-acting analogs of luteinizing hormone-releasing hormone. Several different luteinizing hormone-releasing hormone analogs are available for the treatment of precocious puberty. Deslorelin (Somagard), the first luteinizing hormone-releasing hormone analog used to treat precocious puberty, is available through a formal treatment investigational new drug exemption (Somagard information service: 1–800–752–4255). The effective dose is 4 μg/kg body weight by daily subcutaneous injection. Leuprolide (Lupron) is the most widely used luteinizing hormone-releasing hormone analog in the United States. Two formulations are available: a short-acting subcutaneous formulation, which is effective in precocious puberty at daily doses of 30 to 100 μg/kg, and a long-acting intramuscular depot formulation, which is effective at the dose of 0.3 mg/kg every 3 to 4 weeks. Other luteinizing hormone-releasing hormone analogs include histrelin (Supprelin; effective dose, 10 μg/kg by daily subcutaneous injection) and nafarelin (Synarel), which is administered as an intranasal spray.

The effectiveness of deslorelin treatment can be monitored by clinical measures. Growth rate usually becomes normal after 6 months of treatment. Bone age advancement is usually normal during the first year of treatment and less than normal (mean, 0.5 bone age year per chronologic year) during the second year. Menses cease within the first

month of treatment. Noticeable regression of breast size and amount of pubic hair often occurs within 6 months. If these clinical signs of effectiveness of treatment are observed, there is little need to confirm suppression of puberty by laboratory tests. If the effectiveness of treatment is not apparent clinically within 6 months, the possibility of noncompliance with treatment or an error in diagnosis should be considered. The most useful laboratory evidence of effective treatment is suppression of the luteinizing hormone response to administered luteinizing hormone-releasing hormone. One may also monitor suppression of plasma estradiol level in girls and plasma testosterone level in boys.

Precocious puberty in the McCune–Albright syndrome may be treated with testolactone (Teslac) in three to four daily oral doses, beginning with 20 mg/kg/d and increasing weekly by 10 mg/kg/d to a maximum dose of 40 mg/kg/d. This is an investigational use of testolactone, which is an aromatase inhibitor that is marketed for the treatment of breast carcinoma.

Two investigational treatments are being evaluated for boys with familial male precocious puberty. The first uses ketoconazole (Nizoral), an antifungal agent that also inhibits adrenal and gonadal steroidogenesis, at oral doses of 17 to 32 mg/kg/d given every 12 hours with food. The second combines the antiandrogen spironolactone (Aldactone) at a dose of 5.7 mg/kg/d and the aromatase inhibitor testolactone (Teslac) at a dose of 40 mg/kg/d, each given three to four times daily.

Side effects have not been observed with any of the luteinizing hormone-releasing hormone analogs that have been used to treat precocious puberty. The ultimate safety of these drugs will not be known, however, until reproductive function of the treated children has been shown to be normal.

The side effects of testolactone are gastrointestinal, usually a transient diarrhea that resolves with temporary dose reduction or discontinuation of the drug.

The side effects of ketoconazole are nausea, gastrointestinal distress, and, less commonly, headache, sommolence, and nervous irritability. Additionally, 0.1 to 1% of patients have developed hepatic dysfunction, which may be severe and which necessitates regular monitoring of liver function.

The side effects of spironolactone are gynecomastia, which appears to be minimized by concurrent use of testolactone to decrease estrogen formation, and mineralocorticoid deficiency related to the antimineralocorticoid activity of spironolactone. Mineralocorticoid deficiency appears to be compensated by increased endogenous mineralocorticoid production if the dose is begun at one-fourth the maximum dose and raised over several weeks. Nonetheless, we ask patients to wear a MedicAlert bracelet while using this drug and to discontinue the drug during intercurrent illness, such as viral gastroenteritis, which might impose an additional stress on volume and electrolyte homeostasis.

Surgery is rarely indicated in children with central precocious puberty. An exception is the child with a progressive central nervous system lesion in which surgery offers the only prospect of curing the lesion or protecting vital brain structures. Hypothalamic hamartoma, the most common central nervous system lesion associated with precocious puberty, should not in general be approached surgically. Surgery may not cure the precocious puberty, and there is a substantial risk of devastating complications.

Our approach in the child with an apparent hypothalamic hamartoma is to make a presumptive diagnosis based on the clinical presentation and characteristic appearance on computed tomography or magnetic resonance imaging. Follow-up computed tomography or magnetic resonance imaging scans are done, initially at yearly intervals, to detect potential enlargement. No progression has occurred in any of our 24 patients with presumed hypothalamic hamartoma over a mean follow-up of 4 years.

Human chorionic gonadotropin-secreting dysgerminomas in the pineal region can be cured by radiotherapy, which I consider to be the treatment of choice (Linstadt et al., 1988).

Surgery is the appropriate treatment for peripheral precocious puberty due to adrenal or gonadal tumor. Surgery should not be performed, however, for the McCune–Albright syndrome. It does not cure the disorder, which will recur in the remaining ovarian tissue, and it exposes the child to unnecessary risk.

The parents whose child has apparent premature thelarche should be told that their daughter appears to have premature thelarche and that this is a harmless disorder of unknown cause. The breast development may remain or it may disappear. In any case it should not progress beyond a midpubertal-sized breast, and it should not be accompanied by any other signs of puberty. The timing of the normal pubertal mechanism is not altered by premature thelarche, and there are no known lasting effects of the disorder. In a small percentage of cases, girls who appear initially to have premature thelarche actually turn out to have early puberty. In this case, other signs of puberty, such as growth spurt, pubic or axillary hair, a vaginal discharge or odor, adult body odor, increased oiliness of the skin with blackheads or acne, and eventually menstruation, will occur. If any of these signs appear, parents should notify the physician. Even if no new signs are noticed, the child should be reexamined every 3 to 6 months until the physician is confident that she is not going to develop any further signs of puberty. Similar advice should be given in the case of premature adrenarche.

The parents of children with central precocious puberty should be told that their child has an early onset of the normal brain mechanism that controls puberty and that this will result, if not treated, in an early occurrence of all the events that normally occur at puberty. The only known lasting consequence of early puberty is that the child will stop growing sooner than normal and will be shorter than he or she would have been if puberty had occurred at the normal time. In general, it appears that a child's adult height will be decreased about 1 inch for each year of puberty below age 9. Precocious puberty can now be treated medically. The treatment appears safe at present, but ultimate proof of safety will not be available for many years. The decision to treat must thus balance the anticipated benefit of treatment against the risk of an unforeseen adverse effect of the drug. In general, we do not recommend treatment unless the onset of puberty was at age 6 or below or the predicted adult height is below the normal range.

Additional information, which is beyond the scope of this chapter, should be given about the nature and prognosis of the specific underlying cause of the precocious puberty.

FOLLOW-UP

Follow-up for premature thelarche and premature adrenarche should be at 3- to 6-month intervals until the diagnosis is firmly established. The physician should repeat the history, physical examination, and bone age determination to look for evidence of precocious puberty. The patient and patient's parents should be instructed in the other symptoms and signs of puberty that should lead to earlier follow-up.

Follow-up for central and peripheral precocious puberty depends to some extent on the specific diagnosis and whether the response to treatment is satisfactory. The most reliable index of a satisfactory treatment response is normalization of growth rate after 6 months of treatment. Thus we routinely follow patients every 6 months for the first year of treatment and at yearly intervals thereafter.

DISCUSSION

Prevalence and Incidence

Reliable information on the incidence and prevalence of precocious puberty is not available. Based on relative referral rates compared with other endocrine disorders, we estimate that between 1 in 5000 and 1 in 10,000 children will have an onset of central precocious puberty at age 6 or below.

Related Basic Science

Physiologic Derangement

The altered physiology in all forms of central precocious puberty involves an early activation of the pubertal (or adult) pattern of luteinizing hormone-releasing hormone secretion (Figure 9–28–1). This increases pituitary gonadotropin secretion, which in turn stimulates gonadal sex steroid secretion and causes the secondary sexual changes of puberty. One of these changes is the pubertal growth spurt. When this growth spurt occurs prematurely, it causes accelerated bone maturation, early epiphyseal fusion, and adult short stature.

The precise mechanisms through which luteinizing hormone-releas-

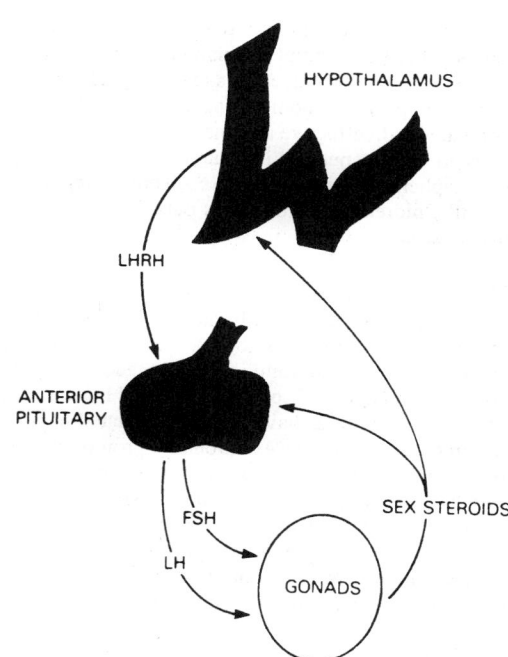

Figure 9–28–1. Physiology of the hypothalamic–pituitary–gonadal axis. Hypothalamic luteinizing hormone-releasing hormone (*LHRH*) stimulates pituitary secretion of luteinizing hormone (*LH*) and follicle-stimulating hormone (*FSH*), and luteinizing hormone and follicle-stimulating hormone stimulate gonadal sex steroid secretion. The sex steroids feed back on the hypothalamus and pituitary to inhibit luteinizing hormone-releasing hormone and gonadotropin secretion. Puberty is believed to result from a primary central nervous system maturational process that leads to increased luteinizing hormone-releasing hormone secretion. *(Source: Muller EE, MacLeod RM, Frohman LA, eds. Neuroendocrine perspectives. vol. 4. New York: Elsevier Science, 1985:74. Reproduced with permission from the publisher and the authors.)*

ing hormone is restrained during normal childhood or released prematurely by certain central nervous system lesions are not known. Luteinizing hormone-releasing hormone cannot yet be measured reliably in peripheral blood. The presence of the pubertal pattern of luteinizing hormone-releasing hormone can be detected indirectly, however, by measuring the gonadotropin response to exogenous luteinizing hormone-releasing hormone (see Plans, Diagnostic). Before puberty, the peak follicle-stimulating hormone level after exogenous luteinizing hormone-releasing hormone (measured in International Units per liter) exceeds the peak luteinizing hormone level. After puberty begins, this ratio is reversed.

The pathophysiologic processes leading to gonadal activation without pubertal hypothalamic–pituitary activation in familial male precocious puberty and in the McCune–Albright syndrome involve activating mutations along the pathway of gonadotropin signal transduction.

Altered Molecular Biology

Familial male-limited precocious puberty results from constitutively activating missense mutations of the luteinizing hormone receptor. The mutations cause amino acid substitutions, in the transmembrane and third intracellular loop domains of the receptor, that activate the G-protein adenylyl cyclase signal transduction pathway.

The McCune–Albright syndrome results from mosaicism for early somatic mutations affecting the alpha subunit of the stimulatory G-protein (G_s). The mutations cause substitution of cysteine or histidine for the arginine at position 201. This destroys the intrinsic GTPase activity of G_s. Without GTPase activity, G_s is unable to switch off after stimulation. This results in autonomous overactivity of the ovary and other endocrine glands, such as thyroid, adrenal, and pituitary, that are regulated by G_s.

Natural History and Its Modification with Treatment

The morbidity of the disorder is related to the dyssynchrony of the child and his or her peers. Precocious puberty, untreated, leads to tall stature throughout childhood and short stature as an adult. Children with precocious puberty may unintentionally hurt their peers because of their greater strength and body size. This leads to pressures to put them in age-inappropriate play or school settings. These problems can be reduced or eliminated with effective treatment.

Mortality in precocious puberty is related to malignant neoplasms of the brain or periphery. Fortunately, these disorders represent a small proportion of all children with precocious puberty, and treatment is effective in many cases.

Prevention

Prevention of precocious puberty is limited to the prevention of head injury (as has occurred from child abuse), the avoidance of factitious causes, genetic counseling for familial male precocious puberty, and early diagnosis and treatment of congenital adrenal hyperplasia. Neonatal thyroid screening programs have all but eliminated hypothyroidism as a cause of precocious puberty. Additionally, prompt recognition and treatment of all forms of peripheral precocious puberty are essential to prevent secondary central precocious puberty associated with somatic or skeletal maturation. Although no prevention is known for many of the disorders associated with precocious puberty, treatment of the precocious puberty can reverse secondary sexual development, reduce age–size dyssynchrony, and improve adult height.

Cost Containment

Significant savings can be achieved by avoiding a complete diagnostic evaluation for precocious puberty in the child with premature thelarche or adrenarche. In the child with precocious puberty, careful clinical evaluation may provide clues to the diagnosis of a central nervous system lesion, McCune–Albright syndrome, or familial male precocious puberty, thereby limiting the need for expensive laboratory tests. In many children, however, there will be no clinical evidence of the cause, and an expensive diagnostic evaluation will be unavoidable. I suggest the sequence luteinizing hormone-releasing hormone test to detect central precocious puberty, computed tomography or magnetic resonance imaging scan of those with a pubertal response to luteinizing hormone-releasing hormone, and tests to exclude peripheral precocious puberty in children with a prepubertal response to luteinizing hormone-releasing hormone or a pubertal luteinizing hormone-releasing hormone response and a normal computed tomography or magnetic resonance imaging scan (to detect central precocious puberty secondary to peripheral precocious puberty). In my view, this is the least costly approach that will yield the correct diagnosis.

Treatment costs can be limited by not treating children whose pubertal onset occurs at age 7 or above and by careful attention to the total duration of treatment.

Frequently ordered tests that have little diagnostic value are plasma estradiol level determinations in girls and plasma testosterone level determinations in boys. These hormones represent the final common pathway leading to secondary sexual development. For a given stage of pubertal development, they are usually similarly elevated irrespective of diagnosis.

REFERENCES

Grumbach MM, Styne DM. Puberty: Ontogeny, neuroendocrinology, physiology, and disorders. In: Wilson JD, Foster DW, eds. Textbook of endocrinology, 8th ed. Philadelphia: Saunders, 1992:1139.

Kasa-Vabu JZ, Kelch RP. Precocious and delayed puberty: Diagnosis and treatment. In: De Groot LJ, editor-in-chief. Endocrinology. 3rd ed. Philadelphia: Saunders, 1995:1953.

Lindstadt D, Wara WM, Edwards MSB, et al. Radiotherapy of primary intracranial germinomas: The case against routine craniospinal irradiation. Int J Radiat Oncol Biol Phys 1988;15:291.

Oerter KE, Uriarte MM, Rose SR et al. Gonadotropin secretory dynamics during puberty in normal girls and boys. J Clin Endocrinol Metab 1990;71:1251.

Pescovitz OH, Comite F, Hench KD, et al. The NIH experience in precocious puberty: Diagnostic subgroups and the response to short-term LHRH analogue therapy. J Pediatr 1986;108:47

Rogol A, Blizzard R. Variations and disorders of pubertal development. In: Kappy MS, Blizzard RM, Migeon CJ, eds. The diagnosis and treatment of endocrine disorders in childhood and adolescence. 4th ed. Springfield, IL: Charles C Thomas, 1994:857.

CHAPTER 9–29

Type I (Insulin-dependent) Diabetes Mellitus

Jay S. Skyler, M.D., and Jennifer B. Marks, M.D.

DEFINITION

Diabetes mellitus is a chronic metabolic syndrome defined by inappropriate hyperglycemia and characterized by relative or absolute deficiency of insulin secretion and/or insulin action, with consequent deranged metabolism of carbohydrates, fats, and proteins, which, as a function of time, leads to the development of chronic complications including accelerated vascular disease, neurologic deficits, and other organ-specific degenerative processes.

Current classification divides primary diabetes into two major categories, known as type I and type II. Type I, or insulin-dependent diabetes mellitus (IDDM), is characterized by absolute insulin deficiency and, thus, a dependence on insulin therapy for the preservation of life. In contrast, in type II, or non-insulin-dependent diabetes mellitus (NIDDM), insulin therapy is not generally required for the maintenance of life, but may be necessary for the control of symptoms or for the correction of disordered metabolism.

ETIOLOGY

Type I diabetes mellitus is a disease of disordered immune function, involving the destruction of pancreatic islet insulin-secreting beta cells. The onset of clinical symptoms of diabetes represents the endpoint of a chronic progressive decline in beta cell function, and occurs when the majority of beta cells have been lost. Evidence suggests that the islet immunopathology begins several years prior to the clinical onset of disease. The antigen that causes T-cell activation and initiates the chronic destructive immune response is not yet known, but a number of candidate autoantigens have been identified. The theory that such an autoantigen may display "molecular mimicry" with an environmental antigen, for example, a virus or toxin to which the host was exposed at some time in the past, has been suggested. Additionally, it is generally accepted that a particular genetic background is prerequisite to, but not sufficient for, the development of type I diabetes.

CRITERIA FOR DIAGNOSIS

Diabetes mellitus, in the untreated state, is recognized on the basis of chronic elevation of plasma glucose (hyperglycemia) (Table 9–29–1). Specifically, diabetes mellitus is defined by fasting plasma glucose greater than 140 mg/dL (on two occasions), by random plasma glucose greater than 200 mg/dL in the presence of symptoms of diabetes, or by plasma glucose levels greater than 200 mg/dL at two time points after a 75-g glucose challenge, including the 2-hour value. This is an oral glucose tolerance test (OGTT). Normal glucose tolerance is defined as a fasting plasma glucose of 115 mg/dL or less and a 2-hour value on OGTT of 139 mg/dL or less. Impaired glucose tolerance is defined as a

TABLE 9–29–1. CRITERIA FOR DIAGNOSIS OF DIABETES

I. Diabetes Mellitus in Nonpregnant Adults
Any one of the following are diagnostic of diabetes:
A. Classic symptoms (e.g., polyuria, polydipsia, ketonuria, rapid weight loss) together with gross and unequivocal elevation of random plasma glucose (>200 mg/dL)
B. Elevated fasting glucose (on more than one occasion):
1. Venous plasma ≥140 mg/dL or
2. Whole blood ≥120 mg/dL
C. Sustained elevated glucose during 75-OGTT on more than one occasion. Both the 2-hour sample and some other sample ($\frac{1}{2}$-, 1-, or $1\frac{1}{2}$hour) must meet the following criteria:
1. Venous plasma ≥200 mg/dL or
2. Venous whole blood ≥180 mg/dL or
3. Capillary whole blood ≥200 mg/dL
II. Diabetes Mellitus in Children
Same as Part I, except both B and C must be met.
OGTT uses 1.75 g/kg body weight.
III. Impaired Glucose Tolerance in Nonpregnant Adults
Three criteria must be met:
A. Fasting glucose below that in Part IB.
B. Two-hour sample on 75-g OGTT must be between normal and diabetic values
C. One other sample ($\frac{1}{2}$-, 1-, $1\frac{1}{2}$hour) must be unequivocally elevated (by criteria in Part IC)
IV. Impaired Glucose Tolerance in Children
Two criteria must be met:
A. Fasting glucose below that in Part IB
B. Two-hour sample in OGTT must exceed values usually used for fasting, i.e., those in Part IB
V. Normal Glucose Levels in Nonpregnant Adults

	Venous Plasma (mg/dL)	Venous Whole Blood (mg/dL)	Capillary Whole Blood (mg/dL)
Fasting	<115	<100	<100
$\frac{1}{2}$, 1-, $1\frac{1}{2}$hour OGTT	<200	<180	<200
2-hour OGTT	<140	<120	<140

VI. Diabetes Mellitus During Pregnancy
Two or more of the following glucose concentrations must be met or exceeded, following a 100-g oral glucose tolerance test:

	Venous Plasma (mg/dL)	Venous Whole Blood (mg/dL)	Capillary Whole Blood (mg/dL)
Fasting	105	90	90
1-hour	190	170	170
2-hour	165	145	145
3-hour	145	125	125

OGTT, oral glucose tolerance test.
Source: From Skyler JS. Insulin-dependent diabetes mellitus. In: Kohler PO, ed. Clinical endocrinology. New York: John Wiley & Sons, 1986:514. Reproduced with permission from the publisher and author.

glycemic response to a standard glucose challenge intermediate between normal and diabetic, and can therefore be determined only by an OGTT. The criteria for impaired glucose tolerance are a fasting plasma glucose between 116 and 139 mg/dL and a 2-hour OGTT glucose between 140 and 200 mg/dL. The above definitions apply for nonpregnant adults. During childhood and during pregnancy, slightly different criteria are used (Table 9–29–1).

Type I diabetes mellitus is usually readily distinguished from type II diabetes by the clinical setting in which it occurs, that is, in childhood or adolescence or in a thin adult less than 30 years of age. There is a tendency to ketosis under basal conditions, if insulin therapy is inadequate. Islet cell antibodies are present in the majority of patients at the time of diagnosis, but are generally not necessary to establish the diagnosis.

CLINICAL MANIFESTATIONS
Subjective

The onset of type I diabetes is generally before the age of 30, although the syndrome may occur at any age. Patients are generally thin, in contrast to those with type II diabetes 80% of whom are obese. There often is a family history of type I diabetes, but only 15% of patients have a first-degree relative with type I diabetes.

The symptoms of type I diabetes vary with the abruptness of onset. There is almost always a history of polyuria and polydipsia, even if only for a few hours or a day. Most patients present with a history of polyphagia, fatigue, and weight loss as well. Symptoms may be present for days or weeks, and these symptoms always lead the patient to seek medical attention in less than 1 month. Another common constellation of symptoms, particularly in patients with a more insidious onset, comprises lethargy, weakness, blurred vision (from altered lens refraction), and gradual but progressive weight loss. Other symptoms in patients with very insidious onset include failure to grow, failure to gain weight, and failure to develop normally. Enuresis, particularly nocturnal, may be seen in younger children. Adolescent girls may develop secondary amenorrhea. Although polyphagia is the classic symptom, some patients have anorexia, particularly if there is listlessness and/or ketosis. Pruritis vulvae from vulvovaginal moniliasis is a not uncommon symptom. The male counterpart, balanitis, is rare. Symptoms of dehydration, including dizziness, postural faintness, and headache, may be seen.

Perhaps 10 to 20% of patients present with diabetic ketoacidosis (see Chapter 9–31). These patients usually manifest drowsiness, air hunger, the smell of acetone on the breath, dehydration, and nausea and/or vomiting. Some have obtundation of consciousness or coma. Occasional patients have severe abdominal pain, which may be difficult to distinguish from pancreatitis. Progression to ketoacidosis is more likely when the onset of diabetes is triggered by an acute infection.

During the course of diabetes, with loss of diabetic control, any or all of the initial symptoms may recur. Indeed, patients need to be particularly alert for the onset of lethargy, tiredness, polyuria and polydipsia, which may herald impending ketosis or ketoacidosis.

Objective
Physical Examination

Physical findings vary with the abruptness and severity of onset. Thus, there may be a paucity of findings or the appearance of an ill, wasted individual with signs of loss of weight from dehydration, fat breakdown, and proteolysis. Signs of dehydration include hypotension (rarely hypovolemic shock); weak, rapid pulse; dry skin and tongue; and loss of orbital turgor. There may be forceful, deep Kussmaul respiration; the smell of acetone on the breath; hyporeflexia or areflexia; hepatomegaly; salivary gland enlargement; and signs of moniliasis.

Routine Laboratory Abnormalities

The diagnosis of diabetes mellitus, by definition, rests on the demonstration of inappropriate hyperglycemia. The current definition of inappropriate hyperglycemia is a fasting venous plasma glucose level greater than or equal to 140 mg/dL, or a sustained plasma glucose level in excess of 200 mg/dL 2 hours after the ingestion of a glucose load and also at some other time between zero time and 2 hours (Table 9–29–1). With type I diabetes, there is usually unequivocal hyperglycemia substantially above this criteria. Glycosuria is usually present as well. Both ketonemia and ketonuria are seen unless onset has been mild and insidious. Other routine laboratory abnormalities present at diagnosis are related to dehydration, electrolyte depletion, acidosis, and generalized manifestations of stress.

PLANS
Diagnostic
Differential Diagnosis

Differential diagnosis is generally not difficult, particularly in the presence of classic symptoms and signs. Transient glycosuria may be seen during severe infection or trauma, and usually remits during recovery.

During acute illness, particularly if food intake is decreased, mild ketosis may develop as a consequence of both starvation and stress. Again, this readily remits during recovery and refeeding. Glycosuria may occur from renal glucosuria, and nonglucose melituria may mimic glucosuria in tests that do not discriminate between various reducing substances. Salicylate intoxication may mimic diabetic ketoacidosis.

Diagnostic Options and Recommended Approach

Generally, patients with type I diabetes present with classic signs and symptoms, accompanied by unequivocal hyperglycemia (random plasma glucose > 200 mg/dL). Further diagnostic testing is not generally needed. In equivocal cases, the diagnostic criteria are those defined in Table 9–29–1.

Therapeutic

The fundamental principle operative in attempting to achieve metabolic control in type I diabetes is the balance between energy expenditure (reflected by activity), energy availability (reflected by food intake), and insulin action (which is necessary for effective energy utilization). From this framework, the three components of therapy emerge: the nutritional plan, exercise, and insulin dosage. Successful treatment of diabetes then, by definition, involves the balancing of these three components and the careful monitoring of that balance. As the patient must be engaged in this balancing on a daily basis, two additional critical principles emerge: (1) patient education is essential to successful therapy, and (2) the treatment program must be sufficiently flexible and dynamic to allow for highly varied and changing lifestyles without sacrificing careful metabolic control.

Given that the underlying principle in management of type I diabetes is the achievement of balance between food intake, energy expenditure, and energy dosage, two important corollaries become evident. The first is that once balance has been achieved, it should be possible to maintain that balance by keeping food intake, energy expenditure, and insulin dosage relatively constant from day to day. Thus, assuming that a given patient's daily activities (and energy expenditures) are relatively constant, then a basic meal plan and basic insulin dosage can be developed that provide balance with the patient's usual energy expenditure. The second corollary is that if energy balance is to be maintained, then any time one of the three components (food, activity, insulin) is altered, there must be a compensatory alteration in at least one other component as well. This dictates that the treatment regimen must be dynamic. It also underscores the need to integrate the three components of therapy.

Targeted Blood Glucose Control

Each patient should have defined blood glucose targets, individualized for her or his needs. The targets must be explicitly defined, to avoid confusion and for the patient to understand what the goal is in self-adjustment. Today the goal of therapy, supported by the results of the Diabetes Control and Complications Trial (DCCT), is meticulous glycemic control with near-normal glycemic targets. This trial showed unequivocally that intensive therapy of type I diabetes with resultant improvement in glycemic control effectively delays the onset and slows the progression of diabetic complications.

Examples of targets for a young, otherwise healthy patient who recognizes hypoglycemic symptoms and spontaneously recovers from hypoglycemia are preprandial blood glucose, 70 to 130 mg/dL; 2-hour postprandial blood glucose, 80 to 150 mg/dL; and overnight (2:00 to 4:00 AM) blood glucose, 70 to 120 mg/dL.

The DCCT clearly showed that intensive diabetic treatment carried with it a threefold increase in severe episodes of hypoglycemia. Such targets as outlined above would be inappropriate in a patient with hypoglycemic unawareness, counterregulatory insufficiency, angina pectoris, or other complicating features. Such patients might require a preprandial blood glucose target of, for example, 150 to 250 mg/dL. It is important to note that the DCCT demonstrated that *any* improvement in glycemic control was associated with a decrease in the risk of diabetic complications. Targets may also be changed with time. For example, when initiating intensive therapy, even if the ultimate goal is meticulous glycemic control, the initial target might be a preprandial blood glucose level of 100 to 200 mg/dL.

Self-monitoring of blood glucose is essential to management of patients with type I diabetes and should be performed several times daily.

Nutritional Plan

The attainment of near normalization of glycemia in type I diabetes entails careful balancing between energy expenditure (activity), energy (calorie) intake, and insulin availability. In contrast to the nondiabetic subject, the patient with type I has little or no beta cell insulin secretory capacity and is therefore dependent on exogenous insulin administration to restrain postprandial hyperglycemia and to promote efficient energy utilization. This involves predicting the exogenous insulin dose prior to eating, to ensure appropriate assimilation of the meal calories. Thus, for patients with type I diabetes, nutritional planning traditionally has been based on four basic principles.

- A basic daily meal plan should be developed, consistent in total energy intake (calories) and distribution of energy-yielding nutrients (carbohydrates, fats, and proteins). A basic insulin dosage is prescribed to provide appropriate insulinemia for the basic meal plan, in balance with the patient's energy expenditure.
- To maintain balance between food, activity, and insulin, nutritional planning must provide for compensatory changes for unusual circumstances. During activity that is not part of the patient's daily routine, extra food intake compensates for increased energy expended. Reduction of insulin dosage should be considered in addition to the dietary supplements. Consumption of the unusually large (or small) meal should be accompanied by a corresponding increase (or decrease) in insulin dose.
- Hyperglycemia must be avoided by omitting rapidly absorbed simple sugars (glucose, sucrose, maltose) from regular meal planning.
- Hypoglycemia must be avoided by maintaining reasonable constancy in timing of meals, with particular emphasis on avoiding long delay between meals and snacking to shorten periods between calorie intake and to provide substrate at times of peak exogenous insulin action or excessive exercise.

In the past, it was common for physicians to recommend an insulin program and dosage, a particular pattern of food intake, and perhaps an exercise or activity prescription. The pattern of food intake almost invariably included three meals (breakfast, lunch, and supper) and one or more (often three) snacks. In addition, the dietary prescription often included a specific calorie intake, proportions of nutrients (carbohydrate, fat, and protein distribution), and even might specify the distribution of calories into meals. Patients also were counseled to eat their meals and snacks at the same time each day. Unfortunately, such dietary prescriptions often conflicted either with the previous habits of an individual patient and/or with patient and family preferences. For example, not everyone prefers to eat three meals per day, every day, at the same time. Many individuals prefer to skip a meal either routinely or occasionally, to be able to eat at somewhat different hours some days, or to vary their portion sizes or meal composition. Thus, there often was an inherent conflict between dietary prescription and patient desires. This frequently led to either patient frustration or abandonment of the dietary prescription. Therefore, it is not surprising that diet therapy of diabetes often was deemed a failure.

Contemporary dietary practices are more flexible. Modern multiple-component insulin regimens permit greater flexibility in meal size and meal timing without sabotaging glycemic control. This may lead to increased patient compliance and improved therapeutic outcome.

A careful dietary history by a skilled dietitian, supplemented by a food intake record maintained by the patient for a few days, permits definition of a patient's preferred eating habits (number and timing of meals) and food preferences, as well as calculation of consumed calories and food composition. With knowledge of the patient's habits and preferences, an "average" or "basic" meal plan can be constructed for that patient, assuming that energy expenditure ("average" activity) is more or less equivalent from day to day. Then, an insulin regimen can be developed that meets the needs of that patient's "average" meal plan. Insulin regimens differ in the degree to which they permit flexibility of meal size, meal timing, and skipping of meals. When an appropriate insulin regimen is selected and implemented, doses can be adjusted during a period that the patient strictly adheres to the "average" meal plan developed. Once satisfactory glycemic control is attained and an "average" insulin dosage established, the patient can learn how to alter insulin dosages and food intake for circumstances when a larger or smaller than "average" meal is consumed or when activity is more or less than "average."

Diabetic patients should follow sound general nutritional practices. Because our therapeutic goals include normalizing nutrition and providing for normal growth and development, it is necessary that the diet of patients with type I diabetes be well balanced, meeting energy and protein requirements for normal growth, avoiding vitamin and other nutritional deficiencies, and avoiding the development of obesity. It is desirable to avoid excess intake of saturated fats and cholesterol, as such consumption adversely influences serum lipids, which also may be elevated if there is suboptimal diabetic control. It also is desirable to limit salt (sodium) consumption, which may aggravate the risk of blood pressure elevation and may alter vascular reactivity. There should be a tendency to avoid foods that have a high "glycemic index" (i.e., foods that cause rapid rises in plasma glucose), while also favoring foods relatively high in fiber. There is no need to disproportionately limit intake of complex carbohydrates or foods that have a low "glycemic index." If the patient is not overweight (most patients with type I diabetes are not), there is no need to limit calorie consumption arbitrarily.

The nutritional principles emphasize primarily meal planning and consistency in daily food intake, assuming that energy expenditure is relatively constant. Thus, the basic meal plan should not be an externally imposed, arbitrarily defined, restrictive "diet." Rather, it is desirable to base total energy intake (calories), distribution of nutrients, and size of meals on information obtained from a carefully taken dietary history. The emphasis is on "meal planning" to balance energy expenditure and insulin dosage. Total energy intake is based on the actual energy the patient has been consuming, provided there is a normal rate of growth and development (if a child or adolescent) and provided obesity is not present. Actual calorie consumption can be estimated from the dietary history and modified upward or downward according to whether the patient loses or gains weight. The recommended calorie level is changed if there is a change in the patient's routine activity expenditure, lifestyle, or eating habits, or if the patient is not satisfied with the calorie recommendation for one reason or another. The dietary history is the predominant determinant of the recommended total energy intake in the basic meal plan. The best long-term guide to actual energy requirement is change in body weight determined at regular intervals, adjusted to ensure normal growth and development.

The best way to develop the basic meal plan is on the basis of a careful dietary history, using this dietary history to determine total energy intake, distribution of nutrients, and size of meals. The dietitian can translate the patient's previous diet into food exchange groups and develop the basic meal plan using some system of substitutes. The various substitution systems facilitate the selection of a variety of food choices while remaining within a basic meal plan. The substitution systems permit equivalent amounts of food to be interchanged. They basically function as bookkeeping systems. Several substitution systems have been developed for this purpose. In the United States, the most widely used system is the Exchange Lists for Meal Planning, developed by the American Diabetes Association and the American Dietetic Association. The Exchange Group System categorizes foods into six groups (milk, vegetable, fruit, bread/starch, meat/protein, and fat exchanges) and provides lists of the quantity of foods that have essentially the equivalent amounts of energy-yielding nutrients (carbohydrates, fats, and proteins) and essentially equivalent amounts of calories. Alternatively, other systems focus only on carbohydrate equivalents, while permitting liberal (virtually unlimited) intake of protein and (to a lesser extent) fat.

With the Exchange Group System, any food within a particular exchange list may be substituted in the proper amount for any other food on that list. Virtually all foods (except concentrated sugars) of known composition can be incorporated into the Exchange Group System using either one or a combination of several exchanges. Thus, the exchange lists can be supplemented to make them more flexible by combining exchanges so that more complex foods can be included in the system; for example, one scoop of ice cream equals one bread and two fat exchanges. The major expenditure of time and energy on the part of the patient and the nutritional counselor should be in understanding and using the Exchange Group System, rather than making major modifications in nutritional habits and preferences.

The use of the Exchange Group System allows for portion sizes to be accurately estimated and facilitates the substitution of foods of approximately equivalent composition to provide variety of choice while maintaining consistency of intake from day to day. Thus, by defining the basic meal plan in terms of given numbers of each exchange for each meal, consistency of calories and proportions of energy-yielding nutrients can be maintained while allowing a wide variety of food choices. When the patient first uses the Exchange Group System, it may be helpful to weigh foods and measure portion sizes. Weighing should be considered only as an educational tool initially and not a permanent activity.

The guiding principle is that the basic meal plan is a dynamic tool that facilitates diabetes management and not a static restraint interfering with the patient's lifestyle.

Insulin

Physiologic insulin secretion includes both continuous basal insulin secretion and substrate-related incremental insulin secretion following meal consumption. Basal insulin secretion restrains hepatic glucose production, keeping it in equilibrium with basal glucose utilization by the brain and other tissues that are obligate glucose consumers. After meals, substrate-related incremental insulin secretion stimulates glucose utilization and storage, while inhibiting hepatic glucose output.

Contemporary insulin regimens have multiple components that attempt to mimic the two normal types of endogenous physiologic insulin secretion, by providing components that give incremental insulin availability coinciding with each meal and one or more components that give continuous insulin availability overnight and between meals. If plasma insulin levels are to be matched with food intake, it is obvious that one or two injections daily of intermediate-acting insulin are not appropriate.

A number of insulin regimens use two to four daily subcutaneous insulin injections. A commonality of all of these insulin regimens is that they have multiple components of insulin availability; however, they vary in (1) the extent to which they mimic the normal pattern of insulin secretion and (2) the amount of flexibility they allow in size, timing, and potential omission of meals.

Split-and-Mixed Insulin Programs. A popular long-standing insulin regimen is the twice-daily administration of mixtures of rapid-onset regular insulin and intermediate-acting insulin (NPH or Lente), the so-called split-and-mixed insulin regimen (Figure 9–29–1A). The advantage of this regimen is that it requires only two injections. Also, the doses of regular insulin before breakfast and supper may be increased or decreased for meals that are larger or smaller than average.

Disadvantages of this regimen are related to the time–action profiles of intermediate-acting insulins, which have onset of action about 2 hours after injection and produce peak insulin levels approximately 8 to 10 hours after injection. Therefore, when intermediate-acting insulin is administered before supper, it often does not sustain its effect throughout the night, a deficiency that results in fasting hyperglycemia in the morning, a time of relative insulin resistance, known as the "dawn phenomenon." Attempts to correct this fasting hyperglycemia by increasing the dose often are complicated by nocturnal hypoglycemia when insulin action peaks.

One solution, which has become increasingly popular in many diabetes centers, is to delay administration of the intermediate-acting insulin until bedtime, when it is given as a third injection (Figure 9–29–1B). This both provides higher prebreakfast serum insulin levels to overcome the dawn phenomenon and reduces the risk of nocturnal hypoglycemia. The disadvantage of this regimen is that the patient still has little flexibility in meal schedule. In addition, some patients are not willing to administer three injections each day.

Another problem, also related to the time–action profile of intermediate-acting insulin, complicates both of these two insulin regimens. The problem is that the daytime intermediate-acting insulin is given before breakfast to provide both daytime basal insulinemia and meal-related insulinemia for lunch. Yet, because the intermediate-acting in-

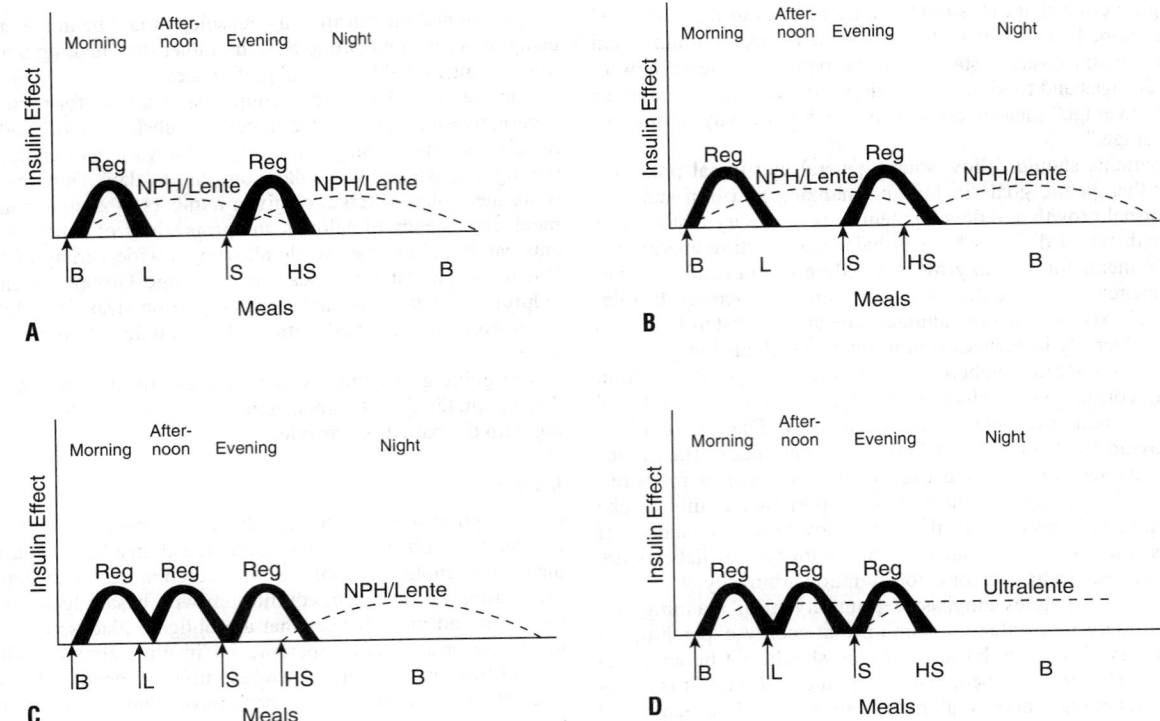

Figure 9–29–1. Schematic representation of ideal insulin effect provided by various subcutaneous insulin regimens using rapid-onset regular (REG) insulin, intermediate-acting (NPH or LENTE) insulins, or long-acting Ultralente insulin. **A.** "Split-and-mixed" insulin regimen consisting of two daily doses of regular insulin and intermediate-acting insulin. **B.** "Split-and-mixed" insulin regimen in which evening intermediate-acting insulin is delayed until bedtime, resulting in peak action coinciding with prebreakfast blood glucose measurement. **C.** Multiple-dose regimen providing three daily injections of regular insulin before meals and one injection of intermediate-acting insulin at bedtime. **D.** Multiple-dose regimen providing regular insulin before meals, and long-acting, relatively peakless Ultralente insulin for basal insulinemia. B, breakfast; L, lunch; S, supper; HS, bedtime snack. Arrows indicate time of insulin injection, 30 minutes before meals. *(Source: Schade DS, Santiago JV, Skyler JS, Rizza R. Intensive insulin therapy. Princeton, NJ: Excerpta Medica, 1983. Reproduced with permission from the publisher and author.)*

sulin has a broad peak, lunch and supper must be eaten on time if the patient is to avoid hypoglycemia. Also, the effect of the insulin usually peaks 8 to 10 hours after administration, a time that is too late to provide optimal insulin availability for lunch. Moreover, because the intermediate-acting insulin is given before breakfast, it is difficult for the patient to make changes in the size or timing of lunch

Multiple-dose Program with Premeal Regular and Bedtime Intermediate-acting Insulin. The problem of perilunch glycemic control can be solved by eliminating (or substantially reducing) the dose of intermediate-acting insulin in the morning and adding an injection of rapid-onset regular insulin before lunch. This regimen uses three preprandial injections of regular insulin and an injection of intermediate-acting insulin at bedtime (Figure 9–29–1C). Each of the doses is adjusted individually.

This provides meal insulinemia at a more appropriate time, and solves the meal flexibility problems to some degree. The size of meals may be altered, and the size of the accompanying premeal insulin dose altered in parallel. If either lunch or supper is substantially delayed, however, hyperglycemia may ensue. A solution to this is to reinstate a small dose of intermediate-acting insulin before breakfast, to provide basal insulinemia only. The prelunch regular insulin provides meal insulinemia.

The multiple-dose premeal regular with bedtime intermediate regimen has become increasingly popular in recent years for a variety of reasons. It is straightforward and easy both to understand and to implement, as each time period of the day has a well-defined insulin component providing primary insulin action. Moreover, the introduction of insulin pens has stimulated its popularity in many countries. As a consequence, this regimen has become the most widely used insulin regimen in several countries in Europe.

Multiple-dose Program with Premeal Regular and Basal Ultralente Insulin. An alternative way to achieve basal insulinemia is by using long-acting Ultralente insulin (Figure 9–29–1D), which in most patients is rela-

tively peakless after steady state has been attained. Use of this insulin is coupled with rapid-onset regular insulin before each meal, by syringe or by pen. The premeal doses permit total flexibility in meal timing. The size and timing of meals may be altered, and meals may be omitted along with the accompanying premeal insulin dose.

The beef and mixed beef–pork Ultralente insulin preparations (soon to be eliminated entirely from availability) have a sluggish onset with an essentially flat action profile extending more than 36 hours. This resulted in the use of Ultralente insulin as a peakless "basal" insulin which in theory should prevent fasting hyperglycemia and ketosis. Several authors found it helpful to divide animal Ultralente insulin preparations into two injections, administering half with the prebreakfast regular and half with the presupper regular insulin. This took advantage of the small peak in action seen in some patients 12 to 15 hours after administration, and limited the total volume of injection.

Human Ultralente has a broad peak at about 12 to 16 hours and action up to 24 hours and sometimes beyond. As a consequence of waning insulin effect around 24 hours, there may be a rise in fasting glucose if human Ultralente insulin is administered in a single morning dose. Thus, it probably is best to use human Ultralente as a twice-daily preparation (or to give it all in the evening, either before supper or at bedtime) when providing basal insulinemia. An important point is that it appears that in most patients the peak of human Ultralente is sufficiently blunted at steady state to still permit use of this preparation as a "peakless" insulin. On the other hand, in some patients who appear to be "fast" absorbers (usually thin individuals) of human insulin (both Ultralente and intermediate-acting insulin), it may be desirable to use human Ultralente as if it were an intermediate-acting insulin preparation.

Continuous Subcutaneous Insulin Infusion. The most precise way available today to mimic normal insulin secretion clinically is to use an insulin pump in a program of continuous subcutaneous insulin infusion (CSII)

(Figure 9–29–2). The pump delivers microliter amounts of regular insulin on a continual basis, thus replicating basal insulin secretion. Many pumps can be programmed to vary the basal rate at times of diurnal variation in insulin sensitivity, if the variation results in disruption of glycemic control. Thus, the basal infusion rate may be programmed either to be decreased overnight to avert nocturnal hypoglycemia or to be increased to counteract the "dawn phenomenon," which often results in hyperglycemia on awakening. Programmability also allows the patient to "suspend" insulin delivery during increased physical activity, thus reducing the risk of exercise-related hypoglycemia.

The pump may be activated before meals to provide increments of insulin as meal "boluses" or "boosts," thus stimulating normal physiology. The meal insulin boluses are given about 30 minutes before a meal. This allows total flexibility in meal timing. If a meal is skipped, the insulin bolus is omitted. If a meal is larger or smaller than usual, a larger or smaller insulin bolus is selected. Thus, CSII patients have the potential of easily varying meal size and meal timing, as well as omitting meals, without sabotaging glycemic control.

Initial Insulin Doses and Distribution. The insulin dosage required for meticulous glycemic control, in typical patients with type I diabetes within 20% of their ideal body weight, in the absence of intercurrent infections or other periods of instability, approximates 0.5 to 1.0 U/kg body weight per day. During the period of relative remission ("honeymoon" period) early in the course of the disease, insulin requirements generally are less. During periods of intercurrent illness, dosage requirement may increase markedly. Dosage also increases during the adolescent growth spurt, and some adolescents may have a sustained increased dose requirement.

Initial insulin distribution is empirically derived from the average distribution requirements of other patients. Each patient then alters the various components individually to attain the desired control. For the split-and-mixed insulin programs, initial distribution provides two thirds of the total daily dose in the morning and one third of the daily dose in the evening. The morning prebreakfast dose is divided as one-third regular insulin and two-thirds intermediate-acting insulin. One half of the evening dose is given as regular insulin before supper, and one half is given as intermediate-acting insulin either mixed with regular insulin before supper or as a separate dose at bedtime. For the multiple-dose programs, basal insulin is given either as 20 to 25% of the total daily dose as bedtime intermediate-acting insulin or 25 to 50% of the total daily dose as Ultralente insulin (generally administering half with the prebreakfast regular and half with the presupper regular); the remainder (regular insulin) is divided as 30 to 45% before breakfast, 25 to 30% before lunch, and 25 to 30% before supper. Some patients desire or require a small additional dose of regular insulin to cover a bedtime snack.

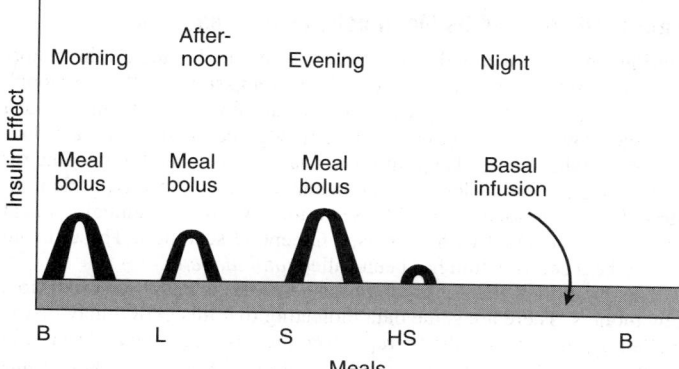

Figure 9–29–2. Schematic representation of ideal insulin effect provided by continuous subcutaneous insulin infusion. B, breakfast; L, lunch; S, supper; HS, bedtime snack. *(Source: Schade DS, Santiago JV, Skyler JS, Rizza R. Intensive insulin therapy. Princeton, NJ: Excerpta Medica, 1983. Reproduced with permission from the publisher and author.)*

For CSII, initially the basal infusion constitutes 40 to 50% of total daily dose, prebreakfast bolus 15 to 25% of total daily dose, prelunch bolus about 10 to 20% of total daily dose, presupper bolus 15 to 20% of total daily dose, and prebedtime snack bolus 0 to 10% of total daily dose.

Obviously, unusual meal distributions may dictate a deviation from the above schemes. Moreover, these dosage distributions are arbitrary and designed for the average or ideal patient. Clearly, they must be individualized for any given patient.

Preprandial injections or activation of preprandial boluses generally should occur at least 20 to 30 minutes before meal consumption, to permit insulin absorption to commence and, it is hoped, to coincide with substrate absorption.

Dose Alteration. Patients are provided with an action plan to alter their therapy to achieve their individually defined blood glucose targets. These actions are guided by self-monitored blood glucose determinations and daily records. The action taken may depend on the answers to several questions the patient needs to ask at the time of any premeal insulin injection: What is my blood glucose now? What do I plan to eat (i.e., usual-size meal, large meal, or small meal)? What do I plan to do after eating (i.e., usual activity, increased activity, decreased activity)? What has happened in these circumstances previously? The answers dictate treatment response. The intervention actions dictated by the plan include food intake (altering the size or content of food), activity, insulin dosage, and timing of injections in relation to meals.

The plan also calls for separate action in response to a pattern of glycemia occurring over several days. Such actions presuppose that the patient has a stable pattern of meals and activities, has no intercurrent illness, and is free from unusual stress.

Exercise

As noted earlier, the fundamental principle of management of type I diabetes is the balance between energy expenditure (activity), energy availability (food intake), and insulin action. Thus, the energy expended in the patient's usual daily routine determines the calorie content of the diet and influences the insulin dose and regimen. Regular physical activity is included in this balance. On the other hand, for sporadic physical activity that represents a departure from the patient's usual daily routine, one needs to take compensatory action to avert hypoglycemia. Such action might include consumption of extra food to provide energy for the increased activity. Initially, this may be 10 to 15 g of carbohydrates every 30 to 45 minutes during increased activity. Blood glucose should be monitored before, during, and after exercise to determine the effectiveness of this intervention. Another option is insulin dose reductions either in addition to or instead of the dietary supplements. All patients should have quick-acting, rapidly absorbed carbohydrate available during activity in case of hypoglycemia.

Exercise-induced hypoglycemia may be less frequent in patients on CSII therapy than on conventional therapy, as CSII eliminates subcutaneous depots of insulin that are mobilized with physical activity.

Patients should realize that moderately intensive exercise may deplete glycogen stores, resulting in a sustained food requirement to replace the glycogen. As a consequence, hypoglycemia may occur well after exercise (e.g., 12 hours after jogging). For this reason, patients should be cautious when planning vigorous physical activity in the evening hours.

FOLLOW-UP

Patients with type I diabetes who are stable should be followed approximately every 3 months. At each visit, glycosylated hemoglobin (HbA1 or HbA1c) is determined to monitor long-term glycemic control. In patients in whom the target is near-normal glycemia, glycosylated hemoglobin values should be within 125% of the upper limit of normal of the assay being used. At each visit, weight, height (if a child or adolescent), and blood pressure are measured. Annually, the patient should have a complete physical examination, including funduscopic examination through dilated pupils; determination of creatinine clearance and urinary albumin excretion; and electrocardiogram in adults over age 30.

The patient with type I diabetes must appreciate that this is a chronic, lifelong disease and that maintenance of glycemic control is important to help prevent the development of many chronic complications. An active role is required of the patient if both short-term complications (ketoacidosis, hypoglycemia) and long-term complications are to be avoided. Ideally, there is an interactive role of the patient and his or her family with the diabetes management "team" (physician, nurse specialist, dietitian, psychologist or social worker). Patient responsibility includes keeping follow-up appointments, having consistent eating habits according to an individualized meal plan, maintaining regular physical activity, taking insulin as prescribed, self-monitoring blood glucose several times daily, and learning to alter insulin and food intake on the basis of the blood glucose results, in an effort to maintain glycemic control as individually targeted. Patients (and their families) must learn to recognize hypoglycemic symptoms and know how to correct them, and should learn to recognize early signs and symptoms of uncontrolled diabetes and to seek medical guidance when appropriate.

The patient should keep a careful diary of daily blood glucose measurements, insulin doses, hypoglycemic episodes, and departures from daily routine (e.g., unusually large meals, increased physical activity, intercurrent illness). The patient record becomes the focus of discussion at each follow-up visit. In particular, it is desirable to determine if the patient has made appropriate changes in insulin dose or meals in response to prevailing blood glucose, meals, and activity. Explanation of hypoglycemic episodes and unusual hyperglycemia is sought.

Clearly, patient motivation is essential for successful implementation of this type of treatment program. Indeed, strong patient motivation may override deficits in educational background that might be deemed by some as necessary for success. An example is our ability to tightly regulate blood glucose in illiterate non-English-speaking refugees who are pregnant.

Psychological support is an important component of diabetes management as well. The major elements of glucose homeostasis for diabetes management are food intake, energy expenditure, and insulin dosage. Yet, in the patient with type I diabetes, endogenous insulin is not available to increase in response to stress-induced hyperglycemia, which is stimulated by glucose counterregulatory hormones (i.e., catecholamines, cortisol, glucagon, growth hormone) all of which are increased by stress. Thus, stress can disrupt glycemic control. Therefore, it may be desirable to learn stress reduction techniques or techniques for otherwise channeling stress, and so facilitate smooth glucose regulation. Moreover, it should be appreciated that just having diabetes is stressful. The treatment program is demanding. The margin for error may be small, with symptomatic hypoglycemia supervening. The risk of serious life-threatening complications is substantial. And the patient is being asked to perform chores that might otherwise be assigned to a laboratory technician, dietitian, nurse, or physician. Treatment involves dealing with everything one eats and all of one's daily activities, while also demanding that one be stuck several times daily to measure blood glucose and to administer insulin. Clearly, the patient labors under considerable pressure, if not outright stress. And if a complication develops, the stress will likely increase. Thus, in our view, psychological support is an important component of diabetes management.

DISCUSSION
Prevalence and Incidence

Type I diabetes is the most common endocrine–metabolic disorder in childhood and the leading cause of chronic disability in childhood. Incidence and prevalence rates of the disease vary in different populations. Current estimates are that in the United States it afflicts approximately 100,000 children under the age of 20, or about 1 of every 600 children in the United States. Type I diabetes usually has its onset in childhood, with a peak incidence between ages 10 and 14, although it may occur at any age. The incidence rate is relatively low for children under the age of 5, increases between the ages of 5 and 15, and then begins to taper off. In the United States, the cumulative risk to age 20 is about 1.5 per 10,000 population per year. Both sexes appear to be nearly equally affected with a very slight excess in males. It would appear that the African-American population has about a 50% reduction

in the risk of developing type I diabetes, while the risk for Asian children is much less.

There is a strong genetic predisposition to type I diabetes. Besides the family tendency of the disease, evidence for this genetic predisposition comes from demonstrations that the concordance rate is higher in monozygotic than in dizygotic twins.

Related Basic Science

Type I diabetes mellitus is a disease of disordered immune function, involving the destruction of pancreatic islet insulin-secreting beta cells. The onset of clinical symptoms of diabetes represents the endpoint of a chronic progressive decline in beta cell function, and occurs when the majority of beta cells have been lost. Pancreases from humans with recent-onset diabetes show the coexistence of various stages of inflammation, termed *insulitis,* consisting primarily of T lymphocytes (mostly cytotoxic/suppressor cells), some B lymphocytes, and macrophages. The lesion of insulitis is consistent with a cell-mediated immune reaction, similar to the lymphocytic infiltration associated with other autoimmune endocrinopathies. Not all islets are involved at the time of diagnosis. Histologically, a few show the pathognomic insulitis lesion, but intact islets with beta cells can be found, as can an occasional hyperplastic islet. The majority of islets are "pseudoatrophic," small islets without mononuclear infiltration and devoid of beta cells, but with intact glucagon-secreting alpha cells and somatostatin-secreting delta cells.

Evidence suggests that the islet immunopathology may begin several years prior to the clinical onset of disease. The antigen that causes T-cell activation and initiates the chronic destructive immune response is not yet known, but a number of candidate autoantigens have been identified. Islet cell antibodies, complement-fixing islet cell antibodies, and insulin autoantibodies have been demonstrated up to 10 years prior to the onset of clinical symptoms in first-degree relatives of probands with type I diabetes. The finding of islet cell antibodies and insulin autoantibodies, together with a measurable decrease in early insulin release after an intravenous glucose load, predicts the future development of type I diabetes in this population at high risk.

That a particular genetic background is prerequisite to, but not sufficient for, the development of type I diabetes is generally accepted. Ninety-five percent of Caucasian individuals who develop type I diabetes carry HLA-DR3 and/or HLA-DR4. Furthermore, recent studies using DNA probe techniques have identified a possible association with an allelic substitution at position 57 of the HLA-DQ B chain, and this region, rather than the DR subregion, may include the gene that contributes to the inheritance of diabetes. It appears likely, however, that a gene or genes outside the major histocompatibility complex region are also necessary for the development of diabetes. Additionally, given the less than 50% concordance rate in monozygotic twins, it is likely that nongenetic (i.e., environmental) factors play a role in disease pathogenesis.

Natural History and Its Modification with Treatment

During the first few months after the onset of type I diabetes, the majority of patients undergo a period of relative remission, the "honeymoon" period, manifested by improvement in carbohydrate tolerance and a tendency toward frequent episodes of hypoglycemia dictating a reduction in insulin dosage. The remission phase is associated with some recovery of pancreatic islet beta cell insulin secretory capacity, as demonstrated by increased C-peptide secretion, whereas eventual clinical relapse is associated with decreased C-peptide secretion. The ultimate loss of beta cell function has been called *total diabetes.*

The duration of the remission phase generally is but a few weeks to a few months. There are some data indicating that this period may be extended by vigorous insulin therapy from the onset of clinical disease. In addition, as noted earlier, recent investigations have suggested that this period may be extended by the use of immune intervention.

As a function of time, many patients suffer the ravages of the chronic complications of the disease: vascular, neurologic, and organ specific. The frequency, severity, and progression of the chronic complications appear to be related to the degree of hyperglycemia and associated metabolic derangements, as well as the duration of the disease.

Prevention

If type I diabetes develops insidiously from an ongoing, immune-mediated destructive process, and it may, in fact, be predicted with some degree of accuracy, then it is possible that intervention at a point in this long prodromal period would prevent the initiation or perpetuation of beta cell destruction. Immune intervention has been successful in preventing or reversing the development of diabetes in the BB rat and the NOD mouse, as well as in animals that have received diabetes by passive transfer of T lymphocytes. These successes, as well as the evidence that immune mechanisms are critical in the pathogenesis of human diabetes and the obvious desirability of preventing the disease, have led to a number of clinical studies of various immunotherapies in early diabetes and prediabetes in humans, involving cyclosporin, azathioprine, nicotinamide, and other agents. To date, studies in recent-onset type I diabetes have demonstrated that immune intervention does indeed alter the natural history of the disease. Yet, these studies have not allowed a conclusion as to the potential long-term clinical benefits of such intervention, largely because of the small sample sizes and relatively short duration of follow-up of the subjects. It is possible that intervention at this stage in the disease process may be effective in halting the destruction of beta cells, resulting in milder disease, certainly a benefit for the patient with diabetes; however, it is more likely that immune intervention at this point is already too late to preserve sufficient beta cell function to be clinically important. Thus, the logical goal of future studies will be to intervene during the stage of "prediabetes," prior to clinical diagnosis.

Cost Containment

The overall health care burden of diabetes is enormous. Yet, most of the expense is related to management of the chronic complications of diabetes. Thus, it makes sense to expend whatever resources are necessary to carefully control glycemia, in an effort to limit the risk of the chronic complications. The goal is to maintain the patient as a productive member of society throughout his or her life span. Unfortunately, too often the emphasis has been on cost containment early in the course of the disease. This is shortsighted and fails to appreciate where the real expense lies.

REFERENCES

Diabetes Control and Complications Trial Research Group. The effect of intensive treatment of diabetes on the development and progression of long-term complications in insulin-dependent diabetes mellitus. N Engl J Med 1993;329:977.
Hirsch IB, Farkas-Hirsch R, Skyler JS. Intensive insulin therapy for the treatment of type I diabetes mellitus. Diabetes Care 1990;13:1265.
Marks JB, Skyler JS. Clinical review: Immunotherapy of type I diabetes mellitus. J Clin Endocrinol Metab 1991;72:3.
National Diabetes Data Group. Classification of diabetes mellitus and other categories of glucose intolerance. Diabetes 1979;28:1039.
National Diabetes Data Group. Diabetes in America. Publication 85-1468. Washington, DC: U.S. Public Health Service, 1985.
Schade DS, Santiago JV, Skyler JS, Rizza R. Intensive insulin therapy. Princeton, NJ: Excerpta Medica, 1983.
Skyler JS. Relationship of metabolic control of diabetes mellitus to chronic complications. In: Rifkin H, Porte D, eds. Ellenberg & Rifkin's Diabetes mellitus: Theory and practice, 4th ed. New York: Elsevier, 1990:856.
Skyler JS, Marks JB. Immune intervention in type I diabetes mellitus. Diabetes Rev 1993;1:15.
Skyler JS, Rabinovitch A. Etiology and pathogenesis of insulin-dependent diabetes mellitus. Pediatr Ann 1987;16:682.

CHAPTER 9–30

Type II (Non-Insulin-dependent) Diabetes Mellitus

William G. Blackard, M.D.

DEFINITION

Type II or non-insulin-dependent diabetes mellitus (NIDDM) can be defined as diabetes mellitus that does not require insulin to prevent death, ketoacidosis, or weight loss. Many non-insulin-dependent diabetic patients, however, may take insulin to control hyperglycemia. In contrast, in type I diabetes (insulin-dependent diabetes mellitus), insulin treatment is required for survival and prevention of ketoacidosis.

ETIOLOGY

Carbohydrate intolerance in the type II diabetic has been attributed to both insulin resistance and insulin deficiency (relative or absolute). Without the diabetic gene impairing beta cell function, insulin secretion may be increased sufficiently to overcome insulin resistance in many patients (nondiabetic obese patient).

CRITERIA FOR DIAGNOSIS
Suggestive

The patient with type II diabetes is frequently asymptomatic. Fifty percent of type II patients do not know that they are afflicted. Consequently, many are detected as a result of routine blood testing. Others may be detected as a result of more focused testing because of known risk factors for diabetes, such as a history of obesity, large babies, or strong family history of diabetes. Half of the patients, however, are detected because of symptoms suggesting the possibility of diabetes, such as polyuria, polydipsia, polyphagia, weight loss or gain, pruritus, dry mouth, visual disturbance, fatigue, and monilial vaginitis or balanitis.

Definitive

The diagnosis of diabetes (type II as well as type I) is based solely on demonstration of hyperglycemia. For specific criteria, see Plans, Diagnostic.

CLINICAL MANIFESTATIONS
Subjective

A family history of diabetes in first-degree relatives is present in 25 to 30% of type II diabetics, roughly twice as often as in type I diabetes. Twin studies (monozygotic) indicate 80 to 100% concordance for type II diabetes, whereas concordance is observed in only 50% of type I diabetes. Nongenetic (environmental) factors such as overeating caused by obesity and increased parity also provide a background partly responsible for diabetes. The fact that diabetes is observed twice as frequently in minority groups may be due to either environmental or hereditary factors.

Polyuria, polydipsia, and polyphagia are the three most characteristic symptoms, leading even the most naive layperson to suspect the diagnosis. Dry skin with pruritus and dry mouth occur as a result of hyperglycemia and polyuria. An increase in skin infections, particularly of the external genitalia (monilial vaginitis and balanitis), is an additional external manifestation of hyperglycemia and glycosuria. Blurred vision, caused by lens refractive changes induced by hyperglycemia, is also a frequent presenting complaint triggering suspicion of diabetes. Less commonly, type II diabetics may present with a complication of diabetes such as a mononeuropathy (third or sixth nerve palsy) or peripheral neuropathy with paresthesias of the legs and feet. Even more rarely, the type II diabetic may present with more severe complications thought to require 10 years' or more duration of diabetes for their development, such as retinopathy and nephropathy (see Chapter 9–31). A number of musculoskeletal conditions (e.g., Dupuytren's contractures, carpal tunnel syndrome, and stiff joints) may also be associated with diabetes, but their specificity for diabetes is so low that they do not serve as specific indicators of the disease.

Objective

Physical Examination

The physical examination in patients with type II diabetes may reveal little other than obesity. The obesity is sometimes centripetal, with supraclavicular fat padding giving the patient the appearance of Cushing's disease, often called the pseudocushingoid appearance of diabetes. Increased upper abdominal obesity (increased waist-to-hip ratio) is known risk factor for diabetes, particularly in women.

Hypertension also occurs more frequently in diabetic patients, being present in 50%.

Epidemiologic and clinical studies have suggested that insulin resistance accompanied by hyperinsulinemia may play important roles in diabetes, hypertension, dyslipidemia, and atherosclerosis. A variety of dermatologic conditions may be present, from necrobiosis lipoidicum diabetocorum and granuloma annulare to the eruptive xanthoma seen as a result of diabetes-associated hypertriglyceridemia. Particular note should be made of acanthosis nigricans (Figure 9–30–1), thought to be a marker for insulin resistance and present in obese insulin-resistant nondiabetics as well as in type II diabetics. The lesion is a creased, sightly elevated hyperpigmented area often with a velvety appearance over the nape of the neck and in the axilla, often associated with accordons (skin tags).

Retinopathy, is present (50% prevalence if duration of disease is > 10 years), will be detected by the presence of microaneurysms, exudates and hemorrhages, and, in some cases, neovascularization and fibrous proliferation.

Involvement of the internal organs rarely gives rise to abnormal physical findings, except for the cardiomegaly of diabetic or hypertensive cardiomyopathy and hepatomegaly secondary to fatty infiltration. Rarely, cirrhosis secondary to diabetes can occur.

Neuropathy is common and presents most commonly with hypesthesia and decreased vibratory sensation over the lower legs with hypoactive or absent reflexes. One of the more important aspects of the physical examination in diabetic patients is examination of the feet. Neurotrophic ulcers over the metatarsal heads as well as gangrenous toes may not be recognized by some patients because of the absence of pain sensation.

An absent or decreased pedal pulse is a common manifestation of premature atherosclerosis.

Routine Laboratory Abnormalities

Routine laboratory tests in the uncomplicated type II diabetic patient may show no more than glycosuria on urinalysis and hyperglycemia on

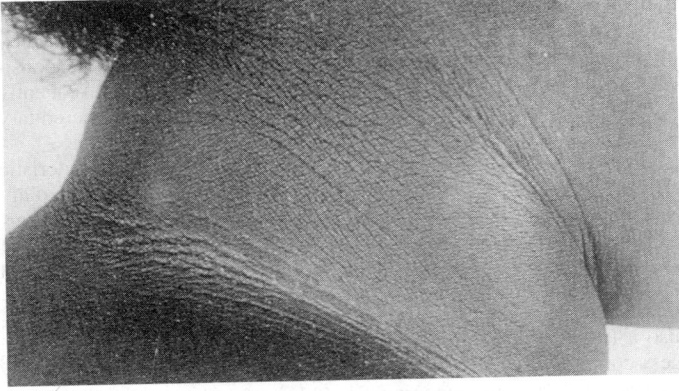

Figure 9–30–1. Acanthosis nigricans in an insulin-resistant patient.

blood analysis. When complications occur, the laboratory findings reflect those complications: proteinuria and increased plasma blood urea nitrogen and creatinine when kidneys are involved, cardiomegaly radiographically and abnormal electrocardiogram when the heart is involved. Lipid profiles are mandatory in diabetic patients because of both the increased association of diabetes and dyslipoproteinemia and the cardiovascular risk stratification. Plasma total cholesterol, low-density lipoprotein cholesterol, and triglycerides are frequently elevated. Testing for microalbuminuria (undetectable by standard dipsticks) may be useful in detecting patients at risk for developing clinical nephropathy.

PLANS

Diagnostic

Differential Diagnosis

Postprandial hyperglycemia must be differentiated from type II diabetes (NIDDM). This can be successfully accomplished by requiring that the blood sample is drawn from the patient who is fasting.

Diagnostic Options and Recommended Approach

Diagnosis of type II diabetes depends solely on the demonstration of hyperglycemia. Internationally accepted criteria for the diagnosis of diabetes require one of the following: fasting venous plasma glucose level greater than 140 mg/dL (7.8 mM) on two occasions or sustained elevated plasma glucose concentration during the oral glucose tolerance test. If the blood glucose level is greater than 140 mg/dL (7.8 mM), the oral glucose tolerance test is not required and is rarely employed today for the diagnosis. If, however, a strong suspicion of diabetes exists and fasting plasma glucose values are nondiagnostic, the oral glucose tolerance test may be useful. Plasma glucose values greater than 200 mg/dL (11.1 mM) at 2 hours and at some other time point within 2 hours of administration of the 75-g glucose dose confirm the diagnosis of diabetes. Caution is urged in performing oral glucose tolerance tests in hospitalized patients admitted for acute illnesses or patients not properly prepared with a 300-g carbohydrate diet for several days prior to testing because of the high incidence of false-positive tests under these conditions.

Glycosylated hemoglobin determinations are now routine in the management of diabetic patients. Glycosylated hemoglobin reflects the integrated plasma glucose over the previous 2-month period. This test is essential in following type I diabetic patients, where random office plasma glucose values rarely reflect accurately glycemic control. It is also extremely useful in the care of type II diabetics to determine that the normal fasting or postprandial glucose values obtained in the office do not simply represent compliance with the therapeutic program for the few days prior to the visit.

Several characteristics distinguish type II from type I diabetes (see Table 9–30–1). These include age of onset (>40 vs <40), greater percentage of first-degree relatives affected, lack of association with HLA antigens, infrequent association with autoimmune diseases, resistance to ketosis, frequent presence of obesity (60–80%), and a frequently excellent response to diet and oral agents. A change in status such as appearance of ketosis years later can result in reclassification of type II diabetes as type I. Conversely, a patient presenting with severe stress and infection with ketosis may be reclassified as type II after alleviation of the acute condition.

Therapeutic

The primary treatment of type II diabetes is dietary. Fifty percent of patients can achieve normoglycemia with weight reduction. If diet fails, a trial of oral hypoglycemics is indicated. These agents are listed in Table 9–30–2. The first four are first-generation sulfonylureas, whereas the last two are second-generation agents characterized by smaller dose requirements and nonionic protein binding. The latter characteristic offers an advantage to patients on numerous drugs, as most protein-binding drugs bind ionically and may displace or be displaced by first-generation drugs, which also bind ionically. Seventy to eighty percent of type II diabetics respond initially to these agents, but secondary

TABLE 9–30–1. A COMPARISON OF INSULIN-DEPENDENT DIABETES MELLITUS (TYPE I) AND NON-INSULIN-DEPENDENT DIABETES MELLITUS (TYPE II)

Characteristic	Type I	Type II
Age of onset	Usually <30 years	Usually >40 years
Ketosis	Common	Rare
Body weight	Nonobese	Obese
Genetics		
Association with histocompatibility antigens?	Yes	No
Monozygotic twin studies, concordance rate	40–50%	Nearly 100%
Circulating islet cell antibodies?	Yes	No
Associated with other autoimmune phenomena?	Occasionally	No
Treatment with insulin necessary	Always	Usually not
Complications	Frequent	Frequent
Insulin secretion	Severe deficiency	Moderate deficiency to hyperinsulinemia
Insulin resistance	Occasional, with poor control or excessive insulin antibodies	Usually, due to receptor and postreceptor defects

failure occurs at a rate of 6% per year. When secondary failure occurs, the physician can try to restore responsiveness to the drug by a short period of intensive dieting or insulin treatment. It is important to emphasize that the maximal *effective* dose is generally half of that stated in Table 9–30–2; that is, patients who fail on 10 mg glyburide or 20 mg glipizide rarely respond to higher doses. The introduction of new drugs, such as metformin, will result in salvage of many patients who are secondary failures on sulfonylureas.

When failure on oral agents occurs, permanent insulin treatment is usually instituted. A popular approach is to start with twice-daily therapy (bedtime insulin, daytime sulfonylurea). Usually, insulin at 0.2 U/kg is begun at bedtime to control overnight hepatic glucose production, and sulfonylurea is administered in the morning to enhance meal-induced insulin secretion. Otherwise, insulin treatment can be initiated at a dose of 0.5 U/kg body weight using intermediate-acting insulin. This dose may be supplemented with rapid-acting insulin if hyperglycemia is excessive before lunch or with evening intermediate-acting insulin if early-morning hyperglycemia persists.

The major side effect of insulin and of the oral antidiabetic agents is hypoglycemia. Mild postprandial hypoglycemia can occur in 25% of patients on oral hypoglycemics, but severe fasting hypoglycemia is less common; however, when severe fasting hypoglycemia occurs in patients on oral agents, the patient must be hospitalized because of the need for intravenous glucose for up to a week. Chlorpropamide and glyburide, because of their greater potency, are the agents most commonly associated with severe hypoglycemia. Caution should be exercised particularly in treating people over the age of 60 with these drugs because of their greater propensity to hypoglycemia. Other than hypoglycemia, the drugs are extremely well tolerated, with less than 2% of patients discontinuing therapy because of gastrointestinal, hematologic, or dermatologic reactions.

In no disease is patient education more important than in diabetes. Patients should have an understanding of the disease process consonant with their ability to comprehend. They must be educated about the complications of diabetes in such a way that they can approach the future optimistically. The patient must also be intensively educated regarding diet, exercise, foot care, and the complications of treatment (hypoglycemic reactions). The advent of glucose self-monitoring for diabetic patients has been perhaps the greatest single advance in the treatment of diabetes in the past three decades. Patients need to be educated on blood glucose testing and how to manipulate therapy accordingly (particularly diet and insulin).

FOLLOW-UP

Diabetic patients, having been taught to recognize early signs and symptoms of complications, should report them promptly to the health care team. Promptness is particularly important in the case of foot problems, where early attention can prevent 50% of the amputations. Patients should also report interim problems with blood glucose control so intervisit adjustments can be made.

Type II diabetic patients should be seen at least semiannually; those patients on insulin or with complications should be seen more frequently. A complete physical examination should be done annually. On interim visits, examination should consist of weight, blood pressure, and areas found abnormal on previous examinations or areas indicated by interim history. The feet should be examined at each visit not only to detect lesions but to emphasize the importance of foot care. Annual examination by an ophthalmologist is recommended for all patients over the age of 35 or younger if diabetes has been present more than 5 years.

Glycosylated hemoglobin should be performed twice yearly. Fasting or postprandial plasma glucose values at each visit are also useful in monitoring control. Patients should be encouraged to bring their glucose monitoring equipment into the office so they can compare glucose values determined simultaneously by the laboratory and by their apparatus. A lipid profile should be obtained annually. Routine urinalysis should be performed yearly to assess proteinuria. If proteinuria is present, serum blood urea nitrogen and creatinine, 24-hour urine protein, and glomerular filtration rate should be assessed at least yearly.

TABLE 9–30–2. COMPARISON OF ORALLY ADMINISTERED SULFONYLUREA HYPOGLYCEMIC AGENTS

Characteristic	Tolbutamide (Orinase)	Acetohexamide (Dymelor)	Tolazamide (Ronase)	Chlorpropamide (Diabinese)	Glipizide (Glibenese)	Glyburide (Micronase)
Relative potency	1	2.5	5	6	100	150
Duration of action (h)	6–10	12–18	16–24	24–72	16–24	18–24
Protein binding						
Type	Ionic/nonionic	Ionic/nonionic	Ionic/nonionic	Ionic/nonionic	Nonionic	Nonionic
Extent (%)	>98	~90	>98	~95	>98	>98
Dose (mg)						
Range	500–3000	250–1500	100–1000	100–500	2.5–40	1.25–20
Average	1500	1000	250	250	10	7.5
Doses per day (No.)	2 or 3	2	1 or 2	1	1 or 2	1 or 2
Frequency of severe hypoglycemia (%)	<1	~1	~1	4–6	2–4	4–6
Usual initial daily dose (mg)	500	250	100	100	5	2.5
Approximate monthly cost of average dose ($)	15	20	20	10	15	15

Source: Gerich JE. Oral hypoglycemic agents. N Engl J Med 1989;321:1235. Modified with permission from the publisher and author.

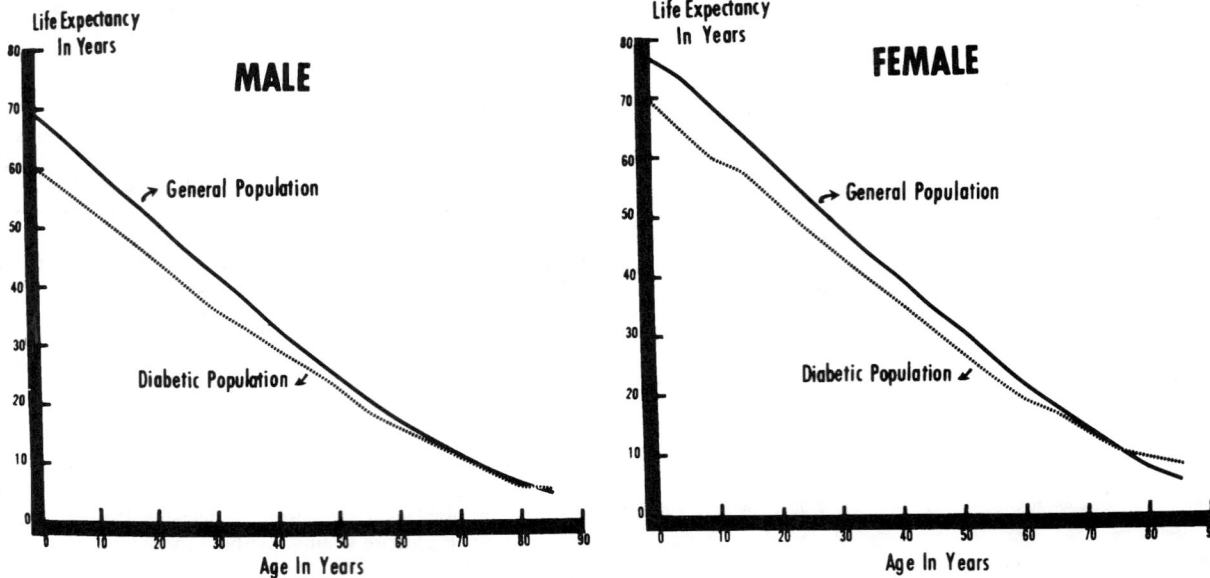

Figure 9–30–2. Estimated life expectancy of diabetics by sex. Diabetic population of Iowa, 1972 to 1973, versus general population of Iowa, 1969 to 1971. *(Source: Bale GS, Entmacher PS. Estimated life expectancy of diabetics. Diabetes 1977;26:437. Reproduced with permission from the publisher and author.)*

DISCUSSION

Prevalence and Incidence

The prevalence of type II diabetes for Caucasians is slightly less than 7%; however, the prevalence in minority groups (African-Americans and Mexican-Americans) is two to two and a half times greater.

Related Basic Science

The pathogenesis of type II diabetes is quite different from that of type I diabetes, although the end result of a relative or absolute deficiency of insulin produces similar manifestations in both. Type II diabetes is due to both insulin resistance and insulin deficiency (relative or absolute). As the most common cause of insulin resistance is obesity, it is not surprising that 80% of type II diabetics in this country are obese. Not all obese people have diabetes, however. It is generally believed that what is inherited in the diabetic is the inability of the beta cell to compensate and hypersecrete insulin to overcome the resistance. The resultant hyperglycemia may perpetuate the defect by further impairing beta cell secretion, so-called "glucose toxicity." Necropsy studies have indicated a severe reduction in beta cell volume and mass in type II diabetics, although not nearly the reduction observed in type I diabetics. "Insulinitis" as observed in type I diabetes due to autoimmunity or infection is not found in the pancreas of type II diabetics. Rather, amyloid deposition in the islets is a common finding. The amino acid composition of islet amyloid has now been determined, and significant homology with calcitonin-related gene protein has been noted. This material has been called diabetes-associated protein or amylin. Speculation as to its role in impairing insulin secretion has created great interest in this protein.

The cause of insulin resistance in type II diabetes has not been clearly established. The defect appears to be more postreceptor than receptor. Abnormalities in autophosphorylation of the beta subunit of the insulin receptor as well as in the ability of the receptor to function as a tyrosine or serine kinase has been demonstrated. It is not clear whether these abnormalities are primary or secondary to the metabolic state. A search for candidate genes for type II diabetes has revealed occasional (rare) cases of mutations in the insulin receptor and even rarer mutations in insulin receptor substrate I. Another contender with limited support as yet is a glycogen synthase gene. Greatest success in the search for a candidate gene for diabetes has been in MODY (maturity-onset diabetes of youth) families, where 50% have been shown to have a mutation in the glucokinase gene. The precise role of these and other postreceptor aberrations in the causation of insulin resistance has yet to be established.

Natural History and Its Modification with Treatment

Cross-sectional population studies indicate that initially hyperinsulinemia is present as the beta cells attempt to compensate for insulin resistance. At this time, hyperglycemia is mild and insulin receptor numbers may be decreased as a result of downregulation by hyperinsulinemia. As loss of beta cells occurs, hyperinsulinemia may revert to normoinsulinemia or hypoinsulinemia with further elevation of plasma glucose. Insulin receptors at this point during hypoinsulinemia may actually be increased. If beta cell loss continues such that insulin secretory capacity is severely impaired, ketosis may result, necessitating reclassification of the patient.

The complications of type II diabetes are generally related to the duration of diabetes (see Chapter 9–31).

The mortality from diabetes is shown in Figure 9–30–2. This figure represents mortality for both type I and type II, but because 90% of diabetics are type II, it generally reflects their mortality rates.

Prevention

A major factor in the pathogenesis of type II diabetes is insulin resistance. Any effort made to reduce insulin resistance will at least delay, if not prevent, the appearance of diabetes. Weight control and exercise are established methods of improving insulin sensitivity and, therefore, should be encouraged in anyone at risk for diabetes (positive family history, history of big babies, obesity).

Cost Containment

The major factor in cost containment is proper patient care to prevent hospitalization for acute and chronic complications costing as much as four times outpatient costs. In this regard, additional costs for glucose self-monitoring equipment to improve patient management is economical. Conversely, failure to use other health care professionals (teaching nurses, dietitians, podiatrists, etc.) is false economy. On the other hand, costs for pumps for constant subcutaneous insulin infusion ($5000 initial outlay plus $1000 per year) may not be justified unless compliance is reasonably ensured by a trial period in pump use before purchase. Studies have shown high attrition rates within the first year of pump use if patients are not adequately selected and prepared.

REFERENCES

American Diabetes Association. Clinical practice recommendations. Diabetes Care 1990;13(suppl. 1):1.

Cooper GJS, Leighton B, Dimitriades GD, et al. Amylin found in amyloid deposits in human type II diabetes mellitus may be a hormone that regulates glycogen metabolism in skeletal muscle. Proc Natl Acad Sci USA 1988;85:7763.

Davidson JK, ed. Insulin Deficiency. In: Clinical diabetes mellitus: A problem-oriented approach. 2nd ed. New York: Thieme, 1991:68.

DeFronzo RA. The triumvirate: β-cell, muscle, liver. Diabetes 1988;37:667.

Harris ML, Hamman RE, eds. National Diabetes Data Group: Diabetes in America (data compiled in 1984). NIH Publication 85-1468. Washington, DC: National Institutes of Health, 1985.

Gerich JE. Drug therapy: Oral hypoglycemic agents. N Engl J Med 1989;321:1231.

National Diabetes Data Group. Classification and diagnosis of diabetes mellitus and other categories of glucose intolerance. Diabetes 1979;28:1039.

CHAPTER 9–31

Acute Complications of Diabetes • Diabetic Ketoacidosis and Hyperosmolar Hyperglycemic Nonketotic Coma (Hyperosmolar Hyperglycemic Syndrome)

Jennifer B. Marks, M.D., and Jay S. Skyler, M.D.

DEFINITION

Diabetic ketoacidosis (DKA) is a life-threatening metabolic acidosis associated with varying degrees of hyperglycemia and ketonemia, the consequence of a relative or absolute deficiency of insulin coupled with counterregulatory hormone excess. Hyperosmolar hyperglycemic nonketotic coma (HHNC), also a life-threatening condition, results from relative insulin deficiency and is characterized by severe hyperglycemia, hyperosmolarity and dehydration, altered sensorium, and the absence of significant ketoacidosis. Mental status changes associated with lesser degrees of hyperosmolarity are also seen, constituting a range of hyperosmolar hyperglycemic nonketotic states that can be referred to as the hyperosmolar hyperglycemic syndrome (HHS).

ETIOLOGY

Diabetic ketoacidosis and HHNC or HHS are the result of uncontrolled diabetes mellitus. DKA is most commonly a complication of type I (insulin-dependent) diabetes mellitus, but may rarely occur in type II (non-insulin-dependent) diabetes, and can be encountered as the first presentation of undiagnosed type I diabetes (see Chapter 9-29). HHNC develops most often in older patients with a history of non-insulin-dependent diabetes or impaired glucose tolerance, but also not uncommonly in the setting of unsuspected type II diabetes.

Both DKA and HHNC most commonly occur as the result of a precipitating stress. In fact, in as many as 75% of patients developing DKA, an underlying contributing cause can be identified. Stress causes an increase in the secretion of the counterregulatory hormones—epinephrine, norepinephrine, glucagon, cortisol, and growth hormone—all with antiinsulin effects, rendering the ambient insulin, whether endogenously produced or supplementally administered, inadequate. Examples of triggers that precipitate DKA are an intercurrent infection, the omission of insulin, a myocardial infarction, pancreatitis, trauma, pregnancy, and emotional stress. Similarly, precipitating factors often underlie the development of HHS. Patients at risk for HHS are often elderly, sometimes infirm or socially isolated, and frequently have underlying medical problems, including cardiac and renal disease. When their already limited mobility is further impaired by a recent infection (urinary tract infection, pneumonia), injury (hip fracture), or other event (myocardial infarction, cerebrovascular accident, gastrointestinal bleed), fluid losses increase, fluid intake is reduced, and a vicious cycle of hyperglycemia, hyperosmolarity, and hyperosmolar diuresis ensues, further augmenting fluid losses.

Both DKA and HHNC result from insulin deficiency. In the former case the deficiency may be virtually absolute, but in either case the deficiency is at least a relative one; in HHS, circulating insulin levels may in fact be elevated. In the presence of an insulin deficiency, relative or absolute, the cells of the body are unable to use glucose, as insulin provides the mechanism that transports glucose into the cell. The body responds to this state of relative starvation by activating counterregulatory mechanisms to produce greater amounts of glucose, resulting in hyperglycemia, and to produce alternative fuels, including ketoacids and fatty acids. Because of this increase in counterregulatory hormone secretion and the altered metabolic environment, DKA and HHS represent states of relative insulin resistance; that is, this altered metabolic milieu causes resistance to the action of any amount of insulin that may be present (relative deficiency) and contributes to the development and worsening of acidosis (DKA) and hyperglycemia (both).

CRITERIA FOR DIAGNOSIS

Suggestive

Diabetic ketoacidosis should be part of the differential diagnosis in a younger patient presenting with hyperglycemia and metabolic acidosis, with or without a history of diabetes.

Definitive

The cardinal diagnostic features of DKA are hyperglycemia, ketosis, and acidosis; volume depletion is also frequently present.

A clinical diagnosis of DKA can be made at the bedside in the patient who presents with hyperglycemia, ketonemia, evidence of volume depletion, and hyperventilation (Kussmaul respirations), from which one can infer the presence of acidosis and quickly confirm it with an arterial blood gas and the demonstration of an elevated anion gap metabolic acidosis. The serum glucose is generally 250 mg/dL or greater, the pH is less than 7.3, the serum bicarbonate is less than 15 mEq/L, and ketonemia is present in undiluted plasma. The degree of hyperglycemia need not be great; a significant proportion of patients with DKA have glucose concentrations less than 350 mg/dL.

In contrast, patients with HHNC or HHS are usually older, with or without a known history of diabetes. They are severely hyperglycemic and profoundly dehydrated secondary to osmotic diuresis and inadequate fluid replacement. The diagnosis of HHNC or HHS is made by the demonstration of severe hyperglycemia (600–2000 mg/dL), elevated serum osmolality (>350 mOsm/kg), and minimal or absent ketonuria in a patient with an abnormal mental status.

CLINICAL MANIFESTATIONS

Subjective

The patient with DKA complains of fairly recent, subacute onset of symptoms of polyuria, polydipsia, nocturia, fatigue, and weight loss despite an increased appetite. The symptoms may follow a viral infection or other stress. At the time of presentation, the patient may complain of dizziness and abdominal pain. The patient with HHS has symptoms that are more insidious in onset, including polyuria, nocturia, polydipsia, weight loss, malaise, and some degree of altered sensorium, which may be identified by a family member rather than the patient. The patient may, in fact, be unable to provide a history, frequently presenting with profound obtundation. The history of the gradual onset of symptoms of hyperglycemia, therefore, as well as symptoms of an underlying precipitating event, may be obtained only in retrospect.

Objective

Physical Examination

Physical findings in DKA include signs of volume depletion (hypotension, orthostasis, tachycardia, dry mucous membranes, diminished urine output), Kussmaul respirations, an odor of acetone on the breath, abdominal tenderness, and altered sensorium. The patient with HHS appears profoundly ill and severely dehydrated, with a markedly abnormal mental status, ranging from mild obtundation to frank coma and seizures, depending on the degree of hyperosmolality. Indeed, the clinical picture may initially suggest a primary neurologic event, and unless the index of suspicion is sufficiently high, the diagnosis may be missed or delayed. The physical examination in both HHS and DKA should be directed not only toward confirmation of the diagnosis, but also toward identification of precipitating causes.

Routine Laboratory Abnormalities

The degree of hyperglycemia in DKA is extremely variable, dependent partly on the degree of hypovolemia present. It can range from nearly normal to levels more characteristic of HHS. A decreased serum pH reflects excessive ketogenesis and decreased levels of bicarbonate in the blood, resulting in an increased anion gap metabolic acidosis. DKA may present without an anion gap (hyperchloremic acidosis) if the extracellular volume status and the renal excretion of ketoacids are relatively well maintained.

The patient with HHS may have a mildly increased anion gap acidemia, usually due to lactic acidosis, but without significant ketoacidosis. Common electrolyte abnormalities to be anticipated in both DKA and HHS include disturbances in sodium and potassium. Despite often elevated serum potassium levels, there is invariably a deficit of total body potassium stores in DKA. In HHS, decreased serum potassium levels result from the profound osmotic diuresis. As a result of the profound diuresis in HHS, there is marked hypertonicity and increased serum sodium levels. In DKA serum sodium levels tend to be low, despite increases in osmolality, due either to a dilutional hyponatremia mediated by hyperglycemia, or to pseudohyponatremia from associated hypertriglyceridemia. Hypertriglyceridemia is often seen with diabetes out of control, secondary to decreased lipoprotein lipase activity due to insulin deficiency. Phosphate levels are usually low in both DKA and HHS, reflecting an actual deficiency resulting from acidosis and diuresis and/or a general catabolic state. Levels of blood urea nitrogen and creatinine are often elevated in both DKA and HHS due to volume depletion, although this may also reflect true underlying renal failure. Spurious elevations in creatinine seen in DKA are secondary to the interference of acetoacetate with certain methods of measurement.

Hyperamylasemia, due to either pancreatitis, increased salivary secretion, or decreased renal clearance, may be present. An elevated hematocrit and a leukocytosis are frequent in both conditions, usually as a result of volume contraction, although the elevated white blood cell count may also reflect the effects of catecholamine and cortisol excess or an underlying infection.

PLANS

Diagnostic

Differential Diagnosis

The differential diagnoses of DKA and HHS include uremia, poisoning, lactic acidosis, and alcoholic ketoacidosis. These all may present with varying degrees of metabolic acidosis, ketonuria, azotemia, anorexia, nausea, vomiting, altered sensorium, and signs of hypovolemia. The diagnosis of alcoholic ketoacidosis is based on clinical history and lack of significant hyperglycemia (although a mild elevation of blood glucose is not uncommon). It is seen in the setting of recently decreased or discontinued alcohol ingestion in a patient with a history

of alcohol abuse, and may also be associated with gastrointestinal symptoms of peptic ulcer disease or pancreatitis. Ketonuria secondary to starvation, but not usually ketonemia, may be present. Difficulty arises when a patient with alcoholic ketoacidosis has a history of diabetes, as the two conditions can coexist. Uremia is a common cause of increased anion gap acidosis, but ketonemia is not present, and acidosis is usually not significant until renal function is severely compromised. Toxin ingestion may cause an increased anion gap, but usually not significant hyperglycemia or ketonemia. Isopropyl alcohol ingestion causes acetone breath and ketonemia and elevated osmolarity, but not an increased anion gap. An increased anion gap metabolic acidosis, without evidence of hyperglycemia, ketonemia, uremia, or alcohol or toxin ingestion, may represent lactic acidosis due to any number of causes, including shock resulting from severe volume depletion and sepsis. The clinical setting as well as an increased blood lactate level should confirm the diagnosis. With severe obtundation as occurs in HHNC, one may also consider a primary neurologic event, for example, a cerebrovascular accident or subarachnoid hemorrhage, as the etiology of the mental status change. The picture usually becomes quite clear as laboratory results become available and as the patient responds to appropriate treatment for hyperosmolarity.

Diagnostic Options and Recommended Approach

A careful physical examination, electrocardiogram, chest x-ray, and appropriate blood, urine, and throat cultures help to elucidate any underlying factors precipitating the development of DKA or HHS. The presence of ketosis, electrolyte disturbances, and the degrees of hyperglycemia and acidosis are confirmed by routine electrolyte, blood urea nitrogen, and creatinine determinations. As therapeutic measures are instituted, one anticipates a fairly predictable course of improvement, if uncomplicated DKA or HHS is the correct diagnosis.

Therapeutic

Patients with DKA and mild degrees of acidemia who are able to tolerate increased oral fluids can be managed at home, with supplemental regular insulin before meals in addition to their usual daily regimen. With moderate to severe ketoacidosis, volume depletion, or vomiting, the patient requires hospitalization. The most critical aspects in the treatment of both diabetic ketoacidosis and hyperosmolar hyperglycemic nonketotic coma include the normalization of fluid status and electrolyte imbalances, the administration of appropriate amounts of insulin, and, not least importantly, careful observation and attention to the ongoing clinical status of the patient.

Fluid Replacement

The first priority of therapy in either DKA or HHS is to restore intravascular volume, to normalize tissue perfusion and aid in the delivery of insulin to target organs. It is important to remember that the severity of ketoacidosis depends on the balance between the rates of production and removal of ketoacids in plasma, and fluid repletion enhances their mobilization and excretion. Fluid replacement also lowers plasma glucose by hemodilution and by improvement in renal blood flow and glucose excretion. An isotonic solution is the fluid of choice; the use of hypotonic solutions, although theoretically most closely replacing the actual deficits, runs the risk of too rapid a reduction of plasma osmolality, with large intracellular fluid shifts precipitating cerebral edema and hypovolemic shock. Either normal saline (0.9% NaCl) or, alternatively, a solution of one ampule (50 mEq) of sodium bicarbonate added to a liter of half-normal saline (0.45% NaCl) can be used. The latter solution affords several advantages. First, it has an osmolality close to physiologic but hypotonic relative to plasma, thus minimizing fluid shifts. Second, it provides more sodium than hypotonic saline alone, and is therefore more effective in replacing extracellular fluid volume. Third, it provides sodium at a higher rate than chloride, thus minimizing the likelihood of the development of hyperchloremic acidosis with treatment. Lastly, when given over an hour or longer, bicarbonate therapy does not cause any of the adverse consequences sometimes associated with its use as a bolus (see Bicarbonate Therapy). The actual rate of fluid replacement in both DKA or HHS is individualized, but should follow some general guidelines (see

Table 9-31-1). In adult patients with DKA, fluid is given at a rate of 1 to 2 L over the first hour, 1 L/h for the next 3 hours, then decreased and maintained according to intake and output measurements, central venous pressure readings, and clinical assessment of the patient's state of hydration.

In HHS, the water losses are generally greater than those of the patient with DKA, but replacement may need to be done more cautiously, because of the age of the patients and the presence of renal and/or cardiac impairments. The initial rate of fluid replacement, therefore, is similar to that outlined for DKA, but is continued at a rate consistent with the cardiac and renal status of the patient, up to 1 L/h, until signs of peripheral perfusion, orthostasis, central venous pressure, and so on have normalized. Then, at a point in treatment when volume status is normal by clinical parameters, a hypotonic (0.45% NaCl) solution can be started, at a rate approximately equal to twice the urine output. The hypotonic fluid provides further sodium to replete remaining deficits and maintain extracellular volume, while providing free water to replace total body water deficits and lower serum osmolality.

In DKA, when the plasma glucose level falls to 250 to 300 mg/dL,

glucose is included in the intravenous fluid, to prevent hypoglycemia, as the insulin therapy is continued until the acidosis is resolved. The goal in either DKA or HHS of *gradually* restoring the normal metabolic state without creating complications due to treatment is foremost; this means no more rapidly than within 24 to 48 hours.

Insulin

Given the central role of insulin deficiency in the development of both DKA and HHNC, insulin administration is obviously vital to treatment and is initiated rapidly, unless there is evidence of severe hypovolemia or hypokalemia. In patients with HHS, who are profoundly volume depleted and often hypotensive, insulin therapy is withheld until the volume status is normalized, as the movement of glucose and water from the extracellular to the intracellular fluid compartment may precipitate shock.

Low doses of insulin are as effective as high doses for treating hyperglycemia and ketoacidosis, and help to avoid the development of hypoglycemia and hypokalemia, which may occur with high doses. After an initial intravenous bolus of 10 U in the patient with DKA, or 5 to 10 U in the patient with HHS, a continuous infusion of regular insulin is started at 5 to 10 U/h, adjusted approximately every 2 hours according to glycemic levels. If serum glucose does not decrease by approximately 10%/h after 2 hours, the infusion rate is doubled, and is continued until a target blood glucose concentration is reached (approximately 200-300 mg/dL). In DKA the insulin infusion rate is then decreased, but maintained at 2 to 5 U/h for at least 6 hours after the acidosis has resolved. The patient is begun on a subcutaneous regimen of insulin, including administration of regular insulin every 4 hours while receiving intravenous fluids and not taking nourishment by mouth, or a combination of intermediate-acting insulin (NPH) twice a day plus regular insulin before meals when the patient is eating a diet. The total daily dose may approximate the patient's previous insulin dose (if a history of diabetes exists) or consist of a regimen of 0.5 to 1.0 U/kg/d in divided doses, based on ideal body weight. It should be emphasized that recurrences of DKA in hospitalized patients are all too often due to inadequate insulin administration after discontinuation of the intravenous insulin infusion, often the result of "sliding scale" dosing regimens, which run the risk of omitting insulin at times when the glycemic level is only minimally elevated. The patient with type II diabetes and HHS can resume a previous diabetic regimen once the hyperglycemia and hyperosmolality have resolved and the glucose infusion has been replaced by an oral diet.

Potassium Replacement

Serum potassium levels do not accurately reflect total body levels. Although actual deficits may result from osmotic diuresis in both DKA and HHS, more often transcellular shifts of potassium occur due to insulin deficiency and acidosis, moving the potassium from the extracellular to the intracellular space, creating an apparent, but not real, deficiency. Patients who have real deficits of potassium are at risk for cardiac arrhythmias or arrest, particularly if levels decrease further with correction of acidosis and hyperglycemia. For these reasons, unless the patient is anuric or has evidence of hyperkalemia, potassium supplementation is initiated immediately in the course of treatment, at a rate of 10 to 40 mEq/h, depending on initial and subsequent repeated potassium determinations, the degree of acidosis, and the development of electrocardiogram changes (Table 9-31-1).

Bicarbonate Therapy

The use of bicarbonate in the treatment of DKA is controversial, despite studies that have demonstrated no improvement in metabolic recovery associated with its use, even in severely acidemic patients. Theoretically, there are good arguments both for and against the use of bicarbonate. Among the adverse consequences of acidosis are depressed cardiac and respiratory function, arrythmias, and hypotension. Conversely, overzealous use of bicarbonate may lead to metabolic alkalosis, aggravate hypokalemia, and contribute to the development of cerebral edema. Recent evidence also suggests that early bolus administration of bicarbonate may, in fact, delay the fall in total blood ketone bodies compared with infusion of saline alone, despite the use of simi-

TABLE 9-31-1. GUIDELINES FOR TREATMENT

Fluid replacement	
DKA	1. 0.9% NaCl or 0.45% NaCl plus 44-50 mEq of NaHCO$_3$/L at 1-2 L/h for first hour, then 0.5-1.0 L/h for next 2-3 hours until BP, P, CVP normal.
	2. 0.45% NaCl at approximately twice the urine output.
	3. Dextrose 5% in 0.45% NaCl when serum glucose is 200-300 mg/dL.
HHNC	1. 0.9% NaCl at 1 L/h for first hour; continue until BP, P, CVP normal; rate according to cardiac and renal status.
	2. 0.45% NaCl at approximately twice the urine output.
	3. Dextrose 5% in 0.45% NaCl when serum glucose is 200-300 mg/dL.
Insulin	
DKA	1. 5-10 U regular insulin IV bolus.
	2. Continuous infusion at 5-10 U/h. If serum glucose does not decrease by approximately 10% per hour after 2 h, double infusion rate and continue until blood glucose is 150-250 mg/dL.
	3. 2-5 U/h until at least 6 h after acidosis has resolved.
	4. Subcutaneous regular insulin every 4 h while on intravenous fluids, or a combination of NPH insulin twice a day plus regular insulin before meals when eating a diet (total daily dose 0.5-1.0 U/kg[IBW]/d).
HHNC	1. Withhold insulin until fluid status adequate and potassium normal.
	2. 5-10 U regular insulin IV bolus.
	3. Continuous infusion at 5-10 U/h. If serum glucose does not decrease by approximately 10% per hour after 2 h, double infusion rate and continue until blood glucose is 200-300 mg/dL.
	4. Combination of NPH insulin twice a day plus regular insulin before meals when eating a diet; may resume previous diabetic regimen.
Potassium replacement	
DKA	1. Goal: serum K$^+$ of 4-5 mEq/L
	For K$^+$ <3 mEq/L, infuse 40 mEq/h.
	For K$^+$ 3-4 mEq/L, infuse 30 mEq/h.
	For K$^+$ 4-5 mEq/L, infuse 20 mEq/h.
	For K$^+$ 5-6 mEq/L, infuse 10 mEq/h.
	For K$^+$ >6 mEq/L or hyperkalemic T-wave changes on electrocardiogram, withhold potassium infusion.
HHNC	1. Initiate as soon as urine output is adequate. Add 40 mEq/L IV fluids. Discontinue for K$^+$ >5 mEq/L or hyperkalemic T-wave changes on electrocardiogram. Continue otherwise as outlined for DKA above.

DKA, diabetic ketoacidosis; HHNC, hyperosmolar hyperglycemic nonketotic coma; BP, blood pressure; P, pulse; CVP, central venous pressure; IBW, ideal body weight.

lar amounts of insulin and similar rates of fall in blood glucose levels in both cases. Specific guidelines for use of bicarbonate are difficult to formulate because of lack of exhaustive studies of its use, but, in general, bolus bicarbonate therapy is generally restricted to use in very severe acidemia (i.e., pH < 7.0) or in less severe acidemia with underlying medical problems that may be adversely affected by the acidosis (myocardial infarction, cardiac arrhythmias, sepsis). To emphasize, the key treatments of acidosis, as outlined above, are to encourage removal of carbon dioxide from tissues through enhanced perfusion, accomplished by vigorous fluid repletion, and to inhibit production of hydrogen ions by the administration of insulin. Bicarbonate therapy is not indicated in the treatment of HHS.

Phosphate Supplementation

Although deficiencies in phosphate invariably exist in DKA and HHS, the issue of phosphate replacement is also unclear. The major concern is the potential to cause hyperphosphatemia and resultant hypocalcemia; however, phosphate levels decrease during the treatment of acidosis and correction of fluid depletion and may be associated with problems, including low 2,3-diphosphoglycerate levels, rhabdomyolysis, and respiratory muscle weakness. If phosphate is used judiciously, with levels checked daily, hyperphosphatemia can be avoided. One of the available intravenous mixtures of potassium and phosphate can be alternated with potassium chloride in a regimen of potassium and phosphate replacement. Phosphate should be withheld during the initial treatment of DKA or HHS to avoid aggravation of preexisting hypocalcemia.

Patient Monitoring

The most important factors in the successful treatment of DKA and HHS are continuous vigilance and careful monitoring of the patient's clinical status both for the desired effects of treatment and for the development of complications related to that treatment. If treatment is gradual and logical, and guided by repeated assessments of all important clinical and laboratory parameters, the risk of doing harm and causing complications is minimized, and the chance of a successful outcome is enhanced. An important tool in the ongoing assessment of the patient with uncontrolled diabetes is the flow sheet, which should be established immediately on institution of treatment and continued until the patient is stable. The intervals of assessment are adjusted according to the status of the patient. The flow sheet can take various forms, but should be established to record all diagnostic and therapeutic parameters followed during treatment. Table 9–31–2 lists the parameters to be recorded when treating patients with DKA; a similar plan can be used in patients with HHS, adapted as appropriate.

FOLLOW-UP

The frequency of follow-up of a patient who has had decompensated diabetes must be individualized, depending on many factors, including age of the patient, level of acceptance and understanding of the diagnosis and the factors that led to metabolic decompensation, ability of the patient to participate in management, extent of family and other available support systems, type of treatment regimen, concomitant aggravating illnesses or conditions, and presence of chronic diabetic complications.

Recurrence of DKA requiring repeated hospitalizations is a serious problem for the patient and the health care delivery system and, in large part, represents a failure to adequately educate and/or provide ongoing follow-up for patients with diabetes. Education and discharge planning should begin as soon as the acute phase of treatment of DKA is completed. The patient needs to understand that diabetes is a chronic, life-long disease and that DKA will recur if insulin is omitted or not adjusted during times of stress or illness. Too commonly patients assume that if they are not eating, they do not need to take insulin.

The patient with either insulin- or non-insulin-dependent diabetes must understand that poor glycemic control and recurrent decompensation are detrimental and associated with the eventual development of many chronic complications, and that an active role is required of the diabetic patient if short-term, as well as long-term, complications are to be avoided. This includes not only the responsibility to keep follow-up appointments and take insulin or oral hypoglycemic agents as prescribed, but in the case of insulin-requiring patients, to self-monitor blood glucose levels and adjust insulin and diet according to algorithms based on those results. Patients and families must learn to recognize early signs and symptoms of uncontrolled diabetes and to seek medical help before the full-blown syndromes of DKA or HHNC are allowed to develop.

DISCUSSION
Prevalence and Incidence

Diabetic ketoacidosis and HHNC are important causes of morbidity and mortality in patients with diabetes. The frequency of DKA requiring hospital admission in the United States is approximately 50,000 episodes per year, significant proportions of which are patients with a known history of diabetes (80%) and patients with recurrent episodes of DKA (20%). With an estimated mortality of 5 to 10%, 2500 to 5000 deaths per year may be attributable to DKA. The frequency of HHS is not known, but it may account for as many as half of the hospital admissions for uncontrolled diabetes. The mortality from HHNC approximates 50%, largely due to the age of the patients, presence of underlying medical problems, and occurrence of often profound hyperosmolality.

Related Basic Science

The history, physical findings, and metabolic derangements of both DKA and HHS reflect the underlying pathophysiology of the conditions. DKA develops as a consequence of a relative or absolute insulin deficiency and an excess of the insulin counterregulatory hormones glucagon, cortisol, growth hormone, and catecholamines. This results in a disturbance in metabolism of both glucose and fatty acids. Insulin deficiency and glucagon excess result in increased glucose production and decreased glucose utilization. Glucagon promotes glycogenolysis and gluconeogenesis in the liver. Insulin deficiency enhances proteolysis, resulting in muscle breakdown and release of amino acids, which are then used by the liver for gluconeogenesis. Hyperglycemia and hyperosmolality develop, a shift of water from the intracellular to the extracellular compartment follows, then glycosuria and an osmotic diuresis accompanied by large urinary losses of potassium and phosphorus ensue, and hypovolemia results. Similarly, because of the relative insulin deficiency and counterregulatory hormone (particularly glucagon) excess and insulin resistance, lipolysis and ketogenesis are stimulated, clearance of ketone bodies is decreased, and ketoacidosis develops due to the accumulation of β-hydroxybutyrate, acetoacetic acid, and acetone. Excess counterregulatory hormone levels are enhanced by the presence of precipitating factors; for example, an infection stimulates secretion of cortisol and glucagon, and myocardial infarction is accompanied by increases in catecholamines, thus contributing to the development of DKA.

In HHS the characteristic derangements develop gradually over a period of days. Hyperglycemia, developing as a consequence of insulin insufficiency and insulin resistance, together with any precipitating fac-

TABLE 9–31–2. GUIDELINES FOR ESTABLISHING A DIABETIC KETOACIDOSIS FLOW SHEET

Diagnostic Parameters

Hourly	Clinical status (mental status, blood pressure, pulse, respiratory rate), electrocardiogram (T waves), urine volume
Every 2 h	Blood glucose and ketones, urine glucose and ketones, temperature
Every 2-4 h	Electrolytes
Every 4-12 h	Blood urea nitrogen; hematocrit; blood gas, i.e., pH, pCO_2 (optional)

Therapeutic Parameters

Hourly	Review therapy—fluid (mL), potassium (mEq), insulin

tors, causes hyperosmolality and results initially in depletion of the intracellular fluid compartment and expansion of the extracellular fluid compartment. The hyperglycemia continues to worsen and osmotic diuresis ensues, resulting in losses of both solute and water, but relatively more water than solute, and depletion of the intracellular and extracellular fluid compartments. As hyperglycemia is present and the loss of water is greater than that of sodium and other electrolytes, plasma osmolality increases further. A vicious cycle of severe insulin resistance, increasing hyperglycemia, ongoing diuresis, and worsening hyperosmolality develops. A decrease in the rate of glomerular filtration and progressive azotemia follow. As hyperosmolality worsens, mental status deteriorates. Hypotension and impaired tissue perfusion can result in lactic acidosis, but ketoacidosis does not develop to any significant degree. Why severe hyperglycemia develops and ketoacidosis does not is probably due to the fact that levels of endogenous insulin are sufficient to inhibit the development of ketoacidosis, but not to prevent hyperglycemia.

As previously mentioned, both DKA and HHS are states of insulin resistance, because of the altered metabolic environment. Because of the increase in counterregulatory hormones (glucagon, catecholamines, cortisol, growth hormone), which have antiinsulin properties, resistance to the action of any endogenous or administered insulin is present and contributes to the development of and worsening of metabolic derangements.

Natural History and Its Modification with Treatment

Morbidity in DKA and HHS is due to the metabolic derangement per se (acidosis, renal failure, vascular thrombosis), to associated underlying illnesses (infection, myocardial infarction, pancreatitis), or to complications of treatment (hypokalemia, hypophosphatemia, pulmonary or cerebral edema). Morbidity is highest in elderly or debilitated patients with coexistent disease. Meticulous attention to detail and careful monitoring of the progress of the patient can reduce the morbidity associated with either condition.

Death in either DKA or HHS may result from many of the same factors that contribute to morbidity. The risk of mortality is higher in the elderly and the patient with underlying cardiac or other serious medical illness. Coma, severe hyperosmolality, hypokalemia, hypothermia, and circulatory failure are bad prognostic signs and are associated with a high mortality rate.

Prevention

As the greatest number of episodes of DKA occurs in patients with known diabetes, and many of these episodes are recurrent, the best

means of prevention are to provide (1) patient education to increase involvement in daily diabetes management and awareness of symptoms of early decompensation, and (2) access to medical advice and follow-up when appropriate. The patient with HHS presents a different problem, as many are newly diagnosed or have a history of only mild glucose intolerance, are often elderly, and have serious coexistent medical problems. It is unlikely in many cases that the unpredictable development of HHS can be prevented. In the patient with previously diagnosed diabetes known to be at risk, however, family and/or patient education centering on increasing awareness of the signs and symptoms of early decompensation and teaching appropriate steps of intervention and, again, ready access to medical advice may help to prevent the development of the full-blown picture of HHNC.

Cost Containment

Patient/family education and careful follow-up aimed at prevention of decompensation are obviously important ways to decrease the cost of hospital admissions for acute treatment of decompensated diabetes. When hospitalization becomes necessary, however, careful evaluation, meticulous attention to detail, and close observation for changes in patient condition help to minimize cost. A logical approach to diagnostic workup, as indicated by the individual patient's history, signs and symptoms, and response to intervention, rather than a "shotgun" approach, will help to maximize cost containment and hasten recovery.

REFERENCES

DeFronzo RA, Matsuda M, Barrett EJ. Diabetic ketoacidosis: A combined metabolic-nephrologic approach. Diabetes Rev 1994;2:209.

Ennis ED, Stahl EJvB, RA Kreisberg. The hyperosmolar hyperglycemic syndrome. Diabetes Rev 1994;2:115.

Foster DW, McGarry JD. The metabolic derangements and treatment of diabetic ketoacidosis. N Engl J Med 1983;309:159.

Geheb MA. Clinical approach to the hyperosmolar patient. Crit Care Clin 1987;5:797.

Kitabchi AE, Murphy MB. Diabetic ketoacidosis and hyperosmolar hyperglycemic nonketotic coma. Med Clin North Am 1988;72:1545.

Walker M, Marshall SM, Alberti KGMM. Clinical aspects of diabetic ketoacidosis. Diabetes/Metab Rev 1989;5:651.

CHAPTER 9–32

Chronic Complications of Diabetes Mellitus

William G. Blackard, M.D.

DEFINITION

Chronic complications of diabetes occur as a result of years of an altered metabolic environment (hyperglycemia and dyslipidemia).

ETIOLOGY

Most of the chronic microvascular complications are thought to be related to glycosylation of proteins in the basement membrane of capillaries. Macrovascular complications are also related in part to the glycosylation process (glycosylation of lipids). The neuropathic disturbances have been attributed by some to the accumulation of sugar alcohols (sorbitol) in a tissue not requiring insulin for glucose uptake.

CRITERIA FOR DIAGNOSIS

Diabetes affects every organ in the body; however, major disability occurs as a result of involvement of only a few organs: retina, kidney, cardiovascular system, and peripheral nerves. Some of the chronic complications are specific to the disease (i.e., retinopathy and nephropathy); others represent an acceleration of the normal aging process (i.e., macrovascular complications). The chronic complications can be divided into three categories: (1) microvascular complications to include retinopathy and nephropathy, (2) neuropathic complications to include the various forms of neuropathy and foot problems, and (3) macrovascular complications to include peripheral vascular disease, cerebrovascular disease, and ischemic cardiovascular disease.

In general, the complications are related to the duration of disease, requiring a minimum of 5 years but often more than 10 years for their appearance. Because of the often asymptomatic nature of the condition, patients with type II diabetes can present with a chronic complication at the time of disease detection. Nevertheless, the metabolic disturbance may have been present for many years. This is particularly true of macrovascular complications for which impaired glucose tolerance not meeting the criteria for diagnosis can be almost as great a risk factor as diabetes itself. An increasing body of evidence suggests that the insulin resistance with resulting hyperinsulinism, whether present in the diabetic or a person with impaired glucose tolerance, may accelerate atherosclerotic complications through its putative effect on hypertension, lipids, and the atherosclerotic process itself.

The chronic complications of diabetes are detected from the history, physical examination, and laboratory data reflecting specific organ involvement (i.e., proteinuria indicates nephropathy). The presence of one complication, however, leads to increased vigilance for detection of other complications.

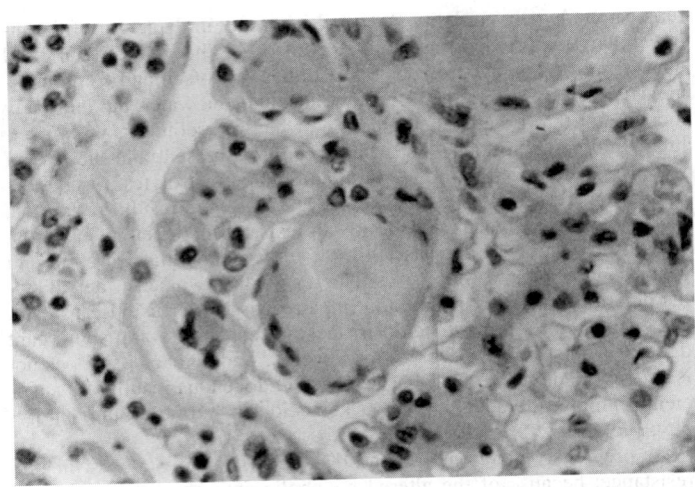

Figure 9–32–1. Nodular glomerulosclerosis in a diabetic patient.

CLINICAL MANIFESTATIONS
Microvascular Complications

Retinopathy

Subjective. Regardless of whether the eye complication is retinopathy, glaucoma, or cataract, the primary symptom is decreased vision. Some patients fail to note early deterioration in visual acuity and may seek medical advice only when damage has been significant.

Objective. The ability of physicians to detect diabetic retinopathy varies depending on their ability, interest, and patience. Studies have shown that generalists are accurate in their assessment less than 50% of the time. The earliest retinal findings are background changes consisting of microaneurysms, hemorrhages, and exudates. Retinopathy may be arrested at the background stage or it may progress to proliferative retinopathy. Capillary dropout (seen only with fluorescein angiography) characterizes the preproliferative phase; however, cotton wool exudates as a result of microinfarction of the nerve layer and venous dilation and tortuosity (seen on routine ophthalmoscopy) also suggest this stage. Finally, neovascularization and formation of fibrous tissue occur during the proliferative phase. At this point, vision is at great risk and acute changes can occur as a result of hemorrhage into the vitreous or retinal detachment. Patients are almost always aware of these changes because they experience a loss of vision or see the blood. One of the acute emergencies in diabetic eye disease is rubeosis due to neovascularization of the iris.

Nephropathy

Subjective. Diabetic nephropathy in its early stages is totally asymptomatic. Only after months to years of proteinuria does the patient develop manifestations of the nephrotic syndrome with massive proteinuria, hypoalbuminemia, and edema.

Objective. Hypertension present in 50% of diabetic patients may precede and, in fact, play an important role in the pathogenesis of diabetic nephropathy. Hypertension precedes the onset of renal disease more commonly in type II than in type I diabetic patients. Most patients with diabetic nephropathy have evidence of retinopathy. Nodular glomerulosclerosis (Figure 9–32–1) or the Kimmelstiel–Wilson lesion is virtually pathognomonic of diabetic nephropathy, but it correlates poorly with renal functional status.

The laboratory hallmark of diabetic nephropathy is proteinuria. Prior to the detection of "clinically detectable" proteinuria (>500 mg/24 h), microalbuminuria (20–450 mg/24 h) may be present. Although microalbuminuria may fluctuate with glycemic control, it is often predictive of significant diabetic nephropathy leading to end-stage renal disease. Once gross proteinuria occurs, glomerular filtration rate decreases variably at an average rate of 1 mL/min/mo. Therefore, several years may intervene before blood urea nitrogen and creatinine elevations occur. Hypercholesterolemia and anemia often accompany the nephrotic syndrome. Hyporenin hypoaldosteronism (type IV RTA) (presenting as hyperkalemia) is most commonly observed in diabetic patients with only modest blood urea nitrogen (30–50 mg/dL) and creatinine elevation.

Neuropathy

Subjective. The diabetic with neuropathy may be asymptomatic or may present with one of three different types of syndromes. In mononeuropathy or mononeuropathy multiplex, a single nerve or several specific trunks are involved respectively. In the former case, the patient may complain of visual problems due to a third or sixth nerve cranial palsy. If the neuropathy involves the peroneal nerve or the ulnar nerve, foot or wrist drop will be recognized by the patient. Rarely, several nerve trunks (pelvic girdle) may be involved causing amyotrophy, in which extreme weakness, atrophy, and pain occur in the lower legs. This is often associated with extreme weight loss mimicking a malignancy and has been called "diabetic cachexia."

The most common neuropathy observed in diabetic patients is symmetric peripheral polyneuropathy. Both motor and sensory elements can be involved. The patient complains of paresthesias of the feet and legs (often considered by the patient to be a circulatory disturbance). In other patients, fortunately not too commonly, the neuropathy causes excruciating pain. In these patients, as well as in other patients having not experienced pain, nerve death with hypesthesia and anesthesia occurs, placing the patient at great risk for injuries requiring normal pain sensation for prevention.

Autonomic neuropathy can be the most devastating form of neuropathy. Symptoms include postural hypotension, impotence, retrograde ejaculation, lower bowel disturbance (constipation more frequently than nocturnal diarrhea), gastroparesis diabetocorum (presenting with nausea and vomiting), and neurogenic bladder, presenting as urinary infection or incontinence. Occasionally, gastroparesis will complicate diabetic management because of delayed and erratic gastric emptying.

Objective. Muscle weakness and wasting and loss of proprioceptive sensation along with visual impairment can result in crippling disability. On physical examination, loss of vibratory sensation and deep tendon reflexes is the most common manifestation. Hypesthesia, decreased muscle strength, and decreased proprioception occur less commonly. Physical findings of autonomic neuropathy consist of postural hypotension, impaired post-Valsalva increase in blood pressure, uneven sweating pattern, and decreased rectal tone. It should, however, be pointed out that none of the signs and symptoms are specific for diabetic neuropathy.

Neuropathy can lead to a number of foot problems such as metatarsal neurotrophic ulcers and Charcot joints (painless swelling and deformity of the foot with loss of normal bony structure). Unrecognized blisters, cuts, and puncture wounds result from loss of sensation. Infection and gangrene are often complications of the insensitive diabetic foot.

Macrovascular Complications

Subjective. An increased incidence of strokes, transient ischemic attacks, myocardial infarctions, angina, and intermittent claudication occur in diabetic patients. The symptomatology resulting from these events is similar to that in nondiabetics, except that diabetic neuropathy results in painless ischemic heart disease and a silent myocardial infarction.

Objective. Carotid bruits and decreased lower-extremity pulses may indicate cerebrovascular and peripheral vascular disease, respectively.

PLANS

Diagnostic

Early detection of diabetic complications improves prognosis. Therefore, testing for complications before the patient is aware of them makes good clinical sense. It is recommended that all diabetics over the age of 35 or those who have had diabetes more than 5 years have yearly ophthalmologic exams. Examination of urine for protein should be performed yearly. The value of yearly testing for microalbuminuria has also been advocated recently, as it permits earlier identification of those patients prone to develop nephropathy. Those with microalbuminuria should be singled out for more aggressive treatment to control their hypertension. Whether to treat normotensive microalbuminuric subjects with angiotensin-converting enzyme inhibitors or low-protein diet remains moot. Once proteinuria has occurred, measurement of glomerular filtration rate, blood urea nitrogen, and serum creatinine should be performed at least yearly. No specific laboratory tests exist for neuropathy. Yearly assessment of respiratory variation in R–R intervals, recommended by some to detect autonomic neuropathy, is not mandatory.

As glycemic control is not of proven benefit for the macrovascular complications of diabetes, analysis and treatment of other risk factors (obesity, lipids, hypertension, exercise, and smoking) is imperative. Yearly lipid profiles are recommended to determine the need for hypolipidemic therapy.

Therapeutic

For retinopathy and nephropathy, conclusive evidence (Diabetes Control and Complications Trial Research Group, 1993) exists that control of plasma glucose and hypertension will decrease the prevalence and severity of these complications. For that reason, both hyperglycemia and hypertension should be treated aggressively. In patients demonstrating neovascularization, retinal photocoagulation will spare vision. For patients suffering vitreous hemorrhages, vitrectomy with removal and replacement of vitreous contents has preserved vision. Traction retinal detachment is the most common indication for vitrectomy.

When end-stage renal disease occurs in diabetic patients, intervention is required by either hemodialysis, peritoneal dialysis, or transplantation. These interventions have been nearly as successful in diabetic patients as in nondiabetic patients. Live related donor transplantation has resulted in an 82% 3-year survival in diabetic patients and has stabilized vision in 85 to 90% of recipients. Three-year rates of survival for cadaveric transplants and hemodialysis are 65 and 39%, respectively.

Therapy for the neuropathic complications has been disappointing. Control of hyperglycemia improves motor nerve conduction time, but thus far convincing evidence of clinical improvement has not been reported. Trials of aldose reductase inhibitors based on the sorbitol pathway theory of pathogenesis have been disappointing. Despite improving motor nerve conduction time, these agents have failed to result in significant clinical improvement and have been associated with significant toxicity. Painful neuropathy may be treated effectively with amitriptyline 25 mg at bedtime in some patients. Occasionally, a phenothiazine may result in additional benefit. In intractable cases, the anticonvulsants phenytoin and carbamazepine have been used with limited success.

Treatment of macrovascular complications is the same as in nondiabetic subjects. In the case of macrovascular complications, peripheral revascularization procedures may be less successful in diabetic patients because of more distal vascular disease.

As with most chronic diseases, education is an important part of therapy for diabetics. Physicians should be honest in discussing diabetic complications with their patients in the hope that the patient will work with them to prevent these complications. This can be done in such a way that they do not live in constant fear of blindness, kidney failure, and gangrene. It can be pointed out that although these complications occur, they do not affect every patient, not even the majority. They should be told that the physician expects to see background retinopathy after 10 to 15 years and that this stage may or may not progress to proliferative retinopathy, and even then, therapy such as photocoagulation and vitrectomy can prevent blindness. Similarly, end-stage renal disease can be treated with dialysis or transplantation. Patients should be told of the complications that necessitate immediate attention: sudden change in vision, any wound or lesion of the feet. The patient should also be educated about other risk factors for macrovascular complications so that they can be reduced to balance the irreducible risks from hyperglycemia itself. Thus, they should be educated about obesity, lipids, hypertension, exercise, and smoking tobacco.

FOLLOW-UP

The frequency of follow-up visits depends on the nature of the complication. Frequency of visits to the ophthalmologist depends on multiple factors: extent of disease, remaining vision, and procedures indicated. Diabetic patients over the age of 35 or those with 5 years' or more duration of the disease should be seen by an ophthalmologist once a year. A diabetic patient with nonazotemic nephrotic syndrome may require visits no more frequently than twice yearly. As a patient becomes azotemic, more frequent visits are required, perhaps three to four times a year. When the creatinine reaches 3 to 4 mg/dL, the patient should be referred to a nephrologist to set the stage for renal transplantation or dialysis. Uncontrolled hypertension, because of its adverse effect on complications, may also require increased physician visits. In arranging for follow-up care, the physician should be aware of visits to other health care professionals. When the patient is seeing an ophthalmologist, nephrologist, and podiatrist, the generalist should work with these other physicians to keep visits to a minimum.

DISCUSSION

Prevalence and Incidence

Thirty percent of new patients with end-stage renal disease are diabetic. Although diabetes is the leading cause of blindness, with more than 8,000 new cases a year, and the risk of blindness after 20 years is increased 15- to 20-fold, only 2% of diabetics become blind. Nephropathy occurs in 35% of type I diabetics and 20% of type II diabetics after 15 years' duration. Diabetic neuropathy is common. If decreased motor nerve conduction time is the criterion for neuropathy, neuropathy is present in 70% of cases. Macrovascular complications are increased in diabetic patients. Coronary artery disease is increased twofold in male diabetics and fourfold in female diabetics. Cerebrovascular accidents occur four times more frequently in diabetics. Atherosclerosis obliterans is present in 8% of diabetics at onset, but in 45% after 20 years of disease. Diabetes accounts for 50% of the nontraumatic amputations, with gangrene being 50 times greater than in nondiabetic patients.

Related Basic Science

The hallmark for microvascular complications is capillary basement membrane thickening. Changes in basement membrane width as well as changes in composition, such as increased glycation and less negatively charged proteins, are thought to be responsible for glomerular protein leakage. Hyperfiltration as well as protein leakage leads to mesangial thickening and destruction with hyalinization of the glomerulus (if nodular, Kimmelstiel–Wilson lesion).

In diabetic retinopathy, the pericytes lining the retinal capillaries die. Microaneurysms, dot hemorrhages, and exudates result. When capillary closure and dropout occur, parts of the retina become anoxic, and according to popular belief supported by studies, an angiogenesis factor is released that is responsible for proliferative retinopathy.

The precise cause of diabetic neuropathy remains unknown. The etiology of diabetic mononeuropathy is probably vascular and is characterized by nerve infarction. Subsequently, regeneration of the nerve occurs, resulting in normalization of nerve function. Peripheral sensory and motor neuropathy and autonomic neuropathy, however, have a different pathogenesis. The sorbitol theory is popular (but not proven) and has led to clinical trials of aldose reductase inhibitors to prevent sorbitol accumulation. According to theory, hyperglycemia leads to sorbitol (sugar alcohol) accumulation in the insulin-insensitive nerve cells. As a result, nerve cell myoinositol concentration is decreased (controversial) and diminished secondary messengers of the phosphyltidylinositol pathway result in decreased sodium potassium ATPase responsible for neurotransmission. Another theory suggests a defect in myelin synthesis and content in diabetic nerves.

The atherosclerosis responsible for the macrovascular complications of diabetes is qualitatively similar to that in nondiabetics, just more severe and of earlier onset. Roles for hypertension (present in 50% of diabetics), hyperlipemia (present in 30%), glycosylation of lipoproteins, and hyperinsulinism have been suggested in the accelerated atherosclerosis of diabetes.

Natural History and Its Modification with Treatment

Most studies suggest a somewhat worse prognosis for diabetics after a vascular event (myocardial infarction or stroke) than for nondiabetics. "Painless ischemia" may delay the patient seeking medical attention and result in greater mortality from coronary artery disease. Nevertheless, diabetic patients do well with cardiac and peripheral revascularization procedures, and the indications for these procedures are the same as in the nondiabetic. The leading cause of death in diabetes is cardiovascular disease, accounting for roughly two thirds of the deaths. In those with onset of diabetes prior to age 20, renal disease is the most common cause of death, accounting for 40% versus 30% for cardiovascular disease. Figure 9–32–2 shows the natural history of diabetic renal disease.

Prevention

The microvascular complications are clearly related to metabolic control. Compelling evidence for the role of glycemic control in microvascular complications is the observation that within 2 to 4 years of renal transplantation, the donor kidney shows diabetic changes; conversely, diabetic kidneys transplanted into nondiabetic patients have shown a loss of the diabetic pathology. Most importantly, the recently completed multicenter Diabetes Control and Complication Trial (1993) has clearly shown a 30 to 60% reduction in microvascular and neuropathic complications in extremely well-controlled patients versus those treated in the standard fashion with suboptimal control.

The macrovascular complications of diabetes can be delayed by reducing other risk factors. Careful attention should be paid to control of hypertension, hyperlipidemia, and weight. Exercise should be encouraged and smoking not allowed. Perhaps it is the greater attention to

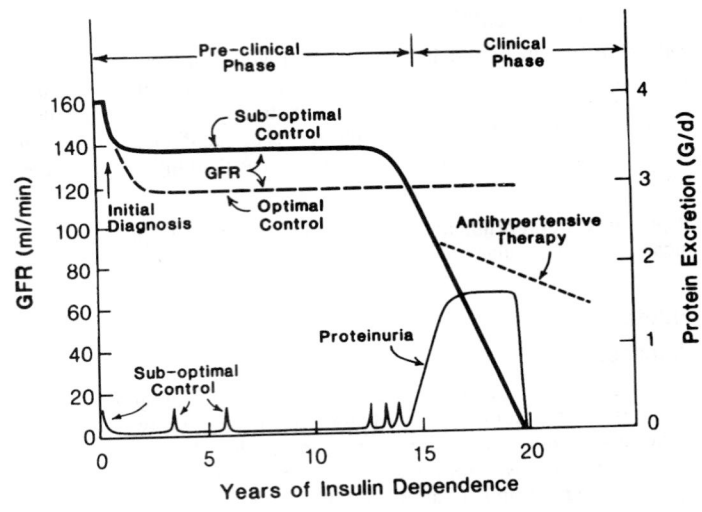

Figure 9–32–2. Natural history of diabetic nephropathy. *(Source: Goetz FC, Hostetter TH. Diabetic kidney disease. In: Davidson JK, ed. Clinical diabetes mellitus: A problem oriented approach. New York: Thieme, 1986:343. Reproduced with permission from the publisher and author.)*

these other risk factors that is responsible for comparable deaths rates in diabetics and nondiabetics after age 70.

Cost Containment

See Chapter 9–30.

REFERENCES

Brownlee M, Gerami A, Vlassara H. Advanced glycosylation end products in tissues and the biochemical basis of diabetic complications. N Engl J Med 1988;318:1315.

Diabetes Control and Complications Trial Research Group. The effect of intensive treatment of diabetes on the development and progression of long-term complications in insulin-dependent diabetes mellitus. N Engl J Med 1993;329:977.

Dyck PJ, Zimmerman BR, Velen TH, et al. Nerve glucose, fructose, sorbitol, myoinositol, and fiber degeneration and regeneration in diabetic neuropathy. N Engl J Med 1989;319:542.

Harati Y. Diabetic peripheral neuropathies. Ann Intern Med 1987;107:546.

Runyan JW Jr, and Committee. Statement on hypertension. Diabetes Care 1987;10:764.

Zavaroni I, Bonora E, Pagliara M, et al. Risk factors for coronary artery disease in healthy persons with hyperinsulinemia and normal glucose tolerance. N Engl J Med 1989;310:702.

CHAPTER 9–33

Hypoglycemia

Philip E. Cryer, M.D.

DEFINITION

Hypoglycemia is an abnormally low plasma (or blood) glucose concentration typically, but not invariably, associated with neurogenic (autonomic) symptoms, neuroglycopenic symptoms, or both.

ETIOLOGY

Hypoglycemia occurs when the rate of glucose efflux from the circulation exceeds the rate of glucose influx into the circulation. In this context, glucose efflux is synonymous with glucose utilization (for storage or metabolism) by body tissues, as external glucose loss per se does not cause hypoglycemia. Influx can be from endogenous (hepatic) glucose production, exogenous glucose delivery (e.g., from a meal), or both. Because of the normal capacity of the liver to increase glucose production substantially, hypoglycemia is usually the result of a rate of hepatic glucose production that is too low relative to that of glucose utilization.

Hypoglycemia is not in itself a disease, but rather a disorder that is a consequence of one or more of a variety of diseases or the treatment of diseases.

CRITERIA FOR DIAGNOSIS
Suggestive

Glucose is the predominant metabolic fuel for the brain. Thus, hypoglycemia is most often suspected clinically because of symptoms (or signs) of brain dysfunction in a setting in which hypoglycemia might occur; however, the symptoms and signs are nonspecific. The definitive diagnosis of hypoglycemia requires documentation of a low plasma glucose concentration.

Hypoglycemia is sometimes suspected when the plasma glucose concentration, measured for other reasons, is found to be relatively low in the absence of symptoms.

Definitive

Hypoglycemia is diagnosed convincingly when typical symptoms are associated with a low plasma glucose concentration and are relieved after the plasma glucose level is raised to normal (Whipple's triad).

Postabsorptive (fasting) hypoglycemia can also be diagnosed in the absence of symptoms when the postabsorptive glucose level is unequivocally, and reproducibly, low. In such cases, the likelihood that the disorder will result ultimately in symptomatic hypoglycemia is so high that definitive diagnosis and treatment of the underlying disease are indicated. After an overnight fast, plasma glucose concentrations less than 45 mg/dL (2.5 mmol/L) are abnormally low; those between 45 and 60 mg/dL (2.5 and 3.3 mmol/L) are suspect and dictate repeated measurements.

Diagnosis of postprandial (reactive) hypoglycemia requires documentation of Whipple's triad after a mixed meal. An oral glucose tolerance test should *not* be used to make this diagnosis.

Except in persons who use drugs that lower the plasma glucose concentration (especially insulin or sulfonylureas used to treat diabetes mellitus), hypoglycemia is an uncommon clinical event. Therefore, in the absence of symptoms, and particularly in the absence of a clinically apparent hypoglycemic mechanism, artifactual lowering of the measured plasma glucose concentration must be considered. This can be the result of continued metabolism of glucose by blood cells after the sample is drawn, especially in the presence of leukocytosis, thrombocytosis, or polycythemia, if the separation of plasma from the formed elements is delayed.

Specific measurement of the plasma (or blood) glucose concentration is critical to the definitive diagnosis of hypoglycemia. Even if the glucose level is estimated to be low with a bedside glucose monitoring device, a sample for glucose measurement *must* be sent to the laboratory; the monitoring devices, which are designed for out-of-hospital self-estimates of blood glucose by patients with diabetes mellitus, are neither accurate nor precise.

CLINICAL MANIFESTATIONS
Subjective
Symptoms

There are both neurogenic (autonomic) and neuroglycopenic symptoms of hypoglycemia. Neurogenic symptoms are the result of the perception of physiologic changes caused by the autonomic discharge triggered by hypoglycemia (both the sympathochromaffin and parasympathetic components of the autonomic nervous system are activated). They include adrenergic (catecholamine-mediated) symptoms such as palpitations, tremulousness, and anxiety. They also include cholinergic (acetylcholine-mediated) symptoms such as sweating, hunger, and paresthesias. Neuroglycopenic symptoms are the direct result of neuronal fuel (glucose) deprivation. They range from subtle behavioral changes and cognitive dysfunction to seizure, coma, and even death. Others include a sense of warmth, weakness, faintness, drowsiness or dizziness, as well as confusion, incoordination, difficulty thinking or speaking, and blurred vision. Focal neurologic deficits can occur, but are rare.

Although symptoms frequently occur in the morning before breakfast (following the longest period without food ingestion) in patients with postabsorptive hypoglycemia, they often occur at other times of the day, especially following exercise. The timing of iatrogenic hypo-

glycemia in patients with drug-treated diabetes mellitus varies in relation to the time course of actions of the insulin preparation or sulfonylurea used, meals, physical activity, and so on, but episodes occur most commonly during the night. Symptoms occur between 1 and 4 hours after a carbohydrate-containing meal in patients with postprandial hypoglycemia.

Past History

In the vast majority of cases the review of systems, social history, or past history discloses the probable, if not the obvious, specific cause of a hypoglycemic episode. These include, particularly, the use of drugs that cause hypoglycemia, most commonly insulin, a sulfonylurea, or alcohol. Others include clues to the presence of a critical illness that can cause hypoglycemia (hepatic, renal, or cardiac failure, sepsis, inanition) or of hormonal deficiencies or a non-beta cell tumor. The absence of such historical features raises the possibility of a rare cause of hypoglycemia such as endogenous hyperinsulinism.

Family History

In general, the family history does not point to a specific cause of hypoglycemia. Diabetes mellitus is, of course, familial, but hypoglycemia occurs only in drug-treated diabetes. A minority of insulinomas, a rare cause of hypoglycemia, are a component of an autosomal dominant familial syndrome such as multiple endocrine neoplasia type I (with hyperparathyroidism, a pituitary tumor that is often functional and a pancreatic islet tumor such as an insulinoma).

Objective
Physical Examination

The physical examination can be normal in a hypoglycemic patient. Neurologic findings—commonly overtly abnormal behavior or cognition, sometimes coma, occasionally focal deficits—are often apparent. Because of cutaneous vasoconstriction and diaphoresis (manifestations of activation of the sympathochromaffin system), the skin is usually pale, cold, and moist. Although heart rate increases and pulse pressure widens during hypoglycemia, prominent tachycardia and systolic hypertension are unusual. Hypothermia can occur during hypoglycemia; posthypoglycemic fever has been described.

Physical findings indicative of the underlying disease that results in hypoglycemia are often evident even between episodes of hypoglycemia.

Routine Laboratory Abnormalities

Aside from a low plasma glucose concentration, routine laboratory tests are not useful in the diagnosis of hypoglycemia per se. Hypoglycemia can elevate the leukocyte count, specifically the granulocyte count; however, routine tests can provide clues to the underlying disease.

PLANS
Diagnostic
Differential Diagnosis

The differential diagnosis of the postabsorptive and postprandial hypoglycemias is outlined in Table 9–33–1. Although a variety of approaches to classification could be used, a clinical classification is used here.

Drugs are, by far, the most common cause of postabsorptive hypoglycemia. Insulin and sulfonylureas, used to treat diabetes mellitus, and alcohol are the most common offending agents. Iatrogenic insulin-induced hypoglycemia in patients with insulin-dependent diabetes mellitus is most common during intensive therapy and in patients with the clinical syndromes of defective glucose counterregulation, hypoglycemia unawareness, or both (discussed later). Risk factors for sulfonylurea-induced hypoglycemia in patients with non-insulin-dependent diabetes mellitus include advanced age, poor nutrition, and renal insufficiency as well as use of relatively long-acting drugs such as chlorpropamide and glyburide (glibenclamide).

Because alcohol inhibits gluconeogenesis but not glycogenolysis,

TABLE 9–33–1. CLINICAL CLASSIFICATION OF HYPOGLYCEMIA

I. Postabsorptive (fasting) hypoglycemia
  A. Drugs, especially insulin, sulfonylureas, and alcohol
  B. Critical organ failure
    1. Hepatic failure
    2. Renal failure
    3. Cardiac failure
    4. Sepsis
    5. Inanition
  C. Hormonal deficiencies
    1. Cortisol, growth hormone, or both
    2. Glucagon and epinephrine
  D. Non beta cell tumors
  E. Endogenous hyperinsulinism
    1. Insulinoma (and related disorders)
    2. Beta cell secretagogue (e.g., sulfonylurea)
    3. Autoimmune hypoglycemia
      a. Antibodies to insulin
      b. Antibodies to the insulin receptor
      c. ? Antibodies to beta cells
  F. Hypoglycemias of infancy and childhood
    1. Neonatal hypoglycemias
    2. Congenital deficiencies of glucogenic enzymes
    3. Ketotic hypoglycemia of childhood
II. Postprandial (reactive) hypoglycemia
  A. Congenital deficiencies of enzymes of carbohydrate metabolism
    1. Galactosemia
    2. Hereditary fructose intolerance
  B. Alimentary hypoglycemia
  C. Idiopathic (functional) postprandial hypoglycemia

alcohol-induced hypoglycemia commonly follows an alcoholic binge in which alcohol is substituted for food for several days (resulting in glycogen depletion).

Infrequently used drugs that commonly cause hypoglycemia include pentamidine and quinine (or quinidine). Both release insulin. Frequently used drugs that rarely produce hypoglycemia include aspirin and sulfonamides. Hypoglycemia has been attributed to a variety of other drugs, including beta-adrenergic antagonists, but the causal relationships are not well documented. Perhaps such drugs are one factor in the pathogenesis of multifactorial hypoglycemia.

Hypoglycemia can occur in the setting of a variety of critical illnesses. The pathogenesis of hypoglycemia is most obvious in hepatic failure, as the liver is the site of endogenous glucose production. Extensive hepatic destruction, as in acute hepatic necrosis, is required to produce hypoglycemia; clinical hypoglycemia does not occur in most instances of hepatitis or even end-stage cirrhosis. The mechanism(s) of hypoglycemia in chronic cardiac failure or chronic renal failure is unknown. Deficient formation of gluconeogenic substrates (e.g., glucogenic amino acids) has been suggested as a factor in patients with the latter. Sepsis regularly results in increased glucose utilization. Failure of hepatic glucose production to increase sufficiently to match utilization results in hypoglycemia. The mechanism(s) of hypoglycemia in inanition is also obscure. It has been speculated that the absence of fat as a source of fuel for extraneural tissues results in excessive glucose utilization by such tissues that exceeds the capacity of the liver, in the setting of limited gluconeogenic substrate provision, to increase glucose production.

Hormonal deficiencies are an uncommon cause of hypoglycemia. Glucocorticoid deficiency, whether the result of primary or secondary adrenocortical insufficiency, can cause hypoglycemia. Glucocorticoids normally limit glucose utilization by extraneural tissues and support hepatic glucose production. Anorexia with consequent glycogen depletion may be a contributing factor to the development of hypoglycemia. Hypoglycemia has been attributed to growth hormone deficiency (with or without adrenocorticotropic hormone deficiency) in young children with hypopituitarism, but does not appear to occur in adults with that disorder. The combination of glucagon and epinephrine deficiencies increases the frequency of iatrogenic hypoglycemia in insulin-dependent diabetes mellitus (as discussed later), but isolated glucagon deficiency

has not been documented in adults and isolated epinephrine deficiency does not cause hypoglycemia.

Retroperitoneal, intraabdominal, or intrathoracic non-beta cell tumors that cause hypoglycemia are usually large and clinically apparent. These mesenchymal or epithelial (e.g., hepatoma) tumors are a rare cause of hypoglycemia. The mechanism often involves overproduction and incomplete processing of the somatomedin insulin-like growth factor II (IGF-II). These result in reduced binding of IGF-II to circulating binding proteins, increased free IGF-II levels, and increased insulin-like actions (increased glucose utilization without appropriately increased glucose production) despite suppressed insulin secretion.

Endogenous hyperinsulinism is a rare cause of hypoglycemia. The critical pathogenetic (and diagnostic) feature of these diseases is relative hyperinsulinism, insulin levels that are inappropriately high relative to the ambient plasma glucose concentration. Absolute hyperinsulinemia need not be present. Causes include insulinoma and related disorders, the presence of an insulin secretagogue, and the autoimmune hypoglycemias.

An insulinoma is a pancreatic islet beta cell tumor that releases insulin in a constitutive, nonexocytotic fashion. Thus, in contrast to normal beta cells, which virtually cease secreting insulin as the plasma glucose concentration falls into the low physiologic range, an insulinoma continues to release insulin as the plasma glucose level falls even below the physiologic range. Thus, during hypoglycemia plasma insulin levels are inappropriately high, as are levels of the connecting peptide (C-peptide) cleaved from the insulin precursor molecule proinsulin. (Inappropriately high C-peptide levels distinguish endogenous hyperinsulinism from exogenous hyperinsulinism in which C-peptide levels are suppressed.) Because of incomplete processing to insulin with nonexocytotic release, proinsulin levels are also elevated in patients with insulinomas even in the absence of hypoglycemia. Although the finding of an insulinoma is the rule in adults with endogenous hyperinsulinism not explicable on the basis of a secretagogue or an autoimmune mechanism, a discrete tumor is not found in some patients, particularly children, with an otherwise similar pathophysiologic mechanism. The latter are assumed to have a functional defect in insulin secretion without a defined anatomic correlate.

Hypoglycemia caused by a beta cell secretagogue, such as surreptitiously ingested sulfonylurea, resembles that caused by an insulinoma except that proinsulin levels are less markedly elevated. (Secretagogues stimulate exocytotic insulin secretion.)

Autoimmune hypoglycemias include those caused by autoantibodies to insulin. Such antibodies bind normally secreted (e.g., postprandial) insulin, which then dissociates slowly, in an unregulated fashion, resulting in inappropriately high insulin levels following the transition from the postprandial to the postabsorptive state. Thus, the history may suggest late postprandial hypoglycemia in affected patients. Endogenous insulin secretion is suppressed and free C-peptide levels are low during hypoglycemia; however, because of cross-reactivity of C-peptide antisera with the C-peptide component of proinsulin, which is also bound by insulin antibodies, total C-peptide levels may not be suppressed. Another rare form of autoimmune hypoglycemia is that caused by autoantibodies to the insulin receptor. Although most of the latter are antagonists and cause resistance to insulin actions, some are agonists and produce hypoglycemia. Again, endogenous insulin secretion, as evidenced by C-peptide levels, is suppressed during hypoglycemia; however, because of reduced clearance, insulin levels tend to be inappropriately high. Finally, beta-cell-stimulating antibodies (analogous to thyroid-stimulating antibodies in Graves' disease) remain a theoretical cause of endogenous hyperinsulinism and hypoglycemia. Although such antibodies have been described in sera from patients with hypoglycemia, clinical hypoglycemia caused by a beta cell autoantibody has not been documented.

Causes of hypoglycemia in infants and children include those just discussed plus several that are unique. The latter include the neonatal hypoglycemias (e.g., that in small-for-gestational-age infants and infants of diabetic mothers), a variety of congenital deficiencies of glucogenic enzymes or those involved in fatty acid oxidation, and the syndrome of ketotic hypoglycemia of childhood.

The causes of postprandial hypoglycemia are different from those of postabsorptive hypoglycemia just discussed. Postprandial hypoglycemia can occur as a feature of rare congenital enzyme deficiencies (galactosemia, hereditary fructose intolerance) or following gastric surgery (alimentary hypoglycemia). The extent to which it occurs as an idiopathic disorder is debated, but it appears to be quite rare.

Diagnostic Options

The first issue is whether or not the patient has hypoglycemia. That diagnosis is suspected much more often than it is confirmed because the symptoms of hypoglycemia are generally nonspecific and the patient is often not symptomatic when seen. If hypoglycemia is documented, the issue becomes determination of the specific cause. The latter is often straightforward. It is sometimes quite challenging.

If the patient is symptomatic when seen, measurement of the plasma glucose concentration and administration of carbohydrate will either confirm the diagnosis of hypoglycemia, by fulfilling Whipple's triad, or provide strong evidence against that diagnosis. A clearly normal glucose level indicates that symptoms at that time were not the result of hypoglycemia, and suggests that previous similar symptoms were also not the result of hypoglycemia.

If hypoglycemia is considered on the basis of the history, but the patient is not symptomatic when seen, the physician must make one of three judgments: (1) The history is not sufficiently compelling to warrant further pursuit of the diagnosis of hypoglycemia. This judgment can sometimes be made safely by a physician experienced in hypoglycemic disorders. (2) Because of the clinical setting, the history is sufficiently compelling and the diagnosis can be assumed. That judgment is commonly made in patients with a plausible reason for hypoglycemia and, often, previously documented hypoglycemia with similar symptoms, for example, in a patient with insulin-treated insulin-dependent diabetes mellitus. (3) Hypoglycemia cannot be assumed but the history is sufficiently compelling to warrant pursuit of that diagnosis. If so, one seeks to demonstrate Whipple's triad or, failing that, to document unequivocally low plasma glucose concentrations.

Given the decision to pursue the diagnosis of hypoglycemia, a decision branch point is whether the history suggests postprandial or postabsorptive hypoglycemia. If it suggests postprandial hypoglycemia, and particularly if there is a plausible reason for postprandial hypoglycemia such as previous gastric surgery, one seeks to demonstrate Whipple's triad after a mixed meal. (The oral glucose tolerance test should *not* be used.) One approach is to measure the plasma glucose concentration and ask the patient to record all symptoms serially after a mixed meal. A common outcome is that a clearly low glucose level is not found and symptoms are not temporally related to the nadir glucose level, thus providing evidence against the diagnosis. A conceptually preferable, but generally impractical, approach is to arrange for the patient to obtain a blood sample, for subsequent glucose measurement in the laboratory (not with a blood glucose self-monitoring device), at the time of postprandial symptoms. When that has been done, low glucose levels have generally not been found in patients suspected to have idiopathic postprandial hypoglycemia. Finally, occasional patients with a disease that causes postabsorptive hypoglycemia have only postprandial symptoms. Thus, because postabsorptive hypoglycemia is generally recurrent and progressive and will ultimately require specific diagnosis and treatment, the physician may elect to pursue that diagnosis even in a patient with postprandial symptoms.

Recommended Approach

Given the decision to pursue the possibility of postabsorptive hypoglycemia, it is worthwhile to first review the differential diagnosis of that disorder in the context of the patient's initial clinical presentation. Is a potentially offending drug being used? Is an underlying disease that could cause hypoglycemia (Table 9–33–1) apparent or readily diagnosable? Critical illnesses that can cause hypoglycemia are apparent on the basis of the history, physical examination, and routine laboratory tests. Given any relevant findings consistent with glucocorticoid deficiency, adrenocortical insufficiency can be confirmed or denied by measurement of the plasma cortisol concentration 30 minutes after parenteral administration of synthetic adrenocorticotropic hormone (cosyntropin). Non-beta cell tumors are usually clinically apparent. If none of these drugs or diseases is apparent, postabsorptive hypoglycemia, if docu-

mented, is likely the result of hyperinsulinism. Therefore, the diagnostic plan should be designed both to document postabsorptive hypoglycemia (preferably Whipple's triad) and to begin to dissect the differential diagnosis of hyperinsulinism with measurements of, at a minimum, plasma insulin and C-peptide levels and a serum sulfonylurea screen at the time of documented hypoglycemia. (This principle also applies to the patient with hypoglycemia of unknown cause when first seen.)

Although a variety of provocative and suppressive tests have been used, the definitive approach to documentation of postabsorptive hypoglycemia is a fast, prolonged if necessary. Assuming a random plasma glucose concentration is not unequivocally low, serial plasma glucose measurements after overnight fasts are a reasonable first step. If these do not document hypoglycemia the patient must be hospitalized for a prolonged (up to 72-hour) fast. More than two thirds of patients with endogenous hyperinsulinism become hypoglycemic within 24 hours, almost all within 48 hours. Although rare affected patients have not become hypoglycemic by 72 hours, for practical purposes the absence of Whipple's triad after a 72-hour fast excludes a diagnosis of postabsorptive hypoglycemia. As noted earlier, plasma glucose measurements during the fast must be made in the laboratory, not at the bedside.

Critical measurements, in addition to plasma glucose, at the time of hypoglycemia include plasma insulin and C-peptide levels and a serum sulfonylurea screen. Proinsulin levels can also be measured then, although they are also often elevated after an overnight fast in the absence of hypoglycemia in patients with insulinomas. It is the author's practice to also measure insulin antibodies in such patients (not necessarily at the time of hypoglycemia but after hypoglycemia has been documented). It could be argued that because with modern insulin preparations exogenous insulin administration may not produce substantial insulin antibody titers and autoantibodies to insulin are a rare cause of hypoglycemia in the United States, this measurement is not necessary. The consequences of misdiagnosis could be substantial (e.g., an unnecessary laparotomy), however. Furthermore, insulin antibodies cause artifactually high insulin values measured with a double-antibody radioimmunoassay, which is the commonly used method.

Although plasma glucose levels less than 45 mg/dL (2.5 mmol/L) during a fast are generally abnormal, and permit interpretation of the data, some normal women and children have lower values without symptoms. Therefore, it is preferable to prolong the fast until Whipple's triad is documented. Given the latter, the following diagnostic patterns emerge:

- *Hypoglycemia with relative or absolute hyperinsulinemia and suppressed C-peptide levels:* This pattern is typical of exogenous hyperinsulinism (e.g., surreptitious insulin injection). It can occur in autoimmune hypoglycemia due to antibodies to insulin, but total C-peptide levels (which are routinely measured), unlike free C-peptide levels, may not be suppressed in that disorder as discussed earlier. Insulin antibodies are invariably measurable in the latter and may be present in the former. This pattern also occurs in the rare patients with autoantibodies to the insulin receptor, although insulin elevations are not marked. As a diagnosis of surreptitious insulin injection needs to be as compelling as possible, insulin receptor antibodies should be shown to be absent before that diagnosis is made.

- *Hypoglycemia with relative or absolute hyperinsulinemia and C-peptide levels that are not suppressed:* (In the laboratory used by the author, plasma insulin levels greater than 10 µU/mL (60 pmol/L) are clearly elevated, and levels of 5 to 10 µU/L suspect; and plasma C-peptide levels greater than 1.5 ng/mL (0.5 nmol/L) are clearly inappropriately high, and levels of 1.0 to 1.5 ng/L suspect during hypoglycemia.) This pattern is typical of insulinoma. It also occurs following sulfonylurea ingestion, but the sulfonylurea screen is positive in that case. Furthermore, proinsulin levels are more distinctly elevated with an insulinoma than with sulfonylurea ingestion. The theoretical possibility of beta cell-stimulating antibodies would be expected to produce a pattern similar to that of a sulfonylurea but, in the absence of a proinsulin measurement, indistinguishable from that of an insulinoma.

Given convincing clinical and biochemical evidence of an insulinoma, attempts to localize the tumor are indicated. Most adults have single, benign (only about 10% are malignant) insulinomas, virtually all within the pancreas. Multiple tumors are the rule in familial insulinoma. The majority of young children with similar pathophysiology, and a few adults, do not have a discrete insulinoma.

Insulinomas are generally small, averaging 1 to 2 cm, but they can be large. Recognizing, therefore, that a negative study does not exclude an insulinoma, abdominal computed tomography scans should be obtained prior to surgery, as the lesion can be demonstrated in up to 80% of cases and metastases, if present, may be identified. Magnetic resonance imaging has not been shown to be superior to computed tomography. The relative utility of octreotide scintigraphy remains to be determined, but some insulinomas are identified with that technique. In the view of experienced surgeons, intraoperative ultrasonography has been an important advance in the localization of insulinomas.

Therapeutic

Therapeutic Options

Symptomatic postabsorptive hypoglycemia requires urgent treatment, diagnostic explanation, and definitive treatment to prevent recurrent hypoglycemia. Because it is self-limited, symptomatic postprandial hypoglycemia rarely requires urgent treatment, but attempts at long-term prevention, such as a diet low in simple sugars and including frequent feedings, may be indicated.

Recommended Approach

For urgent treatment of hypoglycemia plasma glucose must be raised to normal levels and kept there. Mild hypoglycemia in an alert patient (most often an insulin-treated patient with diabetes mellitus) can be treated with approximately 20 g of oral glucose, repeated as necessary. Glucose (dextrose) tablets are available, but soft drinks, candy, fruit juices, and milk are often used. If the patient is unable or unwilling (because of neuroglycopenia) to take an oral treatment, parenteral therapy is needed. Intravenous glucose, 25 g (e.g., 50 mL of 50% dextrose in water), with re-treatment 15 to 20 minutes later if symptoms persist or the plasma glucose level remains low, is the preferred initial therapy. Intravenous glucose infusion may be required to prevent recurrent hypoglycemia in the short term. Stimulation of endogenous glucose production by subcutaneous, intramuscular, or intravenous administration of glucagon (1.0 mg in adults) can be used initially when it is not feasible to give intravenous glucose. Glucagon is virtually ineffective in glycogen-depleted patients and is less effective in those with endogenous insulin secretion, because the latter is stimulated by glucagon. It is used primarily in hypoglycemic patients with insulin-dependent diabetes mellitus.

Resolution of symptoms (and signs) of hypoglycemia typically follows promptly after effective treatment. Rarely, recovery is delayed for hours, or even days, presumably because of cerebral edema. Permanent neurologic, including intellectual, deficits can follow an episode of prolonged (hours) severe hypoglycemia, but this too is very uncommon. Seemingly, complete recovery of brain function is the rule. Some data, however, indicate that recurrent episodes of severe hypoglycemia can cause rather subtle permanent cognitive defects, especially in young children, but also in adults.

The prevention of recurrent postabsorptive hypoglycemia requires correction of the underlying cause (Table 9–33–1). An offending drug should be discontinued or its dose adjusted. Other causative disorders such as critical illnesses, hormonal deficiencies, and non-beta cell tumors should be treated, if possible, and insulinomas should be removed surgically. Patients with unresectable insulinomas can be treated with diazoxide (Proglycem); octreotide (Sandostatin) has been useful in some patients. Immunosuppressive drugs including glucocorticoids have been used to treat autoimmune hypoglycemias.

FOLLOW-UP

The frequency of follow-up plasma glucose measurements must be individualized. It will range from every 15 to 30 minutes initially to days, weeks, and months. The frequency of long-term follow-up will necessarily be based in large part on symptoms in many patients, although those with drug-treated diabetes mellitus should be taught to self-monitor blood glucose.

DISCUSSION
Prevalence and Incidence

Except in persons who use drugs that lower the plasma glucose concentration, hypoglycemia is an uncommon clinical event. Patients with insulin-dependent diabetes mellitus suffer untold numbers of episodes of biochemical hypoglycemia and thousands of episodes of symptomatic hypoglycemia (an average of once or twice per week) in a lifetime of diabetes. Approximately one quarter suffer at least one episode of severe, temporarily disabling hypoglycemia, often with seizure or coma, in a given year. It is estimated that 4% of deaths of patients with insulin-dependent diabetes mellitus are caused by hypoglycemia, an alarming iatrogenic mortality rate. In addition to recurrent physical morbidity, and some mortality, iatrogenic hypoglycemia often causes recurrent or even persistent psychosocial morbidity in insulin-dependent diabetes mellitus. At the other extreme of the spectrum, fewer than one person per million harbors an insulinoma.

Drugs, particularly insulin, sulfonylureas, and alcohol, are by far the most common cause of hypoglycemia. In one series of emergency room admissions for hypoglycemia, two thirds were using medications to treat diabetes mellitus and two thirds had been consuming alcohol. Obviously, this combination of drugs can be devastating. The third most common cause was sepsis. Among hypoglycemic inpatients, drugs are also an important factor although critical illness, particularly renal failure, emerges as a major contributing factor.

Related Basic Science
Physiology of Glucose Counterregulation

Glucose is an obligate, and virtually the exclusive, metabolic fuel for the brain. As the plasma glucose concentration falls below the physiologic range, blood-to-brain glucose transport becomes limiting to brain metabolism and, thus, survival. Therefore, it is not surprising that physiologic mechanisms have evolved that normally are very effective in preventing or correcting hypoglycemia.

The first defense against falling plasma glucose concentrations is decreased insulin secretion; however, the prevention or correction of hypoglycemia is not due solely to dissipation of insulin. It also involves glucose counterregulatory (plasma glucose-raising) factors. Whereas insulin is the dominant glucose-lowering factor, there are redundant glucose counterregulatory factors and a hierarchy among these. Among the counterregulatory factors, glucagon plays a primary role. Epinephrine is not normally critical, but it becomes critical when glucagon is deficient. Thus, insulin, glucagon, and epinephrine stand high in the hierarchy of redundant glucoregulatory factors. Hypoglycemia develops or progresses when both glucagon and epinephrine are deficient and insulin is present despite the actions of other counterregulatory factors. Growth hormone and cortisol are demonstrably involved in defense against prolonged hypoglycemia, but neither is critical to the correction of even prolonged hypoglycemia or to the prevention of hypoglycemia after an overnight fast. There is evidence consistent with the interpretation that glucose autoregulation—hepatic glucose production as an inverse function of the ambient plasma glucose concentration independent of hormonal and neural regulatory factors—is operative in humans albeit only during severe hypoglycemia. Hormones, neurotransmitters, or substrates other than glucose may be involved but they play minor roles.

Pathophysiology of Glucose Counterregulation

The pathogenesis of hypoglycemia in insulin-dependent diabetes mellitus has been studied rather extensively. Iatrogenic hypoglycemia in insulin-dependent diabetes mellitus is the result of the interplay of absolute or relative insulin excess, which must occur from time to time because of the imperfections of all current insulin replacement regimens, and compromised glucose counterregulation. Syndromes of compromised glucose counterregulation in insulin-dependent diabetes mellitus include defective glucose counterregulation (the result of combined deficiencies of the glucagon and epinephrine secretory responses to falling plasma glucose levels), hypoglycemia unawareness (loss of the warning neurogenic symptoms of developing hypoglycemia), and elevated glycemic thresholds (lower plasma glucose concentrations required) for symptoms and counterregulatory hormone secretion during effective intensive therapy. Recent evidence indicates that the last two of these syndromes are largely the result of recent antecedent hypoglycemia, and are reversible during scrupulous avoidance of iatrogenic hypoglycemia. Other, as yet unidentified, factors play more important roles in the pathogenesis of defective glucose counterregulation.

Detailed discussion of the pathophysiologic mechanisms of hypoglycemia in the clinical settings of critical illnesses, hormonal deficiencies, non-beta cell tumors, and endogenous hyperinsulinism is beyond the scope of this chapter. The interested reader is urged to consult the references that follow.

Natural History and Its Modification with Treatment

As mentioned earlier, postabsorptive hypoglycemia is generally a progressive disorder that requires, in addition to urgent treatment, diagnostic explanation and definitive treatment to prevent recurrent hypoglycemia. The rate of progression can be rapid, as with critical illnesses, or gradual, as with glucocorticoid deficiency, non-beta cell tumors, and endogenous hyperinsulinism including that caused by an insulinoma.

Drug-induced hypoglycemia can be cured or minimized by discontinuation of the offending drug or adjustment of the therapeutic regimen. Critical illnesses sufficient to cause hypoglycemia can sometimes be treated as can non-beta cell tumors, but both of these are most often ultimately fatal. Glucocorticoid deficiency can be corrected with hormonal replacement, and most insulinomas can be totally removed surgically. The extent to which resolution of autoimmune hypoglycemia is the result of therapy or spontaneous remission is unknown.

Prevention

Most causes of hypoglycemia cannot be prevented; however, the frequency of iatrogenic hypoglycemia in patients with insulin-dependent diabetes mellitus can be minimized by application of the principles of modern intensive therapy—patient education and professional support, frequent blood glucose self-monitoring, and flexible insulin replacement regimens—coupled with the selection of prudent, individualized glycemic goals.

Cost Containment

Aside from those with critical illnesses, those requiring a prolonged diagnostic fact, and those suffering an episode of sulfonylurea- or alcohol-induced hypoglycemia, patients with hypoglycemic disorders generally do not require hospitalization.

The oral glucose tolerance test should not be used to diagnose postprandial hypoglycemia.

In general, expensive imaging techniques should not be performed in the evaluation of patients with hypoglycemia unless they are clearly indicated *after* the hypoglycemic mechanism (e.g., a probable insulinoma) has been determined.

Efficient diagnostic evaluation, including a well-thought-out plan and early consultation when indicated, can minimize the cost of the care of patients with hypoglycemia. Indeed, prompt referral of a patient with hypoglycemia of obscure cause to a physician experienced in hypoglycemic disorders is undoubtedly cost effective.

REFERENCES

Bailey, CJ, Flatt PR, Marks V. Drugs inducing hypoglycemia. Pharmacol Ther 1989;42:361.

Cryer PE., Glucose homeostasis and hypoglycemia. In: Wilson JD, Foster DW, eds. Williams' textbook of endocrinology. 8th ed. Philadelphia: Saunders, 1992:1223.

Cryer PE. Fisher JN, Shamoon H. Hypoglycemia. Diabetes Care 1994;17:734.

Fisher KF, Lees JA, Newman JH. Hypoglycemia in hospitalized patients. N Engl J Med 1986;315:1245.

Malouf R, Brust JCM. Hypoglycemia: Causes, neurological manifestations and outcome. Ann Neurol 1985;17:421.

Norton JA, Whitman ED. Insulinoma. Endocrinologist 1993;3:258.

Palardy J, Harrankova J, Lepage R, et al. Blood glucose measurements during symptomatic episodes in patients with suspected postprandial hypoglycemia. N Engl J Med 1989;321:1421.

CHAPTER 9–34

Obesity

Mario DiGirolamo, M.D.

DEFINITION

Obesity is an excessive accumulation of body fat. Its clinical relevance derives from the knowledge that obesity predisposes to, or aggravates, other conditions such as hypertension, hyperlipidemia, coronary atherosclerotic heart disease, congestive heart failure, diabetes mellitus, gout, degenerative arthritis, restrictive lung disease, gallbladder disease, and infertility.

ETIOLOGY

Obesity is a multifaceted disorder with several possible etiologies. It develops because energy intake exceeds energy expenditure and thus lipid storage is enhanced, mostly in adipose tissue. Recent studies have indicated a genetic predisposition in 20 to 30% of obese subjects. A more complete list of etiologic possibilities and associated tests or observations is given in Table 9–34–1.

The precise mechanisms by which various etiologies of obesity may influence food intake or the various components of energy expenditure (basal metabolic rate, thermic effect of food, energy loss of physical activity, energy lost in urine and stool) are not known.

CRITERIA FOR DIAGNOSIS
Suggestive

A useful clinical indicator of obesity is the relative body weight (i.e., actual body weight divided by the "desirable" body weight for height and sex). A relative body weight in excess of 120% of desirable body weight has been used as a cutoff point for the presence of significant obesity. Being overweight, however, is not the same as being obese. Measurement of skinfold thickness can help determine the amount of body fat. A more recent index of adiposity is the body mass index (kg/m^2). The normal range of the body mass index (BMI) is 20 to 25 for men and women. Obesity can be defined as a body mass index in excess of 27 for men and women.

Definitive

Assessment of body fat (usually expressed as a percentage of body weight) can give a definitive diagnosis, even in individuals who may be overweight due to overdeveloped lean body mass. The cutoff for presence of obesity is body fat in excess of 22% in the male and 30% in the female. Definition of obesity in terms of percentage body fat can contribute to a better understanding of the severity of obesity.

TABLE 9–34–1. ETIOLOGY OF OBESITY

Diagnostic Possibilities	Diagnostic Tests or Observations
Primary endocrine	
Hyperinsulinemia	Insulinoma; other
Glucocorticoid excess	Andrenocortical tumor or pituitary tumor secreting adrenocorticotropic hormone
Primary (or hypothalamic–pituitary) hypogonadism	See Chapter 9–20
Primary hypothyroidism	See Chapter 9–19
Polycystic ovarian syndrome associated with diabetes mellitus	
Cushing's syndrome	See Chapter 9–6
Hypothalamic–pituitary	
Tumors or inflammatory lesions of hypothalamus or pituitary	
Trauma or surgical injury to the brain	
Pseudotumor cerebri	
Empty sella syndrome	
Genetic syndromes associated with obesity	
Laurence–Moon–Biedl syndrome	
Hyperostosis frontalis interna	
Alstrom's syndrome	
Prader–Willi syndrome	
Pseudohypoparathyroidism	See Chapter 9–38
Possibly genetic in origin	
Down syndrome	
Familial obesity	Severe obesity with familial incidence; associated with diabetes or with familial hyperlipidemia

CLINICAL MANIFESTATIONS

Subjective

The patient is frequently conscious of being overweight, although the perception of being overweight varies according to familial and ethnic background, socioeconomic status, age, sex, and other factors. The patient may complain of easy fatiguability, shortness of breath, limited ambulating capacity, or joint pain. Severity of these symptoms is related to the degree of obesity.

Objective

Physical Examination

Physical examination reveals an excessive accumulation of subcutaneous adipose tissue, with the occasional "yellow striae" of skin stretching. The pattern of obesity may vary from the typical truncal distribution without limb involvement to the involvement of every segment of the body. Body measurements (height, weight, limb span, waist and hip girths, skinfold thickness) and body hair distribution should be noted. Hypertension is frequently present.

Routine Laboratory Abnormalities

Frank hyperglycemia or various degrees of carbohydrate intolerance may be present. Hyperlipidemia, mostly hypertriglyceridemia (with elevated levels of very low density lipoproteins), may be present.

PLANS

Diagnostic

Differential Diagnosis

The diagnostic goal in obesity should be fourfold: definition of severity of obesity; characterization in terms of morphology, cellularity, and metabolic disorders; definition of possible underlying endocrine and nonendocrine etiologies; and identification of behavioral and psychological factors.

Diagnostic Options

Definition of Severity of Obesity. Simple measurements of height and weight can provide the data base for a determination of the body mass index. Mild obesity can be defined as a body mass index between 27 and 30; moderate obesity, as a body mass index between 30 and 40; and severe obesity, as a body mass index in excess of 40. As obesity is defined as an excessive accumulation of fat, methods have been developed to determine body fat content. These techniques vary from simple, inexpensive ones, such as measurement of skinfold thickness by skin calipers, to more complex ones, such as determination of body density by underwater weighing, body water, body potassium, and so on. The desirable amount of fat for optimal health in the adult man is between 9 and 18% of total body weight; in the adult woman, between 18 and 28%. Presence of body fat in excess of 20% in a man and 30% in a woman supports the definition of obesity and provides a quantitative measure of it.

Characterization in Terms of Morphology, Cellularity, and Metabolic Disorders. Recent studies have indicated that a greater link exists between body fat accumulation in the abdominal region and certain systemic disorders (such as hypertension, carbohydrate intolerance, hyperlipidemia) than accumulation in other body regions. Skinfold thickness in at least four districts (biceps, triceps, infrascapular region, and iliac crest) should be measured, together with circumferences (abdominal, hip, femur), to separate the obesity phenotype into an upper-body-segment pattern of obesity (i.e., greater accumulation of fat around the waist, also called "apple") or a lower-body-segment pattern of obesity (i.e., greater accumulation of fat in the thighs and buttocks, also called "pear").

A minimum laboratory evaluation includes determinations of fasting and postprandial blood sugar, uric acid and lipid profile.

In the assessment of the severity of obesity, the presence of other disorders that may be related to, or secondary to, obesity should be noted. Of particular importance is the identification of hypertension, diabetes mellitus, cardiovascular disease, hyperlipidemic disorders, gallbladder disease, pulmonary dysfunction, and osteoarthritis.

Definition of Possible Underlying Endocrine and Nonendocrine Etiologies. Listed in Table 9–34–1 are several endocrine and nonendocrine etiologies. The physician needs to be aware of them, as removal of the underlying cause, when possible, can often ameliorate the obesity state.

Identification of Behavioral and Psychological Factors. A complete diagnostic workup for obese patients requires elucidation of socioeconomic and personal factors that may influence the development of the obesity or its persistence. Knowledge of family environment, financial resources, social and occupational pressures, labor-saving devices, and periods of forced inactivity may often give clues to initiating or perpetuating factors.

Recommended Approach

Assessment of nutritional factors, such as quantity and quality of diet (i.e., proportions of fat, carbohydrate, and protein), pattern of eating (number of meals, snacking, bulimic binges, etc.), and concomitant intake of alcohol-based calories, is useful in identifying important nutritional variables.

Among the factors affecting energy expenditure, the most important are the estimate of type, frequency, and pattern of physical activity and, if possible, a measurement of basal metabolic rate.

Evaluation of possible psychological factors includes exploration of psychological disturbances, either primary or secondary to the obese state, and the attitudes of patient, family, and friends toward probable causes of obesity. Use of anorectic agents or other drugs needs to be investigated.

Therapeutic

Therapeutic Options

Available evaluations of various forms of treatment for obesity offer rather discouraging results, particularly if long-term results are scrutinized.

In view of the complexity of obesity and its causes, important essential information about the patient, family, and environment should be gathered to design the most effective therapeutic measures.

The goal of treatment is to achieve a near-"desirable" body weight by a combination of dietary restraint and physical exercise. The patient must be reeducated regarding dietary and living habits. Patients should be apprised of desirable rates of weight loss, the beneficial effects expected, and the risks of untested diets and of anorectic and other drugs.

Conventional Diet. A diet balanced in its composition of protein, carbohydrate, and fat with emphasis on fruit and vegetables, taken in three to four meals per day, and containing an amount of calories in deficit of approximately 500 kcal from the estimated maintenance diet (for patient's age, sex, weight, and degree of activity) should produce an approximate weight loss of 1 pound per week, 3 to 4 pounds per month. Adjustments may be made if compliance is good but expected rate of weight loss is not maintained. The success of the dietary regimen is probably proportional to the patient's motivation, the dietitian's efforts in education, and the eventual encouragement of group reinforcement. A clear understanding of time, effort, progression, and expected benefits is necessary to ensure compliance and continuity of effort on the part of the patient.

Experimental Diets. The effects of high-protein or high-fat diets have been emphasized in the lay press. Advantages such as rapidity of weight loss and anorexia have been emphasized, but risks inherent to the ingestion of large amounts of fat—persistent ketosis with anorexia and elevated uric acid levels, for example—have not received sufficient scientific attention. A variety of "fad diets" are proposed from time to time, based on imbalance of nutrient composition. Usually these diets are brought to the attention of the consumer with emphasis on their effectiveness but without scientific validation. In most cases, these diets are ineffective and possibly harmful.

When rates of weight loss more rapid than 1 pound per week are desired, total fasting for 1 week or a very low calorie diet (400–800 kcal per day, usually high in protein) have been used. For the long-term effect, the nitrogen sparing of the 600- to 800-kcal high-protein diet, supplemented by electrolytes and vitamins, or a 1200-kcal diet seems to offer some advantages over other experimental diets. Some recent concerns have been raised, however, by reported cardiovascular risks (such as sudden death) associated with certain types of high-protein diets, particularly very low calorie diets consisting mostly of protein of low biological value derived from liquefied animal residues. It has been noted that the long-term goals of nutrition reeducation are not advanced by either fasting or drastically reduced diets.

Physical Exercise. Physical activity is an important adjunct to diet in attempts to reduce excessive body weight and fat. Physical exercise, particularly in the early stages of obesity, can be beneficial because of its effect on body composition (reduced fat mass and increased lean body mass). Although the effect of exercise on lean body mass can be explained by the hypertrophy of muscle fibers resulting from chronic exercise, the effect on body fat mass is harder to explain. Some studies have suggested that chronic exercise may lead to an improved sensitivity and responsiveness of the fat cells to lipolytic hormones, thus contributing to mobilization of adipose tissue lipids and reduction in adipocyte size. In severely obese patients, in whom osteoarthritis and pulmonary impairment have developed, exercise is of limited benefit and may be contraindicated. Properly supervised, the physical effort may provide an additional motivation, even though the energy expenditure of the various forms of exercise is rather limited in comparison to the goals of sizable reduction of excess fat.

Exercise removes the patient from the proximate opportunity to eat and promotes a sense of well-being. It also can reduce elevated insulin levels and contribute to improved carbohydrate tolerance; it may aid in the control of blood pressure and of hyperlipidemia and, to some degree, the prevention of cardiovascular disorders.

Drug Therapy. In view of the difficulty of treating obesity, drug treatment has been advocated, but should always be considered adjunctive to diet, exercise, and behavior modification.

Theoretically, the pharmacologic approach to obesity envisions developing and using drugs that may interfere with fat deposition (by reducing appetite, inhibiting absorption of nutrients, or reducing lipid synthesis) or stimulate energy metabolism (by accelerating fat mobilization and oxidation and/or enhancing thermogenesis).

The most common anorectic agents are mazimdol, amphetamine derivatives, fenfluramine, and fluoxetine. Acarbose prevents absorption of dietary carbohydrate and has been used to improve blood glucose and induce weight loss. Several side effects of these drugs limit their use, but they may be used in helping the patient through difficult times with weight loss or temporary relapses.

The most common thermogenic agents are thyroid hormones, ephedrine, caffeine, and beta-adrenoceptor agonists (among these, β_3-agonists have received recent attention). Thyroid hormones, however, should be used only in the treatment of hypothyroid obese patients.

Careful monitoring of the patients and of possible drug side effects should be routinely done by the physician, when one of the available drugs is used as an adjuvant in treatment of obesity.

Surgical Measures. Wiring of the jaw, gastric stapling or balloon, and other techniques have been applied to the massively obese patient in whom the risk of obesity is greater than the inherent risks of these procedures. In many cases, patients lose weight while the procedure is still operative, but regain weight promptly when normal function is reestablished. In severe obesity, when complications such as diabetes, severely reduced pulmonary function, and thromboembolism may be life-threatening, surgical reduction of stomach size has been a useful therapeutic measure, for which benefits outweigh the risks. Suction lipectomy is ineffective in reduction of the excessive adipose mass in obesity and should be reserved only for the treatment of small, localized, and cosmetically disturbing accumulations of adipose tissue. The reader is directed to specialized literature for a more complete assessment of these therapeutic forms.

Behavior Modification. In recent years, techniques of behavior self-modification have been developed and applied to the treatment of obesity. Early results with these techniques have been encouraging, but they must be individualized and frequently reinforced. It is too early to determine whether this approach, which requires specialized personnel and frequent patient visits, will successfully meet the needs of the very obese and of the increasing number of obese patients in the population.

Recommended Approach

Best results are obtained if a motivated patient is evaluated and followed closely in an environment in which a physician, nurse, and dietitian work closely to educate, support, and guide the patient. Combination of a moderate caloric reduction (about 500 kcal below estimated caloric maintenance) with a low-fat, balanced diet, rich in vegetables and fruit, regular moderate exercise (total of 30–40 minutes per day, at least 5 days per week), and simple measures of behavior modification frequently leads to beneficial weight loss. The education process of understanding quantity and composition of recommended nutrients in the diet assists the patient (and family) in healthier dietary practices during weight loss and maintenance.

FOLLOW-UP

In the first 3 months, follow-up visits every 2 weeks may be necessary for instruction and reinforcement. Body weight changes and dietary and exercise compliance should be reviewed each visit. After the first 3 months, appointments every 2 to 3 months may be necessary to continue the supervision of patient care and reinforcement.

DISCUSSION
Prevalence and Incidence

Obesity is very prevalent in the Western world and is becoming more prevalent in Third World countries that have recently raised standards of living and available food supplies. In the United States, approximately one third of the adult population is considered obese by exceeding 120% of ideal body weight, body mass index of 27, or both. Obesity is on the increase, in adults and adolescents, despite multiple efforts at education and treatment.

Related Basic Science

Many biochemical and pathophysiologic observations are available from studies in spontaneous obesity (in humans and animals), experimental obesity (in humans by forced hypernutrition, in animals by forced hypernutrition or lesions in the ventromedial nuclei of the hypothalamus), and congenital forms of obesity (such as in the *ob/ob* mice or the Zucker fatty rat). The following changes have been observed with the development of obesity: a tendency to eat a large, prolonged meal late in the day; a decrease in the spontaneous physical activity; an increase in plasma levels of cholesterol, triglycerides, free fatty acids, amino acids, insulin, and, frequently, glucose, with a diminished glucose tolerance; a reduced responsiveness to the hypoglycemic and other metabolic effects of insulin; an elevation of cortisol production rate and urinary 17-hydroxycorticoid excretion (with unchanged plasma cortisol); and a diminished growth hormone level, both basally and after various stimuli.

Early-onset obesity appears to be characterized by an increase in the adipose cell number (with some increase in cell size); this has been called *hyperplastic–hypertropic obesity.* Maturity-onset obesity, called *hypertrophic obesity,* shows an increase in cell size with a limited increase in cell number. More recent studies, however, seem to indicate that cell number can increase even in mature subjects if a critical cell size is exceeded.

There is considerable evidence indicating that many, if not all, of the metabolic and endocrine changes described are secondary rather than primary to the development of obesity, and thus they do not appear to be a cause of this condition. It is, however, possible that some of the changes described may perpetuate obesity. For instance, if obesity leads to a decrease in physical activity (or in spontaneous locomotor activity), this may reduce the caloric expenditure and contribute to weight gain if the caloric intake remains unchanged.

Studies also have shown that regional differences exist in the contribution to the total fat mass and that these differences may be related to health risk hazards such as hypertension, hyperlipidemia, diabetes, and atherosclerotic heart disease. A male pattern of obesity (accumulation of fat around the waist) may carry a greater health risk than a female pattern of obesity (accumulation of fat in the thighs and buttocks); the ratio of waist-to-hip circumferences has been used as a predictor of health hazards in obesity. More recently, the abdominal (upper-body-segment) pattern of obesity has been subdivided into predominantly subcutaneous and predominantly visceral. Health risk hazards are associated more with the visceral pattern.

Interestingly, a change in the size of fat cells has been found to alter the rate and pattern of glucose metabolism and of lipolysis. In small fat cells of young rats and children, glucose conversion to fatty acids and the response to insulin are quite active. With cellular enlargement, de novo fatty acid synthesis from glucose is markedly reduced and stimulation of glucose metabolism by insulin declines markedly. Cellular enlargement is also accompanied by accelerated rates of basal lipolysis (as measured by glycerol release per cell) and of glyceride synthesis (as shown by glucose conversion to glyceride–glycerol), and by a progressive increase in the conversion of glucose to lactate, which in obese subjects can reach 70% of total adipocyte glucose metabolism. Thus, large fat cells exhibit, in comparison to smaller fat cells from leaner subjects, an accelerated triglyceride breakdown and triglyceride synthesis. The meaning of this metabolic adaptation in unclear, but it may represent an example of a futile cycle attempting to prevent further accumulation of lipids in an already overdistended fat cell.

Hyperinsulinemia (both fasting and postprandial) almost always is present in the early stages of obesity. Considerable attention has been given to the cellular mechanisms of insulin resistance. Among the possibilities explored are an impaired recognition and/or binding of insulin by cell membrane receptors and also a postreceptor abnormality that would make the cells unable to respond to normal insulin binding and action. In several tissues of the body, including muscle, liver, and blood monocytes, a diminished binding of insulin has been shown in obese subjects; this has been considered the result of a "downregulation" of the insulin receptor, brought about by the hyperinsulinemia itself. Furthermore, fasting appears to return the insulin binding capacity toward normal.

With regard to adipose cells, however, the information on insulin binding is more controversial. In some laboratories, adipocytes from obese rodents and human beings have been found to have a reduced capacity to bind insulin, whereas other laboratories have shown an unchanged or even greater capacity to bind insulin on a per cell basis.

The present understanding of the alterations in insulin action resulting in insulin resistance attributes to postreceptor events a major role, with receptor abnormalities being modest or not contributing to the overall alteration in response to the hormones. It has also been suggested that insulin resistance may be primary to the development of obesity. Obesity is a multifactorial disorder with a variety of clinical presentations, and continuing elucidation of clinical syndromes and underlying metabolic and other disorders will contribute to the clarification of as yet unresolved questions.

Natural History and its Modification with Treatment

The natural history of obesity varies a great deal with the type of obesity. For instance, hyperplastic–hypertrophic obesity begins at an early age (frequently in infancy) and the individuals affected have an excessive body weight in all phases of growth. In contrast, in hypertropic, maturity-onset obesity, the individual accumulates an excess of body weight after maturity has been reached.

When a time can be identified at which a specific cause (hypothalamic disorder, emotional trauma, etc.) begins to operate, usually by hyperphagia, the development of obesity appears to go through an active stage with rapid and progressive weight gain until a plateau is reached and body weight is relatively constant. This is reminiscent of the "set point" of body weight produced in animals by hypothalamic lesions in the "satiety center." In other patients, the body weight accumulation is a progressive one, with 8 to 10 pounds added each year. With age, in sedentary individuals, there is a progressive diminution of the muscle mass and an increase in the fat mass.

Prevention

In view of the limited success in treating obesity and the severe and numerous medical complications associated with it, the prevention of obesity appears to be a desirable goal in an individual or in a population. This goal can be fostered by education, with emphasis on proper nutrition, (use of low-fat diets, enriched in carbohydrates, fruit, and vegetables) and desirable body weight and encouragement of habits of regular physical activity. This education should start in the family and be reinforced in school and through national advertising. Particularly important should be the realization that, after maturity, diminished caloric requirements and reduced opportunities for physical activity require increased efforts to find a balance between caloric intake and caloric expenditure.

Cost Containment

Paradoxically, the prevalence of obesity is higher in economically deprived portions of the population. Suggestions that this may be due to the type of good ingested (cheaper, fatter meats, etc.) have received partial documentation. A preventive therapeutic effort at weight reduction in obesity requires a reduced calorie intake and will almost invariably result in cost containment. Prudent diets, with emphasis on reduced use of fatty meats and dairy products and adundant use of vegetables and fruit, do not cost more than the more common types of diet. Furthermore, the costly "diet" products do not offer particular benefits to justify their purchase. Diet education offered by professional staff can reduce the cost of the excessive, expensive, and often misleading information offered in the lay press and in the numerous "diet" books easily available to patients. Patient education regarding dietary habits should include this type of information.

REFERENCES

Atkinson RL. Proposed standards for judging success of the treatment of obesity. Ann Intern Med 1993;119:677.

Bjorntorp P. Physical exercise in the treatment of obesity. In: Bjorntorp P, Brodoff BN, eds. Obesity. Philadelphia:Lippincott, 1992:708.

Bray GA. Use and abuse of appetite-suppressant drugs in the treatment of obesity. Ann Intern Med 1993;119:707.

Davidson JK, DiGirolamo M. Non-insulin-dependent diabetes mellitus. In: Davidson JK, ed. Clinical diabetes mellitus: A Problem-oriented approach. 2nd ed. New York: Thieme Medical, 1991:17.

Goldstein DJ. Beneficial health effects of modest weight loss. Int J Obes 1992;16:1.

Goldstein,DJ, Potvin JH. Long-term weight loss: The effect of pharmacologic agents. Am J Clin Nutr 1994;60:1101.

Kissebah AM, Peiris AN. Biology of regional body distribution: Relationship to non-insulin dependent diabetes. Diabetes Metab Rev 1989;5:83.

Lerman RH, Cove DR. Medical and surgical management of obesity. Adv Intern Med 1989;36:127.

National Institutes of Health. Consensus Development Conference statement: Health implications of obesity. Ann Intern Med 1985;103:1073.

Weintraub M, Gray GA. Drug treatment of obesity. Med Clin North Am 1989;73:237.

CHAPTER 9–35

Hyperlipoproteinemia (See Section 15, Chapter 1)

CHAPTER 9–36

Hypercalcemia and Hyperparathyroidism

Robert W. Downs, Jr., M.D.

DEFINITION

Hypercalcemia is defined as an abnormally high concentration of ionized calcium in the extracellular fluid.

ETIOLOGY

The causes of hypercalcemia are listed in Table 9–36–1. Hyperparathyroidism is the most common cause, followed by malignancy.

CRITERIA FOR DIAGNOSIS

Suggestive

The diagnosis of hypercalcemia should be considered in patients who present with nephrolithiasis or renal insufficiency, bone pain, refractory peptic ulcer disease, or pancreatitis. Primary hyperparathyroidism is the most common cause of hypercalcemia in the ambulatory patient population, and it is often detected by routine screening laboratory tests in asymptomatic outpatients or in the setting of mild or vague constitutional symptoms.

Definitive

Hypercalcemia is diagnosed if the serum concentration of calcium, corrected for abnormalities of protein concentration, is greater than 10.6 ml/dL. (The exact upper limit of the normal range may vary in different laboratories.) If hypercalcemia is mild (<11.5 mg/dL), it should be confirmed on at least three occasions in blood collected without prolonged venous stasis. As the total serum calcium concentration is usually measured instead of the ionized calcium concentration, it is important to recognize factors in the clinical setting that may affect the distribution of calcium between bound and ionized fractions. The most important of these is variation in the concentration of albumin, which is the major calcium-binding protein in plasma. If serum albumin is abnormal, then the degree of ionized hypercalcemia can be estimated by a crude "correction" of 0.8 mg/dL for each 1g/dL change in albumin concentration from normal, or ionized calcium can be directly measured. Determination of ionized calcium by direct measurement is usually not necessary unless there are complex abnormalities of plasma proteins, changes in acid–base status, or alterations in the concentrations of calcium-binding inorganic anions (phosphate, citrate).

The cause of hypercalcemia is established by careful attention to the details of the medical history and by results of laboratory testing, which define the pathophysiology of hypercalcemia in a particular patient.

CLINICAL MANIFESTATIONS

Subjective

Now that multichannel chemical testing of serum is common, hypercalcemia is often discovered in patients who are asymptomatic or who have only minimal symptoms. When symptoms do occur, most result from the effects of the excess extracellular calcium concentration on cellular function or reflect the tendency for calcium salts to be deposited in tissues (Table 9–36–2).

Past History

There are few symptoms of hypercalcemia that give reliable clues to its etiology, so a careful medical history is critical for recognizing specific underlying diseases that may be responsible for hypercalcemia. Particular attention should be paid to the chronicity of hypercalcemia and the presence of associated concurrent disorders, which might provide a clue to the diagnosis of malignancy, sarcoidosis, or the many other disorders that may cause hypercalcemia (Table 9–36–1).

Family History

A family history of nephrolithiasis or neck exploration may indicate familial hyperparathyroidism.

Objective

Physical Examination

In most patients, hypercalcemia itself is responsible for a few important physical findings. Muscle weakness, particularly of proximal muscle groups, occurs commonly in hyperparathyroidism. Evidence of calcium salt precipitation in the form of bank keratopathy or vascular calcification associated with evidence of tissue ischemia may be found, particularly if both calcium and phosphate levels have been elevated.

As part of the objective evaluation, a careful search for physical signs that may reveal the underlying cause of hypercalcemia should be performed. This would include a search for evidence of primary malignant tumor or lymphadenopathy suggesting metastasis, lymphoma, or sarcoidosis; an examination of the thyroid gland for enlargement and a further examination for associated signs of thyrotoxicosis; evaluation for adrenal insufficiency; and evaluation of the degree of immobilization.

Routine Laboratory Abnormalities

Routine laboratory investigations should first confirm the diagnosis of hypercalcemia. Other routine laboratory studies may provide informa-

TABLE 9–36–1. CAUSES OF HYPERCALCEMIA

Parathyroid hormone-related hypercalcemia
    Primary hyperparathyroidism
    Ectopic production of parathyroid hormone (rare)
    Familial hypocalciuric hypercalcemia
    "Tertiary" hyperparathyroidism
Hypercalcemia not mediated by parathyroid hormone
    Malignancy
        With bone metastasis
        Humoral hypercalcemia
    Vitamin D intoxication
    Sarcoidosis and other granulomatous diseases
    Thyrotoxicosis
    Immobilization
    Milk-alkali syndrome
    Acute renal failure and rhabdomyolysis
    Vitaimin A intoxication
    Addison's disease
Drugs
    Thiazides, lithium

tion that is helpful in the differential diagnosis of the cause of hypercalcemia. Blood chemistry studies and x-ray films may show evidence of excess parathyroid hormone action (hypercalcemia accompanied by hypophosphatemia, hyperchloremic metabolic acidosis, and elevated bone alkaline phosphatase level with evidence on x-ray films of subperiosteal bone resorption, thinning of the trabecular pattern of the distal clavicles, or frank osteitis fibrosa cystica), and in rare instances a parathyroid mass may even be seen in the neck or upper mediastinum on routine chest x-ray in a patient with primary hyperparathyroidism.

Alternatively, routine testing may show evidence of suppressed parathyroid hormone activity (hypercalcemia with normal or high serum phosphorus concentration and normal serum chloride levels) or evidence of an underlying disease responsible for hypercalcemia (bone metastasis or sarcoidosis).

Evidence of mild renal insufficiency is found frequently in patients with hypercalcemia, particularly in cases of nonparathyroid hypercalcemia. Hematuria may indicate the presence of nephrolithiasis. In more severe hypercalcemia, the electrocardiogram may demonstrate an obvious shortening of the QT interval.

PLANS
Diagnostic
Differential Diagnosis

The discovery of hypercalcemia, even if it is mild, should lead to a prompt diagnostic evaluation to determine the cause (see Table 9–36–1). Because primary hyperparathyroidism is such a common cause of hypercalcemia, the first step in the diagnostic evaluation is to establish whether hypercalcemia is mediated by parathyroid hormone. This is accomplished most accurately by determination of the circulating parathyroid hormone concentration.

Recent advances in the parathyroid hormone immunoassay to incorporate two-site immunometric methods have considerably improved the sensitivity of the assay. In addition, the two-site assays are not significantly affected by the decreased clearance of inactive carboxy-terminal parathyroid hormone fragments that occur in patients with renal insufficiency, so that interpretation of parathyroid hormone assay re-

sults is simplified. With modern techniques, low parathyroid hormone levels are reliably demonstrated in patients who have hypercalcemia not mediated by parathyroid hormone, and elevated levels are usually observed in patients with primary hyperparathyroidism. Most commercial laboratories use the immunometric two-site assays now, but not all do. Therefore, it is still important for the clinician to insist that any reputable laboratory supply its own clinical correlation data to allow comparison of the parathyroid hormone result for an individual patient with results in a series of patients with hypercalcemia due to various known disorders. It is particularly important that clinicians recognize that results from assays that recognize single midmolecule or carboxy-terminal antigenic sites may not be interpretable in patients who have even moderate renal insufficiency because of delayed renal clearance of inactive parathyroid hormone fragments.

If a low parathyroid hormone assay result indicates the likelihood of hyercalcemia not caused by excess parathyroid hormone, clues to the cause of hypercalcemia can often be determined from a careful clinical evaluation of the patient. The patient should be questioned particularly about dietary and supplemental calcium and vitamin intake, and a thorough examination should search for evidence of malignancy and granulomatous disease. Evaluation of hypercalcemia of unknown etiology may require a complex series of studies, including laboratory tests for thyrotoxicosis, vitamin D intoxication, and myeloma; a radiologic search for occult malignancy, metastatic bone disease, sarcoidosis, and other granulomatous diseases; and tissue biopsies to determine the presence of hematologic or lymphoproliferative disorders, sarcoidosis, or malignancy.

Diagnostic Options and Recommended Approach

If a high serum parathyroid hormone concentration suggests the diagnosis of primary hyperparathyroidism, alternate diagnoses should be considered before therapeutic decisions are made. First, as noted above, caution must be exercised in the interpretation of parathyroid hormone assay results in patients with renal insufficiency. The clinician will need to be satisfied that the results of the assay really do indicate excess secretion of parathyroid hormone from the parathyroid glands before the diagnosis of hyperparathyroidism can be established. Second, familiar hypocalciuric hypercalcemia must be distinguished from typical primary hyperparathyroidism (see below).

In patients who are found to have primary hyperparathyroidism, several additional diagnostic studies are useful for further care and follow-up. These additional tests are to determine if there are important renal or skeletal complications due to the hyperparathyroidism, and include measurement of creatinine clearance and x-rays to search for evidence of nephrolithiasis or bone resorption. Quantitative bone mineral density is often low, even in patients who appear to have mild asymptomatic hyperparathyroidism, and should be determined periodically if patients are not treated with surgery, to evaluate the need for more definitive treatment. In patients who have severe hyperparathyroidism, x-rays or bone scans should be done to find lytic cystic lesions in weight-bearing bones that may present a risk for pathologic fracture.

There are a number of diagnostic localization procedures to search for enlarged parathyroid glands, including radionuclide scans, high-resolution ultrasonography, computed tomography of the neck and mediastinum, and magnetic resonance imaging with high-resolution surface coil techniques. It is still true, though, that a good surgeon can find abnormal glands more reliably than any of these techniques.

Because of false-negative and false-positive results, such localization studies should never be used to establish a diagnosis of hyperparathyroidism, and are not indicated except prior to re-operative neck exploration.

Therapeutic
Therapeutic Options

Treatment should be directed not only toward the hypercalcemia itself but also toward the underlying disease responsible for the increase in serum calcium. Patients who have mild, minimally symptomatic hypercalcemia may not require acute therapy while the diagnostic evaluation proceeds. In cases of severe hypercalcemia (serum calcium concentration greater than 14 mg/dL) or if there is hypoalbuminemia, dehydra-

TABLE 9–36–2. CLINICAL MANIFESTATIONS OF HYPERCALCEMIA

Neuromuscular	Weakness, fatigue, depression, confusion, somnolence, coma
Gastrointestinal	Constipation, anorexia, nausea, dyspepsia
Cardiovascular	Digitalis sensitivity, shortened QT interval
Renal	Polyuria (concentrating defect), renal colic, renal failure, nephrocalcinosis
Miscellaneous	Soft tissue calcifications (band keratopathy, vascular calcifications, pruritus)

tion, or immobilization, which may be expected to cause the hypercalcemia to worsen, acute therapy to lower the serum calcium concentration is necessary and may be lifesaving.

Rehydration and saline diuresis are the usual first steps in acute therapy. For successful treatment, the saline diuresis must be vigorous enough to result in definite volume expansion, so that proximal renal tubular reabsorption of both sodium and calcium will be minimized. In many patients, this will mean that a loop diuretic will be necessary for management of signs or symptoms of volume overload; however, diuretics are not the principal agent necessary for effective therapy. Too much reliance on diuretic treatment may produce volume depletion and worsening of hypercalcemia. In elderly subjects and in others with compromised cardiovascular function, direct monitoring of hemodynamic status may be required. All patients treated with vigorous diuresis will require replacement of potassium and magnesium.

If saline diuresis fails to produce an acceptable decline in the serum calcium level, other agents can be used.

Bisphosphonates bind to the surface of bone and decrease osteoclastic bone resorption. Of the currently available bisphosphonates, pamidronate (Aredia) is the most potent. For treatment of hypercalcemia, pamidronate is infused intravenously over 6 to 14 hours in a dose of 30 to 90 mg, depending on the severity of the hypercalcemia. Most (but not all) patients become normocalcemic after pamidronate infusion, but the therapeutic effect is temporary. Because of prior parathyroid suppression by hypercalcemia, some patients may develop transient hypocalcemia after treatment. Pamidronate infusion is associated with an "acute phase reaction" characterized by transient malaise, low-grade fever, and leukocytosis. Etidronate, another bisphosphonate, is less potent when administered intravenously. Other potent bisphosphonates are also highly effective in the treatment of hypercalcemia and likely to become available in the near future. Plicamycin (Mithracin) (25 μg/kg intravenous bolus) has direct effects to block osteoclast-mediated bone resorption, and is usually successful in reducing the serum calcium concentration within 24 hours. Now that potent bisphosphonates are available, plicamycin is considered a second-line therapeutic option because of associated nephrotoxicity, hepatotoxicity, and the rare occurrence of an idiosyncratic abnormality of platelet function that can result in severe bleeding complications. Salmon calcitonin (Calcimar, Miacalcin) in doses up to 8 units/kg intravenously or intramuscularly every 6 hours may also effectively decrease elevated serum calcium levels. Calcitonin has a rapid onset of action, and serum calcium levels may fall within 12 hours; however, many patients will "escape" from the beneficial effects of calcitonin within several days.

Gallium nitrate has been demonstrated to be quite effective in reducing serum calcium in patients with hypercalcemia of malignancy; the recommended dose is 200 mg/m^2 body surface area administered as a continuous infusion over 24 hours, daily for 5 days or until the serum calcium concentration falls into an acceptable range. Gallium should not be used in patients with renal insufficiency. Glucocorticoids can provide effective therapy for patients with a vitamin D-mediated mechanism of hypercalcemia or if the underlying disease is responsive to glucocorticoid treatment; however, glucocorticoids are not often used if the diagnosis of the underlying disease is uncertain, because they may interfere with the diagnostic evaluation and because they are only rarely effective in treating hypercalcemia caused by hyperparathyroidism and most nonhematologic cancers.

Recommended Approach

Surgical removal of the parathyroid glands is effective for the treatment of hypercalcemia, of course, if the diagnosis of primary hyperparathyroidism is established. Surgery is definitely indicated if hypercalcemia is significant (>12.0 mg/dL), even if the patient is asymptomatic, if there are definite symptoms attributable to hypercalcemia, or if there is evidence of diminished renal function, active renal stone disease, or bony lesions due to excess parathyroid hormone. Some selected patients who are asymptomatic and who are free of complications of hyperparathyroidism can be carefully followed without surgical intervention.

Recent data from longitudinal studies of patients with mild asymptomatic hyperparathyroidism indicate that such patients can be followed safely without surgical intervention for long periods, and that worsening of disease or development of bone or renal complications is uncommon.

The argument in favor of surgical therapy in most cases is that successful surgery is curative and reduces the risk of later complications of hypercalcemia. In addition, surgery is less risky in the younger patient with mild hypercalcemia than in the elderly patient who has been followed for many years before developing more severe hypercalcemia or symptoms such as declining mental function that might be attributable to hypercalcemia. Surgery should always be performed by a surgeon with particular experience in parathyroid surgery, as a large portion of unsuccessful initial neck explorations are the result of poor surgical strategy. In most series published by experts in parathyroid surgery, approximately 95% of patients are cured with a single operation. Most surgeons advocate that all parathyroid glands be directly visualized at surgery, because there are instances of asymmetric hyperplasia in which some glands may appear to be normal in size but cause recurrent hypercalcemia if left in place in patients with multiple-gland disease. If two or more abnormal glands are identified, then the patient should be recognized as having multiple-gland disease and even the apparently normal glands should be dealt with as if they were hyperplastic. There is an extremely high incidence of persistent and recurrent hyperparathyroidism after surgical treatment of patients with familial multiple endocrine neoplasia type I. A careful preoperative family history and appropriate family screening before surgery will influence the operative strategy to ensure a more favorable surgical outcome; patients who are members of multiple endocrine neoplasia kindreds should be assumed to have parathyroid hyperplasia affecting all glands regardless of the apparent pathology at the time of operation. Some authors have advocated removal of all parathyroid tissue from the neck in such patients, with autotransplantation of a portion of a gland to a more accessible location in a forearm muscle.

For some patients who are not candidates for surgery because of other illnesses, symptomatic hypercalcemia can be managed medically, even though this treatment is less satisfactory than treatment with surgery. The usual medical regimen involves adequate hydration, mobilization, and treatment with oral phosphate in gradually escalating doses to a total of 2 to 3 g of elemental phosphorus daily in divided doses. The patient usually notes some gastrointestinal intolerance, which can often be minimized by beginning with low doses taken with meals. Diarrhea often limits the total dose that can be administered. Most serious side effects of phosphate treatment include congestive heart failure, precipitated by the sodium that accompanies the phosphate, and declining renal function. Serum phosphorus and creatinine levels should be monitored closely during therapy, and the treatment dose should be decreased if the serum phosphorus level exceeds 4.0 mg/dL or if the creatinine level rises. Estrogen can also be used for medical treatment of selected postmenopausal women with hyperparathyroidism. The fall in serum calcium concentration observed after initiation of estrogen treatment is usually only slight, but may be adequate in some patients with mild symptomatic hypercalcemia. Neither phosphate nor estrogen treatment appears to decrease serum parathyroid hormone concentrations, so neither is expected to be effective in reducing bone resorption in patients with hyperparathyroidism.

FOLLOW-UP

The need for follow-up depends on the cause of the hypercalcemia. After a successful neck exploration for primary hyperparathyroidism, little follow-up is necessary for most patients. Patients with a history of parathyroid hyperplasia may be at risk of recurrent hypercalcemia, and regular annual visits should be scheduled for measurement of serum calcium. Patients with hyperplasia and a family history of multiple endocrine neoplasia type I are at risk for the development of pituitary adenomas and pancreatic islet cell tumors, so follow-up of such patients should include an evaluation for signs and symptoms of these disorders. Patients with hypercalcemia caused by malignancy, sarcoidosis, or other chronic diseases need more frequent follow-up to ensure adequate hydration, monitoring of renal function, and treatment of hypercalcemic complications if they occur.

DISCUSSION

Prevalence and Incidence

Primary hyperparathyroidism is the most common cause of hypercalcemia in the ambulatory patient population. Screening of large populations indicates that the incidence of hyperparathyroidism is between 0.1 and 0.2%. The majority of cases diagnosed with such screening are asymptomatic. The incidence of hyperparathyroidism peaks in the fifth and sixth decades of life, and females have a slightly higher incidence than males.

Related Basic Science

Altered Molecular Biology

Calcium is an important ion involved in the control of a variety of cellular processes. Recent research has identified major calcium-dependent intracellular regulatory mechanisms. These include control of a class of protein kinases by calcium and phospholipids, and regulation of the activity of other protein kinases by calmodulin, an important calcium-binding protein. Calmodulin is also involved in the control of cytoskeletal elements. The intracellular calcium concentration important for the activation of these calcium-dependent regulatory mechanisms is carefully maintained by cellular mechanisms that include regulation of the distribution of calcium into the endoplasmic reticulum, sarcoplasmic reticulum, and mitochondria, and by plasma membrane components (calcium pumps, channels, and exchangers) that affect the distribution of calcium across the cell membrane.

An increase in the concentration of extracellular calcium, as occurs in the hypercalcemic states, perturbs this system of tightly controlled intracellular calcium and affects the responsiveness of excitable cells such as nerve and muscle, which depend on membrane polarization or calcium exchange across the sarcoplasmic reticulum for their normal functions. This basic mechanism probably accounts for many of the constitutional symptoms common in patients with hypercalcemia, such as weakness, fatigue, constipation, and depression. Some of the dyspepsia experienced by hypercalcemic patients may be due to abnormal lower esophageal sphincter tone.

Other symptoms of hypercalcemia may be related to the effects of extracellular calcium as a stimulator of hormone secretion. Serum levels of gastrin are slightly higher in hypercalcemic patients than in normal subjects and may result in hyperacidity and a propensity to peptic ulceration.

The concentration of ionized calcium in the extracellular fluid is tightly regulated by the actions of parathyroid hormone and 1,25-dihydroxyvitamin D. These hormones act to regulate the exchange of calcium between skeletal mineral stores and the extracellular fluid, the handling of calcium and phosphorus by renal tubular cells, and the absorption of calcium across the intestinal mucosa. An understanding of the altered physiology in states of hypercalcemia helps to direct an organized approach to the patient.

Physiologic and Metabolic Derangement

Primary Hyperparathyroidism.
In primary hyperparathyroidism, there is inappropriate hypersecretion of parathyroid hormone despite an elevated concentration of ionized calcium in extracellular fluids. Hyperparathyroidism occurs because of hyperfunction of one or more of the parathyroid glands. Single-gland disease (adenoma) accounts for about 75 to 85% of cases, and multiple-gland disease (hyperplasia) accounts for most of the rest. There is a very small (less than 1%) incidence of parathyroid carcinoma.

An important subset of patients with hyperparathyroidism have familial hypercalcemia associated with the syndromes of multiple endocrine neoplasia type I (parathyroid hyperplasia, pancreatic islet-cell tumors, and pituitary adenomas) and type II (medullary thyroid carcinoma, pheochromocytoma, and parathyroid hyperplasia). In 5 to 10% of cases of primary hyperparathyroidism there is a history of prior neck irradiation.

Most of the pathophysiologic consequences of hyperparathyroidism can be deduced from a knowledge of the actions of parathyroid hormone. Parathyroid hormone stimulates osteoclastic bone resorption. In the kidney, parathyroid hormone promotes distal tubular reabsorption of calcium, which tends to increase retention of calcium and also tends to reduce the amount of calcium found in the final urine. Most patients with hyperparathyroidism have slightly elevated 24-hour urinary excretion of calcium despite this action of parathyroid hormone, because of the high filtered load of calcium associated with hypercalcemia. Nevertheless, the increases in urinary calcium in hyperparathyroidism are minimal compared with the major increases found in patients with hypercalcemia who have suppressed parathyroid hormone and who therefore lack the distal tubular effect of parathyroid hormone. At the level of the proximal tubule, parathyroid hormone increases phosphate and bicarbonate clearance, an effect that is responsible for the hypophosphatemia and the hyperchloremic acidosis often observed in patients with hyperparathyroidism. Parathyroid hormone also acts to enhance the conversion of 25-hydroxyvitamin D to its active metabolite, 1,25-dihydroxyvitamin D (calcitriol). Calcitriol then acts to enhance intestinal calcium absorption. All these actions combine to increase the serum concentration of calcium. In patients with parathyroid adenoma, the hypercalcemia suppresses the function of the normal parathyroid glands, so that after successful surgical removal of the adenoma, there is often a brief period of postsuppression hyperparathyroidism.

Ectopic Parathyroid Hormone Production.
Stringent criteria for proof of hypercalcemia caused by etopic production of parathyroid hormone by a neoplasm would include demonstration of immunoreactive parathyroid hormone in plasma, increased parathyroid hormone in tumor extracts compared with extracts of normal tissue, arteriovenous gradients across a tumor bed, and normalization of serum calcium levels after tumor removal. Modern laboratory techniques also make it possible to identify messenger RNA for parathyroid hormone in tumor extracts. There are just a few reported cases that convincingly satisfy such rigid criteria, so that although ectopic secretion of parathyroid hormone certainly does occur, it must be considered to be extremely rare. It is important to recall that hyperparathyroidism is a very common disease, so the coexistence of malignancy and elevated parathyroid hormone levels does not prove that the tumor is producing the parathyroid hormone. Some tumors do produce a related hypercalcemic peptide (see below) that is not identical to parathyroid hormone.

Familial Hypocalciuric Hypercalcemia.
Familial hypocalciuric hypercalcemia is an uncommon autosomal dominant familial syndrome characterized by hypercalcemia that is usually completely asymptomatic

In many families with familial hypocalciuric hypercalcemia, recent studies using genetic probes have shown abnormalities in the messenger RNA that encodes a cell surface calcium receptor important for the recognition of extracellular calcium concentration by parathyroid cells and kidney cells. Affected individuals do appear to have some parathyroid gland hyperplasia as well as a characteristic abnormality of renal calcium handling that causes low urinary calcium excretion despite the relatively large filtered load of calcium. Parathyroid hormone levels may be high in some patients, so patients may appear to have asymptomatic typical primary hyperparathyroidism; however, surgical treatment is ineffective in curing the hypercalcemic state and, therefore, is not indicated. Screening for familial hypocalciuric hypercalcemia in patients who appear to have typical primary hyperparathyroidism is accomplished by determining the ratio of calcium clearance to creatinine clearance in a 24-hour urine specimen. If the ratio of calcium clearance to creatinine clearance ($[U_{ca}/S_{ca}] \times [S_{cr}/U_{cr}]$) is less than 0.010, familial hypocalciuric hypercalcemia must be considered possible and other family members should be screened for asymptomatic hypercalcemia.

"Tertiary" Hyperparathyroidism.
Patients with renal failure may develop a form of semiautonomous hyperparathyroidism. The term "tertiary" has been applied to this condition, but it is somewhat inappropriate because it implies an irreversibility that does not really exist in many patients. Some patients may require parathyroidectomy for hypercalcemia associated with severe osteitis fibrosa cystica or to treat dangerous hypercalcemia in the post-renal transplant period. This is usually not a difficult diagnosis to suspect because of the clinical setting of renal failure in which it occurs.

Hypercalcemia of Malignancy.
Several mechanisms can account for hypercalcemia in patients with malignancy:

- Direct lytic bone metastasis
- Humoral hypercalcemia
- Prostaglandins, osteoclast-activating factors (interleukin-2), other locally acting factors and cytokines
- Production of active vitamin D metabolites
- Coincidental primary hyperparathyroidism

Humoral hypercalcemia of malignancy is caused by a parathyroid hormone-related peptide that is produced by many malignant tumors. The amino-terminal portions of parathyroid hormone-related peptide and parathyroid hormone are similar in amino acid sequence, but parathyroid hormone-related peptide is otherwise distinct and does not react in parathyroid hormone radioimmunoassays. Parathyroid hormone-related peptide does have parathyroid hormone-like actions on parathyroid hormone target tissues, which are mediated through parathyroid hormone receptors. Therefore, patients with humoral hypercalcemia, unlike patients with direct metastatic invasion of bone, have high renal phosphate clearance and elevated levels of urinary cyclic AMP, findings that are usually present in primary hyperparathyroidism.

Vitamin D Intoxication. Although vitamin D is formed in the skin, it is not possible to become hypercalcemic solely from overexposure to ultraviolet light. Clinical vitamin D intoxication results from the ingestion of excessive amounts of vitamin D or its metabolites. Most commonly, patients with vitamin D intoxication are receiving prescribed treatment for hypocalcemia. Occasionally, patients will be taking vitamin D as part of a fad food regimen or even surreptitiously abusing vitamin D as a manifestation of psychiatric disease.

Sarcoidosis. A normal chest x-ray or lack of peripheral lymph-adenopathy does not exclude the diagnosis of sarcoidosis in a patient with hypercalcemia. The granulomatous tissue is responsible for unregulated overproduction of 1,25-dihydroxyvitamin D (calcitriol) from precursors. Hypercalciuria and hypercalcemia result from stimulated bone resorption and intestinal hyperabsorption of calcium, and hypercalcemia can worsen if renal calcium excretion falls because of deteriorating renal function or because of the administration of drugs such as thiazides, which reduce renal calcium excretion.

Similar hypercalcemic syndromes due to unregulated production of 1,25-dihydroxyvitamin D have been described in patients with other granulomatous diseases and in some patients with lymphoma.

Thyrotoxicosis. Thyroid hormones directly stimulate bone resorption. The real incidence of hypercalcemia with thyrotoxicosis is unclear, particularly now that patients with thyroid disease are diagnosed and treated before their disease is severe. Some older series have reported an incidence of hypercalcemia in as many as 15 to 23% of patients.

Immobilzation. Absence of weight bearing alters the balance between bone formation and bone resorption in favor of bone resorption. The result is hypercalciuria, and hypercalcemia will occur in patients with rapid bone turnover (children, persons with Paget's disease, or patients with underlying prior causes of hypercalcemia) and in patients in whom renal insufficiency decreases the ability to excrete the calcium mobilized from bone.

Drugs. Thiazide diuretics may cause hypercalcemia in a substantial group of patients. Thiazides decrease urinary calcium excretion, and in any state of increased bone resorption with high urine calcium excretion, this drug effect can lead to hypercalcemia. A large proportion of patients discovered to be hypercalcemic while receiving thiazides remain hypercalcemic after discontinuation of the drug or redevelop hypercalcemia after a brief period of normocalcemia. All patients with thiazide-induced hypercalcemia should be evaluated to determine the cause of their hypercalcemia.

Natural History and Its Modification with Treatment

The natural history of hypercalcemia depends, of course, on the specific disease that is the cause of the elevated serum calcium concentration. The spectrum of natural history extends from familial hypocalciuric hypercalcemia, which is asymptomatic, not progressive, and not clearly associated with any reduced mortality, to hypercalcemia present in the terminal stages of a metastatic malignancy. In many situations in which there is hypercalcemia, there is some risk for progressive demineralization of bone, hypercalciuria, nephrocalcinosis, and renal failure.

Consideration of the natural history is probably most important in patients with mild or asymptomatic primary hyperparathyroidism. The long-term natural history in this group of patients is still not certain. Recent short-term clinical studies have followed patients with mild hyperparathyroidism and have found no progression of symptoms or definite worsening of skeletal or renal disease during observation. Patients who are being followed without surgical intervention do not generally progress to develop hypercalcemic crisis, but there may be a small risk of this serious complication; patients should be warned of the hazards of dehydration and immobilization, and should know to contact a physician promptly if they become ill.

Prevention

The only causes of hypercalcemia that can be prevented are tertiary hyperparathyroidism in patients with renal failure, which can be prevented in many instances by rigid adherence to a low-phosphate regimen during the early stages of renal insufficiency; and vitamin D intoxication, most instances of which could be prevented by careful monitoring of the patients who are receiving vitamin D prescribed by a physician.

Cost Containment

Strategies for cost containment depend on the etiology of hypercalcemia. No sweeping generalizations can be made, other than that a careful history and thorough physical examination will often yield information that will allow the physician to select an appropriate test for confirmation of a clinical diagnosis rather than a larger series of expensive and undirected laboratory tests.

Cost containment may be important in the care of the patient who has hyperparathyroidism. Redundancy of parathyroid hormone assays after the diagnosis is already established serves no purpose, and the serum concentration of parathyroid hormone is not useful as a test to determine when surgery should be recommended in a patient with mild hyperparathyroidism. Expensive imaging studies to localize parathyroid glands prior to an initial neck exploration are not warranted. The success rates for location of adenomas by such procedures are not yet close to the success rates achieved by skilled and experienced surgeons, and there are no published data that show that tentative localization decreases operative time or improves clinical outcome. In fact, it is possible that excessive reliance on localization imaging could have the reverse effect, because of occasional misleading false-positive results and because tentative localization may embolden an inexperienced surgeon to attempt a neck exploration.

REFERENCES

Broadus AE, Magee JSI, Mallette LE, et al. A detailed evaluation of oral phosphate therapy in selected patients with primary hyperparathyroidism. J Clin Endocrinol Metab 1983;56:953.

Heath H, Hodgson SF, Kennedy MA. Primary hyperparathyroidism: Incidence, morbidity, and potential economic impact in a community. N Engl J Med 1980;392:189.

Marx SJ, Stock JL, Attie MF, et al. Familial hypocalciuric hypercalcemia: Recognition among patients referred after unsuccessful parathyroid exploration. Am Intern Med 1980;92:351.

NIH Conference. Diagnosis and management of asymptomatic primary hyperparathyroidism: Consensus development conference statement. Ann Intern Med 1991;114:593.

Rosenthal N, Insogna KL, Godsall JW, Smaldone L, Waldron JA, Stewart AF. Elevations in circulating 1,25-dihydroxyvitamin D in three patients with lymphoma associated hypercalcemia. J Clin Endocrinol Metab 1985;60:29.

CHAPTER 9–37

Secondary and Tertiary Hyperparathyroidism

Mario DiGirolamo, M.D.

DEFINITION

Secondary Hyperparathyroidism

Secondary hyperparathyroidism is a condition characterized by elevated secretion of parathyroid hormone in the presence of normocalcemia or variable degrees of chronic hypocalcemia.

Tertiary Hyperparathyroidism

Tertiary (or autonomous) hyperparathyroidism is a rare condition characterized by excessive secretion of parathyroid hormone coupled with variable degrees of hypercalcemia.

ETIOLOGY

Secondary Hyperparathyroidism

See Plans, Diagnostic, for a list of conditions in which secondary hyperparathyroidism may occur.

Tertiary Hyperparathyroidism

See Plans, Diagnostic.

CRITERIA FOR DIAGNOSIS

Secondary Hyperparathyroidism

The clinical setting in which the condition is found is one likely to produce chronic hypocalcemia, such as malabsorption or chronic renal insufficiency.

Clues to the presence of secondary hyperparathyroidism can be found in symptoms of hypocalcemia and/or in the presence of many clinical disorders (see Plans, Diagnostic) that produce chronic hypocalcemia and secondary hypersecretion of parathyroid hormone.

Tertiary Hyperparathyroidism

Diagnosis of tertiary hyperparathyroidism requires a history of secondary hyperparathyroidism that persists even when the clinical disorder producing chronic hypocalcemia is corrected.

CLINICAL MANIFESTATIONS

Subjective

Secondary Hyperparathyroidism

Symptoms of secondary hyperparathyroidism vary depending on the underlying clinical disorder (see the list of disease processes likely to produce secondary hyperparathyroidism under Plans, Diagnostic) and the concomitant hypocalcemia, when present. Bone pain is frequently present in advanced stages of renal insufficiency in which bone demineralization and osteitis fibrosa cystica may be present. As in primary hyperparathyroidism, proximal muscle weakness may develop.

When hypocalcemia is present, patients may experience a variety of symptoms that vary in relation to the severity of the hypocalcemia. Malaise and mental torpor, anxiety, and psychoneurosis may be present together with photophobia and diplopia, dysphagia, pylorospasm, and bronchospasm. Only rarely is the hypocalcemia so severe as to produce the prodomes of a tetanic attack (for more details, see Chapter 9–38).

Tertiary Hyperparathyroidism

Symptoms associated with hypercalcemia are often vague (bone pain, frequent urination, etc.) and difficult to explain as specific effects of calcium. The subjective complaints associated with tertiary hyperparathyroidism are to a degree determined by the condition (such as malabsorption or chronic renal insufficiency) that led to secondary hypoparathyroidism and subsequent autonomous parathyroid function.

Objective

Secondary Hyperparathyroidism

Physical Examination. Findings due to hypocalcemia per se include manifestations of carpopedal spasms, flexion of the metacarpophalangeal joints, adduction of the thumb, and spasm of the facial muscles. Latent tetany (rare in patients with secondary hyperparathyroidism) may be recognized by specific signs.

- Chvostek's sign is elicited by tapping the facial nerve anterior to the ear lobe. A positive response occurs when the tapping produces twitching of the muscles innervated by the facial nerve.
- Trousseau's sign is elicited by inflating a blood pressure cuff 10 to 20 mm Hg above the systolic blood pressure. A positive response occurs when a carpal spasm is produced within 3 minutes.
- Erb's sign is elicited by application of a galvanic current to a nerve. A positive response is a motor nerve response produced by a cathodal current of less than 6 mA.

Routine Laboratory Abnormalities. Abnormalities reflect the underlying disorders (see Plans, Diagnostic, and related chapters) that produce chronic hypocalcemia and lead to secondary hyperparathyroidism.

Tertiary Hyperparathyroidism

Physical Examination. Physical findings are usually unremarkable in tertiary hyperparathyroidism.

Routine Laboratory Abnormalities. The important laboratory features of tertiary hyperparathyroidism include the following:

- Hypercalcemia (usually $\geq$ 10.8–12.0 mg/dL. The elevation of calcium is mostly in the ionized fraction.
- A blood level of phosphate that can vary from severe hypophosphatemia (i.e., < 2.5 mg/dL) to normal or even elevated levels of phosphate if chronic renal insufficiency is present.
- Inappropriately elevated parathyroid hormone levels. When hypercalcemia exceeds 10.6 mg/dL, parathyroid hormone levels should be undetectable.
- Bone lesions with advanced demineralization (osteopenia), brown tumors, and, at times, the typical osteitis fibrosa cystica.
- A variety of other lesions such a nephrocalcinosis or nephrolithiasis, peptic ulcer disease, hypertension, and chronic pancreatitis.

PLANS

Diagnostic

Secondary hyperparathyroidism

Differential Diagnosis. When chronic hypocalcemia is produced by a variety of clinical disorders, feedback activation of the parathyroid gland to produce and secrete parathyroid hormone leads to continuous and excessive secretion of parathyroid hormone. Hypersecretion of parathyroid hormone may, in part, correct the hypocalcemia, but it also leads to the chronic complications associated with primary hyperparathyroidism (see Chapter 9–36).

The following clinical disorders (listed in order of frequency) may precede and accompany the hypocalcemia and subsequent parathyroid hormone hypersecretion:

- Chronic renal insufficiency, characterized in early stages by retention of phosphate and in more advanced stages by uremia and deficient calcium transport and absorption.
- Malabsorption of vitamin D and calcium due to diseases of the small bowel or after gastrectomy.
- Deficiency of dietary vitamin D caused by reduced intake or malnutrition.
- Hypomagnesemia, which can be produced by a variety of condi-

tions. The most frequent clinical disorders associated with hypomagnesemia are chronic alcohol abuse, increased losses from the gastrointestinal tract (vomiting or diarrhea, nasogastric suction), diuretic therapy, or renal diseases such as tubular acidosis.

- Drug-induced osteomalacia, frequently associated with laxative abuse, anticonvulsants (phenobarbital, phenytoin), or the hypocholesterolemic agent cholestyramine.
- Pseudohypoparathyroidism.
- Vitamin D-dependent and vitamin D-resistant rickets.
- Fanconi syndrome and renal tubular acidosis.

Diagnostic Options and Recommended Approach. The tests to be used to diagnose the underlying disorder(s) are dictated by knowledge of the disorders associated with production of chronic hypercalcemia. The reader is referred to Chapters 3–41 and 9–36 for pertinent diagnostic tests.

Tertiary Hyperparathyroidism

Differential Diagnosis. Tertiary hyperparathyroidism is suspected when hypercalcemia develops during the course of a disorder (such as malabsorption and chronic renal insufficiency) that produces chronic hypocalcemia and secondary hyperparathyroidism.

Diagnostic Options and Recommended Approach. The diagnosis is confirmed by findings of hypercalcemia that persist even when the underlying condition such as malabsorption or chronic renal insufficiency is corrected by appropriate treatment or, in the latter instance, by kidney transplant.

Therapeutic

Secondary Hyperparathyroidism

Treatment of secondary hyperparathyroidism should be directed mainly at the underlying condition.

In chronic renal insufficiency, when the plasma phosphate level is elevated, treatment includes a low-phosphate diet and the use of phosphate-binding gels together with large doses of absorbable calcium, such as calcium carbonate. Doses of up to 5 g per day can be used, but frequent monitoring of the serum calcium level is necessary to prevent or treat occasional hypercalcemia. Vitamin D in various preparations has been used with variable results. Recently, 1,25-dihydroxyvitamin D_3 has been used with notable success in chronic renal failure, where a renal defect in the 1α-hydroxylation of 25-hydroxyvitamin D_3 prevents formation of the active metabolite. Doses up to 1 to 2 μg per day have been found to be effective.

Deficiency of dietary vitamin D can be easily corrected by vitamin D_3 administration.

Malabsorption may require correction of the underlying etiologic factors.

Hypomagnesemia that leads to hypocalcemia may require not only calcium supplementation but also avoidance of alcohol and administration of magnesium sulfate.

Drug-induced osteomalacia requires removal of the offending agent and temporary calcium supplementation.

Tertiary Hyperparathyroidism

When autonomous hypersecretion of parathyroid hormone produces hypercalcemia with severe complications such as pathologic bone fractures and osteitis fibrosa cystica, surgical removal of three and a half parathyroid glands is recommended to reduce parathyroid hormone levels toward normal (see Plans, Therapeutic, in Chapter 9–36).

FOLLOW-UP

Secondary Hyperparathyroidism

Once the underlying disorder has been diagnosed and treatment has been initiated, the frequency of follow-up is determined. Patients should be seen every 2 months initially and less frequently (e.g., every 4–6 months) once the chronic hypocalcemia has been corrected. At each visit, the physician should determine by history and physical examination the possible symptoms and signs of hypocalcemia (see

above). Laboratory abnormalities, such as hypocalcemia, hyperphosphatemia, and abnormal tests of renal function, should be determined prior to each visit.

The patient should be informed of symptoms to look for (increasing malaise and mental torpor, tingling, numbness, etc.) to indicate worsening of hypocalcemia. A follow-up visit at an earlier interval than planned should be prompted by the patient's perception of worsening of his or her symptoms.

Tertiary hyperparathyroidism

Frequent visits (e.g., every 1–2 months) should be scheduled to monitor the level of hypercalcemia until the autonomous hypersecretion of parathyroid hormone is corrected by surgical means. At each visit, levels of calcium and phosphate should be monitored.

The patient should be made aware of the symptoms of hypercalcemia (frequent urination, malaise, bone pain, etc.). Worsening of the symptoms should lead to an additional physician visit for correction of potential dehydration and additional therapeutic intervention.

DISCUSSION

Prevalence and Incidence

Secondary Hyperparathyroidism

Secondary hyperparathyroidism is a normal physiologic response to any condition that promotes hypocalcemia. Chronic renal disease is probably the most common underlying disease. The incidence of secondary hyperparathyroidism is dependent on the cause.

Tertiary Hyperparathyroidism

The incidence of tertiary hyperparathyroidism is strongly associated with the duration and management of chronic renal failure prior to renal transplantation. Renal failure of long duration with poor control of calcium and phosphate is likely to promote tertiary hyperparathyroidism following renal transplantation.

Related Basic Science

Secondary Hyperparathyroidism

Secondary hyperparathyroidism occurs in clinical conditions associated with hypocalcemia and represents a state of compensatory hypersecretion of parathyroid hormone. In turn, hypersecretion of parathyroid hormone in these clinical conditions can produce hyperparathyroid bone disease with accelerated bone resorption, osteopenia, and osteitis fibrosa cystica.

Depending on the underlying clinical condition, several factors contribute to the development of manifestations of secondary hyperparathyroidism. In the most common form—secondary hyperparathyroidism due to chronic renal failure—the kidney is unable to excrete phosphorus in a normal fashion. This results in hyperphosphatemia, which produces a reduction of the ionized calcium in the extracellular fluid. Chronic hypocalcemia then results in hypersecretion of parathyroid hormone by the parathyroid glands. The blood levels of parathyroid hormone and its fragments are elevated, as decreased renal clearance leads to accumulation of these peptides in the circulation. Hyperphosphatemia is known to inhibit the final 1α-hydroxylation of 25-hydroxyvitamin D_3, the active metabolite of vitamin D_3. Reduced synthesis of 1,25-dihydroxyvitamin D_3 may reduce the intestinal absorption of calcium and thus worsen the hypocalcemia. Renal impairment and uremia also can produce partial peripheral resistance to the effects of parathyroid hormone. Aluminum-gel preparations, used to lower the hyperphosphatemia, can in some cases produce aluminum toxicity, which suppresses parathyroid hormone secretion and can lead to changes of osteomalacia in the bone.

Owing to the variety of conditions leading to chronic hypocalcemia and secondary hyperparathyroidism, the skeletal abnormalities are varied (generalized osteopenia, osteomalacia, osteosclerosis, and osteitis fibrosa cystica) and reflect the sum of the competing factors elicited by the underlying disorder: parathyroid hormone effects on bone, reduced vitamin D metabolism and subsequent reduction in calcium absorption, resistance to parathyroid hormone, aluminum toxicity, and so on.

Tertiary Hyperparathyroidism

Some patients with chronic renal failure, chronic malabsorption, or other causes of secondary hyperparathyroidism develop severe parathyroid hyperplasia, with marked enlargement of all parathyroid glands and 20-to 30-fold elevation of all parathyroid hormone levels. Fortunately, these patients are rare. In these patients, removal of the original stimulus—persistent hypocalcemia or resistance to parathyroid hormone action—does not result in involution of the hyperplastic parathyroid glands, which have reached a state of "autonomous" or "unsuppressible" hypersecretion.

The vast majority of patients who undergo renal transplantation after chronic dialysis for renal insufficiency present a transient state of hypercalcemia, which contributes to the feedback suppression of parathyroid hormone hypersecretion and restoration of parathyroid hormone levels to normal with consequent return to calcium and phosphorus homeostasis. A few patients show persistence of the parathyroid hormone hypersecretion with concomitant elevation of serum calcium levels and continuing damage to the bone and other organs, suggesting the failure of involution of the parathyroids. This occurs despite removal of factors responsible for hormone resistance or therapeutic measures such as restriction of phosphate intake or vitamin D administration.

Natural History and Its Modification with Treatment

Secondary Hyperparathyroidism

The natural history of secondary hyperparathyroidism depends on the nature and severity of the underlying disorder producing chronic hypocalcemia. Complications usually occur when hypocalcemia has persisted long enough to produce continuing hypersecretion of parathyroid hormone with several of the manifestations typical of this disorder.

Tertiary Hyperparathyroidism

The natural history of tertiary hyperparathyroidism is to a large extent unknown. It is not clear why only a few of the patients affected by secondary hyperparathyroidism reach the "autonomous" level of parathyroid hormone hypersecretion. This condition develops slowly over a period of months or years. Severe complications, such as pathologic bone fractures and osteitis fibrosa cystica, are now rare if the disease process is diagnosed early and prompt correction by available therapeutic means is instituted.

Prevention

Secondary Hyperparathyroidism

Prompt recognition of chronic hypocalcemia and its etiology and timely institution of therapeutic measures can reduce and/or prevent the onset of secondary hyperparathyroidism.

Tertiary Hyperparathyroidism

As above, recognition of the transition from secondary hyperparathyroidism to "autonomous" hypersecretion of parathyroid hormone by the parathyroid glands, detected by early rises in blood calcium level from hypocalcemia to eucalcemia and hypercalcemia, should direct the physician to the proper therapeutic measures and thus avoid the serious complications of tertiary hyperparathyroidism.

Cost Containment

Secondary Hyperparathyroidism

An experienced physician should recognize early the development of chronic hypocalcemia. By early identification of the etiologic factors, prompt treatment can reduce the costs of long-term treatment and expenses related to treatment of complications.

Tertiary Hyperparathyroidism

By early recognition of tertiary hyperparathyroidism and prompt and satisfactory treatment, the physician can reduce the development of severe complications and thus reduce costs.

REFERENCES

Arnaud CD Jr, Bordier PJ. Management of secondary hyperparathyroidism. In: DeGroot LJ, ed. Endocrinology. New York: Grune & Stratton, 1979:751.

Conceicao SC, Wilkinson R, Feest TG, et al. Hypercalcemia following renal transplantation: Causes and consequences. Clin Nephrol 1981;16:235.

Cushner HM, Adams ND. Review: Renal osteodystrophy. Pathogenesis and treatment. Am J Med Sci 1986;29:264.

Feinfield DA, Sherwood LM. Parathyroid hormone and $1,25(OH)_2D_3$ in chronic renal failure. Kidney Int 1988;33:1049.

Hanley DA, Sherwood LM. Secondary hyperparathyroidism in chronic renal failure: Pathophysiology and treatment. Med Clin North Am 1978;62:1319.

Parfitt AM. Hypercalcemic hyperparathyroidism following renal transplantation: Differential diagnosis, management, and implications for cell population control in the parathyroid gland. Miner Electrolyte Metab 1982;8:92.

Reiss E, Slatopolsky E. Secondary (adaptive) hyperparathyroidism. In: DeGroot LJ, ed. Endocrinology. New York: Grune & Stratton, 1979:745.

Richards AJ. Vitamin D deficiency and hyperparathyroidism. Proc R Soc Med 1972;65:1018.

CHAPTER 9–38

Hypocalcemia and Hypoparathyroidism

Guillermo E. Umpierrez, M.D.

DEFINITION

In most clinical laboratories the normal total concentration of serum calcium is 8.5 to 10.5 mg/dL. Therefore, a serum calcium concentration less than 8.5 mg/dL indicates hypocalcemia.

ETIOLOGY

Classification of hypocalcemia is shown in Table 9–38–1. The principal causes of hypocalcemia include hypoparathyroidism, hypomagnesemia, deficiency or abnormal metabolism of vitamin D, and acute or chronic renal failure. From a pathophysiologic standpoint, hypocalcemic states can be divided into parathyroid hormone (PTH) deficiency states and failure of PTH action at its target tissues.

CRITERIA FOR DIAGNOSIS
Suggestive

Typically, the hypocalcemic patient presents with numbness and tingling of the lips and extremities or with muscle cramps associated with carpopedal spasm. A similar picture could result from hypokalemia, hypomagnesemia, or respiratory alkalosis; thus, serum calcium, magnesium, potassium, and blood gases should be checked.

Definitive

A total serum calcium concentration less than 8.5 mg/dL indicates hypocalcemia. Approximately 40 to 45% of the total serum calcium is bound to carrier proteins, 5 to 10% is complexed to inorganic anions

TABLE 9–38–1. CAUSES OF HYPOCALCEMIA

Parathyroid hormone deficiency states
    Postsurgical
    Idiopathic
    Hypomagnesemia
Failure of parathyroid hormone action at target tissues
    Vitamin D deficiency or resistance
    Pseudohypoparathyroidism
    Renal failure
    Hypomagnesemia
Miscellaneous
    Acute pancreatitis
    Osteoblastic metastasis
    Rhabdomyolysis
    Sepsis
    Drugs

(citrate, sulfate), and the remaining 50% is present as ionized (unbound) calcium ions. Variations in serum protein therefore alter proportionately the concentration of the protein-bound and total serum calcium. As albumin accounts for 80% of the protein binding of calcium, a simple correction fraction for hypoalbuminemia can be made by adding 0.8 mg/dL to the total serum calcium for every 1.0 g/dL by which the serum albumin is lower than 4.0 g/dL. Changes in pH also affect protein-bound calcium. Acidosis increases ionized calcium (but not total) by decreasing the binding of calcium ions to albumin, whereas alkalosis decreases the ionized fraction by enhancing calcium binding to carrier proteins. Measurement of the level of total serum calcium is usually adequate for most clinical situations, but in complex cases direct measurement of the ionized calcium should be performed.

CLINICAL MANIFESTATIONS
Subjective

The clinical manifestations of hypocalcemia vary greatly among patients and depend not only on the degree of hypocalcemia, but also on the rate of fall in serum calcium levels. Patients with chronic hypocalcemia sometimes have few, if any, symptoms despite quite low serum calcium levels. In contrast, patients with acute hypocalcemia often do have symptoms, although there is no absolute level of serum calcium at which symptoms occurs. Most of the clinical manifestations are due primarily to enhanced neuromuscular irritability attributable to a reduction in ionized calcium concentration in extracellular fluids. In mild cases, patients commonly complain of paresthesias or the sensation of tingling in the tips of fingers and around the mouth. In severe or acute hypocalcemia, patients may experience a life-threatening syndrome known as tetany, which is manifested by diffuse muscle twitching and cramps, carpopedal spasm, dysphagia, bronchospasm, laryngeal stridor, and generalized seizures.

Hypocalcemia may also result in a variety of psychiatric and neurologic abnormalities, including irritability, paranoia, hallucinations, depression, and frank psychosis. Children may develop mental retardation and impaired intellectual abilities. Dementia has been reported in adults. Seizures of all types (syncopal episodes, petit mal, focal or grand mal) can occur in acute or chronic hypocalcemia. Hypocalcemic seizures are usually not associated with loss of consciousness or incontinence and are not preceded by an aura. Increased intracranial pressure occurs in some patients with long-standing hypocalcemia, accompanied by headache and papilledema.

Patients with chronic hypocalcemia due to idiopathic hypoparathyroidism or pseudohypoparathyroidism may also complain of reduced vision (subcapsular cataracts), dental abnormalities (hypoplasia of the enamel, defects in dentin, and delayed eruption of the teeth), dry skin and brittle nails, greasy stools and weight loss (intestinal malabsorption), and extrapyramidal symptoms such as classic parkinsonism or chorea due to basal ganglia calcifications.

Objective
Physical Examination

Overt tetany is not difficult to recognize if witnessed by the physician. Latent tetany may be detected by eliciting certain signs that are suggestive of lesser degrees of neuromuscular irritability. Chvostek's sign is revealed by tapping the facial nerve just anterior to the ear and consists of ipsilateral contraction (twitching) of the muscles supplied by the nerve. Although Chvostek's sign is a classic manifestation of hypocalcemia, it can be seen in up to 25% of normal individuals. Thus, its clinical relevance is best appreciated in the context of known hypocalcemia. Trosseau's sign is elicited by inflation of the blood pressure cuff to just above the systolic blood pressure for 3 minutes. The classic response, adduction of the thumb followed by flexion of the wrist and metacarpophalangeal joints, reflects increased irritability of the nerves due to ischemia in the region of the cuff. A positive Trosseau's sign is rare in the absence of significant hypocalcemia.

The physical examination may also be helpful in determining the etiology of hypocalcemia. Evidence of previous neck surgery would suggest the diagnosis of postsurgical hypoparathyroidism. The presence of exfoliate dermatitis, dry skin, atopic eczema, vitiligo, alopecia, and cutaneous candidiasis would be consistent with immunologic abnormalities seen in idiopathic hypoparathyroidism. Short stature, round face, short thick neck, obesity, and, in particular, shortening of the fourth and fifth metacarpal bones, would indicated Albright's hereditary dystrophy, a common feature of pseudohypoparathyroidism type I. If hypocalcemia is a manifestation of a vitamin D-deficient state, signs of osteomalacia may be present.

Routine Laboratory Abnormalities

Routine laboratory tests such as complete blood count, electrolytes, and urinalysis are usually normal in patients with hypocalcemia, whereas the chemistry screen (renal function tests, and levels of serum of phosphate, total proteins, albumin, lactic dehydrogenase, and magnesium) is critical and may help in the differential diagnosis (see Plans).

Electrocardiographic evidence for hypocalcemia is a prolonged QT interval due to ST-segment prolongation. Ventricular arrhythmias and atrial fibrillation have also been reported in patients with hypocalcemia.

PLANS
Diagnostic
Differential Diagnosis

Various disorders may cause hypocalcemia. Hypocalcemic states occurs either because of failure of secretion of PTH (hypoparathyroid states) or from failure of PTH action at its target tissues (PTH resistance states). Primary hypoparathyroidism is a common cause of symptomatic hypocalcemia. Surgical hypoparathyroidism accounts for 80 to 90% of all causes and results from excision of or trauma to the parathyroid glands or their vascular supply. This may be secondary to parathyroid or thyroid surgery or to neck dissection for laryngeal or esophageal carcinoma. It should be emphasized that some patients may develop transient hypocalcemia after removal of a hyperfunctioning parathyroid adenoma because of the deficient secretion of PTH by the remaining previously suppressed parathyroid glands. Idiopathic hypoparathyroidism (sporadic or familial) often occurs as part of a complex autoimmune syndrome associated with multiple endocrine deficiencies (adrenal insufficiency, hypothyroidism, diabetes mellitus, and hypogonadism). Congenital aplasia of the parathyroid gland may occur, usually in conjunction with defective development of the thymus (DiGiorge's syndrome).

Hypocalcemia may also occur with magnesium depletion. At least two pathogenic mechanisms have been implicated: impaired PTH secretion and peripheral resistance to the action of PTH. In addition, there may also be a defect in the formation of 1,25-dihydroxyvitamin D in association with magnesium deficiency. This hypocalcemia is extremely resistant to treatment but can be completely corrected by magnesium supplements.

In PTH resistance states, hypocalcemia occurs despite normal parathyroid gland function. The most common causes of hypocalcemia with normal or increased PTH secretion are related to deficiencies of vitamin D and/or its active metabolites. The incidence of nutritional vitamin D deficiency varies worldwide, but may be as high as 10 to 25% of the elderly in the United States. It can occur in patients in whom both exposure to ultraviolet light and dietary intake of vitamin D are inadequate. Vitamin D malabsorption may occur in patients with one of several gastrointestinal disorders, including nontropical sprue, Crohn's disease, and pancreatic insufficiency. Acquired abnormalities in vitamin D metabolism, such as in patients with cholestatic liver disease and cirrhosis result from reduced hepatic hydroxylation of vitamin D to 25-hydroxy vitamin D or intestinal malabsorption of vitamin D metabolites. A variety of drugs, such as alcohol and anticonvulsants, may be associated with accelerated metabolism of 25-hydroxyvitamin D to more polar inactive metabolites.

Renal failure is a common cause of hypocalcemia, and is usually associated with hyperphosphatemia and increased PTH levels. The pathogenesis of hypocalcemia in renal insufficiency is multifactorial. In acute renal failure, hypocalcemia results primarily from phosphate retention, causing complexing of calcium into soluble compounds. In chronic renal insufficiency, phosphate retention and impaired production of 1,25-dihydroxyvitamin D_3 are recognized as the two most important factors in the development of hypocalcemia.

Two variants of hereditary disorders of vitamin D function have been recognized: (1) vitamin D-dependent rickets type I (VDDRI), which is characterized by a selective defect in 1α-hydroxylase activity with consequent inability to convert 25-hydroxyvitamin D to 1,25-dihydroxyvitamin D; (2) vitamin D-dependent rickets type II (VDDRII), a rare disorder characterized by target organ resistance to virtually all forms of vitamin D, especially 1,25-dihydroxyvitamin D_3.

Pseudohypoparathyroidism is a rare familial disorder characterized by target tissue resistance to PTH, hypocalcemia, elevated immunoreactive PTH, and a variety of skeletal and somatic defects including short stature, round face, obesity, pseudowebbing of the neck, and short fourth and fifth metacarpals and metatarsals. This syndrome has been subclassified into two types. In pseudohypoparathyroidism type I, there is neither cyclic AMP nor phosphaturic response to exogenous PTH. This blunted response is consistent with a defect in the receptor–adenylate cyclase complex. Some patients with pseudohypoparathyroidism type I have resistance to other hormones and may have multiple endocrine abnormalities (hypothyroidism, hypogonadism) in addition to hypoparathyrodism. Patients with pseudohypoparathyroidism type II show reduced phosphaturic response to administration of PTH, despite a normal increase in urinary cyclic AMP excretion, indicating that hormone resistance in pseudohypoparathyroidism type II results form a defect distal to the receptor–cyclase complex.

Miscellaneous causes of hypocalcemia and secondary hyperparathyroidism include acute pancreatitis, hungry bone syndrome, osteoblastic metastasis to bone, and acute critical illness. In acute pancreatitis, massive pancreatic inflammation and destruction lead to fatty release, saponification, and deposition of calcium soaps. "Hungry bone syndrome," in which bone acts as a sponge and absorbs massive amounts of calcium and phosphate, occurs following resection of large parathyroid adenomas in patients with severe parathyroid bone disease (osteitis fibrosa cystica). Occasionally, osteoblastic metastasis, usually from prostatic cancers, may result in increased calcium flux into osteoblastic lesions to cause hypocalcemia. Finally, toxic shock syndrome, Gram-negative bacteremia, and other critical illnesses have been associated with hypocalcemia.

Diagnostic Options and Recommended Approach

During the workup of a patient with hypocalcemia, a useful initial step is to consider whether the serum phosphate is increased or decreased. The most common cause of hypocalcemia with hyperphosphatemia is renal insufficiency, which is readily detected by measurement of serum creatinine and creatinine clearance. Hypomagnesemia must also be excluded, as it may cause a reversible hypoparathyroidism. In general, the serum magnesium is lower than 1.0 mg/dL (0.4 mmol/L) when hypocalcemia is due to hypomagnesemia. Despite the functional hypoparathyroidism induced by hypomagnesemia, serum phosphate is not always elevated because magnesium depletion often occurs in the setting of nutritional deficiency, alcoholism, or malabsorption.

The finding of hypocalcemia and hyperphosphatemia in the absence of renal failure is virtually diagnostic of hypoparathyroidism. Definitive characterization of the form of hypoparathyroidism requires determination of serum PTH and the response of urinary cyclic AMP and urinary phosphate to exogenous administration of PTH. In patients with primary hypoparathyroidism, PTH levels are low or undetectable, but

following an injection of PTH, patients are able to respond normally by increasing their plasma and urinary cyclic AMP and urinary phosphate levels. Patients with pseudohypoparathyroidism usually present with low serum calcium and high serum phosphate (similar to primary hypoparathyroidism) levels; however, their PTH levels are markedly elevated (resistance to PTH action). In addition, they have an abnormal response to the exogenous administration of PTH. In pseudohypoparathyroidism type I, in which there is a receptor defect, PTH fails to produce an increase in urinary cyclic AMP and phosphate. In contrast, patients with pseudohypoparathyroidism type II, in whom the defect is distal to the receptor–cyclase complex, can generate cyclic AMP but are unable to show a phosphaturic response.

A pattern of low calcium with low phosphorus points to deficient or ineffective vitamin D. Hypocalcemia resulting from a disorder of vitamin D metabolism would lead to secondary hyperparathyroidism (high PTH levels) as a compensation. To determine if the cause is an abnormality in vitamin metabolism, assays for 25-hydroxyvitamin D and 1,25-dihydroxyvitamin D can be quite helpful. Serum 25-hydroxyvitamin D levels are low in patients with nutritional vitamin D deficiency, intestinal malabsorption, and liver disease. Low levels of 1,25-dihydroxyvitamin D might be seen in patients with vitamin D-dependent rickets type I (hereditary deficiency of 1α-hydroxylase activity). In contrast, end-organ resistance to the action of 1,25-dihydroxyvitamin D, or vitamin D-dependent rickets type II, is accompanied by dramatic elevations in circulating 1,25-dihydroxyvitamin D.

Therapeutic

Therapeutic Options

Acute hypocalcemic crisis, manifested by frank tetany, laryngospasm, or seizures, requires emergency treatment with intravenous calcium. Calcium gluconate (90 mg elemental calcium/10-mL ampule) should be infused over 5 to 10 minutes. Because of the short duration of the acute infusion, subsequent calcium infusion is usually required. In general, 15 mg/kg elemental calcium infused over 4 to 6 hours raises the serum calcium by 2 to 3 mg/dL. Frequent determinations of serum calcium level (every 4–6 hours) are necessary to adjust the infusion rate and maintain the serum calcium level at 7 to 8.5 mg/dL.

With respect to long-term management, resolution of hypocalcemia depends on treating the underlying cause. When this is not possible, long-term therapy with vitamin D and calcium salts may be required. The objective of therapy is to restore serum calcium to levels high enough to prevent chronic complications of hypocalcemia, but without the appearance of severe hypercalciuria. In general, the therapeutic endpoint is maintenance of serum calcium levels in the range 8.0 to 9.2 mg/dL. A wide variety of choices for therapy with vitamin D are available (Table 9–38–2). Vitamin D_2 (50,000–100,000 U/d) is effective in treating patients with all forms of hypoparathyroidism and is the least expensive. Vitamin D_2 is lipophilic, and a period of several weeks (4–8 weeks) is required for its full effect to be established on beginning therapy. Likewise, it also has the longest duration of action and can result in prolonged toxicity. More recently, there has been widespread use of more active metabolites, such as 25-hydroxyvitamin D (25–200 µg/d) and 1, 25-dihydroxyvitamin (0.25–2.0 µg/d). These compounds have a more rapid onset of action, and a shorter period is required for their effects to decrease after discontinuation.

In addition, oral calcium salts (1500–2000 mg of elemental calcium per day in divided doses) may be given to patients whose dietary intake is inadequate. Commonly prescribed calcium salts include calcium carbonate, calcium citrate, and calcium gluconate. The most convenient preparation to use is calcium carbonate because it contains a greater

TABLE 9–38–2. VITAMIN D PREPARATIONS

	Daily Dose	$t_{1/2}$	Offset of Action
Ergocalciferol (vitamin D_2)	25,000–100,000 IU	12–24 h	1–3 wk
Dihydrotachysterol	0.2–1 mg	12–24 h	1–3 wk
Calcifediol*	20–200 µg	15 d	1–3 wk
Calcitriol†	0.25–2 µg	6 h	3–14 d

*25-hydroxy vitamin D_3.
†1,25-dihydroxy vitamin D_3.

percentage of elemental calcium (40%) than calcium citrate (21%), or calcium gluconate (9%). In patients with reduced gastric acid production, calcium citrate is preferred because of superior calcium absorption. In patients with severe hypercalciuria (> 400 mg/d), the use of thiazide diuretics may result in lower urinary calcium excretion and reduced risk of stone formation, a potential complication of the long-term management of patients with hypoparathyroidism.

Recommended Approach

In the presence of overt tetany, 10 to 20 mL of calcium gluconate 10% diluted in 50 to 100 mL of 5% dextrose should be infused over 10 minutes. Symptoms are promptly relieved, but because of the short duration of the acute infusion, a continuous infusion of calcium gluconate is usually required. Elemental calcium 10 to 15 mg/kg infused every 4 to 6 hours is recommended with serum calcium monitored closely to adjust the infusion rate and maintain the serum calcium level between 7 and 8.5 mg/dL. If serum magnesium is low, therapy must include replacement of magnesium before the hypocalcemia can be expected to resolve.

Vitamin D is the mainstay of management in virtually all chronic hypocalcemic states. Vitamin D_2 (500,000–100,000 U/day) is the least expensive form of vitamin D, and it is effective in most patients with hypoparathyroidism and disorders associated with ineffective vitamin D action. In most patients with primary hypoparathyroidism and in renal disease, the use of 1,25-dihydroxyvitamin D_3 (0.25–2.0 μg/d) is preferable because its use overcomes the metabolic block to its formation. Oral calcium salts should be given at a dose of 1500 to 2000 mg of elemental calcium per day. The most convenient preparation is calcium carbonate, except in patients with reduced gastric acid production in whom the citrate form is preferred.

FOLLOW-UP

Once the serum calcium level has been stabilized in the low-normal range (8.5–9.2 mg/dL), visits to the physician should be scheduled every 2 to 4 months. It is important to look for clinical evidence of latent tetany (Chvostek's and Trousseau's signs) or hypercalcemia (polyuria, nausea, vomiting, or anorexia). Important laboratory tests include measurement of serum calcium, phosphorus, and creatinine. The serum calcium level should be checked every 1 to 2 weeks at the outset and every 2 to 4 months after a stable level is reached. The urine calcium level should be measured periodically, especially after major therapeutic changes because hypercalciuria may be a complication of calcium and vitamin D therapy.

DISCUSSION
Prevalence and Incidence

The exact prevalence of hypocalcemia is not known. Although chronic hypocalcemia is less common than hypercalcemia, low total and ionized calcium concentration is relatively frequent in hospitalized patients, especially in septic or critically ill patients.

Related Basic Science
Physiologic or Metabolic Derangement

Parathyroid hormone regulates the levels of calcium and phosphate in blood by modulating the activity of specific cells in bone and kidneys; thus, hypocalcemia occurs when there is a failure of the homeostatic action of PTH. This can occur if the hormone is simply absent (hypoparathyroid states) or it is rendered ineffective by any mechanisms that interfere with its action at target tissues (PTH resistance states). Surgical hypoparathyroidism, transient or permanent, is the most common cause of primary hypoparathyroidism. Idiopathic hypoparathyroidism is a rare disease, and often occurs as part of a complex autoimmune syndrome associated with multiple endocrine deficiencies, such as primary adrenal failure, hypogonadism, and diabetes mellitus. Circulating autoantibodies specific for parathyroid and adrenal tissues are frequently present, but correlate poorly with clinical manifestations. Functional hypoparathyroidism can occur in patients with long-standing hypomagnesemia.

The most common cause of hypocalcemia due to impaired PTH action is related to reduced vitamin D effect (as in chronic renal failure, vitamin D deficiency, or abnormal vitamin D metabolism). Calcium

flux from the intestine to blood is decreased; in addition, parathyroid hormone mobilization of calcium from bone to blood is impaired. PTH may also be rendered ineffective if there are abnormalities in the hormone receptor–adenylate cyclase complex (pseudohypoparathyroidism type I) or if there is resistance to 1,25-dihydroxyvitamin D owing to deficiency in 1,25-dihydroxyvitamin D receptors. Hypocalcemia could also occur if the action of PTH is overwhelmed by the loss of calcium from the extracellular fluid at a rate faster than it can be replaced, with accompanying soft tissue calcification (as in acute hyperphosphatemia, rhabdomyolysis, or hungry bone syndrome).

Altered Molecular Biology

In recent years, the development of assays for the components of the PTH receptor–adenylate cyclase enzyme system has shed new light on the pathogenesis of pseudohypoparathyroidism. PTH activates its target cells by binding to specific receptors located on the cell membrane. It is now known that peptide hormone receptor is coupled to the adenylate cyclase enzyme by guanidine nucleotide-binding proteins (G-proteins) that act as transducers of the hormone signal. Interaction of PTH with its receptor triggers G-proteins, which activate signal effector systems that generate intracellular second-messenger cyclic AMP, which mediates the multiple distal effects of PTH. Various forms of pseudohypoparathyroidism have been described. Patients with pseudohypoparathyroidism type IA have a 50% deficiency of the stimulatory G-protein in their cell membranes. As a consequence of this generalized G-unit deficiency, these patients are resistant not only to PTH but also to many other peptide hormones for which cyclic AMP serves as a second messenger, including thyroid-stimulating hormone, glucagon, and gonadotropins. Clinical hypothyroidism and hypogonadism are quite common in these patients. Individuals with pseudohypoparathyroidism type IA also have characteristic physical features of Albright's hereditary osteodystrophy. Patients with type IB, have a normal appearance and normal G-protein activity, and are resistant only to PTH action. Although the molecular basis for reduced PTH receptor activity in pseudohypoparathyroidism type IB has not been defined, it has been suggested that a defect in the PTH receptor could be involved. Recently, pseudohypoparathyroidism type IC has been recognized. Such patients have features of Albright's hereditary osteodystrophy and multiple hormone resistance; however, they have normal G-protein levels, and the defect has been localized to the catalytic subunit of adenylate cyclase. Patients with pseudohypoparathyroidism type II show reduced phosphaturic response to administration of PTH, despite a normal increase in urinary cyclic AMP excretion, indicating that hormone resistance in pseudohypoparathyroidism type II results from a defect distal to the receptor–cyclase complex.

Natural History and Its Modification with Treatment

The acute complication of hypocalcemia is tetany, which is related to the rate of fall and to the degree of hypocalcemia. Although it is frightening to the patient, tetany is completely reversible and rarely life threatening. Chronic hypocalcemia (6.0– 8.5 mg/dL) may be well tolerated by patients with rare episodes of overt tetany. The duration of hypocalcemia is related to long-term complications such as cataracts, basal ganglia calcification, papilledema, and increased intracranial pressure, psychiatric disorders, intestinal malabsorption, dry skin, and congestive heart failure. Long-term restoration of serum calcium to normal or nearly normal levels usually results in improvement in most manifestations of hypoparathyroidism and in prevention of chronic complications of hypocalcemia.

Prevention

Prevention is related to the primary disease that results in hypocalcemia. Improved surgical techniques and the use of parathyroid autotransplantation of a portion of the gland to the forearm may lower the incidence of permanent hypoparathyroidism. If the technology is available, some parathyroid tissue should be preserved for future transplantation.

Cost Containment

Treatment of permanent hypocalcemia requires vitamin D and calcium supplementation. Vitamin D_2 (ergocalciferol) is the least expensive form of vitamin D replacement, and it is effective in treating patients with all forms of hypoparathyroidism and disorders associated with resistance to vitamin D action. The cost of a typical dose of 50,000 to 100,000 U/d would be $0.09 to $0.27 daily; however, the cost benefits must be weighed against the delayed onset (2–4 weeks) and prolonged duration of action (6–18 weeks), as well as the risk of vitamin D toxicity especially in patients with hypoparathyroidism (with its decreased parathyroid hormone-dependent 1α-hydroxylase activity in the kidney). In patients with renal failure, 1,25-dihydroxyvitamin D is the most rational therapy, because its administration overcomes the metabolic block to its formation. 1,25-dihydroxyvitamin D (calcitriol [Rocaltrol]) has a rapid onset (1–2 days) and offset (1–2 days) of action; however, it is the most expensive vitamin D metabolite, with a daily cost of between $2 and $4. The calcium carbonate salt is usually the least expensive source of calcium, but the cost for 1000 mg varies from $0.18 per day for Tums to $0.35 per day for Os-Cal. Calcium citrate (Citracal) is more expensive: $0.5 per day. Once stabilized, patients should be followed quarterly with measurement of serum calcium, phosphate, and creatinine levels and occasional 24-hour urinary calcium levels.

REFERENCES

Aurbach GD, Marx SJ, Spiegel AM. Parathyroid hormone, calcitonin and the calciferols. In: Wilson JD, Foster DW, eds. Williams' textbook of endocrinology. 7th ed. Philadelphia: Saunders, 1992:1397.

Bell NH. Vitamin D endocrine system. J Clin Invest 1985;76:1.

Burckhardt P. Idiopathic hypoparathyroidism and autoimmunity. Horm Res 1982;16:304.

Eastell R, Heath H III. The hypocalcemic states: Their differential diagnosis and management. In: Coe FL, Favus MJ, eds. Disorders of bone and mineral metabolism. New York: New York Press, 1992:1555.

Forman DT, Lorenzo L. Ionized calcium: Its significance and clinical usefulness. Ann Clin Lab Sci 1991; 21:297.

Johnson GL, Dhanasekaran N. The G-protein family and their interaction with receptors. Endocr Rev 1989;10:317.

Tohme JF, Bilezikian JP. Hypocalcemic emergencies. Endocrinol Metab Clin North Am 1993; 22:363.

CHAPTER 9–39

Osteoporosis

Robert P. Heaney, M.D.

DEFINITION

Osteoporosis is defined both as a condition of increased skeletal fragility and as a reduction in the amount of bony material per unit volume of bone as a structural member. The fragility, once attributed exclusively to the reduced mass, is now recognized as due to varying combinations of decreased skeletal mass, defective skeletal architecture, and accumulated fatigue damage in the bony material.

ETIOLOGY

Etiology is multifactorial. Bone mass may be reduced because of failure to achieve the genetically programmed peak mass (mainly from low calcium intake and decreased physical activity during growth); alternatively, low bone mass can result from excess bone loss after the peak has been reached (mainly because of gonadal hormone deficiency, low calcium intake, vitamin D insufficiency, disuse, smoking, alcohol abuse, medical diseases such as iatrogenic hyperthyroidism, and medical treatments such as corticosteroid therapy). Etiology of the disordered architecture and of the accumulated fatigue damage is unknown.

CRITERIA FOR DIAGNOSIS

Suggestive

Fractures occurring with minor trauma at any bony site indicate weakness of the skeletal structures. In the elderly most such fractures are due to osteoporosis, as are most vertebral body compression fractures in postmenopausal women. Back pain without fracture is almost never due to osteoporosis.

Definitive

There are no specific clinical chemical tests on blood or urine that are abnormal in osteoporosis. Prior to fracture, osteoporosis is asymptomatic, but low bone mass can be detected by bone mass measurement. Recent World Health Organization criteria define bone mass values between −1 and −2.5 standard deviations of the young adult mean as osteopenia (i.e., a shortage of bone); values more than 2.5 standard deviations below the young adult mean are defined as osteoporosis, whether or not fracture is present.

The presence of a low trauma fracture indicates fragility, and establishing osteoporosis as its basis requires ruling out other causes, principally multiple myeloma, metastatic malignancy, radiation necrosis, and vertebral osteomyelitis.

CLINICAL MANIFESTATIONS

Subjective

The first symptom of osteoporosis is fracture, which may present either as a backache (mild or severe) or as the pain, disability, and deformity associated with an extremity fracture, such as of the hip. The pain of spine compression fractures ranges from excruciating to so mild that the patient may be unaware of the fracture. After several fractures, the patient will notice a shortening of stature, with bowing of the back, forward thrust of the head, abdominal protrusion, and inability to get clothes to fit well. With multiple compressions, there is exaggeration of the usual dorsal kyphosis ("dowager's hump") or loss of the normal lumbar lordosis. Backache is the most common complaint in women with the crush fracture syndrome. Acutely, it is due to the hematoma and soft tissue damage of the fracture, and chronically, to muscle spasm, ligamentous stretching, and degenerative arthritis associated with the malalignment of weight-bearing forces which follows from the fracture deformity. When kyphosis becomes advanced, the lower ribs become angled nearly vertically and impinge on the pelvic brim, with resulting local tenderness. Family history is often positive, but osteoporosis is so common that this is not particularly helpful.

Objective

Physical Examination

Physical findings of vertebral body fractures are confined to point tenderness over the fracture region in the acute phase, muscle spasm and general tenderness in the region both acutely and chronically, and kyphosis or loss of lumbar lordosis. Acutely, compression fractures may also produce some degree of ileus as a reaction to retroperitoneal hemorrhage. Additionally, hip, wrist, rib, ankle, or proximal humerus fractures exhibit the characteristic pain and deformity of these injuries (e.g., external rotation of the fractured hip). Osteoporotic fractures heal quite normally, except in extreme cases where the bone loss is so advanced that the residual bony scaffolding is inadequate to produce a mechanically stable union.

Routine Laboratory Abnormalities

On x-ray films, there is evidence of fracture and an apparent decrease in bone density. Lateral spine radiographs characteristically show reduction in height of one or more vertebral bodies, either at the anterior edge (wedge fracture) or both anteriorly and posteriorly (crush fracture). Sometimes there will also be herniation of the nucleus pulposus of an intervertebral disk into the body of a vertebra (Schmorl's node). Decreased bone mass can be detected by most of the methods currently available for such measurement (see below).

All the usual blood and urine tests are entirely normal unless osteoporosis is secondary to other disorders, such as hyperthyroidism and hyperparathyroidism, which produce the expected laboratory abnormalities.

PLANS
Diagnostic
Diagnostic Options Prior to Fracture

Patients thought to be at risk for fragility fracture can now have bone mass (and density) assessed by a number of techniques based on absorption by bone mineral of photons in the x-ray range of the electromagnetic spectrum. These include single-photon absorptiometry of distal forearm bones or calcaneus; dual-energy x-ray absorptiometry of spine, hip, or total body; x-ray absorptiometry of hand bones; and quantitative computed tomography of trabecular bone in the vertebral bodies. Results of such measurements are commonly expressed in terms of both the young adult normal range (a so-called T score), and the age-adjusted value Z scores). The young adult referent (T) is the more useful for assessing fracture risk.

The velocity and attenuation of an ultrasonic pulse through accessible bones (calcaneus, tibia, patella) also measure the density of the bone in the transmission path of the pulse, and exhibit about the same degree of diagnostic discrimination as does measurement by absorptiometry. Further, ultrasound velocity is sensitive to some of the qualitative changes in bone structure (trabecular disconnection and unrepaired fatigue damage) that the densitometric methods miss.

Not all persons found to have decreased bone density (or low ultrasound values) will sustain a fracture and it should be stressed that, with the exception of ultrasound velocity, these techniques do not detect the architectural or bone quality components, which are also important risk factors. Bone mass or density values in one region are generally well correlated with bone mass in other skeletal regions. Hence, measurements at any site using any of the foregoing techniques usually suffice for detecting persons at increased risk of fracture.

Recommended Approach Prior to Fracture

Women at greatest risk for future fracture are those who are thin, small, inactive, have had relatively low calcium intake, and have had intermittent periods of amenorrhea and/or short luteal phase cycles. All such women should be screened for bone mass prior to menopause to establish their level of risk. It is likely that a low value will be found, and the evidence thereof can be an important motivator in a decision to initiate and sustain estrogen replacement therapy at menopause, as well as to make such other life style changes as may be required (e.g., increased physical activity, increased calcium intake).

Diagnostic Options Following Fracture

Fracture on minor trauma, particularly of the spine, and particularly in white postmenopausal women, is almost always due to osteoporosis. It is necessary, however, to exclude the relatively less common but important conditions that may produce the same initial manifestation, but may either be remediable (such as hyperthyroidism and hyperparathyroidism) or may have more immediate life-threatening significance to the patient (such as multiple myeloma). Women with anorexia nervosa and amenorrheic performance athletes commonly have some degree of osteoporosis and may have several compression fractures, even at ages as young as 20 to 30.

Osteomalacia may occur in the population susceptible to osteoporosis, especially the elderly. In most such cases, it is an additional disorder superimposed on and complicating the underlying osteoporosis. Finding normal values for serum calcium, phosphorus, and alkaline phosphatase, normal thyroid function tests, normal serum proteins, and normal urinalysis usually suffices to exclude these other conditions, but in some cases more extensive diagnostic evaluation may be required, including bone marrow biopsy, serum protein electrophoresis, and,

more rarely, undecalcified bone biopsy, taken at the iliac crest. All laboratory tests remain normal throughout the course of the disorder. Only bone mass or density is reduced. A baseline value for bone mass (or density) can be useful in subsequent follow-up.

Recommended Approach Following Fracture

Typically, a postmenopausal woman with a vertebral compression fracture needs a workup consisting of only a history and physical; a lateral spine x-ray; blood tests to ensure normal serum calcium, phosphorus, and alkaline phosphatase levels; a normal serum protein electrophoresis; and, if she is receiving thyroid replacement therapy, a determination of thyroid-stimulating hormone level to rule out overtreatment with thyroid hormone. Low trauma extremity fractures should be considered signs of generalized skeletal fragility and should trigger a whole-person approach to this problem.

Therapeutic

There is no approved curative therapy that will increase bone mass and restore damaged structures, particularly deformed vertebral bodies. The principal trophic factor for maintaining or restoring the skeleton after completion of growth is the mechanical stress incurred in the course of everyday activities. In the absence of this stimulus, bone undergoes atrophy. The pain, fear, and disability associated with osteoporotic fracture usually reduce physical activity and hence tend to aggravate the underlying problem, whatever its original cause. Thus, most therapy is inevitably somewhat unsatisfactory, and any treatment that ignores the basic importance of mechanical loading will usually be quite unsatisfactory.

Therapeutic Options

Therapy should be directed at several levels. First is the control of acute discomfort following fracture. Mild analgesics, a tight corset or binder, and often short-term bed rest may be required for the crush fracture patient. Increasing abdominal pressure (by voluntary contraction of the diaphragm, the levator ani, and the rectus abdominus muscle groups) will splint the spine and aid the patient in moving in and out of bed or onto the toilet during the acute phase following fracture. The patient with a hip or other extremity fracture requires orthopaedic management. Following the acute phase, effort must be directed toward physical therapy, rehabilitation, and change in habits of daily living.

Several drug therapies are available, most of them able to produce at best only a slowing or cessation of further bone loss, but not an appreciable increase in bone mass. Approved therapies include mainly calcium supplements, estrogen, and calcitonin. An intake of at least 1.5 g per day of calcium should be ensured, whether or not other agents are used, and in many patients even that quantity will not be adequate because of inefficient absorption. Dietary calcium sources are to be preferred, but supplements are usually necessary as well. Calcium carbonate is the most inexpensive supplement form. It is well absorbed if taken with meals, even in patients with achlorhydria. Optimally, calcium should be given in divided doses, with meals and at bedtime. Estrogen may be used in a dose of 0.625 mg conjugated equine estrogens per day (or equivalent). If the patient still has her uterus, most authorities recommend a concomitant progestogen (e.g., 2 to 10 mg medroxyprogesterone acetate given either cyclically or continuously); this approach reduces the risk of endometrial carcinoma. Many synthetic progestogens, however, also reduce the beneficial effect of estrogens on blood lipids (and hence on the risk of cardiovascular disease). There is no need either for a progestogen or for cycling of the estrogen in women without a uterus.

Sodium fluoride is currently an investigational therapy and not yet approved for general use. Fluoride is the only drug currently available that substantially increases bone mass in certain involved regions. It is an osteoblastic stimulant that usually results in steady, continuing increases in trabecular bone density, particularly in the spine; its effect on cortical bone is less certain. It is associated with a number of troublesome side effects, including gastrointestinal irritation and various rheumatic complaints in the feet and legs, the full extent and severity of which vary with dosage and with formulation. The gastrointestinal side effects seen with plain sodium fluoride are minimal to absent with newer slow-release or intestinal-release preparations. When bony response to fluoride is exuberant, bone hunger may result, creating a demand for high calcium intakes (2000–3000 mg/d), and in the absence of adequate oral calcium, appendicular bone may be eroded to feed the appetite of the central skeleton.

Bisphosphonates are widely used to treat patients with osteoporosis in the United States and abroad. The principal such agents today are etidronate and alendronate. Dosage regimens vary from agent to agent. All bisphosphonates inhibit bone remodeling and thereby slow remodeling-related bone loss. Additionally, alendronate produces a small, steady increase in bone density.

Calcitonin is also a remodeling suppressor, and produces effects qualitatively similar to those of the bisphosphonates. Calcitonin is available either by injection or by nasal spray. It also has intrinsic analgesic properties that can be very helpful in some patients, particularly in the acute phase following vertebral compression. The principal side effects are nausea and nasal irritation (for the nasal form only). The injectable form is used daily to three times weekly.

As bone remodeling is often elevated in patients with osteoporosis, any remodeling inhibitor reduces the volume of bone that is temporarily "out of service" while undergoing remodeling (the so-called "remodeling space") and thereby produces a one-time increase in usable (and measurable) bone, amounting to several percent of the starting value. In high-remodeling osteoporoses, this can amount to a 15 to 20% increase. This one-time gain, plus the slowing of further loss, is the basis for the therapeutic benefit produced by these agents.

Tailoring Therapy. Bone remodeling may be high, low, or normal in patients with osteoporosis, reflecting the diverse pathogenesis of this disorder (just as marrow activity can vary in patients with anemia). Although approved agents available to treat osteoporosis in the United States are still limited in number, there is a wide spectrum of pharmacologic agents potentially available, each of which may have differing effects on remodeling. In part for this reason, it can be useful to characterize the basal state of bone remodeling before selecting a therapy. Several biomarkers are available for this purpose, including serum osteocalcin and bone-specific alkaline phosphatase (reflecting bone formation), and urinary levels of collagen breakdown products (reflecting bone resorption), such as hydroxyproline, pyridinoline cross links, and *N*-telopeptides. High values for any or all of these markers indicate high bone turnover and suggest use of a remodeling-suppressive agent. Low values predict poor response to a suppressor and suggest instead a stimulator, such as fluoride. Combination therapy offers many theoretical benefits, but has not been carefully studied.

Recommended Approach

For vertebral osteoporosis the core of the approach is a comprehensive physical therapy program designed to strengthen back muscles and correct postural problems. Vitamin D 800 IU/d and calcium at least 1500 mg/d are essential. Drug therapy consists of estrogen, calcitonin, a biphosphonate, or fluoride, alone or in combination.

FOLLOW-UP

The physician should stress to the patient the importance of maintaining a regular exercise program, remaining physically active (walking, swimming), and adopting habits of daily living that may protect against fracture. These include bending at the knees when picking something up off the floor, using special exercise regimens that strengthen the posterior back muscles, and employing similar measures that, although undramatic, are crucially important. For most patients, the condition can be stabilized and thus worsening avoided, but even this will usually not be possible if the patient does not remain physically active. The physician should also emphasize maintenance of good nutrition, to include an adequate intake of calcium and vitamin D, and describe various ways, without an undue reliance on supplements, that the patient can increase the calcium content of the daily diet from normal and fortified food sources. The patient should also be helped to realize that her skeleton is already weakened and that she should not be discouraged if additional fractures occur.

Frequency of follow-up depends on the presenting complaint and

generally is specific to the fracture. Because the crush fracture syndrome produces permanent deformity and often chronic discomfort, follow-up is determined by the severity of the patient's complaints and by the desire of the physician to assess compliance with the prescribed regimen. The patient will naturally seek further attention if additional symptomatic fractures occur. Although a goal of therapy is to reduce risk of further fractures, the physician and patient should not be discouraged if further fractures occur. By the time the first fracture appears, bony fragility is, manifestly, present. Hence the skeleton will be prone to further fractures. Successful therapy reduces their number and severity, but should not be expected to eliminate them entirely.

Monitoring patient progress is important in motivating compliance with treatment regimens for chronic disorders, and can give the physician a sense of whether the patient is responding. This is especially important in disorders where episodes (e.g., fractures) are intermittent. Looking for changes in bone mass in response to treatment would seem a logical way to do this. Unfortunately, although bone absorptiometry is more accurate than most biological measurements, it does not reliably detect changes in bone mass less than a few percentage points. Bone mass, unlike blood pressure, blood sugar, or other markers for underlying diseases, changes only very slowly. Hence it is not usually helpful to measure bone mass more often than every 2 to 3 years. Inferences drawn from measurements over shorter time intervals are often seriously misleading. If, however, the physician has based therapy on measurement of biomarkers, these can be expected to change in a matter of only a few weeks or months and are the best way to tell whether the agent chosen is doing what was intended.

DISCUSSION
Prevalence and Incidence

As noted previously, the spine crush fracture syndrome is predominantly a disease of white women in the United States. Still, 10 to 15% of all cases of vertebral osteoporosis and 25 to 35% of hip fractures occur in men. Although as many as 25% of all women over age 65 will have one or more compression fractures, many are asymptomatic, and the real prevalence of symptomatic crush fracture syndrome is probably less than 15%. The risk of most extremity fractures rises exponentially with age, so that by age 85, a white woman has about a 30% chance of sustaining at least one hip fracture. The extremity and the spine crush fracture syndromes appear to be somewhat distinct inasmuch as the prevalence of spine fracture in hip fracture patients is not much greater than in the general population of the same age.

Osteoporosis is less common in blacks and Hispanics as well as in women (of all races) who have relatively high body mass indices. Body weight is strongly protective against fracture, both because bone density is higher in overweight individuals and because soft tissue padding over vulnerable bony parts protects the bone.

Related Basic Science
Physiologic and Anatomic Influence

The higher incidence of osteoporotic fractures in the elderly is only partly due to the fact that bone is lost with age. Even at constant bone mass values, individuals over age 75 have an order-of-magnitude higher risk of a fragility fracture than individuals 45 to 55 years of age. This is due to many factors, including the probability of accumulated architectural defects and fatigue damage in the bony material, more frequent falling among the elderly, poor postural accommodation during falling, and weight loss (with its consequent loss of soft tissue padding).

Like anemia, carcinoma, or coronary artery disease, osteoporosis is not so much a specific disease as an end state, and thus it has no single pathogenesis. But like those other disorders, all forms of osteoporosis exhibit certain common features. For a normal skeleton to become osteoporotic, there must be a sustained imbalance in the remodeling process such that new bone formation is less than old bone resorption. Estrogen loss at menopause is associated with an acceleration of this imbalance. The cellular mechanisms for this estrogen effect are not known.

The remodeling imbalance of aging and of osteoporosis may have many causes, from a defect in osteoblastic impetus (as in immobilization or disuse atrophy) to a parathyroid hormone-mediated excess of resorption caused by inadequate calcium intake and/or intestinal malabsorption of calcium. Interestingly, the remodeling imbalance of osteoporosis is site specific. At the periosteal surface, even in severe osteoporosis, new bone formation generally exceeds old bone resorption. By contrast, at the trabecular and endosteal surfaces, resorption exceeds formation. This is true both in normal individuals and in those with osteoporotic fractures, although the imbalance is greater in those with osteoporosis.

The geometry of various bones also determines fracture susceptibility. Even after adjusting for body size and bone density, Asian women have only about half the hip fracture rate of Caucasians. This is now believed to be due to a short hip axis length, that is, the length of the lever arm from the lateral surface of the trochanter to the inner surface of the acetabulum. Hip axis length is shorter in Asians than in Caucasians. Accordingly, for the same bone density, the structure is stronger.

In most cases, osteoporosis is a disorder of the entire skeleton, although patterns of loss and bone remodeling differ somewhat in the several fracture syndromes. An example is found in the different patterns of trabecular loss in men and women. The loss that occurs with age in men consists primarily of a thinning of trabeculae, with preservation of most of the major architectural elements. By contrast, bone loss in many women, and particularly in those with the crush fracture syndrome, exhibits a reduction in the number of trabeculae and notably a loss of the horizontal, bracing structures. This disproportionately weakens the bone.

Natural History and Its Modification with Treatment

Bone mass in the total body peaks at about age 30, and at the hip, by age 18. It remains stable to about age 50, and declines thereafter, generally in parallel with a corresponding decline in muscle mass. In both sexes, as we become more sedentary with age, we inevitably lose bone. Thus, the longer a person lives, the higher is the risk for osteoporotic fracture. At menopause, or whenever there is a substantial reduction in gonadal hormone levels, bone mass declines sharply, coming into equilibrium at a new steady-state mass about 15% below the hormonally replete state. Estrogen (or hormone) replacement therapy completely abolishes this exaggerated loss, but does not prevent the slower, age-related loss that occurs in both sexes. Achieving maximal bone mass at age 30 is probably the best protection against fracture later in life. A woman at one standard deviation above the young adult mean can lose 15% of her skeleton at menopause and still have about as much bone at age 65 as the average premenopausal woman.

Once fracture has occurred, as noted previously, the disorder often follows a progressive course, largely because of the superimposition of decreased physical activity on the already weakened skeleton. Further, there is a tendency for certain of the fractures to occur in clusters; thus, a group of spine fractures may occur within a period of 2 to 3 years, following which the rate of further fracture slows.

Osteoporosis is not itself generally a fatal disorder; however, it is widely held that perhaps as much as one sixth of all hip fracture patients die as a consequence of the fracture, with its associated hospitalization, surgery, and other adverse impacts on life adjustment. Most of these deaths occur in globally fragile individuals past age 85, and the extent of the real excess mortality is uncertain.

Prevention

Because osteoporosis is a multifactorial disorder, no single preventive measure will work in all persons. Estrogen replacement therapy in postmenopausal women has been clearly shown to prevent the sex differential in age-related bone loss between men and women, as well as to re-

duce subsequent risk of both spine and hip fractures. Estrogen's effect is to stabilize bone mass and prevent further bone loss; it will not replace lost bone, and for maximum bony effect, it is thus best started at the time of menopause. Even when started late in life, however, estrogen has been shown to reduce fracture risk, possibly because of its established effect on improving body handling of calcium or because of improved neuromuscular tone and coordination (or both).

An adequate calcium intake is also of great importance. Calcium and vitamin D supplements have been shown to reduce fracture risk by from 20 to 40%, even when started in 80+-year-old women. Several factors influence the calcium requirement, but these may be difficult to assess in individual patients. They include calcium absorption efficiency, vitamin D status, intake of other nutrients (e.g., protein, sodium, fiber, caffeine), as well as use of various drugs, such as steroids, diuretics, and aluminum-containing antacids. Thus, ensuring an adequate calcium intake (at least 1000 mg/d in estrogen-replete perimenopausal women and 1500 mg/d in estrogen-deprived women) is the safest course for most women, even though calcium deficiency will not be the principal causal factor in all of them. Optimal calcium intake for men is now considered to be 1000 mg/d from ages 24 to 65 and 1500 mg/d thereafter.

The maintenance of good mechanical loading by a vigorous lifestyle and a regular pattern of exercise is crucial. The skeleton maintains only as much mass as is needed to sustain routine activities. A vigorous exercise program has secondary benefits as well: it results in higher levels of growth hormone, which is trophic for bone, and it permits a higher level of nutrient intake and thus helps to ensure a nutritionally adequate diet.

Alcohol abuse must be mentioned. Although the precise mechanism of the alcohol effect is not clear, alcohol is known to be toxic to osteoblasts, and the skeletons of alcoholics commonly exhibit severe osteoporosis. Unrecognized alcoholism, particularly in middle-aged, suburban housewives, may be a major contributing factor to the crush fracture syndrome seen in such patients. This type of problem is potentially preventable, but it must first be recognized. Cigarette smoking also contributes to bone loss and fragility. Hip fracture risk is several times greater in smokers than in nonsmokers.

Cost Containment

If simple screening tests are negative, usually there is no need for expensive determinations of parathyroid hormone or vitamin D metabolites. Estrogen, calcium, exercise, and even fluoride are inherently inexpensive treatments. Certain other proposed therapies (e.g., parenteral calcitonin) are not only of less utility, but are inherently more expensive.

REFERENCES

Chapuy MC, Arlot ME, Duboeuf F, et al. Vitamin D_3 and calcium to prevent hip fractures in elderly women. N Engl J Med 1992;327:1637.

Consensus Development Conference statement: Optimal calcium intake. JAMA 1994;272:1942.

Heaney RP. Nutritional factors in osteoporosis. Annu Rev Nutr 1993;13:287.

Kanis JA, Melton LJ III, Christiansen C, et al. The diagnosis of osteoporosis. J Bone Miner Res 1994;9:1137.

Kleerekoper M, Villanueva AR, Stanciu J, et al. The role of three-dimensional trabecular microstructure in the pathogenesis of vertebral compression fractures. Calcif Tissue Int 1985;37:594.

Pak CYC, Sakhaee K, Piziak V, et al. Randomized controlled trial of slow-release sodium fluoride in the management of postmenopausal osteoporosis. Ann Intern Med 1994;120:625.

Rigotti NA, Nussbaum SR, Herzog DB, Neer RM. Osteoporosis in women with anorexia nervosa. N Engl J Med 1984;311:1601.

Osteomalacia

Rajiv Kumar, M.B., B.S.

DEFINITION

Osteomalacia is defined as a reduction in the mineralization rate of bone. Normally, bone matrix or osteoid is synthesized by osteoblasts; osteoid is then mineralized at the mineralization front by the deposition of calcium and inorganic phosphorus. In osteomalacia, unmineralized osteoid accumulates and forms a disproportionately large proportion of bone. A mineralization defect of bone results in osteomalacia in adults and rickets in children. This disorder needs to be carefully distinguished from a much more common disorder, osteoporosis, in which bone mineralization is normal.

ETIOLOGY

Osteomalacia is most frequently due to a lack of adequate amounts of calcium and phosphorus in extracellular fluid. Deficits in extracellular fluid and plasma concentrations of these minerals are commonly due to a decrease in the efficiency of their absorption from the intestine or due to excessive loss of these minerals from the kidney. Rarely, the deposition of these minerals at the mineralization front is interfered with by the accumulation of toxic substances, such as aluminum, at the mineralization front. Table 9–40–1 lists the mechanisms by which, and the conditions in which, osteomalacia occurs.

CRITERIA FOR DIAGNOSIS

Suggestive

The diagnosis of osteomalacia is suggested by the presence of bone pain and muscle weakness, which is reflective of a proximal myopathy found in this condition. These symptoms, especially within the context of diseases that might cause osteomalacia such as malabsorption disorders, should alert the physician to the possible presence of osteomalacia. Severe cases of osteomalacia may present with symptoms of hypocalcemia such as tetany, carpopedal spasm, circumoral tingling and paresthesias, and, on rare occasions, laryngeal stridor and generalized seizures.

Definitive

A definitive diagnosis of osteomalacia can be made only on bone biopsy following double tetracycline labeling of bone; however, hypocalcemia, hypophosphatemia, elevated serum alkaline phosphatase concentrations, and an elevated parathyroid hormone concentration together with a low urinary calcium and an appropriate clinical setting strongly suggest the diagnosis of osteomalacia. X-ray evidence of pseudofractures of the pubic rami, ribs, or bones of the extremities is useful in establishing a diagnosis of osteomalacia. Alterations in vitamin D metabolite concentrations detailed later (Table 9–40–2) are also helpful in establishing a diagnosis.

CLINICAL MANIFESTATIONS

Subjective

Symptoms of osteomalacia are subtle, frequently mimicked by other conditions, and are often dismissed as trivial and of no consequence. The practitioner must be alert to the importance of these symptoms, especially within the context of the disease states mentioned in Table 9–40–1. Symptoms of osteomalacia include bone pain and generalized aches. Myopathy occurs and manifests as proximal muscle weakness. Subjects have difficulty in getting up out of a chair, climbing stairs, and abducting their arms above their head, as frequently occurs in day-to-day tasks such as combing hair and lifting objects onto a shelf. Fractures can occur and manifest as pain at the site of fracture. Severe hypocalcemia can result in symptoms such as circumoral tingling, car-

popedal spasm, and, rarely, grand mal seizures. Severe hypophosphatemia has on occasion has been reported to cause cardiac dysrhythmias, manifest as palpitations; diminished cardiac output, manifest as dyspnea or orthopnea; and on occasion, rhabdomyolysis, manifest as dark pigmented urine with or without renal failure. Past medical history may reveal a history of diarrhea with fatty stools, use of drugs such as phenobarbital and phenytoin that induce cytochrome P450 enzymes; or use of drugs such as ketoconazole and isoniazid that inhibit the formation of 25-hydroxyvitamin D, 1,25-dihydroxyvitamin D, or both. Family history is important in diseases such as X-linked hypophosphatemia, autosomal dominant hypophosphatemia, and the various vitamin D-dependent rickets. Patients frequently report that their relatives had a short stature, failed to grow normally, or had other manifestations of osteomalacia.

Objective

Physical Examination

On physical examination, bone tenderness may be elicited. Proximal muscle weakness may manifest as a waddling gait. Weakness during abduction of the upper extremities and during flexion of the leg at the thigh may be observed. In subjects with the various forms of hereditary

TABLE 9–40–1. MECHANISMS BY WHICH OSTEOMALACIA OCCURS

Defects in the absorption of calcium
  Vitamin D deficiency or resistance
    Decreased availability of vitamin D
      Low exposure to sunlight
      Failure of formation of vitamin D from 7-dehydrocholesterol in the skin
      Low intake of vitamin D
      Malabsorption of vitamin D from the intestine
    Enhanced metabolism of vitamin D and 25-hydroxyvitamin D to nonactive compounds, caused by drugs such as phenytoin, phenobarbital, and rifampin
    Failure of formation of 25-dihydroxyvitamin D
      Liver diseases (alcoholic cirrhosis, primary biliary cirrhosis)
      Drugs such as isoniazid
    Failure of formation of 1,25-dihydroxyvitamin D
      Renal failure
      Renal tubular disorders (X-linked vitamin D-resistant rickets, sporadic hypophosphatemia, Fanconi's syndrome)
      Tumor-induced osteomalacia
      Hypoparathyroidism and pseudohypoparathyroidism
      Drugs that inhibit 25-hydroxyvitamin D_3 1α-hydroxylase activity such as ketoconazole and isoniazid
      Aging
      Acidosis (?)
    End-organ resistance of 1,25-dihydroxyvitamin D (type II vitamin D-dependent rickets)
Defects in bone matrix that result in osteomalacia
  Treatment with biphosphonates
  Treatment with fluoride
  Heavy metals such as strontium and cadmium
  Metals such as aluminum
Defects in the intestinal absorption or renal reclamation of phosphate
  Treatment with phosphate binders
  Fanconi's syndrome
  X-linked hypophosphatemia
  Sporadic hypophosphatemia
  Tumor-induced osteomalacia

Source: Audran M, Kumar R. The physiology and pathophysiology of vitamin D. Mayo Clin Proc 1985;60:851. Reproduced with permission from the publisher and author.

TABLE 9–40–2. SERUM AND URINE CONCENTRATIONS OF RELEVANT ANALYTES IN VARIOUS PATHOLOGIC CONDITIONS CAUSING OSTEOMALACIA OR RICKETS

Condition	Serum Calcium	Serum Phosphate	Urine Calcium	Urine Phosphate	Serum Alkaline Phosphatase	Serum Parathyroid Hormone	Plasma 25-Hydroxy-vitamin D*	Plasma 1,25-Dihydroxyvitamin D†
Nutritional vitamin D deficiency, malabsorption	Decreased	Decreased	Low	Normal or low, fractional excretion‡ high	High, especially bone alkaline phosphatase	Increased	Decreased	Decreased, normal, or sometimes elevated
Renal failure (creatinine clearance < 30–50 mL/min)	Decreased	Increased	Low, fractional excretion of calcium may be normal or high	Low, fractional excretion high	High	Increased	Normal	Decreased
Hypoparathyroidism, pseudohypoparathyroidism	Decreased	Increased	Low, fractional excretion is high	Low, fractional excretion low	Normal	Decreased in hypoparathyroidism; increased in pseudohypoparathyroidism	Normal	Decreased
X-linked hypophosphatemic rickets	Normal	Decreased	Low	High, fractional excretion high	Normal	Normal	Normal	Decreased or normal
Tumor-induced osteomalacia	Normal	Decreased	Low	High, fractional excretion high	Normal or elevated	Normal	Normal	Decreased
Vitamin D-dependent rickets Type I (autosomal recessive)	Decreased	Decreased or normal	Low	Variable, fractional excretion high	High	Increased	Normal	Decreased
Type II	Decreased	Decreased	Low	Variable, fractional excretion high	High	Increased	Normal	Increased

*Normal range is generally 10–40 ng/mL, but normal values are variable; individual seasonally adjusted ranges should be established in each laboratory.
†Normal range is 20–60 pg/mL.
‡Fraction of filtered inorganic phosphate that appears in the urine. The tubular maximum for phosphate/glomerular filtration rate is low when the fractional excretion is high.
Modified from Audran M, Kumar R. The physiology and pathophysiology of vitamin D. Mayo Clin Proc 1985;60:851. Reproduced with permission from the publisher and author.

or acquired rickets, growth retardation is seen, and deformities of the long bones as a result of rickets are apparent. During infancy and early childhood, rickets manifests with objective physical signs such as widening of the bones of the forearm and wrists and hypertrophy of the costochondral junctions of the ribs, which produces a rachitic rosary. In childhood and adolescence, subjects manifest bowing of the legs. When subjects have severe hypocalcemia, tetany and carpopedal spasm may be observed. Chvostek's sign and Trousseau's sign may be positive. Papilledema may be observed.

Routine Laboratory Abnormalities

Routine laboratory abnormalities for each condition causing osteomalacia or rickets are listed in Table 9–40–2.

PLANS
Diagnostic

Differential Diagnosis

The conditions that may cause osteomalacia are listed in Table 9–40–1. Several conditions can present with bone pain including osteoporosis with associated fractures, degenerative joint disease, and Paget's disease.

There are two types of osteoporosis: one occurs in the immediate postmenopausal period; the second occurs after the age of 70 years and is referred to as senile osteoporosis. Osteoporosis can occur in all age groups, although it is frequently found in individuals younger than those with osteoporosis. Recent evidence suggests that elderly nursing home residents may indeed be vitamin D deficient and may suffer from subclinical osteomalacia.

Bone pain in osteoporosis is present only when a fracture has occurred. As in the case of osteomalacia, in osteoporosis bone mineral density is diminished. Skeletal x-ray films show a decrease in the density of bone. Bone densitometry reveals a decrease in the total content of bone mineral. In osteoporosis, however, pseudofractures are not seen on skeletal radiography. Moreover, serum calcium and phosphate concentrations are generally normal. Parathyroid hormone concentrations are generally not altered in osteoporosis. Serum 25-hydroxyvitamin D concentrations are normal. 1,25-Dihydroxyvitamin D concentrations may be normal, decreased, or sometimes elevated. The 24-hour urinary calcium is generally not as low as seen in osteomalacia.

Degenerative joint disease is seen in elderly individuals and can manifest as diffuse bone pain. A careful history and radiologic assessment will differentiate degenerative joint disease from osteomalacia. Generally, bone demineralization is not seen in degenerative joint disease. Serum calcium, phosphorus, parathyroid hormone, and vitamin D concentrations are normal. Urinary calcium concentrations are also normal.

Paget's disease of the bone can also cause bone pain. Generally, calcium and phosphorus concentrations are normal, and alkaline phosphatase concentrations are elevated. Skeletal radiography will show the typical features of Paget's disease of bone. Paget's disease is usually not diffuse and is generally confined to one or, at the very most, several bones.

Diagnostic Options

Various noninvasive laboratory tests required to establish a diagnosis of osteomalacia and its etiology are listed in Table 9–40–2. In addition, skeletal x-ray films will reveal pseudofractures of the upper humerus, ribs, tibia, and metatarsals. Signs of secondary hyperparathyroidism with phalangeal tuft resorption and erosions of the shafts of the metacarpals and phalanges may be seen. To confirm a diagnosis of os-teomalacia, a bone biopsy is necessary. This is performed after giving a tetracycline label (commonly demeclocycline, 300 mg PO bid) for 3 days; no drug is given for the next 14 days. Two weeks after the first course of demeclocycline (day 17), demeclocycline is given for another 3 days at the same dose as noted earlier. Three days after the last dose of tetracycline, a bone biopsy is performed from the iliac crest. This is then processed, stained with Goldner's stain, and examined by fluorescence microscopy to determine the mineralization rate.

Recommended Approach

A careful history is most important in establishing a diagnosis of osteomalacia. The presence of malabsorption syndrome is often not suspected. Family histories must be carefully elicited. Dietary intake of vitamin D and calcium should be assessed. A history of intake of various medications also needs to be carefully determined. A diagnostic algorithm is given below.

1. History, family history, physical examination
↓
2. Serum calcium, inorganic phosphorus, and alkaline phosphatase concentrations; hemoglobin; mean corpuscular volume; urinalysis; and 24-hour urine calcium and phosphorus concentrations
↓
3. Skeletal x-rays, whole molecule parathyroid hormone and assay, serum/plasma 25-hydroxyvitamin D and 1,25-dihydroxyvitamin D concentrations
↓
4. Bone biopsy after double tetracycline labeling of bone

Therapeutic

Therapeutic Options

Therapy is aimed at providing sufficient amounts of calcium and phosphorus for adequate mineralization to occur. If osteomalacia is due to the presence of toxins such as aluminum, then every effort should be made to remove such toxins from the medication schedule and the patient's dietary intake. If the osteomalacia is associated with the use of drugs, alternative drugs might be considered. For example, if osteomalacia is associated with the use of anticonvulsants such as phenytoin and phenobarbital, another agent such as sodium valproate, which is not associated with a reduction in the plasma levels of 25-hydroxyvitamin D, can be tried for seizure control. Similarly, if malabsorption syndrome is due to a treatable disease such as gluten-sensitive enteropathy or blind-loop syndrome with bacterial overgrowth, then appropriate therapeutic measures should result in elimination of the cause of osteomalacia. Tumor-induced osteomalacia can be treated by removal of the offending tumor.

Recommended Approach

Despite the preceding comments, it is clear that osteomalacia will need to be treated initially, at least, with adequate amounts of calcium, phosphorus, and vitamin D preparations.

Calcium. Osteomalacia associated with the malabsorption of calcium from the bowel due to any reason will not be cured with vitamin D therapy unless adequate amounts of calcium are provided in the diet. Various oral calcium preparations are available as shown in Table 9–40–3. These should be administered in order to provide at least 1000 to 2000 mg of elemental calcium per day. If hypocalcemia does not respond, then more oral calcium may need to be given.

Symptomatic, severe hypocalcemia may need to be treated with intravenous preparations of calcium, such as calcium gluconate (10% solution, 1 g or 10 ml IV slowly over 5 minutes). Calcium chloride can be used instead.

Phosphorus. Phosphorus, as neutral sodium phosphate, 1 to 2g orally is required for the treatment of hypophosphatemic rickets and tumor-induced osteomalacia.

TABLE 9–40–3. CALCIUM PREPARATIONS USED IN TREATING OSTEOMALACIA

	Elemental Calcium (per g)	To Supplement Calcium
Calcium carbonate	400 mg	1–2 g between meals
Calcium acetate	250 mg	1–2 g between meals
Calcium citrate	200 mg	
Calcium lactate	130 mg	Sufficient to provide 1–2 g elemental calcium
Calcium glubionate	115 mg/5 mL	Sufficient to provide 1–2 g elemental calcium

Vitamin D Preparations. Most cases of osteomalacia need to be treated with vitamin D. Various vitamin D preparations are available as shown in Table 9–40–4.

Specific Conditions Associated with Osteomalacia and Their Treatment. Nutritional osteomalacia occurs infrequently in the United States as dairy products are fortified with vitamin D. This is not the case in other countries such as the United Kingdom, where milk is not fortified with vitamin D. The Asian immigrant population has a high incidence of rickets and osteomalacia in the United Kingdom on account of diminished sunlight exposure, dark skin pigmentation, and nutritional deficits. In the United States, the occurrence of osteomalacia or rickets should lead one to suspect a malabsorption syndrome or one of the hereditary rickets. Nutritional osteomalacia of dietary origin is usually treated with the administration of vitamin D_2 in a dose of 2000 to 4000 IU/d (0.05–0.1 mg/d). This should produce satisfactory healing within a period of 6 to 12 weeks. Higher doses (50,000 IU/d) can be used but are not generally needed. As noted earlier, if dietary calcium intake is low, calcium supplements must be given, because in the absence of requisite amounts of calcium, the healing of bone will not occur. With therapy, symptoms of osteomalacia should disappear. Serum alkaline phosphatase levels should diminish after an initial increase and radiologic abnormalities should heal. Therapy with the recommended dietary allowance of vitamin D, 400 IU/d should be continued indefinitely.

Osteomalacia associated with malabsorption syndromes and hepatic disorders requires a specific approach. In patients with steatorrhea and hepatic disorders, vitamin D may need to be given in larger amounts on account of the malabsorption of the orally administered vitamin. A dosage of vitamin D_2 between 25,000 and 50,000 IU/d is given until a definite response is noted. Supplemental calcium preparations are needed. In patients with hepatic disorders, 25-hydroxyvitamin D_3 is theoretically a more suitable agent to use, as the conversion of D_3 to 25-hydroxyvitamin D_3, which may be abnormal in hepatic diseases, is circumvented; however, it is more expensive and initial therapy with vitamin D should be tried.

Bone disease in patients with chronic renal failure and in patients on long-term hemodialysis also requires a specific approach. Virtually all patients with chronic renal failure and end-stage renal disease have secondary hyperparathyroidism; however, a subset of patients have a mineralization defect. Osteomalacia in the context of renal failure and end-stage renal disease is often associated with the exposure of patients to aluminum present in phosphate binders such as aluminum hydroxide. Patients who use corticosteroids, those with diabetes, immobilized patients, and patients who have undergone a parathyroidectomy are at particular risk for aluminum-associated osteomalacia. Some patients have a mixture of secondary hyperparathyroidism and osteomalacia. The treatment of renal bone disease due to secondary hyperparathyroidism consists of the use of phosphate binders such as calcium acetate and calcium carbonate, given with meals, and the use of various vitamin D analogs, usually 1,25-dihydroxyvitamin D_3 given either orally or intravenously. The treatment of osteomalacia or low-turnover bone disease in patients with renal failure is more difficult. Aluminum-containing phosphate binders should be eliminated and exposure to aluminum in intravenous solutions should also be eliminated. Exposure of patients to aluminum via aluminum-containing dialysate should be avoided. As these patients tend to be hypercalcemic, vitamin D analogs and calcium preparations should be used cautiously. Desferrioxamine therapy to chelate aluminum and the subsequent removal of the desferrioxamine

TABLE 9–40–4. USUAL DOSE REQUIREMENT AND DURATION OF TOXICITY OF VITAMIN D ANALOGS IN CHRONIC RENAL FAILURE

| Vitamin D Analog | Potency Relative to Vitamin D$_3$ | Daily Dose (μg) | | Duration of Toxicity |
		Prevention	*Treatment*	
Vitamin D$_3$*	1	250–2500	750–10,000	17–30
Dihydrotachysterol	10	100–200	200–1000	17–30
Calcidiol, 25-hydroxyvitamin D$_3$	50		50–200	15–30
1α-Hydroxyvitamin D$_3$†	5000	0.5–1.0	0.5–2.0	5–15
Calcitriol, 1,25-dihydroxyvitamin D$_3$	5000	0.5–1.0	0.5–3.0	2–7

*1 IU = 25 ng.

†Not available in the United States.

Source: Johnson WJ. Use of vitamin D analogs in renal osteodystrophy. Semin Nephrol 1986;6:31. Reproduced with permission from the publisher and author.

aluminum complexes by sorbent methods of dialysis with high-flux dialyzers is the preferred form of treatment.

Osteomalacia associated with anti-convulsant or anti-tuberculous medications requires a specific approach. These patients may have low 25-hydroxyvitamin D levels. Where practical, anticonvulsants can be changed to those not associated with alterations in vitamin D metabolism, such as sodium valproate. In general, however, patients will require therapy with a vitamin D preparation. Four thousand units of vitamin D given daily should result in a reversal of osteomalacia.

Osteomalacia associated with phosphate depletion requires a specific approach. Osteomalacia occurs in patients who have hypophosphatemia. This can be due to a renal tubular defect that can either be hereditary or acquired. Treatment of this condition requires 1 to 2 g of oral neutral phosphate per day and the administration of 1,25-dihydroxyvitamin D$_3$ until such time as phosphate concentrations come into the normal range and alkaline phosphatase concentrations decrease.

FOLLOW-UP

Treatment of patients with osteomalacia requires careful monitoring of therapy. The following tests should be obtained, initially every 2 weeks and subsequently every month until the patient's symptoms and signs have normalized. The following tests are required for monitoring:

- *Serum calcium, phosphorus, alkaline phosphatase, and creatinine:* Serum calcium and phosphorus concentrations should increase with therapy. Alkaline phosphatase should diminish. In the treatment of patients with nutritional osteomalacia or osteomalacia associated with hepatic disease or steatorrhea, there is frequently an increase in alkaline phosphatase initially because of an increase in osteoblastic activity. This tends to return toward normal within a few weeks. Serum creatinine is monitored to ensure the maintenance of normal renal function.
- *Urinary calcium excretion:* This is initially low and comes into the normal range following therapy. Hypercalciuria may be the first sign of toxicity and 24-hour urine calcium determinations are especially important in monitoring therapy. They should be performed every 2 to 4 weeks until a stable dose is achieved or a cure is effected.
- *Immunoreactive Parathyroid Hormone, 25-Hydroxyvitamin D, and 1,25-dihydroxyvitamin D concentrations:* These measurements may also be useful, although they are less practical than the preceding measures.

DISCUSSION
Prevalence and Incidence

Nutritional osteomalacia is uncommon in the United States. The most common cause of osteomalacia is malabsorption or hepatic disease. Osteomalacia is seen in approximately 5% of patients with end-stage renal disease. Its incidence is diminishing with the decreased use of aluminum binders.

Related Basic Science
Metabolic Derangement

The vitamin D endocrine system plays a central role in the genesis of osteomalacia. Vitamin D is synthesized in the skin or obtained from the diet and is metabolized in the liver to 25-hydroxyvitamin D$_3$ and in the kidney to 1,25-dihydroxyvitamin D$_3$. 1,25-Dihydroxyvitamin D is the active metabolite of the vitamin. Synthesis of 1,25-dihydroxyvitamin D in the kidney is measured in states of calcium demand. Parathyroid hormone increases the activity of the enzyme.

Tumors associated with osteomalacia are thought to elaborate a new hormonal factor known as phosphatonin that causes osteomalacia. Removal of these tumors is associated with cure of the disease.

Genetics

Individuals with X-linked hypophosphatemia have a genetic abnormality that may be due to the same factor elaborated by patients with tumor-induced osteomalacia, although this is not certain. Expression of the sodium phosphate transporter involved in sodium-dependent phosphate transport in the proximal tubule is diminished in patients with X-linked hypophosphatemia. Individuals with vitamin D-dependent rickets type I have a congenital absence of the 25-hydroxyvitamin D$_3$ 1α-hydroxylase enzyme. Subjects with vitamin D-dependent rickets type II have abnormalities in the vitamin D receptor that cause either imperfect binding of 1,25-dihydroxyvitamin D$_3$ to the receptor or an inappropriately low binding of the receptor to promoter elements of various genes induced by 1,25-dihydroxyvitamin D$_3$.

Natural History and Its Modification With Treatment

This is noted in the individual sections above.

Prevention

Nutritional osteomalacia can be prevented by fortification of milk and dairy products with the vitamin. Individuals with poor intakes of food, such as individuals in nursing homes, the elderly, or institutionalized patients, should receive adequate quantities of vitamin D either as a supplement or in their diet.

Cost Containment

Nutritional osteomalacia is most easily treated with vitamin D$_2$ or vitamin D$_3$. These medications have the virtue of being much cheaper than other vitamin D preparations such as 1,25-dihydroxyvitamin D$_3$ and 25-hydroxyvitamin D$_3$. In my opinion, there is no reason for the treatment of nutritional osteomalacia or osteomalacia secondary to malabsorption syndromes with anything other than vitamin D$_2$ or vitamin D$_3$ as the vitamin D preparation. The cheapest form of calcium is calcium carbonate. Unless patients cannot tolerate calcium carbonate, it is the preferred form of calcium supplementation. In the long run, from the public health standpoint, prevention of osteomalacia in nursing home populations and in the elderly will yield the most significant benefit by reducing the number of unnecessary fractures.

REFERENCES

Audran M, Kumar R. The physiology and pathophysiology of vitamin D. Mayo Clin Proc 1985;60:851.

Cai Q, Hodgson SF, Kao PC, et al. Inhibition of renal phosphate transport by a tumor product in a patient with oncogenic osteomalacia. N Engl J Med 1994;330:1645

Johnson JA, Kumar R. Renal and intestinal calcium transport: Role of vitamin D and vitamin D-dependent calcium binding proteins. Semin Nephron 1994;14:119.

Kumar R. Osteomalacia. In: Bardin CW, ed. Current therapy in endocrinology and metabolism—3, Toronto: Decker, 1988:361.

Lobaugh B, Burch WM Jr, Drezner MK. Abnormalities of vitamin D metabolism and action in the vitamin D-resistant rachitic and osteomalacic diseases. In: Kumar R, ed. Vitamin D: Basic and clinical aspects, Hingham, MA:Martinus Nijhoff, 1986:665.

CHAPTER 9–41

Renal Stones (See Section 16, Chapter 16 and Section 18, Chapter 35)

CHAPTER 9–42

Diabetes Insipidus

Gary L. Robertson, M.D., László Kovács, M.D., D.Sc., and Tamara Vokes, M.D.

DEFINITION

Diabetes insipidus is a syndrome characterized by the excretion of abnormally large volumes (>50 mL/d) of dilute urine (polyuria) and increased intake of fluid (polydipsia). This combination of abnormalities can result from one of three basic defects: a deficiency of the antidiuretic hormone vasopressin, in which case it is designated as *neurogenic, central, cranial,* or *vasopressin-sensitive diabetes insipidus;* decreased renal sensitivity to the antidiuretic effect of vasopressin, which is referred to as *nephrogenic* or *vasopressin-resistant diabetes insipidus;* and excessive intake of water, which is called *primary polydipsia.* There is a subdivision of the first type of diabetes insipidus which is also due to a deficiency of vasopressin, but in this case the deficiency results from increased metabolism as well as decreased secretory capacity of the hormone. It has been observed only during pregnancy and is called *gestational diabetes insipidus.*

ETIOLOGY

The diseases responsible for the syndrome of diabetes insipidus differ depending on which of the three types is involved. Neurogenic diabetes insipidus often results from diseases of the pituitary and/or hypothalamus, but it may also occur as an isolated idiopathic effect in individuals or as a familial disease transmitted in an autosomal dominant mode (Table 9–42–1). The familial disorder has been linked to a number of different mutations in exons of the gene that codes for the protein precursor of vasopressin. Nephrogenic diabetes insipidus is usually caused by certain metabolic disturbances or drugs, but it also may occur as an isolated idiopathic defect or as a familial disorder transmitted in either an X-linked or an autosomal recessive mode. These two familial disorders have been linked to a number of different mutations in exons of the genes that code, respectively, for the vasopressin-2 receptor or for aquaporin II, the protein that forms the water channels in renal collecting tubules. Finally, primary polydipsia (or primary polydipsic diabetes insipidus) results from excessive intake of water with consequent suppression of vasopressin release and water diuresis. The latter syndrome can result from a defect in thirst mechanism, in which case it may be called *dipsogenic diabetes insipidus,* or it may be a manifestation of a more general cognitive defect, in which case it is often referred to as *psychogenic polydipsia* or *compulsive water drinking.* Dipsogenic diabetes insipidus can result from the same diseases of the pituitary hypothalamus as neurogenic diabetes insipidus, and the former sometimes progresses to the latter, resulting in a dual or combined defect. Gestational diabetes insipidus results when increased metabolism of vasopressin by the placenta is superimposed on a subclinical deficiency in the capacity to secrete vasopressin.

CRITERIA FOR DIAGNOSIS
Suggestive

The diagnosis of diabetes insipidus should be suspected in any patient who reports excessive thirst, frequent urination, nocturia, or enuresis or who, on routine examination, has a urinary specific gravity less than 1.010.

Definitive

Definitive diagnosis requires documentation that under basal conditions of ad libitum fluid intake, the 24-hour urine is abnormally voluminous

TABLE 9–42–1. CAUSES OF DIABETES INSIPIDUS

Vasopressin deficiency (neurogenic diabetes insipidus)
  Acquired
    Trauma (accidental, surgical)
    Tumors (craniopharyngioma, metastases, lymphoma)
    Granuloma (sarcoid, histiocytosis, tuberculosis, syphilis)
    Infectious (meningitis, encephalitis, Guillain–Barré syndrome)
    Vascular (Sheehan's syndrome, aneurysms, aortocoronary bypass, cerebral thrombosis)
    Idiopathic
  Familial (autosomal dominant)
Excessive water intake (primary polydipsia)
  Dipsogenic
    Granuloma (sarcoidosis)
    Tuberculous meningitis
    Multiple sclerosis
    Idiopathic
  Psychogenic
Vasopressin insensitivity (nephrogenic diabetes insipidus)
  Acquired
    Infectious (pyelonephritis)
    Postobstructive (prostatic, ureteral)
    Vascular (sickle cell disease, trait)
    Infiltrative (amyloid)
    Cystic (polycystic disease)
    Metabolic (hypokalemia, hypercalcemia)
    Granuloma (sarcoid)
    Toxic (lithium, demeclocycline, methoxyflurane)
    Solute overload (glucosuria)
  Familial (X-linked recessive)
Gestational

Adapted from Robertson GL. Posterior pituitary. In: Felig P, Baxter J, Broadus AE, Frohman LA, eds. Endocrinology and metabolism. 2nd ed. New York: McGraw-Hill, 1987:339. Reproduced with permission from the publisher and author.

(more than 3.5 L/day) and dilute (osmolality less than 300 mosm/kg) in the absence of glucosuria or other forms of increased solute excretion (normal urinary solute excretion less than 1 mosm/mg creatinine per day).

CLINICAL MANIFESTATIONS
Subjective

A family history of diabetes insipidus is absent except in the rare patient who has one of the inherited forms of the disorder. Occupational or environmental factors play a role only through their association with diseases such as sarcoidosis and lung carcinoma.

The symptoms of diabetes insipidus are polyuria, polydipsia, and thirst. Nocturia is usually present and may interfere with sleep. In children, the disease may present with enuresis. In secondary forms (see Table 9–42–1), the symptoms of the underlying disease are frequently apparent. If diabetes insipidus is associated with insufficiency of anterior pituitary function, the polyuria and polydipsia may not manifest until the corticosteroid deficiency is treated. In contrast to patients with neurogenic, nephrogenic, and dipsogenic forms, patients with psychogenic polydipsia usually do not complain of thirst. Instead, they explain the extremely high rates of water intake by other reasons, such as the need to cleanse their body of poisons and to relieve anxiety. In patients with gestational diabetes insipidus, the polyuria and polydipsia usually begin at the end of the first trimester and remit a few weeks after delivery of the placenta. The symptoms may be mistaken for urinary frequency of pregnancy.

Objective

Physical Examination

Physical examination is unremarkable in a patient with diabetes insipidus as long as fluid intake is sufficient to match urinary losses. If, however, drinking is restricted by neurologic impairment, altered mental status, or external events, there may be signs of dehydration such as tachycardia, orthostatic hypotension, and, in severe cases, circulatory collapse and death. The physical manifestations of associated anterior pituitary or hypothalamic defects also may be present.

Routine Laboratory Abnormalities

On routine laboratory tests, the most characteristic finding is decreased urine specific gravity (<1.010). The plasma sodium level tends to be at the upper limit of the normal range in patients with neurogenic and nephrogenic diabetes insipidus and at the lower limit in primary polydipsia. Usually, however, the values are not diagnostically useful because of considerable overlap between the groups. Hypernatremia is not a feature of diabetes insipidus in an ambulatory patient on ad libitum fluid intake unless there is an associated defect in the osmoregulation of thirst. Similarly, true hyponatremia rarely occurs in dipsogenic diabetes insipidus unless there is an associated defect in vasopressin secretion and/or urinary dilution. In gestational diabetes insipidus, basal plasma osmolality and sodium concentration are usually at the lower limit of the normal range because the osmotic threshold for thirst is also significantly reduced in pregnancy.

PLANS
Diagnostic

The diagnosis is usually established by the history of polydipsia, polyuria, and thirst in patients with normal blood glucose levels. See Criteria for Diagnosis.

Differential Diagnosis

Once the presence of diabetes insipidus is established, it is necessary to differentiate between the neurogenic, nephrogenic, and primary polydipsic types. Often this distinction can be made simply by considering the clinical setting. Not infrequently, however, this approach is ambiguous or misleading because several diseases are associated with more than one type of diabetes insipidus (see Table 9–42–1). Differentiation also may be possible by conducting a closely monitored therapeutic

trial with (1-deamino-8-D-arginine vasopressin (DDAVP) or another antidiuretic drug (see below); however, such a trial can also be misleading and, in a patient with primary polydipsia, carries a hazard of inducing water intoxication. Usually, therefore, some other approach to determining the type of diabetes insipidus is necessary.

The simplest and most reliable method of differential diagnosis is a standard dehydration test supplemented, when necessary, by measurement of the plasma vasopressin level. The precise way that this test is performed and interpreted varies depending on the patient (Figure 9–42–1). The first step should always be to measure plasma osmolality and sodium levels under conditions of ad libitum fluid intake. If they are high (above the upper limit of normal, usually 295 mosm/kg and 143 mEq/L, respectively) in the presence of polyuria, the diagnosis of primary polydipsia is excluded and it is unnecessary and potentially hazardous to attempt further dehydration. In such a patient, the workup should proceed directly to the administration of aqueous vasopressin or DDAVP to differentiate between neurogenic and nephrogenic diabetes insipidus (see below). In all other cases, however (i.e., in patients in whom plasma osmolality and sodium concentration are within the normal range), the next step should be to stop all intake of fluid for a period sufficient to produce significant dehydration. The test is continued until either urine osmolality reaches a plateau (as indicated by three consecutive hourly increases of less than 30 mosm/kg) or body weight decreases by 3%. If fluid deprivation does not result in concentration of the urine (osmolality > 300 mosm/kg) despite evident dehydration (plasma osmolality and/or sodium levels above the upper limit of normal), aqueous vasopressin or injectable DDAVP should be given subcutaneously and measurements of urine osmolality repeated 30, 60, and 120 minutes later. If the highest postvasopressin value is less than 150% of the highest urine osmolality before vasopressin, a diagnosis of complete nephrogenic diabetes insipidus is virtually certain. In contrast, if the highest postvasopressin value is more than 150% of the prevasopressin osmolality, the most likely diagnosis is severe neurogenic diabetes insipidus. Rarely (about 1 in 20 patients), the latter response is also seen in a patient with partial nephrogenic diabetes insipidus. If fluid deprivation results in neither urinary concentration, weight loss, nor hypertonic dehydration, the patient may be drinking surreptitiously and should be retested under closer observation.

A different diagnostic approach must be used if the dehydration test results in concentration of the urine (i.e., a rise in urine osmolality to 300 mosm/kg or greater). This response is consistent with any of three possibilities (partial neurogenic diabetes insipidus, partial nephrogenic diabetes insipidus, or primary polydipsia), which cannot be differentiated reliably by measuring the change in osmolality following an injection of aqueous vasopressin or DDAVP. In this situation, it is best to collect venous blood for measurement of plasma vasopressin, osmolality, or sodium and plot the relationship between the values on a suitable nomogram (Figure 9–42–2). This approach usually provides a clear diagnosis in patients with neurogenic diabetes insipidus even if the vasopressin deficiency is incomplete. It is most effective, however, if vasopressin is measured when plasma osmolality and sodium are greater than 295 mosm/kg and 145 to 150 mEq/L (by corrected and uncorrected ion-specific electrode, respectively). If this level is not achieved by the time the patient begins to concentrate his or her urine, prolonging the fluid restriction is usually not sufficient to reach the desired endpoint promptly. Therefore, to minimize further discomfort to the patient, it is best to shorten the test by adding an infusion of hypertonic (3%) saline (0.1 mL/kg/min) and repeating the measurements of plasma osmolality and vasopressin as soon as the requisite level of hypertonicity has been achieved (usually 45–90 minutes).

Differentiation of dipsogenic from partial nephrogenic diabetes insipidus can sometimes be achieved by examining the relationship between plasma vasopressin level and the concurrent urine osmolality during dehydration (Figure 9–42–3). Because polyuria of any kind significantly alters renal function (see below), however, this distinction is sometimes difficult and may require special procedures that are best handled by referral centers with a particular interest and expertise in water metabolism.

The diagnosis of diabetes insipidus during pregnancy is similar except for three things. First, the desired endpoints for plasma osmolality and sodium concentration during the fluid deprivation and/or hyper-

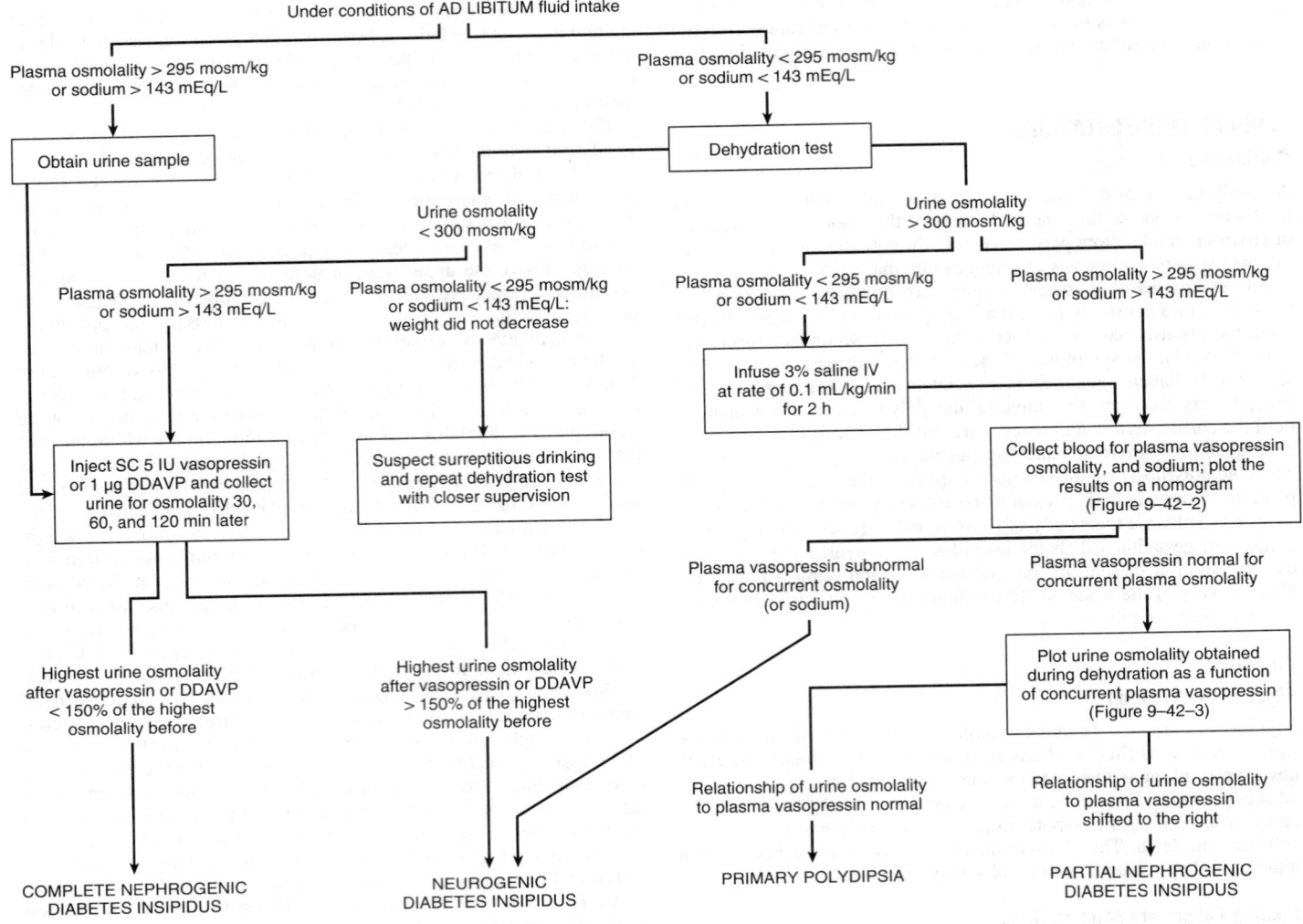

Figure 9–42–1. Evaluation of polyuria.

tonic saline infusion tests are about 10 mosm/kg and 5 mEq/L lower than in the nongravid subject because the osmotic threshold for vasopressin release as well as that for thirst is reduced by this amount in a normal pregnancy. Second, if the patient fails to concentrate her urine during an adequate fluid deprivation test, the antidiuretic hormone challenge should be performed only with DDAVP, as aqueous vasopressin itself may be relatively ineffective because of a markedly increased rate of metabolism of the native hormone that occurs during normal pregnancy. Third, if plasma vasopressin is assayed to make or confirm the diagnosis, the blood sample should be collected in phenanthroline or a similar protease inhibitor to prevent rapid, in vitro degradation of the hormone by the plasma vasopressinase produced by the placenta.

A careful search for the cause of the diabetes insipidus should also be undertaken. In patients with the neurogenic form, this search should include, in addition to routine laboratory tests, a computed tomography scan or magnetic resonance imaging of the brain. If these procedures are unrevealing, a lumbar puncture should be considered because certain causes, such as neurosarcoid, may be detected only by examination of cerebrospinal fluid. Other hypothalamic–pituitary functions also should be evaluated (see Chapter 9–2). In patients with nephrogenic diabetes insipidus, the cause will usually be evident from routine history and physical and laboratory tests; however, special procedures such as hemoglobin or serum electrophoresis, urinary calcium determination, and tissue biopsies may sometimes be necessary to detect causes such as sickle cell trait, hypercalciuria, and amyloidosis. In patients with psychogenic water drinking, the underlying psychosis is almost always grossly evident on routine examination. In others, particularly those who attribute drinking to thirst, hypothalamic and other neuropathology

should be sought using the same methods as in patients with neurogenic diabetes insipidus.

Therapeutic

Neurogenic diabetes insipidus can be treated by administration of vasopressin, a vasopressin analog, or certain oral drugs with antidiuretic effects.

Vasopressin itself can be given intramuscularly or subcutaneously as a short-acting aqueous solution (aqueous pitressin). In standard doses of 5 to 10 units intramuscularly, its antidiuretic effect lasts 2 to 4 hours. Therefore, its use is usually limited to diagnostic testing or short-term postoperative therapy.

An analog of vasopressin, DDAVP, has recently been developed. Because of two modifications in the molecule, it has a much longer duration or action than the native hormone, and, unlike the latter, it is virtually devoid of pressor effects. It comes in two preparations. One (DDAVP) is given by nasal insufflation in doses of 10 to 25 µg two or three times daily. The other (injectable desmopressin, Stimet) may be given subcutaneously or intravenously in doses of 1 to 2 µg once or twice a day. Resistance is unusual and is confined largely to intranasal administration, where absorption may be impaired by rhinitis or other local pathology. Side effects, mostly irritation of nasal mucosa, are rare. As with all preparations of antidiuretic hormone, water intoxication may develop if the polydipsia persists during treatment; however, this complication is uncommon and is usually seen only in patients with severe, long-standing diabetes insipidus in whom polydipsia has become a habit. In these patients, the hyponatremia is almost always tran-

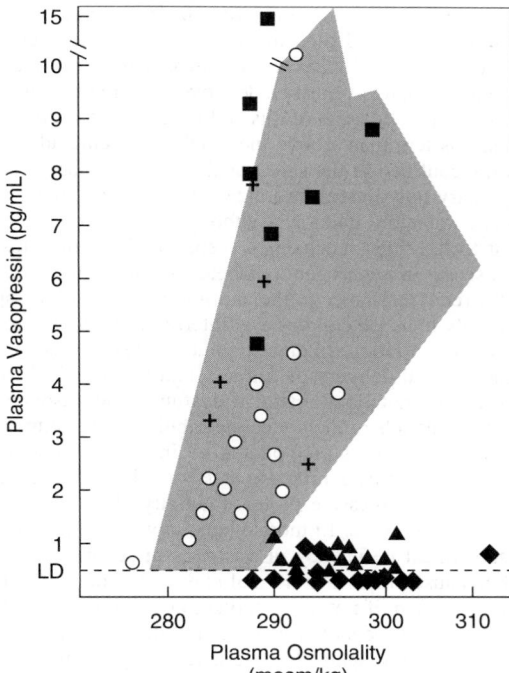

Figure 9–42–2. Relationship of plasma vasopressin level to concurrent plasma osmolality in patients with polyuria of diverse etiology. All measurements were made at the end of a standard dehydration test. The shaded area represents the range of normal. In patients with severe (◆) or partial (▲) neurogenic diabetes insipidus, the plasma vasopressin level was almost always subnormal relative to plasma osmolality. In contrast, the values from patients with dipsogenic (○) or nephrogenic (■) diabetes insipidus were consistently within or above the normal range. *(Source: Robertson GL. Diagnosis of diabetes insipidus. Front Horm Res 1985;13:176. Reproduced with permission from the publisher S. Karger AG, Basel, and author.)*

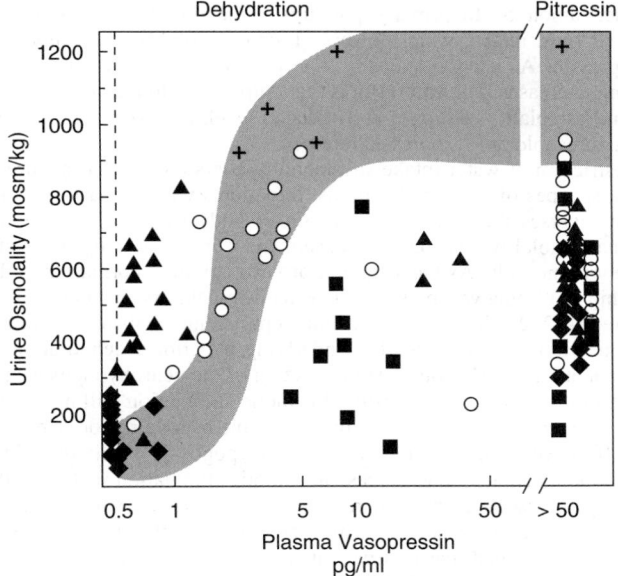

Figure 9–42–3. Relationship of urine osmolality to concurrent plasma vasopressin level in patients with polyuria of diverse etiology. All measurements were made at the end of a standard dehydration test. The shaded area represents the range of normal. In patients with severe (◆) or partial (▲) neurogenic diabetes insipidus, urine osmolality is normal or supranormal relative to plasma vasopressin level when the latter is submaximal. In patients with nephrogenic diabetes insipidus (■), urine osmolality is always subnormal for the plasma vasopressin level. In patients with dipsogenic diabetes insipidus (○), the relationship is often normal but may be subnormal due to blunting of concentrating capacity. *(Source: Robertson GL. Diagnosis of diabetes insipidus. Front Horm Res 1985;13:176. Reproduced with permission from the publisher S. Karger AG, Basel, and author.)*

sient and subsides with continued treatment. Severe or sustained hyponatremia is an indication to stop treatment and repeat diagnostic studies, as it usually indicates that the patient has some primary defect in the regulation of water intake. Patient acceptance of DDAVP is generally good, although difficulty with intranasal administration and the relatively high cost of the drug (currently about $2000 a year compared with about $250 a year for the other agents) remains a problem for some. DDAVP is particularly appropriate for the treatment of gestational diabetes insipidus because the analog is resistant to degradation by placental vasopressinase and has no known oxytocic or teratogenic effects. It should be discontinued several weeks after delivery to determine if endogenous production of vasopressin is sufficient to maintain antidiuresis once the hypermetabolic state ceases.

Oral drugs with antidiuretic effect include chlorpropamide (Diabinese), clofibrate (Atromid-S), and carbamazepine (Tegretol). They probably work by potentiating the renal effects of subthreshold amounts of endogenous vasopressin. The oral hypoglycemic chlorpropamide has been used and studied most widely. At conventional doses of 250 to 500 mg per day, it improves urinary concentration in nearly all patients with neurogenic diabetes insipidus regardless of the severity of their disease; however, as urine output decreases by an average of only about 50%, the residual degree of polyuria may be tolerable in patients with mild disease but not in those with severe forms of the disease. In the latter, the addition of chlorothiazide (250 mg twice a day) almost always provides satisfactory if not complete control of the polyuria (see below). The onset of action of chlorpropamide is considerably slower than that of vasopressin analogs and may require several days to manifest. Like vasopressin and its analogs, chlorpropamide is ineffective in patients with nephrogenic diabetes insipidus. The major side effects of chlorpropamide are hypoglycemia, which most frequently occurs in children or patients with anterior pituitary insufficiency, and flushing after ingestion of alcohol. Because of possible teratogenic effects, the drug should not be used in pregnancy. Patient acceptance of chlorpropamide is generally quite good because it is relatively inexpensive and convenient. Clofibrate, in a dose of 0.5 to 1 g three times a day, or carbamazepine, in a dose of 400 to 600 mg daily, also decreases urine output in patients with neurogenic diabetes insipidus; however, these drugs are usually less effective and more toxic than chlorpropamide and are used infrequently for treatment of diabetes insipidus.

Several other measures may be helpful in reducing polyuria in diabetes insipidus of any etiology. Restricting salt intake reduces urine output by reducing solute load. A similar effect may be achieved with thiazide diuretics, which deplete body sodium by inhibiting its reabsorption in the ascending limb of Henle's loop. Because this step is necessary for maximum urinary dilution, the thiazides also raise urine osmolality and impair the ability to excrete a water load. For this reason, they may precipitate water intoxication if given to a patient with primary polydipsia. As thiazides can cause severe hypokalemia, potassium supplementation is necessary for most patients treated with these compounds.

The management of neurogenic diabetes insipidus in comatose and/or postoperative patients presents a special problem because medications cannot be given orally or intranasally and water intake is not regulated by the thirst mechanism. In this situation, the best approach is to maintain a relatively fixed level of antidiuresis by giving desmopressin (1 to 2 µg subcutaneously or intravenously every 12–24 hours) and adjusting parenteral fluid intake to match renal and extrarenal losses. The latter can vary considerably depending on such factors as respiratory rate and temperature, but usually averages about 10 mL/kg per day.

Treatment of nephrogenic diabetes insipidus is considerably more difficult. In some patients it is possible to eliminate the drug or disease responsible for the disorder. In others, however, particularly those with familial or idiopathic forms, the only available therapy is to decrease sodium intake and/or administer thaizide diuretics. In standard doses, the latter have a paradoxical antidiuretic effect in nephrogenic as well as neurogenic diabetes insipidus (see above). Patients with partial nephrogenic diabetes insipidus can be treated by administering doses of desmopressin 10-fold higher than those used for neurogenic diabetes insipidus; however, the great expense of this approach makes it impractical at present.

Treatment for dipsogenic diabetes insipidus is currently unavailable. In the psychogenic form, treatment of the underlying psychosis occasionally corrects the polydipsia. Antidiuretic substances or thiazides should not be given because these agents diminish water excretion without reducing intake and thus can precipitate water intoxication. For the same reason, if primary polydipsia has not been clearly excluded as a cause of polyuria, any therapeutic trial with antidiuretic drugs should be conducted in the hospital with careful monitoring of fluid balance and plasma osmolality and sodium.

Surgery and radiotherapy play no role in the treatment of diabetes insipidus per se; however, they may be indicated for management of the underlying disease such as hypothalamic craniopharyngioma or dysgerminoma. Even if complete, removal of a tumor rarely if ever corrects the underlying vasopressin deficiency.

The patient should be informed that diabetes insipidus is a relatively benign condition that poses no threat to his or her well-being as long as water intake is unrestricted. The diagnosis should be carried in the wallet or on a MedicAlert bracelet so that the need for special therapy will be recognized promptly in the event of an emergency. The patient should also be informed of manifestations of hyponatremia, such as headache, confusion, and convulsion, and any other side effects of the therapy. If diabetes insipidus is due to some underlying disease, the nature and prognosis of the latter should be explained as well.

FOLLOW-UP

Once the diagnosis is firmly established and appropriate therapy prescribed, the patient should be reevaluated every 3 months during the first year and every 6 months thereafter. At each visit, the patient is questioned about the magnitude of polyuria and polydipsia, and body weight, plasma osmolality, and sodium level are measured. If there is any doubt regarding efficacy of therapy, 24-hour urine volume and osmolality are determined. If the patient is treated with oral drugs, the common side effects should be monitored as well. The patient is instructed to contact the physician if signs of hyponatremia (headache, confusion) develop or if polyuria is not controlled by a preciously effective dose of the medication. A significantly reduced need for antidiuretic therapy also should be carefully evaluated, as it usually signals the development of some serious complication (such as adrenal insufficiency or damage to the thirst mechanism) that masks the effect of the underlying vasopressin deficiency. In patients with a recognized cause for diabetes insipidus, the progress of the underlying disease also should be monitored. In those with idiopathic diabetes insipidus of short duration (<12 months), repeat searches for a cause should be made every 6 to 12 months for 2 to 3 years because they occasionally will uncover a previously undetected and potentially treatable disease such as lung carcinoma, dysgerminoma, neurosarcoid, or histiocytosis.

DISCUSSION

Prevalence and Incidence

All three types of diabetes insipidus are thought to be uncommon; however, the true frequency of their occurrence is unknown because the syndrome often goes unrecognized by physician and patient alike. This is particularly true of patients with the inherited forms of neurogenic diabetes insipidus who usually regard their symptoms as a normal variant even when their polyuria and polydipsia are quite severe.

Related Basic Science

The pathogenesis of diabetes is not completely determined in most cases because histologic and/or biochemical studies of the organs involved are necessarily very limited and few animal models are available; however, a variety of indirect evidence such as the clinical setting, radiologic imaging, hormonal testing, and autopsy studies all indicates that most if not all cases of neurogenic diabetes insipidus are due to destruction of the magnocellular neurohypophyseal neurons that normally make vasopressin. This appears to be true even in the idiopathic forms of the disorder, although the "toxin" in those instances is unknown. In other, secondary forms of neurogenic diabetes insipidus such as those due to head trauma, pituitary hypothalamic tumors, surgery, or neu-

rosarcoid, the neurohypophysis is thought to be interrupted by shearing, cutting, or compression and then to undergo retrograde degeneration similar to other neurons. Whatever the mechanism, more than 75 to 80% of the neurohypophysis must be destroyed before clinically appreciable polyuria begins. Because of this and the fact that many neurohypophyseal neurons terminate above the diaphragm sella, adenomas or other pathology confined to the sella usually do not cause diabetes insipidus. In primary polydipsia, the fundamental cause of the excessive fluid intake is completely unknown, although destruction of some inhibitory input to the thirst mechanism seems likely in the dipsogenic form of the disease. In nephrogenic diabetes insipidus, the mechanism responsible for renal resistance to the antidiuretic effect of vasopressin is understood only in sickle cell disease (interference with formation of the medullary concentration gradient), solute diuresis (washout effect due to increased distal delivery of filtrate), and the inherited forms of the disease (genetic mutations result in dysfunctional vasopressin receptors or water channels in the collecting tubules of the kidney). Gestational diabetes insipidus is precipitated by increased metabolism of endogenous vasopressin by a protease that is made in the normal placenta. In some cases, excessive protease activity alone may be sufficient to cause the syndrome. In most others, however, there is also an underlying subclinical deficiency of vasopressin secretion that is not great enough to cause polyuria at normal rates of hormone metabolism. This deficiency is often, if not always, due to partial destruction of the neurohypophysis by an adenoma or other pituitary hypothalamic disease. There are no demographic characteristics that predispose to its development.

The pathophysiology of diabetes insipidus differs depending on the type. In the neurogenic form, the primary defect is a reduction of vasopressin secretion. The resultant deficiency of plasma vasopressin leads to excretion of large volumes of dilute urine and a loss of body water, which increases plasma osmolality. This stimulates thirst and increased intake of fluid, which prevents further dehydration and stabilizes plasma osmolality around the thirst threshold, usually at the upper limit of normal range. In nephrogenic diabetes insipidus, the pathophysiology is similar, but the pathogenic mechanism is an absent or deficient renal response to vasopressin, which is secreted in normal or even increased amounts. In primary polydipsia, the initial event is the increased fluid intake, which lowers plasma osmolality and suppresses vasopressin. As a consequence, urine osmolality also falls and urine volume increases. The end result is that output rises to match intake and plasma osmolality stabilizes at a reduced level, approximating the osmotic threshold for vasopressin release.

Restriction of water intake substantially alters the clinical picture in all three types of diabetes insipidus. In patients with primary polydipsia, it reverses the underlying dilution of body fluids. Consequently, plasma osmolality, plasma vasopressin, and urine osmolality rise while urine volume falls. As the secretion of vasopressin is normal, the relationship of plasma vasopressin to plasma osmolality is also normal (see Figure 9–42–2). In neurogenic and nephrogenic diabetes insipidus, fluid restriction exacerbates the underlying hypertonic dehydration. If the patient has nearly complete destruction of the neurohypophysis, the resultant increase in the intensity of osmotic stimulation will have little or no effect on plasma vasopressin level, urine osmolality, or urine volume. If, however, destruction of the neurohypophysis is only partial (as it is in most patients), the increase in osmotic stimulation will force the neurohypophyseal remnant to release enough vasopressin to concentrate the urine. In absolute terms, the level of plasma vasopressin achieved may equal that in a patient with primary polydipsia, yet will always be subnormal relative to the concurrent level of plasma osmolality (see Figure 9–42–1). In a patient with nephrogenic diabetes insipidus, the rise in plasma osmolality produced by fluid restriction always stimulates a very large increase in the plasma vasopressin level. If resistance to the antidiuretic effects of the hormone is complete, urine osmolality and volume are little affected. If, however, the resistance is partial (as it is in many patients with acquired and congenital forms of the disorder), plasma vasopressin may reach supraphysiologic levels (see Figure 9–42–2) sufficient to concentrate the urine (see Figure 9–42–3). In absolute terms, the level of urine osmolality achieved may equal that in patients with primary polydipsia or partial neurogenic diabetes insipidus, but is always subnormal relative to the concurrent plasma vasopressin level.

It should be noted that the levels of urine osmolality achieved during acute dehydration and/or vasopressin administration are almost always subnormal in patients with dipsogenic as well as neurogenic or nephrogenic diabetes insipidus (see Figure 9–42–3). This is so because polyuria of any cause reduces maximum concentrating capacity by "washing out" the renal medullary gradient on which it depends. Because of this and other reversible changes in renal sensitivity to vasopressin, dehydration and/or large doses of vasopressin often increase urine osmolality by a similar amount in patients with primary polydipsia, partial neurogenic, and partial nephrogenic diabetes insipidus.

Natural History and Its Modification with Treatment

Morbidity due to diabetes insipidus per se is very low as long as fluid intake is appropriate. Extreme dehydration and death can occur, however, if the patient is unconscious, is unable to obtain fluids, or has an impaired thirst mechanism. In infants and children, particularly those with severe diabetes insipidus (usually nephrogenic), growth impairment, mental retardation, and even death may result if the need for increased fluid intake is not recognized early.

Neurogenic diabetes insipidus is a lifelong disease, an exception being gestational diabetes insipidus or transient polyuria following head trauma or a neurosurgical procedure. Therefore, the reduction in urine output in a patient with established diabetes insipidus usually indicates occurrence of another pathology such as renal insufficiency, loss of thirst, development of anterior pituitary failure, or, rarely, the syndrome of inappropriate antidiuresis due to malignancy. Nephrogenic diabetes insipidus may be reversible if it is due to a drug or a treatable disease. After many years of untreated polyuria of any etiology, patients may develop dilation of the urinary tract and hydronephrosis, resulting in chronic infection and renal failure.

Treatment with DDAVP or the oral agents does not correct the underlying deficiency of vasopressin secretion or action and usually must be continued for the life of the patient. The only recognized exception occurs in a few men with familial neurogenic diabetes insipidus. For an unknown reason, they may have a spontaneous remission of their polyuria in middle age despite a continuing severe deficiency of vasopressin. Otherwise, a spontaneous remission or reduction of polyuria is usually a sign of superimposed adrenal insufficiency or damage to the thirst mechanism.

Prevention

There is no known prevention for familial or idiopathic diabetes insipidus. The secondary forms may be prevented by measures that prevent or treat the underlying diseases (see Table 9–42–1).

Cost Containment

The cost of managing diabetes insipidus can be reduced by avoiding the diagnostic tests that are now known to be unreliable and by using the less expensive, oral forms of therapy. We believe, however, that a thorough search for underlying disease should be made in a patient with newly diagnosed neurogenic diabetes insipidus, particularly if a family history of diabetes insipidus is negative. In our opinion, the benefit of finding a serious disease that is potentially treatable justifies the relatively high cost involved in the workup.

REFERENCES

Bichet DG, Birnbaumer M, Lonergan M, et al. Nature and recurrence of AVPR2 mutations in X-linked nephrogenic diabetes insipidus. Am J Hum Genet 1994;55:278.

Blotner H. Primary idiopathic diabetes insipidus. A systemic disease. Metabolism 1958;7:191.

Durr JA. Diabetes insipidus in pregnancy. Am J Kidney Dis 1987;9:276.

McLeod JF, Kovacs L, Gaskill MB, et al. Familial neurohypophyseal diabetes insipidus associated with a signal peptide mutation. J Clin Endocrinol Metab 1993;77:599A.

Richardson DW, Robinson AG. Desmopressin. Ann Intern Med 1985;103:228.

Robertson GL. Differential diagnosis of polyuria. Annu Rev Med 1988;39:425.

Robertson GL. Dipsogenic diabetes insipidus: A newly recognized syndrome caused by a selective defect in the osmoregulation of thirst. Trans Assoc Am Physicians 1987;C:241.

Robertson GL. Posterior pituitary. In: Felig P, Baxter JD, Broadus AE, Frohman LA, eds. Endocrinology and metabolism. 3rd ed. New York: McGraw-Hill, 1995:385.

Van Lieburg AF, Verdijk MAJ, Knoers VVAM, et al. Patients with autosomal nephrogenic diabetes insipidus homozygous for mutations in the aquaporin 2 water-channel gene. Am J Hum Genet 1994;55:648.

Zerbe RL, Robertson GL. A comparison of plasma vasopressin measurements with a standard indirect test in the differential diagnosis of polyuria. N Engl J Med 1981;305:1539.

CHAPTER 9–43

Syndrome of Inappropriate Antidiuresis

Gary L. Robertson, M.D., László Kovács, M.D., D.Sc., and Tamara Vokes, M.D.

DEFINITION

The syndrome of inappropriate antidiuresis is characterized by hyponatremia and impaired urinary dilution in the absence of renal insufficiency, adrenal insufficiency, hypovolemia, hypotension, or any other nonosmotic stimulus for vasopressin release.

ETIOLOGY

The syndrome results from an impaired ability to dilute the urine and develop a water diuresis in the presence of an inappropriately high rate of water intake. Failure to dilute the urine is usually due to impaired osmotic inhibition of vasopressin secretion, but, in a few cases, it may also result from some as yet undefined vasopressin-independent mechanism. Inadequate suppression of vasopressin secretion can result from a large number of different causes including ectopic production by a malignancy and eutopic production induced by various acute or chronic diseases of brain or lung or the administration of various drugs (Table 9–43–1).

CRITERIA FOR DIAGNOSIS

Suggestive

The syndrome of inappropriate antidiuresis should be suspected in any patient who develops hyponatremia in the absence of hyperglycemia or overt historical or physical evidence of volume depletion, renal insufficiency, congestive failure or liver disease.

Definitive

The diagnosis can be confirmed by demonstrating that the hyponatremia is associated with a proportionate reduction in plasma osmolality and impaired urinary dilution (urine osmolality greater than 100 mosm/kg) in the absence of azotemia, hypokalemia, hyperuricemia, or hemoconcentration.

CLINICAL MANIFESTATIONS

Subjective

Symptoms may or may not be present. When present, they are usually attributable to hyponatremia per se. They include weakness, anorexia,

TABLE 9–43–1. DISORDERS ASSOCIATED WITH THE SYNDROME OF INAPPROPRIATE ANTIDIURESIS

Malignant Tumors	**Diseases of the lung**
Carcinoma of the lung	Pneumonia
Carcinoma of the duodenum	Tuberculosis
Carcinoma of the pancreas	Cavitation
Thymoma	Empyema
Mesothelioma	Cystic fibrosis
Carcinoma of the bladder	Pneumothorax
Carcinoma of the ureter	Asthma
Prostatic carcinoma	Positive pressure breathing
Lymphoma	**Drugs**
Ewing's sarcoma	Vasopressin and DDAVP
Disorders of the central nervous system	Oxytocin
Meningitis	Vincristine, vinblastine
Encephalitis	Chlorpropamide
Brain abscess	Thiazide diuretics
Guillain–Barré syndrome	Phenothiazines
Head trauma	Monoamine oxidase inhibitors
Subarachnoid hemorrhage	Tricyclic antidepressants
Cerebrovascular accident	Carbamazepine
Cavernous sinus thrombosis	Clofibrate
Brain tumors	Nicotine
Olfactory neuroblastoma	"Idiopathic"
Cerebellar and cerebral atrophy	
Hypoplasia of corpus callosum	
Hydrocephalus	
Neonatal hypoxia	
Multiple sclerosis	
Delirium tremens	
Wernicke's encephalopathy	
Shy–Drager syndrome	
Acute intermittent porphyria	
Rocky Mountain spotted fever	
Tetanus	
Acute psychosis	

DDAVP, 1-deamino-8-D-arginine-vasopressin.
Source: Adapted from Vokes T, Robertson GL. Clinical effects of altered vasopressin secretion. In: Muller EE, McLeod RM, Frohman LA, eds. Neuroendocrine perspectives, vol. 4. Amsterdam: Elsevier Science, 1985:1. Reproduced with permission from the publisher and author.

nausea with or without vomiting, headaches, irritability, muscle cramps, lethargy, and confusion. Patients may or may not give a history of increased fluid intake and weight gain. The severity of symptoms is variable and depends on the degree of hyponatremia, the rate of its development, and the age of the patient. The symptoms of underlying disease may be present as well.

Family history is absent. Occupational and environmental associations may be present if the syndrome is caused by certain malignant or infectious diseases (see Table 9–43–1).

Objective

Physical Examination

Physical signs may or may not be present. If they are, neurologic signs of hyponatremia predominate. These include altered mental status (lethargy, confusion), pathologic reflexes, extrapyramidal signs, pseudobublar palsy, Cheyne–Stokes respirations, and, in severe cases, convulsion and coma. By definition, patients with this syndrome do not have edema or signs of intravascular volume depletion such as tachycardia and orthostatic hypotension; however, a coincidental finding of localized edema, such as is seen in inflammation or in obstruction of lymphatic or venous drainage, does not exclude the diagnosis of the syndrome of inappropriate antidiuresis.

Routine Laboratory Abnormalities

Routine laboratory tests reveal hyponatremia (sodium usually < 130 mEq/L), low or low-normal serum concentrations of urea and uric acid, and a urine specific gravity above 1002 or osmolality above 100 mosm/kg. (Exceptions to the latter are described below in the Basic

Science section.) Usually, serum uric acid is low and urinary sodium excretion is increased.

PLANS

Diagnostic

See Criteria for Diagnosis.

Differential Diagnosis

In evaluating a patient with hyponatremia, the first step is to rule out factitious causes such as hyperlipidemia, hyperproteinemia, and hyperglycemia. The best way is to measure plasma osmolality, as true hyponatremia is invariably associated with hyposmolemia (plasma osmolality < 270 mosm/kg), whereas factitious hyponatremia is not.

Diagnostic Options and Recommended Approach

If the hyponatremia is associated with hyposmolality of body fluids, urine osmolality should be measured to verify that it is less than maximally dilute (i.e., > 100 mosm/kg). This measurement should also be made while the patient is still hyponatremic. Concentration of the urine (i.e., an osmolality > 300 mosm/kg) is *not* necessary for the diagnosis, as values above 100 mosm/kg markedly reduce the rate of urine production and are clearly inappropriate in the presence of hyponatremia. Similarly, a urine osmolality below 100 mosm/kg does not exclude the diagnosis because inappropriate secretion of vasopressin is often due to a reduction in the threshold or "set" of the osmoregulatory mechanism (see below). This variant of the syndrome can be recognized by repeating the measurement of urine osmolality during therapeutic fluid restriction and finding that it rises above 100 mosm/kg before plasma osmolality and sodium concentration return to the normal range.

The next step is to exclude conditions in which hyponatremia is due to a decreased effective blood volume, decreased total blood volume, or hypotension. This can be done by a careful physical examination and a few simple laboratory tests. A decrease in effective blood volume is associated with conditions such as congestive heart failure, cirrhosis, and nephrotic syndrome and is characterized by the presence of generalized edema. Decreased total blood volume is usually associated with a history of fluid-depleting factors such as nausea, vomiting, diarrhea, and diuretic abuse and may be recognized by signs of dehydration such as orthostatic hypotension, tachycardia, and prerenal azotemia. The syndrome of inappropriate antidiuresis is characterized by the absence of symptoms and signs of decreased effective or total blood volume. If volume status is doubtful, plasma renin activity should be measured, as it is more sensitive to volume depletion than is clinical examination. Measurement of the urinary sodium level also may be helpful, as it is characteristically high (>20 mEq/d) in this syndrome and low (<20 mEq/d) in edematous and hypovolemic hyponatremia. An exception to the latter rule is hypovolemic hyponatremia due to diuretic (ab)use or salt-losing nephropathies, in which the urinary sodium level may be high, and the recovery phase of the syndrome of inappropriate antidiuresis hormone secretion, where the urinary sodium level is usually low (see below). In addition, the serum cortisol level should be measured in an early morning sample, as adrenal insufficiency, particularly if it is secondary to hypothalamic or pituitary disease, may not be associated with hyperkalemia or signs of volume depletion. If the morning cortisol level is low, further evaluation of adrenal function is indicated (see Chapter 9–11). The serum thyroxine level and a free thyroxine index should be determined as well because hypothyroidism, if severe, can be associated with hyponatremia.

Measurement of the plasma vasopressin level is of no help in differential diagnosis, as it is usually elevated to the same extent in this syndrome as in other forms of hyponatremia. Likewise, a water-loading test is not indicated in a patient who currently has hyponatremia. It may, however, be useful in determining the need for continuous treatment in patients with chronic syndrome of inappropriate antidiuresis in whom sodium has been normalized by fluid restriction or drug therapy. The test is performed by giving 20 mL/kg tap water orally over 20 minutes and measuring the plasma sodium level as well as plasma and urine osmolality every 30 minutes for 4 hours. If the patient responds normally—that is, excretes at least 80% of ingested water in 4 hours, dilutes urine to below 100 mosm/kg, and remains eunatremic—the syndrome is no longer present.

In a patient who has this syndrome without an obvious cause, it is important to search for an underlying potentially treatable disease, particularly malignancy. The minimal workup should include routine chemistry panels, total and differential blood count, roentgenogram of the chest, and computed tomography or magnetic resonance imaging of the brain.

Therapeutic

A patient with significant hyponatremia should be hospitalized until the condition is corrected. In patients with the syndrome of inappropriate antidiuresis, the most rational therapy would be to correct the underlying abnormality in vasopressin secretion. If present, drugs known to cause the syndrome should be stopped. When the syndrome is associated with infection, antimicrobial treatment of lung abscess, pneumonia, or tuberculosis usually results in gradual clearing of the disorder. In a patient with the syndrome due to malignancy, surgical resection, irradiation, or chemotherapy may alleviate hyponatremia even if the underlying disease is only partially treated. In many patients, particularly those with strokes, the syndrome remits spontaneously in 7 to 14 days.

In many patients, however, the underlying defect in vasopressin secretion cannot be remedied, and therapy must be directed at reducing the excess of body water that is responsible for the hyponatremia. In a patient with chronic and/or asymptomatic hyponatremia, the therapy of choice is to restrict water intake. To be effective, the total intake of water must be at least 500 mL per day less than the total urinary and insensible loss. As the amount of water contained in food usually approximates insensible loss, discretionary intake of fluids should be kept at least 500 mL per day below urine output.

In practice, satisfactory fluid restriction is difficult, if not impossible to achieve in many patients because they also have inappropriate thirst. Moreover, even when fluid restriction is effective, the improvement in plasma sodium is slow (about 2–3 mEq/L/d) unless the defect in urinary free water excretion is minimal or improves spontaneously. Therefore, if the hyponatremia is severe and/or symptomatic, more rapid treatment is usually indicated. This is best achieved by infusing hypertonic (3%) saline at a rate of 0.05 to 0.1 mL/kg per minute. At this rate, plasma sodium concentration rises by about 1–2% per hour and the infusion should be continued only until it reaches asymptomatic levels (usually around 125 mEq/L). This approach appears to be quite safe in patients with this syndrome. A few patients, however, have developed central pontine myelinolysis, a rare and often fatal neurologic disorder characterized by quadriparesis, dysphagia, and dysarthria. It is still unclear whether this complication is due to the disease per se or to raising the plasma sodium level too far or too fast.

It should be noted that some therapeutic measures described for this syndrome may be ineffective or even harmful in other forms of hyponatremia. Thus, in edematous states, fluid restriction is appropriate, but the administration of hypertonic saline may be dangerous because it only aggravates sodium retention and/or cardiac overload. In contrast, in patients with hypovolemic hyponatremia, the administration of hypertonic saline may be appropriate, whereas fluid restriction is clearly contraindicated.

If the syndrome persists longer than 2 weeks, therapeutic measures other than fluid restriction with or without hypertonic saline infusion may be necessary. In this situation, drugs that interfere with the antidiuretic effect of vasopressin are most often useful. Among these, the most effective is the tetracycline derivative demeclocycline (Declomycin). When given in a dose of 0.9 to 1.2 g per day, it causes reversible nephrogenic diabetes insipidus in almost all patients. The side effects include reversible elevation in blood urea nitrogen level and photosensitivity. Other drugs reported as successful in interfering with vasopressin release or action include diphenylhydantoin (Dilantin), narcotic antagonists, and lithium carbonate; however, because they are effective less consistently and/or are more toxic, these drugs are used rarely, if at all, for treatment of the syndrome of inappropriate antidiuresis. Selective antidiuretic antagonists of vasopressin have been developed, but their safety and efficacy in treating this syndrome and other forms of hyponatremia in humans have not been determined.

Other measures that can be useful in treating the chronic form of the syndrome include fludrocortisone, 0.1 to 0.4 mg twice a day, with or without salt tablets.

Patients with the chronic form of this syndrome should be taught to monitor their water balance and adjust fluid intake accordingly. The simplest and most effective method is to assign a target weight corresponding to the normonatremic state and instruct the patient to weigh daily and reduce fluid intake by a specified amount (e.g., 250 mL or one 8-oz glass) for every pound in excess of the target. In addition, the patient should be familiarized with various symptoms of hyponatremia and instructed to contact the physician promptly if they occur. The nature and prognosis of the underlying disease should be explained as well.

FOLLOW-UP

If treated on an ambulatory basis, a patient with this syndrome should be seen initially every 1 to 2 weeks. At each visit, weight, plasma electrolytes, and plasma osmolality should be assessed to determine the efficacy of treatment. Once the proper regimen is established, the patient can be seen monthly or less often until the disorder remits.

The patient should be instructed to contact the physician if he or she develops symptoms of hyponatremia. In addition, patients should be advised to monitor their weight daily and notify the physician if it increases by more than 1 to 2% as the latter usually indicates fluid retention and development of hyponatremia.

Because many patients with this syndrome recover spontaneously, it is important to evaluate periodically the need for continued therapy. This is best done by stopping the current regimen and performing a water-loading test (see above). A normal response to water loading indicates that the syndrome is no longer present and that the therapy may be discontinued.

DISCUSSION

Prevalence and Incidence

Hyponatremia is a relatively common disorder. Its prevalence in hospitalized patients is about 2.5%, and approximately a third of these have the syndrome of inappropriate antidiuresis.

Related Basic Science

In healthy people, even extremely high rates of fluid intake do not produce hyponatremia because suppression of vasopressin secretion results in maximal urinary dilution and a marked increase in urinary free water excretion that effectively prevents more than a slight increase in total body water. Similarly, the administration of maximum doses of antidiuretic hormone alone also does not produce significant hyponatremia because the initial, slight fall in plasma osmolality and sodium suppresses thirst and inhibits water intake to exactly counterbalance the fall in urine output. It follows, therefore, that hyponatremia develops only if *both* fluid intake and urinary concentration are inadequately suppressed.

The pathogenesis of the excessive fluid intake and impaired free water excretion varies depending on the type of hyponatremia and other factors peculiar to individual patients. In the edematous and hypovolemic forms, vasopressin secretion is thought to be stimulated by a marked reduction in "effective" or total blood volume and water intake may be stimulated by a similar mechanism. Urinary free water excretion is further reduced by increased reabsorption of glomerular filtrate in proximal tubules. In contrast, an identifiable osmotic or nonosmotic stimulus to thirst or vasopressin secretion is usually lacking in the syndrome of inappropriate antidiuresis and distal delivery of filtrate is increased. In some cases, excessive fluid intake, impaired urine dilution, or both abnormalities are iatrogenic. In others, however, thirst is increased inappropriately and vasopressin is produced endogenously either by a tumor or by the neurohypophysis as a result of some as yet undetermined aberrant stimulus or defect in secretory control.

Consistent with the heterogeneity of the pathogenesis, the pattern of inappropriate vasopressin secretion in this syndrome may assume one of several forms (Figure 9–43–1). In type a, which is encountered in

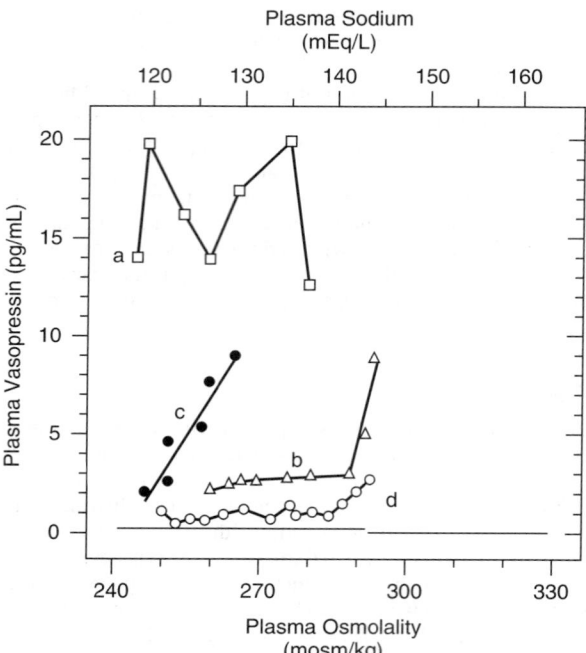

Figure 9–43–1. Relationship of plasma vasopressin level to osmolality during hypertonic saline infusion in four different patients with the clinical syndrome of inappropriate antidiuresis. *(Modified from Robertson GL. Thirst and vasopressin function in normal and disordered states of water balance. J Lab Clin Med 1983;101:351. Reproduced with permission from the publisher and author.)*

about 25% of patients, there are large and erratic fluctuations in vasopressin level unrelated to changes in plasma osmolality or sodium levels. This type of defect is probably due to total loss of osmoregulation or intermittent stimulation by some unrecognized nonosmotic influence. In another 25%, exemplified by line b in Figure 9–43–1, plasma vasopressin remains fixed at an inappropriately high level while plasma osmolality and sodium levels are low. When the latter are raised to or above the normal range, however, vasopressin level rises appropriately and in close correlation with the rise in plasma osmolality and sodium levels. The pattern is probably caused by a nonsuppressible leak of vasopressin in the face of otherwise normal osmoregulatory function. The type c defect, also known as reset osmostat, is the most common, occurring in at least 35% of all patients. It is characterized by plasma vasopressin levels that rise and fall in close correlation with changes in plasma osmolality and sodium levels; however, the level at which vasopressin begins to be secreted (osmotic threshold for vasopressin release) is significantly below normal. In the type d defect, which is considerably less common than the other three, vasopressin secretion is normal but urine osmolality remains inappropriately elevated in the face of hyponatremia and in the absence of detectable vasopressin. In these patients, urinary concentration may be due to a yet unidentified antidiuretic substance or to increased renal sensitivity to subthreshold levels of vasopressin. There is no apparent association between the type of osmoregulatory defect and the underlying cause of this syndrome, as all four patterns, including reset osmostat, have been described in association with a variety of malignant and nonmalignant diseases.

The pathophysiology of hyponatremia in the syndrome of inappropriate antidiuresis is exemplified by the changes that occur when vasopressin is administered to healthy volunteers. If water intake is normal—1 to 2 L per day—producing a fixed antidiuresis has little or no effect on total body water or plasma sodium levels. If, however, fluid intake rises even slightly, a commensurate rise in output does not occur because plasma vasopressin and urine osmolality levels do not fall in response to the fall in plasma sodium level. Consequently, a portion of ingested water is retained and, if it is continued for several days, sufficient water may accumulate to cause a progressive expansion of body fluids and hyponatremia. When body fluids are expanded by more than 10%, the urinary excretion of sodium increases apparently because of

suppression of renin–angiotensin–aldosterone, increased atrial natriuretic peptide, and decreased sodium reabsorption in the proximal tubule. This natriuresis partially corrects the hypervolemia and prevents occurrence of edema but further aggravates hyponatremia. In many subjects, however, water retention and urinary sodium loss cannot account fully for the magnitude of the fall in plasma sodium level. Hence other factors such as sequestration of sodium and inactivation of intracellular solute may contribute to the development of hyponatremia.

It should be noted that clinical manifestations in this syndrome depend primarily on the rate of water intake. For example, vasopressin hypersecretion and antidiuresis will not result in hyponatremia unless accompanied by increased fluid intake. Similarly, the magnitude of hyponatremia depends primarily on the rate of water intake rather than on the level of antidiuresis or the extent of vasopressin hypersecretion. In this respect, the role of vasopressin is different from that of many other hormones, such as adrenocorticotropic hormone and parathyroid hormone, where hypersecretion per se results in a clinical syndrome and determines the severity of its manifestations.

The rate of water intake also influences other features of this syndrome, such as natriuresis. The latter is a characteristic finding of the developmental phase of hyponatremia, while body fluids are expanding. If, however, water intake is curtailed for any reason, the rate of urinary sodium excretion falls rapidly to very low levels well before the plasma sodium level returns to normal. For this reason, finding a low urinary sodium level does not exclude this syndrome as a cause of hyponatremia.

The clinical manifestations of the syndrome of inappropriate antidiuresis can also be influenced by the type of defect in vasopressin secretion. In patients in whom the level of antidiuresis is more or less fixed (as in types a, b, and d above), the pathophysiology is probably very similar to that induced experimentally by administering vasopressin to normal subjects (see above). Patients with reset osmostat (type c defect), however, exhibit one important pathophysiologic difference: their plasma vasopressin level and urinary concentration can be maximally suppressed, albeit at levels of plasma osmolality and sodium considerably below normal. The clinical consequences of this difference are twofold. First, an underlying abnormality in vasopressin secretion cannot be excluded by demonstrating that plasma vasopressin and/or urine osmolality levels are less than 0.5 pg/mL and/or 100 mosm/kg, respectively. In such a case, it is also necessary to determine whether plasma vasopressin and/or urine osmolality levels begin to rise before plasma osmolality and/or sodium levels reach the normal range. Second, the severity of the hyponatremia in patients with reset osmostat is limited even if their fluid intake increases or remains abnormally high.

Natural History and Its Modification with Treatment

In most patients, the course of this syndrome follows that of the underlying disease. For unknown reasons, however, the syndrome sometimes improves even if the causative disorder deteriorates or improves only partially. This dissociation is particularly evident in patients with strokes and other brain injuries.

Prevention

Some cases of this syndrome may be prevented by avoiding the drugs or preventing and treating the diseases that have been associated with the disorder (see Table 9–43–1). In hospitalized patients, particularly those recovering from recent surgery and anesthesia, hyponatremia may be prevented by avoiding excessive administration of hypotonic intravenous solutions.

Cost Containment

To minimize costs, the tests used to differentiate this syndrome from other forms of hyponatremia should be limited to clinical examination and routine laboratory tests, supplemented only when necessary by more expensive measurements such as plasma renin activity. A patient who presents with this syndrome without an obvious cause also deserves a careful search for underlying disease, particularly malignancy, because this syndrome may be the first manifestation of a serious but potentially treatable disease.

REFERENCES

Berl T. Treating hyponatremia. Kidney Int 1990;37:1006.

Cheng J-C, Zikos D, Skopicki HA, et al. Long-term neurologic outcome in psychogenic water drinkers with severe symptomatic hyponatremia: The effect of rapid correction. Am J Med 1990;88:561.

Forrest JN Jr, Cox M, Hong C, et al. Superiority of demeclocycline over lithium in the treatment of chronic syndrome of inappropriate secretion of antidiuretic hormone. N Engl J Med 1978;298:173.

Kamoi K, Ebe T, Kobayashi O, et al. Atrial natriuretic peptide in patients with the syndrome of inappropriate antidiuretic hormone secretion and with diabetes insipidus. J Clin Endocrinol Metab 1990;70:1385.

Kovacs L, Robertson GL. Syndrome of inappropriate antidiuresis. In: Veldhuis J, ed. Endocrinology and Metabolism Clinics of North America: Neuroendocrine Issue. Philadelphia: Saunders, 1992:859.

Oelkers W. Hyponatremia and inappropriate secretion of vasopressin (antidiuretic hormone) in patients with hypopituitarism. N Engl J Med 1989;321:492.

Robertson GL, Berl T. Water metabolism. In: Brenner BM, Rector FC, eds. The kidney. 5th ed. Philadelphia: Saunders, 1995.

CHAPTER 9–44

Short Stature and Delayed Puberty

John S. Parks, M.D., Ph.D.

DEFINITION

Short stature is defined as a height below the range appropriate for a child's or adolescent's age, gender, and genetic background. Delayed puberty denotes an absence of breast development in girls by age 13 or a lack of testicular enlargement in boys by age 14.

ETIOLOGY

Birth weight and length do not predict growth during childhood or adult stature. Instead, children tend to resemble their parents in timing and extent of growth, with 70% of the variance in stature during childhood being attributable to parental heights. Children usually enter their genetically determined growth channels between the ages of 2 and 3 years. With good health and adequate nutrition, they stay in these channels until puberty. Early maturers tend to become relatively short adults, whereas late maturers tend to become relatively tall. Most short or tall children are growing normally for their genetic backgrounds.

Significant short stature or growth arrest may reflect malnutrition, underlying chronic illness (e.g., anemia, malabsorption, pulmonary disease, cystic fibrosis, cyanotic or high-output congenital heart disease, renal failure, inflammatory diseases); genetic limitations in the ability to respond to normal growth signals (e.g., achondroplasia, Turner syndrome); or endocrine disease. Acquired hypothyroidism, growth hormone deficiency, adrenal insufficiency, and Cushing syndrome are in the latter category. Variants of normal growth include genetic short stature and constitutional delay of growth and pubertal development.

CRITERIA FOR DIAGNOSIS
Suggestive

The basic tools for evaluation of growth are a device for measuring standing height, a tape measure, a scale, and a set of age- and gender-appropriate National Center for Health Statistics (NCHS) growth charts. Two-year to maturity charts depict standing height, weight, and weight for stature. Serial measurements add an important dimension to one-time measurements in that they indicate patterns of growth.

In evaluating growth, all available measurements are plotted to address the following questions:

- How tall is the child compared to other children of the same age and gender?
- How tall is the child compared to the parents?
- How did the child arrive at his or her current height?
- Is the child's pubertal status appropriate for age?

Criteria for beginning to think that there is a problem with growth or puberty follow:

- Height between the 5th and 1st percentiles for age and gender.
- Height between one and three channels (isopliths) below the sex-adjusted midparental height percentile. An example would be a child at the 5th percentile whose parents are at the 50th percentile.
- Crossing of one height percentile channel after 2 years of age. An example would be crossing from the 50th to below the 25th percentile.
- Pubertal delay of 1 to 2 years compared with the average.

Definitive

The following patterns should be considered abnormal and demand investigation:

- Height below the 1st percentile. There is a reasonable chance of detecting a disease process at this extreme degree of short stature. There is a much lower probability of a treatable disease process in children between the 5th and 1st percentiles.
- Height more than three channels (isopliths) below the midparental channel. For example, if both parents are in the 90th percentile for height, there is a reasonable chance that their 10th-percentile son is not meeting his genetic potential for growth.
- Crossing of two or more channels after 2 years of age. The large baby of short parents will usually grow at a "subnormal" rate in infancy while seeking his or her genetically determined growth channel. Deviations of this magnitude after age 2 years usually indicate a disease process.
- Absence of breast development in girls by age 13 or lack of testicular enlargement in boys by age 14.

CLINICAL MANIFESTATIONS
Subjective

The family history is important in sorting out causes of short stature and delayed puberty. Moderate shortness in one or both parents suggests polygenic inheritance of short stature; however, extreme or disproportionate shortness in one parent may indicate inheritance of a dominant, single-gene disorder such as hypochondroplasia, vitamin D-resistant rickets, or growth hormone deficiency. Extreme shortness in a sibling may provide a clue to recessive inheritance of growth hormone deficiency. In children with constitutional delay of growth and pubertal development, parents, aunts, and uncles may have a history of late puberty and late completion of growth. Questioning of the mother about age at menarche and the father about significant growth beyond age 18 is helpful in this regard. Children with Kallmann syndrome of anosmia and central hypogonadism often have first-degree relatives with one or both findings.

A 24-hour dietary history can be instructive, particularly with regard to qualitative abnormalities of feeding. The child who steals food from siblings' plates, eats from the dog's bowl, or gorges and vomits may be expressing the syndrome of psychosocial dwarfism. Low food intake and significant weight loss may reflect chronic illness, anorexia nervosa, or anorexia athletica. The last term denotes a condition in which low caloric intake, strenuous physical activity, and concern about obesity combine to limit growth. It is seen in ballet dancers, gymnasts, and wrestlers, among others. Inflammatory bowel disease is a very important cause of growth failure during late childhood or adolescence. Weight loss and growth arrest tend to precede specific bowel symptoms by many years. Diminished food intake and early satiety tend to precede abdominal pain. Constipation is a symptom of hypothyroidism, but loose, frequent, or bulky bowel movements are insensitive features of malabsorption. Easy fatigability can be a sign of chronic illness, adrenal insufficiency, or hypothyroidism. The hypothyroid child tends to restrict extracurricular activities while maintaining good grades in school Craniopharyngioma is the most common cause of acquired hypopituitarism in childhood. Children with this disorder tend to present with visual loss and headache, lethargy, or other signs of increased intracranial pressure rather than with specific hormonal complaints.

Objective
Physical Examination

Accurate height and weight measurements are critically important. Height should be plotted versus age, and height percentile should be estimated. Is the child in the 50th or the 5th percentile of height for age? If the child is below the 5th percentile, then calculate how far below, remembering that the 1st percentile is about 2 in. below the 5th. Plot parents' heights in percentile channels at the right of the chart. When possible, measure the parents because the average adult "rounds up" his or her height by 1.5 in. Add 5 in. to put a mother on the male chart or subtract 5 in. to put a father on the female chart. This adjustment reflects the mean difference in adult heights between men and women. Women, on average, experience 2 fewer years of childhood growth at a rate of 2.5 in. per year and this accounts for the 5-in. difference in adult height. Estimate the midpoint between the parents' height percentiles and compare this with the child's height percentile. Plot past measurements to distinguish between slow but steady growth and growth arrest.

Height and weight should be compared by plotting weight for stature on the back of the growth chart. These percentile plots are valid only for prepubertal children. Special concern should be raised by shortness together with weight for stature above the 95th or below the 5th percentiles. The former might indicate hypothyroidism or the rare case of Cushing syndrome, whereas the latter could reflect malnutrition or systemic illness.

Determine whether the pubertal stage is appropriate for chronologic age. Examine breasts, pubic hair, and genitalia and record the Tanner stage. Be alert to shortness with no signs of puberty by age 13 in girls or by age 14 in boys. Either breast budding or pubic hair appears at an average of 11 years of age in girls, whereas subtle enlargement of the testes appears at an average of 11 years in boys. The 13- and 14-year figures allow for two standard deviations of 1 year. In genetic short stature, pubertal development is appropriate for chronologic age. These children are short for age, but they do not appear young for age. Absence of age-appropriate pubertal development in a girl, together with very mildly dysmorphic features, may reflect Turner syndrome. Children with hypopituitarism or with constitutional delay of growth tend to look young for age during childhood and fail to enter puberty at a normal age. In addition, the boy with hypopituitarism may have an abnormally small penis measuring less than 4 cm in stretched length. Hypothyroidism may present with premature puberty without an appropriate pubertal growth spurt.

Additional body measurements provide useful information. Measurement and plotting of head circumference are necessary to detect either microcephaly or hydrocephalus as contributors to growth disturbance. Arm span is normally a bit less than height before age 8 and a bit more thereafter. It is conveniently plotted on height charts. Measurement of span is very useful for tracking growth in children with abnormalities of the lower extremities, such as, for example, in children with spina bifida. The lower body segment, measured from the top of the symphysis pubis to the floor, is normally less than the upper segment through age 8 and more than the upper segment thereafter. Retention of a younger child's body proportions occurs in acquired hypothyroidism and in the many varieties of short-limbed short stature.

Routine Laboratory Abnormalities

Many of the disorders responsible for growth impairment are obvious during a careful history and physical examination. In this event, laboratory studies are ordered to test clinical hypotheses. In other cases, the cause of growth restriction is not obvious, and certain screening tests are indicated.

Appropriate screening studies include a complete blood count, an erythrocyte sedimentation rate, urinalysis, and serum chemistries. Occult anemia is detected as a low hemoglobin level and hematocrit and may reflect deficient iron intake, chronic blood loss, hemolysis associated with sickle cell disease or thalassemia, renal failure, inflammatory bowel disease, or celiac disease. An elevated erythrocyte sedimentation rate can provide a clue to regional enteritis, ulcerative colitis, rheumatoid arthritis, or other inflammatory disease as a cause of growth arrest. The urinalysis should be done on a second-voided morning specimen to assess urinary concentrating ability, which is impaired in renal failure, hypercalcemia, and diabetes insipidus. Glycosuria may reflect a renal tubular defect or indicate diabetes mellitus. The presentation of insulin-dependent diabetes mellitus usually includes unintentional weight loss of duration too short to produce detectable arrest of linear growth. Elevated blood urea nitrogen and creatinine levels can prompt a diagnosis of occult renal failure. Serum carbon dioxide content tends to be low in renal tubular acidosis, but most instances of low carbon dioxide content tend to be laboratory artifacts due to prolonged storage of samples before assay. Both low and high serum calcium levels should be investigated as clues to specific diseases impairing growth. The serum inorganic phosphorus level is higher in children than in adults, and values below 4 mg/dL can reflect either vitamin D-deficient or vitamin D-resistant rickets. Children have moderately elevated lactate dehydrogenase and alkaline phosphatase levels compared with adults, and these values do not indicate disease. A low serum albumin level can reflect malnutrition or renal or intestinal protein loss.

PLANS
Diagnostic
Differential Diagnosis

Most children with mildly short stature are between the 5th and 1st percentiles for height, and few have classic growth hormone deficiency or any other specific disorder of growth. The majority of these children have either constitutional delay or genetic short stature. The operational distinction is that those with constitutional delay have a bone age 2 or more years behind chronologic age. They have a greater predicted mature height than genetic short stature children with similar heights and no delay in bone age. The group is heterogeneous with respect to family history, growth rate, extent of delay, and final height attainment. Use of the Greulich and Pyle bone age method and the Bayley tables for height prediction overestimates attained adult height by greater than 2 in. in more than 50% of such children.

Diagnostic Options

In children less than the 1st percentile for height, history and physical examination, together with routine laboratory tests, will identify many of the specific syndromes and chronic diseases that can cause growth failure or delayed puberty. Thyroid function studies should be obtained in any child or adolescent with otherwise unexplained short stature. Growth arrest is the cardinal sign of hypothyroidism in children and may precede the development of myxedematous facies by several years. The serum thyroxine level is low and the serum thyroid-stimulating hormone level is high in primary hypothyroidism. Thyrotropin-releasing hormone stimulation of thyroid-stimulating hormone is indicated if the thyroxine level is low and the thyroid-stimulating hormone level is normal. This test can detect both compensated primary hypothyroidism and central hypothyroidism. An upper gastrointestinal series with small bowel follow-through and/or barium enema are probably indicated to search for inflammatory bowel disease in any slender child with diminished food intake and unexplained interruption of growth, particularly in the presence of an elevated erythrocyte sedimentation rate. Girls below the first percentile in height should have a buccal smear and/or lymphocyte karyotype done to establish or exclude the diagnosis of Turner's syndrome. Serum luteinizing hormone and follicle-stimulating hormone levels are elevated in Turner syndrome and in other cases of primary hypogonadism. Low gonadotropin levels do not discriminate between delayed puberty and permanent, secondary, or tertiary hypogonadism.

Recommended Approach

A bone age estimate is useful to determine whether the child is destined to be a late maturer and has a greater potential for adult stature than is indicated by the present height channel. A greater than 2-year delay in bone age and normal results in the other tests suggest a need for additional studies, which may include insulin-like growth factor I (IGF-I) levels and tests of growth hormone reserve.

The diagnosis of growth hormone deficiency is usually suspected in one of three clinical settings: (1) hypoglycemia, micropenis, and prolonged jaundice in a newborn; (2) subnormal height velocity and height far below the first percentile in an older child; (3) a decline in height velocity prior to or following treatment of an intracerebral mass lesion.

Potential thyroid-stimulating hormone, adrenocorticotropic hormone, and antidiuretic hormone deficiency as parts of multiple pituitary hormone deficiency should be evaluated (see Chapter 9–2) and treated before definitive testing of growth hormone reserve. Hormone deficiencies presenting in early infancy or following surgical treatment of craniopharyngioma are usually multiple. In contrast, hypothalamic irradiation on the order of 5000 rad usually affects only the growth hormone axis. Instances of isolated growth hormone deficiency and multiple pituitary hormone deficiency are roughly equal in the other settings.

Classic growth hormone deficiency is diagnosed through failure to raise growth hormone levels above 7 μg/L in response to two or more pharmacologic tests of growth hormone reserve. The clonidine stimulation test is a useful test that poses little risk or discomfort to the child. Several different dosage schedules have been proposed for the clonidine test. A single oral dose of 0.075 mg/m^2 of body surface area with sampling at 0, 30, and 60 minutes usually provokes adequate growth hormone release without causing hypotension, but patients should lie in bed during the test. Other tests that are reasonably safe to do on an outpatient basis include arginine infusion and L-dopa administration.

Therapeutic

Therapeutic Options

Treatment of nonendocrine diseases causing growth failure depends on the specific diagnosis. Hypothyroidism requires replacement with L-thyroxine in doses sufficient to maintain a normal serum thyroxine level and suppress thyroid-stimulating hormone. Human growth hormone injections provide specific treatment for growth hormone deficiency and may eventually find a place in management of other forms of short stature.

Recommended Approach

Biosynthetic human growth hormone has been available in the United States since 1985. The maximum recommended dose is 0.3 mg/kg/wk, divided into six or seven subcutaneous injections. This dosage level probably represents twice the normal daily production of growth hormone. Children with complete deficiency and a greater sensitivity to growth hormone grow nearly as well at doses on the order of 0.15 mg/kg/wk. Growth rates typically increase to 8 to 12 cm per year during the first year and decline in subsequent years. If there is a favorable growth response, treatment should be continued through puberty and until the growth rate slows to less than 2.5 cm per year.

Several important side effects of growth hormone treatment have been described. Most children show an early and temporary increase in total body water. Clinically evident edema is rare. Induction of glucose intolerance is also rare. Like other children in a rapid phase of growth, children receiving growth hormone treatment are at risk for development of slipped capital femoral epiphysis. Scoliosis can progress rapidly during treatment. Headaches can reflect increased intracranial pressure and pseudotumor cerebri. Reports from Japan of a two- to fourfold increase in the risk of leukemia among children treated with

growth hormone have not been confirmed in the United States or Europe.

In managing constitutional delay patients (where a need for treatment is often mandated by psychosocial problems), it is wisest to wait until a chronologic age of 14 and a bone age of 11 is attained and then use repository intramuscular testosterone (testosterone enanthate 50–100 mg/mo) in 3- or 4-month treatment cycles to achieve a narrowing of the gap in pubertal development.

Delayed or absent puberty can be present without short stature. The therapeutic approach depends on the precise diagnosis and on the time at which this diagnosis is made. Children known to have a condition (e.g., anorchia, gonadal failure with high luteinizing hormone and follicle-stimulating hormone, or Kallmann syndrome) that precludes spontaneous pubertal development should be helped through puberty at an appropriate chronologic age and not allowed to fall behind their peers. In boys, it is appropriate to begin monthly intramuscular testosterone injections in a dose of 25 to 50 mg at age 12 and advance to an adult maintenance dose of 200 mg every 2 weeks by age 18. In girls, one can begin hormone replacement at age 11 with oral ethinyl estradiol (200 ng/kg/d for 6 months and then increase to 20 μg/d accompanied by a progestational agent such as medroxyprogesterone (10 mg/d) for 14 days of a 28-day cycle.

FOLLOW-UP

The endocrinology consultant to the family of a short child has the responsibility of evaluating growth patterns in the context of genetic and societal backgrounds, detecting and treating diseases when present, providing a realistic estimate of projected mature height, and tracking subsequent growth with or without therapeutic intervention. Diagnosis and treatment should be made comprehensible to the child as well as his or her family. Most families are able to absorb only a limited amount of information in a single office visit, so the educational process should be spread over several visits. Follow-up is important in determining that the predicted changes do, in fact, occur.

Scheduled follow-up should be at yearly intervals during childhood and every 6 months during adolescence. Following therapeutic intervention, there should be a visit at 1 month to determine understanding, compliance, and side effects and at 3-month intervals thereafter.

DISCUSSION
Prevalence and Incidence

By definition the prevalence of moderately short stature (height between the 5th and 1st percentiles) is 4%. The prevalence of severe shortness (height below the 1st percentile) is 1%. These figures assume that the reference values for height distributions are accurate reflections of heights in the population at risk. When there are differences in genetic background or nutritional status, far more than 1% of a population may be below the first percentiles for height or weight according to NCHS charts. The prevalence of acquired hypothyroidism may be as high as 2% in adolescence and estimates of the prevalence of growth hormone deficiency range from 0.1 to 0.01%.

Related Basic Science
Genetics

The most important contributions to differences in the tempo and extent of growth appear to be genetic. More than 70% of the variation in children's heights can be accounted for by midparental heights. We do not know which genes exert major effects on variation in growth within the normal range and whether the variation is caused by differences in the level of expression or in the potency of the gene products. The greatest attention has been devoted to study of the components of the growth hormone axis. Many of the participating genes have been cloned and sequenced. Two types of heritable defect have been characterized at the molecular level.

Isolated growth hormone deficiency type IA (IGHD IA) is an autosomal recessive disorder caused by homozygosity for deletion of the GH-1 gene encoding pituitary growth hormone. Growth impairment is early and severe, resulting in lengths more than four standard deviations below the mean by a year of age. Serum human growth hormone levels are undetectable after pharmacologic stimuli and after stimulation with growth hormone-releasing hormone. Early reports emphasized antibody formation and secondary growth arrest during growth hormone treatment. More recent studies indicate that antibody formation is variable and that many of these children continue to grow well and attain normal heights when treated with growth hormone. The condition should be suspected and Southern blotting or polymerase chain reaction studies should be done for diagnosis in children with particularly severe forms of growth hormone deficiency. Single base substitutions in the *GH-1* gene have been associated with hormone deficiency. Autosomal recessive IGHD IB in some families is caused by mutations in the fourth intron of *GH-1,* and autosomal dominant IGHD II has been attributed to mutations in the third intron of *GH-1.* These intronic mutations interfere with posttranscriptional splicing of *GH-1* messenger RNA. Although the molecular defects responsible for most forms of autosomal recessive multiple pituitary hormone deficiency have not been identified, explanations have been found for disorders involving deficiencies of growth hormone, prolactin, and thyroid-stimulating hormone (TSH). Embryonic differentiation and mature function of somatotropes, lactotropes, and thyrotropes require the participation of a transcriptional activation factor known as *Pit-1.* Some mutations of this gene disrupt binding of *Pit-1* protein to growth hormone, prolactin, and β-TSH promoters and cause autosomal recessive deficiency of the three hormones. Others bind normally, but inhibit transcriptional activation and cause autosomal dominant growth hormone, prolactin, and TSH deficiency. The recognition of these new categories of disease mandates assessment of prolactin release during investigation of hypopituitarism.

Laron's syndrome is an autosomal recessive disorder involving abnormalities of the gene encoding the growth hormone receptor. Growth retardation is similar to that observed in IGHD IA. Circulating human growth hormone levels are high, but IGF-1 and IGF-2 levels are very low. Serum growth hormone-binding protein activity, reflecting a circulating form of the extracellular domain of the growth hormone receptor, is markedly reduced or absent. Several patients with Laron syndrome have been found to have deletion of three exons encoding a part of the extracellular domain. Others have mutations in the growth hormone receptor gene that require polymerase chain reaction amplification and sequencing for detection. As patients with growth hormone insensitivity lack a vital component for recognizing growth hormone, they do not respond to administered growth hormone. Adult heights range from 105 to 130 cm. Treatment with biosynthetic IGF-I offers a means of bypassing the missing receptor.

Physiology

Clinical studies that compare short with normally growing and tall children have shown positive correlations between height standard deviation score for age and a number of components of the growth hormone axis. These include mean serum growth hormone levels with frequent sampling over 12- or 24-hour intervals, serum growth hormone-binding protein levels, serum IGF-I levels, and levels of IGF-binding protein 3. All of these parameters increase with age and physical maturity during childhood and adolescence. It is not clear whether the positive correlations with height reflect advanced maturity in the taller children or hormonal contributions to greater adult height. None of the measurements has been proven to have consistent diagnostic value in identifying children who will benefit from growth hormone treatment. The explanation for this may lie in the fact that more than 80% of short children show a significant, greater than 2 cm per year, short-term increase in growth rate when given growth hormone in currently recommended dosage schedules. Carefully controlled studies are needed to determine whether the measurements identify children who need treatment to attain a normal adult height.

Natural History and Its Modification with Treatment

The best predictor of adult height is probably the height percentile that is followed during midchildhood. For example, a male who follows the 10th percentile from ages 4 to 10 is likely to attain a height of about 67 in. (170 cm). Early maturers have a shorter period of childhood growth but a more intense pubertal growth spurt. Late maturers have a longer period of childhood growth, but less intense growth at puberty. The child whose growth is impaired by systemic illness will be a short adult if the disease is not diagnosed and treated. Timely recognition and appropriate treatment of even the most severe forms of thyroid hormone deficiency or growth hormone deficiency enable a child to attain a normal height. It remains to be seen whether perturbation of growth with growth hormone treatment alters the final height in other types of short stature.

In the teenager who has not begun pubertal development, it is very difficult to determine whether puberty is simply delayed or will not occur spontaneously, no matter how long one waits. Extreme delay in puberty interferes with peer relationships and social development as well as having a lasting effect on body proportions. It is probably best to begin sex hormone replacement at no later than age 14 in girls or 15 in boys, with the knowledge that treatment can be stopped when signs of endogenous pubertal progression appear.

The child with growth hormone deficiency requires growth hormone replacement to approach his or her genetically determined height. Early recognition and consistent treatment may enable these children to exceed the adult heights predicted on the basis of bone age and height at the beginning of therapy. Long-term studies of girls with Turner's syndrome suggest that combined treatment with growth hormone and oral androgens may succeed in increasing adult height beyond genetic potential. Chronic renal failure may be another circumstance in which growth hormone treatment improves adult height. In other forms of short stature, growth hormone treatment produces an increase in growth rate but there is little evidence that it improves adult height.

Androgen treatment has been used in constitutional delay and genetic short stature children for more than 30 years. There is general agreement that androgens can produce a growth spurt similar to that seen in puberty. Few studies have suggested an improvement in adult height, but many endocrinologists have witnessed induction of inappropriately early puberty, with an adverse effect on adult height, when doses are excessive or when androgens are begun before a bone age of 11 years. Enthusiasm for oral androgen treatment has waned since the appearance of reports detailing cholestatic jaundice and rare induction of hepatic neoplasms.

Prevention

Prevention of extreme short stature involves early recognition of severe growth disturbances. Each visit to a physician should entail measurement and plotting of length (0–3 years) or height (2–18 years) and weight. There is also a role for school or community-based screening for short stature, with identification and referral of children below the first percentile.

Cost Containment

Direct costs related to short stature involve medical visits, diagnostic tests, and medications. The primary physician can reduce costs by having a good understanding of normal growth and reasonable criteria for suspecting a growth disturbance. The boy with delayed puberty whose height dips below the first percentile should not have extensive tests of spontaneous growth hormone secretion in an effort to demonstrate a subtle neurosecretory disturbance. Androgen treatment of delayed puberty is three orders of magnitude less expensive than growth hormone treatment. At $50/mg, and with a dose of 0.3 mg/kg/wk, growth hormone treatment of a person weighing 50 kg costs $39,000 per year.

There is continuing debate about the use of growth hormone in treatment of short stature. At one extreme, some authorities have emphasized diagnostic limitations in identifying children who might respond to treatment and have suggested that all children below the first percentile for height are entitled to growth hormone. Treatment would be continued until height exceeds the 5th percentile. In this context, the height deficit is considered to be more relevant than a specific disease diagnosis. At the other extreme, treatment would be limited to the one child in several thousand who fulfills traditional criteria for growth hormone deficiency. Guidelines for prescribing growth hormone continue to evolve. It is hoped the next decade will see the completion of studies addressing long-term physical and psychological benefits of growth hormone and the development of more specific and less costly strategies for managing the more common types of short stature.

REFERENCES

Albertson-Wikland K. Growth hormone treatment in short children: Short-term and long-term effects on growth. Acta Paediatr Scand (Suppl) 1988;343:77.

Allen DB, Fost NC. Growth hormone therapy for short stature: Panacea or Pandora's box? J Pediatr 1990;117:16.

Amselem S, Duquesnoy P, Duriez B, et al. Spectrum of growth hormone receptor mutations and associated haplotypes in Laron syndrome. Hum Mol Genet 1993;2:355.

Blethen SL, Gaines S, Weldon V. Comparison of predicted and adult heights in short boys: Effects of androgen therapy. Pediatr Res 1984;18:467.

Cogan JC, Phillips JA III, Sakati N, et al. Heterogeneous growth hormone (GH) gene mutations in familial GH deficiency. J Clin Endocrinol Metab 1993;76:1224.

Frasier SD, Lippe BM. Clinical review 11: The rational use of growth hormone during childhood. J Clin Endocrinol Metab 1990;71:269.

Guevara-Aguirre J, Rosenbloom AL, Fielder PJ, et al. Growth hormone receptor deficiency in Ecuador: Clinical and biochemical phenotype in two populations. J Clin Endocrinol Metab 1993;76:417.

Lesage C, Walker J, Landier F, et al. Near normalization of adolescent height with growth hormone therapy in very short children without growth hormone deficiency. J Pediatr 1991;119:29.

Neely EK, Rosenfeld RG. Use and abuse of human growth hormone. Annu Rev Med 1994;45:407.

Parks JS, Abdul-Latif H, Kinoshita E, et al. Genetics of growth hormone gene expression. Horm Res 1993;40:54.

Rosenfield RL. Clinical review 6: Diagnosis and management of delayed puberty. J Clin Endocrinol Metab 1990;700:559.

CHAPTER 9–45

Excessive Growth

John S. Parks, M.D., Ph.D.

DEFINITION

Excessive growth is a process leading to stature above the range appropriate for a child or adolescent's age, sex, and genetic background.

ETIOLOGY

The most common explanation for tall stature is tall parents. In this context, growth is appropriate for genetic background but may be excessive in the eyes of the family or of society. Other explanations for growth excess are listed in Table 9–45–1. The mechanisms driving excessive growth are not known in most syndromes involving tall stature. Sometimes, a child may be tall because of early pubertal development, and very rarely, their growth is driven by excessive pituitary growth hormone production.

CRITERIA FOR DIAGNOSIS

Suggestive

The tools for assessing growth are a device for measuring height, a scale, and a set of age- and sex-appropriate National Center for Health Statistics (NCHS) growth charts. Suggestive criteria for growth excess include a height between the 95th and 99th percentiles for age and sex, a height one to three channels above the midparental height percentile, or a crossing of more than one channel on the growth chart after 2 years of age.

Definitive

The definitive criteria for growth excess involve more extreme deviations. They include a height above the 99th percentile for age and sex, a height more than three channels above the midparental height, or a crossing of more than two channels on the growth chart after 2 years of age.

CLINICAL MANIFESTATIONS

Subjective

An understanding of growth relative to family history is crucial to the analysis of growth excess. The patient's height and the measured heights of all other available family members should be plotted on appropriate charts. Midparental height percentile is estimated as the midpoint between the height of the like-sex parent and the adjusted height of the opposite sex parent (add 5 in. to plot maternal height on a male chart and subtract 5 in. from paternal height to plot on a female chart).

Children of very tall parents tend to be tall, but closer to the mean than their parents because of the phenomenon of regression to the mean. Selectivity results in referral of children who are taller for age than their tall parents. Family history of pace and timing of puberty is also important. The tall child may be expressing a familial tendency for early maturation rather than for tall adult height.

Environmental as well as genetic factors enter into tall stature associated with obesity. Histories should include maximum nonpregnant weights as well as current weights for adult relatives and caretakers. Marfan's syndrome is an autosomal dominant condition with a high spontaneous mutation rate. It should be suspected when one parent has been tall and died prematurely of a dissecting aortic aneurysm.

Excessive birth weight and length are features of conditions in which growth excess begins during fetal life. These conditions include cerebral gigantism (Soto syndrome), Beckwith–Wiedemann syndrome, and hyperinsulinism. Symptoms of hypoglycemia (e.g., seizures, confusion, etc., see Chapter 9–33) can provide a clue to hyperinsulinism. Crossing of height percentiles is a feature of sex hormone excess. The parents may have noted definite signs of puberty and an increase in appetite

TABLE 9–45–1. CATEGORIES OF EXCESSIVE GROWTH

Polygenic
    Constitutional tall stature
Monogenic and chromosomal
    Cerebral gigantism
    Beckwith–Wiedemann syndrome
    Marfan's syndrome
    Klinefelter's syndrome
    XYY chromosome constitution
Hormonal
    Sex hormone excess
        Premature puberty
        Gonadal or adrenal tumor
        Congenital adrenal hyperplasia
        McCune–Albright syndrome
    Growth hormone excess
        Pituitary somatotroph adenoma
        McCune–Albright syndrome
        Growth hormone-releasing hormone hypersecretion
    Thyroid hormone excess
    Insulin excess
        Obesity
        Pancreatic beta cell tumor/hyperplasia

concomitantly with the pubertal growth spurt. Learning disabilities may be a prepubertal marker for cerebral gigantism, Klinefelter syndrome, or 47,XYY chromosome constitution.

Objective

Physical Examination

The phenotypes of specific named syndromes are fairly characteristic. Large, irregular café-au-lait spots are characteristic of McCune–Albright syndrome. In cerebral gigantism, there is macrocephaly and dolicocephaly with disproportionately large hands and feet, coarse facial features, and prognathism. Accelerated bone maturation and relatively early puberty generally lead to a normal adult height. Beckwith–Wiedemann syndrome combines fetal and early childhood overgrowth with variable combinations of unusual ear creases, macroglossia, omphalocele, visceromegaly, and skeletal asymmetry. Marfan syndrome has objective findings of arachnodactyly with hyperextensibility of joints, scoliosis, pectus deformity of the chest, narrow face and palate, and upward subluxation of the lens. Some of the same features are seen in homocystinuria and in lysyl hydroxylase deficiency. Klinefelter syndrome is difficult to recognize before puberty, when disproportionately small and firm testes together with gynecomastia can suggest the diagnosis.

During the physical examination, particular emphasis should be placed on determining whether the child has inappropriately early signs of pubertal development. A growth spurt, increased muscularity, and advancement of bone age generally precede phallic enlargement and pubic hair growth in boys with virilizing congenital adrenal hyperplasia. Girls with congenital adrenal hyperplasia may also have genital ambiguity or clitoral enlargement. Isosexual precocious puberty involves the appearance of any sign of puberty before age 8 (see Chapter 9–28).

Pituitary growth hormone excess is a rare cause of excessive growth during childhood or adolescence; however, it accounts for many of the instances of adult height over 7 ft, particularly in females. Clinical suspicion is increased when growth continues after age 16 or when the distinctive physical findings of acromegaly appear. The child with hyperthyroidism tends to be tall for age and have advanced skeletal maturity. Impaired weight gain may exaggerate the appearance of tall stature in hyperthyroid children. Endogenous obesity is frequently associated with rapid linear growth and rapid bone maturation. The fat, tall child tends to have excessive insulin secretion as a consequence of overeating, but such a child is very unlikely to have a specifically treatable endocrine disorder.

Routine Laboratory Abnormalities

Routine laboratory tests are of very little value in discriminating between alternative explanations for tall stature.

Chest x-rays may show aortic dilation in Marfan syndrome and scoliosis in this as well as several other named syndromes.

PLANS
Diagnostic

Differential Diagnosis

The differential diagnosis of growth excess is depicted in Table 9–45–1. Pertinent categories include polygenic or constitutional tall stature and specific named syndromes and conditions involving inappropriately high levels of sex hormones, growth hormone, thyroid hormones, or insulin.

Diagnostic Options

History and physical examination may suffice for making the diagnosis of genetic tall stature. In this case, no further studies are needed except for a radiograph of the hand and wrist. Estimation of bone age is useful in predicting mature height. Children with advanced bone ages will be shorter as adults than they are in comparison to their age peers during childhood, and the problem will take care of itself without medical intervention.

Recommended Approach

A general approach to diagnosis is outlined in Table 9–45–2. There is no specific laboratory test to confirm the diagnosis of cerebral gigantism (Soto syndrome), but computed tomography of the brain may show enlargement of the cerebral ventricles. The diagnosis of Beckwith–Wiedemann syndrome is also made on clinical grounds. Abdominal ultrasonography is indicated to detect the presence of Wilms tumor or other embryonal neoplasms. Diagnosis of Marfan syndrome is also clinical, aided by finding long metacarpal bones on x-ray films of the hand. Klinefelter syndrome is diagnosed by finding a sex chromatin-positive buccal smear or a 47,XXY karyotype. Karyotyping of tall males is indicated if there is no family history of tall stature or if there are other physical findings suggestive of Klinefelter syndrome.

Diagnostic paradigms for precocious puberty, virilizing tumors, and congenital adrenal hyperplasia are presented in Chapters 9–28, 9–26, and 9–8, respectively. Growth hormone excess is suspected in cases of tall stature without a family history of tallness and in situations in which there is visual field impairment or continuation of rapid growth beyond age 15 in girls or age 17 in boys. Insulin-like growth factor I (IGF-I) levels are a useful screening test, but there is overlap between the high values of gigantism and the high values attained during normal puberty. Specific strategies for evaluation of growth hormone dynamics and pituitary tumor are discussed in Chapters 9–3 and 9–1, respectively. Thyroid hormone excess is suspected on clinical grounds and confirmed by measurement of serum thyroxine, triiodothyronine, and thyroid-stimulating hormone levels (see Chapter 9–17).

The strategies for diagnosis and management of premature puberty, congenital adrenal hyperplasia, growth hormone excess, hyperthyroidism, and beta cell overactivity are provided in Chapters 9–28, 9–8, 9–3, and 9–17.

Therapeutic

Therapeutic Options

Endocrinologists differ in their opinions about what constitutes excessive stature in girls. Some consider treatment when predicted mature height is greater than 5 ft 10 in., whereas others raise the issue only when predicted heights are greater than 6 ft 2 in. Treatment for the genetic forms of tall stature is limited to early and/or excessive provision of sex hormones to limit growth and accelerate bone maturation. There is a considerable literature on the use of estrogens and progestins to treat tall stature in girls. Different series estimate reductions in mean adult heights of 1 to 3 in. Theoretically, one could use fairly small doses of estrogen in a young girl to induce premature puberty. In practice, most authors have used quite large estrogen doses to slow growth after endogenous puberty has begun but before the beginning of menses. Treatment regimens involve use of the equivalent of 100 to 500 µg of ethinyl estradiol (e.g., Lynoral) on a daily basis, together with a progestational agent, for example, medroxyprogesterone (Provera) 10 mg orally, given 14 days of each month to promote menses.

Side effects include increased appetite, weight gain, and nausea.

TABLE 9–45–2. DIAGNOSTIC EVALUATION OF TALL STATURE

Test	Observation and Action	
Height measurement	>95th percentile for age	
Comparison with parents	<1 SD above midparent Probably constitutional	>1 SD above midparent Possibly pathological
Assessment of puberty	Advanced	Normal for age
Bone age	Advanced >2 years	Normal ± 2 years
Consider and test for	Premature puberty Gonadal tumor Congenital adrenal hyperplasia	Cerebral gigantism Beckwith–Wiedemann syndrome Marfan's syndrome Hyperthyroidism Growth hormone excess

Thromboembolic complications are rare. There have been several reports of ovarian cysts requiring operative intervention during treatment. Hepatic tumors are a theoretical complication of treatment, but they have not been described in several large series dealing with estrogen treatment of tall stature. Contraindications to treatment are the same as with birth control pills.

Recommended Approach

The decision to treat tall girls with estrogen should not be taken lightly. Realistic predictions of adult height with and without treatment should be provided. It is advisable to provide the girl and her family with copies of scientific articles and book chapters describing the diverse experiences with treatment. The final decision for intervention is left up to the girl and her family.

Once initiated, estrogen treatment is generally continued until bone age 15 or until there has been less than 0.5 in. of growth in two successive 6-month intervals. Reports of tall girls treated with estrogen include more than 1000 patients, and there has been no evidence for increased risks of neoplasia or cardiovascular disease. Some authors contend that estrogens limit the risk of cardiovascular complications as well as tall stature in Marfan syndrome. Posttreatment menstrual and reproductive histories tend to be normal. Much less is known about the use of testosterone to truncate the growth period in tall boys.

FOLLOW-UP

Follow-up of the tall child should be at yearly intervals during childhood, increasing to every 6 months during puberty. With estrogen treatment, there should be a visit at 1 month to assess understanding, compliance, and side effects and every 3 to 6 months thereafter. There should be provision for pretreatment and yearly pelvic examinations and Pap smears.

DISCUSSION

Prevalence and Incidence

Adult heights above the 95th percentile for age are observed in 5% of the normal population. Early puberty can produce heights above the 95th percentile during childhood, but these children tend to be short adults. Klinefelter syndrome has an incidence of about 1 in 1000 live male births. The prevalence of pituitary gigantism is much lower, being on the order of one in one million individuals.

Related Basic Science

Pituitary somatotroph adenomas are thought to arise from mutations in a single somatotroph cell. The best recognized are activating mutations of the gene encoding the G-protein alpha stimulatory subunit (Gαs). With heterozygosity for this mutation, the cell becomes independent of growth hormone-releasing hormone stimulation, outgrows other somatotroph cells, and overproduces growth hormone. Similar mutations occurring at an early stage of embryonic development and influencing the growth and function of multiple cell lineages are responsible for McCune–Albright syndrome, a condition that can produce excessive growth through ovarian or testicular autonomy and through pituitary hypersection of growth hormone. With the exception of pituitary gigantism, the mechanisms underlying other categories of excessive growth are poorly understood. There are some reports of quantitative increases in spontaneous growth hormone secretion and in circulating levels of IGF-I in tall children and adolescents. Recombinant DNA probes for each of the hormones in the growth hormone axis provide a possibility for understanding the genetic basis of normal variation in the pace and extent of growth.

Estrogen treatment tends to increase spontaneous secretion of growth hormone; however, high doses of estrogen suppress bioassayable IGF-I activity and immunoassayable IGF-I levels and actually slow growth while promoting rapid epiphyseal maturation.

Natural History and Its Modification with Treatment

Children with constitutional tall stature may either benefit or suffer from their tallness, depending on involvement in sports, development of self-esteem, and social experiences. Depending on skeletal maturity at starting treatment, up to 80% can expect a 1-in. or greater reduction in adult height, and up to 20% can expect a 3-in. or greater reduction in adult height.

The child with precocious puberty is much taller than his or her peers during the early school years but, because of a truncation of the time available for growth, tends to be short as an adult. Potential handicaps in syndromes associated with growth excess include mental slowness in cerebral gigantism, dislocation of the lens and dissecting aortic aneurysm in Marfan syndrome, and difficulties in social and vocational adjustment in Klinefelter and 47,XYY syndromes.

The long-term effects of pituitary gigantism are devastating. A study of pituitary giants living in the London area indicated that practically all were handicapped by kyphoscoliosis and other complications and that all led reclusive lives. Hyperthyroidism predisposes to emotional and learning difficulties if untreated.

Prevention

In American society, tall stature tends to be considered a desirable characteristic in females as well as males up to a point. There is general agreement among endocrinologists that adult female heights in excess of 74 in. are undesirable and that predicted heights in excess of this value should at least raise the issue of treatment.

Cost Containment

Costs may be contained by considering genetic tall stature to be a positive diagnosis rather than a diagnosis by exclusion. This means that tall children of tall parents who have no other signs of disease should not be tested for growth hormone excess or, in boys, for Klinefelter syndrome.

REFERENCES

Cutler L, Jackson JA, Uz-zafar S, et al. Hypersecretion of growth hormone and prolactin in McCune–Albright syndrome. J Clin Endocrinol Metab 1989;68:1148.

Daughaday WH. Pituitary gigantism. Endocrinol Metab Clin North Am 1992;21:633.

Dodge PR, Holmes SJ, Sotos JF. Cerebral gigantism. Dev Med Child Neurol 1983;25:248.

Lu PW, Silink M, Johnston I, et al. Pituitary gigantism. Arch Dis Child 1992;67:1039.

Moran A, Asa SL, Kovacs K, et al. Gigantism due to pituitary mammosomatotroph hyperplasia. N Engl J Med 1990;323:322.

Pyeritz RE, McKusick VA. The Marfan syndrome: Diagnosis and management. N Engl J Med 1979;300:772.

Schlesinger S, MacGillivray MH, Muschauer RW. Acceleration of growth and bone maturation in childhood thyrotoxicosis. J Pediatr 1973;83:233.

Wettenhall HNB. The tall child. In: Brook GD, ed. Clinical paediatric endocrinology. Oxford: Blackwell Scientific, 1981:134.

Whitaker MD, Scheithaver BW, Hayles AB, et al. The hypothalamus and pituitary in cerebral gigantism: A clinico-pathologic and immunocytochemical study. Am J Dis Child 1985;139:679.

Whitehead EM, Shalet SM, Davies D, et al. Pituitary gigantism: A disabling condition. Clin Endocrinol 1982;17:271.

CHAPTER 9–46

Multiple Endocrine Neoplasia Syndromes

Suzanne S. P. Gebhart, M.D.

DEFINITION

The multiple endocrine neoplasia (MEN) syndromes are a group of familial disorders characterized by hyperfunction in two or more endocrine organs. The pathologic defect may consist of hyperplasia, adenoma, or carcinoma. Three distinct syndromes have been described (Table 9–46–1). MEN I is associated with adenomas or hyperplasia of the parathyroid glands, pancreatic islet cells, and anterior pituitary. Adrenal cortical hyperplasia, carcinoid tumors, colonic polyposis, and lipomas also have been described with this syndrome.

Multiple endocrine neoplasia IIa is characterized by medullary carcinoma of the thyroid, pheochromocytoma, and parathyroid adenomas.

Multiple endocrine neoplasia IIb consists of medullary carcinoma of the thyroid, pheochromocytoma, mucosal neuromas, corneal nerve thickening, and a marfanoid appearance. This is the only multiple endocrine neoplasia syndrome that does not involve the parathyroid gland.

ETIOLOGY

Multiple endocrine neoplasia I (Wermer's syndrome) and IIa (Sipple's syndrome) have autosomal dominant inheritance with variable penetrance. MEN I tumors have been shown to have allele losses on chromosome 11. Genetic linkage analysis has assigned the MEN I marker to chromosome band 11q13. MEN IIa has been shown to be associated with a locus near the centromeric region of chromosome 10. MEN IIb is rare, with only 50% of cases showing a familial incidence.

CRITERIA FOR DIAGNOSIS

Suggestive

A family history compatible with any of these syndromes or the presence of any two characteristics of one of the MEN syndromes merits consideration of the diagnosis.

Definitive

Multiple Endocrine Neoplasia I

Evidence of hyperfunction of the parathyroid, pancreatic islet cells, or anterior pituitary in an individual with a family history of MEN I syndrome is sufficient to make the diagnosis. Neoplasia of two characteristic endocrine organs in an individual without a family history of the disorder is highly suspect and merits further evaluation.

Multiple Endocrine Neoplasia IIa

The diagnosis of MEN IIa must be considered in any individual with medullary thyroid carcinoma or pheochromocytoma with or without hyperparathyroidism, especially if the medullary thyroid carcinoma is multifocal or the pheochromocytoma is bilateral.

TABLE 9–46–1. MULTIPLE ENDOCRINE NEOPLASIA SYNDROMES

Neoplasia Multiple Endocrine Syndrome	Typical Clinical Features
I	Adenomas or hyperplasia of parathyroid, pancreatic islets, and anterior pituitary
IIa	Medullary thyroid carcinoma Pheochromocytoma Parathyroid adenomas
IIb	Medullary thyroid carcinoma Pheochromocytoma Mucosal neuromas

Multiple Endocrine Neoplasia IIb

The physical features of this syndrome are virtually diagnostic. Unfortunately, medullary thyroid carcinoma develops early and is often found in small children before the appearance of submucosal neuromas or before marfanoid habitus becomes apparent.

CLINICAL MANIFESTATIONS

Subjective

Multiple Endocrine Neoplasia I

Onset of symptoms is typically during the third or fourth decade, although the syndrome has been reported in infants as well as the elderly. The presenting symptoms depend on the substance secreted by the hyperplastic or neoplastic tissue.

Historical clues to the presence of hyperparathyroidism include nephrolithiasis, weakness, headache, and anorexia; however, half the patients with this disorder are asymptomatic.

Tumors of the pancreatic islets of Langerhans occur in approximately 80% of patients with MEN I and produce a constellation of symptoms and physical findings dependent on the hormone that is produced. Gastrinomas, the most common islet cell tumors, increase gastric acid production, leading to epigastric pain, upper gastrointestinal bleeding, and recurrent peptic ulceration. Insulin-producing tumors produce hypoglycemia, with symptoms of palpitations, sweating, hunger, and syncope classically unrelated to meals. Because the symptoms are relieved with food, many patients have a history of weight gain. Vasoactive intestinal polypeptide hypersecretion produces a syndrome sometimes called pancreatic cholera, consisting of voluminous watery diarrhea and weakness associated with hypokalemia and achlorhydria. Glucagon-producing tumors are associated with the development of stomatitis, skin rash, and glucose intolerance. Gastrinomas are twice as common as insulinomas. Tumors producing glucagon, or a mixture of gastrin and insulin combined, constitute only about 5% of the total islet cell tumors.

The most common hormone secreted by adenomas of the anterior pituitary is prolactin, which can produce menstrual disturbances and/or galactorrhea in premenopausal women and decreased libido in men or postmenopausal women. Much less frequent are hypersecretion of growth hormone, producing the characteristic symptoms and physical features of acromegaly, and adrenocorticotropic hormone excess, producing symptoms and physical features of Cushing's syndrome. Both secretory and nonsecretory pituitary tumors may also present with local symptoms such as headache and visual field loss. It is believed that virtually all patients who inherit the genetic defect in MEN I will eventually express defects in the parathyroid, pancreatic islets, and anterior pituitary; however, decades may intervene before the development of symptoms.

A family history of endocrine surgery, renal stones, or peptic ulcer disease can usually be obtained.

Multiple Endocrine Neoplasia IIa

Patients may have no symptoms. Medullary thyroid carcinoma is asymptomatic in early stages. Tracheal compression, dysphagia, and hoarseness occur as the tumor advances. Distant metastases may cause pain.

Pheochromocytoma, found in 50% of patients with MEN IIa, can produce episodic palpitations, headache, syncope, or hypertension; however, these symptoms are often absent in MEN IIa.

The symptoms of hyperparathyroidism were discussed under Multiple Endocrine Neoplasia I. Only 10 to 30% of patients with the MEN IIa syndrome and hyperparathyroidism are symptomatic.

Multiple Endocrine Neoplasia IIb

Mucosal neuromas on the lips and tongue may produce cosmetic complaints. Gastrointestinal neuromas may cause symptoms such as constipation, diarrhea, and abdominal distention.

Objective

Multiple Endocrine Neoplasia I

Physical Examination. Physical examination may be entirely normal. Secretory tumors of the islets of Langerhans and of the anterior pituitary can most readily be suspected based on the clinical history. Acromegaly and Cushing's syndrome, although occurring rarely in this disorder, produce classic physical findings which are discussed in separate chapters (Table 9–46–2).

Routine Laboratory Abnormalities. Hyperparathyroidism should be suspected when serum calcium is persistently elevated, and is often associated with a decrease in serum phosphate level and an elevation in alkaline phosphatase level.

Multiple Endocrine Neoplasia IIa

Physical Examination. Medullary carcinoma of the thyroid is often multifocal, but it may present as a single palpable nodule, most commonly in one of the upper lobes. Occasionally, dense, irregular calcification can be seen on x-ray films. Diffuse c-cell hyperplasia, the premalignant condition characteristic of MEN IIa and IIb, cannot be detected by physical examination.

Episodic, severe elevations in blood pressure, when present, suggest pheochromocytoma, but hypertension may be sustained or absent. Orthostasis may be present.

Routine Laboratory Abnormalities. This condition cannot be detected by the use of routine laboratory procedures. The presence of hypercalcemia suggests hyperparathyroidism. As in MEN I, phosphate may be low and alkaline phosphatase high.

Multiple Endocrine Neoplasia IIb

Physical Examination. The physical features of this syndrome are characteristic and may lead to the diagnosis before the development of medullary thyroid carcinoma or pheochromocytoma. Early recognition is important, as medullary thyroid carcinoma has occurred before 5 years of age.

Affected individuals have marfanoid features with thickened lips. Submucosal nodules are present on the lips or anterior tongue. These ganglioneuromas actually extend throughout the gastrointestinal tract, and colonic distension is a common feature. Skeletal abnormalities such as increased joint laxity, scoliosis, and pectus excavatum may be present. Neurogenic weakness with poor muscle development may be present. Keratitis and decreased visual acuity from thickened corneal nerves have been reported.

Routine Laboratory Abnormalities. Routine laboratory procedures are not helpful in making the diagnosis.

TABLE 9–46–2. CROSS-REFERENCES FOR SPECIFIC EVALUATION OF NEOPLASMS ASSOCIATED WITH MULTIPLE ENDOCRINE NEOPLASIA SYNDROMES

	Chapter
Hyperparathyroidism	9–36, 9–37
Islet cell tumors	
Gastrinoma	19–30
Insulinoma (see Hypoglycemia)	9–32
Pituitary neoplasms	
Prolactinoma	9–4
Cushing's syndrome	9–6
Acromegaly	9–3
Medullary carcinoma of thyroid	9–14
Pheochromocytoma	14–8

PLANS

Diagnostic

Differential Diagnosis

The differential diagnosis is usually centered around the identification of the type of multiple endocrine neoplasia present.

Multiple Endocrine Neoplasia I

The diagnosis of hyperparathyroidism rests with the documentation of hypercalcemia with an inappropriately elevated serum parathyroid hormone level. Hyperparathyroidism without involvement of other endocrine organs is a common disorder which can be familial.

Gastrinoma (Zollinger–Ellison syndrome) may be diagnosed by the documentation of elevated serum gastrin levels and gastric hyperacidity. If there is a history of previous gastric surgery, retained gastric antrum or G-cell hyperplasia must be ruled out. Basal gastrin levels greater than 300 pg/mL with no prior surgical intervention are virtually diagnostic; however, many patients with gastrinomas have basal gastrin levels that fall below the diagnostic range, requiring the use of provocative tests. Usually, calcium as calcium gluconate is infused over 3 hours at a rate of 3 to 5 mg/kg per hour; if this produces a rise in gastrin greater than 400 pg/mL at any point during the infusion, it is diagnostic of a gastrinoma. Secretin has also been used as a provocative agent, given as an intravenous bolus of 2 U/kg. Samples for gastrin are taken at 2-minute intervals for 10 minutes. Normal responses range up to 100 pg/mL, and higher levels are suggestive of a gastrinoma.

The diagnosis of insulinoma rests on the documentation of fasting hypoglycemia with an inappropriately high plasma insulin level. Under basal conditions, the normal ratio of plasma insulin (μU/mL) to glucose (mg/dL) is less than 0.3 and either decreases or remains constant during a fast. In the presence of an islet cell tumor, this ratio increases to greater than 0.3 during a fast. When factitious insulin administration is a consideration, elevation of proinsulin and C-peptide may confirm the diagnosis of insulinoma. Other islet cell tumors are quite rare. Fasting glucagon levels, which are normally quite low, are elevated in the presence of glucagonomas. Vasoactive intestinal polypeptide can also be measured if secretory diarrhea is present.

Diagnostic procedures to localize the site of adenomas in either the parathyroids or the pancreas are frequently inconclusive. Magnetic resonance imaging may disclose a mass. Technetium/sestamibi parathyroid scanning can often demonstrate parathyroid enlargement when other studies are not helpful. Computed tomography of the pancreas with selective angiography may help in localizing islet cell neoplasia. Selective venous sampling has also been useful, as has been intraoperative ultrasound for pancreatic tumors. In the MEN I setting, however, islet cell tumors are frequently multiple, and all may not be visualized. Pituitary adenomas secreting prolactin or growth hormone produce elevated serum or plasma levels of these hormones. Measurement of the plasma adrenocorticotropic hormone level may be less helpful. The diagnostic workup for adrenocorticotropic hormone hypersecretion can be found in Chapter 9–6. Computed tomography or magnetic resonance imaging of the pituitary can detect an adenoma in most cases.

Carcinoid tumors are found in 5 to 10% of patients with MEN I syndrome and can occur intrabronchially, in the thymus, or within the duodenum. Tumors may be benign or malignant and may be detected by measurement of 5-hydroxyindoleacetic acid in urine. In addition to serotonin, carcinoid tumors sometimes secrete calcitonin or adrenocorticotropic hormone, and a carcinoid tumor should be considered in a patient with the MEN I who presents with Cushing's syndrome. Flushing is a rare finding in carcinoid tumors that are not of gastrointestinal origin with liver metastases.

Multiple Endocrine Neoplasia IIa

An elevated basal calcitonin level (greater than 300 pg/mL) suggests the presence of medullary thyroid carcinoma and is diagnostic in family members at risk for MEN IIa. Normal or moderately elevated calcitonin levels are compatible with the diagnosis, but patients with medullary thyroid carcinoma characteristically exhibit an exaggerated calcitonin response to calcium or pentagastrin infusion. A combined test of calcium (2 mg/kg) infused over 1 minute followed by a bolus of pentagastrin (0.5 µg/kg) should produce a fivefold increase in calcitonin if medullary carcinoma of the thyroid is present.

The diagnosis of pheochromocytoma is based on documentation of increased catecholamine production measured by 24-hour urine collection of vanillylmandelic acid, catecholamines, and/or metanephrines. Measurement of plasma catecholamines may also be useful, but samples must be collected under controlled conditions with the patient supine and unstressed, and the specimens handled carefully. Bilateral pheochromocytoma occurs in 60 to 70% of patients. Approximately 85% of pheochromocytomas in adults occur in the adrenal medulla, and the remainder develop along the sympathetic chain. Computed tomography is the most sensitive technique to detect adrenal enlargement. Imaging with [^{131}I]metaiodobenzylguanidine, which is taken up by catecholamine vesicles, also may be useful for both diagnosis and localization.

In MEN IIa, the first indication of hyperparathyroidism may be enlarged parathyroid glands at the time of thyroid surgery.

Multiple Endocrine Neoplasia IIb

Medullary thyroid carcinoma is much more aggressive in association with this syndrome than with MEN IIa, and occurs at an earlier age. Diagnosis is based on serum calcitonin levels. Pheochromocytoma occurs in about 40% of patients with this disorder. Diagnosis is the same as with MEN IIa. Hyperparathyroidism is not associated with this disorder.

Therapeutic

Multiple Endocrine Neoplasia I

In MEN I, the primary therapy is surgery. The treatment of choice for hyperparathyroidism is subtotal parathyroidectomy. Multiple tumors of the parathyroids tend to develop over time so the recurrence of hypercalcemia is quite high, dependent on the amount of remaining parathyroid tissue. In addition, hypercalcemia may stimulate gastrin production and may contribute to development or exacerbation of gastrinomas. Removal of all parathyroid tissue with autotransplantation of small fragments of parathyroid tissue into the muscles of the forearm has been used to avoid the difficulties of reexploration of the neck should hypercalcemia develop at a later time.

Management of pancreatic islet cell tumors is extremely difficult. Many patients with elevated serum gastrin levels may respond to medical therapy with various H_2 receptor blockers, like cimetidine (Tagamet) and ranitidine (Zantac). Should medical therapy be unsuccessful, surgical intervention is necessary. Surgery is curative when an isolated adenoma is present; however, these tumors are often multiple or may involve generalized hyperplasia of the islets without adenoma formation. This may also be true for insulin-secreting tumors. In this situation, partial pancreatectomy may be the procedure of choice. Medical management of insulin-producing tumors is often less successful. Diazoxide (Proglycem) in a divided daily dose of 3 to 8 mg/kg may be effective in blocking insulin release, but fluid retention is an unpleasant side effect. Injections of streptozotocin, doxorubicin, or dacarbazine have been used, but these drugs are highly toxic and have limited success. Octreotide, a synthetic somatostatin analog, has been used successfully to reduce production of gastrin, vasoactive intestinal peptide, and, in some cases, insulin and improve symptoms associated with islet secretory tumors. Some carcinoid tumors also appear responsive to this drug. Octreotide is given subcutaneously two or four times a day or by infusion pump. The effective dose is variable, but the range is 100 to 600 µg/d.

Management of prolactin-secreting pituitary adenomas must be individualized. There are several options. Close observation without specific therapy, bromocriptine therapy, and surgical removal are reasonable choices depending on the clinical situation (see Chapter 9–4). Adrenocorticotropic hormone- and growth hormone-producing tumors require surgical intervention.

Multiple Endocrine Neoplasia IIa

The appropriate therapy for medullary thyroid carcinoma is total thyroidectomy with regional node dissection, because the disease tends to be multifocal with early lymph node metastases. Occult pheochromocytoma must be diligently sought prior to neck surgery. If a pheochromocytoma is present, it should be removed first.

The management of parathyroid hyperplasia can be more conservative, as symptoms and complications are rare. Adenomas or parathyroid enlargement at the time of thyroid surgery should be removed. Normal-appearing parathyroid glands may be left in place or implanted in the forearm.

Multiple Endocrine Neoplasia IIb

As with MEN IIa, surgical management is required for medullary thyroid carcinoma and pheochromocytoma.

FOLLOW-UP

Patients with MEN I need lifelong follow-up. Recurrent hyperparathyroidism is a frequent problem, and routine calcium determinations should be made. In addition, the development of other endocrine neoplasias should be considered during follow-up and provocative testing should be done. The major morbidity and mortality associated with MEN I are due to the gastrointestinal effects of hypersecretion of gastrin.

Lifelong follow-up is also necessary for patients with MEN IIa and IIb. Surgery for medullary thyroid carcinoma confined to the thyroid (MEN IIa and IIb) can be curative. After successful surgery, serum calcitonin levels will be normal with a normal response to provocative tests. Many patients with elevated postoperative serum calcitonin levels remain asymptomatic over the long term; no further medical or surgical intervention is indicated unless there is clinical evidence of recurrence. Local recurrence should be resected. Distant recurrence is generally unresponsive to radiation or chemotherapy. Twenty-four-hour urine collections for vanillylmandelic acid and metanephrines also should be done.

Because of the frequency of MEN I in first-degree relatives, family members should be screened for asymptomatic hypercalcemia and for the presence of gastrinoma. It is recommended that family members of patients affected by the syndrome be screened with calcium and gastrin measurements every 2 years from ages 15 to 65. Patients affected should be aware of the need for monitoring serum calcium levels, as recurrence of hyperparathyroidism is high. They should also be aware of the other organs affected in this syndrome and the symptoms that would suggest involvement.

Early detection of abnormal calcitonin secretion through basal and provocative tests is essential in family members of patients with MEN IIa. Patients should be aware of the symptoms of catecholamine excess. It has been recommended that provocative testing for calcitonin, urine screening for pheochromocytoma, and serum calcium level be obtained at yearly intervals from ages 3 to 35 among family members at risk. DNA probes developed for genetic linkage testing the MEN I and MEN IIa alleles have demonstrated clinical utility in identifying individuals at risk for development of disease among unaffected family members. This may allow for earlier disease detection in affected individuals and spare needless testing for other individuals.

The earlier age of onset in MEN IIb requires screening for abnormal calcitonin secretion in family members beginning at 1 year of age. Medullary thyroid carcinoma and pheochromocytoma have not been known to occur in adults who do not also exhibit the submucosal neuromas; however, because affected children may not develop submucosal abnormalities until 3 or 4 years of age, and by then may have incurable medullary thyroid carcinoma, all children at risk should be screened. Genetic linkage in MEN IIb is unclear.

DISCUSSION

Prevalence and Incidence

Although the multiple endocrine neoplasia syndromes are rare, many members of an affected family develop the syndrome because of the autosomal dominant inheritance. High penetrance, close to 50% among offspring of individuals with the disease, has been reported for MEN I. Lower familial incidence occurs in MEN IIa and IIb.

Related Basic Science
Metabolic Derangement

Despite a number of theories, there is no clear explanation to account for the development of multiple endocrine neoplasia. A defect in endocrinologic precursor cells arising from the neural crest (termed amine precursor uptake and decarboxylation [APUD], i.e., peptide-producing cells) would explain the development of medullary thyroid carcinoma and pheochromocytoma in MEN II. The parathyroid glands, however, are not of neural crest origin and figure prominently in this disorder.

Alternatively, inherited carcinomas could result from two independent cellular events. A genetic mutation could first occur in a stem cell, making all later cells susceptible to neoplastic transformation. A second mutation or chromosomal break could occur in a later clone of cells, resulting in neoplasia. This has been termed the *two-hit model*. It does not account for the involvement of only certain endocrine organs.

A third speculation is that a single defect in multiple endocrine neoplasia syndromes results in hormone hypersecretion and produces the subsequent lesions found in other endocrine organs. For example, excess gastrin can lower calcium levels with resultant stimulation of the parathyroids. Or, in reverse, elevated calcium levels might stimulate secretion of gastrin, calcitonin, and insulin. Supporting this hypothesis, there have been reports that plasma from patients with MEN I induces increased mitotic activity in cultured parathyroid cells. This increased mitotic activity was not seen in parathyroid cells exposed to normal plasma or plasma from patients with other causes of hypercalcemia (Brandi et al., 1986).

Genetics

Gene analysis of tumors associated with MEN I have shown missing or abnormal alleles on chromosome 11 at the 11q13 locus. It has been suggested that the MEN I gene acts as a tumor suppressor. Likewise, MEN IIa has been associated with several loci on chromosome 10 in the centromeric region. In some, but not all, MEN IIa cohorts, germline mutations of the RET protooncogene located at the 10q11.2 locus have been identified.

Because of the large percentage of cases of MEN IIb without family history, very little is known about genetic markers in this syndrome.

Natural History and Its Modification with Treatment

In MEN I, most of the morbidity is associated with the effects of islet cell tumors. Gastrinomas, the most common tumor type, cause gastrointestinal bleeding from recurrent peptic ulcer disease. Pheochromocytomas produce the most life-threatening risk in MEN IIa. In MEN IIb, medullary carcinoma of the thyroid is associated with high mortality. Unfortunately, most patients with MEN IIb die of medullary thyroid carcinoma before the age of 30 years.

Prevention

Family screening before disease is symptomatic is paramount, particularly in MEN IIa and IIb.

Cost Containment

Provocative testing and yearly screening are expensive, but early detection can significantly decrease morbidity and prolong life.

As genetic screening becomes more widely available, the need for hormonal screening of all family members should be largely eliminated and targeted only to individuals at high risk.

REFERENCES

Brandi ML. Multiple endocrine neoplasia type 1: General features and new insights into etiology. J Endocrinol Invest 1991;1 14:61.
Brandi ML, Aurbach GD, Fitzpatrick LA, et al. Parathyroid mitogenic activity in plasma from patients with familial multiple endocrine neoplasia type 1. N Engl J Med 1986;314:1287.
Larson C, Nordenskjold M. Multiple endocrine neoplasia. Cancer Surv 1990;9:703.
Lips CJM, Landsvater RM, Hoppener JWM, et al. Clinical screening as compared with DNA analysis in families with multiple endocrine neoplasia type 2A. N Engl J Med 1994;331:828.
Rane F, Zink A. Clinical features of multiple endocrine neoplasia type 1 and type 2. Horm Res 1992;38(suppl 2):31.
Skogseid B, Eriksson B, Lundquist G, et al. Multiple endocrine neoplasia type 1: A 10 year prospective screening study of four kindreds. J Clin Endocrinol Metab 1991;73:281.
Sobol H, Narod SA, Nakamura Y, et al. Screening for multiple endocrine neoplasia type 2a with DNA-polymorphism analysis. N Engl J Med 1989;321:996.
Tsai MS, Ledger GA, Khosla S, et al. Identification of multiple endocrine neoplasia, type 2 gene carriers using linkage analysis and analysis of the RET proto-oncogene. J Clin Endocrinol Metab 1994;78:1261.
Vaser HFA, Lamers CBH, Lips CJM. Screening for the multiple endocrine neoplasia syndrome type I. Arch Intern Med 1989;149:2717.

CHAPTER 9–47

Ectopic Hormone Syndromes

Imad M. El-Kebbi, M.D.

DEFINITION

Ectopic hormone production is defined as the production of a hormone by a tissue, usually a neoplasm, that normally does not synthesize that hormone. The hormone thus produced can result in the development of a constellation of signs and symptoms termed ectopic hormone syndrome. There are a variety of ectopic hormone syndromes, but those resulting from ectopic adrenocorticotropic, antidiuretic, and parathyroid hormone-related protein production are clinically more significant and are discussed in some detail. For other hormone syndromes, refer to Table 9–47–1.

ETIOLOGY

Several theories have been suggested to explain ectopic hormone production by tumors. The most likely mechanism is that the process of neoplastic transformation is accompanied by derepression or enhanced expression of the gene encoding for the ectopic protein.

Ectopic Adrenocorticotropic Hormone Syndrome

CRITERIA FOR DIAGNOSIS
Suggestive

Signs and symptoms of hypercortisolism, hyperpigmentation, and hypokalemia, and presence of a tumor, most commonly in the lung (50%), are suggestive criteria. Less frequently associated tumors include

We thank Dr. Y. Khalid Siddiq for permission to update the chapter he wrote on the same subject in the third edition of *Medicine for the Practicing Physician.*

TABLE 9–47–1. UNCOMMON ECTOPIC HORMONE SYNDROMES

Ectopic Hormone	Associated Tumors	Clinical Features	Diagnostic Tests
Melanocyte-stimulating hormone	Same as ACTH-producing tumors	Hyperpigmentation	Melanocyte-stimulating hormone assay
Growth hormone or growth hormone-releasing hormone	Lung carcinoma, pancreatic and carcinoid tumors	Acromegaly	Growth hormone or growth hormone-releasing hormone assay, IGF-I assay
Human chorionic gonadotropin	Carcinoma of lung, ovary, stomach and pancreas	Gynecomastia in males, irregular vaginal bleeding in females	Human chorionic gonadotropin assay
Calcitonin	Thymic, oat cell lung, carcinoid, and pancreatic tumors	Asymptomatic	Calcitonin assay
Erythropoietin	Renal carcinoma, cerebellar hemangioblastoma, uterine fibroma, hepatoblastoma	Polycythemia	Erythropoietin assay
Insulin-like growth factor (mainly IGF-II)	Mesenchymal tumors, hepatoma, adrenocortical carcinoma	Hypoglycemia	IGF-II assay (less commonly IGF-I)

ACTH, adrenocorticotropic hormone; IGF, insulin-like growth factor.
Adapted from Siddiq YK. Ectopic hormone syndromes. In: Hurst JW, editor-in-chief. Medicine for the practicing physician. 3rd ed. Boston: Butterworth-Heinemann, 1992:642. Reproduced with permission of the author.

pheochromocytomas and pancreatic, thymic, gastrointestinal, and thyroid medullary tumors.

Definitive

Increased urinary free cortisol and 17-hydroxycorticosteroids, with inadequate suppression after high-dose dexamethasone administration in most though not all patients; increased circulating levels of cortisol and adrenocorticotropic hormone (ACTH); evidence of an ACTH arteriovenous gradient across the tumor bed; and detection of ACTH immunoreactivity in tumor tissue confirm the diagnosis.

CLINICAL MANIFESTATIONS

Subjective

Patients may lack the classic manifestations of prolonged hypercortisolism, especially if the associated tumor is malignant. In such cases, the duration of symptoms usually does not exceed 6 months, and they include muscle weakness, skin pigmentation, weight loss, hirsutism, polyuria, polydipsia, and hypertension. Complaints related to the underlying tumor may predominate.

Objective

Physical Examination

Physical examination may reveal the presence of hypertension, wasting, hirsutism, hyperpigmentation, and proximal muscle weakness. Sodium retention is occasionally reflected as peripheral edema and pulmonary congestion.

Routine Laboratory Abnormalities

Hypokalemia, metabolic alkalosis, and hyperglycemia are common findings.

PLANS

Diagnostic

Differential Diagnosis

The differential diagnosis includes exogenous glucocorticoid or mineralocorticoid intake, Cushing's disease, and steroid-secreting adrenal tumors.

Diagnostic Options

Diagnostic tests are performed to confirm hypercortisolism, to establish the ectopic and autonomous nature of ACTH. Twenty-four-hour urinary free cortisol, 17-hydroxycorticosteroids, and 17-ketosteroid levels and circulating levels of cortisol and ACTH are all elevated. High-dose dexamethasone (2 mg every 6 hours for 2 days), which suppresses ele-

vated urinary 17-hydroxycorticosteroids in 80 to 90% of patients with pituitary-dependent Cushing's syndrome, fails to do so in most patients with ectopic ACTH-producing tumors; however, some ACTH-producing tumors, and specifically bronchial carcinoids, may be suppressed by high-dose dexamethasone. Corticotropin-releasing hormone administration leads to stimulation of ACTH in patients with Cushing's disease; however, it rarely does so in ACTH-producing tumors. Corticotropin-releasing hormone stimulation with selective petrosal or peripheral vein sampling for ACTH level may be helpful. Staining of tumor biopsy material for ACTH protein or mRNA confirms the diagnosis.

Recommended Approach

It is recommended to document first that a 24-hour urine collection shows elevated free cortisol levels on at least two occasions. Serum cortisol and ACTH levels should be elevated. To differentiate an ectopic from a pituitary source of ACTH, a Liddle test may be performed. These studies, along with the presence of hypokalemia, hyperpigmentation, and a tumor with a known association with ectopic ACTH production, are usually enough to establish the diagnosis. In problematic cases, corticotropin-releasing hormone testing with peripheral or petrosal vein sampling may be needed.

Therapeutic

Therapy should be aimed primarily at eliminating the source of ectopic ACTH production. Surgical resection of the tumor, tumor debulking, radiotherapy, or chemotherapy may be used depending on the tumor type and stage. Potassium or spironolactone administration, sodium restriction, and antihypertensive therapy may be necessary. In the presence of advanced disease, drugs that inhibit cortisol synthesis may be used cautiously so as not to precipitate acute adrenal insufficiency. Ketoconazole (400–1200 mg/d) inhibits the P450 enzyme system, blocking steroid synthesis. It may be combined with metyrapone (500–1000 mg/d), which inhibits the enzyme 11β-hydroxylase. Aminoglutethimide (1–2 g/d), which inhibits conversion of cholesterol to pregnenolone, may be helpful. Mitotane, an adrenal cytotoxic drug, or surgical adrenalectomy may be used in refractory cases. Hydrocortisone may need to be coadministered with the drugs mentioned above to prevent symptoms of adrenal insufficiency.

FOLLOW-UP

The patient's 24-hour urine cortisol and serum potassium levels should be followed periodically, every 6 to 12 weeks, especially when changes in drug therapy are made.

Ectopic Antidiuretic Hormone Syndrome

CRITERIA FOR DIAGNOSIS
Suggestive

Suggestive findings are hyponatremia, urine osmolality higher than that of serum, and presence of a tumor, most commonly small cell lung carcinoma; squamous cell carcinoma of the lung, leiomyosarcoma of the stomach, carcinoma of the pancreas, thymus, and bladder, and tumors of the central nervous system have been also reported to cause this syndrome.

Definitive

Hyponatremia and serum hypoosmolality in the presence of an inappropriately high urine osmolality; continued renal excretion of sodium; no clinical evidence of intravascular volume depletion; normal renal, thyroid, and adrenal function; elevated circulation levels of antidiuretic hormone (ADH); and detection of ADH mRNA or protein in tumor tissue confirm the diagnosis.

CLINICAL MANIFESTATIONS
Subjective

The patient may remain asymptomatic until serum sodium concentration falls to less than 120 mEq/L, when a variety of symptoms attributable to hypotonicity of body fluids appear. These include anorexia, nausea, vomiting, headache, fatigue, confusion, convulsions, and coma.

Objective
Physical Examination

Physical examination may reveal findings related to the primary tumor or its metastasis. Neurologic changes manifesting as impaired memory, disorientation, and impaired consciousness may be found if hyponatremia is severe.

Routine Laboratory Abnormalities

Hyponatremia, serum hypoosmolality, low blood urea nitrogen reflecting the mild degree of volume expansion, urine osmolality higher than that of serum, and urine sodium above 20 mEq/L are common findings.

PLANS
Diagnostic
Differential Diagnosis

The differential diagnosis includes drug-induced hyponatremia and hyponatremia related to intravascular volume depletion, hypocortisolism, hypothyroidism, and renal disease.

Diagnostic Options and Recommended Approach

It is recommended to document first the absence of intravascular volume depletion (related to impaired cardiac output, cirrhosis, or the nephrotic syndrome) and the absence of drugs known to stimulate ADH secretion, such as vincristine, cyclophosphamide, barbiturates, and morphine, all of which are commonly used in cancer patients. Hypothyroidism and hypocortisolism should be ruled out. In the absence of any of the above conditions, and in the presence of an inappropriately elevated serum ADH, the diagnosis of inappropriate ADH secretion is established. If in doubt, a water loading test may be performed; it is considered diagnostic if it fails to dilute the urine. Detection of ADH in the tumor tissue confirms the diagnosis.

Therapeutic

Therapy should be aimed primarily at eliminating the source of ectopic ADH production. Surgical resection of the tumor, tumor debulking, radiotherapy, or chemotherapy may be used depending on the tumor type and stage. Restriction of fluid intake to less than 1 L per day is often necessary to raise the serum sodium concentration. In severe cases, especially when neurologic abnormalities are present, acute administration of 3% (hypertonic) saline and furosemide has been found effective; however, rapid correction of hyponatremia can result in neurologic deterioration, known as central pontine myelinolysis. Therefore severe hyponatremia, especially if chronic, should be corrected at a rate no faster than 2 mEq/L per hour to bring serum sodium above 120 mEq/L; correction rates of 25 mEq/L or more in the first 48 hours should be avoided. Demeclocycline (600–1200 mg/d) counteracts the effects of ADH on the renal tubule and is useful for chronic management. Lithium acts similarly but has considerable side effects, limiting its use.

FOLLOW-UP

The patient's serum sodium level should be followed periodically, every 2 to 4 weeks, especially when changes in drug therapy are made. Renal function should be monitored if demeclocycline is used.

Ectopic Parathyroid Hormone-related Protein Syndrome

CRITERIA FOR DIAGNOSIS
Suggestive

Hypercalcemia and hypophosphatemia in the presence of known or suspected malignancy, mainly squamous cell tumors of the lung, kidney, and urogenital tract, suggest the diagnosis.

Definitive

Hypercalcemia and hypophosphatemia associated with a malignancy, with no evidence of local bone destruction; and elevated serum parathyroid hormone (PTH)-related protein and low serum PTH levels confirm the diagnosis.

CLINICAL MANIFESTATIONS
Subjective

Hypercalcemia-related symptoms tend to occur when serum calcium is above 11.5 mg/dL. They may manifest as malaise, anorexia, nausea, vomiting, polyuria, and confusion, and may progress to coma and death.

Objective
Physical Examination

Physical examination may reveal findings related to the primary tumor or its metastasis. Muscular weakness, hyporeflexia, and alteration in mental status may be found in moderate to severe hypercalcemia.

Routine Laboratory Abnormalities

Hypercalcemia, hypophosphatemia, and hypercalciuria are common; hypercalcemic nephropathy may lead to elevation in blood urea nitrogen, creatinine, phosphorus, and uric acid levels; serum alkaline phosphatase of bone origin may be elevated.

PLANS
Diagnostic
Differential Diagnosis

The differential diagnosis includes primary hyperparathyroidism and tumor hypercalcemia mediated by factors other than PTH-related protein (such as 1,25-dihydroxyvitamin D in lymphoma, osteoclast activation factor and cytokines in multiple myeloma, and prostaglandins in breast carcinoma).

Diagnostic Options and Recommended Approach

It is recommended to rule out primary hyperparathyroidism first by documenting that serum PTH level is suppressed; a bone scan would be helpful to rule out local bony resorption, and an elevated serum PTH-related protein level would confirm hypercalcemia induced by PTH-related protein.

Therapeutic

Therapy should be aimed primarily at eliminating the source of production of PTH-related protein. Surgical resection of the tumor, tumor debulking, radiotherapy, or chemotherapy may be used depending on the tumor type and stage. Hypercalcemia is initially treated with intravenous saline administration coupled with furosemide-induced diuresis. In severe cases, pamidronate, 30 to 90 mg given intravenously over 24 hours, or gallium nitrate, 200 mg/m^2 daily for 5 consecutive days, is recommended. Serum calcium, phosphorus, magnesium, and creatinine levels should be closely monitored. Mithramycin 0.025 mg/kg intravenously should be reserved for resistant cases in view of its toxicity. Calcitonin is poorly effective in hypercalcemia of malignancy.

FOLLOW-UP

Serum calcium, phosphorus, magnesium, and creatinine levels should be monitored every 2 weeks.

Ectopic Hormone Syndromes

DISCUSSION
Prevalence

Ectopic ACTH-producing tumors account for 15 to 20% of patients with Cushing's syndrome. Among patients with small cell lung cancer, 20 to 40% have the syndrome of inappropriate ADH secretion. Close to 10% of patients with squamous cell lung cancer have tumor-induced hypercalcemia.

Related Basic Science

The exact mechanisms involved in the pathogenesis of ectopic hormone syndromes are unclear. During development, all cells contain totipotential genetic material. Most of this information is repressed as normal cells undergo differentiation and acquire specialized functions; however, it is postulated that with the development of neoplastic changes, "derepression" of certain genes may occur, leading to unregulated excessive production of their corresponding proteins.

Natural History and Its Prevention with Treatment

The course of the disease is determined by the nature of the underlying malignancy and the type of ectopic hormone being produced.

Prevention

These diseases cannot be prevented; however, the adverse effects of ectopic hormones can be minimized by early detection and treatment.

Cost Containment

A thorough workup may be expensive. Management outside the hospital and avoiding unnecessary repetition of hormone assays once the disease has been established would help in limiting cost.

REFERENCES

Moses AM, Scheinman SJ. Ectopic secretion of neurohypophyseal peptides in patients with malignancy. *Endocrinol Metab Clin North Am* 1991;20:489.

Mundy GR. Ectopic secretion of calciotropic peptides. *Endocrinol Metab Clin North Am* 1991;20:473.

Schteingart DE. Ectopic secretion of peptides of the proopiomelanocortin family. *Endocrinol Metab Clin North Am* 1991;20:453.

CHAPTER 9–48

Autoimmune Polyglandular Syndromes

Suzanne S. P. Gebhart, M.D.

DEFINITION

Autoimmune polyglandular syndromes are a group of disorders characterized by the autoimmune destruction of two or more endocrine organs. Two distinct forms of this disease have been described. Type I polyglandular syndrome is characterized by the triad of chronic mucocutaneous candidiasis, hypoparathyroidism, and autoimmune adrenal insufficiency (Addison's disease). Type II polyglandular syndrome (Schmidt's syndrome) is defined as the presence of Addison's disease plus at least one other endocrine organ dysfunction.

A third category of patients have no evidence of adrenal dysfunction but do have two autoimmune diseases, commonly thyroid disease and either diabetes mellitus or nonendocrine autoimmune dysfunction, such as pernicious anemia or myasthenia gravis. Whether this group represents a true syndrome is unclear at present. Most of these patients, however, do not progress to adrenal insufficiency.

ETIOLOGY

Both type I and II autoimmune polyglandular syndromes are associated with detectable antibodies directed against cellular components (usually enzymes) of endocrine organs. The presence of antibodies, however, does not carry direct correlation with endocrine function. For the most part, it is felt cell-mediated autoimmunity, also active in both autoimmunity syndromes, produces cellular damage.

Type I syndrome is usually sporadic in occurrence but has also been shown to occur as an autosomal recessive trait. The inheritance pattern of type II syndrome is stronger and appears to be autosomal dominant with incomplete penetrance.

CRITERIA FOR DIAGNOSIS
Suggestive

Autoimmune polyglandular syndrome type I has onset in childhood. Recurrent mucocutaneous candidiasis and other fungal infections are often present during infancy. Peak age of onset is 12 years. The most common endocrine abnormality is hypoparathyroidism.

Type II autoimmune polyglandular syndrome generally does not develop until adulthood. The presence of adrenal insufficiency is necessary for the diagnosis. Autoimmune thyroid disease—either hypothyroidism, Hashimoto's thyroiditis, or Graves' disease—is the most common second endocrinopathy. Insulin-dependent diabetes mellitus is also quite common and occurs at a somewhat older age when associated with this syndrome. Table 9–48–1 lists the clinical features of each syndrome according to frequency of occurrence.

Definitive

The criterion for the diagnosis of type I polyglandular syndrome is the presence of two of the three classic conditions: mucocutaneous candidi-

TABLE 9–48–1. POLYGLANDULAR FAILURE SYNDROMES: CLINICAL MANIFESTATIONS IN ORDER OF FREQUENCY

Type I	Type II
Hypoparathyroidism	Addison's disease
Chronic mucocutaneous candidiasis	Autoimmune thyroid disease
Addison's disease	Insulin-dependent diabetes mellitus
Gonadal failure	Gonadal failure
Gastrointestinal malabsorption	Pernicious anemia
Pernicious anemia	Hypoparathyroidism
Alopecia	Myasthenia gravis
Chronic active hepatitis	Vitiligo
Sjogren's syndrome	Diabetes insipidus
Vitiligo	
Autoimmune thyroid disease	
Insulin-dependent diabetes mellitus	

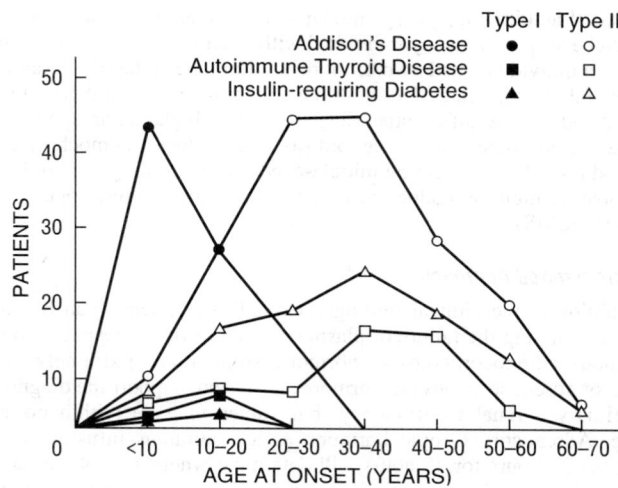

Figure 9–48–1. Occurrence of autoimmune disease associated with polyendocrine syndrome type I (solid lines) is compared with that associated with polyendocrine syndrome type II (dotted lines). Circles, Addison's disease; squares, autoimmune thyroid disease; triangles, insulin-requiring diabetes. *(Source: Neufeld M, MacLaren NK, Blizzard RM. Two types of autoimmune Addison's disease associated with different polyglandular autoimmune (PGA) syndromes. Medicine 1981;60:355. Reproduced with permission from Williams & Wilkins and the author.)*

asis, hypoparathyroidism, and adrenal insufficiency. If the patient is a member of an affected family, then the presence of one of these major components may be sufficient to make the diagnosis.

The criterion for the diagnosis of type II polyglandular failure is the documented presence of autoimmune adrenal insufficiency and either autoimmune thyroid disease or diabetes mellitus.

CLINICAL MANIFESTATIONS
Subjective

The most common presenting symptom for type I polyglandular syndrome is mucocutaneous candidiasis. This may range from abnormalities of the nail beds to pain and redness associated with candidal infections of the skin or mucosal surfaces. Hypoparathyroidism, which can present with a range of symptoms varying from mild tingling in the fingers to tetany, laryngeal stridor, or seizures, is usually the second abnormality to occur. Both are often present before the age of 5 years and precede the development of Addison's disease. Symptoms of Addison's disease are weakness, hypoglycemia, weight loss, hyperpigmentation, postural hypotension, and/or syncope. In all reports, the first manifestation of type I polyglandular failure occurs before the age of 15 years. As most cases are sporadic, there may be no family history.

The onset of various components of type II polyglandular syndrome is more variable, although it tends to occur at a later age. Addison's disease, found (by definition) in 100% of patients with this syndrome, occurs as the presenting symptom in approximately 40 to 50% of patients. It is preceded by either diabetes mellitus or autoimmune thyroid disease in 30 to 40% of patients, and the two diseases occur simultaneously in 20%. Many years may separate the development of each component of this disorder (Figure 9–48–1).

Autoimmune thyroid disease may be asymptomatic. If metabolism is low, symptoms of weight gain, lethargy, dryness of the skin or hair, constipation, hoarseness, or menstrual irregularity may be present. If Graves' thyrotoxicosis is present, symptoms of hypermetabolism such as weight loss, palpitations, nervousness, and heat intolerance may predominate. Sometimes, thyroid enlargement causes the individual to seek medical attention. Autoimmune thyroiditis is painless but may be associated with transient hypo- or hyperthyroidism with associated symptoms.

Diabetes mellitus presents with weight loss, polyuria, thirst, weakness, and ketosis.

Type II syndrome is often associated with a family history of other autoimmune problems.

Objective
Physical Examination

In type I polyglandular syndrome, chronic candidiasis may cause pitting, thickening, and irregularities of the nail beds and hyperkeratotic lesions of the scalp, face, and hands. Mucosal surfaces may show maceration and leukoplakia.

Physical manifestations of hypoparathyroidism are muscle spasms and tetany. Muscle irritability may manifest as a facial twitch elicited by tapping over the facial nerve (Chvostek's sign) or carpopedal spasm during constriction of the circulation to the arm (Trousseau's sign).

Addison's disease may present with orthostatic hypotension, muscle wasting, and hyperpigmentation. Nausea, vomiting, and vascular collapse are signs of adrenal crisis and warrant emergency intervention with steroid administration. Fasting hypoglycemia may occur.

The thyroid gland in autoimmune thyroid disease is nontender and usually enlarged. Hashimoto's thyroiditis may involve all or only part of the gland, producing diffuse enlargement or asymmetric nodularity. In Graves' disease, the thyroid is smooth and diffusely enlarged. There may be evidence of ophthalmopathy or dermopathy. Hypothyroidism may be detected as a delay in relaxation after eliciting deep tendon reflexes.

New onset of diabetes mellitus usually produces physical findings of dehydration and ketosis.

Routine Laboratory Abnormalities

In hypoparathyroidism, the plasma calcium level is low, the inorganic phosphate level is high, and the alkaline phosphatase level is normal. Serum albumin levels should always be checked in conjunction with the calcium level to determine if the hypocalcemia is based on reduced calcium binding. Addison's disease is associated with hyperkalemia, acidosis, and prerenal azotemia. In Hashimoto's thyroiditis serum thyroxine is usually normal, but it may be high or low. Total and free thyroxine levels are elevated in Grave's disease. Thyroid-stimulating hormone is suppressed. Laboratory diagnosis of hypothyroidism is based on a low total thyroxine with elevated thyroid-stimulating hormone. Hyperglycemia with severe ketoacidosis and coma may be the initial presentation of diabetes mellitus.

PLANS
Diagnostic
Differential Diagnosis

The diagnosis of both types of autoimmune polyglandular syndrome is based on the clinical presentation. Because of the early age of onset and distinct features of mucocutaneous candidiasis, type I disease rarely presents a diagnostic problem.

Type II autoimmune polyglandular syndrome may be more subtle. It should be suspected in any individual with a family history of the disorder or in individuals with two or more autoimmune endocrine diseases.

Several diseases can affect multiple endocrine organs and need to be considered in the differential diagnosis of polyglandular syndrome. These include tuberculosis, sarcoidosis, amyloidoses, hemochromatosis, and a syndrome affecting middle-aged men consisting of peripheral neuropathy, multiple endocrine organ failure, and sclerotic plasmacytoma (POEMS).

Recommended Approach

In addition to the clinical findings, adrenal insufficiency can be confirmed by noting the failure of plasma cortisol to rise in response to intravenous adrenocorticotropic hormone stimulation. Extremely high levels of adrenocorticotropic hormone, if present, support the diagnosis of primary adrenal insufficiency, but values may be within normal range. Adrenocorticotropic hormone as a continuous infusion of 40 units per 24 hours for 48 hours will determine whether an abnormality exists in the hypothalamic–pituitary axis. The normal response is an increase in 24-hour urinary free cortisol and 17-hydroxysteroid levels, which will not occur if primary adrenal disease is present.

In general, measuring circulating antibodies directed against endocrine tissue is not a useful clinical tool. These tests are difficult to obtain and do not correlate well with endocrine dysfunction. One possible exception, however, is the measurement of antibodies against thyroid peroxidase, the antigen measured in antithyroid microsomal antibody assays. This antibody is present in high titer in Hashimoto's thyroiditis and in somewhat lower titer in Graves' disease. The presence of Addison's disease with normal thyroid function tests but elevated antithyroid microsomal antibodies would confirm polyglandular disease.

Therapeutic

Recommended Approach

Chronic mucocutaneous candidiasis is refractory to topical antifungal therapy. Amphotericin B and ketoconazole have been successful in a few patients.

Treatment of patients with both types of polyglandular syndrome is dependent on the endocrinopathy involved (Table 9–48–2). Adrenal insufficiency is a life-threatening condition that is commonly present in both polyglandular failure syndromes. Recognition of this disorder and initiation of replacement therapy are essential. Both mineralocorticoid replacement and glucocorticoid replacement are required.

In children, the dose of hydrocortisone must be closely regulated to avoid growth retardation. Glucocorticoid replacement with hydrocortisone, 12 to 20 mg/m^2 per day, and mineralocorticoid replacement with fludrocortisone (Florinef), 0.05 to 0.2 mg per day, must be adjusted individually. A diet liberal in salt is recommended.

It is essential that each patient with Addison's disease understand the absolute necessity of taking cortisol regularly. Stress or illness increases steroid requirements. Minor illnesses can usually be managed by instructing the patient to double his or her usual maintenance steroid dose. All patients with Addison's disease should carry identification with their diagnosis and their doctor's name. An emergency kit of dexamethasone for intramuscular injection may be appropriate for some patients and their families.

The management of hypoparathyroidism relies on giving vitamin D or its metabolites and oral calcium. Synthetic parathyroid hormone is not used therapeutically. Vitamin D in 25,000 to 150,000 units per day is the least expensive form of therapy and is effective. Because it is stored in fat, however, if vitamin D toxicity occurs, it is long-lasting. Calcitriol (Rocaltrol), a 1,25-dihydroxyvitamin D analog, is the active form of vitamin D and is a potent stimulator of calcium absorption. It has a shorter duration of action (3–5 days). Dosage must be titrated carefully to prevent hypercalcemia and ranges from 0.25 to 2 μg per day. Calcium supplement in the range of 2 to 3 g elemental calcium per day is usually adequate in combination with vitamin D therapy to maintain the serum calcium level in the low-normal range.

Management of autoimmune thyroid disease is dependent on the form of the disease. In Graves' disease, metabolism should be returned to normal. In Hashimoto's thyroiditis, if thyroid function is normal, only observation may be required. Hypothyroidism requires replacement therapy using levothyroxine in the range of 0.05 to 0.2 mg per day. Dose should be based on maintaining serum levels of thyroid-stimulating hormone within normal range. Diabetes mellitus requires insulin therapy and adjunctive training and support to maintain lifelong glycemic control.

FOLLOW-UP

Lifelong periodic follow-up is necessary in both syndromes. Many patients with type I polyglandular syndrome are diagnosed when they are children. Following growth curves is useful in ascertaining appropriate replacement therapy. Growth retardation is a sensitive indicator of excessive glucocorticoids, as well as of the new development of Addison's disease. Serum calcium levels should be maintained at the lower range of normal with adjustments to vitamin D and calcium supplements. Chronic active hepatitis occurs in approximately 10% of patients with type I polyglandular syndrome, requiring periodic checks of hepatic function.

As in type I autoimmune polyglandular syndrome, follow-up in patients with type II syndrome is geared to detecting developing autoimmune disease and assessing appropriate replacement therapy. In patients with autoimmune thyroid disease who are not hypothyroid at the time of diagnosis, the development of hypothyroidism during the course of their illness is likely, and levels of thyroid-stimulating hormone and total thyroxine should be checked at yearly intervals or when the patient develops symptoms suggestive of low metabolism. As pernicious anemia can occur in both disorders, yearly blood counts also may be appropriate as part of routine follow-up. It is generally not useful to follow antibody titers directed to endocrine organs. There is no good correlation between antibody levels and actual organ function. Changes in body weight, skin or hair, menstrual patterns in women, and sexual function are helpful in evaluating the development of endocrinopathies.

As both autoimmune polyglandular syndromes can be familial, family members with this disorder can have undiagnosed endocrine disease; therefore, it is wise to screen first-degree family members.

DISCUSSION

Prevalence and Incidence

Type I polyglandular syndrome is a rare disorder that is usually sporadic, but in some families inherited in an autosomal recessive pattern. Circulating immunoglobulins directed against the adrenal, thyroid, ovary or testes, gastric parietal cells, and anterior pituitary have been detected, although the presence of antibodies has not invariably resulted in end-organ dysfunction. Males and females are equally affected.

Type II polyglandular syndrome, originally called Schmidt's syndrome, is more common than polyglandular syndrome type I, with a frequency of approximately 20 per million in the general population. Its mode of inheritance has not been consistent; some families exhibit an autosomal dominant pattern with variable penetrance, whereas others show an autosomal recessive pattern. Females predominate in this disorder, being two to three times more likely to develop this syndrome than males.

TABLE 9–48–2. THERAPEUTIC MANAGEMENT OF ENDOCRINOPATHY

Defect	Chapter
Hypoparathyroidism	9–38
Adrenal insufficiency	9–11
Hypothyroidism	9–19
Hashimoto's thyroiditis	9–15
Graves' thyrotoxicosis	9–18
Insulin-dependent diabetes mellitus	9–29
Primary gonadal failure	9–20, 9–21, 9–24, 10–2

Related Basic Science

Genetics

Many autoimmune diseases are associated with specific allelic patterns of the HLA complex located on the short arm of chromosome 6. HLA-B8/DR3 loci have been linked with Addison's disease, diabetes mellitus, and Graves' disease in Caucasians, but do not appear to be associated with the transmission of polyglandular syndrome type II. Increased risk for type II syndrome has been described with the HLA-A1/B8 haplotype and with the expression of HLA-DR4.

Altered Molecular Biology

Antibodies directed against several endocrine organs are detectable in both syndromes. Circulating immunoglobulins capable of altering growth and function by binding to thyroid-stimulating hormone receptors and adrenocorticotropic hormone receptors have been detected in autoimmune thyroid disease and Addison's disease. Tissue-specific antibodies directed toward cellular enzymes such as thyroid peroxidase and islet cell glutamic acid decarboxylase, found in autoimmune endocrine disease, may serve as sensitive markers of the disease process, but also may shed insight into underlying pathophysiologic mechanisms.

There is evidence of altered cellular immunity in both syndromes, as evidenced by the increased susceptibility to candidal infections in patients with the type I syndrome and by the decreased suppressor cell number and increased cell-mediated cytotoxicity in the type II syndrome.

Despite expanding knowledge of the immune system, much needs to be learned about the underlying defects resulting in autoimmune disease. The etiology is almost certainly multifactorial. Although there is clearly a genetic predisposition, environmental exposure to infection, stress, and dietary variation may also play a role. In addition, physiologically insignificant autoimmune reactivity is found in the normal population.

The contribution of the endocrine system to susceptibility to autoimmune disease is poorly understood. Many autoimmune diseases show a female predominance. It is most pronounced in autoimmune thyroid disease, where there is a female:male predominance of 4:1. This is true to a lesser degree in type II polyendocrine syndrome. Activity of autoimmune mechanisms appears to be modulated by pregnancy and the postpartum period. Animal studies suggest that androgens may suppress autoimmunity, while estrogens may stimulate it. Glucocorticoids have long been recognized as immunosuppressants. The recent observation that the lymphokine interleukin-1 stimulates adrenal cortisol production provides intriguing possibilities for immune–hormone interaction.

A proposed mechanism for the development of autoimmune disease postulates organ damage in a genetically susceptible individual that results in a low but persistent level of immune activation. Failure of normal mechanisms to suppress this response leads to increasing recruitment of cytoxic lymphocytes and development of antigen-specific immunoglobulins, which result in clinically apparent disease. Secondary factors such as the hormonal milieu, local factors inhibiting suppressor activity, or endocrine cell membrane antigen expression may further augment the immune response. Ultimately, there may be sufficient expansion of the immune response to induce cross-reactivity and damage to other organs.

Natural History and Its Modification with Treatment

Prompt recognition of endocrinopathies and initiation of appropriate replacement therapy have resulted in low morbidity associated with these disorders. The primary complication is adrenal crisis.

Prevention

No preventive measures are currently available. Clinical trials using immunosuppression in the early management of diabetes, if successful, may be applicable to these disorders as well. More research is needed.

Cost Containment

Replacement therapy for endocrinopathies is generally inexpensive. Careful history and physical examination and follow-up visits should indicate when provocative testing for end-organ failure is required.

REFERENCES

Ahonen P, Myllarniemi S, Sipila I, Perheenturpa J. Clinical variation of autoimmune polyendocrinopathy-candidiasis-ectodermal dystrophy (APECED) in a series of 68 patients. N Engl J Med 1990;322:1829.

DeGroot LJ, Quintans J. The causes of autoimmune thyroid disease. Endocr Rev 1989;10:537.

Karlsson FA, Kampe O, Winqvist O, Burman P. Autoimmune endocrinopathies: 5. Autoimmune disease of the adrenal cortex, pituitary, parathyroid glands and gastric mucosa. J Intern Med 1993;234:379.

Muir A, Maclaren NK. Autoimmune diseases of the adrenal glands, parathyroid glands, gonads and hypothalamic–pituitary axis. Endocrinol Metab Clin North Am 1991;20:619.

Neufeld M, Maclaren NK, Blizzard RM. Two types of autoimmune Addison's disease associated with different polyglandular autoimmune (PGA) syndromes. Medicine 1981;60:355.

Uibo R, Aavik E, Peterson P, et al. Autoantibodies to cytochrome P450 enzymes P450scc, P450c17 and P450c21 in autoimmune polyglandular disease types I and II and in isolated Addison's disease. J Clin Endocrinol Metab 1994;78:323.

CHAPTER 9–49

Abnormal Endocrine Measurements in Nonendocrine Chronic Illness

John T. Nicoloff, M.D.

DEFINITION

Characteristic alterations in endocrine indices, including thyroid, growth, and sex hormones, occur in a wide variety of chronic illnesses. These illnesses include sepsis, trauma, surgery, advanced malignancies, and metabolic disorders such as diabetes mellitus. Similar endocrine alterations may also be observed with dietary caloric restriction (protein and carbohydrates), undernutrition, and advancing age.

ETIOLOGY

Changes in systemic endocrine function associated with chronic illnesses are usually orchestrated through the systemic actions of circulating cytokines such as interleukins (IL-1, IL-2, IL-6, and IL-12), tumor necrosis factor, and interferons that are released from activated immune system cells (macrophages and monocytes). Various bacterial toxins, as well as trauma itself, may serve as inciting agents for cytokine release. The mechanism underlying similar endocrine responses associated with metabolic disorders and undernutrition is unclear.

CRITERIA FOR DIAGNOSIS

Suggestive

Endocrine alterations associated with chronic disease should be entertained in any patient with a systemic illness persisting beyond 1 week.

Definitive

Reductions in serum thyroid hormone levels provide the most accessible and cost-effective method for establishing a biochemical diagnosis. A persistent depression of serum total triiodothyronine (T_3) values to less than 50 ng/dL or a T_3/thyroxine (T_4) ratio less than 10 indicates that such endocrine abnormalities of chronic illnesses or undernutrition are present. In critically ill populations, depression of total T_4 values to less than 4 μg/dL also serves as an excellent predictor of mortality. Conversely, increasing T_3, T_4 and T_3/T_4 ratio values serve as indicators of recovery.

CLINICAL MANIFESTATIONS

Subjective

There is a paucity of specific clinical findings indicating the presence of endocrine abnormalities in these patients. Surprisingly, there are no clinical features of thyroid hormone deficiency despite substantial reductions in serum T_3 levels; however, depressions in gonadal function, as reflected by a decline or absence of libido, testicular atrophy, or cessation of menstruation, are not uncommon. With prolonged chronic illnesses, evidence for impairment of general somatic growth occurs as reflected by losses in lean body mass and retarded growth of hair, nails, and skin. This impaired anabolism is most dramatically evidenced in children, in whom slowing or cessation of linear growth may be seen.

Objective

Physical Examination

On physical examination, weight loss and decrease in lean body mass may be displayed by reductions in skeletal muscle strength. The magnitude of this problem usually parallels the duration and severity of the illness. With prolonged chronic illness, testicular atrophy may be evidenced. Wound healing is not affected in the early phases of chronic illness, but if the general wasting is severe, it too may be retarded.

Routine Laboratory Abnormalities

This catabolic state of chronic illness may be reflected in depressed serum albumin levels. Otherwise, there are no alterations in routine chemistries.

PLANS

Diagnostic

The changes in endocrine tests for this disorder are summarized in Table 9–49–1. Depressions in serum T_3, T_3/T_4 ratio, and T_4 values provide the best integrated index of this phenomenon. Specifically, the measurement of serum T_3/T_4 ratio values is recommended as the best screening test. A

TABLE 9–49–1. ENDOCRINE ALTERATIONS IN CHRONIC NONENDOCRINE ILLNESSES

Measurement	Severity of Illness	
	Mild	Severe
Total and free triiodothyronine	↓	↓↓
Total thyroxine	→	↓↓
Free thyroxine index	→	↓↓
Free thyroxine	↑→	→
Thyroid-stimulating hormone	→	→↓
Testosterone	↓	↓↓
Estrogens	↓	↓↓
Luteinizing hormone and follicle-stimulating hormone	↓	↓↓
Growth hormone	↓→	↑→↓
Insulin-like growth factor 1	↓	↓↓
Cortisol	↓→	↑→↓
Renin	↑→	↑→
Aldosterone	→	↓

↓=decreased, →=unchanged, ↑=increased.

lack of elevation in serum thyroid-stimulating hormone helps to distinguish this condition from primary hypothyroidism. As gonadotropin and sex hormone levels are also frequently depressed, some diagnostic confusion with hypopituitarism may occur; however, the presence of normal or elevated serum free thyroxine and cortisol levels with nonendocrine illnesses distinguishes this disorder from pituitary disease. Measurements of other endocrine indices, as listed in Table 9–49–1, are of interest in showing the breadth of alterations occurring in endocrine metabolism, but are not of particular diagnostic utility.

Therapeutic

There is no evidence that endocrine therapy plays a role in the treatment of nonendocrine chronic illnesses. In some patients, however, empiric therapy may be indicated until adequate laboratory assessment becomes available for ruling out intrinsic endocrine disease. In those instances, the intravenous administration of 500 μg of levothyroxine and 40 to 300 mg of hydrocortisone, or its equivalent, daily should be used until laboratory data become available to establish a definitive diagnosis. In critically ill patients displaying hyperreninemic hypoaldosteronism syndrome associated with hyperkalemia, potassium restriction usually suffices. Serious consideration of parenteral alimentation should be considered in most cases if oral nutrition is not feasible, as undernutrition may be playing an important role in perpetuating this disorder.

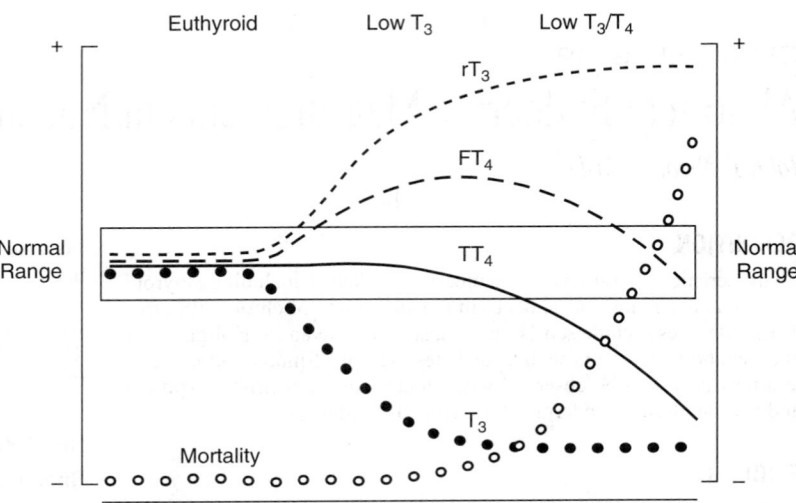

Figure 9–49–1. Schematic representation of the relative alterations in serum total thyroxine (TT_4), total triiodothyronine (T_3), total reverse triiodothyronine (rT_3), and free thyroxine (FT_4) values in relationship to the severity of nonthyroidal illness and mortality.

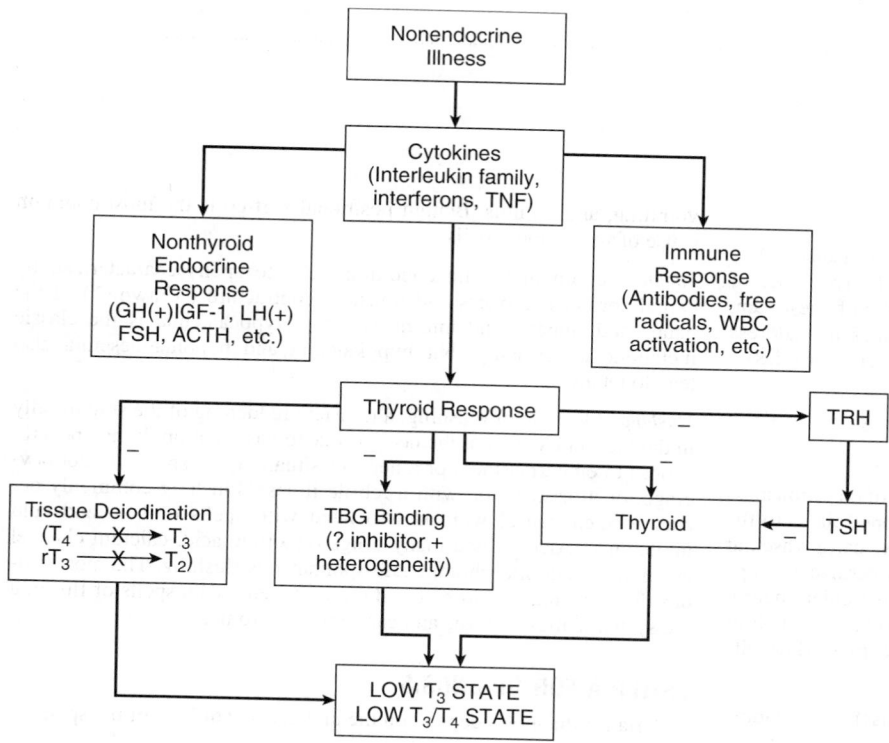

Figure 9–49–2. Schematic representation of the putative role of the cytokine system in initiating both immunologic and endocrine responses to nonendocrine illnesses. TNF, tumor necrosis factor; WBC, white blood cell; GH, growth hormone; IGF-1, insulin-like growth factor I; LH, luteinizing hormone; FSH, follicle-stimulating hormone; ACTH, adrenocorticotropic hormone; TBG, thyroxine-binding globulin; TRH, thyrotropin-releasing hormone; TSH, thyroid-stimulating hormone; T_4, thyroxine; T_3, triiodothyronine; rT_3 total reverse T_3; T_2, diiodothyronine.

FOLLOW-UP

Serial measurements of serum T_3/T_4 ratio values serve as a most practical prognostic indicator of clinical status, as is shown in Figure 9–49–1. As a patient's condition worsens, this ratio value may progress into a low T_3/T_4 state, which indicates a high risk for a fatal outcome. If alimentation therapy is employed, an increase in the serum T_3/T_4 ratio value also serves as an indicator of therapeutic benefit.

DISCUSSION

Prevalence

The array of endocrine alterations, as listed in Table 9–49–1, may occur in all patients with acute or chronic systemic illnesses or injuries to some degree. In hospitalized populations, approximately 50% of patients achieve the criteria for a low T_3 state, whereas about 5% display the low T_3/T_4 state associated with critical illness.

Related Basic Science

At present, these endocrine alterations represent a part of a complex cascade of events orchestrated by cytokines, as graphically shown in Figure 9–49–2. These cytokines are also responsible for producing many, if not all, of the clinical and chemical features that are associated with acute and chronic illness including fever, anorexia, and local inflammatory responses. Associated with this cytokine response is the induction of a generalized catabolic state which, in part, is mediated by the elevations in adrenocorticotropic hormone and cortisol. This catabolic state is further accelerated by reductions in circulating insulin-like growth factor 1 levels, which are principally responsible for determining the rate of somatic growth. Lowering of serum T_3 concentrations, in contrast, appears to be a conservation measure that helps to minimize muscle mass losses as the correction of low serum T_3 levels with exogenous T_3 leads to an acceleration of muscle breakdown. A few days of such a catabolic condition following an acute illness in a previously healthy individual is usually well tolerated and is rapidly reversed as cytokine levels fall and recovery proceeds. In contrast, continued catabolism occurring with chronic illnesses may lead to wasting, frailty, and impairment of the immune system's response to superinfection. Ulti-

mately, this may result in secondary infection and a progressive downhill clinical course.

Natural History and Its Modification with Treatment

The abnormalities of endocrine measurements may continue to be present in patients with nonendocrine disease. No specific endocrine therapy is indicated (see Plans, Therapeutic). At present there is no well-defined mechanism to reverse this endocrine-mediated catabolic state associated with chronic illness other than treatment of the primary disorder, good supportive care, and optimal nutrition. With respect to the last item, the anorexia associated with chronic illness often interferes with effective oral alimentation. Recently, infusions of human insulin-like growth factor 1 have been used experimentally in an attempt to reverse this catabolic course but with only modest success.

Cost Containment

The early recognition of these endocrine alterations associated with chronic illnesses may be important in developing an effective initial management strategy, that is, antibiotics, nutrition, and supportive care. Further, by monitoring these alterations, such as assessing the T_3/T_4 ratio values, the physician can objectively determine whether the program is successful or needs to be altered. Such monitoring may avoid inappropriate treatment programs, prolonged hospitalizations, and even fatal outcomes.

REFERENCES

Isselbacher K, Braunwald E, Wilson J, et al., eds. Harrison's principles of internal medicine. 30th ed. 1994:486, 511, 1543, 1937.

Nicoloff JT. Thyroid function in nonthyroidal disease. In: DeGroot L, Besser G, Cahill G, et al., eds. Endocrinology. Philadelphia: Saunders, 1989:640.

Nicoloff JT, LoPresti JS. Nonthyroidal illness. In: Braverman LH, Utiger RD, eds. The thyroid. 6th ed. Philadelphia: Lippincott, 1995:357.

Spencer CA, LoPresti JS, Guttler RB, et al. Applications of a new chemiluminescent thyrotropin assay to subnormal measurement. J Clin Endocrinol Metab 1990;70:453.

Zipser RD, Davenport MW, Martil KL, et al. Hyperreninemic hypoaldosteronism in the critically ill: A new entity. J Clin Endocrinol Metab 1981;53:867.

CHAPTER 9–50

The Patient with "Spells"

Warner M. Burch, M.D.

DEFINITION

Spells are defined as a period of bodily or mental distress/disorder. Any event that a patient experiences may be called a "spell." Examples of spells include a spell of coughing, an episode (or "spell") of chest pain, a fainting spell, or a "nervous" spell. This chapter does not address spells of pain (e.g., headache, chest, or abdominal pain, or arthritides).

ETIOLOGY

Conditions Associated with Unconsciousness

Syncope. Syncope is defined as a sudden transient loss of consciousness with loss of postural tone. The classification of syncope relates to the cause of transient interruption of cerebral blood flow: cardiovascular (reflex syncope due to right-sided heart underfilling or cardiac syncope due to inadequate left-sided heart output); noncardiovascular (neurogenic, such as vertebrobasilar artery ischemia, or psychiatric, such as hysteria); and those syncopal episodes that remain unexplained despite in-depth evaluation.

Seizures. Seizures are defined as abnormal neuronal discharges leading to easily recognized and highly stereotyped patterns such as unconsciousness, muscle stiffening and jerking, and postictal signs seen in typical tonic–clonic, generalized major motor seizures. A thorough knowledge of seizure types helps in evaluating spells. For example, complex partial seizures consist of a motionless stare followed by some repetitive behavior such as chewing, lip smacking, picking at clothes, dressing and undressing, or opening and closing a door.

Pseudoseizures. Pseudoseizures or hysterical seizures mimic seizures but, on careful history taking and observation, differ; for example, the "aura" represents a buildup of anxiety, emotion, and hyperventilation; the person undergoing a simulated grand mal seizure rolls from side to side, thrusts, thrashes arms and legs, often for a prolonged period, but almost never has fecal incontinence and rapidly returns to consciousness following "seizure." The electroencephalogram is normal. These spells occur in patients with emotional overlay, secondary gain, and stress.

Spells That Occur in Alert and Conscious Patients

Hyperadrenergic Spells. Increased sympathetic tone and catecholamine secretion ("fright or flight" reaction) cause spells of palpitations, rapid heart rate, perspiration, trembling, choking, abdominal pain, and anxiety. Most often, acute anxiety reaction accounts for these spells. These patients may hyperventilate secondary to air hunger, which can lead to a syncope spell. Patients who have dramatic, repeated attacks of anxiety often with sense of impending doom or terror have panic syndrome (panic attacks). Neuroglycopenia increases catecholamine secretion; hypoglycemia in diabetics taking insulin (insulin reaction) is the classic example. Postprandial or reactive hypoglycemia is the catch-all category characterized by adrenergic symptoms that develop within a few hours of eating (e.g., idiopathic reactive hypoglycemia, hereditary fructose intolerance). Thyrotoxic patients have spells of palpitations, anxiousness, and nervousness because of increased sensitivity of the sympathetic nervous system in hyperthyroidism. Very rarely, a pheochromocytoma (a tumor of the sympathetic ganglia) secretes excessive catecholamines leading to hypertension and symptoms of increased sympathetic tone.

Presyncope. Many of the causes of reflex syncope (such as orthostatic hypotension) lead to spells of light-headedness, blurred vision, dizziness, and staggered gait without loss of consciousness.

Vertigo. Vertigo and dizziness from vertebral artery insufficiency and Meniere's disease are causes of spells that are associated with nausea, vomiting, and tinnitus. Benign positional vertigo is the most common cause of vertiginous spells.

Tetany. Certain metabolic conditions lead to spells characterized by carpal spasm, numbness and transient contracture ("drawing") of the hands and fingers, and muscle cramps. Hypocalcemia is the classic metabolic abnormality, but hypokalemia and hypomagnesemia also lead to tetany.

Flushing. Flushing or blushing, a transient reddening of the skin usually in the face and V area of the neck, is due to vasodilation. It may be a response to embarrassment or a nervous situation, a response to hot beverage, or in association with a febrile illness. Flushing commonly occurs in menopausal women associated with spells of heat and cold intolerance. Alcohol and many drugs (nicotinic acid, calcium channel antagonists, and morphine) cause spontaneous flushing. The most serious diseases that should be ruled out in patients with spells of flushing are systemic mastocytosis and carcinoid syndrome.

CRITERIA FOR DIAGNOSIS

Criteria for diagnosis depend on the underlying etiology of the spell.

CLINICAL MANIFESTATIONS

Subjective

Describing spells in the context of consciousness or unconsciousness, posture, and precipitating factors helps place the patient into one of the diagnostic categories discussed earlier. The patient should be asked to list in detail the actual spells and the events surrounding the spells so that data from multiple spells may be used to produce a composite picture. Whenever possible, an eyewitness account of a patient's spell is most helpful. The following points should be noted.

Consciousness. Did the patient remain alert or was there an interval of unconsciousness? Loss of consciousness due to syncope requires a diligent search as to its cause (Table 9–50–1).

Effect of Position. Spells occurring on arising from a sitting or recumbent posture suggest orthostatic hypotension. More important is the documentation of spells while recumbent. If the patient's spells occur while lying down, two of the most common differential diagnoses, orthostatic hypotension and vasovagal syncope, can be eliminated.

Relation to Effort. Recurrent spells in relation to effort suggest a cardiac cause including aortic stenosis, primary pulmonary hypertension, and cardiac arrhythmias.

Aura. Patients often state that their spells come on without warning; however, if this point is pursued in detail by asking questions about the moments just prior to the spell, helpful information may be obtained. For example, the most helpful aura is that of pancerebral hypoperfusion: a feeling of giddiness or wooziness, weakness, disequilibrium with true vertigo, and finally dimming of vision prior to loss of consciousness. Such aura is strong evidence against seizures and vertebrobasilar ischemia. A history of an abrupt transition from normal wakefulness to unconsciousness suggests a generalized seizure. Stiffness, jerking, or numbness may indicate a focal motor or sensory seizure that progresses to a major seizure. The auras of temporal lobe epilepsy include bizarre taste or smell sensations and visions.

Description of Patient During the Spell. Major motor seizure with typical tonic–clonic posturing lasting usually less than a minute can be easily diagnosed by lay observers. Pseudoseizures, however, often lasting much longer with purposeless thrashing about or rolling, must be differentiated from major motor epilepsy. The automatisms of temporal lobe epilepsy can be quite helpful in making that diagnosis.

TABLE 9–50–1. CLASSIFICATION OF SYNCOPE

Cardiovascular
  Reflex
    Vasovagal (simple faint)
    Vasovagal (situational)
      Micturition
      Deglutition
      Defecation
      Glossopharyngeal neuralgia
      Postprandial
      Tussive
      Supine hypotensive syndrome of near-term pregnancy
      Valsalva
      Oculovagal
    Orthostatic
      Hyperadrenergic (e.g., volume depletion)
      Hypoadrenergic
        Primary autonomic insufficiency
        Secondary autonomic insufficiency (e.g., neurologic disorders or drugs)
    Carotid sinus
      Cardioinhibitory
      Vasodepressor
  Cardiac
    Mechanical (obstructive)
      Aortic stenosis
      Hypertrophic cardiomyopathy
      Pulmonary embolism
      Aortic dissection
      Myocardial infarction
      Mitral stenosis
      Left atrial myxoma
      Pulmonic stenosis
      Cardiac tamponade
      Prosthetic valve malfunction
      Global myocardial ischemia
      Tetralogy of Fallot
      Pulmonary hypertension
    Electrical (dysrhythmic)
      Atrioventricular block
      Sick sinus syndrome
      Supraventricular or ventricular arrhythmias
      Long-QT syndrome
      Pacemaker-related
Noncardiovascular
  Neurologic
    Vertebrobasilar transient ischemic attack
      Atherosclerosis
      Mechanical
    Subclavian steal syndrome
    Takayasu disease
    Normal pressure hydrocephalus
    Unwitnessed seizure
  Metabolic
    Hypoxia
    Hypoglycemia
    Hyperventilation
  Psychiatric
    Panic disorders
    Major depression
    Hysteria
Unexplained

Modified from Manolis AS, Linzer M, Salem D, Estes NAM. Syncope: Current diagnostic evaluation and management. Ann Intern Med 1990;112,850. Reproduced with permission from the publisher.

Recovery Period Following Spell. Following pancerebral hypoperfusion, unless prolonged, the patient regains consciousness and full orientation within a brief interval (few seconds). A generalized or complex partial seizure is characterized by a return to consciousness with many minutes of confusion before full orientation is regained. The postictal confu-

sional state, characteristic of seizure disorder, provides a clue as to differential diagnosis of spells caused by syncope or seizure.

Objective

Physical Examination

Occasionally, health personnel will observe a spell. The cause of the spell may be easily discerned (such as major motor epilepsy; posttussive syncope; the confused, agitated and sweaty diabetic patient having a hypoglycemic reaction). Obtaining vital signs is imperative (heart rate, pulse, respiratory rate, and blood pressure, both supine and standing). Assess whether the patient is conscious or unconscious, oriented or confused, sweaty or without perspiration, and whether there is fecal or urinary incontinence. Note any circumstance surrounding the spell such as hot, stuffy environment or a situation of fear, anxiety, or emotional stress. The typical simple faint is usually associated with pallor and perspiration. While sitting down or standing up, the patient suddenly feels weak, apprehensive, and nauseated, becomes pale, and breaks out in a cold perspiration; these symptoms are followed by giddiness and clouding of vision, and the patients slumps to the floor unconscious. By this time, the blood pressure and heart rate have fallen; respiration is shallow; pulse is weak; and the patient is pale, cold, clammy, and sweaty; the pupils may respond poorly to light. Within seconds after being supine, the patient returns quickly to previous status. In spells of "syncope" due to hysteria, most of these autonomic symptoms are missing, including a fall in blood pressure. The physical examination may reveal factors that cause the spell, such as orthostatic hypotension, carotid sinus hypersensitivity, aortic outflow murmur, and absent deep tendon reflexes (peripheral neuropathy leading to reflex syncope). Nystagmus helps localize the process to the vestibular apparatus as in benign positional vertigo. Café-au-lait spots or neurofibroma in a hypertensive patient with spells suggests pheochromocytoma.

Routine Laboratory Abnormalities

Occasionally, it is possible to obtain urine and blood for routine analysis. One of the conditions noted previously may be identified in the routine laboratory tests.

PLANS

Diagnostic

Laboratory studies are performed in cases in which the spell cannot be explained or in conditions that predispose one for spells. The history and physical examination should key appropriate studies so that not every possible study is ordered. Table 9–50–2 lists the appropriate studies that should be performed in patients with unexplained spells. If the spell is due to syncope, often the precipitating event is obvious (e.g., micturition, Valsalva, tussive, oculovagal). The physical examination establishes a cause (e.g., orthostatic hypotension). Cardiac syncope is discussed in Chapter 15–3.

Postprandial hypoglycemia can be diagnosed when the symptoms of hypoglycemia are associated temporally with plasma glucose levels less than 50 mg/dL after a meal. Many patients desire a medical diagnosis with which they can allay their spells of anxiety. In such patients,

TABLE 9–50–2. STUDIES FOR PATIENTS WITH SPELLS

Study	Reason
Hemoglobin and hematocrit	Anemia
Blood glucose	Hypoglycemia
Electrocardiogram and 24-hour Holter monitor	Dysrhythmias
Serum electrolytes (K, Na)	Hypokalemic paralysis, hyponatremia
Serum calcium	Tetany or seizures
Thyroid function tests	Hyperthyroidism
24-Hour urine for catecholamines	Pheochromocytoma
24-Hour urine for 5-hydroxyindoleacetic acid	Carcinoid syndrome
Electroencephalogram	Seizures; normal in pseudoseizures

an oral glucose tolerance test is rarely helpful and is best avoided. In a subset of patients who have had gastric surgery, alimentary hypoglycemia appears to be due to excessive glucose loads within the duodenum, which leads to quick absorption and rapid release of insulin, with resultant fall of plasma glucose to a nadir within 2.5 hours of eating.

Therapeutic

Therapy is directed to the cause of the spells. Some spells have a remediable treatment (such as anticonvulsants for seizure disorders and estrogen for "hot flashes" in menopausal women). Often the cause of the spell is unexplained. In such situations, continual observation, a sympathetic physician, and symptomatic remedies such as antianxiety medications for the nervous patient are indicated.

Many patients with "hypoglycemia" do not have hypoglycemia (blood glucose < 50 mg/dL) as a cause of their spells. What to say and what to recommend to these people who are looking for a label for and a means of controlling their symptoms requires clinical discernment. All of these patients (most often women aged 20 to 45) have stresses that are either recognized or not acknowledged. Many have chronic fatigue and somatic complaints lasting days and weeks that do not conform to typical episodic spells of true hypoglycemia. How well these patients are handling stress is reflected in the "hypoglycemic" symptoms.

FOLLOW-UP

Follow-up depends on the underlying etiology of the spell and its treatment.

DISCUSSION

Prevalence and Incidence

"Spells" are common. The exact prevalence and incidence of "spells" are not known.

Related Basic Science

"Spells" with a transient loss of consciousness are a common problem accounting for 3% of emergency room visits and 6% of medical admissions to the hospital (Day et al., 1982). Some syncope spells are benign and self-limited (simple faint); however, considerable morbidity may occur as a result of trauma from falls in the elderly patient. The incidence of syncope increases with age, with an annual occurrence of 6 to 7% and recurrence rate of 30% (Kapoor et al., 1983).

Most syncope is due to hypoperfusion of the brainstem (vertebrobasilar artery ischemia) or panhypoperfusion of both cerebral hemispheres as in cardiovascular syncope. Syncope caused by atherosclerotic carotid artery disease is uncommon and must be the result of severe, bilateral disease. Transient interruption of cerebral blow flow results in loss of consciousness within 8 to 10 seconds. Generally, a fall in systolic blood pressure below 70 mm Hg produces syncope.

The cause of flushing spells of carcinoid syndrome is unknown; they are not due to serotonin or its major metabolite, 5-hydroxyindoleacetic acid.

Natural History and Its Modification with Treatment

When the cause of syncope is ventricular tachycardia, the prognosis is poor if untreated (one third experience sudden death in a year). In up to 50% of patients with syncope, a cause cannot be identified despite extensive evaluation (Manolis et al., 1990). The prognosis in such patients is good and, in some studies, has been no different from that of age-matched control patients. The 1-year mortality for cardiac syncope is 20 to 30%, and that for noncardiac causes, only 5% (Kapoor et al., 1983).

Prevention

The prevention of spells relates to their cause.

Cost Containment

Before ordering studies by "knee jerk" reasoning, the physician should be certain that the history is clear and detailed and the physical examination is thorough.

REFERENCES

Day SC, Cook EF, Funkenstein H, Goldman L. Evaluation and outcome of emergency room patients with transient loss of consciousness. Am J Med 1982;73:15.

Kapoor WN, Karpf M, Wieand S, et al. A prospective evaluation and follow-up of patients with syncope. N Engl J Med 1983;309:197.

Manolis AS, Linzer M, Salem D, Estes NAM. Syncope: Current diagnostic evaluation and management. Ann Intern Med 1990;112:850.

Soniat TLL, Rarron RE. Recurrent falling spells: Differential diagnosis. South Med J 1969;62:855.

Volow MR. Pseudoseizures: An overview. South Med J 1986;79:600.

CHAPTER 9–51

The Weak and Tired Patient

Warner M. Burch, M.D.

DEFINITION

Fatigue is mostly subjective, difficult to describe, and almost impossible to quantitate in terms of laboratory data. The patient who complains of weakness, tiredness, lack of energy, and fatigue is a common scene in any practitioner's office. The nonspecificity of such complaints opens a Pandora's box of possible causes ranging from being up most of the night with a sick child, to incipient diabetes mellitus, to a severe illness. To make any sense out of these symptoms, the physician must integrate them with other symptoms and physical signs.

ETIOLOGY

In many circumstances, it is reasonable to experience weakness and tiredness; that is, fatigue may be normal and physiologic. Prolonged physical and mental exertion without adequate rest leads to fatigue. Sedentary lifestyle leads to deconditioning (poor cardiopulmonary reserve), which fosters a vicious cycle of more fatigue and less activity. Similarly, severe obesity causes fatigue. Inadequate or restless sleep often leads to fatigue. Acute and chronic dieting with negative nitrogen balance and ketosis is associated with lassitude and weakness. Advancing age with decreasing physiologic reserve may lead to fatigue.

Acute fatigue of recent or sudden onset is often the prodrome or sequela of acute infections, such as viral infection, mononucleosis, urinary tract infection, and meningitis. Metabolic states of any fluid or electrolyte imbalance, such as hypokalemia and dehydration, are causes of weakness. Hemolytic anemia and acute leukemia lead to acute fatigue. Finally, circulatory failure may lead to acute onset of fatigue.

Longer, more insidious causes of chronic fatigue are legion. The differential diagnosis includes the following:

- Chronic infection (e.g., subacute bacterial endocarditis, Lyme disease, tuberculosis, fungal and parasitic infestation, chronic pyelonephritis or osteomyelitis)

- Disease related to HIV infection
- Anemias (e.g., megaloblastic and iron deficiency anemias)
- Autoimmune disease (e.g., systemic lupus erythematosus, rheumatoid arthritis)
- Chronic intoxication of endogenous sources (e.g., uremia and hepatic insufficiency)
- Chronic intoxication of exogenous sources (e.g., alcohol, barbiturates, minor tranquilizers, and, rarely, heavy metals, pesticides, or solvents)
- Endocrine disorders (e.g., diabetes mellitus, hyperthyroidism and hypothyroidism, hypercortisolism and hypoadrenalism, hyperparathyroidism and hypoparathyroidism)
- Malignancies (fatigue commonly accompanies middle- and end-stage carcinoma)
- Neurologic disease (e.g., myasthenia gravis, amyotrophic lateral sclerosis, intracranial tumors including hematomas, narcolepsy)
- Chronic fatigue syndrome and fibromyalgia

Tired patients who do not have a definite physical disorder present with several major patterns. Patients with depression have fatigue as a major complaint and often somatize with gastrointestinal symptoms (usually irritable bowel syndrome). Patients with hysteria usually have a complicated or dramatic medical history, a positive review of systems, and a minimum of 25 symptoms without a medical explanation of their etiology. A third group of tired patients exhibit situational exhaustion. These patients are often "workaholics" who are appropriately fatigued and who lack proper rest, relaxation, and sleep. Some of these patients have had chronic stress such as caring for ill and dying family members or live in families with considerable emotional conflict. Finally, a large group of patients have chronic anxiety with and without hyperventilation. These patients are those who may have cardiac neurosis and panic attacks.

CRITERIA FOR DIAGNOSIS

Criteria for diagnosis depend on the underlying etiology of the patient's fatigue.

CLINICAL MANIFESTATIONS

Subjective

Crucial to the differential diagnosis of the weak and tired patient is a careful history taken by an attentive physician. The interaction of the patient and physician at this stage is important, particularly in the patient with chronic fatigue. The last thing a tired health care worker wants to meet is another weak and tired patient. Subtle facial expression, vocal tones, and genuine interest are recognized by the patient. Diligence, persistence, and patience are required to interrogate such patients. Thus, while running the list of "organic" causes (the informational aspect of the complaint), be careful to recognize the transactional side of the complaint. Detailed information on the following should be obtained.

Onset of Tiredness and Weakness. Is there a relationship to known factors such as initiation of medications, increased activity, decreased sleep, and important life changes (new job, new family, or divorce)?

Careful Family History of Diabetes, Anemia, Endocrine Disorders, Depression, or Alcoholism. A history of tick bite is relevant to Lyme disease; and a history of intravenous drug use and sexual partners to HIV infection.

Full Review of Systems. Has the patient lost weight or had a fever, skin rash, or other systemic symptoms or signs? If symptoms are present for every organ system ("positive review of symptoms"), then chronic fatigue of psychiatric origin or chronic fatigue syndrome is likely.

Oral Intake History. This includes dietary history and ingestion of alcohol, caffeine, and prescribed, over-the-counter, or recreational drugs. Such history may reveal "incidental" facts of excessive vitamin A ingestion (hypercalcemia), kelp intake (causing hyperthyroidism or hypothyroidism in a patient with nodular goiter), or excessive intake of nonsteroidal antiinflammatory agents (exacerbating nephropathy).

Objective

Physical Examination

A complete, unhurried physical examination is both informative and therapeutic. Special attention should be directed to evidence of muscle wasting, strength testing (including repetitive muscle fatigue of myasthenia), localizing zones of tenderness over muscles of the torso (e.g., looking for "trigger points" in the fibromyalgic patient), organomegaly, lymph node enlargement, and skin changes (e.g., hyperpigmentation of primary adrenal insufficiency).

Routine Laboratory Abnormalities

Laboratory examination routinely includes a complete blood count with differential; urinalysis; and serum chemistry profile to include electrolytes, glucose, calcium, liver and renal function studies, and thyroid levels.

When scientific data are lacking but the clinician senses that "something is up," he or she should trust that intuitive skill because chronic fatigue may precede any positive physical or laboratory findings.

PLANS

Diagnostic

Special studies may be performed depending on the clinical index of suspicion. Unexplained weight loss or cough prompts a chest x-ray. Nausea with weight loss prompts a short adrenocorticotropic hormone study to exclude adrenal insufficiency. Thyroid function studies, an HIV screen, and PPD skin test should also be performed.

Epstein–Barr virus titers are not helpful nor useful in most patients with chronic fatigue. The incidence of "significant titers" in such patients is similar to that in control patients. Furthermore, the pathogenetic relationship of Epstein–Barr virus to chronic fatigue (or postviral) syndrome is not established. Chronic fatigue syndrome and fibromyalgia have similar clinical features of fatigue, muscle aches, and pain, and often a positive review of systems. The latter two conditions merit discussion in any patient with chronic fatigue whose physical examination and laboratory evaluation are unremarkable.

Because of the nonspecific nature of the symptoms and the lack of a diagnostic test, a consensus of what constitutes chronic fatigue syndrome has been proposed (Holmes et al., 1988) Two major criteria are as follows: (1) new onset of persistent or relapsing, debilitating fatigue in a person who had no previous symptoms that does not resolve with bed rest, and is severe enough to impair daily activity below 50% of premorbid activity for a period of at least 6 months; (2) exclusion of other clinical conditions that cause chronic fatigue. Other minor symptoms include mild fever or chills, sore throat, painful lymph nodes, unexplained generalized muscle weakness, muscle discomfort or myalgia, prolonged (24 hours or greater) generalized fatigue after levels of activity that premorbidly would have been easily tolerated, generalized headaches, migratory arthralgia without joint swelling or redness, neuropsychological complaints (photophobia, visual scotoma, forgetfulness, excessive irritability, confusion, inability to concentrate, and depression), sleep disturbance; often, these symptoms follow a severe flu-like illness. The physical examination should document a low-grade fever (37.6–38.6°C orally) on two occasions 1 month apart; nonexudative pharyngitis or palpable or tender anterior and posterior cervical or axillary lymph nodes. Lymph nodes greater than 2 cm suggest a more serious disorder (e.g., lymphoma, metastatic disease) that requires further evaluation.

Therapeutic

Management of the tired and weak patient who has a specific medical diagnosis such as adrenal insufficiency, side effect of drugs, hyperthyroidism, or acute infection requires specific treatment of the underlying disorder. Such therapy is usually rewarding, with a return of normality for the patient. The ameliorations of fatigue due to severe medical illnesses such as congestive heart failure and carcinomatosis follows the successful treatment of the underlying disorder.

Most physicians are more comfortable managing tired and weak patients who have a physical illness than handling the same complaints in patients who have no obvious disease, such as those with chronic anxiety, depression, hysteria, or chronic fatigue syndrome. For some patients with mild anxiety and apprehension, a thorough history and physical examination and appropriate laboratory studies, followed by encouraging reassurance, are all that is necessary. Others with severe anxiety may require antianxiety medication (e.g., alprazolam 0.25–0.5 mg tid, buspirone 5 mg tid, or lorazepam 0.5–1mg tid). Patients with depression need frequent visits and a psychopharmacologic approach. Involving the family and treating aggressively with antidepressants for several weeks help some patients, but I prefer consultation with a psychiatrist for most patients with chronic fatigue due to depression. The hysterical patient is a difficult problem. Such patients may be so angry and frustrated that no one can help them. Often, medications cause "untoward" side effects. Recognizing these hysterical patients allows a countertransference of problems (patient ventilating and clinician sympathizing) and often saves the patient the pain and expense of a nonproductive workup. The weak and tired patient with fibromyalgia may have nonrestorative sleep; often, amitriptyline 25 to 75 mg at bedtime may help.

Management of the patient with chronic fatigue syndrome is exasperating for both patient and clinician. The conventional approach has been to tell the patients they have a poorly understood disease; they should limit physical and mental activity to prevent further deterioration of their status; they should approach physical activity with caution; and if they experience an upsurge in symptoms, they should get further rest until the symptoms resolve or a treatment becomes available. A better approach is that suggested by Wessely et al. (1989). His message is paraphrased as follows. "You have had an acute illness (80–90% of cases of chronic fatigue syndrome start with flu-like illness) which has forced you to become inactive. Subsequently, you have begun to experience fatigue on exertion and as a result you have started to limit or avoid all activity. Whenever you attempt activity, you begin to encounter symptoms, but never pursue the activities long enough to allow the symptoms to resolve. By doing this you lose tolerance to everyday activity due to increasing unfitness and poor cardiovascular condition leading to symptoms at lower levels of activity that previously were not as difficult. When you experience these symptoms, you also undergo thoughts such as 'If I proceed with this activity, I may get worse' or 'there must be something seriously wrong to make me feel this way.'" This leads to a vicious cycle of increasing avoidance, inactivity and fatigue.

A behavioral program must be tailored to each patient. Regular exercise (gradually increased to involve walking, swimming, etc.), gradual exposure to all avoided activity, cognitive strategies to involve alternative explanations of symptoms (e.g., "I feel tired, I must have done too much" versus "I may be tired because I haven't been doing much lately"), and treatment by a psychotherapist offer a reasonable approach to a difficult problem.

FOLLOW-UP

Follow-up depends on the underlying etiology of the fatigue and the treatment.

DISCUSSION

Prevalence and Incidence

The condition is common but no scientific data are available to indicate its exact prevalence and incidence.

Related Basic Science

There are few scientific data related to this particular symptom. With respect to the weak and tired patient, not much has changed since Allen's (1944) classic review 50 years ago of 300 consecutive patients who presented to the Lahey Clinic with weakness, fatigue, or weak spells. Twenty percent of these patients had a physical ailment (which was obvious in about half of these cases and hidden in about one third); the other 80% had a nervous disorder characterized then as psychoneurosis, depression, or "benign nervous states." These "benign nervous states," which constituted most of the nonphysical causes of fatigue, fit with today's diagnosis of anxiety.

Natural History and Its Modification with Treatment

Many patients obtain relief with the approaches discussed here. This is especially true when an illness can be identified and treated. When the condition has no identifiable cause, the symptoms tend to persist.

Prevention

The prevention of fatigue relates to its cause and, regrettably, the course is not always apparent.

Cost Containment

Before ordering studies by "knee jerk" reasoning, the physician should be certain that the history is clear and detailed and that the physical examination is thorough.

REFERENCES

Allen FN. The differential diagnosis of weakness and fatigue. N Engl J Med 1944;231:414.

Greenberg DB. Neurasthenia in the 1980's: Chronic mononucleosis, chronic fatigue syndrome, and anxiety and depression. Psychosomatics 1990;31:129.

Hench PK. Evaluation and differential diagnosis of fibromyalgia. Rheum Dis Clin North Am 1989;15:19.

Holmes GP, Kaplan JE, Gantz NM, et al. Chronic fatigue syndrome: A working case definition. Ann Intern Med 1988;108:387.

Wessely S, David A, Bulter S, Chalder T. Management of chronic (post-viral) fatigue syndrome. J Coll Gen Pract 1989;39:26.

Common Gynecologic Disorders

Dorothy E. Mitchell-Leef, M.D.

CHAPTER 10–1

Dysmenorrhea

Dorothy E. Mitchell-Leef, M.D.

DEFINITION

Dysmenorrhea may be defined as lower abdominal and back pain with associated radiation to the sacrum and upper thighs coincident with menstruation. It usually occurs just prior to the onset of menses and may continue during the remainder of the period. Primary dysmenorrhea refers to pain associated with intrinsic uterine factors. Secondary dysmenorrhea involves pain arising from abdominal pathology.

ETIOLOGY

Release of prostaglandins from endometrial necrosis and tissue breakdown are the events that lead to the absorption of prostaglandins into the uterine musculature and blood supply. Secondary dysmenorrhea is usually noted in patients later in menstrual life owing to acquired organic disease. The pain is usually associated with longer time intervals and may occur even after menses has been completed.

CRITERIA FOR DIAGNOSIS
Suggestive

A patient who presents with a complaint of cyclic onset of pelvic or back pain associated with the onset of menses should be considered to have dysmenorrhea. When a patient is known to have other pelvic pathology including uterine leiomyoma with associated pain, dysmenorrhea should be diagnosed.

Definitive

Primary dysmenorrhea can be diagnosed only after all other diagnoses have been ruled out definitively. Patients who have undergone diagnostic laparoscopy and have had absolute diagnosis of endometriosis along with the complaint of dysmenorrhea should be considered as having secondary dysmenorrhea. Also, patients who have documented uterine leiomyoma or pelvic inflammatory disease with extensive adhesion formation or the presence of an intrauterine device may be considered as having definitive dysmenorrhea, caused by a presenting secondary factor.

CLINICAL MANIFESTATIONS
Subjective

Complaints of dysmenorrhea must be evaluated by the physician as to severity, onset, and duration.

Symptoms

Primary dysmenorrhea is seen mostly in women under the age of 25; however, it may occur in any age group. Young girls may have dysmenorrhea after ovulatory cycles are established. Some degree of dysmenorrhea is experienced by 50% of all premenopausal women. The pain is characterized as low midline, suprapubic, and may be either sharp or cramplike. The symptom may begin up to 12 hours before menses is recognized and may be associated with nausea, vomiting, backache, and diarrhea. Five major factors contributing to secondary dysmenorrhea are adenomyosis, endometriosis, chronic pelvic inflammatory disease, uterine leiomyomas, and intrauterine devices. In certain types of secondary dysmenorrhea, usually associated with endometriosis, there is a history if increasing cyclic menstrual pain, dyspareunia, or pain on defecation. Secondary dysmenorrhea may also be associated with prolonged or profuse menses.

Past History

Individuals who have been previously diagnosed with endometriosis, with or without dysmenorrhea, who present with these symptomatologies must be considered as having recurrent endometriosis. These patients require a follow-up evaluation including diagnostic laparoscopy to rule out recurrent disease and need to be evaluated and treated for this recurrence. Patients who have a previous history of uterine leiomyoma and present with recurrent dysmenorrhea should be evaluated with a thorough pelvic examination and possible vaginal ultrasound to determine whether or not uterine leiomyomas have recurred. Diagnostic laparoscopy may be an aid in evaluating whether or not smaller leiomyomas have recurred; however, state-of-the-art ultrasound evaluation may be the most cost-effective evaluation prior to treatment rather than a laparoscopic approach.

Family History

Approximately 7% of first-degree relatives of affected patients with endometriosis may have the disease. Knowledge that a first-degree relative has had documented endometriosis may be used in counseling individuals who present with dysmenorrhea and may thereby facilitate early diagnosis and treatment of this disease state.

Polygenic or multifactorial inheritance has been implicated as a causative factor for uterine leiomyomas. If family members have a positive history for uterine leiomyomas, the patient with the presenting dysmenorrhea should be evaluated for this finding.

Objective
Physical Examination

Primary dysmenorrhea may present on examination as uterine tenderness and/or adnexal discomfort only during the menses. The dysmenor-rhea associated with hematocolpos or cryptomenorrhea is usually retropubic and is diagnosed by detecting the bulging, intact hymen.

The diagnosis of endometriosis is somewhat elusive due to the fact that earlier stages are not detectable by pelvic examination. Patients may complain of pelvic tenderness or discomfort during the examination of the adnexae and uterus; however, this is very subjective. A more objective finding is that of adnexal masses or nodularity in the cul-de-sac; however, the definitive diagnosis cannot be made until laparoscopic visualization of the disease state is carried out. Occasionally, patients may have a finding of an extrapelvic lesion, such as bleeding in an incision site, that may lead to the verification that endometriosis is present in this area with secondary diagnosis of endometriosis at the time of laparoscopy.

Patients having uterine leiomyomas that are significantly enlarged may be evaluated easily by pelvic examination. Quantification of the number of leiomyomas and their position and size is easily documented by physical examination alone. For those structures that remain somewhat elusive, diagnosis by vaginal probe ultrasound may be an adjunct to the pelvic examination.

Individuals with pelvic infections may complain of pelvic tenderness and discomfort during physical examination. A prolapse of endometrial polyps may occur through the cervix that can be adequately visualized at the time of speculum examination of the cervix.

Routine Laboratory Abnormalities

There are no specific laboratory abnormalities that would reveal a definitive diagnosis of dysmenorrhea. Physical examination or ultrasound confirmation of uterine leiomyoma can document a fibroid uterus. Evidence of pelvic infection can easily be documented with an elevated white blood cell count on a routine hematologic profile. Individuals with an intact, bulging hymen may need ultrasound confirmation of hematocolpos.

Primary dysmenorrhea is documented only when all other factors are ruled out. A thorough evaluation of the patient's symptoms and physical findings must be made to differentiate primary and secondary causes of dysmenorrhea.

PLANS
Diagnostic

Primary dysmenorrhea is a diagnosis made by exclusion. Diagnosis of secondary dysmenorrhea is based on a definitive causative factor.

Differential Diagnosis

Primary dysmenorrhea occurs in ovulatory cycles. No pelvic lesion is usually found, and primary dysmenorrhea may or may not resolve after pregnancies have occurred. Secondary dysmenorrhea may occur as a consequence of endometriosis, pelvic infections, prolapse of an endometrial polyp, or degenerating leiomyoma; secondary dysmenorrhea may also be due to a rudimentary uterine horn caused by obstructed menstrual fluid and is cramplike and unilateral. Dysmenorrhea associated with hematocolpos or cryptomenorrhea is usually retropubic and is diagnosed by detecting the bulging, intact hymen. Individuals with an intact, bulging hymen may need ultrasound confirmation of hematocolpos.

After multiple diagnoses have been considered and ruled out, diagnostic laparoscopy remains the most important adjunct in final diagnosis in patients who have elusive findings of dysmenorrhea.

Diagnostic Options

Patients with findings of a leiomyoma or endometrial polyps present no dilemma. Pelvic inflammatory disease is frequently suggested by past history or present physical findings. In the case of secondary dysmenorrhea, when no pathology is obvious by either history or pelvic examination, laparoscopy must be performed. Endometriosis and chronic pelvic inflammatory disease involving extensive scar tissue may be adequately diagnosed with laparoscopy. Endometriosis should never be diagnosed unless a thorough laparoscopy has been performed, usually using a second puncture technique for complete investigation of pelvic structures.

In individuals who may have a uterine leiomyoma but are not diagnosed definitively at the time of pelvic examination, a vaginal probe ultrasound may be used to define the number, size, and position of the structures. The finding of an intact hymen with associated dysmenorrhea requires further evaluation for hematocolpos by ultrasound or magnetic resonance imaging. A noncommunicating rudimentary horn may be seen on vaginal probe ultrasound or at laparoscopy.

Patients who may have no associated pelvic pathology but who have associated menorrhagia may be suffering from adenomyosis, a form of endometriosis. In these patients, the uterus is usually found to be enlarged. Diagnosis is not made until the time of hysterectomy, when the pathologic specimen is examined.

Patients who present with primary dysmenorrhea may initially be placed on prostaglandin synthetase inhibitor medication unless overt abnormalities such as ovarian cysts and uterine leiomyomas are detected at the initial examination. If medical therapy does not improve symptomatology, further diagnostic options should be instituted, including diagnostic laparoscopy and ultrasound visualization of pelvic structures.

Recommended Approach

Diagnosis of dysmenorrhea may initially be approached with caution, that is, attempting medical therapy first with either birth control pills or prostaglandin synthetase inhibitors. One must incorporate information about familial history of endometriosis or uterine leiomyoma before proceeding on with diagnostic laparoscopy. When hematocolpos or a noncommunicating uterine horn is diagnosed, surgery is mandatory. Individuals who are infertile and who have the findings of dysmenorrhea should be counseled as to their possibility of having endometriosis or uterine leiomyoma and that the diagnosis should be made not only for the discomfort that they experience but also as a possible causative factor of their infertility. Patients with progressive symptomatology should definitely be evaluated more aggressively for endometriosis, as increasing symptomatology may herald advancing stages of disease.

Therapeutic

Therapeutic Options

Primary dysmenorrhea may be ruled out by inhibiting ovulation through birth control pills. Combined oral contraceptive medications with at least 35 µg estrogen should be used, beginning on the third to the fifth day of the menstrual cycle and continuing for 21 days. Another simple method of testing for primary dysmenorrhea is to administer prostaglandin synthetase inhibitors during menses. Approximately 80% of dysmenorrheic women are relieved by prostaglandin inhibitors. There is no surgical management of primary dysmenorrhea. The only exception to this is that of resolving an intact hymen with a stellate incision of the hymenal membrane and allowing efflux of the hematocolpos. Staging of endometriosis at the time of laparoscopy is important, according to the American Fertility Society Classification (see Chapter 10–21) Whenever possible, laser ablation of endometriosis is performed. If all endometriosis is not ablated, further medication for 3 to 6 months may be needed in the form of gonadotropin-releasing hormone agonists. These preparations may cause menopausal symptomatology such as vaginal dryness, hot flushes, insomnia, and night sweats. Gonadotropin-releasing hormone agonists are effective in significantly diminishing estrogen levels. If the staging of endometriosis is extensive, conservative surgery with laser ablation or excision of lesions is the therapy of choice. Definitive hysterectomy and bilateral salpingo-oophorectomy are rarely indicated and should be performed only if the patient has no desire to maintain fertility.

Rudimentary uterine horns need removal if symptoms occur. These structures do not communicate with the normal uterine structures and must be excised if accumulation of blood has caused dysmenorrhea. Leiomyomas may be removed with conservation of the uterus with a myomectomy if dysmenorrhea is significant or if dysfunctional bleeding occurs. Endometrial polyps can be removed by a dilation and curettage procedure.

Dysmenorrhea secondary to acute infection is usually successfully treated with combination antibiotic therapy administered over a 7- to 10-day period. Chronic disease states can be relieved secondary to adhesions by lysis of the adhesions via the laparoscope or laparotomy, depending on the severity of the disease state and the desire for future fertility. When acute disease causes severe infection with tubo-ovarian abscesses, either drainage transvaginally via the cul-de-sac or laparotomy with excision of these structures may be necessary.

Recommended Approach

A trial of medications may first be attempted if the diagnosis is unclear. If symptoms do not resolve, further diagnostic tests with appropriate therapy are then indicated.

FOLLOW-UP

Depending on the basis for the dysmenorrhea, pelvic examination must be performed on either an annual or semiannual basis. If primary dysmenorrhea is diagnosed, follow-up evaluation with oral contraceptive therapy, including blood pressure and SMA-18 determinations, may be necessary, depending on whether any contraindications arise while on these preparations. Follow-up of prostaglandin synthetase inhibitor preparations should be reevaluated after two to three cycles of medication.

For secondary dysmenorrhea, depending on whether the patient has endometriosis and the stage of the disease, close follow-up examinations must be performed. If the patient is taking a gonadotropin-releasing hormone agonist, monthly follow-up evaluations are recommended during therapy to rule out any problems on the agonist.

Uterine leiomyomas that perhaps are mildly symptomatic may change over the course of a year, and the patient should be reevaluated at 6-month intervals for this problem.

If patients have recurring symptoms associated with pelvic inflammatory disease, immediate attention should be paid to rule out acute exacerbations; otherwise, annual follow-up examinations may be sufficient depending on other pathology present.

DISCUSSION
Prevalence

Very few studies are available to document the prevalence and incidence of dysmenorrhea. Approximately 60% of menstruating adolescents have dysmenorrhea. Approximately 45% of women report moderate or severe dysmenorrhea. Of adolescents reporting dysmenorrhea, approximately 15% limit their activity or miss school because of their symptoms.

Related Basic Science

Investigations and research regarding dysmenorrhea are limited. Ongoing research in the area of endometriosis continues to show no definitive etiology for endometriosis.

Genetics

There is no associated genetic inheritance for primary dysmenorrhea. Patients who have first-degree relatives with endometriosis as a cause of secondary dysmenorrhea have a 7% incidence of the disease. Endometriosis is inherited as a single mutant gene with possible transmission due to polygenetic or multifactorial inheritance; however, no specific gene has been delineated as the causative factor for this disease. Genetic inheritance of uterine leiomyomas that cause secondary dysmenorrhea are in the polygenetic or multifactorial group.

Altered Molecular Biology

Women with primary dysmenorrhea have greater endometrial production of prostaglandin compared with asymptomatic women.

Physiologic or Metabolic Derangement

Prostaglandin $F_{2\alpha}$ has been found to cause contraction of the myometrium. Found in large amounts in the nonpregnant state, prostaglandin E_2 causes inhibition of uterine contractions. It is known that in the secretory phase of the cycle, the prostaglandin $F_{2\alpha}/E_2$ ratio increases markedly. This is secondary to estrogen stimulation of the endometrium, which increases prostaglandin synthetase levels. In addition, at the time of ovulation, estrogen is required to effect a significant increase in prostaglandin synthetase levels. At the time of menstrual endometrial necrosis, arachidonic acid is released with endometrial breakdown, causing prostaglandin $F_{2\alpha}$ to be formed in increasing amounts. Absorption causes intense uterine contractions associated with primary dysmenorrhea. Use of antiprostaglandin agents is important prior to the time bleeding occurs so that this cascade of events can be diminished. Combination oral contraceptive pills are effective in diminishing menstrual cramps caused by atrophic decidualized endometrium.

It is now recognized that nonsteroidal antiinflammatory compounds are effective inhibitors of prostaglandin synthesis. Approximately 70 to 80% of patients with primary dysmenorrhea are relieved of their menstrual pain if medication is started prior to the onset of menses.

Anatomic Derangement

Endometriosis may cause enlargement of the ovaries as well as pelvic adhesions, deranging the normal anatomy of the pelvis. This, in turn, causes secondary dysmenorrhea. Adhesions resulting from pelvic infections may change normal anatomy as well.

Natural History and Its Modification with Treatment

Patients with primary dysmenorrhea continue to produce prostaglandin as long as endometrial and myometrial stimulation by estrogen occurs.

Individuals with endometriosis-caused dysmenorrhea continue to have persistent problems if there is no medical or surgical intervention (see Chapter 10–21).

Prevention

Early onset of therapy prior to the menses may aid in decreasing the severity of the pain. Patients who have secondary dysmenorrhea and who may have endometriosis as a possible cause of their pain should undergo early diagnostic laparoscopy to rule out this disease process. If endometriosis is diagnosed early and appropriately treated, problems with further dysmenorrhea, dyspareunia, and eventual infertility will be diminished.

Cost Containment

Considering the time lost from school or work on a monthly basis because of dysmenorrhea, it is important that patients be evaluated fully for this problem. Patients should be given medication for their dysmenorrhea and be adequately followed up so that further organic causes can be ruled out if medication is not effective. Prostaglandin synthetase inhibitors and oral contraceptives should be initiated first, and then further evaluation should be performed if therapy has not solved the problem. Diagnosis of endometriosis at an early stage is especially cost-effective, owing to the time lost and problems involved in infertility and other organ involvement in the future if this disease is allowed to progress.

REFERENCES

Speroff L, Glass RH, Kase NG. Clinical gynecologic endocrinology and infertility. 4th ed. Baltimore: Williams & Wilkins, 1994.

Thompson JD, Rock JA. Operative gynecology. 7th ed. Philadelphia: Lippincott, 1992.

Wallach EE, Kempers RD. Modern trends in infertility and conception control. vol. 4. Chicago: Year Book Medical, 1988.

Yen SC, Jaffe RB. Reproductive endocrinology. 3rd ed. Philadelphia: Saunders, 1991.

CHAPTER 10–2

Amenorrhea

Dorothy E. Mitchell-Leef, M.D.

DEFINITION

Patients presenting with the following should be considered as having amenorrhea: no evidence of onset of menses by age 14 with the absence of secondary sexual characteristics or growth; lack of menses by age 14 regardless of secondary sexual characteristics and normal growth; absence of menses, equal to three or more cycles, in women who have had otherwise normal menstrual histories.

ETIOLOGY

Causes of amenorrhea may be considered in four different areas that may be disordered: (1) abnormal uterine factors and outflow tract obstruction; (2) ovarian dysfunction; (3) abnormalities involving the central nervous system and its integration with hypothalamic control mechanisms; (4) abnormalities of the anterior pituitary.

CRITERIA FOR DIAGNOSIS
Suggestive

Absence of menses at an expected age during early adolescence and secondary amenorrhea longer than 3 months in women with a prior history of normal function based on accurate history are suggestive of the diagnosis. Pregnancy must be ruled out in all cases of amenorrhea.

Definitive

Documentation of amenorrhea by history combined with physical examination confirms the diagnosis. A positive pregnancy test also definitively confirms secondary amenorrhea.

CLINICAL MANIFESTATIONS
Subjective

The diagnosis of amenorrhea requires lack of menses as a solitary symptom or associated with the following:

- *Uterine and vaginal congenital anomalies* (usually in women with normal ovarian function and normal pubertal development): This may include vaginal agenesis alone, with or without normal uterine development. An intravenous pyelogram should be ordered in these patients, with abnormalities usually being found in 30 to 45% of patients.
- *Cryptomenorrhea* (imperforate hymen): This may occur with normal vagina, uterus, and secondary sexual development. Bulging of the hymenal area is observed in these patients.
- *Ovarian insensitivity:* Gonadotropin-resistant ovaries are present with normal secondary sexual development.
- *Hypogonadotropic hypogonadism (Kallmann's syndrome):* This is associated with sexual infantilism and anosmia.

- *Androgen insensitivity, complete (46,XY):* This is associated with a female phenotype, breast development, absent axillary and pubic hair, blind vagina, absent uterus, and abdominal or inguinal testes.
- *Partial androgen insensitivity (46, XY):* This differs from the preceding with only minimal or no breast development, normal pubic hair, and clitoromegaly with vagina and uterus usually present. Gonads may be intraabdominal or inguinal.
- *Gonadal dysgenesis (Turner's syndrome):* The patient is usually eunuchoid, less than 60 in. in height, and may have webbing of the neck, coarctation of the aorta, and a shieldlike chest. Depending on mosaicism, varying from the strict 45,X karyotype, development and clinical symptoms may differ.
- *Primary ovarian failure:* This patient has undergone surgery for ovarian tumors or radiation before the menarche or has had embryonic ovarian growth failure. She has sexually immature development and is taller than normal.

These remaining types of amenorrhea are usually secondary:

- *Pregnancy:* Normal cycling women with abrupt onset of amenorrhea need pregnancy ruled out.
- *Premature ovarian failure:* This may be complete or incomplete. The patient usually has a 46,XX karyotype; however, occasional Y chromosome variations may occur. Therefore, any patient under age 30 with this disorder should have a karyotype completed to rule out a Y component. If this is present, bilateral oophorectomy should be performed so that malignant dysgerminomas may be avoided.
- *Pituitary tumors, craniopharyngiomas:* These patients usually present with either arrest of growth or accelerated growth involving the growth hormone. Extensive thirst or impaired temperature regulation may be present if secretion of pituitary hormones is impaired.
- *Prolactin-producing pituitary tumors:* These patients may have galactorrhea in addition to the symptomatology of hypothyroidism.
- *Hypothalamic disorders:* Emotional distress is the most common cause of hypothalamic dysfunction. Anxiety in many circumstances may be the trigger or factor. In addition, patients with depression and other mental illnesses may be amenorrheic. Anorexia nervosa, extensive weight loss, nutrition deficits, and loss of fat in, for example, extensively training athletes may produce similar problems. Obesity alters hypothalamic functions as well.
- *Systemic diseases:* The most probable cause of amenorrhea in these patients is multifactorial rather than singular.
- *Drug abuse:* Excessive use of marijuana may suppress hypothalamic function.
- *Asherman's syndrome:* This is seen in women with a history of multiple and vigorous uterine curettage. Tuberculosis also may be a rare causative factor.
- *Polycystic ovarian disease (Stein–Leventhal syndrome):* Patients complain of hirsutism and oligomenorrhea. The abnormal hair growth usually occurs on the upper lip, face, nipples, and abdomen. Patients may or may not be obese. Ovaries may be enlarged bilaterally on bimanual examination.
- *Thyroid diseases:* Most patients will not have overt hypothyroid symptomatology; occult changes are more common. Galactorrhea may or may not be present if associated with prolactin-producing tumors. Hyperthyroid symptomatology is more frequently classic for this disease state.
- *Postpill amenorrhea:* Patients who do not resume regular menses 3 to 6 months after discontinuing oral contraceptives cannot be considered normal and must be evaluated for additional pathology.
- *Radiation and/or chemotherapy:* Ablation of ovarian and/or uterine tissue may cause amenorrhea.

The only significant family history that is of importance in the diagnosis of amenorrhea is that of premature ovarian failure. Women whose family members initiated menopause early or experienced early ovarian failure may have an increased risk of a similar occurrence. Early evaluation with follicle-stimulating hormones on day 3 of the cycle may herald changes of early ovarian failure in those individuals who are in question of early ovarian failure.

Objective
Physical Examination

Full evaluation of multiple system presentations must be considered in the diagnosis of amenorrhea. Physical examination may include one or more of the following: absence of the vagina and uterus on abdominal/rectal examination, varying degrees of hirsutism, large ovaries (up to 7 cm in diameter), atrophic ovaries (usually not palpable), visual field defects, galactorrhea, and evidence of intercurrent chronic disease processes such as diabetes and/or tuberculosis.

Routine Laboratory Abnormalities

There are no specific routine laboratory abnormalities.

PLANS
Diagnostic

A thorough examination and laboratory studies must be performed before a final diagnosis can be made.

Differential Diagnosis

See Table 10–2–1 for the differential diagnosis of amenorrhea.

Diagnostic Options

A follicle-stimulating hormone level greater than 40 mIU/mL indicates ovarian failure. Luteinizing hormone: follicle-stimulating hormone concentration ratios greater than 3:1 are indicative of polycystic ovarian disease. Subnormal levels of either follicle-stimulating hormone or luteinizing hormone, or both, are indicative of hypogonadotropic hypogonadism. Gonadotropin-releasing hormone stimulation tests will show no normal stimulatory changes of follicle-stimulating hormone and luteinizing hormone in patients with Kallman's syndrome or hypogonadotropic hypogonadism. Hypothyroidism is diagnosed with elevated levels of thyrotropin-stimulating hormone levels; hyperprolactinemia requires further evaluation for a pituitary tumor. Karyotyping results that do not coincide with phenotypic appearance are pathognomonic of intersex disorders. Mosaic patterns as well as deletions or extra chromosome findings on karyotyping must be evaluated and compared with phenotypic appearance and presentation of symptoms. Elevated levels of androgens such as total testosterone, dehydroepiandrosterone sulfate, and 17-hydroxyprogesterone must be further evaluated and used in the differential diagnosis of individuals having either primary or secondary amenorrhea. Pituitary tumors noted on computed tomography or magnetic resonance imaging scans must be correlated with appropriate prolactin, thyroid, and adrenocorticotropic hormone levels.

Recommended Approach

After a physical examination and evaluation of all organ systems relating to amenorrhea, one must integrate appropriate laboratory tests for either exclusion of the diagnosis or inclusion of certain types of amenorrhea. Many diagnoses of amenorrhea are considered simplistic; however, those involved with multiple system abnormalities, including abnormal laboratory findings as well as physical abnormalities, must be thoroughly evaluated prior to making a definitive diagnosis.

Therapeutic

Each separate diagnosis of the type of amenorrhea as described under Differential Diagnosis must be individually approached and therapy administered depending on the presenting symptom complex.

Therapeutic Options

If the vagina is the only absent structure, a vaginoplasty may be performed with normal menses occurring. The artificial vagina results in a satisfactory sexual adjustment for the patient and her partner. If the uterus is absent and a vaginal pouch is present, serial dilation may be used with dilators to create a normal vaginal depth. If this fails, a vaginoplasty may be performed.

If an imperforate hymen is present, a surgical incision must be made

TABLE 10–2–1. DIFFERENTIAL DIAGNOSIS OF AMENORRHEA

Absence of vagina and/or uterus	Pelvic examination reveals no vagina and/or uterine structures; pelvic ultrasound confirms these findings. Intravenous pyelography should be obtained to rule out congenital urinary tract anomalies that coexist with these findings.
Cryptomenorrhea	Ultrasound visualizes a normal uterus, vagina, and ovaries with fluid-filled vagina.
Ovarian insensitivity	Levels of follicle-stimulating hormone and luteinizing hormone are elevated; ovaries appear normal at examination and laparoscopy.
Hypogonadotropic hypogonadism	Patient has anosmia; levels of follicle-stimulating hormone and luteinizing hormone are low, with one possibly being selectively unresponsive over the other. Gonadotropin-releasing hormone stimulation test should be done to determine if a hypothalamic or pituitary defect is present.
Androgen insensitivity syndrome	Karyotype is 46,XY, possibly with mosaicism. Gonads are visualized on ultrasound or in inguinal hernia. Total testosterone level is in the normal male range. Vaginal pouch is absent or small.
Gonadal dysgenesis	Karyotype is 45,X with specific emphasis on mosaicism. It is necessary to rule out presence of Y chromosome. If Y chromosome is present, gonadectomy should be performed. Consider cardiac evaluation and thyroid testing.
Primary ovarian failure	If follicle-stimulating hormone and luteinizing hormone levels are high, bone age should be determined. Karyotyping should be done.
Premature ovarian failure	Follicle-stimulating hormone and luteinizing hormone levels are elevated. As failure may be transient, patient should be periodically tested, especially after estrogen–progesterone therapy. Karyotype should be done to rule out presence of a Y chromosome in patients under age 30. Testing for thyroid antibodies and autoimmune diseases especially should be performed to rule out Hashimoto's thyroiditis, which is frequently associated with this disease state.
Pituitary tumors and prolactin-producing tumors	Levels of prolactin and thyroid-stimulating hormone should be measured, and computed tomography or magnetic resonance imaging of the sella turcica performed. Pap smears of galactorrhea should be done to rule out carcinoma of the breasts. Visual field evaluation should be performed.
Hypothalamic disorders/chronic anovulation	Follicle-stimulating hormone and luteinizing hormone levels may be normal to low. Gonadotropin-releasing hormone may show selective follicle-stimulating hormone or luteinizing hormone secretion failure. This also rules out hypothalamic versus pituitary failure. Weight gain or loss may be associated with this abnormality as may stress and excessive exercise.
Systemic disease states	Testing for underlying disease states is usually done preceding a final diagnosis of amenorrhea.
Asherman's syndrome	Follicle-stimulating hormone and luteinizing hormone levels are normal. Estradiol levels are also normal. If a pregnancy test is negative, patients are given progesterone for withdrawal flow with negative results. Hysterosalpingogram with subsequent hysteroscopy should be performed to evaluate for scarring or uterine synechiae.
Polycystic ovarian disease/chronic anovulation with androgen excess	Luteinizing hormone level is greater than follicle-stimulating hormone level by a ratio of 3:1. Endometrial biopsy shows proliferative endometrium and rules out adenomatous hyperplasia. Total testosterone and dehydroepiandrosterone sulfate levels should be obtained. Free testosterone level is usually elevated. Total testosterone level should be less than 2 ng/mL to rule out ovarian tumors.
Hypothyroidism	Thyroid-stimulating hormone level is elevated. Prolactin level may be elevated because of dual role of thyrotropin-releasing hormone in stimulating both thyroid-stimulating hormone and prolactin. Galactorrhea, if present, dictates cytology to rule out carcinoma of the breasts.
Postpill amenorrhea	If menses do not recur within 3 to 6 months and if pregnancy test is negative, medroxyprogesterone acetate withdrawal therapy should be instituted. Follicle-stimulating hormone, luteinizing hormone, prolactin, and thyroid-stimulating hormone levels should be determined to rule out further pathology.
Endocrine diseases	Thyroid-stimulating hormone screen and free thyroxine, prolactin, or associated pituitary hormone levels should be determined. Galactosemia 17 α-hydroxylase or 17/20-lyase deficiency should be ruled out.
Radiation/ chemotherapy	Levels of follicle-stimulating hormone and luteinizing hormone are elevated. Progesterone withdrawal should be given; if no response, estrogen and progesterone should be given to determine endometrial responsiveness.

in a stellate fashion to allow normal afflux of menstrual flow. No other therapy is necessary.

In patients with either hypothalamic, pituitary, or ovarian failure, estrogen and progesterone replacement therapy must be administered. In those individuals under the age of 40 with no contraindications, combination oral contraceptive preparations may be given. If the patient wishes an alternative therapy, medications should include cyclic estrogen and progesterone therapy in the form of at least 0.625 mg conjugated estrogen or its potency equivalent, such as ethinyl estradiol. This should be given, at most, on days 1 through 25 per month. A progestational agent in the form of medroxyprogesterone acetate (Provera 10 mg/d for at least 12 days per month) should be given during the last days of the estrogen therapy. Withdrawal flow is then eventuated, and therapy is restarted on the first of each month. If the patient has any dysfunctional uterine bleeding, an endometrial biopsy should be performed to rule out any problems with adenomatous hyperplasia.

In those patients with premature ovarian failure, cyclic therapy should be given and followed on a 3- to 6-month basis with discontinuation of the medication for at least 6 weeks and repeated follicle-stimulating hormone and luteinizing hormone determinations to see if transient failure had occurred with resumption of normal ovulatory function.

In patients who have either androgen insensitivity syndrome, complete or incomplete, or a karyotype containing a Y chromosome component, bilateral gonadectomy must be performed to avoid malignant dysgerminoma development.

In patients with macroadenomas of the pituitary greater than 10 mm or other pituitary tumors, transsphenoidal resection by a neurosurgeon may be an option depending on individual patient problems. If the patient has a prolactin-producing macroadenoma less than 10 mm as determined by computed tomography or magnetic resonance imaging, therapy with bromocriptine (2.5 mg twice daily) may be given. Repeat prolactin level determinations at 6-month intervals should be performed, with yearly computed tomography or magnetic resonance imaging follow-up to rule out the tumor. Patients with hypothalamic disorders should have the underlying disease states or etiologies corrected, including weight gain or loss or change in environmental status.

In those patients with systemic disease, the underlying etiology must be corrected, with ovulation resuming after therapy is initiated.

Patients with Asherman's syndrome should undergo hysteroscopy with lysis of adhesions. High-dose estrogen and progesterone therapy in a cyclic form for one cycle should be given after the procedure to restore normal endometrial status. Antibiotics also should be given postoperatively. A pediatric Foley catheter balloon may need to be left in place for 3 to 5 days.

If the patient desires fertility, polycystic ovarian disease is most often treated with clomiphene citrate (Clomid), beginning with 50 mg/d on days 3 to 7 of the cycle. This must be followed by an endometrial biopsy to determine if ovulation has occurred; if not, increased dosages, up to 150 mg, can be given. Additional human chorionic gonadotropin therapy in the form of 10,000 units intramuscularly must be given to individuals who require 150 mg clomiphene citrate for initiation of ovulation. Those individuals who do not desire fertility should be placed on combination oral contraceptive medication with at least a 35-μg dosage of an ethinyl estradiol preparation. Hirsutism may be partially resolved with this preparation. Ovarian wedge resections are rarely used as a therapeutic modality.

Treatment of the underlying thyroid disease abnormality usually results in resumption of normal menses.

In patients who are obese and have no need for additional estrogen therapy or who are overweight and have the additional risk of adenomatous hyperplasia, medroxyprogesterone acetate should be given in the form of 10 mg daily for 14 days per cycle. If dysfunctional bleeding occurs, an endometrial biopsy should be performed to rule out adenomatous hyperplasia. A pretreatment endometrial biopsy may be considered for those at high risk for hyperplasia.

In patients who have not resumed normal menses 3 to 6 months after discontinuing birth control pills, a pregnancy test must be performed. If this is negative, medroxyprogesterone acetate (10 mg/d for 10 days) may be given and normal menses expected. Observation may continue for at least three more cycles. Concomitant follicle-stimulating hormone, luteinizing hormone, prolactin, and thyroid-stimulating hormone levels should be determined if menses does not occur 6 months after discontinuation of the oral contraceptives.

In patients receiving radiation and/or chemotherapy medication (cyclic estrogen–progesterone preparations) should be given as if ovarian failure had occurred. If fertility is desired in the future and if uterine function does occur with cyclic estrogen and progesterone therapy, then a donor embryo or donor egg may be a possibility.

Calcium replacement to prevent osteoporosis in those patients at high risk must be discussed with the patient, with up to 1500 mg calcium replacement given per day, depending on the diagnostic problem.

Recommended Approach

Therapy must not be considered until a complete evaluation has been performed. Careful observation, administration of appropriate therapy, and continued surveillance of expected results must be done in a systematic fashion so as not to miss salient points of diagnosis. It is important to recognize causes of amenorrhea that involve intersex disorders such as androgen insensitivity syndrome, for which gonadectomy is recommended to decrease chances of malignant gonadal changes.

Once the more common etiologies of amenorrhea (such as emotional stress or anxiety) have been ruled out, further discussion with the patient is warranted according to the particular abnormalities:

- Depending on the options available, if patients have structural anatomic abnormalities, such as vaginal agenesis, one may discuss vaginoplasty versus serial manual manipulations, such as the "bicycle seat" technique for manual dilation.
- Patients with ovarian failure must be placed on monthly estrogen and progesterone therapy with an option for possible embryo or egg donation when fertility is desired.
- The patient with a prolactin-producing tumor is instructed that continuous bromocriptine (Parlodel) therapy, along with yearly computed tomography or magnetic resonance imaging evaluation, is necessary.
- Psychotherapy for anorexia, weight loss, or weight gain should be carried out to reverse the present disease state.
- Psychological support is recommended for patients with intersex abnormalities or for those who have the diagnosis of ovarian failure and consequent infertility.

FOLLOW-UP

Generally, once amenorrhea is diagnosed according to its respective etiology, the patient requires no more follow-up than the usual recommended annual visit. The exceptions to this are patients with polycystic ovarian disease, who require clomiphene citrate therapy for ovulation induction, and those who are excessively overweight, who require serial endometrial biopsies to rule out adenomatous hyperplasia or carcinoma. Patients with galactorrhea who have proven hyperprolactinemia must be reevaluated at 6-month intervals. Those individuals with endocrinologic disease states must be at least serially evaluated depending on the underlying etiology.

DISCUSSION
Prevalence and Incidence

Varying forms of amenorrhea may be seen in women of all reproductive ages; however, statistics specific to each category of amenorrhea are elusive. The more unusual forms of amenorrhea, including resistant ovary syndrome and hypogonadotropic hypogonadism, are low in incidence, whereas the incidence of postpill amenorrhea and chronic anovulation due to secondary events such as stress, weight loss, or excessive exercise is considered high in women of different reproductive ages.

Related Basic Science

The most salient causes of amenorrhea are chromosomal abnormalities, in particular, presence of the Y chromosome in patients with no obvious evidence of masculinization. Technology such as computed tomography and magnetic resonance imaging to detect early pituitary tumors is essential in making a diagnosis that otherwise might remain elusive.

Genetics

Kallman's syndrome, or hypogonadotropic hypogonadism, occurs five to seven times more frequently in males than in females. Three modes of transmission have been considered: X-linked, autosomal dominant, and autosomal recessive. Its greater frequency in males indicates that X-linked transmission is the more common mode. The X-linked transmission can be associated with disorders due to deletions or translocations.

Deletions of the X chromosome can be responsible for premature ovarian failure. Finding this deletion is not essential; however, because this abnormality is known to occur in families, knowledge of its presence would allow other family members to be tested and make appropriate family planning decisions. Patients with complete androgen insensitivity (testicular feminization) have a 46,XY karyotype. This is considered to be a maternally X-linked recessive disorder, with a 25% risk of an affected child and a 25% risk of being a carrier.

Thirty to forty percent of patients with primary amenorrhea have gonadal dysgenesis. Of these patients, 50% are 45,X; 25% are mosaic; and 25% have a normal 46,XX karyotype.

Individuals with secondary amenorrhea and gonadal dysgenesis may have a normal 46,XX karyotype; a 46,XX karyotype with mosaic deletions of the short and long arms of the X, or a 47,XXX karyotype. Women who experience ovarian failure before age 30 require a complete karyotypic evaluation to rule out the presence of a Y chromosome. Although patients may not manifest virilization or masculinization, they require gonadectomy to avoid the neoplastic changes induced by the Y chromosome. In women with premature ovarian failure, the more common abnormalities are 45,X and 47,XXY followed by mosaicism.

Physiologic or Metabolic Derangement

Menstruation occurs as a result of rather rapidly declining estrogen and progesterone tissue levels and results in a thinning of the endometrium. This, in turn, causes increased coiling of spiral arterioles and disruption of their capillary connections to decidual sinusoids, which results in bleeding into the stroma, breakage of basement membranes into endometrial glands, and exuding of stroma and blood via the gland lumen into the endometrial cavity. Estrogen withdrawal bleeding also occurs in nonovulatory cycles, where the mechanism is somewhat similar.

Virtually all types of amenorrhea occur because of a failure to build up a thickened endometrial layer, whether this stems from an infection, mechanical destruction of the basalis layer, or deficient production of estrogen and progesterone. Releasing and inhibiting factors from the hypothalamus and, more immediately, the ability of the pituitary gland to produce gonadotropin hormones have been extensively discussed in Section 9. Possible roles of endorphins and neurotransmitters must be considered at this time.

Anatomic Derangement

Individuals who have an imperforate hymen may have different variations of anatomic derangement; the spectrum can vary depending on the degree of occlusion. Individuals with Mayer–Rokitansky–Kuster–Hauser syndrome, or vaginal agenesis, have what appears to be an imperforate hymen; no vaginal structures are detected after repair of the imperforate hymen.

Anatomic intersex abnormalities, such as a blind vaginal pouch, absence of pubic and axillary hair, but normal breast development, are pathognomonic of androgen insensitivity syndrome. Patients with inguinal hernias may have gonads in the hernia sacs. Other intersex abnormalities must be differentiated depending on the complete physical findings. An enlarged thyroid requires a full evaluation, as hyperthyroidism may cause secondary amenorrhea.

Natural History and Its Modification with Treatment

The natural history of amenorrhea varies according to the underlying pathology. In the absence of a uterus, menstruation cannot be established, but an artificial vagina can be created. If the uterus is absent, vaginal serial dilation may be an alternative to surgical intervention.

Menses can easily be produced by cycling with estrogen and progesterone, with the ovaries mostly remaining refractory to gonadotropic stimulation.

In primary hypogonadotropic hypogonadism, cyclic bleeding can be established by estrogen–progesterone therapy, but the deficient ovarian tissue cannot be replaced.

Polycystic ovarian disease frequently responds satisfactorily to the use of clomiphene for fertility purposes. If not, menotropin (Pergonal) therapy needs to be initiated.

Hypothalamic amenorrhea associated with pituitary adenoma may recur when definitive surgery on the pituitary has been completed. It appears that recurrence following the use of bromocriptine is likely. Patients remaining on the medication will in most instances have suppression of the tumor.

Hysteroscopy has been used successfully to reestablish a normal uterine cavity in Asherman's syndrome, following which regeneration of endometrium usually occurs.

If endometriosis is sufficient to cause amenorrhea, general resumption of ovarian function depends on the stage of the ovarian disease.

Patients experiencing premature ovarian failure can achieve cyclic bleeding through the use of exogenous ovarian steroids in the form of estrogen and progesterone therapy. Patients may occasionally resume normal menses after estrogen–progesterone therapy.

Amenorrhea responds rather promptly to regulation of diabetes, hypothyroidism, and hyperthyroidism.

Postpill amenorrhea occurs only if the patient had irregular cycles prior to the use of oral contraceptives. If oral contraceptives are prescribed again, discontinuation will result in reversion to amenorrhea.

Persons with radiation- or chemotherapy-induced amenorrhea may achieve cyclic bleeding with exogenous ovarian steroids.

Prevention

Most types of amenorrhea are nonpreventable in the light of present understanding of hypothalamic–pituitary–ovarian relationships. Stressful exercise, weight gain, and weight loss, along with anorexia nervosa, are exceptions. Some cases of Asherman's syndrome result from overenthusiastic curettage or repeated induced abortion. Patients should be made aware of this possibility. Patients undergoing pelvic radiation may have their ovaries surgically repositioned out of the radiation fields to allow continuation of normal steroid function.

Cost Containment

Testing must be differentiated in those individuals who have specific etiologies or symptomatology warranting endocrine testing. Usual screening of follicle-stimulating hormone, luteinizing hormone, prolactin, and thyroid-stimulating hormone selectively rules out a major portion of these disease states. When clinical observation warrants, karyotyping is mandatory.

REFERENCES

Huffman JW, Dewhurst CJ, Capraro VJ. The gynecology of childhood and adolescence. 2nd ed. Philadelphia: Saunders, 1981.

Speroff L, Glass RH, Kase NG. Clinical gynecologic endocrinology and infertility. 4th ed. Baltimore: Williams & Wilkins, 1994.

Yen SSC, Jaffe RB. Reproductive endocrinology. 3rd ed. Philadelphia: Saunders, 1991.

CHAPTER 10–3

The Menopause

R. Don Gambrell, Jr., M.D.

DEFINITION

Menopause is the cessation of menses due to estrogen deficiency. The climacteric encompasses the premenopausal, perimenopausal, and postmenopausal periods, during which women may experience symptoms of estrogen deficiency. Postmenopause is 1 year without menstrual periods.

ETIOLOGY

As a woman approaches menopause, a number of biological changes take place. The number of oocytes declines progressively from before birth but reaches critically low levels by the time of menopause. Menstrual cycles may become irregular as follicle-stimulating hormone (FSH) levels increase and ovarian steroid levels decrease. At birth, there are 1,000,000 to 2,000,000 oocytes; this number decreases to 400,000 at menarche. By menopause there are only a few hundred oocytes, which results in declining estrogen levels.

CRITERIA FOR DIAGNOSIS

Suggestive

The diagnosis of menopause can be established based on symptoms and confirmation of estrogen deficiency by various parameters. Most women seek medical attention because of vasomotor symptoms as manifested by hot flushes, hot flashes, or night sweats. Menstrual periods will at least be irregular or have ceased completely. Other patients may notice vaginal dryness or irritation; a few women will present with psychosomatic complaints.

Definitive

Estrogen deficiency can be confirmed by vaginal hormonal cytology, failure to respond to the progestogen challenge test (if the uterus is intact), or a serum FSH level above 30 mIU/mL.

CLINICAL MANIFESTATIONS

Subjective

The average age of menopause is 50 years, although some women experience symptoms in their early forties and others may not have hot flushes until their midfifties. Of course, if the ovaries are removed during the reproductive years, menopausal symptoms begin at that time. About 25% of postmenopausal women never experience any symptoms, although their menstrual periods cease at midlife.

The most prevalent symptoms of menopause are vasomotor, manifested by the hot flush, hot flash, or night sweat. The severity of vasomotor symptoms depends on the rapidity of declining estrogen levels. Therefore, if the ovaries are removed surgically during the reproductive years, hot flushes are severe and frequent. With a natural menopause, onset of symptoms may be insidious and gradually increase as serum estrogens decline. If untreated, the hypothalamus and autonomic nervous system gradually adjust to the lower levels of estrogen, and eventually hot flushes will abate.

Atrophy of the genital epithelium may result in atrophic vaginitis with symptoms of irritation, dryness, pruritus, leukorrhea, dyspareunia, and, occasionally, even vaginal bleeding. Vaginal secretions decrease; the vaginal epithelium may become thin, atrophic, and easily traumatized; and the vagina may shorten and become less distensible. To a lesser extent, vulvar epithelium also becomes thin and may be irritated. As the integrity of the lower urinary tract mucosa is estrogen dependent, irritative symptoms such as dysuria and burning on urination may occur, and episodes of cystitis become more frequent. Urethral caruncles and nongonococcal urethritis occur entirely in postmenopausal women.

Many postmenopausal women complain of increased nervousness, depression, anxiety, insomnia, and headaches. Preexisting psychosomatic problems may be intensified simply because of hot flushes. Libido may be decreased due to dyspareunia as a result of atrophic vaginitis. Carefully controlled double-blind and crossover studies indicate that estrogens have a tonic mental effect—patients had higher scores on psychometric evaluation—alleviating the psychogenic manifestations independent of vasomotor symptoms. Sexual dysfunction, long regarded by psychologists and sex therapists as entirely psychogenic in origin, repeatedly has been shown to be responsive to hormone therapy. Relief may be afforded by estrogens, including estrogen vaginal cream, for such complaints as vaginal dryness and dyspareunia, and by androgens, when loss of sex interest is the basis of the problem. Vascular headaches such as migraine usually decrease at menopause. These may return with estrogen replacement but usually abate when androgens are added.

Objective

Physical Examination

Atrophic vaginal mucosa will eventually be the principal physical finding in postmenopausal women; however, this may take 5 to 10 years to manifest, and usually occurs after the onset of vasomotor and psychosomatic symptoms. The vaginal mucosa appears pale, is thinned, and loses much of the rugae normally present throughout the reproductive years. Vaginitis is more frequent, evidenced by leukorrhea, but dryness may be the presenting finding. Urethral caruncles occur almost entirely with long-term estrogen deficiency. Even vulvar skin may become thinned and lose some of its elasticity. Pubic hair may decrease because of the decreased levels of androgens associated with menopause.

Routine Laboratory Abnormalities

The routine examination of the blood and urine reveals no abnormality. High density lipoprotein cholesterol declines prior to menopause, while low density lipoprotein cholesterol and total cholesterol may increase at menopause.

PLANS

Diagnostic

Differential Diagnosis

The differential diagnosis of menopause should not be difficult if an adequate history is taken. Pregnancy is very rare but possible at this time in a woman's life. Perfectly regular menses with sudden amenorrhea in the absence of menopause symptoms should arouse suspicion. A pregnancy test would confirm or deny this diagnosis. Other causes of amenorrhea such as a pituitary microadenoma would be diagnosed on the basis of an elevated prolactin level and normal FSH level. Cushing's syndrome, hypothyroidism, and other endocrine disorders would also be confirmed or denied with the appropriate endocrine test. When any uncertainty exists, a serum FSH level above 30 mIU/mL confirms the diagnosis of menopause.

Diagnostic Options and Recommended Approach

The diagnosis of menopause can usually be made based on symptoms, physical findings, and vaginal hormonal cytology. Papanicolaou smears usually report the estrogen index or hormone reading, and if not, a maturation index can be requested from either the cytologist or pathologist. This reports the percentage of superficial, intermediate, and parabasal cells. High percentages of superficial and intermediate cells indicate normal endogenous estrogen production, whereas mostly parabasal cells predict estrogen deficiency. If the woman has an intact uterus, cervical mucus can be taken for presence or absence of the fern pattern. Ferning of the cervical mucus also indicates normal estrogen levels; however, absence occurs after ovulation and during pregnancy so a careful history must be taken. Another good predictive test if the patient still has her uterus and is not menstruating regularly is the progestogen challenge test. This is performed by administering a progestogen, such as medroxyprogesterone acetate 10 mg or norethindrone acetate 5 mg (Table 10–3–1), for 13 days to the amenorrheic woman. Withdrawal bleeding would indicate that normal endogenous estrogens are present. A negative response in the presence of menopausal symptoms diagnoses estrogen deficiency.

Estradiol and estrone levels fluctuate widely during the perimenopausal years, and menopausal symptoms are almost always present before estradiol levels drop below the 50 pg/mL diagnostic level. The most accurate laboratory test, the serum FSH level, is diagnostic above 30 mIU/mL. During the reproductive years, the serum FSH level is 10 mIU/mL or below; it begins to rise prior to menopause.

Therapeutic

Therapeutic Options and Recommended Approach

Not all postmenopausal women need estrogen therapy, as many produce sufficient endogenous estrogens to remain asymptomatic and prevent the consequences of long-term estrogen deficiency such as osteoporosis, coronary artery disease, and Alzheimer's disease. Within this group, however, are certain patients who may benefit from cyclic progestogen therapy to prevent endometrial hyperplasia, which may lead to cancer. If the patient has a positive response to the progestogen challenge test, manifested by withdrawal bleeding, then the progestogen should be continued for 13 days each month for as long as withdrawal bleeding follows.

Patients with menopausal symptoms, in the absence of contraindications, should be prescribed estrogens and progestogens. Conjugated estrogens 0.625 mg or equivalent dosages of other estrogens (Table

TABLE 10–3–1. AVAILABLE PROGESTOGENS

Brand Name	Progestogen	Doses Available (mg)	Minimum Effective Dosage
Provera	Medroxyprogesterone acetate	2.5, 5, 10	10 mg daily
Curretab	Medroxyprogesterone acetate	10	10 mg daily
Cycrin	Medroxyprogesterone acetate	10	10 mg daily
Amen	Medroxyprogesterone acetate	10	10 mg daily
Aygestin	Norethindrone acetate	5	2.5 mg daily
Norlutate	Norethindrone acetate	5	2.5 mg daily
Norlutin	Norethindrone	5	2.5 mg daily
Megace	Megestrol acetate	20, 40	40 mg daily
Ovrette	Norgestrel	0.075	0.150 mg daily
Micronor	Norethindrone	0.35	1.05 mg daily
Nor-Q.D.	Norethindrone	0.35	1.05 mg daily
	Progesterone vaginal suppositories	25, 50	25 mg b.i.d.
	Oral micronized progesterone	50, 100	300 mg in divided doses

TABLE 10–3–2. CURRENTLY RECOMMENDED ESTROGENS

Brand Name	Estrogen	Doses Availble (mg)	Minimum Effective Dosage
Premarin	Conjugated estrogens	0.3, 0.625, 0.9, 1.25, 2.5	0.625
Estrace	Micronized estradiol	0.5, 1.0, 2.0	1.0
Estratab	Esterified estrogens	0.3, 0.625, 1.25, 2.5	0.625
Ogen	Estropipate	0.625, 1.25, 2.5, 5.0	1.25
Estraderm	Transdermal estradiol	0.05, 0.1	0.05

10–3–2) can be given cyclically from the 1st through the 25th of the month, and the progestogen added during the last 13 days of estrogen therapy, from the 13th through the 25th. Estrogen–progestogen therapy for postmenopausal women with an intact uterus is not without consequence, as 97% experience withdrawal bleeding until age 60. Withdrawal bleeding from combination estrogen–progestogen therapy gradually declines from ages 60 to 65, at which time 60% continue with a bleeding response. Most women can accept these light 3- to 4-day periods, but for those who cannot, alternate methods are available (Table 10–3–3).

Several methods of hormone replacement are suitable for treating menopausal symptoms, and each has its advantages and disadvantages. Therapy should be individualized to fit each woman's need. The method preferred for new patients with an intact uterus is the cyclic sequential regimen. This has the fewest side effects except for withdrawal bleeding; however, if women on this regimen have menopausal symptoms during the days off estrogen at the end of each month, the estrogen can be given continuously and the progestogen added for the first 12 to 14 days each month (continuous sequential).

Some women object to resumption or continuation of menstruation, so the continuous combined and cyclic combined regimens have been devised to produce amenorrhea (Table 10–3–3). With the continuous combined method, low dosages of estrogen, such as 0.625 mg conjugated estrogens, are given along with medroxyprogesterone acetate 2.5 mg or norethindrone acetate 2.5 mg, every day for 365 days a year. For the first 4 to 6 months, there is a lot of spotting or breakthrough bleeding, but by 6 months, 60 to 65% of women using continuous combined therapy become amenorrheic. The other 35 to 40% need to use one of the sequential methods.

After 2 to 3 years of amenorrhea with the continuous combined method, some women will start spotting or have breakthrough bleeding again. Until December 1992, all endometrial biopsies performed by this author showed atrophic endometrium. These are difficult to manage and increasing the dosage of progestogen to 5 mg, even 7.5 mg, rarely helps the breakthrough bleeding, so these patients usually must be given one of the sequential regimens. In December 1992, an 81-year-old patient of mine was found to have poorly differentiated adenocarcinoma of the endometrium. Four other cases of endometrial cancer have been reported, and I am aware of 32 more, for a total of 37 cases with the continuous combined regimen. This may be only the tip of the iceberg after a decade of experience with this method. It seems to be very important to interrupt the progestogen for a few days each month to allow any buildup of endometrium to be shed.

The cyclic combined regimen is superior clinically to the continuous combined regimen, as 75% of patients will become amenorrheic by 4 months, compared with 60 to 65% with the continuous combined regimen at 6 months. Low-dosage estrogen and low-dosage progestogen

TABLE 10–3–3. METHODS OF HORMONE ADMINISTRATION

Regimen	Estrogen	Progestogen
Cyclic sequential	1st–25th/month	13th–25th/month
Continuous sequential	Every day	1st–14th/month
Continuous combined	Every day	Every day
Cyclic combined	1st–25th/month	1st–25th/month

are given from the 1st through the 25th of each month (Table 10–3–3). After a comparable amount of spotting the first month of therapy, there is less breakthrough bleeding, usually only 1 or 2 days of spotting on the 26th or 27th of the month, or both, which occurs in only 25% of women. Most patients can accept this minimal withdrawal bleeding when a full explanation and reassurance are given. Whether the cyclic combined method is more endometrial-protective than the continuous combined regimen remains to be proven, as we have only 5 years of experience. Theoretically, it should be, because discontinuing the progestogen should allow for shedding any built-up endometrium.

Prevention of Endometrial Cancer

Unopposed estrogens have a role in the development of endometrial hyperplasia, which may lead to adenocarcinoma (Figure 10–3–1), primarily because of incomplete shedding of the endometrium. Progesterone or progestogen therapy ensures more complete sloughing of the endometrium, which in turn prevents the continued proliferation that may result in hyperplasia or endometrial cancer. In fact, progestogen therapy can reverse 98% of endometrial hyperplasias to normal proliferative or secretory endometrium. The protective action of progestogens on the endometrium is believed to be primarily physical, in that more cells and glands are shed, thus leaving behind fewer glands for continued proliferation. This is why the cyclic combined regimen should be more endometrium-protective than the continuous combined method. Stopping the progestogen allows any proliferation of endometrium to be shed. Any abnormal or unscheduled bleeding, including the bleeding from the initial progestogen challenge test, should be promptly investigated by endometrial sampling. In the Wilford Hall USAF Medical Center studies, the incidence of endometrial cancer was significantly lower in the estrogen–progestogen users (49.0 per 100,000) when compared with both unopposed estrogen users (390.6 per 100,000) and untreated women (245.5 per 100,000) (Table 10–3–4). (Gambrell, 1995)

Reduction in Risk of Breast Cancer

There is no evidence that estrogen replacement therapy increases the risk of breast cancer, although this has been of considerable concern for a number of years. Figure 10–3–2 shows that the relative risk of breast cancer with estrogen therapy hovers around 1.0. There is increasing evidence that added progestogen will significantly reduce the risk of breast cancer for some women. In the Wilford Hall USAF Medical Center studies (Gambrell, 1995), the incidence of breast cancer in the unopposed estrogen users (142.3 per 100,000) was actually a little lower than that expected for this age group according to both the Third National Cancer Survey (188.3 per 100,000) and the National Cancer Institute SEER data (261.6 per 100,000) (Table 10–3–5). The incidence of breast cancer in the estrogen–progestogen users (66.8 per 100,000) was significantly lower than that of the nonusers (343.5 per 100,000) and than that expected from both the Third National Cancer Survey and National Cancer Institute SEER data. This has been confirmed in a 20-year study from Germany, where the incidence in estrogen–progestogen users was 123.4 per 100,000, and in a 22-year study from New York, where there were no breast cancers in the estrogen–progestogen users, compared with six cases in the never users.

The recently published Nurses' Health Study purports to show an increased risk of breast cancer in current estrogen users (RR=1.46; 95% confidence interval, 1.22 to 1.74; Colditz et al., 1995). The risk was the same for 5 to 9 years (RR=1.46; 95% confidence interval, 1.22 to 1.74) as it was for 10 or more years (RR=1.46; 95% confidence interval, 1.20 to 1.76), which is not biologically probable. Also, if estrogen replacement increased the risk of breast cancer, this risk should remain for several years; yet in their past users it was gone within 2 years (RR=0.90; 95% confidence interval, 0.77 to 1.05). Like other epidemiologic studies, all the variables for carcinoma of the breast cannot be evaluated. Alcohol use increases the risk of breast cancer two-fold and obesity increases the risk 1.5-fold, yet neither of these variables were included in the Nurses' Health Study. Detection bias was also evident in that screening mammography was 14% higher among women currently using hormones.

The Nurses' Health Study did not observe a decreased risk of breast

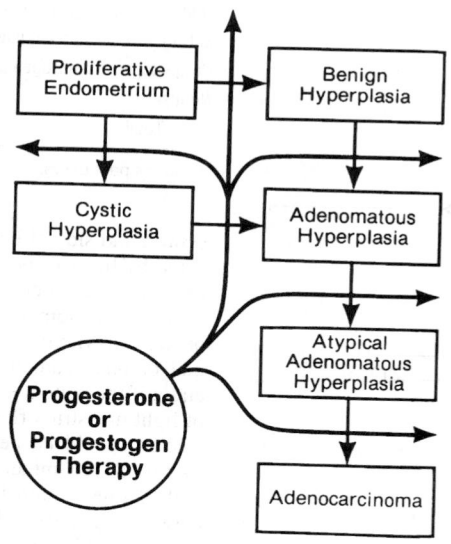

Figure 10–3–1. Schematic representation of the role of unopposed estrogens in the development of endometrial hyperplasia and neoplasia (left) and the effect of progestogens in preventing these changes (right). (*Source: Gambrell RD Jr. The menopause: Benefits and risks of estrogen–progestogen replacement therapy. Fertil Steril 1982;37:457. Reproduced with the permission of the publisher, the American Society for Reproductive Medicine (The American Fertility Society).)*

cancer in their estrogen–progestogen users (RR=1.41; 95% confidence interval, 1.15 to 1.74). They admitted that widespread use of progestogens was a recent phenomenon in their cohort so they were unable to examine associations with risk according to dose or duration. In our studies, a significant reduction in breast cancer incidence was not observed until the ninth and tenth year of ever-increasing addition of progestogens to estrogen therapy. Confirming the benefit of added progestogen to estrogen therapy was the publication of the study from Australia in the summer of 1995 where patients with breast cancer were treated with hormone replacement (Eden et al., 1995). Among the 90 estrogen–progestogen users, there were no deaths and only 7% developed a recurrence, compared to 17% of the non-users (RR=0.40; 95% confidence interval, 0.17 to 0.93).

Side Effects

Side effects of combination estrogen–progestogen therapy occur in 5 to 10% of patients but usually are minimal and frequently transient. Some of the untoward reactions to estrogens, such as breast tenderness, may be alleviated by adding progestogens. Ironically, added progestogens may aggravate mastodynia the first few months of therapy, but this usually abates with time. Other side effects include edema, bloating, premenstrual irritability, lower abdominal cramps, dysmenorrhea, and headaches. Edema, bloating, and irritability are more frequent in

women using unopposed estrogens, but at times are aggravated by added progestogens. These symptoms are best managed by decreasing the estrogen dosage if more than 0.625 mg is being used, but sometimes it is necessary to add a mild diuretic, such as spironolactone 25 mg or hydrochlorothiazide 25 mg, for the last 7 to 10 days of progestogen therapy. Lower abdominal cramps and dysmenorrhea usually respond to a change to another progestogen (Table 10–3–1), but it may be necessary to add a prostaglandin-inhibiting analgesic such as aspirin, ibuprofen, naproxen sodium, or mefenamic acid. Some women cannot tolerate any oral progestogen, so it may be necessary to substitute progesterone vaginal suppositories, 25 mg twice daily, for the 13 days.

There is no evidence that estrogen replacement has any adverse effect on coagulation factors or increases thromboembolic phenomena, although some clotting factors may increase with aging. The synthetic estrogens in the original high-dosage oral contraceptives were associated with vascular thrombosis; however, the low-dosage natural estrogens needed by postmenopausal women do not have this effect. The progestogen in birth control pills tends to mediate the estrogen-induced clotting changes. Prothrombin time and partial thromboplastin time are not affected by estrogen replacement, and although fibrinogen values rise, they remain within the normal range. Coagulation factor V decreases during estrogen therapy, but factors VII and X do not change. Antithrombin III is significantly decreased in pregnant women and oral contraceptive users, but only slightly decreased with conjugated or other natural estrogens, remaining within the normal range. Several clinical studies in long-term estrogen users indicate decreased cerebral vascular accidents and myocardial infarction.

Patients know the benefits of estrogen replacement therapy but are concerned about the risk of endometrial and breast cancer. The Food and Drug Administration requires a patient package insert be given by the pharmacist with all prescribed estrogens. In this are listed the dangers of estrogens (endometrial cancer, blood clots, etc.). The physician must become familiar with the patient package insert so it can be discussed in advance with the patient. When progestogens are added to estrogen therapy, not only is the risk of endometrial cancer not increased, the risk is reduced to less than that of those not receiving any hormone replacement. A major compliance problem is the resumption or continuation of menstrual periods; however, when patients are told that taking the progestogen reduces the risk of endometrial cancer, most can accept

TABLE 10–3–4. INCIDENCE OF ENDOMETRIAL CANCER AT WILFORD HALL USAF MEDICAL CENTER: 1975–1983

Therapy Group	Patient-Years of Observation	Patients with Cancer	Incidence (per 100,000)
Estrogen–progestogen users	16,327	8	49.0
Unopposed estrogen users	2,560	10	390.6
Estrogen vaginal cream users	2,716	2*	73.6
Progestogen or androgen users	1,160	0	—
Untreated women	4,480	11	245.5
Total	27,243	31	113.8

*Includes past estrogen vaginal cream users.

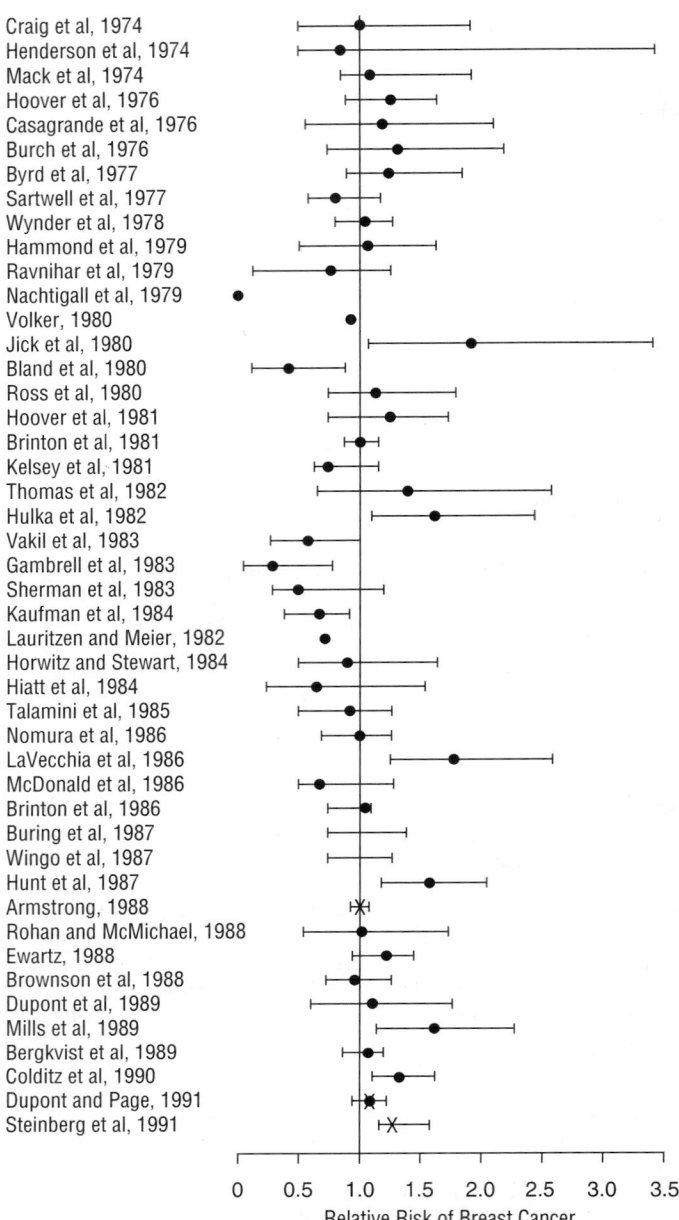

Figure 10–3–2. Schematic representation of 46 studies, including 3 meta-analyses (×) regarding the effect of estrogen therapy on breast cancer risk. Shown are the relative risk (solid circles) and 95% confidence interval (horizontal lines). (Sources for the data are available from the chapter author on request.)

TABLE 10–3–5. INCIDENCE OF BREAST CANCER AT WILFORD HALL USAF MEDICAL CENTER: 1975–1983

Therapy Group	Patient-Years of Observation	Patients with Cancer	Incidence (per 100,000)
Estrogen–progestogen users	16,466	11*	66.8
Unopposed estrogen users	19,676	28*	142.3
Estrogen vaginal cream users	4,298	5*	116.3
Progestogen or androgen users	1,825	3*	164.4
Nonusers	6,404	22	343.5
Total	48,669	69	141.8

*Includes past users.

essary, and side effects, if any, can be treated. Patients should be reassured by further discussion of the benefit/risk ratio. Thereafter, follow-up at 6-month intervals is recommended.

Annual endometrial biopsies are not necessary if progestogens are prescribed with cyclic estrogen therapy for the last 13 days. Any abnormal or unscheduled bleeding should be promptly investigated, especially if the patient experiences any bleeding other than the 3 to 4 days of light menstrual flow expected at the end of the month. Papanicolaou smears should be performed annually. Mammograms should be performed as recommended by the American Cancer Society: for women with normally palpable breasts, baseline at age 40, every 1 to 2 years between ages 40 and 50, then annually after age 50. Breast examinations should be done at the 6-month visit and anytime the patient notes any changes in her mammary tissue. Of course, any dominant mass or discrete nodule requires biopsy or at least an early mammogram.

In addition to routine blood tests, urinalysis, blood pressure, weight, and so on, if total cholesterol is elevated, fractionation of the lipoproteins into high- and low-density lipoproteins should be done every 1 to 2 years.

DISCUSSION
Prevalence
All women go through menopause.

Related Basic Science
At the time of menopause, ovarian function declines and gonadotropin release by the pituitary correspondingly increases. The age of menopause ranges from the early forties to the late fifties. In our studies of more than 2000 women undergoing a natural menopause, the mean age was 49.1 years. Postmenopausally, serum FSH and luteinizing hormone values are markedly elevated, with FSH in the range 75 to 200 mIU/mL and luteinizing hormone in the range 60 to 90 mIU/mL. Postmenopausal women produce little, if any, progesterone. This deficiency of progesterone may lead to improper shedding of the endometrium, so that continuous unopposed exposure to estrogen may lead to hyperplasia and even endometrial cancer. There is also some evidence that long-term progesterone deficiency increases the risk of breast cancer.

Natural History and Its Modification with Treatment
A wide variety of symptoms and physical changes are associated with menopause. Some patients may experience only cessation of menses; others experience severe reactions that are occasionally disabling. Several factors influence development of symptoms during the postmenopausal years. The most important factor is probably the degree of estrogen deficiency and the rate at which estrogen levels decrease. A second factor may be the inherited or acquired propensity to withstand or succumb to the aging process. A third factor may be the psychological impact of aging and the woman's ability to accept or deny the emotional changes of menopause.

Estrogen deficiency contributes to the development of osteoporosis, a skeletal disorder affecting primarily trabecular bone, at least in the early postmenopausal years, in which a reduction in the quantity of bone predisposes to vertebral fractures. We are learning that estrogen deficiency is also related to type II or age-related osteoporosis, affect-

the light 3- to 4-day menses with hormone replacement. With new methods such as the cyclic combined regimen (Table 10–3–3), they may safely remain amenorrheic. The other major compliance issue is fear of breast cancer. Breast cancer risk is not increased with even unopposed estrogen therapy, and added progestogen may reduce the risk for mammary malignancy in some women. There is no evidence that postmenopausal estrogen therapy adversely affects coagulation factors. There is currently considerable publicity about osteoporosis, so in discussing hormone replacement therapy, the benefits—prevention of osteoporosis, heart disease, genital atrophy, and Alzheimer's disease—should be emphasized and the risks adequately covered.

FOLLOW-UP
After initiation of hormone replacement, the patient should be reevaluated in 3 months. At this time, hormone dosages can be adjusted, if nec-

ing cortical bone, which predisposes to hip fracture. Although both sexes have loss of bone mass with aging, it is rare for men to develop symptomatic osteoporosis before age 70. This is a major public health problem affecting 20,000,000 older Americans, of which 90% are postmenopausal women. It has been estimated that there are 1,700,000 fractures each year from osteoporosis at an annual public health cost in excess of $6 billion. Approximately 25% of white women over age 60 have spinal compression fractures, and this proportion increases to 50% by age 75. The incidence of hip fracture doubles every 5 years after the age of 60 so that by the time women reach age 90, 40% of white women have sustained a hip fracture. With increasing longevity, a woman reaching age 50 now has a life expectancy of 80.4 years, at which age the already serious morbidity and mortality associated with postmenopausal osteoporosis become even greater. Of all hip fractures, 80% are associated with osteoporosis, and 34% of all patients with hip fracture die within 6 months. Other fractures also occur, including those of the wrist and long bones, secondary to relatively minor trauma, and may be the first presenting sign of postmenopausal osteoporosis.

Myocardial infarction rarely occurs in women prior to menopause. Consequently, it has been suggested that normal endogenous estrogens provide a protective effect against atherosclerosis. Younger women who have had bilateral oophorectomy (surgical menopause) demonstrate a higher incidence of coronary artery disease unless estrogen replacement is begun soon after the ovaries are removed. Both surgical menopause and natural menopause appear to be related to changes in blood lipid profiles, development of atherosclerosis, increased hypertension, and the incidence of coronary artery disease. An increase in total cholesterol and low density lipoprotein is associated with coronary artery disease, whereas high density lipoprotein seems to have some protective effect. High density lipoprotein decreases with estrogen deficiency and increases to within the normal range with estrogen replacement therapy.

Prevention

Several studies have demonstrated that estrogen therapy together with adequate dietary or supplemental calcium prevents osteoporosis, decreases vertebral and hip fractures, and prevents loss of height. The recommendation of the National Institutes of Health Consensus Development Conference on Osteoporosis is that estrogen therapy is the best prevention and treatment of osteoporosis. Calcium supplementation, which should be begun by age 40 or approximately 10 years prior to menopause, should be given in dosages of 1000 mg of elemental calcium daily. Weight-bearing exercises are the best activity to prevent osteoporosis. The dosage of conjugated estrogens that has been shown to prevent osteoporosis in more than 90% of postmenopausal women is 0.625 mg daily (Table 10–3–2). Higher dosages of estrogen (1.25 mg) and calcium (1500 mg) are required if osteoporosis is already present.

Oral or injectable progestogens are also effective in preventing bone loss. Where most studies indicate that estrogen therapy inhibits the resorption of calcium from bone, most likely by restoring calcitonin levels that are decreased after menopause, several studies have shown that combination estrogen–progestogen therapy may actually increase bone mass by promoting new bone formation. In a crossover double-blind study comparing the effects of estrogen–progestogen therapy with placebo, bone mineral mass increased during 3 years of combination therapy but continued to decline in the placebo-treated group. When some patients in the estrogen–progestogen group were changed to placebo, bone density decreased; the placebo-treated women had increased bone mass after being changed to active hormone therapy. Long-term studies of 10 years' duration revealed ever-increasing bone density with estrogen–progestogen therapy.

The proven and almost universally accepted benefits of estrogen–progestogen replacement therapy include relief of vasomotor symptoms, prevention of atrophic vaginitis, and prevention of osteoporosis. Hormone therapy may also help alleviate some of the psychogenic manifestations that are aggravated by menopause. The greatest benefit that will accrue to postmenopausal estrogen users is a 50% reduction in

heart attacks by preventing coronary artery disease. This is partially mediated by the estrogen-induced rise in high density lipoprotein cholesterol; however, estrogens directly affect coronary arteries by increasing blood flow, promoting vasodilation, and reducing plaque formation. The latest benefit to be shown with estrogen replacement is a 30 to 40% reduction in Alzheimer's disease. This is manifested by increasing dendritic spines and increasing the cholinesterase enzymes necessary to reconvert the neurotransmitters to acetylcholine.

Thirteen days of cyclic progestogens reduces the risk of endometrial cancer by preventing or treating estrogen-induced hyperplasia. The risk of breast cancer is well shown not to be increased with estrogen therapy, and addition of progestogens may provide additional protection from this tumor. There is no evidence that either estrogens or progestogens, in the small dosages needed for menopause, increase the risk of thromboembolic disease. As with any therapy, the physician should weigh the benefits against the risks, discuss these fully with the patient, and individualize therapy. Finally, not all postmenopausal women need estrogen therapy. Some are asymptomatic but nonetheless produce sufficient endogenous estrogen to require cyclic progestogens only to reduce the risk of endometrial cancer.

Cost Containment

Diagnosis and treatment of menopause need not be expensive. Simple noninvasive tests, based on symptoms and physical findings, such as vaginal hormonal cytology, cervical mucus for fern pattern, and the progestogen challenge test, are usually all that is needed. It is not necessary to do elaborate and expensive tests to screen for osteoporosis. Quantitative computed tomography will detect early bone loss within 2 months of bilateral oophorectomy; however, nearly all women whose ovaries are removed during the reproductive years become estrogen deficient immediately and, so, should be started on therapy. Dual-energy x-ray absorptiometry is very accurate in diagnosing osteoporosis; however, if the physician identifies and treats estrogen deficiency as outlined above, more than 90% of postmenopausal osteoporosis will be prevented, thus making these expensive tests unnecessary except for clinical research. About the only clinical use for dual-energy x-ray absorptiometry is to convince reluctant patients that they are losing bone. Of course, calcium supplementation should be started by age 40 and estrogen–progestogen replacement added when estrogen deficiency is diagnosed. Fortunately, estrogens have been available for many years, so medication is relatively inexpensive. More expensive routes of administration such as injectables and subcutaneous pellets are usually not required by most women. Unfortunately, progestogens are a little more expensive than estrogens, but the cost/benefit ratio (prevention of endometrial cancer, reduction in breast cancer, promotion of new bone formation) still is very favorable.

REFERENCES

Cobleigh MA, Berris RF, Bush T, et al. Estrogen replacement therapy in breast cancer survivors: A time for change. JAMA 1994;272:540.

Colditz GA, Handinson SE, Hunter DJ, et al. The use of estrogens and progestins and the risk of breast cancer in postmenopausal women. N Engl J Med 1995;332:1589.

Dupont WD, Page DL. Menopausal estrogen replacement therapy and breast cancer. Arch Intern Med 1991;151:67.

Eden JA, Bush T, Nand S, Wren BG. A case-control study of combined continuous estrogen–progestin replacement therapy among women with a personal history of breast cancer. Menopause: J N Am Menopause Soc 1995;2:67.

Gambrell RD Jr. Hormone replacement therapy. 4th ed. Durant, OK: Essential Medical Information Systems, 1995:1.

Lobo RA. Treatment of the postmenopausal woman: Basic and clinical aspects. New York: Raven Press, 1994;1.

Paganini-Hill A, Henderson VW. Estrogen deficiency and the risk of Alzheimer's disease in women. Am J Epidemiol 1994;140:256.

Stampfter MJ, Colditz GA. Estrogen replacement therapy and coronary heart disease: A quantitative assessment of the epidemiologic evidence. Prev Med 1991;20:47.

Uterine Bleeding Prior to Menopause

Carlene W. Elsner, M.D.

DEFINITION

Any uterine bleeding other than regular menstrual bleeding is considered abnormal.

ETIOLOGY

Abnormal uterine bleeding can occur because of hormonal, mechanical, infectious, or neoplastic reasons. A spectrum of disordered hormonal stimulation of the endometrium ranging from anovulation with bleeding from an estrogen-primed endometrium, to deficient luteal phase support of the endometrium by progesterone, to threatened abortion may result in irregular spotting or bleeding. Endometrial or endocervical polyps, submucous fibroids, endometritis, and cervicitis may all produce bleeding. Finally, neoplasia of the cervix, endocervix, and endometrium also causes bleeding.

CRITERIA FOR DIAGNOSIS

Suggestive

History of any vaginal bleeding other than regular cyclic menses is suggestive of uterine bleeding.

Definitive

Visualization on pelvic examination of blood coming from the cervical os establishes the diagnosis.

CLINICAL MANIFESTATIONS

Subjective

Most women cannot reliably distinguish the source of perineal bleeding. Rectal, perineal, or urinary bleeding can be confused with vaginal bleeding because of the proximity of the respective orifices.

Uterine bleeding may or may not be associated with cramping or pain. The pattern of bleeding, particularly the frequency, duration, and amount of blood loss, may give clues to the diagnosis. Irregular and heavy bleeding of prolonged duration with an interval of less than 18 days from onset of bleeding to onset of next bleeding suggests luteal phase dysfunction. Postcoital bleeding as well as bleeding or spotting at other times is suggestive of endocervical polyps, cervicitis, cervical erosions, and cervical cancer. Bleeding that is very heavy and prolonged, resulting in anemia, is compatible with submucous fibroid. Cramping is severe in these instances, particularly if the fibroid prolapses through the cervical os. Bleeding with endometrial polyps or with endometrial cancer ranges from spotting to frank bleeding without any particular pattern.

Objective

Physical Examination

Careful pelvic examination is necessary to rule out vaginal or perineal lacerations as a possible source of bleeding. Visualization of blood per os establishes the uterus as the site of bleeding. Examination of the cervix may reveal a friable cervical lesion, an endocervical polyp, or a dilated cervix with products of conception protruding through the os. Endometrial casts are sometimes passed in ectopic pregnancies. Uterine tenderness to palpation suggests endometritis. Sometimes uterine fibroids are palpable on bimanual examination; however, submucous fibroids responsible for bleeding may be small and therefore easily missed.

Routine Laboratory Abnormalities

A negative pregnancy test, preferably beta human chorionic gonadotropin, rules out abnormal pregnancy, intrauterine or ectopic, as the reason for bleeding. Complete blood count determines if the patient is anemic. Basal body temperatures are an inexpensive indirect indicator of ovulation. The absence of a thermal shift suggests anovulation.

PLANS

Diagnostic

Differential Diagnosis

Benign causes of uterine bleeding include complications of pregnancy, such as threatened, incomplete, or complete abortion and ectopic pregnancy; anovulation; infection, like pelvic inflammatory disease or endometritis; and mechanical factors, including submucous fibroids and endometrial polyps. Malignant causes of uterine bleeding include cervical, endocervical, and endometrial cancer.

Diagnostic Options

A pregnancy test will be positive in the presence of viable trophoblast. A negative quantitative beta human chorionic gonadotropin rules out pregnancy as a reason for bleeding. Endocervical polyps are frequently seen on pelvic examination. Friable cervical lesions should be biopsied. A fractional dilation and curettage with cervical, endocervical, and endometrial samples taken in that order is the best way to rule out cancer, or if present, to stage it. Endometrial biopsy will also detect other reasons for bleeding such as endometritis, anovulation, and endometrial hyperplasia. Hysterosalpingogram detects intrauterine filling defects like endometrial polyps and submucous fibroids and, rarely, may suggest adenomyosis. Sonographic hysterogram combines ultrasound with saline instillation into the uterine cavity to determine if intrauterine filling defects are in fact fibroids. Hysteroscopy allows direct visualization of the endometrial cavity to determine the source of bleeding.

Recommended Approach

First, rule out pregnancy, even in a woman who has not missed a period. Biopsy any suspicious lesions; then finish the workup. Basal body temperatures document anovulation. If temperature charts are ovulatory, bleeding episodes can be correlated to the phase of the cycle to detect patterns of occurrence.

Therapeutic

Therapeutic Options

Irregular anovulatory bleeding is common in the year following menarche and requires no treatment unless bleeding is heavy or prolonged. In such instances, oral contraceptives provide regular withdrawal bleeds that are self-limited; however, on discontinuance of medication, anovulation may recur.

If anovulation is the reason for abnormal bleeding, the patient's current desire for fertility determines treatment. Low-dose combination oral contraceptive medication provides regular withdrawal periods for those who choose to delay fertility. Women desiring pregnancy should be treated with ovulation induction agents. Alternative therapy for women who do not tolerate or do not need oral contraception includes medroxyprogesterone acetate (Provera), 10 mg daily days 16 through 26 of the cycle, or oral micronized progesterone (Oragest), 100 mg mornings and 200 mg evenings for the same period. Women who lack adequate estrogenic stimulation of the endometrium may require estrogen (Premarin or Estrace) as well as progesterone to maintain regular menstrual periods.

Polyps should be removed surgically either by direct visualization hysteroscopically or by dilation and curettage.

Submucous fibroids can be reduced in size temporarily by treatment with gonadotropin-releasing hormone agonists. Maximal effect is achieved in 2 to 3 months. Bleeding usually stops, allowing recovery from anemia. Myomas return to pretreatment size rapidly following discontinuance of medication, rendering this therapy most useful as a preoperative measure to facilitate surgical removal and minimize blood loss at surgery. For women desiring fertility, myomectomy via hysteroscopy or laparotomy provides relief of symptoms while improving fertility potential. Older women, whose families are complete, may prefer definitive treatment by hysterectomy.

Threatened abortion in the absence of fever is treated expectantly with pelvic rest and limitation of activity. Progesterone supplementation, if begun early enough, may result in cessation of bleeding. Progesterone levels in pregnancy above 30 ng/mL are adequate and do not require supplementation. Frequently, bleeding will stop and such pregnancies will proceed normally to term. Patients may resume normal activity after bleeding has stopped for 24 hours.

Bleeding associated with infection clears when the infection is satisfactorily treated.

Dilation and curettage is sometimes viewed as therapy for abnormal bleeding; however, it is primarily a diagnostic procedure and, unless the underlying cause of bleeding is treated, the abnormal bleeding pattern frequently recurs within a few months. Treatment of cervical and uterine cancer is discussed elsewhere (see Chapters 10–8 and 10–9).

Recommended Approach

Anovulatory patients desiring pregnancy require ovulation induction. In the absence of hormonal abnormalities, clomiphene citrate is the drug of choice. Beginning with 50 mg a day orally on cycle days 5 to 9, the dosage is increased monthly until ovulation occurs or to a maximum of 250 mg a day. Prolonged use of clomiphene citrate is to be avoided because of recent reports of increased risk of ovarian cancer in women using this drug longer than 1 year. Anovulatory patients not desiring pregnancy are best managed on low-dose combination oral contraceptives.

Polyps and submucous fibroids should be removed hysteroscopically if possible. Large submucous fibroids (>6 cm) require laparotomy and myomectomy for removal.

Progesterone therapy is not useful to maintain a pregnancy in cases of threatened abortion if the serum progesterone level is more than 30 ng/mL. When serum progesterone is less than 30 ng/mL, progesterone supplementation may result in cessation of bleeding and continuance of pregnancy to term. Progesterone supplementation will not maintain an abnormal pregnancy indefinitely. No matter how much progesterone is given, ultimately the abnormal pregnancies will be lost.

FOLLOW-UP

After therapy is initiated, follow-up visits at 3- to 6-month intervals are appropriate to review menstrual calendars and alter treatment until abnormal bleeding is eliminated. Then routine visits can be reinstituted. If symptomatology recurs, reevaluation is necessary. Patients with infertility may require further workup. Women who have had myomectomies are followed with yearly pelvic examinations and ultrasounds, if appropriate, to monitor for recurrence.

DISCUSSION
Prevalence

Abnormal bleeding is one of the most frequent gynecologic complaints encountered by practitioners providing health care to women. Bleeding in early pregnancy indicates threatened miscarriage. Ultimately, 20 to 25% of all pregnancies end in early miscarriage. Leiomyomas, the most common tumor of the female genital tract occurring in 20% of women over 30, are frequently associated with abnormal bleeding. Bleeding due to anovulation and related hormonal abnormalities occurs with greatest frequency at the extremes of reproductive life, 50% in the premenopause and 20% following menarche.

Related Basic Science
Genetics

Leiomyomas are cytogenetically abnormal, resulting from somatic mutations of individual muscle cells. Each myoma results from the prolifera-

tion of genetically abnormal clones of cells derived from a single cell. Myomas are multicentric in origin. The number of myomas in a uterus, as well as the likelihood of recurrence following myomectomy, relates directly to the endogenous somatic mutation rate for the effected individual. Therefore, an individual with a solitary myoma has a low endogenous mutation rate and a low likelihood of recurrence following myomectomy. An individual with many myomas has a high endogenous mutation rate and a high likelihood of recurrence following myomectomy.

Metabolic Derangement

In anovulatory women, bleeding occurs from an estrogen-primed proliferative endometrium. Unopposed estrogenic stimulation of the endometrium results in lush endometrial growth, which sheds incompletely. Over time, if the condition is left untreated, progression to adenomatous hyperplasia and eventually to endometrial carcinoma may occur. Cyclic treatment with progesterone results in development of secretory endometrium. Progesterone withdrawal causes complete shedding of the endometrium to the basalis, greatly reducing the risk of development of hyperplasia and carcinoma.

Progesterone production by the corpus luteum of pregnancy is necessary for the maintenance of the pregnancy for the first 12 weeks. Following that, the ovaries may be removed and the pregnancy will proceed to term. If for any reason progesterone production is insufficient during the first trimester, spotting or bleeding will occur. There are many other reasons for threatened abortion discussed elsewhere (see Chapters 10–19 and 10–20).

Anatomic Derangement

Endometrial polyps result from proliferation of the endometrium and are frequently associated with ovulatory disorders or anovulation. Polyps are most common in patients with unopposed estrogenic stimulation of the endometrium. Recurrence of polyps is reduced with the use of cyclic progesterone to shed endometrium completely.

Pelvic inflammatory disease and malignancies are discussed elsewhere (see Chapter 8–26 and other chapters in this section).

Natural History and Its Modification with Treatment

During the first year following menarche, ovulation is not well established and frequently menses are anovulatory and irregular. This irregular bleeding pattern changes to that of regular monthly menses when ovulation is established. No treatment is required unless bleeding is heavy or prolonged. If the irregular bleeding pattern is of concern to the patient or her mother, oral contraceptives will provide predictable monthly withdrawal bleeds. If regular monthly menses are not established within 2 years of menarche or on discontinuance of oral contraceptives, endocrine workup should be considered.

Temporary anovulation can occur during periods of stress. Classically this is seen in girls going away to college for the first time, but may also occur with sudden weight loss or gain, with job stress, or illness or death in the family. Once the stress is over, generally regular ovulation and menses return.

If anovulation continues, workup is appropriate to rule out systemic disease as a cause for anovulation. Hypothyroidism, hyperprolactinemia, and androgen excess in women all can result in anovulation. Treatment of the underlying disease allows return of regular ovulatory menses.

Persistent anovulation in an estrogen-producing individual results in irregular shedding of the endometrium with unpredictable and sometimes heavy bleeding. This is a progressive disorder that over a period of years leads to the development of adenomatous hyperplasia and even endometrial carcinoma. This progression may be reversed by the use of cyclic progesterone.

Myomas grow under the influence of ovarian hormones. They may recur following myomectomy. Myomas enlarge during pregnancy and regress after the menopause.

Prevention

Many causes for uterine bleeding cannot be prevented. One exception is persistent anovulatory bleeding progressing to adenomatous hyperplasia, which can be prevented with the use of cyclic progesterone.

Cost Containment

Abnormal uterine bleeding should be addressed promptly. Timely institution of therapy reduces the risk of anemia and progression of underlying disease which ultimately could prove costly in terms of patient morbidity, costs of medical therapy, and lost time from work or other activities. Tissue diagnosis should be obtained in anyone in whom the reason for bleeding is unclear. Long periods of anovulation require treatment so that dilation and curettage, anemia, and progression to adenomatous hyperplasia do not occur. Dilation and curettage should not be regarded as curative for abnormal bleeding. If the underlying cause is not treated, bleeding will recur. In anovulatory patients who have a dilation and curettage, institution of therapy is indicated in their next cycle.

REFERENCES

Barbieri RL. Leiomyomata uteri. Semin Reprod Endocrinol 1992;10:301.

Carson KJ, Miller BA, Fowler FJ. The Maine Women's Health Study. II: Outcomes of nonsurgical management of leiomyomas, abnormal bleeding, and chronic pelvic pain. Obstet Gynecol 1994;83(4):566.

Jones HW, Jones GS. Novak's textbook of gynecology. Baltimore: Williams & Wilkins, 1981.

Mattox JH. Abnormal uterine bleeding. In: Wilson JR, Carrington E. Obstetrics and gynecology. St. Louis: Mosby, 1991;85.

Pernoll ML, Benson RC. Current obstetrics and gynecologic diagnosis and treatment. Norwalk, CT: Appleton & Lange, 1987.

Speroff L, Glass RH, Kase NG. Clinical gynecologic endocrinology and infertility. Baltimore: Williams & Wilkins, 1994.

CHAPTER 10–5

Uterine Bleeding After Menopause

Sarah L. Hosford, M.D.

DEFINITION

Uterine bleeding after menopause affects only a subset of patients who in fact come under the more general heading of women with postmenopausal bleeding. Postmenopausal bleeding refers to any bleeding in a menopausal woman, whether the source be from the perineum or internal gynecologic structures. Postmenopausal uterine bleeding is a subset of postmenopausal bleeding whose cause can be attributed to uterine sources. Menopause is defined as the complete cessation of menstrual bleeding, spanning a period of 6 to 12 months from the last spontaneous menses. The average age of menopause in the United States is 51 years.

ETIOLOGY

The etiology of postmenopausal bleeding is quite varied. Up to one third of women with postmenopausal bleeding have a premalignant or malignant condition of the uterus itself. Another one third of women with postmenopausal bleeding demonstrate no clear pathologic cause except atrophic changes of the endometrial lining. The etiology of uterine bleeding is attributed to hormonal fluctuations of the endometrial lining itself, either atrophic, hyperplastic, or frank malignant changes, as well as structural abnormalities such as polyps and submucous leiomyomas.

CRITERIA FOR DIAGNOSIS

Suggestive

Any bleeding from the perineal area in a menopausal woman demands complete evaluation by a physician. The exact amount or timing of bleeding is not as important as the presence of absence of bleeding. *Any* bleeding, whether reported to be minimal or excessive by the patient, requires a thorough evaluation. Likewise, excessive menstrual bleeding in a perimenopausal female requires the same thorough workup.

Definitive

As a component of postmenopausal bleeding, the definitive diagnosis of bleeding from the uterus after menopause requires exclusion of causes from the perineum (urethra, vulva, and anus), as well as vaginal and cervical sources. Only at that point can the bleeding be attributed to the uterus.

CLINICAL MANIFESTATIONS

Subjective

As stated above, any bleeding after the complete cessation of menstruation is abnormal. The quantity, quality, and duration of bleeding are not as important as the presence or absence of bleeding itself.

Objective

Physical Examination

The mainstay of evaluation in a woman with postmenopausal bleeding is a complete gynecologic evaluation. A careful history is important, with attention to drugs that may cause bleeding, such as anticoagulants. The physical examination should begin with a thorough visualization and palpation of the external structures. This includes the clitoris, urethra, and vulva, including both labia majora and labia minora, and the anus. A speculum examination to visualize the vaginal walls is critical, particularly to evaluate for atrophic changes or any evidence of injury. The cervix should be visualized to rule out any obvious tumors or polyps. A digital rectovaginal examination is crucial to evaluate the size and mobility of the uterus, as well as any adnexal pathology.

Routine Laboratory Abnormalities

Laboratory studies that might be helpful at this point include a stool guaiac for blood, possibly a urinalysis to screen for hematuria if a urinary source is suspect, and, if significant bleeding has occurred, a complete blood count to screen for anemia.

PLANS

Diagnostic

Differential Diagnosis

The differential diagnosis of postmenopausal uterine bleeding includes frank malignancy, endometrial hyperplasia, atrophic changes, and any structural changes such as endometrial polyps and submucosal myomas.

Diagnostic Options and Recommended Approach

The absolute minimum evaluation for a patient with a suspected uterine abnormality is a Pap smear, endocervical curettage, and endometrial biopsy. These can easily be done in the office at the initial evaluation when no other lesions are seen to account for the bleeding. Another helpful test is a pelvic ultrasound, with attention paid to the thickness of the endometrial lining itself. This is particularly important when the endometrial biopsy reveals only atrophic changes or minimal tissue, to help confirm whether further evaluation is needed. If cellular atypia is found on the endometrial biopsy, a fractional dilation and curettage of the uterine cavity is critical to confirm that, in fact, no frank malignancy is present. If no cause of the bleeding is found on examination, Pap smear and biopsies, followed by hysteroscopy, are indicated to evaluate the uterine cavity for other possible sources of bleeding. These would include endometrial polyps, a focal abnormality of the endometrial lining, and submucous leiomyomas.

Therapeutic

Treatment for postmenopausal bleeding is dictated by the etiology of the bleeding itself. The most common cause of uterine bleeding due to malignancy, as well as the most common gynecologic malignancy, is adenocarcinoma of the endometrium. Sarcomas are also seen, but with much less frequency. Further workup and treatment of malignancies should be left in the hands of a qualified oncologist. Another common source of uterine bleeding after the menopause is endometrial hyperplasia, which represents a wide spectrum of hormone stimulation of the endometrial lining. The normal endometrium should be atrophic in the menopausal state and glands should be inactive. Stimulation by estrogen can be from a variety of sources, the most likely being ingestion of oral estrogens or use of topical estrogen preparations without cyclical progesterone withdrawal. Increased circulating estrogens can also be found in patients with liver disease and obesity, with problems of decreased clearance and increased endogenous production, respectively. Simply identifying the source of estrogen and eliminating it may be the entire treatment needed in this situation, as long as no atypical features were seen on biopsy.

Frank hyperplasia of the endometrial lining deserves more specific intervention. Simple or complex hyperplasia without cytologic atypia has low malignant potential, and can be easily treated with progestational agents to reverse these changes. Medroxyprogesterone acetate, 10- to 20-mg tablets daily, can be used in either cyclical fashion or continuous fashion for 3 to 6 months with repeat biopsy being done at the end of this period to confirm the reversal of the hyperplastic changes. An alternate method is to use medroxyprogesterone acetate in its long-acting form (Depo-Provera), 400 mg intramuscularly every 2 to 4 weeks for the same period. Careful follow-up and repeat biopsy are essential. When cytologic atypia is present, whether in conjunction with simple or complex architecture, then malignant potential is increased and hysterectomy is the appropriate therapy.

If atrophic changes are seen on the endometrial biopsy, then no therapy and consideration of hormone replacement therapy are appropriate choices. Other benign pathology such as endometrial polyps and submucous myomas can be evaluated hysteroscopically. Endometrial polyps can be easily removed with the hysteroscope. Hysteroscopic resection and hysterectomy are both reasonable alternatives for treatment of symptomatic myomas in a postmenopausal patient.

FOLLOW-UP

Patients who are placed on hormone therapy for reversal of hyperplastic changes must be seen at regular intervals, with a careful history and repeat examination, including an endometrial biopsy, performed. Appropriate treatment will reveal that the endometrial changes are reversed with the progestational effect. If persistent bleeding occurs in a patient with atrophic changes or no specific etiology on initial evaluation, then hysteroscopy and fractional dilation and curettage are indicated to look for missed causes of postmenopausal bleeding. Again, the goal must always be to consider the possibility of malignancy and evaluate with that in mind.

DISCUSSION
Prevalence and Incidence

The exact prevalence and incidence of postmenopausal uterine bleeding are not known, but it is not an uncommon finding in an active gynecologic practice.

Related Basic Science

Causes of uterine bleeding after menopause fall most easily in the category of physiologic or metabolic derangement of a normal process. Most of the changes originate from abnormal stimulation of the endometrial lining, either by exogenous sources such as hormone replacement therapy or by other endogenous sources. These include an increase in precursor androgens that can be seen in liver disease, endocrine tumors, and stress; increased aromatization and production of estrogen as seen in obesity, hyperthyroidism, and liver disease; direct secretion of estrogen as seen in ovarian tumors; and increased availability of estrogen caused by decreased levels of sex hormone-binding globulins, commonly seen with administration of steroids or androgen excess.

Natural History and Its Modification with Treatment

More than 95% of patients with hyperplasia regress with therapy. As stated above, the most important criterion for malignant potential appears to be the presence of cytologic atypia. There is close to a 10% risk of malignant potential in simple endometrial hyperplasia with cytologic atypia, which increases to a 25% risk of malignant progression with complex architectural changes associated with cytologic atypia.

Prevention

Little can be done to eliminate endogenous sources of estrogen, but the use of unopposed oral estrogens as estrogen replacement in the postmenopausal woman continues to be a source of endometrial carcinomas. A woman who uses unopposed estrogen has four to eight times the risk of developing endometrial carcinoma as a nonuser. With this unacceptably high risk of malignant potential, unopposed estrogen should not be used in women who have not had a hysterectomy.

Cost Containment

Relatively little can be done to prevent endometrial cancers, but appropriate evaluation to include a thorough physical examination and use of office Pap smear and biopsies will reduce the overall cost and increase the early detection and treatment of uterine pathology, particularly malignancies.

REFERENCES

Herbst AL, Mishell DR, Stenchever MA, Droegemueller W. Comprehensive gynecology. 2nd ed. St. Louis: Mosby, 1992.
Morrow CP, Curtin JP, Townsend DE. Synopsis of gynecologic oncology. 4th ed. New York: Churchill Livingstone, 1993.
Speroff L, Glass RH, Kase NG. Clinical gynecologic endocrinology and infertility. 5th ed. Baltimore: Williams & Wilkins, 1994.

CHAPTER 10–6

Carcinoma of the Breast (See Section 3, Chapter 16)

CHAPTER 10–7

Carcinoma of the Ovary (See Section 3, Chapter 17)

CHAPTER 10—8

Cervical Carcinoma

Cyril O. Spann, M.D.

DEFINITION

Cervical carcinoma is a malignancy of the cervix uteri. It can be in the form of adenocarcinoma, squamous carcinoma (most common), or adenosquamous carcinoma. There are other reported histologic types, but these are quite rare.

ETIOLOGY

Cervical carcinoma has long been thought to be a venereal disease. The herpes simplex virus for many years was thought to be a causal agent, but recent studies have suggested that this is not the case. The human papillomavirus is now thought to be the major offending agent. There are numerous subtypes, but types 16, 18, 31, 33, 35, and 51 are the ones most commonly implicated in causing cervical dysplasia and/or carcinoma. Immune status, use of steroid medications, and history of cigarette smoking are considered cofactors in the development of cervical carcinoma.

CRITERIA FOR DIAGNOSIS

Suggestive

The diagnosis of cervical carcinoma is suggested by a patient history of postcoital bleeding and bloody discharge, especially with pelvic pain. Patients can also present with abnormal vaginal bleeding but, it must be pointed out that most with this symptom alone do not have a diagnosis of cervical carcinoma.

Definitive

The definitive diagnosis is established by histologic evaluation.

CLINICAL MANIFESTATIONS

Subjective

The symptoms are those as mentioned above. Patients with more advanced disease may present with pelvic or leg pain because of tumor volume or nerve involvement. Some may have a previous history of dysplasia or poor history of cervical carcinoma screening (Pap smears). There is no familial inheritance, but women who were exposed to diethylstilbestrol (DES) in utero may be at a slightly increased risk for adenocarcinoma of the cervix.

Objective

Physical Examination

Patients classically have a gross cervical lesion. The lesion may be exophytic, endophytic, or ulcerative. The astute clinician, however, must be aware that cancer is not the only condition of the cervix that may present with a gross lesion. Condylomata, venereal diseases, and abnormalities of the cervix caused by DES exposure also lead to gross lesions. Patients with very early disease may have no lesion at all, thus illustrating the importance of a properly obtained Pap smear. On bimanual examination the parametrial tissues (the tissues lateral and posterior to the cervix providing its support) should be assessed for induration or involvement. This is confirmed by rectovaginal examination. The areas bearing lymph nodes, particularly the supraclavicular and inguinal nodes, should be assessed for enlargement. The lower extremities are examined for the presence or absence of edema.

Routine Laboratory Abnormalities

There is no laboratory abnormality that is routinely abnormal. Premenopausal patients should have pregnancy ruled out. An SMA-18 and complete blood count allow the clinician to assess whether the patient is anemic and can give a clue as to whether there is disease in the liver or if there is renal compromise. A chest x-ray film may reveal metastatic lesions.

PLANS

Diagnostic

Differential Diagnosis

The differential diagnosis for cervical carcinoma includes metastatic carcinoma from other sites including the uterus and ovary.

Diagnostic Options and Recommended Approach

During the initial evaluation the examiner must discern whether the tumor is confined to the upper vagina only, which would dictate a diagnosis of primary vaginal cancer. Any tumor involving the cervix and vagina should be assigned as a primary cervical tumor with metastasis to the vagina. The diagnosis again is confirmed by histologic evaluation. A stage is assigned for the patient based on physical examination and radiographic studies (Table 10–8–1).

Most gynecologic oncologists feel that an examination under anesthesia with a radiation oncologist be done to establish the patient's stage. Cystoscopy and proctoscopy are done to establish whether there is bladder or rectal involvement. An intravenous pyelogram establishes whether there is involvement of the urinary tract. Abdominopelvic computed tomography with contrast has become more popular over the last decade in evaluating patients with newly diagnosed cervical carcinoma. It not only gives information about the urinary tract, but also can help assess nodal status and the presence or absence of liver metastases. Nodal or liver involvement detected in this manner can be used to modify treatment but not to assign a stage.

Therapeutic

The primary mode of therapy for cervical carcinoma is radiation therapy. Patients with minimal invasion (<3 mm) can be treated by cervical conization alone if future fertility is desired. A cervical cone biopsy is the acquisition of a large biopsy of the cervix. Patients with minimal invasion who do not desire future fertility and others with stage I and IIa disease are candidates for simple or radical hysterectomy with upper vaginectomy. The cure rates for surgery and radiation therapy are comparable for early-stage disease. Surgery has the advantage of ovarian preservation with minimal to no long-term complications as seen with radiation therapy in 3 to 5% of cases (bowel obstruction, hemorrhagic cystitis, diarrhea, proctitis). Radiation offers the advantage of avoiding major surgery with its inherent short-term complications (bladder atony, pulmonary embolism, infection, fistula, etc.). It is especially useful in those patients who have medical problems placing them at high risk for surgery. Radiation is administered by external beam over a 4- to 5-week period followed by intracavitary treatment to the vagina and cervix. Some investigators have achieved more success treating advanced disease by adding chemotherapy to radiotherapy protocols. Gynecologic oncologists are now looking into the efficacy of placing patients with large-lesion stage I disease (>4 cm) and small-lesion stage II disease on neoadjuvant chemotherapy before proceeding with radical hysterectomy.

FOLLOW-UP

Patients should be evaluated at 3-month intervals. A Pap smear should be obtained and the cervix (if radiation alone) and upper vagina carefully inspected. A rectovaginal examination is mandatory to assess the parametria for nodularity. Lymph node-bearing areas should be assessed for enlargement and extremities evaluated for edema. Most rec-

TABLE 10–8–1. INTERNATIONAL FEDERATION OF GYNECOLOGY AND OBSTETRICS (FIGO) STAGING OF CARCINOMA OF THE CERVIX UTERI

Preinvasive Carcinoma

Stage 0 Carcinoma in situ, intraepithelial carcinoma (cases of Stage 0 should not be included in any therapeutic statistics).

Invasive Carcinoma

Stage I	Carcinoma strictly confined to the cervix (extension to the corpus should be disregarded).
IA	Preclinical carcinomas of the cervix, that is, those diagnosed only by microscopy.
IA1	Minimal microscopically evident stromal invasion.
IA2	Lesions that can be measured are detected microscopically. The upper limit of the measurement should not show a depth of invasion of more than 5 mm taken from the base of the epithelium, either surface or glandular, from which it originates. A second dimension, the horizontal spread, must not exceed 7 mm. Larger lesions should be staged as 1B.
IB	Lesions of greater dimensions than stage 1A2, whether seen clinically or not. Preformed space involvement should not alter the staging but should be specifically recorded so as to determine whether it should affect treatment decisions in the future.
Stage II	The carcinoma extends beyond the cervix but has not extended onto the wall. The carcinoma involves the vagina, but not the lower third.
IIA	No obvious parametrial involvement.
IIB	Obvious parametrial involvement
Stage III	The carcinoma has extended onto the pelvic wall. On rectal examination, there is no cancer-free space between the tumor and the pelvic wall. The tumor involves the lower third of the vagina. All cases with hydronephrosis or nonfunctioning kidney.
IIIA	No extension to the pelvic wall.
IIIB	Extension to the pelvic wall and/or hydronephrosis or nonfunctioning kidney.
Stage IV	The carcinoma has extended beyond the true pelvis or has clinically involved the mucosa of the bladder or rectum. A bullous edema does not permit a case to be allotted to Stage IV.
IVA	Spread of the growth to adjacent organs.
IVB	Spread to distant organs.

Source: International Federation of Gynecology and Obstetrics. Annual report on the results of treatment in gynecological cancer, vol. 20. Stockholm: FIGO, 1988. Reproduced with permission from the publisher.

ommend a chest x-ray yearly. Patients with large-volume disease who are at high risk for recurrence or persistence should have a computed tomography scan yearly. The TA-4 antigen is elevated in some patients with squamous cell carcinoma, but is used mainly in the research setting. Appropriate patients with recurrent central disease are candidates for exenterative procedures.

DISCUSSION

Prevalence and Incidence

There are approximately 14,000 to 15,000 new cases of cervical carcinoma per year. This is unfortunate because, theoretically, cervical carcinoma is a preventable disease. Advanced disease at the time of diagnosis appears to be decreasing, whereas the incidence of dysplasia is increasing. The mean age at diagnosis is 52 years.

Related Basic Science

Patients with squamous cell carcinoma often will have human papillomavirus genetic material incorporated into the chromosomes of the squamous carcinoma cells.

Natural History and Its Modification with Treatment

Patients with cervical carcinoma who go untreated will complain of vaginal bleeding because of the expanding mass. Pain may develop and patients with very advanced disease are at risk for ureteral obstruction. A malodorous discharge often accompanies advanced disease, which causes the patient discomfort and or embarrassment. With no treatment, patients die of uremia and renal failure or bleeding. Patients who are treated successfully are spared these unpleasant complications.

Prevention

Cervical carcinoma is best prevented by regular Pap smear screening. The interval is addressed by the clinician and patient and depends on her history of cervical cytology and social habits. The more sexual partners a patient has, the more at risk she is for contracting the papillomavirus. Pap smears should detect patients with precancerous conditions, which can be treated conservatively without hysterectomy.

Cost Containment

Costs are contained by detecting dysplasia before it transforms to malignancy. Patients who are infected with HIV should be screened twice yearly, and those on chronic steroid therapy at least yearly.

REFERENCES

Berek J, Hacker N. Practical gynecologic oncology. Baltimore: Williams & Wilkins, 1994:243.

Boring CC, Squires TS, Tong T. Cancer statistics, 1994. CA Cancer J Clin 1994;44:7.

FIGO Cancer Committee in Gynecologic Oncology. Staging announcement. 1986;25:383.

Katu H, Miyauc HI, Morio KA. Tumor antigen of human cervical squamous cell carcinoma: Correlation of circulating levels with disease progress. Cancer 1979;43:585.

Panici PB, Scambia G, Baiocchi G, et al. Neoadjuvant chemotherapy and radical surgery in locally advanced cervical cancer: Prognostic factors for response and survival. Cancer 1991;67:372.

Thomas G, Dembo A, Fyles A, et al. Concurrent chemoradiation in advanced cervical cancer. Gynecol Oncol 1990;38:446.

CHAPTER 10–9

Uterine Carcinoma

Sarah L. Hosford, M.D.

DEFINITION

Cancers arising from the uterine corpus include adenocarcinomas and sarcomas. Adenocarcinomas originate from the endometrial lining itself, and are by far the most common histologic type, constituting greater than 90% of uterine cancers. Uterine sarcomas account for about 5% of all uterine cancers and take their origin from the myometrium and connective tissues of the uterine wall. In general, they are more aggressive tumors and fortunately constitute a small percent-

age of total uterine cancers. In this chapter, we discuss adenocarcinoma of the endometrium, as it is by far the most commonly encountered uterine malignancy.

ETIOLOGY

The etiology of endometrial adenocarcinoma is essentially unknown. Hormonal stimulation of the endometrial lining can result in hyperplasia, and if cellular atypia is present, there is a definite risk of progression to malignancy. Unopposed estrogen use increases the risk of endometrial hyperplasia and progression to malignancy fourfold compared with nonuse of estrogen. Although the addition of progesterone to postmenopausal estrogen replacement therapy is now the most common situation, endometrial adenocarcinoma still originates in a small population of women who are taking unopposed estrogen. A prior history of pelvic radiation therapy is also a risk factor for the development of both endometrial adenocarcinomas and uterine sarcomas.

CRITERIA FOR DIAGNOSIS
Suggestive

Any bleeding in a postmenopausal woman or irregular bleeding in a perimenopausal woman is a criterion for consideration and investigation of possible endometrial adenocarcinoma. Less than 5% of endometrial adenocarcinomas are found in reproductive age women, but this must always be a consideration when bleeding persists despite institution of a treatment program. The setting of chronic anovulation found in polycystic ovarian disease is the one example where very young women can develop endometrial adenocarcinomas. As discussed in Chapter 10–5, prompt evaluation of any abnormal bleeding in a female patient is mandatory.

Definitive

Definitive diagnosis of endometrial adenocarcinoma is done by biopsy, both endocervical curettage and endometrial sampling. This most often is easily accomplished in an office setting, but fractional dilation and curettage may be necessary for a definite diagnosis. The endocervical curettage is done to evaluate for a primary tumor of the endocervix, which can closely resemble an endometrial primary.

CLINICAL MANIFESTATIONS
Subjective

The most consistent presenting symptom of endometrial adenocarcinoma is some form of irregular bleeding. The vast majority of women, approximately 90%, experience some type of vaginal bleeding, either postmenopausal bleeding or irregular perimenopausal bleeding. In a majority of patients, this will be the only presenting symptom, as these tumors tend to present very early in their clinical course and most women report abnormal bleeding very promptly to their physician. Other rare symptoms include an enlarging abdomen secondary to ascites or metastatic tumor to the vulva that bleeds easily and alerts the patient to an abnormality. These are very uncommon findings and usually represent widespread disease.

Objective
Physical Examination

The most common setting for evaluation is a patient who presents with abnormal bleeding and on endometrial biopsy is found to have an adenocarcinoma. At that point, further evaluation should include a thorough history and physical examination, evaluation of supraclavicular and inguinal lymph nodes, and a thorough gynecologic examination. This includes a visual inspection of the vagina and cervix, a Pap smear and endocervical curettage, if they have not already been performed, and a thorough rectovaginal examination to evaluate uterine size and any suggestion of adnexal pathology or pelvic mass.

Routine Laboratory Abnormalities

There are no routine laboratory tests that accompany the initial evaluation. If the patient reports excessive bleeding, a complete blood count may be helpful to screen for anemia.

PLANS
Diagnostic
Differential Diagnosis

The differential diagnosis of endometrial adenocarcinoma includes an endocervical primary versus other tumors, most likely an ovarian primary or synchronous tumors arising in the ovary and endometrium. It is also helpful to review the pathology specimen to evaluate for components of more aggressive histologic subtypes including adenosquamous, clear cell, or papillary serous adenocarcinomas, which will require a more extensive metastatic evaluation.

Diagnostic Options and Recommended Approach

Metastatic evaluation should include a Pap smear and endocervical curettage, if not already done, and consideration of a pelvic ultrasound if the pelvic examination was abnormal. General preoperative evaluation should include a chest x-ray, electrocardiogram, and routine chemistries to screen for liver and kidney function as well as any evidence of metastatic disease. Barium enema and mammography are routinely included to screen for other commonly associated cancers, as well as to evaluate for any possible involvement of the tumor with the gastrointestinal tract. An abdominal/pelvic computed axial tomography scan may be considered if advanced disease is expected, to further evaluate for intraabdominal spread of tumor. An intravenous pyelogram may be done to further delineate the location and status of the ureters, but if an abdominal/pelvic computed axial tomography scan has been done, this is not needed, as the ureters are visible in this study. Specialized laboratory tests including a CA-125 may give evidence of extrauterine spread in light of a normal examination. The general purpose of the metastatic evaluation is to screen a patient for any signs of extrauterine spread as well as evaluate the patient for surgery, as this is the primary mode of treatment.

Therapeutic

The standard treatment for a patient with endometrial adenocarcinoma is a total abdominal hysterectomy, bilateral salpingo-oophorectomy, and tailored surgical staging depending on the risk factors for extrauterine disease. A comprehensive surgical staging includes pelvic washings for cytologic evaluation, selective pelvic and periaortic lymph node sampling, thorough abdominal exploration, and omental biopsy. The current staging classification of uterine cancer is based on data obtained at surgical staging, and this will help identify patients with intermediate or high-risk features that require postoperative treatment.

Postoperative radiation therapy is the mainstay of adjuvant treatment given to patients with intermediate- or high-risk endometrial adenocarcinomas. There has been a shift from preoperative radiation therapy (brachytherapy or whole-pelvis radiation) to postoperative radiation therapy tailored to the patient and her particular risk features. With comprehensive surgical staging information, up to three quarters of all women will need no further therapy and their cure rate will be greater than 90%. Women with intermediate- or high-risk features include those with grade II to III tumors, positive lymphatic or vascular channel involvement, significant myometrial invasion (greater than one third), lesions involving the lower uterine segment or cervix, or any evidence of extrauterine spread, including pelvic cytology, lymph node involvement, or widespread intraabdominal or extraabdominal disease. Radiation therapy or chemotherapy can be tailored to the exact location of metastatic spread that will afford the highest chance of long-term survival.

FOLLOW-UP

As with most gynecologic malignancies, the follow-up of these patients is centered on the first several years, with frequent and regular screening office visits. Recurrence of endometrial adenocarcinoma should be evident within the first 2 to 3 years, with the pelvis being the most common site. During the first year, the patient is seen every 3 months for physical examination and Pap smear, and this progresses to every 4 months during the second year. From the third to the fifth years after initial treatment, Pap smear and physical examinations are done every 6 months, and then can be done on a yearly basis after a 5-year disease-free survival. It is also important to continue surveillance for other commonly associated cancers such as breast and colon cancer. Yearly mammography according to the guidelines of the American Cancer Society, as well as stool guaiac, should be done at regular intervals.

DISCUSSION
Prevalence and Incidence

The American Cancer Society (1994) predicted 31,000 new cases of uterine cancer in 1994 and 5900 deaths from the disease. There is a 2.4% lifetime risk of endometrial adenocarcinoma for white women compared with a 1.3% lifetime risk for black women.

Related Basic Science

The basic mechanism involved in endometrial adenocarcinoma appears to be a physiologic derangement of a normal situation. The common denominator most likely involves abnormal stimulation of the endometrial lining. This may occur through the use of exogenous hormones (unopposed estrogen), increased peripheral conversion of adrenal steroids to estrone (associated with obesity), and, in patients with prior breast cancer, the use of tamoxifen, which exerts a weak estrogenic effect on the endometrium. Some of these effects can be counteracted and some are purely related to genetic predisposition and body habitus.

Natural History and Its Modification with Treatment

If left untreated, there is a definite rate of progression and growth of endometrial adenocarcinoma that will most likely result in widespread metastatic disease in almost all patients. The histologic grade of the tumor plays an important role in the rate of progression, as well-differentiated tumors may be very slow growing and poorly differentiated tumors may grow rapidly. When treated, the overall cure rate for endometrial adenocarcinoma is excellent if no extrauterine spread is found at the initial time of treatment. As mentioned previously, recurrences should be evident within the first 2 to 3 years, with the pelvis being the most common initial site. When patients with intermediate- or high-risk features have been treated with adjuvant pelvic radiation therapy, the recurrence rate in the pelvis is lower, with distant sites of metastatic disease becoming more common.

Prevention

The majority of cases of endometrial adenocarcinoma cannot be prevented, as we are unsure of why they develop. The use of unopposed estrogen for postmenopausal hormone replacement therapy in women who have their uterus should be abandoned, as a consistent number of women develop endometrial adenocarcinoma when using estrogen alone. Altering risk factors such as obesity may decrease the incidence of endometrial adenocarcinoma, and recent data have suggested that combination oral contraceptives used during the childbearing years decrease the risk of endometrial adenocarcinoma up to 50%.

Cost Containment

Endometrial adenocarcinoma by its location and natural history presents early in the disease. Prompt evaluation of any abnormal bleeding in menopausal or perimenopausal patients will result in early diagnosis. In addition, evaluation of endometrial cells on Pap smear of any postmenopausal woman, as well as abnormal glandular cells on a reproductive age or perimenopausal patient, will aid in early detection of this disease. With surgical therapy resulting in a high cure rate in the majority of patients, the cost containment is obvious, as a cancer cure is achieved and further therapy is unnecessary.

REFERENCES

Cancer facts & figures, Atlanta: American Cancer Society, 1994.
Disai PJ, Creasman WT. Clinical gynecologic oncology. 4th ed. St. Louis: Mosby, 1993.
Morrow CP, Curtin JP, Townsend DE. Synopsis of gynecologic oncology. 4th ed. New York: Churchill Livingstone, 1993.

CHAPTER 10–10
Pelvic Inflammatory Disease (See Section 8, Chapter 26)

CHAPTER 10–11
Vaginitis (See Section 8, Chapter 25)

CHAPTER 10–12
Vulvar Neoplasia

R. Allen Lawhead, Jr., M.D.

DEFINITION

The term *vulvar neoplasia* refers to new growths arising on the vulva that are typified by abnormal cell proliferation. Vulvar neoplasia may be classified as benign, premalignant, or malignant as shown in Table 10–12–1.

ETIOLOGY

As with most neoplasms the etiology of vulvar neoplasm is unknown.

CRITERIA FOR DIAGNOSIS
Suggestive

Vulvar neoplasm should be suspected when an abnormal growth of tissue is seen or felt on the vulva.

Definitive

The only acceptable criteria for the diagnosis of vulvar neoplasia is a histologic diagnosis based on a biopsy specimen.

TABLE 10–12–1. CLASSIFICATION OF VULVAR NEOPLASIA

Benign	Premalignant Potential	Malignant
Hemangioma	VIN*	Squamous cell carcinoma (invasive)
Fibroma	VIN-1 (mild dysplasia)	Adenocarcinoma
Lipoma	VIN-2 (moderate dysplasia)	Melanoma
Neurofibroma	VIN-3 (severe dysplasia/ carcinoma in situ)	Sarcoma
		Verrucous carcinoma
Leiomyoma	Intraepithelial Paget's disease	Extramammary Paget's disease with underlying adenocarcinoma
	Condyloma acuminatum†	Bartholin's gland carcinoma (squamous cell carcinoma, adenocarcinoma, transitional cell carcinoma)
		Basal cell carcinoma
		Metastatic cancer

*Vulvar intraepithelial neoplasia.
†See Chapter 10–13.
Source: Lawhead RA. Neoplasms of the vulva. In: Rakel RE, ed. 1994 Conn's current therapy. Philadelphia: Saunders, 1994:1080. Reproduced with permission from the publisher and author.

CLINICAL MANIFESTATIONS

Subjective

Women with symptoms relating to the vulva or vulvar lesions require evaluation to rule out vulvar neoplasia. More than 90% of patients with vulvar malignancies are symptomatic at the time of diagnosis, and virtually all patients with invasive malignancies will have visible lesions (Morrow and Townsend, 1987). The most common symptoms are pruritus, pain, bleeding, dysuria, presence of a growth on the vulva, and discharge. All complaints of abnormal pigmentation on the vulva should also be evaluated. No familiar tendency is associated with vulvar carcinoma; however, patients with a history of squamous cell lesions of the cervix or vagina and smokers have an increased incidence of vulvar neoplasia. Patients with a history of human papillomavirus infection of the lower genital tract may also be at increased risk.

Objective

Physical Examination

There is no classic appearance of vulvar neoplasia, and all patients who have significant vulvar lesions require biopsy for definitive diagnosis. Physical findings include the presence of lesions such as exophytic growth, wart, ulcer, and an area of atypical pigmentation, either white, black, brown, or red. The lesions may extend into the vagina, the perineum, the perianal area, or the periurethral area. Examination of the vagina and cervix may also detect metastatic or separate primary lesions, as patients with squamous cell lesions of the vulva have an increased incidence of similar lesions in the vagina and cervix.

Routine Laboratory Abnormalities

No abnormalities are found in the routine laboratory tests.

PLANS

Diagnostic

It is essential that patients with vulvar lesions have a careful visual inspection of the vulva, speculum inspection of the vagina and cervix, and careful bimanual and rectovaginal examinations to complete the evaluation. The inguinal lymph nodes are the primary sites of the lymphatic drainage from vulvar lesions, and careful assessment of these nodes is mandatory. Bartholin's gland enlargement that persists or occurs in postmenopausal women requires careful evaluation.

Patients with significant vulvar lesions should be evaluated with a colposcopic examination of the lower genital tract and appropriate biopsies to confirm the diagnosis.

Therapeutic

In most instances, neoplasms of the vulva are best treated surgically. For patients with benign neoplasms such as fibroma and lipoma, complete excision is generally curative. The treatment of condyloma acuminatum, the most common vulvar neoplasm, is described in Chapter 10–13. Precancerous diseases of the vulva such as vulvar intraepithelial neoplasia are generally treated by wide excision or laser vaporization. This allows for a cure rate of 85 to 90% and conservation of female sexual function and body image. Although total vulvectomy was used liberally in the past to treat women with vulvar intraepithelial neoplasia, it is rarely indicated now, even with multifocal disease.

Invasive malignancies of the vulva generally require more extensive treatment. Patients with advanced vulvar malignancies may require radical vulvectomy with bilateral groin dissection or, rarely, pelvic exenteration. Women with small lesions, however, may be treated with radical excision and ipsilateral groin dissection. Patients with medical contraindication to surgery or extremely large lesions are often treated with primary radiation therapy or a combination of chemotherapy and radiation therapy. Very superficial lesions with minimal stromal invasion may be treated by wide excision only, sparing the essential elements of vulvar anatomy and function. Such a lesion is defined as a squamous cell carcinoma measuring less than 1 mm in depth from the basic membrane of the nearest adjacent dermal papillae and less than 2 cm in diameter without vascular/lymphatic space involvement. Conservative treatment is possible only after a thorough review of the histologic specimen and the patient's clinical condition. A cure rate of 90% or better should be expected with conservative treatment if the patient is properly selected (Berek and Hacker, 1989). Superficial melanomas may also be treated in this fashion. All patients with invasive vulvar malignancies should be referred to a gynecologic oncologist for the definitive decision regarding radical or conservative therapy. Locally invasive malignancies such as basal cell carcinoma and verrucous cell carcinoma are generally treated with wide excision.

Extramammary Paget's disease of the vulva may also be treated with wide excision unless there is an underlying adenocarcinoma, in which case the patient must be treated for invasive carcinoma. Generally, the main complication of surgery is suboptimal healing in an area of the body that is often moist and subject to significant tension. Laser vaporized and wide excisions usually heal nicely; however, patients who undergo radical vulvectomy and groin dissection often have significant wound breakdown. Those with groin dissection are often at risk for chronic lymphedema. With proper treatment, patients with early invasive carcinomas without lymph node metastases may expect an 85 to 90% cure rate (Disais, 1989).

FOLLOW-UP

Generally, patients treated for vulvar neoplasia are followed up every 3 months for the first year, every 4 months for the second year, and every 6 months thereafter. Follow-up includes a thorough pelvic examination as previously described and colposcopic examination of the lower genital tract with biopsies as indicated, in addition to the items dealt with on general physical examination.

DISCUSSION

For more than 100 years the medical literature has repeatedly documented two major obstacles to the successful treatment of vulvar neoplasia: delayed patient presentation and delayed physician evaluation. As recently as 1950, Parsons described vulvar carcinoma as the "most badly diagnosed and poorly treated condition in the field of malignant disease" (Newell and McKay, 1952).

Prevalence and Incidence

Currently, the incidence of precancerous and cancerous disease of the vulva is increasing in all women, but especially in younger women. Vulvar carcinoma has been reported to be more common in lower socioeconomic groups, smokers, and postmenopausal women, and is often associated with granulomatous disease of the vulva. Recently, however, the incidence of squamous cell lesions of the vulva has increased significantly in younger women.

Related Basic Science

The cause of vulvar carcinoma is not known, but the human papillomavirus has been implicated as a possible etiologic cofactor, and the rapidly increasing incidence of this virus in the general population is parallelling the increasing incidence of squamous cell neoplasia.

Natural History and Its Modification with Treatment

The objective for successful diagnosis and treatment of vulvar neoplasia should be to promote early detection, allowing for curative therapy that can spare female identity and sexual function.

Vulvar neoplasia may begin as a pigmented lesion, ulcer, mass, or wart and generally grows to significant size locally prior to detection. Regional lymph node metastases and distant metastases are usually late phenomena; however, they can occur more rapidly in poorly differentiated lesions and melanomas.

Prevention

Almost all vulvar malignancies are visible to the naked eye at the time of diagnosis, and more than 90% of patients with vulvar carcinomas are symptomatic (Morrow and Townsend, 1987). Nevertheless, over the last 135 years, delayed patient presentation and delayed physician evaluation continue to be the major obstacles confronting the treatment of vulvar malignancy. The increasing incidence of vulvar neoplasia, the persistent historical problem of delayed patient presentation and physician evaluation, and the availability of successful conservative therapy for early lesions of the vulva mandate further attention to screening for vulvar neoplasia. In this regard, the practice of regular vulvar self-ex-

amination has been suggested for all women who are sexually active or are 18 years or older. Vulvar self-examination should be performed on a monthly basis or whenever symptoms related to the vulva occur. This technique has been well described and involves a careful visual inspection and palpation of the vulva using a hand-held mirror and adequate lighting. Patients are encouraged to report significant changes, warts, bumps, ulcers, or abnormal pigmentation to their physician. Clinical experience has shown that patients using this technique have successfully found lesions that led to the early diagnosis of vulvar neoplasia, allowing conservative, life-saving therapy that preserved female identity and sexual function.

Cost Containment

The key to successful conservative therapy as well as cost containment is early diagnosis, and the key to early diagnosis is vulvar self-examination.

REFERENCES

Berek JS, Hacker NF. Practical gynecologic oncology. Baltimore: Williams & Wilkins, 1989:401.

DiSaia PJ, Creasman WT. Invasive cancer of the vulva. In: DiSaia PJ, Creasman WT (eds.) Clinical gynecologic oncology. St. Louis: Mosby, 1989:241.

Hacker NF. Current treatment of small vulvar cancers. Oncology 1990;4(8):21.

Lawhead RA Jr. Vulvar self examination. Am J Obstet Gynecol 1988;158(5):4.

Lawhead RA Jr, Majmudar B. Early diagnosis of vulvar neoplasia as result of vulvar self examination. J Reprod Med 1990;35(12):1134.

Morrow CP, Townsend DE. Tumors of the vulva. Syn Gynecol Oncol 1987;3:63.

Newell JW, McKay DG. Vulva and vagina: A clinical review of carcinoma of the vulva. J Obstet Gynecol Surv 1952;2:84.

CHAPTER 10–13

Abnormalities of the Vulva

R. Allen Lawhead, Jr., M.D.

DEFINITION

Abnormalities of the vulva include infections and neoplastic and idiopathic lesions.

ETIOLOGY

Abnormalities of the vulva may be caused by infections, dystrophies, and other abnormalities including neoplasia and trauma (see Table 10–13–1).

CRITERIA FOR DIAGNOSIS

Candida vulvitis may be diagnosed by observation of hyphae in saline or a 10% potassium hydrochloride preparation of the vaginal discharge under the microscope. A positive fungal culture from the vagina or vulva may also establish the diagnosis.

Herpes genitalis is classically diagnosed by a viral culture of the

TABLE 10–13–1. COMMON ABNORMALITIES OF THE VULVA

Infectious Diseases	Dystrophies	Other Abnormalities
Candidiasis	Lichen sclerosis	Benign neoplasms
Condyloma acuminatum	Hypertrophic dystrophy	Sebaceous cysts
Herpes genitalis		Vitiligo
Folliculitis		Physical or chemical trauma
		Vulvodynia

vesicles or ulcers noted during the acute phase of infection. Cytology samples from these areas may be helpful, but they are less reliable.

Condyloma acuminatum should be documented by biopsy diagnosis, and in general, all new growths on the vulva require biopsy diagnosis prior to treatment.

A biopsy diagnosis is also required to establish the diagnoses of hypertrophic dystrophy and lichen sclerosis.

Vulvodynia is defined as a symptom of chronic burning, vulvar pain, or discomfort.

CLINICAL MANIFESTATIONS

Subjective

Patients with vulvar candidiasis, lichen sclerosis, and hypertrophic dystrophy present with the complaint of severe and progressive vulvar pruritus and burning. There is often a history of thick white discharge with candidiasis.

Condyloma acuminatum is often asymptomatic and may be noted first by the patient as a new growth that is usually painless, but may also be associated with irritation, discharge, or large painful masses.

Herpes vulvitis is generally associated with painful ulcers or vesicles, and there may be an antecedent history of sexual exposure to the virus.

Objective

Physical Examination

Patients with candidiasis often display a reddened friable vulva with a thick white discharge. Women with condylomata acuminata generally display the classic genital warts, which may be found on the vulva, vagina, and cervix.

Clusters of small painful vesicles or ulcers are generally noted in patients with acute herpes vulvitis.

Examination of patients with lichen sclerosis usually reveals areas of hypopigmentation or abnormal pigmentation, either white, purple, or red, which are associated with pruritus or chronic irritation. Secondary infections and inflammation may also be present because of excessive scratching.

Vulvodynia may be produced by a variety of diseases such as chronic candidiasis, vestibulitis, hypersensitivity condition, inflammatory condition, or neoplasia, or it may be idiopathic.

Routine Laboratory Abnormalities

There are no diagnostic routine laboratory abnormalities. The blood glucose level may be elevated in patients with bacterial or fungal infection.

PLANS

Diagnostic

All patients with symptoms or complaints relating to the vulva or with vulvar lesions should be evaluated with a careful history and physical examination. This should include careful visualization and palpation of the vulva, speculum examination of the vagina and cervix with cytology and cultures as indicated, and a bimanual examination with a recto-vaginal examination.

Vulvar colposcopy is recommended prior to biopsy of vulvar lesions or dermatoses to assess the extent of the lesion, look for satellite lesions, and select the optimal site(s) for biopsy. Vulvar colposcopy with biopsy is often a useful adjunct in the evaluation of vulvodynia or chronic pruritis.

Therapeutic

Candida infections of the vulva are generally treated with topical creams such as miconazole (Monistat), clotrimazole (Gyne-Lotrimin, Mycelex), terconazole (Terazol), butoconazole (Femstat), and nystatin (Mycostatin).

Although there is no cure of genital herpes, the symptoms associated with the formation, rupture, and healing of painful vesicles may be treated with acyclovir (Zovirax). A topical ointment consisting of 5% acyclovir may be applied every 3 to 4 hours for 7 days or oral acyclovir 200-mg tablets may be taken every 4 hours (maximum 5 per day) during the initial outbreak and in certain cases of recurrent outbreaks. The use of topical or oral acyclovir in acute painful infections may decrease the duration of pain and viral shedding and increase the healing rate.

When a patient presents with vulvar dystrophy, the diagnosis must be established by biopsy, allowing for the appropriate topical therapy. Lichen sclerosis is treated with 2% testosterone propionate in petrolatum gel prescribed once or twice a day. If an initial response is noted, the patient may continue to take this two to three times per week indefinitely. Side effects include increased hair growth, increased libido, and clitoromegaly. Patients with *hypertrophic dystrophy* may be treated with 0.1% betamethasone valerate cream (Valisone) twice daily for 1 to 3 weeks. As the symptoms subside the cream is withdrawn to be reapplied in episodes of significant symptomatology. An alternative to this is 0.1% hydrocortisone cream (Hytone) used in a similar fashion.

Patients with a histologic diagnosis of condyloma acuminatum should be informed that this disease may be transmitted sexually and they should be encouraged to perform regular vulvar self-examinations. Colposcopic examination of the lower genital tract is essential to rule out any underlying precancerous or cancerous condition. Patients with documented condylomata acuminata on the vulva should be evaluated for the virus in the cervix and vagina. Treatment for condylomata acuminata of the lower genital tract must be individualized, but should proceed as follows. Patients with precancerous or cancerous conditions are treated appropriately for those conditions. If there is no associated neoplastic condition, then the large warts may be treated with laser vaporization, excision, cryotherapy, or fulguration. Smaller warts can be treated with topical therapy, such as trichloracetic acid or podophyllin

(Cantharone Plus, Verrex) therapy. Podophyllin should not be used in pregnant patients. Currently, there is no known way of eliminating the human papillomavirus, which causes condyloma acuminatum, from the lower genital tract. Therefore, the goals of treatment should be realistic and aimed at removing the undesired warts, alleviating symptoms, and treating a neoplastic condition. Asymptomatic patients with no visible warts and no associated neoplasia should be followed with pelvic examination and Pap smears every 6 months and should practice regular vulvar self-examination. Women with large exophytic growths on the vulva or those with lesions refractory to topical treatment should be referred for specialized gynecologic evaluation.

In general, symptoms of vulvodynia are best treated by treating the specific disease causing the symptoms. Patients with idiopathic vulvodynia often respond well to oral amitriptyline 10 mg at bedtime or twice daily. Therapy may be discontinued after resolution of these symptoms. Patients with intractable vulvodynia or difficult vulvar problems may be referred to vulvologists through the International Society for the Study of Vulvar Disease (ISSVD).

Patients with infectious disease of the vulva should be given basic instructions in vulvar hygiene, which include warm tub baths or sitz baths followed by careful drying with a towel or hair dryer on the cool cycle. Sometimes a whirlpool bath is required for extensive inflammatory conditions of the vulva. Patients treated for common abnormalities should be educated in vulvar self-examination, and patients with condyloma and herpes should be made aware of the possibility of sexual transmission. The male partners of patients with herpes and condylomata acuminata may find it useful to be evaluated by a urologist, especially if any lesions are noted on the genital organs. Evaluation of a male for condylomata acuminata should include a colposcopic or hand-lens evaluation of the penis with acetic acid staining similar to the evaluation required for the female.

FOLLOW-UP

Patients should perform vulvar self-examination monthly or whenever symptoms are noted, and they should be encouraged to report abnormalities to their physician. Patients with significant vulvar dystrophy or condylomata acuminata are usually seen every 3 to 4 months the first year and every 6 months thereafter. Patients with condylomata acuminata may benefit from Pap smears every 6 months.

DISCUSSION

Prevalence and Incidence

The exact prevalence and incidence of vulva abnormalities are now known. Abnormalities are known to be common and some are increasing dramatically (see below).

Related Basic Science

Patients with recurrent candidiasis should be considered for evaluation of systemic diseases such as immunodeficiency and diabetes mellitus. Condyloma acuminatum is caused by the human papillomavirus, more than 40 subtypes of which are known. In addition, it has been stated that types 6 and 11 are more associated with benign genital warts, and types 16 and 18 are more associated with warts in areas of cancerous or precancerous changes of the lower genital tract. Condyloma acuminatum is increasing in epidemic proportions, with the incidence having increased 500% over the last 15 years. This virus is a cofactor in the development of squamous cell neoplasia of the cervix, vagina, and vulva, and currently the presence of this virus in the lower genital tract is believed to carry a slightly increased risk for cervical carcinoma. Following biopsy diagnosis, patients with small condylomata can be treated with simple excision or with 50 to 80% trichloracetic acid. Excisional therapy is also an option. Laser vaporization is preferred for the treatment of large areas of condyloma or condyloma resistant to topical therapy.

Women of all ages are risk for condyloma acuminatum; however, the disease is most prevalent in the age range 18 to 35. One must suspect an underlying precancerous or cancerous condition in all patients with large condylomata, especially postmenopausal women. Because there is no known method that eliminates the virus from the lower genital tract, treatment is aimed at relief of symptoms, removal of large warts, and monitoring and therapy of precancerous and cancerous conditions. Condyloma acuminatum is not transmitted exclusively through sexual intercourse; however, it is highly sexually transmissible, with 60 to 85% of the partners of infected women having evidence of the virus (Baggish, 1985). These are often asymptomatic in males and may have a prolonged latent phase. The incidence of genital herpes, the presence of herpesvirus, and the development of cervical carcinoma are all increasing. Patients with herpes and condyloma acuminatum should have a Pap smear and a pelvic examination every 6 months. Patients with vulvar dystrophy generally respond well to the appropriate topical hormone preparations; however, refractive vulvar dystrophy should be further evaluated to rule out any underlying intraepithelial neoplasia or malignancy.

Natural History and Its Modification with Treatment

Natural history of the infectious disease is varied according to the type of infection. Human papillomavirus generally begins in small areas of condyloma that tend to enlarge and multiply. In this regard, the use of regular vulvar self-examination may be helpful to detect condyloma early, for less extensive treatment. Most patients with vulvar dystrophy, however, complain of chronic itching and irritation that has been present for years and often have a history of unsuccessful treatment because the correct diagnosis was not established by biopsy.

Prevention

There is no known method of preventing vulvar dystrophy, but careful evaluation and treatment of symptoms of vulvar irritation and pruritus

may lead to early diagnosis and prevent the spread of this local condition. Increased public awareness of the consequences of irresponsible sexual behavior may lead to a decrease in the incidence of diseases such as herpes and condyloma acuminatum; however, those conditions have been shown to be transmitted at birth. Patients in labor with active herpes genitalis infections are best delivered by cesarean section to reduce the incidence and consequences of neonatal infection. On the other hand, there is no indication for cesarean delivery in patients with human papillomavirus infection of the lower genital tract unless the sheer mass of bulky condyloma impedes delivery.

Cost Containment

Careful vulvar hygiene, annual pelvic examination, monthly vulvar self-examination, and early diagnosis are encouraged as means of cost containment for the common abnormalities of the vulva.

REFERENCES

Baggish MS. Basic and advanced laser surgery in gynecology. Norwalk, CT: Appleton-Century-Crofts, 1985:133.

Dickson FJ, Moore RA. Tumors of the male sex organs. In: Atlas of tumor pathology, sect. 8, fasc. 31B and 32. Washington, DC: Armed Forces Institute of Pathology, 1952:127.

Droegemueller W, Herbst A, Mishell D, Stenchever M. Comprehensive gynecology. St. Louis: Mosby, 1987.

Friedrich EG Jr. Vulvar diseases, vol. 9. Philadelphia: Saunders, 1983.

Lawhead RA. Early detection of vulvar disease. Med Aspects Hum Sex, June 1990;24:43.

CHAPTER 10–14

Vaginal Carcinoma

Cyril O. Spann, M.D.

DEFINITION

Vaginal carcinoma is defined as a malignancy of the vaginal epithelium. It may be squamous cell, adenocarcinoma, melanoma, or clear cell adenocarcinoma. Invasive disease is characterized by demonstrating malignant cells beneath the basement membrane on histologic examination.

ETIOLOGY

Squamous carcinoma is thought to arise from vaginal dysplasia, although the association is not as clear as with cervical dysplasia and squamous cell cervical cancer. The length of time required to progress from dysplasia is variable and highly subject to the patient's immune status. Patients who take steroids, smoke, or are infected with HIV are thought to be at increased risk.

CRITERIA FOR DIAGNOSIS

Suggestive

The diagnosis is suggested in patients who have persistent vaginal discharge and bleeding. The clinician should note that this diagnosis is quite rare and should not be at the top of the differential diagnosis when a patient presents with these symptoms. Cervical carcinoma is more common, and vaginitis due to infectious agents such as *Trichomonas* is highly prevalent in our society.

Definitive

The definitive diagnosis is made by histologic evaluation.

CLINICAL MANIFESTATIONS

Subjective

The common presenting symptoms include vaginal bleeding and discharge. Patients with disease in the lowermost portion of the vagina may complain of a bulge at the vaginal introitus although most patients present with lesions in the posterior upper vagina. Some complain of postcoital spotting. Those with advanced disease often complain of pelvic or leg pain because of disease extension to bony or neural tissues. Many with advanced disease also complain of anorexia or weight loss. They can also present with anemia symptoms if vaginal bleeding has been persistent over a long period.

Objective

Physical Examination

On physical examination, the classic finding is a mass in the vagina. Most often it is friable and bleeds readily on manipulation. One must be careful to ascertain whether there are any other lesions on the cervix or vulva. If the cervix is without gross lesion, then colposcopic evaluation of the cervix may be indicated to rule out the cervix as the primary source of the tumor.

On further examination, the patient may have palpable inguinal or supraclavicular lymphadenopathy. Bimanual or rectovaginal examinations in those with advanced disease can demonstrate thickening or induration to the pelvic sidewall. Also, the rectum or bladder can be involved with tumor by direct extension. Rectal involvement can be detected by proctoscopy and bladder involvement by cystoscopy.

Routine Laboratory Abnormalities

Laboratory abnormalities in patients with vaginal cancer are nonspecific. Liver enzymes may be elevated in patients with metastatic disease to the liver. The serum creatinine can be increased for those patients who have significant obstruction of the ureters or urethra. The hematocrit may be low in patients who have had persistent bleeding over an extended period. A chest radiograph and intravenous pyelogram are routinely ordered to rule out metastatic disease to those sites.

PLANS

Diagnostic

Differential Diagnosis

Vaginal carcinoma must be differentiated from other malignant diseases, vaginitis, and cervical carcinoma.

Diagnostic Options and Recommended Approach

Over the past decade the computed tomography scan and magnetic resonance imaging have been used with increasing frequency to study the collecting system as well as the lymphatic chains. In many centers an examination under anesthesia is recommended to give a more accurate assessment of the extension of the malignancy. Also, proctoscopy and urethrocystoscopy may be done to ascertain whether there is tumor extension to these organs.

Once the diagnosis is made by pathologic evaluation and the appropriate staging procedures performed, the patient can be assigned a stage. This allows for treatment planning and gives the patient and the clinician an indicator for prognosis. The staging of vaginal carcinoma based on the annual report of the International Federation of Gynecology and Obstetrics (1988) is as follows:

Stage 0	Carcinoma in situ
Stage I	Limited to the vaginal wall
Stage II	Involves the paravaginal tissues, but has not extended to the pelvic sidewall or other organs.
Stage III	Has extended to the pelvic sidewall
Stage IV	Has extended beyond the true pelvis or has involved the mucosa of the bladder or rectum

Therapeutic

The treatment of invasive vaginal carcinoma is highly individualized. Most patients are treated with radiation therapy; however, patients with small stage I lesions confined to the upper vagina may be treated primarily by surgery. This would include radical hysterectomy with upper vaginectomy and pelvic lymph node dissection. In younger patients with the squamous cell type, efforts should be made to preserve the ovaries at time of surgery to protect patients from the long-term consequences of estrogen deprivation. If the ovaries are removed, then the patient should be placed on estrogen replacement.

If radiotherapy is chosen as the primary treatment it is administered by one or a combination of whole-pelvis, interstitial, or intracavitary therapy. Side effects of radiotherapy include a decrease in vaginal caliber (especially in those patients who do not use dilators or have regular intercourse) and the risk of the development of vesicovaginal fistulas. Chemotherapy is generally ineffective for invasive disease and is reserved for those patients with recurrent or persistent disease.

FOLLOW-UP

The patient is made aware of the symptoms and signs that suggest recurrent disease. These include the appearance of growths or lumps in the groin or supraclavicular node-bearing areas. Vaginal bleeding can be an early indicator of recurrent disease. Anorexia, weight loss, and pelvic pain are other symptoms that suggest failure of treatment. Rectal bleeding or bleeding from the urinary tract may suggest recurrent disease in these areas. The TA-4 antigen has been detected in a fair number of patients with squamous cell carcinoma of the cervix. Perhaps it can provide useful information in the follow-up of these patients.

On visits with the clinician, the patient should be asked about her general well-being and questioned regarding the above symptomatology. The physical examination should include weight. The node-bearing areas should be palpated and a careful pelvic examination performed. Any differences from previous examinations should be noted and investigated. The onset of leg edema may indicate lymphatic or venous obstruction due to tumor. Serum chemistries should be obtained periodically. This will allow for the detection of elevated liver enzymes and abnormalities in renal function. Chest x-rays and computed tomography scans (magnetic resonance imaging may be substituted) are obtained at least once a year for the first several years as these may be used to diagnose pelvic or paraaortic lymphadenopathy that could not be detected on physical examination.

DISCUSSION

Prevalence and Incidence and Related Basic Science

On examination of the patient, a cervical primary lesion should always be ruled out. If carcinoma is found to involve the cervix, then she should be given a diagnosis of cervical cancer with metastasis to the vagina. It is also important that the colon be evaluated by barium enema or colonoscopy to rule out a coexisting primary lesion. Mammography is always recommended yearly in patients over the age of 50 by the American Cancer Society.

Related Basic Science

Vaginal carcinoma is a relatively rare genital tract carcinoma. It constitutes approximately 2% of all genital tract malignancies. The disease is more likely to occur in patients who have had some form of neoplasia in the lower genital tract. This can be from dysplasia or malignancies of the cervix, vagina, or vulva. The vast majority of vaginal carcinomas are of the squamous cell variety. Women whose mothers took diethylstilbestrol during pregnancy are at increased risk for adenocarcinoma of the vagina. The human papillomavirus has been implicated as being at least a cofactor in the development of genital tract dysplasia. Patients who have been treated for dysplasia of the cervix and those with a history of genital warts should be advised of their potential increased risk for vaginal carcinoma. The age of presentation in most patients is between 50 and 60. Adenocarcinoma due to diethylstilbestrol exposure usually occurs in women below the age 25.

Natural History and Its Modification with Treatment

The survival rate of vaginal carcinoma worsens with advanced stages of the disease. Approximately 60 to 70% of patients diagnosed with stage I carcinoma of the vagina survive 5 years. The 5-year survival for stage III disease is approximately 20 to 30%.

Prevention

Patients exposed in utero to diethylstilbestrol should be followed carefully to colposcopic evaluation at least yearly. Others should get regular pelvic examinations and Pap smears.

Cost Containment

The best way to contain costs is to prevent the occurrence of the disease process. Counseling on the prevention of sexually transmitted diseases should be emphasized to older and younger patients alike. This is achieved by routine pelvic examinations and performance of Pap smears at regular intervals.

REFERENCES

Berek JJ, Hacker N. Vaginal carcinoma. In: Practical Gynecologic Oncology. Baltimore: Williams & Wilkins, 1994:441.

Gusberg S, Shingleton H, Deppe G, et al. Cancer of the vagina: Female genital cancer. New York. Churchill Livingstone, 1988:253.

International Federation of Gynecology and Obstetrics. Annual report on the results of treatment in gynecological cancer, vol. 20, Stockholm: FIGO, 1988.

Johnson G, Klotz J, Boutsells J. Primary invasive carcinoma of the vagina. Surg Gynecol Obstet 1983;156:34.

Manetta A, Gutrecht EL, Berman ML, DiSaia PJ. Primary invasive carcinoma of the vagina. Obstet Gynecol 1990;7776:639.

Stock RG, Mychalczak B, Armstrong JG, et al. The importance of brachytherapy technique in the management of primary carcinoma of the vagina. Int J Radiat Oncol Biol Phys 1992;24:7747.

Ueda G. Immunohistochemical demonstration of tumor antigen TA-4 in gynecologic tumors. Int J Gynaecol Pathol 1984;3:291.

CHAPTER 10–15

Pruritus Vulvae and Vulvodynia: Itching and Burning

Marilynne McKay, M.D.

DEFINITION

Pruritus vulvae translates from the Latin as vulvar itching, and this term is usually reserved for clinical situations in which itching localized to the vulva is the patient's chief complaint. Vulvodynia (from the Greek *odynia* for "pain") has been defined by the International Society for the Study of Vulvovaginal Disease (ISSVD) as chronic vulvar discomfort, especially that characterized by the patient's complaint of burning, stinging, irritation, or rawness.

ETIOLOGY

In most cases, pruritus vulvae and vulvodynia will be found to be distinctly different diagnostic and management problems. The most important considerations are vulvar dermatoses (see Section 11), recurrent vulvovaginal candidiasis, and pudendal neuralgia or dysesthesia.

CRITERIA FOR DIAGNOSIS
Suggestive

Because pruritus is often associated with vaginitis, especially candidiasis, most women consult their gynecologists for therapy. The internist is likely to see only the most recalcitrant problems or symptoms that have persisted for weeks or months. Pruritus vulvae or vulvodynia may extend to the perineum or anus, but if itching or burning is generalized on the body, these diagnoses are probably not applicable and Section 11 should be consulted.

Definitive

Pruritus vulvae (and/or vulvodynia) is defined as chronic vulvar itching (and/or burning) that has been present for several months. Symptoms may wax and wane, but these conditions return spontaneously and persistently.

CLINICAL MANIFESTATIONS
Subjective

As with most cutaneous problems, symptoms vary considerably in severity from patient to patient (see Table 10–15–1). Uncontrollable itching results in excoriation of the skin, and the patient will describe bouts of scratching that may result in bleeding or scarring. On the other hand, the patient who complains of vulvar burning or irritation may not be able to tolerate even the contact of clothing on the skin. Some degree of dyspareunia may also be present, and it is important to differentiate severe and consistent pain on penile entry from irritation only following intercourse, especially if symptoms seem to be episodic. Patients with symptomatic genital disorders are often extremely anxious and upset. Agitation may result from fear of sexually transmitted diseases, anger at physicians who have suggested that the problem is psychosomatic, and frustration at the inability to achieve resolution of the problem.

Objective

Any physical conditions that require frequent antibiotic therapy (sinusitis, urinary tract infections, acne) or immunosuppressed states may predispose to *Candida* superinfection. The complaint of episodic itching, swelling, or irritation, especially if related to the menstrual cycle, is often associated with cyclic vulvovaginitis or *Candida* hypersensitivity.

Physical Examination

Internists should become familiar with vulvar anatomy; normal variation is considerable, and it may thus be difficult to recognize pathologic changes. A systematic approach to the vulvar examination, proceeding from the labia majora inward, is important. The examination should be performed routinely in the same fashion for all genital complaints, so that the physician will be better able to recognize anatomic variations. The outer portions of the labia minora contain tiny sebaceous glands that may give a "cobblestone" appearance, and the posterior introitus may exhibit fine papillations that should not be taken for genital warts (although this location is susceptible and typically involved in human papillomavirus infection). During the examination, the physician can reassure the patient by verbalizing normal findings, and an office hand mirror may be used to help the patient and physician discuss specific areas of concern.

Although some patients describe elements of itching *and* burning, the two conditions may usually be differentiated on physical examination. Cutaneous changes of lichenification (leathery thickening) or excoriation (scratch marks) are more typical of pruritus vulvae, because the patient with burning skin rarely rubs or scratches the affected area. Without evidence of scratching, the patient with vulvodynia may appear to have a normal examination.

Routine Laboratory Abnormalities

There are no routine diagnostic findings.

PLANS
Diagnostic
Differential Diagnosis

Table 10–15–1 lists the major morphologic criteria and supporting data from symptomatic vulvar disorders. In many cases, the differential diagnosis will include one or more problems.

Diagnostic Options

Careful history and physical examination are the keys to diagnosis of pruritus vulvae and vulvodynia. A vaginal culture for *Candida* is helpful in patients who describe cyclic symptoms, even if there is no typical "cottage cheese" discharge. Some of these patients are colonized with *Candida* and overgrowth occurs with use of antibiotics or steroids. The use of vinegar or 5% acetic acid solution has been recommended to facilitate the visualization of human papillomavirus but this technique is not diagnostic; acetowhitening may be seen on any hyperkeratotic epithelium and does not indicate the presence of human papillomavirus (HPV).

Unless there is a visible cutaneous change, biopsy is unlikely to be of any diagnostic benefit. Raised lesions should be biopsied, however, and the thickest part of the lesion should be evaluated. Multiple biopsies may be required in multifocal disease. Most cancers are not symptomatic (although ulcerated lesions may be sensitive to touch), so it is unusual for a patient to complain of itching or burning as a primary symptom of malignancy.

TABLE 10–15–1. DIFFERENTIAL DIAGNOSIS OF PRURITUS VULVAE AND VULVODYNIA

Location	Clinical Appearance	Symptoms	Diagnosis	Supporting Data
Labia majora	White hyperkeratotic or atrophic, friable "keyhole" pattern around vulva and anus	Itch or burn	Lichen sclerosus (et atrophicus) (LSA)*	Cutaneous biopsy
	Lichenified, dermatitic, often excoriated with pigmentary changes	Severe itch	Contact/irritant dermatitis* Lichen simplex chronicus*	Careful history and patch testing, if indicated; flares and remits
	Lilac plaques (see also Vagina, below)	May itch	Lichen planus (LP)*	Cutaneous biopsy
	Pink plaques, may be scaling or fissuring	May itch	Psoriasis* or seborrhea*	Typical distribution on rest of body
	Intertriginous; papular border, clearing center	May itch	Tinea* (rare in women)	KOH preparation of scale shows hyphae
	Red, eczematous, swollen, satellite pustules	Severe itch	Candida*	Gram stain of pustule or vaginal smear
	Recurrent ulcerated papule or grouped vesicles	Burn	Recurrent herpes simplex*	Lasts 5–8 days; viral culture confirms
	Erythema	Burn	Steroid withdrawal dermatitis	History of potent topical steroid use
	Verrucous papules; may be smooth, sessile	May itch	Condylomata acuminata*	Cutaneous biopsy
	Irregular rough-surfaced plaques, may ulcerate	May itch	Vulvar intraepithelial neoplasia (VIN)*	Cutaneous biopsy
Labia minora	Yellowish plaques–normal variant	Asymptomatic	Sebaceous hyperplasia	Recognition by observation
	Acetowhite papillae, mosaic vessel pattern	May burn	Papillomatosis	Acetowhitening, colposcopy and/or biopsy
Vulvar vestibule	Dyspareunia; red, tender gland openings	Burn, pain	Vestibulitis	Gland orifice tender to cotton swab palpation
Vagina	Thick white discharge	Itch, burn	Candidiasis	KOH or culture positive vaginal smear
	Erosive vaginitis	Burn	Lichen planus, bullous diseases (pemphigus, pemphigoid)	Cutaneous biopsy for pathology and direct immunofluorescence
	Recurrent symptoms, may vary with menses	Burn	Cyclic, recurrent vulvovaginitis	Improvement with long-term anticandidal agents
Diffuse	Unremitting burning, older patient	Burn	Dysesthetic vulvodynia	Both symptom patterns improve with low-dose tricyclic antidepressants
	Radiation of pain down one or both legs		Pudendal neuralgia	

*See Index for location of sections presenting more detailed discussion of these conditions.

Cyclic symptoms with a history of frequent Candida vaginitis are reason enough to consider a trial of Candida suppression therapy. The complaint of constant unremitting perineal burning, especially in an elderly patient, is more likely to be related to a pudendal neuralgia or dysesthesia, possibly associated with relaxation of the pelvic floor. It is also important to ascertain what the patient has been doing for self-treatment, as long-term use of even midpotency steroids on the vulva can result in rebound erythema and burning that imitate a contact or irritant dermatitis.

Recommended Approach

The physician should be especially concerned with the possibility of malignancy in lesions that do not respond to therapy or that persist after an overlying dermatitis has resolved. Elderly patients who mention vulvar symptoms should always be examined before prescribing therapy; they are particularly likely to have neglected gynecologic visits and may deny the presence of remarkably large ulcers or growths. Simple punch biopsies should be taken from the thickest portions of the lesion(s) or from the borders of an ulcer.

Therapeutic

Therapeutic Options

The vulvar dermatoses are generally responsive to topical steroids. For severe pruritus vulvae with thickened, lichenified skin, a high-potency topical preparation (clobetasol proprionate 0.05% [Temovate] or betamethasone dipropionate 0.05% [Diprolene]) may be applied twice daily for 1 month then daily for 1 month. Thereafter it may be used as needed for symptomatic relief, which should not exceed the equivalent of 1 week's worth of medication a month. This same dosage can be used for the treatment of biopsy-proven lichen sclerosus et atrophicus. For other vulvar conditions, the use of high-potency steroids is strongly discouraged because of the tendency of the vulva to develop steroid rebound dermatitis with erythema and burning.

For patients with cyclic vulvar symptoms and a history of frequent Candida vulvovaginitis, Candida suppression can be achieved with a topical (azole [Terazol] or clotrimazole [Gyne-Lotrimin]) or systemic (fluconazole [Diflucan] or ketoconazole [Nizoral]) antifungal agent. If symptoms improve on a Monday–Wednesday–Friday dosage schedule for 2 to 4 months (150 mg weekly for fluconazole), the patient may be tapered off the medication. In many cases, this is all that is needed to control cyclic symptoms that have been recurrent for many months or even years.

Menopausal or elderly patients with dysesthetic burning in the perineal area are most likely to respond to low-dose tricyclic antidepressant therapy. Amitriptyline (Elavil) or nortriptyline (Pamelor) is the first choice, beginning with 10 mg at bedtime and gradually increasing the dosage to 40 to 50 mg a day. This is the same regimen that has been used to treat postzoster neuralgia and other cutaneous dysesthesias. If amitriptyline is not well tolerated, trazodone (Desyrel), desipramine (Norpramin), or clonazepam (Klonopin) may have fewer side effects. Fluoxetine (Prozac), although well tolerated, has not been useful in pudendal neuralgia.

Recommended Approach

Long-standing symptoms, whether itching or burning, will not resolve rapidly. False expectations from the patient or the physician may cause discontinuation of an entirely appropriate therapeutic regimen. Successful treatment of a vulvar dermatosis will gradually result in resolution of symptoms, but therapy may have to be continued for weeks or months. Section 11 of this text should be consulted for treatment of specific dermatoses (see Table 10–15–1). Treatment programs should not be abandoned until a fair trial has been given (usually 6–8 weeks). If symptoms persist after 2 months of what seems to be appropriate therapy, the possibility of another diagnosis should be considered and a biopsy performed.

In addition to explaining how the medication should be applied and the expected time frame of treatment response, the physician should understand the psychological factors critical to the success of any treatment program. Patients with chronic genital discomfort or pain are often anxious and hypersensitive, and patience should be emphasized by the physician. This clinical problem is often multifactorial, and the patient and her physician should work together to find the best treatment modality.

A treatment trial of anticandidal therapy is of less benefit if the patient is elderly and not on replacement estrogen therapy. Young patients with primary dyspareunia rarely benefit from low-dose tricyclic antidepressants as recommended for dysesthesia. Because of the emotional nature of a chronic pain disorder in the genital area, psychiatric consultation should be considered; in some cases, the problem is similar to that of vaginismus.

FOLLOW-UP

Vulvar dermatoses should be reexamined on return visits to assess response to therapy. Persistent symptoms may not be treatment failures, but may actually represent new problems: topical steroids, for example, may promote candidiasis; sensitivity to medication may develop; or papillomavirus infection may spread. Patients should be followed regularly and encouraged as small increments of progress are made. Patients with a known history of human papillomavirus infection should be examined regularly, both with vulvar examination and Pap smears, because of the risk of vulvar intraepithelial neoplasia.

DISCUSSION
Prevalence and Incidence

The prevalence and incidence of pruritus vulvae and vulvodynia are unknown, but many aspects of these problems are similar to other chronic pain disorders. Patient visits to multiple specialists and multiple physician contacts by frustrated patients with chronic complaints probably gives these problems a higher perceived profile than warranted by the actual incidence.

Related Basic Science

Inflammatory dermatoses (contact or irritant dermatitis, lichen simplex chronicus, lichen planus, lichen sclerosus, psoriasis, tinea, candidiasis, recurrent herpes simplex) have been associated to a greater or lesser degree with itching and are discussed in detail in Section 11 of this text. Human papillomavirus infection, vulvar intraepithelial neoplasia, and vaginal candidiasis have been associated with both itching and burning, and are presented in detail in Section 10.

The symptom of vulvar burning (vulvodynia) should be characterized as diffuse or localized by history. Diffuse unremitting burning is most likely to be due to some form of dysesthesia, and will often respond to tricyclic antidepressant therapy. Localized burning, especially with the complaint of entry dyspareunia, is typical of vulvar vestibulitis, a recently described and still poorly understood condition characterized by persistent tenderness of the openings of the major (Skene's and Bartholin's) and minor glands of the vulvar vestibule.

From personal experience we all recognize the difference between sensations of itching and burning, but from the standpoint of basic science, this is not simple to explain. For this discussion, it may help to think in terms of three levels of sensory information processing: nerves, mediators, and perception.

Nerves. "Itch nerve" endings have been generally considered to be polymodal nociceptors that transmit disagreeable sensations, including "burning," along unmyelinated C fibers. Receptors for itching and pain, which seem to be located at the dermoepidermal junction or just within the epidermis, are physiologic, rather than anatomic, entities. The means by which these sensations are produced and the precise structures responsible for their perception are not firmly established.

The more diffuse state of "itchy skin" may be the result of activation of a facilitating circuit of adjacent neurons within the sensory relay areas of the cord following low-intensity stimulation of pain fibers. An interesting property of these fibers seems to be the phenomenon of sensitization, in which a prolonged stimulus can result in a random background firing that persists despite the withdrawal of the original stimulus. In most cases, itching initiates and is overcome by scratching,

apparently through stimulation of larger nerve fibers, which in turn inhibit the smaller itch fiber stimuli. The symptom of burning, however, virtually precludes a scratch response, and may be a self-protective mechanism enabling damaged tissues to heal themselves without outside interference. Postinflammatory cutaneous hyperalgesia resulting from sensitized nerve endings is an appealing explanation for vulvodynia.

Mediators. It has also been proposed that sensory nerve facilitation might be peripheral, due to local release in the skin of pharmacologic agents. Diffusible mediators have long been thought to be an essential link between the itch-producing stimulus applied to the skin and elicitation of low-grade impulses in the free sensory nerve endings, but the scientific basis for this universal assumption has not been clearly established.

The biogenic amines (prostaglandins, histamine) and polypeptides (bradykinin, serotonin) are present in inflamed tissues, and each is known to cause itching and burning when injected into the skin. Chemical stimuli may act directly on receptors or indirectly by release of endogenous histamine. Ischemia and tissue pH have been implicated in the sensation of burning as well, and evidence is increasing for the role of opioid peptides of the central nervous system in the perception of itch.

Perception. The existence of tertiary neurons (thalamocortical tracts) relaying itch or pain to the cortex has been inferred, but these have not been precisely identified. The phenomenon of referred itch is probably due to the spread of excitation in the thalamus. The therapeutic success of low-dose tricyclic antidepressants in the treatment of cutaneous dysesthesias such as postzoster neuralgia and "essential" or dysesthetic vulvodynia may be the result of altering the perception of peripheral stimuli.

Natural History and Its Modification with Treatment

With most acute inflammatory conditions, symptoms parallel the activity of the disease process. Chronic inflammation is more likely to lead to chronic symptomatology, so every effort should be made to find and treat underlying conditions that may be contributing to ongoing symptoms. Resolution of symptoms will eventually occur in a great majority of cases, but treatment may be required for months at a time. Recurrences are common in susceptible individuals, and the patient should learn to recognize the onset of symptoms and self-initiate effective treatment.

Prevention

Little can be done to prevent most of the noninfectious vulvar dermatoses associated with itching and burning, except to encourage maintenance therapy of chronic inflammatory conditions and evaluate symptom flares carefully for acute infections, such as *Candida*. Long-term use of potent topical steroids may lead to "steroid withdrawal" dermatitis with rebound erythema and burning when these medications are discontinued. A cycle of genital dermatitis is then perpetuated as the patient continues to relieve erythema and discomfort with potent topical steroids. The physician should bear in mind that patients rarely medicate or overscrub normal or asymptomatic skin. Discovery of a dermatitis induced by a topical agent should initiate careful examination for a preexisting or concurrent problem that may still require appropriate therapy. Discontinuation of irritating cleansing habits, use of bland emollients (such as vegetable shortening), and reassurance are often all that is needed to soothe dermatitis secondary to overuse of topicals.

Cost Containment

Careful diagnostic testing to determine appropriate treatment is the mainstay of economical therapy. Compounding mixtures of topical medications is expensive for the patient; 2% testosterone propionate ointment is no longer recommended for the treatment of lichen sclerosis. Probably the best first-line topical for chronic itching is generic triamcinolone 0.1% ointment used for up to a month, and followed by hydrocortisone 1% cream or ointment (Hytone) for maintenance. Intermittent itching or burning may be due to hypersensitivity to *Candida*, and vaginal creams such as terconazole (Terazol) and clotrimazole (Gyne-Lotrimin) are preferred to vaginal suppositories, as the creams can be applied to the vulvar skin as well as intravaginally.

There seems to be a tendency to expect "overnight cure" with topical agents prescribed for vulvar disease, and the patient's money is often wasted on new prescriptions of different brands of the same type of medication (topical steroids, anticandidals). Although tachyphylaxis (resistance to a medication used over a long period) may occur in some cases, it is more often true that the patient has simply not used the medication for a long enough period for an effect to be seen. Chronic dermatoses may take many weeks to resolve; recurrence of symptoms is usually not a sign of treatment failure, but of the need for ongoing maintenance therapy.

REFERENCES

Fitzpatrick TB, Eisen AZ, Wolff K, et al., eds. Dermatology in general medicine. 4th ed. New York: McGraw-Hill, 1993.

Lynch PJ, Edwards L. Genital dermatology. New York: Churchill Livingstone, 1994.

McKay M. Genital disorders. In: Newcomer VD, Young EM, eds. Geriatric dermatology. New York: Igaku-Shoin, 1988:477.

McKay M. Vulvar dermatoses. Clin Obstet Cynecol 1991;34:614.

McKay M. Vulvitis and vulvovaginitis: Cutaneous considerations. Am J Obstet Gynecol 1991;165:1176.

McKay M. Vulvodynia: Diagnostic patterns. Dermatol Clin 1992;10:423.

McKay M. Vulvodynia, scrotodynia, and other dysesthesias of the anogenital region (including pruritus ani). In: Bernhard JD, ed. Itch: Mechanisms and management of pruritus. New York: McGraw-Hill, 1993.

McKay M. Dysesthic ("essential") vulvodynia: Treatment with amitriptyline. J Reprod Med 1993;38:9.

McKay M. Vulvodynia and pruritus vulvae. In: Black MM, McKay M, Braude P, eds. Color Atlas and Text of Obstetric and Gynecologic Dermatology. London: Mosby–Wolfe, 1995.

CHAPTER 10–16
Family Planning

Robert A. Hatcher, M.D., M.P.H.

DEFINITION

Family planning is the sum of the voluntary contraceptive decisions made by women and men together or individually throughout the reproductive years.

ETIOLOGY

The need for birth control emanates from the basic desire to do something very pleasurable, that is, to have sexual intercourse, *without* becoming pregnant. Family planning services have been demonstrated to decrease maternal mortality rates, infant mortality rates, and early childhood death rates.

CRITERIA FOR DIAGNOSIS
Suggestive

The need for contraception is *suggested* whenever a woman in her reproductive years is in a sexual relationship with a man (or when a man is in a sexual relationship with a woman who is in her reproductive years).

Definitive

The need for voluntary contraception is *confirmed* when any woman or man states that she or he wishes to use a contraceptive.

CLINICAL MANIFESTATIONS
Subjective

Women needing family planning may be as young as 10 and as old as their early fifties. Men from age 10 on may need contraception.

Questions about a person's current sexual relationship with an individual of the opposite sex, desire for pregnancy at the present time, desired family size, current/past use of contraception, complications from contraceptives used, past history of sexually transmitted infections, consistency of condom use when exposed to the risk of a sexually transmitted infection, and likelihood of exposure at the present time to HIV infection will usually identify individuals in need of contraceptives, will suggest the relative importance of condom use, and may very quickly identify the method a person wishes to continue using. History is far more important than physical examination or laboratory tests in determining the best contraceptive option for an individual or couple.

Objective
Physical Examination

A complete physical examination is desirable but usually is *not essential* to determine the appropriate contraceptive. Pelvic examination to look for pelvic pathology of any kind and specifically for an enlarged uterus and other signs of pregnancy, as well as to screen for sexually transmitted diseases, is important for some women.

Routine Laboratory Abnormalities

The routine family planning encounter *may* include obtaining a hematocrit annually; a Pap smear for cervical cancer; screening for gonorrhea, chlamydia, or HIV infection as indicated; routine urinalysis annually; a sensitive urine pregnancy test (sensitive to 25–50 mIU) if it is important to rule out pregnancy; and screening for cholesterol, particularly late in the reproductive years or if a woman has risk factors for cardiovascular disease. Mammography to screen for breast cancer is recommended for women late in their reproductive years and, of course, after menopause.

PLANS
Diagnostic

The clinician and the individual wishing to use a contraceptive must be in agreement regarding the need for a contraceptive.

Therapeutic
Therapeutic Options

Sterilizaton is the method chosen most often by couples in the United States. Tubal sterilization is more commonly selected than vasectomy despite the fact that vasectomy is less expensive, safer, and more effective. Although sterilization procedures are sometimes reversible, for the most part they should not be considered unless an individual/couple is certain they want no more children.

Oral contraceptives are almost as popular as sterilization. Serious complications have become extremely rare as (1) the doses of estrogens and progestins have fallen dramatically; (2) pills have not been prescribed to women over 35 who smoke; and (3) women have been taught to look for these warning signals; headaches, eye problems such as blurred vision or sudden loss of vision, chest pain, severe abdominal pain, and severe leg pain. Additional warning signs are depression, loss of interest in sex, jaundice, and a breast mass.

The effects of oral contraceptives on coagulation can be minimized in smokers and nonsmokers by the use of pills with the smallest amount of ethinyl estradiol (20 μg pills) (Fruzetti et al., 1994). If a woman is already at increased risk for thromboembolic complications because of age, history of diabetes, smoking, or hypertension, it may be particularly wise to prescribe a pill with only 20 μg of estrogen.

The use of currently available oral contraceptives in two high doses (4 pills at a time repeated in 12 hours) is the most commonly used emergency contraceptive following unprotected intercourse. Combined oral contraceptives are used for many noncontraceptive purposes, including control of dysmenorrhea, dysfunctional uterine bleeding, treatment of functional ovarian cysts, and treatment of acne. Pill use is associated with a decreased risk for endometrial and ovarian cancer, which appears to persist long after a woman discontinues pills.

Norplant contraceptive implants consist of six small (match stick-sized) capsules made of silicone rubber, which are placed just under the skin of the upper arm under local anesthesia. They elaborate very low levels of the progestin levonorgestrel, and provide extremely effective contraception for 5 years. Irregular bleeding must be explained in advance.

Norplant removal clearly is more difficult than insertion, particularly if implants were inserted too deeply. Removal occasionally requires more than one visit. In one U.S. study of 143 removals, removal of implants took from 4 to 215 minutes; slightly more than 19% of 143 removals took more than 1 hour, and in 24% of cases, women described the pain at the time of removal as "significant" (Frank et al., 1993).

If Norplant implants have an Achilles heel, it is the problems associated with removal. Some women are having difficulty finding a physician to remove implants. Others have it inserted at no cost and then have to have it removed when they are no longer eligible for public support. Some physicians who insert implants do not remove them. When clinicians insert implants but do not remove them themselves, they may not insert them correctly. Complications at the time of removal include slight disfiguration due to scarring from the incision(s), cutting of the median or ulnar nerve, infection, and one death from general anesthesia.

When women have difficulties getting their implants removed, it raises the question: Is this a completely voluntary method of contraception? It is the convergence of these two issues—difficult and possibly unaffordable removals, and the ever-present concern that each method we provide not be coercive—that is causing some clinicians, women's groups, and journalists to question the wisdom of using this superb contraceptive at all. Therefore, despite the effectiveness, safety, convenience, privacy, and long-term protection afforded by Norplant implants, a cloud now hangs ominously over this method.

Contraceptive implants are a safe and effective method, an important and desirable contraceptive option; however, the role of implants over time depends on two factors. First, commitment to the principles of informed consent and voluntarism is essential. And second, improved techniques for removing implants, such as the Emory technique for rapid Norplant removal (Sarma and Hatcher, 1994), must be developed and promulgated. The development of a one-rod or a two-rod implant system will greatly simplify the removal of contraceptive implants.

Intrauterine devices (IUDs) are the second most popular method of contraception worldwide but are much less popular in the United States. The Copper T 380A is the primary device used in the United States and is now formally approved for 10 years of use. Cramping and irregular vaginal bleeding are the most common side effects of intrauterine devices. Postcoital insertion of the Copper T 380 during the 5 to 7 days following unprotected intercourse is the most effective emergency contraceptive available. When RU 486 (mifepristone) is available in the United States, it will be as effective as the insertion of a Copper T 380A as an emergency contraceptive.

Condoms provide excellent protection against both pregnancy and infection when used correctly with each act of intercourse. In a prospective study of HIV-negative individuals whose only risk of HIV infection was a heterosexual relationship with an HIV-infected partner, there was no transmission of HIV infection after 15,000 acts of sexual intercourse over an average of 20 months (DeVincenzi, 1994). There

are now myriad other studies demonstrating a decreased relative risk for the transmission of other sexually transmitted infections in couples using condoms consistently (Hatcher et al., 1994). In addition to latex condoms, polyurethane and tactylon condoms are being developed which are acceptable to individuals allergic to latex. The Reality female condom is made of polyurethane and is effective in preventing pregnancy and infections. The female condom covers the vaginal vault and part of the outside of the vagina or vulva.

Diaphragms are a barrier contraceptive that must be used with a spermicide. The diaphragm requires fitting, and is difficult for some women to insert and/or remove. Failure rates for the diaphragm and the female condom are somewhat higher than for the other contraceptives noted above (Hatcher et al., 1994).

Cervical caps are another barrier/spermicide contraceptive with higher failure rates than pills, sterilization, intrauterine devices, or condoms (Hatcher et all, 1994). Fitting is fairly complicated. Caps can be fairly effective for 2 to 5 days, but leaving a cervical cap in for more than 48 hours is generally not recommended.

Spermicidal suppositories, jellies, creams, and foam are approaches that are somewhat less effective (Hatcher et al., 1994), but may be obtained from pharmacies without a prescription. In vitro, spermicides kill most of the bacteria and viruses that cause sexually transmitted infections (including HIV). These preparations may cause annoying irritations for either the man or the woman.

Fertility awareness methods include a variety of techniques used to determine when in her cycle a woman is able to become pregnant. Abstinence must be practiced when a woman is fertile. Hence this method is often called *periodic abstinence*. The most effective technique is for a woman to avoid having intercourse until there has been a rise in her basal body temperature for 3 days; however, this approach demands abstinence for a major portion of the cycle. Couples depending on fertility awareness methods, who will not avoid intercourse when abstinence is dictated, experience extremely high failure rates.

Future methods with promise include the levonorgestrel intrauterine device; a silicone rubber cap called the FemCap; contraceptive implants that require only one or two rather than six implants; condoms made of tactylon rather than latex; and an oral contraceptive for men derived from cottonseed oil called Gossypol (Hatcher et al., 1994).

Recommended Approach

Women usually have a fairly clear idea of the contraceptive(s) they wish to use. Effectiveness is an important consideration for couples considering contraceptive options, and the failure rates of current contraceptives are summarized in Table 10–16–1 (Hatcher et al., 1994). Although most contraceptives are safe for most women, with some contraceptives, definite precautions or contraindications should be taken into consideration. It is important, in general, to prescribe the method a woman *wants to use and thinks that she will use consistently and correctly.* Often the highest priority in her mind will be use of *the most effective contraceptive,* whereas the clinician may be wanting her to add to contraceptive considerations the need for prevention of sexually transmitted infections. In actual practice, this may mean encouraging her to use both an effective contraceptive like oral contraceptives *and also condoms.*

FOLLOW-UP

It is generally recommended that all women in their reproductive years have a pelvic examination annually. Following insertion of an intrauterine device, a woman should return after her first menstrual period to make sure that there has been no expulsion or partial expulsion of the device. An extra visit is also recommended shortly after a woman has been shown how to insert her diaphragm or cervical cap, to be sure she is inserting it properly. Women are sometimes asked to return 2 to 3 months after first starting pills to see if they have any questions and to check blood pressure. This is optional. Women must return each 3 months for injections of 150 mg medroxyprogesterone acetate (Depo-Provera), and it is important to ask about weight gain at each visit. Women receiving Norplant contraceptive implants are asked to return at 1 month to check the insertion site and to answer the many questions

TABLE 10–16–1. PERCENTAGE OF WOMEN EXPERIENCING A CONTRACEPTIVE FAILURE DURING THE FIRST YEAR OF PERFECT USE AND THE FIRST YEAR OF TYPICAL USE AND THE PERCENTAGE CONTINUING USE AT THE END OF THE FIRST YEAR, UNITED STATES

Method	% of Women Experiencing an Accidental Pregnancy Within the First year of Use		% of Women Continuing Use at 1 Year‡
	Typical Use*	Perfect Use†	
(1)	(2)	(3)	(4)
Chance§	85	85	
Spermicides″	21	6	43
Progestin only		0.5	
Combined		0.1	
Periodic abstinence	20		67
Calendar		9	
Ovulation method		3	
Symptothermal#		2	
Postovulation		1	
Withdrawal	19	4	
Cap¶			
Parous women	36	26	45
Nulliparous women	18	9	58
Sponge			
Parous women	36	20	45
Nulliparous women	18	9	58
Diaphragm¶	18	6	58
Condom**			
Female (Reality)	21	5	56
Male	12	3	63
Pill	3		72
Intrauterine device			
Progesterone T	2.0	1.5	81
Copper T 380A	0.8	0.6	78
LNg 20	0.1	0.1	81
Depo-Provera	0.3	0.3	70
Norplant (6 capsules)	0.09	0.09	85
Female sterilization	0.4	0.4	100
Male sterilization	0.15	0.10	100

Emergency contraceptive pills: Treatment initiated within 72 hours after unprotected intercourse reduces the risk of pregnancy by at least 75%††

Lactational amenorrhea method: This is a highly effective, temporary method of contraception.‡‡

*Among typical couples who initiate use of a method (not necessarily for the first time), the percentage who experience an accidental pregnancy during the first year if they do not stop use for any other reason.

†Among couples who initiate use of a method (not necessarily for the first time) and who use it perfectly (both consistently and correctly), the percentage who experience an accidental pregnancy during the first year if they do not stop use for any other reason.

‡Among couples attempting to avoid pregnancy, the percentage who continue to use a method for one year.

§The percentages failing in columns (2) and (3) are based on data from populations where contraception is not used and from women who cease using contraception to become pregnant. Among such populations, about 89% become pregnant within one year. This estimate was lowered slightly (to 85%) to represent the percentage who would become pregnant within 1 year among women now relying on reversible methods of contraception if they abandoned contraception altogether.

″Foams, creams, gels, vaginal suppositories, and vaginal film.

#Cervical mucus (ovulation) method supplemented by calendar in the preovulatory phase and basal body temperature in the postovulatory phase.

¶With spermicidal cream or jelly.

**Without spermicides.

††The treatment schedule is one dose as soon as possible (but no more than 72 hours) after unprotected intercourse and a second dose 12 hours after the first dose. The hormones that have been studied in clinical trials of postcoital hormonal contraception are found in the following brands of oral contraceptives: Nordette, Levlen, Lo/Ovral (one dose is 4 pills), Triphasil, Tri-Levlen (one dose is 4 yellow pills), and Ovral (one dose is 2 pills).

‡‡However, to maintain effective protection against pregnancy, another method of contraception must be used as soon as menstruation resumes, the frequency or duration of breastfeedings is reduced, bottle feedings are introduced, or the baby reaches 6 months of age.

Source: Hatcher RA, Trussell J, Stewart F, et al. Contraceptive technology. 16th rev. ed. New York: Irvington, 1994. Reproduced with the permission of Contraceptive Technology Communications, Inc.

that may be arising about the pattern of bleeding. Several visits are important if a woman is using one of the fertility awareness methods, as these techniques are difficult to learn.

DISCUSSION

Prevalence and Incidence

Most women start having periods at about age 12 and stop at about age 51. Intercourse begins several years before most women want to have their first child, and then the average woman has only two children in the United States. So for approximately 30 years she may be having intercourse when she does not wish to become pregnant. It is during these years that she will be considering her family planning options.

Related Basic Science

Genetics

There are few if any genetic differences in women's ability to tolerate different contraceptives. Contraceptives may be indicated for individuals with some genetically determined diseases such as muscular dystrophy, cystic fibrosis, and sickle cell disease; however, each contraceptive decision must be completely voluntary.

Physiologic or Metabolic Derangement

Contraceptives dramatically affect the physiology of the hypothalamic–pituitary–ovarian–endometrial axis through changes in the primary female hormone, estradiol, and through changes in gonadotropin-releasing hormones, gonadotropins, progestins, androgens, and sex hormone-binding globulins.

Anatomic Derangement

Uterine abnormalities may eliminate intrauterine device insertion as an option.

Natural History and Its Modification with Treatment

In most instances clinicians and clients have no difficulty agreeing on the appropriate contraceptive(s) to be used. When a woman strongly expresses the desire to use a method the clinician deems to be inappropriate or dangerous, referral to a second clinic or physician may be the best course of action.

Prevention

Close to 90% of failures related to the use of contraceptives arise from the errors couples make using them. Hence, it is essential that couples choose the method they will use consistently and then commit themselves to using the method without fail. The provider can foster this commitment by encouraging, answering questions, listening to concerns, and making suggestions as to approaches known to have helped other couples.

Cost Containment

The cost of contraception and approaches to preventing sexually transmitted infections pales in comparison to the financial consequences of sex without these therapeutic modalities. For example, the cost of pregnancy and raising a child to the age of 18, of a single person becoming infected with HIV, or of infertility can quickly run to many thousands of dollars. Contraception is very cost effective even when the client or a clinic is paying the highest price charged for methods or supplies. Contraceptives and means of preventing sexually transmitted infections should be available to all who wish to use them. Here are three suggestions of the many ways that might be employed to lower the cost of contraception:

- Generic oral contraceptives are perfectly acceptable and may cost $5 per cycle when other brands are costing a woman $20 to $25 per cycle of pills.
- Condoms cost 5 cents apiece when an order of as little as $500 worth of condoms are purchased. Hospitals, HMOs, clinics, and individual

physicians' offices can easily make this investment to facilitate condom use.
- In the long run, the methods that provide long-term contraception from a single decision, such as the Copper T 380A, Norplant contraceptive implants, vasectomy, and tubal sterilization, are far less expensive than methods that must be used over and over again.

REFERENCES

De Vincenzi I. A longitudinal study of human immunodeficiency virus transmission by heterosexual partners. N Eng J Med 1994;331:341.

Frank ML, Poindexter AN, Cornin LM, et al. One-year experience with subdermal contraceptive implants in the United States. Contraception 1993;48:229.
Fruzzeti F, Ricci C, Fioretti P. Haemostasis profile in smoking and nonsmoking women taking low-dose oral contraceptives. Contraception 1994;49:579.
Hatcher RA, Trussell J, Stewart F, et al. Contraceptive technology. 16th rev. ed. New York: Irvington, 1994.
Sarma SP, Hatcher RA. The Emory method: A modified approach to Norplant® implant removal. Contraception 1994; 49:551.

CHAPTER 10–17

Pelvic Pain

Carlene W. Elsner, M.D.

DEFINITION

Deep pain that localizes between the umbilicus and the symphysis is properly referred to as pelvic pain. This pain may be acute in onset or chronic, intermittent or constant, and may or may not be associated with rebound tenderness.

ETIOLOGY

The etiology of pelvic pain relates to infections or other disease processes of the structures lying within the pelvis. Most important to consider are disorders of the reproductive tract (uterus, tubes, and ovaries), the lower urinary tract (ureters and bladder), and the lower gastrointestinal tract (small and large bowel and appendix). Pelvic pain is almost always related to a disorder of one of these three systems. Only rarely does musculoskeletal or neurologic disease present as pelvic pain.

Infections of the reproductive tract include endometritis, acute or chronic pelvic inflammatory disease, and pelvic abscesses. Noninfectious reproductive tract causes of pelvic pain include ovarian cysts, particularly if they undergo torsion, ectopic pregnancy, endometriosis, dysmenorrhea, and, in some instances, uterine fibroids.

Nongynecologic causes of pelvic pain are discussed elsewhere.

CRITERIA FOR DIAGNOSIS
Suggestive

Pelvic pain that is acute in onset and severe in nature may be associated with rebound tenderness. Fever greater than 101°F in this instance suggests pelvic inflammatory disease with or without abscess formation. Low-grade fever or normal temperature, with delayed or irregular menses and syncope is a classic description of ectopic pregnancy. Acute severe abdominal pain relieved or improved by changes in position is characteristic of a torsed ovarian cyst.

Chronic pelvic inflammatory disease leads to chronic pelvic pain that exacerbates with menses and is associated with low-grade fever. Endometriosis is associated with increasing pain before and during menses, as well as dyspareunia, but normal temperature. Classically dysmenorrhea begins within hours of onset of menses and abates within 48 hours. Functional ovarian cysts arise at ovulation and cause low abdominal discomfort until onset of menses, when they regress.

Definitive

A quantitative beta human chorionic gonadotropin (βHCG) greater than 5000 mlU/mL with no gestational sac visualized in the uterus on transvaginal ultrasound with or without free fluid in the cul-de-sac on ultrasound represents an ectopic pregnancy until proven otherwise.

Acute salpingitis manifests by fever, elevated white cell count, and tender uterus and adnexae on pelvic examination. If Gram-negative intracellular diplococci are seen on cervical Gram stain, the causative organism is *Neisseria gonorrhoeae.*

Endometriosis can be definitively diagnosed only by visualization of lesions at laparoscopy or laparotomy.

Painful fibroids are diagnosed when palpation of the fibroid on pelvic examination reproduces the patient's pain.

Ovarian cysts are diagnosed on pelvic examination or by transvaginal ultrasound. Torsion is suggested by careful history taking.

Dysmenorrhea is primarily a historical diagnosis. It is a diagnosis of exclusion and can be made with confidence only after endometriosis has been ruled out by laparoscopy.

CLINICAL MANIFESTATIONS
Subjective

Ectopic pregnancy may or may not be associated with irregular or delayed menses, so it should be considered in the differential diagnosis of every woman of reproductive age who presents with pelvic pain. The description of the pain may be acute in onset, severe, and associated with pain on defecation and syncope or it may be described as a dull ache in the lower abdomen that increases gradually over days or even weeks. There may be a history of previous pelvic infection, tubal disease, tubal surgery, ectopic pregnancy, or infertility.

Pelvic inflammatory disease frequently becomes worse with menses or shortly thereafter. There may or may not be a history of prior intercourse. Infertility is common in individuals with a history of repeated episodes of pelvic inflammatory disease.

Endometriosis is a great masquerader. Severe disease may be associated with little or no symptomatology, whereas minimal disease may result in severe symptoms. When symptoms are present they include pelvic pain, worse with menses, but frequently present at other times of the cycle as well. Dyspareunia and infertility are common. Occasionally, pain on urination or defecation is present. Frequently, there is a family history of endometriosis.

Functional ovarian cysts arise with ovulation, persist throughout the luteal phase of the cycle, and regress with menses. Pain related to these cysts is dull low abdominal discomfort generally localized to the side containing the cyst. Positional changes resulting in torsion of these cysts can cause acute onset of severe pain relieved by changes in position. Large ovarian cysts may rupture with intercourse and result in acute onset of severe pain that lasts up to 24 hours.

In patients with leiomyoma, low abdominal discomfort, fullness, heaviness in the pelvis, menorrhagia, and dysmenorrhea are common. Menses are frequently heavy enough to cause anemia. Decreased bladder volume as well as vague bowel complaints and dyspareunia are described by some patients. Others describe sharp knifelike pains localized to the site of the fibroid. Acute degeneration of leiomyoma is associated with increased pain over the tumor as well as low-grade fever. There may be a history of fibroids in other female relatives.

Primary dysmenorrhea is menstrual cramps in the absence of pelvic pathology. It is a diagnosis of exclusion and can therefore be made only after other possible causes of pain have been excluded. Classically, pain begins within hours of onset of menses and persists for less than 48 hours. This pain is dramatically relieved by prostaglandin antagonists. Frequently there is a positive family history for primary dysmenorrhea.

Objective

Physical Examination

Patients with ruptured ectopic pregnancies represent true medical emergencies. They present in acute distress with an acute abdomen, hypotension, and tachycardia. Depending on the amount of abdominal bleeding that has occurred, the abdomen may be distended, with low abdominal tenderness to palpation and dramatic rebound tenderness. There may be a small amount of vaginal bleeding on pelvic examination. The cervix and uterus are normal in size but very tender to palpation. Adnexae are tender to palpation, sometimes worse on the side of the ectopic pregnancy. Adnexal masses may or may not be palpable. Culdocentesis yields nonclotting blood in ruptured ectopic pregnancies as well as in other instances of intraabdominal bleeding. This procedure is very painful and is frequently replaced by vaginal ultrasound. Patients with unruptured ectopic pregnancies are dramatically different. They may have only slight lower abdominal tenderness to deep palpation localized to the side of ectopic. Findings on pelvic examination may be limited to unilateral adnexal tenderness with or without palpation of an adnexal mass. Following rupture, the hemoglobin falls.

The physical examination in acute pelvic inflammatory disease is very similar to that of ruptured ectopic pregnancy. Such patients present in acute distress with fever, abdominal tenderness to palpation, worse in the lower abdomen, and rebound tenderness. Pelvic examination may reveal a purulent vaginal discharge. Cervical and uterine tenderness is exquisite, with bilateral adnexal tenderness with or without palpable adnexal masses.

Patients with endometriosis may have a normal pelvic examination. Physical findings on pelvic examination suggestive of endometriosis are ovarian cysts and tender nodularity of the uterosacral ligaments.

Fibroids are frequently palpable on pelvic examination as a hard nodule on the uterus. If they are the source of pain, they will be tender to palpation.

Ovarian cysts are palpable on pelvic examination as cystic adnexal masses that may be tender to palpation. If these cysts undergo torsion, they become exquisitely tender to palpation.

The pelvic examination in patients with primary dysmenorrhea is normal.

Routine Laboratory Abnormalities

Hemoglobin and hematocrit fall in ruptured ectopic pregnancy as intraperitoneal bleeding continues. These two parameters are often chronically low with submucous fibroids. Sedimentation rate is elevated with pelvic infection. White blood count is elevated with increased polymorphonuclear lymphocytes in acute pelvic inflammatory disease. Occasionally, white count elevations may also be seen with ruptured ectopic pregnancy, torsion of ovarian cysts, and acute degeneration of a fibroid.

PLANS

Diagnostic

Differential Diagnosis

Pelvic pain may be either acute, that is, sudden in onset and severe in nature, or chronic with a duration of days, weeks, or months.

Acute Pelvic Pain. The differential diagnosis of appendicitis, ruptured ectopic pregnancy, and acute pelvic inflammatory disease is sometimes very difficult. A quantitative beta human chorionic gonadotropin, a complete blood count with differential, and a transvaginal ultrasound are most useful in making the distinction. Transabdominal ultrasound may also be used, but it is not as sensitive.

Chronic Pelvic Pain. Unruptured ectopic pregnancy, chronic pelvic inflammatory disease, ovarian cysts, endometriosis, degenerating leiomy-

omata, primary dysmenorrhea, as well as nongynecologic reasons for pain such as cystitis, trigonitis, ureteral colic, regional enteritis, and ulcerative colitis, must all be considered in the differential diagnosis of pelvic pain.

In the presence of low levels of beta human chorionic gonadotropin in serum, interval blood samples obtained 48 to 72 hours apart are helpful in establishing the viability of the trophoblast. Levels should double every 48 to 72 hours in a healthy intrauterine pregnancy. A slow rise, plateau, or falling level is often seen in ectopic pregnancy or threatened abortion. Beta human chorionic gonadotropin doubling times in conjunction with vaginal ultrasound when beta human chorionic gonadotropin levels reach 5000 mIU/mL are most useful in ruling out unruptured ectopic pregnancy as a reason for pelvic pain.

With chronic pelvic inflammatory disease, cervical cultures for *Chlamydia* and *Neisseria gonorrhoeae* may or may not be positive. White cell count elevations are mild. Sedimentation rate is generally elevated. Laparoscopy is essential to the diagnosis of endometriosis and often provides the definitive diagnosis in chronic pelvic infection, unruptured ectopic pregnancy, and torsion of ovarian cysts. Hematuria on clean-catch or catheterized urine samples is suggestive of ureteral calculi or hemorrhagic cystitis. Pyuria and positive urine cultures are present in cystitis, whereas cultures are usually negative in trigonitis.

Diagnostic Options and Recommended Approach

Acute Pelvic Pain. A positive beta human chorionic gonadotropin establishes the existence of a pregnancy. It does not determine its location. An intrauterine gestational sac with a positive fetal heart on ultrasound rules out the possibility of an ectopic pregnancy, except in women who have recently used fertility drugs or assisted reproductive techniques (in vitro fertilization or genetic intrafallopian transfer) to conceive, where a heterotopic pregnancy (concomitant intrauterine and ectopic) is possible. A beta human chorionic gonadotropin over 5000 mIU/mL in the absence of an intrauterine gestational sac on transvaginal ultrasound is an ectopic gestation until proven otherwise. Free fluid in the cul-de-sac on ultrasound strongly suggests intraperitoneal bleeding. A falling hemoglobin also is frequently present with acute bleeding into the abdomen. A marked elevation in white blood cell count with leukocytosis is consistent with the diagnosis of acute pelvic inflammatory disease with or without abscess formation. White count elevations with appendicitis are usually not as high as they are with acute salpingitis.

Chronic Pelvic Pain. Quantitative beta human chorionic gonadotropin, complete blood count with differential, sedimentation rate, and cervical cultures should be done initially. If beta human chorionic gonadotropin is positive but low and physical examination and complete blood count are normal, doubling times should be done as should an ultrasound when appropriate. If the patient's clinical condition deteriorates, a transvaginal ultrasound and laparoscopy are imperative.

Therapeutic

Therapeutic Options

Ruptured ectopic pregnancy requires immediate surgical intervention via laparotomy or laparoscopy, with appropriate measures to establish hemostasis and remove the ectopic gestation. Most of the time this can be accomplished on an outpatient basis through laparosopy. Unruptured ectopic pregnancy may be removed laparoscopically most frequently by linear salpingostomy. Medical treatment using intramuscular methotrexate is an alternative only if the patient is completely asymptomatic.

Acute pelvic inflammatory disease in the absence of tubo-ovarian abscesses is treated with 4.8 million units of aqueous penicillin intramuscularly given in two sites with 1 g probenecid orally. In individuals sensitive to penicillin, administer tetracycline 500 mg orally every 6 hours for 7 to 10 days, or doxycycline 100 mg orally twice a day for 7 to 10 days, or erythromycin 500 mg orally every 6 hours for 7 to 10 days. For individuals with acute pelvic inflammatory disease and evidence of tubo-ovarian abscesses, that is, adnexal masses on pelvic examination or ultrasound, hospitalization with intravenous antibiotics is appropriate. The choice of antibiotics must cover enteric aerobes and anaerobes including *Bacteroides*. After the patient has been afebrile for

24 hours, antibiotics may be administered orally until the course of therapy is complete. Occasional patients with chronic or recurrent pelvic infection may require long-term antibiotics (3–4 weeks) to treat their disease adequately. Only rarely is surgical intervention required to remove tubo-ovarian abscesses refractory to treatment. In a young woman desirous of future fertility, every reasonable effort should be made to preserve the uterus, even if both tubes must be removed. In vitro fertilization and, if necessary, donor oocyte technology make it possible for these women to become pregnant in the absence of tubes or even in the absence of ovaries.

The treatment of choice in most cases of endometriosis is laparoscopy and laser vaporization or excision of the lesions with or without medical treatment of residual disease using long-acting gonadotropin-releasing hormone agonists (Lupron or Synarel) for 3 to 6 months. Alternative therapies include medical treatment with long-acting gonadotropin-releasing hormone agonists or danazol or the use of oral contraceptives.

Laparoscopy can be used to relieve ovarian torsion. If good color returns, the cyst can be removed and the ovary preserved. If, however, the ovary is gangrenous, it must be removed. Unless malignancy is suspected, most ovarian cysts can be removed laparoscopically. Functional cysts will resolve on their own and do not require surgical intervention. An ultrasound obtained during the menstrual period will show reduction in size or complete resolution of these cysts.

Primary dysmenorrhea classically responds dramatically to the use of prostaglandin antagonists, as the pathophysiology of this disorder relates directly to increased menstrual fluid prostaglandin levels. If symptoms do not respond to treatment with these drugs, the diagnosis is suspect.

Uterine leiomyomata may be treated by myomectomy or hysterectomy depending on the patient's desire for future fertility. Large myomas may be treated preoperatively with long-acting gonadotropin-releasing hormone agonists to reduce myoma size and facilitate removal surgically. If myomectomy is performed, myomas may recur, so desired pregnancies should be attempted expediently.

Recommended Approach

Once the diagnosis is established, treatment is straightforward. Laparoscopic removal of unruptured ectopic pregnancies under 3 cm in diameter is the treatment of choice. The use of laparoscopy otherwise to treat ectopic pregnancy is dependent on the condition of the patient and the technical skill of the treating physician and must be decided on a case-by-case basis. Laser vaporization of endometriotic implants at time of initial diagnostic laparoscopy is adequate and appropriate treatment for 80% of patients with endometriosis. Most ovarian cysts can be safely removed on an outpatient basis laparoscopically. Myomectomy is appropriate for women desiring pregnancy who have large painful fibroids. Women whose childbearing is complete may prefer hysterectomy.

Acute pelvic inflammatory disease in the absence of abscess formation should be treated with 4.8 million units of aqueous penicillin intramuscularly plus 1 g of probenecid orally. Pelvic abscesses require hospital admission for administration of intravenous antibiotics.

Primary dysmenorrhea should be treated first with oral prostaglandin antagonists like Anaprox 275 to 550 mg orally every 4 hours or Motrin 600 to 800 mg orally every 4 hours.

FOLLOW-UP

Following removal of an ectopic pregnancy when the tube is left in situ or if methotrexate is used, quantitative beta human chorionic gonadotropin determinations should be obtained weekly until negative. Two months after treatment, a hysterosalpingogram should be obtained to determine the patency of the affected tube. Individuals with a history of previous ectopic pregnancy, pelvic inflammatory disease, endometriosis, or other tubal disease who become pregnant deserve careful monitoring with quantitative beta human chorionic gonadotropin doubling times and appropriately timed transvaginal ultrasound until the site of the pregnancy is established, because these women are at increased risk (10–15%) of ectopic pregnancy. In women with previous

myomectomies, ultrasounds obtained at intervals of 6 months to a year are very effective in monitoring recurrence or growth of existing myomas.

Following completion of treatment for pelvic inflammatory disease, pelvic examination should be repeated to ensure return to normal. Appropriate counseling to make sure the patient understands transmission of disease plus the regular use of condoms may decrease the risk of recurrence.

Sometimes the etiology of pelvic pain is unexplained, and in those circumstances psychological evaluation should be considered.

All women undergoing treatment for pelvic pain, regardless of the cause, should undergo follow-up pelvic examination to ensure adequate response to treatment.

DISCUSSION

Prevalence and Incidence

Pelvic pain is a very frequent gynecologic complaint. The prevalence of endometriosis has been estimated to be 7.5 to 10% in women of reproductive age. The risk of ectopic pregnancy is increased in women with a history of previous pelvic infection, endometriosis, pelvic adhesion, previous abdominal surgery, septic abortion, or appendicitis. The incidence of ectopic pregnancy is estimated at 16.8 per 1000 pregnancies and was responsible for 12% of national deaths in 1987.

Related Basic Science

Genetics

Fibroids are the result of mutations in individual muscle cells. Karyotypes of myomas usually show aneuploidy. Individuals who have large numbers of fibroids have high somatic mutation rates and a higher incidence of recurrence following myomectomy than do women with a single myoma.

Physiologic Derangement

Functional ovarian cysts arise from the site of ovulation. If follicular rupture does not occur, the fluid is clear. If ovum release from the follicle occurs and bleeding at the site of ovulation follows, a hemorrhagic corpus luteum cyst results. Both types of functional cysts regress with the subsequent menses. Complete resolution may require a few additional weeks.

Metabolic Derangement

Primary dysmenorrhea results from smooth muscle contractions of the uterus caused by increased levels of prostaglandin in the menstrual effluent. These increased prostaglandins may also cause contraction of smooth muscle of other systems, especially gastrointestinal and vascular, resulting in nausea and vomiting, diarrhea, and headache.

Anatomic Derangement

Pelvic infection damages tubal endothelium, causing intratubal agglutination as well as tubal occlusion and adnexal adhesions. This damage interferes with tubal mobility and ovum transport, which predisposes the affected individual to ectopic pregnancy or infertility.

No single mechanism completely explains the development of endometriosis. Retrograde menstruation, transformation of coelomic epithelium, and immunologic factors may all play a role in the development of endometriosis.

Natural History and Its Modification with Treatment

Repeated or persistent pelvic infection results eventually in infertility or an increased risk of ectopic pregnancy. Timely definitive treatment may decrease this risk. Celibacy, monogamous relationships, and regular use of condoms reduce the risk of developing pelvic infection.

Untreated ectopic pregnancy usually results in tubal rupture, intraperitoneal bleeding, and death. In these cases timely surgical intervention is lifesaving. Occasionally, a tubal abortion will occur, the bleeding will stop, and the symptoms eventually will spontaneously resolve.

Endometriosis grows under the influence of ovarian hormones, becoming more severe with time. Following cessation of hormonal stimulation at the menopause, lesions regress unless replacement hormonal therapy is instituted, in which case endometriosis may persist. Pregnancy causes endometriosis to regress. Laparoscopic treatment of endometriosis may result in long periods of remission, though eventually disease usually recurs.

Fibroids, like endometriosis, grow under the influence of ovarian hormones. Fibroids also enlarge during pregnancy. Removal of hormonal stimulation at menopause results in regression of fibroid size. Fibroids are multicentric in origin and therefore may recur after removal. Following myomectomy, many women reach menopause before their fibroids recur.

Prevention

Celibacy is the only preventive factor for pelvic inflammatory disease and ectopic pregnancy, although condom usage is protection against both as well. Other causes for pelvic pain are not preventable.

Cost Containment

Pelvic pain can be debilitating, causing interference with normal marital relations and lost time from work and other activities. Laparoscopy should not be delayed when the diagnosis is in doubt or when symptoms persist following treatment. Early laparoscopic diagnosis and treatment of endometriosis or unruptured ectopic pregnancy make management of these diseases on an outpatient basis possible. Laparoscopic surgery in these cases avoids the need for laparotomy with hospital admission and allows return to work in only a few days instead of a 4- to 6-week recovery period following laparotomy. Initial surgical and hospital costs are lower with laparoscopic procedures and return to work is much quicker than with standard surgical procedures.

REFERENCES

Barbieri RL, Leiomyomata uteri. Semin Reprod Endocrinol 1992;10:301.

Carson KJ, Miller BA, Fowler FJ. The Maine Women's Health Study: II: Outcomes of nonsurgical management of leiomyomas, abnormal bleeding, and chronic pelvic pain. Obstet Gynecology, 1994;83(4):566.

Jones HW, Jones GS. Novak's textbook of gynecology. Baltimore: Williams & Wilkins, 1981.

Pernoll ML, Benson RC. Current obstetrics and gynecologic diagnosis and treatment. Norwalk, CT: Appleton & Lange, 1987.

Speroff L, Glass RH, Kase NG. Clinical gynecologic endocrinology and infertility. Baltimore: Williams & Wilkins, 1994.

CHAPTER 10–18

Pelvic Relaxation and Genital Prolapse

Louis W. Goolsby, M.D., and A. Gatewood Dudley, M.D.

DEFINITION

Pelvic relaxation and genital prolapse describe both symptomatic and asymptomatic defects of vaginal and uterine supportive tissues. Multiple anatomic defects usually result with pelvic organs protruding into the vagina or beyond the introitus. Pelvic floor dysfunction often accompanies anatomic defects.

ETIOLOGY

Genital prolapse results when intraabdominal pressure exceeds the resistance of vaginal and uterine supports. Possibilities include increased intraabdominal pressure, decreased resistance, or combinations of both. Obesity, chronic cough, and strenuous activity produce increased intraabdominal pressure. Inadequate or abnormal vaginal and uterine support probably indicates both congenital and acquired conditions. Congenital factors include absence of support structures, abnormal connective tissue, and inadequate innervation of pelvic musculature. Acquired factors include obstetric trauma, menopause, and pudendal neuropathy.

CRITERIA FOR DIAGNOSIS

Suggestive

Pelvic relaxation and genital prolapse may or may not produce symptoms. Symptoms of genital prolapse do not reliably correlate with severity or location of support defects.

Complaints of pelvic fullness or pressure suggest pelvic relaxation. Additional symptoms may indicate voiding, anorectal, and sexual dysfunction. Complaints of a mass or protrusion from the vagina usually indicate genital prolapse.

Definitive

Pelvic examination demonstrates downward displacement or protrusion of pelvic organs into the vagina or beyond the introitus. As intraabdominal pressure and gravity influence pelvic relaxation, correct diagnosis requires examination at rest and during maximal straining. Examination with the patient standing provides the most accurate information.

CLINICAL MANIFESTATIONS

Subjective

Symptoms

Most patients with symptomatic pelvic relaxation report general symptoms of pelvic pressure, pelvic fullness, and low backache. Often patients report a sensation of something "falling out" of the vagina. General symptoms characteristically worsen at day's end and just before and during menstruation. Symptoms do not improve with voiding or defecation.

Table 10–18–1 describes symptoms that indicate specific sites of genital prolapse. Urinary symptoms occur with defective support of the anterior vaginal segment. A pure cystocele may produce voiding difficulty requiring the patient to void standing or to replace the prolapsed bladder digitally before successfully voiding. More commonly, a cystourethrocele produces stress urinary incontinence, an involuntary loss of urine with increased intraabdominal pressure without bladder detrusor contraction.

Anorectal symptoms occur with defective support of the posterior vaginal segment and perineum. Rectocele may produce difficulty with defecation requiring the patient to replace the prolapsed rectum digitally before defecation. Anal incontinence usually indicates complete perineal laceration with disruption of the sphincter mechanism. With significant perineal defects, the patient and her partner may report the vagina is too loose for adequate sexual function.

Defective support of the superior vaginal segment usually produces general symptoms of pelvic relaxation already described. Uterine prolapse and enterocele result from inadequate support of the superior vaginal segment.

TABLE 10–18–1. PELVIC RELAXATION: ANATOMIC DEFECTS, DEFECT SITES, AND ASSOCIATED SYMPTOMS

Anatomic Defect and Site	Associated Symptoms
Urethrocele/urethra	Stress incontinence Falling out
Cystocele/bladder	Voiding difficulty Falling out
Prolapse/cervix or cuff	Falling out Heaviness
Enterocele/cul-de-sac	Pelvic fullness Falling out
Rectocele/rectum	True bowel pocket Falling out
Laceration/perineum	Anal incontinence Too loose

Modified from Baden WF, Walker T. Surgical repair of vaginal defects. Philadelphia: Lippincott, 1992:12. Reproduced with permission from the publisher and author.

Past History

Previous vaginal delivery near term represents the most common risk factor for pelvic relaxation. Previous pelvic and abdominal surgery, especially reparative surgery and hernia repairs, may indicate defective connective tissue. Estrogen replacement may improve symptoms if the patient experienced surgical or natural menopause. Pulmonary disorders producing chronic cough predispose development of pelvic relaxation.

Objective

Physical Examination

Pelvic examination performed at rest, during straining or Valsalva, and during contraction of pelvic musculature allows proper evaluation of vaginal and uterine support defects. Sometimes examination with the patient standing reveals significant abnormalities not detected in the dorsal lithotomy position. Two Sims specula assist with evaluation of each vaginal segment. The Sims speculum replaces the prolapsed portion, allowing visualization of each vaginal segment. During the examination the physician determines which vaginal segment descends first. After replacing this prolapsed segment with the Sims speculum the physician determines support in the remaining two vaginal segments. Documentation of the examination provides descriptions of each vaginal segment. In addition a grade assigned to each defect provides further explanation. The Halfway System, outlined in Table 10–18–2, provides uniform and reproducible descriptions of pelvic relaxation and genital prolapse.

TABLE 10–18–2. HALFWAY SYSTEM FOR GRADING RELAXATIONS

Urethrocele, Cystocele, Uterine Prolapse, Enterocele, and Rectocele: Grade Descent of Site with Patient Straining Firmly
Grade 0: Normal position for each site
Grade 1: Descent halfway to the hymen
Grade 2: Descent to the hymen
Grade 3: Descent halfway past the hymen
Grade 4: Maximal possible descent for each site

Perineal Laceration: Grade with Patient Contracting Perineal Muscles
Grade 0: Normal or superficial epithelial laceration
Grade 1: Laceration halfway to the anal sphincter
Grade 2: Laceration to the anal sphincter
Grade 3: Laceration involving anal sphincter
Grade 4: Laceration involving rectal mucosa

Modified from Baden WF, Walker T. Surgical repair of vaginal defects. Philadelphia: Lippincott, 1992:14. Reproduced with permission from the publisher and author.

Routine Laboratory Abnormalities

Urinary symptoms require urinalysis and urine culture to exclude urinary tract infections. Symptoms of vaginal discharge, odor, or vulvar irritation require examination of saline preparations and potassium hydroxide preparations from vaginal discharge. As complete uterine prolapse may result in cervical ulceration and abnormal vaginal bleeding, evaluation may require Pap smear, cervical biopsy, and endometrial biopsy.

PLANS
Diagnostic
Differential Diagnosis

Pelvic relaxation and genital prolapse produce general symptoms and site-specific symptoms that occur with disease processes involving other organ systems. Pelvic pressure and low backache may accompany gynecologic conditions such as uterine leiomyomata and endometriosis. Other possibilities include urologic, intestinal, orthopaedic, and neurologic diseases.

Diagnostic Options

Urinary incontinence requires evaluation to determine the etiology. A history of involuntary urine loss associated with increased intraabdominal pressure may indicate stress urinary incontinence. Confirmation requires reproducing urine loss during the examination and demonstrating loss of the acute angle at the urethrovesical junction. A cystometrogram provides further support for a diagnosis of stress urinary incontinence. Detrusor instability may mimic stress incontinence and represents the most common cause of urinary incontinence. Although stress incontinence responds to proper surgical treatment, detrusor instability is treated medically. As detrusor instability develops after certain surgical procedures for pelvic relaxation, many surgeons prefer performing urodynamic studies before surgery in continent women with pelvic relaxation.

Anal incontinence may result from complete perineal laceration with sphincter disruption. If the perineal body appears normal, then anorectal function studies may reveal neurologic disease as the cause of anal incontinence.

Recommended Approach

Most patients with pelvic relaxation receive adequate evaluation with complete history and physical examination, urinalysis and urine culture, and simple urologic evaluation. Patients with urge incontinence, mixed urge and stress incontinence, and prior failed surgery require multichannel urodynamic evaluation. Patients with an abnormal screening neurologic examination need complete neurologic evaluation. Neurologic disorders frequently explain the occurrence of urinary and anal incontinence with a normal perineal body.

Therapeutic
Therapeutic Options

Treatment goals include relief of symptoms with restoration of anatomy and function. Pelvic floor exercises, vaginal cones, and electrical stimulation increase strength and awareness of pelvic floor musculature. Correction of estrogen deficiency may improve symptoms. Alpha-adrenergic agonists may improve stress urinary incontinence. Weight reduction and treatment of chronic cough may produce symptomatic relief. Pessaries provide some women satisfactory symptom relief from pelvic relaxation and genital prolapse.

Surgery for pelvic relaxation requires careful evaluation of the entire patient with particular attention to specific pelvic support defects. Numerous corrective procedures exist using the patient's own tissue for repair or grafts from fascia or synthetic materials. Depending on the patient's individual needs, a vaginal, abdominal, or combined approach may become necessary. Operative goals include relief of symptoms, restoration of normal anatomy, and restoration of normal function. Considerable controversy exists on the correct operation for each de-

TABLE 10–18–3. THERAPEUTIC OPTIONS FOR SPECIFIC SITE DEFECTS, NONSURGICAL AND SURGICAL

Defect	Nonsurgical	Surgical
Urethrocele and cystocele	Pelvic floor exercises Electrical stimulation Vaginal cones Estrogen replacement Alpha-adrenergic agonists Pessary	Anterior colporrhaphy Needle suspension procedures Paravaginal repair Marshall–Marchetti–Krantz repair Burch colposuspension
Prolapse and enterocele	Pelvic floor exercises Estrogen replacement Pessary	Hysterectomy and vault suspension Sacrospinous ligament fixation Abdominal sacrocolpopexy Moschcowitz or Halban culdoplasty
Rectocele	Pelvic floor exercises Estrogen replacement Pessary	Posterior colporrhaphy
Perineal laceration	Pelvic floor exercises	Perineorrhaphy Anal sphincter repair

fect. Table 10–18–3 summarizes general procedures utilized for specific site defects.

Recommended Approach

Proper identification and correction of each support defect promise optimal results. In general, stress urinary incontinence requires a retropubic procedure with an abdominal approach. As anterior vaginal suspension increases the posterior cul-de-sac, the successful procedure must include adequate attention to the superior vaginal segment. Possibilities include obliteration of the posterior cul-de-sac with the Moschcowitz or Halban procedure. Vaginal vault suspension with sacrocolpopexy or sacrospinous ligament fixation produces excellent results. Posterior vaginal segment defects require a vaginal approach. Perineorrhaphy and posterior colporrhaphy produce good long-term results. Anal incontinence due to sphincter disruption is treated with anal sphincter repair.

FOLLOW-UP

Patients treated medically return frequently to evaluate compliance and response. Pessary use requires weekly follow-up initially and every 1 to 3 months later to detect vaginal or cervical ulceration or infections. Postoperative patients return for evaluation 2 and 6 weeks after surgery and then resume routine examination at 6 or 12 months.

DISCUSSION
Prevalence and Incidence

Clinically detectable pelvic relaxation follows approximately 50% of vaginal deliveries at term. About 10 to 20% of women develop symptoms or prolapse severe enough to require surgery.

Related Basic Science

No one etiology or mechanism adequately explains pelvic relaxation and genital prolapse. Evidence suggests that anatomic, biochemical, histologic, and neurologic changes influence the disease process. These changes reflect genetic influence and acquired factors.

Anatomic Derangement

The vaginal wall consists of an inner mucosa surrounded by an outer sheath of endopelvic fascia. Extensions of endopelvic fascia, or sheath supports, attach the vaginal sheath to the pelvic wall, or bony pelvis. Three paired tendinous arches participate in attachment of the sheath anteriorly, superiorly, laterally, and posteriorly. Anatomic defects may result from disruption of the fascial sheath or detachment of sheath supports.

The cervix and upper vagina receive suspensory and attachment support from the uterosacral and cardinal ligaments. Pubocervical fascia supports the bladder and urethrovesical junction. Rectovaginal fascia prevents anterior bulging of the rectum. The lower vagina fuses with the levator ani, urogenital diaphragm, and perineal body. Anatomic defects include loss of one or more mechanisms from suspension, attachment, and fusion.

Altered Molecular Biology

Biopsies from pubococcygeal muscle and pubocervical fascia indicate muscle damage, decreased fibroblasts, and increased collagen fibers in patients with genital prolapse compared with patients without genital prolapse. The quality of connective tissue may influence the severity of pelvic relaxation and the response to nonsurgical and surgical treatments.

Physiologic or Metabolic Derangement

Measurements of pudendal and perineal nerve motor terminal latencies demonstrate significant prolongation in women with prolapse compared with women without prolapse. Pudendal nerve damage contributes to urinary incontinence, fecal incontinence, and prolapse. Predisposing factors for pudendal nerve damage include multiparity, forceps delivery, prolonged second stage of labor, and third-degree perineal laceration, and macrosomia.

Natural History and Its Modification with Treatment

Anatomic defects usually worsen with time due to aging, menopause, and acquired medical conditions. Estrogen replacement and conservative measures may retard progression of pelvic relaxation, but the condition never spontaneously disappears. Appropriate surgical treatment successfully improves or eliminates most symptoms or defects. Some patients experience recurrences despite appropriate, well-performed procedures.

Prevention

Effective preventive strategies remain unconfirmed or unidentified. As effective nonsurgical treatments exist for pelvic relaxation, it appears reasonable to use the same strategies for prevention. Many physicians recommend pelvic floor exercises after vaginal delivery as a prophylactic measure. No study confirms or rejects the effectiveness of routine pelvic floor exercises.

A review of predisposing factors indicates several recommendations appropriate for general health. Proper diet and exercise prevent obesity and chronic constipation. Avoidance or elimination of cigarette smoking reduces risk of chronic lung disease and chronic cough. Strenuous physical exertion requires attention to posture and correct lifting methods. These general health recommendations address the predisposing factors of obesity, chronic cough, constipation, and strenuous occupation.

Iatrogenic factors contribute to pelvic relaxation. Proper repair of episiotomy and obstetric lacerations may prevent future development of pelvic relaxation. Adequate evaluation and management of vaginal support with hysterectomy provide an opportunity to prevent pelvic relaxation.

Cost Containment

Symptomatic pelvic relaxation includes urinary and fecal incontinence. Patients avoid reporting these symptoms out of shame or fear. In the elderly, incontinence represents the second most common cause for nursing home placement. Astronomic costs result from purchase of absorbent products and diapers, medications for skin breakdown and urinary infections, and materials and personnel time used in changing bedding. Chronic urethral catheterization and associated complications contribute to medical expenses related to pelvic relaxation. The majority of incontinent patients improve with proper evaluation and treatment. Physicians must ask patients about incontinence and institute proper evaluation and management to effectively reduce costs.

Proper evaluation and management need not involve expensive testing or surgery. Simple office tests and nonsurgical treatments produce satisfactory results. Effective surgical treatment requires proper preoperative evaluation and a comprehensive operation that addresses all anatomic defects.

REFERENCES

Baden WF, Walker T. Surgical repair of vaginal defects. Philadelphia: Lippincott, 1992.

Benson JT. Female pelvic floor disorders. New York: Norton Medical Books, 1992.

DeLancey JO. Anatomic aspects of vaginal eversion after hysterectomy. Am J Obstet Gynecol 1992;166:1717.

Rosenzweig BA, Pushkin S, Blumenfeld D, Bhatia NN. Prevalence of abnormal urodynamic test results in continent women with severe genitourinary prolapse. Obstet Gynecol 1992;79:539.

CHAPTER 10–19

Pregnancy

Paul C. Browne, M.D., and Lewis H. Hamner III, M.D.

DEFINITION

Pregnancy is defined as a successful fertilization of the human oocyte followed by implantation in the human body. The overwhelming majority of pregnancies diagnosed in the United States (97–99%) result from sexual intercourse, spontaneous fertilization, and intrauterine implantation. Extrauterine pregnancies are abnormal pregnancies where successful fertilization has occurred, but implantation has occurred outside of the uterine cavity. These include tubal ectopic pregnancies, cornual ectopic pregnancies, primary abdominal pregnancies, and secondary abdominal pregnancies. Molar pregnancy (gestational trophoblastic disease) and choriocarcinoma represent an abnormal fertilization process that results in neoplastic placental tumors. These tumors are almost always intrauterine.

ETIOLOGY

Pregnancy is not a disease process. Approximately 50 to 75% of pregnancies in the United States result from intentional conception by the parent couple. A small percentage of pregnancies in the United States result from assisted reproductive technology (ART). These processes include ovulation induction, intrauterine insemination of sperm, and intrauterine instillation of fertilized embryos through in vitro fertilization (IVF) and gamete intrafallopian transfer (GIFT). The remaining pregnancies are unplanned and are diagnosed based on the patient's clinical history, physical examination, and laboratory findings.

CRITERIA FOR DIAGNOSIS

Suggestive

The triad of amenorrhea, breast tenderness, and nausea represent the most common presenting complaints of pregnant women. The pregnant patient's uterus is abnormally large. Most parent couples who are attempting pregnancy have confirmed the diagnosis of pregnancy with a home urine laboratory test (urinary human chorionic gonadotropin, beta subunit). Amenorrhea without other symptoms is also highly suggestive of pregnancy, especially if the patient has a normal menstrual history. Pregnancy must be considered in the differential diagnosis in any female patient of reproductive age who presents with abnormal bleeding. Symptoms such as presyncope, syncope, nausea, vomiting, and breast tenderness are suggestive of pregnancy in a woman of reproductive age, but are not diagnostic.

Definitive

The definitive diagnosis of pregnancy can be made by confirming the presence of human chorionic gonadotropin in maternal blood or urine. Definitive diagnosis can also be achieved with ultrasound of the female pelvis. Ultrasound images confirming the presence of intrauterine placental tissue, fetal tissue, and cardiac activity would give equivalent accuracy in diagnosis. A pelvic ultrasound examination that fails to confirm intrauterine pregnancy in a patient with a positive human chorionic gonadotropin should be considered highly suspicious for ectopic pregnancy.

CLINICAL MANIFESTATIONS

Subjective

Most pregnant women present to their physician with amenorrhea following voluntary attempts at conception. Menstrual cycle duration in normal human women ranges from 21 to 35 days. Cycle intervals longer than 35 days are highly suspicious for pregnancy. Breast tenderness and nausea are common symptoms of pregnant women in their early first trimester.

The patient's past medical history is extremely important, especially in the diagnosis of extrauterine pregnancy. Ectopic pregnancies are much more common in patients with previous pelvic inflammatory disease, severe endometriosis, and infertility. Ectopic pregnancies are also more common in patients who have had gamete intrafallopian transfer. The physician should seek pertinent history regarding these risk factors for ectopic pregnancy. Also pertinent in the patient's past medical history is her past reproductive performance. Patients with recurrent pregnancy loss or previous ectopic pregnancy are at high risk for spontaneous abortion and recurrent ectopic pregnancy.

The patient's family history is important to determine risks for pregnancy-related conditions such as gestational diabetes and pregnancy-induced hypertension. A strong family history of glucose intolerance or hypertension places the patient at risk for pregnancy complications. The family history is critical to determine the patient's risk for fetal genetic diseases. Family histories of trisomy 21 (Down syndrome), sickle cell trait, and cystic fibrosis are examples of genetic risk factors for the pregnant woman. (See Discussion, Related Basic Science, Genetics.)

Objective

Physical Examination

The most common diagnostic physical finding for pregnancy is a central pelvic mass. During early pregnancy, the mass may not be appreciated on abdominal examination. By the midtrimester, the pelvic mass enlarges above the symphysis pubis, and can be felt abdominally. The cervix develops a cyanotic coloring (Chadwick's sign). The breasts are tender and mildly edematous.

An adnexal mass found on examination during early pregnancy may represent a corpus luteum cyst of the ovary; however, an adnexal mass may also be a positive physical finding in ectopic pregnancies and should be immediately evaluated in a patient in the first trimester. Doppler ultrasound can be used to confirm the presence of fetal heart tones in patients greater than 10 weeks' gestation. In patients prior to 10 weeks of gestation, fetal cardiac activity can be confirmed by B-mode ultrasound.

Routine Laboratory Abnormalities

The majority of pregnant women develop a mild anemia in the third trimester. This anemia is a multifactorial anemia resulting from iron deficiency and hemodilution in most cases. Serum platelet count rises in early pregnancy, but returns to normal levels in the late third trimester. White blood cell counts remain unchanged, and can be used as an indicator of infection if elevated.

Mild elevations in levels of liver enzymes, specifically alkaline phosphatase and lactate dehydrogenase (LDH), are also seen during normal pregnancy; however, other liver enzymes such as serum aminotransferases (aspartate transaminase, glutamic–oxaloacetic acid transaminase) remain in the normal range, as does serum bilirubin. Approximately 3% of all pregnant women develop glucose intolerance during pregnancy. The diagnosis is made by elevations in postprandial blood sugars (Rapid Glucose Screen [RGS] or 3-hour glucose tolerance test [GTT]). Gross elevations in serum glucose (greater than 120 mg%) are abnormal and should prompt testing for gestational diabetes. Glycosuria is a fairly common finding in normal pregnant women and should not be used to diagnose glucose intolerance during pregnancy.

Renal function studies reflect an increase in glomerular filtration. Creatinine clearance increases to supernormal levels by the second trimester (125–175 mL/min). Urea nitrogen (BUN) and creatinine levels fall slightly during pregnancy. Twenty-four-hour urine protein collections should reflect protein values of less than 200 mg in normal pregnancy. Microalbuminuria (24-hour protein values of 200–500 mg) has been associated with an increased risk of gestational hypertension or preeclampsia. Gross proteinuria (greater than 500 mg/24 h) is always associated with significant pathology such as preeclampsia, glomerulonephritis, or pyelonephritis. Semiquantitative urine chemistry tests for glucose, protein, and ketones should remain negative throughout pregnancy. Ketonuria is a common finding in hyperemesis gravidarum and in clinical infectious states. Proteinuria is found most commonly with urinary tract infections and preeclampsia. Persistent proteinuria may indicate underlying glomerulonephritis in patients with no evidence of urinary tract infections or hypertension.

Chest radiography shows a mild, symmetric cardiomegaly from early pregnancy. The electrocardiogram is not altered by pregnancy, but reflects a slight increase in baseline heart rate.

The presence of pregnancy can be confirmed by elevation in human chorionic gonadotropin, found either in serum or in urine. Elevation of human chorionic gonadotropin in serum is found most commonly in pregnancy. Rarely, human chorionic gonadotropin may be elevated in patients with malignant germ cell neoplasms of the ovary. Other fetal-specific proteins include alpha-fetoprotein and human placental lactogen. Elevations in estriol and progesterone are associated with placental production of these hormones during pregnancy.

PLANS

Diagnostic

Differential Diagnosis

The differential diagnosis of pregnancy concerns primarily exclusion of abnormal pregnancies such as spontaneous abortion, extrauterine (ectopic) pregnancy, and gestational trophoblastic disease (molar pregnancy). Elevations in human chorionic gonadotropin are rarely seen in the absence of pregnancy and most likely represent laboratory error. Rarely, diagnosis of malignant germ cell tumors is made by elevation in human chorionic gonadotropin.

Diagnostic Options

Table 10–19–1 details the recommended laboratory studies to be performed at a first obstetric visit.

An increase in thyroxine-binding globulin alters the normal range for thyroid function tests during pregnancy. The triiodothyrodine uptake (T_3U) values are lower and the thyroxine (T_4) values higher in normal pregnancy. Values for thyroid index (T_7) and thyroid-stimulating hormone remain normal in pregnancy. Thyroid stimulating hormone is the most sensitive indicator of abnormal thyroid function during pregnancy.

During a first encounter visit for pregnancy, the most important diagnoses to confirm are the intrauterine location of the pregnancy and the presence of positive fetal cardiac activity. If the patient has risk factors for extrauterine pregnancy, diagnostic pelvic ultrasound should be performed immediately to exclude the presence of adnexal masses,

TABLE 10–19–1. DIAGNOSIS OF PREGNANCY BY COMMON CLINICAL AND LABORATORY FINDINGS

	Subjective	Objective	Laboratory
Early pregnancy	Amenorrhea Breast tenderness Nausea/ vomiting	Central pelvic mass	Elevated human chorionic gonadotropin Ultrasound
Late pregnancy	Amenorrhea Quickening (fetal movement)	Abdominal mass Fetal heart tone auscultation	Elevated human chorionic gonadotropin Ultrasound

hematoperitoneum, and so on. The use of Doppler ultrasound (fetoscope) or B-mode ultrasound should accurately confirm the presence of fetal heart tones in patients with a viable pregnancy. If diagnostic ultrasound fails to confirm the presence of intrauterine pregnancy, the patient should undergo an evaluation for an ectopic pregnancy.

The diagnosis of spontaneous abortion is usually suspected based on the absence of fetal cardiac activity or the onset of bleeding in early pregnancy. Patients with a confirmed intrauterine pregnancy and lack of fetal heart tones must be presumed to be at risk for spontaneous abortion. Although fetal cardiac activity may not be detected accurately by diagnostic ultrasound prior to 6 weeks from the last menstrual period, patients with gestational ages greater than 6 weeks should have positive fetal cardiac activity on ultrasound. Disorganized echo patterns within the uterus in early pregnancy may suggest the possibility of incomplete spontaneous abortion or ectopic pregnancy. Even small amounts of vaginal bleeding (spotting) may be suggestive of spontaneous abortion. The evaluation for a patient with suspected spontaneous abortion should include a quantitative human chorionic gonadotropin, a diagnostic pelvic ultrasound to confirm fetal cardiac activity, and a pelvic examination to exclude dilation of the cervix. Patients with abnormally low human chorionic gonadotropin levels, absent fetal cardiac activity, or cervical dilation in early pregnancy should be considered to be at high risk for spontaneous abortion.

In the midtrimester, cervical dilation in the absence of other symptoms of spontaneous abortion may suggest incompetent cervix. Vaginal bleeding in the absence of other symptoms of spontaneous abortion may result from postcoital trauma, vaginal infection, or hemorrhoidal bleeding. Absent fetal cardiac activity without other signs of spontaneous abortion is only normal in patients at extremely early gestational ages (5–6 weeks). Follow-up ultrasound 7 to 10 days after the initial evaluation should confirm fetal cardiac activity in patients whose pregnancies are viable.

Recommended Approach

The recommended diagnostic approach for confirmation of pregnancy is as follows: pelvic examination; cervical examination; qualitative human chorionic gonadotropin (serum, urine); and ultrasound if patient is thought to be at risk for spontaneous abortion or extrauterine pregnancy.

Therapeutic

Therapeutic Options

If the diagnosis of pregnancy is incidental to a medical evaluation for other cause, an obstetrician should be consulted regarding patient management. The obstetrician should assist in determining which medical therapies are appropriate. In patients undergoing evaluation for surgery, obstetric consultation is mandatory. Nonessential surgical operations should be postponed until after the patient's delivery. Essential surgical procedures (appendectomy, trauma, etc.) should never be delayed in pregnant patients, regardless of gestational age. In these instances, the health of the mother is the most important factor in preserving a viable pregnancy.

In nonemergent patient encounters, the patient should be prescribed prenatal vitamins. These vitamin supplements should contain at least 1 mg of folic acid and at least 60 mg of elemental iron daily. The patient should be advised that the prenatal vitamins may cause mild nausea and mild constipation, and may change stool color to green-black.

If patients are experiencing nausea, dizziness, and other vagal symptoms, antiemetic medication may be given to improve the patient's hyperemesis. The most common treatments include promethazine 12.5 to 25 mg orally every 6 to 8 hours, or promethazine (rectal suppositories) 25 mg every 6 hours. An alternative antiemetic medication is prochlorperazine 10 mg orally every 4 to 6 hours. The patient may also take prochlorperazine as a 25-mg rectal suppository every 6 hours. Both promethazine and prochlorperazine may cause tardive dyskinesia. The patient should be warned of these possible side effects. Patients who cannot tolerate the extrapyramidal side effects of these phenothiazines may be given haloperidol 1 to 2 mg orally every 8 hours. Haloperidol may also be given as an intramuscular injection of 1 mg every 6 to 8 hours. Patients with intractable nausea and vomiting in early pregnancy may also benefit from metoclopramide 10 mg orally every 6 hours to accelerate gastric emptying.

Recommended Approach

Following the confirmation of intrauterine pregnancy, the patient should be referred to an appropriate obstetric provider (obstetrician, family practitioner, or certified nurse-midwife) for prenatal care. Nonemergent laboratory studies (such as those outlined in Table 10–19–2) can be safely postponed until the initial obstetric evaluation.

If the diagnosis of pregnancy is made in association with a medical/surgical evaluation for a nonrelated condition, then consultation with an obstetrician is necessary. Guidance regarding appropriate radiographic tests, laboratory tests, and medical/surgical therapies should be offered by the obstetrician to assist in the care of the patient by a nonobstetrician.

Diagnosis of spontaneous abortion or extrauterine (ectopic) pregnancy demands immediate consultation with a gynecologist for surgical treatment.

FOLLOW-UP

Routine prenatal care for uncomplicated pregnant patients includes a monthly physician's visit during the first 6 months of the pregnancy. During the final 3 months of the pregnancy, the frequency of the visits gradually increases from monthly to weekly. The frequency of visits is determined by the complexity of the patient's pregnancy. Routine laboratory studies detailed in Table 10–19–2 can be postponed until the patient's first outpatient obstetric visit if the initial diagnosis of pregnancy is made in the emergency room.

If ectopic pregnancy is suspected, a gynecologic surgeon should be consulted regarding surgical diagnosis and treatment. The majority of ectopic pregnancies can be removed laparoscopically. Laparoscopic treatment decreases patient morbidity and shortens hospitalization.

When spontaneous abortion is suspected, the gynecologic surgeon must advise the patient regarding her options: surgical treatment or conservative management.

TABLE 10–19–2. STANDARD PRENATAL LABORATORY TESTS DURING PREGNANCY

New Visit	16–20 Weeks	26–28 Weeks
Hematology panel	Maternal serum alpha-fetoprotein	Diabetes screen
Blood type, Rh	Genetic studies—amniocentesis*	
Antibody screen	Ultrasound*	
Rubella IgG		
Syphilis serology		
Hepatitis B surface antigen		
Urine culture		
Cervical cytology		
Gonorrhea culture*		
Chlamydia antigen*		
Genetic studies—chorionic villus sampling*		

*Where indicated.

DISCUSSION

Prevalence and Incidence

Consistently, 2 to 5% of women of reproductive age are pregnant in most industrialized countries. Approximately 85% of parent couples attempting to achieve pregnancy are successful without medical intervention. In the remaining 15% of couples, approximately half are found to have a female etiology for infertility and half are found to have a male etiology for infertility. Based on the accuracy of diagnostic methods, 15 to 33% of early pregnancies are spontaneously aborted. One to two percent of pregnancies have ectopic implantation. In pregnancies that enter the third trimester, the perinatal mortality averages 6 to 15 per 1000, depending on geographic location in the United States.

Related Basic Science

Genetics

Genetic studies of products of conception are important in cases of spontaneous abortion or molar pregnancy (gestational trophoblastic disease). Approximately 50% of spontaneously aborted pregnancies are found to have chromosomal abnormalities by karyotype. Common genetic abnormalities include monosomy X (Turner's syndrome), autosomal trisomies, and triploidy. In cases of gestational trophoblastic disease, placental tissue may be found to be diploid (usually two copies of paternal chromosomes) or triploid (one copy of maternal chromosomes, two copies of paternal chromosomes).

With the explosive advance of technology for antepartum genetic diagnosis, it is now possible to make antepartum diagnosis of literally thousands of familial genetic diseases. In most cases, the patients have a family history suggestive of a particular autosomal recessive illness. Using karyotype analysis, restriction length fragment polymorphism, and family linkage studies, patients not only can obtain information about their carrier status for genetic diseases, but may also obtain informative studies regarding the genetic status of their fetus. The three most common genetic diseases that should prompt carrier status testing in adult women are cystic fibrosis, sickle cell anemia, and Tay-Sach's disease. Currently, there is intense debate within the medical community regarding the utility of "routine" carrier status testing of adult females for genetic diseases. Patients should be informed about the possibility of voluntary carrier status diagnosis and antepartum diagnosis in their fetus. Formal genetics counseling is usually indicated for patients with a family history of genetic disease.

Altered Molecular Biology

The molecular biological changes of the female body that occur to accommodate pregnancy are beyond the scope of this textbook. The reader is referred to the References for literature regarding biochemical changes that occur during normal pregnancy.

Physiologic or Metabolic Derangement

Over the 266-day human pregnancy, the uterus increases in mass dramatically to accommodate the growing fetus(es). This is accomplished solely by muscle hypertrophy. The combined actions of progesterone and prostaglandin gradually thin or efface the myometrial wall. Blood flow through the uterus at term may constitute 15% of total cardiac output. Even more remarkably, the uterus resumes its normal shape and size within 40 days of delivery.

The cardiovascular system adjusts to the increased oxygen demands of the pregnant woman by increasing cardiac output. This is done by a combination of increased chamber size, increased heart rate, and decreased peripheral resistance. A 40% increase in blood volume is experienced during pregnancy. This hefty increase is made possible by peripheral venous dilation, although much of this blood resides in the growing uterus and placenta. The pregnant woman is therefore in a state of maximum cardiac efficiency. Significant cardiovascular disease reduces maternal ability to accommodate increased cardiovascular demands and may result in disability or death.

Functional residual capacity decreases during pregnancy in response to the enlarging uterus. In contrast, tidal volumes are relatively unaffected. The most common compensatory mechanism of the pregnant woman is a slight rise in respiratory rate late in pregnancy. Oxygenation and ventilation are rarely affected by pregnancy in the absence of underlying pulmonary disease. The most common pulmonary complications found during pregnancy are bronchospasm, pneumonia, and influenza. Patients with these complications may develop respiratory insufficiency in the third trimester of pregnancy.

Many hematologic changes occur during the first 5 months of pregnancy. The dramatic increase in blood volume requires that red blood cell mass increase by 25 to 50%. This almost always results in a degree of anemia in the normal pregnant woman. Iron deficiency results in an exacerbated microcytic hypochromic anemia. Free water retention increases late in pregnancy, resulting in a physiologic "dilutional" anemia. Evaluation of anemia in pregnancy is therefore complex, as the contribution of these varying influences must be assessed. Blood losses of up to 1000 mL during labor and delivery are well tolerated by the normal pregnant woman. White blood cell counts are not significantly altered during pregnancy. Platelet counts increase early in pregnancy, then gradually fall in late pregnancy due to increased consumption. A well recognized cellular immune deficiency that occurs in pregnancy results from alterations in T-cell distribution; however, humoral immunity is unaffected, as are plasma cell numbers.

Alterations in other organ systems during pregnancy are less dramatic. Gastrointestinal discomforts are common during pregnancy, but are related to mechanical obstruction and motility. There are minor musculoskeletal changes thought secondary to hormonal levels of progesterone that include laxity of tendons and joint relaxation. These changes are reversed promptly after delivery. There are no known alterations in neurologic function during pregnancy except in the presence of maternal disease.

Anatomic Derangement

The most common anatomic changes during pregnancy include enlargement of the uterus, enlargement of the breasts, enlargement of the heart, and physiologic edema. The approximate gestational age of the pregnancy can be estimated by uterine size in the first trimester. By 6 weeks' estimated gestational age, the uterus is the size of a tennis ball or tangerine. By 8 weeks' gestation, the uterus is baseball size or orange size. By 10 to 12 weeks' gestation, the uterus is usually the size of a softball or grapefruit. The uterine fundal height (measured from the cephalad portion of the symphysis pubis to the highest point of the myometrium) reaches the umbilicus by 20 weeks' gestation in most uncomplicated pregnancies. As a usual rule of thumb, the fundal height increases 1 cm per week from 16 weeks until 36 weeks.

Chest radiograms performed on patients after the first trimester show mild symmetric cardiomegaly. In advanced pregnancies, there may be mild elevation of the diaphragm. Breast size gradually increases from early pregnancy until the early third trimester. The patient may begin having leakage of breast fluid (colostrum) in the late third trimester. Most patients have a slow and progressive onset of edema in the lower extremities, hands, and face from 20 weeks until term. Much of the weight gain in the third trimester can be attributed to physiologic edema and fluid retention in pregnant women.

Natural History and its Modification with Treatment

The average duration of human pregnancy is 280 days from the onset of the patient's last menstrual period. In the United States, approximately 75 to 80% of patients deliver vaginally at the completion of their pregnancy. The remaining patients deliver by cesarean section for a variety of reasons including cephalopelvic disproportion, abnormal progress of labor, fetal distress, and malpresentation. Following delivery, most patients experience 3 to 4 weeks of postpartum bleeding (lochia). The bleeding, initially heavy, rapidly decreases within 48 to 72 hours of delivery. The onset of spontaneous menses is delayed in patients who breastfeed. In patients who do not breastfeed, the resumption of spontaneous menses usually occurs 6 to 8 weeks following delivery.

The anemia of pregnancy can be dramatically improved by supplementing the patient with folic acid and iron. This single intervention has improved pregnancy outcome for the majority of patients in industrialized countries. The physiologic edema of pregnancy can be improved with increasing bed rest. Knee-length support stockings can often be used to alleviate lower-extremity paresthesias from peripheral edema.

Prevention

Pregnancy prevention is a major public health goal in many parts of the world. Contraception and abortion technology have stirred religious, political, and moral debate; however, there is excellent epidemiologic evidence that pregnancy poses a greater threat to maternal health than contraception. Several maternal conditions pose grave threats to maternal health during pregnancy, such as Eisenmenger's syndrome, aortic stenosis, mitral stenosis, pulmonary hypertension, polymyositis, severe lupus erythematosus, muscular dystrophy, and cystic fibrosis. Patients with these conditions should be strongly encouraged to practice contraception and avoid pregnancy.

There are six major categories of contraceptive technology: surgical sterilization, endocrine contraception, intrauterine devices, barrier contraception, abortion, and male contraception. All are discussed in detail in Chapter 10–16.

Cost Containment

Universal prenatal/neonatal care would likely be the most cost-effective measure that could be instituted regarding pregnancy. Lack of prenatal and neonatal care significantly increases the risk of poor maternal and neonatal outcomes; however, current efforts at cost containment in obstetrics have been aimed at limiting available technology.

Expensive maternal screening programs such as serum α-fetoprotein testing and genetic amniocentesis have been shown to be cost effective when directed at appropriate subpopulations. Universal use of these screening programs may not, however, be cost effective in certain populations. In the next 20 years, a large number of genetic probes (restriction fragment length polymorphism) will become available to test for autosomal and sex-linked diseases such as cystic fibrosis, sickle cell disease, muscular dystrophy, and hemophilia. This technology will likely be expensive and may only be cost effective in certain, defined patient groups. Careful scrutiny of proposed maternal screening programs may appropriately reduce expenditure on prenatal care.

Ultrasound has been targeted as one area where pregnancy costs could be contained. The American College of Obstetricians and Gynecologists does not recommend routine ultrasound examinations during pregnancy. Controversial studies such as the RADIUS study have concluded that routine obstetric ultrasound does not alter pregnancy outcome in low-risk patients (LeFevre, et al., 1993). Currently, the majority of patients in the United States undergo obstetric ultrasound during their pregnancy (92% in the RADIUS study). Certainly, the high cost of multiple ultrasound procedures during pregnancy can be reduced by judicious use of ultrasound imaging in selected patients.

REFERENCES

Creasy RK, Resnik R. Maternal–fetal medicine: Principles and practice. Philadelphia: Saunders, 1994.

Cunningham FG. Williams' obstetrics. Norwalk, CT: Appleton & Lange, 1993.

Gabbe SG, Niebyl JR, Simpson JL. Obstetrics: Normal and problem pregnancies. New York: Churchill Livingstone, 1991.

LeFevre ML, Bain RP, Ewigman BG, et al. A randomized trial of prenatal ultrasound screening: Impact on maternal management and outcome. Am J Obstet Gynecol 1993;169:483.

Ultrasonography in pregnancy. American College of Obstetricians and Gynecologists Technical Bulletin, 1993:187.

Ectopic Pregnancy

Lewis H. Hamner III, M.D., Michael D. Graubert, M.D., and Paul C. Browne, M.D.

DEFINITION

Ectopic pregnancy may be defined as the implantation of a fertilized ovum outside of the uterine cavity. Approximately 95% of ectopic pregnancies occur within the fallopian tubes, the majority being in the distal or ampullary portion. Nontubal ectopic gestations are most likely to be found in the ovaries, abdominal cavity, or cervix.

ETIOLOGY

The etiology of ectopic pregnancy includes infection, prior tubal surgery, and peritubal adhesions from prior pelvic surgery. The increased occurrence of pelvic inflammatory disease is largely responsible for the dramatic increasing incidence of ectopic pregnancy. It has been postulated that the use of antibiotics has actually increased ectopic gestations by allowing patency in a scarred tube. *Chlamydia* infection may cause irreparable damage to the tube without history of pelvic inflammatory disease. The damage is most likely the result of an untreated, subclinical infection. The association between prior use of an intrauterine device and ectopic pregnancy is most likely due to the increased incidence of pelvic inflammatory disease and subclinical infections in intrauterine device users.

Functional tubal defects leading to ectopic implantation include poor ciliary activity and hormonal imbalances that alter normal tubal transport.

CRITERIA FOR DIAGNOSIS

Subjective

Ectopic pregnancy must be suspected when a woman of reproductive age presents with abdominal pain combined with amenorrhea or irregular vaginal bleeding. A sensitive beta human chorionic gonadotropin test will confirm pregnancy.

Definitive

Ultrasound may assist in the diagnosis of ectopic pregnancy by identifying the lack of an intrauterine gestation, but a definitive diagnosis can be made only by visualization of an extrauterine embryo on ultrasound, by laparoscopy, or by exploratory laparotomy.

CLINICAL MANIFESTATIONS

Subjective

Greater than 95% of all patients with ectopic gestation complain of abdominal or pelvic pain. The pain may be generalized, bilateral, or even contralateral to the ectopic site. Localized pelvic pain is thought to indicate distention of the fallopian tube, whereas tubal rupture is suggested by shoulder pain occurring from irritation of the diaphragm due to hemoperitoneum. Ectopic pregnancies implanted in the isthmic or proximal portions of the tube present earlier and are more likely to rupture than implantations in the distal tube, because the ampullary portion is capable of sustaining a larger gestational mass.

Greater than 75% of patients present with amenorrhea in conjunction with abdominal symptoms, usually several weeks after a missed period. More than half the patients may complain of abnormal vaginal bleeding and may describe their last period as "light" or irregular in duration or onset. This most likely represents endometrial shedding and may be confused with a normal period by the patient and the physician. Other symptoms that are associated with ectopic pregnancy but occur with less frequency include nausea, vomiting, syncope, dizziness, and shoulder pain due to referred pain from diaphragmatic irritation.

Ectopic pregnancy is a diagnostic challenge for many practicing clinicians due to the extreme variability of the presenting symptoms. A majority of women with ectopic pregnancy are seen by a physician at least once before the hospital admission that establishes the diagnosis. Even more alarming is the finding that of the women who die of ectopic pregnancy each year, more than 50% are misdiagnosed by their physician. Risk factors for ectopic pregnancy include the presence of pelvic inflammatory disease, use of an intrauterine device, prior tubal surgery, infertility, and prior ectopic pregnancy. These risk factors should be listed in a careful history.

Objective

Physical Examination

Findings on physical examination are also highly variable among patients. Tubal rupture will be associated with orthostatic blood pressure and pulse changes if greater than 10% of blood volume is lost. This surgical emergency is uncommon. Other signs suggestive of less dramatic hemoperitoneum include a low-grade fever, rebound tenderness, and abdominal wall guarding from peritoneal irritation. Half of the patients with ectopic pregnancy have a palpable adnexal mass on pelvic examination that may be tender. Greater than 10% of patients have a contralateral adnexal mass most likely from an enlarged corpus luteum cyst. There is often cervical motion tenderness. The uterus is often soft and normal in size, but may be enlarged slightly from a deciduation or pooling of blood.

Routine Laboratory Abnormalities

A complete blood count assists in the workup, but a sensitive beta human chorionic gonadotropin assay is the most important biochemical test used in the initial diagnosis of ectopic pregnancy. A positive test confirms the existence of pregnancy, but a single beta human chorionic gonadotropin level does not differentiate an intrauterine from an extrauterine pregnancy. Serial beta human chorionic gonadotropin measurements have been quite useful in the detection of abnormal pregnancy including ectopic gestation. As stated earlier, ultrasound may assist in the diagnosis of ectopic pregnancy by identifying the lack of an intrauterine gestation, but a definitive diagnosis can be made only by visualization of an extrauterine embryo.

PLANS

Diagnostic

Differential Diagnosis

Ectopic pregnancy is frequently misdiagnosed as pelvic inflammatory disease. Pelvic inflammatory disease is associated with leukocytosis, fever, and often cervical discharge, but this may not be the case in low-grade infections. Appendicitis is also included in the differential diagnosis. Again, a complete blood count assists in the workup. Other clinical disorders difficult to distinguish from ectopic pregnancy include ruptured corpus luteum cyst with an intrauterine pregnancy and threatened or incomplete abortion.

Diagnostic Options

Serial beta human chorionic gonadotropin measurements are useful in recognizing an abnormal gestation. Ultrasound assists in the diagnosis of intrauterine contents, but the diagnosis of incomplete abortion is definitively made from the finding of chorionic tissue on intrauterine curettage. The finding of decidua without chorionic tissue on endometrial sampling indicates ectopic gestation. Because dilation and curettage will interrupt a potentially normal intrauterine pregnancy, it should not be used to assist the diagnosis of an abnormal pregnancy unless the clinical suspicion is extremely high.

Ultrasound examination of the pelvis may provide a definitive diagnosis of ectopic pregnancy by demonstrating extrauterine fetal cardiac activity. This, unfortunately, is a late finding. Traditionally, ultrasound has been most useful at identifying the presence of an intrauterine pregnancy, which would almost always exclude the diagnosis of ectopic pregnancy in women who had a positive beta human chorionic gonadotropin test. Kadar et al. (1981) developed the notion of a "discriminatory zone" of human chorionic gonadotropin in which an intrauterine pregnancy becomes detectable by abdominal ultrasound. The inability to visualize an intrauterine gestational sac in women with a discriminatory zone between 6000 and 6500 mIU/mL human chorionic gonadotropin is strongly suggestive of ectopic pregnancy. The absence of an intrauterine gestational sac by abdominal ultrasound had little significance when human chorionic gonadotropin values were below the zone; however, visualization of an intrauterine sac in conjunction with human chorionic gonadotropin levels below the zone are indicative of missed abortion or potentially an ectopic pregnancy. In additional studies, the presence of an adnexal noncystic mass in women with beta human chorionic gonadotropin titers below 6000 mIU/mL predicted ectopic pregnancy 80% of the time.

The development of transvaginal sonography has tremendously improved resolution of the adnexal and intrauterine structures and, in contrast to transabdominal ultrasonography, has allowed the visualization of a normal intrauterine pregnancy and early embryonic structures almost 1 week earlier. This has effectively lowered the "discriminatory zone" at which extrauterine and intrauterine pregnancies may be detected. Transvaginal scanning has allowed the visualization of intrauterine gestational sacs at beta human chorionic gonadotropin levels of 1400 to 2000 mIU/mL in several studies. Transvaginal sonography not only improves visualization of intrauterine structures, but allows high resolution of complex adnexal masses in comparison to transabdominal ultrasound. Transvaginal ultrasound is very sensitive in detecting free fluid in the cul de sac, which is a consistent finding in patients with ectopic pregnancy. Vaginal ultrasound may also detect fetal cardiac activity in the adnexa as soon as 6 weeks' gestational age. The sensitivity of transvaginal ultrasound in patients with clinically suspected ectopic pregnancy approaches 100%.

Recommended Approach

In the management of hemodynamically stable patients with the provisional diagnosis of ectopic pregnancy, serial beta human chorionic gonadotropin and initial ultrasound examination of the pelvis are appropriate. If the sonogram is nondiagnostic, beta human chorionic gonadotropin titers should be closely monitored until the "discriminatory zone" is reached or the titers strongly suggest an abnormal pregnancy. Sonography may be repeated, and if the diagnosis remains unclear, diagnostic laparoscopy allowing direct visualization of the tubes and ovaries is indicated.

Therapeutic

Therapeutic Options

Several means of nonsurgical management are currently being explored to improve potential fertility in patients with unruptured ectopic pregnancies. Studies using systemic methotrexate chemotherapy with or without citrovorum rescue have resulted in the successful resolution of ectopic pregnancies. Intratubal injections of methotrexate, potassium chloride, and $F_{2\alpha}$ prostaglandin under ultrasonographic guidance is currently being investigated, and preliminary results have been promising. It is hoped that intratubal medical treatment will avoid the potential toxicity of systemic medical treatment. Women with ectopic pregnancies who are Rh negative run the risk of Rh sensitization and should receive 50 μg of Rh immune globulin. In the past, surgery has been the modality of choice for treating ectopic pregnancy. The hemodynamic stability of the patient determines the need for emergency operative treatment or more conservative surgical treatment. If the patient is unstable, fluid and blood component therapy should be instituted before exploratory laparotomy. In hemodynamically stable patients, salpingectomy and salpingostomy through the laparoscope have become common procedures. Laparoscopic intratubal injection of the gestational toxins previously discussed has also shown promising results. Salpingectomy, once the standard treatment for tubal pregnancies, is re-

served for emergent cases where hemostasis must be quickly achieved, future fertility is not desired, and the tubal gestation is larger than 4 cm in diameter.

Recommended Approach

Patients who are hemodynamically stable with unruptured tubal pregnancies that are less than 4 cm in diameter are candidates for conservative surgical management or nonsurgical medical therapy. The absence of positive fetal cardiac activity is a good prognostic indicator for success with medical therapy. In those patients receiving surgical therapy, salpingostomy is the most common procedure performed. Salpingostomy is performed by making a linear incision over the protuberant surface of the gestation using scissors, cautery, or laser. This may be done via laparoscopy. The ectopic mass is removed, and hemostasis is achieved with cautery or laser. The incision heals by secondary intention. Because tubal patency may remain intact, patients who have had salpingostomy may have an increased probability of achieving an intrauterine pregnancy. Unfortunately, salpingostomy is associated with a higher repeat ectopic rate than other surgical procedures. Hysterectomy and oophorectomy are not indicated in patients desiring future fertility who may undergo in vitro fertilization techniques to achieve an intrauterine pregnancy.

FOLLOW-UP

Appropriate follow-up for patients who have received treatment for ectopic pregnancy includes examination of beta human chorionic gonadotropin titers. After conservative surgical management of an ectopic pregnancy, the level should fall to zero by 25 days after surgery. In patients treated medically, the time may extend to as long as 40 days. Failure of the titers to follow this pattern may indicate a persistent ectopic pregnancy or persistent trophoblastic tissue. Patients in this category may be eligible for second-look laparoscopy or repeat systemic treatment with methotrexate.

DISCUSSION
Prevalence and Incidence

Data collected by the Centers for Disease Control and Prevention from 1987 revealed an ectopic pregnancy rate of 16.8 per 1000 reported pregnancies, almost a fourfold increase since 1970. As in the past, the incidence of ectopic pregnancy was highest in women greater than 30 years of age. The incidence of ectopic pregnancy is 40% higher among African-Americans and other minority groups in comparison to whites. Geographically, the ectopic rate is highest in the South and lowest in the Northeast.

Related Basic Science
Anatomic Derangement

Implantation of the fertilized ovum into the endometrium requires normal fallopian tube function. The fallopian tube is necessary for pickup of the ovum, transport of spermatozoa, and provision of an appropriate milieu for fertilization and development of the early conceptus. The pathophysiology of ectopic pregnancy lies in the potential structural and functional defects in the tube along this pathway. Intraluminal narrowing due to scarring and fibrosis impairs tubal transport and leads to implantation of the developing embryo in the fallopian tube wall.

Physiologic or Metabolic Derangement

High levels of estrogen found in women taking ovulation-stimulating drugs may affect tubal smooth muscle contractility within the fallopian tube. Women enrolled in in vitro fertilization programs have ectopic rates that range from 2 to 10%. Explanations include hormone dysfunction and tubal damage that occurs during embryo transfer.

Natural History and Its Modification with Treatment

Ectopic pregnancy is associated with significant maternal morbidity, the most likely being a decrease in fertility. Following an ectopic pregnancy, only about one third to one half of women will bear a living child. Approximately 10% of women with a history of ectopic pregnancy have a second one. Untreated ectopic pregnancy may be maternally resorbed with few complications. This has been documented through the use of serial beta human chorionic gonadotropin; however, trophoblastic tissue, by its nature, is invasive, and a more likely sequela of an untreated ectopic pregnancy is arteriolar invasion with subsequent hemorrhage and death. Ectopic pregnancy is the second leading cause of maternal death in the United States. Fortunately, the death rate has declined almost 90% since 1970, the death rate being 3.4 deaths per 10,000 ectopic pregnancies in 1987. The decrease in the mortality associated with ectopic pregnancy is the result of our ability to diagnose this disorder at an earlier stage. Improved sensitivity of beta human chorionic gonadotropin assays and diagnostic ultrasound have made this possible.

Prevention

It is hoped that new techniques in both medical treatment and surgical intervention will further decrease maternal mortality and morbidity; however, the true key to prevention of ectopic pregnancy lies in our ability to educate the public concerning the prevention of sexually transmitted disease with its resulting tubal damage. Increased usage of oral contraceptives and barrier methods of contraception (such as condoms) may greatly decrease the incidence of tubal disease and, subsequently, the risk of ectopic pregnancy.

Cost Containment

The diagnosis of ectopic pregnancy is based mainly on patient history and physical examination in the face of a positive pregnancy test. Transvaginal sonography is the easiest and most cost-effective measure to improve diagnostic accuracy. The earlier a diagnosis of ectopic pregnancy is made, the greater the likelihood of successful treatment with decreased maternal morbidity and mortality. Earlier diagnosis results in less tubal damage and may prevent loss of future fertility, which, in the long run, is the greatest cost of ectopic pregnancy.

REFERENCES

DeCherney AH. Ectopic pregnancy. Clin Obstet Gynecol 1987;30:148.
Centers for Disease Control. Ectopic pregnancy: United States, 1987. MMWR 1990;39:401.
Kadar N, Caldwell B, Romero R, et al. A method of screening for ectopic pregnancy and its indications. Obstet Gynecol 1981;58:162.
Kadar N, DeVore G, Romero R, et al. Discriminatory hCG zone: Its use in the sonographic evaluation for ectopic pregnancy. Obstet Gynecol 1981;58:146.
Timor-Tritsch IE, Yeh MN, Piesner DB, et al. The use of transvaginal ultrasonography in the diagnosis of ectopic pregnancy. Am J Obstet Gynecol 1989;161:157.

CHAPTER 10–21

Endometriosis

Dorothy E. Mitchell-Leef, M.D.

DEFINITION

Endometriosis may be described as the aberrant growth of viable endometrial tissue found in the peritoneal cavity involving the ovary and pelvic structures. Displaced endometrial tissue also may be found in more remote areas of the body, including intestinal structures, scars from previous laparotomies, lung pleura, and lymph nodes.

ETIOLOGY

There have been multiple suggestions as to the etiology of endometriosis; however, the most commonly held mechanism is Sampson's theory: that retrograde flow of endometrial tissue through the fallopian tubes and, thus, into the abdominal cavity causes endometriosis. The facts that endometriosis is found in dependent portions of the pelvis and that endometrial fragments can grow on the peritoneum and pelvic structures substantiate these conclusions.

Other theories are concerned with possible deficiencies of the immune response or humoral antibodies that may be directed against endometrial tissue. With respect to the diagnosis of extrapelvic endometriosis, one must consider the possibility that endometrial tissue may have been inadvertently transplanted during a previous surgical procedure or that vascular or lymphatic transport of endometrial tissue may have occurred.

CRITERIA FOR DIAGNOSIS
Suggestive

The complaint of dysmenorrhea is highly suggestive of endometriosis; however, it must be understood that many women who have endometriosis are asymptomatic and present with no complaints except infertility. There is no direct correlation between the stage of the disease and the pain experienced. This leads to difficulty in diagnosing endometriosis, especially in those individuals who have only mild symptoms. The physician must ascertain whether there are some other abnormalities caused by endometriosis that would produce symptoms only in the bladder or rectal areas. Cyclic pain or symptomatology is the main indicator for considering endometriosis as the disease process.

Definitive

Laparoscopic visualization and staging of endometriosis provide the most definitive diagnosis. Pathologic diagnosis may be used in questionable areas. Other indirect diagnoses may be made when evaluating complaints of the genitourinary or gastrointestinal tract that involve cyclic pain or bleeding. Endometriosis may be found to be the etiology of the initial genitourinary or gastrointestinal complaints. For tissue in more remote areas of the body that is suggestive of endometriosis, pathologic diagnosis means would be the only form of definitive diagnosis.

CLINICAL MANIFESTATIONS
Subjective

Patients who present with dysmenorrhea, dyspareunia, and other forms of cyclic abdominal or pelvic pain must be evaluated to rule out endometriosis.

Symptoms

Endometriosis should be suspected in any woman who complains of dysmenorrhea and/or dyspareunia, especially if the symptoms are progressive and have not responded to combination oral contraceptives or prostaglandin synthetase inhibitors for the dysmenorrhea. Other complaints include diffuse pelvic pain, usually associated with or occurring prior to menstruation, painful defecation associated with menstruation, diarrhea associated with menstruation, an acute abdomen caused by spontaneous rupture of an endometrioma usually in the luteal phase, and obstruction of the ureter or bowel at the time of menstruation. Symptomatology during the time of menses may be noted in a cyclic fashion in unusual sites in the body, for example, incisional pain, cyclic pneumothorax, or hemoptysis during menses.

Endometriosis also must be considered in any woman who has been evaluated for infertility and has had an otherwise normal evaluation or who has been adequately treated for otherwise existing infertility problems and has not had a diagnostic laparoscopy to exclude this diagnosis.

Adolescents with persistent and aggressive dysmenorrhea need to be evaluated for endometriosis, especially if first-degree relatives have been diagnosed with this disease.

Past History

Patients with a significant history of endometriosis who have had therapy in the past or who have had a pregnancy must still be considered for recurrent disease. Endometriosis is a recurrent disease; therefore, anyone with a history must be considered strongly for further evaluation. There is no cure for endometriosis except total abdominal hysterectomy and bilateral salpingo-oophorectomy. Even in those patients, occasional residual disease may cause further growth of endometriosis if they receive estrogen replacement therapy, which may induce growth of endometrial implants. Therefore, in those women who have pelvic pain or other gastrointestinal or genitourinary complaints, it is very important to keep in mind their history of this disease, even if they have undergone total abdominal hysterectomy and bilateral salpingo-oophorectomy.

Family History

Approximately 7% of first-degree relatives of affected patients with endometriosis may have the disease. Knowledge that a first-degree relative has had endometriosis may be useful in counseling the individual about childbearing (e.g., suggesting early rather than delayed childbearing), and if symptomatology is present, an early diagnosis should be made so that progression of the disease can be avoided.

Objective
Physical Examination

Physical examination of the pelvic structures will not elucidate mild forms of the disease. When the ovaries are enlarged or pelvic fixation is present along with nodularity, a more advanced stage of the disease may be considered; however, definitive diagnosis must rest on confirmatory laparoscopy.

Other findings on physical examination may reveal distant sites of endometriosis that bleed cyclically coincident with the patient's menses. These findings may be missed unless the patient returns for examination during her menses and reveals lesions that show these cyclic changes. Individuals who have involvement of the pleura may complain of cyclic hemoptysis. Definitive diagnosis is made only with a confirmatory pathology report on the material produced.

It may be pointed out that individuals who have a retroverted uterus do not necessarily have endometriosis.

Routine Laboratory Abnormalities

No definitive laboratory tests can routinely be performed to diagnose endometriosis. Specimens of distant-site endometriosis can be evaluated only by definitive pathologic criteria. CA-125 has been implicated as a possible useful marker in endometriosis; however, the assay cannot be used as a screening test. It has been indicated as a possible marker for response to medications; however, cross-reactivity with other disease states does not warrant its use for diagnosis of endometriosis.

PLANS
Diagnostic

Endometriosis must be definitively evaluated by surgical visualization, at the time of either laparoscopy or laparotomy. Pathologic confirmation of distant-site endometriosis must be definitive as well.

Differential Diagnosis

Patients with dysmenorrhea must first be treated medically with antiprostaglandin medications or continuous birth control pill therapy. If

these treatments do not improve symptoms, definitive diagnosis of endometriosis is warranted.

In patients who have had a history of unexplained infertility despite thorough evaluation, diagnostic laparoscopy must be performed to rule out endometriosis. Approximately half of women undergoing laparoscopy for unexplained infertility are found to have endometriosis. When cyclic bleeding occurs in sites distant from the pelvis, definitive diagnosis must be performed using pathologic diagnosis to confirm the disease. Individuals who have cyclic complaints of gastrointestinal or genitourinary origin may need further elucidation of specific etiologies regarding their symptoms. If other evaluation reveals no abnormalities in the gastrointestinal or genitourinary tract, then laparoscopy should be considered to define whether or not endometriosis is the causative factor.

Diagnostic Options

Few definitive options are available short of laparoscopy. Those patients with a history of cyclic bladder or bowel complaints at the time of menses may have additional intravenous pyelography and/or a barium enema to rule out other possible diagnoses. The findings of these tests must be correlated with the findings at the time of diagnostic laparoscopy. If cyclic bleeding occurs in scar tissue, or if hemoptysis is present, a biopsy specimen should be sent for pathologic determination of endometrial tissue.

Recommended Approach

The pelvic structures must be visualized by diagnostic laparoscopy to rule out endometriosis. Many times, patients have evidence of old fibrosis and reaction left behind by endometriosis that is no longer active and would not be pathologically demonstrable if a biopsy were performed. Experienced practitioners usually do not perform confirmative biopsies in these patients, but they must evaluate the patient completely according to the stage of the existing disease. Early lesions appear clear or red. Intermediate-age lesions are brown. Black lesions are the most advanced. Careful evaluation of all such lesions is vital to accurate diagnosis. Endometriosis must be classified at the time of laparoscopy according to the American Fertility Society classification for endometriosis (Figure 10–21–1). Once evaluation of the patient is completed, a staging of the disease must be provided for the patient record so that appropriate therapy may be initiated. It is important to remember that although a couple may have infertility abnormalities in their initial evaluation, laparoscopy should still be performed. The etiology of infertility is often multifactorial. Endometriosis is found in approximately half of women undergoing laparoscopy for infertility.

If the patient has had enlarged ovaries, either unilaterally or bilaterally, along with the symptomatology described above, pelvic ultrasound may be an adjunctive diagnostic tool to confirm enlargement of the ovaries. Ultrasound or computed tomography scan evaluation alone, however, is not reliable to confirm or rule out the diagnosis of endometriosis.

Therapeutic
Therapeutic Options

Once appropriate staging has been performed at the time of diagnostic laparoscopy, decisions on therapy modalities can be made. Therapy may be either medical, surgical, or a combination of both. The armamentarium available includes laser ablation and fulguration of endometriosis implants. A gonadotropin-releasing hormone agonist or danazol (Danocrine) may be considered as follow-up medical therapy once the disease is diagnosed. If a gonadotropin-releasing hormone agonist or danazol is not a consideration, medroxyprogesterone acetate (Depo-Provera) or continuous birth control pill therapy may be considered. Total abdominal hysterectomy with bilateral salpingo-oophorectomy is the most definitive therapy; however, it is left only for those individuals with no other options and for whom further childbearing is not a concern.

Recommended Approach

Laparoscopic laser ablation of endometriosis implants, or fulguration if a laser is unavailable, should be performed whenever possible so that

Stage I (Minimal):   1–5
Stage II (Mild):   6–15
Stage III (Moderate): 16–40
Stage IV (Severe): > 40

Laparoscopy _____ Laparotomy _____ Photography _____
Recommended Treatment _____
_____

Total _____   Prognosis _____

PERITONEUM ENDOMETRIOSIS	< 1 cm	1–3 cm	> 3 cm
Superficial	1	2	4
Deep	2	4	6
R Superficial	1	2	4
Deep	4	16	20
L Superficial	1	2	4
Deep	4	16	20

Posterior Cul de Sac Obliteration	Partial	Complete
	4	40

ADHESIONS	< 1–3 Enclosure	1/3–2/3 Enclosure	> 2–3 Enclosure
R Filmy	1	2	4
Dense	4	8	16
L Filmy	1	2	4
Dense	4	8	16
R Filmy	1	2	4
Dense	4*	8*	16
L Filmy	1	2	4
Dense	4*	8*	16

*If the fimbriated end of the fallopian tube is completely enclosed, change the point assignment to 16.

Additional Endometriosis _____ | Associated Pathology _____
_____ | _____

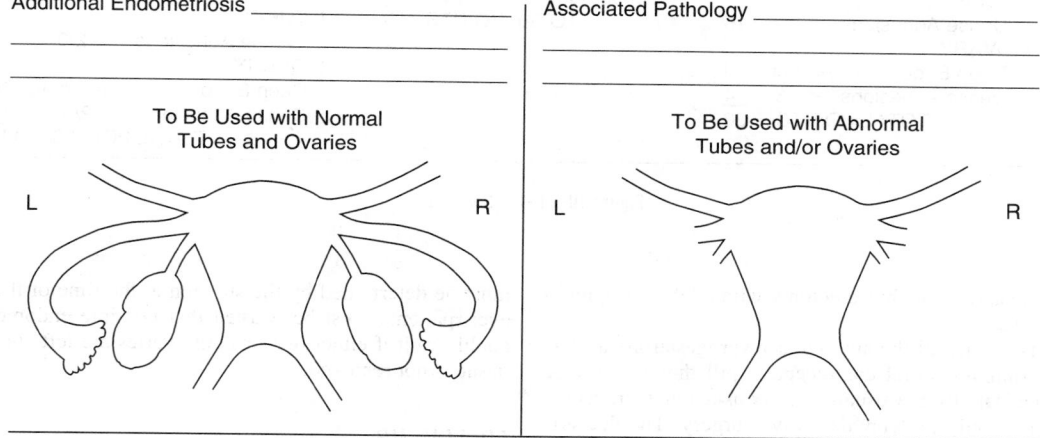

To Be Used with Normal Tubes and Ovaries   To Be Used with Abnormal Tubes and/or Ovaries

Figure 10–21–1. The American Fertility Society revised classification of endometriosis. *Point assignment changed to 16; **point assignment doubled. *Source: The American Fertility Society. Revised American Fertility Society Classification of Endometriosis: 1985. Fertil Steril 1985;43:351. Reproduced with permission of the publisher, the American Society for Reproductive Medicine.*

the residual disease is minimal. If the endometriosis is advanced, further conservative surgery at laparotomy must be considered. Laparotomy is performed to remove only those areas involved with endometriosis, with the goal of restoration of the pelvic anatomy to its normal state. In some instances, postoperative gonadotropin-releasing hormone agonist therapy may be indicated. Opinions differ as to whether pre- or postoperative suppressive therapy is best. If the surgeon feels that there may be residual endometriosis, a gonadotropin-releasing hormone agonist or danazol may be administered for 3 to 6 months. If laser ablation or fulguration is unavailable at the time of laparoscopy, 6 months of medical therapy with a gonadotropin-releasing hormone agonist or danazol should be prescribed. Patients should return monthly to be evaluated for any side effects. Gonadotropin-releas-

ing hormone agonists are given either as an intranasal spray taken twice daily or as a depot injection administered once a month. Side effects include hot flushes, night sweats, vaginal dryness, and insomnia. If they are taken longer than 6 months, bone loss may occur. Danazol is administered orally in a total dose of 800 mg daily. This synthetic androgen preparation suppresses ovarian function, causing a hypoestrogenic state. Side effects may include weight gain, mild acne, hirsutism, and voice changes. Resumption of menses may occur 1 to 2 months after discontinuing gonadotropin-releasing hormone agonist therapy or danazol.

If patients are no longer interested in reproduction and endometriosis has been diagnosed at laparoscopy, the patient may be advised as to options for therapy. If she has extensive disease and does not desire fur-

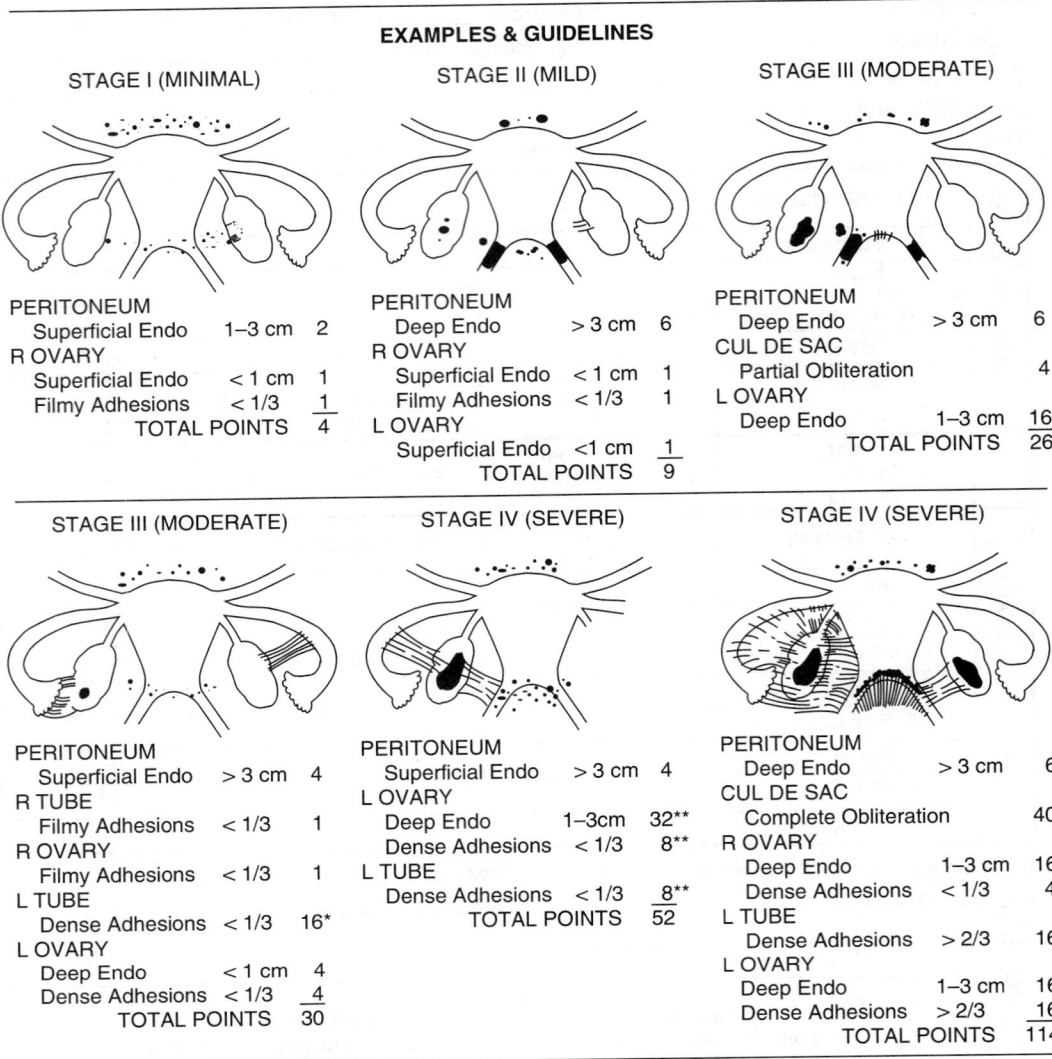

EXAMPLES & GUIDELINES

STAGE I (MINIMAL)

PERITONEUM		
Superficial Endo	1–3 cm	2
R OVARY		
Superficial Endo	< 1 cm	1
Filmy Adhesions	< 1/3	1
TOTAL POINTS		4

STAGE II (MILD)

PERITONEUM		
Deep Endo	> 3 cm	6
R OVARY		
Superficial Endo	< 1 cm	1
Filmy Adhesions	< 1/3	1
L OVARY		
Superficial Endo	<1 cm	1
TOTAL POINTS		9

STAGE III (MODERATE)

PERITONEUM		
Deep Endo	> 3 cm	6
CUL DE SAC		
Partial Obliteration		4
L OVARY		
Deep Endo	1–3 cm	16
TOTAL POINTS		26

STAGE III (MODERATE)

PERITONEUM		
Superficial Endo	> 3 cm	4
R TUBE		
Filmy Adhesions	< 1/3	1
R OVARY		
Filmy Adhesions	< 1/3	1
L TUBE		
Dense Adhesions	< 1/3	16*
L OVARY		
Deep Endo	< 1 cm	4
Dense Adhesions	< 1/3	4
TOTAL POINTS		30

STAGE IV (SEVERE)

PERITONEUM		
Superficial Endo	> 3 cm	4
L OVARY		
Deep Endo	1–3cm	32**
Dense Adhesions	< 1/3	8**
L TUBE		
Dense Adhesions	< 1/3	8**
TOTAL POINTS		52

STAGE IV (SEVERE)

PERITONEUM		
Deep Endo	> 3 cm	6
CUL DE SAC		
Complete Obliteration		40
R OVARY		
Deep Endo	1–3 cm	16
Dense Adhesions	< 1/3	4
L TUBE		
Dense Adhesions	> 2/3	16
L OVARY		
Deep Endo	1–3 cm	16
Dense Adhesions	> 2/3	16
TOTAL POINTS		114

Figure 10–21–1. (*Continued*)

ther childbearing, total abdominal hysterectomy with bilateral salpingo-oophorectomy is advised.

If the patient refuses surgical therapy, medroxyprogesterone acetate (Depo-Provera) or continuous oral contraceptive pill therapy may be instituted. These medications are usually not considered therapeutic, however; they are used only to delay definitive surgery. The decision rests on the amount of endometriosis present at the time of staging. Medroxyprogesterone acetate is not used in the infertile patient because of the length of time it takes for ovulation to resume after discontinuation of the medication.

Gonadotropin-releasing hormone therapy has been developed for pseudomenopausal treatment of endometriosis. A gonadotropin-releasing hormone agonist is given either as a spray intranasally twice a day, intramuscularly in depot form once a month, or subcutaneously daily. This treatment suppresses the disease process but does not cure the endometriosis. Patients who desire future fertility but at present are not interested in childbearing need to be followed closely and given suppressive therapy during the interim from diagnosis to the time at which they wish to conceive. These patients may be first placed on gonadotropin-releasing hormone agonist therapy for 6 months and then treated continuously with a combination oral contraceptive medication to eliminate menstruation, thereby diminishing the chance of endometriosis recurring. In those individuals who have minimal to moderate endometriosis and require hysterectomy, conservation of ovaries may be a rare possibility, depending on the extent of the disease. This

must be determined by the surgeon at the time of the procedure; however, patients must be warned that possible endometriosis recurrence could result if either one or both ovaries are left and all endometriosis tissue is not removed.

FOLLOW-UP

In those individuals who have had a complete diagnostic evaluation, including a laparoscopy, close follow-up is mandatory. If the patient desires fertility, conservation of the pelvic structures is advised, and medical or hormonal suppression of ovulation and menses must be continued until childbearing is desired. If the patient has undergone surgery for endometriosis and desires fertility afterward or in the future, the patient must be reevaluated at 6-month intervals to decide whether or not there has been a recurrence. Reevaluation may include repeat laparoscopy, depending on whether the patient has received adjunctive medical therapy. If the patient does not conceive within at least 12 to 15 months of surgery or medical therapy, laparoscopy definitely should be repeated to reevaluate for recurrent disease. In a patient who is a candidate for danazol therapy, follow-up must be made with an SMA-18 determination every 6 weeks, along with a pelvic examination to rule out liver enzyme changes while on the medication and to evaluate for any side effects. Oral contraceptives, if given continuously, also must be monitored at least every 3 months, with pelvic examinations and laboratory tests as indicated. If the patient has had definitive surgery for endometriosis in the form of total abdominal hysterectomy and bilateral salpingo-oophorectomy, then reevaluation should still continue at 6 months to a year, owing to possible microscopic recurrence not discovered at the time of laparotomy. If the patient has bowel or gastrointestinal tract symptoms, then an intravenous pyelogram and barium enema must be performed. In particular, patients placed on estrogen 6 months after total abdominal hysterectomy and bilateral salpingo-oophorectomy must be observed for recurrence of the disease.

DISCUSSION
Prevalence

Approximately 10% of all women and 30% of infertile women have endometriosis. It is important to refute the previous belief that endometriosis is limited to women over 30 who are Caucasian, high strung, and intellectual. In fact, endometriosis has been found in teenagers; 50 to 60% of adolescents with complaints of chronic pelvic pain were found to have endometriosis at the time of laparoscopy. Black women are also found to have this disease. Another fallacy that has been reversed is that this problem occurs only in nulliparous women. If secondary infertility occurs, endometriosis must be considered as well. If endometriosis is a factor in infertility, patients must be made aware not only that endometriosis will cause difficulty with conception because prostaglandin production alters tubal motility, but also that multifactorial problems, such as anovulation, luteal phase deficiency, and autoimmune disease, may be implicated. The incidence of spontaneous abortions may be increased in patients with endometriosis.

Related Basic Science

The exact etiology of endometriosis and its effect on reproductive potential remains elusive.

Genetics

A single mutant gene with possible transmission due to polygenic or multifactorial inheritance has been implicated as a causative factor in endometriosis. This may be a trait that results from a combination of effects of single genes or the composite of both genetic and environmental factors.

Altered Molecular Biology

Levels of prostaglandin metabolites and peritoneal macrophages are markedly elevated in individuals who have endometriosis implants. It has been speculated that the peritoneal reaction from endometriosis implants causes release of prostaglandins with secondary alterations in tubal motility, resulting in infertility as well as dysmenorrhea. Increased prostaglandin concentrations in the peritoneal fluid of patients with endometriosis cause irritation of the peritoneal lining, resulting in dysmenorrhea and altering ovarian function and tubal motility.

In addition, endometriosis may cause dysfunction of the corpus luteum, thereby producing a luteal phase deficiency, which in turn is a causative factor in patients with infertility and endometriosis.

Anatomic Derangement

Retrograde menstruation that undergoes implantation seems to be an accepted etiology based on clinical observation and induction experiments in animal models, first provided by Sampson in 1927. Other theories have been enumerated; however, this has been the most valid one, owing to the facts that blood flow from the fimbriated end of the tube has been observed in menstruating women at the time of laparoscopy and endometriosis is most commonly found in the most dependent portion of the pelvis. That distant sites of endometriosis have been found indicates that vascular or lymphatic transport may be an additional causative factor. Also, a combination of genetic and immunologic factors may increase the risk of developing endometriosis. Decreased cellular immunity or immunologic defects may cause some individuals to have increased susceptibility to the disease as well.

Natural History and Its Modification with Treatment

In individuals who have documented endometriosis, the problem may, if left untreated, spontaneously regress or it may remain, resulting in fibrosis and scarring and leaving the patient infertile. In these patients, surgical intervention is necessary to remove adhesions and restore the anatomy to its normal state; otherwise, infertility will continue.

If the individual chooses not to obtain treatment and her disease progresses, there is no way to predict whether the process will involve the bladder, bowel, tubes, ovaries, and other adjacent structures. In those individuals who have been noted to have this involvement, time intervals are variable and no adequate determinant or scale can be used to predict the timing or progression of the disease process. In some instances, if left alone, patients develop complete extrinsic bowel obstruction and ureteral obstruction with subsequent bowel and renal complications. Bladder involvement could destroy mucosa, as well as ureteral surfaces, and cause urinary tract dysfunction. If left untreated, extrinsic endometriosis involving the gastrointestinal tract would result in the need for resection of involved bowel. Those patients with hemoptysis and involvement of the lung pleura warrant resection of the affected tissue. Mild disease may or may not progress further, varying in individual patients.

The recurrence rate of endometriosis is approximately 40% within 5 years of diagnosis and treatment. Depending on the initial stage of the disease, women treated with gonadotropin-releasing hormone agonists had recurrence rates at 5 years of 37% with minimal disease and 74% with severe disease (Speroff, et al.).

Prevention

As a definite etiology for endometriosis has not been determined, preventive methods cannot be discussed. It is hoped that early diagnosis and therapy, especially in adolescents and young women, can decrease progression of the disease process. Continued surveillance for recurrence can help to diagnose early stages of the disease so that adequate suppressive therapy can be instituted until pregnancy is desired.

Cost Containment

If one considers the time lost from either school or work because of dysmenorrhea, it is advisable that patients who have a genetic predisposition for this problem be counseled. Those with any symptomatology should be properly evaluated so that infertility and dysmenorrhea therapy can be obtained at an early stage. This would reduce the time lost to the patient, as well as decrease the eventual cost of medical and surgical therapy.

REFERENCES
Sampson JA. Peritoneal endometriosis due to menstrual dissemination of endometrial tissue into the peritoneal cavity. Am J Obstet Gynecol 1927;14:422.
Speroff L, Glass RH, Kase NG. Clinical gynecologic endocrinology and infertility. 4th ed. Baltimore: Williams & Wilkins, 1994.
Wallace EE, Kempers RD. Modern trends in infertility and conception control, vol. 4. Chicago: Year Book Medical, 1988.
Yen SC, Jaffe RB. Reproduction endocrinology. 3rd ed. Philadelphia: Saunders, 1991.

Infertility

Dorothy E. Mitchell-Leef, M.D.

DEFINITION

Infertility is defined as 1 year of unprotected coitus with failure to achieve a pregnancy. *Secondary infertility* implies that pregnancy has not occurred after at least 1 year of attempting conception with proven past fertility, including ectopic pregnancies and spontaneous abortions. *Fecundity* is the ability to achieve a live birth in one menstrual cycle.

ETIOLOGY

Infertility may be considered as having a single cause, either ovulatory dysfunction, tubal disease, or hormonal imbalance in the female partner. Male factor infertility may account for more than 50% of infertility in a couple. Many times, the cause of infertility is multifactorial.

CRITERIA FOR DIAGNOSIS

Suggestive

Couples not achieving pregnancy after 6 months of well-timed intercourse with no obvious medical problems require a full evaluation.

Definitive

Couples who have known factors causing infertility require immediate evaluation.

CLINICAL MANIFESTATIONS

Subjective

As couples presenting with the problem of infertility rarely have subjective complaints except for the inability to conceive, it is important to take a complete history to elucidate any complaints the couple may not otherwise classify as a problem. It is for this reason that the initial interview for infertility should include the couple, so that both partners are involved in the investigation and are fully aware of all questions being asked. The male partner is extremely valuable in providing past medical information not only for himself, but also for the couple, and may shed light on important aspects of their infertility.

Symptoms

The woman should be asked for a menstrual history, including onset of menarche and regularity of her cycle. If amenorrhea has been a problem in the past, this must be elucidated by previous laboratory tests obtained at that time and should become part of the permanent medical record of the couple. Any medical reason for amenorrhea or oligomenorrhea should be discussed at this time. Further questioning should concern coital timing and frequency, especially at the time of ovulation; use of lubricants; postcoital activities, such as douching; prior forms of contraception, especially intrauterine devices and any pertinent sequelae such as infections; and previous pregnancies, including ectopic gestations and spontaneous abortions with pertinent sequelae. Significant questioning should address such complaints as dysmenorrhea, dyspareunia, premenstrual spotting, onset of hirsutism, galactorrhea, history of sexually transmitted diseases and their sequelae, and any important genetic history such as chromosomal abnormalities.

Information about such medical problems as diabetes, lupus, and liver, thyroid, or renal disease should be obtained. Noting any previous abdominal or pelvic surgical procedure is important in the evaluation of a couple who are infertile because postoperative adhesions may be a problem in the woman. Medications that may interfere with ovulation should be determined.

The history from the male partner should include any conceptions with either his present partner or previous partners and the timing of those conceptions. It is important to note whether there have been any

changes in his health since the prior pregnancies. Other information to obtain at this time includes pertinent urologic abnormalities such as varicocele, undescended testicles, or trauma in the past; childhood illnesses (e.g., mumps, tuberculosis) or radiation; and history of retroperitoneal surgery, in which sterilization could perhaps have inadvertently occurred. Sexually transmitted diseases such as gonorrhea with strictures should be discussed, as should herpetic lesions that may have caused significant urethral damage. A history of chronic prostatitis or environmental exposures to toxins, radiation, or extensive heat should be determined. Medications that may lower sperm count or motility are of special importance, and this discussion should include any abused drugs, such as marijuana, alcohol, and tobacco, which are implicated in lowering motility. Cimetidine (Tagamet) may decrease sperm production. Any history of diethylstilbestrol (DES) exposure or significant genetic abnormality must be noted. Patients with emotional or physical stress may see changes in their seminal quality, and therefore, any history of work or physically related stress, such as illnesses, may be of significance. Additional questioning concerning libido may help define hyperprolactinemia.

The male or female partner may have had sterilization procedures performed and may desire reversal of a vasectomy or tubal ligation.

Past History

A past history of endometriosis, luteal phase defect, uterine leiomyoma, habitual abortions, tubal occlusion, ovulatory dysfunction, and male factor infertility is significant to evaluation for secondary infertility.

Family History

A family history of endometriosis involving first-degree relatives is important, especially for women who have dysmenorrhea, dyspareunia, or unexplained fertility. Uterine leiomyomas have polygenic inheritance and may be a cause of habitual abortions or tubal occlusion. Familial history of early menopause or ovarian failure would warrant early attempts at completing a family. Women with family members experiencing early menopause may require close evaluation for early ovarian failure.

Objective

Infertility is most times multifactorial and diagnosis is achieved in large part by performing all recommended basic tests.

Physical Examination

Physical examinations of the couple should be performed, and the most salient findings for the infertility evaluation listed.

In women, hirsutism on the upper lip, nipples, and abdomen should be noted, as it may indicate polycystic ovarian disease. Visual field defects may indicate microadenomas of the pituitary gland. Any evidence of galactorrhea or thyroid enlargement may be important because either hyperprolactinemia or hypothyroidism can cause ovulation dysfunction and may be the cause of infertility. Anosmia is experienced by individuals with hypogonadotropic hypogonadism. On pelvic examination, vaginal stenosis and evidence of vaginismus or other pelvic pathology may be of significance, as it may cause a decrease in sexual activity or dyspareunia, resulting in coital infrequency. Cervicitis may cause problems with poor mucus and should be evaluated at the time of initial examination. Those women with previous conizations or cryosurgery may be noted to have significant cervical stenosis with poor to no cervical mucus production at the initial examination. Bimanual examination of the pelvis may reveal a significantly retroverted uterus with problems involving deposition of semen in the posterior vaginal vault, especially in women whose partners have low-motility sperm. If the uterus is fixed with either unilateral or bilateral adnexal masses, one must be highly suspicious of either previous pelvic inflammatory disease, possibly unknown to the patient, or endometriosis. Evidence of nodularity of the uterosacral ligaments may indicate endometriosis; however, the examination is not diagnostic for this. Patients who have had previous pelvic surgery may have significant adhesive disease with immobilization of the uterus and adnexa, either unilaterally or bilaterally. At the time of examination, one would be unable to determine the exact etiology of the pelvic findings. Rectovaginal examination in those patients with advanced-stage endometriosis may show significant rectal narrowing or induration in the area of the rectovaginal space.

In men the examiner should pay attention to secondary sexual development (i.e., axillary and pubic hair), looking for any eunuchoid body habitus and other aberrations from normal male pattern sexual hair. The neurologic examination should include visual fields to rule out any possibility of pituitary tumor and a test for anosmia to rule out hypogonadotropic hypogonadism. The penis should be carefully examined, and meatal size and location noted. Presence of a hydrocele or undescended testicle should be determined, as should evidence of healed surgical scars and size and consistency of each testicle. Testicular size should be measured bilaterally with an orchidometer: the lower limit is 20 cm^3 volume ($4.0 \times 2.7 \text{ cm}$). Presence of a varicocele must be determined, and any evidence of other scrotal abnormality noted.

Routine Laboratory Abnormalities

There are no routine diagnostic abnormalities.

PLANS
Diagnostic

The basic tests include the following.

More than one test is required to diagnose men with an abnormal semen analysis as having true male factor infertility. Abnormalities identified include a low sperm count (< 20 million), less than 50% sperm motility, and less than 50% normal morphology. Very low seminal volumes, less than 2 to 3 mL, may also be considered abnormal. After the semen analysis is obtained, evaluation by a urologist is recommended.

Hysterosalpingograms that illustrate a septate versus a bicornuate uterine defect require further evaluation by simultaneous diagnostic laparoscopy and hysteroscopy to differentiate the diagnosis of the defects. Endometrial polyps, uterine leiomyomas, and residual intrauterine devices can be diagnosed at the time of the hysterosalpingogram. As for tubal occlusion, illustration of cornual occlusion versus distal hydrosalpinges is valuable information in an infertility evaluation.

Postcoital tests demonstrating sperm that do not move, swim in a circular motion, or shake in place may indicate the possibility of sperm antibodies, which necessitates further testing. Both partners would need evaluation to elucidate whether the abnormality lies in the man, woman, or both. Evidence of infection or lack of sperm in postcoital tests represents a positive finding necessitating further investigation of cervical mucus quality. Fewer than five sperm per high-power field or a sperm motility less than 50% would be considered an abnormal result.

Endometrial biopsy may show a 2-day or longer lag of the endometrium, endometritis, or anovulation.

The diagnosis of infertility cannot be made until all appropriate basic tests are completed on both partners. After this basic evaluation, further testing may be needed to elucidate more specific etiologies of the couple's combined problem of infertility. Even after all tests have been completed and have been found to be within normal range, further therapy may need to be considered in the form of in vitro fertilization, at which time a cellular (egg or sperm quality) problem may be elucidated.

Differential Diagnosis

At each step of the evaluation of each partner, multiple examinations/tests must be performed with respect to the different possible problems; for example, diagnosis of a bicornuate versus septate uterus by hysterosalpingogram requires further elucidation with simultaneous laparoscopy and hysteroscopy. Each evaluation must be thorough to rule out an abnormality; however, not until there is extensive evaluation would a differential diagnosis be a consideration. Therefore, differential diagnosis is discussed under Diagnostic Options.

Diagnostic Options

For semen analysis, the specimen is obtained by masturbation in a clean container, left at room temperature, and brought to the laboratory within 1 hour of collection. It is important that the man abstain from ejaculating for at least 48 hours prior to the analysis. Normal semen has a sperm count greater than 20 million per milliliter, with at least 50 to 60% of the sperm exhibiting 4+ forward motility. The volume should be 3 to 5 mL with normal liquefaction present. Morphologic evaluation is also important; at least 60% of the sperm should have normal form. In patients found to have severe azoospermia, an endocrine evaluation must be performed to determine levels of follicle-stimulating hormone, luteinizing hormone, prolactin, total testosterone, and thyroid-stimulating hormone. These should be done as a screen to rule out the most significant reasons for azoospermia. Additional karyotyping to rule out Klinefelter's syndrome with 47,XXY also must be considered in these individuals, as should testicular biopsies to determine whether maturation arrest is the etiology of the azoospermia. It is also most important to note the presence of agglutination and white blood cells.

In the female partner, a hysterosalpingogram is done after menses has been completed and prior to ovulation. If the patient has a history of pelvic inflammatory disease, a sedimentation rate is obtained, and if it is elevated, antibiotic therapy is administered prior to repeating the sedimentation rate. Under fluoroscopy, a water-soluble dye is injected through the cervix via a cannula to outline the uterine and tubal structures. Tubal patency and mucosal pattern are evaluated. The outline of the uterine cavity is important to determine whether there is any evidence of abnormal uterine structures, including a T-shaped uterus associated with diethylstilbestrol exposure, Asherman's syndrome, bicornuate or septate uterus, bilateral cornual obstruction secondary to salpingitis isthmic nodosa, or hydrosalpinx (distal occlusion) associated with pelvic inflammatory disease or adhesive disease. Occasionally, tubal spasm occurs, and atropine (Donnatal) may be used effectively just prior to the study to rule out tubal occlusion. Sometimes, an oil-base dye (Ethiodol) is the preferred medium in those individuals with no history of pelvic inflammatory disease who may have unexplained infertility. For women who have undergone tubal ligation, the extent of tubal occlusion must be documented by hysterosalpingogram.

A postcoital (Huhner's) test is performed at the time of ovulation, which is determined either by basal body temperature graph or by luteinizing hormone antibody testing (ovulation detection kit). This is done when the cervical mucus is optimal, which is usually within 2 to 3 days of ovulation. The couple abstains from intercourse at least 48 hours prior to the test and the woman returns to the office within 2 to 6 hours of intercourse. At that time, cervical mucus is removed with forceps or by cervical aspiration. Spinnbarkeit is measured to determine the stretchability of the mucus; it should be at least 8 to 20 cm. The specimen is placed on a slide to test for ferning, which is a determination of estrogen content. Once this has been done, the number of sperm per high-power field must be counted. A normal finding is at least five sperm with fast-forward motility per high-power field. It is important to note the direction of sperm motility and whether the sperm are moving in place or dead. The presence of white cells also must be appreciated. For couples who have had a poor postcoital test or in whom the male partner had a low semen analysis, Huhner's test is often performed 2 hours after artificial insemination using the man's sperm to determine if faulty coital technique resulted in abnormal tests.

Endometrial biopsies are performed in the second half or secretory phase of the cycle, usually 2 to 3 days prior to the expected onset of menses. With a small curette, a specimen is obtained from the anterior or lateral wall of the uterus. The specimen must be histologically evaluated according to the criteria outlined by Noyes et al. (1950). If the patient is unable to have an endometrial biopsy owing to cervical stenosis, the serum progesterone level should be determined for 3 successive days, starting 8 days after ovulation. The average of these levels should be at least 10 ng/mL to indicate normal corpus luteum function. A luteal phase defect is ruled out if the patient is within 1 day or less of endometrial dating, as determined by the date of menses after the biopsy. If the biopsy is more than 2 days out of phase, then the patient is determined to have a luteal phase defect. Patients found to have proliferative endometrium on a biopsy or a progesterone level less than 3 to 4 ng/mL are considered to be anovulatory and are candidates for ovulation induction therapy.

Basal body temperature graphs are employed to determine ovulation. Basal body temperature thermometers must be used; these are available commercially. Patients use the thermometer daily and record their temperature findings on a graph each morning.

Ovulation can be timed by determining luteinizing hormone monoclonal antibodies. Home urine tests are now available to determine the luteinizing hormone surge using monoclonal antibodies. Instead of using basal body temperature charts, the patient tests the urine each day prior to the time of expected ovulation and determines the luteinizing hormone peak, which signals that ovulation will occur within 24 to 36 hours. This is much more specific than basal body temperature charts and is less stressful for the couple. It is useful in determining timing for artificial inseminations, human chorionic gonadotropin injections, and coitus.

If agglutination is noted on semen analysis, an immunobead assay to rule out sperm antibodies must be considered, especially if agglutination correlates with an abnormal postcoital test showing sperm that are shaking in place or are not motile. This can determine whether there may be an immunologic cause for infertility.

Patients who have evidence of normal ovulation and who have had an otherwise normal evaluation may undergo serial ultrasound determinations of follicular size to determine whether the follicle is actually expelled. Vaginal ultrasounds may be used to follow follicular development prior to ovulation and to determine whether, on the day after ovulation, fluid is in the cul-de-sac and the follicle had indeed ruptured. This is also helpful in determining follicular size at the time of menotropin therapy for ovulation induction and in timing human chorionic gonadotropin injections.

Laparoscopy is performed when all other test results are normal in the woman. In women who have had abnormal hysterosalpingograms, laparoscopy must be performed to rule out tubal occlusion. If endometriosis had been detected on past laparotomies or on diagnostic laparoscopies prior to infertility evaluation, this procedure must be performed concomitantly with other infertility evaluations to rule out recurrent disease. In those women who undergo laparoscopy, adhesion disease must be ruled out, as must endometriosis, leiomyomas, uterine malformations that may be clarified further with adjunctive hysteroscopy, and any other intraabdominal abnormalities that may cause infertility. Lysis of adhesions may be performed at this time, as ablation of endometriosis implants, depending on the extent of disease. Chromotubation with indigo carmine dye may be performed to observe tubal patency if a hysterosalpingogram has not been performed because of iodine allergy. Diagnosis and staging of endometriosis can be performed only during laparoscopy or laparotomy. Moreover, length of tube remaining for possible reanastomosis can be determined only by laparoscopy.

A hysteroscopy is performed in women who have abnormal uterine findings at the time of hysterosalpingogram or who are known to have had Asherman's syndrome. During hysteroscopy, adhesions can be lysed and uterine contour fully evaluated. If a uterine septum is diagnosed, and a bicornuate uterus has been ruled out, hysteroscopic resection of the septum can be performed with either the resectoscope or hysteroscopic scissors.

In patients with habitual abortion or otherwise unexplained infertility, it is important to rule out by cervical culture such infections as *Chlamydia, Mycoplasma,* and even gonorrhea, which may be causative agents in tubal infection and cervicitis.

If women have had two successive spontaneous abortions, normal hysterosalpingograms, and no luteal phase defects or significant cervical infections, karyotyping of both partners is required to rule out genetic abnormalities that may be the etiology of repeated miscarriage. Levels of anticardiolipins, lupus anticoagulants, thyroid-stimulating hormone, and prolactin should also be determined.

Recommended Approach

The basic evaluation, including semen analysis, hysterosalpingogram, postcoital test, and endometrial biopsy, must be performed prior to a follow-up consultation with the couple to coordinate information about the basic tests and pertinent findings. During the consultation, further therapy and/or further testing are discussed. If there are no abnormal laboratory findings, a diagnostic laparoscopy to elucidate endometriosis, adhesions, or other pelvic pathology needs to be considered. If the laparoscopy and all other tests are within normal limits, then in vitro fertilization may need to be the next step to elucidate whether abnormal sperm–egg interaction is causing infertility. This, however, would be the last approach only after the thorough evaluation described above is completed.

Therapeutic

The therapeutic options are discussed as they relate to each individual test and its outcome. The cause of infertility may be multifactorial, requiring complex coordination of therapeutic modalities depending on the specific diagnoses elucidated.

Therapeutic Options

Abnormal Semen Analysis. Further therapy must address the specific problem. If a testicular biopsy shows maturation arrest with azoospermia, further therapy may be considered depending on access to centers performing assisted reproductive technology with in vitro fertilization. In patients with Klinefelter's syndrome with hyalinization of the tubules, sperm production will not be improved by any therapeutic modality. Men whose vasectomy reversals have failed or who do not desire the reversal procedure may now be candidates for direct testicular sperm aspiration or microscopic epididymal sperm aspiration combined with intracytoplasmic direct sperm injection through in vitro fertilization procedures. One sperm can be directly inserted into an egg even if the sperm is immobile or has low normal morphology.

Secondary Testicular Disease. Men who have a secondary testicular disease caused by pituitary dysfunction, resulting in low follicle-stimulating and luteinizing hormone levels, may be given clomiphene citrate (Clomid) if hypothalamic function is intact. In patients who have pituitary tumors, bromocriptine (Parlodel) therapy or a transsphenoidal resection may help, depending on the extent of the tumor.

Low Sperm Counts/Low Sperm Motility. For couples who have otherwise normal evaluations but low sperm counts or low-motility sperm with no etiology, intrauterine insemination can be considered. In this treatment, sperm are washed and then placed into the uterine cavity at the time of ovulation to enhance the chances of fertilization. Drugs for ovulation induction may be added to the regimen to increase the number of potential follicles for fertilization. If these procedures are performed and pregnancy still is not achieved with both partners being fully evaluated prior to these attempts, two options remain. One is gamete intrafallopian transfer (GIFT), in which sperm are washed, mixed with the aspirated follicles at the time of laparoscopy, and replaced into the ampullary portion of the tube, where fertilization may possibly occur. The other option is in vitro fertilization (IVF), where follicles aspirated via vaginal ultrasound are mixed with semen, allowed to fertilize into an embryo, and then transferred into the uterus. New techniques including intracytoplasmic sperm injection are available in a few centers for cases of severe oligospermia. As stated before, artificial donor insemination is an option for those couples who desire fertility and in whom the female partner is completely normal or is being treated for her other infertility problems.

Abnormal Uterine Cavity. Women with abnormal uterine cavities as a result of Asherman's syndrome or uterine synechia can undergo hysteroscopy to remove the adhesions. Patients are placed on high-dose estrogen therapy and then allowed to have normal menses thereafter. Patients with submucous, leiomyomas who have had problems with spontaneous abortions may need myomectomy for treatment of this abnormality. Diethylstilbestrol-exposed women with a T-shaped uterus do not usually have infertility problems, but may have cervical incompetence and may need a Shirodkar or a McDonald's cerclage for this problem; they also may have an increased incidence of second-trimester abortion. These individuals do not need any surgical intervention except, possibly, cerclage.

Habitual Abortions. Women found to have a septate uterus need to undergo surgical intervention for this abnormality via hysteroscopic resection. The procedure allows normal uterine architecture to be restored with, it is hoped, a decrease in recurrent abortions. In those women with distal tubal occlusion or hydrosalpinx, microsurgical salpingostomy is performed to provide tubal patency. If individuals have patent tubes but are found at laparoscopy to have peritubal or periovarian adhesions that decrease tubal motility, the adhesions may be lysed at the time of the laparoscopy. If cornual or proximal occlusion of the tubes has been noted, tubal catheterization via hysteroscopy or radiologically directed catheterization may be attempted. If that attempt fails, in vitro fertilization may be the best option.

Poor Huhner's Test. If the sperm motility is low or the sperm count is below normal, then full evaluation is required. The most likely reason for a poor Huhner's test is incorrect timing with poor mucus and ovulation that is either presumptively early or late. Usually, if this is the case, luteinizing hormone monoclonal antibody testing may be used in addition to Huhner's test to determine more specifically the timing of ovulation. If agglutination or no sperm motility is found, further evaluation for sperm antibodies must be done, and the cervical mucus penetration test performed. If evidence of infection is present, or the male partner has been found to have prostatitis with evidence of white blood cells in his semen, then treatment of both partners with doxycycline (100 mg twice daily) for a total of 10 to 14 days, starting the first day of the woman's period, should be considered. Huhner's test can then be performed during that cycle, and if improvement occurs, the most likely etiology was infection. If Huhner's test does not improve after antibiotic therapy, then testing for sperm antibodies is required. If the mucus is abnormal with good timing illustrated by basal body temperature determination and/or luteinizing hormone surge testing, intrauterine insemination should be considered. If improvement occurs, this medication should be continued on a monthly basis. If all therapeutic modalities have been attempted, then intrauterine insemination with washed sperm must be considered. If sperm antibody testing is positive for either the woman or man, intrauterine insemination might be considered, although therapy for this problem does not lead to a high pregnancy rate.

Anovulatory Cycles. For women found to have anovulatory cycles, by either progesterone or endometrial biopsy determination, clomiphene citrate must be used to initiate ovulation. The dose is 50 mg per day starting on day 3 of each cycle and continued for 5 days per month. Ovulation should occur between days 12 and 16, and an endometrial biopsy should be performed or a progesterone level drawn during the luteal phase of the cycle in the initial month of therapy to determine whether ovulation has indeed occurred. If ovulation has not occurred, then dosage is usually increased to 100 mg the next cycle. Until ovulation occurs, therapy can be increased to 150 mg clomiphene plus an additional 10,000 units of human chorionic gonadotropin given at the time of ovulation (determined by follicular size). If follicular development or ovulation still has not occurred, then therapy with human menopausal gonadotropin (Pergonal) should be initiated. If pregnancy does not occur after four well-timed cycles of clomiphene, Pergonal therapy must be considered.

Luteal Phase Deficiency. A woman who does ovulate but is found to have a luteal phase deficiency may be given progesterone vaginal suppositories, beginning with 50 mg daily or 25 mg twice daily on the fourth day after ovulation, or oral progesterone, 100 mg twice daily. Initiation of the medication can be determined by either basal body temperature graph or luteinizing hormone surge testing. Endometrial biopsy or serial progesterone level determination is necessary the first month on the medication to ascertain whether the deficiency has been corrected. Increasing doses must be administered when adequate levels have not been achieved. If the cause of the luteal phase deficiency is hyperprolactinemia or hypothyroidism, bromocriptine or thyroid medication is administered rather than progesterone. A patient who misses her period should be tested for pregnancy and continued on progesterone until either the pregnancy is negative or 12 weeks of gestation have occurred. Bromocriptine is discontinued with a positive pregnancy test.

Endometriosis. Therapeutic modalities are determined by the stage of the disease. Patients may be treated at the time of laparoscopy or may require laparotomy to remove endometriosis implants and restore the anatomy to normal (see Chapter 10–21). Medical therapy with gonadotropin-releasing hormone agonists or danazol (Danocrine) is used in mild or moderate cases.

Chromosomal Abnormalities. Patients with habitual abortions caused by chromosomal abnormalities must seek counseling and determine abnormalities of recurrence. If there is a male factor, donor insemination may be an alternate course in attempting pregnancy.

Other Etiologies. For those individuals with nonoperable tubal occlusion, unexplained infertility, or male factor infertility, in vitro fertilization may be the only course available. This therapy is not a panacea. Success rates vary from 18 to 28% in centers throughout the world; however, it may be one of the last modalities considered by individuals who continue to desire fertility evaluation and therapy.

Recommended Approach

It is important that the practitioner complete all basic testing on a couple prior to consulting with them regarding further therapy. Semen analysis, hysterosalpingogram, postcoital test, and endometrial biopsy must be completed on any couple who seeks infertility testing. It would be remiss for a practitioner to perform tests on only the woman or only the man. Once the basic evaluation is completed, further testing at the second level of evaluation may be considered. After evaluating his or her own expertise in this area, the practitioner may refer couples to appropriate centers where advanced technology is available. It is important that couples are counseled as to all of their options. For example, with respect to male factor infertility, donor insemination should not be considered until the couple is apprised of other available options. Also, women with tubal ligations may choose to undergo less expensive and less involved in vitro fertilization procedures rather than a surgical procedure to bypass tubal occlusion. It is important to present all options to the couple so they can make an informed decision. Couples must also be apprised of the costs, which range from minimal to extensive depending on the particular problems.

FOLLOW-UP

Those individuals who have been interviewed for infertility are usually counseled at that time as to the testing and therapeutic modalities that are available and may be necessary. Often there is no way to determine the etiology of the infertility at the first visit; therefore, follow-up is frequent until all possible problems are evaluated. This may continue for months to years depending on the cause of infertility. During this time, the couple requires not only medical therapy but also emotional support. The extreme stress and emotional upheaval often affects not only their relationship, but also their relationships with friends, peers, and close family members. Counseling the couple, taking stress into consideration, paying close attention to detail in the evaluation, and updating the couple on their progress are exceedingly important. The problem should not be taken lightly. For women over 30, infertility should be evaluated every 6 months rather than yearly because every month is precious in terms of attempting pregnancy. When a couple approaches a physician for this complaint, they usually have delayed the visit a long time and are exceedingly concerned when they enter the office. Asking patients to take vacations, to decrease stress, or to change their work or telling them it is "all in their heads" is not appropriate; the problem must be taken seriously. When the basic evaluation has been performed and the physician feels that a more detailed investigation should be carried out, referral is advisable and is usually well accepted by the couple.

DISCUSSION

The field of infertility is constantly changing because of advances in assisted reproduction technology. Couples should continue to follow breakthroughs that may assist in their pursuit of achieving a pregnancy.

Prevalence

Today, 10 to 15% of all married couples are infertile. The reasons for increasing infertility are complex. Couples are delaying pregnancy to an older age. Also, there has been an increase in the incidence of sexually transmitted diseases, which in turn affects tubal abnormalities and pelvic adhesion disease. In addition, because abortion has been legal for more than 17 years, the number of adoptable babies has decreased, reducing the possibility of this option for couples who cannot have children. Technology has allowed more couples to seek evaluation. Again, the cause of infertility is often multifactorial, and because two individuals are involved, the problem becomes even more complicated.

Related Basic Science

Assisted reproduction technology represents the future in treating those individuals with some form of egg–sperm interaction abnormality. It is in this area where rapid advances are being made, for example, in vitro fertilization procedures, intracytoplasmic direct egg injection or sperm injection, egg donation programs, and embryo cryopreservation.

Physiologic or Metabolic Derangement

Basic abnormalities of egg–sperm interaction underlie the major reasons for infertility. Sperm capacitation and cervical mucus, tubal motility, absence of or problems with tubal ciliogenesis, distal fimbrial disease, sperm motility or dysfunction, and other factors constitute the complex array of possible factors in infertility. A singular derangement or a spectrum of abnormalities may have resulted in infertility. One must dissect each segment of the reproductive system to rule out the possible abnormalities causing infertility. Some etiologies are quite apparent; others are elusive. Therefore, constant vigilance and conscientiousness are required in diagnosis and treatment of the infertile couple.

Anatomic Derangement

As discussed, anatomic abnormalities include uterine defects (septate versus bicornuate, tubal occlusion, cornual versus distal, cervical stenosis), pelvic pathology (endometriosis, adhesions, tubal disease), abnormal sperm morphology and function, and variation in egg quality with the aging process.

Natural History and Its Modification with Treatment

Depending on the problems involved, if a couple elect not to seek therapy, their status will most probably remain unchanged. Women with polycystic ovarian disease occasionally ovulate spontaneously, but infrequently. Men who have had a borderline to low semen analysis may sporadically have counts high enough to allow adequate fertilization of a normal egg. Patients with anatomic defects such as occluded fallopian tubes usually remain infertile unless surgical intervention is performed.

There are many anecdotal cases of infertile couples achieving a pregnancy after discontinuing therapy or adopting a child. In truth, a small percentage of individuals do so. Infertility itself is not a health problem. Marital relationships may either strengthen or falter depending on the emphasis placed on the problem. Women with endometriosis as a cause of their infertility should seek further medical or surgical therapy; otherwise, this disease state can cause further complications involving bowel, ureters, or adjacent pelvic structures (see Chapter 10–21).

Prevention

Prevention of infertility can be considered only in individuals who are at greatest risk, namely, those who may be exposed to sexually transmitted disease and must be counseled concerning this possibility. The increase in evidence of *Chlamydia* and *Mycoplasma* as etiologic agents of tubal occlusion is important to relate to patients when they become sexually active. Nulliparous women or women who have not completed their family should be discouraged from using intrauterine devices to prevent infections that may cause tubal damage or disease. Women who are at risk for developing endometriosis because they have a first-degree relative with endometriosis or who have significant dysmenorrhea or dyspareunia should be evaluated by laparoscopy at an early age to minimize future problems. Although infertility is not usually considered a problem until past the age of 40, couples in their late twenties or early thirties should be advised that women over the age of 35 are at high risk for having infants with Down syndrome and must take this fact into consideration when postponing pregnancy or infertility evaluation. Success rates decline markedly starting at age 35, especially in women whose husbands have male factor infertility. Couples must evaluate their problems and consider pursuit of therapy.

Cost Containment

The infertility evaluation must comprise basic testing of both the man and woman, including semen analysis, hysterosalpingogram, postcoital test, and endometrial biopsy. Only after a thorough basic evaluation should diagnostic laparoscopy or surgical intervention (second-level diagnostic studies) be considered. Women with significant disease that may contribute to infertility, such as a history of endometriosis, uterine leiomyoma, intrauterine device use, or pelvic inflammatory disease, should not wait before being evaluated. Because infertility is usually not covered by most insurance companies and can be expensive, the couple must be made aware of all aspects of the procedures, the costs involved, and the ultimate percentage success rates. They can then make an educated decision regarding their desire to proceed with evaluation and possible therapy.

Prevention of sexually transmitted disease, avoidance of intrauterine devices by nulliparous women, and careful tissue handling of pelvic anatomy and structures in the reproductive-age woman could all be considered areas of eventually decreasing cost. Planning to do one test at a time over a period of years is not cost effective because patients grow older and more frustrated. Evaluation for infertility is expensive, and this must be made clear to couples at their initial visit.

REFERENCES

Noyes RW, Hertig AT, Rock J. Dating the endometrial biopsy. Fertil Step 1950;1:3.

Speroff L, Glass RH, Kase NG. Clinical gynecologic endocrinology and infertility. 5th ed. Baltimore: Williams & Wilkins, 1994.

Tucker MJ, Wright G, Morton PC, et al. Practical evolution and application of direct intracytoplasmic sperm injection for male factor and idiopathic fertilization failure infertilities. Fertil Steril 1995;63(4):82.

Yen SC, Jaffe RB. Reproductive endocrinology. 3rd ed. Philadelphia: Saunders, 1991.

Dermatologic Problems

Marilynne McKay, M.D., Robert L. Rietschel, M.D.

CHAPTER 11–1

Skin Disease Localizing to a Body Region

Marilynne McKay, M.D.

DEFINITION

Certain parts of the body are more likely to be affected by one skin disorder than by others, and a skin disease limited to one area of the body can sometimes be diagnosed primarily on the basis of its distribution.

ETIOLOGY

Localization of lesions can be the result of environmental factors, such as sunlight or exposure to allergens and chemicals; infections, such as sexually transmitted diseases on the genitalia; or common skin pathogens entering through a traumatized area, such as the hands or feet. Some parts of the body are more susceptible to specific problems: examples include hairy areas, intertriginous zones, the lower extremities where circulation is poor, mucosal surfaces, dermatomes, and areas where sebaceous glands are more concentrated. In some cases, the rea-

son for the distribution of a skin disease is unknown, even though the pattern is typical of that disorder.

CRITERIA FOR DIAGNOSIS
Suggestive

Lesion location is only one aspect of disease categorization, because the pattern and morphology of lesions also offer important diagnostic clues (see Chapters 11–3 to 11–20).

The localization or concentration of skin lesions on certain areas of the body may provide valuable diagnostic clues to the physician. Obviously, the entire body should be examined, and particular attention should be given to the morphology and configuration of the lesions. Only in this complete context can proper emphasis by given to regional involvement. Careful evaluation of the distribution of cutaneous disease frequently helps to eliminate similar-looking diseases in the same morphologic category, and beginning with regional involvement may be helpful in expanding the physician's thinking toward a broader differential diagnosis.

Definitive

Biopsy and/or culture for bacteria, virus, and/or fungi can be very helpful in some cases, but it is not necessary for most common dermatologic problems.

CLINICAL MANIFESTATIONS
Subjective

The patient often comes to the physician with the complaint of a skin eruption involving a particular body region. Many times a careful examination reveals a much more generalized problem, but the patient tends to focus on areas of the body important to him or her. The face is probably the most cosmetically significant area, but involvement of the hands and feet may render the patient functionally immobile. Genital lesions are often frightening to patients and may evoke fear of carcinoma or sexually transmitted diseases.

It is very likely that the patient will have developed his or her own ideas about what has caused the problem, and it should be assumed that the patient will have attempted some form of treatment. The latter may have exacerbated the problem or changed the lesion morphology, making diagnosis more difficult. It is important to seek out new "primary" lesions or to ask the patient to describe the original outbreak.

The history should include exposures to a chemical, drug, or other agent as well as what treatment the patient may have tried on his or her own. The length of time the problem has been present is important, as is the determination of whether the patient has had this or a similar skin problem in the past. Family history is less important in the adult patient, who usually volunteers whether other family members have a similar skin disorder.

Objective
Physical Examination

See Table 11–1–1. These morphologic criteria should lead the reader to the appropriate chapter for further details.

Routine Laboratory Abnormalities

There are no routine diagnostic laboratory abnormalities.

PLANS
Diagnostic
Differential Diagnosis

See Table 11–1–1.

Diagnostic Options

Careful observation of the patient's entire skin should enable the examiner to decide which morphologic category best describes the typical lesions.

Skin biopsy is a helpful means of distinguishing one dermatologic disorder from another, but nonspecific "rashes" typically produce nondiagnostic histology. Culture of an infectious process is important, but bacterial, fungal, and viral media should be considered at the time of the initial evaluation. Secondary infection of inflamed or eroded skin is typical, and *Staphylococcus, Streptococcus,* and *Candida* often represent only invasion of skin already compromised by inflammation.

Recommended Approach

By matching the lesion morphology to the affected area of the body, the reader should be able to determine the appropriate chapter in this section to read for more detailed description of the disorder.

Therapeutic
Therapeutic Options

Suggestions for proper evaluation and therapy are given in subsequent chapters under the appropriate morphologic category heading for each condition.

Recommended Approach

The reader should attempt to narrow the diagnostic possibilities to decide on the simplest therapeutic option. Multiple medications are discouraged as they may interfere with one another and the patient may become confused about frequency or sites of application.

FOLLOW-UP

Except for tumors and infections, skin disorders tend to be chronic and recurrent. It is often necessary for patients to learn to use topical medications to control flares and remissions of disease. Patient education is an important aspect of management for dermatologic disorders.

DISCUSSION
Related Basic Science

There are many reasons for localization of cutaneous reactions. Exposure of a small area of skin to a contact allergen will limit the T cell–mediated reaction to a very specific location and pattern, making the diagnosis of contact dermatitis relatively obvious. Photosensitive reactions will be evident on sun-exposed areas of the skin. The malar face is classically involved, but in a true photoeruption one should additionally look for sparing of relatively shaded areas on the face, such as the upper lip and eyelids. Vasculitic and stasis-related lesions tend to be more obvious on the lower extremities, where gravity increases the venous pressure and the vessel becomes more "leaky." Mucous membranes are especially susceptible to blistering and erosive processes, and hyperkeratotic or scaling disorders in moist areas in general will appear white as a result of maceration or overhydration of the stratum corneum. The localization of certain pigmented lesions such as lentigines to specific areas of the body appears to have little rationale, except as a helpful aid to diagnosis. Similarly, involvement of the palms and soles seems to be surprisingly nonspecific, except when there is a generalized eruption, when the presence or absence of lesions in these areas becomes a significant factor in differential diagnosis.

In evaluating the patient with a localized dermatitis, the physician should additionally evaluate areas on the body spared by the eruption. For example, a severe dermatitis may begin in one area, such as the hands, and spread further up the arms and then to the rest of the body in a generalized flare. It may be difficult to differentiate such a chronic hand and arm contact dermatitis from a photosensitive disorder, but involvement of the sun-protected inner upper arm or axilla will make photoeruption a less likely possibility. Similarly, the white lacy buccal mucosal lesions of lichen planus are rarely noticed by the patient, but they are most helpful to the physician seeking oral involvement as a confirmation of the diagnosis of lichen planus in its typical distribution on the wrists.

Many disorders look alike at the lesion level and differ greatly on similar areas of involved skin. The experienced dermatologist knows that diagnosis depends on completeness in physical examination and considers all three aspects of the patient's problem: lesion morphology, configuration, and distribution.

Natural History, Prevention, and Cost Containment

These items are discussed in the chapters in which morphologic characteristics are discussed (i.e., papules, pustules).

REFERENCES

Callen JP, Greer KE, Hood AF, et al. Color atlas of dermatology. Philadelphia: Saunders, 1993.
Lawrence CM, Cox NH. Physical signs in dermatology: Color atlas and text. London: Mosby-Year Book Europe, 1993.

TABLE 11–1–1. REGIONAL DERMATOLOGIC DIAGNOSES

Location/Lesion Morphology	Supporting Data	Probable Diagnosis
Scalp		
Papules and nodules		
Rough-surfaced	Since birth or childhood	Nevus verrucosus, nevus sebaceous,* verruca vulgaris, prurigo nodularis
	Recent onset	Seborrheic keratosis
Smooth, dome-shaped	Changing or recent onset	Basal cell carcinoma,* metastasis,* epidermoid or pilar cyst, cylindroma
Erythematous, red	Stable size	Hemangioma, nevus, mastocytoma
Pigmented	Changing or recent onset	Melanoma,* dermatofibroma
Erythematous plaques	Lesions on elbows, knees, nail pits	Psoriasis
with scaling	Lesions on central face	Seborrheic dermatitis
	KOH+, fungal culture+	Tinea capitis
Hair loss (alopecia)		
Smooth scalp	Round areas, acute onset	Alopecia areata → totalis → universalis
	Diffuse or patchy	Telogen effluvium, traction alopecia, secondary syphilis, endocrine problems, cytotoxic drugs, male or female pattern baldness
With scarring	Irregular pattern	Scarring alopecias (various)
	Follicular plugging, ANA+	Discoid lupus erythematosus
Face		
Macules		
Brown	Sun-exposed areas	Freckles, lentigo, melasma, berloque dermatitis, lentigo maligna*
White	Periorificial	Vitiligo, Chediak–Higashi syndrome, Vogt–Koyanagi–Harada syndrome
	Forehead, may include lock of hair	Piebaldism, Waardenburg's syndrome
Papules		
Yellow to white	Adult onset, multiple	Xanthoma, xanthelasma, milia, amyloid, senile sebaceous hyperplasia, syringoma, molluscum contagiosum, closed comedones
Red to blue	Present since birth or childhood	Hemangioma, nevi, urticaria pigmentosa
	Adult onset, multiple	Hydrocystoma, syphilis, lichen planus, lymphocytoma cutis, mycosis fungoides* sarcoidosis, eccrine tumors
Flesh-colored	Present since birth or childhood	Adenoma sebaceum (tuberous sclerosis)
	Adult onset, multiple	Basal cell carcinoma,* syringoma, keloids, trichoepithelioma, nevi, flat warts, molluscum, amyloidosis, cutaneous tuberculosis
Brown to black	Dark-skinned, malar region	Dermatosis papulosa nigra (seborrheic keratoses)
	Single or multiple	Basal cell carcinoma,* seborrheic keratosis, nevi, sarcoidosis
Erythematous plaques		
"Malar rash"	Symmetric	Seborrheic dermatitis, steroid rosacea, systemic lupus erythematosus, photoeruption, polymorphous light eruption, pemphigus, collagen–vascular diseases
	Asymmetric	Contact dermatitis, erysipelas, tinea, granuloma faciale, lymphocytic infiltrate, actinic keratoses
With pustules	Adult onset	Acne vulgaris, acne rosacea, steroid acne, pseudofolliculitis barbae, tinea, folliculitis
Mouth and tongue		
Blisters and erosions	Localized to oral cavity	Aphthae, Behçet's, herpangina, aphthae, contact, trauma, syphilis, squamous cell carcinoma,* erosive lichen planus; methotrexate reaction
	Lesions elsewhere on body	Pemphigus vulgaris, pemphigoid, erythema multiforme (Stevens–Johnson syndrome), epidermolysis bullosa, hand/foot/mouth, cyclic neutropenia, leukemia, systemic lupus erythematosus
White lesions	Acute	Aphthae, candidiasis, trauma, syphilis
	Chronic	Candidiasis, leukoplakia, psoriasis, lichen planus, Darier's disease, oral papillomatosis, geographic tongue, squamous cell carcinoma,* discoid lupus erythematosus
Pigmentation	Localized	Peutz–Jeghers syndrome, Addison's disease, lentigo, nevi, heavy metals, drugs
Papules/plaques	Usually red	Condylomata acuminata, lichen planus, trauma, psoriasis, pyogenic granuloma, Fordyce spots, squamous cell carcinoma,* Bowen's disease,* metastatic carcinoma,* Kaposi's sarcoma,* amyloidosis, histoplasmosis, phlebectasia, hemangioma, varicosities, telangiectasias
Gingival thickening		Dilantin therapy, pregnancy, lymphoma, leukemia, periodontal disease, scurvy
Genitalia		
Ulcers	Sexually transmitted	Syphilis, chancroid, granuloma inguinale, herpes simplex, candidiasis, scabies
	Noninfectious	Behçet's syndrome, factitia, trauma, fixed drug, erythema multiforme, squamous cell carcinoma,* aphthae, pemphigoid, pemphigus, pyoderma gangrenosum
Papules		
Pink to flesh color	Multiple	Lichen planus, lichen nitidus, vulvar papillae, pearly penile papules, condylomata acuminata, molluscum
Red to black	Multiple, scrotum or vulva	Angiokeratoma, nevi, seborrheic keratoses
Plaques		
"White lesions"	Localized	Lichen sclerosus, Bowen's disease,* Paget's disease,* lichen simplex chronicus
	Lesions elsewhere on body	Psoriasis, seborrhea
Axillae and groin		
Macules	Freckling	Crowe's sign (neurofibromatosis)
	Blue-gray 1-cm spots	Maculae cerulae (pubic lice)
	Diffuse darkening	Postinflammatory pigmentation, ochronosis

(continued)

TABLE 11–1–1. (*Continued*)

Location/Lesion Morphology	Supporting Data	Probable Diagnosis
Dermatitis/eczema	Acute onset	Contact dermatitis
	Chronic	Hailey–Hailey disease
Papules	Flesh-colored or dark	Fox–Fordyce disease, flat warts, epidermal nevi, skin tags
	Red	Angiokeratomas, candidiasis
Plaques	Pigmented, "velvety"	Acanthosis nigricans,* pseudoacanthosis
	Pigmented, scaly	Erythrasma, tinea, lichen simplex
Pustules	Inflammatory	Candidiasis, tinea, pustular psoriasis
Cysts	Multiple, chronic	Steatocystoma multiplex
	With inflammation	Hidradenitis suppurativa
Cutaneous atrophy	Striae distensae	Cushing's disease, steroid therapy (including topical)
	With yellowish papules	Pseudoxanthoma elasticum
Palms and soles		
Macules		
Yellow	Diffuse, also behind ears	Carotenemia
Brown	Irregular margins	Tinea nigra, acral lentiginous melanoma*
Black	Punctate spots	Plantar wart, black heel (secondary to trauma)
Vesicles/pustules	Acute onset	Scabies, tinea, orf, hand/foot/mouth
		Dyshidrosis (pompholyx), Reiter's syndrome, pustular psoriasis, pustulosis plantaris/palmaris, epidermolysis bullosa simplex
Erythema/pupura	Chronic and recurrent	Secondary syphilis, Rocky Mountain spotted fever, gonococcal sepsis, graft-vs-host, lupus, erythema multiforme, rheumatoid arthritis
Hyperkeratosis		
Localized	Dermatoglyphs intact	Callus, corn, clavus
	"Black dots"	Verruca vulgaris/plantaris
	Chronic	Arsenical keratoses, Darier's disease
Extensive	Thick scaling	Psoriasis, tinea, Reiter's syndrome, hereditary keratodermas, hyperkeratosis plantaris/palmaris, secondary to lymphoma or carcinoma*
Acral sclerosis		Arteriosclerosis obliterans, Buerger's disease, cryoproteinemia, Raynaud's disease, sclerodactyly secondary to scleroderma (progressive systemic sclerosis), emboli, ergot toxicity
Lower extremities		
Painful nodules	Multiple	Erythema nodosum, angiolipoma, leiomyoma, lupus profundus, superficial thrombophlebitis, Weber–Christian panniculitis, eccrine poroma, Kaposi's sarcoma,* Majocci granuloma (tinea)
Ulcers	Vascular	Arteriosclerosis obliterans, stasis, sepsis, leukocytoclastic vasculitis, arterial
	Infectious	Deep fungus, ecthyma, anthrax, atypical mycobacterium, tropical ulcer, treponemal
	Hematologic	Cryopathies, sickle cell, thalassemia
	Neurologic	Tabes dorsalis, mal perforans, Hansen's disease
	Neoplasia	Squamous cell carcinoma,* Kaposi's sarcoma,* melanoma,* mycosis fungoides,* metastatic carcinoma,* basal cell carcinoma,* angiosarcoma*
	Miscellaneous	Trauma, factitial, chemical, bites/stings, pyoderma gangrenosum, necrobiosis lipoidica diabeticorum
Trunk and generalized ("rashes")		
Erythematous reactions	Macular (flat)	Sunburn, drug eruption, viral exanthem, measles, typhoid, Kawasaki's, infectious mononucleosis and hepatitis, rheumatic fever, juvenile rheumatoid arthritis
	Papular (elevated)	Urticaria (hives), erythema multiforme
Papulosquamous	Multiple small plaques	Pityriasis rosea, secondary syphilis, guttate psoriasis, lichen planus, seborrhea, tinea versicolor, parapsoriasis, lupus
	Entire body ("exfoliative erythroderma")	Eczematous dermatitis, psoriasis, lymphoreticular malignancy, drug eruption
Dermatitis/eczema	Acute, odd patterns	Contact dermatitis, factitial
	Annular (round) lesions	Nummular dermatitis, tinea corporis
	Antecubital, popliteal especially	Atopic dermatitis
	Fingerwebs, axillae, genitals	Scabies
Vesicles and pustules	Acute	Miliaria rubra ("prickly heat"), drug eruptions, pustular psoriasis, candidiasis, folliculitis
Purpura	Coagulopathy	Drug-induced, infectious, tumor
	Vasculitis	Allergic, collagen-vascular disease, Henoch–Schönlein syndrome, thrombocytopenic purpura (TTP), dysproteinemia
	Infectious	Meningiococcemia, Rocky Mountain spotted fever

ANA, antinuclear antibody. *Malignancy or associated with neoplasia. + = positive (test confirms diagnosis).

CHAPTER 11–2

Infections of the Skin and Soft Tissue (See Section 8, Chapter 29)

CHAPTER 11–3

Pigment Abnormalities

Marilynne McKay, M.D.

DEFINITION

A macule is a flat skin lesion that can be perceived visually, but cannot be palpated. Most macular skin disorders are the result of pigment abnormalities.

ETIOLOGY

Normal reddish-brown to blue-black cutaneous pigmentation is due to melanin produced by epidermal melanocytes. Whitening of the skin is due to loss of normal pigment. Deposition of metabolites or heavy metals can also produce yellow or bluish skin pigmentation.

CRITERIA FOR DIAGNOSIS

Macular lesions without a papular component are likely to be due to pigment abnormalities. Flat lesions that blanch with pressure are considered to be erythematous, not macular: this is an important distinction. (See Chapters 11–11 and 11–12 for discussion of erythematous and vascular lesions.) Elevated or scaly lesions are also discussed in other chapters (11–4, 11–5, 11–6).

Suggestive

Pigmentary change may be primary or secondary. The mere presence of macules does not indicate that the skin problem is due to alteration in pigment, as postinflammatory changes may result in lightening or darkening of the skin after an inflammatory process has resolved.

Definitive

Macular lesions that have been present from birth or have arisen de novo without preceding dermatitis or inflammation are typical of pigmentary abnormalities. Congenital pigmentary aberrations are generally constant throughout the patient's lifetime. Acquired pigment disorders are noticed by the patient as a visible change in skin color that is not usual for him or her. Either type may be local or generalized, and borders may be well circumscribed or diffuse.

CLINICAL MANIFESTATIONS

Subjective

Most pigment changes are asymptomatic, but some may be related to a preceding inflammation, which may have been pruritic. Associated skin lesions, age of onset, and variation over time are significant historical elements. Systemic disease may be responsible for pigmentary changes, as may ingestion or application of certain drugs or chemicals.

Objective

Physical Examination

Pigment changes of normal brown to black skin tones may be observed as darkening (hyperpigmentation) or lightening (hypopigmentation). The degree of change or contrast depends to a large extent on the overall skin tone of the individual, as lightening or darkening lesions may be far more obvious on dark skin than on fair skin. Blue-gray or yellow pigmentation of the skin also may be seen, although less commonly. All pigmentary abnormalities may occur as individual lesions or may be generalized to the entire integument. The distribution should be noted carefully, as should the configuration of individual macules or patches. Patterns should be sought; the hair, nails, mucous membranes, and genitalia should be examined as well.

Routine Laboratory Abnormalities

Except for tests for specific systemic diseases which may typically present with alteration of skin pigmentation (e.g. Addison's disease) there are no routine laboratory tests for this category of skin disorders.

PLANS

Diagnostic

Differential Diagnosis

The differential diagnosis of pigmentary disorders is given in Table 11–3–1.

Diagnostic Options

Wood's light (ultraviolet light A of 320 to 400 nm) is often a helpful diagnostic tool for examining skin. Epidermal hyperpigmentation is accentuated under Wood's light examination; dermal pigment is not distinguishable. Hypopigmentation due to normal numbers of melanocytes with decreased capacity for melanin synthesis (hypomelanosis) appears "off white" under Wood's light; in the absence of melanocytes (amelanosis), the skin appears chalk white.

Biopsy is indicated when malignant melanoma is a possibility or when color alteration is thought to be due to deposition of material (e.g., xanthoma) or an underlying skin disorder (e.g., scleroderma). Biopsy can also differentiate between epidermal (melanocytic) and dermal pigmentation.

Recommended Approach

When a patient presents with a pigmented macule that has changed in color, size, shape, or sensation or that bleeds easily, a biopsy should be performed to rule out malignancy. Other, more diffuse, pigmentation changes can usually be diagnosed by observation of the distribution and pattern of pigment (see Table 11–3–1).

Therapeutic

Therapeutic Options

If the cause can be determined, treatment should be directed to the underlying problem. Photosensitive hyperpigmentation may respond slowly to regular application of hydroquinone-containing "bleaching creams" and concomitant use of sunscreens. Extensive hypopigmentation such as generalized vitiligo (more than 40% of the body) may be treated by depigmentation of normal skin with monobenzyl ether of hydroquinone; the goal of therapy is not to restore the original skin color, but to achieve a uniform one. Localized vitiligo may be treated with photochemotherapy or oral 8-methoxypsoralen and ultraviolet A (PUVA). This may require several months of therapy two to three times per week, but it is successful in a majority of patients. Topical psoralens are also effective, but they must be used with extreme caution.

Most pigmentary abnormalities are distressing to the patient. Reassurance and interest are important. Sunscreens (SPF15) help prevent

TABLE 11–3–1. DIFFERENTIAL DIAGNOSES OF PIGMENTARY CHANGES

Characteristic Appearance	Associated Findings	Likely Diagnosis
Localized hyperpigmentation		
Small brown macules in sun-exposed areas	Wood's light accentuates	Freckles (ephelides)
Well-circumscribed brown macules on hands and face, middle-aged or older	Persistent	"Age spots" (lengito, lentigines)
Variegated mottling, irregular border, sun-exposed, palms/soles in blacks	Enlarging, changing appearance, hemorrhage or pigment loss	Lentigo maligna
Brown-black "stain" on palm or sole	Potassium hydroxide positive for hyphae	Tinea nigra
Millimeter-sized, variable shades, some raised	Present many years	Pigmented junctional nevi
Centimeter-sized, uniform, irregular border	Single common, multiple rare (rule out neurofibromatosis, Albright's syndrome)	Café-au-lait spots
Palm-sized, brown-black, hairy, irregular	Onset at adolescence, occurrence familial	Becker's nevus
Symmetric "butterfly" blotch, women	Pregnancy or oral contraceptives, Wood's light accentuates	Melasma
Dark line, publis/umbilicus, occasionally to xiphoid	Associated with pregnancy	Linea nigra
Irregular margins, "wrinkly" surface	History of previous dermatitis, Wood's light fades	Postinflammatory hyperpigmentation
Brown geometric patterns	Spares non-sun-exposed areas	Tanning
Symmetric line anterior upper arms, posterior lateral legs, black people	Present since childhood	Futcher's line
Brown "drippy" patterns, acute onset	History of contactant: lime juice, chemicals such as silver nitrate	Berloque dermatitis, photoactivated "stain"
Generalized hyperpigmentation		
Uniform skin darkening, pale intertriginous	Nude sunbathing, tanning booth	Tanning
Bronze, increased in sun-exposed areas	Diabetes, cirrhosis, hemosiderin in skin biopsy	Hemochromatosis
Sun-exposed darkening, blisters on dorsal hands	Hirsutism, estrogens, cirrhosis	Porphyria cutanea tarda
General darkening	History of systemic medication (busulfan, etc.)	Drug induced
Brownish, especially over pressure points	Weakness, orthostatic hypotension	Addison's disease
Darker in intertriginous areas, new scars, mucous membranes, genitalia, palmar creases	Diabetes, obesity, hypertension, weight loss, tremor, sweating	Cushing's syndrome, hyperthyroidism
Mottled "raindrops in a dusty road"	Palmar/plantar keratoses, skin and visceral carcinoma	Arsenic ingestion (chronic)
Generalized dark brown to blue-black	History of melanoma and metastasis	Melanosis
Localized hypopigmentation		
Oval "ash-leaf" macule on trunk, congenital	Adenoma sebaceum, shagreen patch, periungual fibromas, Wood's light pale	Tuberous sclerosis
Geographic patch, often involves scalp	May be familial, Wood's light white	Piebaldism
Enlarging patches, acral and periorificial	May be familial, high-risk thyroid disease	Vitiligo
Acral pigment loss, "bleaching"	History of exposure, especially phenols	Chemical depigmentation
Pigment loss around a mole	Adolescence, pregnancy	Halo nevus
Pigment loss within an enlarging mole	Variegated change in appearance	Malignant melanoma
Irregular pale macule	Unresponsive constricted blood vessels	Nevus anemicus
Anesthetic pale macules	Exposure history, nerve lesions, biopsy	Leprosy
Mottled hypopigmentation or hyperpigmentation	Exposure history, serology/darkfield positive	Pinta
"Salt and pepper" follicular pattern	Sclerosis, esophageal motility, biopsy	Scleroderma
2- to 4-mm macules on anterior shins	Usually female, often black, no associated systemic findings	Idiopathic guttate hypomelanosis
Irregular macules, "wrinkly" surface	History of previous dermatitis	Postinflammatory hypopigmentation
Generalized hypopigmentation		
Congenital completely white skin and hair	Nystagmus, photophobia, melanocytes without melanin	Albinism
White skin and hair, residual pigment	Acquired, no melanocytes	Vitiligo
Pale skin, blond hair	Eczema, seizures, mental retardation	Phenylketonuria
Blotchy pigment fading, dyschormic hair	Evidence of protein malnutrition	Kwashiorkor
Localized blue-gray pigmentation		
Solitary blue-black macule, often has depth	Typical biopsy	Blue nevus
2- to 5-cm, slate color, ill-defined, on back and buttocks of infants, fades as adult	Congenital, blacks/Asians (rule out ecchymosis)	Mongolian spot
Palm-sized ill-defined blue-gray area, unilateral face or shoulder	Congenital, may involve sclera, typical dermatome pattern	Nevus of Ota (eye) or Ito (shoulder)
Gray-brown cartilage, sclera, skin	Homogentisic acid in urine	Ocronosis
Irregular gray-blue pigmentation	History of antimalarial agents, minocycline, phenothiazine, mercury, etc.	Medications
Blue to red-brown irregular splotches	History of trauma, anticoagulants	Ecchymosis
Discrete blue-black stippling	History of decorative/traumatic tattoo	Tattoo (foreign material)
Black punctate spots on heel, acute	History of running/start–stop activity	"Black heel" (blood)
Less than 1-cm blue-gray macules on trunk, pubis	Demonstrate body or pubic lice	Maculae cerulae (lice)
Bizarre swirls and stripes over trunk	Congenital, female, history of blisters and raised lesions early	Incontinentia pigmenti
Generalized blue-gray pigmentation		
Dusky gray-blue skin	History of bismuth, silver, mercury, or phenothiazine therapy	Medications
Blue-black darkening	History of melanoma and metastasis	Melanosis
Localized yellowish pigmentation		
Yellow palms/soles, behind ears	Intake of yellow vegetables, β-carotene	Carotenemia
Yellowish opaque plaques	Elevated serum lipid/triglycerides	Plane xanthoma
Discrete artistic macules	History of tattoo with cadmium sulfide	Tattoo
Generalized yellowish pigmentation		
Yellow to yellow-green skin	Yellow sclerae	Jaundice
Greenish yellow-brown	Normal sclerae, use of antimalarials	Medications
Opaque "powdery" yellowish skin	Elevated serum lipid/triglycerides	Plane xanthoma

further contrast between photosensitive skin and lighter areas, and opaque cosmetic coverups (Dermablend, Covermark) may be used successfully, especially by women.

Recommended Approach

An effort should be made to help the patient understand the cause of the problem, because therapeutic measures (if available) generally take considerable time and effort on the patient's part. Avoidance of sunlight and the use of sunscreens to decrease contrast due to tanning are important in both photosensitive disorders and normally pigmented skin surrounding areas of hypopigmentation. Sun-exposed depigmented skin may be more susceptible to actinic damage and skin carcinomas. Pigmentation due to systemic causes should be explained to the patient, as should the absence of associated findings if this is the case. Patients may believe that their problem is due to an infection such as venereal disease or leprosy, and they should be encouraged to discuss their fears so that appropriate reassurances may be given. The likelihood of familial inheritance should be discussed when appropriate.

FOLLOW-UP

The frequency of follow-up visits depends on the cause and treatment of the pigment abnormality. Extensively hypopigmented patients at risk for sun-induced skin carcinomas should be examined at yearly intervals or more frequently if carcinomas have begun to develop.

DISCUSSION
Prevalence and Incidence

Each of the many causes of cutaneous pigmentation abnormalities has a different prevalence and incidence. Postinflammatory hyper- and hypopigmentation is extremely common, especially in dark-skinned individuals. Intensive efforts to educate patients about sun damage to the skin seem to be slowing the rate of sun-induced skin damage and cancers. The future will show whether this approach continues to be effective.

Related Basic Science
Genetics

Melanin is the brownish black pigment responsible for the normal color of the human epidermis. It is produced from tyrosine and bound to the melanosome, an organelle synthesized in the melanocyte and then transferred to epidermal keratinocytes. The melanocyte and surrounding keratinocytes form the epidermal melanin unit. Abnormalities of melanocytes, melanosomes, or melanin itself may result in changes in skin coloration. The difference between normal light and dark skin is the number and functional activity of the epidermal melanin units and the packaging of the melanosomes.

Physiologic or Metabolic Derangement

Ultraviolet light stimulation increases the rate of melanosome synthesis. Melanosomes are gradually lost as keratinocytes are transported up-

ward in the epidermis and desquamated, accounting for the transient nature of ultraviolet-induced tanning. Other factors affecting skin pigmentation include local genetic regulator mechanisms, hormones, drug ingestion, blood flow, epidermal turnover, nutrition, and metabolism.

Hypopigmentation, or leukoderma, may be due to the absence or decreased production of melanin or melanosomes by the epidermal melanin unit.

Blue-gray pigmentation is most often due to the abnormal presence of melanin in the dermis. Scattering of reflected light by the overlying epidermis results in a characteristic slate or blue color. Foreign or biologic material lodged in the skin also may appear bluish or black, for example, hemoglobin, hemosiderin, metal salts, carbon from tattooing, and injectable metals (bismuth, silver, mercury).

Generalized yellow pigmentation may be caused by an accumulation of carotenes, bilirubin, biliverdin, and antimalarial therapeutic agents. Plane xanthomas are localized yellow deposits of lipids.

Anatomic Derangement

Decreased blood flow may cause an apparent lightening of skin in the affected area, an effect best seen in light-skinned individuals.

Natural History and Its Modification with Treatment

Each of the many causes of cutaneous pigmentary abnormalities has its own natural history. Some conditions are self-limited and resolve with time, whereas others seem to worsen with age. Resolution or response to therapy is generally slow.

Prevention

No preventive measures are currently available for the majority of pigmentary disorders. When inflammation is a factor, control of the associated dermatitis may be helpful. Discontinuation of pigment-inducing medications may prevent further changes, and protection from sunlight may lessen contrast between normal and abnormal skin.

Cost Containment

Treatment of cutaneous hypopigmentation (vitiligo) is most likely to incur the greatest expense to the patient. The need for months of continuous office therapy with special ultraviolet light units (PUVA) can be discouraging. Fair-skinned patients should be urged to consider the use of sunscreens and opaque cosmetic coverage rather than PUVA, as this therapeutic modality increases the likelihood of premature aging and skin carcinoma. The use of topical psoralens with natural sunlight is somewhat risky, for sunburn can occur with overexposure times of less than a minute.

REFERENCES

Champion RH, Burton JL, Ebling FJG, eds. Textbook of dermatology. Oxford, England: Blackwell Scientific, 1991.

Fitzpatrick TB, Eisen AZ, Wolff K, et al., eds. Dermatology in general medicine. 4th ed. New York: McGraw-Hill, 1993.

CHAPTER 11–4

Scaling and Flaking

Marilynne McKay, M.D.

DEFINITION

Scaling is dry desquamation of a thickened stratum corneum, or horny layer. Scales may range in appearance from fine powdery flakes to thick shell-like plates that crack and fissure.

ETIOLOGY

The primary scaling (ichthyosiform, "fish scale") dermatoses are relatively rare genetic diseases. Far more common is xerosis, dry flaky skin due to lack of emollients; this is typically seen in elderly patients, especially on the lower extremities. Also common is secondary postinflammatory scale developing with resolution of an inflammatory dermatosis. Dry scaly skin is also a problem for patients with systemic disease such as HIV infection, chronic graft-versus-host disease (GVHD), and some malignancies.

CRITERIA FOR DIAGNOSIS
Suggestive

The presence of flakes or scales on the skin is very common, and when the problem is persistent and recalcitrant the diagnosis of a scaling dermatosis should be considered. On the other hand, scaling is a major component of the hyperproliferative disorders (e.g., psoriasis, seborrheic dermatitis, eczema), in which the underlying morphologic change is an elevated papule with secondary scale. In these cases, the lesion is elevated and scaly or "papulosquamous" and is discussed in Chapter 11–6.

Definitive

Persistent scaling and flaking in the absence of localized inflammation should elicit a differential diagnosis of one of the scaling dermatoses.

CLINICAL MANIFESTATIONS
Subjective

"Dryness," flaking, and itching are the patient's primary complaints. Lack of skin pliability may be severe enough in some areas to cause painful fissures and bleeding. Generalized scaling disorders may be hereditary and begin in early childhood, but are usually associated with aging skin. In either case, symptoms generally worsen during the winter or in low-humidity environments.

Objective
Physical Examination

The major morphologic criteria and characteristic distributions of scaling conditions are listed in Table 11–4–1.

Routine Laboratory Abnormalities

There are no routine laboratory abnormalities.

PLANS
Diagnostic
Differential Diagnosis

A family history or examination of other family members is helpful in the congenital ichthyosiform dermatoses. New mutations may be identified by the unrelenting pattern of the disorder. Skin biopsy of lesions may show characteristic changes, such as large keratohyalin granules with granular layer vacuolization in epidermolytic hyperkeratosis and absence of the granular layer in ichthyosis vulgaris.

In noncongenital scaling and flaking conditions, appearance and history are most important. The diagnosis of postinflammatory desquamation obviously requires a history of earlier skin inflammation or dermatitis. Xerosis is associated with accentuation of scaling on the lower extremities and the lack of ongoing emollient therapy in dry weather in older persons. Drugs associated with skin scaling and flaking include gold, penicillin, allopurinol, and lithium salts, to name just a few. Acquired ichthyoses may develop as a result of chronic malabsorption, and scaling and flaking may be seen in essential fatty acid and zinc deficiencies. The relatively recent onset of diffuse scaling and flaking in a previously normal individual, however, should prompt an investigation for systemic problems.

Diagnostic Options

A careful history of the onset and duration of the disorder, as well as any rashes preceding the scaling, is important. If the condition has been present since childhood, it should be determined if other family members have been affected. A drug history should be obtained, as should laboratory testing if an underlying systemic disease is suspected.

In addition to genetic counseling for heterozygous parents at risk of having children affected with severe ichthyosis, prenatal diagnosis is possible in some cases.

Recommended Approach

Hereditary or acquired ichthyosiform skin disorders are distinctly different from the dry xerotic skin seen commonly in advancing age. The latter responds well to emollient therapy, and may not be present at all in summer or a higher-humidity environment. It is not necessary to work up simple xerosis, but the acute onset of severe ichthyosis should prompt a thorough evaluation.

TABLE 11–4–1. SCALING AND FLAKING LESIONS

Possible Diagnosis	Onset	Associated Findings
Ichthyosis vulgaris	Childhood	Autosomal dominant; fine light scale; palms/soles involved; spares flexures; associated with atopy; relatively common
X-linked ichthyosis	Birth or infancy	X-Linked recessive; sterol sulfatase deficiency; large dark "dirty" scales, especially on sides of neck, flexures; normal palms/soles; corneal opacities on posterior capsule
Lamellar ichthyosis	Birth	Autosomal recessive; large thick scales all over; verrucous, especially around joints; ectropion; hyperpyrexia; nail thickening; alopecia; frequent skin infections
Epidermolytic hyperkeratosis	Birth	Autosomal dominant; coarse verrucous scales, especially flexural; blisters or clear spots in involved areas; frequent skin infections
Acquired ichthyosis	Adult	Fine scales; generalized over body; associated with certain drugs, hypothyroidism, and malignancy, especially lymphoma
Linear ichthyosis (ichthyosis hystrix)	Childhood	An area of scaling, sometimes verrucous, with a dermatome-like segmental distribution; actually a hyperkeratotic epidermal nevus
Xerosis	Adult	Mosaic-tile pattern of scaling; no erythema; pruritic, especially lower extremities; wintertime; older patients
Postinflammatory desquamation	Any age	Generalized fine scaling, frequently seen during resolution of erythema group conditions (measles, sunburn, drug eruption)
Scarlet fever	Childhood	History of pharyngitis, fever, red skin with "sandpaper" feel; marked desquamation 4 to 5 days after rash; begins on face, includes palms and soles approximately 2 weeks later
Kawasaki disease (mucocutaneous lymph node syndrome)	Early childhood	Five of six of following criteria: (1) indurated edema and erythema of palms/soles followed by desquamation, (2) erythema of oropharynx/tongue, (3) polymorphous exanthem, (4) fever more than 7 days, (5) conjunctival injection, (6) cervical lymphadenopathy; myocarditis by electrocardiogram in 70%; coronary aneurysms; etiology unknown

Therapeutic

Therapeutic Options

Treatment of chronic ichthyotic conditions and xerosis is directed primarily toward hydration of the thickened horny layer to increase pliability and removal of excess keratin, if possible. Simple emollient creams and lotions (such as Eucerin, Aquaphor, and Nivea) restore oil to the skin and retard evaporation of water. They should be massaged into the affected areas immediately after bathing as well as periodically during the day. An emollient agent will conceal scale edges, and this optical effect is extremely important in making the skin appear smooth. Bath oils should be added to the water about 10 minutes after immersion to allow the skin to hydrate maximally, but it should be noted that oils generally do not slow evaporation as well as creams and must be applied more often.

Urea-containing creams and lotions (10–20%) are hygroscopic, help to maintain hydration, and are somewhat keratolytic as well. Salicylic acid preparations are useful in scale removal, especially in ichthyosis vulgaris, but they must be used with caution because cutaneous absorption of salicylates may occur. Lactic acid preparations are well accepted by patients, and propylene glycol (40% in water under occlusion) has been reported to have good results.

To date, systemic therapy for scaling and flaking conditions has been disappointing. Antibiotics are used for secondary infection when necessary (lamellar ichthyosis, epidermolytic hyperkeratosis), and corticosteroids for episodes of severe erythroderma. Clinical trials of 13-*cis*-retinoic acid, a vitamin A analog, have shown it to be remarkably efficacious in lamellar ichthyosis and certain cases of epidermolytic hyperkeratosis and ichthyosis vulgaris. Currently, the drug is approved only for short-term therapy of cystic acne. Side effects such as cheilitis, skin fragility, abnormalities of bone growth, and elevation of serum triglycerides are major limitations to the long-term use of oral retinoids, especially in children.

Recommended Approach

Most patients with dry, itching, scaling skin realize that cold, wind, and dehydration increase their symptoms. Most also use some type of body lotion from time to time. The success of topical therapy depends on patient compliance: not only must the proper agents be applied, but they must be applied correctly. An effort must be made to explain the principles of skin hydration.

Water is the only agent that imparts flexibility to skin keratin. A good example for the patient is the ease with which toenails may be clipped after softening in the bath or shower. Normal skin produces and retains oils that slow evaporation of water and, therefore, keep the skin supple and pliant. Sweating also contributes to hydration. Long hot baths, especially with soaps that are degreasing agents, remove natural skin oils, allowing subsequent evaporation of water and resultant dry skin. In the scaling and flaking disorders there is often less skin oil and sweat, either because of the inherited ichthyotic defect or because of decreased production associated with aging. Patients may bathe often, enjoying the feel of hot water on their dry skin, but not realize that they are worsening the condition by scrubbing away what little oil is available to prevent evaporation and dryness. The patient must understand that baths must be only long enough for skin hydration (15–20 minutes) with brief use of a cream-containing soap (e.g., Dove) to preserve natural oils. In addition, on leaving the bath, the patient must immediately apply an emollient to "seal in" the moisture that has been absorbed. This after-bath application is the most important one of the day, as subsequent cream applications prevent further evaporation but do little to actually hydrate the skin.

An inexpensive room humidifier may make the immediate environment more comfortable, and avoidance of "scratchy" materials such as wool can decrease itching.

FOLLOW-UP

Periodic visits to evaluate and review therapy during winter flare or episodes of secondary infection may be required.

DISCUSSION

Prevalence and Incidence

Banal xerosis affects almost everyone in low-humidity winter environments, and is more common with advancing age. It is one of the most frequent skin findings in advancing HIV disease, with an incidence of 75%. Chronic graft-versus-host disease occurs in about 25 to 50% of patients who survive at least one year after transplantation.

The congenital ichthyosiform disorders are rare, with the exception of ichthyosis vulgaris, which affects 1 in 300 persons. X-linked ichthyosis affects 1 in 6000 males, and epidermolytic hyperkeratosis and lamellar ichthyosis 1 in 300,000 persons.

Related Basic Science

Genetics

The inherited ichthyotic conditions have been studied extensively and show different pathophysiologic characteristics. There is an increased cell turnover time in lamellar ichthyosis and epidermolytic hyperkeratosis and increased adhesiveness or failure of separation of stratum corneum cells in ichthyosis vulgaris and X-linked ichthyosis. Scaling skin may occur with alterations in lipid metabolism and has been reported with certain drugs (e.g., triparanol), essential fatty acid deficiency in malabsorption, and genetic disorders (phytanic acid accumulation in Refsum disease).

Physiologic or Metabolic Derangement

The stratum corneum is a tough, resistant barrier membrane formed by the keratinization of epidermal cells during the last stage of cell maturation. Although this membrane is highly resistant to chemical and physical insult, it acts as a semipermeable osmotic barrier. Accumulated lipids in the dead corneal cells aid in the movement of water in and out. Factors affecting scaling and dryness of the skin include the rate of cell production and loss, cell adhesiveness, epidermal lipid and protein synthesis, and possibly sweat and sebum production. Abnormal keratin has not been shown to be a significant factor.

Many of the xerotic and inflammatory skin changes seen in patients with HIV disease share histologic features similar to those of GVHD. Although clinical features tend to be nonspecific, follicular involvement is common.

Natural History and Its Modification with Treatment

The ichthyotic conditions are lifelong, and symptoms wax and wane with seasons and the patient's attention to maintenance of topical therapy. Psychological problems may develop in patients with the more severe disfiguring disorders, especially in adolescence. Genetic counseling should be made available. Prenatal diagnostic techniques such as fetoscopy and prenatal skin biopsy have been used to diagnose epidermolytic hyperkeratosis (bullous congenital ichthyosiform erythroderma).

Prevention

There is no known means of prevention of the inherited disorders, but symptoms respond well to therapy when it is instituted early. "Winter itch" may be controlled by "autumn emollients."

Cost Containment

Continued maintenance of therapy with simple emollients and keratolytic agents is desirable. Expensive steroid-containing preparations are usually unnecessary.

REFERENCES

Champion RH, Burton HL, Ebling FJG, eds. Textbook of dermatology. Oxford, England: Blackwell Scientific, 1991.

Fitzpatrick TB, Eisen AZ, Wolff K, et al., eds. Dermatology in general medicine, 4th ed. New York: McGraw-Hill, 1993.

Smith KJ, Skelton HG, Yeager J, et al. Clinical features of inflammatory dermatoses in human immunodeficiency virus type 1 disease and their correlation with Walter Reed stage. J Am Acad Dermatol 1993;28:167.

Smith KJ, Skelton HG, Yeager J, et al. Cutaneous findngs in HIV-1-positive patients: a 42-month prospective study. J Am Acad Dermatol 1994:31:1746.

Papules

Marilynne McKay, M.D.

DEFINITION

A papule is a smooth- or rough-surfaced palpable skin elevation that may range in size from barely perceptible to several millimeters in height, but is always less than 1 cm in diameter. (Larger lesions are nodules or tumors.) Small papules are almost always due to an epidermal or superficial dermal process of some kind (hyperplasia, inflammation, infiltration, deposition, or neoplasia). Prominent follicles or pores on the skin surface frequently account for the papular appearance of an erythematous vasodilatory cutaneous "rash."

CRITERIA FOR DIAGNOSIS

Palpable "bumps" on the skin surface that may be single or multiple, but each of which is less than 1 cm in diameter, constitute the criteria for diagnosis. In some conditions, papules may coalesce into plaques, which are raised, flat-topped lesions larger than 1 cm in diameter. Crusts or scabs on the surface of papules usually indicate that the condition is pruritic and the patient has excoriated the lesions. Scaling, however, is not a component of lesions in this category; and scaly papules and plaques are discussed in Chapter 11–6. Follicular papules should be examined carefully for the presence of pus; if present, the lesion is a pustule and is discussed in Chapter 11–9.

Suggestive

Papular dermatoses are characterized by single or multiple skin lesions composed of small elevations which can be palpated or which can be seen to rise above the normal skin surface when viewed from the side. Lesions that are scaly or primarily pigmentary in nature are less likely to represent one of the papular skin disorders.

Definitive

Smooth- or rough-surfaced palpable "bumps" on the skin surface—they may be single or multiple, tiny or up to 1 cm in diameter—confirm the diagnosis. Lesion color may vary from flesh-colored to yellow, red, brown, or black, depending on the diagnosis.

CLINICAL MANIFESTATIONS

Subjective

Papules may itch or burn, but symptoms vary with the disorder. Many are completely asymptomatic and are noted by patients only when they feel or see a change in the texture of their skin. Papular conditions may be acute or chronic, and the history will help to establish the duration and pattern of the disorder.

Objective

Physical Examination

Careful examination of the size, shape, and color of individual papules is important, but equal attention should be given to the configuration and distribution of multiple lesions. A relatively simple approach is to determine whether papules have a smooth or rough surface and then to look for additional lesions. If there are multiple papules, are they discrete or do they tend to coalesce into plaques? Where are they located? Table 11–5–1 lists the major morphologic criteria of the papular disorders.

Routine Laboratory Abnormalities

There are no routine diagnostic laboratory abnormalities.

PLANS

Diagnostic

Differential Diagnosis

Table 11–5–1 lists the major morphologic criteria of the papular disorders.

Diagnostic Options

Careful examination of the entire skin surface for similar lesions to identify a characteristic distribution pattern is a useful approach to the evaluation of a papular eruption, along with the history of what the patient has done to change the appearance of the lesions.

A skin biopsy is probably the single most helpful procedure for diagnosing the papular cutaneous disorders. In the case of a single small papule, the entire lesion may be removed; if the papule is large or in a cosmetically significant area, only a portion may be taken. In the latter case, the remainder would be removed in a manner appropriate to the diagnosis, for example, expression of the contents of molluscum contagiosum versus wide excision of a carcinoma. The choice of biopsy technique is based on clinical diagnostic impression, experience, and therapeutic considerations. For example, a "shave" biopsy is quite adequate for diagnosis of a basal cell carcinoma, but it would be inappropriate if malignant melanoma were a consideration. Because depth of involvement is critical to melanoma staging and prognosis, the original biopsy should include deep tissue. In disorders with multiple lesions, selection of a typical fresh papule is important, and it may help the pathologist if more than one lesion is taken for interpretation.

Another diagnostic maneuver is diascopy: direct pressure on the papule with a glass slide. A vascular lesion will blanch with pressure, or the "apple jelly" appearance of sarcoidosis may be appreciated.

Recommended Approach

Begin with a careful history and physical examination followed by discussion with the patient about the major concerns he or she has about the lesion(s).

As many papular disorders have a similar appearance, patients may self-treat extensively with a variety of medications. In chronic disorders characterized by multiple papules, confirmation of the diagnosis by cutaneous biopsy may help the physician to explain the condition to the patient, who may then understand therapeutic principles for the particular problem. The patient who is highly concerned about the possible malignancy of skin lesions may be expressing fears raised by discovery of carcinoma in a friend; in this case, evaluation of lesions by a dermatologist may be most appropriate for the patient's peace of mind.

Therapeutic

Therapeutic Options

For a single lesion, removal of the entire papule by biopsy serves as treatment, the exception being a malignancy requiring further excision of margins after the diagnosis has been established. In most cases, appropriate therapy depends on the diagnosis. Inflammatory papules may respond to topical or intralesional corticosteroids. Viral papules may disappear spontaneously, but destruction is usually required to prevent further spread. Papules associated with systemic disorders may respond to appropriate therapy of the underlying problem. In many cases, no treatment is currently available.

Recommended Approach

Determine what the patient expects from therapy: in asymptomatic conditions, a name for the disorder may be all that is required. If a malig-

TABLE 11–5–1. PAPULES

Appearance	Supporting Data	Likely Diagnosis
Smooth papules		
Single or scattered		
Pale or flesh color	Present for years, ± hairs, not changing	Intradermal nevus
	Pedunculated, intertriginous, older patient	Acrochordon (skin tag)
	Pearly, telangiectatic, may ulcerate	Basal cell carcinoma*
With central core	Large, facial, especially around eyes; puberty	Syringoma
	Acute onset, childhood; also adult genitalia	Molluscum contagiosum
	Associated with acne, blackheads	Closed comedo (whitehead)
Yellowish	Tiny, irregular, especially around eyes	Milia
	Childhood: head, trunk, iris of eye	Xanthogranuloma
	Irregular shape, eyelids, older patient	Xanthelasma
Pink to red	Acute onset, pruritic; consistent history	Insect bite
	Firm maroon papules on trunk, older patient	Cherry angioma
	Painful lesion tip of digit, often under nail	Glomus tumor
Red-brown	Present for years, ± hairs, not changing	Junctional or compound nevus
	Wheals when stroked, may be multiple	Mastocytoma
	Fast-growing, moist-looking, may bleed	Pyogenic granuloma
Blue-black	Present for years, not changing	Blue nevus
	Irregular borders, uneven color, ulceration	Malignant melanoma*
	Irregular borders, uneven color, palm/sole	Acral lentiginous melanoma*
	Firm, central core that may be expressed	Giant comedone
	Compressible lesion on lip of elderly patient	Venous lake
Multiple		
Pale or flesh color	Flat-topped, grouped on face or extremities	Verrucae plana (flat warts)
	Pruritic, axillae and groin, especially female	Fox–Fordyce disease
	Pedunculated, associated with café-au-lait spots	Neurofibromas
Pink to red	Firm, follow trauma in susceptible patients	Hypertrophic scar or keloid
	Crops of firm-domed papules, older patient	Metastatic carcinoma*
	Pruritic urticarial papules on face, upper trunk HIV-positive status	Pruritic papular eruption of HIV disease (HIV-associated eosinophilic folliculitis)
	Nondescript persistent lesions in AIDS	Kaposi's sarcoma*
	Pruritic, serpiginous, history of beach visit	Cutaneous larva migrans
	Face, hands, mucosae, and polyarthritis	Multicentric reticulohistiocytosis
Yellowish	Extensor surfaces, elevated serum lipids	Eruptive xanthoma
	Small, central dell; sun-exposed elderly patient	Sebaceous hyperplasia
Red-brown	Males (X-linked), midabdomen to knees, oral	Fabry's disease (angiokeratomas)
	Grouped around nasolabial fold, chin	Adenoma sebaceum (tuberous sclerosis)
Blue-black	Scattered in patient with known melanoma	Metastatic melanoma*
	Especially on lower extremities of elderly men	Kaposi's sarcoma (classic)*
Coalescing into plaques		
Pale or flesh color	Localized flat cobblestone pattern	Connective-tissue nevus
	Firm cobblestoning, lower legs	Pretibial myxedema
Pink to red	Annular pattern, especially on dorsal hands or feet	Granuloma annulare
	Purplish, symmetrical: extensors, palms, soles	Erythema elevatum diutinum
	Single irregular plaque: usually face, stable	Granuloma faciale
	Multiple irregular plaques: face, recurrent	Lymphocytic infiltrate of skin
	Prominence in sun-exposed skin, adults	Polymorphous light eruption
	Pruritic transient lesions last only hours	Urticaria (hives)
	Velvety red genital plaque; especially older male	Erythroplasia of Queyrat
	Small papules: around eyes, nose, within scars	Sarcoidosis
	Asymmetric, occur in crops, may ulcerate	Malignancy: lymphoma, leukemia, mycosis fungoides*
Rough-surfaced papules		
Single or scattered		
Pale	Cauliflower (verrucoid) surface; especially hands	Verruca vulgaris
	Pointed (acuminate) surface; genitalia	Condyloma acuminatum
	Irregular shape, sessile; especially on genitalia	Bowenoid papulosis (carcinoma in situ)*
Red	Palms and soles, history of arsenic ingestion	Arsenical keratoses
	Sun-exposed areas, fair-skinned older patient	Actinic keratosis
Brown	Dark red, genitalia, especially scrotum; older patient	Angiokeratoma
	Waxy, "stuck-on," especially trunk of elderly patient	Seborrheic keratosis
	Over malar area of blacks, may pedunculate	Dermatosis papulosa nigra
	Soft, present for years, ± hairs, not changing	Junctional or compound nevus
	Firm, attached deeply, usually arm or leg	Dermatofibroma
Multiple		
Pale or flesh color	Very tiny, common on male genitalia	Lichen nitidus
	Tiny, localized in "streak" pattern, especially face	Lichen striatus
Pink to red	Tiny, upper lateral arm, buttocks	Keratosis pilaris
	Pruritic, occurs after insect bites, especially fleas	Papular urticaria
	Child, acral distribution, hepatitis B surface antigen positive	Gianotti–Crosti syndrome
	Arms, trunk in hot, humid environment	Miliaria rubra (heat rash)

(continued)

TABLE 11–5–1. (*Continued*)

Appearance	Supporting Data	Likely Diagnosis
Brown	Geometric pattern, present since childhood Yellow-brown, verrucoid, overlie vesicles Firm, generalized, patient on renal dialysis	Epidermal nevus Lymphangioma circumscriptum Kyrle's disease

Coalescing into plaques
  Yellowish
  Pink to red
  Brown
	Localized verrucoid plaque in scalp
	Annular groups on face, neck, ears
	Waxy, symmetric; scalp, neck, face, torso
	Purpuric; body folds, periorbital, pretibial
	Velvety plaques in axillae, groin, sides of neck
	Linear down an extremity, present in childhood
		Nevus sebaceous*
		Elastosis perforans serpiginosa
		Darier's disease
		Amyloidosis (several types)
		Acanthosis nigricans*
		Linear epidermal nevus

*Malignancy or associated with neoplasm.

nancy or progressive cutaneous disorder has been identified on biopsy, consultation may be an important consideration.

FOLLOW-UP

Follow-up depends on the cause of the problem: patients with cutaneous malignancies usually require 6-month or 1-year checkups, as new lesions tend to develop on affected (usually sun-damaged) skin. Warts may be particularly hard to eradicate, and patients should return for therapy as new lesions develop to prevent spread.

DISCUSSION

Prevalence and Incidence

Papular lesions represent a spectrum of dermatologic disease from the common (warts, nevi, insect bites, seborrheic keratoses) to the esoteric. The practicing physician soon comes to recognize the common lesions in his or her patient population, and with careful observation, the practitioner gradually learns to see when the lesion is "not quite right" for the expected diagnosis.

Related Basic Science

Elevation of the skin surface to form a papule may be the result of a variety of pathophysiologic mechanisms affecting the epidermis, the dermis, or in some conditions both. Palpable "bumps" may represent the accumulation of inflammatory cells or edema fluid, proliferation of neoplastic or hyperplastic cells, or deposition of material not normally found in the skin. Smooth papules that retain normal skin surface markings indicate dermal changes, whereas rough-surfaced papules are usually due to epidermal processes.

The classic description of a "maculopapular eruption" is not part of the dermatologist's lexicon, for the morphologic basis of diagnosis requires distinguishing whether the condition actually fits into the category of macular (nonpalpable) or papular (palpable). Use of the term *maculopapular* is on observation of papules with surrounding erythema due to vascular dilation. This appearance is simply the result of inflammation, which may have a variety of causes. In some cases, however, nonerythematous "microinflammation" of the papillary dermis results directly in the formation of papules. These discrete elevations reflect focal vascular inflammation of dermal papillae with edema limited by the epidermal rete pegs. Extension of inflammation into the epidermis

results in surface changes, often with enlargement and coalescence of individual lesions. It is the inflammatory group of lesions that responds best to treatment with topical and intralesional corticosteroids.

The etiology of a papule may determine its color. Deposition of lipids in the epidermis results in yellowish smooth papules and plaques (xanthomata), whereas proliferations of pigmented nevus cells are brown. Local, discrete proliferations of blood vessels may be seen as red papules, and pooling of blood in a dilated vessel may appear blue or even black. Pressure on a vascular lesion causes blanching by forcing red blood cells into adjacent vessels. Epidermal tumors or epidermal proliferative disorders, such as warts, are characteristically pale or flesh-colored. Itchy papules excoriated by the patient may develop postinflammatory changes such as hyperpigmentation and scaling (lichenification).

Natural History and Its Modification with Treatment

Natural history is determined to a great extent by the etiology of the papule.

Prevention

With the possible exception of lesions associated with sun exposure (actinic keratoses, basal cell carcinoma, melanoma), little can be done to prevent the development of these cutaneous disorders.

Cost Containment

Determination of the correct diagnosis by biopsy is recommended, for this is the most important determinant of appropriate therapeutic measures.

REFERENCES

Bason MM, Berger TG, Nesbitt LT Jr. Pruritic papular eruption of HIV-disease. Int J Dermatol 1993;32:784.

Champion RH, Burton HL, Ebling FJG, eds. Textbook of dermatology. Oxford, England: Blackwell Scientific, 1991.

Fitzpatrick TB, Eisen AZ, Wolff K, et al., eds. Dermatology in general medicine. 4th ed. New York: McGraw-Hill, 1993.

Rosenthal D, LeBoit PE, Klumpp L, Berger TG. Human immunodeficiency virus-associated eosinophilic folliculitis: A unique dermatosis associated with advanced human immunodeficiency virus infection. Arch Dermatol 1991;127:206.

Papulosquamous Lesions

Robert L. Rietschel, M.D.

DEFINITION

Papulosquamous lesions constitute a collection of disorders characterized by scale formation, usually in discrete patches that are palpable.

ETIOLOGY

The causes of most of the diseases in this category are unknown. Genetic factors are suspected to play a role in the pathogenesis of psoriasis. Recent investigations of lichen planus have focused on a possible role for hepatitis C virus. *Pityrosporum* yeasts are implicated as an etiologic factor in seborrheic dermatitis.

CRITERIA FOR DIAGNOSIS

Suggestive

Papulosquamous change implies that the lesion is above the normal skin plane and is scaling. Usually, the lesions are inflammatory and have an erythematous quality, but oozing or crusted exudate is not significant in this category. If seen at all, eczematous change is minimal and secondary to scratching or a low-grade bacterial superinfection. The presence of vesicles or bullae would exclude placement of the disorder in the papulosquamous morphologic category.

Definitive

Histologically, the papulosquamous group of disorders does not manifest microvesicle formation or spongiosis, with the exception of acute tinea corporis, pityriasis rosea, seborrheic dermatitis, and lichen simplex chronicus. When microvesiculation proceeds to a macroscopically evident state, the disease resembles an eczema; therefore, some papulosquamous diseases have features of two morphologic categories.

These conditions are commonly located on the trunk and extremities, and many individual lesions are present, frequently coalescing into plaques of papulosquamous change.

Table 11–6–1 gives the disease-specific definitive data needed to support a specific diagnosis.

CLINICAL MANIFESTATIONS

Subjective

The family history is helpful only with psoriasis in this group of diseases. Approximately two thirds of all patients with psoriasis have a close family member who is affected. Occupational history does not provide a clue in distinguishing among the diseases in the category. Environmental factors such as sunlight are helpful for psoriasis, pityriasis rosea, and pityriasis lichenoides chronica and harmful for discoid and subacute cutaneous lupus erythematosus.

Pruritus may or may not be present. It is characteristically absent in secondary syphilis, and this is a helpful differential point. Pruritus is commonly present in tinea corporis and pityriasis rosea and variably present in the other forms of papulosquamous change. In lichen planus the sensation, although described as pruritus by some, is poorly categorized by others and tends to evoke rubbing rather than scratching. The lesions of lichen planus are seldom excoriated because of this peculiar sensation. In lichen simplex chronicus, the pruritus may be severe enough to awaken one from sleep, or rubbing may occur at a subconscious level.

Objective

Major morphologic criteria for distinguishing the various papulosquamous disorders are noted in Table 11–6–1. In this group of diseases, histologic examination is more commonly necessary to distinguish between the diagnostic possibilities. Characteristic histologic findings occur in cutaneous T-cell lymphoma (CTCL), mycosis fungoides (plaque stage), pityriasis lichenoides et varioliformis acuta, lichen planus, and lupus erythematosus. Histologic findings are extremely helpful in distinguishing secondary syphilis, psoriasis, pityriasis rosea, seborrheic dermatitis, and lichen simplex chronicus.

TABLE 11–6–1. DIFFERENTIAL DIAGNOSIS OF PAPULOSQUAMOUS PAPULES OR PLAQUES

Supporting Data	Likely Diagnosis
Positive potassium hydroxide preparation or fungal culture	Tinea corporis
Positive VDRL and FTA-ABS tests; annular facial lesions; hyperpigmented macules on palms and soles; nonpruritic	Secondary syphilis
Histology: lymphohistiocytic perivascular and/or periappendageal infiltrate with liquefaction degeneration of basal cell layer; may have positive lupus band test on direct immunofluorescence	Discoid lupus erythematosus or subacute cutaneous lupus erythematosus
Violaceous, flat-topped, polygonal papules; lacy white lines and papules on buccal mucosa; histology: bandlike infiltrate of predominantly lymphocytes with thickened granular layer, sawtoothing of epidermis	Lichen planus
Original patch is largest lesion, followed in 7 to 14 days by multiple other papules between neck and knees; tends to follow skin cleavage lines on trunk; histology: focal spongiosis of epidermis; pruritic	Pityriasis rosea
Scale may resemble mica; nails have pits, ridges, or onychlolysis; plaques coalesce on elbows, knees, scalp, gluteal fold, histology: subcorneal microabscesses, regular acanthosis and parakeratosis	Psoriasis
Scalp, eyebrows, nasolabial grooves; occasionally presternal region, axilla, and groin involved; greasy scaling; histology: like psoriasis but with spongiosis	Seborrheic dermatitis
Looks like psoriasis but lacks characteristic clustering at elbows, knees, scalp; has nondiagnostic histology; acute form resembles chickenpox	Pityriasis lichenoides et varioliformis acuta
Chronic form is a diagnosis of exclusion	Pityriasis lichenoides chronica
Single or multiple plaques with telangiectasias, hyper- and/or hypopigmentation; histology: Pautrier's microabscesses in epidermis and scattered Lutzner cells infiltrating epidermis	Cutaneous T-cell lymphoma (CTCL), mycosis fungoides (plaque stage)
Single or multiple plaques with much lichenification; histology: spongiotic dermatitis with vertical streaking of collagen in elongated dermal papillae; very pruritic	Lichen simplex chronicus
Total body red, scaling, with islands of normal skin and hyperkeratosis of palms and soles	Pityriasis rubra pilaris
Total body red and scaling with no normal skin	Erythroderma

VDRL, Venereal Disease Research laboratories; FTA-ABS, flourescent treponemal antibody aborption.

When this group of diseases involves the scalp, hair loss may occur with the following: secondary syphilis, in a moth-eaten pattern; discoid lupus erythematosus, with scarring; and tinea capitis. Hair loss is not characteristic of psoriasis or seborrheic dermatitis, but it may occur to a minimal extent when the diseases are severe. A rare form of lichen planus (lichen planopilaris) may result in hair loss.

PLANS
Diagnostic
Differential Diagnosis

The diseases listed in Table 11–6–1 constitute the proper differential diagnostic possibilities for the papulosquamous group of diseases.

Diagnostic Options

If the disorder producing the papulosquamous lesion cannot be identified by the patient's history and the morphologic examination, it is necessary to perform a microscopic examination of a potassium hydroxide preparation of a scraping of the lesion. If this is negative, a biopsy from involved skin for routine histologic processing is the next step. If lupus erythematosus is suspected, the specimen may be split in half, with half processed routinely and the other half sent for direct immunofluorescence. Serologic testing for syphilis may be done at the same time. If the cutaneous disorder resembles lupus erythematosus (or one of the many subsets of this disorder), a serologic profile, including antinuclear antibody, anti-native double-stranded DNA, antiribonucleoprotein, Ro (SSA), and La (SSB), may be necessary for complete evaluation. In general, the antinuclear antibody test is an adequate screening procedure, but there are subsets of lupus in which this test may be negative or positive in only a low titer; thus, more extensive serologic evaluation is required for adequate prognostic and therapeutic considerations.

If the patient is erythrodermic, the examination should include a biopsy to look for evidence of cutaneous T-cell lymphoma. A history of any gradually progressive dermatitis militates against lymphoma and in favor of the preexisting dermatitis as the cause. The presence of lymphadenopathy with erythroderma is not uncommon, and lymph node biopsy is necessary to evaluate the presence or absence of lymphoreticular malignancy. In most cases, dermatopathic lymphadenopathy is the diagnosis. If occult lymphoreticular malignancy is suspected by history and physical examination to be the cause of the erythroderma, the physician must choose between lymphangiography and abdominal computed tomography scanning to evaluate periaortic and retroperitoneal lymph node involvement. The causes of erythroderma and the frequency of its occurrence in adults are listed in Table 11–6–2.

Recommended Approach

The first test to perform is the potassium hydroxide examination of scale taken from the periphery of a lesion. A skin biopsy would be the next step in most cases, unless the clinical presentation is strongly suspicious for syphilis. In the case of syphilis the serologic test would take precedence over a biopsy. Serologic studies and a skin biopsy would be done simultaneously if lupus is the prime consideration.

TABLE 11–6–2. FREQUENCY OF ERYTHRODERMA AS RELATED TO DIAGNOSIS

Diagnosis	Frequency (%) in Adults
Eczematous dermatitis (includes contact, atopic, stasis, and seborrheic dermatitis)	40
Psoriasis	35
Lymphoreticular malignancy and leukemia	15
Drug eruptions (most notable: penicillin, barbiturates, mercury, gold, organic arsenic)	10
Undetermined causes	8
Other skin disorders (lichen planus, ichthyosiform erythroderma, dermatophytosis, pityriasis rubra pilaris, scabies, pemphigus foliaceus)	2

Therapeutic
Therapeutic Options

Tinea corporis. Tinea corporis is usually treated with topical agents when convenient. Among the most effective topical antifungal agents are clotrimazole (Lotrimin), econazole (Spectazole), miconazole (Monistat), ciclopirax olamine (Loprox), oxiconazole (Oxistat), naftifine (Naftin), and terbinafine (Lamisil). The only appropriate systemic antifungal agents are griseofulvin (Grisactin) and ketoconazole (Nizoral). Itraconazole (Sporanox) is an effective, but not currently approved, medication that merits selective consideration based on the individual's experience with other treatment options. There is no specific time frame for treatment with any of these drugs; rather, the patient is followed until there is no evidence of infection. For cutaneous infections, a dose of 400 mg per day of ketoconazole is commonly required. Patients treated with this agent should be followed for liver function abnormalities.

Lupus erythematosus. Discoid and subacute cutaneous forms of lupus erythematosus are usually treated with potent fluorinated topical corticosteroids. When these prove to be inadequate, hydroxychloroquine (200 mg) or chloroquine (250 mg) daily or twice daily are used. Occasionally, a patient requires systemic corticosteroids for severe scarring forms of these disorders, but topical or intralesional treatment is preferable. Treatment with antimalarial drugs requires close monitoring for ocular toxicity by an ophthalmologist.

Lichen planus. Lichen planus is usually treated with potent fluorinated topical corticosteroids or a brief course of systemic corticosteroids. Occasionally, lichen planus responds to oral griseofluvin in doses similar to those used to treat tinea corporis. The reason for this is unknown.

Pityriasis rosea. Generally no treatment is required, as pityriasis rosea is a self-limited condition that resolves in 6 to 8 weeks. Simple lubrication generally keeps the patient comfortable, although the course may be shortened somewhat by erythemogenic doses of ultraviolet light.

Psoriasis. Psoriasis is often treated with topical corticosteroids, although these drugs do not produce any lasting remission. Topical treatment with various tar preparations, such as tar gel, crude coal tar, and liquor carbonis detergens in various vehicles, produces a slower but more sustained response. Topical calcipotriol (Dovonex) is a vitamin D_3 derivative used in psoriasis; its effect is similar to that of topical corticosteroids but without the tendency to produce atrophy. Ultraviolet light in the sunburn (UVB) range, when combined with tars, is one of the most effective management tools available for this condition. This treatment, commonly referred to as the Goeckerman regimen, when effectively applied for a period of 3 to 4 weeks, may produce remissions of 1 year or longer. Anthralin has been found to have a similar beneficial effect on psoriasis. This product is somewhat more irritating and tends to stain the skin a brownish color at the periphery of the psoriatic lesions, but these side effects are minimized by use of 1% concentrations of cream or ointment applied for 15 to 30 minutes and then washed off.

When psoriasis fails to respond to topical measures, the clinician is then left with a choice of methotrexate or psoralen plus ultraviolet light A (PUVA) therapy. Methotrexate is given in either single or divided doses of 12.5 to 25 mg per week. Liver fibrosis, which may occur without any abnormality in chemical profile testing, has necessitated periodic liver biopsies in methotrexate-treated patients. The psoralen that is most commonly used in PUVA therapy is 8-methoxypsoralen. Doses of approximately 40 mg orally are administered hours prior to irradiation with high-output ultraviolet light A bulbs. This treatment clears psoriasis in approximately 90% of patients within 2 months when conducted two to three times per week. Squamous cell carcinoma has been seen more commonly in patients on chronic PUVA therapy.

Two other considerations for systemic treatment of psoriasis are available. Etretinate (Tegison) in doses ranging from 0.5 to 1.0 mg/kg per day can be effective, but the onset of benefit in plaque-type psoriasis may be slow (from 6 to 8 weeks). This aromatic retinoid ethyl ester is more impressive with pustular and erythrodermic forms of psoriasis. Hypertriglyceridemia is a unique toxic effect, but dry skin and mucous membranes are the most common. Cyclosporine (Sandimmune) can clear psoriasis in as little as 1 week in dosages ranging from 3 to 6 mg/kg per day. At present, this immunosuppressant drug is considered experimental for psoriasis. Hypertension and nephrotoxicity are potential side effects.

Seborrheic dermatitis. Seborrheic dermatitis usually responds to frequent shampooing with tar shampoos or selenium sulfide shampoos. Cutaneous lesions generally respond to 1% hydrocortisone; because these lesions commonly are located on the face, stronger corticosteroid preparations and concentrations are generally not indicated. Topical ketoconazole cream is also effective.

Pityriasis lichenoides. Management of the acute form of pityriasis lichenoides is occasionally successful with ultraviolet light, 2 g daily of tetracycline, or 1 g daily of erythromycin. It is unclear why these antibiotics are effective in some cases of this disorder. The chronic form of pityriasis lichenoides is managed somewhat similarly to psoriasis.

Mycosis fungoides. Plaque-stage mycosis fungoides, CTCL, is usually treated with either topical nitrogen mustard or electron beam therapy. The use of topical nitrogen mustard is usually accomplished by diluting 10 mg (the contents of one vial) in 60 mL of water and applying this to the entire integument. This treatment produces extensive contact dermatitis after several weeks in approximately 50% of patients so treated. The ability of treatment to alter survival has not yet been established, although favorable response rates are seen. Cutaneous T-cell lymphoma has also been managed by PUVA therapy, as noted above for psoriasis. This is effective in the early stages of the disease. The most effective treatment for the leukemic stage of the disease has been photopheresis in which 8-methoxypsoralen is administered to the patient and then the buffy coat is harvested with a cell separator. The buffy coat is irradiated extracorporeally with UVA light after which the cells are reinfused into the patient. Interferon alfa alone and in combination with PUVA has also been shown to be of benefit at various stages of cutaneous T-cell lymphoma.

Lichen simplex chronicus. Lichen simplex chronicus is usually treated by application of a topical corticosteroid preparation of intermediate strength to the area of dermatitis whenever the itch sensation becomes apparent. This requires that the patient carry the medication with him or her at all times.

Pityriasis rubra pilaris. Pityriasis rubra pilaris may be treated identically to psoriasis; however, successful management with megadoses of vitamin A (1 million units daily for a total of 2 weeks) is occasionally useful in producing remission. Isotretinoin (Accutane) in doses of 1 to 2 mg/kg is also helpful.

Erythroderma. Erythroderma is usually treated with topical corticosteroids under occlusion unless it is caused by cutaneous lymphoma, in which case other specific antilymphoma treatment is used.

Recommended Approach

For the noninfectious inflammatory disorders the preferred treatment is topical prior to the use of systemic agents whenever possible. Systemic antibiotic treatment is preferred for all stages of syphilis. Systemic antifungal agents are generally required for scalp and nail infections. Stage 1 and 2 mycosis fungoides is generally treated with either topical nitrogen mustard, total skin electron beam, or PUVA. The value of photopheresis at the earlier stages of this disease is under investigation.

FOLLOW-UP

All patients should be seen every 3 to 4 weeks until the disorder has either cleared or stabilized.

DISCUSSION
Prevalence

The prevalence of every disorder discussed in this chapter is not known; however, statistics do exist for several of the diseases. The prevalence of psoriasis is about 5 per 1000, and for seborrheic dermatitis, about 30 per 1000. All forms of dermatophytosis have a prevalence of about 80 per 1000.

Related Basic Science

Tinea corporis may be self-limited and resolve within 2 to 3 months without treatment. In atopic individuals, however, tinea may become widespread and chronic, involving the entire integument. In such individuals, the role of histamine and immediate hypersensitivity in interfering with the development and expression of routine delayed hypersensitivity to the infecting organisms is thought to be crucial to the development of a host–parasite relationship.

The causes of the noninfectious disorders are unknown. Pityriasis rosea is a condition that demonstrates a propensity to outbreaks in the spring and fall. This clustering suggests that there is an infectious agent, although none has been found.

One of the most intriguing disorders in the papulosquamous group is psoriasis. Although a great deal is known about the hyperproliferative state of the epidermis in this condition, and many analogies can be drawn to neoplasia in general, the condition remains an enigma. Some investigators feel that the pathologic process originates within the epidermis and is due to a loss of normal differentiation in favor of proliferation. Other investigators hold that the defect arises within the dermis and may be centered on the dermal blood vessels, which become dilated and tortuous with extension of the postcapillary venule and leakage of material into the dermal papillae. Still other investigators focus on the development of the spongiform pustule high in the epidermis. This event begins with the exudation of polymorphonuclear leukocytes from the dermal papillae and subsequent migration to a location immediately beneath the stratum corneum, where aggregates of polymorphonuclear leukocytes are commonly referred to as Munro's microabscesses. Immunologists have found multiple defects in the behavior of polymorphonuclear leukocytes from people with psoriasis; however, the relationship of this to the pathogenesis of the condition is still a mystery. Studies using peritoneal dialysis suggest that psoriasis has circulating factors; when these factors are removed, the psoriasis improves. It is intriguing that hemodialysis does not cause a similar improvement in psoriasis; it has been postulated that different molecular weight substances are being removed by the two different dialysis procedures. It is still unclear why the plaques of psoriasis tend to be so distinctly localized and so sharply marginated in view of any of the preceding hypotheses. Some investigators feel that pityriasis ruba pilaris is simply a variation of psoriasis.

Erythroderma has a mortality rate that varies from 15 to 20%. The usual cause of mortality includes acute infectious complications. Because of the high metabolic rate and excessive water loss from the cutaneous surface, the patient may be septic yet manifest a normal or below-normal core body temperature. Infection may not manifest as fever until exceedingly late in the course of the disease. Occasionally, individuals with erythroderma develop high-output cardiac failure, but this occurs in only one third to one half of such patients. Skin blood flow in individuals with erythroderma is generally increased from 1 liter per minute in the normal state to 2.7 to 4.8 liters per minute in the erythrodermic state, occupying from 52 to 72% of the cardiac output. Hepatomegaly may be present in 20 to 40% of these individuals, and splenomegaly is variably present in up to one fifth. This may or may not be associated with the lymphoma–leukemia group of disorders. Metabolic disturbances in erythroderma include decreased renal blood flow, increased plasma volume, hypoalbuminemia, and an increased venous pressure. These factors contribute to the peripheral edema that commonly accompanies erythroderma. Hematologically, an elevated white blood cell count and erythrocyte sedimentation rate can routinely be anticipated with a volume dilutional anemia and, not uncommonly, low serum iron and folate levels. Patients may exhibit an increased thirst but usually retain normal osmolarity, blood urea nitrogen levels, and a balanced electrolyte profile. Although renal blood flow is diminished, creatinine clearance remains normal, and there is no tendency to inappropriate antidiuretic hormone release. When erythroderma is chronic, hyperestrogenism may manifest as gynecomastia, and this may be present even in the absence of increased urine estrogen levels. The uric acid level also may be elevated.

Natural History and Its Modification with Treatment

Tinea corporis and pityriasis rosea are self-limited diseases. Psoriasis is a chronic disorder. Erythroderma is a very serious disease with a mortality rate ranging from 15 to 20%. The 5-year survival for biopsy-proven mycosis fungoides is about 45%. With ulcerated lesions, median survival in CTCL (mycosis fungoides) is between 2 and 3 years, and with systemic involvement, median survival is 1 year.

Prevention

Among the preventable diseases in this category, syphilis is the most obvious. Use of a condom during intercourse can significantly alter the risk of contracting this disorder. The other papulosquamous disorders discussed in this section are not preventable. Exacerbations of various forms of lupus erythematosus may be minimized by avoiding excessive sun exposure and using sunscreens with skin protective factors of 8 to 15.

Cost Containment

To date, no studies have been done regarding cost containment in the treatment of papulosquamous lesions.

REFERENCES

Cunliffe WJ, Berth-Jones J, Claudy A, et al. Comparison study of calcipotriol (MC903) ointment and betamethasone 17-valerate ointments in patients with psoriasis vulgaris. J Am Acad Dermatol 1992;26:736.

Edelson R, Berger C, Gasparro F, et al. Treatment of cutaneous T-cell lymphoma by extracorporeal photochemotherapy. N Engl J Med 1987;316:297.

Jones HE, Reinhardt JH, Rinaldi MG. Immunologic susceptibility to chronic dermatophytosis. Arch Dermatol 1974;110:213.

Kuzel TM, Gilyon K, Springer E, et al. Interferon alpha-2a combined with phototherapy in the treatment of cutaneous T-cell lymphoma. J Natl Cancer Inst 1990;82:203.

Olsen EA, Rosen ST, Vollmer RT, et al. Interferon alpha-2a in the treatment of cutaneous T-cell lymphoma. J Am Acad Dermatol 1989;20:394.

Sontheimer RD, Thomas JR, Gilliam IN. Subacute cutaneous lupus erythematosus. Arch Dermatol 1979;115:1404.

Weinstein GD, Voorhees JJ, eds. Symposium on psoriasis. Dermatol Clin 1983;2:3.

Wentzell IM, Baughman RD, O'Connor GT, et al. Cyclosporine in the treatment of psoriasis. Arch Dermatol 1987;123:163.

CHAPTER 11–7

Dermatitis–Eczema

Robert L. Rietschel, M.D.

DEFINITION

Eczema means to weep. In the acute stage this happens and is morphologically identified by vesicles and bullae.

ETIOLOGY

The causes of most of the diseases in this category are either unknown or multifactorial. A genetic predisposition combined with an environmental insult results in several of the conditions discussed in this chapter. Specific environmental chemicals account for contact dermatitis.

CRITERIA FOR DIAGNOSIS
Suggestive

The lesions that are commonly grouped under the heading dermatitis–eczema have a tendency to ooze early in the course of their development. As the eczematous process becomes more entrenched, less weeping and a more lichenified appearance follows, mimicking the papulosquamous category of skin disorders. Eczematous changes may occur on any area of the skin surface.

The eczematous lesion must be accompanied histologically by an inflammatory process with a spongiotic change within the epidermis. When the process remains microvesicular, the disease is correctly categorized as an eczema; however, when this condition becomes more extreme, vesiculobullous changes may result.

Definitive

The specific features needed to support a diagnosis are listed in Table 11–7–1.

CLINICAL MANIFESTATIONS
Subjective

The family history is not helpful in distinguishing among the various types of dermatitis; however, more than three fourths of patients with atopic dermatitis have an immediate family member with either asthma, hayfever, or atopic dermatitis. The occupational history is important in patients with contact dermatitis. Certain manufacturing and outdoor occupations permit exposure to known allergic sensitizers. Examples include electrical and telephone workers exposed to poison ivy/oak, construction workers exposed to chromates in powdered cement, rubber industry workers exposed to a variety of antioxidants and accelerators added in the manufacturing process, and electrical and semiconductor workers exposed to epoxy resins. These and many other occupational and environmental factors should be examined in searching for the cause of dermatitis. The most common subjective symptom of an eczema is the presence of pruritus. In most cases, this is at its zenith in the evening. Nocturnal pruritus is alleged to be most characteristic of scabies; however, pruritus of any cause is greatest and least tolerated at night. When the eczemas become severe and intractable, normal daily function may be impaired, particularly if the hands and feet are involved.

Objective

Major morphologic criteria for distinguishing the various eczemas are listed in Table 11–7–1. It should be borne in mind that the eczematous process is one in which an early exudative state either resolves or evolves into a more chronic, more lichenified appearance. This is easily confused with a papulosquamous process, but this should not dissuade the observer from correct categorization.

PLANS
Diagnostic
Differential Diagnosis

The diseases to consider that have eczematous or dermatitic features are listed under the heading Likely Diagnosis.

Diagnostic Options

The patient's history is very important in diagnosing the various types of eczema. Onset in early infancy with a family history or a personal history of asthma, hayfever, or eczematous dermatitis suggests an atopic dermatitis or, at the least, an atopic diathesis. A thorough knowledge of products applied to the skin is necessary to evaluate the major

TABLE 11–7–1. MORPHOLOGIC CRITERIA FOR THE DIAGNOSIS OF THE VARIOUS ECZEMAS

Morphologic Change	Supporting Data	Likely Diagnosis
Eczematous change with annular patches common or predominating, widely distributed	KOH preparation from border of lesion shows branching, septate hyphae	Acute tinea corporis
	Burrows noted, especially in webs of fingers, toes; KOH shows mites or eggs	Scabies
	Purulent draining lesions with surrounding eczema and similar eczema distant from draining lesion	Infectious eczematous dermatitis
	Repetitive applications of potential sensitizer to localized dermatitis or wound with development of widespread, patchy eczema; no grossly draining wound or lesion	Autoeczematization reaction
	Negative KOH; no draining lesions; coin-shaped patches especially about extensor surfaces of distal extremities	Nummular eczema
	Similar to above with tendency to lichenify; commonly involves penis, perioral areas	Exudative discoid and lichenoid dermatitis
Localized or more discretely confined patches of eczema	Dry, xerotic skin with irregularly distributed patches of eczema that at times have a cracked-pavement appearance	Asteatotic eczema
	Flexural body areas involved; sometimes cheeks, extensors; personal or family history of asthma, hayfever, or eczema in childhood	Atopic dermatitis
	Linear streaks of papulovesicular change; potential exposure to common sensitizers or irritants	Contact dermatitis
	Predominantly sun-exposed skin involved; sparing of covered skin, eyelids, infranasal areas	Photosensitivity state
	Clear, tense, fluid-filled vesicles on palms, lateral aspects of digits and soles; KOH negative	Dyshidrosis (pompholyx)
	Vesicles to bulla on palms, soles; with positive KOH from blisters on feet but not from hands	Dermatophytid reaction
	Unilateral nipple eczema with pagetoid cells on biopsy	Paget's disease of breast
	Edematous lower leg with hyperpigmented eczematous change	Stasis dermatitis
	Localized plaque most commonly on extremity or nape of neck; lichenified with fairly discrete margins and biopsy showing subacute to chronic dermatitis	Lichen simplex chronicus
	Localized plaque to widely scattered, fairly discrete patches with biopsy showing Pautrier's microabscesses or infiltration of epidermis with atypical lymphocytes	Patch- or plaque-stage mycosis fungoides (cutaneous T-cell lymphoma, CTCL)

causes of contact dermatitis. This will be dealt with further under Discussion. A history of the bathing pattern of the individual is helpful in distinguishing what role xerosis and irritants may play. The presence or absence of similar signs and symptoms in other family members may suggest a diagnosis such as scabies.

Most eczematous change requires microscopic examination of the lesional stratum corneum using potassium hydroxide to rule out fungal disease. Scabies can be searched for with the same procedure. (Many individuals prefer to use mineral oil to make the preparation as a substitute for potassium hydroxide in this setting.) Culture of cutaneous eczematous dermatitis frequently yields *Staphylococcus aureus,* which commonly colonizes eczematous skin. This should not be construed as etiologic unless the lesion is grossly purulent. Staphylococcal colonization of eczema is generally considered an aggravating factor, and anti-staphylococcal systemic antibiotics are frequently helpful in alleviating the dermatitis, but this should not be implicated as the primary etiologic agent.

A biopsy is frequently required to rule out patch- or plaque-stage mucosis fungoides, CTCL. In most eczemas, a perivascular lymphohistiocytic inflammatory infiltrate is found with or without eosinophils. This is most commonly located around the superficial vascular plexus of the dermis near the dermal–epidermal interface. There is very little interface dermatitis present in the majority of the eczemas, and no disruption of the dermal–epidermal junction as seen in lichenoid reactions. Within the epidermis, varying degrees of intercellular edema account for the amount of oozing noted clinically. When the epidermis is infiltrated with atypical lymphocytes, as seen in cutaneous T-cell lymphomas, a similar eczematous-type process may be observed clinically. Infiltration of the epidermis with pagetoid cells in the areola (Paget's disease) likewise mimics eczematous dermatitis, although these cells are histologically distinct.

Should the diagnosis of contact dermatitis be suspected on the basis of the history and no clear etiology found, patch testing should be performed by a dermatologist thoroughly familiar with the pitfalls of this procedure and the likely causes of contact dermatitis. Patch testing by novices with little regard for avoiding the application of irritant concentrations of materials has resulted in misinformation, incorrect diagnoses, and chemical burns.

Should the clinician suspect photosensitivity, a history of exposure to topical materials with photosensitizing capability, such as the halogenated salicylanilides, musk ambrette (a fragrance), and, paradoxically, sunscreen agents, should be sought. Oral medications that are capable of photosensitizing, such as the sulfonamides, tetracycline, and phenothiazines, should be investigated and eliminated if possible. If there is no history of exposure to these materials and there are no signs or symptoms suggestive of a lupuslike state, an antinuclear antibody test is still indicated to eliminate the possibility that the individual is in a prodromal phase of lupus. Distinguishing lupus erythematosus from polymorphous light eruption can be very difficult on the basis of clinical and historical information. Likewise, histologic findings may be very similar. Skin biopsy from the involved area, obtained for cutaneous immunofluorescence, will show a positive lupus band test in more than 90% of patients with lupus, but a positive lupus band is seen in specimens from patients with polymorphous light eruption only rarely.

Recommended Approach

A potassium hydroxide examination is always a good starting point. If the dermatitis has persisted and required two or more physician visits, then diagnostic patch testing would be in order. A persistent dermatitis that is unresponsive to treatment should be biopsied. If the condition is confined to sun-exposed skin, the patient should be photo tested and photopatch tested.

Therapeutic

Therapeutic Options

Potentially curable sources of eczematous dermatitis include acute tinea corporis, scabies, infectious eczematoid dermatitis, autoeczematization reaction, and some cases of contact and photosensitivity-induced dermatitis.

Acute tinea corporis frequently responds to topical preparations such as miconazole (Monistat) and clotrimazole (Lotrimin), but if the lesions are widespread, the use of oral microsized griseofulvin (Fulvicin) at 500 mg daily following meals is usually curative within 1 month.

Successful treatment of scabies requires a correct diagnosis. Application of lindane (Kwell), permethrin (Elimite), or crotamiton (Eurax) nocturnally following a hot shower or bath; the wearing of clean, freshly laundered clothing; and the use of clean, freshly laundered bed linens are usually sufficient. Occasionally, the treatment must be repeated 7 days later. It is not at all uncommon for patients who have had scabies to itch for several weeks following successful treatment, so this is not necessarily an indication for additional therapy.

Infectious eczematous dermatitis is usually cured if the source of infection is eradicated through adequate antibiotic therapy coupled with a brief course of systemic corticosteroids. The appropriate antibiotic is determined by the organism cultured.

The autoeczematization reaction most commonly results from repetitive application of an allergen to an area of abnormal skin. Cure of such patients requires diagnostic patch testing and successful reeducation of the patient to avoid the sensitizer. Likewise, appropriate diagnostic testing for other sources of contact dermatitis and photosensitive contact dermatitis can lead to appropriate patient reeducation and elimination of continued eczematous dermatitis.

Acute, self-limited, but severe eczema may occur. This is most notable after contact with poison ivy, poison oak, and poison sumac. When eczema is so intense that it interrupts daily functioning due to involvement of extremities, genital skin, or generalized dermatitis or when eyelid edema interferes with vision, a course of systemic corticosteroids is required. In these cases, topical steroids are of no value. Daily doses of prednisone in the range of 60 mg per day are usually required to suppress the eruption. Acute poison ivy-like eruptions usually persist for approximately 3 to 4 weeks. More rapid tapering of prednisone frequently leads to a recurrence of the dermatitis. Prednisone should be administered as a single morning dose on a daily basis for a 3-week period. Alternate-day therapy is not indicated, as this is reserved for maintenance therapy rather than clearing of acute disease.

The more chronic forms of eczema are generally not treated with systemic corticosteroids. In the weeping state, compresses with solutions that are nonirritating and mildly bactericidal are helpful. The purpose of a compress is to allow for enhanced evaporative cooling of the skin; this produces vasoconstriction and subsequently decreases the edema. The compresses should not be soaking wet, but rather only damp and of a fairly porous gauzelike material. Tap water should be used to moisten the compress, as tap water is as good as more expensive agents, unless antibacterial activity is required. Soaking or immersing eczematous dermatitis for protracted periods leads to maceration. The compresses should be left in place for approximately 15 to 20 minutes every 3 to 4 hours until the lesion has become dry. Treatment with topical corticosteroids is usually quite helpful. There are many topical steroid preparations from which to choose. The physician should make a selection on the basis of three considerations: the steroid molecule, the vehicle, and the patient setting. If a dry eczematous process such as asteatotic eczema is being treated, the physician should select an ointment-based topical corticoid. If the eczema involves a great deal of hair-bearing skin, such as the scalp, a lotion may be selected. If the patient lives in a warm, moist climate, ointments may be poorly tolerated, if at all, and cream-based vehicles may be necessary; patients in arid climates may require exactly the opposite. Gel-based vehicles are generally designed to optimize steroid solubility and enhance the efficacy of the steroid molecule. The disadvantage of most gel preparations is that the vehicle tends to burn or sting acute eczematous dermatitis, and this limits therapy in many instances.

Hydrocortisone (1%) is usually considered to be the least potent of the presently available topical corticosteroids, but the 1% concentration is considered effective. This product is very useful for maintenance therapy, once clearing or near-clearing has been achieved. It is the corticosteroid of choice for genital and facial skin and for most childhood eczemas. Fluorination of the corticosteroid molecule results in increased potency. The intermediate-strength topical corticosteroids are generally those in the triamcinolone, betamethasone category. These products are adequate for most eczematous dermatitides. They are generally used in a 0.1% concentration, and when used excessively or oc-

cluded with plastic wrap, they can produce purpura and striae. Application of fluorinated steroids to the face produces a rosacea-like dermatitis, militating against this use. When intermediate-strength corticosteroids are occluded with plastic wrap, their penetration through skin is greatly enhanced, as are both their therapeutic and side effects. This may be desirable on a short-term basis to induce clearing of the dermatitis. More potent topical fluorinated corticosteroid preparations are generally not necessary for eczematous dermatitis on a prolonged basis. In fact, after approximately 1 week of therapy, a diminished response, known as tachyphylaxis, is noted. Examples of preparations in this category are fluocinonide (Lidex), halcinonide (Halog), and betamethasone dipropionate (Diprosone). After a patient's dermatitis has improved significantly, a lower-strength corticosteroid may be substituted with very little loss of efficacy. In general, the lowest-strength corticosteroid that adequately keeps the patient comfortable is the correct one.

Recommended Approach

Topical treatment is advised whenever possible. Severe and extensive eczematous eruptions cannot be treated adequately with topical medications and will require systemic medication, usually corticosteroids. Acute or self-limited dermatitis is more amenable to systemic treatment.

FOLLOW-UP

Monitoring patients with chronic eczematous dermatitis is necessary to detect abuses in the use of topical steroids. The earliest sign of excessive steroid use may be purpura followed by atrophy and striae. The striae are permanent. Likewise, the patient must be observed for accidental use of fluorinated steroids on facial or genital skin. Depending on the severity of the dermatitis and the amount of medication being used, the patient should be seen at intervals ranging from 1 to 6 months.

DISCUSSION
Prevalence

The prevalence of atopic dermatitis is almost 20 per 1000. Other eczemas are less prevalent.

Related Basic Science

The cause of eczemas due to infectious agents is fairly clear-cut. In general, the infectious agent is thought to produce an eczematous state by stimulating the development of delayed hypersensitivity. The causes of such eczematous states as atopic dermatitis, nummular eczema, exudative discoid and lichenoid dermatosis, and dyshidrosis are far from clear. These diseases are chronic with frequent exacerbations and remissions. It is common to blame emotional stress as a cause of these disease processes, but the mechanism by which this occurs is not clear.

Both histamine and proteinases have been implicated as causative factors in atopic dermatitis. The individual with atopic diathesis has a lowered itch threshold to chemical, thermal, and mechanical stimuli. Scratch and intradermal skin tests to various allergens are found to be positive in 52 to 97% of patients with atopic dermatitis. In one series, 78% of patients with dermatitis alone demonstrated immediate hypersensitivity to one or more allergens. When patients who had asthma or rhinitis (in addition to dermatitis) were added to the study, 95% of the patients reacted to one or more allergens (Rajka, 1975). Unfortunately, elimination of the offending allergen, even when identified by radioabsorbent techniques (RAST), seldom produces improvement in the dermatitis. Food allergies to fish, oranges, tomatoes, and apples are commonly identified in patients with atopic dermatitis, but when compared with patients with other causes of dermatitis, there was no significant difference.

Most dry skin conditions itch, but the cause is unclear. Thus, skin moisture enhancement is generally considered an adjunctive therapy in management of these forms of eczema. Approximately three quarters of patients with atopic dermatitis ultimately "outgrow their eczema"; however, many of these individuals return as adults with problems of asteatotic eczema or chronic hand eczema.

The pathophysiology of contact dermatitis is better understood. Not all individuals are equally susceptible to the various haptens that are present in the environment. Dinitrochlorobenzene sensitizes approximately 95% of individuals challenged, and the urushiol antigen present in poison plant rashes sensitizes approximately 70%. Less potent allergens cause the greatest degree of difficulty in diagnosis. These substances are the ones that generally produce contact dermatitis of a more chronic and subtle degree and require patch testing for confirmation. Among the most notorious in this category are nickel, benzocaine, chromates, ethylenediamine, and various rubber additives such as the thiurams, mercaptobenzothiazole, carbamates, and paraphenylenediamine derivatives. Formaldehyde and formaldehyde-releasing preservatives are becoming an increasing problem, as are certain perfume ingredients. When a sensitizer is applied to skin, it penetrates through the strateum corneum and is picked up by dendritic cells located high in the epidermis (Langerhans cells). These cells process the antigen in conjunction with interleukin-1 and summon lymphocytes, which make contact with the Langerhans cells. Lymphocytes and macrophages then travel to the lymph node and recruit additional sensitized lymphocytes, which ultimately return to the Langerhans cells, where their lysosomal contents are released, producing a spongiotic, inflammatory dermatitis. This delayed hypersensitivity mechanism is now fairly well characterized for contact dermatitis, but its broader role in host defense is yet to be clarified.

Natural History and Its Modification with Treatment

Eczema tends to be chronic, but improvements can be achieved if patients follow the therapeutic instructions discussed above.

Prevention

At present, no preventive measures are guaranteed to be successful. Avoidance of ear piercing may minimize the risk of sensitization to nickel. Avoidance of the use of ethylenediamine-containing medicants such as Mytrex cream will minimize the risk of contact dermatitis to these specific agents. Rather notorious allergens such as neomycin, thimerosal, and benzocaine may be avoided by the judicious selection of alternative products.

There is controversy regarding the significance of breastfeeding in reduction of the incidence of atopic dermatitis in infancy. Studies to date have not demonstrated a clear-cut benefit. Likewise, dietary manipulations have failed to demonstrate conclusively that infantile atopic dermatitis can be prevented with these manipulations.

Cost Containment

The most prudent method of reducing expense in this group of diseases and all other corticosteroid-responsive skin conditions is to use generic preparations of hydrocortisone or triamcinolone for maintenance therapy. More expensive and more potent forms of topical steroid therapy may be indicated for brief periods, but they offer less benefit for chronic maintenance therapy owing to the phenomenon of tachyphylaxis (diminishing response with repeated application).

REFERENCES

Adams RM. Occupational skin disease. Philadelphia: Saunders, 1990.

Fisher AA. Contact dermatitis. Philadelphia: Lea & Febiger, 1986.

Fregert S. Manual of contact dermatitis. Copenhagen: Munksgaard, 1974.

Haustein U-F, Hlawa B. Treatment of scabies with permethrin versus lindane and benzyl benzoate. Acta Derm Venereol (Stockh) 1980;69:348.

Rajka G. Atopic dermatitis. Philadelphia: Saunders, 1975.

Silbergberg I, Baer RL, Rosenthal SA. The role of Langerhans' cells in allergic contact hypersensitivity: A review of findings in man and guinea pig. J Invest Dermatol 1976;66:210.

Storrs FJ. Symposium on contact dermatitis. Dermatol Clin 1984;2:4.

CHAPTER 11–8

Vesicles and Bullae

Marilynne McKay, M.D.

DEFINITION

A blister is a circumscribed elevation of the epidermis containing a macroscopic cavity filled with a clear fluid. A vesicle is a blister less than 1 cm in diameter; a bulla is larger than 1 cm.

ETIOLOGY

Blister formation occurs when fluid accumulates in the epidermis in response to disruption of interepidermal coherence or dermal–epidermal adherence. Blister depth ranges from superficial to deep, depending on the mechanism of the pathogenic process.

CRITERIA FOR DIAGNOSIS
Suggestive

Almost any fluid-filled lesion should prompt the consideration of a vesiculobullous disorder, especially if there are multiple lesions greater than 1 cm in diameter. Although the classic blister contains clear fluid, lesions more than a few days old may accumulate cellular debris that resembles pus. Hemorrhagic blisters are rare unless there has been trauma to the underlying basement membrane zone. The blister roof may slough from mucosal lesions, leaving moist round erosions; drying blisters may leave a ring of scale. Erosions or scales may suggest the presence of earlier blisters; a background of postinflammatory hyperpigmentation suggests a chronic and recurring blistering process.

Definitive

Fresh intact vesicles or bullae that contain clear fluid establish the diagnosis of a blistering disorder.

CLINICAL MANIFESTATIONS
Subjective

Symptoms are variable in vesiculobullous disorders. The patient may not have noticed blister formation in early lesions, because of either early rupture of superficial lesions (especially on mucous membranes) or excoriation of blister roofs secondary to extreme pruritus. Not all vesiculobullous lesions are pruritic; the symptom of "burning" is said to be characteristic of early lesions of herpesvirus (simplex and varicella–zoster) and staphylococcal infections, as well as dermatitis herpetiformis, an immune-mediated disorder.

Objective
Physical Examination

Individual blisters may have a round or oval shape, and confluence of vesicles or bullae may result in polycyclic or scalloped lesion borders. Fresh blisters are more tense and tend to become flaccid with time, but this finding also depends on the depth of the blister and the integrity of adjacent tissue. Deep bullae (e.g., bullous pemphigoid) have a thicker epidermal roof and remain tense for days. Superficial vesicles (e.g., bullous impetigo and pemphigus foliaceous) tear easily and the entire roof may be lost, leaving a red, moist erosion that may crust. The clue to a bullous etiology of such a lesion is persistence of the blister remnant as a "collarette" at the periphery of the erosion. In the mouth, vesicles lose their tops early and appear as aphthae, small round erosions with a fibrinous yellow exudate at the base.

A central depression or umbilication, due to an area of necrosis, is the hallmark of a viral vesicle. Umbilicated herpesvirus vesicles characteristically occur in clusters. Irregular or linear patterns of smooth-topped vesicles suggest an extrinsic contactant cause (friction, poison ivy, burn, chemical irritant, adhesive tape). The patient's age may be significant in bulla formation, as children tend to blister more easily in response to inflammation (insect bites, scabies). Blister fluid is usually clear, but it may become turbid with cellular debris if bullae remain intact for days. Whitish or cloudy fluid may indicate secondary infection, and reddish or black fluid is due to hemorrhage.

Some of the vesiculobullous diseases are chronic and recurrent; a few are almost asymptomatic. The inherited blistering disorders usually present in childhood; there may be a history of other family members with similar lesions or a related infant with a severe skin disease who died shortly after birth.

Routine Laboratory Abnormalities

There are no routine diagnostic laboratory abnormalities.

PLANS

Diagnostic

Differential Diagnosis

See Table 11–8–1. A skin biopsy is extremely useful in differentiating between the various vesiculobullous disorders. In some cases, immunofluorescence of skin (direct) or serum (indirect) may be necessary to confirm a diagnosis (dermatitis herpetiformis, pemphigus, bullous pemphigoid). Elicitation of a bulla by firm sliding pressure on nonlesional skin is called a positive Nikolsky sign. This may be evoked in acantholytic disorders such as epidermolysis bullosa and pemphigus, as well as in the more severe generalized blistering disorders such as toxic epidermal necrolysis and staphylococcal scalded skin syndrome (SSSS). Rapid differentiation between drug-induced toxic epidermal necrolysis and staphylococcal scalded skin syndrome may be performed by examination of a frozen section to determine the level of the epidermal split:

TABLE 11–8–1. VESICLES AND BULLAE

Type of Blister	Probable Diagnosis	Diagnostic Tests or Observations
Subcorneal	Miliaria crystallina	Pinpoint, superficial at entrance of sweat duct
	Bullous impetigo	*Staphylococcus aureus*-positive culture; bullae due to exotoxin may generalize (staphylococcal scalded skin syndrome [SSSS])
Intracellular degeneration	Dominant congenital ichthyosiform erythroderma (epidermolytic hyperkeratosis)	Hereditary; generalized erythema; thick brown verrucous scaling, especially flexures; SB-D
	Epidermolysis bullosa (Cockayne form)	Hands and feet; dominant inheritance; initiated by mild trauma; SB-D
	Friction blisters	Normal individual; history of trauma
Spongiotic (intercellular edema)	Dermatitis (eczema)	See Chapter 11–7
	Allergic contact dermatitis, acute	Patch test confirmatory, history consistent (e.g., poison ivy)
	Dyshidrotic eczema	Sides of fingers, palms, and soles; chronic, recurrent, pruritic
	Insect bite reaction	History helpful; frequently lower extremities
Acantholytic (dissolution of intercellular cement)	Pemphigus foliaceous	Subcorneal bullae, frequently on sun-exposed areas; occasionally associated with penicillamine therapy; SB-D, DIF
	Pemphigus vulgaris	Includes mucous membranes, generalized; SB-D; DIF; InIF; associated with myasthenia gravis
	Paraneoplastic pemphigus	Oral erosions, erythematous lesions that develop blisters, especially in patients with lymphoma or thymoma; SB-C; DIF; InIF shows IgG of all desmosome-containing epithelia
	Familial benign chronic pemphigus (Hailey–Hailey disease)	Dominant inheritance; intertriginous and neck; erosive, nonscarring; SB-C
	Keratosis follicularis (Darier's disease)	Often dominant; hyperkeratotic, crusted follicular papules in seborrheic distribution; SB-C
	Transient acantholytic dermatosis (Grover's disease)	Usually males more than 40 years of age; chest, back hyperkeratotic; SB-C
Viral blisters (ballooning degeneration of epidermal cells), umbilicated vesicles	Herpes simplex	Localized, recurrent; Tzanck smear shows multinucleated giant cells; SB-C
	Varicella	Chickenpox; generalized, especially torso; vesicles cloudy second day
	Varicella–zoster (shingles)	Grouped vesicles; dermatome distribution; older patients
	Hand, foot, and mouth	Coxsackie virus A-5, -10, -16; acral lesions
Degeneration of basal cells	Epidermolysis bullosa simplex	Dominant inheritance; nonscarring; SB-D
	Erythema multiforme, epidermal	Iris lesions, may generalize (toxic epidermal necrolysis); associated with drugs, herpes; *Mycoplasma* pneumonia; SB-C
	Herpes gestationis	Pregnancy; pruritic; SB-C
	Comatose bullae	Large 4 × 6-cm, oval areas of pressure; sweat gland necrosis on SB; history suggestive
Degeneration of basement membrane zone	Epidermolysis bullosa dystrophica	Dominant or recessive; scarring; mucosal and nail involvement; recessive more severe; SB-D
	Bullous pemphigoid	Large tense bullae, especially flexural surfaces; older patients; usually self-limited; SB-C; DIF
	Benign mucosal pemphigoid (cicatricial)	Mucous membranes; scarring, especially on conjunctiva
	Dermatitis herpetiformis	HLA-B8/-DRw3; symmetric grouped vesicles; pruritus and burning; SB-D; DIF
	Porphyria cutanea tarda	Blisters on light-exposed areas; scarring; hirsutism; uroporphyrin in urine; onset middle age; associated with alcoholism

SB, skin biopsy; D, diagnostic; C, consistent with diagnosis; IF, immunofluorescence; DIF, direct immunofluorescence (skin biopsy); InIF, indirect immunofluorescence (serum).

at the granular zone for staphylococcal scalded skin syndrome, below for toxic epidermal necrolysis.

Diagnostic Options

Skin biopsy is recommended in widespread disease, especially if the disorder is chronic and/or recurrent. Specimens should be taken for both routine histopathology and immunofluorescence microscopy, (the latter should be preserved in Michel's medium, a special tissue fixative, rather than formalin. For best results, the specimen should be directed to a laboratory specializing in cutaneous immunofluorescence studies, which will also provide the medium and shipping container for the tissue sample.)

Another helpful diagnostic technique is the Tzanck smear, which is a scrape from a blister base after the roof has been removed with scissors. The smear is then stained with Wright's or Giemsa stain and observed microscopically. Presence of multinucleated giant cells confirms a viral blister. Acantholytic cells (rounded-up epidermal cells that have lost their attachment to one another) may be seen in pemphigus.

Bacterial culture of blister fluid is rarely helpful, unless phage type 71 staphylococcus is cultured from a suspected staphylococcal scalded skin syndrome. Viral culture may be extremely useful, especially when herpes is suspected in immunocompromised or dermatitic patients with widespread lesions. If porphyria is likely, urine porphyrin studies should be obtained. Patch testing should be done if a contact dermatitis is suspected, so that the patient may avoid the offending substance in the future.

Recommended Approach

Depending on the patient's history (acute onset versus chronic disorder, episodic or ongoing, etc.) and the distribution of lesions (localized, dermatomal, generalized), biopsy or viral cultures should be considered to establish the diagnosis. Tzanck smear should be performed in the office if herpesvirus infection is suspected.

Therapeutic

Therapeutic Options

A detailed discussion of therapy for each of the vesiculobullous disorders is beyond the scope of this chapter, and the reader is referred to a current dermatologic reference text. In most cases, consultation with a dermatologist is recommended for management of chronic bullous disorders.

Systemic steroids are of limited, specific usefulness is vesiculobullous disorders. In some cases, corticosteroids are definitely life-saving (pemphigus), but in others (erythema multiforme, toxic epidermal necrolysis) no firm evidence exists that they are efficacious. They continue to be used in these conditions, however, and many investigators are convinced that they decrease morbidity. There is a definite indication for systemic steroid therapy in pemphigus, bullous pemphigoid, herpes gestationis, and cicatricial pemphigoid. Before the advent of systemic steroid therapy, pemphigus was almost uniformly fatal. Mortality is now around 25% and is due primarily to the complications of steroid therapy. The usual corticosteroid dosage is 60 mg per day, although initial control of pemphigus lesions may require as much as 300 mg per day. When blister formation stops, steroid dosage should be tapered to a level permitting only occasional blisters. Should it become apparent that prolonged corticosteroid therapy at significant dosages will be needed, an immunosuppressive agent (azathioprine [Imuran], cyclophosphamide [Cytoxan], methotrexate [Folex]) or gold compounds may be used to reduce the requirement for corticosteroids in pemphigus. Alternate-day administration of steroids is a desirable goal. Herpes gestationis and bullous pemphigoid are generally self-limited, and periodic trials of steroid tapering should be attempted.

Dermatitis herpetiformis is associated with gluten-sensitive enteropathy, although this is often asymptomatic. A gluten-free diet may successfully control skin symptoms, but is sometimes difficult for patients to maintain. Oral therapy with sulfones or sulfapyridine is generally effective in dermatitis herpetiformis. Dapsone (Avlosulfon) is usually begun at 100 to 200 mg per day and raised or lowered to control

blistering eruptions. The mechanism of action is unknown. Before therapy, a complete blood count and a test for glucose-6-phosphate dehydrogenase deficiency should be performed. Hemolysis and methemoglobinemia regularly occur with sulfone treatment, and patients with glucose-6-phosphate dehydrogenase deficiency should not take sulfones. Systemic steroids are usually ineffective.

The inherited blistering disorders are quite resistant to therapy. Recently, the oral retinoids (synthetic vitamin A analogs) have been found helpful in epidermolytic hyperkeratosis and Darier's disease; however, this treatment is experimental. The various forms of epidermolysis bullosa are also recalcitrant, but phenytoin (Dilantin) has shown promise in some recent reports. Present therapy is directed toward prevention of trauma to the epidermis (soft diets help esophageal abrasion) and local care with topical antibiotics.

Porphyria cutanea tarda may be effectively controlled by avoidance of continued liver damage by alcohol, phlebotomy to reduce iron load, elimination of exacerbating drugs, and sunscreens for protection from ultraviolet light. Antimalarial agents may induce remissions in some cases.

A 3-week tapering course (60 mg per day for a week, then 40 mg per day, then 20 mg) of systemic corticosteroids is helpful for severe cases of acute contact dermatitis. Topical steroids are generally of little use in the blistering disorders.

For acute primary herpes simplex virus outbreaks, oral acyclovir (Zovirax) has been shown to be effective in a dosage of 200 mg every 4 hours, 5 doses daily for 10 days. Recurrences should be treated with the same dosage schedule of oral acyclovir for 5 days, beginning at the onset of the prodrome. Topical acyclovir ointment reduces viral shedding in primary herpes simplex virus infections, but has not been found to be effective in recurrent disease. For herpes zoster, the dosage of acyclovir is 800 mg, 5 doses daily for 10 days; treatment should be started as close to the onset of vesicle development as possible. Systemic steroids have not been proven to be effective in preventing post-zoster neuralgia in elderly patients.

Recommended Approach

Appropriate therapy of vesiculobullous diseases depends entirely on accurate diagnosis. As immunosuppressive drugs may be required, it is extremely important to be certain of the diagnosis. In some cases, rebiopsy is recommended when response to therapy does not seem to occur as expected. Dermatologic consultation should be strongly considered.

Genetic counseling should be performed as appropriate for the hereditary chronic vesiculobullous diseases (epidermolytic hyperkeratosis, familial benign chronic pemphigus, Darier's disease, epidermolysis bullosa). The patient should understand that many of the chronic bullous diseases (cicatricial pemphigoid, pemphigus, dermatitis herpetiformis) may be controlled only with medications that have potentially serious side effects. The goal of therapy is adequate disease control on the lowest possible dosages of medications, which may mean occasional blister formation.

The vesicle fluid of herpes simplex and varicella–zoster (shingles) contains active virus, and other individuals may become infected by lesional contact until drying and crusting occur. Lesions of herpes zoster expose others to varicella; individuals who have had chickenpox previously are apparently not at risk. Lesions of herpes simplex, however, may infect others at the point of contact despite a past history of herpes simplex in the exposed individual.

FOLLOW-UP

Patients on long-term immunosuppressive therapy should have regularly scheduled follow-up appointments. Assessment of developing side effects to steroids, antimalarial agents, retinoids, sulfones, and other systemic medications should be performed at each visit, and tapering of dosages should be considered as the disease stabilizes. A drug monitoring protocol and flow sheet in the patient's chart can facilitate appropriate data collection.

DISCUSSION

Prevalence and incidence

The prevalence of pemphigus vulgaris and pemphigus foliaceous is similar in men and women; The mean age of disease onset is 50 to 60 years, but ranges from childhood to old age. Pemphigus vulgaris is more common in Jews and probably in people of Mediterranean descent, so incidence is higher in areas where these populations predominate. (For example, in Jerusalem, the prevalence of pemphigus vulgaris is 1.6 per 100,000; in Connecticut, 0.42 per 100,000; and in Finland, 0.76 per 1,000,000. In the United States the ratio of pemphigus vulgaris to pemphigus foliaceus cases is about 5:1.

Related Basic Science

Genetics

Epidermolysis bullosa is the term used for a group of disorders with the common feature of blister formation after minor skin trauma. Both dominant and recessive forms occur, with epidermolysis bullosa simplex and dystrophic epidermolysis bullosa representing the dominant inheritance pattern. Most cases of recessive epidermolysis bullosa are either recessive dystrophic epidermolysis bullosa or junctional epidermolysis bullosa; severity ranges from generalized mutilating disease to relatively mild localized lesions. Sporadic cases may be difficult to classify.

Dermatitis herpetiformis is associated with a high occurrence of HLA antigens B8, DR3, and DQw2 and other alloantigens thought to be related to the pathogenesis of the disease, possibly as a consequence of an abnormally overactive immune response to naturally occurring antigens. The gluten-sensitive enteropathy seen in dermatitis herpetiformis patients probably relates to the immunoglobulin (Ig) A deposits found in the skin of these patients, but the pathophysiology of blister formation remains unknown at present. Granular IgA deposits are associated with enteropathy, but linear IgA deposits are not; thus, dermatitis herpetiformis and linear IgA disease are thought to be different disorders.

A functional genetic defect of the cell membrane and desmosomal complex is the basis of the acantholysis seen in familial benign pemphigus (Hailey–Hailey disease), inherited as an autosomal dominant trait with a family history obtainable in about two thirds of patients. Friction and infection cause acantholytic damage to the epidermis, accounting for its usual localization in intertriginous areas.

Physiologic or Metabolic Derangement

Blister formation occurs when fluid accumulates in the epidermis in response to disruption of interepidermal coherence or dermal–epidermal adherence. In the horny layer, the intercellular bond is stable, consisting of desmosomes and an intercellular cement substance. In the malpighian layers, this bond is dynamic, formed by maturing epidermal cell cytomembranes as they migrate from the basal layer upward. At the dermal–epidermal junction, epidermal adherence depends on a complex system of hemidesmosomes, anchoring fibrils, and cement substance.

The basic morphologic patterns of blister formation reflect common features of pathogenesis, but are not necessarily specific to any one disease entity. Spongiosis is a nonspecific pattern of intercellular edema, widening the space between cells and stretching points of desmosomal attachment into "intercellular bridges." This is the most common pattern of epidermal vesicle formation and, accompanied by dermal inflammation, is seen in eczemas, allergic contact dermatitis, insect bite reactions, and some fungal infections.

Ballooning is intracellular edema that causes swelling and degeneration of epidermal cells and is seen especially in viral blistering diseases. This particular pattern is seen in association with multinucleated epidermal giant cells in herpesvirus (herpes simplex and varicella–zoster) infections.

Acantholysis is a loss of intercellular coherence, resulting in a "rounding up" and separation of epidermal cells. In the pemphigus group of diseases, an immune reaction is directed against elements of the epidermal cell membrane. Immunofluorescence may demonstrate a specific pemphigus IgG antibody in the intercellular space as well as in the serum. A functional genetic defect of the cell membrane and desmosomal complex is the basis of the acantholysis seen in familial benign pemphigus (Hailey–Hailey disease) and, possibly, in Darier's disease as well. Superficial acantholysis also occurs in response to exotoxin production in staphylococcal scalded-skin syndrome.

Cytolytic blisters form as a result of fluid accumulation occurring in spaces formed by epidermal cell rupture and death. These processes are seldom specific and can range from genetic defects (epidermolytic hyperkeratosis, epidermolysis bullosa simplex) to physical trauma (heat, cold, friction) and inflammation (erythema multiforme). The location of the cytolytic process in the epidermis is a helpful diagnostic feature.

Blisters occurring the vicinity of the dermal–epidermal junction may be characterized by specific ultrastructural target sites. Immunoglobulin deposition with accompanying complement activation limited to the lamina lucida is seen in bullous pemphigoid and herpes gestationis. Lesions of cicatricial pemphigoid show additional damage to the lamina densa. Damage to the papillary dermis with subsequent vesiculation beneath an intact basal lamina may occur in severe inflammatory disorders or segmental necrosis (leukocytoclastic angiitis). Papillary tip vesiculation is seen in dermatitis herpetiformis, a genetic-associated autoimmune disorder associated with HLA-B8 antigen and gluten-sensitive enteropathy. There is granular deposition of IgA immune complexes and fibrin in the dermal papillae, where reticulin fibers may share an antigen with gluten. Epidermolysis bullosa dystrophica is due to an inherited defect in anchoring fibrils, resulting in easy mechanical dislodgement of the epidermis at the level of the basal lamina. Collagen degeneration is the predominant finding in porphyria cutanea tarda, correlating with the mechanical and actinic sensitivity of this disorder.

Natural History and Its Modification with Treatment

Unless the cause is determined to be infectious or traumatic and, therefore, self-limited, the bullous disorders are, for the most part, chronic. Recurrences are not uncommon (herpes simplex, erythema multiforme). Severe scarring may occur in the dystrophic mechanobullous disorders, and epidermal loss may lead to fluid imbalance and death in toxic epidermal necrolysis and pemphigus. The chronicity and potential morbidity of the vesiculobullous diseases require early and continuous medical intervention.

Prevention

Careful padding and minimization of rubbing or chafing are helpful in preventing the formation of friction blisters in normal individuals. Such precautions are essential in treatment of patients with hereditary blistering disorders, as repeated traumatic bullae will lead to progressive scarring and loss of function. If the cause of a vesicular process (allergic contact dermatitis, drug-induced erythema multiforme) can be determined to be due to a specific agent, avoidance of that substance is in order. Unfortunately, no method of prevention is known for the great majority of vesiculobullous diseases.

Cost Containment

Careful outpatient monitoring of disease progress and therapeutic side effects may decrease the necessity of hospitalizations for disease flares or complications.

REFERENCES

Anhalt GJ, et al. Paraneoplastic pemphigus: An autoimmune mucocutaneous disease associated with neoplasia. N Engl J Med 1990;323:1729.

Callen JP. Internal disorders associated with bullous disease of the skin. J Am Acad Dermatol 1980;3:107.

Champion RH, Burton HL, Ebling FJG, eds. Textbook of dermatology. Oxford, England: Blackwell Scientific, 1991.

Fine J-D, et al. Revised clinical and laboratory criteria for subtypes of inherited epidermolysis bullosa. J Am Acad Dermatol 1991;24:119.

Fitzpatrick TB, Eisen AZ, Wolff K, et al., eds. Dermatology in general medicine. 4th ed. New York: McGraw-Hill, 1993.

Stanley JR. Pemphigus. In: Fitzpatrick TB, Eisen AZ, Wolff K, et al., eds. Dermatology in general medicine. 4th ed. New York: McGraw-Hill, 1993:606.

Pustules

Marilynne McKay, M.D.

DEFINITION

Pustules are eruptive focal epidermal elevations containing purulent material (inflammatory cells and serum). Puncture of the cavity with a needle or blade yields white, yellow, or greenish yellow material.

ETIOLOGY

The formation of a pustule results from the epidermal or dermal accumulation of leukocytes in response to one or several stimuli, generally inflammatory in nature.

CRITERIA FOR DIAGNOSIS

Suggestive

A cutaneous pustule is familiar to patients as well as physicians, so the history of "pus bumps" can be helpful when lesions have been altered by time or the patient's manipulation. *Staphylococcus* and *Streptococcus* often colonize normal skin. When the skin's normal barrier function is compromised by injury, lesions may become secondarily infected; pustules may thus be seen with scabies, insect bites, minor skin wounds, varicella, herpes simplex, and atopic dermatitis. The latter are not considered to be primarily pustular disorders, however, and are discussed elsewhere. Fluid in vesicles and bullae of primary blistering diseases may accumulate cellular debris, giving the appearance of leukocytes.

Definitive

Inflammatory red-rimmed papules that develop rapidly into pustules are typical of the pustular disorders. They are usually acute in onset.

CLINICAL MANIFESTATIONS

Subjective

Pustules usually arise rather quickly over a day or two; even in chronic pustular dermatoses that are characterized by ongoing eruptions, individual lesions rupture or dry out in a few days to be replaced by yellow or brownish crusts. Active crops of pustules may become confluent and involve extensive areas of the skin. Involved areas may be pruritic or asymptomatic. Recurrent pustules on the palms and/or soles are often recalcitrant and may be difficult to manage.

The patient's history may be beneficial to the evaluation of pustular conditions, especially psoriasis. The onset of folliculitis may be related to occlusive clothing or tars, although lesions should also be cultured for bacteria and fungus. Drug-related eruptions are most commonly associated with corticocosteroids, iodides, bromides, and isoniazid.

Objective

Physical Examination

The major morphologic criteria for distinguishing the various pustular dermatoses are listed in Table 11–9–1.

Routine Laboratory Abnormalities

Routine laboratory tests reveal no diagnostic information.

PLANS

Diagnostic

Differential Diagnosis

See Table 11–9–1.

Diagnostic Options

It should be borne in mind that not all pustular skin conditions are infectious in origin, so it is important to examine purulent material carefully. A Gram stain of pustule contents should be examined for bacteria and Gram-positive budding yeast forms. A potassium hydroxide preparation of the cavity roof may reveal fungal hyphae. Bacterial cultures should be done on aspirates of cleaned, intact pustules.

Isolated pustules occurring in association with sparse acral palpable purpuric lesions should always suggest septic vasculitis, and cultures of blood and lesions should be obtained immediately.

Sterile pustules in symmetric acral, flexural, and genitocrural distribution may be seen in pustular psoriasis. High fevers, leukocytosis, hypocalcemia, and hypoalbuminemia may obscure the noninfectious etiology of this condition, but blood cultures remain sterile unless secondary infection occurs. Reiter's disease is similar but usually has more mucosal and joint involvement. In contrast, subcorneal pustular dermatosis has few associated problems, with mild pruritus as the chief complaint.

The major determination to be made is whether the pustules are of infectious or noninfectious origin. The laboratory is an ally in examination of pustule contents, and a skin biopsy may be helpful in establishing a histologic pattern such as psoriasis.

Recommended Approach

A careful history should be taken to determine if this is the first episode of skin disease or if another cutaneous problem antedated the development of pustules. Extensive fungal or bacterial infection should raise the consideration of HIV disease, especially if there are risk factors.

Therapeutic

Therapeutic Options

Bacterial pyodermas respond most rapidly to oral antibiotics. Unless specific bacterial sensitivities have been established, a penicillinase-resistant penicillin or erythromycin is the drug of choice. Topical antibiotics may be helpful for superficial pyodermas after the application of cleansing tap water soaks three times daily and gentle debridement to remove crusts. Treatment of sepsis is based on the results of blood cultures.

The antifungal imidazole derivatives (clotrimazole [Lotrimin], miconazole [Monistat]) are effective topical treatments for both fungal and candidal skin infections. Twice daily application for 4 weeks is sufficient for most infections. Oral griseofulvin (Fulvicin) is useful only in the treatment of fungal infections, but oral ketoconazole (Nizoral) and fluconazole (Diflucan) are also active against *Candida*.

Drug-related disorders remit when therapy is discontinued, assuming discontinuation is possible.

Pustular psoriasis of von Zumbusch requires hospitalization and careful monitoring of fluids and electrolyte levels as well as multiple blood cultures to rule out initial or secondary bacteremia. Fulminant, recurring waves of pustules may respond to etretinate (Tegison), the drug of choice, or low weekly doses of methotrexate (Folex).

Systemic corticosteroids have been reported to precipitate pustular reactions in plaque-type psoriasis and are best avoided.

Reiter's disease is generally treated with antiinflammatory agents such as aspirin, steroids, and indomethacin (Indocin) acutely. Methotrexate and other immunosuppressive agents have been reported to be effective in some cases.

If bacterial, fungal, and yeast infections have been excluded from the diagnosis of a pustular dermatosis (such as palmoplantar pustulosis), a trial of topical steroids should be given. It may be necessary to occlude areas at night to enhance penetration of the medication.

TABLE 11–9–1. PUSTULES

Major Morphologic Change	Likely Diagnosis	Physical/Additional Findings	Supporting Data
Discrete individual pustules			
Sparse, acral			
With central hemorrhage	Gonococcemia	Arthralgia; fever; leukocytosis; periarthritis	Blood culture positive if early
With purulent purpura	Staphylococcal sepsis		Gram-positive cocci in pus aspirate, culture positive
Grouped pustules			
With crusting	Impetigo	Face, preexisting dermatitis	Gram-positive cocci, culture *Streptococcus* or *Staphylococcus aureus*
Follicular	Bockhart's impetigo	Lower extremities and scalp especially; superficial yellow pustules	Culture *Staph. aureus*, superficial yellow pustules
	Drug-related eruption	Trunk; symmetric superficial pustules	Lesions sterile; history of systemic steroids, halides
	Folliculitis	Hairy areas: proximal extremities, chest, buttocks	History of occlusion
Associated with erythematous plaques	Dermatophyte	Usually groin or feet	Potassium hydroxide, fungal culture positive
Associated with scaling, redness	Candidiasis	Moist intertriginous areas; mouth; penis; vagina; satellite lesions at periphery	Gram stain: budding yeasts; fungal culture positive
Numerous symmetric pustules			
Superficial; flaccid in arcuate patterns	Subcorneal pustular dermatosis of Sneddon–Wilkinson	Intertriginous areas; flexors; trunk	Sterile pustules
Spreading pustules, coalescing into lakes	Pustular psoriasis of von Zumbusch	Acral, flexures; groin; may generalize; fever; leukocytosis	Sterile pustules; history of psoriasis
Hyperkeratosis with pustules (keratosis blenorrhagica)	Reiter's disease	Primarily acral with arthritis, conjunctivitis, urethritis	HLA-B27
Palms and soles			
Pustules with scaling and plaques	Dermatophyte	Asymmetric, arcuate; toe web involvement	Potassium hydroxide–positive
	Barbers' psoriasis	Chronic, recurrent; proximal palm, soles especially	Lesions sterile; nail pitting; plaques; history of psoriasis
	Palmoplantar pustulosis		Without psoriatic stigmata

Recommended Approach

Once the etiology of the pustular eruption has been determined, appropriate therapy can be initiated. Elements of soap and water hygiene should be explained to patients with secondary pyodermas.

FOLLOW-UP

Most bacterial infections improve within a week of oral antibiotic therapy. Fungal treatment should be reevaluated in 3 to 4 weeks to confirm eradication. Chronic hand and foot dermatitis should be followed on demand, as flares and remissions are the rule.

DISCUSSION

Prevalence and Incidence

Superficial skin infections such as impetigo and folliculitis are extremely common problems. Pustular psoriasis, on the other hand, is rare, even in psoriatics (see Chapter 11–6). Palmoplantar pustulosis is also rare, but occurs more commonly in women than men (3:1).

Related Basic Science

Genetics

Generalized pustular psoriasis has been associated with HLA-B27, as have psoriatic arthritis and Reiter's disease. Neither pustular psoriasis of the palms and soles nor palmoplantar pustulosis is associated with HLA antigens.

Physiologic or Metabolic Derangement

The formation of a pustule results from the accumulation of leukocytes in response to one or several stimuli, presumably for the purpose of ingesting and destroying material harmful to the organism. Movement of polymorphonuclear leukocytes is a complex process initiated by such factors as random migration, concentration gradients of attractants, secretory products of sensitized lymphocytes and polymorphonuclear leukocytes, denatured proteins, and functional changes in the polymorphonuclear leukocytes affecting orientation (chemotaxis) and locomotion (chemokinesis). Complement activation is considered to be a general source of chemotactic substances, set off by such diverse agents as bacteria (pyodermas), fungi, yeasts, and epidermal cells themselves (psoriasis).

The cause of psoriasis remains unknown, although research is progressively uncovering pathophysiologic mechanisms. Chemotactic factors apparently derived from complement-binding immune complexes have been found in psoriatic scale, and the polymorphonuclear leukocytes themselves may contain highly specific immunoglobulin membrane antibodies directed against epidermal cell nuclei. In pustular psoriasis, the characteristic subpapillary dermal inflammatory infiltrate is the most conspicuous process. Polymorphonuclear leukocytes move from the dilated papillary capillaries into the epidermis, forming multilocular "spongiform" pustules with epidermal cell degeneration. Subcorneal focal accumulations of these cells are called Munro's microabscesses and are consistent features of psoriasis. The microabscesses of pustular psoriasis, however, rapidly enlarge into pustules, coalesce, and form lakes of pus beneath the horny layer.

Natural History and Its Modification with Treatment

The single most common isolate from childhood impetigo in the United States is group A *Streptococcus*. Normal skin apparently is colonized from close contact with an infected individual. Although superficial pyodermas are generally uncomplicated, the frequency of acute glomerulonephritis following infection with a known pyoderma-associated nephritogenic strain of group A *Streptococcus* (serotypes 2, 49, 55, 57, 60) is 10 to 15%. These serotypes differ from the ones reported for pharyngitis-associated nephritis, and the latent period is longer, about 3 weeks after the pyoderma.

Staphylococcal skin infections are also spread by contact with carriers who may or may not have active lesions. As with streptococcal pyodermas, skin trauma is a predisposing factor, but follicular colonization with *Staphylococcus* also occurs. Superficial folliculitis (Bockhart's impetigo) is a relatively mild condition, but deeper inflammation of a follicle may result in a furuncle or boil. In an otherwise healthy young person, recurrent furunculosis may represent reinfection from close contact with members of the family or peers, especially if the latter are sexually active. Early treatment with penicillinase-resistant penicillin is effective in preventing the development of a painful draining furuncle, which may spread infection to others.

Pustular psoriasis, whether rising de novo or as a complication of plaque-type psoriasis, is a difficult therapeutic problem. Waves of pustules progress peripherally, leaving the edematous epidermis denuded and oozing. Significant fluid loss as well as infection can occur at this stage until lesions dry. The pustular process may repeat itself many times until the flare runs its course or is controlled by medication.

Prevention

Elements of good skin hygiene and health maintenance are instrumental in the prevention of bacterial and fungal skin infections. Perspiration and maceration in intertriginous areas, especially in obese individuals, are important in recurrent candidal and fungal infections. Avoidance of occlusive clothing, cleanliness, and deliberate air exposure at home should be encouraged.

The sterile pustular dermatoses are very recalcitrant to treatment, and no preventive measures are known at the present. As flares of psoriasis may be set off by skin trauma, care should be taken to prevent sunburn, for example. Systemic steroids should be avoided in psoriasis; withdrawal may precipitate a "rebound flare," which sometimes presents as pustular psoriasis.

Cost Containment

After the appropriate diagnostic procedures have been done to establish the etiology of the pustule (i.e., infectious versus sterile), therapy should be directed toward rapid resolution of the condition.

Most staphylococcal skin infections are caused by penicillinase producers, so the semisynthetic penicillins and erythromycin are the oral antibiotics of choice. The latter is the most economical.

Patient compliance is an important factor in the resolution of this condition, and careful explanation of how to apply a topical agent will result in less waste and more effective use of a cream or ointment.

REFERENCES

Champion RH, Burton HL, Ebling FJG, eds. Textbook of dermatology. Oxford, England: Blackwell Scientific, 1991.

Fitzpatrick TB, Eisen AZ, Wolff K, et al., eds. Dermatology in general medicine. 4th ed. New York: McGraw-Hill, 1993.

CHAPTER 11–10

Acneiform Eruptions

Robert L. Rietschel, M.D.

DEFINITION

Acneiform eruptions comprise follicular papules and pustules with or without cyst formation.

ETIOLOGY

The conditions listed in Table 11–10–1 are felt to have a strong genetic component, with the exception of those conditions caused by specific microbiologic agents.

CRITERIA FOR DIAGNOSIS
Suggestive

An acneiform eruption is a constellation of "blackheads" (comedones), erythematous papules, pustules, and cysts generally involving the face and/or upper trunk and extremities.

Definitive

The specific findings needed to support a diagnosis are given in Table 11–10–1.

CLINICAL MANIFESTATIONS
Subjective

The family history is not usually helpful in arriving at a diagnosis of acne vulgaris, although the patient's parents frequently have had acne. The acneiform condition steatocystoma multiplex, however, is autosomal dominant. Occupations involving machinery that uses cutting oils can be of importance in the development of chloracne (acne venenata). Additional environmental and occupational factors in the development of acneiform eruptions are listed in Table 11–10–1.

Objective

See Table 11–10–1.

PLANS
Diagnostic
Differential Diagnosis

The diagnostic possibilities are listed under Likely Diagnosis in Table 11–10–1.

Diagnostic Options

See Table 11–10–1. Few laboratory tests are necessary to evaluate an acneiform eruption. If the patient develops pustules about the nose and mouth within days of discontinuation of broad-spectrum antibiotics, culture of the lesion is useful to establish a diagnosis of Gram-negative folliculitis. Cultures of the purulent discharge in hidradenitis suppurativa are of little value, because the microbial flora that is present is secondary; the primary defect is excess keratinization of the follicular orifice.

Recommended Approach

Physical examination coupled with history leads to diagnosis in this category of disorders. A bacterial culture is done only in the clinical setting outlined under Objective for Gram-negative folliculitis (Table 11–10–1).

Therapeutic
Therapeutic Options

Acne vulgaris is treated with multiple agents. Topical therapy with either salicylic acid preparations or tretinoin (Retin-A) is directed at eliminating the follicular retention of keratin. Various concentrations are used, according to the ability of the individual's skin to withstand

TABLE 11–10–1. CLINICAL MANIFESTATIONS OF ACNEIFORM ERUPTIONS

Predominant Primary Lesions	Subjective	Objective	Likely Diagnosis
Blackheads (comedones)	Teenager, young adult; no prior antibiotics, other drugs; possible exacerbation around menses in women	Face, trunk, upper arms likely involved; papules, pustules; some cysts may be present	Acne vulgaris
	Prior history of acne and/or prolonged use of broad-spectrum antibiotics	Pustules, especially around nose, within 24 to 48 hours of discontinuing antibiotics; culture of pustule reveals Gram-negative organisms	Gram-negative folliculitis
	Discrete localization of lesions to areas not usually solely involved in acne; contact with cutting oils, chlorinated hydrocarbons, sunlight, cosmetics	Areas of physical contact with suspected etiologic agent are only areas of lesions	Acne venenata
Inflammatory papules or pustules with rare blackheads		Papulopustules on trunk but not face in young adult on no medication	Pityrosporum folliculitis
		Papules on back and chest	
	Middle-aged adult; relatively asymptomatic; may be exaggerated by spicy foods, coffee, tea	Central facial involvement; oily to ruddy complexion; telangiectasia, papules, large sebaceous glands; possible keratitis	Rosacea
	May be febrile or afebrile; use of medication such as iodine, bromide, isoniazid, phenytoin, phenobarbital, steroids	Papules or pustules all in same stage of development predominate	Drug eruption
	Aggravated by shaving; resolved by growing a beard	Ingrown hairs evident	Pseudofolliculitis barbae
	Onset in childhood or adolescence; possible history of atopy or ichthyosis	Keratotic papules on upper arms; fewer lesions on thighs	Keratosis pilaris
	Young adult, usually female; lesions only around mouth; may use fluoride toothpaste, moisturizers, or topical steroids on face	5-mm zone of normal skin surrounds vermilion border of lips; papulopustular lesions	Perioral dermatitis
Cysts predominate	Family history of similar problem; involves sternum, axilla, groin	Noninflamed cysts until traumatized; no discharge of material without mechanical trauma	Steatocystoma multiplex
	Adolescent onset	Double or triple blackheads overlying cysts; predominately on trunk	Acne conglobata
	Chronic draining cysts	Multiple sinus tracts of axilla and groin; possibly scalp cysts with fluctuant nature and purulent discharge	Hidradenitis suppurativa

the irritation that accompanies these drugs. Mild soaps and minimal face washing are the rule when tretinoin is used. When either of the agents is combined with 5 or 10% benzoyl peroxide gel, a highly effective program of therapy may be achieved within 6 to 8 weeks. Topical use of antibiotics such as tetracycline, clindamycin, and erythromycin is increasing, as some studies show that these preparations approach the efficacy of systemic antibiotics. *Pityrosporum* folliculitis resembles acne vulgaris but is confined to the trunk of young adults and does not form cysts but rather papulopustules. Although this condition is suppressed partially by tetracycline therapy, ketoconazole (Nizoral), topically or systemically, is more effective.

Some acneiform eruptions such as those induced by corticosteroids, chlorinated hydrocarbons, sunlight, and cosmetics are most effectively treated with tretinoin. Others, such as rosacea, perioral dermatitis, and cystic acne, respond more favorably to oral antibiotic management. The tetracyclines appear to offer the greatest response in doses ranging from 250 mg to 1 g daily. Topical metronidazole (Metrogel) is effective for rosacea and is used singly or in combination with tetracycline class antibiotics. For severe cystic acne, isotretinoin (Accutane) may produce prolonged remissions or cures. The usual course of therapy is 4 months, and relapse rates vary inversely with the dosage used. Treatment with 1 to 2 mg/kg per day produces the lowest relapse rates, but doses as low as 0.1 mg/kg per day also are effective. Side effects include cheilitis, sun sensitivity, conjunctivitis, hair loss, and elevation of serum triglycerides. These changes reverse with discontinuation of therapy, but skeletal hyperostosis and premature closure of the epiphyses, which occur more frequently with prolonged therapy, do not appear reversible. Isotretinoin is teratogenic. Alternative drugs include erythromycin, minocycline, dapsone (Avlosulfon) (for severe cystic acne), and clindamycin (Cleocin) (only when the risk of pseudomembranous colitis is outweighed by the possible benefit). In Gram-negative folliculitis, treatment is determined by the sensitivities obtained on culturing the causative organism.

Individual acne lesions may be opened with a 25-gauge needle or scalpel and the contents expressed with a comedo extractor. Surgical treatment is the only definitive therapy in steatocystoma multiplex and in many cases of hidradenitis suppurativa.

Recommended Approach

Topical treatment should be the starting point for this group of disorders.

FOLLOW-UP

Follow-up depends on the severity and type of treatment selected. When a program of therapy is instituted, 3 to 4 weeks is generally required before any judgment may be passed on the effectiveness. In women of childbearing age a negative blood pregnancy test prior to and monthly during isotretinoin therapy is recommended.

DISCUSSION
Prevalence

The prevalence of acne vulgaris is about 70 per 1000, and that of cystic acne, about 2 per 1000.

Related Basic Science

A number of biological events collide in the skin of the young adult or adolescent and result in the clinical state of acne vulgaris. These involve keratinization, lipid production, bacterial proliferation, and hormonal influences. The importance given each of these events varies, and a simple cause-and-effect role for each is lacking. A compact form of keratin is generated and retained within the pilosebaceous units of the face and upper torso. This progresses to an occlusion of the pilosebaceous duct. Sebaceous gland lipids are produced at an accelerated rate, but the path from sebaceous gland to surface is occluded with a keratinaceous plug. There is no feedback inhibition of sebum production, which continues even under enormous pressure. In high enough concentrations, these sebaceous lipids induce inflammatory reactions.

The bacterial organism that thrives in this environment is *Propionibac-terium acnes*. This organism is present to a much lesser degree in the pilosebaceous units of individuals without acne. This sequence of events appears to be triggered by an increase in the androgen-to-estrogen ratio. Total plasma and urine testosterone levels are normal in men and women with acne, but skin from these individuals shows an increased conversion of testosterone to the more active metabolite dihydrotestosterone. Several recent studies have shown increased free testosterone levels in women with acne.

Rosacea is most common in the age group 30 to 50. Sebaceous gland hypertrophy and vascular dilation are prominent features, which may be aggravated by ingesting hot beverages. Heat (not caffeine) has been demonstrated to cause the central facial flushing common in these individuals. Although *Demodex folliculorum* (a mite) can frequently be isolated in the dilated sebaceous glands, its etiologic significance is disputed. Sebaceous hypertrophy may result in rhinophyma.

Natural History and Its Modification with Treatment

The natural history of this sequence of events is follicular enlargement and rupture with the possibility of scarring. After several years a spontaneous remission is customary, but it is not uncommon for acne to continue into the third and fourth decades of life.

Prevention

Prevention of acneiform eruptions is not possible in all cases. Avoiding cosmetics and pomades and drugs that are known to produce this type of eruption and limiting contact with cutting oils and other chlorinated hydrocarbons may be helpful.

Cost Containment

The measures listed under Prevention provide the basis for cost containment of acne and acneiform eruptions. Use of over-the-counter forms of salicylic acid, sulfur, and benzoyl peroxide for common acne is reasonable and cost-effective. If these measures prove inadequate, consultation with a dermatologist should be sought.

REFERENCES

Beck O, Faergemann J, Hornqvist R. *Pityrosporum* folliculitis: A common disease of the young and middle-aged. J Am Acad Dermatol 1985;12:56.

Cunliffe WJ, Cotterill JA. The acnes: Clinical features, pathogenesis and treatment. Philadelphia: Saunders, 1975.

Peck GL, Olsen TG, Butkus D, et al. Isotretinoin versus placebo in the treatment of cystic acne. J Am Acad Dermatol 1982;6:735.

Plewig G, Kligman AM. Acne morphogenesis and treatment. New York: Springer-Verlag, 1975.

Pochi PE, Ceilley RI, Coskey RJ, et al. Guidelines for prescribing isotretinoin (Accutane) in the treatment of female acne patients of childbearing potential. J Am Acad Dermatol 1988;19:920.

Schiavone FE, Rietschel RL, Sgoutas D, Hams R. Elevated free testosterone levels in women with acne. Arch Dermatol 1983;119:799.

Shelley WB, Shelley ED. Unilateral demodectic rosacea. J Am Acad Dermatol 1989;20:915.

Stein RS, Poss TM, Komaroff AL. Topical versus systemic agent treatment for papulopustular acne: A cost-effectiveness analysis. Arch Dermatol 1984;120:1571.

Wilkinson DS, Kirton V, Wilkinson JD. Perioral dermatitis: A 12-year review. Br J Dermatol 1979;101:245.

CHAPTER 11–11

Erythema-group Reactions

Robert L. Rietschel, M.D.

DEFINITION

Disorders characterized by red, raised, nonscaling lesions of various geometric patterns are classified as erythema-group reactions. Wheals are also encompassed within this group.

ETIOLOGY

The causes of erythema-group reactions range widely. Medications, infections, collagen–vascular disease, and internal malignancy must be considered. Table 11–11–1 gives additional considerations.

CRITERIA FOR DIAGNOSIS

Suggestive

Erythema-group reactions are cutaneous eruptions characterized by erythema and edema that persist for varying lengths of time. The lesions may assume any size or shape.

Definitive

The specific findings necessary for a specific diagnosis are found in Table 11–11–2.

CLINICAL MANIFESTATIONS

Subjective

The family history is not helpful in determining the cause or differential diagnosis within the erythema-group reactions. Occupational and environmental events are of prime importance in discovering the cause of the eruption. The etiology of the erythema-group reactions may be discovered in the history (Table 11–11–1).

Pruritus may or may not accompany the lesions described in this chapter. When pain is part of the erythematous eruption, leukocytoclastic vasculitis frequently is present. Erythematous lesions in which pain is pronounced are usually in the process of evolving to a more extensive morphologic category.

Objective

The major morphologic criteria for distinguishing the various erythema-group reactions are enumerated in Table 11–11–2. It is noteworthy that erysipelas cannot be distinguished from cellulitis by any morphologic characterization or laboratory examination. Cellulitis merely represents a more extensive, deeper version of the same pathophysiologic process manifested in erysipelas.

The duration of the lesion is useful information in evaluating the erythema-group reactions. When an erythematous, edematous lesion of any size or shape fades completely within 24 hours, the nature of the eruption is urticarial. If that same lesion maintains its position longer than 24 hours, the term *erythema multiforme* may be invoked. Occasionally, the term *erythema perstans* is used to describe single or multiple erythematous, edematous lesions that remain stable for several days at a time.

The erythema-group reactions should not be accompanied by scaling except near the periphery of the papule, patch, or plaque. If scaling is prominent, then the disease is a papulosquamous eruption and not an erythema-group reaction.

TABLE 11–11–1. ETIOLOGY OF ERYTHEMA-GROUP REACTIONS

Infection	
Viral	Herpes simplex, psittacosis, variola, vaccinia, orf, milkers' nodules, mononucleosis, mumps, poliomyelitis, adenovirus, Coxsackie B5, echovirus, hepatitis, lymphogranuloma venereum
Bacterial	Syphilis, diphtheria, typhoid, tuberculosis, bacille Calmette–Guérin vaccination, gonorrhea, leprosy, *Pseudomonas, Salmonella typhimurium, Staphylococcus, Streptococcus Yersinia, Vibrio parahemolyticus*
Fungal	Histoplasmosis, coccidioidomycosis, dermatophytosis
Other	*Mycoplasma,* trichomoniasis
Drugs	Antibiotics, anticonvulsants, heavy metals (gold, mercury, arsenic), barbiturates, corticosteroids, hydralazine, nitrogen mustard, phenolphthalein, phenylbutazone, sulfonamides, opiates, radiocontrast media, aspirin, azo dyes, benzoates
Internal malignancy	Carcinoma, reticulosis, leukemia, myeloma
Collagen–vascular disease	Lupus erythematosus, polyarteritis nodosa, Wegener's granulomatosis, dermatomyositis, rheumatoid arthritis, hypocomplementemic vasculitis
Miscellaneous	X-ray therapy, pregnancy, sarcoidosis, contact dermatitis, cold, sunlight, menstruation, polycythemia, foods

PLANS

Diagnostic

Differential Diagnosis

The differential diagnostic possibilities are listed under Likely Diagnosis in Table 11–11–2.

Diagnostic Options

When a single erythematous, sharply marginated plaque suddenly appears and is accompanied by fever, the likelihood of the diagnosis of erysipelas or cellulitis is so great that antibiotics are routinely administered. The presence of fever with other erythema-group reactions, however, is not uncommon. Typically one is faced with an overtly ill patient who is on multiple medications and develops a multiform erythema. No morphologic criteria allow distinctions to be drawn between erythema-group reactions due to infection and those due to drugs. The cutaneous reactions listed in Table 11–11–3 have morphologic features that distinguish one from another, but an etiologic diagnosis cannot be based on the morphologic features. The causes of these eruptions are listed in Table 11–11–1. In general, drugs that have been added within the past 48 hours are most suspect, but the actual offend-

TABLE 11–11–3. CUTANEOUS REACTION PATTERNS

Erythema multiforme
Erythema annulare centrifugum
Urticaria
Morbilliform erythema
Scarlatiniform erythema
Toxic epidermal necrolysis

ing agent may have been added any time in the previous 14 days. Unfortunately, the cutaneous eruptions that may accompany multiple types of infection may resemble a drug-induced erythema. When fever is not a manifestation of an erythema-group reaction, infection is still a possible cause, but noninfectious causes are more likely (see Table 11–11–1). Proper evaluation of patients for internal malignancy and collagen–vascular disease is covered elsewhere in this text.

Occasionally, the patient's history gives a clue to the cause of the eruption. For example, typical herpes labialis may have occurred 2 weeks prior to the onset of the cutaneous reaction. Herpes simplex commonly produces this delayed form of erythema multiforme. The development of a nonproductive cough in conjunction with erythema multiforme may suggest *Mycoplasma* pneumonia. Another infectious agent that has a tendency to produce characteristic findings is *Staphylococcus aureus,* group 2, phage type 70–71, which typically produces staphylococcal scalded skin syndrome (SSSS). Seen most commonly in children and in patients who have renal failure or are on immunosuppressive therapy, staphylococcal scalded skin syndrome produces a diffuse erythema that rapidly desquamates at a very superficial level of the epidermis. Inflammatory *Trichophyton* infections of the feet may produce erythema annulare centrifugum. The infection may be documented as the cause through skin testing with *Trichophyton* antigen. The skin reaction to this antigen is an erythematous papule that expands to produce a ring with a clearing center and gradual peripheral enlargement, thus mimicking the natural disease state of tinea.

The history can provide a clue to the diagnosis of many of the erythema-group reactions. Erythematous plaques accompanied by a fever unresponsive to antibiotics indicate that a biopsy should be performed. The problem may be Sweet's syndrome, in which case treatment with corticosteroids results in a very dramatic clearing of the condition. Alternatively, an erythematous plaque may be cellulitis secondary to cryptococcosis rather than a bacterial agent. If the erythematous reaction tends to be nummular, always recurs in the same place, and heals with profound hyperpigmentation, drug ingestion is the likely cause. When the eruption resembles an exaggerated sunburn response, a photosensitizing drug becomes the most likely cause. A history of a tick bite with the development of a spreading annular erythema surrounding

TABLE 11–11–2. MORPHOLOGIC CRITERIA FOR DISTINGUISHING ERYTHEMA-GROUP REACTIONS

Major Morphologic Criteria	Supporting Data	Likely Diagnosis
Plaquelike erythema	Fever; sharp margin; rising antistreptolysin-O titer	Erysipelas or cellulitis
	Fever, polymorphonuclear leukocytosis; histology; dense band of polymorphonuclear leukocytes in superficial dermis	Acute neutrophilic dermatosis (Sweet's syndrome)
Erythema with geometric patterning	Annular to irregular lesions with dusky centers resembling targets; tendency to acral distribution	Erythema multiforme
	Annular to arcuate lesions with central clearing; peripheral extension; faint scale on central side of erythema	Erythema annulare centrifugum
	Same as above but single lesion associated with tick bite and arthritis	Erythema chronicum migrans
	Waves of rippled erythema on trunk resembling the grain of lumber	Erythema gyratum repens
	Annular lesions that always recur in the same place, heal with hyperpigmentation	Fixed drug eruption
	Confined to sun-exposed skin, resembles exaggerated sunburn	Phototoxic eruption
	Evanescent lesions of any size or shape lasting less than 24 hours as any one discrete lesion	Urticaria
	Centrifugally spreading erythema that may center around intertriginous skin; peripheral faint scale; circumoral crusting; weight loss; usually diabetes mellitus; elevated plasma glucagon levels	Necrolytic migratory erythema
Generalized erythema	Measleslike, "maculopapular" eruption	Morbilliform erythema
	Erythema with measleslike quality and fine, keratotic sandpapery papules	Scarlatiniform erythema
	Erythema with skin peeling off in sheets	Toxic epidermal necrolysis

the area with or without the onset of arthritis is strongly suggestive of erythema chronicum migrans (Lyme arthritis).

If the history and physical findings suggest necrolytic migratory erythema as one of the diagnostic considerations, a biopsy should be taken from the peripheral scaling area, where superficial dyskeratotic cells are likely to be found histologically. Plasma glucagon levels should be obtained. Occasionally, acquired acrodermatitis enteropathica may resemble necrolytic migratory erythema morphologically, and zinc blood levels may help distinguish these two entities.

Toxic epidermal necrolysis embodies two separate disease categories. These may be distinguished rapidly by examining a frozen section of a skin biopsy. When the biopsy is taken from the leading edge of the superficial desquamating area, a split located high in the epidermis near the granular layer indicates staphylococcal scalded-skin syndrome. If the split occurs between the epidermis and dermis near the basement membrane zone, the disease is not staphylococcal scalded-skin syndrome, but rather drug-induced toxic epidermal necrolysis. Most investigators believe this to be a variant of the Stevens–Johnson syndrome or a severe erythema multiforme.

Recommended Approach

Newly introduced medications should be withdrawn if at all possible. If fever is present, the appropriate laboratory investigations for the signs and symptoms present should be ordered. Persistent, unexplained erythema-group reactions may require evaluation for occult malignancy. This is a low-yield exercise if the diagnosis is erythema annulare centrifugum; however, specific elements of the medical history can serve to guide the extent of the investigations ordered.

Therapeutic

Therapeutic Options

In most of the erythema-group reactions, treatment is not directed at the cutaneous eruption, but rather at the cause. Treatment of the eruptions secondary to infection consists of appropriate antimicrobial selection and administration.

In Sweet's syndrome, systemic corticosteroids are used; however, there is controversy regarding the role of steroids in erythema multiforme and toxic epidermal necrolysis. Supportive therapy is advocated by some as equally efficacious and less hazardous than intervention with corticosteroids. Convincing data on which to base sound treatment decisions in this area are not available. In practice, corticosteroids are commonly given with rapid defervescence of cutaneous signs and symptoms, but this is seldom done in the absence of other manipulations, such as withdrawal of drugs thought to be implicated in the etiology and treatment of infections when they seem to be present. When systemic steroids are administered to patients with toxic epidermal necrolysis of the staphylococcal scalded-skin syndrome variety, mortality actually increases. Whether or not this is true for drug-induced toxic epidermal necrolysis is far from clear.

Treatment of urticaria is usually accomplished with a single antihistamine drug administered in adequate doses. Occasionally it is necessary to use multiple antihistamines in combination. Antihistamine therapy is limited by the sedative action of these drugs. Hydroxyzine hydrochloride is frequently administered in this setting at dosages of 25 mg four times a day. This is increased or decreased depending on the patient's response and may be combined with antihistamines from other classes. Doxepin (Sinequan) has recently been shown to be significantly more effective and less sedating than diphenhydramine (Benadryl) for chronic urticaria in dosages of 10 mg three times a day. Nonsedating H_1-blocking antihistamines may also be beneficial, in some cases combined with other antihistamines.

Recommended Approach

Topical treatment can be helpful in the more limited erythema-group reactions and should be tried prior to systemic treatment. As medications cause most of the disorders considered in this group, it is helpful to keep the addition of further systemic medications to a minimum as cross-reactions between medications occur with some frequency.

FOLLOW-UP

Most patients with erythema-group reactions require weekly follow-up until a stable pattern is recognized and the appropriate searches have been made for the causes. After the condition has stabilized to a more chronic form, monthly follow-up for a few visits is sufficient.

DISCUSSION

Prevalence and Incidence

The prevalence of persons with significant skin pathology ranges from 200 to 400 per 1000 population, with an increase occurring with increasing age. Erythematous conditions represented 1.9% of dermatologic diagnoses (Mendenhall, 1977).

Related Basic Science

The pathophysiologic events that lead to the erythema-group reactions are predominantly vasodilatory stimuli. In some cases, direct histamine release is involved, whereas in others, complement activation and Arthus-like reactions may occur. Vasoactive amines are thought to be involved in the vasodilation of erythema-group reactions. As vasodilation increases, exudation of fluid and subsequently of cells into the superficial dermis enhances the edematous quality seen clinically. Histologically, in most of these disorders there is a perivascular inflammatory infiltrate. In some cutaneous reaction patterns, such as erythema multiforme, there is evidence of cell death within the epidermis. When this proceeds to a more extensive involvement, total loss of the epidermis follows, as in toxic epidermal necrolysis. The predominant cell type noted in the inflammatory infiltrate is the lymphohistiocytic series; however, eosinophils may accompany the drug-induced forms of erythema, and polymorphonuclear leukocytes tend to predominate in infections or complement-mediated events.

The ability of such diverse stimuli as deep x-ray therapy for treatment of malignancy and common tinea pedis to produce erythema-group reactions at sites that are located some distance from the site of primary involvement remains an intriguing riddle, but it suggests an immunologic response. In erythema multiforme, immunoglobulin M, complement, and fibrin may occasionally be seen deposited around dermal vessels, noted on direct immunofluorescence. Hypocomplementemia is evident is some forms of urticaria. These findings, however, do not explain all the events found within the erythema-group reactions. It is important to remember that events as far removed as 2 weeks prior to the presentation of the erythema-group reaction may have etiologic significance, as is most dramatically noted in patients with erythema multiforme following herpes simplex infections.

Natural History and Its Modification with Treatment

The natural history of erythema-group reactions depends on their cause. Drug reactions and erythema due to infections usually clear, whereas conditions such as toxic epidermal necrolysis are extremely serious, with mortality rates ranging from 20 to 50%. Blindness from corneal scarring, esophageal web formation, pneumothorax, and renal failure have all been associated with severe toxic epidermal necrolysis.

Prevention

It is not possible to prevent erythema-group reactions; however, identification of the causes of these conditions may enable the patient to prevent further contact with the drugs or other substances that may be involved in the development of the eruption.

Cost Containment

No specific information is available regarding cost containment. Obviously, cost can be decreased when a condition can be prevented, for example, by avoiding contact with drugs known to cause the condition in a patient.

REFERENCES

Amon RB, Diamond RL. Toxic epidermal necrolysis. Arch Dermatol 1975;111:1433.

Champion RH, Burton JL, Ebling FJG, eds. Textbook of dermatology. Oxford, England: Blackwell Scientific, 1991.

Elias PM, Fritsch PO. Erythema multiforme. In: Fitzpatrick TB, Eisen AZ, Wolff K, et al., eds. Dermatology in general medicine. New York: McGraw-Hill, 1987:555.

Green SL, Reed CE, Schroeter AL. Double-blind crossover study comparing doxepin with diphenhydramine for the treatment of chronic urticaria. J Am Acad Dermatol 1985;12:669.

Mendenhall RC. Dermatology practice study report. Washington, DC: Department of Health, Education, and Welfare, Sept. 28, 1977.

Skolnick M, Mainmann ER. Erythema gyratum repens with metastatic adenocarcinoma. Arch Dermatol 1975;111:227.

Swenson KH, Amon RB, Hanifin JM. The glucagonoma syndrome, a distinctive cutaneous marker of systemic disease. Arch Dermatol 1978;114:224.

CHAPTER 11–12

Telangiectasias and Purpuras

Robert L. Rietschel, M.D.

DEFINITION

Telangiectasias are dilated capillaries that are visible to the naked eye. Purpura is the term used for a group of disorders than include bruiselike, ecchymotic lesions that may be palpable or nonpalpable.

ETIOLOGY

Most of the disorders in this category have a genetic component, but excess hormones of endogenous or exogenous origin may stimulate telangiectasias. Collagen–vascular disorders are prime factors in the development of purpura, as are infection and metabolic disorders.

CRITERIA FOR DIAGNOSIS

Suggestive

Telangiectasias are blanchable dilations of vascular structures in which there may be an increase in vessel size or in vessel number. Purpura represents hemorrhage into the skin and may occur in a variety of sizes and shapes. The distinction between telangiectasias and purpuras is generally based on diascopy. This simple procedure requires a glass or plastic instrument that, when pressed against the skin, allows the observer to determine whether the lesions blanch under pressure. Blanching is characteristic of telangiectasias but not of purpuras.

Purpuras range from petechial hemorrhages of pinpoint size to large ecchymotic, bruiselike lesions. The purpuras are divided into palpable and nonpalpable types. The ability to close one's eyes and outline the lesion with the fingertip places the lesion in the palpable category.

Definitive

Tables 11–12–1 and 11–12–2 list the morphologic criteria and supporting data for diagnoses of telangiectasia or purpura.

CLINICAL MANIFESTATIONS

Subjective

The family history may reveal a tendency to some of the telangiectatic states that are autosomal dominant, such as the common nevus flammeus of the neck and hereditary hemorrhagic telangiectasia. Autosomal recessive conditions with telangiectasia include ataxia telangiectasia, Wiskott–Aldrich syndrome, some forms of histiocytosis X, Cockayne's syndrome, Rothmund–Thompson syndrome, and Bloom's syndrome. Occupational exposure to aluminum has been associated with telangiectasia, but other environmental factors have not been identified. Telangiectasias generate patient complaints because of their appearance or because of bleeding. Lesions on mucous membranes may cause epistaxis or melena depending on their location.

Purpuric lesions of the nonpalpable type generate complaints similar to those of telangiectasias, whereas the palpable purpuras, due to vasculitic causes, are frequently painful.

Objective

Major morphologic criteria for distinguishing the various telangiectasias and purpuras are noted under Criteria for Diagnosis and in Tables 11–12–1 and 11–12–2.

PLANS

Diagnostic

Differential Diagnosis

The diagnostic possibilities are listed under Likely Diagnosis in Tables 11–12–1 and 11–12–2.

Diagnostic Options

Multiple telangiectasias of unexplained etiology should prompt a search for liver abnormalities or sources of increased estrogen. If no etiology can be determined, idiopathic telangiectasia is diagnosed by exclusion. Periungual telangiectasias, although commonly seen with collagen–vascular diseases, are not themselves sufficient to warrant workup for these conditions in the absence of other complaints. Mucosal telangiectasias may be accompanied by petechiae under the nail plate or small petechiae on palmar surfaces, and this should prompt an evaluation for hereditary hemorrhagic telangiectasia. A thorough search for internal organ arteriovenous fistula formation and evidence of visceral hemorrhage is warranted.

Telangiectasia macularis eruptiva perstans may be accompanied by lytic bone lesions or peptic ulcer disease. Episodes of flushing with evidence of increased 5-hydroxyindoleacetic acid production should prompt a search for carcinoid, bronchial adenoma, or ovarian tumors.

Telangiectatic change may accompany growth disturbances. These syndromes frequently are associated with immunodeficiency and photosensitivity. Many of these conditions are detected in the pediatric age group. A history of photosensitivity may suggest a porphyrin abnormality.

Occurrence of nonpalpable purpura in acral regions should prompt a search for abnormalities of platelet number and function, episodes of recent infection, dysgammaglobulinemias, and amyloidosis. The presence of purpuric changes within areas of eczema or dermatitis should trigger a search for a history of topical corticosteroid use. Should this be negative, a history of thrombocytopenia or recurrent infections should suggest Wiskott–Aldrich syndrome. Should this additional history be negative, a biopsy should be performed to look for evidence of histiocytosis X.

Palpable purpura frequently occurs in acral or dependent areas of the body. When palpable purpura is accompanied by episodes of fever, a Gram stain may demonstrate the etiologic bacteria more rapidly than any other test. Cultures of skin lesions in this setting have a variable yield of positivity. It may be not be possible to distinguish between an acutely ill patient with lupus erythematosus and a patient with subacute bacterial endocarditis, as both may have palpable purpura about the hands and feet. When central pustulation occurs in small purpura over

TABLE 11–12–1. CLINICAL MANIFESTATIONS OF TELANGIECTASIAS

Secondary Morphologic Change/Distribution	Supporting Data	Likely Diagnosis
Macular, erythematous, discrete		
Solitary lesion	None	Nevus araneus (spider)
Multiple lesions, widely distributed	Liver abnormality, increased estrogen, or no abnormality	Secondary or idiopathic
Dermatomal pattern	Liver abnormality, increased estrogen, or no abnormality	Unilateral nevoid telangiectasia syndrome
Periungual	Arthritis, muscle weakness, sclerotic skin, multiple system complaints	Collagen–vascular disease (systemic lupus erythematosus, scleroderma, dermatomyositis)
Palmar	Liver abnormality, increased estrogen, multiple system complaints, or no abnormality	Secondary or idiopathic
Facial	Middle-aged adult, possible sebaceous gland hyperplasia	Rosacea
Mucosal	Epistaxis, gastrointestinal hemorrhage, arteriovenous fistulas in lung, brain	Hereditary hemorrhage telangiectasia (Rendu–Osler–Weber syndrome)
Macular, erythematous, confluent		
Stainlike quality	None	Nevus flammeus
Serpiginous border, stippled appearance	Buttock or extremities from childhood, early adult life	Angioma serpiginosum
Papular		
Bluish	Compressible	Venous lake
Erythematous	Stuck-on appearance	Cherry angioma
Accompanied by color changes		
Widely scattered over body as discrete hyperpigmented lesions	Pruritus and whealing when lesion stroked	Telangiectasia macularis eruptiva perstans
Face and upper torso with cyanosis	Bronchial adenoma, ovarian tumor; 5-hydroxyindoleacetic acid excretion in the urine	Carcinoid syndrome
Accompanied by growth abnormality		
Oculocutaneous telangiectasia	Frequent infections, cerebellar ataxia, decreased immunoglobulin A and cell-mediated immunity	Ataxia telangiectasia (Louis–Bar syndrome)
Dwarfism, facial telangiectasia in childhood	Photosensitive; decreased immunoglobulins	Bloom's syndrome
Telangiectasias on exposed surfaces; hyperpigmented face; loss of subcutaneous fat	"Birdlike" facies, photosensitive, "Mickey Mouse" ears	Cockayne's syndrome
Dwarfism, poikilodermatous exposed skin	Cataracts	Rothmund–Thomson syndrome

the joints, with or without tenosynovitis, a presumptive diagnosis of gonococcemia is appropriate.

Palpable purpuric change may be due to ischemic infarction secondary to fragments of atheromatous plaques. These lesions tend to occur on digits in the most acral end arteries. A search should be undertaken at the bedside for bruits that may identify the source of the atheromatous material.

Leukocytoclastic histologic findings with palpable purpura should guide the physician to look for one of the following causes: (1) drug ingestion; (2) infection, (3) collagen–vascular disease, (4) dysproteine-

TABLE 11–12–2. CLINICAL MANIFESTATIONS OF PURPURAS

Secondary Morphologic Change/Distribution	Supporting Data	Likely Diagnosis
Nonpalpable		
Follicular	Low vitamin C	Scurvy
Lower legs, with/without scaling; cayenne pepper spots; hyperpigmentation common; large patches	None	Progressive pigmented purpuric dermatoses
Lower legs, erythema and warmth common, 1- to 2-cm-diameter lesions	Monoclonal or polyclonal gammopathy	Dysgammaglobulinemia
Acral areas, punctate, petechial	Decreased platelet function, exertion, trauma, Valsalva, infection	Secondary
Acral, 1 to 4 cm, ecchymotic	Elderly individual	Senile purpura
Eyelid purpura	Pinching produces purpura	Amyloidosis
Nonanatomic distribution	Abnormal mental status	Psychogenic
Areas of prior dermatitis	Use of potent fluorinated topical corticosteroids	Corticoid purpura
Purpura within areas of eczema	Recurrent infections, thrombocytopenia, immunoglobulin M deficiency	Wiskott–Aldrich syndrome
Seborrhea-like eczema, purpura	Histologic identification of abnormal cells with Langerhans granules	Histiocytosis
Palpable		
Small 2- to 6-mm lesions about hands and feet	Positive blood cultures	Subacute bacterial endocarditis (etc.)
	Signs and symptoms of lupus or rheumatoid arthritis	Collagen–vascular disease
	Central pustule, tenosynovitis	Gonococcemia
Acral to widespread varying sites	Extreme distal digit	Atheromatous infarction
	Histology: leukocytoclastic	Cutaneous systemic vasculitis
	Tick bite fever, Weil–Felix test positive for OX-19 and OX-2	Rocky Mountain spotted fever
Large lesion with central hemorrhagic bullae	Consumptive coagulopathy	Disseminated intravascular coagulation
	Coumadin recently instituted	Coumadin necrosis
	Dark urine intermittently; positive acid hemolysis test	Paroxysmal nocturnal hemoglobinuria

mias due to macroglobulins and cryoglobulins, and (5) thrombotic thrombocytopenic purpura. Regardless of etiology, it is important to look for evidence of systemic vasculitic change in organs such as the kidney and lung. Rocky Mountain spotted fever may closely mimic cutaneous–systemic vasculitis.

The onset of large necrotic purpura that undergoes central bulla formation should prompt an immediate search for disseminated intravascular coagulopathies if there is no history of coumadin ingestion or signs and symptoms suggestive of paroxysmal nocturnal hemoglobinuria.

Recommended Approach

Telangiectasias are generally diagnosed on the basis of history and physical findings with laboratory investigations done only as listed in Table 11–12–1. Purpura is generally confirmed by skin biopsy as an initial investigation. Serologic investigations to evaluate collagen–vascular disorders, infection, or metabolic diseases would then follow as appropriate.

Therapeutic

Therapeutic Options

Telangiectasias usually require no treatment, but electrocautery, laser treatment, or sclerosing solution accurately applied to the central feeder vessel may ablate the lesion. Photosensitivity states in which telangiectasias become prominent may be managed with sunscreens with skin protection factors of 8 to 15.

Although scurvy can be corrected with vitamin C ingestion, patients with the more common progressive pigmented purpuras such as Schamberg's disease are frequently given ascorbic acid as well as a topical corticosteroid such as 0.1% triamcinolone acetonide cream (Aristocort). Therapy for dysproteinemias, amyloidosis, and platelet abnormalities is discussed elsewhere in this book. When purpuras are produced by exogenous corticosteroid applications, it is often sufficient to reduce the potency and frequency of application. Use of nonfluorinated corticosteroids or simple hydrocortisone or the occlusive therapy may reverse this early sign of steroid abuse.

Palpable purpura due to septic thrombi is best corrected by appropriate antibiotic therapy. The organism producing the gonococcemia dermatitis–arthritis syndrome is exquisitely sensitive to penicillin, and acceptable oral outpatient management has been achieved.

Atheromatous infarction of skin is corrected by surgical removal of the involved vessels and replacement with an appropriate vascular implant.

Palpable purpuras with leukocytoclastic histologic characteristics improve with oral prednisone, but treatment may be prolonged and side effects profound if correctable causes are overlooked. The cutaneous lesions associated with disseminated intravascular coagulopathies, coumadin necrosis, and paroxysmal nocturnal hemoglobinuria may produce full-thickness sloughs that ultimately may require skin grafting. This should not be performed until it is clear which material is actually becoming a firm sclerotic mass that will require debridement and grafting.

Recommended Approach

Topical therapy has little to offer in the management of these disorders. Treatment should focus on the underlying cause rather than the symptom whenever possible. Systemic corticosteroids should be used at the lowest effective dose and on an alternate-day schedule when control of the disease is established.

FOLLOW-UP

Follow-up is unnecessary for most patients with telangiectasias once the diagnosis is made. Patients with hereditary hemorrhagic telangiectasias may require frequent visits if the workup reveals evidence of active gastrointestinal hemorrhage. Likewise, patients with telangiectasia macularis eruptive perstans and peptic ulcer disease may require monthly visits until control is demonstrated. If immunodeficiency accompanies telangiectasia, patients require follow-up depending on the seriousness of their infection. Follow-up for specific diseases identified under the purpura group may be found in the discussion of those entities. Patients given fluorinated corticosteroids require follow-up at intervals of 3 to 6 months, to watch for early signs of cutaneous toxicity in the form of purpuras and striae.

DISCUSSION
Prevalence

The prevalence of telangiectasias and purpura is unknown; they are extremely common.

Related Basic Science

Although the etiology of many telangiectatic states is still unknown, research with angiogenic factors has shown that there is a heat-labile, diffusible, but nondialyzable protein known as epidermal angiogenic factor. This factor somewhat resembles tumor angiogenic factor. Tumor angiogenic factor produces more tortuosity and vasodilation more rapidly than epidermal angiogenic factor in animal model systems. Angiogenic factors appear to be mitogenic for capillary endothelial cells, and it is thought that they may interfere with endothelial chalones that normally suppress endothelial cell proliferation. The role of angiogenic factors in a vast group of telangiectatic states is still uncertain.

Natural History and Its Modification with Treatment

Telangiectasias, once established, are not expected to regress. Those that develop as a result of exposure to the sun may be prevented by a sunscreen. The natural history of purpuras is that of the causative disorder.

Prevention

It is not possible to prevent most telangiectasias. Prevention of the telangiectasia related to cirrhosis is linked to prevention of the cirrhosis. Telangiectasia related to sunrays may be prevented by sunscreen. The prevention of purpuras is related to the prevention of the disease that caused them.

Cost Containment

To date, nothing is known about cost containment for this group of disorders.

REFERENCES

Braverman IM. Skin signs of systemic disease. Philadelphia: Saunders, 1970:119.

Garden JM, Tan OT, Parrish IA. The pulsed dye laser: Its use at 577 nm wavelength. J Dermatol Surg Oncol 1987;13:134.

Moschella SL. Diseases of the peripheral vessels and their contents. In: Moschella SL, ed. Dermatology. Philadelphia: Saunders, 1975:837.

Rietschel RL, Lewis CW, Simmons RA, et al. Skin lesions in paroxysmal nocturnal hemoglobinuria. Arch Dermatol 1978;114:560.

Uhlin SR, McCarthy KS Jr. Unilateral nevoid telangiectatic syndrome: The role of estrogen and progesterone receptors. Arch Dermatol 1983;119:226.

Wilkin JK, Smith JG Jr, Cullison DA, et al. Unilateral dermatomal superficial telangiectasia. J Am Acad Dermatol 1983;8:468.

Wolff JE Jr, Hubler WR Jr. Tumor angiogenic factor and human skin tumors. Arch Dermatol 1975;111:321.

CHAPTER 11–13
Atrophic Changes of the Skin
Robert L. Rietschel, M.D.

DEFINITION
The disorders in this category are characterized by a loss of substance from one or more of the layers of the epidermis, dermis, or subcutaneous tissue.

ETIOLOGY
The etiology of the atrophic skin diseases is largely unknown.

CRITERIA FOR DIAGNOSIS
Suggestive
Atrophic changes are due to the loss of all (or part of) the substance of the integument. Thinning of the epidermis may be identified by the cigarette-paper wrinkling appearance, whereas loss of the deeper structures of the skin may lead to depressions, striae, loss of elasticity, or laxity.

Definitive
The specific features needed for the diagnosis of an atrophic disorder are listed in Table 11–13–1.

CLINICAL MANIFESTATIONS
Subjective
The family history is helpful in some of the diseases discussed in this chapter. Cutis laxa may be autosomal dominant, in which case pulmonary and other internal complications are mild or absent. There is also an autosomal recessive form. Ehlers–Danlos syndrome types I to IV are autosomal dominant, but type V is X-linked and types VI and VII are autosomal recessive. Pseudoxanthoma elasticum has four inheritance patterns: two autosomal dominant and two autosomal recessive. In each inheritance pattern there are two presentations: one with retinopathy and serious vascular complications, and the other with generalized skin change with minimal internal disease. No occupational or environmental factors are critical for diagnosis in the group, save for the role of sunlight (Table 11–13–1). There are usually no symptoms, except for the altered appearance of the skin and the psychological impact this produces. Preceding inflammatory eruptions may provide clues to the diagnosis.

Objective
The atrophies can be divided into six morphologic subgroups: (1) macular atrophies (with and without visible inflammation), (2) subcutaneous atrophies, (3) poikilodermatous atrophies, (4) panatrophies, (5) atrophies with laxity, and (6) atrophies with sclerosis. Macular atrophies are extremely superficial and generally unaccompanied by pigment alterations. Poikilodermatous atrophies are also superficial, but they include telangiectasias and hyperpigmentation as well as hypopigmentation. Subcutaneous atrophies involve the loss of deeper structures and are easily recognized as depressions. Atrophies accompanied by a sclerosing process tend to be very firm, with obvious depressions, whereas those accompanied by laxity may have no apparent cutaneous alterations. Table 11–3–1 gives the morphologic clues required to distinguish these entities.

PLANS
Diagnostic
Differential Diagnosis
The diseases to consider in the differential diagnosis of atrophic skin changes are listed in Table 11–13–1 under Likely Diagnosis.

Diagnostic Options
Histologic examination of most atrophic conditions usually confirms the absence of the structures noted to be diminished on physical examination. In the poikilodermatous atrophies, histologic examination is crucial to the diagnosis of cutaneous T-cell lymphoma; in lichen sclerosus et atrophicus, the histologic examination is diagnostic. Serologic evaluation of the collagen–vascular subset of atrophies is useful, and diabetes should be suspected in necrobiosis lipoidica.

Recommended Approach
A skin biopsy would be the first study to order for most of the atrophies to correctly categorize the substance that is altered. Additional studies would be based on the biopsy findings and the information in Table 11–13–1.

Therapeutic
Therapeutic Options
No effective therapy is available for macular atrophies. Surgical reconstruction is of temporary benefit in such conditions as blepharochalasis, and dermabrasion may benefit cutis laxa. Acrodermatitis chronica atrophicans is treated with penicillin for 7 to 14 days in its early stages.

Sunscreens are of benefit in lupus, dermatomyositis, poikiloderma of Civatte, and radiodermatitis. Topical corticosteroids are beneficial in collagen–vascular disease and in lichen sclerosus et atrophicus and necrobiosis lipoidica, even though corticosteroids paradoxically may produce atrophy and striae. When these diseases are in their end stages and inflammatory activity is minimal, corticosteroids are of less benefit.

Therapy for most of the hereditary or congenital atrophies is poor or nonexistent; however, studies on two conditions—linear scleroderma (Nelder, 1978) and pseudoxanthoma elasticum—have shown promise. Linear scleroderma is improved by physical therapy and occasionally by surgical release of constricting bands. Significant reversal of the sclerosis was achieved with phenytoin, 100 mg three times a day, in a series of five patients (Nelder, 1978). An initial response was seen in the first 2 to 3 months of therapy, with recurrences when the medication was discontinued.

In pseudoxanthoma elasticum, the abnormal elastic fibers become calcified, leading to prematurely brittle arteries and vascular accidents. Restricting calcium intake and avoiding calcium-containing antacids retard the onset of this vascular fragility and prolong survival.

Recommended Approach
This is a largely untreatable group of disorders. What can be done is disease specific and listed above. The treatment of mycosis fungoides is discussed in Chapter 11–6.

FOLLOW-UP
Those atrophies for which there is no treatment require no specific follow-up. The poikilodermatous atrophies require 3- to 6-month follow-up visits to look for progression to plaques of cutaneous T-cell lymphoma (mycosis fungoides).

DISCUSSION
Prevalence
The prevalence of atrophic skin diseases is unknown; they are rare.

Related Basic Science
The atrophies are a diverse group of diseases, and atrophy may be the end stage of other inflammatory conditions. In general, once the end stage of the disease is reached, the atrophied tissues cannot regenerate.

TABLE 11–13–1. CHARACTERISTICS OF ATROPHIC CHANGES

Major Morphologic Alteration	Secondary Morphologic Changes	Localization and Supporting Subjective Data	Likely Diagnosis
Macular atrophy (skin bulges under slight tension)	Preceding erythema or urticaria; no pigment changes	10-mm oval to round lesions; upper half of body; second to fourth decades	Anetoderma of Jadassohn–Pellizari
Macular atrophy	No inflammation antecedent; skin looks normal in color and vascular pattern; but lax with gravitational pull	10- to 20-mm annular to oval lesions on upper body	Anetoderma of Schweninger–Buzzi
Poikilodermatous atrophy	Bluish hue; skin appears transparent; veins easily seen	Lower leg or extremities; European and Asian areas; tick *Ixodes ricinis* as possible vector	Acrodermatitis chronica atrophicans
	Telangiectasia predominates over atrophy	Localized to neck with submental sparing; no systemic symptoms	Poikiloderma of Civatte
	Erythema and telangiectasia prominent	Sun-exposed skin and upper eyelides; muscle weakness and malaise	Dermatomyostitis
	Plaques of poikiloderma; salmon-colored erythema	Persistent, pruritic, often in bathing trunk areas	Mycosis fungoides (plaque stage)
	Hyperkeratotic papules may be present; atrophy and pallor obvious	Geometric pattern; history of x-ray therapy	Chronic radiodermatitis
Subcutaneous atrophy with color change or pigmentation	"Cliff drop" border; blue-brown to violaceous plaques	Backs of young women	Atrophoderma of Pasini and Pierini
	Linear; initially purple; gradually become pale	Puberty; pregnancy; deltoid, breast, buttocks; Cushing's disease; steroid therapy	Striae distensae
	Plaquelike; yellow to orange hue	Lower legs; diabetes mellitus	Necrobiosis lipoidica
Subcutaneous atrophy without color change	Localized to injection sites	Diabetes mellitus	Insulin atrophy
		Corticosteroid use	Corticosteroid atrophy
	Localized	Present from birth; multiple defects of skin, bones, eyes, and soft tissue	Focal dermal hypoplasia
	Localized	No associated defect; present from birth	Aplasia cutis congenita
	Localized	Linear; possibly hemifacial	Linear scleroderma; facial hemiatrophy
	Generalized	Insulin-resistant; nonketotic diabetes; hyperlipidemia	Total lipoatrophy (Lawrence–Seip syndrome)
	Generalized	Face, back, chest, neck, upper extremities	Partial lipoatrophy
Atrophy with laxity	Generalized loose skin hanging in folds	Abnormal elastic fibers; emphysema; pneumothorax; aneurysms; diverticuli	Cutis laxa
	Loose skin with yellowish papules at body folds	Early adult onset; angioid streaks; cardiovascular accidents; gastrointestinal hemorrhage	Pseudoxanthoma elasticum
	Scars about joints from minor trauma; ecchymoses; calcified subcutaneous nodules	Joint hyperextensibility	Ehlers–Danlos syndrome
Atrophy with sclerosis	White papules coalescing into plaques	Predisposed to genital orifices	Lichen sclerosus et atrophicus
	Hyperpigmented periphery; hypopigmented center with large patulous follicles and hyperkeratotic plugs	Favors sun-exposed skin	Discoid lupus erythematosus
	Fibrous constricting band around digit	Progression to amputation	Ainhum
	Generalized atrophy of skin and nails; sclerotic plaques on abdomen; alopecia	Dwarfism; birdlike appearance	Progeria
	Atrophy of subcutis and muscle; scleroderma-like plaques on feet; aged appearance	Short stature; cataracts; atherosclerosis prematurely	Werner's disease
	Sclerotic bands in flexural areas; generalized poikiloderma; sclerosis of palms and soles	Autosomal dominant; clubbing	Hereditary sclerotic poikiloderma

An occasional patient with discoid lupus erythematosus may regrow hair in an old atrophic plaque of alopecia, but this is the exception rather than the rule.

Several of the atrophies overlap into a sclerotic disease. At times, lichen sclerosus et atrophicus cannot be distinguished from morphea. In some patients, histologic evidence of both diseases can be found in different anatomic sites with no distinguishing clinical features. In a similar paradox, the same impurities present in insulin that produce lipoatrophy will in other persons give a hypertrophic response. The relationship of atrophy to sclerosis is poorly understood.

Natural History and Its Modification with Treatment

The fact that atrophic skin does not regenerate is of major importance in the management of these disorders.

Prevention

Atrophy of the skin is not preventable except when it is due to corticosteroid or insulin injections. Corticosteroid atrophy is prevented by giving the injection deep in the gluteal muscle, and atrophy due to insulin can be prevented by using purified single-component insulin.

Cost Containment

Nothing is known that will help contain costs associated with these disorders. Money is saved when it is realized that medication is of little value in treating patients with these conditions.

REFERENCES

Badame AJ. Progeria. Arch Dermatol 1989;125:540.
Braverman IM. Skin signs of systemic disease. Phildelphia: Saunders, 1970:398.

Fleischmajer R, Matus NR. Diseases of the corium and subcutaneous tissue. In: Moschella SL, Pillsbury DM, Hurley JH, eds. Dermatology. Philadelphia: Saunders, 1975:960.

Kalvoustian VM der, Kurban AK. Genetic diseases of the skin. New York: Springer-Verlag, 1979.

Nelder KH. Treatment of localized linear scleroderma with phenytoin. Cutis 1978;22:569.

Pullara TJ, Lober CW, Fenske NA. Idiopathic atrophoderma of Pasini and Pierini. Int J Dermatol 1984;23:643.

Uitto J, Ryhaenen L, Tan EML. Collagen: Its structure, function and pathology. In: Fleischmajer R, ed. Progress in diseases of the skin, vol. 1. New York: Springer-Verlag, 1979.

CHAPTER 11–14

Cicatricial and Sclerotic Changes of the Skin

Robert L. Rietschel M.D.

DEFINITION

The diseases in this morphologic category are scarlike in quality. The skin has an abnormal firmness that is palpable.

ETIOLOGY

The causes of most of the disorders in this chapter are unknown. Eosinophilic fasciitis is an exception; a spirochete has been associated with this disorder. Heredity plays a dominant role in the porphyrias.

CRITERIA FOR DIAGNOSIS
Suggestive

The predominant abnormalities seen with cicatricial and sclerotic changes are thickening and hardening of the skin. There is necessarily some overlap with those conditions in which atrophy and sclerotic change exist concomitantly.

Definitive

The specific features needed to support a diagnosis in the cicatricial category are listed in Table 11–14–1.

CLINICAL MANIFESTATIONS
Subjective

With the exception of erythropoietic protoporphyria, the family history is not helpful in this group of disorders. Erythropoietic protoporphyria is autosomal dominant, and the environmental factor of sunlight causes stinging and burning sensations of exposed skin within minutes.

An occupational history is not generally helpful in making a diagnosis.

Historical data such as past trauma, x-ray treatment, and past history of visceral cancer may be helpful clues (Table 11–14–1). Patients most often complain of a tightening of the skin and a limitation of flexibility. Alternatively, if the condition is producing redundant skin in a firm, scarlike fashion, as is seen with keloids, this sclerotic change may be that of a nodulotumorous growth.

Objective

The major morphologic criteria for distinguishing the various sclerotic and cicatricial skin disorders are listed in Table 11–14–1.

TABLE 11–14–1. CLINICAL MANIFESTATIONS OF CICATRICIAL AND SCLEROTIC SKIN DISORDERS

History	Physical Examination	Diagnosis
Localized disease		
Trauma	Confined to area of trauma	Hypertrophic scar
	Extension beyond area of trauma	Keloid
Prior x-ray treatment	Atrophy, telangiectasias	Radiodermatitis
No explanation for change	White papules; ivory white sclerosis; atrophy; or follicular plugging	Lichen sclerosus et atrophicus
	Pearly to eczematous border on sclerotic plaque	Basal cell carcinoma (morphea type)
	Lilac border to flesh-colored plaque	Morphea
	Ropelike cord on chest, penis, etc.	Mondor's disease
Possible past history of visceral malignancy, especially breast carcinoma	Truncal plaque, possible eczematous-like changes	Carcinoma en cuirasse
Widespread disease		
Onset at 3 to 4 days of life	Progression from leg upward of stony induration	Sclerema neonatorum
Recent streptococcal pharyngitis; possibly diabetic	Upper trunk involved with nonpitting induration	Scleredema
Graves' disease	Anterior lower leg thickened	Pretibial myxedema
No helpful history	Linear thickening with possible hyperpigmentation	Linear scleroderma or morphea
No helpful history	Annular thickening around digits with autoamputation	Ainhum
Raynaud's phenomenon; dysphagia	Acral thickening with contractures; restrictive lung disease	Systemic scleroderma
No helpful history	Diffuse thickening of skin with many papules, histologically mucopolysaccharides	Scleromyxedema
Onset after increased exercise or tryptophan ingestion	Fascia thickened, peripheral eosinophilia	Eosinophilic fasciitis
Flushing	Sclerodermoid facies	Carcinoid syndrome
Photosensitivity within minutes, with stinging and burning as complaints	Thickening in sun-exposed areas only	Erythropoietic protoporphyria
Bone marrow transplant recipient	Sclerodermoid facies	Graft-versus-host reaction
Easy bruising and blistering on back of hands	Facial hirsutism and sclerodermoid facies	Porphyria cutanea tarda

PLANS
Diagnostic
Differential Diagnosis

The differential diagnostic possibilities are listed in Table 11–14–1 under Diagnosis.

Diagnostic Options

No diagnostic workup is required for hypertrophic scars or keloids. Although keloids are more common in blacks, they are not confined to this racial group. Occasionally, dermatofibromas mimic keloids, but these can be distinguished histologically.

Histologic findings on biopsy easily distinguish metastatic carcinomas, morphea-type basal cell carcinomas, true morphea, lichen sclerosus et atrophicus, pretibial myxedema, scleredema, and scleromyxedema. Although scleroderma cannot be definitively diagnosed histologically, it can be suspected and differentiated from the preceding inflammatory and neoplastic conditions. An extremely deep fascial biopsy is required to distinguish eosinophilic fasciitis from scleroderma.

Diagnostic evaluation of patients with systemic scleroderma includes evaluation of restrictive lung disease, esophageal and intestinal dysmotility, and renal failure. Scleroderma may be mimicked by several other disorders, including the carcinoid syndrome, graft-versus-host reactions, and several of the porphyrias. These sclerodermoid states may be distinguished by urinary evaluation for 5-hydroxyindoleacetic acid (for the diagnosis of carcinoid), uroporphyrins, coproporphyrins, and appropriate medical history. Erythropoietic protoporphyria cannot be detected by urine test, but it may be confirmed by red cell protoporphyrin levels or the observation of fluorescent red blood cells on immunofluorescence of a direct peripheral blood smear.

Recommended Approach

A skin biopsy to the depth of the visible and palpable pathologic changes is a good first step in the evaluation of these disorders. Exceptions are the porphyrias and carcinoid syndrome, for which the tests listed above for those diagnostic possibilities would supersede the skin biopsy.

Therapeutic
Therapeutic Options and Recommended Approach

Localized sclerotic conditions such as hypertrophic scars and keloids are responsive to intralesional triamcinolone (Aristocort) injections. The concentration required to produce atrophy in these lesions varies from 5 to 40 mg/mL. The frequency of injections varies depending on the corticosteroid salt chosen. In general, monthly injections are sufficient with the acetonide salt.

Lichen sclerosus et atrophicus may at times be indistinguishable from morphea, and histologic confirmation of both conditions may be seen within any given patient when samples are taken from different areas. These particular conditions may respond to superpotent topical corticosteroids, like clobetasol (Temovate).

The morphea type of basal cell carcinoma is very difficult to treat by simple surgical excision or curettage and electrodesiccation. All treatment modalities except for microscopically controlled surgical excision (Mohs' micrographic technique) have exceedingly high recurrence rates. Micrographic surgery is the treatment of choice.

At present, no good treatment programs are available for the management of sclerema neonatorum or scleredema.

Pretibial myxedema may be treated with a series of intralesional corticosteroid injections.

The treatment of scleroderma itself is difficult. Reports have appeared of responses of patients to griseofulvin (Grisactin), azathioprine (Imuran), colchicine (Doloral), and penicillamine (Cuprimine). None of these drugs can be depended on to produce an improvement in any given patient, but among the choices, penicillamine offers the greatest hope. Treatment with penicillamine must be protracted, as a response may not appear for months to 1 to 2 years. Investigations of a new extracorporeal treatment known as photopheresis have shown encouraging results at reversing the skin sclerosis of systemic scleroderma when treatment is initiated within 2 to 4 years of the onset of disease (Rook et al., 1989). This therapy was initially used to treat cutaneous T-cell lymphoma (see Discussion in Chapter 11–6). Linear forms of scleroderma are improved by physical therapy to help prevent contractures.

Eosinophilic fasciitis may very closely resemble the acrosclerotic changes of systemic scleroderma. This particular entity is more responsive to treatment than true scleroderma, and intervention with systemic prednisone may produce a remission. Reports of a link between tryptophan ingestion and eosinophilic fasciitis-like illness have led to speculation and investigations pointing to a link between this illness and contaminants in tryptophan and alterations in tryptophan metabolism (Belongia et al., 1990). The finding of spirochetes of *Borrelia burgdorferi* in the fascia of eosinophilic fasciitis patients is promising and will likely alter the management of this disease (Granter et al., 1994). This connects the condition to Lyme disease.

Follow-up

Follow-up of most of the sclerotic conditions should not be more frequent than once per month. Responses tend to occur slowly, and monthly visits can generally provide sufficient opportunity to observe the patient's response. When penicillamine is being used for treatment of scleroderma in the early stages, more frequent visits to check for idiosyncratic adverse reactions such as blood dyscrasias would be prudent.

DISCUSSION
Prevalence and Incidence

The prevalence of skin disease ranges from 200 to 400 per 1000 population. Hypertrophic and atrophic skin diseases account for about 5% of diagnoses in dermatologic practice.

Related Basic Science

Hypertrophic scars more commonly occur over the upper back, shoulders, and anterior chest. When lesions of this type occur without trauma, the general tendency is to accept the phenomenon as a keloid. Occasionally, histologic findings confirm the lesion to be a dermatofibroma. As dermatofibromas are not responsive to intralesional steroids, this distinction may have some clinical relevance. Dermatofibromas of a large plaque type may occur over the presternal region, mimicking keloid formation.

The causes of morphea, scleroderma, and lichen sclerosus et atrophicus are unknown. The earliest histologic events in scleroderma are inflammation of the capillaries of the dermis and subcutis with lymphocytes, plasma cells, macrophages, and fibroblasts. An increase in prolylhydroxylase occurs and is thought to be involved in the excessive production of collagen. The ratios of type 1 to type 3 collagen in scleroderma are similar to those in normal adult human skin.

Scleredema frequently follows an upper respiratory streptococcal infection. There is a sudden onset of nonpitting, symmetric thickening of the skin of the upper back, which may then spread to the face, arms, and neck. The skin becomes so firm that it can no longer be folded. Spontaneous resolution may occur in several months to several years, but thickening may persist indefinitely in one quarter of patients. The persistent cases are frequently associated with obesity and adult-onset diabetes mellitus. Most of these patients are insulin resistant, and antidiabetic therapy has been shown to have no effect on the resolution of their scleredema.

Eosinophilic fasciitis is a condition in which a peripheral eosinophilia and skin induration resembling scleroderma occur. Intense periods of physical exertion or tryptophan ingestion are occasionally related to the onset of the disease. Is it not yet clear to what extent an altered metabolism of tryptophan is responsible for this syndrome. The finding of *Borrelia* spirochetes in the fascia of these patients will likely change the concepts of this disease and link it to Lyme disease. A contaminant found in some batches of tryptophan has been linked to the closely related eosinophilia–myalgia syndrome in some cases. Raynaud's phenomenon and systemic involvement are generally absent, and improvement is seen with corticosteroid therapy. Histologic examination of the fascia may occasionally reveal eosinophils within the diffusely thickened fascia. When patients with suspected localized or systemic scleroderma are studied with deep fascia biopsies and peripheral eosinophil counts, occasional cases are found to fit this syndrome.

Natural History and Its Modification with Treatment

Cicatricial and sclerotic conditions are chronic disorders, and little change or gradual progression is to be expected.

Prevention

At present, no preventive measures are available for these conditions. Patients who are known to form keloids would be well advised to avoid ear piercing.

Cost Containment

At present, nothing is known that would limit the cost of diagnosing and treating this disorder. When the diagnosis is established, it is possible to save money be limiting the use of worthless drugs.

REFERENCES

Belongia EA, Hedberg CW, Gleich Gl, et al. An investigation of the cause of the eosinophilia–myalgia syndrome associated with tryptophan use. N Engl J Med 1990;323:257.

Fleishchmajer R. Scleredema. In: Fitzpatrick TB, Eisen AZ, Wolff K, et al., eds. Dermatology in general medicine. New York: McGraw-Hill, 1979:1313.

Fleischmajer R, Dessau W, Timpl R, et al. Immunofluorescence analysis of collagen, fibronectin, and basement membrane protein in scleroderma skin. J Invest Dermatol 1980;75:270.

Fleischmajer R, Perlish JS, Duncan MR. Regulatory mechanisms and collagen metabolism in scleroderma skin. In: Fleischmajer R, ed. Progress in diseases of the skin, vol. 2. New York: Grune & Stratton, 1984:125.

Granter SR, Barnhill, RL, Hewins ME, Duray PH. Brief report: Identification of Borrelia burgdorferi in diffuse fasciitis with peripheral eosinophilia: Borrelial fasciitis. JAMA 1994;272:1283.

Rook AH, Frundlich B, Nahass GT, et al. Treatment of autoimmune disease with extracorporeal photochemotherapy: Progressive systemic sclerosis. Yale J Biol Med 1989;62:639.

Uitto J, Santacrus DJ, Bauer EA, et al. Morphea and lichen sclerosus et atrophicus. J Am Acad Dermatol 1990;3:271.

Wahl SM. Immunologically induced fibrosis. In: Fleischmajer R, ed. Progress in diseases of the skin, vol. 2. New York: Grune & Stratton, 1984:111.

CHAPTER 11–15

Nodules and Tumors

Robert L. Rietschel, M.D.

DEFINITION

Discrete lesions greater than 1 cm in diameter are considered in this category.

ETIOLOGY

The causes of most of the conditions considered in this chapter are unknown.

CRITERIA FOR DIAGNOSIS
Suggestive

A nodule is described as a palpable lesion greater than 1 cm in diameter. This lesion may involve any or all parts of the integument. By definition, a tumor is generally 2 cm or greater in diameter. In practice, the terms *nodule* and *tumor* are often used interchangeably. A diagnosis may be suspected by the morphologic appearance of the lesion (Table 11–15–1), but it is confirmed by histologic identification of the lesion.

Definitive

The features found in Table 11–15–1 and histologic examination form the basis for a firm diagnosis.

CLINICAL MANIFESTATIONS
Subjective

Distinguishing malignant from benign lesions by history and physical examination requires a great deal of experience. Among the more common lesions, the seborrheic keratoses have an extremely variable appearance. These lesions can, in their black, rough state, appear similar to malignant melanoma. Subtleties such as recognition of pseudohorn cysts when the lesion has been lightly frozen assist in making a diagnosis and provide the opportunity to render treatment without the necessity of a biopsy. Pseudohorn cysts have the appearance of small, keratinous spherules studded throughout the rough texture of the lesion. A sudden shower of seborrheic keratoses on previously normal skin is the sign of Leser–Trelat. This is considered a sign of occult malignancy and should provoke the physician to search for neoplasia.

When visceral malignancies metastasize to the skin, the carcinoma usually underlies the general body region in which the cutaneous metastasis has occurred. Some tumors, such as breast carcinoma and renal carcinoma, have a predilection for the face and scalp. Cutaneous metastases of this type usually do not ulcerate, and their color will vary from reddish brown to bluish plum. Occasionally, an erysipelas-like reaction may be seen around the metastasis or may be the sole presenting sign of the metastasis, such as in carcinoma en cuirasse. The family history is particularly helpful in some of the malignant conditions discussed in this chapter. Familial forms of melanoma exist and may or may not be preceded by lesions known as atypical nevi (formerly dysplastic nevi). Dysplastic nevi may occur within families, and diagnosis of this condition should prompt a careful search for both melanoma and dysplastic nevi in other family members.

People of Celtic origin are at great risk for sunlight-induced malignancy, and a family history of basal cell or squamous cell carcinoma may be encountered.

Nodulotumorous lesions may produce such complaints as pruritus, spontaneous hemorrhage, disfigurement, discoloration, displacement of other structure, pain, and rapid increase in size.

Objective

Abnormalities that support a preliminary diagnosis are listed in Table 11–15–1. They include color (primarily brown-black, reddish, or plum), surface architecture (ulcerated/crusted, protruding appendages, rough or warty), onset of pain, and degree of firmness (hard, fleshy, or soft). The actual diagnosis, however, depends on histologic confirmation.

PLANS
Diagnostic

Differential Diagnosis

The differential diagnostic possibilities are listed in Table 11–15–1 by morphologic features.

TABLE 11–15–1. NODULES AND TUMORS

Characteristic	Major Diagnostic Possibilities	Additional Features Supporting Diagnosis
Color		
Blue, brown, black	Acrochordon (skin tag)	Traumatized lesion, turned black "overnight"; flexural region of body
	Seborrheic keratosis	Rough surface, warty looking; lesion looks pasted on, sitting above normal skin; colors from yellow to black
	Dermatofibroma	Firm feel, present years without change; tan to black
	Hematoma	History of trauma; blue to black
	Nevi	Discrete, soft, fairly uniform pigmentation; may contain hairs; tan, brown, black, and flesh-colored
	Dysplastic or atypical nevi	Nevus with irregular border; somewhat more red than brown; usually large (about 1 cm in diameter)
	Melanoma	Irregular pigmentation, rapid growth, spontaneous hemorrhage; red, black, blue, and slate gray
	Pigmented basal cell carcinoma	Ulcerated center, rolled border, deeply pigmented racial group; black-colored lesion
	Solitary angiokeratoma	Black in color but rough surface
	Blue nevus	Regular to round lesion with black color
	Kaposi's sarcoma	Bluish nodule, often multiple on lower legs
Reddish	Squamous cell carcinoma	Pink to red; rapid growth; bleeds easily
	Epidermoid cyst	Flesh-colored to red; central pore; discharges foul-smelling material
	Pyogenic granuloma	Dome shaped, easily bleeding nodule; rapid growth
	Hemangiomas	Bright red to bluish
	Dermatofibrosarcoma protuberans	Trunk or extremities; brown to reddish blue color
	Atypical fibroxanthoma	Elderly individuals; preauricular location common; reddish brown color
	Spindle and epithelioid cell nevus (benign juvenile melanoma)	Children and young adults; pink to red; dome-shaped
Plum	Leukemia cutis	Known or suspected leukemia
	Mycosis fungoides (cutaneous T-cell lymphoma)	May resemble a "rotten tomato"
	Pseudolymphoma	Usually on face
Surface		
Ulcerated/crusted	Keratoacanthoma	Central keratin volcano-like core; rapid growth
	Squamous cell carcinoma	Pink to red; rapid growth; bleeds easily
	Basal cell carcinoma	Rolled, pearly border; telangiectasia
	Melanoma	Irregular pigmentation; rapid growth; spontaneous hemorrhage; red, black, blue, and slate gray
	Metastatic carcinoma	Variable color and body location; often on scalp
Hairy	Nevi	In scalp, pigment often absent and tufts of hair protrude
Warty	Verruca vulgaris	Flesh-colored, rough surface
	Seborrheic keratosis	Rough warty surface; looks pasted on; yellow to black
Spontaneous pain	Eccrine spiradenoma	Skin-colored
	Neuroma/neurilemmoma	Skin-colored
	Glomus	Bluish, extremities
	Angiolipoma	Similar to ordinary lipoma
	Leiomyoma	Flesh-colored; truncal
Firmness		
Hard	Pilomatrixoma	Solitary; young adult; face, neck
	Osteoma cutis	Stony hard
	Calcinosis cutis	Frequently widespread
Fleshy	Keloid	History of trauma
	Neurofibroma	Tend to be pedunculated
	Lipoma	Rubbery feel; discrete
	Nevi	Pigment may be absent
	Lymphangioma	Sometimes pulsatile
	Gouty tophi	Soft early; hard later
Inflammatory	Rheumatic nodules	Skin biopsy helps to confirm diagnosis
	Rheumatoid nodules	
	Erythema nodosum	
	Iododerma, bromoderma	
	Prurigo nodularis	
	Foreign-body granuloma	
	Sarcoid	
	Necrobiosis lipoidica	
	Deep granuloma annulare	
Infectious	Syphilis	Serologic testing, skin biopsy, and/or tissue culture when appropriate
	Tuberculosis	
	Leprosy	
	Milkers' nodules	
	Deep fungal infection	
	Leishmaniasis	

Diagnostic Options

In all nodulotumorous lesions, the diagnosis depends on histopathologic examination of the tissue.

Recommended Approach

A biopsy is indicated for all lesions that are not clinically diagnosable.

Therapeutic

Therapeutic Options

The patient may want total surgical removal of the lesion. Lesions such as warts and seborrheic keratoses are easily removed by such methods as liquid nitrogen cryosurgery and curettage and desiccation. Hemangiomas, particularly those seen in young children, are best left untreated unless they are impinging on vital structures or consuming platelets, at which time corticosteroids may be indicated to induce a rapid decrease in the size of the lesion.

Nevi in general do not require removal, unless the clinician is sufficiently uncertain of their true nature that histologic confirmation is required. Nevi on the palms or soles are no more likely to undergo malignant degeneration than those on other parts of the body. Nevi that are present at the time of delivery are felt to be a distinct group of congenital nevi with a greater likelihood to undergo transformation to melanoma nevi and are as likely to undergo malignant change as are the larger "bathing trunk" nevi. When malignancy develops in a congenital nevus of a young patient, it tends to develop in the deeper portion of the lesion. With congenital nevi, the physician should perform a full-thickness surgical excision as soon as possible, if he or she feels compelled to treat the patient rather than observe the lesion for possible changes.

Atypical nevi should be removed and the patient followed carefully for the development of melanoma. Careful photographic records may be required to properly monitor the progression of the multiple nevi present in cases of multiple atypical (dysplastic) nevi.

Malignant lesions such as the common basal cell carcinoma and squamous cell carcinoma are best treated by one of two surgical methods: curettage and electrodesiccation or surgical excision. Although both modalities have cure rates of approximately 95% in the hands of a well-trained dermatologic surgeon, cure rates diminish when the physician is not familiar with both the lesion and the technique. Recurrences are best treated by a technique known as Mohs' chemosurgery. This technique is more accurately described as microscopically controlled surgical excision. Routine excisions, performed while the pathologist checks the margins, do not deliver the cure rates of Mohs' chemosurgery, which approach 100%. As small islands of malignant cells stream between the collagen bundles in the skin to surrounding normal-appearing skin, the small outcroppings from the main body of the tumor are frequently missed in routine histologic sectioning and checking of margins.

Melanoma is managed primarily by surgical excision. The decision to perform lymph node dissection depends on the location of the lesion and its depth. Depth is defined as the distance in millimeters from the granular layer of the epidermis to the deepest levels of the tumorous infiltrate. When the depth of the tumor exceeds 1.5 mm, lymph node dissection is usually performed; studies show a 64% 5-year survival rate in cases with lymph node dissection as opposed to 31% 5-year survival without. Chemotherapeutic programs involving dacarbazine (DTIC-Dome) have shown some responses in patients with melanomas, and adjuvant immunotherapy has occasionally been beneficial.

Nodulotumorous lesions due to inflammatory dermatoses or conditions generally require identification of the underlying disease and treatment of that entity. In the case of prurigo nodularis, intralesional steroids such as triamcinolone acetonide (Kenalog) in concentrations of 5 to 10 mg/mL are often beneficial. This same type of treatment may be used in such conditions as deep granuloma annulare, necrobiosis lipoidica, foreign-body granulomas, and sarcoidosis. Iododermas and bromodermas produce nodulotumorous lesions and can be cured by removal of the inciting iodide or bromide. Nodulotumorous lesions due to infectious diseases may be treated successfully with the appropriate antimicrobial agents.

Recommended Approach

If treatment is medically unnecessary, such as in the case of seborrheic keratosis or skin tags, reassurance can be offered and the patient can participate in the decision to treat or not. If a nonscarring treatment is available, such as liquid nitrogen in the case of warts, it should be given preference. Incisional or if possible excisional biopsy is advised for suspected malignant lesions.

FOLLOW-UP

Follow-up of patients with benign conditions is generally not required. Patients with nevi are frequently instructed to watch these lesions for change. In general, the patient is capable of performing this examination and returning to the physician when he or she detects alterations in size, configuration, color, spontaneous hemorrhage, increased pruritus, or other unexplainable symptomatology. Patients with malignant diagnoses should be followed at frequent intervals shortly after their diagnosis; it is customary to see these patients within 1 month of treatment to observe the healing process for adequacy of wound closure. Over the following 2 years, patients should be seen at intervals of 3 to 6 months for the uncomplicated case. Additional base cell carcinomas will develop in one of every five patients within 2 years of the primary diagnosis. Patients with dysplastic atypical nevi should be seen annually or more frequently if indicated by an unusual change in specific lesions.

DISCUSSION
Prevalence

The prevalence of malignant skin tumors is 5 to 9 per 1000. Basal cell carcinoma has a prevalence of about 2 per 1000.

Related Basic Science

Very little specific information is known regarding the basic science background of nodules and tumors that is unrelated to the specific cause. Please see the chapters on specific diagnoses, such as sarcoid, rheumatic fever and rheumatoid arthritis, gout, and neoplastic diseases, for further discussion.

Natural History and Its Modification with Treatment

The natural history of nodules and tumors is, or course, linked directly to the specific disease with which they are associated. Please see specific diagnoses for further discussion.

Prevention

Most of the malignancies due to ultraviolet light can be prevented by the appropriate use of sunscreens and prudence in exposure to ultraviolet light sources. Unnecessary exposure to ultraviolet light is to be shunned. No preventive measures are presently available for the benign nodulotumorous group of diseases.

Cost Containment

Other than the preventive measures mentioned above, there are no cost containment measures to suggest. As always, the sooner an accurate diagnosis is made, the more likely one is to save money by avoiding the cost of worthless treatment.

REFERENCES

Andrade R, Gumport SL, Popkin GL, Reese TD, eds. Cancer of the skin: Biology, diagnosis, management. Philadelphia: Saunders, 1976.

Caro WA. Tumors of the skin. In: Moschella SL, Pillsbury DM, Hurley HJ, eds. Dermatology. Philadelphia: Saunders, 1975:1323.

Cawley EP. Genetic aspects of malignant melanoma. Arch Dermatol 1952;65:440.

Clark WH Jr, Reimer RR, Green MH, et al. Origin of familial malignant melanoma from heritage melanocytic lesions: The B-K mole syndrome. Arch Dermatol 1978;114:732.

Greene MH, Clark WH, Tucker MA, et al. High risk of malignant melanoma in melanoma-prone families with dysplastic nevi. Ann Intern Med 1985;102:458.

Koft AW, Friedman JR, Rigel DS. Atypical mole syndrome. J Am Acad Derma-
　tol 1990;22:117.

Revalence, morbidity and costs of dermatologic disease. J Invest Dermatol
　1979;73:395.

CHAPTER 11–16

Malignant Melanoma (See Section 3, Chapter 27)

CHAPTER 11–17

Skin Erosions, Excoriations, and Ulcerations

Robert L. Rietschel, M.D.

DEFINITION

This group of diseases are characterized by the absence of a normal
epidermal layer and/or deeper layers of the skin. These conditions are
further characterized by lack of other primary lesions to account for the
loss of normal surface integrity.

ETIOLOGY

The causes of these disorders vary from vascular occlusion to inflammatory vascular compromise, neuropathy with secondary trauma, infections, and physical injury.

CRITERIA FOR DIAGNOSIS

Suggestive

The distinction between an erosion and an excoriation is somewhat artificial. In both conditions, skin is denuded in a superficial manner. An
erosion implies that the denudation was caused by the offending disease process. An excoriation implies that the patient has scratched or
manipulated a lesion until a superficial erosion was produced. Ulceration of the skin is a similar process, but is deeper and more extensive
(Table 11–17–1).

Definitive

The specific criteria required to support a diagnosis are listed in Table
11–16–1.

CLINICAL MANIFESTATIONS

Subjective

A family history of such disorders as sickle cell disease, thalassemia,
and diabetes mellitus can be helpful in evaluating potential causes of
cutaneous ulceration. Environmental factors such as stress, psychosocial dynamics, and potential for secondary gain are important in assessing the possible diagnosis of factitial cutaneous ulceration. Major historical points that may be crucial to the diagnosis of cutaneous
ulceration include evidence for the ingestion of bromides, iodides, or
ergot compounds. Sexual history and preference can have a bearing on
ulceration secondary to herpes simplex, chancroid, granuloma inguinale, and syphilis (see Table 11–17–1).

Generalized pruritus may lead to multiple excoriations (see Chapter
11–18). Any pruritic dermatosis may be excoriated by the patient in an
attempt to relieve the pruritus and pain. In general, pain is a more tolerable symptom than pruritus. Erosions may be seen following various
insults that produce blisters.

For the purpose of this text, cutaneous conditions are categorized
under their primary lesions. Blistering diseases that often produce erosions and denudation of skin are discussed in Chapter 11–8.

Ulceration is most commonly accompanied by the sensation of pain.
On occasion, the absence of sensation is a clue to the cause of the ulceration. The mere presence of cutaneous ulceration is often the presenting
complaint.

Objective

The major morphologic and historic criteria distinguishing the various
causes of cutaneous ulceration are enumerated in Table 11–16–1.

PLANS

Diagnostic

Differential Diagnosis

The differential diagnostic possibilities are listed under Likely Diagnosis in Table 11–17–1.

Diagnostic Options

The subjective and objective data required to consider a diagnosis of
cutaneous ulcers are provided in Table 11–17–1.

Investigation of the ulcer should include the use of Gram's stain and
the microscopic examination of a preparation using potassium hydroxide. Under local anesthesia, a small amount of tissue should be excised
and divided into halves. Half this material may be sent for routine histologic examination; the other half should be ground and cultured for
aerobic and anaerobic bacteria, typical and atypical acid-fast bacilli,
and fungi. These studies should be performed only when the history,
physical examination, and appropriate laboratory investigations noted
in the table are not diagnostic. With appropriate histologic preparation
the material may be examined under polarized light for evidence of foreign particulate matter. This may be of some help in evaluation of factitious cases.

Recommended Approach

When the cause cannot be determined by history and physical examination alone, the first step is a skin biopsy for both routine histology and
culture. Appropriate serologic investigation would be done at the time
of the skin biopsy in cases where the suspected diagnosis is of metabolic, connective tissue disease, or infectious origin.

Therapeutic

Therapeutic Options

Therapy for ulcerative and excoriated skin disease revolves around
treatment of any underlying or complicating conditions. Leg ulcers are
most often seen with venous insufficiency. Although there are many
proposed therapeutic maneuvers for the treatment of these ulcers, only
one maneuver is relevant: the removal of back pressure and edema.

TABLE 11–17–1. CUTANEOUS ULCERS

	Subjective	Objective	Likely Diagnosis
On relatively normal skin	Painful	Evidence of atherosclerotic cardiovascular disease	Atherosclerosis; hypertension
		Vasculitis on biopsy; collagen–vascular disease	Vasculitic origin
		Excessive smoking	Thromboangiitis obliterans
	Pain less prominent	Young adult or child	Sickle cell disease; thalassemia
		X-ray shows calcium deposits	Calcinosis cutis
		Ingestion of halide	Bromoderma; iododerma
		Bizarre shape, pattern; or abnormal psychological status	Factitial
		Cultural evidence of pathogen	Infectious etiology
	Pain variable	Crohn's disease: rheumatoid arthritis; negative cultures; biopsy nonspecific with many polymorphonuclear leukocytes	Pyoderma gangrenosum
On relatively abnormal skin	Variable	Vasculitis; inflammatory plaques or papules	Lupus erythematosus; polyarteritis nodosa; rheumatoid vasculitis; scleroderma
			Stasis dermatitis
		Lower legs; inflammatory plaques; edema	
		Lower legs; inflammatory plaques; granulomatous histology with negative cultures	Necrobiosis lipoidica; sarcoidosis; pancreatitis; Wegener's granulomatosus
		Atrophic plaque	Radiodermatitis; squamous cell carcinoma
		Nodule with or without inflammation	Gout; erythema induratum; basal cell carcinoma; squamous cell carcinoma; metastatic carcinoma
		Histology of vascular occlusion; purpuric lesions	Disseminated intravascular coagulopathy; thrombotic thrombocytopenic purpura
With anesthetic skin	Painless	Abnormal glucose tolerance	Diabetes mellitus; malum perforans
		Positive STS on lumbar puncture	Tabes dorsalis
		Positive Fite stain on biopsy	Leprosy
		Other neurologic signs and symptoms	Any sensory neuropathy
Genital ulcers	Recent sexual contact	Positive darkfield examination; relatively painless lesion	Syphilis
		Erythematous beefy ulcer with rolled border; crush preparation positive for Donovan bodies	Granuloma inguinale
		Painful dirty ulcer with necrotic, overhanging edges	Chancroid
		Began as pain; small vesicles coalesced	Herpes simplex
		Recurrent lesions, uveitis, oral ulcers	Bheçet's syndrome
Oral ulcers	Variable, but usually painful	Recurrent, small, shallow	Aphthous stomatitis
		Genital ulcers; uveitis	Behçet's syndrome
		Cyclic low white blood cell count	Cyclic neutropenia
		Positive viral culture; lesions on mucosa adherent to bone	Herpes simplex
		Pustules on hands and feet	Hand, foot, and mouth disease
		Immunofluorescence shows deposits of immunoglobulin on intercellular cement substance of stratified squamous epithelium; blisters on skin	Pemphigus vulgaris
		Signs and symptoms of lupus erythematosus	Systemic lupus erythematosus
		Recent positive STS or rising titer	Syphilis
		Leukemia	Leukemia
		Positive cultures	Sporotrichosis; actinomycosis
		Inflammatory bowel disease	Crohn's disease
		Positive patch tests to orally used agents	Contact stomatitis
		Positive heterophile antibody	Infectious mononucleosis
		Biopsy shows malignancy	Squamous cell carcinoma
Digital	Usually painful	Ergot ingestion	Ergotism
		Positive cryoglobulins or cryofibrinogens	Cryoglobulinemia
		Atherosclerotic disease	Cholesterol emboli
		Bacterial sepsis	Bacterial emboli
		Cold exposure	Frostbite

STS, serologic test for syphilis.

This can be achieved by strict and prolonged bed rest, leg elevation, and simple cleansing with hydrogen peroxide. Topical antibiotics and debriding agents may occasionally be useful, but their role is secondary. When the base of the ulcer is clean, grafting may be achieved by either pinch grafts or split-thickness grafts. Pinch grafts offer an advantage over split-thickness grafts. Low-grade overgrowth may cause loss of a small island of grafted tissue, but it will not cause loss of the entire graft, as would more commonly occur with solid split- or full-thickness grafts.

Pyoderma gangrenosum is difficult to treat and heals with scarring, regardless of management. The drugs most effective in producing clinical improvement are the corticosteroids (usually in high doses), azathioprine (Imuran), salicylazosulfapyridine (Azulfidine), and clofaz-imine (Lamprene). Improvement usually begins within 1 to 2 weeks of starting an effective agent. Pulse therapy with 1 g methylprednisolone has been effective in refractory cases. Several pulses are usually required.

Self-limited ulcerative disorders such as herpes simplex and aphthous stomatitis require symptomatic management. Although many therapies for herpes simplex have been proposed, double-blind studies fail to document any improvement in recurrence rates. Systemic acyclovir has been shown to be effective in acute herpes simplex infections (200 mg five times daily for 10 days), as well as in preventing recurrences (200 mg three times daily). Acyclovir ointment is effective, but healing is no faster with this antiviral agent in recurrent herpes simplex infection than with many less expensive, nonspecific topical ointments.

Treatment with mild compresses of tap water, saline, Burrow's solution, or other agents designed to induce a more rapid drying of the lesions is superior to no treatment at all. Recurrent aphthous stomatitis may be symptomatically improved by tetracycline powder compresses. Alternatively, oral corticosteroid preparations may be useful. An occasional patient with severe recurrent episodes may require brief bursts of systemic prednisone to achieve control.

Recommended Approach

It is necessary to start with both good wound care externally and appropriate systemic treatment in this group of disorders. The systemic treatment depends on the diagnosis.

FOLLOW-UP

Patients with cutaneous ulceration who are undergoing active therapy frequently require hospitalization with daily encouragement that bed rest and elevation of the part involved are vital to their improvement. On an outpatient basis, patients who understand their treatment can be evaluated adequately at intervals of 1 to 2 weeks.

DISCUSSION

Prevalence

The prevalence of skin erosions, excoriations, and ulcerations is not known, but they are common.

Related Basic Science

Cutaneous ulceration tends to occur with vascular compromise or local tissue destruction of an exogenous origin. Exogenous causes include caustic agents, trauma, and infectious agents (Table 11–17–2). Vascular compromise may be embolic, such as is seen with septic thrombi from systemic infections, cholesterol, emboli from atheromatous plaques, fibrin thrombi in disseminated intravascular coagulopathy, and thrombotic thrombocytopenic purpura. Alternatively, vascular compromise may be produced by prolonged vasoconstriction, such as may occur in ergotism, Raynaud's phenomenon, exogenous compression via depositional states, or vascular destruction by inflammatory mediators.

In stasis dermatitis, prolonged edema and persistent low-grade inflammation lead to vascular compromise and ultimate tissue destruction. When edema and inflammation are removed, healing can begin. This compromised skin of the lower leg is extremely susceptible to allergic contact dermatitis. Many medicaments may have been applied in an attempt to promote healing or prevent infection. It is not uncommon to see an increasing erythema around a stasis ulcer misinterpreted as cellulitis, when in fact it is an allergic contact dermatitis and a reaction to the topical preparation in use. In this setting, simple ingredients, such as the preservative or the active agents themselves, may be the offending allergens. Thus it is important to avoid the application of medicaments frequently required for serious systemic diseases to this skin lest the patient become sensitized. Neomycin, ethylenediamine (*not* in Mycolog II cream), and parabens are the most notorious allergens encountered in stasis dermatitis.

Natural History and Its Modification with Treatment

The natural history of skin erosions, excoriations, and ulcerations depends on the cause, and duration ranges from a few days (aphthous

TABLE 11–17–2. INFECTIOUS CAUSES OF SKIN ULCERS

Diagnosis	Organism Involved
Anthrax	*Bacillus anthracis*
Botryomycosis	*Staphylococcus aureus; Pseudomonas*
Buruli ulcer	*Mycobacterium ulcerans*
Yaws	*Treponema pertenue*
Leprosy	*Mycobacterium leprae*
Tularemia	*Francisella tularensis*
Amebiasis	*Entamoeba histolytica*
Leishmania	*Leishmania tropica, L. brasiliensis*
Blastomycosis	*Blastomyces dermatitidis*
South American blastomycosis	*Paracoccidioides brasiliensis*
Coccidioidomycosis	*Coccidioidomycosis immitis*
Cryptococcosis	*Cryptococcus neoformans*
Sporotrichosis	*Sporothrix schenkii*
Chromomycosis	*Cladosporium, Phialophora, Fonsecae*

stomatitis) to weeks and months (stress ulcer) to persistence (sensory neuropathy).

Prevention

Patients with chronic vascular insufficiency may avoid the morbidity of cutaneous ulceration by wearing support stockings. Often these need to be applied in the morning before arising from bed. Patients with neuropathies may avoid cutaneous ulceration by avoiding smoking (which may produce severe burns), attaching large wooden handles to cooking utensils, and frequently inspecting the soles of the feet to detect any early signs or symptoms of cutaneous ulceration. If changes such as areas of persistent erythema, are noted in the soles, a change in footwear to displace weight may prevent neurotrophic ulceration. The use of condoms during sexual intercourse can be an effective method of preventing the acquisition of venereal ulcerations. Appropriate protection from cold injury can prevent the cutaneous ulcerations of frostbite.

Cost Containment

No organized study has been done on limiting the cost of the management of these skin disorders. Obviously, money is saved when a condition can be prevented (see Prevention).

REFERENCES

Jarratt M, Smith R, Knox JM. Therapy of herpes simplex infection. Int J Dermatol 1979;18:357.

Johnson RB, Lazarus GS. Pulse therapy: Therapeutic efficacy in the treatment of pyoderma gangrenosum. Arch Dermatol 1982;118:76.

Mandell GL, Alexander ER, Amdt KA. Guidelines for sexually transmitted diseases. J Am Acad Dermatol 1983;8:589.

Rogers RS. Recurrent aphthous stomatitis: Clinical characteristics and evidence for immunopathogenesis. J Invest Dermatol 1977;69:499.

Ryan TJ, Wilkinson DS. Diseases of the veins: Venous leg ulcers. In: Rook A, Wilkinson DS, Ebling FJG, et al., eds. Textbook of dermatology. Oxford, England: Blackwell Scientific, 1979:1077.

CHAPTER 11–18

Pruritus

Robert L. Rietschel, M.D.

DEFINITION

The conditions considered under the heading of pruritus are those in which itch is present and persistent but unaccompanied by visible morphologic changes.

ETIOLOGY

The causes of unexplained itch include metabolic disorders, polycythemia, occult malignancy, and the skin diseases listed in Table 11–18–1.

CRITERIA FOR DIAGNOSIS
Suggestive

Persistent or paroxysmal pruritus in the absence of dermatologic lesions are considered under this heading. Persistent pruritus may lead to the development of multiple excoriations. The diseases discussed in this chapter tend to have minimal skin excoriations, and when present, the excoriations are extremely small.

Definitive

Pruritus unaccompanied by skin lesions but associated with a disease known to be capable of producing this symptom complex is generally accepted as an adequate explanation for this event. Correction of the underlying metabolic (or other) disturbance that results in elimination of the pruritus would be conclusive, but this is not always possible.

CLINICAL MANIFESTATIONS
Subjective

The family history is not helpful in evaluating pruritus, but environmental factors that favor the development of dry skin are important. Frequency of bathing, type of soap product used when bathing, season of year, and relative humidity of the home and/or work environment can play a role in increasing or decreasing pruritus. Frequent hot baths or showers, especially more than one per day, with or without soap, may be detrimental. Cleansing bars with moisturizers added tend to alleviate pruritus. The winter season and low ambient relative humidity aggravate pruritus.

Pruritus is a common skin complaint. It is not uncommon for the itching to be most bothersome at night. Occasionally, a patient relates that pruritus is most severe following a hot bath or shower; this suggests that polycythemia rubra vera may be present. Pruritus may be purely seasonal and most severe in the winter.

Objective

At times, the patient with pruritus may have transient cutaneous lesions that are not present at the time of examination. Xerotic skin changes may be noted in some patients.

Conditions in which primary lesions may be easily missed include dermatitis herpetiformis, pediculosis corporis, scabies, insect bites, and chronic urticaria. Careful questioning of patients may reveal that the earliest skin change was in fact a small blister, erythematous papule, or wheal. Nits may be found within the clothing of patients with pediculosis corporis.

Objective findings that may be a clue to the etiology of chronic pruritus include the presence of jaundice, uremic frost, palpable lymphadenopathy, organomegaly, goiter, and exophthalmos. In general, the pruritic diseases considered in this chapter are characterized by a lack of objective skin findings.

Skin biopsy of normal-appearing skin may reveal histologic changes of a very specific dermatologic disorder. The presence of typical histologic findings in the absence of overt skin disease indicates an invisible dermatosis. Conditions that occasionally exhibit this phenomenon are listed in Table 11–18–1.

PLANS
Diagnostic
Differential Diagnosis

The disorders listed in Table 11–18–1 as well as the metabolic disturbances noted under Clinical Manifestations, Objective, form the appropriate considerations.

Diagnostic Options

Elimination of any direct histamine-releasing agents such as the opiates should be performed as a diagnostic maneuver. If the skin is xerotic, lubrication with occlusive emollients such as petrolatum (Aquaphor) should be beneficial and, therefore, of diagnostic value.

Laboratory evaluation should consist of complete blood count to rule out polycythemia, creatinine and blood urea nitrogen levels to evaluate renal status, liver function tests to rule out obstructive biliary disease, fasting and 2-hour postprandial blood sugar levels to rule out diabetes mellitus, thyroid function test for both hyperthyroidism and hypothyroidism, and 5-hydroxyindoleacetic acid test for carcinoid syndrome. Additional considerations include stool samples for ova and parasites and lymph node biopsy of any palpable adenopathy. Should leukemia be suspected, bone marrow examination may be necessary.

If no cause is found, the last procedure worthy of consideration is a biopsy of the symptomatic skin, which may reveal a dermatosis or evidence of a subclinical drug eruption.

Recommended Approach

A complete blood count and screening chemistry panel (with thyroid-stimulating hormone) forms a good survey for the disturbance of note in this symptom complex. Additional studies may be appropriate based on the medical history.

Therapeutic
Therapeutic Options

Therapy of xerotic pruritus is directed toward skin moisturization, which can be achieved by the use of occlusive moisturizers such as petrolatum or, alternatively, by the use of moisture-enhancing skin lubricants such as those containing high concentrations of glycerine or 10% urea, alpha hydroxy acids, or lactic acid.

Antihistamines are a useful adjunct in the management of pruritus; however, their tendency to produce sedation limits their general applicability. The proper dose of antihistamine is the one that relieves the pruritus but does not produce adverse side effects. Hydroxyzine (Atarax) tends to produce the most symptomatic improvement in the pruritic patient. Terfenadine (Seldane), astemizole (Hismanal), and loratadine (Claritin) may be tried if sedation is a problem. A topical antipruritic agent based on doxepin (Zonalon) has been introduced specif-

TABLE 11–18–1. SKIN DISORDERS THAT MAY CAUSE PRURITUS WITHOUT VISIBLE SKIN LESIONS

Pseudoxanthoma elasticum	Psoriasis
Sarcoidosis	Lupus erythematosus
Lepromatous leprosy	Necrotizing vasculitis
Lichen planus	Dermatitis herpetiformis
Amyloidosis	Erythropoietic protoporphyria
Hunter's and Hurler's syndromes	Lipoid proteinosis
Thyroid diseases	Ceroid lipofuchsinosis
Mycosis fungoides	

ically to address this symptom complex; however, systemic absorption can lead to sedation in some patients. Cholestyramine (Questran) may relieve the severe pruritus of biliary disease.

Metabolic causes of pruritus such as renal failure and obstructive biliary disease may be improved by suberythema doses of ultraviolet light B (the sunburn spectrum) administered two to three times per week for 4 weeks. Whether this mode of therapy can be extended to other metabolic causes of pruritus is uncertain. Therapy of the neoplastic causes of pruritus is directed primarily at the neoplasm by chemotherapy and radiotherapy.

Winter itch is one of the most common causes of generalized pruritus. The daily bath is the most common culprit in this setting. As the human body ages, the skin becomes less tolerant of daily bathing with or without soap. Many patients have the impression that a daily bath is required for hygiene; this is not so. Decreasing the frequency of bathing during the winter months avoids the development of winter itch in many patients, and mineral oil should be applied to the skin while bathing.

Recommended Approach

Topical moisturization with therapeutic moisturizers with or without the use of topical or systemic antihistamine is the customary starting point. Light treatment is generally reserved for resistant cases.

FOLLOW-UP

Patients with generalized pruritus of undetermined cause (in whom malignancies may be suspected, yet no objective findings are available) should be followed at intervals of 3 to 6 months. At follow-up visits, close inspection of the skin for subtle changes suggestive of cutaneous lymphoma or underlying dermatologic disease and palpation of lymph nodes, liver, and spleen are mandatory.

DISCUSSION
Prevalence and Incidence

The prevalence of skin disease ranges from 200 to 400 per 1000 population. Pruritus and related disorders accounts for about 2% of dermatologic diagnoses.

Related Basic Science

Itching due to most of the pathologic conditions described in this chapter is mediated through nerve fibers of the C class, and the sensation is poorly localized. Impulses are carried through the spinothalamic tract to the thalamus and on to the sensory cortex. Scratching seems to interrupt the rhythm of afferent impulses to the spinal column and relieves the sensation of pruritus.

Chemical mediators such as histamine and the endopeptidases can produce pruritus on injection. Kinins may or may not produce pruritus, but prostaglandins of the E1 series are not pruritogenic.

It has been suggested that retained bile salts cause cutaneous irritation and pruritus in obstructive biliary disease. This is supported by the observation that cholestyramine, which binds bile salts, may relieve pruritus. Although bile acids have been found within the skin of these pruritic patients, no relationship between the concentration of these substances and the severity of the pruritus can be found. It is not uncommon for pruritus to disappear in the patient with terminal liver failure.

Observations in the pruritus of chronic renal failure suggest that microangiopathy may be present. The relationship of this finding to the pruritus and successful management with ultraviolet light are uncertain.

Natural History and Its Modification with Treatment

The natural history of pruritus is determined by its specific cause. Winter itch is persistent but is relieved by treatment. Pruritus due to metabolic disorders is relieved as the metabolic disorder is corrected. Pruritus due to biliary obstruction is severe and is relieved by cholestyramine, but it is persistent until the biliary obstruction is relieved. Pruritus is likely to persist unless the underlying cause can be eliminated.

Prevention

Pruritus cannot be prevented unless the patient is aware of and can avoid the factors that have produced the itching in the past.

Cost Containment

Winter itch can be prevented with decreased bathing and the application of emollients after the bath. Petrolatum is quite helpful and is cheaper than many other preparations.

REFERENCES

Bernhard JD, ed. Itch: Mechanisms and Management of Pruritus. New York: McGraw-Hill, 1994.

Gilchrest BA. Pruritus: Pathogenesis, therapy, and significance in systemic disease states. Arch Intern Med 1982;142:101.

Herndon JH Jr. Itching: The pathophysiology of pruritus. Int J Dermatol 1975;14:465.

Rietschel RL, Lewis CW. Invisible dermatoses. Cutis 1978;21:378.

Sinclair D. Mechanisms of cutaneous sensation. New York: Oxford University Press, 1981.

Valsecchi R, Cainelli T. Generalized pruritus: A manifestation of iron deficiency. Arch Dermatol 1983;119:630.

Winkelman RK. Perspectives on dermatopathology. Arch Dermatol 1976; 112:1674.

CHAPTER 11–19

Nail Changes

Robert L. Rietschel, M.D.

DEFINITION

The disorders considered in this chapter include those with derangement in the physical appearance of the nail plate and surrounding support structures.

ETIOLOGY

The causes for nail changes include metabolic disturbances, genetic factors, infections, and external environmental exposures.

CRITERIA FOR DIAGNOSIS
Suggestive

Major types of changes in the appearance of the nail or surrounding tissue include absence or atrophy of the nail plate, hypertrophy of the nail plate, derangements in the surface architecture of the nail plate (pits, lines, grooves, clubbing, spooning), color changes, nail plate separation, periungual inflammatory changes, periungual neoplasm, and subungual hemorrhage.

Definitive

The findings necessary to support a diagnosis of specific nail disorders are listed in Table 11–19–1.

CLINICAL MANIFESTATIONS

Subjective

The family history can be helpful with genodermatoses, such as nail–patella syndrome, congenital ectodermal defects, pachyonychia congenita, psoriasis, and especially clubbing. Occupational and environmental exposure to moisture, irritants and allergens, and ionizing radiation may result in nail changes, as noted in Table 11–19–1. Nail changes seldom produce symptomatic complaints, except for the patient's awareness of the altered appearance. Occasionally, hypertrophic or tumorous lesions produce pain or acute or chronic inflammatory changes.

Objective

The various objective morphologic alterations in nail appearance are enumerated in Table 11–19–1. These, along with the supporting data, lead to a tentative diagnosis.

PLANS

Diagnostic

Differential Diagnosis

The differential diagnostic possibilities to consider are listed under Likely Diagnosis in Table 11–19–1.

Diagnostic Options

A guide for the diagnostic interpretation of nail changes is included in Table 11–19–1. Cultural evidence of fungi or bacteria cannot necessarily be construed as etiologic, as it is not uncommon for multiple organisms to colonize defective nails, as is seen in onycholysis or other traumatically induced conditions.

Nail diseases in general require the physician to look elsewhere in the body or environment for an etiology. All too often the inexperienced clinician rapidly accepts a positive fungal culture as explanation for the changes present. As treatment of fungal disease of the nails requires 6 to 8 months of systemic therapy with griseofulvin (Grisactin) or ketoconazole (Nizoral), it is important to remain skeptical. As pointed out earlier, diseased nails are a fertile ground for secondary colonization. When all 10 nails are involved in a process, fungal disease becomes less likely.

There are times when onycholysis or nail pitting may be the sole evidence of a condition such as psoriasis. Nail involvement with psoriasis is commonly associated with psoriatic arthritis, and this may be a clue in the patient with rheumatologic complaints.

Linear pigmented bands in lightly pigmented individuals present a problem in diagnosis. Often a biopsy of the nail matrix leads to a permanent deformity in the nail plate; however, this is the only way to ascertain whether the lesion is secondary to a nevus, melanocytic hyperplasia, or an early melanoma. Persistent tumorous lesions with a verrucous appearance should likewise arouse suspicion of malignancy. Bowen's disease and squamous cell carcinoma may mimic verruca vulgaris in this region.

Recommended Approach

Culture of the nail for fungi, yeast, and sometimes bacteria is a good starting point and should be given even greater emphasis when the diagnosis is not clear-cut. Tumors and new pigmented lesions require a biopsy diagnosis.

Therapeutic

Therapeutic Options

There is no effective treatment for end-stage atrophy or absence of the nail plate. When scarring processes such as lichen planus are treated early in the course with intralesional steroids, obliteration of the nail matrix is occasionally prevented. Hypertrophic conditions of the nail plate are best treated by mechanical filing when the etiology is not infectious. Occasionally, psoriasis may respond to injections of corticosteroids into the nail matrix, but this is painful and may be of only temporary benefit. Antimicrobial treatment of fungal infections of the nail plate requires therapy in excess of 6 months and is seldom effective in toenails; fingernails are somewhat more responsive to this management.

One of the most vexing problems is onycholysis. Subungual debris should be cultured to rule out fungal infections, which are often overdiagnosed. If no thyroid function abnormalities have been determined and there is no history of use of harsh chemicals, nail hardeners, or trauma, the clinician is left with the possible diagnosis of psoriasis or will be unable to identify an etiology (idiopathic). This condition may be somewhat responsive to injections of corticosteroids into the nail matrix. Triamcinolone acetonide suspension (Kenalog) in a concentration of 5 mg/mL or less is generally used. Either direct injection with a 30-gauge needle or air injection, such as with a Dermajet, may be attempted.

Acute paronychia is usually secondary to *Staphylococcus aureus* of the penicillinase-producing type and is responsive to appropriate antimicrobial agents. Surgical excision and drainage are seldom required with early antimicrobial treatment. Chronic paronychia may be exacerbated by mechanical manipulations of the posterior nailfold and perpetuated by the patient who may be under the impression that this is a useful technique. Continued exposure to water tends to keep a small film of moisture in the proximal nailfold region by capillary action. Therapy is directed toward drying with topical anticandidal and antibacterial agents as well as topical corticosteroids.

One of the most difficult periungual neoplasms to treat is the myxoid cyst. This tumor is an outpouching of synovium from the distal interphalangeal joint and may respond to intralesional injections of corticosteroids, but a high rate of recurrence is expected. Simple repeated incision and draining may be equally effective. With total surgical extirpation, the tumor also may frequently recur, unless the small bony spur that is triggering synovial hyperplasia is also removed.

Treatment of periungual warts is very difficult. Occasionally, these are perpetuated by mechanical trauma and nail biting and do not respond to treatment until the trauma ceases. Combinations of salicylic acid and lactic acid and flexible Collodion are occasionally successful.

True fungal infection of the nail plate and nailbed may be treated topically with clotrimazole (Lotrimin) or miconazole (Monistat) solutions; ciclopirox olamine cream or lotion (Loprox); or naftifine (Naftin). If systemic therapy is used, the choice is between griseofulvin, ketoconazole, fluconazole, and itraconazole. Ketoconazole has a higher cure rate with fingernail infections than griseofulvin, but both do a poor job on toenail disease. Liver toxicity may occur with both medications but has received more attention with ketoconazole, especially in women over age 40. Both fluconazole and itraconazole appear more effective in the clearing of toenail infections based on published reports. It is not clear if the long-term cure rates will be as encouraging.

Recommended Approach

Topical treatment is frequently disappointing. As systemic treatments are preferred, a firm diagnosis is all the more important prior to instituting care.

FOLLOW-UP

If a patient is placed on protracted griseofulvin or ketoconazole therapy for fungal infection of the nails, follow-up should be no more often than every 2 to 3 months, as it is difficult to assess the natural growth of the nail over a shorter term. The usual course of therapy for fingernail disease would be a 6- to 8-month course of therapy; for toenails, 1 to 2 years. At 2- to 6-month intervals, screening laboratory blood work including liver function testing is indicated.

If a patient has a nail condition necessitating intralesional injections of triamcinolone acetonide suspension, follow-up is required at intervals of 3 to 4 weeks. In general, the pharmacologic activity of these injections persists for approximately 3 weeks. More frequent injections may lead to atrophy of the nail matrix and nail plate.

TABLE 11–19–1. ABNORMALITIES OF THE NAILS

Major Morphologic Alteration	Supporting Data	Likely Diagnosis
Absence or atrophy of nail	Absence of patella; renal abnormalities and iliac spurs	Nail–patella syndrome
	Hyperhidrosis or hypohidrosis; alopecia; dental abnormalities; palmar hyperkeratosis	Congenital ectodermal defect (both anhidrotic and hidrotic types)
	Atrophic surrounding skin; history of x-ray exposure	Radiodermatitis
	History or presence of inflammatory skin disease	Secondary to matrix involvement in dermatoses (especially lichen planus)
Hypertrophy	All nails involved from early age; negative fungal culture; leukokeratosis; cataracts; alopecia	Pachyonychia congenita
	All nails involved; culture positive for *Candida*	Chronic mucocutaneous candidiasis
	Increasing hand and head size with endocrine dysfunction	Acromegaly
	Localized to several nails, especially toenails; positive fungal culture	*Trichophyton* infection
	All toenails involved; elderly patient; negative fungal culture	Secondary to aging; altered blood supply
	Papulosquamous plaques elsewhere; history of psoriasis	Psoriasis
Pits	Papulosquamous plaques elsewhere	Psoriasis
	Hair loss; no other abnormality	Alopecia areata; normal variant
Lines	Single line of pits or depression running left to right	Beau's line (secondary to major metabolic slowdown)
	Two parallel white bands against normal pink background	Muehrcke's lines (hypoalbuminemia)
	Left to right white band	Leukonychia (usually secondary to trauma)
	White bands running left to right	Mees' lines (arsenic)
	Brown or black line running proximal to distal	Matrix nevus: melanoma: or racial trait in darkly pigmented individuals
	Red line running proximal to distal; keratotic truncal lesions	Darier's disease
Grooves	Midline of nail split	Habit tic (median canal dystrophy)
	Indentation in nail running proximal to distal with proximal papular lesion	External compression of matrix; likely due to myxoid cyst
Clubbing	Family history; gradual onset	Familial
	No family history; gradual to rapid onset	Pulmonary disease (infectious or neoplastic); cyanotic cardiovascular disease; cirrhosis; chronic diarrhea
Spooning (koilonychia)	Anemia	Iron deficiency; Plummer–Vinson syndrome
Color	Black	Hair dyes; mercuric sulfide; pinta; B$_{12}$ deficiency; Peutz–Jeghers syndrome
	Gray-black	Melanoma
	Blue-brown	Wilson's disease; chloroquine
	Brown	Hydroquinone
	Gray	Argyria; phenolphthalein; mercuric chloride
	Green	*Pseudomonas*
	Yellow	Yellow nail syndrome (chronic edema)
Nail plate separation (onycholysis)	Positive potassium hydroxide and fungal culture	Fungal infection
	Use of nail hardeners	Chemical or allergic etiology
	Trauma in past	Altered physical structure of matrix
	Psoriasis elsewhere	Psoriasis
	Abnormal thyroid functions	Hyperthyroidism or hypothyroidism
Periungual inflammatory changes	Acute or chronic erythema; edema; pus discharged from proximal nailfold; positive bacterial or fungal culture	Acute or chronic paronychia
Periungual neoplasm	Cystic with clear jelly on puncture	Myxoid cyst
	Bluish color	Glomus
	Firm papule	Enchondroma
	Verrucous surface	Warts; Bowen's disease or squamous cell carcinoma
Subungual hemorrhage	May be seen with:	Subacute bacterial endocarditis; trauma; vasculitis; psoriasis; cirrhosis; other chronic infections

DISCUSSION
Prevalence

The prevalence of nail problems is unknown; they are relatively uncommon as signs of systemic disease.

Related Basic Science

The matrix produces the nail plate and is partially covered by the posterior nail fold. Very little nail plate substance comes from the nailbed. The slow growth of the fingernail (about 0.1 mm per day) is about three times the speed of growth of the toenail.

Natural History and Its Modification with Treatment

Diseases of the matrix and posterior nailfold are noted proximally and progress distally over several months, whereas extrinsic agents such as fungi begin distally and progress proximally. Effective treatment of a nail disease will not be detected for 3 to 6 months on fingernails and 1 to $1\frac{1}{2}$ years on toenails because of the rate of growth.

Prevention

It is important to keep the patient's expectations in line with current treatment potential when attempting to manage fungal diseases of the toenails. As a long-term cure cannot be expected, it is often beneficial to instruct the patient in a program of nail care designed to mechanically file down hypertrophic tissue to minimize pain. Trimming of the nail as short as possible minimizes the trauma that may extend the onycholysis, when this is the patient's condition. Applications of bleaching creams, hair dyes, and other topical products may lead to nail staining, and awareness of these possibilities may minimize patient confusion as to why their nails are becoming discolored. Artificial nails and nail hardeners frequently contain methacrylates, formaldehyde, toluene formaldehyde, sulfonamide resin, and other sensitizers that may lead to allergic contact dermatitis or chemical onycholysis. Avoidance of these materials is prudent.

Many individuals are under the impression that an orange stick or other agent should be used to push back the cuticle to maintain healthy nails. This advice is ill-conceived, and patients should be instructed not to manipulate the posterior nailfold; this, as well as avoidance of protracted water immersion, should minimize the difficulties in managing chronic paronychia.

Patients given drugs with photosensitizing potential should be counseled to avoid excessive sun exposure, as not only photosensitivity of the skin but also light-induced onycholysis may occur in patients taking drugs such as tetracycline and 8-methoxypsoralen.

Cost Containment

To date, nothing is known about cost containment measures for these nail disorders.

REFERENCES

Coldiron B. Recalcitrant onychomycosis of the toenails successfully treated with fluconazole. Arch Dermatol 1992;128:909.

Kechijian P. Onycholysis of the fingernail: Evaluation and management. J Am Acad Dermatol 1985;12:552.

Pardo Castello V, Pardo OA. Diseases of the nail. Springfield, IL: Charles C Thomas, 1960.

Samman PD. The nails in disease. Springfield, IL: Charles C Thomas, 1979.

Scher RK. Cosmetics and ancillary preparations for care of nails. J Am Acad Dermatol 1982;6:523.

Zaias N, Baden HP. Nails. In: Fitzpatrick TB, Eisen AZ, Wolff K, et al., eds. Dermatology in general medicine. New York: McGraw-Hill, 1979:418.

Zaias N, Drachman D. A method for the determination of drug effectiveness in onychomycosis. J Am Acad Dermatol 1983;9:912.

CHAPTER 11–20

Abnormalities of Hair

Robert L. Rietschel, M.D.

DEFINITION

The disorders considered in this chapter include increased and decreased amounts of hair as well as structural defects in the hair shaft.

ETIOLOGY

Causes of hair abnormalities include endocrine disorders, infections, hereditary factors, metabolic disturbances, and inflammatory dermatoses.

CRITERIA FOR DIAGNOSIS
Suggestive

An increase or decrease in the quantity or quality of hair diffusely or in localized areas suggests an abnormality.

Definitive

The specific changes needed to support a diagnosis of hair abnormalities are listed in Table 11–20–1.

CLINICAL MANIFESTATIONS
Subjective

A family history of pattern (androgenetic) baldness in both men and women is easily elicited in this most common cause of hair loss.

Monilethrix, which is a structural defect that results in beaded hairs, is autosomal dominant. A family history of minimal sweating may be found in women who are carriers of the X-linked recessive trait that results in anhidrotic ectodermal dysplasia with diminished or absent hair in affected male offspring.

Environmental factors such as how tightly the hair is rolled or styled or how it is brushed, combed, or permed can result in physically induced forms of hair loss such as traction alopecia and trichorrhexis nodosa. Psychosocial history plays a role in both trichotillomania and telogen effluvium. A perceived increase or decrease in the amount, color, or rate of growth of the hair constitutes the principal symptom. A 30% loss of scalp hair can be detected by patients, whereas the physician may not perceive the loss until 50% of hairs are absent.

Objective

Increases in the amount of hair (hypertrichosis) are noted in areas where hair is normally sparse or absent. There are two basic hair types: soft, babylike lanugo hair, and coarser, adult terminal hair (Table 11–20–1).

Decreases in the amount of hair (alopecia) are categorized into two types: scarring (cicatricial) and nonscarring (noncicatricial).

The most common color change is routine graying, referred to as *canities;* the occurrence of localized clusters of white hair is termed *poliosis.*

TABLE 11–20–1. ABNORMALITIES OF THE HAIR

Major Morphologic Change	Additional Physical Findings	Supporting Data	Likely Diagnosis
Hypertrichosis Lanugo type	Generalized distribution	Look for occult malignancy	Hypertrichosis lanuginosa
Terminal type	Localized	Possibly present from birth: possible pigment increase	Nevoid hypertrichosis
	Female with increase in areas of male pattern	Associated with endocrine hyperproliferative states, drugs, porphyria cutanea tarda	Hirsutism
Alopecias Nonicatricial	Localized to frontal, vertex, or frontotemporal areas	Family history of baldness; young male (occasionally in women)	Male pattern alopecia
	Circumscribed patches, total scalp, or total body	Exclamation point hairs	Alopecia areata
	Moth-eaten; patchy	Positive STS	Secondary syphilis
	Geometric pattern, especially at temples	Use of tight hair roller, tight braids	Traction alopecia
	Generalized poor hair growth with loss	Microscopic: beaded hairs	Monilethrix
		Microscope: fractured hairs resembling two brooms pushed together	Trichorrhexis nodosa
		History of poor sweating and abnormal teeth	Anhidrotic ectodermal dysplasia
	Generalized thinning with increased hair loss	Recent major illness, high fever, pregnancy, or psychological trauma; increased telogen count on pull test	Telogen effluvium
		Abnormal thyroid tests	Hyperthyroidism or hypothyroidism
		Signs and symptoms of pituitary dysfunction	Hypopituitarism or panhypopituitarism
		Decrease iron stores	Iron deficiency anemia
		Severe restriction of protein or calorie intake	Dietary alopecia
		Drugs: thallium, chemotherapeutic agents, colchicine, anticoagulants, iodine, borax, bismuth, vitamin A, allopurinol, thiouracil, trimethadione, amphetamines, gold	Drug-induced alopecia
Cicatricial	Circumscribed with stubble of hair within the patch	KOH or fungal culture positive	Tinea capitis
	Localized with tumorlike mass associated	Histology of lesion	Nevi; basal or squamous cell carcinoma; lymphoma; metastatic carcinoma
	Localized	History of physical or chemical trauma	Burns: radiodermatitis; etc.
	Localized with boggy purulent mass	Fungal culture positive; KOH positive or negative	Kerion
	Localized with:	Positive culture for TB	Lupus vulgaris
		Positive Fite stain of biopsy; acid-fast culture negative	Leprosy
		Positive STS	Tertiary syphilis or yaws
	Papulosquamous lesions elsewhere; atrophy	Positive lupus band test on biopsy and compatible histology	Lupus erythematosus
	Papulosquamous lesions elsewhere: follicular accentuation	Biopsy with lichenoid infiltrate	Lichen planus
	Sclerotic skin elsewhere		Scleroderma
	Scarring of cornea, mucosal surfaces	Positive direct immunofluorescence	Cicatricial pemphigoid
	Follicular pustules	Variable bacterial flora	Folliculitis decalvans
Color change	Graying	Family history of early graying	Canities
		Abnormal thyroid tests	Hyperthyroidism
		Recent patches of hair loss	Alopecia areata
	White patches	Present from birth	Piebaldism

STS, serologic test for syphilis: TB, tuberculosis.

PLANS

Diagnostic

Differential Diagnosis

The differential diagnostic possibilities are listed in Table 11–20–1 under Likely Diagnosis.

Diagnostic Options

Diagnostic evaluation for hypertrichosis most commonly revolves around evaluation of hirsutism. A family history of hirsutism is most common. Any signs or symptoms suggestive of acromegaly, adrenogenital syndrome, Cushing's disease, iatrogenically administered androgens or glucocorticoids, or menstrual cycles longer or shorter or less than 28 days should prompt endocrinologic evaluation. Additionally, endocrine tumors may secrete hormones that produce this type of change. A history of sensitivity to sunlight, skin fragility or blistering, or a propensity to bruise easily over the dorsum of the hands and forearms should direct the physician toward porphyria cutanea tarda. A history of ingestion of phenytoin, penicillamine, streptomycin, or minoxidil may give a clue to the origin of the hirsutism.

The noncicatricial alopecias have many potential causes, and appropriate diagnostic evaluation revolves around the ability to examine the hair adequately. The initial test to be performed is a pull test. Approximately 10 hairs are firmly grasped and extracted with a smooth, steady stroke. In conditions such as telogen effluvium, virtually all the hairs are extracted with this procedure and more than 30% of the hairs have a whitish club on the proximal end. The hair should then be examined under the dissecting microscope for structural abnormalities. Additionally, hairs should be studied in a 10% potassium hydroxide solution and cultured to rule out fungal infection. If these examinations have not provided adequate information for a diagnosis, serologic tests for syphilis, thyroid function tests, and evaluation of iron status would be appropriate. If the diagnosis of trichotillomania is suspected, it may be necessary to paint flexible Collodion or some other impermeable material over the area of alopecia and observe this area for regrowth of hair; this will prevent the patient from being able to continually extract the short hairs as they grow out.

Cicatricial alopecias often require a biopsy with routine hematoxylin and eosin as well as immunofluorescence staining for the evaluation of potential causes. If infectious diseases are suspected, the skin biopsy should be ground and cultured for deep fungi and typical and atypical acid-fast bacilli. Serologic tests for syphilis as well as collagen–vascular disorders also are appropriate for scarring alopecia.

Recommended Approach

Hair loss of short duration is frequently due to hair breakage. A pull test should yield broken hairs devoid of root structures. Massive hair loss of a diffuse nature present for less than 4 months is usually due to telogen effluvium, and a history accompanied by a positive pull test for club hairs is sufficient for diagnostic purposes. Diagnosis of diffuse hair loss of moderate amounts, present for greater than 6 months, is more difficult. Medical history may provide a clue to the next reasonable diagnostic step. Endocrine disorders, particularly thyroid diseases, and iron deficiency anemia should be investigated. If these studies are normal, androgenetic alopecia becomes a more likely possibility. Generally, alopecia should be present longer than 1 year for this diagnosis.

Hair loss in patches or patterns that are not classic for androgenetic alopecia or that are accompanied by an inflammation of the scalp should be biopsied to gain insight into the disease process. If the pattern is "moth-eaten" then a serologic test for syphilis would take presidence over the scalp biopsy.

If the abnormality is a change that affects primarily the ability to style hair, the first test should be surface microscopy of the hair shafts for structural defects.

Cultures of the scalp for fungi are appropriate for patchy hair loss in children prior to scalp biopsy. Fungal infection of the scalp is sufficiently rare in adults that a biopsy will be more helpful.

Therapeutic

Therapeutic Options

Therapy for the hypertrichoses revolves around identification of underlying etiologies. Male pattern alopecia may be treated by hair transplantation, which is an expensive and time-consuming procedure. Medical management of male pattern alopecia can be undertaken with 2% minoxidil solution (Rogaine) applied twice daily to the scalp. Approximately 40% of patients treated with the solution experience demonstrable hair growth in formerly bald areas. The best candidates for this treatment are mild to modestly affected individuals who present within 5 to 7 years of onset of balding and those with some vellus hair remaining within balding areas. Stabilization of hair growth occurs in approximately 90% of treated patients, offering some benefit to those wishing to retard further losses.

Alopecia areata may respond to intralesional or systemic steroid administration, but the benefits of systemic treatment are debatable in mild cases. Spontaneous regrowth may occur in some cases, whereas an initial response to steroids may eventually give way to repeated alopecia when the steroid effect is lost. In general, intralesional steroid therapy carries minimal risks and has a reasonable chance of success, whereas systemic therapy may be required for protracted periods and carries much greater risks to the patient, but may be the only effective option. Other treatments for alopecia areata include topical anthralin (Lasan), topical minoxidil, and topical or systemic psoralen combined with ultraviolet light A (PUVA).

Structural defects in general are untreatable at this time. Traction alopecia may become permanent if the traction is not alleviated at an early stage. The telogen effluvium seen after a major metabolic disturbance usually has its onset approximately 2 to 3 months following the disturbance, with an increase in hair loss for approximately 6 months. This hair loss is usually temporary and no treatment is necessary, although the patient may require some form of scalp care for reassurance. Correction of underlying endocrine or other metabolic disturbances and withdrawal of inciting drugs for drug-induced alopecias usually lead to regrowth of hair.

Treatment of tinea capitis requires oral griseofulvin (Grisactin).

There is no specific time frame for treatment; rather, the patient must be followed until signs of regrowth appear throughout the area of alopecia, at which time the medication can usually be discontinued. Topical treatment of tinea capitis has been uniformly disappointing.

The cicatricial alopecias are difficult to treat, and regrowth of hair is generally not expected. An occasional patient with cicatricial lesions of discoid lupus may experience hair regrowth after prolonged treatment with chloroquine (Aralen) or other agents. Folliculitis decalvans may be improved to some extent with antibiotic therapy similar to that used for the management of acne.

Recommended Approach

Topical antifungal agents are not effective in the treatment of fungal infections of the scalp; systemic antifungal agents are required. Inflammatory disorders can be treated topically prior to use of systemic treatment. Alopecia areata responds faster to intralesional corticosteroids than to topical corticosteroids. If a systemic disease is identified, treatment should be directed at the systemic disease rather than the scalp.

FOLLOW-UP

No routine follow-up is required, except that patients with tinea capitis should be followed at 1-month intervals when treatment with griseofulvin has been instituted. Patients with cicatricial alopecias requiring systemic immunosuppressive therapy, such as patients with cicatricial pemphigoid, also require frequent follow-up for monitoring of hematologic and immunologic function. Patients on topical minoxidil are routinely evaluated after 1 month of treatment and at 6- to 12-month intervals thereafter.

DISCUSSION

Prevalence and Incidence

The prevalence of skin disease ranges from 200 to 400 per 1000 population. Hair diseases and related follicular disorders account for 2 to 3% of dermatologic diagnoses.

Related Basic Science

The most common hair abnormality is male pattern alopecia. Prepubertal castration of men from families with strong tendencies toward male pattern alopecia prevents development of this condition; institution of testosterone replacement therapy brings about the onset of male pattern alopecia. It is an intriguing paradox that the same hormone produces excessive hair growth in other areas of the body. The mechanism by which minoxidil reverses this genetic trait is not known. The drug is concentrated in cells lining the dermal papillae of the hair root. There is no known antiandrogenic action of minoxidil. A transient increase in blood flow occurs following application of topical minoxidil, but this alteration is not persistent enough to explain the overriding of genetic programming.

Alopecia areata exhibits several unique features, one of which is the sparing of depigmented, gray, or white hairs. Stories of individuals turning gray overnight are generally instances of acute onset of alopecia areata in which all the pigmented hairs are lost in a rapid fashion. It is not uncommon for the lost hair to regrow and be totally gray. Although the cause of this condition is unknown, one study (Happle et al., 1978) suggests that immunologic therapies such as sensitization to dinitrochlorobenzene with subsequent applications of this same material to the areas of alopecia will produce a regrowth of hair. The mechanisms for this form of therapy are uncertain, and the condition may occasionally respond to simple irritants applied in a similar fashion, but less consistently.

Tinea captitis has two forms: common epidemic ringworm, which is often due to fungi that fluoresce under Wood's light, and the subtle black dot ringworm infection, which does not fluoresce under Wood's light. Over the past decade, black dot ringworm has become the more common of the two. This condition may at times be difficult to distinguish from seborrheic dermatitis. The hairs are broken off at the surface, leaving residual small fragments within the follicle and giving rise to the so-called black dot appearance. Cultural evidence of the fungus most commonly producing this infection requires plucking of these small fragments from the follicles. Wood's light examination cannot be relied on to rule out tinea capitis. Nor should Wood's light be used to evaluate ringworm of the body surfaces. When the ringworm lesions of the scalp are of an acute type, a boggy pustular plaque known as a *kerion* is formed. The intensity of the inflammatory reaction may destroy the fungi, so that it is difficult to find a positive potassium hydroxide preparation and culture the organism. These lesions may produce a cicatricial alopecia due to the inflammatory destruction of hair follicles within this region. The pustular nature of the lesions suggests bacterial superinfection, but this is seldom the case. Treatment with griseofulvin and prednisone for suppression of this intense inflammatory reaction may result in prevention of scarring alopecia.

Natural History and Its Modification with Treatment

The natural history of disorders that produce an excess or decrease in hair depends on the cause of the conditions. Some of the conditions produce permanent hair loss or excessive hair growth, whereas others are self-limited or treatable.

Prevention

Some of the hair loss due to chemotherapeutic agents may be prevented by tourniquets about the scalp or icepacks placed over the scalp to induce vasoconstriction. This may also diminish delivery of the intended medication to this area, and this possibility must be weighed against the psychological benefits to the patient of minimizing the drug-induced alopecia. Topical 2% minoxidil appears capable of retarding male pattern alopecia in approximately 90% of cases over the course of 1 year, but the degree of success this will have in prevention has not been eval-uated in any long-term studies. Severe caloric restriction, as in fad diets, will result in a temporary alopecia in some individuals, and this may be prevented by a more gradual form of dietary restriction.

Cost Containment

Avoidance of over-the-counter remedies for hair restoration is prudent. Only the self-limited conditions respond. Likewise, physicians should refrain from prescribing expensive treatments for the self-limited (temporary) forms of hair loss.

REFERENCES

DeVillez RL. Topical minoxidil therapy in hereditary androgenetic alopecia. Arch Dermatol 1985;121:197.

DeVillez RL. Androgenetic alopecia treated with topical minoxidil. J Am Acad Dermatol 1987;16:669.

Happle R, Cebulla K, Happle KE. Dinitrochlorobenzene therapy for alopecia areata. Arch Dermatol 1978;114:1629.

Jarrett A. The physiology and pathophysiology of the skin. Vol. 4: The hair follicle. New York: Academic Press, 1977.

Mitchell AJ, Krull EA. Alopecia areata: Pathogenesis and treatment. J Am Acad Dermatol 1984;11:763.

Munro DD, Darley CR. Hair. In: Fitzpatrick TB, Eisen AZ, Wolff K, et al., eds. Dermatology in general medicine. New York: McGraw-Hill, 1979:395.

Olsen EA, DeLong ER, Weiner MS. Long-term follow-up of men with male pattern baldness treated with topical minoxidil. J Am Acad Dermatol 1987;16:688.

Price VH. Testosterone metabolism in skin. Arch Dermatol 1976;111:1496.

Weiss VC, West DF, Fu TS, et al. Alopecia areata treated with topical minoxidil. Arch Dermatol 1984;120:457.

Hematologic Disorders

Maurie Markman, M.D., Alan E. Lichtin, M.D.

CHAPTER 12–1

Normochromic Normocytic Anemias

Alan. E. Lichtin, M.D.

DEFINITION

The normocytic normochromic anemias are defined as anemias with a mean corpuscular volume (MCV) within the normal range. In most laboratories, the normal range is 80 to 100 femtoliters (fL).

These disorders are summarized in Table 12–1–1. Several topics related to normocytic normochromic anemias, such as aplastic anemia and myelophthisic disorders (lymphomas, leukemias, and myelofibrosis), are covered in other chapters of this textbook.

ETIOLOGY

Because so many disorders cause normochromic normocytic anemias, etiology is discussed with respect to each disorder.

CRITERIA FOR DIAGNOSIS

Suggestive

All anemic patients should have a careful review of the peripheral blood smear. Modern laboratory instruments that give complete blood counts will give a MCV. Anemic patients with a MCV between 80 and 100 would be defined as having a normochromic normocytic anemia. Some of these patients have elevated reticulocyte counts and may have an immune hemolytic anemia with spherocytes on the peripheral smear but a normal MCV; this situation is discussed under immune hemolysis (see Chapter 12–4). Most patients with normochromic normocytic anemias have a low or low-normal reticulocyte count. This means that their erythroid lineage in the bone marrow has a hypoproliferative status. They are anemic, but do not compensate properly for their anemia and do not produce enough red cells to meet the demands of oxygen consumption peripherally.

Definitive

Patients who are anemic with a hemoglobin below the normal range (at the Cleveland Clinic the normal range for men is 13.5–17.5 g% hemoglobin, and for women, 12–16 g% hemoglobin) and a normal MCV (80–100 fL), by definition, have a normochromic normocytic anemia.

TABLE 12–1–1.   CAUSES OF NORMOCHROMIC-NORMOCYTIC ANEMIA

Aplastic anemia
Pure red cell aplasia
Anemia of chronic renal failure
Anemia of endocrine disorders
Myelophthisis
Myelodysplasia
Membrane/cytoskeletal abnormalities
Hereditary spherocytosis
Anemia of chronic disease
Heart valve hemolysis

Again, review of the peripheral blood smear is important in assigning a cause. The reticulocyte count must be obtained to prove a hypoproliferative state.

CLINICAL MANIFESTATIONS

Subjective

Most patients who are anemic note symptoms of lassitude, fatigue, dizziness, feeling cold, or dyspnea on exertion. In patients diagnosed with anemia it is critical to review the past record for analysis of previous complete blood counts. Patients who have been anemic their entire life often have a hemoglobinopathy or inborn error of hemoglobin synthesis. Patients who were normal in the past, but have become anemic have an acquired state. Most patients with a normochromic normocytic anemia have an acquired anemia and do not have a family history suggestive of an inborn error in hemoglobin synthesis or red cell membrane structure.

Certain individuals with membrane or cytoskeletal abnormalities such as hereditary spherocytosis and elliptocytosis may present with a normochromic normocytic anemia. These individuals usually have a lifelong history of mild jaundice and other family members with a lifelong history of mild jaundice. Also, a history of gallstone removal at ages 20 to 30 in other family members might lead the physician to work up the patient for a membrane or cytoskeletal abnormality.

Patients with the anemia of chronic disease usually complain of problems related to their known chronic ailment. Some of these can be subtle, especially in the elderly. One must be aware that disorders such as miliary tuberculosis, giant cell arteritis, and polymyalgia rheumatica may present primarily as an anemia of chronic disease.

Objective

Physical Examination

Most patients with the normochromic normocytic anemias appear pale. Patients with aplastic anemia may also have evidence of infection or bruising. Patients whose anemia is related to endocrine disease may have physical findings characteristic of the underlying endocrine disease; for example, hypothyroid individuals may manifest myxedematous changes in the skin of the legs or arms. Most of these patients have a normochromic normocytic anemia, although some may have macrocytosis. Patients with myelophthisic (myelofibrosis, lymphoma, or leukemia) disorders may present with splenomegaly.

Routine Laboratory Abnormalities

Review of the peripheral blood smear is important in determining the etiology of the anemia. Patients with aplastic anemia have pancytopenia, and the peripheral smear shows normochromic normocytic red cells without fragmentation, along with a low white blood cell count and thrombocytopenia. Patients with pure red cell aplasia have normal white blood cell counts and platelet counts, but have a low reticulocyte count, lack of evidence of polychromasia, and a peripheral smear without alterations in the red blood cell morphology. Patients with the anemia of chronic renal failure have a fairly normal smear but are anemic. Patients with the anemia of endocrine disease, as stated, have a fairly normal peripheral blood smear but are anemic as well. Patients with myelophthisis have teardrop cells as well as a left-shifted white cell series with myelocytes, metamyelocytes, and bands on peripheral blood smear. They may even have blasts, promyelocytes, and nucleated red blood cells. Patients with myelophthisis due to the myeloproliferative disorders may also have basophilia. Patients with myelodysplasia have hypogranular polymorphonuclear leukocytes, Pelger–Huet anomaly, and, usually, leukopenia. Patients with hereditary disorders of the membrane or cytoskeleton have abnormal red cell shapes. For example, patients with hereditary spherocytosis have an increased number of spherocytes on the peripheral smear along with an abnormal osmotic fragility curve, and patients with hereditary elliptocytosis have elliptocytes on peripheral smear. Patients with microangiopathic hemolytic anemia (this is described in more detail in Chapter 12–38 on disseminated intravascular coagulation and Chapter 12–15 in the discussion of thrombotic thrombocytopenic purpura) have evidence of red cell fragmentation with schistocytes and helmet cells; they also may have left-shifted granulopoiesis. Patients with disseminated intravascular coagulation have elevated prothrombin and partial thromboplastin times and evidence of fibrin degradation products, along with a low fibrinogen level. Patients with the anemia of chronic disease have a low serum iron level, low total iron binding capacity, a low percentage saturation, and a normal or elevated ferritin level. Their peripheral blood smear may appear normal.

PLANS
Diagnostic
Differential Diagnosis

In evaluating a patient with a normochromic normocytic anemia one needs to keep in mind all the diagnoses in Table 12–1–1. Reviewing the smear and reticulocyte count, eliciting a good history, and performing a physical examination usually pinpoint the diagnosis.

Diagnostic Options

One may be able to diagnose the cause of the normochromic normocytic anemia without pursuing bone marrow aspiration and biopsy; in aplastic anemia, bone marrow aspiration and biopsy are usually necessary to confirm this diagnosis. Patients with myelophthisis require bone marrow aspiration and biopsy to establish the diagnosis. Patients with myelodysplasia usually require a bone marrow examination with chromosome analysis to determine the French–American–British (FAB) subtype of myelodysplasia. Patients with red cell membrane or cytoskeletal abnormalities usually do not need to undergo bone marrow aspiration and biopsy because they all have an erythroid hyperplasia and most diagnoses can be established by reviewing the peripheral smear. Bone marrows of patients with microangiopathic hemolytic anemia usually demonstrate erythroid hyperplasia. It is more important to take the history, perform the physical examination, and obtain other laboratory data, for example, blood cultures and coagulation parameters, to determine the cause of microangiopathy. Echocardiography may be important to rule out heart valve-related hemolysis. In affected individuals, the valve causes turbulence in the stream of blood flowing through the heart and this causes red cell injury, an elevated lactate dehydrogenase level, indirect hyperbilirubinemia, a low haptoglobin level, microangiopathy on peripheral smear, and elevation of the reticulocyte count. Bone marrow aspiration is usually not required.

Recommended Approach

The normochromic normocytic anemias can be diagnosed on the basis of the information provided by the complete blood count, review of the peripheral blood smear, the reticulocyte count, the history, the physical examination, and, sometimes, a bone marrow examination. Special circumstances, as found in persons with hereditary disorders of the red cell membrane, require further testing, such as the osmotic fragility test and more detailed analysis of the amino acid structure of the proteins involved in the cytoskeleton (e.g., spectrin and ankyrin).

Therapeutic
Therapeutic Options

If patients are severely anemic and compromised by their anemia to the point of having angina or high-output heart failure, an immediate transfusion of red blood cells may be necessary; however, the more important therapeutic options depend on the outcome of the diagnostic workup. If patients have aplastic anemia, are below the age of 20, and have an HLA-compatible sibling, bone marrow transplantation may be the aim of therapy. About half of patients with pure red cell aplasia have a thymoma and its removal may be beneficial. If the patient has anemia of chronic renal failure but is not severely anemic, administration of erythropoietin may correct the anemia. In a patient with lymphoma or leukemia, chemotherapy directed to eradication of the neoplastic disease is indicated. Patients with hereditary abnormalities of the cytoskeleton usually can be observed without any specific treatment. Splenectomy may ameliorate the anemia if it is severe enough to cause symptoms. Patients who have a heart valve (usually artificial) causing significant degrees of hemolysis may require valve replacement to reduce the turbulence in the red blood cell stream.

Recommended Approach

It is necessary to establish the cause of the normochromic normocytic anemia before instituting therapy. The most commonly used directed therapies are listed above. When physicians are confronted by an anemic patient the impulse is to transfuse or administer a hematinic. It is very important to establish the cause of the underlying normochromic normocytic anemia before proceeding to transfusion. Red blood cell transfusions carry the risk of transmitting hepatitis and HIV and causing immunologic perturbations, such as antibodies to minor red cell antigens, making future transfusions problematic. Thus, it is important to stress the need for accurate review of the history, previous complete blood counts, physical examination, peripheral smear and bone marrow examinations, and ancillary tests before ordering a transfusion.

There is also an impulse to use erythropoietin in several settings other than the anemia of chronic renal failure. At this point the Food and Drug Administration has approved erythropoietin for use only in the anemia of chronic renal failure, the anemia associated with HIV infection and its treatment (with AZT), and the anemia associated with chemotherapy administration. Even in the latter two settings, erythropoietin is an expensive therapy compared with blood transfusion.

FOLLOW-UP

Each cause of normochromic normocytic anemias listed in Table 12–1–1 would require a different form of follow-up. Patients with aplastic anemia who have a bone marrow transplant need to be followed carefully in the posttransplant period for evidence of cytomegalovirus infection, opportunistic infections, and so on. Patients with pure red cell aplasia who have a thymoma may benefit from thymectomy; however, half of these patients continue to have pure red cell aplasia. If a drug is causing the pure red cell aplasia and it is stopped, usually the red cell count rises within 1 month and remains normal thereafter. Phenytoin is one of the more common drugs to do this.

Patients on dialysis who require erythropoietin simply need periodic complete blood counts. Iron administration has to accompany erythropoietin administration to keep erythropoiesis active. The patient with hypothyroidism who is anemic usually becomes nonanemic once the hypothyroidism is treated. Patients with myelophthisic disorders such as myelofibrosis usually need to be monitored fairly closely by hematologists to make sure the blood counts do not drop to such a point that transfusion is necessary. There is no specific treatment at this time that reverses myelofibrosis. In patients with hereditary spherocytosis who undergo a splenectomy, often the anemia improves, and no specific follow-up is required unless they notice worsening jaundice or fatigue. The presence of these symptoms usually means hemolysis has increased; this is seen during viral infections. Patients with the anemia of chronic disease improve when the underlying chronic disease (inflammatory, infectious, or neoplastic) is properly treated.

DISCUSSION
Prevalence

The normochromic normocytic anemias, especially the anemia of chronic disease, are very common. There have been articles bemoaning the misdiagnosis and nonrecognition of anemia in hospitalized patients. Not only can nonrecognition cause diagnoses to be missed, but unnecessary and potentially morbid testing might be carried out on patients inappropriately without proper recognition of the cause of anemia.

Related Basic Science

Recent research into the anemia of chronic disease has uncovered several potential mechanisms for this common problem. When red cells senesce and die, they break down into their component parts and the iron is reused for the production of new red cells. In the anemia of chronic disease, there is a low serum iron level, a low total iron binding capacity, and a low percentage saturation; however, there are adequate reticuloendothelial iron stores as demonstrated by normal ferritin levels and the ease in visualizing iron on specially stained specimens of bone marrow and other organs. It was initially felt that the release of reticuloendothelial iron was blocked; however, experiments with radiolabeled iron showed that this was not the case. Recent studies of the cytokines interleukin-1, tumor necrosis factor, and interferons beta and gamma have demonstrated that each has an effect on erythropoietin production, reticuloendothelial iron release, and the development of erythroid progenitors. Exogenous erythropoietin can potentially improve the anemia of chronic disease in some patients; however, it has not yet become the standard of care. Rather, attempting to reverse the cause of the chronic disease is the more important therapeutic step.

Natural History and Its Modification with Treatment

In those patients with anemia of chronic disease related to some underlying chronic inflammatory disorder that is completely correctable, such as osteomyelitis or tuberculosis, treatment of the underlying condition often completely eliminates the anemia. For those disorders that may be altered but not completely reversed, such as rheumatoid arthri-tis, the patient may manifest a partial improvement in the associated anemia of chronic disease. Some of these patients require transfusion therapy (or erythropoietin) as long as the underlying disease is active.

In those patients with hereditary inborn errors of membrane or cytoskeletal proteins, the normal life span may be interrupted by cholecystectomy at a young age and, possibly, splenectomy. Once a splenectomy is performed, there is a 1% risk of fulminant pneumococcal sepsis for the remainder of the lifespan of the patient.

Prevention

Many causes of the normochromic normocytic anemias are not preventable. Specific prevention strategies for aplastic anemia are discussed in Chapter 12–19.

Cost Containment

Although there are no supporting data, swift recognition, diagnosis, and treatment without performing excessive laboratory tests or procedures probably constitute the most cost-conscious approach to patients with normochromic normocytic anemias. In the present age of health care reform, primary care practitioners may take on a greater role in working up these patients. This is appropriate in the majority of patients as long as the importance of the above-stated elements of the evaluation of these patients is recognized.

REFERENCES

Agre P. Hereditary spherocytosis. JAMA 1989;262:2887.

Erslev AJ. Erythropoietin. N Engl J Med 1991;324:1339.

Means RT, Krantz SB. Progress in understanding the pathogenesis of the anemia of chronic disease. Blood 1992;80:1639.

Palek J, Sahr KE. Mutations of the red blood cell membrane proteins: From clinical evaluation to detection of the underlying genetic defect. Blood 1992;80:308.

Self KG, Conrady MM, Eichner ER. Failure to diagnose anemia in medical patients: Is the traditional diagnosis of anemia a dying art? 1986;81:786.

CHAPTER 12–2

Microcytic Hypochromic Anemias

Ralph Green, M.B., B.Ch., M.D.

DEFINITION

A microcytic anemia is any anemia in which the mean cell volume (MCV) is below the normal reference range for the patient's age. In most laboratories, the lower limit of normal for MCV in adults is 80 fL. As is the case in macrocytic anemias (see Chapter 12–3), when microcytic anemia is acquired, MCV may appear normal during the early stages of the disease, particularly when the patient's initial MCV was in the upper normal range. Microcytosis may also occur in the absence of anemia. Frequently, the red cells in patients with microcytic anemia are also hypochromic. The total amount of hemoglobin (mean cell hemoglobin [MCH]) is decreased in microcytic red cells because of their decreased volume, but in addition there is also a decrease in the mean cell hemoglobin concentration (MCHC). Because of the frequent association of microcytosis with hypochromia, the term *microcytic hypochromic anemia* is frequently used to describe most anemias that are characterized by microcytic red cells.

ETIOLOGY

Microcytic hypochromic anemias result from several disorders in which there is a quantitative defect in hemoglobin synthesis. This can result either from deficiency of iron or its defective utilization or from a quantitative defect in hemoglobin synthesis, such as occurs in the tha-lassemias. There are some situations in which microcytosis may result from red cell membrane loss, in which there is no associated hypochromia. These conditions can be caused by mechanical or immune-mediated hemolytic mechanisms and may be congenital or acquired. Examples include traumatic hemolysis and hereditary spherocytosis, which are discussed in Chapter 12–6. In hereditary spherocytosis, the sphering that results from red cell membrane loss is frequently associated with *hyper*chromic red cells and an increased MCHC.

CRITERIA FOR DIAGNOSIS
Suggestive

The diagnosis of a microcytic anemia depends, ultimately, on the laboratory demonstration of microcytosis in a patient with anemia which prompts a search for the cause of the microcytic anemia. Microcytic anemias are far more common than macrocytic anemias because of the high prevalence of the three major causes of microcytic anemias, namely, iron deficiency anemia, the anemia of chronic disease, and thalassemia minor. This is particularly true of iron deficiency, which results from chronic blood loss, a disease more commonly encountered in certain target groups, and of thalassemia, which has a higher incidence in certain geographic areas. Consequently, iron deficiency anemia may be suspected in an individual with a history or suggestion of possible chronic blood loss (usually gastrointestinal or gynecologic) and whose blood smear shows hypochromic microcytic red cells. Alternatively, thalassemia minor may be suspected when microcytosis, with or without mild anemia, is discovered in a patient whose blood smear contains microcytes and target cells and who is of Mediterranean, African, or Asian descent. Finally, in patients with known or suspected underlying chronic infection, inflammatory disease, or cancer, the presence of anemia suggests that it may be caused by the anemia of chronic disease.

Definitive

Diagnosis of a specific cause of a microcytic anemia proceeds through a stepwise consideration of the patient's' clinical presentation and risk factors, strengthened or confirmed by appropriate clinical laboratory tests. These tests include the blood count with red cell indices as well as tests to confirm or exclude abnormalities in iron metabolism or thalassemia. In clear-cut cases, typical findings render diagnosis straightforward. For example, low serum ferritin and serum iron with high iron binding capacity in simple iron deficiency anemia; low serum iron with normal or raised ferritin and normal or lowered iron binding capacity in anemia of chronic disease; normal iron studies with raised hemoglobin A_2 and/or hemoglobin F in thalassemia minor. Often the picture is not so straightforward, however. Coexistence of more than one process (iron deficiency and chronic disease or iron deficiency and thalassemia minor) complicates the picture and renders diagnosis more difficult.

CLINICAL MANIFESTATIONS
Subjective

As with any anemia, patients with a microcytic anemia may complain of a variety of symptoms resulting from the hypoxemic effects of anemia. These include weakness, tiredness, fatigue, decreased exercise tolerance, palpitations, and shortness of breath. The severity of these symptoms depends on the rate of onset and progression of anemia. When anemia is caused by iron deficiency, the cause is usually pathologic blood loss either from the gastrointestinal tract or, in women, from gynecologic or previous obstetric causes. Subjective features of the underlying cause may be present, such as abdominal pain and discomfort relating to lesions at various levels of the gastrointestinal tract including hiatal hernia, peptic ulceration, inflammatory bowel disease, neoplasms, and hemorrhoids. There may be a history of ingestion of salicylates or other nonsteroidal antiinflammatory drugs. A history of frank gastrointestinal blood loss, including melena is unusual, gastrointestinal blood loss more frequently being occult. Women of childbearing age who develop iron deficiency anemia usually provide a history of epimenorrhagia.

Iron deficiency may have additional effects unrelated to, but difficult to distinguish from, those of anemia. The best recognized but least understood of these is pica, a perverted appetite for bizarre items like dirt, paper, chalk, ice, and other nonnutritious materials. Behavioral defects may occur in children, most notably learning disabilities associated with a diminished attention span. Complaints relating to food ingestion such as a painful tongue, cracked corners of the mouth, and dysphagia, reported previously in iron deficiency, are now quite rare.

In patients with the anemia of chronic disease, any of the myriad symptoms that may be associated with the underlying disorder may be present. Patients with thalassemia minor are usually asymptomatic.

Objective

Physical Examination

Physical signs and laboratory findings in microcytic hypochromic anemias vary with the severity of anemia and its underlying cause. In early, mild iron deficiency anemia, there may be no physical findings. As the anemia progresses, conjunctival and skin pallor become apparent. The patient may demonstrate tachycardia and tachypnea at rest. Occasionally, changes in the mucosal surface of the oral cavity may be evident in the form of the red, raw beefy tongue of glossitis or the split corners of the mouth of angular cheilosis. Spooning of the nails (koilonychia) is rarely seen. Slight splenomegaly is found in about 10% of patients.

Laboratory findings consist of anemia with microcytic and hypochromic red cell indices (lowered MCV, MCH, and MCHC). The red cell distribution width (RDW), a measure of anisocytosis, is elevated in iron deficiency anemia and the anemia of chronic disease, but in thalassemia minor, it is usually though not invariably normal. The leukocyte count is usually unremarkable except that in the anemia of chronic disease, it may be elevated, reflecting underlying infection or chronic inflammation. In both iron deficiency anemia and the anemia of chronic disease, the platelet count is usually elevated. In severe iron deficiency, however, thrombocytopenia may occur. Some modern automated blood counters that use light scatter to measure red cells provide a direct measurement of individual red cell hemoglobin content and concentration, both of which show early changes in iron deficiency.

Routine Laboratory Abnormalities

Microcytosis is usually quite evident in the blood smear (Color Plates 12–2–1 and 12–2–2, after page 826). Microcytic red cells have a diameter less than that of the nucleus of a small lymphocyte. Hypochromasia, in which the area of central pallor of the red cell exceeds two thirds of its diameter, may also become evident as the iron deficiency progresses. The red cells in iron deficiency anemia also show variations in size and shape, and elliptocytes are quite commonly seen. Target cells (Color Plate 12–2–3, after page 826) may also be seen, but are usually more prominent in thalassemia minor. In the majority of cases, iron deficiency anemia is associated with occult gastrointestinal blood loss which may be detected by guaiac testing of the stool for occult blood.

PLANS
Diagnostic
Differential Diagnosis

Iron deficiency anemia is not only the most common cause of microcytic hypochromic anemias, but is also the single most common cause of all anemias. It is important to confirm or exclude iron deficiency for several practical reasons. First, if iron deficiency is confirmed, then a cause must be established so that both the cause and the iron deficiency may be treated. Second, it is important to know when microcytic anemia is not due to iron deficiency to avoid unnecessary, unhelpful, and potentially harmful effects of iron administration to a non-iron-deficient individual. Other causes of microcytic hypochromic anemias include the common anemia of chronic disease and the thalassemia syndromes, as well as the uncommon congenital sideroblastic anemias. Presumptive differential diagnosis between these disorders can generally be accomplished by the use of blood count information and definitively, in most cases, by the use of various measurements of iron metabolic status, sometimes including stainable bone marrow iron and hemoglobin studies. The general algorithmic approach to a patient with a microcytic anemia is shown in Figure 12–2–1, and the typical test results to differentiate the major causes of microcytic hypochromic anemias are summarized in Tables 12–2–1 and 12–2–2. In general, red cell indices can be used to distinguish iron deficiency anemia from thalassemia minor (Table 12–2–1). For any particular level of anemia, the degree of microcytosis is generally more marked in thalassemia minor, whereas anisocytosis is mild or absent. Also, the red cell count in thalassemia minor is usually normal or may even be elevated. Differences in numerical values for MCV, RDW, and red cell count between thalassemia minor and iron deficiency anemia have been used, either singly or in combination in calculated red cell discriminant functions, to help in distinguishing iron deficiency anemia from thalassemia minor.

To distinguish iron deficiency anemia from the anemia of chronic disease, information from the blood count is generally not helpful and it is necessary to resort to measurements of iron status including serum iron, total iron binding capacity, transferrin saturation, erythrocyte protoporphyrin, and serum ferritin. A patient with typical iron deficiency anemia has a low serum iron with elevated total iron binding capacity resulting in low transferrin saturation. Red cell protoporphyrin is increased and serum ferritin low. The distinguishing features between iron deficiency and the anemia of chronic disease using these and other tests are summarized in Table 12–2–2. The single most helpful labora-

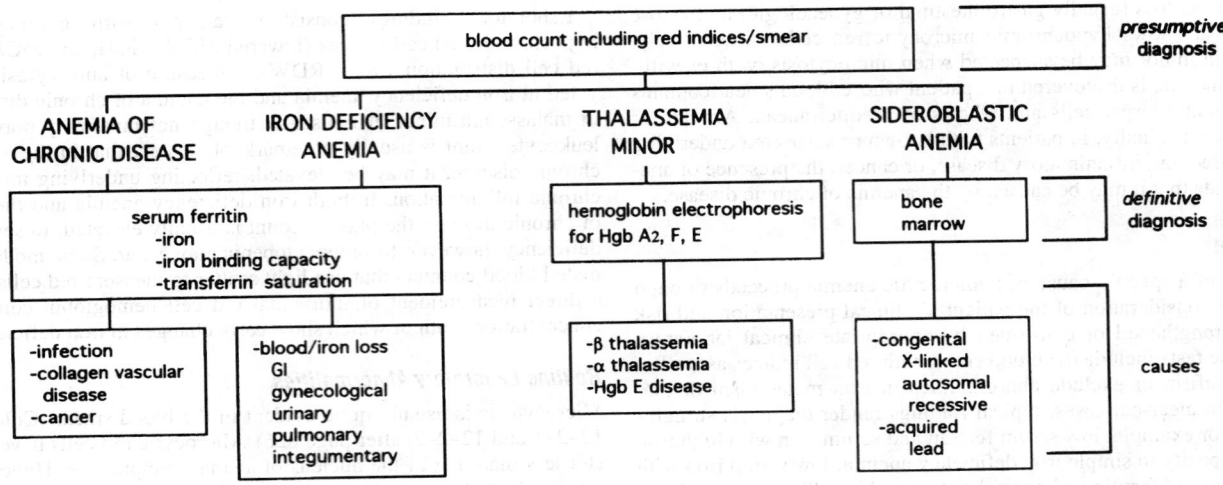

Figure 12-2-1. Simplified algorithmic-based plan for the diagnostic approach to a patient with microcytic hypochromic anemia.

tory test for distinguishing iron deficiency anemia from the anemia of chronic disease is the serum ferritin, which is generally greater than 50 μg/L in the anemia of chronic disease. Also useful is the plasma total iron binding capacity, which is decreased in the presence of inflammation.

It is usually possible to distinguish simple iron deficiency anemia from the anemia of chronic disease on the basis of these noninvasive tests, but it is sometimes necessary to resort to a bone marrow biopsy, in particular for assessing storage iron and its distribution. In iron deficiency, there is usually a mild to moderate increase in erythroid precursors. When iron deficiency is severe, erythroid elements may show cytoplasmic maturation defects including a reduction in volume, irregular borders, and vacuolization. It is the iron stain, however, that provides the most useful information. Iron is normally visible (blue by the Perl stain) in bone marrow histiocytes in the form of stainable hemosiderin granules. These range from fine and sparse to coarse and numerous, depending on the state of reticuloendothelial iron stores. Additionally, it is usually possible to discern occasional fine powdery blue granules in later nucleated erythroid precursors (normal sideroblasts). In iron deficiency, storage iron is absent and normal sideroblasts are markedly reduced or absent. By contrast, in the anemia of chronic disease, iron stores are present and often appear increased, although normal sideroblasts are, again, lacking. In the rare sideroblastic anemias, the iron

stain is the linchpin for diagnosis. Not only are the iron stores increased, but the iron granules in erythroid precursors are large and are conspicuous for partly or completely encircling the nucleus, giving rise to the term *ringed sideroblasts*.

The differential diagnosis of the common causes of microcytic anemias is rendered more difficult when two or more of the conditions coexist. In a practical sense, the most vexing and clinically important situations arise in patients with iron deficiency anemia who have a coexistent chronic disease or in patients with an underlying thalassemia minor who develop iron deficiency anemia. The effects of such coexisting disorders are listed in Tables 12-2-1 and 12-2-2.

In a patient with iron deficiency anemia, if the cause is not obvious, gastrointestinal blood loss should be suspected, and if confirmed by stool guiac testing, a lesion should be sought diligently with the help of radiologic and fundoscopic studies. In the vast majority of cases, iron deficiency is caused by gastrointestinal or uterine blood loss, but in rare situations iron deficiency may be caused by iron losses sustained through other sites and by other mechanisms (see Figure 12-2-1). Examples include urinary iron loss in the form of hemosiderin in paroxysmal nocturnal hemoglobinuria and other causes of chronic intravascular hemolysis or as transferrin-bound iron in the nephrotic syndrome. Urine hemosiderin, urine iron measurement, and other tests for paroxysmal nocturnal hemoglobinuria may be carried out as deemed appro-

TABLE 12-2-1. DIFFERENTIATION OF IRON DEFICIENCY ANEMIA FROM THALASSEMIA MINOR

	Iron Deficiency Anemia	Thalassemia Minor	Combined Thalassemia Minor and Iron Deficiency Anemia
Mean corpuscular volume	Low	Very low	Very low
Red cell distribution width	High	Normal or high	High
Red cell count	Low	Normal	Normal or low
Stainable marrow iron	Absent	Normal	Absent
Serum iron	Low	Normal	Low
Total iron binding capacity	High	Normal	High
Serum ferritin	Low	Normal	Low
Serum transferrin receptors	High	Normal	High
Hemoglobin A$_2$	Low	High*	Normal

*Hemoglobin A$_2$ is usually high in β-thalassemia minor. Hemoglobin F is increased in about 30% of individuals with β-thalassemia minor. Thalassemia minor caused by α-thalassemia can be detected by molecular biologic techniques (deletion of two α-globin genes).
Source: Green R. Disorders of inadequate iron. Hosp Pract 1991;26(suppl. 3):28. Reproduced with permission from the publisher and author.

TABLE 12-2-2. DIFFERENTIATION OF IRON DEFICIENCY ANEMIA FROM ANEMIA OF CHRONIC DISEASE

	Iron Deficiency Anemia	Anemia of Chronic Disease	Combined Iron Deficiency Anemia and Anemia of Chronic Disease
Stainable marrow iron	Absent	Normal or increased	Absent
Serum ferritin	Low	Normal or high*	Normal†
Serum iron	Low	Low	Low
Total iron binding capacity	High	Low	Low
Transferrin saturation index	Very low	Low	Low
Transferrin receptors	High	Normal	Not known
Serum ferritin	Low	Normal	Low
Mean corpuscular volume	Low	Low or normal	Low
Red cell distribution width	High	High or normal	High

*Usually >50 μg/L.
†Usually <50 μg/L.
Source: Green R. Disorders of inadequate iron. Hosp Pract 1991;26(suppl. 3):28. Reproduced with permission from the publisher and author.

TABLE 12–2–3. DIAGNOSIS OF THE THREE STAGES OF IRON DEFICIENCY

	Depletion of Iron Stores	Iron-Deficient Erythropoiesis	Iron Deficiency Anemia
Stainable marrow iron	Absent	Absent	Absent
Serum ferritin	Low	Low	Low
Transferrin saturation	Normal	High	Low
Free erythrocyte protoporphyrin	Normal	High	High
Transferrin receptors	Normal	High	High
Hemoglobin	Normal	Normal	High
Mean corpuscular volume	Normal	Normal	Low
Red cell distribution width	Normal	Normal	Low

Source: Green R. Disorders of inadequate iron. Hosp Pract 1991;26(suppl. 3):26. Reproduced with permission from the publisher and author.

priate. Protein-losing enteropathy, iron sequestration in the lungs in pulmonary hemosiderosis, and severe exfoliative dermatitis are extremely rare causes of iron deficiency. Rarely, microcytic hypochromic anemias may be the result of congenital sideroblastic anemia. This disorder may be suspected in children or young adults with a microcytic anemia characterized by the presence on the blood smear of pronounced anisocytosis and poikilocytosis, including minuscule hypochromic red cells and basophilic stippling. The hallmark of this condition, as mentioned above, is the presence, on a bone marrow iron stain, of "ringed" sideroblasts. In these patients there is a block in porphyrin synthesis or in iron incorporation into heme, which results in iron accumulation in bone marrow erythroid precursors, high serum iron and transferrin saturation, and increased iron stores with raised serum ferritin. Sideroblastic anemia may also occur in association with a variety of hematologic and other diseases including myelodysplasia, some of the symptomatic thalassemia syndromes, and following ingestion of certain drugs and toxins (e.g., lead, benzene, alcohol). In general, however, anemia in patients with acquired sideroblastic anemia is normocytic or macrocytic except in lead poisoning, in which some microcytosis is often present. As with the thalassemia syndromes, patients with hereditary sideroblastic anemia may provide a family history positive for these conditions.

Iron deficiency in younger female patients usually results from excessive menstrual blood loss, which is usually ascertainable by careful clinical history taking (duration of bleeding, number of pads or tampons, their saturation and the passage of clots). Uncommonly, such a history may not be elicited or there may be other grounds to doubt that menstrual blood losses can account for intractable or recurrent iron deficiency anemia. In such instances, when other potential avenues for pathologic blood or iron loss including paroxysmal nocturnal hemoglobinuria have been excluded, the possibility of factitious blood loss should be entertained. Self-inflicted blood loss is not easy to uncover. Perpetrators of this deception who may have knowledge and training in the health care field often go to great lengths to conceal their act. Indirect proof may be obtained that there is a source of blood loss by measuring radiochromium-tagged red cell survival. The finding of stepwise decrements in blood radioactivity provides strong presumptive evidence of blood loss, even though the site is obscure. Actual proof of factitious blood loss is usually impossible to obtain. Gentle suggestions or confrontations fail equally to elicit an admission. These patients may flit from one physician to another, leaving a trail of suspected but not proven diagnoses of self-inflicted blood loss.

Exceedingly rare patients with lack of transferrin (congenital atransferrinemia) or with defective cellular uptake of iron have been described.

Diagnostic Options

In a patient with a microcytic hypochromic anemia, careful scrutiny of the red cell indices usually discloses the likely presence of thalassemia minor. Microcytosis with a raised red cell count, pronounced microcytosis with only a mild degree of anemia, and little or no anisocytosis are pictures that suggest thalassemia minor. Microcytic erythrocytosis may

also be seen in a patient with iron-deficient polycythemia vera. If there is any uncertainty regarding the diagnosis of thalassemia minor, then a hemoglobin electrophoresis screen including quantitation of hemoglobin A_2 and F can be carried out. Hemoglobin A_2 is usually raised in β-thalassemia, except if there is concurrent iron deficiency or coexistent α- or δ-thalassemia. Hemoglobin F is raised in about one third of the patients with β-thalassemia. To confirm the presence of α-thalassemia, it is necessary to carry out DNA analysis to determine the α-globin genotype or to measure reticulocyte globin chain synthesis ratios. Detailed discussion of the diagnosis of the thalassemia syndromes may be found in Chapter 12–7.

Iron deficiency evolves through several stages, from iron stores depletion to iron-deficient erythropoiesis and, finally, to iron deficiency anemia (Table 12–2–3). The relative usefulness of the various tests to assess iron status depends on several considerations. No single test consistently provides sufficient information on which to base a diagnosis. Of all the available tests, however, the serum ferritin is probably the single most useful of the noninvasive tests. Low serum ferritin signals depletion of the body iron stores, the very earliest stage of evolving iron deficiency. Unlike the serum iron, the serum ferritin is uninfluenced by time of day or recent food intake. The finding of a low serum ferritin is also highly specific for iron deficiency compared with low serum iron, which can occur even when iron stores are increased but are not being released. For detection of iron-deficient erythropoiesis, which precedes the development of frank iron deficiency anemia, it is necessary to demonstrate decreased transferrin saturation, increased total iron binding capacity, or increased red cell protoporphyrin in addition to lowered serum ferritin. Several of these tests are also useful for distinguishing iron deficiency anemia from the anemia of chronic disease as shown in Table 12–2–2. The single least reliable test is the serum iron, as it cannot be used to distinguish iron deficiency anemia from the anemia of chronic disease and, also, because it is prone to marked circadian variation as well as being influenced by recent dietary intake of iron. It is therefore inadvisable to make diagnostic decisions that are based on single determinations of serum iron.

Recommended Approach

In a patient with a microcytic anemia, I try to make a presumptive diagnosis of iron deficiency anemia, anemia of chronic disease, or thalassemia minor based on the subjective and objective clinical findings, and I then order other confirmatory tests as appropriate (Figure 12–2–1). The red cell indices can be quite helpful for distinguishing iron deficiency and the anemia of chronic disease, on the one hand, from thalassemia minor, on the other. MCV and RDW tend to be lower and red cell count higher in thalassemia. I make use of these differences in the form of a discriminant function, $MCV^2 \times RDW/hemoglobin$ $(g/dL) \times 100$. In our laboratory, a numerical value for this term of 73 or greater is indicative of iron deficiency (or anemia of chronic disease); a value less than 73 is compatible with thalassemia minor. Slight adjustments to this cutoff need to be made depending on the type and calibration of the automated blood counter. If I feel reasonably certain that the patient does not have thalassemia minor, or if I strongly suspect, on clinical grounds, that the patient may have iron deficiency anemia, then I measure the serum ferritin concentration, and if this is below normal, then I proceed with the further investigation of the cause of iron deficiency and its treatment.

If the serum ferritin concentration is normal or elevated, I order the serum iron and binding capacity from which the transferrin saturation may be calculated. These tests usually enable me to distinguish between iron deficiency anemia and the anemia of chronic disease. If the results of these tests are equivocal and I cannot resolve the issue, then I do a bone marrow biopsy with an iron stain. I also obtain a bone marrow examination in patients whose anemia persists following treatment and who do not have continuing or demonstrable gastrointestinal blood loss.

Therapeutic

The critical question in a patient with a microcytic hypochromic anemia is whether there is iron deficiency, because this determines whether the patient should be treated with iron. The objectives of iron replacement therapy are to correct the anemia and to reinstate some normal quantity of iron stores without causing undesirable side effects. Oral iron is safer than parenteral iron. Regarding form and dosage of the oral iron preparation, the considerations of relative cost, efficacy, and rate of repletion of iron should be taken into account. On balance, ferrous sulfate is the preferred form, with a total dose of 100 to 300 mg iron daily, administered in three divided doses. Iron absorption is more efficient when tablets are taken on an empty stomach, but the trade-off is a higher frequency and severity of gastrointestinal side effects. Because the efficiency of absorption of iron salts may be reduced to less than 20% by certain foods, it is better for the patient to take lower doses on an empty stomach, providing this can be tolerated.

The dose of iron may be adjusted up or down depending on the occurrence and severity of side effects. Side effects, when they occur, are predominantly gastrointestinal and include dyspeptic symptoms of heartburn, nausea, and upper abdominal discomfort as well as troublesome changes in bowel habits, either constipation or diarrhea. There is evidence to suggest that these symptoms can have an organic basis or may be psychological. For example, although some patients receiving placebo iron tablets experience gastrointestinal intolerance, other studies show that escalating doses of iron are associated with a higher rate of untoward effects. The upper gastrointestinal problems are believed to be related to direct irritation by the iron compound, whereas changes in stool frequency are probably secondary to the effects of iron on intestinal bacterial flora.

Although numerous alternative formulations of iron have been heavily promoted by the pharmaceutical industry, few have been shown to be absorbed more efficiently than ferrous sulfate, and when the added cost of alternative preparations is taken into account, there is little justification for using anything other than ferrous sulfate. Ferrous succinate and ferrous ascorbate are certainly absorbed more efficiently than ferrous sulfate. The reason for the enhanced absorption of the succinate salt, which is absorbed about 30% better than ferrous sulfate, is obscure. On the other hand, ascorbic acid is know to maintain iron in the reduced, ferrous state as well as to form a soluble complex with the iron. Reduction and solubility are two key luminal factors that are known to enhance iron absorption. The increment in efficiency of iron absorption usually comes with a double cost—more money and more side effects.

On the other side of the coin are those iron preparations for which it is claimed that there are fewer side effects. Various nostrums are marketed in which clever strategies are employed such as enteric-coating and sustained-release preparations. Even if they work to reduce side effects, these too have a double cost—more money and reduced efficiency of absorption. The site of maximum iron absorption is the upper small intestine. Delivery of the iron to lower sites is of little or no avail.

Although there are ample grounds for skepticism about expensive, alternative novel iron formulations, I do not totally dismiss their use. Because of the psychological component of side effects, when these become troublesome it is justifiable to administer a different iron preparation together with a strong dose of suggestion that the symptoms may be ameliorated. If this strategy does not at first succeed, then it may be worth trying a second or even a third iron formulation. If the side effects persist, and are intolerable to the patient, then desist from oral iron therapy.

Another facet of therapy concerns the adequacy of response to iron replacement. Several factors influence response, including the severity of the anemia, the persistence of the underlying cause (bleeding), the coexistence of other causes of anemia (e.g., infection), and the efficiency of absorption of the administered iron. Response to therapy usually begins on the third to fourth day after treatment although the peak reticulocyte count usually occurs only on the sixth or seventh day of treatment. An adequate response to therapy consists of a daily rise in hemoglobin concentration of 0.1 to 0.2g/dL starting on day 4 (or 2 g/dL or more over a 3-week period). Depending on the initial hemoglobin level, recovery is usually complete within 8 to 12 weeks. Failure to meet these benchmarks usually implies one of the following possibilities: (1) an incorrect initial diagnosis; (2) persistent blood loss; (3) coexistent other disease, most often infection or some other cause of anemia of chronic disease; (4) patient noncompliance or failure to absorb the particular oral iron preparation; (5) actual malabsorption of iron,

(although rare, this must also be considered as a possible cause of failure of oral iron therapy). Attention should be paid to each of these possibilities and suitable steps taken to elucidate or correct them in the event of failure to respond to treatment with oral iron.

The response to treatment with oral iron also represents a means to confirm the diagnosis and a therapeutic trial is indeed sometimes used for that purpose when the diagnosis is in doubt.

Wherever possible, oral iron is preferable to parenteral iron because of serious potential risks associated with injection of iron. These range from potentially fatal anaphylactic reactions to skin discoloration. The only approved form of injectable iron in the United States is iron dextran.

Indications for parenteral iron include some of the causes of failure to respond to oral iron such as poor compliance, severe gastrointestinal intolerance, malabsorption, and persistent uncontrolled blood loss. There is also a need to rapidly correct the iron status of patients with severe anemia, as in patients requiring surgery or in late pregnancy when intravenous iron may be administered. Parenteral iron may also be indicated in patients with inflammatory bowel disease in whom oral iron preparations may exacerbate symptoms and in some patients with anemia of chronic disease such as rheumatoid arthritis, in whom there is some evidence to suggest that parenteral iron may partially overcome the reticuloendothelial block in iron utilization and also because these patients may have decreased iron absorption. When parenteral iron is given (intramuscular or intravenous), the dose should be obtained from the estimated iron deficit. This is calculated as iron deficit (mg) = [15 − patient's hemoglobin (g/dL) × body weight (kg) × 3]. A test dose of 0.5 mL should be administered in case of possible anaphylaxis.

Although strictly speaking not a side effect of treatment, acute iron poisoning should be mentioned in the context of the use of oral iron therapy, because the widespread use of oral iron preparations is inevitably tied to its intentional and accidental misuse. Iron poisoning remains one of the most common causes of accidental poisoning in young children and also features prominently as a cause of attempted suicide in young women. Depending on age, and the form of the iron, lethal doses may range from 1 to 10 g.

The indications for blood transfusion to treat severe iron deficiency anemia should be restricted to dire emergencies, considering the major risks associated with transfusion and the ultimate efficacy of iron preparations. Therefore, only if bleeding is severe and uncontrollable or if a patient requires lifesaving surgery is it necessary to treat iron deficiency anemia with blood transfusion.

Other major causes of microcytic hypochromic anemia are either not amenable to specific treatment, in the case of the anemia of chronic disease, or do not require treatment, in the case of thalassemia minor. There are reports of some patients with anemia of chronic disease responding to administration of recombinant human erythropoietin or to parenteral iron. Generally, however, a response is elicited only if the underlying cause can be treated effectively.

Some patients with congenital sideroblastic anemia respond to the administration of high doses of pyridoxine by mouth. When this diagnosis is made, a trial of pyridoxine (100 mg daily) should be administered and the patient monitored for a reticulocyte and hemoglobin response while other forms of treatment, including transfusion, are withheld.

FOLLOW-UP

There are several aspects to the follow-up of patients found to have and treated for iron deficiency anemia. First, it is very important to impress on the patient the need to take iron. Then, following the institution of iron replacement therapy, it is important to ensure that the hemoglobin returns to normal and is maintained. A suboptimal or incomplete response to treatment or a recurrence of the microcytic anemia indicates that there is either a persistence or a recurrence of the underlying cause, usually blood loss, or that there is some other complicating cause of anemia. The patient's response to treatment should be monitored every 2 weeks for up to 8 to 12 weeks after initiation of iron treatment.

Following treatment with iron, recovery usually, but not always, confirms that the anemia was caused by iron deficiency. Exceptions occur, such as in patients undergoing spontaneous remission from the anemia of chronic disease caused by infection or a self-limiting collagen–vascular disease (e.g., temporal arteritis).

Patients with thalassemia minor should be made aware that their red cells are smaller than normal. Accordingly, before they follow any recommendations to receive iron therapy in the future, they should make sure that adequate steps are taken to confirm that they do, in fact, have iron deficiency.

The duration of treatment with iron depends on its initial severity as well as assessment of the risk of persisting negative iron balance in a particular patient. This depends on such variables as age, diet, and the possible presence of chronic factors predisposing to gastrointestinal or menstrual blood loss. In general, 6 months of treatment with oral iron is sufficient to replace the red cell deficit and to replenish normal iron storage reserves. Excessive treatment with iron should be avoided, as there is considerable and mounting evidence to suggest that redundant intracellular iron may be harmful. It is also a consideration that unnecessarily large iron reserves may allow a patient to sustain longer periods of chronic blood loss, thus postponing the diagnosis of an underlying condition that might otherwise have been revealed through the development of a microcytic anemia.

DISCUSSION

Prevalence and Incidence

Iron deficiency is the single most important cause of anemia throughout the world. The incidence is highest in the tropics as a result of hookworm and other parasitic infestation and because of the generally lower bioavailability of dietary iron in developing countries. Age and sex are the other important determinants of susceptibility to iron deficiency. Several estimates of the prevalence of iron deficiency have been reported from different parts of the world. In the United States a series of detailed surveys have been carried out during the past three decades. The National Health and Nutrition Examination Survey (NHANES), now in its third iteration, includes an assessment of iron status among representative age and gender samples of the population. These and other surveys have provided similar estimates of the prevalence of iron deficiency in various demographic groups. Depletion of iron stores, assessed through lowered plasma ferritin levels, precedes and is more common than frank iron deficiency anemia.

Groups particularly susceptible to iron deficiency include infants and young children, adolescents, women of childbearing age, particularly during pregnancy, and the elderly. Socioeconomic factors including dietary factors also play a role so that even within demographic groups, prevalence of iron deficiency varies. Premature infants and those fed cow's milk are more susceptible to iron deficiency. Estimates of the prevalence of iron stores depletion and iron deficiency anemia vary widely in different pediatric populations, sometimes affecting more than 50% of the survey population. The prevalence of iron deficiency among women during their reproductive years varies from about 5 to 20% as assessed by plasma ferritin values, but generally, less than half of these individuals are anemic. During pregnancy, the occurrence of iron deficiency is directly related to standards of nutrition and prenatal health care so that estimates vary widely, from 10 to 60%. Among the elderly, the common occurrence of gastrointestinal blood loss in both sexes, together with suboptimal dietary intake, contributes to an overall prevalence of iron deficiency of approximately 5%, half of whom have associated anemia. Adult men are least susceptible to iron deficiency anemia. In the United States, around 3% of this group are iron deficient and only about 1% actually have anemia.

The overall incidence of iron deficiency anemia has been lowered in the United States and other countries that practice food iron fortification.

Related Basic Science

The principal manifestations of iron deficiency result from anemia, which is caused by an inadequate supply of iron required for normal hemoglobin synthesis. Two thirds of the 3–4 g of total iron normally present in an adult are contained within maturing and circulating erythroid cells. The remainder is widely distributed, usually in association with proteins that either require iron for their function or are concerned with the regulation, transport, or storage of this essential element. In the former category are hemoglobin, myoglobin, and other heme-containing proteins and enzymes, as well as nonheme iron-requiring enzymes such as aconitase and ribonucleotide reductase. The two major storage forms of iron are ferritin and hemosiderin. Plasma transport and cellular uptake of iron depend on the plasma iron-binding protein transferrin and its specific cellular receptor. Each single polypeptide molecule of transferrin has two iron binding sites and when one or both are occupied, transferrin binds with high affinity to the transferrin receptor, present more abundantly on the surface of erythroid precursors. Once engaged, the receptor internalizes transferrin by endocytosis and iron is released from transferrin at the lower pH within the endocytic vesicle. The transferrin receptor, still clasping transferrin, is recycled to the cell surface in a reversal of endocytosis, and transferrin devoid of iron is returned to the plasma.

The amount of iron present in the plasma represents less than one-thousandth of the total body iron, yet its turnover is rapid. External iron exchange is relatively small, excretion being normally limited to obligatory daily losses that average 1 mg in adult men and 2 mg in women of reproductive age.

Endogenous and exogenous mechanisms are involved in regulating iron absorption. The major endogenous factors are the size of the body iron store and the rate of erythroid marrow activity. Absorption, attuned to body iron needs, is inversely related to the amount in stores. When stores are depleted, absorption increases, and when stores are increased, absorption is diminished. To a lesser extent, absorption is also influenced by the rate of erythropoiesis; it is increased following blood loss or acute hemolysis, and decreased when erythropoiesis is suppressed following transfusion or in aplastic conditions of the bone marrow. The effect of erythroid activity on iron absorption is, however, inconsistent; absorption is increased in conditions like thalassemia and sideroblastic anemia, but generally not in the membrane and enzyme-related congenital hemolytic anemias like hereditary spherocytosis and glucose-6-phosphate dehydrogenase deficiency. In general, conditions characterized by ineffective erythropoiesis are associated with enhanced iron absorption.

It is unknown how signals relating to the size of the body iron store or the rate of activity of the erythroid bone marrow are translated into altered absorption in the intestinal mucosa. Earlier studies assigned a regulatory role to ferritin in the mucosal cell. More recently, a variety of intestinal iron-binding proteins in addition to transferrin and ferritin have been identified and studied, but no unifying hypothesis for the role of these proteins has been proposed.

There is evidence that cellular iron metabolism is controlled at the level of the mRNAs for ferritin and the transferrin receptor. Regulation of the rate of synthesis of these proteins occurs through a factor known as the iron-regulatory protein (IRP) which can bind to specific nucleotide sequences or iron response elements (IREs) in the untranslated regions of the mRNAs for ferritin and the transferrin receptor. When cellular iron levels are low, IRP binds tightly to both IREs. The effects, however, are reciprocal. In the case of ferritin mRNA, the IRE is in the 5′ untranslated region and translation is blocked. With the transferrin receptor, IRP binds in the 3′ untranslated region, which stabilizes the mRNA. Consequently, transferrin receptor levels will be increased but ferritin levels will be diminished, a situation favoring iron capture from the environment. Conversely, when intracellular iron levels are high, the affinity of IRP for IRE is lowered, and ferritin mRNA translation is allowed to occur, while transferrin receptor mRNA is destabilized. This situation diminishes iron uptake and promotes storage. The discovery of this control mechanism has provided important insights into the regulation of iron metabolism. The IRE–IRP system is also linked to the control of erythropoiesis through the enzyme δ-aminolevulinate synthase, and may turn out to be involved in the regulation of iron absorption.

The exogenous factors that influence iron absorption include the form of dietary iron, the presence of substances in the diet that influence iron absorption, and other intraluminal factors such as pH. In general, heme iron (derived from animal foods) is better absorbed than nonheme or inorganic iron (derived from plant sources), which is much more strongly influenced by dietary composition. The bioavailability of food iron is affected by many factors and conditions. Overall, the absorption of food iron in an individual with normal iron stores is generally less than 10%. The typical daily Western diet contains 15 to 20 mg iron, of which 1 to 2 mg must be absorbed to maintain iron balance, depending on sex. Women are doubly disadvantaged because not only is their daily requirement greater but their food intake is less. Iron intake is closely related to caloric intake, being approximately 6 mg/1000 kcal. Factors known to enhance iron absorption include citric, malic, and tartaric acids present in fruits, fructose, and other sugars and certain amino acids. In general, these factors improve the solubility of iron and/or reduce it from the ferric to the more soluble ferrous form. They may also form soluble complexes with iron. Alcohol also enhances iron absorption through a number of possible mechanisms such as the stimulation of gastric acid production and the presence of lactate in beer and other fermented beverages. Meat not only contains heme iron that is better absorbed than nonheme iron, but also has been shown to enhance the absorption of iron from nonheme sources. This property has been attributed to the cysteine content of meat proteins. Factors that reduce iron absorption include polyphosphates, phytates, and fiber present in plant foods as well as tannins and other plant polyphenols found in tea and red wines. These compounds either render iron insoluble or form chelates that are poorly absorbed.

Apart from anemia with its consequent hypoxia, other deleterious effects of iron deficiency anemia are also described. It is not known exactly how the nonhematologic complications of iron deficiency arise, but they are presumed to be related to the cofactor requirements for iron of several reactions involved in DNA synthesis, electron transport, and catecholamine metabolism. There is convincing evidence that links iron deficiency with impairment of physical work performance, cognitive functions, and immunity. In addition, immune tolerance may also be impaired in iron deficiency. Work performance of iron-deficient subjects and experimental animals is compromised, and in animals this can be reversed by iron administration, independently of the correction of anemia. Iron deficiency is associated with cognitive defects in young children, including behavioral problems and learning disabilities. The relationship between iron and infection is complex and controversial. On the one hand, excessive amounts of iron can predispose to certain infections, particularly in immunocompromised individuals. On the other hand, iron deficiency can result in impairment of cell-mediated immune functions, including superoxide-mediated bacterial killing in phagocytic cells and interference with T-lymphocyte function.

Excessive iron is also associated with deleterious effects. In hereditary hemochromatosis and other forms of iron overload, progressive accumulation of iron results in organ damage including cardiac failure, cirrhosis, multiple endocrine dysfunction including diabetes and hypogonadism, and arthropathy. The harmful effects of iron are believed to result from the generation of free radicals. Evidence is now mounting that these harmful effects of iron may not be restricted only to situations in which iron is present in vast excess. Several studies have shown that there is an increased odds ratio for development of heart disease and cancer among individuals with higher iron stores, even within the range considered to be normal. Although not all studies have confirmed this association, because it is possible that there may be an increased risk of neoplasia as well as cardiovascular and other degenerative diseases in individuals with higher iron stores, iron supplements should be administered judiciously, only where indicated, and only for as long as is necessary to correct the deficiency.

Natural History and Its Modification with Treatment

Iron deficiency anemia results from imbalance between absorption and loss. Except among malnourished populations or those subsisting on predominantly vegetarian diets, the cause of deficiency is usually pathologic blood loss, which is frequently occult and may go unnoticed until iron deficiency anemia develops. In this typical situation, anemia occurs only after iron stores have become depleted. During the stage of iron-deficient erythropoiesis, which immediately precedes frank iron deficiency anemia, vague subjective complaints related to tissue iron deficiency may occur, such as reduced exercise tolerance. At this early

stage, objective evidence of iron deficiency is limited to abnormal laboratory tests of iron status (Table 12–2–3).

Once the state of iron deficiency has been recognized, and its cause identified, iron replacement can be instituted and the iron deficiency corrected. A sense of improved well-being is associated with, but may precede, correction of the anemia. This could, in part, be related to amelioration of tissue iron deficiency. When the cause of iron deficiency is blood loss, providing the underlying cause can be corrected, iron deficiency should not recur; however, when nutritional factors play a major role, as is the case in developing countries, iron deficiency may frequently recur.

Prevention

Preventive measures to avoid iron deficiency can be carried out to a limited extent in target groups. For example, prolonged bottle feeding of infants with cow's milk should be discouraged. For reasons of cost and logistics, it is unfortunately not possible to implement widespread public health measures designed to improve the diet or to eradicate hookworm and other intestinal parasitic diseases in those parts of the world most afflicted by iron deficiency anemia. In practical terms, therefore, iron deficiency and its accompanying anemia can be prevented only by iron supplementation or by fortification. Supplementation with an oral iron preparation is directed to specific target groups such as pregnant women and infants. In this setting, motivation is generally high and compliance good. For other segments of the population, however, compliance is poor.

Because of the widespread prevalence of iron deficiency, with or without anemia, and its potential effects on health and productivity, the alternative strategy of food iron fortification has been implemented in some countries, including the United States. To be effective, the iron compound must have good bioavailability, and the chosen food vehicle for fortification should be a staple item of diet, which is consumed by the population at large and by target groups in particular. The appearance and palatability of food should not be compromised. Unfortunately, in countries where it is most needed, centralized facilities to prepare, distribute, and monitor fortification are lacking. Most evidence suggests that iron fortification programs have been safe and effective; however, there is a substantial risk of iron fortification to those segments of the population who have iron-loading diseases, including hereditary hemochromatosis and thalassemia major. Furthermore, with mounting evidence of the possible deleterious effects of higher iron levels, the risk:benefit ratio of iron fortification programs will probably grow.

Cost Containment

Three measures can be directed toward cost containment for the diagnosis and treatment of iron deficiency anemia. First, laboratory tests should be limited, wherever possible. Laboratory test utilization should be restricted to what is necessary for making or excluding the diagnosis of a cause of microcytic hypochromic anemia, as outlined in Tables 12–2–1 and 12–2–2 and in Figure 12–2–1. If a patient does not respond to oral iron, then noncompliance should be considered before expensive tests for rare disorders are undertaken. Second, simple, inexpensive iron medication, usually ferrous sulfate, should be used whenever possible. Third, unnecessary and unduly prolonged iron treatment should be avoided. This practice is not only potentially harmful, but is also wasteful.

REFERENCES

Ascherio A, Willett WC, Rimm EB, et al. Dietary iron intake and risk of coronary disease among men. Circulation 1994;89:969.

Baynes RD, Bothwell TH. Iron deficiency. Annu Rev Nutr 1990;10:133.

Casey JL, Hentze MW, Koeller DM, et al. Iron-responsive elements: Regulatory RNA sequences that control mRNA levels and translation. Science 1988;240:924.

Dallman PR. Biochemical basis for the manifestations of iron deficiency. Annu Rev Nutr 1986;6:13.

Dallman P. Iron deficiency: Does it matter? J Intern Med 1989;226:367.

DeMaeyer E, Adiels-Tegman M. The prevalence of anaemia in the world. World Health Statist 1985;38:302.

Green R. Disorders of inadequate iron. Hosp Pract 1991;26(suppl. 3):25.

Green R, King R. A new red cell discriminant incorporating volume disperson for differentiating iron deficiency anemia from thalassemia minor. Blood Cells 1989;15:481.

Skikne BS, Flowers CH, Cook JD. Serum transferrin receptor: A quantitative measure of tissue iron deficiency. Blood 1990;75:1870.

CHAPTER 12–3

Macrocytic Anemias

Ralph Green, M.B., B.Ch., M.D.

DEFINITION

For purposes of diagnosis, it is convenient to classify anemias according to the mean volume of individual red cells (mean cell volume [MCV]). A macrocytic anemia is any anemia in which the MCV exceeds the normal reference range for the patient's age. In most laboratories, the upper limit of normal for MCV is 100 fL. It is important to bear in mind that in the early stages of an anemia, because of the 120-day life span of red cells, MCV may be normal, even when there is an underlying disease process that ultimately will result in a macrocytic anemia. Furthermore, in a given patient with anemia, the initial "normal" MCV for that individual affects the time lag between onset of disease and appearance of macrocytosis. Macrocytosis may occur in the absence of anemia.

ETIOLOGY

Macrocytic anemia can result from several conditions that cause an abnormality of DNA synthesis in blood cell precursors in the bone marrow (megaloblastic anemia). The most commonly encountered causes of megaloblastic macrocytic anemia are deficiencies of either folic acid or vitamin B_{12}.* Macrocytic anemia may also occur in association with a variety of hematologic and systemic diseases and without any apparent defect in DNA synthesis (nonmegaloblastic macrocytic anemias). The several causes of megaloblastic and nonmegaloblastic macrocytic anemias are listed in Table 12–3–1. In general, greater degrees of macrocytosis (MCV > 110 fL) are more likely to be the result of a megaloblastic rather than nonmegaloblastic macrocytic anemia. The converse, however, does not hold. Anemia associated with only a slight or modest degree of macrocytosis is quite frequently present in folate or vitamin B_{12} deficiency, particularly, but not exclusively, during the early stages of the deficiency.

CRITERIA FOR DIAGNOSIS
Suggestive

The diagnosis of macrocytic anemia is definitional and proceeds in three steps: first, the diagnosis of anemia; second the determination that anemia is macrocytic; third, the establishment of a cause for the macrocytic anemia. The diagnosis of some of the more common specific causes of macrocytic anemias, for example pernicious anemia, may be suggested in a patient with a macrocytic anemia who has neurologic problems, a sore tongue, or gastrointestinal complaints and whose blood smear contains hypersegmented neutrophils.

Definitive

The diagnosis of a specific cause of a macrocytic anemia is confirmed by clinical laboratory tests including morphologic appearances of the blood and bone marrow, which make it possible to differentiate megaloblastic from nonmegaloblastic macrocytic anemia and by which it

may be possible to identify particular underlying disease. Again, using the example of pernicious anemia, a definitive diagnosis can be made by the finding of a low serum vitamin B_{12} level or a raised serum or urine level of methylmalonate followed by the demonstration of serum antibodies to intrinsic factor or an abnormal Schilling's urinary excretion test corrected by the oral administration of intrinsic factor. Other specific examples are discussed below.

CLINICAL MANIFESTATIONS
Subjective

Patients with a macrocytic anemia, regardless of its cause, may complain of any of the common symptoms of anemia of gradual onset such as lack of energy, diminished exercise tolerance, weakness, tiredness, dyspnea, and palpitations. In addition, patients with either folate or vitamin B_{12} deficiency, and in particular those who owe their deficiency of these vitamins to malabsorption, may give a history of various gastrointestinal complaints including sore tongue, anorexia, dyspepsia including flatulence and disturbances in bowel habits, particularly constipation. Neurologic symptoms are present in more than 75% of patients with vitamin B_{12} deficiency and may be the predominant or the only manifestations in approximately 25% of such patients. These symptoms, usually slow in onset, include paresthesias and other sensory as well as motor disturbances. Less commonly there may be cognitive changes ranging from memory loss and disorientation to frank dementia and disturbances of affect including irritability, mood swings, and depression. Other symptoms, such as insomnia, visual disturbances, impotency, and autonomic disturbances, may also occur. In patients with a macrocytic anemia caused by folate deficiency, on the other hand, apart from depression, neurologic complaints are rare. A patient with a macrocytic anemia caused by one of the conditions listed in Table 12–3–1, such as liver disease or hypothyroidism, may also experience the symptoms associated with these underlying illnesses.

Patients with the autoimmune disease pernicious anemia may have other associated autoimmune diseases, notably those involving functional disorders of the thyroid or other endocrine glands, myasthenia gravis, adult-onset diabetes, and vitiligo. These patients may also manifest the features of the associated autoimmune disorder in their past medical history. In addition, there is a strong genetic component in susceptibility to pernicious anemia and its associated autoimmune diseases so that a family history of these illnesses is often present.

TABLE 12–3–1. PATHOLOGIC CAUSES OF MACROCYTIC ANEMIAS

Nonmegaloblastic	Megaloblastic
Raised reticulocyte count	Folate deficiency
Alcohol	Cobalamin deficiency
Liver disease	Drugs
Myelodysplasia	Inborn errors of metabolism
Aplastic anemia	
Hypothyroidism	

Source: Green R. The diagnostic approach to macrocytic anemias. Sangre 1993;38(suppl. 2):40. Reproduced with permission from the publisher and author.

---

*In keeping with widespread use in the medical literature, the term vitamin B_{12} is used in this chapter to refer, generically, to cobalamin and all its congeners. In the recommended biochemical nomenclature, vitamin B_{12} should refer only to cyanocobalamin.

Objective

Physical Examination

The objective manifestation of anemia, regardless of its cause, is pallor. Apart from pallor, physical findings in a patient with a macrocytic anemia depend on the underlying cause of the macrocytic process. Patients with megaloblastic anemia often have mild degrees of jaundice because of hemolysis. Together with the marked pallor that may be present, the patient's skin may have a peculiar "lemon-yellow" hue. In general, in megaloblastic macrocytic anemia, diminished cell production is not restricted to the red cell series because the underlying defect in DNA synthesis affects other bone marrow elements as well. Patients may therefore present with petechiae or purpura resulting from a low platelet count and may have fever or other signs of infection resulting from neutropenia.

A variety of epithelial changes may occur in vitamin B_{12} and folate deficiency. Pernicious anemia patients also often show premature graying of the hair and about 20% have a smooth tongue caused by papillary atrophy; there is patchy skin hyperpigmentation in about 10% of patients. Patients with pernicious anemia may have hypopigmentation caused by associated vitiligo.

Neurologic changes are the most prominent objective organ system manifestations associated with megaloblastic anemia when the anemia is caused by vitamin B_{12} deficiency; only rarely do these occur in folic acid deficiency. In vitamin B_{12} deficiency neurologic findings are not only frequent (75–90%), but may also be the first manifestations of the deficiency (25%). It is being increasingly recognized that neurologic changes may be the most prominent or the *only* clinical manifestations of vitamin B_{12} deficiency. The more classic findings consist of both sensory and motor problems ("combined system disease"), most frequently in the lower extremities. These are related to the pathologic changes of demyelination affecting the long posterior and lateral columns of the white matter in the spinal cord that have been described in early reports of patients dying with untreated pernicious anemia. Neurologic findings include a variety of sensory deficits, most prominent of which are position and vibration sense loss. The former is associated with ataxia, Romberg's sign, and abnormalities of gait. Vibration sensory loss first becomes apparent in the ankles and later extends toward the trunk. It is most reliably elicited with a 256/s frequency tuning fork. Less frequently, deficits in other sensory modalities may also be elicited. These include light touch, pin-prick and deep pain, pressure, and temperature. Cranial nerve involvement is rare. A variety of other neurologic findings have been reported in vitamin B_{12} deficiency, including cognitive deficits shown by psychological testing and visual field defects. Given the prevalence of vascular and other neurodegenerative diseases that occur among the elderly, caution should be exercised before attributing impairments of mentation to vitamin B_{12} deficiency. Objective improvement in neurologic abnormalities following treatment with vitamin B_{12} provides after-the-fact evidence that the abnormalities were attributable to the deficiency.

Routine Laboratory Abnormalities

Laboratory findings consist of anemia with macrocytic red cell indices (raised MCV and MCH), and with the possible exceptions of macrocytosis associated with liver disease and alcohol abuse, a raised red cell distribution width (RDW), reflecting the presence of anisocytosis. In megaloblastic macrocytic anemia, some degree of neutropenia and/or thrombocytopenia is often also present and, typically, the blood smear contains oval macrocytes and teardrop forms as well as other abnormally shaped red cells. The number of nuclear lobes in neutrophil polymorphonuclear leukocytes (PMNs) is increased and cells with five or more lobes (hypersegmented PMNs) are conspicuous (Color Plate 12–3–1, after page 826). This feature is reported to be the earliest morphologic change to appear in the blood in megaloblastic anemia as well as the last to disappear after treatment. Performing an actual lobe count is laborious, but the presence of more than 5% PMNs with 5 lobes (the "rule of fives") or the presence of even one PMN with more than five lobes represents good presumptive evidence of an underlying megaloblastic process.

In patients with megaloblastic anemia, serum levels of lactic dehydrogenase (isoenzyme LDH-I) are almost invariably raised, and there is a mild elevation of unconjugated bilirubin. Both are caused by a combination of hemolysis and ineffective hematopoiesis. The ineffective erythropoiesis is also responsible for impaired iron utilization, which results in raised levels of serum iron and ferritin, regardless of the patient's underlying iron status.

PLANS

Diagnostic

Differential Diagnosis

Deficiency of folic acid or vitamin B_{12} is the most commonly encountered cause of macrocytic and megaloblastic anemia and, being a deficiency disease, is treatable and usually correctable. Depending on the features in a given patient at presentation, however, other causes of macrocytic anemia, megaloblastic anemia, or pancytopenia should be considered in the differential diagnosis. Thus, after vitamin B_{12} and folic acid deficiencies have been excluded on the basis of assays of these vitamins in the blood and on the basis of serum methylmalonic acid and homocysteine levels, then other causes of macrocytic anemias should be considered. In the absence of megaloblastic changes in the blood or bone marrow, the several other causes of macrocytosis should be excluded on the basis of appropriate testing. The reticulocyte count should be determined to exclude hemolysis or recent acute blood loss and thyroid and liver function tests should be done to exclude those systemic diseases. In a patient with macrocytic anemia that is associated with other cytopenias, it is important to exclude the myelodysplastic syndromes, acute leukemia, aplastic anemia, and other causes of pancytopenia. Although the diagnosis of myelodysplastic syndrome and acute leukemia is usually obvious from examination of the blood smear (see Chapters 12–30 and 12–31), confirmation of these primary hematologic disorders, including aplastic anemia and myelophthisic disorders, requires bone marrow examination. A form of myelodysplastic syndrome known as the 5q– syndrome (see Chapter 12–30) is usually associated with macrocytic anemia. The morphologic changes in bone marrow erythroid precursors that occur in myelodysplastic syndromes and following exposure to some drugs and toxins may resemble and sometimes closely mimic megaloblastic changes. To distinguish these changes from the fine lacelike nuclear chromatin pattern seen in true megaloblastic change, the term *megaloblastoid* is sometimes applied. Megaloblastoid changes consist of irregularly clumped chromatin, giving a speckled appearance that has been compared to sliced salami. Differentiation of megaloblastic anemia from myelodysplasia and acute leukemia is most easily carried out by examination of the stained bone marrow aspirate smear. On the biopsy section, it is much more difficult to make this distinction, as differences may be subtle. In a patient who has a macrocytic anemia and megaloblastic change but no evidence of either vitamin B_{12} or folic acid deficiency, the possibility of drugs or inborn errors of metabolism must be considered. When megaloblastic anemia is caused by drugs, this is usually ascertainable from the patient's record or history. Exposure to certain drugs and toxins may cause dysplastic, megaloblastoid changes in erythroid marrow precursors. Examples include benzene, arsenic, and the anticonvulsants diphenylhydantoin and valproic acid. A rare cause of megaloblastic anemia associated with pancytopenia is erythroleukemia, in which there is often marked dyserythropoiesis with bizarre multinucleated forms and pronounced megaloblastoid changes. This may be confused with severe megaloblastosis caused by vitamin B_{12} or folate deficiency (see Chapter 4–4). Congenital dyserythropoietic anemias, which occur in children or in young adults, have several variants, one of which (Type 1) is associated with macrocytic anemia, megaloblastoid changes, and binucleated erythroblasts, some of which display internuclear chromatin bridges.

If the diagnosis of vitamin B_{12} or folic acid deficiency is in doubt, then the response to specific therapy with either vitamin B_{12} or folic acid can be determined. The reticulocyte count (%) rises to reach a peak within 5 to 8 days of starting daily doses of the appropriate vitamin. In the case of vitamin B_{12} deficiency, because the cause is usually a defect in absorption, 100 μg of vitamin B_{12} should be administered by intramuscular injection daily. Folic acid may be administered by mouth (1 mg daily). Other than the early rise in reticulocyte count, evidence of a response may also be provided by one or more of several changes in blood count after initiation of a course of treatment. An increase in hematocrit of at least 5% or a decrease in MCV of 5 fL or more constitutes objective evidence of a therapeutic response. This is not, however, indicative of a *complete* response.

Diagnostic Options

The basic algorithmic approach to a patient with a macrocytic anemia is shown in Figure 12–3–1. When faced with a patient who has macrocytic anemia, the first step is to determine whether there is an underlying megaloblastic process. This can frequently, but not always, be established with information that is obtained from a complete blood count and examination of the blood smear. The presence of macrocytosis with a high RDW, signifying marked anisocytosis of red cells, together with hypersegmentation of neutrophil polymorphonuclear leukocytes, is strong presumptive evidence of megaloblastosis.

Bone marrow biopsy is not considered necessary as a first-line test, except where the diagnosis is in doubt. The marrow is usually markedly hypercellular with erythroid hyperplasia and left shift. All hematopoietic elements, but particularly the erythroid series, show delayed nuclear maturation with resulting asynchrony between nuclear and cytoplasmic development. Cells and nuclei are larger than normal and this is most conspicuous in the granulocytic series at the metamyelocyte and band stages, where "giant forms" occur. Marrow iron stores appear increased and abnormal sideroblasts, including ringed forms, may be present.

When a macrocytic anemia is known or suspected to be due to a megaloblastic process, it is essential to identify or exclude deficiency of vitamin B_{12} or folic acid. In general, serum levels of either or both of these vitamins are low, depending on the particular deficiency. There are problems with the specificity and sensitivity of these assays, however. Because serum folate fluctuates with recent dietary intake, red cell folate is more reliable for identifying folic acid deficiency. Although red cell folate is low in both folic acid and vitamin B_{12} deficiencies, it may be used to distinguish between the two deficiencies. A low red cell folate when both the serum folate and vitamin B_{12} levels are normal points to folate deficiency.

Evidence to suggest an underlying megaloblastic process should therefore prompt measurement of vitamin B_{12} and folate levels in the blood. Although the presence of hypersegmented neutrophils is a useful and fairly reliable indicator of megaloblastosis, with the general trend toward automated differential leukocyte counting, examination of the blood smear is requested or done less commonly. In practice, blood levels of vitamin B_{12} and folic acid should therefore be ordered on any patient with an unexplained macrocytic anemia.

The particular importance of accurately identifying folate or vitamin B_{12} deficiency rests in the fact that they are correctable nutrient deficiencies and that vitamin B_{12} deficiency, if unrecognized and untreated, ultimately leads to debilitating and potentially irreversible neurologic damage. For these reasons, as well as the fact that patients with deficiencies of folate or, particularly, vitamin B_{12} may have unusual clinical presentations, a high level of awareness and vigilance for these vitamin deficiencies is advisable. Several atypical presentations may be encountered among patients with vitamin B_{12} or folate deficiency. Patients may not display macrocytosis, either as a result of a coexisting microcytic disorder, such as iron deficiency or thalassemia minor, or when the deficiency is early. Normal red cells, with a life span of 120 days, may not yet have been replaced by macrocytic cells. Frequently, patients with vitamin B_{12} deficiency may have no anemia and may present only with neurologic features. There is evidence to suggest that the severity of neurologic involvement may be inversely related to the degree of anemia.

In recent years, sensitive and reliable assays have become available for measurement of compounds that accumulate in the serum or urine during vitamin B_{12} or folic acid deficiencies. The two most widely used are methylmalonic acid, which is raised only in vitamin B_{12} deficiency, and homocysteine, which can be increased in either vitamin B_{12} or folic acid deficiency. In patients with renal impairment, however, serum levels of these metabolites show nonspecific elevation. The combined usefulness of blood levels of the vitamins themselves or of the metabolites that accumulate during their deficiencies is shown in Table 12–3–2. When a macrocytic anemia cannot be explained on some other basis but there is a high index of suspicion that the patient may have vitamin B_{12} or folate deficiency, despite normal blood levels of the vitamins, then measurements of methylmalonic acid and homocysteine should be carried out in the serum (methylmalonic acid may also be measured in the urine). The finding of low levels of serum vitamin B_{12}—with or without low levels of serum or red cell folic acid—may also require confirmation by measurement of serum or urine metabolites. This is because the finding of low blood levels of vitamin B_{12} may be nonspecific, and there are several causes of falsely low serum vitamin B_{12}. Conversely, patients who are vitamin B_{12} deficient may have a normal serum vitamin B_{12} level. The several possible reasons for this are summarized in Table 12–3–3. Sometimes the cause relates to the distribution of vitamin B_{12} on its plasma binding proteins. The physiology of plasma vitamin B_{12} binding and its relevance to diagnosis of vitamin B_{12} deficiency is discussed below.

Serum levels of methylmalonic acid and homocysteine do not return to normal for approximately 1 week after replacement of the deficient vitamins. Consequently, these tests may be used to diagnose vitamin B_{12} or folic acid deficiency retrospectively, for several days after vitamin treatment has been initiated.

As in any nutrient deficiency anemia, there is a sequence of changes that occurs in deficiency of vitamin B_{12} or folic acid. At progressive stages during the evolution of the deficiency state, abnormalities in various laboratory tests occur. These sequential changes begin to develop after a critical level of depletion of body stores of the vitamin has occurred. Lowering of serum levels of the vitamin is usually followed by

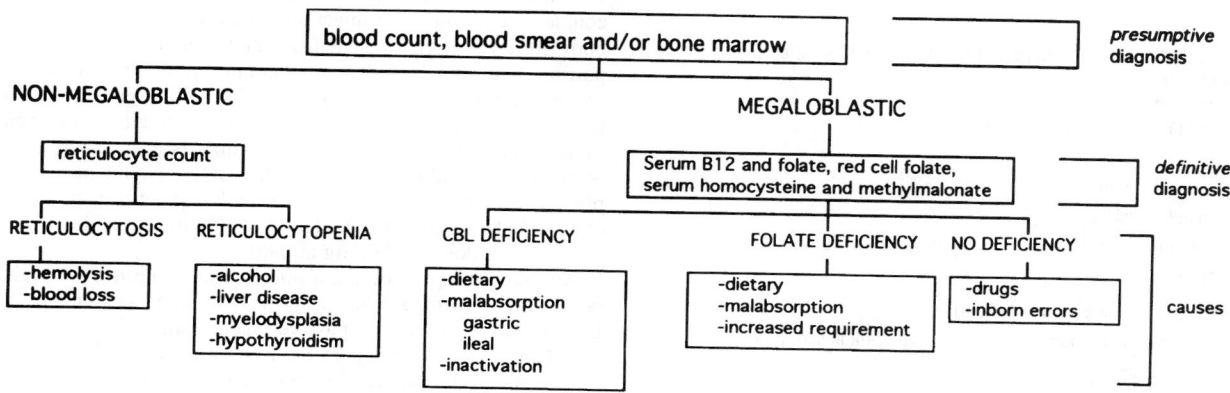

Figure 12–3–1. Simplified algorithm-based plan for the diagnostic approach to a patient with a macrocytic anemia. *(Modified from Green R. The diagnostic approach to macrocytic anemias. Sangre 1993;38(suppl. 2):43. Reproduced with permission from the publisher and author.*

TABLE 12–3–2. CORRELATION OF SERUM VITAMIN B$_{12}$, FOLATE, AND METABOLITE LEVELS WITH CLINICAL STATUS

Test	B$_{12}$ Deficiency	Folate Deficiency	Combined Deficiency
Serum B$_{12}$	Low	Normal	Low
Serum folate	Normal or high	Low	Low
Red cell folate	Low	Low	Low
Serum methylmalonic acid	High	Normal	High
Serum homocysteine	High	High	High

Source: Green R. The diagnostic approach to macrocytic anemias. Sangre 1993;38(suppl. 2):42. Reproduced with permission from the publisher and author.

biochemical effects which can be demonstrated by changes in the levels of metabolites in the blood and urine. Finally, tissue effects occur, such as megaloblastic changes, macrocytosis, and anemia. In some conditions, such as pernicious anemia, laboratory evidence of the underlying autoimmune process and its effect on vitamin B$_{12}$ absorption may be demonstrable before vitamin B$_{12}$ deficiency has occurred. This temporal sequence of events is shown in Figure 12–3–2.

A specific test to identify vitamin B$_{12}$ or folate deficiency and to distinguish each from the other is the so-called deoxyuridine suppression test. The test requires bone marrow for short-term culture and is not routinely available. Its basis is discussed below.

In pernicious anemia, some laboratory evidence of the autoimmune process is usually present. Serum antibodies are present against parietal cells (90%) and against intrinsic factor (60%) among patients with pernicious anemia. Unfortunately, false-positive results for the gastric parietal cell test are quite common (10% of people over age 70). Though it lacks sensitivity, the test for intrinsic factor antibodies is much more specific. Direct measurement of gastric output of intrinsic factor following pentagastrin stimulation can be carried out, but is not warranted for routine diagnosis. Measurement of serum gastrin level is preferred and may be useful for establishing the presence of achlorhydria, which is almost invariably associated with pernicious anemia.

In the absence of laboratory evidence of gastric autoimmunity, pernicious anemia may be diagnosed using Schilling's urinary excretion test, by demonstrating vitamin B$_{12}$ malabsorption that can be corrected with intrinsic factor.

Recommended Approach

In a patient who either has an unexplained macrocytic anemia or has evidence of megaloblastic change (in the blood or bone marrow), I recommend measurement of serum vitamin B$_{12}$ and folic acid levels as first-line investigations, because they are relatively inexpensive and generally reliable as far as sensitivity goes. (There are exceptions, as has been indicated above and for the reasons given below.) I would also measure red cell folate in a hospitalized patient, particularly if the patient is old, socioeconomically disadvantaged, or alcoholic. Such pa-

TABLE 12–3–3. PROBLEMS IN THE INTERPRETATION OF SERUM VITAMIN B$_{12}$ MEASUREMENT

False Negative (normal level in a deficient patient)

- Assay artifact
- Prior vitamin B$_{12}$ injection
- Transcobalamin II deficiency
- Elevated levels of transcobalamin I (e.g., chronic granulocytic leukemia)
- Nitrous oxide exposure

False Positive (low level in a normal patient)

- Interference by other radioisotopes (e.g., gallium) present in serum
- Transcobalamin I deficiency
- Folate deficiency (occasionally)

Source: Green R. The diagnostic approach to macrocytic anemias. Sangre 1993;38(suppl. 2):42. Reproduced with permission from the publisher and author.

tients are more likely to have nutritional folate deficiency, so that serum folate may be spuriously normal because of recent dietary folate intake while in hospital. Even in the presence of anemia without macrocytosis or macrocytosis without anemia I recommend serum vitamin B$_{12}$ measurement if there is clinical suspicion of possible deficiency, for example, if there are associated neurologic manifestations.

I caution, however, that there are technical problems with red cell folate assays which limit their usefulness. Also, a recent trend toward less expensive non-isotopic assays for vitamin B$_{12}$ and folate has introduced more potential problems with sensitivity (normal values in deficient patients), because these assays have not yet been adequately validated.

I consider the finding of a subnormal vitamin B$_{12}$ or folic acid level alone sufficient to arrive at a presumptive diagnosis of deficiency of the vitamin if this fits with the clinical picture in a particular target group (e.g., vitamin B$_{12}$ deficiency in an older patient or following gastrectomy or folate deficiency in someone who is malnourished). If I consider it necessary to confirm the presence of deficiency, particularly in a patient with low serum vitamin B$_{12}$ (a somewhat nonspecific finding), I measure serum methylmalonic acid; if folic acid is low, then I measure homocysteine; if both vitamins are low then I measure both metabolites. The other situations where I would measure methylmalonic acid and homocysteine are where blood levels of folic acid and vitamin B$_{12}$ are normal yet I suspect that there may still be a deficiency of one of these vitamins, and when there has been an incomplete or failed response following treatment with one or both vitamins.

To pursue the cause of deficiency, I like to confirm that a patient has pernicious anemia (by far the most common cause of vitamin B$_{12}$ deficiency) before committing them to lifelong injections of vitamin B$_{12}$. I start with the test for serum antibodies to intrinsic factor (present in about 60% of pernicious anemia patients), and only if the test is negative do I proceed to Schilling's urinary excretion test. If abnormal, then I do part II (with intrinsic factor). If this is also abnormal, then I repeat part II after 8 weeks of vitamin B$_{12}$ treatment to make sure that the intestinal malabsorption was not a secondary complication of vitamin B$_{12}$ deficiency.

It is not necessary to always do a bone marrow biopsy, but I do recommend it in the following circumstances: if the patient presents with pancytopenia or severe anemia; if the clinical or hematologic features are unusual; if there is persistence of anemia, macrocytosis, or other hematologic abnormality 3 months after treatment.

Therapeutic

Once a diagnosis of vitamin B$_{12}$ or folic acid deficiency has been made, specific replacement therapy should be initiated. It is important to ensure that requisite blood specimens for measurement of vitamin levels and metabolites are taken before specific treatment is started. Metabolite levels actually may remain abnormal for up to 1 week following treatment. Megaloblastic changes in the bone marrow revert to normal within hours of treatment. Therefore, if a bone marrow examination is to be carried out it should be done before treatment is instituted.

In the case of vitamin B$_{12}$ deficiency, treatment should consist of a course of intramuscular injections of cyanocobalamin to replenish the body store followed by regular maintenance injections for life. Only a portion of the injected dose of vitamin B$_{12}$ is retained, the remainder being excreted in the urine. The fraction of an injected dose that is retained varies inversely with the dose. Although cyanocobalamin is more widely available, hydroxocobalamin is a more physiologic form of the vitamin and better retained. A standard course of treatment to replenish stores consists of three daily injections of 1000 μg of cyanocobalamin followed by twice weekly injections for 1 month and a maintenance dose of 1000 μg monthly.

Although the physiologic absorption of vitamin B$_{12}$ requires an intact intrinsic factor-mediated pathway, a small percentage of vitamin B$_{12}$ can be absorbed by a passive mechanism in the upper small intestine. Consequently, it is possible to treat patients with pernicious anemia by mouth if sufficiently large doses are given. Because of the potential risk of neurologic complications arising in noncompliant patients, this alternative should be used only in extremely frail individuals or those who refuse injections. Also, rare patients may have a hy-

Autoimmune diathesis
↓
Immune destruction of gastric parietal cells and their contents
(gastric parietal cells and intrinsic factor antibodies)
↓
B_{12} malabsorption   (abnormal Schilling's test)
↓
Cobalamin depletion   (low serum cobalamin, holo-transcobalamin II)
↓
Functional cobalamin deficiency   (raised serum methylmalonic acid and homocysteine)
↓
Structural cobalamin deficiency
(megaloblastic change, demyelination)

Figure 12–3–2. Stages in the pathogenesis of pernicious anemia, showing the sequential development of laboratory features. *(Source: Green R. Typical and atypical manifestations of pernicious anemia. In: Bhatt R, Besser M, James VHT, Keen H, eds. Thomas Addison and his diseases. Bristol: Journal of Endocrinology Ltd, 1994;1:383. Reproduced with permission from the publisher and author.)*

persensitivity to parenteral vitamin B_{12}. In these circumstances, daily oral doses of 500 µg of vitamin B_{12} may be used, which will provide the 2 to 3 µg necessary to satisfy the daily requirement. This approach should be used only for maintenance therapy, and stores should first be replenished using a course of injections.

In the case of folate deficiency, unless there is malabsorption, folic acid may be given by mouth. A daily dose of 5 mg should be given for 2 to 4 months until a new population of red cells has been produced. Inadequate dietary intake is responsible for a large proportion of patients with folate deficiency. In a minority of patients, the cause may be intestinal malabsorption. Patients with adult celiac disease or those who have had extensive resections of small bowel need to be given folic acid by injection. When folate deficiency is caused by persistently increased demands for the vitamin, as in thalassemia major, sickle cell disease, and other congenital hemolytic anemias, it is necessary to continue folic acid supplementation indefinitely to prevent the recurrence of deficiency.

The administration of therapeutic doses of folic acid to a patient with vitamin B_{12} deficiency may result in a partial or temporary remission of the hematologic and other megaloblastic complications of vitamin B_{12} deficiency. The administration of folic acid to a patient with vitamin B_{12} deficiency therefore carries the potential risk of masking the true underlying vitamin B_{12} deficiency. Nervous system deprivation of vitamin B_{12} will continue and may therefore result in progressive and irreversible neurologic damage. For this reason, it is critically important to exclude vitamin B_{12} deficiency before starting treatment with doses of folic acid in excess of 1 mg daily.

The standard form of folic acid (pteroylmonoglutamic acid) cannot be used to reverse toxic effects of methotrexate and other dihydrofolate reductase inhibitors. To overcome the block of these folate analogs, folinic acid or citrovorum factor (5-formyl tetrahydrofolic acid) must be used.

Treatment with both vitamin B_{12} and folic acid should be avoided, unless there is clear evidence of deficiency of both vitamins or if the patient is extremely ill with profound anemia or pancytopenia. Blood transfusion should be used only in the most severely anemic patients and, even then, should be administered slowly to avoid circulatory overload. Administration of a fast-acting diuretic may also be necessary.

FOLLOW-UP

In the case of vitamin B_{12} or folate deficiency, after specific treatment has been given and depleted body stores of the vitamin have been replaced, the patient should be reassessed 3 months later. If any persistent abnormalities are discovered on the blood count, then these should be investigated appropriately. Persistence of anemia may indicate the presence of some other underlying or coexistent hematologic disease. Often, and particularly in patients with pernicious anemia, there is associated iron deficiency that is not apparent before vitamin replacement because fewer erythroid precursors reach the stage of maturation at which iron utilization takes place. Coexistent iron deficiency should be suspected if the reticulocyte response is blunted, if the rise in hemoglobin concentration is suboptimal, and, in particular, if the MCV drops

below the normal range following treatment. In any of these circumstances, iron status should be assessed along standard lines as discussed in Chapter 12–2. In some circumstances, as in infection or the anemia of chronic disease, the failure to respond to treatment may be due not to a lack of iron, but to an impairment of iron reutilization. Posttreatment microcytosis also occurs in patients with thalassemia minor.

Failure to respond to treatment with folic acid or vitamin B_{12} or failure to sustain remission may be due to inadequate dosage, incorrect route of administration (in the case of oral folate given to a patient with intestinal malabsorption), or administration of the inappropriate vitamin. To confirm a failure of response to treatment before investigating these possibilities, it is helpful to study serum methylmalonic acid and homocysteine levels. Complete failure of response to treatment usually signifies a misdiagnosis in the first instance, and suggests that there is some other explanation for the macrocytic anemia. Additional testing is then required, and if not done previously, a bone marrow examination is indicated.

DISCUSSION

Prevalence and Incidence

The prevalence of vitamin B_{12} and folic acid deficiencies varies with a number of demographic factors. The most common cause of vitamin B_{12} deficiency is pernicious anemia. The mean age at diagnosis is 60 years among Caucasian populations (younger among patients of Hispanic and African origin); and the female-to-male ratio is approximately 1.5:1. The incidence of the disease rises with increasing age. Among patients over age 65, reported prevalence figures for pernicious anemia in various populations in Europe have varied from 1 to 3%. Comparable figures for populations in the United States are not available, but if the European figures are applied to the population over age 60 in the United States, then the total number of cases would be from 300,000 to 1,000,000. Certainly, the prevalence of low serum vitamin B_{12} levels in the elderly population is high, reports varying between 5 and 20%.

The highest incidence of folate deficiency resulting from nutritional lack occurs among particular target populations including the poor, the elderly, and alcoholics. Infants and pregnant or lactating women are also at greater risk for developing folate deficiency. Folate deficiency during early pregnancy may play a role in causing neural tube defects and supplementation with 400 µg of folate or more daily lowers the prevalence of neural tube defects among women who are at risk for recurrence of this problem.

Related Basic Science

The characteristic feature of all megaloblastic macrocytic anemias is a phenotypic change affecting rapidly dividing cells in the bone marrow and other tissues which results from a defect in DNA synthesis. Although the molecular basis for megaloblastosis has not been fully elucidated, all conditions that give rise to megaloblastic changes have in common a disparity in the rate of synthesis or availability of the four purines and pyrimidines required for DNA replication during the S phase of the cell cycle. In both folate and vitamin B_{12} deficiencies, the defect in DNA synthesis is caused by a failure to convert adequate amounts of deoxyuridine to thymidine. This conversion requires folate in a form that is produced via a reaction that needs vitamin B_{12}. Therefore, in vitamin B_{12} deficiency there is a state of functional folate deficiency through "trapping" of folate in the methyl form. This explains the high serum folate levels frequently encountered in vitamin B_{12} deficiency. The biochemical block in DNA synthesis that occurs in either folate or vitamin B_{12} deficiency can be demonstrated in short-term bone marrow culture and has been adapted in the form of a test for distinguishing folate from vitamin B_{12} deficiency (the deoxyuridine [dU] suppression test). In this test bone marrow is cultured in the presence of [^{3}H]thymidine, which becomes incorporated into DNA. In normal bone marrow, preincubation with deoxyuridine, which results in the formation of large amounts of deoxythymidine (dT), dilutes the [^{3}H]thymidine incorporation into DNA. In either folate or vitamin B_{12} deficiency, however, the conversion of deoxyuridine to deoxythymidine is interdicted, which results in a failure of suppression of [^{3}H]thymidine incorporation into DNA. This can be corrected in vitro by the addition of vitamin B_{12} when the underlying cause is vitamin B_{12} deficiency or by folate in the form of 5-methyltetrahydrofolate when the cause is folate deficiency.

In either folate or vitamin B_{12} deficiency, the inadequate amount of thymidine production results in an abrogation of the normal rate of DNA synthesis. There is also evidence that the shortage of deoxythymidine triphosphate (dTTP) for pairing with dATP during DNA replication may result in its substitution by deoxyuridine triphosphate (dUTP), which is present in abundant amounts because of the block in dTTP production (normally, base pairing of dUTP and dATP occurs only in RNA). There is a mechanism for recognition of the faulty sequence in DNA, but repair is not possible as long as dTTP remains in short supply. This situation results in repeated cycles of futile excision and misrepair, with consequent interruption of the normal program of DNA synthesis, and ultimately apoptotic cell death.

Although deficiency of either folate or vitamin B_{12} ultimately result in the same biochemical abnormality in rapidly dividing cells, there are considerable and important differences between these B-group vitamins with respect to their nutrition, physiology, and causes of deficiency. Whereas folate is widely distributed in various foods and is particularly abundant in green leafy vegetables as well as liver, vitamin B_{12} is restricted to foods of animal origin. Vitamin B_{12} is heat stable, whereas folate is destroyed by cooking. In the absence of intake or absorption, depletion of body stores takes only 3 to 5 months for folate but 3 to 5 years for vitamin B_{12}. Consequently, folate deficiency caused by lack of dietary intake is common, whereas for vitamin B_{12} it is rare, occurring only in strict vegetarians who eat no animal foods, including dairy products and eggs.

Folate is absorbed mainly in the jejunum, by an active transport mechanism. In the intestinal mucosa, folate is converted to methyltetrahydrofolate, which enters the plasma from where it is taken up by tissue cells. This form of folate participates in the methionine synthase reaction in which homocysteine is converted to methionine, and in the process, it is converted to tetrahydrofolate. Within cells, tetrahydrofolate is converted to and retained as polyglutamates. Therefore, in vitamin B_{12} deficiency, where conversion to tetrahydrofolate is impaired, cellular folate including red cell folate is low. Vitamin B_{12} is absorbed in the terminal ileum by a mechanism that requires intrinsic factor, a glycoprotein that is produced by gastric parietal cells. Food vitamin B_{12} must first be released by peptic digestion before it is bound in the stomach by a salivary vitamin B_{12}-binding protein (cobalophillin). In the alkaline milieu of the small intestine, salivary cobalophillin is destroyed by tryptic digestion and vitamin B_{12} is more efficiently bound by intrinsic factor. The vitamin B_{12}-intrinsic factor complex is taken up by ileal enterocytes through absorptive endocytosis.

Folate malabsorption results from disease or resection of the middle third of the small intestine and is relatively uncommon, occurring in such diseases as tropical sprue and gluten-associated enteropathy (celiac disease). On the other hand, vitamin B_{12} deficiency is frequently the result of defective absorption, resulting from abnormalities of the gastric component more often than the intestinal component. The most frequent cause of vitamin B_{12} deficiency is pernicious anemia, caused by failure of intrinsic factor production, and that appears to have an au-

toimmune basis. It is associated with gastric atrophy and achlorhydria. Rarely, intrinsic factor may be defective or absent on a congenital basis. Affected individuals (usually children) have normal gastric acid production. Total gastrectomy results in a failure of vitamin B_{12} absorption, which leads inevitably to deficiency within 5 years. Following partial gastrectomy, the outcome is variable, as there is a considerable reserve capacity of intrinsic factor production.

Ileal causes of vitamin B_{12} malabsorption are less common, occurring in Crohn's and other inflammatory bowel disease affecting the terminal ileum, as well as following resection of bowel for these diseases or for other reasons. Rare congenital absence of the ileal intrinsic factor receptor occurs (Immerslund–Gräsbeck syndrome). There are several causes of vitamin B_{12} malabsorption arising within the gut lumen. For the normal intrinsic factor-mediated mechanism of vitamin B_{12} absorption, certain requirements in the gastrointestinal lumen must be met. There must be adequate gastric output of acid and pepsin to ensure release of food vitamin B_{12}. Failure of this mechanism is believed to be responsible for a condition known as food vitamin B_{12} malabsorption. This is associated with low serum vitamin B_{12} levels, with or without evidence of vitamin B_{12} deficiency but with apparently normal vitamin B_{12} absorption as measured by the standard Schilling test (which measures only the absorption of crystalline vitamin B_{12}).

Some patients with food vitamin B_{12} malabsorption later develop pernicious anemia but the exact relationship between these two conditions is not clear. The use of H_2 blockers for treatment of peptic ulcer disease causes a decrease in vitamin B_{12} absorption, and continued use may lead to lowering of the serum vitamin B_{12} level. Excessive output of gastric acid can also impair vitamin B_{12} absorption by decreasing the affinity of intrinsic factor for vitamin B_{12}. This occurs in hypergastrinemia associated with the Zollinger–Ellison syndrome. Disruption of the optimal intraluminal alkaline pH that is necessary for release of vitamin B_{12} from cobalophillin and its binding to intrinsic factor can also result from chronic pancreatic disease. Diminished output of pancreatic bicarbonate as well as failure of the tryptic digestion of salivary binding protein contributes to the malabsorption of vitamin B_{12} seen in chronic pancreatic disease. Finally, within the gut lumen, there may be competition for vitamin B_{12} by abnormal bacterial flora. This occurs following intestinal surgery that results in blind loops of bowel. Competition for vitamin B_{12} is also responsible for the deficiency caused by infestation with the fish tapeworm *Diphylobothrium latum*. Resection of the terminal ileum or surgery resulting in bypass of this portion of the bowel results in vitamin B_{12} malabsorption. In general, the extent of the resection determines the degree of impairment.

In all situations resulting from impairment of vitamin B_{12} absorption, the time to onset of deficiency depends on several factors, including the size of the body store, the extent of impairment of absorption (partial or complete), and, in diseases like pernicious anemia or those affecting all of the intestine, the rate of progression of the disease. In general, however, vitamin B_{12} deficiency resulting from malabsorption develops sooner (3–5 years) than is the case in the dietary deficiency encountered among vegans (10–20 years). This difference may be explained by the existence of a considerable enterohepatic recirculation of vitamin B_{12}. Biliary vitamin B_{12} is efficiently reabsorbed in vegans compared with patients with pernicious anemia or other forms of malabsorption.

During normal absorption, after vitamin B_{12} attached to intrinsic factor has entered the mucosal surface of the ileal epithelial cell, the intrinsic factor is broken down and the vitamin attaches to a plasma binding protein, transcobalamin II (TCII), which is produced in endothelial cells. TCII is the binding protein that is responsible for cellular uptake of vitamin B_{12}, but it normally binds only 10 to 20% of the total serum vitamin B_{12}. Transcobalamin I (TCI), and to a minor extent transcobalamin III (TCIII), related glycoproteins known as the haptocorrins, bind the major portion of vitamin B_{12} in plasma. The function of haptocorrins is not known, but rapidly proliferating cells including bone marrow precursors can obtain vitamin B_{12} only from TCII. Consequently, the critical fraction of the serum vitamin B_{12} is the TCII-bound portion, known as holo-TCII. Conditions that alter the amount or distribution of vitamin B_{12} on these binding proteins can critically affect delivery and transport of the vitamin. Therefore, conditions that lead to an increase in haptocorrins, such as chronic granulocytic

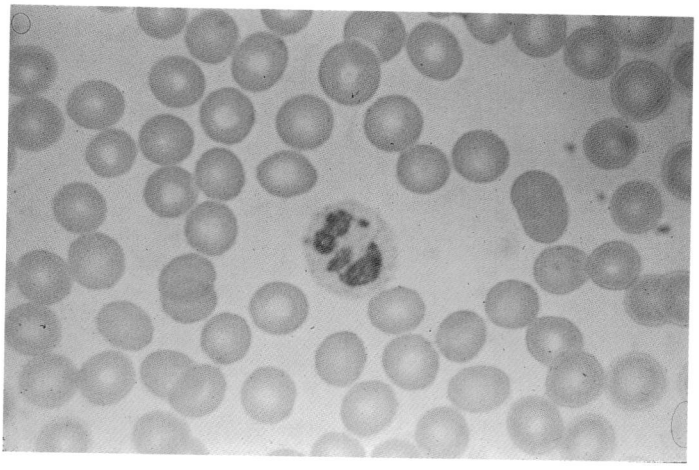

Color Plate 12–2–1. Normal peripheral blood smear.

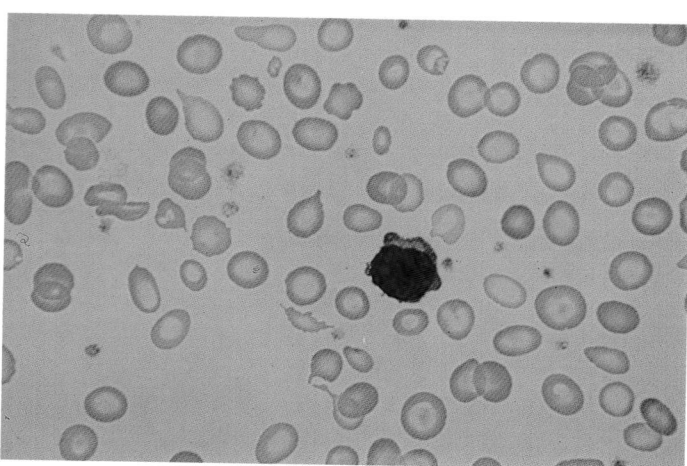

Color Plate 12–2–2. Hypochromic microcytic peripheral smear, such as that seen in iron deficiency anemia.

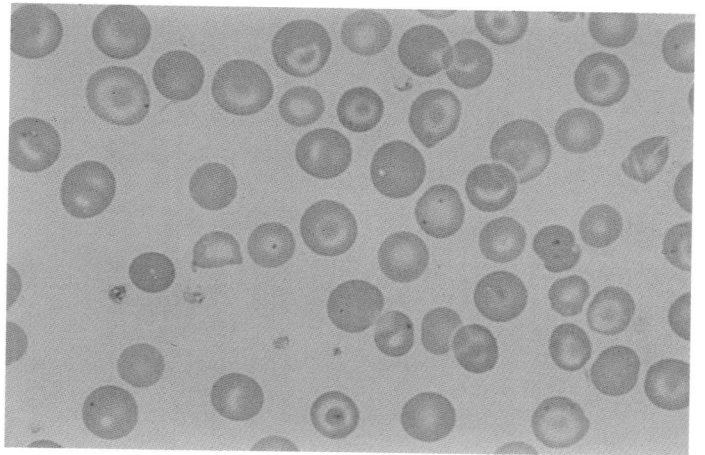

Color Plate 12–2–3. Target cells. These are seen in liver disease.

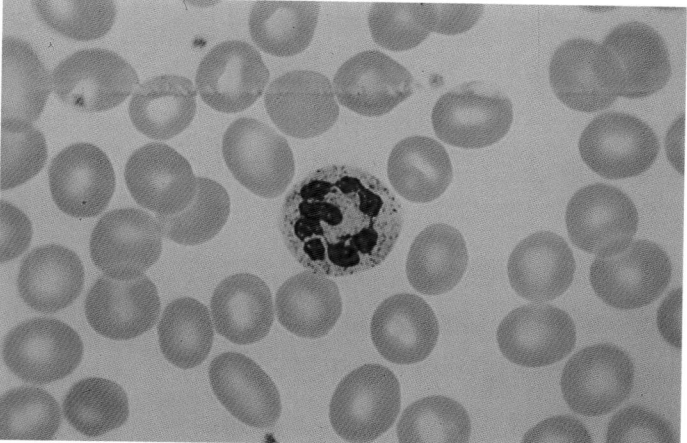

Color Plate 12–3–1. Macrocytic red blood cells (mean cell volume, 124 fL) and hypersegmented neutrophil, such as seen in vitamin B_{12} or folate deficiency.

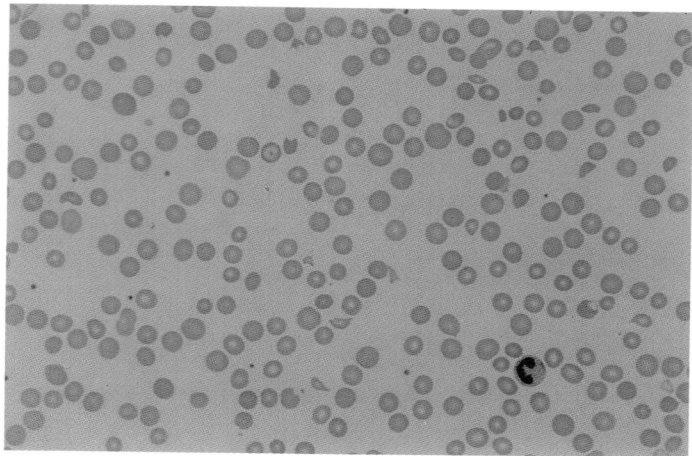

Color Plate 12–4–1. Autoimmune hemolytic anemia with polychromasia and spherocytes.

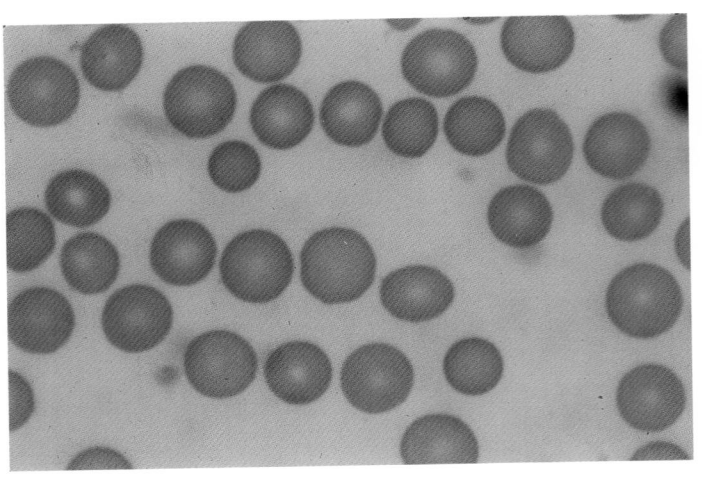

Color Plate 12–6–1. Hereditary spherocytosis.

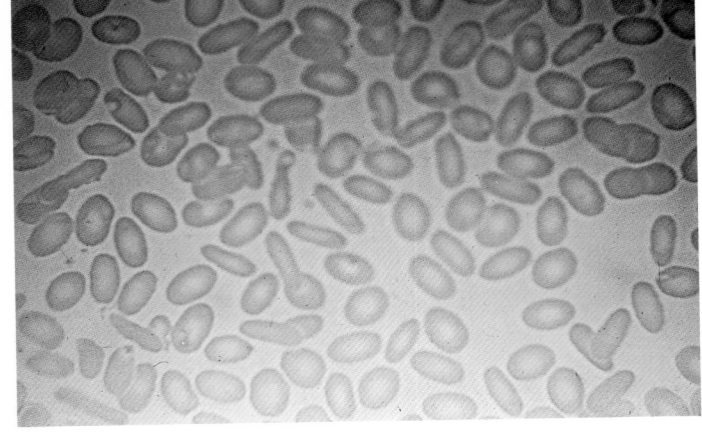

Color Plate 12–6–2. Hereditary elliptocytosis.

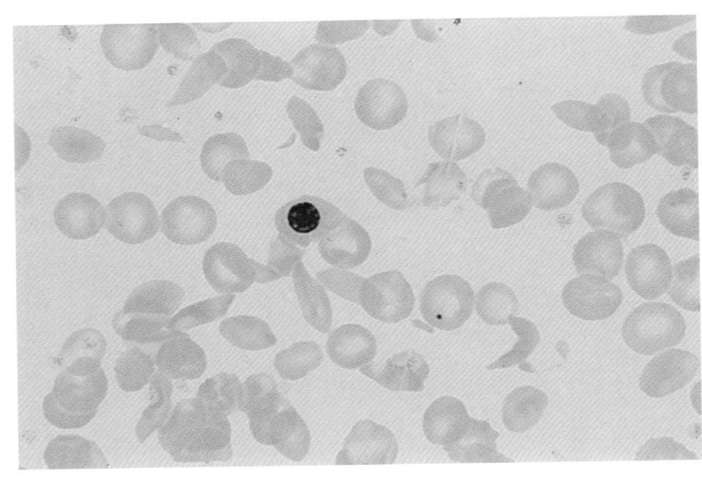

Color Plate 12–7–1. Sickle cells.

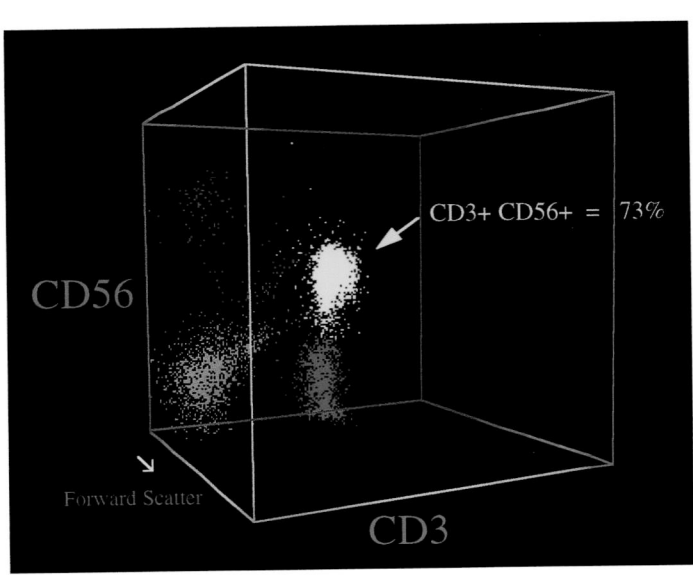

A

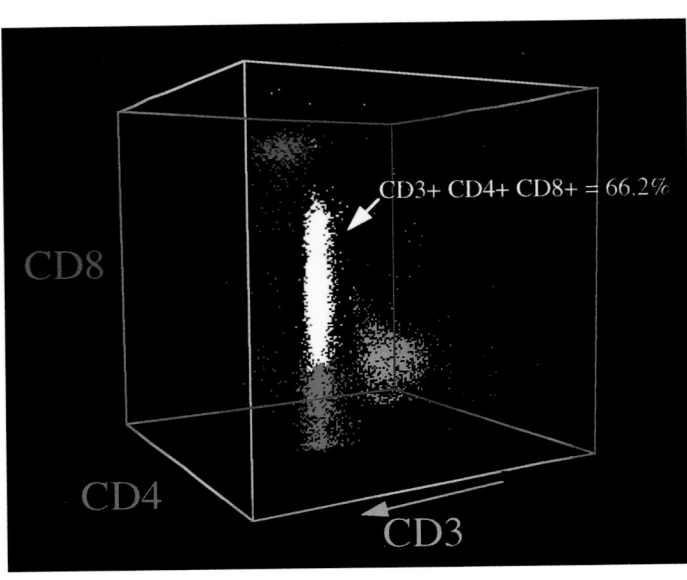

B

Color Plate 12–13–1. Multiparameter analysis (by flow cytometry) of an unusual variant of large granular lymphocytosis. An abnormal population of CD3+ CD56+ lymphocytes (**A**) which coexpress CD4 and CD8 (**B**) is illustrated.

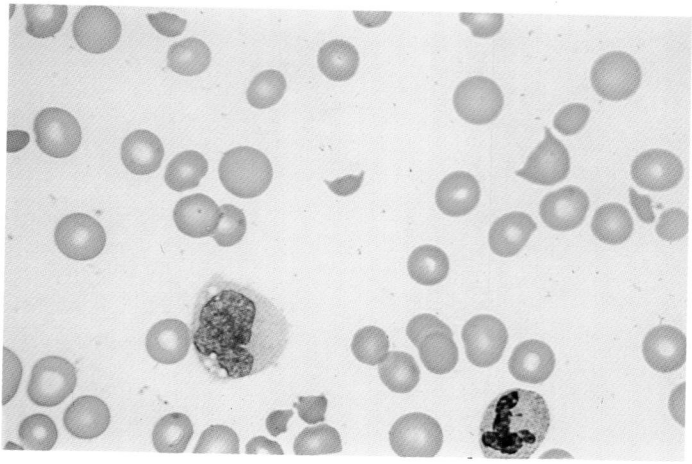

Color Plate 12–15–1. Thrombotic thrombocytopenic purpura. Note the schistocytes, thrombocytopenia, and microangiopathy.

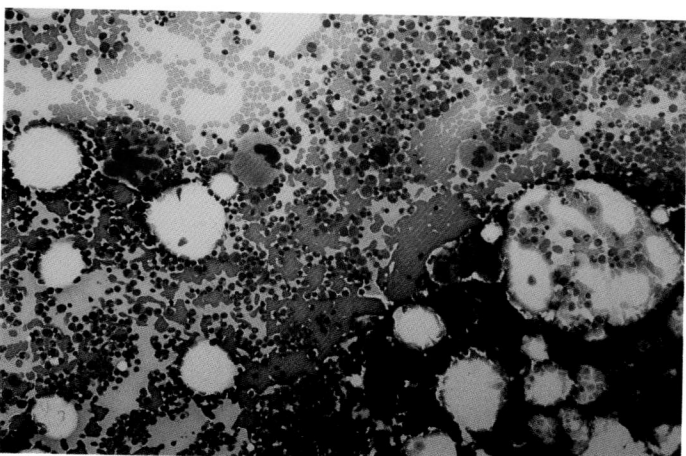

Color Plate 12–15–2. Bone marrow with an increased number of megakaryocytes, as seen in idiopathic thrombocytopenic purpura.

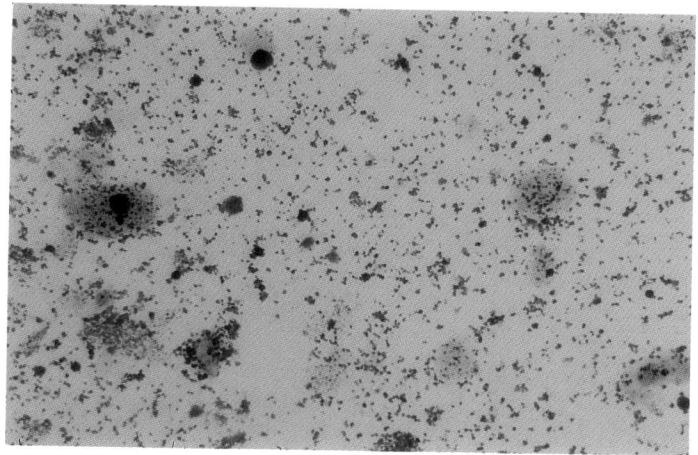

Color Plate 12–19–1. Urine hemosiderin. This sort of Prussian blue stain positivity would be seen in paroxysmal nocturnal hemoglobinuria or any disorder with intravascular hemolysis.

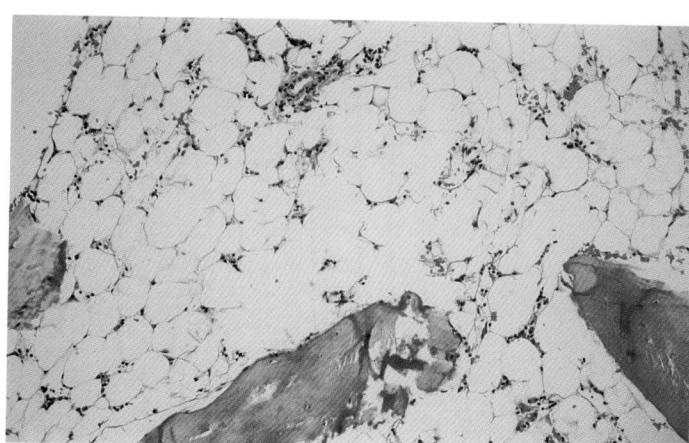

Color Plate 12–19–2. Bone marrow of a patient with aplastic anemia.

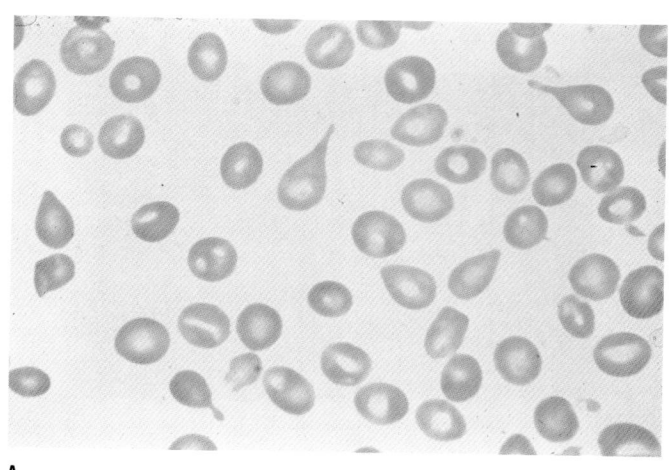

A

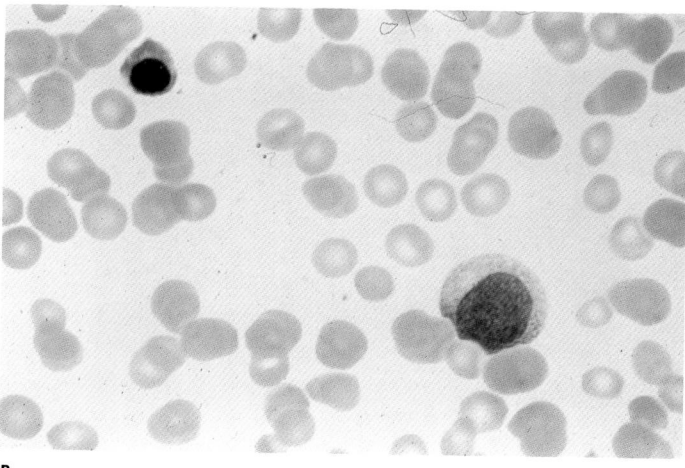

B

Color Plate 12–22–1. Peripheral blood smear changes in myelophthisic disorders. **A.** Teardrop cells. **B.** Leukoerythroblastic changes.

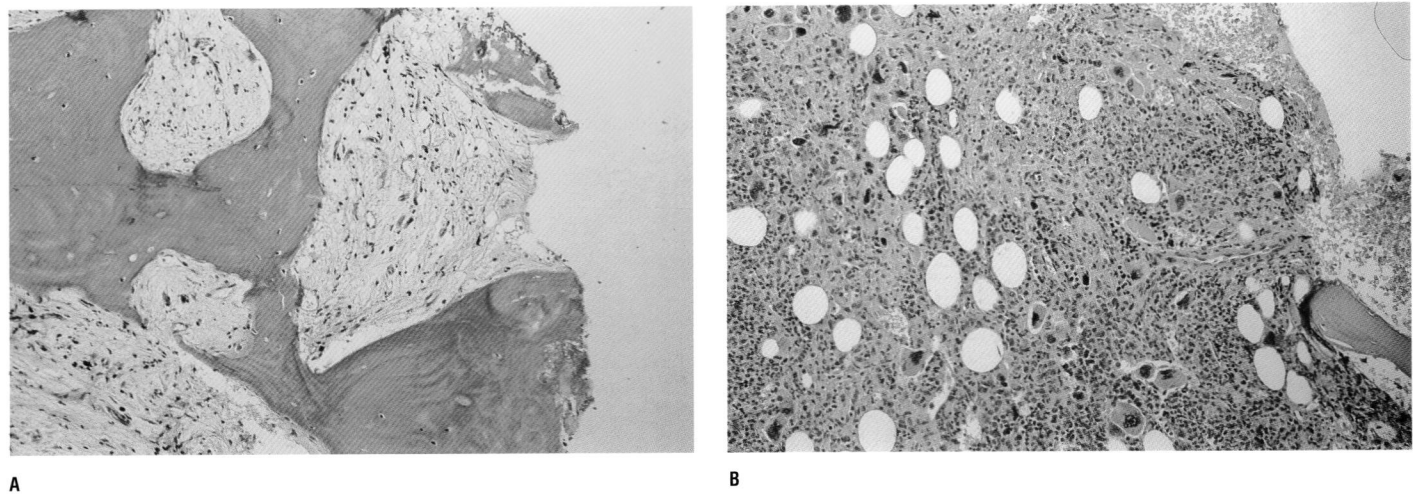

A

B

Color Plate 12–22–2. Bone marrow appearance of myelofibrosis. **A.** Increased fibrosis. **B.** Increased overall cellularity with increased fibrosis.

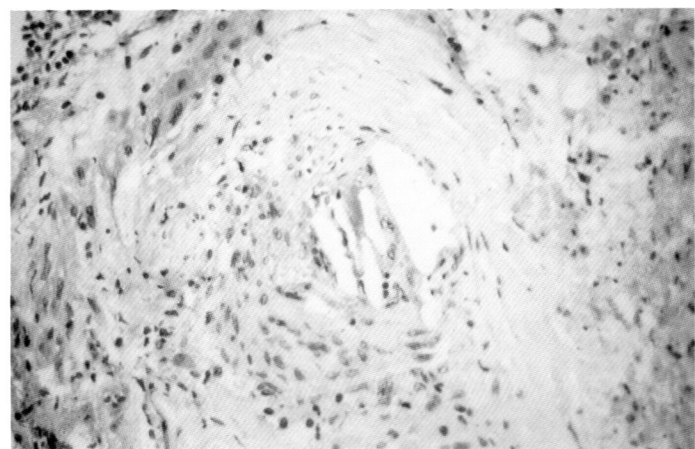

Color Plate 16–22–1. Cross section of a renal interlobular artery containing ghostlike clefts of several cholesterol crystals. (*Photomicrograph courtesy of Dr. Angelo Ucci, Pathology Department, New England Medical Center Hospital.*)

leukemia (TCI and TCIII are produced in granulocytes), can give rise to an apparently normal serum vitamin B_{12} level even in patients who have pernicious anemia or some other cause of vitamin B_{12} deficiency. Conversely, a decrease in holo-TCII can result in vitamin B_{12} deficiency even if the serum vitamin B_{12} level is apparently normal. This is known to occur in infants and children affected by congenital TCII deficiency which is associated with severe megaloblastic anemia. Levels of TCII, which is produced mainly in endothelial cells, may be affected by a number of factors. Lowering of holo-TCII can result in tissue vitamin B_{12} deficiency with a normal serum vitamin B_{12} level. Although holo-TCII has been measured, and appears to correlate well with serum metabolite levels and other parameters of vitamin B_{12} deficiency, routine assays sufficiently sensitive to measure the small fraction of vitamin B_{12} that occurs as holo-TCII are not currently available.

In a patient with vitamin B_{12} deficiency, the cause of the underlying deficiency can usually be established by carrying out tests of vitamin B_{12} absorption using Schilling's urinary excretion method. Typically, patients with classic pernicious anemia have an abnormal test result when radioactive vitamin B_{12} alone is given by mouth (part I). This abnormality is corrected when the test is repeated with intrinsic factor (part II). Failure to correct vitamin B_{12} malabsorption in part II of the Schilling test signifies an intestinal cause for the vitamin B_{12} malabsorption. Part II of the Schilling test may be repeated, after giving antibiotics or a vermicide to exclude bacterial overgrowth ("blind loop syndrome") or fish tapeworm, respectively, both of which cause vitamin B_{12} deficiency by competition with the host. Vitamin B_{12} malabsorption can be attributed to chronic pancreatic disease if an abnormal part II of the Schilling test can be corrected by the administration of pancreatic extract and bicarbonate. If none of these measures succeed in correcting part II of the Schilling test, then the cause lies in the wall of the terminal ileum (e.g., Crohn's disease). A normal part I of the Schilling test in a patient with vitamin B_{12} deficiency may be observed in total vegetarians and in patients with food vitamin B_{12} malabsorption, who show normal absorption of crystalline vitamin B_{12}, but are unable to digest and absorb vitamin B_{12} present in food. This defect can be identified using a modified Schilling test in which radioactive vitamin B_{12} is administered with food. In nitrous oxide-induced vitamin B_{12} deficiency, part I of the Schilling test is also normal.

The Schilling test and its various modifications can be extremely helpful in arriving at a definitive diagnosis of the cause of vitamin B_{12} deficiency; however, several problems can interfere with the interpretation of the tests. These are summarized in Table 12–3–4. Recent injection or administration of vitamin B_{12} dilutes the radiolabeled tracer vitamin and can cause spuriously low test results. In some patients with pernicious anemia and severe megaloblastic changes affecting the small intestine, there may be a failure of intrinsic factor to correct vitamin B_{12} malabsorption. Recovery from this secondary malabsorption may take 6 to 8 weeks following the start of treatment.

Whereas the mechanism of megaloblastic change in folate and vitamin B_{12} deficiency is reasonably well understood, the biochemical basis of the neurologic damage that occurs in vitamin B_{12} deficiency remains uncertain. Of the two enzymatic reactions that require vitamin B_{12} in mammalian cells, the methionine synthase reaction is the more likely candidate for playing a critical role in the nervous system. The product of this reaction, methionine, is converted to *S*-adenosylmethionine, which is required for all methylation reactions, including myelin

phospholipids. What is puzzling, however, is that neurologic complications are rare in folate deficiency even though methionine synthase requires folate as a cosubstrate. The other reaction that requires vitamin B_{12} involves the conversion of methylmalonyl coenzyme A to succinyl coenzyme A. Accumulation of methylmalonate and its precursor, propionate, may provide unusual substrates for fatty acid synthesis, resulting in abnormal odd-carbon and branched-chain fatty acids, which may be incorporated into the myelin sheath.

A number of rare inborn errors of metabolism have been identified that result in megaloblastic anemia either through interference with folate or vitamin B_{12} or because of some other derangement of DNA synthesis. These genetic disorders should be considered in infants or young children with unexplained megaloblastic anemia. Abnormalities include orotic aciduria, which affects pyrimidine metabolism; the Lesch–Nyhan syndrome, which affects purine metabolism; and a variety of defects involving the absorption, transport, activation, or metabolism of vitamin B_{12} or folate. Detailed consideration of these rare but interesting disorders is beyond the scope of this chapter.

Several drugs can produce macrocytic anemia. Purine and pyrimidine analogs that interfere with DNA synthesis, such as azathioprine (Imuran) and cytosine arabinoside (Ara-C), cause megaloblastic changes. In addition, there are a number of drugs that interfere with folate metabolism, including methotrexate and other dihydrofolate reductase inhibitors, phenytoin and related anticonvulsants, and oral contraceptive agents. Several drugs interfere with vitamin B_{12} absorption, but it takes years to exhaust the body store of vitamin B_{12}. Consequently, although some drugs such as colchicine and *p*-aminosalicylic acid may cause vitamin B_{12} malabsorption, these drugs are usually not taken over a long enough period to induce deficiency. Drugs such as cimetidine and other H_2 blockers as well as oral antidiabetic agents can interfere with vitamin B_{12} absorption and may be administered over a sufficiently long period to cause, or contribute to, vitamin B_{12} deficiency. The anesthetic gas nitrous oxide, which oxidizes methylcobalamin, one of the coenzyme forms of vitamin B_{12}, can produce vitamin B_{12} deficiency after repeated exposure or can accelerate the onset of deficiency in patients with borderline vitamin B_{12} stores. Patients exposed to nitrous oxide who display the effects of vitamin B_{12} deficiency may at first have normal serum vitamin B_{12} levels. Later, however, the serum vitamin B_{12} falls as a result of irreversible oxidation and destruction of the vitamin B_{12} molecule.

Natural History and Its Modification with Treatment

Megaloblastic anemia caused by folate or vitamin B_{12} deficiency is usually gradual in onset so that the patient may adapt well to the anemia. Very severely anemic patients, though rare nowadays, may be remarkably well compensated for their level of anemia. The natural history of pernicious anemia was well documented in the era before vitamin B_{12} was identified and specific treatment became available. At that time, it was noted that the progression of the disease was sometimes erratic. Temporary and partial remissions may have been related to either waxing and waning of the autoimmune process or, possibly, to dietary intake of food rich in folate that might have intermittently ameliorated the block in DNA synthesis.

It is possible that this folate effect may also be responsible for the inverse correlation between neurologic and hematologic complications in vitamin B_{12} deficiency. Patients who have better folate nutrition may manifest fewer or no hematologic effects of vitamin B_{12} deficiency, yet neurologic complications may be unaffected.

In this regard, the proposal to fortify staple foods with folic acid to protect women at risk from having children with neural tube defects may carry with it a potential risk of masking hematologic manifestations in patients with pernicious anemia. This may result in progression to irreversibility of neurologic complications.

Following treatment with the appropriate vitamin, patients with megaloblastic anemia show a prompt response in both subjective and objective manifestations. Patients often report a dramatic improvement in their sense of well-being. This does not apply to neurologic complications, which usually show a slow improvement after treatment and, in the case of long-standing neurologic complications, may show little or no improvement.

TABLE 12–3–4. PROBLEMS IN THE INTERPRETATION OF THE SCHILLING TEST

- Incomplete urine collection
- Renal disease
- Recent injection of vitamin B_{12} (within 48 hours)
- Food B_{12} malabsorption
- Intestinal megaloblastosis resulting from vitamin B_{12} deficiency caused by pernicious anemia
- Isotope exchange in the combined double-isotope Schilling test

Source: Green R. The diagnostic approach to macrocytic anemias. Sangre 1993;38(suppl. 2):44. Reproduced with permission from the publisher and author.

Patients with pernicious anemia or other irreversible forms of vitamin B_{12} malabsorption require continuation of treatment for life.

Prevention

For socioeconomic reasons, nutritional folate deficiency often recurs in individuals at risk. Improvement in diet and education regarding the importance of not overcooking vegetables is important for the prevention of recurrence. Food fortification with folic acid, presently being contemplated in the United States to prevent neural tube defect pregnancies, will doubtless also contribute to a lowering of the incidence of nutritional folate deficiency. Although this will carry the risk of masking vitamin B_{12} deficiency, there are other potential advantages of improved folate nutrition in the U.S. population, including a lowering of the plasma homocysteine concentration. High plasma homocysteine has been linked to premature vascular disease and thrombosis. There is also evidence to suggest that folate deficiency may be associated with premalignant changes in the cervical epithelium and in the colon.

In association with some diseases and following certain surgical procedures, it is predictable that folate or vitamin B_{12} deficiency may develop. Therefore, following ileal resection or gastrectomy, either patients should be monitored for possible onset of vitamin B_{12} deficiency or, when the resection is extensive, patients should be given prophylactic vitamin B_{12} supplements. In patients with chronic hemolytic anemias or myeloproliferative disorders, in whom folate requirements are increased, similar vigilance may be exercised with respect to folate.

Cost Containment

Ideally, the object of reaching an accurate diagnosis in a patient with a macrocytic anemia is to do so with a minimum of laboratory tests. This is frequently possible in straightforward, typical cases. It is false economy, however, to skimp on laboratory tests when the diagnosis is not clear.

The cost of doing additional tests to firmly establish a diagnosis of vitamin B_{12} deficiency should be balanced against the cost and inconvenience of lifelong injections of vitamin B_{12} in the event that these may not be necessary. Also, timely detection of vitamin B_{12} deficiency in atypical cases can reduce the subsequent cost of protracted care for patients who develop irreversible neurologic damage.

REFERENCES

Allen RH, Stabler SP, Savage DG, et al. Diagnosis of cobalamin deficiency. I. Usefulness of serum methylmalonic acid and total homocysteine concentrations. Am J Hematol 1990;34:90.

Carmel R. Subtle and atypical cobalamin deficiency states. Am J Hematol 1990;34:108.

Green R. Typical and atypical manifestations of pernicious anemia. In: Bhatt R, Besser M, James VHT, Keen H, eds. Thomas Addison and his diseases. Bristol: Journal of Endocrinology Ltd, 1994;1:377.

Green R. Metabolic assays in cobalamin and folate deficiency. In: Wickramasinghe SW, ed. The megaloblastic anemias: Balliére's clinical haematology 1995;8:533.

Healton EH, Savage DG, Brust JCM, et al. Neurologic aspects of cobalamin deficiency. Medicine 1991;70:229.

Herbert V. The 1986 Herman Award Lecture. Nutrition science as a continually unfolding story: The folate and vitamin B_{12} paradigm. Am J Clin Nutr 1986;46:387.

Herbert V. Don't ignore low serum cobalamin (vitamin B_{12}) levels. Arch Intern Med 1988;148:1705.

Schilling RF. Vitamin B_{12} deficiency: Underdiagnosed, overtreated? Hosp Prac 1995;30:47.

Spivack JL. Masked megaloblastic anemia. Arch Intern Med 1982;142:2111.

CHAPTER 12–4

Immune Hemolysis

Ronald E. Domen, M.D.

DEFINITION

Hemolytic anemia, in general, is characterized by the premature destruction of the red blood cell. The immune hemolytic anemias are further defined as disorders in which red blood cell survival is shortened by antibody(ies). The immune hemolytic disorders can be classified into three basic categories: autoimmune hemolytic anemia (AIHA), drug-induced hemolytic anemia, and alloimmune hemolytic anemia (Table 12–4–1).

ETIOLOGY

Antibodies directed against the red blood cell can be produced secondary to a known antigenic stimulus (e.g., a drug or an allogeneic red

TABLE 12–4–1. CLASSIFICATION OF THE IMMUNE HEMOLYTIC ANEMIAS

I. Autoimmune hemolytic anemia (AIHA)
   A. Warm antibody AIHA
   B. Cold antibody (agglutinin) AIHA
   C. Paroxysmal cold hemoglobinuria

II. Drug-induced immune hemolytic anemia
   A. Immune complex mechanism
   B. Drug adsorption mechanism
   C. Autoantibody mechanism
   D. Nonimmunologic mechanism

III. Alloimmune hemolytic anemia
   A. Hemolytic disease of the newborn
   B. Hemolytic transfusion reaction

blood cell transfusion) or may be produced without a known antigenic stimulus (e.g., AIHA).

Warm antibody AIHA is idiopathic in approximately one half to two thirds of cases and secondary to an underlying lymphoproliferative disorder or other autoimmune disorder (e.g., systemic lupus erythematosus or rheumatoid arthritis) in the remaining cases. Typically, warm AIHA is characterized by immunoglobulin (Ig)G autoantibodies with specificity usually directed against antigens in the Rh blood group system.

Cold AIHA has a much lower incidence than warm AIHA and is usually characterized by an IgM autoantibody with specificity directed against the I blood group system. Cold AIHA can be idiopathic or secondary to an underlying disorder. Classically, cold AIHA has been described in association with either *Mycoplasma pneumoniae* pneumonia or infectious mononucleosis.

Paroxysmal cold hemoglobinuria is a relatively rare disorder that historically was associated with congenital or late syphilis. It is characterized by a cold-reacting IgG autoantibody, also referred to as the Donath–Landsteiner antibody, directed against antigens in the P blood group system. Paroxysmal cold hemoglobinuria has also been described in association with various viral infections.

Drug-induced immune hemolytic anemia can cause immune hemolysis through three basic mechanisms: immune complex formation (e.g., quinine and quinidine), drug adsorption (e.g., penicillin and cephalosporin), and autoantibody formation (e.g., methyldopa). A fourth mechanism, membrane modification or nonimmunologic protein adsorption (e.g., as caused by some of the cephalosporins), has so far not been proven to cause immune hemolysis. In the immune complex mechanism, the drug carrier protein–IgM antibody complex binds nonspecifically to the red blood cell ("innocent bystander"), leading to destruction. In the drug adsorption mechanism, IgG antibodies are directed against the drug that has been adsorbed onto the red cell membrane. In the autoantibody mechanism, clinical and laboratory features are similar to those of warm AIHA.

There have been an increased number of reports in recent years of immune hemolysis due to the second- and third-generation cephalosporins. Some of these reports were associated with fatal immune hemolysis. In addition, all three mechanisms of drug-induced immune hemolysis have been reported to occur simultaneously in the same patient with these drugs (e.g., cefotetan). Such unusual cases have prompted some investigators to rethink and reevaluate the pathophysiology underlying the drug-induced immune hemolytic anemias.

Alloimmune hemolytic anemia occurs in two clinical situations: hemolytic transfusion reaction and hemolytic disease of the newborn. In both situations, red cell alloantibodies are stimulated to form secondary to exogenously administered (i.e., transfused) red blood cell antigens. The antibody, which is usually IgG, attaches to those transfused red cells positive for the corresponding antigen with resultant cellular destruction and hemolysis.

CRITERIA FOR DIAGNOSIS
Suggestive

Immune hemolysis should be considered in any patient with evidence of a hemolytic anemia associated with a positive direct antiglobulin test (or Coombs test).

Definitive

Antibody, complement, or both attach to the red blood cell membrane, resulting in cellular destruction and hemolysis. A positive direct antiglobulin test and other laboratory evidence for hemolysis are the main features that support a diagnosis of immune hemolytic anemia.

CLINICAL MANIFESTATIONS
Subjective

The patient's clinical symptoms and physical signs are often a result of the anemia itself and can be highly variable depending on such factors as the rapidity of hemolysis and the presence of any other underlying associated diseases. Shortness of breath, angina, fatigue, dizziness, pallor, and jaundice may be present.

A patient with cold AIHA may have signs and symptoms referable to acrocyanosis of the peripheral extremities following exposure to cold ambient temperatures. Similarly, cold exposure may precipitate hemoglobinuria in paroxysmal cold hemoglobinuria.

Clinical signs and symptoms of drug-induced immune hemolysis secondary to antibiotics may be overshadowed by the underlying infectious process being treated.

Certain historical data may be helpful in determining an immune basis when approaching a patient with an undiagnosed anemia. A prior history of immune hemolysis or of another immunologically mediated cytopenia (e.g., autoimmune thrombocytopenic purpura), a history of an underlying autoimmune disorder, pregnancy history and any associated episodes of hemolytic disease of the newborn, and transfusion history and associated complications should be detailed.

A family history of similar disorders may indicate possible inheritance and familial patterns. In general, however, such information is usually of a nonspecific and noncontributory nature.

Objective
Physical Examination

The physical examination is generally not very helpful. Hepatosplenomegaly and lymphadenopathy may be variably present in one to two thirds of patients. Jaundice secondary to the hemolytic process may be seen in only approximately 20% of patients. Any objective physical findings may be related more to an associated underlying disease (e.g., a lymphoproliferative disorder).

Routine Laboratory Abnormalities

Automated blood cell counts demonstrate the degree of anemia. The mean corpuscular red cell volume (MCV) may be elevated, as may the reticulocyte count. The reticulocyte count may actually be normal to low in as many as one fourth of cases. The white blood cell and platelet counts are not particularly helpful in establishing the diagnosis of immune hemolysis. Examination of the peripheral blood smear may reveal characteristics typical of any hemolytic process such as spherocytes and nucleated red blood cells (Color Plate 12–4–1, after page 826). In cold agglutinin AIHA, red cell agglutination or rouleaux formation may be evident on the peripheral smear. Rarely, the first indication of the cold agglutinin nature of the AIHA comes from the hematology laboratory when the agglutinated red cells cause problems with the automated cell counters. Morphologic examination of the peripheral blood and bone marrow is helpful if an underlying lymphoproliferative or other malignant process is present. Elevated indirect serum bilirubin and lactic dehydrogenase levels are commonly seen as part of a hemolytic process.

PLANS
Diagnostic
Differential Diagnosis

The history, physical examination, and laboratory studies are all important in establishing the presence of a hemolytic anemia. Congenital causes of hemolysis (e.g., sickle cell anemia, glucose-6-phosphate dehydrogenase deficiency) are usually self-evident from the history. Disseminated intravascular coagulation, thrombotic thrombocytopenic purpura, and the hemolytic–uremic syndrome can be causes of hemolysis that may be confused with immune hemolysis at initial presentation. The antiglobulin test will establish the immune nature of the hemolytic process. It is important to remember that other causes of a hemolytic anemia (e.g., sickle cell anemia) may also have a superimposed immune hemolytic anemia (e.g., a transfusion reaction, warm antibody AIHA).

Diagnostic Options

Laboratory testing determines the etiology of the patient's hemolytic process and helps guide therapy.

The single most important test for establishing and characterizing an immune hemolytic anemia is the antiglobulin test. First described in 1945 by Coombs, Mourant, and Race (Petz and Garratty, 1980), the antiglobulin test is used to demonstrate immunoglobulin or complement bound to the red blood cell (direct antiglobulin test) or red blood cell antibody(ies) circulating free (unbound) in the serum (indirect antiglobulin test). Thus, the direct antiglobulin test is used to demonstrate the in vivo coating of red blood cells with antibody and/or complement, whereas the indirect antiglobulin test is used to detect the in vitro attachment of serum antibody and/or complement to commercially prepared, reagent red blood cells.

Anti-human globulin reagents used in the direct and indirect antiglobulin tests can be polyspecific or monospecific. Polyspecific anti-human globulin contains antibody to human IgG and to the C3d component of human complement. Other anticomplement antibodies (e.g., anti-C3b, anti-C4b, and anti-C4d) may occasionally be present in this preparation. In general, there is no activity against IgM or IgA. Monospecific anti-human globulin (AHG), on the other hand, contains specifically either anti-IgG, or anti-C3b, -C3d activities. Monospecific AHG anti-human globulin with anti-IgM or anti-IgA activity is not commercially available for use as an immunohematologic reagent.

Probably fewer than 5% of patients with AIHA have a negative direct antiglobulin test. The direct antiglobulin test is a very sensitive diagnostic tool, being able to detect as few as 150 to 200 molecules of IgG per red blood cell. A negative test, therefore, does not necessarily rule out clinically significant AIHA, but it does make the diagnosis suspect. Conversely, a positive test does not necessarily indicate the presence of clinically significant immune hemolysis. Those few patients who have AIHA due to an IgM or IgA antibody often have a positive direct antiglobulin test because of the presence of complement. In general, the intensity or degree of positivity of the direct antiglobulin test directly correlates with the amount of antibody coating the red blood cell.

If the direct antiglobulin test is positive, the antibody can be eluted off the red cells and its specificity determined. This is not always necessary, especially if the indirect antiglobulin test is positive and the serum antibody's specificity has already been determined. In cases of alloimmunization, recently transfused patients, possible hemolytic transfusion reaction, or hemolytic disease of the newborn, elution and characterization of the antibody may provide useful information.

In the case of cold antibody AIHA, determination of the antibody's titer and thermal amplitude (i.e., its highest temperature of reactivity as determined in vitro) may be clinically useful. In suspected paroxysmal cold hemoglobinuria, a Donath–Landsteiner test should be performed.

Recommended Approach

In suspected immune hemolytic anemia both direct and indirect antiglobulin tests should be performed. If the direct test is positive, an antibody elution study may be indicated to characterize further the antibody(ies) coating the red blood cell.

Therapeutic
Therapeutic Options

Therapy may include glucocorticosteroids, immunosuppressive drugs, splenectomy, discontinuation of a drug causing hemolysis, plasma exchange, or some combination of all of these.

Recommended Approach

Glucocorticosteroid therapy is the mainstay for warm antibody AIHA. Daily doses of 60 to 100 mg of prednisone in the adult patient usually achieve a response in approximately 80 to 90% of cases. The onset of a response is usually evident in the first few days, and is maximal in 2 to 3 weeks. The first indication of a response may be a rise in the hematocrit. Once the hematocrit starts rising or shows signs of stabilizing, which is indicative of a decreased rate of hemolysis, the prednisone can be gradually tapered. Those patients experiencing life-threatening hemolysis may benefit from larger doses in the form of intravenous therapy equivalent to 400 mg of hydrocortisone over 24 hours.

If, after 3 weeks of glucocorticosteroid therapy, remission has not been achieved, splenectomy or immunosuppression with cytotoxic drugs should be considered. Treatment with azathioprine (Imuran) or cyclophosphamide (Cytoxan) in combination with prednisone will cause a remission in about half of those patients not responding to prednisone alone. Splenectomy is potentially effective only in those cases of warm AIHA due to IgG antibody.

As the liver is the major site of antibody attachment resulting in subsequent red cell destruction in those cases of immune hemolytic anemia due to IgM antibody, splenectomy is not of therapeutic benefit in such patients. Patients with cold (IgM) antibody AIHA also do not generally have a good response to glucocorticosteroids. Keeping the patient warm and warming intravenous fluids prior to infusion are beneficial.

Drug-induced immune hemolytic anemia usually responds to withdrawal of the offending drug. There has been an increasing number of fatal cases caused by the second- and third-generation cephalosporins, so early recognition and discontinuation of the offending drug are important.

The use of therapeutic plasma exchange for the treatment of immune hemolytic anemia has not generally shown great promise. Those cases caused by IgM antibody would, theoretically, benefit the most from plasma exchange therapy.

Hemolytic transfusion reactions should be treated by general supportive measures. Major blood group incompatibility (i.e., involving the ABO system) is more likely to result in acute hemolysis and the severe complications of renal failure, disseminated intravascular coagulation, and/or cardiovascular collapse. Most fatal hemolytic transfusion reactions occur as a result of an ABO mismatch. An incompatibility involving a minor blood group antigen system (e.g., Rh, Duffy, Kidd) is usually the cause of a delayed hemolytic transfusion reaction and is only rarely complicated by more than shortened survival of the transfused blood. In either case, at the first indication of a possible he-molytic transfusion reaction it is important to discontinue the red cell transfusion, monitor the patient, and notify the blood bank/transfusion service.

Red blood cell transfusions should generally be avoided in the immune hemolytic anemias, particularly warm and cold antibody AIHA. In general, transfused red cells will have the same shortened lifespan as the patient's own red cells and any anticipated benefit from the transfusion is most likely to be short-lived. Maintenance of blood volume with intravenous fluids and volume expanders, administration of oxygen therapy, and maintenance of renal function are important supportive measures. Cardiovascular, central nervous system, or pulmonary decompensation due to inadequate tissue oxygenation may necessitate red cell transfusion. It is extremely important that blood samples for diagnostic and red cell crossmatching purposes be obtained before any blood is transfused into the patient. A clinical pathologist specialized in blood banking and transfusion medicine should be consulted early in the course of treatment.

FOLLOW-UP

Close clinical observation of the patient and monitoring of laboratory parameters are critical. The critically ill and decompensated patient may require treatment in an intensive care setting. Diagnosis and treatment of any underlying condition (e.g., infection, systemic lupus erythematosus, malignancy) should be performed concurrently with treatment of the hemolytic anemia. Patients with warm or cold antibody AIHA can potentially have unpredictable relapses and thus should be watched closely for a period after going into remission. Idiopathic cases of warm or cold AIHA should be clinically observed for the future development of associated autoimmune or lymphoproliferative disorders. The patient should be educated about the immune hemolytic anemia and the importance of self-screening and examination, as well as prognostic considerations.

DISCUSSION
Prevalence and Incidence

Warm antibody AIHA has a reported incidence of approximately 1 in 50,000 to 80,000 individuals. Persons of any age can be affected and there is no race predilection. Cold antibody AIHA is more frequently seen in middle-aged or elderly patients, and it has a lower incidence as compared with warm antibody AIHA. Both males and females appear to be equally prone to develop cold antibody AIHA. Paroxysmal cold hemoglobinuria is an uncommon disorder.

Hemolytic anemia secondary to drugs is not that common, but should always be considered in the patient with no other ready explanation for a positive direct antiglobulin test and hemolysis, or in the patient receiving drug therapy and no other explanation for a low blood cell count. Approximately 10 to 15% of patients receiving methyldopa develop a positive direct antiglobulin test, but less than 1% actually develop a hemolytic anemia. Methyldopa produces a clinical picture indistinguishable from that of warm antibody AIHA and the pathophysiology is incompletely understood.

Fatalities secondary to acute hemolytic transfusion reactions are not common. The current estimated incidence of a fatal acute hemolytic transfusion reaction is approximately 1 in 600,000 to 800,000 red blood cell transfusions. Fatalities are most commonly related to clerical, system, or managerial errors, rather than technical mistakes, and most often involve an ABO-incompatible transfusion. Delayed hemolytic transfusion reactions occur with greater frequency and are rarely associated with significant morbidity or mortality.

Related Basic Science

The binding of an antibody to an antigen, or antigen–drug complex, on the surface of the red blood cell membrane does not, by itself, adversely affect the lifespan of the red blood cell. Otherwise normal individuals (e.g., blood donors), as well as an occasional patient, may be found to have a positive direct antiglobulin test without evidence of immune hemolysis. Basically, two mechanisms have been identified to explain the immune destruction of antibody-coated red blood cells: (1)

complement activation and red cell lysis, and (2) adherence of antibody Fc receptors to cells of the monocyte/macrophage system (primarily the spleen or liver) followed by phagocytosis and red cell destruction.

Red cells coated with IgG are destroyed primarily in the spleen, whereas IgM-mediated hemolysis occurs through complement activation and/or phagocytosis by liver macrophages. IgG subclasses 1 and 3 (i.e., IgG1 and IgG3) are also capable of complement fixation. Although exceptions exist, as a general rule the stronger the direct antiglobulin test reaction, the higher the concentration of antibody and the more severe the immune hemolysis. IgM cold agglutinins must have a high thermal range or amplitude (i.e., above 30°C) to be a cause of clinically significant hemolysis.

The etiology and basic pathophysiology underlying the diverse causes of immune red cell destruction are far from being completely understood.

Natural History and Its Modification with Treatment

Morbidity and mortality are highly variable and unpredictable in the immune hemolytic anemias. Rapidity of onset and degree of red cell destruction, associated underlying conditions, antibody class and subclass, and required treatment modality(ies) are all significant variables affecting the clinical outcome in individual cases. Hemolysis associated with renal failure or disseminated intravascular coagulation is also a cause of significant morbidity and mortality.

Prevention

Few preventive measures exist for this type of hemolysis. Drugs known to induce immune hemolysis in a particular patient should be avoided in any future therapy. The patient with paroxysmal cold hemoglobinuria with chronic disease may need to avoid those exposures to cold that induce hemolysis. In those patients with red cell alloantibodies, exposure to the corresponding antigen should be avoided.

Cost Containment

With close observation, patients with immune hemolysis can occasionally be managed as outpatients. Once the diagnosis is made, laboratory testing can usually be kept at a minimum. As noted above, transfusion therapy should be individualized and kept at a minimum.

REFERENCES

Ballas SK. The pathophysiology of hemolytic anemias. Transfus Med Rev 1990;4:236.

Engelfriet CP, Overbeeke MAM, von dem Borne AEGKr. Autoimmune hemolytic anemia. Semin Hematol 1992;29:3.

Garratty G, Nance S, Lloyd M, Domen R. Fatal immune hemolytic anemia due to cefotetan. Transfusion 1992;32:269.

Petz LD. Drug-induced autoimmune hemolytic anemia. Transfus Med Rev 1993;7:242.

Petz LD, Garratty G. Acquired immune hemolytic anemias. New York: Churchill Livingstone, 1980.

CHAPTER 12–5

Hemoglobinopathies • Nonsickling Disorders

Andrew J. Fishleder, M.D.

DEFINITION

Hemoglobinopathies are inherited abnormalities of hemoglobin structure or production.

ETIOLOGY

These disorders result from either qualitative or quantitative defects in the globin chain component of hemoglobin. The qualitative or structural hemoglobinopathies are characterized by amino acid substitution, deletion, or addition within the alpha or beta globin chain amino acid sequence. These structural changes may or may not have clinical consequence depending on the type and location of amino acid alteration within the globin chain. The quantitative hemoglobinopathies, in contrast, are characterized by an imbalance in globin chain production that results from an inherited decrease in the production of a normally structured globin chain. These abnormalities are termed *thalassemia syndromes* and are individually named for the specific globin chain that is reduced in quantity (e.g., alpha thalassemia secondary to reduced alpha globin chain production). A third type of hemoglobinopathy that is neither qualitative nor quantitative in nature is hereditary persistence of fetal hemoglobin. This disorder results from a failure of the red blood cell to switch from gamma globin chain (fetal) to beta globin chain (adult) production, resulting in elevated hemoglobin F and reduced hemoglobin (Hb) A levels. This disorder is beyond the scope of this chapter and therefore is not further described.

CRITERIA FOR DIAGNOSIS
Suggestive

The structural hemoglobinopathies typically do not present with a peripheral blood count or red blood cell morphology that suggests their diagnosis, with the exception of Hb C, which demonstrates target cells and may be mildly microcytic (and Hb S associated with sickling disorders). Patients with Hb C disease (homozygous state) may also display condensed hemoglobin segments termed *Hb C crystals* in the peripheral blood. Hemoglobinopathies that increase or decrease the oxygen affinity of hemoglobin may present with erythrocytosis or anemia, respectively, but typically demonstrate normal red blood cell morphology. Finally, those structural defects that result in unstable hemoglobins may present with chronic hemolysis and reticulocytosis. Evaluation of red blood cell morphology may reveal "bite cells," and Heinz bodies may be demonstrable by special stains.

The thalassemia syndromes can be subdivided into thalassemia minor (heterozygous state) and thalassemia intermedia/thalassemia major (homozygous state). Thalassemia minor is characterized by a blood count demonstrating a microcytic erythrocytosis with either a normal or slightly reduced hemoglobin. Red blood cell mean corpuscular hemoglobin (MCH) is also reduced, although the red cell distribution width (RDW) is typically normal. Red blood cell morphology may be abnormal with target cells, poikilocytosis, and basophilic stipling. Thalassemia intermedia and thalassemia major demonstrate a more pronounced microcytic anemia that varies in severity depending on the etiologic molecular defect. Hemoglobin may range from 5 to 9 g/dL with prominent poikilocytosis and red blood cell polychromasia indicative of a reticulocyte response. Circulating nucleated red blood cells may also be noted.

Definitive

Hemoglobin electrophoresis enables identification of many but not all of the clinically significant hemoglobinopathies. The more common disorders such as Hb S, Hb C, Hb E, Hb D, and Hb G can all be identified by this technique. In contrast, many of the structurally abnormal hemoglobins that cause altered oxygen affinity or hemoglobin instability cannot be differentiated from normal Hb A by this technique. The unstable hemoglobins may be specifically identified by performing an isopropanol denaturation test (Carrel test) or heat stability test that causes unstable hemoglobins to precipitate. Identification of Heinz bodies may be helpful but is less specific, as they can be present in other causes of oxidative hemolysis such as red blood cell enzyme defects. Definitive identification of hemoglobinopathies that alter oxygen affinity may require more detailed study of red blood cell oxygen dissociation; however, this is typically not performed.

Definitive diagnosis of the thalassemias can be achieved by evaluation of Hb A, Hb A_2, and Hb F in conjunction with the patient's peripheral blood count. Hb A_2 and Hb F are mildly elevated in beta thalassemia minor, and Hb F alone is mildly elevated in delta–beta thalassemia minor with a slightly reduced Hb A_2. Alpha thalassemia minor, on the other hand, demonstrates normal percentages of Hb A, Hb A_2, and Hb F in conjunction with the typical thalassemic blood picture (microcytic erythrocytosis). Alpha thalassemia minor is most commonly a diagnosis of exclusion, although definitive diagnosis can be achieved by DNA analysis for the specific inherited molecular defect. In the homozygous forms of beta thalassemia and delta–beta thalassemia, the percentages of Hb F are more prominently elevated with little or no normal Hb A present. Alpha thalassemia intermedia (Hb H disease) can be diagnosed by hemoglobin electrophoresis with demonstration of the abnormal Hb H. Hb H inclusions can also be demonstrated by special stains of the peripheral blood.

CLINICAL MANIFESTATIONS

Subjective

Symptoms resulting from the various hemoglobinopathies described above parallel the patient's degree of anemia. In addition, in those individuals with unstable hemoglobins, chronic hemolysis may result in presentation with symptoms of cholelithiasis. Family history should reveal similar chronic hemolysis in the patient's parent as these are dominantly inherited disorders. As the thalassemia syndromes are of clinically significant severity only in the homozygous state, family history may fail to reveal previous familial clinical problems. Because of the inherited nature of these disorders, siblings may or may not have similar clinical abnormalities.

Objective

Physical Examination

Physical examination in most hemoglobinopathies is normal. Splenomegaly may be identified in those individuals with hemoglobinopathies that result in chronic hemolysis (e.g., unstable hemoglobins). Cyanosis may also be apparent with hemoglobinopathies that cause reduced oxygen affinity of hemoglobin.

As with most structural hemoglobinopathies, physical examination is noncontributory in patients with thalassemia minor. These patients are usually identified during a routine peripheral blood screen and are clinically asymptomatic. On the other hand, patients with thalassemia intermedia or thalassemia major present with severe anemia early in life and demonstrate splenomegaly and jaundice as a result of chronic hemolysis. Patients with thalassemia major demonstrate skeletal abnormalities, caused by bone marrow expansion, and growth retardation, as well as endocrine or cardiac dysfunction.

Routine Laboratory Abnormalities

As described previously, chronic hemolysis may be present in patients with a variety of hemoglobinopathies or thalassemia syndromes. Laboratory abnormalities typical of chronic hemolysis include elevated total and unconjugated bilirubin levels, elevated lactate dehydrogenase (LDH) level (particularly isoenzyme LDH-2), and reduced haptoglobin level, as well as chronic reticulocytosis. The degree of anemia varies with each of the different hemoglobinopathies.

In thalassemia minor, the peripheral blood count with a microcytic erythrocytosis with or without a mild degree of anemia will be the sole laboratory abnormality. On the other hand, patients with thalassemia

intermedia or thalassemia major have a moderate to severe hemolytic anemia with prominent microcytosis.

PLANS
Diagnostic
Differential Diagnosis

The differential diagnosis for those structural hemoglobinopathies that result in chronic hemolysis includes a long list of inherited and acquired defects. The inherited disorders include red blood cell membrane defects such as hereditary spherocytosis and hereditary elliptocytosis and red blood cell enzyme defects such as pyruvate kinase deficiency and glucose-6-phosphate dehydrogenase deficiency. The most common causes of acquired chronic hemolysis include immune hemolytic anemia, traumatic hemolytic anemia, and drug-induced hemolysis.

The differential diagnosis of thalassemia minor includes iron deficiency, anemia of chronic disease, some other structural hemoglobinopathies, and polycythemia of any cause complicated by iron deficiency. In contrast to thalassemia minor, thalassemia intermedia and thalassemia major must be differentiated from severe iron deficiency.

Diagnostic Options

Assessment of red blood cell morphology in conjunction with a Coombs test and osmotic fragility test should enable differentiation of structural hemoglobinopathies from red blood cell membrane defects. When red blood cell enzyme defects are suspected, specific enzyme assays may be necessary. Peripheral blood evaluation in conjunction with a Coombs test also enables identification of immune hemolysis, and the identification of red blood cell fragments confirms traumatic hemolysis. Drug-induced oxidative hemolysis may morphologically mimic hemolysis due to unstable hemoglobins and requires clinical history to rule out the use of drugs with oxidant capacity. These are usually sulfa and antimalarial drugs.

A peripheral blood count with red blood cell indices helps to differentiate iron deficiency from thalassemia. Typically, the indices in iron deficiency reveal a mean corpuscular volume that is reduced in parallel to the degree of anemia, and there is prominent variation in red blood cell size reflected by an elevated red cell distribution width. In patients with iron deficiency complicating polycythemia of any etiology, the red blood cell indices more closely resemble those of thalassemia minor except for the elevated red cell distribution width. Serum iron studies should suffice to establish the diagnosis of iron deficiency, although serum ferritin may also be helpful. Anemia of chronic disease may, at times, present with a decreased mean corpuscular volume, but typically not in conjunction with an erythrocytosis. Again, serum iron studies or ferritin may be helpful. In contrast to thalassemia minor, thalassemia intermedia and thalassemia major may present with red blood cell indices similar to those of severe iron deficiency. The presence of nucleated red blood cells and reticulocytes in addition to the clinical history should help to differentiate these thalassemic disorders from iron deficiency.

Recommended Approach

Initial review of a patient's peripheral blood count and red blood cell morphology should significantly narrow the diagnostic possibilities. In the presence of chronic hemolysis, an unstable hemoglobin test and Coombs test should also be performed. Hemoglobin electrophoresis and Hb A_2 quantitation along with serum iron studies enable diagnosis of beta-thalassemia and differentiation from iron deficiency.

Therapeutic

In patients with chronic hemolysis due to structural hemoglobinopathies, splenectomy may be helpful in improving red blood cell survival. Patients should also avoid the use of drugs with oxidant capacity such as sulfa drugs. Blood transfusions may be necessary in those patients with chronic hemolysis who develop an aplastic crisis caused by parvovirus infection.

Therapy for patients with thalassemia major is aimed at treating the severe anemia with blood transfusions and preventing iron overload by the use of iron chelating agents, for example, desferrioxamine. The use of hypertransfusion regimens that maintain hemoglobin levels above 12 g/dL has been shown to reduce skeletal abnormalities and growth retardation that result from bone marrow expansion. Concomitant iron chelation is necessary to prevent complications due to hemosiderosis. Bone marrow transplantation is the only potential cure for this disorder, but is associated with its own morbidity and mortality risk.

FOLLOW-UP

Most difficult decisions dealing with patients with thalassemia intermedia or major are confronted by pediatric hematologists. These decisions include timing of transfusions, when to initiate desferrioxamine therapy, monitoring of iron overload status, and role of splenectomy.

For the adult hematologist or primary care physician following a patient with thalassemia minor, it is usually important to recommend folic acid supplementation at a dose of 1 mg per day to support the hyperactivity of the erythroid series in the bone marrow. If gallstones occur, a cholecystectomy may prevent cholecystitis or having a stone becoming lodged in the cystic duct or common bile duct.

For patients with structural variants of hemoglobin, such as Hg C disease, there is usually no particular clinical problem. Some patients may have splenomegaly and complain of abdominal pain. These patients also may benefit from chronic folate supplementation.

DISCUSSION
Prevalence

Worldwide, the various hemoglobinopathies are extremely common, although the specific incidence of different hemoglobinopathies varies with the genetic background of individual populations. For example, Hb E is extremely common in individuals of Oriental descent, and Hb C and Hb G are common in African-Americans. The thalassemia syndromes are also extremely common in descendants from Asia, Africa, and the Mediterranean basin. As with Hb S, the high prevalence of thalassemia is linked to its ability to protect red blood cells from invasion by malaria.

Related Basic Science

Normal adult hemoglobin comprises two alpha globin chains and two beta globin chains, as well as an oxygen-carrying heme molecule. The alpha chains are coded for by four alpha globin genes, and the beta chains are coded for by two beta globin chains. Structural hemoglobinopathies result from mutations that alter the nucleotide sequence of one of these genes, thereby causing a change in amino acid sequence of the globin chain product. Amino acid substitutions may occur anywhere on a globin chain. Those that occur within sequences in or near the heme-binding portion of a globin chain can result in unstable hemoglobins and/or hemoglobins with altered oxygen affinity. Defects that occur on one beta gene result in approximately 50% normal Hb A and 50% abnormal hemoglobin. When the abnormal hemoglobin is unstable, its percentage is typically less than 50%. Inheritance is autosomal dominant, and patients who are heterozygous for a beta chain defect that is unstable have chronic hemolysis. In contrast to the beta globin gene system, normal individuals possess four alpha globin genes (two inherited from each parent). The product of a single defective alpha gene, therefore, typically results in approximately 25% of the abnormal hemoglobin and 75% normal Hb A. Chronic hemolytic anemia may still result if the amino acid substitution in the abnormal alpha chain affects the heme-binding portion of hemoglobin; however, most unstable hemoglobins result from beta globin chain defects. There are numerous other structural hemoglobinopathies that are not clinically significant. These result from inherited globin chain defects that alter globin chain sequence in locations that do not affect hemoglobin function or stability. Many of these are identifiable by hemoglobin electrophoresis. In contrast, many of the unstable hemoglobins result from amino acid substitutions that do not alter the charge of the hemoglobin molecule and, therefore, are not distinguishable from Hb A by electrophoretic techniques.

The thalassemia syndromes result from mutations that decrease the production of the associated globin chain. The beta thalassemias typically result from one of many point mutations in the DNA sequence in or around the beta globin gene that decreases gene transcription and, therefore, synthesis of the beta globin chain. In contrast, alpha thalassemia and delta–beta thalassemia typically result from deletion of all or a portion of the affected globin gene with a similar result: decreased globin chain production. In either case, the reduction in globin chain synthesis results in an imbalance between alpha and nonalpha globin chains that is characteristic of thalassemia and in some way linked to the red blood cell microcytosis. There are several forms of beta thalassemia with varying severity in the homozygous state dependent on the degree of reduced beta globin chain production. In the heterozygous state, however, all forms result in a thalassemia minor blood picture that is indistinguishable from other forms of thalassemia. The presence of four alpha globin genes makes the genetics of alpha thalassemia somewhat more complicated. Single-gene-deletion alpha thalassemia (three fourths functioning alpha globin genes) is clinically silent with a normal peripheral blood picture. This is because the globin chain imbalance is minimal with three functioning alpha globin genes. Two-gene-deletion alpha thalassemia may result from two patterns of inheritance: heterozygosity for two alpha genes deleted from one chromosome or homozygosity for a single gene deleted from each chromosome. In either case, a thalassemia minor blood picture results; however, in the former pattern, one of the patient's parents will also have thalassemia minor. In the latter pattern, homozygosity for single-gene deletion, both parents may be normal as single-gene-deletion alpha thalassemia is clinically silent. The form of alpha thalassemia with two alpha genes deleted from one chromosome is extremely common in Southeast Asians but rare in African-Americans. Single-gene-deletion alpha thalassemia, however, is very common in both populations. For this reason, Hb H disease with three of four alpha genes deleted is common in Southeast Asians but rare in African-Americans. The term *hemoglobin H* refers to the tetramers of beta globin chain that are able to form due to the severe imbalance between alpha and beta chain production in three-gene-deletion alpha thalassemia. This abnormal hemoglobin molecule can be identified by hemoglobin electrophoresis or by special stains of red blood cells.

Natural History and Its Modification with Treatment

The unstable hemoglobins result in lifelong chronic hemolysis that may improve following splenectomy. As with other forms of chronic hemolytic anemia, parvovirus infection may precipitate an aplastic crisis that temporarily results in severe anemia. This may require transfusion support. Drugs that have an oxidant effect may worsen hemolysis secondary to unstable hemoglobins and should be avoided.

Patients with thalassemia major are transfusion dependent unless cured by bone marrow transplantation. Hypertransfusion therapy significantly lessens skeletal abnormalities and growth retardation; however, rigorous chelation therapy is necessary to prevent end-organ damage due to iron overload.

Prevention

The only form of disease prevention is genetic counseling. Prenatal DNA analysis can also be used to identify a fetus that will have thalassemia major when born.

Cost Containment

The use of esoteric tests to specifically identify individual abnormal hemoglobins is unnecessary. Generic identification of an unstable hemoglobin in most instances is sufficient diagnostically. Likewise, a positive isopropanol denaturation test does not need to be confirmed by a heat stability test, particularly in a patient with chronic hemolysis.

In thalassemia minor, another source of wasted laboratory testing is extensive evaluation for iron deficiency. Patients with a typical thalassemic blood picture that demonstrates a normal hemoglobin with prominent microcytosis do not require additional iron testing nor a therapeutic trial with oral iron. In those individuals with less characteristic red blood cell indices, iron studies may be helpful to exclude iron deficiency or anemia of chronic disease. Alternatively, a trial of iron therapy with follow-up peripheral blood count may suffice to differentiate thalassemia minor from iron deficiency. Bone marrow examination is unnecessary.

REFERENCES

Fosburg MT, Nathan DG. Treatment of Cooley's anemia. Blood 1990;76:435.

Merkel PA, Simonson DC, Amiel SA, et al. Insulin resistance and hyperinsu-linemia in patients with thalassemia major treated by hypertransfusion. N Engl J Med 1988;318:809.

Miale JB. Laboratory medicine: Hematology. 6th ed. St. Louis: Mosby, 1982.

Stabler SP, Jones RT, Head C, et al. Hemoglobin Denver: A low-oxygen-affinity variant associated with chronic cyanosis and anemia. Mayo Clin Proc 1994;69:237.

Steinberg MH, Adams JG. Hemoglobin A$_2$: Origin, evolution, and aftermath. Blood 1991;78:2165.

CHAPTER 12–6
Congenital Hemolytic Anemia

Andrew J. Fishleder, M.D.

DEFINITION

Congenital hemolytic anemia encompasses a broad range of inherited red blood cell defects that result in decreased red blood cell survival. Hemoglobinopathies causing chronic hemolysis are discussed in Chapter 12–5. In this chapter, red blood cell membrane defects and red blood cell enzyme defects are discussed.

ETIOLOGY

Congenital hemolytic anemia is caused by defects intrinsic to the red blood cell that either directly or indirectly alter the integrity of the red blood cell membrane. This may be directly through the production of abnormal membrane proteins or deficiencies in red blood cell enzymes that normally provide energy necessary for membrane function and cellular integrity.

CRITERIA FOR DIAGNOSIS
Suggestive

The presence of persistent anemia and reticulocytosis suggests ongoing hemolysis that may be congenital or acquired in nature. Red blood cell morphology can help rule out traumatic hemolysis, and other etiologies such as immune and drug-induced hemolysis must be excluded with appropriate laboratory tests and history. Red blood cell morphology may demonstrate certain characteristic morphologic abnormalities such as spherocytes and elliptocytes; however, further testing is required for definitive diagnosis. A positive Heinz body stain suggests an unstable hemoglobin or a red blood cell enzyme defect.

Definitive

The presence of numerous spherocytes or elliptocytes in conjunction with a negative Coombs test and a positive family history for chronic hemolysis is consistent with a diagnosis of hereditary spherocytosis or hereditary elliptocytosis (Color Plates 12–6–1 and 12–6–2, after page 826). Sophisticated assays for red blood cell membrane protein defects can definitively identify the specific abnormality, but are typically not necessary. Red blood cell enzyme defects can be detected by enzyme assays to identify the specific abnormality.

CLINICAL MANIFESTATIONS
Subjective

The congenital hemolytic anemias vary greatly in their clinical features. The degree of anemia may be mild to severe, with splenomegaly noted in association with red blood cell membrane defects. Mild jaundice may also be noted. Family history will reveal hemolytic anemia in parents of those individuals with dominantly inherited causes of hemolysis. History may also reveal exacerbation of anemia by oxidant drugs in patients with glucose-6-phosphate (G6PD) deficiency and selected other enzymopathies. In G6PD deficiency, infection may be a presenting cause for acute hemolysis.

Objective
Physical Examination

Splenomegaly and mild jaundice may be the only abnormalities noted on physical examination of patients with chronic hemolysis. Hepatomegaly may also be present on occasion. These findings are, however, nonspecific, and diagnosis requires appropriate laboratory testing.

Routine Laboratory Abnormalities

A peripheral blood count and red blood cell morphology review provide the initial suggestion of chronic hemolysis with the presence of persistent unexplained anemia and reticulocytosis. Morphologic review demonstrating the presence of spherocytes or numerous elliptocytes in conjunction with a negative Coombs test strongly suggests hereditary spherocytosis or hereditary elliptocytosis, respectively.

PLANS
Diagnostic
Differential Diagnosis

The differential diagnosis in patients with chronic hemolysis includes a broad range of inherited and acquired defects. Hemoglobinopathies comprise the most common form of congenital abnormality that must be differentiated from red blood cell membrane and enzyme abnormalities. Acquired causes of hemolysis most commonly result from immune hemolytic anemia, drug-induced hemolytic anemia, and traumatic hemolysis. The latter causes include cardiac valve disease, disseminated intravascular coagulation, thrombotic thrombocytopenic purpura, and microangiopathic anemias, all of which are discussed in other chapters.

Diagnostic Options

In the absence of red blood cell morphologic abnormalities, hemoglobin electrophoresis and tests for unstable hemoglobin exclude hemoglobinopathies as a cause of chronic hemolysis, whereas specific enzyme assays identify red blood cell enzyme defects such as G6PD deficiency and pyruvate kinase deficiencies. A less common enzymopathy, pyrimidine-5'-nucleotidase deficiency, may be suggested by the presence of prominent coarse basophilic stippling of red blood cells in the absence of lead toxicity. As with other causes of chronic hemolysis, all of these disorders may demonstrate elevations in unconjugated and total bilirubin and lactate dehydrogenase.

Recommended Approach

Review of peripheral blood morphology can be the most helpful starting point in the diagnosis of chronic hemolysis. Identification of spherocytes should be followed by a Coombs test to exclude immune hemolysis. An autohemolysis test or osmotic fragility test is not necessary when spherocytes are morphologically identified; however, the latter is commonly used to confirm their presence.

The presence of numerous elliptocytes (greater than 25% of red blood cells) is indicative of hereditary elliptocytosis. Patients with hemolytic hereditary elliptocytosis also demonstrate scattered spherocytes and schistocytes with prominent polychromasia indicating a reticulocytosis. Although other conditions such as iron deficiency and thalassemia may also demonstrate circulating elliptocytes, these abnormal red blood cells are never as numerous as in hereditary elliptocytosis.

In the absence of characteristic red blood cell morphologic abnormalities, an isopropanol precipitation test should be performed to rule out an unstable hemoglobin, and specific assays for red blood cell G6PD and pyruvate kinase should be performed to rule out these two common enzyme disorders. Reference laboratory tests are available to identify less common red blood cell enzyme deficiencies should the above testing be nonproductive.

Therapeutic

Therapeutic Options

In patients with red blood cell membrane defects such as hereditary spherocytosis and hemolytic hereditary elliptocytosis, the only available therapy is splenectomy. This prevents subsequent hemolysis even though the characteristic red blood cell morphologic abnormality persists.

In patients with red blood cell enzyme deficiencies such as G6PD deficiency, the only therapeutic options are transfusion during an episode of acute hemolysis and avoidance of drugs that are known to precipitate hemolysis in susceptible individuals. The latter list includes sulfa drugs and antimalarial agents, as well as a variety of other drugs that may have oxidant activity. In pyruvate kinase deficiency, on the other hand, reduced red blood cell survival may be improved following splenectomy; however, the effectiveness of this therapy is extremely variable. As with any congenital hemolytic anemia, splenectomy should be avoided during the first few years of life because of the increased risk of infection. Red blood cell transfusions may be required if anemia is severe.

Recommended Approach

As described, the therapeutic options for the treatment of red blood cell membrane and enzyme defects are few. Splenectomy improves red blood cell survival in hereditary spherocytosis and hemolytic hereditary elliptocytosis and, therefore, is recommended. It can also be useful in deficiencies of certain enzymes such as pyruvate kinase. Otherwise, acute hemolytic episodes and disorders such as G6PD deficiency should be supported by red blood cell transfusion.

FOLLOW-UP

Patients with hereditary spherocytosis who have significant anemia and splenomegaly do benefit from splenectomy. Once the spleen is removed, they have a 1% risk of fulminant pneumococcal sepsis. They need to be alert to the risk of this infection and seek medical treatment immediately if they develop a flulike syndrome in the future. Alternatively, patients who have had a splenectomy should always have antibiotics available to them to initiate treatment once they feel an infection occurring. Immunization with pneumococcal vaccine is recommended 4 weeks prior to spleen removal. Prophylactic penicillin has been shown to prevent pneumococcal sepsis in children.

Because the inherited red blood cell membrane defect persists after splenectomy, there is still erythroid hyperplasia in the bone marrow and increased erythroid activity. Therefore, folic acid supplementation should be provided.

Patients with hereditary membrane disorders need to be aware of the risk for a drop in hemoglobin accompanying infections or fevers in the future. Parvovirus can cause the prototypic loss of erythroid progenitor cells in the bone marrow, which may last up to 10 days. if patients do develop a viral syndrome and feel much weaker, they should seek medical attention immediately because transfusion may be necessary to get them through this episode.

Patients with membrane disorders also need to be alert to the possibility of gallstones. If they develop right upper quadrant pain or worsening jaundice accompanied by right upper quadrant pain, they should seek medical attention to determine whether a stone has lodged in the biliary tree. Prophylactic cholecystectomy may be indicated for individuals who develop gallstones at a young age.

DISCUSSION

Although a long list of inherited red blood cell membrane and red blood cell enzyme defects can result in chronic hemolysis, inheritance patterns and disease frequency are extremely variable. This discussion focuses on the more commonly inherited defects: hereditary spherocytosis, puruvate kinase deficiency, and G6PD deficiency.

Hereditary Spherocytosis
Prevalence

The incidence of hereditary spherocytosis in the United States is approximately 0.02%. There is no sex predilection, and the disease is encountered in individuals of all races. Hereditary elliptocytosis is equally as common; however, hemolysis occurs in only 10 to 15% of individuals with this disorder.

Related Basic Science

Hereditary spherocytosis is inherited as an autosomal dominant disorder, although incomplete penetrance and sporadic mutations have been reported and account for families in which parents of affected children are hematologically normal. The genetic defects responsible for hereditary spherocytosis result in either a quantitative decrease in red blood cell membrane spectrin levels or the incorporation of a qualitatively abnormal spectrin into the red blood cell membrane. This structural defect alters the red blood cell membrane function and compromises its integrity with resulting decreased red blood cell survival in individuals with an intact spleen. Following splenectomy, however, red blood cell survival is normal or near normal despite persistent spherocytosis.

Natural History and Its Modification with Treatment

Hereditary spherocytosis is associated with a variable degree of anemia, jaundice, and splenomegaly. Both age of onset and severity of disease vary greatly among individuals. In addition to splenomegaly, cholelithiasis is commonly encountered, as is typical of many chronic hemolytic disorders. The degree of a patient's anemia typically remains stable with ongoing compensated hemolysis. An acute aplastic crisis, however, can result in acute onset of severe anemia. Human parvovirus is typically the offending agent for these crises, and anemia resolves in 7 to 10 days. Splenectomy in the vast majority of cases is curative of the hemolytic anemia, although circulating spherocytes remain. In fact, failure to correct anemia postsplenectomy should prompt examination for an accessory spleen.

Prevention

No method of prevention is known.

Cost Containment

A few basic laboratory tests and family history should suffice to establish the diagnosis of hereditary spherocytosis. Sophisticated red blood cell membrane assays to document the spectrin defect are unnecessary clinically and are not cost-justifiable. Likewise, the presence of jaundice does not necessitate a battery of liver enzyme screens and viral hepatitis markers unless a significant change in the patient's condition is noted.

Glucose-6-phosphate Dehydrogenase Deficiency
Prevalence

Glucose-6-phosphate dehydrogenase deficiency has a worldwide distribution. It is common in African-Americans and in individuals of Mediterranean and Asian origin. Overall, it is estimated that more than 100,000,000 people worldwide are affected by this enzyme deficiency.

Related Basic Science

Glucose-6-phosphate dehydrogenase is a key enzyme within the pentose phosphate pathway of red blood cell glycolysis. This biochemical system is responsible for protecting the red blood cell from oxidant damage. The gene that codes for glucose-6-phosphate dehydrogenase is located on the X chromosome. Deficiency of this enzyme, therefore, is inherited as an X-linked recessive disorder: males fully express the deficiency and females have 50% enzyme activity. There are more than 380 variants of G6PD deficiency with different effects and, therefore, differing clinical importance. The most common G6PD deficiency variants, the African-American black and Mediterranean forms, typically present with hemolysis of varying severity caused by certain drugs or precipitated by infection or metabolic stress. Typically, these individuals are not anemic until their red blood cells are challenged, at which time oxidative denaturation of hemoglobin and red blood cell membrane damage result in reduced red blood cell survival and hemolysis. A long list of drugs including antimalarial agents and sulfa-containing compounds such as sulfonamides are well known to precipitate acute hemolysis. Hemolysis induced by infection, however, is probably equally as common in these individuals. In other G6PD deficiency variants, chronic hemolytic anemia occurs in the absence of infection or drug-induced oxidant damage.

Natural History and Its Modification with Treatment

In patients with the more common forms of G6PD deficiency, acute hemolytic episodes occur following ingestion of certain drugs or infection. The severity of anemia is variable, and patients may be jaundiced with dark urine. Hemolysis occurs approximately 3 days following ingestion of an offending drug, and hemoglobin levels may decrease by 3 to 4 g/dL. Bone marrow response and reticulocytosis raise the hemoglobin level within 1 week, even if the offending drug continues to be administered. In patients with chronic hemolysis, aplastic crises due to parvovirus or other etiology may require transfusion therapy for support.

Prevention

Avoidance of drugs known to precipitate hemolysis is the key to disease prevention in G6PD-deficient individuals. This will not, however, prevent hemolysis that may acutely occur during infection. As long as the patient's bone marrow is intact, however, the ensuing hemolysis should be self-limited and correction of the infection or metabolic insult will remove the offending agent.

Cost Containment

As with other causes of chronic hemolysis, laboratory testing aimed at specifically identifying G6PD variants is expensive and unnecessary. Simple screening tests and assay should suffice except during episodes of acute hemolysis when reticulocytosis may mask enzyme deficiency.

Pyruvate Kinase Deficiency

Prevalence

Pyruvate kinase deficiency is second only to glucose-6-phosphate dehydrogenase deficiency in worldwide prevalence. Most cases have been reported in individuals from northern Europe, the United States, and Japan; however, the defect has been described in diverse groups in broad geographic distribution.

Related Basic Science

Pyruvate kinase is a key enzyme in the production of ATP within the red blood cell. Deficiency of this enzyme therefore leads to inadequate ATP production with subsequent red blood cell membrane damage and loss of membrane function. Pyruvate kinase deficiency is inherited as an autosomal recessive trait, and hemolysis therefore occurs only in individuals inheriting a defective gene from both parents.

Natural History and Its Modification with Treatment

The clinical severity of pyruvate kinase deficiency is extremely variable. Some patients have mild chronic hemolysis, whereas others have severe hemolytic anemia. Neonatal jaundice secondary to hemolysis may be present. As with other forms of chronic hemolysis, splenomegaly is commonly detectable and cholelithiasis may develop. Some patients are transfusion dependent and may develop complications of iron overload. Splenectomy may be helpful in some individuals with severe anemia, but is not as effective as in hereditary spherocytosis.

Prevention

Genetic counseling is the only means of disease prevention in families with pyruvate kinase deficiency. Once inherited, the disease cannot be prevented although its severity is variable.

Cost Containment

As with other forms of chronic hemolysis, cost containment should be focused on using a limited battery of laboratory tests that can specifically identify the enzyme defect. Simple screening and quantitative assays for this enzyme are available, and less specific tests such as the autohemolysis test are of limited utility.

REFERENCES

Beutler E. Glucose-6-phosphate dehydrogenase deficiency. N Eng J Med 1991;324:169.

Miale JB. Laboratory medicine: Hematology. 6th ed. St. Louis: Mosby, 1982.

Palek J, Sahr KE. Mutations of the red blood cell membrane proteins: From clinical evaluation to detection of the underlying genetic defect. Blood 1992;80:308.

Valentine WN, Paglia DE. Erythroenzymopathies and hemolytic anemia: The many faces of inherited variant enzymes. J Lab Clin Med 1990;115:12.

Williams WJ. Hematology. New York: McGraw-Hill, 1990.

CHAPTER 12-7

Sickle Cell Anemia

Michael L. Miller, D.O.

DEFINITION

Sickle cell anemia (SCA) is a hereditary disease characterized by sickled erythrocytes and moderate to severe chronic hemolytic anemia with multiple-organ-system injury due to recurrent vaso-occlusive events.

ETIOLOGY

Normal adult hemoglobin (Hb A) is composed of an oxygen-carrying heme molecule and four globin chains (two alpha and two beta chains), designated $\alpha_2\beta_2$. Production of alpha and beta globin chains is controlled by four alpha chain genes and two beta chain genes. Hb S is the result of a genetic mutation involving the beta chain gene, which gives rise to the amino acid substitution of valine for glutamic acid at the sixth position of the beta globin chain ($\beta^{6glu} \rightarrow {}^{val}$). SCA is caused by the homozygous state for the abnormal beta globin chain gene (β^{s}), resulting in the production of only hemoglobin S (Hb S). No normal beta globin chain genes are inherited; therefore, no normal hemoglobin (Hb A) is formed. Because of the abnormal molecular structure of Hb S deleterious structural changes occur during deoxygenation, causing polymerization of the hemoglobin molecule. This results in the formation of sickled red cells, which cause predominantly extravascular hemolysis, splenic and hepatic red cell sequestration, and the occlusion of microvasculature with tissue infarction.

CRITERIA FOR DIAGNOSIS
Suggestive

Individuals with SCA develop evidence of the disease within the first year of life; however, many patients are diagnosed at birth because of neonatal screening programs for the disease. The disease should be suspected in any infant or child when both parents are known to have sickle cell trait (hemoglobin A/S) or when there is anemia with marked reticulocytosis, splenomegaly, and/or episodes of acute localized pain due to vaso-occlusive crises. The red cell morphologic changes typical of the disease are not usually seen until after 6 months of age. It is rare for an individual with SCA to reach adulthood before the diagnosis is made.

Definitive

A definitive diagnosis of SCA is made by laboratory studies that establish that the red cell hemoglobin composition is predominantly Hb S. The finding of sickled cells in the peripheral blood is not diagnostic of SCA, but does indicate the presence of a "sickle syndrome" (see Routine Laboratory Abnormalities, Diagnostic Options, and Differential Diagnosis).

CLINICAL MANIFESTATIONS
Subjective

Symptomatology develops in infancy and is caused primarily by painful vaso-occlusive events, a moderate to severe hemolytic anemia, infection, and organomegaly. Patient complaints are for the most part related to the severity and location of the occlusive events and may include musculoskeletal pain, abdominal pain, chest pain, cough, dyspnea, fever, weakness, fatigue, and neurologic deficits. Among the painful crises experienced by patients with SCA, the most common are those involving the musculoskeletal system, but crises involving the spleen, kidneys, brain, bone, liver, intestine, penis, and lungs also occur. Frequently the earliest sign of SCA in an infant is irritability and refusal to bear weight, with fever and swelling of the hands and feet due to dactylitis, the so called "hand–foot syndrome."

Objective
Physical Examination

Physical examination of the newborn or infant younger than 6 months may be unremarkable, but physical evidence of the disease should be present thereafter. One of the earliest findings is the hand–foot syndrome previously described. Splenomegaly always develops but regresses due to autoinfarction of the spleen. Hepatomegaly may develop at this time as the hepatic reticuloendothelial cells compensate for the loss of splenic function. A rapidly enlarging spleen associated with hypotension and cardiac decompensation may be seen in children and is termed *acute splenic sequestration crisis*. This life-threatening complication is due to the entrapment of a large portion of the blood volume in the spleen.

The sudden onset of chest pain, fever, dyspnea, and cough with pulmonary infiltrates is known as the *acute chest syndrome*. This is caused by infection and/or pulmonary infarction and is associated with a high rate of mortality.

Pallor and fatigue with worsening anemia and reticulocytopenia should suggest the possibility of an "aplastic crisis." This complication is due to human parvovirus B19 infection of early erythroid precursors, causing red cell aplasia, and is usually preceded 4 to 6 weeks by a viruslike syndrome.

Priapism is a common occurrence in males of all ages. It presents as multiple short episodes, which may progress to prolonged episodes (> 24 hours). Complications include sexual dysfunction and urinary retention.

Vaso-occlusive events involving the brain are uncommon but can be devastating when they occur. They often cause seizures, paraplegia, speech and visual defects, coma, and even death.

Chronic organ system damage is inevitable, most frequently involving the heart (systolic and diastolic murmurs and cardiomegaly with left ventricular hypertrophy), the kidneys(nephrotic syndrome and uremia), the hepatobiliary system (cholelithiasis, infarction and hepatitis), the eyes (retinal infarction, hemorrhage, and proliferative retinopathy), the skin (ulcers), the skeletal system (infarction and expanded marrow space), and the lungs (chronic lung disease).

Routine Laboratory Abnormalities

Review of the peripheral blood smear from a patient older than 6 months reveals the characteristic morphologic changes in the erythrocytes (Color Plate 12–7–1, after page 826). The most obvious is sickled red cells, which are always present. As splenic function decreases the red cells also exhibit features of hyposplenia, which include Howell–Jolly bodies, Pappenheimer bodies(siderocytes), target cells, spherocytes, and schistocytes. There is also prominent polychromasia, indicating moderate to marked reticulocytosis. If no reticulocytosis is observed and the patient's anemia is worsening, then an aplastic crisis must be considered, as previously discussed. The complete blood count and leukocyte differential demonstrate moderate to severe anemia with variable neutrophilic and/or lymphocytic leukocytosis and a leukoerythroblastic reaction.

PLANS
Diagnostic
Differential Diagnosis

The differential diagnosis of SCA includes any hemolytic anemia that occurs early in life. Sickled cells in the peripheral blood are not diagnostic of SCA, but do indicate the presence of a sickle syndrome. Sickle syndromes include SCA and other hemoglobinopathies in which Hb S represents at least 50% of the hemoglobin content of the red cells. These patients exhibit variable degrees of sickling and the associated clinical stigmata. The other hemoglobinopathies responsible for the sickle syndrome are doubly heterozygous for the Hb S gene and another abnormal alpha or beta globin gene. These include Hb S–C disease, Hb S–beta thalassemia, Hb SS–alpha thalassemia, Hb S–D disease, Hb S–E disease, Hb S–O disease, and Hb S–Lepore.

Diagnostic Options

To confirm the diagnosis of SCA laboratory studies must be performed to identify the homozygous state for the sickle cell gene (Hb SS). A "sickle solubility test" will detect the presence of Hb S, but the test is not specific for SCA and it does not distinguish between sickle cell trait(Hb A/S) and SCA. Nor can it be used in infants younger than 6 months due to interference by Hb F causing a false-negative result. Confirmation of the diagnosis requires further testing, such as hemoglobin electrophoresis, isoelectric focusing, or high-performance liquid chromatography. These methods can distinguish SCA from sickle cell trait and the doubly heterozygous hemoglobinopathies involving Hb S.

Recommended Approach

The recommended approach to identifying and confirming the diagnosis of SCA is described under Routine Laboratory Abnormalities and Diagnostic Options. Once the diagnosis has been established, baseline studies should be obtained at a time when the patient is clinically stable and asymptomatic. These studies should include complete blood count with differential, reticulocyte count, sedimentation rate, creatinine, chest x-ray, PO_2, and electrocardiogram. A thorough physical examination should also be performed at this time. This information is invaluable in assessing and diagnosing problems as they arise.

Therapeutic

The treatment of SCA is directed at preventive care, the management of painful crises, surgery, pregnancy and the complications of acute splenic sequestration, acute chest syndrome, and aplastic crisis. To improve survival and reduce morbidity it is critical that patients be diagnosed as early as possible, using prenatal and neonatal screening. Those families affected should be educated in the natural history of the disease, learning to recognize infections and avoid activities that predispose to vaso-occlusive episodes. Certainly the major cause of mortality in children is infection (especially *Pneumococcus*) which is preventable through vaccination (especially for *Pneumococcus, hemophilus influenzae,* and hepatitis B) and prophylactic penicillin therapy for children less than 5 years of age.

The majority of painful vaso-occlusive crises experienced can be treated at home with hydration and analgesics. Oxygen therapy is usually not valuable unless the patient is hypoxic and may be detrimental due to suppression of erythropoiesis. If home therapy is not effective in stopping the pain or if hydration is inadequate, then the patient may require hospitalization. Narcotics should be used when necessary to control pain, but the side effects of addiction and hypoventilation with hypoxia must always be taken into consideration.

Patients experiencing the more serious complications of SCA, such as an acute sequestration crisis or aplastic crisis, should receive supportive therapy, primarily through blood transfusions. Patients having a prolonged aplastic crisis because of chronic parvovirus infection frequently benefit from intravenous immunoglobulin. Both conditions are transitory. The acute chest syndrome may require blood transfusions and oxygen if the patient is hypoxic. Appropriate cultures must also be performed to determine if a pulmonary infection is present, and antibiotic treatment should be started empirically (once cultures have been obtained) if the clinical suspicion of infection is high.

Surgery poses a significant risk to these patients because of the potential for hypoxia, dehydration, and acidosis. Therefore, careful attention must be paid to these potential problems intraoperatively and postoperatively. Prior to major surgery it may be advisable to perform an exchange transfusion or give simple transfusions to reduce the percentage of Hb S in circulation to 50% or less.

The pregnant SCA patient is "high risk" and represents a special problem because of the potential for increased frequency and severity of vaso-occlusive events and the acute chest syndrome. Anemia is worsened and the risk of toxemia and death is significantly increased. The mother and fetus must be carefully monitored during the pregnancy. The mother should receive folate. Blood transfusions should be given as needed to prevent the escalation of vaso-occlusive events, worsening anemia, or fetal distress.

The chronic organ system damage experienced by these patients should be monitored with the appropriate studies and treatment provided as deemed necessary.

Various types of antisickling therapy are currently under investigation and some are being used to a limited extent. These forms of therapy are directed primarily at inhibiting Hb S polymer formation. The two most promising are the stimulation of Hb F formation by hydroxyurea or 5-azacytidine and the development of gene therapy to replace the β^s globin gene in bone marrow stem cells with a normal gene.

FOLLOW-UP

Because of the unpredictability of the clinical course in SCA, it is recommended that these patients be seen on a routine basis.

DISCUSSION
Prevalence and Incidence

Hemoglobin S is the most common abnormal hemoglobin. The Hb S gene is most prevalent in west-central Africa, Saudi Arabia, and east-

central India. In African-Americans, the frequencies of sickle cell trait (Hb A/S) and SCA (Hb SS) are approximately 9 and 0.1%, respectively.

Related Basic Science
Genetics

Sickle cell anemia is caused by the homozygous state for Hb S (Hb SS), which results when two Hb S genes are inherited. If one Hb S gene is inherited, then the heterozygous condition exists (Hb A/S) and the individual has sickle cell trait.

Physiologic Derangement

The red cell structural changes seen in SCA are dependent on deoxygenation, which results in decreased solubility of Hb S with the formation of liquid crystals or "tactoids." The sickled red cells thus formed are composed of parallel Hb S fibers that are aligned with the long axis of the cell. The solubility of Hb S is also dependent on its concentration, which is why patients with sickle cell trait (Hb A, 60%; Hb S, 40%) do not form sickle cells unless the O_2 saturation is less than 40%. Hemoglobin F inhibits sickling as evidenced by the fact that the majority of infants do not exhibit evidence of SCA until the Hb F levels have significantly decreased (<10–20%) between 4 and 6 months of age. In fact, patients who are double heterozygotes for Hb S and hereditary persistence of fetal hemoglobin (HPFH) are asymptomatic despite Hb S levels of 70%. In contrast, Hb S can copolymerize more easily with some hemoglobins, such as hemoglobins C, D, and O-Arab. This accounts for the sickle syndrome seen in patients who are double heterozygotes for Hb S and one of these hemoglobins.

The chronic hemolysis seen in SCA is caused primarily by extravascular red cell destruction. The vaso-occlusive phenomena so characteristic of this disease are the result of sickle cell formation with occlusion of arterioles. These events can be precipitated by acidosis, hypoxia, and dehydration.

Of interest is the relationship between the presence of the Hb S gene and protection from falciparum malaria, termed a balanced polymorphism. In fact, there is an inverse relationship between the gene frequency of Hb S and the incidence of falciparum malaria in Africa. The mechanism for the protective effect is unclear.

Natural History and Its Modification with Treatment

Patients with SCA have a variable clinical course, with a few patients experiencing minimal or no clinical symptomatology but most having recurrent vaso-occlusive episodes of varying frequency and severity throughout life with chronic organ system damage. There is a bimodal pattern of mortality, with the peak incidence occurring between 1 and 3 years of age, most often caused by pneumococcal infection. A second increase in deaths is observed beginning in late adolescence and is due to acute chest syndrome, chronic organ system failure, or sudden death of uncertain etiology. The life expectancy of patients with SCA is significantly shortened; approximately 50% survive to age 40 and only 1% into their sixties.

Patient education and preventive care in these patients, in conjunction with the therapeutic options previously discussed, can prolong to a limited extent their life expectancy. But the cumulative effect of recurrent vaso-occlusive events on multiple organ systems is devastating and ultimately fatal. Only the development of therapies (see Therapeutic) that inhibit Hb S polymer formation in red cells will be successful in finally conquering this disease.

Prevention

Sickle cell anemia can be prevented only through genetic counseling of those individuals who have the disease or are carriers of the Hb S gene (Hb S trait). A reduction in mortality and morbidity can be achieved by neonatal diagnosis, educating patients and family to recognize the signs and symptoms of complications and those activities that predispose them to vaso-occlusive episodes, seeking treatment early before serious complications develop, routine immunizations (especially for *Pneumococcus, H. influenzae,* and hepatitis B), and prophylactic penicillin therapy for children younger than 5 years.

Cost Containment

Unfortunately, SCA is a lifelong disorder having a clinical course that is punctuated by acute and chronic complications that require a variety of studies to establish a diagnosis and to monitor the cumulative effects of the disease. Avoidance of overutilization of studies needed for diagnosis and follow-up is an important means of achieving cost containment in these patients. Neonatal diagnosis contributes to cost reduction by early recognition of the disease, which can significantly reduce morbidity and mortality as previously discussed. The establishment of a "Clinical Practice Guideline" for SCA by the U.S. Department of Health and Human Services is an important step in improving the quality of care and controlling costs (see References).

REFERENCES

Charache S, Lubin B, Reid C, eds. Management and therapy of sickle cell anemia. NIH Publication 89-2117. Washington, DC: U.S. Government Printing Office, 1989.

Jandl JH. Hemoglobin S and the sickle cell syndromes. In: Jandl JH, ed. Blood: Textbook of hematology. Boston: Little, Brown, 1987:368.

Platt OS, Dover GJ. SCA. In: Nathan DG, Oski FA, eds. Hematology of infancy and childhood. 4th ed. Philadelphia: Saunders, 1993;21:732.

Sickle cell anemia. Clinical practice guideline, No. 6. Publication 93-0562, Washington, DC: U.S. Dept. of Health and Human Services, Agency for Health Care Policy Research, 1993.

CHAPTER 12–8

Neutrophilia

Amy S. Gewirtz, M.D., and Ronald M. Bukowski, M.D.

DEFINITION

The normal neutrophil count may vary with age and race. Published values for neutrophilia reflect these variations, and for adults values greater than 7.0 to 7.5×10^9/L are consistent with this diagnosis. Neutrophilia may consist of only mature forms or be "left shifted" and include immature granulocytes. The absolute neutrophil count should include both mature and immature circulating granulocytes.

ETIOLOGY

The most important issue facing the clinician in determining the etiology of the neutrophilia is whether the increased neutrophil count is reactive, when it is referred to as a leukemoid reaction, or is neoplastic. The following is a discussion of the various conditions associated with neutrophilia.

Physiologic Stimuli

Strenuous exercise, painful stimuli, acute hypoxia, severe emotional stress, and endogenous epinephrine release can all increase the peripheral neutrophil count in minutes. The increase is transient and consists of mature neutrophils. This phenomenon is thought to be secondary to demargination of neutrophils.

Infection

Bacterial infections commonly produce an increase in circulating neutrophils. Generally, the neutrophilia is associated with a leukocytosis and a left shift. Some infectious processes, particularly those associated with septicemia, produce an increase in neutrophils with toxic granulations, cytoplasmic vacuolization, and Dohle bodies. Not all bacterial infections, however, produce neutrophilia. As an example, infections with *Salmonella* or *Brucella* may produce neutropenia. In addition, the elderly patient may not have the classic laboratory finding of an associated leukocytosis or a left shift. Viral infections may also be associated with a neutrophilia in the early stages.

Noninfectious Inflammatory Processes

Neutrophilia may be associated with various inflammatory disorders such as collagen–vascular diseases, glomerulonephritis, thyroiditis, and hypersensitivity reactions. Extensive tissue damage and necrosis as is seen with burns and organ infarction may also produce neutrophilia.

Malignant Tumors

Hematologic neoplasms are often characterized by peripheral neutrophilia, with chronic myelogenous leukemia being the most common. Neutrophilia may also be present in other chronic myeloproliferative disorders such as polycythemia vera, primary myelofibrosis, as well as acute myelogenous leukemia and chronic neutrophilic leukemia. Occasionally, certain solid tumors such as carcinomas of the lung, thyroid, and gallbladder may be associated with neutrophilia.

Metabolic Disorders

Neutrophilia may accompany uremia, diabetic ketoacidosis, acute gout, thyroid storm, and eclampsia.

Drugs, Hormones, Poisons

Epinephrine causes mobilization of neutrophils from the marginating pool into the circulation. This neutrophilia is brief and is not associated with a left shift. Glucocorticoid administration is also associated with an increase in peripheral neutrophils. This type of neutrophilia occurs several hours following the administration of corticosteroids and is the result of increased marrow release as well as decreased migration of neutrophils from the circulation into the tissues. It may be left shifted and associated with lymphopenia and a decrease in eosinophils and basophils. Pharmaceutical agents such as lithium, digitalis, and heparin can also produce persistent neutrophilia. Granulocytosis can also be seen with ingestion of metals and toxins such as lead, mercury, and ethylene glycol. Cytokine therapy (granulocyte and granulocyte–macrophage colony-stimulating factors) will be associated with a neutrophilia that is often left shifted with accompanying toxic granulation and Dohle bodies.

Pregnancy

Pregnant women may experience a left-shifted leukocytosis in the third trimester of pregnancy. This occurs in up to 25% of individuals and may be secondary to increased endogenous glucocorticoid levels.

Benign Hematologic Disorders

Neutrophilia with a left shift may be associated with hemorrhage and hemolysis.

CRITERIA FOR DIAGNOSIS
Suggestive

There are no suggestive criteria for the diagnosis of neutrophilia.

Definitive

An absolute neutrophil count greater than 7.0 to 7.5×10^9/L confirms the diagnosis.

CLINICAL MANIFESTATIONS
Subjective

The clinical presentation and attendant symptoms vary with the cause of the neutrophilia.

Objective
Physical Examination

Abnormalities in the physical examination are determined by the cause of the neutrophilia. There are no findings specific for increased levels of granulocytes.

Routine Laboratory Abnormalities

To make the diagnosis a blood count must demonstrate an increase in the absolute granulocyte count. This may or may not be associated with an increase in immature forms and a generalized leukocytosis. Lactate dehydrogenase levels may be mildly elevated in association with high rates of neutrophil production.

PLANS
Diagnostic
Differential Diagnosis

The initial fork on the decision tree rests between a leukemoid reaction due to causes previously mentioned and neutrophilia due to a neoplastic hematologic process. Reactive neutrophilia as seen in a leukemoid reaction usually produces absolute neutrophil counts less than 30×10^9/L; however, occasionally counts as high as 60×10^9/L may be seen. A reactive leukocytosis may be associated with a left shift, but generally more mature forms such as mature neutrophils, bands, and metamyelocytes predominate. When infection is the cause of neutrophilia, toxic granulation and Dohle bodies may be present. Increases in the more immature elements such as myelocytes, promyelocytes, and even occasional myeloblasts make the diagnosis between reactive conditions and a neoplastic hematologic disorder, particularly a myeloproliferative disorder, more difficult. Toxic granulation and Dohle bodies are uncommonly seen in chronic myelogenous leukemia, which is often accompanied by eosinophilia and/or basophilia. A leukocyte alkaline phosphatase score can be helpful in distinguishing reactive neutrophilia from chronic myelogenous leukemia. Chronic myelogenous leukemia is almost always associated with a decreased leukocyte alkaline phosphatase score, whereas reactive processes are associated with an increased score. Concurrent infection or blast crisis in patients with chronic myelogenous leukemia causes some elevation of the leukocyte alkaline phosphatase score. Other myeloproliferative disorders should have a normal score. Definitive diagnosis of chronic myelogenous leukemia may require cytogenetic analysis to demonstrate the Philadelphia chromosome. Bone marrow examination may be helpful in distinguishing leukemoid reactions from the myeloproliferative syndromes or an acute myelogenous leukemia.

Diagnostic Options

A thorough history and physical examination may shed light on the cause of the neutrophilia. A history of any of the previously mentioned physiologic stimuli, noninfectious inflammatory conditions, solid tumors, metabolic disorders, or drug ingestion should be sought. Laboratory evaluation should include evaluation of the peripheral smear and perhaps the bone marrow. A leukocyte alkaline phosphatase score can be helpful as previously discussed. Other tests that can aid in the diagnosis of chronic myelogenous leukemia have previously been mentioned. Blood and bone marrow cultures may be helpful if an obvious source of infection cannot be determined from physical examination.

Recommended Approach

The recommended approach to the workup of a patient with neutrophilia is discussed under Diagnostic Options.

Therapeutic

Therapy for neutrophilia itself is not required except in patients with leukemias who develop exceptionally high white blood counts that may produce microcirculatory impairment.

FOLLOW-UP

Follow-up depends on the cause of the neutrophilia. In cases where the neutrophilia appears to be reactive, it may be helpful to reassure the patient as to the benign nature of the process.

DISCUSSION
Prevalence and Incidence

The prevalence and incidence of the neutrophilia vary depending on the cause.

Related Basic Science

The mechanisms responsible for producing neutrophilia include those factors that result in an increase in the circulating pool of granulocytes. Mechanisms responsible for this increase include increased production, mobilization from the marrow, demargination, decreased migration of neutrophils into the tissues, and extramedullary hematopoiesis. Granulopoiesis in the bone marrow is regulated by a number of cytokines, most notably granulocyte colony-stimulating factor (G-CSF) and granulocyte–macrophage colony-stimulating factor (GM-CSF). Granulocyte colony-stimulating factor appears to act primarily on lineage-committed progenitor cells, whereas granulocyte–macrophage colony-stimulating factor acts on uncommitted progenitor cells. Mobilization of bone marrow granulocytes to the periphery appears to be related to changes in cell surface adhesion properties and, perhaps, alterations in cell surface glycoproteins. This phenomenon is seen with infection and acute corticosteroid administration. Demargination is the most rapid mechanism for increasing the peripheral granulocyte count, resulting in the release of neutrophils that previously adhered to the vascular endothelium. This has been referred to as *pseudoneutrophilia* due to compartment shifting rather than a true increase in the total number of neutrophils. This change is seen with physiologic stimuli and epinephrine administration, occurs minutes following the insult, and usually cannot achieve neutrophil numbers of more than twice normal. Extramedullary hematopoiesis occurring in the spleen or liver is seen in response to inadequate marrow production of mature hematopoietic cells. This may be reactive or a component of a malignant hematologic disorder.

Genetic abnormalities and associated metabolic derangement at a cellular level occur in chronic myelogenous leukemia and the acute leukemias. This is discussed in Chapters 12–21 and 12–31.

Natural History and Its Modification with Treatment

The natural history of neutrophilia varies with the etiology. For those conditions associated with a transient increase in circulating neutrophils, removal of the implicated agent results in a return to normal laboratory levels. For other conditions, particularly those associated with an underlying malignancy, the treatment and prognosis are discussed in the individual chapters.

Cost Containment

Cost containment in the workup or therapy for a patient who presents with neutrophilia depends on the cause. Examination of the peripheral smear and determination of the leukocyte alkaline phosphatase score may be the most helpful studies in determining the etiology of the neutrophilia.

REFERENCES

Athens JW. Variations of leukocytes in disease. In: Lee GR, Bithell TC, Foerster J, et al., eds. Wintrobe's clinical hematology. 9th ed. Philadelphia: Lea & Febiger, 1993:60.

Cline MJ. Laboratory evaluation of benign quantitative granulocyte and monocyte disorders. In: Bick RL, ed. Hematology clinical and laboratory practice. St. Louis: Mosby, 1993:75.

Davey FR, Nelson DA. Leukocytic disorders. In: Henry JB, ed. Clinical diagnosis and management by laboratory methods. 18th ed. Philadelphia: Saunders, 1991:27.

Hugley CM. Neutrophilic leukocytosis (neutrophilia) and leukemoid reactions. In: Hurst JW, editor-in-chief. Medicine for the practicing physician. 3rd ed. Boston: Butterworth-Heinemann, 1992:13.

Peterson L, Foucar K. Granulocytosis and granulocytopenia. In: Bick RL, ed. Hematology clinical and laboratory practice. St. Louis: Mosby, 1993:74.

CHAPTER 12–9

Neutropenia

Amy S. Gewirtz, M.D., and Ronald M. Bukowski, M.D.

DEFINITION

The normal range of neutrophil counts varies with patient age and race. The absolute granulocyte values consistent with neutropenia reflect these variations. In adults, neutropenia is present when the absolute count is less than 1.5 to 2.0×10^9/L. In contrast, 1.0×10^9/L is the lower limit of normal for African-Americans. The most important consequence of neutropenia is development of infection. There is a direct correlation between the risk of infection and the degree and duration of neutropenia. Granulocyte counts between 0.5 and 1.0×10^9/L may increase this risk slightly. Severe neutropenia with granulocyte counts below 0.5×10^9/L can result in serious and potentially fatal bacterial infections. Additionally, the duration of neutropenia is very important, with episodes lasting over several days having the most serious consequences.

ETIOLOGY

Infection, drug exposure, and malignancies involving the bone marrow are the most common causes of neutropenia. Inherited syndromes producing neutropenia are also recognized, but are less prevalent. The conditions associated with neutropenia are discussed individually.

Infections

Infections account for the majority of cases of neutropenia in children and young adults. Overwhelming infection with septicemia can lead to neutropenia, particularly in those individuals whose bone marrow function may already be compromised. The cause of the neutropenia in this setting is complex and may include proliferative abnormalities secondary to bone marrow suppression by bacterial toxins, maturation abnormalities resulting in the premature release of granulocytes from the bone marrow into the peripheral blood, and alterations of normal granulocyte distribution with increased migration of neutrophils to infected tissues as well as decreased neutrophil survival. Infections produced by bacterial, viral, rickettsial, and protozoal organisms can all lead to neutropenia. The classic infectious diseases associated with neutropenia are typhoid, brucellosis, yellow fever, viral hepatitis, measles, rubella, Rocky Mountain spotted fever, and malaria.

Drug-Induced Neutropenia

Pharmaceutical agents are the most common cause of neutropenia in adults. The mechanism responsible for neutropenia varies with the drug. The mechanisms responsible include dose-related causes of neutropenia, immune-mediated neutropenia, and idiosyncratic reactions. The types of idiosyncratic reactions include toxic injury to the bone marrow precursor cells and antibody-mediated destruction of circulating granulocytes. Chemotherapeutic agents and other pharmaceuticals that alter DNA and/or RNA synthesis, including folic acid antagonists, purine or pyrimidine antimetabolites, and alkylating agents are most commonly implicated. The neutropenia secondary to chemotherapeutic agents is usually accompanied by pancytopenia. The majority of non-chemotherapeutic-related cases of agranulocytosis are due to analgesics, sedatives, anticonvulsants, antithyroid agents, and antiinflammatory drugs. These include agents such as phenylbutazone, aminopyrine, phenacetin, phenothiazines, sulfonamides (antibacterial), thiouracil, and phenytoin.

Idiosyncratic drug-induced neutropenia of a chronic variety may be seen with agents producing aplastic anemia. These drugs include chloramphenicol, sulfonamides, and phenylbutazone.

Neutropenias of Infancy and Childhood

Neutropenia in neonates can be the result of sepsis in newborn infants or a variety of maternal factors. Maternal antibodies directed against both maternal and infant granulocyte antigens can cross the placenta and produce isoimmune neutropenia, a condition resembling Rh-induced hemolytic anemia of newborn infants. These antibodies can persist in the circulation for up to 4 months.

Childhood causes of neutropenia include both congenital and acquired etiologies. Infantile genetic agranulocytosis (Kostman's syndrome) is an autosomal recessive disease associated with severe neutropenia from birth and life-threatening infections. The bone marrow demonstrates arrest of normal granulocytic maturation. Patients usually die within the first year of life. Congenital aleukocytosis is a rare disorder associated with thymic hypoplasia, hypogammaglobulinemia, absence of both granulocytes and lymphocytes, and death within the first year of life secondary to infections. Chronic benign granulocytopenia of infancy and childhood begins a few months after birth and affects females more than males. The patients have a normal white blood cell count with isolated neutropenia. Infections in these patients can be successfully treated with antibiotics. The vast majority of these children spontaneously recover normal neutrophil counts by age 4. Familial benign neutropenia is another form of inherited granulocytopenia in which patients present with limited symptoms of infection. Many individuals are asymptomatic; others have mainly periodontal disease and a predisposition to furuncle formation. Finally, cyclic neutropenia results in recurrent, cyclical episodes of severe neutropenia occurring every 15 to 35 days associated with various infections. These infections involve the skin and mucosal surfaces, and are associated with fever and cervical lymphadenopathy.

Chronic Idiopathic Neutropenia

Chronic idiopathic neutropenia can develop at any age, but is most common in adults. Neutrophil counts may be as low as 0.5×10^9/L. This illness is most common in females and is not associated with splenomegaly. Approximately 25% of patients develop infectious complications, but septicemia is rare. Bone marrow examination in these individuals may be normal or may demonstrate a decrease in mature granulocytes.

Autoimmune Neutropenia

Primary autoimmune neutropenia produced by antineutrophil antibodies is most common in children less than 3 years of age. Secondary autoimmune neutropenia may occur in patients with other autoimmune disorders such as idiopathic thrombocytopenic purpura, autoimmune hemolytic anemia, collagen–vascular disorders such as systemic lupus erythematosus, and lymphoproliferative diseases.

Hypersplenism

Splenomegaly can result in sequestration of granulocytes and produce neutropenia. Common causes of so-called "splenic neutropenia" are portal hypertension, storage diseases, lymphoma, sarcoidosis, and chronic infections. The triad of rheumatoid arthritis, splenomegaly, and neutropenia is referred to as Felty's syndrome. This occurs infrequently in patients with advanced rheumatoid arthritis and may predispose patients to recurrent infections.

Other Hematologic Disorders

A wide variety of hematologic disorders can present with neutropenia. Most of these conditions are also associated with other hematologic abnormalities such as anemia, leukopenia, and thrombocytopenia. Hairy cell leukemia, myelodysplastic syndromes, aplastic anemia, acute leukemia, and disorders of large granular lymphocytes are examples of such hematologic syndromes. Neutropenia may also occur with megaloblastic anemia in patients who are vitamin B_{12} or folate deficient. Ineffective granulopoiesis results in intramedullary cell death. Frequently, patients with the Chédiak–Higashi syndrome have neutropenia. In this inherited disorder, neutrophils and lymphocytes contain giant cytoplasmic granules causing cellular dysfunction, for example, impaired chemotaxis.

CRITERIA FOR DIAGNOSIS
Suggestive

A clinical history of repeated superficial infections involving primarily the skin and oral mucosa, as well as carbuncle and furuncle formation, suggests the diagnosis.

Definitive

An absolute neutrophil count below the normal range, usually less than 1.5 to 2.0×10^9 cells/L, confirms the diagnosis. Usually, patients with severe recurrent infections have neutrophil counts less than 0.5×10^9/L.

CLINICAL MANIFESTATIONS
Subjective

Symptoms vary depending on the severity and the etiology of the neutropenia. Patients with severe neutropenia are at increased risk for infections, particularly bacterial infections. Acute symptoms are those associated with infection such as chills and high fever. Sites such as the skin and mucous membranes are most commonly affected, with resultant carbuncle and furuncle formation. Patients may, however, be asymptomatic. A past history of recurrent superficial bacterial infections may be elicited. In patients with hereditary neutropenias, family history may be helpful. It is important to remember that infection may be a cause of, as well as a result of, neutropenia. Prior drug exposure or malignancy may be an important aspect of the history.

Objective
Physical Examination

Physical examination requires adequate examination of the skin and mucosal surfaces. Splenomegaly may be present in individuals who have neutropenia based on sequestration. Concurrent organomegaly and lymphadenopathy may be present in patients with secondary causes of neutropenia.

Routine Laboratory Abnormalities

The only specific finding associated with diagnosis of neutropenia is a low neutrophil count. Examination of a peripheral blood smear may provide additional clues in diseases where maturational or structural abnormalities of neutrophils are present.

PLANS
Diagnostic
Differential Diagnosis

The differential diagnosis of isolated neutropenia in the absence of pancytopenia includes possible infection, drugs, various hematologic disorders, splenomegaly, and finally congenital and acquired primary neu-

tropenic disorders. When neutropenia is part of pancytopenia, the differential diagnosis may be similar.

Diagnostic Options and Recommended Approach

It is important to document the chronicity and periodicity of the neutropenia with sequential white blood cell counts. A complete blood count and examination of granulocyte morphology may contribute additional information. Serial blood counts may be necessary to determine if a cyclic pattern is present or to establish chronicity. A detailed history including drug exposure, duration and type of infections, and family history may prove beneficial. Testing of family members may be helpful if a hereditary abnormality is suspected. Bone marrow examination may be helpful to assess qualitative and quantitative granulocytic maturation abnormalities. In addition, it allows assessment of other hematopoietic precursors and excludes the possibility of a primary hematologic abnormality as a cause of the neutropenia. If required, additional testing may be performed and includes evaluation of neutrophil release from the bone marrow, presence of neutrophil antibodies, and ability of the neutrophils to undergo chemotaxis in response to various factors. These tests are complex and should be used in a highly selective manner.

Therapeutic

Treatment of patients with neutropenia is generally required when the neutropenia is severe and/or is associated with infectious complications. Initially, identifying and discontinuing the responsible agent or treating the underlying cause of the neutropenia is necessary. In the presence of fever and/or infection, appropriate antibiotic therapy should be instituted. Granulocyte transfusions have been used in the past, but are rarely beneficial. In general, prophylactic antibiotic treatment in the absence of fever is not recommended. For patients with severe neutropenia, fever, and/or infection, the use of recombinant colony-stimulating factors such as granulocyte and granulocyte–macrophage colony-stimulating factor, may be of value. These agents are continued until satisfactory granulocyte recovery occurs. In patients with cyclic neutropenia, chronic administration of granulocyte colony-stimulating factor is beneficial and decreases the incidence and severity of infections. The use of these factors in selected patients receiving cytotoxic chemotherapy may decrease the frequency of neutropenic episodes associated with fever or infection. The colony-stimulating factors may shorten the duration of neutropenia; however, supportive therapy with antibiotics remains the mainstay of treatment.

FOLLOW-UP

A single neutropenic episode must be evaluated to determine the cause. Once an etiology has been established, follow-up should be tailored to the clinical situations and the diagnosis. Patients with persistent neutropenia should be counseled on the importance of fever and early treatment of potential infectious complications.

DISCUSSION
Prevalence and Incidence

Prevalence, incidence, and etiology of neutropenia are influenced by the age of the patient population. Congenital varieties are rare and occur in infants and children, whereas secondary neutropenia is most common in adults. The prevalence of drug-induced neutropenia varies with the offending agent; for example, it has been estimated at 1 in 250,000 chlorpromazine-treated patients.

Related Basic Science

The mechanisms resulting in neutropenia include granulocyte destruction, proliferative abnormalities, and redistribution of circulating granulocytes. Proliferative abnormalities occur at the stem cell level of hematopoietic development. Some cases demonstrate qualitatively normal maturation of granulocytic cells with a quantitative decrease in cells at all stages of myeloid maturation. Other proliferation abnormalities result in qualitative maturation defects. Survival abnormalities of peripheral blood granulocytes may be due to either increased destruction or removal. Distribution abnormalities may be reflected by a change in the concentration of granulocytes present in the circulating pool, the marginated pool, and the bone marrow. Despite the ability to subclassify the mechanisms of neutropenia, there is often overlap in a given clinical situation.

Natural History and Its Modification with Treatment

Depending on the severity and cause of the neutropenia, patients behave differently. Any patient in whom the absolute neutrophil count decreases to less than 0.5×10^9/L is at severe risk for infection. Selected individuals, however, may have granulocyte counts of 0.2×10^9/L for years without developing serious infections.

Prevention

Prevention of neutropenia is rarely possible as most patients develop this condition without a prior history or exposure to a known causative agent. Recognition of patients with this hematologic complication is most important.

Cost Containment

Cost containment in the workup of a neutropenic patient is reviewed under Diagnostic Options. The use of colony-stimulating factors plus appropriate antibiotics may decrease the duration and severity of infections and the costs associated with treatment. Analyses conclusively demonstrating this, however, are not yet available.

REFERENCES

Athens JW. Neutropenia. In: Lee GR, Bithell TC, Foerster J, et al., eds. Wintrobe's clinical hematology. 9th ed. Philadelphia: Lea & Febiger, 1993:61.

Cline MJ. Laboratory evaluation of benign quantitative granulocyte and monocyte disorders. In: Bick RL, ed. Hematology clinical and laboratory practice. St. Louis: Mosby, 1993:75.

Davey FR, Nelson DA. Leukocyte disorders. In: Henry JB, ed. Clinical diagnosis and management by laboratory methods. 18th ed. Philadelphia: Saunders, 1991:27.

Finch SC. Neutropenia. In: Williams WJ, Beutler E, Erslev AJ, Lichtman A, eds. Hematology. 3rd ed. New York: McGraw-Hill, 1983:773.

Foucar K, Duncan MH, Smith KJ. Practical approach to the investigation of neutropenia. Clin Lab Med 1993;13:4.

Hugley CM. Granulocytopenia (neutropenia). In: Hurst JW, editor-in-chief. Medicine for the practicing physician. 3rd ed. Boston: Butterworth-Heinemann, 1992:13.

Peterson L, Foucar K. Granulocytosis and granulocytopenia. In: Bick RL, ed. Hematology clinical and laboratory practice. St. Louis: Mosby, 1993:74.

CHAPTER 12–10

Basophilia

Beth A. Overmoyer, M.D.

DEFINITION

Basophils normally constitute less than 0.5% of the circulating leukocytes. Their numbers are increased in pathologic states, such as chronic myeloproliferative disorders (4–10%). Immediate hypersensitivity reactions are not usually associated with an elevation in basophil count; however, an elevated immunoglobulin E level is associated with an increased risk of developing immediate hypersensitivity reactions. The diagnosis is usually made on the basis of clinical manifestations.

ETIOLOGY

Basophilia may accompany myeloproliferative disorders and hypersensitivity states.

CRITERIA FOR DIAGNOSIS

Suggestive

Atopic individuals may manifest immediate hypersensitivity to a host of allergens, such as pollen, dander, and food. The symptoms reflect the pathophysiology of anaphylaxis described below: bronchospasm, hypotension, edema, and abdominal colic. A family history of hypersensitivity reactions is often present. Genetic studies have demonstrated a 50% risk of developing hypersensitivity among children with two allergic parents.

Definitive

See Definition. Anaphylactic reactions can manifest as upper or lower airway obstruction, or both. Vascular collapse may also be present. Urticaria and other cutaneous signs are due largely to degranulation of mast cells, rather than basophils.

CLINICAL MANIFESTATIONS

See Plans, Diagnostic, (below) and appropriate chapters elsewhere in the book.

PLANS

Diagnostic

Type I or Immediate Hypersensitivity

Type I or immediate hypersensitivity occurs within seconds or minutes of contact with an antigen (allergen). Accurate diagnosis depends on the history of exposure to an allergen and the presence of anaphylactic symptoms.

Immunoglobulin E Related

These reactions are usually associated with known allergens, such as pollens, foods, drugs, and fungi. Exercise or cold-related events are also mediated by immunoglobulin E.

Complement Mediated

Hereditary C1 inhibitor deficiency is an autosomal dominant condition characterized by a family history of episodic attacks of gastrointestinal colic and laryngeal edema not associated with urticaria. A nonhereditary form is often associated with B-cell malignancies.

Nonimmunologic

Mast cell degranulation contributes to the majority of these attacks. They are precipitated by exposure to antibiotics, opiates, or drugs that mediate arachidonic acid metabolism, such as nonsteroidal antiinflammatory agents.

Idiopathic

The majority of immediate hypersensitivity reactions are idiopathic.

The clinical manifestations of hypersensitivity do not differ among the various etiologies, which supports the importance of the history in diagnosing the underlying condition. The classic skin test is the hallmark of diagnosing a type I response to an allergen.

Therapeutic

Therapeutic Options

Epinephrine can be used to control the symptoms of immediate hypersensitivity. Intravenous corticosteroids do not ameliorate the immediate symptoms, but control persistent bronchospasm and hypotension. Diphenhydramine and aminophylline are additional therapeutic agents.

Recommended Approach

Immediate hypersensitivity reactions can be controlled with subcutaneous epinephrine (0.2–0.5 mL of a 1:1000 dilution) given at 3-minute intervals. Volume expanders and vasopressors are often needed to control hypotension. Bronchospasm can be ameliorated with diphenhydramine or aminophylline with inhaled bronchodilators. Oxygen may be given by nasal cannula or intubation.

FOLLOW-UP

Once an immediate hypersensitivity reaction has resolved, the follow-up consists of determining the cause of the reaction and preventing future attacks.

DISCUSSION

Prevalence and Incidence

The exact prevalence and incidence of immediate hypersensitivity reactions are not known. An elevated immunoglobulin E level does not always predict a risk for allergic responses. Skin tests may also suggest an elevated prevalence of individuals at risk, since approximately 30% of all individuals undergoing skin testing exhibit a type I response without ever manifesting systemic features.

Related Basic Science

Basophils are the least common granulocyte and are related in function to the mast cell. Basophils differ from mast cells in that their lifespan in the circulation is approximately 2 weeks, whereas mast cells live longer within tissue and are capable of division. Both function similarly in hypersensitivity reactions (immediate and cutaneus). Basophils are bilobed and possess coarse purple-black, nonuniform granules.

Basophils originate from myeloid stem cells. Less is known about the basophil than any other leukocyte. Their growth appears to be stimulated by interleukin-3, interleukin-1, and granulocyte–macrophage colony-stimulating factor.

Type I or immediate hypersensitivity occurs following degranulation of basophils and mast cells. Basophil cell surface contains receptors that bind with the high-affinity Fc portion of the immunoglobulin E antibody. Basophil degranulation occurs when di- or multivalent antigens bridge immunoglobulin E receptors or when immunoglobulin E alone is present. Certain allergens such as narcotics may also directly cause basophil degranulation.

Histamine is the major mediator of the type I response, and the majority of histamine is stored and released from circulating basophils. Histamine functions to induce tissue and vascular changes as well as the influx of eosinophils. Basophil granules also contain other eosinophil chemoattractants, such as the slow-reacting substance of anaphylaxis, PAF-acether, and eosinophil chemotactic factor of anaphylaxis.

Tissue damage and increased vascular permeability are mediated by the release of trypsin and chymotrypsin-like enzymes stored within basophil granules. Basophil kallikrein stimulates blood coagulation and activates complement. Heparin is also stored within basophil granules, although the amount released is not sufficient to affect coagulation.

Natural History and Its Modification with Treatment

Repeated exposure to offending allergens results in progressively more severe immediate hypersensitivity reactions. Hyposensitization can be used to limit the severity of symptoms when allergenic exposure is unavoidable. Patients receive repeated subcutaneous injections of escalating concentrations of the presumed allergen. The benefit of this preventive strategy is due to complex interactions, including a rise in immunoglobulin G antibodies.

Hyposensitization should be used only for individuals who are unable to control their allergic symptoms with medication. Antihistamines are the mainstay of medical management of allergic reactions; however, their side effects (e.g., drowsiness) are often prohibitive. Inhaled cromolyn sodium can be used to control pulmonary symptoms.

Prevention

The hallmark of prevention is avoidance of exposure to the effecting allergen.

Cost Containment

The continued development of medications that control and avert immediate hypersensitivity will limit the expense of controlling an anaphylactic reaction in an emergency situation.

REFERENCES

Austen KF. Disease of immediate type hypersensitivity. In: Braunwald E, Isselbacher KJ, Petersdorf RG, et al., eds. Harrison's principles of internal medicine. 11th ed. New York: McGraw-Hill, 1987:1407.

Brostoff J, Hall T. Hypersensitivity—type I. In: Roitt I, Brostoff J, Male D, eds. Immunology. 2nd ed. St. Louis: Mosby, 1980:19.1.

Galli SJ. New concepts about the mast cell. N Engl J Med 1993;328:257.

Serafin WE, Austen KF. Current concepts: Mediators of immediate hypersensitivity reactions. N Engl J Med 1987;317:30.

Shurin SB. Eosinophil and basophil structure and function. In: Hoffman R, Benz EJ Jr, Shattil SJ, et al., eds. Hematology. New York: Churchill Livingstone, 1991:538.

CHAPTER 12–11

Eosinophilia

Beth A. Overmoyer, M.D.

DEFINITION

Eosinophilia is defined as an absolute blood eosinophil count greater than 0.45×10^9/L (450 /μL). Reactive hypereosinophilia is defined as a persistent eosinophil count greater than 1.5×10^9/L (1500/μL).

ETIOLOGY

Eosinophilia may be primary (rare) or secondary to other diseases. (See Clinical Manifestations for a list of causes.)

CRITERIA FOR DIAGNOSIS

Suggestive

The presence of allergic or immunologic diseases (as listed below) may suggest the concurrent presence of hypereosinophilia.

Definitive

See Definition.

CLINICAL MANIFESTATIONS

The subjective and objective manifestations of eosinophilia are determined by the characteristics of the underlying diseases as listed below. See the appropriate chapters elsewhere in the book.

Allergic Disorders

Several common etiologies of eosinophilia include hayfever, asthma, and skin rashes; with or without urticaria. Drug allergies may also cause eosinophilia. Eosinophilia may also occur with rare conditions, such as angioedema, serum sickness, allergic vasculitis, and Stevens–Johnson syndrome. A recent disorder, identified as the eosinophilia–myalgia syndrome, is related to the ingestion of L-tryptophan.

Dermatologic Disorders

Underlying dermatologic disorders may be accompanied by eosinophilia. The diagnosis is based on clinical and/or pathologic changes in the skin. These diseases include psoriasis, eczema, pemphigus vulgaris, pityriasis, and dermatitis herpetiformis.

Parasitic Infection

Eosinophilia occurs as a response to parasitic invasion of tissue and is a reflection of the degree of invasion. Parasitic cysts are associated with the maximal level of eosinophilia. The most common cause of eosinophilia throughout the world is parasitic infection. Several types of parasites are listed here:

- *Protozoan:* toxoplasmosis, amebiasis, malaria, *Pneumocystis.*
- *Nematodes:* strongyloidiasis, enterobiasis, hookworm, filariasis, ascariasis, toxocariasis (visceral larva migrans).
- *Trematodes:* schistosomiasis, clonorchiasis, paragonimiasis.
- *Arthropods:* scabies.
- *Cestodes:* echinococcosis, sparganosis, taeniasis.

Tropical Eosinophilia

Tropical eosinophilia is prevalent in India and Southeast Asia, where it is caused by filarial infestation. This disease has a male predominance (80%) and is characterized by pulmonary infiltrates and granulomas within the spleen, liver, and lymph nodes. Unlike other eosinophilic diseases, tropical eosinophilia is resistant to glucocorticoids, but is responsive to treatment with diethylcarbamazine (Banoside).

Pulmonary Disorders

Pulmonary infiltrates with eosinophilia may represent a hypersensitivity reaction due to reactive eosinophils, rather than distinct pathologic conditions. The spectrum of disease can be categorized by the following conditions: Loffler's pneumonia is characterized by transient pulmonary infiltrates, which may spontaneously resolve within a month. The symptom complex consists of malaise, cough, bronchospasm, and dyspnea. Pulmonary infiltrates with eosinophilia (PIE) has more severe manifestations, and is often fatal. This syndrome is associated with asthma, pulmonary infiltrates, central nervous system involvement, peripheral neuropathies, and periarteritis nodosa. These disorders are responsive to treatment with glucocorticoids.

Gastrointestinal Disorders

Eosinophilia may be due to a range of gastrointestinal diseases such as eosinophilic gastroenteritis, milk precipitin disease, regional enteritis, ulcerative colitis, protein-losing enteropathy, and allergic granulomatosis.

Hereditary Disorders

These constitute a familial type of eosinophilia.

Malignancy

Lymphoma. Hodgkin's disease, non-Hodgkin's lymphoma, and mycosis fungoides (T-cell lymphoma) can cause eosinophilia.

Leukemia. Acute lymphocytic leukemia and acute myelomonocytic leukemia associated with an inversion of chromosome 16 can cause eosinophilia.

Solid Tumors. Carcinomatosis, melanoma, and brain tumors can cause eosinophilia.

Eosinophilic Leukemia/Hypereosinophilic Syndrome. There is ongoing debate about the capability of eosinophilia to transform into primary eosinophilic leukemia. It is often difficult to differentiate between a hypereosinophilic syndrome of unknown etiology and eosinophilic leukemia, as both manifest eosinophil counts greater than 1.5×10^9/L and leukocyte counts greater than 20×10^9/L. The clinical characteristics are also similar; fever, vasculitis, polyserositis, pulmonary infiltrates, cardiac involvement (Loffler's endocarditis), and granulocytic and eosinophilic hyperplasia within the bone marrow. Both diseases are often resistant to glucocorticoids or chemotherapy. Cytogenetic abnormalities may be helpful in the diagnosis of eosinophilic leukemia; however, often the clinician must take the "watch and wait" approach until the disease severity declares itself.

PLANS

Diagnostic

See appropriate chapters elsewhere in this book on the conditions listed under Clinical Manifestations.

Therapeutic

Therapy is aimed at the underlying cause of the condition or elimination of the offending agent.

The hypereosinophilic syndrome requires discussion concerning treatment recommendations. Often cases are mild and can be managed by observation every 3 to 6 months. Once organ system dysfunction is noted, prednisone should be started. The dose is 1 mg/kg every day followed by conversion to an every-other-day regimen. Once disease stabilization or improvement occurs, the prednisone may be tapered to the smallest amount required for disease control. Patients who fail to respond to prednisone may have a trial of hydroxyurea (Hydrea) added to the glucocorticoids. The dose of hydroxyurea ranges from 0.5 to 2.0 g/d titrated to maintain a leukocyte count less than 10,000/mm³. Leukopheresis may be required if the level of eosinophils is equal to or greater than 100,000/mm³. Recent reports have also demonstrated efficacy in using inteferon-alfa or cyclosporin A in patients with the hypereosinophilic syndrome.

Treatment of patients manifesting characteristics of eosinophilic leukemia is identical to that of acute myelogenous leukemia. Chemotherapy with an aminoglycoside and cytidine arabinoside is effective.

FOLLOW-UP

The specific follow-up is determined by the underlying cause of eosinophilia.

DISCUSSION

Prevalence and Incidence

Eosinophilia is rare. In the United States and Europe, the most common cause of eosinophilia is allergic disorders, whereas parasitic infestations account for the majority of cases of eosinophilia worldwide.

Related Basic Science

Mature eosinophils are terminally differentiated cells containing bilobed nuclei which are often obscured by overlying red-staining granules. These granules are composed primarily of major basic protein, eosinophil peroxidase, eosinophil cationic proteins, and eosinophil-derived neurotoxin. Other smaller granules may also contain acid phosphatase and arylsulfatase.

Eosinophils originate from myeloid stem cells. Proliferation can be stimulated by several cytokines, namely, interleukin-3, interleukin-5, and granulocyte–macrophage and granulocyte colony-stimulating factors. Interleukin-5 appears to be the principal cytokine responsible for the production of eosinophils. Eosinophils develop within the bone marrow and remain there for approximately 9 days before entering the circulation. They exist primarily within tissue (gastrointestinal tract, lungs, and skin) rather than blood, and circulate for only approximately 3 to 8 hours.

The eosinophil participates in host defense; however, the mechanisms used during activation often result in damage to adjacent normal cells.

Although eosinophils are similar to neutrophils in having the potential to phagocytose and kill bacteria, they are directed primarily toward defending against nonphagocytosable organisms, such as parasites. Eosinophils bind to parasites via antiparasite immunoglobulin G or E antibodies or through C3b deposited on the parasite surface. The eosinophils then release their granular contents consisting of cationic proteins (major basic protein and eosinophil cationic protein), which are deposited on the parasite surface and function as potent toxins. They also contain eosinophil peroxidase, which, when released, generates hypophalous acids that also kill parasites. Unfortunately, the oxidative products of eosinophil granules, such as superoxide anions, hydroxyl radicals, and singlet oxygen, result in damage to normal host tissue.

Eosinophils also produce leukotriene C_4 and platelet-activating factor, which contract smooth muscle, promote mucus secretion, alter vascular permeability, and promote eosinophil and neutrophil infiltration. Major basic protein can also stimulate the release of histamine from basophils and mast cells. The products of eosinophil activation during an allergic response result in a cascade cellular response that leads to dysfunction of adjoining cells in normal tissue.

Natural History and Its Modification with Treatment

The natural history is dependent on the individual cause. Severe cases of hypereosinophilic syndromes may be fatal; however, often more than 70% of patients respond to glucocorticoids, and 60% of the remaining individuals may respond to hydroxyurea. The availability of interferon-alfa may improve the response rate among hydroxyurea-resistant patients.

Prevention

Eosinophilia may be prevented only when allergies and parasitic infestations are prevented.

Cost Containment

A careful history and physical examination aid in selecting patients who require minimal diagnostic intervention and treatment. This eliminates unnecessary and costly testing to determine a diagnosis in a relatively asymptomatic patient with mild eosinophilia. Of course, patients with severe illness associated with eosinophilia must be thoroughly evaluated to determine a diagnosis.

REFERENCES

Fauci AS. The idiopathic hypereosinophilic syndrome: Clinical, pathophysiologic, and therapeutic considerations. Ann Intern Med 1982;97:78.

Shurin SB. Pathologic states associated with activation of eosinophils and with eosinophilia. Hematol Oncol Clin North Am 1988;2:171.

Shurin SB. Eosinophil and basophil structure and function. In: Hoffman R, Benz EJ Jr, Shattil SJ, et al., eds. Hematology. New York: Churchill Livingstone, 1991:538.

Varga J, Uitto J, Jimenez SA. The cause and pathogenics of the eosinophilia–myalgia syndrome. Ann Intern Med 1992;116:140.

Weller PF. The immunobiology of eosinophils. N Engl J Med 1991;324:1110.

CHAPTER 12–12

Lymphocytopenia

Thomas E. Olencki, D.O.

DEFINITION

There is general agreement that absolute lymphocytopenia occurs at or below 1.0×10^9/L or 1000/µL. This chapter reviews entities associated with a decrease in lymphocytes, but does not discuss specific subsets or conditions of pancytopenia of which lymphocytopenia may be a part.

The absolute number of lymphocytes is age dependent; the highest levels are found in infancy, with a low normal of 5.0×10^9/L at 4 to 8 months, declining in late childhood to 1.5×10^9/L at 10 years and 1.0×10^9/L by 18 to 21 years of age.

In the adult human, approximately 65 to 80% of lymphocytes are T cells, 10 to 15% are B cells, and the remaining 5 to 10% are natural killer cells.

ETIOLOGY

See Table 12–12–1.

CRITERIA FOR DIAGNOSIS

The absolute lymphocyte count as determined by the hematology analyzer is required to make the diagnosis of lymphocytopenia (see Definition).

CLINICAL MANIFESTATIONS
Subjective

Lymphocytopenia is asymptomatic. Patients may have symptoms secondary to their underlying diagnoses.

Objective

There are no unique objective findings on physical examination or laboratory evaluation other than the lymphocytopenia noted on the complete blood count with differential.

PLANS
Diagnostic

The complete blood count with differential is necessary and sufficient to make the diagnosis of lymphocytopenia. The diagnostic challenge is to determine the specific underlying etiology responsible for the low absolute lymphocyte count. Possible causes are shown in Table 12–12–1. See other chapters in which these causes are discussed.

Therapeutic

No specific treatment is indicated for lymphocytopenia. Therapy is to be guided by the underlying etiology.

FOLLOW-UP

The frequency and nature of follow-up are dependent on the underlying etiology of the lymphocytopenia.

DISCUSSION
Prevalence and Incidence

There are no accurate data regarding the prevalence and incidence of lymphocytopenia.

TABLE 12–12–1. ETIOLOGY OF LYMPHOCYTOPENIA

Immunodeficiency syndromes
  Severe combined immunodeficiency (SCID)
    X-linked SCID
    Autosomal recessive—Swiss type
  Reticular dysgenesis
  Severe combined immunodeficiency
    with normal B cells
  Adenosine deaminase deficiency
  Rare lymphocyte syndrome
  Interleukin-2 production defect
  Major histocompatibility syndrome class II deficiency
  Purine nucleoside phosphorylase deficiency
  DiGeorge's syndrome
  Ataxia telangiectasia
  Wiskott–Aldrich syndrome
  Immunodeficiency with short-limbed dwarfism
    (cartilage hair hypoplasia)
  Absence of CD4+ cells
  Thymoma/myasthenia gravis
Connective tissue—autoimmune diseases
  Systemic lupus erythematous
  Felty's syndrome
  Sjögren's syndrome
  Mixed connective tissue disease
  Dermatomyositis
  Rheumatoid arthritis
Treatment related
  Radiation therapy
  Chemotherapy
  Drugs
    Glucocorticoids
    Antithymocyte globulin, OKT3 antibody
  Major surgery
Infection
  Retroviral (HIV-1, HIV-2, human T-lymphotropic
    virus type 1)
  Herpesvirus (varicella zoster, cytomegalovirus)
  Mycobacterium tuberculosis
  Mycobacterium avium–intracellulare
  Measles virus
  Hepatitis B
  Fungal (histoplasmosis, cryptococcosis,
    coccidioidomycosis)
  Rickettsial (Rocky Mountain spotted fever)
  Leishmaniasis
  Brucellosis
  Severe bacterial infection
Neoplastic
  Hodgkin's disease
  Aplastic anemia
  Cancer in advanced state
Other
  Unexplained CD4+ lymphocytopenia (HIV-1 and
    HIV-2 negative)
  Sarcoidosis
  Zinc deficiency
  Severe malnutrition
  Protein-losing enteropathy
  Renal insufficiency
  Chronic alcoholism
  Myocardial infarction

Related Basic Science

Whether lymphocytopenia is due to the failure of lymphocyte development and maturation, peripheral destruction, apoptosis (energy-dependent programmed cell death), redistribution of lymphocytes to the lymph node, or adhesion to the endothelial cell wall is unknown. Research to answer this question is currently underway and includes evaluation of the lymphocyte receptor, cytoplasmic signal transduction, nuclear DNA binding proteins, and genetic mutations.

Natural History and Its Modification with Treatment

The natural history of lymphocytopenia is directly related to the underlying etiology.

Prevention

Prevention must be directed to the underlying etiology.

Cost Containment

The definitive diagnosis is made on the basis of the absolute lymphocyte count as determined by the complete blood count with differential. Pathology review of the peripheral smear and bone marrow biopsy adds little clinical information. Peripheral blood lymphocyte subset evaluation, other than determination of the absolute CD4+ level, is not indicated outside of a clinical trial or research setting. See chapters dealing with diseases listed in Table 12–12–1.

REFERENCES

Schoentag RA, Cangiarella J. The nuances of lymphocytopenia. Clin Lab Med 1993;13:923.
Smith DK, Neal JJ, Holmberg SD, et al. Unexplained opportunistic infections and CD4+ T-lymphocytopenia without HIV infection. N Engl J Med 1993;328:373.
Soriano V, Hewlett I, Heredia A, et al. Idiopathic CD4+ T-lymphocytopenia. Lancet 1992;340:607.
Thompson SD, Gibbons RJ, Smars PA, et al. Incremental value of the leukocyte differential and the rapid creatinine kinase - MB isoenzyme for early diagnosis of myocardial infarction. Ann Intern Med 1995;122:335.
Williams WJ. Lymphocytopenia. In: Williams WJ, Beutler E, Ersler AJ, Lichtman MA, eds. Williams' Hematology, 4th ed. New York: McGraw-Hill, 1990.

CHAPTER 12–13

Lymphocytosis

Abdelghani I. Tbakhi, M.D., and Raymond R. Tubbs, D.O

DEFINITION

Lymphocytosis is an increase in the absolute number of lymphocytes in the peripheral blood.

ETIOLOGY

The etiology of lymphocytosis is outlined in Table 12–13–1.

CRITERIA FOR DIAGNOSIS

Absolute lymphocyte counts are at their highest normal levels in infants and children and diminish with age: at birth, the absolute number of lymphocytes is 2.0 to 11.0×10^9/L; at 14 days, 2.0 to 17.0×10^9/L; at 4 years, 2.0 to 8.0×10^9 /L; and at > 16 years, 1.5 to 4.0×10^9/L. A lymphocytosis exists when the absolute lymphocyte count exceeds 11.0 to 17.0×10^9/L in infants, 8.0×10^9/L in young children, and 4.0×10^9/L in adults.

CLINICAL MANIFESTATIONS

Subjective and *objective* clinical manifestations are variable and are determined by the underlying cause.

PLANS

Diagnostic

Chronic Lymphocytic Leukemia

The disease is a neoplastic, clonal proliferation of a subset of small lymphocytes that express B-cell-associated antigens (CD19, CD20) and are CD5+ and CD23+. There is usually persistent absolute lymphocytosis exceeding 15×10^9/L, with or without lymphadenopathy, hepatosplenomegaly, anemia, or thrombocytopenia in an adult.

Acute Lymphocytic Leukemia

The disease is a malignant bone marrow-derived proliferation of lymphocyte precursors with characteristic morphologic, cytochemical, and immunologic features.

Large Granular Lymphocyte Lymphocytosis

See Color Plates 12–13–1A and 12–13–1B, after page 826.
   T large granular lymphocyte (LGL) *leukemia* is a clonal proliferation of CD3+ LGLs, typically associated with chronic neutropenia and autoimmune disease.
   Natural killer-LGL leukemia is a clonal proliferation of CD3– LGLs, with an acute clinical presentation marked by massive hepatosplenomegaly and systemic illness.
   Polyclonal LGL lymphocytosis is marked by increased numbers of CD3– LGLs and has a chronic clinical course.

Acute Infections

Infectious Mononucleosis. Peripheral smear demonstrates large atypical lymphocytes. The diagnosis is confirmed by the detection of heterophil antibodies and Epstein–Barr virus-specific serologic markers of infection.

Bordetella pertussis. The lymphocyte count in whooping cough is usually approximately 10.0×10^9/L. The lymphocytes appear mature and are predominantly helper-T cells.

Cytomegalovirus Infections. These infections are associated with atypical lymphocytes resembling those seen in infectious mononucleosis. The virus can be demonstrated in tissues by its characteristic morphologic appearance, immunohistochemistry, and/or in situ hybridization.

Acute Infectious Lymphocytosis. This rare benign disease of children is characterized by persistent lymphocytosis. The lymphocytes are of normal morphology and the count may be quite high and persist up to 3 months.

Persistent polyclonal B lymphocytosis. This rare benign lymphoproliferative disorder is seen in females who are smokers, have an HLA-DR7 phenotype and have evidence of Epstein–Barr virus infection.

Chronic Infections

Diagnostic tests are determined by the infection suspected clinically. The lymphocytosis is usually relative rather than absolute.

Therapeutic

There is no specific treatment for lymphocytosis. Treatment should be targeted at the underlying cause.

TABLE 12–13–1. ETIOLOGY OF LYMPHOCYTOSIS

Infections
   Viruses
      Infectious mononucleosis
      Cytomegalovirus
      Infectious hepatitis
      HIV
      Mumps
      Varicella
      Rubeola (measles)
      Rubella
      Herpes simplex
      Herpes zoster
      Roseola infantum
      Influenza
      Others
   Bacteria
      Brucellosis
      Tuberculosis
      Pertussis
   Spirochetes
      Syphilis
   Rickettsiae
   Toxoplasmosis
Drugs
   para-Aminosalicyclic acid
   Phenytoin
   Mephenytoin
Neoplasms
   Leukemia
   Lymphoma
Critical clinical conditions
   Cardiac arrest
   Acute myocardial infarction
   Severe traumatic injuries
   Status asthmaticus
   Status epilepticus
Other causes
   Persistent polyclonal B lymphocytosis
   Radiation
   Poisoning (lead, TNT, trichloroethane, arsenic)
   Agranulocytosis
   Severe dermatitis herpetiformis
   Letterer–Siwe disease
   Stress

FOLLOW-UP

Follow-up depends on the cause of lymphocytosis.

DISCUSSION

Prevalence and Incidence

The prevalence and incidence of lymphocytosis are highly variable and depend on the underlying disorder.

Related Basic Science

Lymphocytes, the principal cells of the immune system, are produced in the primary lymphoid organs (thymus and adult bone marrow) at a high rate (10^9 per day). The average human adult has about 10^{12} lymphoid cells, and the lymphoid tissue as a whole represents about 2% of total body weight. Lymphoid cells represent about 20% of the total white blood cells in the adult circulation. Many mature lymphoid cells are very short-lived, but some are long-lived and may persist as memory cells for several years, or even for the lifetime of an individual. Lymphocytes are generally divided into three subtypes: B cells, T cells, and natural killer cells. Morphologically, however, there are two distinct types of lymphocytes. The smaller of the two is typically agranular and has a high nuclear:cytoplasmic ratio. This type includes B cells and some T cells. The larger cells have a lower nuclear:cytoplasmic ratio and contain intracytoplasmic azurophilic granules. These are currently referred to as LGLs. These LGLs may be T cells (CD3+) or natural killer cells (CD3−).

Physiologic Clonal Expansion of Lymphocytes. Lymphocytes that have been stimulated by binding to their specific antigens take first steps toward cell division. There are early biochemical events that result in the generation of secondary messengers within B or T cells. These are responsible for changes at the molecular (DNA) level. Both B and T cells use a GTP-dependent (G-protein) component that induces intracellular signals. Two secondary messengers are generated: inositol 1, 4, 5-triphosphate and diacylglycerol. The former triggers the release of Ca^{2+} whereas the latter activates protein kinase C. This is accompanied by the expression of surface receptors (e.g., interleukin-2 receptor). Exposure to sufficient concentrations of cytokines, mainly interleukin-2, leads to clonal expansion of the lymphocytes.

Neoplastic Clonal Expansion of Lymphocytes. Altered expression of proto-oncogenes by chromosomal translocation has been implicated in the pathogenesis of certain lymphomas and leukemias. One example is that seen in mantle cell lymphoma, a condition associated with lymphocytosis. In this disease, there is a chromosomal translocation, t(11;14), that involves the immunoglobulin heavy chain locus and the *BCL-1* locus on the long arm of chromosome 11. This translocation results in over-expression of a gene known as *PRAD1*, which encodes for cyclin D1, a cell protein that is not normally expressed in lymphoid cells and may be oncogenic by altering progression through the cell cycle.

Role of Epstein–Barr Virus Infection. The main target of Epstein–Barr virus is the B cell. When Epstein–Barr virus infects B cells binding to the CD21 molecule on the cell surface, its linear genome circularizes to form an episome, or extrachromosomal element, in the nucleus of the cell. The result is transformation of the infected B cells, which acquire the capacity to proliferate indefinitely. In addition, infected B cells express an antigen known as lymphocyte-determined membrane antigen (LYDMA). This antigen is specifically recognized by the cytotoxic/suppresser (CD8) T cells. These activated T cells, which proliferate and appear in the circulation as large atypical lymphocytes, are responsible for preventing the unchecked expansion of Epstein–Barr virus-transformed B lymphocytes.

Natural History and Its Modification with Treatment

The natural history of lymphocytosis and its modification with treatment are determined by the underlying condition.

Prevention

Prevention of lymphocytosis is determined by the cause. Some acute infections can be prevented, whereas others cannot (see chapters dealing with infectious diseases). Many chronic infections can be prevented (see chapters dealing with infectious diseases). Lymphocytosis associated with leukemias and lymphomas cannot be prevented. Lymphocytosis caused by drugs can be prevented by discontinuing the drug if possible.

Cost Containment

Cost containment is usually influenced by the disease or condition associated with the lymphocytosis (see specific chapters).

REFERENCES

Davey FR, Nelson DA. Leukocytic disorders. In: Henry JB, ed. Clinical diagnosis and management by laboratory methods. Philadelphia: Saunders, 18th ed. 1991:984.

Harris NL, Jaffe ES, Banks PM, et al. A revised European–American classification of lymphoid neoplasms: A proposal from the International Lymphoma Group. Blood 1994;84:1361.

Loughran TP. Clonal diseases of large granular lymphocytes. Blood 1993;82:1.

Roitt I, Brostoff J, Male D. Immunology. 3rd ed. St. Louis: Mosby, 1993:2.10.

Strauss SE, Cohen JI, Tosato G, Meier J. Epstein–Barr virus infections: Biology, pathogenesis and management. Ann Intern Med 1993:118:45.

Hematologic Manifestations of HIV Infection

Michael L. Miller, D.O.

DEFINITION

The hematologic abnormalities associated with HIV infection manifest primarily as cytopenias, myelodysplastic syndromes, and hemostatic abnormalities.

ETIOLOGY

Impaired hematopoiesis and autoantibodies are the mechanisms primarily responsible for mediating the development of the cytopenias and hemostatic defects seen in HIV-infected patients, although infections, antimicrobial drugs, neoplasms, and chemotherapeutic agents are also contributing factors.

CRITERIA FOR DIAGNOSIS

Suggestive

The diagnosis is suggested when patients with risk factors for HIV infection but not yet diagnosed or those known to be HIV infected present with clinical findings suggesting a hematologic abnormality.

Definitive

The diagnosis is confirmed when HIV-infected patients present with one or more of the following hematologic abnormalities: normocytic or macrocytic anemia, leukopenia, thrombocytopenia, pancytopenia, a myelodysplastic syndrome, or evidence of a hemostatic abnormality, such as a bleeding episode or prolonged activated partial thromboplastin time (aPTT), prothrombin time (PT), and/or bleeding time.

CLINICAL MANIFESTATIONS
Subjective

All HIV-infected patients develop hematologic abnormalities at some point during the course of the disease. The degree to which these manifest clinically is dependent on the severity and type of abnormality. Fatigue, lassitude, fever, frequent infections, and easy bruisability or, less often, a bleeding episode (e.g., epistaxis) are symptoms that may be noted by the patient.

Objective

Physical Examination

The physical examination of the HIV-infected patient may be noncontributory early in the course of the disease. As the disease progresses, however, physical findings related to the hematologic abnormalities may become evident: pallor and/or tachycardia related to anemia; pulmonary abnormalities secondary to opportunistic infections and petechial hemorrhages, ecchymoses, or clinically significant bleeding secondary to thrombocytopenia and/or a functional platelet defect.

Routine Laboratory Abnormalities

The most common routine laboratory abnormalities found in HIV-infected patients are cytopenias, which are easily identified by a complete blood count with leukocyte differential. Anemia is found in most patients at presentation and is usually normocytic, with an increased red cell distribution width and essentially normal red cell morphology. Macrocytic anemia (>110 fL) may be seen in more than two thirds of patients receiving zidovudine (AZT) after just 2 weeks of therapy. The reticulocyte count is characteristically low in all anemic patients.

Leukopenia is common and frequently occurs in conjunction with anemia. Lymphopenia is uniformly present due to a progressive reduction of CD4 lymphocytes and granulocytopenia occurs in the majority of patients. Leukocyte morphology may be normal but abnormalities are not infrequently seen and include atypical lymphocytes, toxic changes in granulocytes, and dysplastic granulocytes characterized by nuclear hyposegmentation (Pelgeroid neutrophils) or hypogranulation.

Thrombocytopenia is frequently found in conjunction with anemia or granulocytopenia, but may be an independent finding and one of the first indications of HIV infection. It has been reported in more than half of symptomatic patients.

Although a variety of hemostatic abnormalities have been reported in HIV infection the most common, excluding thrombocytopenia, is prolongation of the activated partial thromboplastin time, usually due to the presence of a lupus anticoagulant. The prothrombin time is usually normal. A lupus anticoagulant may be found in two thirds of patients.

Several cases of thrombotic thrombocytopenic purpura have also been reported. The laboratory abnormalities are characterized by a microangiopathic hemolytic anemia (red cell fragments), decreased fibrinogen level, and consumptive thrombocytopenia. Clinically these patients have fluctuating neurologic signs, progressive renal failure, and fever.

PLANS
Diagnostic

Differential Diagnosis

The differential diagnosis includes any disease state that can cause the cytopenias or hemostatic abnormalities described; however, a clinical suspicion of HIV infection based on the clinical history and risk factors followed by appropriate confirmatory testing for the virus should eliminate most other diagnostic possibilities.

Diagnostic Options

The hematologic abnormalities associated with HIV infection are easily identified for the most part with routine laboratory tests; however, additional laboratory studies may be desired as follow-up to routine testing when an abnormal result is encountered or to define further the etiology of the abnormality. Serum erythropoietin levels are useful in assessing the potential responsiveness of an anemia to exogenous erythropoietin. Serum iron studies are normal in the early stage of HIV infection in an otherwise healthy patient, but, in advanced disease, resemble anemia of chronic disease with increased serum ferritin, decreased serum iron, and total iron binding capacity. Serum vitamin B_{12} levels are low in approximately 20% of HIV-infected patients, but no clinical or morphologic evidence of B_{12} deficiency is usually found. Schilling's test may also be abnormal in some patients, with and without low serum B_{12}, and is felt to be secondary to an enteropathic effect of the virus. The Coombs test (direct antiglobulin test) is positive in about 20% of HIV-infected patients with hypergammaglobulinemia. The antibodies react as polyagglutinins and rarely cause a hemolytic anemia in the absence of sepsis.

Thrombocytopenia is usually immune mediated, as evidenced by increased platelet-associated immunoglobulin and increased megakaryocytes in the bone marrow, indicating peripheral consumption.

A patient with dysplastic neutrophils with or without a macrocytic anemia probably should undergo bone marrow examination because of the frequent occurrence of myelodysplastic syndrome in HIV-infected patients. Although the presence of myelodysplastic syndrome does not seem to have the same implications with respect to the development of acute leukemia as in non-HIV-infected patients, it may contribute to the refractory cytopenias and granulocyte dysfunction common to these patients.

A prolonged activated partial thromboplastin time in an HIV-positive patient should be further evaluated for a factor deficiency or a circulating anticoagulant. A variety of tests are used for this purpose; therefore, the hematology laboratory should be consulted as to the proper test to order. If a lupus anticoagulant is present and the prothrombin time is also prolonged, it is advisable to perform a factor II assay. Inhibitors to factor II are occasionally encountered in association with lupus anticoagulant and are known to be responsible for bleeding diasthesis. Of interest is the observation that anticardiolipin antibodies of the immunoglobulin G type have been found to be increased in the majority of symptomatic HIV-infected patients.

Patients experiencing bleeding when the platelet count, activated partial thromboplastin time, and prothrombin time are within normal limits may benefit from a bleeding time. A prolonged bleeding time may indicate a functional platelet defect, possibly caused by a drug, lupus anticoagulant, or dysplastic megakaryopoiesis.

An important laboratory study that is routinely performed is determination of the absolute CD4 and CD8 lymphocyte counts and the CD4/CD8 ratio using flow cytometric analysis. The progressive lymphopenia seen in these patients is due to loss of CD4 lymphocytes. A patient with less than 0.2×10^9/L CD4 lymphocytes is at significant risk for opportunistic infections.

Recommended Approach

The recommended approach to defining the various hematologic abnormalities found in these patients is described under Routine Laboratory Abnormalities and Diagnostic Options.

Therapeutic

The strategy for treating the anemia associated with HIV infection is dependent on several factors. In many patients the bone marrow does not produce red cells because the serum erythropoietin levels are depressed. Some of these patients respond to AZT therapy as reflected by significantly increased erythropoietin levels; however, approximately two thirds continue to have depressed erythropoietin levels while on AZT. These patients may benefit from AZT dose reduction and/or treatment with recombinant human erythropoietin if the baseline erythropoietin level is less than 500 mU/mL. In contrast, if the erythropoietin level is high, the bone marrow will probably not be responsive due to erythroid progenitor aplasia/hypoplasia. In this situation, blood transfusion therapy may be necessary with the potential complications of immune hemolysis and transmission of infectious agents.

Leukopenia or, more specifically, granulocytopenia is most effectively treated using colony-stimulating factors, such as granulocyte and granulocyte–macrophage colony-stimulating factors (G-CSF and GM-CSF). It is well documented that these agents are helpful in overcoming the hematopoietic toxicity of the antiviral drugs and chemotherapy these patients receive.

The treatment of thrombocytopenia is usually disappointing because of the lack of a durable response. AZT has been shown to increase the platelet count in some groups of patients. Systemic steroids achieve an initial response in many patients, but a lasting effect is seen in less than 20%. With this approach the potential risk for further immunosuppression must be considered. If the patient has active bleeding or is being prepared for an invasive procedure, then intravenous immunoglobulin is recommended. A normal platelet count may be obtained within a few days but the median duration is only approximately 3 weeks. Because even severe thrombocytopenia is rarely associated with clinically significant bleeding, it has been suggested that no treatment may be the most appropriate approach.

No therapy is warranted for the presence of a lupus anticoagulant. Unlike HIV-negative patients, the development of thrombosis is an uncommon occurrence in HIV-positive patients with a lupus anticoagulant. In contrast, thrombotic thrombocytopenic purpura should be treated aggressively with plasmapheresis using fresh-frozen plasma.

FOLLOW-UP

Once a patient is known to be HIV positive, he or she should be periodically examined for clinical evidence of hematologic abnormalities. A complete blood count with differential, activated partial thromboplastin time, and prothrombin time should be performed to assess the patient's status and to establish baseline laboratory values. The absolute CD4 and CD8 lymphocyte counts and the CD4/CD8 ratio should also be determined at this time. If abnormalities are found, then additional studies may be warranted as previously described. These tests should be repeated approximately every 6 months if the patient is asymptomatic and more frequently if warranted by the clinical circumstances. Therapeutic decisions depend on the clinical and laboratory findings at different stages of the disease and have to be modified accordingly.

DISCUSSION
Prevalence

All HIV-infected individuals will exhibit hematologic manifestations during the course of the disease, and the frequency and severity of these abnormalities increase significantly as the disease progresses.

Related Basic Science

Human immunodeficiency virus is a cytopathic retrovirus that infects primarily CD4 lymphocytes, but has also been found in hematopoietic

progenitors. The virus causes CD4 lymphopenia, derangements in the normal immune system giving rise to autoantibodies, and impaired hematopoiesis. It is these mechanisms that individually or in concert are responsible for the cytopenias and hemostatic abnormalities observed in the disease. The severity and type of hematologic findings in HIV infection are also dependent on the stage of the disease, the effects of antiviral, antimicrobial, and chemotherapies, and the presence of infection or neoplasm.

Natural History and Its Modification with Treatment

Infection with HIV is a progressive disease that is uniformly fatal despite treatment. Therefore, although the hematologic abnormalities can be ameliorated with variable success, prolonging the life of the patient for a period of time, treatment is only palliative and the eventual outcome is unchanged.

Prevention

The hematologic abnormalities associated with HIV infection cannot be prevented.

Cost Containment

Avoidance of overuse of laboratory tests for the diagnosis and follow-up of hematologic abnormalities is an important means of achieving cost containment in these patients. Another is the careful selection of those cytopenic patients who need to receive expensive forms of therapy, such as, recombinant erythropoietin, colony-stimulating factors (G-CSF and GM-CSF), and intravenous immunoglobulin. The establishment of practice guidelines for managing HIV-infected patients would be an important step in improving the quality of care and controlling costs.

REFERENCES

Aboulafia DM. Hematologic abnormalities in AIDS. Hematol Oncol Clin North Am 1991;5:195.

Karcher DS, Frost AR. The bone marrow in human immunodeficiency virus (HIV)-related disease. Am J Clin Pathol 1991;95:63.

Miles SA. Golde DW. Mitsuyasu RT. The use of hematopoietic hormones in HIV infection and AIDS-related malignancies. Hematol Oncol Clin North Am 1991;5:267.

Perkocha LA, Rodgers GM. Hematologic aspects of human immunodeficiency virus infection: Laboratory and clinical considerations. Am J Hematol 1988;29:94.

Stricker RB. Hemostatic abnormalities in HIV infection. Hematol Oncol Clin North Am 1991;5:249.

CHAPTER 12–15

Thrombocytopenia Secondary to Increased Destruction of Platelets

Alan E. Lichtin, M.D.

DEFINITION

Thrombocytopenia secondary to increased destruction of platelets is a low platelet count resulting from reduction of the lifespan of platelets in the circulation.

ETIOLOGY

Normally, platelets survive around 10 days in the circulation. Once platelets are produced by megakaryocytes and enter the circulation, they may be destroyed prematurely by several different mechanisms. Often, an immune mechanism is operative. An immunoglobulin is pro-

duced against the platelet surface that accelerates the destruction of platelets by macrophages recognizing the Fc receptor of the immunoglobulin on the surface of the platelet. Premature destruction of platelets may also be drug related. Many drugs lead to premature destruction of platelets, especially quinine, quinidine, and H_2 blockers such as cimetidine; however, practically any drug may cause thrombocytopenia in some patients. Many of these drug-induced cases have been proven to be the result of immune mechanisms, but other mechanisms may operate as well, such as a direct effect on the megakaryocyte. The causes of thrombocytopenia secondary to platelet destruction are outlined in Table 12–15–1.

Nonimmunologic
  Infection
    Sepsis
    Disseminated intravascular coagulation
    Protozoa (malaria, trypanosomiasis, toxoplasmosis)
  Thrombotic thrombocytopenic purpura
  Hemolytic uremic syndromes
  Preeclampsia
  Peritoneovenous shunting
  Fat embolism
  Glomerulonephritis
  Renal transplant rejection
  Hemangiomas (Kasabach–Merritt syndrome)
  Snake bites
  Fever or hypothermia
Immunologic
  Drug-induced immunologic thrombocytopenia
  Allergy
  Anaphylaxis
  Posttransfusion purpura
  Immune complexes
  Acute idiopathic thrombocytopenic purpura
  Chronic idiopathic thrombocytopenic purpura
  HIV infection
  Heparin-associated thrombocytopenia

CRITERIA FOR DIAGNOSIS

Suggestive

For each cause of thrombocytopenia secondary to platelet destruction, there are suggestive criteria for diagnosis. Review of the peripheral blood smear is important in discriminating some of these disorders. For example, in patients with disseminated intravascular coagulation or thrombotic thrombocytopenic purpura (TTP), not only is the platelet count low, but the red cell morphology is altered with the development of schistocytes, nucleated red blood cells, and helmet cells (Color Plate 12–15–1, after page 826). A normal red cell morphology and low platelet count suggest idiopathic thrombocytopenic purpura (see below) or a drug effect.

Other clinical findings suggest other causes of the thrombocytopenia. For example, if a pregnant woman in labor develops thrombocytopenia, the clinician would probably consider preeclampsia. A history of an underlying autoimmune disease such as systemic lupus erythematosus would lead the clinician to consider autoimmune mechanisms (or immune complexes) as a cause of the thrombocytopenia.

If clinical findings do not suggest a certain cause of the thrombocytopenia, the peripheral blood smear shows only a decrease in platelet count, and drugs have been ruled out as a cause, the patient may have idiopathic thrombocytopenic purpura (ITP). This is a diagnosis of exclusion, meaning that other causes of increased destruction of platelets must be excluded.

Definitive

A careful history and physical examination are important in confirming diagnosis of enhanced platelet destruction in a thrombocytopenic individual. If all other acquired causes listed in Table 12–15–1 are ruled out and the peripheral smear shows a decrease in the number of platelets, it is likely the patient has ITP. Of course, HIV infection should be ruled out serologically before the diagnosis of ITP is made. Also, a careful drug history must be elicited. Patients should be asked if they consume quinine-containing beverages such as tonic water and over-the-counter medicines for leg cramps. It will be obvious if renal transplant rejection or a fat embolus (e.g., after trauma or an orthopaedic procedure) is causing thrombocytopenia.

CLINICAL MANIFESTATIONS

Subjective

Most patients with thrombocytopenia present with complaints of bleeding. Bleeding manifests as easy bruisability, epistaxis, mucosal bleeding, menometrorrhagia, or petechiae or ecchymoses. With the advent of automated complete blood counts, many patients are referred to a hematologist for thrombocytopenia that is detected without the patient noticing any problem. These patients usually have platelet counts in the moderately thrombocytopenic range, 50,000 to 100,000.

It is important to review the medical record to determine whether the platelet count had been low before. Patients may have a slightly decreased platelet count for quite a long period because the mild nature of the thrombocytopenia would not arouse suspicion in physicians or patients.

A past history of previous episodes of bleeding may be relevant to a person who has intermittent episodes of thrombocytopenia. This might be the case in a person with chronic ITP who has exacerbations of the illness.

The family history is usually not contributory. There are congenital or familial causes of thrombocytopenia, such as Bernard–Soulier syndrome (see Chapter 12–16). In most of these familial forms of thrombocytopenia, destruction of platelets is not increased.

Objective

Physical Examination

Certain aspects of the physical examination are important in individuals with thrombocytopenia. Examining the skin for patterns of bleeding is critical. Petechiae on the lower extremities anteriorly would indicate thrombocytopenia with a platelet count less than 20,000. Ecchymosis or "easy bruising" of the thighs, arms, or trunk is usually seen with platelet counts between 20,000 and 50,000, although it may be seen even at platelet counts of 100,000 to 150,000. In a person with a very low platelet count, a skin rash, if present, will be redder or pinker than in those with higher counts because of concomitant bleeding into the area of the rash.

Other pertinent aspects of the physical examination include searching for evidence of lymphadenopathy or hepatosplenomegaly to exclude lymphoma or leukemia. If the person is pale, he or she likely has an associated anemia such as might be seen in TTP. A fever would suggest an infection. Large hemangiomas of the skin, often seen in children, might be associated with the Kasabach–Merritt syndrome. These may be internal, in the liver or spleen, so it is important to palpate these organs as well. In a near-term pregnant woman who is also thrombocytopenic, it is important to measure blood pressure to check for preeclampsia. The neurologic examination may demonstrate hyperactive reflexes or irritability.

As HIV-positive individuals may have many findings on physical examination, it is important, when seeing a thrombocytopenic person for the first time, to check for evidence of candidiasis of the oral cavity, Kaposi's sarcoma, lymphadenopathy, and so on.

Routine Laboratory Abnormalities

The most important laboratory criterion with respect to enhanced platelet destruction is a low platelet count on peripheral blood smear. A bone marrow examination must usually be performed to rule out some marrow-infiltrative disease, thereby differentiating decreased production of platelets from increased destruction (Color Plate 12–15–2, after page 826). Bone marrow examination is not always necessary, even in cases of ITP, if all other lines of evidence point to a known cause of the thrombocytopenia. For example, if the clinical history is consistent with TTP (presentation with the pentad findings of fever, renal abnormalities, neurologic abnormalities, microangiopathic hemolytic anemia, and thrombocytopenia), and disseminated intravascular coagulation is ruled out on the basis of a normal prothrombin time, partial thromboplastin time, and fibrinogen level, treatment of the TTP may proceed without a bone marrow test.

PLANS

Diagnostic

Differential Diagnosis

When a person is thrombocytopenic, it is important to differentiate enhanced platelet destruction from decreased production, hypersplenism, pseudothrombocytopenia, and dilution of platelets. These other topics are discussed in Chapter 12–16. Table 12–15–1 lists the causes of thrombocytopenia secondary to enhanced platelet destruction.

Diagnostic Options and Recommended Approach

The first step in the diagnosis of a patient with thrombocytopenia secondary to enhanced platelet destruction who is taking several medicines is discontinuation of the medicines. So many individuals have a drug-induced thrombocytopenia that it should be the first thing the physician thinks of when working up such an individual. Discontinuation of medicines may even be considered part of the therapeutic approach. It may raise the platelet count within a few days and, thus make the diagnosis of drug-induced thrombocytopenia more likely. One must always review the peripheral blood smear. Usually a bone marrow examination is done to determine if the number of megakaryocytes is normal or elevated.

If the patient is on heparin and the platelet count falls, a heparin-dependent antibody may be causing the thrombocytopenia. These individuals are, paradoxically, at increased risk for thromboses, even arterial ones (the "white clot syndrome"). The heparin-dependent antibody can be assayed. If this assay is positive, the heparin should be discontinued.

Determination of the prothrombin time, partial thromboplastin time, fibrinogen level, and fibrin degradation products is usually necessary in all thrombocytopenic patients to rule out disseminated intravascular coagulation as the cause. This is particularly true in hospitalized, critically ill or postsurgical patients.

Therapeutic

Therapeutic Options

As stated above, if a person is taking certain medicines and also has thrombocytopenia, it is important to discontinue all medicines. Some patients cannot tolerate the cessation of all drugs. Usually discontinuation of all drugs and substitution with other pharmacologic agents of different classes are recommended, so that cross-reactivity of one drug with another as a cause of thrombocytopenia can be excluded.

In patients with ITP who are severely thrombocytopenic, one first uses corticosteroids to raise the platelet count (prednisone 1–2 mg/kg orally per day). Some clinicians advocate only observation in children because in the vast majority of children with ITP, the disease resolves without therapy. Most adults respond to steroids initially and then, if the platelet count returns to normal, the dose of steroid is tapered. The majority of adult patients with ITP will experience a drop in their platelet count during tapering of the steroid dose; in such cases, splenectomy is often the next step. Eighty percent of individuals with classic ITP who have a splenectomy will thereafter have a normal platelet count. Note that in such patients, the surface of the platelets remains coated with antibody, but removing the spleen reduces the number of macrophages ingesting the antibody-coated platelets, resulting in a normal platelet count.

In the patient who cannot undergo splenectomy or is completely intolerant of corticosteroids, one might use infusions of intravenous immunoglobulin at a dose of 1 to 2 g/kg.

Recommended Approach

The preceding discussion applies usually to adults with ITP. Overall, it is recommended that the physician be certain of the cause of the enhanced platelet destruction. This means reviewing the diagnoses in Table 12–15–1 and confirming that one is not dealing with an underlying disease state requiring a different approach. For example, in the individual with TTP, plasmapheresis must be initiated and, perhaps, antiplatelet agents instituted. In persons with disseminated intravascular coagulation, however, the problem causing the disseminated intravas-

cular coagulation must be eliminated (e.g., treatment of sepsis, evacuation of uterus in abruptio placentae).

In an HIV-infected patient with thrombocytopenia, treatment of the HIV infection is based on the stage of progression to AIDS. For the thrombocytopenia, infusions of intravenous immunoglobulin improve humoral immunity as well as elevate the platelet count. Long-term use of steroids may place an HIV-infected individual at increased risk of infection.

FOLLOW-UP

The majority of patients with ITP who have been treated with steroids and then splenectomy (because the platelet count fell when the steroid dose was tapered) will have a normal platelet count for the rest of their life. They need to be followed relatively frequently soon after the splenectomy to ensure that the platelet count does not fall again. After 6 to 12 months, if the platelet count remains normal, yearly or less frequent follow-up is sufficient.

Individuals whose TTP resolves after a course of plasmapheresis must be taught to return immediately if their symptoms recur. Persons with a drug-induced thrombocytopenia should be warned never to take the offending drug. In some individuals who are very sensitive to quinine, the platelet count can drop to a life-threatening level. Quinine is available in several beverages and affected individuals need to be counseled not to drink anything containing quinine, for example, mixed drinks (such as gin and *tonic*).

DISCUSSION

Prevalence and Incidence

It is impossible to give numbers for the prevalence and incidence of enhanced platelet destruction. It is useful to point out that TTP is a relatively rare disorder; in some institutions it may be seen more frequently. Usually these patients are referred to tertiary care centers so they might receive daily plasmapheresis.

Related Basic Science

Altered Molecular Biology

Quite a bit of research has been devoted to determining why patients develop ITP and why the treatments work. Prednisone improves the platelet count probably by increasing the platelet production by megakaryocytes, whereas splenectomy prolongs platelet survival. Some centers can measure platelet turnover and platelet localization in organs such as the liver as a way of predicting response to prednisone or to splenectomy.

Recently there have been reports that quinine and quinidine cause not only thrombocytopenia but also a hemolytic uremic state. It is possible that quinine-dependent antibodies react not only with platelet membranes but also with neutrophil membrane antigens. Some of these patients have renal failure, rhabdomyolysis, and thrombocytopenia.

Physiologic or Metabolic Derangement

Platelet-associated immunoglobulin G has been explored as a way of helping diagnose immune thrombocytopenia and measuring its level as a way of following the course of the illness. To date, measurement of platelet immunoglobulin G has *not* become part of the standard of care for patients with immune thrombocytopenia. Some studies show that when platelets are destroyed, they absorb nearby immunoglobulin, which may not be directed to platelet antigens. Platelet surface immunoglobulin G may not only represent antiplatelet antibody, but may also be elevated in individuals whose thrombocytopenia is not immune. Thus, it is not a reliable indicator of a cause of thrombocytopenia.

Natural History and Its Modification with Treatment

In adults, ITP is cured up to 80% of the time by splenectomy. For those individuals in whom thrombocytopenia returns after splenectomy, periodic treatment with steroids or intravenous immunoglobulin G may be necessary. Chemotherapeutic drugs such as cytoxan, alone or in combination, are sometimes used for these individuals. It is usually necessary for a hematologist to be involved with the care of these refractory or relapsing patients.

Patients with other disorders such as TTP may experience a fulminant full-blown illness once in their life that after treatment never returns. Up to 20% of individuals with TTP have a recurrence. The role of splenectomy in these individuals is unclear, but if they fail to respond optimally to plasmapheresis, splenectomy may be performed. Disseminated intravascular coagulation is usually a fulminant process associated with infection or some other cause and, once treated, resolves.

In patients with a drug-induced thrombocytopenia who avoid the drug, the thrombocytopenia usually does not return.

Prevention

There is no way to prevent ITP. Once it occurs it needs to be treated as described above. Drug-induced thrombocytopenia is preventable and patients need to be educated about what drugs to avoid. Prescribing physicians should avoid drugs known to cause thrombocytopenia, particularly quinine, quinidine, trimethoprim–sulfamethoxazole, sulfonylureas, and salicylates.

Cost Containment

Steroids are the first choice in treatment of ITP. They are much less expensive than intravenous immunoglobulin, which may cost $2000 to $3000 per treatment. If patients relapse with ITP after splenectomy, they may be handled very appropriately with very low doses of steroids on an every-other-day basis, thus reducing the risk of long-range side effects of steroids.

REFERENCES

George JN. Platelet immunoglobulin G: Its significance for the evaluation of thrombocytopenia and for understanding the origin of alpha granule protein. Blood 1990;76:859.

George JN, El-Harake MA, Raskob GE. Chronic idiopathic thrombocytopenia purpura. N Engl J Med 1994;334:1207.

Gernsheimer T, Stratton J, Ballem PJ, Slichter SJ. Mechanisms of response to treatment in autoimmune thrombocytopenic purpura. N Engl J Med 1989;320:974.

Kaufman DW, Kelly JP, Johannes CB, et al. Acute thrombocytopenic purpura in relation to the use of drugs. Blood 1993;82:2714.

Stoncek DF, Vercellotti GM, Hammerschmidt DE, et al. Characterization of multiple quinine dependent antibodies in a patient with episodic hemolytic uremic syndrome and immune agranulocytosis. Blood 1992;80:241.

CHAPTER 12–16

Thrombocytopenia due to "Pseudothrombocytopenia," Diminished Platelet Production, Hypersplenism, and Dilution

Alan E. Lichtin, M.D.

DEFINITION

Below normal platelet counts caused by mechanisms other than enhanced destruction (discussed in Chapter 12–15) are described in this chapter. Each mechanism is discussed separately.

ETIOLOGY

Thrombocytopenia may be *factitious*, designated as "pseudothrombocytopenia." There are rare individuals who, when their blood is drawn into an vial containing EDTA (ethylenediamine tetraacetic acid), will have an immediate clumping of all the platelets. When the technician places the blood sample into an automated complete blood cell counter, the platelet count is read as very low. These patients have no bleeding or petechiae. If the blood is drawn into a heparinized tube or a citrated tube, the platelet count is usually normal.

Thrombocytopenia due to *decreased platelet production* may be either hereditary or acquired. Hereditary mechanisms include mostly pediatric syndromes such as Fanconi's anemia and thrombocytopenia with absent radius syndrome. Some entities, however, may reach the attention of an internist or adult hematologist. These include May–Hegglin anomaly, which is associated with moderate thrombocytopenia, large platelets, and the presence of Dohle bodies in the polymorphonuclear leukocytes. Bernard–Soulier syndrome is associated with giant platelets, abnormal lack of glycoprotein Ib, and a slight bleeding tendency.

The acquired thrombocytopenias, which are secondary to *decreased production* of platelets, include any disorder with poor marrow function, such as aplastic anemia and myelodysplasia. Many viral infections including varicella, Epstein–Barr virus, and cytomegalovirus depress the hematopoietic elements and may lead to thrombocytopenia. Fever alone can account for thrombocytopenia due to decreased production of platelets.

Alcohol may cause *decreased megakaryocyte function* and lead to thrombocytopenia.

Probably the most common cause of *drug-associated thrombocytopenia* in the United States is thiazide diuretics.

Thrombocytopenia may occur because of *overactivity of the spleen*. This is seen in individuals with cirrhosis, portal venous hypertension, or other disorders leading to enlarged spleens. Usually these individuals have a normal bone marrow or even an increased number of megakaryocytes. The thrombocytopenia is usually mild to moderate.

Patients may develop thrombocytopenia if they receive massive transfusions of red blood cells but not platelets during surgery. The bone marrow cannot keep up with the acute demand, and the platelet count drops because of *dilution*. After transfusion of 6 units of red blood cells at the time of surgery, there is almost always a decrease in the platelet count below the normal range, and if further bleeding is anticipated, platelet transfusions are indicated.

CRITERIA FOR DIAGNOSIS
Suggestive

Thrombocytopenia that is not due to enhanced destruction, as described in Chapter 12–15, might be caused by one of the above-described disorders. Review of the history and physical examination are important in ruling out previous bleeding episodes as seen in hereditary disorders such as Bernard–Soulier syndrome. The important point in the physical examination is determining the size of the spleen. An enlarged spleen may indicate thrombocytopenia caused by hypersplenism.

Reviewing the peripheral blood smear is also important. Several congenital thrombocytopenias associated with decreased production of platelets are characterized by giant platelets.

Definitive

Confirmation of diagnosis of the hereditary disorders of platelet production, such as Bernard–Soulier syndrome and May–Hegglin anomaly, may require the assistance of a research laboratory. Glycoprotein analysis of the surface of platelets is often the definitive test to prove that the patient has such a disorder.

Confirming the diagnosis of pseudothrombocytopenia requires drawing the patient's blood into an EDTA tube, a citrated tube, and a heparinized tube. If only the blood sample in the EDTA tube has a low platelet count and the other tubes yield a normal platelet count, the person has pseudothrombocytopenia.

To be absolutely sure that hypersplenism is causing thrombocytopenia, the physician must detect splenomegaly on the physical examination. It is sometimes difficult to determine the size of the spleen in obese persons. These individuals require a computed tomography scan or a nuclear medicine study (liver/spleen scan). The latter scan can be enhanced by newer techniques involving single-photon-emission computed tomography (SPECT) imaging, which provides a better estimate of the extent of portal hypertension. These patients usually require a bone marrow test to be certain that there is no other abnormality with platelet production.

Review of the transfusion history of patients who become thrombocytopenic after surgery is necessary to determine whether the thrombocytopenia is caused by dilution. Disseminated intravascular coagulation, which can also account for a decreased platelet count, is a postoperative complication.

CLINICAL MANIFESTATIONS
Subjective

Patients with a hereditary decreased platelet count due to May–Hegglin anomaly or Bernard–Soulier syndrome have no symptoms. They may have a history of bleeding episodes. The family history is important, and often drawing platelet counts on the mother, father, and siblings is helpful. The May–Hegglin anomaly is transmitted as an autosomal dominant trait, so other members of the family may be affected.

Patients who have thrombocytopenia caused by a viral syndrome usually feel sick, have a fever, or have a characteristic rash, as in varicella infection.

Eliciting a drug history is very important, especially with respect to the use of thiazide diuretics and abuse of alcohol.

Hypersplenic patients may have no symptoms. The patient with portal hypertension may have a history of variceal bleeds or jaundice.

Objective
Physical Examination

For all of these disorders, it is important to search for signs of bleeding in the skin. Patients with petechiae usually have platelet counts below 20,000/μL. Patients who have moderate thrombocytopenia may manifest only easy bruisability or no skin manifestations of bleeding. Asking patients if they experience epistaxis or bleeding from their gums after flossing can also help determine how low the platelet count is. Menometrorrhagia may also occur.

Some patients may also have hypersplenism from portal vein thrombosis or splenic vein thrombosis. Certain hypercoagulable states contribute to this. These are also sites of thrombosis in patients with paroxysmal nocturnal hemoglobinuria, and this diagnosis, though rare, must be kept in mind.

Routine Laboratory Abnormalities

The platelet count is reported to be lower than normal. The patient who has thrombocytopenia secondary to hypersplenism may have abnormal liver function tests if the spleen is enlarged because of cirrhosis or some other liver problem.

PLANS
Diagnostic
Differential Diagnosis

When a patient is thrombocytopenic, it is important to differentiate thrombocytopenia secondary to enhanced platelet destruction (described in Chapter 12–15) from thrombocytopenia caused by the disor-

ders described in this chapter. Table 12–16–1 lists those disorders that cause thrombocytopenia through diminished production of platelets. Table 12–16–2 lists those disorders that might contribute to hypersplenism.

Diagnostic Options

The patients with the disorders listed in this chapter are usually brought to the attention of a hematologist when thrombocytopenia is noted on the complete blood count. The best approach is to elicit a careful history especially highlighting drug exposures. On physical examination, the physician must search for evidence of lymphadenopathy or hepatosplenomegaly. Skin rash or previous evidence of viral infection is important to note as well. If the lymph nodes, liver, and spleen are enlarged, acute leukemia or lymphoma may be the cause of the thrombocytopenia and appropriate biopsies must be carried out.

Recommended Approach

As discussed above, the history, physical examination, and laboratory data including complete blood count, liver function tests, peripheral smear, reticulocyte count, and, possibly, bone marrow tests will help determine the cause of the thrombocytopenia. It is important to review the peripheral blood smear because in many of these conditions, especially the hereditary thrombocytopenias, the platelets are of abnormal size. Hypersplenic patients often require liver/spleen scanning to determine the extent of liver derangement and secondary enlargement of the spleen.

Therapeutic
Therapeutic Options

Many patients with these disorders do not require any therapy. Persons with hereditary thrombocytopenia need to be aware that they have the disorder so that on future complete blood counts, doctors do not become alarmed and repeat unnecessary testing. Patients must be informed if drugs and alcohol are contributing to the thrombocytopenia, so that they can discontinue using these substances. Patients who have hypersplenism caused by cirrhosis have limited therapeutic options to raise their platelet count. These patients respond neither to steroids nor to intravenous immunoglobulin; there may be a rare patient who requires splenectomy to raise the platelet count.

Recommended Approach

Patients whose platelet count decreases because of a viral infection require supportive care to maintain hydration, antipyretics, and, possibly, antiviral drugs as indicated. Patients with an intact immune system recover from these infections on their own and the platelet count rises.

The approach to the individual with thrombocytopenia caused by thiazides or other drugs usually involves stopping the medicine.

TABLE 12–16–1. CAUSES OF THROMBOCYTOPENIA SECONDARY TO DIMINISHED PRODUCTION OF PLATELETS

Hereditary
  Fanconi's anemia
  Thrombocytopenia with absent radius syndrome
  Bernard–Soulier syndrome
  Alport's syndrome
  May–Hegglin anomaly
  Gray platelet syndrome
  Wiskott–Aldrich syndrome
Acquired
  Aplastic anemia
  Myelophthisic disorders
  Chemotherapeutic drugs
  Radiation therapy
  Viral infections
  Alcohol
  Drugs (thiazide diuretics)
  Vitamin B_{12} or folic acid deficiency

TABLE 12–16–2. CAUSES OF THROMBOCYTOPENIA ASSOCIATED WITH HYPERSPLENISM

Any pathologic process of the liver causing cirrhosis
and resulting in portal hypertension
Hemoglobinopathies, particularly sickle cell disease
Leukemias
Lymphomas
Myelofibrosis
Metastatic cancer
Malaria
Gaucher's disease
Miliary tuberculosis
Histiocytosis-X
Kala azar
Hamartomas of the spleen
Brucellosis

In thrombocytopenia caused by hypersplenism, an attempt should be made to determine if the the problem is reversible. If there is a way to decrease the pressure in the portal venous system, it may be indicated. Surgical decompression has been a controversial area and is usually not recommended. The goal in transjugular intrahepatic portal stenting (TIPS), a new procedure, is to decrease bleeding from varices. Low platelet counts are usually *not* raised with this procedure.

FOLLOW-UP

The patient with thrombocytopenia caused by a hereditary decreased platelet count needs to be followed to ensure there is no change over time. Patients with Bernard–Soulier syndrome may have bleeding from mucocutaneous areas. They must be aware of their problem and should avoid aspirin. Oral contraceptives may be used to control menorrhagia. If such patients require surgery, they may need platelet transfusions, although this should be avoided if possible because of the risk of transmission of viral infections.

Patients with thrombocytopenia secondary to hypersplenism may be at increased risk of developing esophageal varices and bleeding. Because many of the clotting factors are made in the liver, these patients often have elevated prothrombin and partial thromboplastin times, which, together with the thrombocytopenia, place them at significantly increased risk for even fatal bleeding with rupture of esophageal varices. Usually, these patients undergo sclerosis of their varices by a gastroenterologist through endoscopy.

For the patient with thrombocytopenia secondary to hypersplenism from causes other than portal hypertension, splenectomy may be of benefit. Prior to the use of enzyme replacement therapy, persons with Gaucher's disease experienced amelioration of their thrombocytopenia after a splenectomy.

Patients who develop thrombocytopenia after surgery and require a platelet transfusion usually do not require follow-up once they recover. It may, however, be important to screen such persons for hepatitis or HIV infection over time, as it would be in anyone who receives multiple transfusions.

DISCUSSION

Prevalence and Incidence

Studies have reported the frequency of pseudothrombocytopenia caused by EDTA-dependent platelet agglutinins to range from 0.1 to 0.9% (Payne and Pierre, 1984).

Fanconi's anemia, Bernard–Soulier syndrome, and May–Hegglin anomaly are very rare.

There are many mechanisms for cirrhosis and hypersplenism and it is impossible to estimate the prevalence and incidence.

Related Basic Science

Elegant studies using chromium-51-labeled platelets have been carried out to prove whether reduced levels of platelets are due to a decrease in production of platelets or a decrease in the lifespan of platelets in the circulation. These studies are not part of the routine workup of patients. Using formulas, one can determine the total body platelet mass in normal subjects and in patients with thrombocytopenia secondary to splenic pooling. Normal subjects, patients with cirrhosis and congestive splenomegaly, and patients with chronic lymphocytic leukemia and secondary splenomegaly all have a platelet mass of approximately 2.8 to 2.95×10^{10} platelets/kg body weight.

There is exciting, new research on the nature of thrombopoietin. This substance is called the ligand for c-mpl and has been demonstrated in mice. Whether this research will eventually lead to a commercially available product that can be used to raise platelet counts remains to be seen. Interleukins-6 and -11 can lead to a rise in platelet count in some settings.

Natural History and Its Modification with Treatment

Practically all patients whose platelet count decreases because of a viral infection will have a normal count once they recover from the viral infection. Patients with hepatitis C infection with precirrhotic changes may benefit from interferon, which may, over time, decrease their risk of developing varices and other stigmata of liver failure and cirrhosis. Alcohol ingestion may lead to thrombocytopenia acutely; however, over time, as in chronic alcoholism, liver damage may lead to cirrhosis and hypersplenism.

Prevention

Immunization of children to prevent mumps, rubella, and measles may decrease their chance of developing thrombocytopenia from these infections. Prescribing drugs for hypertension that do not induce thrombocytopenia will prevent a decrease in the platelet count of many patients. This is particularly true of the thiazide diuretics. Glucocerebrosidase deficiency (Gaucher's disease) may be prevented through genetic counseling; however, the hypersplenism may be prevented by infusions of the commercially available alglucerase (Ceredase).

Cost Containment

The two treatments discussed above, interferon for hepatitis C infection and alglucerase for Gaucher's disease, are very expensive but have been found to be effective in reducing the rate of development of cirrhosis and improving the lives of patients with Gaucher's disease, respectively.

The majority of patients with portal hypertension and moderate thrombocytopenia do not require any costly interventions. Transjugular intrahepatic portal stenting may decrease portal hypertension and is certainly less expensive than a surgical procedure such as portacaval shunting.

REFERENCES

George JN. Thrombocytopenia due to diminished or defective platelet production. In: Beutler E. Lichtman MA, Coller BS, Kipps TJ. William's Hematology. 5th ed. New York: McGraw-Hill, 1995.

George JN. Thrombocytopenia: Pseudothrombocytopenia, hypersplenism, and thrombocytopenia associated with massive transfusion. In: Beutler E, Lichtman MA, Coller BS, Kipps TJ. William's Hematology. 5th ed. New York: McGraw-Hill, 1995.

Hoffman R. Regulation of megakaryocytopoiesis. Blood 1989;74:1196.

Kunicki TJ, Newman PJ. Molecular immunology of human platelet proteins. Blood 1992;80:1386.

Payne BA, Pierre RV. Pseudothrombocytopenia: A laboratory artifact with potentially serious consequences. Mayo Clin Proc 1984;59:123.

Sabath DF, Drachman JG, Kaushansky K, Broudy VC. Development of a cell line dependent on MPL ligand for proliferation. Blood 1994;84(suppl. 1):325a.

CHAPTER 12–17

Thrombocytosis

Robert J. Pelley, M.D.

DEFINITION

Thrombocytosis is defined as a platelet count greater than 400,000/μL.

ETIOLOGY

Causes of thrombocytosis can be divided into two major categories: *primary thrombocytosis* (or *thrombocythemia*) is the clonal, autonomous production of platelets as part of a malignant myeloproliferative syndrome; *secondary thrombocytosis* (*reactive thrombocytosis*, referred to as simply *thrombocytosis*) results from the stress from any number of a diverse list of other diseases.

CRITERIA FOR DIAGNOSIS

A patient has thrombocytosis when his or her platelet count is greater than 400,000/μl. The diagnosis of reactive thrombocytosis requires the identification of a primary associated disease. The diagnosis of thrombocythemia requires the presence of a sustained platelet count greater than 600,000/μL, the exclusion of other myeloproliferative diseases, and the exclusion of reactive thrombocytosis.

CLINICAL MANIFESTATIONS
Subjective

Patients with secondary thrombocytosis are asymptomatic except for very rare occasions when thrombocytosis contributes to venous thrombosis. Almost all symptoms are attributable to the primary disease. Patients with thrombocythemia have an increased tendency for bleeding manifestations, including recurrent gastrointestinal hemorrhage and epistaxis. Signs of venous thrombosis including erythromelalgia (painful red swelling in the distal extremities), neurologic symptoms, and embolic events may occur at an increased frequency.

Objective

Patients with thrombocythemia may have signs of venous thrombosis or arterial occlusion. Thrombocythemia is associated with palpable splenomegaly in one third of patients.

Patients with secondary thrombocytosis have no objective findings other than those for their primary disease.

PLANS
Diagnostic
Differential Diagnosis

Thrombocythemia (Primary Thrombocytosis). Polycythemia vera, chronic myelogenous leukemia, myelofibrosis, and myeloproliferative syndrome (unclassifiable) are diagnostic possibilities.

Secondary Thrombocytosis. The differential diagnosis includes acute hemorrhage, iron deficiency anemia, hemolytic anemia, tuberculosis, rheumatic fever, osteomyelitis, septic arthritis, rheumatoid arthritis, inflammatory bowel disease, sarcoidosis, Wegener's granulomatosis, carcinoma, mesothelioma, lymphomas, splenectomy, postoperative stress, and bone marrow recovery from ethyl alcohol, vitamin B_{12} deficiency, and chemotherapy.

Diagnostic Options and Recommended Approach

Thrombocythemia (Primary Thrombocytosis). Extreme thrombocytosis (platelet count greater than 1×10^6/μL), which is chronic, is associated with thrombocythemia or myeloproliferative syndromes more than 90% of the time. In myeloproliferative syndromes, the platelets usually appear large and morphologically abnormal on smear, and are dysfunc-

tional as evidenced by prolonged bleeding times and abnormal platelet aggregation studies. Aggregation studies help distinguish thrombocythemia from secondary thrombocytosis, in which function is always normal. Clinical thrombosis or bleeding does not distinguish secondary from primary thrombocytosis.

One myeloproliferative syndrome can be distinguished from another on clinical grounds and by laboratory means. The presence of high leukocytosis, marked splenomegaly, a low leukocyte alkaline phosphatase score, and the Philadelphia chromosome identifies chronic myelogenous leukemia (see Chapter 12–21). Massive splenomegaly, myelophthisic red cell abnormalities on the smear, and fibrosis on bone marrow biopsy identify myelofibrosis (Chapter 12–22). Polycythemia vera is distinguished from thrombocythemia by an increased red cell mass (Chapter 12–20).

Secondary Thrombocytosis. The diagnosis depends on the demonstration of an underlying disorder. Platelet counts usually do not exceed 1×10^6/μL; however, more than 80% of acute and transient extreme thrombocytosis is reactive. Platelet morphology is normal on the peripheral blood smear. Bleeding times are normal and platelet aggregation studies are normal. Bone marrow biopsy reveals increased megakaryocytes with variable size and ploidy. Leukocyte count is usually normal unless also stimulated by the underlying disease process. Splenomegaly is unusual unless associated with the underlying disease. Bleeding and thrombosis are uncommon.

Therapeutic

Thrombocythemia (Primary Thrombocytosis). Patients with thrombocythemia may have a benign course and require no therapy. In patients with a platelet count greater than 1×10^6/μL and thrombotic or hemorrhagic complications, prompt treatment with cytotoxic agents should be started. Alkylating agents such as melphalan, busulfan, thiotepa, and chlorambucil are traditional treatments; however, their association with the development of secondary leukemias has led to the use of hydroxyurea (Hydrea) in doses of 500 to 3000 mg per day. Anagrelide is an investigational agent that selectively suppresses the platelet count by an unknown mechanism. Despite promising activity, it is currently an orphan drug. In those patients with possibly life-threatening complications, or who require emergent surgery, plateletpheresis is used acutely to lower the platelet count. Hydroxyurea must be instituted simultaneously to maintain the effect.

Secondary Thrombocytosis. Patients with secondary thrombocytosis do not require specific therapy to lower the platelet count but should have their underlying disease treated. There is no evidence that secondary thrombocytosis results in increased thrombotic complications. The question of using prophylactic aspirin or heparin in patients with thrombocytosis is often raised, especially in the postsplenectomy patient. There are no controlled trials addressing this question and little evidence in favor of treatment.

FOLLOW-UP

Patients with thrombocythemia require careful monitoring during episodes of extreme thrombocytosis or while suffering thrombotic or hemorrhagic complications. During treatment, blood counts are monitored on a monthly basis if the platelet count is stable.

Patients with secondary thrombocytosis require no specific follow-up for their platelet elevations after identification of the primary disorder.

DISCUSSION
Prevalence

Thrombocythemia is a rare disorder affecting men and women equally in middle and late life. The incidence is similar to that of polycythemia vera, 7 per million population.

Secondary thrombocytosis is common and has been increasingly recognized due to the use of automated complete blood cell counters.

Related Basic Science

Except for the transient rise in platelet count that commonly follows exercise or treatment with epinephrine, all thrombocytoses result from overproduction of platelets by increased numbers of megakaryocytes within the bone marrow. Platelet production in thrombocythemia is autonomous and clonal, reflecting an abnormality in a hematopoietic stem cell. Platelet production in secondary thrombocytosis is regulated, as evidenced by decreases in platelet counts in response to treatment of the underlying disorder.

Natural History and Its Modification with Treatment

The prognosis in thrombocythemia is variable, with 60 to 80% of patient having a normal life expectancy. Morbidity and mortality result primarily from thrombohemorrhagic complications. A small fraction of patients develop other myeloproliferative syndromes or acute leukemia.

The prognosis in secondary thrombocytosis is identical to that of the underlying disease.

Prevention

Thrombocythemia cannot be prevented. Secondary thrombocytosis can be prevented by preventing or treating the underlying disease.

Cost Containment

Unless a patient with thrombocythemia is suffering acutely from thrombohemorrhagic complications, the elevated platelet count should be treated pharmacologically rather than with plateletpheresis. Secondary thrombocytosis requires no specific treatment for the elevated platelet count.

REFERENCES

Bithell TC. Thrombocytosis. In: Lee GR, Bithell TC, Foerster J, et al., eds. Wintrobe's clinical hematology. 9th ed. Philadelphia: Lea & Febiger, 1993:1390.

Buss DH, Cashell AW, O'Connor ML, et al. Occurrence, etiology, and clinical significance of extreme thrombocytosis: A study of 280 cases. Am J Med 1994;96:247.

Frenkel EP. The clinical spectrum of thrombocytosis and thrombocythemia. Am J Med Sci 1991;301:69.

Mitus AJ, Schafer AI. Thrombocytosis and thrombocythemia. Hematol Oncol Clin North Am 1990;4:157.

Murphy S. Primary thrombocythemia. In: Williams WJ, Beutler E, Erslev AJ, Lichtman MA, eds. Hematology. 4 ed. New York: McGraw-Hill, 1990:232.

Williams WJ. Thrombocytosis. In: Williams WJ, Beutler E, Erslev AJ, Lichtman MA, eds. Hematology. 4th ed. New York: McGraw-Hill, 1990:232.

CHAPTER 12–18

Essential Thrombocytosis

David M. Peereboom, M.D.

DEFINITION

Essential thrombocytosis is a clonal myeloproliferative disorder characterized by thrombocytosis, platelet dysfunction, and hemorrhagic and thrombotic complications.

ETIOLOGY

The etiology of this clonal disorder is unknown.

CRITERIA FOR DIAGNOSIS

Suggestive

Essential thrombocytosis should be considered in any patient with thrombocytosis.

Definitive

Essential thrombocytosis is a diagnosis of exclusion. Definitive diagnostic criteria are listed in Table 12–18–1.

CLINICAL MANIFESTATIONS

Subjective

Many patients (up to two thirds in some series) present without symptoms, but are found to have an elevated platelet count on routine hemogram. Symptoms may be noted in retrospect, however. Patients with essential thrombocytosis may have a wide variety of symptoms which result from hemorrhage and/or thrombosis. Bleeding in such patients is usually cutaneous or mucosal and is often provoked by trauma or the use of antiplatelet drugs. Patients may also bleed from the gastrointestinal tract, urinary tract, or surgical wounds. Thrombosis and ischemia occur more frequently than hemorrhage and may involve large vessels or microvasculature, both arterial and venous. Patients may complain of digital symptoms such as paresthesias, pain, coldness, and erythromelalgia. Additional symptoms are headaches, transient ischemic attacks, angina, abdominal pain (from mesenteric ischemia), lower extremity claudication, and symptoms related to deep venous thrombosis.

A minority of patients have constitutional symptoms including weight loss, fever, sweats, and pruritis.

Objective

Physical Examination

The physical examination is usually unremarkable. About one half of patients have mild splenomegaly; a minority have hepatomegaly. Otherwise, physical findings may disclose vascular phenomena such as acrocyanosis and digital gangrene.

Routine Laboratory Abnormalities

All patients have thrombocytosis and most have platelet counts above $1 \times 10^6/\mu L$. Many have leukocytosis and a normal hemoglobin concentration. The peripheral smear is notable for large, often clumped platelets with abnormal shapes. Howell–Jolly bodies and target cells may be seen and represent splenic atrophy. Serum tests may demonstrate pseudohyperkalemia and elevations of phosphate, uric acid, and lactate dehydrogenase.

TABLE 12–18–1. DIAGNOSTIC CRITERIA FOR ESSENTIAL THROMBOCYTOSIS

Platelet count > 600,000/μL

Absence of other causes of thrombocytosis (inflammatory diseases, infections, solid tumors)

Normal serum ferritin or stainable iron in bone marrow

Normal red cell mass (< 36 mL/kg in males, < 32 mL/kg in females) if hemoglobin > 13 g/dL

Absent Philadelphia chromosome in bone marrow

Absence of significant fibrosis of bone marrow (less than one-third the area of biopsy specimen)

PLANS
Diagnostic
Differential Diagnosis

The differential diagnosis includes any cause of thrombocytosis (see Differential Diagnosis, Thrombocythemia [Primary Thrombocytosis], in Chapter 12–17). The distinction between essential and reactive thrombocytosis is usually straightforward. Patients with reactive thrombocytosis usually have platelet counts under $1 \times 10^6/\mu L$. The degree of thrombocytosis usually parallels the severity of the underlying cause and the platelets function normally. Thus, patients with reactive thrombocytosis do not have hemorrhagic complications. Thrombotic complications are also much less frequent in reactive thrombocytosis than in essential thrombocytosis. The differentiation between essential thrombocytosis and other myeloproliferative disorders can be difficult (see Recommended Approach).

Diagnostic Options

Diagnostic options include red cell mass determination, bone marrow aspiration, biopsy and cytogenetics, platelet aggregation studies, and assays for endogenous erythroid and megakaryocytic colonies.

Recommended Approach

The initial evaluation of a patient with suspected essential thrombocytosis should be a thorough history and physical examination to evaluate for secondary causes and a review of prior hemograms. Although the list of secondary causes of thrombocytosis is extensive, the subsequent workup should focus on those diagnostic possibilities elicited by the history and physical examination. If the patient is asymptomatic and no clues are apparent, serial hemograms every 2 weeks for 4 to 8 weeks may reveal a decline in platelet count suggesting a reactive process. In addition, during this interval, the underlying cause of thrombocytosis may declare itself. If the platelet count remains elevated, a bone marrow aspirate and biopsy should be performed to rule out other myeloproliferative disorders and myelodysplastic syndromes. The aspirate in patients with essential thrombocytosis should reveal megakaryocyte hyperplasia. Cytogenetic analysis of the bone marrow (or peripheral blood) is necessary to rule out chronic myelogenous leukemia; the karyotype may also suggest myelodyplasia. If the biopsy reveals fibrosis of greater than one-third the area of the specimen, myelofibrosis should be considered. If the hemoglobin exceeds 13 g/dL, the red cell mass should be determined to rule out polycythemia vera. Finally, the presence of stainable iron in the bone marrow rules out iron deficiency.

Therapeutic
Therapeutic Options

Antiplatelet aggregating agents and nonsteroidal antiinflammatory drugs (NSAIDs) can be used to control microvascular thrombotic symptoms. Options for the long-term control of platelet counts include hydroxyurea, anagrelide, interferon-α_2, busulfan, melphalan, and phosphorus-32.

Recommended Approach

Patients who present with a life-threatening hemorrhage or thrombosis in the setting of essential thrombocytosis require immediate plateletpheresis. Hydroxyurea, 15 mg/kg/d orally, should be started as well with the goal of achieving and maintaining a platelet count below 500,000/μL. For patients with a history of hemorrhage or thrombosis, those with cardiovascular risk factors, and those with symptomatic thrombocytosis, hydroxyurea, 15 mg/kg/d orally, should be started and the dose titrated to reach a normal platelet count or a count at which symptoms resolve. Second and third choices for patients who do not respond or who cannot tolerate hydroxyurea are anagrelide and interferon-α_2, respectively. The dose of anagrelide is 0.5 mg four times a day orally, with 0.5 mg/d added weekly if the platelet count does not fall. The initial dose of interferon-α_2 is 3 to 5×10^6 units per day subcutaneously. Phosphorus-32, 2.9 mCi/m^2, is recommended for patients in whom compliance or frequent follow-up is not ensured. Asymptomatic patients below 60 years of age without cardiovascular risk factors should not receive therapy. Pa-

tients with intermittent ischemic or neurologic symptoms such as erythromelalgia should receive aspirin 500 mg/d, provided they have no history of bleeding. These symptoms may improve despite persistent thrombocytosis. Antiplatelet drugs should be avoided in patients with essential thrombocytosis and a history of bleeding.

FOLLOW-UP

Follow-up intervals vary according to patient status. Asymptomatic patients should be seen every 3 months. The important parameters to monitor are any symptoms of ischemia or neurologic symptoms that suggest thrombocytosis is becoming symptomatic. Symptomatic patients on therapy need follow-up visits every 1 to 3 weeks to monitor symptomatic and hematologic response to therapy.

DISCUSSION
Incidence

The annual incidence of essential thrombocytosis is fewer than 5 cases per one million population.

Related Basic Science

Essential thrombocytosis is a clonal disorder of the hematopoietic stem cell. Megakaryocyte number and volume are increased, although the exact reason remains unclear. Platelet production may be up to 15 times the normal rate. Platelet lifespan, however, is normal. The mechanism of hemorrhagic complications is likely related to a wide array of abnormalities in platelet function. These functional abnormalities vary, as some patients have predominantly thrombotic complications whereas others have both hemorrhagic and thrombotic complications. Similarly, thrombotic complications are not well correlated to platelet number, suggesting an interplay between abnormal quantity and function.

Natural History and Its Modification with Treatment

The average age of patients at diagnosis is 50 to 60 years. The natural history differs among age groups. Most patients with essential thrombocytosis have normal lifespans. Unlike other myeloproliferative disorders, transformation to acute leukemia is rare. The natural history of this disease is marked by thrombotic and hemorrhagic complications. More than one third of patients develop major thrombohemorrhagic complications. Younger patients tend to have fewer complications and seem able to live with marked thrombocytosis for years. Overall, therapy probably decreases the risk of subsequent complications, although the impact of therapy on the natural history has not been formally studied.

Prevention

Essential thrombocytosis has no known prevention.

Cost Containment

Costs can be minimized by appropriate patient selection for therapy. In addition, appropriate drug therapy will contain costs. Of the possible drugs, interferon-α_2 is the most expensive.

REFERENCES

Anagrelide Study Group. Anagrelide, a therapy for thrombocythemic states: Experience in 577 patients. Am J Med 1992;92:69.

Bithell TC. Thrombocytosis. In: Lee GR, Bithell TC, Foerster J, et al., eds. Wintrobe's clinical hematology. 9th ed. Philadelphia: Lea & Febiger, 1993:1390.

Hoffman R, Silverstein MN. Primary Thrombocythemia. In: Hoffman R, Benz EJ, Shattil SJ, et al., eds. Hematology: Basic principles and practice. New York: Churchill Livingstone, 1991:881.

Iland H, Laszlo J, Murphy S. Essential thrombocythemia. In: Wasserman LR, Berk PD, Berlin NI, eds. Polycythemia vera and the myeloproliferative disorders. Philadelphia: Saunders, 1995:292.

Tefferi A, Hoagland HC. Issues in the diagnosis and management of essential thrombocythemia. Mayo Clin Proc 1994;69:651.

Zuckerman KS, Bagby GC, Emanuel PD, Schafer AI. Myeloproliferative disorders. In: McArthur JR, editor-in-chief. Hematology—1992. Washington, DC: American Society of Hematology, 1992:7.

CHAPTER 12–19

Aplastic Anemia

Alan E. Lichtin, M.D.

DEFINITION

The term *aplastic anemia* refers to a heterogenous group of disorders that lead to a hypocellular bone marrow with peripheral pancytopenia. Different texts describe how low counts must drop before aplastic anemia is said to exist. Severe aplastic anemia is usually defined by the presence of at least two of the following:

- $<0.5 \times 10^9$/L granulocytes
- $<1\%$ reticulocytes
- $<20 \times 10^9$/L platelets

ETIOLOGY

Aplastic anemia can be inherited or acquired. The inherited forms usually present in the pediatric clinic (these entities include Fanconi's anemia, Shwachman–Diamond syndrome, and reticular dysgenesis). The acquired forms are those disorders more frequently encountered by internists and hematologists taking care of adult patients. The most common disorder is idiopathic aplastic anemia, that is, aplastic anemia for which no underlying cause is discovered. The secondary aplastic anemias are those disorders for which an underlying cause may be discovered. These are listed in Table 12–19–1.

Idiopathic cases account for up to 80% of patients with aplastic anemia. Aplastic anemia may arise either from a lack of pluripotent hematopoietic stem cells or from deficient function of these stem cells. It may also result from an abnormality in the microenvironment of the marrow. The stromal cells on which marrow elements sit may be defective in cytokine signaling (to the stem cell) to produce all lineages. There are other patients who may be particularly susceptible to an environmental insult (e.g., benzene) such that, even at low concentrations of exposure, aplastic anemia might result.

Stem cell defects may be the cause of marrow failure. Clonal growth of an abnormal stem cell may result in aplastic anemia. Among patients with aplastic anemia observed over a long period, some develop clonal disorders such as parosyxmal nocturnal hemoglobinuria (Color Plate 12–19–1, after page 826) and acute leukemia. Some of these disorders are associated with chromosomal abnormalities.

Lymphocytes may become activated against stem cells or there may be an immunoglobulin-based reaction against pluripotent stem cells leading to aplastic anemia. Studies of patients who have aplastic anemia have demonstrated both cell-mediated immune suppression of stem cells and humoral antibodies directed against stem cell membrane determinants.

TABLE 12–19–1. CAUSES OF ACQUIRED APLASTIC ANEMIA

Idiopathic aplastic anemia
Aplastic anemia secondary to some exposure or illness
  Drugs and chemicals
    Chemotherapy
    Benzene
    Chloramphenicol
    Nonsteroidal antiinflammatory agents
    Antiseizure Drugs (felbamate)
    Heavy metals (e.g., gold)
    Antithyroid drugs (propylthiouracil)
  Viruses
    Hepatitis
    Epstein-Barr virus
    HIV
  Paroxysmal nocturnal hemoglobinuria
  Pregnancy
  Immunologic disorders (eosinophilic fasciitis)

CRITERIA FOR DIAGNOSIS

Suggestive

Any patient who is pancytopenic to the levels described under Definition should be considered to have aplastic anemia.

Definitive

The definitive tests to prove aplastic anemia, besides inspection of the peripheral blood smear and determination of the complete blood count, is bone marrow aspiration and biopsy. The combination of pancytopenia and hypocellular bone marrow confirms the diagnosis of aplastic anemia.

CLINICAL MANIFESTATIONS

Subjective

Some patients with aplastic anemia have very few complaints. They may be slightly fatigued, may present with easy bruising, or may have an infection (fevers, pharyngitis, chills, urinary infection, etc.).

Most patients have a past history that is noncontributory; however, a careful questioner attempts to elicit potential occupational exposures or medications that could have contributed to the development of aplastic anemia. The family history may shed some light, for example, if siblings died in childhood from a blood disorder. This might bring to light one of the congenital aplastic anemia disorders such as Fanconi's anemia.

A careful drug history must be taken. Nonsteroidal antiinflammatory agents are now available over the counter and patients must be asked in detail about use of ibuprofen, naprosyn, and the other prescription nonsteroidal antiinflammatory agents. A patient who received previous x-ray therapy or chemotherapy might have aplastic anemia. Chloramphenicol is available over the counter in developing countries, and a recent travel history should include asking whether the patient took any over-the-counter antibiotics.

Objective

Physical Examination

Patients with aplastic anemia may have a completely normal physical examination. Others may demonstrate bleeding either from mucous membranes or into the skin, with petechiae reflecting the thrombocytopenia. Other patients with aplastic anemia might be quite pale from their anemia. The skin should be examined carefully for furuncles or any areas of cellulitis. Pharyngitis or gum inflammation may be a manifestation of granulocytopenia. Perirectal inflammation may also be seen. Patients usually do not have lymphadenopathy or hepatosplenomegaly. A blood clot in an unusual organ at the same time the patient presents with aplastic anemia might lead the examiner to suspect paroxysmal nocturnal hemoglobinuria. Patients with this disorder may have Budd–Chiari syndrome, portal vein or splenic vein thrombosis with resultant portal hypertension.

Patients with some of the pediatric syndromes will have congenital anomalies. Abnormalities in thumb development are often seen with Fanconi's anemia (absent digit or absent metacarpal).

Routine Laboratory Abnormalities

The complete blood count of patients with aplastic anemia shows the white count, hemoglobin, and platelet count all depressed. Most patients are anemic at presentation with a hemoglobin less than 7 g%.

Review of the peripheral blood smear reveals paucity of platelets and granulocytes. Red cell morphology usually is normal. Observation of teardrop cells, nucleated red blood cells, or schistocytes places the diagnosis of aplastic anemia into question. Many patients have macrocytosis at presentation.

Usually hepatic and kidney function is normal. In those patients who have hepatitis-associated aplastic anemia, transaminase and bilirubin levels may be elevated or there may be serologic evidence of exposure to hepatitis.

Diagnostic

Differential Diagnosis

As stated previously, most patients with aplastic anemia can be diagnosed with a complete blood count, review of the peripheral smear, and bone marrow analysis. Pediatric syndromes such as Fanconi's anemia may also be confused with aplastic anemia. Tests to provoke chromosome damage such as those using diepoxybutane may be used to distinguish Fanconi's anemia from other forms of marrow failure.

Patients with acute leukemia may present with pancytopenia, but usually the peripheral blood smear shows evidence of blasts or other immature white cells. Myelodysplasia may present with pancytopenia to the degree described under Definition. Most patients with myelodysplasia have hypercellular bone marrow with dysplasia. Hairy cell leukemia might present with severe pancytopenia, but usually atypical lymphoid cells with "hairy" projections can be seen on the peripheral smear.

Diagnostic Options and Recommended Approach

The bone marrow analysis should include an aspirate and biopsy. Bone marrow biopsy usually has a cellularity that is close to 0% (Color Plate 12–19–2, after page 826). If a marrow aspirate is diluted by peripheral blood, it may appear to be quite hypocellular but the biopsy might even be hypercellular. Therefore, the aspirate and biopsy must be analyzed together. It is usually not necessary to do much more than review the peripheral blood smear and obtain a complete blood count, reticulocyte count, and bone marrow tests.

If some degree of dysplasia is suspected, chromosome analysis might be indicated to rule out a myelodysplasia. Ham's test rules out paroxysmal nocturnal hemoglobinuria.

Therapeutic

Therapeutic Options

After a careful history is elicited to rule out drug exposure as a cause of aplastic anemia, the approach to this disorder depends on the age of the patient. Individuals under the age of 20 who have an HLA-compatible sibling usually undergo an allogeneic bone marrow transplant. Individuals over the age of 45, especially those who do not have an HLA-compatible sibling, usually receive immunosuppressive treatment, such as antithymocyte globulin, steroids, cyclosporine, or some combination of these. Treatment for those patients between 20 and 45 depends on how sick the person is and how close a tissue type match might be found. The rate and severity of graft-versus-host disease, an immunologic complication of bone marrow transplantation, rise with age of the recipient as well as with the disparity between donor and recipient in histocompatibility testing. Up to 80% of patients younger than 20 who have a bone marrow transplant survive and are free of significant graft-versus-host disease for up to 15 to 20 years.

Other therapeutic options include simple observation for those individuals with blood counts that are compatible with a fairly good lifestyle. There are patients with an extremely hypocellular marrow who maintain a granulocyte count around 500, platelet count around 10,000, and hemoglobin above 5. Such individuals, if asymptomatic and free of infection and bleeding, can be followed without any treatment for a long time.

Androgens have been used for patients with symptomatic aplastic anemia. Androgens have many side effects, especially liver damage. The virilizing side effects are usually poorly tolerated by female patients. The androgen most commonly used is oral oxymetholone at a dose of 1 to 3 mg/kg per day.

Supportive care is necessary in most cases of severe aplastic anemia. This includes transfusions of red blood cells for relief of anemia and transfusions of platelets for bleeding. Patients with infections need to have appropriate cultures drawn and then receive antibiotics. Patients who are candidates for allogeneic bone marrow transplant should be transfused sparingly and receive blood products that have been screened and found not to come from cytomegalovirus-seropositive donors. The blood products need to be irradiated.

Immunosuppressive Therapy. Assays for committed stem cells (CFU-GM [colony-forming unit, granulocyte–macrophage], BFU-E [burst-forming unit, erythroid], and CFU-E [colony-forming unit, erythroid]) can demonstrate a cell-mediated or humoral cause of aplastic anemia in some cases. Out of these studies grew the rationale of using an antilymphocyte globulin or antithymocyte globulin as a pharmacologic intervention. Indeed, for patients over the age of 40, antithymocyte globulin has become the treatment of choice, particularly for patients who do not have HLA-compatible siblings for bone marrow transplantation.

Antithymocyte globulin has many side effects, including skin rash, joint pain, fever, chills, and, occasionally, anaphylactic reaction. Overall survival of patients who receive antithymocyte globulin might be as high as 60% depending on the series one reads. Cyclosporine gives results comparable to those of antithymocyte globulin for patients who do not receive a bone marrow transplant.

Cytokine Therapy for Aplastic Anemia. With the advent of recombinant DNA technology, hematologists now have granulocyte colony-stimulating factor (G-CSF), granulocyte–macrophage colony-stimulating factor (GM-CSF), erythropoietin, and the experimental interleukin-3 and stem cell factor. These agents have undergone trials in aplastic anemia for the past 10 years. As yet, no standard use of these agents has been found. Several patients have transient rises in blood counts with these agents. No long-term sustained cures have been documented. It is hoped that agents such as stem cell factor might act on a more primitive stem cell and lead to better resolution of aplastic anemia. It could be that some patients with severe aplastic anemia will not respond to any hematopoietic growth factor because the earliest pluripotent stem cells are so deranged that they would not respond to even the earliest acting growth factor.

Recommended Approach

If a patient has an apparently nonreversible, non-drug-induced aplastic anemia and is young, that is, less than 20 years of age, and has an HLA-compatible sibling, allogeneic bone marrow transplantation is the treatment of choice. For those individuals who have a nonreversible, non-drug-induced severe aplastic anemia and are between the ages of 20 and 45, the risks and benefits of antithymocyte globulin therapy must be weighed against those of allogeneic bone marrow transplantation. If an excellent match can be found by histocompatibility testing and the patient has an excellent performance status, allogeneic bone marrow transplantation might still be the treatment of choice.

For those individuals over the age of 45, and certainly those individuals over age 60, who have a nonreversible, non-drug-induced aplastic anemia, the treatment of choice is antithymocyte globulin or cyclosporine. If one agent fails to elicit a response, the other agent can be tried. Either of these agents may be combined with methylprednisolone, which may lead to a more rapid response. The major risk of adding steroids is a possible increase in opportunistic infections.

FOLLOW-UP

The severity of the aplastic anemia dictates the frequency of follow-up. Patients who receive an allogeneic bone marrow transplant are usually seen every week for 2 months, every other week for 2 months, and then monthly thereafter. At each visit up to 6 months, intravenous immunoglobulin is administered to prevent cytomegalovirus infection. The patient who engrafts rapidly and feels well may require less frequent follow-up visits.

Most patients who receive antithymocyte globulin do not respond immediately and may require transfusions or admission to the hospital for antibiotics for infections. The major part of the follow-up visit is determining the complete blood count and monitoring for a response by documentation of a reticulocytosis or a rise in the platelet or white cell counts. Patients who are asymptomatic might be followed infrequently, but must be instructed to see the physician immediately if they experience a fever or bleeding.

DISCUSSION
Prevalence

In developed countries the prevalence of aplastic anemia is about 2 cases per million.

Of great interest is the geographic distribution of aplastic anemia. Because of different environmental exposures, and because of different rates of hepatitis, the Orient has been found to be a site where the risk of developing aplastic anemia is increased. Chinese series and data from Thailand show that the rate can be as high as 6 per million. Young males seem to be more affected than other groups in Thailand. These regional differences may be due to certain drugs that are used more commonly in different parts of the world. Exposure to benzene and other agents may also play a role.

Related Basic Science

Recently, interferon gamma has been shown to inhibit hematopoietic colony formation in vitro. T cells growing in tissue culture also release other cytokines which have been shown to suppress all marrow cellular components. T cells grown from patients with aplastic anemia have a high expression of interferon gamma, as well as tumor necrosis factor. Local production of interferon gamma within the bone marrow of patients with aplastic anemia has been documented using sensitive messenger RNA gene amplification techniques.

This new knowledge of interferon gamma has provided insights into how the hepatitis virus may cause aplastic anemia. Hepatitis C virus has been shown to infect hematopoietic stem cells. Viral antigens appear on the surface of these cells. A cytototoxic T-lymphocyte response is mounted against these new antigens on the surface of the hematopoietic stem cells. Interferon gamma has been shown to be a result of this cytotoxic T-lymphocyte response and may lead to inactivity or death of the hematopoietic stem cell.

Natural History and Its Modification with Treatment

Patients with aplastic anemia may be followed without any treatment as long as their blood counts are compatible with life. Among such patients followed over a long period, some developed clonal hematologic disorders such as paroxysmal nocturnal hemoglobinuria, myelodysplasia and acute leukemia. The patient who has a successful bone marrow transplant with engraftment, no significant graft-versus-host disease, and no graft failure probably has the best outcome.

Prevention

All one has to do is review the causes of aplastic anemia secondary to some exposure to determine the circumstances in which aplastic anemia might be prevented. The workplace must be made safe from agents known to cause marrow failure such as benzene. If exposure is unavoidable it should be below the Occupational Safety and Health Administration's tolerance limits.

Nonsteroidal antiinflammatory agents should be avoided unless absolutely necessary. If a patient needs an antithyroid drug or antibiotic, the prescribing physician should choose an agent with a low risk of causing aplastic anemia. Patients at risk for acquiring hepatitis B should be immunized against it. The environment should also be free of exposure to tuberculosis. Communities should institute infection control mechanisms to decrease the risk of tuberculosis.

Cost Containment

Sometimes the most inexpensive treatment is no treatment. The Cooperative Group for the Study of Aplastic and Refractory Anemia's observation that long-term survival might be achieved in nongrafted aplastic anemia patients might dictate that a no treatment approach be used with patients with aplastic anemia characterized by counts compatible with a fairly normal existence.

For patients with severe aplastic anemia who are actively bleeding, are actively infected, are so fatigued from anemia that they are unable to function, some treatment is certainly necessary. It is at this point that the benefits of the various treatment options discussed above must be weighed against the cost to the patient.

REFERENCES

Gillio AP, Gabrilove JL. Cytokine treatment of inherited bone marrow failure syndromes. Blood 1993;81:1669.

Najean Y, Haguenauer O. Long term (5–20 years) evolution of nongrafted aplastic anemias. Blood 1990;76:2222.

Storb R, Champlin RE. Bone marrow transplantation for severe aplastic anemia. Bone Marrow Transplant 1991;8:69.

Young NS, Alter BP. Aplastic anemia, acquired and inherited. Philadelphia: Saunders, 1994.

CHAPTER 12–20

Polycythemia Vera

David M. Peereboom, M.D.

DEFINITION

Polycythemia vera is a myeloproliferative disorder characterized by an increased red cell mass. Like other myeloproliferative disorders, this clonal disease involves multiple hematopoietic lineages and has a propensity to evolve into acute myelogenous leukemia. Unlike other myeloproliferative disorders, however, most patients can survive prolonged periods if the red cell and platelet populations can be controlled.

ETIOLOGY

Polycythemia vera results from neoplastic proliferation of the hematopoietic stem cell. The etiology of this neoplastic transformation is felt to be an acquired mutation, although definitive proof of this etiology is lacking.

CRITERIA FOR DIAGNOSIS
Suggestive

Polycythemia vera should be considered in any patient with an elevated hematocrit and must be strongly suspected in any patient with erythrocytosis and splenomegaly.

Definitive

Diagnostic criteria for polycythemia vera have evolved in recent years with the development of assays for erythropoietin and for bone marrow erythroid colonies. These criteria should allow the clinician to distinguish polycythemia vera from other causes of erythrocytosis.

Definitive diagnosis of polycythemia vera requires that the patient have an absolute (not relative) increase in red cell mass. Diagnostic criteria are listed in Table 12–20–1.

CLINICAL MANIFESTATIONS

The clinical manifestations of polycythemia vera reflect excess hematopoietic cell production with secondary hyperviscosity and tissue hypoxia.

Subjective

Patients with polycythemia vera can be asymptomatic or may report headache, visual disturbances, dizziness, tinnitus, erythromelalgia (burning pain of the extremities associated with erythema, pallor,

TABLE 12–20–1. DIAGNOSTIC CRITERIA FOR POLYCYTEMIA VERA*

1. Elevated red blood cell mass (≥ 36 mL/kg for males, ≥32 mL/kg for females)
2. Normal arterial oxygen saturation (≥ 92%)
3. Splenomegaly
4. Thrombocytosis (platelet count ≥ 400,000/µL) and leukocytosis (white blood cell count ≥ 12,000/µL)
5. Bone marrow hypercellularity associated with megakaryocytic hyperplasia and absent iron stores
6. Low serum erythropoietin concentration (<30 mU/mL) in the presence of increased red blood cell mass
7. Abnormal marrow proliferative capacity as manifested by formation of erythroid colonies in the absence of exogenous erythropoietin.

*The presence of any four of these criteria or of 1 + 2 + (3 or 4) is diagnostic of polycythemia vera. Criterion 1 *must* be present.
Adapted from Hoffman R, Boswell HS. Polycythemia vera. In: Hoffman R, Benz EJ, Shatil WJ, et al. eds. Hematology: Basic principles and practice. New York: Churchill Livingstone, 1991:834. Reproduced with permission from the publisher.

cyanosis, and gangrene), ruddiness, pruritis especially after warm bathing, paresthesias, weight loss, arthralgias, or epigastric distress. The interval between symptoms and diagnosis may be several years. The past medical history may include thromboembolic events, gout, peptic ulcer, and hemorrhagic events such as gastrointestinal bleeding. The family history is usually unremarkable.

Objective

Physical Examination

Physical examination may be normal, but findings may include hypertension, plethora, ruddiness, engorgement of retinal veins, acrocyanosis, and splenomegaly. About three fourths of patients have splenomegaly. Skin findings occur gradually and can mimic robust health.

Routine Laboratory Abnormalities

Laboratory findings usually include erythrocytosis, leukocytosis, thrombocytosis, and hyperuricemia. Hyperkalemia may occur as an artifact of thrombocytosis.

The peripheral blood smear may show several abnormalities. Erythrocytes may demonstrate anisocytosis, basophilic stippling, and an occasional nucleated red blood cell. Immature leukocytes such as metamyelocytes and myelocytes are frequently seen. The platelets may be strikingly enlarged.

TABLE 12–20–2. CAUSES OF POLYCYTHEMIA

Polycythemia vera (primary polycythemia)
Secondary polycythemia (increased erythropoietin production)
  Physiologically appropriate
    Chronic obstructive pulmonary disease
    Smokers' polycythemia
    Pickwickian syndrome
    Cardiac shunt (right to left)
    Others: postural hypoxemia, hemoglobinopathy, decreased 2,3, DPG
  Physiologically inappropriate
    Tumors: renal cell carcinoma, ovarian carcinoma, cerebellar hemangioblastoma, hepatoma, adrenal cortical adenoma, uterine fibroid
    Renal: cysts, hydronephrosis, Bartter's syndrome, transplantation
    Cobalt
Relative polycythemia (also called stress polycythemia, spurious polycythemia, pseudopolycythemia, and Gaisbock's syndrome)

Adapted from Wasserman LR, Berk PD, Berlin NI. Polycythemia vera and the myeloproliferative disorders. Philadelphia: Saunders, 1995:23. Reproduced with permission from the publisher and author.

PLANS

Diagnostic

Differential Diagnosis

The differential diagnosis for polycythemia vera includes any cause of erythrocytosis (Table 12–20–2). It is important to distinguish erythrocytosis (an increase in hematocrit) from an increase in red cell mass (discussed under Recommended Approach). The goal of the workup is to distinguish primary polycythemia (i.e., polycythemia vera) from secondary polycythemia.

Diagnostic Options

Measurement of chromium-51-labeled red blood cell mass is mandatory. The arterial oxygen saturation detects those patients with polycythemia secondary to decreased oxygen hemoglobin saturation. The serum erythropoietin concentration is elevated in secondary polycythemia, but normal or low in polycythemia vera. A bone marrow culture for erythroid proliferation in the absence of erythropoietin is very specific for polycythemia vera. Leukocyte alkaline phosphatase is elevated in polycythemia vera with leukocytosis, whereas in chronic myelogenous leukemia it is low. Additional diagnostic studies that may detect other secondary causes of polycythemia are carboxyhemoglobin (elevated in smokers' polycythemia), $P_{50}O_2$ (abnormal in hemoglobinopathies), and intravenous pyelogram to detect renal causes.

Recommended Approach

An algorithm for the recommended approach to suspected polycythemia vera is provided in Figure 12–20–1. For most patients with polycythemia vera who present with erythrocytosis, leukocytosis, thrombocytosis, and splenomegaly, the diagnosis is clear. Such patients need only a red blood cell mass determination to confirm the diagnosis. The first step in the evaluation of suspected polycythemia vera is measurement of the red blood cell mass. This test separates patients with true or absolute polycythemia from those with relative polycythemia. After confirmation of an increased red cell mass (≥36 mL/kg in males, ≥32 mL/kg in females), it is necessary to separate secondary from primary polycythemia. The next test should be an arterial blood oxygen saturation. Patients with reduced arterial oxygen saturation (<92%) have secondary polycythemia, the underlying cause of which should be determined. Patients with a normal arterial oxygen saturation should have a serum erythropoietin assay. Patients with polycythemia vera have a low serum erythropoietin concentration (<30 mU/mL). The vast majority of patients who fulfill these criteria have polycythemia vera. Patients who do not fulfill these criteria need to be evaluated for secondary polycythemia. This workup should be individualized according to the most likely diagnoses among those causes of secondary polycythemia listed in Table 12–20–2.

An occasional patient will have isolated polycythemia without splenomegaly, thrombocytosis, leukocytosis, or evidence of secondary polycythemia. Such patients may have a variant form of polycythemia vera and should undergo a bone marrow culture for endogenous erythroid colonies. If this assay is negative, the patient should be followed closely for complications of polycythemia vera.

Therapeutic

Therapeutic Options

The optimal therapy for polycythemia vera is unclear, and management of this disease must be individualized according to the patient's age, symptoms, performance status, history of thrombotic complications, and status of the bone marrow. The primary goal of therapy is to prevent thrombotic complications of the disease. This goal is achieved in most patients by maintaining a hematocrit of 42 to 45%.

Phlebotomy is the most rapid and least toxic method for reducing the hematocrit. The potential disadvantage, however, is that pruritis, thrombocytosis, and growth of the malignant stem cell population are unaffected. Myelosuppressive agents for this disease include hydroxyurea, busulfan, and phosphorus-32. Thrombocytosis with repeated thrombosis can be managed with hydroxyurea, anagrelide, interferon-α, aspirin, or plateletpheresis. Patients with hepatic vein thrombosis

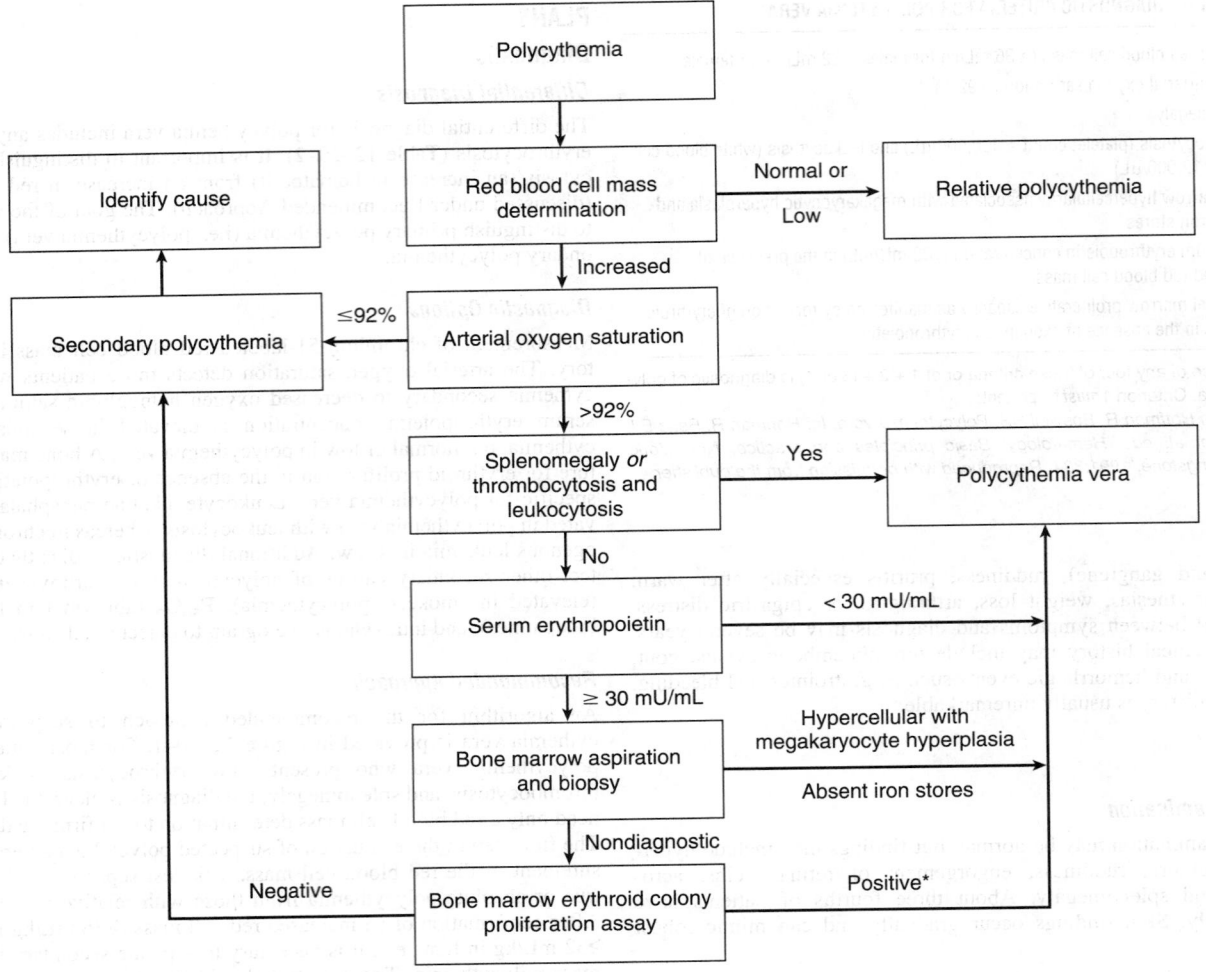

Figure 12–20–1. Diagnostic algorithm for suspected polycythemia vera.* Growth of erythroid colonies in absence of exogenous erythropoietin.

(Budd-Chiari syndrome) can be managed with a portosystemic shunt or, in selected cases, liver transplantation.

Options for the management of thrombotic complications include anticoagulants and, in life-threatening cases, thrombolytic therapy.

Recommended Approach

Initial treatment for polycythemia vera is phlebotomy of 500 mL every 1 to 3 days until the hematocrit is 40 to 45%. Patients above 65 years of age or those with cardiovascular diseases should have smaller volumes (250 mL) removed with each phlebotomy. Thereafter, periodic phlebotomy should be performed to maintain the hematocrit below 45%. Most patients can be managed with phlebotomy alone every 1 to 4 months. Phlebotomy alone is the treatment of choice for patients below age 40 and for older patients who have had no complications of their disease.

Patients who require phlebotomy more frequently or who have persistent symptoms, severe pruritis despite antihistamines, painful splenomegaly, or a history of thrombosis or hemorrhage should receive myelosuppressive agents. The drug of choice is hydroxyurea, 15 mg/kg/d orally. Secondary choices are busulfan and phosphorus-32. With any myelosuppressive therapy, supplemental phlebotomy should be performed if the hematocrit exceeds 47% to minimize drug requirements and potential side effects.

Because of the thrombotic and hemorrhagic complications associated with polycythemia vera, concomitant vascular insults should be minimized. Patients who smoke should be strongly encouraged to stop; hypertension, hypercholesterolemia, and diabetes mellitus need meticulous attention.

Patients with polycythemia vera and hyperuricemia should receive allopurinol 100 to 300 mg daily to maintain serum uric acid below 6 mg/dL. Pruritis is treated with histamine antagonists such as cyproheptadine 4 mg three times daily, diphenhydramine 25 to 50 mg three or four times daily, or famotidine 20 to 40 mg daily.

Surgical procedures in patients with polycythemia vera have high rates of morbidity and mortality due to thrombosis and hemorrhage. All efforts should be made to correct hematologic parameters before surgery. Elective surgery should be delayed until the disease is stable for several months. Emergency surgery should be preceded by phlebotomy.

Therapy for postpolycythemic myelofibrosis and acute leukemia is discussed in Chapters 12–22 and 12–31, respectively.

FOLLOW-UP

After the hematocrit has been normalized, complete blood counts should be monitored every 4 to 6 weeks for three visits to assess the pace of the disease. Thereafter, clinical and laboratory monitoring should focus on maintenance of hematologic control, detection and management of thrombotic complications, and progression to myelofibrosis and myeloid leukemia. The history should focus on thromboembolic or ischemic events such as angina and transient neurologic deficits. Hemorrhage due to qualitative defects in platelet function manifest as epistaxis, ecchymosis, or gastrointestinal bleeding. Follow-up visits should be scheduled every 4 to 8 weeks depending on the therapy used. Spleen size should be followed. Laboratory monitoring should include complete blood counts every 4 to 12 weeks. The serum uric acid concentration should be checked every 3 to 6 months during the first year to verify control of hyperuricemia.

DISCUSSION
Prevalence and Incidence

Polycythemia vera is rare, with an annual incidence of 5 to 17 per million population.

Related Basic Science

Polycythemia vera is a disease of both neoplastic growth and hypersensitivity of the erythroid progenitor to normal growth stimuli. In polycythemia vera, erythroid colony-forming units (CFU-E) grow in the absence of exogenous erythropoietin; the growth of CFU-E in normal patients, however, requires exogenous erythropoietin. Consistent with this result is the finding that erythropoietin concentrations are uniformly low in patients with polycythemia vera, thus confirming that the erythrocytosis in this disease does not result from excess erythropoeitin production. These two assays (CFU-E growth and erythropoietin concentration) have allowed much greater accuracy in the classification of patients with erythrocytosis. A current avenue of research focuses on abnormalities in the structure and function of the receptor for erythropoietin as a possible additional defect in this disease. The high rate of thromboembolic events in patients with polycythemia vera results from increased whole blood viscosity secondary to the elevated red cell mass. The contributions of thrombocytosis and disordered platelet function to this tendency are unclear.

Natural History and Its Modification with Treatment

Although original accounts of this disease suggested an untreated median survival of approximately 18 months, current therapies afford median survivals of 10 years. The most common early cause of death from this disease is thromboembolism. Polycythemia very evolves through three well-defined stages: The erythrocytotic phase, during which the red cell mass is increased and during which the typical presenting symptoms occur, lasts 5 to 20 years. Thereafter, patients enter the spent phase of postpolycythemia myeloid metaplasia, which is characterized by progressive myelofibrosis, extramedullary hematopoiesis with marked hepatosplenomegaly, and anemia. Finally, acute leukemia can complicate the late stages of this disease, Therapy for polycythemia vera prevents the complications of the erythrocytotic phase, but cannot prevent the progression to myelofibrosis or leukemia.

Prevention

Polycythemia vera has no known prevention.

Cost Containment

The most effective cost containment measure is prevention of thromboembolic events, as such events usually require hospitalization and can necessitate significant rehabilitation and possibly long-term home care.

REFERENCES

Athens JW. Polycythemia vera. In: Lee GR, Bithell TC, Foerster J, et al., eds. Wintrobe's clinical hemotology. 9th ed. Philadelphia: Lea & Febiger, 1993:1999.

Hoffman R, Boswell HS. Polycythemia vera. In: Hoffman R, Benz EJ, Shattil SJ, et al., eds. Hematology: Basic principles and practice. New York: Churchill Livingstone, 1991:834.

Prchal JT, Prchal JF. Evolving understanding of the cellular defect and polycythemia vera: Implications for its clinical diagnosis and molecular pathophysiology. Blood 1994;83:1.

Wasserman LR, Berk PD, Berlin NI. Polycythemia vera and the myeloproliferative disorders. Philadelphia: Saunders, 1995.

CHAPTER 12–21

Chronic Myelogenous Leukemia

Brian J. Bolwell, M.D.

DEFINITION

Chronic myelogenous (granulocytic) leukemia (CML) is a clonal hematologic neoplasm caused by a mutation of the pluripotent hematopoietic stem cell. This results in an expansion of the myeloid stem cell compartment, as well as extramedullary hematopoiesis in the spleen and liver. Untreated, the disease evolves into a malignancy identical to acute leukemia.

ETIOLOGY

The association between the Philadelphia chromosome and CML was first discovered in 1960. The Philadelphia chromosome is a reciprocal translocation between chromosome 9 and chromosome 22, shown in Figure 12–21–1. More than 95% of patients with CML have the Philadelphia chromosome present in hematopoietic cells; however, the Philadelphia chromosome can also be found in patients with acute lymphoblastic leukemia and, less frequently, patients with acute myelogenous leukemia. Abundant evidence indicates that this chromosomal translocation is directly responsible for the development of CML.

CRITERIA FOR DIAGNOSIS
Suggestive

Patients with CML invariably present with an elevated white blood cell count. The diagnosis is suggestive if a patient has a persistently elevated white blood cell count over a period of several weeks. Additionally, the white blood cell differential resembles that of a bone marrow aspirate, in that metamyelocytes, myelocytes, promyelocytes, and occasionally blast forms are seen in the peripheral smears. Additionally, increased numbers of basophils and eosinophils are often seen on the peripheral smear.

Definitive

Cytogenetic studies of bone marrow cells that reveal the presence of the Philadelphia chromosome confirm the diagnosis. This translocation can be demonstrated in peripheral blood cells using current molecular biologic techniques.

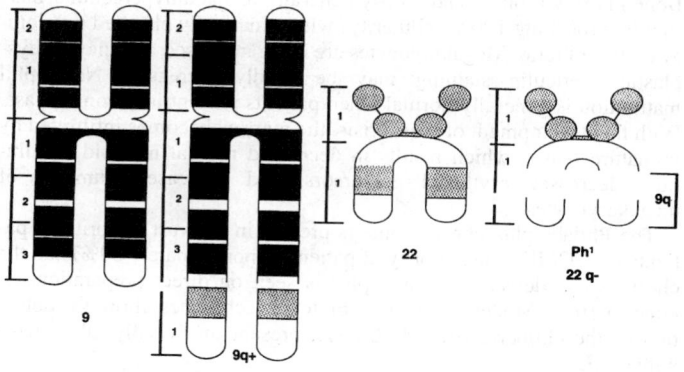

Figure 12–21–1. The Philadelphia chromosome.

CLINICAL MANIFESTATIONS

Subjective

Chronic myelogenous leukemia is characterized by two phases: a chronic phase and an acute phase (evolution to acute leukemia or "blast crisis"). The chronic phase evolves into the acute phase within 5 years in the majority of patients.

Most patients who present in chronic phase have nonspecific symptoms such as malaise. Other presenting symptoms include weight loss, abdominal fullness (secondary to splenomegaly), bleeding, thrombosis, bone pain, headache, and blurred vision. Often patients present with no specific symptoms and the disease is discovered on a "routine" complete blood count. Symptoms of the acute phase of CML, or blast crisis, include localized or generalized bone pain, fever, sweats, weight loss, and abdominal pain secondary to splenic infarcts. The acute phase of CML resembles acute leukemia and is associated with pancytopenia, which results in severe anemia and associated dyspnea and fatigue; leukopenia, which results in fevers and infections; and thrombocytopenia, which results in the development of bleeding and bruising.

Objective

Physical Examination

Physical examination reveals splenomegaly in the majority of patients with CML. Hepatomegaly is unusual. Rarely, lymphadenopathy may be detected.

Routine Laboratory Abnormalities

Chronic myelogenous leukemia is characterized by leukocytosis. This may be mild or may be dramatic with white cell counts grossly elevated to more than 1 million per microliter. As stated above, the white blood cell differential includes myelocytes, metamyelocytes, promyelocytes, and occasional blast forms. Additionally, the differential frequently reveals an elevated percentage of basophils and eosinophils. Patients often present with anemia, and as CML evolves into blast crisis, anemia is universal. Thrombocytosis is seen in many patients at presentation; however, with the development of blast crisis, thrombocytopenia occurs. Serum level of lactate dehydrogenase is often elevated, as is the serum level of uric acid. The morphology of red blood cells and platelets is generally normal.

PLANS

Diagnostic

Differential Diagnosis

Elevated peripheral white blood cell counts may be seen in infections, carcinomas, and a variety of other conditions. Basophilia, eosinophilia, myelocytes, metamyelocytes, and promyelocytes in the peripheral blood, together with thrombocytosis, are strongly suggestive of CML rather than a leukemoid reaction. A low leukocyte alkaline phosphatase level is highly suggestive of CML as these levels are usually normal or raised in leukemoid reactions.

Diagnostic Options and Recommended Approach

Bone marrow aspirate and biopsy generally reveal a hypercellular marrow (approaching 100% cellularity) with a markedly elevated myeloid-to-erythroid ratio. Megakaryocytes are often increased and may be dysplastic. Reticulin staining may be mildly increased. Neutrophil maturation is generally normal when patients present in chronic phase. With the development of blast crisis, the marrow becomes infiltrated by immature blasts, which results in decreased normal myeloid maturation, decreased erythroid precursors, and decreased numbers of megakaryocytes.

The Philadelphia chromosome is present in the vast majority of patients with CML. The majority of patients (approximately 80%) had the chromosome defect in all metaphases seen on direct preparations of bone marrow. Modern molecular biologic techniques allow for detection of the chimeric *BCR–ABL* gene, present in virtually all patients with CML.

Therapeutic

The first question one faces when addressing a patient with newly diagnosed CML is whether or not to initiate any treatment. Although a circulating white blood cell count greater than 100,000 per microliter might be alarming, it does not pose any significant threat to the patient (unless the majority of the cells are blasts, which is extremely unusual at diagnosis). Additionally, conventional doses of chemotherapy have not been shown to improve survival. As such, initial treatment of CML is palliative; however, as most patients do present with objective symptoms such as fatigue and abdominal pain from splenomegaly, systemic therapy is usually initiated at diagnosis to reduce the tumor burden and relieve symptoms.

Initial management of CML is usually with either oral hydroxyurea or busulfan. Hydroxyurea is a cycle-specific inhibitor of DNA synthesis and now the agent of choice for disease control. Generally, a daily dose of 1 to 3 g of hydroxyurea is adequate to control circulating elevated white blood cell counts and circulating elevated platelet counts. Busulfan, an alkylating agent, given at a dose 2 to 8 mg daily may also be used for disease control; however, busulfan is longer acting than hydroxyurea and may be associated with more serious side effects, such as pulmonary, cardiac, and bone marrow fibrosis. Combination chemotherapy has never been shown to be clearly superior than single-agent chemotherapy.

The treatment of choice for patients less than 50 years of age (and perhaps less than 60 years of age) is allogeneic bone marrow transplantation. In fact, allogeneic bone marrow transplantation remains the only known curative modality in the treatment of CML.

The principle of allogeneic bone marrow transplantation is straightforward. Antitumor chemotherapeutic agents, or radiation, or both, if given in sufficient doses, can totally eradicate a given tumor. The dose of antitumor agents is largely limited by toxicity of normal bone marrow. If normal bone marrow is available for transplantation, higher, and potentially curative, antitumor doses of drugs, radiation, or both can be administered, and the donor marrow can save the patient from iatrogenic death. Thus, the fundamental principle of bone marrow transplantation is that of dose intensity.

Allogeneic bone marrow transplantation offers the potential for cure for patients with CML. The best results are those with fully HLA-matched sibling donors, who are transplanted in chronic phase and within the first year of diagnosis. In this setting, 50 to 80% of patients are cured with allogeneic bone marrow transplantation. Relapse rates increase with increasing time from diagnosis to transplant. Relapse rates are highest when patients are transplanted in blastic phase, with greater than 50% of patients relapsing despite allogeneic bone marrow transplantation.

Graft-versus-host disease (GVHD) and opportunistic infections remain the most important complications of allogeneic bone marrow transplantation. GVHD is an immunologic reaction caused by immunocompetent donor T cells reacting against antigens contained within the recipient that are deemed to be "foreign" by these T cells. The T cells then mount an immunologic attack against these antigens, which results in the syndrome known as GVHD. Acute GVHD generally involves the skin, gastrointestinal tract, and liver. Acute GVHD occurs in approximately 50% of HLA-matched sibling donor transplants, and is fatal in approximately 10 to 30% of such transplants. The incidence of acute GVHD increases with unrelated donor transplants and also increases with patient age. Chronic GVHD occurs in approximately 25 to 50% of patients receiving HLA-identical marrow transplants and usually begins within 3 to 12 months of transplantation. The clinical manifestations resemble a collagen–vascular disease with the potential for sclerodermatous changes of the skin and gastrointestinal system, chronic elevations of hepatic enzymes, abnormalities of oral mucosa, and the possibility of pulmonary insufficiency.

Prophylaxis for acute GVHD includes treatment with cyclosporine, with or without methotrexate and corticosteroids. Therapy of established GVHD includes cyclosporine, corticosteroids, and azathioprine. Although many patients respond to GVHD therapy, approximately 25% with either acute or chronic GVHD die as a result of the syndrome or a complication of associated infections.

Opportunistic infections occur with frequency in allogeneic bone marrow transplant recipients for several reasons. Total immune competence takes months to years after allogeneic bone marrow transplantation. The prophylaxis and treatment of GVHD with immunosuppressive agents further reduce the integrity of the immune system. Additionally, GVHD itself predisposes to opportunistic infections. Historically, cytomegalovirus pneumonitis has been a major cause of morbidity and mortality. Recently, the routine use of prophylactic ganciclovir has reduced the morbidity and mortality of cytomegalovirus infections within the first several months of transplantation.

A concept known as the graft-versus-leukemia effect is increasingly recognized as a major contributing factor leading to cure with allogeneic bone marrow transplantation. Many studies have shown that patients with GVHD have a lower risk of relapse than do patients who do not have GVHD. Additionally, T-cell depletion of bone marrow, which reduces the risk of GVHD, is associated with higher relapse rates in patients with CML compared with non-T-cell-depleted transplants. A precise mechanism in which an immunocompetent allogeneic marrow graft reduces the risk of leukemic relapse has not been identified; however, this graft-versus-leukemia reaction is now so well documented that it is used for possible therapy for patients who relapse after transplantation. There are preliminary anecdotal reports suggesting that the reinfusion of donor white blood cells, without any specific chemotherapy, into patients who relapse after allogeneic bone marrow transplantation may result in the induction of the GVHD syndrome, which results in a graft-versus-leukemia effect and clinical remission. These exciting preliminary results are currently undergoing more widespread investigation.

If a patient does not have a matched sibling donor, then the optimal treatment of choice for CML is not known. Three treatment options are acceptable. The first is allogeneic bone marrow transplantation using a matched, unrelated donor. Early morbidity and mortality are higher with unrelated donor transplants than with matched sibling transplants. The incidence of acute GVHD approaches 80%; however, a recent report from the National Marrow Donor Program showed that 45% of patients who were transplanted for CML in the first year of diagnosis had a 2-year disease-free survival with unrelated donor transplantation (Kernan et al., 1993). The actual incidence of hematologic relapse at 2 years was 11%. The 2-year disease-free survival was lower if patients were transplanted in chronic phase more than 1 year from diagnosis, and was zero if patients were treated in blast crisis. Although early mortality rates approach 40% with unrelated donor transplantation, the curative potential is clear, and if a suitable unrelated match is found, early transplantation for young patients with CML in first chronic phase is clearly justified and, in fact, represents the treatment of choice.

Many patients do not have an HLA-matched donor available. As a result, several institutions across the world have explored the use of autologous transplantation in CML, in which patients have their own marrow harvested and stored and used as a source of hematopoietic reconstitution after the delivery of myeloablative therapy. A recent report compiled the experiences of eight such transplant centers and demonstrated that autologous transplantation may prolong survival in patients with CML. In fact, median survival time (with a follow-up of 30 months) for chronic phase CML patients treated with autologous bone marrow transplantation has not been reached. The majority of survivors had evidence of persistent CML manifested by the Philadelphia chromosome, but most patients had normal activity levels. Although it may be unlikely that autologous transplantation represents a curative modality, the treatment may change the natural history of the disease and delay the onset of blast crisis, and warrants continued investigation.

Interferon alfa clearly has a role in the management of patients with CML. Approximately 70% of patients achieve hematologic control with interferon alfa with a dose of 3 to 12 million units daily. Of interest, a minority of patients treated with interferon alfa achieve either partial or complete cytogenetic remission, resulting in the disappearance of the Philadelphia chromosome. A large multiinstitutional trial investigating the use of interferon alfa in patients with chronic phase CML has been published (Ozer et al., 1993). Fifty-nine percent of patients achieved at least a partial hematologic remission, and 40% achieved a partial cytogenic response. The median time to first cytogenetic response was 9 months. Toxicity from interferon was significant and included fever, hepatic abnormalities, diarrhea, weight loss, neuro-

logic changes (dizziness and/or vertigo), as well as hematologic effects including leukopenia and thrombocytopenia. The toxic effects required a dose reduction of interferon at some time during treatment in 38% of patients. The median survival for the 107 treated patients was 66 months. Interestingly, survival for patients achieving a cytogenetic response was not significantly different from survival for patients who did not receive a cytogenetic response. Thus, although the ability to generate cytogenetic remissions is intriguing, there are no definitive data from multiinstitutional trials documenting that the development of such a cytogenetic remission improves survival.

Figure 12–21–2 is a scheme for the management of patients with CML. Given that CML is essentially a fatal disease without allogeneic transplantation, the author's personal preference is to proceed with matched, unrelated donor transplantation if a suitable donor is found for young patients in the chronic phase.

The management of patients with blast crisis is problematic. Untreated survival is measured in weeks. Combination chemotherapy results in hematologic remissions in approximately 20% of patients. These remissions are transient and median survival is only 2 to 10 months. A minority of patients who present in blast crisis have lymphoid markers on the surface of marrow blasts. Such patients may be treated with vincristine and prednisone, which is less toxic than many other forms of traditional antileukemic chemotherapy. Approximately 60% of such patients achieve a hematologic response, which lasts for 2 to 9 months.

FOLLOW-UP

The follow-up for patients with CML depends entirely on the therapeutic approach. Patients treated with bone marrow transplantation need to be followed extremely closely to monitor and treat GVHD and infections. Patients treated with interferon alfa need to be monitored for toxic effects of interferon, including influenza-like syndromes, abnormal liver functions, and allergic reactions. Bone marrow cells should be sampled and analyzed for cytogenetic analysis every 3 to 6 months. Patients treated with hydroxyurea for symptom management should be seen every 4 to 8 weeks with a physician visit, as well as a complete blood count with differential.

DISCUSSION
Prevalence and Incidence

The incidence of CML is approximately 1 per 100,000 population, which appears to be constant worldwide. The peak age incidence of CML is in the fifth and sixth decade of life. Although the incidence of CML was significantly increased in the survivors of the atomic bomb explosions at Hiroshima, there is no clear-cut evidence at this time that chemicals or viruses are risk factors for CML.

Related Basic Science

The Philadelphia chromosome, which represents a reciprocal translocation between chromosomes 9 and 22, is pathognomonic for CML. The exchange of chromosomal material between the long arms of chromosomes 9 and 22 results in the BCR–ABL gene rearrangement. Breaks within the ABL gene from chromosome 9 are variable, whereas the breaks in BCR on chromosome 22 occur within a relatively restricted 5.8-kb portion of the gene. Other molecular events may be associated with progression from chronic phase to blast crisis.

Natural History and Its Modification with Treatment

Median survival in untreated CML is 3 to 4 years. Twenty to twenty-five percent of patients in chronic phase develop blast crisis per year. Allogeneic bone marrow transplantation offers a potential for cure in 40 to 80% of patients, depending on age and other prognostic variables. Treatment with busulfan or hydroxyurea does not change the natural history of CML. It remains to be seen from large clinical trials whether cytogenetic responders to interferon alfa will have an improvement of overall survival.

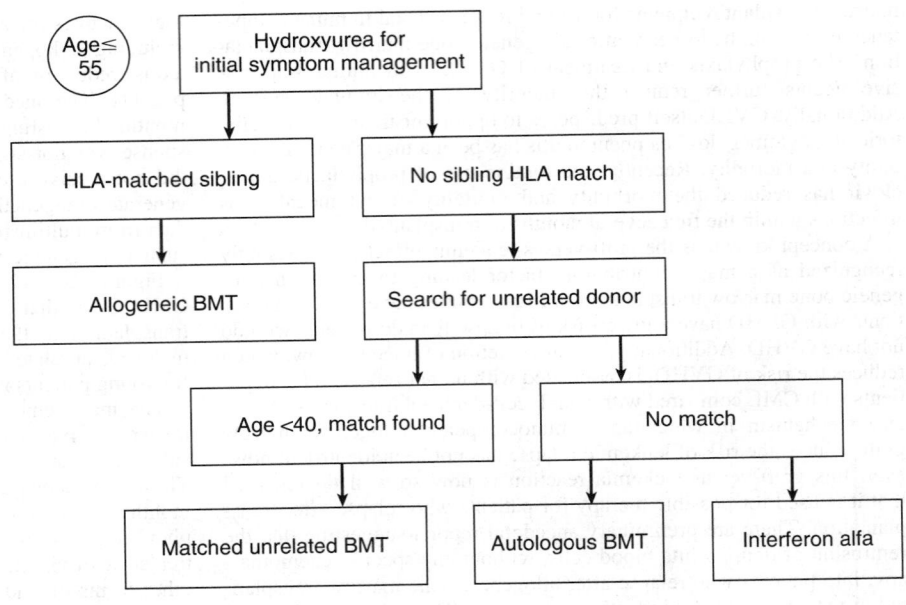

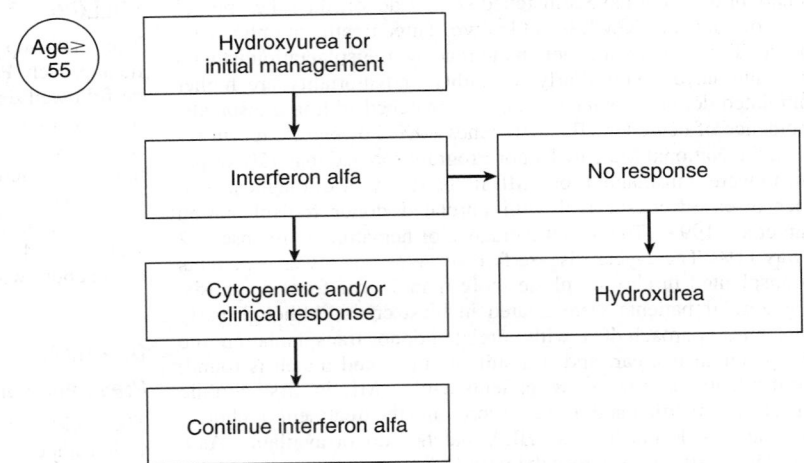

Figure 12–21–2. Therapeutic approach to chronic myelogenous leukemia. BMT, bone marrow transplantation.

Prevention

As there are no known risk factors for CML, there are no specific recommendations for prevention of this disease at this time.

Cost Containment

The major issue in cost containment concerns patient selection for bone marrow transplantation, as well as the costs of interferon alfa. Interferon alfa is an expensive drug and, after an initial trial of 6 to 12 months, should be continued only in those patients who achieve remissions, either hematologic or cytogenic. Although it is clearly expensive, the fact that it remains the only curative modality and offers a potential for patients to return to normal health and serve as productive citizens makes allogeneic bone marrow transplantation cost efficient in the treatment of this disease.

REFERENCES

Champlin R. Bone marrow transplantation for chronic myelogenous leukemia. *Curr Opin Oncol* 1990;2:258.

Goldman JM. Molecular biology and treatment of chronic myelogenous leukemia. *Curr Opin Oncol* 1990;2:49.

Kernan NA, Bartsch G, Ash, RC, et al. Analysis of 462 transplantations from unrelated donors facilitated by the National Marrow Donor Program. N Engl J Med 1993;328(9):593.

McGlave PB, Beatty P, Ash R, Hows JM. Therapy for chronic myelogenous leukemia with unrelated donor bone marrow transplantation: Results in 102 cases. *Blood* 1990;75:1728.

McGlave PB, DeFabritis P, Deisseroth A, et al. Autologous transplants for chronic myelogenous leukaemia: Results from eight transplant groups. *Lancet* 1994;343:1486.

Ozer H, George SL, Schiffer CA, et al. Prolonged subcutaneous administration of recombinant α2b interferon in patients with previously untreated Philadelphia chromosome-positive chronic-phase chronic myelogenous leukemia: Effect on remission duration and survival: Cancer and Leukemia Group B study 8583. *Blood* 1993;82:2975.

Idiopathic Myelofibrosis

David M. Peereboom, M.D.

DEFINITION

Myelofibrosis is a nonspecific term for fibrosis of the bone marrow from any cause. Idiopathic or primary myelofibrosis, also called agnogenic myeloid metaplasia or myeloid metaplasia with myelofibrosis, refers to a specific chronic myeloproliferative disorder characterized by marrow fibrosis and extramedullary hematopoiesis. Like other myeloproliferative disorders, idiopathic myelofibrosis may evolve into acute leukemia. This chapter focuses on idiopathic myelofibrosis.

ETIOLOGY

The etiology of idiopathic myelofibrosis is unknown. The etiology of other causes of myelofibrosis is given in Table 12–22–1.

CRITERIA FOR DIAGNOSIS

Suggestive

Idiopathic myelofibrosis should be considered in any patient with splenomegaly, teardrop forms on the peripheral blood smear, or a "dry" tap on attempted bone marrow aspiration.

Definitive

The definitive diagnosis of idiopathic myelofibrosis requires (1) the absence of other causes of myelofibrosis, (2) fibrosis on bone marrow biopsy, and (3) clinical evidence of extramedullary hematopoiesis. Extramedullary hematopoiesis is manifested on the peripheral blood smear by teardrop poikilocytosis and by leukoerythroblastosis, the combination of immature myeloid elements (commonly called "left shift") and nucleated red blood cells (Color Plates 12–22–1A and 12–22–1B, after page 826). Extramedullary hematopoiesis can also be seen on biopsy of the spleen, liver, and, occasionally, other organs or masses that contain ectopic hematopoietic elements.

CLINICAL MANIFESTATIONS

Subjective

About one third of patients are asymptomatic and present with splenomegaly on routine physical examination or with an abnormal peripheral blood smear. Symptoms (Table 12–22–2) result from anemia (asthenia, fatigue, dyspnea), splenomegaly (early satiety, anorexia, pain, altered bowel habits), abnormal platelet number and function (bleeding, thrombosis, ischemia), and increased cell turnover (gout, fever, weight loss). The past medical history may uncover conditions predisposing to secondary myelofibrosis, in which case the presumptive diagnosis of idiopathic myelofibrosis should be questioned. The family history is noncontributory.

Objective

Physical Examination

Almost all patients with idiopathic myelofibrosis have splenomegaly. Thus, the absence of splenomegaly nearly excludes the diagnosis. Frequently the spleen is massively enlarged. About one half of patients have hepatomegaly. Other less common findings include pallor, jaundice (due to ineffective erythropoiesis), hearing loss, weight loss, petechiae, ecchymoses, and lymphadenopathy.

Routine Laboratory Abnormalities

Although laboratory values can vary widely in idiopathic myelofibrosis, patients generally have anemia, mild leukocytosis, and thrombocytosis. The peripheral blood smear nearly always demonstrates leukoerythroblastosis and teardrop cells (Color Plates 12–22–1A and 12–22–1B, after page 826). Large platelets are also common.

Serum chemistries often reveal elevated uric acid, alkaline phosphatase, and lactate dehydrogenase levels. Pseudohyperkalemia may occur.

PLANS

Diagnostic

Differential Diagnosis

The differential diagnosis includes any cause of myelofibrosis listed in Table 12–22–1. Causes of splenomegaly that can be confused with idiopathic myelofibrosis are Felty's syndrome and liver disease with portal hypertension.

TABLE 12–22–1. CAUSES OF MYELOFIBROSIS

Benign	
Infections	Tuberculosis
	Histoplasmosis
	HIV
	Other viruses
Metabolic bone disorders	Renal osteodystrophy
	Osteopetrosis
	Paget's disease
Endocrine	Vitamin D deficiency
	Hyper- or hypoparathyroidism
Autoimmune	Systemic lupus erythematosus
	Systemic sclerosis
Exposures	Thorium dioxide
	Benzene
	Radiation
Other	Gaucher's disease
	Gray platelet syndrome
Malignant	
Hematologic	Idiopathic myelofibrosis
	Transitional myeloproliferative syndrome
	Polycythemia vera
	Chronic myelogenous leukemia
	Acute leukemia
	Hairy cell leukemia
	Myeloma
	Hodgkin's Disease
	Non-Hodgkin's lymphoma
	Systemic mastocytosis
Solid tumors	Prostate
	Breast
	Lung
	Stomach

Table constructed from data reported by Athens (1993) and Hoffman and Silverstein (1991).

TABLE 12–22–2. SYMPTOMS AND SIGNS OF IDIOPATHIC MYELOFIBROSIS

Cause	Symptoms
Anemia	Asthenia, fatigue, dyspnea
Splenomegaly	Early satiety, anorexia, weight loss, abdominal pain, diarrhea, dyspepsia
Abnormal platelet number and function	Bleeding, thrombosis, ischemia
Hyperuricemia	Gout, renal stones

Table constructed from data reported by Athens (1993), Hoffman and Silverstein (1991), and Rupoli et al. (1994).

Diagnostic Options

Diagnostic options in the evaluation of patients with suspected idiopathic myelofibrosis include any tests required to rule out secondary causes of myelofibrosis. The possible diagnostic tests are bone marrow aspiration, biopsy, culture, and cytogenetics; determination of leukocyte alkaline phosphatase level; tartrate-resistant alkaline phosphatase (TRAP) stain of the peripheral blood (diagnostic of hairy cell leukemia); and biopsies of the spleen, liver, lymph node, or other abnormal masses.

Recommended Approach

When a patient presents with splenomegaly and a leukoerythroblastic peripheral blood smear, a careful review of systems and physical examination will direct the subsequent workup. All patients, however, require bone marrow aspiration and biopsy to confirm the presence of myelofibrosis and to rule out bone marrow disorders that cause myelofibrosis (Color Plates 12–22–2A and 12–22–2B, after page 826). The workup for secondary causes of myelofibrosis should be individualized. A bone marrow culture is recommended in those patients for whom tuberculosis or histoplasmosis is a clinical possibility. If the leukocyte count exceeds 100×10^9/L, bone marrow or peripheral blood cytogenetics should be performed to diagnose chronic myelogenous leukemia. A review of any prior hemograms may help uncover any antecedent hematologic disorders; prior erythrocytosis suggests the diagnosis of postpolycythemia myeloid metaplasia. Women with myelofibrosis should undergo careful breast examination and mammogram; a patient with a dominant lymph node on examination should have a biopsy to rule out Hodgkin's disease or non-Hodgkin's lymphoma as these disorders represent reversible causes of myelofibrosis.

Idiopathic myelofibrosis can be difficult to distinguish from other myeloproliferative disorders. Some of the characteristic features of other myeloproliferative disorders not seen in idiopathic myelofibrosis are listed in Table 12–22–3.

Therapeutic

Therapeutic Options

Although idiopathic myelofibrosis has no cure, therapeutic options are broad. Table 12–22–4 lists the options according to the therapeutic problem.

Recommended Approach

Because idiopathic myelofibrosis remains incurable, patients should be treated only if symptomatic. All patients, however, should receive a pneumococcal vaccine as they may eventually have splenic dysfunction or the need for splenectomy. Patients with anemia should be evaluated prior to therapy as anemia in these patients has multiple possible causes for which therapy differs. Dilutional anemia secondary to hypersplenism requires no therapy. Folate, B_{12}, and iron deficiencies should be corrected. Patients with hemolytic anemia should receive prednisone, 1 mg/kg/d orally, until maximum response, at which time the dose should be tapered to the lowest dose needed to maintain the hemoglobin. Patients with inadequate erythrocyte production should receive a 4-month trial of oxymetholone 50 mg four times daily orally. Ery-

TABLE 12–22–4. THERAPEUTIC OPTIONS IN IDIOPATHIC MYELOFIBROSIS

Anemia
  Red cell transfusions
  Folate, B_{12}, and iron replacement
  Prednisone (autoimmune mechanisms)
  Androgens (ineffective erythropoiesis)
  Therapy for hypersplenism (see below)
Thrombocytopenia
  Transfusions
  Prednisone
  Therapy for hypersplenism
Symptomatic splenomegaly or severe hypersplenism
  Splenectomy
  Hydroxyurea, busulfan, chlorambucil, interferon, phosphorus-32
  Splenic irradiation
Thrombocytosis
  Plateletpheresis
  Antiplatelet agents
  Hydroxyurea, busulfan, chlorambucil, interferon, phosphorus-32
  Anagrelide
Myelofibrosis
  Allogeneic bone marrow transplantation
  Collagen antagonists (hydroxyproline analogs, colchicine, vinblastine, D-penicillamine, 1,25-vitamin D_3)

Source: Table constructed from data reported by Athens (1993) and Hoffman and Silverstein (1991).

thropoietin is used only in conjunction with interferon or hydroxyurea. Transfusions of packed red blood cells are the mainstay of therapy for symptomatic anemia in idiopathic myelofibrosis.

For patients with symptomatic thrombocytopenia, the prothrombin and partial thromboplastin times should be checked to exclude disseminated intravascular coagulation. Thereafter, they should receive a trial of prednisone, 1 mg/kg/d orally, for 3 weeks. If no response occurs, splenectomy should be considered. Platelet transfusions are temporizing.

Patients with thrombocytosis (>600,000/μL) and major symptoms (e.g., bleeding, digital ischemia, neurologic symptoms) should have immediate plateletpheresis. These patients should begin hydroxyurea, 15 mg/kg/d orally chronically to maintain platelet counts under 500,000/μL. Aspirin, 325 mg/d should be used only for patients with a history of thrombotic episodes and without a history of bleeding. Patients with asymptomatic thrombocytosis should not receive antiplatelet therapy but should have strict control of any cardiovascular risk factors.

Symptomatic splenomegaly is best managed by splenectomy except in those patients who are not operative candidates. Such patients should receive chemotherapy with hydroxyurea, 10 to 15 mg/kg/d orally. Splenectomy is indicated for the patient with refractory symptomatic splenomegaly; thrombocytopenia or hemolytic anemia refractory to medical measures; or portal hypertension with gastrointestinal bleeding.

Patients under 40 years of age should be evaluated for allogeneic bone marrow transplantation.

TABLE 12–22–3. DISTINGUISHING FEATURES OF MYELOPROLIFERATIVE DISORDERS

	Idiopathic Myelofibrosis	Chronic Myelogenous Leukemia	Polycythemia Vera	Essential Thrombocytosis	Myelodysplastic Syndrome
Red cell morphology	Teardrops	Normal	Normal	Normal	
Cytogenetics		Ph+			
Prior hemograms			↑↑ Hct*		
Bone marrow morphology					Dysplastic cells

*Hematocrit—may be elevated concurrently with myelofibrosis.
Source: Rosenthal DS. Myeloid metaplasia with myelofibrosis (agnogenic and postpolycythemia vera). In: Wasserman LR, Berk PD, Berlin NI, eds. Polycythemia vera and the myeloproliferative disorders. Philadelphia: Saunders, 1995:259. Adapted with permission from the publisher and author.

The role of inhibitors of collagen metabolism such as 1,25-vitamin D_3 is evolving.

FOLLOW-UP

Patients with asymptomatic idiopathic myelofibrosis should be followed with physical examinations and blood counts every 3 months initially to assess the pace of their disease progression. The important parameters to follow are symptoms of splenomegaly, spleen size, and blood counts.

DISCUSSION

Prevalence and Incidence

Idiopathic myelofibrosis is uncommon, with probably fewer than 5 cases per 1 million population per year. Most patients are 50 to 70 years old at the time of diagnosis.

Related Basic Science

Idiopathic myelofibrosis is a clonal disorder of an early hematopoietic progenitor. Growth factors such as platelet-derived growth factor are secreted from megakaryocytes, which are abnormal in this disease. These factors stimulate fibroblast proliferation and the production of collagen. Sinusoids of the fibrotic marrow are distorted, possibly allowing the release into the circulation of hematopoietic progenitors, which then lodge in the spleen, liver, and other sites of extramedullary hematopoiesis.

Natural History and Its Modification with Treatment

The median survival time after diagnosis is about 5 years, but varies widely. About one half of patients have significant morbidity from bleeding and up to one fourth die of bleeding complications. Thrombosis occurs in almost one half of patients and accounts for about one fifth of deaths. The main causes of death are thrombotic events, bleeding, acute leukemia, and infection. Transformation to acute leukemia or "blast crisis" occurs in up to 20% of patients. Therapy for idiopathic myelofibrosis can forestall complications of the disease. With the possible exception of bone marrow transplantation, however, no treatment can reverse the fibrotic process.

Prevention

There are no known preventive measures.

Cost Containment

The workup of a patient with myelofibrosis should be directed according to clues derived from the history and physical examination. A nondirected approach is time consuming, expensive, and likely to be of low yield. Similarly, although certain metastatic malignancies can cause myelofibrosis the patient should not be subjected to computed tomography scans, nuclear medicine scans, or endoscopic procedures to "look for a malignancy" in the absence of specific symptoms. The workup should be limited to those procedures that have a reasonable likelihood of disclosing a readily treatable cancer (e.g., Hodgkin's disease).

REFERENCES

Athens JW. Myelofibrosis. In: Lee GR, Bithell TC, Foerster J, et al., eds. Wintrobe's clinical hematology. 9th ed. Philadelphia: Lea & Febiger, 1993:2018.

Dickstein JI, Vardiman JW. Issues in the pathology and diagnosis of the chronic myeloproliferative disorder and the myelodysplastic syndromes. Am J Clin Pathol 1993;99:513.

Hasselbach HC. Idiopathic myelofibrosis: An update with particular reference to clinical aspects and prognosis. Int J Clin Lab Res 1993;23:124.

Hoffman R, Silverstein MN. Agnogenic myeloid metaplasia. In: Hoffman R, Benz EJ, Shattil SJ, et al., eds. Hematology: Basic principles and practice. New York: Churchill Livingstone, 1991:870.

Rosenthal DS. Myeloid metaplasia with myelofibrosis (agnogenic and postpolycythemia vera). In: Wasserman LR, Berk PD, Berlin NI, eds. Polycythemia vera and the myeloproliferative disorders. Philadelphia: Saunders, 1995:259.

Rupoli S, Da Lio L, Sisti S, et al. Primary myelofibrosis: A detailed statistical analysis of the clinicopathologic variables influencing survival. Ann Hematol 1994;68:205.

Zuckerman KS, Bagby GC, Emanuel PD, Schafer AI. Myeloproliferative disorders. In: McArthur JR, editor-in-chief. Hematology—1992. Washington, DC: American Society of Hematology, 1992:7.

CHAPTER 12–23

Hodgkin's Disease

Brad Pohlman, M.D.

DEFINITION

Hodgkin's disease is a malignant neoplasm involving primarily lymphoid tissue that has a characteristic histologic appearance including Reed–Sternberg cells or their variants.

ETIOLOGY

The etiology of Hodgkin's disease is unknown. Epidemiologic, serologic, and genetic studies have implicated Epstein–Barr virus.

CRITERIA FOR DIAGNOSIS

Suggestive

Hodgkin's disease should be considered in a patient with single or multiple enlarged lymph nodes, a mediastinal mass, fever, night sweats, or weight loss.

Definitive

The diagnosis of Hodgkin's disease requires a tissue biopsy, preferably of a lymph node, and the histologic identification of (1) disrupted nodal architecture, (2) neoplastic Reed–Sternberg cells or their variants, and (3) a background of nonmalignant reactive immune cells. Rarely, immunophenotyping may help establish the diagnosis.

CLINICAL MANIFESTATIONS

Subjective

Symptoms

The most common initial complaint is painless enlargement of cervical, supraclavicular, axillary, or, less often, inguinal lymph nodes. Although lymph nodes often continue to enlarge, some may temporarily remain stable or even decrease in size. Rarely, patients describe lymph node pain after drinking alcohol. The majority of patients are asymptomatic, but up to one third of patients have systemic "B" symptoms (fevers, night sweats, weight loss). Infrequently, patients experience generalized or less commonly localized pruritis, which may be associated with a skin rash. Some patients complain of cough, chest pain, dyspnea, or diminished exercise tolerance attributable to mediastinal or, less commonly, pericardial or pulmonary involvement. Less common symptoms, usually associated with more advanced disease, may be due to retroperitoneal, gastrointestinal, bone, skin, or neurologic involvement.

Past History

Patients with a history of mononucleosis, autoimmune disease, or immunodeficiency (including HIV infection) have an increased incidence of Hodgkin's disease.

Family History

Siblings of young adults with Hodgkin's disease have an increased incidence.

Objective

Physical Examination

Enlargement of supradiaphragmatic lymph nodes is present in most patients. Lymphadenopathy exclusively below the diaphragm occurs in only 5 to 10% of patients. Lymph nodes are usually firm, rubbery, mobile, and nontender. They may be barely appreciable but are often bulky. The spleen may be palpable. Superior vena cava syndrome is rare.

Routine Laboratory Abnormalities

Routine laboratory abnormalities are not diagnostic. A moderate to marked leukemoid reaction, monocytosis, eosinophilia, and thrombocytosis are common. Anemia due to impaired iron utilization, lymphopenia, and thrombocytopenia usually occurs in patients with more advanced disease. Elevation of the erythrocyte sedimentation rate is present in about half of patients.

Chest x-ray commonly demonstrates mediastinal or hilar adenopathy. Massive mediastinal enlargement may be present in minimally symptomatic patients.

PLANS

Diagnostic

Differential Diagnosis

The differential diagnosis is extensive and includes both benign and malignant disorders. Patients with non-Hodgkin's lymphomas may also have lymphadenopathy and/or B symptoms. Other possibilities include neoplasms of the head and neck, lungs, gastrointestinal tract, thymus, and thyroid; infections (e.g., streptococcal pharyngitis, mononucleosis, HIV, histoplasmosis, tuberculosis, toxoplasmosis); and collagen–vascular diseases (e.g., systemic lupus erythematosus, Sjogren's syndrome). The pathologist must distinguish Hodgkin's disease from other lymphadenopathies. For example, classic Reed–Sternberg cells may be seen in mononucleosis, dilantin-induced lymphadenopathy, and non-Hodgkin's lymphomas. In addition, the pathologist must distinguish the subtypes of Hodgkin's disease: nodular sclerosis, lymphocyte predominant, mixed cellularity, or lymphocyte depleted.

Diagnostic Options

A definitive diagnosis of Hodgkin's disease requires a biopsy of an involved lymph node or an extralymphatic site. If possible, an entire lymph node should be excised. Occasionally, multiple biopsies may be required to make a diagnosis. If a superficial lymph node is not accessible, a percutaneous true-cut needle biopsy may occasionally be adequate; however, a more invasive procedure (such as mediastinoscopy, thoracotomy, or laparotomy) is often necessary to obtain a large enough tissue sample to make a definitive diagnosis. Fine-needle aspiration may be adequate to identify other malignancies such as metastatic carcinoma, but this technique does not distinguish Hodgkin's disease from non-Hodgkin's lymphoma or most benign etiologies.

Once a diagnosis is made, all sites of disease must be identified in order to stage, plan, and monitor therapy. Clinical stage (CS) I–IV indicates no invasive staging procedure has been performed, and pathologic stage (PS) I–IV indicates an invasive procedure and tissue biopsies have been performed in an effort to identify Hodgkin's disease on both sides of the diaphragm. For example, supradiaphragmatic PS I–II indicates that a staging laparotomy and splenectomy have been performed and that microscopic examination of multiple lymph nodes, liver, and spleen has failed to identify any evidence of Hodgkin's disease. In ad-

dition, the stage includes a letter, designating the absence (A) or presence (B) of defined systemic symptoms (Table 12–23–1). The staging process should include a detailed history with particular attention to B symptoms, pruritis, HIV risk factors, and performance status; a complete physical examination including the size of lymph nodes, liver, and spleen; laboratory evaluation including a complete blood count and differential, Westergren erythrocyte sedimentation rate, liver tests (aspartate transaminase, alkaline phosphatase), creatinine, calcium, lactate dehydrogenase, and HIV screening (if risk factors are present); radiologic studies including a computed tomography scans of the chest, abdomen, and pelvis; and bilateral iliac crest bone marrow biopsies. Many experts recommend bipedal lymphangiography in all patients as it may occasionally detect retroperitoneal lymphadenopathy not detected by computed tomography and it may be useful for monitoring therapy; others reserve this test for patients in whom the identification of pathologic lymph nodes below the diaphragm will affect further management decisions. Other imaging studies such as magnetic resonance imaging, bone scan, ultrasonography, echocardiography, and gallium scan may be useful in identifying and/or monitoring other suspected sites of disease. Staging laparotomy may be performed on some patients. The indications for its use are controversial. Approximately one third of patients with supradiaphragmatic CS I–II will have disease detected below the diaphragm by staging laparotomy. The procedure should be restricted to patients in whom the findings will alter treatment—usually patients with CS I–II who will be treated with radiation therapy alone if no disease is detected below the diaphragm. Pneumococcal vaccine should be given to any patient that is going to have a splenectomy.

Recommended Approach

Whenever possible, the largest, most accessible lymph node should be excised. Cervical, supraclavicular, and axillary nodes are preferred over inguinal nodes. When an enlarged lymph node is not present or easily accessible, other diagnostic procedures as outlined above may be pursued. Staging should include a history; physical examination; complete blood count with differential; erythrocyte sedimentation rate; lactate dehydrogenase; aspartate transaminase; alkaline phosphatase; calcium; creatinine; HIV screening; computed tomography of chest, abdomen, and pelvis; gallium scan; and bilateral bone marrow biopsies. If these studies detect no disease below the diaphragm, bipedal lymphangiography and staging laparotomy may be considered.

Therapeutic

Therapeutic Options

The initial treatment of Hodgkin's disease depends primarily on the stage, but also may be influenced by the histologic subtype, other prog-

TABLE 12–23–1. ANN ARBOR STAGING SYSTEM OF HODGKIN'S DISEASE

Stage I	Involvement of a single lymph node region or of a single extralymphatic organ or site
Stage II	Involvement of two or more lymph node regions on the same side of the diaphragm *or* localized involvement of a single extralymphatic organ or site and of one or more lymph node regions on the same side of the diaphragm
Stage III	Involvement of lymph node regions on both sides of the diaphragm, which may be accompanied by localized involvement of a single extralymphatic organ or site or by involvement of the spleen
Stage IV	Diffuse or disseminated involvement of one or more extralymphatic organs or tissues with or without associated lymph node enlargement
A	Absence of the symptoms defined below
B	Unexplained weight loss of more than 10% of the body weight in the previous 6 months
	Unexplained fever with temperatures above 38°C
	Night sweats

Adapted from Carbone PP, Kaplan HS, Musshoff K, et al. Report of the committee on Hodgkin's disease staging classification. Cancer Res 1971;31:1860. Reproduced with permission from the publisher and author.

nostic features, and physician/patient preference. In general, patients with early-stage disease are treated with radiotherapy and patients with more advanced disease are treated with chemotherapy. Certain circumstances require treatment with a combination of chemotherapy and radiation therapy. Patients with supradiaphragmatic PS I–II Hodgkin's disease are usually treated with extended-field radiation therapy. Some centers also treat CS I–II patients with radiation therapy or a combination of chemotherapy and radiation therapy. Studies have suggested that combination chemotherapy alone may be as effective. Stage I–II subdiaphragmatic disease may sometimes be treated with extended-field radiation therapy, but is usually treated with chemotherapy. Radiation therapy alone is inadequate for most patients with advanced-stage disease (i.e., bulky CS I–II, CS or PS III–IV, or presence of fevers and weight loss). Instead, they should receive combination chemotherapy. MOPP (mechlorethamine, vincristine, procarbazine, and prednisone) was the first well-studied combination chemotherapy regimen used in the treatment of Hodgkin's disease, but it has significant potential side effects including sterilization and secondary leukemia. Subsequently, ABVD (doxorubicin [Adriamycin], bleomycin, vinblastine, and dacarbazine) has been shown to have a better response rate and survival and fewer side effects. The MOPP/ABV hybrid regimen also has demonstrated very good preliminary results. Patients are usually treated with six to eight cycles of chemotherapy. Patients with massive mediastinal Hodgkin's disease have approximately a 50% risk of relapse when treated with either chemotherapy or radiation therapy alone. This subgroup of patients should therefore receive chemotherapy followed by radiation therapy. Patients who relapse following radiation therapy should receive combination chemotherapy. Patients who relapse following chemotherapy may be cured with another regimen; however, high-dose chemotherapy with autologous bone marrow or stem cell transplantation appears to offer the best chance for long-term disease-free survival.

Recommended Approach

Patients with nonbulky PS I–IIA Hodgkin's disease should receive radiation therapy. Patients with CS or PS III–IV disease should receive combination chemotherapy. Patients with bulky mediastinal Hodgkin's disease should receive combination chemotherapy followed by radiation therapy. Other situations are more complicated and the patient should be referred to an experienced medical or radiation oncologist for a discussion regarding the risks, benefits, and costs of staging laparotomy with splenectomy and radiation therapy with or without chemotherapy.

FOLLOW-UP
Monitoring for Relapse

The majority of patients who relapse following either radiation therapy or chemotherapy do so within 2 to 3 years. As the majority of relapsed patients can be salvaged with conventional chemotherapy or high-dose chemotherapy with autologous bone marrow or stem cell transplantation, they should be monitored closely by history, physical examination, laboratory tests (i.e., complete blood count with differential, erythrocyte sedimentation rate, aspartate transaminase, alkaline phosphatase), and radiographic studies (i.e., computed tomography of chest, abdomen, and pelvis) for evidence of relapse. These evaluations should be repeated every 3 months during the first 2 years after treatment and less frequently thereafter. Because of the risk of second malignancies following treatment of Hodgkin's disease, it is essential that suspicious lesions be biopsied and not assumed to be Hodgkin's disease.

Monitoring of Complications

In addition to relapse, patients who have been treated for Hodgkin's disease are susceptible to a variety of disease- and treatment-related complications. Because of disease-associated cell-mediated immunodeficiency, prior splenectomy, chemotherapy-induced neutropenia, or steroid administration, these patients are at risk for developing serious bacterial and fungal infections, herpes zoster, *Pneumocystis carinii* pneumonia, and other opportunistic infections. These infections, especially pneumococcal sepsis and herpes zoster, may occur long after

treatment. Up to 50% of patients who receive mantle irradiation develop clinical or subclinical hypothyroidism, which may not be apparent for several years. In addition, up to half of these patients develop benign, or rarely malignant, thyroid neoplasms 20 years or more after treatment. Therefore, these patients should have regular examination of the thyroid gland and thyroid-stimulating hormone monitoring. Cardiopulmonary complications from chemotherapy, especially doxorubicin (Adriamycin) and bleomycin, and mantle irradiation may occur during or months after treatment. These complications are more likely to occur in patients who have received both chemotherapy and radiation therapy. Acute pneumonitis may cause fever, cough, dyspnea, and/or an abnormal chest x-ray, whereas chronic restrictive fibrosis may cause progressive dyspnea on exertion, restrictive changes in pulmonary function tests, a reduction in diffusion capacity, and/or an abnormal chest x-ray. Cardiac complications include acute pericarditis, chronic constrictive pericarditis, acute myocarditis, myocardial dysfunction, and accelerated coronary artery disease, especially in smokers. MOPP chemotherapy leads to permanent azoospermia in nearly 100% of males and ovarian dysfunction including ammenorrhea, sterility, and premature menopause in a large majority of women. The incidence is significantly higher in women over 25 years of age and those who receive chemotherapy and pelvic irradiation. Permanent gonadal dysfunction is less common in patients who receive ABVD chemotherapy. The risk of second malignancies following treatment of Hodgkin's disease is significantly higher than expected for age-matched controls. Solid tumors develop as a complication of radiation therapy in approximately 13% of patients followed for 20 years. The risk continues to increase with time. These tumors, which usually occur within the radiation field, include soft tissue sarcoma, head and neck cancer, melanoma, and cancer of the lung, breast, and gastrointestinal and urogenital tracts. Non-Hodgkin's lymphoma develops in approximately 5% of patients and is more likely in older men treated with combined modality therapy. Myelodysplastic syndrome and acute nonlymphocytic leukemia occur mainly as complications of chemotherapy, particularly alkylating agents, in 3 to 10% of patients 2 to 10 years after treatment. The risk may be higher in older patients, those who have had a splenectomy, and those treated with combined modality therapy. The short- and long-term psychosocial sequelae of the diagnosis and treatment of Hodgkin's disease are often not discussed. These patients face problems with body image and self-esteem, marriage and relationships, sexuality, employment and career, socioeconomic advancement, and insurability.

DISCUSSION
Prevalence and Incidence

Nearly 8000 new cases and 1550 deaths from Hodgkin's disease were estimated in the United States in 1994. A bimodal distribution is present with peak incidences occurring in the third and ninth decades. The incidence of nodular sclerosing Hodgkin's disease, which accounts for 40 to 60% of cases, appears to be increasing modestly.

Related Basic Science

Most evidence suggests that the Reed–Sternberg cell and its variants are the etiologic neoplastic cells of Hodgkin's disease and the background cells are reactive. The immunophenotype, genotype, cytokine expression, and other data suggest a probable lymphoid origin; however, the exact nature of the Reed–Sternberg cell remains elusive.

Hodgkin's disease is classified by the Rye system into four subtypes based primarily on the cellular background and the number of lymphocytes. Nodular sclerosis Hodgkin's disease is characterized morphologically by bands of collagen that traverse the lymph node and a tendency for the Reed–Sternberg cells to assume the lacunar morphology. Lymphocyte-predominant Hodgkin's disease is characterized by a diffuse infiltrate of mature lymphocytes admixed with variable numbers of histiocytes, few inflammatory cells, and no necrosis. Mixed-cellularity Hodgkin's disease is marked by a diffuse infiltrate of lymphocytes, histiocytes, eosinophils, and plasma cells that obliterates the underlying architecture. Lymphocyte-depleted Hodgkin's disease is characterized by the presence of multilobed Reed–Sternberg cells in a background characteristically deplete of lymphocytes and other reactive cells.

Natural History and Its Modification with Treatment

Patients with PS I–II treated with radiation therapy have nearly a 100% complete remission rate and a 15 to 30% relapse rate. Most relapsed patients can be cured with combination chemotherapy and the 10-year survival is 80 to 95%. Compared to patients with PS I–II, patients with CS I–II treated with radiation therapy alone are more likely to relapse; however, as most of these patients can also be salvaged with chemotherapy, the overall survival of pathologically and selected clinically staged patients with supradiaphragmatic disease is probably the same.

Patients with advanced-stage disease have a greater than 50% relapse rate if treated with radiation therapy alone. In contrast, combination chemotherapy results in 65 to 85% complete response rate, and at 5 years, 50 to 65% remain in remission and 65 to 75% are alive. For patients who have failed standard or salvage chemotherapy, high-dose chemotherapy with autologous bone marrow or stem cell transplantation may cure approximately 50%

Prevention

No specific preventive measures can be recommended at this time.

Cost Containment

Studies performed over the past 30 years have helped establish the principles used in the diagnosis, staging, treatment, and follow-up of patients with Hodgkin's disease. Recent studies have attempted to minimize both short- and long-term complications without compromising disease-free survival. These efforts may ultimately translate into cost savings as well. For now, the recommendations outlined above are generally considered the standard of care in the United States.

REFERENCES

DeVita VT, Hubbard SM. Drug therapy: Hodgkin's disease. N Engl J Med 1993;328:560.

Hoppe RT. Radiation therapy in the management of Hodgkin's disease. Semin Oncol 1990;17:704.

Longo DL, Urba WJ. Medical progress: Hodgkin's disease. N Engl J Med 1992;326:678.

Mauch PM. Controversies in the management of early stage Hodgkin's disease. Blood 1994;83:318.

Yellen SB, Cella DF, Bonomi A. Quality of life in people with Hodgkin's disease. Oncol 1993;7:41.

CHAPTER 12–24

Non-Hodgkin's Lymphoma

Brad Pohlman, M.D.

DEFINITION

Non-Hodgkin's lymphoma (NHL) is a heterogeneous group of malignant neoplasms arising from the immune system. Although these disorders are discussed together, they actually constitute an array of clinico-pathologic entities with widely variable features, behavior, treatment, and prognosis.

ETIOLOGY

With few exceptions, the etiology of NHL is unknown. Epstein–Barr virus is strongly implicated in the pathogenesis of African Burkitt's lymphoma and NHL that occurs in patients with immunodeficiencies. Human T-cell lymphotropic virus type 1 (HTLV-1) probably causes adult T-cell leukemia/lymphoma. Epidemiologic studies have implicated irradiation and some environmental exposures.

CRITERIA FOR DIAGNOSIS

Suggestive

Non-Hodgkin's lymphoma should be considered in any patient with lymph node enlargement, fevers, night sweats, weight loss, mediastinal mass, splenomegaly, peripheral blood cytopenias, or suspected neoplasm of any site. Atypical lymphoid cells identified in a biopsy specimen or fine-needle aspiration may suggest a diagnosis of NHL.

Definitive

The definitive diagnosis of NHL requires a biopsy of involved nodal or extranodal tissue. The specific histologic subtype can be determined only by examining lymph node architecture. In poorly differentiated specimens, pathologic techniques that establish lymphoid origin of tissue may be necessary. A demonstration of clonality by kappa or lambda light-chain restriction, immunoglobulin or T-cell receptor gene rearrangement, or cytogenetic abnormalities supports the diagnosis of NHL. Specific subtypes of NHL may be further characterized by immunophenotypic, cytogenetic, and molecular analysis.

CLINICAL MANIFESTATIONS

Subjective

Symptoms

As NHL may involve any lymphatic or extralymphatic tissue, virtually any presenting symptom is possible. The majority of patients complain of painless enlargement of one or more superficial lymph nodes. This abnormality may have been present for weeks or months and may have been stable or progressing. Mediastinal lymphadenopathy may cause chest pain, cough, dyspnea, or superior vena cava syndrome. Retroperitoneal or mesenteric lymphadenopathy or splenomegaly may cause abdominal pain or fullness, early satiety, or back pain. Although extranodal involvement is often a manifestation of more extensive nodal disease, some extranodal sites may be the only site involved: gastrointestinal lymphoma may lead to abdominal pain or fullness, early satiety, symptoms of complete or partial bowel obstruction, hemorrhage, or perforation; central nervous system lymphoma may cause headaches, change in mental status, seizures, or focal neurologic deficits; and cutaneous lymphoma may result in localized or extensive lesions. Symptoms may be due to involvement of less common sites such as bone, testis, spinal cord, orbit, and sinus. Patients may complain of symptoms due to anemia or thrombocytopenia. Approximately 20% of patients have B symptoms (i.e., fever, night sweats, and/or weight loss).

Past History

The past medical history does not usually suggest a diagnosis of NHL. Exceptions include patients with known, or sometimes unrecognized, altered immune systems (e.g., congenital immunodeficiencies, HIV infection, immunosuppression following bone marrow or solid organ transplantation, celiac sprue, and collagen–vascular diseases); patients from areas in which human T-cell lymphotropic virus 1 is endemic (e.g., southwestern Japan, the Caribbean, and the southeastern United States); patients in certain occupations (e.g., construction, agriculture, forestry, and fishing); and patients with exposure to chemicals linked to the development of NHL (e.g., benzene, pesticides, and dark hair dyes).

Family History

Some rare families have multiple members with NHL.

Objective

Physical Examination

The most common physical finding is single or multiple firm enlarged, nontender cervical, supraclavicular, axillary, and/or inguinal lymph nodes. Waldeyer's ring and epitrochlear lymph nodes may be involved. Splenomegaly is common. Occasionally, a mass may be palpable in the abdomen or pelvis. The skin may be the only site of disease, that is, cutaneous T cell lymphoma, or it may be part of more extensive disease. In either situation, the skin lesions may be localized or extensive and in various stages of evolution ranging from erythematous macules to diffuse erythroderma as well as papules, plaques, and tumors. In short, physical findings due to tumor involving any lymphatic or extralymphatic site are possible.

Routine Laboratory Abnormalities

The complete blood count is often normal; however, patients may have mild to moderate anemia (due to gastrointestinal involvement and hemorrhage, poor iron utilization, or bone marrow involvement); thrombocytopenia (due to bone marrow involvement or hypersplenism); or, less commonly, leukopenia. Liver involvement or biliary tract obstruction may cause elevated liver tests (i.e., aspartate transaminase, alkaline phosphatase, or bilirubin). An abnormal alkaline phosphatase may also suggest bone involvement. Retroperitoneal lymphadenopathy may lead to ureteral obstruction and an elevated creatinine. Lactate dehydrogenase may be mildly or markedly elevated. Chest x-ray or computed tomography may show a mediastinal mass, hilar lymphadenopathy, or pulmonary parenchymal lesions. Abdominal computed tomography may demonstrate retroperitoneal, porta hepatis, or mesenteric lymphadenopathy. Less commonly, abdominal imaging studies may show isolated or multiple, focal or diffuse parenchymal lesions involving the liver, spleen, kidneys, adrenal glands, pancreas, or bowel wall. The appearance may be indistinguishable from that of other benign and malignant neoplasms.

PLANS

Diagnostic

Differential Diagnosis

Non-Hodgkin's lymphoma must be distinguished from other benign and malignant causes of lymphadenopathy, B symptoms, and other less common manifestations. The differential diagnosis includes a variety of infectious, collagen–vascular, and neoplastic diseases including mononucleosis, HIV, toxoplasmosis, tuberculosis, systemic lupus erythematosus, Sjogren's syndrome, Hodgkin's disease, and cancer of virtually any organ. The specific subtypes of NHL must also be distinguished. For nononcologists, NHL can be divided into two broad categories: indolent and aggressive. The indolent lymphomas include small lymphocytic, follicular small cleaved cell, follicular mixed small cleaved and large cell, marginal zone, and MALTomas. The aggressive lymphomas include mantle cell, follicular large cell, diffuse small cleaved cell, diffuse mixed small and large cell, diffuse large cell, anaplastic large cell, immunoblastic, lymphoblastic, and small noncleaved cell.

Diagnostic Options

A definitive diagnosis of NHL requires a tissue biopsy. Several techniques are available. An excisional lymph node biopsy provides the most information. A percutaneous true-cut needle biopsy of otherwise inaccessible tissue may provide a specific histologic diagnosis, although it does not usually allow further characterization. Fine-needle aspiration may allow a cytologic diagnosis of carcinoma or sarcoma, obviating the need for a more invasive biopsy; however, this technique is inadequate for diagnosis and histologic classification of NHL. For this reason, fine-needle aspiration should be reserved for situations in which tissue is not accessible without a potentially risky invasive procedure, another diagnosis is more likely, and further diagnostic and/or prognostic information that might be provided by histologic classification and further characterization will not alter the therapeutic approach. If the diagnosis remains elusive, a more invasive procedure such as mediastinoscopy, thoracotomy, or exploratory laparotomy may be necessary.

Once a diagnosis is made, all sites of disease must be identified in order to plan and monitor therapy. This process should include the following: (1) a detailed history including the presence or absence of B symptoms, HIV risk factors, and performance status; (2) a complete physical examination including lymph node regions, liver, and spleen; (3) laboratory evaluation including a complete blood count and differential, liver tests (aspartate transaminase, alkaline phosphatase, bilirubin), creatinine, calcium, lactate dehydrogenase, and HIV screening (if risk factors are present); (4) radiographic studies including chest x-ray or computed tomography, abdomen and pelvis computed tomography, and/or other imaging studies (magnetic resonance imaging, bone scan, or ultrasonography) that may define other suspected sites of disease; and (5) bilateral iliac crest bone marrow biopsies. Unlike Hodgkin's disease, staging laparotomy is not necessary in patients with NHL.

Recommended Approach

Whenever possible, the largest, most accessible lymph node should be excised. Cervical, supraclavicular, and axillary nodes are preferred over inguinal nodes. When an enlarged lymph node is not present or easily accessible, other diagnostic procedures as outlined above may be pursued. As formalin and other preservatives may prevent the appropriate and complete analysis of a suspected lymphoma, biopsied nodal or extranodal tissue should be kept fresh, sterile, and moist. The necessary staging procedures are outlined above.

Therapeutic

Therapeutic Options

The indolent lymphomas are generally considered incurable and treatment is by definition palliative. An exception is the 5 to 10% of patients with indolent lymphoma that is localized to a single lymphatic or extralymphatic site. Approximately 50% of these patients, when treated with involved or extended-field radiation therapy, may be cured. The role of chemotherapy in this situation is unclear. Patients with more advanced disease are not curable with conventional chemotherapy. In 50% of cases, a patient may not require any treatment initially, and expectant monitoring of symptoms, physical findings, and radiographic abnormalities may be all that is required. When the patient develops deleterious signs or symptoms (e.g., bulky lymphadenopathy, pain, fever, night sweats, weight loss, anemia, or thrombocytopenia) or progressive disease with impending problems, treatment should be initiated. Studies comparing radiation therapy, single-agent chemotherapy, and combination chemotherapy for the initial treatment of patients with indolent NHL have not demonstrated any difference in overall survival. Some patients may experience a longer disease-free interval following more aggressive treatment. Several newer agents (e.g., fludarabine and 2-chlorodeoxyadenosine) have been used successfully in the treatment of patients with relapsed or refractory indolent NHL. These drugs are now being compared with standard chemotherapy for initial treatment. Younger patients with indolent lymphoma have received high-dose chemotherapy with autologous bone marrow or stem cell transplantation. Whether this approach is better than standard treatment is unknown.

The diagnosis of aggressive NHL is usually an indication to treat. Elderly patients or patients with multiple medical problems may not be candidates for aggressive chemotherapy. In these cases, a palliative approach with radiation therapy or mild chemotherapy may provide temporary symptom control but will not prolong survival. In fact, any reduction from standard chemotherapy doses will substantially reduce the chance of remission and cure. Among patients in whom the goal is cure, radiation therapy alone is inadequate, even with clinically localized disease, as the relapse rate is greater than 75%. In general, patients with aggressive NHL are treated with six to eight cycles of an anthracycline-containing chemotherapy regimen. The first-generation regimens such as CHOP, (cyclophosphamide, doxorubicin (Hydroxydauno-mycin), vincristine (Oncovin) and prednisone) were studied extensively in the 1970s. During the 1980s many second- and third-generation chemotherapy regimens, which incorporated additional chemothera-peutic drugs into treatment plans, were developed and appeared to have better results than first-generation regimens; however, a large study failed to confirm the superiority of these new regimens. Therefore, CHOP is the most widely used chemotherapy regimen for the treatment of aggressive NHL. Some studies have suggested that treatment of lo-calized, aggressive NHL with a shortened course of chemotherapy fol-lowed by involved-field radiation therapy may be as effective as a full course of chemotherapy. Patients with very aggressive histologies, for example, lymphoblastic and small noncleaved cell lymphoma, may benefit from additional therapy including central nervous system pro-phylaxis and high-dose chemotherapy with autologous bone marrow or stem cell transplantation. Patients with relapsed, aggressive NHL may respond to a number of salvage chemotherapy regimens; however, no one is cured. In contrast, patients who receive high-dose chemother-apy with autologous bone marrow or stem cell transplantation may be cured.

Recommended Approach

The appropriate management of an individual with NHL depends pri-marily on the histologic subtype. In addition, the stage, the patient's age and performance status, and many other clinical and prognostic fac-tors contribute to the treatment plan. Therefore, specific treatment rec-ommendations cannot be made, and the patient should be referred to an experienced oncologist.

FOLLOW-UP

While receiving treatment, patients should be monitored for potential complications, especially bacterial, fungal, and other opportunistic in-fections that result primarily from chemotherapy-induced neutropenia and, less often, prolonged use of steroids. Patients who develop febrile illness while neutropenic need to be fully evaluated for a source of in-fection and treated urgently with broad-spectrum antibiotics. Other common complications that may occur during or soon after the comple-tion of chemotherapy include nausea, vomiting, anorexia, fatigue, alopecia, and sterility. Many other short- and long-term complications are possible.

Patients should be followed for evidence of recurrent disease. Pa-tients with indolent lymphoma may relapse years after diagnosis and treatment. These patients should be followed expectantly with serial history, physical examination, and, in some cases, imaging studies. Be-cause of the potential for transformation to a more aggressive histol-ogy, lesions presumed to be recurrent NHL should be rebiopsied. Re-lapse of aggressive lymphoma usually occurs within 3 years. As many of these relapsed patients can be salvaged with high-dose chemother-apy and autologous bone marrow or stem cell transplantation, they should be monitored closely by history, physical examination, and radi-ographic studies.

DISCUSSION
Prevalence and Incidence

The incidence of NHL has increased by more than 50% over the past 20 years. According to the American Cancer Society, 45,000 new cases and 21,300 deaths were estimated in 1994. The disease may occur at any age but the incidence increases logarithmically beyond the second decade.

Related Basic Science
Pathology

As knowledge of the pathobiology of NHL expands, the systems used to classify the various subtypes continue to evolve. The Working For-mulation is the most widely used system and is based on a morphologic description of lymph nodes and the overall survival of similarly treated patients. The International Lymphoma Study Group has proposed a new classification based on morphologic, immunologic, and genetic

characteristics. The pathologic description of the increasing number of NHL subtypes is beyond the scope of this text, and the reader is re-ferred to the references.

Altered Molecular Biology

Cytogenetic abnormalities have been associated with some types of NHL. In certain cases, the corresponding molecular alterations and pathobiology have been elucidated. For example, Burkitt's lymphoma is the result of a reciprocal translocation, t(8;14), that places the *MYC* proto-oncogene next to the immunoglobulin heavy-chain gene. This re-arrangement leads to the constitutive expression of MYC, a DNA-bind-ing protein that is important in the regulation of cell proliferation. Fol-licular lymphomas are frequently the result of a translocation, t(14;18), that juxtaposes the *BCL-2* proto-oncogene and the immunoglobulin heavy-chain gene leading to the constitutive expression of BCL-2 and interruption of apoptosis or programmed cell death.

Natural History and Its Modification with Treatment

The indolent lymphomas usually have a slowly progressive course. Pa-tients have a median survival of 5 to 10 years, but are rarely curable with conventional therapy. These lymphomas may initially remain rela-tively stable for months of even years without therapy. When treatment is necessary, the disease frequently responds to "mild" chemotherapy but invariably recurs months to years later. Subsequent remissions are obtainable but may require more aggressive chemotherapy and are usu-ally of shorter duration. Many older patients will die *with* their lym-phoma but of unrelated causes. In a minority of patients, the lymphoma will transform to a more aggressive histology, most commonly diffuse large lymphoma.

The aggressive lymphomas have a more rapid course. Without ther-apy, patients usually die within months; with therapy, median survival is less than 3 years. Control of the disease usually requires aggressive chemotherapy. Depending on the specific subtype and other prognostic factors, 40 to 90% of patients may achieve an initial complete remis-sion and 25 to 75% of patients may be cured. Patients with aggressive histology who do not achieve a first complete remission or who relapse after achieving a first remission are incurable with conventional ther-apy. Up to 50% of these patients can be salvaged with high-dose chemotherapy and autologous bone marrow or stem cell transplanta-tion. Many clinical and pathologic characteristics predict which pa-tients are most likely to fail initial therapy. One model, the International Index, identified five independent poor prognostic factors including age greater than 60, serum lactate dehydrogenase above normal, Eastern Cooperative Oncology Group (ECOG) performance status 2 to 4, stage III or IV, and more than one site of extranodal involvement.

Prevention

The vast majority of patients with NHL have no obvious inciting factor. Therefore, preventive measures for the general population cannot be prescribed.

Cost Containment

Patients with relapsed NHL are often salvaged with high-dose chemotherapy and autologous bone marrow or stem cell transplanta-tion. As the associated mortality and morbidity have declined and over-all survival has improved, this therapy has been increasingly applied to patients with what had previously been considered "incurable" indolent lymphomas and to patients with "high-risk" aggressive lymphoma in first complete or partial remission. Whether this approach leads to bet-ter outcomes than the traditional therapies remains unknown. Studies attempting to define the most appropriate patients and timing of this ex-pensive therapy should also address questions pertaining to costs and resource utilization.

REFERENCES

Armitage JO. Drug therapy: Treatment of non-Hodgkin's lymphoma. N Engl J Med 1993;328:1023.

Fisher RI, Gaynor ER, Dahlberg S, et al. Comparison of a standard regimen

(CHOP) with three intensive chemotherapy regimens for advanced non-Hodgkin's lymphoma. N Engl J Med 1993;328:1002.

Harris NL, Jaffe ES, Stein H, et al. A revised European–American classification of lymphoid neoplasms: A proposal from the International Lymphoma Study Group. Blood 1994;84:1361.

International Non-Hodgkin's Lymphoma Prognostic Factors Project. A predic-

tive model for aggressive non-Hodgkin's lymphoma. N Engl J Med 1993;329:987.

Longo DL, Mauch P, DeVita VT, et al. Lymphocytic lymphomas. In: DeVita VT, Hellman S, Rosenberg SA, ed. Cancer: Principles & practice of oncology. 4th ed. Philadelphia: Lippincott, 1993:1859.

CHAPTER 12–25

Chronic Lymphocytic Leukemia

Mohamad A. Hussein, M.B., B.Ch., M.D.

DEFINITION

Chronic lymphocytic leukemia (CLL) is a progressive accumulation of lymphocytes that are functionally incompetent but morphologically appear mature.

ETIOLOGY

The etiology of CLL is unknown. Relatives of CLL patients have an increased frequency of lymphomas and autoimmune disorders.

CRITERIA FOR DIAGNOSIS

Suggestive

Patients with a persistent lymphocytosis, lymphadenopathy, hepatosplenomegaly, or hypogammaglobulinemia should be evaluated for chronic lymphocytic leukemia.

Definitive

Patients should be phenotyped and found to have B-cell-type CLL. Given this prerequisite of B-cell phenotype, the threshold blood lymphocyte count of 5×10^9/L should be adequate to define lymphocytosis. The threshold for bone marrow lymphocytosis is 30% of all nucleated cells.

CLINICAL MANIFESTATIONS

Subjective

The usual complaints of CLL patients are weakness, easy fatigability, night sweats, fever without infections, weight loss, frequent bacterial and viral infections, increased bleeding tendencies, and exaggerated responses to mosquito or other insect bites. Symptoms may be entirely absent, or all may be present in varying degrees of severity. Autoimmune complications are known to occur frequently in CLL; however, autoimmune diseases may precede CLL.

Objective

Physical Examination

Lymphadenopathy is the most frequently noted abnormal finding on physical examination. The size of the lymph nodes may vary from small (1 cm in diameter) to massively enlarged glands. The lymph nodes in CLL are almost always nontender, discrete, firm, and easily movable on palpation. Splenomegaly, which is present in approximately 50% of the patients, may range from a barely palpable spleen below the left costal margin to a massively enlarged spleen. Hepatomegaly is elicited less often. Infiltration by CLL may be manifested in virtually all other parts of the body, including meninges, pleural space, and skin. These infiltrative processes would result in physical findings related to the organs infiltrated.

Routine Laboratory Abnormalities

Blood Count. Lymphocytosis as defined by a persistent absolute lymphocyte count of 5×10^9/L for more than 4 weeks may be as high as 500×10^9/L and even as high as $1,000,000 \times 10^9$/L. In most cases it is

in excess of 20×10^9/L. Platelets could be normal or decreased, with the thrombocytopenia either secondary to an immune destructive process, where the number of giant and large-size platelets is increased, or heavy infiltration of the marrow with leukemia, or both. Anemia, if present, could be secondary to an autoimmune hemolytic process, where the peripheral blood film demonstrates microspherocytes, increased reticulocytes, and occasional red cell fragments. Anemia secondary to bone marrow infiltration or pure red cell aplasia should be investigated. The peripheral blood film demonstrates lymphocytes that are usually small, with the nucleus filling almost the entire cell, and the nuclear chromatin is dense and clumped and without any discernible nucleoli. Occasionally, the CLL lymphocyte may be a large cell with a round or somewhat notched nucleus, there may be a distinct nucleolus, and the cytoplasm may be abundant and slightly basophilic or orthochromatic. CLL lymphocytes are very fragile and the mechanical trauma induced in the preparation of blood films may cause severe morphologic deformities recognized as smudge cells.

Blood Chemistries. There is no characteristic abnormality of the blood chemistry profile in CLL, although hypercalcemia, abnormal liver enzymes, and abnormal kidney functions may be encountered.

PLAN

Diagnostic

Differential Diagnosis

Malignant lymphoma in leukemic phase may sometimes be indistinguishable from CLL. T-cell CLL and morphologic variants of CLL (prolymphocytic leukemia, Sézary syndrome, hairy cell leukemia, etc.) are distinguished by their respective characteristic phenotypic and microscopic appearances.

Diagnostic Options and Recommended Approach

Flow Cytometry. The peripheral blood should demonstrate B cells expressing a low cell surface density of immunoglobulins, usually immunoglobulin (Ig) M or IgM with IgD, which are monoclonal as revealed by expression of only one light chain, either kappa or lambda. The B cells of B–CLL stain positively for CD–5, while simultaneously staining with at least one of the B-cell monoclonal antibodies, CD–20, CD–19, or CD–24. The overall interpretation of this phenotypic expression is that CLL B cells are arrested or frozen at an intermediate stage in the pathway of B-cell differentiation.

Bone Marrow Aspiration and Biopsy. The overall cellularity of the bone marrow is normal or increased. A hypocellular bone marrow is not a typical finding in CLL unless it is the result of cytotoxic chemotherapy. Depending on the extent of lymphocytic infiltration, myeloid and erythroid precursors as well as megakaryocytes may be decreased or normal. Pure red cell aplasia may also occur in CLL. The biopsy specimens are helpful in defining the pattern of infiltration, which may be diffuse, nodular, or interstitial.

Rai Staging System. The Rai system is based on clinical and laboratory findings and correlates very well with overall survival. Also, it is a major component of the management plan (Table 12–25–1).

TABLE 12–25–1. RAI STAGING OF CHRONIC LYMPHOCYTIC LEUKEMIA

0	Lymphocytosis in blood and marrow only
I	Lymphocytosis and lymphadenopathy
II	Lymphocytosis and lymphadenopathy and splenomegaly
III	Lymphadenopathy and anemia
IV	Lymphadenopathy and thrombocytopenia

Source: Rai KR, Savitsky A, Cronkite EP, et al. Clinical staging of chronic lympho-cytic leukemia. Blood 1975;46:219. Reproduced with permission from the publisher and author.

Therapeutic

Therapeutic Options

One of the main decisions in the management of chronic lymphocytic leukemia is when to treat CLL. To understand the rationale behind the current guidelines for treatment an understanding of the different prognostic factors is essential. Clinical stage remains the strongest predictor of survival in patients with CLL. The substantial heterogeneity even within a clinical stage has lead to a search for laboratory and clinical prognostic factors to improve on currently available staging systems.

Cellular Morphology. A number of morphologic variants appear to be associated with a poor prognosis, that is, larger lymphocytes, larger number of prolymphocytes, clefted cells, or granular cells. It is not clear, however, how many of the cases studied to define these morphologic criteria as a poor prognostic factor are not CLL and represent other low-grade lymphoproliferative disorders.

Pattern of Bone Marrow Involvement. The bone marrow in CLL has traditionally been considered to be diffusely infiltrated by mature-appearing lymphocytes; however, a substantial number of patients exhibit a nondiffuse (nodular, interstitial mixed) pattern of involvement. A retrospective analysis of 329 cases of CLL (227 without prior therapy) demonstrated that patients with a diffuse pattern of bone marrow involvement had a shorter survival than those with a nondiffuse pattern (Rozman et al., 1984). Moreover, the pattern of bone marrow involvement appeared to be a stronger predictor of survival than hepatomegaly, hemoglobin level, lymphadenopathy, age, or thrombocytopenia. The bone marrow pattern did not appear to add to the predictive value of clinical stage, however; although it separated patients within clinical stage, only in stage B patients was the difference significant.

Age. Older age has consistently been shown to confer a poorer prognosis in CLL. Nevertheless, the outlook for younger patients is still unsatisfactory.

Cytogenetics. Recent technologic advances have permitted satisfactory cytogenetic analysis in the majority of cases of CLL (Han et al., 1987; Juliusson et al., 1990). An increasing body of data supports the prognostic importance of cytogenetics in CLL, as in other forms of acute and chronic leukemias. Chromosome abnormalities occur in approximately 50% of cases of CLL. The most frequently reported abnormality is trisomy 12. Patients with a normal karyotype have a more favorable outcome than patients with single abnormalities, who live longer than those with complex karyotypic abnormalities.

Cell Kinetics. Not only has the absolute number of peripheral blood lymphocytes been reported by some investigators to correlate with survival, but the rate at which the lymphocyte count increases has been suggested to have prognostic importance as well. Montserrat and coworkers (1986) performed a retrospective analysis of 100 previously untreated cases and noted that cases with a lymphocyte doubling time shorter than 12 months had a median survival of 5 years, whereas the median was not yet reached for those with a doubling time longer than 12 months. A similar distinction was apparent when 6 months was used as the cutoff, but the cases were not as evenly distributed.

Recommended Approach

At the time of diagnosis of CLL, disease activity is relatively indolent in about 80% of cases. These patients fall mostly in stage 0 and some in stage 1. It is preferable to withhold institution of cytotoxic therapy in these cases for a period ranging from several weeks to a few years. Regular follow-up clinical visits provide the opportunity to evaluate the lymphocyte doubling time as well as the clinical progression of the disease.

In 1988, a National Cancer Institute-sponsored working group developed a series of guidelines for CLL protocols (Cheson et al., 1988). A definition of active disease was developed that includes weight loss of 10% or more of body weight during the previous 6 months, extreme fatigue, fevers higher than 100.5°C for 2 or more weeks unrelated to infection, night sweats, development of anemia, thrombocytopenia, and autoimmune anemia and/or thrombocytopenia that does not respond to corticosteroid therapy. In addition, massive splenomegaly, lymphadenopathy, and progressive lymphocytosis with a greater than 50% increase over a 2-month period or lymphocyte doubling time less than 6 months were indications to start treatment. Marked hypogammaglobulinemia and development of a monoclonal protein were not considered sufficient causes for initiation of therapy.

Treatment Based on Clinical Stage.

LOW RISK GROUP: STAGE 0. When therapy is indicated, single-agent therapy with oral chlorambucil 20 to 30 mg/m² in one day to be repeated every 3 to 4 weeks, with or without steroids at a dose of 30 to 40 mg/m² per day for 5 to 7 days, should be continued until the symptoms or signs that required this intervention have resolved. For younger patients, investigational protocols should be recommended.

INTERMEDIATE RISK GROUP: STAGES I AND II. If evidence of active disease (defined above) develops, therapy with a regimen similar to that for the low-risk group should be instituted. Cyclophosphamide 500 to 700 mg/m² at intervals ranging from 2 to 4 weeks, with or without steroids, is another alternative.

HIGH-RISK GROUP: STAGES III AND IV. There is limited information to support the use of multiple agents, and the combination of chlorambucil and steroids is a reasonable option. A reasonable alternative therapy would be the combination of cytoxan 500 to 700 mg/m² on day 1; vincristine 1.4 mg/m², not to exceed 2.0 mg intravenously, on day 1; and prednisone 40 mg/m² on days 1 to 5, with the cycle to be repeated every 2 to 4 weeks. An anthracycline (daunorubicin or mitoxantrone) might be beneficial in some cases.

OTHER GROUPS. In all different groups if institutional studies or intergroup studies are available to evaluate different new treatment modalities, it is quite justifiable to encourage the patient to participate in these trials.

Treatment of Refractory Chronic Lymphocytic Leukemia. Fludarabine, which is an adenine nucleoside analog, has been approved for treatment of CLL for patients who have failed initial therapy with an alkylating agent. It is an effective drug for the control of refractory CLL. A dose of 25 mg/m² per day intravenously for 5 days to be repeated every month appears to be well tolerated. As patients with CLL are already immunocompromised and fludarabine is an immunosuppressive agent, the possibility of opportunistic infection should be kept in mind if the patient develops fever of unknown origin or pulmonary infiltrates. The latter is complicated by the fact that fludarabine could result in unspecific noninfectious pneumonitis.

Treatment of Complications Secondary to Chronic Lymphocytic Leukemia. The causes of anemia and thrombocytopenia in CLL are not always clearly identifiable, but in a small minority of cases they result from autoimmune phenomena. Diagnosis of autoimmune hemolytic anemia is relatively easy because of the ready availability and reliability of the Coombs test. On the other hand, the diagnosis of immune thrombocytopenic purpura requires a certain degree of clinical judgment. In most cases, autoimmune hemolytic anemia and immune thrombocytopenia respond to therapy with prednisone. The initial starting dose of prednisone should be 1 mg/kg, which could be tapered when there is a clinical response to therapy. Therapy for autoimmune hemolytic anemia requires a longer duration of steroid therapy and a slower tapering schedule than does therapy for immune thrombocytopenia. If steroids fail in management, intravenous immunoglobulins should be added to therapy at a dose of 0.4 g/kg to be repeated at 3-week intervals after an initial loading dose given daily for 5 days. Pure red cell aplasia is a relatively rare cause of anemia in CLL and it seems to be mediated by the inhibitory effect of suppressor/cytotoxic T cells on erythropoiesis. Therapy with steroids and, in resistant cases, with cyclosporine has been found to induce a reticulocyte response and, eventually, a significant increase in hemoglobin concentration.

Patients who have previously suffered at least one major bacterial infection (such as pneumonia) and/or have a markedly decreased level of serum immunoglobulin G should be considered for therapy with intravenous immunoglobulin. The dose is 0.4 g/kg every 3 weeks for 1 year. There are no data available documenting whether maintenance therapy beyond 1 year, either at a lower dose or on a less frequent schedule, is beneficial.

FOLLOW-UP

Patients should be evaluated every 4 to 8 weeks by physical examination, complete blood count with differential, and review of the peripheral blood smear, SMA–16, and coagulation studies. Body weight, temperature, night sweats, adenopathy, splenomegaly, hepatomegaly, leukocytosis, anemia, thrombocytopenia, and levels of lactate dehydrogenase and uric acid should be monitored. Occasional evaluation of the quantitative immunoglobulin, especially if normal at the time of onset, might be helpful in predicting patients who could be susceptible to infections in the future.

DISCUSSION

Prevalence and Incidence

The annual incidence of chronic lymphocytic leukemia is 1.8 to 3.0 per 100,000 population in the United States. Incidence is age related, with 5.2 per 100,000 persons between the ages of 35 and 59 and 30.4 per 100,000 persons between 80 and 84 years of age (Surveillance Epidemiology and Results Incidence and Mortality Data, 1981). It affects twice as many men as women. CLL is less common in Japanese and other Asian populations. Clusters of CLL in families have been reported and first-degree relatives of patients with CLL have a threefold increased risk of CLL and other lymphoid neoplasms, compared with the general population.

Related Basic Science

The majority of CLL patients are of B-lineage derivation, by virtue of the expression of B-cell-restricted and -associated cell surface antigen. CLL B cells are not the neoplastic counterparts of normal resting B cells. Similar to the peripheral blood B cell, CLL B cells express CD19, CD20, CD21, CD24, CD29/49D, CD40, CD44, CD45R, L-select, and sIgM/D; however, unlike peripheral blood B cells, CLL B cells generally do not express C3b complement receptor (CD35), CD11a/18, or CD22. In addition, CLL B cells express the T-cell-associated antigen CD5 and a number of antigens induced on normal B cells following in vitro activation. Normal CD5+ B cells, which phenotypically resemble CLL B cells, are present in fetal lymphoid tissue and in small numbers in the peripheral blood of adults. Moreover, normal CD5+ B cells are present in increased numbers in patients with autoimmune diseases. These findings support the hypothesis that CLL B cells are the neoplastic counterpart of one or more unique subpopulations of normal B cells.

Natural History and Its Modification with Treatment

The natural history of the disease varies according to stage, with a median survival ranging from 1½ years to 12+ years. Different treatment regimens at this time have not proven to change the overall survival; however, different studies have shown that progression to a higher stage can be delayed with different therapeutic approaches. The introduction of new drugs such as fludarabine, which induces complete remission in a significantly larger percentage of previously untreated patients, could possibly have an impact on disease-free survival and overall survival; however, current studies have to mature before this conclusion can be reached.

Prevention

Chronic lymphocytic leukemia does not appear to be associated with any particular risk factors and at this time no specific preventive measures are available.

Cost Containment

During routine follow-up, only routine complete blood counts and SMA-16 are indicated. In patients with a long doubling time, clinical follow-up visits could be scheduled every 12 to 16 weeks. Evaluating the peripheral smear when there are symptoms or signs suggestive of disease progression is usually a cost-effective method of providing important information.

REFERENCES

Cheson B. Chronic lymphocytic leukemia: Scientific advances and clinical developments. New York: Marcel Dekker, 1993.

Cheson BD, Bennet JM, Rai KR, et al. Guidelines for clinical protocols for chronic lymphocytic leukemia: Recommendations of the National Cancer Institute-sponsored Working Group. Am J Hematol 1988;29:152.

DeVitta VT Jr. Cancer: Principles and practice of oncology. 4th ed. Philadelphia: Lippincott, 1994.

Han T, Henderson ES, Emrich LJ, Sandberg AA. Prognostic significance of karyotypic abnormalities in B cell chronic lymphocyte leukemia: An update. Semin Hematol 1987;24:257.

Hoffman R. Hematology: Basic principles and practice. 2nd ed. New York: Churchill Livingstone, 1994.

Juliusson G, Oscier DG, Fitchett FM, et al. Prognostic subgroups in B-cell chronic lymphocytic leukemia defined by specific chromosomal abnormalities. N Engl J Med 1990;323:720.

Montserrat E, Sanchez-Bisono J, Vinolas N, Rozman C. Lymphocyte doubling time in chronic lymphocytic leukaemia: Analysis of its prognostic significance. Br J Haematol 1986;62:567.

Rozman C, Montserrat E, Rodriquez-Fernandez JM, et al. Bone marrow histologic pattern: The best single prognostic parameter in chronic lymphocytic leukemia: A multivariate survival analysis of 329 cases. Blood 1984;64:642.

Surveillance epidemiology and results incidence and mortality data, 1973–1977. NCI Monograph 57. Bethesda, MD: National Cancer Institute, 1981.

CHAPTER 12–26

Waldenström's Macroglobulinemia

G. Thomas Budd, M.D.

DEFINITION

Waldenström's macroglobulinemia is a disorder characterized by the proliferation and accumulation of immunoglobulin (Ig) M-secreting plasmacytoid malignant cells of lymphocytic origin.

ETIOLOGY

The etiology of Waldenström's macroglobulinemia is unknown, though a familial susceptibility may be present in some cases.

CRITERIA FOR DIAGNOSIS
Suggestive

Waldenström's macroglobulinemia is suggested by signs and symptoms related to plasma hyperviscosity, tissue infiltration by atypical lymphocytes, or an immunologic disorder that can be related to the monoclonal paraprotein. The finding of a monoclonal gammopathy on serum protein electrophoresis in such a setting would lead to more definitive testing. It should, however, be remembered that an IgM paraprotein may represent a monoclonal gammopathy of uncertain significance, and that for a malignant diagnosis to be made, some manifestation of malignancy must be present.

Definitive

To make a definite diagnosis of Waldenström's macroglobulinemia, it is necessary to demonstrate the production of a monoclonal protein of the IgM class and the presence of malignant lymphocytes of B-cell origin. The laboratory studies necessary to accomplish this are discussed below.

CLINICAL MANIFESTATIONS
Subjective

Waldenström's macroglobulinemia may present with a variety of signs and symptoms. The classic symptom complex associated with this disease is the constellation of findings associated with plasma hyperviscosity: mucosal bleeding, fatigue, dizziness, visual changes, and sausage-shaped retinal veins on fundoscopic examination. Tissue deposition of circulating paraprotein may produce a sensorimotor peripheral neuropathy. The paraprotein may also be associated with an immunologic disorder, such as cryoglobulinemia, hemolytic anemia, or immune thrombopenia. Tissue infiltration by the malignant B-cell clone produces hepatosplenomegaly or lymphadenopathy in about one third of patients. The presence of a cytopenia as a result of an immunologic disorder or infiltration of the hematopoietic system by atypical lymphocytes may produce thrombocytopenia and consequent bleeding or fatigue and other symptoms of anemia. Nowadays, many cases are detected after an abnormal complete blood count or serum total protein is noted.

Usually, the past medical history and family history give no suggestion of the diagnosis of macroglobulinemia, though familial clusters have been described. The disease occurs at a median age of 63 years and there is a slight male predominance (55%).

Objective
Physical Examination

Lymphadenopathy or splenomegaly is present in approximately one third of cases. Fundoscopic examination may reveal sausage-shaped retinal veins, which suggests the presence of plasma hyperviscosity. A peripheral neuropathy may be present in 5% of cases; this is usually of the mixed sensorimotor type.

Routine Laboratory Abnormalities

The most important routine laboratory abnormality is an elevation of the total protein on the serum chemistry profile due to paraproteinemia. Anemia is noted in 70% of cases, and thrombopenia in 30%.

PLANS
Diagnostic
Differential Diagnosis

A monoclonal gammopathy of the IgM class is essential for a diagnosis of Waldenström's macroglobulinemia, so that the differential diagnosis for this disorder is the differential diagnosis of IgM monoclonal gammopathy. Only about one fourth of patients with an IgM paraprotein will have Waldenström's macroglobulinemia. Rarely, lytic bone lesions are seen, in which case the disorder is termed IgM multiple myeloma rather than Waldenström's macroglobulinemia. In states other than Waldenström's macroglobulinemia or IgM myeloma, the quantity of the M-spike is usually less than 2.0 g/dL. Such an IgM M-component may be present in chronic lymphocytic leukemia, non-Hodgkin's lymphoma, or the cold hemagglutinin syndrome. A monoclonal gammopathy of uncertain significance (MGUS) may also be of the IgM class.

Diagnostic Options and Recommended Approach

To establish the presence of and characterize the monoclonal protein, initial serum protein electrophoresis should be followed by immunoelectrophoresis and quantitative immunoglobulin studies to demonstrate that the M-protein is of the IgM class and to characterize the disease as to light-chain type. Urine protein analysis should be performed, though only about 10% of patients will have urinary light-chain excretion. The serum viscosity should be determined, and monitored closely at levels greater than 3. Bone marrow aspiration and biopsy should be performed to demonstrate the presence of malignant lymphoid cells, which classically appear as plasmacytoid lymphocytes.

Therapeutic

In the event of symptomatic hyperviscosity syndrome, cryoglobulinemia, cold agglutinin hemolytic anemia, or peripheral neuropathy, plasmapheresis is the procedure most likely to reduce rapidly the quantity of circulating paraprotein. Although the value of the serum viscosity may not be strictly predictive of symptoms, patients with a serum viscosity (relative to normal) of 3 or greater should be monitored closely for signs and symptoms of hyperviscosity and plasmapheresis instituted in the event of symptoms.

Patients with symptomatic or progressive disease may also benefit from systemic chemotherapy. A combination of an alkylating agent, generally chlorambucil or cyclophosphamide, and a corticosteroid, generally prednisone, has been the standard regimen, inducing responses in approximately 50 to 60% of patients. After a stable remission has been induced, therapy may be discontinued and reinstituted at the time of recurrent symptoms or progressive disease. With this approach, the median survival for patients with Waldenström's macroglobulinemia is approximately 5 years. Interferon alfa may also be useful in selected cases. Great enthusiasm has developed for the use of the newer nucleoside analogs fludarabine and 2-chlorodeoxyadenosine. These agents produce objective responses in approximately 40% of patients with primary resistance to front-line therapy with the combination of an alkylating agent and a corticosteroid. Because of this activity, fludarabine and 2-chlorodeoxyadenosine have been studied as primary therapy, where initial reports have suggested that objective responses can be produced in 80% of patients. The long-term consequences of such therapy remain to be determined, however. It is anticipated that combination chemotherapy regimens employing these new agents will be developed.

FOLLOW-UP

While undergoing active therapy, patients with Waldenström's macroglobulinemia should be monitored closely to assess their disease status and the toxicity of therapy. Because pancytopenia may be a consequence of both the disease and its treatment, close monitoring of the complete blood count may be necessary during treatment. Disease activity may best be monitored by serial quantitation of the M-component. This may be accomplished by serum protein electrophoresis or laser nephelometry. Although the correlation between serum viscosity and the clinical manifestations of hyperviscosity is not strong, patients whose relative viscosity is greater than 3 are at increased risk of developing symptoms, and serial monitoring of viscosity should be performed if a patient is symptomatic or has a viscosity greater than 3. Because Waldenström's macroglobulinemia can have a long natural history, patients will experience periods of remission during which they receive no active therapy. Follow-up with physical examination, complete blood count, assessment of renal function, serum viscosity, and M-component quantitation should be performed every 2 to 3 months during these times, so that treatment can be reinstituted appropriately.

DISCUSSION
Prevalence and Incidence

Waldenström's macroglobulinemia is an uncommon disorder. It represents approximately 2% of hematologic malignancies, and is diagnosed in about 1500 Americans annually. It tends to affect the elderly, so that its incidence may vary with changes in the age distribution of the population in question.

Related Basic Science

The cause of Waldenström's macroglobulinemia is unknown. Familial clusters of macroglobulinemia and IgM monoclonal gammopathy of uncertain significance have been noted, suggesting a genetic component, but a family history is lacking in most cases and exposure to common environmental influences might also be invoked as an explanation for such clusters. No specific karyotypic abnormality has been described, though chromosomal abnormalities are relatively common and often complex in the disease. Gains or losses of chromosome 10, 12, or 20 are the most common findings, with occasional patients having the t(8;14) or t(14;18) translocations described in other lymphoid malignancies and which are associated with activation of the *C–MYC* or *BCL–2* oncogenes. Exposure to chronic antigen stimulation might be postulated as a cause of the disorder, but data to support such an hypothesis are scanty.

Natural History and Its Modification with Treatment

Waldenström's macroglobulinemia has a relatively long natural history, with the median survival being approximately 5 years. Treatment is most important in relieving the symptoms of the disease, and probably favorably affects survival. Patients who respond to chlorambucil have been reported to have survivals superior to those of nonresponders, but such analyses are subject to the length–time bias; that is, patients who respond to therapy must necessarily live long enough to manifest a response. Studies of prognostic factors for the disease have suggested that older age (>60 years), male sex, presence of general symptoms, and cytopenias are adverse prognostic factors. Interestingly, the initial tumor burden, as determined by the degree of marrow infiltration, organomegaly, or IgM level, does not seem to be an important prognostic factor. The causes of disease-related mortality are most often infection and pancytopenia.

Prevention

Because the cause of the disease is unknown, no preventive measures can be taken. Patients in whom a monoclonal gammopathy of uncertain significance is detected should be monitored, as progression to hematologic malignancy is common in such patients.

Cost Containment

Waldenström's macroglobulinemia is a rare disorder, so that it contributes little to the total health care budget. But, because of its chronic nature, attention must be paid to the cost consequences of diagnostic testing and therapy in individual patients. Once the disease is characterized, its activity is best monitored by relatively simple tests. Because therapy with the newer nucleosides is more expensive than therapy with an oral alkylating agent and a corticosteroid, it is important that the usefulness of early treatment with the more costly alternatives be clearly demonstrated in clinical trials.

REFERENCES

Dellagi K, Dupouey P, Brouet JC, et al. Waldenström's macroglobulinemia and peripheral neuropathy: A clinical and immunologic study of 25 patients. Blood 1983;62:280.

Dimopoulos MA, Alexanian R. Clinical review article: Waldenström's macroglobulinemia. Blood 1994;83:1452.

Dimopoulos MA, Kantarjian H, Estey E, et al. Treatment of Waldenström's macroglobulinemia with 2-chlorodeoxyadenosine. Ann Intern Med 1993;118:195.

Dimopoulos MA, O'Brien S, Kantarjian H, et al. Fludarabine therapy in Waldenström's macroglobulinemia. Am J Med 1993;95:49.

Facon T, Brouillard M, Duhamel A, et al. Prognostic factors in Waldenström's macroglobulinemia: A report of 167 patients. J Clin Oncol 1993;11:1553.

CHAPTER 12–27

Hairy Cell Leukemia

David J. Adelstein M.D.

DEFINITION

Hairy cell leukemia is a chronic B-cell lymphoproliferative malignancy originally called *leukemic reticuloendotheliosis* when first described in 1958. The name hairy cell leukemia comes from the appearance of the malignant cell, an atypical lymphocyte found in the peripheral blood with irregular cytoplasmic projections suggestive of hair (Figure 12–27–1).

ETIOLOGY

The etiology of this disease is unknown. There is no recognized contagious risk nor clear environmental exposure that can be considered responsible. Familial associations have been reported.

CRITERIA FOR DIAGNOSIS

Suggestive

The diagnosis of hairy cell leukemia is suggested by the clinical presentation of pancytopenia, splenomegaly, and the presence of atypical circulating lymphocytes in a middle-aged man.

Definitive

The diagnosis of hairy cell leukemia can be confirmed only after pathologic analysis of blood, bone marrow, and/or spleen.

CLINICAL MANIFESTATIONS

Subjective

Most patients with this disease are men in their fifth or sixth decade. The disease has not been reported in children.

The most common subjective complaints result from one or several of the hematologic cytopenias: anemia, leukopenia, or thrombocytopenia. Unlike other lymphoproliferative disorders, constitutional symptoms such as fever, night sweats, and weight loss are uncommon unless infection is present. Bleeding and/or symptoms of anemia can occur. Patients may also present with symptoms related to splenomegaly, such as abdominal fullness, discomfort, and early satiety. A distinct minority of patients are asymptomatic at presentation, with the diagnosis being considered only because of the detection of splenomegaly or a hematologic cytopenia on a routine or other examination.

Past medical history and family history generally do not contribute to the diagnosis of this illness.

Objective

Physical Examination

The most reproducible finding on physical examination is splenomegaly. This can, on occasion, be massive. A minority of patients, however, present with no clinically evident splenomegaly. Hepatomegaly and lymph node enlargement have also been described, but generally represent later manifestations of more advanced disease.

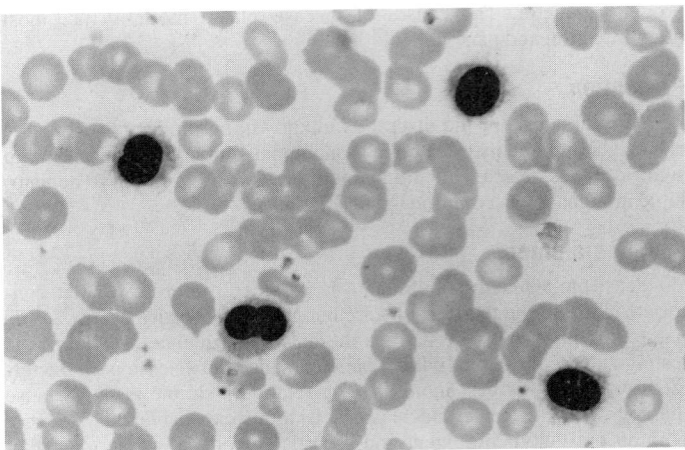

Figure 12–27–1. Photomicrograph of a peripheral blood smear from a patient with hairy cell leukemia. Note the cytoplasmic projections on the atypical lymphocyte suggestive of "hairs."

Bone and/or skin involvement, as well as other extranodal disease, may occur, but is distinctly uncommon. Other disease manifestations may result from complications of the presenting cytopenias.

Routine Laboratory Abnormalities

Laboratory evaluation is notable for the pancytopenia, although the degree of abnormality can be quite variable. Mild asymptomatic thrombocytopenia and/or anemia may be the only clinical clues to diagnosis, or patients may present with profound symptomatology from anemia, infection, or thrombocytopenic purpura. Despite the name *hairy cell leukemia,* most patients are leukopenic. Specifically, neutropenia and very marked monocytopenia are the rule. Circulating hairy cells may be infrequent or abundant. Only a minority present with circulating hairy cell counts above 10,000/μL. There are no diagnostic biochemical abnormalities in the peripheral blood and it is uncommon for patients to present with significant elevations in uric acid or lactate dehydrogenase levels, as in the more aggressive lymphoproliferative disorders.

PLANS

Diagnostic

Differential Diagnosis

Although the diagnosis should be considered in any middle-aged man with pancytopenia and splenomegaly, the presence of hairy cell leukemia cannot be confirmed without more specific testing. Differential diagnostic possibilities are multiple depending on the nature and extent of the clinical manifestations. Pancytopenia and splenomegaly are not uncommon presenting manifestations of multiple hematologic neoplasms, including other lymphoproliferative disorders, myeloproliferative disorders, and myelodysplastic syndromes. Aplastic anemia, acute leukemia, and even mast cell diseases, as well as some of the more uncommon true histiocytic disorders, must be considered. If circulating atypical lymphocytes are found, particularly if their appearance is consistent with circulating hairy cells (Figure 12–27–1), a low-grade lymphoproliferative malignancy such as hairy cell leukemia is suggested.

Diagnostic Options and Recommended Approach

This clinical presentation, however, mandates a bone marrow examination, and bone marrow involvement is virtually universal in patients with hairy cell leukemia. It is not infrequent to find the bone marrow aspiration difficult and a "dry tap" may occur. This is a result of the associated fibrosis that is common in this disorder. Bone marrow biopsy, however, is often diagnostic. There may be a diffuse or patchy leukemic infiltrate with monotonous-appearing mononuclear cells. Although the hairlike projections seen in the peripheral blood cannot be

appreciated on bone marrow biopsy, a characteristic halo of pale-staining cytoplasm surrounds and separates the leukemic cell nuclei. This feature is readily apparent and has been described as a "fried egg" appearance. It is quite distinctive from the more densely packed nuclei found in other chronic low-grade lymphoproliferative malignancies. Although the marrow is most frequently hypercellular, on occasion hypocellular and even aplastic bone marrow biopsies have been described. Silver staining often demonstrates an increase in reticulin fibers, although gross fibrosis is uncommon.

If a sufficient number of malignant cells are present in the peripheral blood or can be obtained on bone marrow aspiration, cytochemical staining of the malignant cells is most useful. Hairy cells will stain positively for acid phosphatase, which is then resistant to digestion by tartrate. Tartrate-resistant acid phosphatase (TRAP) negative staining of hairy cell leukemia cells and positive staining in other lymphoproliferative malignancies, however, have been described, suggesting a need for further diagnostic confirmation. Similarly, a characteristic, but not completely diagnostic immunophenotype of these neoplastic cells has been described. Although multiple cytogenetic abnormalities have been reported, no pattern appears diagnostic.

Splenectomy is being performed less frequently in this disease, but the splenic morphology is also diagnostic. A diffuse infiltration of splenic red pulp cords and sinuses by hairy cells is seen. Similarly, the diagnosis can be suggested by the pathologic appearance of lymph node or liver biopsies.

Therapeutic

Therapeutic Options and Recommended Approach

The treatment of hairy cell leukemia has undergone dramatic improvement over the last decade. The disease has changed from a chronic incurable malignancy with a number of relatively ineffective treatments, to a highly treatable disease with several options available that may be capable of eradicating the neoplasm.

For decades, the initial treatment of choice was a splenectomy. The rationale was based on the recognition that at least some of the pancytopenia present in patients with hairy cell leukemia was due to hypersplenism. Particularly in those individuals with markedly enlarged spleens, splenectomy was often very effective in producing partial and complete hematologic remissions; however, this procedure did not address the underlying malignancy and its bone marrow involvement. As such, hematologic relapse eventually occurred in most patients. Furthermore, patients presenting without splenomegaly tended to have a considerably less impressive hematologic response, and splenectomy has now been largely replaced by the current systemic treatment options. Nonetheless, for those individuals with significant abdominal discomfort, splenic infarction, or rupture, splenectomy still remains a reasonable treatment consideration.

For those patients failing splenectomy, conventional chemotherapeutic agents such as corticosteroids and the alkylating agents, specifically low-dose daily chlorambucil, have been used. These have been only modestly successful, often producing significant toxicity by aggravating either the cytopenias or the immunologic dysfunction present in these patients. Treatment with these agents is, in general, no longer recommended.

The first of the modern treatments for hairy cell leukemia was recombinant interferon alfa. The efficacy of this intervention has been well established. Relatively low doses of interferon alfa can be given three times weekly and are capable of producing significant hematologic improvement in more than 80% of patients. Only a small fraction of these patients, however, experience complete disappearance of tumor. Treatment is often required for 6 months or longer and, although usually well tolerated, is associated with transient flulike symptoms and fatigue. Numerous mechanisms of action have been proposed, but this remains unclear. Unfortunately, after discontinuation of interferon therapy, disease recurrence is the rule.

Two new chemotherapeutic agents, both purine analogs, are currently approved for the treatment of patients with hairy cell leukemia. Deoxycoformycin (Pentostatin), an adenosine deaminase inhibitor, has produced responses in up to 100% of patients with hairy cell leukemia. These responses are complete in between 33 and 89% of patients and may be durable in more than half. Normalization of blood counts occurs quickly, although treatment may be complicated by profound neutropenia and severe viral infections, most notably with herpes simplex and zoster. Abnormalities of immune function, including T-lymphocyte depression, have persisted for significant periods after treatment is discontinued. Both complete response rates and relapse-free survival were superior when previously untreated patients treated with deoxycoformycin were compared with an untreated population treated with interferon alfa.

2-Chlorodeoxyadenosine is the newest purine analog released for the treatment of hairy cell leukemia. A single course of therapy with this drug, given as a 7-day continuous intravenous infusion, has produced complete responses in up to 80% of patients. These responses appear durable and the suggestion that this treatment may be curative has been made. Treatment is well tolerated, with the major side effect being a fever which is often related to the resultant transient neutropenia. Immunologic suppression also appears to result from treatment with this agent, although its duration and clinical significance are unclear.

As such, there are now three nonsurgical alternatives that can be chosen as the initial management in patients with this disease. The excellent tolerance and ease of administration of 2-chlorodeoxyadenosine suggest that it may emerge as the treatment of choice. Longer-term follow-up is required. The durability of the remissions induced by 2-chlorodeoxyadenosine and deoxycoformycin, however, suggest that neither splenectomy nor interferon is an intervention of first choice. Furthermore, the former practice of deferring intervention until symptomatic cytopenias develop must also be questioned. The ability to produce long-term, if not permanent, remission with the use of chemotherapy suggests that early treatment, immediately after diagnosis, is the preferable strategy.

The availability of growth factors, such as granulocyte colony-stimulating factor and granulocyte-macrophage colony-stimulating factor, provides an additional dimension to our treatment capability. Leukopenia and monocytopenia may pose significant hazards in the treatment of patients with hairy cell leukemia. The use of growth factors has been shown to reduce the degree of myelosuppression and may prove a valuable adjunctive treatment in the initial phases of disease management.

FOLLOW-UP

The frequency of patient follow-up visits is entirely dependent on the patient's clinical status. Significant myelosuppression is common immediately after initial therapeutic intervention and requires close monitoring. Hematologic and antibiotic support may be required. After remission induction, however, less frequent follow-up is appropriate. This disease is indolent in its progression and is unlikely to produce sudden hematologic deterioration.

DISCUSSION

Prevalence and Incidence

Hairy cell leukemia is an uncommon disease representing less than 2% of adult leukemias. Only 500 to 600 cases are diagnosed annually. Its unique morphology as well as the recent improvements in its treatment have produced considerable interest in this disorder, however.

Related Basic Science

No clear normal counterpart has been identified for the malignant hairy cell. It appears to be a preplasma cell of B-cell lineage, although occa-

sional cases of hairy cell leukemia with T-cell characteristics have been identified. The etiology of the profound monocytopenia found in this disease is unknown. Other immunologic derangements common in patients with this disorder include a reduction in total T lymphocytes, or a reversal of the CD4/CD8 ratio, and defective natural killer cell function. This lymphocyte dysfunction, the monocytopenia, and the not infrequent neutropenia all contribute to a heightened risk of infectious complications in the untreated patient. In particular, an association with infections by atypical mycobacteria such as *Mycobacterium kansasii* has been noted. The additional association between hairy cell leukemia and a number of autoimmune disorders, including several vasculitides, may also reflect disease-induced immune dysfunction.

Natural History and Its Modification with Treatment

Before the recent development of effective systemic therapy, the median survival for patients with hairy cell leukemia was between 4 and 5 years, although very mild disease manifestations requiring no treatment were seen in up to 10% of patients. There can be no doubt, however, that recent treatment success has dramatically changed the natural history of this illness. The expectations from these interventions are unknown, given the short-term follow-up of most patients treated with newer agents such as deoxycoformycin and 2-chlorodeoxyadenosine. It does, however, appear that long-term, unmaintained remission is possible with both of these medications and that the potential for cure may exist. Whether this will result from single-agent therapy or will require further treatment combinations or innovations is unclear at present; however, the restoration of a normal life expectancy is a reasonable treatment goal for these patients. Indeed, the issues of greater concern may be the long-term effects of these immunosuppressive agents on the risk of infection, autoimmune disorders, and second malignancies.

Prevention

In the absence of a clear etiology, no preventive measures are available.

Cost Containment

The cost of disease management has also evolved dramatically in the past decade. Hairy cell leukemia has changed from a chronic disease requiring multiple interventions and hospitalizations to a potentially curable disease after treatment with a single course of chemotherapy. The implications for cost control are profound. The diagnosis can be established relatively simply, and early effective treatment can be rapidly initiated. Cost issues may ultimately prove most important in deciding among the effective available treatments.

REFERENCES

Bouroncle BA, Wiseman BK, Doan CA. Leukemic reticulendotheliosis. Blood 1958;13:609.

Chang KL, Stroup R, Weiss LM. Hairy cell leukemia. Current status. Am J Clin Pathol 1992;97:719.

Jaiyesimi IA, Kantarjian HM, Estey EH. Advances in therapy for hairy cell leukemia: A review. Cancer 1993;72:5.

Saven A, Piro L. Newer purine analogues for the treatment of hairy-cell leukemia. N Engl J Med 1994;330:691.

CHAPTER 12–28

Multiple Myeloma

Mohamad A. Hussein, M.B., B.Ch., M.D.

DEFINITION

Multiple myeloma is a prototype of a group of conditions known as plasma cell neoplasms. Plasma cell neoplasms are a group of related disorders, each of which is associated with proliferation and accumulation of immunoglobulin-secreting cells that are derived from the B-cell series.

ETIOLOGY

There is no clear etiologic factor; however, radiation exposure may be implicated, as people who entered Hiroshima within 3 days of the blasts had nearly a 60% greater risk of dying of myeloma than those not exposed. It was known that radiologists experienced an excess of myeloma deaths 30 years ago, and even with modern equipment and protective gear, they still have a twofold excess myeloma risk.

CRITERIA FOR DIAGNOSIS

Suggestive

Unexplained weakness or fatigue, anemia, macrocytosis, elevation of the erythrocyte sedimentation rate, back pain, osteoporosis, osteolytic lesions or fractures, immunoglobulin deficiency, hyperglobulinemia, hypercalcemia, renal insufficiency, and recurrent infections suggest the diagnosis. It should be considered in adults with sensory or motor peripheral neuropathy, carpal tunnel syndrome, refractory congestive heart failure, nephrotic syndrome, orthostatic hypotension, or malabsorption.

Definitive

No single test differentiates benign from malignant plasma cell proliferation (Table 12–28–1). The most dependable method involves serial measurements of the monoclonal protein in the serum and urine as well as periodic evaluation of pertinent clinical and laboratory features to determine whether multiple myeloma, systemic amyloidosis, macroglobulinemia, or another plasma cell proliferative disease has developed. The diagnostic features of monoclonal gammopathy of unknown significance, smoldering myeloma, indolent myeloma, and multiple myeloma are detailed in the table. The multiplicity of criteria reflects the lack of a single reliable diagnostic test to distinguish the entities.

CLINICAL MANIFESTATIONS

The clinical features of multiple myeloma develop from tissue damage by multiple bone tumors, complications from the monoclonal component, and an increased vulnerability to infection due to depressed normal immunoglobulin levels. These complications provide the first clues to the diagnosis and form the basis for defining the stage and prognosis.

Subjective

All patients who present with monoclonal gammopathy of unknown significance are asymptomatic relative to the monoclonal protein. Long-term follow-up of these patients demonstrates that over a 10-year period, 25% develop multiple myeloma, macroglobulinemia, amyloidosis, or related diseases. The interval from recognition of the monoclonal gammopathy to the diagnosis of multiple myeloma ranges from 2 to 20 years (median, 10 years).

Bone pain, the most common symptom, results from pathologic fractures. Compression fractures of the thoracic and lumbar vertebral bodies usually result in severe spasms and back pain. Multiple compression fractures may culminate in painless dorsal kyphosis and loss of as much as 6 in. of height. Pleuritic pain from pathologic rib and clavicle fractures is also common and is associated with marked local tenderness.

Destruction of the proximal bones of the extremities is less frequent, and distal bones of the extremities are rarely affected.

Bandlike or radicular pain should alert the clinician to impending spinal cord compression, which is a serious complication representing an emergency requiring immediate diagnosis and treatment.

Nausea, confusion, polyuria, and constipation are common symptoms secondary to hypercalcemia, which occurs in 25% of patients at diagnosis.

Easy fatigability or dyspnea on exertion is usually secondary to anemia, which is present in most patients at presentation.

When immunoglobulins (Igs) are present at concentrations greater than 5 g/dL some IgG or IgA myeloma globulins can produce features of the hyperviscosity syndrome. Symptoms and signs of this condition are generally not seen unless the relative serum viscosity is greater than 4.0 units. Lassitude, confusion, headaches, transient disturbances of vision, and increased bleeding tendency could be related to this syndrome.

Recurrent bacterial infections are a major cause of illness and the most frequent cause of death in patients with advanced myeloma. Infections result primarily from the marked depression of production of normal immunoglobulins that occurs in more than 75% of the patients.

TABLE 12–28–1. DIAGNOSTIC CRITERIA FOR MULTIPLE MYELOMA, MYELOMA VARIANTS, AND MONOCLONAL GAMMOPATHY OF UNKNOWN SIGNIFICANCE

Multiple Myeloma*
Major Criteria
    Plasmacytoma on tissue biopsy
    Bone marrow plasmacytosis with >30% plasma cells
    Monoclonal globulin spike on serum electrophoresis exceeding 3.5 g/dL for IgG peaks or 2.0 g/dL for IgA peaks; Bence Jones protein excretion ≥ 1.0 g/24 h; or light-chain excretion on urine electrophoresis in the presence of amyloidosis
Minor Criteria
    Bone marrow plasmacytosis with 10–30% plasma cells
    Monoclonal globulin spike present, but less than the level defined above
    Lytic bone lesions
    Residual normal IgM < 50 mg/dL, IgA < 100 mg/dL, or IgG < 600 mg/dL

Indolent Myeloma
No bone lesions or limited to 2 or 3 small lytic lesions; no compression fractures
Bone marrow plasma cells 20–30%
Monoclonal component level: IgG < 7.0 g/dL *or* IgA < 5.0 g/dL
No symptoms or associated features, i.e.,
    performance status > 70%, hemoglobin > 10 g/dL, serum calcium normal, serum creatine < 2.0 mg/dL, no infections

Smoldering Myeloma
Bone marrow plasma cells 10–20%
    No bone lesions
    Monoclonal component level:
        IgG > 3.5 g/dL or IgA > 2.0 g/dL or BJ ≤ 1.0 g/24 h
    No symptoms or associated disease features

Monoclonal Gammopathy of Unknown Significance
    Monoclonal gammopathy
    Monoclonal component level:
        IgG ≤ 3.5 g/dL *or* IgA ≤ 2.0 g/dL
    Bence Jones protein excretion ≤ 1.0 g/24 hours
    Bone marrow plasma cells ≤ 10%
    No bone lesions
    No symptoms, no anemia, no hypercalcemia or renal failure

*Diagnosis of multiple myeloma in symptomatic patients with clearly progressive disease requires a minimum of one major and one minor criterion (bone marrow plasmacytosis is not sufficient with plasmacytoma), or three minor criteria that must include bone marrow plasmacytosis and monoclonal globulin spike.

Systemic amyloidosis occurs in approximately 15% of patients with multiple myeloma. The presenting symptoms of amyloidosis with or without multiple myeloma include weakness, weight loss, ankle edema, dyspnea, paresthesia, lightheadedness, and syncope. Aching in the hands, particularly at night, can signify median nerve compression associated with carpal tunnel syndrome caused by amyloid infiltration of the transverse carpal ligament.

Objective

Physical Examination

No specific physical abnormality may be detected. Most patients with symptomatic myeloma have tenderness on pressure over an involved bone, kyphoses, or a pathologic fracture to indicate the site of bone lesions. In approximately 15% of patients, firm plasma cell tumors arise from areas of underlying bone destruction and may be palpated on the skull, sternum, clavicles, and ribs, where the affected bone is close to the skin. Fundal examination, especially in patients with suspected hyperviscosity syndrome, could reveal segmental dilation of retinal veins with retinal hemorrhages. Mouth, throat, and neck examination might reveal extramedullary plasmacytomas, which usually develop in the nasopharyngeal area or paranasal sinuses. Signs of lobular pneumonia could be detected on auscultation and palpation of the chest. In the rare instances where pleural effusion may develop from plasmacytomas and plasmacytosis, pleural effusion could be detected clinically and radiologically. Cardiac examination could reveal ventricular gallop as a sign of failure secondary to severe anemia, hyperkalemia, or amyloid heart disease. Neurologic signs could be caused by spinal cord or nerve root compression, sensorimotor peripheral neuropathy, or myelomatosis meningitis. Spinal examination could reveal kyphoses and, on palpation, tenderness at the areas of fractures or plasmacytomas; also, palpation could trigger radiculopathy, which could help in localizing the site of an imminent cord compression. Upper extremities could demonstrate signs of carpal tunnel syndrome. Skin plaques secondary to amyloid deposits and joint effusions may be presenting features. Generalized edema secondary to nephrotic syndrome and/or congestive heart failure could be elicited on the physical examination.

Routine Laboratory Abnormalities

Routine laboratory screens, complete blood count, SMA–16, urinalysis, and chest x-ray are usually nonspecific with respect to reaching a diagnosis; but are extremely helpful in pointing to specific diagnostic procedures.

Cytopenias. Anemia is present in most patients and is a major diagnostic clue. Several factors account for anemia, such as bone marrow infiltration by plasma cells, renal failure, and chronic disease. Low serum B_{12} levels may occur without signs of functional B_{12} deficiency; however, evaluation for B_{12} deficiency should be sought. High levels of IgA or IgG frequently increase the plasma volume and the hematocrit may be 6% points less than the value expected from the measured red cell volume.

Thrombocytopenia. Thrombocytopenia is uncommon at the time of diagnosis and usually reflects a marked degree of bone marrow replacement by plasma cells.

Mild Granulocytopenia. Mild granulocytopenia occurs frequently for reasons that are unclear and usually persists throughout the clinical course. Plasma cell leukemia with more than 2×10^9 plasma cells/L usually signifies extensive bone marrow infiltration and is seen primarily during the late phase of the disease.

Chemical and Metabolic Abnormalities. Elevated total globulins, hypoalbuminemia, or overall hypoproteinemia secondary to nephrotic syndrome may be observed, as may hypercalcemia, hyperuricemia, increased serum creatinine secondary to the multiple myeloma, protein or metabolic changes. An increased level of lactate dehydrogenase is noted in 10 to 15% of patients and usually signifies a poor prognosis. The serum alkaline phosphatase is usually normal but may be elevated in patients with healing pathologic fractures or osteosclerotic lesions. Proteinuria is detected in approximately 65% of patients.

Chest X-Ray. The chest radiograph may reveal osteolytic lesions in the clavicles, scapulae, or ribs; a subpleural plasmacytoma attached to a rib; or a pleural effusion. Cardiomegaly may be seen in patients with cardiac amyloidosis.

PLANS
Diagnostic
Differential Diagnosis

Lytic bone lesions must not be related to metastatic carcinoma, connective tissue diseases, chronic infections, or lymphoma.

Patients with multiple myeloma must be differentiated from those with monoclonal gammopathy of unknown significance and smoldering multiple myeloma (see Table 12–28–1).

Bone pain, anemia, and renal insufficiency constitute a triad strongly suggestive of multiple myeloma. Minimal criteria for the diagnosis of multiple myeloma are a bone marrow with more than 10% plasma cells or a plasmacytoma plus one of the following: M-protein in the serum (usually at a level above 3 g/dL) and M-protein in the urine.

Diagnostic Options

When plasma cell dyscrasia is suspected the following tests should be performed to confirm the diagnosis, detect complications, assess the stage of disease, and establish baseline values for following the treatment progress:

- Serum and urine protein electrophoresis, supplemented by immunoelectrophoresis and immunofixation, when multiple myeloma, macroglobulinemia, amyloidosis, or other related disorders are suspected
- 24-hour urine collection for total protein (grams per 24 hours)
- Serum β_2-microglobulin
- Quantitative immunoglobulins
- C-reactive protein
- Bone marrow aspiration and biopsy with cytogenetics
- Complete skeletal survey (skull, ribs, vertebrae, pelvis, long bones of the arms and legs)
- Magnetic resonance imaging of the spine if spinal cord compression is suspected to confirm the site and extent or to differentiate between early myeloma that requires therapy and early myeloma that can be monitored without treatment
- Myelogram to evaluate for cord compression if magnetic resonance imaging is not available
- Cerebrospinal fluid examination with cytospine and protein electrophoresis in patients with neurologic symptoms unexplained by metabolic changes. (The detection of plasma cells in the cerebrospinal fluid indicates meningeal involvement by myeloma cells.)

Recommended Approach

The hallmark of plasma cell dyscrasias is a monoclonal immunoglobulin in the serum, urine, or both, which occurs in approximately 99% of cases. In 1% of patients, nonsecretory multiple myeloma occurs secondary to a defect in the synthesis or assembly of light or heavy chains. Immunoelectrophoresis and immunofixation are rather expensive; however, they are very sensitive when compared with protein electrophoresis, which could miss up to 15% of monoclonal gammopathies.

Urine should always be evaluated for M-protein, even if no abnormal M-protein is detected in the serum, as a significant number of patients could be missed if this procedure is ignored.

Serum β_2-microglobulin is the light chain of the major histocompatibility complex in the cell membrane. Serum β_2-microglobulin levels are found to be elevated in patients with active multiple myeloma. A close relationship is noted between serum β_2-microglobulin (uncorrected for serum creatine) and measured myeloma cell mass. Patients can be assigned to low-risk, medium-risk, and high-risk groups on the basis of serum β_2-microglobulin. Levels greater than 6 mg/dL are indicative of a large tumor mass and poor prognosis.

C-reactive protein production is controlled by interleukin-6 (IL-6) in vivo and is a convenient and direct indicator of IL-6 production. IL-6 promotes growth of fresh human myeloma cells in vitro, and patients with terminal myeloma, especially plasma cell leukemia, have higher serum IL-6 levels than patients with stable myeloma.

Bone marrow aspiration and biopsy are helpful in evaluating the different etiologies of the cytopenias and are also crucial in diagnosing multiple myeloma as well as evaluating cell morphology for prognosis. If available, a plasma cell labeling index on the bone marrow could add important prognostic information and possibly aid in structuring the management plans for the patient. A labeling index less than or equal to 0.8% usually indicates a good prognosis. Bone marrow plasmacytosis may be spotty, but an increase in bone marrow plasma cells is usually easy to demonstrate from most bone marrow sites. Cytogenetic abnormalities occur in 30% of multiple myeloma patients. Numeric anomalies occurred most often in chromosome 11, and structural aberrations occurred most often in chromosomes 1, 11, and 14. Irrespective of treatment status, patients with an abnormal karyotype had a significant shorter median survival than patients with a normal karyotype.

A complete skeletal survey does aid diagnosis; however, more importantly, it helps in evaluating lytic lesions in stress areas that might require radiation treatment to prevent pathologic fractures.

Magnetic resonance imaging or a myelogram, if the former is not available, is crucial to evaluating suspected spinal cord compression as well as in managing this emergency complication. In patients with early multiple myeloma, a magnetic resonance imaging scan of the lumbosacral area could aid in treatment decisions, in that patients with a normal bone marrow signal could be watched without treatment without any detrimental effects regarding complications or overall survival. Over the long run this might be cost effective.

Note that diffuse osteoporosis is one of the radiologic signs of multiple myeloma. About 1% of patients with multiple myeloma develop osteosclerotic bone lesions, a sensorimotor polyneuropathy. The combination of polyneuropathy, organomegaly, endocrinopathy, and M-protein with skin changes is known as POEMS syndrome.

Therapeutic

Patients with monoclonal gammopathy of unknown significance do not require any specific therapy; however, because over a 10-year period 25% of these patients will progress to some form of lymphoproliferative disorder, follow-up is necessary.

Patients with smoldering multiple myeloma require no specific therapy and should be watched carefully to determine the time to initiate therapy. Therapy within the scope of an investigational protocol could be considered.

Indolent multiple myeloma should be carefully evaluated to determine if early therapy is indicated. Otherwise, careful follow-up or enrollment in an investigational protocol is recommended.

Therapy for multiple myeloma can be artificially classified into definitive treatment of the disease and treatment of complications related to the disease.

Therapeutic Options for Definitive Treatment of Multiple Myeloma

Chemotherapy at standard doses is the mainstay of treatment of multiple myeloma. Chemotherapy with regimens comprising a single or multiple alkylating agents are available for therapy. The melphalan/prednisone regimen, introduced over 20 years ago and not significantly modified since that time, remains a simple, effective regimen to improve upon. Combination chemotherapy was introduced in the early 1970s on the strength of theoretic and experimental evidence. Despite strong arguments in its favor, combination chemotherapy has not led to a significantly longer survival than therapy with melphalan and prednisone in most randomized trials, although there is not complete agreement regarding this point. The VAD combination regimen comprises vincristine 0.4 mg by intravenous continuous infusion daily for 4 days; Adriamycin [doxorubicin] 9 mg/m^2 per day by intravenous continuous infusion for 4 days; and dexamethasone 40 mg daily for 4 days to be repeated every 4 weeks. The VBAP regimen consists of vincristine 2.0 mg intravenously on day 1, carmustine (BCNU) 30 mg/m^2 intravenously on day 1, Adriamycin 30 mg/m^2 on day 1, and prednisone 60 mg daily for 5 days, with the entire regimen being repeated every 3 to 4 weeks. These are two of several combinations.

Recommended Approach for Definitive Treatment

Patients should be encouraged to participate in investigational protocols.

The recommended regimen consists of melphalan 0.25 mg/kg/d orally for 4 days and prednisone 100 mg orally daily for 4 days, to be repeated every 4 to 6 weeks. It is crucial to check blood counts in 2 weeks, at which point the dose of melphalan should be altered until modest midcycle cytopenia occurs. This regimen should be continued for 1 to 2 years and discontinued when the M-protein levels in serum and urine have been stable for at least 6 months without any evidence of active disease.

Chemotherapy is the preferred initial treatment for symptomatic multiple myeloma; however, palliative radiation in a dose of 2000 to 3000 cGy should be limited to patients with disabling pain who have a well-defined focal process that has not responded to chemotherapy.

Analgesics plus chemotherapy usually can control the pain. Methadone 5 to 10 mg orally every 6 hours is usually adequate. This should be combined with a bowel regimen to avoid constipation; Colace 100 mg twice daily and encouraging oral fluid intake are usually adequate.

Recommended Approach for Primary and Secondary Resistance

A common and challenging clinical problem is that resistance to treatment can be primary or secondary. High doses of pulse glucocorticoids appear to be the best treatment, with an expected response rate of 40% (defined as a reduction in the monoclonal protein concentration of 50% or more). Pulse steroids could be given as methylprednisolone 2 g intravenously three times weekly for a minimum of 4 weeks; if there is a response, then administration of methylprednisolone is reduced to once or twice weekly. Another approach would be decadron 40 mg orally every day for 4 days, to be repeated every 2 weeks and to be reduced to every month. Both regimens should be accompanied by sucralfate (Carafate), or H-pump blocker, or H$_2$ blocker as well as Bactrim DS once a day.

If an investigational protocol is available, these patients should be strongly encouraged to participate.

In *secondary resistance,* patients are sub-divided into two groups. For patients who relapse during therapy or within 6 months of discontinuation of therapy, the combination of vincristine, doxorubicin, and dexamethasone is one of the most effective salvage therapies, resulting in approximately 75% response rates. For patients who relapse more than 6 months after stopping therapy (an unmaintained remission), restarting the initial therapy leads to recontrol 60 to 70% of the time. If progression is observed or if there is a response and then relapse in this setting, vincristine, doxorubicin, and dexamethasone chemotherapy can be administered. If an investigational protocol is available, these patients should be strongly encouraged to participate.

Recommended Approach for Maintenance Therapy

The ideal duration of chemotherapy is unknown. Cessation of chemotherapy usually results in relapse, but continued chemotherapy may lead to the development of a myelodysplastic syndrome or acute leukemia. In a randomized trial no difference in survival was found between patients receiving continuous melphalan and prednisone and those receiving no maintenance therapy. Chemotherapy should be continued for 1 to 2 years and then discontinued if serum and urine M-protein levels have been stable for at least 6 months and the patient has no further evidence of active disease. The patient should be followed closely and chemotherapy reinstituted when relapse occurs.

Interferon alfa might be beneficial in prolonging the plateau phase in patients with multiple myeloma.

Recommended Approach in the Management of Complications Related to Multiple Myeloma

Bone Destruction. The physician should encourage physical activity and supervise its progress regularly, especially in disabled, hospitalized patients. For most patients with mild or moderate back pain due to vertebral compression fractures, rational use of analgesics, corsets, and walkers is sufficient. Radiotherapy (approximately 2500 cGy given over 7–10 days) may be necessary to relieve severe localized pain, but should be delayed in patients with newly diagnosed multiple myeloma until the benefits from the first course of chemotherapy have been assessed. Radiation therapy to lytic lesions occupying 50% or more of long bones should be given prophylactically to prevent pathologic fractures.

Preventing paraplegia. When cord compression is suspected an emergency dose of dexamethasone, 20 mg intravenously should be given, followed by 10 mg intravenously or orally every 6 hours for maintenance until the diagnosis is ruled out or confirmed, at which point the regimen is discontinued or continued, respectively. Radiation therapy is to be initiated immediately at the site of cord compression secondary to plasmacytoma. Sucralfate, H_2 blockers, or H-pump blockers should be used simultaneously with steroids.

Hypercalcemia. Hydration, diuresis, corticosteroids, and chemotherapy should be of help, especially in previously untreated patients. Bedridden patients with pathologic fractures from advanced myeloma refractory to all available therapies may have increased pain and may need more narcotic analgesics when hypercalcemia is controlled; therefore, control of hypercalcemia in this setting may be unjustified.

Hyperviscosity. Plasma exchange with albumin in which a volume and a half is exchanged at each treatment alleviates symptoms. Tumor control with chemotherapy reduces myeloma globulin levels and the risk of hyperviscosity. If remission is not achieved, regular plasma exchange is necessary to prevent and control serum hyperviscosity. Anemic patients should be transfused cautiously to prevent worsening of hyperviscosity signs and symptoms.

Renal Failure. The combination of hydration, glucocorticoids for hypercalcemia, and chemotherapy rapidly reverses mild renal failure in approximately 50% of the patients.

Infections. *Streptococcus pneumoniae* and *Hemophilus influenzae* are the most common pathogens in previously untreated myeloma patients and in nonneutropenic patients who respond to chemotherapy. Depending on the clinical picture, therapy with oral or intravenous antibiotics should be instituted. In neutropenic patients and in those with refractory disease, *Staphylococcus aureus* and Gram-negative bacteria are the predominant organisms. Vaccines containing live organisms are contraindicated in patients with myeloma because of their immunodeficiency, which permits infections to disseminate.

FOLLOW-UP

Patients should be evaluated every 4 to 6 weeks. The physical examination should assess height, weight, and temperature, as well as how well the pain is controlled and the amount of pain medications required to keep the patient comfortable. Blood work should include blood counts, blood chemistries, serum protein electrophoresis, and, if demonstrated at the time of diagnosis, 24-hour urine for protein quantitation.

During the maintenance period, off any therapy, patients should be evaluated every 2 to 3 months by physical examination, blood counts, blood chemistries, serum protein electrophoresis to evaluate the amount of M-protein, and 24-hour urine to evaluate the amount of M-protein if documented at the time of diagnosis. A complete bone survey is recommended every 12 to 18 months or sooner if clinically indicated.

DISCUSSION
Prevalence and Incidence

Multiple myeloma accounted for about 1% of all malignant neoplasms in whites and double that in African-Americans in the United States. In whites, the average incidence rate is almost 5 in men and slightly less in women per 100,000 population. The incidence is almost double these figures in African-Americans. Multiple myeloma accounts for about

one third of the lymphoproliferative neoplasms among African-Americans and almost 15% among the white population. There is no clear explanation for the difference in incidence between African-Americans and whites. Exposure to radiation is the only known risk factor associated with the increased incidence of multiple myeloma. The strongest evidence linking radiation to myeloma comes from studies of atomic bomb survivors. Radiologists are observed to have excess myeloma deaths and, despite recent advances in machinery and protective measures, these professionals still have a two-fold excess myeloma risk. First-degree relatives of myeloma patients appear to have a higher incidence and familial myeloma has been the subject of case reports.

Related Basic Science

Interleukin-6 promotes growth of fresh human multiple myeloma cells in vitro, making it possible to obtain myeloma cell lines whose proliferation depends completely on exogenous IL-6. Patients with terminal myeloma, especially plasma cell leukemia, have higher serum IL-6 levels than patients with stable myeloma. Overproduction of IL-6 in multiple myeloma patients is directly evident by increased production of C-reactive protein. IL-6 also appears to interact with other hematopoietic growth factors and cytokines, such as granulocyte and granulocyte–macrophage, colony-stimulating factors, Interleukin-1β, and tumor necrosis factor. In multiple myeloma patients, treatment with anti-IL-6 monoclonal antibody blocks C-reactive protein production but also results in clinical remissions.

Natural History and Its Modification with Treatment

The medium survival of persons with multiple myeloma without any treatment is 7 months. Since the introduction of chemotherapy, the median survival has improved to 36 to 48 months. Secondary acute leukemia develops in approximately 2% of patients who survive 2 years, which is 50 to 100 times more frequently than in normal individuals. Cytogenetic studies almost always confirm loss or deletion of the long arm of chromosome 5 or 7, or both. These karyotypic patterns are similar to those of patients with acute myeloid leukemia treated previously with radiation, chemotherapy, or both, or with other malignant or nonmalignant diseases. Fewer than 5% of patients with multiple myeloma have acute leukemia at diagnosis or acquire it within several months of starting chemotherapy. The frequency of solid tumors in multiple myeloma patients is no higher than in persons of similar age or sex.

Prevention

There have been substantial advances in our understanding of multiple myeloma and related plasma cell neoplasms over the past two decades. Unfortunately, at this time no clear factors are known that cause or influence the incidence of the disease, and development of preventive strategies awaits such discoveries.

Cost Containment

The management plan outlined for diagnosis and treatment is cost effective; however, the following procedures are of no or little value and should be requested only in special circumstances: bone scans; and resection of solitary plasmacytomas or repair of lytic lesions with bone grafts and bone cement.

REFERENCES

Hoffman R. Hematology: Basic principles and practice. 2nd ed. New York: Churchill Livingstone, 1994.
Hussein MA. Multiple myeloma: An overview of diagnosis and management. Cleveland Clin J Med 1994;61:285.
Malpas JS, Bergsagel DE, Kyle RA. Myeloma: Biology and management. New York: Oxford Medical, 1995.

CHAPTER 12–29

Amyloidosis

Mohamad A. Hussein, M.B., B.Ch., M.D.

DEFINITION

Amyloid is a substance that has a homogenous, amorphous appearance under the light microscope and stains pink with hematoxylin and eosin. Under polarized light, amyloid stained with Congo red produces an apple-green birefringence. The patient is said to have amyloidosis when the material is deposited in the tissues.

ETIOLOGY

Amyloidosis results from the interplay of many factors. Its cause is unknown.

CRITERIA FOR DIAGNOSIS

Subjective

The clinical diagnosis is usually delayed either because the initiating mechanism is unclear (as in primary amyloidosis) or the signs and symptoms of the primary disease mask or merge with those of the deposition of amyloid itself. Amyloidosis should be suspected with the insidious onset of unexplained proteinuria or renal failure, hepatomegaly, splenomegaly, macroglossia, peripheral neuropathy, malabsorption, or cardiomyopathy.

Definitive

The diagnosis is established by the demonstration of amyloid in tissue specimens (abdominal fat aspirate 80% of the time, bone marrow biopsy 50% of the time, rectal biopsy 80% of the time, or a specific organ). All amyloid deposits exhibit an apple-green birefringence when observed with the Congo red stain under polarized light microscopy.

CLINICAL MANIFESTATIONS

Subjective

Weakness or fatigue and weight loss are the most frequent symptoms. Dyspnea, pedal edema, angina pectoris, arrhythmias, syncope, and lightheadedness occur secondary to the congestive heart failure and orthostatic hypotension that often develop during the course of the disease. Paresthesias, peripheral neuropathy, and sensorimotor neuropathy, as well as autonomic neuropathy manifesting as gastrointestinal symptoms, are observed, especially in the neuropathic hereditary familial amyloidosis. Amyloidosis can involve paraarticular structures and produce the shoulder pad syndrome. Large amyloid deposits may produce osteolytic lesions and cause pathologic fractures. Extensive deposits of amyloid produce pseudohypertrophy of skeletal muscles, which may be impressive. A strong family history is suggestive of familial amyloidosis except for the familial Mediterranean fever.

Objective

Physical Examination

Orthostatic hypotension often develops during the course of the disease. This could be due to direct vascular involvement, infiltration, and/or dysfunction of the autonomic nervous system. Vitreous opacities are noted in type I and II familial amyloidosis. Purpura and flesh-colored, waxy, nonpruritic papular lesions could be widely distributed with a predilection for eyelids, ears, and body folds. Macroglossia is present in only 10% of patients. Generalized lymphadenopathy is infrequent but may be the initial manifestation of primary amyloidosis. Signs of fluid overload or congestive heart failure may be elicited by lung examination. Cardiovascular signs are those of a restrictive cardiomyopathy with or without congestive heart failure or cardiomegaly. Abdominal examination is significant for hepatomegaly and splenomegaly. Ascites may be noted, and although hepatic involvement

is common, liver failure is rare. Neurologic signs are related to sensorimotor peripheral neuropathy characterized by dysesthetic numbness involving the lower extremities; muscle wasting also may be noted. Involvement of the skin in systemic amyloidosis may manifest as petechiae, ecchymoses, papules, plaques, nodules, tumors, bullous lesions, alopecia, dystrophy of the nails, or skin thickening resembling scleroderma. Rarely, amyloid may be found in the external auditory canal.

Routine Laboratory Abnormalities

Hematology. Anemia is not a prominent feature in primary amyloidosis. When present it is usually due to renal insufficiency, multiple myeloma, or gastrointestinal bleeding. Thrombocytosis occurs in 5 to 10% of patients and may be a clue to the diagnosis.

Blood Chemistry. Levels of serum alkaline phosphatase are increased in about one fourth of patients. Hyperbilirubinemia is an infrequent finding but, when present, is an ominous sign. Hypoalbuminemia is associated with the nephrotic syndrome, and cholesterol and triglyceride levels are generally elevated in patients with this syndrome. Twenty-five percent of patients have an elevated creatine level at the time of diagnosis. The prothrombin time is increased in about 15% and the thrombin time in about 60% of patients.

Electrocardiogram. The electrocardiogram may reveal low-voltage QRS complexes and signs of pseudoinfarction.

Diagnostic

Differential Diagnosis

Primary Amyloidosis. There is no evidence of preceding or coexisting disease except for multiple myeloma. The amyloid fibrils from patients with primary amyloidosis are virtually identical to the variable portion of a monoclonal light chain. Primary amyloidosis can be divided into two categories: primary and primary with multiple myeloma.

Secondary Amyloidosis. Secondary amyloidosis is associated with inflammatory processes (rheumatoid arthritis and its variants, inflammatory bowel disease), infectious diseases (tuberculosis, bronchiectasis, osteomyelitis), drug abuse, malignant diseases (Hodgkin's disease, macroglobulinemia, lymphoma, renal cell carcinoma, heavy-chain disease), as well as rare diseases such as Gaucher's. A monoclonal protein is not found in the serum or urine. The amyloid type is AA and the major protein is protein A.

Familial Amyloidosis. Familial or hereditary amyloidosis in all forms except familial Mediterranean fever has an autosomal dominant inheritance pattern. Clinical familial amyloidosis can be classified most easily as neuropathic—amyloid is AF and main protein is prealbumin; nephropathic—amyloid is AA and major protein component is protein A; and cardiopathic—major protein is prealbumin (transthyretin).

Localized Amyloidosis. Localized amyloidosis is associated with medullary carcinoma of the thyroid and islets of Langerhans. In the former the major protein component is calcitonin, and in the latter the major protein component is insulin-associated polypeptide with amyloid type AE.

Senile Amyloidosis. Senile amyloidosis is subdivided into senile cardiac amyloidosis—amyloid type is ASC1 and major protein is prealbumin—and isolated atrial amyloidosis—amyloid type is IAA and major protein is atrial natriuretic peptide.

Dialysis Arthropathy. The amyloid type is AB and the major protein component is β_2-microglobulin.

Amyloidosis should be considered in all conditions that could result in nephrotic syndrome, cardiomyopathy and congestive heart failure, arrhythmias, hepatosplenomegaly, peripheral neuropathy, sensorimotor neuropathy, or periorbital skin lesions.

Diagnostic Options and Recommended Approach

Establish the Diagnosis of Amyloidosis. The initial diagnostic procedure should be to obtain an abdominal fat aspirate, as this aspirate is positive in more than 80% of the patients. Experience in the staining technique and interpretation are important before the technique can be used routinely. A bone marrow aspirate and biopsy specimen should be obtained to determine the degree of plasmacytosis. With bone marrow specimens, stains for amyloid are positive in slightly more than 50% of patients. If the abdominal fat and bone marrow biopsies are negative, a rectal biopsy specimen should be taken that must include the submucosa; this biopsy is positive in approximately 80% of patients. If these sites are negative, tissue should be obtained from a suspected involved organ. Renal biopsy results in a high incidence of positive findings in patients with nephrotic syndrome or renal insufficiency. Liver biopsy frequently discloses amyloid. Tissue obtained at carpal tunnel decompression should always be examined for amyloid because it is positive in a large percentage of patients with primary amyloidosis. The sural nerve is an excellent source of biopsy material in patients with peripheral neuropathy.

Establish the Presence of Occult or Covert Plasma Dyscrasia. Serum protein immunoelectrophoresis and urine protein immunoelectrophoresis should be performed. If these tests are positive, further workup is required to rule out the presence of multiple myeloma. Most patients with biopsy-proven amyloid deposition have small paraprotein components; only a few have frank multiple myeloma.

Therapeutic

Therapy of primary amyloidosis is not satisfactory. Because amyloid fibrils consist of the variable portion of a monoclonal immunoglobulin light chain, treatment should be attempted with alkylating agents that are known to be effective against plasma cell proliferative processes. Treatment with melphalan 0.25 mg/kg orally per day for 4 days and prednisone 100 mg orally daily for 4 days, to be repeated every 4 to 6 weeks, is a reasonable approach in the absence of a well-designed clinical trial. Treatment of secondary amyloidosis depends on the underlying disease. Resorption of amyloid after therapy of osteomyelitis, tuberculosis, or empyema has been reported. Nephrectomy for hypernephroma may result in the disappearance of amyloid. Dimethyl sulfoxide has apparently helped some patients with rheumatoid arthritis or ankylosis spondylitis. Renal transplantation may be of benefit.

Familial Amyloidosis. Specific treatment does not exist for *neuropathic familial amyloidosis,* and management is limited to symptomatic care. Colchicine is effective in controlling the symptoms and preventing the development of *nephropathic familial amyloidosis.* There is no specific treatment for *cardiopathic familial amyloidosis.*

Dialysis-associated Amyloidosis. Hemodialysis-associated arthropathy rarely occurs when porous membranes, such as those of polyacrylonitrile, are used. Renal transplantation leads to dramatic improvement in joint symptoms.

FOLLOW-UP

The frequency of visits and clinical evaluation is usually dictated by the patient's clinical condition and different syndromes at the time of diagnosis.

DISCUSSION

Prevalence and Incidence

Amyloidosis is a rare disease. About two thirds of patients with amyloid have primary (AL), of which about one fifth are localized (AE), less than 5% have secondary (AA), less than 5% have familial (AF and AA), and less than 5% have senile (ASC, IAA) amyloidosis. In patients with primary amyloidosis, only a small percentage (<5%) are under the age of 40 and two thirds are men.

Related Basic Science

Amyloid fibrils from a patient with primary amyloidosis are virtually identical to the variable portion of a monoclonal light chain. The light-chain class is more frequently lambda than kappa in primary amyloidosis. The mechanism for the deposition of monoclonal light chains in amyloidosis is unclear.

In secondary amyloidosis, the major component of the amyloid fibril is protein A, which has a molecular weight of 8500, consists of 76 amino acids, and is not related to any known immunoglobulin. With the use of antiserum to amyloid A, an antigenically related larger molecule (molecular weight 12,500) known as serum amyloid A-related protein (SAA), has been found in the serum of normal patients as well as in those with amyloidosis. The SAA level corresponds to the incidence of secondary amyloidosis. SAA is synthesized by the liver and is found in the rough endoplasmic reticulum in the Golgi apparatus of hepatocytes.

Amyloid P (AP) is a glycoprotein composed of 10 identical glycol-related polypeptide subunits, each with a molecular weight of 23,500 and arranged into pentamers. Human serum amyloid P (SAP) is produced in the liver, is present in normal persons, and shows 50 to 60% homology with C-reactive protein. SAP is bound to the amyloid fibrils in a calcium-dependent fashion, but is not an integral part of the fibrillar structure. It is found in all types of amyloid, including the vessel walls in Alzheimer's disease patients. Neither the physiologic role nor the pathologic role of SAP in amyloidosis is known.

The catabolism or breakdown of amyloid fibrils is an important factor in pathogenesis. It has been noted that patients with amyloidosis fail to degrade AA, suggesting that different patterns of proteolysis may predispose one to the development of amyloidosis. Human neutrophil elastase has been identified on amyloid fibrils of AL, AA, and AF origin, indicating that this enzyme might play a role in amyloid precursor protein degradation.

Amyloidosis results from the interplay of many factors, including excessive deposition of amyloid and degradation of the amyloid fibrils.

Natural History and Its Modification with Treatment

Primary Amyloidosis. Currently the median survival of patients with primary amyloidosis is almost 2 years. The longer survival is due to several factors: earlier diagnosis, improved supportive care, and superior chemotherapy. Patients with only peripheral neuropathy have a median survival of more than 5 years. Cardiac involvement accounts for death in almost 50% of the patients. The presence of congestive heart failure, urinary monoclonal light chain, and hepatomegaly, and the extent of weight loss have a significant influence on survival during the first year.

Secondary Amyloidosis. The natural history of secondary amyloidosis depends on the primary diagnosis.

Familial Amyloidosis. In neuropathic familial amyloidosis, death usually occurs within 10 years. In cardiopathic familial amyloidosis, progressive congestive heart failure begins in the fourth or fifth decade of life and leads to death in 2 to 6 years.

Senile Amyloidosis. Senile cardiac amyloidosis is commonly recognized antemortem and is characterized by congestive heart failure with a mean survival after diagnosis of 26 months, which is much longer than that seen with cardiac primary amyloidosis.

Prevention

Effective management of the primary disease should prevent secondary amyloidosis; however, no preventive measures are currently available for the different types of amyloidosis.

Cost Containment

The cost of medical care for patients with amyloidosis is high. Caring for the patient with secondary amyloidosis entails the expense of caring for the primary disease (see chapters related to the diseases in which amyloidosis occurs) and the complications of amyloidosis itself. Patients with primary amyloidosis require costly diagnostic testing. The cost can be somewhat contained if the disease is suspected and *appropriate* testing is used early in the course of the disease. Tests need not be repeated too often because it is usually possible to follow the clinical course of the patient without excessive testing.

REFERENCES

Barlogie B. Multiple myeloma. Hematol Oncol Clin North Am 1992;6:2.

Hoffman R. Hematology: Basic principles and practice. 2nd ed. New York: Churchill Livingstone, 1994.

CHAPTER 12–30

Myelodysplasia

Alan E. Lichtin, M.D.

DEFINITION

Myelodysplasia, or myelodysplastic syndromes (MDS), is the term used to describe disorders in which the production of blood elements is suboptimal. These disorders are usually associated with a hypercellular bone marrow and morphologic abnormalities, which are described below.

Table 12–30–1 summarizes the French–American–British subtypes of MDS with respect to what aspects on the peripheral smear and in the marrow are necessary to define the conditions.

ETIOLOGY

Most patients develop MDS de novo. Certain exposures predispose populations to development of MDS. These include nuclear explosions and radiation. Exposures to certain chemicals such as benzene predispose to development of MDS. Also, administration of alkylating agent chemotherapy predisposes individuals to develop MDS (therapy-related MDS).

Most patients with MDS are older than 60 years. It is likely that there are derangements in the control of hematopoiesis as individuals age that may promote the development of MDS.

CRITERIA FOR DIAGNOSIS
Suggestive

In older patients who have anemia not related to nutritional deficiency and also of recent onset (meaning that they were not always anemic or had a known hemoglobinopathy), MDS should be suspected. The most likely presentation is a person who is bicytopenic or pancytopenic.

Definitive

Definitive criteria for diagnosis can be obtained by examination of the peripheral blood smear and bone marrow.

CLINICAL MANIFESTATIONS
Subjective

Most patients with MDS complain of a gradual onset of fatigue, dizziness, easy bruising, or infections. These symptoms reflect the development of anemia, thrombocytopenia, and leukopenia. If a patient who has been treated with radiation therapy or chemotherapy (usually within the past 5 years) for a malignancy develops pancytopenia, MDS should be considered. Usually, the family history is not contributory.

Other symptoms include bone pain, usually in the sternum or the tibia ("shin splints"), night sweats, and weight loss.

Objective
Physical Examination

Patients usually are pale and bruise easily. Lymphadenopathy is usually not present. The liver and spleen are often of normal size. Some patients might have extramedullary hematopoiesis and one or both of these organs might be enlarged. The skin might demonstrate ecchymoses from easy bruising.

Routine Laboratory Abnormalities

The important findings on laboratory analysis are some combination of anemia, thrombocytopenia, and granulocytopenia. One might see blasts or a left-shifted change on the peripheral smear. The term *dysgranulopoiesis* describes morphologic abnormalities in granulocyte maturation that might be prominent on the peripheral blood smear. These include hypogranular polymorphonuclear leukocytes (Figure 12–30–1) and Pelger–Huet anomaly (Figure 12–30–2). Bone marrow examination may reveal dyserythropoiesis, which includes megaloblastic changes in red cell morphology and bilobed or multilobed nucleated red blood cells. As patients with MDS evolve toward acute leukemia, levels of uric acid and lactate dehydrogenase may rise.

12–30–1. CLASSIFICATION OF MYELODYSPLASTIC SYNDROMES

Myelodysplastic Syndrome	% Marrow Blasts	% Peripheral Blood Blasts	Auer Rods	Monocytes > 10³/L	% Marrow Ring Sideroblasts
Refractory anemia (RA)	<5	≤1	No	≤1.0	≤15
Refractory anemia with ringed sideroblasts (RARS)	<5	≤1	No	≤1.0	>15
Refractory anemia with excess blasts (RAEB)	5-20	<5	No	≤1.0	Any*
Chronic myelomonocytic leukemia (CMML)	<20	<5	No	≥1.0	Any*
Refractory anemia with excess blasts in transformation (RAEB-T)	>20–30	0–30†	Yes†	Any†	Any*

†≥5% blasts in peripheral blood in MDS indicates RAEB-T; >30% blasts in marrow indicates acute leukemia. Presence of Auer rods in MDS indictes RAEB-T. Monocytosis may be present in RAEB-T.

*Ring sideroblasts may be present in higher grades of MDS, but do not affect subclassification.

Source: Bennett JM, Catovsky D, Daniel MT, et al. Proposals for the classification of the myelodysplastic syndromes. Br J Haematol 1982;51:189. Reproduced with permission from the publisher and author.

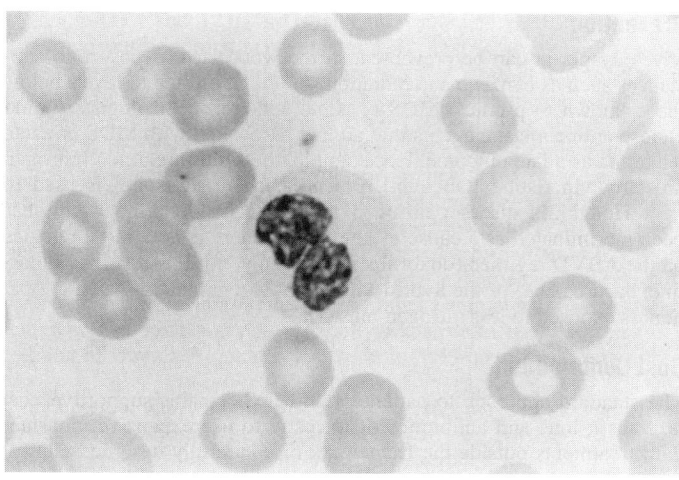

Figure 12–30–1. Hypogranular polymorphonuclear leukocyte.

PLANS
Diagnostic
Differential Diagnosis

The differential diagnosis of a bicytopenic or pancytopenic patient includes many disorders. Aplastic anemia may appear identical to MDS on peripheral smear, but the marrow in aplastic anemia is hypocellular. The bone marrow in MDS is usually hypercellular. The presentations in certain inflammatory disorders, such as tuberculosis and HIV infection, can be confused with that of MDS. Vitamin B_{12} and folate deficiency need to be ruled out.

Diagnostic Options and Recommended Approach

A clinician need not rush to do a bone marrow when a patient presents with a *mildly* depressed red cell, white cell, or platelet count. Such patients should be instructed to return to the clinic promptly if there are changes in their health status. These patients have early MDS. The prudent approach is to follow them periodically and, if the counts worsen, perform a marrow examination.

If, however, a patient is significantly anemic, thrombocytopenic, and leukopenic, and the peripheral blood smear reveals changes consistent with a MDS, bone marrow aspiration and biopsy with chromosome analysis are important. Chromosomal abnormalities are seen in about

50% of patients with MDS. The most common are loss of part of the long arm of chromosome 5, monosomy 7, trisomy 8, and loss of part of the long arm of chromosome 20.

Therapeutic

Patients who have mild forms of MDS, such as refractory anemia and refractory anemia with ringed sideroblasts, often require no treatment. Some patients have been followed for decades without any interventions besides a periodic visit to the doctor. Most patients with refractory anemia with excess blasts or refractory anemia with excess blasts in transformation require more frequent follow-up evaluations and may require transfusions of red cells to keep them from becoming too anemic. Some patients need to be transfused rather frequently. When patients develop thrombocytopenia along with their MDS, platelet transfusions might be necessary. If patients develop infections, admission to the hospital and administration of intravenous antibiotics may be necessary.

There is much in the literature about the use of growth factors in this disorder. There are also studies demonstrating the utility of differentiating agents such as retinoids. At the time of this writing, however, there is as yet no clear understanding that either group of agents has a role in the standard care of these patients. It is known that MDS evolves toward acute leukemia, and there is a concern that the use of certain growth factors might accelerate the development of acute leukemia. In trials with these agents in MDS, patients developed acute leukemia, but apparently not at a greater rate than the natural history might imply. Great caution must be exercised in interpreting these data. In a patient with MDS being treated with granulocyte colony-stimulating factor, usually for symptomatic neutropenia, an increase in the percentage of blasts on the peripheral smear or bone marrow would be an indication to interrupt treatment.

For the younger patient, especially less than 45 years of age, who has an HLA-compatible donor, allogeneic bone marrow transplantation offers the only chance for cure of MDS. There is a better prognosis for younger patients and for patients who have few blasts in the marrow at the time of transplantation.

Chemotherapy usually leads to unsatisfactory outcomes in MDS. Based on in vitro data demonstrating that exposure of myelodysplastic cells to low concentrations cytosine arabinoside induced differentiation, patients have been treated with low doses of this drug. This has not proven to be effective; neither has treatment with another differentiating agent, 5-azacytidine. Standard antileukemia agents, such as daunorubicin and cytosine arabinoside, have been used in MDS patients. In general, the rates of complete remissions are lower and the duration of remission is shorter in MDS patients compared with de novo acute leukemia patients.

As patients with MDS are transfused with red cells, they become iron overloaded. Deferoxamine therapy is indicated once the ferritin rises significantly above the normal range.

FOLLOW-UP

Because these patients are very heterogeneous in their progression toward acute leukemia or toward worsening cytopenias requiring more intense monitoring, follow-up must be tailored to the needs of the patient. It is wise, once the diagnosis is made, to follow the patient rather frequently with history, physical examination, and complete blood count initially. If the patient demonstrates stability, then the frequency of follow-up can be reduced (even to several months between visits). Patients need to be instructed to return to clinic if they are progressively fatigued, if their temperature rises above 38°C and is associated with a shaking chill, or if any pronounced bleeding occurs.

DISCUSSION
Prevalence and Incidence

Most textbooks of hematology do not state the prevalence and incidence of MDS. In our ever increasingly industrialized society, there is exposure to greater numbers of potential leukemogens. Still there is no

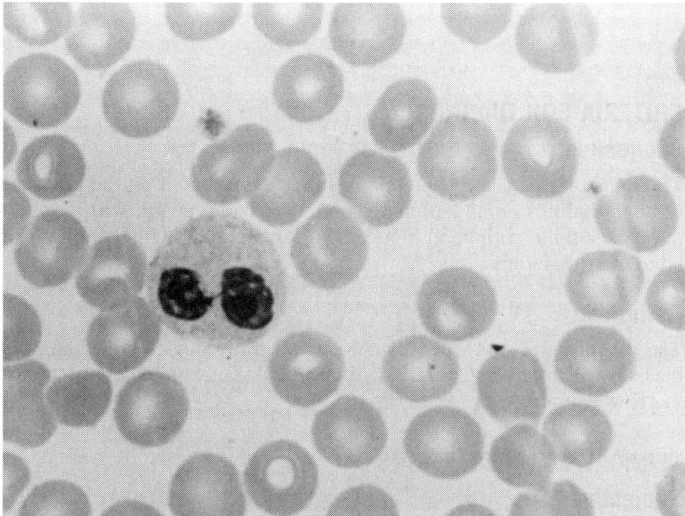

Figure 12–30–2. Pelger–Huet anomaly.

clear indication from the medical literature that the incidence of MDS has increased.

Related Basic Science

Molecular Biology

Myelodysplasia is an exciting subject for molecular biologists. Myelodysplastic cells have been studied as a model for leukemogenesis.

Myelodysplasia appears to be a clonal disorder that arises from one cell, either a pluripotent stem cell or a cell committed to myeloid lineage. Methods by which this has been documented include glucose-6-phosphate dehydrogenase isoenzymes, isotype analysis of Epstein–Barr virus-transformed B cells, and, lately, fluorescence in situ hybridization.

Genetics

Chromosomal aberrations in MDS have also been an area of exciting research. The genes for growth factors and growth factor receptors are found on some of these chromosomes, especially the long arm of chromosome 5, where one finds the genes for interleukins-3, -4, -5, and -9. It is likely that loss of these genes plays a role in the development of MDS and leukemia.

The gene for an interferon regulatory factor, IRF-1, is also located on the long arm of chromosome 5. The protein, IRF-1, has antioncogenic activity. It is possible that its loss may have a role in the development of MDS and acute leukemia.

Natural History and Its Modification with Treatment

The median survival for patients with MDS depends on the subtypes. Some patients with RA, RARS, and CMML can have very long survivals, even longer than 10 years. Most patients with RAEB or RAEB-T who are elderly will have a median survival of 10 or 6 months, respectively. For the younger patient who receives an allogeneic bone marrow transplant, the probability of disease-free survival at 4 years is 40%.

Prevention

Myelodysplasia can be prevented. In the workplace, exposure to substances such as benzene and radiation should be limited to levels below those known to produce MDS or acute leukemia. Oncologists should choose antineoplastic agents that are not associated with MDS or acute leukemia as a late outcome. For example, the MOPP regimen (nitrogen mustard, vincristine [Oncovin], procarbazine, prednisone) is used to treat Hodgkin's disease; nitrogen mustard, an alkylating agent, has been incriminated as a cause of late MDS. There is now more reliance on the ABVD regimen (doxorubicin [Adriamycin], bleomycin, vinblastine, dacarbazine) or the hybrid MOPP/ABV regimen, in which the patient is exposed to less nitrogen mustard.

Cost Containment

The standard approach to patients with MDS remains supportive, that is, transfusions and antibiotics. It is costly to use expensive, nonstandard treatments outside the framework of a carefully designed clinical trial.

REFERENCES

Anderson JE, Appelbaum FR, Fisher LD, et al. Allogeneic bone marrow transplantation for 93 patients with myelodysplastic syndrome. Blood 1993;82:677.

Bennett JM, Catovsky D, Daniel MT, et al. Proposals for the classification of the myelodysplastic syndromes. Br J Haematol 1982;51:189.

Boultwood J, Fidler C, Lewis S, et al. Allelic loss of IRF-1 in myelodysplasia and acute myeloid leukemia: Retention of IRF-1 on the 5q- chromosome in some patients with the 5q- syndrome. Blood 1993;82:2611.

Gerritsen WR, Donohue J, Bauman J, et al. Clonal analysis of myelodysplastic syndrome: Monosomy 7 is expressed in the myeloid lineage, but not in the lymphoid lineage as detected by fluorescent in situ hybridization. Blood 1992;80:217.

Noel P. Management of patients with myelodysplastic syndrome. Mayo Clin Proc 1991;66:485.

CHAPTER 12–31

Acute Leukemia

Matt E. Kalaycioglu, M.D.

DEFINITION

Normal hematopoietic progenitor cells are polyclonal cells that mature and differentiate into mature blood elements by complex and tightly controlled processes. Acute leukemia is the malignant proliferation of clonal (originating from a single cell) progenitor cells that escape hematopoietic control and thus fail to differentiate.

ETIOLOGY

The cause of acute leukemia is unknown, but both congenital and acquired factors may predispose to the development of acute leukemia (Table 12–31–1). These predisposing factors probably cause several sequential somatic gene defects that ultimately lead to the neoplastic transformation of hematopoietic progenitor cells. Viruses have been implicated as causative agents in Burkitt's type acute lymphocytic leukemia (ALL) and in human T-lymphotropic virus type 1-related adult T-cell leukemia/lymphoma (which is not really an acute leukemia), but not in acute nonlymphocytic leukemia (ANLL).

CRITERIA FOR DIAGNOSIS

Suggestive

The diagnosis of acute leukemia is subjectively based on the presence of abnormalities on an automated complete blood count, with or without blasts in the peripheral blood smear, in a patient with symptoms of bone marrow failure.

Definitive

The diagnosis is confirmed by the demonstration of greater than 30% blasts by histology and special cytochemical stains on review of a bone marrow aspirate.

CLINICAL MANIFESTATIONS

Subjective

The symptoms of acute leukemia are usually of brief duration and reflect bone marrow failure. Malaise, fatigue, and dyspnea from anemia

TABLE 12-31-1. FACTORS ASSOCIATED WITH AN INCREASED INCIDENCE OF ACUTE LEUKEMIA

	Leukemia	
	Lymphocytic	**Nonlymphocytic**
Congenital Factors		
Familial	+	+
Down syndrome	++	+++
Kleinfelter's syndrome	+	+
Fanconi's anemia	+	+
Ataxia telangiectasia	+	+
Bloom's syndrome	+	+
Neurofibromatosis	+	+
Acquired Factors		
Ionizing radiation	+	++
Chemical exposure	+	++
Cigarette smoking	−	+
Viruses	+(?)	−
Chemotherapy	−	++
Myeloproliferative disorders	+	++
Myelodysplasia	−	+++
Plasma cell dyscrasias	−	+
Paroxysmal nocturnal hemoglobinuria	−	+
Aplastic anemia	−	+

are common. Bleeding gums and a petechial rash from thrombocytopenia are also common presenting symptoms. Less commonly, but of more concern, are symptoms related to either leukocytosis or leukopenia. When the absolute peripheral blast count approaches 100,000K/μL symptoms related to leukostasis may become evident. The white cell mass occludes smaller capillaries and ischemic symptoms may result. These are particularly pronounced in the central nervous system and manifest as focal neurologic deficits, alterations in mental status, and headache. Other common leukostatic symptoms include blurred vision, dyspnea, and ischemic pain. When the absolute neutrophil count falls below 1000k/μL, the risk of infection increases. Although fevers and night sweats are often noted in ALL, it is important to realize that fever is not a common presentation of ANLL and more likely represents occult infection in the neutropenic host. Rarely, a patient will present with a mass, and local symptoms related to it, from a leukemic tumor (chloroma).

A history considering the factors potentially predisposing to acute leukemia should be obtained (Table 12-31-1). The past medical history should consider previous hematologic and oncologic disorders as well as their treatment. Nonneoplastic disorders such as rheumatic fever and glomerulonephritis are often treated with chemotherapeutic agents including alkylating agents. A family history of a congenital disorder should be specifically sought. History of tobacco use is a common finding.

Objective

Physical Examination

Objective findings on physical examination include fever, tachycardia, and tachypnea. Gum hyperplasia is a characteristic feature of monocytic ANLL. Mucosal hemorrhages, ecchymoses, and petechiae are common manifestations of thrombocytopenia. Lymphadenopathy and hepatosplenomegaly can be seen in ALL, but are less common in ANLL. Rashes are common and may reflect drug effect, thrombocytopenia, or cutaneous involvement with leukemia. Mass lesions may represent chloromas in ANLL or local deposits of leukemia in ALL, especially when discovered in the testes.

The leukemic blasts of ALL have a greater tendency to infiltrate areas of the body that are relatively protected from chemotherapy. The most common "sanctuary sites" are the central nervous system and the testicles. The examination of a patient with acute leukemia, particularly

ALL, must take into consideration the propensity of the disease to involve these sites. Nerve deficits and alterations in mental status suggest leukemic meningitis that should be confirmed with a lumbar puncture and cytologic examination of the spinal fluid.

Routine Laboratory Abnormalities

Laboratory findings may be dramatic and are often out of proportion to clinical findings. Anemia and thrombocytopenia, often severe, are almost universal. The leukocyte count may be either elevated or reduced. Red blood cell indices are generally normal and the reticulocyte count is low. The differential often demonstrates a "leukemic hiatus" characterized by a low percentage of neutrophils and high percentage of blast forms, with few or no intermediate myeloid cells. The blood elements are usually normal in morphology with the exception of the blast cells, which may have large, bizarre nuclei with prominent nucleoli. Eosinophilic spindle-shaped cytoplasmic inclusions, called Auer rods, may be seen within the blast cells and are virtually diagnostic of ANLL.

Chemistry panels are often normal but may reflect a high cell turnover rate with elevated potassium, lactate dehydrogenase, uric acid, and phosphorus levels. Leukemic infiltration may cause elevated hepatic transaminase levels and hyperbilirubinemia.

Even in the absence of significant bleeding, coagulation tests should be obtained. ANLL, particularly promyelogenous leukemia, is often associated with a coagulopathy that usually manifests as bleeding but may cause thrombosis. The prothrombin and activated partial thromboplastin times are usually elevated and the fibrinogen level is usually low. The D-dimer is also usually elevated, which has historically led to the conclusion that the coagulopathy is due to disseminated intravascular coagulation; however, relatively normal antithrombin III and low antiplasmin levels suggest that fibrin(ogen) lysis may also be playing a role. Coagulopathy is less common with ALL, but may occur, especially with the onset of treatment.

PLANS

Diagnostic

Differential Diagnosis

There are few other disorders that are characterized by circulating blast cells. Possibilities include chronic myelogenous leukemia and myelodysplastic syndromes. Generally the presence of peripheral blasts in these disorders heralds the onset of either blast crisis in chronic myelogenous leukemia or frank acute leukemia in myelodysplasia. Peripheral blasts do not result from the use of hematopoietic growth factors.

Diagnostic Options and Recommended Approach

A bone marrow aspirate and core biopsy obtained from the posterior iliac crest allows the diagnosis of acute leukemia. The most important aspect of the diagnosis is differentiating ALL from ANLL. This is usually done by histologic appearance and the use of specific cytochemical stains that help identify hematopoietic lineages. These diagnostic maneuvers have helped classify the acute leukemias. The French–American–British (FAB) classification system has identified three subcategories of ALL and eight subcategories of ANLL based on histologic and staining characteristics. One category is defined by flow cytometry or electron microscopy in the absence of diagnostic staining (FAB M0). These categories, associated clinical characteristics, typical cytogenetic findings, and prognoses are listed in Table 12-31-2. The presence of Auer rods is diagnostic of ANLL, as is the positivity of myeloid-specific cytochemical stains. Unfortunately, Auer rods are not always present and the stains are not always diagnostic.

Specific cytogenetic abnormalities are diagnostic of certain types of ANLL, but are present in only about half of all cases and take up to 2 weeks to determine. Flow cytometry to identify populations of nonlymphoid versus lymphoid antigen-bearing cells is quick and has become a useful tool in differentiating nonlymphoid from lymphoid blasts. The application of this new technology has identified acute leukemias that often defy classification, as they bear both nonlymphoid and lymphoid

TABLE 12–31–2. FRENCH–AMERICAN–BRITISH (FAB) CLASSIFICATION OF THE ACUTE LEUKEMIAS AND THEIR CHARACTERISTIC CLINICAL FEATURES, CYTOGENETIC FINDINGS, AND PROGNOSTIC CORRELATES

FAB Class	Type	Characteristics	Cytogenetics	Prognosis
AML, M0	AML with minimal evidence of myeloid maturation	Requires flow cytometry		Poor
AML, M1	AML without maturation			Standard
AML, M2	AML with maturation		t(8;21)	Good
AML, M3	Promyelocytic leukemia	Coagulopathy, responds to retinoic acid	t(15;17)	Good
AML, M4	Myelomonocytic leukemia			Standard
AML, M4e	Myelomonocytic leukemia with eosinophilia	Central nervous system involvement	inv16	Good
AML, M5	Monocytic leukemia	Gum hypertrophy, skin involvement, tissue infiltration	del or t(11q)	Standard
AML, M6	AML with erythroid differentiation	Associated with Down syndrome	Trisomy 21	Poor
AML, M7	Megakaryoblastic leukemia	Associated with Down syndrome and myelofibrosis		Poor
ALL, L1	Small cell ALL	Childhood ALL		Good
ALL, L2	Large cell ALL	Childhood and adult ALL		Standard
ALL, L3	Burkitt's type	Bone tumors, associated with HIV infection	t(8;14)	Poor

AML, acute myelogenous or acute nonlymphocytic leukemia; ALL, acute lymphocytic leukemia.

antigens. These "biphenotypic" or "mixed lineage" acute leukemias demonstrate the hematopoietic "lineage infidelity" of malignant hematopoietic cell proliferations.

Karyotypic analysis allows the differentiation of chronic myelogenous leukemia in blast crisis (Philadelphia chromosome positive) from ANLL (Philadelphia chromosome negative) and identifies a poor prognostic group in ALL (Philadelphia chromosome positive). The cytogenetic profile and leukemic expression of certain antigens also provide prognostic information that has been used to guide therapy. Given the diagnostic and prognostic information afforded by modern cytogenetics and flow cytometry, the usefulness of the FAB classification system has been called into question, but it remains routinely applied.

Therapeutic

Therapeutic Options

The initial and supportive management of acute leukemia is often the most crucial. Therapy must begin while the diagnosis is being established and clinical data are being collected. Adequate hydration must be ensured to allow renal excretion of cellular by-products and to avoid the tumor lysis syndrome. The urine is often alkalinized to promote the solubility of uric acid, and allopurinol 300 to 600 mg orally daily is routinely added to reduce the production of uric acid. These precautions are begun even in the absence of an elevated uric acid, as cytotoxic treatment increases cellular turnover and may provoke tumor lysis syndrome.

Fever in the neutropenic host is always treated empirically with broad-spectrum antibiotics, most commonly an extended-spectrum penicillin (i.e., piperacillin 4 g intravenously every 6 hours) combined with an aminoglycoside (i.e., gentamicin 2 mg/kg intravenously as a loading dose, then maintenance dosing based on the creatinine clearance), while awaiting the results of cultures. Vancomycin (1 g intravenously every 12 hours) is often added, particularly if an indwelling central venous catheter is present. Persistent or recurrent fever despite the use of antibiotics for 4 days justifies the empiric addition of amphotericin B (1 mg/kg intravenously daily). Prior to or concurrent with the onset of fever, acyclovir (250 mg/m^2 intravenously daily) is often started, particularly in patients previously exposed to herpes simplex virus, to prevent acute herpes infection.

Transfusion support is critical to the success of initial treatment. Red cell transfusions are generally administered to maintain a hemoglobin greater than 9 g/dL. These transfusions are usually irradiated to prevent transfusion-associated graft-versus-host disease. In the potential bone marrow transplant patient, cytomegalovirus negative or leukocyte-depleted transfusions are usually given to prevent cytomegalovirus seroconversion. Platelet transfusions are given to prevent and control bleeding due to thrombocytopenia. Typically, platelets are given to keep the platelet count greater than 20,000k/μL, especially in patients with fever

or evidence of sepsis. Patients who become refractory to platelet transfusions may benefit from single-donor or HLA-matched platelets. White cell transfusions are rarely used today.

Hypofibrinogenemia (fibrinogen < 150 mg/dL) is treated with cryoprecipitate, and prolongations of the prothrombin and activated partial thromboplastin times are treated with fresh-frozen plasma. Low-dose heparin is often added to control disseminated intravascular coagulation, although this is controversial. Persistent bleeding in the setting of refractory thrombocytopenia justifies the addition of ε-aminocaproic acid (100 mg/kg intravenously as a loading dose, then 1 g/h intravenously as a maintenance infusion) to reduce plasmin activation.

Leukostasis is a medical emergency that necessitates a prompt reduction in peripheral blast counts. Leukophereses will quickly, but temporarily, reduce counts and relieve symptoms. The simultaneous addition of hydroxyurea (4–6 g orally every 4–6 hours) or cytarabine (Ara-C, 500 mg intravenously) is necessary to control counts and symptoms longer while awaiting the preparations for induction chemotherapy to be completed. Prophylactic cranial radiation is sometimes used to destroy leukemic blasts in the brain parenchyma and vasculature, but this treatment is controversial.

The definitive treatment of acute leukemia can be divided into two components: remission induction and postremission therapy. Remission induction therapy for ANLL has remained largely unchanged over the past 20 years. The treatment is built on cytarabine, the single most active agent in ANLL. Cytarabine is S phase specific and is therefore administered as a continuous infusion (100 mg/m^2/d) for 7 days. An anthracycline or anthracycline derivative (daunorubicin 45 mg/m^2/d, idarubicin 12 mg/m^2/d, or mitoxantrone 12 mg/m^2/d) is also given for 3 days (thus the "7 + 3" regimen). This regimen results in a complete remission in 60 to 70% of patients. Unfortunately, without additional therapy, all will relapse, hence the need for postremission therapy.

The optimal postremission therapy for patients with ANLL in their first complete remission is controversial. The best results reported are with allogeneic bone marrow transplantation, with a 45 to 55% disease-free survival at 5 years of follow-up. This approach is limited by the eligibility of patients (age, performance status) and the relative lack of a suitable bone marrow donor. Autologous bone marrow transplantation results in a 40 to 50% 3-year disease-free survival because of a lower treatment-related mortality despite a higher relapse rate. Recently, postremission therapy with very high doses of cytarabine C (3 g intravenously every 12 hours × 6–12 doses) has provided results similar to those achieved with bone marrow transplantation, particularly in the subgroups of ANLL with a favorable prognosis (see Table 12–31–2). Studies are ongoing to identify the optimal postremission treatment.

The treatment of ALL in the adult is similar to that in children but with poorer results. Initial therapy usually consists of vincristine (2 mg intravenously every week) and prednisone (60–120 mg orally every day) combined with any or all of cyclophosphamide, daunorubicin, and

L-asparaginase in various dosages and treatment schedules. Complete remission is achieved in nearly 80% of patients with induction therapy, but similar to ANLL, all relapse without additional therapy.

Postremission therapy generally consists of intensive consolidation, central nervous system prophylaxis, and maintenance chemotherapy. Intensive consolidation usually incorporates cytarabine and either etoposide or teniposide in addition to the same drugs used in induction. Central nervous system prophylaxis is provided by intrathecal injections of methotrexate or cytarabine with or without cranial irradiation. Oral methotrexate and 6-mercaptopurine are usually given for 1 to 2 years after completion of consolidation as maintenance therapy. This standard treatment regimen results in long-term disease-free survival in 30 to 40% of patients treated.

The role of bone marrow transplantation in ALL is as controversial as it is for ANLL. The relatively better prognosis of ALL compared with ANLL has led some to recommend bone marrow transplantation only after relapse of ALL. In fact, retrospective reviews have failed to demonstrate an advantage for transplant in first complete remission compared with waiting until relapse or second complete remission; however, for ALL with poor prognostic features such as high initial leukocyte count, the presence of the Philadelphia chromosome, aberrant nonlymphoid antigen expression, and delayed onset of complete remission, most authorities recommend allogeneic bone marrow transplantation in first complete remission to those with a suitable bone marrow donor. The role of autologous bone marrow transplantation is even less clearly defined but is a suitable alternative to repeated cycles of intensive consolidation in ALL.

Relapsed, refractory, and transformed (see Table 12–31–1) acute leukemia in adults is incurable without bone marrow transplantation. Allogeneic bone marrow transplantation is the preferred postremission treatment modality, as cures have clearly been demonstrated with this approach. Autologous bone marrow transplantation provides up to 25% long-term disease-free survival in relapsed patients transplanted with marrow that was stored in first complete remission and is a suitable alternative in patients lacking a bone marrow donor. In general, patients receive intensive reinduction chemotherapy prior to autologous transplant to reduce their leukemic burden.

Recommended Approach

Standard therapy for acute leukemia is inadequate and therefore the recommended approach is that all patients be treated in clinical trials if at all possible. If a patient is ineligible or a clinical trial is unavailable, the recommended treatment for ANLL is induction chemotherapy with cytarabine and idarubicin, followed by allogeneic bone marrow transplantation if a suitable donor can be identified. If no donor is available, autologous bone marrow should be harvested and the patient should be treated with either a high-dose cytarabine regimen or autologous bone marrow transplantation. In ALL, patients should be induced with a combination of vincristine, prednisone, and daunorubicin, followed by intensive postremission chemotherapy including central nervous system prophylaxis and oral maintenance chemotherapy. If the patient has high-risk ALL, allogeneic bone marrow transplantation in first remission is recommended if a donor is available.

FOLLOW-UP

Patients are examined daily for evidence of infection and treatment side effects such as nausea, vomiting, diarrhea, stomatitis, and rash. Daily peripheral blood counts help monitor therapeutic progress and guide transfusion support. Daily monitoring of electrolytes and renal function is required to rule out tumor lysis syndrome and to guide replacement therapy. Coagulation studies are obtained daily for the first week of treatment to monitor for worsening coagulopathy. Bone marrow aspiration is performed as often as weekly to guide therapy and document response.

DISCUSSION
Prevalence and Incidence

Approximately 13,000 new cases of adult acute leukemia are diagnosed per year. Ninety percent of adult leukemias are ANLL. ANLL affects 2.3 persons per 100,000 population, with an incidence that rises with age to as high as 15 per 100,000 in those 75 years and older.

Related Basic Science
Genetics

Characteristic acquired chromosomal abnormalities are found in several of the acute leukemias. Several of these karyotypic abnormalities are associated with specific histologic variants of ANLL and correlate with prognosis (Table 12–31–2). The molecular biology of these chromosomal abnormalities is being actively investigated for clues not only to pathogenesis, but also to genetic regulation. The potential for new therapeutic strategies directed toward the genetic alterations in the acute leukemias is best exemplified by acute promyelogenous leukemia (FAB M3). This type of ANLL is characterized by the specific chromosomal translocation t(15;17). In more than 90% of cases of promyelogenous leukemia, the retinoic acid receptor α gene *(RARA)* located on chromosome 17 is translocated to chromosome 15, where it juxtaposes the *PML* oncogene. This juxtaposition results in the creation of a novel fusion *PML/RARA* mRNA that in turn is transcribed into a leukemogenic fusion protein of uncertain function. The independent discovery that the administration of all-*trans*-retinoic acid to patients with t(15;17) somehow leads to a complete remission in nearly 100% of cases has led to considerable excitement that similar results might be achieved in other forms of acute leukemia.

Altered Molecular Biology

The identification and synthesis of hematopoietic growth factors have given the basic research scientist new tools with which to investigate the biology of acute leukemia. Hematopoietic growth factors induce ANLL blasts to proliferate just as they do normal progenitors. The differentiation machinery, however, is dysfunctional, leading to a proliferation of undifferentiated blasts. Large doses of hematopoietic growth factors can overcome this "maturation arrest" in certain ANLL cell lines, but this has not been successful clinically.

The increased proliferation induced by growth factors may be useful in combination with chemotherapy, however. As cytarabine is active only against proliferating cells, one new strategy is to administer growth factors before the administration of cytarabine in an attempt to increase the susceptibility of the leukemic blasts to the chemotherapy. This strategy has met with only limited success thus far, but is an active area of clinical research. Another area where growth factors may play a role is accelerating the recovery of peripheral blood counts following aggressive chemotherapy. The morbidity of chemotherapy for ANLL is particularly great in the elderly and anything that reduces the period of neutropenia following chemotherapy in these patients is likely to improve results. Growth factors may have a role in this population of patients with ANLL. Interestingly, there is no evidence that growth factors accelerate leukemic relapse and no evidence for shortened remission in patients treated with growth factors.

Natural History and Its Modification with Treatment

Untreated acute leukemia is fatal in most patients within weeks of diagnosis. Modern treatment prolongs survival in the majority of patients by the induction of complete remission. Unfortunately, treatment is curative in only a minority of patients. As only about 70% of patients with acute leukemia achieve complete remission, if all patients in complete remission receive an allogeneic bone marrow transplant (with a disease-free survival of about 50%), less than 40% of all patients will be cured. Moreover, less than 30% of patients have a suitable bone marrow donor. Other modalities are not more effective than bone marrow transplantation, which means that current standard therapy is unlikely to cure more than 35% of all patients who are diagnosed with acute leukemia. New approaches are needed.

Prevention

There is currently no proven method to prevent the development of acute leukemia. The risk can be reduced, however, by avoidance of environmental leukemogens such as benzene and radiation (radon). The role of chemotherapy and therapeutic radiation in increasing the risk of secondary acute leukemia has led to treatment protocols that attempt to reduce cancer patients' exposure to each modality. Whenever possible, less leukemogenic drugs are substituted for more leukemogenic ones (i.e., hydroxyurea for busulfan).

Cost Containment

The costs of treating acute leukemia are very high and reflect the duration of hospital stay necessary following intensive chemotherapy, the use of expensive pharmaceuticals, and the necessity of blood product support. When patients relapse and become refractory to chemotherapy, supportive care measures remain expensive, as transfusions are often necessary to palliate symptomatic thrombocytopenia and anemia. Only new approaches to cure the disease are likely to reduce the costs associated with treating acute leukemia. On the other hand, recognizing populations of patients unlikely to benefit from a standard treatment approach and withholding aggressive therapies from them will spare those patients the morbidity and cost inherent in their use.

REFERENCES

Geller RB. Post-remission therapy of acute myelocytic leukemia in adults: Curability breeds controversy. Leukemia 1992;6:915.

Miller KB. Clinical manifestations of acute nonlymphocytic leukemia. In: Hoffman R, Benz EJ Jr, Shattil SJ, et al., eds. Hematology: Basic principles and practice. New York: Churchill Livingstone, 1991:715.

Poplack DG. Clinical manifestations of acute lymphoblastic leukemia. In: Hoffman R, Benz EJ Jr, Shattil SJ, et al., eds. Hematology: Basic principles and practice. New York: Churchill Livingstone, 1991:776.

Preti A, Kantarjian HM. Management of adult acute lymphocytic leukemia: Present issues and key challenges. J Clin Oncol 1994;12:1312.

Stone RM, Mayer RJ. Treatment of the newly diagnosed adult with de novo acute myeloid leukemia. Hematol Oncol Clin North Am 1993;7:47.

CHAPTER 12–32

The Bleeding Patient

Steven W. Andresen, D.O.

DEFINITION

The need to evaluate a patient with a bleeding disorder is not a rare event in clinical medicine. Patients requiring assessment fall into three categories: those who are currently bleeding or have a history of bleeding, patients about to undergo surgery, and those patients with abnormal coagulation screening studies.

ETIOLOGY

Systemic disorders of hemostasis may be produced by abnormalities of platelet number or function; a deficiency of, or inhibitor to, coagulation factors; a mixture of both; or a vascular defect. These disorders may be inherited or acquired.

CRITERIA FOR DIAGNOSIS

Suggestive

Abnormal bleeding is a common manifestation of disease. The physician must determine whether the patient is bleeding as a result of a local problem, such as peptic ulcer or dysfunctional uterine bleeding, or whether a systemic disorder of hemostasis exists. Bleeding manifestations are usually apparent in the patient with a severe defect in systemic hemostasis. The character of bleeding is important in that petechiae, retroperitoneal bleeding, hemarthroses, hematomas, and large ecchymoses are more frequently associated with a systemic disorder of hemostasis. Hemorrhage most commonly occurs from multiple sites, is spontaneous, and is severe.

Definitive

Once a generalized defect in hemostasis is considered, the history and physical examination provide information that is instrumental in determining whether the defect is inherited or acquired and whether the underlying mechanism is related to platelet dysfunction, an abnormality in a coagulation factor(s), a combination of both, or a vascular defect. The results of screening laboratory tests provide the information necessary for pursuing further and more specific laboratory studies.

CLINICAL MANIFESTATIONS

Subjective

A careful history is the most important tool in the accurate diagnosis of bleeding disorders. Inquiry should be made about bleeding at the time of previous surgery such as tonsillectomy, abdominal operations, and circumcision. Problems associated with tooth extractions and previous trauma should be sought. In the female, the character of menstruation should be determined. A detailed medication history should be taken. The physician should ask about potential symptoms associated with an underlying disorder such as a connective tissue disease or malignancy.

Inherited abnormalities of hemostasis usually present in infancy and are associated with a positive family history, and bleeding will have occurred with previous trauma. Acquired hemostatic defects generally begin in adult life, are associated with a negative family history, and have had no bleeding associated with previous trauma or operation. Often an underlying associated illness is present.

Patients with thrombocytopenia or qualitative platelet disorders present with petechiae or bleeding from mucous membranes. As the platelet provides the initial hemostatic plug, bleeding occurs immediately and may continue for some time. The patient with an abnormality of a plasma coagulation factor presents with deep bleeding such as a hematoma, hemarthrosis, or retroperitoneal hemorrhage. Disorders related to an abnormality in blood vessels present similarly to those illnesses involved with altered platelet number or function. In patients with inherited disorders of hemostasis, the pattern of transmission is helpful in making a specific diagnosis. Autosomal recessive inheritance is the pattern in kindred with deficiencies of factors V, VII, X, XI, and XII. Autosomal dominant inheritance is the pattern most commonly seen in von Willebrand's disease and hereditary hemorrhagic telangiectasia. Sex-linked recessive inheritance is the pattern seen in the hemophilias.

Objective

Physical Examination

The physical examination is directed toward detecting evidence of bleeding such as petechiae, purpura, which is confluent petechiae, ecchymoses, hematomas, or hemarthroses. In addition, if a vascular disorder is suspected one should search for telangiectasia and angiomas.

Routine Laboratory Abnormalities

A complete blood count is used to determine the adequacy of platelet numbers. Spontaneous bleeding is uncommon with a platelet count greater than 50,000 but frequent and often severe when the platelet count is below 15,000. Screening laboratory studies are used to suggest the mechanism of the bleeding (see Plans).

PLANS
Diagnostic

The screening tests for hemostatic disorders are listed in Table 12–32–1.

Diagnostic Options. The partial thromboplastin time (PTT) is measured by adding kaolin and phospholipid to plasma. Kaolin activates factors XII and XI. Phospholipid substitutes for platelets and accelerates the reactions involving factors V and VIII. An intact intrinsic and common pathway is necessary for a normal PTT. The PTT is abnormal with deficiencies of high-molecular-weight kininogen, prekallikrein, prothrombin, and fibrinogen. It is also abnormal in deficiencies of or in the presence of inhibitors to factors XII, XI, IX, VIII, X, and V. Factor VII is not involved in the intrinsic pathway and, therefore, the PTT is normal in patients with deficiency or an inhibitor to factor VII.

Prothrombin time (PT) is a screening test that evaluates the extrinsic and common pathways of coagulation. The test is performed by adding an extract of tissue and calcium to plasma. This activates factor VII, which in turn activates the common pathway. Deficiencies or inhibitors to factor VII and the common pathway factors cause a prolongation of the prothrombin time.

The bleeding time (BT) reflects the effectiveness of the primary hemostatic plug produced by platelets. It is measured by determining the time required for bleeding from a small incision in subcutaneous tissue to stop. It is abnormal or prolonged in thrombocytopenia and in qualitative platelet disorders.

A screening test for disorders associated with a vascular defect is not available.

Subsequent to the finding of an abnormal screening test, specific tests are used to define the exact nature of the defect.

A bone marrow aspirate and biopsy are used to determine if inadequate bone marrow production or excessive peripheral destruction of platelets is operative.

Thrombocytopenia

Differential Diagnosis. Thrombocytopenia results from either inadequate bone marrow production or excessive peripheral destruction.

TABLE 12–32–1. SCREENING TEST PATTERNS IN HEMOSTATIC DISORDERS

Test	Disorder
Prolonged PT	Factor VII deficiency
Isolated prolonged PTT	Factor VIII deficiency
	Factor IX deficiency
	Factor XI deficiency
	Factor XII deficiency ⎫
	High–molecular-weight kininogen deficiency ⎬ Negative bleeding history
	Prekallikrein deficiency ⎪
	Lupus anticoagulant ⎭
Prolonged PT and PTT	Factor X deficiency
	Factor V deficiency
	Prothrombin deficiency
	Vitamin K-dependent factor deficiency
	Coumarin therapy
	Disseminated intravascular coagulation
Prolonged PTT and BT	Von Willebrand's disease
Prolonged BT, normal platelet count	Qualitative platelet disorder
Normal screening tests and positive bleeding history	Mild factor deficiency
	Factor XIII deficiency
	α₂- Antiplasmin deficiency
	Vascular defect
	Hereditary hemorrhagic telangiectasia
	Ehlers–Danlos syndrome
	Schönlein–Henoch purpura
	Amyloidosis
	Senile purpura

PT, prothrombin time; PTT, partial thromboplastin time; BT, bleeding time.

Recommended Approach. A careful history and physical examination are instrumental in determining the presence of a drug or underlying illness that may be associated with thrombocytopenia. Thrombocytopenia is discussed in Chapters 12–15 and 12–16.

Qualitative Platelet Defects

Differential Diagnosis. Qualitative platelet defects may be primary or associated with an underlying disorder. The abnormality may lie in the failure of platelets to adhere to subendothelium; produce or release ADP; synthesize thromboxane A_2, which mediates ADP release; or aggregate with ADP.

Von Willebrand's protein acts as an intercellular bridge between the platelet and subendothelium. In its absence or in the presence of an abnormal protein as in von Willebrand's disease, a failure of adhesion occurs. In Bernard–Soulier syndrome platelet glycoproteins 1a and 1b, which are the receptors for Von Willebrand's protein, are absent. Accordingly, there is a deficiency in adhesion to subendothelium in this disorder. In diseases such as multiple myeloma and Waldenström's macroglobulinemia, the excess gamma globulin present may coat platelets and interfere with their ability to adhere.

Storage pool disease results from a decrease in the number of ADP storage granules (dense granules) and is associated with deficient release of ADP. Aspirin acetylates cyclooxygenase, which decreases the production of thromboxane A_2, resulting in defective ADP release. A similar defect is seen following cardiopulmonary bypass and in myeloproliferative disorders. These defects in production or release of ADP produce deficient aggregation and potential bleeding. Glanzman's thromboasthenia results from the absence of platelet glycoproteins 2b and 3a, which interact with ADP to produce aggregation. Ill-defined defects in platelet function occur in renal failure and the myeloproliferative disorder and may be associated with bleeding.

Diagnostic Options. Platelet function tests that measure adhesion and aggregation often are helpful in identifying the specific defect in platelet function so that an exact diagnosis may be made. Not infrequently, platelet dysfunction exists yet an exact diagnosis cannot be made.

Recommended Approach. In the patient with a history and/or physical findings suggestive of platelet-associated bleeding, that is, petechiae and mucous membrane hemorrhage, bleeding time should be measured. If this is abnormal, platelet function tests should be done. Levels of factor VIII and Von Willebrand's protein may need be determined to exclude Von Willebrand's disease.

Deficiency of or Inhibitors to Coagulation Factors

Differential Diagnosis. When the history and/or physical examination reveal evidence of hematoma, hemarthrosis, hematuria, or retroperitoneal bleeding, an abnormality of a plasma coagulation factor is suspected. Coagulation factors apart from factor VIII are synthesized in the liver. Factors VII, IX, and X and prothrombin are vitamin K dependent. Bleeding may occur from either decreased synthesis of a coagulation protein or synthesis of an abnormal molecule. Deficiencies in plasma coagulation factors produce an abnormality in either the PT, PTT, or both. Inhibitors, generally immunoglobulins, may arise to any coagulation factor. The pattern of findings on the PT and/or PTT with inhibitors is similar to that seen when a deficiency or abnormal molecule is present.

Diagnostic Options. With the finding of an abnormal PT and/or PTT, the first study is a mixing test. Here, an equal amount of normal plasma is mixed with the patient's plasma. Should this mixture correct the abnormal coagulation test, the diagnosis of a deficiency may be made. Should this not result in correction of the abnormal test, the presence of an inhibitor is suggested. The identification of the specific biochemical lesion in either case is made by factor assay.

An isolated prolongation of the PT indicates factor VII deficiency. This is confirmed by factor assay.

Isolated prolongation of the PTT occurs with deficiency of or inhibitor to factor XII, XI, IX, or VIII. Deficiencies in high-molecular-weight kininogen and prekallikrein also produce a prolonged PTT. Hemophilia A and hemophilia B caused by deficiencies in factor VIII and factor IX, respectively, are covered in detail in Chapter 12–33. Interestingly, deficiencies of factor XII, high-molecular-weight kininogen, and prekallikrein are not associated with clinical bleeding. This is likely a result of multiple alternative mechanisms for activating the intrinsic system. Deficiency of factor XI is associated with a bleeding tendency. Although inhibitors may develop to any plasma coagulation factor, they most commonly arise to factor VIII. Inhibitors are discussed in detail in Chapter 12–35.

Prolongation of both the PT and PTT occurs with deficiencies of or inhibitors to factors X and V, prothrombin, and fibrinogen. Disseminated intravascular coagulation is also associated with a prolongation of the PT and PTT. This occurs because of the development of fibrin degradation products, which inhibit coagulation, and is exacerbated by the potential depletion of coagulation factors, particularly fibrinogen. Deficiency of vitamin K-dependent factors and anticoagulation with coumarin derivatives also produce prolongation of the PT and PTT.

The lupus anticoagulant is an immunoglobulin directed against phospholipid. When it binds to the phospholipid in the PTT test system, artificial prolongation of the PTT occurs. This antibody may also cause prolongation of the PT with or without an associated hypoprothrombinemia. In the absence of associated hypoprothrombinemia and/or thrombocytopenia, bleeding is not associated with the lupus anticoagulant, but rather in some patients, a hypercoagulable state is present.

Recommended Approach. When a deficiency of or an inhibitor to a plasma coagulation factor is suspected by the history and physical examination, the pattern of the PT and PTT should be examined and a mixing study performed. Diagnostic possibilities should be confirmed by specific coagulation factor assay.

Combined Defects

Differential Diagnosis. The most common disorder of hemostasis that presents as a combined disorder of platelet function and plasma coagulation factor deficiency is von Willebrand's disease. As discussed above, von Willebrand's protein is the intercellular bridge between the platelet and subendothelium. It participates in the mechanism by which the primary hemostatic plug is produced. The bleeding time is prolonged, and bleeding such as seen in platelet dysfunction, for example, petechiae, or excessive menstrual loss is seen. In addition, von Willebrand's protein acts as a carrier molecule for factor VIII and protects it from proteolytic degradation. Accordingly, a severe decrease or abnormal Von Willebrand's protein may cause a significant decrease in factor VIII and a prolonged PTT and bleeding consistent with a plasma coagulation factor deficiency such as hemarthrosis.

Disseminated intravascular coagulation is often associated with thrombocytopenia and also may present as a mixed disorder.

Diagnostic Options. When von Willebrand's disease is suspected, it may be confirmed by measurement of factor VIII, von Willebrand's protein, ristocetin cofactor activity, and the individual subtype determined by crossed immunoelectrophoresis.

Recommended Approach. As von Willebrand's disease is the most likely disorder associated with a combined disorder of hemostasis, it should be looked for specifically in this setting. It is important to remember that the level of von Willebrand's protein may fluctuate in time and increase with situations such as stress and pregnancy. When the index of suspicion for the disorder is high, multiple testings may be necessary. Von Willebrand's disease and disseminated intravascular coagulation are covered in Chapters 12–34 and 12–38, respectively.

Vascular Disorders

Differential Diagnosis. Vascular disorders, characterized by easy bruising and bleeding from small vessels, result either from structural abnormalities of small vessels or by inflammation caused by a secondary process. The diagnosis is most frequently made after thrombocytopenia or a qualitative platelet disorder has been excluded.

These disorders may be either inherited or acquired. The most common inherited disorder is hereditary hemorrhagic telangiectasia. This disease is autosomal dominant in inheritance. Telangiectasias in the skin and mucous membrane are noted in early adult life. There is an ab-

normality or defect in subendothelial connective tissue that produces dilation and thinness of vessels and resultant easy bleeding. The most common symptoms are epistaxis and gastrointestinal bleeding. The diagnosis should be considered in patients with iron deficiency. Lesions blanch with pressure and become more frequent with advancing age. Other inherited vascular disorders are unusual and include Ehlers–Danlos syndrome and osteogenesis imperfecta.

Acquired vascular defects include such disorders as Schönlein–Henoch purpura and connective tissue disorders such as rheumatoid arthritis and amyloidosis. Schönlein–Henoch purpura is thought to be an acute hypersensitivity vasculitis associated with inflammation of capillaries and small arterioles. Patients present with rash, purpura, arthralgias, hematuria, and abdominal pain. It is generally self-limiting but may be recurrent. Symptoms likely result from an increase in vascular permeability and hemorrhage into tissues. Amyloid deposition in perivascular tissue causes increased fragility and leads to purpura and intradermal hemorrhage. Bleeding in the vascular disorders is generally not severe and occurs mainly into skin. The platelet count and bleeding time are normal. The tourniquet test used in the past lacks sensitivity and specificity.

Recommended Approach. When bleeding suggestive of platelet dysfunction such as petechiae and purpura occur in the presence of a normal platelet count and bleeding time, the vascular disorders of hemostasis should be suspected. There are no specific laboratory tests at present to diagnose these disorders, and accordingly, the history and physical examination are of most importance.

Therapeutic

Patients with thrombocytopenia and platelet levels greater than 50,000 do not frequently have spontaneous bleeding yet may bleed excessively with trauma. When bleeding occurs, platelet transfusions should be administered. The patient with a platelet count less than 15,000 should receive platelet transfusions prophylactically to avoid hemorrhage. In some disorders such as thrombotic thrombocytopenic purpura (TTP) platelet transfusion may actually aggravate the underlying disorder and should be used cautiously. Thrombotic thrombocytopenic purpura is discussed in detail elsewhere in this section.

The patient with life-threatening bleeding secondary to a qualitative platelet disorder should be treated with platelet transfusion. If secondary to a drug, the offending agent should be discontinued. Vasopressin (DDAVP) has been used with benefit in some forms of von Willebrand's disease likely by releasing preformed von Willebrand's protein from endothelial cells. It has been used in other disorders of bleeding related to platelet dysfunction with mixed results.

The therapy of disorders associated with plasma coagulation factor deficiencies revolve around replacement of the deficient factor. The treatment of hemophilia, Von Willebrand's disease, and patients with inhibitors is covered elsewhere in this section (Chapters 12–33, 12–34, and 12–35). Replacement of other plasma coagulation factors is accomplished by specific transfusion products such as fresh-frozen plasma and cryoprecipitate.

There is no specific therapy for bleeding associated with vascular disorders other than therapy directed at the underlying disorder in patients with acquired disease.

FOLLOW-UP

Patients with inherited qualitative platelet defects require lifelong follow-up, treatment of bleeding episodes, and perhaps prophylactic preparation prior to invasive procedures. Those who have acquired dysfunction may need no further follow-up if an offending agent can be removed or an underlying illness treated.

Patients with deficiencies in plasma coagulation factors also require lifelong follow-up, treatment during bleeding episodes, and perhaps prophylactic therapy prior to invasive procedures. The abnormal screening test, for example, PTT, and specific assay may be useful during treatment and in the preparation for invasive procedures.

The follow-up of Von Willebrand's disease, which is the most common disorder of hemostasis to present as a mixed bleeding problem, is similar to that of a patient with a deficiency and a plasma coagulation factor and is discussed in detail in Chapter 12–34.

Patients with inherited vascular defects require lifelong follow-up, although there is no specific therapy or laboratory study to follow. A similar situation exists in those with acquired disorders, although specific therapy of an underlying disorder may prove helpful.

DISCUSSION

Prevalence

Thrombocytopenia related to primary hematologic disease is somewhat rare. Thrombopenia related to an infection, drug, or underlying disorder is much more common.

Inherited deficiency of plasma coagulation factors or the development of inhibitors to these factors is relatively rare. Acquired deficiencies of coagulation factors secondary to vitamin K deficiency or the use of coumarin anticoagulants are common.

Although more common than what once was realized, von Willebrand's disease is also an unusual hematologic disorder.

Inherited vascular defects that produce bleeding are very rare. Acquired disorders such as those that occur in the connective disorders or amyloidosis are much more common.

Related Basic Science

The coagulation pathway is shown in Figure 12–32–1. The basic mechanisms of the disease processes involved in thrombocytopenia are discussed in detail in Chapters 12–15 and 12–16.

Inherited qualitative platelet disorders produce bleeding most commonly because of abnormalities in platelet glycoprotein receptors. A better understanding of the molecular biology of these receptors and, accordingly, the genetic aberrations that produce them will be helpful from a diagnostic and, perhaps, treatment standpoint.

Deficiencies of plasma coagulation factors, for example, the hemophilias, may be approached with gene therapy once full characterization of the genetic process that produces the disorder is accomplished. Similarly, the inherited disorders involving vascular defects may also be approached some day with gene therapy following similar investigation.

Natural History and Its Modification with Treatment

Bleeding disorders, whatever the etiology, may produce hemorrhagic death. An accurate diagnosis concerning the specific etiology of the process may make possible specific therapy which may be lifesaving. Despite accurate diagnosis and specific therapy, the disease and/or its treatment may produce secondary associated chronic problems that require significant medical attention. A good example is the health care of the hemophiliac, which is discussed in detail in Chapter 12–33.

Prevention

In the future, some inherited disorders, particularly those involving single genetic lesions, may be treated or prevented by the use of gene ther-

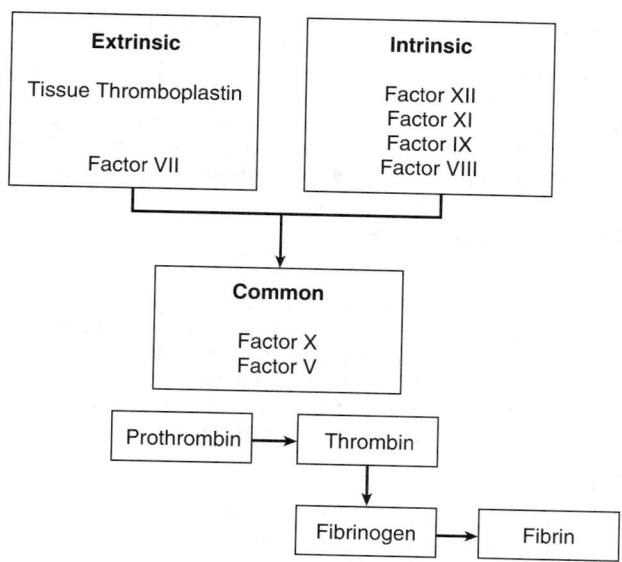

Figure 12–32–1. Coagulation pathways.

apy. Acquired disorders related to drugs or underlying illnesses may be prevented with avoidance of medication or more successful therapy of the underlying disorder.

Cost Containment

An accurate, complete, and specific history and physical examination and prudent use of screening coagulation tests will commonly eliminate the need for many needless and expensive specific laboratory testing procedures.

REFERENCES

Bick RL. Acquired platelet function defects. Hematol Oncol Clin North Am 1992;6(6):1203.

Coleman RW, Hirsh J, Marder UJ, Salzman EW. Hemostasis & thrombosis: Basic principles and clinical practice. Philadelphia: Lippincott, 1994.

Hassouna HI. Laboratory evaluation of hemostatic disorders. Hematol Oncol Clin North Am 1993;7(6):1161.

Kitchens CS. Approach to the bleeding patient. Hematol Oncol Clin North Am 1992;6(5):983.

Williams WJ, Beutler EB, Erslev AJ, Lichtman MA. Hematology. New York: McGraw-Hill, 1990.

CHAPTER 12–33

Hemophilia

Kandice Kottke-Marchant, M.D., Ph.D.

DEFINITION

Hemophilia A is a genetically inherited abnormality of coagulation factor VIII that leads to severe bleeding abnormalities. Hemophilia B is similar to hemophilia A, but is an inherited abnormality of coagulation factor IX.

ETIOLOGY

Factor VIII is a protein coded for by a gene on the X chromosome, which participates in the coagulation cascade as a part the tenase complex where it is a cofactor to activated factor IX in the conversion of factor X to activated factor X. Hemophilia A is a congenital coagulation disorder resulting from a deficiency or defect of factor VIII. It is inherited in an X-linked recessive fashion and males are affected almost exclusively.

Factor IX is a serine protease that participates in the coagulation cascade in the conversion of factor X to activated factor X, as mentioned above. Hemophilia B, also called Christmas disease, is a deficiency or defect of factor IX inherited in an X-linked fashion analogous to hemophilia A.

CRITERIA FOR DIAGNOSIS
Suggestive

Suggestive criteria for the diagnosis of both hemophilia A and B include a moderate to severe, lifelong bleeding diathesis in male patients characterized by spontaneous bleeding into joints, muscles, and soft tissues and prolonged bleeding from skin wounds. In patients with such a history, an isolated prolongation of the activated partial thromboplastin time suggests the diagnosis of either hemophilia A or hemophilia B.

Definitive

Definitive diagnosis of hemophilia A or B relies on the performance of specific coagulation assays for factor VIII or IX. The severity of hemophilia A or B is classified by the level of factor VIII or IX activity: less than 2%, severe; 2 to 5%, moderate; 5 to 30%, mild disease. Some authors consider severe factor VIII defects to be those with factor VIII or IX levels of less than 5%.

CLINICAL MANIFESTATIONS
Subjective

Patients with hemophilia A and B have similar clinical manifestations. Bleeding problems often start at birth, with excessive bleeding during circumcision. Patients with hemophilia A and B have hemorrhagic problems most often characterized by deep bleeding, such as internal hematomas and joint bleeding, rather than mucosal bleeding. Long-term complications of the hemorrhagic disorder include hemarthosis with crippling joint fibrosis and the risk of intracranial hemorrhage. Both hemophilia A and B are inherited in an X-linked recessive fashion and affected individuals are almost always males. Mothers of hemophiliacs are often asymptomatic carriers, although up to 30% of hemophilia A cases are thought to be due to spontaneous mutations. Finding laboratory values consistent with hemophilia A in a female is unusual, but may suggest a symptomatic carrier state, a rare homozygote, a chromosomal abnormality such as 46XY, or von Willebrand's disease type Normandy.

Objective
Physical Examination

Early in the course of the disease, the physical examination may be normal between bleeding episodes. Joint pain or swelling can be found and suggests hemarthrosis. Joints typically involved include the knees, elbows, ankles, and wrists. In patients with long-standing hemophilia, joint fixation, flexion contractures, and muscle atrophy may indicate chronic degenerative joint changes due to repeated hemarthrosis. Indications for muscular hematomas on physical examination include superficial bruising and painful intramuscular swelling occasionally accompanied by skin necrosis or gangrene. Deep hematomas are more difficult to diagnose on physical examination and may require ultrasound or computed tomography scans for detection.

Routine Laboratory Abnormalities

Patients with hemophilia A or B will present with a normal PT and a prolonged aPTT. The routine laboratory examination of the blood and urine is usually normal, except that a normocytic anemia may be seen if hemorrhage is severe.

The chest x-ray film is usually normal, as is the electrocardiogram.

PLANS
Diagnostic
Differential Diagnosis

Male patients who present for medical attention with a characteristic bleeding pattern, prolonged activated partial thromboplastin time

(aPTT) and a sex-linked family history of bleeding diathesis pose little difficulty in the diagnosis of either hemophilia A or B after appropriately decreased factor levels are documented. Other disorders to consider in patients with a bleeding diathesis and elevated aPTT are von Willebrand's disease and factor XI deficiency. Bleeding is usually less severe in patients with factor XI deficiency, the inheritance pattern is autosomal, and the defect is more common in the Jewish population. The bleeding pattern in mild von Willebrand's disease more often involves mucocutaneous sites than deep tissue sites, the inheritance is usually autosomal dominant, and the bleeding time is often prolonged. Patients with severe type III von Willebrand's disease may present identically to those with severe hemophilia, except for the autosomal inheritance pattern. To distinguish type III von Willebrand's disease from severe hemophilia A, an assay of von Willebrand's factor antigen is suggested. Patients with deficiencies of factor XII, prekallekrein, or high-molecular-weight kininogen present with an isolated elevation of the aPTT, but their history is usually devoid of bleeding episodes.

Diagnostic Options

The definitive diagnosis of hemophilia A or B is arrived at with specific laboratory tests. In general, a panel of screening hemostasis tests (prothrombin time, aPTT, platelet count, bleeding time) point to the diagnosis of either hemophilia A or B. Definitive diagnosis of hemophilia A requires the demonstration of a low level of factor VIII coagulant activity. Definitive diagnosis of hemophilia B requires the demonstration of a low level of factor IX coagulant activity.

Recommended Approach

In patients with strong, documented family histories of either hemophilia A or B, diagnostic laboratory studies would include only a PT, aPTT, and either factor VIII or IX level. In patients without a family history, testing needs to be more extensive to eliminate other coagulopathies. In these patients, diagnostic tests should include prothrombin time, aPTT, platelet count, bleeding time, factor VIII coagulant activity, factor IX coagulation activity, and von Willebrand factor antigen. Exclusion of circulating factor inhibitors should be sought as outlined in Chapter 12–35 in patients with severe hemophilia who experience an increased requirement for factor replacement therapy.

Therapeutic
Therapeutic Options

Patients with hemophilia A can be treated with fresh-frozen plasma, cryoprecipitate, factor VIII concentrates, or 1-amino-8-D-arginine vasopressin (DDAVP). In general, factor VIII concentrates have been the mainstay of therapy for hemophilia A; however, these concentrates historically have been responsible for viral transmission to patients, as they are prepared from a pool of hundreds or thousands of donors. Unfortunately, many patients with hemophilia A have been infected with HIV and have developed AIDS due to use of factor VIII concentrates. Once this devastating complication was realized, manufacturers devised many processes to sterilize the concentrates, including pasteurization, solvent/detergent treatment, filtration, and purification using immunoaffinity chromatography. Most of the currently used concentrates are purified using immunoaffinity chromatography followed by a viral attenuation process. Examples include Monoclate (Armour), Hemofil-M (Hyland), and Antihemophilic Factor Method-M (American Red Cross). With these products the transmission of hepatitis and HIV is negligible. Recently, recombinant factor VIII has become available and use of this product is expected to nearly eliminate risk of viral transmission. DDAVP is an analog of arginine vasopressin and causes the release of factor VIII and von Willebrand's factor from endothelial storage sites. It is an effective treatment in patients with mild to moderate hemophilia A, but is generally ineffective in patients with severe hemophilia A. Patients with hemophilia A who have developed inhibitors to factor VIII present further challenges in therapy, which are discussed in Chapter 12–35.

Factor IX deficiency can be treated with fresh-frozen plasma, newly available concentrates of factor IX, or prothrombin complex concentrates (factor IX together with other vitamin K-dependent coagulation factors). Factor IX levels are negligible in cryoprecipitate and DDAVP does not influence plasma factor IX levels, so neither of these are therapeutic options for patients with hemophilia B. Carefully screened fresh-frozen plasma carries a low, but still present risk of viral transmission, and the high volume of this therapy is a consideration when large doses of factor IX are required. Many of the prothrombin complex concentrates contain activated vitamin K-dependent coagulation factors and have been associated with a risk of thrombotic complications, but these remain the mainstay of therapy for hemophilia B due to the increased cost of the more highly purified factor IX concentrates.

Recommended Approach

Factor replacement in hemophilia A should be limited to treatment of bleeding episodes and coverage during surgical procedures or after trauma. For severe hemophilia A, factor VIII concentrates (either virally inactivated or recombinant) are the recommended primary therapeutic agents. The amount of factor VIII replacement needed may vary depending on the patient's basal factor VIII level, the potency of the replacement product, and the type and extent of the bleeding episode. The actual amount of factor VIII contained in any replacement product varies per batch and is listed on the product label. In general, cryoprecipitate contains approximately 20 to 30 U/mL factor VIII and the concentrates contain approximately 300 to 1000 U/mL factor VIII. In calculating factor replacement, 1 U of factor VIII activity is defined as the amount of factor VIII contained in 1 mL of normal plasma (also defined as 100% activity). In general, the infusion of 1 U of factor VIII per kilogram of body weight increases the patient's factor VIII level by 2% (or 0.02 U/mL). For example, in a 50-kg hemophiliac with a basal factor VIII level of 0%, the infusion of 2500 U of factor VIII would be required to raise the factor VIII level to 100%. Target factor VIII levels for severe bleeding episodes would be 70 to 100%, whereas 30 to 50% would be adequate for minor bleeding episodes. The half-life of infused factor VIII obtained from all available plasma-derived products is approximately 8 to 12 hours, so plasma factor VIII levels would be expected to be half-maximal 12 hours after the original infusion. A repeated infusion of approximately half of the initial bolus amount would be needed every 12 hours to maintain the increased levels of factor VIII. During prolonged factor VIII replacement therapy, factor VIII coagulant activity levels should be measured daily to monitor the efficacy of therapy. Instead of giving repeated bolus doses of factor VIII, a constant plasma level can be obtained using an initial bolus dose followed by continuous infusion. A continuous infusion rate of 3 U/kg/h usually results in a plasma factor VIII level of 50%.

As in hemophilia A, treatment for hemophilia B should be given for bleeding episodes and during surgery. The recommended replacement products are either the prothrombin complex concentrates or the more expensive, purified factor IX. The half-life of factor IX is longer than that of factor VIII, approximately 24 hours, so plasma replacement needs to be given less frequently. Factor IX is a smaller protein than factor VIII (56,000 daltons versus 330,000 daltons) and factor IX distributes in both the intravascular and extravascular spaces, so the volume of distribution for factor IX is twice that of factor VIII. Thus, twice as much concentrate must be given to achieve a similar increase in factor levels. For the example above, a 50-kg patient with hemophilia B with a basal factor IX level of 0% would require the infusion of 5000 U of factor IX to raise the factor IX level to 100%. Target factor IX levels for severe bleeding episodes would be 70 to 100%, whereas 30 to 50% would be adequate for minor bleeding episodes. During prolonged factor IX replacement therapy, factor IX coagulant activity levels should be measured daily to monitor the efficacy of therapy.

FOLLOW-UP

Patients with severe hemophilia need to be followed for long periods by their physician to treat recurring bleeding episodes effectively. A close relationship needs to be established between the physician, patient, and family to ensure proper education of the patient and his family as well as to treat bleeding. Many patients can be maintained on home factor replacement therapy, but they should still report the incidence of any bleeding episodes to their physician. Periodic visits to a physician or hemophilia center should be scheduled, even in the absence of overt bleeding episodes, to evaluate the presence of joint disease or psychosocial problems. Laboratory evaluation should include tests to determine the development of plasma inhibitors or viral infections.

DISCUSSION
Prevalence and Incidence

Approximately 1 in 10,000 males are affected by hemophilia A in Great Britain, the United States, and Europe. The disorder is less common in African and among African-Americans. Hemophilia B is one fifth to one tenth as common as hemophilia A. Hemophilia B is more common in some select population groups, such as the Amish of Ohio and Pennsylvania.

Related Basic Science

Factor VIII is a glycoprotein present in trace quantities (0.2 µg/mL) in plasma that is a cofactor in the activation of factor X. It is coded for by a gene 186 kb long on the long arm of the X chromosome. Factor VIII exists in plasma as a two-chain protein with a light chain of about 80,000 daltons and a heavy chain with a variable molecular weight of 90,000 to 210,000 daltons. Factor VIII circulates in plasma bound to von Willebrand's factor, and formation of this complex is thought to protect factor VIII from proteolytic degradation. Factor VIII binds von Willebrand's factor via its light chain, which must be cleaved by thrombin to release factor VIII into plasma for procoagulant activity. For factor VIII to possess cofactor activity, factor VIII itself must be activated, primarily by thrombin. Thrombin cleaves several sites on the heavy chain of factor VIII, which activates the cofactor function of the molecule. Although it has no proteolytic activity, factor VIII accelerates the activation of factor X by activated factor IX, presumably by altering the conformation of one or more proteins. The complex of factors VIII, IX, and X, called the tenase complex, also requires phospholipid and calcium for full activity. Activated factor VIII is inactivated via proteolytic degradation by activated protein C.

Mutations in patients with severe hemophilia have been found to be frameshifts and deletions, whereas mildly affected patients are more likely to have one of many possible point mutations. Because of the high frequency of gene deletions in severe hemophiliacs, up to 90% of patients do not have detectable antigen levels and thus have a true deficiency and not merely a dysproteinemia. Recent studies have detected a "hotspot" for mutations, with up to 40% of patients with severe hemophilia A having a mutation in intron 22 of the factor VIII gene.

Factor IX is a single-chain protein containing 415 amino acids, coded for by a gene located on the long arm of the X chromosome. It is a vitamin K-dependent factor, and requires posttranslational gamma carboxylation of N-terminal glutamyl residues for maximal procoagulant activity. Factor IX is activated by the cleavage of two peptide bonds with the formation of a two-chain activated protein. This activation takes place in the absence of phospholipids and is carried out by either factor XIa or VIIa. Once activated, factor IX has a serine protease activity and, in turn, activates factor X with the participation of the tenase complex, as described above. Most patients with hemophilia B have a true deficiency of factor IX due to gene deletions, insertions, and nonsense mutations, but the rest have a dysproteinemia with detectable antigen levels caused by point mutations. Many different mutations have been described in patients with hemophilia B.

Natural History and Its Modification with Treatment

Before the advent of factor replacement therapy, hemophilia was often a fatal disease. The availability of factor concentrates for therapy of bleeding episodes and coverage during surgery has had a major impact on the survival of patients with both hemophilia A and B. Most patients lead normal, productive lives and many can administer replacement therapy at home. There is still severe morbidity associated with the disease, especially joint disease and, more recently, the transmission of HIV. Most of the currently marketed factor concentrates and the recently available recombinant factor VIII should eliminate the fear of life-threatening viral transmission in this population of patients.

Prevention

Hemophilia A and B are both X-linked genetic disorders that cannot be prevented. As mothers and daughters of known hemophiliacs are for the most part obligate carriers, chorionic villous sampling can be used to diagnose hemophilia in the first trimester of pregnancy and genetic counseling may influence the number of hemophiliacs born.

Cost Containment

Patients with severe hemophilia require factor replacement for life. Although many of the newer recombinant or highly purified products are more expensive for the amount of factor infused, they are significantly safer than older products, cryoprecipitate, or unfractionated plasma in the risk of viral transmission, which is extremely costly, in both monetary and human terms. The use of home infusion therapy for hemophilia has resulted in cost savings compared with administration of factor replacement therapy in the hospital.

REFERENCES

Forbes CD, Madhok R. Genetic disorders of blood coagulation: Clinical presentation and management. In: Ratnoff OD, Forbes CD, eds. Disorders of hemostasis. 2nd ed. Philadelphia: Saunders, 1991:141.

Furie B, Limentani ST, Rosenfield. A practical guide to the evaluation and treatment of hemophilia. Blood 1994;84:3.

Kottke-Marchant K. Laboratory diagnosis of hemorrhagic and thrombotic disorders. Hematol Oncol Clin North Am 1994;8:809.

Westphal RG, Smith DM. Treatment of hemophilia and von Willebrand's disease: New developments. Arlington, VA: American Association of Blood Banks, 1989.

CHAPTER 12–34

von Willebrand's Disease

Kandice Kottke-Marchant, M.D., Ph.D.

DEFINITION

Von Willebrand's disease is a heterogeneous group of genetic disorders resulting in dysfunction or deficiency of von Willebrand's factor. It is the most common of the congenital hemorrhagic disorders and usually manifests as a mild bleeding diathesis. More than 20 different subtypes have been described, most of which are quite rare. The von Willebrand's disease subtypes can be divided into three main categories: type I, an autosomal dominant disorder characterized by a quantitative decrease in normal-appearing von Willebrand's factor; type II, variably inherited qualitative defects in von Willebrand's factor structure and function; and type III, an autosomal recessive severe bleeding disorder with virtually absent von Willebrand's factor levels.

ETIOLOGY

Von Willebrand's factor is a large, multimeric protein produced by endothelial cells and megakaryocytes that is stored in Weibel–Palade bodies and platelet alpha granules. Von Willebrand's factor plays a central role in the interaction of various elements of the hemostasic system and is a principal factor in primary hemostasis. Von Willebrand's factor acts as a carrier for factor VIII, mediates platelet adhesion to subendothelium via binding to several platelet surface glycoproteins, and is a component of the extracellular matrix. Abnormalities in the amount or function of von Willebrand's factor lead to defects of platelet adhesion and the clinical manifestation of platelet-type or mucosal-related bleeding symptoms. Because of the protective role of von Willebrand's factor as a carrier protein for factor VIII, patients with abnormalities of von Willebrand's factor also have decreased factor VIII levels in plasma due to a rapid proteolytic inactivation of factor VIII. Rarely, von Willebrand's disease can be acquired in association with clinical settings such as plasma cell dyscrasias, lymphoproliferative disorders, and autoimmune disorders, usually due to an antibody to von Willebrand's factor. Acquired von Willebrand's disease may also be seen in patients with diverse disorders such as congenital heart disease, Wilms' tumor, Ehlers–Danlos syndrome, and myeloproliferative syndromes.

CRITERIA FOR DIAGNOSIS
Suggestive

Suggestive criteria for the diagnosis of von Willebrand's disease include a clinical history compatible with a mild, mucocutaneous or platelet-type bleeding disorder in a patient with abnormalities of screening coagulation assays, particularly the bleeding time and the activated partial thromboplastin time (aPPT). Because of the autosomal inheritance patterns of many of the von Willebrand's disease subtypes, a history of a mild bleeding disorder in both male and female members of the patient's family is helpful. The recent onset of clinical symptoms and laboratory abnormalities consistent with von Willebrand's disease may suggest an acquired type of von Willebrand's disease.

Definitive

Diagnosis of von Willebrand's disease can be inferred from the patient's personal and family history, as well as routine screening coagulation assays, but definitive diagnosis requires the use of very specific laboratory assays. In patients with the most common type of von Willebrand's disease (type I), the typical laboratory findings include a prolonged aPTT, prolonged bleeding time, decreased factor VIII coagulant activity, decreased von Willebrand's antigen level, and decreased functional activity of von Willebrand's factor (ristocetin cofactor assay). Analysis of the multimer size distribution of the von Willebrand's factor protein can be performed by sodium dodecyl sulfate–agarose gel electrophoresis and can be used to help determine the disease subtype. The different subtypes of von Willebrand's disease are due to different abnormalities of the protein, and their typical laboratory findings are listed in Table 12–34–1.

Although cumbersome, the differentiation of the various subtypes of von Willebrand's disease is clinically useful, as the recommended therapy varies with the subtypes.

CLINICAL MANIFESTATIONS
Subjective

The majority of patients with von Willebrand's disease have a mild bleeding diathesis that is more similar to that of patients with platelet dysfunction than hemophilia, as they complain of purpura, easy bruisability, mucosal bleeding, epistaxis, prolonged bleeding with cuts or trauma, and menorrhagia. More unusual forms of bleeding include gastrointestinal bleeding, tonsillar hemorrhage, pulmonary hemorrhage, and postpartum bleeding. Some patients with mild von Willebrand's disease are asymptomatic, even with challenges to the hemostatic system, such as trauma and surgery. The bleeding tendency may vary in a patient over a period of time. Von Willebrand's factor levels are known to fluctuate with time, and this fluctuation may account for the variable presence or absence of bleeding symptoms experienced by persons with von Willebrand's disease. Additionally, the bleeding diathesis may wane as the patient ages or during pregnancy, when levels of von Willebrand's factor tend to increase. Patients with some of the subtypes

TABLE 12–34–1. LABORATORY FINDINGS IN VON WILLEBRAND'S DISEASE

Disorder	aPTT	BT	fVIII:C	vWF:Ag	Ristocetin: Cofactor	vWF Multimers
Type I	Slightly elevated	Prolonged or normal	Decreased	Decreased	Decreased	Normal
Type IIA	Elevated	Prolonged	Decreased or normal	Usually normal	Decreased	Loss of high- and intermediate-MW multimers
Type IIB*	Elevated	Prolonged	Decreased or normal	Usually normal	Decreased or normal	Loss of high-MW multimers
Pseudo-vWD*,+	Elevated	Prolonged	Decreased or normal	Decreased or normal	Decreased	Loss of high-MW multimers
Type Normandy	Elevated	Normal	Decreased	Normal	Normal	Normal
Type III	Elevated	Prolonged	Markedly decreased	Absent (or<3%)	Absent	Usually absent

aPTT, activated partial thromboplastin time; BT, bleeding time; fVIII:C, factor VIII coagulant activity; vWF:Ag, von Willebrand's factor:antigen; vWD, von Willebrand's disease; MW, molecular weight.
*Demonstrates increased susceptibility to ristocetin-induced aggregation (RIPA).
+Platelet aggregation demonstrable with addition of cryoprecipitate.

of von Willebrand's disease (particularly type IIb and pseudo-von Willebrand's disease) may have thrombocytopenia, especially after treatment with 1-desamino-8-D-arginine vasopressin (DDAVP). Patients with severe (type III) von Willebrand's disease may additionally have major bleeding symptoms similar to those observed in severe hemophiliacs, such as hemarthrosis, due to their very low levels of factor VIII. Patients with von Willebrand's disease type Normandy have a defect in the ability of von Willebrand's factor to bind factor VIII. This results in decreased plasma levels of factor VIII with normal von Willebrand's factor levels. This disorder may explain some of the cases of "autosomal hemophilia" described in the literature.

Most of the subtypes of von Willebrand's disease are inherited in an autosomal dominant fashion. Mild bleeding symptoms are often reported in family members of both sexes. Three subtypes—type IIc, type III, and type Normandy—appear to be inherited in an autosomal recessive fashion, so parents of affected patients are usually normal by clinical and laboratory criteria.

Objective

Physical Examination

Physical examination in patients with von Willebrand's disease is often normal, but signs of mucocutaneous bleeding or ecchymoses may be present. Examination should include the nares and the gingiva for signs of recent bleeding. Evidence of gastrointestinal bleeding should be sought by evaluating the presence of occult blood in stool. Joint pain or swelling may indicate the presence of hemarthosis in patients with severe von Willebrand's disease.

Routine Laboratory Abnormalities

Abnormalities of several routine laboratory tests can be seen in patients with von Willebrand's disease. The most common abnormality seen is an elevation of the aPTT, with a normal prothrombin time. The complete blood count is usually normal, but if bleeding is severe, the patient may have a normocytic anemia. Some of the rare subtypes of von Willebrand's disease are associated with thrombocytopenia. The urinalysis may show erythrocytes in the urine, but should be normal otherwise. Abnormalities of the chest x-ray, electrocardiogram, and routine chemistry tests are unusual.

PLANS
Diagnostic

Differential Diagnosis

The combination of a mild mucocutaneous bleeding diathesis with an elevated aPTT and bleeding time, together with a decreased factor VIII coagulant activity, decreased von Willebrand's factor antigen, and decreased ristocetin cofactor is characteristic of von Willebrand's disease. Some patients with mild von Willebrand's disease, however, may not

have bleeding symptoms or may have a normal aPTT or bleeding time. In patients with only a prolonged bleeding time, the presence of platelet dysfunction should be sought. Patients with bleeding abnormalities and an isolated prolongation of aPTT should be evaluated for abnormalities of the intrinsic pathway, such as deficiencies of prekallikrein and factors XII, XI, IX, and VIII, in addition to evaluation for von Willebrand's disease. Patients with type III von Willebrand's disease may present with severe neonatal bleeding and be clinically mistaken for hemophiliacs. The diagnosis of type III von Willebrand's disease will be missed in these patients if laboratory evaluation is limited to analysis of factor VIII coagulant activity.

Diagnostic Options

The definitive diagnosis of von Willebrand's disease is established with proper laboratory testing. In general, a screening hemostatis panel (prothrombin time, aPTT, platelet count, bleeding time) suggests the diagnosis of von Willebrand's disease.

Typical laboratory findings of type I von Willebrand's disease are listed in Table 12–34–1. Von Willebrand's factor multimer analysis will show a normal distribution of multimer sizes with a decreased total amount. Caution should be exerted in diagnosing type I von Willebrand's disease in individuals with blood type O, as factor VIII coagulant activity and von Willebrand's factor antigen levels are normally lower in these individuals.

Numerous type II von Willebrand's disease subtypes have been described, but the two that merit discussion include types IIA and IIB. The laboratory features of type IIA von Willebrand's disease have been summarized in Table 12–34–1 and are distinctive for a disproportionately decreased ristocetin cofactor activity compared with von Willebrand's factor antigen levels and a loss of both high- and middle-molecular-weight von Willebrand's factor multimers. Type IIB von Willebrand's disease is characterized by loss of only the highest-molecular-weight multimers and by an enhanced aggregation to ristocetin. With the establishment of a panel of known mutations for type IIA and IIB von Willebrand's disease, the laboratory diagnosis of these subtypes of von Willebrand's disease may be done by molecular techniques in the near future. Clinically, type IIB von Willebrand's disease is important to diagnose because patients may become thrombocytopenic if treated with DDAVP. Platelet-type von Willebrand's disease or pseudo-von Willebrand's disease is a rare subtype that is really a platelet disorder rather than a von Willebrand's factor abnormality, but it bears striking resemblance to type IIB von Willebrand's disease in laboratory tests. This disorder can be distinguished from type IIB von Willebrand's disease by the ability of cryoprecipitate to stimulate aggregation of platelets in platelet-type von Willebrand's disease and by the presence of large platelets.

The laboratory findings seen in patients with type III von Willebrand's disease are listed in Table 12–34–1. Unlike other von Willebrand's disease subtypes, patients with type III defects may develop antibodies to von Willebrand's factor. These antibodies usually interfere with ristocetin cofactor activity and are usually not detectable by aPTT mixing studies.

Persons with type O blood may have lower von Willebrand's factor antigen levels than persons with type A, B, or AB blood. Evaluation of blood type is suggested in evaluating persons for possible von Willebrand's disease. Von Willebrand's factor levels may fluctuate in both normal individuals and those with von Willebrand's disease. Thus, to completely exclude von Willebrand's disease, laboratory evaluation of von Willebrand's factor should be performed more than once with an interval of at least a month.

Recommended Approach

The recommended diagnostic approach in a patient suspected of having von Willebrand's disease is first to evaluate a screening hemostasis panel (prothrombin time, aPTT, platelet count, bleeding time). If the aPTT and bleeding time are prolonged, then all of the specific assays for von Willebrand's disease (factor VIII coagulant activity, von Willebrand's factor antigen, ristocetin cofactor, ristocetin-induced platelet aggregation, multimeric analysis) should be performed on a single specimen to eliminate difficulties due to temporal variability of von Willebrand's factor levels.

Therapeutic

Therapeutic Options

Most of the subtypes of von Willebrand's disease respond therapeutically to infusion of DDAVP; however, the bleeding diathesis in most subtypes of von Willebrand's disease is mild and treatment is usually necessary only in preparation for surgery or to treat bleeding complications of trauma. DDAVP is a vasopressin analog and, because it is not derived form human plasma, carries no risk of viral transmission. Intravenous infusions of 0.3 to 0.4 µg/kg DDAVP usually result in elevation of von Willebrand's factor antigen or ristocetin cofactor levels three- or fourfold above baseline within 1 hour of infusion. Von Willebrand's factor antigen levels usually decrease back to baseline within 6 to 8 hours and repeated infusions of DDAVP should be given every 8 to 12 hours when increased hemostasis is necessary for prolonged periods. Not all patients respond equally to DDAVP and a trial of DDAVP is often recommended before the first use of DDAVP, especially if it is to be given during a surgical procedure. Because of problems with thrombocytopenia, patients with type IIB and platelet-type von Willebrand's disease should not be given DDAVP. DDAVP is usually ineffective in patients with type III von Willebrand's disease. Side effects of DDAVP are usually mild and include facial flushing due to cutaneous vasodilation, headache, mild tachycardia, mild decrease in blood pressure, and hyponatremia. Tachyphylaxis has been reported occasionally with repeated use of DDAVP. Rare cases of thrombosis have been reported with DDAVP, but usually in patients with preexistent cardiovascular disease.

If DDAVP does not give the desired improvement in von Willebrand's factor levels, plasma-based therapy is available for von Willebrand's disease. The most commonly used plasma product for treatment of von Willebrand's disease is cryoprecipitate, although fresh-frozen plasma may be used if cryoprecipitate is not available. Cryoprecipitate contains both coagulant factor VIII and von Willebrand's factor. Currently, cryoprecipitate is produced from virally screened plasma. It does not undergo viral inactivation, and there is a risk of viral transmission. Therapy is usually empiric, but recommended starting dosages are one "bag" of cryoprecipitate per 10 kg body weight per day. Cryoprecipitate should not be used in patients with platelet-type von Willebrand's disease. Rather, these patients should be treated with platelet transfusions. Most currently available factor VIII concentrates do not contain the desired concentration of high-molecular-weight von Willebrand's factor multimers and are ineffective in treating von Willebrand's disease. Some success has been achieved with Humate P, which has more of the high-molecular-weight multimers. Patients with inhibitors to von Willebrand's factor pose a difficult therapeutic problem. Cryoprecipitate transfusion is often ineffective, especially with high-titer inhibitors. Other options include high-dose intravenous gamma globulin, plasmapheresis, and immunoadsorption.

Recommended Approach

When improved hemostasis is required in patients with most subtypes of von Willebrand's disease, the recommended therapy is DDAVP, as discussed above. DDAVP is not recommended for patients with type IIB, type III, or platelet-type von Willebrand's disease. If DDAVP does not provide the expected therapeutic results, cryoprecipitate should be tried next. The first line of therapy for patients with type IIB and III von Willebrand's disease is cryoprecipitate. Patients with platelet-type von Willebrand's disease should be treated with platelet transfusions, when necessary.

FOLLOW-UP

Most patients with von Willebrand's disease have very mild hemostatic problems and do not require close follow-up; however, patients with type III von Willebrand's disease may require long-term follow-up to optimize therapy. Patients with acquired inhibitors to von Willebrand's factor are often difficult to treat and require close observation and flexibility in changing therapeutic approaches.

DISCUSSION
Prevalence and Incidence

The incidence of the autosomal dominant forms of von Willebrand's disease ranges from 1 per 100 in Italy to 3 per 100,000 in Great Britain. Type III von Willebrand's disease is much more uncommon, being seen in only 1 per 1,000,000 individuals. The true incidence of von Willebrand's disease is difficult to determine due to the variability in the laboratory and clinical manifestations of the disease.

Related Basic Science
Genetics

The gene for von Willebrand's factor is located on the short arm of chromosome 12. It is translated to a 8.7-kb-long strand of mRNA that is transcribed to a protein of 2813 amino acids, which is processed to a mature von Willebrand's factor subunit of 2050 amino acids. Von Willebrand's factor is synthesized in megakaryocytes and endothelial cells and is stored in the Weibel–Palade bodies of endothelial cells or the alpha granules of platelets prior to release. Some of von Willebrand's factor is released into plasma, where it complexes with coagulation factor VIII and circulates in the bloodstream. Von Willebrand's factor is also released into the subendothelial matrix, where it complexes with other extracellular matrix proteins such as collagen and fibronectin. Stimuli for release of the Weibel–Palade bodies include thrombin, histamine, and the vasopressin derivative DDAVP.

Biological Derangement

Von Willebrand's factor plays a central role in the interaction of various elements of the hemostatic system and is a principal factor in primary hemostasis. Von Willebrand's factor acts as a carrier for factor VIII and extends factor VIII's half-life in plasma, most likely by protecting factor VIII from proteolytic degradation. The N-terminal portion of factor VIII is associated with the N-terminal region of von Willebrand's factor. Patients with mutations in the N-terminal region of von Willebrand's factor have been described to have decreased von Willebrand's factor/factor VIII binding and decreased plasma factor VIII levels (von Willebrand's disease type Normandy). The mechanism of platelet adhesion to subendothelium is thought to involve binding of von Willebrand's factor to either GPIb or GPIIb/IIIa on the platelet membrane and to collagen or other extracellular matrix components. Patients with type IIA and IIB von Willebrand's disease have abnormalities in the binding of von Willebrand's factor to GPIb. At high-shear conditions, von Willebrand's factor is also able to bind to GPIIb/IIIa, although this receptor usually binds to fibrinogen. Under unstimulated conditions, von Willebrand's factor does not bind to either GPIb or GPIIb/IIIa. On binding to subendothelium or interaction with the antibiotic ristocetin or botrocetin, a conformational change occurs in von Willebrand's factor and binding to the platelet surface glycoproteins can occur.

Natural History and Its Modification with Treatment

Most patients with von Willebrand's disease have only a mild bleeding diathesis and treatment does not markedly prolong their life; however, treatment can decrease morbidity during surgery or treatment of major trauma. Patients with type III von Willebrand's disease have a life-threatening bleeding disorder. Without proper treatment with plasma products, their prognosis is similar to that of persons with untreated severe hemophilia.

Prevention

Classic von Willebrand's disease is a genetic abnormality and prevention is not possible. The genetic abnormalities have not been determined for most of the subtypes of von Willebrand's disease, so carrier detection is not yet possible and genetic counseling is not useful. Acquired forms of von Willebrand's disease are usually seen with hematologic or other malignancies, and again, prevention is not possible.

Cost Containment

In general, von Willebrand's disease produces only mild symptoms and can be treated in a cost-effective manner with DDAVP. Laboratory testing for von Willebrand's disease is expensive because a number of different assays must be employed. Complete testing for von Willebrand's disease should be undertaken only in persons with suggestive clinical histories and appropriate abnormalities of screening coagulation tests.

REFERENCES

Bloom AL. Von Willebrand factor: Clinical features and inherited and acquired disorders. Mayo Clin Proc 1991; 66:743.

Ginsburg D, Bowie EJW. Molecular genetics of von Willebrand's disease. Blood 1992;79:2507.

Ruggeri ZM, Ware J. The structure and function of von Willebrand factor. Thromb Haemost 1992;67:594.

Ruggeri ZM, Zimmerman TS. Von Willebrand factor and von Willebrand disease. Blood 1987;70:895.

Scott JP, Montgomery RR. Therapy of VWD. Semin Thromb Hemost 1993;19:37.

CHAPTER 12–35

Coagulation Inhibitors

Kandice Kottke-Marchant, M.D., Ph.D.

DEFINITION

Circulating coagulation inhibitors are acquired substances, usually immunoglobulins, that bind to coagulation proteins or inhibit the formation of coagulation complexes.

ETIOLOGY

Coagulation inhibitors can be divided into two general classes. The first class consists of immunoglobulins (Igs), usually IgG, that bind to coagulation proteins. These are often referred to as specific factor inhibitors. They are not infrequently observed in patients with severe deficiencies of a coagulation factor, such as hemophilia A and B. The production of these inhibitors is thought to arise when patients who are deficient in a coagulation protein are exposed to a "foreign" protein through transfusion of the deficient factor. This transfusion then stimulates antibody production against the replaced factor. Rarely, specific factor inhibitors arise de novo in patients without coagulation factor deficiencies. These de novo inhibitors may be seen in elderly persons, postpartum, or in patients with plasma cell dyscrasias, autoimmune disorders, or lymphoproliferative disorders. These specific factor inhibitors are often associated with severe bleeding problems and are therapeutically problematic.

The second class of acquired inhibitors are those that do not bind to specific coagulation proteins, but rather have activity against phospholipids. These antibodies disrupt the formation of phospholipid-dependent coagulation complexes, such as the tenase or prothrombinase complex. Both lupus anticoagulants and anticardiolipin antibodies are separate, but related types of antiphospholipid antibodies. Unlike specific factor inhibitors, antiphospholipid antibodies are associated with increased risk of thrombosis rather than a bleeding diathesis. Rarely, nonspecific heparin-like inhibitors have been described in patients with malignancy. These inhibitors display heparin-like activity, and are not considered further because of their rarity.

CRITERIA FOR DIAGNOSIS

Suggestive

Suggestive criteria for the diagnosis of de novo specific factor inhibitors include an acquired bleeding diathesis, together with a newly prolonged prothrombin time (PT) or activated partial thromboplastin time (aPTT). In patients with hemophilia, the presence of a factor inhibitor is suggested by an increased requirement for factor replacement products or the inability of standard doses of factor replacement products to increase factor levels to expected concentrations.

The presence of an antiphospholipid antibody may not be obvious clinically, as many patients with an antiphospholipid antibody are asymptomatic. Findings suggesting an antiphospholipid antibody include recurrent venous or arterial thrombosis and repeated spontaneous abortions, with an elevated aPTT and thrombocytopenia. Although all types of antiphospholipid antibodies can be associated with thrombosis, only the lupus anticoagulant is associated with abnormalities of coagulation assays.

Definitive

Definitive diagnosis of specific factor inhibitors entails documentation of an elevated PT and/or aPTT together with an isolated decrease in a coagulation factor, such as factor VIII or IX. The presence of the inhibitor is documented by mixing the patient's plasma in a one-to-one mixture with normal plasma and repeating the PT, aPTT, or factor assay. This test is referred to as a *mixing study*. An inhibitor in the plasma will cause the PT or aPTT to remain prolonged even after mixing, whereas a simple factor deficiency will be corrected by the mixing and the PT or aPTT should revert to normal. Specific factor inhibitors often require incubation of the mixture for 1 to 2 hours to demonstrate the persistence of the prolonged aPTT, a characteristic termed a *delayed-acting inhibitor*. Likewise, assay of the coagulation factor activity remains depressed even after mixing if an inhibitor is present. The inhibitor can be titered using either the Bethesda or New Oxford assays. In the Bethesda assay, inhibition of a fixed amount of an added factor is quantified. One Bethesda Unit is defined as the amount of an inhibitor that inhibits 50% of the added factor during a specified incubation period.

Diagnosis of lupus anticoagulants is often very difficult because of the heterogeneity of the antibodies and because no single "gold standard" assay is available. Testing should include three levels: (1) a screening test, (2) a test to demonstrate an inhibitor, and (3) a phospholipid-specific test. A sensitive screening test, such as the aPTT with a sensitive reagent, will be elevated in the presence of a lupus anticoagulant. Tests to demonstrate the inhibitor, such as incubated mixing studies, should be performed if the screening test is abnormal. Lupus anticoagulants are most often immediate-acting inhibitors, compared with specific factor inhibitors, which are delayed-acting inhibitors, although this finding is not absolute. The third level of testing for diagnosis of the lupus anticoagulant should include lipid-specific tests, such as the platelet neutralization procedure, tissue thromboplastin inhibition test, and hexagonal phase phospholipid neutralization procedure. In the presence of a lupus anticoagulant, the addition of excess phospholipid to the plasma in these tests will bind the antibody, thus inhibiting its effect and correcting the clotting time toward normal.

Anticardiolipin antibodies usually are not detectable using the clotting-based assays described for the lupus anticoagulant. IgG, IgA, and IgM anticardiolipin antibodies can be detected by enzyme-linked immunosorbent assay. Some patients have both lupus anticoagulant and anticardiolipin activities in their plasma simultaneously, whereas others have either lupus anticoagulant or anticardiolipin activity demonstrable.

CLINICAL MANIFESTATIONS

Subjective

Patients with specific factor inhibitors can be divided into those with underlying coagulation protein deficiencies and those who were previously normal. The symptoms experienced in patients in whom the inhibitor develops as a result of treatment for a coagulation protein deficiency are often very similar to those of the underlying coagulopathy, but increased in intensity. In patients with hemophilia A, the development of an inhibitor can be suggested by increased frequency and intensity of bleeding episodes and by lack of response of factor VIII coagulant activity to previously effective doses of factor VIII concentrate. Patients with de novo coagulation inhibitors often present for medical attention because of the recent onset of bleeding problems, such as hemarthrosis, gastrointestinal bleeding, increased bruising, and deep tissue hematomas. The past medical history in these patients is usually devoid of bleeding episodes, but pertinent associated historical findings would be recent childbirth, history of autoimmune or connective tissue disorders, use of medications such as penicillin, and history of malignancy. Inhibitors to factor V and bovine thrombin have occurred in patients who received bovine thrombin preparations as a hemostatic agent during cardiac surgery, so history of previous surgeries should be sought.

Unlike the specific factor inhibitors mentioned above, antiphospholipid antibodies are not associated with a bleeding diathesis, but can predispose to both venous and arterial thrombosis. Patterns of thrombosis common in these patients include deep vein thrombosis, pulmonary embolism, stroke, myocardial infarction, and recurrent spontaneous abortions. Clinical conditions associated with antiphospholipid antibodies and the lupus anticoagulant include systemic lupus erythematosus, drugs (chlorpromazine, hydralazine, quinidine, etc.), infectious diseases, and lymphoproliferative disorders. There is usually no family or lifelong history of thrombosis in affected patients, as these antibodies are acquired.

Objective

Physical Examination

Physical examination of patients with specific factor inhibitors often reveals evidence of a hemorrhagic diathesis similar to that of a severe factor deficiency with superficial bruising, evidence of gastrointestinal bleeding, or signs of deep tissue hemorrhage, such as painful swelling of limbs. In patients with an underlying factor deficiency, the physical examination is not markedly changed with the presence of an inhibitor.

Patients with antiphospholipid antibodies may exhibit signs of thrombosis, which include pain and swelling in the legs, stroke, shortness of breath, recurrent spontaneous abortions, and chest pain. The reader is referred to Chapter 12–36 for a more detailed discussion.

Routine Laboratory Abnormalities

Patients with coagulation inhibitors often present with abnormalities of either the PT or aPTT. Patients with inhibitors against a specific coagu-

lation factor who present with bleeding abnormalities may also present with a normocytic anemia or hematuria. Patients with the lupus anticoagulant usually have a normal complete blood count and urinalysis, but may occasionally have thrombocytopenia. In patients with a coagulation inhibitor associated with a lymphoproliferative disorder, the leukocyte count is often elevated with an absolute lymphocytosis. Abnormalities of the chest x-ray film, electrocardiogram, and routine chemistry tests are unusual, unless there are other underlying diseases.

PLANS
Diagnostic
Differential Diagnosis

In patients with preexisting coagulation factor deficiencies, such as hemophilia A and B, the development of an inhibitor is often anticipated after prolonged factor replacement therapy. As such, laboratory assays to detect the development of an inhibitor are often part of the routine follow-up of these patients. When inhibitor activity is detected in the laboratory in these patients, there is little else in the differential diagnosis. Lupus anticoagulants or other inhibitors are very unusual in this patient population.

Patients without known coagulation factor deficiencies who develop a de novo specific factor inhibitor often present with recent onset of a bleeding disorder together with elevation of the PT and/or aPTT. The differential diagnosis should include a previously undetected factor deficiency, von Willebrand's disease, consumptive coagulopathy, liver disease, or vitamin K deficiency. In all of these disorders, the mixing study corrects the abnormality in the PT and/or aPTT to normal. The specific diagnosis can then be reached by performing panels of factor assays. Inhibitors to fibrinogen or factor II, V, or X usually give rise to an elevated PT and aPTT. Patients with inhibitors to most of these factors have a bleeding diathesis, but occasional patients with inhibitors to factor V have been reported to experience thrombotic episodes. Inhibitors to factor VIII, IX, XI, or XII or prekallikrein demonstrate a prolonged aPTT with a normal PT. Only inhibitors to factors VIII, IX, and XI usually result in a hemorrhagic diathesis. Inhibitors to factor VII are very rare, but give rise to an elevated PT and a normal aPTT. Inhibitors to von Willebrand's factor often give rise to laboratory findings similar to those in type IIa von Willebrand's disease, except that the ristocetin cofactor assay does not revert to normal with the mixture of the patient's plasma (one-to-one) with normal plasma.

The differential diagnosis of antiphospholipid antibodies is often complex. Patients with lupus anticoagulants can be detected by an elevated aPTT, the presence of an immediate-acting inhibitor, and abnormalities of the phospholipid-based assays listed previously. There is, however, considerable variability in the pattern of abnormal laboratory tests between lupus anticoagulants and often definitive diagnosis is not possible. Specific factor inhibitors should be excluded if the results of laboratory tests are not conclusive for the lupus anticoagulant. Many patients with lupus anticoagulant and thrombosis are on heparin therapy. Heparin is an anticoagulant with activity directed against the prothrombinase and tenase complexes, and the effect of heparin is nearly identical to that of the lupus anticoagulant in every coagulation test. If a heparin effect is suspected, heparin can be neutralized with polybrene or protamine or removed using a heparin filter. Tests for the lupus anticoagulant can also be repeated once the patient has been switched from heparin to coumadin therapy.

Diagnostic Options

Laboratory abnormalities in patients with specific factor inhibitors include an elevated PT and/or aPTT together with an isolated decrease in a coagulation factor. Mixing studies, described under Criteria for Diagnosis, Definitive, usually reveal a delayed-acting inhibitor. Assay of the affected coagulation factor activity remains depressed even after mixing if an inhibitor is present. Quantification of the inhibitor by an assay such as the Bethesda assay reveals either a low (<10 Bethesda Units) or high (≥10 Bethesda Units) titer. Response of the inhibitor to therapeutic intervention is best followed with the Bethesda assay. Factor assays are not useful in following the inhibitor titer, as patients with underlying factor deficiencies have low factor levels, even in the absence of the inhibitor, and patients with de novo inhibitors often have undetectable factor levels with an inhibitor titer as low as 1 Bethesda Unit. Inhibitors to von Willebrand's factor are often more difficult to detect. Laboratory abnormalities in patients with inhibitors to von Willebrand's factor are often similar to those in type IIa von Willebrand's disease, except for the fact that the ristocetin cofactor assay does not revert to normal with the mixture of the patient's plasma (one-to-one) with normal plasma. For more information, please see Chapter 12–34. Another unusual inhibitor is the inhibitor to bovine thrombin that develops in patients exposed to this agent during cardiac surgery. In these patients, the PT and aPTT are normal, as is the factor II level, because the inhibitors usually have little cross-reactivity to human factor II. The one laboratory test that is abnormal in these patients is the thrombin clotting time, if performed with bovine thrombin as the reagent. Some rare patients have nonneutralizing antibodies that do not inhibit the function of the coagulant protein, but cause increased clearance from plasma. The presence of nonneutralizing antibodies is difficult to detect, but can be accomplished by finding that a column of protein A–Sepharose beads, which normally removes IgG from plasma, removes a specific factor activity from plasma as well.

The aPTT is usually prolonged in patients with lupus anticoagulant, and the PT is normal. Occasional patients with lupus anticoagulant have elevations of both PT and aPTT. In some patients, acquired factor II deficiencies and factor II inhibitors have been described, so the finding of an elevated PT should prompt evaluation of factor II levels. These patients are unusual among patients with lupus anticoagulants in that they may experience bleeding abnormalities. The aPTT remains elevated long after mixing the patient's plasma with normal plasma. This effect is demonstrable immediately after mixing the patient's plasma with normal plasma, and is often referred to as an immediate-acting inhibitor. Patients with lupus anticoagulants also have abnormalities of phospholipid-specific tests, such as the platelet neutralization procedure, tissue thromboplastin inhibition test, and hexagonal phase phospholipid neutralization procedure. Anticardiolipin antibodies generally have no activity in the clotting-based assays for the lupus anticoagulant, but can be detected using enzyme-linked immunosorbent assay for detection of IgG, IgA, and IgM anticardiolipin antibodies.

Recommended Approach

In patients in whom a specific coagulation factor inhibitor is suspected, the recommended diagnostic approach is to perform a screening PT or aPTT to localize the defect to the intrinsic, extrinsic, or common pathway. An incubated mixing study based on the abnormal screening test (PT or aPTT) should be performed next. Demonstration of a delayed acting inhibitor will then prompt assay of specific factor levels. For an inhibitor in the intrinsic pathway, factors VIII, IX, XI, and XII can be assayed. It is usually not necessary to assay factors other than the congenitally deficient factor in a known hemophiliac who develops an inhibitor. Fibrinogen and factors II, V, and X can be assayed for an inhibitor in the common pathway. For an inhibitor in the extrinsic pathway, factor VII can be assayed. Demonstration of a single decreased factor level should next suggest the performance of a Bethesda assay to titer the inhibitor. Response to therapy should be followed exclusively using the Bethesda assay or other quantitative assay of inhibitor strength.

The recommended approach to the diagnosis of an antiphospholipid antibody is twofold, as patients may have either a lupus anticoagulant, an anticardiolipin antibody, or both. To detect and quantify anticardiolipin antibody activity, a specific enzyme-linked immunosorbent assay is recommended, with measurement of IgG, IgA, and IgM activities. Diagnosis of a lupus anticoagulant should include three levels of testing: (1) a screening test, (2) a test to demonstrate an inhibitor, and (3) a phospholipid-specific test. A sensitive screening test, such as the aPTT with a sensitive reagent, is elevated in the presence of a lupus anticoagulant. An elevation of the aPTT should lead to incubated mixing studies, where an immediate-acting inhibitor is often detected. Detection of an immediate-acting inhibitor should lead to performance of a phospholipid-sensitive confirmatory test for lupus anticoagulant, as described under Criteria for Diagnosis, Definitive. A laboratory screen for

heparin should also be performed to exclude a heparin effect, especially in hospitalized patients.

Therapeutic

Therapeutic Options

Patients with specific factor inhibitors, especially inhibitors against factor VIII or IX, pose a difficult therapeutic challenge. Simple factor replacement is often futile, as the inhibitor binds to the infused factor, rendering it ineffective. Furthermore, repeated infusion of the factor against which the inhibitor is directed may result in an anamnestic response with an increase in the titer of the inhibitor. In patients with hemophilia A who develop inhibitors or those with de novo inhibitors to factor VIII, therapy should be limited to treatment of bleeding episodes or prophylaxis for surgery. For minor bleeding episodes or in patients with low-titer inhibitors, factor replacement may be effective on a short-term basis. For major bleeding episodes, therapies that bypass either factor VIII or the inhibitor are often used. Porcine factor VIII may be useful in patients in whom the inhibitor does not cross-react with porcine factor VIII, as demonstrated by a modification of the Bethesda assay. Therapies that bypass factor VIII include concentrates that contain some activated clotting factors, such as prothrombin complex concentrate. Inhibitor titers can be reduced temporarily using plasmapheresis or immunoadsorption using a column filled with protein A attached to Sepharose beads. Immunosuppression is occasionally successful using agents such as corticosteroids, methotrexate, azathioprine, and cyclophosphamide. Attempts to induce immune tolerance by prolonged infusion of factor VIII have met with some limited success.

Patients with inhibitors to factor IX can be treated with prothrombin complex concentrates, although an anamnestic response may be seen. The therapeutic modalities aimed at decreasing the inhibitor titers through plasmapheresis, immunoadsorption, or immunosuppression may also be used.

Specific inhibitors to other coagulation factors are unusual, but the therapeutic approach is generally similar to that for factors VIII and IX. When possible, therapy to restore coagulation should be used that does not provoke an anamnestic response. For example, patients with inhibitors to factor V can often be treated using platelet transfusions. In patients with de novo inhibitors associated with malignancy, inhibitor titers often respond to treatment of the underlying malignancy. In some patients with de novo inhibitors, the inhibitor titer may resolve spontaneously without therapy. This is more commonly observed in inhibitors that develop postpartum or those associated with a drug therapy.

Antiphospholipid antibodies rarely give rise to hemorrhagic episodes, but are often associated with thrombotic events. Therapy in these patients is directed at preventing further thrombotic episodes and in controlling the titer of the antibody. Antiphospholipid antibodies often arise in patients with underlying autoimmune or connective tissue disorders and the levels of the antibody may respond to immunosuppressive therapy in some individuals. Usually, therapy in patients with antiphospholipid antibodies is limited to preventing and treating thrombotic episodes. Coumadin is often used in the prevention of thrombotic episodes. Treatment of acute venous and arterial thrombotic episodes is discussed in Chapter 12–36. Treatment of pregnant women with lupus anticoagulants and a history of recurrent spontaneous abortions has included heparin, aspirin, and steroids.

Recommended Approach

There is no single recommended therapeutic approach to patients with specific coagulation factor inhibitors. In patients with inhibitors to factor VIII, minor bleeding episodes or low-titer inhibitors can be treated with factor VIII concentrates, but the risk of an anamnestic response exists. Recommended therapy for major bleeding episodes includes either porcine factor VIII or prothrombin complex concentrates, with the addition of plasmapheresis to temporarily lower antibody titers. Long-term therapeutic strategies for all types of specific coagulation factor inhibitors should be aimed at lowering the antibody titers through immunosuppressive drugs. It is important to tailor the therapeutic approach to each individual patient, as not all therapies are equally effective in every patient with an inhibitor.

Patients with antiphospholipid antibodies often pose a therapeutic challenge. Immunosuppressive therapy may be successful in lowering the antibody titers in occasional patients. Most therapy in these patients is designed to treat or prevent thrombotic events. Prophylactic anticoagulation treatment with coumadin in patients with antiphospholipid antibodies without a history of thrombosis is controversial, and most physicians would reserve prophylactic anticoagulation therapy for persons with a previously documented thrombotic episode. In patients with antiphospholipid antibodies and a single thrombotic episode, the length of anticoagulation therapy is controversial. Most patients with two or more thrombotic episodes are recommended to continue oral anticoagulation for life. Treatment of acute venous and arterial thrombotic episodes is discussed in Chapter 12–36, but heparin is currently the mainstay of treatment for acute thrombosis.

FOLLOW-UP

Patients with specific factor inhibitors usually require close clinical follow-up due to their frequency and intensity of bleeding events. Monitoring the inhibitor titer to detect an increasing or decreasing trend is often useful.

Patients with antiphospholipid antibodies who are on prophylactic or therapeutic oral anticoagulant therapy require follow-up to monitor their coumadin level. Monitoring can be done by measuring the patient's PT using the International Normalized Ratio (INR). Therapeutic INR levels are 2 to 3 for thrombosis prophylaxis or therapy in this group of patients.

DISCUSSION

Prevalence

Specific factor inhibitors are seen in approximately 6 to 15% of patients with severe hemophilia A and in approximately 3% of patients with severe hemophilia B. Inhibitors are more likely to develop in patients with gene deletions than in those with point mutations or mild hemophilia. In patients who develop inhibitors, the inhibitor usually develops at a relatively young age. Studies are underway to determine if the newer, more highly purified or recombinant factor VIII concentrates are associated with an increased incidence of inhibitor development. The incidence of de novo inhibitors to coagulation proteins is extremely low, and with the exception of inhibitors to factor VIII, they are usually the subject of single case reports. These inhibitors are more likely to be seen in the elderly, postpartum, and in individuals with malignancy or underlying autoimmune or connective tissue disorders.

The prevalence of the lupus anticoagulant in the general population is approximately 2%. The prevalence of the lupus anticoagulant among patients with systemic lupus erythematosus is much higher, approximately 30 to 40%. Approximately 50% of patients with the lupus anticoagulant also have anticardiolipin antibody activity demonstrable in their plasma.

Related Basic Science

Specific factor inhibitors are immunoglobulins, usually IgG_4. These antibodies develop either in patients with coagulation factor deficiencies as an immune response to the transfusion of "foreign" protein or de novo in patients without an underlying coagulation disorder. Inhibitors tend to develop most often in patients with true gene deletions compared with those with point mutations. Most of the antibodies to factor VIII bind to either the light chain or heavy chain of factor VIII and inhibit its coagulant activity. These are known as neutralizing antibodies. Some antibodies to factor VIII and other coagulation factors are nonneutralizing. These antibodies may not inhibit the protein's function, but form antibody–antigen complexes that are removed by the reticuloendothelial system and result in a decrease in the level of the protein in plasma. Although many patients with severe hemophilia develop an inhibitor after repeated factor replacement, it is unclear why some patients develop inhibitors and others do not. The reason why inhibitors spontaneously resolve in some patients and persist in others is also not known.

The lupus anticoagulant is a heterogeneous group of immunoglobulins which are a subclass of antiphospholipid antibody. Another subclass of antiphospholipid antibody, distinct from the lupus anticoagulant but often seen in the same patient population and also associated with the thrombosis, is anticardiolipin antibodies. The binding of antiphospholipid antibodies to phospholipid has been shown to require the presence of β2-glycoprotein I, a protein present in plasma. The lupus anticoagulant interferes with the in vitro activation of prothrombin by the prothrombinase complex, presumably through its interaction with negatively charged phospholipid. The precise mechanism of this activity of the lupus anticoagulant has not been elucidated, but is thought to be responsible for the prolongation of the aPTT seen in affected patients. Many pathophysiologic mechanisms have been proposed for the thrombotic action of the lupus anticoagulant, including impairment of prostacyclin production by endothelium, increased platelet activation and adhesiveness, interference with protein C activation, and abnormal antithrombin III activity. Because of the heterogeneity of the lupus anticoagulant, it is likely that different antibodies have different mechanisms of action.

Natural History and Its Modification with Treatment

Specific factor inhibitors can resolve without therapy, decrease in intensity with therapy, or increase in titer despite therapy. It is often difficult to predict which course an inhibitor will follow for an individual patient. In general, most specific factor inhibitors persist despite therapy, but often inhibitors arising postpartum or those associated with drug therapy spontaneously resolve. Immunosuppressive therapy may lower the titer of the antibody, and development of immune tolerance has been accomplished in some patients.

Response of antiphospholipid antibodies to immunosuppressive therapy is unpredictable. Anticoagulant therapy does nothing to alter the amount or presence of the antiphospholipid antibody, but may prevent devastating thrombotic episodes.

Prevention

Development of inhibitors in patients with hemophilia cannot currently be prevented. Studies are underway to determine if one type of factor replacement therapy is associated with a lower incidence of inhibitor development. Likewise, de novo factor inhibitors and antiphospholipid antibodies cannot be prevented.

Cost Containment

Patients with specific factor inhibitors are very expensive to treat as they often need frequent intervention for bleeding episodes. Additionally, therapy with agents such as porcine factor VIII is extremely expensive. If a reliable immunosuppressive or immune tolerance regimen could be developed that would lower antibody titers for extended periods, it would result in considerable cost savings.

Patients with antiphospholipid antibodies are at increased risk for thrombotic episodes with their attendant morbidity. Acute thrombotic events usually require costly hospital-based treatment. Prophylactic therapy to decrease the incidence of thrombotic episodes may require more office visits for anticoagulant therapy monitoring, but may prevent hospital admissions for acute thrombotic events.

REFERENCES

Brandt JT, Triplett DA, Alving B, Scharrer I. Criteria for the diagnosis of lupus anticoagulants: An update. Thromb Haemost 1995;74:1185.

Kasper CK. Laboratory tests for factor VIII inhibitors, their variation, significance, and interpretation. Blood Coag Fibrinolysis 1991;2(suppl. 1):7.

Love PE, Santoro SA. Antiphospholipid antibodies: Anticardiolipin and the lupus anticoagulant in system lupus erythematosus (SLE) and non-SLE disorders. Ann Intern Med 1990;112:682.

Nilsson IM, Berntorp E, Freiburghaus C. Treatment of patients with factor VIII and IX inhibitors. Thromb Haemost 1993;70:56.

Shapiro SS. Antibodies to blood coagulation factors. Clin Haematol 1979:2:207.

CHAPTER 12–36

Arterial Thrombosis

Carmen M. Fonseca, M.D.

DEFINITION

Arterial occlusion is usually caused by a thrombus within a vessel. A thrombus is an aggregation of fibrin, platelets, cellular elements, and coagulation factors. When the thrombus, or part of it, migrates to a distal vessel, it is called an embolus. Thrombi may occur in arteries, veins, and cardiac chambers, and may be occlusive or nonocclusive.

ETIOLOGY

The most common cause of arterial occlusion is thrombus that forms in an area of preexisting extensive atherosclerosis. Other causes of arterial occlusion are not that uncommon and must be evaluated thoroughly in patients who show no evidence of atherosclerosis or in the younger population. The causes of arterial occlusion are classified into the following categories: thrombosis in situ, embolus, vasculitis, obliterative process, drugs, and miscellaneous (Table 12–36–1).

CRITERIA FOR DIAGNOSIS
Suggestive

Acute thrombosis of large vessels is easily diagnosed by history and physical examination. Acute arterial occlusions usually cause catastrophic events, that is, myocardial infarction, strokes, organ infarction, gangrene. Chronic occlusion of smaller vessels may require more careful evaluation. The clinical presentation varies according to the organ involved and the percentage reduction in blood flow. Pain is the hallmark of arterial thrombosis.

Definitive

The diagnosis of arterial occlusion in the extremities is made on physical examination. Noninvasive studies are performed to confirm the diagnosis and quantify the severity of disease. They include Doppler, pulse volume recordings, ankle:brachial index, sequential systolic pressure measurements, and ultrasound imaging.

With the availability of accurate noninvasive studies, arteriography is not recommended to diagnose atherosclerosis. Arteriography is indicated when the diagnosis is uncertain and other diseases are being considered, for example, dissection, vasculitis, thoracic outlet, entrapment syndromes. Arteriography is essential prior to reconstruction to plan adequate treatment, and is necessary in thrombolytic therapy to determine the site of lysis and to place the delivery catheter.

Ultrasonography has been increasingly used for the evaluation of peripheral arterial disease. Several modalities are combined and include B-mode imaging, color flow, and Doppler velocities. The arterial wall, intima, and lumen are clearly seen and atherosclerotic plaques may be easily identified. Cross-sectional views can be obtained and diameter reduction observed. Dissections and fibromuscular disease may be diagnosed on duplex. The Doppler is also used to calculate velocities of blood flow through different segments of an artery. An area of stenosis causes faster flow or increased velocity. The narrower the artery, the higher the velocity. This phenomenon has helped categorize the degree of stenosis in the carotid arteries with remarkable accuracy. The addition of color helps determine presence of flow, direction of flow, and areas of turbulence and may suggest areas of stenosis which could be further investigated with the Doppler.

CLINICAL MANIFESTATIONS
Subjective

Patients with an acute arterial occlusion of the extremities present with signs and symptoms that are called the *six P's* (Table 12–36–2).

Patients with acute occlusions develop sudden, severe symptoms.

Patients with chronic ischemia or good collateral flow develop symptoms gradually. Patients with chronic ischemia usually give a history of claudication. They notice pain or cramping of the legs when walking. The pain is usually relieved within 5 to 10 minutes by rest. They do not need to sit down or move or lean against something for the pain to subside.

A detailed history provides information that is helpful in determining the etiology of the occlusive process. A past history of atherosclerosis in other organs, presence of risk factors for coronary disease (smoking, diabetes, hypercholesterolemia, hypertension, etc.), and a family history of arteriosclerosis should raise the suspicion of atherosclerosis. Patients with a history of arrhythmias such as atrial fibrillation should alert the physician to the possibility of an embolism. A patient with systemic illness and constitutional symptoms may have vasculitis. Young

TABLE 12–36–1. CAUSES OF ARTERIAL OCCLUSION

Thrombosis in situ
  Antistreptolysin-O
  Lupus anticoagulant
  Anticardiolipin antibodies
  Homocystinuria
  Myeloproliferative disorders
  Paroxysmal nocturnal hemoglobinuria
  Extrinsic compression
  Hypercoagulable state
  Protein C, protein S, antithrombin III deficiencies
  Sickle cell anemia
  Trauma (catheters, vibrating tools)
Embolus
  Cardiac chamber
  Cardiac valves
  Myxoma
  Atheromatous embolization
  Aneurysms
  Arrhythmias (atrial fibrillation)
  Dilated cardiomyopathies
  Paradoxical embolus (patent foramen ovale, atrial septal defect, ventricular septal defect, patent ductus)
Vasculitis
  Takayasu's arteritis
  Giant cell arteritis
  Kawasaki disease
  Polyarteritis nodosa
  Wegener's granulomatosis
  Vasculitis associated with rheumatoid arthritis or systemic lupus erythematosus
  Cryoglobulinemia
  Thromboangiitis obliterans (Buerger's disease)
Obliterative Processes
  Scleroderma
  CREST (calcinosis, Raynaud's phenomenon, esophageal dysmotility, sclerodactylia, telangiectasia)
  Radiation
Drugs
  Ergotamine
  Cocaine
  Chemotherapy (5-fluorouracil)
  Heparin-induced thrombocytopenia with thrombosis
Miscellaneous
  Dissection
  Popliteal entrapment syndrome
  Thoracic outlet syndrome
  Phlegmasia cerulea dolens
  Compartment syndrome

Pain
Pallor
Paresthesias
Paralysis—loss of motor function
Polar—coolness
Pulselessness

patients who are heavy smokers and have distal disease may have thromboangiitis obliterans. Young females with constitutional symptoms who have decreased blood pressure or absent pulses in their arms may have Takayasu's arteritis. Thrombosis that occurs after interventional procedures may be the result of atheroemboli.

Objective

Physical Examination

The physical examination is fundamental to make the diagnosis of arterial occlusive disease. Careful examination of the pulses may provide information on the site and extent of disease. The superficial temporal pulse is located in front of the ear and is felt in the temporal area. The carotid pulses are located on each side of the neck. They should be palpated one at a time and gently. Palpation at the base of the neck is preferable to avoid the carotid body, which could cause bradycardia. The subclavian artery is felt behind the clavicles. The axillary pulse is located at the axilla. The brachial artery runs medially and is palpable proximally under the biceps muscle and distally at the antecubital fossa. The radial pulse is located laterally on the ventral side of the wrist, whereas the ulnar pulse is medial. Allen's test is helpful in evaluating occlusion of the radial and ulnar arteries. It should be done routinely prior to inserting an arterial line in the radial artery. Allen's test is performed by asking the patient to make a fist. With the patient's hand closed, the physician milks the blood from the palm and occludes both radial and ulnar arteries. The patient is then asked to open the hand gently so as to avoid hyperextension. The pressure is then released from one of the arteries while occluding the other. In normal patients, Allen's test is negative. A negative test is determined by prompt filling of the entire hand via either one of the arteries alone while the other is kept occluded. A positive test indicates occlusion of the radial or ulnar arteries or incomplete palmar arches. A positive Allen's test is determined by showing adequate filling of the hand when the patent artery is released, but delay or nonfilling when the occluded artery is released. A positive Allen's test is found in patients with scleroderma, CREST syndrome, and thromboangiitis obliterans. The cardiac examination is an important part of the vascular evaluation. The abdominal aorta can be palpated in patients who are not obese. To determine its size, the examiner rolls the fingers over the contour of the aorta or approaches the aorta laterally from both sides with the tip of the fingers and estimates the distance between them. The femoral pulses are located in the groin. An absent femoral pulse indicates occlusion of the aortoiliac or common femoral artery. The popliteal pulse is found in the popliteal space somewhat laterally. An absent popliteal pulse, when the femoral pulse is present, indicates a superficial femoral artery occlusion. If the popliteal pulse is present but the pedal or ankle pulse is absent, the corresponding tibial artery is likely to be occluded. The posterior tibial pulse is found behind the medial malleolus. It may be easier to find by gently dorsiflexing the foot and slightly everting it. The anterior tibial pulse is located anteriorly at the ankle. The peroneal pulse is sometimes palpable anterior to the lateral malleolus. The dorsalis pedis pulse is found in the dorsum of the foot, but may be absent in about 5% of the population. When feeling pulses, one should compare both sides and note any difference. After the pulses are felt and recorded, one listens for bruits. Bruits can be heard at the carotids, subclavians, epigastrium (aorta), renals (both upper quadrants), iliacs (both lower quadrants), and femoral arteries.

In addition to decreased or absent pulses, the appearance of the extremity provides clues to the severity and chronicity of the disease. In an acute large-branch arterial occlusion, the extremity will be pale, cold, and pulseless. The motor and sensory functions may become impaired. Severe pain accompanies arterial occlusions. Chronic arterial insufficiency causes atrophy of the subcutaneous tissue, hair loss, brittle toenails, dry skin, and decreased nail growth. With more severe ischemia, the extremity becomes cooler. The skin may look mottled with a livedo reticularis pattern. One may observe dependent rubor. The toenails lose their nutrition, become thickened, and frequently develop fungal infection. The skin gradually turns shiny and paper thin. These patients are prone to develop ulcerations at sites of trauma or pressure, between the toes ("kissing ulcers"), and distally at the tip of the toes. Ischemic ulcers are necrotic, lack granulation tissue, and fail to heal despite treatment. The base is black or yellow and covered with fibrous material. Arterial ulcers are painful. Ischemia to the nerves may cause decreased sensation to touch and vibration. As ischemia progresses, gangrene occurs.

Routine Laboratory Abnormalities

None of the routine laboratory tests suggest arterial thrombosis; however, tissue necrosis usually causes elevations in levels of lactate dehydrogenase and serum glutamic–oxalacetic transaminase. A mild leukocytosis can occur.

PLANS

Diagnostic

Differential Diagnosis

The differential diagnosis of an acute arterial occlusion varies in accordance with the organ involved. The challenge lies in identifying the cause of arterial thrombosis, especially when neither atherosclerosis nor embolus seems to be playing a role. Dissection should always be kept in mind in patients who present with an acute ischemic limb.

Diagnostic Options and Recommended Approach

The diagnosis of an arterial occlusion should be made by physical examination and history. Pulse volume recordings, ankle:brachial index, and duplex are used to confirm the diagnosis and quantify the severity of ischemia. Angiography is recommended prior to revascularization to define the anatomy and best treatment plan. Angiography can unveil the diagnosis in patients who have no evidence of atherosclerosis and the history suggests other possibilities, for example, vasculitis, dissection, fibromuscular disease, radiation arteritis, or entrapment syndrome. Arteriography is also used to determine the source of atheroemboli. Patients who present with an embolic event warrant a search for the site of origin. Workup may include transthoracic echocardiography, transesophageal echocardiography, arteriography, ultrasonography, and Holter monitoring. Patients who present with spontaneous thrombosis and without evidence of atherosclerosis warrant laboratory studies to investigate a hypercoagulable state.

Therapeutic

The therapy chosen should be guided by the severity of the symptoms and degree of ischemia. The goal of treatment is to prevent end-organ damage, restore blood supply, and, if possible, treat the underlying disease to prevent recurrence.

Patients presenting with an acute embolic event can be managed with anticoagulation if adequate perfusion is still present. For more severe ischemia, prompt surgical removal via embolectomy catheters is the preferred approach. In recent years, thrombolysis has also been used successfully. A catheter is placed within the thrombus for delivery of the lytic agent. Urokinase is commonly used at a dose of 2,200 U/kg/min via continuous infusion until dissolution of the clot. For patients in whom thrombolysis is contraindicated, embolectomy remains the best approach. Patients with arterial embolism should remain anticoagulated indefinitely or until the source is identified and corrected. Eighty percent of arterial emboli are thought to originate in the heart.

For patients in whom the underlying pathology is atherosclerosis, the therapeutic approach varies according to the severity and location of the disease. Acute occlusions with severe ischemia are usually treated surgically via bypasses. A selective group of patients can be treated with thrombolysis or angioplasty. Some arteries are best treated with endarterectomy and patching. Indications for revascularization in the extremities include severe ischemia or impending gangrene, rest pain, disabling claudication, and nonhealing arterial ulcers.

In patients with vasculitis, steroid therapy and occasionally cytotoxic agents are necessary to stop the inflammatory process. Patients with a hypercoagulable state, anticardiolipin antibody, lupus anticoagulant, atrial fibrillation, and severe cardiomyopathy may require long-term anticoagulation. Patients with thromboangiitis obliterans do well if they quit smoking. Ergotamines and cocaine must be discontinued.

For patients with adequate perfusion, a regular walking exercise is recommended. Several studies have shown improved walking distance with this therapy alone. Cessation of smoking is strongly recommended. Diabetics should strive for good glycemic control. Attempts at lowering cholesterol by either diet, pharmacologic treatment, or a combination of the two should be initiated. Many extremities are lost because of poor care of the feet in patients with impaired circulation. It is crucial that patients understand the potential serious consequences of minor trauma to their feet. Patients should be advised against application of local heat to their feet. Feet should be cleaned, dried, moisturized, and inspected daily. If athlete's foot occurs, prompt treatment with an antifungal cream or lotion is advised. Lamb's wool can be placed between the toes to prevent ulcers.

Pharmacotherapy for claudication is evolving. The first drug approved specifically for claudication is pentoxyphylline (Trental), 400 mg to be taken three times a day after meals. It works by lowering blood viscosity and improving erythrocyte flexibility. It is reported to improve walking distance in patients with claudication. Other therapies are currently under investigation.

FOLLOW-UP

On follow-up visits, the level of activity and the walking distance before the onset of claudication are recorded. Also, each pulse should be documented and graded. Patients with atherosclerosis of the lower or upper extremity can be followed clinically. There is no need to obtain pulse volume recordings unless there is a change in the clinical picture. An assessment of the risk factors is made and recommendations are discussed to continue modification. Careful inspection of the extremities must occur at each visit, with special attention to the ischemic area. Symptoms of arterial insufficiency in other organs may occur and need evaluation. Follow-up with pulse volume recordings is recommended after intervention and surgical procedures to evaluate response to therapy.

The carotid, renal, and mesenteric arteries can be followed by duplex. In general, carotid stenosis is followed by duplex on a yearly basis. Patients with embolic events need to be followed for recurrence. They are kept on long-term anticoagulation, so the international normalized ratio needs to be monitored at least monthly. Patients with vasculitis need periodic visits to document control of the inflammatory process. In addition to clinical assessment, laboratory parameters like the Westergren sedimentation rate and C-reactive protein are followed.

DISCUSSION
Prevalence and Incidence

Claudication secondary to atherosclerotic occlusive disease is said to affect 10% of the U.S. population over the age of 70 and 1 to 2% of those under 69 (Droller and Pemberton, 1953; Peabody et al., 1974). The true prevalence of peripheral arterial disease in the general population is unknown because of the lack of information in asymptomatic patients. The prevalence of atherosclerosis increases with age and the presence of risk factors. The incidence of peripheral arterial disease in diabetics ranges from 16 to 58% (Report of the National Commission on Diabetes, 1976). The prevalence of cerebrovascular disease in patients with peripheral arteriosclerosis has been reported to be between 10 and 15% (Dormandy et al., 1989). The incidence of coronary atherosclerosis has been reported around 90% in patients with peripheral arterial disease who have been evaluated by coronary angiography (Hertzer et al., 1984).

The incidence of hypercoagulable states in arterial thromboembolism is unknown. Recent studies are looking at this entity as a cause of arterial occlusive disease in the younger population (<50 years of age). Hypercoagulability may play a role in patients who present with recurrent graft thrombosis. Patients with atrial fibrillation have a high risk of thromboembolic events. In patients with underlying rheumatic valvular disease, this may be at least 8 to 10% per year (Dunn et al., 1989). Patients with nonvalvular atrial fibrillation who have had a thrombotic event are at high risk of having a second event. Older patients with atrial fibrillation and history of hypertension and congestive heart failure are also at increased risk.

Related Basic Science

Atherosclerosis is basically a disease of the intima. The initial triggering event that leads to the atherosclerotic plaque remains unknown. Several theories are under investigation, and several factors seems to be playing a role. An interaction between hemodynamic changes, endothelial cells, monocytes, lipids, oxidized low-density lipoprotein, and exposed collagen, along with other factors that are not yet known, may contribute to atherosclerosis. Hypercoagulable states are discussed in Chapter 12–37.

Natural History and Its Modification with Treatment

The clinical course of patients with atherosclerosis is usually progressive. The rate of progression, however, is highly variable and depends on many factors. Patients who present with limb-threatening ischemia at a younger age have a more aggressive form of the disease. The presence of multiple risk factors is associated with accelerated disease progression. Modification of these is likely to slow this process. The single most consistent adverse risk factor for atherosclerosis is cigarette smoking. Cessation of smoking has been shown to improve walking distance, ankle:brachial index, graft patency, and overall outcome. Diabetics usually have extensive diffuse disease and are more likely to require revascularization and amputations. Prevention and control of diabetes are necessary. Hyperlipidemias are also associated with progressive atherosclerosis and thrombosis. Controlling cholesterol has been shown to cause regression of atherosclerosis in several studies. Exercise has also shown beneficial effects in the vasculature, decreasing thrombogenicity and development of collateral circulation.

The natural histories of arterial emboli, vasculitis, hypercoagulable states, entrapment syndromes, fibromuscular dysplasia, and so on are discussed in other chapters. Cessation of smoking basically cures thromboangiitis obliterans. Anticoagulation for cardiac arrhythmias and severe dilated cardiomyopathy markedly decreases embolic events, which are associated with significant morbidity and mortality.

Prevention

Attempts at preventing atherosclerosis are extremely important. Smokers are more likely to develop intermittent claudication compared with nonsmokers and show accelerated atherosclerosis. Cessation of smoking improves the prognosis of patients with atherosclerosis and with Buerger's disease. Patients should be encouraged to be active and walk on a regular basis. A diet low in fat and cholesterol is emphasized. Patients who are diabetic must be closely monitored. They require good glycemic control and correction of other risk factors. Adequate control of the systemic blood pressure is encouraged.

In patients with atrial fibrillation, anticoagulant therapy is usually recommended to prevent thromboembolism. Patients who present with arterial emboli in whom the source is not clear should remain anticoagulated indefinitely. Patients with a hypercoagulable state that have had an arterial thrombotic event may also need to continue anticoagulation indefinitely to prevent further events.

Cost Containment

A detailed history and physical examination help the clinician narrow the diagnostic possibilities and avoid unnecessary studies. Patients with claudication should have a baseline ankle:brachial index and pulse volume recordings to quantify the disease severity. Angiography is not indicated to diagnose atherosclerosis. Pulse volume recordings should be repeated when progressive ischemic symptoms occur. For stable clau-dication, however, there is no need to do serial studies. There is no need to get both arterial duplex and pulse volume recordings/ankle:brachial index, except for a few occasions. Carotid arterial disease can be accu-rately evaluated by duplex. Cerebral angiography is needed only when surgery is planned or if intracranial pathology is suspected. In general, carotid duplex does not need to be repeated any sooner than yearly un-less symptoms change. Unnecessary or premature revascularization should be avoided. Risk factor modification may help delay or prevent expensive surgical reconstruction. Anticoagulation with warfarin ther-apy is essential in patients with atrial fibrillation, unexplained arterial emboli, hypercoagulable states with documented arterial thrombosis, and severe dilated cardiomyopathy. Prevention of thrombotic events decreases the number of hospitalizations, cost of treatment, and rehabil-itation.

REFERENCES

Dormandy J, Mahir M, Ascady G, et al. Fate of the patient with chronic leg is-chemia. J Cardiovasc Surg 1989;30:50.
Droller H, Pemberton J. Cardiovascular disease in a random sample of elderly people. Br Heart J 1953;15:199.
Dunn M, Alexander J, deSilva R, et al. Antithrombotic therapy for cerebrovas-cular disorders. Chest 1989;95(suppl.):118.
Hertzer NR, Beven EG, Young JR, et al. Coronary artery disease in peripheral vascular patients: A classification of 1000 coronary angiograms and result of surgical management. Ann Surg 1984;199:223.
Peabody CN, Kannel WB, McNamara PM. Intermittent claudication: Surgical significance. Arch Surg 1974;109:693.
Report of the National Commission on Diabetes. DHEW Publication (NIH) 76-1022, vol. 3, pt. 2. Washington, DC: U.S. Government Printing Office, 1976:60.

CHAPTER 12–37

Hypercoagulable States

John R. Bartholomew, M.D.

DEFINITION

Hypercoagulable states refer to those conditions in which persons are unusually predisposed to thrombotic events. These events usually affect the venous system as deep vein thrombosis or pulmonary embolism, while less often involving the arterial system as stroke, myocardial in-farction, or an ischemic leg.

ETIOLOGY

The etiology of hypercoagulable states is complex and more easily un-derstood by classification into primary and secondary disorders. Pri-mary hypercoagulable states are generally inherited in an autosomal dominant manner, although they may be acquired in some acute or chronic illnesses. They may be the result of an abnormality involving the fibrinolytic system or a deficiency of one of the inhibitors of the co-agulation cascade. Secondary hypercoagulable states are usually ac-quired and associated with physiologic states that are already well known to predispose to thrombosis. Many of the known primary and secondary hypercoagulable states are listed in Tables 12–37–1 and 12–37–2.

CRITERIA FOR DIAGNOSIS
Suggestive

A hypercoagulable state should be suspected when a patient presents with a swollen arm or leg, acute shortness of breath, pleuritic or non-pleuritic chest pain, an ischemic limb, superficial thrombophlebitis,

manifestations of stroke, or any clinical finding that suggests throm-boembolic phenomenon.

Definitive

A diagnosis for hypercoagulable state relies on both sophisticated and routine laboratory studies in the appropriate clinical setting and identi-fication of those precipitating factors or predisposing conditions that led to the thrombosis.

CLINICAL MANIFESTATIONS
Subjective

Hypercoagulable states may present as either arterial or venous throm-boembolism. A primary hypercoagulable state should be suspected in a patient with a thrombotic event when there is a family history of throm-bosis, thromboembolic event at an early age, thrombosis at an unusual anatomic site (mesenteric veins, hepatic veins, cerebral veins), resis-tance to anticoagulation, and a history of recurrence. In addition, unex-plained neonatal thrombosis, arterial thrombosis under the age of 30, or skin necrosis that develops while the patient is on warfarin should alert the physician to the possibility of a primary disorder (Table 12–37–3).

The secondary hypercoagulable states should be considered in pa-

TABLE 12–37–1. PRIMARY HYPERCOAGULABLE STATES

Antithrombin III
Protein C
Protein S
Hypoplasminogenemia
Dysplasminogenemia
Dysfibrinogenemia
Heparin cofactor II
Factor XII
Homocystinuria
Resistance to activated protein C

TABLE 12–37–2. SECONDARY HYPERCOAGULABLE STATES

Malignancy
Pregnancy and use of oral contraceptives
Nephrotic syndrome
Myeloproliferative disorders
Hyperlipidemia and diabetes mellitus
Heparin-induced thrombocytopenia
Surgery and trauma
Vasculitis
Antiphospholipid-antibody syndrome
Artificial surfaces
Obesity and immobilization
Disseminated intravascular coagulation or thrombotic thrombocytopenic purpura

TABLE 12–37–3. FEATURES SUGGESTING A PRIMARY HYPERCOAGULABLE STATE

Family history of thrombosis
Thrombosis at an early age
Thrombosis at unusual anatomic sites
Resistance to anticoagulation
Recurrent thrombosis
Unexplained neonatal thrombosis
Skin necrosis (while on warfarin)
Arterial thrombosis before age 30

tients who develop thrombosis during an acute or chronic systemic illness; or who have a history of weight loss, recent infection, pregnancy, miscarriage, use of oral contraceptives, or postoperative state; or in the setting of trauma, stroke, or congestive heart failure (Table 12–37–4).

Objective

Physical Examination

The physical examination may be unrewarding in diagnosing a primary hypercoagulable state, except for the thrombosis. Signs of chronic venous insufficiency or symptoms suggestive of pulmonary hypertension may occasionally be present on physical examination. Osteoporosis, ectopia lentis, aberrations of gait, and muscle weakness are noted in those rare individuals with homocystinuria.

In secondary hypercoagulable states, the physical examination reflects the underlying illness. The individual with an underlying malignancy may appear cachectic or have migratory superficial thrombophlebitis or other clinical features suggestive of a tumor. An enlarged spleen or liver or digital ischemia may be seen with myeloproliferative disorders. Recent hip fracture, surgical intervention, catheter placement, stroke, myocardial infarction, or signs of congestive heart failure will be obvious to the examiner and suggest a diagnosis of secondary hypercoagulable disorders.

Routine Laboratory Abnormalities

Sophisticated testing is required for the diagnosis of a primary hypercoagulable state. Routine laboratory tests should be performed, however, and serve as a screening tool for the secondary hypercoagulable states. A complete blood count including an examination of the peripheral blood smear alerts the physician to the possible diagnosis of heparin-induced thrombocytopenia, myeloproliferative disorders such as essential thrombocythemia and polycythemia vera, or thrombotic thrombocytopenic purpura or disseminated intravascular coagulation.

A blood chemistry profile helps to document an underlying liver or renal disorder, whereas a routine urinalysis may help lead to the diagnosis of nephrotic syndrome. A prolonged prothrombin time may suggest a lupus anticoagulant, although this is typically recognized by a prolonged activated partial thromboplastin time.

TABLE 12–37–4. FEATURES SUGGESTING A SECONDARY HYPERCOAGULABLE STATE

Systemic illness
Recent infection
Pregnancy
Miscarriage
Postoperative state
Trauma
Medications including heparin and oral contraceptives
Age (elderly persons)
Recent catheter or pacemaker insertion
Obesity

PLANS

Diagnostic

Differential Diagnosis

Hypercoagulability manifests as arterial or venous thromboembolism, and the differential diagnosis depends on whether the hypercoagulable state is felt to be a primary or a secondary disorder. These are listed in Tables 12–37–1 and 12–37–2.

Diagnostic Options

A number of sophisticated laboratory tests are available to identify the primary hypercoagulable states. These tests are not readily available at all hospitals; however, blood specimens can be sent to a regional laboratory for testing. This may be costly. The primary hypercoagulable laboratory tests most likely to be helpful include analysis for antithrombin III, proteins C and S, and resistance to activated protein C.

Many of the tests needed for the diagnosis of a secondary disorder are routine and readily available. These states often rely more on clinical recognition than laboratory testing, although tests to identify a lupus anticoagulant, anticardiolipin antibodies, heparin-induced thrombocytopenia, or a myeloproliferative disorder are available at most hospitals.

Recommended Approach

At our institution, laboratory tests to assist in the diagnosis of the hypercoagulable states are grouped together and referred to as the hypercoagulation profile (Table 12–37–5). Caution should be used in interpreting these test results in the setting of an acute thrombotic event or on a patient receiving warfarin, heparin, or a thrombolytic agent. Therefore, it is best to order a hypercoagulable profile after the acute event has resolved. At times, this will be impossible, as the patient may require lifelong anticoagulation. In this situation, obtaining studies on immediate family members is recommended for the purpose of determining the existence of a primary disorder.

Limited testing may also be helpful. For example, in patients with severe toxic hepatitis, the nephrotic syndrome, or acute fatty liver of pregnancy, an antithrombin III level is recommended. In the setting of warfarin skin necrosis or purpura fulminans, a protein C or S level is indicated. With a history of unexplained arterial thrombosis, a lupus anticoagulant, anticardiolipin antibody, or homocysteine levels should be ordered.

An area of great laboratory interest is the development of a blood test that may identify individuals at risk for thrombosis, also referred to as the *prethrombotic state*. A number of tests, including prothombin fragment 1 + 2, protein C activation peptide, fibrinopeptide A, D-dimer, thrombin–antithrombin III complex, and factor X activation peptide, are being used for research and in some institutions for clinical care. The aim of these tests is to assist the clinician in diagnosing an acute venous or arterial thromboembolism or in monitoring patients at high

TABLE 12–37–5. HYPERCOAGULATION PROFILE

Prothombin time
Activated partial thromboplastin time
Fibrinogen level
Thrombin time
Reptilase time
D-dimer
Antithrombin III
Protein C
Protein S
Plasminogen levels
Heparin cofactor II
Resistance to activated protein C
Lupus anticoagulant
Anticardiolipin antibodies
Heparin aggregation testing

risk in clinical settings that put them at increased risk for thrombosis. These tests may play an important role in the future by identifying the hypercoagulable patient before the actual thrombotic event.

Therapeutic

Therapeutic Options

With few exceptions, the treatment of hypercoagulable states is medical management. The mainstay of treatment for venous thromboembolism remains heparin and warfarin. Heparin is used initially during the acute management, followed by long-term treatment with warfarin.

Thrombolytic therapy also has a role in the management of the hypercoagulable states. Urokinase and streptokinase, and tissue plasminogen activator (t-PA) are available and may be indicated with massive pulmonary embolism and extensive deep vein thrombosis, and in select individuals with an acute myocardial infarction or an acutely ischemic limb. Superior vena cava or inferior vena cava filters are recommended in the management of venous thrombosis when there is a contraindication to anticoagulation. Surgical intervention is used more often in the setting of arterial thromboembolism and is rarely used in venous thromboembolism.

Commercial products such as antithrombin III concentrate are now available, and proteins C and S may be available in the near future. They will play a role in the management of the primary hypercoagulable states.

Recommended Approach

For the acute thrombotic event, heparin is administered with a bolus of 5000 to 10,000 units intravenously, followed by sufficient amounts to maintain the activated partial thromboplastin time between 1.5 and 2.5 times the baseline value. A number of nomograms are available to assist the clinician in dosing heparin. Warfarin is given to maintain the international normalized ratio between 2 and 3, or higher in patients with arterial events, antiphospholipid-antibody syndrome, or a history of recurrent thromboembolism. With primary hypercoagulable states, lifelong anticoagulation may be indicated when the original event is a massive pulmonary embolism or with extensive deep vein thrombosis. This is especially true in the setting of no known precipitating factors. In the individual who has a thrombotic event with a known precipitating factor, treatment is individualized, but lifelong anticoagulation should not be necessary, once the initiating factor is removed. If the patient has antithrombin III deficiency, administration of antithrombin III concentrate should be considered.

Treatment for the primary hypercoagulable patient with no previous thrombotic event is controversial. Most of these individuals are identified because a family member has had a thrombosis. Current recommendations include the use of prophylaxis in situations that place these individuals at increased risk for thrombosis, including surgical intervention, pregnancy, trauma, and immobilization. No treatment is generally indicated in those individuals identified with a primary disorder who are asymptomatic.

In the secondary hypercoagulable states, length of treatment is often dictated by the underlying disorder. If the patient had a recent surgical procedure and venous thrombosis, treatment for 3 to 6 months is adequate. If the patient has an underlying cancer with Trousseau's syndrome, lifelong treatment with subcutaneous heparin is indicated. Identification and treatment aimed at eliminating the underlying disorder should always be attempted.

FOLLOW-UP

The patient with a primary hypercoagulable state needs close follow-up. Frequent monitoring of the international normalized ratio while the patient remains on warfarin is important. The frequency will vary with both the reliability of the patient and the seriousness of the thrombotic event. Generally following a hospital discharge, a prothombin time every 1 to 2 weeks will suffice. This interval will most likely decrease with time. With the secondary hypercoagulable states, the underlying illness dictates the need for close monitoring. If the patient had a thrombotic event related to a surgical intervention, there is obvious rea-

son to believe that he or she will return to a more normal state once recovered from the inciting event.

Complications can occur from recurrent deep vein thrombosis and can manifest in the form of chronic venous insufficiency. Stasis leg ulcers, swelling, and the postphlebitic syndrome are possible long-term complications. For the individual with recurrent pulmonary embolism, signs and symptoms suggestive of pulmonary hypertension may be expected. For the arterial events, complications vary depending on the thromboembolic event. Patients should be informed about any potential complication and educated in the signs and symptoms of thromboembolic phenomena in order that they may seek medical care at the earliest warning.

DISCUSSION

Prevalence and Incidence

The incidence of the primary hypercoagulable states is unknown and presently a diagnosis is possible in only about 10 to 20% of patients presenting with suspected primary hypercoagulable states. The incidence of secondary hypercoagulable states is probably higher but difficult to compile. For example, up to 70% of patients with hip fractures develop venous thrombosis without prophylaxis, whereas the incidence in hospitalized patients with a myocardial infarction or stroke who are not given routine prophylaxis ranges from 20 to 35%.

Related Basic Science

The etiology for the hypercoagulable states remains complex. New protein deficiency states that contribute to this process are continuing to be identified. Over the last several decades, the identification of antithrombin III, protein C, and protein S has contributed to our better understanding of these disorders. Nevertheless, the principles of Virchow's triad, noted well over a century ago, still contribute to our basic understanding of hypercoagulability. Venous stasis, vascular injury, and hypercoagulability are the basis of our primary and secondary hypercoagulable states. These processes can lead to thrombosis.

Natural History and Its Modification with Treatment

Thromboembolic disease remains a major cause of morbidity and mortality in the United States. Pulmonary embolism may lead to 200,000 deaths annually and is a common cause of unexpected death in hospitalized patients. Deep vein thrombosis contributes to morbidity in the form of venous stasis ulcers, chronic venous insufficiency, and the postphlebitic syndrome. Arterial events such as stroke and myocardial infarction can be devastating to the affected individual. Fortunately, treatment of venous thromboembolism is often very successful and greatly affects the outcome of the disease. Many of the arterial thromboembolic events can also be modified by the appropriate treatment.

Prevention

Many thrombotic events can be prevented. Unfortunately, all too often there is a failure by the physician to recognize the secondary hypercoagulable states in time to prevent venous thromboembolism. Simply using prophylaxis on patients admitted to the hospital will eliminate the majority of venous thrombotic events. Subcutaneous heparin given 2 hours before surgery and then every 12 hours after (the procedure), intermittent compression stockings applied at the time of surgery, or the use of low-molecular-weight heparin after orthopaedic surgery will decrease the incidence of venous thromboembolism. Risk factor modification is important in arterial thromboembolism, and includes cessation of smoking, dietary intervention, lipid modification, and better control of diabetes and hypertension.

In the setting of a primary hypercoagulable disorder, identifying those individuals at risk by studying family members is advisable. Placing these individuals on appropriate prophylaxis during pregnancy and surgical procedures and in the setting of trauma is advised.

Cost Containment

Thromboembolism is a costly problem in the United States. Every year, hospitalizations for deep vein thrombosis, pulmonary embolism, stroke, myocardial infarction, and other thromboembolic disorders take a huge number of our health care dollars. By eliminating venous thromboembolism with the proper use of prophylaxis and surveillance, untold billions of dollars might be saved. Unfortunately, studies continue to show that physicians all too commonly fail to use prophylaxis.

REFERENCES

Heijboer H, Brandjes DP, Buller HR, Sturk A. Deficiencies of coagulation inhibiting and fibrinolytic proteins in outpatients with deep-vein thrombosis. N Engl J Med 1990;323:1512.

Nachman RL, Silverstein R. Hypercoagulable states. Ann Intern Med 1993;119:819.

Schafer AI. The hypercoagulable states. Ann Intern Med 1985;102:814.

Svenson PJ, Dahlback B. Resistance to activated protein C as a basis for venous thrombosis. N Engl J Med 1994;330:517.

CHAPTER 12–38

Disseminated Intravascular Coagulation

Maurie Markman, M.D.

DEFINITION

Disseminated intravascular coagulation (DIC) is an abnormality in the delicate balance within the blood clotting cascade between factors that cause activation and deactivation of clot formation. This imbalance can lead to excessive clot formation, bleeding, or both.

ETIOLOGY

There are a number of causes of DIC including advanced cancer, acute leukemia (particularly the acute promyelocytic subtype), infection, trauma, heat stroke, shock, obstetric complications, surgery, collagen–vascular diseases, snake bites, amyloidosis, aortic aneurysm, large hemangiomas, and major blood transfusion mismatches. Tumors that produce mucin (e.g., prostate, gastric, and ovarian cancers) are particularly likely to be associated with the development of DIC, presumably because the mucin material is capable of entering the systemic circulation and causing subsequent activation of the clotting cascade.

CRITERIA FOR DIAGNOSIS
Subjective

A patient presenting with any type of blood clot for which there is no obvious explanation for its development (e.g., recent trauma to the extremity, use of birth control pills) should be considered a candidate for the presence of DIC. The presence of migratory thrombophlebitis (Trousseau's syndrome) is a serious sign because it is frequently associated with the presence of an underlying malignancy.

Objective

The presence of DIC is confirmed by the performance of coagulation studies that indicate the abnormal activation of the clotting cascade.

CLINICAL MANIFESTATIONS
Subjective

The clinical manifestations depend on whether the imbalance is more to the side of clotting or bleeding, although both manifestations can be present in the same patient. DIC associated with bleeding is frequently associated with acute promyelocytic leukemia, but can also be observed in individuals who develop DIC following surgery, with sepsis, or with liver failure. In patients with severe thrombocytopenia it is often difficult to distinguish bleeding from the low platelets versus abnormal activation of the clotting cascade.

Of particular significance is the finding of spontaneous bleeding, often from multiple sites (e.g., skin, bloody urine, melena) in an acutely ill patient. Bleeding from a number of unrelated sites suggests a systemic process, rather than an isolated structural abnormality.

The development of blood clots in multiple locations (Trousseau's syndrome) is an indication of a hypercoagulable state and strongly suggests the presence of an underlying malignancy, most often a solid tumor, such as gastric, prostate, pancreatic, ovarian, and lung cancers. Although these clots are more common in the venous system of the lower extremities, they can occur in any region of the body and may involve arteries as well as veins.

Objective
Physical Examination

Physical findings of DIC might include bleeding into the skin, hematuria, hemoptysis, melena, deep venous thrombosis, migratory thrombophlebitis, arterial thrombosis.

Routine Laboratory Abnormalities

The most common routine laboratory abnormality in DIC is the finding of a low platelet count.

Microangiopathic anemia may be associated with DIC. Evidence of this process on a peripheral blood smear, however, is insufficient by itself to make a diagnosis of DIC, as such changes may be observed in a number of other conditions, including vasculitis, collagen–vascular diseases, prosthetic heart valves, and cancer.

PLANS
Diagnostic
Differential Diagnosis

The diagnosis of DIC can often be difficult as the process may present in mild or severe forms, be acute or chronic, and result from multiple different causes. In addition, other conditions may mimic DIC and must be considered in the differential diagnosis. These include liver failure (with reduction in multiple coagulation factors), severe thrombocytopenia (with bleeding and subsequent activation of the clotting cascade), systemic vasculitis (with development of localized clot formation at the site of vessel inflammation), microangiopathic hemolytic anemia, thrombotic thrombocytopenic purpura, and the presence of a prosthetic valve.

Diagnostic Options

The hallmark of DIC is evidence of a decrease in clotting factors and their function in association with increased activity of the fibrinolytic pathway.

Thus, abnormalities in DIC include the following findings: increase in fibrinogen–fibrin degradation products (FDPs); low serum fibrinogen; low platelets; inadequate clot formation; prolonged prothrombin (PT), partial thromboplastin (PTT), and thrombin (TT) times; and decreased factor V, factor VII, factor X, antithrombin III, and plasminogen levels. In addition, review of the blood smear frequently reveals an element of microangiopathic hemolytic anemia. The most sensitive test is that for FDPs, as fibrinolysis leading to excessive formation of degradation products is almost always present with abnormal clotting.

The most common aberrations in the clotting profile include reductions in levels of platelets, prothrombin, and factors V, VIII, and XIII. In more severe cases, levels of factors II, X, IX, and VII may also be reduced. Serum levels of FDPs are frequently elevated to 40 μg/mL or higher.

It should be noted that patients with DIC may actually have a normal plasma fibrinogen level despite other evidence of active and abnormal activation of the clotting cascade. This circumstance results from the fact that fibrinogen is an acute phase reactant and is often initially quite elevated in the presence of a number of illnesses that can cause DIC (e.g., sepsis, advanced malignancy).

Recommended Approach

In a patient suspected to have DIC on the basis of both clinical signs and symptoms and routine laboratory evaluation, standard coagulation testing should be performed. This includes reviewing the peripheral smear and measuring PT, PTT, and levels of serum fibrinogen and FDPs, and individual clotting factors.

Therapeutic

Therapeutic Options

It is important to note that not all situations where DIC is documented by laboratory findings require treatment. In certain individuals abnormal activation of the clotting cascade may be compensated effectively by the same degree of activation in the fibrinolytic system. In such circumstances the patient will have laboratory evidence of DIC (e.g., elevation of FDPs, decreased clotting factors), but no evidence of abnormal bleeding or clot formation.

There are several circumstances in which it is appropriate to initiate treatment directed to the clotting abnormalities: (1) Therapy of the underlying cause of DIC does not rapidly reverse the clotting abnormalities (e.g., continued DIC despite the use of appropriate antibiotics in sepsis). (2) Therapy of the underlying disease is not available (e.g., advanced unresectable pancreatic cancer). (3) Initial symptoms of DIC are of such severity (e.g., significant bleeding in a patient with acute promyelocytic leukemia) that it is not possible to wait for a response to treatment of the primary disease abnormality.

The major goal of therapy of DIC is the interruption of abnormal activation of the clotting cascade. One strategy calls for the administration of heparin (used principally to inhibit microthrombus formation), even if bleeding is the principal manifestation of DIC in a particular patient. In an individual who is actively bleeding, platelets and plasma clotting factors should also be administered, even if this may appear to be "feeding the fire." In such situations it is critical that a balance between activation of the clotting and fibrinolytic cascades be reestablished, and the use of heparin (to interfere with clot formation) along with the judicious administration of clotting factors and platelets (to prevent bleeding) may be necessary to interrupt the cycle sufficiently for normal homeostatic mechanisms to come into play.

Unfortunately, the clinical utility of heparin in DIC has never been demonstrated in randomized controlled clinical trials. In addition, there is a natural and appropriate concern with the use of heparin in an individual who is actively bleeding. Thus, this strategy should be employed only after careful consideration of alternatives in a particular situation and with knowledge of the potential for increasing bleeding.

Recommended Approach

The optimal therapeutic approach to the management of DIC depends on the etiology of the process, its severity, and its potential reversibility. In general, the most effective treatment of DIC is that directed toward the underlying disease process (e.g., effective antibiotics for bacteremia, repair of an aortic aneurysm, chemotherapy for acute leukemia).

FOLLOW-UP

Depending on the severity of DIC and the underlying disease process, intensive monitoring may be required. In individuals with a milder or more chronic disease process, outpatient management may be appropriate. As the coagulation abnormalities actually may be the initial presenting feature of an underlying disease process, diagnostic tests to define the cause of the DIC may be required (e.g., search for an underlying malignancy, presence of an occult abscess).

DISCUSSION
Prevalence

As DIC may be very mild and more of a laboratory finding than a symptomatic disease process in many patients, it is impossible to provide an estimate of its prevalence, except to state it is likely to be far more common than recognized clinically. It should, however, be emphasized that the mere presence of laboratory evidence of DIC should not, by itself, be an indication to treat the process with either heparin or plasma clotting factors.

Related Basic Science

In experimental animal systems it can be demonstrated that a number of procoagulant materials, including thrombin, tissue thromboplastin, and snake venom, can produce a clinical state closely resembling acute fulminant DIC in humans. Weaker procoagulant materials present in the circulation in sufficient concentration can overcome the ability of the body to rapidly remove the product, leading to more chronic abnormal activation of the clotting cascade.

It is known that a number of procoagulants can activate specific clotting factors. For example, mucin, produced by certain adenocarcinomas, directly activates factor X. The defibrination observed after certain snake bites is the result of the direct conversion of fibrinogen to fibrin caused by the entry of proteolytic enzymes in the systemic circulation. Following severe brain trauma, prostate surgery, or obstetric complications, DIC can result from the release of tissue thromboplastin factors. Finally, there is evidence that the DIC associated with leukemia may be mediated by interleukin-1.

Natural History and Its Modification with Treatment

It is fortunate that in many circumstances DIC is rapidly reversible following successful treatment of the primary disease process (e.g., sepsis, repair of an aortic aneursym), although in other individuals the abnormalities of the coagulation cascade are only one manifestation of an untreatable and progressive disease entity (e.g., advanced cancer). It is reasonable to conclude that, in general, if the underlying cause of DIC can be discovered and successfully treated, the abnormalities in the clotting cascade will be reversed.

Prevention

The only method available to prevent DIC is avoidance of clinical circumstances that may be associated with its development (e.g., sepsis following the administration of high-dose chemotherapy to an individual with advanced cancer).

Cost Containment

Optimal treatment of DIC should focus on removal of the initiating event. Effective treatment of this primary process will reduce the duration and severity of the clotting abnormalities and decrease the need for expensive blood products (e.g., fresh-frozen plasma, platelets, red cells, plasma clotting factors). Finally, as noted above, it is inappropriate to initiate treatment of DIC (e.g., heparin, clotting factors) solely on the basis of mild laboratory evidence of this disease process (e.g., elevated FDPs, decreased platelets, elevated prothrombin time).

REFERENCES

Baker N. Clinical aspects of disseminated intravascular coagulation: A clinician's point of view. Semin Thromb Hemost 1989;15:1.

Bick RL, Kunkel LA. Disseminated intravascular coagulation syndromes. Int J Hematol 1992;55:1.

Colman RW, Rubin RN. Disseminated intravascular coagulation due to malignancy. Semin Oncol 1990;17:172.

Feinstein DI. Treatment of disseminated intravascular coagulation. Semin Thromb Hemost 1988;14:351.

The Porphyrias

James P. Kushner, M.D.

GENERAL DEFINITION

The porphyrias are a group of disorders characterized by photosensitivity, acute attacks of abdominal pain and neurologic abnormalities, or both. The porphyric disorders, because of their complex and archaic titles, present a confusing problem to most clinicians. At least seven different porphyrias have been described.

GENERAL ETIOLOGY

The porphyrias result from specific enzyme defects in the heme biosynthetic pathway (Figure 12–39–1). The porphyrias differ from one another clinically and in the type of porphyrin or porphyrin precursor excreted. In general, the major compound excreted is the substrate of the defective enzyme. Porphyrins have unique fluorescent properties, and when they are produced in excess, there is associated cutaneous photosensitivity. The porphyrin precursors, δ-aminolevulinic acid (ALA) and porphobilinogen (PBG), do not have fluorescent properties, and when they are produced in excess, there is an associated syndrome of acute attacks of abdominal colic, peripheral neuropathy, paralysis, psychosis,

and even coma. Thus, porphyric disorders in which only porphyrins are produced in excess are characterized clinically by cutaneous photosensitivity, whereas those in which only porphyrin precursors are produced in excess are characterized by attacks of pain and neurologic symptoms. When excessive amounts of both porphyrins and porphyrin precursors are produced, the porphyria is characterized clinically by both photosensitivity and acute attacks. These considerations form the basis for a practical clinical classification given in Table 12–39–1.

Porphyria Cutanea Tarda

DEFINITION

Porphyria cutanea tarda, the most common porphyria in humans, is a liver disease with striking cutaneous manifestations. It is a disease of adults, mainly middle-aged men who use alcohol regularly. In recent

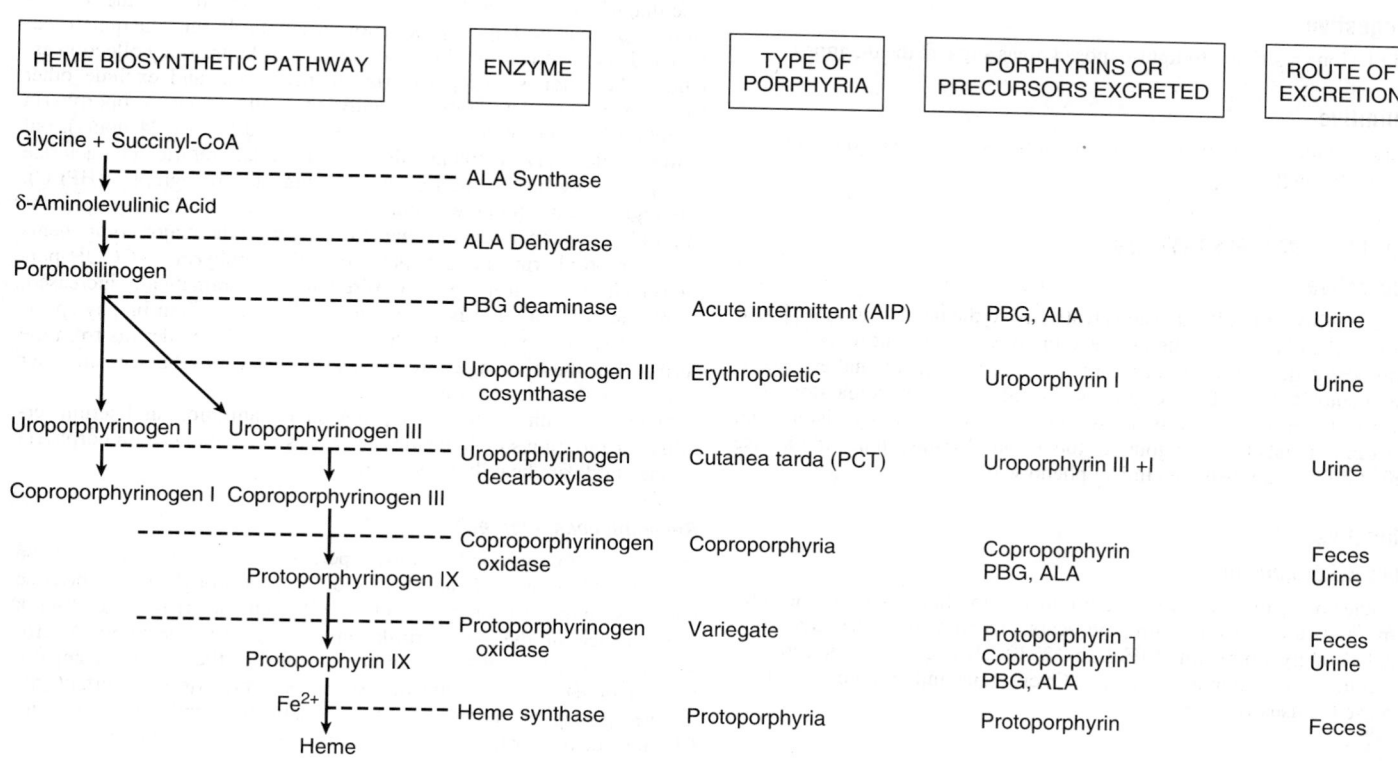

Figure 12–39–1. The heme biosynthetic pathway and the metabolic abnormality in each type of porphyria. Reduced porphyrinogens are the substrates for several of the enzymes, but excreted compounds are always oxidized porphyrins. Mitochondrial enzymes include δ-aminolevulinic acid synthase, coproporphyrinogen oxidase, protoporphyrinogen oxidase, and heme synthase. The remaining enzymes are cytosolic. In the three forms of porphyria associated with acute attacks there is an increase in heptatic δ-aminolevulinic acid synthase activity as a result of derepression and loss of feedback inhibition, both resulting from the primary enzyme defects indicated. ALA, δ-aminolevulinic acid; PBG, porphobilinogen.

TABLE 12–39–1. CLINICAL CLASSIFICATION OF THE PORPHYRIAS

Porphyrias producing cutaneous photosensitivity
   Porphyria cutanea tarda (PCT)
   Protoporphyria
   Congenital erythropoietic porphyria
Porphyrias producing acute painful attacks
   Acute intermittent porphyria (AIP)
Porphyrias producing both photosensitivity and acute attacks
   Variegate porphyria
   Hereditary coproporphyria

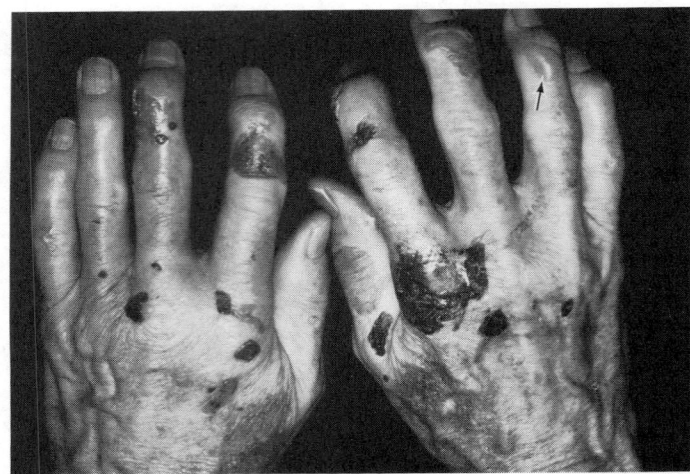

Figure 12–39–2. Porphyria cutanea tarda. Fragile skin with a fresh bullous lesion (*arrow*), erosions, and scars of past lesions.

years, more women with porphyria cutanea tarda have been recognized, many of whom are ingesting estrogenic hormones.

ETIOLOGY

Porphyria cutanea tarda is due to subnormal activity of uroporphyrinogen decarboxylase (Figure 12–39–1). In about one half of the cases, the enzymatic defect is inherited as an autosomal dominant trait, and the enzyme deficiency can be detected in any tissue. This form of porphyria cutanea tarda is designated *familial porphyria cutanea tarda*. Rare instances of homozygous deficiency for uroporphyrinogen decarboxylase have been reported producing striking photosensitivity beginning in early childhood. In the remainder of the cases there is little to suggest an inherited basis for the disease, and most available evidence suggests that the deficiency of uroporphyrinogen decarboxylase is restricted to the liver. The cause of the deficiency appears to be the generation of an inhibitor of enzyme activity in liver cells.

CRITERIA FOR DIAGNOSIS

Suggestive

Skin lesions restricted to light-exposed areas suggest the diagnosis.

Definitive

Markedly increased urinary excretion of uroporphyrin is required to establish the diagnosis.

CLINICAL MANIFESTATIONS

Subjective

Skin fragility and bullous lesions restricted to the hands and face should suggest the diagnosis. When these symptoms are present in association with heavy alcohol intake or with the ingestion of medicinal estrogens, the diagnosis should be strongly considered. In the autosomal dominant form of the disease there is occasionally a positive family history, but most individuals heterozygous for the uroporphyrinogen decarboxylase defect do not manifest the clinical phenotype.

Objective

Physical Examination

Vesicles and bullae form over the dorsa of the hands and on the forearms and drain, leaving atrophic scars that may be either hyperpigmented or hypopigmented (Figure 12–39–2). Facial hypertrichosis is generally most notable in females. Overt signs and symptoms of liver disease are usually not present.

Routine Laboratory Abnormalities

Routine laboratory testing may reveal slight to moderate elevations in serum transaminase levels, but liver function tests vary considerably from one patient to another. The hemoglobin concentration, white blood cell count, and platelet count are generally normal. Antibodies to the hepatitis C virus are detected in most patients.

PLANS

Diagnostic

Differential Diagnosis

The differential diagnosis lies between porphyria cutanea tarda and other forms of photosensitive bullous dermatoses. Drug-associated bullous dermatoses may mimic porphyria cutanea tarda. The most common offending agents are nonsteroidal anti-inflammatory drugs. Rarely, an immunologic disease, epidermolysis bullosa acquisita, may be confused with porphyria cutanea tarda.

Diagnostic Options

The diagnosis of porphyria cutanea tarda is established by the demonstration of increased urinary excretion of uroporphyrin. The quantification and characterization of porphyrins in a 24-hour urine collection establish the diagnosis of porphyria cutanea tarda, and exclude other forms of bullous dermatoses. Usually, the daily urinary uroporphyrin excretion is about 3000 μg (normal, < than 50 μg per 24 hours), but higher values may be found. Most reference laboratories characterize urinary porphyrins by high-pressure liquid chromatography (HPLC). The high-pressure liquid chromatography pattern of urinary porphyrins in porphyria cutanea tarda is characteristic, with the major components being uroporphyrin and a heptacarboxylic porphyrin (7-COOH-porphyrin). If urinary uroporphyrin excretion is not dramatically increased, porphyria cutanea tarda is not a tenable diagnosis. Skin biopsy specimens reveal bullae formed by the separation of the epidermis from the dermis, but these changes are not specific and may be seen in other forms of bullous dermatosis.

The serum iron concentration, transferrin saturation, and serum ferritin concentration should be measured, as some patients with porphyria cutanea tarda are heavily iron-laden.

Recommended Approach

If there are no contraindications, a percutaneous needle biopsy of the liver should be done. If an ultraviolet lamp is brought to the bedside (Wood's lamp), it is simple to observe the characteristic reddish-pink fluorescence in the porphyrin-laden liver biopsy specimen. Microscopic examination of the specimen establishes the degree of hepatocellular damage and hepatic fibrosis (if present). More important, the degree of hepatic siderosis can be established with an iron stain. Chronic active hepatitis due to hepatitis C is a frequent finding.

Therapeutic

Therapeutic Options

Exposure to alcohol or estrogen should be eliminated. Removal of iron by repeated phlebotomy is the most useful therapeutic approach and is effective even if alcohol consumption continues. If there are no contraindications, 500 mL of blood can be removed every 2 weeks. Clinical remissions are usually achieved after the removal of about 3 L of blood (six phlebotomies), but some patients require additional therapy. Patients with very prominent hepatic siderosis should continue therapy until laboratory evidence of iron depletion is documented. Phlebotomy-induced remissions are long (30 months average), and if relapse occurs, a second course of phlebotomy therapy is usually effective.

If phlebotomy therapy cannot be employed (because of another illness or because of inadequate venous access), an alternate form of therapy is the oral administration of low doses of chloroquine phosphate (250–500 mg twice weekly). The drug forms an easily excreted water-soluble complex with hepatocellular porphyrins. Clinical remissions generally occur after a few months of therapy, at which point treatment should be stopped. Because of the potential danger of hematologic and hepatic side effects, and because phlebotomy is safe and effective, chloroquine therapy should be reserved only for patients unsuitable for phlebotomy.

Recommended Approach

Phlebotomy therapy is clearly the recommended approach. Protection of the hands and face from sunlight is important during the early phases of phlebotomy therapy. Conventional sun-screening agents are ineffective as a symptomatic treatment because they do not block the wavelengths in the Soret band of the spectrum (around 400 nm) that are responsible for inducing porphyrin-mediated photosensitivity. Opaque reflective material such as zinc oxide or theatrical makeup may be useful until the beneficial effects of phlebotomy therapy are achieved. The use of protective clothing such as gloves and broad-brimmed hats may be helpful when photosensitivity is prominent.

FOLLOW-UP

The hemoglobin concentration or the volume of packed red cells (hematocrit) should be measured prior to each phlebotomy. A repeat 24-hour urine porphyrin determination should be performed after six phlebotomies. Urine porphyrin excretion rarely returns to normal, and the goal of therapy is to reduce porphyrin excretion to about 300 to 500 µg daily. When this is achieved, follow-up evaluations every 6 to 12 months should suffice. These visits should include a physical examination, the collection of a 24-hour urine sample for porphyrin determination, and the laboratory assessment of liver function. After a year or two, if there are no cutaneous symptoms, urinary porphyrin determinations can be less frequent. The need to monitor liver function should be stressed to the patient, and the follow-up visits offer the opportunity to reemphasize the need to avoid alcohol.

DISCUSSION
Prevalence and Incidence

Porphyria cutanea tarda is recognized in about 1 of 25,000 Caucasians. It is uncommon in blacks, with the exception of the Bantu population of South Africa.

Related Basic Science

The primary defect in all patients with porphyria cutanea tarda is subnormal activity of hepatic uroporphyrinogen decarboxylase (Figure 12–39–1). In familial porphyria cutanea tarda, the enzyme defect is present in all tissues and is inherited as an autosomal dominant trait. Most family members with the enzyme defect express no clinical or biochemical evidence of porphyria cutanea tarda. The development of hepatic siderosis appears to be required for expression of the defect. Rare cases of homozygosity for the genetic defect have been reported, and in these patients, symptoms of porphyria begin in early childhood. In sporadic porphyria cutanea tarda the enzyme defect is restricted to the liver, and there is no strong evidence to support an inherited factor in the pathogenesis of the disease. As in familial porphyria cutanea tarda, hepatic siderosis is present in all patients with the sporadic form of the disease. The role of iron in the pathogenesis of the disease cannot be simply explained, however, as the disease is rarely found in patients

with hereditary hemochromatosis or other iron storage diseases. The complex relationship between genetic factors, exposure to hepatotoxins, and hepatic siderosis has not been resolved.

Natural History and Its Modification with Treatment

If liver iron stores are depleted and liver toxins are avoided, there is little evidence to suggest that porphyria cutanea tarda affects life expectancy. Several reports from Europe have indicated an increased risk of developing hepatocellular carcinoma, but this has not been the experience in North America.

Prevention

Following successful therapy, the likelihood of relapse can be greatly reduced by the avoidance of alcohol, estrogens, and medicinal iron. Some have advocated periodic phlebotomies (three or four annually), but there is no evidence to support the efficacy of such treatment as a preventive maneuver.

Cost Containment

Cost containment can be accomplished only by adherence to the preventive measures described above.

Protoporphyria

DEFINITION

Protoporphyria is an inherited illness characterized by a type of photosensitivity quite unlike that seen in other patients with porphyria. No acute attacks of abdominal pain or neurologic abnormalities occur.

ETIOLOGY

Protoporphyria is inherited as an autosomal dominant trait and is due to mutations of the gene encoding the terminal enzyme in the heme biosynthetic pathway, namely, heme synthase (ferrochelatase) (Figure 12–39–1).

CRITERIA FOR DIAGNOSIS
Suggestive

A history of stinging and burning sensations in the skin occurring after exposure to sunlight suggests the presence of protoporphyria. These symptoms generally begin in childhood.

Definitive

The diagnosis is established by demonstrating a marked increase in the concentration of protoporphyrin in red cells and in the stool.

CLINICAL MANIFESTATIONS
Subjective

A history of photosensitivity beginning in childhood is characteristic, and by early adulthood the skin of the face and hands often appears prematurely aged. Most patients with protoporphyria complain of an intensely unpleasant sensation of prickling, itching, or burning after even brief exposure to the sun. Many patients with protoporphyria develop gallstones. The family history may uncover other relatives with photosensitivity and/or gallstones, but most family members with the genetic defect have no clinical symptoms. Symptoms of photosensitivity are usually most prominent in summer and may be totally absent during the darker winter months.

Objective
Physical Examination

Edema and erythema occur only on sun-exposed areas of the body. Chronic changes include shallow, pitted scars over the cheeks and nose and premature aged-appearing skin over the dorsa of the hands. Signs and symptoms of cholelithiasis may be present, and rare patients develop a rapidly progressive and fatal cirrhosis.

Routine Laboratory Abnormalities

Routine laboratory testing may reveal a mild, slightly hypochromic anemia and evidence of hepatocellular dysfunction.

PLANS
Diagnostic

The free erythrocyte protoporphyrin concentration is greatly increased in symptomatic patients. Free erythrocyte protoporphyrin values ranging from 300 to 4500 μg/dL have been reported (normal, < 50 μg/dL). The free erythrocyte protoporphyrin value may be elevated in patients with iron deficiency anemia, but rarely does the value exceed 300 μg/dL. Fluoresence microscopy reveals the characteristic salmon-pink porphyrin fluorescence in a variable portion of erythrocytes. Fecal protoporphyrin excretion varies widely from patient to patient, but is generally higher than normal and may be as high as 1400 μg/g (dry weight) (normal, <100 μg/g).

Differential Diagnosis

Drug-induced photosensitivity, particularly the type associated with tetracycline ingestion, is a consideration but erythrocyte protoporphyrin levels are normal in these conditions.

Diagnostic Options and Recommended Approach

Once the clinical suspicion is present the diagnosis can be made only by measuring protoporphyrin in red cells and feces.

Therapeutic

Therapy is directed toward reducing the consequences of sun exposure. Topical sunscreens effective in the 400-nm portion of the spectrum (see above) may be useful. The induction of carotenemia (serum carotene levels above 400 μg/dL) may result in increased tolerance to sunlight. Carotenemia is best induced by administering β-carotene beadlets (Solatene) in a dose of 120 to 300 mg per day. Experimental attempts to protect the liver by interrupting the enterohepatic circulation of protoporphyrin have included the administration by mouth of porphyrin-binding compounds such as cholestyramine and activated charcoal. Although preliminary results are promising, these agents cannot be considered as standard therapy.

Cholecystectomy is indicated when gallstones are present. The stones are dark in color and contain protoporphyrin.

FOLLOW-UP

Annual evaluations of liver function should suffice for most patients. Carotene therapy may be required only in summer. Screening of family members is best done by measuring the free erythrocyte protoporphyrin level and fecal porphyrin excretion.

DISCUSSION
Prevalence and Incidence

Protoporphyria is relatively common but the exact incidence has not been determined. Hundreds of cases have been reported throughout the world.

Related Basic Science
Genetics

The disease is due to a dominantly inherited defect in the mitochondrial enzyme heme synthase, but there is great variation in the severity of clinical expression and in the degree to which porphyrin metabolism is detectably altered.

Metabolic Derangement

Excess protoporphyrin is synthesized in young erythrocytes, diffuses into plasma, is rapidly cleared by the liver, and is excreted in the bile.

Cholestasis may occur when the liver is required to clear and secrete large amounts of protoporphyrin. Serious morbidity of the disorder occurs only in those rare patients with hepatocellular disease due to extreme cholestasis.

Natural History and Its Modification with Treatment

Protoporphyria in most patients is a benign disease that progresses very little. The complication of cirrhosis with liver failure is rare, and the only effective therapy for this complication is liver transplantation.

Prevention

No preventive measures, other than minimizing sun exposure, are currently available.

Cost Containment

Reduction of symptoms by prevention is the only necessary cost containment approach. Avoidance of sunshine, use of protective clothing, and application of ultraviolet blocking agents are effective. Induction of carotenemia should be necessary only in those who cannot avoid exposure to the sun, and then perhaps only in the summer.

Congenital Erythropoietic Porphyria

DEFINITION

Congenital erythropoietic porphyria is an exceedingly rare form of porphyria which is inherited as an autosomal recessive trait. In most cases the disease is evident at birth and results in striking photomutilation. Congenital erythropoietic porphyria was one of the first porphyric disorders to be clinically characterized and is also known as Gunther's disease after the clinician who published a comprehensive description of the disorder in 1911.

ETIOLOGY

Congenital erythropoietic porphyria is due to a severe deficiency of uroporphyrinogen III cosynthase (Figure 12–39–1). Mutations in the gene encoding the enzyme result in a gene product with markedly diminished catalytic activity. The disease is characterized biochemically by the urinary excretion of large amounts of uroporphyrin I. The site of uroporphyrin overproduction is the developing erythroblast, and marrow fluorescence is uniformly present.

CRITERIA FOR DIAGNOSIS
Suggestive

Diapers of affected newborns often exhibit pink-to-purple staining. The stains fluoresce when illuminated with long-range ultraviolet light. The development of bullous lesions over light-exposed skin may be noted in the newborn nursery, especially when phototherapy is used to control neonatal jaundice.

Objective
Physical Examination

Extreme photosensitivity is common, and as children grow older almost all display bullous lesions, skin fragility, cutaneous infections, hirsutism, and often severe photomutilation. Hemolytic anemia of varying severity is common, and splenomegaly is present in most cases. Deposition of porphyrins in the dentin of developing teeth results in a brownish discoloration, and the teeth may fluoresce under ultraviolet light.

Routine Laboratory Abnormalities

Routine laboratory testing generally reveals a moderate anemia. The white blood count and platelet count are generally normal.

PLANS
Diagnostic
Differential Diagnosis

The clinical signs and symptoms of congenital erythropoietic porphyria are so striking that very few other diagnoses need be considered. Congenital forms of epidermolysis bullosa might be considered in the neonatal period.

Diagnostic Options

The diagnosis is based on recognition of the clinical syndrome and the detection of massive amounts of uroporphyrin I in the urine. Values exceeding 100,000 µg/d have been reported. In addition to the finding of fluorescence in the bone marrow, the nuclei of affected erythroblasts are dysmorphic. Kinetic studies have demonstrated both ineffective erythropoiesis and peripheral hemolysis.

Recommended Approach

Because this disorder is so rare, the discovery of new cases should prompt referral to a center with experience in dealing with congenital erythropoietic porphyria. Family studies and genetic counseling are required, and if parents desire additional children, it may be advisable to characterize the molecular defect and to perform in utero diagnostic testing in subsequent pregnancies.

Therapeutic

The treatment of congenital erythropoietic porphyria is based on avoidance of exposure to sunlight. Protective clothing coupled with appropriate sunscreens is recommended. Additional therapy depends on the severity of the hemolytic anemia. Splenectomy and transfusions have been employed successfully, but prolonged transfusion therapy carries the risk of transfusion-induced iron overload.

Therapeutic Options

Bone marrow transplantation may be useful in selected cases.

Recommended Approach

Avoidance of sunlight is the cornerstone of patient management.

FOLLOW-UP

Patients with this disorder need frequent evaluations with prompt attention to the treatment of infections occurring in ulcerated areas of photomutilated skin. An aggressive approach to cutaneous infections can prevent severe photomutilation.

DISCUSSION
Prevalence and Incidence

Fewer than 300 cases of congenital erythropoietic porphyria have been reported in the medical literature. In the Middle Ages, unfortunate souls with this disease probably were considered werewolves as they were hirsute, mutilated, and nocturnal. An extensive description of the disease can be found in the review by Kappas et al. (1989).

Related Basic Science

See Etiology.

Natural History and Its Modification with Treatment

Bone marrow transplantation is the only therapeutic option that reverses the disease phenotype, but the procedure is feasible only when normal HLA-matched sibling donors are available. If photomutilation can be avoided, and if the hemolytic anemia is not too severe, affected individuals may lead long, productive lives.

Prevention

Prevention of new cases in a pedigree in which an affected proband has been identified can be achieved only through genetic counseling coupled with in utero diagnostic techniques.

Cost Containment

Bone marrow transplantation is costly and should be reserved for patients with a severe phenotype.

Acute Intermittent Porphyria

DEFINITION

Acute intermittent porphyria is an inherited disorder characterized by episodic attacks of abdominal pain and neurologic symptoms. Acute attacks are often precipitated by the ingestion of specific drugs. Although the disease is inherited as an autosomal dominant trait, most symptomatic patients are women. Attacks rarely occur before puberty.

ETIOLOGY

Mutations in the gene encoding porphobilinogen deaminase (Figure 12–39–1) are responsible for acute intermittent porphyria. As a result of the partial block in the heme biosynthetic pathway, δ-aminolevulinic acid synthase is induced in the hepatocyte, and aminolevulinic acid and porphobilinogen are produced in excess and excreted in urine. The metabolic abnormality is accompanied by the acute attack. Acute intermittent porphyria is transmitted as an autosomal dominant trait, but most carriers of a mutant porphobilinogen deaminase allele never develop clinical symptoms.

CRITERIA FOR DIAGNOSIS
Subjective

Severe abdominal pain, often associated with obstipation, occurring episodically in a female patient should suggest the diagnosis. When these symptoms are present in association with peripheral neuropathy or an acute psychiatric disturbance, the diagnosis should be strongly considered. Suspicion should be heightened if the clinical episode occurred after the ingestion of a barbiturate, a sulfa antibiotic, an antiepileptic, or a hormone preparation. A compilation of the drugs that have been known to precipitate acute attacks is given in the reviews by Kappas et al. (1989) and Moore (1980). The family history may reveal that relatives have suffered with abdominal pains, mental aberrations, and peripheral neuropathies.

Objective
Physical Examination

Acute porphyric attacks usually begin with abdominal pain and are associated with some sign of autonomic dysfunction. Severe attacks may be associated with peripheral motor neuropathy, cranial neuropathy, delirium, seizures, and coma. Respiratory paralysis is a particularly ominous sign.

Routine Laboratory Abnormalities

Leukocytosis is occasionally observed during acute attacks, a finding that may support an erroneous diagnosis of an abdominal condition requiring surgery. Hyponatremia, reflecting inappropriate antidiuretic hormone secretion, is a common finding.

PLANS
Diagnostic
Differential Diagnosis

Attacks of abdominal pain may be associated with any number of disorders. In contrast to diseases requiring surgical intervention, the physical examination during an acute attack of acute intermittent porphyria rarely reveals signs of peritoneal irritation. Bowel sounds are generally markedly diminished.

Diagnostic Options

The characteristic abnormality of porphyrin metabolism is the excessive urinary excretion of the porphyrin precursors porphobilinogen and, to a lesser extent, δ-aminolevulinic acid. A rapid method of detecting excess porphobilinogen in urine is the Watsen–Schwartz test. This test is based on the finding that porphobilinogen forms an intense red color with Ehrlich's reagent (*p*-dimethyl aminobenzaldehyde dissolved in glacial acetic acid and perchloric acid). The resulting chromogen cannot be extracted in organic solvents such as chloroform and *n*-butanol. False-positive results may occur when patients are ingesting a variety of medications, and it is important to verify a positive test with quantification of porphobilinogen and δ-aminolevulinic acid by ion-exchange chromatography. Fecal porphyrin excretion is normal, but it should be measured to exclude the possibility of variegate porphyria or hereditary coproporphyria (see below), both of which may present with an identical clinical syndrome.

Assays of porphobilinogen deaminase activity in lysates of erythrocytes are available in a number of commercial laboratories. The activity is half-normal in patients with acute intermittent porphyria. Unfortunately, the test is often applied incorrectly. The finding of half-normal porphobilinogen deaminase activity merely identifies a heterozygote for the genetic mutation responsible for acute intermittent porphyria. As most heterozygotes never develop the clinical phenotype, an abnormal enzyme assay result does not establish that an acute porphyric attack is occurring. The enzyme assay is useful in identifying other pedigree members who might be susceptible to acute attacks, and such pedigree members should be counseled about avoiding drugs known to precipitate attacks.

Recommended Approach

Hospitalization is usually required for the treatment of an acute attack. The Watson–Schwartz screening test should be performed quickly and surgical disorders excluded.

Therapeutic

Therapeutic Options

Drugs known to be harmful should be withdrawn. Morphine and phenothiazines are effective and safe agents that are useful in treating the pain and anxiety. Hydration should be carefully monitored, and carbohydrates should be administered orally (if possible) or intravenously (as 10% dextrose) so that the equivalent of 300 to 500 g of glucose is given daily. If improvement is not observed within a day, treatment with intravenous hematin (ferric heme) should be initiated. Hematin was made commercially available as an "orphan drug" in 1983 (Panhematin, Abbott Pharmaceutical, 313 mg of hematin per vial) and appears to be effective therapy when administered early in an attack. Hematin is administered in a dose of 4 mg/kg of body weight at 12-hour intervals. Clinical symptoms generally improve within 24 to 48 hours. Hematin, or a more recently introduced preparation of heme-arginate, causes a prompt decrease in the urinary excretion of δ-aminolevulinic acid and porphobilinogen, presumably mediated by the suppression of δ-aminolevulinic acid synthase activity in the liver. It is not known, however, if either hematin or heme-arginate enters neural cells, where the pathophysiology of the acute porphyric attack is centered.

Recommended Approach

The key to managing patients with acute intermittent porphyria is the education of patients concerning exposure to potentially harmful drugs. Patients should be given a list of these agents and should carry it at all times.

FOLLOW-UP

The frequency of follow-up is determined by the frequency of symptoms. Most patients suffer only two or three attacks in a lifetime and, if drugs are avoided, suffer no ill effects of their porphyria. Others may have permanent, disabling sensory and motor neuropathy and require long-term rehabilitation.

DISCUSSION
Prevalence and Incidence

Estimates of the prevalence of the defect have ranged from 1.5 to 10 per 100,000 but most individuals with porphobilinogen deaminase deficiency never develop clinical symptoms.

Related Basic Science

The primary defect in all patients with acute intermittent porphyria is half-normal activity of porphobilinogen deaminase. Immunoquantification usually reveals half-normal porphobilinogen deaminase protein concentration as well. A wide variety of mutations including point mutations and deletions have been identified in the porphobilinogen deaminase gene. A subset of patients (approximately 20%) have porphobilinogen deaminase mutations that affect catalytic activity of the enzyme, but a normal amount of enzyme protein is present.

The relationship between the metabolic abnormality and the symptoms of the acute attack remains obscure. It is clear that all manifestations of the acute attack reflect abnormalities of the nervous system, but neither δ-aminolevulinic acid nor porphobilinogen have been established as neurotoxins. The metabolic defect may result in subnormal heme synthesis in nervous tissue. Heme synthesis is required in all tissues for the production of cytochromes and other critical enzymes. Depletion of heme in nervous tissue and the liver may be a consequence of exposure to certain drugs, and may explain why drugs precipitate attacks. Significant heme depletion induces increased activity of δ-aminolevulinic acid synthase, the first and rate-regulating enzyme in the pathway (see Figure 12–39–1), leading to the production of more δ-aminolevulinic acid and porphobilinogen, the latter being the substrate of the constitutionally deficient porphobilinogen deaminase.

Natural History and Its Modification with Treatment

If acute attacks are successfully prevented, life expectancy is normal. Early effective treatment of the acute attacks that do occur usually prevents permanent nerve damage. The frequency of attacks in women usually declines after the menopause.

Prevention

Patients should be warned that fasting may induce attacks. Maintenance of caloric intake is important enough that parenteral glucose should be administered when oral intake is interfered with by intercurrent disease. Avoiding harmful drugs is of paramount importance.

In some women, attacks may be related to the menstrual cycle. Suppression of ovulation with oral contraceptives may be helpful, but this should be done cautiously because paradoxical worsening of symptoms may occur.

A most important preventive measure is the screening of family members for the disease. Screening is important because latent carriers of the defect also should be instructed to avoid harmful drugs. Most latent carriers do not excrete excess porphobilinogen in the urine, but they can be detected by measuring the activity of porphobilinogen deaminase in circulating erythrocytes.

Cost Containment

Cost containment can be accomplished only by application of the preventive measures described above.

Variegate Porphyria and Hereditary Coproporphyria

DEFINITION

Both of these dominantly inherited porphyrias are due to subnormal activity of enzymes active in the terminal steps of heme biosynthesis. Variegate porphyria is due to subnormal activity of protoporphyrinogen oxidase and hereditary coproporphyria is due to subnormal activity of coproporphyrinogen oxidase (see Figure 12–39–1). Photosensitivity identical to that seen in porphyria cutanea tarda may be present in either disorder. Photosensitivity may be the sole clinical manifestation in some patients with variegate porphyria, whereas acute attacks identical to those seen in acute intermittent porphyria may be the sole manifestation in others. Clinically, hereditary coproporphyria closely resembles variegate porphyria, but in coproporphyria, photosensitivity occurs only during acute attacks. The two disorders can be distinguished by their distinctive patterns of fecal porphyrin excretion. In coproporphyria, coproporphyrin excretion exceeds protoporphyrin excretion, whereas just the opposite occurs in variegate porphyria.

ETIOLOGY

Both disorders are due to the autosomal dominant transmission of mutant alleles encoding the enzymes that are deficient. Five cases of homozygous hereditary coproporphyria have been described and have been characterized by early age of onset of clinical symptoms and, in some cases, hepatosplenomegaly and hemolytic anemia. The human genes encoding the two defective enzymes have only recently been cloned, and the nature of the mutations responsible for these two disorders has not yet been clarified. The acute attacks are associated with the urinary excretion of large amounts of δ-aminolevulinic acid and porphobilinogen (as in acute intermittent porphyria), but urinary findings revert to normal between episodes.

CRITERIA FOR DIAGNOSIS
Suggestive

Photosensitive dermatosis coupled with episodes of abdominal pain suggest the diagnosis. When these symptoms are present in association with a positive family history, the diagnosis should be strongly considered.

Objective
Physical Examination

Vesicles and bullae in light-exposed areas closely resemble those seen in porphyria cutanea tarda but hypertrichosis is generally not as pronounced. During acute attacks, the physical examination of the abdomen and nervous system reveals findings identical to those seen in patients with acute intermittent porphyria.

Routine Laboratory Abnormalities

During acute attacks, routine laboratory testing may reveal leukocytosis and hyponatremia as described above under Acute Intermittent Porphyria.

PLANS
Diagnostic
Differential Diagnosis

The differential diagnosis lies between variegate porphyria, hereditary coproporphyria, porphyria cutanea tarda, and acute intermittent porphyria.

Diagnostic Options

The diagnosis is established by the measurement of fecal porphyrin excretion. Excess excretion of fecal porphyrins is a constant finding in both disorders, even between acute attacks and even when photosensitivity is not prominent. During the acute attacks, urinary excretion of δ-aminolevulinic acid and porphobilinogen is increased.

Recommended Approach

The acute attack is managed in the same fashion as described for acute intermittent porphyria. Phlebotomy therapy is not of value in managing the photocutaneous manifestations. As with acute intermittent porphyria, avoidance of drugs known to precipitate attacks is critical.

Therapeutic

Carbohydrate replacement and infusion of hematin may both be useful during acute attacks. Photosensitivity, when present, is best managed with appropriate sunscreens and protective clothing.

The suggestions listed above for the management of patients with acute intermittent porphyria apply to both variegate porphyria and hereditary coproporphyria.

FOLLOW-UP

As with acute intermittent porphyria, the frequency of follow-up is related to the frequency of acute attacks. In both of these disorders, almost all attacks are precipitated by exposure to harmful drugs.

DISCUSSION
Prevalence and Incidence

Both of these disorders are rare, but variegate porphyria occurs most commonly in South Africans of Dutch descent (however, cases have been recognized worldwide).

Related Basic Science

The isolation and characterization of the genes encoding protoporphyrinogen oxidase and coproporphyrinogen oxidase should lead shortly to the identification of specific mutations associated with these diseases. The photosensitivity is clearly due to the photosensitizing properties of the porphyrin substrates of the two defective enzymes. The basis for the neurologic syndrome has not been defined, and the same considerations discussed under Acute Intermittent Porphyria apply to these two disorders as well.

Natural History and Its Modification with Treatment

The avoidance of offending drugs generally prevents the development of any attacks. If acute attacks are prevented, life expectancy is normal.

Prevention

The same considerations mentioned under Acute Intermittent Porphyria apply to these two disorders.

Cost Containment

Cost containment can be accomplished only by application of the preventive measures described above.

REFERENCES

Elder GH. Porphyria cutanea tarda: Pathogenesis in relationship to therapy. Curr Probl Dermatol 1991;20:91.

Kappas A, Sassa S, Galbraith RA, Nordman Y. The porphyrias. In: Wyngaarden CR, Frederickson DS, eds. The metabolic basis of inherited disease. New York: McGraw–Hill, 1989.

Kauppinen R, Mustajoki P. Prognosis of acute porphyria: Occurrence of acute attacks, precipitating factors and associated diseases. Medicine (Baltimore) 1992;71:1.

Kushner JP. Laboratory diagnosis of the porphyrias. N Engl J Med 1991;324:1432.

Moore MR. International review of drugs in acute porphyria. Int J Biochem 1980;12:1089.

Hemochromatosis

James R. Eckman, M.D.

DEFINITION

Hemochromatosis is a syndrome of iron overload that causes cirrhosis of the liver, diabetes mellitus, arthropathy, cardiac abnormalities, pituitary dysfunction, and increased skin pigmentation. Historically the term refers both to hereditary iron overload caused by increased intestinal absorption of iron and to iron overload associated with transfusion, increased absorption secondary to hematologic and hepatic disease, and intake of dietary or medicinal iron. More recently, hemochromatosis refers primarily to the autosomal recessive inherited genetic disease in which iron overload occurs because of excessive iron absorption from the intestine.

ETIOLOGY

The specific defect responsible for the excessive absorption of iron by the intestinal mucosa is yet to be defined. Affected individuals are homozygous for a recessive gene closely linked to the HLA-A locus on chromosome 6. Variable penetrance and environmental factors such as dietary iron, menstrual bleeding, pregnancy, and blood donation modify the clinical expression of the genetic disease.

CRITERIA FOR DIAGNOSIS

Suggestive

Presenting complaints include abdominal pain, arthralgia, and weakness. Unexplained hepatomelgaly, elevated serum transaminase, increased skin pigmentation, diabetes mellitus, loss of libido or impotence in males, unexplained cardiac dysfunction, and high transferrin saturation suggest this diagnosis. Onset of abdominal pain, unexplained liver test abnormalities, arthralgia, and weakness in a person with a family history of hemochromatosis or history of transfusions should prompt evaluation for hemochromatosis.

Definitive

Increased transferrin saturation, total iron binding capacity greater than 55%, is a sensitive screening test, and serum ferritin is useful in estimating total body iron burden. Liver biopsy demonstrating quantitative increase in the amount of iron per gram wet or dry weight and hepatocellular deposition of iron establishes the diagnosis. Further confirmation is provided when increased mobilization of iron is documented during chronic phlebotomy or chelation therapy.

CLINICAL MANIFESTATIONS

Subjective

Patients with hereditary hemochromatosis often present in their forties or fifties. Males present at a younger age and are more often symptomatic. Up to 40% are detected by chance or family studies. Abdominal pains, joint pains, weakness, fatigue, and malaise are frequent complaints at presentation. Loss of libido and impotence are common in males. Diabetes and liver disease are now less common at presentation than in the past.

Patients with acquired iron overload have a history of thalassemia, hemolytic anemia, or chronic refractory anemia requiring chronic transfusion. Chronic iron administration may be reported in patients with iatrogenic iron overload. Chronic alcoholism is more common in individuals with hereditary hemochromatosis.

The family history is usually positive in hereditary hemochromatosis. Individuals with secondary iron overload may also have a family history of thalassemias, refractory anemias, or other hematologic problems.

Objective

Physical Examination

Hepatomegaly and increased skin pigmentation are still the most common findings leading to the diagnosis of hereditary hemochromatosis. The liver is usually smooth but may become irregular with onset of cirrhosis. Skin color varies from classic bronze pigmentation to the more common dusky gray color. Cardiomegaly, findings of cardiac failure, and irregular pulse occur in about one fourth of patients. Knees, hips, or metacarpophalangeal joints may have findings of degenerative arthritis, acute pseudogout, or, rarely, a symmetric polyarthritis simulating rheumatoid arthritis. Testicular atrophy is common in males.

Routine Laboratory Abnormalities

Liver test abnormalities are common. Serum transaminase and bilirubin levels are mildly elevated in up to one half of patients. Other changes include elevation of lactate dehydrogenase and alkaline phosphatase levels with reduction in serum albumin level. Diabetes detected by elevated fasting or postprandial blood glucose levels is not uncommon at presentation. Abnormalities on electrocardiogram are also present in about one half of patients.

PLANS

Diagnostic

Transferrin saturation is the most useful screening test for hereditary hemochromatosis. A transferrin saturation greater than 50% repeated with an elevated second fasting sample supports the diagnosis with acceptable sensitivity and specificity in family studies. The combination of transferrin saturation and ferritin accurately identifies homozygotes older than 20 most of the time. The serum ferritin is usually greater than 200 µg/L. This test is most specific for iron overload, although a very small percentage of patients with parenchymal iron overload may have normal values and false positives are seen with hepatitis, chronic inflammation, and lymphomas. Findings of both elevated serum ferritin and high transferrin saturation accurately predict increased parenchymal iron on liver biopsy. Increased parenchymal iron is uncommon if both are normal.

Liver biopsy with quantitation of iron confirms iron overload, provides indexes of iron distribution, and allows detection of cirrhosis. Iron levels greater than 30 µmol/g dry liver weight in females and 40 in males are suggestive of hemochromatosis. An iron index greater than 2 (liver iron in micromoles/gram dry weight divided by the patient age in years) is diagnostic of hemochromatosis. In early disease, Prussian blue stains iron primarily in the hepatic parenchyma. Cirrhosis may be present with more advanced disease.

Determination of HLA linkage is useful in detecting presymptomatic homozygotes and heterozygote carriers in family studies. These tests are of no utility in screening or diagnosis outside of family studies.

Assessments of liver density by computed tomography and nuclear magnetic resonance are noninvasive techniques being used to detect iron overload. Present methods are both expensive and lack sensitivity and specificity.

Therapeutic

Phlebotomy is the treatment of choice for hereditary hemochromatosis. Treatment is initiated by venesection of 500 mL of blood twice a week in young patients without cardiac disease. Approximately 250 mg of iron is removed per unit bled. Weekly phlebotomies may be required for up to 2 years to remove the 10 to 40 g of excess iron present at diagnosis. Weekly removal of 500 mL is indicated for older patients, those with cardiac disease, and those who cannot tolerate more intense phlebotomy. Phlebotomies are continued until iron deficiency is established and documented by a serum ferritin less than 20 µg/L. Maintenance phlebotomies are continued for life at 2- to 4-month intervals to maintain a ferritin level less than 50 µg/L. Hemoglobin and ferritin are used to assess the rate of iron accumulation and determine the frequency of maintenance phlebotomy.

Chelation with deferoxamine given by intravenous or subcutaneous infusion is required to treat iron overload accompanied by chronic anemia. Deferoxamine 750 to 2000 mg is infused over 8 to 12 hours, 5 to 7 days a week, using portable, battery-powered pumps. Ascorbic acid 250 mg/d may increase excretion of iron. Cardiac arrhythmias, sudden death, and left ventricular dysfunction are reported with ascorbic acid doses in excess of 500 mg/d. Lack of compliance with therapy and complications compromise therapy in many patients on chronic chelation. Side effects include local irritation, cataracts, sensory neural hearing loss, and *Yersinia* infection. Allergic reactions including anaphylaxis have been reported. Local irritation, urticaria, and induration are common with subcutaneous administration. Placement of the needle in the deep subcutaneous tissue and addition of 10 mg of hydrocortisone may decrease local reactions. Careful rotation of sites is mandatory.

FOLLOW-UP

Hemoglobin levels should be determined before each phlebotomy during treatment initially to remove excess iron. When the hemoglobin is less than 11 g/dL, ferritin levels should be followed every month until less than 20 µg/L. Frequency of phlebotomy is reduced to every 2 to 4 months once iron deficiency is established. Ferritin is measured annually to assess iron burden.

Complications such as diabetes, heart failure, and cirrhosis may require more frequent follow-up. Unexplained weight loss, right upper quadrant pain, hepatomegaly, or changes in liver tests should prompt evaluation of hepatocellular carcinoma.

In patients treated with deferoxamine chelation, annual monitoring for cataracts and hearing loss is indicated.

DISCUSSION

Prevalence and Incidence

The frequency of hereditary hemochromatosis is as high as 1 in 400 or 1 in 500 in whites. The frequency of heterozygotes is about 10% in the United States and parts of Europe. There is the impression that hemochromatosis is less common in individuals from other ethnic groups; however, this impression is not based on systematic, population-based surveys.

Although the gene frequency is identical, clinical expression is 10 times more frequent in males than females. Females also present with symptoms later because they are protected by menstrual losses and pregnancy.

Related Basic Science

Genetics

Clinical expression in hereditary hemochromatosis is a classic example of interaction between a genetic disorder and environmental factors. Hereditary hemochromatosis shows classic autosomal recessive inheritance. The gene is closely linked to the HLA-A complex on the short arm of chromosome 6. The gene is yet to be identified. When homozygous, the gene causes increased and inappropriate absorption of iron from the intestine, leading to iron overload in target tissues.

Phenotypic expression occurs after absorption of 20 to 40 g of extra iron. This occurs frequently in the fifth or sixth decade with the usual American diet. Factors such as dietary iron supplementation, blood donation, menstrual loss, pregnancy, and alcoholism can modify the rate of iron accumulation. There may also be variation in gene penetrance.

Altered Molecular Biology

The molecular defect causing increased intestinal absorption of iron in hereditary hemochromatosis is unknown. Heterozygotes have increased iron absorption but do not accumulate excessive tissue or storage iron.

Physiologic or Metabolic Derangement

The excess tissue iron in homozygotes causes organ failure by oxidant damage to the heart, liver, and endocrine glands. The primary metabolic problem is the excessive accumulation of tissue iron. Iron is avidly conserved by the body, so overload will occur if there is chronic increased absorption as in hereditary hemochromatosis or with ineffective erythropoiesis. Accumulation also occurs if there is administration of excessive iron as with chronic transfusion or inappropriate parenteral administration of medicinal iron.

Anatomic Derangement

Liver changes include iron deposition in periportal hepatocytes and bile duct epithelial cells early and perilobular fibrosis with cirrhosis and dense fibrosis in advanced cases. Hepatomegaly is common.

Cardiac findings include perinuclear deposition of iron pigment in myocardial fibers with cardiomegaly. Cardiac arrhythmias are common and respond to removal of iron. Cardiomyopathy causing heart failure is a late consequence.

Exocrine and endocrine cells show accumulation of iron. Endocrine epithelial cells have increased hemosiderin. Diabetes mellitus is caused by loss of islet cells with pancreatic fibrosis. Testicular atrophy and ovarian dysfunction occur secondary to pituitary failure with deficiency of follicle-stimulating hormone and luteinizing hormone. Skin color changes are caused by increased melanin deposition related to pituitary failure, not iron accumulation in the skin.

The arthritis is characterized by synovial thickening, iron deposits in the synovium and cartilage, and calcium pyrophosphate deposition with chondrocalcinosis in large joints. Involvement of the second and third metacarpophalangeal joints of the hand with sclerosis, cystic changes, and loss of cartilage is an early and characteristic finding.

Natural History and Its Modification with Treatment

The prognosis in hereditary hemochromatosis is markedly improved with early recognition and treatment. Mean survival in the 1930s was about 4.5 years with supportive therapy for diabetes mellitus, liver failure, and cardiac disease. Treatment of established disease with phlebotomy increases 5-year survival to almost 90%, but 25 to 30% of patients with cirrhosis develop hepatocellular carcinoma. Recent series show that survival in treated patients without cirrhosis is similar to that of age- and sex-matched controls.

Skin pigmentation is still seen in more than 90% of cases at presentation. Liver enlargement and hepatic dysfunction are most common in advanced cases. Diabetes mellitus develops in one half of patients, but is uncommon if hemochromatosis is detected and treated early. Cardiac arrhythmias and failure develop in 30% of untreated patients. Joint pains are still prevalent and arthritis occurs in most without treatment. Sexual dysfunction in males and females is common. Decreased libido and impotence are common and do not often improve with therapy.

Treatment improves the common and nonspecific presenting complaints of weakness, fatigue, lethargy, and abdominal pains. Hepatomegaly, skin pigmentation, and cardiac arrhythmias respond well to reduction in iron. Liver failure, diabetes mellitus, arthritis, and impotence are not usually improved by phlebotomy. The risk of hepatocellular carcinoma is also not significantly reduced once cirrhosis is present.

Secondary iron overload is most commonly caused by repeated transfusions for thalassemia major, sickle cell anemia, or other refractory anemias. Both increased iron absorption and loading from transfusion complicate thalassemias and some refractory anemias. Manifestations of iron overload are the same as in hereditary hemochromatosis. Cardiac failure is more problematic because coexistent anemia increases cardiac work and limits ability to use phlebotomy for therapy.

Prevention

Clinical complications in hereditary hemochromatosis can be completely prevented by early diagnosis and treatment. This common genetic disease is often not diagnosed because of the nonspecific nature of initial symptoms and failure of the physician to consider the diagnosis. Because of this and the frequency of the gene, screening the general population using transferrin saturation and ferritin is advocated.

As a minimum, family studies should be undertaken whenever an individual with disease is identified. HLA testing with pedigree analysis to establish HLA linkage to the hemochromatosis gene and use of transferrin saturation are effective means of early diagnosis. Repeated screening using transferrin saturation is indicated in families where HLA linkage is not informative. Ferritin can be used to follow iron burden in individuals known to be homozygous for hereditary hemochromatosis. Use of alcohol should also be discouraged in families with hemochromatosis.

Secondary iron overload can be prevented by minimizing transfusion where possible. Iron deficiency must be documented before chronic administration of oral or parenteral iron and all chronic iron therapy should be monitored by serum ferritin determinations. In situations where chronic aggressive transfusions are indicated, such as thalassemia major and sickle cell anemia complicated by strokes, the serum ferritin should be determined annually and chelation therapy initiated when the ferritin exceeds 1500 μg/L.

Cost Containment

Early diagnosis and treatment reduce costs by preventing complications. Transferrin saturation and ferritin are the most cost-effective screening tests. HLA typing should be used only in family studies where linkage between an HLA haplotype and the gene for hemochromatosis is established. HLA typing is expensive and inaccurate for diagnosis or screening in other settings.

Phlebotomy is the best treatment in patients without severe anemia.

Not only is it cost-effective, but the blood can be used for transfusion. Treatment of secondary hemochromatosis usually requires deferoxamine. Chelation is expensive because of the cost of the drug, pumps, and disposables required to accomplish effective continuous infusion therapy. Because of cost and increased toxicity from deferoxamine with low iron burden, chelation should be deferred until a significant iron overload is documented.

Transfusion therapy in most refractory anemias should be based on symptoms. By minimizing units transfused, costs related to iron overload, exposure to infectious disease, alloimmunization, and transfusion will be reduced.

REFERENCES

Bomford, A, Williams R. Long term results of venesection therapy in idiopathic hemochromatosis. Q J Med 1976;45:611.

Edwards CQ, Kushner JP. Screening for hemochromatosis. N Engl J Med 1993;328:1616.

Finch SC, Finch CA. Idiopathic hemochromatosis, an iron storage disease. Medicine 1955;34:381.

Niederau C, Stremmel W, Strohmeyer GWW. Clinical spectrum and management of haemochromatosis. Clin Haematol 1994;7:881.

Phatak PD, Cappuccio JD. Management of hereditary hemochromatosis. Blood Rev 1994;8193.

Powell LW, Jazwinska E, Halliday J. Changing concepts of haemochromatosis. Adv Exp Med Biol 1994;356:285.

CHAPTER 12–41

Infectious Mononucleosis (See Section 8, Chapter 72)

Pulmonary Disorders

Stephan L. Kamholz, M.D.

CHAPTER 13–1

Sleep Apnea as Viewed by a Pulmonologist

Albert E. Heurich, M.D.

DEFINITION

Sleep apnea is a sleep disorder brought on by recurrent interruptions of sleep related to apnea-induced episodes of transient failure of ventilation. The impaired quality of sleep caused by the sleep interruptions results in a symptom complex in which daytime hypersomnolence is a primary component. The symptom complex induced by sleep apnea is termed the *sleep apnea syndrome*.

Apnea is defined as the cessation of airflow at the mouth for 10 seconds or more. The number of apneas per hour occurring during sleep is termed the *apnea index*. An apnea index exceeding 5 per hour is considered to increase the susceptibility of a patient to development of the syndrome. Also see Chapters 20–26 and 21–37.

ETIOLOGY

Apneas can be obstructive, central, or mixed. These are depicted in Figures 13–1–1, 13–1–2, and 13–1–3. In *obstructive apnea*, airflow cessation is related to upper airway inspiratory obstruction caused by the tongue, uvula, tonsils, vocal cords, or nasopharyngeal obstruction, the last facilitating inspiratory pharyngeal collapse. Respiratory efforts continue during obstructive apneas but are ineffectual in generating airflow due to the obstruction. Airflow cessation in *central apneas* results from absence of respiratory muscle activity. Radiographic studies during central apneas have demonstrated the presence of upper airway obstruction during the apnea. *Mixed apnea* is a sequence of an initial central apnea combined with and terminating in obstructive apnea.

CRITERIA FOR DIAGNOSIS

Suggestive

The significance of snoring as an indicator of sleep apnea has been debated. Heavy snoring that is disturbing to others is characteristic of sleep apnea and warrants investigation as does snoring associated with hypersomnolence. Increased vagal tone can occur at the onset of apneas. This produces a sequence of bradycardia followed by tachycardia related to catecholamine release from worsening hypoxemia and hypercapnia. A Holter monitor pattern of recurring bradycardia followed by tachycardia lasting 10 seconds or longer should make one consider the possibility of sleep apnea.

Definitive

The characteristic individual with sleep apnea is a middle-aged, obese male or a postmenopausal woman who has stentorian snoring. The decibel value of the latter is loud enough to disturb other individuals and can cause deafness in a sleeping partner.

CLINICAL MANIFESTATIONS

Subjective

The main presenting feature of the patient with the sleep apnea syndrome is daytime hypersomnolence. This leads to problems of poor work performance and impaired interpersonal relationships. The conflicts at work and at home can lead to depression and personality changes. Hypersomnolence makes these patients more prone to accidents.

Patients with sleep apnea are often unaware of their problem. They become aware of it when other individuals complain about their loud snoring or inform them that they are falling asleep during the day. Frequently the first encounter with a physician is when pedal edema develops from cor pulmonale. Morning headaches are a frequent complaint in this condition. Patients may describe awakening at night with a choking sensation. Enuresis, nocturnal polyuria, and impotence are common findings.

Personality changes are common, with patients frequently becoming disinterested in daily activities. This may lead to conflicts with other individuals in the home or at work. When the patient's immediate activities are not stimulating enough, sleep ensues. Automatic behavior and forgetfulness are additional conditions experienced by the patient. When cor pulmonale complicates the picture, exercise limitation occurs.

Reports of a familial factor for sleep apnea exist. In the majority of patients, however, a familial factor is usually not identified.

Objective

Physical Examination

The patient may appear plethoric. Systemic hypertension is usually present and signs of pulmonary artery hypertension may be identified. When the patient is left alone for a period, sleep and loud intermittent

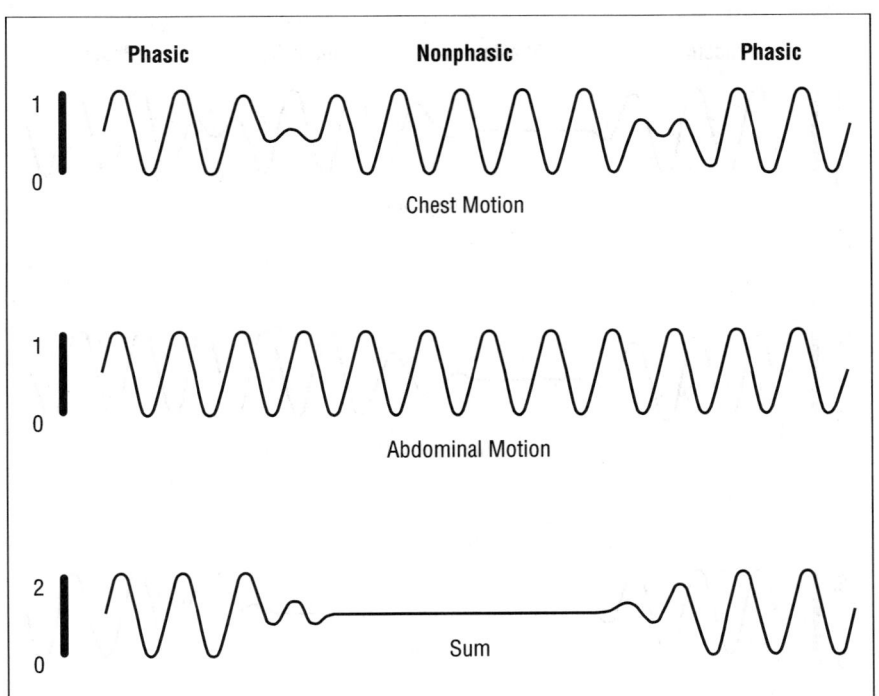

Figure 13–1–1. Depiction of the waveform patterns occurring in obstructive sleep apnea. The waveforms below the sections marked phasic represent normal respiration. The nonphasic segments show reversal of the timing for the maximum and minimum points on the chest motion trace relative to the abdominal motion trace. This represents chest wall paradox during the period of upper airway obstruction. Note the change in scale for the sum trace.

snoring develop. When the patient is sleeping supine, periodic inspiratory chest wall paradox is observed. Marked musculoskeletal activity can be seen at the termination of apneas. In some patients this may take the form of thrashing about that may be severe enough to injure the patient or a bed partner. Sleep walking and disorientation can be additional nocturnal manifestations.

The neck is typically short and thick. The oropharynx has a boggy, redundant mucosa which frequently makes visualization of the posterior pharynx difficult. Enlarged tonsils and adenoids may be contributing factors to upper airway obstruction. Careful examination of the nose and throat is essential identify for potentially correctable causes

such as deviated nasal septum, manifestations of nasal allergy, other anatomic deformities causing nasal obstruction, micrognathia, retrognathia, macroglossia, and vocal cord paralysis. Features of hypothyroidism and acromegaly should be sought as potentially treatable causes of sleep apnea.

Routine Laboratory Abnormalities

Polycythemia may be seen but is more likely in patients who have associated waking hypoventilation.

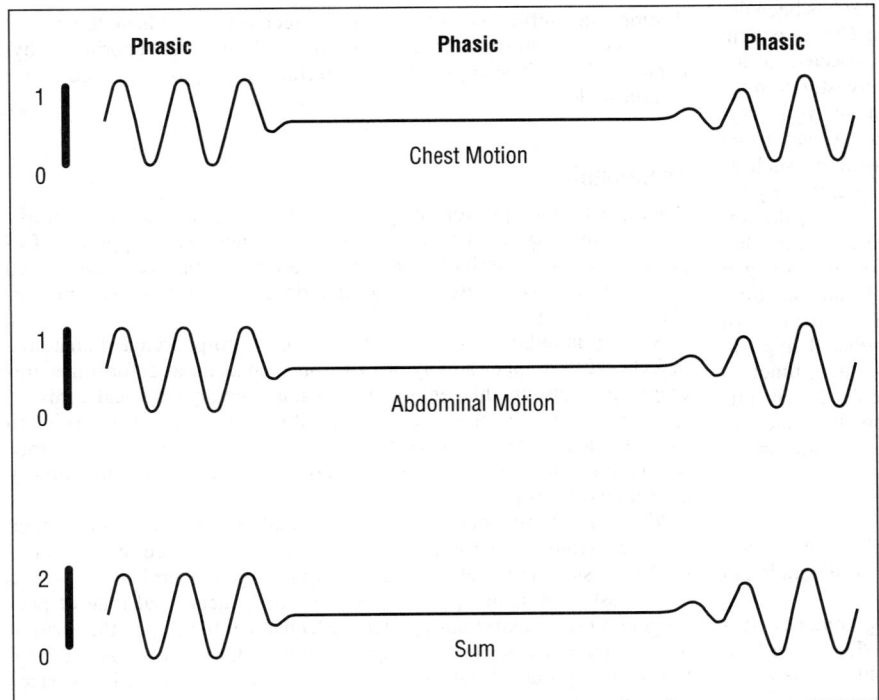

Figure 13–1–2. Depiction of the waveform patterns occurring in central sleep apnea. In this type of apnea the signals remain in phase. The straight lines in the center of the trace represent absence of chest and abdominal motion, indicating absence of respiratory muscle activity. Note the change in scale for the sum trace.

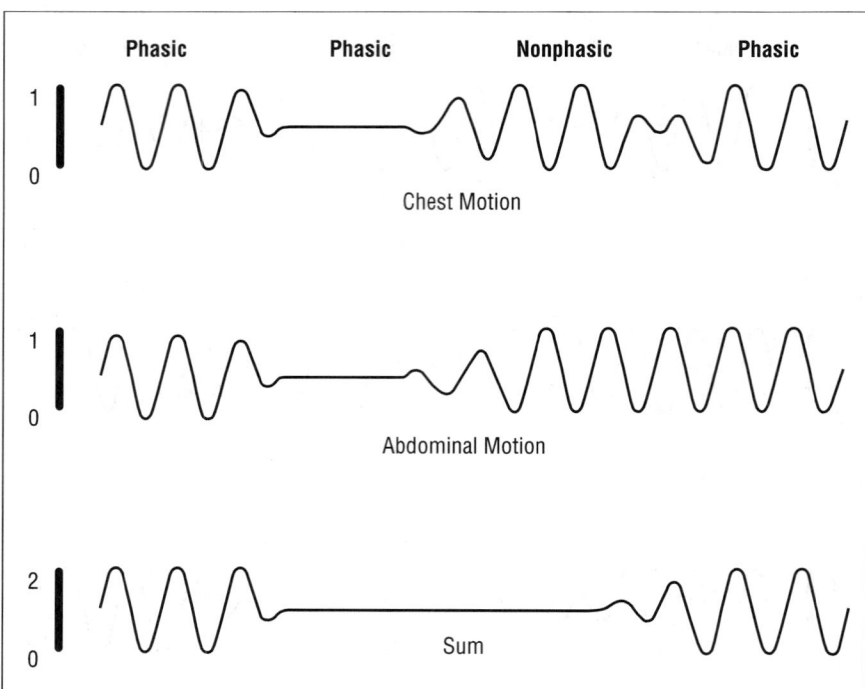

Figure 13–1–3. Depiction of the waveform patterns occurring in a mixed apnea. The initial and last phasic sections represent normal respiration. The center section starts with a phasic section that represents a central apnea. This then transforms into a nonphasic section which represents an obstructive apnea. The combination of a central apnea with an obstructive apnea constitutes a mixed apnea. Note the change in scale for the sum trace.

Electrocardiographic changes associated with systemic and pulmonary hypertension may occur.

PLANS
Diagnostic
Differential Diagnosis

The typical patient with sleep apnea is a middle-aged obese man. In women the condition is usually seen in the postmenopausal state. This has suggested potential hormonal influences. Testosterone administration has been reported to induce sleep apnea.

Several conditions require differentiation from sleep apnea. Waking blood gases are frequently normal in sleep apnea, but a subgroup of patients with chronic obstructive pulmonary disease (COPD) has been described who also have sleep apnea. A hypersomnolent COPD patient with polycythemia or one in whom hypercapnia is not expected for the degree of obstruction that is present should prompt an investigation for sleep apnea. Hypersomnolence with snoring and nonapneic cyclic oxygen desaturation has recently been described as an upper airway resistance syndrome (UARS). Patients with pulmonary disorders such as respiratory neuromuscular restriction, kyphoscoliosis, or extreme obesity may have adequate saturation in the waking state but may desaturate during sleep. When combined with UARS, the desaturation becomes cyclic and is significantly magnified due to the low lung oxygen stores associated with their restriction. Obesity, normal lung function, and hypercapnia in the waking state identify the patient with obesity–hypoventilation syndrome. This patient has reduced hypoxic and hypercapnic drive. In the absence of obesity, normal lung function with hypercapnia defines the condition of primary alveolar hypoventilation. Hypersomnolence is also seen in narcolepsy, hypothyroidism, and acromegaly. Sleep apnea can be associated with these conditions.

Diagnostic Options

Observation of the patient during sleep usually establishes the diagnosis. Intermittent stentorian snoring combined with chest wall paradox is typically present.

Full overnight polysomnographic recording in a sleep center is considered the ideal for identification and differentiation of sleep disorders. The limited availability of such studies for many patients has resulted in modified studies such as multiple sleep latency tests and recordings in the home. The need for and role for specific types of tests remain controversial. For sleep apnea patients with clinically evident disease, any of these types of tests will be able to document the presence of the condition.

A sawtooth pattern may be seen on the flow–volume curve. The recurrent hypoxemia of sleep apnea triggers increased catecholamine release, which can be detected as increased urinary catecholamines. Levels of plasma testosterone and insulin-like growth factor 1 are reduced. Holter monitoring may demonstrate a recurring pattern of bradycardia followed by tachycardia lasting 10 seconds or longer. Oximetry shows a pattern of recurring cyclic oxygen desaturation during sleep.

Recommended Approach

A simple cost-effective initial screening technique is to have the patient tape-record breathing during sleep. This will document snoring. If hypersomnolence is also present, then further testing as discussed above is indicated.

Therapeutic

Appropriate therapy for sleep apnea must often address multiple causes. This may require more than a single therapeutic approach. Depending on the underlying etiologies the options that have been used are surgical therapy, lifestyle modification, medical therapy, and mechanical therapy.

Surgery is indicated for correction of naso-oro-pharyngeal anatomic defects causing upper airway obstruction such as nasal deformities, micrognathia, retrognathia, enlarged tonsils, and paralyzed vocal cords.

Lifestyle modification includes prohibition of alcohol use prior to sleep, dietary modification to facilitate weight reduction, and avoidance of conditions leading to irregular patterns of sleep such as continuously altering work shifts.

Medical therapy should address potential contributory factors such as hypothyroidism, acromegaly, conditions of disordered muscle activity during sleep in the elderly, and nasopharyngeal allergies.

In most sleep apnea patients an abnormally decreased tone of pharyngeal muscles exists during sleep. Mechanical therapy in the form of nasal continuous positive airway pressure is the main therapeutic option in this group of patients, which constitutes the majority of sleep apnea patients.

FOLLOW-UP

A single negative study does not necessarily rule out the presence of sleep apnea. Positive studies require follow-up studies with nasal continuous positive airway pressure (NCPAP), when this is indicated, or postoperatively when therapy has been surgical. Periodic reassessment of NCPAP studies is needed, as changes in the patient's condition, such as weight change, may alter the level of NCPAP required. Even with successful surgical intervention, failure to control weight can cause recurrence of sleep apnea.

DISCUSSION
Prevalence

Obstructive and mixed apneas are the most common forms of apnea encountered clinically. Isolated central apnea is uncommon. Central apneas occurring with obstructive apneas are thought to be a consequence of the latter, as relief of obstructive apnea eventually leads to cessation of central apneas.

Estimates of the prevalence of sleep apnea vary considerably depending on the population evaluated and the methods used for assessment. The prevalence has been estimated to be less than 1% in a study of the general population in Japan to almost 50% of patients in a nursing home population. In the United States, the prevalence in men is estimated to be about 25% and in women, about 10%. In elderly men almost 50% have a significant number of nocturnal apneas. More than 30,000 patients per year receive therapy for sleep apnea.

Related Basic Science
Genetics

Studies of families and of particular neurologic and muscular disorders have demonstrated familial clustering of sleep disorders.

Physiologic or Metabolic Derangement

Obstructive sleep apnea is associated with a decrease in the levels of somatomedin and testosterone that is reversible with NCPAP. Nocturnal catecholamine secretion and atrial natriuretic peptide levels are increased. NCPAP therapy decreases these levels and the systemic and pulmonary hypertension that may be present.

Anatomic Derangement

Excessive decrease of tone in pharyngeal musculature leading to inspiratory collapse and obstruction is the primary derangement in most patients with obstructive sleep apnea. In the obese patient, pharyngeal narrowing is further amplified by a boggy, redundant mucosa. Vocal cord paralysis, increased nasal or pharyngeal resistance, or retroposition of the tongue further enhances the obstruction.

Natural History and Its Modification with Treatment

Much has been learned about sleep apnea disorders in recent years but much remains to be learned. The natural history of the disease is not yet well defined. This probably reflects the heterogeneous nature of the disorder, particularly with respect to waking blood gases and oxygen stores. The number of apneas can vary considerably from one study to another, making the predictive value of a single test poor. NCPAP provides effective therapy when tolerated. Therapeutic compliance is about 75%. Uvulopharyngopalatoplasty is successful in approximately half of the patients. The presence of multiple sites of obstruction may limit the success of a surgical procedure.

Prevention

Snoring is a very common phenomenon in the population and is a prominent feature of sleep apnea. Mass screening of snorers is not feasible from a cost–benefit perspective. Education of the population to enhance awareness of the problem and targeting of high-risk groups for study appear to provide the best approach for dealing with identification of those individuals requiring therapy. Avoidance of alcohol and sedatives will prevent the sleep apnea induced by these agents.

Cost Containment

Technologies that permit adequate assessment in the patient's home environment are being evaluated and, in combination with data transmission to a remote central station, may provide a cost-effective technique for assessing multiple patients simultaneously.

REFERENCES

Kryger MH, Roth T, Dement WC. Principles and practice of sleep medicine. 2nd ed. Philadelphia: Saunders, 1994.
Saunders NA, Sullivan CE. Sleep and breathing. 2nd ed. New York: Marcel Dekker, 1994.
Stradling JR. Handbook of sleep-related breathing disorders. Oxford: Oxford University Press, 1993.

CHAPTER 13–2

Preoperative Evaluation and Perioperative Management of Patients with Lung Disease

Peter R. Smith, M.D.

DEFINITION

Internists and pulmonologists are frequently asked to consult when patients with pulmonary disease require surgery. The concept of "clearing" a patient for surgery is a familiar one. More appropriately, the role of the consultant is assessment of risk and assistance with preoperative evaluation and perioperative management. Prevention of perioperative pulmonary complications is the key issue.

ETIOLOGY

The major risk factors for perioperative pulmonary complications are listed in Table 13–2–1. The type of surgical procedure and the patient's underlying pulmonary illness are the most important. Upper abdominal and thoracic surgery, especially with pulmonary resection, carry the highest pulmonary risk. Advanced pulmonary disease of any sort is of great concern, but severe, chronic obstructive pulmonary disease presents the most important problem because of its relative frequency and broad impact on pulmonary physiology and airway defense mechanisms. The duration of the surgical procedure also has a major impact. Surgery of long duration is often associated with intraoperative problems or complications that impact on the postoperative course. With some exceptions, notably asthma, the anesthetic method is relatively less important in terms of risk. Spinal or epidural anesthesia is often recommended and employed for pulmonary patients, but a reduction in

TABLE 13–2–1. RISK FACTORS FOR PERIOPERATIVE PULMONARY COMPLICATIONS

- Preexisting pulmonary disease   (type, severity)
- Smoking
- Type of surgical procedure
- Duration of surgical procedure
- Type of anesthesia
- Comorbid conditions, ASA class
- Age
- Obesity

respiratory complications compared with general anesthesia has not been proven.

Comorbid conditions and the patient's general health status as assessed by the American Society of Anesthesiologist's (ASA) rating scale may be the ultimate causes of severe morbidity and mortality in pulmonary patients. The negative effects of advanced cardiac or renal disease, or diabetes with vascular complications, can markedly alter outcome in the presence of postoperative pulmonary complications. Obesity has long been thought to be a risk factor for pulmonary complications. There is little objective corroboration for this belief, and more recent data have not shown obesity to be an independent risk factor. Also, preoperative weight reduction has not been shown to reduce the incidence of postoperative pulmonary complications. In several studies, older age has been identified as a risk factor. Obviously, there is no way of modifying age, and older patients should not be denied surgery based on age alone.

CRITERIA FOR DIAGNOSIS

The criteria for diagnosis relate to identifying patients at risk for perioperative pulmonary complications due to underlying pulmonary disease.

Suggestive

A history of smoking, occupational exposures, or pulmonary complications with prior surgery may suggest underlying lung disease in patients without documented pulmonary illness. Respiratory symptoms such as cough, dyspnea, and wheezing, even if only intermittent, should be evaluated.

Definitive

The diagnosis of pulmonary disease and estimation of severity are based on historical data, physical findings, chest radiographic abnormalities, and pulmonary function studies.

CLINICAL MANIFESTATIONS

The clinical manifestations to be considered are those due to postoperative pulmonary complications.

Subjective

The symptoms related to postoperative pulmonary complications are due to the various pulmonary problems that may occur. They are relatively nonspecific. Cough, sputum production, dyspnea, and respiratory distress are most common. Wheezing, chest pain, hemoptysis, and fever are also frequent.

Objective

The most important postoperative pulmonary complications are listed in Table 13–2–2. In addition, the consequences of these complications are often considered as objective outcome measures in clinical studies. These ancillary indicators include days on mechanical ventilation, days spent in intensive care, and length of stay in the hospital.

Atelectasis is most often subsegmental and may not be visible on chest radiographs. Basilar crackles and reduced inspiratory excursion on chest examination may be the only manifestations. On chest radi-

TABLE 13–2–2. SIGNIFICANT POSTOPERATIVE PULMONARY COMPLICATIONS

- Atelectasis
- Bronchitis
- Pneumonia
- Pulmonary embolism
- Respiratory failure

ographs, high diaphragms and the findings of platelike changes in dependent lung zones may be visible. Atelectasis is a central feature in the development of postoperative pulmonary complications. As will be discussed in more detail later, abdominal and thoracic surgery results in a functional reduction in lung volumes and increase in respiratory rate. This rapid-shallow breathing pattern is associated with the development of atelectasis, which in turn results in hypoxemia. In addition, there is reduced clearance of secretions, which may lead to pulmonary infection. The diagnoses of bronchitis and pneumonia are made in the usual fashion. Pulmonary embolism is often a difficult diagnosis. A discussion of clinical manifestations and diagnostic evaluation in suspected pulmonary embolism is dealt with in Chapters 13–36 and 15–57. The main issue is that pulmonary emboli are usually preventable with appropriate prophylactic measures. The diagnosis of respiratory failure is based on arterial blood gas abnormalities. Severe hypoxemia (e.g., $PaO_2 < 60$ mm Hg on room air) or significant hypercapnia ($PaCO_2 > 45$ mm Hg) are frequently used criteria for respiratory failure.

PLANS

Diagnostic

Differential Diagnosis

The differential diagnosis concerns the complications discussed above. Detailed discussions of differential diagnosis are included in the chapters dealing with those conditions.

Diagnostic Options

Preoperative pulmonary evaluation starts with a careful history and physical examination. Chest radiographs should be obtained when abnormalities are identified from the history or physical examination. A baseline chest radiograph is also indicated in patients undergoing major surgery, especially if the type of procedure is associated with an increased risk of pulmonary complications. The value of pulmonary function studies in preoperative assessment of patients undergoing nonpulmonary surgery is not well defined at present. Although it is true that patients with a history of smoking and chronic obstructive pulmonary disease are at increased risk for postoperative pulmonary complications, there is no level of abnormality that reliably identifies patients who will experience significant problems. There have been a number of studies that have shown that pulmonary function tests do not accurately predict complications. In several reports, pulmonary function studies were found to be no more predictive than a history of lung disease, pulmonary symptoms, or smoking. Clinical variables including ASA class, age, and comorbidity may better predict postoperative pulmonary complications than pulmonary physiologic studies.

Despite the failure of pulmonary function studies as a "gold standard" for predicting pulmonary complications, they are still useful for quantitating the level of abnormality and planning perioperative care. Commonly used criteria indicating severe lung disease include FEV_1 under 1.0 L or less than 40% predicted, and $PaCO_2$ greater than 45 mm Hg. The indications for preoperative pulmonary function studies are given in Table 13–2–3. These studies should include spirometry and arterial blood gases drawn while the patient breathes room air. In patients with evidence of airway obstruction, spirometry should be repeated after administration of aerosolized bronchodilator. Additional tests, especially single breath diffusing capacity, may be helpful when the basic studies indicate significant abnormalities.

In patients scheduled to undergo pulmonary resection, preoperative evaluation must be concerned not only with the risks for postoperative

TABLE 13–2–3. INDICATIONS FOR PREOPERATIVE PULMONARY FUNCTION STUDIES

TABLE 13–2–3. INDICATIONS FOR PREOPERATIVE PULMONARY FUNCTION STUDIES

- History, symptoms, or physical findings suggesting pulmonary disease
- History of smoking
- Chest radiographic abnormalities suggesting pulmonary disease
- Pulmonary resection

TABLE 13–2–4. PREOPERATIVE ASSESSMENT FOR PULMONARY RESECTION

- Spirometry and arterial blood gases
- Diffusing capacity
- Quantitative radionuclide lung scan
- Exercise studies

pulmonary complications, but also the impact of the removal of lung tissue on future function. Especially when surgery is done for pulmonary malignancy, the extent of the resection that is necessary may not be known until the exploratory thoracotomy is underway. Therefore, the evaluation usually must assess the patient's ability to undergo pneumonectomy even when preoperative staging suggests that a lesser resection would be sufficient to remove all tumor. Most clinical studies investigating preoperative assessment for resection have focused on criteria that would predict the patient's ability to tolerate pneumonectomy.

Patients with pulmonary cancers requiring resection often present a particularly difficult problem because of the frequency of preexisting lung disease. The majority have at least some evidence of chronic obstructive pulmonary disease, as smoking is the most important risk factor for both conditions. About 20% have severe physiologic impairment. In those with advanced lung disease, successful resection might be accomplished only at the cost of severe chronic disability. On the other hand, surgical resection represents the only reasonable chance for cure in patients with non-small cell lung cancer.

In evaluating patients for lung resection, physiologic studies including routine pulmonary function tests, quantitative radionuclide scans, and exercise studies have been used to predict postoperative pulmonary complications and long-term outcome. As in the case of nonpulmonary surgery, however, the predictive value of these tests remains unclear. There are no universally accepted physiologic criteria that are considered prohibitive in terms of future function or accurately predict postoperative pulmonary complications. In fact, mortality in the postoperative period is related mainly to complications that are not predictable by pulmonary physiologic studies. In particular, the main causes of postoperative mortality are myocardial infarction, pulmonary embolism, pneumonia, and empyema.

Despite the failings of physiologic studies in evaluating patients for pulmonary resection, they help to define a subset of patients who are at increased risk and their use is routine among pulmonologists and thoracic surgeons. The studies listed in Table 13–2–4 are those that are most widely used. They are usually applied in stepwise manner, progressing to the more technically complex and costly procedures when the results of spirometry and arterial blood gases are considered insufficient for estimating risk. Figure 13–2–1 summarizes an approach used by several authorities for decision analysis in candidates for resection. Applying this system, resection including pneumonectomy should be well tolerated if the absolute value of FEV_1 is greater than 2.0 L or greater than 60% of predicted and diffusing capacity is greater than 60% of predicted. Below these limits, further testing is recommended. Quantitative radionuclide studies, using either perfusion or ventilation scanning, permit assessment of individual lung function ("split-function") and, thus, calculation of postoperative FEV_1 or diffusing capacity.* A predicted postoperative value for FEV_1 greater than 1.0 L or greater than 40% of predicted and a diffusing capacity greater than 40% of predicted are considered satisfactory to proceed with surgery. Failing this, exercise testing has been advocated as a final step in the decision analysis. Older studies suggested that stair climbing and treadmill exercise could predict outcome after pulmonary resection. More recent work has indicated approximate limits of maximal oxygen uptake ($\dot{V}O_2$ max) which correlate with postoperative results. A $\dot{V}O_2$ max greater than 15 mL/kg/min has been suggested as a minimally accept-

able level. Finally, there is a consensus that patients with lung disease severe enough to result in hypercapnia ($PaCO_2 > 45$ mm Hg) are at great risk for any resection, even if less than lobectomy.

Recommended Approach

A comprehensive history and physical examination are required in all operative candidates. Smokers and patients with pulmonary disease should be evaluated further with chest radiographs and pulmonary function studies, including spirometry and arterial blood gases. Lastly, significant comorbid conditions must always be given careful consideration in the preoperative evaluation process.

The algorithm for physiologic assessment before pulmonary resection discussed above is a reasonable approach based on currently available data; however, these criteria are not absolutes. Comorbidity, the patient's attitude, and even intuitive assessment of risk by the health care professionals involved are factors in the final decision. A patient whose objective evaluation suggests a poor outcome after pneumonectomy might still opt for surgery, understanding that there is a risk for major complications or severe disability. Or, if preoperative staging suggests that lobectomy or less could be curative, the individual might choose a plan where the surgeon will "open and close" without resection, if at surgery only pneumonectomy would be sufficient to remove all tumor.

Therapeutic

Therapeutic Options

The therapeutic options in perioperative management concern prevention of complications. Obviously, risk assessment and preventive interventions apply mainly to elective situations. Emergency surgery for acute, life-threatening conditions is usually undertaken even in high-risk patients with little or no preparation. Interventions to prevent perioperative complications in patients with lung disease can be grouped into preoperative, intraoperative, and postoperative measures as shown in Table 13–2–5.

Recommended Approach

Preoperative. Smokers should always be encouraged to quit and assisted in their efforts. For those who will not stop permanently, 4 to 8 weeks of abstinence before surgery reduces the incidence of respiratory complications. At the very least, stopping for 12 to 24 hours preoperatively provides cardiovascular benefit due to a reduction in carboxyhemoglobin levels. Patients with chronic obstructive pulmonary disease and purulent bronchitis may benefit from a course of antibiotics prior to surgery. Asthmatics and those with chronic obstructive pulmonary disease should receive bronchodilators given by metered-dose inhaler or nebulizer throughout the perioperative period. In asthmatics, the agents of choice are beta agonists. Beta agonists combined with ipratropium bromide are recommended in patients with chronic obstructive pulmonary disease. Asthmatics should receive inhaled corticosteroids and often systemic corticosteroids. This is also appropriate in selected patients with chronic obstructive pulmonary disease, particularly those who have a significant component of bronchospasm. Systemic corticosteroids may be given orally or intravenously, beginning at least 12 hours prior to surgery. Methylprednisolone 40 mg intravenously every 6 hours for a period of 24 to 36 hours, is appropriate. If possible, systemic steroids should not continue past the third postoperative day to avoid effects on wound healing. Prophylaxis for thromboembolism should begin preoperatively. Patients with hypercapnia due to chronic obstructive pulmonary disease or disordered control of respiration

---

*The prediction of postpneumonectomy FEV_1 (or diffusing capacity) using quantitative radionuclide lung scanning is made by using the following formula:

Predicted postop FEV_1 (or diffusing capacity) = preop FEV_1 (or diffusing capacity) ×% perfusion (or ventilation) contributed by the lung to remain.

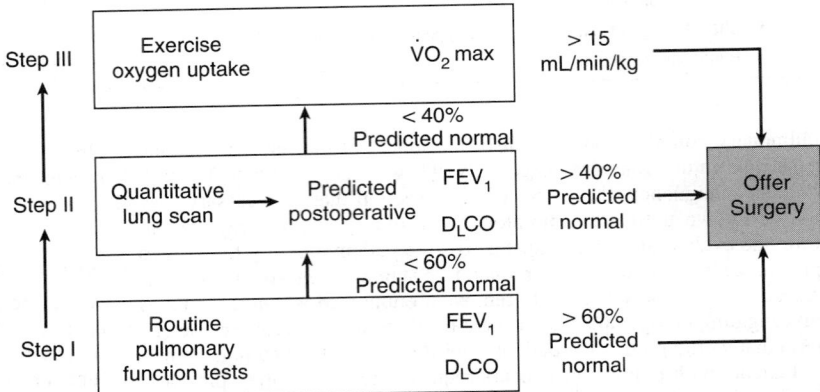

Figure 13–2–1. Physiologic evaluation for pulmonary resection. The evaluation of cardiopulmonary operability is illustrated in its steps of increasing complexity. *(Source: Marshall MC, Olsen GN. The physiologic evaluation of the lung resection candidate. Clin Chest Med 1993;14:318. Reproduced with permission from the publisher and author.)*

should probably not receive preoperative sedation before arriving in the operating room.

Lung expansion techniques are employed postoperatively to prevent and/or reverse atelectasis. To ensure that patients can effectively perform these maneuvers, they should be taught prior to surgery. A variety of techniques have been used. Deep breathing exercises produce satisfactory results in those patients who are well motivated and cooperative. The patient inhales to total lung capacity, breathholds for 4 to 6 seconds, and follows with a triple cough. Those who are less motivated may benefit from incentive spirometry. The maneuver again is maximal sustained inspiration, but the visual feedback provided by the device may help improve effort. Continuous positive airway pressure (CPAP) can be used in patients who are poorly cooperative. CPAP is applied by mask every 30 to 60 minutes at levels from 5 cm H_2O up to 12.5 cm H_2O.

Intraoperative. Patients who are treated with bronchodilators and steroids preoperatively should continue to receive them intraoperatively and postoperatively as described above. Acute asthma can be triggered by airway manipulation during intubation and extubation. Spinal or epidural anesthesia, rather than general anesthesia, may therefore be preferable in these patients. With other pulmonary conditions, the benefit of avoiding general anesthesia has not been proven. Laparoscopic surgery, which requires smaller incisions, might reduce postoperative complications and be of benefit, particularly in high-risk patients. There are some clinical studies supporting this but further investigation is required.

Postoperative. Lung expansion techniques are instituted as soon as the patient is extubated and awake. Those who have undergone thoracic or upper abdominal procedures require the most attention to prevent atelectasis and its sequelae. Thromboembolism prophylaxis is continued

in the postoperative period. Bronchodilators and corticosteroids are continued as indicated. Getting the patient up in a chair and beginning ambulation as soon as possible are helpful for lung expansion and reduce the risk of thromboembolism. As will be discussed in more detail later, epidural analgesia postoperatively may prevent the reflex diaphragmatic inhibition that occurs after upper abdominal procedures. Epidural analgesia may therefore be beneficial in high-risk patients, and further experience with this technique is awaited. Patients with advanced lung disease, particularly those with severe chronic obstructive pulmonary disease, should probably leave the operating room with the endotracheal tube in place. They should be extubated only after they are fully awake and stable in the recovery room or intensive care unit. Two indices of severity that may be used in this context are FEV_1 under 1.0 L or less than 40% predicted and the presence of baseline hypercapnia.

FOLLOW-UP

The role of the medical consultant continues postoperatively. Particularly when patients with advanced lung disease undergo major procedures, evaluation on the day of surgery in the recovery room or intensive care unit is important. Thereafter, patients should be seen regularly until ambulatory and approaching their baseline level of function.

DISCUSSION
Prevalence and Incidence

The reported incidence of postoperative pulmonary complications varies from 3 to 70%. This wide range reflects differences in the definition of complications, the health status of the populations studied, and the surgical procedures performed. Where patients are unselected for the type of surgery, complications in those with abnormal pulmonary function may occur in more than 50%. Conversely, in patients undergoing upper abdominal surgery, but unselected for baseline health status, total morbidity has been estimated at 20 to 25%, and in those with significant respiratory complications, mortality was as high as 3 to 5%.

RELATED BASIC SCIENCE
Effects of Anesthesia

The effects of anesthesia on pulmonary physiology can be divided into four areas: lung mechanics, gas exchange, respiratory control, and mucociliary flow.

Lung Mechanics

Almost immediately after the induction of anesthesia, there is an average decline of 16% in functional residual capacity (FRC). Both inhalational and intravenous anesthetics, with the exception of ketamine, pro-

TABLE 13-2-5. OPTIONS FOR PREVENTION OF PERIOPERATIVE COMPLICATIONS IN PATIENTS WITH LUNG DISEASE

Preoperative	Postoperative
Smoking cessation	Extubation in recovery room or intensive care unit
Antibiotics	Epidural analgesia
Bronchodilators	Bronchodilators, corticosteroids
Corticosteroids	Lung expansion techniques
Teaching lung expansion techniques	Thromboembolism prophylaxis
Thromboembolism prophylaxis	Early ambulation

Intraoperative
Spinal or epidural anesthesia
Bronchodilators, corticosteroids

duce this effect, and it occurs independent of paralytic agents. The etiology remains the topic of some debate. The physiologic alterations that appear to contribute to this phenomenon include a reduction in central respiratory drive, which leads to a decrease in diaphragmatic tone. The diaphragm relaxes and moves cephalad. Inhalational agents also depress synaptic transmission and affect chest wall musculature. As a consequence of the shift in diaphragmatic position, atelectatic plaques develop in dependent lung zones within several minutes of induction. Studies employing computed tomographic scanning during general anesthesia have demonstrated these crescent-shaped areas of "compression atelectasis." These may persist for up to 24 hours after surgery.

Gas Exchange

General anesthesia results in an increase in the alveolar–arterial oxygen difference ($AaDo_2$). Two factors contribute to the widened $AaDo_2$. There is an increase in shunt fraction and an increase in ventilation–perfusion ($\dot{V}/\dot{Q}$) mismatch. Shunt fraction rises to an average of 8% and may be as high as 17% in some patients. Compression atelectasis, described earlier, appears to be the cause of the increased shunt. A loss of hypoxic vasoconstriction with perfusion of poorly ventilated lung zones is the putative mechanism responsible for worsening $\dot{V}/\dot{Q}$ mismatch. This occurs with volatile anesthetics but not with intravenous agents. The widened $AaDo_2$ and risk for arterial hypoxemia may last several hours after anesthesia.

Respiratory Control

Most inhalational and intravenous anesthetics affect respiratory control by blunting oxygen and carbon dioxide responsiveness. Depending on the particular agent, dose, and duration of anesthesia, significant depression may persist postoperatively. Patients with chronic obstructive lung disease and those with sleep-disordered breathing may be at particular risk during the early postoperative period.

Mucociliary Flow

Although the cause remains controversial, a reduction in mucociliary flow is a known consequence of general anesthesia. This may last 2 to 6 days. Individuals with preexisting damage to cilia and the mucous escalator mechanism would be particularly at risk for complications related to decreased clearance of secretions.

Effects of the Surgical Procedure

The type of surgical procedure is the most important risk factor for postoperative pulmonary complications. Abdominal operations, especially upper abdominal surgery, and thoracic procedures including cardiac surgery carry the greatest risk. With thoracotomy and resection of a significant volume of lung tissue, there is a permanent loss of lung function. Abdominal and thoracic surgery alters pulmonary physiology in all patients. The impact in patients with preexisting lung disease is greater and has more effect on clinical outcome.

Abdominal surgery impairs lung function in a predictable way and the decrease depends on the proximity to the diaphragm. Immediately after upper abdominal procedures, there is a reduction in all lung volumes. This is maximal during the first 72 hours and slowly returns to preoperative levels over about 2 weeks. Conversely, respiratory rate increases and returns to normal over the same time course. Minute ventilation remains essentially unchanged. The same alterations occur with lower abdominal procedures but are less marked. This altered breathing pattern promotes atelectasis and the other complications that follow

from it. In patients with underlying lung disease, progressive abnormality leading to respiratory failure may ensue.

The genesis of the alteration in respiratory mechanics after upper abdominal surgery is believed to be due to stimulation of visceral or somatic afferent nerves leading to reflex inhibition of phrenic nerve activity. Data from animal and human studies support this concept. It is of interest that epidural analgesia used postoperatively interrupts this reflex. Further data are needed to assess the benefit of epidural analgesia in high-risk pulmonary patients.

Atelectasis is frequent after thoracotomy, even without lung resection. The mechanism is different from that seen with upper abdominal surgery. Mechanical compression of the lung, an increase in lung water, reduced surfactant activity, and accumulation of bronchopulmonary secretions have been postulated as contributing causes. Atelectasis and pulmonary sequelae are also common after cardiac surgery. With coronary artery bypass, there can be phrenic nerve damage from the iced slush used for cardiac cooling. Direct trauma to the nerve may also occur during mobilization of the internal mammary artery; however, atelectasis after heart surgery is due more often to mechanisms other than phrenic nerve damage. Possible causes include inadequate blood supply to the alveolar epithelium during cardiac bypass and abnormalities in surfactant production.

Natural History and Its Modification with Treatment

Questions persist concerning the true benefit of perioperative measures for prevention of pulmonary complications. Although it would seem reasonable to aggressively manage high-risk pulmonary patients, more clinical data are needed to support this conclusion. Based on the results of older studies and the consensus of authorities in the field, the identification of high-risk patients and perioperative measures to "optimize" their pulmonary status are worthwhile strategies.

Prevention

The central issue in preoperative evaluation and perioperative management is the prevention of complications. It is hoped that the application of the principles and techniques described will be beneficial in this regard.

Cost Containment

As the primary goal is prevention of complications, preoperative evaluation and perioperative management should have a positive effect on cost containment. In general, the diagnostic modalities and pharmacologic and other management strategies are relatively inexpensive. Occasionally, more expensive interventions are required. For example, radionuclide lung scans and/or exercise studies may be necessary before lung resection. Overall, the diagnostic and management strategies discussed in this chapter should yield a net reduction in costs.

REFERENCES

Crapo RO. Pulmonary-function testing. N Engl J Med 1994;331:25.

Gilbreth EM, Weisman IM. Role of exercise stress testing in preoperative evaluation of patients for lung resection. Clin Chest Med 1994;15:389.

Olsen GN, guest ed. Perioperative respiratory care. Clin Chest Med 1993;14(2):205.

Stein M, Koota GM, Simon M, Frank HA. Pulmonary evaluation of surgical patients. JAMA 1962;181:765.

Weiner-Kronish JP, Matthay MA. Preoperative evaluation. In: Murray JF, Nadel JA. Textbook of respiratory medicine. 2nd ed. Philadelphia: Saunders, 1994:29.

CHAPTER 13–3

Health Consequences of Smoking Tobacco

Stephan L. Kamholz, M.D.

DEFINITION

Inhalation of smoke from burning tobacco (cigarette, cigar, or pipe), either directly by the individual smoking (oral route) or passively by those in close contact with the smoker (nasal route), can lead to a broad spectrum of adverse health consequences affecting the respiratory tract, cardiovascular and central nervous systems, digestive tract, and systemic metabolic and immunologic functions (including alterations in the handling of drugs), and can materially affect fetal development during intrauterine gestation.

ETIOLOGY

Tobacco smoke is a complex mixture of hundreds of chemical substances, many of which have unique actions, including proinflammatory, cytotoxic, and carcinogenic effects. In addition to direct toxic effects on the epithelium of the aerodigestive tract, other systems and organs (e.g., cardiovascular, cerebrovascular, peripheral arterial) are adversely affected by tobacco smoke or its constituents. The duration and intensity of exposure (pack-years for cigarette smokers, or the equivalent dose-duration measure for other types of smokers) and individual susceptibility (believed to be genetically controlled) to the effects of smoke are codeterminants of the nature and extent of "damage."

Nonsmokers who suffer environmental exposure to tobacco smoke are believed to be at some increased risk of development of adverse health effects, including alterations in pulmonary function ("small airway disease" detectable by pulmonary function testing), and to have a higher incidence of bronchogenic carcinoma than non-smoke-exposed individuals. It is estimated that about 1 in 10 lung cancers in the United States develops in a nonsmoking woman, and that these tumors were at least partly attributable to "passive smoking."

CRITERIA FOR DIAGNOSIS

Suggestive

Because of the extensive nature of adverse health effects associated with inhalation of tobacco smoke, the occurrence of a disease known to be related to smoking is suggestive of its possible etiologic role in that individual. In obtaining the medical history, information regarding the nature and extent of tobacco use must be sought. It is insufficient to inquire "do you smoke," as patients will often not volunteer a prior smoking history. Rather, "have you ever smoked, how much, and for how long" are the more appropriate questions to be asked. Corroboration of

the smoking history may be sought from relatives if the extent and duration are in doubt.

Definitive

The presence of a smoking-related disease, for example, chronic obstructive pulmonary disease (COPD), bronchogenic carcinoma, and coronary artery disease, in an individual with a smoking history (usually in excess of 15 pack-years) is sufficient in most instances to permit causal attribution. In instances of atherosclerotic cardiovascular disease, the contributions of associated diabetes, hypertension and hypercholesterolemia must be taken into account. In instances of suspected COPD, pulmonary function testing will help to confirm the presence of obstructive airway disease. Radiographic studies and histopathologic examination of biopsy or cytology specimens are required to confirm a diagnosis of bronchogenic carcinoma. Atherosclerotic disease of the coronary, cerebral, or systemic arterial tree is confirmed by relevant imaging studies, in association with organ-specific symptomatology. Definitive criteria for the diagnosis of less frequent smoking-related lesions/diseases appear in Table 13–3–1.

CLINICAL MANIFESTATIONS

Subjective

Among the most common sequelae of prolonged exposure to tobacco are airway disease, bronchogenic carcinoma, and atherosclerotic disease.

Airway Disease. Airway disease (chronic bronchitis and/or pulmonary emphysema [COPD]) usually manifests with variable levels of exertional dyspnea (dyspnea at rest in more advanced cases), cough, and wheezing.

Bronchogenic Carcinoma. Bronchogenic carcinoma may occasionally be detected in the asymptomatic individual solely by chest roentgenogram, but more frequently patients present with cough and/or general systemic complaints including malaise, weakness, weight loss, chest pain, hemoptysis, and dyspnea.

Atherosclerotic Disease. Atherosclerotic disease varies in its symptomatology depending on the site(s) affected. *Coronary artery disease* may present with classic effort angina (substernal chest pressure on exertion), or with acute severe crushing chest pain, diaphoresis, and dyspnea of myocardial infarction, although it is occasionally characterized by a more insidious presentation with chronic progressive dyspnea and peripheral edema attributable to congestive heart failure due to is-

---

TABLE 13–3–1. OTHER DISEASES/ENTITIES OF LOWER FREQUENCY WHOLLY OR PARTLY ATTRIBUTABLE TO TOBACCO SMOKE CAUSATION

Smoking-Related Disease/Entity	Clinical Manifestations	Definitive Criteria for Diagnosis
Nasopharyngeal and oral cavity carcinoma	Hoarseness, dysphagia, dysphonia, oral pain, halitosis, bleeding	Examination including fiberoptic laryngoscopy, biopsy
Esophageal carcinoma	Dysphagia, chest pain, odynophagia, vomiting, recurrent aspiration, weight loss	Esophagram, esophagoscopy, biopsy
Renal cell carcinoma	Flank pain, flank mass, hematuria, metastatic manifestations	Sonographic or computed tomography imaging, biopsy
Bladder carcinoma	Hematuria, suprapubic pain, recurrent cystitis	Radiographic imaging, urine cytology, biopsy
Peptic ulcer disease/reflux esophagitis	Epigastric pain, vomiting, bleeding, retrosternal pain, "water brash" in throat	Gastroscopy, upper gastrointestinal radiography, 24-hour pH monitoring
Pancreatic carcinoma	Weight loss, abdominal pain, jaundice, ascites, migratory phlebitis	Computed axial tomography scan, endoscopic retrograde cholangiopancreatography, biopsy
Fetal injury or fetal loss	Low birth weight, mental retardation, placental abruption, stillbirth	History of smoking by the mother during pregnancy
Altered drug metabolism	Increased or decreased specific drug effects in patients who smoke	Knowledge of the specific drug and the change in its handling or disposition in smokers; observation of altered effect

chemic cardiomyopathy. *Cerebrovascular disease* presents with the acute motor and/or sensory impairments of stroke, or more subtly with transient ischemic attacks or slow progressive cognitive and/or memory losses. *Peripheral vascular disease* involving the systemic arterial tree may present with local ischemic symptoms such as intermittent claudication of the lower extremities, or with an acute catastrophe (low back or severe abdominal pain, orthostatic hypotension or syncope) related to abdominal aortic aneurysm.

Clinical manifestations of other smoking-related problems appear in Table 13–3–1.

Objective

Chronic Obstructive Pulmonary Disease. Obstructive abnormality (reduced expiratory flow rates) on pulmonary function tests, usually accompanied by evidence of air trapping (increased functional residual capacity and residual volume), gas exchange abnormalities attributable to ventilation–perfusion mismatching (detectable by blood gas analysis), including variable degrees of arterial hypoxemia, and, in more advanced cases, hypercapnia are objective manifestations. Reduced single-breath carbon monoxide diffusing capacity is observed in patients with emphysema. Chest roentgenographic findings may include hyperinflation with flattened diaphragms, increased retrocardiac and retrosternal airspaces, and attenuation of vascular markings in the periphery of the lung fields.

Bronchogenic Carcinoma. The presence of bronchogenic carcinoma is established by radiographic imaging studies (routine chest roentgenogram, thoracic computed axial tomography scan/magnetic resonance imaging), and the diagnosis is confirmed by histopathologic examination of biopsy samples obtained by relevant sampling techniques (selected based on site and accessibility of the lesion), which may include fiberoptic bronchoscopy with endo- or transbronchial biopsy, percutaneous fine-needle aspiration biopsy (which usually yields material for cytopathologic examination), mediastinoscopy, and pleural biopsy. In the presence of extrathoracic metastatic disease, these lesions (lymph node, liver, skin, bone marrow) are often biopsied, as the cell type of the lung cancer and inoperability of the primary lesion can be established via a single procedure.

Atherosclerotic Disease. The diagnosis of atherosclerotic disease is established by documenting compromise of arterial inflow (ischemia) in the affected organ (attributable to compromise of the vascular lumen). Coronary artery disease is suggested by the presence of ST and T wave changes on electrocardiography, and confirmed by perfusion scintigraphy with thallium-201 or by contrast arteriography. Related methodologies may be applied to cerebral (single-photon-emission computed tomography [SPECT] scanning before and after administration of acetazolamide to reveal reversible cerebral perfusion defects or cerebral arteriography) and peripheral (duplex Doppler studies, arteriography) arterial beds, where atherosclerotic involvement is suspected. The presence of asymptomatic coronary and cerebral arterial disease should be strongly considered in individuals with smoking-related COPD and lung cancer, as alternative therapeutic approaches for the management of bronchogenic carcinoma may have to be sought.

PLANS

Diagnostic

The differential diagnosis, diagnostic options for, and recommended approaches to smoking-related illnesses are specifically delineated in the chapters dealing with the specific entities.

Therapeutic

Therapy for specific smoking-related illnesses is discussed within the chapters dealing with the specific subjects. Early detection of airway disease may be facilitated by spirometry with methacholine-inhalational challenge testing, which can detect bronchial hyperreactivity that has been associated with an increased likelihood of progression of early airway damage to COPD. In this way, appropriate counseling and vigorous efforts to encourage smoking cessation may be initiated. Many approaches exist to facilitate smoking cessation, but unfortunately, all

are associated with only limited success. Nicotine-containing chewing gum and transdermal (patch) delivery systems that contain nicotine have been used in efforts to "wean" smokers from the addictive effects of nicotine in the tobacco that they smoke. Group therapy sessions, aversion therapies, and hypnosis have also been attempted. Repetitive efforts to ensure smoking cessation are fully warranted and must be recommended as part of routine health maintenance, and must be specifically employed for patients with cardiopulmonary disease.

FOLLOW-UP

In individuals with specific smoking-related illnesses, the follow-up should be disease specific. In those individuals with presymptomatic airway disease detected by screening pulmonary function tests, it is appropriate to repeat the studies sequentially after smoking cessation, to document stabilization (or amelioration) of the obstructive defect.

DISCUSSION

Prevalence and Incidence

In 1991, the National Health Interview Survey estimated that more than 45 million adults in the United States were current smokers. Males (28%) were more likely to be smokers than females (23%). The prevalence of smoking tended to be higher among underrepresented minority populations (African Americans, Native Americans, and Alaskan Natives) than among Caucasians, perhaps because of the aggressive targeted marketing strategies employed by the tobacco industry. Recent estimates suggest that the worldwide death toll from cigarette smoking will triple, reaching 20 per minute during the next 25 years (unless efforts directed at encouraging smoking cessation are broadly successful). Currently, about 3 million deaths per year are attributable to smoking (almost 6 per minute). In the Unites States, cigarette smoking is causal in or significantly associated with the top 15 causes of death.

Related Basic Science

The gaseous and particulate phases of cigarette smoke contain several thousand compounds, many of which are responsible for adverse health effects. Carbon monoxide is an important component of the gaseous phase; it combines to form carboxyhemoglobin (blood levels generally three- to tenfold higher in smokers than nonsmokers), causing episodes of angina in individuals with coronary artery disease. Tobacco smoke can cause coronary artery spasm and thrombosis in some patients. Nicotine is responsible for the addictive qualities of tobacco smoke. Tars, benzo-α-pyrene, N-nitrosamines, and methycholanthrene are among the carcinogenic hydrocarbon components of tobacco smoke. Previously unsuspected disease associations with cigarette smoking have recently been described. It has been estimated that slightly more than 20% of all myeloid leukemias are induced by smoking. Mucociliary transport is directly inhibited by the toxic effects of tobacco smoke, with ciliary paralysis occurring. This inhibition of airway defense mechanisms, when coupled with the effects of smoke particulates and tars (which are concentrated in pulmonary alveolar macrophages) results in the inhibition of resistance to respiratory tract infection. The phagocytic function of pulmonary alveolar macrophages is diminished, reducing the effectiveness of the defense mechanisms against a variety of pathogens, accounting in part for the increased incidence of lower respiratory tract infections in smokers. The smoke-induced inhibition of ciliary beat frequency (of the ciliary columnar airway epithelium) is associated with recurrent episodes of bronchitis as well as lower respiratory tract infections.

Natural History and Its Modification with Treatment

Refer to the chapter dealing with the specific disease entity for data regarding natural history. Smoking cessation may beneficially impact the course (delay or inhibit development or progression of COPD and coronary artery disease) and thus alter the natural history of some of the tobacco smoke-related diseases.

Prevention

Extensive public advertising campaigns highlighting the multiple adverse effects of smoking, the Surgeon General's warnings on each package of cigarettes (and on all tobacco-related advertising), and the institution of laws prohibiting smoking in public places (including restaurants, theaters, public transport conveyances, hospitals, and government buildings) have achieved a slow but measurable decline in the rate of smoking in the United States. The beneficial impact of the prevention of the initiation of smoking (or the encouragement of early cessation before onset of irreversible disease) is important in terms of the reduction of morbidity and mortality.

Cost Containment

Smoking prevention and cessation would be the most important cost containment measures. Estimating the dollar value of time lost from work (reduction in the gross domestic product) because of smoking-related disease/disability (including excess respiratory tract infections, COPD, heart disease, bronchogenic and other carcinomas, as well as less common tobacco smoke-related diseases) and the cost of medical

care for these illnesses is staggering. At least $200 billion could be saved annually in the United States alone!

REFERENCES

Brownson, RC, Alavanja MCR, Hock ET, et al. Passive smoking and lung cancer in nonsmoking women. Am J Public Health 1992;82:1525.
Cigarette smoking among adults—United States, 1991. MMWR 1993;42:230.
Cigarette-smoking attributable mortality and years of potential life lost—United States, 1990. MMWR 1993;42:645.
Fiore MC, Jorenby DE, Baker TB, et al. Tobacco dependence and the nicotine patch: Clinical guidelines for effective use. JAMA 1993;268:2687.
Report of the Surgeon General. The health consequences of smoking: Nicotine addiction. Publication CDC 88-8406. Washington, DC: U.S. Department of Health & Human Services, 1988.
Siegel M. Smoking and leukemia: Evaluation of a causal hypothesis. Am J Epidemiol 1993;138:1.

CHAPTER 13–4

Pleurisy

Linda S. Efferen, M.D.

DEFINITION

Pleurisy is defined as inflammation of the pleura. The term is often used as an equivalent to pleuritic pain, which is a symptom arising from the inflammation. As only the parietal pleura is innervated with pain fibers, pleuritic chest pain specifically indicates inflammation of the parietal pleura.

ETIOLOGY

Pleurisy is a nonspecific condition that can develop in response to a variety of disparate stimuli and can be found in association with a plethora of systemic conditions. It is generally a manifestation of some underlying process and, as such, is a marker for evaluation of the primary problem.

CRITERIA FOR DIAGNOSIS
Suggestive

The diagnosis is suggested by the patient's history. In general patients complain of chest pain that developed acutely or subacutely over several hours. Occasionally the pain may be insidious in onset. The pain is usually fairly well localized, most frequently to the lateral chest wall, corresponding to innervation by intercostal nerves of the area adjacent to the inflammation. Pain that radiates to the diaphragm or ipsilateral shoulder indicates inflammation of the diaphragmatic portion of the pleura, which is innervated by branches of the phrenic nerve.

Definitive

There is no definitive diagnostic symptom, sign, or test that establishes the diagnosis. Other causes of similar pain need to be excluded and additional studies may need to be done to establish an etiology.

CLINICAL MANIFESTATIONS
Subjective

Patients with inflammation of the pleura generally complain of chest pain which may be pleuritic or dull and aching. Pleuritic chest pain is generally described as a sharp, stabbing pain that occurs or is worsened with deep breathing. Individuals may complain of dyspnea if pain is severe and limits normal respiration, but it is not usually present unless pleurisy is related to a significant underlying pulmonary process.

Past or family history is generally noncontributory except in situa-

tions where the pleurisy is a manifestation of a chronic or hereditary disease process.

Objective
Physical Examination

Patients may be tachypneic and they may splint the affected side to minimize pain. Percussion over the affected area may elicit pain. If an associated pleural effusion or parenchymal process is present the percussion note may be dull. Auscultatory findings may reveal decreased breath sounds, inspiratory crackles, or a pleural friction rub, or may be normal.

Routine Laboratory Abnormalities

Abnormalities found on routine laboratory examination may reflect the underlying disease process and support a specific etiology (i.e., abnormal renal function in uremic pleuritis, elevated white blood cell count in parapneumonic effusions) but would not be diagnostic of pleurisy per se.

PLANS
Diagnostic
Differential Diagnosis

The initial diagnostic step is to establish the pleura as the source of pain. The character and nature of the pain must be separated from musculoskeletal, abdominal, cardiac, or esophageal sources. The location of the pain, association with respiration, and the duration and character of the pain can help guide the diagnostician. The etiology for the pleural inflammation should then be determined and infectious, malignant, thromboembolic, and associated collagen–vascular disorders should be considered.

Diagnostic Options

The appropriate diagnostic evaluation should be dictated by the organ system most likely to be involved based on the information contributed by the history and physical examination (Table 13–4–1).

Recommended Approach

Initial evaluation should include a focused history regarding the onset, nature, and character of the pain; relationship of the pain to breathing, movement, or eating; associated symptoms of dyspnea; prior episodes;

TABLE 13–4–1. DIAGNOSTIC OPTIONS

Etiology	History	Physical	Tests
Musculoskeletal			
Rib	Trauma	Point tenderness	Rib films
Muscle	Strain, severe coughing	Superficial, localized tenderness	
Costochondral junction	Aggravated by movement	Point tenderness	
Pleurisy with effusion			
Infection: bacterial, mycobacterial	Fever, cough	Decreased breath sounds, dullness to percussion	Chest films with decubitus views, thoracocentesis
Malignant disease	Weight loss; dull, aching pain	Dullness to percussion, decreased breath sounds	Chest films with decubitus views, thoracocentesis
Collagen vascular diseases	Joint swelling, pain	Dullness to percussion, decreased breath sounds	Chest films with decubitus views, thoracocentesis
Pleurisy, no effusion			
Infection	Fever, cough	May be normal	Chest films
Thromboembolic disease	Acute onset with dyspnea	May be normal	Chest films, ventilation–perfusion scan, impedance plethysmography of lower limbs
Nonpulmonary			
Pericardial	Substernal pain, alleviated in upright and forward position	Pericardial rub	Chest films, electrocardiogram, echocardiography
Mediastinal	Deep pain, may radiate to back	Variable, may be normal	Chest films, computed tomography scan chest, esophagram

and history of trauma. A complete physical examination, with specific attention to the chest, is important. If the most likely diagnosis is musculoskeletal pain and rib fracture is not suspected, no further diagnostic tests would be warranted. Rib series if fractures are suspected should confirm the diagnosis. Radiographic evaluation with posteroanterior and lateral views would be indicated if underlying pulmonary disease is suspected. If cardiac disease is most likely an electrocardiogram and further cardiac evaluation may be warranted.

Therapeutic

Therapeutic Options

Treatment will be definitive if directed to the underlying disease process as established by the diagnostic evaluation. Pain relief is generally indicated unless there is a specific contraindication. The analgesic of choice will be determined by the severity of pain. Severe pain may require narcotics or occasionally intercostal nerve block or epidural anesthesia. Antiinflammatory agents may be the preferred agent in situations where the pain is related to an underlying inflammatory process such as a collagen–vascular disorder.

Recommended Approach

If the pain is mild to moderate acetaminophen or a nonsteroidal antiinflammatory agent can be used. The latter agent should not be administered if an invasive procedure is contemplated due to its potential effects on platelet function. If the pain is severe and limiting normal respiration or effective coughing, or other agents have been nontherapeutic, narcotics can be used. Their potential for respiratory compromise via sedation must be considered.

FOLLOW-UP

The appropriate follow-up is determined by the underlying disease state. In self-limiting conditions the patient should be advised that resolution of the pain is expected to occur over several days (musculoskeletal) to weeks (herpes zoster, rib fracture) and long-term follow-up is rarely necessary. If symptoms worsen or fail to respond, early follow-up and reevaluation may be advised.

DISCUSSION

Prevalence and Incidence

Precise information regarding the prevalence and incidence of pleurisy is not available. It is a process that is associated with many diseases and syndromes. As it generally is a clinical manifestation of an underlying condition or disease, reporting of this as a specific process is not done.

Related Basic Science

The pleura is a serous membrane that covers the lung parenchyma, mediastinum, rib cage, and diaphragm. It is subdivided into the visceral pleura, which covers the entire surface of the lung including the interlobar fissures, and the parietal pleura, which covers the inner surface of the thoracic cage, mediastinum, and diaphragm.

Sensory nerve endings are present in the costal and diaphragmatic parietal pleura. The intercostal nerve innervates the costal and peripheral portion of the diaphragmatic pleura, with pain referred to the adjacent chest wall. The phrenic nerve supplies the central portion of the diaphragmatic pleura, and pain is referred to the ipsilateral shoulder. There are no pain fibers in the visceral pleura. The presence of pleuritic chest pain therefore signifies inflammation or irritation of the parietal pleura.

Natural History and Its Modification with Treatment

The natural history and response to treatment of pleurisy are determined by the underlying etiology. In most cases, pleurisy is a self-limiting and nonrecurring process. Symptomatic treatment with analgesics may modify the expression of the symptom but does not alter the course of the underlying process.

Prevention

There is no available prevention for pleurisy per se. Prevention for some of the diseases associated with pleurisy such as thromboembolic disease and recurrent pneumonia may be indicated.

Cost Containment

Cost containment can be exercised both in limitation of the diagnostic evaluation and in treatment. Diagnostic evaluation should be judiciously guided based on the principles previously discussed. Treatment is determined by the underlying process and symptoms experienced. Aspirin or acetaminophen may be adequate analgesics. Nonsteroidal antiinflammatory drugs may also be used, but this may increase cost and the relative benefits of a given agent should be considered with cost in mind. If narcotic analgesia is required, codeine is a relatively inexpensive option.

REFERENCES

Abramowicz M, ed. Drugs for rheumatoid arthritis. Med Lett 1994;36:101.
Light RW. Pleural diseases. 2nd ed. Philadelphia: Lea & Febiger, 1990.
Loudon R, Murphy R. Lung sounds. Am Rev Respir Dis 1984;130:663.
Murray JF. The normal lung. 2nd ed. Philadelphia: Saunders, 1986.

Empyema

Laura J. Mandel, M.D.

DEFINITION

In simplest terms, the word *empyema* refers to the presence of gross pus or microbial contamination in the pleural space. More technical and varied definitions exist; however, these are of greatest value in addressing specific management issues, and are discussed below. The broad definition given above is the most useful working definition with regard to clear identification of patients with this condition.

ETIOLOGY

The most common category of empyema is that occurring secondary to underlying pulmonary parenchymal infection, pneumonia, or lung abscess. Empyema occurring as a complication of pneumonia accounted for approximately 80% of episodes of empyema in the preantibiotic era and is still responsible for 40 to 60% of episodes. Nosocomial empyema, often associated with thoracic surgery, accounts for 10 to 30% of episodes of empyema in recent series. A third important category includes empyema occurring secondary to intraabdominal pathology including subdiaphragmatic abscesses. Although any organism can cause empyema, most cases are due to bacterial pathogens. Specific bacterial pathogens are implicated with different frequency in various studies, depending on the year the study was performed (pre- or postantibiotic era) and the distribution of predisposing conditions present in the study population.

The frequency with which pleural effusion or empyema complicates the course of pneumonia due to different pathogens is a function of both the organism and the duration of infection prior to the initiation of effective antibiotic therapy. Although most patients with parapneumonic effusions do not go on to develop empyema, recognition of the potential for this complication is very important. *Streptococcus pneumoniae*, implicated in the majority of cases of empyema in the preantibiotic era, is now seen less frequently but still accounts for 5 to 40% of cases. Recent studies have demonstrated that parapneumonic effusions occur in 40 to 60% of patients with pneumococcal pneumonia, much more frequently than previously recognized. Fewer than 5% of patients with pneumococcal pneumonia, however, develop empyema. *Hemophilus influenzae, Streptococcus pyogenes,* and *Staphylococcus aureus* are other important causes of empyema in otherwise healthy individuals. In patients with pneumonia due to *Streptococcus pyogenes,* pleural effusion is present in 55 to 95%, and 30 to 40% have a positive pleural fluid culture. Empyema associated with bronchopleural fistula accounts for 10 to 20% of episodes and is associated with organisms likely to cause pulmonary parenchymal necrosis such as *S. aureus,* Gram-negative bacilli, and anaerobes. In recent years, anaerobic organisms have been isolated from about one third of patients developing empyema secondary to pneumonia or lung abscess. Although less commonly implicated as etiologic agents in published series of cases of empyema, atypical pathogens including *Legionella* species, *Chlamydia pneumoniae,* and *Mycoplasma pneumoniae* may also be associated with significant pleural effusion. Among patients with nosocomially acquired empyema, infections due to *S. aureus* and Gram-negative bacilli are common.

Mycobacterium tuberculosis is another important cause of infection involving the pleural space. With the current increasing incidence of tuberculosis, it is always important to consider the possibility of tuberculous pleuritis in the differential diagnosis of empyema.

CRITERIA FOR DIAGNOSIS
Suggestive

The clinical signs and symptoms associated with empyema are often vague and are often referable to the predisposing condition or underlying disease process. This is particularly true in patients who develop empyema as a complication of pneumonia or lung abscess, where the predominant symptoms are cough, sputum production, and fever. The possibility that an empyema may be present should be considered in all patients with pneumonia or lung abscess at the time they are initially evaluated, as the presence of a complicated pleural effusion or empyema necessitates additional diagnostic and therapeutic interventions. A physician should also suspect that an empyema may be present in any patient with pulmonary parenchymal infection who fails to respond in an expected fashion to appropriate antibiotic therapy. Indices that a patient is not responding as expected include persistent fever (generally beyond 72 hours), persistently elevated white blood cell count, and, less commonly, thrombocytosis. In addition, empyema should be considered in any patient with clinical or radiographic evidence of fluid in the pleural space who has unexplained fever, leukocytosis, or thrombocytosis.

When empyema develops in the setting of pneumonectomy, in addition to the nonspecific indices of infection such as fever and leukocytosis, a shift of the mediastinum toward the contralateral hemithorax may provide an additional suggestion as to the diagnosis. In all circumstances, the presence of a high index of suspicion on the part of the physician is critical to the diagnosis.

Definitive

The diagnosis of empyema is documented by the finding of pus and/or microorganisms in pleural fluid obtained by thoracentesis (see Plans, Diagnostic).

CLINICAL MANIFESTATIONS
Subjective

When empyema occurs in the setting of pneumonia or lung abscess, the signs and symptoms of the associated pulmonary parenchymal process dominate the clinical picture. Patients often present with complaints of fever, cough, sputum production, and dyspnea. Pleuritic chest pain may or may not be present. In patients with a more chronic course, complaints of chills, weight loss, or night sweats may be present or even dominate the clinical picture. This less acute presentation is seen with increased frequency in patients with anaerobic pleuropulmonary infection and in patients with postpneumonectomy empyema.

Objective
Physical Examination

The most important physical findings in patients with empyema are those related to the presence of pleural fluid. These include dullness or flatness to percussion and diminished or absent breath sounds. A pleural friction rub may be present. Chest wall tenderness to percussion or palpation over the affected area is not uncommon. Although most patients with empyema have fever, this is not a universal finding and its absence can never be used to argue definitively against the presence of empyema.

Routine Laboratory Abnormalities

Routine laboratory examinations reveal only nonspecific abnormalities associated with the presence of infection such as leukocytosis, with or without a left shift. Thrombocytosis and anemia of chronic disease may also be present, especially in patients with a more subacute or chronic presentation.

The routine chest radiograph reveals evidence of pleural effusion (blunting of the costophrenic angle) if at least 300 to 500 mL of fluid is present. Lateral decubitus views can detect smaller amounts of fluid (100–200 mL). The chest x-ray film may appear normal in patients with smaller amounts of fluid or if fluid is developing in interlobar or subpulmonic spaces. The presence of pleural effusion may also be difficult to recognize on routine chest radiographs in the presence of extensive pneumonia or when a loculated empyema occurs in a patient with a bronchopleural fistula (giving the radiographic appearance of a peripherally located lung abscess). Additional diagnostic imaging modalities that can be useful in these circumstances are discussed below.

PLANS

Diagnostic

Differential Diagnosis

In addition to bacterial infection, the differential diagnosis of empyema includes pleural infection due to other classes of organisms (including tuberculosis, fungi, and viruses), pulmonary embolism, postcardiotomy syndrome, collagen–vascular disease, malignant effusion (primary and metastatic), congestive heart failure, and sympathetic effusions secondary to intraabdominal processes such as pancreatitis and subdiaphragmatic abscess.

Diagnostic Options

In circumstances where the presence of pleural fluid or empyema is suspected but it is not demonstrated on routine radiographs (including lateral decubitus views), ultrasound and computed tomography provide more sensitive techniques for identifying the presence of pleural fluid. In addition, these techniques provide a safe and effective means of obtaining pleural fluid in situations where thoracentesis might be difficult, such as in patients with small or loculated effusions. Once the presence of pleural fluid is identified by any of the above modalities, analysis of pleural fluid obtained by thoracentesis is mandatory for diagnosis.

Recommended Approach

Posteroanterior and lateral chest radiographs should be obtained in all patients with possible parapneumonic effusion or empyema. If either the posterior or lateral costophrenic angles are blunted or obscured by infiltrate, bilateral decubitus films should be obtained. If the presence of free pleural fluid is demonstrated on lateral decubitus radiographs, an estimate is made as to the amount of fluid present. Most authorities agree that if the amount of fluid seen on the lateral decubitus film is less than 10 mm thick, most patients will respond to antibiotic therapy alone, and a thoracentesis is not indicated. Such patients, however, must be followed carefully for any evidence of failure to respond appropriately to antibiotic therapy or increase in the size of the effusion. If the amount of the effusion as seen on the decubitus x-ray is 10 mm or greater, a diagnostic thoracentesis is indicated. If areas of loculated pleural fluid are suspected, an ultrasonographic examination should be performed. If loculations are visualized, thoracentesis should be performed on all visualized collections under sonographic guidance, because the nature of each collection may vary.

By definition, the presence of microorganisms in pleural fluid by either stain or culture or the presence of gross pus is diagnostic of empyema. In addition, analysis of pleural fluid is important in identifying specific pathogens, in providing bacterial isolates for antibiotic susceptibility testing, and in considering alternative diagnoses. Whenever possible, if empyema is suspected on clinical grounds, diagnostic thoracentesis should be performed prior to initiation of antibiotic therapy to maximize the yield of bacterial cultures. The gross characteristics, including color, odor, and viscosity, of pleural fluid obtained by thoracentesis should be described. A faeculent odor is an indication that anaerobes are likely to be present.

Fluid should always be submitted for Gram stain and aerobic and anaerobic cultures. If clinically indicated, fluid should also be submitted for culture and stain for other organisms including mycobacteria, fungi, and other atypical pathogens including *Legionella, Chlamydia*, and amebae, and for cytologic examination. In the absence of prior antibiotic therapy, most patients with bacterial empyema will have microorganisms identified on either Gram stain or culture. It is important, however, to recognize that smear-negative/culture-negative empyema fluid has been reported in up to 15% of patients. In pleural tuberculosis,

organisms may be identified in pleural fluid by culture or stain in approximately 20% of patients. If the index of suspicion for tuberculosis is high, pleural biopsy is indicated and gives a much higher diagnostic yield.

In addition to microbiologic analysis, aliquots of pleural fluid should be submitted for total cell count and differential and determination of protein, pH, glucose, lactate dehydrogenase, and amylase. The character of the fluid reflects type and duration of infection and the nature of the underlying disease process. Analysis of these biochemical parameters is important in defining the pathophysiologic stage of an empyema if one is present, and this has important therapeutic implications. Established empyema fluid characteristically has a pH less than 7.2, a glucose level less than 40 mg/dL, and lactate dehydrogenase activity greater than 1000 mg/dL. Patients with uncomplicated parapneumonic effusion or with pleural effusion due to malignancy or collagen–vascular disease have negative Gram stains and cultures, and the biochemical profile of the pleural fluid generally reveals a pH of 7.3 or higher, a glucose of 60 mg/dL or greater, and a lactate dehydrogenase of less than 600. Other less specific abnormalities seen in patients with empyema are a pleural fluid protein level greater than 3.0 mg/dL and a specific gravity greater than 1.018. The correlation of pleural fluid leukocyte count with infection is a less reliable determinant of stage of infection than these other parameters; however, many patients with pleural empyema have pleural fluid leukocyte counts greater than 25,000. Those with uncomplicated parapneumonic effusion or other diagnoses tend to have leukocyte counts less than 20,000. Most patients with bacterial infection have a predominance of polymorphonuclear leukocytes. In contrast, pleural effusion or empyema due to organisms such as *Mycobacterium tuberculosis* is more commonly associated with a predominance of mononuclear cells.

Therapeutic

Therapeutic Options

Optimal therapy for empyema requires both administration of antibiotics effective against the isolated or presumed pathogen and drainage of the infected pleural space; however, major controversy exists regarding what constitutes optimal drainage for any individual patient. Pleural involvement due to *Mycobacterium tuberculosis* is a notable exception to this rule because tuberculous empyema usually resolves with effective antituberculous chemotherapy alone.

Recommended Approach

Antibiotic Therapy. Guidelines for the selection of antibiotics to treat patients with empyema are similar to those for the treatment of suppurative infection at other sites. Although general recommendations can be made, the final selection of antibiotics for any given patient should be based on the results of susceptibility testing of the organism or organisms isolated from pleural fluid. For most patients, the initial choice of antibiotics includes a β-lactam drug with activity against the likely pathogen. Penicillin G is an appropriate choice in patients with infection due to *Streptococcus pneumoniae* or *Streptococcus pyogenes*. An antistaphylococcal penicillin such as oxacillin or nafcillin is the treatment of choice in patients with presumed or proven infection due to *Staphylococcus aureus,* unless the likelihood of infection with a methicillin-resistant strain is great. If infection with methicillin-resistant *S. aureus* is likely or proven, or a patient with empyema due to staphylococci or streptococci has a history of hypersensitivity to penicillin, vancomycin is a reasonable alternative. An extended-spectrum penicillin or cephalosporin is an appropriate choice in patients likely or proven to be infected with *Hemophilus influenzae* or other Gram-negative bacilli. Anaerobic infection can be treated with clindamycin or with β-lactam/β-lactamase inhibitor combinations. All of these agents achieve adequate levels in the pleural space with systemic therapy; therefore, local instillation is not necessary. Aminoglycoside antibiotics have a narrow therapeutic margin and poor activity in the milieu of the infected pleural space; therefore, they should not be used as single agents in the treatment of empyema. When combined with appropriate β-lactam antibiotics, however, aminoglycosides may be of value in the treatment of empyema due to *Pseudomonas aeruginosa, Acinetobacter calcoaceticus,* and *Enterobacter cloacae*. Antibiotics should be given at high dose and generally for a duration of 2 to

4 weeks (or until the thoracostomy tube is removed). Some patients may require more prolonged courses of antibiotics. Specifically, infections such as those due to *Nocardia*, actinomycosis, tuberculosis, or fungal infection require more prolonged therapy.

Drainage. Drainage is a critical aspect of the treatment of patients with pleural empyema. The optimal therapeutic modality for achieving drainage in any given patient is an area of continuing controversy. During the initial stage of infection, pleural fluid is usually thin and present in relatively small amounts. At this stage, infection frequently resolves with antibiotics and repeated needle drainage by thoracentesis or small-bore catheter. In some patients, however, drainage by these mechanisms is inadequate and the patient requires more extensive drainage procedures. As delay of adequate initial drainage frequently results in increased morbidity and increased cost and duration of hospitalization, attention has focused on identifying parameters that enable physicians to identify patients who require closed-chest tube drainage early. Pleural fluid pH is often cited as an important parameter to decide whether a patient with an infected but nonpurulent parapneumonic effusion has a complicated effusion that will require thoracostomy tube drainage. Some authorities have suggested that a low or decreasing pleural fluid pH is a marker of the second, fibropurulent stage of infection and is therefore a marker for patients who require more aggressive drainage. Specifically, patients with a pleural fluid pH less than 7.0 (or at least 0.3 pH point less than simultaneously measured arterial pH) usually require closed thoracostomy tube drainage. Patients with pleural fluid pH above 7.3 rarely require such drainage. Although these guidelines are useful in the majority of patients, individual patients do not always conform to these guidelines. Furthermore, in special circumstances such as empyema due to *Proteus mirabilis,* elevations of pleural fluid pH may occur as a result of the metabolism of the organism, giving a false impression of early or uncomplicated effusion in a patient who in fact has a complicated effusion that requires thoracostomy drainage. Patients with a pleural fluid pH between 7.0 and 7.3 require careful repeated clinical evaluation, often including repeat pleural fluid analysis.

When thick, grossly purulent empyema fluid is present, initial drainage with closed thoracostomy tube drainage is indicated. In such patients, therefore, the determination of pleural fluid pH is superfluous. Because attempting to perform measurement of pH on such grossly purulent fluids can damage blood gas analyzers, in this setting, pH should not be determined. Once drainage is established, clinical parameters such as fever and leukocytosis, as well as the amount of pleural fluid drainage, should be measured daily. In patients who respond favorably to this therapy, improvement is generally noted within 48 hours. When the amount of drainage falls to less than 50 mL/d, drainage can be converted from closed to open drainage and the tube can gradually be withdrawn. Closed-chest tube drainage may fail in as many as one third of such patients in whom it used as the initial drainage procedure for parapneumonic empyema. In some patients who fail to improve with antibiotics and thoracostomy tube drainage, streptokinase, administered directly into the pleural space, has been used successfully to facilitate drainage and avoid the need for more extensive surgical procedures such as decortication. The failure rate of thoracostomy tube drainage is even higher in patients in whom empyema develops secondary to pneumonectomy. When thoracostomy drainage fails, open drainage with rib resection or decortication is indicated. Such management decisions should be made in consultation with a thoracic surgeon.

FOLLOW-UP

It is reasonable to discharge patients who have responded well to closed drainage as soon as the drainage is converted to open and the chest tube is being advanced. Such patients should be followed at weekly intervals until the tube is out and the thoracostomy wound healed.

DISCUSSION
Prevalence and Incidence

It is estimated that 1.2 million people in the United States contract pneumonia annually. Of these, approximately 5% go on to develop empyema. Although the rate with which empyema complicates pneumonia has decreased dramatically since the advent of the antibiotic era, current estimates put the incidence of empyema in the order of 0.5 to 0.8 per 1000 hospital admissions.

Related Basic Science

Although the spectrum of pathophysiologic changes seen in the course of development of empyema is a continuum, it is customary to think of the process as occurring in three stages: the exudative phase, the fibropurulent phase and the organization phase. An understanding of these phases is key to understanding why and how different patients respond to different forms of drainage. During the exudative phase there is an initial outpouring of sterile fluid into the pleural space. This occurs because of increased permeability of capillaries in the visceral pleura in areas adjacent to pneumonia. In this phase the pleural fluid is characterized by a low leukocyte count and lactate dehydrogenase, and normal glucose and pH. If the process is allowed to progress, the fibropurulent phase evolves. During this phase there is accumulation of increasing amounts of fluid, leukocytes, bacteria, and cellular debris, and pH and glucose fall progressively and lactate dehydrogenase increases. Fibrin is deposited on both visceral and parietal pleural surfaces, limiting lung expansion and creating an environment favorable to development of loculation of fluid. During the third and final phase, the organization phase, fibroblasts grow into the exudate, producing a thick, leathery membrane that severely limits lung function. This membrane is referred to as a pleural peel.

Natural History and Its Modification with Treatment

If antibiotic therapy is instituted during the first, exudative phase, in most cases further development of the inflammatory process is aborted, and aggressive drainage is not necessary. Once the fibropurulent stage develops, aggressive drainage of the affected area (including all loculations) is necessary to achieve resolution of infection and prevent progression to the organization phase. With early recognition and aggressive therapy most empyemas resolve with little long-term morbidity. In the face of delayed or inadequate therapy, however, hospitalization may be prolonged, often with the additional need for more extensive surgical procedures such as decortication to achieve adequate resolution of infection or improve severe restrictive sequelae.

Prevention

Prevention relies on early recognition and appropriate treatment of pneumonias and associated parapneumonic effusions when they occur.

Cost Containment

The most effective means of limiting the costs of treatment once empyema develops are aggressive early drainage and administration of appropriate antibiotics. This approach will shorten hospital stay and decrease long-term morbidity. In addition, as is true in other types of infection, decisions regarding the choice of antibiotics should include consideration of antibiotic cost, as well as the considerations of microbial susceptibility and drug toxicity mentioned under Plans, Therapeutic.

REFERENCES

Berger HA, Morganroth ML. Immediate drainage is not required for all patients with complicated parapneumonic effusions. Chest 1990;97:731.

Light RW. Parapneumonic effusions and infections of the pleural space. In: Light RW, ed. Pleural diseases. Philadelpha: Lea & Febiger, 1983:101.

Poe RH, Marin MG, Israel RH, Kallay MC. Utility of pleural fluid analysis in predicting tube thoracostomy/decortication in parapneumonic effusions. Chest 1991;100:963.

Robinson LA, Moulton MD, Fleming WH, et al. Intrapleural fibrinolytic treatment of multiloculated thoracic empyemas. Ann Thorac Surg 1994;57:803.

Taryle DA, Potts DE, Sahn SA. The incidence and clinical correlates of parapneumonic effusions in pneumococcal pneumonia. Chest 1978;74:170.

VanSonnenberg E, Nakamoto SK, Mueller PR, et al. CT and ultrasound-guided catheter drainage of empyemas after chest tube drainage. Radiology 1984;151:349.

Benign Pleural Effusions
Linda S. Efferen, M.D.

DEFINITION

A pleural effusion is a collection of fluid within the pleural cavity that exists, under normal conditions, as a potential space between the parietal and visceral layers of the pleura. Benign refers to a nonmalignant etiology and does not imply any information regarding course or prognosis.

ETIOLOGY

Numerous processes and disease states can alter the normal homeostasis controlling the production and removal of fluid in the pleural cavity. Pathophysiologic mechanisms contributing to the development of effusions and associated clinical diagnoses are delineated in Table 13–6–1 and 13–6–2, respectively.

CRITERIA FOR DIAGNOSIS
Suggestive

The presence of a pleural effusion may be suggested by the patient's history, findings on physical examination, or a coincidental finding on a screening chest radiograph. Pleural effusions generally occur as a manifestation of some underlying disease process and symptoms related to the primary process may predominate the clinical picture. The presence of a clinical condition commonly associated with an effusion may increase the suspicion for an effusion.

Radiographic abnormalities suggestive of fluid would include blunting of a costophrenic angle on a posteroanterior or lateral view of the chest, with the superior aspect of the density assuming a meniscus shape. The appearance of pleural thickening or a pleural-based mass may also indicate a possible effusion. At times fluid may accumulate under the lung without spilling into the costophrenic sulcus. Radiographic findings in these cases of subpulmonic effusions may include elevation of the diaphragm, lateral displacement of the apex of the diaphragm, or a sharper slope of the diaphragm as it converges with the lateral costophrenic angle.

Definitive

Lateral decubitus view radiograph demonstrating free-flowing fluid is definitive evidence of an effusion within the pleural cavity. Fluid accumulates in the most dependent portion of the lung. In the upright position, fluid accumulates in the posterior costophrenic sulcus. In the decubitus position, fluid moves within the pleural cavity and accumulates between the inner aspect of the chest wall and the outer aspect of the lung surface.

At times fluid may be loculated and not layer on decubitus films. Ultrasound or computed tomography scan may be required in these cases to confirm the diagnosis. Determining the etiology of the fluid requires clinical correlation and diagnostic thorocentesis.

CLINICAL MANIFESTATIONS
Subjective

The symptoms a patient expresses generally reflect the underlying disease process causing the pleural effusion. When symptoms are related to the effusion per se, they are generally related to inflammation of the parietal pleura (pleurisy), compromise of pulmonary mechanics or interference with gas exchange (dyspnea), or lung compression (cough). Many patients may be asymptomatic. Past history may be informative in the presence of a disease process known to cause pleural effusions, such as renal failure, congestive heart failure, or systemic lupus erythematosus. Care, however, must be exercised to avoid prematurely ascribing the etiology of a new effusion to an antecedent condition without appropriate evaluation.

Objective
Physical Examination

The physical examination of a patient suspected of having a pleural effusion may reveal differences in the relative sizes of the two hemithoraces. In situations where pleural pressure is increased on the side of the effusion, the hemithorax will be larger and the usual concavity of the intercostal spaces will be blunted or possibly convex. Conversely, if pleural pressure on the side of the effusion is decreased, as may occur with obstruction of a major bronchus or a trapped lung, the ipsilateral hemithorax will be decreased in size and the normal concavity of the intercostal spaces will be increased.

Palpation of the chest wall may serve to delineate the extent of the effusion. In areas where the effusion separates the lung from the chest wall, tactile fremitus is decreased or absent as the fluid absorbs the vibrations emanating from the lung. The percussion note over a pleural effusion is dull or flat. If the dullness to percussion shifts as the position of the patient changes, then free-flowing fluid is most likely present. Tactile fremitus may be more sensitive than the commonly used percussion note in identifying the extent of the effusion. With a thin rim of fluid the percussion note may still be resonant, but tactile fremitus is decreased.

Auscultation over pleural fluid reveals decreased or absent breath sounds. Near the superior border of the fluid, breath sounds may be increased due to superior conductance through partially atelectatic lung. A pleural rub may be present or may appear as the amount of fluid decreases.

The remaining physical examination may provide clues to the underlying disease process causing the pleural effusion.

TABLE 13–6–1. ETIOLOGY: PATHOPHYSIOLOGIC MECHANISMS

Transudates
Increased capillary hydrostatic pressure
Decreased plasma oncotic pressure
Decreased intrapleural hydrostatic pressure*

Exudates
Increased permeability of the pleural surface to protein
Decreased lymphatic flow from the pleural space

*May contribute to formation of exudative effusions also.

TABLE 13–6–2. ETIOLOGY: CLINICAL DIAGNOSES

Transudates	
Cirrhosis	Miscellaneous
Nephrosis	Peritoneal dialysis
Congestive heart failure	Hypothyroidism
Pulmonary embolism	Sarcoidosis
Exudates	
Infectious disease	Collagen–vascular disease
Bacterial	Drug-related
Mycobacterial	Miscellaneous
Parasitic	Sarcoidosis
Fungal	Yellow nail syndrome
Viral	Amyloidosis
Malignancy	Ovarian hyperstimulation
Pulmonary embolism	Postpartum
Gastrointestinal disorders	Trauma

Routine Laboratory Abnormalities

Abnormalities on routine laboratory examination would reflect the underlying disease process (i.e., abnormal renal function in uremic pleuritis, elevated white blood cell count in parapneumonic effusions) and may serve to support a particular etiology, but would not be diagnostic of a pleural effusion per se.

PLANS

Diagnostic

Differential Diagnosis

Pleural-based masses or pleural thickening may appear similar to pleural effusions and should be differentiated via radiographic evaluation as previously discussed. As to the etiology of the effusion, a broad and diverse range of diseases must be considered (Table 13–6–2). The initial differentiation of the effusion as a transudate or exudate serves to focus the diagnostic considerations. The etiology of a transudative effusion is frequently readily apparent from history, physical examination, and routine laboratory evaluation. The majority of exudative effusions are due to infection, malignancy, or pulmonary embolization; however, a pleural effusion may be the presenting symptom of a gastrointestinal disease, collagen–vascular disease, drug reaction, or an uncommonly seen disease.

Diagnostic Options and Recommended Approach

If a pleural effusion is suspected based on initial radiography, bilateral decubitus views should be obtained. Bilateral views allow visualization of the underlying lung on the ipsilateral side, which may be obscured by the effusion on routine views, in addition to determining if the effusion is free flowing. Ultrasound should be used for diagnosis in cases where decubitus films are technically inadequate or nondiagnostic and to localize the fluid for thoracocentesis in difficult cases or loculated effusions.

With few exceptions all undiagnosed pleural effusions should be evaluated. A pleural effusion in association with overt congestive heart failure, and in the absence of any clinical suspicion of infection, may be monitored for response to treatment. Similarly, a small effusion, as determined by a measured distance between the inner aspect of the chest wall and the outer aspect of the lung of less than 10 mm on decubitus films, is probably not clinically significant, may be difficult to obtain by thoracocentesis, and should not be sampled.

After it is ascertained by radiographic evaluation that there is a significant free-flowing or loculated effusion, a sample of fluid should be obtained by an experienced operator, with ultrasound guidance as indicated.

A diagnostic thoracocentesis requires removal of at least 50 mL of fluid. The gross appearance of the fluid should be noted: purulent material suggests a complicated parapneumonic effusion; a white, milky appearance suggests chylothorax or pseudochylothorax; and grossly bloody fluid may raise concerns about a hemothorax. The next step is the analysis of the fluid, with a concomitant serum sample, for protein and lactate dehydrogenase (LDH) levels, to determine if the fluid is a transudate or exudate. The most universally accepted criteria to aid in this distinction is the pleural fluid-to-serum LDH and pleural fluid-to-serum protein ratios. If the LDH ratio is greater than 0.6 or the protein ratio is greater than 0.5, the fluid is characterized as an exudate. If neither of these criteria is met, the fluid is considered a transudate. A third criterion for diagnosing an exudate is a pleural fluid LDH value greater than two-thirds the upper limit of the normal serum LDH value, or an absolute level greater than 200 IU/L. This criterion has been generally reported as somewhat less reliable than the pleural fluid-to-serum ratios. Normal values for LDH vary between laboratories and elevated serum levels in some disease states may cause a parallel increase in the pleural value unrelated to a primary pleural abnormality.

If a transudate is present, no further analysis of the fluid is generally required and clinical evaluation should be focused on the diagnosis and treatment of the underlying disease process. If an exudate is present, additional testing of the fluid should be performed and includes pH, glucose, and cell count with differential. As the majority of exudative effusions are infectious or malignant in etiology, appropriate stains with cultures and cytologic examination are generally indicated (Figure 13–6–1). Additional fluid analysis may be helpful in characterizing exudative effusions of unclear etiology (Table 13–6–3). These tests should not be routinely requested but should be considered in select cases. Percutaneous (closed) pleural biopsy may be helpful in cases where malignancy or tuberculosis is suspected (discussed in Chapter 13–7) and is generally indicated in an undiagnosed exudative effusion.

Despite extensive evaluation, the etiology of an exudative effusion remains obscure in up to 20% of cases, many of which resolve spontaneously without sequelae. In patients with an undiagnosed exudative effusion, the need for additional evaluation should be guided by the clinical course and suspected disease. If symptoms are minimal and improve with time, a less aggressive approach may be indicated. In cases where the need for a diagnosis is felt to justify the risks of the procedure, video-assisted thoracoscopic pleural biopsy or traditional open lung pleural biopsy via thoracotomy may be considered. Fiberoptic bronchoscopy may be useful in cases where lung parenchymal abnormalities exist. If the etiology of the effusion remains elusive, evaluation for pulmonary embolism should be considered.

Therapeutic

Treatment should be directed to the underlying disease process as established by the diagnostic evaluation. Pain relief is generally indicated unless there is a specific contraindication. Oxygen supplementation should be given if hypoxemia is demonstrated. If a large effusion is present, a therapeutic thoracocentesis can be performed at the initial tap. This would generally decrease dyspnea. Chest tube drainage may be required for complicated parapneumonic effusions (see Chapter 13–5), malignancy effusions (see Chapter 13–7), or trauma (hemothorax).

FOLLOW-UP

Once an etiology is established, additional diagnostic evaluation of the pleural effusion is generally not required. Two notable exceptions include (1) a new clinical suspicion of infection in the pleural space and (2) follow-up of the progression of an evolving complicated parapneumonic effusion.

Appropriate clinical follow-up is determined by the underlying disease process causing the effusion. In general, chest radiographs should be followed until complete resolution is documented unless the underlying condition is chronic and unremitting.

DISCUSSION

Prevalence and Incidence

Information regarding the prevalence and incidence of pleural effusions is not readily available. In general, reporting is limited to the frequency of this finding occurring in association with a given disease, with the true prevalence of effusion determined by the prevalence of the primary process. Estimates of the occurrence of pleural effusions are variable and range from 5 to 50% based on the disease category.

Related Basic Science

Normally there is a thin layer of fluid between the visceral and parietal pleura, an ultrafiltrate of the serum with similar chemical composition but a lower protein level. The movement of fluid across the pleural membrane is believed to be governed by Starling's law of transcapillary fluid exchange:

$$Q_f = K_f[(P_{cap} - P_{pl}) - \sigma(\pi_{cap} - \pi_{pl})]$$

where Q_f = net liquid flow, K_f = filtration coefficient, P = hydrostatic pressures, σ = colloid reflection coefficient, and π = oncotic pressures. The hydrostatic pressure from the parietal and visceral pleura favors the movement of fluid into the pleural space based on the usual negative intrathoracic pressure and positive capillary blood vessel pressure. Oncotic pressure in the pleural space is lower than capillary blood oncotic pressure, favoring removal of fluid from the pleural space. As hydrostatic pressures are somewhat higher than the opposing oncotic pressures,

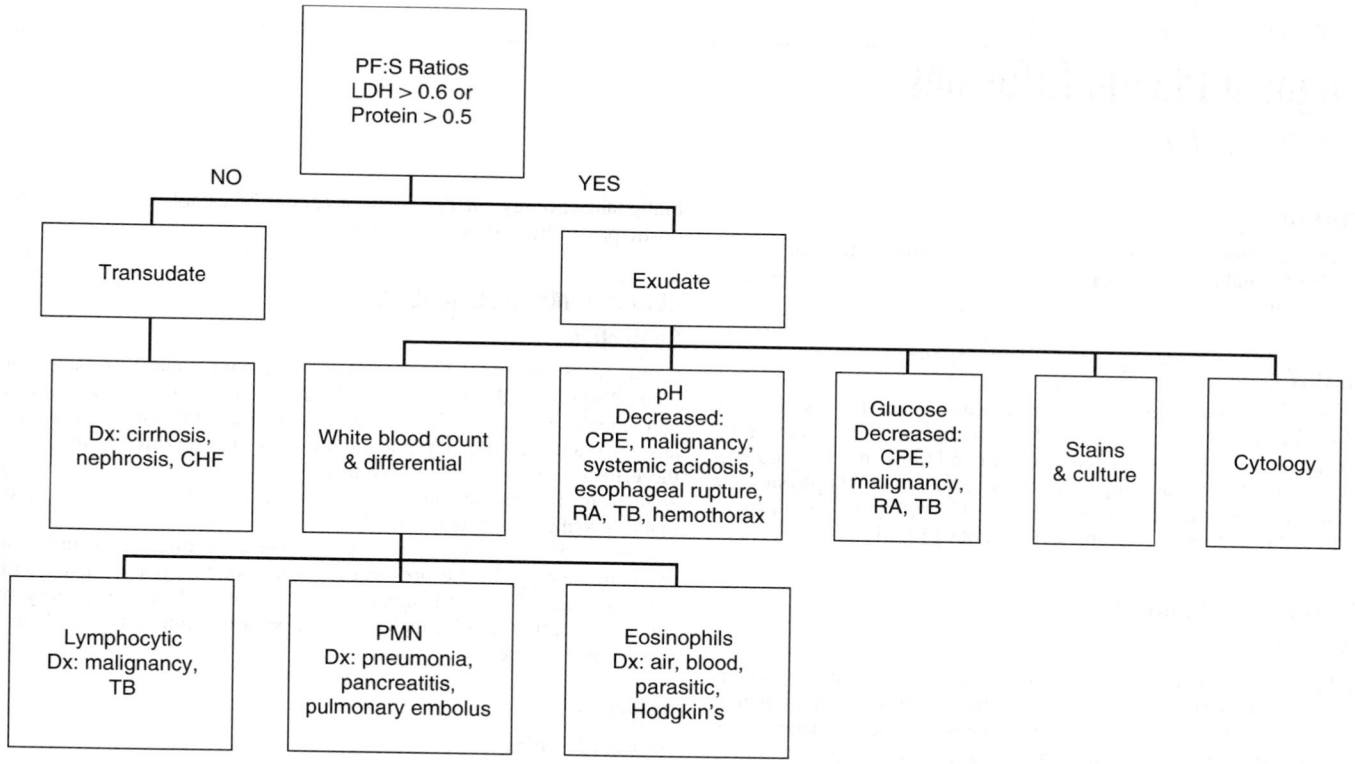

Figure 13–6–1. Diagnostic evaluation. PF:S, pleural fluid: serum; LDH, lactate dehydrogenase; Dx, diagnoses to consider; CPE, complicated parapneumonic effusion; RA, rheumatoid arthritis; TB, tuberculosis; PMN, polymorphonuclear cells.

there is a net movement of fluid into the pleural space. Fluid normally does not accumulate because the rate of removal through parietal pleura stomas and lymphatics can easily accommodate the low volume that is formed.

Pleural fluid and protein exchange can increase substantially in pathologic conditions. A pleural effusion develops when the formation of fluid exceeds the removal capacity. Any alteration in the Starling equation favoring pleural fluid movement into the pleural space in excess of its removal causes fluid to accumulate. The preexisting hydrostatic and oncotic pressure gradients are altered, affecting the ongoing formation and removal of fluid. This dynamic process contributes to fluid accumulation until a new equilibrium point is reached where fluid removal is equal to amount formed.

Natural History and Its Modification with Treatment

The natural history of the pleural effusion depends for the most part on the underlying etiology. In some clinical conditions the pleural effusion is self-limiting and may resolve even in the absence of any treatment (e.g., tuberculous pleuritis, pulmonary embolism, viral infections). In other situations one would expect clinical deterioration and possibly

TABLE 13–6–3. ADDITIONAL DIAGNOSTIC EVALUATION

Test	Clinical Evaluation
Amylase	Esophageal perforation, pancreatitis, malignancy
Immunologic studies	Collagen–vascular diseases
Antinuclear antibody, complement, rheumatoid factor, LE cells	
Hematocrit	Hemothorax
Lipid studies	Chylothorax, pseudochylothorax
Triglycerides, chylomicrons, cholesterol crystals	

even death in the absence of definitive therapy, whereas full recovery can generally be expected with appropriate treatment (e.g., pneumonia and empyema, renal failure, congestive heart failure). Some conditions may follow a chronic, remitting course such as renal failure, congestive heart failure, and lupus. In general, the final outcome is determined by the underlying disease process.

Prevention

There is no primary prevention aimed toward the pleural effusion per se. Direct treatment of the pleural space to prevent reaccumulation of fluid after the initial presentation is not generally indicated in benign pleural effusions. Therapy should be directed to treatment and control of the underlying disease process. Prevention may be appropriate for some diseases associated with pleural effusion, such as isoniazid prophylaxis for tuberculosis, pneumococcal vaccination for bacterial pneumonia, and smoking cessation for modification of lung cancer risk.

Cost Containment

Cost containment can be exercised both in limitation of the diagnostic evaluation and in treatment. The most cost-effective approach in evaluating a patient with a high likelihood of a transudative effusion would be to order only LDH and protein analysis; however, adequate fluid should be removed from the patient at the initial thoracocentesis to fully evaluate the underlying process if an exudative effusion is found. Treatment is directed primarily to the underlying process and the most cost-effective regimen should be used. Direct treatment of the effusion may occasionally be required in specific conditions and is discussed elsewhere (see Chapters 13–5 and 13–7).

REFERENCES

Light R. Pleural diseases. 2nd ed. Philadelphia: Lea & Febiger, 1990.
Murray JF. The normal lung. 2nd ed. Philadelphia: Saunders, 1986.
Sahn SA. The pleura. Am Rev Respir Dis 1988;138:184.
Sokolowski JW (Chair, ATS Practice Committee). Guidelines for thoracocentesis and needle biopsy of the pleura. Am Rev Respir Dir 1989;140:257.

Malignant Pleural Effusions

Linda S. Efferen, M.D.

DEFINITION

A malignant pleural effusion is a collection of fluid within the pleural cavity due to, and containing cytologic or pathologic evidence of, a tumorous origin.

ETIOLOGY

In patients with underlying malignant disease, pleural effusions may develop secondary to direct pleural or mediastinal involvement by tumor; however, other associated clinical conditions may also be present and lead to the development of an effusion. Pathophysiologic mechanisms contributing to the development of effusions, with associated clinical correlates, are delineated in Table 13–7–1.

CRITERIA FOR DIAGNOSIS
Suggestive

A malignant pleural effusion should be suspected in any individual with a known malignancy, or risk factors for developing a malignancy, who presents with signs or symptoms consistent with a pleural effusion. Risk factors for malignancy include a history of cigarette smoking, asbestos or other occupational exposure, or a family history of cancer. As with benign effusions, malignant effusions are generally a manifestation of the underlying condition, and symptoms related to the primary tumor may predominate the clinical picture.

Radiographic abnormalities suggestive of fluid from any etiology are discussed in Chapter 13–6. Massive pleural effusions are more likely to be due to a malignant process. The presence of mediastinal shift due to large volume effusions, an underlying pulmonary parenchymal mass, mediastinal lymphadenopathy, or osteolytic or blastic bone lesions increases the likelihood of a malignant etiology.

A malignant etiology should always be considered when an exudative effusion is present; malignancy is the second most common cause of exudative effusions. A hemorrhagic appearance with a predominance of mononuclear cells should increase the suspicion for a malignant etiology.

Definitive

The method for establishing the presence of an effusion is discussed in Chapter 13–6. The identification of malignant cells in the pleural fluid or on the pleural surface is required to confirm a malignant etiology for the effusion. This is most commonly accomplished by pleural fluid analysis or closed pleural biopsy. Identification of a primary tumor is presumptive evidence of a malignant effusion but is not diagnostic. If a

malignant etiology for the effusion cannot be established, other diagnostic possibilities should be considered.

CLINICAL MANIFESTATIONS
Subjective

Common symptoms associated with malignant pleural effusions include dyspnea, dull aching chest pain, sensation of fullness in the chest, and cough. Systemic complaints may include fatigue, weight loss, anorexia, and malaise. Dyspnea and cough may be directly related to the effusion, may be secondary to parenchymal involvement, or may arise from preexisting lung disease. Some patients may be asymptomatic or symptoms may reflect the primary tumor site.

Past history regarding previous diagnoses, treatment with radiation or chemotherapy, or the presence of other conditions associated with nonmalignant pleural effusions may be helpful. A family history of cancer may provide information for risk stratification and possible primary tumor source.

Objective
Physical Examination

The physical examination of the chest is described in detail in Chapter 13–6. In addition, massive effusions may cause deviation of the trachea to the contralateral side. The general physical examination should attempt to assess the extent of disease by identifying areas of metastatic tumor involvement or the primary site. This information would be useful for prognosis as well as diagnostic purposes. Extrathoracic lymph nodes, especially in the supraclavicular area, may provide a readily accessible biopsy site if present. Organ systems that may be the primary source of the malignant process should be carefully evaluated including the rectum with stool guaiacs, pelvis and breasts, and thyroid.

Routine Laboratory Abnormalities

Abnormalities on routine laboratory examination may be present and suggestive of a malignant process or may implicate other organ system involvement, but would not be useful in specifically diagnosing a malignant etiology for the pleural effusion.

PLANS
Diagnostic
Differential Diagnosis

Pleural-based masses or pleural thickening may appear similar to pleural effusions. Radiographic evaluation with ultrasound or computed tomography scan generally serves to differentiate these processes.

The presence of a pleural effusion carries a broad differential as discussed in Chapter 13–6. In the presence of an exudative, predominantly mononuclear cell effusion, tuberculosis and malignancy are the two most likely diagnoses; however, contributing or alternative etiologies must be considered if clinically indicated, including parapneumonic effusion secondary to a postobstructive pneumonia, pulmonary embolism, radiation injury, and other benign pleural effusions.

The large majority of documented malignant pleural effusions are due to carcinoma of the lung and breast or lymphoma. Metastatic ovarian or gastrointestinal cancers represent a small percentage of the total number of malignant etiologies. Other metastatic malignancies combined make up less than 5% of all diagnosed etiologies. Primary pleural tumors such as mesothelioma and some sarcomas are rare causes of malignant pleural effusions. The etiology remains obscure despite extensive evaluation in approximately 5% of cases.

13–7–1. MALIGNANT DISEASE AND PLEURAL EFFUSIONS (PATHOPHYSIOLOGY : CLINICAL CORRELATE)

Pleural involvement
  Increased permeability :: pleural metastases
  Decreased clearance :: obstruction of parietal stomas
  Decreased intrapleural pressure :: bronchial obstruction with atelectasis
Mediastinal involvement
  Increased capillary hydrostatic pressure :: pericardial involvement
  Decreased clearance :: thoracic duct obstruction
  Decreased clearance :: lymphatic vessel compression from mediastinal lymph node
Other causes
  Malnutrition
  Pulmonary embolism
  Radiation pneumonitis
  Parapneumonic effusion secondary to postobstructive pneumonia

Diagnostic Options

Diagnostic strategies vary somewhat based on local practice and the perceived pretest likelihood of malignancy versus tuberculosis. The initial evaluation establishing the effusion as an exudate is universally supported. The role of pleural biopsy in the evaluation of an undiagnosed exudative effusion is well established, though timing is somewhat arbitrary. Some experts suggest closed pleural biopsy should be performed at the time of the initial thoracocentesis if tuberculosis is considered to be the most likely diagnosis, versus delaying pleural biopsy until three separate samples for cytology are negative when a malignant etiology is suspected. Similarly, the utility of pleural fluid glucose and pH is viewed differently, with some authors recommending routine measurement in all exudative effusions versus measuring these parameters only when evaluating a presumed complicated parapneumonic effusion.

Recommended Approach

There are two related goals in the diagnostic evaluation of a suspected malignant pleural effusion: (1) confirming the etiology of the effusion as malignant and (2) identifying the source of the malignancy.

The general approach and principles of diagnosing a pleural effusion are discussed in Chapter 13–6. If the initial fluid evaluation is nondiagnostic and there is a high clinical suspicion of malignancy, a repeat thoracocentesis for cytology should be considered and a large volume of fluid sent for cytologic evaluation if possible. The overall yield for pleural fluid cytology is estimated to be 60% with a single sample, increasing up to 90% if three separate specimens are submitted. If the diagnosis remains unclear after a second trap, percutaneous (closed) pleural biopsy should be performed. In general, pleural biopsy is less likely to be diagnostic in malignant effusions than pleural fluid cytology, with an approximate yield of 40%. It can, however, be positive in some cases where fluid cytology is negative, thus increasing the overall diagnostic yield. Conversely, if the diagnosis of tuberculosis is considered most likely, pleural biopsy should be considered after the first nondiagnostic thoracocentesis. Pleural biopsy is diagnostic in 50 to 80% on pathologic examination, with the diagnostic yield increasing to more than 90% with culture.

If the etiology for the effusion remains elusive, video-assisted thoracoscopic pleural biopsy or traditional open lung pleural biopsy via thoracotomy may be indicated. Empiric antituberculous therapy may be considered in the appropriate clinical setting.

In addition to diagnosing the effusion as malignant, identification of the primary tumor is indicated to direct therapy. The presence of malignant cells in the pleural space generally indicates disseminated disease. Identification of malignancies with some response to chemotherapy or radiation therapy may allow control of the pleural effusion and primary tumor. It is important to remember that a patient with bronchogenic cancer in whom a malignant etiology for the effusion cannot be established may be an operative candidate.

Appropriate screening to rule out "treatable" malignancies (i.e., lymphoma, small cell lung cancer, breast and prostate cancer) in patients with malignant effusions and an unknown primary is reasonable. In general, patients should have a computed tomography scan of the chest and abdomen. If abnormalities are noted, then further investigation may be indicated. If symptoms referable to a specific organ system exist, then that system should be investigated. In women, mammography and pelvic examination are warranted.

Therapeutic

When possible, treatment should be directed to the underlying malignancy. If the malignancy is likely to respond to radiation or chemotherapy, then these modalities should be used. If the underlying malignancy is not treatable, or is not responding, then primary treatment of the pleural effusion may be necessary.

Prior to initiating direct intervention or treatment of the effusion, the patient's status should be assessed. If the patient is moribund and terminally ill, comfort care alone would be the most logical course of treatment. If the patient has a reasonable life expectancy and the effusion is contributing to the morbidity of the patient, then primary treatment of the effusion may be indicated. Two issues should be addressed: First,

will removal of fluid decrease or alleviate the patient's symptoms? If the patient is asymptomatic or if dyspnea is due to a process other than the effusion, then intervention may not be warranted. In addition to the effusion patients may have underlying heart or lung disease, anemia, marasmus, or pulmonary parenchymal involvement causing the respiratory symptoms, which would not be relieved with aggressive treatment of the effusion. If no reasonable symptom relief is likely, then invasive management of the pleural effusion is not indicated. Second, will the underlying lung be able to reexpand after drainage of the pleural space? If there is any suspicion that an endobronchial lesion or other parenchymal disease may preclude full reexpansion of the underlying lung, chest tube drainage should not be initiated. If the mediastinum is shifted to the side with the effusion, this suggests that the underlying lung is collapsed and may not be able to reexpand. Fiberoptic bronchoscopy to rule out endobronchial obstruction and therapeutic thoracocentesis to evaluate the underlying lung's ability to reexpand may be intermediate measures.

If the patient's symptoms are improved with therapeutic thoracocentesis and the underlying lung reexpands, chest tube drainage and pleurodesis can be considered. If a massive pleural effusion is present, evacuation of the pleural space should be performed at intervals to decrease the likelihood of reexpansion pulmonary edema. Duration of chest tube drainage should be minimized and pleurodesis should be attempted as soon as the lung has fully reexpanded.

Pleurodesis involves creating an intensive inflammatory reaction that can be very painful. Local anesthesia with intrapleural lidocaine at a suggested dose of up to 4 mg/kg is recommended. After the lidocaine is injected through the chest tube, the tube is clamped and the patient is positioned to ensure that the entire parietal pleura is anesthetized. After the anesthetic agent is drained, the sclerosing agent of choice is injected into the pleural space, the chest tube is clamped, and the patient is again positioned to ensure that the entire pleural surface is affected. Systemic analgesia should be employed as needed. Morphine sulfate or meperidine (Demerol) can be used, with titration of dose based on patient need. After 2 hours, the chest tube is unclamped and put back to negative pressure. It is removed after 24 hours or when drainage has decreased to less than 150 mL/d.

The success of pleurodesis is variable and depends to some extent on the sclerosing agent employed. Talc appears to be the most effective agent, but is technically more difficult to use. Doxycycline and minocycline have replaced tetracycline and are reasonably effective. Bleomycin and other agents are possible alternatives but are not widely or routinely recommended. Other factors affecting the success rate of pleurodesis are the pleural fluid glucose level and pH. A pleural fluid glucose level less than 60 mg/dL or a pH less than 7.3 is associated with a success rate of approximately 50%, as compared with an estimated 85% succeess rate with higher values. Pleuroperitoneal shunts or pleurectomy may be considered as alternative measures to control the pleural effusion in select cases failing to respond to pleurodesis.

FOLLOW-UP

Appropriate follow-up is determined by the primary malignancy, response to therapy, and expected course. Patients whose respiratory symptoms recur should be reevaluated for recurrence of effusion or other conditions. Patients undergoing radiation or chemotherapy treatment need routine follow-up to monitor for signs of toxicity and response to treatment. In patients who are receiving supportive care only, follow-up can be arranged as needed.

DISCUSSION

Prevalence and Incidence

The occurrence of malignant pleural effusions varies with the underlying site, cell type, and stage of disease. The incidence of this manifestation is dependent on the background incidence of malignant disease. More than 1 million new cancer cases are expected to be reported in 1994. Lung and breast cancer account for approximately one third of all new cancer cases expected. Approximately 15% of patients with lung cancer present with a malignant effusion and up to 50% develop one during the course of their disease. Breast cancer has an estimated incidence of malignant pleural effusions approaching 50% as well. The overall incidence of this manifestation of malignant disease is dependent on the background incidence of the various malignancies and the relative frequency of associated malignant effusions.

Related Basic Science

Physiologic or Metabolic Derangement

The pathophysiology leading to the development of pleural effusions is discussed in Chapter 13–6. The specific mechanisms operative in malignant effusions are delineated in Table 13–7–1. A low pH and glucose in the pleural fluid are felt to indicate a high tumor burden and have been found to be associated with a poorer prognosis and response to pleurodesis and a higher diagnostic yield for pleural fluid cytology and pleural biopsy.

Genetics and Altered Molecular Biology

There is an expanding pool of information on the genetic and molecular basis of malignancy. Cytogenetic abnormalities, chromosomal deletions, proto-oncogene amplification and expression, and various growth factors have been implicated in altering the expression of promoter and suppressor genes. It seems probable that the development of at least some malignancies results from a combination of inherited mutations, which are unmasked or promoted by environmental factors via activation of proto-oncogenes or inactivation of suppressor genes. Implications for diagnostic and treatment intervention await further investigation but hold the preliminary promise of a means to impact the course and prognosis of malignant disease, based on an improved understanding of the biological and molecular behavior of neoplastic cells.

Natural History and Its Modification with Treatment

In general, the presence of a malignant pleural effusion indicates disseminated disease in nonbronchogenic primaries and at least stage IIIB for primary lung cancer. This precludes surgery as curative therapy, and the utility of treatment with chemotherapy or radiation is determined by the underlying disease. Although some tumors may respond to radiation or chemotherapy, the overall prognosis is generally poor.

Prevention

Prevention is the treatment of choice. Prevention must be directed to those processes or agents that are known to increase the likelihood of malignancy such as cigarette smoking (both direct and second-hand smoke), exposure to asbestos, ionizing radiation, dietary factors, and genetic predisposition. Screening for some malignancies is useful and should be done in an effort to detect disease at an earlier, and potentially curable, stage. "Prevention" of the reaccumulation of an established malignant effusion is merely palliative.

Cost Containment

Cost containment can be exercised both in limitation of the diagnostic workup and in treatment. The most judicious approach in attempting to identify a primary tumor in an individual without an obvious source would be to exclude potentially responsive malignancies as previously discussed. Expeditious and appropriate management of the pleural effusion to limit hospital days is important.

REFERENCES

Birrer MJ, Minna JD. Molecular genetics of lung cancer. Semin Oncol 1988;15:226.

Light R. Peural diseases. 2nd ed. Philadelphia: Lea & Febiger, 1990.

Murphy GP. Cancer statistics 1994. CA Cancer J Clin 1994;44:7.

Murray JF, Nadel JA. Textbook of respiratory medicine. Philadelphia: Saunders, 1988.

Sokolowski JW (Chair, ATS Practice Committee). Guidelines for thoracocentesis and needle biopsy of the pleura. Am Rev Respir Dis 1989;140:257.

Walker-Renard PB, Vaughan LM, Sahn SA. Chemical pleurodesis for malignant pleural effusions. Ann Intern Med 1994;120:56.

CHAPTER 13–8

Pneumothorax

Pratibha Kaul, M.D.

DEFINITION

Pneumothorax is the collection of air in the pleural space as a result of disruption of the parietal or the visceral pleura.

ETIOLOGY

Pneumothorax can be spontaneous without any antecedent trauma or can be traumatic secondary to either a penetrating or a nonpenetrating trauma. Most often the air enters the space from the lung, but sometimes may be introduced from the outside. A classification of pneumothorax by etiology is depicted in Table 13–8–1. The cause of primary spontaneous pneumothorax is most often rupture of a bleb or cyst on the upper lobe near the apex, and is frequently seen in tall and thin patients. Blebs may be congenital, but are more likely acquired as a result of local bronchial inflammation or disturbed collateral ventilation. Secondary spontaneous pneumothorax is associated with formation of subpleural cystic spaces related to diffuse interstitial fibrosis or emphysema. Rupture of one of these is likely the immediate cause of pneumothorax. Catamenial pneumothorax occurs in women between the ages of 30 and 36 during menstrual periods, and can be recurrent. Of all cases of pneumothorax, trauma is the most common. Patients receiving volume cycled mechanical ventilation and positive end-expiratory pressure (PEEP) are at increased risk. High inspiratory peak pressure in patients with severely obstructed airways or noncompliant lungs can cause alveolar rupture and pneumothorax.

CRITERIA FOR DIAGNOSIS

Suggestive

Chest pain, which may be pleuritic, and dyspnea, either alone or together with pleuritic chest pain, suggest the diagnosis.

Definitive

Definitive diagnosis is established on chest radiograph by demonstrating a visceral pleural line displaced away from the chest wall.

CLINICAL MANIFESTATIONS

Subjective

In primary spontaneous pneumothorax, the symptoms usually begin at rest. Ipsilateral pleuritic chest pain which may later become dull and persistent, dyspnea, and cough are predominant symptoms. Symptoms usually resolve within 24 hours, even without therapy. Secondary spontaneous pneumothorax presents with more severe symptoms like dyspnea (100%) and chest pain (74%). The symptoms generally do not abate until treated.

Objective

Physical Examination

Sinus tachycardia is a common finding. On chest examination, the side with the pneumothorax moves less with respiration. In large pneumo-

13–8–1. CLASSIFICATION OF PNEUMOTHORAX BASED ON ETIOLOGY

I. *Spontaneous*
  A. Primary
  B. Secondary
    1. Airway disease
      a. Chronic obstructive pulmonary disease
      b. Asthma
      c. Cystic fibrosis
    2. Infections
      a. Necrotizing pneumonia: *Staphylococcus, Klebsiella,* anaerobes
      b. *Mycobacterium tuberculosis,* atypical mycobacteria
      c. *Pneumocystis carinii* pneumonia
      d. Nocardiosis
      e. Hydatid disease
      f. Subphrenic abscess
    3. Interstitial lung disease
      a. Sarcoidosis
      b. Scleroderma
      c. Pulmonary alveolar proteinosis
      d. Occupational lung diseases
      e. Tuberous sclerosis
      f. HIstiocytosis X
      g. Idiopathic pulmonary fibrosis
    4. Miscellaneous
      a. Catamenial
      b. Lymphangioleiomyomatosis
      c. Xanthomatosis
      d. Biliary cirrhosis
      e. Marfan's syndrome
      f. Berylliosis
      g. Pulmonary infarction
      h. Wegener's granulomatosis
II. *Traumatic Pneumothorax*
  A. Iatrogenic
    1. Central vein line insertion
    2. Mechanical ventilation with or without positive end-expiratory pressure
    3. During cardiopulmonary resuscitation
    4. Pulmonary procedures
      a. Thoracentesis, pleural biopsy
      b. Transbronchial biopsy
      c. Transthoracic needle aspiration
  B. Noniatrogenic
    1. Gunshot wounds and stab wounds
    2. Blunt trauma

Adapted from Conrad S. Pneumothorax and chest wall trauma. In: Pulmonary and critical care medicine. St. Louis: Mosby-Year Book, 1994:Ch. 3, P. O, p. 1. Reproduced with permission of the publisher and author.

thoraces the trachea may be shifted to the opposite side. Tactile fremitus is absent, the percussion is hyperresonant, and breath sounds are absent on the affected side. Hamman's sign (crunching or clicking sound synchronous with the heartbeat) may be associated with left-sided pneumothorax, whereas the liver may be pushed down with right-sided pneumothorax. Horner's syndrome may occur because of traction on sympathetic ganglion by the shifting of the mediastinum. The physical findings are subtle in secondary spontaneous pneumothorax because of underlying hyperexpansion of lungs secondary to emphysema. Tension pneumothorax may present with hypotension, cyanosis, or electromechanical dissociation.

Routine Laboratory Abnormalities

The electrocardiogram may reveal rightward shift of the QRS axis, a diminution of precordial R voltage, a decrease in QRS amplitude, and inversion of precordial T waves. Electrical alternans has been reported in patients with left-sided spontaneous pneumothorax. Arterial blood gas analysis reveals mild hypoxia, hypocarbia, and an increased alveolar–arterial oxygen gradient. The chest radiograph reveals a space of air density devoid of lung markings between the lung and the chest wall. Widening of intercostal spaces and tracheal shift may be seen in very large or tension pneumothoraces. In 25% of all cases there is evidence

of fluid in the pleural space. The fluid is usually eosinophilic. Estimation of size of pneumothorax can be done from a chest radiograph, as shown in Figure 13–8–1.

PLANS
Diagnostic
Differential Diagnosis

In view of the symptomatology of chest pain and dyspnea, pneumothorax must be distinguished from pulmonary thromboembolism, myocardial infarction, aortic dissection, esophageal rupture, and perforated peptic ulcer. On radiographic evaluation, blebs and bullae must be differentiated from pneumothorax. As opposed to pneumothorax, the inner margins of cysts and bullae are concave in relation to the chest wall and do not conform to the contour of the costophrenic sulcus.

Diagnostic Options

In a young, tall and thin male, the diagnosis is usually suggested by clinical history and physical examination. The diagnosis is established by good-quality posteroanterior chest radiographs, especially in expiration, as the lung is decreased in size and the air occupies a larger space in the hemithorax. A lateral decubitus film with the affected side superior can be helpful. In supine position, gas is detected in the ventral portions of the thorax and at the lung bases. Subpulmonic pneumothoraces occur more often on the left side and are manifested by basilar hyperlucency extending deep into the costophrenic sulcus, depression of hemidiaphragm, and visualization of an unusually distinct cardiac apex. Erect or decubitus views should be obtained to confirm the presence of a pneumothorax in such cases. A computed tomography scan of the chest may be necessary to detect pneumothorax in some patients. Air–fluid level may be seen in 25% of cases secondary to pleural effusion. If the fluid accumulates rapidly, a hemopneumothorax or rupture of the esophagus into the pleural space should be suspected. In the latter case, the pH of the fluid is acidic and has high salivary amylase level.

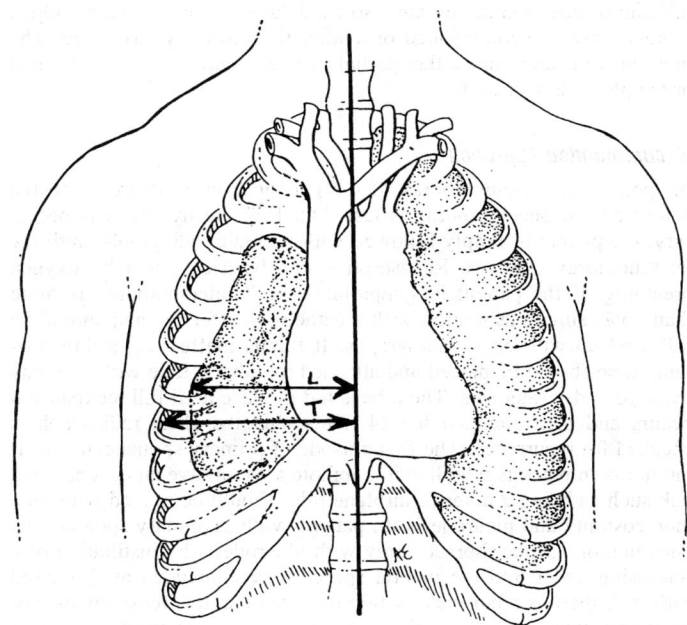

Figure 13–8–1. Measurements used to calculate percentage of pneumothorax, where *L* is the average diameter of the lung and *T* is the average diameter of the hemithorax on the side of the pneumothorax.

$$\% \text{ Pneumothorax} = 100 - L^3/T^3$$

Recommended Approach

Once pneumothorax is suspected, it is confirmed by a chest radiograph obtained at end expiration. Sometimes a computed tomography scan of chest may be required to differentiate pneumothorax from big bullae.

Therapeutic

The goals for therapy are to remove air from the pleural space and to decrease the likelihood of recurrence.

Therapeutic Options

Small spontaneous pneumothorax (< 15%) in an asymptomatic patient can be followed expectantly with serial chest radiographs until resolution. Air in the pleural space is reabsorbed gradually at a rate of 1.25% of hemithorax in 24 hours. Patients with secondary spontaneous pneumothorax have underlying lung disease and are generally symptomatic; thus observation is unlikely to be an option. The administration of supplemental oxygen accelerates the rate of pleural air absorption by at least four times. Continuous oxygen increases the nitrogen gradient between the alveolar and pleural air and enhances absorption of air in the pleural space. The initial treatment for most patients with primary spontaneous pneumothorax greater than 15% of the volume of the hemithorax should be simple aspiration with a small 16-gauge needle. Aspiration is successful in approximately 70% of primary spontaneous pneumothorax and 31% of secondary spontaneous pneumothorax. Tube thoracostomy is indicated for patients with primary spontaneous pneumothorax who have severe dyspnea or chest pain, for patients who have failed catheter aspiration, and for patients with secondary spontaneous pneumothorax greater than 15% of the hemithorax volume. Intrapleural administration of a chemical (chemical pleurodesis) produces adherence of visceral and parietal pleura by intense inflammatory reaction and obliterates the space. It should be reserved for recurrent spontaneous pneumothorax; however, if a chest tube is used for initial therapy, pleurodesis should be considered. Many different agents including quinacrine, talc, tetracycline, bleomycin, doxycycline, and minocycline are used as sclerosing agents. Video-assisted thoracoscopy should be considered in patients whose lungs have not expanded after 7 days, those who have persistent bronchopleural fistula after 7 days, and those who have recurrent pneumothorax after chemical pleurodesis. In addition patients who have an occupation or an avocation such as airplane piloting or deep sea diving are also candidates for thoracoscopy. Open thoracotomy is recommended only after thoracoscopy has failed. The blebs are oversewn, and either partial parietal pleurectomy is performed or the pleura is scarified.

Recommended Approach

In spontaneous pneumothorax, if the patient is in no distress and the percentage of pneumothorax is less than 15%, no treatment is necessary; the patient is simply followed with periodic radiographs until the pneumothorax resolves. Reabsorption can be accelerated by oxygen breathing. If the patient is symptomatic or if pneumothorax is more than 15%, simple aspiration with a catheter is effective and should be followed up with chest radiographs. If this is ineffective, a thoracostomy tube should be placed and attached to either a tube with one-way valve or underwater seal. The tube is left in place until full reexpansion occurs and then clamped for 24 hours, and the chest radiograph is checked for recurrence. The first episode of primary spontaneous pneumothorax in patients who live in a remote area or have an occupational risk such as being a diver or airplane pilot should be treated with tube thoracostomy and pleurodesis. In patients with secondary spontaneous pneumothorax, tube thoracostomy with pleurodesis by instillation of a sclerosing agent into the pleural space is recommended as discussed earlier. If there is recurrence or failure to resolve, thoracoscopy or thoracotomy with ablation of blebs, pleurectomy, or pleurodesis can be done. The diagnosis of tension pneumothorax should be made from physical examination and one should not wait to confirm it with a chest radiograph. A large-bore angiocath inserted into the pleural space is lifesaving while awaiting chest tube placement. Narcotics, particularly codeine, may be necessary for relief of chest pain. Oxygen therapy should be instituted in any patient admitted to the hospital with pneumothorax.

FOLLOW-UP

If pneumothorax is less than 15% and no active treatment is instituted, the patient should be followed up in 24 to 48 hours with a chest radiograph to watch for any increase in pneumothorax. Patients who have had a secondary spontaneous pneumothorax should be treated for their underlying condition, and if there is recurrence of pneumothorax, chemical or operative pleurodesis is indicated. Once sclerosing is done, the chest radiograph is repeated to look for any recurrence within 3 to 4 weeks and after that only if symptoms recur.

DISCUSSION

It is crucial to recognize a pneumothorax in a symptomatic patient to avoid further progression of the pneumothorax, which may result in a tension pneumothorax; however, severe deterioration in respiratory status can occur in patients with compromised lung function with a pneumothorax even in the absence of tension.

Prevalence and Incidence

The reported incidence of spontaneous pneumothorax is 7.4/100,000 for men and 1.2/100,000 for women. The incidence is probably higher than reported because many asymptomatic individuals never seek medical attention. The peak incidence is between the second and third decades, increases with age, and is more likely to occur in tall and thin individuals. The incidence is higher in fall and winter months. There is a strong positive relationship between the amount of tobacco exposure and the incidence of pneumothorax. Most primary spontaneous pneumothoraces are unilateral, but rarely, a simultaneous bilateral pneumothorax can occur. The incidence of traumatic pneumothorax varies with procedures and the type of trauma.

Related Basic Science

A familial incidence of spontaneous pneumothorax has been described and it appears to related to the presence of HLA haplotype $A_2 B_{40}$, and α1-antitrypsin phenotype M_1M_2.

Natural History and Its Modification with Treatment

A primary spontaneous pneumothorax is mainly a nuisance and is rarely life threatening to the patient. In a young individual, the bronchopleural fistula closes promptly and the pneumothorax resolves by itself. The risk of subsequent pneumothorax following an initial primary pneumothorax is substantial. Some reports have shown recurrence rates between 32 and 52% within 2 to 3 years. The majority of recurrences are on the ipsilateral side. The risk of recurrence rises with each subsequent pneumothorax and is not affected by treatment, with the exception of chemical or surgical pleurodesis. Most secondary spontaneous pneumothoraces require tube thoracostomy treatment for longer duration and, if untreated, may progress to tension pneumothorax. A tension pneumothorax develops when alveolar air continues to enter the pleural space through a break in the visceral or parietal pleura, which in this setting acts as a one-way valve, allowing air into but not out of the pleural space. The ipsilateral lung collapses completely and mediastinal shift occurs toward the contralateral side. Patients develop circulatory collapse because of impairment of venous return. The recurrence rate of secondary spontaneous pneumothorax is about 50%. In one study, the recurrence rate was 41% in patients treated with chest tubes without pleural sclerosis and was 25% in patients treated with intrapleural tetracycline.

Prevention

Use of proper technique in procedures that could result in pneumothorax can reduce the incidence of pneumothorax. The use of appropriate levels of positive end-expiratory pressure and smaller tidal volumes in patients on mechanical ventilation may prevent the occurrence of pneumothorax. Early sclerotherapy or surgical intervention in patients with secondary spontaneous pneumothorax would prevent recurrences.

Cost Containment

Asymptomatic patients with less than 15% primary spontaneous pneumothoraces do not require hospitalization and can be treated as outpatients. Video-assisted thoracoscopy is preferable to thoracotomy, as it is less invasive and avoids a prolonged hospital stay.

REFERENCES

Bense L, Eklund G, Wilman LG. Smoking and the increased risk of contracting spontaneous pneumothorax. Chest 1987;92:1009.

Conrad SA. Pneumothorax and chest wall trauma. In: Pulmonary and critical care medicine. St. Louis: Mosby-Year Book, 1994:Ch. 3, Pt. 0, 1.

Jantz MA, Pierson DJ. Pneumothorax and barotrauma. Clin Chest Med 1994;1:75.

Kirby TJ, Ginsberg RJ. Management of pneumothorax and barotrauma. Clin Chest Med 1992;13:97.

Light RW. Management of spontaneous pneumothorax. Am Rev Respir Dis 1993;148:245.

CHAPTER 13–9

Cough

Robert H. Poe, M.D.

DEFINITION

Cough is a normal housekeeping activity of the respiratory system that occurs at one time or another in all persons. Cough is defined by the dictionary as "a sudden noisy expulsion of air from the lungs usually produced to keep the airways of the lungs free of foreign matter." A cough that is effective in clearing secretions, debris, and/or foreign material from the lungs is termed productive. A cough that lasts more than 4 weeks is labeled as being persistent or chronic.

ETIOLOGY

Cough is associated with a variety of disorders and results from a reflex action (Figure 13–9–1). Stimulation of cough receptors in both the upper and lower respiratory tract produces cough. The impulse is conducted by afferent nerves to the cough center located in the medulla. The impulse, once integrated, is passed down the efferent nerves to effector organs (laryngeal, diaphragm, thoracic and abdominal muscles). It is not unusual for cough to occur when the mucociliary clearance mechanism of the lower respiratory tract becomes ineffective or is overwhelmed.

CRITERIA FOR DIAGNOSIS
Suggestive

In some patients with cough, it is acute and self-limiting and most commonly attributable to viral upper respiratory tract infection. Cough that persists is suggestive of underlying disease that may have clinical significance.

Definitive

A persistent cough can be a symptom of numerous diseases affecting a variety of anatomic locations. Hence, a troublesome cough lasting 4 weeks or longer usually warrants investigation. This may not apply to cigarette smokers who cough chronically but do not complain.

CLINICAL MANIFESTATIONS
Subjective

The medical history often suggests the cause of a cough. A morning cough due to an accumulation of secretions overnight, the need to continuously clear one's throat, and nasal discharge suggest postnasal drip. Symptoms of sinusitis including headache may accompany an upper respiratory cause for the cough. Cough that worsens on exposure to cold dry air, perfumes and scents, or smoke and is worse with exertion suggests variant asthma. A paroxysmal cough followed by wheezing or a brief period of dyspnea is typical of asthma. Atopy and/or a family history of asthma can also be elicited. Gastroesophageal reflux can cause cough, yet be clinically silent in early stages. Heartburn, restrosternal burning, a sour taste or regurgitation of food, dysphagia, and odynophagia are clues

encountered with disease progression. Cough due to gastroesophageal reflux is often nocturnal, intensified by lying down and made worse by weight gain. Hoarseness suggests aspiration. Cough seen after a viral upper or lower respiratory tract infection may persist for weeks to months often due to increased bronchial reactivity and has been termed *postinfectious syndrome*. Cough produced by irritants, of which cigarette smoke is the most common, is seen with chronic bronchitis. Environmental irritants, both at home and in the workplace, need to be considered. Cough due to chronic bronchitis is frequently productive. Drugs such as angiotensin-converting enzyme inhibitors may produce cough. Beta blockers including timolol eyedrops may worsen cough-variant asthma.

Sometimes, the character of cough suggests its anatomic origin. A loud and brassy cough suggests a tracheal or large airway source but is also seen with cardiac and mediastinal disease. A productive self-propagating "wet" cough suggests disease of the tracheobronchial tree. Cough associated with interstitial lung disease is usually nonproductive. A nonproductive cough that occurs at the same time every day and not at night suggests a psychogenic cause.

Objective
Physical Examination

A careful physical examination may also provide important clues to the cause of cough. Mucopurulent secretions in the oropharynx or prominent submucosal lymphoid follicles giving a cobblestone appearance to the posterior pharyngeal wall are typical of postnasal drainage. The nose should be examined for congestion or polyps and the ear canals for foreign bodies, hair, or cerumen, which can stimulate cough. Mild wheezing due to asthma may go unnoticed unless the patient is asked to perform a forced expiratory maneuver. At times, wheezing may be unilateral, implicating a possible foreign body or tumor in a large airway. Mediastinal node enlargement may produce wheezing by compression of a bronchus, and a tumor within the trachea may cause both cough and inspiratory stridor.

Early stages of congestive heart failure may escape detection in the absence of suspicion. Inspection of the fingers for clubbing and palpation of the cervical and supraclavicular areas for adenopathy are important with malignancy. The physician should always encourage patients to reproduce the cough and look at a specimen of sputum if produced.

Routine Laboratory Abnormalities

The chest radiograph is pivotal in the evaluation of persistent cough. It may reveal a carcinoma, foreign body (detected best by films taken in both inspiration and expiration), or interstitial lung disease.

PLANS
Diagnostic

An anatomic approach to the diagnosis of cough based on the anatomy of the cough reflex is now generally accepted. History and physical ex-

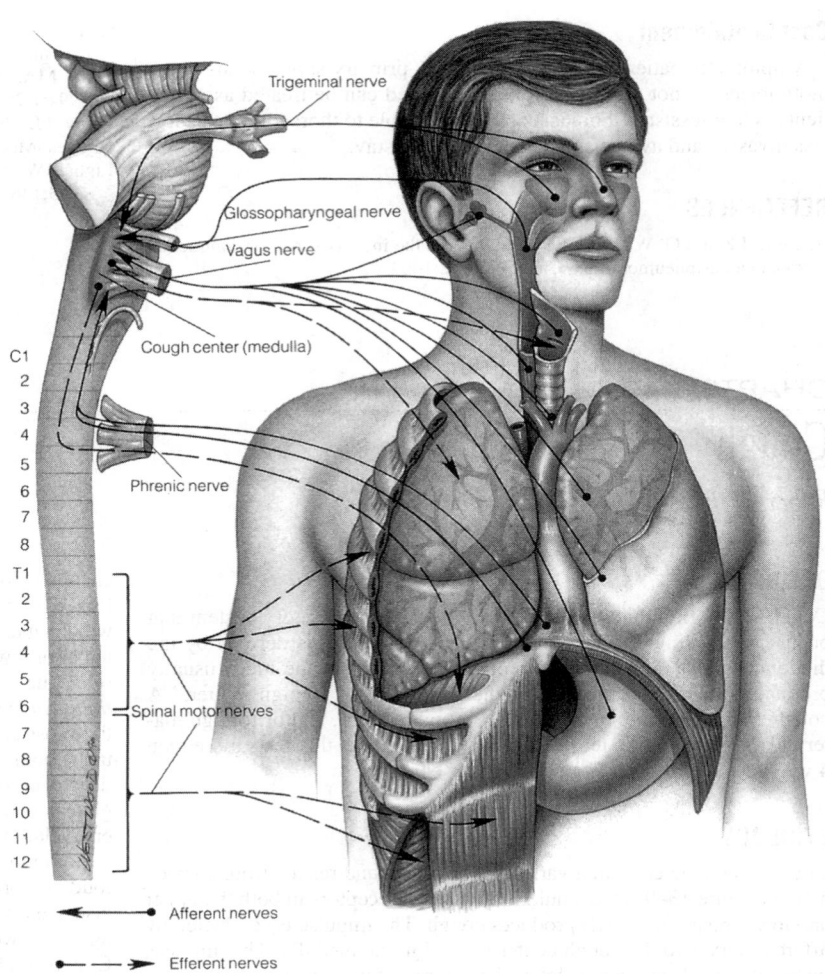

Figure 13–9–1. Anatomy of the cough reflex. (Source: Poe RH, Israel RH. Evaluating and managing that nagging chronic cough. J Respir Dis 1990;11:298. Reproduced with permission from the publisher and artist. © William G. Westwood.)

amination may provide sufficient clinical clues to allow initiation of therapy. Cough associated with acute respiratory illness and mild asthma is an example; however, a chest radiograph is required for the majority of patients. Although its diagnostic value as an isolated test is limited, it is essential to exclude an abnormality that would explain the cough before embarking on a more extensive search.

Differential Diagnosis

Ninety percent of patients with persistent cough and a normal chest radiograph have one of five causes for their cough (see Table 13–9–1). It is important to remember that there may be more than one etiology for cough. For example, postnasal drip and asthma may be active problems in a patient with an underlying allergic diathesis.

Diagnostic Options

Once it has been determined that the chest radiograph is normal, diagnostic options are individualized depending on helpful clinical clues. Although empiric therapy for the suspected cause can be considered, if asthma or gastroesophageal reflux is believed responsible, appropriate confirmatory studies should be obtained.

Spirometry may show reduced expiratory airflow in asthma. If spirometry is normal, asthma is not excluded and a methacholine challenge test is necessary to demonstrate airway hyperreactivity. Sinus radiographs or computed tomography scan may be abnormal in patients with postnasal drip. Upper gastrointestinal contrast studies may show a hiatal hernia or esophagoscopy esophagitis, but the test that best correlates cough with episodes of reflux is the 24-hour esophageal pH monitoring study. Patients with postinfectious cough may have elevated cold agglutinins or elevated serum antibodies to pertussis.

Recommended Approach

When the clinical evalution fails to suggest a lead, routine spirometry is recommended and if airflow is reduced, response to bronchodilator is elicited. At least a 15% improvement in the forced expired volume in 1 second (FEV_1) is necessary to diagnose asthma. If the result is normal, proceed with a methacholine challenge test. A 20% reduction in FEV_1 compared with baseline using a standard challenge protocol is a positive test. Other patients may require additional pulmonary function testing. A reduction in lung volumes with a reduced diffusing capacity suggests early interstitial lung disease at a time when the chest radiograph may still be normal.

If pulmonary function testing is normal, proceed to a 24-hour esophageal pH monitoring test. If gastroesophageal reflux is the cause of cough, this test is less expensive than endoscopy and correlates reflux events with cough. Although it is unusual for pathologic conditions involving the upper airway to be silent, sinus films and/or a thorough ear, nose, and throat evaluation should be considered next. The diagnostic yield for bronchoscopy is small when the chest radiograph is normal. It should be done to complete the sequential testing if no diagnosis has been found. The possibility of psychogenic cough should be considered as a diagnosis of exclusion.

Therapeutic

Therapeutic Options

Patients with postnasal drip are best treated with an antihistamine–decongestant combination. Many sustained-release preparations are available for twice-a-day dosing. Intranasal corticosteroids or cromolyn can be added, especially when signs of allergic rhinitis are present.

Patients with cough-variant asthma are treated just as patients with more flagrant symptoms. A β_2-selective sympathomimetic and an inhaled corticosteroid by metered-dose inhaler are an effective combina-

TABLE 13–9–1. CAUSES OF PERSISTENT COUGH IN PATIENTS WITH NORMAL CHEST RADIOGRAPHS

Causes	Prevalence*
Common	
Postnasal drip	28–41%
Asthma	24–33%
Postinfectious syndrome	11–17%
Gastroesophageal reflux	6–21%
Chronic bronchitis	5–12%
Less Common	**9–10%**
Bronchiectasis	
Occupational factors	
Early stage, interstitial lung disease	
Angiotensin-converting enzyme inhibitor therapy	
Hair or cerumen touching tympanic membrane	
Cardiac disease	
Hyperthyroidism	
Occult carcinoma	
Psychogenic disorders	

*Varies with series, with multiple causes existing in some patients.

tion. Patients with gastroesophageal reflux, when supine, need to avoid foods causing relaxation of the lower esophagel sphincter such as caffeine, nuts, and chocolate: to refrain from lying supine immediately after meals; and to elevate the head of their bed on blocks at night. Pharmacologic therapy consists of both an H_2 blocker and a prokinetic agent such as cisapride or metoclopramide.

Patients with a postinfectious syndrome may respond to a cough suppressant such as benzonatate or codeine. Although the cough eventually clears, a brief tapering 10-day to 2-week course of corticosteroid starting with 30 to 40 mg of prednisone in the morning may hasten healing of the process.

All smokers with cough should be regarded as having chronic bronchitis. Smoking cessation is critical in treating their cough. If sputum is purulent, an antibiotic is indicated. As *Hemophilus influenzae* infection is common in this population, the agent should be one that is effective against β-lactamase-producing strains. If there is evidence of airway obstruction, a bronchodilator and/or corticosteroid can be added.

The treatment of gastroesophageal reflux is discussed in Chapter 19–16.

Recommended Approach

Definitive treatment depends on an anatomic approach to first determine the cause of the cough. If a cause is discovered and specific therapy is rendered, the cough will disappear. Symptomatic therapy alone will fail whenever the cause of the cough is not self-limiting.

FOLLOW-UP

It is important to follow the patient to assess response to the specific therapy prescribed. Depending on the result, the diagnostic evaluation becomes progressively more sophisticated. Fortunately, a precise cause for the cough is usually found. It is important that therapy be sustained until the cough has resolved and the cause corrected. Whenever the cause is not determined, the patient should be followed for signs of organic disease.

DISCUSSION
Prevalence

Cough is one of the most common symptoms for which patients seek medical attention from a wide variety of generalists and specialists. Healthy people rarely cough. Transient cough is usually associated with viral upper respiratory tract infections. Chronic cough can be the result of cigarette, pipe, or cigar smoking. Persistent cough in the nonsmoker is usually related to postnasal drip, asthma, gastroesophageal reflux, or

residual irritation following an infection in either the upper or lower respiratory tract (postinfectious syndrome). The relative prevalence of persistent cough attributed to both common and less common causes is shown in Table 13–9–1.

Related Basic Science

The physician should have a thorough understanding of the pathophysiology of cough to effectively meet patient expectations of symptomatic relief.

Anatomic Derangement

The cough reflex is triggered by irritation of cough receptors (Figure 13–9–1). Some believe bronchoconstriction caused by irritation stimulates the cough receptor. Any disorder, inflammatory or structural, that affects the anatomy where cough receptors are located is capable of producing cough, which once started proceeds according to a fixed pattern. Phase 1 of cough is a deep inspiration. Phase 2 is the compression that results from muscle contraction against a closed glottis. Phase 3 is expiratory. It fulfills the main function of cough, the expulsion of material from the upper and lower respiratory tracts.

Physiologic or Metabolic Derangement

Pathologic conditions that lead to ineffective cough usually interfere with both the inspiratory and expiratory phases of cough. A variety of extrapulmonary neuromuscular and skeletal disorders may render cough ineffective. Pain, generalized weakness, and central nervous system depression can also reduce the effectiveness of cough. Any condition that reduces the expiratory flow including bronchospasm. endobronchial lesions, extrinsic compression by a mass, stricture, a small endotracheal tube, and secretions interferes with clearance of material from the tracheobronchial tree. Patients with emphysema, chronic bronchitis, or bronchiectasis have reduced expiratory airflow due to disproportionately greater dynamic compression of the trachea and large bronchi, resulting in a substantial resistance to flow in the smaller airways. The predominant effect here is on the expiratory phase of cough.

Natural History and Its Modification with Treatment

The natural history of cough depends on its cause, with resolution depending on treatment of any underlying disease. Acute cough, by definition, is self-limited. When inflammation caused by an infection clears, the cough is usually gone. When the precise cause of a persistent cough is discovered, specific therapy can be successful 90% or more of the time. Cough that is severe may produce syncope, trauma to the larynx and chest cage, pneumothorax, subcutaneous emphysema, incontinence, hernias, and a variety of other disorders. When the cause of a cough escapes detection and appears to serve no useful purpose, suppressive therapy may be required to minimize potential complications.

Prevention

Cough that serves the useful purpose of removing secretions from the tracheobronchial tree should not be suppressed. Mucolytics can facilitate expectoration and reduce the frequency of coughing episodes. The underlying cause of a cough, on the other hand, may be amenable to preventive measures. Smoking cessation will prevent many episodes of cough and related illness. Prevention of an occupational cause is appropriate for the workplace. When problems as chronic sinusitis and gastroesophageal reflux are responsible for cough and are not controlled by specific medical therapy, appropriate surgical procedures may be necessary to prevent recurring problems.

Cost Containment

When serious underlying disease is not present and clinical clues point to a cause, a trial of specific but empiric therapy may result in resolution of the cough without an expensive diagnostic workup. These patients have an otherwise normal examination and chest radiograph. For example, were cough believed secondary to postnasal drip, a trial of an antihistamine–decongestant with or without a nasal steroid might suffice and more extensive and expensive otolaryngologic evaluation would be avoided. If treatment of a patient with heartburn eliminates an accompanying cough, additonal investigation of reflux as its cause may be unnecessary. When there are no obvious clues as to cause, systematic implementation of a diagnostic protocol based on the relative prevalence of the more common causes of cough usually results in diagnosis. Implementation of effective therapy at any point would eliminate the need for additional investigation. Fortunately, bronchoscopy can usually be avoided and expensive studies such as computed tomography scanning of the thorax, which is rarely useful for diagnosing cough, need not be done. Patients under the age of 40 who smoke may need nothing more than to quit to experience resolution of their cough.

REFERENCES

Irwin RS, Corrao WM, Pratter MR. Chronic persistent cough in the adult: The spectrum and frequency of causes and successful outcome of specific therapy. Am Rev Respir Dis 1981;123:413.

Irwin RS, Curley JF, French CL. Chronic persistent cough: The spectrum and frequency of causes, key components of the diagnostic evaluation, and outcome of specific therapy. Am Rev Respir Dis 1990;141:640.

Poe RH, Harder RV, Israel RH, et al. Chronic persistent cough: Experience in diagnosis and outcome using an anatomic diagnostic protocol. Chest 1989;95:723.

Poe RH, Israel RH, Utell MJ, Hall WJ. Chronic cough: Bronchoscopy or pulmonary function testing? Am Rev Respir Dis 1982;126:160.

Pratter MR, Bartter T, Akers S, DuBois J. An algorithmic approach to chronic cough. Ann Intern Med 1993;119:977.

CHAPTER 13–10

Hemoptysis

Stuart M. Garay, M.D.

DEFINITION

Hemoptysis is the expectoration of blood. The term is not quantitative, as it includes the spectrum ranging from minimal blood-tinged mucus to grossly bloody sputum to ultimately cupfuls of blood. By definition, blood must originate from a source below the larynx.

ETIOLOGY

For centuries hemoptysis was considered pathognomonic for pulmonary tuberculosis. Hippocrates stated that "the spitting of pus follows the spitting of blood, consumption follows the spitting of this and death follows consumption." It is now recognized that there are numerous causes for hemoptysis, though worldwide tuberculosis remains the most common one. The ranking of etiologies depends on the patient population: medical versus surgical, inner city versus suburban community, inpatient versus outpatient. In the United States, the most common cause of minor or streaky hemoptysis is bronchitis. In addition, most series have found that the more common causes include bronchiectasis, lung carcinoma, tuberculosis, mycetoma (most often due to *Aspergillus* but also *Candida, Nocardia,* and *Allescheria*), bacterial pneumonia (*Streptococcus pneumoniae* as well as necrotizing infections due to *Staphylococcus, Kelbsiella, Pseudomonas,* and *Legionella*), lung abscess, pulmonary infarction, and bleeding diatheses. Depending on geography, primary fungal infections due to *Cryptococcus, Coccidioides, Histoplasma,* or *Blastomyces* may result in hemoptysis. Less frequent fungal infections include actinomycosis, geotrichosis, and allescheriasis. Although parasitic infestation does not commonly cause hemoptysis in the United States, *Paragonimus westermani* is the leading cause of hemoptysis in parts of Asia, Africa, and South America. Other parasitic infections resulting in hemoptysis include invasive strongyloidiasis, schistomiasis, echinococcosis, ascariasis, and ancylostomiasis. Occasionally, hemoptysis results from pulmonary arteriovenous malformations (congenital or acquired), bronchial adenoma, endobronchial foreign bodies, and alveolar hemorrhage syndromes secondary to Goodpasture's syndrome, Wegener's granulomatosis, and idiopathic hemosiderosis. Rare causes include an aortic aneurysm rupturing into a bronchus, pulmonary endometriosis, anomalous systemic vessels communicating with the pulmonary vascular system such as a pulmonary artery originating from the aorta, as well as anomalous pulmonary parenchymal conditions such as a cardiac bronchus (bronchial diverticulum) and an intralobar sequestration.

Although hemoptysis secondary to endobronchial metastases is unusual, these tumors include colon, kidney, thyroid, and breast tumors and melanoma. Choriocarcinoma and osteogenic sarcoma may also result in hemoptysis. Esophageal carcinoma may extend directly into the tracheobronchial tree, resulting in hemoptysis. Patients with hematologic malignancies, especially leukemia, develop pulmonary hemorrhage with or without hemoptysis often associated with fungal infection (i.e., *Aspergillus* or *Mucor*). The latter invade the pulmonary vasculature resulting in thrombosis, infarction, and hemorrhage and may occur in other immunocompromised hosts. Iatrogenic hemoptysis may occur secondary to transthoracic needle biopsy, transbronchial biopsy, or pulmonary artery perforation due to Swan–Ganz catheter use.

Finally, patients with Eisenmenger's syndrome due to congenital heart disease and pulmonary hypertension or patients with mitral stenosis due to rheumatic heart disease may have hemoptysis.

CRITERIA FOR DIAGNOSIS
Suggestive

Although the patient may present complaining of coughing up blood, it is necessary to ascertain that the patient is truly experiencing hemoptysis. Patients may complain of a sudden welling up of blood in their throat or mouth; however, blood may arise from the nasopharynx, throat, or mouth which may simulate hemoptysis. In the latter case, epistaxis and hoarseness may be present. A patient may complain of vague chest pain, burning, bubbling, or chest heaviness prior to expectorating blood. Alternatively, there may be a gurgling noise within the chest or a sensation within the chest or throat stimulating cough. Hematemesis may also be confused with hemoptysis. The former is often preceded by nausea and vomiting; blood may be mixed with food particles; and there may be a history of alcoholism, gastrointestinal or liver disease.

Definitive

True hemoptysis is expectoration of blood. The blood is bright red and a portion may appear frothy. In distinguishing hemoptysis from hematemesis, blood from hemoptysis is alkaline, whereas that from hematemesis is acid. Blood may be mixed with pus; leukocytes, macrophages, and organisms may be visible on microscopic staining. Occasionally, macrophages contain hemosiderin particles. Blood-tinged sputum may persist for days.

CLINICAL MANIFESTATIONS
Subjective

Important information relates to the character and quantity of expectorated blood as well as the duration of symptoms. Patients with tuberculosis, bronchogenic carcinoma, and pulmonary infarction present with frankly bloody sputum without mucus, whereas those with infectious etiologies due to pneumonia, lung abscess, and bronchiectasis have purulent sputum mixed with blood. Frothy pink sputum is suggestive of congestive heart failure. Rusty brown-colored sputum is seen in pneumonia due to *Streptococcus pneumoniae*, whereas bloody and mucoid sputum with a currant jelly-like appearance suggests pneumonia due to *Klebsiella pneumoniae*. Putrid sputum suggests a lung abscess. The presence of gritty particles mixed with blood suggests broncholithiasis. Hemoptysis may be misdiagnosed in two conditions. Pneumonia secondary to *Serratia marcescens,* a Gram-negative rod, may produce red sputum which is hematest negative and contains no red blood cells. Rupture of an amebic abscess into a bronchus may produce sputum resembling anchovy paste, which may be mistaken for "old" blood.

Minimal to mild hemoptysis (arbitrarily defined as <20 mL/d) is more often observed in patients with chronic bronchitis, whereas major or massive hemoptysis (>200 mL/d) is more frequently observed in patients with bronchiectasis, tuberculosis, and mycetoma. Patients with bronchogenic carcinoma usually have mild hemoptysis, though some series have found it to be a significant cause of major hemoptysis. The pattern of hemoptysis should also be ascertained. Brief episodes occurring over months to years are more often observed in chronic bronchitis and bronchiectasis. Recurrent hemoptysis in an otherwise healthy young woman suggests a bronchial adenoma. On the other hand, if it is associated with menses, pulmonary endometriosis should be suspected. The age of the patient is also important to determine, as certain diseases are age related. Lung carcinoma usually occurs after age 40 in a cigarette smoker with a greater than 40-pack-year smoking history. The time of onset of the hemoptysis with respect to other pulmonary symptoms should be assessed. Rarely is hemoptysis the initial symptom in patients with bronchogenic carcinoma, occurring late and often preceded by a change in frequency and character of the patient's cough. Such patients may also describe several months of anorexia and weight loss.

Additional history should be obtained regarding the presence of fever, night sweats, weight loss, prior tuberculosis (exposure or infection), cardiopulmonary symptoms, and travel history. The latter may not only suggest fungal or parasitic etiologies, but prolonged sitting during travel may also predispose to pulmonary embolus and infarction. A history of hematuria suggests Wegener's granulomatosis, Goodpasture's syndrome, or collagen–vascular disease. A history of anticoagulation usage as well as a possible bleeding dyscrasia should be obtained. Acute pleuritic chest pain may be seen in acute pulmonary embolus with infarction, other pleura-based diseases including vasculitis and collagen–vascular disease, pneumonia with a parapneumonic effusion, and metastatic pleural disease. Other historical data should be obtained including family history (Osler–Weber–Rendu syndrome or other blood dyscrasias), known heart murmur or history of rheumatic fever (mitral stenosis), and recent blunt chest trauma (pulmonary contusion).

Objective
Physical Examination

Level of consciousness and hemodynamic stability should be assessed initially. The latter can be evaluated quickly by observing for orthostatic changes in blood pressure and pulse. Next a careful examination of the upper airway is necessary to rule out bleeding from this source. The mouth should be examined for lacerations, foreign bodies, and tumors, remembering to remove dentures when present. The nasal passages should also be inspected for fresh or old blood. Sometimes indirect laryngoscopy or fiberoptic laryngoscopy may be necessary to rule out more distal upper airway bleeding. Observation of the chest wall for evidence of trauma or rib fractures precedes auscultation. A pleural friction rub suggests pulmonary infarction or other pleura-based diseases such as vasculitis and collagen–vascular disease. A localized wheeze suggests narrowing of the airway by a bronchogenic carcinoma, compressing the airway either externally or intraluminally by an endobronchial mass. A foreign body partially obstructing a large airway may also result in a localized wheeze. Diffuse wheezing suggests chronic bronchitis or bronchiectasis. The presence of a continuous murmur or bruit while auscultating the lungs suggests pulmonary arteriovenous malformation as seen in Osler–Weber–Rendu syndrome. Localized crackles or rhonchi, however, are nonspecific and may be

compatible with a blood pneumonitis secondary to aspiration of blood. Jugular venous distension suggests congestive heart failure as well as severe mitral valve disease. Cardiac auscultation may reveal a diastolic rumble and opening snap indicative of mitral stenosis. Evidence of pulmonary hypertension, such as a loud pulmonary valve closure sound, may be seen in patients with Eisenmenger's physiology, primary pulmonary hypertension, as well as recurrent pulmonary emboli.

Extrapulmonary findings are also helpful. Cervical or supraclavicular adenopathy, as well as clubbing, is suggestive of both bronchogenic carcinoma and sarcoidosis. Clubbing may also be observed in patients with Eisenmenger's physiology, chronic bronchiectasis, chronic lung abscess, and, rarely, tuberculosis (in advanced cases only). Ulceration of the nasal septum and other midline structures of the upper airway is suggestive of Wegener's granulomatosis. Ecchymoses and petechiae suggest a coagulopathy, whereas telangiectasia on the lips and buccal mucosa is indicative of Osler–Weber–Rendu syndrome.

Routine Laboratory Abnormalities

Routine hematologic studies include a complete blood count with differential and an estimation of the number of platelets. The hemoglobin level may or may not reflect blood loss through the respiratory tract. The hematocrit is elevated in patients with Eisenmenger's physiology. An elevated white blood cell count may point to a possible infectious process. A blood urea nitrogen and creatinine will determine a possible uremic cause for bleeding. A urinalysis revealing red blood cells suggests Wegener's granulomatosis, Goodpasture's syndrome, or collagen–vascular disease.

An attempt should be made to quantitate the degree of bleeding. Patients should be given a cup and instructed to expectorate all blood into the cup. Patients' and physicians' estimations of the amount of hemoptysis are often erroneous.

All patients expectorating blood must have a chest radiograph (posteroanterior and lateral), regardless of any other clinical features. A patchy infiltrate may represent aspirated blood from a bleeding site elsewhere in the lungs; diffuse infiltrates may also be nonspecific, representing alveolar filling due to hemorrhage. It may take a week or more for this blood to be absorbed. Certain radiographic findings, however, point to a specific etiology. A mass lesion with distal atelectasis suggests a carcinoma, whereas a cavitary infiltrate suggests tuberculosis. A cavity with an air–fluid level more often suggests a lung abscess, but occasionally is seen in tuberculosis or even a squamous cell carcinoma. An old tuberculous cavity with a movable mass within it (best seen on decubitus views) suggests an aspergilloma. Peribronchial cuffing, ring shadows, and tram-track lines suggests bronchiectasis. An enlarged left atrium associated with Kerley B lines in the pulmonary parenchyma is indicative of mitral stenosis. Finally, some patients with hemoptysis have no chest radiographic abnormalities. This should not, however, preclude further diagnostic testing.

PLANS
Diagnostic
Differential Diagnosis

In the 1950s and 1960s, several large series revealed that bronchitis, bronchiectasis, bronchogenic carcinoma, tuberculosis, and lung abscess were the most common causes of hemoptysis. These remain the most common etiologies, though the percentage of each differs among several recent studies. When assessing a patient for a specific etiology, it is important to bear in mind the specific clinical situation from which a patient derives. For example, in the setting of trauma, pulmonary contusion may be responsible for hemoptysis, whereas in a cigarette smoker over age 40, chronic bronchitis and bronchogenic carcinoma are more likely. In approximately 20% of patients no etiology may be found despite extensive workup. The differential diagnosis includes all entities discussed under Etiology.

Diagnostic Options

Microscopic examination of the sputum helps identify patients with acute pneumonia, lung abscess, and active tuberculosis. An acid-fast bacillus sputum smear not only aids in the diagnosis, but helps in assessing infectivity if positive. Sputum should be sent for routine, tuberculosis, and, when indicated, fungal cultures. Cytologic examination of the sputum may prove positive for bronchogenic carcinoma, though a negative result does not exclude carcinoma. A tuberculin skin test should be placed; an anergy panel is optional.

Serologic markers for Wegener's granulomatosis, Goodpasture's syndrome, and systemic lupus erythematosus may be obtained, if suspicion is great. An arterial blood gas determination assesses the degree of hypoxemia and possible hypercapnia, suggesting impending respiratory failure.

The pace of the workup depends on the rate of bleeding. When the bleeding is not massive (i.e., <200 mL of blood in 24 hours), there is sufficient time for evaluation of the etiology and proper management. When hemoptysis is massive, localization of the site of bleeding, identification of the etiology, and specific therapy must progress simultaneously. In such emergent cases specific therapy including intubation and surgical intervention may precede a complete diagnostic workup.

In patients with nonemergent hemoptysis and a nonlocalizing chest radiograph, a high-resolution computed tomography (CT) scan follows in the workup of hemoptysis. CT scanning is extremely sensitive in detecting airway abnormalities. It may also detect both central and peripheral tumors, not apparent radiographically as well as bronchoscopically. Although early studies failed to demonstrate that CT scans had significant clinical impact on patients with hemoptysis, more recent studies have confirmed its utility. High-resolution CT, using thin sections of 5 and 1.5 mm through the central and peripheral airways, may detect specific abnormalities in 50% of cases with normal chest radiographs and normal or nondiagnostic bronchoscopies. One of the more commonly detected diagnoses is bronchiectasis, an entity that is apparent on plain films only when severe, cannot be diagnosed by bronchoscopy, and previously required confirmation by bronchography. High-resolution CT may also provide a road map for the bronchoscopist when searching for the site of bleeding, as well as provide guidance for transbronchial needle aspiration of peribronchial nodes and peripheral masses.

Most patients who present with hemoptysis without a readily identifiable cause should undergo fiberoptic bronchoscopy. Bronchoscopy is not necessary in patients with some diagnoses such as pulmonary infarction, active tuberculosis, and pneumonia; however, if hemoptysis is persistent or recurrent, bronchoscopy is warranted to rule out a coexisting carcinoma. Fiberoptic bronchoscopy has replaced rigid bronchoscopy, as it allows visualization of segmental and subsegmental bronchi. An exception is in patients who present with massive hemoptysis (see below). Rigid bronchoscopy with its larger aspirating channel allows suctioning of blood and clot as well as maintenance of an airway.

The major issues regarding bronchoscopy and hemoptysis are in whom to perform the procedure and when. In patients with localizing findings on a chest radiograph there is a high yield using bronchoscopy. An area of uncertainty concerns which patients with normal chest radiographs should undergo bronchoscopy. It has been suggested in this setting that only patients with risk factors for carcinoma undergo bronchoscopy. Such risk factors include age greater than age 40, male sex, smoking of 40 pack years or more, and hemoptysis lasting longer than 1 week. Bronchoscopy, however, has a low yield in patients with a single episode, normal radiographic findings, and in whom the clinical suspicion bronchogenic carcinoma is low. Early bronchoscopy is two to three times more likely to identify the site of bleeding than bronchoscopy delayed until after the bleeding has stopped; however, studies have not demonstrated any significant clinical impact of early compared with delayed bronchoscopy in patients who do not have massive hemoptysis.

If the source of hemoptysis cannot be identified because the rate of bleeding prevents visualization of the airway, rigid bronchoscopy and/or emergency bronchial arteriography are indicated. Other diagnostic testing is occasionally necessary. In the patient who presents with pleuritic chest pain ventilation–perfusion lung scanning may be necessary to confirm a diagnosis of pulmonary embolus/infarction. If the scan is "indeterminate" and clinical suspicion is high, proceeding to a pulmonary angiogram is necessary in light of the therapeutic need of anticoagulation.

Radionuclide studies using ^{99m}Tc-sulfur colloid isotope-labeled red blood cells have been performed to localize bleeding. Experience is limited, however, and both false-positive and false-negative scans have occurred, the latter due to an insufficient rate of bleeding (<6 mL/min). This type of nuclear imaging has limited clinical impact and should be reserved for patients in whom bronchoscopy has not proved helpful and arteriography is contraindicated.

Recommended Approach

Following completion of a careful history, physical examination, routine laboratory studies, and a plain chest radiograph, most patients should have high-resolution CT followed by bronchoscopy. It must be emphasized that high-resolution CT and bronchoscopy are complementary—not competitive—modalities in patients with hemoptysis. Bronchial arteriography is necessary in patients with continued hemoptysis and in whom a bleeding site has not been identified. It is also necessary in anticipation of embolization therapy (see below).

Therapeutic

Management of hemoptysis depends on the etiology and severity of the bleeding as well as the condition of the patient. The immediate goal is to stop the bleeding and prevent asphyxiation. Usually, mild hemoptysis ceases spontaneously without therapy and treatment is directed at the underlying disease. Thus, in conditions such as acute and chronic bronchitis, pneumonia, lung abscess, and bronchiectasis, antibiotic therapy is initiated and bleeding ceases. In some instances, coughing may be irritative and cause further bleeding; codeine may be helpful in suppressing this cough. Vigorous chest and thoracic movement such as that caused by chest physiotherapy and spirometry should be avoided. If bleeding is more vigorous, bedrest and mild sedation are indicated. Only mild sedation is necessary, as depression of consciousness may result in aspiration of blood into the contralateral lung. If the bleeding site has been identified, the patient is positioned with the bleeding side down to minimize aspiration into the contralateral lung.

Massive hemoptysis is an emergency situation. Rarely does it stop spontaneously and recurrence is often fatal. Control of the airway is critical and may require immediate intubation. Arterial blood gases should be monitored; hypoxemia should be treated with supplemental oxygen. Hypercapnia and respiratory acidosis signify ventilatory failure due to aspirated blood, and immediate intubation with mechanical ventilation is mandatory. Sometimes it is necessary to intubate the patient with a double-lumen endotracheal tube to isolate the bleeding lung and prevent aspiration of blood into the contralateral lung. Following intubation, stabilization of hemodynamics and gas exchange proceeds. Subsequently, bronchoscopy should be performed to identify the site of bleeding as well as aspirate clots from the airway.

Further management of massive hemoptysis is controversial. Medical therapy and surgical resection are the two choices. Interventional medical therapy includes bronchial arterial embolization, laser photocoagulation, tamponade of the bleeding site with a balloon-tipped catheter inserted proximally via a bronchoscope, and endobronchial infusion of fibrinogen–thrombin to plug the airway. To date, embolization therapy is the most proven short-term nonsurgical therapy. When surgery is opted, elective rather than emergency surgery should be attempted. Selection of surgery requires identification of an anatomic basis for the bleeding (such as a bronchogenic carcinoma, a lung abscess, or even localized cavitary tuberculosis). Furthermore, the patient should have adequate pulmonary function to undergo surgical resection.

Emergency surgery should be considered in patients who are operative candidates and embolization is not available or when bleeding continues despite embolization. Whether to proceed with elective surgery in a patient whose massive hemoptysis has ceased is controversial, though conservative nonsurgical therapy has been favored most recently. It should, however, be noted that the long-term prognosis in patients treated with endobronchial tamponade is unknown. Furthermore, although embolization therapy controls bleeding for prolonged periods—and is the treatment of choice in patients with inoperable disease due to limited cardiac or pulmonary reserve or bilateral progressive disease—it is not definitive. In approximately 30% of patients who have undergone embolization therapy, bleeding recurs.

FOLLOW-UP

Follow-up is determined by the specific etiology of the hemoptysis. In approximately 20% of patients the etiology remains cryptogenic. Such patients should be followed every 3 to 4 months over the course of the subsequent year to rule out early bronchogenic carcinoma.

DISCUSSION

Prevalence and Incidence

As discussed earlier the specific causes for hemoptysis appear to have changed during the past 30 years due to the decline in tuberculosis and rise in bronchogenic carcinoma. As the incidence of tuberculosis increases during the 1990s, this may again change. There seems to be a decline in the incidence of bronchiectasis, though this may relate to the failure to use high-resolution CT as well as bronchography to diagnose this condition. Similarly, the etiology of massive hemoptysis has changed. Previously, tuberculosis accounted for greater than half of cases and bronchiectasis for about one quarter of the cases. More recently, bronchogenic carcinoma accounts for approximately one third and bronchiectasis for one quarter of patients who develop massive hemoptysis.

Related Basic Science

The lungs receive two blood supplies: the low-pressure pulmonary arterial and the high-pressure bronchial arterial supplies. The latter, arising from the thoracic aorta, plays a crucial role in patients with hemoptysis due to its position along the entire tracheobronchial tree. Proximally, bronchial arteries anastomose with each other, forming a plexiform arrangement in the peribronchial space. Additionally, bronchial arteries penetrate bronchial walls, forming extensive submucosal plexi. Distally, they anastomose with precapillary veins and pulmonary veins. Disruption of the bronchial circulation leads to "high-pressure" hemorrhage. It is frequently more massive, containing fresh or old blood. Bronchial arterial bleeding is observed in cavitary tuberculosis, bronchiectasis, aspergillosis, and broncholiths. Low-pressure pulmonary arterial bleeding is observed in bronchitis, pneumonia, arteriovenous malformations, and pulmonary infarction. Severe bleeding is occasionally observed in patients with arteriovenous malformations.

Numerous mechanisms may result in bleeding along the tracheobronchial tree. Inflammation of the mucosa as in acute or chronic bronchitis results in bleeding as the mucosa is well vascularized and friable. Endobronchial injury from granuloma formation is seen in sarcoidosis, whereas mucosal ulceration with necrosis of adjacent blood vessels is observed in tuberculosis. In patients with cavitary tuberculosis, the rupture of pulmonary capillaries or dilated aneurysmal bronchial arteries (Rasmussen's aneurysms) adjacent to areas of inflammation and infection results in hemoptysis. In healed tuberculosis, erosion of calcified nodes into the bronchial lumen may also erode the bronchial arterial supply, resulting in massive hemoptysis. In patients with bronchiectasis, whether due to tuberculosis or other processes such as cystic fibrosis, bleeding occurs in the enlarged tortuous bronchial vessels or the rich submucosal plexi in the wall of the bronchiectatic segment following repeated infection. Although the bronchial arterial supply to bronchogenic tumors is increased, rupture of these vessels is unusual. Rather, invasion of the bronchial mucosa by the tumor and/or tumor necrosis are more likely mechanisms for hemoptysis. Direct tumor invasion into pulmonary vessels is rare.

Natural History and Its Modification with Treatment

The prognosis of patients who present with hemoptysis depends on several factors: the rapidity of bleeding, the total amount of bleeding, and the underlying etiology. Minor bleeding has minimal prognostic implications. Massive hemoptysis, however, may prove fatal. Short-term mortality from massive hemoptysis is related to the rate and amount of bleeding rather than the etiology. Patients who bleed in excess of 600 mL per 24 hours have a greater than 50% mortality rate. In addition, inoperable patients have a higher mortality than operable patients who are treated medically or surgically. Surgical and medical mortality rates are comparable in operable patients. At lower bleeding rates medical therapy is slightly superior, whereas at higher bleeding rates (>1000 mL per 24 hours) surgical intervention may improve survival.

Cryptogenic hemoptysis refers to hemoptysis that eludes etiologic diagnosis despite a thorough workup. As discussed, it occurs in 15 to 20% of all cases and 10 to 15% of cases with massive bleeding. Most patients with cryptogenic hemoptysis have either normal airways or bronchitic changes on bronchoscopic examination. Ultimately, bronchogenic carcinoma is found in up to 6% of patients. On the basis of data collected from several series, the prognosis of patients with hemoptysis, a clear chest radiograph, and a negative bronchoscopy is good, with 5-year survival ranging from 85 to 95%.

Prevention

Most episodes of hemoptysis are spontaneous, unexpected, and not preventable. When an etiology and site are identified, specific treatment may prevent recurrence. Thus, resection of a bronchogenic carcinoma prevents repeated hemoptysis. Often, however, definitive therapy cannot be administered, as in patients with bronchiectasis. Supportive therapy of these patients in an effort to reduce infection and inflammation may reduce the severity and shorten the duration of hemoptysis.

Cost Containment

The most cost-effective approach in patients with hemoptysis requires the sequential approach outlined above of routine chest radiograph, high-resolution CT, and bronchoscopy. Often the first two diagnostic tests either obviate the need for the latter or optimize its diagnostic capabilities. These three diagnostic tests diagnose between two thirds and three quarters of all cases of hemoptysis, reducing the need for ancillary studies mentioned above. Identification of a specific etiology helps contain therapeutic costs.

REFERENCES

Adelman M, Haponik EF, Bleecker ER, et al. Cryptogenic hemoptysis: Clinical features, bronchoscopic findings, and natural history in 67 patients. Ann Intern Med 1985;102:829.

Corey R, Hla KM. Major and massive hemoptysis: Reassessment of conservative management. Am J Med Sci 1987;294:301.

Johnston H, Reisz G. Changing spectrum of hemoptysis. Arch Intern Med 1989;149:1666.

McGuinness G, Beacher JR, Harkin TJ, et al. Hemoptysis: Prospective high-resolution CT/bronchoscopic correlation. Chest 1994;105:1155.

Poe RH, Israel RH, Ortiz CR, et al. Utility of fiberoptic bronchoscopy in patients with hemoptysis and a nonlocalizing chest roentgenogram. Chest 1988;92:70.

Santiago S, Tobias J, Williams AJ. A reappraisal of the causes of hemoptysis. Arch Intern Med 1991;151:2449.

Uflaker R, Kaemmerer A, Picon PD, et al. Bronchial artery embolization in the management of hemoptysis: Technical aspects and long-term results. Radiology 1985;157:637.

CHAPTER 13–11

Dyspnea

Peter J. P. Finch, M.D.

DEFINITION

Dyspnea is defined as distressing shortness of breath not attributable solely to level of exertion.

ETIOLOGY

Shortness of breath has a normal protective function to force the termination of exercise that threatens dangerously to stress cardiopulmonary function. A second natural function is to alert us to threatened strangulation or suffocation. As a symptom of disease it signals physiologic dysfunction leading to increased neural stimulation to breathe, out of proportion to that justified by ambient activity.

CRITERIA FOR DIAGNOSIS

Suggestive

The patient shows tachypnea, hyperpnea, or gasping breathing at rest or while exercising with a healthy peer who is not distressed.

Definitive

There are no definite criteria for diagnosis as dyspnea is a symptom.

CLINICAL MANIFESTATIONS

Subjective

Dyspnea usually first manifests on exercise. If not, one should consider paroxysmal cardiac arrhythmia, pulmonary embolism, or emotional causes and look for associated signs and symptoms. History of smoking, occupational exposure, and chest pain are suggestive of various diagnoses that may result in dyspnea. Tuberculosis and lung cancer may have breathlessness as a prominent part of their presentation. Asthma usually shows a prominent cough and wheeze and production of sticky mucus. There are often close relatives affected by this problem or by allergic illness, or a history of previous similar attacks.

Objective

Physical Examination

Expiratory rhonchi are heard throughout the lung fields when asthma is active. Emphysema destroys alveolar walls allowing expiratory airway collapse, air trapping, and the overexpansion of poorly functional lung spaces. As air is trapped the patient's resting lung volume after tidal expiration (functional residual capacity) gradually increases until it begins to approach total lung capacity. The patient exhibits signs of hyperinflation: absent cardiac dullness to percussion, caudally displaced liver dullness, increased anteroposterior diameter, and loss of the normal outward movement of the rib margin on tidal inspiration. Rhonchi may be heard on forced expiration.

Interstitial lung disease may show prominent tachypnea with widespread crepitations and clubbing of the fingers. Cyanosis and cor pulmonale may be evident. Signs of an underlying rheumatologic process should be sought. Any chronic lung disease may first be brought to the physician's attention when coryza, influenza, or pneumonia occurs; be prepared to make such a double diagnosis if recovery is incomplete. Pulmonary vascular disease diminishes the capillary bed for gas exchange and disturbs the local regulation of perfusion to match ventilation. Blood gases may be abnormal as is pulmonary artery pressure. Both these abnormalities trigger increased impulse traffic to breathe. Increased jugular venous pressure, often with the giant V wave of tricuspid regurgitation, tender liver, and peripheral edema, is likely to be seen, with minimal evidence of parenchymal disease of the lung.

Cardiac disease restricts cardiac output and raises pulmonary venous pressure at rest or on mild exercise. Breathlessness is precipitated by tissue acidosis and hypoxia on exertion, by increased signals from the pulmonary vessels, and by stiffening of the lung caused by pulmonary edema. One often finds extra heart sounds, murmurs, and basal crepitations in addition to jugular venous distension and edema.

Dysfunction of the muscles of the respiratory pump is usually associated with weakness of the limbs or face or with severe generalized malnutrition. Consider amyotrophic lateral sclerosis, dystrophia myotonica, Guillain–Barré syndrome, myasthenia gravis, and so on, and look for associated weakness, fasciculation, or other neurologic signs. Diaphragmatic paralysis may cause much more shortness of breath on recumbency than in an erect posture.

Obesity increases the work of breathing and the energy cost of physical activities. It is often combined with simple muscle deconditioning. If muscles are underused they atrophy and their blood supply involutes. Minor exertion then causes them to exceed their maximal aerobic metabolic rate and release lactate to provoke disproportionate ventilatory drive and symptomatic dyspnea.

Metabolic acidosis causes slow deep breathing without evident obstruction. Look for evidence of diabetes or renal failure. Acute, otherwise unexplained "acidotic" breathing may be due to aspirin overdose or to antifreeze or methanol ingestion.

Dyspnea not related to exertion or attended by irregular sighing or grimacing or grunting and ineffectual cough may be an attention-seeking maneuver or the somatosizing of unacknowledged emotional stress. The patient shows no convincing organic signs, is likely angrily to deny the offered interpretation of her or his symptom, but may have clear-cut evidence of psychosocial maladjustment on simple questioning. Dyspnea may be exaggerated by those malingering to seek disability status or those afraid of the stresses attending their work (or family responsibilities).

Anemia and thyrotoxicosis may present with dyspnea, but usually are immediately suspected in a skilled routine examination.

Routine Laboratory Abnormalities

The complete blood count may disclose anemia. Arterial blood gases may reveal hypoxemia, hypercapnia, or hypocapnia or be entirely normal. A raised hemoglobin suggests polycythemia secondary to hypoxemia. The chemistry profile may demonstrate and explain metabolic acidosis causing dyspnea.

Chest Radiograph. Evidence of overinflation (low flat diaphragms, more air space than usual in front of the heart on the lateral radiograph and below the heart on the posteroanterior radiograph) may be seen in obstructive disease. Loss of peripheral vasculature and prominent central pulmonary arteries suggest pulmonary hypertension. Small, poorly aerated lungs may be seen with fibrosis or with muscle weakness. Increased upper zone fibrosis and hilar lymphadenopathy may be seen in tuberculosis and sarcoidosis.

Electrocardiogram. The electrocardiogram typically shows left ventricular hypertrophy, left-axis deviation of the QRS vector, or left bundle-branch block with left ventricular disease. It often shows right-axis deviation of the QRS vector, P pulmonale, and right bundle-branch block with lung disease causing cor pulmonale. $S_IQ_{III}T_{III}$ and other patterns of acute right ventricular strain may accompany pulmonary embolism. Atrial fibrillation suggests pulmonary embolism, thyrotoxicosis, or mitral stenosis.

Urinalysis. Urinalysis may show evidence of glycosuria and ketonuria in diabetic ketoacidosis, and of proteinuria or infection in renal failure with metabolic acidosis.

PLANS

Diagnostic

Differential Diagnosis

The differential diagnosis includes all the entities discussed under Clinical Manifestations. Crucially important is a carefully taken and considered history.

Diagnostic Options

See Recommended Approach. An electrocardiogram and chest radiograph are usually required, but pulmonary function tests should generally be necessary only if there is evidence of pulmonary disease or an unexplained dyspnea. Chest computed tomography and bronchoscopy are required for the nonresolving infiltrate or for localized masses on the chest radiograph. Sputum gram stain is valuable for clarifying bacterial versus viral infection; culture is less useful, though needed in severe pneumonia. Sputum examination by differential white cell count is underused and raised eosinophil count by this technique strongly suggests asthma. Dyspnea in a previously normal person is a danger signal. We hope to make the diagnosis of a cause, then to treat the underlying pathology, and, almost incidentally, relieve the presenting symptom.

Recommended Approach

Forced expiratory spirometry shows greater reduction of forced expiratory volume in 1 second than of forced vital capacity (low FEV_1:FVC ratio) when the airways are obstructed and blocking the outward flow of air. This is relatively fixed in chronic obstructive pulmonary disease (COPD) and more responsive to inhaled sympathomimetics in asthma. Equal reduction of FEV_1 and FVC (restrictive physiology) occurs when the lung is stiff with fibrosing disease or other interstitial lung disease, but also with disease of the pleural space (pneumothorax, pleural effusion) or fibrothorax following organization of empyema or hemothorax or with disease of the chest wall (kyphoscoliosis, trauma, etc.). Diaphragmatic paralysis, neuromuscular weakness (polio, amyotrophic lateral sclerosis, Guillain–Barré, etc), severe obesity or ascites, or, of course, resectional surgery of the lung can also produce "restriction." Diffusion capacity of the lung for carbon monoxide (DLCO), being low in association with obstruction, suggests emphysema rather than asthma. DLCO is often low with interstitial lung disease and parallels the loss of surface area of blood–air interaction, but especially the loss of adjustment of local blood flow to local ventilation ($\dot{V}$:$\dot{Q}$ mismatch). Lung volumes are increased with airway obstruction and reduced in interstitial diseases.

Arterial blood gases may show a fall in pCO_2 with inflamed lung or abnormal vasculature, pneumonia, pulmonary edema, fibrosis, or anxiety (e.g., with emphysema). Association with low pO_2 especially suggests pulmonary embolism. A raised pCO_2 occurs with sedation or severe COPD of the "blue bloater" type or terminally with emphysema. Normal pCO_2 does not exclude muscle weakness; we follow vital capacity.

Cardiopulmonary exercise testing frequently allows a confident attribution of dyspnea to cardiac or pulmonary mechanisms or to a less specific unfitness or deconditioning of the skeletal muscles and their blood supply—a common major mechanism in older and more obese subjects. It may also be required to add weight to an impression of psychological etiology.

Therapeutics

Therapeutic Options

Asthma and COPD are common pulmonary causes of dyspnea. Smoking cessation, bronchodilators, antibiotics, theophylline, and oxygen are all useful modalities. Cardiac dyspnea is usually due to left ventricular failure, which should be treated appropriately. The options for the various other causes are delineated under Recommended Approach. The guiding principle in the management is to establish a treatable etiology. The symptom will be demystified and less alarming to the patient and his family and will be substantially or totally relieved as normal physiology is restored.

Recommended Approach

The crucial therapeutic step in emphysema and bronchitis is to stop smoking; almost all cases are attributable to tobacco and rational care is not achievable while the habit continues. The vital finding is that addicts can quit if they try repeatedly to quit. The advisor's role is often to help the patient learn from each failure the lesson that will justify another more informed attempt and to encourage his or her hope to achieve health and autonomy. Exacerbations of COPD usually follow respiratory viral infections and may be worsened by bacterial superinfection. Trimethoprim–sulfamethoxazole remains the most appropriate antibacterial agent. An allergic mechanism and the potential to respond to inhaled antiinflammatory agents are more likely than the presence of bacteria resistant to bactrim in patients with prolonged exacerbations of COPD. It is difficult to decide whether theophylline will be helpful to a particular patient. Patients should probably be encouraged to use the agent, say 250 mg every 8 or every 12 hours sustained release, during exacerbations and to try periods on and off the agent when in "chronic stable state." Unfortunately, the side effects (tremor, agitation, dyspepsia, etc.) are often more clear-cut than the benefits. Some patients do, however, show improved ability to sleep through the night or to perform sustained mild exercise. Exercise tolerance and perhaps dyspnea specifically are often helped by relieving the edema of cor pulmonale by a low-salt diet and judicious use of diuretics. Ambulatory patients function better if edema is not demonstrable after a night's sleep but perhaps allowed to accumulate a little during the day. I allow them to experiment with the dosage time—breakfast, lunch, or early evening—that produces the most manageable period of polyuria and the least interrupted sleep.

Oxygen is well established to ameliorate cor pulmonale and help keep patients out of hospital and alive longer when arterial pO_2 at rest is below 55 or below 60 with evidence of cor pulmonale. It is advised as nearly as possible continuously (>18 hours) for this purpose. It is also effective in many dyspneic patients to improve exercise tolerance even with resting PaO_2 above 60 mm Hg (Dean et al., 1992). Here it may be justified if the improved exercise tolerance enables patients to live effectively and care for themselves at home when otherwise they would need an aide or to be institutionalized.

Despite all we can do with classic pharmacologic therapy, many patients with COPD are left with real dyspnea for months or years before death. Managing this period is difficult but can be rewarding (Carrieri-Kohlman et al., 1993). Many relatively independent people benefit from "pulmonary rehabilitation." This is classically a daily program for 3 to 6 weeks built around exercise testing and regular exercise training with a demonstration of the achieved improvement after the course. Education about the disease and its management and readjustment of the person's goals and the grounds of personal satisfaction occur too, and occasionally patients are recognized to have major psychiatric problems and referred for fuller assessment. Breathing exercises, especially pursed lip breathing and inspiratory muscle training, have been shown in various studies to be able to improve exercise tolerance and somewhat to diminish breathlessness. A crucial objective is to slow the respiratory rate on exertion.

With dyspnea and low $PaCO_2$, it is rational to try to downregulate inspiratory effort using sedatives, tranquilizers, or opiates (Light, 1991). A calmer breathing, allowing the $PaCO_2$ to be normal at rest and a little raised during exertion, seems "sensible" if not accompanied by hypercapnia during sleep and the worsening cor pulmonale that would cause. Low-dose oral hydrocodone early in the day may be helpful. The author uses it occasionally, especially in COPD patients who complain also of nonproductive cough, and sometimes in lung cancer patients with cough and dyspnea. Pleural fluid of any real volume reduces the efficiency of ventilation. It should be mobilized by treatment of cardiac failure or hypoalbuminemia. Empyema must be drained, usually with a chest tube, or fibrothorax may lead to permanently damaged breathing and require surgical decortication later.

Interstitial lung disease has more than 100 etiologic mechanisms. Subspecialty referral is almost always appropriate and the most complete diagnosis possible may lead to effective reversal and symptomatic benefit. Ultimately, nonresponsive, deteriorating pneumoconiosis, rheumatoid lung, or lymphangitis carcinomatosa can be palliated only by high concentrations of oxygen and by morphine.

Patients maintained chronically on ventilators may still experience dyspnea and demand an increased minute ventilation, in excess of metabolic need. Some patients with neuromuscular disease reject sedation and respond to addition of dead space in the ventilatory circuit. The neuromuscular experience of "normal" tidal volume and minute ventilation is required for comfort, even when metabolic CO_2 production falls very low. Resting the muscles of some patients who become fatigued with kyphoscoliosis or emphysema by nocturnal cuirass ventilation improves daytime function and sometimes normalizes blood gases after hypercapnia had been established.

Intractable breathlessness attributed to pulmonary fibrosis in relatively young patients should lead to a discussion of possible lung transplantation. Primary pulmonary hypertension, which advances despite cessation of cigarette smoking and contraceptives and administration of low-dose coumadin, may also merit lung or heart lung transplantation. Severe emphysema in younger patients may benefit from double, or recently, single lung transplantation (Kaiser et al., 1991). Lung volume reduction surgery, clamping off and excising the bullous apex and upper outer parts of first one and then the other lung at one surgery, via a median sternotomy, has more real potential. Modern stapling devices and techniques to buttress the flimsy, long wound in the emphysematous lung with denatured bovine pericardium seem, in expert hands, to have solved the problem of persistent air leak that bedeviled earlier surgeries (Cooper, 1994). The smaller lungs allow the chest wall and diaphragm to return to normal "functional residual capacity" and allow the ribs and diaphragm to work comfortably and efficiently. Operative morbidity is "acceptable" in well-selected cases. If intractable breathlessness is attributed to pulmonary thromboembolism, very occasional cases may be able to benefit from pulmonary thromboendarterectomy.

Clearly all these dramatic possibilities require screening and careful evaluation by local and regional subspecialty experts.

FOLLOW-UP

Follow-up varies with the mechanism diagnosed. It is vital in most etiologies that the physician shows his or her ranking of the quitting of smoking as the first priority. Every visit should include inquiry and counseling. Remember to plan with your patient for anticipated seasonal factors, give cromolyn during the pollen season to allergic asthmatics, and give flu shots to COPD patients. If you have given advice or referral about breathing exercise or about relaxation therapy or formal pulmonary rehabilitation, remember to reinforce its anticipated benefit and review the techniques and lessons with interested concern. If obesity or congestive heart failure was important, ensure follow-up inquiry and monitoring weight and edema. If family stress is uncovered in working up dyspnea, check for its resolution or improvement.

DISCUSSION
Prevalence

Chronic obstructive pulmonary disease is the most common cause of disabling dyspnea, and 101,090 deaths were attributed to COPD (of a total of 2,268,000) in the United States in 1993. This number is growing annually. Perhaps 5% of the population has asthma. Many patients with chronic dyspnea suffered repeated premonitory "chest colds" with shortness of breath, yet failed to quit smoking.

Related Basic Science

Recently most experts agree that we are or can be conscious of our "effort" to breathe, of an "efferent copy" of the output from the medulla to the inspiratory muscles being relayed to consciousness "via feedback mechanisms high in the central nervous system" (Cherniack, 1988). Previously it had been felt by many that dyspnea specifically required that muscle tension and length monitoring organs be relaying evidence of vigorous contraction with little effectual shortening. This "inappropriateness" has been the focus of much work and remains part of the explanation with stiff or obstructed lungs. If the reality of direct information from medullary inspiratory centers to the cortex is accepted, however, we can explain dyspnea as precipitated by inappropriately small ventilation, sensed as volume change by receptors in the lungs, chest wall, and diaphragm, in proportion to the intensity of neural drive to contract inspiratory muscles. This primary mechanism is amplified when there is not an evident primary cause for the need to breathe deeply and forcefully. It is more distressing to breathe with a given force in response to metabolic acidosis or to high inhaled pCO_2 than in response to "healthy" vigorous physical exercise. It is devastating to breathe repeatedly against a closed airway shutter or with one's chest and belly bound so that no volume change can be effected. In a few ineffectual breaths, and before blood gases are significantly abnormal, one senses impending suffocation and struggles uncontrollably.

Muscle physiologists have studied the relationship of tension development to initial length, usually with supramaximal stimulation. It has been argued that with hyperinflation, the muscles cannot develop appropriate tension as they are already overshortened. The diaphragm has been analyzed as the arc of a circle. The smaller the radius of the circle, the greater the downward force it can generate on its dome. As hyperinflation develops, the arc describes a circle of greater and greater radius, ultimately approaching a flat disk with no moment to descend at all. Less emphasized is the fact that muscles effect volume change of the thorax by moving bones. The lower ribs droop down sideways from their anterior fulcra, based on the sternum, and their posterior fulcra, on the vertebral column. As the diaphragm pulls up on this curve, from a vertical insertion apposed to the inner chest wall, the ribs pivot out, increasing the lateral dimension of the chest, until they are fully expanded in this plane. This movement, whatever tension is applied, is thereafter ineffective to increase volume. Approaching the horizontal, the diaphragm develops a moment to pull the lower chest inward (paradoxically) and reduce its volume at total lung capacity. As one approaches total lung capacity, the only effectual maneuver is to raise the anterior ends of the ribs with the sternum and deepen the posteroanterior diameter. This involves mainly the use of the sternomastoid, scalenes, and sometimes the pectorals. The action is inefficient, in part because it necessitates the fixation of the extended neck by the erector spinae muscles and sometimes fixation of the elbows on the arms of a chair or the hands grasping a door or table. The volume of muscle stimulated is much greater than that required at a normal, lower functional residual capacity. Again, once the movement is completed, any tension developed is totally ineffective to draw air in; all it can do is to heighten dyspnea and hasten on muscle fatigue. Distress at this lung volume is attributable as much to the position of the ribs and diaphragm as to airway obstruction. Consciously downregulating "effort" reduces "inappropriateness" and dyspnea.

Natural History and Its Modification with Treatment

The most prevalent cause of shortness of breath in our society is COPD. This is best monitored by the FEV_1. Population studies have shown that FEV_1 declines very slowly with age in healthy people and much more steeply with the onset of COPD. We should seek symptoms in smokers, establish obstruction early, and achieve smoking cessation. If smoking is abandoned then the decline in FEV_1 flattens out and severe disability may be greatly postponed or avoided altogether. Weight loss in obese patients improves dyspnea. Treatment of coronary artery disease or left ventricular failure improves dyspnea in patients with those diagnoses.

Prevention

Society would prevent much distress and reduce costs of billions of dollars per year if cigarettes were "educated" or "taxed" out of widespread use. Patients with COPD benefit at all stages of deterioration from quitting cigarette use.

Cost Containment

Education of the individual to understand his or her own pattern of dyspnea and how to prevent or mitigate it improves quality of life and reduces emergency room visits and admissions to hospital. A patient seen within 48 hours of deterioration by the physician who knows her or him can be stabilized much more economically than those who delay going to the emergency room, hoping to get better (or are given an appointment to see an internist 10 days later). Panicky patients repeatedly seeking acute care should be evaluated by mental health colleagues if the clinician suspects pathologic anxiety or depression. Early diagnosis of COPD or coronary artery disease modifies the course of illness and helps contain costs.

REFERENCES

Carrieri-Kohlman V, Douglas MK, Gormley JM, Stulbarg MS. Densensitization and guided mastery: Treatment approaches for the management of dyspnea. Heart & Lung 1993;22:226.

Cherniack NS. Dyspnea. In: Murray, Nadel, eds. Textbook of pulmonary medicine. Philadelphia: Saunders, 1988:389.

Cooper JD. Techniques to reduce air leaks after resection of emphysematous lung. Ann Thorac Surg 1994;57:1038.

Dean NC, Brown JK, Himelman RB, et al. Oxygen may improve dyspnea and endurance in patients with COPD and only mild hypoxemia. Am Rev Respir Dis 1992;146:941.

Kaiser LR, Cooper JD, Trulock EP, et al. The evolution of single lung transplantation for emphysema. J Thorac Cardiovasc Surg 1991;102:333.

Light RW. Treatment of dyspnea with tranquilizers. In: Cherniack NS, ed. Chronic obstructive pulmonary disease. Philadelphia: Saunders, 1991:542.

CHAPTER 13–12

Wheezing

John G. Weg, M.D.

DEFINITION

Wheezing is a continuous adventitial sound longer than 250 milliseconds in duration. High-pitched wheezes (formally sibilant wheezes) are currently referred to simply as wheezes. They have a frequency of 500 Hz (Hz is frequency of oscillation in cycles per second) or more. Low-pitched wheezes (formally sonorous rhonchi) are currently referred to simply as rhonchi. Stridor is a loud crowing or whooping monophonic musical sound caused by upper airway obstruction. In contrast to these musical sounds with a well-defined pitch, noisy inspiration creates so-called "white noise"; this is a nonmusical sound heard best at the mouth in patients with airflow obstruction.

ETIOLOGY

Wheezing is generated by the rapid oscillation of airway walls or intraluminal materials. The pitch is determined by the frequency of the fundamental note and there may be harmonically related overtones. The pitch ranges between 60 and more than 2000 Hz. Oscillation occurs because of the Venturi effect of flow through a narrow lumen or because of dynamic compression of airways due to rising intrathoracic pressure.

CRITERIA FOR DIAGNOSIS

Suggestive

The patient may complain of dyspnea and may notice wheezing.

Objective

High-pitched wheezes or just plain wheezes have a frequency of 500 Hz or more. They may be heard in inspiration, expiration, or both. Polyphonic wheezing is characterized by notes with different pitches all starting at the same time and continuing to the end of expiration. Polyphonic wheezing typifies asthma and can often be heard at some distance from the patient. It is so characteristic that once heard, even lay people can reliably identify such wheezing. As airway obstruction increases, the pitch of the wheeze increases, the volume decreases, and the duration decreases. When airway obstruction is very severe, wheezing may cease; this is an ominous sign in the dyspneic tachypneic patient with asthma.

Paroxysmal monophonic wheezing that is loud and often characterized as whooping or crowing is caused by upper airway obstruction, for example, trachea, larynx, and above. If the site is extrathoracic, the sound is louder in inspiration and may not be heard in expiration. Intermittent episodes of paroxysmal monophonic wheezing originating from the larynx characterize the syndrome of laryngeal dyskinesia. Such wheezing is heard best over the larynx with some transmission to the chest wall; it is not heard from the intrathoracic airways. This wheezing is created by adduction of the vocal cords and narrowing of the glottis. If not recognized, a diagnosis of severe asthma is often made, resulting

in endotracheal intubation of a patient who appears severely ill but usually has normal arterial blood gases.

Short late inspiratory wheezes of varying pitch and amplitude may be heard in patients with idiopathic pulmonary fibrosis. Normal individuals wheeze at the very end of a forced expiratory maneuver due to dynamic compression of the airways.

Rhonchi are low pitched and characteristic of secretions in the airway. They may be heard in inspiration, expiration, or both and are usually polyphonic. They occur randomly throughout the respiratory cycle and usually partially or totally clear with coughing. A localized monophonic rhonchus suggests endotracheal or endobronchial obstruction such as by tumor, foreign body, scar, or granulomata. Such a localized rhonchus can often be heard only in a single position such as supine or prone or lying on one side. This sound may persist when air movement is no longer heard from the remainder of the lung following a deep rapid inspiration or expiration.

The bronchial leak squeak sound is a high-pitched continuous squeaking sound produced by having the patient perform a Valsalva maneuver when there is a bronchopleural fistula. It can be heard after chest tube insertion, if there is continued air leakage even when bubbling is not seen in the underwater drainage system. In the patient who is being mechanically ventilated, a continuous loud nonmusical whooshing sound in inspiration is also characteristic of a bronchopleural fistula.

The sound of noisy inspiration, "white noise" is a nonmusical sound caused by waves of random amplitude with an evenly spread frequency distribution between 200 and 2000 Hz. The sound is easily heard even at some distance from the patient.

CLINICAL MANIFESTATION

Subjective

Although some patients complain of wheezing, others describe chest tightness, a whistling sound, a squeaky sound in the chest, or a gurgling sensation; some appreciate only cough; and some may be oblivious to wheezing.

Objective

Wheezing is a sign of airway obstruction. Airway obstruction can be quantitated with spirometry or a flow volume curve. Loss of peak flow on the flow volume loop is indicative of upper airway obstruction. A semiquantitative measure of the amount of airway obstruction is the forced expired time (FET), the time required to perform a forced vital capacity maneuver as measured by hearing air flow with one's ear near the patient's mouth or with a stethoscope over the cervical trachea. A normal FET is 3 seconds or less; a FET of 4 seconds or more indicates airway obstruction.

It is often necessary to perform varying degrees of the forced expiratory maneuver to identify wheezing. This is especially true in patients with symptomatic asthma who minimize respiratory efforts by breathing with small tidal volumes and low flow rates, which may mask airway obstruction.

Normal Breath Sounds. Table 13–12–1 classifies commonly heard lung sounds. Normal breath sounds are described as vesicular; they are breezy or swishy with a maximum frequency content of 100 to 500 Hz. Inspiration predominates and the pitch is relatively high. There is a silent pause between inspiration and expiration, with expiration heard only as a short faint low-pitched sound about one fourth as long as inspiration. Bronchial or tracheal breathing is characterized by inspiration that is louder and higher pitched and expiration that is longer than inspiration, and with greater amplitude; it contains a wide band of frequencies from audible to more than 1000 Hz. Bronchial or tracheal breathing is heard over the trachea and the main bronchi. An intermediate stage is bronchovesicular breathing, which is normally heard over the second interspace anteriorly, in the intercapsular area posteriorly, and often at the medial right apex. Inspiration is the same as with vesicular breathing but expiration is louder and equal in length to inspiration.

Abnormal Breath Sounds. Discontinuous adventitial sounds are short intermittent explosive sounds usually shorter than 20 milliseconds called *crackles.* They are thought to be produced by the sudden opening of small airways. Fine crackles are due to the intermittent passage of air through a closed airway. Coarse crackles are due to bubbling of air through secretions. Fine late inspiratory crackles are high pitched and have variable intensity in spacing; they have been described as Velcro or cellophane crackles and can be simulated by rubbing strands of hair together. They tend to be more evident at the bases or in the dependent portion of the lung. They are characteristic of idiopathic pulmonary fibrosis, but are also heard in patients with consolidation and early pulmonary edema. Coarse crackles may occur early in inspiration, throughout inspiration, or in expiration. They are low pitched, less frequent and louder than fine crackles, and vary in frequency and loudness. They are characteristic of generalized airflow obstruction such as in patients with chronic bronchitis and emphysema. An even more course low-pitched rattling or bubbling sound is generated by secretions in large airways, especially with coughing. This sound can often be heard without a stethoscope. Simultaneous production of course crackles of varying pitch is characteristic of patients with bronchiectasis.

Routine Laboratory Abnormalities

There are no diagnostic abnormalities noted on routine laboratory tests.

PLANS
Diagnostic

An initial differential diagnosis of the causes of wheezing is provided in Table 13–12–2. The diagnoses have been divided into upper airway obstruction; diseases that cause generalized airway obstruction such as asthma, chronic obstructive pulmonary disease, bronchiolitis, aspiration, congestive heart failure, and pulmonary embolism; and lesions that may cause localized airway obstruction. It should be noted that the wheezing associated with pulmonary embolism and congestive heart failure is not the characteristic polyphonic wheezing heard in asthma, but rather is more likely to be monophonic and low pitched—rhonchi (see chapters dealing with these etiologies).

TABLE 13–12–1. CLASSIFICATION OF COMMON LUNG SOUNDS

Acoustic Characteristics	American Thoracic Society Nomenclature	Common Synonyms	Laennec's Original Term	Representation of Sound at Chest Wall	Time-Expanded Waveforms
Normal					
200–600 Hz Decreasing power with increasing Hz	Normal	Vesicular Pulmonary	Bruit respiratoire pulmonaire ou respiration vesiculaire	Inspiration, Expiration	Inspiration
75–1600 Hz Flat until sharp decrease in power (900Hz)	Bronchial Bronchovesicular	Bronchial Tracheal Bronchovesicular	Bruit respiratoire bronchique Bruit etrangers		Expiration
Adventitious					
Discontinuous, interrupted explosive sounds (loud, low in pitch), early inspiratory or expiratory	Adventitious Coarse crackle	Abnormal Coarse rale	Rale muquex ou garegouillement	Inspiration / Air Flow / Expiration	
Discontinuous, interrupted, explosive sounds (less loud than above and of shorter duration; higher in pitch than coarse crackles or rales), mid- to late inspiratory	Fine crackle	Fine rale, crepitation	Rale humide ou crepitation	Inspiration / Air Flow	
Continuous sounds (longer than 250 m, high-pitched; dominant frequency of 400 Hz or more, a hissing sound)	Wheeze	Sibilant rhonchus	Rale set sonore ou stifflement	Expiration	
Continuous sounds (longer than 250 ms, low-pitched; dominant frequency about 200 Hz or less, a snoring sound)	Rhonchus	Sonorous rhonchus	Rale sibilant sec ou ronflement		

Source: Weg JG. The respiratory system. In: Judge RD, Zuidema CD, Fitzgerald FT, eds. Clinical diagnosis. 5th ed. Boston: Little, Brown, 1989:220. Reproduced with permission from the publisher and author.

TABLE 13–12–2. DIFFERENTIAL DIAGNOSIS OF THE CAUSES OF WHEEZING

Upper Airway Obstruction
Epiglottitis
Retropharyngeal infection or hemorrhage
Laryngeal edema
Laryngospasm
Laryngeal dysfunction syndrome
Vocal cord paralysis
Foreign body
Tracheomalacia
Tracheal stenosis
Tumor

Generalized Airway Obstruction
Asthma
   Occupational asthma
   Allergic bronchopulmonary aspergillosis
Chronic obstructive pulmonary disease
   Chronic bronchitis
   Emphysema
   α_1-Antitrypsin deficiency
Bronchiectasis
   Primary
   Secondary
Bronchiolitis
   Infectious
   Fumes—toxic gas
   Organ transplantation
   Aspiration
   Congestive heart failure
   Pulmonary embolism

**Localized Airway Obstruction
(endobronchial/external compression)**
Foreign body
Adenoma
Carcinoma
Granuloma

Source: Weg JG. The respiratory system. In: Judge RD, Zuidema CD, Fritzgerald FT, eds. Clinical diagnosis. 5th ed. Boston: Little, Brown, 1989:195. Reproduced with permission from the publisher and author.

Therapeutic

See chapters dealing with the etiologies listed above.

FOLLOW-UP AND DISCUSSION

See Chapters 5–1 and 13–20.

REFERENCES

Forgacs P. Lung sounds. London: Cassell and Coller Macmillan Publishers. 1978.
Loudon R, Murphy RLH Jr. Lung sounds. Am Rev Respir Dis 1984;130:663.
Murphy RLH Jr, Holford SK, Knowler WC. Visual lung-sound characterization by time-expanded wave-form analysis. N Engl J Med 1977;296:368.
Nath AR, Capel LH. Inspiratory crackles—early and late. Thorax 1974;29:223.
Weg JG. The respiratory system. In Judge RD, Zuidema CD, Fitzgerald FT (eds): Clinical Diagnosis. Boston: Little, Brown & Co., 1989:195.

CHAPTER 13–13

Arterial Hypoxemia

Alice Beal, M.D.

DEFINITION

Arterial hypoxemia is the state of low oxygen content in the arterial blood. Oxygen content depends on both oxygen saturation, which correlates with the partial pressure of oxygen, and hemoglobin concentration. As oxygen concentration is not conveniently measured, hypoxemia is defined for clinical purposes as a pO_2 less than 70 mm Hg, which corresponds to an oxygen saturation of approximately 93%, when the hemoglobin is normal. Hypoxia refers to low oxygen content in the tissues, and is dependent on both arterial oxygen content and cardiac output.

ETIOLOGY

There are six major etiologies of arterial hypoxemia: (1) hypoventilation, the easiest to determine (inadequate ventilation causes inadequate oxygenation); (2) inhalation of air with a low partial pressure of oxygen (this commonly occurs at high altitudes, including commercial airline travel); (3) displacement of oxygen from the hemoglobin, as occurs in smoke inhalation, especially with carbon monoxide poisoning, or in the presence of some congenital or acquired hemoglobinopathies; (4) right-

to-left shunt (in the presence of a right-to-left shunt, the oxygenated blood mixes with deoxygenated blood before it gets to the arteries); (5) diffusion abnormalities, which occur in the presence of interstitial disease (not as clinically relevant as once thought); (6) ventilation–perfusion mismatch, by far the most prevalent cause of arterial hypoxemia.

Low mixed venous pO_2 and low cardiac output alone do not cause arterial hypoxemia; however, they can exacerbate it in the presence of one of the above listed etiologies.

CRITERIA FOR DIAGNOSIS
Suggestive

The clinical picture of altered mental status, tachypnea and tachycardia, or cyanosis suggests hypoxemia.

Definitive

Diagnosis is made by obtaining an arterial blood gas that reveals a low pO_2. A normal pO_2 is 80 to 100 mm Hg in patients under the age of 60. Because of the shape of the oxygen–hemoglobin dissociation curve, a pO_2 greater than 60 mm Hg is clinically acceptable in the absence of heart disease. The saturation decreases slowly when the pO_2 is greater than 60 mm Hg, but drops precipitously when the pO_2 decreases below that level (Table 13–13–1).

CLINICAL MANIFESTATIONS

Subjective

The clinical symptoms of hypoxemia are often subtle or absent. When symptoms occur, mental status changes such as decreased clarity of thought, irritability, and restlessness may be present. These occur to varying degrees in the setting of hypoxemia. When there is a rapid drop in arterial oxygen, headache, somnolence, and clouding of consciousness can occur. The symptoms of arterial hypoxemia, in conjunction with acute pulmonary symptoms, are easily recognizable. On the other hand, in the setting of chronic obstructive pulmonary disease (COPD), these symptoms may provide the only evidence of decompensation.

Smoke inhalation or occupational exposure such as mining or automobile repair in a poorly ventilated garage makes low oxygen saturation very likely.

Objective

Physical Examination

Tachypnea, tachycardia, and hypertension are the most common signs of mild hypoxemia. The classic sign of cyanosis occurs late and is often difficult to determine in darkly pigmented individuals. Profound acute drops in arterial oxygen can cause seizures, retinal hemorrhages, and hypoxic brain damage. Rarely, hypotension and bradycardia can occur in the setting of a severe rapid drop in arterial oxygen.

Routine Laboratory Abnormalities

Arterial blood gases should be obtained, initially. Once hypercapnia has been ruled out, measurement of oxygen saturation with a pulse oximeter can be substituted for an arterial blood gas. Pulse oximetry is noninvasive and reliable when there is good perfusion, but it does not measure carbon dioxide.

PLANS

Diagnostic

Differential Diagnosis

Arterial hypoxemia is a laboratory result not a clinical diagnosis. The challenge is to determine the etiology, as listed above, and thereby direct treatment. A useful clinical approach to arterial hypoxemia is to first rule out those causes that are easily excluded.

Diagnostic Options

Hypoventilation is confirmed by a high pCO_2 and a normal alveolar–arterial gradient. Therefore, hypoventilation can be diagnosed by an arterial blood gas. Situations of low inspired oxygen should be obvious from the clinical history. When high altitude is the etiology, the arterial blood gas reveals a low pO_2 and a low pCO_2 with a normal alveolar–arterial gradient (in the absence of pulmonary disease). In cases of smoke or toxic gas inhalation, patients must have cooximetry measurements along with arterial blood gases because the pO_2 may be normal with a low O_2 saturation. Cooximetry directly measures oxygen saturation as well as measuring CO and methemoglobin levels. Arterial blood gases

merely calculate the O_2 saturation. Shunting commonly occurs in pulmonary edema, pneumonia, and atelectasis. For patients in whom shunting is suspected, a history, physical examination, and chest x-ray are as important as an arterial blood gas. The hypoxemia will not resolve after the inhalation of 100% oxygen when a shunt is the predominant process.

Ventilation–perfusion mismatch occurs whenever there is uneven ventilation or perfusion in the lungs, and can be seen in almost any pulmonary disease. The classic diseases that cause ventilation–perfusion mismatch are asthma, COPD, pneumonia, interstitial diseases, and cystic fibrosis. When ventilation–perfusion mismatch is the etiology, the pO_2 is low, the pCO_2 is high or normal, and the alveolar–arterial gradient is increased. Low mixed venous saturation occurs when the oxygen consumption is disproportionately high compared with oxygen delivery. This occurs in heart failure and hypermetabolic states in which the heart cannot adequately compensate (e.g., sepsis or systemic inflammatory response syndrome). This can be determined clinically by the typical signs and symptoms of heart failure or, if a pulmonary artery catheter is present, by measurement of cardiac output and/or mixed venous oxygen saturation.

Recommended Approach

A good history and physical examination provide the diagnosis in the majority of cases. An arterial blood gas confirms hypoxemia, and establishes the alveolar–arterial gradient as well as the level of carbon dioxide and the acid–base status. The chest x-ray is the next most useful diagnostic tool.

Next, compare the chest x-ray film with the pCO_2. Table 13–13–2 provides a differential diagnosis of hypoxemia by comparing pCO_2 with "black" versus "white" lung fields on the chest x-ray film.

Therapeutic

Arterial hypoxemia is relatively easy to treat once the underlying diagnosis has been established. Whether the process is acute or chronic, therapy should be directed at the specific disease. Acute hypoxemia may take time to reverse and chronic hypoxemia may never resolve. In either situation, oxygen is the mainstay of therapy. The object of oxygen therapy is to minimize tissue hypoxia. Unfortunately, hypoxemia and hypercapnia often accompany one another and have overlapping signs and symptoms. Treating one without the other can have disastrous consequences.

The object of therapy is to increase the pO_2 above 60 mm Hg, which correlates with an oxygen saturation of 90%. In the absence of carbon dioxide retention, a Venturi mask of 28 to 40% or nasal cannula of 1 to 3 L/min is started. An arterial blood gas must be repeated within half an hour to ensure adequate oxygenation and to rule out the possibility of carbon dioxide retention. Patients with chronic carbon dioxide retention may have a blunted carbon dioxide response curve. They have a predominant hypoxic drive and may hypoventilate in response to high levels of oxygen. If this is not recognized early they may go on to carbon dioxide narcosis and eventual respiratory arrest.

If the oxygen saturation is not above 90% after starting oxygen therapy, the concentration of oxygen must be increased. The oxygen via nasal cannula can be increased to 6 L/min, but above that level it will dry out and irritate the nose. The Venturi mask can be increased to 50%. If that is not enough, then a high-humidity mask, which will deliver close to 70% oxygen, or a nonrebreather, which can deliver close to 100% oxygen, can be used. If more than 70% oxygen is required then mechanical ventilation should be considered.

If patients need oxygen therapy after an acute event, they must be reevaluated after 1 month to determine whether they need long-term oxygen therapy. Long-term oxygen therapy is usually delivered via nasal cannula or transtracheal catheter. The funding for long-term oxygen is strictly regulated in the United States, making its prescription complicated. Patients must meet specific criteria to qualify for reimbursement. The current criterion is a pO_2 less than 55 mm Hg or a pO_2 of 55 to 59 mm Hg with evidence of concomitant right-sided heart failure (including p pulmonale, right ventricular hypertrophy, or pedal edema). This hypoxemia must persist for at least a month after optimal

TABLE 13–13–1. RELATIONSHIP OF PO_2 TO OXYGEN SATURATION*

pO_2 (mm Hg)	Oxygen Saturation (%)
100	98–100
80	95
60	90
40	75

*Assuming a normal oxygen–hemoglobin dissociation curve.

TABLE 13–13–2. DIFFERENTIAL DIAGNOSIS OF HYPOXEMIA

pco₂ < 40 mm Hg		pco₂ > 40 mm Hg	
Black CXR	*White CXR*	*Black CXR*	*White CXR*
Pulmonary embolism	Diffuse	COPD	Diffuse
Other vascular obstruction	ARDS (any cause)	Status asthmaticus	ARDS
Circulatory failure	Cardiac pulmonary edema	Alveolar hypoventilation	Cardiac pulmonary edema
Anatomic right-to-left shunt	Pulmonary fibrosis	Sleep apnea syndrome	Pulmonary fibrosis
	(with acute insult)		End stage (irreversible)
	Localized		With airway disease
	Pneumonia		(some reversibility)
	Atelectasis		Localized
	Infarction		Pneumonia plus
			COPD
			Respiratory depression

CXR, chest x-ray film; ARDS, adult respiratory distress syndrome; COPD, chronic obstructive pulmonary disease.
Modified from Stevens PM. Acute respiratory failure. In: Sahn SA, ed. Pulmonary emergencies. New York: Churchill Livingstone, 1982:77. Reproduced with permission from the publisher and author.

treatment of an acute exacerbation, before long-term oxygen therapy is reimbursable.

FOLLOW-UP

Patients with acute arterial hypoxemia should be treated and followed up as appropriate for their underlying disorders. A significant number of patients have mixed disorders, such as pneumonia superimposed on COPD. When this is the case, follow the patients as appropriate for each of the underlying diseases. After resolution of the underlying cause of acute hypoxemia, no follow-up is necessary until further exacerbation.

Patients should be reevaluated 1 month after initiating long-term oxygen therapy. Many patients with chronic pulmonary disease slowly recover from acute insults and may not require oxygen after 1 month. Patients who remain hypoxemic longer than 1 month qualify for long-term oxygen therapy. When this is the case, patients should be followed with clinical evaluation and blood gases or oxygen saturation measurements every 6 months. Pulse oximetry is very useful in this situation, if pco₂ is not a significant problem.

DISCUSSION
Prevalence

The most common cause of arterial hypoxemia is chronic lung disease, especially COPD. An estimated 5.5 million people over the age of 55 have COPD in the United States. COPD was the fifth leading cause of death in 1990. Arterial hypoxemia is prevalent in severe COPD.

Related Basic Science

Hypoxemia is self-evident when the pO₂ is under 70 mm Hg. More difficult to recognize is hyperventilation with a normal pO₂ and an increased alveolar–arterial gradient and, therefore, inappropriately low oxygenation. Normal oxygenation can be calculated by using the alveolar–arterial gradient (Table 13–13–3). The alveolar–arterial gradient

TABLE 13–13–3. ALVEOLAR-ARTERIAL GRADIENT

Alveolar-arterial gradient =
$(P_B - P_{H2O}) \times F_iO_2 - (pO_2 + 1.25 \times pco_2)$
A-a gradient (on room air, at sea level) =
$150 - (pO_2 + 1.25 \times pco_2)$
Normal A-a gradient = 10–15
Increases with age (up to 1/3 age in years)
Oxygen Content (for clinical purposes):
Oxygen Saturation × HGB × 1.34

widens with age, and should be (in mm Hg) less than one-third the patient's age (in years).

A normal pO₂ does not preclude hypoxemia, as hypoxemia is the state of low oxygen content. It is possible to have hypoxemia with a normal pO₂, for instance, in the setting of severe anemia or carbon monoxide poisoning. Furthermore, hypoxia can occur in the absence of arterial hypoxemia, with a low cardiac output or distributive shock. Finally, hypoxemia occurs in the absence of hypoxia if the cardiac output is high enough. The overall evaluation of hypoxemia requires taking all these variables into account.

Ventilation–perfusion (V/Q) inequality is the most common pulmonary cause of arterial hypoxemia because a high V/Q ratio in some areas of the lung cannot compensate for the low V/Q ratio in other areas of the lung. On average, when the V/Q ratio is 1, venous blood has an oxygen content of 14.6 vol% and arterial blood has an oxygen content of 19.5%. When the V/Q ratio increases tenfold, the oxygen content increases only to 20.0 vol%. On the other hand, when the V/Q ratio decreases tenfold to 0.1, the oxygen content decreases to 16.0 vol%. Therefore, the effect of the low V/Q ratio is proportionately much greater than that of the high V/Q ratio.

Natural History and Its Modification with Therapy

Patients with acute arterial hypoxemia deteriorate if not promptly treated. Oxygen therapy in such cases should be instituted as a supportive measure, but the outcome depends on the underlying etiology. Chronic hypoxemia results in deleterious effects on the right ventricle, such as right heart failure with p pulmonale on the electrocardiogram, right ventricular hypertrophy, and edema. Central nervous system effects also occur. These include altered mentation and personality changes. Long-term oxygen therapy in patients with COPD has been shown to improve exercise tolerance and to prolong survival.

Prevention

The most common cause of COPD, and therefore of arterial hypoxemia, is cigarette smoking. Smoking cessation is a major preventive measure in avoiding hypoxemia. Smoking cessation programs have a low success rate, but when the absolute numbers are evaluated they are staggering. It is estimated that if 50% of U.S. physicians advise their patients to quit smoking, and 10% of those patients successfully quit, there would be 2 million new nonsmokers per year.

Avoidance of exposure to smoke inhalation and to high altitudes also decreases the incidence of arterial hypoxemia.

Cost Containment

In patients requiring prolonged oxygen therapy because of decompensated COPD, a repeat evaluation for arterial hypoxemia in 4 to 6 weeks may demonstrate improvement, at which point oxygen therapy can be discontinued. Proponents of the use of intermittent inspiratory flow devices and expiratory storage devices claim that oxygen usage is decreased by 10 to 75% with these devices. Liquid oxygen, in tanks, is very expensive, but is usually reimbursed by insurance. On the other hand, oxygen concentrators, which concentrate oxygen from room air, are not expensive, but use considerable electricity which is not reimbursed by any insurance.

The use of pulse oximetry to evaluate desaturation of oxygen is noninvasive and less expensive than arterial blood gas analysis. When retention of carbon dioxide is not a concern, serial oxygen saturation measurements are a cost-effective means of following patients' progress.

REFERENCES

Glynn TJ, Manley MW. How to help your patients stop smoking. Bethesda, MD: National Cancer Institute, 1991.

Greene KE, Peters JI. Pathophysiology of acute respiratory failure. Clin Chest Med 1994;15:1–12.

Hodgkin JE. Chronic obstructive pulmonary disease. Clin Chest Med 1990;11(3):ix.

Nocturnal Oxygen Therapy Trial Group. Continuous or nocturnal oxygen therapy in hypoxemic chronic lung disease: A clinical trial. Ann Intern Med 1980;93:391.

Petty TL, Snider GL, et al. Further recommendation by prescribing and supplying long-term oxygen therapy. Am Rev Respir Dis 1988;138:745.

West JB. Respiratory physiology: The essentials. 4th ed. Baltimore: Williams & Wilkins, 1990.

CHAPTER 13–14

Acute Infectious Bronchitis

Aymarah M. Robles, M.D.

DEFINITION

Acute infectious bronchitis is a nonspecific acute inflammation of the tracheobronchial tree that occurs as a result of a respiratory tract infection.

ETIOLOGY

Acute infectious bronchitis is commonly diagnosed by primary care physicians in outpatient community-based clinics. Respiratory viruses as well as bacterial pathogens are implicated in the etiology of acute bronchitis. Infection arising in a previously healthy person is generally caused by respiratory viruses, especially those perceived responsible for the common cold: rhinovirus, respiratory syncytial virus (RSV), parainfluenza virus, coronavirus, adenovirus, and influenza A and B viruses. Nonviral important pathogens include *Mycoplasma pneumoniae, Chlamydia pneumoniae* strain TWAR, and *Bordetella pertussis.*

The role of usual respiratory tract bacterial colonizers and pathogenic bacteria such as *Streptococcus pneumoniae, Hemophilus influenzae, Staphylococcus aureus, Legionella,* and *Moraxella catarrhalis* in the etiology of acute bronchitis, especially in otherwise healthy adults, is uncertain. Patients with underlying medical problems, including those with chronic obstructive pulmonary disease, cardiorespiratory illness, or immunocompromised states, or those with impaired cough reflex, whether from impaired consciousness, neuromuscular disease, or primary esophageal disorders, are at higher risk for infection not only with these organisms but with fungal pathogens as well. Another special situation is acute smoke inhalation that can induce a severe tracheobronchitis producing an intensive aggressive desquamative mucosal ulcerative inflammatory process from acute invasion of dormant herpesvirus infection in the susceptible host.

This chapter is limited to acute infectious bronchitis occurring in previously healthy adults with the absence of any predisposing disease process, who present with upper respiratory tract symptoms and cough to their primary physician.

CRITERIA FOR DIAGNOSIS

Suggestive

The diagnosis of acute bronchitis is based on clinical symptoms. Acute inflammation of the tracheobronchial airways is characterized by cough either nonproductive or productive of sputum. Cough is often persistent and unrelenting and continues in an indolent manner even when other signs and symptoms of the acute infection have ameliorated. Substernal burning like chest pain or discomfort that is aggravated by cough is frequent. Fever may be present. New-onset wheezing may occur. The patient does not appear toxic or severely ill. Chest radiography, if performed, is normal.

Definitive

Diagnosis requires careful clinical evaluation. There is no precise definitive diagnosis; it is a diagnosis of exclusion that relies predominantly on symptoms and the absence of severe adverse clinical findings.

CLINICAL MANIFESTATIONS
Subjective

Nonspecific common symptoms of acute upper respiratory viral infection include headache, facial tenderness, rhinorrhea, sore throat, ear discomfort, cough, and generalized malaise. The appearance of cough, either productive or nonproductive, together with retrosternal discomfort with or without wheezing serves to localize these symptoms to the lower airways.

Mycoplasma pneumoniae infection is characterized by a 2- to 3-week subclinical typical upper respiratory prodrome followed by sudden onset of sore throat, dysphonia, and intractable dry cough that is occasionally productive of scant amounts of mucoid sputum. Fever from 101 to 102°F and headache are prominent.

In *C. pneumoniae* infection, a biphasic pattern is common. Early symptoms are those of an upper respiratory viral illness with pharyngitis and laryngitis as prominent symptoms, followed 2 to 6 weeks later by a protracted dry cough. At the time of presentation to a physician, fever has usually resolved and symptoms of sinusitis may be prominent.

The presentation of pertussis in adults includes all of the usual symptoms of an upper respiratory infection. These occur in the first week. The diagnosis is suggested by greater than 2 weeks' duration of paroxysmal episodes of protracted cough that is usually nonproductive. Sleep disturbance occurs commonly due to paroxysmal nocturnal cough. The characteristic "whoop" is an atypical finding in adults.

Objective
Physical Examination

Physical examination is relatively within normal limits. Fever is usually absent in adults who have rhinovirus, respiratory syncytial virus, or coronavirus infections and, when present, tends to be low grade. In influenza A and B, adenovirus, *M. pneumoniae*, *C. pneumoniae* (TWAR), and *B. pertussis* infections, fever is present.

On auscultation, rhonchi or coarse rales are heard that characteristically either change or clear with cough. This suggests the presence of increased airway secretions. No focal or lobar signs of consolidation are present. Wheezing is another nonspecific finding that may be encountered after viral syndromes and *Mycoplasma* infection, and has recently been reported in patients who have *C. pneumoniae* strain TWAR. Patients with serologically confirmed TWAR showed a strong statistically significant dose–response relationship between *C. pneumoniae* antibody titers ≥ 1:64 and prevalence of asthma (Hahn et al., 1991).

Careful attention to ocular findings and ear, nose, and throat examination yields pertinent findings: a severe conjunctivitis together with pharyngitis and cough may suggest adenovirus, especially in epidemic clustering of infection. Bullous myringitis, though an unusual feature of *M. pneumonia* infection, is highly suggestive of the diagnosis in the appropriate clinical setting. Nonspecific inflammatory changes of nasal and oropharyngeal mucosa are seen and present with pain, erythema, and mild edema.

Routine Laboratory Abnormalities

Routine laboratory tests are essentially normal. Peripheral white cell count is either normal or slightly elevated with a normal differential or a minor left shift. Absolute lymphocytosis greater than 10,000, a feature seen in children with pertussis, is not seen in adults.

PLANS
Diagnostic
Differential Diagnosis

Differential diagnosis of acute bronchitis includes entities that affect all of the mucosa that forms the continuum from the nostrils down into the airways, and includes sinusitis, acute rhinitis, allergic rhinitis, rebound rhinitis secondary to extended use of α-adrenergic agents, laryngitis, and otitis. Many of these conditions have overlapping symptoms with acute infectious bronchitis.

Cough variant asthma may also present with cough, sputum production, and chest pain. Hyperreactivity of the airways may be secondary to an underlying bronchospasm component or occur as a result of postinfectious irritant stimulation of the aiways.

In addition, other lower respiratory tract infections need to be excluded. Chest x-ray may be required to diagnose infiltrates that would confirm pneumonia, or "tram track" dilation of bronchi that would suggest bronchiectasis.

Diagnostic Options

The decision to pursue a definitive diagnosis of an upper respiratory viral infection causing bronchitis is generally unnecessary. Nasopharyngeal washings for viral culture are expensive and require approximately 7 days for the diagnosis of influenza and 14 days or more for other respiratory viruses. Appropriate therapy should not be withheld awaiting diagnostic confirmation. Note that the percentage of positive cultures drops 5 to 7 days after initial presentation.

Nasopharyngeal swabs may be collected for both culture and direct fluorescent antibody for the diagnosis of TWAR and *B. pertussis*. The percentage of positive cultures for pertussis drops percipitously 2 weeks after the onset of symptoms.

Nasopharyngeal swabs or sputum may be cultured for *M. pneumoniae*. The gold standard in diagnosis of *M. pneumoniae* is a fourfold elevation in complement fixation titers between acute and convalescent sera. A single titer of 1:128 or greater is highly suggestive of recent infection.

For TWAR, serologic evidence to determine acute infection is regarded as a fourfold rise in complement fixation antibody titer. Additionally, the microimmunofluorescence test with immunoglobulin (Ig) M and G conjugates requires an IgM greater than 1:16, an IgG greater than 1:512, or a fourfold rise in titers, and helps to determine acute from past infection and primary from reinfection (Hahn et al., 1991). In

acute infection, IgM titers appear within 3 weeks of onset, and IgG at 6 to 8 weeks.

Elevated cold agglutinin titiers greater than 1:32, though nonspecific, are highly suggestive of *M. pneumoniae* infection and may be considered presumptive diagnostic evidence. Results of this test are not rapidly available. A simple bedside rapid cold agglutination test yields diagnostically helpful information. It is performed by placing 1 mL of the patient's whole blood into a tube containing buffered sodium citrate as an anticoagulant (prothrombin tube) and placing the tube in ice for approximately 5 minutes. The tube is removed and observed for clumping of red cells along the glass surface. When it is rewarmed by being held at body temperature, clumping should disappear. This confirms a positive result.

Sputum Gram stain, if performed, may show a predominance of inflammatory cells, especially neutrophils, and no organisms. If a predominant organism is found, it will guide empiric therapy until sensitivities are available. The presence of mixed flora suggests oropharyngeal contamination. The chest x-ray, if performed, shows no infiltrates.

Recommended Approach

A clinical approach to the evaluation of bronchitis is strongly recommended. A thorough history with emphasis on epidemiologic considerations, for example, recent community outbreaks of influenza, patient's living conditions especially those that encourage clustering, concurrent infections in persons who are close contacts, occupation, habits, underlying disease process, and time of onset of current symptoms, is most important. This together with a meticulous physical examination with special attention to ear, nose, throat, and cardiorespiratory system is primordial. Complete blood count with differential, serum electrolytes, and sputum Gram stain with culture and sensitivity are recommended. Nasopharyngeal swabs may be collected for culture and specific direct fluorescent antibody as described; these are more important when a definitive diagnosis is required in a patient with a prolonged course, where a high clinical index of suspicion exists for either pertussis, which requires prophylaxis of close contacts, or TWAR, which can persist for long periods or recur. Acute and convalescent complement fixation titers are not routinely recommended in uncomplicated acute bronchitis. Chest radiography should be obtained in all patients with an underlying disease state or in patients who appear "sick." Spirometry before and after bronchodilator therapy may be useful to determine hyperactivity of the airways and response to therapy.

Therapeutic
Therapeutic Options

Treatment of the majority of cases of acute bronchitis is symptomatic and focused largely on the control of cough. An evaluation of the current literature does not support antibiotic therapy for acute bronchitis (Orr et al., 1993). Antibiotics should be reserved for specific instances where a nonviral etiology is suspected. Inhaled β_2-adrenergic agonists were significant in reducing symptoms of acute bronchitis in patients who presented with wheezing on auscultation or bronchial hyperactivity on spirometry (Melbye et al., 1991). In another study, oral β_2-adrenergic agents, compared with erythromycin, administered to patients with acute bronchitis revealed that patients given bronchodilator therapy reported more rapid subjective improvement as well as resolution of cough (Hueston, 1991). More study in this area needs to be performed, perhaps looking at combinations of erythromycin with β_2 agonists.

Recommended Approach

Therapy is aimed at controlling symptoms: acetaminophen, oral liquids, and bedrest when malaise and fever predominate. Cough suppressants such as dextromethorphan 15 mg every 4 to 6 hours should be employed only for nonproductive cough. Alpha-adrenergic sympathomimetic nasal decongestants for no longer than 3 to 5 days may be used. Inhaled selective β_2 agonists 2 puffs every 6 hours may be prescribed with careful attention to technique to achieve optimal use.

During epidemics of influenza A, when clinical suspicion warrants therapy and when duration of illness is less than 48 hours, treat with amantadine 100 mg orally ever 12 hours. Therapy of *M. pneumoniae* infection requires erythromycin or tetracycline 500 mg orally every 6 hours or doxycycline 100 mg orally every 12 hours. Alternatives include the newer macrolide antibiotics: azithromycin 500 mg orally once per day or clarithromycin 500 mg orally every 12 hours. Quinolones may also be used. A 10- to 14-day course of antibiotic therapy is recommended to prevent relapse. For *C. pneumoniae* (TWAR) infection, institute therapy with first-line drugs such as erythromycin, tetracycline, and doxycycline at dosages equivalent to those for *M. pneumoniae;* however, longer duration of treatment may be required. Quinolones and the newer macrolide antibiotics are also therapeutic alternatives. The organism is resistant to sulfonamides. For pertussis, oral erythromycin is the drug of choice at 500 mg orally every 6 hours for 14 days. Alternatively, trimethoprim–sulfamethoxazole at 160 mg of the trimethoprim component every 12 hours is recommended for adults. Prophylaxis of pertussis is recommended for all close contacts of the index case. Dosage and duration of therapy are equivalent for both prophylaxis and therapy.

A consideration of symptomatic therapy together with a trial of oral erythromycin 500 mg and inhaled bronchodilators, 2 puffs every 6 hours, seems a reasonable approach in the appropriate clinical setting, when nonviral pathogens are suspected, for the treatment of acute bronchitis. Antihistamines, especially the newer, longer-acting medications such as terfenadine and astemizole, should be avoided not only for their limited efficacy in acute bronchitis, but also for their potentially life-threatening interactions with erythromycin.

FOLLOW-UP

Symptoms of acute bronchitis are usually self-limited and patients undergo complete resolution. Follow-up visits are generally not required and should be reserved for those with underlying chronic lung diseases or those who fail to resolve within approximately 6 weeks of initiation of therapy.

DISCUSSION

Prevalence and Incidence

The National Ambulatory Care Survey 1989 summary of physicians reported acute bronchitis as the ninth most common outpatient illness seen in the United States. It represented an annual expenditure of 200 to 300 million U.S. health care dollars, and was responsible for significant absenteeism from the workplace and so represented loss of productivity (Orr et al., 1993).

The highest incidence of acute bronchitis occurs during late fall and winter, occasionally extending into early spring. This seasonal predominance coincides with the high prevalence of upper respiratory infections during these periods.

In acute bronchitis, the most frequent viral etiologies are influenza A virus, influenza B virus, adenovirus, parainfluenza virus, and respiratory syncytial virus. Transmission of upper respiratory viral infections requires close person-to-person contact with an infected person who is in the stage of viral shedding. During this period, a large viral burden is present in respiratory secretions and is preferentially disseminated by coughing, sneezing, talking, and laughing. Inhalation of aerodynamically highly efficient infectious droplet nuclei of less than 10 μm occurs. This reduces the amount of inoculum required to establish infection. Low ambient temperature and humidity also favor transmission. Person-to-person transmission also occurs from contact with contaminated environmental surfaces, that is, door handles, leading to direct autoinoculation of mucosal membranes of the eyes and nose that further subsequent viral spread.

Success rate for infection to occur is multifactorial. Naturally occurring antigenic variability also plays a role. Immunity is strain specific, so that when a new viral strain is introduced into a susceptible population, it results in an acute epidemic. New cases peak within 2 to 4 weeks and then gradually taper off within the following month. The most susceptible groups include the very young and the elderly, as well as patients with underlying cardiorespiratory or immunosuppressive states.

Mycoplasma pneumoniae infection occurs in epidemic proportions. Person-to-person spread via infected droplet nuclei occurs. Most household contacts of the index case become infected in a wavelike manner over the subsequent 2 to 4 months until all susceptible hosts in the population are infected. It is more common in situations where clustering of persons occur: family units, military recruits, boarding schools. Historical information showing several weeks between cases within a family or living unit is an important clue to the diagnosis. Periodicity is present with peaks every 3 to 4 years.

Chlamydia pneumoniae TWAR infection is also transmitted by close person-to-person contact. Thirty to fifty percent of the worldwide adult population is seropositive for *C. pneumoniae* antibody. Antibody response to primary infection is transient and reinfection is common.

The resurgence of pertussis in the United States is a significant and important cause of acute infectious bronchitis: 5457 cases of pertussis were reported from January 3, 1993 to December 4, 1993 to the Centers for Disease Control. This represented an 82% increase as compared with the same period 1 year earlier, and was reported to be the highest annual number of cases in the United States since 1967. This increased incidence coincided with the expected cyclical pattern with peaks expected at 3- to 4-year intervals. Cases reported among persons older than 10 years of age have been noted to increase steadily: 15.1% from 1977 to 1979, 19.8% from 1980 to 1989, and 26.9% from 1992 to 1993 (Resurgence of Pertussis, 1993). This increased susceptibility may be attributable to waning immunity, which occurs approximately 12 years after primary vaccination is completed. It is important to recognize that adults are therefore important reservoirs for infection, especially for unimmunized or underimmunized children.

Related Basic Science

Cough as the defining symptom of bronchitis is a complex physiologic defense mechanism that protects the airway from injury. Cough receptors are numerous and are located throughout the airway mucosal and submucosal surfaces, primarily in the larynx, trachea, and the large bronchi, predominantly at sites of bifurcation. These are mediated by afferent branches of the vagus nerve. Irritation of the pharynx is mediated by the glossopharyngeal nerve. Interestingly, irritation of the external auditory canal can also elicit coughing by direct stimulation of afferent vagal receptors. Irritation of the diaphragm or pericardial surfaces stimulates cough via the phrenic nerve.

A positive correlation exists between cough and many inhaled noxious stimuli including tobacco smoke and air pollutants. Persons involved in dusty trades such as mining and sand blasting and grain workers have a greater incidence of cough. Firefighters, city dwellers, and persons living in homes where carbon is used for heating and cooking also have a higher incidence of cough.

Sleep influences the cough reflex even in healthy persons. Sleep raises the cough threshold, prompting an "asleep" cough reflex leading to decreased incidence of cough especially during sleep stages 3 and 4, including rapid eye movement sleep. This contributes to nocturnal pooling and retention of secretions within the airway.

Pathophysiology

During the acute stages of viral infection the normal ciliated columnar epithelium of the trachea and bronchi appears to be the principal site for viral replication. Marked dysplasia ensues; mucosal degeneration occurs that leads to denudement and desquamation of the epithelium, leaving an exposed basal membrane. This destruction may cause stimulation of submucosal efferent pathways, thereby altering bronchomotor tone.

Mycoplasma pneumoniae is especially notorious for its ability to adhere tightly to epithelial cells, where an intense polymorphonuclear leukocyte reaction together with recruitment of large mononuclear cells occurs, producing an inflammatory exudate at mucosal surfaces. These findings closely correlate with the clinical scenario of persistent cough, mucociliary impairment, and airway hyperreactivity.

Infection-induced cytopathic as well as ciliotoxic effects impair normal lung defense mechanisms. In the airways, the first line of defense at the cellular level is the pulmonary macrophage. It has the ability to ingest viral particles and present antigens to other immunocompetent cells, especially those found along lymphoid aggregates in the submucosa that are densely concentrated at bifurcation sites called bronchus-associated lymphoid tissue. These lymphocytes help generate local mucosal immune responses. Viral-specific IgG, IgM, and IgA neutralize viral infectivity. Natural killer cells as well as activated T lymphocytes are also recruited. This protective immune response occurs within the first 7 to 14 days after infection begins. Maximum histopathologic changes occur during the first 7 to 10 days. Ongoing slow resolution continues until complete healing occurs.

Pulmonary Function Tests

Acute infectious bronchitis may cause short-term abnormalities of airway reactivity. An obstructive ventilatory pattern is seen with increased airway resistance that is reversible with bronchodilators. These findings are most prominent in the first 2 weeks after the onset of symptoms and may persist longer than 6 weeks after initial symptoms resolve.

Natural History and Its Modification with Treatment

Previously healthy adults who are within the age range 20 to 60 who have symptoms of acute bronchitis delay presentation to their family physicians for a mean of 5 to 7 days after the onset of symptoms. Previously healthy smokers further delay presentation for 7 to 10 days after symptoms occur (Boldy et al., 1980). Viral origin of bronchitis is usually self-limited, though cough and postviral irritation of the airways may persist long after viral infection has resolved. Antibiotics shorten the course of *M. pneumoniae;* however, they have no effect on the nasopharyngeal carrier state. TWAR requires a prolonged course of antibiotic therapy, as infection may persist or recur despite appropriate antibiotic therapy. Often, multiple courses of appropriate antibiotics may be required to eradicate infection. Therapy of patients with pertussis is effective in decreasing both severity and transmission of disease.

Prevention

Annual immunization with influenza vaccine for susceptible groups including health care workers who care for these persons is recommended. Public health programs need to promote *B. pertussis* revacci-

nation for adults. New acellular pertussis vaccines are associated with less adverse effects and have serologic responses comparable to or higher than those seen with conventional whole cell vaccines. These should be further investigated in order to halt the U.S. resurgence of pertussis. Environmental pollutants including tobacco should be avoided.

Cost Containment

Prevention of disease in susceptible populations as described above is the single best cost containment method. A careful history and physical examination, together with judicious use of diagnostic modalities applicable to each pertinent clinical setting, are required. Choice of antibiotic therapy with first-line less expensive antibiotics is encouraged. Expensive, newer antibiotics regimens should be reserved for patients who are unable to tolerate first-line drugs either secondary to adverse effects (usually related to gastrointestinal symptoms: nausea, epigastric distress, diarrhea,) or adverse drug interactions, or when a suboptimal clinical response requires antibiotic change. Therapy, however, must be individualized and take into account such factors as ease of administration of once or twice daily regimens that ensue better patient compliance to therapy.

REFERENCES

Boldy DAR, Skidmore SJ, Ayres JG. Acute bronchitis in the community: Clinical features, infective factors, changes in pulmonary function and bronchial reactivity to histamine. Respir Med 1980;84:377.
Hahn DL, Dodge RW, Golubjatnikov R. Association of *Chlamydia pneumoniae* (strain TWAR) infection with wheezing, asthmatic bronchitis, and adult onset asthma. JAMA 1991;266:225.
Hueston WJ. A comparison of albuterol and erythromycin for the treatment of acute bronchitis. J Fam Pract 1991;33:476.
Melbye H, Aasebo U, Straume B. Symptomatic effect of inhaled fenoterol in acute bronchitis: A placebo-controlled double-blind study. Fam Pract 1991;8(3):216.
Orr PH, Scherer K, Macdonald A, et al. Randomized placebo-controlled trials of antibiotics for acute bronchitis: A critical review of the literature. J Fam Pract 1993;36:507.
Resurgence of pertussis—United States, 1993. MMWR 1993;42/49:952.

CHAPTER 13–15
Chronic Bronchitis
Patricia M. Romano, M.D.

DEFINITION

Chronic bronchitis, along with pulmonary emphysema, is part of the spectrum of chronic obstructive pulmonary disease (COPD), a disorder characterized by abnormal tests of expiratory airflow that do not change markedly over short periods of observation. According to the American Thoracic Society, chronic bronchitis is defined by chronic or recurrent excess mucus secretion with sputum production occurring on most days for at least 3 months of the year, for at least 2 successive years. Bronchiectasis or other inflammatory diseases that affect the lung are excluded.

ETIOLOGY

Chronic bronchitis is epidemiologically associated with cigarette smoking and inhalation of other irritants. Cigarette smoke inhalation causes mucus gland hyperplasia in the trachea and large airways; this subsequently leads to chronic sputum production. The earliest pathologic abnormality noted in cigarette smokers is an inflammatory reaction in the respiratory bronchioles. Excess mucous production by goblet cells,

may also cause airflow obstruction. Clara cells, which secrete surfactant, may become metaplastic and lead to bronchiolar collapse.

CRITERIA FOR DIAGNOSIS
Suggestive

Chronic bronchitis should be suspected in a patient who is a chronic cigarette smoker and gives a history of progressive shortness of breath, cough productive of sputum, intermittent or chronic wheezing, and an insidious decline in exercise tolerance. Generally, patients will have definite episodes of clinical deterioration associated with superimposed upper respiratory infections with fever, purulent sputum, and significant decline in their overall performance due to respiratory failure. Between these episodic deteriorations, patients return to their baseline level of respiratory dysfunction; however, unlike patients with asthma, lung function generally never normalizes.

Definitive

A definitive diagnosis of chronic bronchitis is made when patients with a history of chronic cigarette smoking present with the clinical syndrome described previously. This clinical syndrome is supported by objective evidence of expiratory airflow obstruction, demonstrated by formal pulmonary function testing (see Routine Laboratory Abnormalities). Furthermore, other inflammatory pulmonary diseases such as tuberculosis, cystic fibrosis, and other types of bronchiectasis, lung abscess, and acute bronchopulmonary infections must be excluded. Occasionally, patients do not give a history of cigarette smoking; in these patients disease may be due to passive smoke ingestion or to irritant, smoke, or toxic gas inhalation.

CLINICAL MANIFESTATIONS
Subjective

Patients with chronic bronchitis present with cough, chronic baseline sputum production as well as episodic increases in the quantity and changes in the character of their sputum production, wheezing, respiratory distress, and limited exercise capacity. Generally, this condition is most prevalent among smokers older than 35. Symptoms may begin during an acute respiratory infection and persist after the acute infection subsides. Sputum may be either mucoid or mucopurulent, but often it becomes more purulent during intercurrent respiratory infections. During infectious exacerbations, patients may appear cyanotic and in marked respiratory distress due to hypercapnia as well as hypoxemia. When pulmonary hypertension develops, patients present with symptoms of right-sided heart failure with orthopnea, jugular venous distension, hepatomegaly, and lower extremity edema. Then there will be a progressive decrease in exercise tolerance in the absence of evidence of worsening airflow obstruction.

Objective
Physical Examination

Characteristically, chronic bronchitis affects middle-aged and older persons. Physical examination in patients with chronic bronchitis reveals signs of lung overinflation, increased respiratory muscle effort, altered breathing patterns, and abnormal breath sounds. Wheezes, especially during forced expiratory maneuvers, rhonchi, and diminished air entry may be present. During bacterial pulmonary superinfections, localized signs of consolidation with bronchial breath sounds may also be appreciated. With the development of pulmonary hypertension, signs of right-sided heart failure may also be present with palpation of a parasternal or subxiphoid right ventricular lift, auscultation of an accentuated pulmonic component to the second heart sound, or appreciation of a right parasternal fourth heart sound. Late findings include a third heart sound or a murmur of tricuspid valve insufficiency, usually audible as a parasternal systolic murmur that increases in intensity with inspiration. Peripheral edema, indicating the presence of right-sided heart failure, has been associated with a decreased right ventricular ejection fraction.

Routine Laboratory Abnormalities

In uncomplicated chronic bronchitis, there are no characteristic abnormalities of the chest radiograph. If cor pulmonale is present, the main pulmonary arteries are enlarged. Signs of lobar consolidation may be present during bacterial pulmonary parenchymal superinfection.

Electrocardiography may show signs of right ventricular strain with voltage criteria of right ventricular hypertrophy, intraventricular conduction defects, right bundle branch block, and right atrial abnormality of the P wave.

Other laboratory measurements may provide supportive information. Erythrocytosis secondary to chronic hypoxemia may be present with end-stage disease as evidenced by an elevated hemoglobin and hematocrit. Serum bicarbonate levels may also be elevated in renal compensation for chronic hypercarbia. During exacerbations secondary to upper respiratory infections, the usual signs of bacterial superinfection such as leukocytosis and purulent sputum may be present.

PLANS
Diagnostic
Differential Diagnosis

The major differential diagnosis is between COPD and other etiologies of chronic cough and sputum production. Other inflammatory pulmonary disorders such as tuberculosis, lung abscess, cystic fibrosis, and other forms of bronchiectasis can generally be excluded through evaluation of the patient's history, sputum analysis for microbiologic culture, chest radiographs, and high-resolution chest computed axial tomography as needed. Asthma is excluded by a history of episodic, reversible wheezing after a discrete inciting event such as exercise, cold weather, viral illness, or an atopic challenge; lung function is entirely normal between exacerbations. The distinction between emphysema and chronic bronchitis may be less clear and overlap does occur.

Diagnostic Options and Recommended Approach

Generally, patients with "pure" emphysema present with a predominant symptom of progressive worsening dyspnea with exercise intolerance alone. They demonstrate diminished breath sounds despite exaggerated respiratory efforts with pursed lip breathing and less wheezing and sputum production. Signs and symptoms of cor pulmonale are more frequently associated with chronic bronchitis, although they occur with both conditions. The most characteristic symptoms and signs of "pure" chronic bronchitis are evidence of expiratory airflow obstruction (wheezing, dyspnea) and sputum production.

Spirometry establishes the diagnosis of COPD. The abnormalities associated with chronic bronchitis include a reduction in the forced expiratory volume in 1 second (FEV_1) and in the ratio of FEV_1 to forced vital capacity (FEV_1/FVC). Spirometry should also be performed after inhalation of a bronchodilator to assess the extent that the condition is reversible. A 15% increment in FEV_1 after bronchodilator treatment is considered significant; however, failure of forced expiratory flows to improve acutely after bronchodilator inhalation do not preclude a long-term beneficial response to these medications. Unlike patients with emphysema, patients with chronic bronchitis may not demonstrate an increased total lung capacity or a reduced diffusion capacity. The residual volume may be normal or enlarged. Abnormalities in lung mechanics are also seen with increased airflow resistance. Arterial blood gases may be normal or may show evidence of hypoxemia. Hypercapnia is more likely to be present in patients with chronic bronchitis than in patients with emphysema, especially during episodic infectious complications. There may be evidence of chronic renal compensation for the respiratory acidosis.

Echocardiography likewise may show independent right ventricular dilation with preserved left ventricular function.

Therapeutic

Cessation of cigarette smoking is essential. Patients with airflow obstruction should be treated with inhaled bronchodilators including ipratropium bromide (Atrovent) and selective short- and long-acting β_2 agonists. Oral theophylline may provide benefit for some patients. The efficacy of both inhaled and systemic corticosteroids in COPD patients is controversial, but these compounds are generally used in patients who remain symptomatic despite maximal therapy with bronchodilator therapy. Details of a recommended therapeutic regiment for patients with COPD are described in detail in Chapter 13–16 and are summarized in Table 13–15–1. All patients should use spacers (Inspirease, Aerochamber, etc.) with their metered-dose inhalers to maximize actual delivery to the bronchi and minimize deposition of inhaled drugs in the oropharynx.

Additionally, in patients with chronic bronchitis, sputum viscosity is often tenacious, especially when superinfection occurs. Patients should avoid agents that may dry secretions, such as antihistamines. Adequate hydration should be maintained. Mucolytics such as iodinated glycerol (Organidin), guaifenesin-containing compounds (e.g., Humibid LA), and iodinated compounds such as potassium iodide (SSKI) have been used to reduce viscosity and enhance expectoration. Although none of these agents have been shown to reduce airflow obstruction, quality of life may be improved as secretions are expectorated. Patients treated with iodinated compounds should have periodic thyroid function testing performed.

Acute bacterial exacerbations are frequent in patients with chronic bronchitis. These episodes are characterized by increased sputum volume and purulence, with increased evidence of airflow obstruction. Bacteria may be involved in exacerbations either as the primary

TABLE 13–15–1. RECOMMENDED THERAPEUTIC AGENTS FOR USE IN CHRONIC BRONCHITIS

Compound	Dose Regimen
Inhaled anticholinergic therapy	
Ipatropium bromide (Atrovent)	4–6 puffs q4–6h
Inhaled β₂ agonist therapy	
Short-acting	
Albuterol (Proventil, Ventolin)	2 puffs q4–6h
Long-acting (maintenance)	
Salmeterol (Serevent)	2 puffs every q12h*
Long-acting oral theophylline	
(Theodur, Theolair, etc.)	200–300 MG q12h†
Inhaled corticosteroids	
Beclomethasone (Beclovent, Vanceril)	2 puffs q6h‡
Triamcinolone (Azmacort)	2–4 puffs q6h **or** 4–8 puffs q12h‡
Flunisolide (Aerobid)	2 puffs q12h‡
Oral corticosteroids	
Prednisone	5–60 mg/d; generally start with 30–60 mg/d and taper over 7–10 d to off or lowest dose possible; alternate-day steroids may also be tried in doses of 30–60 mg every other day
Guiafenesin Compounds	
(Humibid Long-Acting)	600 mg po bid
Antibiotics for acute exacerbations	See text for details

*For maintenance use only; not for acute relief of bronchospasm.
†Dose to achieve level of 10–15 μg/mL.
‡Instruct patients to gargle after use to avoid oral thrush.

pathogen or as a superinfection after acute viral, chlamydial, or mycoplasma infection. Bacterial species include *Hemophilus influenzae, Streptococcus pneumoniae, Branhamella catarrhalis,* and, to a lesser degree, *Klebsiella* and *Pseudomonas* species. Antibiotics are used to accelerate the recovery from an exacerbation. It is recommended that a sputum Gram stain be performed to guide the choice of antibiotic therapy. Antimicrobial agents that may be used include penicillin V potassium, ampicillin, amoxicillin, amoxicillin/clavulanic acid (Augmentin), ciprofloxacin, ofloxacin, trimethoprim–sulfamethoxazole (Bactrim/ Septra), second- or third-generation oral cephalosporins, and erythromycin among others. Whether prophylactic antibiotic therapy reduces the incidence of exacerbations is less clear; patients who experience frequent, recurrent exacerbations should be considered for prophylactic antibiotic treatment. One prophylactic regimen alternates any of the above oral antibiotics for the first week of each month, especially during the winter season.

Patients whose arterial oxygen levels (PaO_2) are below 55 mm Hg should receive supplemental oxygen therapy for at least 18 hours daily, to reduce pulmonary artery hypertension. Patients whose PaO_2 is 56 to 59 mm Hg should also receive supplemental oxygen when there is evidence of pulmonary hypertension, cor pulmonale, or polycythemia.

Chronic hypercapnia is generally well tolerated. Hypercapnia can be minimized by improving overall lung function with bronchodilator therapy and decreasing the viscosity of pulmonary secretions. More recently, noninvasive mask ventilation with continuous positive airway pressure has been used to improve ventilation and thereby reduce hypercarbia in selected patients, both acutely during exacerbations and in maintenance care.

FOLLOW-UP

Patients should be followed at regular intervals according to the severity of their disease. Patients should be counseled to report acute exacer-

bations promptly so that bronchodilator treatment can be maximized and antibiotic treatment implemented. Preventive measures should include the administration of Pneumovax and yearly administration of influenza vaccine. Pulmonary function testing should be followed at yearly intervals.

DISCUSSION
Prevalence

Up to 10 million people in the United States suffer from COPD. It is largely a disorder associated with cigarette smoking and prolonged inhalation of toxic irritants in the workplace. It is a disease of the middle-aged and elderly.

Related Basic Science

The basic structural abnormality seen in chronic bronchitis is generalized hypertrophy and hyperplasia of the mucus-secreting bronchial glands throughout the trachea and bronchi. There is also evidence of diffuse inflammatory change. Increased numbers of mononuclear cells are present in the thickened tracheobronchial submucosa and metaplastic epithelial changes occur, with the loss of cilia. The physiologic end result of these changes is progressive resistance to airflow and evidence of expiratory airflow obstruction on formal pulmonary function testing.

Natural History and Its Modification with Treatment

The natural history is of progressive deterioration, especially when cigarette smoking continues; however, there is evidence that worsening of lung function may be halted with cessation of cigarette smoking. Moreover, patients develop episodic respiratory failure, usually associated with viral and bacterial superinfection, as characterized by increased sputum volume and purulence. Hospital admissions are generally associated with the infectious episodes. With continued disease, pulmonary hypertension and cor pulmonale develop.

Prevention

Cessation of cigarette smoking is the key to prevention. Additionally, exposure to irritants and toxic gases must be avoided by use of face-mask respirators in the workplace.

Cost Containment

Each patient's management should be individualized to find the optimal therapeutic regimen that will provide bronchodilation and ensure good patient compliance. Antibiotics should be used early for exacerbations and considered for prophylaxis in patients who have frequent flares.

REFERENCES

Chodosh S. Treatment of acute exacerbations of chronic bronchitis: State of the art. Am J Med 1991;91(6A):87S.

Dantzker DR, Pingleton SK, Pierce JA, et al. American Thoracic Society: Standards for the diagnosis and care of patients with chronic obstructive pulmonary disease (COPD) and asthma. Am Rev Respir Dis 1987;136:225.

Ferguson GT, Cherniack RM. Current concepts: Management of chronic obstructive pulmonary disease. N Engl J Med 1993;328:1017.

Murphy TF, Sethi S. State of the art: Bacterial infection in chronic obstructive pulmonary disease. Am Rev Respir Dis 1992;146:1067.

Salvaterra CG, Rubin LJ. Clinical commentary: Investigation and management of pulmonary hypertension in chronic obstructive pulmonary disease. Am Rev Respir Dis 1993;148:1414.

CHAPTER 13–16

Pulmonary Emphysema

Patricia M. Romano, M.D.

DEFINITION

Pulmonary emphysema is defined morphologically. It is defined by the American Thoracic Society as a condition of the lung characterized by abnormal permanent enlargement of the airspaces distal to the terminal bronchiole. It is accompanied by actual destruction of alveolar walls and without obvious evidence of fibrosis. This destruction is not uniformly distributed; the normal order of the lung acinus is lost.

Clinically, pulmonary emphysema and chronic bronchitis (see Chapter 13–15) are referred to as chronic obstructive lung disease (COPD). The dominant clinical feature in COPD is reduction in expiratory airflow as demonstrated by formal pulmonary function testing.

ETIOLOGY

Cigarette smoking is the single most important factor in the development of pulmonary emphysema. Smoking increases respiratory epithelial cell permeability by directly damaging type I pneumocytes in experimental animal models. Inhalation of cigarette smoke also causes a classic inflammatory reaction in the airway with edema formation and neutrophil aggregation. This is followed by tissue repair leading to fibrosis.

Emphysema is more common in lower socioeconomic groups, possibly related to the increased prevalence of cigarette smoking. Occupational exposures including coal mining and exposures to inorganic dusts, irritants, and pollutants (e.g., NO_2) are also associated with the development of emphysema.

Additionally, a small percentage of patients (approximately 2%) are prone to the development of pulmonary emphysema at an early age (30–40 years), especially if they smoke cigarettes, as a result of a congenital deficiency of a naturally occurring antiprotease in the lung, α_1-antitrypsin (AAT). This condition is discussed in detail subsequently (see Related Basic Science). These patients develop emphysema that is most severe in the lower zones of the lung.

CRITERIA FOR DIAGNOSIS

Suggestive

There is a continuum in the clinical diagnosis of pulmonary emphysema and chronic bronchitis. A history of cigarette smoking increases the likelihood that symptoms are due to emphysema or chronic bronchitis. Generally, patients with emphysema complain of progressive dyspnea, reduced exercise tolerance, perhaps wheezing, and generally little sputum production, except in the setting of bacterial superinfection. Dyspnea tends to worsen insidiously over time, without marked change over short periods of observation, which helps to distinguish emphysema from asthma. A family history of obstructive airway disease occurring in younger patients with or without a history of cigarette smoking suggests familial inheritance of AAT deficiency.

Definitive

Definitive evidence of airspace destruction with hyperinflation requires postmortem pathologic examination. Even postmortem pathologic examinations of patients clinically classified as having either emphysema or chronic bronchitis reveal characteristics of both diagnostic categories.

Definitive clinical criteria for pulmonary emphysema are established through pulmonary function tests and chest radiography, in the proper clinical scenario. In pulmonary emphysema, there is evidence of hyperinflation as well as progressive airflow obstruction. Hyperinflation is manifested by an increased total lung capacity, decreased lung elastic recoil, and increased lung compliance. Loss of alveolar surface results in a reduction of carbon monoxide uptake, as performed in the single-breath diffusion test maneuver (DLCO). Chest radiography (Figure 13–16–1) evidence of hyperinflation includes a flattened diaphragm, widened retrosternal airspace, small midline cardiac silhouette, and rapid tapering of central vascular shadows with a sparsity of vascular markings in the periphery and bullous lesions (lucent areas with absence of lung markings).

CLINICAL MANIFESTATIONS

Subjective

Patients with emphysema complain of progressive dyspnea, cough, and some wheezing. There may be a history of recurrent respiratory infections, with intermittent sputum production. Occasionally, dyspnea may be the only presenting symptom; it may be insidious in onset and progressive in severity. As the disease progresses, even normal activity levels such as dressing and eating evoke shortness of breath and the patient may become markedly incapacitated. Patients may acclimate to the insidious development of dyspnea and not present to a physician's attention until the process is markedly advanced. Episodic wheezing, especially in response to various stimuli, with symptom-free, normal lung function between episodes is more characteristic of asthma or "reactive airway syndromes" (e.g., after viral upper respiratory illnesses or an atopic challenge).

Objective

Physical Examination

Patients with advanced disease have marked exercise intolerance secondary to dyspnea. Weight loss is common, perhaps secondary to excessive work of breathing. Psychological disturbances such as anxiety, depression, and lack of concentration are present. Physical examination reveals signs of hyperinflation with a low, flat diaphragm and minimal diaphragm excursion on inspiration and expiration. Breath sounds are markedly decreased. The forced expiratory time is prolonged. There may be signs of increased respiratory muscle effort, with use of accessory muscles of respiration as well as altered breathing patterns (e.g., pursed lip breathing). True wheezing may be absent; in fact, more commonly auscultation reveals distant breath sounds alone. Clubbing is absent and patients are not cyanotic unless a respiratory superinfection with clinical deterioration is present. Rarely, there may be signs of secondary pulmonary hypertension.

Routine Laboratory Abnormalities

Electrocardiography generally reveals low voltage and a vertically directed mean QRS vector. Findings present on conventional chest radiography have been previously described (see Figure 13–16–1).

Other laboratory measurements may provide supportive information. Erythrocytosis secondary to chronic hypoxemia may be present with advanced disease as evidenced by an elevated hematocrit. Serum bicarbonate levels may also be elevated as the kidney compensates for chronic hypercarbia, although this is much more commonly seen in patients with chronic bronchitis and generally only terminally in patients with emphysema.

PLANS

Diagnostic

Differential Diagnosis

The differential diagnosis is between asthma and other forms of COPD, chronic bronchitis, and emphysema. Patients with asthma generally present at a younger age; have evidence of reversible airway dysfunction after a specific challenge (e.g., cold air, exercise, atopic stimuli),

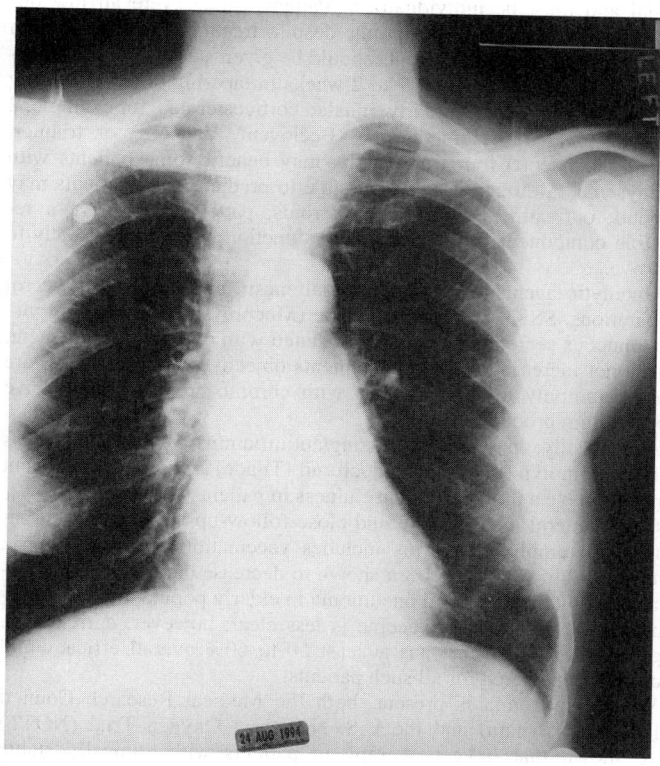

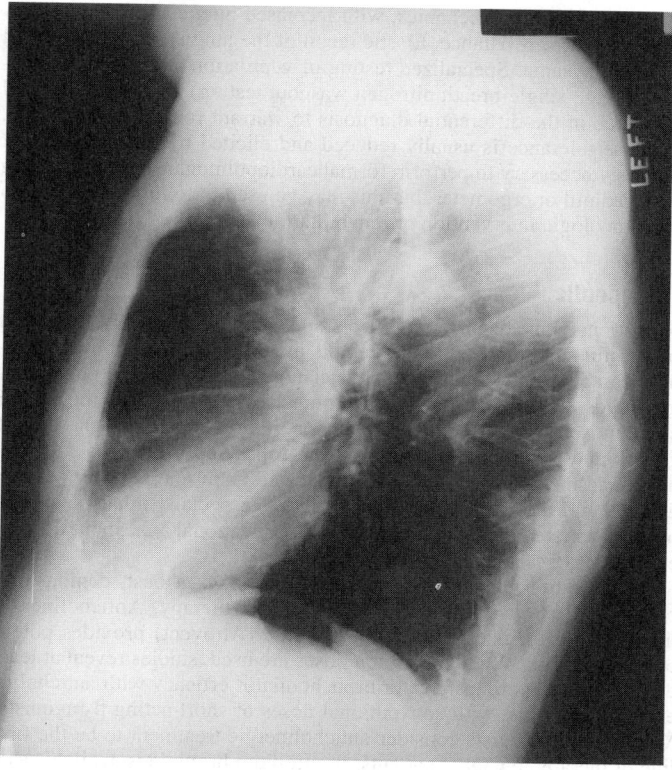

A   **B**

Figure 13–16–1. Posteroanterior (**A**) and lateral (**B**) chest radiographs in pulmonary emphysema. There is evidence of a flattened diaphragm, small cardiac shadow, tapering of central vascular shadows, and increased retrosternal airspace.

with a significant response to bronchodilators; and generally have normal lung function between episodes. There may be considerable overlap between chronic bronchitis and emphysema; in pure emphysema, dyspnea and reduced exercise tolerance with little sputum production, few intercurrent bacterial infections, and preservation of $PaCO_2$ until advanced disease prevail.

Diagnostic Options and Recommended Approach

High-resolution chest computed axial tomography (CAT) has allowed the identification of specific patterns of emphysema (panlobular, centriacinar—see Related Basic Science). CAT reveals patchy areas of reduced attenuation of lung parenchyma, bulla formation, and a paucity of vasculature in abnormal areas (Figure 13–16–2). Rarely, however, is it necessary to obtain CAT to obtain the diagnosis. Spirometry establishes the diagnosis of COPD. By definition, in obstructive airway diseases, the forced expired volume in 1 second (FEV_1) and the ratio of FEV_1 to forced vital capacity (FEV_1/FVC) are reduced. Repeat spirometry is performed after the inhalation of a bronchodilator compound, for example, a short-acting β_2 agonist such as albuterol, to assess whether a reversible component of obstruction exists. Failure to respond does not preclude a long-term benefit from these compounds. Additionally, measurement of lung volumes typically reveals an enlarged total lung capacity, an increased residual volume, and an increased residual volume/total lung capacity ratio. This reflects air trapping, due to early closure of smaller airways from airway obstruction. The DL_{CO} may be reduced due to ventilation/perfusion abnormalities as well as loss of lung surface area.

Arterial blood gases generally reveal some degree of hypoxemia and the arterial oxygen concentration (PaO_2) falls. The arterial concentration of carbon dioxide ($PaCO_2$) may be normal or elevated.

α_1-Antitrypsin levels should be assayed in young patients who present with an emphysema pattern on pulmonary function testing and who have no or an insignificant smoking history and/or a family history of obstructive lung disease.

Chronic obstructive pulmonary disease is usually associated with ab-

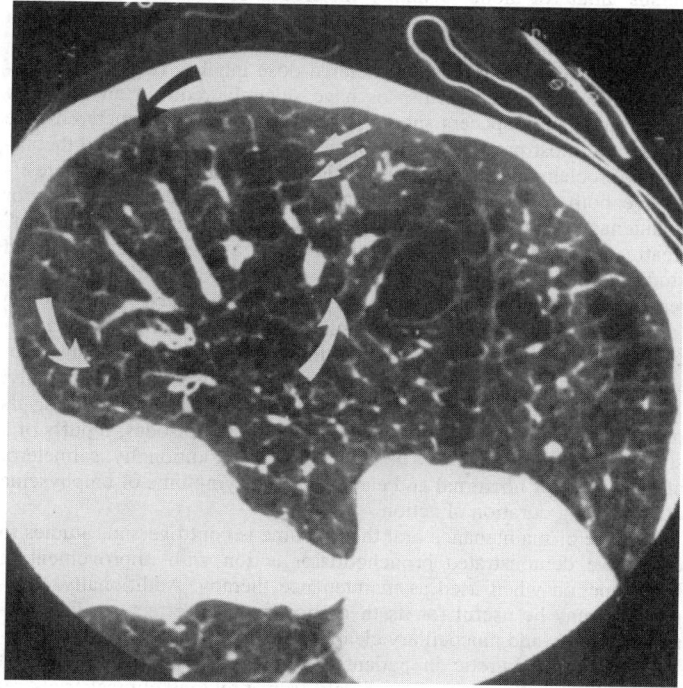

Figure 13–16–2. High-resolution chest computed axial tomography (CAT) in pulmonary emphysema. CAT reveals patchy areas of low attenuation of lung parenchyma separated from surrounding normal parenchyma without clearly definable walls. The straight arrows mark interlobular veins that help define these spaces. The curved arrows mark these vessels cut tangentially. *(Source: Naidich DP, Zerhouni EA, Siegelman SS. Computed tomography and magnetic resonance of the thorax. New York: Raven 1994;382. Reproduced with permission from the publisher and author.)*

normalities in lung mechanics, with increased lung compliance and increased airflow resistance. Elastic recoil of the lung is severely reduced with emphysema. Specialized testing of ventilation and perfusion mismatch (e.g., single-breath nitrogen washout testing) is rarely of clinical relevance in the differential diagnosis to warrant routine performance. Exercise tolerance is usually reduced and elicited by history. It is not routinely necessary to perform formal cardiopulmonary exercise testing via treadmill or ergometer, but this may be used to follow a response to pharmacologic intervention or rehabilitation efforts.

Therapeutic

All patients must be encouraged to stop smoking completely. The most successful smoking cessation attempts include a combination of smoking cessation counseling by a physician/nurse coordinator, pharmacologic aids such as nicotine patches or chewing gum, and the use of clonidine orally or by patch. Behavior modification through support groups may also be helpful. Long-term follow-up is essential. All patients and their families should be educated about the severity of their disease, and the proper use of medications, especially inhalers, should be demonstrated along with provision of educational aids about the disease, its progression, and its prognosis.

By definition, patients with emphysema may, at best, demonstrate only partial reversibility with bronchodilator therapy. Anticholinergic therapy with inhaled ipratropium bromide (Atrovent) provides potent bronchodilation. When maximum doses are used, studies reveal at least equivalent and perhaps greater bronchodilator efficacy than with anticholinergic therapy than with conventional doses of short-acting β_2 agonists. Many pulmonologists consider anticholinergic treatment to be the first line of therapy in COPD patients. Ipratropium bromide is available as a metered-dose inhaler and more recently as a nebulized solution in unit doses (0.5 mg in normal saline). Four to six puffs inhaled four times daily via a metered-dose inhaler or 0.5 mg administered three times daily via nebulized solution is the maximum dose recommended. A recent 12-week study in patients with COPD revealed a synergistic increase in FEV_1 with ipratropium bromide in combination with albuterol versus albuterol alone. Whether metered-dose inhalers or nebulized therapy should be used is also currently under debate; studies show an advantage to the use of nebulized delivery if patients are unable to effectively coordinate the use of metered-dose inhalers (e.g., elderly patients, patients with arthritis) or have severely reduced airway flow rates. Medication spacers should be used routinely with metered-dose inhalers in most patients to maximize medication delivery into the airway (Aerochamber, Inspirease). Inhaled short-acting β_2 agonists are effective both for acute bronchodilation during exacerbations and for maintenance therapy. Controversy exists for "maintenance versus prn" treatment with β_2 agonists for obstructive airway disease in general, but studies to date have not been conclusive. The maximum dose for maintenance treatment should be 2 puffs every 4 to 6 hours. A long-acting (at least 12 hours) inhaled β_2 agonist, salmeterol (Serevent), was recently released in the United States for maintenance treatment of obstructive airway disease. The recommended dose is 2 puffs twice daily. This drug is not indicated for acute bronchoconstrictive episodes, as its onset of action is 18 to 20 minutes. During these episodes, 2 puffs of a short-acting β_2 agonist may be supplemented. Additionally, salmeterol affords relief of nocturnal and early morning symptoms of emphysema due to it long duration of action.

The use of maintenance oral theophylline is controversial. Studies to date have demonstrated bronchodilator action with improvement in lung function when used as maintenance therapy. Additionally, theophylline may be useful for its theoretical positive effect on diaphragmatic motility and mucociliary clearance, as a central respiratory stimulant, and as a diuretic in patients with secondary right-sided heart failure. Moreover, evaluation of data from previous clinical trials reveals that serum levels of 10 to 15 μg/mL are within the therapeutic dose range for bronchodilation while minimizing the toxicity associated with previously recommended higher therapeutic levels (15–20 μg/mL). Long-acting theophylline preparations may be most useful when administered before bedtime in patients with nocturnal or early morning symptoms of airway obstruction.

The use of corticosteroids in COPD, unlike in asthma, is also contro-versial and must be individualized. Patients with severe airflow obstruction and continuing symptoms despite treatment with maximum doses of other therapeutic agents should be given a course of oral prednisone or its equivalent over 1 to 2 weeks in tapering doses guided by response to treatment. Similarly, inhaled corticosteroids, for example, 2 puffs of inhaled beclomethasone (Beclovent, Vanceril) or triamcinolone (Azmacort) four times daily, may benefit some patients with emphysema. Although it is not possible to predict which patients may respond to treatment with corticosteroids, patients who have a reversible component of their airway dysfunction are the most likely to improve.

Mucolytic agents, for example, guaifenesin and iodinated glycerol preparations, SSKI, and acetylcysteine (Mucomyst), by loosening viscous mucous secretions, may be associated with clinical improvement, but do not increase FEV_1 measurements objectively. These agents are more commonly used in patients with chronic bronchitis who have more sputum production.

Additionally, mast cell-stabilizing/antiinflammatory agents such as sodium cromolyn (Intal) and nedocromil (Tilade) are also available, but generally have a more limited usefulness in patients with COPD.

Good general medical care and close follow-up are essential in patients with emphysema. This includes vaccination against influenza virus each fall, which has been shown to decrease the incidence of flu-related hospitalizations and pneumonia in elderly populations. The usefulness of pneumococcal vaccine is less clear; however, current data suggest that this vaccine has at least 50 to 60% overall efficacy and should be considered for all such patients.

When hypoxemia is present, both the Medical Research Council Trial (Great Britain) and the U.S. Nocturnal Oxygen Trial (NOTT) have shown that oxygen therapy in patients with clinically stable COPD may prolong survival. Indications for home oxygen include a PaO_2 less than 55 mg Hg at rest; a PaO_2 of 55 to 59 mm Hg at rest but less than 55 mm Hg with exercise or during sleep; and a PaO_2 of 55 to 59 mm Hg at rest but evidence of cor pulmonale on electrocardiography or secondary polycythemia. Oxygen therapy must be used at least 18 hours per day to prolong survival. In addition to lengthening life span, continuous oxygen therapy also improves the quality of life by improving daytime performance, cognitive skills, and the quality of sleep.

More recently, noninvasive mask ventilation with continuous positive airway pressure (CPAP) has been used in selected patients with hypercarbia, both acutely during exacerbations and in maintenance care.

Rehabilitation programs include respiratory and occupational therapy, exercise programs, nutritional guidance, and psychosocial counseling have all been used to improve lifestyle. Aerobic exercise conditioning, upper extremity training, and respiratory muscle training with inspiratory loading have been employed. No study to date has definitely shown improvement in pulmonary function, though a modest increase in exercise capacity along with a reduction in breathlessness and enhanced psychosocial function may be seen. Patients should be encouraged to remain active and eat well. Undernutrition has been estimated to be present in 25% of outpatients with COPD and up to 50% of hospitalized patients. Respiratory biofeedback and relaxation therapy as well as individual, group, and family group therapy sessions may also be useful, along with mild anxiolytic therapy.

Specific augmentation therapy with AAT is approved for use intravenously in weekly to monthly intervals for patients with levels below 11 μM and who have stopped smoking (see Related Basic Science). Bullectomy may improve dyspnea in selected patients with bullae causing lung compression. Single-lung transplantation for treatment of end-stage emphysema has been performed successfully over the last several years at several centers. To date, long-term survivors are alive at least 2 to 3 years posttransplant, with significant improvement in FEV_1 and PaO_2 seen by 3 months after transplant. Exercise function is also significantly better.

FOLLOW-UP

Good general medical care with emphasis on prophylactic measures as previously mentioned should be the mainstay of the therapeutic program. Periodic spirometry, DLCO, and arterial blood gas measurements may be obtained to chronicle the patient's stability or decline, but need not be obtained more often than yearly.

DISCUSSION
Prevalence and Incidence

Chronic obstructive pulmonary disease is the fifth leading cause of death in the United States and accounted for about 15% of all hospitalizations in 1985. It is a disease of advanced age with peak prevalence rate between 65 and 75 years of age. Although it is more common in men due to increased cigarette smoking, rates in women are increasing. The single most important associated factor is cigarette smoking. The exact mechanism is unclear, as only 15% of all smokers develop clinically significant COPD.

Related Basic Science
Anatomic Derangement

Emphysema develops as lung elastin is degraded by endogenous proteolytic enzymes that overwhelm the body's natural inhibitors and lead to lung autodigestion. AAT provides approximately 90% of all inhibitory capacity against proteolysis of the lung. The type of emphysema associated with cigarette smoking is classically centrilobular. There is an accumulation of dust-laden macrophages in and around respiratory bronchioles. Studies evaluating smokers by bronchoalveolar lavage show that they have a five times increased neutrophil population in the lung. These neutrophils are capable of releasing proteolytic enzymes into the alveoli and airways, leading to emphysema pathologically. In 1963, Laurell and Eriksson recognized the familial deficiency of AAT. Individuals with congenital deficiency of AAT develop a panacinar emphysema in that all components of the lung acinus are equally affected.

Genetics

In the United States, a very small percentage of all patients with emphysema are predisposed to the disorder due to a recessive autosomal defect of the gene that encodes for AAT. AAT deficiency represents one of the most common lethal hereditary disorders of Caucasians in the United States and Europe. Typically, emphysema in these patients becomes evident in the third to fourth decades of life, especially in cigarette smokers. Some adult patients may also present with cholestatic liver disease, which may lead to cirrhosis. Rarely, hepatoma has been associated with this enzyme deficiency. This genetic disorder should be suspected in patients who develop severe airway obstructive disease, especially if they have affected siblings or parents and have a meager cigarette smoking history. The diagnosis is established by measuring serum AAT levels (normal values are 150–350 mg/dL or 20–48 μM). The variants of AAT occur because of point mutations that result in a single amino acid substitution. The normal M alleles (the alleles are assigned a letter code) occur in about 90% of persons of European de-

scent with normal serum AAT levels; their phenotype is designated protease inhibitor MM (PiMM). More than 95% of persons in the severely deficient category are homozygous for the Z allele, designated PiZZ, and have serum AAT levels of 2.5 to 7 μM (16% of normal). Persons with nonexpressing allele genes also exist (Pi null–null), as do heterozygotes (PiMZ). The threshold protective level is 11 μM or 80 mg/dL (35% of normal). Patients with PiZZ phenotype are at risk for emphysema; if these patients smoke cigarettes, their risk is markedly enhanced. Establishment of the diagnosis is crucial, as augmentation therapy by weekly to monthly intravenous infusion of AAT from pooled plasma is available in addition to standard pharmacologic treatment. It is presumed that augmentation therapy will halt progression of the disease.

Natural History and Its Modification with Treatment

The course of pulmonary emphysema is progressive. Smoking cessation slows the progression of disease. Bronchodilator therapy improves quality of life and exercise tolerance but is not curative.

Prevention

Eradication of cigarette smoking and reduction of occupational risks to inhaled inorganic dusts will decrease the incidence of pulmonary emphysema. Genetic counseling for families of patients with AAT deficiency will decrease the incidence of the disease.

Cost Containment

To contain costs, efforts must be made to maximize and individualize each patient's therapeutic regimen with as concise a pharmacologic regimen as possible. The cost of cigarettes will be saved for those who discontinue smoking. Prophylactic measures should be followed to decrease hospitalization and allow the patient to be productive for as long as possible.

REFERENCES

Bone RC, Dantzker DR, George RB, et al. Chronic obstructive pulmonary disease. In: Pulmonary and critical care medicine. 3rd ed. St. Louis: Mosby-Year Book, 1993:1.

Buist AS, Burrows B, Cohen A, et al. American Thoracic Society: Guidelines for the approach to the patient with severe hereditary alpha-1-antitrypsin deficiency. Am Rev Respir Dis 1989;140:1494.

Dantzker DR, Pingleton SK, Pierce JA, et al. American Thoracic Society: Standards for the diagnosis and care of patients with chronic obstructive pulmonary disease (COPD) and asthma. Am Rev Respir Dis 1987;136:225.

Ferguson GT, Cherniack RM. Current concepts: Management of chronic obstructive pulmonary disease. N Engl J Med 1993;328:1017.

Hodgkin JE. Clinics in chest medicine: Chronic obstructive pulmonary disease. Philadelphia: Saunders, 1990.

Laurell CB, Eriksson S. The electrophoretic α1-globulin pattern of serum in α1-antitrypsin deficiency. Scand J Clin Lab Invest 1963;15:132.

CHAPTER 13–17

Pneumomediastinum

Roger Boykin, M.D.

DEFINITION

Pneumomediastinum may be defined as the presence of air or other gas within the mediastinum.

ETIOLOGY

There are multiple causes of pneumomediastinum that can be categorized as in Table 13–17–1.

More common causes include conditions associated with alveolar–

interstitial air leak (asthma, mechanical ventilation) and violation of the oral pharyngeal, tracheobronchial, or esophageal tissue planes.

CRITERIA FOR DIAGNOSIS
Suggestive

Crepitation at the suprasternal notch with or without frank subcutaneous emphysema suggests the diagnosis. This is especially the case when these two observations occur in the proper clinical setting, that is,

TABLE 13–17–1. ETIOLOGY OF PNEUMOMEDIASTINUM

Trauma	Alveolar–Interstitial Air Leak
Penetrating trauma in neck or chest	Secondary to endobronchial neoplasm or foreign body
Dental procedures, e.g., extractions, and air turbine drilling	Emphysema
Facial bone, sinus fracture extractions, and air-turbine drilling	Asthma
Facial bone, sinus fractures	Mechanical ventilation
	Pneumothorax
Associated with Infectious Disease	Spontaneous pneumomediastinum
Head and neck soft tissue infections	
Acute bacterial mediastinitis	**Iatrogenic**
Pneumatosis cystoides intestinalis	Secondary to artificial pneumothorax or pneumoperitoneum
Tonsillitis	Secondary to subcutaneous emphysema associated with chest tube insertion
Osteomyelitis of facial bones	Secondary to dental, oral, pharyngeal, tracheobronchial, esophageal, thoracic, or neck surgery
Sialadenitis	Secondary to pulmonary function testing
Peritonsillar abcess	

in conditions associated with alveolar–interstitial air leak or tissue plane violation.

Definitive

The definitive diagnosis is almost always established radiographically.

CLINICAL MANIFESTATIONS

Subjective

Clinical manifestations vary depending on the cause. Symptoms may be absent or obscured by the associated condition. Substernal pain and dyspnea are usually present if the air is confined to the mediastinum and deep cervical fascia. Sudden intense substernal pain radiating to arm and neck has been described. The pain can be made worse with respiration, movement, swallowing, and activity. As expected, if radiation occurs the pain is experienced in the neck, back, arms, or shoulders. Perilaryngeal air dissection has been reported to result in dysphagia and dysphonia or what has been called a "tinny" or "hot potato" voice. A muffled voice has also been observed. Cough frequently precedes the development of spontaneous pneumomediastinum in as many as 30 to 40% of cases.

Spontaneous pneumomediastinum has important features distinct from secondary pneumomediastinum, that is, cases secondary to trauma or mechanical ventilation. In spontaneous pneumomediastinum, chest pain, dyspnea, or both are present in 82% of cases. Importantly, patients with spontaneous pneumothorax who do not complain of either chest pain or dyspnea complain of characteristic underappreciated symptoms of neck discomfort. This symptom is described in various ways: neck swelling, neck pain, throat pain, or dysphagia. The past medical history and family history are frequently noncontributory. On occasion a history of prior parenchymal lung disease can be elicited. A history of asthma or chronic obstructive lung disease can at times be elicited.

Objective

Physical Examination

The physical examination can be normal depending on the cause, stage of development, and subsequent evolution of the process. Most important clinically are hemodynamic compromise and shock that can occur secondary to tension pneumomediastinum or what has been called mediastinal air block. Cardiac electromechanical dissociation and superior vena caval syndrome have rarely been described. Hamman's sign, a precordial crunching sound with neck swelling first described in 1939, can occur but is not always present. Hamman's sign has also been described with pneumothorax. It has been reported in as many as 40% of cases with spontaneous pneumomediastinum. Hamman's sign has been described as a crunching, bubbling, popping, crackling, or clicking sound. It has been proposed that the Hamman's crunch is caused by the cyclic anteroposterior cardiac motion (cardiac filling and emptying) resulting in channeling pleural air into and out of the lung fissures, thus creating the sound. This explanation has been fostered based on a case where the crunch was present in a patient where pneumomediastinum proved absent but pneumothorax was present by computed axial tomography (CAT) scan. The sound is synchronous with systole, pronounced in the left lateral decubitus position, and fades when the patient assumes erect or supine position. Some have described an increase in the sound with expiration. Expiration increases pressure within the pleura and mediastinal space, which forces air to move within the spaces. The extension of air to subcutaneous and fascial planes can result in dramatic facial deformity and marked subcutaneous emphysema. Crepitation in the suprasternal notch is suggestive of the diagnosis. Subcutaneous emphysema has been reported to be the most common physical finding, being present in 60% of patients with spontaneous pneumomediastinum. It is usually about the neck or chest. If associated pneumothorax exists, one can observe decreased fremitus, decreased breath sounds, and hyperresonance. In neonates, a malignant tension pneumomediastinum with hemodynamic compromise has been described in those requiring mechanical ventilation with high airway pressures.

Routine Laboratory Abnormalities

Radiographically, pneumomediastinum is confirmed by the appearance of a vertical line of radiolucency seen best along the left heart border, representing displacement of the mediastinal pleura. Additional observations include "highlighting" increased radiolucency of the aortic knob, the continuous diaphragm sign (an unbroken radiolucent line extending from one hemidiaphragm to the other beneath the heart), and increased retrosternal air with lucent streaks outlining the aorta or other mediastinal structures on lateral chest film. Subcutaneous emphysema may be seen outlining the tissue planes of the neck, chest wall, and pectoral muscles. A "ring around the artery" sign has been described referring to a well-defined lucency encircling the right pulmonary artery. This sign is apparent on the lateral chest film. Pneumothorax can be distinguished radiographically by taking a lateral decubitus film which reveals air movement to the most elevated portion of the chest cavity. Air located within the mediastinal interstitium will be nearly unchanged with position. In pneumopericardium, the air seldom rises above the aortic knob which is outside the pericardial sack. Of course, the chest x-ray is the gold standard for making the diagnosis of pneumomediastinum. With spontaneous pneumomediastinum, the radiographic findings can be subtle. In fact, up to 50% of cases of spontaneous pneumomediastinum have been missed on standard posteroanterior views of the chest. The lateral chest x-ray is felt to be critically important and often more sensitive than the posteroanterior view.

Nonspecific S-T and T wave electrocardiographic changes have been observed in occasional patients. The most common electrocardiographic change is low-voltage or axis shift.

PLANS

Diagnostic

Differential Diagnosis

The differential diagnosis of pneumomediastinum when unassociated with readily apparent causes is broad. The nonspecific frequent complaints of chest pain with or without radiation and dyspnea raise the differential diagnoses of pulmonary thromboembolic disease, pneumothorax, thoracic musculoskeletal disease with anxiety, myocardial infarction, and pericardial disease. If one is fortunate enough to document the characteristic radiographic appearance on x-ray, then the diagnosis is clinched. Evolution of the process and suboptimal radiographic technique can make the diagnosis elusive. For example, if the mediastinal air has gone on to the pleural space and pneumothorax has developed, one might miss the usual appearance of pneumomediastinum on x-ray and rather observe the features of pneumothorax, that is, decreased lung markings, caudad movement of the hilum, increased radiolucency of the hemithorax.

Diagnostic Options and Recommended Approach

Careful review of the x-ray film is essential with attention to mediastinal contours. As mentioned, the lateral chest x-ray film is often of value. Mediastinal air collection is sometimes best recognized with CAT scan, especially if subcutaneous emphysema overlies endothoracic structures. CAT scan may reveal retrosternal air bubbles in association with pulmonary fibrosis. There have been reports of aerorachia on CAT scan in which pneumomediastinal air has penetrated into cervical spine space.

Therapeutic

Most often conservative management with observation only is appropriate. This is especially the case for nontraumatic cases. Any associated condition, for example, foreign body, bronchospasm, and infection, should be treated. Chest tube thoracostomy and evacuation of air pockets are inappropriate and not recommended. Decompression of the anterior mediastinum has been performed by fine-needle aspiration and cervical mediastinotomy. This has been reserved for cases with tension pneumomediastinum with hemodynamic compromise.

FOLLOW-UP

In a series of cases of spontaneous pneumomediastinum, the mean length of hospitalization was 6.3 days, although asthma and upper respiratory tract infection constituted 24 and 12% of the cases, respectively. Recurrence of spontaneous pneumomediastinum is felt to be uncommon. Many studies of spontaneous pneumomediastinum have identified a predisposing factor in as many as two thirds of the cases (physical exertion, asthma, or upper respiratory tract infection). Follow-up x-rays are not recommended for spontaneous pneumomediastinum. In those secondary cases of pneumomediastinum, the patient's clinical status and associated conditions often dictate the frequency of follow-up x-rays.

DISCUSSION

Prevalence and Incidence

The actual prevalence and incidence of pneumomediastinum are uncertain. Spontaneous pneumomediastinum is rare, estimated at approximately one per 10,000 to 30,000 hospital admissions. An incidence as high as 5.4% of 479 x-rays for children admitted with exacerbation of asthma has been associated with pneumomediastinum. Spontaneous pneumomediastinum, in contrast to pneumomediastinum of other causes, tends to occur in young men age 18 to 30 years. Often there is a predisposing factor; currently, three quarters of the cases are associated with inhalational drug use, often with a history of a Valsalva-type maneuver.

Related Basic Science

Pneumomediastinum frequently occurs secondary to alveolar–interstitial leak or secondary to immediately apparent exogenous causes. Pathophysiologically, exogenous introduction of air into a fascial plane or alveolar–interstitial air leak accounts for the majority of cases. Subdiaphragmatic dissection of air into the mediastinum can occur from beneath the diaphragm, for example, secondary to pelvic and intraab-

dominal pathology. As the iatrogenic or exogenous introduction of air beneath fascial planes is readily apparent, a discussion of the alveolar–interstitial air leak is appropriate. Alveolar rupture into the bronchovascular interstitium occurs secondary to pressure gradient differential between the two spaces. Air in the interstitial space then dissects centrally toward the mediastinal compartment, resulting in pneumomediastinum. A marked predisposition to alveolar disruption has been noted when there is preexisting alveolar infiltration, be it infective or inflammatory. Pulmonary fibrosis, for example, has been associated with alveolar rupture or honeycomb cyst rupture and subsequent air leakage into the surrounding bronchovascular interstitium. This is followed by central air migration, resulting in pneumomediastinum. Honeycombing and violent coughing are recognized risk factors.

Natural History and Its Modification with Treatment

When pneumomediastinum develops spontaneously, a number of studies have shown that it is a benign process and, in fact, does not require hospitalization. Studies have shown that when hospitalization does occur, the length of stay for spontaneous pneumomediastinum varies between 2 and 6 days. For spontaneous pneumomediastinum, the mean duration of symptoms is 2.2 days and the mean duration of the chest x-ray remaining abnormal is 4 days. Although treatment is usually unnecessary, heroic efforts have been described to manage severe sequelae of pneumomediastinum (cardiac electromechanical dissociation and superior vena caval syndrome). Transverse suprasternal incision with digital probing as well as full sternotomy have been described. Percutaneous computed tomography-guided placement of a mediastinal drainage catheter can prove valuable. In neonates with malignant tension pneumomediastinum, a transverse incision 2 cm below the xiphoid down to the anterior sheath, with exposure of the anterior mediastinum, has been described.

Prevention

In most instances it is difficult to prevent pneumomediastinum. Caution should be used when performing pulmonary function tests in patients with opportunistic lung infections, as pneumomediastinum has been reported in a patient with *Pneumocystis carini* pneumonia undergoing such tests.

Cost Containment

In cases of primary or spontaneous pneumomediastinum, considerable financial savings can be attained by avoiding hospitalization. Several studies have demonstrated a low incidence of complications and/or recurrences. In addition, specifically with spontaneous pneumomediastinum, the practice of obtaining serial chest x-rays has not been proven to be of benefit. There is therefore considerable potential for cost savings. Finally, again with spontaneous pneumomediastinum, unless there is a strong history for Boerhaave's syndrome, there is no indication for barium swallow as it has not been shown to be valuable. This also represents a potential for savings. One should be careful not to extrapolate the potential for savings with spontaneous pneumothorax to secondary cases of pneumomediastinum, for example, trauma-induced cases, as adequate studies have not been done.

REFERENCES

Abolnick I, Lossos I, Breuer R. Spontaneous pneumomediastinum: A report of 25 cases. Chest 1991;100:93.

Collins RK. Hamman's crunch: An adventitious sound. J Fam Pract 1994;38:284.

Maunder RJ, Pierson DJ, Hudson LD. Subcutaneous and mediastinal emphysema: Pathophysiology, diagnosis, and management. Arch Intern Med 1984;144:1447.

Minocha A, Richards RJ. Pneumomediastinum as a complication of upper gastrointestinal endoscopy. J Emerg Med 1991;9:325.

Panacek EA, Singer AJ, Sherman BW, et al. Spontaneous pneumomediastinum: Clinical and natural history. Ann Emerg Med 1992;21:1222.

Bronchiectasis

John G. Weg, M.D.

DEFINITION

Bronchiectasis is permanent dilation and destruction of subsegmental bronchi or bronchioles. The diameter of the involved bronchus is larger than that of the accompanying pulmonary artery.

ETIOLOGY

The development and progression of primary bronchiectasis are due to inflammation ("the phlogistic theory"). Following the initial insult, whether infectious, toxic, foreign body, or other, mucociliary clearance is impaired. This permits microorganisms to colonize, persist in, and invade the airways.

CRITERIA FOR DIAGNOSIS

Suggestive

A history of recurrent sinopulmonary infections or chronic cough productive of large amounts of purulent sputum is characteristic of patients with bronchiectasis.

Definitive

A diagnosis of bronchiectasis can be confirmed with the use of a thin-section computed tomography scan; it has replaced bronchography, visualization of the bronchi with iodized oil. The latter is rarely performed because of the appreciable discomfort to the patient and frequent complications of fever, pneumonia, and bronchospasm. In some patients, the bronchiectatic areas can be identified on a plain chest roentgenogram.

CLINICAL MANIFESTATIONS

Subjective

The signal complaint is that of chronic cough productive of copious amounts of purulent sputum, which at times may be mucoid or have blood streaking; wheezing is also common. The onset of symptoms usually occurs at a very young age, less than 7 and often less than 2. Patients may also complain of dyspnea if the disease is extensive. Recurrent, chronic purulent sinus infections are also common. Patients with upper lobe bronchiectasis, usually a complication of tuberculosis or fungal infections, generally do not produce purulent sputum; their disease process is often described as "dry bronchiectasis." Such patients have recurrent hemoptysis as their primary symptom.

Primary bronchiectasis is a disease of the lung. The etiologic associations of primary bronchiectasis are listed in Table 13–18–1. Secondary bronchiectasis is associated with congenital or inherited local or systemic disease processes. The most common cause of secondary bronchiectasis in young adults is cystic fibrosis. Allergic bronchopulmonary aspergillosis (ABPA) and common variable immunodeficiency syndrome are also quite common. In an effort to identify bronchiectasis as secondary, one should obtain a family history of similar recurrent sinopulmonary problems, evaluate for male infertility, and search for evidence of malabsorption. A history of wheezing, coughing up worm-like hard brown casts of small bronchi, and recurrent fever with associated changing pulmonary infiltrates suggests allergic bronchopulmonary aspergillosis. Diseases associated with bronchiectasis are listed in Table 13–8–2.

Objective

Physical Examination

On examination of the chest, coarse crackles are heard in inspiration and expiration over the affected areas. They frequently clear partially with coughing and are louder over dependent areas. Hyperreactive airway disease is very common and clinical asthma is frequent. Crackles of varying pitch and volume are often heard simultaneously, suggesting "popping" in various size bronchi. Rhonchi due to secretions in large airways are also common. The forced expiratory time, the time required to perform a forced vital capacity maneuver as determined by listening to airflow near the patient's mouth or with a stethoscope over the cervical trachea, is usually prolonged, more than 4 seconds.

Routine Laboratory Abnormalities

Hypercarbia occurs with extensive disease. Peribronchial fibrosis and cystic areas are often evident on the plain chest roentgenogram. The peribronchial fibrosis may appear as vertical, parallel lines of a descending bronchus, so-called "tramlines." If seen on end, they may appear as circular shadows with lucent centers in association with the smaller opaque shadows of pulmonary arteries. The cystic areas indicating saccular bronchiectasis frequently have air–fluid levels or they may be opacified, if filled with pus. There may be associated pleural scarring.

TABLE 13–18–1. PRIMARY BRONCHIECTASIS: ETIOLOGIC ASSOCIATIONS

I. Postinfectious (particularly in small children and infants)
   A. Acute
      1. Bacteria: the usual organisms causing acute bronchitis and pneumonia including *Mycoplasma pneumoniae, Hemophilus influenzae,* anaerobes
      2. Viruses (often with superimposed bacterial infection)
        a. Pertussis
        b. Rubeola
        c. Adenovirus
        d. Influenza
   B. Chronic (upper lobe–"dry" bronchiectasis)
      1. Tuberculosis
      2. Fungi
        a. Histoplasmosis
        b. Coccidioidomycosis
        c. Blastomycosis
        d. Aspergillosis
        e. Phycomycosis
II. Aspiration/inhalation
   A. Gastric contents
      1. Alcohol excess
      2. Seizures
      3. Swallowing disorders
      4. Peri-anesthesia/surgery
   B. External
      1. Foreign body: timothy, barley, oats, peanuts, others
      2. Hydrocarbons
      3. Mineral oil
      4. Corrosive gases
        a. Ammonia
        b. Oxides of nitrogen or sulfur
      5. Smoke inhalation
      6. Intravenous drug addicts
III. Trauma
   Transection of trachea or bronchus (particularly partial)

Source: Weg JG. Bronchiectasis. Semin Respir Med 1992;13:177. Reproduced (with modification) from Seminars in Respiratory Medicine by permission of Thieme Medical Publishers.

TABLE 13–18–2. SECONDARY BRONCHIECTASIS: THE ASSOCIATED DISEASES AND DEFECTS

A. Local
1. Generalized cystic bronchiectasis
2. Unilateral hyperlucent lung syndromes (Swyer–James, McLeod's)
3. Bronchial cartilage deficiency (Williams–Campbell)
4. Bronchial stenosis with or without vascular compression
5. Sequestration
6. Tracheobronchomegaly (Mounier Kuhn)
7. Congenital tracheobronchial–esophogeal fistula
8. Distal to neoplasm
9. Nodular amyloidosis
10. Congenital lobar emphysema
B. Systemic
1. Cystic fibrosis
2. Allergic bronchopulmonary aspergillosis
3. Immunoglobulin deficiency
   a. Common variable immunodeficiency syndrome (CVIDS)
   b. Isolated immunoglobulin A deficiency
   c. Agammaglobulinemia (Bruton's)
   d. Combined immunodeficiency syndrome
4. Ciliary dyskinesia (immotile cilia) syndrome
   a. With situs inversus (Kartagener's)
   b. Young's syndrome
5. Phagocytic deficiencies
   a. Chronic granulomatous disease
   b. Chediak–Higashi syndrome
   c. Job syndrome
   d. Infantile agranulocytosis
   e. Cyclic neutropenia (Shwachman–Diamond)
6. α_1-Antitrypsin deficiency
7. Complement deficiencies
8. Acute and chronic leukemia
9. Rheumatoid arthritis
10. Inflammatory bowel disease
11. Schistosomiasis
12. Endometriosis
13. Relapsing polychondritis
14. Bronchiectasis, lymphedema, and yellow nail syndrome

Source: Weg JG. Bronchiectasis. Semin Respir Med 1992;13:177. Reproduced with modification by permission of Thieme Medical Publishers.

PLANS

Diagnostic

Differential Diagnosis

A history of recurrent sinopulmonary infections or chronic purulent sputum production is characteristic of bronchiectasis. The major differential diagnosis lies between primary and secondary bronchiectasis (see Tables 13–18–1 and 13–18–2). The mild cylindrical enlargement of bronchi commonly seen for 6 to 12 weeks following pneumonia or similar changes in patients with chronic bronchitis and emphysema are not associated with chronic purulent sputum production. They are best excluded from the diagnostic category of bronchiectasis as they do not require the same therapeutic interventions.

Diagnostic Options

Most often the history of recurrent sinopulmonary infections and chronic purulent sputum production beginning at very young age is sufficient to make the diagnosis. This is often strengthened by identifying abnormalities on the plain chest roentgenogram. Thin-section computed tomography (or bronchography) confirms the diagnosis.

In the presence of the appropriate history, family history, or other findings, sweat chloride determination with pilocarpine iontophoresis, serum protein immunoelectrophoresis, and IgG subsets should be obtained. A diagnosis of allergic bronchopulmonary aspergillosis can be confirmed by a positive immediate skin test for *Aspergillus,* and an ele-

vated serum IgE or specific IgE for *Aspergillus* species by enzyme-linked immunosorbent assay.

The most common organisms in sputum of patients with bronchiectasis, excluding those with cystic fibrosis, are *Hemophilus influenzae* (approximately 85%), *Streptococcus pneumoniae* (approximately 35%), and *Staphylococcus aureus* (approximately 5%). *Klebsiella pneumoniae, Escherichia coli, Proteus* species, anaerobes, so-called normal flora, *Neisseria catarrhalis, Enterobacter* species, and *Pseudomonas* species are also found. In patients with cystic fibrosis, *Staphylococcus aureus* and *Pseudomonas aeruginosa,* especially the mucoid form, are most common. *Xanthomonas* species and *Burkholderia cepecia* (formerly *P. cepecia*) are also common in patients with cystic fibrosis.

Recommended Approach

In most patients the clinical history supported by the chest roentgenogram is sufficient to make the diagnosis of bronchiectasis. We generally also obtain a sweat chloride, serum immunoelectrophoresis, and sputum culture. If the history is that of current wheezing, changing pulmonary infiltrates, and fever, we evaluate for allergic bronchopulmonary aspergillosis. We perform thin-section computed tomography to document localized bronchiectasis only for the rare patient who may require surgery. Bronchoscopy is reserved for patients with localized disease in whom aspiration of a foreign body or endobronchial obstruction is suspected.

Therapeutic

Therapeutic Options

The mainstay of treatment of patients with bronchiectasis is antibiotics in an effort to eliminate purulence in sputum if possible. The initial treatment for an increase in or the development of purulent sputum is oral antibiotics for approximately 14 days. The least costly drug that is effective and tolerated should be used, such as tetracycline 500 mg four times daily or trimethoprim 160 mg–sulfamethoxazole 800 mg (double-strength) twice daily, ampicillin 500 mg four times daily, or erythromycin 500 mg four times daily. Doubling the trimethoprim to 320 mg and the sulfamethoxazole to 1600 mg has been reported to be effective. If a satisfactory response is not obtained with one of these drugs, amoxicillin 500 mg every 8 hours or amoxicillin–clavulanate 500 mg every 8 hours should be considered. If response is not obtained, amoxicillin 3 g twice daily should be considered. Cefuroxime 250 to 500 mg twice daily or cefaclor 250 to 500 mg three times daily may also be effective. If purulent sputum returns within 1 to 2 weeks after a 14-day course of antibiotics, a repeat course for at least 4 weeks is recommended; some patients require several months of therapy to maintain the sputum free of purulence.

If the response to antibiotic therapy is unsatisfactory or hospitalization is required, Gram stain and culture with susceptibility are obtained. If an individual is acutely ill we initiate therapy with gentamicin 3 mg/kg/d intravenously divided into three doses given every 8 hours or tobramycin 3 mg/kg/d or amikacin 15 mg/kg/d intravenously each divided into three doses given every 8 hours, and Cefazolin 2 g intravenously every 8 hours. Gentamicin serum concentrations should be between 8 and 12 µg/mL at the peak 60 minutes after infusion and less than 2 µg/mL at the trough. In renal failure, the initial or loading dose of the aminoglycosides is the same; however, subsequent doses should be adjusted on the basis of measured or estimated creatinine clearance leading to a reduction in dose or an increased interval between doses. An alternative is ceftazidime 1 to 2 g every 8 hours instead of an aminoglycoside. It may also by used as an initial single-drug regimen. Until susceptibilities are available, initial selection of antibiotics should be used based on knowledge of local drug resistance patterns and the patient's prior organisms and their susceptibility.

Pseudomonas organisms are particularly difficult to eradicate even if susceptible. Once *Pseudomonas* organisms have been identified, a second effective intravenous agent is added such as carbenicillin 40 g/d intravenously divided into six doses every 4 hours, or ticarcillin 24 g/d intravenously divided into 6 doses, or piperacillin 18 g/d intravenously divided into six doses, or imipenem/cilastatin 3 g (as imipenem)/d intravenously divided into three doses. Doses must be adjusted for renal impairment. One should monitor serum aminoglycosides to ensure effective blood levels. In particular, patients with cystic fibrosis have increased clearances and require larger than usual doses; such data are not available on other individuals with bronchiectasis. Ceftazidime 2 g every 8 hours may be used as an alternative. If there is an exacerbation shortly after completing a 14-day course, a second course of two effective intravenous drugs is given along with a nebulized antibiotic.

The oral quinolones, ciprofloxacin or ofloxacin, are the only oral antibiotics effective against *Pseudomonas* species. The usual dose of ciprofloxacin is 750 mg every 2 hours given about 2 hours after eating. An increase in the dose to 1000 or even 1500 mg every 12 hours may be more effective in patients with bronchiectasis. Ofloxacin is given as 400 mg twice a day. The quinolone dosage must be adjusted for renal impairment. This group of drugs increases serum theophylline levels. They may rarely cause central nervous system stimulation or seizures. We reserve the quinolones for outpatient therapy whenever possible.

Nebulized antibiotics are effective in eliminating persistent microbes by raising antibiotic concentration in airways. Gentamicin 80 mg four times daily, tobramycin 80 mg four times daily, or either followed by carbenicillin 1 g two to four times daily (or ticarcillin or piperacillin and ceftazidime 1 g two to four times daily) has been effective in clearing or reducing the amount of purulence in sputum, improving pulmonary function, and reducing the number and duration of hospitalizations in patients with cystic fibrosis. Carbenicillin or piperacillin should be given separately from the aminoglycosides, as gentamycin may inactivate them. There is not uniform agreement on the use of nebulized antibiotics, but they do appear to be effective for *Pseudomonas* species. The antibiotic should be diluted in normal saline and should be preceded by or given with a nebulized beta agonist such as albuterol 2.5 to 5.0 mg (0.5–1.0 mL of the 0.5% solution) or metaproterenol 10 to 20 mg (0.2–0.4 mL of the 5% solution) to avoid bronchospasm. The use of a nebulized antibiotic should be continued for 8 to 12 weeks initially. A blood level should be checked if an aminoglycoside is given by nebulization, as (rarely) up to 20 to 30% systemic absorption may occur. If exacerbations are frequent, then nebulized antibiotics should be considered for 6 months and, in some patients, may be of benefit on an indefinite basis.

If anaerobes are suspected because of foul-smelling sputum or the growth of "normal flora" in a patient not responding to initial antibiotic coverage, oral outpatient treatment with amoxicillin 500 mg every 8 hours, amoxicillin–clavulanate 500 mg every 8 hours, clindamycin 300 mg every 6 hours, or metronidazole 500 mg every 6 hours should be given. If the patient is acutely ill, penicillin G 18,000,000 units intravenously daily divided into six doses is recommended. An alternative is clindamycin 2.4 g/d intravenously divided into four doses every 6 hours or metronidazole with an intravenous loading dose of 15 mg/kg over 1 hour, then 7.5 mg over 1 hour every 6 hours. Serum concentrations may be monitored to ensure satisfactory levels based on susceptibility testing.

Most patients with bronchiectasis obtain clinical important improvement with bronchodilators. A trial of an inhaled beta-agonist bronchodilator by metered-dose inhaler (MDI) such as albuterol or metaproterenol, 2 to 4 puffs approximately every 6 hours can be used for an initial trial.* An attactive alternative is the use of salmeterol 2 to 4 puffs every 12 hours with the addition of albuterol or metaproterenol for acute episodes of bronchospasm. Ipratropium bromide 2 to 10 puffs every 6 hours should be added to the beta agonists to obtain additional relief. The most effective dose of a beta agonist or vagolytic drug such as ipratropium is that which provides the greatest relief of symptoms. This can be best measured objectively with a 6- or 12-minute walking distance test as opposed to relying solely on an increase in the 1-second forced expiratory volume (FEV_1). The most effective dose of albuterol has been shown to be 1 mg, that is, five 200-μg capsules for inhalation or approximately eleven 90-μg puffs. The comparble dose of ipratro-

pium bromide is approximately 0.5 mg by nebulizer or approximately 10 puffs from a metered-dose inhaler. Some patients benefit from a long-acting theophylline with a starting dose of 200 mg every 12 hours. This dose can be increased by 100 mg every 3 days until the patient has evidence of symptomatic improvement or evidence of side effects such as upset stomach, nausea, anorexia, diarrhea, and, rarely, nervousness or tachycardia. A theophylline blood level has been recommended if the dose is increased above 900 mg daily, but clinical monitoring is usually satisfactory up to a dose of 1200 mg daily. If mild side effects occur, the patient is instructed to reduce the dose by 100 to 200 mg; if the side effects are more severe, the patient is instructed to discontinue the drug. A written list of side effects is given to the patient. If side effects occur, a theophylline level should be obtained. Dosing should be according to theophylline levels in individuals who have a potential for more serious side effects such as seizures, if there is a history of epilepsy or alcoholism, if individuals may have a prolonged clearance such as those with underlying liver disease or heart failure, or if individuals are unlikely to identify the side effects. The generally accepted therapeutic concentration is between 10 and 20 mg/L.

Inhaled *N*-acetylcysteine is often of benefit in patients with extremely viscid purulent sputum that does not promptly clear with antibiotics, bronchodilators, and percussion and postural drainage. It should always be given with or following an inhaled beta agonist such as albuterol. The dose is 10 mL of the 10% solution every 6 hours. If the patient indicates that *N*-acetylcysteine improves his or her ability to clear secretions, it is continued. Long-term dornase α has been shown to be effective in improving FEV_1 and decreasing the number of hospitalizations in patients with cystic fibrosis. It is given via a recommended nebulizer in a dose of 2.5 mg once daily. To date there are no data on its use in other patients with bronchiectasis.

Many patients find percussion and postural drainage to be helpful in clearing secretions during exacerbations of bronchiectasis. The most involved area is positioned so as to effect gravity drainage. As the lower lobes are usually involved, a head-down 30° to 45° prone position with the left side elevated for right lower lobe disease or vice versa should be tried. Clapping the back with cupped hands assists drainage. Few patients find this of value on a long-term daily basis.

Surgical resection of bronchiectasis should be limited to patients who have unilateral disease localized to a segment or lobe or occcasionally the lower lobe with the middle lobe or lingula in whom there is a clear-cut failure of full medical management. If surgery is considered, thin-section computed tomography must be done to document that the disease is truly localized to the area considered for resection. In the unusual individual who fails medical therapy the disease is almost always widespread and bilateral. Such individuals are unlikely to benefit from surgery. Surgical intervention has had an operative mortality of 1 to 15% and a complication rate of approximately 20%. If there is massive hemoptysis, most recommend an attempt at bronchial artery occlusion to stop bleeding, if a skilled angiographer is available. An alternative is surgical resection of the segment or lobe involved, if the patient's overall cardiopulmonary status permits.

Sinus drainage may be necessary if there is recurrent purulent sinusitis that does not respond to antibiotics and decongestants. Bronchoscopy to clear secretions or to effect bronchoalveolar lavage is not recommended.

Every effort must be made to have the patient discontinue smoking. A general exercise program and encouragement to lead a full and normal life are also recommended. Annual influenza vaccination and a single pneumococcal vaccination should be given. If the arterial oxygen tension is less than 55 mm Hg or the patient evidences cor pulmonale, long-term oxygen should be given. Exercise training similar to that for patients with chronic obstructive pulmonary disease is provided for patients with limited exercise tolerance.

Recommended Approach

We initially treat exacerbations in patients who have not been *Pseudomonas* carriers with tetracycline, trimethoprim–sulfamethoxazole, or ampicillin for 2 weeks. If symptoms recur within a week or two, a course of these antibiotics is increased to 1 month and, on occasion, to 2 months. These antibiotics are prescribed without obtaining

---

*The current standard recommended dose of beta agonists and anticholingerics is the lower of the ranges indicated in this section.

Gram stain or culture and susceptibility studies. If the acute exacerbation is sufficient to warrant hospitalization and the patient is not known to be infected with *Pseudomonas,* an intravenous aminoglycoside (depending on local susceptibilities or those of the patient) or cefazolin is given. If *Pseudomonas* organisms are likely, intravenous ceftazidime is started or, alternatively, an aminoglycoside along with carbenicillin or ticarcillin based on prior susceptibilities is started. The antibiotics are adjusted according to susceptibility studies when they become available.

For the known *Pseudomonas* carrier who exacerbates but does not require hospitalization, an oral quinolone is prescribed. In patients with *Pseudomonas* in whom it is difficult to clear sputum of purulence a nebulized aminoglycoside is used along with intravenous antibiotics for the acute episode; the nebulized aminoglycoside is continued for 1 month or longer.

We recommend inhaled salmeterol twice daily as the basic beta agonist, with the use of albuterol for superimposed acute symptoms. If this does not satisfactorily eliminate symptoms related to airway obstruction, ipratropium bromide is added. We use percussion and postural drainage for acute episodes when there is evidence that this enhances sputum production.

If massive hemoptysis occurs, we attempt to promptly identify the site and recommend bronchial artery occlusion.

FOLLOW-UP

The frequency of return visits is governed by the severity and frequency of exacerbations of disease. In patients who are relatively stable and well controlled, a visit every 3 to 6 months is sufficient; at this time we obtain a spirogram. With more severe disease, monthly visits with a spirogram may be required. If the disease is sufficiently severe, pulse oximetry is used at each visit to identify hypoxemia. A chest roentgenogram on a routine basis is not likely to be helpful in patient management.

DISCUSSION
Prevalence and Incidence

Although exact figures are not available, primary bronchiectasis is increasingly uncommon in developed countries, with perhaps most cases being related to aspiration of gastric contents or inhalation of a foreign body or toxic substance. The disease is still extremely common in developing countries following bacterial pneumonia or viral infections, often with superimposed bacterial infections such as pertussis, rubeola, adenovirus, and influenza. In such areas upper lobe bronchiectasis related to tuberculosis is also quite common.

Related Basic Science

Bronchi that demonstrate irregular widening and enlargement are described as having varicose or fusiform bronchiectasis. Saccular bronchiectasis is defined as enlarged bulbous terminal sacs, usually in intermediate bronchi. The lumens are filled with purulent mucus. There are varying degrees of infiltration with lymphocytes, macrophages, dendritic cells, and plasma cells along with lymphoid follicles microscopically. As the disease progresses, there is erosion of the mucosa with ulceration and abscess formation and loss of some small airways. Bronchomalacia, airway smooth muscle hypertrophy, and neovascular-

ization of bronchial arteries with bronchopulmonary arterial anastomoses develop. In addition to the changes in and about the airways, there are destruction and fibrosis of lung tissue.

These changes come about because of an interplay between the bacteria and their products, leading to a continuing inflammatory response. Some bacterial products alter ciliary function and release proteins that disrupt epithelium, which impairs bacterial clearance. The persistence of organisms leads to chronic inflammation with increased numbers of neutrophils recruited by chemoattractants in the pus. The chemoattractants are generated by both the host and the organisms. Release of superoxide radicals and elastases further damages the epithelium and engenders mucous gland hyperplasia. A decrease in IgA activity enhances bacterial adherence. The inflammatory process is perpetuated by cell-mediated immunity interacting with the persistent bacteria.

Natural History and Its Modification with Treatment

Primary bronchiectasis usually follows an acute bacterial or viral infection. Recurrent infections lead to progressive destruction of lung tissue, respiratory failure, cor pulmonale, inanition, and death by the fourth or fifth decade, if not earlier. Patients may develop massive hemoptysis, empyema, amyloidosis, and metastatic brain abscesses. With prompt and appropriate antibiotic treatment and the use of bronchodilators, patients with primary bronchiectasis generally stabilize and extension of disease does not occur. In patients with secondary bronchiectasis, the prognosis is related to the underlying disease process.

Prevention

The prime method of prevention is active vaccination programs against the exanthems, pertussis and influenza. In addition the prompt treatment of purulent respiratory tract infections, acute bronchitis and pneumonia, with antibiotics probably reduces the incidence of bronchiectasis.

Cost Containment

The most effective cost containment is prevention with appropriate immunization in childhood and treatment of purulent infections. Limit computed tomography scanning to patients in whom surgical intervention is being considered. Use the least expensive effective antibiotic(s). Providing the patient with a supply of antibiotics and instructions to self-initiate therapy when purulent sputum develops reduces the need for hospitalization and intravenous antibiotics. In the patient who does require hospitalization and requires intravenous antibiotics, discharge the patient when clinically stable to complete a course of intravenous antibiotics at home with the use of home health care services.

REFERENCES

Barker AF, Bardana EJ Jr. State of the art—bronchiectasis: Update of an orphan disease. Am Rev Respir Dis 1988;137:969.

Ip M, Lam WK, So SY, et al. Analysis of factors associated with bronchial hyperreactivity to methacholine in bronchiectasis. Lung 1991;169:43.

McGuinness G, Naidich DP, Leitman BS, McCauley DI. Bronchiectasis: CT evaluation. Am J Radiol 1993;160:253.

Thomassen MJ, Demko DA, Doershuk CF. State of the art—cystic fibrosis: A review of pulmonary infections and interventions. Pediat Pulmonol 1987;3:334.

Weg JG. Bronchiectasis. Semin Respir Med 1992;13:177.

CHAPTER 13–19

Cystic Fibrosis

Lynn Goldowski, M.D.

DEFINITION

Cystic fibrosis is an autosomal recessive genetic disorder of exocrine gland function that causes impaired clearance of secretions, resulting in obstruction of passageways in many organ systems. This leads to an illness characterized by pancreatic insufficiency, malnutrition, failure to thrive, recurrent pulmonary infections, chronic, progressive pulmonary disease, and infertility.

ETIOLOGY

Cystic fibrosis is the most common inherited disease among Caucasians. Although there is multisystem involvement, pulmonary manifestations are the most common cause of morbidity and death. Once thought to be chiefly a gastrointestinal disease, it was originally called cystic fibrosis of the pancreas, also known as mucoviscidosis, which refers to the thick fluid characteristic of the secretions from mucus cells. These secretions lead to obstruction of passages, with the lungs, pancreas, liver, and intestines most often affected.

In the mid-1980s, specific ion channel defects responsible for the mucus abnormalities were elucidated. In 1989, the specific gene and the ion channel protein for which it encodes was described. The protein product of this gene, called cystic fibrosis transmembrane conductance regulator (CFTR), is a chloride channel activated by cyclic adenosine monophosphate (cAMP). Patients with cystic fibrosis have a 3-base-pair deletion in a gene located on chromosome 7 that normally codes for the amino acid phenylalanine at position 508. In most patients with cystic fibrosis, this amino acid residue is deleted from the protein product, resulting in an abnormal CFTR. This genetic deletion is abbreviated ΔF508. Although the remainder of the protein is normal, the missing phenylalanine changes its function enough to cause a chronic, progressive, and ultimately fatal disease. More than 300 mutations have been found to cause cystic fibrosis; however, the ΔF508 deletion is responsible for about 70%.

CRITERIA FOR DIAGNOSIS

Suggestive

Most patients with cystic fibrosis are diagnosed shortly after birth or in early childhood. About 10% present in the neonatal period with meconium ileus. In childhood, patients may develop intestinal obstruction or intussusception. Older children usually present with respiratory symptoms, such as chronic cough, wheezing, or recurrent pulmonary infections. In a small percentage of patients, cystic fibrosis is not diagnosed until after the age of 18. These patients generally have milder symptoms and may present during evaluation of infertility.

Definitive

The Cystic Fibrosis Foundation's criteria for the diagnosis of cystic fibrosis are clinical features suggestive of the disease, for example, pancreatic insufficiency or pulmonary disease, and two sweat chloride tests obtained by pilocarpine iontophoresis with results greater than or equal to 60 mEq/L.

If uncertainty about the diagnosis exists, genetic testing may be required. Being homozygous for the ΔF508 mutation confirms the diagnosis.

CLINICAL MANIFESTATIONS

Subjective

Cystic fibrosis is a multisystem disorder affecting the upper and lower respiratory tracts, pancreas, gastrointestinal tract, hepatobiliary system, endocrine system, sweat glands, and reproductive tract. About 80% of patients are diagnosed before age 5, and about 10% are not recognized until adolescence. It is rare for patients to be diagnosed in late adulthood. A family history of the disease may be present. The clinical severity varies considerably from one patient with cystic fibrosis to another, even in those with identical genetic mutations. This difference may be due to genetic factors other than the cystic fibrosis gene, to environmental factors, or to nutritional status.

Clinical presentation varies with the age of the patient. In neonates, the most common presenting symptom is intestinal obstruction secondary to meconium ileus. This occurs in about 10% of infants with cystic fibrosis and results from inspissation of viscous meconium at the ileocecal junction. Infants and children may present with failure to thrive, with protein- and/or fat-soluble vitamin deficiencies even in the presence of adequate nutritional intake, or with steatorrhea, with complaints of frequent, foul-smelling, bulky stools. In later childhood, patients may present with intestinal obstruction and intussusception. The prevalence of intestinal obstruction complications increases with age, occurring in almost one fifth of the adult population. The obstruction also usually occurs at the ileocecal junction. This is referred to as meconium ileus equivalent and results from a combination of incomplete digestion, abnormal intestinal fluid and electrolyte transport, and abnormal gut secretions which make the fecal material semisolid instead of liquid. Malabsorption from pancreatic insufficiency is seen in 95% of adult patients.

Although gastrointestinal symptoms are the more common presenting features in infancy and early childhood, pulmonary complaints are the most common presentation in older children, who may have chronic cough, wheezing, sinusitis, bronchitis, or recurrent pneumonia.

Some patients have mild disease with a paucity of symptoms and are not diagnosed until adolescence or early adulthood. These cases may represent a failure to recognize symptoms, as most of these patients have pulmonary involvement. Other, less common presenting symptoms may be chronic sinusitis, nasal polyposis, delayed sexual maturation, infertility, cirrhosis, cholelithiasis, cholestasis, or diabetes mellitus.

Objective

Physical Examination

Most patients with cystic fibrosis weigh less than would be predicted for their height. Otherwise, early in the disease, physical examination may be normal. Autopsy findings of infants who die of meconium ileus show normal lungs. The earliest pulmonary abnormalities are hypertrophy of bronchial glands, followed by mucus plugging and obstruction of the small airways. Patients develop bronchiolitis and, with progression, chronic bronchitis. The lungs become colonized, initially with *Staphyloccocus aureus* or *Hemophilus influenzae* in children; then eventually 100% of patients are colonized with *Pseudomonas aeruginosa*. Host defenses are activated, with recruitment of inflammatory cells, mostly neutrophils, and subsequent release of chemical mediators. In an effort to eliminate bacterial pathogens, this inflammatory process is a major contributor to lung tissue destruction. Neutrophils release active oxygen species, neutrophil elastase, and other lysosomal enzymes which directly damage lung tissue. Chemoattractants such as leukotrienes and interleukins are also locally released and recruit more inflammatory cells, which sets up a viscious circle of events. Chronic parenchymal destruction leads to loss of tissue, causing hyperinflation and airway obstruction.

The earliest abnormalities in lung physiology are abnormalities in ventilation and perfusion. Ventilation studies are abnormal before the chest x-ray or pulmonary function tests become abnormal. The upper lobes are first and most severely involved. These ventilatory changes cause an increased alveolar–arterial oxygen difference. In children, the earliest pulmonary function changes are reduced expiratory flow rates at low lung volumes. As the disease progresses, large airway obstruction develops, manifested as reductions in the forced expiratory volume in 1 second (FEV_1) and maximal midexpiratory flow. Loss of elastic recoil accounts for increased residual volume and functional residual capacity, thus reducing vital capacity. Physical examination of the lungs may show wheezing or rhonchi and other evidence of chronic obstructive airway disease, such as an increased anteroposterior chest diameter and hyperinflation. Digital clubbing may be seen. Diffusion capacity usually becomes decreased. Arterial blood gases may show hypoxemia early in the disease. This finding does not correlate with clinical findings or prognosis. Hypercarbia does not develop until late in the course of the disease; however, this finding is correlated with poor prognosis. Even with severe hypoxemia, patients rarely develop polycythemia. Red cell mass is appropriately increased, but there is an associated increase in plasma volume.

Routine Laboratory Abnormalities

The earliest change seen on chest radiographs is hyperinflation, which is secondary to mucus plugging of bronchioles. As inflammation and infection progress, bronchiole thickening occurs, characteristically seen as thick-walled circles on cross-sectional view. Saccular bronchiectasis occurs in almost 100% of patients with cystic fibrosis, most commonly involving the upper lobes first. The end-stage chest radiograph in cystic fibrosis typically shows hyperinflation, small heart, bronchiectatic lesions, cyst formation, fibrosis, and abscesses.

Other abnormalities seen in these patients include those caused by derangements in the sweat glands and gastrointestinal tract, especially secondary to pancreatic insufficiency and resulting nutritional deficits. Hyperglycemia or diabetes mellitus may be present. Serum electrolytes may show hyponatremia, hypokalemia, and hypochloremia. Prolonged prothrombin time may result from vitamin K deficiency. Serum levels of fat-soluble vitamins may be reduced. Qualitative fecal fat analysis and stool trypsin show evidence of malabsorption. Anemia and hypoalbuminemia may result from malabsorption as well.

Additional findings seen in patients with cystic fibrosis may include sinusitis, with opacification of sinuses on radiographs, nasal polyps, acute pancreatitis, rectal prolapse, cholelithiasis, and focal biliary cirrhosis secondary to intrahepatic bile duct obstruction with portal hypertension.

Infertility is seen in almost all men with cystic fibrosis. This occurs because of obstruction of the vas deferens, resulting in azospermia. Women with cystic fibrosis have developmentally normal reproductive tracts, but have reduced fertility, presumably secondary to increased viscosity of cervical mucus, which may hinder sperm penetration. Many women are able to conceive. These women have an increased rate of perinatal death, fetal loss, or prematurity.

PLANS
Diagnostic

The majority of patients with cystic fibrosis are diagnosed in childhood, but some patients are not diagnosed until late adolescence or early adulthood. A family history of cystic fibrosis is helpful. Meconium ileus in the neonatal period is diagnostic. Growth retardation, failure to thrive, or symptoms of malabsorption should alert the physician to consider cystic fibrosis. It is more common for younger patients than adults to present with symptoms of pancreatic insufficiency. Children may present with recurrent bronchitis, recurrent pneumonia, chronic cough, and asthma.

Patients who elude diagnosis before reaching adulthood have usually had respiratory symptoms for years, although these may have been mild, and the diagnosis of cystic fibrosis was not considered. These patients present with sinusitis or nasal polyposis, chronic cough, bronchitis, asthma, or bronchiectasis. Isolation of the mucoid form of *Pseudomonas aeruginosa* in a patient with chronic obstructive lung symptoms is seen almost exclusively in patients with cystic fibrosis and should prompt diagnostic testing if found. Rarely, adult patients can present with acute pancreatitis, cholestasis, cholelithiasis, and liver cirrhosis with portal hypertension. Patients who are not diagnosed before adulthood have usually achieved normal stature. It is important to re-

member that there can be tremendous variability in patients' presentations, in both age range as well as symptomatology, and one should keep this diagnosis in mind when patients present with these problems.

The diagnosis is made by collecting 100 mg of sweat on two separate occasions, using the pilocarpine iontophoresis test. Sweat chloride levels greater than 60 mgEq/L are considered diagnostic in the presence of suggestive symptoms. Entities that cause an elevation of sweat chloride and may yield a false-positive result include hypothyroidism, hypoparathyroidism, adrenal insufficiency, ectodermal dysplasia, renal diabetes insipidus, some forms of glycogen storage disease, mucopolysaccharidosis, and fucosidosis. Almost all patients with cystic fibrosis have a sweat chloride concentration greater than 60 mEq/L, and less than 1% have a sweat chloride concentration in the normal range below 40 mEq/L.

Genetic testing is not required or recommended for confirmation of the diagnosis because of the vast number of mutations responsible for causing cystic fibrosis. If, however, a patient is homozygous for the ΔF508 deletion, found in about three fourths of patients with cystic fibrosis in the United States, the diagnosis is confirmed.

Therapeutic

The approach to the treatment of patients with cystic fibrosis emphasizes maintaining adequate nutrition, improving clearance of bronchial secretions, and treating respiratory infections. Close monitoring of patients is recommended because progression of the disease is slow, often with subtle changes.

Chest physiotherapy has been shown to improve pulmonary function test results in patients with cystic fibrosis. This consists of postural drainage, directed cough, deep breathing, chest percussion, and forced expiration maneuvers with the intended goal of improving removal of purulent secretions from the lung. Regular exercise increases physical fitness in these patients, although there is no evidence to support that it improves pulmonary function or reduces morbidity or mortality. The routine use of bronchodilators in patients with cystic fibrosis is helpful in a subset of patients with a component of reversible airway disease evident on pulmonary function testing. Theophylline has not been shown to be of any benefit in patients with cystic fibrosis. N-Acetylcysteine, an aerosolized mucolytic agent, was formerly recommended to help loosen viscous secretions. This agent is no longer recommended, as it causes bronchospasm and may worsen symptoms.

A new agent, recombinant human deoxyribonuclease (rhDNase) has recently been approved for use in patients with cystic fibrosis, and is aimed at reducing the viscosity of sputum. Retention of purulent secretions in the airways contributes to the ultimate lung destruction in cystic fibrosis. Degenerating host neutrophils release DNA, causing the mucus to become thick and gellike. The rhDNase cleaves only extracellular DNA and decreases the viscoelasticity of the sputum. Early studies have shown that rhDNase, administered via inhalation, eases expectoration, reduces the frequency of pulmonary exacerbations requiring antibiotics, and improves pulmonary function and quality of life. This agent is well tolerated, with minimal side effects, consisting of mild and transient upper airway irritation with symptoms of hoarseness and laryngitis.

Repeated pulmonary exacerbations are related to loss of lung function, so intravenous antibiotic therapy is recommended for treatment in patients during exacerbations. When possible, choice of antibiotics should be guided by results of sputum culture and sensitivity. The responsible organism, usually *P. aeruginosa,* will not be eradicated in most cases, so the goal is to reduce the bacterial load and the inflammatory response. Combination therapy, usually pairing an aminoglycoside or fluoroquinolone with a beta-lactam antibiotic, is recommended. Higher doses and longer courses of treatment are generally necessary. The use of prophylactic antibiotics in these patients is not recommended because it is felt to increase the development of drug resistance.

Treatment for pancreatic insufficiency is recommended in all patients with cystic fibrosis. Oral pancreatic enzyme replacements are dosed individually, aimed at reducing symptoms. Unrestricted, high-calorie, high-protein diets and regular multivitamin and especially fat-soluble vitamin supplements are recommended. Some patients may go on to require supplemental enteral nutrition with a nasogastric tube or a surgically placed abdominal feeding tube. Patients who develop diabetes should be treated with insulin.

FOLLOW-UP

The majority of patients with cystic fibrosis are followed regularly at cystic fibrosis centers accredited by the National Cystic Fibrosis Foundation. Patients are monitored with full history and physical examinations, height, weight, dietary and nutritional assessments, blood counts, sputum cultures, pulmonary function tests, and chest x-rays at routine intervals. In addition, patients and their families are educated about cystic fibrosis, especially regarding life expectancy, infertility, the need for ongoing treatment, and the importance of compliance. These centers also provide other important services, such as social services and financial assistance.

Patients should be seen by their primary physician for changes in their baseline symptoms, ranging from constitutional symptoms, such as weight loss and fatigue, to a change in quality or quantity of sputum production, to intestinal obstruction, which can be minimally symptomatic in cystic fibrosis.

DISCUSSION
Prevalence

Cystic fibrosis is the most common lethal genetic disorder of Caucasians, occurring in 1 in 2000 to 2500 live births. One in twenty (5%) people in this population are carriers of the gene. Cystic fibrosis is much rarer in other populations; it occurs in 1 in 17,000 African-Americans and in 1 in 90,000 North American Indians and Asians.

Related Basic Science
Genetics

The gene responsible for cystic fibrosis was identified in 1989. It is located on the long arm of chromosome 7 and codes for a protein called cystic fibrosis transmembrane conductance regulator (CFTR). This protein product is thought to be a chloride channel activated by cAMP and regulating chloride conductance across epithelial cell membranes. More than 300 different mutations in this gene have been identified in patients with cystic fibrosis. Seventy percent of cases are due to a single mutation located at locus 508 of the gene, causing a deletion of a thymidine triplet encoding for phenylalanine (abbreviated ΔF508). The gene is transmitted by autosomal recessive means. Males and females are equally affected. If both parents are heterozygous, each child has a 1 in 4 or 25% chance of having the disease. It is considered a lethal or semilethal gene because 98% of affected males are infertile and women have reduced fertility.

A heterozygous advantage for the carrier state has been proposed and researched because the gene is so common. Although not proven, the most popular hypothesis is that the carrier state confers protection against infant mortality through an increased resistance to chloride-secreting diarrheas (such as cholera).

Altered Molecular Biology and Metabolic Derangement

The biochemical defect resulting from an abnormal CFTR in patients with cystic fibrosis is caused by an inability of epithelial cells to secrete chloride in response to stimulation by cAMP as normal cells do. This abnormal chloride transport affects exocrine cell function. In the sweat glands, this results in the cell's inability to reabsorb chloride ions and a consequently high level of chloride and sodium in the sweat. This serves as the basis for the pilocarpine iontophoresis sweat test used in making the diagnosis of cystic fibrosis. Pilocarpine is used to provoke local stimulation of the sweat glands. The sweat is collected and analyzed for chloride content. The test is sensitive and specific for cystic fibrosis, as there is usually no overlap between normal (<40 mEq/L) and abnormal (>60 mEq/L) results. As people age, their sweat chloride concentration increases; however, the sweat test remains an excellent diagnostic test and the gold standard for diagnosing cystic fibrosis.

In the pancreas, the failure of chloride secretion from the exocrine glands is associated with a resultant failure of proper water secretion.

The pancreatic ducts become desiccated and proteinaceous material precipitates in the ducts, causing obstruction and consequent fibrosis, resulting in decreased output of digestive enzymes and malabsorption.

There is also a failure of chloride secretion in the lung, as well as a large increase in sodium reabsorption. These two features lead to desiccation of airway secretions and impair the normal upward motion of the respiratory cilia. This, along with changes in airway mucins, leads to plugging of airways and results in trapping of bacteria and subsequent infection. The infection elicits an inflammatory response with release of chemical mediators and a viscious circle ensues, with consequent lung destruction.

Natural History and Its Modification with Treatment

Until recently, cystic fibrosis was considered to be fatal in early childhood. In 1960, the mean survival was 5 years. With improved understanding of this disorder, new therapies, and the availability of more potent antibiotics, the prognosis has greatly improved. Survival has gradually been increasing, with mean survival in 1992 of 29 years.

The clinical severity varies widely among patients, although there are some manifestations found commonly among most individuals with cystic fibrosis. Pansinusitis is found in 95% of patients, pancreatic insufficiency is found in 95%, and 98% of men with cystic fibrosis are infertile. Women also have reduced fertility, most likely because of the production of abnormally viscid cervical mucus that may impair normal mobility of sperm. Sweat chloride concentrations are elevated in 98% of patients.

Pulmonary complications account for most of the chronic morbidity associated with cystic fibrosis and are usually the cause of death in affected adults. Chronic lung disease develops from bacterial colonization, infection, and host inflammation, leading to bronchiectasis in virtually 100% of patients. In childhood, *Staphylococcus aureus* and, to a lesser extent, *Hemophilus influenzae* are the organisms most commonly isolated from the respiratory tract. In older children and adults, *Pseudomonas aeruginosa* colonizes the lower respiratory tract and is responsible for deterioration in lung function. Infections with *Burkholderia cepacia* (formerly *Pseudomonas cepacia*) and mucoid strains of *P. aeruginosa* are being seen with increasing frequency. *Burkholderia cepacia* can lead to a rapidly progressive deterioration in pulmonary function, respiratory failure, and sepsis and is associated with a poor prognosis. Although the lungs are colonized with *S. aureus* or *P. aeruginosa* in almost all patients, sepsis and other hematogenously spread infections are rare. Host immune responses are usually normal and thus contain the infection within the respiratory tract. Less common pulmonary complications occur with increasing frequency as patients enter adulthood. Pneumothorax is rare before age 10, but increases in adolescents and adults. Hemoptysis, ranging from minimal to massive, is also seen more in adults than children. Hypoxemia, pulmonary hypertension, cor pulmonale, and pulmonary hypertrophic osteoarthropathy may be seen. The clinical course is usually gradual with progressive respiratory failure.

Treatment of the pulmonary component of the disease is focused on mobilizing secretions, minimizing bacterial colonization, and treating pneumonias in an effort to preserve lung function. These goals are accomplished by chest physiotherapy, consisting of postural drainage, chest percussion, directed cough, and exercise. Recombinant human DNase (rhDNase) is used to reduce the viscosity of the sputum, enabling patients to expectorate more easily. Early studies with aerosolized recombinant human DNase show reduction in exacerbations of respiratory symptoms and improvement in pulmonary function, as well as a subjective improvement in patients' general sense of well-being. Periodic sputum cultures allow the health care team to know the sensitivity of the organism colonizing their patient's airway so that antibiotic therapy can be specifically directed during an exacerbation. Lung transplant is a final therapeutic option for patients with end-stage lung disease. This is limited by the availability of organ donors.

The second most common cause of chronic morbidity is gastrointestinal involvement. In addition to malabsorption which can lead to severe weight loss, caloric deprivation, and nutritional deficiencies, especially of fat-soluble vitamins, patients may develop intestinal obstruction from the accumulation of abnormal fecal material (called meconium ileus equivalent) or rectal prolapse. Acute, recurrent pancreatitis may occur. Cholelithiasis and/or chronic cholestasis are found in adult patients and occur because of the abnormal bile formation caused by pancreatic insufficiency. There may be fatty liver or intrahepatic bile duct obstruction which can lead to focal areas of biliary cirrhosis in the liver. A small number of these patients with liver involvement develop portal hypertension and hepatic failure. Eventually, pancreatic fibrosis can lead to glucose intolerance or diabetes because of disruption of the islets, producing insulin deficiency. Ketoacidosis is rare.

Treatment of pancreatic insufficiency is accomplished by oral pancreatic enzyme replacement, which virtually eliminates the malabsorption and helps correct nutritional deficiencies. All patients with cystic fibrosis require supplementation with the fat-soluble vitamins A and E. Improvement in nutritional support is associated with increased survival in patients with cystic fibrosis.

Prevention

Generalized screening for the carrier state of cystic fibrosis is not recommended. If an individual has a known relative with cystic fibrosis, carrier testing can be performed by linkage analysis where there is a DNA sample available from the affected family member. This is used in conjunction with the usual test for carrier status, called mutation analysis.

Prenatal screening to determine if a fetus is affected with cystic fibrosis is available, but is recommended only for couples found to have an increased risk of having an affected child (e.g., if they have a child with cystic fibrosis).

Cost Containment

Cystic fibrosis is a chronic disease with severe morbidity. Symptoms manifest early in life and progress throughout the patient's entire lifespan, requiring close, continued follow-up. Ongoing medical care, inpatient and outpatient, as well as inability to regularly attend school or work contribute to the high financial burden placed on patients and their families. A comprehensive approach to patient care is vital. Psychological support and early education, with attention to good nutrition, regular exercise, vigilance to subtle changes in usual symptoms, and prompt therapeutic intervention, may help contain costs. The majority of patients are followed at accredited cystic fibrosis centers. The advent of new therapeutic modalities such as recombinant human DNase, may reduce the severity and/or frequency of exacerbations. Although expensive, these may be found to reduce long-term morbidity by preventing or slowing down the progressive deterioration of lung disease. Home-based hospital care for administration of intravenous antibiotics during mild exacerbations or use of aerosolized antibiotic therapy may reduce the number of hospital admissions and help to reduce costs.

REFERENCES

Fiel SB. Clinical management of pulmonary disease in cystic fibrosis. Lancet 1993;341:1070.

Fuchs HJ, Borowitz DS, Christiansen DH, et al. Effect of aerosolized recombinant human DNase on exacerbations of respiratory symptoms and on pulmonary function in patients with cystic fibrosis. N Engl J Med 1994;331:637.

Koch C, Hoiby N. Pathogenesis of cystic fibrosis. Lancet 1993;341:1065

Sammut PH, Taussig LM. Cystic fibrosis in the adolescent and adult. In: Simmons DH, ed. Current pulmonology. St. Louis: Year Book, 1989;10:377.

Taussig LM. Cystic fibrosis. New York: Thieme–Stratton, 1984.

CHAPTER 13–20

Asthma as Viewed by a Pulmonologist

Michael J. H. Akerman, M.D.

DEFINITION

Asthma is a pulmonary disease with the following characteristics: airway obstruction that is reversible (but not completely reversible in some patients); airway inflammation; and increased airway responsiveness to a variety of stimuli ("twitchy airways"). Asthma is a heterogeneous disease that can vary in signs and symptoms and affect all age and ethnic groups. Asthma can range from mild and intermittent disease to severe and chronic disease. Fatal attacks may occur.

CRITERIA FOR DIAGNOSIS

Suggestive

The diagnosis of asthma may be suggested based on a characteristic history of episodic or chronic wheezing, coughing, dyspnea, or chest tightness and the resolution of these symptoms with specific pharmacologic treatment for asthma. The examination may be normal. Other diseases that can cause these symptoms should be excluded (Table 13–20–1).

Definitive

A definitive diagnosis of asthma can be made when the above suggestive symptoms are present and objective confirmation is made with office measurement of peak expiratory flow rate (PEFR) or spirometry. Classically, asthma presents with a decreased PEFR or decreased forced expiratory volume in 1 second (FEV_1). There is an increase in these measurements after pharmacologic treatment. Asthma, however, may present as an episodic and highly variable disease, with normal PEFR or spirometry. In addition, other diseases may present with asthmalike symptoms (see Table 13–20–1). Therefore, if the patient does not respond appropriately to treatment for asthma based on the suggestive presentation, then the clinician should reconsider the differential diagnosis.

CLINICAL MANIFESTATIONS

Subjective

The patient complains of wheezing, cough, dyspnea, chest tightness, chest congestion, or sputum production.

The physician should determine the frequency and anatomic location of the wheezing. Is it perennial or seasonal, continuous or episodic? Does it occur on a weekday or is there circadian variation?

Conditions associated with an increased asthma frequency include rhinitis, sinusitis, nasal polyposis, and atopic dermatitis.

Precipitating or aggravating triggers include viral infections, environmental allergens (e.g., pollens, molds, dust, pets); occupational exposures (vapors, chemicals); airway irritants (passive or active smoking, air pollutants, aerosols or odors); medications (aspirin, beta blockers [including ophthalmic drops], nonsteroidal antiinflammatory drugs); foods; food additives (e.g., sulfites in wine and salads); weather or humidity changes; exercise; pregnancy or menses; and traumatic social or emotional situations. It is important to note than an asthmatic reaction may occur immediately after exposure or may be delayed for 6 to 8 hours. The age of onset, prior evaluation, and prior treatment (including frequency of emergency department visits, hospitalization, use of steroids, life-threatening episode) must be determined.

TABLE 13–20–1. DIFFERENTIAL DIAGNOSIS OF ASTHMA

- Mechanical obstruction of the airways due to foreign body aspiration, tracheal stenosis, or tumors
- Airway compression from an enlarged thyroid gland or mediastinal structures
- Laryngeal dysfunction (such as due to nerve damage)
- Rhinitis or sinusitis with post nasal drip syndrome
- Chronic bronchitis or emphysema
- Congestive heart failure
- Pulmonary embolism
- Chronic aspiration due to neurologic dysfunction, esophageal reflux, or esophageal diverticula
- Interstitial lung disease such as sarcoidosis, pulmonary eosinophilia, or systemic vasculitis with pulmonary involvement
- Cough secondary to medications such as beta blockers and angiotensin-converting enzyme (ACE) inhibitors.
- Panic disorder or psychogenic dyspnea
- Pneumothorax

It is important to document the patient's fears of beta-agonist overuse or of corticosteroid side effects.

The family history of similar symptoms or related conditions should be determined.

Objective

Physical Examination

The upper airway should be examined for the presence of otitis, rhinitis, sinusitis, or nasal polyps. The pulmonary examination should determine respiratory rate, use of accessory muscles of expiration (sign of severe disease); evidence of hyperinflation (depressed diaphragm by percussion, or increased anteroposterior diameter of the chest); quality of the breathing (absent breath sounds may suggest a pneumothorax or severe asthma with no air movement); presence of wheezing; and presence of cough during forced expiration. Wheezing from asthma may occur during expiration alone or on both inspiration and expiration. Inspiratory wheezing alone without expiratory wheezing may be due to stridor from upper airway obstruction. Localized wheezing may occur with asthma, but alternatively may be due to a localized pulmonary problem other than asthma (see Table 13–20–1). Wheezing is not a reliable indicator of the severity of asthma.

The forced expiratory time is a useful bedside maneuver measured by having the patient take a complete inspiration and then a rapid total expiration. The patient must be coached to expire as fast as possible. The physician auscultates over the trachea until all expiration is ended. Normal forced expiratory time is less than 3 seconds.

In most patients, some of these physical findings are present during symptomatic asthma; however, the absence of all of these physical findings does not rule out the diagnosis of asthma.

Routine Laboratory Abnormalities

The complete blood count may show eosinophilia. There are no characteristic blood chemistry findings.

PLANS
Diagnostic

Differential Diagnosis

Many other diseases may present with signs similar to those of asthma, or may coexist with asthma and require simultaneous treatment. These are listed in Table 13–20–1. Usually, the presence of another disease is suggested by specific historical or physical examination findings; however, asthmatics not responding well to usual therapy may require reconsideration of the differential diagnosis and further diagnostic evaluation.

Diagnostic Options

A chest x-ray is not always required. It may be helpful at the time of first presentation or during severe exacerbations to evaluate for lung infiltrates (due to pneumonia or interstitial lung disease) and to look for thoracic mass lesions or cardiomegaly.

Objective pulmonary evaluation of asthma severity can be done in the clinician's office in less than a minute with a portable, handheld, and inexpensive peak expiratory flow rate meter. This measurement is precise and reproducible when the patient is coached to perform properly.

In difficult cases, complete pulmonary function testing is the most important diagnostic option available. In typical asthma, spirometry should be used to demonstrate findings of airway obstruction (a reduced PEFR or FEV_1). This obstruction should be at least partially reversible after treatment with a bronchodilator. Reversibility of obstruction with treatment may occur at the time of testing in response to inhalation of a beta-agonist spray; however, some asthmatics with significant airway inflammation may not show any improvement until after 6 weeks of aggressive therapy with corticosteroids. Therefore, in cases where asthma is unproven, but still the most likely diagnosis, antiinflammatory treatment would be initiated and pulmonary function testing repeated after 6 weeks (see Therapeutic).

Complete pulmonary function testing also includes measurement of flow volume loops, lung volumes, and diffusion capacity. The flow volume loop evaluates the patient for tracheal external airway compression. The lung volumes and diffusion capacity evaluate the patient for the presence of interstitial lung disease or emphysema (see Appendix 5).

The diagnosis of exercise-induced asthma can be confirmed by measuring spirometry before and after an exercise challenge test on a bicycle or treadmill. This is conducted according to specific protocols and is not available in all pulmonary function laboratories.

Bronchoprovocation (bronchial challenge) testing evaluates the presence of airway hyperreactivity. It is performed by using spirometry before and after the patient has inhaled graduated concentrations of methacholine or another antihistamine. Patients with cough-variant asthma or exercise-induced asthma are candidates for this test. Bronchoprovocation testing can also be used to diagnose occupational asthma, with specific allergens or irritants for the inhalant challenge. Bronchoprovocation testing is done only in tertiary referral centers and entails a small risk of precipitating a severe immediate or delayed asthma attack.

Other diagnostic options may be necessary to investigate alternative diagnoses or to rule out coexisting diseases (see Table 13–20–1) when there are suggestive symptoms, physical findings, or inconsistent treatment responses. These tests include bronchoscopy to evaluate for foreign body aspiration; echocardiography to evaluate cardiac function; nasal endoscopy to evaluate the upper airway, computed tomography of the head to evaluate for chronic sinusitis, gastrointestinal evaluation to evaluate for gastroesophageal reflux, and nuclear scanning to evaluate for pulmonary embolism. Cardiopulmonary exercise testing may occasionally be of value in difficult-to-diagnose cases of dyspnea (see Appendix 6).

Recommended Approach

The vast majority of patients present with a characteristic history and improve with pharmacologic treatment. This is usually adequate for the diagnosis, providing that the differential diagnosis has been carefully considered. Office PEFR monitoring should be done initially and at follow-up visits to guide therapy. A normal PEFR value in the workup of asthma does not eliminate the diagnosis because asthma is typically an episodic disease. Cases who present atypically or who do not respond to appropriate treatment should have complete pulmonary function testing.

If the diagnosis is not confirmed, then a careful review of the differential diagnosis and pulmonary subspecialty consultation are recommended. Pulmonary subspecialty consultation should also be obtained for confirmed asthmatic patients who have uncontrolled symptoms, frequent emergency department visits, problems with medication compliance, or who require high-dosage treatment with corticosteroids. Allergy subspecialty consultation is recommended for asthmatics who have asthma associated with environmental or seasonal allergens.

Therapeutic

Therapeutic Options

Asthma is not curable; however, it can be controlled and the symptoms minimized in approximately 95% of patients. Asthma is treated with combinations of different classes of medications (see Table 13–20–2) aimed at the different components of the asthmatic response: Bronchodilators are used for the treatment of bronchospasm to bring about immediate relief, and antiinflammatory medications are used to attenuate the airway hyperreactivity and underlying inflammation. Antiinflammatory agents are thus important for prevention of recurrent exacerbations and long-term improvement. The stepwise management of chronic asthma is shown in Figures 5–1–1 and 5–1–2.

Most medications for asthmatics are available in inhalation, oral, and parenteral forms. Inhalation forms of medication are always preferred for first-line therapy of the outpatient or of patients with mild or moderate asthma due to their decreased systemic absorption and decreased risk of toxicity. Asthma therapy is applied in a stepwise fashion based on disease severity (see Figure 5–1–2). Concurrent with the use of medications to achieve symptom control, a search should be made for environmental factors to be avoided (see Discussion, Prevention). The drugs commonly used for the treatment of asthma are discussed below.

Rapid-onset Beta-agonist Bronchodilators.
Bronchodilators administered via the inhalation route typically have an onset of action within minutes and may be effective for 4 hours or longer. They are used for acute symptomatic relief when needed (two sprays every 4 hours). Routine usage when asymptomatic should be discouraged. Ephedrine (Primatene Mist, available without a prescription) and isoproterenol inhalers should be avoided because of their increased side effect profile and very short duration of action (1–2 hours).

Long-acting Beta-agonist Bronchodilators.
These drugs are effective for about 12 hours. Long-acting beta-agonist inhalers are *never* to be used for rapid or emergency relief because of their slow onset of action. Long-acting inhalers are typically prescribed for nocturnal asthma symptoms or in severe asthma to improve baseline control.

Some studies have reported increased mortality associated with increased beta-agonist usage. The explanation of this finding is controversial. Nevertheless, all patients should always be given a rapid-acting beta-agonist inhaler to use as needed when symptomatic. In addition, any patient requiring increasing dosage of a beta-agonist inhaler probably has inadequately controlled asthma and should have increased monitoring and be given increased doses of antiinflammatory medication (see Figure 5–1–2).

Theophylline.
This drug is no longer recommended as a first-line choice for treating asthma. Theophylline may still have an important role in treating nocturnal asthma and in treating older patients who cannot use

inhalers and spacers. Theophylline has a narrow therapeutic/toxic ratio. Therefore, blood levels must be monitored on a regular basis. In addition, other medications or diet can substantially affect theophylline metabolism and blood levels. Therefore, theophylline blood levels must be monitored closely whenever other medications are changed. The therapeutic goal is symptom relief with a serum level of 5 to 15 μg/mL.

Anticholinergic Bronchodilators.
These drugs are less potent than the beta agonists and slower in onset in acute emergency treatment. They may provide additive bronchodilatory effects to beta-agonist treatment in some patients.

Antiinflammatory Agents.
These drugs fall into two categories: the corticosteroids and the cromones (See Discussion). Paradoxically, some patients may have an increased cough after using inhalation forms of these medications due to airway irritation. This irritation can sometimes be prevented by pretreatment with a beta-agonist spray.

Corticosteroids.
These drugs are the most potent of the antiinflammatory agents. Oral and intravenous dosages are effective within hours; however, substantial improvement may not be seen for days. Inhaled preparations may take longer to produce substantial improvement in symptoms. Maximum improvement may take 3 to 6 months.

Steroid inhalers may cause side effects such as dysphonia and oral candidiasis. These side effects may be alleviated through the use of a different steroid brand or through the use of a spacer device (see Recommended Approach below). Candidiasis may also be prevented by rinsing the mouth with warm water after each dosage. Long-term usage of high dosages of inhaled steroids may rarely cause adrenal suppression which is usually of no clinical importance. Systemic side effects such as bruising, weight gain, and effects on bone metabolism have also been reported. Therefore, periodically, the effectiveness and requirement for inhaled corticosteroids should be objectively assessed. When stopping a course of corticosteroids, the patient should be observed closely for several weeks since their protective effects may persist for up to two additional weeks.

Inhaled corticosteroids administered by MDI should be added to the treatment regimen of every asthmatic with persistent or frequent symptoms or decreased PEFR. Asthmatics with mild *and intermittent* disease who use their bronchodilator less than two times per week and have normal function in between attacks usually do not need a corticosteroid MDI.

Cromones.
These drugs, specifically cromolyn and nedocromil, are available only by inhalation. They are effective in asthmatics with obvious seasonal or allergic triggers and not usually effective in asthmatics with perennial symptoms and no obvious triggers. They may take up to 6 weeks to show effectiveness. They have little systemic absorption and no known systemic side effects.

Special Treatment Considerations.
The *pregnant asthmatic* is treated with the same step approach as the nonpregnant asthmatic; however, priority is given to specific medications with the least systemic absorption or with the longest worldwide experience and, therefore, the best safety profile. The physician should always remember that the biggest danger to the fetus is hypoxemia due to uncontrolled asthma.

Exercise-induced asthma is best treated with beta-agonist inhalation 15 minutes prior to exercise. This typically provides protection for 90% of individuals and lasts 2 to 4 hours. Inhaled cromolyn is an alternative. It is effective in preventing exercise-induced asthma in approximately 50% of individuals.

Immunotherapy for asthma is discussed under Prevention.

Recommended Approach

Patients with asthma should be classified according to symptom frequency and PEFR as either mild, moderate, or severe (see Table 5–1–1). Medication dosages are stepped up and additional medications are added based on the therapeutic response. Initial therapy in all asthmatics (except the mildest asthmatics with infrequent symptoms) should include the use of a beta-agonist inhaler as needed and an antiinflammatory inhaler two times per day. If symptoms do not improve, the frequency of inhaled corticosteroid usage should be increased. In moderate to severe disease, oral corticosteroids may be added. For better

TABLE 13–20–2. CLASSES OF DRUGS USED TO TREAT ASTHMA

Bronchodilators	
Rapid acting beta-agonists	
Metered-dose inhalers	Albuterol, bitolterol, metaproterenol, pirbuterol, terbutaline
Nebulizer solutions	Albuterol, metaproterenol
Oral syrup or tablets	Albuterol, metaproterenol, terbutaline
Methylxanthines	Theophylline (oral syrup or tablets)
Anticholinergic agents	Ipratroprium bromide (metered-dose inhaler or nebulizer solution)
Long-acting beta agonists	Salmeterol
Antiinflammatory drugs	
Corticosteroids	
Metered-dose inhalers	Beclomethasone, triamcinolone, flunisolide, budesonide,* fluticasone*
Systemic	Prednisone, prednisolone, triamcindone
Cromones	Cromolyn sodium, nedocromil sodium

*Not yet available in the United States.

acute symptom control (especially nocturnal symptoms), inhaled sal-meterol (long-acting beta agonist), oral theophylline, and/or oral beta agonists may be added; however, when improvement is noted after adding these other agents or due to increased antiinflammatory therapy, patients always need to be educated and cautioned against discontinuing their antiinflammatory medication. As improvement occurs, many patients will tolerate stepwise removal or decreased dosage of some of their medications.

Patient education is especially important due to the widespread promotion of different classes of inhaled medications as the first-line treatment for asthma. Studies have shown that up to 50% of physicians and patients do not use an inhaler properly. Thus, in the physician's office this skill must be demonstrated to the patient and practiced *prior* to giving the prescription to the patient. The skill should then be reviewed periodically if the treatment response is inadequate.

A minority of patients after instruction and practice cannot properly coordinate metered-dose inhaler (MDI) activation with their own inhalation. These patients should be given an additional device to allow for aerosolized medication delivery. The devices available include a spacer extension to their MDI, an automatic inhaler, or a nebulizer.

Spacer devices come in several sizes. The larger devices (called holding chambers) are placed on the end of the MDI and allow the aerosolized medication particles to remain suspended for several seconds. With this type of spacer, there is no need for the patient to coordinate inhalation with the MDI.

The automatic inhaler is a new breath-activated device for metered-dose medication delivery. The patient simply turns on the trigger and breathes in, and the medication is automatically delivered. This "auto-haler" device is approximately the same size and cost as the regular MDI and, therefore, just as convenient to carry in the pocket for emergency relief. It can be used successfully by patients who cannot master the standard MDI and obviates the need for a spacer; however, it is currently available only for the beta-agonist pirbuterol. Patients may still need to have a spacer device to be kept at home for their steroid MDI. With either a spacer or an autohaler, patient education is still required. Because of the availability of spacers and "autohalers," expensive and cumbersome nebulizer devices are rarely needed.

The patient should be taught to differentiate the beta-agonist inhaler used for rapid "rescue" relief (and should be carried at all times for urgent usage) from the antiinflammatory inhaler, which is to be used regularly and not to be used for emergency symptom relief. The patient must be taught that the long-acting beta agonist salmeterol, is not for urgent or quick relief. Most of the inhaler brands differ in style or color. Therefore, the physician should keep samples of the inhalers in the office to use while teaching patients. This helps the physician monitor patient compliance during follow-up visits by asking the patient to identify the number of inhalations of each unit which he or she uses daily and by asking the patient to identify the purpose of the different inhalers.

FOLLOW-UP

Untreated asthma may persist with mild symptoms, or may increase in severity causing near-fatal airway obstruction or respiratory arrest. Usually these symptoms are gradual in onset and allow time for therapeutic intervention as an outpatient. If, however, the early signs are ignored, asthma may worsen, leading to emergency hospital visits and admissions.

The response to treatment can be evaluated by monitoring symptoms and PEFR at every office visit. Important questions to be asked at follow-up visits include whether there is a decrease in nocturnal awakening and a decrease in the frequency of usage of the inhaled beta agonist. Monitoring of the PEFR is analogous to monitoring the blood pressure of a hypertensive patient or the glucose level of a diabetic. Any decrease of 15% or more is of medical significance and should prompt a change in therapy. PEFR undergoes diurnal variation with a peak value at 4:00 PM and a nadir at 4:00 AM. Therefore, PEFR monitoring should be done at the same time of day.

Patients who are not improving or are worsening should be reassessed for proper medication compliance and proper inhaler technique and, if appropriate, have a further step-up of medications. The

physician should also reassess the differential diagnosis or consider subspecialty referral. Continued patient and family education is important during follow-up visits.

Patients with frequent exacerbations and with a poor perception of their asthma symptoms should be taught home monitoring of their PEFR. This is analogous to diabetic home monitoring of glucose levels to adjust insulin doses. The patient is given a medication instruction sheet, color coded to match colored zones on the PEFR meter. The patient adjusts the medication and/or calls the physician based on the amount of change in the self-measured home PEFR.

Recent literature suggest that a single measurement of the early morning PEFR may be the most sensitive single measurement to monitor at home. In a small percentage of patients changes in PEFR may lag behind changes in symptoms. The home diary should therefore include documentation of both PEFR and asthma symptoms.

A minority of patients have been reported to have fatal or near-fatal asthma attacks of rapid onset (within minutes to hours of being asymptomatic). These patients need to be extra careful regarding trigger avoidance. It has been suggested that such patients carry a self-activated epinephrine injector for initial rapid treatment in the event of a severe attack. They should also wear a medical identification bracelet.

DISCUSSION
Prevalence and Incidence

The prevalence and morbidity of asthma increased through the 1980s in the United States as well as worldwide. In 1992, the prevalence in the U.S. was almost 5%. Overall, asthma is equally prevalent among both sexes and among all age groups; however, prevalence, hospitalization rate, and mortality are slightly higher below age 18 and above age 65. The prevalence, hospitalization rate, and mortality are higher among African-Americans in the United States and among populations living in inner-city areas. The overall age-adjusted death rate is 1.2 per 100,000. Nearly 20% of people with asthma suffer some limitation in their daily activities due to their disease. Asthma accounts for 4.3% of the prevalence of significant activity limitation due to all chronic conditions for people of all ages and 18% of activity limitation for people younger than age 18.

Related Basic Science

The development of airway obstruction is responsible for the clinical manifestations of asthma. Airway obstruction is caused by differing combinations of muscle spasm, mucus plugging, airway edema, and inflammatory cell infiltration. Morphologic studies show that some bronchial infiltration with inflammatory cells is present even in the mildest cases of asthma.

Asthma is not caused by a single cell or mediator. Asthma results when a stimulus triggers a complex interaction among inflammatory cells, mediators, and the airway. Once this process is initiated the airway becomes susceptible to further inflammation with repeated exposure to triggers. Triggers may be many and varied (listed under Clinical Manifestations). The trigger leads to activation of mast cells, eosinophils, macrophages, and lymphocytes. The trigger may also cause additional bronchospasm through an autonomic nervous system pathway.

The activated inflammatory cells release a variety of interleukins, prostaglandins, leukotrienes, and cytokines which together cause smooth muscle contraction (known as the early phase or immediate asthmatic response), epithelial damage, subepithelial collagen deposition, and additional inflammatory cell chemotaxis into the airways. Eosinophilic protein is thought to play a major role in the initial bronchospasm and epithelial injury. Cytokines from lymphocytes stimulate neutrophilic infiltration and further inflammatory cell activation. This ongoing inflammation causes the late phase (or delayed asthmatic response) and increases susceptibility to inflammation from recurrent trigger exposure. This process may progress into an inflammatory spiral with ongoing airway edema, mucus secretion, increased vascular permeability, and ongoing cellular infiltration. Chronic inflammation may also lead to subepithelial fibrosis.

Phase 3 trials have been conducted investigating the salutary effects of a specific 5-lipoxygenase (leukotriene) synthesis inhibitor (zileuton) on asthma control. This medication has been shown to improve control of mild to moderate asthma and to prevent asthmatic reactions induced by aspirin or nonsteroidal antiinflammatory drugs. Zileuton is currently pending Food and Drug Administration approval and its role in step therapy of asthma would need to be further defined. Trials are also well underway with specific leukotriene receptor antagonists.

Beta agonists have multiple effects on the airway. Their primary mechanism of bronchodilation is thought to occur through stimulation of the beta receptors of smooth muscle cells. Regular daily usage of beta agonists may lead to downregulation of the number of beta receptors and decreased bronchodilatory effectiveness. With regular beta-agonist use, the airways may then become more hyperreactive and sensitive to triggers. Corticosteroids modulate the inflammatory process and also improve the effectiveness of bronchodilators. The precise mechanism, however, is unknown.

Natural History and Its Modification with Treatment

Asthma is a chronic disease that can be controlled but not cured. Some patients are asymptomatic most of the time and do not consider themselves as asthmatic. These patients experience mild, very occasional symptoms in response to a specific trigger (e.g., viral respiratory illness) and may require treatment for only a few weeks after this event. At the other extreme are the patients with chronic lifelong symptoms and the need for multiple medications. Perhaps 80% of asthmatics have mild, easily controlled disease.

Children with mild asthma may "outgrow" their disease; however, children with severe asthma or chronic cough are likely to have persistent or recurrent symptoms during adult life. During pregnancy, one third of asthmatics worsen, one third of asthmatics improve, and one third of asthmatics remain unchanged. It is postulated but not proven that untreated inflammation in asthma is one cause of chronic obstructive pulmonary disease. It is unknown whether chronic treatment with inhaled steroids can prevent this disease outcome.

Prevention

Risk factors for the primary development of asthma have not been delineated; however, asthma exacerbation can be prevented by comprehensive *patient education to avoid triggers and institute environmental control measures.* It is currently not possible to identify in advance all asthmatics who can benefit from this process. Environmental control requires a substantial effort. It can involve removal from the household of molds, animal proteins and dander (left by cats, dogs, birds), dust and dust mites, rodents, cockroaches, chemical sprays, humidifiers, and exposure to odors such as cigarette smoke and perfume. (Housedust

mites are controlled by encasing the mattress and pillows in plastic covers, washing bed linen every week in hot water (130° F), avoiding lying on upholstered furniture, decreasing indoor humidity to less than 50%, and removing carpets and draperies.) Not all patients require all these measures. Conversely, many of these measures are difficult and impractical for patients to implement.

Immunotherapy has been shown to be helpful to some patients with asthma caused by housedust, cat dander, grass pollen, and alternaria. Immunotherapy treatment should be instituted only if the history suggests a particular allergen and this specific allergen is confirmed by dermal testing. In addition, immunotherapy must be maintained for at least several years to be continually effective. Immunotherapy should not be continued if there is no evidence of protection through two allergy seasons. Immunotherapy requires availability of personnel to treat any (rare) potentially life-threatening reaction.

Asthma exacerbation can also be prevented through community or emergency department outreach and identification of asthmatics not receiving regular office-based care. All patients need to be educated regarding proper step therapy of asthma and how to prevent exacerbations from progressing to medical emergencies.

Cost Containment

Proper asthma management can decrease loss of time from school or work. Studies have suggested that spending extra money on patient education and medication can save on the total costs of asthma care over several years. The education leads to successful prevention of severe asthma exacerbation and a decrease in overall financial and social costs to society through a decrease in emergency department visits and a decrease in activity restriction.

REFERENCES

Beasley R, Roche WR, Roberts JA, et al. Cellular events in the bronchi in mild asthma and after provocation. Am Rev Respir Dis 1089;139:807.

Burrows B, Lebowitz MD. The beta-agonist dilemma. N Engl J Med 1992;326:560.

Global Initiative for Asthma. National Heart, Lung and Blood Institute; National Institutes of Health; Bethesda, MD 20892. Publication No. 95–3659, January, 1995. To order telephone 301–251–1222.

Juniper EF, Kline PA, Vanzieleghem MA, et al. Effect of long-term treatment with an inhaled corticosteroid (budesonide) on airway hyperresponsiveness and clinical asthma in nonsteroid-dependent asthmatics. Am Rev Respir Dis 1990;142:832.

Management of Asthma During Pregnancy. National Heart, Lung and Blood Institute; National Institutes of Health; Bethesda, MD 20892. Publication No. 93–3279, September, 1993. To order telephone 301–251–1222.

CHAPTER 13–21

Pulmonary Hypertension and Chronic Cor Pulmonale as Viewed by a Pulmonologist

Richard K. Albert, M.D.

DEFINITION

Pulmonary hypertension is defined by a mean pulmonary arterial pressure greater than 25 mm Hg. The term *cor pulmonale* has been used to indicate right ventricular failure, as well as pulmonary hypertension due to pulmonary disease in the *absence* of left ventricular failure.

ETIOLOGY

Pulmonary hypertension can occur secondary to numerous diseases or conditions as categorized in Table 13–21–1. Patients with elevated pulmonary arterial pressures in the *absence* of any of these associated dis-

eases or conditions are given the diagnosis of primary pulmonary hypertension.

CRITERIA FOR DIAGNOSIS
Suggestive

Pulmonary hypertension is suggested by finding signs of right ventricular failure on physical examination, enlarged pulmonary arteries and right ventricular hypertrophy or lung disease on chest roentgenograms, or manifestations of right ventricular hypertrophy, right-axis deviation, and/or right atrial abnormality on the electrocardiogram.

TABLE 13-21-1. CAUSES OF PULMONARY HYPERTENSION

Secondary to pulmonary venous hypertension
    Left ventricular failure from any cause (e.g., aortic valve disease, subaortic stenosis, cardiomyopathy)
    Mitral valve stenosis or insufficiency
    Left atrial myxoma
    Fibrosing mediastinitis impinging on the pulmonary veins
    Pulmonary venoocclusive disease
Secondary to hypoxia
    High altitude
    Obstructive or restrictive pulmonary diseases
    Sleep apnea
    Abnormal ventilatory drives (e.g., hypothyroidism, medication-induced, primary central hypoventilation)
Secondary to systemic disease
    Portal hypertension
    Connective tissue diseases (e.g., systemic lupus erythematosus, scleroderma, rheumatoid vasculitis)
    HIV infection
Secondary to congenital cardiac disease
    Atrial septal defect (with Eisenmenger's reaction)
    Ventricular septal defect (with Eisenmenger's reaction)
    Patent ductus arteriosus (with Eisenmenger's reaction)
Secondary to emboli
    Pulmonary thromboemboli (central or peripheral)
    Foreign body (i.e., talc or cotton fibers as seen in intravenous drug abusers)
    Parasites (e.g., schistosomiasis)
    Amniotic fluid
    Tumor
Primary pulmonary hypertension

Definitive

Echocardiography or right-sided heart catheterization is needed for a definitive diagnosis of pulmonary hypertension. Distinguishing between primary and secondary pulmonary hypertension generally requires right-sided heart catheterization, arterial blood gases, and a number of additional studies seeking evidence supporting or excluding the various diagnoses listed in Table 13-21-1.

CLINICAL MANIFESTATIONS

Subjective

The symptoms of pulmonary hypertension are nonspecific but, in the earlier stages, include dyspnea on exertion and lightheadedness. Chest pain, presyncope, and syncope can occur as the disease progresses. Hemoptysis is rare but is seen more commonly in patients with pulmonary venous hypertension and in patients with Eisenmenger's syndrome (Table 13-21-1). Raynaud's syndrome occurs in a small minority of patients.

Patients may also present with symptoms that are specifically related to pulmonary disease, cardiac disease, or systemic diseases that are known to cause pulmonary hypertension (e.g., paroxysmal nocturnal dyspnea and orthopnea in patients with pulmonary venous hypertension, snoring and spousal reports of choking or gasping in patients with sleep apnea).

When patients present with pulmonary hypertension in the absence of any of the associated conditions listed in Table 13-21-1, the physician should search for evidence of previous lower extremity trauma, venous thrombosis, and/or pulmonary emboli.

A careful family history should be obtained for evidence of hypercoagulation or possible pulmonary vascular problems. Risks for HIV infection should be sought.

Objective

Physical Examination

Physical findings include those resulting from the pulmonary hypertension per se and those attributable to any of the associated conditions (e.g., emphysema, aortic or mitral stenosis, scleroderma). Jugular ve-

nous distension occurs when right atrial pressure increases or when right ventricular failure has developed. Tricuspid valve regurgitation produces prominent *v* waves in the jugular venous pulse as a result of right ventricular dilation. The *a* wave becomes prominent because of the poor compliance of the right ventricle. Palpation may yield a parasternal heave. The pulmonary component of the second heart sound is increased. The holosystolic murmur of tricuspid insufficiency is distinguished by its increasing intensity with inhalation and its location along the left sternal border. A diastolic murmur of pulmonary regurgitation (Graham Steell) and a fourth heart sound emanating from the right ventricle may be heard as the pulmonary hypertension progresses and right ventricular failure ensues. Hepatic congestion can result in hepatosplenomegaly and/or ascites. Pedal edema is common. Patients with atrial or ventricular septal defects may present with marked cyanosis if the pulmonary hypertension has progressed to the point that the left-to-right shunt has reversed (i.e., the Eisenmenger reaction). Patients with the Eisenmenger's syndrome due to patent ductus may exhibit more cyanosis of the toes than of the fingers due to the reversal of the shunt in the ductus. Obesity, systemic hypertension, and a neck circumference greater than 38 cm suggest the possibility of sleep apnea.

Routine Laboratory Abnormalities

Laboratory tests that may be abnormal include an elevated hematocrit or hemoglobin (seen primarily in patients with Eisenmenger's syndrome); lymphopenia (in patients with pulmonary hypertension associated with HIV infection); an increased or decreased serum bicarbonate (compensating for a chronic respiratory alkalosis, which may accompany hypoxemia, or for chronic respiratory acidemia associated with abnormal ventilatory drives); and abnormal liver enzymes, bilirubin, albumin, or prothrombin time (which might result from hepatic congestion or from any type of primary liver disease with associated pulmonary hypertension).

Common electrocardiographic abnormalities are summarized on Table 13-21-2. Because the left ventricle is markedly thicker than the right in normal circumstances, considerable right ventricular hypertrophy must occur before it is apparent on the electrocardiogram.

The chest roentgenogram may be particularly helpful in that evidence of an enlarged pulmonary outflow track and/or enlarged pulmonary arteries that taper promptly are quite specific for pulmonary hypertension. Many of the conditions resulting in secondary pulmonary hypertension may also have distinctive roentgenographic abnormalities (e.g., mitral stenosis, emphysema).

PLANS

Diagnostic

Differential Diagnosis

The differential diagnosis for pulmonary hypertension centers around determining whether the problem is primary or secondary to any of the diseases or conditions listed in Table 13-21-1.

Diagnostic Options

Four questions must be answered: Does the patient have pulmonary hypertension? If so, is the problem primary or secondary? What is the extent of the pressure elevation? And, if the condition is primary, is the pulmonary vascular bed reactive to one or more vasodilating medications? Given the numerous causes of secondary pulmonary hyperten-

TABLE 13-21-2. ELECTROCARDIOGRAPHIC FINDINGS IN PATIENTS WITH PULMONARY HYPERTENSION

Right-axis deviation of the QRS complex and right ventricular hypertrophy
    Axis > 100°
    $R/s \geq 1$ with an $R > 5$ mm in V_1
    $S > 3$ mm in left precordial leads
    rSR', or incomplete right bundle-branch block in V_1
Right atrial abnormality
    P wave > 2.5 mm in II, III, aVF, V_1
    Tall P wave in V_1 and lower-than-usual P wave in V_6

sion, a multiplicity of tests could be indicated and the order in which they are obtained could and should vary depending on the clinical presentation of a given patient. Nonetheless, considering issues of cost, risk, and diagnostic yield, the following approach seems most reasonable.

Recommended Approach

If the history, physical examination, chest roentgenogram, and/or electrocardiogram suggest pulmonary hypertension in the *absence* of overt cardiac or pulmonary disease, echocardiography with Doppler should be obtained. This test provides a noninvasive method by which to screen for abnormalities in right ventricular or right atrial dimensions, ventricular wall thickness and motion, and tricuspid and/or pulmonary regurgitation. If tricuspid regurgitation is present, systolic pulmonary arterial pressure may be rather accurately estimated. In addition, pericardial disease and left-sided cardiac abnormalities may be apparent, as may right-to-left shunts. If the echocardiogram points to left-sided cardiac abnormalities, the diagnostic and therapeutic approach should subsequently focus on the specific abnormality observed. If only right-sided abnormalities are found, a number of studies may be needed and the order in which they are obtained may vary depending on clinical suspicion.

If the patient is obese or has a clinical evaluation compatible with sleep apnea or abnormal ventilatory drives a sleep study should be ordered. Ventilation–perfusion (*V/Q*) lung scan should be obtained seeking evidence of recurrent, unresolved emboli (multiple lobar *V/Q* mismatches). *V/Q* scans in patients with primary pulmonary hypertension are generally normal or only show areas of patchy, peripheral hypoperfusion.

Patients thought to have pulmonary hypertension on the basis of systemic disease, congenital cardiac disease, or emboli, and those thought to have primary pulmonary hypertension require right-sided heart catheterization to determine the degree of pulmonary hypertension, to assess cardiac function, and to seek evidence of intracardiac shunts. The procedure should be done by physicians experienced in evaluating patients with pulmonary hypertension to avoid subjecting patients to the expense and risk of *two* procedures (as occurs when the data obtained on the initial studies are incomplete). On occasion, specially designed catheters are needed to obtain pulmonary arterial and wedge pressures in these patients and these are not commonly available in many catheterization laboratories or intensive care units. In addition, administering vasodilating medications is not without risk as, in the setting of a relatively fixed pulmonary vascular bed, the systemic vasodilation that occurs may result in life-threatening hypotension. Finally, experienced centers may have access to one or more experimental vasodilating agents that are not yet generally available.

Patients suspected of having collagen disease such as scleroderma or lupus should have the appropriate test to support the diagnosis.

Therapeutic

Therapeutic Options

Therapy for secondary pulmonary hypertension is directed at the underlying cause whenever possible. The treatment of chronic obstructive lung disease is discussed in Chapter 13–16. The treatment of other secondary causes of pulmonary hypertension is discussed in chapters dealing with specific etiologies.

The standard approach to treatment of primary pulmonary hypertension consists of administering long-term anticoagulation to all; calcium channel blockers, nitrates, or other pulmonary vasodilators to the relatively small fraction (perhaps 25%) of patients who respond to these medications with pulmonary vasodilation; and lung or heart-lung transplantation for those who do not respond to medications or for those in whom vasodilators fail to prevent disease progression. In some centers continuous intravenous infusion of prostacyclin is available on an experimental protocol. In others, type 5 phosphodiesterase inhibitors are being combined with other vasodilators.

Digitalis may improve right ventricular contractility, but the modest beneficial effects must be weighed against an increased risk of digitalis toxicity in these patients. Although diuretics are commonly administered to reduce ascites and edema, they may adversely affect right ven-

tricular function by diminishing right ventricular preload and, therefore, must be used judiciously. Atrial septostomy improved the clinical status in a small number of patients. The procedure comes with associated risks of paradoxical embolism and, if the communication is too large, of severe hypoxemia.

Recommended Approach

General measures include ensuring that the PaO_2 exceeds 55 to 60 mm Hg at rest during sleep and with exercise, and that the erythrocythemia that may accompany chronic hypoxemia does not result in hyperviscosity, thereby further reducing cardiac function. If phlebotomy is needed (generally not until the hematocrit exceeds 50–55%) it must be done under isovolume conditions so as to maintain right ventricular preload. Diuretics may be used with care. Pedal edema may be effectively treated without reducing right ventricular preload by use of elastic compression stockings that are appropriately sized to fit the patient's calf and thigh dimensions. Warfarin is generally recommended (aiming for an INR of 1.5 to 2.5) based on a sound pathophysiologic rationale (i.e., patients may be hypercoagulable on the basis of one or more endothelial abnormalities and/or very low flow going through markedly narrowed pulmonary vessels); the results of two uncontrolled clinical trials; and the high mortality associated with the condition.

As above, most should undergo right-sided heart catheterization including determination of wedge pressure, right atrial pressure, and cardiac output; collection of blood from different positions in the right heart seeking evidence of left-to-right intracardiac or intrapulmonary shunts; and trials of several vasodilators. Initially, short-acting vasodilators should be given (e.g., nitroglycerin, adenosine, or acetylcholine to assess the guanyl cyclase pathway; prostacylin, when it becomes available, to assess the adenyl cyclase pathway, and nifedipine to assess the response to calcium channel blockers). Nitroglycerin is generally preferred over acetylcholine as it has less serious side effects, and is also used more commonly than adenosine as it is less expensive. Nitroglycerin may be started at 0.5 g/kg/min intravenously and increased 0.5 g/kg/min every 10 to 15 minutes to a maximum of 5 g/kg/min, or until the patient becomes nauseated, develops a severe headache, or drops his or her systemic vascular resistance by 25%. A positive response is one in which pulmonary arterial pressure or pulmonary vascular resistance falls at least 25%. Smaller changes may represent nothing more than random variation. Prostacyclin may be started at 2 ng/kg/min, increasing 1 to 2 ng/kg/min every 5 to 10 minutes until resistance improves 25% or headache, flushing, or hypotension develops. Nifedipine may be tried at a dose of 10 mg sublingually, repeating 15 to 20 minutes later if no response occurs. If patients respond favorably to intravenous nitroglycerin and/or to nifedipine they should be considered candidates for long-term therapy with nitrates (nitroglycerin ointment 0.5–2 in. every 4 hours or isosorbide 5–20 mg orally every 4–6 hours) and/or calcium channel blockers (nifedipine 10–60 mg orally every 6–8 hours or diltiazem 30–240 mg three times daily). Doses should be titrated in an intensive care unit setting over the subsequent 36 to 48 hours to obtain a maximal reduction in pulmonary vascular resistance without adversely affecting systemic vascular resistance.

In selected centers, prostacyclin is available for continuous infusion, as is combined therapy with nitrates, calcium channel blockers, and/or phosphodiesterase inhibitors (type 3 or 5 to augment intracellular cyclic AMP and/or cyclic GMP, respectively). Inhaled nitric oxide causes pulmonary vasodilation without affecting systemic vascular resistance. Long-term use of nitric oxide awaits demonstration of its lack of toxicity when used chronically and development of safe delivery devices.

Lung transplantation is presently the only available option for those patients who do not respond favorably to vasodilators or for those in whom vasodilation fails to halt progression of disease.

FOLLOW-UP

Patients should be closely monitored (every 2–4 months) to ensure that oxygenation is adequate ($SaO_2 > 90\%$) and that hyperviscosity does not develop. Right ventricular function should be monitored by following the degree of edema, ascites, and jugular venous pressure elevation and by listening for the development of a right ventricular S_4. Static or orthostatic hypotension may indicate inadequate left ventricular function resulting from right ventricular dilation and/or from bulging of the ventricular septum into the left ventricle, thereby diminishing left ventricular compliance, and may suggest that right ventricular preload is suboptimal. Atrial dilation may result in supraventricular arrhythmias. Those patients with primary pulmonary hypertension who are receiving vasodilators should be monitored for medication-associated hypotension, nausea, headache, or flushing. The pulmonary vasodilating effect should be monitored every 4 to 6 months by repeat echocardiography.

The clinical condition of patients with secondary pulmonary hypertension may progress to the extent that they need frequent follow-up. The specific interval depends on the condition, its severity and rate of progression, and the various therapeutic options available. Patients with primary pulmonary hypertension should be referred to centers experienced in caring for this problem, most of which will also have the option of lung transplantation available.

DISCUSSION

Prevalence and Incidence

Secondary pulmonary hypertension is a common problem given the prevalence of the various conditions with which it is associated (e.g., emphysema, left ventricular failure). In fact, cor pulmonale due to obstructive lung disease is the third most common cause of heart failure, exceeded only by coronary disease and hypertension.

Primary pulmonary hypertension is rare but is being identified more commonly now than in the past.

Related Basic Science

The basic science related to chronic obstructive lung disease is discussed in Chapter 13–16.

Genetics

A small number of families with primary pulmonary hypertension have been reported. The inheritance pattern is that of autosomal dominance with complete penetrance. An association with HLA-DR3, -DRW52, and -DQW2 has been reported. If a familial association is discovered, *all* family members should have echocardiography, even if they are asymptomatic.

Altered Molecular Biology

A number of vasoactive mediators have been implicated in the pathophysiology of primary pulmonary hypertension, including prostacyclin (which causes vasodilation by stimulating adenyl cyclase, thereby increasing smooth muscle cAMP, and inhibits platelet aggregation as well as their adherence to endothelial cells); nitric oxide (which causes vasodilation by stimulating guanyl cyclase, increasing smooth muscle cGMP, and also inhibits platelet aggregation and adherence); and endothelin (one of the most potent vasoconstrictors yet described). A small series of patients with hypoxemic congenital heart disease respond to nitrates (nitric oxide generators) with pulmonary vasodilation but have no such effect in response to acetylcholine or adenosine (nitric oxide synthase activators). These disparate results suggest the possibility of abnormalities in endothelial nitric oxide synthase. The endothelial cells of patients with primary and secondary pulmonary hypertension have increased expression of endothelin mRNA, and hypoxia has been shown to increase mRNA for endothelin precursors. The fawn-hooded rat spontaneously develops pulmonary hypertension and suffers from a genetically determined platelet storage abnormality that results in an increased production of endothelin.

Physiologic or Metabolic Derangement

Patients with primary pulmonary hypertension produce more thromboxane, a vasoconstrictive prostaglandin, and less prostacyclin than do patients with pulmonary hypertension resulting from other causes. Continuous nitric oxide release from the pulmonary endothelium seems to contribute to the low resistance inherent in the normal pulmonary circulation. The interrelationship between these systems is apparent as endothelin increases nitric oxide release, which, in turn, decreases endothelin release from the pulmonary endothelium.

Anatomic Derangement

Several histologic findings are pathognomonic for pulmonary hypertension but none can specifically distinguish between the various causes. Although the angiopathy generally affects pulmonary arteries or arterioles, pulmonary venules or veins may also be abnormal. The arterial histopathology consists predominantly of medial hypertrophy (resulting from thickening of the medial smooth muscle and the elastic laminae in larger arteries, muscularization of smaller arterioles, and replacement of smooth muscle by fibrous tissue); plexogenic lesions (characterized by medial hypertrophy, intimal atheromas and/or myofibrosis, and matrix deposition); or thrombotic pulmonary arteriopathy (consisting of medial hypertrophy with concentric or eccentric intimal fibrosis). Although patients with medial hypertrophy may be at an earlier stage of disease, and may be more responsive to vasodilating medications than those with plexogenic lesions, the clinical, prognostic, and therapeutic implications of the different classifications are not clear. Regardless of which vascular lesion predominates, the chronically increased right ventricular afterload results in marked right ventricular hypertrophy and, subsequently, right ventricular dilation.

Natural History and Its Modification with Treatment

The natural history of patients with chronic obstructive lung disease is discussed in Chapter 13–16.

The median survival of patients with primary pulmonary hypertension (generally untreated) is about 3 years after the diagnosis is established. Survival clearly relates to the subjective and objective findings at the time of presentation (Table 13–21–3).

The small fraction of patients who respond to high doses of calcium channel blockers by reducing their pulmonary arterial pressure or pulmonary vascular resistance by at least 20% have a much better prognosis than those who do not respond and are, accordingly, not treated. Whether this difference is due to the medication or the fact that the patients receiving treatment are capable of pulmonary vasodilation has not yet been determined. Unfortunately, the risk of giving vasodilators to unresponsive patients precludes a truly randomized clinical trial, and the low incidence and overall poor prognosis of primary pulmonary hypertension have thus far precluded treating responsive patients with placebo. Uncontrolled, retrospective studies also suggest (but do not establish) that long-term anticoagulation may also be beneficial. Although prostacyclin is not yet generally available, its use has been associated with a reduced mortality when used as a bridge to transplant. Of note is the fact that the patients given long-term prostacyclin were only minimally responsive to the medication when it was given as a test dose.

13–21–3. RELATIONSHIP OF CLINICAL PRESENTATION TO SURVIVAL IN PRIMARY PULMONARY HYPERTENSION

Variable	Survival (months)
New York Heart Association status	
Class 1 or 2	59
Class 3	32
Class 4	6
Raynaud's syndrome	
Present	12
Absent	44
Right atrial pressure	
< 10 mm Hg	45
≥ 20 mm Hg	2
Pulmonary arterial pressure	
< 55 mm Hg	48
≥ 85 mm Hg	12
Cardiac index	
> 4 L/min·m²	43
< 2 L/min·m²	12

Data from Barst et al, 1994.

Recent data suggest that the 3-year survival following lung transplant for pulmonary hypertension is between 50 and 60%. More importantly, the large majority have little if any exercise limitation and many can return to full-time employment.

The benefits of continuous oxygen supplementation on mortality of patients with hypoxemia secondary to emphysema and/or chronic bronchitis have been well documented.

Prevention

The pulmonary hypertension resulting from some of the conditions listed in Table 13–21–1 can be prevented by aggressively treating the primary disorder (e.g., left ventricular failure, sleep apnea, hypothyroidism, emphysema) and/or the hypoxemia that might result. No measures are known to prevent primary pulmonary hypertension.

Cost Containment

The most cost-effective treatment plan involves treating the primary problem as aggressively as possible. This is commonly the case when dealing with chronic obstructive lung disease. In some instances this requires a decision regarding aortic or mitral valve replacement, use of continuous positive airway pressure versus tracheostomy for patients with sleep apnea, or pulmonary thromboendarterectomy for patients with large vessel thrombi.

The high mortality of patients with primary pulmonary hypertension dictates that they be evaluated and treated by specialists experienced with the condition as well as with the indications for lung transplantation.

REFERENCES

Barst RJ, Rubin LJ, McGood MD, et al. Survival in primary pulmonary hypertension with long-term continuous intravenous prostacyclin. Ann Intern Med 1994;121:409.

D'Alonzo GE, Barst RJ, Ayres SM, et al. Survival in patients with primary pulmonary hypertension: Results from a national prospective registry. Ann Intern Med 1991;115:343.

Nocturnal Oxygen Therapy Trial Group. Continuous or nocturnal oxygen therapy in hypoxemic chronic obstructive pulmonary disease: A clinical trial. Ann Intern Med 1980;93:391.

Packer M, Greenberg B, Massie B, Dash H. Deleterious effects of hydralazine in patients with pulmonary hypertension. N Engl J Med 1982;306:1326.

Rich S, Kauffmann E, Levy PS. The effect of high doses of calcium-channel blockers on survival in primary pulmonary hypertension. N Engl J Med 1992;327:76.

CHAPTER 13–22

Asbestosis

Robert N. Jones, M.D.

DEFINITION

Asbestosis is diffuse interstitial fibrosis of the lung caused by inhaled asbestos. Asbestos can separately cause pleural fibrotic conditions, which should not be called "asbestosis."

ETIOLOGY

Asbestos is the common term for a group of naturally occurring fibrous minerals that have had commercial value. They are silicate minerals that can occur in both solid ("rock") and fibrous forms, depending on the geologic influences at their formation. The fibers are in the micrometer to submicrometer diameter range, and so can be inhaled and deposited in the fine air passages and airspaces of the lung. Asbestos fibers are relatively durable in tissue, and are cleared or broken down only slowly. The most common type of asbestos is chrysotile, which is least durable in tissues. The other types are classified as amphiboles, which include amosite, crocidolite, and anthophyllite. The amphiboles are much more durable in tissues, which probably accounts for their greater toxicity.

Asbestos exposure does not always cause asbestosis. The risk of asbestosis increases with increasing cumulative exposure, which means exposure intensity times exposure duration.

CRITERIA FOR DIAGNOSIS
Suggestive

A patient with diffuse, basilar-predominant interstitial lung disease (diagnosed radiographically) has a history of past occupational exposure to asbestos.

Definitive

- There is a history of lengthy work in a trade or setting associated with a significant risk of asbestosis.
- There is radiographic evidence of diffuse, basilar-predominant interstitial lung disease.
- There is no good reason to believe that some other disease explains the radiographic abnormality.

In recording the exposure history, document the industry (manufacturing, construction, shipbuilding, seafaring, building maintenance); the craft or job (welder, machine operator, insulator, boilermaker); the setting (for a shipyard machinist, shop versus shipboard, or for a carpenter or plumber/pipefitter, residential versus commercial versus industrial); the history of direct handling versus bystander exposures to asbestos-containing materials; and, of course, the starting and ending years of each different exposure situation. Remember to ask the patient what his or her construction jobs have actually involved. There are pipefitters who have done only pipe welding, and boilermakers who have never worked on boilers, and brickmasons who have done firebrick instead of common brick work.

It is freely conceded that asbestosis can exist in a preradiographic stage and, in fact, must do so prior to becoming sufficiently advanced for radiographic diagnosis. Also, a few reported patients have had lung function or physical examination evidence, in the form of restriction or rales or clubbing, with negative or nondiagnostic radiographs but positive lung biopsies. But they were reported (reportable = rare), and biopsy was required to prove the diagnosis. The clinical criteria given above simply acknowledge the fact that without radiographic disease, histopathologic findings are required to prove the diagnosis.

The third criterion deals with potential confounders. There is no need to order tests to exclude possibilities not suggested by a complete history and physical examination. Conversely, a patient with inflammatory polyarthritis or Raynaud's phenomenon should be evaluated for connective tissue diseases.

According to a widely accepted system formulated by a committee of the College of American Pathologists and the U.S. National Institute of Occupational Safety and Health, minimal histopathological criteria are peribronchiolar fibrosis plus (multiple) asbestos bodies. Asbestos bodies are fibers that have become coated with iron-rich proteins, and the finding of multiple ones on ordinary sections establishes an asbestos exposure that may plausibly explain coexisting lung fibrosis. The tissue must be presumably representative of the whole lung; transbronchoscopic and needle biopsies are inadequate. Fibrosis in the immediate vicinity of cancer is often a "desmoplastic" reaction to the tumor itself and cannot be taken as evidence of diffuse fibrosis. Some authorities require alveolar wall fibrosis for a diagnosis of asbestosis, because peribronchiolar fibrosis can be a chronic response to many irritating industrial dusts and smokes.

A problem for both radiographic and histopathologic diagnosis is the entirely nonspecific appearance of the fibrosis. The collagenous fibrosis of asbestosis is indistinguishable from that of many other causes. Histopathologic diagnosis thus does not involve demonstration of a pathognomonic lesion. It involves an inference that the asbestos exposure caused the nonspecific-appearing scar tissue. In some cases, that inference will be wrong, as when the exposures were too recent to cause disease (the latency principle), or when the fibrotic process is too rapid to be asbestosis (asbestosis is very slowly progressive), or another cause is more likely (e.g., amiodarone, bleomycin, therapeutic irradiation, scleroderma).

CLINICAL MANIFESTATIONS

Because occupational exposure levels have greatly declined, most cases are now diagnosed in elderly men whose causative exposures occurred prior to 1970. It is often diagnosed at an early stage, when there are few or no symptoms and when lung function is not significantly impaired.

Unfortunately, asbestosis is also a marker of increased lung cancer risk, and some cases are diagnosed when the patient presents with symptoms of carcinoma.

Subjective

The cardinal symptom of advanced asbestosis is exertional shortness of breath. Another frequent symptom is a persistent and highly annoying dry cough. Clearly, these symptoms are so nonspecific as to be of no use as diagnostic criteria. Most patients have either no symptoms or have symptoms resulting from other conditions: productive cough from smoking, chest pains from coronary disease, exertional shortness of breath from the classic retirement-age factors of aging, weight gain, and reduced activity levels.

Objective

Physical Examination

The direct nonradiographic signs of lung fibrosis (again, in the more advanced cases) are restriction of chest expansion, crackling rales, restrictive abnormality and reduced diffusing capacity on lung function tests, and arterial hypoxemia. Clubbing occurs in a minority of cases. All of these signs may be absent in a given case, yet the clinical diagnosis will be sound if the plain chest radiograph is consistent with asbestosis and the other criteria are met.

Routine Laboratory Abnormalities

Radiographically, asbestosis produces a diffuse, linear interstitial process that starts and remains most advanced in the lung bases. On plain radiographs, it is notably uniform in its apparent distribution from deep to peripheral areas. It is bilaterally symmetric, except where pleural disease or bullae have altered the appearance.

Asbestos can also cause diffuse pleural fibrosis and pleural plaques. The diffuse fibrosis is indistinguishable from that caused by more common agents, including infections and trauma. Diffuse pleural fibrosis thus provides no support for a diagnosis of asbestosis in the same patient, and may hinder diagnosis by making the lungs difficult to image and by providing an alternate explanation for rales and restriction. Fibrotic hyaline plaques are highly specific for asbestos causation, but are not found in every case of asbestosis and are often found in workers who do not have asbestosis. Plaques can develop from exposures lower than those causing asbestosis, and so are not markers of sufficient exposure to cause asbestosis. Thus plaques do not bolster a diagnosis of asbestosis in the same patient, but their absence does not weaken it (unless exposure is in doubt, in which case it is fatally weak, anyway).

Lung asbestos burdens can be estimated after digestion of adequate (surgical or autopsy) tissue specimens. Finding fiber levels in the range associated with proven asbestosis cases may buttress a diagnosis made in the presence of other causes of lung fibrosis. It does not establish the diagnosis when fibrosis is absent (see Definition).

PLANS

Diagnostic

Differential Diagnosis

The list is long and includes most chronic diffuse interstitial conditions, fibrotic and otherwise. Only those that present a distinctly nodular appearance (e.g., silicosis) or are found exclusively or predominantly in the upper lung zones (e.g., sarcoidosis) rate low consideration. The most troublesome confounders include idiopathic pulmonary fibrosis and related conditions (usual and desquamative and lymphocytic interstitial pneumonias); connective tissue diseases; adverse effects of drugs and radiation; and a few other pneumoconioses, such as hard metal disease. Congestive heart failure can closely simulate interstitial lung disease and can even cause it, when severe and chronic. Centrilobular and bullous emphysema produce radiographic shadowing by compressing, and diverting blood flow to, the lung bases, and they are often responsible for erroneous diagnosis of diffuse fibrosis. Mere obesity is responsible for some diagnostic errors: the diaphragm is high, the lung bases appear dense, the patient is short of breath and has rales, and testing shows reduced lung volumes. (Asbestosis diagnostic schemes that award points for various symptoms and laboratory findings usually flunk the challenge posed by congestive heart failure or morbid obesity.) Finally, diffuse pleural thickening can cause atelectasis of subpleural lung, and this can be mistaken for lung fibrosis.

Diagnostic Options

Clinical diagnosis is sound when based on the criteria given above. Computed tomography (CT) scans have been advocated for early diagnosis but have not yet become an accepted modality. The advocates of CT diagnosis often rely on abnormalities that may in fact represent effects of pleural scarring on subpleural lung. CT comes to the rescue when pleural disease prevents a good look at lung details on the plain radiograph, and when in such cases it shows a diffuse lung disease, that criterion is adequately met. CT scans rarely provide persuasive evidence of asbestosis when the lungs look normal on the plain radiographs.

Biopsy should not be needed unless there is a substantial likelihood of another condition.

Recommended Approach

The chest radiograph is the most important item in clinical diagnosis. Many clinicians can recognize advanced interstitial fibrosis, with small lungs and honeycomb appearance, but relatively few are equipped by training and experience to detect confidently the mild interstitial abnormality found in most cases. When relying on a radiologist's interpretation, it must be clear that a positive reading means that the radiologist thinks that diffuse interstitial disease is present. Many radiologists fall into the habit of describing "increased interstitial (or bronchovascular) markings" in an implausibly large percentage of older patients. Some describe "fibrotic changes" in a large number of emphysema patients. Such reports are not helpful. What is needed is a true consultation, in which the clinician poses the question: Is this radiograph consistent with diffuse interstitial lung disease? In most cases the answer should be a plain yes or no. In the few cases that are radiographically borderline, it is appropriate to weigh all the other clinical information, including exposure data, physical examination, and lung function tests, to make or reject the diagnosis.

The diagnosis is made when it is "more likely than not"; otherwise, it should not be given. Asbestosis is a disease for which there is no treatment, and is the result of exposures long past, so there is no benefit from premature diagnosis. It is also a diagnosis that can jeopardize the patient's employability and lead to claims and lawsuits. A premature diagnosis can lead to hasty legal decisions that actually preclude later recovery of damages for more severe illness.

Biopsy is not indicated for the sole purpose of diagnosing or excluding asbestosis. If lung tissue is going to be obtained surgically from a patient who might have asbestosis, the histopathologic diagnosis should be made from tissue that is (1) not subpleural and (2) not in the immediate vicinity of a neoplasm or an inflammatory process. Iron stains may help in finding asbestos bodies. The surgeon and pathologist should have advance warning of the possibility of asbestosis, a point frequently overlooked when the operation is for suspected cancer.

Complete lung function tests (spirometry, lung volumes, diffusing capacity) should be obtained at the time of diagnosis.

Therapeutic

There is presently no effective treatment to retard or reverse lung scarring.

FOLLOW-UP

At the time of diagnosis, inform patients that they are unfit for further occupational exposures to asbestos or other fibrogenic dusts. Patients should be told that they have an occupational disease and that they should obtain legal advice. The purpose is not to encourage litigation, but rather to preserve the patient's option of later bringing a claim. In many jurisdictions, the diagnosis of an occupational disease establishes a period (often 1 to a few years) in which the patient must take some action, or else a future claim will be barred. Failure to understand this can have disastrous consequences for the person whose disease is mild at diagnosis but later becomes complicated or severe. If lung function is more than mildly impaired (from asbestosis and/or other causes), it is imprudent to work around strongly irritating or sensitizing inhalants. Smoking cessation should be urged and aided, to prevent independent damage to lung function and to reduce risk of lung cancer. The (one-time) immunization against pneumococci should be given to old or impaired patients, who should also receive annual influenza immunization. Interview and examine the patient yearly, preferably in late fall to administer the new influenza vaccine. Obtain a plain chest radiograph yearly.

Spirometry is adequate for lung function follow-up and can be repeated at long intervals (3–5 years) or when there is a change in symptoms or the radiograph.

DISCUSSION
Prevalence and Incidence

There are no good data on rates in the general population. Most patients with asbestosis "die with it, not of it," and so the condition is greatly underreported on death certificates. Cases show geographic clustering according to past differences in distribution of industries. There is virtually no asbestos mining in the United States, nor much manufacturing (any more) of asbestos products. The current cases are mostly from remote exposures in manufacturing and shipbuilding and remote and more recent exposures in construction and maintenance work, particularly ship repair and industrial plant maintenance.

Asbestos usage has greatly declined, and fewer workers are exposed in the industries that accounted for most of the cases. Exposure levels have also been dramatically lowered. New cases must therefore inevitably decline in both numbers and severity.

Related Basic Science

Mild asbestosis is compatible with normal lung function. More advanced disease is associated with reductions in total lung capacity (TLC), vital capacity (VC), and forced vital capacity (FVC). In smokers who have both asbestosis and chronic airway obstruction, increased residual volume (RV) caused by obstruction may offset the reduced VC caused by scarring, leaving a normal TLC (TLC = VC + RV). VC is then a better measure of the impact of asbestosis on lung function. Diffusing capacity is highly variable in asbestosis, as it is in general. Diffusing capacity testing is complicated and thus highly subject to errors, is abnormal in nonpulmonary conditions (anemia, cardiovascular diseases), reflects airway dysfunction (not just interstitial disease), and is further depressed by smoking itself. Exercise testing in patients referred for asbestos evaluations usually turns up evidence of cardiovascular limitations.

Natural History and Its Modification with Treatment

There is no effective treatment. The disease is very slowly progressive—so slowly, in fact, that today death from asbestosis itself is a rarity. Most asbestosis patients die of unrelated causes. Asbestosis increases the risk of lung cancer, multiplying the risk from habitual smoking. The risk of pleural and peritoneal mesothelioma is also higher in asbestosis, but these tumors are relatively rare (and unrelated to smoking). Trials of early cancer detection and dietary cancer prevention have been disappointing.

Prevention

Asbestosis is a dose-related disease, and limitation of exposure can prevent it. This is accomplished by avoidance or reduction of exposure, through substitution of materials, engineering controls of dust levels, hygienic work practices, and use of personal respiratory protective devices.

Cost Containment

There is no proven value of routine follow-up at intervals shorter than 1 year. Simple spirometry is preferred to follow the course of lung function.

REFERENCES

American Thoracic Society. The diagnosis of nonmalignant diseases related to asbestos. Am Rev Respir Dis 1986;134:363.

Craighead JE, Abraham JL, Churg A, et al. The pathology of asbestos-associated diseases of the lungs and pleural cavities: Diagnostic criteria and proposed grading schema. Report of the Pneumoconiosis Committee of the College of American Pathologists and the National Institute for Occupational Safety and Health. Arch Pathol Lab Med 1982;106:544.

Mossman BT, Bignon J, Corn M, et al. Asbestos: Scientific developments and implications for public policy. Science 1990;247:294.

Roggli VL, Greenberg SD, Pratt PC. Pathology of asbestos-associated diseases. Boston: Little, Brown, 1992.

Solomon A, Kreel L, eds. Radiology of occupational chest disease. New York: Springer-Verlag, 1989.

CHAPTER 13–23

Byssinosis

Stephan L. Kamholz, M.D.

DEFINITION

Byssinosis is a respiratory tract disease with both acute and chronic manifestations that results from occupational exposure to cotton, flax, or hemp dusts. A characteristic complex of symptoms and respiratory impairment occurs, and indeed, it may be classified as a form of occupational asthma. A chronic bronchitis-like form of respiratory impairment is found in chronically exposed individuals.

ETIOLOGY

The exact component of cotton (flax or hemp) dust that is responsible for the induction of respiratory symptoms is still a matter of debate. It is known that an endotoxin-like component (perhaps attributable to bacterial contamination of cotton) may in part be responsible for some of the manifestations of the disease. Inhalation of water-soluble extracts of cotton dust can provoke many of the symptoms associated with byssinosis itself. Histamine release from bronchial mast cells has been postulated to play a role in the development of bronchoconstriction after exposure to cotton dust, although administration of histamine receptor antagonists does not consistently prevent the response. Two forms of byssinosis are recognized: the acute form which, when it does develop, characteristically occurs on the first day at the workplace after an absence; and the more chronic form, which develops after years of repeated exposure and is a form of chronic bronchitis.

CRITERIA FOR DIAGNOSIS
Suggestive

The occurrence of a typical complex of symptoms (chest tightness, shortness of breath, and cough) that occurs on the first workday of the week, accompanied by a decrease in pulmonary function, in individuals occupationally exposed to cotton dust is suggestive of the diagnosis of byssinosis.

Definitive

The definitive diagnosis of byssinosis is made in the presence of the clinical criteria that are listed above as suggesting the diagnosis. Spirometric determinations that demonstrate a reduction in the 1-second forced expiratory volume (FEV_1) after 6 to 8 hours of workplace exposure to cotton dusts are confirmatory. The federal Occupational Safety and Health Administration (OSHA) has defined a fall (during a single work shift) in FEV_1 of 5% or 200 mL as indicative of a positive response. Inhalation challenge tests using various extracts of cotton dusts are useful in epidemiologic and immunologic investigations, but are not essential to the clinical diagnosis in the affected individual.

CLINICAL MANIFESTATIONS
Subjective

Patients with early byssinosis are asymptomatic while away from the workplace (weekends and holidays) and develop symptoms and bronchoconstriction within several hours of return to the workplace. Symptoms are often maximal by the end of the first working day, and may abate (but not disappear) during the rest of the work week, perhaps due to tachyphylaxis to the inciting agent(s). Interestingly, decrements in expiratory airflow rates of similar magnitude to those observed in workers who have the symptom complex of byssinosis can often be demonstrated in asymptomatic cotton workers. The duration of work exposure prior to the onset of symptomatology is highly variable. Cigarette smoking is clearly a "cofactor" in the development of respiratory symptoms, including wheezing, cough, and sputum production.

Objective
Physical Examination

Physical examination, if performed when the individual is acutely symptomatic, may reveal wheezes and rhonchi characteristic of obstructive airway disease.

Routine Laboratory Abnormalities

Routine laboratory data, including the chest x-ray film, are noncontributory. In the late stages of the disease, radiographic abnormalities consistent with chronic bronchitis may be found.

PLANS
Diagnostic
Differential Diagnosis

Idiopathic asthma and chronic bronchitis must be considered in the differential diagnosis of byssinosis; however, the definitive history of occupational exposure will be lacking in the other entities.

Diagnostic Options

Complete history, physical examination, chest roentgenogram, and worksite spirometry throughout a work shift must be performed. Spiro-

metric measurements may have to be obtained on more than one day, as symptomatology and bronchoconstriction are variable. Assessment of the workplace for cotton dust levels is important from an epidemiologic and occupational health standpoint. In selected cases, inhalation challenge studies using cotton dust extracts may be required to substantiate claims for compensation or disability payments.

Recommended Approach

Complete history including the exact nature of worksite involvement with cotton processing, physical examination, chest roentgenography, and spirometry should be performed. To establish the diagnosis of the acute bronchoconstrictor reaction to cotton dusts, pulmonary function evaluation at the worksite, with baseline preexposure spirometry and repeat measurements through the shift, is indicated. Postbronchodilator spirometry is useful in establishing the reversibility of airflow obstruction and in selecting the appropriate class of therapeutic agent, for example, β_2-adrenergic bronchodilators.

Therapeutic
Therapeutic Options

Procedures to reduce the amount of dust generated during cotton processing are important in reducing the likelihood of development of byssinosis among workers in a plant. These interventions include washing or steam cleaning of cotton prior to processing. Treatment for reversible airflow obstruction should be prescribed for workers who have developed byssinosis. The treatment may include aerosol β_2 bronchodilators (e.g., albuterol, metaproterenol, or pirbuterol, 2 puffs every 3–4 hours), anticholinergic aerosols (e.g., ipratropium bromide, 2 to 4 puffs every 4 hours), and aerosol corticosteroids, with the dose adjusted based on severity of symptoms and potency of the specific drug. Pretreatment with β_2-adrenergic aerosol or with an antihistaminic agent may partly abolish the bronchoconstrictor response on exposure to the offending cotton dusts. The role of disodium cromoglycate and nedocromil in byssinosis remains to be established. In patients with chronic bronchitis resulting from chronic exposure to cotton dusts, therapy is similar to that employed for patients with smoking-related chronic bronchitis.

Recommended Approach

Preventive measures are most important, as delineated above. Use of specific dust/mist/fume respirator masks may be helpful. Treatment of reversible airflow obstruction, as delineated above, is recommended.

FOLLOW-UP

Followup is indicated for individuals with bronchoconstrictive byssinosis, to reassess the response to interventions aimed at ameliorating bronchoconstriction. Similarly, aggressive treatment of those individuals with advanced byssinosis (chronic bronchitis) may require regularly scheduled visits. The OSHA cotton dust standard requires ongoing annual surveillance of exposed workers, and this is usually carried out at the worksite.

DISCUSSION
Prevalence and Incidence

Recent data suggest that an increasing incidence of byssinosis can be detected at a single worksite if longitudinal studies of the pulmonary function of exposed workers are carried out. Between 40 and 50% of long-term exposed workers may have some manifestations of the disease. The prevalence of byssinosis can be limited by the application of dust-limiting and dust-protective interventions.

Related Basic Science

Acute decrements in airway function have been documented in cotton workers exposed to crude cotton and its dusts, particularly those workers involved in the separation and carding of fibers. In contrast, workers exposed to steam-cleaned or washed cotton experience less bronchoconstriction. This suggests that the inciting agent(s) is in the cotton bract (or trash) that contaminates crude cotton. The exact mechanism(s) by which these substances induce bronchoconstriction is not clear, but it differs from classic antigen (immunoglobulin E)-mediated bronchospasm in time course, with immunoglobulin E asthma being almost immediate and with the bronchoconstrictor form of byssinosis occurring 1.5 to 2 hours after the onset of exposure in reactive individuals. Some of the response may be attributable to bacterial endotoxin (contaminating crude cotton), as inhalation of endotoxin has been shown to induce bronchoconstriction in animal models. Inhalation of endotoxin-free aqueous bract extracts has, however, been shown to produce bronchoconstriction in healthy volunteers, casting some doubt on the role of endotoxin. The possibility that an inflammatory response is evoked by inhalation of cotton dusts is currently being explored. Cotton bract extracts do exhibit neutrophil chemotactic activity, and bronchoalveolar lavage from exposed individuals does contain increased numbers of polymorphonuclear leuckocytes. Inflammatory mediators released from the polymorphonuclear leukocytes locally in the airways may then induce the bronchoconstriction. Nonspecific airway hyperreactivity may also play a role in byssinosis, increasing the likelihood that an exposed worker will develop a bronchoconstrictor response; that is, it is both a risk factor for and an effect of the response to cotton dust. Atopic individuals exposed under laboratory conditions to cotton dust demonstrate a greater decrease in FEV_1 after exposure than nonatopic individuals. The histopathology and physiologic manifestations of bronchitic (advanced) byssinosis are identical to those found in chronic bronchitis attributable to smoking.

Natural History and Its Modification with Treatment

Byssinosis is totally reversible when the affected individual is removed from contact with the offending cotton dust. Inhalational bronchodilators reverse the bronchoconstriction, returning flow rates to normal values. Long-term exposure results in chronic airflow limitation, with the structural changes of chronic bronchitis. This should be largely preventable through application of federally mandated surveillance of cotton workers.

Prevention

Industrial approaches that limit the amount of cotton dust that enters respirable air in the workplace are among the most important preventive measures. Enclosing dusty operations, use of air conditioning and air filtration systems, and efficient removal of dusts from work surfaces all contribute to the reduction of ambient dust levels. The use of personal dust/mist/fume respiratory masks should also be considered as adjunctive. Federally required surveillance programs, identification of individuals at risk, and removal from the worksite, or modification of specific tasks in an effort to eliminate exposure, are all important steps in the prevention of advanced disability from byssinosis.

Cost Containment

Chronic disability due to byssinosis limits the productivity of the affected worker and often requires expensive long-term medical care. Thus, the most effective cost containment intervention is the careful application of the mandated surveillance programs that will identify workers at risk before permanent disability develops.

REFERENCES

Glindmeyer HW, Lefante JJ, Jones AN, et al. Exposure-related declines in the lung function of cotton textile workers: Relationship to current workplace standards. Am Rev Respir Dis 1991;144:675.

Gordon T, Balmes J, Fine J, et al. Airway oedema and obstruction in guinea pigs exposed to inhaled endotoxin. Br J Ind Med 1991;48:629.

Jacobs RR, Boehlecke B, Van Hage-Hamsten M, et al. Bronchial reactivity, atopy and airway response to cotton dust. Am Rev Respir Dis 1993;148:19.

Schachter EN, Zuskin E, Buck M. Airway reactivity and cotton-bract induced bronchial obstruction. Chest 1985;87:51.

Zuskin E, Ivankovic D, Schachter EN, et al. A ten-year follow-up study of cotton textile workers. Am Rev Respir Dis 1991;143:301.

CHAPTER 13–24

Coal Workers' Pneumoconiosis

Stephan L. Kamholz, M.D.

DEFINITION

Coal workers' pneumoconiosis (CWP), also known as black lung disease, results from the chronic deposition of coal dust in the lungs of occupationally exposed individuals, most often encountered in workers at the coal seam who are directly involved in cutting or drilling. Other individuals involved in "support" occupations within the coal mine are also at risk of dust inhalation, with the severity of the exposure varying with their role and location. Characteristic radiographic abnormalities (see later) are noted, and individuals with more significant disease suffer respiratory symptoms.

ETIOLOGY

It is now known that coal dust itself is the cause of CWP; however, the presence of varying quantities of quartz (silica) in the inhaled dust has made it difficult to entirely separate CWP from silicosis, and indeed, in some cases the lesions of both entities coexist. A distinct pathologic lesion, the coal macule, characterizes both the mild ("simple") and more severe (progressive massive fibrosis or "complicated") types of CWP, and develops on the accumulation of considerable amounts of dust within the lung. The exact mechanism by which coal dust provokes an inflammatory and fibrotic response within the lung is not known, but the interplay between dust burden and host response (immunologic factors) is believed to be a critical factor in the development of the lesions.

CRITERIA FOR DIAGNOSIS
Suggestive

The presence of an abnormal chest roentgenogram characterized by small rounded nodular opacities predominantly in the upper lobes, in association with an appropriate history of occupational exposure to coal dust, is suggestive of the diagnosis of CWP. More advanced and extensive lesions are found in complicated CWP.

Definitive

The definitive diagnosis of CWP is made employing the same criteria that are suggestive. Usually the small rounded opacities develop during the course of exposure to coal dust, the duration of which has in most instances exceeded 10 years. Occasionally the radiographic abnormality is noted after the exposure has ceased. Thin-section computed axial tomography scan may then be helpful in confirming the presence of nodules, but is usually not necessary. Histopathologic confirmation is not routinely sought.

CLINICAL MANIFESTATIONS
Subjective

Most patients with simple CWP are asymptomatic, unless they have associated lung disease of a different etiology, such as chronic bronchitis (attributable to smoking), or have advanced involvement with a profusion of nodular opacities. In complicated CWP, dyspnea or exertion (sometimes noted at rest in more advanced states), cough, and the occasional production of black sputum are the classic manifestations. In the most severe cases of complicated CWP, symptoms of cor pulmonale including peripheral edema may be noted. The history of occupational exposure to coal dust is essential for diagnosis. The family history is generally noncontributory, although the history of CWP in a first-order relative may suggest a heightened familial susceptibility to the effects of coal dust.

Objective

Physical Examination

In simple CWP the physical examination is usually normal. For those patients with concomitant chronic bronchitis, the auscultatory findings of coarse rhonchi and wheezing may be noted. In patients with complicated CWP, auscultatory findings over the larger parenchymal lesions are those of consolidation (percussion dullness, bronchial breath sounds, enhanced tactile fremitus) or those of atelectasis. When pulmonary hypertension and cor pulmonale are present in advanced complicated CWP, neck vein distension, inferolateral displacement of the cardiac apex, right parasternal lift, accentuation of the pulmonic component of the second heart sound, hepatomegaly (occasionally pulsatile), and peripheral edema may all be noted.

Routine Laboratory Abnormalities

Routine laboratory data are nonrevealing. Specific chest roentgenographic abnormalities are delineated under Plans, Diagnostic.

PLANS

Diagnostic

Differential Diagnosis

Silicosis must be considered in the differential diagnosis of CWP, although knowledge of the dust composition at the worksite (coal dust, quartz) and of the specific task(s) in which the coal worker was/is involved is helpful in separating the entities. Other causes of small nodular pulmonary opacities (granulomatous inflammatory disease, metastatic carcinomatosis) do not contribute to diagnostic confusion because of the irrefutable history of exposure to coal dust and the absence of symptoms expected with these other entities.

Diagnostic Options

Complete history (including the nature and duration of occupational exposure), physical examination, and chest radiography are the essential components of the diagnostic evaluation. Pulmonary function tests, including spirometric determination of flow rates, lung volume determination, and diffusing capacity measurements, are all indicated when there is respiratory symptomatology or when prospective monitoring of exposed workers is conducted as part of industrial hygiene surveillance measures. With the earliest stages of simple CWP, pulmonary function tests are normal or show very slight ventilatory impairment. In significantly affected individuals, pulmonary function testing documents reduced lung volumes, impairment of expiratory flow rates, and reduction of carbon monoxide diffusing capacity. Arterial blood gases may reveal hypoxemia with hypocapnia, and will show evidence of worsening hypoxemia with oxyhemoglobin desaturation during exercise. As the pathologic lesions in CWP may be predominantly fibrotic (reduced volumes and diffusion) or may encroach on airways (reduced expiratory flow rates), it is not possible to predict in advance which pattern of respiratory impairment will predominate. The characteristic radiologic lesions seen in simple CWP are small (usually 4 mm; range, 1–10 mm) rounded nodular opacities which predominate in the upper lobes. Though not usually required, thin-section chest computed axial tomography scanning will confirm the presence of these small nodular opacities in the upper lobes before these can be detected on routine chest roentgenograms. The extent and severity of radiographic involvement in CWP are graded according to the scheme developed by the International Labor Organization–Union Internationale Contra Cancer (ILO–UICC).

The size and profusion of nodules are reflected by the classification, with category 1 reflective of the findings in most cases of simple CWP. More advanced levels of apparent parenchymal involvement (categories 2 and 3) are associated with a higher risk of development of progressive massive fibrosis (complicated CWP). For those individuals with systemic complaints, including fever, weight loss, and sweats, and for those individuals with progressive massive fibrosis who have cavitary lesions (with or without referable symptoms), studies to exclude complicating infection with *Mycobacterium tuberculosis* are indicated.

Recommended Approach

Complete history, physical examination, chest roentgenography, and screening spirometry should be performed. More complete pulmonary function evaluation, including exercise testing, is indicated when symptomatology is severe or when compensation/disability payments are sought.

Therapeutic

Therapeutic Options

There is no specific therapy for CWP. Individuals who have early lesions detected incidentally or those who are found to have abnormalities during regularly scheduled surveillance examinations may be counseled to change their task or workplace to preclude further dust exposure. Preventive measures including the use of dust/mist/fume respirator masks and methods of ventilation control to reduce the workplace dust burden are efficacious. Symptomatic treatment of associated chronic bronchitis or cor pulmonale is indicated.

Recommended Approach

Preventive measures are most important, as delineated above. As specific therapies are not available, symptomatic relief of bronchospasm, cough, intercurrent airway infection, and hypoxemia should be prescribed when indicated.

FOLLOW-UP

Specific follow-up is not indicated for individuals with simple CWP, especially those with category 1 involvement. When treatment is required for associated chronic bronchitis, cor pulmonale, intercurrent infection, or tuberculosis, the frequency of visits should be predicated on the therapeutic requirements for those problems.

DISCUSSION

Prevalence and Incidence

Almost 200,000 individuals are employed in coal mining in the United States; however, the specific prevalence of CWP is not readily determined. Rates of radiographic detection of CWP vary from region to region within the United States, ranging from a low of less than 5% (Colorado) to more than 40% in eastern Pennsylvania. Mining tasks with relatively high dust exposure (cutting machine operators, continuous mining machine operators, loading machine operators, and roofbolters) have the highest association with the development of CWP. Mining tasks with lower-density dust exposure (motorman, driver, mechanic, electrician) have a reduced but definite association with the development of disease. Coal trimmers (who load and stow coal in stores or ship holds), graphite miners and millers, and manufacturers of carbon electrodes are all at risk of developing a pneumoconiosis identical to CWP. Rates of CWP have been steadily dropping since the introduction of the 1969 Federal Coal Mine Health and Safety Act ("Black Lung Act"), which mandated certain personnel protective policies and surveillance measures. Increasing concentrations of quartz in mine dust are associated with a greater likelihood of the development of progressive massive fibrosis, which can be expected in about 2% of those with category 2 or more severe CWP.

Related Basic Science

The basic lesion of CWP is the coal macule, which is surrounded by focal emphysema. The macule is a small pigmented lesion, which is usually distributed evenly through the upper lobes of the lungs. Dust-laden alveolar macrophages and fibroblasts constitute the lesion, which tends to develop around respiratory bronchioles and extend into the interstitial spaces. Cytokines released by the macrophages result in chemotaxis of neutrophils, which in turn release proteolytic enzymes that contribute to local tissue destruction, weakening of the adjacent bronchiolar wall, and subsequent dilation and the creation of a focal area of emphysema. Periarteriolar and subpleural coal dust deposits may develop. Progressive massive fibrosis is attributable to the coalescence of perivascular lesions, usually in the posterior upper lobes or superior segments of the lower lobes. These lesions can impinge on airways or vessels, and may cavitate. An unusual association of a nodular pneumoconiosis with rheumatoid arthritis in coal miners has been described, and is known as *Caplan's syndrome.* Serologic markers of rheumatoid arthritis are often present in this entity, and lung lesions tend to be of the progressive massive fibrosis type (though nonpigmented nodules can also be seen). As noted above, the severity and pattern of pulmonary functional impairment vary with the extent and location of parenchymal lesions. A predilection for infection with *Mycobacterium tuberculosis,* though more frequent in silicosis, is also noted in CWP, attributable to the diminution in pulmonary alveolar macrophage function caused by the dust burden.

Natural History and Its Modification with Treatment

Therapeutic measures are not available for CWP. Careful adherence to preventive measures and frequent surveillance of the risk group can be expected to reduce the development of new disease, and to provide the opportunity for workplace or task modification that will halt progression of pneumoconiosis. Simple CWP is not associated with reduction in life expectancy. Individuals with progressive massive fibrosis, however, suffer reduced lifespan and progressive respiratory insufficiency and may die of respiratory failure.

Prevention

With the advent of mechanized coal mining, the number of at-risk employees exposed to coal dust has dropped; however, dust levels at worksite have not uniformly decreased. Careful attention to the protective and surveillance measures required by the Black Lung Act is the most important preventive measure. Efforts to encourage miners to comply with safety measures are also vital.

Cost Containment

As the morbidity of CWP is largely preventable, cost containment measures are embodied in the use of personnel protective devices, improvements in mine ventilation and dust control, and surveillance of workers. Compensation for advanced disability due to CWP is currently borne by the employers and the federal government, and these costs can be expected to decrease as preventive measures are more widely employed.

REFERENCES

Derickson A. The United Mine Workers of America and recognition of occupational respiratory diseases, 1902–1968. Am J Public Health 1991;81:781.

Kusaka Y, Brown GM, Donaldson K. Alveolitis caused by exposure to coalmine dust: Production of interleukin-1 and immunomodulation by bronchoalveolar leukocytes. Environ Res 1990;53:76.

Mejers JMM, Swaen GMH, Slangen JJM, et al. Long term mortality in miners with coal workers' pneumoconiosis in The Netherlands: A pilot study. Am J Ind Med 1991;19:43.

Rom WN. Basic mechanisms leading to focal emphysema in coal workers' pneumoconiosis. Environ Res 1990;53:16.

Seaton A. Coal mining, emphysema and compensation. Br J Ind Med 1990;47:433.

CHAPTER 13–25

Silicosis

Robert N. Jones, M.D.

DEFINITION

Silicosis in its ordinary form is a chronic, nodular, diffuse scarring condition of the lungs.

"Simple silicosis" is the radiographic stage in which there are rounded small (2–6 mm) opacities, usually most profuse (concentrated) in the upper lung zones. "Complicated silicosis" is the radiographically advanced stage that results from the coalescence of these nodular small opacities to form large masses (>10 mm in diameter) of scar tissue. Occasional cases are rapidly progressive ("accelerated silicosis") or even "acute," and in these the radiographic abnormalities are more extensive, and the nodules are less discrete. In acute silicosis there may be no visible nodulation, only large consolidations resembling pulmonary edema.

ETIOLOGY

Silicosis is caused by the inhalation of minute particles of silicon dioxide, SiO_2, in crystalline form. Naturally occurring pure forms are quartz and cristobalite. Crystalline silica is a major constituent of the earth's crust. Sand is mostly quartz, and many clays are rich in quartz. Rocks with high silica concentrations include sandstone, slate, granite, and feldspars. Noncrystalline or amorphous silica (e.g., diatomite, fused silica, ordinary glass) does not cause silicosis.

Silica in rocks, and even in fine sands, is in particles too large to be inhaled deeply into the lung. Silicosis results from mining or industrial processes that break down the crystals into respirable sizes (less than 10 μm) and disperse large concentrations in the air. Silicosis is therefore a disease of certain occupations: mining (and quarrying and tunneling), processing (cutting, carving, milling, crushing, or grinding of rocks/sands), abrasive operations (sandblasting, polishing, compounding of abrasives), and other uses of finely divided crystalline silica (e.g., for making foundry molds, pottery, ceramics). Amorphous silica can be converted into crystalline silica by heating, as when diatomite is heated above 800°C to produce calcined diatomite, which is rich in fine crystals of quartz and/or cristobalite.

The risk of silicosis is related to the cumulative exposure to respirable-sized crystals, that is, to the average concentration times the total duration of exposures. It is generally a disease of long latency, the latent period being defined as the interval between first exposure and disease onset. The latent period is inversely related to intensity of exposure, with larger concentrations producing earlier disease onset.

CRITERIA FOR DIAGNOSIS

Suggestive

The chest radiograph (see below) shows abnormalities consistent with silicosis, in a patient with past work in a dusty trade.

Definitive

- There is a history of work in a trade or setting associated with risk of silicosis.
- The chest radiograph shows abnormalities consistent with silicosis.
- There is no good reason to believe that the radiographic abnormalities are the result of some other disease or condition.

Pathologic diagnosis requires a representative sample of lung tissue that contains silicotic nodules, or silicotic nodulation of massive scar tissue, or silicolipoproteinosis. The silicotic nodule, described below, is a pathognomonic lesion whether in the form of isolated nodules separated by normal lung tissue or incorporated into larger masses of collagen. Silicolipoproteinosis is found in the rare instances of acute silicosis.

CLINICAL MANIFESTATIONS
Subjective

Symptoms are usually absent in early simple silicosis. There may be a mild cough, with mucoid sputum. Shortness of breath either is absent or is attributable to other conditions. Some cases, however, are first diagnosed when silicosis is complicated by mycobacterial or fungal lung infections, to which silicotics are predisposed in even the preclinical stage of disease. As silicosis worsens, exertional shortness of breath appears and is later followed by dyspnea at rest. In advanced complicated silicosis, there may be a need for continuous oxygen supplementation, and symptoms of cor pulmonale can occur.

The history of occupational exposure to finely divided crystalline silica is an essential element of the clinical diagnosis of silicosis. Otherwise, information from the medical history is useful mainly in excluding other diagnostic possibilities.

Objective
Physical Examination

Mild silicosis usually produces no detectable physical examination findings. Advanced cases may show tachypnea, limited chest expansion, and vague alterations in percussion note and transmission of voice sounds and vibrations. Signs of airway obstruction (prolonged expiratory phase, wheezing) are common, but they correlate poorly with the amount of lung scarring. Cyanosis and signs of cor pulmonale (venous distention, enlarging liver, edema) are seen in far-advanced disease.

Routine Laboratory Abnormalities

Radiographic abnormality is essential for the clinical diagnosis of silicosis. In simple silicosis there are discrete, sharply outlined round densities, usually in the diameter range 2 to 6 mm. The upper lung zones are affected sooner and more severely than the lower zones. In contrast with tuberculosis (except miliary tuberculosis) and with most cases of metastatic spread of cancer to the lungs, silicotic "small opacities" are uniform in size and are evenly dispersed within the affected lung zones. In complicated silicosis there are larger masses of confluent scar tissue, also usually in the upper zones. The threshold size for diagnosis of complicated silicosis is 1 cm, but these masses, silicotic "large opacities," are usually larger and may reach 8 to 10 cm in longest dimension. They tend to be bilaterally symmetric, which helps to distinguish them from primary lung cancer or the residual scars of old tuberculosis. Of even greater help, vis-à-vis tuberculosis, is the tendency of silicotic large opacities to be separated from the pleura by air-containing lung tissue, whereas tuberculous scars usually extend to the pleura and even spread out along it.

Thoracic lymph node enlargement is rare in silicosis, but a peripheral or "eggshell" pattern of lymph node calcification is seen in perhaps 10 to 15% of cases. Eggshell calcifications are extremely rare in other diseases (sarcoidosis, irradiated Hodgkin's lymphoma) and, when found, indicate that a nodular lung disease is probably silicosis. They can be found, however, in a few silica-exposed persons who do not have radiographic lung nodulation, in which cases they only indicate silicotic inflammation of the lymph nodes.

Silicosis is not notable for causing pleural disease. Ragged, patchy pleural thickening may be seen adjacent to coalescing lung nodules. Pneumothorax sometimes occurs in complicated silicosis, and the scarred lung may be difficult to reexpand. Pleural effusions or empyemas can result from complicating infections. Silicosis itself does not cause pleural plaques; in a silicotic patient, plaques indicate past exposure to asbestos.

Lung function abnormalities in silicosis are nonspecific and not helpful in diagnosis. Simple silicosis may produce no abnormality.

PLANS
Diagnostic
Differential Diagnosis

Coal workers' pneumoconiosis, China clay (kaolin) pneumoconiosis, and a few other mineral dust diseases can mimic both simple and complicated silicosis on radiographs and must be distinguished by either the exposure history or tissue examination. Inert dust ("macular") pneumoconioses, such as siderosis (welders' pneumoconiosis) or some miners' diseases (caused by ores of tin, barium), tend to involve all parts of the lung from the outset and do not predominate in the upper zones, nor progress to form large opacities.

The major diagnostic challenges are tuberculosis and sarcoidosis, both of which are upper-zone-predominant, nodular diseases that can progress to massive scarring. Silicosis does not produce uveitis, granulomatous hepatitis, or focal skin or bone lesions, any of which help to identify sarcoidosis. Tuberculosis and silicosis may coexist; fever, hemoptysis, rapidly evolving consolidations, and cavitations indicate infection. Tuberculosis alone (especially treated or inactive cases) may simulate silicosis but is usually less symmetric, less uniform in size and distribution of nodulation, and more apt to have conspicuous pleural lesions. Hematogenous "miliary" tuberculosis or carcinomatosis progresses too rapidly to be confused (for long) with simple silicosis. Bronchogenic carcinoma may complicate silicosis and escape early detection because of silicotic nodulation.

Diagnostic Options

Clinical diagnosis, using the plain radiograph and exposure history, is adequate in the great majority of cases. Computed tomography scans are not standard in the diagnosis. If biopsy is needed to diagnose or exclude silicosis, it should be open biopsy, by thoracotomy or thoracoscopy. Bronchoscopic biopsy is acceptable for the exclusion of other conditions such as sarcoidosis and carcinoma.

Although silicosis is a scarring process, obstruction (reduced flow rates), either alone or combined with some restriction (reduced exhaled volumes or total lung capacity), is the usual pulmonary function test finding. Reduced volumes dominate ventilatory function in only the most severe cases. Diffusing capacity is highly variable, with significant reductions found mainly in patients who also have severe abnormalities of ventilatory function. Arterial blood gas values are also highly variable. The functional effects of past smoking are often greater than those of silicosis, except in severe cases.

Recommended Approach

Demonstrate the characteristic radiographic abnormality, establish that the patient has had occupational exposures in a trade associated with silicosis, and affirm the clinical diagnosis if there is no good reason to suspect a confounding condition. Resort to biopsy when there is a potential confounder. Evaluate every silicotic for tuberculous disease or infection.

Therapeutic
Therapeutic Options

There is currently no effective treatment to reverse or retard scarring, or to remove retained silica. Tuberculous or fungal infections aggravate silicotic scarring, and their prevention or rapid treatment can limit this effect.

Recommended Approach

See below.

FOLLOW-UP

Newly diagnosed patients should have an intradermal PPD skin test, and it should be repeated at least annually while negative. If it is positive, sputum should be cultured and treatment or prophylaxis given.

The patient should receive immunizations against pneumococci (one-time) and influenza virus (yearly). The radiograph should be repeated yearly and in any intercurrent respiratory illness. Lung function tests can be repeated at longer intervals or with radiographic or symptomatic worsening. The patient must be warned to seek early examination for any new or changed respiratory symptom and for any unexplained or lingering febrile illness. Ordinary respiratory infections should be treated as bacterial unless the physician is certain that they are merely viral. Any suspicion of a mycobacterial or fungal disease requires that it be promptly ruled out, or ruled in and treated. Smokers should be urged to quit, to limit the independent lung function damage and the cancer risk. The silicotic, who is usually male, must be warned that he is medically unfit for further occupational exposures to silica or other fibrogenic dusts. If lung function is impaired, it is imprudent to work around potent irritants or sensitizers.

At the time of diagnosis, the patient should be told that he has an occupational disease and should obtain legal advice. The purpose is not to encourage litigation, but to preserve the patient's option of later bringing a claim. In many jurisdictions, the diagnosis of an occupational disease establishes a period (often, one to a few years) in which the patient must take some kind of action or else a future claim will be barred. Failure to understand this can have disastrous consequences for the person whose disease is mild at diagnosis but later becomes complicated or severe.

DISCUSSION

Prevalence and Incidence

Cases are distributed unevenly, according to geographic differences in the kinds of work and workplace exposures. Rates of occurrence in the general population are not accurately known. The disease is underdiagnosed and grossly underreported, especially on death certificates (most silicotics die of cardiovascular or neoplastic diseases unrelated to occupation).

Related Basic Science

Pathogenesis

Crystalline silica particles are deposited in the periphery of the lung and enter the interstitium before or after being ingested by macrophages. The particles cause leakage of lysosomal enzymes, leading to cell death. They are then spilled back into the interstitium and undergo repeated cycles of macrophage phagocytosis and cytolysis. This cycle in some way leads to collagen deposition.

Anatomic Derangement

The silicotic nodule has concentric layers of acellular collagen, presenting an "onionskin" appearance. Surrounding this is a zone rich in chronic inflammatory cells. The cellular zone contains most of the silica particles, which are weakly birefringent under polarized light. When nodules coalesce, the concentric architecture of individual nodules is preserved in the larger masses of acellular collagen. Mature nodules and masses are hyalinized, and in a few patients the nodules become calcified. Ischemic necrosis can occur in large masses but is rare.

Extensive areas of collagen contract and distort the parenchyma, bronchi, and pulmonary vessels. Emphysema develops in the wake of contracting scars and is prominent at the lung bases and around the edges of upper zone masses. Particles cleared to hilar and central lymph nodes cause granulomatous lymphadenitis. Particles and silicotic nodules have been found in distant organs, usually without clinical effect.

Natural History and Its Modification with Treatment

Most cases are first diagnosed many years after the start of exposure and in the stage of simple silicosis. The tendency of the scarring to worsen over time is associated with higher average and cumulative exposures, earlier age at onset, unknown host factors, and the contraction of granulomatous infections. And, the more advanced the radiographic stage, the greater the risk of worsening. The only specific intervention is prophylaxis or treatment of granulomatous infection. Silicosis may increase the risks of developing connective tissue diseases and lung cancer, although these issues are not settled.

Prevention

Silicosis is preventable, by avoidance or limitation of exposure through substitution of materials, engineering controls of dust levels, hygienic work practices, and use of personal respiratory protective devices. The continuing occurrence of the disease is the result of ignorance of the hazard and failure to apply effective preventive measures. Early diagnosis can aid prevention by identifying hazardous workplaces, leading to protection of similarly exposed workers.

Cost Containment

It is safer and less costly to have the silicosis patient promptly report any respiratory and febrile illness, rather than depend on frequent scheduled "checkups." Routine annual visits for interview, chest radiograph, and PPD skin test can be scheduled for late fall to permit administration of the new influenza immunization. Spirometry is adequate for following functional change and can be obtained at long intervals (3–5 years). Tuberculosis prophylaxis is cost effective and could be lifesaving. Chest computed tomography scans are not needed unless there is a suspicion of lung cancer.

REFERENCES

Bretland PM, Parkes WR. Imaging in occupational disease of the lung. In: Parkes WR, ed. Occupational lung disorders. 3rd ed. Oxford: Butterworth-Heinemann, 1994:160.

Churg A, Green FHY, eds. Pathology of occupational lung disease. New York: Igaku-Shoin, 1988.

Silicosis and Silicate Disease Committee, National Institute for Occupational Safety and Health. Diseases associated with exposure to silica and nonfibrous silicate minerals. Arch Pathol Lab Med 1988;112:673.

Solomon A, Kreel L, eds. Radiology of occupational chest disease. New York: Springer-Verlag, 1989.

Weill H, Jones RN, Parkes WR. Silicosis and related diseases. In: Parkes WR, ed. Occupational lung disorders. 3rd ed. Oxford: Butterworth-Heinemann, 1994:285.

CHAPTER 13–26

Smoke Inhalation

Sotirios Kassapidis, M.D.

DEFINITION

Smoke inhalation occurs when an individual is exposed, often in a confined space, to the products of combustion. The nature of the substance or substances burning determines the potential toxic components of the smoke.

ETIOLOGY

See definition.

CRITERIA FOR DIAGNOSIS

Suggestive

Smoke inhalation can be defined as any pulmonary and/or airway damage that arises from exposure to toxic gases of combustion. Patients may present with or without skin burns. Signs and symptoms may be absent immediately following exposure, and the diagnosis is usually guided by the history alone. Physicians should be especially suspicious if the patient has been exposed for a significant length of time or has been in an enclosed, poorly ventilated area.

Definitive

Documented history of exposure and evidence of respiratory consequences from that exposure (see below) confirm the diagnosis.

CLINICAL MANIFESTATIONS

Subjective

The symptomatology associated with smoke inhalation is dependent on what part of the tracheobronchial tree is involved, and this in turn depends on the chemical compositon of the inhalation. Smoke acts as a chemical irritant and can cause both airway and alveolar injury. Symptoms such as cough, dyspnea, wheezing, and sputum production are not diagnostic, but merely suggestive of smoke inhalation. Hoarseness and stridor should alert the physician to evaluate the upper airway for injury and edema formation. Quite often patients may remain asymptomatic for up to 36 hours before developing any signs of respiratory compromise. Patients may quickly decompensate due to the development of laryngeal edema, tracheobronchitis, bronchiolitis, or alveolitis. Management of these patients may range from supplemental oxygen to emergent intubation. It is therefore recommended that patients with prolonged or significant smoke inhalation should be hospitalized and monitored for 36 to 48 hours.

Systemic absorption of poisons via the alveoli can occur during smoke inhalation. It is impossible to identify all the toxic products that are released during a fire. Two major components are carbon monoxide and cyanide. Carbon monoxide is generated by the incomplete combustion of carbon-containing material, whereas cyanide is generated when synthetic materials are burned. Both work synergistically in causing local pulmonary compromise and systemic hypoxia. Carbon monoxide binds to hemoglobin and forms carboxyhemoglobin, causing a decrease in the oxygen-carrying capacity of hemoglobin, which produces a leftward shift of the oxyhemoglobin dissociation curve. As carboxyhemoglobin levels rise, patients may experience severe headaches, palpitations, confusion, weakness, syncope, seizures, a change in mental status, tachypnea, and tachycardia. Loss of consciousness is highly suggestive of carbon monoxide poisoning, which has a high risk of morbidity and mortality. Measurement of carboxyhemoglobin levels and supplemental use of 100% oxygen are required as initial treatment in patients with suspected carbon monoxide poisoning.

Objective

Physical Examination

When evaluating a patient for smoke inhalation, the physician must remember that the pulmonary sequelae may be divided into two categories: *thermal* and *chemical*. The occurrence of thermal injuries depends on the temperature of the inhaled gases and the patient's distance from the source of origin. Patients who present with facial and cervical burns, singed nasal hairs, or soot in the nares, throat, and posterior pharynx are likely to have suffered thermal burns of the upper airway. Direct laryngoscopy is recommended, as thermal injuries may cause mucosal edema leading to upper airway obstruction. Inspiratory stridor signifies that significant airway narrowing has occurred and the patient may require intubation. Thermal burns rarely cause direct damage to pulmonary parenchyma and structures located below the trachea. The sparing of the lower airway is thought to be secondary to the low heat capacity of dry air and the efficiency of heat exchange that occurs in the upper airway. The lower airway may on occasion be subject to thermal injury if it comes in contact with hot particulate matter and partially oxidized gases that continue to burn in the respiratory tract.

Chemical burns from smoke inhalation arise from the toxic products of combustion as they make their way into the lower airway. These products can be differentiated into local irritants and systemic poisons. Chemical irritants lead to the formation of tracheobronchitis, bronchiolitis, and alveolitis. The auscultation of crackles and wheezes heralds the presence of bronchospasm and increased airway secretions. The occurrence of noncardiogenic pulmonary edema signifies that alveolar damage and destruction have occurred.

Routine Laboratory Abnormalities

There are no diagnostic routine laboratory abnormalities.

Carbonaceous sputum is considered the sine qua non of respiratory injury. This may not occur over the first 12 to 24 hours postexposure, and may arise in only a minority of patients with significant pulmonary injuries.

PLANS

Diagnostic

Diagnostic Options

The diagnosis of smoke inhalation is guided by the history alone. Laboratory data and specific diagnostic procedures may be useful in determining the extent of injury and the clinical course of the patient. Data that may be of use on presentation include chest roentgenograms, arterial blood gas, carboxyhemoglobin level and an electrocardiogram.

Recommended Approach

The following should be obtained:

Roentgenographic studies. Patchy atelectasis and pulmonary edema may be present, but generally the roentgenogram is normal early in the course of smoke inhalation. Often, as in other diseases, the chest radiograph will lag behind the physical examination and is often used as a baseline for later comparison. As most admission studies are normal, it has been suggested that roentgenograms be performed on hospitalized patients only.

Arterial Blood Gases. Severe injury may lead to a marked decrease in the partial pressure of arterial oxygen (PaO_2) and a widened alveolar–arterial oxygen gradient, but mild hypoxemia is often seen. Delayed hypoxemia can occur, and early measurements of the patient's PaO_2 can be insensitive indicators of injury and do not predict outcome.

Carboxyhemoglobin Levels. Elevated levels of carboxyhemoglobin may help identify patients with carbon monoxide poisoning and may implicate other toxins (i.e., cyanide). Because carboxyhemoglobin levels are influenced by the half-life of carbon monoxide and supplemental oxygen therapy, normal levels do not exclude inhalation injury.

Electrocardiogram. As with most other tests on admission, the electrocardiogram is generally unremarkable. In patients with severe carbon monoxide intoxication, the electrocardiogram may reveal arrhythmias or signs of cardiac ischemia and infarction. The formation of cardiac dysrhythmias and manifestations of cardiac ischemia are often delayed, and therefore, a normal electrocardiogram does not rule out cardiac involvement.

Other Tests. Other diagnostic tests that may be helpful in patients with smoke inhalation injuries include pulmonary function testing, fiberoptic bronchoscopy, and xenon ventilation–perfusion testing. These tests are useful in specialized cases and are not required in every patient with smoke inhalation.

Therapeutic
Therapeutic Options

The injury associated with smoke inhalation vary from a benign cough and shortness of breath to laryngeal edema and asphyxia. Therefore, it is mandatory for every emergency room physician who comes in contact with a smoke inhalation victim to remember the ABCs of basic life support: airway, breathing, and circulation. Once these parameters are evaluted, the use of supplemental oxygen is crucial in preventing damage from hypoxia and carbon monoxide poisoning. The use of bronchodilators may be beneficial to patients suffering from acute bronchospasm.

Recommended Approach

In addition to the foregoing, it is important to note that patients suffering from thermal burns may develop laryngeal edema and require intubation. The development of pulmonary edema may necessitate the use of high fractions of inspired oxygen and positive end-expiratory pressure. Corticosteroids have no use in the management of inhalation injury, especially in patients who have suffered thermal burns. Studies have shown an increase in morbidity and mortality associated with steroid use in these patients. Prophylactic use of antibiotics is not recommended, and administration should be withheld until an obvious source of infection is identified.

The use of hyperbaric oxygen has been recommended for patients with symptoms of acute carbon monoxide poisoning, especially in the setting of neurologic sequelae. Anecdotal reports suggest clinical improvement from hyperbaric oxygen, although there have been no controlled studies to support this. Limitations include the absence of specific guidelines and a paucity of hyperbaric chambers.

FOLLOW-UP

Most patients who suffer from smoke inhalation require supportive care and are usually discharged from the hospital in less than 36 hours. These patients have a low morbidity and rarely develop further problems. Other patients whose initial injury was more severe may require long-term follow-up including multiple chest roentgenograms, pulmonary function testing, and possible fiberoptic bronchoscopy.

DISCUSSION
Prevalence and Incidence

As most cases of smoke inhalation do not require hospitalization, it is difficult to determine the actual incidence and prevalence. In evaluating the cases, one may be able to use the number of exposures and injuries incurred by firefighters as the upper end of the scale, as smoke inhalation can be considered an occupational hazard. In a major eastern city there have been approximately 250 cases of smoke inhalation over a 2-year period leading to more than 2000 working days lost.

Related Basic Science

Smoke is composed of all airborne products that arise from the combustion of material located in a fire. Smoke can be thought of as a suspension of small and large particles in various gaseous combinations. These gases are acids and aldehydes which are absorbed onto particles and thus can be absorbed into the respiratory system. Once inhaled they are deposited onto the mucosa of the respiratory tract and the net result is a chemical injury. In general, the larger the particle, the higher up it is deposited in the respiratory tract. The amount of damage that occurs varies according to the pH and solubilityof the gases. The spectrum of chemical products can be divided into two groups: local irritants and systemic poisons. Systemic poisons include carbon monoxide and cyanide. Most other gases produced are local pulmonary irritants, most notably hydrochloric acid, acrolein, and phosgene.

Once gas particles are deposited onto the mucosal surface of the respiratory tract they may combine with water to form corrosive acids. The chemical injury that occurs may cause tracheobronchitis, alveolitis, and pulmonary edema. The primary mechanism of pulmonary edema is not actual stromal damage to the alveolar epithelium, but a microvascular injury that causes increased permeability. It is postulated that margination of white blood cells to smoke by-products may be responsible for these microvascular changes.

Carbon monoxide and cyanide work synergistically in producing cellular asphyxia and hypoxia. The toxic effects of carbon monoxide result from its binding to hemoglobin and associated decrease in its oxygen-carrying capacity. The relative affinity of carbon monoxide for hemoglobin is approximately 200 times greater than that of oxygen. This produces a leftward shift of the oxygen-hemoglobin dissociation curve, resulting in a lowered PaO_2 for any given level of hemoglobin saturation and less oxygen delivery to the periphery. By this process, the affinity of hemoglobin for any bound oxygen will increase, thus causing a reduction in peripheral hemoglobin desaturation and oxygen release. Carbon monoxide can also affect the heme-containing proteins, most notably myoglobin. By binding to myoglobin, carbon monoxide can interfere with oxygen utilization by muscle cells. It is suggested that the effect on muscle oxygen stores is responsible for cardiac sequelae, that is, arrhythmias, myocardial necrosis, and cardiac arrest.

Natural History and Its Modification with Treatment

The evolution of smoke-induced lung injury is modified by early removal of the subject from the site of burning substances and prompt resuscitation. No known interventions, however, prevent the ultimate development of fibrotic lung disease in those destined to suffer this complication.

Prevention

More widespread application of fire safety standards to homes and businesses should reduce the number of fires and, thus, the number of cases of smoke inhalation.

Cost Containment

The initial evaluation and diagnosis of patients who suffer smoke inhalation rarely require the use of complex diagnostic testing. Routine testing on presentation should be limited to chest roentgenography, arterial blood gases, carboxyhemoglobin levels, and electrocardiography. Sophisticated testing such as fiberoptic bronchoscopy and xenon lung perfusion scanning should be used judiciously and when deemed appropriate.

REFERENCES

Clark WR. Smoke inhalation: Diagnosis and treatment. World J Surg. 1992;16:24.

Coleman DL. Smoke inhalation (medical staff conference UCSF). West J Med 1981;135:300.

Fein A, Leff A, Hopewell PC. Pathophysiology and management of the complications resulting from fire and the inhaled products of combustion. Crit Care Med 1980;8:94.

Heimbach DM, Waeckerle JF. Inhalation injuries. Ann Emerg Med 1988;17:1316.

Herdon DN, Thompson PB, Traber DL. Pulmonary injury in burned patients. Crit Care Clin 1985;1:79.

Inhalation of Toxic Gases and Fumes

Sotirios Kassapidis, M.D.

DEFINITION

This condition is defined as occupational, avocational, environmental, or accidental exposure to potentially noxious gases that have the ability to damage airway epithelium and/or lung parenchyma.

ETIOLOGY

See definition.

CRITERIA FOR DIAGNOSIS

Suggestive

Exposure to toxic fumes and gases with the subsequent development of pulmonary complaints is sufficient evidence to assume a chemically induced injury has occurred.

Definitive

Unlike smoke inhalation, the offending agent can often be identified and treated. The treatment in most cases is supportive, although specific antidotes may be required for patient survival. Treatment problems may arise due to the inexperience of the treating physician in recognizing the exposures.

CLINICAL MANIFESTATIONS

Subjective

The symptomatology associated with the inhalation of toxic gases and fumes is dependent on the offending agent's solubility, concentration, and size. A gas is defined as a material without a definitive volume or shape that can expand indefinitely if unconstrained. Fumes are defined as small suspensions of gases, usually submicrometer particles, that can penetrate deeply into the lung.

The absorption of a gas in the respiratory tract is determined primarily by its water solubility. Gases with a high solubility are absorbed in the upper respiratory tract, whereas less soluble gases reach the lower tract. The deposition of particulate matter is dependent on particle size. Large particles are deposited proximally, whereas those 5 mm or smaller reach the lower airways.

It is important to keep these concepts in mind when evaluating a patient exposed to toxic irritants. Immediate and intense irritation of the eyes, nose, and throat causing lacrimation, rhinnorhea, conjunctivitis, and cough are signs of upper airway involvement. Patients may present complaining of occasional cough and progressive shortness of breath, bronchospasm, and/or pulmonary edema, implying lower tract involvement.

Objective

Physical Examination

The physical findings are dependent on the length of the exposure and subsequent lung injury. Mucosal irritation, conjunctivitis, and rhinitis are frequently present. Chest auscultation may reveal diffuse wheezing, crackles, and a decreased inspiratory:expiratory ratio.

Routine Laboratory Abnormalities

There are no diagnostic routine laboratory abnormalities. Chest roentgenography may initially be normal or may show signs of atelectasis and pulmonary edema.

PLANS

Diagnostic

Differential Diagnosis

Respiratory signs and symptoms following the exposure to a toxic gas are generally nonspecific. A careful exposure history (environmental and occupational) is necessary to help identify the offending agent. Table 13–27–1 lists some of the more prevalent gases and their sources. These agents have been divided into three categories: direct irritants, asphyxiants, and pulmonary antigens/sensitizers.

Diagnostic Options and Recommended Approach

After a specific exposure history is elicited, arterial blood gases, and carboxyhemoglobin level, and a chest roentgenogram should be obtained. Arterial blood gas measurements invariably show some degree of hypoxemia, indicative of altered ventilatory mechanics. The diffusing capacity, as evaluated by the diffusing capacity of the lung for carbon monoxide (DLCO), may be normal or decreased, especially in pulmonary edema. Pulmonary function testing frequently demonstrates reversible disease and possible airway obstruction.

Therapeutic

Therapeutic Options

Despite the fact that various clinical syndromes are associated with toxic gas inhalation, the therapy is usually the same and consists of supportive care.

Recommended Approach

Prehospital treatment should include decontamination, supplemental oxygen, and irrigation of irritated surfaces (skin and eyes) with water or normal saline. On presentation to the hospital, airway maintenance and administration of supplemental oxygen are of immediate concern. As previously stated, gases with a high solubility affect the upper airway and may cause airway obstruction due to laryngeal edema. Emergent intubation and occasional tracheostomy may be necessary to secure the

TABLE 13–27–1. SOME TOXIC GASES AND THEIR SOURCES

Gas	Source
Irritants	
Ammonia	Refrigeration, fertilizer production, cleaning, paper production
Sulfur dioxide	Extensively in chemical industry, paper industries, bleaching, fumigation; a by-product of ore smelting
Chlorine	Pharmaceutical industry, chemical industry, water purification, disinfectants, swimming pool maintenance
Ozone	Arc welders, paper bleaching, industrial waste treatment
Phosgene	Chlorinating agent in the synthesis of dyes, firefighters, welding, metallurgy
Nitrogen oxides	Silo fillers, fertilizer production, welding, metal cleaning
Acrolein	Plastic manufacturing, textile finishing, synthetic fibers, pharmaceuticals
Asphyxiants	
Carbon monoxide	Combustion of organic material, steel workers, fires, home heaters
Cyanides	Gold ore extraction, blast furnace workers, metal plating and polishing
Pulmonary antigens/Sensitizers	
Toluene diisocyanate	Production of polyurethane foam, automobile upholstery, furniture coatings

airway. Adequate oxygenation with humidified oxygen is warranted in all patients with inhalation injury. Development of pulmonary edema and subsequent acute respiratory distress syndrome may necessitate the use of mechanical ventilation and positive end-expiratory pressure. Adequate chest physiotherapy with vigorous suctioning should be used to control secretions. Bronchodilators may help with patients suffering acute bronchospasm, and high-dose corticosteroids are recommended for their antiinflammatory effect. With phosgene inhalation, carboxyhemoglobin may be elevated and should be measured.

FOLLOW-UP

Follow-up care is dependent on the initial injury and subsequent pulmonary parenchymal damage. Most acute exposures cause very little permanent damage and therefore minimal follow-up care and testing is required. Significant pulmonary damage can occur secondary to continuous prolonged exposure to a toxin. It is in these patients that long-term follow-up is required along with periodic chest roentgenography and pulmonary function testing.

DISCUSSION

Prevalence and Incidence

As with smoke inhalation, the actual incidence and prevalence seen with the inhalation of toxic gases and fumes are difficult to determine. According to a major eastern city poison control center, more than 2700 cases were reported over a 1-year period. The number of patients requiring hospitalization is unfortunately unknown.

Related Basic Science

Despite the similarity among most toxic gases and their treatment, the following deserve special attention.

Ammonia. A colorless, extremely soluble, highly irritant alkaline gas, ammonia is used extensively in industries, oil refining, and refrigeration. Most exposures occur as a result of ruptured or leaky tanks. Harmful effects include burning of mucosal surfaces, airway obstruction, and pulmonary edema. Long-term sequelae include bronchiectasis and bronchiolitis obliterans.

Chlorine. A greenish-yellow, water-soluble gas that is irritating to mucous membranes, chlorine is used in many chemical industries and processes. The gas can be formed by mixing a chlorine bleach with an acid cleaner. Irritant effects include tracheobronchitis and pulmonary edema. The effects of exposure depend not only on the concentration of the gas but also on the duration of exposure and the presence of preexisting disease.

Nitrogen Oxides. Nitrogen oxides may be generated in many oxidative processes, including welding and fertilizer production. Nitrogen dioxide may evolve during the decomposition of plants with a high nitrate content (i.e., silo filler's disease). The color of the gas is variable but may be clear, red, or orange-brown. Symptomatology is usually immediate and frequently involves the lower airway. Pulmonary edema may be delayed for up to 12 hours. Asthma may occur immediately or over the first few days. Relapse may occur up to 3 weeks after resolution of initial symptoms. Close follow-up for the development of late sequelae is necessary.

Ozone. A highly toxic gas with a characteristic pungent odor, ozone is one of the most powerful oxidizing substances known. It is used as a bleaching agent and in the sterilization of water. Pulmonary damage includes tracheobronchitis, pulmonary edema, and pulmonary hemorrhage.

Phosgene. A colorless gas with a sweet, pungent smell resembling freshly mowed hay, phosgene is used as a chlorinating agent and found in paint removers. It may be formed by the combustion of polyvinyl chloride during a fire. Phosgene is less soluble than chlorine and ammonia; therefore, there is less mucosal involvement and more involvement of the lower respiratory tract (i.e., alveoli and capillaries). Pulmonary edema and respiratory distress may develop 24 to 48 hours after exposure. Chronic exposure may lead to the development of interstitial pneumonitis and fibrosis.

Sulfur Dioxide. The most commonly encountered toxic gas, sulfur dioxide is colorless and is recognized at low concentrations by its characteristic rotten-eggs odor. It is an intense respiratory irritant because it is first hydrated and then oxidized to sulfuric acid in the mucosal surfaces. The onset of symptoms can be within seconds. Keratoconjunctivitis is often noted on physical examination. Loss of consciousness, seizures, cardiogenic and noncardiogenic pulmonary edema, and respiratory arrest are common. Chronic toxicity may cause fatigue, headaches, dizziness, and irritability.

Toluene Diisocyanate. A well-studied chemical that produces occupational asthma, toluene diisocyanate is used in the production of polyurethane plastics. Inhalation leads to bronchoconstriction via an immunologic response. The predominant symptom is cough rather than wheezing. Treatment with bronchodilators and steroids is beneficial; however, successful treatment hinges on permanent removal from the occupation.

Natural History and Its Modification with Treatment

Most exposures to toxic gases can be classified as acute versus chronic. Most acute intoxications lead to symptom delays of only a few hours. Chronic exposure to low doses of toxic gases (i.e., mercury fumes) may lead to the development of pulmonary fibrosis. Supportive therapy with a detailed occupational and exposure history is the key to successful treatment.

Prevention

Exposure to toxic gases occurs on a daily basis. The best method of prevention is by improved education and strict adherence to safety precautions for those individuals who come in contact with these agents regularly.

Cost Containment

Preventing injury via improved education and following recommended safety measures is the key to cost containment.

REFERENCES

Hryhorczuk D. Ammonia and chlorine. Clin Toxicol Rev 1986;9:1.
Karr RM, Davies RJ, Butcher BT, et al. Occupational asthma. J Allergy Clin Immunol 1978;61:54.
Rorison DG, McPherson SJ. Acute toxic inhalations. Emerg Med Clin North Am 1992;10:409.
Schwartz DA, Smith DD, Lakshminarayan S. The pulmonary sequelae associated with accidental inhalation of chlorine gas.Chest 1990;97:820.

CHAPTER 13–28

Aspiration of Foreign Bodies

Stephan L. Kamholz, M.D.

DEFINITION

Accidental inhalation of a foreign body, when not immediately expelled by coughing, is followed by the lodging of that object in the airways, a serious and potentially lethal occurrence. Consequences of endobronchial lodgement of a foreign body are related to its size, structure, and chemical composition and to the duration it remains in the airway.

ETIOLOGY

Most instances of foreign body aspiration are accidental, and the problem is encountered much more frequently in children than in adults. Infants and young children often insert small objects or pieces of toys into their mouths, setting the stage for possible aspiration. This is followed by inadvertent inhalation, and the development of symptoms and signs described below (see Clinical Manifestations). In adults, alterations in level of consciousness (alcohol and drug intoxication, general anesthesia, seizure disorder) are often the precursors of episodes of foreign body aspiration. Trauma to the head and neck area, especially involving the face and oral cavity, may result in dislodging of teeth or dental appliances, which then may be aspirated. The spectrum of objects that may be inhaled is vast, limited only by the relationship of the internal dimensions of the oral cavity to the external dimensions of the object. Foreign bodies concealed in food (e.g., bone fragments in meat, fish, or poultry) present a special problem in that they may have sharp edges, and may thus cause oropharyngeal or laryngeal trauma during the episode of aspiration.

CRITERIA FOR DIAGNOSIS

Suggestive

The acute onset of protracted coughing, gagging, wheezing, or choking unassociated with obvious respiratory tract infection should raise the suspicion of foreign body aspiration. This is especially true in infants and children, as the vast majority of episodes of foreign body aspiration are either witnessed or felt to be highly likely from the circumstances surrounding the presentation. With regard to delayed recognition of the aspirated foreign bodies, persistent localized pulmonary infection, hemoptysis, and segmental or lobar atelectasis should raise the suspicion of a foreign body, prompting bronchoscopic investigation.

Definitive

Roentgenographic demonstration of an endobronchial foreign body on plain chest films is feasible when the object is radiopaque (metallic, calcified bony fragment), and is definitive evidence of the presence of a foreign body. Thin-section computed axial tomography scan is also a useful diagnostic adjunct, and may delineate the presence of a foreign body when performed as part of the investigation of an unresolving infiltrate, hemoptysis, or atelectasis. Bronchoscopic visualization and extraction of the foreign body provide definitive evidence for the diagnosis.

CLINICAL MANIFESTATIONS

Subjective

Coughing and wheezing are the most common symptoms encountered in patients with foreign body aspiration, especially in the period immediately following the event. Shortness of breath, throat or chest pain, choking, and the development of fever are also frequently encountered. Many adults will be able to relate a history of aspiration, or will at least recall an episode of difficulty swallowing or "a bone getting struck in the throat." Family members of the patient with an unresolving local-

ized pulmonary infection (lobar or segmental pneumonitis) may recall a remote episode during which the patient had a choking fit or coughing spell. Elderly patients in chronic care facilities may present with indolent fever and pulmonary infiltrates as a manifestation of foreign body aspiration. Occasionally the presence of an endobronchial foreign body may not stimulate any symptomatology whatsoever. In the acute setting where the aspirated object is large (frequently a large bolus of incompletely chewed food, e.g., steak), the victim will be noted to have the classic signs of complete upper airway obstruction, that is, choking, inability to speak, frantic pointing to the throat region, development of cyanosis, and progressive unconsciousness. With incomplete obstruction, stridor may be audible. The Heimlich maneuver may be lifesaving in such circumstances.

Objective

Though many patients are afebrile early in the course after foreign body aspiration, those with subacute or chronic presentations have fever. Tachypnea is frequently noted. The focused examination should include careful palpation and inspection of the neck (looking for crepitus and lymphadenopathy that may be associated with local trauma induced by the foreign object immediately prior to traversing the glottis); close inspection of the oropharynx is indicated to look for evidence of mucosal lacerations. On chest examination, localized wheezing over the area of the foreign body is often noted. There may be diminished breath sounds over the lung fields that are distal to the foreign body, and coarse ronchi may be heard, as some types of foreign bodies provoke a brisk airway inflammatory reaction with the development of mucosal edema and increased airway secretions. If pneumonia has developed, then the physical findings may include the presence of bronchial breath sounds, crackles, enhanced tactile fremitus, and localized percussion dullness. With "pure" atelectasis, dullness to percussion and decreased breath sounds over the area of affected lung parenchyma may be the only findings. Pleural changes, including effusion, may ensue in those individuals who have developed an associated pneumonia, which may be accompanied by the classic findings of effusion. In subacute and chronic cases, leukocytosis, leftward shift of the white blood cell differential count, and elevation of erythrocyte sedimentation rate may all be found, though these are nonspecific. Plain chest radiologic studies may directly demonstrate the foreign body (if radiopaque) or may reveal secondary findings such as alveolar infiltration or consolidation, localized atelectasis, hypoaeration or overinflation (obstructive emphysema) of a portion of the lung field (with or without shift of midline structures), and, on occasion, pleural effusion. In those patients with dyspnea, determination of arterial blood gases is indicated, and usually reveals hypoxemia with widening of the alveolar–arterial oxygen gradient, and hypocapnia. Blood gas abnormalities may be more severe in those patients with underlying cardiopulmonary disease or more severe parenchymal involvement.

PLANS

Diagnostic

Differential Diagnosis

The acute symptomatology of foreign body aspiration may be mimicked by anaphylaxis. For those patients presenting with subacute or chronic complaints, obstructive pneumonitis and/or atelectasis due to endobronchial neoplasia (benign or malignant) must be considered in the differential diagnosis. Within this spectrum, patients with antecedent postinflammatory calcified mediastinal lymphadenopathy may present with recurrent episodes of pneumonia, atelectasis, or hemoptysis because of migration of one or more of the nodes into the airway (broncholithiasis). This possibility must be considered in patients with a prior history of tuberculosis or histoplasmosis, especially if there is roentgenographic evidence of right middle lobe involvement (the most common location for a broncholith).

Diagnostic Options

After appropriate plain radiographic studies, most patients undergo bronchoscopic examination, which is both diagnostic and potentially therapeutic. The choice of flexible versus rigid bronchoscopy is often guided by the age of the patient (rigid bronchoscopy under anesthesia is more feasible in children) or the size/dimensions of the object that must be removed. Anesthesia can be achieved and ventilation maintained through a rigid bronchoscope. For initial assessment of the airways in adults in whom foreign body is suspected, inspection fiberoptic bronchoscopy can be rapidly performed, and the nature of the foreign body (if any) can be determined. Computed axial tomography scans of the thorax may be useful in suggesting an unexpected foreign body in association with an infiltrate or lesion that is undergoing evaluation.

Recommended Approach

Initial evaluation via fiberoptic bronchoscopy is preferred in adults. A wide variety of retrieval forceps, baskets, and balloons are available for use with the fiberoptic bronchoscope, expanding the utility of this instrument in the management of foreign bodies. When a very large or jagged foreign body is suspected in the adult, and/or when respiratory insufficiency limits the patient's ability to tolerate the procedure without ventilatory assistance, rigid bronchoscopy is chosen as the initial procedure. After the nature and location of the foreign body are confirmed, and the retrieval device to be used is determined, the patient undergoes attempted retrieval of the foreign body.

Therapeutic

Therapeutic Options

Successful removal of the foreign body identified via initial evaluation, and localized and visualized via the bronchoscope, is the goal of the procedure. In most instances, retrieval of hard objects may be accomplished using grasping forceps or basket forceps, inserted through either the flexible or rigid bronchoscope. Some operators pass the fiberoptic bronchoscope through the rigid scope and perform the initial inspection and mobilization of the foreign body with the more maneuverable flexible scope, then complete the removal with the rigid bronchoscope. When softer objects are encountered, especially those composed of vegetable matter, care must be taken not to pulverize or fragment the foreign body. An additional consideration is that foreign bodies of this nature (e.g., peanuts) may evoke an exuberant inflammatory and exudative response in the airway, which may lead to adherence to the bronchial musosa and to further softening of an already friable foreign body. An inflatable balloon catheter may be employed to cautiously reposition the object in a larger airway, where other removal instruments can be more effectively maneuvered. On occasion, pretreatment with oral and inhalational corticosteroids may be employed to decrease the inflammatory response associated with some foreign bodies, thereby reducing surrounding mucosal edema and facilitating removal. Several investigators have reported the use of the neodymium YAG laser via the fiberoptic bronchoscope as an adjunct in foreign body retrieval. Bursts of laser energy have been used to fragment large calcified foreign bodies, thereby facilitating removal of smaller pieces. Thoracotomy with bronchotomy and removal of the foreign body is occasionally required in the most difficult cases.

Recommended Approacch

The skill and the experience of the bronchoscopist are as crucial as the choice of instrument, and the approach must be individualized for each situation. The patient's general condition and cardiopulmonary status must be carefully assessed prior to the procedure, permitting the determination as to whether general anesthesia and/or a ventilating rigid bronchoscope will be required. Radiographic studies will have been performed and usually, in association with the findings on physical examination, will have provided a general localization of the foreign body. After careful inspection, the appropriate removal forceps is se-

lected, and the foreign body is extracted. In instances where the outer dimensions of the foreign body exceed those of the bronchoscope lumen, the entire bronchoscope may have to be removed while the object is grasped by forceps that extend beyond the distal end of the scope. Extreme caution is required in these circumstances to avoid upper airway/laryngeal laceration, and to avoid dislodgement of the foreign body from the grasping forceps while in the trachea or larynx. In instances where pneumonia has developed in association with endobronchial foreign body, pre- and postoperative antibiotic treatment is indicated, with the choice of agent(s) predicated on the results of cultures. When culture data are not available, broad-spectrum therapy including agents with anaerobic and Gram-negative specificity should be chosen.

FOLLOW-UP

After successful extraction of an endobronchial foreign body, patients should be followed until symptomatic and roentgenographic resolution of atelectasis and pneumonia have occurred. In instances where multiple fragments of a friable object have been encountered, repeat bronchoscopies may be required to completely remove all residua.

DISCUSSION

Prevalence and Incidence

Although the total number of episodes of foreign body aspiration is not known, it has been estimated that in the United States, more than 2000 deaths are attributable to this diagnosis each year, predominantly in children.

Related Basic Science

Acute airway obstruction results in marked ventilation–perfusion inequality in the lung units distal to the involved bronchus. Blood gases initially reveal hypoxemia with hypocapnia, but the hypoxemia is reversible with supplemental oxygen. When pneumonia or atelectasis occurs, an significant right-to-left intrapulmonary shunt may develop, with worsening arterial hypoxemia that is at least partly refractory to supplemental oxygen. In the affected airway, bronchial mucosal hyperemia and edema develop, accompanied by an increased mucus secretory rate. This may result in impaction of the foreign body in an inflamed swollen bronchus, which complicates attempts at extraction. The release of cytokines and other inflammatory mediators is responsible for systemic symptoms, including fever and chills. The long-term sequelae of endobronchial foreign body may include localized, segmental or lobar bronchiectasis and localized pulmonary fibrosis. Patients are at risk for significant hemoptysis while the foreign body is in situ, and the extraction procedure itself may be complicated by bleeding.

Natural History and Its Modification with Treatment

It is generally desirable to remove the foreign body as soon as possible after inhalation. In this manner the sequelae of infection, bleeding, and bronchiectasis, as well as the complications associated with more difficult late extraction, may be avoided.

Prevention

Foreign body aspiration by children may be largely preventable. More attentiveness on the part of parents or child care personnel is crucial. Parents should avoid purchasing toys or other objects that have small detachable components. Industry has provided age recommendation labels on children's toys and other products that are designed to reflect concerns regarding the potential for inhalation or ingestion of component pieces. In some instances, dangerous toys have been voluntarily recalled from the market by the manufacturers. Greater awareness among adolescents and adults regarding the potential dangers of such "innocent" acts as "popping peanuts" may also lead to a reduction in episodes of foreign body aspiration in these groups.

Cost Containment

Early recognition and intervention in cases of foreign body aspiration are the most important factors in cost containment. The costs of medical care for patients with advanced pulmonary complications of unrecognized aspiration may thus be avoided. The indirect costs to society of time lost from productive work among adult victims of foreign body aspiration is difficult to estimate. Although specific cost containment measures are not applicable to the problem, educational efforts delineated above (see Prevention) are likely to have the largest impact, as children represent the greatest risk group for this problem.

REFERENCES

Kamholz SL, Rothman NI, Underwood PS. Fiberbronchoscopic retrieval of iatrogenically introduced endobronchial foreign body. Crit Care Med 1979;7:346.

Lan RS, Lee CH, Chiang YC, et al. Use of fiberoptic bronchoscopy to retrieve bronchial bodies in adults. Am Rev Respir Dis 1989;140:1734.

Moisan TC. Retained endobronchial foreign body removal facilitated by steroid therapy of an obstructing inflammatory polyp. Chest 1991;100:270.

Rees JR. Massive hemoptysis associated with foreign body removal. Chest 1985;88:475.

Vera-Hernando H, Garcia-Quijada RC, Ruiz de Galareta AA. Extraction of foreign bodies with fiberoptic bronchoscopy in mechanically ventilated patients. Am Rev Respir Dis 1990;142:258.

CHAPTER 13–29

Near Drowning

Lawrence Glaubiger, M.D.

DEFINITION

Drowning is when death occurs from suffocation in a liquid medium. *Near drowning* is defined as recovery, at least temporarily, after submersion in a liquid medium. Most authors agree that there must be an episode of loss of consciousness while submerged to meet the criteria for near drowning. *Wet drowning* occurs if the victim has glottic relaxation with continued aspiration of fluid. The glottic relaxation is thought to be due to asphyxia and subsequent loss of consciousness. In *dry drowning,* which occurs 10 to 15% of the time, the glottis remains in spasm beyond the point of asphyxia without fluid aspiration. In *secondary drowning,* the victim makes an apparent full recovery but relapses into fulminant respiratory failure.

ETIOLOGY

The near drowning episode begins with panicking and aspiration of a minimal amount of fluid, resulting in laryngospasm. The initial laryngospasm is due to a reflex parasympathetic response to fluid in the larynx. This response is exaggerated in dry drowning, where relaxation of the laryngospasm does not occur. Loss of consciousness seen during a near drowning episode is due to hypoxia and hypercarbia. While the victim is struggling, a huge catecholamine response occurs that accelerates depletion of oxygen stores and potentiates cardiac arrhythmias. Hypothermia, hypoxia, hypercarbia, and lactic acidosis contribute to the occurrence of fatal arrhythmias.

CRITERIA FOR DIAGNOSIS

Suggestive

Victims seen submerged or unconscious in a body of water most likely fit the criteria for a near drowning episode. The diagnosis is strongly suspected if the victim demonstrates associated clinical manifestations of neurologic, cardiac, or respiratory dysfunction.

Definitive

Definitive diagnosis is established by finding fluid in the victim's alveoli similar to the fluid in which the victim was submerged.

CLINICAL MANIFESTATIONS

Subjective

Dyspnea, cough, and vomiting are the primary symptoms. A history of alcohol intake is found in approximately half of teenage and adult drownings. Alcohol and other recreational drug use is often involved not only in submersion injuries to the intoxicated victim but to children whom they were supervising. Divers who hyperventilate before swimming underwater are at risk for a near drowning incident. A past history of a seizure disorder might indicate that the victim may have had a convulsion while swimming. A myocardial infarction could be suspected in an individual with a history of coronary artery disease. Determining what medications the victim had been prescribed might assist in the evaluation of what precipitated the near drowning incident.

Objective

Physical Examination

Neurologic examination performed 1 to 2 hours after resuscitation is a useful prognostic indicator and is classified into three categories: (A) awake, (B) blunted sensorium, (C) comatose. Respiratory examination might often reveal tachypnea and cyanosis. The patient might also cough a pink frothy fluid significant for lung injury and washout of surfactant from alveoli. Aspiration of fluid can lead to rales as well as rhonchi or wheezing. An asthmatic attack might be triggered by simple aspiration of fluid or an inflammatory reaction to suspended debris in the fluid. Localized absence of breath sounds might represent plugging of airways from the debris. The development of severe respiratory insufficiency from an apparently asymptomatic patient can occur insidiously.

Cardiac findings are closely related to the hypothermia that is associated with near drowning episodes. The immediate cause of death in a drowning episode is mostly cardiac arrhythmias. When the body temperature is below 32°C, there is greater susceptibility to ventricular fibrillation and asystole. At these temperatures the heart is more irritable and any slight agitation can induce arrhythmias. The most frequent cardiac rhythm is atrial fibrillation and profound sinus bradycardia. Some advocate waiting a full minute before declaring that a victim is pulseless and requires cardiopulmonary resuscitation (CPR). Renal insufficiency presenting as acute tubular necrosis occurs rarely and is usually due to hypoxemia and hypotension. Rhabdomyolysis and hemoglobinuria have also been thought to precipitate renal dysfunction.

Routine Laboratory Abnormalities

The alveolar–arterial gradient on arterial blood gas will demonstrate the severity of pulmonary injury. The degree of acidosis, which is often a combined metabolic and respiratory acidosis, is also thought to be an important prognostic indicator. An elevated blood urea nitrogen and creatinine or abnormal urinalysis is a rare finding. Initial chest radiographs are normal about 20% of the time. Most show varying degrees of pulmonary edema. Confluent alveolar opacification is usually bilateral and symmetric, but less severe aspirations may present only with parahilar or midzonal opacities. The electrocardiogram might show a cardiac arrhythmia or changes manifested from hypothermia, such as prolongation of the PR, QRS, and QT intervals along with elevation of the J point (Osborne wave). Rarely, disseminated intravascular coagulation can occur, manifested as abnormal prothrombin and partial thromboplastin times and low platelet counts. Hypoglycemia has rarely been found as well. The alcohol and drug toxicology screen should be evaluated routinely and is often positive. Hemoglobin, hematocrit, and serum electrolytes are usually normal.

PLANS

Diagnostic

Differential Diagnosis

Near drowning from aspiration alone should be differentiated from associated disorders such as cervical spine injury myocardial infarction, cerebrovascular accident, and intracranial hemorrhage leading to the incident. Scuba divers might have a near drowning episode while suffering from an arterial gas embolus to the central nervous system.

Diagnostic Options

With the slightest suspicion of cervical neck injury a cervical spine radiograph should be obtained. Patients with focal neurologic deficits, which are uncharacteristic of near drowning, should have a computed tomography examination of the head. An abnormal electrocardiogram may indicate an acute myocardial infarction, and cardiac enzymes may confirm the diagnosis.

Recommended Approach

The recommended diagnostic approach is shown in Figure 13–29–1.

Therapeutic

Therapeutic Options

Initial Resuscitative Options and Recommended Approach. On reaching the victim, if necessary, resuscitative efforts should begin while in the body of water. Chest compressions should not be started until the victim is brought to a flat, stable surface. On moving the victim from the site of the incident, the cervical spine should be stabilized until the possibility of cervical spine injury can be evaluated. All victims should immediately be placed on 100% oxygen. Endotracheal intubation should be considered in the apneic patient. An initial evaluation of body temperature should be made rapidly, preferably with a rectal probe. Electrical defibrillation is futile at core temperatures less than 29°C, and aggressive measures at rewarming should be attempted. In the event the victim has ventricular fibrillation, intravenous lidocaine or bretylium should be given until the core temperature rises. No victim should be declared dead until he or she is warmed to near-normal core temperatures, as revival of victims who had prolonged absence of vital signs has occurred. Intensive cardiopulmonary resuscitation should be performed on all near drowning victims, as extraordinary recovery with minimal sequelae has been documented on many occasions on apparently lifeless patients. There is no indication to follow intracranial pressure or do an immediate computed tomography scan of the head.

In-Hospital Resuscitative Options. The only accepted therapy to curtail neurologic sequelae is hyperventilation and supportive care. The early use of positive end-expiratory pressure has proved beneficial in reducing morbidity and mortality. As loss of surfactant is important in the process of worsening respiratory insufficiency, a new approach to poorly ventilating victims is the use of aerosolized artificial surfactant. Fever 2 to 7 days after resuscitation, with a new infiltrate on chest radiography, probably heralds a pneumonia. Organisms such as *Pseudomonas* and *Vibrio* species are associated with saltwater drowning. Coliform bacteria are associated with drowning in swimming pools. The use of prophylactic antibiotic therapy has not been shown to improve survival, but instead increases the incidence of infections due to bacteria highly resistant to antibiotics. Bronchial obstruction from aspiration of mud, teeth, and debris could be the cause of lack of improvement in ventilatory status. In these cases, bronchoscopy for inspection and removal of any foreign body is warranted. Bronchospasm and wheezing should be treated with inhaled bronchodilators and intravenous theophylline. If arterial gas embolism is suspected, transfer to a facility capable of recompression and hyperbaric oxygen therapy should be considered. In view of the complications associated with it, hypothermia often needs aggressive treatment. Initially, heating blankets should be used. Administration of heated humidified oxygen at 40°C, warmed intravenous fluids, and warm gastric lavage might be attempted if blanket warming is unsuccessful. Unresponsive hypothermia has been treated by peritoneal, pleural, and mediastinal lavage as well. Recently, successful resuscitation of severely hypothermic victims has been done using cardiopulmonary bypass. Occasionally, temporary hemodialysis is required for victims in renal failure. The use of bicarbonate infusion is controversial, as it has not been shown to improve survival. Most authors agree that it should be administered in cases of extreme acidosis (pH < 7.1). The recommended in-hospital therapeutic approach to the near drowning victim is summarized in Figure 13–29–2.

FOLLOW-UP

If the patient's neurologic status immediately postresuscitation is awake or obtunded (category A or B), then there is a 90% chance of survival without clinical sequelae. Those who are comatose (category C) have a higher morbidity and mortality. The prognosis worsens as the neurologic findings change from decerebrate to flaccid. The most reliable indicator for good prognosis is the presence of spontaneous respirations immediately following cardiopulmonary resuscitation. Postresuscitation improvements in the patient's neurologic status portend a good prognosis and should be followed by frequent determination of pupillary response and Glasgow Coma Scale score. Severe metabolic acidosis following resuscitation is indicative of poor prognosis. Pulmonary function testing in adults has not demonstrated any chronic pulmonary sequelae. Rarely, there will be residual fibrosis or linear opacities.

DISCUSSION

Prevalence and Incidence

Approximately 6000 to 9000 deaths from drowning occur in the United States each year. Near drowning is thought to occur 10 to 50 times more frequently. There is a bimodal incidence according to age. One peak is at age less than 4 to 5 years, where the incident is most often due to an unattended or poorly supervised toddler. The second peak occurs between ages 15 and 24. This is thought to be due to adolescents who undergo swimming or aquatic sports while intoxicated. Males have a higher incidence than females. Southern states of the United States have a higher incidence than northern states.

Related Basic Science

It is now recognized that the amount of fluid aspirated during a near drowning incident is almost never enough to affect the volume or electrolyte status of the victim. More importantly, aspiration of either fresh or salt water will create washout or destabilization of surfactant. This creates atelectasis of the involved ventilatory units as well as decreased lung compliance. The development of noncardiogenic pulmonary edema following the near drowning episode is thought to be due to destruction of the pulmonary ultrastructure caused by passage of water through the alveolar epithelium, basement membrane, and endothelial capillaries. The end result of these processes is varying degrees of ventilation–perfusion mismatch and inadequate ventilation.

Divers have learned that by hyperventilating, their partial pressure of carbon dioxide ($PaCO_2$) decreases significantly without much change in the partial pressure of oxygen (PaO_2). By lowering her or his baseline $PaCO_2$ before swimming, the diver can swim longer underwater. Unfortunately, as the diver swims, the PaO_2 can decrease to 30 to 40 mm Hg. This would lead to cerebral hypoxia and loss of consciousness.

Why some survivors can remain submerged for extraordinary lengths of time that logically should have caused severe anoxic brain damage is unclear. Many believe that the diving reflex present in mammals operates in these instances. The reflex is initated by placing the subject's face in liquid. Profound bradycardia and increased systemic vascular resistance occur with shunting of blood to the brain and heart. Hy-

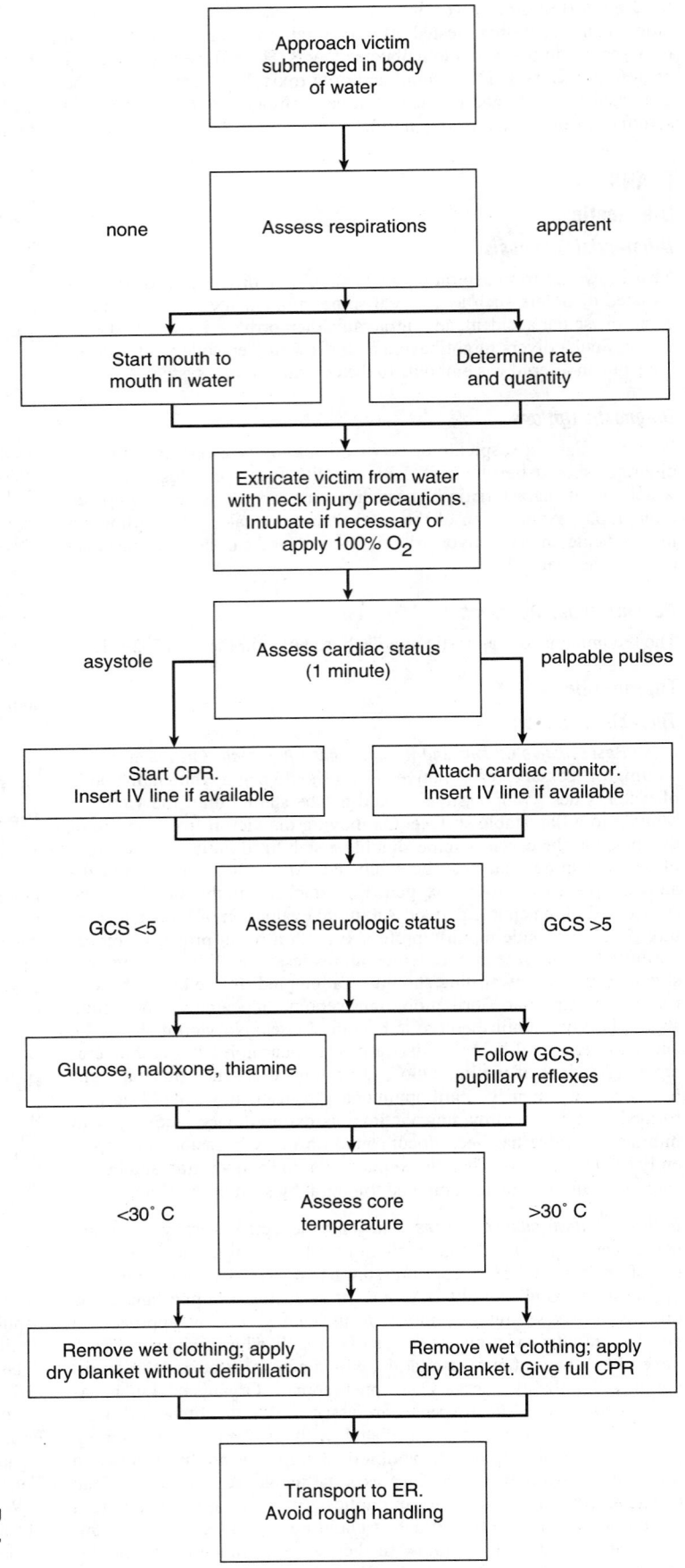

Figure 13–29–1. Recommended initial diagnostic approach to near drowning patient. GCS, Glasgow Coma Scale; CPR, cardiopulmonary resuscitation; ER, emergency room.

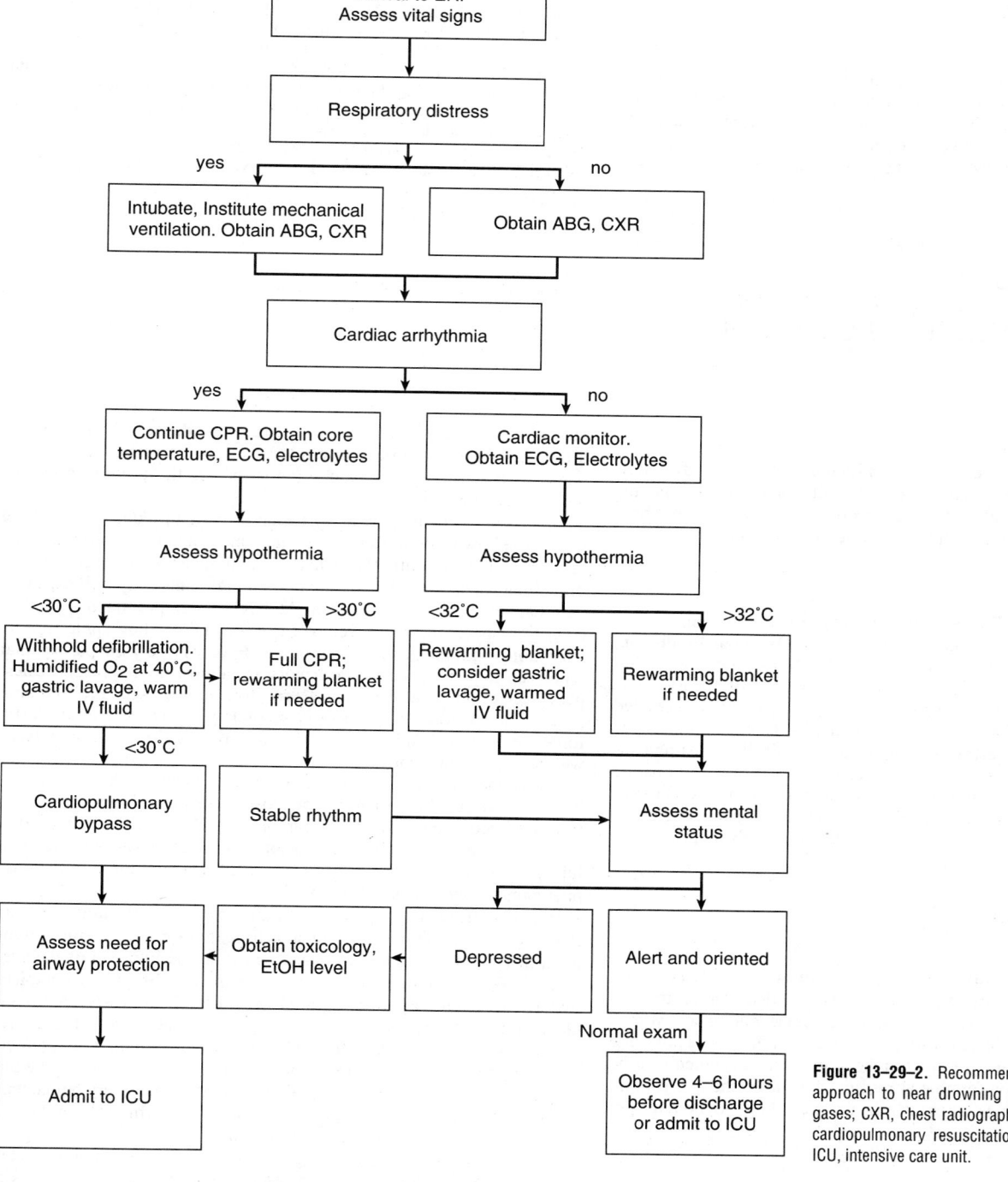

Figure 13–29–2. Recommended in-hospital therapeutic approach to near drowning patient. ABG, arterial blood gases; CXR, chest radiograph; EtOH, ethyl alcohol; CPR, cardiopulmonary resuscitation; ECG, electrocardiogram; ICU, intensive care unit.

pothermia was thought to help survival by slowing cerebral metabolism and postponing the deleterious effects of cerebral anoxia. Most recent studies do not show evidence of an operative diving reflex in humans, and hypothermia most often has an adverse effect on survival.

Natural History and Its Modification with Treatment

Most survivors of a near drowning episode have no significant neurologic or respiratory dysfunction and the event has no impact on the individual's quality of life. Some degree of neurologic damage occurs occasionally and might present as mild incoordination or motor deficits. Factors that are thought to prevent permanent sequelae are the duration of submersion, delay in initiation of effective cardiopulmonary resusci-

tation, severe metabolic acidosis, asystole, and poor initial neurologic signs (fixed dilated pupils and low Glasgow Coma Scale score).

Prevention

Legislation that requires fencing around home pools still has not prevented a significant number of toddlers from undergoing a submersion injury. Education of the need for constant supervision of children near a body of water is necessary. Proper flotation devices while in water and undertaking aquatic sports should be encouraged. Swimming lessons and instilling a proper attitude concerning the dangers of water related sports or exercise should be started at an early age. The disastrous effects of indulging in intoxicating beverages or drugs while interacting with water should be reemphasized, especially at public swimming pools and beaches.

Cost Containment

The most important factor in cost containment is prevention of the event. As good prognosis from the near drowning event is related to the rapidity with which the victim is resuscitated, public awareness and education of cardiopulmonary resuscitation might circumvent or limit the need for extensive hospitalization and intensive care unit stay.

REFERENCES

Bohn DJ, Biggar WD, Smith CR, et al. Influence of hypothermia, barbiturate therapy, and intracranial pressure monitoring on morbidity and mortality after near drowning. Crit Care Med 1986;14:259.

Cohen DS, Matthay MA, Cogan MG, et al. Pulmonary edema associated with salt water near drowning: New insights. Am Rev Respir Dis 1992;146:794.

Gonzalez-Rothi RJ. Near drowning: Consensus and controversies in pulmonary and cerebral resuscitation. Heart Lung 1987;16:474.

Modell JH. Drowning. N Engl J Med 1993;328:253.

Olshaker JS. Near drowning. Emerg Med Clin North Am 1992;10:339.

CHAPTER 13–30

Diffuse Interstitial Lung Disease

Ethan D. Fried, M.D.

DEFINITION

Diffuse interstitial lung disease is a syndrome of pulmonary infiltration composed of inflammatory tissue, as in alveolitis or vasculitis. The initial insult may either heal or form a fibrotic scar composed of fibroblasts in a stroma of collagen and other structural elements.

ETIOLOGY

The specific causes of diffuse interstitial lung disease are summarized in the decision-making flowchart (Figure 13–30–1). Ionizing radiation, pneumoconioses, toxins like nitrogen dioxide (NO_2—silo fillers' disease), neoplastic infiltrates like lymphangitic spread of breast carcinoma, infections as in the "atypical" pneumonias, immune-mediated disease like rheumatoid arthritis (see Chapter 13–31), and other entities all cause syndromes of restrictive lung disease clinically indistinguishable from each other. The specific diagnostic criteria for the idiopathic form of diffuse interstitial lung disease is that none of these other syndromes can be demonstrated clinically, serologically, or histologically. In Great Britain, the term *cryptogenic fibrosing alveolitis* represents the same entity.

CRITERIA FOR DIAGNOSIS
Suggestive

The typical patient is relatively young, is otherwise healthy, and tells a remarkably consistent story of progressive, slowly debilitating, respiratory disease marked by ever-diminishing exercise tolerance. After a careful history of possible exposures to toxic or injurious factors like ionizing radiation or fumes or dusts in the workplace, it is noted that the patient reports being comfortable at rest, even as he or she is breathing shallow breaths at a rate approaching or exceeding 30 breaths per minute.

Definitive

A chest radiograph solidifies the suspicion for some kind of interstitial lung disease. The infiltrate is not lobar or segmental in its distribution, but is seen as wispy shadows of a delicate reticular lace. Where reticular strands cross, the resulting granule is called a *micronodule*. Thus, a reticulonodular infiltrate represents a thickening of the pulmonary architectural elements. In the absence of chubby vascular markings or the appearance of free extrapulmonary fluid, this reading signifies diffuse interstitial lung disease.

CLINICAL MANIFESTATIONS
Subjective

The main symptom of this family of slowly progressive restrictive pulmonary interstitial fibrotic illness is progressive dyspnea on exertion. Exercise tolerance decreases and documentation of this diminishing ex-

ercise tolerance is a guide one can use to gauge the severity of the syndrome. Improvement in exercise tolerance, however, may reflect a reponse to therapy, a spontaneous remission, or the training effect of more efficient exercise.

Other symptoms include a dry cough or cough productive of white, gray, or yellow sputum. Hemoptysis may mean an infection (bronchitis, pneumonia), a vasculitis (Wegener's granulomatosis), or even primary inflammatory disease like allergic bronchopulmonary aspergillosis. Occasional fever with or without night sweats may prompt many clinicians to suspect miliary tuberculosis to explain the radiographic appearance along with the patient's symptoms. Fever is rarely the paroxysmal type seen in acute pneumonia. Rigors are almost never present. Chest pain may occur as a result of pleural involvement with the fibrosing process, local areas of atelectasis secondary to the increased elastic forces, or musculoskeletal pain from the increased muscle activity as well as the constant cough.

Occasionally, patients complain of an acute pleuritic chest pain. This has been attributed to inflammation close to the pleural surface or often to a localized pneumothorax (Figure 13–30–2). Rheumatoid lung disease can manifest as a pleural effusion (see Chapter 13–31). Systemic lupus erythematosus can manifest as pleuritis in addition to interstitial pneumonitis (see Chapter 13–32).

When confronted by a patient with this progressive respiratory insufficiency the first job of the clinician is to search for the systemic symptoms that might allow one to place the syndrome into one of the systemic inflammatory processes (see Figure 13–30–1). A complete review of systems is often required to gather all the associated data. Generalized questions include whether or not the patient has fever, chills, or night sweats. Appetite and weight changes should be inquired about. Failure to thrive in a very young or a very old patient may be the only presenting complaint. Complaints of joint stiffness, erythema, tenderness, loss of range of motion, effusions, or deformities may be the only clues one has to focus on one of these processes. Raynaud's phenomenon may also occur and suggest lupus, progressive systemic sclerosis, or mixed connective tissue disease. Patient complaints of skin rashes or nodular eruptions may represent the necrobiotic nodules of rheumatoid disease or the erythema nodosum of sarcoidosis. Neurologic complaints are not uncommon in systemic inflammatory disease. Symptoms of cloudy, bloody, or decreased urine output must be specifically sought, as must the general symptoms related to renal insufficiency, as many of these systemic illnesses involving antigen–antibody excess or antibody production to host tissue can result in both pulmonary and renal inflammatory processes.

In advanced lung disease, patients may complain of bone pain which is secondary to hypertrophic osteopathy. This finding is generally accompanied by clubbing of the digits.

Family history can occasionally give the clinician a clue as to the type of inflammatory process causing the syndrome. This is especially true of the patients who have a family history for lupus or have rheumatoid arthritis and are HLA-B40 positive (see Chapter 13–31).

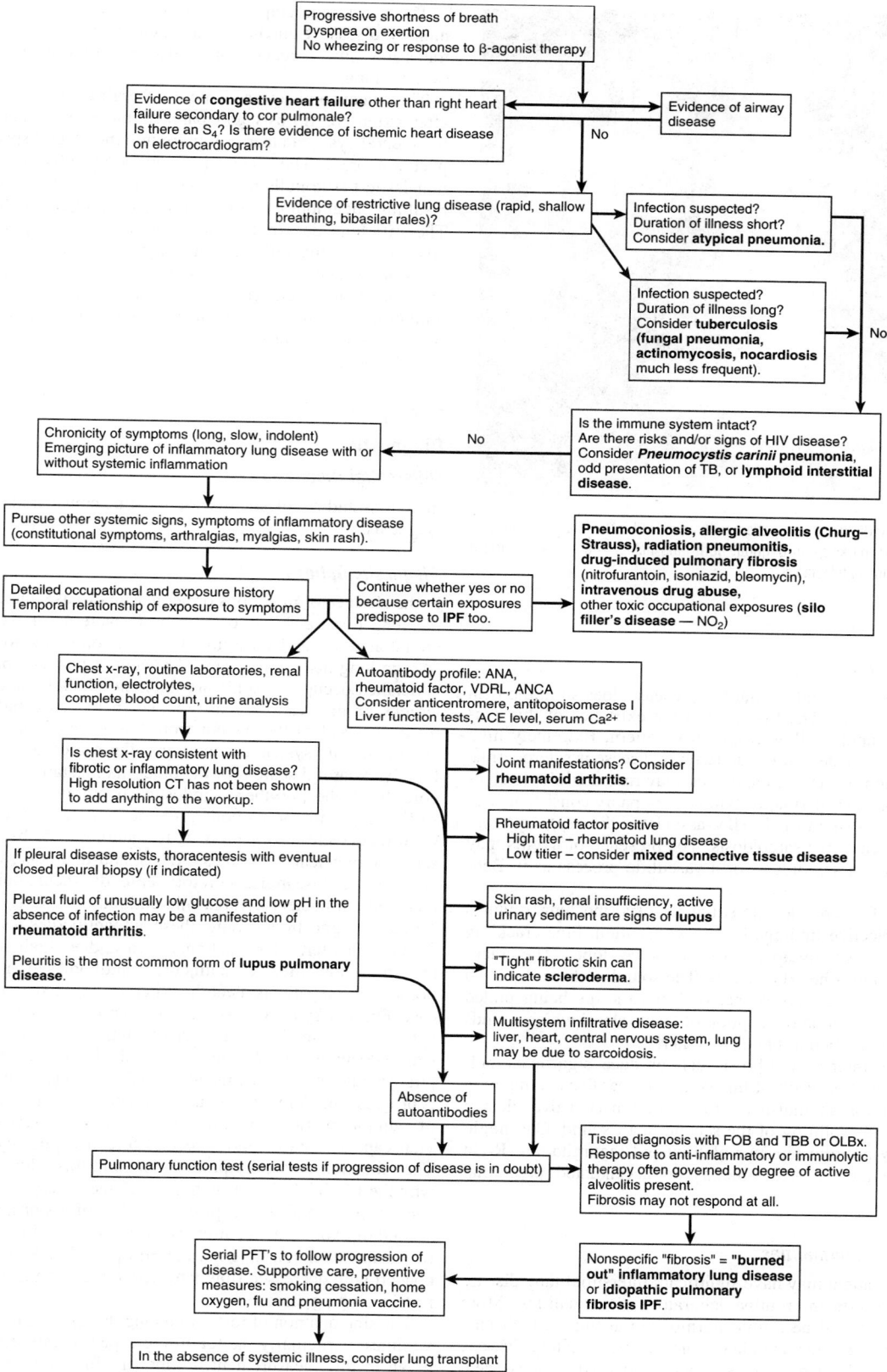

Figure 13–30–1. Proposed scheme for the identification, characterization therapy, and follow-up of interstitial lung disease. Differential diagnoses are in **bold**. Dashed arrows and boxes indicate optional. TB, tuberculosis; IPF, idiopathic pulmonary fibrosis; ANA, antinuclear antibodies; VDRL, Venereal Disease Research Laboratory antigen; ANCA, antineutrophile cytoplasmic antibody; ACE, angiotensin converting enzyme; PFT, pulmonary function test; FOB, fiberoptic bronchoscopy; TBB, transbronchial biopsy; OLBx, open lung biopsy; CT, computed tomography; RAST, radioallergosorbent test.

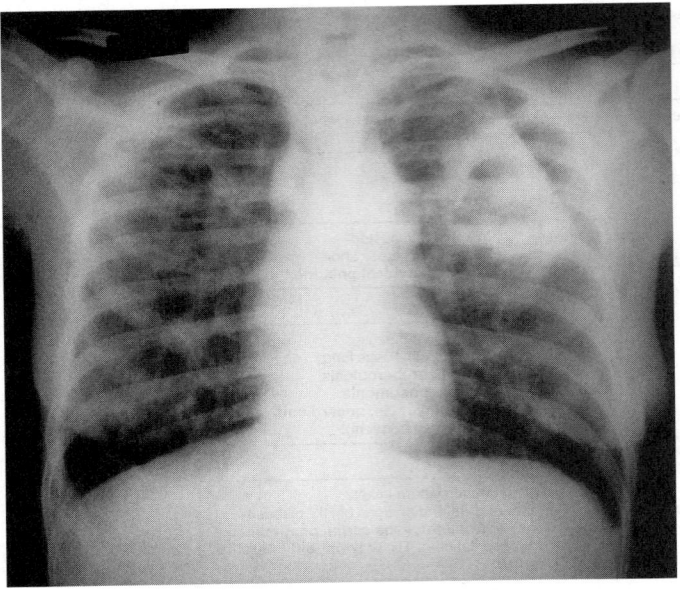

Figure 13–30–2. Chest radiograph of a patient with advanced interstitial lung disease. There are reticulonodular markings throughout both lung fields. There is a left apical pneumothorax with proximal atelectasis.

Objective

Physical Examination

The patient presenting with interstitial lung disease does so in the fifth to seventh decades of life. The first clue to the existence of this syndrome is often the rapid shallow respiratory pattern. Extremely high blood pressure may indicate that the underlying disease is scleroderma. A careful examination of the head and neck may reveal etiologic clues like the tight skin of scleroderma, or lymphadenopathy consistent with an abnormal immune system (as in HIV-associated disease), or a systemic infiltrative disease like sarcoidosis. The presence of uveitis may suggest the existence of sarcoidosis or a vasculitic process as in Behçet's disease.

In the presence of idiopathic interstitial fibrosis, the lung findings may be the only objective findings in the examination. Fine crackling rales occur and are especially apparent in the lower lobes. The crackling is high pitched and is heard in sheets. The sound of these so-called "dry rales" has been described as that of Velcro strips being pulled apart rather than the common description of "wet rales," which sounds more like a pinch of hair being rubbed together.

In its late stages interstitial fibrosis can produce significant pulmonary hypertension. The result of this is that the cardiac examination may be significant for an unusually loud pulmonary valve closure sound, as well as wide splitting of the second heart sound. One might even hear the early systolic murmur of tricuspid regurgitation. Right ventricular enlargement is detectable as an accentuated precordial thrust.

Routine Laboratory Abnormalities

It is possible that a patient may have significant interstitial lung disease and there be no significant routine laboratory abnormalities. More likely, however, there will be a mild normocytic anemia, which may eventually be attributed to the anemia of chronic inflammatory disease. In severe hypoxemic lung disease, secondary polycythemia is seen. White blood cells and platelets are normal most of the time, rising only as an acute phase reactant. The routine chemistries are normal most of the time. It is conceivable that a picture of inappropriate secretion of antidiuretic hormone will be seen with low sodium and chloride levels. In the presence of severe systemic inflammation with immune complex deposition and glomerulonephritis, serum electrolytes, renal function tests, and urine analysis reflect more extensive renal disease and an active urinary sediment.

The chest radiograph can exhibit a full range of infiltrative pulmonary disease from linear to reticulonodular to ground grass infiltrates and, finally, coarse fibrotic disease with loss of volume and "honeycomb lung."

The honeycomb cysts, which are epithelium-lined cysts, are seen after extensive fibrosis and parenchymal destruction have occurred. Subpleural cysts can tear or rupture into the pleural space, resulting in a pneumothorax. This happens more frequently when the fibrotic, nonelastic tissue pulls more vigorously on its pleural attachment. The resulting pneumothorax often has a rather unique self-limiting property. The stiff lung does not collapse as easily as the pliant healthy lung. Also, the chronic inflammatory stage often promotes sclerotic adhesions of parietal and visceral pleura. The pneumothorax remains localized, often not even requiring hospitalization. Adjacent to the pneumothorax is often a ridge of atelectasis. It will resolve spontaneously or remain a fixed feature of the patient's chest radiograph for years (Figure 13–30–2).

PLANS

Diagnostic

Differential Diagnosis

Infections and neoplastic disease must be considered in the differential diagnosis.

Diagnostic Options

In the absence of infectious or neoplastic disease, the causes of interstitial lung disease fall into three basic patterns of pathology: fibrotic, granulomatous, and vasculitic. Often the only clue to the etiology of a fibrotic lung disease is a careful review of past and present exposures. A detailed occupational history, including hobbies and exposures to allergens or medications that are known to cause pulmonary fibrosis, often declassifies the patient from "idiopathic." A careful search for granulomatous systemic conditions like sarcoidosis is useful as well. Finally, a careful search for the other manifestations of vasculitis (temporal headaches, erythema nodosum, hemoptysis, hematuria, renal insufficiency with or without proteinuria or an active sediment) may yield diagnostic information. A full autoimmune battery consisting of serum antinuclear antibodies (ANA), anti-double-stranded DNA, Veneral Disease Research Laboratory antibody, rheumatoid factor (RA factor), and antinuclear cytoplasmic antibody (ANCA) needs to be done. To have diagnostic meaning, these autoantibodies need to be of a relatively high titer. Many patients with and without interstitial fibrosis may have low titers of antinuclear antibodies or rheumatoid factor. Some of these patients meet the criteria for mixed connective tissue disease. Pulmonary fibrosis is often a complication of this disorder.

Once the suspicion of a restrictive lung disease is raised, it is important to document the degree to which the lungs are impaired. Serial respiratory rates offer some insight into the rapidity with which the disease is progressing. A more standardized method of investigation is a full set of pulmonary function tests. Spirometry may reveal reduced forced vital capacity (FVC) and 1-second forced expiratory volume (FEV_1). The reduction is usually proportional and this allows us to understand why the FEV_1/FVC% is such a useful measurement. As a normal person ought to be able to expire 75 to 80% of his or her FVC in the first second of expiration, a patient with stiff fibrotic lungs with high elastic recoil may exhibit a supernormal FEV_1/FVC%. A high FEV_1/FVC% in concert with decreased flow rates and forced volumes can be a hint that restrictive lung disease exists.

The sine qua non of restrictive lung disease is a reduction in the lung volumes, particularly the total lung capacity. Particular care should be given to this measurement. Pulmonary function laboratories that employ multiple methods for the measurement of total lung capacity (i.e., helium dilution and body plethysmography) may be more subject to error. Diffusion capacity should be decreased in terms of both the absolute value and the value corrected for the alveolar volume. This is in contrast to whole lung diffusion, which is reduced while the value corrected for volume is normal and which is associated more with extrapulmonary restrictive disease. The pulmonary function tests are also an ideal way of documenting disease activity. Mild to moderate restrictive lung disease that is static in serial pulmonary function tests over a period of months to years may be "burned out" and not worth pursuing for a final diagnosis, particularly in an older patient.

On the other hand, serial pulmonary function tests that show a decline in function are best approached aggressively for any proposed treatment to make a difference. In this case, the clinician needs to confirm the absence of infectious disease before initiating immunolytic therapy. More often, however, serial sputum examinations looking for acid-fast bacilli either in stained smears or in culture in concert with skin testing with purified protein derivative of *Mycobacterium tuberculosis* (PPD) and control skin tests (*Candida,* mumps virus, *Histoplamsa,* etc.) are not enough to confidently rule out other chronic infectious processes. This is when fiberoptic bronchoscopy and transbronchial biopsy (TBB) may be helpful.

Fiberoptic bronchoscopy is a low-level invasive method for sampling the alveolar tissue. Its shortfalls include the fact that this maneuver is actually less effective in the diagnosis of tuberculosis than serial sputum samples held for 8 weeks in culture. Additionally, one of the goals of transbronchial biopsy is to obtain alveolar tissue while avoiding vascular tissue (to avoid the complication of excessive bleeding). This fact makes the fiberoptic bronchoscope a relatively poor tool in the diagnosis of vasculitis, which can appear clinically indistinguishable from idiopathic pulmonary fibrosis.

Other diagnostic maneuvers accomplished through the fiberoptic bronchoscope include bronchoalveolar lavage. This procedure is adequate to diagnose certain pulmonary infections, including *Pnemocystis carinii.* A differential cell count can be done on the bronchoalveolar lavage fluid. The normal cellular composition of bronchoalveolar lavage fluid includes a majority of pulmonary macrophages. Chronic inflammatory states may produce a flood of lymphocytes. Further analysis may reveal a predominance of a particular series of lymphocytes, such as the appearance of helper T cells in the bronchoalveolar lavage fluid of sarcoidosis patients. Idiopathic fibrosis patients have a large number of pulmonary macrophages in their bronchoalveolar lavage fluid. Further studies may show that the cells are actively secreting inflammatory mediators such as leukotriene B_4 and interferon gamma, but this is not a routine measurement.

Other diagnostic tools may one day include polymerase chain reaction testing of respiratory secretions including bronchoalveolar washings and bronchoalveolar lavage fluid. This tool may soon become useful in the diagnosis of many infections.

Beyond fiberoptic bronchoscopy, a more invasive but fairly definitive diagnostic procedure is open lung biopsy. Although technically the easiest area to biopsy is the lingular division of the left upper lobe, the *recommended* area to biopsy is the border of the most recently affected region of the lung. This "leading edge" tissue is the most likely to yield a distinctive diagnosis. Most interstitial inflammatory diseases that do not heal eventually progress to pulmonary fibrosis, at which point the causes are indistinguishable from each other.

Although the increased use of thoracoscopic biopsy is making this procedure more tolerable, it is still not recommended unless there is clinical evidence that the disease process is active or the patient is young. In the absence of progressive symptoms or pulmonary function test evidence of worsening restrictive lung disease, invasive diagnostic procedures stand little chance of leading to a treatable diagnosis. Once permanent scarring and fibrosis have occurred, there is little medical therapy has to offer. If a tissue diagnosis is required as a prelude to lung transplantation, however, open lung biopsy may be the most definitive and controlled method of acquiring the tissue.

Recommended Approach

The author's approach is summarized in Figure 13–30–1. First, I attempt to fully classify the patient's serologic picture. I also collect sputum samples for culture of acid-fast bacilli. A PPD and controls should be placed as well. Then I try to establish whether the patient's disease is active and advancing by conducting serial pulmonary function tests over a period of 2 to 3 months and again 6 months later if there is no change on the initial pair. If there is evidence of progressive disease and the sputum I have collected is negative after 2 months I schedule a biopsy procedure (either mediastinoscopy for mediastinal lym-

phadenopathy or fiberoptic bronchoscopy with transbronchial biopsy or open lung biopsy for parenchymal disease). Of course, if the syndrome is rapidly progressing and cannot wait for these studies, then a quicker biopsy is indicated.

Therapeutic

Having established the diagnosis of idiopathic pulmonary fibrosis and documented that lung restriction is progressing or that the patient's symptoms or exercise tolerance is worsening, corticosteroids can be used to attempt to stop further inflammation and further fibrosis. The typical regimen consists of prednisone 40 to 100 mg (1 mg/kg) in single or divided doses. If the disease process seems to be under control, this regimen should be continued for up to 6 months before slowly tapering it as tolerated. If steroids do not help, salvage immunolytic therapy consists of cyclophosphamide (1–5 mg/kg for at least 2 days per week, watching out for the known hematologic, gastrointestinal, reproductive, urinary, and integumental side effects) or azothiaprine (1 mg/kg twice per week then increasing by 0.5 mg/kg per week to a maximum of 2.5 mg/kg), but these drugs are not officially indicated for idiopathic pulmonary fibrosis.

A patient with advancing pulmonary fibrosis who is not responding to antiinflammatory or immunolytic agents, however, should be referred for lung transplant. Lung transplant candidates should generally be less than 65 years of age and be free of significant comorbidities. Transplant is generally only recommended in patients with disease limited to the lung. Patients with pulmonary fibrosis secondary to systemic inflammatory diseases, like sarcoidosis and rheumatoid arthritis, therefore, would not necessarily be eligible. There have, however, been cases of successful transplant in some of these patients. Patients with cor pulmonale may be eligible for heart–lung transplant. Additionally, most centers that do lung transplants require patients to have an adequate social support network, as the procedure and follow-up are intense and require the patient to be able to stay close to the center for prolonged periods.

FOLLOW-UP

Patients with advanced disease awaiting lung transplant or those who are not eligible for whatever reason can best be managed with measures to limit cor pumonale, secondary polycythemia, and the other complications of chronic hypoxemia. Home oxygen therapy via an electric concentrator or tanks of liquid or compressed oxygen delivering at rates of 2 to 3 liters per minute via nasal cannula or transtracheal catheter can be used to improve oxygenation and limit or delay the onset of cor pulmonale. Patients with a resting partial pressure of oxygen (PO_2) less than 55 on room air, a PO_2 of 60 or less with evidence of cor pulmonale, or oxygen saturation that drops below 85% with activity are eligible for this treatment. Home oxygen needs to be applied for at least 18 hours per day to effect a prolongation of survival. Patients should be instructed to wear their supplemental oxygen as much as possible.

Patients should report yearly for influenza virus vaccine and should receive the 23-valent pneumococcal pneumonia vaccine at least every 5 to 6 years. These steps limit the risk of pneumonia, which would be disastrous in these patients. An emergency supply of oral antibiotics, such as ampicillin, trimethoprim–sulfamethoxazole, and erythromycin, in case patients develop a productive cough, may reduce the morbidity of respiratory infections. If symptoms persist or worsen (development of lethargy, edema, persistent fever, rigors, cyanosis), the patient should waste no time in getting inpatient attention. Secondary polycythemia with a hematocrit greater than 55% can be managed with therapeutic phlebotomy to reduce blood viscosity. Lastly, patients who receive prolonged courses of corticosteroids are subject to adrenal suppression and Addisonian crisis. This can happen especially in time of stress (trauma, infection, myocardial infarct, etc.). Patients in this category must remember to tell physicians who treat them about their steroid use. If these occasions arise, patients should receive "stress dose steroids" at about 40 mg of prednisone per day. Addisonian crisis can occur during times of stress even 2 years after high-dose steroids.

Smoking imposes an increased hazard for decreasing the total lung capacity and diffusion of CO, but not for lowering survival itself.

Smoking should be strongly discouraged in idiopathic pulmonary fibrosis patients, as should exposure to industrial dusts (metal workers) or agricultural products or solvents.

DISCUSSION

Prevalence and Incidence

Although autopsy studies have advanced a cause-specific mortality rate of up to 7 per 1000, the bias of selection of cases that died relatively young and tragically might account for this number. In any event, there is not likely to be much incidence–prevalence bias (overrepresentation of long survivors) in this estimate, as the average survival appears to be rather short (less than 5 years).

Related Basic Science

Genetics

Although no particular genetic linkage is apparent in this disease, there is familial form, where children of patients have been shown to have the alveolitis thought to precede the scarring.

Cellular and Molecular Biology

Idiopathic pulmonary fibrosis was originally described by Hamman and Rich in 1944 as a rapidly progressive restrictive lung disease leading to irreversible gas-exchange abnormalities and death within months. It is now clear that when most patients with idiopathic pulmonary fibrosis reach a clinical horizon, they have already undergone extensive damage to the alveolar compartment and they are developing their fibrotic lung disease as a late consequence of diffuse alveolitis. The current mean survival of 4 to 5 years after diagnosis is probably due to better diagnostic accuracy than better treatment.

The alveolar inflammatory response is probably a by-product of immune complex deposition, which attracts acute and chronic inflammatory cell populations and begins a process of cell-mediated cytotoxicity. These observations have driven the use of antiinflammatory drugs to combat idiopathic pulmonary fibrosis. Steroids with and without cyclophosphamide have been the most widely used drugs, with limited success in prolonging survival. Azathioprine up to 3 mg/kg (not to exceed 200 mg/d) has been used with prednisone to produce a marginal survival advantage.

Other inhibitors of chemotaxis and inflammatory mediators may one day play a part in the treatment of idiopathic pulmonary fibrosis. These include leukotriene B_4 inhibitors as well as therapy aimed at limiting oxidant damage, such as desferoxamine, superoxide dismutase, and reduced glutathione (GSH).

Other aspects of the biology of idiopathic pulmonary fibrosis include the postinflammatory laying down of collagen to produce the fibrotic scarring. Both colchicine and false analog proline-laden liposomes have had some demonstrable affect in animal models, but in the case of the former, enjoy only anecdotal success. The latter has not been used in human systems as of yet.

Much of the biology of idiopathic pulmonary fibrosis has been learned by studying the cell populations found in the bronchoalveolar lavage fluid of these patients. Macrophage secretion of prostaglandin E_2 and an abundance of polymorphonuclear cells and eosinophils have been thought to portend ill for the idiopathic pulmonary fibrosis patient. Recent studies, however, stratifying for age, sex, and pack-years of smoking, have not shown these to be reliable predictors of disease activity.

Anatomic Derangement

The pathophysiology of this manifestation is twofold. First, the elastic recoil of the lungs is stronger. By definition, therefore, lung compliance is decreased. Because it takes more negative pressure or more frequent respiration to maintain the same alveolar minute volume, the work of breathing is progressively increased. This is perceived by the patient as dyspnea. The other pathophysiologic principle at work is the increase in the transit time for oxygen to be absorbed from the alveoli through the diseased, infiltrated interstitium. At rest, the patient may have adequate gas exchange as blood lazily perfuses the alveolar spaces. As the

patient begins to move about, the speed at which the alveolus is perfused begins to increase. With the longer transit time of diffuse interstitial disease, there may not be enough time for gases to be exchanged. The percentage of blood that passes through the lungs without participating in gas exchange is defined as the shunt fraction.

Specific structural damage has been demonstrated in the epithelial cell layer of the alveoli. Flat, high-transport, type I epithelial cells are damaged and are replaced by cuboidal type II cells. This is matched by disruption of the endothelial cell layer, allowing capillary leak and increased migration of leukocytes. The basement membrane between the two cell layers becomes thickened and, in some places, duplicated. The leakage of fluid and inflammatory cells into the alveoli accounts for the beginning of fibrosis, whereas the earliest diffusion abnormalities are explained by the basement membrane changes.

Fibrosis occurs when connective tissue masses fill the alveoli, obliterate the distal airspaces, and are reepithelialized in the interstitial and bronchiolar areas.

The milieu of increasing collections of collagen may trigger the proliferation of mesenchymal fibroblasts and smooth muscle cells. The appearance of mature woven bone has even been described in cases of interstitial fibrosis.

Natural History and Its Modification with Treatment

Predictions about the natural history of this disease are best made by measuring the degree of restrictive ventilatory defect as manifested in the total lung capacity and diffusing capacity of the lung for carbon monoxide (DLCO). Biopsy specimens should be judged for how much fibrosis is present. Patients with less fibrosis and less derangement in DLCO or limitation of total lung capacity have the best prognosis.

Response to corticosteroid therapy and/or immunolytic therapy has been shown to preserve activities of daily living (as measured with standardized tools like the Sickness Impact Profile), but has made less of an impact on survival time. The cause of death is usually respiratory failure. As lung cancer is more prevalent in the setting of idiopathic pulmonary fibrosis, this should be monitored, especially in smokers.

Prevention

Some of the known causes of pulmonary fibrosis related to specific occupational exposures or to inflammatory conditions can be avoided and/or treated. Fibrosis related to mechanical ventilation can be avoided by strict attention to the fraction of inspired oxygen used in mechanical ventilation and attempts to keep this fraction and mean airway pressures at a minimum. The idiopathic form of the disease cannot be prevented.

Cost Containment

Probably the most effective form of cost containment in this disease is the prudent use of invasive diagnostic tests. A patient who presents with a protracted history of restrictive lung disease may have disease that is entirely fibrotic without histologic evidence of the specific etiology. The phrase *burned out inflammatory lung disease* implies that whatever the agent of injury was, the process has run its course. It will get neither better nor worse as time goes on unless the patient is young and otherwise well. This patient may not need expensive invasive diagnostic procedures, but only documentation that there is no progression of disease. Two sets of pulmonary function tests showing similar levels of impairment over a 4- to 6-month period probably indicates that the disease has run its course, whereas a patient who tells of a more rapid decline in function may have a disease that is still at a stage that responds to antiinflammatory therapy. These are the cases worth pursuing for tissue diagnoses.

Most, if not all, of this diagnostic workup can be done on an ambulatory basis. Only mediastinoscopy or open lung biopsy should require hospitalization. Flexible fiberoptic bronchoscopy can be done in the setting of an ambulatory invasive procedure unit in a hospital, in case complications arise from the procedure.

End-of-life hospitalizations, on the other hand, will likely be expensive as the patient waits for lung transplant or is futilely intubated and maintained in the intensive care setting. It is useful to discuss advanced directives with such patients well before this inevitable stage.

REFERENCES

Crystal RG, Ferrans VJ, Basset F. Biologic basis of pulmonary fibrosis. In: Crystal RG, West JB, eds. The lung: Scientific foundations. New York: Raven Press, 1991:2031.

Fried ED, Godwin TA. Extensive diffuse pulmonary ossification. Chest 1992;102:1614.

Iwai K, Mori T, Yamada N, et al. Idiopathic pulmonary fibrosis: Epidemiologic approach to occupational exposure. Am J Respir Crit Care Med 1994;150:670.

Poiani GI, Greco M, Choe JK, et al. Liposome encapsulation improves the effect of antifibrotic agent in rat lung fibrosis. Am J Respir Crit Care Med 1994;150:1623.

Schwartz DA, Helmers RA, Galvin JR, et al. Determinants of survival in idiopathic pulmonary fibrosis. Am J Respir Crit Care Med 1994;149:450.

Schwartz DA, Van Fossen DS, Davis CS, et al. Determinants of progression in idiopathic pulmonary fibrosis. Am J Respir Crit Care Med 1994;149:444.

CHAPTER 13–31

Rheumatoid Lung Disease

Ethan D. Fried, M.D.

DEFINITION

This entity is defined as pulmonary disease associated with the diagnosis of rheumatoid arthritis (RA). Rheumatoid arthritis is a systemic inflammatory process characterized by chronic relapsing inflammatory arthritis of multiple, frequently symmetric diarthrodial joints. This usually, but not necessarily, includes high serum titers of rheumatoid factor and existence of diarthrodial joint disease. The syndrome can be manifested in one or more of a few distinct patterns of pathology (see below).

ETIOLOGY

The true etiology of rheumatoid arthritis is not known. It is most likely an autoimmune phenomenon with a higher prevalence in families who possess the HLA-DR4 class II major histocompatibility complex. The genetic sequence of HLA-DR4 bears some resemblance to Epstein-Barr virus, and genetic mimicry may play some role in the pathogenesis of rheumatoid arthritis. As in many autoimmune lung diseases, rheumatoid lung disease is most likely a result of immune complex deposition in the lung. The complexes trigger an inflammatory reaction, which is both acute and chronic. This can appear in the alveolar epithelium, the pleural membranes, the perivascular area, or parenchymal necrobiotic nodules. Each tissue affected produces a lung disease of a different type.

CRITERIA FOR DIAGNOSIS
Suggestive

A patient who manifests the joint deformities and dysfunction of RA and who also has pulmonary complaints is likely to have rheumatoid lung disease. Pleuropulmonary disease has been reported in up to 50% of rheumatoid arthritis patients. It is most common in patients with other extraarticular manifestations of RA.

Definitive

The clinical diagnostic criteria (see Chapter 6–1) are related mostly to the arthritic manifestations but also include the development of systemic inflammatory signs (i.e., subcutaneous nodules). In addition, there is frequently (80%) a high latex agglutination titer of rheumatoid factor: immunoglobulin M complexes with specificity for the Fc fragment of immunoglobulin G. Patients with rheumatoid lung disease are more likely to be rheumatoid factor seropositive. The disease takes on one or more of four well-known patterns: pleural disease: interstitial disease including fibrosis and bronchiolitis obliterans organizing pneumonia; parenchymal necrobiotic nodules (which, when occurring in the setting of pneumoconiosis, is called Caplan's syndrome); pulmonary arteritis. Of these, only the interstitial disease and the pleural disease are routinely symptomatic. Although the patient may show the usual signs of chronic systemic inflammatory disease with all of these, the interstitial disease typically causes symptomatic restrictive lung disease, whereas the pleural form may cause pain. It is possible for a patient with necrobiotic nodules to manifest with hemoptysis, but the nodules are more frequently incidental in RA patients.

CLINICAL MANIFESTATIONS
Subjective

Occasionally, a patient may present with seemingly isolated pulmonary disease due to RA. In the case of the interstitial form, this may take the form of dyspnea on exertion which is progressive (see Chapter 13–30). There will generally be some indication of systemic inflammation, with weight loss despite an adequate appetite, fever, or night sweats. Joint disease may take some directed inquiry or may be perfectly obvious. Pleural RA may present with complaints of shortness of breath or of a "congestion" or "heaviness" in the chest. There may or may not be pleuritic chest pain depending on the degree of inflammation within the fluid collection. Pulmonary arteriolitis due to RA may be detected during the workup of an RA patient or may present with mild hemoptysis due to the arteriolar infiltrates. As stated above, the necrobiotic nodules usually remain clinically silent and are identified only by routine chest x-ray in a rheumatoid arthritis patient.

As there is a familial tendency toward developing RA, the family history is extremely important in the initial workup. Furthermore, there is evidence to suggest that HLA-B40 predisposes RA patients to lung involvement, which would certainly make the family history particularly important.

Although a detailed history of possible exposures to dusts of silicon, asbestos, or aluminum may invoke a diagnosis of Caplan's syndrome, there is little else outside of the general and rheumatologic review of systems of importance in the history.

Objective
Physical Examination

The respiratory physical examination of the RA interstitial lung disease patient will be indistinguishable from that of the other forms of interstitial lung disease. The differences are mostly related to the joint manifestations that go along with this diagnosis. As the pleural disease can accompany the interstitial disease, a thorough search for signs of effusion is warranted.

Routine Laboratory Abnormalities

Routine laboratory tests should include an erythrocyte sedimentation rate, complete blood count, electrolytes, renal function, liver function, urine analysis, and chest x-ray. These tests are nonspecific, but reveal the extent of systemic involvement of this disease.

PLANS
Diagnostic
Differential Diagnosis

A battery of serum markers will help the clinician to sort out the various causes of inflammatory lung disease. Serum antinuclear antibodies, anti-DNA antibody, antineutrophil cytoplasmic antibody, rheumatoid factor, and Venereal Disease Research Laboratory antibody can be obtained. Low titers of multiple markers may point more to a diagnosis of mixed connective tissue disease, which is not as responsive to therapy as is rheumatoid arthritis. Lupus can present as pneumonitis with a restrictive ventilatory defect. Systemic lupus erythematosus can also present with a pulmonary vasculitis so it is particularly important to tell these disorders apart. The vasculitic presentation of Wegener's granulomatosis can be confused with that of RA. Finally, interstitial fibrosis secondary to particular exposures, oxygen toxicity, or no identifiable agent (see Chapter 13–30) have different natural histories and degrees of responsiveness to therapy than does pulmonary RA.

Additionally, sputum for acid-fast bacilli and a tuberculin skin test (PPD) should be obtained. This helps to separate the cavitating necrobiotic nodules from tuberculous granulomata. The pleural effusion of primary tuberculosis may be indistinguishable in many ways from that of RA. The difference is that with tuberculosis, an effusion forms only during initial infection, which occurs in a significantly lower age group than the fourth and fifth-decade patients who present with RA.

Diagnostic Options

A set of pulmonary function tests is a nonspecific way of quantifying the extent of disease. Studies have suggested that up to 40% of RA patients have demonstrable restrictive ventilatory defects. Smoking worsens pulmonary function. It is not clear whether or not this effect is increased or out of proportion in RA patients compared with non-RA patients.

The chest radiograph appearance allows the clinician to document one or more of the types of pulmonary RA.

Pleural disease. Pleural disease appears as pleural effusions and/or thickening. This is the most common form of rheumatoid lung disease. The effusions tend to be right-sided, but left-sided and bilateral effusions occur. Symptoms of pleuritic chest pain may occur and they should hasten the performance of a thoracentesis. Thoracentesis may be done blindly if free-flowing pleural effusions can be demonstrated on lateral decubitus chest radiographs with at least 1 cm of layered fluid along the chest wall. Complicated pleural effusions may require ultrasonographic or computed tomographic guidance. The fluid of RA effusions is decidedly exudative, with a fluid-to-serum protein ratio greater than 0.5 and a fluid-to-serum lactate dehydrogenase ratio greater than 0.6. The typical rheumatoid pleural effusion will have an alarmingly low glucose (often less than 30 mg%) and low pH (as low as 6.8). These findings may even cause the clinician to wonder whether an infection is responsible, but in the absence of other signs of infection and with other corroborating indicators of RA present, a comfortable diagnosis of pleural RA can be established with these data alone. The absence of positive cultures from the fluid and demonstration of rheumatoid factor in the fluid confirm the diagnosis. In the event that a pleural biopsy becomes necessary, as in the ruling out of tuberculosis, rheumatoid nodules may be seen.

Interstitial Pneumonitis. Interstitial pneumonitis can occur in many systemic inflammatory processes including RA and lupus erythematosus. Indeed, obtaining histologic data on the interstitial process is often unnecessary and requested only when the inflammatory damage is ongoing and must be distinguished from the granulomatous forms of interstitial lung disease like sarcoidosis. Biopsy material via flexible fiberoptic bronchoscopy or by open lung biopsy may need to be obtained to qualify a patient with a nonsystemic illness for a lung transplant. Transplants are usually not done for RA, as this syndrome is felt to go beyond the lung and transplanted tissue would be at as much risk as native lung.

Necrobiotic Nodules Necrobiotic nodules occur in sizes up to 1 cm or more and are found predominantly in the periphery of the lung fields. They can cavitate and can look exactly like tuberculosis. Patients with subcutaneous nodules are more likely to display these findings.

Pulmonary vasculitis. Inflammation around the small pulmonary arterioles can present with hemoptysis. The radiologic appearance might be the same as that of interstitial disease. Histologically, necrobiotic nodules can be demonstrated within the walls of the vessels.

Recommended Approach

The recommended approach to the workup for pulmonary RA would first be to establish the diagnosis of RA with clinical findings and serology. Symptomatic interstitial pulmonary and pleural disease would call for definitive diagnosis and treatment. Biopsy is unnecessary is the diagnosis was clear from noninvasive data. As with any other interstitial or pleural disease that is symptomatic and rapidly progressing, tissue diagnosis should be obtained if the diagnosis is not apparent from other criteria. Once other causes of interstitial or pleural disease (granulomatous—sarcoidosis; infectious—tuberculosis, *Pneumocystis carinii*; neoplastic—lymphangitic spread of cancer) are ruled out, patients can begin a therapeutic regimen.

Therapeutic

The therapy for mild rheumatoid arthritis is directed mostly at the limitation of inflammation and control of pain. Nonsteroidal antiinflammatory drugs are sufficient for patients with mild to moderate joint pain alone, but therapy of progressive extraarticular disease may require the use of disease-modifying antirheumatic drugs. This set of chemically and pharmacologically unrelated agents includes gold compounds, D-penicillamine, the antimalarial drugs, and sulfasalazine. There is no literature that specifically addresses the use of these agents in rheumatoid lung disease.

Progressive disabling pneumonitis or vasculitis of the lung due to rheumatoid arthritis has been treated with high doses of systemic corticosteroids. Prednisone at 1 mg/kg/d, administered orally in divided doses and after 1 week consolidated into a single daily dose, is one valid approach. This drug should be given in concert with some form of gastric peptic prophylaxis like an H_2 blocker or a cytoprotective agent.

Cytotoxic agents that reduce inflammatory conditions, such as methotrexate and cyclosphamide, have also been used with varying success in severe rheumatoid disease of the lung.

The occurrence of painful disabling exudative pleural effusions may require the use of chest tube drainage, but this in itself can be quite disabling as it requires a prolonged hospitalization. Chest tube drainage has no guarantee that the fluid will not reaccumulate and chemical sclerosis of the pleural cavity may be necessary. Doxycycline 500 to 1000 mg diluted in 1% lidocaine and brought to a volume of 100 to 150 mL is infused through the chest tube after drainage has stopped or is less than 100 to 150 mL per day. The mixture is allowed to sit for at least an hour and then drained. Narcotic analgesics are recommended for the immediate procedure, as well as for the few days following while an exuberant scar seals the pleural space and prevents further accumulation.

FOLLOW-UP

Patients with rheumatoid arthritis and especially those with extraarticular manifestations should be evaluated for evidence of pulmonary disease with a chest x-ray and pulmonary function tests. Follow-up pulmonary function tests and chest x-rays can be obtained whenever there is a significant change in status or at 6-month intervals until stability is reached. On the other hand, patients who present with only lung involvement who are found to suffer from pulmonary RA should be told that the joint disease may not be far away. As pulmonary RA patients have an increased risk of carcinoma of the lung, it may be worthwhile to do annual or semiannual screening chest x-rays, especially in smokers. There is no evidence, however, that early detection of lung carcinoma on routine chest x-ray has an effect on mortality from that disease. In addition, some measure of disease activity like the erythrocyte sedimentation rate or rheumatoid factor may be helpful to follow the progression of the disease. The joint manifestations can be monitored with range-of-motion (goniometer) devices and by documentation of joint swelling, redness, and deformity. Other aspects of RA are covered elsewhere in this book.

DISCUSSION
Prevalence and Incidence

The prevalence of RA has been estimated at 1% of the population. Evidence exists that in up to 50% of RA patients, respiratory involvement can be demonstrated. It is clear that many of these patients do not present to physicians for care so the range of illness from pulmonary RA must be very broad.

Related Basic Science

Anatomic derangement

Like many inflammatory lung diseases, the pathophysiology of rheumatoid lung disease is most likely related to the deposit of circulating immune complexes and rheumatoid factor particles, which then act as an attractant for inflammatory cells. The resulting damage to the alveolar epithelium, basement membrane, and pulmonary capillary endothelium is what is responsible for the interstitial lung disease that follows. Histologically, this is similar to any other inflammatory infiltrate. Focal disease, when it occurs, is in the form of necrobiotic nodules composed of acute and chronic inflammatory tissue. Cavitation may or may not occur within these nodules.

Genetics

Although not specific to the pulmonary manifestations of RA, there is a known familial predisposition for RA, with first-degree relatives of seropositive individuals having a fourfold increase in the incidence of RA. There are several well-known alterations in the HLA-DR4 allele that have implications in the incidence of RA. A study of these is referenced below.

Natural History and Its Modification with Treatment

Even if the pain and dysfunction of rheumatoid joint disease can be mitigated, the lung manifestations are unpredictable. Interstitial disease may stabilize, remit, or progress to respiratory failure even while being treated with the disease-modifying antirheumatic drugs. Nodules may remain as chronic granulomata, heal, or cavitate and cause hemoptysis or even pneumothorax. Effusions may spontaneously remit or require drainage and pleurodesis. Even when the lung disease precedes the other systemic manifestations, the lung disease is not necessarily the most prominent feature.

Prevention

There is no measure that can be taken to prevent rheumatoid lung disease. As in the other inflammatory lung diseases, it is wise to avoid other injurious problems by removing patients from dust exposures, advocating diligent use of influenza and 23-valient pneumonia vaccines, screening for tuberculosis, and paying prompt attention to even minor pulmonary problems. Smokers should be strongly urged to quit, and referral to a no-smoking support group might be useful. Lung cancer can be screened for, but there may be no survival advantage to this.

Cost Containment

As with the other interstitial diseases, the invasive workup of patients with rheumatoid lung disease is only worth pursuing if there is evidence of active, treatable inflammation. Once the diagnosis is established, there should be no reason to repeat invasive diagnostic procedures unless indicated by the onset of a new set of signs and symptoms. Periodic pulmonary function tests and x-rays can be used to assess disease activity and to assess the success of therapy.

REFERENCES

Helmers R, Galvin J, Hunninghake GW. Pulmonary manifestations associated with rheumatoid arthritis. Chest 1991;100:235.

Leavitt RI, Fauci AS. Pulmonary vasculitis.Am Rev Respir Dis 1986;134:149.

Lipsky PE. Rheumatoid arthritis. In: Isselbacher KJ, ed. Harrison's principles of internal medicine. 13th ed. New York: McGraw-Hill, 1994;1648.

Nepom GT, Mansen JA, Nepom BS. The molecular basis for HLA class II associations with rheumatoid arthritis. J Clin Immunol 1987;7:1.

CHAPTER 13–32

Lung Disease due to Systemic Lupus Erythematosus

Ethan D. Fried, M.D.

DEFINITION

The diagnosis of systemic lupus erythematosus (SLE) depends on the existence of 4 of 11 criteria from the American Rheumatological Association's list of diagnostic criteria (see Chapter 7–1). Lung disease occurring in conjunction with these criteria allows a diagnosis of SLE to be made. Pleuritis, the most common of the pulmonary manifestations of SLE, is one of the criteria, so only three others are needed if pleuritis and/or pericarditis are present.

ETIOLOGY

Systemic lupus erythematosus is an autoimmune disorder. There is a clear genetic component, with 10% of patients having more than one affected family member. Various haplotypes are associated with certain manifestations of this systemic inflammatory disease. Drug-induced lupus like disease is more self-limited than the spontaneous form. Women of childbearing years have three times the likelihood of developing lupus than postmenopausal women and nine times the likelihood when compared with men. Undoubtedly estrogen has some influence on its occurrence.

CRITERIA FOR DIAGNOSIS

Suggestive

To the astute clinician, it is not hard to recognize patients with "full-blown" SLE. They are usually young women, often African-American. They complain of the usual constitutional symptoms of a chronic inflammatory state. On directed questioning, they may report myalgias, Raynaud's phenomenon, joint paint and swelling, or an odd erythematous skin rash that is activated by sun exposure and takes on a peculiar distribution of the cheeks and the bridge of the nose. There is often a mild cognitive dysfunction with signs of depression or anxiety. Rarely, there will be more overt central nervous system disease with psychosis or seizures.

Up to 60% of SLE patients are found to manifest pulmonary disease. Chest pain, shortness of breath on exertion or at rest, and peripheral edema may be the clinical clues to the existence of pleural or pericardial inflammation of effusion, interstitial inflammation or fibrosis, or right heart failure due to pulmonary hypertension.

Definitive

Once the diagnosis of SLE is made, a careful review of the respiratory system may disclose the pulmonary disease. To say definitively that it is lupus and not infection, neoplasia, or some other process causing the symptoms, the clinician must, to a reasonable degree, rule these other etiologies out. Patients with pleural effusions may have diagnostic thoracentesis with or without pleural biopsy to check for the absence of malignant cells and stainable or cultured organisms. The glucose level and pH of the fluid will be higher than found in rheumatoid arthritis. Any biopsy material collected should not include tumor, granulomata, or infectious processes. When lupus erythematosus (LE) cells (leukocytes with phagocytized erythrocytes in them) are found in pleural fluid, they should also appear in peripheral smears. The LE cells are not very specific. If other causes of pulmonary disease can be effectively ruled out and the patient has lupus by separate criteria, then the diagnosis of lupus lung disease can be made.

CLINICAL MANIFESTATIONS

Subjective

As mentioned, patients complaints may range from chest pain to shortness of breath at rest or with exertion. The symptoms may come and go throughout the course of the disease. Occasionally, pulmonary symptoms may precede the other symptoms of SLE, so one must be on the lookout for serologic or biopsy confirmation of SLE in any patient with unexplained infiltrative or pleural disease. As pleurisy occurs in up to 50% of lupus patients the most common complaint is chest pain, which may be peripheral rather than central and is characterized as burning or searing rather than knifelike or aching. Pain is usually exacerbated by deep inspiration or coughing; consequently, patients may splint one side of the chest.

Shortness of breath and dry cough may be signals to a more extensive pleural reaction with effusion or an active pneumonitis. Lupus vasculitis may present with hemoptysis that is scanty, whereas extensive pneumonitis may cause alveolar hemorrhage and massive hemoptysis. Insidious slowly progressive dyspnea on exertion is the hallmark of interstitial fibrosis (see Chapter 13–30) or pulmonary hypertension. Rapidly progressive dyspnea that leads to respiratory failure and death is more indicative of severe pneumonitis or pulmonary hemorrhage.

Patients with SLE often have a familial history of SLE. Patients with otherwise unexplained pulmonary disease should be asked whether any relatives suffered from skin rashes, arthritis, mysterious weight loss and swollen lymph nodes, chest pain of pleuritis or pericarditis, mysterious positive blood tests for syphilis, or kidney failure.

Objective

Physical Examination

Patients should be examined for signs of systemic inflammatory disease. Findings outside the chest consistent with pulmonary involvement of SLE include clubbing of the fingers and rapid shallow breathing. With right heart failure, peripheral edema, jugular venous distention, and hepatic congestion occur. In severe pneumonitis, central cyanosis may be seen and indicates an emergency. On chest examination, one must pay particular attention to asymmetric movement of the chest secondary to splinting. There is also decreased diaphragmatic excursion, leading to platelike atelectasis (also called *shrinking lung syndrome*) and thoracoabdominal dissociation (paradoxical inward movement of the diaphragm with inspiratory effort) due to bilateral phrenic neuritis with diaphragmatic weakness. Unilateral phrenic nerve involvement or pleural disease would be seen as asymmetric diaphragmatic excursion. Pleural disease may produce an audible pleural rub.

Other findings include radiographic confirmation of effusion of pleural thickening as well as infiltrative lung disease. Hilar and mediastinal adenopathy might be observed.

Routine Laboratory Abnormalities

See Chapter 7–1.

PLANS

Diagnostic

Differential Diagnosis

Pulmonary infection and neoplastic disease must be ruled out with appropriate tests (see Criteria for Diagnosis).

Diagnostic Options and Recommended Approach

Outside of the special serologies one would check for in SLE, there is no additional special blood work to do for pulmonary disease of SLE. When interstitial disease is suspected, pulmonary function tests should be obtained. A restrictive ventilatory defect with low diffusion of car-

bon monoxide and low total lung capacity are the hallmarks of interstitial lung disease. Serial tests performed a few months apart can track progression of disease or response to therapy. The value of biopsy and culture of sputum and tissue is that other causes of interstitial disease can be ruled out (see Chapter 13–30). If the underlying disease is unclear or the disease is rapidly progressing and tissue diagnosis is needed, then invasive procedures are called for. If mediastinal adenopathy is present, then mediastinoscopy should be considered. If parenchymal lung disease is predominant, then fiberoptic bronchoscopy with transbronchial biopsy is in order. If the prevailing defect is vasculitis, then it may be better to try open lung or thoracoscopic biopsy.

Therapeutic

The goal of therapy of SLE lung disease is to limit inflammation in active cases. Simple pleurisy can be relieved by nonsteroidal antiinflammatory drugs. Patients without a systemic indication for treatment and serial pulmonary function tests that do not show progression of disease may not require antiinflammatory therapy. Those in whom it is necessary to treat can receive high-dose corticosteroids (1 mg/kg up to 100 mg of prednisone orally or methylprednisolone 100 mg every 6 hours intravenously). It is important to protect the gastric mucosa with sucrafate or an H_2 blocker. Pulse steroids have been anecdotally used for life-threatening complications of SLE and consist of 50 mg of methylprednisolone intravenously over 30 minutes every 12 hours. Failing this, the patient will probably not be amenable to steroids.

Second-line therapy for SLE consists of cytolytic immunosuppressive therapy such as azathioprine or cyclophosphamide. The effect on SLE of these drugs is described elsewhere, but it should be said that results may take a few weeks to become evident although "pulse" cyclophosphamide $(0.5–1 \text{ g/m}^2(\times)1)$ has been known to work more quickly. This can be repeated monthly. Plamapheresis could theoretically filter the immune complexes out of the system, but has never been shown to alter the course of this disease.

FOLLOW-UP

Aside from the markers one might follow in SLE, in general, some specific recommendations in patients with lung disease are as follows. Depending on disease activity, repeat chest radiographs and pulmonary function tests can be used to monitor the progression of disease or the response to therapy. In the case of the patient with long-standing stable pulmonary fibrosis, good lung health habits are strongly recommended. This includes quitting smoking, yearly screening tuberculosis and control skin tests (*Candida, Histoplasma,* coccidioidomycosis, etc.), yearly influenza vaccine, and streptococcal pneumonia vaccine every 5 to 6 years. Home oxygen may be indicated and can prolong survival if used appropriately (See Chapter 13–30).

DISCUSSION

Prevalence and Incidence

The prevalence of SLE in the United States is thought to be 15 to 50 per 100,000. Ninety percent of its victims are women, with African-Americans outnumbering whites. As up to 60% can be demonstrated to have cardiac or pulmonary disorders, the prevalence of SLE lung disease approaches 10 to 30 per 100,000.

Related Basic Science

The mechanisms of injury seems to be the deposition of circulating immune complexes. These tend to attract inflammatory cells, which release proteolytic enzymes, oxidants, and more chemotaxic factors, which all produce tissue damage. The acute parenchymal inflammatory stage causes restrictive lung disease and interferes with gas exchange by causing exudative secretions to fill the alveoli and interstitium. This form of pulmonary disease is sometimes amenable to therapy, but sometimes progresses unremittingly to respiratory failure. The pleural disease may simply cause discomfort and extrapulmonary restriction. The late-stage fibrosis can be the most difficult to deal with as it does not respond to therapy.

Natural History and its Modification with Treatment

The natural history of SLE can be unpredictable. Each of its manifestations can spontaneously remit, progress, or remain stable. Ultimately when patients die they do so with renal failure. Patients are also susceptible to infection, and the drugs used to treat lupus are immunolytic and invite infection as well.

Much rarer complications of pulmonary vasculitis in SLE are alveolar hemorrhages, which appear as quickly enlarging infiltrates on chest radiographs. One interesting confirmatory diagnostic test for this condition is a rise in the diffusion of carbon monoxide. This finding is, however, misleading as it represents blood absorbing carbon monoxide but staying within the lung and not circulating throughout the body. Massive alveolar hemorrhage is frequently fatal.

Prevention

There are no preventive measures in classic SLE. Drug-induced SLE can be monitored by following serum antinuclear antibody in patients on hydralazine, procainamide, isoniazid, D-penacillamine, and other drugs. The syndrome causes less systemic complications than does spontaneous lupus. Both serum markers and symptoms generally resolve within a few weeks of withdrawing the offending drug. A short course of steroid treatment is rarely necessary. Prevention of pulmonary complications are outlined under Follow-up.

Cost Containment

As not all SLE patients develop pulmonary complications, cost may vary. An initial chest x-ray is a reasonable beginning. In the absence of radiologic disease in the chest and without respiratory symptoms, no further tests are needed. In patients who present with dyspnea in the absence of systemic signs or symptoms, part of the workup might involved obtaining autoimmune serologies, and because there can be much overlap in these between the various syndromes, the whole battery of serologies should be ordered. As in all immune-related pulmonary fibrosis, a patient who is stable might be simply observed without expensive attempts at tissue diagnosis.

REFERENCES

Brasington RD, Furst DE. Pulmonary disease in systemic lupus erythematosus. Clin Exp Rheumatol 1985;3:269.

Pines A, Kaplinsky N, Olchovsky D, et al. Pleuro-pulmonary manifestations of systemic lupus erythematosus: Clinical features of its subgroups: Prognosis and therapeutic implications. Chest 1985;88:129.

Stevens WM, Burdon JG, Clemens LE, Webb J. The 'shrinking lungs syndrome': An infrequently recognized feature of systemic lupus erythematosus. Aust NZ J Med 1990;20:67.

CHAPTER 13–33

Pulmonary Disease due to Progressive Systemic Sclerosis (Scleroderma)

Ethan D. Fried, M.D.

DEFINITION

Progressive systemic sclerosis (PSS) is a fibrotic syndrome with manifestations in the skin and visceral organs. The etiology of this fibrosis is unknown but has been shown to involve the cell-mediated immune system and may be autoimmune in nature. This disease occurs in one of several patterns. Fibrosis may be limited to the skin and superficial tissues and muscles. Fibrosis may involve the skin primarily but also have features of the CREST syndrome (calcinosis, Raynaud's phenomenon, esophageal dysmotility, sclerodactyly, and telangiectasia). Fibrosis may be truly systemic in addition to the cutaneous features. Finally, fibrosis may involve visceral organs without cutaneous manifestations.

The pulmonary involvement may take one of several forms. There may be interstitial fibrosis or vascular fibrosis with pulmonary hypertension. Finally, there may be frequent aspiration due to esophageal dysfunction.

ETIOLOGY

The precise etiology of PSS is probably multifactorial. A familial form does exist and there is some evidence for an association with certain HLA types. There also seems to be an exposure risk in that people affected generally can be traced to a mineral or organic compound exposure. In Spain in 1981, a syndrome resembling scleroderma occurred in many people who ingested rapeseed oil. In 1989, a series of cases of eosinophilia–myalgia syndrome with scleroderma-like skin changes were traced to the ingestion of a particular brand of L-tryptophan. The manufacturer of this otherwise harmless amino acid used frequently as a sleep aid had recently changed the manufacturing process and an impurity was introduced. Women who had been given silicon breast implants began to report a disturbing number of scleroderma-like symptoms, but a large retrospective study published in 1994 found no statistical link between the implants and the development of this or any other collagen–vascular disease-like syndrome. Other substances linked to the development of PSS have been certain aromatic compounds.

CRITERIA FOR DIAGNOSIS
Suggestive

The patient with pulmonary disease of PSS may present the same way as patients with many other fibrotic lung disorders. A person presenting with progressive shortness of breath, complaints of joint pain and stiffness, and the firm, indurated skin changes of scleroderma probably has the associated visceral fibrosis including pulmonary fibrosis.

Definitive

The patient should manifest some of the prominent features of PSS. Raynaud's phenomenon, skin changes, esophageal dysmotility with weight loss, and multiple episodes of aspiration pneumonia in the clinical history are highly suggestive. A high erythrocyte sedimentation rate is too nonspecific to rely on for diagnosis. Antinuclear antibodies, particularly antitopoisomerase I, or anticentromere antibodies are less sensitive but highly specific for PSS. In the pulmonary disease, restrictive ventilatory defects are found with bibasilar rales and signs of pulmonary hypertension. Lung biopsy may show fibrosing alveolitis but may just show the fibrosis, which is nonspecific. The other prominent but very late signs of PSS include renal failure with proteinuria, microangiopathic hemolytic anemia, and malignant hypertension. Like the pulmonary hypertension, these latter manifestations occur quite late in the disease and indicate that the patient will soon die.

CLINICAL MANIFESTATIONS
Subjective

The usual early symptoms are patient complaints of dysphagia, with or without Raynaud's phenomenon. Fingers and hands may be swollen at this early stage along with the forearms and face. Patients are usually in the third to fifth decades and women in childbearing years are at least three times more likely to be affected than men. There may be a familial distribution. Another key point in the history is a thorough occupational history looking for exposure to minerals such as silicon or to organic compounds such as vinyl chloride, benzene, and toluene. Furthermore, one should inquire about possible exposures to medicinal agents such as bleomycin and L-tryptophan (now removed from the market).

Objective

Physical Examination

Rapid shallow breathing in a patient with tight, fibrotic skin of the fingers and the face is often the first objective sign of this often fatal syndrome. Bibasilar inspiratory crackles and a loud pulmonary component of the second heart sound with or without the murmur of tricuspid valve regurgitation indicate advanced lung disease with pulmonary hypertension.

Routine Laboratory Abnormalities

The electrocardiogram may reveal right ventricular hypertrophy and right atrial abnormality.

The chest radiograph shows bibasilar reticulonodular infiltrates.

The erythrocyte sedimentation rate is elevated. Renal function may be decreased, and the blood creatinine and urea nitrogen may be elevated. Urine protein may be elevated.

PLANS
Diagnostic
Differential Diagnosis

The typical abnormalities shown on the x-ray film in a patient with obvious progressive systemic sclerosis is diagnostic and a differential diagnosis is not needed.

Diagnostic Options and Recommended Approach

The battery of autoantibodies might include a positive rheumatoid factor or antinuclear antibodies in low titer. Anticentromere or antitopoisomerase I antibodies may be positive and would be most specific for PSS. When many different autoantibodies are present, a diagnosis of mixed connective tissue disease or overlap syndrome may be invoked. Anemia workup may reveal normochromic anemia secondary to microangiopathic hemolysis with helmet and teardrop cells present. Hypochromic iron deficiency anemia may develop secondary to gastrointestinal blood loss. Macrocytic anemia might result from gastrointestinal dysmotility, bacterial overgrowth, and B_{12}/folic acid deficiency.

Biopsied skin of the PSS patient may show the abnormal accumulation of mucopolysaccharides and can be used to differentiate the PSS patient from one with primary amyloidosis. Lung biopsy may show alveolitis, which may be amenable to antiinflammatory treatment, or fibrosis, which is permanent. Vasculitis is also potentially treatable, but the late stage of arteriolitis obliterans is not.

The most logical approach in a patient who is not progressing rapidly is, after the initial chest x-rays and routine laboratory tests, to take serial pulmonary function test measurements to determine if the disease is still active and worth doing a biopsy or treating. Next might be an investigation into whether an aspiration pneumonia might be present and a simultaneous erythrocyte sedimentation rate might be obtained. A battery of serum autoantibodies might be ordered, and then if no other tissue is available, lung biopsy via the fiberoptic bronchoscope might be planned. It would not be unusual in this procedure to come up with nothing but nonspecific fibrosis and require an open lung biopsy to determine a tissue diagnosis. Even then the workup may reveal end-stage disease not amenable to treatment.

Therapeutic

If after empirical treatment for aspiration pneumonia the patient is making no recovery, and other tests reveal PSS, it may be best to attempt to limit immune-mediated damage. Prednisone and cyclophosphamide, as well as D-penicillamine, have been used alone and in combination with variable success. The most productive efforts can be in the preventive

medicine area with home oxygen therapy, annual influenza vaccines, and pneumonia vaccine and quick effective treatment for respiratory infections. Treatment for the other manifestations of PSS is discussed in Chapter 7–4. It has recently been found that angiotensin-converting enzyme inhibitors clearly prolong life in the most severely ill PSS patients with renal failure.

FOLLOW-UP

Occasional pulmonary function tests and chest x-rays, or at least regular assessments of respiratory rates and character, can be obtained. Therapy with the antiinflammatory drugs should take effect within a few weeks. If the effect cannot be observed then it is time to go on to something else or to stop and provide comfort care only to the patient.

DISCUSSION
Prevalence and Incidence

It has been estimated that about 15 cases per million are diagnosed in the United States per year. Fewer cases are diagnosed in the less industrialized areas. As disease severity varies, it is difficult to estimate prevalence. Once patients develop pulmonary hypertension, death comes within 2 years. Patients with malignant hypertension and renal failure have an even shorter life expectancy.

Related Basic Science

The earliest detectable damage in PSS seems to be damage to the endothelium. This precedes the diffuse perivascular fibrosis that marks advanced disease. Von Willebrand's factor is released with endothelial injury and is followed by a cascade of other factors, including platelet-derived growth factor and transforming growth factor β. Smooth muscle cell proliferation and collagen deposition produce the intimal thickening that characterizes PSS. Later arteriolitis gives way to fibrosis and the development of collateral vessels. The proliferating vessels attract chronic inflammatory cells such as monocytes and macrophages in the lung and lots of interleukin-2. This continues to drive the inflammatory reaction, which is eventually replaced by fibrosis.

There is evidence to suggest that chromosomal abnormalities may lead to chromatid breaks, eccentric fragments, and ring chromosomes, which may influence the development of this syndrome.

The primary lung manifestation is the alveolitis, which soon leads to fibrosis. Perivascular infiltrates lead to pulmonary hypertension. Finally, repeated aspiration in a patient with PSS esophageal dysmotility may lead to restrictive lung disease too.

Natural History and Its Modification with Treatment

The pulmonary involvement of PSS is highly variable. Lung disease may stabilize, worsen, or remit. Chronic aspiration can be treated with rotating chronic antibiotics, but this has limited value. Simple percutaneous access to the gastrointestinal tract as in a gastrostomy does not necessarily prevent aspiration of oral secretions. Progressive dyspnea indicates the development of pulmonary hypertension and death will soon follow.

Prevention

As no measures can prevent the onset of lung disease in PSS, the best strategy is to prevent other respiratory complications like pneumonia and to prevent the onset of cor pulmonale with home oxygen used at least 16 hours per day.

Cost Containment

Because only patients with active alveolitis can be helped, it is most prudent to reserve expensive biopsy procedures for those patients who manifest rapid progression and new infiltrates. In addition to ruling out other causes of lung disease, these procedures help to distinguish active alveolitis from "burned out" fibrosis. Patients with only systemic signs and symptoms without pulmonary function test evidence of restrictive lung disease or chest x-ray changes can be treated without pulmonary biopsy altogether.

REFERENCES

Lomeo RM, Cornella RJ, Schabel SI. Progressive systemic sclerosis sine scleroderma, presenting as pulmonary interstitial fibrosis. Am J Med 1989;87:525.

Young RH, Mark GJ. Pulmonary vascular changes in scleroderma. Am J Med 1978;64:998.

CHAPTER 13–34

Allergic Alveolitis

Ghassan W. Jamaleddine, M.D.

DEFINITION

Extrinsic allergic alveolitis, also known as hypersensitivity pneumonitis, is an immunologic inflammation involving the distal lung parenchyma, particularly the distal bronchioles, interstitium, and alveoli. This inflammation is the result of repeated inhalation of organic dust and other agents by a sensitive host.

ETIOLOGY

More than 50 different occupational and environmental sources of antigen exposure have been identified. Some of the agents implicated are listed in Table 13–34–1. The common sources of causative agents can be (1) plant products, such as moldy hay, silage, or grain; (2) animal products, like pigeon droppings and duck feathers; and (3) heating, cooling, and humidification systems. In addition, reactive simple chemicals like isocyanate can cause hypersensitivity pneumonitis. These lung diseases are often referred to in the context of specific clinical entities, for example, farmer's lung, pigeon breeder's disease, and humidifier lung.

CRITERIA FOR DIAGNOSIS
Suggestive

The disease can present in an acute, subacute, or chronic form. In the acute form, the diagnosis is suggested in patients who present with shortness of breath, dry cough, fever, chills, and malaise, with bilateral end inspiratory rales on physical examination, 3 to 8 hours after exposure to an offending agent. In the subacute form, the symptoms are more insidious in onset; they appear over a period of weeks, are marked by dyspnea and cough, and may worsen enough to require hospitalization. In the acute and subacute forms, usually the symptoms ameliorate if there is no further exposure to the antigen. If exposure to the antigen continues, the disease progresses to a chronic form, where the presentation is that of progressive interstitial lung disease with chronic dry cough and worsening exertional dyspnea. In this form irreversible lung damage has occurred.

Definitive

The diagnosis is established with a consistent history, physical findings, pulmonary function tests, exposure to a recognized antigen, and finding of antibody to that antigen.

CLINICAL MANIFESTATIONS
Subjective

In the acute variety, symptoms start 3 to 8 hours after exposure to the offending agent; they diminish and disappear after cessation of contact. Fever and chills are the more transient symptoms, lasting a few hours at the most. Malaise is variable and includes fatigue, muscle pain, and chest tightness. Cough is present in most cases; however, it may not be a predominant symptom. It is usually dry initially, but may become productive after the febrile illness. Dyspnea is often severe and it can persist for days or weeks after the end of the febrile phase of the illness. In most instances, acute febrile episodes recur after each contact; patients with farmer's lung, for example, often present with daily evening

febrile illnesses over weeks or months. In the subacute form of allergic alveolitis, the bouts of chills and fever are not present; the patient becomes progressively short of breath and often has a chronic nonproductive cough. Progressive weight loss may be seen. In the advanced chronic form, patients present with chronic worsening shortness of breath and respiratory failure.

TABLE 13–34–1. ALLERGIC ALVEOLITIS

Disease	Source of Antigen	Antigen
Animal sources		
Pigeon breeder's disease	Pigeon droppings	Pigeon serum
Bird-fancier's lung	Bird products	Bird proteins
Laboratory worker's disease	Rat fur and urine, mice	Rat proteins
Turkey handler's lung	Turkey products	Turkey proteins
Pituitary snuff taker's disease	Pituitary proteins	Bovine or porcine proteins
Plant sources		
Farmer's lung	Moldy hay	Thermophilic actinomycetes
Bagadssosis	Moldy pressed sugarcane	Thermophilic actinomycetes
Mushroom worker's lung	Moldy compost	Thermophilic actinomycetes
Maple bark disease	Contaminated maple logs	*Cryptostroma corticale*
Aspen tree peelers	Contaminated wood dust	Thermophiles
Malt worker's lung	Contaminated barley	*Aspergillus clavatus* and *A. fumigatus*
Sequoiosis	Contaminated wood dust	*Graphium, Pullularia*
Paprika splitter's lung	Paprika dust	*Mucor stolonifer*
Cheese washer's lung	Cheese particles	*Penicillium caseii*
Grain handler's lung	Moldy grain	Thermophiles
Detergent worker's lung	Detergent powder	*Bacillus subtilis* enzymes
Humidifier lung, heating and air conditioning	Contaminated home humidifier and air conditioner, refrigerator defrosters, mist vaporizers	Thermophilic actinomyctes, amebae, *Aspergillus, Bacillus cereus.*
Wine grower's lung	Mold on grapes	*Botrytis cinerea*
Saxophone lung	Saxophone mouthpiece	*Candida albicans*
Tobacco worker's lung	Mold on tobacco	*Aspergillus* species
Hot tub lung	Mold on ceiling	*Cladosporium* species
Miller's lung	Wheat weevils	*Sitophilus granarius*
Reactive chemicals		
Toluene diisocyanate hypersensitivity pneumonitis	Toluene diisocyanate	Altered proteins
Trimellitic anhydride hypersensitivity pneumonitis	Trimellitic anhydride	Altered proteins
Epoxy resin lung	Heated epoxy resin	Phthalic anhydride

Objective

Physical Examination

On physical examination, fever most often is absent at the time the patient is seen; tachypnea and cyanosis can be seen in severe cases. Clubbing may be observed in the chronic form of the disease, and it has been associated with poor prognosis. Chest auscultation reveals bibasilar fine inspiratory rales; in the chronic phase, rhonchi and squeaks are heard. Signs of cor pulmonale and respiratory failure are seen in the advanced stages of the chronic form.

Routine Laboratory Abnormalities

The chest radiograph may be normal in the early stages. Acute and subacute forms of the disease are usually characterized by interstitial and alveolar nodular infiltrates appearing in patchy or homogeneous distribution. In the more chronic form, diffuse interstitial fibrosis is seen. With increasing fibrosis, there is loss of lung volume and cardiomegaly.

In the acute form, a mild leukocytosis with increased neutrophil count can be present. Eosinophilia is variable and is not a feature of this disease.

PLANS

Diagnostic

Differential Diagnosis

The differential diagnosis of the acute and subacute presentations includes drug-induced interstitial pneumonitis, sarcoidosis, eosinophilic pneumonia, and allergic asthma. The chronic form might be indistinguishable from advanced idiopathic pulmonary fibrosis.

Diagnostic Options

Arterial blood gases show hypoxia associated with respiratory alkalosis when the hypoxia is severe ($PaO_2 < 55$ mm Hg). A nonspecific polyclonal rise in gamma globulins with a normal immunoglobulin E level, an increased sedimentation rate, and a positive rheumatoid factor with antinuclear antibodies are often observed. Although there is no single diagnostic test of hypersensitivity pneumonitis, a number of helpful diagnostic options are available. Pulmonary function tests should be done on all patients in whom the diagnosis is suspected; they show a restrictive ventilatory defect with decrease in forced vital capacity (FVC), total lung capacity, and diffusion capacity of the lung for carbon monoxide. The 1-second forced expiratory volume (FEV_1) is reduced; however, the FEV_1/FVC ratio is normal. This pattern distinguishes hypersensitivity pneumonitis from asthma, where there is an obstructive impairment.

A high-resolution chest computed tomography scan might be helpful in distinguishing the disease from sarcoidosis, in the cases where bilateral hilar lymphadenopathy is not very obvious on the chest radiograph.

A number of immunologic tests are available, including skin tests, precipitating antibody tests, and inhalation challenge test. Skin tests are rarely helpful, because few antigens are available, and when available, they often give a nonspecific irritation due to impurities. Precipitating antibody to the offending antigen is found in more than 90% of affected patients; however, many normal people may have the same antibodies, so precipitating antibody can be used as a marker of exposure. Inhalation challenge tests to the offending antigen are available in certain centers; however they are not well standardized and may be dangerous in some patients as a severe reaction may develop.

Fiberoptic bronchoscopy with transbronchial biopsy and bronchoalveolar lavage should be considered when the noninvasive measures fail to make the diagnosis. Bronchoalveolar lavage is characterized by an increased lymphocyte count in the acute phase of the disease.

The lymphocytes are the CD8+ T-cell type; thus, the CD4/CD8 ratio is decreased. This is helpful in distinguishing extrinsic allergic alveolitis from sarcoidosis, where the CD4/CD8 ratio is elevated, and from idiopathic pulmonary fibrosis, where neutrophils are predominant.

Lung biopsy is not diagnostic, yet a distinctive histopathology is seen depending on the stage of the disease. In the acute phase there is accumulation of neutrophils and macrophages in the interstitium and alveoli, in the subacute phase there is a predominant lymphocytic and plasma cell infiltration of the interstitium with formation of noncaseating granulomas, and the chronic phase shows varying degrees of fibrosis.

Recommended Approach

The disease should be suspected in patients presenting with repeated influenza-like illness and in patients with signs and symptoms of active interstitial lung disease. A good environmental and occupational history is of utmost importance. A presumptive diagnosis could be made on the basis of a history of exacerbation associated with exposure to a specific antigen. An initial workup should include pulmonary function tests. If clinical, radiologic, and pulmonary function tests are consistent with the diagnosis and they improve after avoidance of the antigen source, then the diagnosis is established. Presence of antibody to the antigen is supportive of the diagnosis. Bronchoalveolar lavage and lung biopsy should be reserved for patients in whom the diagnosis remains unclear and other diagnoses are considered.

Therapeutic

The management is dependent on the identification and elimination of the antigen from the environment of the affected patient. Avoidance of exposure may not be easy; patients may have to change jobs, change hobbies, or even change their homes. In certain instances, changes in industrial procedures should be suggested to protect other individuals at risk. Improved ventilation, use of masks, and air filtering systems have proved to be helpful in some situations.

In severe acute cases supplemental oxygen should be given as needed ($PaO_2 < 55$ mm Hg); systemic steroids, prednisone 1 mg/kg/d, in conjunction with contact avoidance will assist recovery. With improvement, the prednisone should be tapered and discontinued in 1 to 2 weeks. In the subacute presentation, a longer period of prednisone treatment is usually needed; the starting dose of 1 mg/kg/d is decreased in 3 to 4 weeks to the lowest dose that controls symptoms, usually 0.3 mg/kg/d. A course of 3 to 6 months may be required. In the chronic fibrotic stage, treatment is not effective; however, a steroid trial is warranted.

FOLLOW-UP

Patients with acute allergic alveolitis who respond to contact avoidance do not need long-term follow-up. Repeat chest x-rays and pulmonary function tests should be done to document recovery. In the subacute form, a longer follow-up period is needed until symptoms ameliorate. This might vary from 3 months to more than a year; the frequency of follow-up depends on the severity of symptoms and response to treatment. Subjects who decide to stay in the environment that causes hypersensitivity pneumonitis should be instructed about all preventive measures discussed above, and should be followed closely with pulmonary function tests and chest x-rays. Patients with permanent fibrotic changes need chronic follow-up; chest x-rays and pulmonary function tests should be done periodically to assess the course of the disease.

DISCUSSION

Prevalence and Incidence

The prevalence of allergic alveolitis is hard to establish and it is variable in different states and countries. The incidence of farmer's lung has been reported to be between 0.4 and 8.5%. Females are at greater risk than males (5:1) when exposed to the same antigen. Age is not a factor in increasing the risk. There is no specific racial, genetic, or familial prevalence. The incidence of seropositive normal farmers is approximately 10% in endemic regions. In pigeon breeders, the incidence is reported to be between 40 and 50%.

Related Basic Science

The development of extrinsic allergic alveolitis is dependent on the inhalation of an organic dust of an appropriate size that is able to reach the distal bronchioles and alveoli of the immunosensitive host. The inhaled particle must be smaller than 5 to 6 μm to reach the terminal bronchioles; larger particles are trapped in the upper airways. These particles, some of which are listed in Table 13–34–1, may be fungal spores, animal products, bacterial products, or any aerosolized proteins. Once they reach the terminal bronchioles and the alveoli, these antigens are recognized by the memory lymphocytes, which are activated and trigger the start of a lymphocytic inflammatory process. During this process the activated lymphocytes secrete various intercellular signaling molecules (cytokines), which cause more activation of lymphocytes and macrophages, leading to tissue damage. If the antigen exposure continues, the process is magnified, and in addition, the fibroblasts are stimulated to start laying extracellular matrix proteins leading to fibrosis. So the pathogenesis involves both immune complex-mediated disease (type III or Arthus-type reaction) and cell-mediated immunity (type IV reaction). These immunologic reactions explain the lymphocytic inflammatory process observed in the alveoli and the terminal bronchioles.

Natural History and Its Modification with Treatment

The natural history depends on the stage of disease at the time of presentation. In the acute stage, complete recovery is expected after localizing the antigen and controlling exposure. In the subacute stages, marked improvement will occur over longer period; residual damage to the lung is variable depending on repeated exposure. If exposure continues, fibrosis will ensue, leading to irreversible damage and eventually to respiratory failure.

Prevention

Prevention is discussed under Plans, Therapeutic.

Cost Containment

A high index of suspicion and a careful detailed occupational and environmental history are the keys to avoiding unnecessary tests and repeated hospitalizations for recurrent pneumonia. Avoidance of contact with the antigen will control the disease and reduce medical costs.

REFERENCES

Reynolds HY. Hypersensitivity pneumonitis: Correlation of cellular and immunologic changes with clinical phases of disease. *Lung* 1988;166:189.

Richerson HB, Bernstein IL, Fink JN, et al. Guidelines for the clinical evaluation of hypersensitivity pneumonitis. *J Allergy Clin Immunol* 1989;84:839.

Salvaggio JE. Recent advances in the pathogenesis of allergic alveolitis. *Clin Exp Allergy* 1990;20:137.

Silver SF, Miller NL, Miller RR, Lefcoe MS. Computed tomography in hypersensitivity pneumonitis. *Radiology* 1989;173:441.

CHAPTER 13–35

Idiopathic Pulmonary Hemorrhage (Pulmonary Hemosiderosis)

Stephan L. Kamholz, M.D.

DEFINITION

Idiopathic pulmonary hemorrhage (idiopathic pulmonary hemosiderosis [IPH]) is a rare condition, seen predominantly in children (< 10 years of age) and adolescents, in which recurrent episodes of bleeding into the pulmonary parenchyma are associated with dyspnea, cough, and hemoptysis. The diagnosis of IPH is made after exclusion of all known immunologic, inflammatory, and cardiovascular etiologies, as well as systemic diseases that can cause pulmonary bleeding.

ETIOLOGY

The etiology of IPH is unknown. IPH is distinguished from other causes of diffuse alveolar hemorrhage by the absence of histologic evidence of capillary inflammation on review of open lung biopsy specimens; circulating antiglomerular basement membrane antibody, or autoantibodies associated with systemic lupus erythematosus; glomerulonephritis (focal segmental) or other evidence of extrapulmonary involvement; and evidence of pulmonary veno-occlusive disease, pulmonary venous hypertension, or mitral valve stenosis.

CRITERIA FOR DIAGNOSIS
Suggestive

The most common symptoms are dyspnea, cough, and hemoptysis (although expectoration of blood may be absent early in the disease and, when present, may range from mere blood streaking of phlegm to massive hemoptysis). Occasionally, symptoms of anemia, such as lethargy, weakness, and pallor, call attention to the problem in advance of specific respiratory symptomatology. Past medical history is noncontributory, and in contrast to cases of classic Goodpasture's syndrome, there is no temporal relationship to an antecedent viral respiratory tract infection. Family history is generally noncontributory, although there are a few isolated reports of familial occurrence of IPH. Approximately three quarters of the cases of IPH occur in children and adolescents; there is a 2:1 male preponderance among adults (usually over age 30) with IPH.

Definitive

The diagnosis is made in a patient with characteristic symptomatology on exclusion of other etiologies of diffuse alveolar hemorrhage. During acute episodes, the chest roentgenogram reveals diffuse alveolar infiltrates; the repetitive episodes result in pulmonary fibrosis (interstitial infiltrates) and respiratory failure. Essential features include recurrent episodes of diffuse alveolar hemorrhage, alveolar infiltrates on chest roentgenogram, iron deficiency anemia, histopathologic evidence of the presence of blood, and hemosiderin-laden alveolar macrophages in alveolar spaces (also demonstrable on cytocentrifuge preparations of bronchoalveolar lavage), accompanied by hyperplasia of type II pneumocytes, without evidence of intraalveolar inflammation or capillaritis, and without deposition of immune complexes in the lung. Changes of interstitial fibrosis and collagenization are found in more advanced cases.

CLINICAL MANIFESTATIONS
Subjective

The clinical picture is variable, though most patients have episodes of cough, dyspnea, and hemoptysis, often accompanied by fever. The extent of bleeding may range from mere streaking of sputum to massive life-threatening hemoptysis. These symptoms are common to all causes of diffuse alveolar hemorrhage and do not uniquely characterize IPH. Less commonly, patients present with dyspnea in the absence of hemoptysis, and are found to have an abnormal chest roentgenogram. The iron deficiency anemia may be the initial manifestation detected because of related symptoms (see Criteria for Diagnosis, Suggestive).

Objective
Physical Examination

Physical findings during initial acute episodes of IPH are usually restricted to the chest. Crackles are heard over the affected lung fields, and the patient is often tachypneic. Occasionally, pallor of the conjunctivae and nailbeds is the only clue to the presence of IPH. In more chronic cases, when interstitital fibrosis has supervened, dry "velcro" rales may be heard, and nail clubbing may be present. In children, lymphadenopathy and hepatosplenomegaly may be noted in less than one quarter of the cases of IPH.

Routine Laboratory Abnormalities

Rarely, the related anemia is discovered on routine laboratory examination in an otherwise asymptomatic child. The only consistent finding on routine laboratory examination is that of hypochromic microcytic anemia.

In early IPH, the chest x-ray films reveal an alveolar filling process. Later in the course of disease, interstitial infiltrates may predominate, and Kerley B lines (thickened interlobular septa) may be noted.

PLANS
Diagnostic
Differential Diagnosis

The differential diagnosis of IPH includes all the causes of diffuse alveolar hemorrhage. Those in which capillaritis is absent include IPH, Goodpasture's syndrome, pulmonary venous hypertension (including veno-occlusive disease), mitral valve disease, and coagulopathies. Extremely rare causes include industrial exposure to trimellitic anhydride (the occupational history is essential here) and therapeutic use of penicillamine (again revealed by history). In Goodpasture's syndrome, circulating antiglomerular basement membrane antibody is present, and linear deposits of immunoglobulin G may be detected in renal and lung biopsies by immunofluorescence staining; additionally, the urinary sediment is usually abnormal. Mitral stenosis may be suspected on physical examination and confirmed by echocardiography. Similarly, pulmonary venous hypertension of other etiologies is associated with an accentuated pulmonic component of the second heart sound, right parasternal lift or heave, occasionally with a pulmonic insufficiency (Graham Steele) murmur, and/or with tricuspid regurgitation. Veno-occlusive disease mimics mitral stenosis, but the murmur is absent, and the chest roentgenogram may reveal chronic alveolar infiltrates and/or Kerley B lines. In diffuse alveolar hemorrhage related to coagulopathy, the platelet count and/or prothrombin/partial thromboplastin time(s) are abnormal.

Entities causing diffuse alveolar hemorrhage in which capillaritis is present include collagen vascular disease (primarily systemic lupus erythematosus), systemic necrotizing vasculitis (i.e., microscopic polyarteritis syndrome), Wegener's granulomatosis, focal segmental necrotizing glomerulonephritis with alveolar hemorrhage, and Henoch–Schönlein purpura. Patients with systemic lupus erythematosus usually have other systemic manifestations, including renal disease, cutaneous disease, and arthritis. Antinuclear and anti-DNA antibodies and reduction in total hemolytic complement are detectable in the serum of systemic lupus erythematosus patients, and urine sediment and renal function are abnormal. Interestingly, the spectrum of histopathologic changes in diffuse alveolar hemorrhage complicating systemic lupus erythematosus may include examples with and without capillaritis, the latter being found more frequently. In systemic necrotizing vasculitis with diffuse alveolar hemorrhage, necrotizing glomerulonephritis is frequently present, cutaneous and nervous system involvement is frequent, antinuclear and anti-DNA antibodies are absent, but antineutrophil cytoplasmic antibody is often detected in the serum. Wegener's granulomatosis may occasionally present as diffuse alveolar hemorrhage, and capillaritis can be found in slightly less than one third of lung biopsies from affected patients. Sinusitis, upper airway involvement, and renal disease frequently develop later in the course of Wegener's granulomatosis, but antineutrophil cytoplasmic antibody is usually detectable in active cases. Nodular pulmonary infiltrates, often with cavitation, are the more classic radiographic manifestations of Wegener's granulomatosis. Necrotizing glomerulonephritis with alveolar hemorrhage is distinguished from microscopic polyarteritis syndrome by the absence of involvement of organs other than kidney and lung. Henoch–Schönlein purpura is associated with palpable purpura; renal, joint, and gastrointestinal involvement; and the presence of granular immunoglobulin A deposits (detected by immunofluorescence staining) on the capillary

basement membrane in affected tissues. Pulmonary involvement (diffuse alveolar hemorrhage) in Henoch–Schönlein purpura is uncommon.

Diagnostic Options

Complete evaluation is directed at confirming the diagnosis of IPH in a patient with a compatible clinical presentation by excluding other etiologies of diffuse alveolar hemorrhage. Studies include hemogram (which reveals iron deficiency anemia), platelet count, prothrombin and partial thromboplastin time determinations (to exclude coagulopathy), standard posteroanterior and lateral chest roentgenograms, arterial blood gases on room air (and supplemental oxygen, if indicated), and pulmonary function tests. Occasionally, it is helpful to perform a thin-section chest computed axial tomography scan to confirm the patchy alveolar distribution of the hemorrhage. Blood gases reveal hypoxemia with hypocapnia. Pulmonary function tests reveal a restrictive ventilatory abnormality (reduced total lung capacity, forced vital capacity, 1-second vital capacity) without airway obstruction. Single-breath carbon monoxide diffusing capacity is elevated during and immediately after episodes of bleeding, because the extravasated red cells in the alveoli serve as a "sink" for carbon monoxide. Microscopic analysis of urine sediment and blood urea nitrogen/creatinine determinations are performed to exclude active renal involvement. Serum antiglomerular basement membrane, antinuclear and anti-DNA antibodies, antineutrophil cytoplasmic antibody, quantitative serum immunoglobulin (serum immunoglobulin A is frequently elevated in IPH), and total hemolytic complement determinations should be obtained. Bronchoalveolar lavage may be performed as part of the fiberbronchoscopic assessment of the patient with hemoptysis. Red blood cells and hemosiderin-laden macrophages will be noted on examination of the cytocentrifuge preparation of bronchoalveolar lavage. Histopathologic examination of lung biopsy specimens is necessary to exclude capillaritis and an intraalveolar inflammatory component. Immunofluorescence staining of the lung biopsy for immunoglobulins G and A should be performed.

Recommended Approach

The essential components of the diagnostic workup (selected from the options listed above) include chest roentgenograms; pulmonary function tests and blood gases; hemogram; coagulation profile; antibody, immunoglobulin, and complement determinations; and the lung biopsy (with requisite stains).

Therapeutic
Therapeutic Options

There is no specific therapy for IPH. Supportive care includes supplemental oxygen, fluid and blood replacement, and administration of supplemental iron. Corticosteroids have shown some benefit during acute bleeding, but long-term response is unlikely. Azathioprine has been used occasionally, though data are insufficient to recommend its use. Plasmapheresis has been attempted, with anecdotal reports of benefit.

Recommended Approach

Correction of hypoxemia and blood and volume replacement are essential during the acute episode. Iron therapy is important in patients with microcytic hypochromic anemia. Corticosteroid administration should be tried during acute episodes of bleeding that do not cease spontaneously.

FOLLOW-UP

The frequency of visits is determined by the severity of IPH and the recurrence of episodes of bleeding. Pulmonary function tests and serial measurements of single-breath carbon monoxide diffusing capacity can be used to follow alveolar hemorrhage in patients in whom the chest roentgenogram does not provide adequate evidence of changes in status.

DISCUSSION

Prevalence and Incidence

The disease is quite rare and the exact prevalence and incidence are not known.

Related Basic Science

The etiology of IPH remains obscure, as does the pathogenesis. The presence of elevated serum immunoglobulin A in many patients and the numerous reports of improvement after administration of immunosuppressive drugs are suggestive of an "immunologic" disease. The histologic findings in the affected lung are important, in that they serve to exclude other diagnoses. Hyperplasia of type II pneumocytes is found in association with intraalveolar hemorrhage and hemosiderin-laden macrophages. Electron microscopy reveals degeneration of type I alveolar lining cells and various types of disruption in the continuity of the alveolar capillary basement membrane. Linear deposits of immunoglobulins A and G are absent from the capillary basement membrane when immunofluorescence staining of the biopsy is obtained. Neutrophilic inflammation of the capillary walls, necrosis, and interstitial inflammation are absent.

Natural History and Its Modification with Treatment

Most patients with IPH are children, frequently less than 10 years old. It is unclear that therapeutic intervention is beneficial in changing the natural history of the disease, which may be indolent or very aggressive. The mean survival (especially in children) is in the range 3 to 5 years. Among adults, the prognosis is somewhat better, with only one quarter succumbing to relentless progression of IPH. About half of adults with IPH have some symptoms related to progressive interstitial fibrosis, and the remaining quarter suffer only a single episode of diffuse alveolar hemorrhage.

Prevention

Specific preventive measures are not known.

Cost Containment

Limitation of acute hospitalization to acute episodes of IPH is the only cost-saving measure. The rarity of the disease and the requisite complexity of the initial evaluation do not readily lend themselves to cost containment measures.

REFERENCES

Albeida SM, Gefter WB, Epstein DM, et al. Diffuse pulmonary hemorrhage: A review and classification. Radiology 1985;154:289.

Chryssanthopoulos C, Cassimos C, Pangiotidou C. Prognostic criteria in idiopathic pulmonary hemosiderosis in children. Eur J Pediatr 1985;140:123.

Donlan CJ Jr, Strodes CH, Duffy FD. Idiopathic pulmonary hemosiderosis: Electron-microscopic, immunofluorescent and iron kinetic studies. Chest 1975;68:577.

Gonzales-Crussi F, Hull MT, Crosfeld JL. Idiopathic pulmonary hemosiderosis: Evidence of capillary basement membrane abnormality. Am Rev Respir Dis 1976;114:689.

Thaell JF, Greipp PR, Stubbs SE, et al. Idiopathic pulmonary hemosiderosis: Two cases in a family. Mayo Clin Proc 1978;53:113.

Soergel KH, Sommers SC. Idiopathic pulmonary hemosiderosis and related syndromes. Am J Med 1962;32:499.

Yeager H, Powell D, Winberg RM, et al. Idiopathic pulmonary hemosiderosis: Ultrastructural studies and response to azathioprine. Arch Intern Med 1976;136:1145.

CHAPTER 13–36

Pulmonary Embolism and Infarction (See Section 15, Chapter 57)

CHAPTER 13–37

Sarcoidosis

Linda S. Efferen, M.D.

DEFINITION

Sarcoidosis is a multisystem disorder of unknown etiology characterized pathologically by the presence of nonnecrotizing granulomatous lesions.

ETIOLOGY

Anecdotal information concerning sarcoidosis and solid organ transplantation lends support to the concept of a transmissible, bloodborne agent, refocusing attention on a viral antigenic stimulus as a possible cause for sarcoidosis. Other investigators, using polymerase chain reaction techniques, are reexamining the role of mycobacteria in this disease. Information from both avenues of investigation is interesting and potentially promising; however, more than a century after its first description, the etiology of sarcoidosis remains unknown.

CRITERIA FOR DIAGNOSIS

Suggestive

Sarcoidosis generally affects young, previously healthy adults. Approximately 80% of patients are between 20 and 40 years of age on initial presentation. Incidence appears to vary with race and gender. In the United States, African-American women have the highest risk for developing disease.

Most patients present with typical clinical (Table 13–37–1) and/or radiographic (Table 13–37–2) features. Approximately one half of patients are asymptomatic, with characteristic abnormalities found on routine chest radiographs. In symptomatic patients, an insidious onset of symptoms from pulmonary, ocular, or cutaneous involvement is usual. Rarely, individuals may experience the acute onset of a constellation of symptoms suggestive of Lofgren's syndrome (fever, polyarthritis, iritis, and erythema nodosum). A typical clinical and radiographic presentation in a young, previously healthy individual is highly suggestive of sarcoidosis.

Definitive

Sarcoidosis is a diagnosis of exclusion. Demonstration of nonnecrotizing granulomatous lesions in pathologic specimens in an appropriate clinical setting, and in the absence of evidence supporting alternative etiologies known to produce similar pathologic lesions, clinical symptoms, or radiographic changes, would be considered diagnostic. At times, the clinical presentation may be sufficiently typical to preclude the need for tissue confirmation.

TABLE 13–37–1. CLINICAL MANIFESTATIONS

Organ System	Symptoms/Signs
Intrathoracic: lungs and/or lymph nodes (90%)*	Asymptomatic, shortness of breath, nonproductive cough, chest pain, radiographic abnormalities
Ocular (20–30%)	Iridocyclitis, chorioretinitis, keratoconjunctivitis, glaucoma, cataract, blindness, Heerfordt's Syndrome†
Cutaneous (20–30%)	Maculopapular, nodular, plaquelike (lupus pernio)
Reticuloendothelial system	Peripheral lymphadenopathy (40%), hepatosplenomegaly (20%)
Musculoskeletal (10–15%)	Polyarthritis, bone cysts, myositis
Myocardial (5%)	Palpitations, syncope, dizziness, chest pain, arrhythmia, sudden death
Nervous system (5%)	Seizures, basal granulomatoid meningitis, hypothalamic hypopituitarism or hypothyroidism, cranial nerve palsies, hydrocephalus
Exocrine glands (4%)	Painless swelling parotid glands, keratoconjunctiva sicca‡
Renal	Hypercalcemia (10–20%), hypercalciuria (20–25%), nephrocalcinosis

*Percentage of patients with involvement.
†Anterior uveitis, parotid gland enlargement, facial palsy, fever.
‡Lacrimal gland enlargement, xerostomia, xerophthalmia.

CLINICAL MANIFESTATIONS

Subjective

Characteristic symptoms from pulmonary, ocular, or cutaneous involvement predominate the majority of patients' clinical presentations (Table 13–37–1). Unusual signs or symptoms from commonly affected organs or less frequently involved organs may delay the clinical suspicion for the disease. Systemic complaints including fever, chills, myalgias, arthralgias, weight loss, and fatigue are not uncommon and their presence does not exclude the diagnosis.

A prior history of sarcoidosis or abnormal chest radiograph, exposure to tuberculosis, travel or residence in areas endemic for fungal disease, occupational exposures, or drug use may provide clinically useful information. Family history is unlikely to be contributory, though sporadic reports exist of sarcoidosis occurring in members of the same family.

Objective

Physical Examination

Findings on physical examination depend on the organ system involved (Table 13–37–1). Examination of the chest is usually normal, though end-inspiratory crackles or wheezing may be present. Ocular and cutaneous manifestations of the disease are common and fairly character-

TABLE 13–37–2. CHEST RADIOGRAPHIC STAGES IN SARCOIDOSIS

		Frequency (%)	
Description		Presentation	Spontaneous Remission
0.	Normal chest radiograph	10	
I.	Bilateral hilar adenopathy; paratracheal adenopathy possible	50	65–95
II.	Adenopathy with pulmonary parenchymal involvement	30	35–60
III.	Pulmonary parenchymal involvement without adenopathy	10	< 25%
IV.*	Pulmonary fibrosis with honeycombing		

*Variably delineated separately from stage III.
Source: The percentages shown in this table were compiled from data obtained from several sources.

istic. Hepatosplenomegaly and extrathoracic lymphadenopathy can occur.

Routine Laboratory Abnormalities

Routine laboratory tests may reveal abnormalities suggestive of sarcoidosis. Hypercalcemia or hypercalciuria, evidence of abnormal calcium metabolism, and elevated liver enzymes, especially alkaline phosphatase, may be present (Table 13–37–1). Polyclonal hypergammaglobulinemia is variably reported in 25 to 80% of patients and leukopenia occurs in 5 to 15%.

The chest radiograph may reveal bilateral hilar or mediastinal lymph node enlargement and/or pulmonary parenchymal involvement. Pulmonary fibrosis and honeycombing, or a normal chest radiograph, may be seen (Table 13–37–2).

PLAN

Diagnostic

Differential Diagnosis

Sarcoidosis is generally distinguished from other etiologies based on clinical presentation, radiographic appearance, and supporting data. Other diagnoses to be considered include infectious diseases (tuberculosis and fungal disease), hypersensitivity pneumonitis, pneumoconioses, foreign body granulomatosis, and lymphomas.

Diagnostic Options and Recommended Approach

At times the clinical and radiographic appearances are sufficiently characteristic that additional diagnostic studies are not required. A baseline evaluation, including ocular screening, liver function tests, serum calcium level, and pulmonary function tests should be performed, even in the absence of symptoms, to exclude subclinical organ involvement and to serve as a reference for monitoring progression or remission of disease. In symptomatic patients, evaluation of other organ systems in addition to the baseline assessment may be indicated by the clinical presentation. Tuberculin skin testing with controls is generally performed and usually reveals cutaneous anergy. Pulmonary function tests show evidence of restrictive lung disease, with decreased lung volumes and diffusion capacity in 40 to 70% of patients tested. Evidence of airflow obstruction may be present in up to one third of patients, and airway hyperreactivity to methacholine challenge is demonstrable in a smaller percentage of patients.

The need for tissue diagnosis should be determined clinically. Pathologic confirmation of the diagnosis is not always required. This is especially true in an asymptomatic patient without clinical evidence to suggest lymphoma or an infectious etiology. When tissue diagnosis is required, fiberoptic bronchoscopy with transbronchial biopsy of the lung is the method most frequently employed. It is diagnostic in 75 to 90% of patients with abnormal chest radiographs (stages I–III) and in up to 50% with normal radiographs (stage 0). If other organ involvement is apparent and readily accessible, alternative biopsy sites to establish the diagnosis can be considered (i.e., skin, conjunctiva). Although mediastinoscopy is reported to be diagnostic in up to 95% of patients with intrathoracic lymphadenopathy and liver biopsy may be positive in 75 to 90% of patients, these procedures are generally not required or routinely employed. Similarly, open lung biopsy is rarely needed.

The Kveim test has been used as a diagnostic tool. Variable results based on the source of antigen and a long delay (4–6 weeks) in diagnosis have limited the test's clinical utility. Serum angiotensin converting enzyme and gallium-67 scanning have been extensively evaluated but have not fulfilled their earlier promise of providing a reliable, noninvasive method of diagnosis. Serum angiotensin converting enzyme is neither sensitive nor specific. It is variably elevated in 40 to 80% of sarcoid patients and may be elevated in association with a variety of other disorders, including infections (tuberculosis, fungal, HIV), intravenous drug use, Gaucher's disease, and liver cirrhosis. Gallium scan is positive in 60 to 80% of patients but is also nonspecific. The distribution of uptake may be suggestive with bilateral hilar uptake more commonly seen in sarcoidosis, and extrathoracic lymph node uptake more commonly seen in lymphoma, but overlap exists and the overall diagnostic utility of this information is limited.

Bronchoalveolar lavage in sarcoidosis characteristically demonstrates an alveolar lymphocytosis. The increase in lymphocytes is due almost exclusively to an increase in the helper T-cell subset. Although a great deal of information has been forthcoming from bronchoalveolar lavage studies, its precise role in diagnosis and treatment decisions remains to be determined. Persistence of alveolitis appears to be a poor prognostic indicator, but is neither diagnostic nor an established indication for treatment independent of clinical and physiologic correlation.

High resolution computed tomography (HRCT) provides superior anatomic detail compared with conventional chest radiography. It may play a role in predicting response to therapy by demonstrating evidence of active alveolitis versus end-stage lung disease. In sarcoidosis, characteristic findings on HRCT include parenchymal lesions in a peribronchovascular distribution, with relative sparing of lower lobes; and focal, nodular, or ground glass opacities. In idiopathic pulmonary fibrosis, subpleural and basilar regions of the lung are preferentially affected. Focal nodules are rare and linear, reticular opacities or honeycomb cysts are the predominant lesions. HRCT does not provide information regarding etiology and is not a diagnostic tool. Its role in the clinical management of sarcoidosis requires further study.

Therapeutic

No definitive therapy exists for sarcoidosis. Corticosteroids have been used in an attempt to ameliorate symptoms and prevent progression of disease. Estimation of treatment efficacy has been favorably biased by the overall benign clinical course and prognosis of the disease and the high rate of remission even in the absence of therapy. Corticosteroids are generally effective in suppressing the clinical and physiologic manifestations of disease in 70 to 90% of patients; however, relapse is common (30–50%) when treatment is stopped, and demonstration of long-term benefit is lacking. Treatment should therefore be reserved for patients with significant symptoms not controlled with other therapy or with evidence of vital organ involvement (i.e., ocular, heart, and central nervous system). Asymptomatic patients with progressive deterioration of lung function should also be considered for therapy.

The optimal dose and duration of corticosteroid therapy is poorly defined. A maximum dose of 1 mg/kg/d prednisone or equivalent for life-threatening organ system involvement (cardiac, ocular, or central nervous system), with lower doses (30–40 mg/d) suggested for non-life-threatening organ involvement (hypercalcemia, pulmonary), can be generally surmised from current recommendations. Duration of therapy for a minimum of 1 year, with an average treatment duration of 18 to 36 months, has been suggested but may unnecessarily prolong exposure to corticosteroids. In the absence of any evidence indicating that therapy alters the course or eventual outcome of disease, a more rational approach may be to follow patients' response to therapy, with gradual withdrawal and discontinuation of corticosteroids when clinically and physiologically stable. If relapse occurs, therapy may be reinstituted. Conversion to alternate-day dosing should be attempted if prolonged treatment with corticosteroids is required.

In certain instances, systemic corticosteroids are unnecessary. Inhaled corticosteroids have relatively low toxicity and, when used in relatively high doses (i.e., budesonide 1600 µg/d or equivalent), may suppress markers of alveolitis. In patients with mild pulmonary sarcoid, especially if cough, wheezing, or signs of bronchial hyperreactivity are present, this form of therapy may be beneficial. Ocular involvement manifested by anterior uveitis may be managed with topical corticosteroid drops and ointments. Cutaneous sarcoid may be controlled with hydroxychloroquine or topical therapy. Hypercalcemia may be controlled with hydroxychloroquine in some cases. Spontaneous remission occurs in approximately 90% of patients presenting with an acute onset of symptoms and stage I chest radiographs. In this group, corticosteroid treatment can generally be avoided, with nonsteroidal agents used for symptomatic treatment.

Other agents have been used with variable success in patients with refractory disease or those unable to tolerate corticosteroids (Table 13–37–3). These agents have been used in anecdotal cases, in small series of patients, or with a presumed benefit based on the drug's mecha-

TABLE 13–37–3. THERAPEUTIC ALTERNATIVES IN REFRACTORY DISEASE

Agent	Dose	Toxicity
Methotrexate	10 mg/wk to 20 mg twice weekly	Liver
Azathioprine	200 mg/d	Bone marrow
Cyclophosphamide	1–2.5 mg/kg/d	Bone marrow, bladder
Chlorambucil	4–12 mg/d	Bone marrow
Cyclosporin A	5–7 mg/kg/d	Renal, hypertension
Chloroquine	250–500 mg qd*	Ocular
Hydoxychloroquine	200 mg bid	Ocular

*May be administered bid.
Source: The figures shown in this table were compiled from data obtained from several sources.

nism of action. Although no strong recommendation can be made for any particular agent or regimen, these drugs may be considered for use in select cases as an adjunct or alternative to corticosteroid therapy.

Transplantation may be considered in appropriate candidates with progressive deterioration in specific organ function. Recurrence of disease in transplanted donor lungs has occurred, despite treatment with corticosteroids and immunosuppressive agents, but is of unclear clinical significance.

FOLLOW-UP

Asymptomatic patients without evidence of significant organ involvement should be considered for follow-up at 6- to 12-month intervals for 2 to 3 years. Pulmonary function tests should be performed to detect subclinical deterioration in function, and liver enzyme and serum calcium determinations should be considered annually. In symptomatic patients or individuals receiving therapy, follow-up should be more frequent and determined by the degree of clinical acuity. Pulmonary function tests are followed to monitor response to therapy or to detect physiologic deterioration. Diffusing capacity is the most common variable monitored. Spirometry and lung volumes should also be followed. Normal variability in test results should be taken into account when interpreting changes in lung function.

Serum angiotensin converting enzyme has not been found to be a reliable marker of disease activity, although peak level may correlate with prognosis. Serial determinations are performed by some clinicians but are probably of little clinical utility. Chest radiograph changes may not reflect disease state or functional level and are similarly unreliable. Radiographic improvement or deterioration can be seen without parallel changes in functional status.

DISCUSSION
Prevalence and Incidence

Sarcoidosis has a worldwide distribution. The prevalence of disease varies significantly between geographic regions. To some extent this may reflect medical practice and the relative frequency with which routine chest x-rays are obtained in a specific region. The highest reported incidence rate is from Sweden (64/100,000), and the disease appears to be rare in Africa and Central and South America. The reported rate from North America, Europe, Japan, and the United Kingdom is 10 to 20 per 100,000, and from New York City, 40 per 100,000.

Related Basic Science
Immunology

At sites of disease activity increased numbers of activated mononuclear phagocytes (macrophages, monocytes) and helper/inducer T cells (Leu 3+ or CD4+), reduced numbers of suppressor/cytotoxic cells (Leu 2+ or CD8+), and an increased CD4+:CD8+ ratio have been demonstrated. Interactions between activated macrophages and T lymphocytes lead to the production and release of cytokines that dictate the evolution and immunoregulation of the granulomatous lesion. In the peripheral blood, a decrease in T lymphocytes and a blunted immune response are noted.

Activated helper T lymphocytes and/or loss of regulation by suppressor T cells appear to play a role in the activation of B lymphocytes, resulting in hypergammaglobulinemia.

Genetics

Sporadic reports of the occurrence of sarcoidosis in families and some association between specific HLA antigens with various manifestations of sarcoidosis have lent support to a genetic predisposition for sarcoidosis. Major histocompatibility loci and HLA-DR antigens may modulate the evolution and expression of disease in genetically susceptible individuals.

Pathology

The granulomatous lesion in sarcoidosis is typical but not specific. In the lung, activated T lymphocytes and alveolar macrophages infiltrate the airspace and interstitium. Interactions between the lymphocytes, alveolar macrophages, fibroblasts, and other cells in the lung dictate the course of disease. Alveolar macrophages may amplify inflammation and fibrogenesis via release of various biochemical markers and cytokines (fibronectin, alveolar macrophage-derived growth factor, oxygen radicals, tumor necrosis factor, interleukin-1, hyaluronate, neopterin, procollagen, collagenase) or may suppress or downregulate the inflammatory response. Resolution of the alveolitis or progression with development of granulomatous lesions may occur. The central core of the granuloma, composed of epithelioid cells and multinucleated giant cells, is surrounded by lymphocytes with an admixture of plasma cells. Central necrosis is rare. These granulomatous lesions may resolve or progress to fibrosis and permanent scarring.

Natural History and Its Modification with Treatment

Sarcoidosis is generally presumed to follow a benign clinical course. Although estimates vary, probably at least in part based on the population surveyed, up to 80% of patients have a mild to moderate course, with resolution of disease possible even in the absence of treatment.

Progressive, unremitting disease with significant organ dysfunction and morbidity may occur in approximately 20% of patients. Treatment may alleviate symptoms and laboratory evidence of disease, but the overall course of the disease and clinical outcome does not appear to be affected. Predicting the course an individual patient will experience is difficult, though older age, multisystem organ involvement, and radiographic stage III have been associated with a worse prognosis.

Prevention

In the absence of an identifiable cause for the disease, primary prevention is not possible. Therapy to limit progression of disease appears to be unsuccessful in altering the clinical outcome. Morbidity related to treatment should be minimized by avoiding prolonged or unnecessary therapy.

Cost Containment

The diagnostic evaluation should be performed as expeditiously as possible. Ancillary tests should be ordered only when additional information is expected to be of clinical relevance. Studies that are unlikely to impact on patient care should probably be deferred, except in research settings.

REFERENCES

Fanburg BL, Pitt EA. Sarcoidosis. In: Murray JF, Nadel JA, eds. Textbook of respiratory medicine. Philadelphia: Saunders, 1988.

Hunninghake GW, Gilbert S, Pueringer R, et al. Outcome of the treatment for sarcoidosis. Am J Respir Crit Care Med 1994;149:893.

Muthiah MM, Macfarlane JT. Current concepts in the management of sarcoidosis. Drugs 1990;40(2):231.

Sharma OP. Pulmonary sarcoidosis and corticosteroids. Am Rev Respir Dis 1993;147:1598.

Takada K, Ina Y, Noda M, et al. The clinical course and prognosis of patients with severe, moderate or mild sarcoidosis. J Clin Epidemiol 1993;46:359.

CHAPTER 13–38

Solitary Pulmonary Nodule

Urmila Shivaram, M.D.

DEFINITION

A solitary pulmonary nodule can be detected on the chest x-ray film. It is defined as a solitary opacity within pulmonary parenchyma that measures between 1 and 4 cm in the maximum diameter. It is fairly well circumscribed without hilar enlargement or atelectasis.

ETIOLOGY

The nodules seen on the chest x-ray film can be of varied etiology and can be classified as benign or malignant nodules (Table 13–38–1). The benign lesions can be grouped into infectious, neoplastic, and miscellaneous varieties, whereas malignant lesions can be primary or metastatic.

CRITERIA FOR DIAGNOSIS

Suggestive

Certain clinical and radiologic features may distinguish between benign and malignant lesions (Table 13–38–2). Certain characteristics such as increased age, smoking history, prior history of malignancy, larger size of the nodule, and shagginess of the borders are associated with increased likelihood of malignancy. If the lesion grows over time, it does

not necessarily indicate malignancy, as some pulmonary hamartomas and granulomas have been reported to grow over time.

Definitive

Definitive diagnosis is obtained by histologic evaluation in most cases. Certain features on computed tomography (CT) scan of the chest are diagnostic of granulomas and hamartomas.

CLINICAL MANIFESTATIONS
Subjective

The solitary pulmonary nodules are usually asymptomatic and present as an incidental finding on a chest radiograph. On rare occasions, patients present with a history of cough, hemoptysis, or wheezing. A past history of having had a similar lesion on a chest roentgenogram is suggestive of benign nature of the lesion. A history of tuberculosis, fungal disease, or residence in endemic areas for these infections suggests the etiology of granuloma. Occupational history of exposure to asbestos is important in the diagnosis of rounded atelectasis. Travel history is essential in making a diagnosis of uncommon conditions such as echinococcal or dirofilarial infections. Patients with a history of smoking are more likely to have a malignant nodule.

TABLE 13–38–1. CAUSES OF SOLITARY PULMONARY NODULE

Malignant
Bronchogenic carcinoma
Metastatic nodule
Other
    Kaposi's sarcoma
    Lymphoma
    Carcinoid

Benign
Granulomas
    Tuberculosis
    Histoplasmosis
    Coccidioidomycosis
    Cryptococcosis
    Blastomycosis
    Aspergillosis
Other Infections
    Ecchinococcal cyst
    Dirofilaria immitis
Neoplastic
    Hamartomas
    Fibroma
    Lipoma
    Teratoma
    Chondroma

Miscellaneous
Sequestration
Silicotic nodule
Pulmonary hematoma
Arteriovenous malformation
Pulmonary infarction
Wegener's granulomatosis
Bronchial cyst
Rheumatoid nodule
Nodular pulmonary amyloidosis
Pseudotumor
Rounded atelectasis
Bronchogenic cyst

Objective

Physical Examination

Physical examination is usually normal. Rarely, localized wheezing may be present on examination. Diagnosis is based on historical and radiologic presentation.

Routine Laboratory Abnormalities

The routine laboratory test results are usually normal except for chest roentgenogram that shows the solitary pulmonary nodule.

PLANS

Diagnostic

Differential Diagnosis

The characteristics of the nodule on chest roentgenogram are useful in the differential diagnosis. The crucial factor in the differential diagnosis

TABLE 13–38–2. CRITERIA FOR DIAGNOSIS

Features suggestive of benignity
    Age less than 30 years
    Nonsmoker
Features diagnostic of benignity
    Patterns of calcification
        Popcorn-like calcification in hamartoma
        Laminated calcification in granuloma
        Homogeneous dense calcification
    Absence of growth of the lesion over 24 months

is to determine whether the lesion is benign or malignant. In some cases a previous film showing an identical lesion may have been overlooked. Absence of growth over time in comparison to a previous film is characteristic of benign nodules and may obviate the need for any further diagnostic tests. Lobulation and shagginess of the margins of the lesion on the chest radiograph suggest malignancy. The presence of satellite lesions is common in granulomatous lesions. The majority of lesions larger than 3 cm in diameter are malignant. Most benign lesions are smaller; less than 5% of benign nodules are larger than 3 cm in diameter. The characteristics of the lesion are better defined on CT scan of the chest, which may reveal definite patterns of calcification. Hamartomas may reveal fat density tissue and popcorn pattern of calcification. CT densitometry, which involves the assessment of the CT number from thin sections of CT scans in apparently noncalcified nodules, has been found to differentiate benign from malignant lesions. High CT numbers (164 Hounsfield units or greater) are reported in benign lesions, whereas malignant lesions have a relatively lower CT number.

Diagnostic Options

A CT scan of the chest that reveals a benign variety of calcification obviates the need for any further workup. In all other cases of a new nodule or nodule increasing in size, an attempt at histologic diagnosis should be made. In patients in whom a benign diagnosis is likely, fiberoptic bronchoscopy with directed biopsy provides histologic diagnosis. Bronchoscopic biopsy is preferable in patients presenting with hemoptysis or localized wheezing, as it allows examination of the airways. The diagnostic yield of bronchoscopy is poor in lesions less than 2 cm in diameter. Percutaneous transthoracic aspiration of the lung is an alternative to bronchoscopy in providing a definite diagnosis if the lesion is accessible, and it has a greater yield with larger lesions. If an infectious etiology is identified by either of these procedures, a thoracotomy can be avoided. Excisional biopsy by thoracoscopy or thoracotomy is a reliable method of obtaining a histologic diagnosis and represents the preferred approach when malignancy is considered likely. When pulmonary arteriovenous malformation is suspected, a pulmonary angiogram is indicated.

Recommended Diagnostic Approach

A proposed scheme of diagnostic evaluation is depicted in Figure 13–38–1.

Therapeutic

Therapeutic Options

Surgical resection is the procedure of choice for all patients with a solitary pulmonary nodule that is new or growing with no clear features of benignity on radiologic or histologic evaluation. This can be accomplished by video-assisted thoracoscopic resection, which is less invasive than thoracotomy. In some cases, open thoracotomy and resection may be required. In those patients with mediastinal adenopathy seen on CT scan of the chest, biopsy of the lymph nodes is indicated prior to resection of the nodule. If the lymph nodes are positive for malignancy, more extensive resection may be required. When carcinoma of the lung is diagnosed prior to surgery, a lobectomy is performed. In patients with a single metastatic lesion, wedge resection is performed if there are no other metastases. In patients with malignant nodules who are inoperable because of comorbid conditions or unresectable because of metastases elsewhere, radiation therapy or chemotherapy may be indicated. In those patients with a benign diagnosis, observation is adequate in many instances. In some patients, specific therapy is directed to the etiologic factor, as in tuberculosis or fungal infections. Those patients with positive reaction to PPD and a granuloma in the chest x-ray are candidates for isoniazid chemoprophylaxis if not previously treated for tuberculosis.

Recommended Approach

Excision is recommended in all malignant lesions and those lesions with no definite features of benignity. In cases of primary bronchogenic carcinoma, a lobectomy is indicated. Further therapy is directed by the histologic features. A single metastasis to the lung is best approached

Solitary Pulmonary Nodule

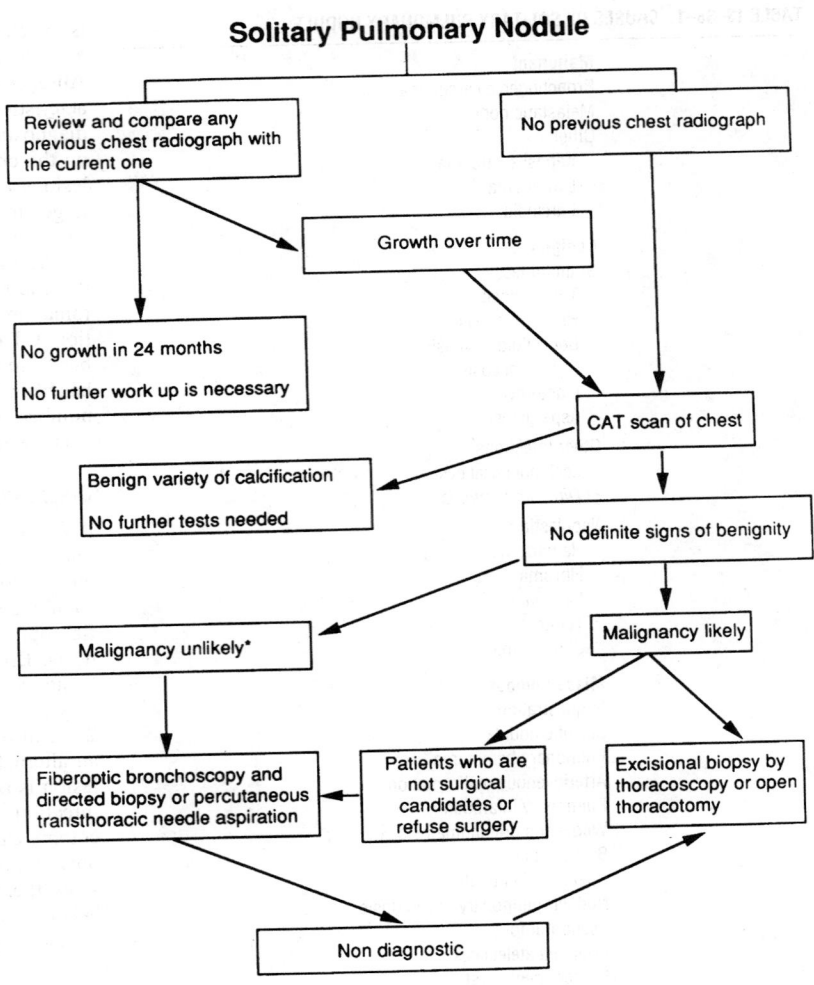

Figure 13–38–1. Proposed scheme for evaluation of solitary pulmonary nodule. *In a nonsmoker under age 30 whose nodule is less than 2 cm in diameter, observation with follow-up chest radiograph is appropriate. CAT, computed axial tomography.

by resection of the nodule by thoracoscopy or thoracotomy. Benign lesions do not require surgical resection. The indications for treating the specific granulomatous lesions are covered in the respective chapters.

FOLLOW-UP

A patient with a small nodule, no significant smoking history, and age less than 30 may be followed without a histologic diagnosis because of the low probability of malignancy. Periodic chest radiographs for 2 to 3 years following the original presentation are indicated in these patients. If the lesion remains stable, no further follow-up is necessary. Patients with resection of malignant nodules require close follow-up. In some studies, measurement of tumor markers such as tissue polypeptide antigen and neuron-specific enolase has been noted to reliably indicate recurrence after complete resection of bronchogenic carcinoma. In instances where a benign diagnosis has been established and specific therapy is not indicated, further follow-up is generally not required.

DISCUSSION

The major concern in the management of a solitary pulmonary nodule is to differentiate a malignant from a benign lesion. Early resection of malignant lesions and avoidance of surgical excision of the benign lesions are the primary objectives in these cases.

Prevalence and Incidence

Among all solitary pulmonary nodules approximately 35% of the total are primary bronchogenic carcinoma, 9% are metastatic nodules, and the remaining nodules are benign. According to the American Cancer Society, the estimated incidence of bronchogenic carcinoma for 1994 is

approximately 172,000 cases, and one third of these present as a nodule on the initial chest roentgenogram (Verbal communication, American Cancer Society). Based on this, the estimated incidence of bronchogenic carcinoma for 1994 presenting as a solitary pulmonary nodule is 57,000. The incidence of malignancy increases with age, and in patients over 50 years, 65% of the nodules are malignant. Of the benign nodules, the granulomata constitute the largest group of lesions, up to 80% in one series. The etiology of the granuloma depends on the endemicity of tuberculosis and fungal infections in the area.

Related Basic Science

Genetics

There is a genetic predisposition to bronchogenic carcinoma, and the trait is expressed in the presence of environmental insults. Altered expression of certain growth factors like bombesin, transforming growth factor α, and insulin-like growth factor has been reported in bronchogenic carcinoma. Mutation of *ras* and p53 oncogenes and amplification of *myc* oncogene have been noted in some lung cancer cell lines. Increased expression of proto-oncogenes like P185C-*erb*B-2 is associated with poor survival in patients with adenocarcinoma of lung. Polymerase chain reaction has been useful in identifying *Mycobacterium tuberculosis* and can be useful in the diagnosis of granulomas of tuberculosis origin.

Immunology

When Wegener's granulomatosis is considered a diagnostic possibility, antineutrophil cytoplasmic antibody has a high degree of confirmatory specificity and sensitivity.

Natural History and Its Modification with Treatment

An asymptomatic patient with a benign nodule generally requires no therapy. Patients with an infectious nodule and clinical features of infection may progress if not treated. Radiologic reduction or resolution is the expected outcome of therapy in the absence of calcification. In solitary malignant pulmonary nodules, the operability and curative resectability rate is much higher than in lung cancer as a whole. In untreated patients, however, it results in death. Outcome of surgical resection of solitary metastasis is more favorable in an asymptomatic patient.

Prevention

Abstinence from or cessation of smoking decreases the incidence of bronchogenic carcinoma, which is the most common cause of malignant solitary pulmonary nodule. Avoiding exposure to ionizing radiation and asbestos decreases the chance of development of bronchogenic carcinoma.

Cost Containment

Review of available chest radiographs or CT scans is essential. If the lesion is unchanged over 24 months, no further workup is necessary. A CT scan showing a benign variety of calcification also saves further diagnostic procedures. In a patient with low probability of carcinoma, follow-up chest x-ray is a cost-effective approach. A benign diagnosis obtained by either fiberoptic bronchoscopy or percutaneous needle aspiration saves the expense of thoracoscopy or thoracotomy. Overall cost effectiveness is not proven, however, because of the increased length of stay associated with bronchoscopy, which may be due to unrelated causes.

REFERENCES

Mack MJ, Hazelrigg SR, Landreneau RJ, Acuff TE. Thoracoscopy for the diagnosis of the indeterminate solitary pulmonary nodule. Ann Thorac Surg 1993;56:825.

Midthin DE, Sweasen SJ, Jett JR. Approach to the solitary pulmonary nodule. Mayo Clin Proc 1993;68:378.

Stoller JK, Ahmad M, Rice TW. Solitary pulmonary nodule. Cleve Clin J Med 1988;55:68.

Templeton PA, Zerhouni E. Computed tomography of the solitary pulmonary nodule and focal pulmonary disease. Curr Opin Radiol 1989;1:25.

Toomes H, Delphendahl A, Manke HG, Moykopf IV. The coin lesion of the lung, a review of 955 resected coin lesions. Cancer 1983;51:534.

CHAPTER 13–39

Carcinoma of the Lung

Spiro Demetis, M.D.

DEFINITION

The term *lung cancer* applies to malignant transformation of any cellular element from the tracheobronchial tree or lung parenchyma. The greatest proportion of lung cancers arise from the bronchial tree, hence the term *bronchogenic carcinoma*.

ETIOLOGY

Tobacco smoke is clearly the most important risk factor for the development of bronchogenic carcinoma. Only about 2% of lung cancers occur in nonsmokers. In the United States, 80% of lung cancers in women and 90% in men are attributed to smoking. Many carcinogens have been identified in tobacco smoke including aromatic hydrocarbons, nitrosamines, peroxides, vinyl chloride, and nickel. The risk for developing lung cancer is directly related to the cumulative amount of exposure to tobacco smoke (number of cigarettes and years of use), as well as younger age of initiation, high tar and nicotine content, increasing depth of smoke inhalation, and use of filterless cigarettes. Previous reports that after 10 to 15 years of smoking cessation, the risk for developing lung cancer is that of a lifelong nonsmoker may be inaccurate. Although the risk for lung cancer drops significantly after a decade of smoking cessation, in a recent study from Japan, the risk in subjects who stopped smoking from 20 to 24 years was ten times that of lifetime nonsmokers.

Passive smoking as a risk factor is a topic of controversy. Although there is a trend toward increased risk for lung cancer with significant exposure to environmental tobacco smoke, when compared with "non-exposed" nonsmokers, only 3 of 13 studies reported a statistical significance. The present consensus is that significant and prolonged exposure to environmental tobacco smoke results in an overall odds ratio for lung cancer of 1.34. It is believed that 3000 to 5000 lung cancer deaths annually are secondary to exposure to environmental tobacco smoke.

The list of potential lung carcinogens in the workplace is long and includes arsenic, asbestos, ionizing radiation, nickel, vinyl chloride, aromatic hydrocarbons, and synthetic fibers. Most of these probably act as cocarcinogens with tobacco smoke, and the risk for lung cancer in exposed smokers is multiplicative. Nonoccupational exposure to asbestos is not a public health problem and produces a negligible lifetime risk for lung cancer. Occupational exposure in a nonsmoker results in an odds ratio of 3 to 5 for lung cancer. This increases to 90 in an active smoker.

Radon is a decay product of naturally occurring radium in the ground. It produces alpha particles that have a direct carcinogenic effect on the respiratory epithelium. Levels in U.S. homes range from 1 to 100 pCi/L of ambient air. Lung cancer deaths attributed to radon in nonsmokers range from 5000 to 10,000. Remedial measures are recommended for homes consistently testing greater than 4 pCi/L air. Radon probably acts synergistically with tobacco smoke.

Pulmonary fibrosis and chronic bronchitis/emphysema are chronic lung diseases that independently carry an increased risk for the development of lung cancer after correcting for other risk factors. Poor clearance of carcinogens, squamous metaplasia and atypial epithelial proliferation, and/or chronic oxidative exposure are the probable reasons for the increased risk for lung cancer in these disease states.

CRITERIA FOR DIAGNOSIS
Suggestive

Lung cancer should be suspected in any patient who presents with an unexplained lung mass, regardless of the presence or absence of symptoms. Pulmonary infiltrates persisting after 6 to 8 weeks of proper antibiotic therapy for pneumonia should raise the possibility of bronchogenic carcinoma. Lung cancer should always be included in the differential diagnosis of chest pain and chronic cough in a smoker, especially when complicated by hemoptysis, even in the presence of a normal chest radiograph.

Definitive

The ultimate diagnosis of lung carcinoma, in a patient suspected of having the disease, requires the detection of malignant cells in a cytologic specimen (sputum, pleural fluid, lymph node aspirate, or bronchial washings) or areas of malignancy in a biopsy specimen by an experienced pathologist.

CLINICAL MANIFESTATIONS

Subjective

As early detection of lung cancer is probably the single most important factor in determining prognosis, recognizing its clinical manifestations is imperative. Only about 15% of patients with lung cancer are asymptomatic at the time of diagnosis, and as a group have a better prognosis. The clinical presentation of lung cancer is diverse and is dependent on cell type, tumor location and its relation to surrounding structures, biological behavior of the tumor, and presence or absence of other coexisting diseases.

Reviews of most studies indicate that cough is the most frequent symptom, followed by dyspnea, chest pain, and hemoptysis (Table 13–39–1). Symptoms are typically ignored initially or attributed to benign disease processes by the patients, resulting in significant delays before consulting a physician. Hemoptysis is the most alarming symptom, and patients who experience it usually seek help expeditiously. Loss of appetite, weakness, and some loss of weight are almost always reported at the time of diagnosis. Critical narrowing of a bronchus by endobronchial tumor or extrinsic compression may result in postobstructive pneumonia with the possible accompanying symptoms of fever, dyspnea, nonproductive cough or hemoptysis, pleuritic chest pain, and so on. Localized chest wall pain may be secondary to direct thoracic wall invasion or by hematogenous metastases to the ribs, sternum, vertebral bodies, pleura, muscles, or skin. Referred pain to the shoulders, neck, and arms, along with weakness of the shoulder muscles, may be seen when there is direct invasion of the brachial plexus (apical or pulmonary sulcus tumors). Dysphagia and hoarseness of voice are ominous signs that usually indicate significant extension of the tumor to the mediastinum. By the same mechanism, headache, facial fullness, flushing, and edema of the upper extremities may be reported if there is superior vena cava compression with intraluminal thrombosis (superior vena cava syndrome). Not infrequently, the initial clinical manifestations of lung cancer may be the signs and symptoms of cardiac tamponade resulting from direct or hematogenous spread to the pericardium.

The clinical manifestations of metastatic disease are variable but most commonly involve bone pain and neurologic symptoms such as difficult-to-control headaches, cranial nerve palsies, hemiparesis, seizures, and paralysis from spinal cord or nerve root compression. Although hematogenous spread to the liver and adrenals is commonly seen, only rarely and in very advanced cases, does one see evidence of hepatic or adrenal insufficiency. Symptoms from the multitude of paraneoplastic syndromes associated with bronchogenic carcinoma may be reported (Table 13–39–2).

Objective

Physical Examination

The physical examination findings are variable and depend on the extent of intrathoracic spread of tumor and the presence/location of distant metastases. Examination of the chest and lungs may be normal.

TABLE 13–39–1. SYMPTOMS AND SIGNS OF LUNG CANCER AT INITIAL PRESENTATION

Symptoms/Signs	Frequency (%) (range)
No symptoms	15
Cough	75 (30–87)
Dyspnea	46 (8–58)
Hemoptysis	43 (6–57)
Chest pain	35 (30–60)
Weight loss	32 (8–69)
Bone pain	8 (0–25)
Clubbing	7 (0–20)
Hoarseness	7 (1–18)
Superior vena cava syndrome	4 (0–7)

Data obtained from Hyde and Hyde (1974).

TABLE 13–39–2. PARANEOPLASTIC SYNDROMES ASSOCIATED WITH BRONCHOGENIC CARCINOMA

Endocrine	Cutaneous
Hypercalcemia	Acanthosis nigricans
Syndrome of inappropriate ADH secretion	Erythema multiforme
Cushing's syndrome	Hyperpigmentation
Hypoglycemia	Hematologic
Galactorrhea	Anemia
Gynecomastia	Leukemoid reaction
Carcinoid syndrome	Eosinophilia
Hyperthyroidism	Thrombocytopenia
Neuromuscular	Dysproteinemia
Eaton–Lambert syndrome	Other
Mononeuritis	Nonbacterial endocarditis
Polyomyositis	Arterial thrombosis
Encephalopathy	Venous thrombosis
Myelopathy	Pulmonary embolism
Skeletal	Constitutional symptoms
Pulmonary hypertrophic osteoarthropathy	Fevers
Digital clubbing	Anorexia
	Weight loss

Localized inspiratory wheezes may be heard with partial obstruction of a bronchus. Lack of air entry to a particular lung segment and percussion dullness suggest complete bronchial obstruction with postobstructive collapse of that segment or the presence of very large pleural effusion with compressive atelectasis. Deviation of the trachea and heart may also be noted. The presence of single or multiple hard, fixed, painless, cervical or supraclavicular nodes is an important clinical finding confirming advanced inoperable disease. Vocal cord paralysis may be detected by indirect laryngoscopy. It is secondary to invasion of the recurrent laryngeal nerve, and implies extensive mediastinal spread of tumor. Phrenic nerve paralysis may result in dyspnea and may be confirmed by fluoroscopy. Impressive jugular venous distension may be seen with compression of the superior vena cava or pericardial tamponade. Fullness of the face, upper extremity edema, and superficial venous collaterals of the lateral neck and upper extremities suggest the obstructed superior vena cava syndrome. Enlarged cardiac silhouette, severe dyspnea (oftentimes with unimpressive lung parenchymal radiologic findings), narrow pulse pressure, and low cardiac output state (progressive increased anion gap metabolic acidosis) all suggest cardiac tamponade. These findings should prompt the urgent request for an echocardiogram. Pain may be elicited on palpation of the skeletal structures at any location from metastases.

Variable neurologic deficits may be detected on examination depending at the level of involvement and the presence of paraneoplastic syndromes. Fundoscopic evidence of papilledema, even in the absence of symptoms, should encourage the performance of cranial computed tomography to rule out brain metastases.

Routine Laboratory Abnormalities

The radiologic presentation of bronchogenic carcinoma is understandably diverse. A variable size mass may be seen clearly separated from the hilar structures on the chest radiograph. Pathologically, these tumors are most likely to represent the adenocarcinoma and large cell carcinoma varieties. Similarly, central tumors and endobronchial tumors are most likely to be of the squamous or oat cell types. Partial or complete atelectasis of a lung segment may be seen, and this usually indicates proximal endobronchial obstruction. Tracheal, mediastinal, or cardiac silhouette deviations, along with ipsilateral diaphragmatic elevation, strongly suggest a postobstructive process. Large tumors may cavitate secondary to autoinfarction of central blood supply, and may be confused with lung abscess. In addition, central cavitation and colonization of bronchogenic carcinoma with *Aspergillus* species have been repeatedly reported. Variable size pleural effusions may be seen. Often there may be evidence of contiguous spread of tumor to the mediastinum. Hilar and mediastinal nodes may be enlarged. Careful observation of the bony structures may reveal rib, sternum, or vertebral body erosions by direct tumor spread.

Other laboratory abnormalities may be seen. Spread to the liver usually results in early elevation of alkaline phosphatase and later elevation of other liver enzymes. The alkaline phosphatase may also be elevated secondary to bone metastases.

Hyponatremia secondary to inappropriate antidiuretic hormone secretion may be present. Hypercalcemia may be seen, usually in association with epidermoid carcinoma. Mild anemia may be present, but severe anemia should raise the suspicion of bone marrow invasion (seen most often with small cell carcinoma).

PLANS

Diagnostic

Differential Diagnosis

The differential diagnosis of a lung mass includes primary or metastatic malignancy, benign primary tumors, infectious processes (mycobacterial, fungal, bacterial, etc.), and noninfectious inflammatory processes (sarcoidosis, rheumatoid arthritis, Wegener's granulomatosis).

Diagnostic Options

In the process of evaluation of a patient with an intrathoracic mass, it is important to first prove the diagnosis of malignancy and then determine the clinical stage as accurately as possible.

When the clinical extent of disease is limited to the intrathoracic area, the main diagnostic tests available to the clinician include sputum cytology, fiberoptic bronchoscopy, and transthoracic needle aspiration. In advanced cases of lung cancer the diagnosis may sometimes be obtained by sampling peripheral sites such as lymph nodes, cutaneous nodules, bone, and bone marrow.

Sputum cytology is a noninvasive technique that should be used routinely. A positive result may spare the patient an invasive diagnostic study. Ideally, five consecutive morning specimens, after tooth brushing and mouth rinse, are needed to achieve maximum diagnostic yield. Squamous cell carcinoma, central location, and large tumor size are associated with a positive sputum cytology result. Although false-positive results are rare (1%), false-negative results occur with significant frequency (30–40%). Because of this poor negative predictive value, further diagnostic studies must always be ordered in a patient with a lung mass and negative sputum cytology.

The types of specimens obtained with fiberoptic bronchoscopy include bronchial washings, bronchial and transbronchial brushings, bronchoalveolar lavage, endobronchial or transbronchial forceps biopsies, and transtracheal or transbronchial needle aspirates. Samples from endoscopically visible tumors have the highest diagnostic yield (90–100%). The diagnostic yield with peripheral tumors is variable (30–60%) and depends primarily on the size of the lesion and the expertise of the bronchoscopist in the performance of transbronchial forceps biopsy and transbronchial needle aspiration. Possible complications with transbronchial forceps biopsy or needle aspiration include bleeding or pneumothorax. With peripheral tumors, computed tomography (CT) scan of the chest may be of some help in guiding the bronchoscopist. With peripheral lesions, even when a diagnosis is not established, fiberoptic bronchoscopy yields important information regarding staging and operability and, in the author's opinon, should always be performed before surgery is contemplated. Transbronchial needle aspiration, in experienced hands, can be used to sample mediastinal, subcarinal, and hilar nodes, further providing staging information.

For peripheral lesions, especially when small and in close proximity to the chest wall, transthoracic needle aspiration has the highest diagnostic yield; however, compared with fiberoptic bronchoscopy, transthoracic needle aspiration carries a significantly higher risk for pneumothorax. The risk of pneumothorax is directly related to the distance of the mass from the chest wall. The person performing this procedure should be proficient in the use of the Heimlich valve or other methods of treating clinically significant transthoracic needle aspiration-related pneumothoraces.

Recommended Approach

The evaluation of all patients with suspected lung cancer should begin with a thorough physical examination, with special attention to the cervical and supraclavicular nodes. Enlarged nodes should be aspirated. Involved nodes have a high diagnostic yield. If involved, they prove advanced disease (stage IIIB), and exclude surgery as a therapeutic option. Sputum cytology should be performed in all patients with suspected lung cancer. If negative, sputum cytology is followed by fiberoptic bronchoscopy or transtracheal needle aspiration depending on the location and size of the lesion. A CT scan is usually performed by this time, and may help with this selection.

The most important task for the pathologist is to distinguish between small cell lung carcinoma (SCLC) and non-small cell lung carcinoma (NSCLC). This distinction is important, as subsequent staging procedures, therapy, and prognosis vary drastically. The new staging system for NSCLC as proposed by Mountain (1987) and accepted by the World Health Organization is shown in Tables 13–39–3 and 13–39–4 and Figure 13–39–1. The most important study in the staging of NSCLC includes a CT scan of the chest that extends down to include the liver and adrenals. Whether or not contrast is necessary depends on the appearance of the mediastinum and the presence of liver or adrenal abnormalities. The unequivocal presence of mediastinal tumor extension indicates that a patient is not a surgical candidate. In cases where it is difficult to judge, magnetic resonance imaging may be of help, especially in evaluating for possible pulmonary artery involvement. Large mediastinal nodes (> 1 cm), usually indicate further evaluation with mediastinoscopy. Incidental benign primary adrenal tumors pose a common differential diagnostic problem. Whether all adrenal masses should be aspirated preoperatively is controversial. Tumors smaller than 2 cm that image "benign" by CT scan criteria should not be sampled. Larger size tumors should probably be routinely aspirated. Bone scans should be performed if symptoms of localized bone pain are present. Likewise CT of the head is usually performed in patients with neurologic deficits attributable to central nervous system pathology. An area of controversy is whether CT scans of the head should be routinely performed preoperatively in patients with the adenocarcinoma variety of NSCLC. The author performs this study preoperatively in adenocarcinoma patients with large size primary tumors and all surgical candidates with marginal lung function.

The staging of SCLC patients includes CT of chest/liver/adrenals, CT of head, bone scan, and bone marrow evaluation if anemia is present. SCLC is staged as limited or extensive. Limited disease is disease confined to one hemithorax with or without nodal involvement (N1–N3) and with or without ipsilateral malignant effusions. Extensive

TABLE 13–39–3. DEFINITIONS OF PRIMARY TUMOR AND NODAL INVOLVEMENT

Primary Tumor (T)

TX	Positive sputum cytology; tumor cannot be localized by chest x-ray or bronchoscopy
TIS	Carcinoma in situ
T1	Tumor < 3 cm and surrounded by lung or visceral pleura; on fiberoptic bronchoscopy, no evidence of invasion proximal to lobar bronchus
T2	Tumor > 3 cm or any size tumor that invades the visceral pleura or has associated atelectasis extending to the hilar region; on fiberoptic bronchoscopy, the tumor must be at least 2 cm away from the main carina
T3	Any size tumor with direct extention to the chest wall, diaphragm, mediastinal pleura, pericardium *without* invasion of the heart, great vessels, trachea, esophagus, or vertebral bodies
T4	Any size tumor with invasion of the mediastinum (heart, great vessels, trachea, esophagus, vertebral bodies) or carina, or the presence of a malignant pleural effusion

Nodal Involvement (N)

N0	No nodal involvement
N1	Peribronchial and/or ipsilateral hilar metastases
N2	Ipsilateral mediastinal or subcarinal nodal involvement
N3	Contralateral hilar or mediastinal or ipsilateral/contralateral scalene or supraclavicular nodal metastases

Source: Mountain FC. *The new International Staging System for lung cancer. Surg Clin North Am* 1987;67:925. Reproduced with permission from the publisher and author.

TABLE 13-39-4. TNM STAGING SYSTEM OF NON-SMALL CELL LUNG CANCER

Occult carcinoma	TX	N0	M0
Stage 0	TIS (carcinoma in situ)		
Stage I	T1	N0	M0
	T2	N0	M0
Stage II	T1	N0	M0
	T2	N0	M0
Stage IIIa	T3	N0,N1	M0
	Any T	N2	M0
Stage IIIb	Any T	N3	M0
	T4	Any N	M0
Stage IV	Any T	Any N	M1

Source: Mountain FC. The new International Staging System for lung cancer. Surg Clin North Am 1987;67(5):925. Reproduced with permission from the publisher and author.

disease refers to involvement of the contralateral hemithorax and/or distal sites.

Therapeutic

Therapeutic Options

The best chance for a cure in patients with NSCLC is surgical resection in patients with limited intrathoracic disease. This corresponds to stages I and II. The "gold standard" procedure is lobectomy along with extensive mediastinal lymph node dissection. More limited resections (seg-

mentectomies) have been performed in patients with very poor pulmonary reserve, but should be avoided in patients who can tolerate lobectomy. In very elderly debilitated patients with poor lung function, small (< 3 cm) peripheral tumors may be resected thoracoscopically. The obvious disadvantages with this procedure are inability to secure clean surgical margins and inability to sample the peribronchial or hilar/mediastinal nodes. Five-year survival rates with surgically documented stage I and II NSCLC are 70 and 45%, respectively. From these figures the prognostic significance of N1 (hilar nodes) involvement is obvious. Oftentimes, postoperative mediastinal radiation is given to patients with epidermoid cancers with positive hilar/mediastinal nodes. Although this practice has been shown to prevent local recurrence, there are no studies that document improved survival. In stage I and II patients who, for other reasons, cannot undergo resection, radiation therapy is an option. High doses (6000 rad) should be given. Survival can be significant at 3 to 5 years, if patients with small tumors have a good response to radiation therapy and are able to tolerate the regimen. Concomitant administration of *cis*-platinum may improve tumor response to radiation therapy.

Stage IIIA and IIIB patients are not considered surgical candidates. Stage IIIB patients probably have a survival similar to that of stage IV patients. A small select group of patients with stage IIIA disease may be surgical candidates. Five-year survival in patients with T3N0M0 (stage IIIA) may be comparable to that of stage II patients, after complete resection of the tumor and en bloc resection of the chest wall. This is especially true if the tumor is of the epidermoid variety. Several trials have been conducted, and others are still ongoing, to study the survival impact of preoperative chemotherapy/radiotherapy to N2M0 disease. The results to date have shown only a small improvement in survival, and today these therapies must be considered experimental until further

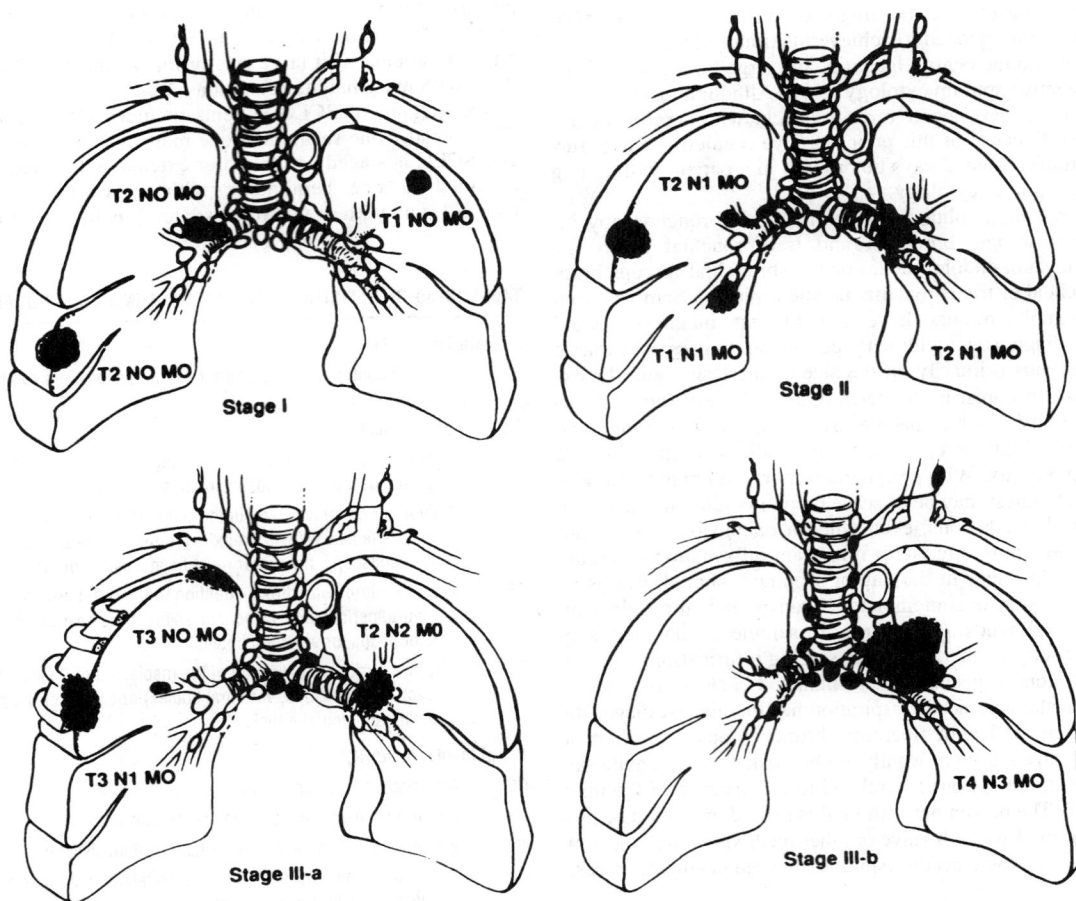

Figure 13-39-1. International Staging System for lung cancer. Diagrammatic representation of TNM subsets in each stage. *(Source: Mountain CF. Staging of lung cancer. In: Roth JA, Cox JD, Hong WK, eds. Advances in the diagnosis and therapy of lung cancer. 4th ed. Cambridge: Blackwell Scientific, 1993:112. Reproduced with permission of Blackwell Scientific Publications, Inc.)*

data are available. Inoperable stage III patients should be offered radiation therapy.

The management of stages IIIB and IV depends on the extent of disease and the patient's performance status. It must be individualized and, in each case, approved by an informed patient who understands the goals of such therapy. Palliative therapies may include conventional radiation therapy or brachytherapy for control of pain, mass effect, hemoptysis, or bronchial obstruction. Bronchoscopic laser therapy may be used to relieve obstruction resulting from large endobronchial/endotracheal tumors. For the same purpose, endobronchial stents may be placed by experienced physicians with rigid bronchoscopy.

Recommended Approach

Surgery should be aggressively pursued for patients with stage I and II disease, even in cases of marginal lung function. Lung perfusion scans should be used to predict the postoperative forced expiratory volume in 1 second (FEV_1) in patients undergoing lobectomy with marginal lung function or patients undergoing pneumonectomy. Usually an estimated postresection FEV_1 that is about 40% of predicted or greater, should allow one to undergo surgery. Preoperative carbon dioxide retention is a recognized risk factor for increased perioperative morbidity but is not an absolute contraindication to surgery. Surgery should also be aggressively pursued for patients with the T3N0 subtype of stage IIIA disease.

N2 stage IIIA patients should not undergo surgery unless they are enrolled in some investigational protocol as mentioned above. These are usually large-scale cooperative studies, and it is likely that an academic center near one's institution is participating. Finally there comes a time when there is very little we can offer our patients, and our approach should be aimed at supportive care and judicious use of palliative treatments, always considering the patient's quality of life.

Most patients with SCLC have extensive disease at the time of diagnosis. Surgery is not an option in this group of patients. Chemotherapy and judicious use of radiation therapy are the only options. Two-year survival is poor in this group. Surgery may be considered for some patients with limited disease. Some reports have demonstrated improved survival (30% at 5 years) for patients with limited disease who underwent surgery combined with chemotherapy/chest radiotherapy.

FOLLOW-UP

Patients who underwent successful complete resections should be followed with regular visits (every 3 months) for the first 2 to 3 years, with detailed physical examinations and laboratory evaluations (chemistries including calcium and liver function tests, as well chest x-rays). The frequency of visits should decrease over the next 2 to 3 years. Patients may be considered cured if they are disease free at 5 years, although some exceptions exist. Local or distant recurrence should be detected promptly so that further interventions may be instituted early. Epidermoid cancer is most likely to recur locally, whereas adenocarcinoma is most likely to present with distant metastases, usually brain or skeletal.

Inoperable patients undergoing radiation therapy or other experimental protocols should be followed more frequently, so that complications from treatment and/or tumor progression (mass effect with local invasion of tissues, segmental lung collapse, pneumonia, hemoptysis, respiratory failure, spinal cord compression, or central nervous system metastases) may be treated as early as possible. Not enough can be said about the value of a good doctor–patient and doctor–family relationship in the management of these terminal patients, especially near the time of expected death.

DISCUSSION

Prevalence and Incidence

Lung cancer is most prevalent in industrialized countries. The overall annual incidence in the United States is 80 cases per 100,000 population; however, there are geographic, racial, and sex differences. One of the highest rates in the world is in the African-American citizens of the New Orleans area (107 cases per 100,000). The male-to-female ratio was very high initially, reflecting the difference in smoking habits be-

tween the sexes. With the reversal in smoking trends over the last 30 years, the incidence gap between the sexes has narrowed significantly. It is projected that lung cancer rates in men will plateau and begin to decline in the late 1990s, mostly reflecting the lack of tobacco use by young white men. The same is not expected for women until the year 2010.

Related Basic Science

Histopathology of Lung Cancer

The histologic classification of lung cancer is shown in Table 13–39–5. The most important distinction to be made by the pathologist is that between NSCLC and SCLC. This is usually not a difficult task. The subclassification of NSCLC, on the other hand, may be problematic (although not as important for therapeutic decisions). When closely studied, most tumors contain elements of more than one cell type, and the pathology report reflects the one that predominates.

Squamous cell (epidermoid) carcinomas account for 30 to 35% of all lung cancers. They arise from bronchial epithelial areas where squamous metaplasia is present, reflecting areas of damaged or chronically inflamed epithelium. This cell type is strongly associated with tobacco use. They are typically central in origin (65%); consequently sputum cytology may be positive. Clinically they often present with hemoptysis or obstructive atelectasis. Central cavitation is seen most often with this cell type of NSCLC. The histologic hallmarks of these tumors include keratin "onion pearls" and intercellular bridges. Within the NSCLC group, patients with well-differentiated epidermoid carcinoma have the best survival. Postoperatively these tumors tend to recur locally.

Adenocarcinomas tend to occur peripherally as solitary nodules or large masses sometimes invading the chest wall. Their prevalence is increasing, and they may account for 30% of all lung cancers. Tobacco use is also a risk factor for the development of these cancers. For unknown reasons, they are more common in women. This is the cell type most often seen in patients with a history of exposure to ionizing radiation. Glandular formation of variable extent is usually seen histologically, and they stain positive with mucin carmen. It is sometimes difficult to distinguish primary bronchogenic adenocarcinoma from adenocarcinoma metastatic to the lungs. The most frequent pattern of recurrence postresection is that of distant metastases (brain and bone). Bronchoalveolar carcinoma is considered a subtype of adenocarcinoma. It originates at the terminal bronchioles and extends to involve the alveolar spaces. Clinically these cancers present as peripheral nodules or peripheral "pneumonic" infiltrates that continue to enlarge despite use of antibiotics. Oftentimes, sputum cytology is diagnostic.

Large cell carcinomas account for 10 to 15% of lung cancers. They are typically "large" in size and peripheral in location. They represent all the NSCLCs that despite careful review and the use of special immunohistochemical stains cannot be classified as either squamous carcinomas or adenocarcinomas.

Neuroendocrine cancers account for about 20 to 25% of all lung can-

TABLE 13–39–5. HISTOPATHOLOGY OF LUNG CANCER

Cell Type	Frequency (%)
Non-small cell carcinoma	
Squamous cell carcinoma	30–35
Adenocarcinoma (and bronchoalveolar)	25–30
Large cell carcinoma	10–15
Neuroendocrine tumors	
Small cell carcinoma	20–25
Carcinoid (typical or atypical)	2–5
Uncommon primary malignant lung cancers	
Malignant melanoma	
Adenoid cystic carcinoma	
Epithelioid hemangioendothelioma	
Papillomas of the tracheobronchial tree	
Pulmonary blastoma	
Fibrosarcoma and leiomyosarcoma	
Primary pulmonary hemangiopercytoma	

cers. The three subtypes in this group are SCLC, typical carcinoid, and atypical carcinoid. SCLC is by far the most prevalent (carcinoid tumors account for only 2–4% of all lung cancers). They most often occur centrally, and present clinically with postobstructive pneumonia, cough, and hemoptysis. These tumors have the potential to produce many humoral substances (serotonin, bombesin, somatostatin, vasoactive intestinal polypeptide, etc.), and may produce several neuroendocrine syndromes. Carcinoid syndrome is rarely seen with bronchial carcinoid tumors (2–5% incidence).

Other rare primary malignant neoplasms may occasionally be seen (Table 13–39–5) and collectively account for less than 5% of all lung cancers.

Molecular Pathogenesis of Lung Cancer

Carcinogenesis of the bronchial epithelium is believed to be related to either the activation of protooncogenes to oncogenes or the lack of expression of tumor suppressor genes.

In more than 80% of smokers with NSCLC, activated oncogenes have been found. Many families of activated oncogenes have been associated with lung cancer, but the most important are the *ras* and *myc* families. Detection of activated oncogenes may predict the incidence of distal metastases in patients with adenocarcinoma, and may imply a poor prognosis, independent of clinical stage. Similarly, protein p21, which is a product of *ras* family oncogene activation, may be seen in 60 and 80% of squamous cell carcinomas and adenocarcinomas, respectively, and is associated with poor survival.

Tumor suppressor genes appear to be located on chromosome 3, and deletions of the short arm of this chromosome as well as deletions of the short arm of chromosomes 17 and 11 have been reported in patients with SCLC. The clinical utility of this information at present is unclear. It is possible that routine chromosomal analysis may become part of the pretreatment evaluation of bronchogenic carcinoma. The potential role of DNA analysis in the early detection of lung cancer is also unclear.

Natural History and Its Modification with Treatment

It is clear that untreated lung cancer is uniformly fatal. The survival interval in patients unable or unwilling to undergo any form of therapy depends on the disease stage, performance status, biological behavior of the tumor, and presence of other organ system disease.

Despite aggressive treatment regimens over the last 30 years, the case fatality ratio for lung cancer remains very high (90%). The most important reason for this is advanced disease at the time of diagnosis. The biggest survival impact with surgery is seen with stage I patients (Figure 13–39–2). As a group they have a 65 to 70% 5-year survival and a chance for a cure. The survival impact on stage II disease is also significant; however, the same cannot be conclusively stated for patients with stage III or IV disease.

Prevention

The most important measure in the prevention of lung cancer is smoking cessation. Patient education about available methods for smoking cessation should be routinely offered to all smokers by their physicians. Measures should also be taken to minimize exposure to potential lung carcinogens in the workplace.

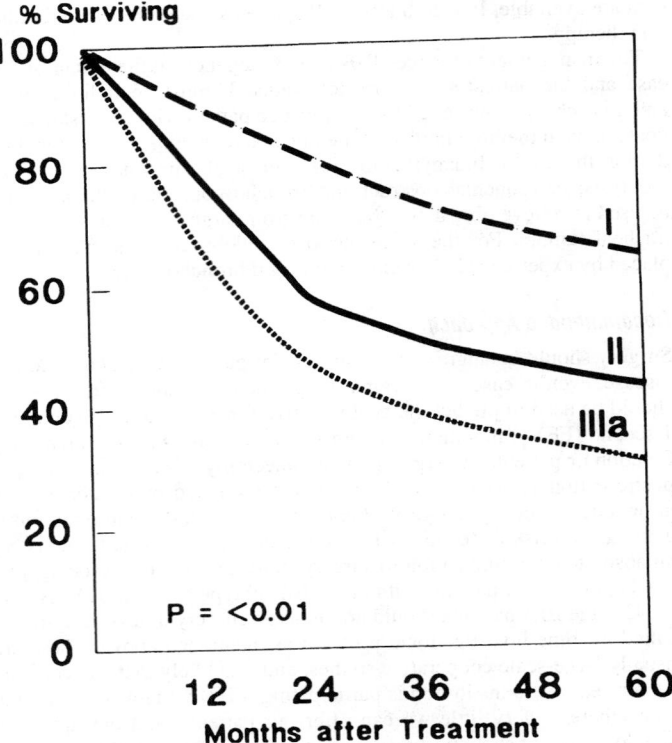

Figure 13–39–2. Cumulative proportion of patients with non-small cell lung cancer expected to survive 5 years or more according to surgical (pathologic) stage, operative deaths excluded (1975–1982 collected series). (*Source: Mountain CF. Lung cancer staging classification. Clin Chest Med 1993;14:48. Reproduced with permission from the publisher and author.*)

Cost Containment

Indirectly, the best cost containment method is also smoking cessation, as smoking is associated with greater than 80% of all lung cancers. Judicious use of available diagnostic procedures with consideration of cost and potential yield is very important. Laboratory investigations should be narrowed to specific information needed, and the least expensive test should be chosen whenever possible.

REFERENCES

Grippi MA. Clinical aspects of lung cancer. Semin Roentgenol 1990;25:12.

Hyde L, Hyde CI. Clinical manifestations of lung cancer. Chest 1974;65:299.

Mackay B, Lukeman JM, Ordonez NG. Tumors of the lung. Philadelphia: Saunders, 1991.

Matthay RA, guest ed. Lung cancer. Clin Chest Med 1993;14(1).

Mountain CF. The new International Staging System for lung cancer. Surg Clin North Am 1987;67:925.

Symposium on Intrathoracic Neoplasms. Mayo Clin Proc 1993;68.

CHAPTER 13–40

Superior Vena Cava Syndrome

A. Ross Hill, M.D., C.M.

DEFINITION

Superior vena cava syndrome (SVCS) refers to the clinical picture that develops when venous return from the territory of the superior vena cava (SVC) is impeded for whatever reason. It is nearly always due to partial or complete obstruction of the SVC or of the brachiocephalic (innominate) veins bilaterally. Mild to moderate SVC obstruction is usually subclinical and would not merit the term SVCS.

ETIOLOGY

More than 50 underlying diseases or mechanisms have been described, including most processes known to affect the superior mediastinum (Table 13–40–1). Since 1950 most series from general hospitals attribute 10 to 25% of cases to benign disorders; malignant neoplasms account for the remainder (Table 13–40–2).

Bronchogenic carcinoma is the single most common cause, underlying 50 to 80% of all adult cases. Of these, 80% or more arise in the right lung and 30 to 60% are small cell carcinomas. *Lymphomas* are the second leading malignant cause in adults (5–15%) and are the foremost acquired cause in children.

Fibrosing mediastinitis is the leading benign cause of SVCS in the United States (2–5%). In regions where *Histoplasma capsulatum* is prevalent, a chronic immunologic reaction to this fungus or its residual antigens is believed to underlie most cases, but many are idiopathic. Other infectious agents that invade mediastinal lymph nodes can also cause SVCS: tuberculosis and syphilis were once prominent causes (proven or presumed), and a variety of other bacterial and fungal agents are incriminated rarely.

Iatrogenic thrombosis induced by central venous or pulmonary artery catheters, chronic indwelling (Hickman, Broviac) catheters, pacemaker wires, or any other intravascular device has accounted for a growing proportion of cases over the last 25 years. Though thrombi often develop along the path of central venous "lines," especially those present longer than 48 hours, the vast majority go undetected. Venous instrumentation may now be the leading nonneoplastic cause in some centers. Other cases of primary thrombosis of the great veins are due to hypercoagulable states or remain idiopathic.

Rarely, SVCS is due to volume overload without venous obstruction; this may occur when a fistula from the ascending aorta (aneurysm, aortitis) to the SVC produces a large arteriovenous shunt.

The distribution of causes of SVCS has shifted dramatically over the decades. In a review up to 1946, 30% of 504 published cases were due to aneurysms of the ascending aorta, mostly syphilitic in origin (Table 13–40–1). Tuberculosis was once the presumed etiology in 5 to 10%, but is now a very rare cause.

CRITERIA FOR DIAGNOSIS

Suggestive

Mild or incomplete SVCS may be suspected when there is unexplained bilateral neck vein distension, mild periorbital or facial edema, or subtle prominence of superficial veins on one or both sides of the upper torso, particularly in a patient with apparent mediastinal disease. Imaging of the great veins is needed to confirm their involvement.

Definitive

Physical examination affords definitive diagnosis of SVCS in fully developed cases (Table 13–40–3). The cardinal signs are prominent subcutaneous collateral veins that descend over the upper thorax and

TABLE 13–40–1. MECHANISMS AND CAUSES OF SUPERIOR VENA CAVA SYNDROME

Category	Disorder	Comments/Examples
Malignant neoplasms	Lung cancer	Leading cause (50–80% of all superior vena cava syndrome cases), small cell carcinoma most common type
	Non-Hodgkin's lymphomas	Next most common malignancy (5–15%)
	Hodgkin's lymphoma	Uncommon complication
	Extrathoracic primary with mediastinal metastases	5–10% of superior vena cava syndrome cases; breast, renal cell, and gastrointestinal cancers, sarcomas, etc.
	Mediastinal primary	Thymoma, germ cell tumors, etc.
Inflammatory/infectious	Granulomatous infections	Histoplasmosis most common; rarely, tuberculosis, syphilis, blastomycosis
	Idiopathic fibrosing mediastinitis	Extrathoracic involvement in some patients
	Other bacterial or fungal infections	Aspergillosis, nocardiosis, actinomycosis
	Pyogenic mediastinitis, abscess	Following surgery, esophageal perforation
	Sarcoidosis	Rare complication
Other fibrosing conditions	Radiation therapy	Rare
	Drugs	Methysergide
Primary thrombosis	Intravascular devices	Central venous, pulmonary artery, or long-term catheter; pacemaker wire
	Behçet's disease	Vasculitis; superior vena cava thrombosis develops in 5–10%
	Hypercoagulable states	Systemic lupus erythematosus, cancer, inherited deficiencies, etc.
	Hyperviscosity	Polycythemia vera
	Idiopathic	
Benign mass lesions	Benign neoplasms	Teratoma, thymoma, etc.
	Substernal goiter	Radioiodide scan sometimes useful
	Trauma	Mediastinal hematoma or emphysema, pneumothorax (rarely)
	Developmental	Bronchogenic cyst, cystic hygroma
Cardiovascular disorders	Aneurysm of ascending aorta	Tertiary syphilis, Marfan's syndrome
	Congenital heart disease	Mustard procedure, Glenn anastomosis, etc.
	Acute aortic dissection	
	Aortocaval fistula	Volume overload of superior vena cava circulation
	Right atrial mass	Myxoma, thrombus, metastasis to heart

TABLE 13–40–2. SUPERIOR VENA CAVA SYNDROME: UNDERLYING DISEASES IN LARGE RETROSPECTIVE SERIES

Reference	Number of Cases	Place, Period	Malignant Neoplasm (%)	Lung Cancer (%)	Lymphomas (%)	Benign Disorders (%)	Comments
McIntire, Sykes Ann Intern Med 1949	250	World literature 1904–1946	30	≥9	12	62	Aortic aneurysm in 24%
Effler, Groves J Thorac Cardiovasc Surg 1962	64	Cleveland Clinic 1950–1961	75	"Overwhelming majority"	—	25	Adults
Banker, Madison Dis Chest 1967	438	literature 1951–1966	82	65	4	18	
Schraufnagel et al. Am J Med 1981	107	Montreal 1961–1979	85	63	9	15	Adults; no major sequelae from superior vena cava obstruction per se
Parish et al. Mayo Clin Proc 1981	86	Mayo Clinic 1960–1979	78	52	9	22	Adults; 5% iatrogenic (thrombosis)
Issa et al. Pediatrics 1983	150	literature 1951–1976	16	0	11	84	Children; 71% following surgery for congenital heart lesions
Bell et al. Med J Aust 1986	159	Sydney 1970–1979	~99	≥81	≥2	~1	Adults; malignancy suspected but unconfirmed in 13%
Yellin et al. Am Rev Respir Dis 1990	63	Israel 1972–1987	83	48	21	18	Includes 7 children

edema of the upper body. An exact anatomic diagnosis requires imaging of the great veins, traditionally by contrast venography (see Diagnostic Options), though such studies are unnecessary in most cases.

CLINICAL MANIFESTATIONS
Subjective

Two aspects of symptomatology require evaluation in patients with SVCS: symptoms attributable to the underlying disease, which are most often respiratory and/or constitutional in nature, and symptoms caused by the venous obstruction per se (Table 13–40–3).

Dyspnea and swelling are the most frequent complaints encountered in SVCS. Dyspnea may be present at rest, an unusual finding in most chest diseases, and is aggravated by bending over or recumbency. As edema develops, patients notice a puffiness of the eyes and face or tightness of the shirt collar or hat. When venous obstruction is acute or severe, a variety of neurologic symptoms may ensue, ranging from headache or lightheadedness to confusion or obtundation. Hoarseness may reflect vocal cord paralysis or laryngeal edema. Exertional syncope is an uncommon but alarming occurrence.

TABLE 13–40–3. SYMPTOMS AND SIGNS OF SUPERIOR VENA CAVA SYNDROME* (SVCS)

Clinical Findings	Frequency (%)	Comments
Symptoms		
Dyspnea	>40	Increased by recumbency (due to superior vena cava syndrome or thoracic disease)
Increased neck girth	>50	
Swelling of eyes, face, arms	>50	Worse after recumbency
Cough	20–60	Underlying disease
Headache, "fullness"	5–40	
Dizziness, visual disturbance, impaired thinking, drowsiness	~5	
Dysphagia	5–10	
Syncope	~5	With exertion or bending over
Chest pain	5–20	Underlying disease
Signs		
Venous collaterals over upper trunk	40–90	Prominence and location vary
Neck vein distension (bilateral)	60–100	
Edema of upper body	50–90	Usually decreases as collateral veins develop
Proptosis, chemosis		
Facial plethora	~20	
Cyanosis	10–20	Limited to SVC territory
Hoarseness	~5	Vocal cord paralysis, rarely edema
Horner's syndrome	~2	Malignant cases
Impaired cognition	<5	Rule out brain metastases, etc.
Obtundation, coma	<2	Rule out brain metastases, etc.
Seizures	Rare	Other factors involved?

*Clinical features vary among patients; rarely, severe superior vena cava obstruction may be clinically inapparent. The stated frequencies are typical of published series; as the literature on superior vena cava syndrome is retrospective, some may be underestimates.

Objective
Physical Examination

The sign with the greatest diagnostic specificity is the presence of dilated and tortuous superficial veins distributed over the shoulders and upper thorax; they provide collateral flow toward the abdomen (inferior vena cava territory). Distension of the cervical and arm veins is usually apparent; the arm veins exhibit delayed emptying when the hand is elevated. Jugular venous pulsations are characteristically damped or absent. Edema varies in degree, depending on the effectiveness of collateral drainage; periorbital puffiness is a frequent early sign. Ruddy suffusion or plethora of the face or (less often) frank cyanosis restricted to the SVC territory is typical of full-blown SVCS. Focal central nervous system abnormalities should not be attributed to SVCS alone.

Routine Laboratory Abnormalities

Routine chemical and hematologic tests have no role specific to SVCS itself, except in occasional patients with a clotting disorder; any abnormalities reflect the associated disease process(es). Chest radiography usually shows widening of the superior mediastinum, except in primary thrombosis of the SVC.

PLANS
Diagnostic
Differential Diagnosis

The physical findings are pathognomonic in full-blown SVCS. Subtle, incomplete, or asymmetric presentations must be carefully distinguished from other disorders, including unilateral obstruction of a subclavian or axillary vein. Congestive heart failure and valvular or other lesions involving the right side of the heart can usually be diagnosed by bedside evaluation plus radiographic, electrocardiographic, or echocardiographic evidence of primary cardiac dysfunction. These disorders produce neck vein distension, often with abnormal venous pulsations, but do not produce upper body edema or differential cyanosis.

Cardiac tamponade and constrictive pericarditis also produce SVC congestion and should be excluded, especially because malignant pericardial effusion is not rare in the typical setting for SVCS.

Dyspnea is a prominent symptom in SVCS but is quite nonspecific. Before attributing it to venous obstruction one should consider possible associated disorders: other pathophysiologic effects of the underlying lung cancer, mediastinitis, and so on; background lung disease such as chronic obstructive pulmonary disease; pulmonary thromboembolism or tumor emboli; and/or impaired cardiac output. Cardiorespiratory disorders manifest mainly as exertional dyspnea. It is particularly important to rule out large airway obstruction (malignant stenosis of trachea and/or main bronchi, laryngeal paralysis), which sometimes accompanies SVCS. Auscultation for wheezing or stridor, thoracic imaging, and above all bronchoscopy will clarify the status of the main airways.

Diagnostic Options

The nonspecific diagnosis of SVCS is usually made at the bedside. Several imaging techniques afford a more precise demonstration of the site and mechanism of obstruction, as well as the distribution and function of collateral pathways. Contrast venography is the classic method; it involves bilateral injection into arm veins and is usually well tolerated. Radionuclide angiograms reveal flow patterns safely but lack anatomic detail. Computed tomography (CT) is currently the leading radiographic approach; it often provides useful information about the underlying disease but requires optimal contrast injection to demonstrate venous anatomy. Magnetic resonance imaging, an alternative to CT that is more expensive and often less practical, can provide images in any plane and display vascular lumens without contrast injection. Transesophageal echocardiography depicts the SVC, is portable to the bedside, obviates contrast material, and also evaluates the heart and pericardium.

Given the diverse spectrum of underlying causes, an accurate diagnosis is crucial to optimal management. Occasionally a rapid noninvasive diagnosis can be made by sputum cytology or culture. Though diagnostically adequate for many carcinomas, sputum cytology has limited sensitivity (~50%); tissue biopsy is preferred and is often essential for definitive diagnosis. The invasive procedures most often fruitful include superficial lymph node biopsy, fiberoptic bronchoscopy, and cervical mediastinoscopy or anterior mediastinotomy. Full thoracotomy interrupts venous collaterals and should be avoided if possible, except when a curative (e.g., thyroidectomy) or palliative procedure is planned; thoracoscopy is an alternative last resort for diagnosis.

Recommended Approach

The goal is to secure a specific (usually histologic) diagnosis as efficiently as possible. The approach selected should combine a high yield, little time delay, and a relatively low risk of complications.

Historically, SVCS has been regarded as an "oncologic emergency"; urgent radiation therapy, even without diagnosis, was commonly recommended. This view has been revised for several reasons. First, SVCS, though often a source of morbidity, is generally well tolerated; there is virtually no evidence that it causes permanent organ damage. Second, fear of bleeding from invasive procedures was probably exaggerated; numerous reports support the relative safety of bronchoscopy and surgical procedures (mediastinoscopy, thoracotomy) provided they are conducted with care and expertise. Third, specific diagnosis is needed to select the optimal initial therapy, which for small cell carcinoma and lymphomas is usually chemotherapy, not irradiation. Finally, "blind" radiation therapy can obscure subsequent histologic diagnosis and carries its own risks: we are aware of more than one patient irradiated inappropriately for aortic aneurysm (in the pre-CT era) with fatal results. A firm diagnosis can and should be safely obtained in the great majority of patients before embarking on therapy.

One should take care to recognize concomitant obstruction of the central airways and cardiac tamponade. These true emergencies can be life threatening and require immediate management.

If there is palpable lymphadenopathy in the supraclavicular fossa or neck, excisional biopsy or fine-needle aspiration is the preferred approach. If radiography suggests lung cancer or other extramediastinal mass, fiberoptic bronchoscopy is indicated, both for tissue diagnosis and to inspect the airways.

Expeditious CT or magnetic resonance imaging can help by suggesting the cause of SVCS, guiding the choice of diagnostic route, or revealing the site and nature of venous obstruction, particularly the presence of thrombus. Primary mediastinal masses can sometimes be diagnosed by transthoracic needle aspiration or by bronchoscopy with transbronchial aspiration, but cytologic diagnosis of such lesions is often unreliable. Cervical mediastinoscopy, anterior mediastinotomy, or thoracoscopy is appropriate when less invasive approaches have failed.

Vascular imaging is unnecessary in most patients, but should be performed when there is no apparent mass or other lesion involving the superior mediastinum.

Benign diagnoses typically take longer to confirm, but there is less urgency than in malignancy, as SVC obstruction is usually gradual in onset and well compensated. A wide array of imaging, serologic, microbiologic, and histologic studies may be called on for diagnosis.

Therapeutic

Therapeutic Options

Table 13–40–4 lists the gamut of procedures, both established and experimental, that have been employed in SVCS. Chemotherapy is the primary treatment for patients with small cell carcinoma, lymphoma, or drug-sensitive germ cell tumors. Nonsensitive malignancies are managed with radiation, delivered initially in high dose fractions (3–4 Gy).

Surgical bypass or reconstruction has received variable enthusiasm; it successfully relieved the venous obstruction in more than 50% of patients reported, with some recurrences thereafter. Recently, less inva-

TABLE 13–40–4. MANAGEMENT OPTIONS FOR SUPERIOR VENA CAVA SYNDROME (SVCS)

	Method	Comments
Treatment of underlying cause	Radiation therapy	Most commonly used modality, partial or complete response in 70–90% of malignant cases
	Chemotherapy	Indicated for small cell carcinoma, lymphomas, sensitive germ cell cancers
	Antibiotics	Drugs specific for bacterial, tuberculous, or fungal mediastinitis
		?Role in fibrosing mediastinitis associated with histoplasmosis
	Anticoagulants, thrombolytic drugs	Primary thrombosis associated with coagulation disorder, intravascular device, or vasculitis
		?Useful in any acute superior vena cava syndrome precipitated by thrombosis
Relief of venous obstruction	Surgical bypass	Spiral (saphenous) vein graft, synthetic grafts
		Benign causes, malignancy only if prolonged survival expected and good performance status
		Variable long-term success (limited data)
	Intravascular stents, balloon angioplasty, thrombectomy	Percutaneous, intravascular procedures
		Applicable in malignant cases
		Limited experience
Nonspecific symptomatic treatment	Elevation of head, bed rest	Nursing routine
	Oxygen	Arterial hypoxemia
	Diuretics, glucocorticoids	Efficacy uncertain

sive approaches have included a variety of mechanical dilation and/or stenting procedures as well as thrombolytic therapy.

Recommended Approach

Once malignancy is confirmed (or highly likely based on imaging studies, bronchoscopy, etc.), immediate irradiation is appropriate for most patients; however, small cell lung cancers, lymphomas, or other neoplasms that respond well to chemotherapy are better managed from the start with chemotherapy, which treats the disease systemically and is as rapid and effective as radiation in relieving the mediastinum.

The therapeutic implications of thrombus formation in SVCS are poorly defined. It is unclear how often embolization from the SVC territory may occur (the view that the obstruction is protective is unconfirmed); moreover, these patients are often at high risk of thrombosis in the inferior vena cava territory. On the other hand, their risk of bleeding complications may also be increased. With careful monitoring anticoagulants may be beneficial in selected cases, but data regarding their effect on overall prognosis are sparse, and anticoagulation cannot be recommended routinely. Thrombolytic agents are an effective option for primary thrombosis; their value for SVCS due to neoplasms and other stenosing conditions is questionable.

Diuretics and corticosteroids have traditionally been used as symptomatic treatment, but their utility is questionable and must be weighed against possible volume depletion and metabolic and infectious complications. Some practitioners believe that a brief course of high-dose glucocorticoid can prevent exacerbation of venous or large airway obstruction during initial cytotoxic therapy, but the evidence for benefit is anecdotal.

Nonsurgical procedures aimed at decompressing the SVC territory are evolving and can bring symptomatic relief even in advanced malignancy. Surgery is appropriate mainly for stable patients with a benign cause or with an expected survival of many months. The choice of procedure is dictated by the anatomy of the obstruction and by local expertise and experience.

FOLLOW-UP

After specific treatment is initiated, patients recovering from SVCS should be followed for at least 6 months for possible recurrence; those with chronic SVCS may need monitoring indefinitely. Long-term anticoagulation may be beneficial for selected patients with a coagulation disturbance, an indwelling catheter, or following palliative surgery, but otherwise has no established prophylactic role in compensated patients with persistent SVC narrowing.

DISCUSSION

Prevalence and Incidence

Superior vena cava syndrome develops in 3 to 10% of patients with bronchogenic carcinoma. SVCS is an uncommon complication of most benign diseases with which it is associated, and statistics regarding its incidence are lacking. Exceptions include fibrosing mediastinitis, in which SVCS arises in 10 to 40% of cases, and Behçet's disease, which is the most common nonneoplastic cause in communities where it is endemic.

Thrombosis frequently occurs along the course of central venous "lines." More than 50% of Swan–Ganz catheters induce local thrombi, though SVCS or subclavian vein obstruction has been recognized clinically in only about 2%.

Related Basic Science

Physiologic or Metabolic Derangement

The physiologic effects of SVC obstruction reflect venous hypertension and stagnant blood flow in the upper body. The normal mean SVC pressure in recumbent humans at rest is about 5 mm Hg (7 cm H_2O). In patients with SVCS, pressures measured in arm veins range from 20 to more than 60 cm H_2O (normal, <15 cm H_2O). The degree of venous hypertension depends on the efficiency of collateral pathways; hence, SVCS tends to be severe when it develops acutely (e.g., thrombosis of a previously patent SVC) and milder when obstruction develops slowly, as is often the case in benign disorders.

Venous hypertension raises intracranial pressure, which in turn reduces cerebral blood flow and produces edema (the extracranial soft tissues tolerate venous obstruction better than the brain). The low-flow state results in oxygen desaturation and respiratory acidosis at the venous and tissue levels, which no doubt contributes to dyspnea (central chemoreceptors) as well as to the brain dysfunction sometimes seen in SVCS.

Anatomic Derangement

The SVC is a thin-walled, low-pressure conduit that extends 7 to 8 cm from behind the first right costochondral junction to the right atrium. It abuts the ascending aorta, is encircled by lymph nodes, and normally accommodates all the venous drainage from the head, neck, arms, and upper torso. A variety of collateral drainage routes are available when the SVC becomes obstructed (Table 13–40–5). The relative importance of these pathways varies among patients, depending on the site(s) of venous obstruction and normal variations in venous anatomy. A key factor is whether the obstruction involves the azygos vein (or the SVC downstream from their confluence); if so, the major collateral pathway is unavailable and the resultant SVCS is more severe. In classic canine studies, Carlson (1934) found that acute ligation of the SVC cephalad to the azygos vein produced severe SVCS, which subsided spontaneously over days as collateral channels expanded. In contrast, ligation below the azygos was rapidly fatal.

The mechanism of SVC obstruction in a given case may include extrinsic compression (mass effect or fibrosis), direct invasion (malignancy), and/or thrombosis. SVC obstruction also blocks the normal flow of lymph from the upper body, thus contributing to edema formation and possibly to the pleural effusions that are infrequently seen in SVCS.

Luminal thrombus is commonly present upstream from the main site of obstruction. Whether thrombosis was the event precipitating SVCS (in a previously narrowed or injured SVC) or a secondary phenomenon is often unclear.

Natural History and Its Modification with Treatment

The natural course of SVCS is one of gradual improvement over days, weeks, or even months, which one should bear in mind when interpreting the apparent response rates to radiation and other therapies. The final degree of compensation, as judged from benign cases, varies between individuals: some achieve complete relief of symptoms with a well-developed venous collateral network, whereas a minority remain

TABLE 13–40–5. PATHWAYS FOR COLLATERAL VENOUS DRAINAGE OF THE SUPERIOR VENA CAVA (SVC) TERRITORY

Azygos route (most important route when not obstructed)	
SVC obstruction upstream from azygos	SVC tributaries → intercostal veins → azygos and accessory hemiazygos veins (antegrade flow) → SVC
SVC obstruction downstream from azygos	SVC or its tributaries → azygos and accessory hemiazygos veins (retrograde flow) → lumbar veins → IVC
Vertebral route	Brachiocephalic veins → vertebral venous plexus → intercostal and lumbar veins → IVC
Internal thoracic (mammary) route	Internal thoracic veins → superior and inferior epigastric veins → external iliac veins → IVC
Lateral thoracic route (observed on physical examination)	Axillary veins → lateral thoracic veins, other superficial SVC tributaries → thoracoepigastric veins → superficial abdominal veins → great saphenous veins → femoral veins → IVC
Esophageal route	"Downhill" varices of upper ± lower esophagus → left gastric vein → portal vein → IVC

IVC, inferior vena cava.

permanently distressed (and disfigured) and are candidates for invasive restoration of outflow.

The underlying disease largely determines the outcome for patients with SVCS. As most have inoperable malignancies, the average prognosis is poor. Median survival with bronchogenic carcinoma is about 6 months, tending to be longer in patients with small cell carcinoma who respond to chemotherapy. Patients with underlying lymphoma or breast cancer fare better. Though a sign of locally advanced neoplasia, SVCS does not imply a prognosis worse than that of other inoperable cases, suggesting that SVCS per se is rarely life threatening.

Radiation therapy is associated with partial or complete relief of malignant SVCS within 1 to 2 weeks in most patients, although response depends on the radiosensitivity of the tumor and the anatomy and mechanism of the venous obstruction. Response rates to chemotherapy, when this is an appropriate initial therapy, are at least as good. It is unlikely that antineoplastic therapies have any short-term effect when thrombosis is the final mechanism of occlusion.

Superior vena cava syndrome caused by lung cancer recurs in up to 25% of patients during the months following initial treatment. Radiation is a useful rescue therapy in such cases.

Prevention

The development of SVCS is unpredictable in most instances, although patients with right-sided malignant lymphadenopathy or a mass involving the superior mediastinum are at substantial risk (>10%). Prompt treatment directed at this region may be preventive.

Benign thrombotic SVCS may be prevented by avoiding unnecessary venous catheters or by minimizing their duration of residence in the SVC. Patients with a hypercoagulable state (e.g., chronic disseminated intravascular coagulation associated with cancer) or congestive heart failure or who are bedridden due to illness should receive low-dose anticoagulation, usually with subcutaneous heparin, unless a contraindication exists. There are no established guidelines for preventive management of patients with incomplete or threatened SVC obstruc-

tion; the use of anticoagulants in such situations is a matter of individualized judgment.

Cost Containment

Expeditious diagnostic investigation, avoidance of redundant imaging studies, and the use of outpatient radiation or chemotherapy (where appropriate) can reduce management and hospitalization costs.

REFERENCES

Ahmann FR. A reassessment of the clinical implications of the superior vena cava syndrome. J Clin Oncol 1984;2:961.

Banker VP, Maddison FE. Superior vena cava syndrome secondary to aortic disease. Dis Chest 1967;51:656.

Bell DR, Woods RL, Levi JA. Superior vena caval obstruction: A 10–year experience. Med J Aust 1986;145:566.

Carlson HA. Obstruction of the superior vena cava: An experimental study. Arch Surg 1934;29:669.

Effler DB, Groves LK. Superior vena caval obstruction. J Thor Cardiovasc Surg 1962;43:574.

Gray BH, Olin JW, Graor RA, et al. Safety and efficacy of thrombolytic therapy for superior vena cava syndrome. Chest 1991;99:54.

Issa PY, Brini ER, Janin Y, Slim MS. Superior vena cava syndrome in childhood: Report of ten cases and review of the literature. Pediatrics 1983;71:337.

McIntyre FT, Sykes EM, Jr. Obstruction of the superior vena cava: A review of the literature and report of two personal cases. Ann Intern Med, 1949;30:925.

Nieto AF, Doty DB. Superior vena cava obstruction: Clinical syndrome, etiology, and treatment. Curr Probl Cancer 1986;10:441.

Oudkerk M, Heystraten FMJ, Stoter G. Stenting in malignant vena cava obstruction. Cancer 1993;71:142.

Parish JM, Marschke RF, Dines DE, Lee RE. Etiologic considerations in superior vena cava syndrome. Mayo Clin Proc 1981;56:407.

Schraufnagel DE, Hill R, Leech JA, Paré JAP. Superior vena caval obstruction: Is it a medical emergency? Am J Med 1981;70:1169.

Yellin A, Rosen A, Reichert N, Lieberman Y. Superior vena cava syndrome: The myths–the facts. Am Rev Respir Dis 1990;141:1114.

CHAPTER 13–41

Tuberculosis (Including Chemoprophylaxis and Nontuberculous Mycobacterial Lung Infections)

A. Ross Hill, M.D., C.M.

DEFINITION

The name *tuberculosis* (TB), originally a descriptive term from pathology, now denotes clinically identifiable disease caused by *Mycobacterium tuberculosis*. TB is distinguished from infection by *M. tuberculosis*, that is, invasion of host tissues by this mycobacterial pathogen with or without resultant disease. TB, a multifaceted disease which takes both localized and disseminated forms, can affect most organs in the body (Table 13–41–1). Pulmonary TB is the most common presentation and is emphasized in this chapter.

As most infections by *M. tuberculosis* remain asymptomatic and subclinical, the infected state is demonstrated by evidence of the host's immune response to the mycobacterium. In clinical practice, infection is identified by a positive tuberculin skin test, evidence of delayed-type hypersensitivity to specific mycobacterial antigens. Healthy tuberculin-positive persons are assumed to harbor a relatively small number of viable but dormant bacilli (latent infection).

ETIOLOGY

More than 20 mycobacterial species are known to be potential human pathogens. For clinical purposes they fall into three groups: *M. leprae,* the agent of leprosy; *M. tuberculosis,* the agent of TB; and the remain-

der, which are referred to collectively as nontuberculous mycobacteria (NTM [Table 13–41–2]; the terms potentially pathogenic environmental mycobacteria, MOTT bacilli, and atypical mycobacteria have also been used). Most of the NTM cause disease (*mycobacteriosis*) which resembles TB and can be distinguished only by identifying the specific agent in laboratory culture. *Mycobacterium bovis,* the agent of bovine TB, is classified within the *M. tuberculosis* complex; formerly a common cause of human TB (usually acquired from unpasteurized milk), it is now rare in developed countries.

CRITERIA FOR DIAGNOSIS
Suggestive

The diagnosis is suggested by demonstration of acid-fast bacilli (AFB) in sputum, biopsy material, or other samples from a patient having clinical abnormalities consistent with TB. *Caveat*: NTM cannot be distinguished from *M. tuberculosis* by this means.

Necrotizing granulomas in any histologic specimen, together with negative special stains for acid-fast bacilli and other microorganisms plus a clinical response to antituberculous drugs also suggest the diagnosis (again, NTM can produce identical findings).

A compatible clinical illness plus response to antituberculous drugs, particularly in a tuberculin-positive patient, suggest TB. One is often

TABLE 13–41–1. ANATOMIC DISTRIBUTION OF TUBERCULOSIS (TB)*

	Percentage of All TB Cases	Percentage of Extrapulmonary TB Cases
Pulmonary	82.5	—
Extrapulmonary	17.5	(100)†
Lymphadenitis	5.4	31
Pleural	4.0	23
Genitourinary	2.1	12
Bone and joint	1.7	10
Miliary	1.3	7
Meningitis	0.8	5
Peritonitis	0.6	3
Other sites combined	—	10

*Cases reported to the Centers for Disease Control and Prevention for United States, 1986 (Rieder et al., 1990).
†Statistics represent the major clinical site reported for each patient; patients presenting with extrapulmonary TB may have one or more additional sites of involvement, including pulmonary TB in some. The proportion of extrapulmonary cases may be higher (~20–40%) in populations with a high prevalence of HIV coinfection.

left with a presumptive diagnosis in those presentations of TB in which the sensitivity of routine mycobacterial cultures is relatively low (25–75%): serositis, meningitis, minor pulmonary disease, and so on. The response of NTM to standard anti-TB therapy varies among species; some, such as *M. kansasii,* usually respond well and might therefore be confused with TB.

Definitive

Cultivation of *M. tuberculosis* from any source proves disease (TB), as this mycobacterium is never a nonpathogenic commensal (false-positive results due to cross-contamination do occur infrequently in laboratories that process many positive specimens). About 20% of all TB cases in the United States are diagnosed presumptively, with no positive culture obtained.

Definitive diagnosis of disease due to NTM (mycobacteriosis) also requires cultural identification by a laboratory with expertise in the speciation of mycobacteria. Because most NTM can be harmless colonizers as well as pathogens of the respiratory tract, a positive sputum culture does not in itself prove disease (see below).

CLINICAL MANIFESTATIONS
Subjective

The symptoms of TB fall into two categories: constitutional symptoms reflecting the systemic inflammatory state (fever, night sweats, fatigue,

TABLE 13–41–2. NONTUBERCULOUS MYCOBACTERIA (NTM)

Species	Environmental sources	Pathogenicity in humans	Prevalence of disease	Saprophyte or environmental contaminant*	Typical disease syndromes	Response to drug therapy	Laboratory features†
MAC‡	water, soil, birds, animals	yes	most common	yes (most isolates)	pulmonary, lymph node, disseminated§	variable	SG, nonpigmented
M. kansasii	water, animals	yes	2nd commonest	infrequently	pulmonary	good	SG, photochromagen
M. xenopi	water (heated)	yes	uncommon	yes	pulmonary	variable	SG, scotochromagen, 42°C
M. scofulaceum	soil, water, food	yes	uncommon	yes	lymph node (children)	limited?	SG, scotochromagen
M. malmoense	?	yes	rare	no	pulmonary	variable	SG, nonpigmented
M. szulgai	?	yes	rare	yes	pulmonary	poor?	SG, scotochromagen
M. simiae	primates, ? water	yes	rare	yes	pulmonary	limited?	SG, photochromagen
M. haemophilum	?	yes	rare (immunocompromised)	?	skin, soft tissues	limited?	SG, nonpigmented, <32°C, hemin for growth
M. marinum	sealife, fresh and salt water	yes	uncommon	rarely	skin lesions, regional lymphatics	variable	SG/RG, photochromagen, 30–32°C
M. ulcerans	? (tropical)	yes	uncommon	no	skin nodule → ulcer	variable	SG, nonpigmented, 33°C
M. fortuitum	water, soil	yes	uncommon	yes (usually)	skin, ST, pulmonary, surgical wound	good	RG, nonpigmented
M. chelonae	water, soil	yes	uncommon	yes (usually)	skin, ST, surgical wound	variable	RG, nonpigmented
M. abscessus‖	water, soil	yes	uncommon	yes (usually)	pulmonary, skin, ST, wound	variable	RG, nonpigmented
M. gordonae	water	rarely	very rare (AIDS)	almost always	pulmonary, disseminated	good?	SG, scotochromagen, cntm¶
M. smegmatis	environment (urogenital isolates historically)	rarely	very rare	almost always	skin, ST, surgical wound	?	RG, nonpigmented
M. terrae	soil, water	rarely	very rare	almost always	pulmonary	?	SG, nonpigmented, cntm¶
M. gastri	soil, water	rarely	very rare	almost always	?	?	SG, nonpigmented

*If not, laboratory isolation is generally taken to indicate active disease.
†Slow growth (SG, >7 days) or rapid growth (RG, <7 days), usual color formation of colonies *in vitro,* optimal temperature if not 37°C.
‡MAC: *M. avium* complex, including *M. avium* and *M. intracellulare* (*M. scrofulaceum* is now regarded as a distinct species).
§Disseminated MAC infection occurs in 20–50% of AIDS patients but is otherwise rare.
‖*M. abscessus* was formerly classified as a subspecies of *M. chelonae.*
¶Cntm = common environmental contaminant in clinical specimens
ST, soft tissues

malaise, anorexia, and weight loss) and local symptoms reflecting injury to the target organ(s) (these are nonspecific and vary widely from case to case).

The cardinal local symptoms of pulmonary TB are cough and sputum production. Sputum is highly variable, in both quantity and gross appearance. It is usually absent in patients with minor lung lesions. Most patients with cavitary disease produce mucoid or mucopurulent sputum. A few produce copious purulent secretions, which can lead to the misdiagnosis of routine bacterial bronchitis or pneumonia. Patients with advanced (often bilateral) lung TB develop exertional dyspnea. Pleuritic chest pain occurs occasionally and usually signals the development of TB pleuritis, which is readily diagnosed from the radiogaphically visible effusion. Pleurisy should be distinguished from the nonspecific chest discomfort (usually bilateral) associated with chronic cough. In the era of effective chemotherapy, hemoptysis complicates fewer than 5% of fresh cases of pulmonary TB and is rarely life threatening. It now occurs more often as a complication of an inactive residual lesion: bronchiectasis, colonization of an old cavity by a fungus ball, or, rarely, the erosion of a calcified lymph node (broncholith) into a bronchus. Hemoptysis is occasionally massive in these settings.

The symptoms of TB are typically subacute to chronic in duration (2 weeks to a few months), an important point in differential diagnosis. Nonetheless, a minority of patients date their illness to a week or less, particularly those with TB pleuritis or acute pneumonia due to bronchogenic spread of acid-fast bacilli from a cavity or eroding lymph node.

Information regarding the patient's possible past experience with the TB bacillus and his or her general health and immune status should be sought. The patient's geographic history is often helpful in estimating the likelihood of prior exposure to *M. tuberculosis* and to relevant fungi (*Histoplasma, Coccidioides, Blastomyces*) and NTM.

One should also seek a history of household or other close, sustained contact with a family member or acquaintance who has had active pulmonary TB (or a suggestive chronic illness).

Objective

Physical Examination

The findings vary widely, depending on the severity of disease and its anatomic location. Patients with pulmonary or disseminated TB often appear chronically ill and become cachectic with advanced disease ("consumption"). Localized extrapulmonary TB typically has less systemic impact, but this varies and major constitutional illness can develop.

Fever is an important diagnostic clue but can be absent in 20 to 40% of hospitalized TB patients for a variety of reasons: small burden of lesions, old age, corticosteroid therapy, prior (partially effective) antituberculous therapy, or severe inanition. Patients with underlying AIDS nearly always mount a fever (usually >39°C) despite their profoundly impaired cell-mediated immunity.

In pulmonary TB the breath sounds over the lesion(s) become bronchovesicular and sometimes harsh in quality. With extensive disease, crackles can be elicited and signs of lung consolidation are exhibited over areas where alveolar filling reaches the pleura. Nonetheless, the chest examination is often unimpressive or normal, even with moderately extensive radiographic abnormalities. Wheezing due to endobronchial TB is a rare finding in adults.

Because TB is a disease affecting the mononuclear phagocyte system, one should seek enlargement of the lymph nodes, liver, and spleen. Lymphadenopathy can occur at any site, as an isolated lesion or secondary to another tuberculous focus in the same lymphatic territory. Supraclavicular and cervical nodes are the most often detected on physical examination. Tuberculous nodes are characteristically firm and matted, with inflammation often extending into the surrounding soft tissues; warmth, tenderness, suppuration, and sinus formation are common features. Mild splenomegaly can develop, usually in the setting of disseminated TB. Diffuse enlargement or focal masses (tuberculomas) of the liver occur infrequently and may be difficult to detect at the bedside.

Pleural effusion complicates about 10% of TB cases, with or without clinically identifiable lung involvement. Effusions are usually unilateral and small to moderate in volume, though massive effusion occurs rarely.

A myriad of extrapulmonary lesions have been described in TB, making this disease another "great imitator." Focal extrapulmonary presentations include lymphadenitis, subacute or chronic meningitis, peritonitis, pericarditis, soft tissue abscesses (paravertebral, anterior chest wall, various other sites), monoarticular arthritis, osteomyelitis (vertebrae, ribs, long bones), renal foci (detected by urinalysis, often with associated ureteral lesions and stricture), scrotal mass, intestinal obstruction, cerebral tuberculoma, and cutaneous nodules and ulcers, among others. Rare immunologic (noninfectious) epiphenomena include erythema nodosum, erythema induratum (a "tuberculid"), and phlyctenular keratoconjunctivitis.

Routine Laboratory Abnormalities

The chest radiograph in pulmonary TB can show any of several characteristic abnormalities. Primary TB (Table 13–41–3) produces a nonspecific alveolar or nodular opacity, often in the periphery of the mid-or lower lung zones. Unilateral hilar and/or mediastinal lymphadenopathy is the hallmark of primary TB, and pleural effusion is also relatively

TABLE 13–41–3. STAGES IN THE NATURAL HISTORY OF *MYCOBACTERIUM TUBERCULOSIS* INFECTION AND DISEASE

Stage	Timing After Initial Infection	Typical Age	Frequency	Characteristic Locations of Disease	Characteristic Clinical Features
Latent	Anytime (duration: years to lifelong)	Any age	Most common	Ghon focus (lung "primary"), metastatic foci (all quiescent)	Asymptomatic, no active lesions (healed granulomas)
Primary*	Initial months to 2–3 years	Childhood and adolescence; Adults in low-prevalence regions	Common where TB is endemic	1. Lung, intrathoracic lymph nodes, pleura 2. Lung apices (Simon foci), extrapulmonary metastases	1. Focal lung infiltrate, hilar and/or mediastinal lymphadenopathy 2. Upper zone fibrocavitary disease, other focal lesions, miliary disease
Post-primary (Secondary)†					
Reactivation	Years to decades	Adulthood (comorbid conditions)	Common	Lung apices (Simon foci), extrapulmonary sites	Upper zone fibrocavitary lung lesions; focal extrapulmonary lesions, miliary disease
Reinfection	Years to decades	Adulthood (impaired defenses)	Uncommon	Lung apices, extrapulmonary sites (?)	Upper zone fibrocavitary lung lesions; ? extrapulmonary lesions‡

*Primary TB may (1) resolve spontaneously (the usual course), (2) progress locally, sometimes with cavitation ("progressive primary" TB), or (3) progress at one or more metastatic sites following early lymphohematogenous dissemination.

†In severe immunodeficiency (e.g., AIDS), reactivation or reinfection disease can resemble progressive primary disease in the immunologically naïve.

‡Clinical descriptions of disease due to reinfection have been limited, as proof of a new strain of *M. tuberculosis* requires special investigative techniques or epidemiologic circumstances. Reinfection pulmonary TB appears to resemble reactivation disease.

frequent. In postprimary TB (i.e., after specific cell-mediated immunity has developed and the primary lesion has resolved), lung infiltrates are characteristically located in upper zones (apical and posterior segments of the upper lobes or, less often, the superior segments of lower lobes) and are bilateral in about 50%. The infiltrates are often "fibronodular" in appearance, and one or more cavities are noted in 40 to 80% of cases. Though generally a reliable diagnostic tool in pulmonary TB, plain radiography often fails to demonstrate endobronchial lesions, minor lymphadenopathy, and early miliary disease.

In moderate to severe TB, nonspecific abnormalities characteristic of a systemic inflammatory state and/or nutritional deprivation are present: reduced serum concentrations of albumin, cholesterol, triiodothyronine (euthyroid sick syndrome), transthyretin (prealbumin), and various other proteins. Serum proteins that are acute phase reactants increase, as may angiotensin-converting enzyme activity. The globulin fraction is often increased, reflecting a polyclonal gammopathy. Mild to moderate hyponatremia (range, 120–135 mEq/L) occurs in 30 to 60% of patients sick enough to be hospitalized, usually reflecting "inappropriate" vasopressin secretion (SIADH).

Anemia of chronic disease, usually mild, is present in the majority of hospitalized TB patients. The total peripheral blood leukocyte count may be normal, mildly increased (10,000–15,000/mm^3), or decreased because of an underlying disorder such as AIDS. Leukemoid reactions occur rarely. Lymphopenia (500–1500/mm^3) is common, as is a mild reactive thrombocytosis. CD4+ lymphocytes can decline to as few as 200/mm^3 due solely to severe TB, but a CD4/CD8 ratio less than 1.0 usually indicates background HIV disease. In disseminated TB one may encounter major anemia, leukopenia, thrombocytopenia, and/or disseminated intravascular coagulation.

Liver enzymes are often increased because of scattered hepatic foci of TB (hepatic granulomas are found on biopsy in up to 25% of patients with pulmonary TB) or, perhaps more often, because of concomitant disorders such as fatty liver and alcoholic hepatitis. Increases in serum alkaline phosphatase and γ-glutamyl transferase (GGT) are typical of granulomatous hepatitis, but mild, nonspecific elevations of aspartate and alanine transaminases and lactate dehydrogenase are also frequent in TB.

Hypercalcemia, usually mild and asymptomatic, occurs in TB as in other granulomatous diseases. This abnormality varies widely in reported prevalence (0–40%) and tends to arise during the weeks following initiation of treatment. The mechanism involves the local production of 1,25-dihydroxyvitamin D$_3$ by mononuclear inflammatory cells within granulomas.

These biochemical and hematologic changes all resolve over a course of weeks to months during successful treatment.

PLANS

Diagnostic

Differential Diagnosis

Tuberculosis overlaps many other infectious and noninfectious diseases in its protean clinical presentations. Other granulomatous diseases (systemic fungal infections, sarcoidosis, Crohn's disease, etc.), which can resemble TB both clinically and histologically, are prominent in the differential diagnosis. Patients with sarcoidosis usually lack major constitutional illness and are afebrile in over 80% of cases.

A healed *calcified granuloma* is often discovered incidentally on chest roentgenogram and is the most common clinical footprint of prior infection. This represents an inactive primary lesion (the Ghon focus) and is attributed to remote tuberculous infection in purified protein derivative (PPD)-positive persons; however, identical lesions due to *Histoplasma capsulatum, Coccidioides immitis,* and other fungi or NTM are common in regions where these organisms are endemic. Specific skin tests aid in presumptive diagnosis, which is mainly important for guiding preventive therapy against TB. When a nodule does not appear extensively calcified by plain radiography or computed tomography scan, neoplasm must be considered (see Chapter 13–38).

Primary TB can progress to resemble subacute or chronic necrotizing pneumonia of any etiology, as well as noninfectious diseases such as vasculitis. Ipsilateral hilar and/or mediastinal lymphadenopathy, if pre-sent, suggests TB as the diagnosis, but this pattern can also be seen with fungal diseases, bronchogenic carcinoma, lymphoma, and uncommon infections such as actinomycosis, nocardiosis, and tularemia.

Chronic cavitary TB can usually be surmised at first glance of the chest radiograph, but may be mimicked by NTM (most often *M. avium* complex [MAC] or *M. kansasii*), systemic fungi (coccidiomycosis, chronic histoplasmosis), nocardiosis, chronic bacterial lung abscess, sarcoidosis, necrotic lung cancer, pneumoconioses, melioidosis, localized *Pneumocystis carinii* pneumonia, and ankylosing spondylitis, among others.

Miliary TB presents initially with radiographically normal or questionably abnormal lungs in 25 to 50% of cases. The telltale picture of disseminated 1- to 5-mm nodules may evolve over the following days to weeks and is better detected by high-resolution computed tomography. Hematogenous fungal and viral infections, early *P. carinii* pneumonia, and some noninfectious interstitial lung diseases can also produce a diffuse micronodular ("miliary") pattern.

Tuberculosis remains a leading infectious cause of *fever of unknown origin.* Occult miliary disease and deep-seated extrapulmonary foci are the forms usually responsible.

Tuberculosis often presents in atypical fashion in adults with HIV disease, due to varying degrees of failure of the cellular immune response. With moderate immunodeficiency (200–500 CD4+ cells/μL), the lung picture often resembles that in HIV-negative patients: upper zone lung cavities are common (~25%) and a reaction to PPD is elicited in more than 50%. With severe immunodeficiency (<200/μL), noncavitary lung infiltrates predominate (often in lower zones, often mimicking other pneumonias) and cutaneous anergy is the rule (>80%). As circulating CD4+ cells decline from moderately to severely reduced levels, lymphohematogenous dissemination becomes increasingly frequent. Thus, regional or disseminated necrotizing lymphadenitis is a clinical hallmark of AIDS-related TB (well demonstrated by computed tomography). The majority of TB patients with frank AIDS have detectable extrapulmonary involvement.

A variety of agents enter the differential diagnosis of AIDS-related TB: routine bacterial, *Pneumocystis,* or nocardial pneumonias; disseminated histoplasmosis or other fungal infections; NTM; toxoplasmal cerebritis; and so on. One useful exclusion is that disseminated MAC infection, though common, virtually never causes clinical lung disease in advanced AIDS (see Chapter 8–76).

The clinical findings in pulmonary and lymphatic disease due to NTM are similar to those in TB, but the illness tends to be milder. The radiographic appearances of lung disease due to NTM largely overlap those of TB, so that cultural identification is essential to specific diagnosis. Upper zone disease and cavitation are typical, just as in postprimary TB. Infection with NTM often develops in the setting of chronic lung disease, such as chronic obstructive pulmonary disease or bronchiectasis. NTM also account for a substantial fraction of solitary lung nodules and healed granulomas in regions where they are prevalent, such as the southeastern United States.

Diagnostic Options

The *chest roentgenogram* is the most important tool in the initial diagnostic evaluation. A posteroanterior lordotic view can help to reveal small apical abnormalities. The chest film is also essential to the evaluation of patients with suspected extrapulmonary TB, as active pulmonary involvement or inactive residual lesions often coexist.

Once pulmonary TB is suspected, three to five *fresh sputum specimens* are obtained for acid-fast bacillus (AFB) smear and culture (one per day, preferably a pooled collection of early-morning sputum). Sputum should also be cultured in patients with only intrathoracic lymphadenopathy or pleural effusion and in suspected miliary disease (even if the radiograph appears normal). If necessary, one can induce sputum using aerosolized 3 to 5% saline in an appropriately ventilated space. Early-morning gastric aspirates are useful mainly in children, but also have a role in adults who cannot cooperate to produce sputum.

Sputum culture is a much more sensitive (and specific) diagnostic test than sputum acid-fast bacillus smear, which may require 10,000 or more acid-fast bacilli/mL for detection. Growth of mycobacteria *in vitro* is usually apparent by 3 weeks but can take as long as 6 to 8 weeks. New technologies such as radiometric culture systems (Bactec) and DNA probes have substantially decreased the average delay to detection and speciation.

Bronchoscopic specimens (biopsy, brushings, lavage fluid) increase the short-term rate of diagnosis in patients who have lung involvement but three or more negative sputum acid-fast bacillus smears; however, most of these patients will have a positive sputum culture within 2 to 6 weeks, so that bronchoscopy is best reserved for those in whom a secure diagnosis is urgently needed or alternative diagnoses are suspected. Urgent bronchoscopy is appropriate in suspected miliary TB, where the diagnostic yield exceeds 70%. Postbronchoscopy sputum has an excellent yield and should always be collected.

Blood cultures for mycobacteria are useful (though growth may require several weeks) in disseminated TB (miliary disease, multifocal lymphadenitis, etc.) and in all forms of AIDS-related TB, where the sensitivity may exceed 25% when a lysis–centrifugation method is employed.

Any other site that appears diseased is an appropriate source for *histologic and/or culture material*. Pleural fluid should be cultured (centrifuging a large-volume sample improves sensitivity) and is an indication for closed (or occasionally thoracoscopic) pleural biopsy. Fine-needle aspiration is the initial approach to lymphadenitis, soft tissue abscesses, or solid organ lesions and often obviates tissue biopsy. Urine should be cultured in suspected genitourinary TB or when there is unexplained microscopic hematuria or pyuria: three daily collections of early-morning urine suffice.

Many NTM are found in the environment and can colonize the respiratory tract as saprophytes, especially in abnormal lungs (see Table 13–41–2). As a rule, therefore, pulmonary disease is ascribed to NTM only when there are compatible clinical and radiographic abnormalities together with repeated isolation of the same species from sputum (at least two to four isolates, preferably over 2 or more weeks). A positive sputum acid-fast bacillus smear and numerous (>100) colonies on culture are supportive evidence (however smear-positive patients should be managed as having TB until proven otherwise). Cultivation of NTM from any normally sterile site (blood, lymph node, bone marrow, etc.) is diagnostic of infection.

As a rule any specimen cultured for mycobacteria should also be *cultured for fungi and routine bacteria*, the main exception being sputum in "obvious" cases of pulmonary TB.

The standard *tuberculin skin test* entails the intracutaneous injection of 0.1 mL of purified protein derivative (PPD, 5 tuberculin units; other doses are not recommended). After 48 to 72 hours the largest diameter of *induration* at the site is measured. The criteria for a positive test (Table 13–41–4) have been chosen to identify most true positives while eliminating most of the false positives caused by environmental exposure to cross-reacting NTM.

This is a diagnostic test for infection by *M. tuberculosis,* not for disease (TB). A positive reaction requires a sufficient level of cellular immunity (delayed-type hypersensitivity) in the patient, so the test may be falsely negative due to global (or occasionally PPD-specific) anergy. The PPD test is often negative at the time of diagnosis of active TB (in about 20% of pulmonary and 50% of miliary cases in the pre-AIDS era), reflecting transient anergy associated with the illness. These patients become tuberculin-reactive during recovery unless there is a persisting cause of anergy, such as AIDS. Thus, the PPD test can neither rule in nor rule out the diagnosis of TB, which must always be based on other grounds.

Once PPD-positive, most persons remain PPD-reactive for many years and often lifelong. Persisting reactivity is believed to indicate either low-grade latent infection (the rationale for chemoprophylaxis) or repeated unrecognized exposures to *M. tuberculosis.* The PPD response wanes over the years in some individuals, presumably because their immune system is no longer exposed to specific mycobacterial antigens. The administration of PPD to such a person can reawaken the delayed-type hypersensitivity response, the so-called "booster effect" (however, tuberculin testing does not induce reactivity by itself). It is therefore recommended that persons who will be screened periodically be retested 1 to 2 weeks following a negative or "borderline" result; this modestly increases the sensitivity of testing and reduces the likelihood that the individual will be incorrectly labeled a "new converter" on subsequent testing.

Vaccination against TB is practiced in most of the world's countries using bacille Calmette–Guérin (BCG, live attenuated strains derived from *M. bovis*), a moderately effective vaccine. BCG induces PPD reactivity, but the reaction tends to be smaller and wane faster than that due to natural infection, especially when vaccination is performed in infancy. In general, BCG-induced reactions cannot be reliably distinguished from "true positives," though they infrequently exceed 20 mm in size. It is recommended to discount the BCG history in managing PPD-positive persons who are at substantial epidemiologic risk of *M. tuberculosis* infection.

Skin test reagents specific to selected NTM have been available but are not in general clinical use. They have proved valuable mainly in epidemiologic investigation.

Recommended Approach

Every effort should be made to optimize the likelihood of obtaining a positive culture: this not only confirms TB (or NTM infection) but also permits *in vitro* tests of drug sensitivity, which are critical to subsequent management. In TB, in contrast to many bacterial infections, cultures obtained after initiation of specific chemotherapy are still useful; they often remain positive (albeit with a steeply declining yield) for days or weeks. In most cases of localized TB, it is safe to complete diagnostic studies before initiating therapy. Drugs should be administered without delay in the devastating forms of TB, such as meningitis, miliary or far-advanced lung disease, pericarditis, and uveitis.

Therapeutic

Therapeutic Options

The use of streptomycin against TB (1946) marked the advent of effective chemotherapy for mycobacterial diseases. By the mid-1950s the cardinal principles of drug management were established:

- A minimum of two effective drugs must be given; resistance develops rapidly (initial weeks) during monotherapy.
- Treatment must be prolonged to prevent relapse. Subpopulations of dormant or slowly replicating mycobacteria ("persisters") can be eliminated only with months of chemotherapy. At present, the shortest standard regimen lasts 6 months.
- Never add a single drug to a regimen that appears to be failing clinically and/or microbiologically, or after which the patient's disease has relapsed. This is a corollary to the development of acquired (secondary) resistance during monotherapy.

TABLE 13–41–4. INTERPRETATION OF THE TUBERCULIN SKIN TEST

Recommended Criteria for a Positive Test (PPD, TU)*

1. High risk of tuberculous infection: induration (≥)5 mm
- HIV infection (or risk factor with unknown serology)
- Recent close contact with an infectious TB case
- Chest radiograph consistent with old healed TB

2. Moderate risk of tuberculous infection: induration (≥)10 mm
- Foreign-born persons from high-prevalence countries
- Medical conditions that increase the risk of TB†
- Intravenous drug users
- Medically underserved, low-income populations, especially minorities
- Residents of long-term care facilities

3. Low risk of tuberculous infection: induration (≥)15 mm
- All other persons

PPD, purified protein derivative; TU, tuberculin units.
*The three strata of risk take into account the epidemiologic risk of infection by *Mycobacterium tuberculosis,* the risk of progression to disease once infected, and/or the likelihood of diminished test sensitivity due to anergy (all three factors apply in HIV disease).
†Medical risk factors include silicosis, chronic renal failure, diabetes mellitus, high-dose corticosteroid or immunosuppressive therapy, hematologic malignancies, uncontrolled carcinoma, loss of ≥10% of ideal body weight, gastrectomy, jejunoileal bypass, and possibly other conditions (such as alcoholism) that compromise immune function.
Adapted from American Thoracic Society. Diagnostic standards and classification of tuberculosis. Am Rev Respir Dis 1990;142:725.

- Maintaining the patient's compliance throughout the regimen is the main challenge in achieving cure.

The combination of isoniazid and rifampin is the bedrock of modern chemotherapy; all other agents play secondary or reserve roles (Tables 13–41–5, 13–41–6). In the current "short-course" (i.e., <1 year) regimen for pulmonary TB, the early sterilizing activity of pyrazinamide is employed for the first 2 months to reduce the total duration of treatment to 6 months. Table 13–41–7 outlines standard and alternative regimens, which are also appropriate for the treatment of extrapulmonary TB.

Treatment must be altered and prolonged when *drug resistance* is present. Resistance to antituberculous drugs develops by spontaneous mutation in any population of *M. tuberculosis*. For example, resistance to isoniazid occurs in approximately 1 per 10^6 bacilli. As resistance to different drugs arises independently, the probability of encountering a bacillus resistant to two first-line drugs approximates 1 in $10^{11–14}$, an unlikely occurrence given the total bacillary population in a typical TB patient.

A drug-resistant isolate from a patient who has never taken antituberculous drugs (*primary resistance*) reflects prior transmission of a resistant strain (or possibly spontaneous mutation after the patient was infected.) Primary resistance to one or more first-line agents is common worldwide, being encountered in 10% or more of new cases in most nations. Resistance to isoniazid is most frequent, with rates exceeding 20% in some locales. In the United States, primary drug resistance varies widely among communities (from <5% to 30%), averaging about 10%. Drug resistance cannot be predicted reliably at diagnosis in a given patient, so that susceptibility testing should always be performed.

Acquired (secondary) drug resistance develops when chemotherapy for initially susceptible bacilli has been inadequate or irregular, usually due to poor compliance in drug taking. In general, a history of prior therapy (for >2–4 weeks) is the strongest risk factor for drug resistance. Rates of acquired resistance are typically two-fold higher than primary resistance and have reached 40% or more in some communities.

Multidrug-resistant TB escalated dramatically from 1980 to the early 1990s. Multidrug resistance is operationally defined as resistance to two or more drugs including both isoniazid and rifampin. Its prevalence in the United States varies greatly but has recently reached 10 to 20% of new isolates in some urban locales. Multidrug-resistant TB has proved to be incurable in up to half of cases and is often fatal, especially in the immunocompromised.

Antiinflammatory therapy with systemic corticosteroids (e.g., prednisone 20–60 mg daily for 2–4 weeks, then tapered rapidly), although controversial and not rigorously studied, may be beneficial in specific situations by reducing tissue damage, systemic illness, and/or late fibrotic sequelae. Glucocorticoids are currently favored in ocular, meningeal, and pericardial TB. Their potential value in severe pulmonary or miliary TB remains unestablished.

Surgery can be curative in patients who do not respond to the available drugs. Resection of localized disease (lobectomy or pneumonectomy, lymphadenectomy) has long been a mainstay of management for selected cases of recalcitrant NTM disease (*M. scrofulaceum*, MAC, etc.) and has seen a recent resurgence for refractory multidrug-resistant TB.

The management of other pulmonary mycobacterioses follows principles similar to those for TB, except that contagion is not a concern. In general, optimal drug regimens are less well defined due to limited clinical trials and, for some species, refractoriness to available antibiotics. *In vitro* susceptibility testing of NTM has not been as well correlated with clinical response as for *M. tuberculosis*, and its value is controversial.

Recommended Approach

The treatment guidelines published periodically by the American Thoracic Society (1990, 1992, 1994) are recommended. It is crucial to make an appropriate selection of drugs and their doses at the start. Errors in management prove costly in terms of prolonged hospitalization, morbidity, or even death, besides fostering drug-resistant strains in the community.

Given the widespread prevalence of primary resistance to isoniazid and/or other drugs, initial treatment in most communities should comprise a minimum of four drugs. The combination of isoniazid, rifampin, pyrazinamide, and ethambutol, all taken orally, is preferred. Patients

TABLE 13–41–5. FIRST-LINE ANTITUBERCULOUS DRUGS*†

Drug	Usual Formulation	Usual Daily Dose (Adults)	Usual Twice-weekly Dose (Adults)	Main Adverse Effects	Recommended Routine Monitoring	Comments
Isoniazid (INH)‡	300-mg tablet	5 mg/kg (300 mg)	15 mg/kg (750–900 mg)	Increased liver enzymes, hepatitis, neuropathy	Symptoms, AST/ALT in selected patients	Cornerstone of therapy Drug interactions (phenytoin, carbamazepine)
Rifampin (RIF)	300-mg capsule	10 mg/kg (600 mg)	10 mg/kg (600 mg)	Hepatitis, flulike syndrome, nephritis (rare),	Symptoms, AST/ALT in selected patients	Cornerstone of therapy Key to short-course therapy Liver enzyme inducer: many drug interactions
Pyrazinamide (PZA)	500-mg tablet	25 mg/kg (1.5–2.5 g)	40–60 mg/kg (2.5–3.5 g)	Arthralgias, gastrointestinal upset, rash, hepatitis (with high doses)	Symptoms	Enhances early sterilizing activity Increases serum urate (usually asymptomatic)
Ethambutol (EMB)	400-mg tablet	15 mg/kg§ (800–1400 mg)	50 mg/kg (2.4–3.6 g)	Optic neuropathy (especially at high doses), rash	Color vision and acuity monthly	Possibly bactericidal at high doses Main role: prevention of acquired resistance
Streptomycin (SM)‖	Vial, 400 mg/mL	15 mg/kg IM (0.75–1.0 g)	25–30 mg/kg (1.2–1.6 g)	Ototoxicity, renal toxicity	Audiometry q1–2 mo, blood urea nitrogen/creatinine	First-choice injectable Main role: therapy of drug-resistant tuberculosis

AST, aspartate transaminase; ALT, alanine transaminase.
*All except EMB are bactericidal at the usual daily dose. INH and RIF are believed to be active against both rapidly multiplying and dormant bacilli, whether intra- or extracellular in location. SM is active at neutral or alkaline pH, as found in lung cavities; PZA is believed to be active against intracellular bacilli in an acid environment.
†Fixed-dose combination tablets are available for INH + RIF (Rifamate) and INH + RIF + PZA (Rifater); these are especially recommended for patients on a self-administered outpatient regimen.
‡Vitamin B_6 (25–50 mg) is commonly given with INH to prevent pyridoxine deficiency.
§High-dose ethambutol (25 mg/kg) may be used initially, especially for TB meningitis or drug-resistant strains (retinal toxicity is increased).
‖SM is available free-of-charge in the United States from Pfizer Pharmaceuticals (800–254–4445).

TABLE 13–41–6. SECOND-LINE ANTITUBERCULOUS DRUGS*

Agent	Usual Formulation	Usual Daily Dose (Adult)	Main Adverse Effects	Comments
Ofloxacin[†]	200-, 300-, 400-mg tablets	600 mg (range 400–800)	CNS (dizziness, headache, etc.), GI upset	Usually well tolerated Active against many bacteria Drug interactions (theophylline, warfarin)
Cycloserine	250-mg capsules	500–1000 mg in 2–3 doses/d	CNS (impaired mentation, depression, seizures, etc.), rash	Increase dose gradually Monitor mental status
Ethionamide	250-mg tablets	500–1000 mg in 2–4 doses/d	GI upset, metallic taste, increased liver enzymes	Often poorly tolerated Start with 250 mg and increase gradually
Capreomycin	1-g vial, powder	15 mg/kg IM (up to 1 g)	Ototoxicity, renal toxicity, decreased K and Mg	Second-choice injectable Useful for streptomycin-resistant strains Monitor audiogram and blood urea nitrogen/creatinine
Amikacin	1-g vial, 250 mg/mL	15 mg/kg IM or IV (up to 1.2 g)	Renal toxicity, ototoxicity, decreased K and Mg	Similar to kanamycin Alternative to streptomycin (cross-resistance)
Kanamycin	Vials, 250 or 333 mg/mL	15 mg/kg IM or IV (up to 1.2 g)	Renal toxicity, ototoxicity, decreased K and Mg	Alternative to streptomycin (cross-resistance) Pain at injection sites
para-Amino salicylic acid[‡]	Granules in 4-g packet	4 g tid or bid	GI upset, hypersensitivity, increased liver enzymes	New formulation well tolerated Drug interactions
Clofazimine	100-mg capsules	100–300 mg	Orange/brown skin discoloration, rare visual disturbance	Efficacy in TB questionable (used for leprosy, some nontuberculous mycobacteria) Long tissue half-life (weeks)

CNS, central nervous system; GI, gastrointestinal

*In general, these agents are less effective and less well tolerated than first-line drugs. Their use for intermittent therapy is not established and should be considered only for the injectables.

[†]Ciprofloxacin 750–1250 mg qd is an alternative quinolone.

[‡]PAS was relicensed for use in the United States in 1995. (Jacobus, Princeton, NJ).

with possible drug-resistant TB are given five or six drugs, including at least two not taken previously, pending new sensitivity data. Streptomycin and a quinolone are usually the next drugs of choice. Known or suspected drug-resistant TB should be managed in consultation with an expert.

The major obstacle to success in managing TB is not limited effectiveness of therapy but rather limited adherence to the prescribed regimen. Faulty compliance with pill taking is common even among patients who seem reliable and who attend follow-up appointments regularly. *Directly observed therapy,* in which patients take their medications under supervision (usually 2, 3, or 5 days per week) in a clinic or other outpatient setting, has proved quite effective in improving the rate of successful completion. Directly observed therapy should be mandatory for any patient on an intermittent regimen or with drug-resistant TB; it is also urged for the routine management of all TB patients where logistically feasible.

In HIV disease TB tends to arise before other opportunistic infections and is often the first major complication of the immunodeficiency. Routine consideration of underlying HIV infection is therefore appropriate (Table 13–41–8), and serology and counseling are recommended for all persons with newly diagnosed TB.

The reader is referred to Havlir and Ellner (1995), Friedman (1994), and Reichman and Hershfield (1993) and to specialty sources regarding treatment of mycobacterioses due to NTM.

FOLLOW-UP

Modern TB chemotherapy is rapidly bactericidal and brings clinical recovery within days to a few weeks. Early indicators of a favorable response include improvement in appetite and malaise, abatement of fever, and correction of hyponatremia. In contrast, radiographic infiltrates and granulomatous inflammation are slow to resolve. Failure of

TABLE 13–41–7. RECOMMENDED DRUG REGIMENS FOR TUBERCULOSIS*

Clinical Situation	Initial Intensive Phase[†]	Continuation Phase[‡]	Comments
Isolate sensitive to first-line drugs	INH, RIF, PZA, and EMB daily for 2 mo	INH and RIF daily for 4 mo	Standard daily regimen ("short course")
Isolate sensitive to first-line drugs	INH, RIF, PZA, and EMB daily for 2 mo	INH and RIF twice weekly for 4 mo	Standard intermittent regimen
Isolate sensitive to first-line drugs	INH, RIF, PZA, SM daily for 2 wk, then twice weekly for 6 wk	INH and RIF twice weekly for 18 wk	Alternative "Denver regimen" using intermittent therapy (only 62 doses in all)
Isolate sensitive to first-line drugs	INH, RIF, PZA, and EMB thrice weekly for 2 mo	INH and RIF ± PZA thrice weekly	Intermittent therapy throughout Some authorities add SM or continue PZA for >2 mo
Resistance to INH only	RIF, PZA, EMB daily (consider adding SM or quinolone)	Continue 3–4 drugs for 6–9 mo total or for 6 mo after culture conversion	High cure rate Use daily therapy
Resistance to INH and RIF only	PZA, EMB, SM, and quinolone daily	Continue 4 drugs daily for 12–18 mo after culture conversion	Reduced cure rate
Resistance to INH, RIF, + other drugs	Minimum of three drugs with *in vitro* sensitivity	Continue all drugs daily for 18 mo after culture conversion	Reduced cure rate Consider surgery if no response

*See Table 13–41–5 for drugs.

[†]Daily therapy is given for the first 1–2 months, except as noted ("Denver regimen"). A minimum of four drugs are recommended until susceptibility data become available, unless the local prevalence of drug-resistant strains is <4% and the patient has no risk factor for drug resistance.

[‡]Supervised intermittent therapy is recommended for the continuation phase, provided the isolate is drug sensitive; EMB is discontinued once susceptibility to INH and RIF is confirmed. Some authorities recommend prolonged therapy (9 months) for patients with underlying AIDS or with TB involving bone or central nervous system.

TABLE 13-41-8. EPIDEMIOLOGY OF TUBERCULOSIS: SELECTED STATISTICS

	Number	Comments	Source
Global statistics			
Number of persons infected (prevalence)	1,700,000,000	WHO estimate, 1990	Sudre, Bull WHO 1992;70:149
Number of active TB cases (prevalence)	15,000,000–20,000,000		
New TB cases per year (incidence)	8,000,000	WHO estimate, 1992	Bloom (1994)
Deaths from TB per year	2,700,000	WHO estimate, 1992	Bloom (1994)
TB with HIV infection	>5,100,000	WHO estimate, mid 1994	Raviglione, JAMA 1995;273:220
U.S. statistics			
Number of persons infected (prevalence)	10,000,000	CDC estimate (conservative)	Rosenblum, Ann Intern Med 1994;121:786
Overall incidence (cases/100,000/year)	~10	Local rates vary widely	CDC; Bloom (1994), Reichman and Hershfield (1993)
HIV coinfection in TB patients (adults aged 15–44, 1985–1990)	21%	Hospital discharge data (underdiagnosis of HIV)	CDC; Rosenblum, Ann Intern Med 1994;121:786
HIV seroprevalence in new TB patients	21%* (range <1–60%)*	1985–1991, several prospective surveys in urban centers	Bates (1994), Pitchenik and Fertel (1992), Reichman and Hershfield (1993)

WHO, World Health Organization; CDC, Centers for Disease Control and Prevention.
*21% = pooled seroprevalence in 33 urban TB clinics (20 cities) in 1991; median clinic value = 9.5% (Oronato, IXth International Conference on AIDS, 1993; abstract WS-C18-6); range includes other studies.

fever to diminish within 1 to 2 weeks or any sign of clinical worsening should arouse concern about drug resistance, a different or additional diagnosis, or noncompliance with pill taking. Although occasional patients with drug-sensitive TB have prolonged fever (>2 weeks, usually in advanced cavitary disease) or transient exacerbation of a lesion during successful therapy, any potentially adverse trend should prompt the addition of two or three new drugs until susceptibility results are available.

Follow-up sputum cultures are obtained weekly during early therapy and monthly after a favorable response is evident. The density of acid-fast bacilli on smear should diminish during the first 2 weeks of therapy, but final conversion of cultures to negative may take 2 months or longer in advanced cavitary disease.

Outpatients who are taking medications either for active TB or for its prevention should be seen at least monthly to evaluate their progress, review compliance, and exclude significant side effects. Prescriptions should be limited to 1 month's supply of pills.

Tuberculosis patients satisfactorily completing therapy do not need further follow-up provided their isolate was drug-sensitive and their clinical response was uncomplicated. Patients with multidrug-resistant strains, underlying immunodeficiency, or other special considerations are followed at 6-month intervals for another 2 years.

DISCUSSION

Prevalence and Incidence

Mycobacterium tuberculosis is endemic worldwide, infecting an estimated one third of humans (see Table 13-41-8). Although its prevalence has declined tremendously in many nations since the 19th century, TB remains the world's leading infectious cause of death.

Tuberculosis has long been recognized to be a "social disease" in that it flourishes endemically given predisposing social, hygienic, and economic factors: poverty, crowded living conditions, malnutrition, inadequate maintenance of personal and public health, alcoholism, drug abuse, and so on. New cases are diagnosed in about 10 per 100,000 persons (~25,000 cases) per annum in the United States. Case rates vary dramatically according to local epidemiologic conditions, as illustrated in New York City, where annual case rates range by neighborhood from less than 10 to more than 150 per 100,000 inhabitants.

In most of the world other mycobacterioses (leprosy aside) are much less prevalent than TB, though collectively they now rival TB in some "developed" regions. The ratio of NTM disease to TB is roughly 1:10 in some American reports, but reliable statistics are sparse.

Mycobacterial diseases are arguably the foremost infectious complications of HIV disease. TB is 20- to 100-fold more likely to develop in HIV-seropositive persons. Similarly, HIV-infected individuals who harbor latent *M. tuberculosis* run a 5 to 15% annual risk of developing TB and a lifetime risk of up to 50% unless preventive therapy is given. Worldwide, an estimated 40% of HIV-positive persons are coinfected by *M. tuberculosis;* hence, TB is the leading AIDS-related infection in some regions, especially sub-Saharan Africa. In North America HIV seroprevalence among TB cases varies widely, from less than 5% to 40% or more in communities where HIV flourishes.

Nontuberculous mycobacteria are also well-recognized opportunists in AIDS patients, typically causing disseminated mycobacteriosis. MAC is by far the most common, afflicting 20 to 50% of patients with advanced AIDS (CD4 count < 100/µL) in the United States (see Chapter 8–76).

Related Basic Science

Genetics

The innate susceptibility of humans to TB varies among individuals and among ethnic and racial groups. Host resistance to virulent *M. tuberculosis* is believed to be determined by multiple genes which are as yet unidentified. Death rates are high when *M. tuberculosis* first invades a previously unexposed population (e.g., Eskimos or Pacific Islanders). In contrast, many nationalities have acquired substantial herd immunity through centuries of culling by this lethal parasite. Variability in resistance remains, however; for example, African-Americans appear to be twofold more likely than Caucasian Americans to become infected when exposed to this microbe.

Altered Molecular Biology

Mycobacterium tuberculosis contains no known endo- or exotoxins. Rather, the clinical disease that it provokes represents the host's inflammatory response to these tenacious bacilli. Tissue injury may result from several mechanisms, including proteolytic enzymes and reactive oxygen species released from activated mononuclear phagocytes and neutrophils, as well as cytolytic T-cell activity. Tumor necrosis factor, interleukin-1, and other inflammatory cytokines derived from macrophages and T lymphocytes produce the constitutional abnormalities, including fever, weight loss, and altered serum proteins.

Physiologic or Metabolic Derangement

Most patients with moderate to severe TB exhibit the euthyroid sick syndrome (manifest mainly as a low serum triiodothyronine, but with normal or reduced triiodothyronine resin uptake) and mild, asymptomatic hyponatremia due to osmotically inappropriate vasopressin secretion (SIADH). Fulminant (usually miliary) TB occasionally produces the clinical picture of septic shock and can lead to adult respiratory distress syndrome and multisystem organ failure.

Pulmonary TB leaves permanent lung sequelae of varying severity. Spirometry in treated patients commonly discloses a restrictive and/or obstructive ventilatory defect.

Anatomic Derangement

The necrotizing granuloma is the histologic hallmark of TB (and most NTM infections), reflecting the concerted activity of helper T lymphocytes, activated macrophages, cytolytic T lymphocytes, and possibly other cells (*cell-mediated immunity*). Acid-fast bacilli within granulomas vary in number from extremely scarce to copious, depending on the efficacy of local cellular defenses. The host's intense inflammatory response (*delayed-type hypersensitivity*) causes central necrosis within tubercles, the devitalized region classically transforming into a solid cheeselike (caseous) mass which heals by fibrosis. For reasons that are not well understood, the necrotic material sometimes liquefies. Liquefaction within the lung results in an open cavity which, because of the enormous number of extracellular bacilli present (estimated at 10^{7-8} per cavity), plays a key role in contagion and hence in the maintenance of this parasite within human populations.

Pyogenic abscesses containing neutrophils are another familiar pathologic response in TB; these may be "hot" or "cold" in clinical appearance. They can arise from suppurating lymph nodes or other solid foci, whence they form sinus tracts to a body surface or dissect along fascial planes (psoas abscess, parasternal abscess, etc.).

Tuberculous lesions are highly destructive, effacing the tissue architecture at involved sites. Common thoracic sequelae include gross scarring of the lung and adjacent pleura, chronic cavities, bronchiectasis (often in the upper lobes and "dry," i.e., without persistent sputum production), bronchostenosis (especially in children), and local obliteration of pulmonary vasculature. Residual cavities often become colonized by saprophytic microbes: aspergillomas eventually develop in up to 20% and provoke hemoptysis (usually minor) in more than half of cases.

Natural History and Its Modification with Treatment

Mycobacterium tuberculosis is an aerobic intracellular parasite of humans that is not found elsewhere in nature. Naturally occurring infection is acquired only through exposure to a person with active TB. The route of transmission is virtually always by inhalation of one or more viable mycobacteria into the lung.

Person-to-person transmission becomes possible when organisms are aerosolized by someone with active pulmonary TB, especially during cough. Factors favoring transmission include a high bacillary load in the airway secretions of the index (source) case, as evidenced by a positive sputum smear for acid-fast bacilli and/or the presence of lung cavities; prolonged close contact in an indoor space, especially by living in the same household; and relatively low innate resistance in the recipient (innate resistance varies even among normal humans). This bacterium is only moderately infectious; thus, the likelihood of transmission from one brief contact is usually minimal, and repeated inhalations of virulent bacilli may be required before one or more is successful in establishing infection. Nonetheless, whether transmission will result from a given exposure is unpredictable, whence the importance of applying respiratory isolation precautions consistently.

Infection occurs when *M. tuberculosis* eludes the innate nonimmune defenses of the lung and survives within phagocytes. During the 2 to 4 weeks needed for the host to mount a primary cell-mediated immune response, bacilli multiply locally and are carried to the regional lymphatics, these disseminating via the bloodstream. With the development of an effective immune response, a macroscopic granulomatous lesion (a tubercle) appears at the initial locus of infection, curtailing the further multiplication and dissemination of bacilli. Granulomas also develop at minute metastatic lesions throughout the body. Such lymphohematogenous deposits are common in the lungs (especially in the apices, where alveolar oxygen tension is highest), lymph nodes, spleen, liver (Kuppfer cells), bone marrow, kidneys, and brain and meninges, but can occur at virtually any site. They provide the nidus for recrudescent pulmonary or extrapulmonary disease later in life.

Any patient with active TB is at one of three possible stages in the natural history of this infection (see Table 13–41–3). Where *M. tuberculosis* is endemic, primary TB develops mainly in children and adoles-

cents. During the last century the prevalence of TB has declined steadily throughout the world, particularly in "developed" nations, the main exception being a recent resurgence in communities hard-hit by HIV. Thus, reactivation of latent infection acquired years or decades earlier accounts for the majority of new cases in adults. In the United States about 90% of adult cases in recent decades have been ascribed to reactivation; however, recent studies using "DNA fingerprinting" suggest that one third of new TB cases in selected urban centers result from recent transmission, reflecting a shift in epidemiologic influences (AIDS, homelessness, suboptimal TB control programs, recent immigrants, etc.).

By conventional wisdom, tuberculin-positive persons with an intact immune system are highly resistant to repeated infection; however, recent studies confirm that reinfection with a new strain of *M. tuberculosis* can sometimes occur and produce disease, especially (but not exclusively) in immunodeficient individuals. It has been traditional to categorize TB cases as "primary" or "reactivated" based on certain clinical and epidemiologic features (see Table 13–41–3), but it is now clear that such associations are unreliable, particularly in immunodeficient patients. In most patients one cannot be certain of the route to active disease, though one can reasonably presume reactivation if there is a known history of prior TB or tuberculin reactivity.

In the natural history of tuberculous infection, about 5% of persons develop active TB within several years of initial infection ("early" disease), and reactivated TB afflicts another 5% more than 5 years after infection ("late" disease); the remainder never develop clinical TB.

Pleural TB develops when a (caseous) lung lesion erupts through the visceral pleura, as can happen during primary or postprimary disease. In most cases of pleural involvement the local hypersensitivity reaction to mycobacterial components produces an outpouring of serous fluid, which tends to resolve even without therapy. TB can also cause frank empyema and fibrothorax, but these are uncommon in the era of effective therapy.

In about 15% of all TB cases, the sole or dominant focus of disease is extrapulmonary in location (including the pleural space [see Table 13–41–1]); extrapulmonary sites account for a greater proportion where HIV-related TB is common. Extrathoracic TB reflects prior lymphohematogenous dissemination and is usually due to late reactivation.

Miliary TB arises when a necrotizing focus seeds the bloodstream massively with bacilli, producing a syndrome—often overwhelming—in which thousands of minute hematogenous lesions develop synchronously in many organs. It can arise at any stage in the natural history of *M. tuberculosis* infection: within weeks of infection in an infant, after months of pulmonary or extrapulmonary disease in an immnocompetent adult, or following recent or reactivated infection in an AIDS patient.

The course of TB in a given patient may wax or wane according to the complex interaction between the bacillus, the host's immune system, and the pathologic consequences of the disease. The clinical pace of TB varies widely, ranging from fulminant miliary disease or tuberculous pneumonia, which can be fatal in days, to a contained focus that smolders for years. Untreated, TB is often lethal, even in populations with a high "herd immunity." In the preantibiotic era pulmonary TB was ultimately fatal in about half of cases. Another quarter followed a chronic course with recurrent sputum positivity; the remainder achieved cure.

Modern chemotherapy cures more than 95% of drug-sensitive cases, given reasonable adherence. Cure rates are lower if there is resistance to rifampin or to two or more first-line drugs, but even then most cases can be arrested with appropriate supervised therapy. The overall case fatality rate for TB in the United States is about 5 to 10%. Drug-sensitive pulmonary TB is fatal in about 2 to 5%, mainly in advanced cavitary disease; mortality is higher in miliary and meningeal TB. Mortality may be increased somewhat in persons with underlying HIV disease, but most die from other complications of AIDS within 2 years of TB diagnosis.

Failure to consider and pursue the diagnosis of TB may be the foremost factor leading to death; 5% of cases reported in the United States in 1985–1988 died without benefit of treatment. Failure of physicians to "think TB" is a problem particularly in atypical pulmonary presentations and in occult miliary, meningeal, and other extrapulmonary forms.

Disease due to NTM is not considered to be contagious; transmission between humans remains to be proven, although it is conceivable, especially to an immunocompromised recipient. The environmental reservoirs of NTM vary, including fresh water, soil, food and milk, and domestic or wild animals and birds (see Table 13–41–2); for some species the sources of infection are poorly understood. Most NTM infections are believed to occur by inhalation; some occur by aspiration, enteric invasion, or inoculation through the skin. Progression from respiratory tract colonization to disease typically occurs when lung defenses are impaired, often from chronic obstructive pulmonary disease, though healthy persons (especially the elderly) also fall victim to the more virulent species. Latent infection and reactivation disease are believed to occur and may explain the prevalence of upper zone fibronodular and cavitary disease, as in TB.

In immunocompetent patients, NTM pulmonary disease is generally less lethal than TB. As with TB, the natural history varies, but most infections are chronic and slowly progressive. Response to chemotherapy depends on the species (see Table 13–41–2); cure rates may exceed 90% for *M. kansasii,* but have been less (30–80%) for MAC. New antibiotics, such as clarithromycin for MAC, should improve the outcome.

Prevention

Tuberculosis is among the most important of communicable diseases. Clinicians play a key role in preventing its spread in several ways: by correctly diagnosing patients with active disease; by enforcing respiratory isolation for those whose disease involves the lungs, upper airways, or intrathoracic lymph nodes; by identifying infected individuals through appropriate skin testing and contact investigation; and by prescribing preventive chemotherapy for selected individuals with infection or at substantial risk of infection (Table 13–41–9).

Standard preventive therapy consists of isoniazid 300 mg daily (or 900 mg twice weekly as directly observed therapy), taken for 6 to 12 months. There is much interest in developing briefer multidrug regimens to address the problems of noncompliance and drug resistance, but none has been established by adequate clinical trials.

The PPD status of all persons should be determined as a routine part of health maintenance. PPD-negative persons who are at significant risk for infection (health care workers, HIV-seropositive persons, drug addicts, inhabitants of geographic "hot spots" for TB, etc.) should be monitored periodically (e.g., annually) for conversion. The close contacts of every patient with newly diagnosed TB should be screened by skin testing. Contacts who are PPD negative remain candidates for prophylaxis until retesting 2 to 3 months after last exposure excludes recent infection.

Cost Containment

An effective program for outpatient care allows hospitalization to be curtailed. Except for severe cases of TB, 1 to 2 weeks in hospital usually suffices. Medical criteria for discharge include negative sputum examinations for acid-fast bacilli (or a confirmed major reduction in bacillary load), a definite clinical response (improved appetite and well-being, resolution of fever), and no suspicion of drug-resistant infection. Patients with mild disease can receive their entire treatment as outpatients provided they can be sequestered initially in a stable home environment and seem capable of adhering to therapy (directly observed therapy is preferred). The major risk to household contacts occurs before diagnosis (~25–50% have already been infected by then), and their subsequent risk fades rapidly during the initial days to weeks of chemotherapy.

Directly observed therapy of TB is economical in endemic areas, as the savings from preventing new infections and new active (especially drug-resistant) cases among contacts can far exceed the costs of administering the program. Intermittent therapy, which should always be supervised (directly observed therapy), is recommended for the continuation phase (see Table 13–41–7). It is at least as effective as daily therapy and reduces the total cost of the regimen, but is generally restricted to patients with isolates sensitive to isoniazid and rifampin.

TABLE 13–41–9. HIGH-PRIORITY CANDIDATES FOR TUBERCULOSIS-PREVENTIVE CHEMOTHERAPY (TUBERCULIN REACTORS, NO EVIDENCE OF TB)*

Prevention Recommended Regardless of Age

Known or suspected HIV infection[†]

Close contacts of person with infectious TB[‡]

Recent tuberculin skin test converters[§]

Medical conditions that increase the risk of TB[‖]

Prevention Recommended for Individuals <35 years old and Without Additional Risk Factors for TB

Foreign-born persons from high-prevalence countries

Medically underserved low-income populations, including high-risk racial or ethnic groups (African-Americans, Hispanics, Native Americans, etc.)

Residents of long-term care facilities (correctional institutions, nursing homes, mental institutions)

Staff of public institutions and health care facilities in whom TB would pose a risk to many susceptible persons

*Mutidrug therapy for 4 months is now recommended for persons whose chest radiograph is consistent with old TB and who have not received adequate chemotherapy.

[†]Preventive therapy may be offered in the absence of a positive tuberculin test if the person is at high risk of infection and is anergic.

[‡]Preventive therapy should be considered if the initial tuberculin reaction is <5 mm, pending repeat testing 2–3 months after cessation of contact.

[§]"Recent conversion" includes (1) change from unreactive to positive skin test within the last 2 years, (2) all children <2 years old with reaction ≥10 mm, and (3) an *increase* in reaction size of ≥10 mm (≥15 for persons ≥35 years old) within the last 2 years.

[‖]See Table 13–41–4 for medical risk factors.

Adapted from American Thoracic Society. Control of tuberculosis in the United States. Am Rev Respir Dis 1992;146:1623.

Computed tomography scans (CT), though sometimes invaluable in revealing extrapulmonary foci, are generally unnecessary for thoracic TB, as is bronchoscopy. Avoidance of overly frequent sputum samples and chest radiographs helps to minimize follow-up costs.

Preventive measures, when applied with appropriate prioritization, reduce both morbidity and cumulative health care costs.

REFERENCES

American Thoracic Society. Diagnostic standards and classification of tuberculosis. Am Rev Respir Dis 1990;142:725.

American Thoracic Society. Control of tuberculosis in the United States. Am Rev Respir Dis 1992;146:1623.

American Thoracic Society. Treatment of tuberculosis and tuberculosis infection in adults and children. Am J Respir Crit Care Med 1994;149:1359.

Bates JB, ed. Tuberculosis. Med Clin North Am 1994;77:1205.

Bloom BR, ed. Tuberculosis: Pathogenesis, protection, and control. Washington: ASM Press, 1994.

Ellner JE. Multidrug-resistant tuberculosis. Adv Intern Med 1995;40:155.

Friedman LN, ed. Tuberculosis: Current concepts and treatment. Boca Raton, FL: CRC Press, 1994.

Haas DW, Des Pres RM. *Mycobacterium tuberculosis.* In: GL Mandell, JE Bennett, R Dolan, eds. Principles and practice of infectious diseases. 4th ed. New York: Churchill Livingstone, 1995:2213.

Havlir DV, Ellner JJ. *Mycobacterium avium* complex. In: GL Mandell, JE Bennett, R Dolan, eds. Principles and practice of infectious diseases. 4th ed. New York: Churchill Livingstone, 1995:2250.

Pitchenik AE, Fertel D. Tuberculosis and non-tuberculosis mycobacterial disease. In: White DA, Gold JWM, eds. Medical management of AIDS patients. Med Clin North Am 1992;76:121.

Raviglione MC, Snider DE, Jr., Kochi A. Global epidemiology of tuberculosis: Morbidity and mortality of a worldwide epidemic. JAMA 1995;273:220.

Reichman LB, Hershfield ES, eds. Tuberculosis: A comprehensive international approach. New York: Marcel Dekker, 1993.

Rieder HL, Snider DS, Jr., Cauthen GM. Extrapulmonary tuberculosis in the United States. Am Rev Respir Dis 1990;141:347.

Rom WN, Garay SM. Tuberculosis. Boston: Little, Brown and Co., 1996.

CHAPTER 13–42

Pulmonary Infection • Community-Acquired Pneumonia

Ronald F. Grossman, M.D.

DEFINITION

Pneumonia is an infection of the terminal portion of the lungs, which comprises the respiratory bronchioles, alveolar ducts and sacs, and alveoli. Community-acquired pneumonia originates outside the hospital setting and can be distinguished from nosocomial or hospital-acquired pneumonia, which is conventionally defined as developing after 48 to 72 hours following admission to hospital for any other reason.

ETIOLOGY

Although an early diagnosis is optimal in the management of community-acquired pneumonia, the etiology of pneumonia is frequently not ascertained and empiric therapy must be selected. Understanding the epidemiology of pneumonia facilitates the choice of antimicrobial agent. Many studies examining the frequency of pathogens have been published, but many, unfortunately, have important limitations such as limited duration of observation (less than 1 year), which would bias the results in favor of certain pathogens occurring in an epidemic fashion (e.g., influenza, respiratory syncytial virus), and reliance on a limited number of diagnostic tests, or were completed before the recognition of *Legionella* species or *Chlamydia pneumoniae* as important respiratory pathogens. Virtually all studies have reported findings in patients ill enough to require hospitalization. The etiology of pneumonia treated in the community setting is less well defined.

An etiologic agent is found in approximately one half of the patients. A declining role for *Streptococcus pneumoniae* and increasing importance of atypical pathogens have been noted. The most common pathogens in patients under the age of 65 and without co-morbid illnesses are *Mycoplasma pneumoniae, Streptococcus pneumoniae*, respiratory tract viruses, *Chlamydia pneumoniae*, and *Hemophilus influenzae*. Patients over age 65 and with comorbid illnesses are likely to be infected with *S. pneumoniae*, respiratory tract viruses, *H. influenzae*, aerobic Gram-negative bacilli, and *Staphylococcus aureus*. Less common pathogens include *Moraxella catarrhalis, Legionella* species, mycobacterial species, and endemic fungi. In patients ill enough to require intensive care unit admission, the two most common organisms found are *S. pneumoniae* and *Legionella pneumophila*.

CRITERIA FOR DIAGNOSIS

Suggestive

Once the clinical diagnosis of pneumonia has been made based on the clinical presentation and the roentgenographic findings, the most important investigations center on establishing an etiologic agent. A presumptive diagnosis of an etiologic agent can be made if there is a heavy or moderate growth of a predominant bacterial pathogen on sputum culture. Other findings that would permit a presumptive diagnosis include a light growth of a respiratory pathogen in which the sputum Gram stain reveals a bacterium compatible with the culture results; a bacterium isolated on multiple sputum cultures within 3 days of admission; a single elevated titer of 1:320 to *Legionella pneumophila* by enzyme-linked immunosorbent assay or 1:512 or higher titer by indirect immunofluorescence assay; or a *Chlamydia pneumoniae* immunoglobulin M antibody titer of 1:32 or higher.

Definitive

A definitive diagosis of an etiologic bacterium can be made if blood cultures or pleural fluid yields a pathogen. If bronchoalveolar lavage reveals *Pneumocystis carinii* or an open lung biopsy indicates a pathogen, then the causative agent has been isolated. Definitive studies

for atypical organisms include a fourfold rise in antibody titer to *Mycoplasma pneumoniae* (or isolation of the organism from respiratory tract samples), positive direct fluorescent antibody test for *Legionella* species plus an elevated *Legionella* titer, and a fourfold or greater rise in antibody titer for *Chlamydia pneumoniae*.

CLINICAL MANIFESTATIONS

Subjective

Traditionally physicians have used the syndromic approach to make an etiologic diagnosis of pneumonia. Patients have been divided into those with a classic bacterial pneumonia syndrome or those with an atypical presentation. In the former, best exemplified by pneumococcal pneumonia, patients present with the acute onset of a high fever, cough productive of purulent sputum, pleuritic chest pain, and abnormal findings on physical examination of the chest. In contrast, patients with the atypical pneumonia syndrome as typified by *Mycoplasma pneumoniae* tend to have an illness with a more insidious onset, low-grade temperature, a nonproductive cough, and, often, a normal physical examination of the chest. Unfortunately, this approach is limited as the clinical features of many infections overlap with clinical symptoms, being as much a reflection of the host as a reflection of the pathogen. In general, in prospective studies, the clinical features of pneumonia cannot be sufficiently well defined to allow an accurate etiologic diagnosis of pneumonia to be made.

The signs and symptoms of pneumonia are easily recognized but not unique to pneumonia. The most common symptoms were cough (88%), dyspnea (71%), sputum production (69%), chest pain (64%), hemoptysis (17%), and mental confusion (14%) in a British Thoracic Society Research Committee (1987) study. Patients with community-acquired pneumonia infected with *Mycoplasma pneumoniae* tend to have a mild illness, but *Legionella*- and *Streptococcus pneumoniae*-infected patients cannot be reliably distinguished from those with *Mycoplasma* infection. Even use of an elaborate discriminate multivariate analysis of signs, symptoms, and laboratory investigations only allows the correct microbial etiology to be predicted in less than half of cases (Farr, et al. 1989). Several investigators have suggested the abandonment of the syndromic approach to the etiologic diagnosis of pneumonia.

Objective

Physical Examination

Fever is usually present but the fever pattern is not sufficiently unique to suggest a specific etiologic agent. Uncommon but suggestive findings include bullous myringitis for *Mycoplasma* infection; furuncles associated with bacteremic staphylococcal infection; herpes labialis associated with pneumococcal infection; and the presence of poor dentition associated with necrotizing pneumonia caused by aspiration of anaerobic organisms. The physical examination of the chest is rarely helpful in pinpointing an etiologic diagnosis, but signs of consolidation are usually associated with bacterial infection. Using physical examination or roentgenographic techniques does not allow distinction of viral from bacterial etiologies for childhood pneumonia.

Routine Laboratory Abnormalities

Prospective studies indicate that patients with community-acquired pneumonia of all etiologies present with an average leukocyte count slightly higher than 13,000/mm^3. In elderly patients with bacterial pneumonias, counts above 10,000/mm^3 occur 70% or more of the time. In half of the remaining patients, a left shift in the differential is seen. Abnormalities of liver and renal function reflect the severity of the systemic illness but are not unique to any pathogen.

PLANS
Diagnostic

Differential Diagnosis

A wide variety of noninfectious disorders may present with cough, fever, dyspnea, constitutional symptoms, and pulmonary infiltrates. Some of these include bronchiolitis obliterans organizing pneumonia, eosinophilic pneumonias, collagen–vascular diseases, pulmonary infarction, drug reactions, granulomatous disorders such as sarcoidosis, and hypersensitivity pneumonitis (Table 13–42–1). Although most disorders that mimic community-acquired pneumonia are rare, atypical features or a lack of response to appropriate antibiotics should arouse suspicion of an alternate diagnosis.

Diagnostic Options

An abnormal chest roentgenogram is the only way to absolutely confirm the diagnosis of pneumonia and, at times, may confirm the presence of coexisting conditions such as bronchial obstruction and pleural effusions. Although homogeneous alveolar infiltration is more common in bacterial etiologies, other findings such as atelectasis and pleural effusion can be seen in all etiologies. No one organism always produces the same roentgenograpic abnormality, and similar roentgenographic patterns may be produced by different organisms. A panel of expert radiologists were better at diagnosing *Mycoplasma* pneumonia compared with bacterial and viral pneumonia, but agreement on etiology was present in less than one third of cases.

A properly performed Gram stain of expectorated sputum examined by an experienced observer may be diagnostic in infections caused by mycobacteria, endemic fungi, *Legionella,* and *Pneumocystis carinii;* however, false-positive and false-negative rates of 88 and 38 %, respectively have been reported. Failure to visualize a predominant organism on Gram stain despite the presence of many leukocytes should suggest the possibility of atypical pathogens. The results with expectorated sputum cultures are even worse, with less than half of samples processed by the usual clinical methods yielding reliable results. A properly obtained sputum sample with more than 25 neutrophils and fewer than 5 squamous epithelial cells per low-power field on Gram stain may be helpful in identifying the likely etiologic agent. Sputum culture and sensitivity may be useful if experience dictates that penicillin-resistant pneumococci are likely. Blood cultures are positive in only 15 to 25% of hospitalized patients with pneumococcal pneumonia and less frequently with other pathogens.

TABLE 13–42–1. DIFFERENTIAL DIAGNOSIS OF PNEUMONIA

Bronchiolitis obliterans organizing pneumonia
Eosinophilic pneumonias
    Acute eosinophilic pneumonia
    Chronic eosinophilic pneumonia
    Tropical pulmonary eosinophilia
    Allergic bronchopulmonary aspergillosis
Hypersensitivity pneumonitis
Drug-induced pneumonitis
    Methotrexate
    Gold
    Nitrofurantoin
    Amiodarone
Pulmonary vasculitis
    Wegener's granulomatosis
    Lymphomatoid granulomatosis
Alveolar hemorrhage syndromes
    Goodpasture's syndrome
    Systemic necrotizing vasculitis
Collagen–vascular diseases
    Systemic lupus erythematosus
    Rheumatoid vasculitis
Pulmonary infarction
Sarcoidosis
Pulmonary alveolar proteinosis

Streptococcus pneumoniae elaborates a series of toxins (pneumolysin, purpura-producing principle, neuraminidase, autolysins) and type- or species-specific surface markers (pneumococcal capsular polysaccharide antigens, pneumococcal C polysaccharide, M-protein antigen, R-protein antigen). Immunoassays have been developed to detect pneumococcal C polysaccharide (species-specific antigen) and pneumococcal capsular polysaccharide antigens (type-specific antigens). These antigens can be found in sputum, pleural fluid, serum, and urine during acute pneumococcal pneumonia. Urine and serum antigen detection is specific but not sensitive for pneumococcal pneumonia. Detection of pneumococcal antigen in sputum is plagued by colonization of respiratory tract secretions with *S. pneumoniae* in about one third of children, one fifth of healthy adults, and slightly less than half of adults with chronic bronchitis.

Acute and convalescent serologic testing against atypical pathogens such as *Legionella, Mycoplasma,* and *Chlamydia* may retrospectively confirm a suspected diagnosis and could be used for epidemiologic purposes.

The technique of nucleic acid hybridization has developed to the point of being useful in clinical microbiology laboratories. These new methodologies offer rapid, sensitive, and specific diagnostic results for *Mycoplasma* species, *Legionella* species, *Mycobacterium tuberculosis,* and other *Mycobacterium* species. For common bacterial pathogens such as *S. pneumoniae* and *H. influenzae,* difficulties similar to that seen with the detection of pneumococcal antigens can be anticipated.

Transtracheal aspiration bypasses the upper airway and helps eliminate the problem of upper airway contamination. The test is invasive and complications of the test include bleeding, puncture of the soft posterior tracheal wall, subcutaneous emphysema, pneumothorax, and infection at the puncture site. In comparative studies of transtracheal aspirates with direct needle aspirates of the lung, significant false-positive and false-negative rates have been found.

Bronchoscopy with bronchoalveolar lavage and transbronchial lung biopsy is useful in the management of immunocompromised patients because the detection of opportunistic pathogens is considered to be diagnostic. Unfortunately, contamination of the bronchoscopy with upper airway bacteria renders the results of routine bacterial culture of specimens obtained through the bronchoscope unreliable. A protected specimen brush technique has been introduced to avoid the difficulties associated with routine bronchoscopy. Using a cutoff of at least 10^3 colony-forming units (CFU)/mL to distinguish between colonization and infection, high rates of sensitivity and specificity have been reported so long as patients are not receiving antibiotics and are not being mechanically ventilated.

By use of a cutoff of 10^4 to 10^5 CFU/mL to distinguish colonization from infection for bronchoalveolar lavage samples, sensitivity and specificity rates as good as those for the protected specimen brush technique have been obtained. Bronchoalveolar lavage samples a far larger area of the lung than does protected specimen brush, thus decreasing sampling error.

The presence of elastin fibers by potassium hydroxide preparation appears to be specific for the presence of necrotizing pneumonia in patients without adult respiratory distress syndrome, but has a sensitivity of about 50%. In patients with adult respiratory distress syndrome, the test is unreliable. To date the antibody-coated bacterial test has not been shown to be consistently accurate, with sensitivities ranging from 48 to 73% and specificities from 50 to 100%.

Transthoracic lung puncture has largely been avoided because of the risk of pneumothorax; however, a sensitivity of 46% using a 20-gauge needle under fluoroscopic guidance and a sensitivity of 38% and a false-positive rate of 8% using a 22-gauge needle without fluoroscopic guidance have been reported. Fewer then 10% of patients have developed a pneumothorax.

Recommended Approach

A chest roentgenogram should be performed in all patients suspected of having pneumonia. It may assist in the evaluation of severity of illness, as multilobar infiltrates and rapid roentgenographic extension of disease are a harbinger of a complicated hospital course.

A properly performed Gram stain of expectorated sputum is useful in the initial management of patients with pneumonia. This should be supplemented with routine bacterial cultures of sputum. Although these investigations may be useful, their limitations should be recognized. Blood cultures should be routinely sought in patients ill enough to require hospitalization. Patients with a pleural effusion should have a diagnostic thoracentesis. All hospitalized patients should have routine laboratory tests (complete blood count, serum electrolytes, hepatic enzymes, and tests of renal function) to assist in determining the severity of illness. Serologic testing and cold agglutinin measurements are not helpful in the initial evaluation of patients with community-acquired pneumonia. Viral cultures are not useful and should not be routinely performed. Other more invasive investigations should be reserved for more critically ill patients or those who fail to respond to initial empiric therapy.

Therapeutic

Therapeutic Options

The ideal approach would involve the selection of an antimicrobial agent targeted specifically at the causative agent. Unfortunately, in the majority of cases this information is not available and empiric therapy is required. If *Streptococcus pneumoniae* is identified, the agent of choice remains penicillin, unless allergy or high-grade resistance is identified. Alternatives in cases of penicillin allergy include macrolides (erythromycin, clarithromycin, azithromycin), first-generation cephalosporins, clindamycin, trimethoprim–sulfamethoxazole, and tetracycline. Vancomycin may be required for penicillin-resistant pneumococci.

Hemophilus influenzae may be treated with a β-lactam such as amoxicillin unless the organism produces β-lactamase or there is a high community prevalence. Acceptable alternatives include amoxicillin–clavulanic acid, trimethoprim–sulfamethoxazole, second-generation cephalosporins, ciprofloxacin, and tetracycline.

Atypical organisms such as *Mycoplasma pneumoniae, Chlamydia pneumoniae,* and *Legionella* species should be treated with a macrolide such as erythromycin, clarithromycin, or azithromycin. Tetracycline could be used in the setting of macrolide allergy.

Recommended Approach

Patients without significant comorbid illnesses and not severely ill with pneumonia are prone to be infected with *M. pneumoniae, S. pneumoniae, C. pneumoniae,* and *H. influenzae.* An orally administered macrolide antibiotic, such as erythromycin or clarithromycin, should be considered for initial therapy, with tetracycline considered as an alternative. In patients not severely ill but with significant comorbid illness such as chronic obstructive lung disease, the most common organisms are *S. pneumoniae, H. influenzae,* oral anaerobes, Gram-negative rods, *Staphylococcus aureus,* and, in some areas, *Legionella* species. Reasonable initial choices would include second-generation cephalosporins, trimethoprim–sulfamethoxazole, and β-lactam/β-lactamase inhibitors with or without a macrolide. A β-lactam antibiotic such as amoxicillin alone may not be successful because of the increasing prevalence of β-lactamase-producing strains of *H. influenzae* throughout the world.

In patients without comorbid illness requiring hospitalization, a combination of a parenteral macrolide and a second- or third-generation cephalosporin will cover the commonest pathogens. In patients with comorbidity, the macrolide may be omitted if *Legionella* is unlikely. For critically ill patients, a combination of a macrolide plus a third-generation cephalosporin with antipseudomonal activity is appropriate. Alternatives to the latter include imipenem/cilastatin and a quinolone.

FOLLOW-UP

Although these choices are reasonable for initial empiric therapy, close follow-up is required to ensure that a response is achieved. If the etiology of infection is obtained, then targeted therapy with narrow-spectrum antimicrobial agents is warranted.

DISCUSSION

Prevalence and Incidence

In the National Health Interview Survey of 1981 it was estimated that 3.3 million cases of pneumonia occurred in ambulatory children and adults, for a rate of 1.5 episodes per 100 persons per year. In 1981 there were more than half a million admissions to hospital with community-acquired pneumonia in the United States (National Center for Health Statistics, 1982). The attack rates for pneumonia are highest at the extremes of age. The problem is considerably magnified in the elderly (greater than age 65), for whom the admission rate to hospital is 11.5 per 1000 population, compared with 1.0 per 1000 population in the 15 to 44 age group. In Nottingham, England, from October 1984 to September 1985, pneumonia counted for 5.6% of all lower respiratory tract infections for which antibiotics were prescribed (National Center for Health Statistics, 1983). The incidence of pneumonia was 4.7 per 1000 adult population per year in the United Kingdom and 2.6 cases per 1000 adult population in Barcelona, Spain.

Related Basic Science

Approximately 10% of strains of *Streptococcus pneumoniae* in North America exhibit intermediate resistance to penicillin (MIC90 ranging from 0.5 to 1.0 μg/mL), and 1% of strains have high-level resistance (MIC90 ≥ 2.0 μg/mL). This contrasts sharply with reported resistance rates of up to 50% in Spain and Hungary. Approximately 30% of strains of *Hemophilus influenzae* are resistant to β-lactam antibiotics, whereas up to 75% of strains of *Moraxella catarrhalis* exhibit this trait. Identification of resistant strains of common organisms has led to revised recommendations for empiric management of patients with community-acquired pneumonia.

Natural History and Its Modification with Treatment

In the outpatient setting, the mortality rate of pneumonia remains low, below 5%, but among those requiring hospitalization, the mortality rate approaches 25%. Mortality is higher in patients developing acute respiratory failure. Mortality has been linked to inadequate antibiotic therapy before intensive care unit admission, requirement for mechanical ventilation, use of positive end-expiratory pressure, fraction of inspired oxygen greater than 0.6, coexistence of adult respiratory distress syndrome, radiographic spread of pneumonia during intensive care unit admission, septic shock, bacteremia, and *Pseudomonas aeruginosa* as the causative agent. Of all these, radiographic spread of pneumonia and the presence of septic shock accurately predict mortality in the majority of patients.

Prevention

Influenza Vaccine

More than 10,000 excess deaths due to influenza have been reported in each of 19 different epidemics between 1957 and 1986 (Centers for Disease Control, 1993). Secondary bacterial pneumonia is a frequent complication and is often due to *S. pneumoniae, H. influenzae,* and, less frequently, *S. aureus.* When vaccine antigens closely match the prevalent strain, the vaccine may be more than 70% effective in preventing influenza-related pneumonia, hospitalization, and death. Despite proven efficacy, less than a third of those at risk are immunized annually. During outbreaks, the vaccine may be ineffective if the infecting strain varies substantially from the vaccine. Chemoprophylaxis with amantadine or rimantadine offers protective rates similar to that of the vaccine, but both are ineffective against influenza B, which may be responsible for 20% of all epidemics.

Pneumococcal Vaccine

Most of the serotypes identified with bacteremic pneumococcal infection are included in the polyvalent vaccine. Overall efficacy rates in the range 50 to 70% have been reported, with age at vaccination, time since vaccination, and immune status being the most influential factors determining efficacy. The Centers for Disease Control and Prevention recommends immunization of all persons more than 65 years old.

Cost Containment

Respiratory tract infections including pneumonia are responsible for more days of bed disability, restricted activity, and loss of time from work than any other acute illness. It has been estimated that the direct costs of lower respiratory tract infections requiring hospitalization approached $4 billion in 1984 in the United States. If appropriate empiric therapy is initially selected and treatment failures are detected early, economic savings should follow. Some antibiotics, particularly aminoglycosides, have been dosed too often and can be given less frequently with no loss of efficacy and, perhaps, even less toxicity. Many antimicrobial agents are highly bioavailable (e.g., clindamycin, ciprofloxacin) and can be given orally. Commonly, institutions are implementing an intravenous to oral stepdown program whereby health care professionals assess the need for intravenous therapy and suggest early substitution to equivalent oral therapy as soon as it is feasible. The most expensive antibiotic is the one that fails, leading to prolongation of therapy, second or third prescriptions, and/or the development of complications. Antimicrobial choices should not depend solely on acquisition cost; rather, a more sophisticated view encompassing acquisition cost, administrative costs, cost of potential side effects, and cost of failure should be adopted.

REFERENCES

Centers for Disease Control. Prevention and control of influenza. Recommendation of the Immunization Practices Advisory Committee (ACIP). MMWR 1993;43:1.

Current estimates from the National Health Interview Survey, United States, 1981. National Centers for Health Statistics, USDHHS, Data from the National Health Survey. Series 10, No. 141 (DHEW Pub. No. PHS-82-1569) Washington: US Government Printing Office, 1982.

Dixon RE. Economic costs of respiratory tract infections in the United States. Am J Med 1985;78 (suppl. 6B):45.

Fang GD, Fine M, Orloff J, et al. New and emerging etiologies for community-acquired pneumonia with implications for therapy: A prospective multicenter study of 359 cases. Medicine 1990;69:307.

Farr BM, Kaiser DL, Harrison BDW, Connolly CK. Prediction of microbial aetiology at admission to hospital for pneumonia from the presenting features. Thorax 1989;44:1031.

In-patient utilization of short-stay hospitals by diagnosis. United States 1982 annual summary. National Center for Health Statistics, USDH data from the National Health Survey, Series 13, No. 72 (DHS publication No. PHS-83-1733). Washington: US Government Printing Office, 1983.

Niederman MS, Bass JB Jr, Campbell GD, et al. Guidelines for the initial management of adults with community-acquired pneumonia: Diagnosis, assessment of severity, and initial antimicrobial therapy. Am Rev Respir Dis 1993;148:1418.

Research Committee of the British Thoracic Society and the Public Health Laboratory Service. Community-acquired pneumonia in adults in British hospitals in 1982–1983: A survey of aetiology, mortality, prognostic factors and outcome. Q J Med 1987;239:195.

CHAPTER 13–43

Atypical Pneumonia

Charles L. Hyman, M.D.

DEFINITION

Community-acquired pneumonia has traditionally been divided into the two syndromes of typical pneumonia, caused by bacteria such as *Streptococcus pneumoniae,* and atypical pneumonia, classically associated with *Mycoplasma pneumoniae.* Over the past decade or so, numerous studies have shown that neither clinical nor radiologic features are able to differentiate reliably between these syndromes, nor predict a specific etiologic agent. Atypical pneumonias are, however, caused by a variety of infectious agents that share three clinically relevant characteristics that serve to distinguish them as a group from the usual pyogenic bacterial pneumonias: (1) they do not respond to beta-lactam antibiotics, (2) they cannot be detected on a Gram stain of the sputum, and (3) they cannot be isolated by routine methods in a microbiology laboratory.

ETIOLOGY

The spectrum of organisms associated with atypical pneumonia is extensive and includes viruses, bacteria, fungi, and parasites. The most common agents of atypical pneumonia, which are the focus of this chapter, include *Mycoplasma pneumoniae, Chlamydia pneumoniae* (TWAR), *Legionella* species, especially *L. pneumophila* (Legionnaires' disease), and the respiratory viruses such as influenza A and B. Although uncommon in the United States, in certain epidemiologic settings *Chlamydia psittaci* (ornithosis) and *Coxiella burnetii* (Q fever) are important causes of pneumonia that also need to be considered (also see Chapter 8–15).

CRITERIA FOR DIAGNOSIS
Suggestive

Atypical organisms must be considered in all patients, irrespective of age, with community-acquired pneumonia. A prior history of receiving but not responding to beta-lactam antibiotics and a Gram stain of the sputum, if any can be produced, showing abundant leukocytes without organisms should further raise the clinician's index of suspicion that the patient's pneumonia is caused by an atypical organism. Information gathered from the history, physical examination, and routine laboratory and radiographic evaluation is not specific enough to permit an etio-

logic diagnosis, yet as discussed below in the following sections may provide clues to a particular agent (Table 13–43–1).

Definitive

Definitive diagnosis is based either by the detection or isolation of the organism from respiratory tract specimens or the serologic demonstration of an appropriate antibody response to the organism.

CLINICAL MANIFESTATIONS
Subjective

The cardinal symptoms of atypical pneumonia, as for typical pyogenic pneumonia, are cough, sputum production, chills, fever, and malaise. Duration of prodrome and tempo of onset are useful neither in defining nor differentiating the syndromes. Complaints of headache, sputum production, pleuritic chest pain, or gastrointestinal disturbances are common features of community-acquired pneumonia of all etiologies. Upper respiratory tract symptomatology is common and nonspecific; however, complaints of otalgia and hoarseness should raise the suspicion of *Mycoplasma* and *C. pneumoniae* infection, respectively. A history of prior antibiotic therapy, especially with beta-lactams, should suggest infection with an atypical organism, in particular *Legionella* and *Mycoplasma.* Other important historical clues include a history of bird exposure and significant contact with animals, such as cattle husbandry, working in an abattoir, or veterinary work, which if present should prompt the clinician to consider the respective possibilities of ornithosis and Q fever.

Objective
Physical Examination

Fever, headache, and an elevated respiratory rate are common findings in pneumonia. Relative bradycardia has been reported with Legionnaires' disease and ornithosis. The presence of a rash should suggest *Mycoplasma,* but may also be seen in ornithosis and viral infections. Bullous myringitis is typically associated with *Mycoplasma* infections but is seen in less than a quarter of cases. Examination of the chest may be unremarkable, but usually reveals localized abnormal or adventitious

TABLE 13–43–1. CLUES TO ETIOLOGY

Clue	Organism
History	
Prior beta-lactam treatment	*Mycoplasma pneumoniae*
	Legionella sp.
	Chlamydia pneumoniae
Exposure to birds	Ornithosis
Exposure to animals	Q fever
Known epidemic	Legionnaires' disease
	Influenza
Signs and symptoms	
Hoarseness	*C. pneumoniae*
Bullous myringitis	*M. pneumoniae*
Relative bradycardia	Legionnaires' disease
	Ornithosis
Splenomegaly	Ornithosis
Rash	*M. pneumoniae*
	Ornithosis
Encephalitis	*M. pneumoniae*
	Legionnaires' disease
	Q fever
Neurologic dysfunction	*M. pneumoniae*
Ataxia	
Transverse myelitis	
Guillain–Barré syndrome	
Radiographic	
Hilar adenopathy	*M. pneumoniae*
Round opacities	Q fever
Cavitation	Alternative agents
	Rarely *Legionella* sp.
Laboratory	
Hemolytic anemia	*M. pneumoniae*
Cold agglutinin ≥ 1:32	*M. pneumoniae*

breath sounds. Signs of consolidation, thought to be suggestive of pyogenic pathogens, have been noted in pneumonias caused by *Legionella* species, *M. pneumoniae*, and *C. pneumoniae*. In combination with a history of bird exposure, splenomegaly is suggestive of ornithosis, but may also be rarely seen with Q fever. Encephalitis has been reported with *Legionella*, *Mycoplasma*, and Q fever. Neurologic dysfunction such as ataxia, transverse myelitis, and Guillain–Barré syndrome should suggest infection with *M. pneumoniae*.

Routine Laboratory Abnormalities

Abnormalities of routine laboratory tests, such as serum electrolytes and liver enzymes, are common but nonspecific. Such derangements reflect the severity of the infectious process in a given patient, and as such are more useful in providing prognostic, rather than diagnostic, information. The white blood cell count is usually within normal range or only moderately elevated; counts above 15,000/mm³ are less common and should suggest infection with a pyogenic organism. Hemolytic anemia may rarely occur with *M. pneumoniae* infection.

Chest radiography is important for confirming the diagnosis, and defining the extent of the pneumonia. *Mycoplasma*, *Chlamydia*, and viral pneumonias are usually a unilateral subsegmental patchy bronchopneumonia that emanates from the hilum and involves a lower lobe. *Legionella* is more likely to be extensive and bilateral. Bilateral, multiple rounded peripheral opacities are considered characteristic of Q fever pneumonia, but seen in less than half of the cases. Extensive, bilateral pneumonia with and without pleural effusions and progression to adult respiratory distress syndrome are recognized to occur with all of these agents. Therefore, for the individual patient the pattern of pulmonary parenchymal involvement is of little help in refining the etiologic differential diagnosis. Hilar adenopathy is rarely if ever noted with any of these agents, except with *M. pneumoniae*, where it is reported to occur in up to 20% of cases. Lung cavitation is extremely un-

common even with *Legionella*, and if present in the immunocompetent host should suggest an alternative spectrum of organisms.

PLANS

Diagnostic

Differential Diagnosis

The differential diagnosis of fever and a new or progressing pulmonary infiltrate includes noninfectious causes such as pulmonary infarction and immunologically mediated pulmonary disease such as hypersensitivity pneumonitis, collagen–vascular diseases, as well as granulomatous disorders such as sarcoidosis.

Diagnostic Options

Isolation of atypical organisms by culture requires specialized media or cell culture techniques that are not available to most clinical microbiology laboratories. *Legionella* species can be grown readily in BCYE (buffered charcoal yeast extract) medium; however, unless specifically requested, many laboratories do not routinely inoculate specimens onto this medium. *Mycoplasma pneumoniae* can be cultured from sputum, throat, or nasopharyngeal swab specimens but may take up to several weeks of incubation. Special culture medium is required and generally unavailable except at commercial or reference laboratories. *Chlamydia pneumoniae* and the respiratory viruses need to be isolated by cell culture. It is not recommended to attempt to isolate either *Chlamydia psittaci* or *Coxiella burnetti* because of the infectious hazard they represent to laboratory personnel.

Fluorescent antibody staining, antigen detection, and nucleic probes are the methods currently used for direct detection. Commercially available tests include assays for the detection of *Legionella pneumophila* antigen in urine and pleural fluid, direct fluorescent antibody staining for *Legionella*, and nucleic probes for *M. pneumoniae* and *Legionella* in respiratory specimens. The sensitivities of these tests are variable, but the specificities are high and permit diagnosis.

Serology remains the mainstay of establishing a definitive etiologic diagnosis for these organisms. Because the standard criteria for serologic diagnosis requires the demonstration of a fourfold rise in antibody titer between acute and convalescent serum specimens, diagnosis is necessarily retrospective. A presumptive diagnosis of Legionnaires' disease can be made with a single titer of 1:128 or greater. Elevated cold agglutinins can be found in association with several respiratory tract pathogens, but a titer of 1:32 or greater is considered highly suggestive of *Mycoplasma* infection. Table 13–43–2 lists the standard tests most commonly used, and provides a guide to their use with respect to the timing of convalescent serum and interpretation.

Recommended Approach

Specific diagnosis is pursued to guide therapy (see Table 13–43–2). For community-acquired pneumonias encountered in the ambulatory setting, and in particular those caused by the atypical organisms, diagnostic tests rarely provide information in a timely enough manner to influence choice of initial therapy. Given that the majority of outpatients with pneumonia respond to empiric therapy, additional testing beyond obtaining a chest radiograph is of limited benefit.

The approach should be directed toward establishing the need for hospitalization. The decision to hospitalize a patient should be based on the patient and the severity of the pneumonia. In general, it is considered prudent to hospitalize patients older than 65 and those with underlying cardiopulmonary, renal, hepatic, neoplastic, or metabolic disease because of increased risk for a complicated course. The severity of the infection is best reflected by a respiratory rate greater than 30, hypotension, and more than one lobe involvement noted on the chest radiograph. When a patient is hospitalized it is recommended to obtain two sets of blood cultures, routine chemistries, a hemogram, and an arterial blood gas analysis. If a moderate to large pleural effusion is present, thoracentesis should be performed and the fluid sent for evaluation and culture and, possibly, *Legionella* antigen if this is a consideration. Sputum, if obtainable, may be submitted for *Legionella* direct fluorescent antibody and culture, but should not be sent for routine bacterial or

TABLE 13–43–2. DIAGNOSTIC TESTS AND THERAPEUTIC REGIMENS

Organism	Diagnostic Method	Comments	Treatment
Mycoplasma pneumoniae	Culture	Respiratory tract specimen, requires up to 3 wk incubation	Macrolide for 2–3 wk
	Nucleic probe	Respiratory tract specimen	Erythromycin 500 mg PO qid
	Serology		Clarithromycin 500 mg PO bid
	CF	Fourfold rise in titer, antibody rise occurs 2–3 wk after onset of illness	Azithromycin 500 mg initial dose, then 250 mg PO qd
	ELISA	Greater than reference range	Tetracycline 500 mg PO qid
			Doxycycline 100 mg PO bid
Chlamydia pneumoniae	Culture	Not commercially available	Tetracycline (doses as above), 2–3 wk
	Serology		Doxycycline (as above)
	CF	Fourfold rise, single titer ≥ 1:64	Macrolide (as above)
		Unable to distinguish between different Chlamydia spp.	
	MIF	Specific but not commercially available	
		Fourfold rise, single IgM ≥ 1:16 or IgG ≥ 1:512	
		Antibody rise from 3 to 8 wk after onset of illness	
Legionella pneumophila	Culture	Requires BCYE (buffered charcoal yeast extract) medium	Erythromycin 1 g IV q6h ± rifampin 600 mg PO/IV q12h; change to oral therapy with improvement for total 10–14 d
	Nucleic probe	Positive test	
	Antigen detection	Specific for *L. pneumophila* serotype 1	
		Urine and pleural fluid	Trimethoprim–sulfamethoxazole 160 mg/800 mg IV q8h or PO q12h
	DFA	Respiratory specimen, correlates with degree of involvement seen on chest radiograph	Tetracycline
	Serology		Quinolone
	IFA	Fourfold rise, may require up to 8 wk	
		>1:128 presumptive	
Chlamydia psittaci	Culture	Not recommended	Tetracycline for 2–3 wk
	Serology		Doxycycline
	CF	Fourfold rise	
		Unable to distinguish between different Chlamydia spp.	
Coxiella burnetii	Culture	Not recommended	Tetracycline for 2–3 wk
	Serology		Doxycycline
	CF	Fourfold rise, antibody response peaks at 3 mo	
	IFA	IgM > 1:20, response peaks between 4 and 8 wk	

CF, complement fixation; ELISA, enzyme-linked immunosorbent assay; MIF, microimmunofluorescence; DFA, direct fluorescent antibody; IFA, immunofluorescence assay.

viral cultures as the yield is low and provides limited information. The value and utility of a sputum Gram stain are controversial; however, it is a quick and inexpensive test that may provide a clue of an atypical pathogen if no organisms are seen despite the presence of leukocytes. Serologic testing should be pursued only if the patient does not respond to initial therapy or if there is an epidemiologic reason for establishing a specific diagnosis. Even when extensive testing is systemically applied, a definite etiology for community-acquired pneumonias can only be established in approximately half the time.

Therapeutic

Therapeutic Options

The standard therapeutic regimens for the atypical pathogens are provided in Table 13–43–2. The cornerstone of therapy is either a macrolide or tetracycline antibiotic. The macrolide antibiotics erythromycin, clarithromycin, and azithromycin have equal clinical efficacy against *Legionella* species, *C. pneumoniae,* and *M. pneumoniae.* Clarithromycin and azithromycin have the advantages of a broader spectrum of activity against other pathogens of community-acquired pneumonia, such as *Hemophilus influenzae,* and pharmacokinetics that allow for once- or twice-a-day dosing. Quinolones have also been shown to be clinically effective against all of these organisms and *Coxiella burnetii;* however, their role as a standard therapy for community-acquired pneumonia has not been established. The combination of trimethoprim–sulfamethoxazole has been used successfully to treat Legionnaires' disease. The antibiotic of choice for Q fever and ornithosis is a tetracycline, although erythromycin has been used successfully. Amantadine and rimantadine are recommended for the treatment of influenza A and are effective in reducing the duration and severity of illness, if started promptly within 24 to 48 hours of the onset of symptoms.

Recommended Approach

For outpatients who neither have comorbid conditions nor require hospitalization, a macrolide antibiotic is the therapy of choice. If Q fever or ornithosis is a consideration because of an epidemiologic risk factor, tetracycline or doxycycline can be used. Hospitalized patients should be treated with a beta-lactam antibiotic in combination with a macrolide to provide coverage for other bacterial pathogens, and rifampin should be added to the regimen if severe *Legionella* pneumonia is being treated.

FOLLOW-UP

After the institution of appropriate antibiotic treatment, clinical improvement should be evident within 48 hours for infections caused by most of these organisms and by day 5 for Legionnaires' disease. Patients not requiring hospitalization should be seen in 3 to 5 days to confirm improvement and again at completion of therapy. If symptoms fail to resolve, or worsen, more frequent encounters are necessary, and hospitalization should be considered. Hospitalized patients should be seen no less frequently than daily. Once symptoms and fever have abated, antibiotic therapy can be converted from parenteral to oral administration and completed as an outpatient. The radiographic resolution of pneumonia is a slow process that requires weeks to months. Hence, follow-up chest roentgenograms need not be repeated prior to 4 to 6 weeks unless the patient fails to improve, relapses, or deteriorates. Parenchymal abnormalities that fail to resolve and persist beyond 4 to 6 weeks need further evaluation to exclude other pathologies such as an underlying malignancy.

DISCUSSION

The syndrome approach to community-acquired pneumonia has been used to predict etiology and thereby guide therapy. This classification developed as a result of the recognition of a clinical syndrome that was distinct from that typically caused by *Streptococcus pneumoniae.* This "atypical" syndrome was characterized by an insidious onset, prominent upper respiratory tract and systemic complaints, nonproductive cough, a paucity of physical findings on examination of the chest, and patchy lower lobe opacities noted on the chest radiograph. *Mycoplasma pneumoniae* was identified and found to be the cause of many such cases. In succeeding years, *L. pneumophila* and *C. pneumoniae* were isolated and added to the list of agents causing this atypical syndrome. Subsequently, numerous studies have shown that the clinical and radiographic presentations of pneumonias caused by these agents as well as those caused by *S. pneumoniae* and other "typical" pathogens can overlap with each other to such a degree as to be indistinguishable. As a result, it has been proposed by the American Thoracic Society that the syndrome approach to community-acquired pneumonia be replaced by a classification that guides therapy according to the patient's age, presence of coexisting disease, need for hospitalization, and severity of illness.

Prevalence and Incidence

Mycoplasma pneumoniae and *C. pneumoniae* each account for approximately 15 to 20% of all community-acquired pneumonias. Although these organisms cause pneumonia in all ages, the incidence of *M. pneumoniae* peaks between the ages of 5 and 20 and subsequently tapers, whereas the incidence of *C. pneumoniae* pneumonia increases steadily with age. In closed populations, such as university students and military recruits, between 25 and 50% of radiographically confirmed pneumonias can be attributed to *C. pneumoniae* and *M. pneumoniae*, respectively. Infection with both of these organisms occurs endemically, as well as in epidemic cycles. In contrast, the incidence of *Legionella* pneumonia is substantially lower, but more frequently requires hospitalization. Ornithosis and Q fever are uncommon diseases in the United States; however, in parts of Canada and Europe these infections are more common and encountered with sufficient frequency as to warrant their routine consideration. In studies of patients hospitalized for pneumonia, the frequency with which these atypical organisms are identified varies greatly depending on the methods used, the criteria for hospital admission, and the demographic and epidemiologic profile of the populations studied. On average, *M. pneumoniae*, *C. pneumoniae*, influenza viruses, and *Legionella* each account for between 5 and 15% of cases, whereas *Coxiella* and *Chlamydia psittaci* usually account for less than 2% each.

Related Basic Science

When first identified, *M. pneumoniae* was thought to be a virus because of its small size and ability to pass through filters that retain bacteria. Subsequent genetic and structural analyses have placed mycoplasmas in a class of organisms, the Mollicutes, that is distinct from viruses and bacteria. Although *M. pneumoniae* is an extracellular pathogen, it is also able to establish intracellular infection in the host. This intracellular parasitism is thought to explain why *M. pneumoniae* can be persistently isolated from patients' respiratory secretions for extended periods after adequate and clinically effective antimicrobial therapy.

The chlamydiae are obligate intracellular parasites that possess an outer membrane structurally similar to that of Gram-negative bacteria. The life cycle of *Chlamydia* is unique, and involves two distinct forms: the elementary body, which is the metabolically inert but infectious form, and the reticulate body, the intracellular, noninfectious productive form. Whereas *C. psittaci*, the agent of ornithosis, was isolated more than 60 years ago, *C. pneumoniae* has only recently been identified, and respiratory tract disease associated with this organism was first described in the mid-1980s. *Chlamydia pneumoniae* is now recognized to be one of the most common infectious agents, and serologic studies suggest that virtually all persons are infected by *C. pneumoniae* at some time. Although a leading cause of community-acquired pneumonia, the majority of infections with *C. pneumoniae* are asymptomatic or so mild as to go unnoticed.

Coxiella burnetii, the agent of Q fever, is also an obligate intracellular parasite. In contrast to other rickettsiae, *Coxiella burnetii* has a spore stage, which enables the organism to survive outside the host and contaminate the environment for prolonged periods. *Legionella pneumophila*, an intracellular pathogen, is an important cause of nosocomial pneumonias as well as community-acquired pneumonias. Both *Coxiella burnetii* and *L. pneumophila* are Gram-negative organisms; however,

neither stain as such in clinical specimens and are better identified with the Gimenez stain.

Whereas the route of infection for all of these organisms is thought to be via the inhalation of aerosolized infectious material, the mode of transmission and the reservoirs differ. *Mycoplasma pneumoniae*, *C. pneumoniae*, and the respiratory viruses are spread from person to person. *Chlamydia psittaci* and *Coxiella burnetii* are transmitted from their respective avian and animal hosts to humans, and the reservoir for *L. pneumophila* is aquatic, such as water distribution systems and potable water sources. The incubation periods for these pathogens vary from 24 to 48 hours for *L. pneumophila* and the influenza viruses, to weeks for *Chlamydia* and Q fever, to a month for *M. pneumoniae*.

Natural History and Its Modification with Treatment

Mycoplasma pneumonia is usually a mild illness that may resolve without treatment. Mortality is low and generally below 1%; however, infection with *M. pneumoniae* can be severe, especially in patients with sickle cell anemia, and also accompanied by serious extrapulmonary complications, such as myocarditis, neurologic dysfunction, and digital gangrene secondary to cold agglutinin disease. Although *C. pneumoniae* produces a mild disease in younger persons, because it more frequently affects an older age group, mortality is noted to be higher than with *Mycoplasma*. Treatment decreases duration and severity of symptoms, and may need to be continued for up to 3 weeks to prevent relapse of clinical illness. Infection with *C. pneumoniae* has also been associated with the development of asthma, sarcoidosis, and, more recently, coronary artery disease. Mortality from *Legionella* pneumonia is appreciable, but reduced with prompt and appropriate treatment. Clinical improvement is generally noted within 5 to 7 days; however, a feature of severe *Legionella* pneumonia is radiographic progression of disease even after therapy has been instituted. Q fever pneumonia is a self-limiting process that usually resolves even without therapy. Treatment shortens the duration of fever and symptoms by several days. *Coxiella burnetii*, the agent of Q fever, can also cause endocarditis, hepatitis, osteomyelitis, and neurologic dysfunction. Ornithosis may be a severe systemic illness with mortality rates in excess of 10% when untreated. Influenza infection may lead to primary pneumonia, which can be a fulminant process culminating in the adult respiratory distress syndrome, but the more common complication is a supervening bacterial pneumonia.

Prevention

Influenza vaccine can be effective in reducing the incidence, severity of illness, and mortality from influenza. In addition, amantadine and rimantadine are effective chemotherapeutic agents against influenza A, and are recommended to be used as adjunctive prophylactic therapies during outbreaks for those who either cannot receive vaccine or are immunosuppressed and for closed environments such as nursing homes.

Although it would be ideal to place patients with influenza in respiratory isolation to prevent transmission, this is generally impractical especially during outbreaks. Person-to-person transmission with ornithosis is rare but has been reported to occur; therefore, it may be prudent to isolate such patients until clinical improvement is noted. Patients with *Mycoplasma*, *Chlamydia*, *Legionella*, and *Coxiella* pneumonias do not need to be placed in respiratory isolation. Cases of *Legionella* should prompt a search to identify and eradicate a contaminated water source.

Cost Containment

Strategies to reduce costs should be directed toward prevention and more efficient resource utilization. Effective influenza vaccination programs, particularly for the elderly (the age group with the highest rates of hospitalization from pneumonia) and those with chronic cardiopulmonary disease, should result in reducing the rate of complications due to influenza respiratory tract infection and hence hospitalization. For the hospitalized patient with pneumonia, once clinical improvement is established, parenteral antibiotic therapy can be converted to an equivalent oral agent, thereby allowing for completion of therapy as an outpatient, earlier discharge, and reduced length of hospital stay. Diagnostic testing for *Mycoplasma*, *Chlamydia*, respiratory viruses, and *Legionella* can be expensive, does not provide the clinician with clinically useful information when therapy is first instituted, and therefore should not be routinely ordered, but reserved for patients who do not respond to initial therapy. Judicious selection of antibiotic therapy can result in cost savings. Although the newer macrolide and quinolone antibiotics offer a broad spectrum of antibacterial activity and convenient dosing schedules, they have not been shown to be more clinically effective in the treatment of these organisms than standard and less expensive agents, such as erythromycin and the tetracyclines.

REFERENCES

Foy HM. Infections caused by *Mycoplasma pneumoniae* and possible carrier state in different populations of patients. Clin Infect Dis 1993;17(suppl. 1):S37.

Grayston JT. Infections caused by *Chlamydia pneumoniae* strain TWAR. Clin Infect Dis 1992;15:757.

Macfarlane JT, Miller AC, Roderick Smith WH, et al. Comparative radiographic features of community acquired Legionnaires' disease, pneumococcal pneumonia, *Mycoplasma* pneumonia, and psittacosis. Thorax 1984;39:28.

Niederman MS, Bass JB Jr, Campbell GD, et al. Guidelines for the initial management of adults with community-acquired pneumonia: Diagnosis, assessment of severity, and initial antimicrobial therapy. Am Rev Respir Dis 1993;148:1418.

Woodhead MA, Macfarlane JT. Comparative clinical and laboratory features of *Legionella* with pneumococcal and *Mycoplasma* pneumonias. Brit J Dis Chest 1987;81:133.

CHAPTER 13–44

Pulmonary Disease in Human Immunodeficiency Virus Infection

Walfredo J. Leon, M.D.

DEFINITION

Pulmonary complications of HIV infection are episodic or chronic occurrences of respiratory symptomatology (cough, dyspnea, chest pain, etc.) attributable to infectious, immunologic, or neoplastic processes (also see Chapter 8–76 and the chapters dealing with infections and neoplastic disease).

Clinical manifestations of HIV lung diseases are divided into early and late manifestations. Conditions that occur before the actual development of AIDS (with higher CD4 T-cell counts > 200) are early, and those conditions that occur after development of AIDS are late (when the CD4 T-cell counts < 200). The cardinal manifestations of HIV-related lung disease are not specific and can be found in persons with HIV and non-HIV infections.

ETIOLOGY

Specific etiologies of the pulmonary complications of HIV infection are described individually in the following sections: viral etiologies, bacterial etiologies, opportunistic pathogens, noninfectious pulmonary complications.

CRITERIA FOR DIAGNOSIS

Suggestive

Risk factors for acquiring HIV should be considered; these are listed in Chapter 8–76. If no definable risk factor can be identified, then immunosuppression may be suspected in the individual with recurrent infections (such as recurrent respiratory infection or vaginal infection in women). Serious infections such as meningitis and active tuberculosis, especially extrapulmonary tuberculosis, should raise the possibility of immunosuppression. Unexplained chronic constitutional symptoms such as weight loss and chronic fever are also suggestive of immunosuppression.

Definitive

When the patient is diagnosed with an opportunistic infection such as *Pneumocystis carinii* pneumonia (PCP), or the CD4 T-cell count drops below 200, or the proportion of CD4 lymphocytes is less than 14%, the diagnosis of AIDS is established in the HIV-seropositive individual. AIDS is the terminal stage of HIV infection. The following section describes infections and inflammatory processes that affect the lung in patients with HIV infection.

Viral Infections and Nonspecific Pneumonitis (Early Manifestations)

Etiology

Viral infection and nonspecific pneumonitis (a pulmonary inflammatory process where no specific pathogen or neoplastic process can be found) are part of HIV infections. Although most viruses may cause respiratory infections and pneumonia, common viruses such as influenza A and B, respiratory syncytial virus, and rhinovirus are usually the offending agents. Unusual viruses such as those in the herpes–varicella–zoster group and rubeola (which occurs with community outbreaks) are more serious.

Clinical Manifestations

Subjective

Symptoms are fever, myalgia, minimally productive cough, and dyspnea. There is little variation in symptoms between HIV- and non-HIV-infected persons. Historical information may suggest immunosuppression. An HIV-infected person may give a history of recurrent respiratory infections, recurrent sinusitis, or otitis. The family history is not helpful, unless there is a history of a concurrent respiratory infection in the household.

Objective

Physical Examination. The physical examination of a person with viral infections complicating early HIV infection is nonspecific and not impressive. There may be temperature elevation and tachypnea. The lung examination generally is without signs of consolidation. There may be occasional wheezing. Rales and egophony are usually not heard.

Routine Laboratory Abnormalities. The laboratory abnormalities are also nonspecific in early HIV infection. The complete blood count is often at the lower level of normal, with a marginally elevated white blood cell count (generally, < 15,000). The arterial blood gases reveal mild hypoxemia.

The chest radiograph often shows no abnormalities or occasionally a fine reticular or reticular nodular infiltrate.

Plans

Diagnostic

Differential Diagnosis. For persons with CD4 counts greater than 200, confirming a specific virus is not likely. Because the person is relatively immunocompetent, the risk, discomfort, and expense of identifying a specific virus are not justified, unless there is progressive clinical deterioration. The exceptions are viruses in the herpes–varicella–zoster group and influenza. A rapid diagnosis of the herpes group can be made by cytologic examination of the infected tissue such as nasal or oral vesicles, as well as viral culture techniques. Influenza can also be cultured from respiratory secretions, including nasal swabs and sputum in suspected lower respiratory tract infections. Specific and early identification of these two viruses may be helpful as both of them respond to antiviral therapy (acyclovir and amantadine, respectively).

Diagnostic Options. The diagnostic interventions are guided by the severity of the illness. If there is progression of disease, imaging options may include a gallium-67 scan directed at discovering a specific uptake pattern. The uptake pattern may direct diagnostic sampling of lung secretions or tissue. Respiratory secretion may be sampled by either natural or induced sputum or by bronchoscopy (with lavage and biopsy). Bronchoscopy is usually not warranted in early disease.

Recommended Approach. Most of the viral respiratory infections in early HIV disease are self-limited. The approach for diagnosis is to exclude more serious pulmonary processes with routine cultures of blood and sputum. Secondary bacterial infections should also be considered in the management and treated as needed.

If the clinical condition fails to improve or worsens, the patient should undergo a diagnostic study such as a gallium scan, to assess the pattern of lung involvement (diffuse or localized).

Lung specimens can be obtained by bronchoscopy with bronchoalveolar lavage and biopsy for histologic analysis. Lavage specimens should be submitted for acid-fast bacillus culture and stains and special stains for PCP and fungi (and fungal cultures).

Therapeutic

Therapeutic Options. Therapeutic options are geared toward providing relief of the respiratory and other symptoms. These include antipyretics, bronchodilators, and perhaps corticosteroids (if bronchospasm and hypoxemia are severe). In the case of influenza A, amantadine may provide relief of symptoms if begun within 48 hours of the illness. If clinical findings or diagnostic culture and histology suggest herpes infection, acyclovir may be of benefit. Secondary bacterial infections should not be overlooked. They can be a serious and even fatal complication if left untreated.

Recommended Approach. The recommended approach followed at our institution is to assess the possibility of communicable respiratory infections, especially tuberculosis, in all patients. If there is a high index of suspicion, the patient is isolated and sputum is collected for mycobacterial stains and culture. If three sputums are negative for acid-fast bacilli and the patient improves, follow-up for secondary bacterial infections is all that is needed. If the patient fails to improve or deteriorates, bronchoscopy is performed and therapy is guided by results of the cytologic and histologic specimens and special stains.

VIRAL INFECTIONS AND NONSPECIFIC PNEUMONITIS (LATE STAGE)
Etiology

In late-stage HIV infections, the most common viral infection affecting the lung is cytomegalovirus (CMV). Clinical manifestations of late-stage viral infection with CMV are much more severe.

Clinical Manifestations
Subjective

The symptoms of a CMV pneumonia take several days to manifest. There is also an explosive, rapidly progressive presentation with a rapidly fatal course (hours to days). The cardinal symptoms are dyspnea and a dry nonproductive cough. The dyspnea becomes severe as the pneumonia progresses. Historical information such as the diagnosis of AIDS and other opportunistic infections (which occur with CD4 counts < 200) is suggestive but not specific for this pneumonia. There is a high incidence of coinfection with CMV and other respiratory pathogens. Therefore, the

true incidence of pure infection with CMV and its role as a sole pathogen are not known; hence historical factors are poor predictors of CMV pneumonia. Familial disorders do not contribute to this infection.

Objective

Physical Examination. On physical examination the patients usually appear toxic with fever, dyspnea, a dry cough, and respiratory distress. Rales are usually heard. Signs of consolidation are not present. There is an urgency to make the diagnosis and distinguish CMV from other infections or noninfectious processes.

Routine Laboratory Abnormalities. The chest roentgenogram is rarely normal and usually shows a diffuse fine reticular infiltrate. The laboratory analysis reveals the common derangements seen with AIDS, anemia, leukopenia, and lymphopenia, none of which are specific. An elevated level of lactate dehydrogenase is often observed. This is not specific and is seen with various pneumonic processes. Hypoxemia becomes severe with progression of the pneumonia.

Plans
Diagnostic

Differential Diagnosis. Viral infections in late disease, such as CMV and other opportunistic infections including PCP, *Mycobacterium avium* complex, Cryptococcus *Neoformans,* as well as Kaposi's sarcoma, must be considered. Their presentations are similar with a progressive course that ends in respiratory failure.

Diagnostic Options. Cytomegalovirus is reliably diagnosed only by the identification of viral inclusion bodies on a histologic specimen. Sputum analysis gives a low and unreliable yield and should not be used. Bronchoscopic specimens are usually required, especially if empiric therapy for PCP or other pathogens fails. Although transbronchial lung biopsy is the procedure of choice, open lung biopsy is an option in patients from whom larger amounts of tissue may be needed (e.g., multiple cultures and to rule out intestinal pathology or neoplasm).

Recommended Approach. The recommended approach for diagnosis is based on clinical assessment of the degree of illness. Basic laboratory analysis such as arterial blood gases, a complete blood count, and a chest roentgenogram help define the severity of disease. The CD4 count, if below 100, makes the presence of CMV, PCP, and *M. avium* complex more likely. If the patient is severely ill (hypoxic), empiric therapy should begin. As the most common and most readily treatable condition is PCP, all regimens should include treatment for PCP. For those patients who fail to respond to treatment within 48 hours, a diagnostic bronchoscopy with biopsy should be considered. If CMV is found as the sole pathogen, treatment should be modified accordingly.

Therapeutic

Treatment with gancyclovir should be instituted when CMV is documented as the only pulmonary pathogen identified. The dose is usually 5 mg/kg twice daily, but higher doses may be needed if the patient fails to respond. The dose must be adjusted in patients with abnormal renal function. The response to gancyclovir alone is not well documented, and because of the late stage of disease (CD4 often < 100) and the recalcitrant hypoxemia, treatment does not greatly change mortality. The combination of immunoglobulin and gancyclovir has been used in patients with CMV pneumonia who are immunosuppressed because of bone marrow transplantation. The combination appears to be more efficacious than gancyclovir alone; however, this has not been established in AIDS patients.

Bacterial Infections of the Lung in HIV Patients

Etiology

Bacterial infections are common and can sometimes be overlooked as a complication of HIV infection. Most bacterial pneumonias are caused by, but not limited to, encapsulated bacteria such as *Streptococcus pneumoniae* and *Hemophilus influenzae*. The manifestations are quite similar in HIV- and non-HIV-positive patients. The infections may occur at any stage but are generally seen in early disease (CD4 > 200).

Clinical Manifestations

Subjective

Symptoms are acute in nature with productive cough, pleuritic chest pain, fever, chills and rigors, and dyspnea. Historical data that may be of value are prior admissions for a similar or the same type of pneumonia, unusual manifestations of pneumonia (e.g., empyema), or an unusual complication such as meningitis, as a result of bacteremia. The family history is not of great value.

Objective

Physical Examination. The physical examination is that of a consolidating pneumonia. The patient looks toxic and tachypneic, and fever is usually present. The chest examination shows increased tactile fremitus and dullness on percussion, bronchial or bronchovesicular breathing with rales, and egophony.

Routine Laboratory Abnormalities. Routine laboratory abnormalities include a relative leukocytosis with band forms. Leukocyte counts can reach as high as 20,000. The arterial blood gas ranges from mild to severe hypoxemia with a widened alveolar–arterial gradient. Chest radiographs usually show typical segmental or lobar consolidation, especially with *S. pneumoniae*, although there can be multilobar involvement with AIDS. When organisms other than *S. pneumoniae* (e.g., *Staphylococcus* or group B streptococci) are the causative agents, a diffuse consolidation pattern with multilobar involvement can be seen. *Hemophilus influenzae* may cause a multilobar and even bilateral infiltrate.

Plans

Diagnostic

Differential Diagnosis. In the setting of an acute pneumonic process, differential diagnosis usually centers around typical pyogenic infection or an atypical or opportunistic infection. Infection or coinfection with opportunistic organisms such as *Pneumocystis carinii*, *M. tuberculosis*, *Legionella*, and fungi and inflammatory processes such as Kaposi's sarcoma and alveolar proteinosis should not be overlooked because many of these conditions respond well to treatment. Among bacterial pathogens, *S. pneumoniae* and *H. influenzae* remain the most common bacteria; however, *Staphylococcus aureus*, group B streptococci, *Moraxella catarrhalis*, *Legionella*, and *Mycoplasma* have all been reported as pulmonary pathogens in patients with HIV (Murry and Mills, 1990). *Rhodococcus equii* has recently been described as causing a cavitary pneumonia, and *Pseudomonas aeruginosa* is seen with low CD4 counts (<50) (Witt et al., 1987; Murry and Mills, 1990).

Diagnostic Options. The diagnosis of bacterial pneumonias complicating HIV infection is usually made by culturing the organism from the blood or sputum or identifying the organism on Gram stain. If this fails to yield a working diagnosis, and the patient does not respond to initial treatment, a diagnostic sampling of pulmonary secretions via bronchoscopy may be required. Routine lavage sampling of bronchial secretions is not of great value, as the bacterial flora colonizing the upper airway contaminate the specimen. A protected catheter specimen brush should be used to obtain a pure culture specimen of lower airway secretions. Bronchoalveolar lavage specimens from the same procedure can be sent for *P. carinii*, acid-fast bacillus, *Legionella*, and fungal staining. If it is felt that tissue samples are required (i.e., in the case of CMV), a transbronchial biopsy can be obtained during the same procedure. The transtracheal aspiration requires a cooperative patient and some degree (albeit minor) of sedation. At our institution most patients present with hypoxia (po$_2$<60). The discomfort and the relative risk of the procedure mitigate against its use. Another option is transthoracic needle aspiration of the lung, but because of the potential seriousness of the complications (bleeding, pneumothorax, air embolism), this procedure is re-

served (by some experts) for the deteriorating patient in whom no other technique can establish the diagnosis.

Recommended Approach. The recommended approach for diagnosing a pyogenic pneumonia is relatively similar to that for patients with viral infections. Establishing the causative organism and instituting appropriate antibiotics are both essential. If diagnostic cultures are not obtained from the blood or sputum, the patient should undergo bronchoscopy with a protected specimen brush, and the specimens sent for routine bacterial culture as well as acid-fast bacillus culture and the bronchoalveolar lavage for special stains.

There is a high relapse recurrence of bacteremia in HIV-positive individuals, particularly that resulting from *S. pneumoniae* infection. Therefore, bacteremia may be an indicator of the degree of immunosuppression or of previously undiagnosed immunosuppression. In a patient of unknown HIV status who develops bacteremia (especially if recurrent), HIV testing should be considered (Redd et al., 1990).

Therapeutic

Trimethoprim–sulfamethoxazole (TMP–SMX), which effectively treats PCP, will also treat infection with *S. pneumoniae*, *H. influenzae*, and many other pyogenic pathogens. The dose used in PCP (20 mg/kg TMP) is adequate against most pyogenic pathogens. Addition of a macrolide antibiotic to all regimens is indicated for community-acquired infection. This covers pulmonary pathogens such as *Mycoplasma* and *Legionella*.

Investigations to determine dissemination of infection (e.g., central nervous system) are warranted, even if symptoms are not obvious on presentation. If the patient is in extremis, treatment of opportunistic infection such as PCP should begin without delay. Persons who fail to stabilize or show clinical deterioration (of pulmonary status) within a short period (48 hours) should be considered for diagnostic bronchoscopy. If a tissue specimen is needed, a transbronchial biopsy should be obtained at the time of the bronchoalveolar lavage. The tissue specimen can be sent for culture for acid-fast bacilli and histologic analysis.

Treatment depends on the organism that is suspected and isolated. The sensitivities of the organisms are not altered by the immune status. The abnormal immune state makes treatment more difficult. There may be multisystem involvement because of the likelihood of bacteremia. In a community-acquired pyogenic pneumonia, TMP–SMX and a macrolide antibiotic constitute a very good combination. It can be used to treat most community-acquired pneumonias as well as PCP. For extreme manifestations of pneumonia in patients with a low CD4 count (<50), antibiotic coverage for *Pseudomonas* should be considered. An antipseudomonal penicillin or a third-generation cephalosporin and an aminoglycoside should be used in conjunction with TMP–SMX until culture data are available.

OPPORTUNISTIC LUNG INFECTIONS

Etiology

Opportunistic lung infections are lung infections caused by pathogens of low virulence, not usually causative of disease in healthy persons. See below for each pathogen. Opportunistic lung infections occur in late-stage disease and define the AIDS state. Persons with opportunistic lung infections, unlike those with acute bacterial or viral pulmonary infections, have a more indolent subacute course with gradual dyspnea and cough that occurs over weeks.

Clinical Manifestations

Subjective

Historical information confirms a gradual decrease in exercise tolerance along with the usual cough, chest tightness, and small amounts of expectoration in addition to constitutional symptoms of fever and sweats. The degree of immunosuppression is suggested by a history of associated conditions such as oral candidiasis, wasting, and chronic diarrhea or a prior infection with an opportunistic organism. The family history adds little to the diagnosis of opportunistic lung infections.

Dyspnea usually brings the person to medical attention. The dyspnea is accompanied by cough. The nature of expectorated sputum may be suggestive of the pathogen (e.g., persons with PCP usually have a minimally productive cough, tuberculosis or other mycobacterial infections may be accompanied by hemoptysis).

Objective

Physical Examination. The physical examination in most opportunistic lung infections (PCP, cryptococcal pneumonia, M. avium complex infection) is generally nonspecific and reflects the severity of the lung involvement. There are invariably tachypnea and tachycardia with a temperature elevation. In severe cases, there are diffuse areas of lung consolidation on auscultation due to the widespread inflammation and atelectasis. If unattended, these patients eventually develop respiratory failure and require intubation and mechanical ventilation.

Routine Laboratory Abnormalities. As with both bacterial and viral infections, the main physiologic derangement is in gas exchange. There is generally frank hypoxia. Laboratory blood analysis shows nonspecific abnormalities; however, in diseases such as PCP, tuberculosis, and M. avium complex infection, the level of lactate dehydrogenase is usually elevated (at least three times normal).

Radiographic studies (x-rays) show varying abnormalities, but generally the infection begins as a reticular infiltrate, especially in PCP, that can evolve to alveolar infiltrates or consolidation with air bronchograms. There is a radiographic pattern specific to PCP: alveolar consolidation with lucent cysts. This cystic pattern generally occurs in the peripheral lung fields and is seen in severe cases. Gallium scanning of the lung is a technique that may be helpful in diagnosing PCP.

Plans

Diagnostic

Differential Diagnosis. The differential diagnosis is guided by the level of immunosuppression and may include both bacterial infections (especially H. influenzae because of the diffuse radiographic pattern), mycobacterial infections, fungal pneumonia, and inflammatory processes, including alveolar protenosis and Kaposi's sarcoma. The infection of major concern (and the one occurring with greatest frequency) is PCP. It occurs during the course of illness in 80% of patients with AIDS in the United States and is the AIDS-defining diagnosis in approximately 65% of patients (Murray and Mills, 1990).

Diagnostic Options. A gallium scan usually gives a homogenous uptake pattern in the lungs; a nonhomogenous pattern may suggest a more localized process such as tuberculosis, M. avium complex infection, or other inflammatory processes, but does not exclude PCP. Although gallium scanning is only suggestive for PCP, a negative gallium scan is strong evidence against PCP. The most widely accepted method of establishing the diagnosis of an opportunistic lung infection is bronchoscopy with bronchoalveolar lavage or a transbronchial lung biopsy. The yield for such organisms as M. tuberculosis and M. avium complex is variable; by contrast, the yield for P. carinii exceeds 90% in most series.

Bronchoscopy is an invasive diagnostic procedure. There has been an attempt to reproduce the yield achieved by bronchoscopy and bronchoalveolar lavage using secretions obtained by sputum induction. The results for PCP via sputum induction at our institution have not approached those of bronchoalveolar lavage. Hence, for PCP, bronchoscopy is the diagnostic procedure of choice. For tuberculosis and M. avium complex infection, the yield of studies on natural sputum and induced sputum is relatively high and may obviate the need for bronchoalveolar lavage.

Recommended Approach. Because of the possibility of pulmonary tuberculosis, the recommended approach at our institution is immediate respiratory isolation until tuberculosis has been ruled out with three negative expectorated sputum specimens. If the patient is not stable, four antituberculous medications (assuming that there is no prior history of treatment or prophylaxis for tuberculosis, which would increase the likelihood of drug-resistant isolates and mandate a different approach to presumptive therapy) are begun at the time of initial evaluation or if the sputum is positive for acid-fast bacilli. The patient is also started on

TMP–SMX for PCP. If the diagnosis of tuberculosis is not confirmed in 48 hours (after three negative sputum samples for acid-fast bacilli) and the patient fails to improve, he or she is considered for bronchoscopy. Depending on the radiographic pattern (e.g., reticular pattern versus modular or cavity pattern) and the clinical picture, the decision to perform a transbronchial lung biopsy (in addition to bronchoalveolar lavage) is made. Most conditions require only bronchoalveolar lavage; however, if Kaposi's sarcoma, or alveolar proteinosis, or invasive fungal infection is suspected, tissue sampling is required. Following the pathology results, drug therapy is tailored to the specific disease entity.

Therapeutic

Therapeutic Options. The therapeutic options used depend on the organism(s) suspected in the differential diagnosis. Because of the high frequency of PCP as an opportunistic infection, unless there is overwhelming evidence to the contrary, all regimens should include TMP–SMX in doses sufficient to treat PCP (pentamidine in those with sulfa sensitivity). Likewise, because of the potential spread of pulmonary tuberculosis, all persons should be isolated. If sputum is positive for acid-fast bacilli, four antituberculous drugs should be used.

Mycobacterium avium complex has also proven to be a frequent respiratory pathogen in our institution. When a sputum specimen is reported positive for acid-fast bacilli, however, patients are preferentially placed on an antituberculosis regimen rather than an anti-M. avium complex regimen. The only circumstance in which this may change is if there is an acid-fast bacillus-positive blood culture (which is more common with M. avium complex). In these circumstances (and in the appropriate setting), therapy for disseminated M. avium complex is instituted with ethambutol, ciprofloxin, clarithromycin, and rifabutin or clofazimine.

Although fungal (*Cryptococcus* and *Candida*) lung infections are not infrequently found at our institution, because therapy generally involves systemic amphotericin, we do not empirically treat for fungal infection unless it is proven either by culture or by histology.

Recommended Approach. When an opportunistic lung infection is suspected, the patient is treated with TMP–SMX at a dose of 20 mg/kg/d TMP and 100 mg/kg/d SMX in four divided doses. If hypoxemia (pO_2 < 70) exists and there is an alveolar–arterial gradient greater than 35, then steroids are added: prednisone 40 mg or methylprednisolone 32 mg twice daily for 7 days, then tapered to 40 mg once daily for 7 days, then 20 mg once daily for 7 days. The patient completes a course of 21 days of TMP–SMX therapy and is discharged on prophylactic therapy (see Prevention). If the patient has a contraindication to or develops a complication of TMP–SMX therapy, pentamidine is used. Pentamidine is given as a single daily intravenous dose (generally 4 mg/kg) 280 to 300 mg/d. These patients require pentamidine (or dapsone) prophylaxis on discharge (see Prevention).

Mycobacterium tuberculosis, when found on smear, then confirmed by culture, is treated with four antituberculous drugs: isoniazid, rifampin, pyrazinamide, and ethambutol. Treatment is generally continued for 9 to 12 months and for at least 6 months following the first negative culture report. Multidrug-resistant tuberculosis requires special attention, in that the high degrees of resistance carry a high mortality rate. The treatment regimen should be individualized based on susceptibility patterns. Fungal infections, if confirmed by culture or histology, are initially treated with amphotericin 0.5 to 0.8 mg/kg/d until a total dose of 800 to 1000 mg has been given. Prophylaxis should follow with fluconazole 200 mg daily.

Neoplastic and Other Less Common Pulmonary Manifestations of HIV

Etiology

These conditions are defined as noninfectious pulmonary complications encountered in HIV patients attributable to neoplastic or immunologic reactions. The scope of HIV-related lung diseases is not limited to infections. Four entities—Kaposi's sarcoma, alveolar proteinosis, lymphoid interstitial pneumonia, and pleural effusions (associated with AIDS)—are discussed.

Clinical Manifestations

Subjective

Unlike the infective disorders associated with HIV, the inflammatory and neoplastic diseases present with a slow, indolent course, with some patients showing a decrease in exercise tolerance over months. Cough is common, with minimal, if any sputum production, but occasionally patients with Kaposi's sarcoma complain of hemoptysis. The past history is helpful if there has been an episode of PCP or tuberculosis, which may suggest development of alveolar proteinosis. If there is a history of cutaneous Kaposi's sarcoma, pulmonary Kaposi's sarcoma lesions should be considered.

Objective

Physical Examination. In advanced disease, tachypnea is the most consistent physical finding. Rales may be heard with alveolar proteinosis, and in Kaposi's sarcoma there may be wheezing secondary to bronchospasm, but these findings are variable. There are few, if any, consistent findings, and fever is often absent.

Pleural effusions are not uncommonly seen in patients with AIDS. Effusions occur in the setting of a pyogenic infectious, pulmonary process, but they are also seen with noninfectious causes such as Kaposi's sarcoma, as a result of other inflammatory processes such as lymphocytic interstitial pneumonitis, or as a manifestation of malnutrition. In our experience a pleural effusion is often present at the time of initial presentation to the hospital. Analysis of the fluid may lead to the diagnosis prior to other procedures being employed. The size of the effusion varies with the etiology, as do the physical findings. There may be a large effusion and, thus, a dull percussion note of the entire hemithorax (often seen in Kaposi's sarcoma), or the effusion may be small enough to go undetected by clinical examination.

Routine Laboratory Abnormalities. There is a significant difference in the radiographic patterns of these diseases. Kaposi's sarcoma usually presents with moderate to large nodules spread diffusely throughout the radiograph; effusions are often present. Alveolar proteinosis presents with a fine nodular alveolar pattern (almost ground glass), which can be mistaken for PCP, and lymphocytic interstitial pneumonitis presents as a reticular nodular infiltrate on the chest roentgenogram.

The primary abnormality with interstitial pulmonary pathology is the arterial blood gases. All these conditions (Kaposi's sarcoma, alveolar proteinosis, lymphocytic interstitial pneumonitis) are associated with hypoxia. With alveolar proteinosis, however, the hypoxia is very severe. A shunt effect is created that does not respond to supplemental oxygen. Hypoxia is a common cause of death in these patients.

Plans

Diagnostic

Differential Diagnosis. The differential diagnosis includes all the pathologic entities previously described, in addition to most opportunistic infections and nonopportunistic infections.

Diagnostic Options and Recommended Approach. The diagnosis (in almost all cases) can be made only by sampling tissue; therefore, a bronchoscopy with biopsy or an open-lung biopsy is the only way to confirm the diagnosis. For alveolar proteinosis and lymphocytic interstitial pneumonitis, some experts suggest that an open biopsy be obtained; however, in our experience these entities have been diagnosed by transbronchial lung biopsy on several occasions.

Therapeutic

On presentation, the patients are usually treated empirically with a regimen consisting of an antibiotic (usually TMP–SMX) to cover most bacterial pathogens, as well as to cover PCP (steroids may or may not be used depending on the suspicion of PCP). The patient is usually treated for active tuberculosis with four antituberculous medications. If no improvement occurs within 48 hours, the patient is referred for bronchoscopy with bronchoalveolar lavage and biopsy.

Sometimes the patient requires intubation and mechanical ventilation prior to bronchoscopy. In our experience, this has not been a deterrent to transbronchial biopsy.

Therapeutic options are determined by the pathology found. With the exception of lymphocytic interstitial pneumonitis, for which steroids are used, the response to treatment for these conditions is not favorable. Kaposi's sarcoma is treated with antineoplastic agents and interferon. Alveolar proteinosis is also treated with steroids and occasionally whole-lung lavage under general anesthesia (this is not usually done in AIDS patients).

Lymphocytic interstitial pneumonitis is generally reported as a manifestation of AIDS in children; however, we have made the diagnosis in adults with AIDS, using transbronchial biopsy. The response of lymphocytic interstitial pneumonitis to steroid therapy is encouraging. Patients may have a reduction in dyspnea and, in some cases, an improvement in lung function.

FOLLOW-UP

Once the acute illness is over, little immunity develops. The patient is again at risk for developing repeated infection with the same or different organisms. Hence, all persons should be considered for prophylaxis for the most preventable respiratory infections (see Prevention).

In addition, routine follow-up with periodic skin testing (every 6 months) for tuberculosis should be performed, and if anergic, the patient should be evaluated by chest roentgenogram twice a year.

DISCUSSION

Prevalence and Incidence

Of the respiratory processes occurring most frequently in HIV infection, tuberculosis and PCP deserve special comment. These are the most common and well-studied processes affecting the lungs.

The increase in the number of tuberculosis cases has been directly linked to the HIV epidemic, along with a relaxation of surveillance and treatment strategies and the growing poverty and homelessness in urban cities. Prophylaxis against tuberculosis has been proven effective in reducing reactivation of tuberculosis. The current Centers for Disease Control and Prevention recommendation is that all HIV-positive persons receive a skin test with 5 tuberculin units of purified protein derivative (PPD), and if positive, isoniazid prophylaxis be given for 1 year (see Prevention).

It is estimated that 80% of HIV-positive patients have at least one episode of PCP. The strongest immunologic indicator for the development of PCP is a CD4 T-cell count less than 200 (Masur, et al., 1989). Without prophylactic treatment, patients are estimated to have an additive risk of developing PCP of approximately 12% per year. The mortality from the first episode of PCP is between 5 and 20% and doubles for each subsequent episode.

Related Basic Science

Human immunodeficiency virus is a retrovirus that infects by attaching to the CD4 receptor molecule of various cells. The cells most affected are T lymphocytes (monocytes, macrophages, and brain tissue are also particularly susceptible).

Once attached, the viral genome is integrated into the host DNA by the essential enzyme reverse transcriptase. This leads to production of more virus and eventual death of the infected cell. When the immune system is so debilitated and the number of CD4 T cells falls below 200, or opportunistic infections such as PCP occur, AIDS is defined. T lymphocytes, monocytes, and macrophages are the body's main defenses against organism such as, *P. carinii, M. tuberculosis,* fungi, and parasites. B-cell abnormalities also exist. These include dysregulation of chemotaxis, hypergammaglobulinemia, ineffective antibody production, and production of autoantibodies. The foregoing prevent adequate defense against pyogenic bacteria.

Human immunodeficiency virus also generates many other protein markers, one of which is P24 (a core protein), which can be used as a marker of disease activity. Other immunologic abnormalities are associated with HIV, but they are beyond the scope of this chapter.

Natural History and Modification with Treatment

Although there are various therapeutic options (particularly directed toward prophylaxis of infection), the underlying process is immunodeficiency caused by HIV destruction of CD4 cells.

Until HIV can be effectively controlled, these therapies will only provide a temporary stay from the various infections to which the lung and body will eventually succumb.

Prevention

The immunocompromised host develops little effective immunity following most respiratory infections. They often require chronic suppressive therapy and vaccinations to prevent primary or recurrent infections. Most patients with early HIV disease mount an antibody response to pneumococcal vaccine. This vaccine should be administered once HIV positivity is established. The vaccine should be administered even after an episode of pneumococcal pneumonia. Other bacterial vaccines are not well studied, and none are commonly used.

Preventive therapy is well established against *Pneumocystis carinii*. Patients who receive primary or secondary prophylaxis have a reduced risk of developing repeated episodes of PCP. The most effective agent used for prophylaxis is TMP–SMX. The major drawback with this agent is the high frequency of adverse reactions. Dapsone is a sulfone compound used primarily in the prophylaxis of PCP in those persons unable to tolerate TMP–SMX. Its major drawback is the development of anemia and methemoglobinemia, especially in persons who are glucose-6 phosphate dehydrogenase deficient. Aerosol pentamidine is also used as prophylaxis against PCP when administered on a monthly or biweekly basis. The major drawback is the administration of the drug. A jet nebulizer (which produces at least 60 pounds pressure) is required. Ventilation to the outside atmosphere or the use of a chamber or hood to prevent spread of the medication or coughed aerosols is required, as is a unidirectional breathing circuit with an expiratory filter (Marquest Respigard II). This makes the drug cumbersome and expensive to administer. Patients should be screened for active tuberculosis prior to receiving aerosol pentamidine therapy, as coughing induced by the medicine may spread mycobacterial organisms.

Influenza vaccine imparts some immunity to HIV-infected persons who receive it and should be given annually. There are no other commonly used vaccines or medications to prevent viral infections, however.

Prevention of tuberculosis in persons who are HIV positive can be highly effective and is accomplished by prophylactic isoniazid therapy. Any HIV-infected person with a reactive tuberculin skin test (5 tuberculin units of PPD) greater than 5 mm or any person who is anergic and has close daily contact with persons with active pulmonary tuberculosis, or lives in a communal living area such as shelter, should receive isoniazid for 12 months (issues of prophylaxis in those exposed to multidrug-resistant tuberculosis are beyond the scope of this chapter).

Mycobacterium avium complex, unlike *M. tuberculosis*, is not as easily treated or prevented. As yet, there is no definitive regimen for the treatment or prophylaxis of *M. avium* complex. Current prophylaxis includes rifabutin alone or in combination with clarithromycin. Current studies are underway to determine efficacy.

Fluconazole is usually given to prevent recurrence of serious fungal infections such as cryptococcal meningitis and pneumonia. It is also used to prevent recurrence of *Candida* infections. Secondary prophylaxis of fungal infections including pneumonias is generally lifelong.

Cost Containment

The expense of treating HIV disease and all the aspects of HIV lung disease far exceed the scope of this chapter. The cost, however, has been a major expenditure in every aspect of the health care system.

REFERENCES

Masur H, Ognibene FP, Yarchoan R, et al. CD4 counts as predictors of opportunistic pneumonias in human immunodeficiency virus (HIV) infection. Ann Intern Med 1989;111:223.

Murray JF, Mills J. Pulmonary infectious complications of HIV infection. Am Rev Respir Dis 1990;141:1356.

Redd S, Rutherford GW III, Sande MA, et al. The role of human immunodeficiency virus (HIV) infection in pneumococcal bacteremia in San Francisco residents. J Infect Dis 1990;162:1012.

Witt D, Craven DE, McCabe WR. Bacterial infections in adult patients with AIDS and AIDS-related complex. Am J Med 1987;82:900.

CHAPTER 13–45

Primary Lung Abscess

Martin Kramer, M.D.

DEFINITION

A lung abscess is a suppurative process affecting the lung parenchyma that results in one or more cavitary lesions demonstrable by chest radiography. A primary lung abscess occurs when an individual is otherwise healthy without underlying diseases. Secondary lung abscesses are complications of local disease (i.e., pulmonary neoplasms) or systemic immunosuppressive diseases.

ETIOLOGY

Aspiration is the underlying mechanism in most cases. Conditions associated with decreased consciousness (i.e., alcohol use, seizure disorder, general anesthesia), especially in the presence of poor oral hygiene (i.e., gingivitis) and/or the presence of gastrointestinal disorders such as achalasia and esophageal stricture, are present in the majority of cases. The predominant bacteria are anaerobes which, in the presence of gingivitis, may be present in numbers as high as 10^{12} organisms/g in gingival crevices. Anaerobes are present in 80 to 90% of cases, whereas aerobic organisms are present in 30 to 50%, either alone or more frequently together with anaerobes. In the hospital setting, nosocomial organisms (i.e., *Pseudomonas, Staphylococcus aureus, Klebsiella pneumoniae*) are frequently found.

Inhalation of certain organisms may occasionally result in an abscess. *Mycobacterium tuberculosis* is one example.

CRITERIA FOR DIAGNOSIS
Suggestive

A lung abscess should be suspected when a patient presents with a risk factor for aspiration in the presence of abnormal pulmonary findings (see below). About 10 to 20% of cases have no predisposing factor ("cryptogenic lung abscess").

Definitive

The diagnosis is made by the demonstration of one or more cavitary lesions with an air–fluid level on a chest roentgenogram.

CLINICAL MANIFESTATIONS
Subjective

The patient usually presents with an insidious course over 2 or more weeks. Anorexia, weight loss, malaise, fever to 101 to 102°F, cough, hemoptysis, and productive purulent sputum are usually present. In 50% of cases, the sputum is foul smelling.

The patient may give a history of partial or complete loss of consciousness. A history of an initial acute illness that then subsides and becomes chronic may occasionally be elicited. Eliciting a history of drug use, especially alcohol, should be carefully done. A history of dysphagia, symptoms of gastroesophageal reflux, "atypical" chest pain, scleroderma, and so on may suggest a predisposing gastrointestinal disorder.

Objective
Physical Examination

The patient appears chronically ill with weakness and malaise. Fever is usually present. On examination, evidence of poor dental hygiene is often present. A foul odor of the breath (nonspecific) or sputum may be noted. Chest examination reveals findings typical of pneumonia. Amphoric breath sounds may be heard over a large cavity. A pleural friction rub and/or findings consistent with a complicating empyema may be present. Clubbing may be present. Neurologic examination may reveal an abnormal gag reflex or an altered state of consciousness.

Routine Laboratory Abnormalities

Laboratory abnormalities consist of an anemia compatible with an anemia of chronic disease unless other conditions such as iron or folate deficiency are present (i.e., alcoholism). There is a moderate leukocytosis with a left shift. Blood cultures are usually negative.

The chest radiograph reveals an infiltrate associated with the abscess. The right lung is more frequently involved, with the gravity-dependent areas (superior segments of the lower lobes and posterior segments of the upper lobes) affected. Evidence of a pleural effusion may be present.

PLANS
Diagnostic
Differential Diagnosis

Many other diseases may simulate a primary lung abscess.

Infections with mycobacteria (especially *M. tuberculosis*) can present with many of the above features. Although classically involving the apical segment of the upper lobe, many exceptions occur.

Infections with fungi such as *Histoplasma, Aspergillus,* and *Coccidioides* must be considered. An epidemiologic history and evaluation of underlying diseases will dictate the need for investigation.

Malignancy is usually not associated with systemic findings of infection. A pulmonary infarct may occasionally cavitate and superinfection may rarely occur. Septic emboli are usually multiple and bilateral and are associated with bacteremia. The latter may occur in right-sided endocarditis (especially in intravenous drug users) or septic thrombophlebitis (i.e., pelvis, Lemierre's syndrome). Blood cultures are usually positive. Rheumatoid arthritis and Wegener's granulomatosis may be associated with necrobiotic nodules. Various pulmonary anatomic structures such as bronchogenic cysts, bullae, and sequestrations may be superinfected. Prior chest films may reveal these abnormalities.

Subdiaphragmatic infections such as amebiasis and intraabdominal pyogenic infection may present with a lower lobe pneumonia/abscess.

Immunocompromised patients present an expanded differential diagnosis. For example, a cavitary lesion in advanced HIV disease may be due to *Aspergillus* species, *Rhodococcus equii,* or even (rarely) *Pneumocystis carinii*. Transplant patients may present with *Nocardia asteroides.*

Diagnostic Options

Microbiologic diagnosis can be made by a sputum Gram stain and culture. Specimens may also be obtained by transtracheal aspiration, bronchoscopy with qualitative/quantitative cultures, percutaneous needle aspiration, blood cultures, and aspiration of pleural fluid (if present).

A computed tomography scan of the chest can give better anatomic definition of the abscess as well as differentiate parenchymal from pleural disease (if necessary).

Serologic tests may be helpful if certain fungal diseases, Wegener's granulomatosis, or rheumatoid arthritis is suspected.

Sputum cytology may lead to the diagnosis of a neoplasm.

Recommended Approach

If the findings are compatible with a primary lung abscess, a sputum Gram stain and culture and blood cultures should be done. If a pleural effusion is present, thoracentesis must be done to rule out an empyema. The pleural fluid should be cultured for aerobic and anaerobic organisms. Excluding tuberculosis with smears and cultures, as well as performing a tuberculin skin test, is advisable. Antimicrobial therapy is then started. If the response to therapy is good, no further workup is necessary.

If the response to therapy is inadequate after 7 to 10 days (i.e., persistent fever, anorexia, weakness, leukocytosis, no improvement on the chest film radiograph), further evaluation is necessary. It should be noted that the chest radiograph may "normally" worsen during the first week of therapy; this, in itself, should not be considered a therapeutic failure. If empyema was present, adequacy of drainage must be ensured. Bronchscopy should be performed to evaluate for an endobronchial obstruction (i.e., foreign body, carcinoma), to obtain material for culture, and to promote drainage. Transtracheal aspiration is rarely done today. If bronchoscopy is unsuccessful, evaluation for a percutaneous needle aspiration should be undertaken. A chest computed tomography scan often gives valuable information as to the location and anatomic detail of the abscess (and pleural effusion, if present). If a needle aspiration is done, material should be cultured for aerobic and anaerobic bacteria, mycobacteria, and fungi. Cytology should also be sent. The laboratory should be alerted if organisms such as *Nocardia, Legionella,* and *Rhodococcus* are possible. Serologic tests as noted above should be sent. If all of the above fail, a thoracotomy may very rarely be necessary.

Therapeutic
Therapeutic Options

Therapeutic options include antimicrobial therapy, hydration, chest physiotherapy including postural drainage, and surgical drainage.

Recommended Approach

Antimicrobial therapy is based on the microbiology. Treatment has become more complicated, as a significant proportion of anaerobes now produce a penicillinase that inactivates penicillin.

Penicillin is acceptable therapy if the patient's course has been indolent and the patient is not very ill. If used, high doses (10–20 million U/d) should be used. Adding metronidazole to penicillin should be a highly efficacious regimen. Metronidazole by itself is associated with a high failure rate and should not be used alone. Clindamycin is superior to penicillin alone and is very efficacious.

Many other antibiotics are also likely to be effective. Most are very expensive and have an unnecessarily broad antibacterial spectrum, which may predispose patients to colonization with highly resistant bacteria. If cultures grow organisms such as *S. aureus* and *Klebsiella* species or other bacteria known to cause necrotizing pneumonia, the antibacterial spectrum should be expanded accordingly.

Chest physiotherapy may help ensure proper drainage of the abscess.

In complicated cases, surgical drainage by either percutaneous tube drainage or thoracotomy may rarely be indicated.

FOLLOW-UP

Clinical improvement should be seen in 4 to 7 days. Once the patient is afebrile, the white blood cell count is normal, and clinical improvement has occurred, she or he may be placed on oral therapy with penicillin VK with or without metronidazole, clindamycin, amoxicillin/clavulanate, or other antibiotics as appropriate. Therapy is given until the infiltrate has completely cleared or only a small residual lesion remains. Six to twelve weeks of total therapy is usually necessary.

DISCUSSION
Prevalence and Incidence

The prevalence and incidence of lung abscess are not known.

Related Basic Science

A lung abscess results when bacteria are aspirated into the lung and necrosis of lung tissue ensues. The mouth contains large numbers of predominantly anaerobic bacteria. These bacteria predominate in the gingival crevices, where concentrations as high as 10^{12} organisms/g may be reached. Aspiration normally occurs in healthy individuals while asleep, but the small number of aspirated bacteria are cleared by ciliary action and pulmonary defense mechanisms. In debilitated patients, aspiration is more frequent and host defenses are compromised. Thus, the most important factors determining the outcome with aspiration are the state of dental hygiene, degree of altered consciousness, and status of host defenses.

The areas of lung involvement are determined by the patient's position when aspiration occurs. In the supine position, the gravity-dependent portions of the lungs are involved (see Plans, Diagnostic). Most cases of lung abscess are caused by the normal oral flora. The most important anaerobes appear to be peptostreptococci (Gram-positive) and Gram-negative bacteria such as *Bacteroides melaninogenicus* (now reclassified as *Prevotella* species and *Porphyromonas* species), *Bacteroides* species, and *Fusobacterium*. A significant percentage (30–50%) of the Gram-negative anaerobes produce penicillinase. Aerotolerant organisms such as *Streptococcus intermedius* and *Streptococcus parvulus* are also involved. Hospitalized and nursing home patients may be infected with such organisms as *S. aureus*, *Klebsiella* species, *Pseudomonas*, and *Enterobacter* species.

Natural History and Its Modification with Treatment

Most patients with a lung abscess do very well. Antibiotics with ancillary measures to promote drainage are highly successful with a survival rate of about 90%. Surgical intervention is very rarely necessary.

Prevention

The key to prevention is reversal of as many of the predisposing factors as possible. Practicing good dental hygiene as well as altering personal habits that result in an altered state of consciousness (i.e., alcohol use) must be emphasized. Patients with disorders such as achalasia and seizures should be optimally managed.

Cost Containment

Antibiotics such as penicillin, metronidazole, and clindamycin are relatively inexpensive. Parenteral medications such as cefoxitin, ticarcillin/clavulanate, ampicillin/sulbactam, and imipenem/cilistatin are effective but are very expensive and offer no advantages in treating primary lung abscess (also see Plans, Therapeutic). Other oral antibiotics such as amoxicillin/clavulanate should be effective but are also very expensive.

Ensuring proper drainage of the abscess is important to maximize initial success, thereby decreasing the length of hospital stay. Education of the patient is critically important with respect to the preventive measures outlined above and to compliance with outpatient antimicrobial therapy. Emphasizing the duration of the therapy and discussing possible side effects of the medications are necessary.

A computed tomography scan of the chest and bronchoscopy should be ordered only if specific indications are present.

REFERENCES

Bartlett JG. Anaerobic bacterial infections of the lung and pleural space. Clin Infect Dis 1993;16(suppl. 4):S248.

Bartlett JG, Gorbach SL, Tally FP, et al. Bacteriology and treatment of primary lung abscess. Am Rev Respir Dis 1974;109:510.

Gudiol F, Manresa F, Pallares R, et al. Clindamycin vs. penicillin for anaerobic lung infections: High rate of penicillin failures associated with penicillin-resistant *Bacteroides melaninogenicus*. Arch Intern Med 1990;150:2525.

Levison ME, Mangura CT, Lorber B, et al. Clindamycin compared with penicillin for the treatment of anaerobic lung abscess. Ann Intern Med 1983;98:466.

Marina M, Strong C, Civen E, et al. Bacteriology of anaerobic pleuropulmonary infections: Preliminary report. Clin Infect Dis 1993;16(suppl. 4):S256.

CHAPTER 13–46

Aspiration Pneumonitis

Abraham Sanders, M.D.

DEFINITION

Aspiration pneumonitis refers to the syndrome caused by the abnormal entry of oropharyngeal bacteria, gastric contents, foreign objects, inhaled chemicals, smoke, or particulate matter into the lower airways, causing inflammation of the parenchyma of the lung. The aspiration of oropharyngeal bacteria leads to aspiration pneumonia, necrotizing pneumonitis, lung abscess, and empyema.

The aspiration of gastric contents of low pH leads to chemical pneumonitis. Foreign objects aspirated into the airways lead to obstruction and postobstructive pneumonia. Chemicals and smoke can cause airway and parenchymal damage, pulmonary edema, and the adult respiratory distress syndrome.

This discussion focuses on the aspiration of oropharyngeal bacteria, the most common cause of aspiration pneumonia.

ETIOLOGY

The aspiration of the bacterial flora of the oropharynx into the lower airways, overwhelming the local defenses, causes bacterial pneumonia; however, although these organisms are normally resident and aspirated, they do not always cause pneumonia. The normal flora in the healthy population contains 10^8 anaerobes and 10^7 aerobes per milliliter of secretions. Individuals with poor oral hygiene have larger numbers of organisms, and chronically ill patients in hospitals or nursing homes, as well as alcoholics or patients receiving antacids, often are colonized by Gram-negative bacilli. Most normal hosts aspirate during sleep, yet do not develop pneumonia.

Conditions associated with aspiration pneumonia are listed in Table 13–46–1.

CRITERIA FOR DIAGNOSIS
Suggestive

Various conditions are suggestive of aspiration pneumonia, including pneumonia, lung abscess, or empyema in the appropriate host; a witnessed aspiration; foul-smelling sputum; infiltrates or cavities on chest radiograph in gravity-dependent portions of the lungs; and multiple organisms seen on Gram stain of expectorated sputum and nondiagnostic cultures.

Reduced consciousness
  Alcoholism
  Sedation and drug overdose
  General anesthesia
  Seizure
  Cerebrovascular accident, intracranial trauma and tumor
Gastrointestinal disease causing reflux
  Gastrointestinal reflux
  Esophageal dysmotility
  Diverticular disease of hypopharynx and esophagus
  Esophageal carcinoma
Neurologic and neuromuscular disease affecting glottis
  Cerebrovascular accident
  Guillian–Barré
  Multiple sclerosis
  Botulism
  Myasthenia gravis
  Muscular dystrophies
Mechanical reasons for aspiration
  Nasoenteric tube
  Endotracheal tube
  Tracheostomy tube
Factors that increase anaerobic flora
  Periodontal disease
  Gingivitis
Pulmonary conditions impairing airway clearance
  Bronchogenic carcinoma
  Foreign body aspiration

Definitive

Certain diagnosis of aspiration pneumonia is difficult to determine. Anaerobic cultures are not usually done, and many of the aerobic organisms are frequent residents of the oropharynx and may not be pathogens. Culture of organisms from blood, pleural fluid, or sputum obtained by transtracheal aspiration or bronchoscopy with protected brush catheters and quantitative cultures are more likely to represent true infections.

CLINICAL MANIFESTATIONS

Subjective

The signs and symptoms of aspiration pneumonia are nonspecific and cannot be used to separate it from other causes of pneumonia. It can present as acute pneumonia with fever, weakness, and nonproductive or productive cough, or as an insidious process with weeks of low-grade fever, weight loss, and anemia.

It is important to note the presence of preexisting conditions that predispose an individual to aspiration (see Table 13–46–1), such as alcoholism, drug use, gastroesophageal reflux, neurologic disease, and the presence of a nasogastric, endotracheal, or tracheostomy tube. These conditions have in common an adverse effect on swallowing, closure of the epiglottis, or cough, aiding aspiration and decreasing the ability of the patient to clear secretions. In addition, one should note the place where the patient aspirates, such as at home, in a nursing home, or in a hospital, as the organisms involved can differ, determining the course of treatment.

Objective

Physical Examination

Patients exhibit the signs of a local pneumonia with fever, tachypnea, nonproductive or productive cough with foul-smelling sputum, rales, and decreased breath sounds in those with pleural effusions. Examination of the chest can also be normal. Decreased consciousness, poor oral hygiene, decreased or absent gag reflex, or generalized weakness may be present.

Routine Laboratory Abnormalities

Chest radiographs can vary from normal, immediately following the aspiration, to diffuse bilateral infiltrates later. Usually there are infiltrates in the most gravity-dependent segments, basilar and superior segments of the lower lobes and/or the posterior segments of the upper lobes, but any area can be involved. Multiple small and occasionally large cavities (>1 cm) may be seen and are especially suggestive of the diagnosis.

Sputum Gram stain reveals many neutrophils with both Gram-positive and Gram-negative organisms. Occasionally one organism predominates. The white blood cell count is elevated with neutrophilia. Serum chemistries are nonspecific and may show an elevated blood urea nitrogen. The arterial blood gas at rest, on room air, may show hypoxemia.

Cultures of sputum may be negative, if not transported and cultured anaerobically, or may show an aerobic organism. These results may be misleading as these organisms are normal inhabitants of the oropharynx. If only one organism is cultured, it should be suspected as a pathogen.

Blood cultures are usually negative. Pleural fluid is an exudate with a predominance of neutrophils and, if infected, may be foul-smelling (like rotten eggs), with decreased pH and glucose and elevated lactate dehydrogenase.

PLANS

Diagnostic

Differential Diagnosis

The differential diagnosis includes all forms of bacterial pneumonia as well as tuberculosis. Carcinoma should also be considered when individuals have chronic symptoms or infiltrates.

Diagnostic Options and Recommended Approach

All patients should have a complete blood count, serum chemistries, and an arterial blood gas. A chest radiograph in the frontal and lateral projections should be done with attention to the presence of a pleural effusion and the pattern of the infiltrates. If fluid is suspected, chest computed tomography is useful in determining its presence and location.

Blood and sputum cultures should be obtained and a Gram stain of the sputum reviewed. If pleural fluid is present, it should be aspirated as soon as possible and its characteristics of odor and color noted, if foul-smelling or turbid infection is suspected. Fluid should be sent for Gram stain; cultures, both aerobic and anaerobic; pH; lactate dehydrogenase; glucose; and protein, to determine if the fluid is infected.

Therapeutic

Antibiotics and drainage of the infected pleural fluid are the treatments for aspiration pneumonia. The chosen antibiotics must be effective against anaerobes, the predominant organisms. Additional considerations include the possibility of β-lactamase-producing organism, penicillin resistance, and the presence of aerobic Gram-positive organisms such as *Staphylococcus aureus* and Gram-negative organisms such as *Pseudomonas aeruginosa*.

Penicillin G has long been considered the drug of choice and still offers excellent coverage for most anaerobes except *Bacteroides fragilis*. The emergence of penicillin-resistant strains as well as the considerations stated above have led to new recommendations for therapy. Most penicillins, such as ampicillin, penicillin, amoxicillin, and ticarcillin, are equal in efficacy. Clindamycin (600 mg every 8 hours intravenously) has been shown to have excellent activity against anaerobes. Similarly, either cefuroxime, a β-lactamase-resistant agent (750 mg to 1.5 g every 8 hours intravenously), or cefoxitin (1.0–2.0 g every 8 hours intravenously) is also acceptable. The newer β-lactam/β-lactamase inhibitor combination agents such as ampicillin/sulbactam (3.0 mg every 6 hours intravenously) and ticarcillin/clavulanate (3.1 g every 4 hours intravenously) are effective against most anaerobes as well as aerobes.

Some authorities recommend metronidazole (500 mg every 8 hours intravenously), but there appears to be some resistance among anaerobes; therefore, a combination of penicillin G (1–2 million units every 4–6 hours intravenously) and metronidazole can be used.

Erythromycin, popular for community-acquired pneumonia therapy, should not be used alone for aspiration pneumonia because of the lack of clinical studies demonstrating its efficacy in anaerobic infections.

Pleural effusions should be aspirated and if infected, as demonstrated by foul-smelling organism on Gram stain or culture, pH less than 7.0, lactate dehydrogenase greater than 1000 U/mL, or glucose less than 30 mg/dL, drained via a chest tube. Surgery with decortication may be required if the fluid cannot be drained and signs and symptoms persist.

Therapy must be individualized based on clinical response. Patients with pneumonia can be treated for 2 to 3 weeks; those with abscesses and empyema, for up to 4 months. Therapy should begin with intravenous antibiotics, preferably a β-lactam/β-lactamase inhibitor combination, and continued until the patient is afebrile and the white blood count returns to normal, usually within a week. At that time, treatment can be changed to oral agents, such as amoxicillin/sulbactam (500 mg every 8 hours) until the chest radiograph clears or a stable scar remains.

Adjunctive therapies such as chest physical therapy and vigorous suctioning are desirable, but have not been shown to change outcome.

FOLLOW-UP

Therapy should be continued until the patient is symptomatically improved, white blood count is normal, and the radiograph is clear or stable. With an empyema, all fluid should be drained and the pleural space sterile and obliterated. Cure is usually obtained in 1 to 3 months.

DISCUSSION

Prevalence and Incidence

The incidence of aspiration pneumonia is unknown, although aspiration is the most common mode of bacterial entry into the lung.

Related Basic Science

Fifty percent of normal hosts aspirate during sleep; patients with conditions listed in Table 13–46–1 aspirate even more often. These events lead to pneumonia by overwhelming the local defense mechanisms of the lung. Factors such as amount of aspirate and number and virulence of organisms and local factors such as ciliary dysfunction, decreased cough, and macrophage dysfunction aid in the establishment and progression of infection.

Bacterial organisms, mainly anaerobes, are normally resident in the oropharynx in large numbers. Hundreds of species have been identified; the most common are pigmented Gram-negative *Prevotella* and *Porphyromonas, Prevotella oris* and *P. buccae,* and *Fusobacterium nucleatum. Bacteroides fragilis* is seen in less than 5% of cases. Common aerobic bacterial causes of pneumonia are *Staphylococcus aureus, Streptococcus pyogenes,* and Gram-negative bacilli such as *Pseudomonas aeruginosa.*

The sudden aspiration of large amounts of gastric contents can cause a chemical pneumonitis, leading to respiratory failure with capillary leak and the adult respiratory distress syndrome. This event is usually a sterile inflammation, although bacterial superinfection can occur within days.

Natural History and Its Modification with Treatment

In the preantibiotic era, the natural history of anaerobic pneumonia was well described. Initially, local pneumonitis is present; the patient suffers from cough, sputum production, fever, and mild-to-moderate systemic symptoms. As the pneumonia progresses over the next 7 to 14

days to involve adjacent areas, tissue necrosis occurs and foul-smelling sputum can be noted. The process can continue and cause a necrotizing pneumonia with multiple small cavities (< 1 cm), or a larger cavity (> 1 cm) may develop. In addition, spread to the pleura with empyema may occur. These patients have more symptoms and signs.

The manifestations of the disease depend on the point at which the patient is seen within the evolutionary process from local pneumonitis to necrosis. Untreated, the infection can progress through all stages and ultimately cause death in the majority of patients. Modern antibiotic therapy has altered the course of the disease, with cure expected in 70 to 80% of patients with pneumonitis, empyema, or abscess.

The aspiration of gastric contents can lead to respiratory failure and death in up to 60% of patients. Many patients have rapid improvement within 1 week. Some improve only to relapse with new infiltrates, probably due to infection. Important negative prognostic factors include larger volume, acidic pH of the aspirate, and biology of the host, especially increased age.

Prevention

With the knowledge that aspiration of either oropharyngeal or gastric contents is the precipitating event, strategies to decrease the incidence and amount of aspiration are key to its prevention.

Patients with predisposing conditions such as alcoholism, seizure disorders, and neurologic dysfunction should be identified. All patients scheduled for procedures should be kept from eating or drinking for at least 6 to 8 hours before. Patients' ability to swallow properly and cough should be assessed to avoid orally feeding those at high risk for aspiration. Those with nasogastric tubes should be kept with their head in an elevated position. Proper position in the stomach should be checked prior to feeding. Poor oral hygiene should be corrected, if possible.

The presence of an endotracheal or tracheostomy tube does not preclude aspiration. The use of high-volume, low-pressure cuffs, the most common in use today, with meticulous attention to cuff pressures, can decrease, but not prevent, the incidence of aspiration.

Chest physical therapy and vigorous pulmonary toilet in susceptible patients may also decrease the incidence of pneumonia.

Cost Containment

The cost of care can be reduced by properly selecting antibiotics with review of cultures and changing antibiotics accordingly; switching from intravenous to oral agents as the patients improve; carefully monitoring for complications such as empyema and instituting prompt therapy; and judiciously using laboratory and radiographic studies.

Patients should have radiographs every 3 to 4 days for the first week. If the patient is improving, films can be obtained again at discharge, with a follow-up film taken in 1 to 3 months.

White blood cell counts can also be determined less frequently, initially every 3 to 4 days, then discontinued when normal.

REFERENCES

Bartlett JG. Anaerobic infections of the lung and pleural space. Am Rev Respir Dis 1974;110:56.

Bartlett JG. The triple threat of aspiration pneumonia. Chest 1975;68:560.

Bartlett JG. Aspiration pneumonia. Pulm Crit Care Update 1987;2(lesson 20):1.

Bartlett JG. Aspiration pneumonia. In: Gorbach S, Bartlett JG, Blacklow NR, eds. Infectious diseases. New York: Saunders, 1992:512.

Finegold SM. Aspiration pneumonia, lung abscess and empyema. In: Pennington JE, ed. Respiratory infection: Diagnosis and management. 3rd ed. New York: Raven Press, 1994:311.

CHAPTER 13–47

Adult Respiratory Distress Syndrome

D. Robert McCaffree, M.D.

DEFINITION

The adult (or acute) respiratory distress syndrome (ARDS) is a severe form of acute lung injury that usually arises as a complication of another severe illness; is characterized pathologically by inflammation and diffuse damage to the alveolar epithelium and vascular endothelium, with increased permeability pulmonary edema and decreased lung compliance; and is characterized clinically by severe hypoxemia and diffuse radiographic abnormalities. Although left atrial and pulmonary capillary pressures are usually normal, ARDS can coexist with these increased intravascular pressures, but cannot be explained by them.

ETIOLOGY

Considerations of etiology can be separated into clinical settings associated with the development of ARDS, the inflammatory processes that create the damage, and the healing process, which can create different problems later in the course.

A variety of clinical settings are commonly associated with the development of ARDS (Table 13–47–1), but ARDS can develop in many other settings and there may not be a readily identifiable associated condition. There is some disagreement over including the pulmonary infections, but there are circumstances in which the degree of lung injury exceeds the damage attributable directly to the infection; it is in these settings that the term *ARDS* is used. Among the indirect insults, hypertransfusion refers to greater than 10 units over 12 hours.

Adult respiratory distress syndrome is the result of diffuse damage, usually due to inflammation. This process is complex and multifactorial, involving in part macrophages, the complement system, cytokines, eicosanoids, oxygen radicals, the endothelium and the activated neutrophil. The neutrophil–endothelial cell interaction is central to creating the increased endothelial permeability in most cases, and is a likely common pathway in sepsis, ARDS, and multiple organ system failure. It should be pointed out, however, that ARDS can occur in severely neutropenic patients.

At some point, usually after 2 to 3 days, the healing process begins. Hyperplasia of the alveolar type II cells is seen initially. Later, fibroblasts, increased collagen deposition, and thickening of the septae are seen and may be accompanied by vascular obliteration; these then contribute to the pathophysiology of the disorder.

CRITERIA FOR DIAGNOSIS

Suggestive

The diagnosis is usually made clinically (Table 13–47–2) and is suggested by the presence of severe acute dyspnea progressing over a matter of hours to 3 or 4 days, frequently in one of the clinical settings in Table 13–47–1. Laboratory evaluation reveals severe hypoxemia (PaO_2 / FIO_2 < 200), which is poorly responsive to supplemental oxygen. The chest radiograph is diffusely abnormal with evidence of interstitial thickening, alveolar filling, and sometimes pleural effusions. This all occurs in the absence of any evidence of elevated left atrial or pulmonary capillary pressure.

Definitive

If the pulmonary capillary occlusion pressure is less than 18 cm H_2O with the other findings as described above, further credence is given the diagnosis. A pulmonary capillary occlusion pressure greater than 18 cm H_2O, however, does not exclude the diagnosis if the findings cannot be explained by the elevated pressures. Rarely is a biopsy needed to confirm the diagnosis. Should a biopsy be done, the appearance will be that of diffuse alveolar damage, but the exact findings will depend on the timing of the biopsy in the course of the disease (Figure 13–47–1). The earliest changes are those of interstitial and alveolar edema, hyaline membranes, and variable amounts of alveolar hemorrhage and fibrin deposition (exudative phase). Usually, by 2 or 3 days, healing begins. This is initially marked by alveolar type 2 cell hyperplasia, which is followed by fibroblast proliferation, predominantly in the septal regions but also in the alveolae. In some patients fibrosis may also be peribronchial, contributing to the airflow obstruction seen in some patients. If the patient lives long enough, fibrosis can lead to significant restructuring and formation of "honeycombing." Medial hypertrophy of the vessels may also be seen with subsequent vascular obliteration. This model of exudative and proliferative phases and the timing is convenient in understanding the disease but can be highly variable.

CLINICAL MANIFESTATIONS

Subjective

The principal symptom is dyspnea. Other symptoms related to associated conditions, for example, sepsis, trauma, surgery, may also be present and may mask the mild dyspnea that may mark early stages of the disease. The past history is important principally for recognizing associated conditions that increase the risk of ARDS. Family history is of no significance.

TABLE 13–47–1. UNDERLYING CONDITIONS AND SUBSEQUENT RELATIVE RISK OF ADULT RESPIRATORY DISTRESS SYNDROME

Clinical Setting	Relative Risk*
Direct lung injury	
Aspiration	High
Pulmonary infections	Moderate
Near drowning	Moderate
Toxic inhalation	Variable
Lung confusion	Moderate
Indirect lung injury	
Sepsis, sepsis syndrome	High
Hypertransfusion	Moderate–high
Severe nonthoracic trauma	Low–moderate
Cardiopulmonary bypass	Low
Burns	Low
Drug reactions	Low

*Relative Risk: Likelihood of developing ARDS in patients in these settings (high, >20%; moderate, 5–20%; low, <5%).

TABLE 13–47–2. CRITERIA FOR THE DIAGNOSIS OF ADULT RESPIRATORY DISTRESS SYNDROME

Appropriate clinical setting
Severe illness
Trauma
Severe hypoxemia
PaO_2/FIO_2 < 200
Widespread chest radiographic changes
Interstitial thickening
Alveolar rosettes
Pleural effusions
No evidence of increased pulmonary capillary pressure
Pulmonary artery occlusion pressure < 18 mm Hg
(Or if increased, cannot explain findings)

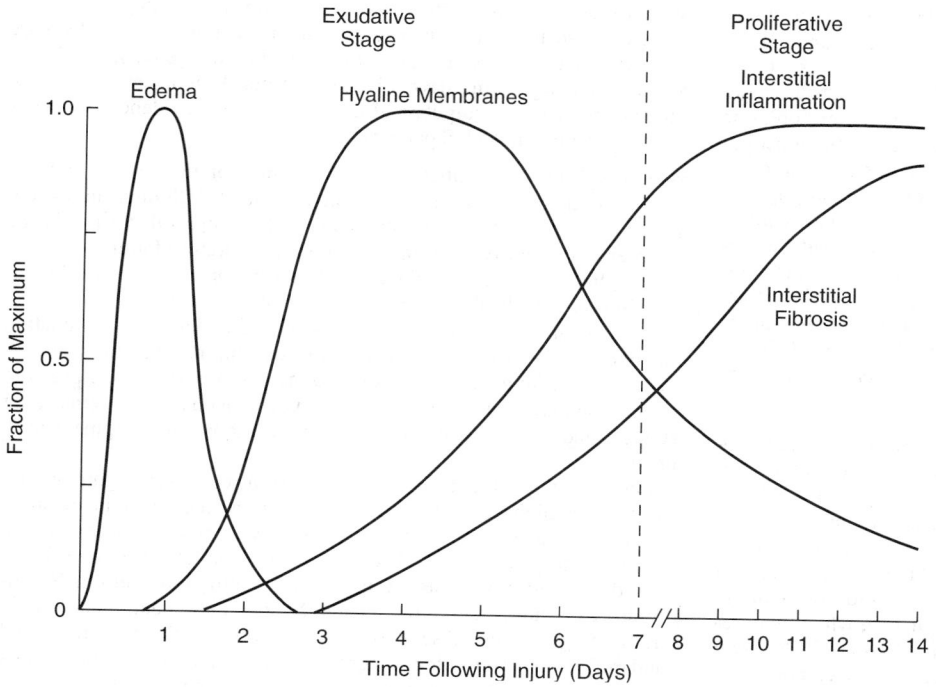

Figure 13–47–1. General time course of histologic findings in adult respiratory distress syndrome. This can, however, be quite variable. *(Source: Katzenstein AA, Askin FB. Surgical pathology of non-neoplastic lung disease. 2nd ed. Philadelphia: Saunders, 1990:12. Reproduced with permission from the publisher and author.)*

Objective

Physical Examination

On observation, the patient is tachypneic, often using accessory muscles of respiration, and may be cyanotic. On auscultation of the chest, crackles and wheezing may be heard but often are not prominent. Consolidation or pleural effusion is usually not found.

Routine Laboratory Abnormalities

Severe hypoxemia is a consistent finding in ARDS, with the PaO_2 / FIO_2 ratio less than 200.

The chest radiograph reveals diffuse abnormalities as described above. If for some reason, one does a computed tomographic scan of the chest, the diffuse pattern evident on the routine chest radiograph is shown to actually be patchy; that is, areas of abnormality are interspersed with normal lung.

Results of other routine laboratory tests such as the complete blood count and urinalysis are nonspecific and not helpful in the diagnosis of ARDS, although they may reflect an associated condition such as sepsis.

PLANS

Diagnostic

Differential Diagnosis

The primary differential diagnostic consideration is high-pressure pulmonary edema such as would be seen in congestive heart failure. In rare instances, acute interstitial pneumonia might be considered in the differential diagnosis.

Diagnostic Options and Recommended Approach

Generally, the presence of one of the known associated conditions, the clinical findings, and the absence of evidence of elevated pulmonary artery pressure are sufficient to establish the diagnosis. Occasionally, additional information may be needed such as measurement of the pulmonary capillary occlusion (wedge) pressure or biopsy of the lung.

Therapeutic

There is no specific or definitive treatment for ARDS. The goals of therapy are threefold. First, treat the underlying or associated condition,

such as sepsis. Second, maintain tissue oxygenation while allowing the lungs to heal. Third, prevent or treat complications that may arise, such as pneumothorax, infection, and multiple organ system failure (Table 13–47–3). The first goal is too broad to discuss in this chapter; therefore, only the second and third goals are discussed.

Maintain Tissue Oxygenation. Tissue oxygenation is the difference between oxygen delivery and uptake. Many factors influence this, including ventilation–perfusion relationships in the lung, intravascular volume, cardiac filling, myocardial contractility, afterload, tissue blood flow distribution, hemoglobin concentration and oxygen affinity, and tissue oxygen uptake.

Three basic strategies are employed to improve and maintain tissue

TABLE 13–47–3. THERAPEUTIC APPROACHES WITH POSSIBLE BENEFITS AND RISKS

Treat the underlying condition (sepsis, shock, etc.).
Maintain tissue oxygenation.
  Improve intrapulmonary gas exchange.
    Positive pressure ventilation (often with PEEP*), oxygen
      Benefit: Improved oxygenation
                 Airspaces recruited
                 Reduced afterload
      Risk: Reduced cardiac filling
                 Lung damage due to distension
                 Oxygen toxicity
  Bronchodilators
      Benefit: Improved airflow
      Risk: Cardiac arrhythmias
  Reduce lung water (fluid management, diuretics, vasoactive inotropic Agents).
      Benefit: Improved lung mechanics, gas exchange
      Risk: Reduced intravascular volume
                 Reduced cardiac output
  Alter blood flow (vasoactive and inotropic agents, fluid management).
      Benefit: Improved tissue oxygen delivery
      Risk: Arrhythmias
                 Increased shunt
                 Maldistributed blood flow
Prevent or treat complications.

*Positive end-expiratory pressure.

oxygenation: (1) improve respiratory function using oxygen, mechanical ventilation, and bronchodilators; (2) reduce lung water; and (3) enhance cardiac output using vasoactive agents or cardiotonics. These strategies are generally employed in concert, although each has both potential benefit as well as detriment to the patient, and therefore, one strategy may work against the goals of another. For example, most patients with ARDS have mechanical ventilation with positive end-expiratory pressure (PEEP). This improves oxygenation of blood going to the tissues, but can cause further lung damage and can reduce cardiac output. Diuretics can reduce pulmonary edema but could reduce preload and thus cardiac output. Inotropic agents can increase cardiac output but may increase shunt and exacerbate the hypoxemia. Therefore, any approach requires careful, frequent monitoring and evaluation of fluid balance, gas exchange, and cardiovascular performance. This can be aided by the use of a pulmonary artery catheter (Swan–Ganz catheter) or other advanced monitoring techniques.

IMPROVE RESPIRATORY FUNCTION. Typically, patients are placed on increasing levels of inspired oxygen while breathing spontaneously until they can no longer maintain acceptable partial pressures of oxygen (PO_2). They then are placed on mechanical ventilation, frequently requiring the addition of PEEP. The exact mechanisms by which PEEP increases PaO_2 are not known but PEEP does increase lung volume and may recruit poorly ventilated areas of the lung and prevent airway closure. In doing the latter it can increase respiratory system compliance, which may reduce the risk of damage to the lung due to overdistension. PEEP may also alter alveolar vessels to improve gas exchange. It does not affect vascular permeability or lymphatic function and does not reduce lung water.

Another potential benefit of PEEP is a reduction in left ventricular afterload, which will help reduce the deleterious effect of positive airway pressure on cardiac output, if the preload is adequate.

A beneficial effect of mechanical ventilation with PEEP is not seen in all patients. Those who do not have an increase in PaO_2 seem to have more severe disease and a worse prognosis. There are two principal detrimental effects of positive intrathoracic pressure including PEEP: (1) a reduction in cardiac output, and (2) damage to the more normal lung due to overdistension. There are several possible mechanisms for the reduction of cardiac output by PEEP. The major mechanism is a reduction in cardiac filling due to the increased intrathoracic pressures. Other proposed mechanisms include a reduction in contractility due to humoral or neural factors, shifts in the intraventricular septum causing changes in left ventricular compliance, and heart–lung mechanical interactions causing alterations in cardiac performance.

Damage to the lung by overdistension may be very apparent (pneumothorax, pneumomediastinum, or subcutaneous emphysema) or may be insidious and may present clinically as slow deterioration of lung function or lack of improvement. The latter presentation is also true of oxygen toxicity and can be suspected, but usually not definitively proven.

In addition to mechanical ventilation, bronchodilators such as albuterol and metaproterenol may improve lung mechanics and possibly gas exchange, as reversible bronchoconstriction has been demonstrated in some patients with ARDS.

REDUCE LUNG WATER. As the hallmark of ARDS is high-permeability edema and it is this edema that contributes to many of the pathophysiologic changes observed, reducing the pulmonary edema is a logical goal. Because at this time there are no interventions that can be used in a timely way to reduce the inflammatory response or reduce the vascular permeability, fluid management, including the appropriate use of diuretics, becomes important in trying to reduce the lung water while maintaining sufficient cardiac filling. Many of the conditions associated with ARDS are accompanied by alterations in intravascular volume, which can affect preload either to increase pulmonary edema or to reduce cardiac output. In addition, there may be changes in pulmonary arterial and aortic pressures, which can either increase or decrease ventricular afterload. Thus, one must carefully balance the effects on lung water and cardiovascular performance of intravenous volume administration, fluid restriction, and volume reduction using diuretics.

ALTER BLOOD FLOW. If there is evidence of tissue hypoperfusion or if the cardiac output is impaired, inotropic agents such as dobutamine or af-terload-reducing vasodilators such as nitroprusside may be useful. Some of these agents may increase the shunt fraction and thus decrease the PaO_2, so a careful evaluation of the effect on oxygen delivery is important. Although some have advocated using these agents to provide supranormal cardiac outputs and oxygen delivery, evidence of an improved outcome in ARDS patients is lacking.

Prevent or Treat Complications. The importance of this goal is emphasized by findings that most people who die with ARDS die from the underlying disease or from complications such as sepsis that arise during treatment. A minority die from unremitting respiratory failure.

Complications can be divided into two categories: mechanical complications and medical complications. (Table 13–47–4).

Mechanical complications include those of endotracheal intubation and tracheotomy (bleeding, edema, mucosa injury, infection, aspiration), those of lung overdistension and increased intrathoracic pressure (pneumothorax, pneumomediastinum, subcutaneous emphysema, lung damage, and decreased cardiac output), and those of equipment malfunction.

Medical complications are common, can affect every organ system, and carry a high risk of mortality. Infection, including nosocomial pneumonia and sepsis or sepsis syndrome with multiple organ system failure, is the greatest risk. The risk of nosocomial pneumonia is increased fourfold in patients on mechanical ventilation, and this is usually due to Gram-negative organisms. Nosocomial pneumonia is difficult to diagnose in these patients, however, as there is no "gold standard" for the premortem diagnosis. Sepsis and multiple organ system failure are particularly ominous in these patients. With sepsis, the risk of nonpulmonary organ system failure is increased, and with each organ system involved, the mortality increases. The two most common sites of origin of sepsis are the lungs and the peritoneal cavity, although the multiple vascular catheters in these patients also carry significant risk.

FOLLOW-UP

Overall the mortality rate is high, being around 50%. This will vary depending on age, severity of the underlying disorder, and presence of extrapulmonary organ failure or other complications. In those who survive, however, pulmonary function improves over the next 6 months and residual abnormalities tend to be mild as are any functional impairments. These abnormalities tend to correlate with the length of mechanical ventilation and oxygen administration rather than initial severity of the ARDS.

TABLE 13–47–4. SOME COMMON COMPLICATIONS

Mechanical
    Complications of endotracheal intubation and tracheotomy
    Lung volutrauma (e.g., pneumothorax)
    Equipment malfunction
Medical
    Infection
        Nosocomial pneumonia
        Sepsis syndrome
        Intravascular line infections
        Intraabdominal infections
    Multiple organ system failure
    Gastrointestinal
        Gastrointestinal bleeding
        Meteorism
        Ileus
    Renal dysfunction
    Hematologic
        Disseminated intravascular coagulation
        Thrombocytopenia
        Anemia
        Thrombosis, Emboli

DISCUSSION

Prevalence and Incidence

The overall incidence is unknown. Estimates have ranged from 1.5 to 75 cases per 100,000 population per year, although those estimates at the extremes have been in different populations. If one looks at those with known predisposing risk factors (e.g., sepsis, aspiration, disseminated intravascular coagulation), the risk of developing ARDS is approximately 5% if there is a single risk factor. With multiple risk factors, this risk increases to approximately 25%. There is a wide range of incidences even with single risk factors. The risk following cardiopulmonary bypass is less than 2%, whereas that following pulmonary aspiration exceeds 30%.

Related Basic Science

Physiologic Derangement

The hallmark of early ARDS is injury to the alveolar epithelium and vascular endothelium and pulmonary edema due to increased permeability. The edema fluid collects initially in the bronchovascular bundle, but eventually overwhelms the ability of the lymphatic system to remove it and alveolar flooding occurs. This is accompanied by surfactant abnormalities, which include both displacement of surfactant and alterations in surfactant composition. All these changes lead to lungs with decreased compliance and the increased venous admixture and hypoxemia that mark ARDS.

Anatomic Derangement

At autopsy, the lungs appear congested and are heavy. The histologic appearance is that of diffuse alveolar damage as described above. With healing, one can find areas of complete resolution or extensive fibrosis with "honeycombing."

Natural History and Its Modification with Treatment

Adult respiratory distress syndrome is associated with disorders that have a high mortality and only add to the risk. There is some evidence that the mortality in patients with ARDS has decreased somewhat over the last two decades, for reasons that are unclear, but may be related to more knowledgeable supportive care and early recognition and intervention of complications. Specific attempts to alter the course (Figure 13–47–2) or severity of the disease, however, have been unsuccessful. Specifically, early administration of corticosteroids or institution of PEEP does not prevent or ameliorate ARDS. There is some evidence that administering corticosteroids in the proliferative phase (clinically, after several days on the ventilator) may be of some benefit, presumably by reducing the fibrotic reaction.

Prevention

There are currently no effective methods of preventing ARDS. There is hope that in the future interfering at some point in the inflammatory

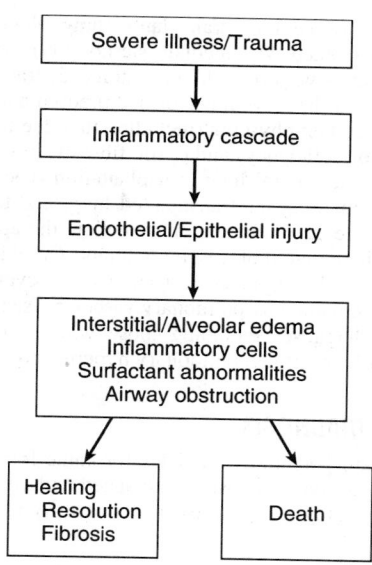

Figure 13–47–2. General progression of events in adult respiratory distress syndrome.

cascade, probably with immunomodulation, may prevent or ameliorate the damage, but this has not yet been demonstrated.

Cost Containment

Because these patients are critically ill, usually from both the underlying disease and the ARDS, they require use of high-intensity, high-cost resources such as intensive care units. Its is unlikely that significant savings will be effected until there is some progress in prevention.

REFERENCES

Bernard GR, Artigas A, Brigham KL, et al. The American–European Consensus Conference on ARDS. Am J Respir Crit Care Med 1994;149:818.

Kollef MH, Schuster DP. The acute respiratory distress syndrome. N Engl J Med 1995;332:27.

Petty TL. Acute respiratory distress syndrome (ARDS). Disease–A–Month 1990;36:1.

Sloane PJ, Gee MH, Gottlieb JE, et al. A multicenter registry of patients with acute respiratory distress syndrome. Am Rev Respir Dis 1992;146:419.

Suchyta MR, Clemmer TP, Elliott CG, et al. The adult respiratory distress syndrome. Chest 1992;101:1074.

Worthen GS. 36th Annual Thomas L. Petty Aspen Lung Conference. Chest 1994;105:43S.

CHAPTER 13–48

Lung Transplantation

Stephan L. Kamholz, M.D.

DEFINITION

Lung transplantation is the surgical replacement of pulmonary tissue for patients with advanced, end-stage pulmonary or cardiopulmonary disease. The "unit of tissue" replaced varies with the nature of underlying disease and its severity (which in part defines the "volume" of lung replacement required), as well as with the availability of appropriate donor organ(s). Lung transplantation may involve (1) lobar, (2) unilateral lung, (3) bilateral or double lung, or (4) combined heart–lung replacement.

ETIOLOGY

During the past 10 years, pulmonary replacement by transplantation has been applied to an ever-increasing spectrum of pulmonary and cardiopulmonary diseases in which the "candidate" has been judged to have irreversible disease with no hope of substantive improvement through "medical" therapy and an unacceptable quality of life. Chronic obstructive pulmonary disease (COPD), idiopathic pulmonary fibrosis, and primary pulmonary hypertension are the three most common underlying disorders in patients receiving unilateral (often called "single") lung transplants. Double lung transplants (lung block with tracheal anastomosis transplanted via median sternotomy) or bilateral-lung transplants (two lungs with bronchial anastomoses transplanted via bilateral thoracotomies) have been performed predominantly for patients with severe advanced emphysema (including that due to hereditary α_1-proteinase inhibitor deficiency) and cystic fibrosis, in which the fear of a poor outcome of unilateral lung transplantation (because of chronic infection in the remaining nontransplanted lung, and the immunosuppressed state of the recipient on antirejection therapy) dictates the choice of a method that replaces both lungs. Combined heart–lung transplantation, initially employed for patients with cyanotic congenital heart disease accompanied by pulmonary vascular disease, has been extended to other diagnoses including those with primary pulmonary parenchymal involvement and pulmonary hypertension.

CRITERIA FOR DIAGNOSIS

In patients who are potential candidates for some form of lung transplantation, the definitive diagnosis of advanced underlying lung disease and a careful physiologic assessment of its severity are important prerequisites.

Suggestive

Severe limiting dyspnea is found in virtually all patients who are candidates for pulmonary replacement. The ability to complete the activities of daily living is universally impaired, even with supplemental oxygen therapy. Well more than 90% of all recipients of lung transplants have symptomatology of New York Heart Association class 3 or 4 severity. Other associated symptoms are referable to the specific underlying disease that has produced the advanced disability. These may include cough, chest pain, syncope, and palpitations.

Definitive

The complete assessment of patients who are potential candidates for lung transplantation involves documentation of the nature and severity of the underlying cardiopulmonary disease with physical examination, routine laboratory investigation, chest roentgenography, complete pulmonary function tests including rest and exercise blood gases (with and without supplemental oxygen, occasionally formal cardiopulmonary exercise testing may be required), lung biopsy (in instances where the nature of parenchymal lung disease has not previously been established), exclusion of active bronchopulmonary infection by appropriate microbiologic studies, and assessment of cardiac function by echocardiography, nuclear scintigraphy, and, occasionally, cardiac catheterization. The criteria for specific diagnosis of the defined cardiac and pulmonary diseases that may be ameliorated by lung transplantation are dealt with in the relevant chapters on those entities.

Although no absolute criteria have been widely accepted that establish the need for pulmonary transplantation, it is generally agreed that the demonstrated pathology and physiologic impairment should be consistent with no more than a 6- to 12-month survival (in the absence of transplantation).

CLINICAL MANIFESTATIONS

Subjective

Progressive dyspnea on exertion and at rest, compromising the individual's ability to complete the activities of daily living, is the most important subjective clinical manifestation in patients who may be benefited by lung transplantation. Chest discomfort, chronic cough, and symptoms of cor pulmonale including peripheral edema are often found. In patients with primary pulmonary hypertension, episodes of syncope and palpitations are commonly encountered.

Objective

Physical Examination

Abnormalities are almost always detectable on cardiopulmonary physical examination. Findings are generally related to the nature of the underlying disease, for example, signs of hyperinflation and expiratory airflow obstruction in patients with COPD/emphysema; dry rales, decreased respiratory excursion, and digital clubbing in patients with fibrosing lung disease; and accentuated pulmonic component of the second heart sound with right ventricular lift (heave) in the absence of specific findings suggesting lung abnormalities in patients with primary pulmonary hypertension.

Routine Laboratory Abnormalities

The radiographic, pulmonary physiologic and cardiac studies mentioned above (See Criteria for Diagnosis, Definitive) reveal abnormalities specific to the underlying disease state.

PLANS

Diagnostic

Differential Diagnosis

The type of end-stage lung or cardiopulmonary disease in the transplant candidate will have previously been established for the patient. When necessary, further workup may be requested by the evaluating transplant center prior to accepting a patient as a candidate. These tests are often requested based on the nature of the underlying lung disease.

Diagnostic Options

Serologic tests to exclude active collagen–vascular disease may have to be performed in patients with pulmonary fibrosis, as there is a concern that the underlying systemic disease may recur in the transplant. Similar concerns exist regarding lung transplantation in patients with sarcoidosis. Studies to establish the level of disease activity in such instances may therefore include gallium-67 lung scintiscanning, enumeration of cell populations (and their functional activity) on bronchoalveolar lavage specimens obtained during fiberoptic bronchoscopy, and open lung biopsy to assess the relative proportion of active inflammation versus fibrosis in the diseased lung. In instances where inflammatory disease activity is documented, transplantation may be deferred pending the outcome of a final aggressive trial of pharmacologic antiinflammatory therapy. Active (or recent) malignancy (pulmonary or extrapulmonary) is generally felt to be a contraindication to pulmonary replacement because of fears of recurrence in the immunosuppressed individual. Most transplant centers insist that all possible efforts be made to wean prospective recipients off corticosteroid therapy prior to transplantation because of the confounding effects of chronic preoperative steroids on wound healing and early perioperative infectious complications. Virtually all recipients receive corticosteroids as part of maintenance immunosuppression after transplantation.

Recommended Approach

In preparation for referral for evaluation by a transplant program, in addition to the studies delineated above (see Criteria for Diagnosis, Definitive, and Plans, Diagnostic, Diagnostic Options) all patients will have had a determination of ABO and Rh blood grouping. Determination of histocompatibility antigens is also performed and reviewed after transplantation in an effort to determine the influence of haplotype matching on graft outcome; however, attempts to match recipient and donor human leukocyte (HLA) antigens are generally not made preoperatively. Measurements are made of the potential recipient's thoracic dimensions, and these are carefully recorded by the transplant center, as there is a need to avoid significant disproportion between donor and recipient dimensions. Careful and complete psychological and psychosocial assessment of the candidate is essential to determine the individual's ability to withstand the emotional impact of the high risk of the procedure, the possibility of demise while awaiting an organ donor, the requirement for protracted hospitalization, the need for constant vigilance in the posttransplant period, and the likelihood of ultimate graft failure. A strong family support structure (or a committed "significant other") must be present before a candidate is accepted by a transplant program. Mounting evidence suggests that an extensive program of physical and occupational rehabilitative therapy prior to contemplated lung transplantation is associated with a better posttransplant outcome and is, thus, essential. Patients who are cachectic or who have significant wasting disease have a very poor prognosis. The financial requirements for lung transplantation are also daunting as this is a tremendously costly medical intervention. Health insurance plans are far from uniform in their willingness to reimburse for the entire costs of the pretransplant evaluation, procedure itself, and years of postoperative care.

Therapeutic

Therapeutic Options

The type of transplant procedure performed is determined by the transplant team after complete evaluation of the patient, taking into account some of the considerations delineated above (see Etiology). Availability of a suitable donor organ (or organs) may also determine the exact type of operation performed. The limited supply of suitable donor organs is the single greatest impediment to more widespread application of lung transplantation as a therapeutic intervention for patients with end-stage lung disease. In contrast to the technology available for remote harvest and efficacious preservation of other organs (which provide for prolonged viability *ex vivo*), the maximal duration of successful lung preservation is about 6 hours, limiting the geographic area from which a donor organ can be retrieved for a specific recipient. Recipient age, underlying diagnosis, and general physical condition prior to transplantation all influence outcome. The highest likelihood of success is in females receiving a single lung transplant for emphysema, with 1-year actuarial survival approaching 80%. Transplants performed for idiopathic pulmonary fibrosis and primary pulmonary hypertension currently are associated with a 60 to 70% 1-year actuarial survival. Four-year survival rates of single lung transplants for emphysema, fibrosis, and pulmonary vascular disease are 40 to 50%. Technical problems account for most early graft loss in the 2 weeks after transplant. Infectious complications are the major cause of morbidity and graft loss from 2 weeks to 3 months posttransplant. Virtually all patients experience one or more episodes of allograft rejection in the first few posttransplant weeks. Beyond 3 months, the cumulative effects of acute and chronic rejection are the most significant factors in graft loss.

Recommended Approach

Lung transplantation should be reserved for those patients in whom no other therapy will meet with clinical improvement. The operative procedure should be performed in a transplant center with an established track record of success, particularly if the underlying disease is one of the less common indications for lung replacement. In the perioperative and postoperative periods, careful attention to the details of immunosuppression (usually employing cyclosporine, azathioprine, and prednisone) is essential. Prophylaxis for certain opportunistic infections is indicated, including trimethoprim–sulfa (or aerosolized pentamidine) for *Pneumocystis carinii*, and ganciclovir for cytomegalovirus if the recipient or donor is seropositive for cytomegalovirus. Physiotherapy should be employed as soon as practical to ensure that the patient regains maximal functional capacity as rapidly as possible.

FOLLOW-UP

After hospital discharge, patients are instructed in the therapeutic regimen, and monitor themselves for signs of infectious complications, graft dysfunction (rejection), and adverse effects of the treatment regimen. Many transplant programs employ home spirometry to document pulmonary function, with twice daily measurements of 1-second forced vital capacity (FEV_1). If the recipient notes a sustained decrease in FEV_1 from baseline, the transplant center is notified, and most often the patient is brought in for evaluation. Assessment for rejection may well include fiberoptic bronchoscopy with multiple transbronchial lung biopsies (to be reviewed for the histologic changes of allograft rejection) and with bronchoalveolar lavage samples sent for appropriate microbiologic studies (to exclude infection). Indeed, it is extremely difficult to distinguish rejection from infection on clinical grounds. Some laboratories have suggested that functional studies of lavage lymphocytes may be useful in the assessment for possible rejection. In some instances, patients develop progressively worsening pulmonary dysfunction attributable to bronchiolitis obliterans, most likely a consequence of chronic rejection. Several patients have undergone retransplantation when respiratory failure has supervened because of this (or other) complication.

DISCUSSION
Prevalence and Incidence

The frequency of the underlying cardiopulmonary diseases that may be treated with lung transplantation is discussed in the chapters on those entities. As of 1993, registry data indicated that approximately 2000 single-lung transplants and more than 700 bilateral or double-lung transplants had been reported. It is known that only a small fraction of the patients who could be benefited by pulmonary replacement ever receive such therapy.

Related Basic Science

A full discussion of the relevant basic science issues of transplant physiology, immunology of allograft rejection, immunosuppression, and histocompatibility matching is beyond the scope of this chapter. Of greatest significance to the generalist physician caring for a patient with a pulmonary transplant is the recognition that graft rejection begins as a subtle process, with minimal derangement of respiratory mechanics and gas exchange. This is attributable to the fact that scant lymphocytic infiltrates in the walls of small airways and in the perivascular space surrounding small pulmonary blood vessels are the earliest lesions of rejection. This may slightly reduce parameters of expiratory airflow, and will cause mild ventilation–perfusion inequality (hypoxemia with hypocarbia). Thus, subtle changes in patient performance or pulmonary symptomatology should prompt consultation with the transplant pulmonologist.

Natural History and Its Modification with Treatment

Lung transplantation may offer the only hope of prolongation of useful life for patients with end-stage pulmonary or cardiopulmonary diseases. Thus, the natural history of otherwise fatal lung disease is altered by this intervention. Single-lung transplant recipients have survived more than 8 years after surgery, with 40 to 50% 4-year survival being relatively characteristic.

Prevention

As COPD constitutes one of the most frequent indications for pulmonary replacement, this requirement is largely preventable. Smoking prevention and smoking cessation would effectively reduce the large numbers of patients with end-stage COPD who are potential candidates for lung replacement. Most of the other diseases that result in indications for lung transplantation are not specifically preventable.

Cost Containment

Lung transplantation is a very expensive therapeutic modality, with costs varying from center to center. Though no general agreement exists, estimates range from $100,000 to $250,000 per case. Complications in the postoperative period, which result in protracted hospital stay, may increase costs markedly. Careful selection of recipients is the most important step in cost containment. The likelihood of compliance with the treatment regimen and the degree of motivation of the potential recipient both contribute to the potential cost-effectiveness of the procedure. Efforts to prevent cigarette smoking-induced lung disease are also likely to reduce overall costs by limiting the number of candidates for the procedure.

REFERENCES

Cooper JD. The evolution of techniques and indications for lung transplantation. Ann Surg 1990;212:249.

Dauber JH, Paradis IL, Drummer JS. Infectious complications in pulmonary allograft recipients. Clin Chest Med 1990;11:291.

Egan TM. Lung preservation. Semin Thorac Cardiovasc Surg 1992;4:83.

Kamholz SL, Goldsmith J, Veith FJ. Lung transplantation: Critical problems and follow-up. In: Kapoor AS, Laks H, Schroeder J, Yacoub MH, eds. Cardiomyopathies and heart lung transplantation. New York: McGraw-Hill, 1991:441.

Schafers H-J, Wagner TOF, Demertzis S, et al. Preoperative corticosteroids: A contraindication to lung transplantation? Chest 1992;102:1522.

Sibley RK, Berry GJ, Tazelaar HD, et al. The role of transbronchial biopsies in the management of lung transplant recipients. J Heart Lung Transplant 1993;12:308.

Trulock EP. Lung transplantation. Annu Rev Med 1992;43:1.

CHAPTER 13–49

Aspergillosis (See Section 5, Chapter 3 and Section 8, Chapter 52)

CHAPTER 13–50

Pneumocystis Carinii Infection (See Section 8, Chapter 63)

Hypertension

W. Dallas Hall, M.D.

CHAPTER 14–1

Borderline Hypertension

Stevo Julius, M.D., Sc.D.

DEFINITION

Borderline hypertension is the "gray zone," where an individual's blood pressure is not clearly normal, but the value is not high enough to mandate antihypertensive treatment.

ETIOLOGY

Borderline hypertension frequently appears in families of subjects with essential hypertension. Furthermore, a large proportion (greater than 70% after 20 years) of subjects with borderline hypertension eventually develop clinical essential hypertension. This suggests that borderline hypertension is of equally complex and unknown etiology as essential hypertension; however, signs of increased sympathetic tone are more readily found in borderline than in established essential hypertension.

CRITERIA FOR DIAGNOSIS
Suggestive

As borderline hypertension is not associated with specific symptoms, its detection is usually a by-product of periodic health examinations, blood pressure screening, or medical evaluations for other complaints. The only clinical clues to borderline hypertension are signs of vasolability (tachycardia, flushing, and occasional lightheadedness) if they occur in slightly overweight (up to 30% over ideal weight), young (aged 18–35 years) men.

Definitive

The diagnosis of the condition is based on three consecutive blood pressure readings taken while the individual is sitting comfortably 5 minutes with the arm bared. The blood pressure should not be measured immediately after a physically taxing or emotionally stressful situation. Borderline hypertension is diagnosed if the average systolic pressure is 140 to 150 mm Hg and the average diastolic pressure is 90 to 95 mm Hg, or if the average is less but one single reading exceeds 140 and/or 90 mm Hg.

CLINICAL MANIFESTATIONS
Subjective

Family history for hypertension is present in about 50% of subjects with borderline hypertension. History is considered positive only if one or both parents have been diagnosed as treatment-requiring hypertensives before they reached 55 years of age. Hypertension in the elderly is not heritable at a young age.

The majority of borderline hypertensives have no symptoms, but if symptoms are present, they are nonspecific. Most frequent are complaints of palpitation, facial flushing, or excessive sweating in stressful situations. Some patients complain of occasional lightheadedness, but this is never a true vertigo with spinning, nystagmus, and nausea. During the diagnostic interview the patients are likely to display characteristic personality traits. They are outward-oriented, sociable, and interested, but unable to express anger even if irritated. They are also submissive. Consequently, they may appear to accept the physician's advice while internally registering dissatisfaction, suspicion, or even dissent.

Objective

Physical Examination

In a patient with borderline hypertension, the physical examination serves to exclude secondary causes of hypertension and ensure that there are no signs of blood pressure-related target organ damage.

The following items in the physical examination help to rule out secondary causes:

- Absence of an abdominal bruit in the area between the umbilicus and the xyphoid speaks against renal artery stenosis. The index of suspicion increases if the bruit is high-pitched and radiates to one or both sides. A low-pitched midline bruit is usually of no consequence. Bruits extending throughout systole into diastole point to a high-grade stenosis in one of the abdominal vessels, however, not necessarily the renal artery. If the bruit can be clearly heard in the flanks, it is diagnostic of renal artery stenosis. A bruit is present in 80% of patients with renal artery stenosis. False-positive bruits are present in about one fifth of young normotensive individuals.
- Signs of coarctation of the aorta, for example, a loud ejection systolic murmur, systolic murmurs over the ribs, and a delayed or decreased femoral artery pulse, are absent. A leg blood pressure 20 mm Hg or more below the forearm pressure is typical of coarctation. The pulse delay in the leg is assessed by simultaneous palpation of the radial and femoral or dorsalis pedis arteries.

Routine Laboratory Abnormalities

Patients with secondary hypertension tend to have severe hypertension. Consequently, in borderline hypertension it is sufficient to perform only routine blood chemistry and urinalysis. Low potassium levels suggest primary aldosteronism. Elevated blood sugar levels call for further workup for diabetic nephropathy, pyelonephritis, and, if the clinical picture is compatible, pheochromocytoma. Albuminuria, hematuria, pyuria, and granular casts mandate further investigation for renal causes of hypertension. Similarly, abnormal serum creatinine levels are often indicative of a primary renal disease.

PLANS

Diagnostic

Differential Diagnosis

See Criteria for Diagnosis. When these criteria are followed there is no differential diagnosis. Obviously, a search for secondary causes of hypertension is always indicated.

Diagnostic Options and Recommended Approach

Medical history and laboratory tests in borderline hypertension serve to eliminate secondary causes of hypertension and assess possible target organ damage. In addition, one must assess risk factors for coronary heart disease.

Secondary Causes. Medical history may suggest secondary causes of hypertension. Attacks of sweating, palpitation and occasional flushing combined with spells of very high blood pressure in a subject who is normotensive between attacks suggest pheochromocytoma. Muscle weakness, paresthesias, and transient paresis of extremities are suggestive of primary aldosteronism. History of hematuria, dysuria, or periods of edema necessitates a workup for renal causes.

Only routine laboratory tests are needed in patients with borderline hypertension (See Routine Laboratory Abnormalities).

All patients must have a careful assessment of the cardiac size by chest x-ray and electrocardiogram.

Target Organ Damage. Echocardiography is becoming increasingly popular to assess left ventricular wall mass, but it is useful only if a laboratory has its own age- and sex-matched normal values.

Risk Factors. Assessment of the risk for atherosclerosis and coronary heart disease is indispensable in the development of individualized management plans in patients with borderline hypertension. For this purpose, fasting plasma cholesterol, triglyceride, and high-density lipoprotein determinations should be obtained. Where available, fasting insulin values should be obtained and, if greater than 22 μU, the patient should be considered at a higher risk of coronary heart disease.

Therapeutic

All patients with borderline hypertension require management, but only a few need antihypertensive medication. A large number of blood pressure readings must be obtained in every patient with borderline hypertension. We prefer to teach patients to measure their own blood pressure. Readings in the physician's office fluctuate, whereas average home blood pressure readings are highly reproducible and can be used for therapeutic decisions, evaluation of treatment, and future follow-up of untreated patients.

Other elements in the management of borderline hypertension are weight control, reduction of sodium intake to 3 g or less sodium per day, cessation of smoking, and limitation of alcohol intake (less than two drinks per day) with a drink defined as 1.25 oz whiskey, 12 oz beer, or 5 oz table wine). Patients should be encouraged to exercise, namely, to engage in activities that, for 20 minutes every day, raise and maintain the heart rate above 130 beats per minute. Isometric exercise is not useful; it raises the blood pressure excessively but does not cause cardiovascular conditioning.

Biobehavioral methods (progressive muscle relaxation, biofeedback, relaxation response, yoga, and transcendental meditation) are helpful in controlling symptoms of vasolability and in enhancing the feeling of well-being; however, they have not been proven efficacious in reducing blood pressure levels.

Treatment should be considered only in a minority of patients with borderline hypertension. Beta-adrenergic blocking drugs are first-line agents for patients with borderline hypertension, based on the theory that they have a proven record of long-term safety; however, they interfere with the patient's ability to exercise and benefit from exercise training. They also negatively affect dyslipidemia and may increase plasma insulin levels. New, "modern" antihypertensive agents (converting enzyme inhibitors, alpha blockers, and calcium antagonists) are preferred if small doses of beta blockers fail, negatively affect blood chemistry, or cause adverse effects. There are no data to indicate that diuretics are not useful in these patients; however, because a large proportion of subjects with borderline hypertension are overweight, have lipid abnormalities, and may have insulin resistance, and because diuretics negatively affect these variables, we now prefer not to use them.

Beta-blocking agents are contraindicated in patients with asthma or Raynaud's syndrome. They should not be given to insulin-requiring diabetics. A high level of habitual exercise (distance runners) also is a practical contraindication because exercise performance and endurance decrease with beta-adrenergic blockade.

Three elements enter into the therapeutic decision: (1) risk factors for hypertension and atherosclerosis, (2) the patient's average blood pressure, and (3) signs of target organ damage. An integrated management and treatment approach is given in Figure 14–1–1. The scheme pertains only to patients who do not have signs of target organ damage. As mentioned earlier, subjects with target organ damage are classified as hypertensive and require treatment. Risk factors are discussed under Natural History and Its Modification with Treatment.

Education is a very important component of the overall approach to the patient with borderline hypertension. Its goal is to explain the asymptomatic nature of the disease, including that the blood pressure may substantially increase without any subjective symptoms; to explain the excessive morbidity in hypertension; and to counsel the patient about the chance of future morbidity. The last point is particularly important, as patients must understand that they are at higher risk and that their blood pressure must be monitored regularly even though drugs

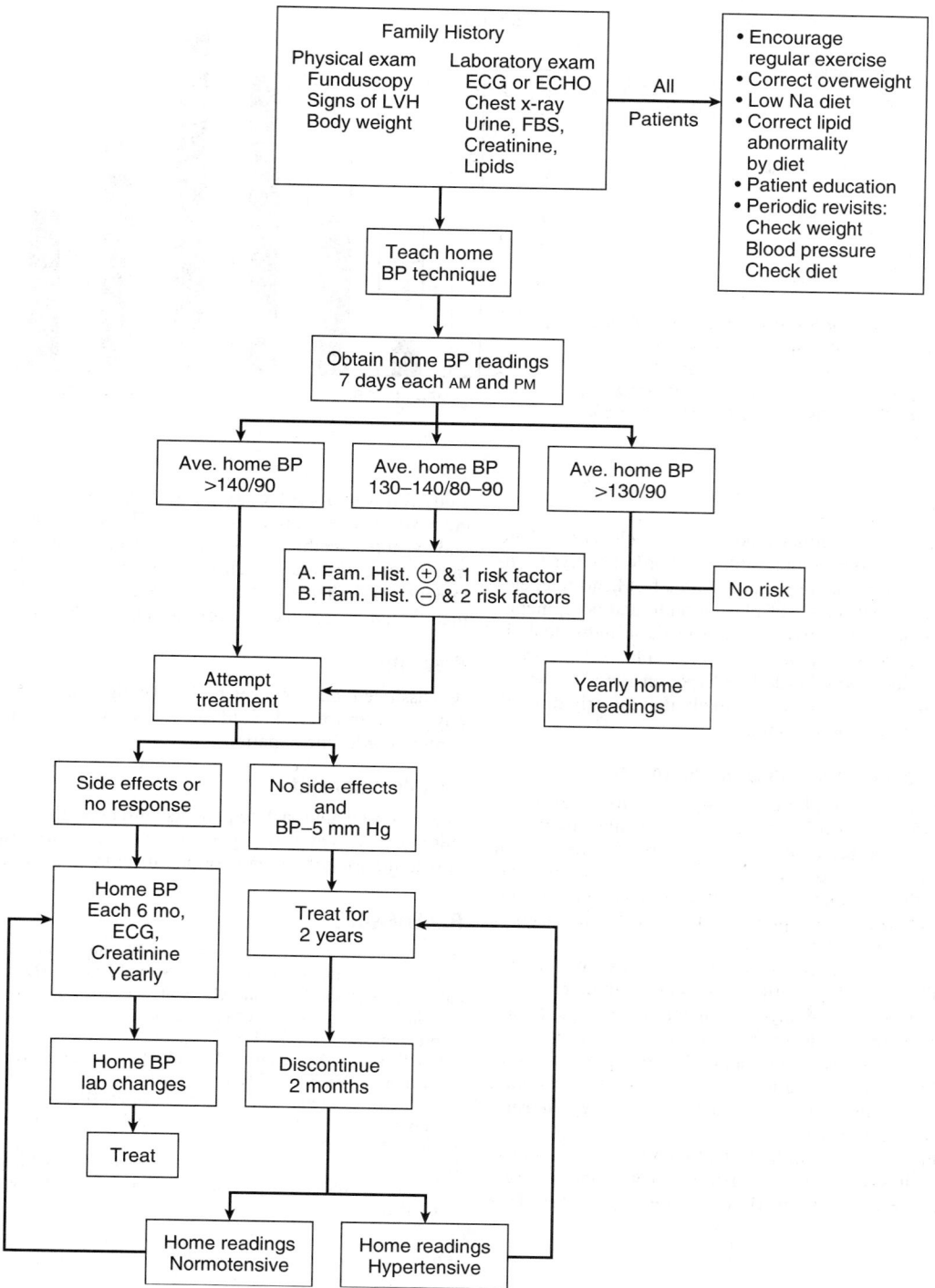

Figure 14–1–1. Proposed scheme for evaluation and follow-up of borderline hypertension. ECG, electrocardiogram; ECHO, echocardiogram; FBS, fasting blood sugar; LVH, left ventricular hypertrophy; BP, blood pressure. *(Adapted from Julius S. Borderline hypertension: An overview. Med Clin North Am 1977;61:508. Reproduced with permission from the publisher and author.)*

against high blood pressure may not yet be necessary. Patient education also should include explanations about the importance of weight control, exercise, and proper diet.

FOLLOW-UP

A systematic approach to the follow-up and treatment of a patient with borderline hypertension is given in Figure 14–1–1. At the beginning of treatment, biweekly visits for dose adjustment may be necessary. Once the blood pressure is satisfactory, semiannual return visits are in order.

DISCUSSION

Prevalence and Incidence

The prevalence of borderline hypertension is depicted in Figure 14–1–2. Obviously, borderline hypertension is widely prevalent; it is estimated that it affects about 18 million adult Americans. Prevalence of borderline hypertension among men aged 20 to 30 years is around 15%, and in women, 3%. The incidence is in the range of 0.5 to 1% per year.

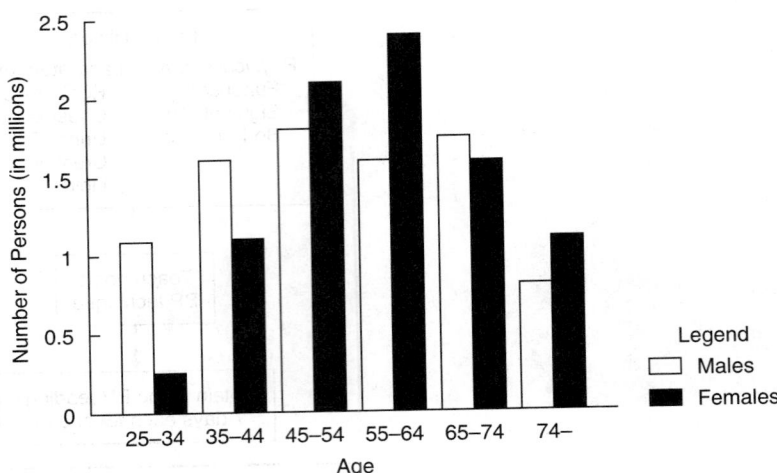

Figure 14–1–2. Distribution of borderline hypertension in the United States by age and sex. The figure is constructed by applying the prevalence of borderline hypertension in Alameda County, California, to the population profile from the U.S. Census. *(Adapted from Julius S. Borderline hypertension: An overview. Med Clin North Am 1977;61:496. Reproduced with permission from the publisher and author.)*

Related Basic Science

Besides the facade of only a minimal blood pressure elevation, there are a number of pathophysiologic abnormalities in borderline hypertension. Most interesting is the subset of patients with a fast heart rate, elevated cardiac output, and high levels of plasma renin and norepinephrine. There is good evidence that hypertension in these individuals is secondary to an excessive sympathetic cardiovascular drive. Since these "hyperkinetic" patients with borderline hypertension also show a characteristic personality and behavior, it is likely that the origin of the excessive sympathetic drive is psychosomatic.

Natural History and Its Modification with Treatment

About 20% of young people with borderline hypertension (age below 35 years) will within 15 years develop more severe, sustained hypertension. One study suggests that between 15 and 20 years of follow-up, an additional 50% of patients will develop hypertension requiring treatment. Risk factors for the development of hypertension (in order of importance) are higher average blood pressure, positive family history, black race, overweight, and resting tachycardia.

Patients with borderline hypertension suffer from excessive cardiovascular morbidity. The morbidity profile is the same as in more severe hypertension, that is, an excess of myocardial infarction, stroke, and renal failure. On average, the frequency of these morbid events is threefold higher than in normotensive individuals; however, the absolute levels of this excessive morbidity are not overwhelming. For example, over 20 years, 10% of young patients with borderline hypertension might develop coronary heart disease.

The situation with mortality is similar to that with morbidity. An example comes from studies of the natural history of cardiovascular diseases in Framingham, Massachusetts (Leitschuh et al., 1991). This study followed for 14 years a cohort of men and women whose age at entry was between 30 and 62 years. The age-adjusted ratio of observed and expected deaths was 100 in borderline hypertensives and 53 in normotensives. Thus, although experiencing double the mortality of normotensives, patients with borderline hypertension had a mortality ratio that did not exceed the average mortality in the whole population.

Prevention

It is assumed, but not proven, that weight reduction, a low-sodium diet, physical exercise, and avoidance of psychic stress may be useful in preventing borderline hypertension.

Cost Containment

The proposed approach to patients with borderline hypertension will result in cost containment by avoiding unnecessary tests and by selecting only a minority of patients for pharmacologic treatment.

REFERENCES

Esler M, Julius S, Zweifler A, et al. Mild high-renin essential hypertension: Neurogenic human hypertension? N Engl J Med 1977;296:405.

Julius S, Jamerson K, Mejia AD, et al. The association of borderline hypertension with target organ changes and higher coronary risk: Tecumseh blood pressure study. JAMA 1990;264:354.

Julius S, Krause L, Schork NJ, et al. Hyperkinetic borderline hypertension in Tecumseh, Michigan. J Hypertens 1991;9:77.

Leitschuh M, Cupples LA, Kannel W, et al. High-normal blood pressure progression to hypertension in the Framingham hypertension study. Hypertension 1991;17:22.

Lund-Johansen P. Central haemodynamics in essential hypertension at rest and during exercise: A 20-year follow-up study. J Hypertens 1989;7(Suppl 6):552.

CHAPTER 14–2

Mild, Moderate, Severe, and Resistant Hypertension

W. Dallas Hall, M.D.

DEFINITION

Table 14–2–1 provides the most current definitions of the levels of systolic or diastolic blood pressure that classify adult hypertensive patients as mild (stage 1), moderate (stage 2), or severe (stages 3 and 4). The term *mild* does not adequately convey the twofold or more increased risk of cardiovascular events in this subset of patients.

There is no widely accepted definition for resistant hypertension. A useful one is a blood pressure of 160/100 mm Hg or more in patients who are compliant to three antihypertensive drugs prescribed in proper combinations and dosage. Severe hypertension is not necessarily resistant to therapy.

ETIOLOGY

Ninety percent of cases of hypertension have no known cause and are referred to as "essential" or primary hypertension. Ten percent of cases

TABLE 14–2–1. CLASSIFICATION OF THE SEVERITY OF HYPERTENSION

Category	Systolic (mm Hg)		Diastolic (mm Hg)
Mild (stage 1)	140–159	or	90–99
Moderate (stage 2)	160–179	or	100–109
Severe (stage 3)	180–209	or	110–119
Very severe (stage 4)	≥ 210	or	≥ 120

have identifiable causes and are referred to as secondary hypertension. The two most common causes of secondary hypertension are renal artery stenosis and chronic renoparenchymal diseases.

CRITERIA FOR DIAGNOSIS
Suggestive

Occasional or transient elevations of systolic blood pressure to 140 mm Hg or more, or of diastolic blood pressure to 90 mm Hg or more, are suggestive of the diagnosis of hypertension. Repeated blood pressure levels in the high-normal range (i.e., 130–139 mm Hg systolic or 85–89 mm Hg diastolic) convey an increased risk for developing hypertension (also see Chapter 14–1).

Definitive

The diagnosis of the various stages of hypertension requires documentation of the levels of blood pressure (specified in Table 14–2–1) on three consecutive occasions.

Resistant hypertension should not be diagnosed until the elevated blood pressures are reproduced outside the office setting and medication compliance is documented. Up to 50% of hypertensive patients who appear to have resistant hypertension demonstrate adequate control of blood pressure at home or when hospitalized and given their prescribed medications. In general, monotherapy controls 30 to 50% of compliant patients, two-drug therapy controls 65 to 85%, and triple therapy controls 90 to 94%. This implies that only about 10% of compliant hypertensives are resistant to triple therapy.

CLINICAL MANIFESTATIONS
Subjective

A genetic component accounts for about 40 to 60% of the population variance in the level of blood pressure. Hence a positive family history of hypertension in first-degree relatives strongly predicts the risk of hypertension. The family history is positive in one half to two thirds of patients with essential hypertension. When both parents are hypertensive, the onset of hypertension can be up to 10 years earlier in their children.

Environmental factors associated with hypertension include residence in coastal areas, urban settings, and industrialized countries. Certain occupations may be associated with a higher than expected prevalence of hypertension. Those reported include air traffic controllers, bus drivers, and jobs associated with continuous, high-intensity noise exposure.

Hypertension is usually asymptomatic, but some studies have noted dizziness, nocturia, headache, and depression in untreated hypertensive individuals as compared with normotensive controls of similar age. A history of weight gain, diabetes, sedentary lifestyle, or alcohol abuse is also associated with hypertension. The medication history should include oral contraceptives, over-the-counter cold remedies, nonsteroidal antiinflammatory drugs, and any steroidal compound or nasal spray. The diet history should include an estimate of salt intake, and the social history should include any history of drug abuse or tobacco use, including chewing tobacco (see Chapter 14–9).

Objective
Physical Examination

The three most common abnormalities on physical examination are obesity (30–60% of patients with essential hypertension), arteriolar

constriction or arteriovenous nicking in the ocular fundus (30–40% of patients), and an audible fourth heart sound (50–70% of patients). Less frequent abnormalities include carotid, abdominal, or femoral bruits and a sustained apical impulse due to left ventricular hypertrophy.

Routine Laboratory Abnormalities

The complete blood count is usually normal except for elevation of the hematocrit (e.g., 51–56 vol%) in a small subset of patients who have a greater long-term risk of cardiovascular complications. The standard biochemical profile should be normal except that dyslipidemia is present in about 40% of patients. Abnormalities in the chemistry panel provide clues to other diseases (Table 14–2–2). The urinalysis is normal except for a mild concentration defect, proteinuria less than 2+ on a dipstick (4–10% of patients), and occasional hyaline casts in the sediment.

The electrocardiogram and chest x-ray film should be normal unless the duration or severity of untreated hypertension has resulted in the development of left ventricular hypertrophy or coronary disease.

PLANS
Diagnostic
Differential Diagnosis

The diagnosis is established when the diagnostic criteria are met.

Diagnostic Options and Recommended Approach

The recommended initial screening laboratory tests are listed in Table 14–2–3. Many authorities also obtain posteroanterior and lateral chest x-rays. Indications for more specialized tests are discussed in the chapters on secondary causes of hypertension.

Therapeutic

Therapy may be nonpharmacologic, pharmacologic, or both. Initial drug therapy is recommended for patients with moderate or severe hypertension (i.e., stage 2, 3, or 4), whereas a 3- to 6-month trial of lifestyle modifications with or without pharmacologic therapy is appropriate for the initial treatment of many patients with mild (stage 1) hypertension (i.e., a systolic blood pressure of 140 to 159 mm Hg and/or a diastolic blood pressure of 90 to 99 mm Hg).

Lifestyle Modifications. The advantage of lifestyle modifications is that they avoid the adverse effects and costs of drugs. The disadvantage is that they often result in less reduction of blood pressure than single-drug therapy. Also, ongoing modifications of lifestyle are more difficult for most patients than taking a few pills each day. Recommended lifestyle modifications are summarized in Table 14–2–4. If lifestyle modifications have not reduced systolic blood pressure to below 140 mm Hg and diastolic blood pressure to below 90 mm Hg within 3 to 6 months, then drug therapy should be started.

Pharmacologic Therapy. Drug therapy also can be selected initially for patients with mild (stage 1) hypertension. It may be particularly appropriate in higher-risk subgroups including older patients, as well as patients of any age with coronary artery disease, left ventricular hypertro-

TABLE 14–2–2. ABNORMALITIES IN BLOOD CHEMISTRIES THAT PROVIDE CLUES TO OTHER DISEASES IN HYPERTENSIVE PATIENTS

Abnormality	A Clue to
Elevated creatinine	Primary renal disease; obstructive uropathy; nephrosclerosis
Hyperchloremic acidosis	Interstitial renal disease
Hypokalemia	Primary or secondary aldosteronism, other mineralocorticoid excess syndromes
Elevated glucose	Diabetes mellitus
Elevated uric acid	Gout; alcoholism; nephrosclerosis
Elevated calcium	Primary hyperparathyroidism
High cholesterol	Hyperlipidemia

TABLE 14–2–3. INITIAL SCREENING LABORATORY TESTS RECOMMENDED IN PATIENTS WITH ESSENTIAL HYPERTENSION

Hematocrit and hemoglobin	Plasma glucose*
Urinalysis	Cholesterol
Serum potassium	High-density-lipoprotein cholesterol
Serum creatinine	Triglycerides*
Serum uric acid	Electrocardiogram

*Fasting

phy, left ventricular dysfunction, diabetes, dyslipidemia, transient ischemic attacks, stroke, advanced retinopathy, peripheral vascular disease, serum creatinine of 1.5 mg/dL or greater, or proteinuria. Insisting on the presence of target organ damage to initiate drug therapy for mild hypertension is not in keeping with most clinical trials, which demonstrate the most benefit when there is the least evidence of target organ damage at baseline. Once target organ damage has developed, the prognosis is generally worse and the benefits of antihypertensive drug therapy are less.

The Joint National Committee on the Detection, Evaluation, and Treatment of High Blood Pressure (JNC V, 1993) recommended either diuretics, beta blockers, calcium channel blockers, angiotensin-converting enzyme inhibitors, alpha blockers, or alpha–beta blockers as choices for first-line therapy of hypertension. Diuretics and beta blockers, however, were listed as preferred initial therapy because of their use in earlier long-term clinical trials that documented reduction in cardiovascular morbidity and mortality, especially stroke. In the Treatment of Mild Hypertension Study (TOMHS), the overall efficacy of the five classes of recommended antihypertensive drugs was very similar over a 5-year period (Neaton et al., 1993).

The Medical Research Council trial was a landmark study for comparison of diuretic, beta blocker, and placebo therapy in patients with hypertension; however, approximately 1040 of the 8700 drug-treated patients (12%) withdrew because of adverse reactions (Medical Research Council Working Party, 1985). Table 14–2–5 gives a breakdown of these reactions in men and women, as well as a comparison of diuretic and beta blocker. The numbers in the table represent the ratio of the incidence of adverse reactions on drug therapy compared with placebo therapy. Note, for example, that lethargy was 6 to 28 times more frequent with either drug than with placebo therapy and that impotence in men was 5 times more likely with beta blocker and 10 times more likely with diuretic than with placebo therapy. These comparative data should be interpreted with caution, however, because supplemental therapy with methyldopa (Aldomet) was used more often in men who were randomized to diuretic therapy.

Table 14–2–6 shows the distribution of biochemical abnormalities reported by Greenberg and associates (1984) after 3 years of diuretic, beta blocker, or placebo therapy. The level of serum potassium fell by 0.5 mEq/L in the diuretic group and rose by 0.2 mEq/L in the beta

TABLE 14–2–4. LIFESTYLE MODIFICATIONS RECOMMENDED FOR PATIENTS WITH HYPERTENSION

- Reduce sodium intake to less than 2300 mg (100 mEq) daily.
- Reduce total calorie intake to lose weight if ideal body weight exceeds 110%.
- After appropriate medical evaluation, gradually begin regular aerobic physical activity such as 30 to 45 minutes of brisk walking three to five times weekly. Other examples of aerobic exercise include jogging, swimming, basketball, tennis, handball, squash, and golf. Hypertensives should generally avoid strenuous isometric (static) exercise.
- Reduce fat intake to less than 30% of total calories; reduce cholesterol intake to less than 225 to 300 mg daily.
- Maintain adequate dietary potassium, calcium, and magnesium intake.
- Limit alcohol intake to no more than 1 oz of ethanol per day.*
- Quit smoking.

*This is equivalent to 2 oz of 100-proof whiskey, 8 oz of wine, or two 12-oz beers.

blocker group. No significant increase in ventricular ectopic beats was noted after 9 to 10 weeks in the group treated with diuretics and no supplemental potassium. In contrast, over a 2-year period, diuretic therapy was associated with an increased number of ventricular ectopic beats, even though the serum level of potassium was the same as in the short-term study (i.e., 3.6 mEq/L). These results suggest that factors other than the serum level of potassium may be associated with the increase in ventricular ectopy that can occur in certain patients following therapy with relatively high doses of thiazide-like diuretics. Use of lower doses of diuretics reduces the risk of hypokalemia, while maintaining efficacy.

Impaired glucose tolerance led to withdrawal from therapy more often in patients treated with diuretics than with beta blockers, once again demonstrating that diuretic therapy can impair insulin sensitivity and glucose tolerance. Serum uric acid rose by 1.1 mg/dL in patients taking diuretics and by 0.3 to 0.5 mg/dL in those taking beta blockers.

Levels of serum cholesterol did not rise after 3 years of either diuretic or beta blocker therapy. These data contrast with most short-term studies that show a deleterious effect of diuretic or beta blocker therapy on the level of serum cholesterol. A slight decrease (4–5 mg/dL, or 1–2%) was noted in the placebo group, and it is possible that drug therapy might have negated this presumably diet-mediated improvement. In addition, some clinical trials have shown persistence of the adverse lipid effects for several years. Of note, however, is the Systolic Hypertension in the Elderly Program (SHEP), where diuretic- and beta blocker-based therapy was associated with a modest ($P < .05$) rise in serum cholesterol but a 27% reduction in coronary heart disease incidence. These data suggest that a significant reduction in systolic blood pressure can overshadow a mild increase in serum cholesterol.

Certain types of patients often respond better to diuretic than to beta blocker therapy. These are summarized in Table 14–2–7. As mentioned earlier, however, other classes of antihypertensive drugs have a similar overall efficacy in lowering blood pressure. Hence, the selection of initial therapy is often predicated more on the adverse effect profile and cost than on the blood pressure-lowering efficacy of a particular class of antihypertensive drug. For example, both the angiotensin-converting enzyme inhibitors and calcium channel blockers have fewer adverse effects than do the diuretics and beta blockers. Table 14–2–8 provides a summary of the relative positive and negative features of the five different classes of antihypertensive drugs that are recommended by JNC V as initial therapy.

If the elevated blood pressure *does not* respond to reasonable doses of the initial drug selected (or if there are limiting adverse effects), it is reasonable to switch to another class that has a different mechanism of action. If the blood pressure *does* respond to reasonable doses of the initial drug selected but the patient is still not controlled (i.e., 50–70% of the patients), then it is usually more effective to add a second drug than to proceed to the highest dose of the first drug. Note that both the systolic *and* the diastolic blood pressure should be controlled.

Triple-drug therapy should be needed by only 15 to 30% of compliant patients. Lack of response to triple-drug therapy in compliant patients is most often due to volume expansion in patients receiving no diuretic. Diuretics enhance the blood-pressure-lowering efficacy of alpha blockers, beta blockers, alpha–beta blockers, and angiotensin-converting enzyme inhibitors. They can be added effectively in very low doses such as 12.5 mg daily of hydrochlorothiazide or chlorthalidone or 1.25 mg daily of indapamide. This need for addition of low-dose diuretic therapy is typical of obese hypertensives, hypertensive African-Americans, and hypertensive patients with renal impairment.

Central-acting alpha agonists such as clonidine (Catapres) and guanfacine (Tenex) are often effective in patients who are incompletely responsive to usual triple-drug therapy. They often should be tried prior to considering more potent drugs. Common adverse effects include dry mouth, sleepiness/fatigue, and bradycardia.

Patients with resistant hypertension need to have 24-hour ambulatory blood pressure monitoring to document that the high blood pressure readings are not just on office visits. If both office and home readings are high, then they should have reevaluation for secondary causes. If none are apparent and diuretic therapy is optimal, then therapy with minoxidil (Loniten) should be considered, beginning with a dose of 2.5 mg daily followed by weekly or biweekly titration to as much as 20 mg

TABLE 14–2–5. MEDICAL RESEARCH COUNCIL TRIAL: ADVERSE REACTIONS* TO DIURETIC (BENDROFLUMETHIAZIDE, 5 MG TWICE DAILY) VERSUS BETA BLOCKER (PROPRANOLOL, UP TO 240 MG DAILY) IN 8700 PATIENTS WITH DIASTOLIC BLOOD PRESSURES OF 90 TO 109 MM HG

Adverse Reaction	Number of Withdrawals	Men ($n = 4523$)		Women ($n = 4177$)	
		Diuretic	*Beta Blocker*	*Diuretic*	*Beta Blocker*
Nausea, dizziness, or headache	194	3.0[†]	2.9[†]	4.1[†]	5.2[†]
Impaired glucose tolerance test	149	2.3[†]	1.0[†]	3.0[†]	1.1
Impotence	148	9.7[†]	4.8[†]	—	—
Lethargy	145	7.2[†]	10.6[†]	5.7[†]	27.7[†]
Gout	124	14.2[†]	1.7	> 10	1.5
Exertional dyspnea	113	0	17.8[†]	1.5	35.5[†]
Raynaud's phenomenon	77	0	25.5[†]	1.0	15.0[†]
Skin disorder	30	2.7	5.0[†]	4.0	12.0[†]

*Adverse reactions that required withdrawal of the drug. Rates represent the ratio of the incidence of reactions on drug therapy versus placebo therapy.
[†]$P < .05$ compared with placebo.
Adapted from Medical Research Council Working Party. MRC trial of treatment of mild hypertension: Principal results. Br Med J 1985; 291: 100. Reproduced with permission of the publisher and author.

twice daily. The use of minoxidil is fraught with hazards, however; the major hazard is acute fluid retention if the dosage of loop diuretics is inadequate. Concomitant therapy with an angiotensin-converting enzyme inhibitor partly blunts this (aldosterone-mediated) fluid retention. Either a beta blocker or clonidine is also usually necessary to block minoxidil-induced reflex tachycardia. Other adverse effects of minoxidil include hirsutism (poorly tolerated by most women) and an increased risk for occult pericardial effusion.

Isolated resistance of the systolic blood pressure is relatively common in elderly individuals with advanced arteriosclerosis and a stiff aorta. In addition to the usual drug therapies, it is sometimes useful to add long-acting nitrates (oral or patch) and reduce any evening wine intake that exceeds one glass.

FOLLOW-UP

Schedule a follow-up visit within 2 to 4 weeks of initial therapy. If a diuretic was prescribed, repeat the serum potassium level at this visit and again within 4 weeks of any increase in dosage. In patients with mild or moderate hypertension, allow a minimum of 4 weeks before stepping up therapy to the next level. Measure blood pressure in the sitting (or supine) position and after 2 minutes standing at each visit because of the increased occurrence of orthostatic hypotension with most antihypertensive drugs.

Once blood pressure is controlled, schedule maintenance visits at 3- to 6-month intervals, depending on the patient's status. Repeat the baseline blood chemistries and lipids at least annually. Consider reduc-

tion in drug dosages ("step-down therapy") in patients whose blood pressure remains controlled below 130/85 mm Hg on at least four visits over a 12-month period, as it is unclear at this time whether treatment to levels below these is more beneficial or harmful, especially in older patients and those with coronary artery disease. Step-down therapy is facilitated by weight reduction in overweight hypertensive patients and by sodium restriction in nonoverweight patients. Make specific appointments for follow-up visits and send reminder postcards. Use telephone calls or postcards for follow-up of missed appointments.

DISCUSSION
Prevalence

There currently are about 50 million adult Americans with hypertension, defined as a systolic blood pressure of 140 mm Hg or more, a diastolic blood pressure of 90 mm Hg or more, or taking antihypertensive medications. The overall prevalence averages about 25%, ranging from 4% of adults aged 18 to 29 years, to 65% of adults aged 70 years or more.

Related Basic Science

Essential hypertension is synonymous with idiopathic hypertension. Nonetheless, much has been learned about physiologic and metabolic abnormalities in hypertension. Following is a summary that provides a *hypothetical* framework within which new discoveries can be placed.

Approximately 25 to 30% of individuals may be born with a genetic

TABLE 14–2–6. BIOCHEMICAL ABNORMALITIES BEFORE AND AFTER 3 YEARS OF THERAPY WITH DIURETIC, BETA BLOCKER, OR PLACEBO THERAPY FOR HYPERTENSION

	Bendrofluazide ($n = 1853$)		Propranolol ($n = 1765$)		Placebo ($n = 3620$)	
	Men	*Women*	*Men*	*Women*	*Men*	*Women*
Potassium (mEq/L)						
Before	4.08	4.03	4.09	4.04	4.11	4.05
3 years	3.58*	3.52*	4.28	4.25*	4.17	4.13
Cholesterol (mg/dL)						
Before	241.3	257.3	239.0	256.1	240.2	256.1
3 years	241.3	256.5	236.7	252.7	234.8	252.3
Uric acid (mg/dL)						
Before	6.43	5.04	6.32	4.91	6.28	4.92
3 years	7.54*	6.16*	6.64*	5.40*	6.35	5.12
Blood urea nitrogen (mg/dL)						
Before	11.6	11.3	11.6	11.0	11.5	11.1
3 years	12.9*	12.5*	12.4*	12.1*	11.9	11.5

*$P < .01$ for comparison between the change in treatment versus placebo group (i.e., not for within-treatment-group comparisons).
Adapted from Greenberg G, Brennan PJ, Miall WE. Effects of diuretic and beta-blocker therapy in the Medical Research Council trial. Am J Med 1984;76(2A): 45. Reproduced with permission of publisher and author.

TABLE 14–2–7. HYPERTENSIVE PATIENTS IN WHOM DIURETICS ARE OFTEN PREFERABLE TO BETA BLOCKERS AS INITIAL THERAPY

African-Americans

Isolated systolic hypertension

Renal insufficiency

Known low-renin hypertension

Patients with concomitant disorders that may benefit from diuretic therapy, such as
  Congestive heart failure
  Idiopathic hypercalciuria

defect (as yet undiscovered) in vascular reactivity. This could be related to factors that enhance vasoconstriction or impair vasodilation. For example, an M235T mutation in the angiotensinogen gene has been reported to be associated with 3 to 5% of cases of hypertension in Caucasians. There also could be anatomic or enzymatic defects in membrane transport of ions such as Na^+, Ca^{2+}, and Cl^-. Defects could be generalized or involve only certain organs. For example, insulin resistance in vascular smooth muscle could impair the function of insulin-sensitive Na^+, K^+–ATPase and Ca^{2+}–ATPase pumps, leading to intracellular accumulation of sodium and calcium. Renal defects could impair the ability to excrete salt, leading to expansion of the intravascular and plasma volume and increase in the venous return to the heart. The expanded cardiopulmonary blood volume would distend the atria and cause release of atrial natriuretic peptide to help regain sodium balance, provided that renal receptors are intact.

The increased venous return would dilate and stretch the fibers of the left ventricle, which would respond (via the Frank–Starling law) with an increase in cardiac output. Alternatively, the cardiac output could be increased directly by sympathetic outflow from the brainstem and hypothalamus in response to blockade of inhibitory central alpha receptors or stimulation of other receptors. An increase in central nervous system sympathetic outflow would evoke secretion and a high turnover rate of norepinephrine at sympathetic nerve terminals. The norepinephrine would stimulate its postsynaptic alpha receptor to cause venular and arteriolar constriction; it also would stimulate cardiac beta receptors to increase myocardial contractility and heart rate. Central nervous system-mediated release of epinephrine from the adrenal medulla also would stimulate β_1-receptors in the heart. A high cardiac output could

result from more vigorous contractility induced by an increase in the amount, availability, or binding kinetics of intracellular calcium in the myocardium.

The net result from any of these mechanisms would be an increase in the cardiac output, associated with a modest rise in heart rate; the total peripheral resistance would remain normal or low. Mean arterial blood pressure would be elevated primarily because of the increased cardiac output. This is the early, or first, stage of essential hypertension.

The increase in cardiac output would cause a transient increase in blood pressure that would enhance natriuresis ("pressure natriuresis") and excrete the retained salt. Baroreceptors in the carotid sinus would try to slow the heart rate and reduce the blood pressure, but their efficacy might be blunted. If any anatomic or physiologic component of the system went awry at this time, then hypertension would become fixed and progressive.

Retention of salt would raise the sodium content in the walls of blood vessels, reflected by an elevated intracellular sodium content of peripheral blood cells. Volume expansion also would enhance the contractility of the vessel wall in response to vasoconstrictors such as norepinephrine and angiotensin II.

The intracellular milieu is not accustomed to sodium and would try to pump it out, but the pump might be inhibited or defective. Calcium would exchange for sodium via the Na–Ca and other exchange mechanisms. The gain in intracellular calcium would cause a further constriction of the vascular smooth muscle wall. Natriuretic hormones would emerge to assist in the membrane exchange of Na for K, but would have vasoconstrictive effects per se. The vessel wall might demonstrate an impaired ability to vasodilate, an exaggerated ability to vasoconstrict, or both. The increased vascular reactivity would manifest clinically as excessive increases in blood pressure in response to a variety of emotional or physical stimuli, such as mental stress, pain, cold temperatures, and isometric exercise.

Sympathetic outflow from the brain would cause the renal sympathetic nerves to release renin. Renin would cleave angiotensinogen to angiotensin I, converted readily (intrarenally and extrarenally) to the vasoconstrictor angiotensin II. The cycle would become more vicious as angiotensin II activated its receptors and stimulated adrenal secretion of aldosterone, which would further increase sodium retention and vascular reactivity.

Intense arteriolar vasoconstriction would be mediated in part by increased vascular wall sodium and calcium, as well as stimulation from

TABLE 14–2–8. POSITIVE AND NEGATIVE FEATURES* OF FIVE DIFFERENT CLASSES OF ANTIHYPERTENSIVE DRUGS RECOMMENDED FOR INITIAL THERAPY OF PATIENTS WITH HYPERTENSION

	Thiazide-like Diuretics	Beta Blockers	Alpha Blockers	Calcium Channel Blockers	Converting Enzyme Inhibitors
Efficacy					
General	+2	+2	+2	+2	+2
Elderly	+3	+1	+2	+3	+3
Young hyperkinetic	+1	+3	+2	+2	+2
African-Americans	+3	+1	+2	+3	+1
Coronary disease	0	+3	0	+2	+1
Congestive heart failure	+2	−2	0	−1	+3
Adverse metabolic effects					
Hypokalemia	−3	+1	0	0	+2
Hyperkalemia	+1	−1	0	0	−2
Hyperuricemia	−3	−1	0	0	0
Insulin resistance	−2	−1	+1	0	+2
Hyperlipidemia	−2	−1	+1	0	0
Adverse quality-of-life effects					
Fatigue	−2	−3	0	0	0
Dyspnea/bronchospasm	0	−2	0	+1	0
Impotence	−2	−2	0	0	0
Rash	0	0	0	−1	−2
Gastrointestinal	0	−1	0	−1	0
Orthostasis	−1	0	−2	0	0
Cardioprotective effect	−1	+3	0	0	0
Cost	+3	−1	−1	−2	−2

*+ = positive feature, 0 = neutral or negligible effect, − = negative feature.

catecholamines, angiotensin II and endothelin. The arteries and veins would attempt to relax by endothelial secretion of prostacyclin (prostaglandin I_2) and endothelium-derived relaxing factor with activation of the nitric oxide pathway, but these vasodilator systems could be defective. Continued vasoconstriction would narrow the radius (*r*) of the arteriolar wall, exponentially increasing the resistance (*R*) to flow according to Poiseuille's law: $R = 8vl/\pi r^4$. Mean arterial blood pressure, the product of cardiac output and total peripheral resistance, would now be increased primarily because of a high total peripheral resistance. This is the second, or fixed, stage of essential hypertension. Fixed elevation of blood pressure causes structural changes in the vascular wall and accelerated atherosclerosis. These eventually damage the small vessels of target organs such as the heart, brain, and kidney, leading to myocardial infarction, stroke, and renal failure.

Chronic elevation of the total peripheral resistance creates a significant workload ("afterload") on the left ventricle. The left ventricle responds by augmenting its protein synthesis to increase myofibril size (hypertrophy) and, thereby, the thickness of its posterior and septal surfaces. The purpose of the hypertrophy is to normalize the stress placed on its walls ("wall stress") from the high tension within the left ventricular cavity. Vascular smooth muscle cells also hypertrophy, further encroaching on the already reduced lumen.

The first sign of impaired left ventricular performance occurs during diastole. It is characterized by slowing of the peak rate of left ventricular filling and delay in the opening of the mitral valve as a result of delayed ventricular relaxation during early diastole. Systolic dysfunction usually occurs later and is characterized by a decrease in the ejection fraction and cardiac output. Systolic dysfunction eventually leads to incomplete ejection of blood so that there is an increase in left ventricular end-diastole volume. The hypertrophied left ventricle now begins to dilate with the appearance of clinical signs of congestive heart failure.

Natural History and Its Modification with Treatment

Mild (stage 1) and moderate (stage 2) essential hypertension are usually first diagnosed between the ages of 30 and 40 years. Left untreated, 10 to 17% of patients progress to more severe levels of blood pressure over a period as short as 5 years, and at least 1% develop a morbid event annually. Death is due to cardiovascular disorders in 55 to 70% of patients, primarily coronary artery disease, congestive heart failure, and stroke. The overall 20-year mortality of untreated patients is approximately 80%. Death preempts life expectancy by an average of 6 to 20 years, depending on the age at diagnosis.

Treatment of hypertension clearly reduces these long-term risks, but the relative risk usually remains somewhat above that of the general population, even with "adequate" control of blood pressure.

Prevention

There are no established methods for the prevention of essential hypertension. Primary prevention studies have assessed the impact of dietary changes in individuals at greater risk of developing hypertension (e.g., those with diastolic blood pressures between 78 and 89 mm Hg). Interventions have included low-sodium, high-potassium, and calorie-restricted diets in overweight individuals. Compared with a control group with no intervention, effective dietary reduction of sodium and calories is associated with a modest reduction in blood pressure and a lower risk of subsequent blood pressure elevation (i.e., diastolic or systolic blood pressure levels of 90 or 140 mm Hg or more, respectively) or the need for antihypertensive drug therapy.

Cost Containment

Table 14–2–9 provides a rough estimate of the dollar costs for the initial evaluation and first year of therapy in the usual patient with hyper-

TABLE 14–2–9. APPROXIMATE DOLLAR COSTS FOR THE INITIAL YEAR OF EVALUATION, THERAPY, AND FOLLOW-UP OF PATIENTS WITH HYPERTENSION

Test/Procedure	Number	Total Cost
Initial history and physical	1	$116
Complete blood count, SMA, urinalysis	2	118
High-density lipoproteins	2	34
Electrocardiogram	1	56
Chest x-ray	1	50
Medications	2*	250
Office visits	4	232
Total		$856

*Assumes that 40 to 60% of patients will require two-drug therapy (including the use of potassium supplement).

tension. The cost for subsequent years would be somewhat lower. Special diagnostic tests should be reserved for patients with specific clinical indications. They include intravenous pyelography ($150), plasma renin ($75), plasma aldosterone ($60), plasma catecholamines ($100), renal angiography ($1750), renal vein renins ($850), 24-hour ambulatory blood pressure monitoring ($300), and echocardiography ($200–$400). The annual cost of effective antihypertensive therapy is low relative to the average annual cost for the cardiovascular complications of hypertension. For example, the average annual U.S. direct cost for the 450,000 cases of stroke is $3 billion, or almost $7000 per patient. A 30 to 40% reduction in the risk of stroke is a bargain for $856 a year.

For resistant hypertensives with documented medication compliance, it is useful to reevaluate the patient for secondary causes, as the yield is considerably higher than in the 90% or more of compliant hypertensive patients whose blood pressure can be controlled with three drugs or less.

REFERENCES

Flack JM, Sowers JR. Epidemiologic and clinical aspects of insulin resistance and hyperinsulinemia. Am J Med 1991;91(suppl 1A):11S.

Greenberg G, Brennan PJ, Miall WE. Effects of diuretic and beta-blocker therapy in the Medical Research Council trial. Am J Med 1984;76(2A):45.

Hall WD. Hypertensive crisis. In: Hurst JW, ed. Current therapy in cardiovascular disease. 4th ed. St. Louis: Mosby-Year Book, 1994:307.

Hypertension Prevention Trial Research Group. The Hypertension Prevention Trial: Three-year effects of dietary changes on blood pressure. Arch Intern Med 1990;150:153.

Joint National Committee on Detection, Evaluation, and Treatment of High Blood Pressure. The Fifth Report of the Joint National Committee on Detection, Evaluation, and Treatment of High Blood Pressure (JNC V). Arch Intern Med 1993;153:154.

Kaplan NM. Treatment of hypertension: Drug therapy. In: Kaplan NM, ed. Clinical hypertension. 6th ed. Baltimore: Williams & Wilkins, 1994:191.

Materson BJ, Reda DJ, Cushman WC, et al. Single-drug therapy for hypertension in men: A comparison of six antihypertensive agents with placebo. N Engl J Med 1993;328:914.

Medical Research Council Working Party. MRC trial of treatment of mild hypertension: Principal results. Br Med J 1985;291:97.

National High Blood Pressure Education Program Working Group. Report on primary prevention of hypertension. Arch Intern Med 1993;153:186.

Neaton JD, Grimm RH Jr, Prineas RJ, et al. Treatment of Mild Hypertension Study (TOMHS): Final results. JAMA 1993;270:713.

Hypertensive Crises

C. Venkata S. Ram, M.D.

DEFINITION

Any form of hypertension may be associated with the development of hypertensive crisis, the chief determinant being the level of blood pressure rather than the etiology of hypertension. A major factor in the development of hypertensive crisis is the abruptness with which the blood pressure rises, as this factor seems to be more important than the absolute level of blood pressure in certain clinical situations, for example, onset of hypertension as in children with acute glomerulonephritis, toxemia of pregnancy, and drug-induced hypertension. In some clinical circumstances, immediate reduction of blood pressure is indicated not because of its absolute level but because the coexisting complications (e.g., aortic dissection, acute left ventricular failure) may make even moderate hypertension dangerous.

ETIOLOGY

Hypertensive crises are conveniently categorized into *emergencies* and *urgencies* (Tables 14–3–1 and 14–3–2). Hypertensive emergencies carry poor prognosis unless the blood pressure is reduced quickly, whereas hypertensive urgencies pose less immediate danger, yet they may become emergencies if the blood pressure is not vigorously controlled. Hypertensive emergencies typically are conditions in which the blood pressure should be reduced in a few hours, whereas in hypertensive urgencies, blood pressure reduction can be accomplished in several hours or days. There is no arbitrary level of blood pressure separating hypertensive emergencies and urgencies, although in the former, the blood pressure levels tend to exceed 200/130 mm Hg.

In the management of hypertensive crises, prompt therapy should take precedence over diagnostic studies. Valuable time should not be lost in the pursuit of an etiology. The complications of hypertensive crisis are largely reversible, but the degree of reversibility depends on how soon appropriate treatment is instituted.

CRITERIA FOR DIAGNOSIS

Several different syndromes are classified as hypertensive emergencies. They are discussed under Clinical Manifestations.

CLINICAL MANIFESTATIONS
Accelerated and Malignant Hypertension

The most striking difference between uncomplicated and accelerated/malignant hypertension is the presence of acute vascular lesions in the kidney and in other target organs in the latter. Accelerated hypertension is identified by the presence of severe retinopathy (without papilledema): exudates, hemorrhages, arteriolar narrowing, and spasm. Malignant hypertension, an extension of the accelerated form, is distin-

guished by the presence of papilledema. Both the accelerated and malignant forms of hypertension are associated with clinical evidence of severe vascular injury to the kidney and other target organs. The manifestations of accelerated and malignant hypertension are listed in Table 14–3–3.

The blood pressure level in malignant hypertension is usually quite high, with diastolic levels often greater than 130 to 140 mm Hg, but the degree of blood pressure elevation is not the only diagnostic factor. The elevation of the blood pressure has to occur abruptly, and most importantly, it is the extent of vascular injury that determines the nature of clinical manifestations. Headache with or without coexisting encephalopathy is the most common symptom. Usually, the headache is occipital in location and more intense in the morning hours. Weight loss may occur in some patients with malignant hypertension as a result of salt and water loss. A majority of patients with malignant hypertension report visual symptoms ranging from blurring to blindness. Drowsiness and altered mental status are commonly observed in patients with malignant hypertension. Any worsening of these symptoms may indicate progression to encephalopathy or other cerebral malfunction.

Congestive heart failure can be a presenting feature of malignant hypertension as a direct consequence of left ventricular dysfunction or of volume retention from associated renal insufficiency. Azotemia, a common feature of malignant hypertension, may be associated with proteinuria. Renal function deteriorates rapidly without proper therapy. Even with appropriate treatment, renal function may decline at times due to reduced renal perfusion. Although hypertension can result from chronic renal disease, renal failure in patients with malignant hypertension is a result rather than the cause of severe hypertension. Anemia is a common finding in malignant hypertension. The degree of anemia may give a clue as to the proximate cause: severe anemia suggests underlying chronic renal disease, whereas modest degrees may reflect microangiopathic hemolysis.

The diagnosis of accelerated and malignant hypertension can be made at the bedside on the basis of history and clinical examination. Simple investigations such as chest x-ray, electrocardiogram, complete blood count, blood urea nitrogen, creatinine, electrolytes, and urinalysis are sufficient for the initial management of malignant hypertension.

Patients with accelerated/malignant hypertension should be treated in the hospital, as the goal is not simply to lower the blood pressure but to monitor, stabilize, and reverse the damage to target organs and to exclude reversible causes. Preferably, the patients should be treated in an intensive care unit; however, in the absence of significant target organ dysfunction, they can be managed safely on the wards.

Although parenteral therapy is widely used in the initial treatment of malignant hypertension, various oral therapies can also be successfully used. Captopril, minoxidil, clonidine, prazosin, labetalol, and nifedipine have all been used for initial treatment of malignant hypertension. The choice between oral and parenteral therapy depends on the monitoring facilities, condition of the patient, and coexisting complications. Once the blood pressure is brought to safe levels, long-term therapy must be initiated with an appropriate agent(s) based on the renal, cardiac, and neurologic status of the patient.

TABLE 14–3–1. EXAMPLES OF HYPERTENSIVE EMERGENCIES

Accelerated/malignant hypertension*
Hypertensive encephalopathy
Acute left ventricular failure
Acute aortic dissection
? Intracranial hemorrhage
Pheochromocytoma crisis
Monoamine oxidase inhibitor + tyramine interaction
Eclampsia
Substance/drug-induced acute hypertension

*Can also be considered as an urgency.

TABLE 14–3–2. EXAMPLES OF HYPERTENSIVE URGENCIES

Accelerated/malignant hypertension*
Severe hypertension associated with coronary artery disease
Severe hypertension in the kidney transplant patient
Preoperative hypertension
Hypertension associated with burns

*Can also be considered as an emergency.

TABLE 14–3–3. CLINICAL MANIFESTATIONS OF ACCELERATED AND MALIGNANT HYPERTENSION

- Marked elevation of blood pressure
- Malaise; weight loss
- Headache
- Retinopathy
- Renal failure (azotemia, proteinuria, hematuria, etc.)

Hypertensive Encephalopathy

Hypertensive encephalopathy is one of the most serious complications of severe hypertension. Although encephalopathy occurs mainly in patients with malignant hypertension, it can also complicate hypertension of short duration. Hypertensive encephalopathy should be quickly recognized and effectively treated, as it carries a poor prognosis if untreated but is rapidly reversible with proper treatment. The clinical manifestations of hypertensive encephalopathy are precipitated not only by severity of blood pressure elevation but also by the abrupt onset of hypertension in a previously normotensive individual. It is generally recognized that hypertensive encephalopathy occurs more frequently when the hypertension is complicated by renal insufficiency than when kidney function is normal. The full clinical syndrome may take 12 to 48 hours to develop.

Clinical manifestations of hypertensive encephalopathy are listed in Table 14–3–4. Severe generalized headache is a prominent clinical symptom. Neurologic dysfunction consisting of confusion, somnolence, and stupor may appear simultaneously with or following the onset of headache. If untreated, progressive worsening of the sensorium occurs, culminating in coma and death. The patient may be quite restless during the initial stages of the syndrome. Other clinical features may include projectile vomiting, visual disturbances ranging from blurring to frank blindness, and transient focal neurologic deficits. Sometimes (especially in children), generalized or focal seizures may dominate the clinical picture.

On physical examination, the blood pressure is invariably elevated but there is no certain level of blood pressure above which encephalopathy is likely to occur. The fundi reveal generalized arteriolar spasm with exudates/hemorrhages. Although papilledema is present in most patients with this complication, its absence should not exclude the diagnosis of hypertensive encephalopathy.

When a patient with poorly controlled hypertension presents with severe headache, altered mental status, papilledema, and variable neurologic deficits, the most likely initial diagnosis is hypertensive encephalopathy, which, of course, must be distinguished from other acute neurologic complications of hypertension such as cerebral infarction or hemorrhage and uremic encephalopathy. A thorough but quick evaluation of the patient should be carried out to consider these differential diagnoses. The only definitive criterion to confirm the diagnosis of hypertensive encephalopathy is a prompt response of the patient's condition to antihypertensive therapy. The syndrome reverses within 1 to 12 hours with appropriate control of hypertension.

Once the diagnosis of hypertensive encephalopathy is suspected, the blood pressure should be lowered rapidly to near-normal levels, yet the diastolic blood pressure should probably remain at or slightly above 100 mm Hg. Rapid reduction in the blood pressure produces prompt, dramatic, and significant relief of symptoms of hypertensive en-

cephalopathy. The patient should be treated in an intensive care unit. The most important goal of therapy is to prevent permanent neurologic damage. Specific details concerning this and other antihypertensive agents are discussed elsewhere. Although potent orally effective agents like minoxidil, nifedipine, and captopril can control severe hypertension, parenteral drugs are preferred in treating a potentially dangerous condition such as hypertensive encephalopathy.

Severe Hypertension and Cerebrovascular Accidents

Patients with acute stroke and severe hypertension pose a challenging management dilemma. When intracerebral pressure rises as a result of hemorrhage or thrombotic infarction, cerebral blood flow may no longer be under normal autoregulation. Therefore, a reduction in the systemic blood pressure may conceivably further compromise cerebral blood flow. Conversely, persistent severe hypertension may worsen the stroke process. In many patients with acute stroke, initial hypertension may resolve spontaneously within 48 hours. There are no definitive data in the literature that provide the practicing physicians with a standard approach in managing these patients.

With the present state of our knowledge, no specific guidelines can be given about the management of hypertensive crises occurring in patients with cerebrovascular accidents. Based on the pathogenesis of these conditions, especially intracerebral hemorrhage, and if the patient has severe hypertension, it is advisable to reduce the blood pressure to near-normal levels or to a degree that will not compromise the cerebral function. If there is evidence of progression of the disease or worsening of the neurologic manifestations, however, then one has to reassess this therapeutic approach. Appropriate precautions should be taken to avoid hypotension in these patients and it is advisable not to lower the diastolic blood pressure to less than 100 mm Hg, usually. In any event, the reduction should be no more than 20% of the baseline blood pressure level.

Acute Aortic Dissection

Of all the symptoms that have been listed in Table 14–3–5, severe pain is the most important manifestation of acute dissection. It is easily confused with the pain of acute myocardial infarction. There are certain subtle qualitative differences between the pain of aortic dissection and that of myocardial infarction. The pain of dissection is abrupt in onset and is quite severe right from the onset, whereas patients with acute myocardial infarction rarely report that the pain began abruptly. The pain of myocardial infarction may wax and wane, whereas aortic dissection pain occurs abruptly and persists. Although the patient's description of the pain may not indicate the site of dissection, it might sometimes reflect the extent of dissection. It is the quality of pain rather than its precise location that characterizes the patient with acute aortic dissection. Certain terms, such as tearing, lacerating, throbbing, ripping, excruciating, and burning, have been used by patients with acute dissection. The onset of pain is almost always sudden and is unremitting in most patients, and the fear of death is imminent.

The clinical diagnosis of aortic dissection is based on a high index of suspicion and the presenting features. Once the diagnosis is suspected, immediate medical therapy should be implemented pending the diagnostic tests.

Two-dimensional echocardiography, transesophageal echocardiogra-

TABLE 14–3–4. CLINICAL FEATURES OF HYPERTENSIVE ENCEPHALOPATHY

- Marked elevation of blood pressure
- Headache
- Nausea, vomiting
- Papilledema
- Visual complaints
- Transient neurologic deficits (seizures)
- Altered mental status

TABLE 14–3–5. CLINICAL FEATURES OF ACUTE AORTIC DISSECTION

- Severe pain in the chest, intrascapular region, neck, midback, sacral area
- Syncope
- Confusional state or headache
- Blindness
- Hemoptysis
- Dyspnea
- Nausea and vomiting
- Melena or hematemesis
- Oliguria, anuria, or hematuria
- Paralysis

phy, and magnetic resonance imaging (MRI) have all been used to diagnose aortic dissection. MRI combined with transesophageal or transthoracic echocardiography yields considerable information; however, MRI is recommended only for patients who are hemodynamically stable and who can be transported to the MRI suite. Digital and/or conventional angiography provides more thorough information concerning the anatomy of dissection and the course taken by the dissecting hematoma.

Once the diagnosis of acute aortic dissection is apparent, the following steps should be undertaken. If the patient is hypertensive, blood pressure should be reduced to near-normal levels with an agent that causes the blood pressure to come down smoothly rather than drastically. Direct vasodilators that reflexly stimulate the heart should be avoided and, in fact, are contraindicated in acute aortic dissection. When instituting antihypertensive therapy, one should keep in mind that the force and velocity of ventricular contraction (dp/dt) and the pulsatile flow are important determinants of the shearing force acting on the aortic wall. Attempts should be made to decrease the dp/dt with a suitable agent; drugs that reflexly stimulate the heart should be avoided.

The blood pressure should be reduced to near-normal levels, and the ideal agent in this situation would be trimethaphan, which has a smooth action and is rapidly effective. As this drug is a ganglion-blocking agent, it decreases the neural transmission at the myocardial contractility sites and has a negative inotropic effect; therefore, it decreases the pulsatile flow and also blunts the sharpness of the pulse wave generated by the heart. This mode of pharmacologic approach in the management has been shown to reduce mortality. The other options include labetalol, a combined alpha and beta blocking drug, and the ultrashort acting beta blocker esmolol.

Acute Left Ventricular Failure

Severe uncontrolled hypertension may precipitate acute left ventricular failure. The higher the blood pressure, the harder the left ventricle must work. Decreasing the workload of the failing myocardium can improve the cardiac function. In acute left ventricular failure, myocardial oxygen requirements increase due to increased end-diastolic fiber length and left ventricular volume. This could be particularly dangerous in patients with concomitant coronary artery disease. Prompt reduction of blood pressure with a balanced vasodilating agent such as nitroprusside is indicated in this circumstance. Sodium nitroprusside decreases both pre- and afterload with restoration of myocardial function and cardiac output. Although the angiotensin-converting enzyme inhibitors, by the virtue of their pharmacologic actions, may be useful in this situation, there is paucity of clinical experience concerning the therapeutic response to angiotensin-converting enzyme inhibition in patients with acute left ventricular failure.

Severe Hypertension Associated with Ischemic Heart Disease

Systemic hypertension increases myocardial oxygen consumption by increasing the left ventricular tension. Patients with myocardial infarction and severe hypertension should, therefore, theoretically benefit from blood pressure reduction, but there are no conclusive data to prove that treatment is beneficial. Reduction of systemic blood pressure reduces the cardiac work, wall tension, and oxygen demand and may thus limit myocardial necrosis in the early phase of infarction. With a reduction in the afterload, the hemodynamic status improves significantly in myocardial infarction. Cautious treatment of hypertension in patients with acute myocardial infarction is, therefore, likely to be beneficial.

Miscellaneous Conditions

Pheochromocytoma Crisis

A patient with pheochromocytoma crisis may present with striking clinical features. The blood pressure is markedly elevated during the paroxysm and the patient may have profound sweating, marked tachycardia, pallor, numbness, tingling, and coldness of the feet and hands. A single attack will last from a few minutes to hours and may occur as often as several times a day to once a month or less.

If pheochromocytoma is suspected, the alpha-adrenergic blocking drug phentolamine should be given in the dose of 1 to 5 mg intravenously, to be repeated in a few minutes if needed. An alternative to phentolamine would be sodium nitroprusside, but the former is more specific. A beta blocking drug may be useful if the patient has a concomitant cardiac arrhythmia. Administration of beta blocking agents should always be preceded by either phentolamine or phenoxybenzamine. If this is not done, beta blockade can aggravate the unopposed alpha-mediated peripheral vasoconstriction. Labetalol, a combined alpha- and beta-receptor-blocking drug has also been successfully used in this condition.

Clonidine Withdrawal Syndrome

A hyperadrenergic state mimicking pheochromocytoma crisis has been reported following abrupt discontinuation of the antihypertensive drug clonidine. Clonidine stimulates the alpha receptors in the brain stem, thus reducing peripheral sympathetic activity. When clonidine is abruptly discontinued (especially high doses) or even sometimes rapidly tapered, a syndrome has been noted consisting of nausea, palpitations, anxiety, sweating, nervousness, and headache, along with marked elevation of the blood pressure.

Symptoms of clonidine withdrawal can be relieved by reinstitution of clonidine. If there is marked elevation of blood pressure and the patient is experiencing such symptoms as palpitations, chest discomfort, and epigastric discomfort, intravenous administration of phentolamine or labetalol is recommended.

Hypertensive Crisis Associated with Drug and Food Interactions: Monamine Oxidase Inhibitors

Patients receiving monamine oxidase inhibitors are at risk of developing hypertensive crisis if they also take drugs such as ephedrine and amphetamines or consume foods containing large quantities of tyramine. In the presence of an inhibitor of monoamine oxidase, tyramine and indirectly acting sympathetic amines escape oxidative degradation, enter the systemic circulation, and potentiate the actions of catecholamines. Sympathomimetic amines such as those contained in nonprescription cold remedies can also provoke this response.

Hypertensive Crisis Induced by Metoclopramide

Hypertensive crisis induced by metoclopramide has been reported in previously normotensive subjects and in patients with pheochromocytoma. The exact mechanism by which metoclopramide, a dopamine agonist, causes the hypertensive response is not known. It could sensitize the vascular endothelium to the pressor effects of catecholamines or cause a release of catecholamines from the adrenal medulla or adrenergic neurons.

Severe Hypertension Associated with Erythropoietin

Erythropoietin therapy has been reported to cause hypertension, which can be severe at times. With the increasing use of erythropoietin, the problem of hypertension in recipients will likely increase. Erythropoietin therapy can result in the development of hypertensive crisis. The mechanisms of erythropoietin-induced hypertension are complex and include elevation of systemic vascular resistance due to blunted hypoxic vasodilation from the correction of anemia, hypervolemia, increased blood viscosity, and activation of the sympathetic nervous system.

Severe Hypertension Associated with Cyclosporine

Severe hypertension can result from the use of cyclosporine. Routine use of cyclosporine A in transplant patients has resulted in the development of severe hypertension. Possible causes of cyclosporine-induced hypertension include augmented sympathetic neuronal activity.

Calcium antagonists have proven to be very effective in controlling cyclosporine-induced hypertension. Whether the therapeutic effect is a nonspecific consequence or due to a reversal of cyclosporine-induced hypertensive mechanisms by calcium antagonists is not fully understood.

Cocaine-Induced Hypertensive Crisis

Cocaine use can cause an abrupt sudden increase in the systemic blood pressure, resulting in a hypertensive emergency. Neurohumoral factors triggered by cocaine likely cause intense vasoconstriction, thus increasing the vascular resistance and the blood pressure level. Sudden rise of blood pressure in a previously normotensive individual may result in serious cardiovascular complications, and cocaine use has resulted in cardiovascular crisis. The blood pressure should be lowered to safe limits without much delay.

Eclampsia

Eclampsia is a potentially serious cardiovascular complication in a pregnant patient. Although the definitive therapy is delivery of the fetus, the blood pressure should be reduced to prevent neurologic, cardiac, and renal damage. Although other antihypertensive drugs may be effective in reducing the blood pressure, the agent of choice is hydralazine, which has a long record of safety. Animal studies have shown that nitroprusside can cause problems in the fetus; therefore, its use should be reserved for hypertension refractory to hydralazine or methyldopa. The ganglion-blocking drug trimethaphan should be avoided because of the risk of meconium ileus. In pregnancy-induced hypertension, volume depletion may be present and diuretics should be avoided. Angiotensin-converting enzyme inhibitors should be avoided due to possible fetal/placental toxicity.

PLANS

Diagnostic

See Clinical Manifestations. Because of the nature of the problem therapeutic measures are more important than immediate diagnosis of the cause of the abrupt rise in blood pressure.

Therapeutic

The need to hospitalize the patient, therapeutic options and objectives, and parenteral versus oral therapy depend on the clinical evaluation of the patient. Patients with hypertensive emergencies should be hospitalized, and those with hypertensive urgencies may not require admission to the hospital. A therapeutic principle underlying the management of hypertensive crisis is not only to lower the blood pressure quickly but to prevent, arrest, and reverse target organ dysfunction and damage. Therefore, close supervision of the patient is mandatory while the blood pressure is being lowered. There are no firm guidelines as to the degree of desired blood pressure reduction, but a reasonable goal for most hypertensive emergencies is to lower the diastolic blood pressure to 100 (or to reduce the mean arterial pressure by 25%) over a period of minutes to hours. Hypertensive emergencies should be preferably managed in an intensive care unit to permit continuous monitoring of the general hemodynamic status of the patient. Although a secondary form of hypertension such as renal artery stenosis or adrenal hypertension may be a causative factor, the immediate goal should be to lower the blood pressure to a safe level instead of launching a big workup, which can be undertaken subsequent to stabilization of the clinical situation at hand. Once the critical situation is resolved, appropriate diagnostic plans should be considered. An important consideration in treating pa-

tients with hypertensive emergencies is the rapidity of onset and duration of action of the chosen drug. The physician should be cognizant of the hemodynamic and pharmacologic actions of the drug to be used, as blood pressure reduction should be accomplished with minimal adverse effects.

Parenteral Drugs

Parenteral drugs for rapid control of severe hypertension are listed in Table 14–3–6.

Nitroprusside. Sodium nitroprusside is one of the most potent blood pressure-lowering drugs and possesses the distinct property of rapid onset and offset of action. The hypotensive response occurs within seconds after infusion is started and dissipates almost as rapidly when the infusion is discontinued. The initial infusion rate should be no higher than 0.3 µg/kg/min, and this can be increased every 5 minutes until the desired blood pressure level is obtained. Once the desired effect of nitroprusside is achieved, the infusion usually can be maintained with minimal adjustment, but the blood pressure should be continuously monitored. Hypotension is the most common but an avoidable side effect of nitroprusside therapy.

Cyanide toxicity from nitroprusside, although extremely rare, has occurred. Prophylactic infusion of hydroxocobalamin (vitamin B_{12a}) 25 mg/h, has been shown to decrease the cyanide concentration and tissue hypoxia resulting from nitroprusside infusion during surgery.

Thiocyanate toxicity secondary to nitroprusside is uncommon and occurs only with high doses and in the presence of renal failure. Treatment should be interrupted when the thiocyanate level is close to 10 mg/dL. Monitoring of plasma thiocyanate levels is not mandatory as long as the patient's clinical status is closely assessed. Treatment of thiocyanate toxicity demands discontinuation of the drug and institution of dialysis.

Intravenous Labetalol. Labetalol is a combined alpha- and beta-adrenergic blocking drug that can be used parenterally or orally for the treatment of hypertensive emergencies. Intravenous labetalol administered as either a continuous infusion or bolus injections reduces the blood pressure promptly because of its rapid onset of action. Controlled smooth reduction in blood pressure may be obtained by continuous infusion of labetalol at the rate of 0.5 to 2 mg/min. As with nitroprusside, close monitoring of the patient is required during the infusion of labetalol therapy. Rapid (but not abrupt) lowering of blood pressure can also be accomplished with bolus injections of labetalol. Labetalol should not be used in patients who may have contraindications to the use of beta blockers such as heart failure, atrioventricular block, asthma, and chronic obstructive pulmonary disease.

Nicardipine Infusion. Nicardipine is a dihydropyridine calcium antagonist that has been shown to exert a prompt hypotensive effect when given intravenously in patients with severe hypertension. Nicardipine infusion is 5.0 mg/h, which can be titrated up gradually to obtain the desired therapeutic effect. Once a stable blood pressure level is reached, most patients do not require dosage alterations. Thus, nicardipine pharmacodynamics resemble those of nitroprusside in terms of the onset, duration, and offset of action. Because of its mechanism of action (calcium channel blockade), nicardipine may be beneficial in preserving tissue perfusion. This property may be particularly

TABLE 14–3–6. PARENTERAL DRUGS USEFUL IN THE IMMEDIATE CONTROL OF SEVERE HYPERTENSION

Drug	Route and Dosage	Onset	Offset	Comments
Nitroprusside	IV infusion, 0.25–8 µg/kg/min	Seconds	3–5 min	Thiocyanate toxicity may occur with prolonged (> 48 h) or high-dose infusion (> 15 µg/kg/min), particularly in renal insufficiency
Labetalol	IV, 20 mg q10min (can increase to 80-mg doses)	≤ 5 min	3–6 h	Prompt response; can be followed with same drug taken orally
Nicardipine	IV, 5–15 mg/h	5–15 min		
Hydralazine	IM/IV, 10–20 min	10–30 min	2–4 h	May precipitate angina, myocardial infarction

advantageous in patients with ischemic disorders, for example, coronary, cerebrovascular, and peripheral vascular disease. From my clinical experience with the use of nicardipine, I believe that it may turn out to be a useful therapeutic option in the management of severe hypertension with or without target organ damage.

Trimethaphan. Trimethaphan camsylate is a ganglion-blocking agent. It is the drug of choice for the medical treatment of acute aortic dissection. Like nitroprusside, trimethaphan should be administered as a continuous intravenous drip, and constant monitoring is necessary, preferably in the intensive care unit. The usual starting dose of the drug should be 1 mg/min titrated to obtain the desired blood pressure level. After prolonged infusion, tachyphylaxis may result from intravascular volume expansion, which can be partially overcome by effective diuretic therapy.

Diazoxide. Diazoxide has a direct relaxant effect on the vascular smooth muscle, causing a rapid fall in arterial blood pressure. The hypotensive effect of diazoxide is associated with striking increases in heart rate and cardiac output.

Diazoxide produces a rapid fall in blood pressure within 1 minute, and the maximum effect is achieved within 2 to 5 minutes. The hypotensive effect of a single injection of diazoxide may last 3 to 15 hours, but if there is no effect from the first injection, an additional dose can be given within 30 minutes. Smaller bolus injections and slow intravenous infusions of diazoxide for the treatment of severe hypertension have been used hoping to reduce the dangers of drastic and precipitous reduction in blood pressure. The need to use diazoxide has been nearly eliminated by the availability of safe alternative drugs.

Hydralazine. The hypotensive action of hydralazine results from a direct relaxation of the vascular smooth muscle and is accompanied by reflex increases in stroke volume and heart rate, which can precipitate myocardial ischemia. Intramuscular or intravenous administration of hydralazine results in an unpredictable but definite fall in blood pressure. In the treatment of hypertensive emergencies, the initial dose should be 10 to 20 mg. The onset of the hypotensive effect occurs within 10 to 30 minutes and its duration of action ranges from 3 to 9 hours. The dose and frequency of administration necessary to control the blood pressure are highly variable. The delayed onset and unpredictable degree of hypotensive effect present difficulties in titration. Nevertheless, hydralazine continues to be successfully employed in the treatment of eclampsia.

Phentolamine. Phentolamine, an alpha receptor-blocking agent, is specifically indicated for treating hypertensive crises associated with increased circulating catecholamines, for example, pheochromocytoma crisis, certain cases of clonidine withdrawal syndrome, and crises resulting from monoamine oxidase inhibitor and drug–food interaction. The hypotensive effect of a single intravenous bolus injection is short-lived and lasts less than 15 minutes.

Nitroglycerin. Nitroglycerin is a weak systemic arterial dilator with a greater effect on large arteries than on smaller arteries. Low doses cause venodilation; much higher doses are required to produce a fall in systemic blood pressure. Because of its pharmacologic actions, nitroglycerin infusion may be particularly beneficial in patients with coronary artery disease with or without hypertension. Although there are no controlled studies, nitroglycerin therapy can be considered in the management of severe hypertension associated with coronary artery disease. The usual initial dosage of nitroglycerin is 5 to 15 µg/min, and it

is titrated upward to a desired therapeutic endpoint. It has a rapid onset (within 2–5 minutes) and offset of action. Although nitroglycerin has been used to achieve controlled hypotension, its main use continues to be in patients with unstable angina and acute myocardial infarction.

Transition from Parenteral to Oral Therapy

After the immediate management of a hypertensive emergency or urgency with parenteral therapy, oral agents should be initiated at the earliest opportunity. Generally, oral therapy can be begun while tapering off the parenteral drug. If possible, oral drugs should be started with a low dose which can be increased gradually depending on the clinical response. It is important to detect and prevent postural hypotension during transition to oral therapy.

Role of Concomitant Diuretic Therapy

Diuretics per se have a limited role in the management of hypertensive emergencies; however, they potentiate the therapeutic response to nondiuretic agents. When the blood pressure does not respond satisfactorily to an adequate dose of the primary agent, adding a diuretic (furosemide) may be helpful. Certainly in volume overloaded states such as heart failure, concomitant administration of a loop diuretic is indicated for optimal results. Diuretics should not be used routinely in the management of hypertensive crises, as prior volume depletion may be present in some conditions such as malignant hypertension. The need for diuretic therapy, therefore, should be individualized on the basis of the hemodynamic and renal function status of the patient.

Oral Drugs

Clinical experience has suggested that antihypertensive drugs given orally Table 14–3–7 as either single or multiple doses lower the blood pressure immediately in patients with severe hypertension. Oral administration of a variety of antihypertensive drugs has been used in patients with or without concomitant target organ damage. Obviously, this approach is most suitable for patients with hypertensive urgencies, not emergencies.

Nifedipine. Nifedipine, a calcium channel blocker, given orally or sublingually, has been shown to reduce the blood pressure rapidly and has been found to be useful in the management of hypertensive crisis. Immediate reduction in blood pressure can be accomplished with sublingual (punctured capsule, or nifedipine liquid drawn out of the capsule with a syringe) or oral administration of the capsules. The drug is also effective when the capsule is bitten and then swallowed. The advantages of nifedipine are rapid onset of action and lack of central nervous system depression. It may cause reflex tachycardia. As the duration of action of nifedipine is short, patients who receive this drug for hypertensive emergencies should be monitored for several hours to consider readministration of the drug. Nifedipine is a useful choice for the management of hypertensive urgencies.

Abrupt fall in the blood pressure induced by nifedipine administration can cause certain adverse effects: symptomatic hypotension, tachycardia, and ischemic events. Therefore, the clinical need to use nifedipine capsules to lower the blood pressure urgently should be carefully assessed.

Clonidine. Clonidine therapy has been shown to produce an immediate antihypertensive effect with repetitive dosing. Typically, clonidine loading was accomplished in the emergency room by administering

TABLE 14–3–7. ACUTE ORAL THERAPY FOR THE IMMEDIATE CONTROL OF SEVERE HYPERTENSION

Drug	Route and Dosage	Onset	Offset	Comment
Nifedipine	10–20 mg PO or sublingually	5–15 min	3–5 h	Generally good response; short duration of action for optimal dosage not standard
Clonidine	0.2 mg PO initially, then 0.1 mg/h, up to 0.8 mg total	0.5–2 h	6–8 h	Prominent sedation
Captopril	6.5–25 mg PO	15 min	4–6 h	Generally good, sometimes excessive response
Minoxidil	5–10 mg PO	30–60 min	12–16 h	Tachycardia, fluid retention

clonidine orally 0.1 mg every hour until the desired goal was obtained. Since nifedipine became available, clonidine loading has been used infrequently and is on the decline. Both clonidine and nifedipine are equally effective in the treatment of hypertensive urgencies.

Angiotensin-Converting Enzyme Inhibitors Captopril, an angiotensin-converting enzyme inhibitor, has been found to be effective in the immediate treatment of severe hypertension and hypertensive crises. Captopril lowers the blood pressure promptly without causing tachycardia and, thus, offers a distinct hemodynamic advantage over direct arteriolar dilators; however, the maximal effect from orally administered captopril may not be attained for as long as 2 hours. On the other hand, there are some reports documenting the effectiveness of sublingual captopril in the treatment of hypertensive crisis. As experience with sublingual captopril is rather limited, further data have to be generated to define its role in the acute management of hypertensive crisis.

Minoxidil. Minoxidil is a powerful direct vasodilator and has been successfully used in the treatment of refractory or severe hypertension. Because of its relatively rapid onset of action and sustained duration, this drug has been used for the treatment of hypertensive crises. Minoxidil in doses ranging from 2.5 to 10 mg can be given every 4 to 6 hours initially in the treatment of severe hypertension. It works best when given along with a diuretic, and an adrenergic blocker is necessary to counteract the reflex tachycardia.

Oral Labetalol. Labetalol, a combined alpha- and beta-adrenergic blocker, can be administered orally (100–300 mg) in the treatment of hypertensive urgencies. Because of its dual adrenergic blockade, the fall in blood pressure is not accompanied by reflex tachycardia, which can be beneficial especially in patients with coronary artery disease.

FOLLOW-UP

Once the hypertensive crisis has resolved and the patient's condition is stable, we should look into possible factors that might have contributed to the dangerous elevation of blood pressure, such as nonadherence to prescribed therapy or the presence and/or progression of a secondary form of hypertension such as a renal artery stenosis.

After the patient's condition has been stabilized, the physician should discuss long-range and periodic outpatient follow-up plans.

DISCUSSION
Prevalence and Incidence

Despite the high prevalence of hypertension in the community, hypertensive crises occur only infrequently. The incidence of hypertensive crises has decreased significantly in the last 25 years, probably due to the widespread use of antihypertensive drugs. It is estimated that no more than 1 to 2% of hypertensive patients develop hypertensive crises.

Related Basic Science

Hypertensive crises usually develop in patients with chronic hypertension, but may also occur in patients with newly discovered or short duration of hypertension. In the previously normotensive individuals, acute elevations in arterial pressure cause complications to a greater degree at any given level of blood pressure than in those with chronic hypertension.

Natural History and Its Modification with Treatment

The prognosis, without treatment, is poor. With appropriate immediate treatment, the outlook is good. The following admonitions are germane to this subject.

The most critical decision in the management of hypertensive emergencies is to assess the patient's clinical state and to ascertain whether the patient's condition truly needs emergency management. A patient with a real hypertensive crisis should be ideally treated in an intensive care unit. The choice of oral versus parenteral drug depends on the urgency of the situation, as well as the patient's general condition. The level to which the blood pressure should be lowered varies with the type of hypertensive crisis and should be individualized. The choice of

TABLE 14–3–8. PARENTERAL DRUGS IN THE TREATMENT OF SEVERE HYPERTENSION

	Nitroprusside	Labetalol	Nicardipine
Severe hypertension	Yes	Yes	Yes
Chronic heart failure	Yes	No	Yes
Atrioventricular block	Yes	No	Yes
Asthma and COPD*	Yes	No	Yes
Renal insufficiency	No	?	Yes
Vascular disease	?	?	Yes
Cerebrovascular accident	?	Yes	Yes
Aortic dissection	?	Yes	—
Switch to same drug orally	No	Yes	Yes

*Chronic obstructive pulmonary disease.

parenteral drug is dictated by the clinical manifestations and concomitant medical problems associated with hypertensive crisis (Table 14–3–8). There is no predestined level for the goal of therapy. Complications of therapy, mainly hypotension and ischemic brain damage, can occur in patients given multiple potent antihypertensive drugs in large doses without adequate monitoring. Such complications can be minimized by gentle lowering of blood pressure, careful surveillance, and individualization of therapy. A relatively asymptomatic patient who presents with severe hypertension, that is, a diastolic blood pressure of 130 to 140 mm Hg, need not be treated with parenteral drugs. These patients should be managed on an individual basis and the usual course would be to intensify or alter the previous antihypertensive therapy. All too often, asymptomatic patients or those without an acute problem are unnecessarily subjected to immediate therapy. Acute alteration of the height of the mercury column does little good and may cause harm. A significant immediate change in the patient's blood pressure may be self-gratifying to the physicians, but is not indicated for most patients with asymptomatic severe hypertension. Indiscriminate use of therapeutic options such as nifedipine and furosemide should be strongly discouraged.

Prevention

The importance of sustained blood pressure control should be emphasized to prevent the recurrence of hypertensive crisis.

Cost Containment

One way to control the expenditure on hypertensive patients is to enforce a disciplined therapeutic approach to chronic hypertension so that the need for hospitalization is significantly reduced. It is very expensive to treat complications of severe hypertension, such as stroke, encephalopathy, and aortic dissection. From a pharmacoeconomic point of view, it makes sense to prevent a crisis than to treat it. Additionally, prevention of recurrent hypertensive crises is not only of prognostic significance but also a cost-saving measure.

REFERENCES

Bertel O, Conen D, Radu E, et al. Nifedipine in hypertensive emergencies. Br Med J 1983;286:19.

Biollaz J, Waeber B, Brunner HR. Hypertensive crisis treated with orally administered captopril. Eur J Clin Pharmacol 1983;25:145.

Clifton CG, Cook ME, Bienvenu GS, Wallin JD. Intravenous nicardipine in severe systemic hypertension. Am J Cardiol 1989;64:16H.

Cohn JN, Burke LP. Nitroprusside. Ann Intern Med 1979;91:752.

Crawford ES. The diagnosis and management of aortic dissection. JAMA 1990;264:2537.

Davis VA, Crook JE, Vestel RE, Oates JA. Prevalence of renovascular hypertension in patients with grade III or IV hypertensive retinopathy. N Engl J Med 1979;301:1273.

Papademetriou V, Notargiacomo AV, Khatri IM, et al. Treatment of severe hypertension with intravenous labetalol. Clin Pharmacol Ther 1982;32:431.

Ram CVS. Hypertensive encephalopathy: Recognition and management. Arch Intern Med 1978;138:1851.

Ram CVS. Diagnosis and management of hypertensive crisis. In: Rippe JM, Irwin RS, Alpert JS, Fink MP, eds. Intensive care medicine. 2nd ed. Boston: Little, Brown, 1991;228.

Ram CVS. Management of hypertensive emergencies: Changing therapeutic options. Am Heart J 1991;122:356.

Ram CVS, Boldrick RW, Heller J, et al. Rapid control of severe hypertension with intravenous infusion of nicardipine: A new therapeutic approach. J Clin Pharmacol 1989;29:835.

Wallin JD, Fletcher E, Ram CV, et al. Intravenous nicardipine for the treatment of severe hypertension. Arch Intern Med 1989;149:2662.

CHAPTER 14–4

Isolated Systolic Hypertension

William McFate Smith, M.D., M.P.H.

DEFINITION

Isolated systolic hypertension is usually defined as systolic blood pressure equal to or greater than 160 mm Hg with an accompanying diastolic blood pressure of less than 90 mm Hg.

ETIOLOGY

Decreased distensibility of the aorta and major vessels due to loss of elasticity is the major factor responsible for the age-related changes in systolic blood pressure leading to isolated systolic hypertension (ISH).

CRITERIA FOR DIAGNOSIS

Suggestive

Isolated systolic hypertension is most commonly seen in older adults, both male and female, its prevalence becoming clinically important after age 60. It is otherwise only seen in young males with the relatively rare idiopathic hyperkinetic heart syndrome.

Definitive

The diagnosis is readily made with standard blood pressure management procedures and equipment; however, owing to the great lability of blood pressure (particularly systolic) in the elderly, it is advisable to limit the diagnosis to those individuals who meet the criteria based on an average of several determinations, recorded on two or more occasions.

CLINICAL MANIFESTATIONS

Subjective

There are no symptoms specifically attributable to the disorder of ISH. Nonetheless, in the elderly, in whom ISH commonly occurs, it may be associated with complaints of faintness on standing, shortness of breath, and ankle swelling. As do other forms of hypertension, ISH usually remains silent (except for the manifestations of concomitant cardiovascular disease) until a serious complication such as stroke or myocardial infarction occurs. A history of diabetes mellitus is present more often than in normotensive patients. ·

Objective

Physical Examination

The most important physical finding (often the only abnormality) is the elevated systolic blood pressure. It is often so labile as to vary up to 30 mm Hg between determinations on a single visit and as much as or more between visits. A fall in systolic pressure greater than 20 mm Hg on standing is common. Falls of 30 to 40 mm Hg are occasionally seen with or without symptoms. Visible pulsations of rigid "pipestem" brachial arteries may be seen in the upper arm, but these are not highly specific for ISH.

Routine Laboratory Abnormalities

The chest x-ray usually demonstrates an uncoiling and widening of the aorta. It is much more likely to reveal the presence of calcification in the aortic wall than in normotensive individuals of the same age.

The electrocardiogram may indicate left ventricular enlargement (hypertrophy). Abnormalities of other routine laboratory tests must be attributed to concomitant disease.

PLANS

Diagnostic

Differential Diagnosis

Hyperthyroidism, arteriovenous fistulas, complete heart block and marked sinus bradycardia, aortic valvular insufficiency, and the aforementioned hyperkinetic heart syndrome, which is seen only in young males, are included in the differential diagnosis. Common to these diagnoses is the wide pulse pressure with elevated systolic and normal diastolic pressures.

Diagnostic Options

Hyperthyroidism may be difficult to recognize in the elderly so it must be excluded by measures of thyroid function. Aortic valve regurgitation is readily excluded on physical examination, as may be arteriovenous anastomosis if a history of injury or surgery is present or there are findings of increased blood flow to an extremity or regional vascular bed.

Echocardiography, however, is more sensitive than electrocardiography in detecting early left ventricular hypertrophy, with the additional value of providing an estimate of left ventricular function.

Recommended Approach

The diagnosis of ISH is questionable only if the blood pressure criteria are not sustained on multiple visits. Failure to meet criteria on subsequent visits is nearly always due to the systolic pressure falling rather than diastolic pressure rising. It is justifiable to follow such suspected patients for many months before labeling them, but when the systolic pressure consistently exceeds 160 mm Hg and the diastolic pressure is consistently below 90 mm Hg, the diagnosis is established. "Borderline" isolated systolic hypertension, defined as systolic pressure of 140 to 159 mm Hg with a diastolic pressure less than 90 mm Hg, is likely to progress to definite ISH and is itself associated with an increased risk for cardiovascular complications. Ambulatory 24-hour pressures are not more useful than clinic pressures in establishing the diagnosis of ISH.

If the patient has not been under prior medical management, a routine evaluation including chest x-ray, electrocardiogram, urinalysis, hemogram, and blood chemistries (fasting glucose, potassium, uric acid, blood urea nitrogen, and creatinine) would be appropriate and a useful baseline for beginning treatment. Inclusion of an echocardiogram, a more sensitive indicator of left ventricular hypertrophy than the electrocardiogram, may be helpful in arriving at the decision to initiate therapy.

Therapeutic

Therapeutic Options

Systolic blood pressure responds successfully to most classes of antihypertensive agents, including diuretics, adrenergic inhibitors, angiotensin-converting enzyme inhibitors, and calcium channel blockers.

Successful regimens are usually simple, the guiding principles being to begin with smaller than usual dosages and increase them at less frequent intervals than in younger patients. Nonpharmacologic measures should also be considered, but are usually no more successful than in younger patients and those with essential hypertension.

Recommended Approach

Systolic blood pressure can be safely lowered to desirable levels with simple drug regimens (Table 14–4–1). The minimum goal should be to reduce systolic blood pressure to the range 140 to 159 mm Hg. In practice, this means lowering it to less than 160 mm Hg or by 20 mm Hg, whichever results in the lower value. Often, the systolic blood pressure falls (even with low drug dosage) to levels less than 140 mm Hg, and if there are no symptoms or deterioration of renal function (a progressive rise in blood urea nitrogen and creatinine is rare), these lower levels are entirely acceptable. Many studies corroborate the effectiveness of diuretics, with and without beta blockers, in the management of ISH, with most reviewers considering them the regimen of choice.

Individualizing the treatment of hypertension in older patients, based on clinical characteristics and concomitant disease, may be even more important than in younger patients. Angiotensin-converting enzyme inhibitors, for example, not only are effective agents for lowering systolic pressure in the elderly, but also are a particularly good choice in patients with congestive heart failure or diabetes mellitus.

In the absence of concomitant ischemic heart disease with anginal syndrome, ventricular arrhythmias, or diabetes mellitus, treatment should be initiated with a low dose of thiazide or thiazide-like diuretic. Loop diuretics should be avoided. Chlorthalidone (Hygroton) 25 mg, hydrochlorothiazide (Esidrex) 25 mg, or an equivalent other diuretic once daily is the recommended starting regimen. The 12.5-mg dose may actually be the preferred starting dose for many patients (particularly those with only mild elevations of systolic pressure in the range 160–179 mm Hg and a maintenance dose for some. The 12.5-mg dose of chlorthalidone has a similar blood pressure-lowering effect and results in less potassium loss than the 25-mg dosage.

The combination of hydrochlorothiazide (25 mg) and amiloride (Moduretic 5 mg) or triamterene (Dyazide 50 mg or Maxzide 25 or 50 mg) will minimize the potential for hypokalemia.

TABLE 14–4–1. ANTIHYPERTENSIVE AGENTS FOR ISOLATED SYSTOLIC HYPERTENSION

Agent	Usual Dosage Range (total mg/d)
Diuretics	
Chlorthalidone	12.5–50
Hydrochlorothiazide	12.5–50
Indapamide	2.5–5
Potassium-sparing	
Amiloride	5–10
Triamterene	50–150
Angiotensin-converting enzyme inhibitors*	
Benazepril	10–40
Enalapril, Captopril	10–40
Fosinopril	10–40
Lisinopril	5–40
Quinapril	5–50
Adrenergic inhibitors	
Beta blockers	
Atenolol	25–50
Metoprolol†	50–100
Central alpha agonists	
Clonidine†	0.2–0.8
Methyldopa†	500–1000
Peripheral antagonist	
Reserpine	0.1–0.25

*Frequency: one or two times daily.
†Usually given in divided doses twice daily.

For individuals with angina pectoris or certain ventricular arrhythmias and ISH, the dose of beta blocker or calcium channel blocker in use for the heart disease manifestation may be adequate to control the systolic hypertension. If not, the lowest available dose of diuretic should be added.

The initial dose of diuretic should be continued for at least 4 weeks and then doubled. If after a total of 12 weeks of treatment with a diuretic the therapeutic goal for the blood pressure has not been achieved, the addition of a second drug is preferable to increasing the dosage of the diuretic beyond 50 mg. More than 75% of patients respond to the diuretic alone, the majority to the starting dose.

Suitable choices of second-step drugs are found in the angiotensin-converting enzyme inhibitor, calcium channel blocker, and adrenergic inhibitor classes (Table 14–4–1). Examples are enalapril (Vasotec), nifedipine (Procardia), the beta blockers atenolol (Tenormin) and metoprolol (Lopressor), and the rauwolfia alkaloid reserpine (Serpasil). Those effective in a single daily dose are preferred for patient convenience and compliance. These drugs have comparable effectiveness and acceptable side effect profiles.

Central adrenergic inhibitors (e.g., clonidine [Catapres], methyldopa [Aldomet]) are also effective, but their frequent side effect of drowsiness makes them less desirable for use in the elderly. Elderly patients may be more susceptible to volume depletion and more sensitive to sympathetic inhibition than younger patients, hence the principle of "start low and go slow." Drugs that have a propensity to cause orthostatic hypotension such as guanethidine (Ismelin), guanadrel (Hylorel), and prazosin (Minipress) should be avoided.

The principal side effects of diuretics are chemical and include hypokalemia, hyperuricemia, and glucose intolerance. Sexual dysfunction also may occur. Angiotensin-converting enzyme inhibitors are virtually free of unfavorable side effects, except for an annoying cough in some patients and the rare instance of angioneurotic edema. They have the added advantage of metabolic neutrality. The calcium channel blockers are also well tolerated, the most annoying side effect, at least in the elderly, being constipation. They are contraindicated in heart block and "sick sinus" syndrome. The adrenergic inhibitors have more symptomatic side effects, including bradycardia, cold extremities, and insomnia (beta blockers); drowsiness, dry mouth, and fatigue (central inhibitors); and lethargy and nasal congestion (rauwolfia alkaloids). All may be associated with sexual dysfunction. Beta blockers are contraindicated in patients with asthma, congestive heart failure, chronic obstructive pulmonary disease, heart block, and sick sinus syndrome. Rauwolfia alkaloids are contraindicated in patients with a history of depression. Angiotensin-converting enzyme inhibitors are contraindicated in patients with bilateral renal artery stenosis.

FOLLOW-UP

Follow-up visits should be monthly until the therapeutic goal is reached, usually in 3 to 6 months. Once the maintenance schedule of medications is established, in the absence of any adverse drug effects, return visits need be no more frequent than every 3 months. As most elderly patients have ready access to blood pressure measurement at community sites, if the pressure remains controlled, they may need to be seen in the physician's office only at 6- to 12-month intervals unless otherwise dictated by concomitant disease.

The serum potassium and blood urea nitrogen or creatinine levels should be checked 1 month after initiating diuretic therapy, after an increase in dose, and again after reaching the maximum dose. Potassium supplements or sparing agents should be prescribed if serum potassium level falls below 3.2 mEq/L and to all patients concomitantly receiving digitalis. A serum glucose and uric acid determination is usually included in the follow-up battery of tests, but in the absence of known diabetes mellitus or gout, it can be limited to annual follow-up examination.

Patients should be instructed to return for follow-up whenever there is an intercurrent illness, in particular if syncope, chest pain, unusual shortness of breath or weakness, gout, or a transient neurologic deficit should occur. Often a phone call rather than an office visit will suffice to provide patient assurance and to exclude serious problems.

DISCUSSION

Prevalence

The prevalence of ISH in the population aged 60 and over is between 5 and 10%, rising to more than 20% of both sexes over age 80. Isolated systolic hypertension is more common in women than in men and in blacks than in whites. Isolated systolic hypertension is the most common form of hypertension in persons over 70 years of age, and is estimated to affect more than 4 million people in the United States. This number is increasing as the mean age of the population continues to shift upward.

Related Basic Science

Decreased distensibility of the aorta and major vessels due to loss of elasticity is the major factor responsible for the age-related changes in systolic blood pressure leading to ISH. The reduced arterial compliance is accompanied by a smaller but significant increase in peripheral vascular resistance. Associated findings in elderly persons with hypertension may include reduced baroreceptor reflexes, low normal plasma volume, low plasma renin levels, and diminished renal blood flow, but none of these is thought to play a role in the genesis of ISH. These findings do influence the response to treatment and account for the variability in blood pressure noted in untreated patients and the heightened responsiveness to certain antihypertensive agents.

Despite considerable understanding of the pathophysiology of ISH, the reason the condition develops in some persons and not others remains unknown.

Natural History and Its Modification with Treatment

It is clear from actuarial data and from numerous prospective population studies that elevated systolic blood pressure is associated with substantial excess cardiovascular risk, particularly for men. A 6-year prospective study found a sevenfold excess cardiovascular mortality in 72 elderly Californians with ISH as compared with age- and sex-matched controls—excess mortality largely attributable to stroke and myocardial infarction. In the Framingham study, subjects aged 55 to 74 with ISH had a twofold excess risk of death from all causes in men and up to a nearly fivefold excess risk in women compared with normotensive subjects. In another prospective study of all causes of cardiovascular disease mortality in a community of older adults who were followed an average of 6.4 years, men with ISH had the highest age-adjusted death rate from all causes (22%) of all groups. These men were more than three times more likely to die from stroke than normotensive men. It should be noted that ISH is strongly correlated with carotid stenosis. In this study, survival was poorest for men with ISH. Normotensive men and women with ISH had comparable survival. Normotensive women had the best survival (Figure 14–4–1).

The Systolic Hypertension in the Elderly Program (SHEP) demonstrated that ISH can be treated effectively, safely, and at low cost using the low-dose stepped-care approach described here. The treatment program resulted in a highly significant 36% reduction in total stroke incidence. Favorable findings were also demonstrated for coronary heart disease (−27%) and multiple cardiovascular events (−32%).

Studies in Sweden (STOP-Hypertension) and England (MRC Working Party) using primarily diuretics with and without beta blockers experienced similar reductions in cardiovascular complications.

Prevention

No preventive measures are currently available.

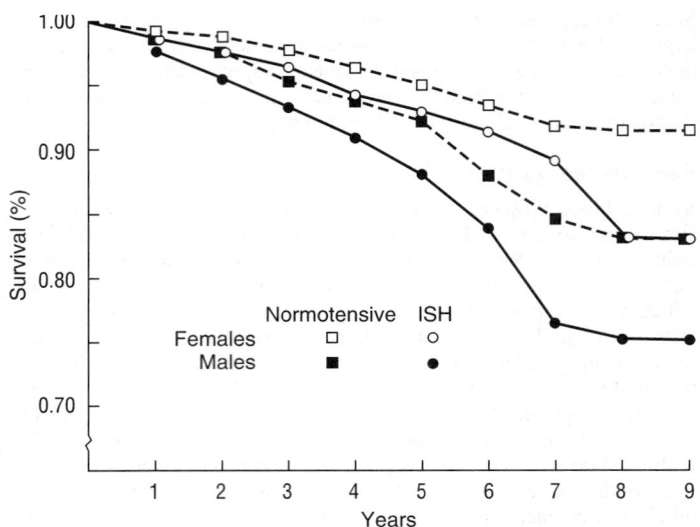

Figure 14–4–1. Survival rates from all causes according to blood pressure at initial visit, adjusted for age, cigarette smoking, diabetes, plasma cholesterol, and obesity. *(Based on data from Garland C, Barrett-Connor E, Suarez L, Criqui MH. Isolated systolic hypertension and mortality after age 60 years. Am J Epidemiol 1983;118:365.)*

Cost Containment

The diagnosis of ISH requires no more than the measurement of blood pressure. It may be necessary to order laboratory tests for hyperthyroidism in some patients, but all other causes of systolic hypertension can be excluded by physical examination. An expensive "workup" is not needed. Diuretics are the primary treatment and are inexpensive. Their combination with a potassium-sparing agent is more expensive and unnecessary for most patients. For the second-step drug, reserpine is the most cost-effective and convenient, and it is as safe as any other.

REFERENCES

Colandrea MA, Friedman GD, Nichaman MZ, Lynd CN. Systolic hypertension in the elderly: An epidemiologic assessment. Circulation 1970;41:239.

Garland C, Barrett-Connor E, Suarez L, Criqui MH. Isolated systolic hypertension and mortality after age 60 years. Am J Epidemiol 1983;118:365.

Hansson L. Future goals for the treatment of hypertension in the elderly. Am J Hypertens 1993;6:40S.

Joint National Committee on Detection, Evaluation and Treatment of High Blood Pressure: The fifth report . . . (JNC-V). Arch Intern Med 1993;153:154.

Kannel WB, Wolf PA, McGee DL, et al. Systolic blood pressure, arterial rigidity, and risk of stroke: The Framingham Study. JAMA 1981;245:1225.

O'Rourke MF. Arterial stiffness, systolic blood pressure and logical treatment of arterial hypertension. Hypertension 1990;15:339.

SHEP Cooperative Research Group. Prevention of stroke by antihypertensive drug treatment in older persons with isolated systolic hypertension. JAMA 1991;265:3255.

SHEP Cooperative Research Group. Implications of the systolic hypertension in the elderly program. Hypertension 1993;21:335.

Renovascular Hypertension

W. Dallas Hall, M.D.

DEFINITION

Renovascular hypertension is a condition where the high blood pressure is due primarily to stenosis of the renal artery. Renovascular hypertension is *not* synonymous with anatomic renal artery stenosis because the latter can often occur in the absence of hypertension.

ETIOLOGY

There are two major causes of renovascular hypertension: atherosclerosis and fibrous dysplasia. The etiology of atherosclerosis and its associated risk factors are discussed in Chapters 15–1 and 15–43 through 15–47.

The etiology of fibrous dysplasia is not known, although at least 10% of cases are hereditary with a dominant pattern of inheritance.

CRITERIA FOR DIAGNOSIS
Suggestive

Seven clinical clues suggest the diagnosis of renovascular hypertension. They are outlined in Table 14–5–1.

Definitive

In clinical terms, the diagnosis is usually made when a suspicious (see Table 14–5–1) patient has high blood pressure, plus 50% or more narrowing of one or both renal arteries, plus elevated renal vein renin levels that lateralize to the stenotic side with unilateral renal artery disease or to the more stenotic (or occluded) side with bilateral renal artery disease.

A definitive diagnosis of renovascular hypertension can be made only after the stenosis is removed by angioplasty or surgery, and the blood pressure is clearly improved or normalized.

CLINICAL MANIFESTATIONS
Subjective

Like essential hypertension, patients with renovascular hypertension are usually asymptomatic unless the hypertension becomes very severe and provokes headache, blurred vision, chest pain, and other symptoms. Hence, symptoms such as edema, exercise intolerance, sleepiness, and cough usually reflect adverse effects of antihypertensive medications, especially when high doses of multiple drug types are needed to control the blood pressure.

Unlike essential hypertension where the blood pressure creeps up slowly each year, patients with renovascular hypertension often give a history of normotension or easily controlled blood pressure prior to an abrupt onset or worsening of hypertension. Symptoms of generalized atherosclerotic disease (angina pectoris, transient ischemic attacks, intermittent claudication) are typical in the older group.

Patients with the autosomal dominant type of fibrous dysplasia often have a striking family history of early-onset hypertension, especially in the mother or sisters.

Objective
Physical Examination

Patients with the fibrous dysplasia type of renovascular hypertension are usually otherwise healthy, nonobese women between the ages of 21 and 49. An upper abdominal bruit that radiates laterally can be detected in about 60% of cases if the clinician listens for more than 30 seconds and peristalsis is not too active. In a young woman, an asymptomatic carotid bruit is an excellent clinical clue to fibrous dysplasia of the renal arteries because the disease can also involve extrarenal arteries (carotid, mesenteric, iliac, etc.) and the abdominal bruits are sometimes heard only intermittently.

Unlike patients with fibrous dysplasia, those with atherosclerotic renovascular hypertension are usually older (50–80) with vascular bruits over the carotid, ophthalmic (over the eyeballs), subclavian (below the midclavicle), aortic (abdominal) or femoral arteries. Abdominal bruits are of less diagnostic value (than in patients with fibrous dysplasia) because the atherosclerotic process often involves other arteries (splenic, mesenteric, etc.). Hypertensive retinopathy and evidence of left ventricular hypertrophy (i.e., a sustained and displaced cardiac apical impulse) are noted more often than in patients with fibrous dysplasia.

Routine Laboratory Abnormalities

Most patients with renovascular hypertension have a normal complete blood count, urinalysis, and chemistry profile. The three most common abnormalities that can occur, however, are hypokalemia, elevated level of serum creatinine, and proteinuria.

Hypokalemia can sometimes be severe and masquerade as primary aldosteronism. It is due to extreme hyperreninemia (and the associated stimulation of aldosterone) and can be easily provoked by aggressive diuretic therapy.

Hypercreatininemia and proteinuria (< 1 g/d) are more common with the atherosclerotic than the fibrous dysplasia type of renovascular disease and usually reflect uncontrolled chronic hypertension with underlying nephrosclerosis. Sudden increases in the level of serum creatinine can be caused by the use of angiotensin-converting enzyme inhibitors in patients with *bilateral* renal artery stenosis or stenosis in a solitary kidney.

Dyslipidemia occurs with the same high frequency as in patients with other atherosclerosis-related end-organ disease.

PLANS
Diagnostic
Differential Diagnosis

Diagnostic evaluation should be reserved for patients in whom there is a moderate to high index of suspicion (see Table 14–5–1) and who are judged to be candidates for intervention if a functional lesion is identified.

Diagnostic Options

A rapid-sequence intravenous pyelogram is normal in about 25% of patients with renovascular hypertension, so the test is too insensitive. A better screening method is the captopril scintiscan, which has a sensitivity and specificity of 90 to 95%. Scintigraphic estimations of glomerular filtration rate demonstrate a decrease in glomerular filtration rate and slowing of the time to peak activity on the affected side

TABLE 14–5–1.   CLINICAL CLUES TO RENOVASCULAR HYPERTENSION

- Abrupt onset of hypertension before age 30 or after age 50
- Resistant hypertension or the abrupt worsening of hypertension
- Systolic abdominal bruit with lateral radiation
- Carotid bruit(s) in a young woman
- Accelerated or malignant hypertension
- Doubling (or more) of serum creatinine level shortly after starting an angiotensin-converting inhibitor.
- Underweight

following oral administration of 25 to 50 mg captopril or intravenous administration of enalapril.

Digital subtraction angiography creates subtraction images of the abdominal arteries. Visualization of the main renal arteries can be achieved in 80% or more of cases. Arterial digital subtraction angiography (DSA) has largely replaced venous digital subtraction angiography because it is more sensitive and specific.

Magnetic resonance angiography of the renal arteries is a noninvasive test that requires no contrast medium. The sensitivity and specificity are thought to be in the range 80 to 85%, but important branch stenoses can be missed. Moreover, most surgeons still require a renal angiogram before intervention.

Once anatomic renal arterial disease has been confirmed, the functional significance of the stenosis should be evaluated with the "renal vein renin ratio," the ratio of plasma renin activity in blood samples obtained from each renal vein. A ratio of 1.5 or greater favoring the stenotic side is abnormal, and about 90% of selected patients respond to technically adequate angioplasty or surgery. It is also desirable that the renin level from the unaffected kidney is "suppressed," that is, the same as or no more than 30% higher than a sample obtained from the inferior vena cava below the renal veins. There are, however, patients who respond to intervention despite nonlateralizing renal vein renin ratios. In addition, the renal vein renin ratio is not as useful in bilateral lesions.

The unstimulated peripheral vein renin activity is often not very useful because of the renin-stimulating or renin-suppressing effects of most antihypertensive drugs required by the patient.

The administration of a single oral dose of 25 to 50 mg captopril 30 to 90 minutes prior to obtaining renal vein renin studies enhances lateralization in patients with unilateral renal artery disease and avoids having to withhold important antihypertensive medications prior to angiography.

Recommended Approach

Once renovascular hypertension is suspected clinically, decide first if the patient is a candidate for surgery or balloon angioplasty if an anatomic and function lesion is identified. If the answer is no, then stop. If the answer is yes, then proceed to captopril scintigraphy unless the clinical clues are so strong that a 5 to 10% false-negative rate is unacceptable, in which case you would proceed to renal angiography even with a negative captopril scan. If the captopril scan is positive, proceed to renal angiography or intraarterial digital subtraction angiography. Continue the preprocedure antihypertensive medications but order either 25 or 50 mg oral captopril on call to the radiology suite.

If the angiogram is negative, the patient does not have renovascular hypertension. If the angiogram is positive, then proceed with the therapeutic options described below.

Therapeutic

Therapeutic Options

The type of renal artery lesion is of major importance in the choice between medical or surgical management. Patients with fibrous dysplasia are likely to benefit from surgery and have a lower operative risk than do patients with atherosclerotic renovascular disease, but balloon angioplasty is generally preferable to medical or surgical treatment because of the excellent results and relatively low risks. In patients with atherosclerotic renal artery disease, medical management is generally preferred because of the lesser yield of surgical cure or improvement and the higher operative risks; however, balloon angioplasty (when the stenosis is not ostial) or surgery may be preferred in selected patients with atherosclerotic renal artery stenosis, generally in the setting where blood pressure cannot be controlled adequately by drug therapy. Revascularization can sometimes lead to improvement in renal function if the kidney on the involved side is not already very small or if the renal failure is not already too advanced (i.e., serum creatinine level above 3–4 mg/dL).

The age of patients is also an important consideration, but a healthy 65-year-old angina-free patient with a serum creatinine of 1.2 mg/dL is probably a better candidate for intervention than is a 44-year-old patient with atherosclerotic renal artery disease, diabetes, angina, claudication, and a serum creatinine of 2.4 mg/dL.

Recommended Approach

If the angiogram is positive and the lesion is appropriate for angioplasty, there are two options. One is to collect renin samples from the low inferior vena cava and left and right renal veins and proceed with the angioplasty. This might be quite appropriate for a young patient with fibrous dysplasia and a high-grade stenosis (and a high pressure gradient across the stenosis) amenable to angioplasty. The second option is to collect the renins and await documentation of lateralization to the stenotic (or more stenotic) side, deciding in the interim whether angioplasty or surgery is the preferred option. This choice might be most appropriate for an older patient with atherosclerotic renal artery stenosis that is bilateral or ostial in location.

Medical therapy must be used in patients who are not candidates for intervention. *If* the stenosis is unilateral, therapy with angiotensin-converting enzyme inhibitors is usually effective and associated with no more than a 10% increase in the level of serum creatinine. Concomitant therapy with loop diuretics is usually necessary if the serum creatinine exceeds 2 mg/dL.

FOLLOW-UP

Patients should be seen again within 2 weeks or less after hospital discharge following balloon angioplasty or surgery. This is because an apparent excellent short-term blood pressure response can occasionally be deceptive in patients who have been sedated, diuresed, or at bed rest. In the initial year after successful intervention, patients should be seen every 3 months or less. In those with recurrence of severe hypertension, the baseline (preintervention) captopril scan and renal vein renin levels are very useful in the interpretation of repeat screening tests to decide if the risk of repeat angiography is justified.

If the decision is made that the risk of surgery or balloon angioplasty is too high and that the patient's hypertension should be managed medically, then the clinician must make every effort to maintain adequate blood pressure control and observe the patient for evidence of renal deterioration. Progressive renal failure due to atherosclerotic renovascular disease may account for 5 to 15% of patients with end-stage renal disease. Serum creatinine levels should be rechecked at least two to four times annually.

DISCUSSION

Prevalence and Incidence

Renovascular hypertension is the most common curable cause of high blood pressure. The prevalence ranges from 2 to 5% of the hypertensive population; it is less common in hypertensive African-Americans.

Related Basic Science

In unilateral renal artery stenosis, the ischemic kidney senses underperfusion. To compensate, it avidly reabsorbs sodium and increases renin (and angiotensin II) production to help raise perfusion pressure; however, despite the efforts of the nonstenotic contralateral kidney to enhance sodium excretion and shut off its own renin production, the elevated angiotensin II level causes intense vasoconstriction, elevated total peripheral resistance, severe hypertension, and other adverse local effects on the kidney and myocardium.

The same physiology occurs with bilateral renal artery stenosis, but there is no compensation available from a more normal kidney. Hence the sodium retention becomes progressive, the total peripheral resistance and blood pressure rise even more, and the patient is susceptible to episodes of pulmonary edema.

Natural History and Its Modification with Treatment

The natural history of patients with renovascular hypertension is an abrupt onset of high blood pressure, followed by initial responsiveness to drugs but subsequent progressive worsening of the levels of blood pressure and relentless resistance to the efficacy of blood pressure-lowering medications. In the worst scenario (i.e., bilateral renal artery stenosis), patients can become refractory to seemingly adequate doses of five or six antihypertensive medications. If the proper diagnosis goes undetected or the appropriate treatment is delayed too long, then the patient can develop a hypertension-associated myocardial infarction or stroke or can progress to end-stage renal disease.

Prevention

There is no known method to prevent the fibrous dysplasia type of renovascular hypertension. Although the occurrence of the atherosclerotic type of renovascular disease is known to be associated with risk factors for atherosclerosis (dyslipidemia, smoking, etc.), there are no studies on control of these risk factors with regard to the incidence or rate of progression of the disease.

Cost Containment

Because 95% of cases of high blood pressure are not due to renovascular hypertension, the greatest cost savings occur by reserving diagnostic evaluation for patients in whom the yield is likely to be high and who, a priori, are potential candidates for balloon angioplasty or surgery. Table 14–5–2 provides rough estimates of the costs (technical plus professional) of a variety of related diagnostic or therapeutic procedures. The relatively high costs must be considered in the context of the long-term risks and the costs of hypertension-related cardiovascular or renal complications associated with uncontrolled hypertension.

Superfluous diagnostic tests should be avoided. For example, the clinician should proceed directly to renal arteriography in a thin 35-year-old woman who has a radiating abdominal bruit and poorly controlled hypertension despite compliance to two medications. The diagnostic yield and potential benefit would be so high that other preliminary screening tests are not indicated. In contrast, diagnostic investigation would be inappropriate for a 75-year-old with a blood pressure of 230/80 mm Hg, a loud abdominal bruit, and past cardiovascular complications such as myocardial infarction and stroke. Although renal artery stenosis would likely be present, it only rarely (if ever) would be the cause of isolated systolic hypertension.

TABLE 14–5–2. RENOVASCULAR HYPERTENSION: COST ESTIMATES OF DIAGNOSTIC AND THERAPEUTIC PROCEDURES

Procedure	Approximate Cost
Antihypertensive medications (annually)	$400–800
Plasma renin activity	75
Split renal vein renin sampling	850
Captopril scintiscan	1,400
Magnetic resonance angiography	1,450
Renal arteriography	1,750
Renal artery angioplasty	3,000
Renal artery surgery	20,000

REFERENCES

Hrick DE, Dunn MJ. Angiotensin-converting enzyme inhibitor induced renal failure: Causes, consequences, and diagnostic uses. J Am Soc Nephrol 1990;1:845.

Mann SJ, Pickering TG. Detection of renovascular hypertension: State of the art: 1992. Ann Intern Med 1992;117:845.

Martinez-Maldonado M. Pathophysiology of renovascular hypertension. Hypertension 1991;17:707.

Rimmer JM, Gennari FJ. Atherosclerotic renovascular disease and progressive renal failure. Ann Intern Med 1993;118:712.

Setaro JF, Chen CC, Hoffer PB, Black HR. Captopril renography in the diagnosis of renal artery stenosis and the prediction of improvement with revascularization: The Yale Vascular Center experience. Am J Hypertens 1991;4:698S.

CHAPTER 14–6

Primary Aldosteronism

Babatunde Olutade, M.D.

DEFINITION

Primary aldosteronism is a syndrome of hypertension, renal potassium wasting, and hypersecretion of aldosterone in the presence of suppressed renin activity.

ETIOLOGY

Primary aldosteronism is due to aldosterone-producing adrenal adenomas in about 65% of cases and bilateral adrenal hyperplasia in about 35%. A familial form is the glucocorticoid-remediable aldosteronism caused by a hereditary defect in an 11β-hydroxylase/aldosterone synthase gene (8q22).

CRITERIA FOR DIAGNOSIS
Suggestive

Most cases due to primary adenoma are diagnosed between the ages of 30 and 50, more frequently in women than men (almost 3:1); however, patients with bilateral hyperplasia are usually older, and men and women are equally affected. The familial type is usually diagnosed in childhood or adolescence and is suggested clinically by a positive family history of hypokalemia and hypertension. Unprovoked hypokalemia with a serum potassium less than 3.5 mEq/L or diuretic-induced hypokalemia with a potassium level less than 3.0 mEq/L and the presence of excessive urinary potassium excretion, hypernatremia, and metabolic alkalosis highly suggest the diagnosis in a hypertensive patient.

Definitive

Definitive diagnosis is made by demonstrating autonomous overproduction of aldosterone (i.e., an elevated plasma aldosterone that does not suppress with adequate volume expansion) and a low plasma renin activity.

CLINICAL MANIFESTATIONS
Subjective

Patients usually have no symptoms specific for primary aldosteronism; however, they often present with symptoms of hypokalemia including nocturia, polyuria, paresthesia, proximal muscle weakness, and fatigue. Symptoms may be precipitated by diuretic use. Patients are hypertensive and may have a history of difficulty with control of their blood pressure. A family history of hypertension with or without hypokalemia in early childhood or adolescence suggests glucocorticoid-remediable aldosteronism.

Objective
Physical Examination

The physical examination is usually remarkable only for hypertension, which is usually mild or moderate. Severe hypertension can occur, but accelerated or malignant hypertension is rare. Proximal muscle weakness, postural decreases in blood pressure without compensatory tachycardia, and decreased or absent deep tendon reflexes may be seen in those with severe hypokalemia.

Routine Laboratory Abnormalities

The precipitation of severe hypokalemia (serum K$^+$ < 3.0 mEq/L) by diuretic therapy is suggestive. Hypokalemia is usually present and can be severe. It is typically associated with metabolic alkalosis, hypomagnesemia, and mild hypernatremia.

Hyperglycemia is sometimes seen secondary to decreased pancreatic insulin secretion as a result of hypokalemia. Hypokalemia can also predispose to rhabdomyolysis. The electrocardiogram usually shows changes consistent with hypokalemia.

PLANS
Diagnostic
Differential Diagnosis

Excess of mineralocorticoids other than aldosterone can also cause hypertension and hypokalemia. Table 14–6–1 lists many of these conditions and the specific mineralocorticoid in excess.

Secondary aldosteronism often occurs with renovascular hypertension or malignant hypertension, but plasma renin activity is high rather than low. Bartter's syndrome and Gitelman's syndrome are rare disorders associated with hypokalemia and marked hyperaldosteronism but normal blood pressure. Liddle's syndrome is a familial disorder that presents with hypertension, hypokalemia, and metabolic alkalosis but subnormal aldosterone secretion. Its clinical presentation may mimic primary aldosteronism.

Diagnostic Options

Hypokalemia and low plasma renin activity are important clues to primary aldosteronism, but both have low specificity when used as screening tests. Hypokalemia and inappropriate urinary potassium excretion (UK$^+$V > 30 mEq/24 h when serum K$^+$ < 3.5 mEq/L) also suggest mineralocorticoid hypertension. Urinary potassium excretion is low (UK$^+$V < 30 mEq/24 h) with hypokalemia due to diuretics or gastrointestinal loss. A random, ambulatory plasma renin activity is usually suppressed.

The ratio of plasma aldosterone concentration to plasma renin activity may be helpful in diagnosis. Most cases of untreated primary aldosteronism have a ratio of plasma aldosterone (ng/dL) to plasma renin activity (ng/mL/h) greater than 20, whereas the ratio is less than 10 in patients with essential hypertension.

The diagnosis of primary aldosteronism is confirmed by demonstrat-

ing autonomous secretion of aldosterone and suppressed renin activity. Autonomous secretion is demonstrated by lack of suppression of aldosterone following volume expansion. Several methods have been used to assess suppressibility. These include volume expansion by the administration of deoxycorticosterone or fludrocortisone, oral salt loads, or intravenous saline. I recommend the intravenous saline method. Usually the patient has been off medications for 24 hours or longer. Blood is drawn for baseline plasma renin activity, plasma aldosterone, and serum potassium after being supine for at least 20 minutes. Two liters of normal saline is given intravenously over 4 hours, with a blood pressure check every hour. Plasma renin activity, plasma aldosterone, and serum potassium are repeated at the end of the 4-hour infusion. A positive test is a lack of aldosterone suppression, with plasma aldosterone of 10 ng/dL or higher.

In patients suspected of having glucocorticoid-remediable aldosteronism, elevated 24-hour urine 18-hydroxycortisol and 18-oxotetrahydrocortisol levels are diagnostic. This test may replace dexamethasone suppression of aldosterone in the workup of these patients. Increased urinary excretion of these steroids is more specific for the diagnosis of glucocorticoid-remediable aldosteronism.

Once the diagnosis of primary aldosteronism is established, the next step is to differentiate between adrenal adenoma and adrenal hyperplasia, and localize the tumor. The diagnostic options useful in differentiating between adrenal adenoma and hyperplasia are outlined in Table 14–6–2.

Plasma aldosterone concentration tends to decrease with standing in patients with adrenal adenoma, whereas it increases in patients with bilateral adrenal hyperplasia. During head-out water immersion, plasma aldosterone and plasma renin activity levels tend not to change in patients with adenoma but decrease in patients with hyperplasia. Overnight recumbent plasma 18-hydroxycorticosterone levels greater than 100 ng/dL are highly suggestive of adenoma. Metoclopramide and cyproheptadine tests are not very useful.

Initial localization of the adrenal tumor is usually achieved by a computed tomography (CT) scan or magnetic resonance imaging (MRI) of the adrenal. One comparative study of CT and MRI of adrenal adenomas showed a better diagnostic accuracy with MRI (81% MRI versus 69% CT scan). The sensitivity and specificity were 100 and 64%, respectively, for MRI and 62 and 77%, respectively, for CT scan. A sensitive localization technique is adrenal vein sampling (90% accuracy) for the measurement of aldosterone. Samples are obtained from both left and right adrenal veins and the low inferior vena cava. Concurrent documentation of adrenal vein epinephrine levels greater than 1500 pg/mL is necessary to confirm that the sample was indeed from the adrenal vein. This is important because the right adrenal vein is often difficult to localize and cannulate. The aldosterone level in venous blood from an adrenal gland with an adenoma is usually increased tenfold or more above that from the contralateral uninvolved gland. Bilateral and unsuppressed (relative to the level in the inferior vena cava) elevation of aldosterone levels is suggestive of bilateral hyperplasia, even when the imaging procedures suggest unilateral disease.

TABLE 14–6–1. CAUSES OF MINERALOCORTICOID EXCESS AND HYPERTENSION

Primary aldosteronism
  Aldosterone-producing adenoma
  Bilateral (idiopathic) adrenal hyperplasia
  Unilateral (primary) adrenal hyperplasia
Adrenal carcinomas
Excess of mineralocorticoids other than aldosterone
  Congenital adrenal hyperplasia
    11β-Hydroxylase deficiency
    17α-Hydroxylase deficiency
  Cushing's syndrome
Dexamethasone-suppressible forms of mineralocorticoid excess
  Glucocorticoid-remediable aldosteronism
  Apparent mineralocorticoid excess
    11β-Hydroxysteroid dehydrogenase deficiency (hereditary)
    Excessive licorice ingestion (active ingredient glycyrrhetinic acid, inhibits 11β-hydroxysteroid dehydrogenase)
    Chewing tobacco
    Carbenoxolone (derivative of glycyrrhizic acid, inhibits 11β-hydroxysteroid dehydrogenase and reductase)
Secondary aldosteronism
  Hypertensive
    Renovascular hypertension
    Malignant hypertension
  Normotensive
    Bartter's syndrome
    Gitelman's syndrome

TABLE 14–6–2. DIFFERENTIATING BETWEEN ADRENAL ADENOMA AND BILATERAL ADRENAL HYPERPLASIA

Test	Adrenal Adenoma	Bilateral Hyperplasia
Plasma aldosterone (PA)	High	Less high
Plasma renin activity (PRA)	↓ (90%)	↓ (90%)
Post 2 L normal saline over 4 hours (PA)	> 8–10 ng/dL	> 8–10 ng/dL
Postural change in PA	Decreases	Increases
Plasma 18-hydroxycorticosterone	> 100 ng/dL	< 40 ng/dL
Head-out water immersion (PA and PRA)	No change	Decrease
Adrenal iodo-cholesterol scan	Unilateral uptake	Bilateral uptake
Adrenal CT scan and MRI	Unilateral mass	Bilateral, full, enlarged
Adrenal vein aldosterone	↑ on affected side	↑ in both glands

Recommended Approach

Suspect primary aldosteronism in a hypertensive patient with unprovoked hypokalemia or diuretic-induced severe hypokalemia that is difficult to replete. Perform the saline suppression test as described above as a screening test. If positive (plasma aldosterone postinfusion > 10 ng/dL), obtain an abdominal CT scan or MRI. If there is definite unilateral adenoma, proceed to recommend adrenalectomy in patients who are surgical candidates. If CT is inconclusive or shows possible bilateral adrenal enlargement, proceed with adrenal vein sampling. Obtain adrenal vein aldosterone and epinephrine from both adrenal veins and the low inferior vena cava.

Adolescents with hypertension and hypokalemia should be screened for glucocorticoid-remediable aldosteronism by obtaining 24-hour urine 18-hydroxycortisol and 18-oxotetrahydrocortisol levels. If the measurement of these compounds is not available, dexamethasone, given in a dose of 0.5 mg four times daily for 7 to 10 days, will normalize blood pressure and the elevated aldosterone.

Therapeutic

Therapeutic Options

Surgical treatment is the therapy of choice for patients with adrenal adenoma. Unilateral adrenalectomy of the affected gland is often curative, although some patients have only improvement because of underlying essential hypertension. Preoperatively, the patient should be treated with spironolactone 200 to 400 mg a day for 4 to 6 weeks as both a therapeutic and further diagnostic agent. Response to spironolactone usually predicts a good result from surgery. Hypokalemia should be corrected prior to surgery.

For patients with bilateral adrenal hyperplasia, medical therapy with spironolactone in doses of 100 to 200 mg twice daily is the treatment of choice. Medical therapy should also be considered for patients with adenoma who are unable or unwilling to undergo surgery and in patients with bilateral adrenal adenoma who may require bilateral adrenalectomy.

Adverse effects of spironolactone, especially frequent with high doses, include gastrointestinal symptoms, breast tenderness, gynecomastia, menstrual irregularities, and impotence. Addition of a thiazide diuretic such as hydrochlorothiazide 12.5 to 50 mg/d to lower doses of spironolactone may allow control of blood pressure with reduced adverse effects. Other potassium-sparing diuretics such as triamterene 50 to 150 mg/d and amiloride 10 to 20 mg/d can be used; however, they are less effective than spironolactone. Calcium channel blockers are additional alternatives because intracellular calcium is necessary for synthesis of aldosterone.

For patients with glucocorticoid-remediable aldosteronism, minimum effective doses of prednisone are recommended. This usually reduces the aldosterone level and lowers the blood pressure. It is important to watch for evidence of glucocorticoid excess.

Recommended Approach

For patients with adenoma, surgical removal is the treatment of choice. Preoperatively, treatment with spironolactone up to 200 mg twice a day for 4 to 6 weeks is indicated.

For patients with bilateral adrenal hyperplasia, use spironolactone therapy. For patients unwilling or unable to undergo surgery, and those who may otherwise require bilateral adrenalectomy, medical therapy is recommended, whatever the adrenal pathology. Patients with glucocorticoid-remediable aldosteronism may benefit from the smallest effective dose of a short-acting glucocorticoid such as prednisone.

FOLLOW-UP

Following surgery, some patients develop a transient state of hypoaldosteronism and hyperkalemia. It is thus recommended not to routinely administer potassium supplements postoperatively. Other patients can occasionally present with symptomatic hypotension up to a year later, with low plasma cortisol, adrenaline, and aldosterone levels. Schedule an initial postoperative visit within 4 to 6 weeks. If the patient remains normotensive, schedule return visits every 3 to 4 months for the first

year. Any signs of adrenal insufficiency should be evaluated, and supplemental glucocorticoids or mineralocorticoids given if necessary.

Patients on medical therapy should be seen at 2- to 4-week intervals initially, adjusting therapy until blood pressure and hypokalemia are adequately controlled. Subsequently, schedule 3- to 4-month follow-up visits. Spironolactone dosages may be gradually decreased as blood pressure control improves.

DISCUSSION
Prevalence

Primary aldosteronism is an uncommon form of secondary hypertension. It is found in 0.5% or less of hypertensives. Most patients are adults 30 to 50 years of age. Aldosterone-producing adenomas are more common in women. Bilateral adrenal hyperplasia shows no gender difference.

Related Basic Science

Physiologic Derangement

Primary aldosteronism invariably results in hypertension and hypokalemia from autonomous aldosterone production. The increased aldosterone results in increased sodium reabsorption in the kidney. This results in increased total body and exchangeable sodium and expansion of the plasma volume. After a certain amount of volume expansion, increases in renal perfusion pressure and atrial natriuretic factor inhibit further sodium reabsorption so that patients "escape" from progressive sodium reabsorption despite increased aldosterone secretion. The expanded plasma volume is associated with increased cardiac output initially, but total peripheral resistance increases long term. The sodium reabsorption in the distal tubules is in exchange for potassium secretion, resulting in increased urinary potassium loss and hypokalemia. Expanded plasma volume and high aldosterone production both suppress renin production. Other important actions of aldosterone include increased sodium influx into vascular smooth muscle, increase in the number of cardiac calcium channels, and enhancement of vasopressin effects in the collecting tubules. Thus, the hypertension in primary aldosteronism is volume dependent, and the patients have increased sodium stores and reduced potassium stores.

The major types of primary aldosteronism are aldosterone-producing adenoma (65%); bilateral hyperplasia, also known as idiopathic hyperaldosteronism (30%); and unilateral (primary) hyperplasia (5%). Aldosterone-producing adrenal carcinomas are a rare cause of primary aldosteronism, usually suspected when the CT scan shows a mass of 6 cm or more in size. For unknown reasons, there appears to be a high prevalence of renal cysts in patients with primary aldosteronism.

Aldosterone-producing adenomas are tumors with histologic features of both the zona glomerulosa and zona fasciculata. They produce large quantities of aldosterone and 18-hydroxycorticosterone. They are usually associated with higher levels of plasma aldosterone, more pronounced hypokalemia, and hyporeninemia than bilateral hyperplasia. They are usually small, most less than 3 cm in diameter. Bilateral hyperplasia usually affects the zona glomerulosa, showing focal or diffuse hyperplasia, with micronodular and/or macronodular lesions. It causes less severe laboratory abnormalities. Unilateral (primary) hyperplasia has clinical and laboratory characteristics of an aldosterone-producing adenoma.

Ectopic aldosterone-producing tumors are reported in the kidney and the ovary. Primary aldosteronism also has been reported in association with primary hyperparathyroidism and the multiple endocrine neoplasia type I syndrome.

Apparent mineralocorticoid excess is a rare syndrome of hypertension with hypokalemia, suppressed plasma renin activity, and low aldosterone. Clinical features are hypertension, short stature, failure to thrive, polyuria, and polydipsia. The hereditary form is a result of 11β-hydroxysteroid dehydrogenase deficiency, which causes an impaired conversion of cortisol to the inactive cortisone, resulting in physiologic levels of cortisol acting on mineralocorticoid receptors. Characteristically, there is increased urinary excretion of cortisol compared with cortisone metabolites. Licorice (active ingredient glycyrrhetinic acid) inhibits 11β-hydroxysteroid dehydrogenase, resulting in a similar clinical syndrome. A type II of the apparent mineralocorticoid excess syndrome has been reported. It is associated with impairment of both dehydrogenase and reductase functions of 11β-hydroxysteroid dehydrogenase. This is identical to the action of carbenoxolone (a therapy for peptic ulcer disease), which produces a similar clinical picture.

Genetics

A genetic form of hyperaldosteronism is the glucocorticoid-remediable aldosteronism. It is rare, familial, and inherited in an autosomal dominant pattern. Glucocorticoid-remediable aldosteronism is secondary to chimeric gene duplication in which the 11β-hydroxylase promoter is fused to the aldosterone synthase coding sequence, resulting in expression of aldosterone synthase in the zona fasciculata, where it is regulated by adrenocorticotropic hormone.

The onset of hypertension is usually during early childhood or adolescence. Glucocorticoid-remediable aldosteronism has typical features of primary aldosteronism, but the clinical and laboratory abnormalities are reversed with the administration of dexamethasone. A characteristic finding is the urinary excretion of large amounts of 18-hydroxycortisol and 18-oxotetrahydrocortisol. The histology often shows bilateral adrenal hyperplasia, especially of the zona fasciculata, with atrophy of zona glomerulosa.

Natural History and Its Modification with Treatment

Hypertension in patients with primary aldosteronism can be very severe. One study in the United Kingdom showed that 23% of 136 patients with primary aldosteronism developed vascular complications including stroke, angina pectoris, myocardial infarction, intermittent claudication, and dissecting aortic aneurysm over a follow-up period of 5.9 years. Others have also reported significant renal damage.

Prevention

There are no known means of preventing primary aldosteronism.

Cost Containment

Primary aldosteronism occurs in no more than 1 in 250 hypertensive patients. Extensive investigations for primary aldosteronism should be reserved for patients in whom the diagnostic yield is likely to be high (i.e., mainly patients with unprovoked hypokalemia or those with severe diuretic-induced hypokalemia that is difficult to replete).

REFERENCES

Arteaga E, Klein R, Biglieri EG. Use of the saline infusion test to diagnose the cause of primary aldosteronism. Am J Med 1985;70:722.

Beevers DG, Brown JJ, Ferris JB, et al. Renal abnormalities and vascular complications in primary aldosteronism: Evidence of tertiary hyperaldosteronism. Q J Med 1976;45:401.

Biglieri EG. Spectrum of mineralocorticoid hypertension. Hypertension 1991;17:251.

Conn JW. Primary aldosteronism: A clinical entity. Trans Assoc Am Physicians 1955;68:215.

Dluhy RG, Lifton RP. Glucocorticoid remediable aldosteronism. Endocrinol Metab Clin North Am 1994;23:285.

Weinberger MH, Fineberg NS. The diagnosis of primary aldosteronism and separation of two major subtypes. Arch Intern Med 1993;153:2125.

CHAPTER 14–7

Renoparenchymal Hypertension

W. Dallas Hall, M.D.

DEFINITION

Renoparenchymal hypertension is present when hypertension accompanies primary renal disease.

ETIOLOGY

The etiology of the hypertension is usually volume expansion due to the inability of the diseased kidney to excrete salt and water adequately. The etiology of the primary renal disease may be hereditary (e.g., polycystic kidney disease), anatomic (e.g., obstructive uropathy with pyelonephritis), or immunologic (e.g., chronic glomerulonephritis).

CRITERIA FOR DIAGNOSIS

Suggestive

The possibility of renoparenchymal hypertension is suggested by an abnormal urine sediment or proteinuria of 3+ or more in a patient with hypertension.

Definitive

Hypertension is confirmed by a systolic blood pressure of 140 mm Hg or more or a diastolic blood pressure of 90 mm Hg or more on three consecutive occasions. Primary renal disease is confirmed when an abnormal urinalysis and elevated level of serum creatinine are accompanied by anatomic defects on the intravenous pyelogram or renal ultrasound.

CLINICAL MANIFESTATIONS

Subjective

The history taken from patients with renoparenchymal hypertension ordinarily gives little or no hint of prior renal disease. Patients with chronic pyelonephritis or interstitial nephritis, however, may have long-standing nocturia, repeated urinary tract infections, intermittent flank pain, stones, analgesic abuse, or previous urinary tract surgery. Those with chronic glomerulonephritis may remember recurrent tonsillitis or "strep throats" during childhood, intermittent edema of the legs, or albuminuria detected at the time of a camp, military, or insurance examination. Patients with polycystic kidney disease may have a past history of intermittent gross hematuria and, because adult polycystic kidney disease is inherited as an autosomal dominant trait, a strong family history of renal disease. Patients with renal involvement from collagen-vascular diseases are usually symptomatic (arthralgia, rash, and so forth) by the time that hypertension is documented. Any of the above varieties of primary renal disease can progress to chronic renal failure with fatigue, anorexia, nausea, and vomiting.

Objective

Physical Examination

The physical examination is typically normal except for elevation of blood pressure, funduscopic arterial narrowing or arteriovenous nicking, and, often, left ventricular hypertrophy. If renal failure is advanced and chronic, however, examination can reveal pallor, muscle wasting, asterixis, exudative retinopathy, signs of congestive heart failure, pericarditis, and Muehrcke's lines or half-and-half nails.

Routine Laboratory Abnormalities

The urinalysis is abnormal in approximately 90% of patients with hypertension secondary to renoparenchymal disease, whereas it is relatively unimpressive in patients with renal disease secondary to hypertension (nephrosclerosis). Microscopic hematuria, persistent proteinuria, and coarse granular or red blood cell casts are typical of glomerular diseases, whereas pyuria, bacteriuria, and white blood cell casts are typical of pyelonephritis and other interstitial diseases.

The concentrations of serum urea nitrogen and creatinine are not useful for differentiating whether the hypertension is due to primary renal disease (renoparenchymal hypertension) or whether the renal disease is secondary to the hypertension (nephrosclerosis), because azotemia and creatininemia occur characteristically with both disorders. Hyperchloremic acidosis provides a clue to the presence of interstitial renal disease.

PLANS
Diagnostic
Differential Diagnosis

The five major diagnostic possibilities for renoparenchymal hypertension are listed in Table 14–7–1.

Diagnostic Options

The diagnostic options are given in Table 14–7–1.

Recommended Approach

Renal ultrasonography is the recommended initial approach in hypertensive patients with an abnormal urine sediment or proteinuria of 3+ or more. Patients with significant proteinuria should also have a 24-hour urine collection for protein and creatinine, a fasting blood glucose, a serum complement level, and an antinuclear antibody (ANA) titer.

Therapeutic
Therapeutic Options

Chronic glomerulonephritis includes a variety of immunologic disorders that are primarily of unknown etiology. Only a few respond to corticosteroid or other immunosuppressive therapy. Chronic pyelonephritis usually results from an anatomic abnormality of the upper or lower urinary tract, and various procedures (cystoscopy, intravenous pyelography, retrograde pyelography, urethrography, voiding cystogram, etc.) should be considered to ensure that there is no residual deformity that could be treated surgically. When no obstructive disease is present, chronic antimicrobial therapy may be effective for the prevention of recurrent bacteriuria.

Diabetic nephropathy is one of the most progressive of the primary renal diseases. The lower urinary tract should be investigated for any treatable condition such as prostatic hypertrophy, periurethral duct abscesses, and autonomic bladder dysfunction. The urine should be examined frequently for signs of urinary tract infection that can be treated. Papillary necrosis or renal lithiasis is suggested whenever flank pain and hematuria occur together. Lowering of the blood pressure, especially with the use of angiotensin-converting enzyme inhibitors in patients with a serum creatinine level below 2.6 mg/dL, slows the progression of diabetic nephropathy. Plans for chronic dialysis therapy should begin when the serum creatinine concentration reaches 5 to 7 mg/dL.

Polycystic kidney disease is a slowly progressive disorder that is not very amenable to therapy. Patency of the ureters should be considered with each episode of gross hematuria. Hypertension is usually present and must be treated. Plans for chronic dialysis or renal transplantation should begin when the serum creatinine concentration reaches 7 to 10 mg/dL.

Recommended Approach

Certain considerations apply to the selection of antihypertensive drugs for the patient with renal failure. First and foremost is that diuretic therapy should be used aggressively because the hypertension of renal failure is classically responsive to volume depletion. Thiazide and thiazide-like diuretics (with the exception of metolazone) are relatively ineffective when the glomerular filtration rate is reduced below 20 to 30 mL per minute. Hence it is usually necessary to use a loop diuretic such as furosemide (Lasix) or bumetanide (Bumex) to induce a significant natriuresis in patients who have serum creatinine concentrations of 2.0 mg/dL or higher. The risk of ototoxicity from higher doses of furosemide, however, is increased in patients with renal failure. Potassium-sparing diuretics are contraindicated in patients with any significant degree of renal failure.

Vasodilators are effective antipressor agents in patients with renal insufficiency. Hydralazine (Apresoline) can be used in usual doses without undue toxicity despite a twofold or more increase in the plasma half-life when the creatinine clearance is in the range 6 to 40 mL per minute. The relative preservation of renal blood flow is a potential advantage of hydralazine. Minoxidil (Loniten) is a potent vasodilator that is effective in reducing the blood pressure of patients with renal failure and hypertension that is resistant to the usual therapeutic efforts. Major side effects, particularly in patients with renal failure, include volume retention and pericarditis. Minoxidil is partially removed during hemodialysis.

Beta blockers (e.g., propranolol in doses of 160–480 mg/d) have been used effectively as the sole antihypertensive agent to control blood pressure in hypertensive patients on chronic hemodialysis. In general, minimal or no adjustment of the usual dosage regimen is necessary in patients with renal failure, although nadolol (Corgard) has a long plasma half-life and is excreted primarily by the kidneys such that the dosage interval approaches 48 hours as the creatinine clearance decreases to 10 mL per minute or less.

Clonidine is a centrally acting sympatholytic agent that is also effective for blood pressure control in many patients with renal failure. Because the plasma half-life of clonidine increases as the creatinine clearance falls, it can be administered in a once-daily dosage in patients with advanced renal failure or receiving maintenance hemodialysis. The hemodialysance of clonidine (27–48 mL per minute) is low enough that postdialysis rebound hypertension has not been reported, and no significant alteration of the dosage is necessary.

Angiotensin-converting enzyme (ACE) inhibitors are effective antihypertensive agents in many patients with chronic renal failure; however, the half-life of most of these compounds is prolonged such that

TABLE 14–7–1. RENOPARENCHYMAL HYPERTENSION

Diagnostic Possibility	Diagnostic Options
Nephrosclerosis	Urinalysis is usually negative but occasionally shows 1+ or 2+ proteinuria, with hyaline or fine granular casts. Intravenous pyelography (IVP) or renal ultrasonography (US) shows symmetric kidneys of low-normal or reduced size.
Chronic glomerulonephritis	Urinalysis has 3+ to 4+ proteinuria with hematuria and granular or red blood cell casts. IVP or US shows small and symmetric kidneys. Serum complement is reduced in some cases.
Chronic pyelonephritis	Urinalysis has pyuria, bacteriuria, and white blood cell casts. IVP or US shows small, asymmetric, or atrophic kidneys. Hyperchloremic acidosis is usually present.
Diabetic nephropathy	Urinalysis has 3+ to 4+ proteinuria. Pyuria, bacteriuria, and white blood cell casts are frequent, but hematuria is unusual without superimposed cystitis, renal infarction, or papillary necrosis. IVP or US shows kidneys that are usually symmetric and normal or slightly reduced in size.
Polycystic kidney disease	Urinalysis has intermittent gross or microscopic hematuria. IVP or US shows enlarged kidneys with large, multiple cysts.

doses should be decreased by about 50% if the serum creatinine is 2.5 to 3.0 mg/dL or more. Adverse effects include hyperkalemia, which limits the use of ACE inhibitors in more advanced cases of renal failure. Angioneurotic edema has been reported with the concurrent use of ACE inhibitors and polyacrylonitrile dialyzers. Postdialysis orthostatic hypotension can become exaggerated during therapy with converting enzyme inhibitors. As mentioned previously, ACE inhibitor therapy has been documented to slow the progression of renal disease in patients with diabetic nephropathy and a serum creatinine level below 2.6 mg/dL.

Calcium channel blockers, especially the dihydropyridines, are also very useful for the control of hypertension in patients with renal failure. Initial oral doses or nifedipine (Procardia) should not exceed 10 mg.

FOLLOW-UP

The guidelines for follow-up of patients with hypertension due to renoparenchymal disease are basically the same as those for patients with uncomplicated hypertension. When blood pressure is controlled, return appointments are generally made at intervals of 2 to 4 months, whereas more frequent appointments are indicated when blood pressure is uncontrolled or when renal failure is more advanced.

DISCUSSION
Prevalence and Incidence

Renovascular hypertension and renoparenchymal hypertension are the two most common secondary causes of hypertension, accounting for a total of 5 to 10% of all cases of hypertension.

Related Basic Science

In early-stage renal failure, prior to the development of anemia, hypertension is characterized by a high cardiac output and a relatively normal total peripheral resistance, reminiscent of the hemodynamic profile of early-stage hypertension in the absence of renal failure. Elevated blood volume and a significant increase in total body exchangeable sodium correlate directly with blood pressure in patients with early renoparenchymal hypertension. The volume expansion of renoparenchymal hypertension contrasts with the volume reduction characteristic of essential hypertension without renal failure.

In patients with end-stage renal disease, the physiology of hypertension includes an increase in both cardiac output and total peripheral resistance. The cardiac output returns toward normal if the anemia is corrected, yet hypertension and the increase in total peripheral resistance persist. Elevated levels of plasma renin, angiotensin II, and catecholamines undoubtedly contribute to vasoconstriction and an increase in the total peripheral resistance of some patients. Moreover, if bilateral nephrectomy is done, total peripheral resistance decreases in most patients. The hypertension of end-stage renal disease, however, is usually volume dependent, so that the blood pressure of 90% of patients can be controlled with appropriate regulation of volume.

Del Greco et al. (1967) compared the peripheral venous renin activity of 33 patients with essential hypertension and 30 patients with a wide variety of relatively advanced parenchymal renal diseases. The average renin activity of 2.0 ng/mL per hour in the group with renal disease was significantly higher than that of 0.5 ng/mL per hour in the group with essential hypertension. These levels of plasma renin activity, however, were within their normal limits in 17 of the 30 patients (57%) with advanced renal disease, including 12 of 18 patients with chronic glomerulonephritis and 4 of 5 patients with chronic pyelonephritis. Hence, absolute elevation of the peripheral venous renin activity occurs in some cases, but is not typical of the hypertension associated with either the glomerular or interstitial varieties of chronic parenchymal renal disease. Others have found no significant difference between the supine, unstimulated peripheral renin activities of hypertensive and normotensive patients with early-stage renal failure due to parenchymal kidney disease.

Hypertension occurs in most patients with end-stage renal disease. The majority of those with normal blood pressure have diseases that involve primarily tubular or interstitial structures, whereas most with ele-

vated blood pressure have diseases that involve primarily the glomeruli or arterioles.

Impaired renal function is not a necessary prerequisite for the development of hypertension in patients with parenchymal renal disease. For example, elevated blood pressure occurs in most patients with polycystic kidney disease at a time when their serum creatinine is normal. Blood pressure elevation in the early stages of renal parenchymal disease is also a relatively common feature of diabetic nephropathy and the various types of glomerulonephritis.

Natural History and It Modification with Treatment

The natural history of renoparenchymal hypertension is that it becomes more severe and more difficult to manage as renal failure worsens. This is likely related to the development of a progressive increase in the total peripheral resistance and a decrease in the efficacy of the usual diuretic therapy to counteract incremental salt and water retention. When renal failure is advanced to such a point that no diuretic program works, the hypertension becomes resistant to all therapeutic efforts other than dialysis. Following the institution of maintenance dialysis, however, many of these same patients become normotensive and require only low-dose or no antihypertensive drugs.

Prevention

The only means available to prevent renoparenchymal hypertension is to prevent development of the primary renal disease. Avoidance of the inordinate use of phenacetin-containing analgesic mixtures should contribute to the prevention of analgesic nephropathy. A decrease in the occurrence of this disease has been noted in countries that have instituted procedures to reduce easy access to analgesic compounds containing phenacetin.

Genetic counseling is recommended for adults with polycystic kidney disease or other renal disorders with an autosomal dominant (type I renal tubular acidosis and hereditary osteoonychodystrophy) or X-linked (Alport's syndrome and Fabry's disease) pattern of inheritance, with a 50% chance of disease in the offspring.

Early and adequate treatment of streptococcal infections of the throat and skin is important in the prevention of poststreptococcal glomerulonephritis.

At least three methods may help prevent the occurrence of renal failure from obstructive disease: early detection and investigation of lower urinary tract symptoms, pursuit of the etiology of recurrent urinary tract infections, and chemical analysis of renal stones to determine if specific measures (in addition to high fluid intake) may help to reduce the risk of future stones. Alkalinization of the urine is generally indicated for patients with uric acid or cystine stones; thiazide therapy may be prescribed for patients with stones associated with idiopathic hypercalciuria.

For patients with diabetes mellitus, long-term control and careful regulation of the blood glucose concentration is recommended. ACE inhibitors usually reduce micro- or macroproteinuria and retard the progression of renal disease if the serum creatinine is below 2.6 mg/dL. For patients with chronic gout, control of the serum uric acid, reduction of the total body uric acid pool and urinary uric acid excretion, and alkalinization of the urine in the event of urate stones are generally recommended.

Once renal disease and renoparenchymal hypertension have developed, vigorous control of the blood pressure and dietary protein restriction are appropriate for the prevention of known complications of hypertension, such as congestive heart failure and stroke. In some cases, these measures also slow the progression of chronic renal failure.

Cost Containment

The hypertension associated with chronic renoparenchymal disease is typically volume dependent, and the appropriate use of diuretic therapy (or dialysis ultrafiltration) often saves both physician time and patient costs relative to use of the more expensive antihypertensive drugs.

The greatest cost savings, however, would be accomplished by reducing the number of patients who develop end-stage renal failure requiring chronic dialysis or renal transplantation. The best current recommendations include tight control of the blood pressure and the use of the previously listed preventive and dietary measures.

REFERENCES

Bennet WM. Guide to drug dosage in renal failure. Clin Pharmacokinet 1988;15:326.

Del Greco F, Simon NM, Goodman S, Roguska J. Plasma renin activity in primary and secondary hypertension. Medicine 1967;46:475.

Hall WD. Renal issues in the management of hypertension. Am J Hypertens 1993;6:245S.

Klahr S, Levey AS, Beck GJ, et al. The effects of dietary protein restriction and blood-pressure control on the progression of chronic renal disease. N Engl J Med 1994;330:877.

Lewis EJ, Hunsicker LG, Bain RP, Rohde RD for the Collaborative Study Group. The effect of angiotensin-converting-enzyme inhibition on diabetic nephropathy. N Engl J Med 1993;329:1456.

National High Blood Pressure Education Program. National High Blood Pressure Education Program working group report on hypertension and chronic renal failure. Arch Intern Med 1991;151:1280.

Zucchelli P, Zuccala A. Pharmacological treatment of renal parenchymal hypertension. Contrib Nephrol 1994;106:198.

CHAPTER 14–8

Pheochromocytoma

Ray W. Gifford, Jr., M.D., Emmanuel L. Bravo, M.D., and William Muir Manger, M.D., Ph.D.

DEFINITION

Pheochromocytoma is a tumor of chromaffin tissue that secretes catecholamines and is usually located in the adrenal medulla, but it can occur wherever chromaffin tissue is found (e.g., along the paravertebral sympathetic chain in the abdomen and thorax, in the organ of Zuckerkandl, and, rarely, in the urinary bladder and neck).

ETIOLOGY

As is true for so many neoplastic diseases, the etiology is unknown.

CRITERIA FOR DIAGNOSIS

Suggestive

The diagnosis should be considered for patients who have hypertension, paroxysmal or persistent, with any of the symptoms listed in Table 14–8–1, and especially for patients who have unusually labile hypertension. Even if blood pressure is normal, patients who complain of discrete symptomatic episodes should have a diagnostic workup; so should patients who have paradoxical responses to some antihypertensive agents (e.g., hydralazine, reserpine, guanethidine, beta blockers), and patients who have hypertensive responses to the induction of anesthesia or during operations or parturition. Patients with malignant hypertension or whose hypertension is unusually resistant to a good medical regimen should also be suspected of having pheochromocytomas. Finally, members of families who have multiple endocrine neoplasia types II and III should be evaluated, even if they have normal blood pressure.

Definitive

The diagnosis is confirmed by finding elevated levels of catecholamines in the blood or urine or high concentrations of catecholamine metabolites (metanephrines or vanillylmandelic acid) in the urine). Magnetic resonance imaging (MRI) or computed tomography (CT) scans of the abdomen (rarely the thorax) usually identify the site of the tumor(s).

CLINICAL MANIFESTATIONS

Subjective

Symptoms of catecholamine excess suggesting this diagnosis are listed in Table 14–8–1. At least 90% of patients with pheochromocytoma have one or more of the following: headache, palpitations, or diaphoresis.

Past history is not usually helpful except in the rare case when patients with Sipple's syndrome (see below) have had medullary thyroid carcinoma or primary hyperparathyroidism.

No more than 10% of patients with pheochromocytoma have a family history of this tumor. Less than one half of these have Sipple's syndrome, characterized by family members who have pheochromocytoma, medullary thyroid carcinoma, or parathyroid adenoma in various combinations (multiple endocrine neoplasia type II). Multiple endocrine neoplasia type III (or IIb) also includes thickening of corneal nerves, mucosal neuromas, marfanoid habitus, and alimentary tract ganglioneuromatosis in various combinations.

Objective

Physical Examination

Hypertension is the most consistent finding on physical examination. Usually it is severe, although it is characteristically labile and may be intermittent with paroxysms lasting from a few minutes to several hours. Tachycardia, hyperactive precordium, tremor, diaphoresis, and pallor of the skin may be observed only paroxysmally, even in patients with persistent hypertension. Tumors are rarely large enough to be palpable, although attempts at deep palpation of the abdomen may induce a paroxysm of hypertension with characteristic symptoms. Flexion of the spine or twisting movements of the torso also may precipitate a symptomatic paroxysm. Hypertensive changes in the optic fundi are unusual in patients with intermittent hypertension, but they can be quite severe, including retinal hemorrhages, exudates, and papilledema (malignant hypertension) in patients with persistent hypertension.

TABLE 14–8–1. SYMPTOMS IN 76 PATIENTS WITH PHEOCHROMOCYTOMA

Symptoms	Paroxysmal Hypertension (37 patients)	Persistent Hypertension (39 patients)
Headache	92%	72%
Excessive and inappropriate sweating	65	69
Palpitations ± tachycardia	73	51
Anxiety (impending doom)	60	28
Pallor (usually of face)	60	28
Tremor	51	26
Pain in chest and/or abdomen	48	28
Nausea ± vomiting	43	26
Weakness, fatigue, prostration	38	15
Weight loss (severe)	14	15
Dyspnea	11	18
None	3	5

Adapted from Manger WM, Gifford RW Jr. Pheochromocytoma. New York: Springer-Verlag, 1977. Reproduced with permission from the publisher and authors.

Routine Laboratory Abnormalities

The electrocardiogram is usually normal, although it may reflect left ventricular hypertrophy in patients who have severe hypertension and/or evidence of catecholamine effects such as sinus tachycardia, with or without atrial or ventricular ectopy and sometimes runs of atrial, junctional, or ventricular tachycardia. Myocardial infarction may occur rarely. Hyperglycemia is not unusual in patients with sustained hypertension. Hypercalcemia is occasionally encountered in patients who have multiple endocrine neoplasia type II with parathyroid adenoma or hyperplasia or whose tumors seem to produce ectopic parathyroid hormone.

PLANS
Diagnostic
Differential Diagnosis

The most frequently encountered differential diagnoses include anxiety tension states, panic disorder, hyperthyroidism, cardiac arrhythmias, menopausal syndrome, migraine and cluster headaches, and unstable angina, all of which are frequently accompanied by hypertension. When symptoms of these conditions are not accompanied by hypertension, the diagnosis of pheochromocytoma is unlikely.

Diagnostic Options

Determination of plasma catecholamines in the fasting, resting state is the most reliable test for confirming the diagnosis of pheochromocytoma. The vast majority of patients with a tumor have plasma catecholamine (epinephrine plus norepinephrine) levels in excess of 2000 ng/L, even at a time when they are normotensive and asymptomatic. In contrast, patients with primary hypertension seldom have plasma catecholamine concentrations greater than 1000 ng/L. Abrupt clonidine withdrawal, drug and food interactions with monoamine oxidase inhibitors, and excessive use of sympathomimetic amines can be associated with hypertension and catecholamine concentrations in the pheochromocytoma range.

When the plasma catecholamine concentration is less than 500 ng/L at a time when the patient is hypertensive, pheochromocytoma can be ruled out. When the catecholamine concentration is between 500 and 2000 ng/L, pharmacologic tests to substantiate or exclude the diagnosis are indicated. If blood pressure is less than 160/100 mm Hg and plasma catecholamines are less than 700 or 800 ng/L, the glucagon stimulation test is indicated. Blood pressure and plasma catecholamines are measured before and 2 minutes after the rapid intravenous administration of 2 mg of glucagon. If a pheochromocytoma is present, plasma catecholamines should increase to more than 2000 ng/L. A hypertensive blood pressure response is frequently seen, but is not necessary for the diagnosis and can be prevented by prior oral administration of nifedipine 10 mg.

If blood pressure is 160/100 mm Hg or higher and plasma catecholamines are between 800 and 2000 ng/L, 0.3 mg clonidine (Catapres) is administered orally. Failure of suppression of plasma catecholamines to less than 500 ng/L and by at least 50% at the end of 3 hours suggests the presence of pheochromocytoma. Clonidine reduces blood pressure whether or not a pheochromocytoma is present.

Plasma catecholamines should be measured in the fasting, resting state. Patients should rest in a supine position for at least 30 minutes after an indwelling needle has been inserted into an antecubital vein before blood is drawn.

When laboratory facilities for measuring plasma catecholamines are not readily available, 24-hour urinary metanephrines (metanephrine plus normetanephrine) can be determined as an alternative. Much less reliable are determinations of urinary catecholamines and vanillylmandelic acid. Of 43 patients with pheochromocytoma, 25 had false-negative values for urinary vanillylmandelic acid and 9 had false-negative values for urinary metanephrines (Bravo and Gifford, 1984). Of 64 patients with pheochromocytoma, only 4 had plasma catecholamine levels that were within the 95% confidence limits of values for patients with essential hypertension (sensitivity, 94%), and none were in the normotensive range (< 500 ng/L) (Bravo and Gifford, 1984). Urinary

catecholamines were diagnostically elevated in only 47 of 60 patients with pheochromocytoma in a Mayo Clinic series (Remine et al., 1974) (sensitivity, 79%) and in only 18 of 27 in a Cleveland Clinic series (Deoreo et al., 1974) (sensitivity, 67%).

When measured by high-pressure liquid chromatographic methods, urinary free catecholamines have been highly sensitive, but this methodology is not widely used.

For patients with evidence of excessive catecholamine secretion, localization of the tumor is essential in planning definitive therapy. MRI is emerging as the procedure of choice in localizing the tumor(s). There are several reasons for this preference: sensitivity is close to 100% and as good as that of CT scanning; unlike CT scanning, MRI usually does not require administration of contrast medium and does not expose the patient to ionizing radiation. It is therefore the only imaging modality, other than ultrasonography, suitable for pregnant women. MRI is superior to CT scanning in detecting cardiac pheochromocytomas. Moreover, pheochromocytomas, benign or malignant, have a high signal intensity on T2-weighted images that distinguishes them from most other benign and some other malignant tumors. The only disadvantage of MRI compared with CT scanning is its greater cost; however, its advantages outweigh this small cost differential (see below). If MRI reveals no tumor in the abdomen, thorax, or neck, CT scanning of those areas is indicated.

A third imaging modality is scintigraphy using ^{131}I-MIBG, an isotope that is specifically concentrated in pheochromocytomas, adrenal or extraadrenal, but not in normal chromaffin tissue, at least to the extent that it is easily visualized on scintigrams. Because it is an expensive test, it is reserved for cases in which the diagnosis is strongly suspected when high levels of catecholamines or their metabolites are present in blood or urine, but MRI and CT scanning fail to reveal a tumor. ^{131}I-MIBG also should be considered if multiple tumors are identified or strongly suspected (e.g., in children and in patients with familial or malignant or recurrent pheochromocytomas). ^{131}I-MIBG scintigraphy is highly specific for pheochromocytoma, but it is not as sensitive as the other two modalities. Figure 14–8–1 demonstrates the three imaging procedures in a patient with pheochromocytoma in the right adrenal gland.

Only rarely is it necessary to localize pheochromocytomas by obtaining blood from multiple levels within the inferior and superior vena cava to determine catecholamine concentrations.

Hypercalcitoninemia may occur in patients with multiple endocrine neoplasia II or III when medullary thyroid carcinoma or hyperplasia is present.

Recommended Approach

It is recommended that when available, determination of plasma catecholamines as described above is optimal. A satisfactory alternative is measurement of 24-hour urinary metanephrines or urinary free catecholamines by high-pressure liquid chromatography. Urinary catecholamines measured by the conventional method and urinary vanillylmandelic acid are not sensitive enough to be reliable screening tests for pheochromocytoma. For reasons described in the previous section, MRI is the recommended approach for imaging.

Therapeutic
Therapeutic Options

The options for managing pheochromocytoma include appropriate antihypertensive drug therapy, surgical extirpation, and, in cases of malignant and metastatic pheochromocytoma, chemotherapy and/or radiation therapy.

Recommended Approach

Surgical extirpation is recommended unless the patient has widespread metastases or presents an unacceptable surgical risk. In patients with obvious metastatic disease, debulking a large tumor is often advisable to relieve symptoms and make hypertension easier to control. Even when symptoms are minimal and hypertension can be controlled with medication, surgical extirpation is recommended, because approximately 10% of tumors are malignant.

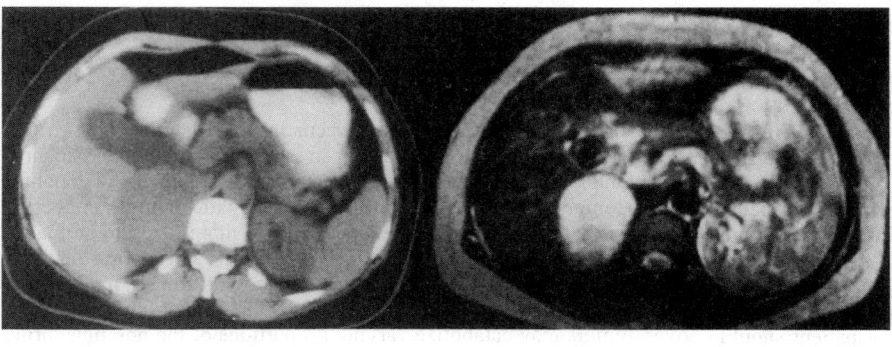

A   B

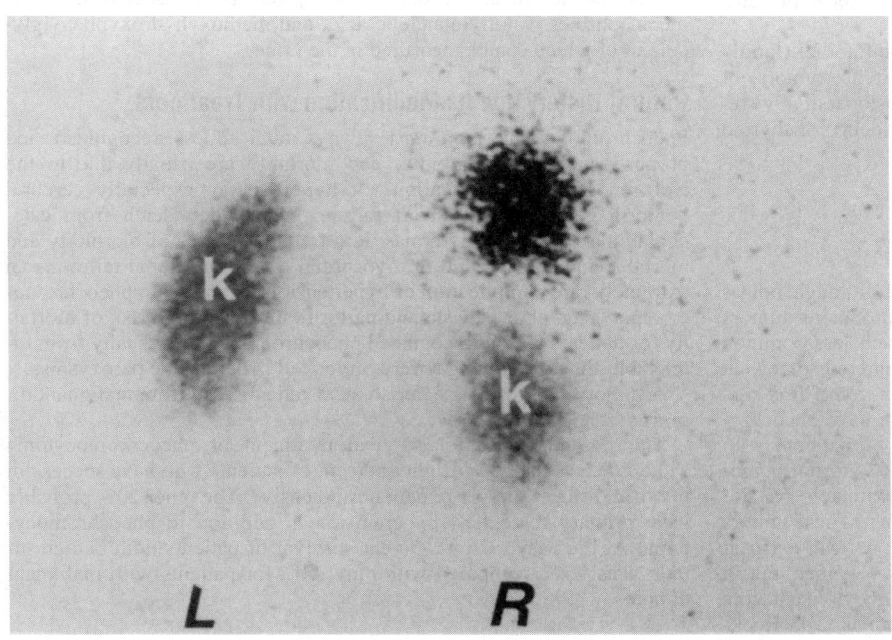

C

Figure 14–8–1. Localization of pheochromocytoma in a patient with a tumor in the right adrenal gland by abdominal CT scan (**A**), MR T_2-weighted image (**B**), and ^{131}I-MIBG scintigraphy 72 hours after radioisotope injection (**C**). K, kidney; L, left; R, right. *(From Bravo EL. Pheochromocytoma: New concepts and future trends. Kidney Int 1991;40:544. Reproduced with permission from the publisher and author.)*

With an experienced team of surgeons, anesthesiologists, internists, and nurses, the surgical mortality rate should be less than 2%. Most surgeons prefer the anterior transperitoneal approach through a transverse subcostal incision so that both adrenals and the paraaortic areas can be fully explored. Many physicians prefer to establish alpha blockade with phenoxybenzemine (Dibenzyline), 10 to 20 mg four times daily, or prazosin (Minipress), 1 to 3 mg three times daily, or doxazosin (Cardura), 2 to 5 mg daily, for 6 or 7 days before the operation. This controls hypertension during the preoperative period and blunts hypertensive responses to induction of anesthesia, intubation, and intraoperative manipulation of the tumor. If complete, or nearly so, preoperative alpha blockade may deprive the surgeon of clues to the presence of an additional tumor(s), because if blood pressure is normal under the influence of alpha blockade, it will not fall when the tumor is removed and will not rise when a small tumor is palpated during exploration of the abdomen. This objection to preoperative alpha blockade is less important now that CT or MRI scans nearly always identify multiple tumors preoperatively. There is, however, no evidence that preoperative alpha blockade has lessened surgical mortality or morbidity, and it delays operation. Its chief value is to replenish intravascular volume, which is usually low in patients with pheochromocytoma. This can be accomplished more expeditiously, but with slightly greater risk, by transfusing 2 units of whole blood within 12 hours of the operation. To eliminate the small risk of transmitting HIV, a blood substitute is preferable. This makes postoperative hypotension less frequent and less severe when it does occur.

Beta-adrenergic blockade is indicated only when tachycardia or cardiac arrhythmias are troublesome during the preoperative or intraoperative period, and should always follow alpha blockade because beta blockade by itself can aggravate hypertension by blocking vasodilator β_2 receptors, leaving vasoconstrictor α receptors unopposed. Propranolol can be administered orally in doses of 40 to 120 mg twice a day or intravenously in doses of 1 to 2 mg during the operation. Most anesthesiologists now prefer the shorter-acting beta blocker esmolol (Brevibloc) in doses of 50 to 300 µg/min intravenously.

Labetalol (Trandate, Normodyne), being both an alpha blocker and a beta blocker, would seem to be the ideal drug to manage hypertension secondary to pheochromocytoma, but there have been case reports of paradoxical hypertension when the drug was administered to such patients. The dose is 200 to 400 mg twice daily.

For managing severe hypertensive spikes due to pheochromocytoma, either preoperatively or intraoperatively, phentolamine (Regitine) can be given by bolus intravenous injection in doses of 5 to 20 mg or sodium nitroprusside can be given by intravenous infusion at a rate of 4 to 10 µg/kg/min. Nitroglycerine administered intravenously is also effective.

When pheochromocytoma is malignant and cannot be resected or metastases occur later, hypertension can usually be controlled by α_1 blockade, labetalol, or a dihydropyridine calcium antagonist. Rarely, these tumors are radiosensitive to x-ray or ^{131}I-MIBG, and some tumors temporarily respond to combination chemotherapy. Metyrosine (Demser) in doses of 0.25 to 1 g four times daily inhibits catecholamine synthesis and will control hypertension secondary to metastatic or inoperable pheochromocytoma, but it may cause diarrhea, crystalluria, extrapyramidal symptoms, and psychic disturbances.

FOLLOW-UP

At the time of discharge from the hospital, the patient should be instructed to have his or her blood pressure measured at weekly intervals for the next 6 weeks and to report any elevations above 160/100 mm Hg or any symptoms that would suggest another pheochromocytoma. Patients should also report any evidence of wound infection to the surgeon.

The patient should be seen by the surgeon and primary physician within 2 to 3 months of surgery. The surgeon should inspect the wound to be certain it is well healed. The primary physician should measure the blood pressure, inquire about symptoms that would suggest the presence of another tumor, and obtain blood for measurement of catecholamines or urine for metanephrines. Thereafter, the patient should be seen again at 6 and 12 months, and then annually for at least 5 years. Blood pressure and plasma catecholamines (or urinary metanephrines) should be monitored at each visit.

Any evidence that the pheochromocytoma might be familial (family history of multiple endocrine neoplasia, bilateral adrenal tumors, or presence of hypercalcitoninemia or hypercalcemia postoperatively) requires subsequent investigation and follow-up for evidence of thyroid or parathyroid disease.

DISCUSSION

Prevalence and Incidence

Pheochromocytoma is a rare cause of hypertension, although not as rare as some other endocrine causes, such as renin-producing tumors and adrenocortical hydroxylase deficiencies. It is much less common than renovascular hypertension and is probably encountered somewhat less often than primary aldosteronism or Cushing's syndrome. It is estimated that 0.05 to 0.1% of patients with hypertension have pheochromocytoma, but it should be noted that only 50% of patients with pheochromocytoma have persistent hypertension; 45% are normotensive between paroxysms of hypertension, and approximately 5% remain relatively normotensive. The incidence is unknown. These tumors occur most frequently in the fourth and fifth decades, but can occur at any age. Among adults there is a slight predilection for women, but in children about two thirds occur in boys. Pheochromocytoma occurs much more frequently in patients with neurofibromatosis (von Recklinghausen's disease) or von Hippel–Lindau disease than in the general population.

Related Basic Science

Genetics

Probably no more than 10% of patients with pheochromocytoma have a family history of this tumor. The multiple endocrine neoplasia syndromes that have been discussed previously are usually familial and probably represent inherited defects in neuroectodermal development because chromaffin tissue and perifollicular C cells are both of neuroectodermal origin.

Physiologic or Metabolic Derangement

Pheochromocytomas synthesize the catecholamines norepinephrine and epinephrine autonomously. Consequently, central nervous system-mediated suppression of the sympathetic nervous system with clonidine does not decrease the concentrations of plasma catecholamines in the presence of a tumor, as it does in patients with primary hypertension. Some tumors secrete only norepinephrine and some only epinephrine, but the vast majority secrete both these amines. In addition, the precursors of norepinephrine, dopamine and dopa, are rarely secreted and most often by malignant tumors.

Although some patients with pheochromocytoma have orthostatic decreases in blood pressure, there is appropriate tachycardia when this occurs and Valsalva overshoot is normal, suggesting that the sympathetic nervous system is functioning normally and the orthostatic decrease in blood pressure is probably the result of hypovolemia (which is a frequent finding in patients with pheochromocytoma).

Following removal of a pheochromocytoma, the plasma catecholamine concentration may not return to normal for 4 to 7 days, suggesting that excessive tissue stores of these amines are dissipated slowly.

Anatomic Derangement

Extraadrenal pheochromocytomas occur in 10% of patients with this disorder, often in addition to a tumor in the adrenal medulla. Pheochromocytomas occur in both adrenal glands in 10% of patients with nonfamilial tumors but in nearly 100% of patient with multiple endocrine neoplasia syndromes. Extraadrenal tumors are more likely to be malignant than adrenal medullary tumors. There is no correlation between the size of the tumor and its catecholamine output. In fact, many of the large tumors have cystic or necrotic centers that do not function. Moreover, tumors may catabolize varying proportions of the norepinephrine and epinephrine they produce before the amines reach the circulation, giving rise to metabolic degradation products: metanephrines, normetanephrines, vanillylmandelic acid, and methoxyhydroxyphenylglycol, all of which can be measured in the urine.

Natural History and Its Modification with Treatment

Pheochromocytoma is almost always fatal unless recognized and properly managed. Morbidity and mortality are usually due to the well-recognized complications of hypertension, especially cerebral hemorrhage, congestive heart failure, and sudden death from catecholamine-induced arrhythmias; less frequent causes of morbidity and mortality include cerebral or myocardial infarction. Renal failure is an extremely rare complication of hypertension secondary to pheochromocytoma. General anesthesia and parturition carry a high risk of mortality for patients with unrecognized pheochromocytoma, usually from intractable shock following severe prolonged hypertensive paroxysms.

A minority of deaths are due to metastatic disease from malignant tumors.

The mortality rate for surgical treatment of pheochromocytoma should be less than 2%. Eighty percent of patients who have successful removal of these tumors remain normotensive. The other 20% probably have primary (essential) hypertension in addition to pheochromocytoma. At the Mayo Clinic, 5-year survival of patients with benign tumors was 96%, compared with only 44% for patients with malignant tumors.

Prevention

There is at present no way to prevent pheochromocytoma.

Cost Containment

Because pheochromocytoma is rare and the vast majority of patients with this tumor have symptoms (Table 14–8–1), it is not cost-effective to screen those patients who are asymptomatic and whose blood pressure is well controlled for pheochromocytoma. When the diagnosis is suspected clinically, the most effective way to confirm it is measurement of plasma catecholamines ($50–100). An alternative is measurement of 24-hour excretion of urinary metanephrines ($35–75), which is more widely available. In our experience, the measurement of plasma catecholamines is more sensitive as a screening test. The imaging procedure of choice is MRI of the abdomen ($1050), which is more expensive than but has advantages discussed previously over CT scanning ($850),

Except in unusual situations, it is not necessary to order urinary catecholamines or vanillylmandelic acid; an intravenous pyelogram; plain films of the kidney, ureters, and bladder; or abdominal angiography. Phentolamine and histamine tests are no longer recommended. The glucagon stimulation test or the clonidine suppression test is indicated only when plasma catecholamines are equivocal, and for this purpose, there is no alternative.

REFERENCES

Bravo EL. Pheochromocytoma: New concepts and future trends. Kidney Int 1991;40:544.

Bravo EL, Gifford RW Jr. Pheochromocytoma: Diagnosis, localization and management. N Engl J Med 1984;311:1298.

Deoreo GA, Stewart BH, Tarazi RC, Gifford RW Jr. Preoperative blood transfusions in the safe surgical management of pheochromocytoma: A review of 46 cases. J Urol 1974;111:715.

Gifford RW Jr, Manger WM, Bravo EL. Pheochromocytoma. Endocrinol Metab Clin North Am 1994;23:387.

Manger WM, Gifford RW Jr. Pheochromocytoma. New York: Springer-Verlag, 1977.

Manger WM, Gifford RW Jr. Clinical and Experimental Pheochromocytoma, 2nd ed. Boston: Blackwell Scientific, 1996.

Remine WH, Chong GC, Van Heerden JA, et al. Current management of pheochromocytoma. Ann Surg 1974;179:740.

Sheps SG, Jiang NS, Klee GG, van Heerden JA. Recent developments in the diagnosis and treatment of pheochromocytoma. Mayo Clin Proc 1990;65:88.

Stein PP, Black HR. A simplified diagnostic approach to pheochromocytoma: A review of the literature and report of one institutions's experience. Medicine 1991;70:46.

CHAPTER 14–9

Unusual Causes of Hypertension

W. Dallas Hall, M.D.

DEFINITION

Unusual causes of hypertension are those that are neither idiopathic ("essential") nor due to the usually recognized secondary causes of hypertension.

ETIOLOGY

The 45 unusual causes of hypertension described in this chapter all have separate etiologies, but share the common physiology of either an increase in cardiac output or an increase in total peripheral resistance.

CRITERIA FOR DIAGNOSIS

Suggestive

Occasional or transient elevations of systolic blood pressure of 140 mm Hg or more or of diastolic blood pressure of 90 mm Hg or more are suggestive of hypertension and often referred to as labile or borderline hypertension.

Definitive

In adults, hypertension is defined as a systolic blood pressure of 140 mm Hg or more or a diastolic blood pressure of 90 mm Hg or more on three consecutive occasions. Most cases of hypertension are idiopathic (i.e., "essential hypertension"), but 5 to 10% are due to known causes, such as renoparenchymal diseases, renovascular hypertension, primary aldosteronism, pheochromocytoma, Cushing's syndrome, and coarctation of the aorta. In addition to these idiopathic and known secondary etiologies of hypertension, there are other rare causes. Forty-five of these are listed in Table 14–9–1. Their presence is often detected only when an astute clinician has a high index of suspicion in the appropriate clinical setting.

CLINICAL MANIFESTATIONS

The subjective and objective clinical manifestations differ for each of the clinical settings (see Discussion).

PLANS AND FOLLOW-UP

The diagnostic and therapeutic plans and the follow-up vary with each of the clinical settings (see Discussion).

DISCUSSION

Prevalence and Incidence and Related Basic Science

By definition, unusual causes of hypertension are relatively rare with a low prevalence and incidence.

Intrinsic Renal Diseases

Large *solitary renal cysts* and *unilateral hydronephrosis* can rarely be associated with ipsilateral renin production and hypertension that responds to removal of the cyst or relief of the obstruction.

A *horseshoe kidney* is a condition in which the two kidneys are fused over the spine, typically at the lower poles. It occurs in approximately 1 of 400 births. Complications include urinary tract infections, renal calculi, ureteropelvic obstruction, and malignancy. Several cases of renal artery stenosis have been reported in patients with a horseshoe kidney. Evaluation is difficult because 60 to 80% of horsehoe kidneys have an anomalous blood supply (multiple arteries, etc.), complicating the collection and interpretation of segmental venous samples for the measurement of renin.

The *Ask–Upmark kidney* is usually detected during evaluation of young or adolescent children for hypertension or vesicourethral reflux. The renal hypoplasia is characterized by a kidney that is contracted by segmental bands of extensive scarring. The condition can be predominantly unilateral and associated with excess renin production and cure of the hypertension by nephrectomy.

Atheroembolic renal infarction presents as severe hypertension with oliguric or nonoliguric renal failure following surgery for aortic aneurysm or trauma in 60- to 90-year-old patients. It can also follow any type of manipulation (including renal arteriography or percutaneous transluminal renal angioplasty) of an aorta with atheromatous plaques that have eroded through an ulcerated intima. Acute embolic pancreatitis, gastrointestinal bleeding, and distal extremity emboli are associated findings. The diagnosis is suspected by the presence of eosinophilia and eosinophiluria (Hansel's stain) and can be confirmed by identifying embolized intraarterial cholesterol crystals in renal biopsy or a frozen section from a gastrocnemius biopsy stained specially for sterols or viewed under polarized light for the characteristic birefringence of the crystals.

The *renal crisis of scleroderma* often presents abruptly with malignant hypertension in a patient with known progressive systemic sclerosis. The bilateral intrarenal vasculitis is often, but not always, associated with cortical ischemia and marked activation of the renin–angiotensin system. Therapy with angiotensin-converting enzyme inhibitors, potent vasodilators (e.g., minoxidil), and interim dialysis can reverse a downhill course in selected patients.

Hypertension occurs in approximately one third of patients with the *Grönblad–Strandberg–Touraine* syndrome, an autosomal recessive disorder associated with pseudoxanthoma elasticum and funduscopic angioid streaks. In addition to peripheral vascular arterial calcifications, these patients can also have unilateral renal angiomas producing renovascular hypertension.

Reninomas (Robertson–Kihara syndrome) are small (0.2–4.0 cm), benign renal cortical tumors of the juxtaglomerular apparatus. Histo-

TABLE 14-9-1. UNUSUAL CAUSES OF HYPERTENSION

Intrinsic renal diseases
  Solitary cysts, unilateral hydronephrosis
  Horseshoe kidney
  Ask–Upmark kidney
  Atheroembolic renal infarction
  Renal crisis of scleroderma
  Grönblad–Strandberg–Touraine syndrome
  Reninoma (Robertson–Kihara syndrome)
Neurologic disorders
  Intracranial hypertension
  Ruptured intracranial aneurysms
  Cerebellar tumors
  Colloid cysts or choroid plexus lesions of the third ventricle
  Sleep apnea
  Neurovascular compression
  Autonomic hyperreflexia of paraplegics and quadriplegics
  Sympathetic storm of tetanus
  Acute intermittent porphyria
Endocrine disorders
  Acromegaly
  Hyperthyroidism
  Hypothyroidism
  Extraadrenal pheochromocytoma
  Page's syndrome (dopamine surges)
  Liddle's syndrome
  Endothelin-secreting hemangioendothelioma
Posttraumatic clinical settings
  Head trauma
  Renal hematoma, traumatic renal artery thrombosis
  Shock-wave lithotripsy
  Burns
Heavy metal and chemical poisonings
  Lead poisoning
  Barium poisoning
  Thallium poisoning
  Sodium poisoning
  Parathion poisoning
Drug-induced hypertension
  Chewing tobacco
  Exogenous mineralocorticoids
  Cyclosporine and tacrolimus (FK 506)
  Erythropoietin
  Anabolic steroids
  Nonsteroidal anti-inflammatory drugs
  Amphetamines and cocaine
  Phencyclidine
  Phenylpropanolamine
  Ketoconazole
Miscellaneous
  Takayasu's arteritis
  Midaortic syndrome
  Scorpion stings
  Black widow spider bites

logically, they resemble hemangiopericytomas, except for the secretion of renin. Clinically, they resemble primary aldosteronism (but the renin level is high) or renovascular hypertension (but the renal arteries are patent). Marked lateralization of the renal vein renins can produce a diagnostic dilemma if the size and vascularity of the peripheral cortical tumor do not allow detection by angiograpy or computed tomography scan. When a proper diagnosis is made, the hypertension is usually cured by partial or total nephrectomy.

Primary reninism also can occur with any renin-secreting tumor and has been reported with Wilms' tumors and hypernephromas, renal and hepatic hamartomas, hemangiopericytomas, oat cell carcinoma of the lung, and adenocarcinoma of the pancreas, ovary, and lung. Renal arteriovenous malformations (e.g., due to renal biopsy or within hypernephromas) also can be associated rarely with a renin-dependent hypertension.

Neurologic Disorders

Intracranial hypertension was described initially by Cushing (Cushing's "phenomenon," "reflex," "response," "physiology," or "law") as a rise in blood pressure and peripheral vascular resistance that accompanied an increase in intracranial pressure. The high intracranial pressure induces an increase in cerebrovascular resistance with resultant hypoxic ischemia of the medullary vasomotor center. *Primary or metastatic brain tumors* produce Cushing's phenomenon when papilledema is present and the cerebrospinal fluid pressure is above 450 mm H_2O. The only consistently effective therapy is reduction of the high intracranial pressure by removal of the cause or by a variety of temporizing measures, such as hyperventilation, dexamethasone, and mannitol. Caution should be exercised with the use of nitroprusside in patients with intracranial hypertension and mass lesions because there are reports of increasing intracranial pressure associated with a reduction in cerebrovascular resistance induced by vasodilator therapy.

Ruptured intracranial aneurysms and certain posterior fossa lesions (e.g., cerebellar tumors or cysts) can cause a hyperadrenergic state that can mimic pheochromocytoma, including elevated levels of urinary metanephrine and vanillylmandelic acid. The elevated blood pressure often responds to alpha blockade with drugs such as prazosin (Minipress), terazosin (Hytrin), and doxazosin (Cardura). Either plasma catecholamine measurements or a clonidine suppression test should be performed prior to the use of alpha blockers in this setting. This is so because alpha-receptor blockade induces feedback elevation of plasma norepinephrine (as well as urinary vanillylmandelic acid excretion) that could be confused with the diagnosis of pheochromocytoma.

Other central nervous system lesions that can occasionally simulate pheochromocytoma (i.e., paroxysms of hypertension and central nervous system symptoms) include *colloid cysts or choroid plexus tumors* of the third ventricle and autonomic epilepsy manifested by surges of autonomic overactivity related to lesions in or adjacent to the hypothalamus.

Sleep apnea may be associated with hypertension more often than has been appreciated in the past. The association persists after controlling for age and obesity. The hypertension is mediated with sympathetic discharge and often improves after treatment with nasal continuous positive airway pressure (CPAP) or uvulopalatopharyngoplasty. Appropriate screening of overweight, sleepy, hypertensive, gaspy snorers includes nocturnal home oximetry (to document hypoxemia) and polysomnography.

Neurovascular compression of the left ventrolateral medulla oblongata by tortuous vertebral arteries has been associated with sympathetically mediated hypertension and reported to respond to surgical decompression.

Autonomic hyperreflexia is characteristic of patients with quadriplegia or paraplegia due to high thoracic (above T_6) or cervical cord lesions. These patients lack central nervous system control of sympathetic outflow below the level of the lesion. Clinical manifestations can include severe paroxysmal hypertension due to spinal sympathetic discharge evoked by manipulation of the bladder, urethra, or rectum. For example, blood pressure can rise by 100/50 mm Hg from bladder distention or even bladder percussion. Bladder distention also can induce significant blood pressure elevations, averaging 15–28/10–14 mm Hg, in nonquadriplegic patients. We have occasionally observed striking elevations of blood pressure in patients with massive hematuria (due to bladder or prostate disease) causing recurrent obstruction of the Foley catheter.

The mechanism of autonomic hyperreflexia includes denervation hypersensitivity with a two- to sevenfold increase in the magnitude of the blood pressure rise in response to norepinephrine. Acute rises in blood pressure can be accompanied by profuse sweating, reflex bradycardia, vasoconstriction of the extremities, and vasodilation with flushing of the face. These autonomic sympathetic discharges can sometimes be controlled with alpha blockers or combined alpha–beta blockers such as labetalol; interestingly, they also may be reduced by chronic therapy with low doses of a calcium channel blocker such as nifedipine (Procardia). Marked, acute elevations of blood pressure also respond to passive upright tilt. Autonomic hyperreflexia also may partially account for the hypertension noted in occasional severe cases of poliomyelitis.

Tetanus can be associated with severe hypertension related to massive sympathetic discharge. Tachycardia also can occur from clostridial involvement of the sympathetic innervation of the heart. Sudden elevations of blood pressure do not correlate with the tetanic muscle spasms. Similar blood pressure crises have been reported with other diseases that involve the peripheral nervous system, including Guillain–Barré syndrome, Riley–Day syndrome, and acute intermittent porphyria. Indeed, acute intermittent porphyria should always be considered in the clinical setting of unexpected blood pressure elevation, especially in a confused patient with tachycardia, abdominal pain, coma, hyponatremia or unexplained neurologic signs.

Endocrine Disorders

Acromegaly is associated with hypertension in 20 to 40% of cases; blood pressure is related to the level of growth hormone. The hypertension is characterized by an expanded extracellular fluid volume, an increase in exchangeable sodium, and a decrease in plasma renin activity.

Hyperthyroidism is characterized by a mild and predominantly high-renin, systolic hypertension associated with excess sympathetic nervous system activity and a good response to high doses of beta blockers. In contrast, *hypothyroidism* can be associated with mild elevations of both systolic and diastolic blood pressure and a low plasma renin activity. The elevated blood pressure may respond to either diuretic or thyroid replacement therapy, although normotension does not always follow return to the euthyroid state.

Extraadrenal pheochromocytomas represent approximately 10% of all chromaffin tumors. Anatomic locations can include the bladder (micturition-induced hypertension), the kidney, the carotid body, the glomus jugulare near the middle ear, the vagus nerve, the pericardium, the atrial septum, and the organs of Zuckerkandl located between the origin of the inferior mesenteric artery and the aortic bifurcation.

Page's syndrome mimics pheochromocytoma except that attacks are usually accompanied by flushing (rather than blanching), nausea, and polyuria. The cause is unexplained, episodic discharges of dopamine. The symptoms and hypertensive episodes usually improve following therapy with beta blockers, combined alpha–beta blockers, or clonidine.

Liddle's syndrome is a rare type of familial, low-renin, volume-dependent hypertension associated with renal sodium retention and potassium loss but subnormal levels of aldosterone and no evidence of an increase in any other known mineralocorticoids. Therapy with aldosterone antagonists is ineffective, but triamterene results in reduction of blood pressure.

Hypertension has been associated with marked elevations of plasma endothelin 1 levels in patients with malignant hemangioendotheliomas of the scalp.

Posttraumatic Clinical Settings

Head trauma is sometimes associated with hypertension, presumably mediated by the previously discussed Cushing's phenomenon. Reduction in intracranial pressure and the use of hypotensive agents such as sublingual nifedipine and miniboluses of labetalol are probably preferable to drugs such as intravenous methyldopa that can suppress the level of consciousness and interfere with clinical evaluation of the patient.

Subcapsular or perirenal hematomas with excess renin production from the involved kidney can occur following abdominal or flank trauma. For example, we have observed a case of severe hyperreninemic hypertension associated with unilateral renal artery thrombosis in a 38-year-old mechanic who was crushed when the jack released while he was working under a car; blood pressure normalized following unilateral nephrectomy.

New-onset hypertension occurs within 1 to 3 years in 1 to 9% of patients following *extracorporeal shock-wave lithotripsy*. Excessive shock waves during one treatment session induce renal damage, including edema, perirenal hematoma, and significant proteinuria, with a long-term risk of chronic renal parenchymal fibrosis.

Burn hypertension occurs in 10 to 25% of patients with extensive thermal injuries. Diuretics are not attractive initial therapeutic options because of the associated tachycardia, volume depletion, hyperreninemia, and elevated levels of urinary catecholamines.

Heavy Metal and Chemical Poisonings

Lead intoxication should be suspected in patients with occupational lead exposure or in past moonshine drinkers who present with hypertension, gout, proteinuria, and renal insufficiency. Serum lead levels may exceed 50 to 80 µg/dL, but the best test is a 72-hour urinary lead level above 600 µg following two doses of EDTA (calcium disodium versenate) given intramuscularly at 12-hour intervals. Lead intoxication is associated with suppression of plasma renin activity whether hypertension is present or absent. It also can cause selective hypoaldosteronism. The mechanism of plasma renin activity suppression may relate to the property of lead to inhibit angiotensin-converting enzyme or impair the adenylate cyclase system. Plasma renin activity returns toward normal following effective chronic therapy with EDTA.

Barium (Ba^{2+}) poisoning can occur from accidental ingestion of barium chloride or barium carbonate. Hypertension results from a direct arterial vasoconstrictor effect of the barium. Profound hypokalemia also occurs, presumably from an intracellular shift of potassium. Associated symptoms include tachycardia and salivation.

Thallium poisoning (thallotoxicosis) from rodenticides can masquerade as alcohol withdrawal hypertension with tachycardia, fever, dysesthesias, and peripheral neuropathy. The diagnosis is often missed until acute alopecia occurs 2 to 4 weeks after the toxic ingestion. Urinary thallium excretion exceeds 1 mg/d, and treatment includes potassium chloride and chelation therapy.

Sodium poisoning can rarely induce acute hypertension if infants receive erroneous formulas or if adults ingest massive quantities of baking soda. We have observed transient acute hypertension (diastolic blood pressure of 220/142 mm Hg and a reflex bradycardia of 48 beats per minute) in a 17-year-old youth who drank a jar of pig's feet juice at a Labor Day barbecue. His blood pressure returned to normal after 40 mg furosemide (Lasix) and a single 500-mg dose of methyldopa (Aldomet); it remained normal on no therapy.

Hypertension was reported in almost 50% of the cases of *parathion poisoning* observed in Greece, where parathion is used extensively for spraying the olive trees against dakus.

Drug-Induced Hypertension

Most popular chewing tobaccos (Beechnut, Brown's Mule, Levi Garrett, Red Man, Workhorse) contain 2 to 8% by weight of *licorice extract* to enhance the flavor.* Approximately 15 to 25% of the licorice consists of glycyrrhizin, the potassium–calcium salt of glycyrrhizinic acid. Glycyrrhizinic acid exerts significant mineralocorticoid activity such that as little as 2 to 4 g daily can induce sodium retention and potassium wasting. The mechanism is related to intrarenal inhibition of 11β-hydroxysteroid dehydrogenase such that cortisol cannot be inactivated to cortisone, which has much less mineralocorticoid activity in the kidney. (Childhood hypertension due to hereditary deficiency of 11β-hydroxysteroid dehydrogenase is referred to as the syndrome of "apparent mineralocorticoid excess.") A typical 3-oz pouch of chewing tobacco contains 1.7 to 7 g licorice, or 0.3 to 1.7 g glycyrrhizin. Chronic abuse of chewing tobacco can thus lead to significant mineralocorticoid hypertension with all the biochemical features of primary aldosteronism except that the plasma and urinary aldosterone levels are low-normal. It either improves or responds dramatically within 1 to 2 weeks of discontinuation of the chewing tobacco.

A similar clinical picture can occur from *overzealous ingestion of licorice candies* (usually in 6-oz or 170-g packages) or from nonproprietary licorice-containing medications such as Lydia Pinkham's Compound, which contains 65 mg licorice per teaspoon. In contrast, most snuff contains less than one sixth as much licorice as chewing tobacco, and hypokalemic hypertension can probably not be attributed to snuff abuse.

---

*Havana Blossom and Leiberman are apparently two brands of chewing tobacco that are reported by the manufacturers to have minimal or no licorice content (personal communication, Dr. Gary Wollam).

Mineralocorticoid hypertension also has been reported rarely with chronic use of excessive dosages of carbenoxolone (an antacid with mineralocorticoid-like activity) or following prolonged exposure to skin ointments or nasal sprays containing 9α-fluorinated steroids or absorbable steroid nasal drops such as dexamethasone. Hypertension has not been reported as an adverse effect of the less well absorbed steroid nasal sprays such as beclomethasone and flunisolide.

Cyclosporine and tacrolimus (FK 506) are immunosuppressive drugs commonly associated with a dose-dependent elevation in blood pressure. The hypertension is mediated primarily through enhanced sympathetic discharge and is worsened by the associated nephrotoxicity of both drugs.

Erythropoietin corrects anemia in patients with end-stage renal disease on dialysis; however, hypertension and even hypertensive encephalopathy can occur as hematocrit improves.

Anabolic steroids are testosterone derivatives with a high ratio of anabolic-to-androgenic activity. Examples of oral preparations include ethylestrenol (Maxibolin), stanozolol (Winstrol), methandrostenolone (Dianabol), and oxandrolone (Anavar). Usual doses often taken by athletes (powerlifters, etc.) can induce salt and water retention with a mild increase in systolic blood pressure, as well as a marked decrease in the level of high-density lipoprotein cholesterol.

Controversy surrounds the issue of whether oral therapy with *nonsteroidal antiinflammatory drugs* (NSAIDs) has blood pressure-raising effect in hypertensive patients. The issue is confounded by the known effect of some NSAIDs to reduce the diuretic efficacy of hydrochlorothiazide, spironolactone (Aldactone), furosemide (Lasix), and bumetanide (Bumex); NSAIDs also can blunt the blood pressure-lowering efficacy of angiotensin-converting enzyme inhibitors and many beta blockers. More frequent measurements of blood pressure are indicated whenever any nonsteroidal antiinflammatory drug is prescribed in hypertensive patients.

Amphetamine abuse is demonstrated most overtly in drug addicts using oral or intravenous methamphetamine ("speed"). These patients can present with hypertension, tachycardia, headache, agitation, fever, seizures, and even subarachnoid or intracerebral hemorrhage. Methylphenidate (Ritalin) and *cocaine* (sometimes "cut" with amphetamines) also can be abused intravenously and result in hypertensive crises. In inner-city emergency departments, it is now common to see patients with cocaine abuse manifested by acute hypertension, tachycardia, and chest pain, sometimes accompanied by dilated pupils, seizures, or altered mental status. Therapy often includes diazepam (Valium) or labetalol (Trandate, Normodyne).

Phencyclidine (PCP or "angel dust") intoxication occurs most often in youngsters experimenting with marijuana or street drugs. The clinical presentation is similar to amphetamine overdosage, but nystagmus and a blank stare due to loss of lid reflexes are more frequent. As with amphetamines, renal excretion of phencyclidine is enhanced by acidifying the urine with oral ammonium chloride or intravenous ascorbic acid.

Phenylpropanolamine is a sympathomimetic amine that can induce pressor responses. It is contained in many cold remedies and over-the-counter appetite suppressants, as well as street drugs marketed falsely as "speed" or cocaine. Single, oral 50-mg doses can raise systolic blood pressure by 18 to 26 mm Hg, and 100-mg doses can cause marked increases in both systolic and diastolic blood pressure in hypertensive patients. Pressor effects can last up to 4 hours. The Food and Drug Administration has recommended that the use of phenylpropanolamine be limited to a maximum of 100 mg daily in divided doses. Phenylpropanolamine-induced hypertension generally responds to beta blockers.

Hypertension has been reported as a complication of long-term therapy with high-dose *ketoconazole*. The mechanism appears to be related to an increase in deoxycorticosterone secretion.

Miscellaneous

Takayasu's arteritis ("pulseless disease") is a disorder characterized by arteritis and focal fibrosis of the subclavian and carotid branches of the aortic arch. It also can involve the superior mesenteric and renal arteries. Classic symptoms include syncope on neck extension, angina, carotidynia, or jaw/arm claudication in young women. Abnormal physical findings include hypertension (50%), absent radial and often ulnar and carotid pulses, supraclavicular bruits, a face-down posture to avoid ocular ischemia, and wreathlike arteriovenous anastomoses near the ocular disk, described originally by Takayasu, a Japanese ophthalmologist. First noted in teenage Oriental women, ethnic heterogeneity is now acknowledged, but the female preponderance of cases remains 80 to 90%. Therapy with angiotensin-converting enzyme inhibitors can be beneficial in hyperreninemic patients in whom angioplasty or surgery is not indicated.

The *midaortic syndrome* is a condition in which fibrotic lesions occur at the origin of the renal, celiac, and/or mesenteric arteries. It usually presents as severe hypertension in childhood.

Stings from the yellow *scorpion, Buthus quinquestriatus* (found in Israel, North Africa, and South America), can induce massive sympathetic discharge (and elevated urinary excretion of total catecholamines and vanillylmandelic acid) with tachycardia, diaphoresis, myocarditis, and severe transient hypertension. Similar findings (i.e., severe hypertension with elevation of urinary catecholamines) have been reported following *black widow spider bite* or lactrodectism. Nonselective beta blockers should be used with caution because of their propensity to induce bronchospasm and, rarely, laryngospasm. Pharmacologic therapy is otherwise similar to that recommended for pheochromocytoma.

Natural History and Its Modification with Treatment

The natural history is determined by the etiology (See Discussion).

Prevention

The risk of atheroembolic renal infarction can be reduced by careful and nonaggressive manipulation of the intraarterial catheter in patients with advanced aortic atherosclerosis. Intracranial hypertension often can be alleviated by hyperventilation, dexamethasone, or mannitol. Intracranial hemorrhage can be lessened by appropriate detection and treatment of hypertension. The hypertension of autonomic hyperreflexia can be reduced by more gentle manipulation of the bladder, urethra, or rectum. It is also suppressed during surgery by the use of halothane anesthesia, and its occurrence may be lessened with the use of calcium channel blockers. Tetanus should be prevented by appropriate immunization.

Head and body trauma is best prevented by the use of seat belts and the avoidance of alcohol. Accidental poisonings are best avoided by home safety precautions. Exogenous mineralocorticoid hypertension can be avoided by the advising against chewing tobacco or by the selection of nonabsorbable steroid nasal sprays. Weightlifters and bodybuilders should be advised that anabolic steroids have serious adverse effects. Drug abusers should receive psychiatric counseling with enrollment in rehabilitation programs. Hypertensive patients should be advised to read the labels of nonproprietary medications and to generally avoid using phenylpropanolamine.

Cost Containment

Costs can be curtailed considerably by application of the preventive measures mentioned. Renal cysts, hydronephrosis, horseshoe kidney, and the Ask–Upmark kidney can be detected by renal ultrasonography. A good medical history will most often lead to the diagnosis and appropriate management of pheochromocytoma and licorice-induced hypertension. Appropriate school educational programs and early counseling may reduce drug abuse.

REFERENCES

Brody SL, Slovis CM, Wrenn KD. Cocaine-related medical problems: Consecutive series of 233 patients. Am J Med 1990;88:325.

Buckner FS, Eschbach JW, Haley NR, et al. Hypertension following erythropoietin therapy in anemic hemodialysis patients. Am J Hypertens 1990;3:947.

Cuthbert MF, Gleenberg MP, Morley SW. Cough and cold remedies: A potential danger to patients on monoamine oxidase inhibitors. Br Med J 1969;1:404.

Farese RV, Biglieri EG, Shackleton CHL, et al. Licorice-induced hypermineralocorticoidism. N Engl J Med 1991;325:1223.

Hla KM, Young TB, Bidwell T, et al. Sleep apnea and hypertension: A population-based study. Ann Intern Med 1994;120:382.

Hoff JT. Neurovascular compression and essential hypertension. J Neurosurg 1992;77:101.

Johnson AG, Nguyen TV, Day RO. Do nonsteroidal anti-inflammatory drugs affect blood pressure? A meta-analysis. Ann Intern Med 1994;121:289.

Kuchel O, Buu NT, Larochelle P, et al. Episodic dopamine discharge in paroxysmal hypertension: Page's syndrome revisited. Arch Intern Med 1986;146:1315.

Lewis DV III, Meranze SG, McLean GK, et al. The midaortic syndrome: Diagnosis and treatment. Radiol 1988;167:41.

Messerli FH, Frohlich ED. High blood pressure: A side effect of drugs, poisons, and food. Arch Intern Med 1979;139:692.

Smith LH, Drach G, Hall P, et al. National High Blood Pressure Education Program (NHBPEP) review paper on complications of shock wave lithotripsy for urinary calculi. Am J Med 1991;91:635.

U.S. Multicenter FK 506 Liver Study Group. A comparison of tacrolimus (FK 506) and cyclosporine for immunosuppression in liver transplantation. N Engl J Med 1994;331:1110.

Cardiovascular Problems

Robert C. Schlant, M.D.

CHAPTER 15–1

Hyperlipidemia

Peter H. Jones, M.D., and Antonio M. Gotto, Jr., M.D., D. Phil.

DEFINITION

Hyperlipidemia is defined as an elevated concentration of plasma total or low-density lipoprotein (LDL) cholesterol and/or triglyceride. A low level of high-density lipoprotein (HDL) cholesterol also constitutes a major dyslipidemia. The hyperlipidemias can be characterized according to the phenotypes given in Table 15–1–1.

ETIOLOGY

Hyperlipidemias are classified as primary (genetic) or secondary. In the preponderance of cases, hyperlipidemia is polygenic and multifactorial in origin; hyperlipidemia that is strictly genetic is uncommon. Major primary hyperlipidemias are described in Table 15–1–2; the genetic lipid disorders most often identified in clinical practice are familial

combined hyperlipidemia, polygenic hypercholesterolemia, familial hypercholesterolemia, and type III hyperlipidemia. Common causes of secondary dyslipidemia are listed in Table 15–1–3. Hypercholesterolemia is commonly associated with excessive intake of dietary fat; hypertriglyceridemia often accompanies diabetes mellitus, central obesity, or excessive alcohol intake. Searching for causes of secondary dyslipidemia is critical to the clinical workup.

CRITERIA FOR DIAGNOSIS
Suggestive

The clinical guidelines issued by the second Adult Treatment Panel (ATP II) of the National Cholesterol Education Program are stratified according to whether coronary heart disease (CHD) or other atheroscle-

TABLE 15–1–1. FREDRICKSON CLASSIFICATION OF THE HYPERLIPIDEMIAS*

Phenotype	Lipoprotein(s) Elevated	Plasma Cholesterol Level	Plasma Triglyceride Level	Atherogenicity	Relative Frequency[†] (%)
I	Chylomicrons	Normal to ↑	↑↑↑↑	None seen	<1
IIa	LDL	↑↑	Normal	+++	10
IIb	LDL and VLDL	↑↑	↑↑	+++	40
III	IDL	↑↑	↑↑↑	+++	<1
IV	VLDL	Normal to ↑	↑↑	+	45
V	VLDL and chylomicrons	↑ to ↑↑	↑↑↑↑	+	5

IDL, intermediate-density lipoprotein; LDL, low-density lipoprotein; VLDL, very low density lipoprotein.

*The Fredrickson classification does not consider levels of high-density lipoprotein (HDL) cholesterol. It is not an etiologic classification and does not differentiate primary and secondary hyperlipidemias.

[†]Approximate percentages of U.S. patients with hyperlipidemia.

Source: International Lipid Information Bureau. The ILIB lipid handbook for clinical practice: Blood lipids and coronary heart disease. Houston: International Lipid Information Bureau, 1995. Reproduced with permission from the publisher and author.

rotic disease is present. In primary prevention (CHD absent), three categories are provided for identifying hypercholesterolemia (National Cholesterol Education Program, 1994). Total blood cholesterol levels less than 200 mg/dL are classified as desirable, levels of 200 to 239 mg/dL are classified as borderline high, and levels of 240 mg/dL or greater are classified as high. Patients with desirable blood cholesterol and HDL cholesterol levels less than 35 mg/dL, patients with borderline-high blood cholesterol and HDL cholesterol levels less than 35 mg/dL or at least two other risk factors, patients with high blood cholesterol, and patients with established CHD or other atherosclerotic disease should have a fasting lipoprotein analysis performed to determine their LDL cholesterol levels.

Additional risk factors in the ATP II's algorithm are age (45 years or older in men; 55 years or older or premature menopause without estrogen replacement therapy in women), family history of premature CHD (definite myocardial infarction or sudden death before 55 years of age in father or other male first-degree relative, or before 65 years of age in mother or other female first-degree relative), current cigarette smoking,

TABLE 15–1–2. SELECTED PRIMARY HYPERLIPIDEMIAS

Disorder	Fredrickson Phenotype	Transmission and Mechanism	Major Clinical Findings and Estimated U.S. Prevalence
Familial chylomicronemia	I	Autosomal recessive; lipoprotein lipase or apo C-II deficiency	Usually diagnosed in childhood by recurrent abdominal pain and pancreatitis. Lipemia retinalis, eruptive xanthomas, and hepatosplenomegaly may occur. Heterozygotes: Normal TG or mild hypertriglyceridemia in absence of other conditions associated with hypertriglyceridemia. Homozygotes: Fasting TG may exceed 1000 mg/dL. Not believed to increase CHD risk. Extremely rare.
Heterozygous familial hypercholesterolemia	IIa (IIb rare)	Autosomal dominant; LDL receptor defect	TC elevated at birth, eventually reaches 350–500 mg/dL. Tendon xanthomas, corneal arcus, and premature atherosclerosis are typical. Prevalence 1/500.
Homozygous familial hypercholesterolemia	IIa (IIb rare)	Autosomal dominant; LDL receptor defect	TC elevated at birth; TC reaches 600–1200 mg/dL. Cutaneous xanthomas, tendon xanthomas; corneal arcus. Severe, widespread early atherosclerosis, including aortic stenosis. Prevalence $1/10^6$.
Familial defective apo B-100	IIa	Autosomal dominant; apo B mutation	Lipoprotein levels and clinical features may be similar to heterozygous familial hypercholesterolemia; in some cases, may be more moderate. Definitive diagnosis by molecular analysis. Prevalence varies by ethnicity; 1/700 in Caucasians.
Polygenic hypercholesterolemia	IIa	Mode of transmission unknown; various genetic defects	TC elevation generally less than in heterozygous familial hypercholesterolemia, 240–300 mg/dL. Xanthomas are very rare. As many as 80% of patients with isolated hypercholesterolemia due to LDL cholesterol have polygenic hypercholesterolemia. Prevalence uncertain; 1/20 to 1/100 estimated.
Familial combined hyperlipidemia	IIa, IIb, IV	Unknown if monogenic or polygenic; mechanism unknown; associated with overproduction of apo B	Elevated TC or TG (or both) in patient and family members. When TC elevated, typically 250–350 mg/dL; when TG elevated, two thirds of patients have mild to moderate hypertriglyceridemia, but elevation may be severe. No unique clinical features. May or may not be expressed in childhood. Increased CHD risk. Prevalence approximately 1/100.
Type III hyperlipidemia (familial dysbetalipoproteinemia)	III	Usually mimics autosomal recessive mode; homozygous for apo E₂ usually requiring other metabolic factors for full expression	Typically, TC 300–600 mg/dL, TG 400–800 mg/dL (TG may be much higher). Palmar xanthomas and tuberoeruptive xanthomas may occur. Disorder is exacerbated by diabetes mellitus and hypothyroidism. Not commonly expressed in childhood. Specialized laboratory can provide definitive diagnosis (apo E isoform). Premature CHD, peripheral vascular disease, and stroke. Prevalence 1/5000.
Familial endogenous hypertriglyceridemia	IV, V	Often dominant; mechanism not established	Typically, TG 200–500 mg/dL in phenotype IV, TG > 1000 mg/dL in phenotype V. HDL cholesterol usually decreased. Early CHD in some families but not in others. Type IV may be associated with modest chylomicronemia, giving a type V pattern in which the VLDL fraction remains predominant. Prevalence of type IV approximately 1/300; type V rare.

apo, apolipoprotein; CHD, coronary heart disease; HDL, high-density lipoprotein; LDL, low-density lipoprotein; TC, total cholesterol; TG, triglyceride.

Source: International Lipid Information Bureau. The ILIB lipid handbook for clinical practice: Blood lipids and coronary heart disease. Houston: International Lipid Information Bureau, 1995. Reproduced with permission from the publisher and author.

TABLE 15–1–3. SELECTED CAUSES OF SECONDARY HYPERLIPIDEMIA

Total and Low-Density Lipoprotein Cholesterol Elevation	Plasma Triglyceride Elevation
Diet rich in saturated fatty acids	Diet rich in carbohydrates
Hypothyroidism	Excessive alcohol consumption (more than 40 g/d ethanol)
Nephrotic syndrome	
Chronic liver disease (mainly primary biliary cirrhosis)	Obesity
	Pregnancy
Cholestasis	Diabetes mellitus
Dysglobulinemia	Hypothyroidism
Cushing's syndrome	Chronic renal failure
Oral contraceptives	Pancreatitis
Pregnancy	Cushing's syndrome
Anorexia nervosa	Hypopituitarism
Acute intermittent porphyria	Dysglobulinemia
	Glycogen storage disease
	Lipodystrophy
	Acute intermittent porphyria
	Systemic lupus erythematosus
	Beta blockers, thiazide diuretics
	Estrogen (contraceptive or replacement)
	Glucocorticoids
	Isotretinoin

Source: International Lipid Information Bureau. The ILIB lipid handbook for clinical practice: Blood lipids and coronary heart disease. Houston: International Lipid Information Bureau, 1995. Reproduced with permission from the publisher and author.

hypertension (140/90 mm Hg or greater or on antihypertensive medication), HDL cholesterol less than 35 mg/dL, and diabetes mellitus; an HDL cholesterol level of 60 mg/dL or greater is a negative risk factor, decreasing by 1 the total number of risk factors.

Definitive

The combination of LDL cholesterol level and overall risk level is used to determine the need for intervention, as shown in Table 15–1–4. In primary prevention, LDL cholesterol less than 130 mg/dL is classified as desirable, 130 to 159 mg/dL is classified as borderline-high risk, and 160 mg/dL or greater is classified as high risk. In secondary prevention (CHD present), LDL cholesterol greater than 100 mg/dL is considered nonoptimal.

In both primary and secondary prevention, the ATP II classifies triglyceride levels less than 200 mg/dL as normal, 200 to 400 mg/dL as borderline high, 400 to 1000 mg/dL as high, and greater than 1000 mg/dL as very high.

TABLE 15–1–4. LOW-DENSITY LIPOPROTEIN CHOLESTEROL TREATMENT LEVELS: NATIONAL CHOLESTEROL EDUCATION PROGRAM ADULT TREATMENT PANEL II

	LDL Cholesterol Level (mg/dL)			
	Dietary Therapy		Drug Therapy	
Risk	Initiation Level	Goal	Consideration Level	Goal
Without CHD, risk factors <2	≥160	<160	≥190*	<160
Without CHD, risk factors ≥2	≥130	<130	≥160	<130
With CHD or other atherosclerotic disease	>100	≤100	≥130†	≤100

CHD, coronary heart disease; LDL, low-density lipoprotein.
*In younger patients (men <35 years of age and premenopausal women) with LDL cholesterol levels of 190–220 mg/dL, drug therapy should be delayed except in high-risk patients such as those with diabetes.
†In patients with CHD and LDL cholesterol levels of 100–130 mg/dL, the physician should exercise clinical judgment in deciding whether to initiate drug therapy.
Source: National Cholesterol Education Program. Second report of the Expert Panel on Detection, Evaluation, and Treatment of High Blood Cholesterol in Adults (Adult Treatment Panel II). Circulation 1994;89:1329.

CLINICAL MANIFESTATIONS

Subjective

Patients with hyperlipidemia, particularly hypercholesterolemia, may present with evidence of atherosclerotic disease, such as angina, myocardial infarction, intermittent claudication, transient ischemic attacks, or stroke. In patients with greatly elevated triglyceride levels, episodes of acute abdominal pain with or without pancreatitis may occur. When triglyceride levels are already high, dietary or alcohol excesses may send them into the range of several thousand within days and induce abdominal pain.

The patient should be questioned about a possible family history of dyslipidemia, which can be confirmed by screening first-degree relatives. It is essential to attempt to determine whether the patient's hyperlipidemia is of a primary or secondary nature. In most cases of secondary hyperlipidemia, treatment of the underlying disease or removal of the offending drug can control the hyperlipidemia.

Family history of cardiovascular disease, hypertension, diabetes mellitus, and central obesity should also be determined. The patient's diet, namely, daily intake of calories, total fat, saturated fat, other types of fat, cholesterol, alcohol, simple carbohydrates, and sodium, should be evaluated. Physical exercise, smoking habits, and stress should also be assessed.

Objective

Physical Examination

The physician should look for manifestations of dyslipidemia, such as tendinous and/or tuberous xanthomas, xanthelasma, corneal arcus, and hepatosplenomegaly. Eruptive xanthomas of the skin and lipemia retinalis may occur in individuals with severe chylomicronemia or severe hypertriglyceridemia. A complete examination of the carotid and peripheral arterial systems, including auscultation for bruits, may detect atherosclerotic involvement.

Physical examination should also include weight, height, calculated body mass index, waist:hip ratio, blood pressure, and examination for manifestations of thyroid abnormalities. Optimal body mass index (weight:height^2 in kg/m^2) is 20 to 25. Desirable waist:hip ratio is less than 0.9 in men and less than 0.8 in women.

Routine Laboratory Abnormalities

Besides abnormal plasma lipid levels, there are no routine laboratory abnormalities that commonly accompany dyslipidemias; however, certain laboratory tests are helpful to diagnose possible secondary causes of hyperlipidemia. Fasting glucose and/or glycosylated hemoglobin, as well as a glucose tolerance test, may be helpful to assess for diabetes or the degree of glucose control. Liver function tests are helpful to consider obstructive liver disease. Thyroid function tests, especially thyroid-stimulating hormone, are useful to consider hypothyroidism. A urinalysis may detect protein, and quantitative 24-hour urine collections can determine if nephrosis is present. Serum creatinine can be used to assess for chronic renal insufficiency.

PLANS

Diagnostic

Differential Diagnosis

Appropriate diagnostic tests should be performed to rule out disease states such as diabetes mellitus, hypothyroidism, nephrotic syndrome, renal failure, and obstructive liver disease, which can be associated with significant lipid disorders.

Diagnostic Options

At the time of lipid screening, a patient should have a stable weight, be on a stable diet, and be free of illness or recent surgery, all of which may affect blood lipids. In patients with myocardial infarction, lipids should be measured within 12 hours of onset of chest pain or 4 to 6 weeks after myocardial infarction. Testing should be deferred for 3 months after other major illness or surgery and for 3 weeks after minor illness. Because pregnancy is associated with physiologic hyperlipidemia, testing should be deferred until after delivery except in patients with a history of hypertriglyceridemia.

Total cholesterol and HDL cholesterol may be measured in the non-fasting state, but to avoid postprandial lipemia, blood samples for triglyceride determination should be collected after a 12-hour fast. Levels of total cholesterol, triglyceride, and, if accuracy can be ensured, HDL cholesterol should be measured. Lipoprotein electrophoresis may be performed to determine the hyperlipidemic phenotype, particularly if the patient has combined hyperlipidemia and if an elevation of intermediate-density lipoprotein (IDL) is suspected. Electrophoretic mobility is as follows: chylomicrons remain at the origin, very low density lipoprotein (VLDL) has pre-beta mobility, IDL has broad-beta mobility, LDL has beta mobility, and HDL has alpha mobility. Alternatively, a plasma aliquot refrigerated at 4°C for several hours can help determine the type of hyperlipidemia. Hypercholesterolemia due to elevated LDL results in a clear plasma. When elevation of VLDL leads to hypertriglyceridemia in excess of 400 mg/dL, there will be uniform turbidity throughout the tube; the presence of chylomicrons is seen as a creamy supranatant.

The level of LDL cholesterol (mg/dL) can be estimated from the Friedewald formula:

$$\text{LDL cholesterol} = \text{total cholesterol} - \text{HDL cholesterol} - (\text{triglyceride}/5)$$

The formula is invalid, however, if the patient has a triglyceride level greater than 400 mg/dL, type III hyperlipidemia, or apolipoprotein $E_{2/2}$ phenotype. In each of these circumstances, measurement of LDL cholesterol by ultracentrifugation in a specialized laboratory is required for accuracy.

Recommended Approach

In our opinion, all adults should undergo a lipoprotein analysis in which their fasting lipid levels are measured. If the values do not fall outside the optimum range, then retesting every 5 years is sufficient. In most people, this schedule will still allow primary preventive intervention when indicated. Lipid screening is also advisable in high-risk children, particularly in those with a family history of premature CHD, hyperlipidemia, diabetes, or hypertension. A separate panel has developed guidelines for children and adolescents (National Cholesterol Education Program, 1992). In all patients, at least two separate measurements should be taken for definitive diagnosis before therapeutic intervention is considered.

Therapeutic

Therapeutic Options

The rationale for treating hypercholesterolemia rests on abundant observational epidemiologic, experimental, genetic, and interventional studies that link total cholesterol and LDL cholesterol in a direct causal fashion to the incidence of CHD. Dietary therapy (Table 15–1–5), which should include weight control and increased physical activity, should be the initial therapy for all patients with hypercholesterolemia (Table 15–1–4). The majority of patients with borderline-high cholesterol may be satisfactorily treated with diet. If diet fails to achieve a sufficient reduction in the cholesterol level, drug therapy may be added. The LDL cholesterol levels for drug treatment consideration as recommended by the ATP II are outlined in Table 15–1–4. Drug therapy supplements but does not replace dietary therapy.

Although strong associations between plasma triglyceride elevation and increased CHD risk have been found in some studies, evidence supporting a causal relation is still incomplete (Austin, 1989). Clinical trials designed specifically to lower triglyceride levels have not been reported. Treatment of hypertriglyceridemia is primarily hygienic and should include a diet low in saturated fat, weight reduction if overweight, alcohol restriction, and increased physical activity. For patients with very high triglyceride levels, drug therapy may be indicated because of the high risk for developing acute pancreatitis. Drugs to reduce triglyceride may also be needed in patients with recalcitrant hypertriglyceridemia who are otherwise at high risk for CHD. Framingham Heart Study data identified a subgroup of individuals defined by elevated triglyceride (>150 mg/dL) and low HDL cholesterol (<40 mg/dL) who are at very high risk for CHD (Castelli, 1992). The American Diabetes Association has suggested that persistent hypertriglyceridemia in diabetics should be treated to reduce atherosclerotic risk. No effective drug therapy exists for the rare familial chylomicronemia (type I hyperlipidemia).

High-density lipoprotein cholesterol concentration has an inverse relation to the incidence of CHD. Although the precise mechanism of HDL's beneficial effect on CHD risk is not known, it is presumed to be related to the putative role of HDL in reverse cholesterol transport. In addition, HDL cholesterol level is inversely related to the triglyceride level. In the absence of results of clinical studies designed to determine the effect of modulating the HDL cholesterol level, the ATP II recommends that attempts to increase HDL cholesterol be limited to nonpharmacologic means. Regular vigorous exercise, smoking cessation, and weight loss increase HDL levels; however, if drug therapy is required to lower elevated LDL cholesterol, agents may be selected that also raise HDL cholesterol. Moderate alcohol consumption has been shown to increase HDL, but alcohol consumption should not be recommended for this purpose.

There are five classes of approved lipid-lowering agents: bile acid sequestrants, nicotinic acid, 3-hydroxy-3-methylglutaryl coenzyme A (HMG-CoA) reductase inhibitors, fibric acid derivatives, and probucol. Their lipid effects, mechanisms, and side effects are summarized in Table 15–1–6.

The bile acid sequestrants, cholestyramine and colestipol, are nonabsorbable powdered resins that are very effective in lowering LDL cholesterol, which can be expected to decrease 15 to 30%. Usual doses are 4 to 16 g/d for cholestyramine and 5–20 g/d for colestipol; maximum doses are 24 and 30 g/d, respectively.

Nicotinic acid, or niacin (vitamin B_3), lowers LDL cholesterol 10 to 25%. In addition, triglyceride may be expected to decrease 20 to 50% and HDL cholesterol to increase 15 to 35%. Nicotinic acid is available in both crystalline and sustained-release preparations, although the sustained-release form is not recommended because of increased risk for hepatotoxicity. The crystalline form is usually dosed at 1.5 to 3 g/d, up to a maximum dose of 6 g/d. Care should be taken to monitor glucose levels in patients with glucose intolerance. Plasma uric acid levels should be monitored in patients with hyperuricemia or a history of gout.

The newest class of drugs for reducing hypercholesterolemia is the HMG-CoA reductase inhibitors, competitive inhibitors of the rate-limiting enzyme in cholesterol synthesis. Available agents are fluvastatin, lovastatin, pravastatin, and simvastatin. These drugs are well tolerated and lower LDL cholesterol 20 to 40%, raise HDL cholesterol 5 to 15%, and lower triglyceride 10 to 20%. Usual doses are 20 to 40 mg/d for fluvastatin, 10 to 40 mg/d for lovastatin or pravastatin, and 5 to 20 mg/d for simvastatin; maximum doses are 40 mg/d for fluvastatin, pravastatin, or simvastatin and 80 mg/d for lovastatin. Rare instances of myositis or elevated hepatic transaminase levels have been reported with these drugs at maximum doses.

Fibric acid derivatives available in the United States are gemfibrozil and clofibrate; fenofibrate is approved but is not yet available. Bezafibrate, ciprofibrate, and fenofibrate are used in other countries. These

TABLE 15–1–5. DIETARY THERAPY OF HIGH BLOOD CHOLESTEROL

Nutrient	Step I Diet	Step II Diet
Total fat	≤30% of total calories	
Saturated fat	8–10% of total calories	<7% of total calories
Polyunsaturated fat	≤10% of total calories	
Monounsaturated fat	≤15% of total calories	
Carbohydrates	≥55% of total calories	
Protein	~15% of total calories	
Cholesterol	<300 mg/d	<200 mg/d
Total calories	Sufficient to achieve and maintain desirable weight	

Source: National Cholesterol Education Program. Second report of the Expert Panel on Detection, Evaluation, and Treatment of High Blood Cholesterol in Adults (Adult Treatment Panel II). Circulation 1994;89:1329.

TABLE 15-1-6. LIPID-LOWERING AGENTS: MECHANISMS, LIPID EFFECTS, AND SIDE EFFECTS

Drug Class and Agents	Mechanism of Action and Lipid Effects	Selected Biochemical Side Effects	Selected Systemic Side Effects
Bile acid sequestrants (resins) Cholestyramine, 4–24 g/d Colestipol, 5–30 g/d	Increase excretion of bile acids in the stool; increase LDL receptor activity; effectively decrease LDL cholesterol; HDL cholesterol increases slightly; may *increase* triglyceride	Binding and decreased absorption of certain other drugs; may prevent absorption of fat-soluble vitamins	No systemic toxicity; upper and lower gastrointestinal complaints common, (e.g., constipation, bloating)
Nicotinic acid (niacin), 1.5–6 g/d	Decreases plasma levels of free fatty acids; decreases hepatic VLDL synthesis; possibly inhibits cholesterol synthesis; effectively decreases both LDL cholesterol and triglyceride; effectively increases HDL cholesterol	Altered liver function tests, increased uric acid, increased glucose intolerance	Cutaneous flushing, pruritus, gastrointestinal upset; side effects tend to limit compliance
HMG-CoA reductase inhibitors (statins) Fluvastatin, 20–40 mg/d Lovastatin, 10–80 mg/d Pravastatin, 10–40 mg/d Simvastatin, 5–40 mg/d	Inhibit HMG-CoA reductase, the rate-limiting step in cholesterol biosynthesis; increase LDL receptor activity; effectively decrease LDL cholesterol; have moderate effect in decreasing triglyceride and in increasing HDL cholesterol	Elevated transaminase levels can occur (minor and usually transient); increased creatine kinase (uncommon)	Mild gastrointestinal symptoms; myositis syndrome (rare)
Fibric acid derivatives (fibrates) Gemfibrozil, 1.2 g/d Clofibrate, 2 g/d	Decrease hepatic VLDL synthesis; increase lipoprotein lipase activity; decrease triglyceride effectively; increase HDL cholesterol effectively; effect on LDL cholesterol variable, but may increase, especially in hypertriglyceridemia	Transient transaminase increases not infrequent; can potentiate effects of oral anticoagulants	Increased incidence of cholelithiasis; diarrhea, nausea, skin rash, myositis (rare)
Probucol, 1 g/d	Enhances scavenger pathway removal of LDL; slightly to moderately decreases LDL cholesterol; usually no effect on triglyceride; substantially *decreases* HDL cholesterol	Prolongation of QT interval and serious ventricular arrhythmias have occurred but are rare	Side effects usually infrequent and of short duration; chiefly, diarrhea, nausea, flatulence

HDL, high-density lipoprotein; HMG-CoA, 3-hydroxy-3-methylglutaryl coenzyme A; LDL, low-density lipoprotein; VLDL, very low density lipoprotein.

agents decrease LDL cholesterol by approximately 10 to 15% and decrease triglyceride by 20 to 50%; HDL cholesterol may be raised 10 to 15%. Usual doses are 1.2 g/d for gemfibrozil and 2 g/d for clofibrate. It is recommended that clofibrate not be used routinely.

Probucol reduces LDL cholesterol 5 to 15%, although the response can vary greatly. HDL cholesterol may be reduced 20 to 30%. The long-term effect of simultaneously lowering LDL cholesterol and HDL cholesterol has not been investigated, and as a result, probucol is seldom used. Recommended and maximum dosage is 1 g/d.

Combination drug therapy may enable enhanced efficacy, lower dosages, reduced side effects, and reduced cost. Aggressive lipid lowering can be achieved with combination drug therapy, which may be particularly useful in patients with established CHD to reach the LDL cholesterol goal of 100 mg/dL. Because of the risk for myositis, the use of an HMG-CoA reductase inhibitor in conjunction with a fibric acid derivative is discouraged; this combination should only be used with caution. There is possibly increased risk for myopathy or liver dysfunction with the combination of an HMG-CoA reductase inhibitor and nicotinic acid.

Estrogen replacement therapy may be considered to improve the lipid profile and to decrease CHD risk in postmenopausal women, although estrogens do not have Food and Drug Administration indications for these uses. LDL cholesterol may be decreased up to 15% and HDL cholesterol may be increased up to 15% at oral doses of 0.625 mg/d conjugated estrogen or 2 mg/d micronized estradiol. Triglyceride level may increase, however, particularly in women who already have elevated triglyceride levels, and therefore should be monitored closely. Whether or not oral estrogen replacement therapy reduces CHD risk requires prospective clinical trial proof.

Experimental methods to lower LDL cholesterol, used primarily in familial hypercholesterolemia, include extracorporeal procedures (plasma exchange, heparin-induced extracorporeal LDL precipitation, and LDL apheresis using dextran sulfate–cellulose columns), portacaval shunt, liver transplantation, and partial ileal bypass surgery.

Recommended Approach

Except in uncommon cases, the initial therapy for hyperlipidemia is diet. The ATP II recommends the American Heart Association's stepped diet approach (Table 15–1–5). The Step I Diet is recommended for the general population 2 years of age and older. For patients with CHD or for patients whose LDL cholesterol remains elevated despite several months of adherence to the Step I Diet, the Step II Diet should be instituted. Some patients can reduce total cholesterol 20% by diet; most achieve about a 10% reduction when diet is maintained over a long period, but response is highly variable.

An experienced dietitian is extremely valuable in instituting dietary therapy, especially the Step II Diet, and encouraging patient compliance. Family members should be included in the patient's nutrition counseling sessions. A regular exercise program, individualized to the patient's specific needs and tolerance, is a necessary component of dietary therapy. Weight loss if needed and smoking cessation as appropriate should also be incorporated into the treatment regimen. An adequate trial of diet should be at least 6 months; a longer period is needed if significant weight loss is required.

If, after an adequate trial of dietary therapy, sufficient LDL cholesterol lowering has not been obtained, consideration may be given to the addition of drug therapy. The initiation and goal levels of LDL cholesterol for drug therapy in the primary and secondary prevention of CHD are listed in Table 15–1–4. ATP II recommendations for drug selection by type of hyperlipidemia are shown in Table 15–1–7.

For very high triglyceride levels, the ATP II recommends drug treatment with nicotinic acid or gemfibrozil if dietary measures are insufficient. High triglyceride levels should be treated with drugs in patients with a history of acute pancreatitis. In our opinion, elevated triglyceride levels in the presence of other CHD risk factors should also be aggressively reduced. If cholesterol and triglyceride levels are both elevated, and if the patient smokes or has hypertension, diabetes, or a family history of premature CHD, we believe that hypertriglyceridemia should be vigorously treated.

TABLE 15–1–7. ADULT TREATMENT PANEL II RECOMMENDATIONS FOR DRUG SELECTION

Hyperlipidemia	Single Drug	Combination Drug
Elevated LDL cholesterol and triglyceride <200 mg/dL	Bile acid sequestrant	Bile acid sequestrant + HMG-CoA reductase inhibitor
	HMG-CoA reductase inhibitor	Bile acid sequestrant + nicotinic acid
	Nicotinic acid	HMG-CoA reductase inhibitor + nicotinic acid*
Elevated LDL cholesterol and triglyceride 200–400 mg/dL	Nicotinic acid	Nicotinic acid + HMG-CoA reductase inhibitor*
	HMG-CoA reductase inhibitor	HMG-CoA reductase inhibitor + gemfibrozil†
	Gemfibrozil	Nicotinic acid + bile acid sequestrant
		Nicotinic acid + gemfibrozil

HMG-CoA, 3-hydroxy-3-methylglutaryl coenzyme A; LDL, low-density lipoprotein.
*Possible increased risk for myopathy or liver dysfunction.
†Increased risk for myopathy; must be used with caution.
Source: National Cholesterol Education Program. Second report of the Expert Panel on Detection, Evaluation, and Treatment of High Blood Cholesterol in Adults (Adult Treatment Panel II). Circulation 1994;89:1329.

FOLLOW-UP

Plasma lipid levels and body weight should be determined every 2 to 3 months until desired lipid reduction and weight reduction are achieved. In primary prevention, an adequate trial of diet is at least 6 months if compliance is good; the trial may be shorter in secondary prevention, or according to clinical judgment. If medications are used, plasma lipid analyses should be repeated every 2 to 3 months for the first 12 months, until efficacy and safety have been established. The physician should also monitor levels of hepatic transaminases, glucose, and uric acid as necessary for the drug chosen. After the first year, follow-up lipid determinations may be performed two to three times a year to confirm efficacy and safety and to ensure patient compliance with diet and drug therapy. A fasting lipoprotein analysis should be performed annually.

Diet should be continued even if medications are given; drug therapy is a supplement to dietary therapy. Once drug therapy is initiated, it usually must be continued indefinitely, despite attainment of treatment goals, as lipids will return to pretreatment levels if drugs are stopped.

DISCUSSION
Prevalence and Incidence

According to data from the third National Health and Nutrition Examination Survey (NHANES III), conducted from 1988 to 1991, 29% of Americans 20 years of age or older require lipid-lowering therapy by the ATP II guidelines (Sempos et al., 1993).

Related Basic Science

Lipids are transported through plasma in macromolecular complexes called lipoproteins. These lipoproteins have a hydrophobic central core of cholesteryl ester and triglyceride and a hydrophilic outer layer of phospholipid, free cholesterol, and apolipoproteins.

Lipoproteins may be classified by their density on ultracentrifugation into chylomicrons, VLDL, IDL, LDL, and HDL. Chylomicrons, which are the largest and least dense of the lipoproteins, transport dietary fat (triglyceride) and cholesterol from the intestine. VLDL is synthesized by the liver and carries endogenous triglyceride and cholesterol. Intravascular activation of lipoprotein lipase by apolipoproteins on the lipoprotein surface leads to the removal of triglyceride from chylomicrons and from VLDL and the formation of chylomicron remnants and IDL, respectively. Chylomicron remnants are rapidly cleared by the liver; IDL is either removed by the liver or converted through further lipolysis by hepatic lipase to LDL.

Approximately 70% of plasma cholesterol is carried by LDL. Most of the body's cholesterol pool is derived from hepatic de novo synthesis, although a significant fraction (15–20%) is derived from the diet.

Part of the hepatic cholesterol pool is converted to bile acids, and part is released into the bile as unesterified cholesterol. Clearance of plasma cholesterol is achieved primarily by specific cell surface receptor-mediated uptake of LDL. The liver is a rich source of LDL receptors, which are under feedback control. As the hepatic concentration of cholesterol increases, LDL receptor activity decreases, and vice versa. Medications such as the bile acid sequestrants and HMG-CoA reductase inhibitors, two classes of drugs that decrease the hepatic intracellular concentration of cholesterol, increase LDL receptor activity. A diet rich in saturated fat and cholesterol may chronically suppress hepatic LDL receptors.

An estimated two thirds to three fourths of the LDL particles are cleared from the circulation by LDL receptors. The remainder are thought to be removed by a scavenger pathway present in cells of the reticuloendothelial system. The lipoprotein receptors on cells such as macrophages do not bind to native LDL, but they do actively bind to and lead to the internalization of LDL that has been chemically altered, for example, by acetylation, modification by malondialdehyde, or oxidation. The macrophages can then become lipid-laden foam cells, which are an early transformation in atherogenesis.

High-density lipoprotein is produced by the liver and intestine and acquires components from the lipolysis of the triglyceride-rich lipoproteins (chylomicrons and VLDL), which may account for the inverse relation between HDL cholesterol and plasma triglyceride levels. HDL is thought to be a vehicle for reverse cholesterol transport, allowing the return of cholesterol from peripheral tissues to the liver and subsequent excretion into the bile. Increased levels of HDL would therefore suggest that adequate triglyceride clearance is occurring as well as enhanced reverse cholesterol transport, both of which may reduce atherogenesis.

Natural History and Its Modification with Treatment

Type IIa hyperlipidemia (see Table 15–1–1) is one of the most common lipid disorders and is associated with increased risk for CHD and peripheral vascular disease. Type IIa hyperlipidemia per se does not define a specific disease, as several genetic and environmental etiologies may produce this lipid pattern. One cause is familial hypercholesterolemia, an autosomal dominant inherited disease characterized by LDL receptor deficiency. Patients with heterozygous familial hypercholesterolemia (prevalence about 1 in 500) have a 50% reduction in LDL receptor activity and experience significant premature CHD. Patients with homozygous familial hypercholesterolemia (prevalence about 1 in 10^6) are usually completely deficient in functional LDL receptors and have marked atherosclerosis by age 20. Other genetic origins of type IIa hyperlipidemia include polygenic hypercholesterolemia, familial combined hyperlipidemia, and familial defective apolipoprotein B.

Type IIb hyperlipidemia is also very common and occurs in familial combined hyperlipidemia, rarely in familial hypercholesterolemia, and as a secondary disorder in non-insulin-dependent diabetes mellitus, the nephrotic syndrome, and hypothyroidism. Type IIb hyperlipidemia is associated with decreased levels of HDL cholesterol.

Type III hyperlipidemia, associated with familial dysbetalipoproteinemia, is clinically uncommon; however, the presence of IDL does predispose to accelerated atherosclerosis. Patients with type III hyperlipidemia are characteristically homozygous for one of the isoforms of apolipoprotein E, namely, apolipoprotein E_2. This condition may be detected by isoelectric focusing. Apolipoprotein E_2 exhibits decreased binding to the LDL receptor compared with apolipoproteins E_3 and E_4. As 1% of the general population is homozygous for apolipoprotein E_2 but the incidence of type III hyperlipidemia is about 1 in 5000, additional predisposing metabolic factors must be present for expression of the disorder.

Like the other phenotypes, type IV hyperlipidemia may be the result of either genetic or secondary factors. Secondary causes of type IV hyperlipidemia include obesity, diabetes, chronic renal failure, overconsumption of alcohol, or the actions of thiazides, steroids, and beta-blocking agents. Some patients with type IV hyperlipidemia may be predisposed to atherosclerosis, particularly those with familial combined hyperlipidemia.

Patients with type I or V hyperlipidemia are predisposed to recurrent bouts of pancreatitis. Type I manifests primarily in childhood and can cause hepatosplenomegaly. Type V is frequently associated with poorly controlled diabetes mellitus. Evidence of premature atherosclerosis has not been recorded in type I hyperlipidemia (see Table 15–1–1).

Prevention

The patient should be counseled by the physician on the risks associated with elevated plasma lipids. Genetic counseling may be helpful to patients with familial dyslipidemia.

Extensive data have shown that lowering a patient's plasma cholesterol level reduces his or her CHD risk. In the Lipid Research Clinics Coronary Primary Prevention Trial, a randomized, double-blind, placebo-controlled, multicenter trial conducted in 3806 men with plasma cholesterol levels greater than 265 mg/dL, patients who received cholestyramine experienced a 9% reduction in cholesterol levels and a 19% reduction in definite CHD events during a mean 7.4 years on trial (Lipid Research Clinics Program, 1984). A subgroup of cholestyramine-treated patients who achieved a 25% reduction in cholesterol had an impressive 49% reduction in CHD events.

More recently, cholesterol lowering has been shown to reduce all-cause mortality. In the Scandinavian Simvastatin Survival Study, a double-blind, multicenter trial, 4444 men and women with a history of angina pectoris or myocardial infarction and with total cholesterol levels of 215 to 300 mg/dL and triglyceride levels no greater than 220 mg/dL after dietary therapy were randomized to receive simvastatin or placebo. After a median of 5.4 years of simvastatin treatment (20 mg/d, increased to 40 mg/d in 37% of patients), cardiovascular mortality decreased 42% and total mortality, the primary endpoint, decreased 30%. Simvastatin lowered total cholesterol 25%, LDL cholesterol 35%, and triglyceride 10% and increased HDL cholesterol 8% (Scandinavian Simvastatin Survival Study Group, 1994).

Recent angiographically monitored trials have suggested that the progression of atherosclerotic disease can be retarded or even reversed with cholesterol lowering. The rates of coronary lesion progression and regression vary depending on the intervention, but on average, these trials have reported coronary lesion progression in twice as many control patients and regression in three times as many treated patients. In these trials, treated patients also experienced fewer CHD events.

The results of these studies suggest, and the ATP II recommends, that physicians should screen all adults for cholesterol abnormalities so that early primary prevention measures can be implemented. Physicians should also evaluate lipids in patients with established CHD so that aggressive secondary prevention measures can be taken to slow the progression of the disease.

Cost Containment

Simple measurement of total cholesterol, triglyceride, and HDL cholesterol, combined with observation of refrigerated plasma, should allow the physician to classify the hyperlipidemia. The more costly lipoprotein electrophoresis should be reserved for patients who have both high cholesterol and high triglyceride levels, to determine whether type IIb or type III hyperlipidemia is present. The ability to measure cholesterol quickly and inexpensively will make it feasible for more of the population to know their cholesterol level. At present, the measurement of selected apolipoproteins, such as A-I and B-100, is a research procedure, and the laboratory procedure has not been standardized; however, these measurements may be useful in the near future as good predictors of CHD risk. Lipoprotein[a] is genetically determined and is associated with increased CHD risk at levels above 30 mg/dL. As with the apolipoproteins, standardized laboratory tests are not yet available, and routine measurement of lipoprotein[a] is not recommended.

REFERENCES

Austin MA. Plasma triglyceride as a risk factor for coronary heart disease: The epidemiologic evidence and beyond. Am J Epidemiol 1989;129:249.

Castelli WP. Epidemiology of triglycerides: A view from Framingham. Am J Cardiol 1992;70:3H.

Lipid Research Clinics Program. The Lipid Research Clinics Coronary Primary Prevention Trial results. I. Reduction in incidence of coronary heart disease. II. The relationship of reduction in incidence of coronary heart disease to cholesterol lowering. JAMA 1984;251:351.

National Cholesterol Education Program. Report of the Expert Panel on Blood Cholesterol Levels in Children and Adolescents. Pediatrics 1992;39:525.

National Cholesterol Education Program. Second report of the Expert Panel on Detection, Evaluation, and Treatment of High Blood Cholesterol in Adults (Adult Treatment Panel II). Circulation 1994;89:1329.

Scandinavian Simvastatin Survival Study Group. Randomised trial of cholesterol lowering in 4444 patients with coronary heart disease: The Scandinavian Simvastatin Survival Study (4S). Lancet 1994;2:1383.

Sempos CT, Cleeman JI, Carroll MD, et al. Prevalence of high blood cholesterol among US adults: An update based on guidelines from the second report of the National Cholesterol Education Program Adult Treatment Panel. JAMA 1993;269:3009.

CHAPTER 15–2

Chest Pain

Robert C. Schlant, M.D.

DEFINITION

Chest pain is an unpleasant physical sensation in the thorax. Some patients with myocardial ischemia or angina pectoris have other sensations that are not truly painful. Some of the many terms used by such patients to describe myocardial ischemia include pressure, tightness, compression, fullness, ache, heaviness, discomfort, constricting, swelling, searing, indigestion, soreness, heartburn, choking, strangling, hard, dull, and like a toothache.

ETIOLOGY

The common causes of chest pain are listed in Table 15–2–1.

CRITERIA FOR DIAGNOSIS

Suggestive

Chest pain or discomfort is subjective and currently there are no clinical techniques to measure it objectively. The more the discomfort varies from the usual characteristics or descriptors, the less likely it is to be related to myocardial ischemia. Some types of chest pain or discomfort are associated with paresthesias or hyperesthesias.

In a middle-aged man with risk factors for coronary artery disease, the occurrence of exertional retrosternal heaviness or discomfort during exertion that is relieved in a few minutes with rest or nitroglycerin has more than a 90% likelihood of being associated with obstructive coronary artery disease. The occurrence of chest discomfort during exercise testing that is associated with significant ST segment changes on the electrocardiogram and/or wall motion abnormalities by imaging techniques has a very high likelihood of being associated with obstructive coronary artery disease on coronary arteriography.

See Appendix 7, Exercise Stress Electrocardiogram, by J. David Talley, M.D.

TABLE 15–2–1. COMMON CAUSES OF CHEST PAIN

Cardiac
Myocardial ischemia
  Exertional angina pectoris (from coronary atherosclerosis, aortic stenosis,
    hypertrophic cardiomyopathy, severe systemic arterial hypertension, severe right
    ventricular hypertension, aortic regurgitation, severe anemia/hypoxia)
  Acute myocardial infarction
  Variant angina pectoris
  Syndrome X
  Inadequate coronary vasodilator reserve
Acute pericarditis
Mitral valve prolapse

Aortic
Aortic dissection
Discrete thoracic aortic aneurysm

Pulmonary
Acute pulmonary embolism, with or without infarction
Pulmonary hypertension
Pneumothorax
Mediastinal emphysema
Pleurisy
Chronic obstructive lung disease
Tracheobronchitis
Tumor

Gastrointestinal
Esophageal reflux
Esophageal spasm
Esophageal rupture
Peptic ulcer disease
Acute pancreatitis
Biliary disease
Splenic flexure syndrome

Musculoskeletal
Chest wall pain and tenderness
Cervical vertebral disk
Degenerative joint disease of cervical/thoracic spine
Costochondritis (Tietze's syndrome)
Bursitis
Intercostal neuralgia, muscle cramps
Shoulder–hand syndrome
Scalenus anticus (thoracic outlet) syndrome
Mondor's syndrome (superficial thrombophlebitis of thoracic veins)

Cutaneous
Herpes zoster

Breasts
Pendulous breasts
Tumors

Psychogenic
Anxiety neurosis
Hyperventilation
Depression
Self-gain

Other
Chest wall tumors

Definitive

The definitive cause of chest pain in most instances is dependent on additional data from the physical examination and routine or specialized diagnostic procedures.

CLINICAL MANIFESTATIONS
Subjective

Pain or other sensations due to myocardial ischemia may be associated with weakness, tachycardia, sweating, or hypotension. Prolonged discomfort due to myocardial ischemia or early myocardial infarction is sometimes associated with an urge to defecate.

Important characteristics of chest discomfort or pain that should be determined include location, severity or intensity (oftentimes graded on a scale from 1 to 10), quality, frequency, mode of onset and precipitating and aggravating factors, duration, pattern of disappearance and factors that lessen or relieve the pain, and associated symptoms. In most instances, the detailed description of the discomfort or pain provides an accurate diagnosis. More detailed discussions of the clinical manifestations of many causes of chest pain are provided in individual chapters discussing specific conditions.

The discomfort of *myocardial ischemia* may radiate to the neck, jaw, shoulder, or arms, especially the ulnar aspect of the left arm. The discomfort of angina pectoris is usually precipitated by physical activity or emotional stress and is usually relieved within 3 to 4 minutes by nitroglycerin or spontaneously within 10 minutes. Rarely, it may last up to 15 to 20 minutes. Angina pectoris is considered stable when the pattern of angina is unchanged for more than 60 days, whereas it is considered unstable if it is a recent onset or when there is a change in or increased frequency or duration of attacks or increased severity or spontaneous episodes within 60 days. In some patients angina pectoris may occur at night (nocturnal) or at rest (angina decubitus). Variant (Prinzmetal's) angina pectoris characteristically occurs at rest, particularly in the early morning. Relief may occur spontaneously or following nitroglycerin, as with classic angina pectoris.

Angina pectoris may also occur in patients with syndrome X or in patients with inadequate coronary vasodilator reserve, such as in patients with left ventricular hypertrophy from hypertensive heart disease or hypertrophic cardiomyopathy.

The discomfort of *acute myocardial infarction* is similar to that of angina pectoris, but is characteristically more severe and lasts 30 minutes or longer. There may be associated nausea, vomiting, sweatiness, apprehension, weakness, dyspnea, and urge to defecate. Nitroglycerin may lessen but usually does not produce complete relief of the discomfort.

The discomfort of *acute pericarditis* is usually sharp and may radiate to the shoulder, neck, flank, or epigastrium. Characteristically, sitting and leaning forward diminish the discomfort, whereas lying down or deep breathing may intensify the discomfort. Acute myocarditis can produce pain either from pericarditis or, occasionally, from inflammation of the heart muscle itself. The latter discomfort can even mimic that of acute myocardial infarction.

Mitral valve prolapse occasionally is associated with nonspecific chest discomfort that is often described as sharp, stabbing, or knifelike in the precordium or substernal area. The duration is often brief and episodes occur both at rest and with exercise.

Aortic dissection most often presents with sudden, severe chest pain that is of maximum intensity within seconds or minutes. It may be ripping or tearing and may radiate into the back, abdomen, lower back, neck, or lower extremities. Aortic dissection may be responsible for a cerebral vascular accident, renal (flank) pain, or a cold, pulseless extremity.

As *discrete thoracic aortic aneurysms* expand, they may produce localized boring discomfort of either the anterior chest or the cervical or thoracic spine. At times, this is worsened by exertion.

Acute pulmonary embolism may produce pain that can mimic angina pectoris or can be pleuritic, particularly when there is pulmonary infarction.

Pulmonary hypertension, as in patients with mitral stenosis or Eisenmenger's syndrome, may produce discomfort similar to angina pectoris, although it is less likely to be relieved as promptly by nitroglycerin or rest. The mechanism is often right ventricular ischemia.

Pneumonia, mediastinal emphysema, chest tumors, and *pneumothorax* can also produce chest pain, often with a significant variation with motion or respiration.

Esophageal motility disorders or spasm can produce discomfort similar to angina pectoris that may be relieved by nitroglycerin, although the pain is often not related to exertion. Esophageal reflex can precipitate discomfort mimicking angina pectoris; it is particularly likely to occur during recumbency and to be relieved by sitting or by antacids. Acute pancreatitis, peptic ulcer disease, biliary disease and the splenic flexure syndrome can occasionally mimic the discomfort of myocardial ischemia.

Musculoskeletal disorders can produce discomfort that can mimic myocardial ischemia. Occasionally the pain can be reproduced by palpation or by manipulating the chest wall, spine, arms, shoulders, or neck.

Chest discomfort of *psychogenic origin* is often sharp, fleeting, stabbing, and frequently not associated with exertion.

Objective

Physical Examination

Because of the many causes of chest pain (Table 15–2–1), patients require a detailed history and very careful examination of the thorax, heart, lung, and abdomen. In most instances, this permits an accurate diagnosis. A careful search should be made for any areas in which palpation or pressure reproduces the discomfort and for motions of the upper extremities, shoulders, spine, or neck that reproduce the discomfort. Unequal or absent peripheral pulses (carotid, brachial, or femoral) may occur in aortic dissection. Some patients with chest discomfort or pain have associated paresthesias or hyperesthesias.

Routine Laboratory Abnormalities

Many causes of acute, severe chest pain are associated with a moderate elevation of the white blood cell count. In patients with pneumonia or pleuritis, the elevation may be much more marked. Patients with chest pain from uremic pericarditis have elevated blood concentrations of urea and creatinine.

The chest x-ray film and electrocardiogram may reveal abnormalities or changes that help identify the cause of the chest pain. Whenever possible, repeat electrocardiograms should be obtained during episodes of recurrent chest pain or discomfort. Arterial blood gases may be abnormal in patients with pulmonary disorders or pulmonary embolism but the changes are seldom diagnostic, and about 20% of cases of pulmonary embolism have no significant arterial oxygen abnormalities. Patients suspected of having acute myocardial infarction should have serial determinations of creatine kinase with MB fractions every 6 to 8 hours for the first 2 to 3 days or until the concentration is clearly abnormal. The routine chemistry profile may provide evidence for increased risk of coronary atherosclerosis, such as increased cholesterol concentration.

PLANS

Diagnostic

Differential Diagnosis

The differential diagnosis of chest pain is indicated in Table 15–2–1.

Diagnostic Options

In addition to a detailed history and physical examination, posteroanterior and lateral chest films, and 12-lead electrocardiogram, many additional tests are potentially available to help establish a diagnosis. These include exercise stress testing, transthoracic echocardiography, transesophageal echocardiography, computed tomography, aortography, magnetic resonance imaging, pulmonary ventilation–perfusion scintigraphy (VQ scan), pulmonary arteriography, myocardial perfusion scintigraphy at rest or during stress induced by exercise or pharmacologic means, and cardiac catheterization.

Recommended Approach

The individual recommended approach to the diagnosis of chest pain or discomfort is guided by the individual patient's history, physical examination, and routine laboratory tests. In considering specific tests for patients with chest pain, one should keep in mind the specific question to be asked, as well as the predictive value of a positive or a negative test in the particular patient subgroup to which the patient belongs. In addition, one should always ask the question as to whether or not the results of the diagnostic test will modify management. In general, the predictive value (and clinical usefulness) of a test is least in patients with either a very low or a very high pretest likelihood.

In male patients the predictive value of a positive electrocardio-

graphic exercise test is approximately 20, 70, and 90% in patients with nonanginal, atypical angina, and definite angina chest discomfort, respectively. In women, these corresponding values are 5, 35, and 60%. Exercise electrocardiographic tests, exercise thallium-201 scintigraphy, and technetium-99*m* ventriculography are generally contraindicated both in patients for the first 4 to 5 days after acute myocardial infarction and in most patients with active, unstable angina pectoris. These tests, which have a higher specificity and sensitivity than an exercise electrocardiographic test, are often very useful for the diagnosis of coronary artery disease and for the evaluation of cardiac function in patients with known coronary artery disease. At this time, coronary arteriography remains the gold standard for the evaluation of the presence and severity of coronary atherosclerosis.

Patients suspected of having aortic dissection may be evaluated by aortography, computed tomography, magnetic resonance imaging, or transthoracic or (preferably) transesophageal echocardiography. The selection of an individual technique in this situation is dependent on the individual patient characteristics and the local hospital experience with these diagnostic procedures. Transthoracic echocardiography is also very useful in establishing the diagnosis of pericardial fluid, hypertrophic cardiomyopathy, significant aortic stenosis, or mitral valve prolapse. An abnormal ventilation–perfusion pulmonary scintigram is very helpful in establishing the likelihood of pulmonary embolism. In some patients, pulmonary arteriography is necessary to demonstrate the pulmonary embolism.

Therapeutic

In most instances, patients with prolonged chest pain of more than 20 to 30 minutes compatible with myocardial ischemia should be hospitalized for monitoring and further tests (see Chapter 15–47). Patients with very severe pain may require opiate therapy. Patients with suspected or known aortic dissection should have their blood pressure promptly lowered and controlled. The location and extent of aortic dissection should be determined in patients who are candidates for surgical repair (see Chapter 15–66). Patients with significant pneumothorax should have the air removed as soon as possible. More specific treatments for many of the causes of chest pain are discussed in the corresponding chapters.

FOLLOW-UP

The follow-up of patients with chest pain depends on the etiology and is discussed in the appropriate chapter.

Patients with coronary artery disease should be educated regarding their discomfort and the factors likely to exacerbate the pain as well as factors that may be important in the progression of coronary artery disease. Smoking should be discontinued; the serum low-density lipoprotein (LDL) cholesterol should be lowered to less than 100 mg/dL by dietary and, if necessary, pharmacologic measures. Patients should be educated to come to an emergency hospital facility whenever the discomfort of angina pectoris is not relieved by nitroglycerin and to see their physician whenever there is a significant change in their pattern of angina pectoris. Patients with hypertension should have this controlled to lessen the likelihood of progressive disease of the blood vessels of the brain, heart, kidney, and peripheral circulation and to lessen the likelihood of heart failure, myocardial infarction, aortic atherosclerosis, or aortic dissection.

DISCUSSION

Prevalence and Incidence, Related Basic Science, Natural History, and Prevention

See chapters on specific diseases.

Cost Containment

A very careful history and physical examination combined with routine laboratory tests often provide a proper diagnosis. In other patients, specialized tests are necessary. The physician should choose the test with the highest predictive value in a particular patient rather than use a battery of expensive tests. The diagnostic predictive value of a test may vary from one hospital to another and the physician should be aware of the diagnostic accuracy of various procedures in any particular hospital.

REFERENCES

Dell'Italia LJ. Chest pain. In: Stein JH, Hutton JJ, Kohler PO, et al., eds. Internal medicine. 4th ed. St. Louis: Mosby, 1994:86.

Goldman L, Braunwald E. Chest discomfort and palpitation. In: Wilson JD, Braunwald E, Isselbacher KJ, et al., eds. Harrison's principles of internal medicine. New York: McGraw-Hill, 1991:98.

Levine HJ. Difficult problems in the diagnosis of chest pain. Am Heart J 1980;100:108.

O'Rourke RA. Chest pain. In: Schlant RC, Alexander RW, O'Rourke RA, et al., eds. Hurst's the heart. 8th ed. New York: McGraw-Hill, 1994:459.

Schlant RC, Alexander RW. Diagnosis and management of chronic ischemic heart disease. In Schlant RC, Alexander RW, O'Rourke RA, et al., eds. Hurst's the heart. 8th ed. New York: McGraw-Hill, 1994:1055.

CHAPTER 15–3

Syncope

Richard P. Lewis, M.D.

DEFINITION

Syncope is a sudden transient loss of consciousness. Bodily trauma may occur when syncope is abrupt. *Presyncope* is a term for lesser symptoms in which consciousness is lost very transiently or not at all. Presyncope is far more common than syncope, but many patients have both. Presyncope may be mechanistically identical to syncope, and in patients with heart disease it should be accorded the same significance.

ETIOLOGY

Syncope is due to an acute drop in cerebral perfusion. Because cerebral perfusion is directly related to cerebral blood pressure, syncope should more properly be considered a failure to maintain the latter. Most patients with low cardiac output do not faint because neurohumoral compensatory mechanisms maintain systemic blood pressure. Conversely, the cardiac output is not greatly reduced in neurocardiogenic syncope.

CRITERIA FOR DIAGNOSIS

Syncope is one of the most alarming of medical symptoms to patients and their families. For the physician, evaluation of the mechanism of syncope is a diagnostic challenge. The etiologic basis for syncope may be elusive after routine evaluation in up to half of patients, and in a significant number of patients syncope is recurrent if no treatment is instituted. The problem is compounded by the fact that in certain patients with heart disease, syncope may be a harbinger of sudden death. There also may be medicolegal implications in patients who work with dangerous machinery or are involved in public transportation.

The causes of syncope are listed in Table 15–3–1. Syncope can be

TABLE 15–3–1. MECHANISM OF COMMON CAUSES OF SYNCOPE

Noncardiac Causes
Reflex
  Vasodepressor (neurocardiogenic)
  Hypersensitive carotid sinus
  Glossopharyngeal neuralgia
  Postprandial (elderly)
  Tracheobronchial or gastrointestinal stimulation
  Situational (cough, deglutition, defecation, micturition, post-Valsalva, diving, Jacuzzi, gastrointestinal hemorrhage)
Orthostatic
  Venous pooling and/or volume depletion (fluid or blood loss, excess diuresis, pregnancy, bedrest, prolonged standing, mitral valve prolapse syndrome, severe venous insufficiency)
  Pharmacologic (nitrates and other direct vasodilators, alpha-adrenergic blocking agents, converting enzyme inhibitors, calcium channel blocking agents, diuretics, tranquilizers, and antidepressants)
  Neuropathy (diabetes, aging, alcoholism, primary and secondary autonomic insufficiency, other neuropathies)
Neuropsychiatric
  Cerebrovascular disease (basilar artery syndrome, four-vessel occlusive disease, subclavian steal, cervical spine disease)
  Migraine
  Cerebral emboli (mitral valve prolapse, prosthetic valves, carotid and/or aortic atherosclerosis)
  Hysteria
  Sleep disorders
  Seizure disorders
Metabolic
  Hyperventilation
  Hypoglycemia
  Hypoxemia/anemia
  Ethanol or other depressant drugs

Cardiac Causes
Acute myocardial infarction (inferior)
Intracardiac obstruction (aortic stenosis, hypertrophic cardiomyopathy, pulmonary stenosis, prosthetic valve dysfunction, left atrial myxoma)
Pulmonary hypertension (pulmonary emboli, primary pulmonary hypertension, Eisenmenger's syndrome)
Arrhythmia
  Bradyarrhythmia (sick sinus syndrome, atrioventricular node disease, pacemaker malfunction)
  Supraventricular tachycardia (paroxysmal atrial tachycardia, atrial flutter or fibrillation with rapid ventricular response)
  Paroxysmal ventricular tachycardia
  Torsade de pointes (long QT)
  Pacemaker syndrome (ventricular pacer)

Undetermined Causes
Multiple cause (old age)
Occult arrhythmia
Reflex

divided into three large categories: noncardiac (55% of all cases), cardiac (25%), and undetermined cause (20%). It must be stressed that syncope usually requires the occurrence of a constellation of events either simultaneously or in sequence. Thus syncope may not always occur in apparently similar settings. Syncope related to more than one cause is common, especially in the aged. Failure to recognize this fact is a major reason for inability to establish a diagnosis.

CLINICAL MANIFESTATIONS

Subjective

Definition of the setting in which the syncopal episode occurs and knowledge of underlying disease and medications are crucial to establishing a diagnosis. Attention should be paid to the presence of factors that facilitate syncope, such as fever, the postprandial state, high ambient temperature, debilitation, alcohol ingestion, advanced age, drugs, upright posture, fatigue, fasting, anemia, and hypoxia. Often, it is necessary to question others present at the time of syncope, as the patient may not remember preceding events.

Vasodepressor or neurocardiogenic syncope (the common faint) occurs predominantly in young individuals, usually during adolescence. It occurs as a response to emotional stress or threatened physical injury (e.g., venipuncture). Although it nearly always occurs in the upright position, because the episode is seldom abrupt, injury is rare. Vasodepressor syncope is often preceded by vague symptoms due to autonomic hyperactivity. It may recur if the individual prematurely returns to the upright posture. It is one of the most common forms of syncope, and the diagnosis can usually be made by clinical examination alone.

Syncope in obstructive cardiac disorders is often postexertional. In left atrial myxoma, it may be positional. Arrhythmic syncope is the most common cause of abrupt syncope and one of the few forms that can occur in the supine position. Palpitations may be noted prior to loss of consciousness. Presyncope is commonly caused by arrhythmias. Arrhythmic syncope is usually associated with underlying heart disease, but in older individuals, diffuse degenerative disease of the conduction system is common and may be isolated. A recently reported cause of bradycardic syncope is excessive regular exercise in middle-aged individuals.

Orthostatic syncope is associated with assuming the upright position or standing for prolonged period. Syncope due to a hypersensitive carotid sinus is usually related to certain positions of the neck, as is vertebral artery compression by cervical spine disease.

Focal neurologic signs usually suggest cerebral vascular disease or a seizure disorder, but they may occur transiently during the early phase of unconsciousness. Incontinence or postictal state seldom occur with syncope.

Neuropsychiatric syncope is usually not true syncope. Loss of consciousness is not sudden (except with petit mal epilepsy) and may be more prolonged. The events surrounding these syndromes are usually characteristic enough to lead to an appropriate diagnostic approach.

The various reflex causes of syncope can usually be defined from history alone. Of particular note is the reflex syncope that may be the predominant manifestation of acute inferior ischemia in 10 to 15% of patients.

The history is crucial for unraveling the various factors contributing to syncope from combined causes (e.g., nitroglycerin in the upright posture in an older individual with the sick sinus syndrome).

Objective

Physical Examination

At the time of syncope, the patient usually shows pallor, sweating, cool extremities, and a variably impaired sensorium. Blood pressure is low at the onset of syncope, but is rapidly restored by assuming the supine position. The heart rate is usually slightly increased. If the pulse is slow, either a vasovagal reaction has occurred or a bradyarrhythmia is the cause of syncope.

The presence of obstructive cardiovascular disorders is usually obvious on physical examination (e.g., aortic stenosis), but other forms of heart disease such as ischemic heart disease, cardiomyopathy, and mitral valve prolapse, which are associated with arrhythmic syncope, may be more subtle.

Orthostatic syncope can be diagnosed by measuring the blood pressure in the upright position (an early-morning value is most likely to be diagnostic). Careful carotid sinus massage with electrocardiographic and blood pressure monitoring may identify carotid sinus hypersensitivity. Patients with cough syncope usually have manifest pulmonary disease, and micturition syncope in older subjects is associated with prostatic enlargement. Most other reflex syncopes and neuropsychiatric causes occur in subjects without heart disease, but physical examination may reveal noncardiovascular abnormalities in these patients.

Routine Laboratory Abnormalities

The routine electrocardiogram can reveal abnormalities that predispose to arrhythmic syncope: sinoatrial and atrioventricular node disease, advanced fascicular blocks, Wolff–Parkinson–White syndrome, old infarction, prolonged QT interval, pacemaker malfunction, and frequent ventricular ectopy. Most arrhythmias that produce syncope, however, are transient and will not be revealed by routine electrocardiogram. The chest x-ray is useful for further evaluation of underlying heart disease. Routine blood work may reveal anemia or diabetes. Diuretic-induced hypokalemia and/or hypomagnesemia are major factors predisposing to tachyarrhythmias.

PLANS

Diagnostic

Differential Diagnosis

If the cause of syncope is not apparent after history, physical examination, and routine laboratory evaluation, further testing may be required. The tests ordered depend on two factors: the preliminary diagnosis and the abruptness of the symptoms. Patients with underlying heart disease are at highest risk. Abrupt syncope, especially if associated with bodily injury, demands complete evaluation.

Extensive cardiovascular workup is usually inappropriate for orthostatic syncope, reflex syncope, and neuropsychiatric syncope. Suspected cerebrovascular syncope, orthostatic syncope due to neuropathy, or seizure disorders should be evaluated in consultation with a neurologist. Obstructive cardiac disorders should undergo complete evaluation, including catheterization study if this has not been previously performed.

Diagnostic Options and Recommended Approach

Arrhythmic syncope is the most common cause of cardiac syncope and one of the high-risk forms of syncope. It seldom occurs in individuals without underlying heart disease. Thus, evaluation of the underlying heart disease, usually starting with an echocardiogram, should be performed. The signal-averaged electrocardiogram is useful for identifying patients with ischemic heart disease who are predisposed to ventricular tachycardia, and it should be performed in suspected arrhythmic syncope. An exercise test should be routinely employed only for the small subgroup of patients with exertional syncope.

Arrhythmia monitoring is not routinely indicated when there is no basis for suspecting an arrhythmic cause, especially if no underlying heart disease is demonstrable. In this setting, ambulatory monitoring (even if performed for several days) has poor sensitivity (15–20%) and poor specificity due to the ubiquity of asymptomatic arrhythmias, especially in those over age 65. The sensitivity and specificity rise significantly when monitoring is confined to those with suspected arrhythmia. Unfortunately, because it is often difficult to establish cause and effect when an arrhythmia is found, additional testing is usually required.

Monitoring with patient-activated recording devices is useful in patients who do not have abrupt symptoms (especially mitral valve prolapse syndrome). This type of monitoring has the advantage of recording the rhythm during symptoms. An arrhythmic basis for syncope can be found in up to one third of cases. The upright tilt test (usually at 60° for 30 minutes) is very useful for the diagnosis and management of neurocardiogenic syncope. The sensitivity and, perhaps more importantly, the specificity of this test (with or without autonomic interventions) are still not clear. It also requires a sophisticated laboratory. Despite these concerns, the upright tilt test provides objective evidence for neurocardiogenic syncope and may be used in a serial fashion to establish efficacy of therapy. As neurocardiogenic syncope is often a secondary cause of syncope (see below), the tilt test is becoming widely used as a screening test in patients with undefined syncope.

If the preceding tests have not revealed a reasonable diagnosis, invasive electrophysiologic testing should be considered. This test reveals an arrhythmia responsible for syncope in up to two thirds of patients with suspected but undiagnosed arrhythmic syncope. Such patients constitute a significant number of those categorized as "syncope of unknown cause" in earlier studies. During the testing, the integrity of the conduction system under the stress of pacing can be determined, and both atrial and ventricular tachyarrhythmias can be induced. Recently, the addition of tilting and autonomic interventions has increased sensitivity and specificity.

Occult conduction disease (especially of the sinoatrial node), rapid ventricular tachycardia, and supraventricular tachycardia with rapid ventricular rate are the most common syncope-producing arrhythmias uncovered by invasive electrophysiologic testing. Failure to document an arrhythmia appears to be reasonably specific for excluding an arrhythmic cause of syncope.

There is still debate over the significance of arrhythmias uncovered by invasive electrophysiologic testing. Nonetheless, current evidence suggests that electrophysiologic testing is a major advance in the evaluation of suspected arrhythmic syncope. Although it is expensive, prolonged monitoring (especially in the hospital) can incur equal cost with far less sensitivity and specificity.

Therapeutic

When syncope is a manifestation of underlying disease, the symptom may often be relieved by treating the underlying disease (e.g., aortic stenosis, cough and micturition syncope, neuropsychiatric disorders, subclavian steal). Orthostatic syncope is often caused by drugs that may be withdrawn or whose dosage may be reduced. Neurocardiogenic syncope usually responds to reassurance and avoidance of noxious stimuli, but if it is recurrent, medical management may be required. Selective beta-adrenergic blockade is the most useful. Adjunctive therapy may include florinef, which is also useful in other types of syncope. Syncope due to supraventricular tachycardia is often amenable to radiofrequency catheter ablation (paroxysmal atrial tachycardia, Wolff–Parkinson–White syndrome, some cases of atrial flutter) or atrioventricular node ablation or modification (atrial flutter or fibrillation). Because of their proarrhythmic effect, class I agents are generally avoided for long-term prevention of arrhythmias producing syncope. Digitalis, beta blockers, calcium channel blockers, or low-dose amiodarone can be used to prevent recurrent supraventricular tachycardia. For ventricular tachycardia, therapy should consist of relieving ischemia if present (beta blockers, percutaneous transluminal coronary angioplasty, or coronary artery bypass surgery), maintaining normal serum electrolytes, and administering amiodarone or sotolol; however, implantable defibrillators are becoming standard for patients with life-threatening ventricular tachycardia. Dual-chamber pacemaker therapy is indicated in most patients with syncope due to bradyarrhythmias if sinus rhythm is present. In patients with the hypersensitive carotid sinus syndrome, syncope may be abolished or improved by dual-chamber pacemakers. Many other forms of reflex syncope can be abolished by proper understanding of the cause and use of an appropriate prophylaxis. Severe obstructive cerebral vascular disease can sometimes be relieved by carotid artery surgery. Cardiac emboli can be reduced by warfarin, which is superior to antiplatelet therapy alone (however, the two are often combined for optimal effect).

For some types of syncope, therapy is far from satisfactory. These include orthostatic syncope due to neurologic dysfunction, some cases of vasodepressor and reflex vasovagal syncope, cardiac obstructive syncope for which surgery is not feasible, atherosclerosis of the thoracic aorta, and vertebrobasilar artery disease.

FOLLOW-UP

Regular follow-up is required for arrhythmic syncope, most obstructive syncope, and orthostatic syncope. Generally, history and physical examination suffice, but periodic ambulatory electrocardiographic recordings (24-hour or transtelephonic) may be required. Recurrence of symptoms should be promptly reported by the patient. It is worth noting that although the recurrence rate of syncope is high among those with organic disease, the recurrence rate in patients in whom no disease is found is far lower.

DISCUSSION

Prevalence and Incidence

Syncope is a common symptom, occurring in 5 to 10% of younger individuals. The incidence in the elderly population is undoubtedly higher. Syncope accounts for 1 to 3% of hospital admissions.

Related Basic Science

The autonomic nervous system is normally responsible for blood pressure maintenance, although other neurohumoral substances (i.e., renin–angiotensin, bradykinin, endothelin, prostaglandins) also play a role. The major input to the medullary vasomotor center is via baroreceptors located in the atria, ventricles, and arterial tree. Stimulation of baroreceptors can produce a prompt fall in blood pressure. The output from the vasomotor center is via either the vagus nerve (parasympathetic) or the sympathetic nerve fibers that richly innervate the heart and vasculature. Vagal stimulation slows the sinus rate and atrioventricular node conduction and produces negative inotropy. Sympathetic stimulation produces sinus tachycardia, increased ventricular contractility, arteriolar and venular constriction (alpha), or dilation of skeletal muscle arterioles (beta). The parasympathetic nervous system can modulate or even override the sympathetic nervous system. Thus, parasympathetic stimulation can result in arteriolar dilation via sympathetic inhibition.

The vasodepressor reaction is due to an acute fall in arteriolar resistance and is due mostly to acute alpha sympathetic withdrawal. Characteristically, mild sinus tachycardia ensues. This is in distinction to the vasovagal reaction, in which there is bradycardia and other evidence of vagal hyperactivity. Hypotension, in this case, is due largely to profound bradycardia; however, these two reactions often coexist. Both reactions represent inappropriate autonomic reactions to pain, stress, or hemodynamic aberrations. It now appears that one (or both) of these reactions is a major component of nonreflex types of syncope (i.e., obstructive, orthostatic, and possibly even arrhythmic).

Autonomic dysfunction due to either drugs or disease is the basis for most orthostatic syncope. Cardiac arrhythmias can produce syncope by an acute fall in cardiac output, although an abnormal autonomic response often contributes to the syncope. Although some causes of obstructive syncope can produce decreased cerebral perfusion pressure, a reflex mechanism (aortic stenosis, pulmonary emboli) is often the major mechanism.

Natural History and Its Modification with Treatment

Precise data on natural history of syncope are not available, in large part because in the past it has been difficult to establish etiology. Syncope is recurrent in up to one third of cases. The 1-year mortality for noncardiac syncope is 6 to 12%, and it is 6% for syncope of undetermined cause. The mortalities are lower than for cardiac syncope but probably exceed the expected mortality rate for an asymptomatic population.

The 1-year mortality for untreated cardiac syncope is an alarming 15 to 25% with most deaths being sudden. It is not yet clear whether this high mortality reflects the presence of syncope or the prognosis of the underlying disease. It is likely, however, that the presence of syncope does adversely affect prognosis when left ventricular function is not severely depressed, and that this prognosis can be improved by specific therapy.

The mitral valve prolapse syndrome warrants special mention due to the high prevalence of this disorder in the population and the relatively common occurrence of syncope and, especially, presyncope. Symptoms may persist for many years. These patients often have autonomic dysfunction, which predisposes to orthostatic and reflex syncope or presyncope. In addition, there is a significant incidence of both atrial and ventricular tachycardia.

Prevention

The initial episode of syncope usually cannot be prevented. Recurrence of syncope after diagnosis and therapy is 15 to 25%.

Cost Containment

The challenge to the clinician is to reserve an aggressive laboratory evaluation of syncope for those who are at high risk for death or bodily injury. An initial complete cardiac workup should be confined to patients with high-risk cardiovascular diseases. These include the various obstructive disorders and, when arrhythmia is suspected, patients with conduction system disease, ischemic heart disease, cardiomyopathy, and some patients with mitral valve prolapse and hypertensive heart disease. Neurologic testing (electroencephalogram, brain scans) is indicated only when there is strong evidence by routine evaluation to suspect a neurologic cause.

REFERENCES

Grubb BP, Temesy-Armos P, Hahn H, et al. Utility of upright tilt-table testing in evaluation and management of syncope of unknown origin. Am J Med 1991;90:6.

Kapoor WN, Peterson J, Wiend HS, Karpf M. Diagnostic and prognostic implications of recurrences in patients with syncope. Am J Med 1987;63:730.

Lewis RP, Boudoulas H, Schaal SF, et al. Diagnosis and management of syncope. In: Schlant RS, Alexander RW, O'Rourke RJ, et al, eds. The heart. 8th ed. New York: McGraw-Hill, 1994:927.

Lipsitz LA. Syncope in the elderly. Ann Intern Med 1983;99:92

Manolis AS, Linzer M. Salem D. Estes NAM. Syncope: Current diagnostic evaluation and management. Ann Intern Med 1990;112:350.

CHAPTER 15–4

Cardiac Arrest and Sudden Cardiac Death

Leonard A. Cobb, M.D.

DEFINITION

Abrupt and sustained loss of consciousness due to cessation of circulation is termed cardiac arrest, a condition uniformly fatal without prompt intervention. Sudden cardiac death is said to have occurred when there has been unexpected circulatory arrest, attributed to a cardiac disorder and usually precipitated by a ventricular arrhythmia. Deaths due to chronic lingering illnesses or to major trauma are not considered here to be cardiac arrests.

ETIOLOGY

Whereas cardiac arrest is most often a complication of an underlying cardiac disorder, other causes include drowning, tracheal obstruction ("cafe coronary"), respiratory failure, massive bleeding, and toxic reactions.

Coronary heart disease (CHD) is responsible for approximately 80% of instances of sudden cardiac deaths; cardiomyopathies and valvular lesions predominate in the remaining. Primary electrical abnormalities (e.g., prolonged QT syndromes, preexcitation), metabolic disorders, and drug reactions constitute only a minority of cases. One or two percent of sudden cardiac deaths have no identifiable cause.

CRITERIA FOR DIAGNOSIS
Suggestive

The possibility of cardiac arrest should be considered in any unresponsive or pulseless patient. The victim of sudden cardiac death may experience no apparent symptoms before collapse (instantaneous death) or there may be acute cardiac symptoms of several minutes' duration. Most episodes occur outside the hospital.

Definitive

The recognition of cardiac arrest is confirmed by persistent loss of consciousness, absence of arterial pulse, and loss of normal breathing pattern. Complete apnea ensues, but occasionally not for several minutes.

CLINICAL MANIFESTATIONS
Subjective

In approximately 80% of unexpected, out-of-hospital cardiac arrests there is a history of cardiac disease or hypertension. A "typical" victim is a 63-year-old man who smokes cigarettes and has a history of remote myocardial infarction; he collapses at home. Although patients often have no premonitory symptoms, they may experience weakness, chest pain, dyspnea, or palpitations immediately prior to the arrest. Statistical predictors of patients at risk for sudden cardiac death include left ventricular dysfunction, frequent ventricular ectopy, and risk factors for coronary heart disease; however, no set or predictor has sufficient accuracy to be useful in selecting prophylactic interventions that might incur appreciable physical or financial burden.

Objective
Physical Examination

Victims of sudden death are completely unresponsive and are either apneic or have "agonal" respirations. Arterial pulses are absent. Cyanosis is frequently marked.

Routine Laboratory Abnormalities

The first recognized cardiac rhythm varies according to the time from collapse to the recording of the electrocardiogram. Ventricular fibrillation is likely to be present when a recording is made within 5 minutes of arrest. On the other hand, asystole or very low amplitude fibrillation is typically present if there has been a delay of 10 minutes or more without the application of cardiopulmonary resuscitation. In one fourth or more of cases, so-called electromechanical dissociation may be present.

PLANS
Diagnostic

A cardiac arrest is recognized by clinical findings; additional diagnostic measures are unnecessary. Establishment of sudden cardiac death is facilitated, however, when witnesses are available to describe the events leading to collapse, particularly the condition of the patient immediately before loss of consciousness.

Differential Diagnosis

Cardiac arrest should be differentiated from other conditions resulting in the abrupt loss of consciousness, particularly syncope and seizures and, occasionally, strokes. If the event was not witnessed, any condition leading to unconsciousness might at first glance be confused with a cardiac arrest (e.g., hypoglycemia, profound respiratory depression, substance abuse, as well as a broad array of metabolic and neurologic disorders).

Diagnostic Options and Recommended Approach

Physical examination, as outlined above, will establish the diagnosis of cardiac arrest. The important differentiating points are unconsciousness of more than a few seconds' duration *and* the complete absence of arterial pulses.

Therapeutic

Therapeutic Options

A major implication of cardiac arrest is the need for immediate intervention. When due to ventricular fibrillation, cardiac arrest can be effectively reversed, the principal determinant of survival being the rapidity with which resuscitative measures are initiated.

The identification of cardiac arrest, however, does not always imply the necessity for initiation of resuscitation, particularly for patients in the terminal phases of a lingering illness. In such cases it is appropriate to counsel family members or others to refrain from summoning emergency personnel to attempt resuscitation in the event of an expected death.

Recommended Approach

The development of *effective resuscitation* is one of the major medical advances in the past three decades. Basic life support (closed chest compression with simple airway management and mouth-to-mouth ventilation) has been adopted throughout the world. The standardization of advanced cardiac life support techniques, including tracheal intubation, defibrillation, and emergency drug therapy, has made it possible for thousands of health care professionals to become proficient in these procedures.

The initial approach to resuscitation varies according to the circumstance in which cardiac arrest occurs. An unexpected cardiac arrest in a patient whose cardiac rhythm is monitored calls for immediate delivery of one or more precordial shocks for ventricular fibrillation (or, less commonly, ventricular tachycardia) when present. Cardiopulmonary resuscitation (CPR) should be initiated if the initial three shocks are ineffective in achieving the restoration of circulation. In all other settings, it is imperative to summon assistance and provide CPR. CPR is a temporizing measure which provides only a minimal blood flow to sustain vital functions for a few minutes until the provision of advanced cardiac life support.

In several communities in the United States, 20 to 30% of victims found in ventricular fibrillation outside the hospital can be effectively resuscitated and discharged home after hospitalization. Accordingly, much emphasis has been directed to the victim in whom that rhythm is present (Figure 15–4–1). In contrast, the outcome is extremely poor if asystole or electromechanical dissociation is the first recorded rhythm. Nonetheless, the possibility of survival is not completely hopeless for

these latter conditions, and resuscitation should usually be continued until it is clear that there has been no response to the advanced life support protocol.

Two strategies have been implemented to minimize delays in the application of basic and advanced cardiac life support outside the hospital. First, large numbers of the public have been trained to recognize cardiac arrest, quickly request appropriate help, and initiate CPR. If resuscitation outside the hospital is to be effective, it is critical for bystanders to participate. To this end, millions of Americans have now received some training in the initial management of unexpected cardiac arrest. A 3- to 4-hour period of instruction has become the principal means of providing such instruction.

A *second* strategy is the development of mechanisms to make defibrillation more readily available (Figure 15–4–2). The training of emergency medical technicians to master a single aspect of advanced cardiac life support (i.e., defibrillation) has been shown to be feasible and effective. This concept should be expanded so that automated defibrillators are made available to large numbers of emergency care providers and possibly other persons. For this approach to be maximally effective, it will be necessary to develop inexpensive defibrillators, possibly even for one-time use.

FOLLOW-UP

The prognosis for the long-term survival of patients resuscitated from an aborted episode of sudden cardiac death is closely related to the severity of myocardial dysfunction, particularly the estimated left ventricular ejection fraction. Complex ventricular ectopy on Holter monitoring is another predictor, but of much less significance than ventricular dysfunction. It is important to note that the prognosis may be relatively favorable if ventricular systolic function is normal (Figure 15–4–3). Similarly, the patient whose ventricular fibrillation was precipitated by acute myocardial infarction has a low probability for recurrent cardiac arrest over the following year, about 2%. On the other hand, the resuscitated patient who had chronic congestive heart failure prior to the sudden cardiac arrest has an approximate 20 to 30% likelihood of developing a recurrent cardiac arrest in the next year.

Patients who have been resuscitated from cardiac arrest, particularly when due to conditions other than acute myocardial infarction, require especially careful follow-up. Consultation with a specialist skilled in the management of cardiac arrhythmias is appropriate. Those patients are at risk for recurrences of the sudden cardiac death syndrome and, depending on the initiating event and the underlying heart disease, may be candidates for coronary bypass surgery, implantation of an automatic defibrillator, or antiarrhythmic drug therapy with amiodarone or another agent.

Coronary artery bypass surgery should be strongly considered in pa-

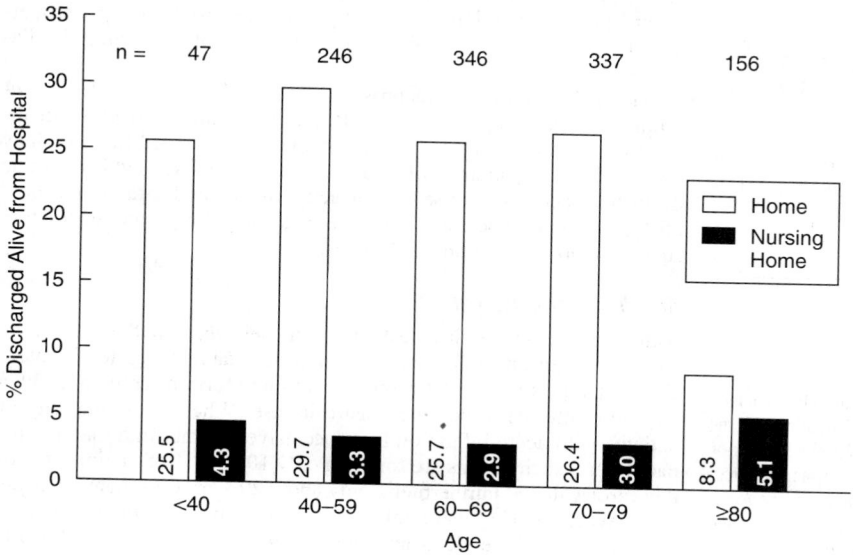

Figure 15–4–1. Relationship between age and survival to hospital discharge in 1132 consecutive patients treated for out-of-hospital cardiac arrest in which the initial rhythm was ventricular fibrillation. *(Source: Longstreth WT, Cobb LA, Fahrenbruch CE, Copass MK. Does age affect outcomes of out-of-hospital cardiopulmonary resuscitation? JAMA 1990;264:2109. Reproduced with permission from the publisher and authors. Copyright 1990, American Medical Association.)*

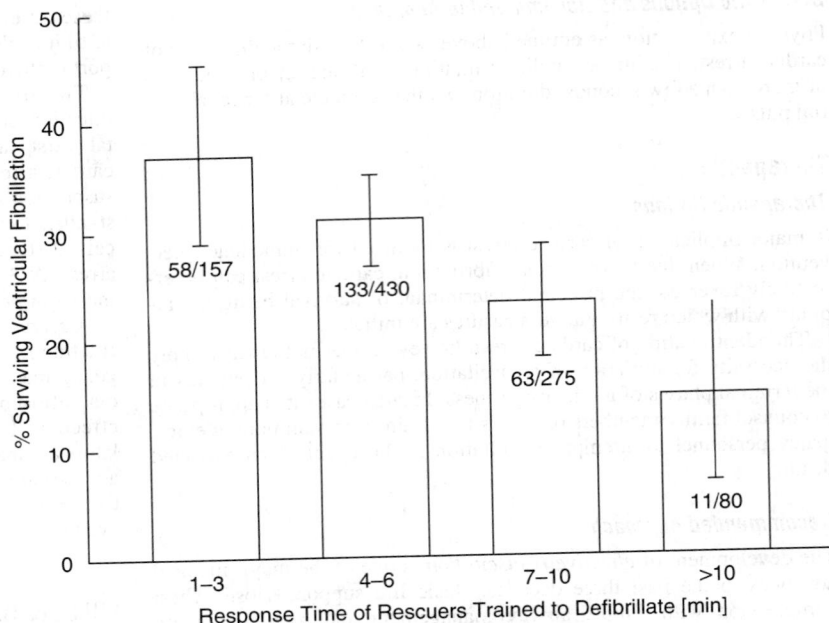

Figure 15–4–2. Nine hundred forty-two patients with out-of-hospital cardiac arrest whose first recorded rhythm was ventricular fibrillation. The patients are grouped according to the response time of the first arriving fire department unit able to provide defibrillation. The proportions of patients who were ultimately discharged home fell proportionately to the delay in providing defibrillation. *(Source: Weaver WD, Cobb LA, Hallstrom AP, et al. Factors influencing survival after out-of-hospital cardiac arrest. J Am Coll Cardiol 1986;7:752. Reproduced with permission from the Journal of the American College of Cardiology 1986;7:752–757.)*

tients whose cardiac arrest appears to have been precipitated by transient myocardial ischemia in the setting of coronary atherosclerosis.

The *implantable cardiac defibrillator* is an innovative device for use in patients at risk for recurrent ventricular fibrillation (or ventricular tachycardia). Clearly, the implantable defibrillator is a device of considerable importance, and in the coming years we may anticipate further technical refinements as well as a clearer definition of its utility.

Although "conventional" *antiarrhythmic drugs* have been extensively used to prevent recurrences of the sudden cardiac death syndrome, it is probable that such agents provide little if any protection, whether used empirically or even with guidance from cardiac electrophysiologic studies. On the other hand, the administration of amiodarone has been shown to provide significantly greater prolongation of life compared with the use of "conventional" antiarrhythmic drugs.

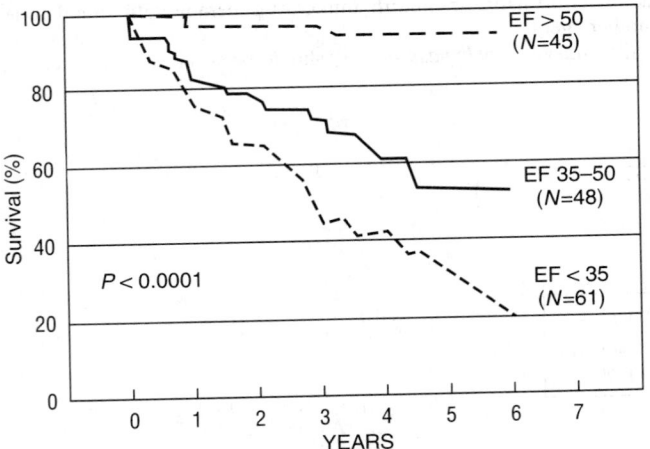

Figure 15–4–3. Survival in 154 patients with coronary atherosclerosis resuscitated from out-of-hospital cardiac arrest. The patients are grouped according to the radionuclide left ventricular ejection fraction (EF) performed an average of 4 months after resuscitation. During follow-up there were a total of 54 fatal events: 42 recurrences of sudden cardiac arrest, 6 other cardiac causes, and 6 noncardiac causes. *(Source: Ritchie JL, Hallstrom AP, Troubaugh GB, et al. Out-of-hospital sudden coronary death: Rest and exercise radionuclide left ventricular function in survivors. Am J Cardiol 1985;55:645. Reproduced with permission from the publisher and authors.)*

DISCUSSION

Prevalence

The burden imposed by sudden cardiac death is enormous, representing one half or more of the mortality attributed to diseases of the heart. In the United States an estimated 750 episodes occur each day.

Related Basic Science

Physiologic or Metabolic Derangement

Ventricular fibrillation can be induced in the experimental laboratory when myocardial ischemia occurs following coronary artery occlusion. In this setting, the consequences of ischemia lead to intracellular and extracellular acidosis, destruction of components of cellular membranes, and lowering of the resting transmembrane potential. As depolarization and conduction are slowed, the conditions are created for fragmented electrical activity, reentrant pathways, and emergence of ventricular fibrillation; however, this ischemic model represents only one of the several clinical settings for sudden cardiac death. It is important to emphasize that more than half of sudden cardiac death victims do not appear to experience ischemic symptoms before the event. In many victims, perhaps most, mechanical (anatomic) factors are implicated in the genesis of ventricular arrhythmias and sudden cardiac death, particularly akinesis, myocardial scars and ventricular aneurysms. In general, nonuniformity of the electrophysiologic properties of the myocardium facilitates the emergence of ventricular fibrillation.

One of the striking characteristics of the sudden cardiac death syndrome is the heterogeneity of the affected population, reflecting the diversity of mechanisms through which ventricular fibrillation may occur. Thus, in patients with coronary heart disease, sudden cardiac death may occur in the setting of acute myocardial infarction (about 25%), transient myocardial ischemia, or deranged myocardial structure such as remote infarction and fibrosis.

Anatomic Derangement

Although sudden cardiac death is often described in the press as a "massive heart attack," acute infarction detectable by currently available techniques accounts for only about one fourth of cases of sudden cardiac death due to coronary heart disease. Whereas the majority of patients with acute infarction have occlusive thrombi in a major coronary artery, such lesions are found in only 10 to 20% of victims of sudden cardiac death. Furthermore, only about 20% of resuscitated patients show evidence of Q-wave infarction in the days following resuscitation. At autopsy, the identification of significant heart disease supports the clinical impression of sudden cardiac death, but the autopsy cannot provide definitive proof for that mode of death. On the other hand, the absence of heart disease at autopsy is strong evidence against sudden cardiac death.

Natural History and Its Modification with Treatment

The incidence of sudden cardiac death appears to be declining in the United States, undoubtedly a reflection of the continued reduction in age-specific mortality attributed to coronary heart disease. It is also noteworthy that the survival experience for patients who have recovered from an episode of aborted sudden cardiac death has also improved substantially over the past two decades.

Prevention

In view of the multifaceted nature of sudden cardiac death, it seems unrealistic to expect the development of a "magic bullet" for the containment of that disorder. Rather, it will likely be necessary to address the specific factors underlying this disorder. For example, hygienic measures, antiischemic interventions, antiarrhythmic therapies, and interventions designed to prevent platelet aggregation may all hold promise. Additionally, the influence of the nervous system in modulating the propensity for ventricular fibrillation has been clearly demonstrated in experimental animals and probably has a similar effect in humans. In this regard, it should be noted that the incidence of sudden cardiac death appears to be influenced by social, economic, and racial considerations.

There is accumulating evidence that the incidence of sudden cardiac death is declining in the United States and in other industrialized nations as well. The basis for this reduction has not been clearly delineated; however, it is likely that there are multiple underlying factors, including hygienic measures (e.g., cessation of smoking, changes in diet) and perhaps also the application of certain medical advances. Several interventions are effective in preventing sudden cardiac death.

Cessation of cigarette smoking, long recognized as a mechanism for primary prevention of coronary heart disease, has also been shown to prevent sudden cardiac death after acute myocardial infarction or after resuscitation from out-of-hospital cardiac arrest. Thus, even following major complications of coronary heart disease, cessation of smoking is still an approach with important benefit.

Coronary artery bypass grafting in selected patients with angina pectoris has been shown to have a salutary effect in extending life, in large part through a reduction in sudden cardiac death. This benefit is most evident in patients who have moderately severe angina, multivessel coronary heart disease, and preserved ventricular function. Survival after coronary artery bypass grafting is also improved in patients who have obstruction of the left main coronary artery; however, that lesion is an infrequent finding in victims of sudden cardiac death.

Several large studies have conclusively demonstrated an improvement in mortality, predominantly a reduction in sudden cardiac death, in patients who received *beta blockers* in the first 2 to 3 years *after acute infarction.* That strategy is limited, however, by the fact that only 10 to 15% of sudden cardiac death victims have had a recognized acute infarction during the 2 years prior to cardiac arrest. A further shortcoming is that beta blockers must be regularly taken by 100 patients to extend the lives of three to four patients during a 1-year period. Although the administration of beta blockers to patients after myocardial infarction is a rational and appropriate measure for many patients, that intervention by itself does not appear likely to effect a major reduction in the overall incidence of sudden cardiac death.

Although antiarrhythmic agents can suppress premature ventricular depolarizations as well as episodes of recurrent ventricular tachycardia, these agents have *not* been shown to be effective in preventing sudden cardiac deaths. Additionally, it is important to note that antiarrhythmic drugs have serious side effects including potentiation of arrhythmias and even the precipitation of sudden death. In this regard, a large clinical trial of antiarrhythmic agents in postinfarction patients (Cardiac Arrhythmia Suppression Trial II Investigators, 1992) demonstrated that three agents—encainide, flecainide, and moricizine—were associated with *enhanced* mortality compared with placebo, despite effective suppression of asymptomatic ventricular ectopy (also see Chapter 15–20).

Cost Containment

It seems unlikely that major cost containment can be achieved in addressing the problem of sudden cardiac death. Despite this, the reduction of premature sudden cardiac death remains an important goal.

REFERENCES

Cardiac Arrhythmia Suppression Trial II Investigators. Effect of the antiarrhythmic agent moricizine on survival after myocardial infarction. N Engl J Med 1992;327:227.

CASCADE Investigators. Cardiac arrest in Seattle: Conventional versus amiodarone drug evaluation (The CASCADE study). Am J Cardiol 1991;67:578.

Cobb LA. The mechanisms, predictors, and prevention of sudden cardiac death. In: Schlant RC, Alexander RW, O'Rourke RA, et al., eds. Hurst's the heart. 8th ed. New York: McGraw-Hill, 1994:947.

Cobb LA, Weaver WD, Fahrenbruch CE, Copass MK. Community-based interventions for sudden cardiac death: Impact, limitations, and changes. Circulation 1992;85(suppl. I):98.

Cummins RO, Eisenberg MS, Hallstrom AP, Litwin PE. Survival of out-of-hospital cardiac arrest with early initiation of cardiopulmonary resuscitation. Am J Emerg Med 1985;3:114.

Eisenberg MS, Horwood BT, Cummins RO, et al. Cardiac arrest and resuscitation: A tale of 29 cities. Ann Emerg Med 1990;19:179.

Emergency Cardiac Care Committee and Subcommittees, American Heart Association. Guidelines for cardiopulmonary resuscitation and emergency cardiac care. JAMA 1992;268:2171.

CHAPTER 15–5

Acute Cardiogenic Pulmonary Edema (Acute Heart Failure)

David T. Kawanishi, M.D., and Shahbudin H. Rahimtoola, M.D.

DEFINITION

Acute cardiogenic pulmonary edema is a disorder characterized by an abnormally elevated pulmonary capillary pressure, which results in fluid accumulation in the extravascular gas-exchanging areas of the lung.

ETIOLOGY

The cause of acute cardiogenic pulmonary edema is an abrupt deterioration of cardiac function that produces a sudden increase in pulmonary venous pressure, which then is reflected in elevation of pulmonary capillary pressure. A number of cardiac disorders may result in acute heart failure (Table 15–5–1). Although in many cases acute heart failure results from an abrupt deterioration in a patient with previously recognized, symptomatic heart disease, it may be the initial manifestation of a cardiac disorder.

CRITERIA FOR DIAGNOSIS
Suggestive

The sudden occurrence of symptoms and signs suggesting compromise of gas exchange, such as shortness of breath, anxiety, tachypnea or

TABLE 15–5–1. CAUSES OF CARDIOGENIC PULMONARY EDEMA

Systemic hypertension
After myocardial infarction (coronary artery disease)
    Left ventricular failure
    Mitral regurgitation
    Left ventricular aneurysm
    Ruptured ventricular septum
    Stiff heart syndrome
Left ventricular outflow obstruction
    Supravalvular aortic stenosis
    Aortic valve disease
        Aortic stenosis
        Aortic regurgitation
    Discrete (membranous) subvalvular aortic stenosis
    Malfunction of prosthetic valve
Cardiomyopathy
    Hypertrophic (with or without outflow obstruction)
    Congestive
    Restrictive
    Obliterative
Mitral valve disease
    Mitral stenosis
    Mitral regurgitation
    Malfunction of prosthetic valve
"Acute" valvular regurgitation
    Aortic regurgitation
        Infective endocarditis
        Trauma
        Dissection of the aorta
    Mitral regurgitation
        Ruptured chordae tendineae
        Infective endocarditis
        Papillary muscle dysfunction or rupture
        Trauma
Other causes of obstruction to left ventricular filling
    Left atrial myxoma
    Cor triatriatum
Constrictive pericarditis
Cardiac tamponade

rales, or any of the other clinical manifestations enumerated below, should suggest the possibility of pulmonary edema. As pulmonary edema may result in obtundation or be associated with a severe cardiac disorder resulting in shock, it may be included in the differential diagnosis of such conditions.

Definitive

The presence of pulmonary edema is confirmed by obtaining evidence of fluid extravasation into the gas-exchanging areas of the lungs. As pulmonary edema may occur as a result of noncardiac disorders, confirmation of acute cardiogenic pulmonary edema requires the presence of elevated pulmonary capillary pressures attributable to a cardiac disorder.

CLINICAL MANIFESTATIONS
Subjective

There is frequently a history of preexisting cardiac disease and the symptoms associated with such diseases should then have been present for a time but often will be increased or worsened recently. The presence of events that may provoke deterioration of a chronic disorder, such as undue exertion or noncompliance with a medical regimen, may also be elicited. Acute pulmonary edema may be the initial manifestation of a cardiac disorder, however, and the symptoms will then be of recent or acute onset. The cardinal symptom is sudden, severe shortness of breath. In its earlier stages, orthopnea, paroxysmal nocturnal dyspnea, exertional dyspnea, and weakness may accompany the pulmonary edema.

Objective
Physical Examination

The patient with acute pulmonary edema is usually extremely anxious and agitated, often sits bolt upright, and is sweating profusely. The skin is usually cool and clammy, and may be cyanotic. Use of the accessory muscles of respiration is frequent, and respirations are rapid and noisy with gurgling or rattling sounds, loud wheezing, and coughing. In the late stages of pulmonary edema, the production of pink frothy sputum is a characteristic sign. The blood pressure may be higher than the patient's normal level and occurs as a result of intense vasoconstriction. Sinus tachycardia is expected, but other tachyarrhythmias or bradyarrhythmias may be precipitating factors. Moist rales, wheezes, and rhonchi are heard on auscultation of the lungs. Auscultation of the heart is usually difficult, but a third heart sound and an increase in intensity of the pulmonic component of the second heart sound may be noted. In addition, the cardiac examination may suggest an underlying abnormality by the presence of murmurs, abnormal valvular opening or closing sounds, or pericardial sounds.

Routine Laboratory Abnormalities

One of the most useful tests for detecting pulmonary edema is the chest x-ray. Redistribution of pulmonary blood flow to the upper lobes, Kerley A and B lines, and peribronchial cuffing may be seen early. In the later stage of alveolar edema, fluid in the alveoli and air bronchograms also may be seen on chest radiograph. In acute cardiac disorders, for example, myocardial infarction, there may be a considerable time lag between the development of severe pulmonary edema and its radiographic appearance. Cardiomegaly suggests the presence of a chronic cardiac disorder. Underlying cardiac disorders, such as calcified aortic and/or mitral valves or a prosthetic heart valve, may be identified.

Findings on the electrocardiogram and blood chemistry are nonspecific for the diagnosis of acute heart failure; however, important clues to the underlying disorder, precipitating factors, and effects on other body organs may be identified.

PLANS
Diagnostic
Differential Diagnosis

Pulmonary edema must be differentiated from other disorders associated with poor gas exchange resulting in dyspnea. Only in pulmonary edema is the disorder a result of fluid extravasated into the interstitial or intraalveolar spaces. Further, acute *cardiogenic* pulmonary edema must be differentiated from noncardiac causes of such fluid extravasation. Finally, accurate cardiac diagnosis may require differentiation of the precise cardiac abnormality responsible for the condition; for example, acute severe mitral regurgitation as a cause may need to be differentiated from deterioration of myocardial function, which is an often concomitant disorder.

Diagnostic Options and Recommended Approach

In some cases, the clinical history, physical examination, and chest x-ray findings alone may be sufficient. The observation of a cardiac structural or functional abnormality on echocardiography may often provide sufficient helpful adjunctive information if the diagnosis is still in question.

Because the physical examination and chest roentgenogram may be equivocal in establishing the cardiac etiology of the pulmonary edema, the definitive diagnosis of acute cardiogenic pulmonary edema may require measurement of the pulmonary artery wedge pressure using a balloon flotation right-sided heart catheter at the bedside. A cardiogenic origin of the pulmonary edema is confirmed by a moderate to severe elevation of pulmonary artery wedge pressure (greater than 20–25 mm Hg in a patient without preceding elevation of pressure). Because of increases in the lymphatic flow that clears fluid rapidly from the interstitial spaces, along with other mechanisms, frank pulmonary edema may not develop at pressures considerably above 25 mm Hg in individuals with chronically elevated pulmonary artery wedge pressures. Hemodynamic monitoring also assists in determining the cardiac output and assessing the efficacy of therapy.

Treatment usually results in reduction of the pulmonary artery wedge pressure and relief of pulmonary edema regardless of the underlying cardiac disorder. An inability to rapidly achieve a pressure reduction suggests the need for further diagnostic evaluation of the disorder. Doppler echocardiography and/or cardiac catheterization with angiography may be necessary to correctly identify the cause of the disorder and state of cardiac function prior to institution of other effective and definitive treatment such as surgery.

Therapeutic

Therapeutic Options

Depending on the extent of clinical and hemodynamic compromise, the range of therapeutic options varies from institution of general supportive measures to invasive diagnostic and interventional procedures such as balloon coronary angioplasty, valvuloplasty, and even cardiac surgery. In general, however, the patient can be stabilized using a combination of supportive measures and pharmacologic treatment. The latter may include diuretics, veno- and arterial dilators, and positive inotropic agents. When indicated, antiarrhythmic drugs, electrical cardioversion, or temporary pacing may be helpful. Importantly, particularly when the initial response to treatment is slow or incomplete, definitive diagnosis of the underlying cardiac disorder and correction of precipitating factors may be crucial to attain relief from pulmonary edema.

Recommended Approach

General supportive measures may be easily and quickly employed and rapidly improve patient comfort. The semiupright position allows easier breathing, facilitates the handling of the copious frothy sputum, and promotes pooling of blood in the lower extremities, thus reducing venous return. Supplemental oxygen is best delivered using a mask and rapid flow rates of 6 to 8 L per minute of 50% oxygen. If respiratory insufficiency is present, intubation and mechanical ventilatory assistance may be required.

Intravenous morphine may produce dramatic improvement of the condition through both a sedative effect and venodilation and is of particular value if the patient is agitated. The drug should be given in small increments and a total of 5 to 15 mg is generally effective. The patient must be carefully observed for respiratory depression, and morphine should not be used if altered consciousness, intracranial bleeding, chronic obstructive airway disease, or carbon dioxide retention is part of the clinical presentation.

The beneficial actions of cardiac glycosides include a positive inotropic effect, a diuretic effect, and a decrease in the ventricular rate in those with supraventricular tachyarrhythmias. If the patient has not previously been receiving digoxin (Lanoxin), an intravenous loading dose of 0.5 mg may be given as an infusion over 15 minutes followed by 0.25 mg every 6 hours to a total of 1.0 to 1.5 mg. A patient previously receiving a glycoside should be examined for manifestations of toxicity, such as nausea and vomiting, an accelerated nonparoxysmal junctional tachycardia, atrial tachycardia with intermittent atrioventricular nodal block, premature ventricular beats, ventricular tachycardia, bradycardia, and heart block. If these are absent, the accelerated ventricular response in supraventricular tachyarrhythmias may be slowed by additional digoxin. Intravenous digoxin and other digitalis preparations should be infused over a 15-minute period; bolus injections produce systemic and coronary vasoconstriction that may be deleterious. In the presence of hypokalemia and severe renal failure, intravenous digitalis preparations should be used with extreme caution. Additional blockade of the atrioventricular node to slow the ventricular rate can be obtained with use of diltiazem. Verapamil may be the drug of choice in atrial flutter, but must be used very cautiously because of its negative inotropic effect.

Specific therapy should be directed at improving cardiac performance (see Table 15–5–2). Left ventricular preload may be reduced through use of diuretics or venodilators. Initial doses of furosemide (Lasix) 40 to 60 mg intravenously or ethacrynic acid (Edecrin) 50 mg intravenously produce diuresis with a peak effect at about 30 minutes. The dosage should be progressively increased to achieve diuresis, up to a maximum single dose of 200 to 250 mg. Furosemide may provide a mild venodilation in addition to its diuretic effect. Both agents produce hyponatremia, hypokalemia, alkalosis, hyperuricemia, and hypovolemia, which, on occasion, can lead to a catastrophic fall in cardiac output.

Nitrates are potent venodilators. A sublingual dose of 0.4 mg nitroglycerin becomes effective within 2 minutes and usually produces a decrease in the pulmonary artery wedge pressure within 5 to 10 minutes. The duration of action is only 15 to 30 minutes, however, and sustained venodilation requires a continuous intravenous infusion of nitroglycerin (Tridil). Beginning with 10 μg/min, the infusion rate can be rapidly increased up to 100 μg/min. Excessive reduction of the elevated pulmonary artery wedge pressure in a patient with a severely diseased left ventricle can result in an abrupt fall of cardiac output and hypotension. Sodium nitroprusside produces both venous and arterial dilation. An initial infusion rate of 8 to 10 μg/min may be increased by increments of 5 to 10 μg/min every 5 minutes until the desired pulmonary artery wedge pressure and cardiac output are achieved or hypotension occurs. The usual maximum dose is 500 μg/min, but it may be considerably less in the setting of renal failure due to accumulation of thiocyanate to toxic levels. Optimal dosing of vasodilators should be carefully determined by hemodynamic monitoring of pulmonary artery wedge pressure and cardiac output.

Use of the positive inotropic agents dopamine (Dopamine) and dobutamine (Dobutrex) may be considered if the previous therapy remains

TABLE 15–5–2. MEASURES TO IMPROVE VENTRICULAR FUNCTION IN HEART FAILURE

Determinant of Left Ventricular Function	Therapeutic Maneuver
Heart rate	Reduce ventricular rate with digitalis, calcium entry-blocking agents, cardioversion, and antiarrhythmic agents. Increase ventricular rate with pacemakers and isoproterenol.
Myocardial contractility	Increase contractility with digitalis, isoproterenol, epinephrine, norepinephrine, dopamine, dobutamine, and amrinone. Reduce contractility with propranolol in special circumstances, such as hypertrophic cardiomyopathy with outflow obstruction and thyrotoxicosis.
Diastolic Function	Improve the stiff heart with relief of myocardial ischemia due to coronary artery disease by drugs or invasive therapy or by use of calcium entry-blocking agents in special circumstances such as hypertrophic cardiomyopathy.
Preload	Reduce with digitalis, diuretics, inotropic agents, venodilators, nitroprusside, captopril, and rotating tourniquets.
Afterload	Reduce with hydralazine, phentolamine, trimethaphan, nitroprusside, captopril, and intraaortic balloon pump.
Regional wall motion	Improve and protect by Increasing arterial oxygen pressure (PaO_2). Decreasing myocardial oxygen consumption (MVO_2) by slowing tachycardias, reducing preload, and reducing afterload. Increasing oxygen supply by correcting reduced cardiac output and hypotension. Increasing coronary blood flow by intraaortic balloon pump and coronary bypass surgery.

ineffective. Intravenous dopamine infusion at rates between 2 and 5 μg/kg/min improves myocardial contractility, produces an increase in renal blood flow and a decrease in peripheral resistance, and facilitates diuresis. At infusion rates between 5 and 10 μg/kg/min, tachycardia and increased peripheral resistance become the dominant effect, and left ventricular end-diastolic and left atrial pressures may increase. At doses exceeding 10 to 15 μg/kg/min, peripheral vasoconstriction may further increase the demands on the diseased heart and may be very deleterious. Dobutamine may also produce a graded increase in cardiac output when infused at rates up to a maximum of 10 μg/kg/min with little increase or a reduction in left ventricular end-diastolic pressures. Both these drugs are sympathomimetic amines and increase myocardial oxygen demand and may produce ventricular arrhythmias. Parenteral amrinone (Inocor) given as a loading dose of 0.75 mg/kg followed by a maintenance infusion of 5 to 10 μg/kg/min shares the properties of dobutamine in having both a positive inotropic and vasodilating effect.

If bronchospasm and wheezing are present, aminophylline may be given (5 mg/kg intravenously over 10–15 minutes, followed by constant infusion at 0.9 mg/kg/h). In addition to bronchodilation, it also has a positive inotropic effect, produces mild venodilation, and acts as a mild diuretic.

A search for precipitating causes of acute heart failure should be made, particularly when the initial response to therapy is less than satisfactory. Hypertension should be treated aggressively. Acute onset of atrial fibrillation in the setting of cardiac states known to be critically dependent on a coordinated atrial systole (such as mitral stenosis, aortic stenosis, hypertrophic cardiomyopathy, and acute myocardial infarction) may require immediate cardioversion. A bradyarrhythmia may necessitate insertion of a pacemaker. Pulmonary embolism, hyperthyroidism, acute infections, and associated renal failure with volume overload are other examples of precipitating causes that may require specific therapy to achieve resolution of acute pulmonary edema.

The nature and severity of the underlying cardiac disorder must be quickly identified because certain conditions need specific therapy urgently and others are exacerbated by some of the therapies that are used. For example, hypertrophic cardiomyopathy is characterized by a dynamic left ventricular outflow tract obstruction that may be severely aggravated by overdiuresis or use of positive inotropic agents or arteriolar dilators. In all cases, if the general measures and pharmacologic therapy are ineffective, the possibility exists that mechanical intervention or surgery may be necessary. Intraaortic balloon pumping may be required to improve acute heart failure. Cardiac tamponade is a cardiac emergency and requires relief with pericardiocentesis or, occasionally, open drainage. Doppler echocardiography can be extremely useful in establishing the underlying cardiac disorder and obtaining an assessment of ventricular function. Thus, when the response to pharmacologic therapy is unsatisfactory despite correction of aggravating factors, emergency echocardiography or cardiac catheterization with angiography may be indicated. In general, if a surgically correctable lesion can be identified and is shown to be responsible for refractory pulmonary edema, the corrective surgery should be performed emergently or semiurgently. Although the risk of morbidity or mortality with surgery under these conditions is higher than in elective cases, it may be the only lifesaving alternative available.

FOLLOW-UP

The appropriate follow-up of patients with acute heart failure is important and essential. It is dependent on the nature of the underlying cardiac disorder or that of the precipitating factors.

In addition to documentation of relief of symptoms, the follow-up should include assessment of any residual hemodynamic compromise such as less than normal functional capacity or dyspnea on exertion. The relationship between such persistent compromise of function and the underlying cardiac disorder will be the basis for planning definitive treatment of the latter. This may be a transitional period between management of acute and chronic heart failure.

As most initial treatment of acute pulmonary edema requires use of intensive care invironment, the patient will have continous monitoring and constant nursing attention. Quantitiative measurement of the hemodynamic response to treatment should document a decrease in pulmonary artery wedge pressures, improved oxygenation, a generally favorable reduction of heart rate, and return of blood pressure to normal. At the same time, the determination should be made as to the urgency of definitive treatment of the underlying cardiac disorder. Acute vavular regurgitation or continuing myocardial ischemia, for example, if identifiable as causing the episode of acute pulmonary edema, may be expected to require further attention in-hospital before the patient can be fully stabilized. Following an initial satisfactory response to treatment, the patient will usually be followed for a period in a nonmonitored area. During this early period of recovery, further diagnostic testing may be directed toward assessment of the severity and correctability of more chronic underlying cardiac disorders.

DISCUSSION
Prevalence and Incidence

The prevalence and incidence of acute cardiogenic pulmonary edema are intimately related to those of the underlying cardiac disorder and also to periods of decompensation in patients with chronic heart failure.

Related Basic Science

The principal mechanism of acute heart failure with resultant pulmonary edema is elevation of the pulmonary capillary pressure that results in accumulation of fluid in the interstitial spaces. In the early stage of pulmonary congestion, increased extravasation of fluid into the interstitial spaces can be removed through increased lymphatic drainage. In more advanced stages, greater amounts of fluid cannot be cleared and interstitial edema forms. The resulting increase in the interstitial oncotic pressure above its normal low level may favor further accumulation of interstitial edema. The lesion that causes the increased pulmonary capillary hydrostatic pressure may be located at any site downstream from the capillary bed and may involve the valves, myocardium, pericardium, or aorta.

Myocardial diastolic dysfunction may result in pulmonary edema even when systolic dysfunction is preserved, for example, in hypertrophic cardiomyopathy or as an early manifestation of acute ischemia. In acute myocardial infarction, decreased ventricular compliance may result in increased end-diastolic pressure. The possible mechanisms include impaired relaxation, ventricular dilation that results in increased intrapericardial pressure, and ventricular interaction. Although systolic dysfunction is usually present concomitantly in acute myocardial infarction, in some cases the diastolic dysfunction may predominate with only mild systolic dysfunction, and severe but transient mitral regurgitation may result in acute cardiogenic pulmonary edema in the absence of shock. Another important mechanism is the occurrence of precipitating events, such as acute volume load, myocardial ischemia, tachycardia, ingestion of substances that may depress ventricular contractility or cause sodium retention, and medical noncompliance, that may aggravate an ongoing condition resulting in acute failure in an otherwise compensated chronic disorder.

Natural History and Its Modification with Treatment

Although in most cases the acute heart failure will improve with initial medical therapy, the immediate outcome may be compromised if effective treatment is not promptly initiated, myocardial function is severely affected, or the underlying disorder or precipitating factors are not quickly identified and treated. When acute cardiogenic pulmonary edema occurs in the setting of acute myocardial infarction, even in the absence of shock, a mortality rate of 30 to 50% may be expected. In situations where the acute failure is largely the result of a reversible alteration of cardiac hemodynamics, such as in malignant hypertension or mitral stenosis with atrial fibrillation in pregnancy, correction of the hypertension or control of ventricular rate and volume overload, respectively, may lead to a rapid return to an asymptomatic state. Subsequently, the morbidity and mortality are those of the underlying disorder. In other cases, the immediate outcome may be poor unless specific, definitive therapy is employed.

Prevention

Prevention of acute heart failure should be aimed at preventing the underlying cardiac disease. Episodes of acute heart failure may be prevented by halting or slowing the progression of disease. Patient compliance with the prescribed medical regimen is critical.

Cost Containment

In a patient with acute heart failure in whom a precipitating cause is obvious, the most direct, specific, and inexpensive approach is rapid correction of that cause. If there is an equivocal response to initial therapy, early institution of hemodynamic monitoring may facilitate the optimization of therapy and, through more rapid improvement, decrease the morbidity, length of hospital stay and cost of care. Definitive therapy of the underlying cardiac disorder by reducing morbidity and loss of employment is of great benefit.

REFERENCES

Chatterjee K. Complications of acute myocardial infarction. Curr Probl Cardiol 1993;Jan.:16.

Cohn JN, Sonnenblick EH. Diagnosis and therapy of heart failure. In: Schlant RC, Alexander RW, O'Rourke RJ, et al., eds. Hurst's the heart. 8th ed. New York: McGraw-Hill, 1994:557.

DeMots H, Rahimtoola SH, McAnulty JH, Murphy ES. Acute pulmonary edema. In: Mason DT, ed. Cardiac emergencies. Baltimore: Williams & Wilkins, 1978:173.

Forrester JS,. Diamond G, Chatterjee K, Swan HJC. Medical therapy of acute myocardial infarction by application of hemodynamic subsets. N Engl J Med 1976;295:1356.

CHAPTER 15–6

Chronic Heart Failure

David T. Kawanishi, M.D., and Shahbudin H. Rahimtoola, M.D.

DEFINITION

Chronic heart failure is a disorder of sustained reduction in cardiac function such that the circulation of blood fails to meet the metabolic needs of the tissues either at rest or during exercise, even at elevated cardiac filling pressures. The syndrome is characterized by a tendency to retain fluids, effort intolerance, and early mortality.

ETIOLOGY

The cardiac disorders associated with chronic heart failure may involve any of the cardiac structures and include disorders of the myocardium, coronary disease, valvular heart disease, pericardial disease, and congenital anomalies. Equally important as causes are precipitating events that may cause an episode of clinical heart failure in an otherwise compensated patient. Clinical heart failure occurs either when the underlying disorder progresses to a point that compensatory mechanisms fail or when the compensatory mechanisms are exhausted or compromised even without a change in severity of the underlying disorder. The causes are essentially the same as those of acute cardiogenic pulmonary edema; the difference in clinical manifestation of the disorder depends largely on the rate at which the cardiac dysfunction occurs and on whether there is sufficient time for compensatory mechanisms to develop.

CRITERIA FOR DIAGNOSIS
Suggestive

The diagnosis of heart failure should be suspected when symptoms due to congestion of the pulmonary or systemic venous system and/or symptoms of low cardiac output occur in a patient with heart disease. A decline in exercise capacity alone may be the only initial clue to the diagnosis. Frequently, the symptomatic state may be precipitated by some factor such as volume overload, upper respiratory tract infection, or an arrhythmia that overcomes the chronic compensatory mechanisms of heart failure (Figure 15–6–1).

The patient usually has evidence of some form of chronic heart disease, with 90% of cases being associated with systemic hypertension or coronary artery disease. In many cases the patient will have had prior symptoms due to the underlying disorder, but in others, the symptoms of congestive heart failure are the initial manifestation of cardiac disease.

Definitive

The constellation of clinical findings required for diagnosis includes evidence of pulmonary and/or systemic venous congestion, a diminished cardiac reserve, and heart disease with impaired cardiac function. Dyspnea on exertion, weakness, and diminished exercise tolerance are common. A history of systemic hypertension, coronary artery disease, valvular heart disease, or cardiomegaly suggests the presence of underlying chronic heart disease.

The essential feature of chronic heart failure is the inability of compensatory mechanisms to maintain adequate cardiac function in the presence of injury to the myocardium or a mechanical lesion resulting in a chronic abnormal load on the heart. The usual consequence is the development of symptoms and signs of congestion in the pulmonary venous or systemic venous system. Also, there is a diminished cardiac reserve with either a decline in exertional capacity or, in more severe

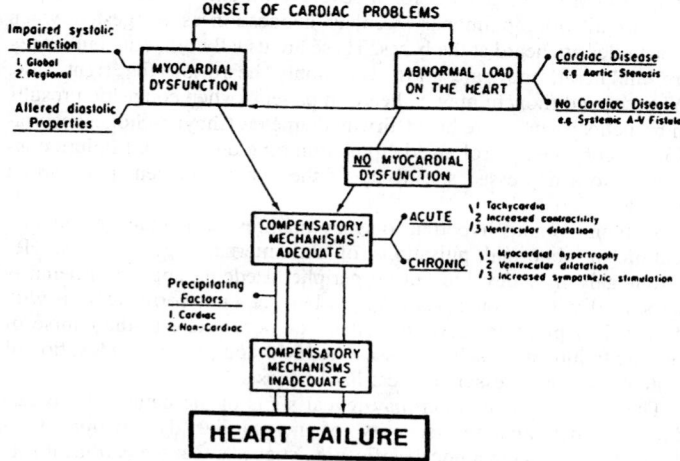

Figure 15–6–1. Pathophysiologic mechanisms in patients with heart failure. *(Source: Rahimtoola SH. Oral vasodilators should not be used routinely in the treatment of congestive heart failure. In: Rapaport E, ed. Current controversies in cardiovascular disease. Philadelphia: Saunders, 1980:613. Reproduced with permission from the publisher and author.)*

states, evidence of diminished organ perfusion even at rest. When these conditions exist, the diagnosis of chronic heart failure is secure.

CLINICAL MANIFESTATIONS
Subjective

The cardinal symptom is dyspnea, which is usually a manifestation of pulmonary venous hypertension, increased pulmonary capillary pressures, and pulmonary congestion. Occasionally, chronic heart failure results from a low cardiac output that is unable to increase adequately on exercise. Early in the course, dyspnea only on exertion may be present; orthopnea, paroxysmal nocturnal dyspnea, and dyspnea at rest develop as the condition worsens. Prominent wheezing associated with paroxysmal nocturnal dyspnea has been called cardiac asthma; it differs from that seen with pulmonary edema in that it occurs in transient paroxysms. Acute heart failure with pulmonary edema may develop if there is an abrupt, severe increase in pulmonary capillary pressure. Symptoms of diminished cardiac output with hypoperfusion of end organs are also common; for example, patients frequently complain of fatigue and at times of weakness of the legs during exertion. Nocturia is a relatively early symptom of chronic heart failure. Central nervous system symptoms also may develop, especially if cerebrovascular disease coexists. Congestion of the systemic venous system may result in right upper quadrant and epigastric discomfort due to congestive hepatomegaly. Anorexia, nausea, constipation, or abdominal pain due to congestion or ischemia of the gastrointestinal tract may develop. In addition, there may be symptoms referable to the underlying cardiovascular disorder or its complications, such as hypertensive end-organ damage and chest pain due to ischemic coronary artery disease. Any past history of cardiac disease should be elicited in detail to clarify where the patient is in the natural course of the disorder.

Objective
Physical Examination

The physical findings associated with chronic heart failure vary with the severity of heart failure and the nature of the underlying cardiac disorder.

In the early stages, when only exertional symptoms exist, the patient may generally appear well at rest. Dyspnea with minimal activity, respiratory difficulty when lying flat, and then obvious respiratory difficulty at rest develop as the heart failure progresses. With chronic severe failure, the patient may become cachectic. Signs of vasoconstriction wtih cool, pale extremities and a resting tachycardia are a result of compensatory mechanisms for a severely diminished cardiac output. On auscultation, pulmonary venous congestion is suggested when moist rales are heard at the bases. These are usually bilateral, but if they are unilateral, they are most commonly heard on the right side. Wheezes and rhonchi may be heard in patients when congestion results in bronchospasm and reduced airway diameter. Cheyne–Stokes respirations occur when a prolonged circulation time due to heart failure contributes to a depressed sensitivity of the respiratory center to carbon dioxide.

Systemic venous hypertension may manifest as jugular venous distention or abnormal pulsations of the internal jugular veins. Hepatomegaly may develop before peripheral edema appears. Edema is associated with chronic heart failure but does not correlate well with the level of pressure elevation. Anasarca occurs late in the course of chronic failure, and ascites is associated with long-standing elevation of systemic venous pressure and cardiac cirrhosis.

The cardiac examination may reveal signs of the nature of the cardiac disorder and the severity of myocardial dysfunction. Cardiomegaly, although a nonspecific sign, suggests that the cardiac disorder is indeed chronic. Some disorders, such as mitral stenosis, restrictive cardiomyopathies, and constrictive pericarditis, may give rise to a chronic heart failure state without cardiomegaly. An S_3 gallop sound suggests abnormal ventricular diastolic properties in an individual older than age 40 unless there is an abnormally large amount of inflow into the ventricle, such as with mitral regurgitation, tricuspid regurgitation, or a left-to-right shunt. When these conditions are absent, an S_3 gallop is a sign of heart failure. Other findings, such as cardiac murmurs, friction rubs, and pericardial knock, may be useful clues to the cardiac disorder underlying the heart failure.

Routine Laboratory Abnormalities

Abnormal findings on the chest roentgenogram include evidence of pulmonary vascular hypertension with pulmonary congestion and abnormalities of the cardiac silhouette. Mild elevation of the pulmonary capillary pressure in the range 15 to 19 mm Hg is associated with equalization of the size of vessels of the upper lobes with that of lower-lobe vessels. In the pressure range of 18 to approximately 23 mm Hg, the upper-lobe vessels appear larger than lower-lobe vessels. In the range 20 to 25 mm Hg or greater, signs of interstitial edema with Kerley A and B lines, peribronchial cuffing, and accumulation of pleural fluid appear. Above 25 mm Hg, alveolar edema becomes apparent (see Chapter 15–5). Specific chamber enlargement may be a clue to the nature of the disorder.

Similarly, the electrocardiogram, although not helpful in the diagnosis of heart failure itself, reflects the nature of the underlying disorder and may be useful in formulating a specific therapeutic plan directed at that disorder. Blood chemistry may reveal prerenal azotemia, hyponatremia, or evidence of congestive hepatomegaly and cardiac cirrhosis. Electrolyte abnormalities such as hypokalemia (the result of chronic diuretic therapy) and hyperkalemia (due to severe heart failure and decreased glomerular filtration rate) or evidence of renal failure as precipitating factors also may be detected.

PLANS
Diagnostic
Differential Diagnosis

The initial differential diagnosis is the determination that the fluid retention or symptoms of circulatory insufficiency are due to a cardiac cause. The presence of other fluid-retaining states (cirrhosis, renal failure) or causes of fatigue and effort intolerance (systemic illnesses such as cancer and endocrine abnormalities) should be excluded. The differential diagnosis of the underlying cardiac etiology may be facilitated by systematically evaluating the various possibly responsible cardiac structural components: myocardium, coronary arteries, valves, pericardium, congenital anomalies. Identification of any precipitating causes is also a part of the differential diagnosis when clinical decompensation occurs. These may include noncompliance with medications or inappropriate reduction of pharmacologic treatment, acute volume loading, arrhythmias, acute infections or other acute illnesses, pulmonary embolism, development of a second cardiac disorder, exposure to drugs that depress ventricular function or facilitate sodium retention, and development of a high-cardiac-output state.

Diagnostic Options

Specific diagnostic tests available beyond the routine chest x-ray and electrocardiogram include echocardiography (either transthoracic or transesophageal), Doppler echocardiography, exercise electrocardiographic treadmill testing, exercise or pharmacologic stress testing with thallium, gated blood pool or echocardiographic imaging, and cardiac catheterization with or without angiography. In some disorders, a positron emission scan, computed tomography scan, or magnetic resonance imaging may provide helpful information.

Recommended Approach

The history, physical examination, and routine laboratory examination usually provide a constellation of findings that are reasonably specific for chronic heart failure. On occasion, however, chronic lung disease or noncardiac causes of peripheral edema may be confused with heart failure. In such cases, direct measurement of the pulmonary artery wedge pressure through right-sided heart catheterization with a balloon flotation thermodilution catheter will establish the diagnosis. When the heart failure is severe or complicated by other severe medical disorders, this catheter may be useful to follow the response to therapy and to permit selection of the most specific drug and most effective dosage.

Furthermore, every effort should be made to establish the nature and severity of the underlying cardiac disorder as early as possible in the management of a patient with heart failure. The most practical and rapid route to a diagnosis depends on the suspected lesion, whether it is hypertension, coronary artery disease, valvular disease, or one of the myriad other causes of heart failure (see Table 15–5–1).

In patients in whom the diagnosis of the underlying cardiac disorder or the state of ventricular function is uncertain, echocardiography is a valuable clinical tool. Cardiac catheterization and angiography may be needed to make a definitive diagnosis and institute appropriate therapy for the underlying cardiac disorder. When the issue of viability of myocardium arises in the setting of a chronic ischemic condition, imaging of provocable myocardial function by echocardiography, a delayed uptake of thallium on late reinjection, or, most definitively, positron emission tomography to confirm the presence of preserved metabolic function despite hypoperfusion may be required.

Therapeutic

In most cases, initial treatment is in the form of pharmacologic support of the failed cardiac function in an attempt to achieve a state of compensation of minimal symptomatology. If a correctable cardiac lesion can be identified, correction should be attempted when practicable and when the benefit of correction outweighs the risk of morbidity or mortality of the corrective procedure. An attempt should be made to avoid excessive delays in definitive treatment, however, because when myocardial dysfunction is due to coronary disease with chronic ischemia or chronic valve regurgitation, such delays may be associated with clinical deterioration and worsen the eventual risk of the corrective procedure.

The approach to therapy of the patient with chronic heart failure is essentially the same as that for the patient with acute heart failure except that it is not quite as emergent a condition as acute heart failure. Correction of the underlying cardiac lesion and removal of precipitating factors should be achieved as soon as possible. The goals of therapy are relief of symptoms and reduced exercise tolerance by correction of the salt and water retention and the depressed myocardial function; correction of precipitating factors; amelioration and correction of the underlying cardiac disease; and prevention of recurrences (see Table 15–6–1). General measures include physical and emotional rest. Dietary sodium should be restricted to 2 g per day or less.

Specific therapy should be directed at each of the determinants of ventricular function (see Table 15–5–2). Most patients benefit from an increase in myocardial contractility with the use of a cardiac glycoside (Figure 15–6–2). Reduction of the ventricular rate with improved diastolic filling of the ventricle must be achieved in the patient with atrial fibrillation. If the failure is mild, digoxin (Lanoxin, 0.25 mg orally each day) may be initiated without a loading dose, with a steady state usually being achieved in 7 to 14 days depending on age, renal function, and other factors. If failure is moderately severe, a loading dose of 1.0 mg may be given in divided doses over the first day, followed by usual maintenance doses of 0.125 to 0.25 mg per day. Higher maintenance

TABLE 15–6–1. MANAGEMENT OF HEART FAILURE

Diagnosis
    Of basic cardiac lesion and its severity
    Of contribution of precipitating factors
Treatment
    Control of excess sodium and water retention with diuretics
    Improve myocardial function with positive inotropic agents
    Change loading conditions of the heart
    Correct underlying cardiac lesion(s)
    Control precipitating factors
Prevention
    Prevention of heart disease is the ideal means, for example, control of rheumatic fever and prevention of recurrences, control of risk factors for coronary artery disease particularly in the young and healthy, and early diagnosis and treatment of systemic hypertension
    Recurrences may be prevented by correcting the underlying cardiac lesion(s) and the precipitating factors

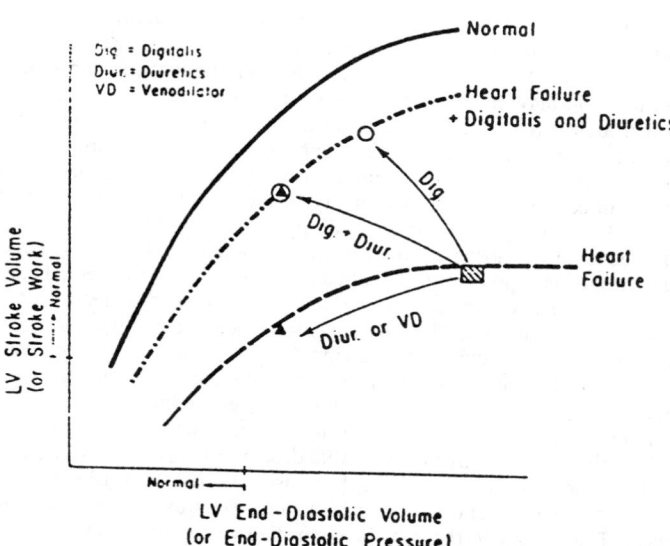

Figure 15–6–2. Shift in left ventricular function showing diminished performance at equivalent or higher-end diastolic volume or pressure in the presence of heart failure. The effects of digitalis, diuretics, and venodilators are also illustrated. LV, left ventricular; Dig, digitalis; Diur, diuretic; VD, venodilator. (*Source: Rahimtoola SH. Oral vasodilators should not be used routinely in the treatment of congestive heart failure. In: Rapaport E, ed. Current controversies in cardiovascular disease. Philadelphia: Saunders, 1980:613. Reproduced with permission from the publisher and author.*)

doses may be needed to control the ventricular rate in atrial fibrillation. If the failure is severe, intravenous therapy may be initiated, as for treatment of acute heart failure. Every patient receiving a cardiac glycoside must be examined carefully for evidence of toxicity on each follow-up visit.

Reduction of preload by use of a diuretic is also indicated for most patients with chronic heart failure; diuretics have this effect by correcting the salt and water retention (Figure 15–6–2). A thiazide diuretic, such as hydrochlorothiazide, in doses of 25 to 50 mg orally once a day, may reduce symptoms and prevent edema formation in patients with mild failure. In moderate to severe failure, however, furosemide (Lasix) in initial oral doses of 40 mg per day may be needed and may be increased to 80 to 160 mg per single dose to control symptoms and edema formation.

Occasionally, a patient such as a diminutive elderly individual may have a satisfactory response to an initial dose as low as 10 mg once a day. A patient who fails to respond to a dose of 240 mg furosemide twice a day may nevertheless respond to substitution of another loop diuretic such as bumetamide (Bumex), starting at 0.5 to 1.0 mg once a day with titration as needed to a maximum of 10 mg once a day, or ethacrynic acid (Edecrin), starting at 50 mg once a day with titration to no more than 200 mg twice a day.

When chronic diuretic therapy is employed, oral potassium supplementation is often needed to avoid hypokalemia, starting in the range of 20 to 40 mEq potassium per day when the milder form or lower doses of diuretic is used. An alternative is the use of a potassium-sparing diuretic such as spironolactone (25 mg four times a day) or triamterene (beginning at 100 mg once a day, up to a maximum of three times a day). These agents should be avoided when there is concomitant renal failure, and combination with oral potassium supplements is usually not advisable. Excessive diuresis to the point of volume depletion should be avoided, particularly when concomitant treatment with a vasodilator is initiated.

If satisfactory resolution of the heart failure cannot be achieved with digoxin and diuretics, vasodilator therapy may be added. Ideally, the choice of vasodilators and optimum dosage of each drug are best achieved with hemodynamic monitoring. Venodilators are useful when venous congestion due to excessive preload is prominent, whereas predominant arterial dilators may be more useful if systemic hypertension or a low-cardiac-output state are present. If both are present, combination therapy or an angiotension-converting enzyme inhibitor may be used. The nitrates are potent venodilators, and several routes of delivery are available. Sublingual nitroglycerin or intravenous nitroglycin via infusion may be used when a very rapid onset of action or a sustained high level, respectively, is desirable in the very ill or unstable patient, as with acute heart failure. For the stable patient with chronic heart failure, oral isosorbide dinitrate (Isordil) may be given, starting at 10 mg three times daily and advancing as tolerated to 40 mg three times daily. The maximum recommended dose is 80 mg three times daily. Headache and orthostatic hypotension are common side effects. Topical nitroglycerin preparations applied once a day are available and convenient for the patient, but their efficacy in treatment of heart failure has come into question. Hemodynamic tolerance to chronic nitrate therapy is a frequent occurrence, and significant tolerance may even occur in the first 24 hours of continuous nitrate therapy. Tolerance may be overcome by providing an 8- to 12-hour nitrate-free interval.

Arterial dilators may be used to reduce afterload. Hydralazine (Apresoline) may be given in an initial dose of 50 mg orally twice a day and increased to 100 to 150 mg per dose. Headaches, flushing, drug fever, rash, nausea and vomiting, and fluid retention with edema may occur. The last side effect may be controlled with concomitant use of a diuretic. A syndrome resembling systemic lupus erythematosus may develop with hydralazine, especially in doses exceeding 200 mg per day, which is commonly needed when treating chronic heart failure. Minoxidil is another arterial dilator, and it may be given in an initial dose of 2.5 mg and increased up to 20 mg three times a day. Prazosin (Minipress) is given initially in a dose 0.5 mg three times a day and may be increased up to 10 mg per dose. It provides both venodilation and arterial dilation, but tachyphylaxis and inability to titrate the individual hemodynamic effects against symptomatology are potential disadvantages. At times, a lower initial dose of 6.25 mg orally three times daily may be necessary; the maximum recommended dose is 100 mg three times daily. Captopril (Capoten) is an angiotensin-converting enzyme inhibitor with a balanced arterial and venodilator effect. It may be started at 12.5 mg orally and increased up to 50 mg three times a day. Captopril in large doses and with mean arterial pressures less than 80 to 90 mm Hg has been associated with deterioration of renal function in patients with coexistent renal insufficiency. In such patients, captopril should be used with great caution and in small doses. Enalapril (Vasotec) is an alternative angiotensin-converting enzyme inhibitor that might be considered. The initial dose is 2.5 mg orally twice daily, with a reasonable target of 10 mg twice daily and a maximum recommended dose of 20 mg twice daily. Lisinopril (Prinivil, Prinzide, Zestoretic, Zestril) and quinapril (Accupril) are alternative angiotensin-converting enzyme inhibitors that have been used successfully in treating chronic heart failure. Any of the arterial dilators may produce marked hypotension, and the patient should be observed or at least cautioned against orthostatic symptoms when therapy is initiated.

The use of beta blockers, carefully titrated, has resulted in clinical improvement and reduced mortality in some series. The first-generation calcium channel blockers appear ineffective in the treatment of chronic heart failure, but the new generation of dihydropyridine calcium channel blockers, amlodipine and felodipine, are distinguished from the former by an apparent lack of negative inotropic effect and are currently under investigation in the treatment of heart failure.

Of the new inotropic agents, parenteral amrinone and milrinone have been useful in the acute setting. As oral treatment of chronic heart failure, milrinone may result in increased mortality according to recent studies.

Pharmacologic antiarrhythmic therapy has not resulted in reduction of mortality in chronic heart failure. Even the implantable cardiac defibrillator, though clearly reducing the incidence of sudden death, may have little benefit for long-term mortality. Some trials using amiodarone have produced some promising results, however.

Cardiac transplantation may be considered for young patients, generally less than 55 years of age, with end-stage disease in whom there has been no significant benefit from standard therapy and who are otherwise healthy and have demonstrated emotional stability and good compliance with their medical regimen. At present, it should not be considered if the patient has a serious systemic disease, such as diabetes or peripheral vascular disease, an active infection, other irreversible organ disease, a history of chemical abuse, or excessive obesity; when the above recommended treatment regimens have been instituted and symptoms persist despite maximal doses, other options may be considered.

When the symptoms of heart failure appear in a patient with an underlying cardiac disorder that is surgically correctable, operation must be seriously considered. If the clinical deterioration is clearly the result of an acute intercurrent event, such as tachyarrhythmia or medical noncompliance, then definitive treatment of the underlying cardiac disorder may occasionally be deferred and the patient followed expectantly if the cardiac disorder is not severe. If, however, there is no such inciting or provoking event, then the clinical appearance of heart failure may be a sign of critical deterioration. In some cases, a low morbidity of corrective surgery and a known progressive natural history suggest that surgery should be recommended without hesitation, as in heart failure associated with left-to-right shunts due to isolated patent ductus arteriosis, ventricular septal defect, or atrial septal defect. In other cases, as in regurgitant valvular lesions with normal ventricular function at rest and a favorable response to minimal drug therapy, then, expectant observation may be appropriate, although surgery must not be delayed to the point of severe irreversible myocardial failure. A precise and thorough assessment of the underlying cardiac disorder is imperative to formulate the most appropriate and complete therapeutic plan.

FOLLOW-UP

In most cases, at least one early follow-up visit after initial treatment is indicated both to assess the continued efficacy of the treatment regimen and, more important, to confirm that a rapidly deteriorating cardiac disorder is not present. Each follow-up visit should include a complete review of symptoms and a search for physical abnormalities. The follow-up interval should vary according to the rapidity of expected deterioration of the underlying condition and the severity of the heart failure at the outset. Reasonable routine parameters to follow include functional capacity, volume status by serial weights and physical examination, and end-organ perfusion and function by appropriate testing, such as blood urea nitrogen and creatinine for renal function.

Because deterioration of the underlying condition or the occurrence of intercurrent problems may rapidly place these patients into life-threatening acute heart failure, patients should be advised to seek medical attention whenever there is recurrence of symptoms of venous congestion or diminished cardiac output.

DISCUSSION
Prevalence and Incidence

It is estimated that there are more than 2,000,000 patients in the United States with heart failure, with around 400,000 new cases diagnosed every year. Approximately 200,000 deaths annually are attributed to heart failure.

Related Basic Science

Heart failure is a common complication of heart disease. Thus, despite a continued improvement in understanding of the pathophysiologic mechanisms involved, heart failure remains a major health problem. Some of the common causes of heart failure are listed in Table 15–5–1; it needs to be reemphasized that 90% of cases are associated with either hypertension or coronary artery disease. Chronic heart failure is a state in which a progressive cardiac disorder results in a decline in cardiac performance beyond the ability of compensatory mechanisms to preserve cardiac output and avoid venous congestion (see Figure 15–6–1). In some patients, there may be no impairment of systolic myocardial function (Kitzman et al., 1991). Disorders such as mitral stenosis, atrial septal defects, and constrictive pericarditis may lead to a chronic deterioration of cardiac function without myocardial dysfunction. Successful, uncomplicated surgical correction of these mechanical problems usually reverses or markedly alleviates the heart failure.

When the heart failure is due to progressive deterioration of myocardial function, a number of biochemical, physiologic, and anatomic changes occur. The failing myocardium is characterized by a decrease in myocardial norepinephrine stores, a reduction in myocardial beta-adrenergic receptor density, a decrease in myosin ATPase activity, and a decrease in calcium transport by the sarcoplasmic reticulum. Whether these changes are a cause of the diminished myocardial contractility or are secondary phenomena, however, has not been established.

The decrease in ventricular contractility is frequently depicted as a downward and rightward shift of the ventricular function curve (see Figure 15–6–2). A higher than normal left atrial pressure is needed to maintain stroke volume and cardiac output. If the myocardial dysfunction is severe, the shift of the function curve may be such that an adequate output cannot be maintained at left atrial pressure levels below that which would result in pulmonary edema. A number of compensatory mechanisms are invoked in heart failure. Myocardial hypertrophy and/or ventricular dilation are common compensatory mechanisms, helping to maintain normal wall stress and tension in the face of chronic pressure or volume overload; however, a diminished diastolic compliance may result in and contribute to venous congestion. An increase in sympathetic tone results in increased heart rate and increased inotropic stimulation of the myocardium. Venoconstriction also may increase fluid return to the heart and augment the ventricular filling pressure. Arterial vasoconstriction helps to maintain blood pressure; however, an undesirable increase in peripheral vascular resistance also may occur. The renin–angiotensin system is activated and further augments ventricular filling pressures through salt and water retention; however, the amount of fluid retention may be excessive and may result in pulmonary congestion and organ engorgement or peripheral edema on the systemic side. Angiotensin II is also an arterial constrictor and may further increase peripheral resistance. The distribution of the vasoconstriction is such that cerebral and coronary flows are preserved at the expense of flow to the splanchnic, renal, skeletal muscle, and cutaneous areas. A compensatory shift in the oxyhemoglobin dissociation curve favoring release of oxygen to the tissues and a shift to anaerobic metabolism in some organs also may occur.

Natural History and Its Modification with Treatment

Overall, congestive heart failure has a very poor prognosis. The survival at 5 years after the onset of heart failure is 50%. Of patients who are in New York Heart Association functional class IV, less than 50% survive 1 year. The prognosis is much better, however, if a mechanical lesion is surgically corrected and irreversible myocardial dysfunction is not a part of the disorder. The only pharmacologic regimens that have been shown to reduce the mortality rate are treatment with the combination of hydralazine and isosorbide dinitrate and treatment with an angiotensin-converting enzyme inhibitor.

Prevention

Prevention of the underlying cardiac disorder is the best means of preventing chronic heart failure. Factors that worsen heart failure, particularly noncompliance with dietary restriction or with medications, can frequently be avoided.

Cost Containment

Prevention of chronic heart failure by early control or correction of the chronic underlying cardiac disorder is the best means of reducing the cost of medical care. Once heart failure develops, effective management of the underlying disorder is usually the least expensive approach. If there is no correctable disorder, or if the severity of left ventricular dysfunction already precludes a definitive corrective approach, the cost of care can be minimized only through strict compliance to an optimal medical regimen designed to minimize rehospitalization for severe symptoms and forestall the development of failure of other organs.

REFERENCES

Arnold SB, Byrd RC, Meister W, et al. Long-term digitalis therapy improves left ventricular function in heart failure. N Engl J Med 1980;303:1443.

Cohn JN, Archibald DG, Ziesche S, et al. Effect of vasodilator therapy on mortality in congestive heart failure: Results of a Veterans Administration Cooperative Study. N Engl J Med 1986;314:1547.

Forrester JS, Waters DD. Hospital treatment of congestive heart failure: Management according to hemodynamic profile. Am J Med 1978;65:173.

Guidelines for the evaluation and management of heart failure. Report of the American College of Cardiology/American Heart Association Task Force on Practice Guidelines (Committee on Evaluation and Management of Heart Failure). J Am Coll Cardiol 1995;26:1376.

Kitzman DW, Higginbothan MB, Cobb FR, et al. Exercise intolerance in patients with heart failure and preserved left ventricular systolic function: Failure of the Frank–Starling mechanism. J Am Coll Cardiol 1991;17:1065.

Pfeffer MA, Braunwald E, Moye LA, et al., for the SAVE investigators. Effect of captopril on mortality and morbidity in patients with left ventricular dysfunction after myocardial infarction: Results of the Survival and Ventricular Enlargement Trial. N Engl J Med 1992;327:669.

Rahimtoola SH. Valvular heart disease: A perspective. J Am Coll Cardiol 1983;1:199.

Schlant RC, Sonnenblick EH. Pathophysiology of heart failure. In: Schlant RC, Alexander RW, O'Rourke RJ, et al., eds. Hurst's the heart. 8th ed. New York: McGraw-Hill, 1994:515.

SOLVD Investigators. Effect of enalapril on mortality and the development of heart failure in asymptomatic patients with reduced left ventricular ejection fraction. N Engl J Med 1992;327:685.

CHAPTER 15–7

Cardiogenic Shock

David T. Kawanishi, M.D., and Shahbudin H. Rahimtoola, M.D.

DEFINITION

Cardiogenic shock is a clinical syndrome of hypoperfusion with hypoxemia of vital organs and hypotension caused by severe cardiac disfunction.

ETIOLOGY

The cardiac functional disturbance that causes cardiogenic shock may be a mechanical disturbance of blood flow involving obstruction or acute severe valvular regurgitation, a clinical event precipitating critical reduction of myocardial function in the setting of a previously compensated chronic cardiac disorder, or an acute myocardial infarction.

CRITERIA FOR DIAGNOSIS
Suggestive

The presence of cardiogenic shock may be suggested when a state of shock occurs in the presence of an acute myocardial infarction or in a patient with a history of, or signs on physical examination of, a severe cardiac disorder. The state of shock is suggested by the presence of hypotension, diminished urine output, altered mental status, cool extremities, and other evidence of organ hypoperfusion. Importantly, only one or a few of the manifestations of severe shock may be present at the earlier stages, and initially, they may be as subtle as an altered state of consciousness in an elderly individual. Characteristically, however, the condition is marked by rapid deterioration of function in multiple organs.

Definitive

The diagnosis of cardiogenic shock is secure when it is demonstrated that in the presence of elevated left ventricular filling pressure represented by a pulmonary artery wedge pressure greater than 18 mm Hg, a cardiac index below 1.8 L/min/m^2 results in systemic hypotension less than 80 mm Hg systolic pressure and hypoperfusion of organs. Cardiogenic shock may result from severe right ventricular failure, which at times may not be associated with significant left ventricular dysfunction.

CLINICAL MANIFESTATIONS
Subjective

The symptoms associated with cardiogenic shock are those of the underlying cardiac disorder and those associated with failure of the mechanisms to compensate in chronic cardiac failure (see Chapter 15–6). As acute pulmonary edema and arterial hypoxemia are part of the cardiogenic shock state, the symptoms of shortness of breath and the rest of the symptoms of that disorder may also be present (see Chapter 15–5). Continuing chest pain frequently accompanies the onset of cardiogenic shock in the patient with acute myocardial infarction. The cerebral hypoperfusion may manifest as mental confusion, obtundation, or somnolence, in which case few other reliable symptoms may be elicitable.

Objective
Physical Examination

The physical findings in cardiogenic shock are those of low cardiac output. These include confusion, agitation or stupor, cool moist skin, a rapid and thready pulse, and a narrow pulse pressure. Hypotension and hypothermia are common. Hypotension may be absent early in the course. Rapid, shallow respirations are typical, and Cheyne–Stokes respirations may be present. The heart sounds are diminished or muffled in quality. All the features of acute heart failure and pulmonary edema may be present. The findings associated with the etiologic or precipitating disorder also should be present and may be very helpful in the initial assessment of the shock state. Examples include a new, prominent cardiac murmur with a thrill due to acute mitral regurgitation or ventricular septal rupture; a new diastolic murmur of acute aortic regurgitation; marked jugular venous distention with minimal pulmonary congestion suggesting either right ventricular infarction, cor pulmonale, acute pulmonary embolism, or cardiac tamponade; and, occasionally, a surprising lack of expected pulmonary or systemic venous congestion if there is coexistent hypovolemia.

Routine Laboratory Abnormalities

Azotemia, elevated liver enzymes, and electrolyte abnormalities on blood chemistry are nonspecific manifestations of hypoperfusion and organ dysfunction or injury. Pulmonary edema and cardiomegaly are commonly present on the chest roentgenogram. An elevated creatine kinase level and the electrocardiographic changes of acute myocardial infarction are often present. The electrocardiogram or bedside cardiac rhythm monitoring may also reveal the nature of the tachyarrhythmia or bradyarrhythmia if this is the precipitating factor of the shock state.

PLANS
Diagnostic
Differential Diagnosis

The diagnosis of cardiogenic shock is usually made when shock coexists with a cardiac disorder; however, the differential diagnosis should at least consider the possibility of causes other than cardiac. At the least, such other problems may be contributing to the cardiac deterioration, if not entirely the cause of the shock state. The cardiac disorders that may result in cardiogenic shock are the same as those that produce acute heart failure without shock (see Table 15–5–1).

Diagnostic Options and Recommended Approach

Because cardiogenic shock is generally a rapidly lethal condition and is particularly so when associated with acute myocardial infarction, rapid accurate diagnosis of the extent of hemodynamic abnormality and the nature of the underlying cardiac disorder is imperative for institution of appropriate specific treatment.

The extent of hypoxia and acidosis should be measured with arterial blood gases and lactate determinations. Direct measurements of the pulmonary artery wedge pressure, cardiac output, and intraarterial pressure are necessary parts of the initial evaluation of the patient in cardiogenic shock. Although these determinations must not be allowed to interfere with immediate institution of general measures to support the patient, they are essential for a complete and secure diagnosis and appropriate management. A low or normal pulmonary artery wedge pressure is not expected in this setting and should suggest the presence of hypovolemia; when it is combined with a "normal" or "elevated" cardiac output, septic shock is a strong possibility.

Depending on the suspected cardiac lesion, echocardiography, radionuclide studies, or cardiac catheterization with left ventricular and/or coronary angiography may be required to establish the nature and severity of the underlying disorder. The spectrum of disorders is the same as that responsible for acute heart failure without shock (see Table 15–5–1); however, as survival in cardiogenic shock is inversely related to the duration of tissue hypoperfusion, and because in the most severe cases improved perfusion cannot be achieved without correction of the underlying disorder, these studies may be needed on an emergency or urgent basis.

Therapeutic
Therapeutic Options

The often rapid deterioration ending in death requires that general supportive measures be instituted immediately and the underlying cardiac disorder identified and corrected as quickly as possible.

Recommended Approach

Therapy is directed at both the general manifestations of shock and the primary cardiac disorder. As in acute heart failure without shock (see Chapter 15–5), general supportive measures should be employed immediately on recognition of the shock state; these include supplemental high-flow oxygen with mechanical ventilatory assistance if indicated. Electrolyte disturbances and metabolic acidosis or other acid–base abnormalities should be corrected. Pain, nausea, vomiting, and fever should be treated appropriately. Aminophylline may be used if bronchospasm is present, as in pulmonary edema.

Effort must be made quickly to improve cardiac output. An optimum preload is important in the severely diseased heart, and a low or normal pulmonary artery wedge pressure is inappropriate. While monitoring the pulmonary artery wedge pressure and the cardiac output, volume should be given to raise this pressure into the range of 18 to 20 mm Hg or, occasionally, up to 25 mm Hg. A pulmonary artery wedge pressure in excess of this may result in pulmonary congestion and pulmonary edema, however, and may necessitate the use of a diuretic or venodilator. Inotropic agents, either dopamine or dobutamine (Dobutrex), in the range 3 to 10 μg/kg per minute may be infused. Isoproterenol (Isuprel), in the dosage range 0.5 to 3 μg per minute infusion, is also a positive inotropic and chronotropic agent and a potent vasodilator; however, the tachycardic response may be excessive, as may the vasodilation, and therefore, it is best reserved for the occasional situation in which bradycardia and severe vasoconstriction coexist. Isoproterenol is likely to be particularly harmful in the setting of acute myocardial infarction. Arrhythmias should be corrected as quickly as possible. Bradyarrhythmias are generally best treated with a temporary pacemaker, either ventricular or atrioventricular sequential pacing may be considered. The bradycardia and hypotension due to excess vagal tone commonly seen with inferior myocardial infarction may be simply treated with atropine (0.5 mg intravenously), and this may be repeated at 3- to 10-minute intervals up to a total dose of 2.0 mg. Inotropic agents should be avoided in shock associated with hypertrophic cardiomyopathy.

If shock cannot be quickly reversed, intraaortic balloon pumping may be of benefit. Pump insertion is contraindicated in the presence of aortic regurgitation and may not be advisable in those conditions considered terminal with no possibility of a definitive maneuver to improve cardiac performance. If a correctable lesion is suspected, it is appropriate to proceed emergently to a definitive diagnostic evaluation, usually cardiac catheterization and angiography, once the intraaortic balloon pump is, in place or as soon as the patient is otherwise stabilized. Emergency percutaneous cardiopulmonary bypass support using femoral cannulation may stablize the patient when other measures have failed and may allow more definitive intervention to be performed, such as emergent percutaneous transluminal coronary angioplasty or surgery.

If a surgically correctable cardiac disorder is identified in a patient with cardiogenic shock, operation is indicated. The risks of surgery may be improved if the shock state can be reversed preoperatively; however, excessive delay may result in further myocardial injury. In some patients who do not improve despite the use of all available nonsurgical measures, the risks of emergency surgery on an unstable patient must be weighed against the risks of a continued state of shock.

FOLLOW-UP

The diagnostic and therapeutic plans described above require an intensity and frequency of monitoring of the clinical and hemodynamic status that can be accomplished only in an intensive care setting. The nature of the follow-up, however, may be modified by the nature and severity of the cardiac and any coexisting disorder, the availability of diagnostic and therapeutic resources, and the desires of the patient and family. Progress in management of the patient should describe the nature and quantification of cardiac and hemodynamic improvement, the response of vital organs to the therapeutic measures, and the status of the underlying disorder at the highest level of resolution possible at the time.

Helpful cardiac and hemodynamic parameters include blood pressure and heart rate, cardiac output, pulmonary artery wedge pressures, augmented and unaugmented, intraaortic balloon pump pressures and arterial and mixed venous oxygen saturations. Although usually not necessary, lactate levels may help to follow the general state of vital organ perfusion and oxygenation.

Once supportive measures have been instituted, the results of some of the more detailed but time-consuming diagnostic testing options, such as transthoracic or transesophageal echocardiography or even cardiac catheterization and angiography, may become available. Documentation of findings is important and correctable lesions should be treated in as timely a manner as practicable. The patient in cardiogenic shock must be seen as frequently, often continuously, as necessary until a *definitive* plan of treatment has been established and implemented.

DISCUSSION
Prevalence

Cardiogenic shock occurs commonly in patients with complications of myocardial infarction, abrupt valve dysfunction, treacherous cardiac arrhythmia, and massive pulmonary infarction.

Related Basic Science

Cardiogenic shock is the result of a profound reduction in cardiac output. Approximately 5 to 10% of hospitalized patients with acute myocardial infarction develop cardiogenic shock. Usually, cardiogenic shock represents a loss of function of at least 40% of the total left ventricular muscle mass. This may be the result of any combination of prior myocardial infarction, acute infarction, and myocardial ischemia. Besides myocardial failure, any mechanical lesion such as acute aortic or mitral regurgitation, ventricular septal rupture, cardiac tamponade, severe aortic stenosis, or severe mitral stenosis may result in cardiogenic shock.

In common with other forms of heart failure, compensatory mechanisms initially invoked to preserve systemic perfusion and cardiac function may contribute to further deterioration through increased myocardial oxygen demands and congestion and ischemia of vital organs.

Natural History and Its Modification with Treatment

The immediate morbidity associated with cardiogenic shock varies with the nature of the cardiac disorder, the duration of tissue hypoperfusion, and the nature and severity of organ damage. There is a wide spectrum in the response to therapy.

The mortality associated with cardiogenic shock is generally high, but it varies significantly according to the nature of the cardiac disorder, the duration of the shocklike state, the inciting factor(s), and the amount of loss of functioning myocardium. Even in cardiogenic shock associated with acute myocardial infarction, where the overall mortality ranges from 70 to 90%, the subset of patients with shock due to right ventricular infarction may have only a 40% mortality, and if the shocklike state is a result of hypovolemia, early correction of the hypovolemia can help effect a very good prognosis. Successful reperfusion through the infarct-related artery by primary angioplasty may improve in-hospital survival from cardiogenic shock to as high as 60 to 100%, compared with a 0 to 33% survival if the artery cannot be recanalized. Early reperfusion within 24 hours appears to be associated with a higher in-hospital survival from cardiogenic shock, on the order of 77%, compared to a delayed reperfusion, where survival falls to 10%. Therefore, when cardiogenic shock is a result of acute myocardial infarction, there is the possibility that application of the principle that earlier reperfusion results in greater salvage of myocardium may have a beneficial effect on patient survival (see treatment of acute myocardial infarction in Chapter 15–47).

Prevention

Prevention of the underlying cardiac disorder is the best means of prevention of cardiogenic shock. Recognition and prompt correction of severe valvular or coronary disease before it progresses to this state are, therefore, imperative. Similarly, efforts to prevent progression of mild or moderate disease may be effective in preventing cardiogenic shock.

Cost Containment

Prompt and effective management of acute heart failure or of severe cardiac disease before shock develops is the most cost-effective measure. Once cardiogenic shock develops, treatment is usually very expensive and invariably is associated with high morbidity and mortality.

REFERENCES

Chatterjee K. Complications of acute myocardial infarction. Curr Probl Cardiol 1993;Jan.: 16.

Ferguson DW, Abboud FM. The recognition and management of shock. In: Hurst JW, ed. The heart. 7th ed. New York, McGraw-Hill, 1990:442.

Gunnar RM, Loeb HS, Rahimtoola SH. Shock in myocardial infarction. New York. Grune and Stratton, 1974.

Lee L, Erbel R, Brown TM. Multicenter Registry of Angioplasty Therapy for Cardiogenic Shock: Initial and long-term survival. J Am Coll Cardiol 1991;17:599.

Moosvi AR, Khaja F, Villanueva L, et al. Early revascularization improves survival in cardiogenic shock complicating acute myocardial infarction. J Am Coll Cardiol 1992;19:907.

Shawl FA, Domanski MJ, Hernandez TJ, Punja S. Emergency percutaneous cardiopulmonary bypass support in cardiogenic shock from acute myocardial infarction. Am J Cardiol 1989;64:967.

CHAPTER 15–8

Sinus Bradycardia

Toshio Akiyama, M.D.

DEFINITION

Sinus bradycardia in the adult is defined as the heart rhythm that arises from the sinoatrial node (sinus node) and that is slower than 60 beats per minute. On the electrocardiogram, the PP interval is longer than 1.0 second, the P wave is normal in morphology, and the P wave is usually followed by a QRS complex. Sinus bradycardia is frequently accompanied by sinus arrhythmia, in which the longest and shortest PP intervals differ by 0.12 second or more.

ETIOLOGY

Enhanced vagal tone and, less importantly, depressed sympathetic tone underlie sinus bradycardia. It may be classified into three forms: physiologic, pharmacologic, and pathologic. Physiologic sinus bradycardia occurs in healthy adults, well-trained athletes (especially endurance athletes), and those engaged in strenuous labor. Sinus bradycardia becomes less frequent with advancing age. Physiologic sinus bradycardia also occurs during sleep and with various vagal maneuvers, the Valsalva maneuver, and carotid sinus massage. Pharmacologic sinus bradycardia occurs commonly in patients treated with beta blockers, calcium channel blockers, d,l-sotalol, and amiodarone. It is important to note that digitalis at therapeutic levels may slow the sinus rate by only 5 to 10 beats per minute but is unlikely to cause severe sinus bradycardia. Pathologic sinus bradycardia occurs under the following conditions: vomiting, elevated intracranial pressure, cervical and mediastinal tumors, cervical cord compression, obstructive jaundice, convalescence from febrile illness, sick sinus syndrome, hypothyroidism, and hypothermia. During the first few hours after acute inferior myocardial infarction, sinus bradycardia is a common finding.

CRITERIA FOR DIAGNOSIS

Suggestive

Sinus bradycardia should be suspected when a pulse rate remains below 60 bpm and fluctuates slightly from time to time, and three distinct positive waves are identified in the neck vein.

Definitive

A simple electrocardiographic recording is sufficient to establish the diagnosis of sinus bradycardia. It is diagnosed when the PP interval is greater than 1.0 second, the P wave is usually followed by a QRS complex, and the P-wave vector is normal and is directed inferiorly to the left and slightly posteriorly (the P wave is upright in I, II, III, aV_F, and aV_L and inverted in aV_R [Figure 15–8–1]). If sinus arrhythmia accompanies sinus bradycardia (sinus bradyarrhythmia), the longest and shortest PP intervals differ by 0.12 second or longer.

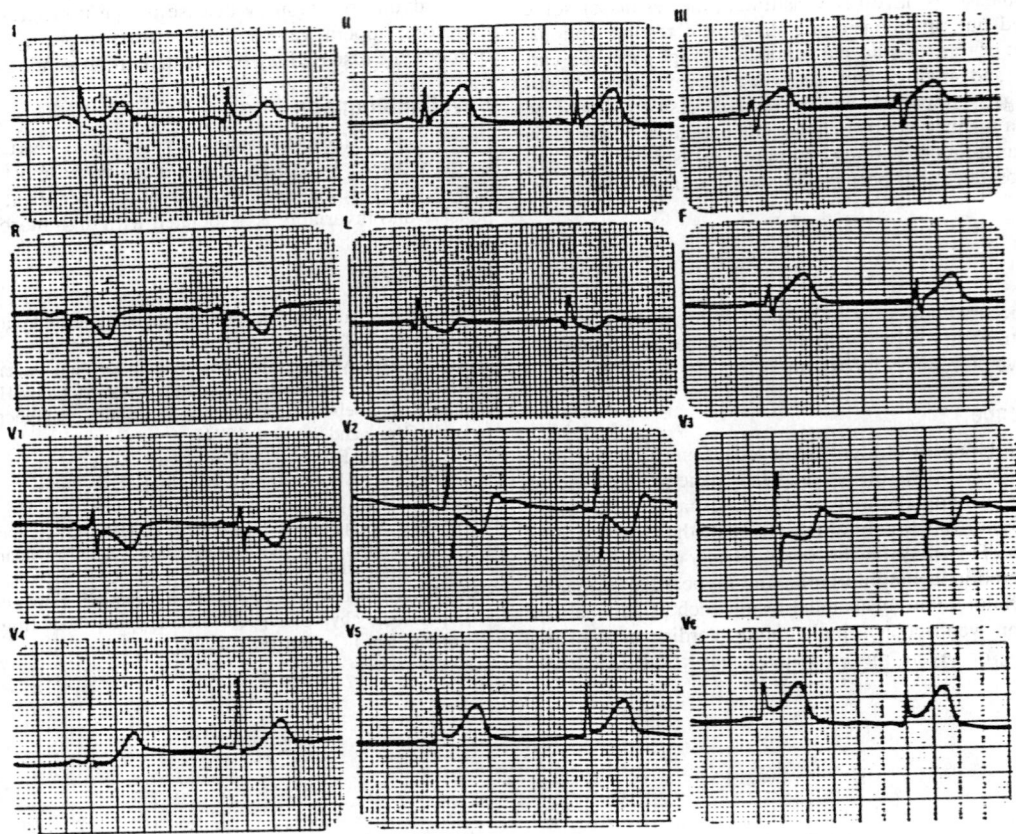

Figure 15–8–1. Sinus bradycardia in a 55-year-old man with hyperacute inferoposterior myocardial infarction extending to the apex. The PP interval ranging between 1.2 and 1.1 seconds along with the normal P-wave vector (directed inferiorly and leftward) establishes the diagnosis of sinus bradycardia, a common finding during the acute phase of the inferior myocardial infarction.

CLINICAL MANIFESTATIONS
Subjective

Usually no symptoms accompany sinus bradycardia. When the rate becomes extremely slow (slower than 40 beats per minute during waking hours) or sinus bradycardia is complicated by cardiac pump failure, the patient may experience malaise, weakness, faintness, dyspnea, disorientation, chest discomfort, or palpitations.

Objective
Physical Examination

There are no abnormal physical findings from sinus bradycardia other than slow pulse and heart rate. In sinus bradycardia, a, c, and v waves and x and y troughs may be easily identified, and their presence along with a pulse rate slower than 60 beats per minute suggests sinus bradycardia.

Routine Laboratory Abnormalities

Normally, however, an electrocardiographic recording is necessary to establish the diagnosis of sinus bradycardia (see Plans, Diagnostic).

PLANS
Diagnostic
Differential Diagnosis

The differential diagnosis of sinus bradycardia includes the following: escape rhythms originating from the AV node, His bundle, or ventricle occurring in the presence of severe sinus bradycardia, or complete AV block; sinoatrial exit block (see Fig. 15–8–2); and hypersensitive carotid sinus syndrome. In the escape rhythms, a beat-to-beat fluctuation in the RR interval is either absent or negligible, which is different from sinus bradycardia, in which a significant beat-to-beat fluctuation exists (Figure 15–8–1). In sinoatrial exit block, while the sinus node beats regularly, there is intermittent failure of impulse conduction from sinus node to atrium. Therefore, in the electrocardiogram the PP interval abruptly lengthens to a multiple of the basic PP interval (Figure 15–8–2). In the hypersensitive carotid sinus syndrome, rather abrupt slowing or cessation of sinus beat occurs frequently in response to head turning or application of pressure to the neck.

Diagnostic Options and Recommended Approach

Only an electrocardiographic recording, either a monitor lead or twelve lead, is necessary to confirm the diagnosis of sinus bradycardia.

Therapeutic

Usually sinus bradycardia does not require therapy (see Table 15–16–2). In fact, its presence often implies good health or good prognosis. In patients with acute inferior myocardial infarction, sinus bradycardia does not have to be treated unless it is extremely slow (well below 50 beats per minute) or is accompanied by cardiac failure.

Pharmacologically induced sinus bradycardia, if it gives rise to a significant reduction in cardiac function, should be treated by discontinuing or reducing the dosage of the causative drug. If symptoms or signs of either reduced cardiac output or myocardial ischemia appear, atropine (0.5 mg) should be given intravenously as an initial dose and may be repeated in about 5 minutes. Side effects of disorientation and agitation are common after its repeated use in elderly patients or patients in cardiac failure. In the absence of myocardial ischemia or infarction, or ventricular arrhythmias, intravenous infusion of isoproterenol may be titrated to obtain its positive chronotropic effect (usually between 0.5 and 5 µg/min). These drugs should be cautiously administered with the patient's symptoms, cardiac rhythm, and blood pressure monitored closely. Sinus tachycardia and, less frequently, ventricular arrhythmia complicate the use of atropine and isoproterenol.

If severe sinus bradycardia resistant to pharmacologic therapy persists for a few hours or longer, temporary cardiac pacing (either transvenous or external) should be considered. If severe sinus bradycardia requiring therapy persists and does not appear to improve after a few days of therapy, implantation of a permanent pacemaker may become necessary. For a relatively young or physically active patient, use of a dual-chamber pacemaker instead of a demand ventricular pacemaker becomes necessary.

FOLLOW-UP

Only those patients with symptomatic sinus bradycardia necessitating a permanent pacemaker implantation need to be followed, usually once or twice a year. At follow-up, not only pacemaker function but also underlying cardiac rhythm should be evaluated.

DISCUSSION
Prevalence

About a quarter of the healthy adult male population exhibit sinus bradycardia (Hiss et al., 1960). Its prevalence decreases with advancing age. Sinus bradycardia along with first-degree atrioventricular block is commonly encountered in endurance athletes (long-distance runners, swimmers, skiers, and basketball players) (Northcote et al., 1989). During sleep, their sinus rate frequently drops below 40 beats per minutes. Sinus bradycardia is also common during the first few hours of myocardial infarction, 30 to 60% in inferior myocardial infarction, resulting from the Bezold–Jarisch reflex (Adgey et al., 1968; Mark, 1993). Hospital mortality of patients with sinus bradycardia is significantly lower (6%) than those without it (15%) (Norris et al., 1972).

Related Basic Science
Histology

The number of nodal cells in the sinoatrial node responsible for rhythmic discharge of an electrical impulse decreases with advancing age (Thery et al., 1977). In the sinoatrial node of patients with abnormal sinus nodal function the following pathologic changes commonly take place: destruction of the node itself with fibrosis, disruption of sinoatrial continuity, inflammatory or degenerative changes in the nerves and ganglia surrounding the node, and fibrotic changes in the atrial wall.

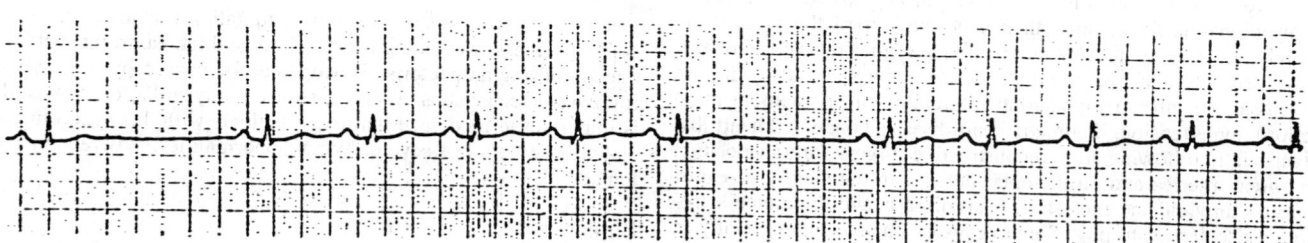

Figure 15–8–2. Intermittent sinoatrial exit block in a 60-year-old man without cardiac symptoms. Except for the two pauses, the PP interval fluctuates only slightly, ranging between 0.76 and 0.73 second. In the beginning and middle of the tracing, the PP interval abruptly lengthens to 1.55 seconds, which is about twice the basic PP interval. It is therefore reasonable to assume that the sinus node beats regularly throughout and that impulse conduction from the sinus node to the atrium fails intermittently.

Electrophysiology

Recent clinical studies on beat-to-beat heart rate variability suggest that reduced heart rate variability, resulting from reduced vagal tone and elevated sympathetic tone, predicts risk for subsequent mortality in patients after myocardial infarction or in a community of elderly patients (Tsuji et al., 1994).

Natural History and Its Modification with Treatment

Reduced cardiac output from sinus bradycardia that requires therapy is uncommon. The availability of drugs and cardiac pacemakers makes it rather unlikely for sinus bradycardia to become a direct cause of permanent morbidity or mortality.

Prevention

Pharmacologic sinus bradycardia can be prevented. For physiologic sinus bradycardia, however, prevention is usually unnecessary. For pathologic sinus bradycardia, prevention of the underlying conditions naturally leads to prevention of the bradycardia.

Cost Containment

The mere presence of moderately severe sinus bradycardia, if asymptomatic, should not constitute a basis for therapy, and unnecessary therapy should be avoided.

REFERENCES

Adgey AAJ, Geodes JS, Mul Holland HC, et al. Incidence, significance and management of early bradyarrhythmia complicating acute myocardial infarction. Lanacort 1968;2:1097.

Hiss RH, Lamb LE, Allen MF. Electrocardiographic findings in 67,375 asymptomatic patients. X, normal values. Am J Cardiol 1960;6:200.

Jordan JL, Karaguezian HS, Gang ES, et al. Normal and abnormal sinus node function. In: El-Sherif N, Samet P, eds. Cardiac pacing and electrophysiology. Philadelphia: Saunders, 1991:114.

Mark AL. The Bezold–Jarisch reflex revisited: Clinical implications of inhibitory reflexes originating in the heart. J Am Coll Cardiol 1993;1:90.

Norris RM, Mercer CJ, Yeates SE. Sinus rate in acute myocardial infarction. Br Heart J 1972;34:901.

Northcote RJ, Canning GP, Ballantyne D. Electrocardiographic findings in male veteran endurance athletes. Br Heart J 1989;6:155.

Thery C, Gosselin B, Lekieffre J, Warembourg H. Pathology of sinoatrial node: Correlation with electrocardiographic findings. Am Heart J 1977;93:735.

Tsuji H, Venditti FJ, Jr, Mandero ES, et al. Reduced heart rate variability and mortality risk in an elderly cohort: The Framingham Heart Study. Circulation 1994;90:878.

Wess SW, Adgey AAJ, Pantridge JF. Autonomic disturbance at onset of acute myocardial infarction. Br Med J 1972;3:89.

CHAPTER 15–9

Sick Sinus Syndrome

Toshio Akiyama, M.D.

DEFINITION

Sick sinus syndrome consists of a variety of sinus nodal dysfunctions and supraventricular tachyarrhythmias. The spectrum of rhythm disturbances includes persistent spontaneous sinus bradycardia, sinus standstill (arrest) and sinoatrial exit block, alternating sinus bradycardia and supraventricular tachyarrhythmias, and frequently atrial fibrillation or flutter (bradytachy syndrome). A significant fraction of patients with this syndrome develop atrioventricular (AV) blocks during the course of the disease, signifying an extensive involvement beyond the sinus node. There is no consensus as to how many of the preceding abnormalities must be present before the terminology of sick sinus syndrome can be applied; however, abnormal sinus nodal function of at least one variety must be present before this syndrome is diagnosed.

ETIOLOGY

This syndrome often occurs in the absence of any structural heart disease (an idiopathic form) other than abnormalities of the sinus node, atria, and, occasionally, the AV conduction system. The syndrome may be associated with many pathologic conditions: coronary artery disease (especially acute inferior myocardial infarction with or without atrial infarction), hypertension, rheumatic heart disease, congenital heart disease (especially following atrial reconstructive surgery for transposition for the great arteries and atrial septal defect), inflammatory diseases, pericarditis, amyloidosis, metastatic heart disease, and Friedreich's progressive muscular dystrophy. Some drugs or chemicals, especially in those with toxic plasma levels, can enhance or produce the electrophysiologic abnormalities of this syndrome; these include beta blockers, digitalis, calcium channel blockers, and amiodarone. Such factors should be removed before diagnosing the idiopathic form of this syndrome.

CRITERIA FOR DIAGNOSIS

Suggestive

Sick sinus syndrome should be suspected when periods of bradycardia or asystole sometimes accompanied by syncope/semisyncope alternate with periods of palpitation of abrupt onset and termination.

Definitive

Sick sinus syndrome is diagnosed when a variety of sinus nodal dysfunctions and supraventricular tachyarrhythmias as described under Definition and Clinical Manifestations, Objective, are demonstrated in such electrocardiographic recordings as ambulatory electrocardiograms and telemetry monitor.

CLINICAL MANIFESTATIONS

Subjective

Common presenting symptoms are palpitations, syncope or near syncope, dizziness, worsening heart failure, and increased intensity or frequency of angina pectoris. Syncope can be caused by any one of the following mechanisms: asystole, severe bradycardia, or tachycardia. It is important to recognize that many patients with this syndrome, especially those with less severe rhythm abnormalities, may remain asymptomatic.

Objective

Physical Examination

The patient with this syndrome may have one or many of the physical abnormalities of various bradycardias and tachyarrhythmias including bradycardia/asystole, regular tachycardia, and irregularly irregular rhythm. Occurrence of these bradycardias and tachyarrhythmias is rather unpredictable, however, and frequently physical examination in these patients may be normal.

Routine Laboratory Abnormalities

Although this syndrome can be suspected from the history and by careful monitoring of the pulse, its definitive diagnosis is usually made from the electrocardiogram, including rhythm strips and ambulatory electrocardiogram recordings. Electrocardiographic abnormalities include the following: sustained severe sinus bradycardia, sinoatrial exit block (intermittent abrupt lengthening of the PP interval to a multiple of the basic PP interval [see Figure 15–8–2]) or sinus standstill (a prolonged period of absent P waves), and any of the supraventricular tachycardias, most commonly atrial fibrillation (Figure 15–9–1) and flutter. Bradycardic periods frequently follow the tachycardic spells.

PLANS
Diagnostic
Differential Diagnosis

Differential diagnosis of sick sinus syndrome includes various supraventricular tachyarrhythmias without sinus node dysfunction, physiologic sinus bradycardia, second- or third-degree AV blocks, frequent ventricular premature complexes, and ventricular tachycardia or fibrillation.

Diagnostic Options and Recommended Approach

A routine 12-lead electrocardiogram (ECG) recording is usually not sufficient to diagnose this syndrome. Either a 24-hour ambulatory ECG recording, a telemetry monitor, or a loop ECG rhythm monitor is recommended.

Therapeutic Options and Recommended Approach

Medical therapy of symptomatic patients with sick sinus syndrome was almost uniformly unsatisfactory prior to the introduction of permanent pacemakers, mainly because oral drugs used for bradycardia were usually ineffective and also because the drugs used to treat supraventricular tachyarrhythmias often made the bradycardia worse. In contrast, since the introduction of dependable permanent pacemakers in the 1960s, symptomatic relief has been realized in many of the symptomatic patients by a combined therapy of permanent pacemaker and antiarrhythmic agents. If cigarettes, alcohol, caffeine, or chocolate appears to be playing a role in precipitating supraventricular tachyarrhythmias, their use should be reduced or discontinued.

No specific therapy other than reassurance is required for asymptomatic patients in whom some of the manifestations of this syndrome are detected by the electrocardiogram. Reassurance and sometimes use of a mild sedative (but usually no specific therapy for the rhythm problem) are required for patients with palpitations; however, patients who have symptoms consistent with cerebral ischemia (syncope, near syncope, lightheadedness), myocardial ischemia (angina), or reduced cardiac output (dyspnea, fatigue, weakness) almost always require specific therapy for their rhythm problems. As bradycardia is usually a part of

the rhythm problems of these patients, and because drugs used for their supraventricular tachycardia frequently make their bradycardia worse, a permanent pacemaker is often required. Therapy with a permanent pacemaker frequently combined with drugs for control of supraventricular tachyarrhythmias has led to symptomatic relief in a great majority of the patients with this syndrome. Although intravenous atropine or isoproterenol (Isuprel) may be used temporarily until permanent pacemaker therapy becomes available, their prolonged use should be avoided (see Chapter 15–8). A dual-chamber pacemaker (DDD pacemaker) is preferred in relatively young patients, physically active patients, or those with significant structural heart diseases unless atrial fibrillation, atrial flutter, or frequent bouts of supraventricular tachycardia are present. For those with persistent or frequent supraventricular tachyarrhythmias, a ventricular demand pacemaker (VVI pacemaker) or its rate-responsive version (rate response VVI pacemaker) is recommended. For those patients in whom AV block is not present and who do not develop AV block with atrial tachy-pacing at a rate faster than their predicted maximal heart rate, use of a simple atrial demand pacemaker (AAI pacemaker) might be considered. As previously noted, however, about one quarter of the patients with this syndrome eventually develop AV blocks of variable severity. When AV blocks beyond the first degree develop in a patient with an atrial demand pacemaker, the pacemaker may have to be modified to a dual-chamber or ventricular demand type. Drug therapy for tachycardia is required for those patients who develop either atrial fibrillation, atrial flutter, or regular supraventricular tachycardia (for such drug therapy, please refer to the appropriate chapters). For those patients with recurrent or persistent atrial fibrillation, anticoagulant therapy with aspirin or warfarin sodium (Coumadin) should be instituted for prevention of stroke unless anticoagulant therapy is contraindicated (see Chapter 15–14).

For patients with drug-resistant atrial flutter or atrial tachycardia, radiofrequency ablation of a reentrant circuit or ectopic focus should be considered. This therapy proves to be effective also for patients with uncontrollably fast ventricular rates in the presence of atrial fibrillation or flutter. Here, complete AV block is produced by radiofrequency ablation of AV node or bundle of His, and the ventricular rate is controlled by an implanted rate-responsive ventricular pacemaker.

FOLLOW-UP

A physician should take time in reassuring the patient with sick sinus syndrome that the problems either do not require therapy, or, if therapy is required, the problems are solved in almost all patients by using a pacemaker occasionally combined with drug(s). It also should be emphasized that patients with the most serious symptom of this syndrome, syncope, do extremely well with pacemaker therapy, and that death as a direct result of this syndrome should not occur in the era of modern pacemakers.

Once appropriate therapy is established, patients require infrequent follow-up, perhaps twice a year. In the follow-up visit, the following areas need to be explored: frequency of the symptoms, side effects of the drugs chosen, and noninvasive assessment of the pacemaker, if implanted. Follow-up of the pacemaker can and should be performed via a telephone monitoring system. Frequency of reimbursable telephone

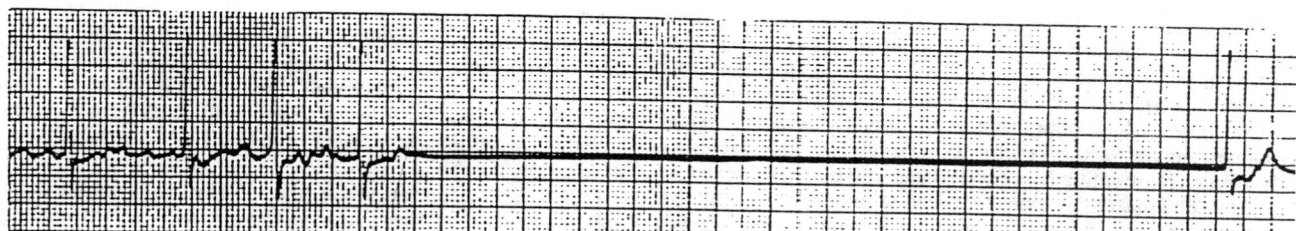

Figure 15–9–1. Bradytachy syndrome. This lead II rhythm strip was recorded from a 66-year-old man with recurrent syncope and palpitation. Following abrupt cessation of atrial flutter with variable atrioventricular block, a prolonged cardiac standstill continued for 6.3 seconds. The sinus node failed to discharge, and finally the atrioventricular junction escaped (the last beat). Other times the patient frequently developed atrial flutter with a 2:1 atrioventricular block (ventricular rate, 145 beats per minute). Syncope has not recurred since implantation of a permanent ventricular demand pacemaker.

monitoring may be variable according to the source of third-party payment; but nevertheless, it should be done normally up to six times a year. Recurrence of any of the major symptoms present prior to initiation of therapy usually necessitates a prompt reevaluation.

DISCUSSION

Prevalence and Incidence

The precise prevalence and incidence of sick sinus syndrome are not known, but the syndrome is most frequently diagnosed between the ages of 50 and 80 (Moss and David, 1974; Benditt and Remole 1994). This syndrome is usually the most common indication for a permanent pacemaker and is a major clinical entity in an arrhythmia clinic.

Related Basic Science

Sick sinus syndrome encompasses abnormalities of the sinus node itself and frequently abnormalities of the atrial and AV conduction system as well. The abnormal function of the sinoatrial node is an essential component of sick sinus syndrome. Abnormalities of the sinus node include persistent spontaneous sinus bradycardia, sinus standstill (arrest), and sinoatrial exit block. These abnormalities can be caused by disease of the sinus node itself, imbalance between the parasympathetic and sympathetic systems, or a combination of these two factors.

Histology

Histologically, various pathologic processes (degenerative changes, fibrosis, and fatty infiltrations) invade the sinus node itself, sinoatrial junction, internodal pathways, and nerves and ganglia to the sinus or AV node (Thery et al., 1977).

Natural History and Its Modification with Treatment

Although syncope is the common symptom in patients with sick sinus syndrome, permanent disability or death in patient without other structural heart disease is rare. Embolic complications, myocardial ischemia

or infarction, and heart failure, however, may be precipitated in the presence of significant structural heart disease. The prognosis for survival with therapy is generally excellent in the absence of significant structural heart disease.

Prevention

Use of cigarettes, alcohol, caffeine, or chocolate should be discouraged if they appear either to exacerbate or to precipitate the patient's supraventricular tachyarrhythmias.

Cost Containment

For those patients who experience no symptoms or in whom palpitation is the lone manifestation, no specific therapy and no further diagnostic tests may be necessary and should be avoided. Reassurance becomes crucial for those patients with no symptoms at all or with the relatively minor symptoms of palpitations alone. Unless sufficient discussion and reassurance are given in a timely fashion, these patients with minimal or no symptoms may perceive themselves as cardiac invalids, as occasionally happens in patients with mitral valve prolapse.

REFERENCES

Benditt DG, Remole SC. Sick sinus syndrome. In: Kastor JA, ed. Arrhythmias. Philadelphia: Saunders, 1994:225.

Bharati S, Nordenberg A, Bauernfiend R, et al. The anatomic substrate for the sick sinus syndrome in adolescence. Am J Cardiol 1980;46:163.

Greenwood RD, Rosenthal A, Sloss LJ, et al: Sick sinus syndrome after surgery for congenital heart disease. Circulation 1975:52:208.

Moss AJ, David RJ. Brady-tachy syndrome. Prog Cardiovasc Dis 1974;16:439.

Tung RT, Shen WK, Hayes DL, et al. Long-term survival after permanent pacemaker implantation for sick sinus syndrome. Am J Cardiol 1994;74:1016.

Thery C, Gosselin B, Ledieffre J, Warembourg H. Pathology of sinoatrial node: Correlations with electrocardiographic findings in 111 patients. Am Heart J 1977;93:735.

CHAPTER 15–10

Sinus Tachycardia

Toshio Akiyama, M.D.

DEFINITION

Sinus tachycardia in the adult is defined as the heart rhythm that arises from the sinoatrial node and that is faster than 100 beats per minute. Its transition from and to normal sinus rhythm is gradual. On the electrocardiogram, the PP interval is shorter than 0.6 second and fluctuates from time to time. The P wave is usually followed by a QRS complex.

ETIOLOGY

Enhanced sympathetic tone and depressed vagal tone mediate sinus tachycardia. Sinus tachycardia may be classified into three forms: physiologic, pharmacologic, and pathologic. Physiologic sinus tachycardia results from exercise, excitement, anxiety, fear, and digestion. The maximal sinus rate achieved on exercise is normally between 150 and 190 beats per minute for the healthy young adult, and this decreases with advancing age, reaching between 120 and 150 beats per minute at the age of 60. Pharmacologic sinus tachycardia may develop with the use of epinephrine, isoproterenol, ephedrine, atropine, amyl nitrate, thyroid hormone, alcohol, caffeine, and nicotine. Pathologic sinus tachycardia may occur as a result of the following conditions: inappropriate sinus tachycardia, fever, deconditioning, hypotension, heart failure, shock, hypoxia, anemia, hyperthyroidism, pheochromocytoma, and myocarditis.

CRITERIA FOR DIAGNOSIS

Suggestive

Sinus tachycardia should be suspected when a patient complains of palpitations faster than 100 beats per minute and the pulse rate fluctuates gradually with time.

Definitive

Definitive diagnosis of sinus tachycardia is usually made from the electrocardiogram. Its onset and termination, if observed, are gradual and are different from those of other forms of tachycardia (many of which start and terminate abruptly). The PP interval fluctuates from time to time more in sinus tachycardia than in other forms of tachycardia. The PP interval is less than 0.6 second. The P wave is usually followed by a QRS complex, and the P-wave vector is directed leftward, inferiorly, and slightly posteriorly (upright in I, II, III, aV_f, and aV_L and downward in aV_R).

Practically, a heart rate greater than 150 beats per minute in the adult not associated with strenuous exercise probably represents a type of tachycardia other than sinus tachycardia. In the presence of sinus tachycardia faster than 150 beats per minute or so, however, the P wave tends to be "buried" in the T wave of the preceding beat, thereby making its identification difficult. Vagal maneuvers, carotid sinus stimulation, and the Valsalva maneuver may slow down sinus rate in sinus tachycardia; however, the sinus rate returns to its previous level over a few cardiac cycles on termination of the maneuver as long as the underlying cause has not been removed.

CLINICAL MANIFESTATIONS
Subjective

No symptoms other than palpitations accompany sinus tachycardia per se. Symptoms experienced are usually from its underlying or accompanying abnormality. In the presence of some forms of heart disease, such as mitral stenosis or ischemic heart disease, the development of sinus tachycardia can give rise to a variety of symptoms; the symptoms that emerge frequently aid in uncovering these heart diseases. In a patient with mitral stenosis, abbreviation of diastole more than systole with tachycardia hinders diastolic emptying of the left atrium. The rise in left atrial pressure may result in pulmonary congestion, thereby bringing about such symptoms as dyspnea and chest discomfort. In a patient with significant coronary atherosclerosis, the stenosed coronary arteries may not be able to meet the increased metabolic demand of myocardium imposed by sinus tachycardia. Consequently, these patients may develop angina pectoris, dyspnea, weakness, and fatigue.

Objective
Physical Examination

There are no abnormal physical findings for sinus tachycardia other than a rapid pulse or heart rate, that is, faster than 100 beats per minute. Abnormal physical findings, if any exist, are manifestations of underlying or accompanying abnormalities. Any form of tachycardia often makes an accurate assessment of jugular venous waveforms difficult. In patients with significant mitral stenosis or ischemic heart disease, pulmonary congestion and an elevation in jugular venous pressure may develop after a sustained period of sinus tachycardia.

Routine Laboratory Abnormalities

Please refer to Criteria for Diagnosis, Definitive.

PLANS
Diagnostic
Differential Diagnosis

Differential diagnosis of sinus tachycardia includes atrioventricular nodal reentrant tachycardia, atrioventricular reentrant tachycardia (of preexcitation syndromes), sinoatrial reentrant tachycardia, ectopic atrial tachycardia, atrial flutter, atrial fibrillation, and multifocal atrial tachycardia. Ventricular tachycardia and flutter need to be differentiated when a patient has a preexisting bundle branch block. Sinus tachycardia is differentiated from these various forms of tachycardia when the tachycardiac rate fluctuates with time and is accompanied by normal P-wave morphology.

Diagnostic Options and Recommended Approach

An electrocardiographic recording of 30 seconds or longer is the only diagnostic test necessary for establishing this diagnosis.

Therapeutic
Therapeutic Options and Recommended Approach

Treatment should be directed at the underlying cause of the sinus tachycardia. The elimination of alcohol, caffeine, and nicotine should be helpful for those patients in whom these pharmacologic agents are a major factor causing the sinus tachycardia. Transient slowing of sinus rate, if it becomes clinically necessary, may be achieved with propranolol or verapamil. When sinus tachycardia persists continually (as in inappropriate sinus tachycardia) for a prolonged period, its rate needs to be reduced to lessen the symptom of palpitation and also to prevent the development of cardiomyopathy. Long-acting beta blockers (metoprolol 25–100 mg by mouth once or twice daily or atenolol 25 mg by mouth once or twice daily) are recommended.

FOLLOW-UP

Only those patients who experience recurrence or persistence of their sinus tachycardia require follow-up. Frequency of follow-up is dictated by the underlying abnormality.

DISCUSSION
Prevalence

The prevalence of sinus tachycardia in the general population is not known. Sinus tachycardia was diagnosed on a resting electrocardiogram in about 3% of U.S. Air Force flying personnel (Hiss and Lamb, 1960, 1962).

Related Basic Science

The sinus node is the predominant pacemaker for the human heart, and at rest it normally discharges an electrical impulse at a frequency of 50 to 90 times per minute. The rate of sinus nodal discharge is under the influence of the autonomic nervous system, circulating humoral factors, and local metabolic factors. The heart is heavily innervated by the parasympathetic and sympathetic nervous systems. The sinus node, along with the atrioventricular node, is much more densely innervated by the parasympathetic system than the atrial or ventricular muscles. The atrial myocardium is richly innervated by both divisions of the autonomic system. The ventricle also receives a rich supply of sympathetic nerves, but it receives much fewer parasympathetic nerves than the atrial myocardium.

Normally, the sinus rate is closely modified by a balance between sympathetic and parasympathetic tones (Levy et al., 1979). Variations in sinus rate tend to occur less often in patients with heart failure than in the normal or well-compensated cardiac patient. Recently, an uncommon atrial tachycardia with inappropriate tachycardia, exaggerated acceleration of heart rate, and normal P wave has been recognized, and is termed inappropriate sinus tachycardia, nonparoxysmal sinus tachycardia, or permanent sinus tachycardia. Possible mechanisms leading to inappropriate sinus tachycardia include a high intrinsic sinus nodal rate, depressed efferent cardiovagal reflex, and beta-adrenergic hypersensitivity. Inappropriate sinus tachycardia in these patients is usually controlled by beta blockers (Morillo et al., 1994).

The sinoatrial nodal cells possess a phase 4 or diastolic depolarization, different from the nonpacemaker cells of ventricular or atrial fibers, which have a stationary flat diastolic potential. The diastolic potential of the sinoatrial nodal cells is around -60 mV during the early phase of diastole. When the diastolic potential climbs to a threshold potential (around -40 to -50 mV), inward channels responsible for depolarization are activated and phase 0 potential ensues (Iriswawa and Giles, 1990). When enough sinoatrial nodal cells depolarize, the depolarization wave is conducted to the surrounding atrial muscle. The steepness of the diastolic depolarization (phase 4) and the level of the threshold potential can be modified by multiple factors, resulting in a varying discharge rate of the electrical impulse from the sinoatrial node. The factors that can influence the sinoatrial nodal discharge rate are listed under Criteria for Diagnosis.

Natural History and Its Modification with Treatment

Mortality does not result from sinus tachycardia alone. Mortality, if it occurs, is usually caused by an underlying serious illness such as shock, heart failure, hypotension, hypoxia, pheochromocytoma, or the development of cardiomyopathy due to persistent tachycardia. When sinus tachycardia complicates an acute myocardial infarction, hospital mortality for these patients is significantly higher (26%) than for those whose heart rate is normal (15%) (Norris et al., 1972). Persistent sinus tachycardia usually responds to medical therapy with beta blockers.

Prevention

Prevention of sinus tachycardia is that of its underlying abnormalities.

Cost Containment

The misdiagnosis of sinus tachycardia, although not common, can lead to unnecessary procedures and therapies. It can be avoided by accurately recognizing the clinical condition surrounding the tachycardia by studying patient response to vagal maneuvers and by carefully analyzing the electrocardiogram.

REFERENCES

Harvey WP, Ronan JA. Bedside diagnosis of arrhythmias. Prog Cardiovasc Dis 1966;8:419.

Hiss RG, Lamb LE. Electrocardiographic findings in 67,375 asymptomatic subjects. Am J Cardiol 1960;6:200.

Hiss RG, Lamb LE. Electrocardiographic findings in 122,043 individuals. Circulation 1962;25:947.

Irisawa H, Giles WR. Sinus and atrioventricular node cells: Cell electrophysiology. In: Zipes DP, Jalife J, eds. Cardiac electrophysiology. Philadelphia: Saunders, 1990:95.

Levy MN, Martin PF. Neural control of the heart. In: Berne RM, Sperelakis N, Geiger SR, eds. Handbook of physiology. Section 2: The cardiovascular system. vol. 1: The heart. Bethesda: American Physiological Society, 1979:581.

Morillo CA, Klein GJ, Thakur RK, et al. Mechanism of inappropriate sinus tachycardia. Circulation 1994;90:873.

Norris RM, Mercer CJ, Yeates SE. Sinus rate in acute myocardial infarction. Br Heart J 1972;34:901.

CHAPTER 15–11

Atrial Premature Complexes

Toshio Akiyama, M.D.

DEFINITION

An *atrial premature complex* (APC), also called an atrial premature beat (APB) or atrial premature depolarization (APD), is defined as a premature beat originating from an ectopic site within the atria. Electrocardiographically, the P wave is premature, the PR interval is usually longer than 0.12 second (or sinus-induced PR interval), and its morphology generally differs from that of the sinus-initiated P wave. The atrial premature complex may be conducted with a normal PR interval or a prolonged PR interval, or it may not be conducted to the ventricles (a blocked atrial premature complex). Generally, atrial premature complexes per se carry a benign prognosis.

ETIOLOGY

Atrial premature complexes are found at all ages and often in the absence of structural heart disease. Some of the structural heart diseases associated with atrial premature complexes are elevated intraatrial pressure or atrial enlargement due to mitral stenosis or heart failure, atrial ischemia or infarction, and cardiac inflammation (including pericarditis). Alcohol, emotion, caffeine, smoking, enhanced sympathetic tone, digitalis toxicity, and toxicity from antiarrhythmic drugs also may trigger atrial premature complexes.

CRITERIA FOR DIAGNOSIS
Suggestive

Atrial and ventricular premature complexes are very common arrhythmias. When intermittent pauses follow regular arterial pulses, either atrial or ventricular complexes should be suspected first. Premature palpable arterial pulse, although weak, and audible first and second heart sounds favor atrial premature complexes over ventricular premature complexes. On the other hand, cannon *a* waves in the neck occurring in the beginning or middle of pauses favor ventricular premature complexes over atrial premature complexes.

Definitive

Atrial premature complexes are usually diagnosed easily by the electrocardiogram (Figure 15–11–1). If the atrial premature complexes are not detected by a routine 12-lead electrocardiogram or a rhythm strip, an ambulatory electrocardiogram tape recording may be necessary. The P wave is premature, the PR interval is the same as or longer than that of the sinus-initiated beat (thus, the PR interval is longer than 0.12 second), and the P-wave morphology usually differs from that of the sinus P wave. The P-wave morphology of the atrial premature complex, however, may be identical to that of the sinus P wave if the atrial premature complex originates from the vicinity of the sinus node or from the sinus node itself. The latter is called sinus premature beat.

CLINICAL MANIFESTATIONS
Subjective

Patients are generally unaware of the presence of atrial premature complexes. If patients are aware of them, this usually happens in a quiet environment at rest or when they retire for the night. Perception of the atrial premature complexes tends to go away with exercise. Symptoms perceived by patients are fluttering, feeling skipped beats, chest discomfort, strong thump in the chest, choking sensation and fullness in the neck.

Objective
Physical Examination

Atrial premature complexes give rise to premature heart sounds of either one or two components: The first heart sound may be snapping; and this is followed by a quiet pause, usually slightly longer than the regular interval. The pause is characteristically not fully compensatory in contrast to ventricular premature complexes (see below). The associated arterial pulse may be slightly weak or may not be palpable, its pulse amplitude being influenced by the degree of ventricular filling, which is in turn determined by the prematurity of the atrial premature complex.

Routine Laboratory Abnormalities

The electrocardiogram is essential for establishing the diagnosis (please refer to Criteria for Diagnosis, Definitive).

When the atrial premature complex is superimposed on the T wave of a preceding beat, its detection might be difficult, requiring a careful search for "deformation" of the T wave in each of the 12-lead electrocardiogram recordings (see Figure 15–11–1, bottom tracing). Occasionally an esophageal electrocardiogram is necessary to aid in identification of P waves. It should be pointed out that an abrupt slowing in the sinus rate (abrupt increase in the PP interval), thus apparent "sinus arrhythmia," sometimes turns out to be the result of a blocked atrial premature complex hidden within the T wave.

Whether the atrial premature complexes are conducted to the ventricles depends on their prematurity relative to the refractory period and conduction velocity of the atrioventricular (AV) conduction system. Thus, a relatively late atrial premature complex and normal AV conduction system result in a normal PR interval (less than 0.20 second), whereas a very early atrial premature complex and an abnormal AV conduction system (prolonged refractory period and/or depressed conduction) lead to a PR interval lengthened beyond that of the sinus beat or to nonconduction of the atrial premature complex (a blocked atrial premature complex; see Figure 15–11–1, bottom tracing). If the atrial premature complex is delayed or blocked, this usually happens at the AV junction (AV node and His bundle); however, this can also happen below the AV junction. At a normal heart rate, the right bundle fibers

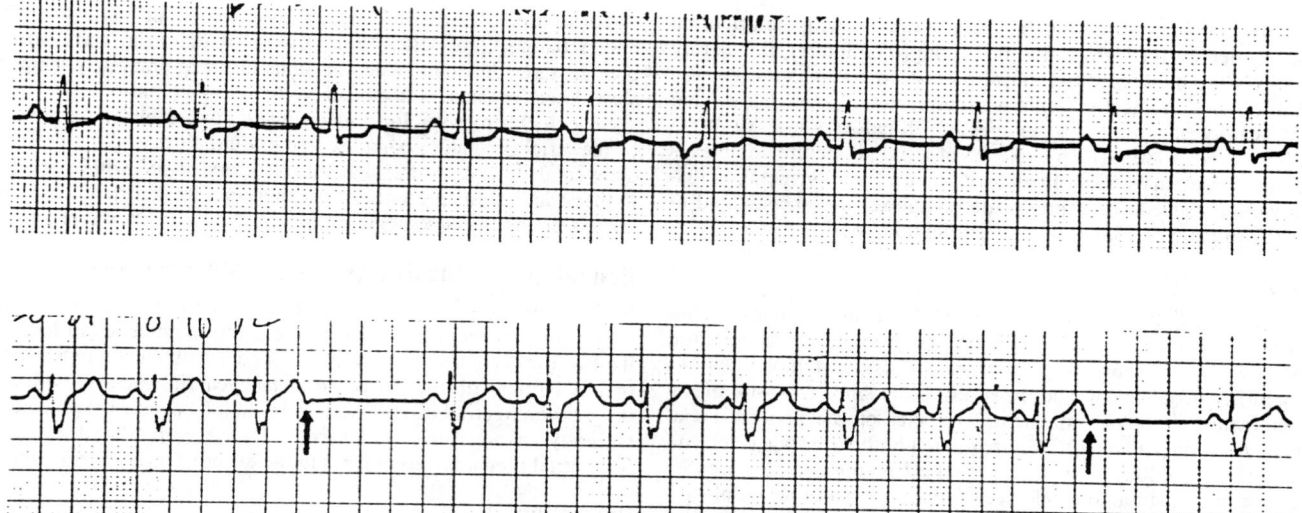

Figure 15–11–1. Atrial premature complexes, recorded in lead II, with sinus node reset (top) and a full compensatory pause (bottom). Top: The P waves are upright except for the inverted P in the middle. The sinus rate fluctuates ony slightly, with the PP interval around 0.88 second and the PR interval 0.18 second. The inverted P wave (the sixth P from the left) is slightly premature, occurring about 0.78 second after the preceding P wave, and the PR wave, and the PR interval is 0.17 second, close to the PR of the sinus beat. The pause following the premature beat is 0.9 second and is very close to the basic sinus cycle length, thereby consistent with resetting of the sinus node by an atrial premature complex. Bottom: except for two occasions, the sinus cycle length remains around 0.65 second. There are two abrupt pauses that last for 1.26 second—about twice the basic sinus cycle length—suggesting sinoatrial exit block; however, closer analysis of the tracing reveals that the terminal portion of the T wave occurring in the beginning of the pause is deformed by a mostly inverted waveform (arrows). This is a case of a blocked atrial premature complex having a full compensatory pause (please refer to the text for further details of a blocked atrial premature complex and full compensatory pause).

take longer to recover their excitability than the left bundle fibers (i.e., the right bundle refractory period lasts longer than the left bundle refractory period). Consequently, a very early atrial premature complex successfully penetrating through the AV junction may be blocked in the right bundle (an aberrantly conducted atrial premature complex).

The pause following the atrial premature complex is under the influence of several factors. The pause may be very short and the atrial premature complex may be sandwiched between two consecutive sinus P waves (interpolated atrial premature complex). The pause may equal the sinus cycle length (see Figure 15–11–1, top tracing). In this instance, the interval between two successive sinus P waves containing the atrial premature complex is less than twice the sinus cycle length, and the pause is called noncompensatory. The pause may be slightly longer, but the interval between the two consecutive sinus P waves may be still shorter than twice the sinus cycle length (noncompensatory). Finally, the pause may be further lengthened so that the interval between the two consecutive sinus P waves may be twice the sinus cycle length. The pause then is called fully compensatory.

PLANS
Diagnostic
Differential Diagnosis

Differential diagnosis of atrial premature complexes include sinus arrhythmia, atrial fibrillation, multifocal atrial tachycardia, atrioventricular nodal premature beats, ventricular premature complexes, and second-degree AV blocks. An electrocardiographic recording is necessary to diagnose atrial premature complexes.

Diagnostic Options and Recommended Approach

A simple electrocardiographic recording, either a 12-lead tracing or a rhythm strip, is necessary to establish the diagnosis.

Therapeutic

Patients with atrial premature complexes usually do not require therapy (see Table 15–16–2). In patients with symptomatic atrial premature complexes or when the complexes are known to precipitate supraventricular tachyarrhythmias (atrial tachycardia, atrial fibrillation or flutter, sinoatrial

reentry tachycardia, AV nodal reentry tachycardia, or AV reentrant tachycardia), therapy to suppress the atrial premature complexes becomes necessary. First, underlying factors including cardiac diseases, emotional stress, caffeine, alcohol, smoking, heightened sympathetic tone, and digitalis toxicity, if present, should be treated or removed. If the symptomatic atrial premature complexes still persist, pharmacologic therapy is indicated. For the symptomatic atrial premature complexes not precipitating supraventricular tachyarrhythmias, a long acting beta blocker should be used as the first-line drug. If a beta blocker alone is not effective, addition of diltiazem or verapamil should be tried. For atrial premature complexes precipitating supraventricular tachyarrhythmias, in addition to the above drugs, the following drugs may be used: quinidine sulfate or gluconate, procainamide, and disopyramide. Use of the latter three drugs should be guided by the electrocardiographic monitoring so as to avoid their proarrhythmic side effects. Please refer to Table 15–16–2 for a listing of these drugs and their usage.

FOLLOW-UP

The majority of patients with atrial premature complexes do not require follow-up. The physician should stress and reassure the patient that atrial premature complexes usually carry a benign prognosis and thus do not require therapy or follow-up. In rare patients with atrial premature complexes requiring drug therapy, however, the physician should take time to point out each of the potentially serious side effects of the drugs prescribed, the appearance of which may necessitate discontinuation of the drugs. In patients requiring drug therapy, follow-up once or twice a year should be adequate once the atrial premature complexes are suppressed or become asymptomatic. Assessment of the patient's symptoms and a 12-lead electrocardiographic recording with a rhythm strip are necessary at each visit. The physician should be contacted if the patient experiences symptoms suggestive of recurring atrial premature complexes or arrhythmias.

DISCUSSION
Prevalence

Atrial premature complexes were recorded rarely in routine 12-lead electrocardiographic recordings from the U.S. Air Force flying personnel (4.3 per 1000) (Hiss and Lamb, 1962); however, with the use of an expanded window for arrhythmia monitoring (continuous ambulatory electrocardiographic recording), atrial premature complexes were detected in 56% of medical students without apparent heart disease and 13% of healthy boys between the ages of 10 and 13 (Brodsky et al., 1977; Scott et al, 1980). The prevalence of atrial premature complexes undoubtedly rises in various illnesses with atrial involvement, as discussed earlier. Indeed, atrial premature complexes are encountered in about 50% of patients with acute myocardial infarction.

Related Basic Science

The pause immediately following the atrial premature complex is controlled by the interactions of several factors: prematurity of the atrial premature complex, refractory period of the tissues (sinoatrial [SA] node, peri-SA nodal fibers, and the atria), basic sinus rate, site of the atrial premature complex, conduction velocity of the peri-SA nodal fibers and the atria, and overdrive suppression of the SA node (Pick and Langendorf, 1979). Responses to the atrial premature complex are discussed briefly in relation to the degree of prematurity of the complex.

First, if the atrial premature complex occurs very early and encounters refractoriness of the peri-SA nodal fibers or of the SA node, the complex fails to discharge (or reset) the SA node. Then the next sinus impulse is discharged, undisturbed by the atrial premature complex. This sinus impulse may or may not be able to activate the atria. In the latter case, a subsequent sinus impulse usually captures the atria, generating a normal sinus P wave. Then the interval between the two sinus-initiated P waves containing the atrial premature complex is twice the sinus cycle length, and the pause is said to be fully compensatory. The former case, where the sinus impulse immediately after the atrial premature complex captures the atria producing a normal P wave, is called an interpolation of the atrial premature complex.

Second, if the atrial premature complex occurs slightly later than in the first instance above, it is likely to be conducted to the SA node across the peri-SA nodal fibers and to reset the SA node (see Figure 15–11–1, top tracing). In this instance, the pause after the atrial premature complex becomes slightly longer than the sinus cycle length owing to a delayed conduction of the atrial premature complex across the peri-SA nodal fibers. Then the interval between the two consecutive sinus P waves embracing the atrial premature complex is slightly shorter than twice the sinus cycle length, and the pause is called noncompensatory.

Third, if the atrial premature complex takes place late and only slightly before the next sinus discharge, the sinus impulse collides with the atrial premature complex and vanishes within the peri-SA nodal fibers. Needless to say, the depolarization front of the atrial premature complex advancing away from the sinus node activates the atria, generating a slightly premature P wave. In this case, with the subsequent sinus impulse generating a regular sinus P wave, a full compensatory pause exists (i.e., the interval between the two consecutive sinus P waves equals twice the sinus cycle length; see Figure 15–11–1, bottom tracing).

These timings may be distorted by concomitant sinus arrhythmias and/or baroreceptor reflex. Furthermore, if the atrial premature complex captures the sinus node, the sinus discharge rate may temporarily slow down for the next few beats (overdrive suppression).

Several electrophysiologic mechanisms are postulated for the genesis of the atrial premature complex: reentry circuit due to the presence of slow conduction and/or prolonged refractory period within or adjacent to the atria, ectopic presence of pacemaker cells, transient afterdepolarization (in digitalis toxicity), and temporal dispersion of repolarization.

Natural History and Its Modification with Treatment

In the course of heart diseases affecting atrial muscle there is a tendency for the frequency of atrial premature complexes to increase as the P wave becomes abnormally widened, accompanied by short bursts of atrial flutter/fibrillation or atrial tachycardia. Finally, with further progression of atrial disease, atrial fibrillation becomes established. It is currently unknown whether pharmacologic therapy retards progression from atrial premature complexes to the eventual atrial fibrillation.

Prevention

The underlying factors should be treated or removed.

Cost Containment

Physicians should accept that a majority of patients with atrial premature complexes do not need to be treated with drugs and that indications for therapy as suggested in this chapter need to be satisfied before therapy is initiated. Frequently, reassurance alone seems to be effective in abolishing the sensation of palpitation in patients with atrial premature complexes.

REFERENCES

Brodsky M, Wu D, Denes P, et al. Arrhythmias documented by a 24-hour continuous electrocardiographic monitoring in 50 male medical students, without apparent heart disease. Am J Cardiol 1977;39:390.

Hiss RG, Lamb LE. Electrocardiographic findings in 122,043 individuals. Circulation 1962;25:947.

Jordan JL, Karaguezian HS, Gang ES, et al. Normal and abnormal sinus node function. In: El-Sherif, Samet P, eds. Cardiac pacing and electrophysiology. Philadelphia: Saunders 1991:114.

Pick A, Langendorf R. Ectopic impulse formation: Specific mechanisms of various disorders of impulse formation, conduction, and their combinations. In: Pick A, Langendorf R, eds. Interpretation of complex arrhythmias. Philadelphia: Lea & Febiger, 1979:367.

Scott O, Williams GJ, Fiddler GI. Results of a 24-hour ambulatory monitoring of electrocardiogram in 131 healthy boys aged 10 to 13 years. Br Heart J 1980;44:304.

Wakida Y, Okamoto Y, Iwa T, et al. Arrhythmias in centenarians. PACE 1994;17:2217.

CHAPTER 15–12

Supraventricular Tachycardias

Toshio Akiyama, M.D.

DEFINITION

The entity of regular supraventricular tachycardia formerly contained only two categories: paroxysmal atrial tachycardia with or without atrioventricular (AV) block, and paroxysmal AV nodal tachycardia. Although no universally accepted classification of supraventricular tachycardia is currently available, an example of supraventricular tachycardia classification based on current knowledge is given in Table 15–12–1. Recognition of these various supraventricular tachycardias by the electrocardiographic pattern is shown in Figure 15–12–1. Atrial

flutter and atrial fibrillation are covered in Chapters 15–13 and 15–14, respectively.

Except for automatic atrial tachycardia and nonparoxysmal AV junctional tachycardia, which are relatively rare, supraventricular tachycardia is usually initiated by an atrial premature contraction and starts and ends abruptly. In these common supraventricular tachycardias, the first P wave (an atrial premature complex) precipitating supraventricular tachycardia differs in morphology from the P waves during the tachycardia. The impulse may be conducted normally, with AV block or

TABLE 15–12–1. SUPRAVENTRICULAR TACHYCARDIA

Reentrant
    Atrioventricular nodal reentrant tachycardia (AVNRT)
    Atrioventricular reentrant tachycardia (AVRT)*
    Sinoatrial nodal reentrant tachycardia (SANRT)
    Intraatrial reentrant tachycardia (IART)
Automatic
    Automatic atrial tachycardia (AAT)
    Nonparoxysmal atrioventricular junctional tachycardia (NPAVJT)
    Multifocal atrial tachycardia (MAT)†

*In the presence of an accessory pathway.
†In contrast to other supraventricular tachycardias listed here, atrial rate in MAT is irregular.

with bundle-branch block depending on the rate of supraventricular tachycardia and the state of the AV conduction system.

Atrioventricular nodal reentrant tachycardia, the most common variety of regular supraventricular tachycardia, is characterized by a regular fast tachycardia (150–250 beats/min). It starts abruptly with an atrial premature contraction and also ends abruptly. The retrogradely conducted P wave is usually buried within the QRS complex, but can appear barely after the preceding QRS complex, and rarely appears in front of the subsequent QRS complex. AV reentrant tachycardia occurs in patients with an accessory pathway, and its orthodromic form is characterized by a narrow QRS tachycardia (150–250 beats/min), with the retrograde P wave being located slightly closer to the preceding than to the subsequent QRS complex (see Chapter 15–15). In sinoatrial nodal reentrant tachycardia, the P waves have exactly the same morphology as normal sinus P waves, and the P wave during tachycardia appears close to the subsequent QRS complex. In *intraatrial reentrant tachycardia,* the P wave differs in morphology from the sinus P wave, and the P wave during tachycardia is located close to the subsequent QRS complex. In *automatic atrial tachycardia* and *nonparoxysmal AV junctional tachycardia,* the tachycardia develops and ends slowly. Automatic atrial tachycardia is often resistant to drug therapy, with its rate

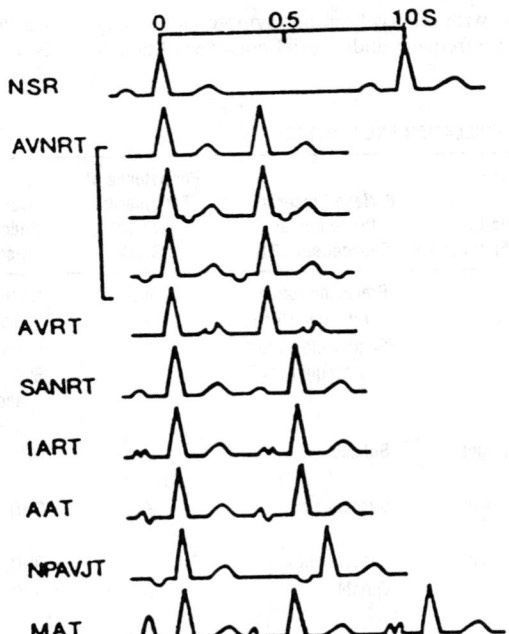

Figure 15–12–1. Electrocardiographic recognition of supraventricular tachycardias using inferior leads (II, III, or aVF). For further details, please refer to the text and Table 15–12–2. AV, atrioventricular; NSR, normal sinus rhythm; AVNRT, AV nodal reentrant tachycardia; AVRT, AV reentrant tachycardia; SANRT, SA nodal reentrant tachycardia; IART, intraatrial reentrant tachycardia; AAT, automatic atrial tachycardia; NPAVJT, nonparoxysmal AV junctional tachycardia; MAT, multifocal atrial tachycardia.

ranging between 100 and 175 beats/min; the P-wave morphology differs from that of the sinus P wave, but remains constant throughout the tachycardia. The rate of automatic atrial tachycardia may be influenced by a change in the autonomic tone. Nonparoxysmal AV junctional tachycardia has a relatively slow rate (70–130 beats/min): its P-wave location relative to QRS complex is variable, and if the P wave becomes visible, it is inverted in inferior leads. Multifocal atrial tachycardia is the easiest tachycardia to diagnose and has constantly changing P-wave shape and rate. Many of the P waves are tall and peaked in inferior leads (P pulmonale).

ETIOLOGY

Atrioventricular nodal reentrant tachycardia occurs in patients who have dual AV nodal pathways but usually have no other structural heart diseases. AV reentrant tachycardia occurs in patients with accessory AV pathway(s). Sinoatrial nodal reentrant tachycardia occurs in normal subjects and also in patients with organic heart diseases. Automatic atrial tachycardia takes place under many conditions, including digitalis intoxication, myocardial infarction, chronic lung disease, and with acute infection and metabolic abnormalities. Nonparoxysmal AV junctional tachycardia usually occurs in patients with digitalis intoxication, acute inferior myocardial infarction, acute rheumatic fever, and open heart surgery. Multifocal atrial tachycardia occurs mainly in patients with severe chronic lung disease but also in patients with diabetes mellitus or digitalis intoxication.

CRITERIA FOR DIAGNOSIS
Suggestive

Supraventricular tachycardias should be suspected for palpitations of sudden onset and offset in patients without structural heart disease or in patients younger than 50. When a patient presents with a tachycardia of abrupt onset and termination at a rate of between 150 and 200 beats/min, normal QRS complexes, and no clearly identifiable P waves, the physician has to assume that the tachycardia is AV nodal reentrant tachycardia, until proved to be otherwise.

Definitive

Supraventricular tachycardias are usually precipitated by an atrial premature complex, and start and end abruptly except for automatic atrial tachycardia and nonparoxysmal AV junctional tachycardia. A specific supraventricular tachycardia is strongly suspected by recognizing the relative position of a P wave in relation to a narrow QRS complex as shown in Figure 15–12–1. Except for multifocal atrial tachycardia, invasive electrophysiologic testing is usually necessary to differentiate definitively one form of supraventricular tachycardias from others. Multiform atrial tachycardia is easily diagnosed from constantly changing P-wave morphology and PP intervals, which are shorter than 0.6 second, many P waves being tall and peaked in inferior leads (P pulmonale), and presence of severe chronic obstructive lung disease.

CLINICAL MANIFESTATIONS
Subjective

Symptoms of patients with supraventricular tachycardias are those of any tachycardias and include palpitations, anxiety, easy fatigability, dyspnea, chest discomfort, and, in some cases, faintness or syncope. The symptoms tend to be more severe and acute in cases of AV nodal reentrant tachycardia and AV reentrant tachycardia, in which very rapid tachycardia starts abruptly. There may be a sudden thump or feeling of skipped beats immediately followed by continuous palpitations and chest discomfort. These symptoms are usually accompanied by anxiety, fear, weakness, or sweating. The patient may develop serious cardiovascular or respiratory decompensation when a rapid supraventricular tachycardia occurs in the presence of significant underlying cardiac or pulmonary disorders. In automatic atrial tachycardia and nonparoxysmal AV junctional tachycardia, in which the tachycardias tend to "warm up" gradually over several beats and their rates tend to be relatively slow, the patient may or may not be aware of the tachycardias.

Objective

Physical Examination

The regular tachycardia is usually the only abnormal physical finding unless the tachycardia occurs in the presence of underlying disorders. When supraventricular tachycardia is very fast and prolonged, the patient is anxious, the pulse is rapid and small, the blood pressure tends to be low, murmurs previously heard may become soft or inaudible, and a summation gallop and pulmonary rales may appear. In some cases, in which the atrial contraction takes place during the ventricular systole, prominent jugular pulsations (cannon *a* waves) may be appreciated; however, in relatively slower supraventricular tachycardia (such as sinoatrial nodal reentrant tachycardia, automatic atrial tachycardia, and nonparoxysmal AV junctional tachycardia), the physical examination may be normal except for the presence of tachycardia. In the patient with multifocal atrial tachycardia, the pulse is irregular and signs of severe chronic lung disease are obvious. The irregular pulse in multifocal atrial tachycardia is often misdiagnosed as that of atrial fibrillation.

When tachycardia persists for a week or longer, it can result in cardiac dilation, decreased ventricular function, and the clinical syndrome of heart failure (see Chapter 15–6).

Routine Laboratory Abnormalities

Please refer to Criteria for Diagnosis, Definitive.

PLANS

Diagnostic

Differential Diagnosis

Differential diagnosis of various forms of supraventricular tachycardias includes sinus tachycardia (see Chapter 15–10), atrial flutter (see Chapter 15–13), atrial fibrillation (see Chapter 15–14), and ventricular tachycardia (see Chapter 15–21). Diagnoses of the various forms of supraventricular tachycardias are usually made from the electrocardiographic findings and the clinical information. In the patient with regular tachycardia the following circumstances favor supraventricular tachycardias over ventricular tachycardia: if the QRS complexes are narrow and normal in configuration, if the tachycardia is initiated by an atrial premature contraction, if the RP interval is very short (< 0.1 second), and if the tachycardic P wave does not have the morphology of the retrogradely conducted P wave (inverted in inferior leads). If these charac-

teristics are present and favor supraventricular tachycardia, the electrocardiogram should be further analyzed for the following characteristics (see Figure 15–12–1): the onset and end of tachycardia in terms of abrupt or gradual, the rate of the tachycardia, morphology of the first P wave relative to other P waves of the tachycardia, whether the P waves are antegradely conducted (upright in inferior leads) or retrogradely conducted (inverted in inferior leads), and the position of the P wave relative to the preceding and subsequent QRS complex. This information from the routine electrocardiogram is useful for the differential diagnosis of supraventricular tachycardia (Table 15–12–2). It should be emphasized that in two thirds of AV nodal reentrant tachycardia (the most common form of supraventricular tachycardia), the P waves are buried within the QRS, in one third the P waves are located immediately after the QRS complexes (RP interval less than PR interval), and rarely the P waves are immediately before the subsequent QRS complexes. Thus, absence of a visible P wave despite the exhaustive search, sometimes including an esophageal electrocardiogram, strongly suggests AV nodal reentrant tachycardia. In many patients, however, invasive electrophysiologic testing may be required to establish the mechanism of supraventricular tachycardia.

Diagnostic Options

As noted above, the position of the P wave in relation to a QRS complex is crucial in the differential diagnosis of supraventricular tachycardias. When P waves are not recognizable during tachycardia on the body surface electrocardiogram, esophageal electrocardiographic recording frequently unmasks previously hidden P waves. Invasive electrophysiologic testing in selected patients is indicated to esablish the diagnosis of a specific supraventricular tachycardia. In this test, intracardiac electrocardiographic waveforms are closely monitored, supraventricular tachycardias are deliberately precipitated by a programmed electrical stimulation, and when supraventricular tachycardias are provoked, their precise electrophysiologic mechanisms as well as the patient's symptoms and cardiac hemodynamics are closely followed. Moreover, if appropriate, the efficacy of antiarrhythmic drugs for the suppression of the supraventricular tachycardia can be evaluated during the electrophysiologic testing.

Recommended Approach

For patients with relatively minor symptoms associated with tachycardias or with infrequent and/or brief episodes of tachycardias, only elec-

TABLE 15–12–2. DIFFERENTIATION OF SUPRAVENTRICULAR TACHYCARDIAS (EXCLUDING ATRIAL FIBRILLATION AND FLUTTER)

SVT	Rate of SVT (beats/min)	Mode of Onset and Termination of SVT	Morphology of First P Wave to Other P Waves During SVT	P Wave in Inferior Leads (After First P)	P Wave Closer to Preceding or Subsequent QRS	Persistence of Tachycardia with AV Block	Common Underlying Diseases
AVNRT	150–250 (mean 180)	Abrupt	Dissimilar	Inverted	Preceding (often buried in QRS)	No	No heart disease
AVRT	150–250 (mean 200)	Abrupt	Dissimilar	Inverted	Slightly closer to preceding QRS	No	Preexcitation, Ebstein's anomaly, MVP
SANRT	80–150 (mean 120)	Abrupt	Dissimilar	Normal and upright	Subsequent	Yes	OHD
IART	100–150 (mean 130)	Abrupt or variable	Dissimilar	Upright or inverted*	Subsequent	Yes	OHD
AAT	100–180	Gradual	Similar	Upright or inverted*	Subsequent	Yes	OHD, digitalis
NPAVJT	70–130	Gradual	Similar	Inverted	Variable†	Yes	OHD, digitalis, IMI, ARF, CPD
MAT	100–130	Gradual	Variable	Variable	Subsequent	Yes	CPD

Abbreviations: AV, atrioventricular; AVNRT, AV nodal reentrant tachycardia; AVRT, AV reentrant tachycardia; SANRT, SA nodal reentrant tachycardia; IART, intraatrial reentrant tachycardia; AAT, automatic atrial tachycardia; NPAVJT, nonparoxysmal AV junctional tachycardia; MAT, multifocal atrial tachycardia; ARF, acute rheumatic fever; CPD, chronic pulmonary diseases; MI, myocardial infarction; IMI, inferior myocardial infarction; MVP, mitral valve prolapse; OHD, organic heart disease.
*The P wave differs in morphology from the sinus P wave.
†Dissociation between sinoatrial and AV nodes is common.

trocardiographic recordings (rhythm strip, 12-lead electrocardiogram [ECG], ambulatory ECG recording, or a loop monitor) are indicated. For patients with relatively severe symptoms or with frequent and/or prolonged episodes of tachycardias, their diagnoses need to be firmly established. Thus, if these body surface electrocardiographic recordings fail to reveal P waves, an esophageal ECG recording or intracardiac ECG recording is indicated. For patients with relatively severe symptoms or infrequent but severely symptomatic tachycardia, an intentional provocation of their clinical tachycardias with programmed electrical stimulation becomes necessary. The information is used not only for establishing the specific mechanism of the patient's tachycardias but also for guiding therapy.

Therapeutic

Therapeutic Options

A wide variety of therapeutic options are available for patients with various forms of supraventricular tachycardias: no therapy other than reassurance and lifestyle modifications; beta blockers and antiarrhythmics; radiofrequency ablation; surgical ablation. In many patients with certain forms of supraventricular tachycardias, radiofrequency ablation is becoming the therapy of choice rather than lifelong pharmacologic therapy (see Recommended Approach).

Recommended Approach

In general, therapy of reentrant tachycardias is more satisfactory than that of automatic tachycardias. Vagal maneuvers such as carotid sinus massage and Valsalva's maneuver may terminate any of the reentrant tachycardias; however, in supraventricular tachycardia of automatic type (automatic atrial tachycardia and nonparoxysmal AV junctional tachycardia), the vagal maneuvers do not terminate the tachycardias but may transiently slow the rates. If vagal maneuvers are not successful initially, they should be repeated after antiarrhythmic drugs are given. Therapy of patients with AV reentrant tachycardia is discussed in detail in Chapter 15–15. Drug therapy is similar among other supraventricular tachycardias and is discussed below. Drug therapy is generally guided by the clinical response, but in some patients experiencing poorly tolerated but infrequent episodes of tachycardia, drug therapy may be guided by the results of serial invasive electrophysiologic tests. The speed and route of drug administration are influenced by the clinical status. Thus, patients with acute hemodynamic decompensation or frequent angina pectoris in association with the onset of supraventricular tachycardias require prompt termination of the supraventricular tachycardias, either by synchronized direct-current countershock or intravenous drugs. It should be pointed out that direct-current countershock therapy is effective only for reentrant tachycardias, but not for automatic tachycardias. For the technique involved in direct-current countershock application, please refer to Chapters 15–14 and 15–22.

Drug Therapy of Supraventricular Tachycardias. The most commonly used drugs are verapamil (Calan, Isoptin), propranolol (Inderal, Inderal-LA), metoprolol (Lopressor), atenolol (Tenormin), quinidine sulfate (Quinidex), quinidine gluconate (Quinaglute), procainamide (Pronestyl, Pronestyl-SR, Procan-SR), disopyramide (Norpace), amiodarone (Cordarone), and flecainide (Tambocor). For these drugs and others in this chapter, please refer to Table 15–16–2. These drugs, often in combination, may not only terminate supraventricular tachycardias, but also may prevent recurring supraventricular tachycardias by suppressing their precipitating atrial premature contractions, by suppressing conduction and prolonging refractoriness of the reentry circuit, and by suppressing the phase 4 depolarization of an ectopic anatomic focus. These drugs have proarrhythmic side effects, however, and supraventricular tachycardia may become more frequent and sustained after drug therapy than before.

For termination of supraventricular tachycardias, adenosine (Adenocard), cholinergic drugs (edrophonium chloride), or pressor amines (phenylephrine or methoxamine) may be given intravenously. Adenosine is an ultrashort-acting drug with a half-life less than 10 seconds, and slows and blocks conduction within the AV node. Among various supraventricular tachyarrhythmias, it is effective for termination of only AV nodal reentrant tachycardia and AV reentrant tachycardia, in which the AV node is an essential component of the reentry circuit. Adenosine should be given as a rapid intravenous bolus injection of 6 mg. If the first dose is ineffective, a bolus injection of 12 mg may be given 1 to 2 minutes after the first dose. Edrophonium chloride (Tensilon) may be given at an initial dose of 5 mg and, if unsuccessful, may be repeated at a dose of 10 mg. Edrophonium is contraindicated in patients with asthma or hypotension. Pressor amines must be used cautiously and are contraindicated in patients with organic heart disease, hypertension, stroke, ischemic heart disease, or aneurysm of the aorta or cerebral arteries. The blood pressure and heart rhythm must be closely monitored during the administration of pressor agents. Phenylephrine (Neo-Synephrine), 0.5 mg, or methoxamine (Vasoxyl), 3 mg, diluted with 10 mL 5% detrose in water may be given intravenously over 1 to 2 minutes. The infusion should be stopped with either termination of supraventricular tachycardia or by a rise of systolic blood pressure over 180 mm Hg.

Radiofrequency Ablation Therapy of Supraventricular Tachycardias. Radiofrequency ablation is curative in about 90% of the patients with atrioventricular nodal reentrant tachycardia and with atrioventricular reentrant tachycardia (preexcitation syndromes). Radiofrequency ablation therapy is also highly successful in the patients with automatic atrial tachycardia and intraatrial reentrant tachycardia. Serious complications such as cardiac perforation, cardiac tamponade, embolic stroke, and development of complete AV block are rare with radiofrequency ablation therapy. Thus, for patients with incapacitating symptoms or with frequent sustained episodes of these tachycardias, radiofrequency ablation has become the treatment of choice over lifelong drug therapy or surgical ablation of an arrhythmic focus or a part of a reentry pathway.

FOLLOW-UP

Patients having frequent, sustained, and relatively fast-rate tachycardias require hospitalization and generally require rather frequent follow-up, monthly for the first few months after discharge, if pharmacologic therapy is chosen. Once the supraventricular tachycardia is well controlled, a follow-up visit two to three times a year is sufficient. The physician should take time to explain the side effects of the antiarrhythmic drugs used and to teach the patient vagal maneuvers (carotid sinus massage and Valsalva's maneuver), as timely and proper application of these maneuvers by the patient may terminate the tachycardia and may help to avoid a hospital visit. In contrast, patients having only rare, brief, or relatively slow supraventricular tachycardias should be told that their conditions usually improve with reassurance and rest.

Patients with significant underlying heart or lung disorders require more frequent follow-up than those without. When the patient experiences symptoms suggestive of drug side effects or increasing frequency or severity of supraventricular tachycardia, the physician should be notified. The possibility of supraventricular tachycardia resulting from the proarrhythmic side effects of the drugs used should always be kept in mind.

After radiofrequency ablation therapy, patients should be evaluated once 2 to 3 weeks after hospital discharge for recurrence of palpitation and complications of radiofrequency ablation. Further cardiac follow-up is not necessary if the patient continues to do well without recurrent palpitation.

DISCUSSION

Prevalence and Incidence

The prevalence of the various forms of supraventricular tachycardia is not known; however, regular supraventricular tachycardia is probably more common than ventricular tachycardia. Among the regular supraventricular tachycardias, AV nodal reentrant tachycardia is by far the most common (about two thirds of the regular supraventricular tachycardias) and then AV reentrant tachycardia involving an accessory pathway (about one third). Other forms of supraventricular tachycardia are rare (Josephson and Seides, 1979).

Related Basic Science

Until about the 1960s, it was generally believed that enhanced automaticity (phase 4 depolarization) was the basis of most tachycardias and premature beats. From the vast amount of both clinical and basic knowledge accumulated over the past 30 years or so, it has become clear that the great majority of tachycardias and premature beats result from the reentrant mechanism, applicable to both supraventricular and ventricular arrhythmias. Furthermore, specialized conduction fibers exposed to toxic doses of digitalis have recently been shown to develop transient depolarization at the beginning of diastole (phase 4). This transient depolarization may be strong enough to reach the threshold potential of these fibers, thereby prematurely discharging them—a premature beat. This transient depolarization may occur in succession, and its clinical counterpart may be a short burst of ectopic tachycardia. Although this mechanism probably explains some of the tachyarrhythmias developing in patients receiving digitalis, it is unclear at this time how often this happens clinically.

As for atrioventricular nodal reentrant tachycardia, it is now believed that these patients have dual AV nodal pathways: slow (α) and fast (β) pathways (Wu et al., 1978). The cells of a slow pathway conduct slowly but recover quickly (thus their refractory periods are short); the cells of a fast pathway, on the other hand, conduct faster than those of a slow pathway but recover slowly (their refractory periods are longer). Thus, this arrangement is rather similar to that present in patients with preexcitation syndromes (see Chapter 15–15). Recent studies suggest the presence of two or more connections between the center of the AV node and the right atrium, with one of the connections ending in the area immediately in front of the ostium of the coronary sinus. This posterior connection appears to be a slow pathway and is a preferred site for radiofrequency ablation.

Natural History and Its Modification with Treatment

The natural history of patients with supraventricular tachycardia is unknown but is probably determined by the underlying heart or lung diseases. In patients with AV nodal reentrant tachycardia and with AV reentrant tachycardia, permanent cure can be accomplished in the majority of patients with radiofrequency ablation therapy.

Prevention

No preventive measures for the initial episode are currently available.

Cost Containment

As already stated, the attacks of supraventricular tachycardia may become more frequent and sustained with drugs than without. Thus, it is important to keep this possibility in mind whenever patients with supraventricular tachycardia are pharmacologically treated.

For patients with drug-resistant symptomatic AV nodal reentrant tachycardia or AV reentrant tachycardia, health care costs are substantial. Radiofrequency ablation therapy in these patients is not only clinically invaluable, but also results in a significant long-term reduction in medical expenses (Kalbfleisch et al., 1992).

REFERENCES

Bauerfeind RA, Wyndham CR, Dhingra RC, et al. Serial electrophysiologic testing of multiple drugs in patients with atrioventricular nodal reentrant paroxysmal tachycardia. Circulation 1980;62:1341.

Josephson ME, Seides SF. Supraventricular tachycardias. In: Josephson ME, Seides SF, eds. Clinical cardiac electrophysiology. Philadelphia: Lea & Febiger, 1979:147.

Kalbfleisch SJ, Calkins H, Langberg JJ, et al. Comparison of the cost of radiofrequency catheter modification of the atrioventricular node and medical therapy for drug-refractory atrioventricular nodal reentrant tachycardia. J Am Coll Cardiol 1992;19:1583.

Kaster J. Multifocal atrial tachycardia. N Engl J Med 1990;322:1713.

Kay GN, Epstein AD, Dailey SM, et al. Selective radiofrequency ablation of the slow pathway after the treatment of atrioventricular nodal reentrant tachycardia. Circulation 1992;85:1675.

McGuire MA, Bourke JP, Robotin MC, et al. High resolution mapping of Koch's triangle using sixty electrodes in humans with atrioventricular junctional (AV nodal) reentrant tachycardia. Circulation 1993;88:2315.

Wellens HJJ. Supraventricular tachycardia with reentry in the atrioventricular node. In: Kastor JA, ed. Arrhythmias. Philadelphia: Saunders, 1994:250.

Wu D, Denes P, Amat-y-Leon F, et al. Clinical, electrocardiographic and electrophysiologic observations in patients with paroxysmal supraventricular tachycardia. Am J Cardiol 1978;41:1045.

CHAPTER 15–13

Atrial Flutter

Toshio Akiyama, M.D.

DEFINITION

Although there are clinical clues to the presence of atrial flutter, the condition can be diagnosed with certainty only by the identification of specific abnormalities in the electrocardiogram. Atrial flutter is a rapid heart rhythm in which the atria are activated at a rate of about 300 beats/min and the ventricles usually beat quite regularly at a rate of 150 or 75 beats/min as a result of 2:1 or 4:1 atrioventricular block.

In classic (type I) atrial flutter, the flutter waves (F waves) are best recorded as regular sawtooth waveforms at a rate between 280 and 320 beats/min in leads II, III, aV_F, and V_1 of the electrocardiogram. In the less common (type II) atrial flutter, the flutter rate is greater than 340 beats/min. Atrial tachypacing is effective in terminating atrial flutter in type I but not in type II. Whereas atrial flutter is more common than atrial fibrillation during the first few years of life, in the adult atrial flutter occurs much less frequently than does atrial fibrillation. There are, however, occasional patients whose rhythms shift back and forth between atrial flutter and atrial fibrillation (atrial flutter–fibrillation or impure atrial flutter).

ETIOLOGY

Atrial flutter occurs under conditions similar to those for atrial fibrillation. Paroxysmal atrial flutter may develop in the absence of underlying heart disease and may be precipitated by excessive use of caffeine, alcohol, cigarettes, or catecholamine bronchodilators. Chronic (or established) atrial flutter, however, occurs almost always in the presence of organic heart disease with right atrial enlargement, such as rheumatic heart disease (especially mitral valve disease), hypertensive heart disease, coronary artery disease, cardiomyopathy, and atrial septal defect. It also occurs with pericarditis, hyperthyroidism, and pulmonary embolism or infection.

CRITERIA FOR DIAGNOSIS
Suggestive

The clinician must consider the possibility of atrial flutter under the following conditions: when supraventricular tachycardia is regular at about 150 beats/min and, especially, when the rate slows abruptly to 75 beats/min (half the basic rate) during carotid sinus massage, promptly returning to the higher rate on discontinuation of carotid sinus massage. Careful inspection of the jugular veins may reveal, though not commonly, regular fast waves ("flutter" waves), much faster than the ventricular rate.

Definitive

The flutter waves (F waves) are easily detected as regular sawtoothed waveforms in leads II, III, aV_F, and V_1 of the electrocardiogram (Figure 15–13–1). The F waves occur typically at a rate between 280 and 320 beats/min in type I atrial flutter and at a rate greater than 340 beats/min in type II atrial flutter in untreated patients. The rate, however, may slow to 200 beats/min after antiarrhythmic therapy, and its distinction from other regular tachycardias becomes nebulous. Usually, the ratio of atrioventricular (AV) block is 2:1 or 4:1, with a resultant ventricular rate of 150 or 75 beats/min, respectively. When a regular 2:1 AV block prevails, every second F wave may be buried within the QRS complex. The hidden F waves may be exposed by transiently intensifying AV block through the use of carotid sinus massage. Should carotid sinus massage fail to reveal the F waves, an esophageal electrocardiogram is often helpful in a patient still suspected of having atrial flutter. Occasionally, the ventricular response may become irregular because of varying AV block or Wenckebach periodicity. In patients with preexcitation syndromes or hyperthyroidism or in infants, a 1:1 AV conduction with the ventricular response at around 300 beats/min may take place. In this case, the QRS complexes may be distorted because of rate-related bundle-branch block, and thus the tachycardia often mimics ventricular tachycardia (see Chapter 15–21). When varying AV block with a pattern of long and short cycles appears, the QRS complex

concluding the short cycle may be conducted aberrantly with right bundle-branch block.

The flutter waves may transform into fine irregular f waves of atrial fibrillation from time to time (flutter–fibrillation or impure atrial flutter). This form is occasionally noted when atrial flutter is treated with digitalis.

CLINICAL MANIFESTATIONS
Subjective

The symptoms of patients with atrial flutter are similar to those experienced by patients with atrial fibrillation: palpitations, anxiety, restlessness, weakness, easy fatigability, dizziness, and dyspnea. Furthermore, the symptoms of underlying cardiac disorders are often magnified in the presence of atrial flutter.

Objective

Physical Examination

In the typical patient with atrial flutter with 2:1 or 4:1 AV block, the heart sounds are regular; however, when a variable AV block or Wenckebach AV block develops, the heart rate and sounds become irregular and the heart sounds may vary in intensity. Flutter waves may be detected, although infrequently, in the jugular veins, and their presence is diagnostic of atrial flutter. It is not uncommon for mitral stenosis to go undiagnosed during the time of tachycardia, including atrial flutter. The clinician should make a habit of reexamining the patient's cardiovascular system when the ventricular rate has slowed, as well as when normal sinus rhythm is restored.

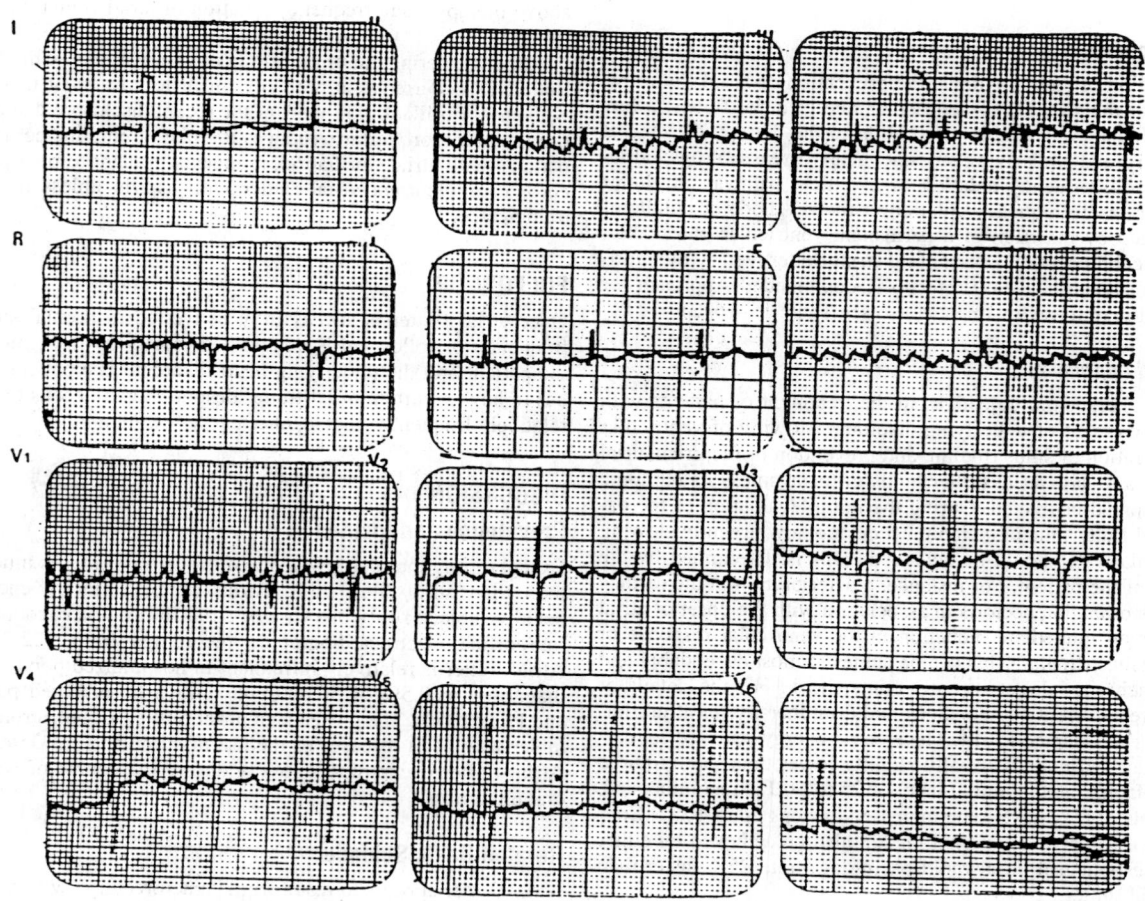

Figure 15–13–1. Atrial flutter with atrioventricular block (4:1 or 3:1 ratio) in a 58-year old man following pneumonectomy. Typical sawtooth flutter waves (F waves) at a rate of 300 beats/min are best seen in II, III, and, a V_F. In V_1, the F waves are seen as distinct upright P waves interspersed with isoelectric baselines.

Routine Laboratory Abnormalities

Generally, the diagnosis of atrial flutter is made from the electrocardiogram (see Criteria for Diagnosis, Definitive).

PLANS

Diagnostic

Differential Diagnosis

Atrial flutter needs to be differentiated from the following tachyarrhythmias: sinus tachycardia, atrial fibrillation, AV nodal reentrant tachycardia, AV reentrant tachycardia (preexcitation syndromes), automatic atrial tachycardia, intraatrial reentrant tachycardia, multifocal atrial tachycardia, and ventricular tachycardia. Presence of a regular atrial rate at 280 beats/min or faster with characteristic sawtooth waveform in the inferior leads separates atrial flutter from other forms of tachyarrhythmias.

Diagnostic Options and Recommended Approach

Clinicians should establish a habit of first suspecting atrial flutter with 2:1 AV block whenever dealing with patients with constant supraventricular rate at around 150 beats/min. Usually, careful analysis of a 12-lead electrocardiogram or a lead II or V$_1$ rhythm strip is the only diagnostic test necessary to diagnose atrial flutter. In patients with atrial flutter having 2:1 AV conduction, every second flutter wave may be buried in the QRS complex and thus its detection may be difficult for untrained eyes. In these patients, enhancement of AV block with such vagal maneuvers as carotid sinus massage or Valsalva maneuver often brings out previously hidden flutter waves. Only rarely do esophageal or intraatrial electrocardiograms become necessary for eliciting atrial flutter waveforms.

Therapeutic

Therapeutic Options

For the restoration of sinus rhythms, the prevention of atrial flutter recurrence, and/or the slowing of ventricular rate of atrial flutter, a few therapeutic options are available in addition to the therapy directed at etiologic factors and underlying organic heart disease: drugs; atrial tachypacing; radiofrequency ablation of a critical pathway of flutter reentrant circuit; radiofrequency ablation of the AV node or bundle of His accompanied by insertion of a permanent ventricular pacemaker; the Maze surgical procedure, interrupting atrial flutter reentry by multiple incisions in the atria. Please refer to Recommended Approach for further discussion of these treatments (also see Table 15–16–2).

Recommended Approach

There are four therapeutic objectives in the treatment of patients with atrial flutter: treatment of underlying disorders, slowing of ventricular response, restoration of sinus rhythm, and prevention of recurrent atrial flutter. Needless to say, atrial flutter tends to recur unless its etiologic factors are removed or treated. During the initial evaluation of the patient with atrial flutter, the clinician must decide how urgently slowing of the ventricular rate should be achieved. This is determined by the clinical status of the patient. For instance, a deterioration in the cardiac hemodynamics or angina pectoris in association with the onset of atrial flutter requires an immediate reduction in the ventricular response or conversion to sinus rhythm. This can be achieved most dependably and rapidly by synchronus direct-current countershock. For the details of synchronus direct-current countershock and drug therapy for atrial flutter, please refer to Chapter 15–14. The electric energy required for cardioversion of atrial flutter is usually slightly lower than that required for atrial fibrillation, and an initial level of 25 to 50 J is recommended. In some patients, it may have to be increased in steps up to 400 J. Conversion of atrial flutter to sinus rhythm can also be achieved by either direct or transesophageal atrial rapid pacing at a rate 25% faster than the rate of atrial flutter.

Slowing of the ventricular rate may be achieved by such drugs as metoprolol (Lopressor), atenolol (Tenormin), and verapamil (Calan, Isoptin).

Please see Table 15–16–2 for drugs used in arrhythmias and AV block. During therapy with these drugs, restoration of sinus rhythm may sometimes occur. For prevention of recurring atrial flutter, removal or effective therapy of etiologic factors appears to be more important than pharmacologic therapy. Indeed, some patients do well when they are not placed on any antiarrhythmic drugs after restoration of normal sinus rhythm.

Commonly used drugs are quinidine sulfate (Quinidex), quinidine gluconate (Quinaglute), and procainamide (Pronestyl, Pronestyl-SR, Procan SR). Less commonly used drugs are diltiazem (Cardizem), flecainide (Tambocor), amiodarone (Cordarone), and disopryamide (Norpace). Please refer to Table 15–16–2 for details of these drugs. It should be emphasized that before the patient is placed on quinidine or disopyramide, a drug slowing the ventricular rate as described above should be initiated. Otherwise, the vagolytic effects of quinidine or disopyramide in association with their slowing of the rate of atrial flutter may result in an acceleration of the ventricular response, in some instances a 1:1 AV conduction. This unexpected acceleration in the ventricular rate due to 1:1 AV conduction resulting from slowing of atrial flutter rate, sometimes deteriorating into ventricular tachycardia or fibrillation, has been observed in occasional patients treated with flecainide alone but not when a beta blocker or calcium channel blocker was used concomitantly. When atrial flutter cannot be converted to sinus rhythm electrically and/or pharmacologically, therapy is directed toward control of the ventricular rate. Although it should be tried only by the experienced physician, for patients with type I atrial flutter, rapid atrial pacing at a rate slightly faster than the rate of atrial flutter for up to 10 seconds may terminate atrial flutter or induce atrial fibrillation, which may revert to sinus rhythm spontaneously or may be electrically converted to sinus rhythm. This atrial stimulation must be done only after confirming that the electrode is positioned in the right atrium, not in the ventricle. This atrial tachypacing is not effective for patients with type II atrial flutter. In some patients with atrial flutter resistant to the above therapy, radiofrequency ablation of atrial flutter should be considered.

Although peripheral embolism occurs in patients with chronic atrial flutter, its occurrence is probably much less frequent than in patients with atrial fibrillation. In view of the recent disclosure that prophylactic use of aspirin or warfarin reduces the rate of embolic complications in patients with atrial fibrillation, it appears prudent to treat patients with chronic or recurrent atrial flutter with aspirin unless its use is contraindicated.

FOLLOW-UP

Once atrial flutter is successfully converted to normal sinus rhythm, frequency of follow-up is determined mostly by the clinical status of the patient and the underlying heart disorder. The patient who continues to have recurrent atrial flutter despite therapy needs to be followed relatively frequently, that is, once every few months.

DISCUSSION

Prevalence and Incidence

Except during the first few years of life, atrial flutter is much less common than atrial fibrillation. Atrial flutter is rarely encountered in healthy subjects; only one case of atrial flutter was encountered in routine office electrocardiographic recordings from 122,043 aviators. Atrial flutter is relatively infrequent in hospitalized populations; it was diagnosed in 0.5% of 50,000 consecutive hospitalized patients (Katz and Pick, 1956). The presence of atrial flutter, indeed, strongly suggests underlying heart diseases or the use of stimulants, as described above. Atrial flutter occurs uncommonly during the course of acute myocardial infarction.

Related Basic Science

Atrial flutter appears to result from "macroreentry" within the atria as a result of areas of nonuniform refractoriness and/or conduction (Waldo and Kastor, 1994). As in most other supraventricular tachycardias, atrial flutter is probably initiated by an atrial premature complex. In the presence of areas of nonuniform repolarization and conduction within the atria, an appropriately timed atrial premature complex may be slowly conducted through an abnormal area of the atria, but it may be blocked in another area because of either its prolonged refractory period or its abnormally depressed conduction. Because of this antegrade conduction block, the impulse proceeding through the first area may be conducted to an area distal to the site of the antegrade block. If the impulse conduction is greatly delayed, by the time the impulse reaches the area proximal to the site of the antegrade block, the cells in this proximal area may have already recovered their excitability, allowing the impulse to conduct retrogradely into this proximal area and to reach the original area of the atrial premature complex. Thus, a complete self-sustaining circuit is established, triggered by an atrial premature complex. In human atrial flutter studied by endocardial mapping, activation was craniocaudal in the anterolateral right atrium and caudocranial in the septum (Cosio et al., 1994). Furthermore, an area of slow conduction as a part of a reentrant circuit was present in the low right atrium (Olshansky et al., 1990). Recent studies suggest a relatively high cure rate by the application of radiofrequency electricity to the local area of a fractionated atrial electrogram, that is, an area of slow conduction (Calkins et al., 1994).

This scheme is only one of many possibilities based on the concept of nonuniform refractoriness and conduction. From the preceding scheme it is apparent that a critical mass of atrial tissue is obviously necessary so that the retrogradely advancing wave does not encounter refractory tissue in the area proximal to the site of antegrade block. The three ingredients—nonuniform refractoriness, slow conduction, and a critical mass—are present in many cardiac diseases. In a proposed model of atrial flutter (the leading-circle concept proposed by Allessie et al. in 1977), however, the area of slow conduction is not required. In this concept, nonuniform refractory periods play a major role in both initiation and maintenance of atrial flutter.

Thus, in theory, to terminate and prevent atrial flutter, it is necessary to lessen the degree of nonuniform refractoriness so that differences in conduction velocity are diminished, and it is necessary to diminish the size of the dilated atria.

Natural History and Its Modification with Treatment

Atrial flutter eventually reverts to normal sinus rhythm or converts to atrial fibrillation. As the underlying cardiac disease of atrial flutter worsens, the latter is likely to recur frequently and probably is transformed into chronic or intermittent atrial fibrillation. It is not clear currently whether or not medical therapy in patients with atrial flutter modifies its natural course.

Prevention

The prevention of atrial flutter involves the prevention of the underlying disorder, which, unfortunately, is not often possible.

Cost Containment

When conversion of atrial flutter to normal sinus rhythm is needed, the pharmacologic therapy should not be continued for more than a day or two because it is less effective, much slower, and has more side effects than direct-current countershock therapy. Specifically, "pharmacologic cardioversion with quinidine" at a much higher dosage schedule than suggested in this chapter is contraindicated. To lessen the length and number of hospitalizations, the physician should search for and treat effectively the underlying disorders of atrial flutter. Although the use of radiofrequency ablative therapy is becoming increasingly common, we need to know more about the safety of this new therapy and its long term benefits before its general use.

REFERENCES

Allessie MA, Bonke FIM, Schopman FJQ. Circus movement in rabbit atrial muscle as a mechanism of tachycardia. Circ Res 1977;41:9.

Calkins H, Leon AR, Dean AG, et al. Catheterization of atrial flutter using radiofrequency energy. Am J Cardiol 1994;73:353.

Cosio FG, Gil ML, Arribas F, et al. Mechanisms of entrainment of human common flutter studied with multiple endocardial recordings. Circulation 1994;89:2117.

Katz LN, Pick A. Clinical electrocardiography. Part I. The arrhythmias. Philadelphia: Lea & Febiger, 1956:43.

Olshansky B, Okumura K, Hess PG, et al. Demonstration of an area of slow conduction in human atrial flutter. J Am Coll Cardiol 1990;16:1639.

Waldo AL, Kastor JA. Atrial flutter. In: Kastor JA, ed. Arrhythmias. Philadelphia: Saunders, 1994:105.

CHAPTER 15–14

Atrial Fibrillation

Toshio Akiyama, M.D.

DEFINITION

Atrial fibrillation is one of the most common cardiac arrhythmias and is characterized by a totally irregular heart rhythm in which atria contract in a disorganized fashion at a rate between 400 and 600 times per minute without an effective atrial contraction. Some of the fibrillatory waves (*f* waves) are conducted to the ventricles resulting in an irregular ventricular response, usually 100 and 180 beats/min in the untreated patient with a normal atrioventricular conduction system. The *f* waves are generally seen best in lead V_1 of the electrocardiogram as fine undulations.

Paroxysmal atrial fibrillation lasts usually less than several hours, but it may last a few days. Before atrial fibrillation becomes established (chronic form), the paroxysmal form occurs for a variable length of time. Atrial fibrillation is said to be chronic when it persists for more than 2 weeks.

ETIOLOGY

Paroxysmal atrial fibrillation can occur in health as well as under stressful situations, with alcohol intake, or during use of bronchodila-tor-containing catecholamines. It may occur with hyperthyroidism, transient left ventricular failure, cardiothoracic surgery, acute pericarditis, pulmonary embolism, acute rheumatic fever, myocarditis, or pneumonia. Chronic atrial fibrillation, however, occurs usually in the presence of significant cardiopulmonary disease such as hypertensive cardiovascular disease, coronary artery disease, and rheumatic heart disease (commonly mitral valve disease). It also develops in thyrotoxicosis, cardiomyopathy, cor pulmonale, chronic pericarditis, syphilitic heart disease, and congenital heart disease (especially atrial septal defect and Ebstein's anomaly). Not infrequently, it is idiopathic.

CRITERIA FOR DIAGNOSIS
Suggestive

The presence of atrial fibrillation should be suspected in patients having an irregular pulse, the arterial pulse rate being slower than the apical heart rate by auscultation ("pulse deficit"); variable amplitudes of the arterial pulses; changing intensities of the heart sounds; and an absent *a* wave in the jugular vein. Whereas the physical findings strongly suggest the presence of atrial fibrillation, its definitive diagnosis is made from the electrocardiogram.

Definitive

Atrial fibrillation is diagnosed in a patient with totally irregular pulse rate when irregularly irregular ventricular response and fine undulating fibrillatory waves are recognized on a routine 12-lead electrocardiogram or rhythm strip.

CLINICAL MANIFESTATIONS

Subjective

Symptoms attributable to atrial fibrillation are usually more noticeable in the paroxysmal form than in the chronic form. Commonly encountered symptoms are palpitations (fast beats, irregular beats, occasionally bothersome or strong beats, skipped beats), anxiety, fatigability, weakness, dyspnea, and lighheadedness. These symptoms may be obscured by the symptoms of the underlying cardiac or pulmonary diseases. At times, the onset of atrial fibrillation may precipitate hemodynamic or respiratory decompensation in patients with underlying diseases; thus, the patient may experience such symptoms as exertional dyspnea, paroxysmal nocturnal dyspnea, orthopnea, and frequent and sustained angina pectoris. Systemic or pulmonary emboli sometimes arise from fibrillating atria, and symptoms attributable to these complications may be experienced.

Objective

Physical Examination

The pulse is irregularly irregular. In untreated patients having a normal atrioventricular (AV) conduction system, the ventricular response generally varies between 120 and 180 beats/min. When the ventricular response in atrial fibrillation exceeds 200 beats/min, the presence of preexcitation syndromes must be considered (see Chapter 15–15). On the other hand, a relatively slow ventricular response (below 100 beats/min) suggests depressed AV conduction caused by either AV conduction disease, enhanced vagal tone, or drugs known to retard AV conduction (digitalis, beta blockers, calcium channel blockers, or type Ic antiarrhythmic agents such as encainide, flecainide, propafenone, and amiodarone). Other physical findings in atrial fibrillation are the "pulse deficit" (the arterial pulse rate being slower than the auscultated apical rate), variable intensities of heart sounds, changing amplitude of the arterial pulse or blood pressure, and absence of an *a* wave in the jugular venous waveform.

An uncontrolled ventricular response often makes the recognition of underlying valvular heart diseases difficult. For instance, mitral stenosis occasionally remains undiagnosed in the presence of a rapid ventricular response. Mitral stenosis is still one of the most common causes of atrial fibrillation. Thus, the patient needs to be reexamined for the presence of mitral stenosis when the ventricular response slows, as well as when sinus rhythm is restored. Murmurs of other valvular lesions also tend to be muffled in the presence of the rapid ventricular rate due to reduced stroke volume. Such murmurs frequently become louder after slowing of the ventricular rate or restoration of sinus rhythm.

Objective evidence of emboli may be apparent.

Routine Laboratory Abnormalities

The electrocardiogram shows atrial fibrillation.

PLANS

Diagnostic

Differential Diagnosis

Differential diagnosis of atrial fibrillation includes the following atrial tachyarrhythmias: sinus arrhythmia; atrial flutter with variable AV block; sinus tachycardia or normal sinus rhythm with frequent atrial or ventricular premature complexes; supraventricular tachycardia or sinus rhythm with Wenckebach AV block; multifocal atrial tachycardia. Electrocardiographic findings of irregular ventricular response and undulating irregular fibrillatory waveforms separate atrial fibrillation from these tachyarrhythmias.

Diagnostic Options and Recommended Approach

The diagnosis of atrial fibrillation is made from the electrocardiogram; a routine 12-lead electrocardiogram is sufficient for diagnosis of chronic atrial fibrillation, but continuous ambulatory electrocardiographic recordings are frequently needed to diagnose paroxysmal atrial fibrillation. The electrocardiogram shows fine undulating *f* waves at a rate between 400 and 600 beats min, usually best recorded in the V_1 chest lead (Figure 15–14–1). Neither P waves nor a discrete straight electrocardiographic baseline exists. In some patients, the fibrillation waves may oscillate between the typical *f* waves (trough-to-peak amplitude less than 0.05 mV) and a regular sawtooth pattern (F waves) of atrial flutter (flutter–fibrillation). Atrial fibrillation is called "coarse" if the amplitude exceeds 0.05 mV. The F waves of atrial flutter, however, are regular sawtooth waves, usually at a rate between 280 and 320 beats/min.

Atypical and wide QRS complexes appearing in patients with atrial fibrillation pose a diagnostic and therapeutic challenge. Differentiation between aberrantly conducted beats and ventricular premature complexes must be made without the diagnostic advantage of a "preceding P wave." It is not uncommon that aberrantly conducted beats are mistaken for ventricular premature complexes, and thus the patient inappropriately receives antiarrhythmic drugs, which may further increase the frequency of aberrancy. Generally speaking, electrocardiographic findings in favor of aberrancy over ventricular premature complexes are as follows: the QRS complex has the typical right bundle-branch block rSR in V_1, the coupling intervals (the interval between the normal QRS and the subsequent abnormal QRS complex) vary, the QRS complex becomes more abnormal as the coupling interval becomes shorter, the initial vector of the abnormal beats resembles that of the normal beats, and when a sequence of a long and short cycle takes place the beat concluding the short cycle is an abnormally wide QRS complex (Ashman's phenomenon, (Figure 15–14–2). Ventricular premature complexes, however, are favored by the presence of fixed coupling intervals, the typical pattern of the left bundle-branch block (QS in V_1), and R or qR in V_1.

Cardiac echocardiographic examinations, transthoracic or esophageal, are usually indicated in patients with both chronic and paroxysmal atrial fibrillation. The test serves two purposes: detection of underlying heart disease and search for atrial thrombi. It is important that hyperthyroidism be included in the differential diagnosis of any newly diagnosed atrial fibrillation. This is especially the case in elderly patients, in whom atrial fibrillation may be the only clinical manifestation of hyperthyroidism ("masked hyperthyroidism"). In these patients with newly diagnosed atrial fibrillation, a screening test for hyperthyroidism (such as triiodothyronine and thyroxine determinations) should be performed.

Therapeutic

Therapeutic Options and Recommended Approach

The cardinal rules in therapy of atrial fibrillation are to restore sinus rhythm or slow the ventricular response and to prevent thromboembolism. Conversion of atrial fibrillation to sinus rhythm is occasionally achieved during an attempt to slow the ventricular rate with drugs. As therapy for slowing the ventricular rate is initiated, it is important that underlying cardiac or other disorders should be evaluated and treated. It is not uncommon, for instance, that successful treatment of hyperthyroidism leads to restoration of sinus rhythm.

In treating the patient with atrial fibrillation, one of the first decisions the physician must make is how urgently slowing of the ventricular response or restoration of sinus rhythm must be achieved. This is determined by the clinical status of the patient. For instance, an immediate slowing of the ventricular rate or restoration of sinus rhythm is imperative for the patient who has developed acute pulmonary edema, hypotension, cardiogenic shock, severe dyspnea, or severe angina pectoris with the onset of atrial fibrillation.

Slowing the Ventricular Rate in Atrial Fibrillation. Digitalis is the drug most commonly used for this purpose. In previously untreated adult patients,

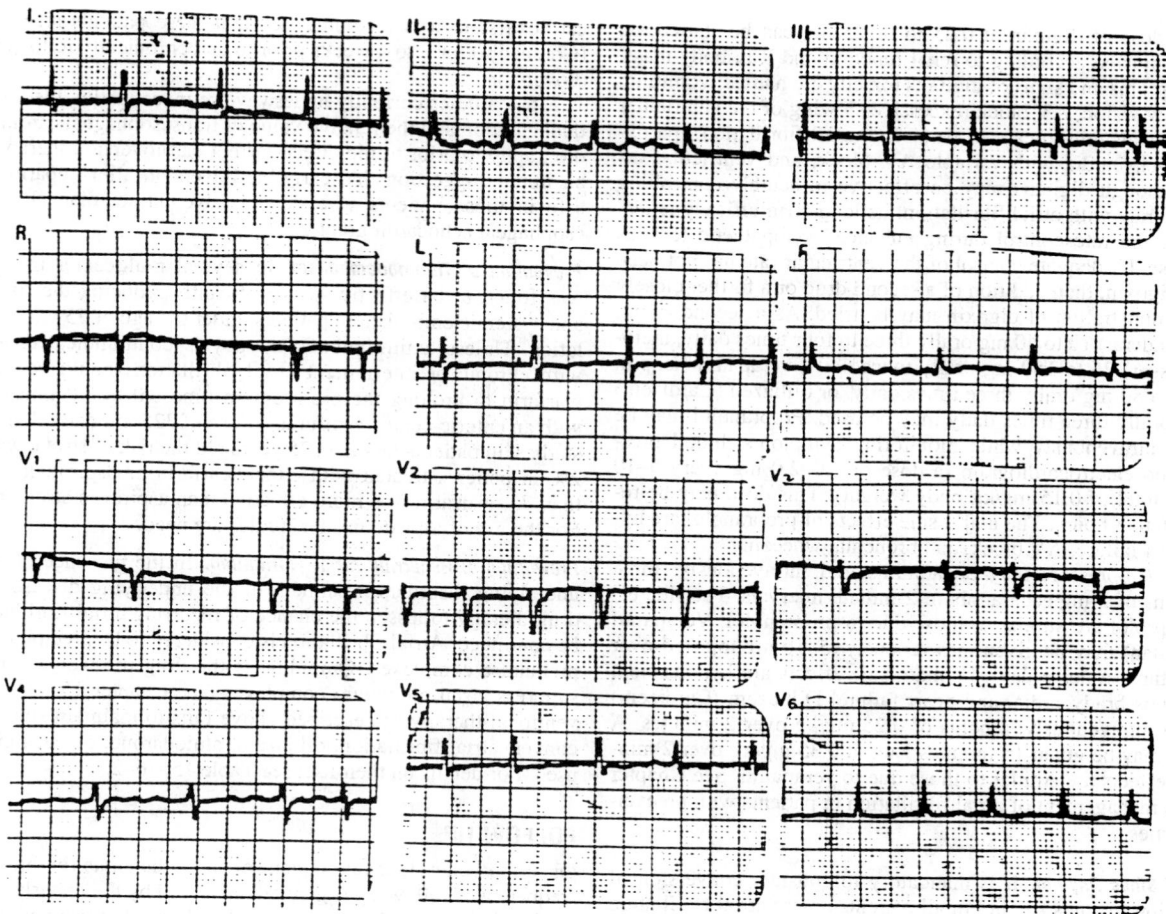

Figure 15–14–1. Atrial fibrillation in a 72-year-old diabetic woman. Fine undulating waves, *f* waves, at a rate of up to 500 beats/min are best seen in leads V_1, II, III, and aV_F. The ventricular response is irregularly irregular and averages about 100 beats/min (range, 63–145 beats/min).

digoxin (Lanoxin) may be administered intravenously or orally. For the intravenous approach, an initial dose of 0.5 to 1.0 mg digoxin may be given over 30 minutes, followed by 0.25 mg every 2 to 4 hours, with a total dose of less than 1.5 mg within the first 24-hour period. Digoxin, when administered intravenously, should be infused slowly, as its rapid injection may transiently produce a hypertensive response. For the oral approach, an initial dose of 0.75 mg may be followed by a dose of 0.5

mg every 6 hours, with a total dose less than 2.0 mg within the first 24-hour period. The dosing schedule must be adjusted according to the response of the patient; achievement of the desired heart rate (generally apical resting rate of 70–90 beats min) or appearance of digoxin's side effects necessitates withholding of further acute loading doses. The acute loading dose also needs to be adjusted according to the lean body mass of the patient. About 12 hours after the last loading dose, a main-

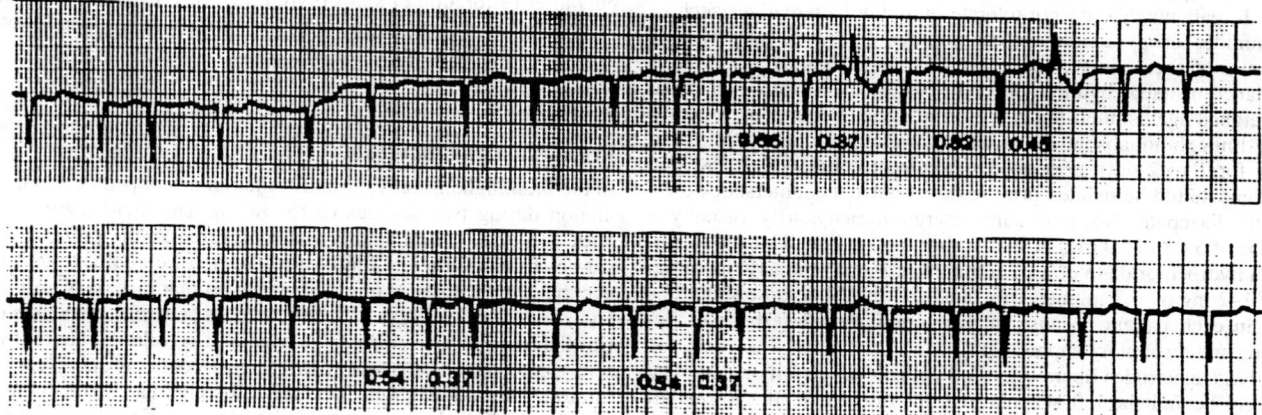

Figure 15–14–2. Ashman's phenomenon in atrial fibrillation (upper and lower tracings are continuously recorded with V_1 lead and coupling intervals are indicated in seconds). Two premature beats in the upper tracing are wide (0.14 second) and in the configuration of right bundle-branch block with coupling intervals of 0.37 and 0.45 second; however, two premature beats with a coupling interval of 0.37 second in the lower tracing are narrow and normal. Further analysis shows that the abnormally wide QRS complexes are preceded by cycle lengths of 0.65 and 0.82 second, which are longer than the two premature but normal QRS complexes in the lower tracing (their preceding cycle length being 0.54 second). Thus, these two beats are the result of Ashman's phenomenon and not of ventricular ectopic impulses.

tenance daily dose of digoxin at 0.25 to 0.125 mg can be started, its dosage to be adjusted according to renal function and lean body mass. Common symptoms and signs of digitalis toxicity are nausea, vomiting, diarrhea, yellow vision, AV block (excessive slowing of the ventricular rate below 50 beats/min in case of persistent atrial fibrillation), paroxysmal atrial tachycardia with variable AV block, and ventricular arrhythmias. Although digitalis may be effective in acutely controlling the ventricular rate with atrial fibrillation, its long-term efficacy is disappointing for the rate control during enhanced sympathetic tone as seen in exercise. If adequate control of the ventricular rate has not been achieved by digoxin, then addition of a second drug or a further closely monitored administration of digoxin may be tried. As a second agent, propranolol (Inderal) 10 to 40 mg orally three to four times daily, metoprolol (Lopressor) 25 to 150 mg orally twice daily, verapamil (Isoptin or Calan) 40 to 80 mg orally three times daily, or diltiazen (Cardizem) 60 to 90 mg orally three times daily may be used. Propranolol may be administered intravenously while monitoring symptoms, blood pressure, pulse, and electrocardiogram (a dose of 1.0–2.0 mg every 5–10 minutes for a total of 0.15 mg/kg body weight). This dose may be repeated every 6 to 8 hours. The major side effects of propranolol are hypotension, heart failure, AV block, and bronchial wheezing.

Metoprolol (Lopressor) may be administered intravenously: three bolus injections of 5 mg each at about 2-minute intervals. The side effects of metoprolol are similar to those due to propranolol. Verapamil (Isoptin or Calan) may be given intravenously (5–10 mg injected over 2–3 minutes three times a day). Its main side effects are hypotension, AV block, sinus bradycardia, and heart failure. Diltiazem (Cardizem) may be given intravenously: a bolus of 0.25 mg/kg over 2 minutes. A second bolus may be given 15 minutes later at 0.35 mg/kg over 2 minutes. Its side effects are similar to those due to verapamil. See Chapter 15–15 for the management of atrial fibrillation in patients with preexcitation syndromes.

Restoration of Sinus Rhythm. It is mandatory to consider conversion of atrial fibrillation to sinus rhythm in all patients unless atrial fibrillation has existed for more than a year. The latter patients are usually considered to be poor candidates for defibrillation because the rate of successful defibrillation is low and sinus rhythm can usually be maintained only briefly even after successful restoration. Restoration of sinus rhythm may be achieved electrically or pharmacologically. The electrical approach is the preferred choice because of its higher success rate, lower rate of complications, and more rapid conversion of atrial fibrillation. For 1 to 2 days prior to application of direct-current countershocks, the patient is given quinidine sulfate (Quinidex) 0.2 g or quinidine gluconate (Quinaglute) 0.325 mg, every 6 hours. This is necessary to lessen the chance of relapse of atrial fibrillation after successful electrical defibrillation, to test the patient's tolerance of quinidine, and, in 10 to 15% of patients, to achieve pharmacologic restoration of sinus rhythm. In patients who do not tolerate quinidine, alternatives such as procainamide, disopyramide, propranolol, and flecainide may be used (for details of these drugs, see Table 15–16–2). Indications for and maintenance of antiarrhythmic drugs in these patients, however, need to be weighed against their potential serious side effects (Coplen et al., 1990). Although not absolutely necessary, we recommend withholding digitalis for 1 to 2 days prior to direct-current countershock therapy. The patient should be sedated prior to direct-current countershock therapy with diazepam (Valium) administered intravenously (usually a total dose of 5.0 to 10.0 mg) or with a short-acting benzodiazepine, midazolam hydrochloride (Versed), administered intravenously (an initial dose of 1–2 mg over 2 minutes to a total of 5 mg). The dose should be titrated in each patient because of their common side effects of hypotension and respiratory suppression.

Two large electrodes liberally coated with electrode jelly are applied posteriorly behind the left scapula and anteriorly over the lower left parasternal area (an anteroposterior application). After appropriate triggering of direct-current countershock by the patient's QRS complex is confirmed, an initial synchronized direct-current impulse of 50 W·s (J) may be discharged. If it is unsuccessful, 100, 200, and finally 400 J should be tried. Direct-current countershock restores sinus rhythm in more than 90% of patients with atrial fibrillation.

For prevention of thromboembolism associated with direct-current

cardioversion, it is recommended that these patients receive warfarin (Coumadin) for 3 to 4 weeks prior to and chronically following the cardioversion.

A few studies currently underway are investigating the length of anticoagulation and the relative value of transesophageal cardiac echocardiography to prior to the direct-current cardioversion therapy. There is an initial suggestion that early cardioversion after heparin therapy is safe in those patients who do not have intracardiac clots by transesophageal echocardiography.

Prevention of Thromboembolism. In several multicenter trials, warfarin was found to be effective in significantly reducing the risk of stroke and systemic embolism in patients under the age of 75 with atrial fibrillation. Unless antithrombotic therapy is contraindicated, all patients with chronic or intermittent atrial fibrillation should be treated with warfarin to prolong the prothrombin time 2.0 to 3.0 times control or with an enteric-coated aspirin in a dose of 325 mg daily. In some recent studies, in patients less than 75 years old the risk of stroke was less than 2% in patients treated with either warfarin or aspirin. In those older than 75, warfarin was more effective than aspirin in stroke prevention. For the use of aspirin, further studies are needed.

Prevention of Recurring Atrial Fibrillation. In the presence of identifiable underlying disorders, treatment of the underlying disease along with drug therapy to lessen the chance of recurring atrial fibrillation should be continued. Atrial fibrillation is considered to be precipitated by atrial premature complexes. Quinidine is the drug most commonly used to suppress atrial premature complexes (see Chapter 15–11). When conventional therapy as described above fails to maintain sinus rhythm or convert atrial fibrillation, diltiazem, amiodarone, or flecainide may be used. For details on their use, see Table 15–16–2.

FOLLOW-UP

Once the ventricular rate is controlled or the sinus rhythm is restored, frequency of follow-up is generally dictated by the underlying disorder. At the clinic, the pulse (both arterial and apical at rest and during usual exercise), the ventricular rate on an electrocardiographic rhythm strip, and the patient's symptoms are used to adjust the drugs. All peripheral arterial pulses should be examined at each visit, and their character should be recorded for future reference.

Patients with paroxysmal atrial fibrillation who use alcohol, caffeine, tobacco, or catecholamine bronchodilators should be instructed to lessen or discontinue the use of these agents. The physician should emphasize the need for long-term drug therapy to prevent recurrences of atrial fibrillation and thromboembolism.

Patients should contact their physician if the resting pulse rate remains constantly above 90 beats/min or below 50 beats/min during waking hours in the presence of atrial fibrillation; if irregular pulse occurs after restoration of sinus rhythm; if exacerbation of the symptoms attributable to underlying disorders occurs; and/or if manifestations of thromboembolism appear.

DISCUSSION
Prevalence and Incidence

In the Framingham study, atrial fibrillation developed in 2% of the population during two decades of follow-up. The incidence rose sharply with age. Atrial fibrillation usually occurred in the presence of other cardiovascular diseases. Thirty-one percent of chronic atrial fibrillation occurred in the absence of other cardiovascular disease. Cardiac failure and rheumatic heart disease were the most powerful predictors of atrial fibrillation, with relative risks in excess of sixfold; however, hypertensive cardiovascular disease was the most common underlying disease of atrial fibrillation, largely because of its high incidence in the general population. The development of chronic atrial fibrillation was associated with a doubling of overall mortality and of mortality from cardiovascular disease (Kannel et al., 1982). These earlier findings were collaborated by the recent study on Medicare-eligible elderly persons, thus over 65 years of age, from four U.S. communities. Atrial fibrillation was diagnosed in 4.8% of women and 6.2% of man, and its prevalence was strongly associated with advancing age in women (Furberg et al.,

1994). Furthermore, a history of congestive heart failure, valvular heart disease and stroke, enlarged left atrium, abnormal mitral or aortic valve function, treated systemic hypertension, or advancing age was independently associated with the prevalence of atrial fibrillation.

Related Basic Science

In atrial fibrillation there is no organized contraction or relaxation of the atria. As in ventricular fibrillation, multiple wave fronts of depolarization are interspersed at any given time with multiple areas of repolarization. The atrial cells discharge at a rate of up to 600 times a minute. The maintenance of atrial fibrillation requires a critical atrial mass, nonuniform repolarization (nonuniform refractory period), and areas of depressed atrial conduction. It should be pointed out that defibrillation can be accomplished by the application of an intense current across the entire heart, such as direct-current countershock, but not by an atrial pacemaker impulse. The direct-current countershock impulse depolarizes all or most of the atrial cells that have already recovered excitability, but not those cells that were activated immediately prior to the direct-current impulse. Then the direct-current impulse essentially aligns all the atrial cells at the starting point of cellular activation. In the absence of persistent severe nonuniformity of refractoriness and conduction, no circulating waves are formed and thus the sinus node can eventually control the atria; however, a pacemaker impulse applied directly to a small area of the atrium can activate only the atrial cells in the immediate vicinity of the pacemaker electrode and not the cells distant from the electrode. Thus, the mixture of multiple depolarization and repolarization wave fronts can persist in the areas of the atria away from the pacemaker electrode, and atrial fibrillation persists despite the atrial pacemaker impulse.

Natural History and Its Modification with Treatment

As the underlying cardiovascular or pulmonary disorder progresses, atrial fibrillation, initially paroxysmal, tends to become chronic. Atrial fibrillation is known to reduce cardiac output by as much as 30% because of the loss of a synchronized atrial contraction. This is called the atrial contribution to the cardiac output, atrial kick, or the atrial booster effect. This reduction in cardiac output often heralds a sudden deterioration in patients with compromised cardiac function.

Atrial fibrillation is documented in about 10% of patients with acute myocardial infarction. In these patients the presence of atrial fibrillation is not an independent predictor of mortality when adjusted for age and severity of myocardial infarction.

In the Framingham study, persons with chronic atrial fibrillation, with or without rheumatic heart disease, were at greatly increased risk of stroke, and the stroke was probably due to embolism. Chronic atrial fibrillation in the absence of rheumatic heart disease is associated with more than a 5-fold increase in the incidence of stroke, whereas chronic atrial fibrillation with rheumatic heart disease has a 17-fold increase.

The Stroke Prevention in Atrial Fibrillation Study Group (1990) found that the event rate for ischemic stroke or systemic embolism in patients with atrial fibrillation from causes other than rheumatic heart disease was 8.3% per year in a placebo group. The event rate was reduced to 1.6% per year in patients treated with either warfarin or aspirin (*P*<.00005); however, no significant reduction was realized in patients over 75 years of age.

In the Stroke Prevention in Atrial Fibrillation II trial, however, warfarin was effective in stroke prevention in those older than 75 (NHLBI Working Group on Atrial Fibrillation, 1993).

Prevention

As the prevalence of various cardiopulmonary diseases has evolved over the past half century, rheumatic heart disease has been replaced as a cause of atrial fibrillation by hypertensive cardiovascular disease, coronary artery disease, cardiomyopathy, and chronic obstructive lung disease. Prevention of these underlying cardiopulmonary illnesses naturally leads to prevention of atrial fibrillation. When etiologic factors or illnesses are identified, their removal or successful treatment may help restore and maintain normal sinus rhythm; however, atrial fibrillation usually recurs soon after defibrillation if it has existed for more than a year.

Cost Containment

Prolonged use of quinidine beyond 2 days specifically for the purpose of converting atrial fibrillation to sinus rhythm should be avoided because of the availability of direct-current countershock therapy, which takes a much shorter time to convert atrial fibrillation. Though a recent study indicated an improved quality of life and cardiac performance after radiofrequency ablation of AV junction for those severely symptomatic patients with drug-resistant atrial fibrillation or flutter (Brignole et al., 1994), it is not clear yet whether this therapy also results in cost savings.

REFERENCES

Brignole M, Gianfranchi L, Menozzi, C, et al. Influence of atrioventricular junction radiofrequency ablation in patients with chronic atrial fibrillation and flutter on quality of life and cardiac performance. Am J Cardiol 1994;74:242.

Collins LJ, Silverman DI, Douglas PS, et al. Cardioversion of nonrheumatic atrial fibrillation. Circulation 1995;92:156.

Coplen SE, Antman EM, Berline JA, et al. Efficacy and safety of quinidine therapy for maintenance of sinus rhythm after cardioversion. Circulation 1990;82:1106.

Furberg CD, Psaty BM, Manolio TA, et al. Prevalence of atrial fibrillation in elderly subjects (for the Cardiovascular Health Study). Am J Cardiol 1994;74:236.

Hunt D, Sloman G, Penington C. Effects of atrial fibrillation on prognosis of acute myocardial infarction. Br Heart J 1978;40:303.

Kannel WB, Abbott RD, Savage DD, McNamara PM. Epidemiologic features of chronic atrial fibrillation: The Framingham study. N Engl J Med 1982;306:1018.

Lindpaintner K, Pfeffer MA. Molecular genetics crying wolf? The case of the angiotensin–converting enzyme gene and cardiovascular disease. J Am Coll Cardiol 1995;25:1632.

Manning WJ, Silverman DI, Gordon SPF, et al. Cardioversion from atrial fibrillation without prolonged anticoagulation with use of transesophageal echocardiography to exclude the presence of atrial thrombi. N Engl J Med 1993;328:750.

Stoke Prevention in Atrial Fibrillation Study Group. Special report: Preliminary report of the Stroke Prevention in Atrial Fibrillation Study. N Engl J Med 1990;322:863.

NHLBI Working Group on Atrial Fibrillation. Atrial fibrillation: Current understanding and research imperatives. J Am Coll Cardiol 1993;22:1830.

Wolf PA, Dawber TR, Thomas HE, Kannel WB. Epidemiologic assessment of chronic atrial fibrillation and risk of stroke: The Framingham study. Neurology 1978;28:973.

Preexcitation Syndromes

Toshio Akiyama, M.D.

DEFINITION

In preexcitation syndromes, the atria and ventricles are connected not only by the normal atrioventricular (AV) conduction system but also by extra-AV nodal accessory pathway(s), frequently resulting in an abbreviated AV conduction and deformation of QRS complexes with delta waves. The clinical significance lies in the complicating tachyarrhythmias to which such patients are prone.

ETIOLOGY

The extra-AV nodal connections are forms of congenital heart disease in which one or more abnormal bands of muscle (termed Kent bundles, "bypass tracts," or "accessory pathways") form additional avenues for electrical communication between atria and ventricles.

CRITERIA FOR DIAGNOSIS

Suggestive

The presence of accessory pathway(s) can lead to any forms of tachyarrhythmias. The clinician needs to exclude first a possibility of preexcitation syndromes as a cause of any tachyarrhythmias. This is especially the case for relatively young patients presenting with recurrent tachycardia, regular or irregular, of sudden onset and termination.

Definitive

The characteristic electrocardiographic signature of sinus rhythm or tachycardia as described below establishes a diagnosis of preexcitation syndromes.

The syndromes are classified according to the anatomic (and hence electrocardiographic) variants. In the most frequent form (Wolff–Parkinson–White [WPW] syndrome), the anomalous communication (Kent bundle) passes directly from atrium to ventricle. Its electrocardiographic signature is that of a shortened (<0.12 second) PR interval, a widened QRS complex introduced by a slurred deflection (the delta wave), and abnormal ST segment and T wave secondary to an abnormal sequence of ventricular activation.

In the Lown–Ganong–Levine syndrome, the anomalous path is presumed to course from atrium to His bundle and gives rise to a shortened PR interval and normal QRS complex. Other anatomic variants include Mahaim fibers, which connect the AV node and ventricle (the electrocardiographic correlate being a normal PR interval, but a widened QRS complex with a delta wave), and fasciculoventricular fibers, which originate in the His bundle or bundle branch. As the latter three variants are less common and less well understood, this chapter focuses on Wolff–Parkinson–White syndrome.

In addition to the electrocardiographic features described above, other clues may suggest the presence of preexcitation: a narrow QRS tachycardia (150–250 beats/min, with the retrograde P wave (inverted in inferior leads) being located slightly closer to the preceding than to the subsequent QRS; atrial fibrillation with a rapid, wide QRS complex response (200 to over 300 beats/min); and the deterioration of a rapid, wide QRS atrial fibrillation to ventricular fibrillation.

Ebstein's anomaly and hypertrophic cardiomyopathy are associated with preexcitation, and these patients should be screened for its presence.

A definitive diagnosis is usually made by the presence of the electrocardiographic abnormalities described above; however, an electrical impulse may not always activate the anomalous pathway. In these patients, still suspected of having preexcitation syndrome, an ambulatory electrocardiographic recording may be useful in which preexcitation beats, especially in response to atrial premature beats, may emerge momentarily.

In occasional patients, diagnostic electrophysiologic testing is necessary to diagnose preexcitation syndromes. This holds especially for patients with a concealed accessory pathway(s), which conducts only retrogradely from the ventricle to the atrium and thus does not generate delta waves.

CLINICAL MANIFESTATIONS

Subjective

Preexcitation syndromes are diagnosed in the adult as frequently as in the pediatric population, supporting a congenital origin. In the absence of tachyarrhythmias, these syndromes are asymptomatic. When tachyarrhythmias occur, symptoms are similar to those of other sustained tachyarrhythmias and include palpitations, anxiety, weakness, fatigue, dizziness, dyspnea, chest discomfort, and syncope. Both the arrhythmia and its symptoms begin and terminate abruptly.

Objective

Physical Examination

The physical examination is normal when tachyarrhythmias or associated diseases are not present. During tachyarrhythmias, the pulse is rapid (regular or irregular), the blood pressure may be reduced, and cannon a waves may be noted in the jugular pulse due to simultaneous atrial and ventricular contraction. When the ventricular rate is extremely rapid (and, of course, during ventricular fibrillation), the pulse may vanish altogether.

Routine Laboratory Abnormalities

Routine laboratory evaluations, other than the electrocardiogram, are normal. Patients with associated heart diseases (Ebstein's anomaly, or cardiomyopathy) may have other laboratory abnormalities (please refer to the appropriate chapters in this book). For electrocardiographic abnormalities please refer to Criteria for Diagnosis, Definitive.

PLANS

Diagnostic

Differential Diagnosis

Unless the clinician forms a habit of first excluding preexcitation as an underlying cause of any tachyarrhythmias, many patients with these syndromes are likely to remain undiagnosed and thereby receive inappropriate treatment. It should be kept in mind that most tachyarrhythmias occur due to the presence of an accessory pathway and that preexcited beats mimic such tachyarrhythmias as frequent ventricular premature complexes, ventricular tachycardia, bundle-branch blocks, AV nodal tachycardia, and atrial tachycardia. AV nodal reentrant tachycardia (AVNRT) is indistinguishable in clinical presentation from the AV reentrant tachycardia of preexcitation syndromes; however, the finding of either no detectable P wave or inscription of a P wave at the end or immediately after QRS complex favors AVNRT. For the relative location of a P wave in relation to a QRS complex in various supraventricular tachycardias, please refer to Figure 15–12–1.

Diagnostic Options

Preexcitation syndromes are essentially electrocardiographic diagnoses, and can be diagnosed from a 12-lead electrocardiogram, a rhythm strip, or an ambulatory electrocardiogram or from the results of invasive electrophysiologic testing.

Recommended Approach

Usually the history and characteristic electrocardiographic findings suffice to establish the diagnosis. In addition to the aforementioned fea-

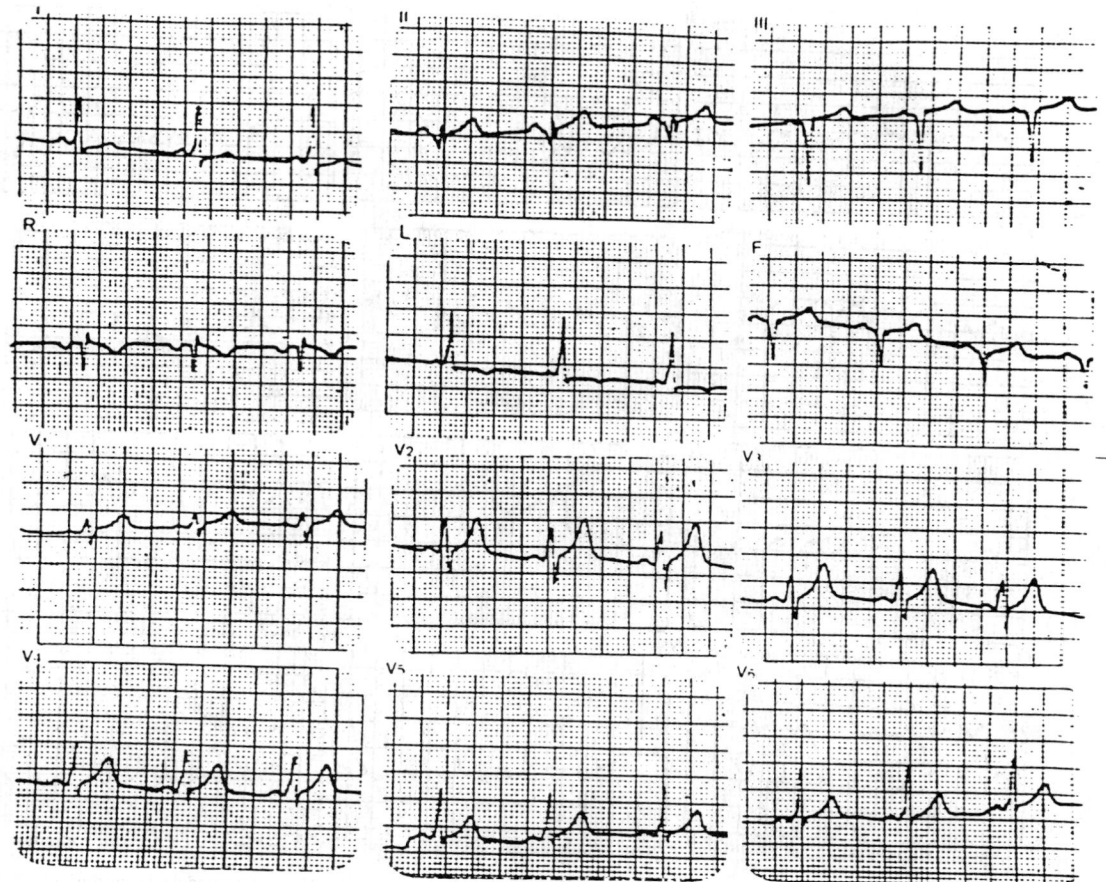

Figure 15–15–1. Typical electrocardiogram for Wolff–Parkinson–White syndrome recorded from a 43-year-old man with a history of recurrent drug-resistant supraventricular tachycardias (see Figure 15–15–2) and atrial fibrillation and flutter. A short PR interval of 0.11 second and a wide QRS complex of 0.10 second with delta wave are diagnostic of Wolff–Parkinson–White syndrome. Please note that the delta waves are upright in I, aV_L, and V_{1-6}, but downward (Q waves) in II, III, and aV_F, mimicking the Q waves of old inferior myocardial infarction (pseudoinfarction pattern).

tures of the electrocardiogram, the width of the delta wave, and hence of the QRS complex, may vary, depending on how large a portion of the ventricles was depolarized by the anomalous tract before arrival of the impulse from the Purkinje fibers of the bundles. There may be abnormalities of the ST segment and T wave, with their vectors commonly being oriented in the opposite direction to those of the delta wave and QRS complex (ST-segment and T-wave abnormalities of secondary type).

In some patients, activation of the anomalous pathway may be intermittent, and the classic electrocardiographic patterns will not always be evident. In such patients, ambulatory electrocardiographic monitoring may help establish the diagnosis by demonstrating transient emergence of the classic electrocardiographic pattern, particularly in response to an atrial premature beat. These wide complexes are sometimes erroneously diagnosed as ventricular premature complexes. The electrocardiographic pattern of preexcitation is a classic example of a fusion beat, with ventricular activation resulting from the combined effects of two separate wave fronts, one emerging quickly from the ventricular insertion of the bypass tract and the other from the arborizations of the Purkinje system. Slow intramyocardial depolarization in the vicinity of the bypass tract insertion causes the delta wave. As the size of this myocardial segment and consequently of the delta wave is dependent on the degree of prematurity of the impulse arrival relative to that arriving from the Purkinje system, atrial premature contractions are likely to elicit or accentuate the preexcitation. Conduction through the AV node is retarded when an atrial premature complex occurs, but conduction velocity is undiminished in the bypass pathway. Thus, because the impulse passing through the bypass tract has a relatively earlier arrival, it captures more of the ventricular mass and favors the appearance of a delta wave. Importantly, these differing electrical properties of the by-

pass tract and the normal AV conduction system account for initiation of AV reentrant tachycardia (AVRT) (Figure 15–15–2).

In some patients suspected of preexcitation, electrophysiologic (EP) testing may be required to establish the diagnosis if the 12-lead and ambulatory electrocardiograms do not disclose it. During electrophysiologic testing, an atrial premature beat is introduced, and the following findings are characteristic of Wolff–Parkinson–White syndrome: First, increasingly premature atrial stimulation causes the delta wave to become gradually larger, until suddenly it disappears and the QRS complex normalizes. The latter signifies a failure of conduction through the Kent bundle (its refractory period has been entered). Second, delta wave size may vary as a function of the position of a stimulating atrial electrode, attaining the largest size when the atrial stimulation is close to the origin of the Kent bundle. Finally, very premature atrial stimulation, encountering a refractory Kent bundle, may conduct extremely slowly through the normal AV node and initiate a rapid, narrow QRS complex tachycardia (AV reentrant tachycardia. Such findings may be used also to choose effective drug(s).

In patients with a concealed accessory pathway conducting only retrogradely, a electrophysiology test is essential and can reveal preexcitation of the atrium with ventricular premature stimulation. The latter may precipitate an orthodromic AV reentrant tachycardia.

Therapeutics

Therapeutic Options

Different forms of therapy are now available for patients and preexcitation syndromes: clinical follow-up only; drugs; radiofrequency or surgical ablation of accessory pathway(s). Radiofrequency therapy has been well established and surgical ablation is now rarely indicated.

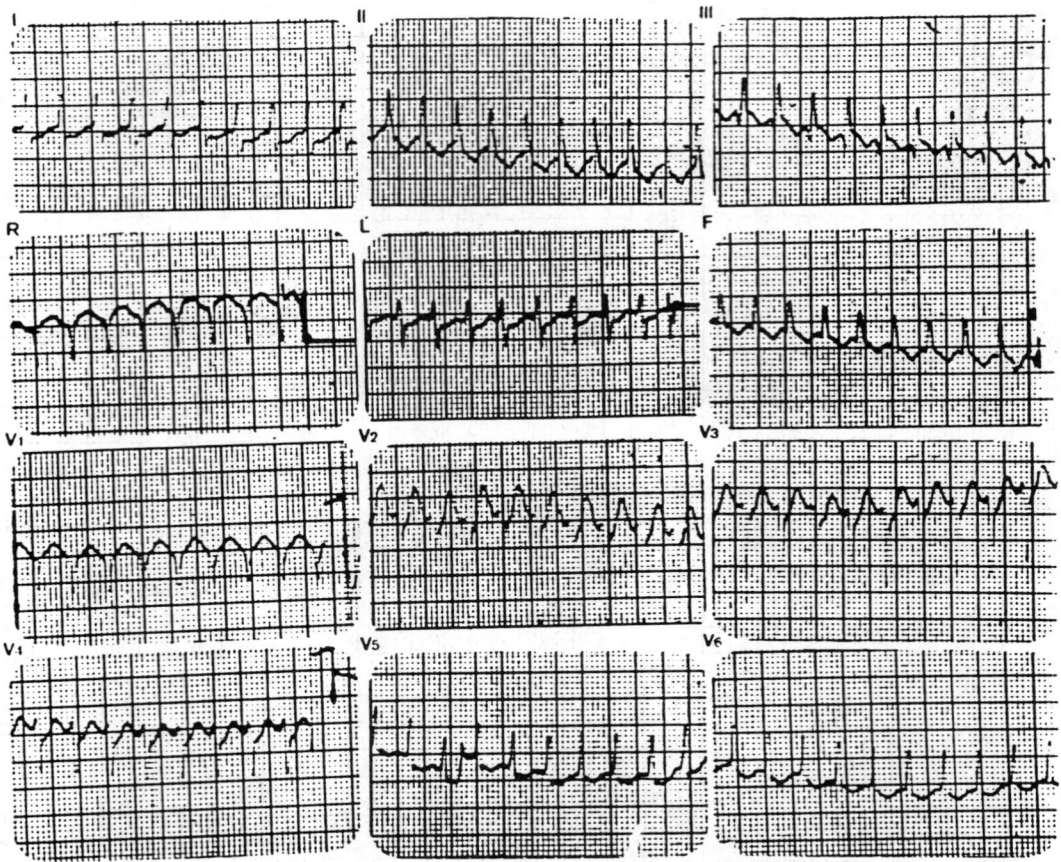

Figure 15–15–2. Rapid, narrow QRS complex tachycardia recorded from the same patient as in Figure 15–15–1. In this regular tachycardia of 230 beats/min, the QRS complex is narrow and is without delta waves. The T waves are inverted and sharply pointed in leads II and III and may be the result of superimposition of an inverted P wave on the inverted T wave. These findings are highly suggestive of the atrioventricular reentrant tachycardia of Wolff–Parkinson–White syndrome. The atrioventricular reentrant tachycardia and atrial fibrillation/flutter were resistant to drug therapy. In the electrophysiologic test, a bypass tract was located at the posterior portion of the left atrium and ventricle. The bypass tract was successfully divided by surgery, and the patient required no further drug therapy.

Recommended Approach

The life-threatening complication in the patient with this syndrome, that is, ventricular fibrillation developing after an extremely rapid ventricular response in the presence of atrial fibrillation, fortunately, is uncommon. Identification of patients who have already developed or are prone to develop this lethal complication is usually the first step in the therapeutic process. Intermittent preexcitation pattern and disappearance of the preexcitation pattern during exercise-induced sinus tachycardia are considered to indicate a relatively long refractory period of the accessory pathway. This is important because maximal ventricular response is slower, and ventricular fibrillation is less likely to develop in case of atrial fibrillation. Although no established guideline is available, these patients, if they have not had a history of palpitation of abrupt onset and termination, may require close follow-up but no drug therapy. Patients who have experienced recurrent symptomatic tachycardia require at least drug therapy. If an electrophysiologic service is available, these patients probably should undergo the electrophysiologic test for the following purposes: to assess the duration of the refractory period of the accessory pathway (generally an antegrade refractory period less than 270 milliseconds identifies patients at high risk of developing ventricular fibrillation), to study directly the ventricular response to electrically induced atrial fibrillation, and to assist in choosing drugs to prevent AV reentrant tachycardia. Patients with preexcitation syndrome who have a history of ventricular fibrillation or of an extremely rapid ventricular response in the presence of atrial fibrillation should have an electrophysiologic test. These patients should undergo radiofrequency catheter ablation of the accessory pathway(s) after the location is identified with the electrophysiologic test.

Once drug therapy is considered, there are four different objectives to be achieved. It is important to realize that the drug therapy directed to meet one therapeutic objective may aggravate other abnormalities.

Prevention of AV Reentrant Tachycardia. Goals of therapy here are suppression of atrial premature complexes, the most common beats precipitating AV reentrant tachycardia; and lengthening of the effective refractory period of the accessory pathway, thereby inhibiting retrograde penetration of the accessory pathway, the process necessary to complete an AV reentrant circuit. Procainamide (Pronestyl, Pronesty-SR, Procan SR), quinidine sulfate (Quinidex, Cin-Quin), quinidine gluconate (Quinaglute, Duraquin), and flecainide (Tambocor) are primary oral drugs for this purpose. Amiodarone (Cordarone) appears to be more effective but may have more serious side effects than procainamide or quinidine (see Table 15–16–2).

Termination of AV Reentrant Tachycardia. Hemodynamically poorly tolerated AV reentrant tachycardia should be promptly cardioverted by direct-current countershock after an adequate level of sedation is achieved. AV reentrant tachycardia that is hemodynamically well tolerated, however, can be treated with vagal maneuvers and/or drugs. Any or all the vagal maneuvers (Valsalva maneuver, squatting, activating the gag reflex, drinking cold water) should be tried before drugs. If vagal maneuvers are unsuccessful, drugs that lengthen the refractory period and/or suppress conduction at some segments of the AV reentrant circuit and make continuation of the circus movement along the reentrant circuit impossible may be used. These include adenosine (Adenocard), verapamil (Calan, Isoptin), metoprolol (Lopressor), and procainamide, and they should usually be given intravenously (see Table 15–16–2). See Drug Therapy of Supraventricular Tachycardias in Chapter 15–12 for the intravenous use of adenosine.

Termination of Atrial Fibrillation or Flutter. Direct-current countershock should be promptly administered for hemodynamically poorly tolerated atrial fibrillation or flutter (see Chapters 15–13 and 15–14). If the arrhythmia is hemodynamically well tolerated, it can be treated by either direct-current countershock or intravenously administered drugs (procainamide) (see Table 15–16–2). Digitalis and verapamil are contraindicated.

Prevention of Atrial Fibrillation or Flutter. Quinidine sulfate or quinidine gluconate is commonly used (see Chapters 15–13 and 15–14). If quinidine is not tolerated because of side effects or is not effective, procainamide or flecainide may be used. Amiodarone is effective but may cause more serious side effects than other commonly used antiarrhythmic agents (see Table 15–16–2). Cardiac glycosides and verapamil should be avoided because these drugs may further shorten the accessory pathway's antegrade refractory period, risking acceleration of the ventricular responses in atrial fibrillation, precipitation of ventricular fibrillation, and death.

Radiofrequency catheter ablation of the accessory pathway(s) should be considered for the following patients, especially if they are relatively young: patients whose atrial fibrillation has deteriorated to ventricular fibrillation, patients with incapacitating recurrent AV reentrant tachycardia despite optimal drug therapy, and patients with uncontrollably rapid ventricular response in the presence of atrial fibrillation despite drug therapy. The procedure is successful in about 90% of the patients, with a serious complication rate of around 2 to 3%.

FOLLOW-UP

At the beginning, the patient should be reassured that the complications of this syndrome, for example, tachyarrhythmias, are usually prevented by drugs, even though the abnormal anatomic substrate is unchanged. Moreover, the patient should be told that a diagnostic or therapeutic electrophysiologic test may be necessary in some patients and that occasional patients may require or benefit from radiofrequency ablation of the accessory pathway(s), which is usually successful and obviates further drug therapy.

Patients should be educated to remain as calm as possible during tachyarrhythmias. The physician should teach the patient various vagal maneuvers, as timely and proper application of these maneuvers by patients frequently terminates tachycardia and precludes hospital visits. If tachycardia recurs, however, the physician should be contacted for further adjustment in the therapy. Many patients can precisely document the exact onset and cessation of their tachycardia, and patients should be encouraged to keep a diary of these events while drugs are being adjusted. This simple record keeping can occasionally circumvent the need for ambulatory electrocardiographic recordings.

Patients with no or rare episodes of tachyarrhythmia can be seen about yearly, and patients with more frequent episodes should be seen every 3 to 6 months. The frequency, duration, and associated symptoms of the tachycardias should be assessed, and adverse drug effects should be evaluated. A 12-lead electrocardiogram should be recorded at each visit; it should be analyzed for preexcitation pattern, AV reentrant tachycardia, and electrocardiographic manifestations of drug toxicity.

The patient should be seen promptly if syncope, dizziness, increasing frequency of tachyarrhythmia, or significant drug side effects occur.

DISCUSSION
Prevalence and Incidence

The preexcitation syndromes have a prevalence of about 2 per 1000, and as such, they constitute one of the more common forms of congenital heart disease.

Related Basic Science

The mechanisms of AV reentrant tachycardia, the most common complicating arrhythmia of Wolff–Parkinson–White syndrome, are now well delineated. The electrical properties of the Kent bundles in Wolff–Parkinson–White syndrome differ from those of the normal AV node in that these bundles conduct faster, but their recovery takes longer than the AV node. This forms the basis for the AV reentrant

tachycardia. As discussed under Plans, Diagnostic, atrial premature contractions are conducted very slowly through the AV node but are transmitted quickly through the Kent bundle (a unique characteristic of the Kent bundle fibers, in that conduction velocity is either not dependent on or only minimally dependent on excitation frequency). An atrial premature complex, therefore, may be accompanied by a large delta wave. When the atrial premature complex occurs even more prematurely, antegrade conduction through the Kent bundle may be blocked due to its relatively long refractory period, causing an abrupt loss of the delta wave; however, the atrial premature complex may still be conducted through the AV node, at an extremely depressed conduction velocity, eventually reaching and depolarizing the ventricles, with a prolonged PR interval. The ventricular activation wave front may then retrogradely enter the Kent bundle and may be conducted to the atrial end of the Kent bundle, thus activating the atrium. This allows the establishment of a reentrant tachycardia, the impulse traveling through the atria, normal AV conduction system (including the AV node), ventricles, and Kent bundle. Then AV reentrant tachycardia is no more than a continuous encirclement of an impulse along this circuit, usually with an antegrade conduction through the normal AV conduction system and a retrograde conduction through the Kent bundle (orthodromic AV reentrant tachycardia). Each component of the reentrant circuit is essential for the maintenance of the AV reentrant tachycardia. Therefore, in a patient with supraventricular tachycardia of unknown etiology, persistence of the atrial tachycardia in the face of vagally induced second-degree or transient third-degree AV block argues against Wolff–Parkinson–White syndrome as its cause and usually favors other mechanisms (see Chapter 15–12).

Natural History and Its Modification with Treatment

The anomalous muscular band of the preexcitation syndrome is a congenital malformation, and the typical electrocardiographic pattern of the preexcitation and its tachyarrhythmic complications may appear at any stage of life.

Prevention

No measures for preventing preexcitation syndromes are currently available; however, attacks of various tachycardias mediated by the accessory pathway may be reduced to some extent by such lifestyle modification as quitting smoking, reducing coffee and caffeine intake, avoiding a hectic lifestyle, and physical conditioning.

Cost Containment

As described above, ventricular fibrillation and recurrent AV reentrant tachycardia can be complications of the preexcitation syndrome; however, exact frequencies of these life-threatening or incapacitating tachycardias are currently not known. Because of the potential for life-threatening arrhythmia, patients strongly suspected of having preexcitation syndromes, especially Wolff–Parkinson–White syndrome, on their 12-lead electrocardiogram or patients with recurrent supraventricular tachycardia of uncertain etiology should usually be referred to a cardiologist experienced with the diagnosis and therapy of these disorders. Effective screening and therapy offer the best hope of avoiding life-threatening arrhythmias and improving quality of life. It is not currently certain whether the preceding approach can reduce the overall frequency of emergency department visits or hospitalization.

The success rate of radiofrequency ablation therapy is around 90% and it is considered to be cost effective over lifelong drug therapy, especially in patients who have experienced life-threatening cardiac arrhythmias or have had frequent symptomatic tachyarrhythmias. The total cost of the ablative procedure ranges from $12,000 to $18,000.

REFERENCES

American College of Cardiology Cardiovascular Technology Assessment Committee: Fisher JD, Cain ME, Ferdinand KC, et al. Catheter ablation for cardiac arrhythmias: Clinical applications, personnel and facilities. J Am Coll Cardiol 1994;24:828.
Buitleir MD, Bove EL, Schmaltz S, et al. Cost of catheter versus surgical ablation in the Wolff–Parkinson–White syndrome. Am J Cardiol 1990;66:189.

Gallagher JJ. Supraventricular tachycardia with reentry in accessory pathways. In: Kastor JA, Arrhythmias. Philadelphia: Saunders, 1994:262.

Jackman WM, Wang X, Friday KJ, et al. Catheter ablation of accessory atrioventricular pathways (Wolff–Parkinson–White syndrome) by radiofrequency current. N Engl J Med 1991;324:1605.

Lown B, Ganong WF, Levine SA. The syndrome of short PR interval, normal QRS complex and paroxysmal rapid heart action. Circulation 1952;5:693.

Wolff L, Parkinson J, White PD. Bundle-branch block with short PR interval in healthy young people prone to paroxysmal tachycardia. Am Heart J 1930;5:685.

CHAPTER 15–16

Atrioventricular Block (First-Degree Heart Block)

Toshio Akiyama, M.D.

DEFINITION

Atrioventricular (AV) block refers to abnormally slow conduction of regular atrial impulses to the ventricles. This may take the form of prolonged conduction time (first-degree AV block), intermittent failure to conduct (Mobitz type I or Wenckebach second-degree AV block and Mobitz type II second-degree AV block), or complete failure to conduct any atrial impulses (complete heart block or third-degree AV block). This chapter focuses on first-degree AV block. The next three chapters explore higher degrees of AV block as defined above.

First-degree AV block is an electrocardiographic diagnosis defined by the presence in the adult of a PR interval greater than 0.20 second for a regular atrial impulse. In extreme cases, the PR interval may extend beyond 0.6 second.

First-degree AV block and Wenckebach AV block appear to be closely related: When serious tachycardia or enhanced vagal tone develops first-degree AV block may be transformed into Wenckebach AV block. When the PR interval is prolonged, the delay is most commonly in the AV node and less commonly in both right and left bundles. This is especially the case if the PR interval is lengthened beyond 0.30 second.

The term *AV block* does not imply that all conduction abnormalities occur in the AV node. Indeed, the four chapters on AV block develop the ideas that conduction abnormalities can occur anywhere in the specialized conduction system, that the site of abnormal conduction can most often be deduced from the clinical setting and the surface electrocardiogram, and that the site of conduction block usually determines prognosis.

ETIOLOGY

The clinical settings in which AV conduction blocks of all degrees occur are listed in Table 15–16–1. The most common causes of acute first-degree AV block are acute inferior myocardial infarction, digitalis intoxication, and administration of beta blockers and/or calcium channel blockers.

CRITERIA FOR DIAGNOSIS

Suggestive

First-degree AV block should be suspected when three venous waveforms of *a*, *c*, and *v* waves are easily separable from each other, the first heat sounds are soft, and the summation gallop is audible. Indeed, it is often possible to recognize prolonged ac intervals in a patient with first-degree AV block.

Definitive

The presence on the electrocardiogram of a PR interval greater than 0.20 second with 1:1 conduction of regular atrial impulse to the ventricles is sufficient to establish the diagnosis of first-degree AV block.

CLINICAL MANIFESTATIONS

Subjective

No specific symptoms are associated with first-degree AV block.

Objective

Physical Examination

The presence of first-degree AV block often makes it relatively easy to recognize the *a* wave and estimate the *ac* interval in the jugular venous waveform. Atrial contraction relatively early in ventricular diastole due to first-degree AV block may augment the early diastolic rapid filling of the ventricle, generating a summation gallop. The relatively closed position of the mitral leaflets at the onset of ventricular systole also results in a diminished intensity of the first heart sound. When *a* waves are easily identifiable, *ac* intervals appear to be prolonged, the summation gallop is audible, and the first heart sound is faint, the physician should suspect the presence of first-degree AV block.

Routine Laboratory Abnormalities

The diagnosis is usually established from electrocardiographic findings. In the presence of regular atrial rhythm, each P wave is followed

TABLE 15–16–1. CAUSES OF ATRIOVENTRICULAR CONDUCTION BLOCK

Structural or infiltrative diseases	Pharmacologic/metabolic/neurohumoral
Chronic ischemic heart disease	Propranolol (Inderal) and other beta blockers
Acute myocardial infarction	Calcium channel blockers, especially verapamil (Calan, Isoptin) and
Degenerative or idiopathic, including Lenegre's disease and old age	diltiazem (Cardizem)
Valvular heart disease, especially calcific aortic or mitral disease in	Digoxin (Lanoxin)
rheumatic heart disease or sclerosis (Lev's disease)	Certain antiarrhythmic agents, especially quinidine, flecainide (Tambocor),
Postoperative	encainide (Enkaid), amiodarone (Cardarone), and propafenone
Congenital heart disease	(Rythmol)
Uncommon infiltrative diseases, e.g., sarcoidosis, amyloid syphilitic	Enhanced vagal tone
gumma, neoplasm	Hyperkalemia
Infectious diseases, especially acute rheumatic fever, myocarditis, Lyme disease,	Uremia
endocarditis with abscess formation, diphtheria, and almost any acute	
systemic infectious disease	
Connective tissue disorders	

by a QRS complex with a constant prolonged PR interval over 0.20 second.

PLANS

Diagnostic

Differential Diagnosis

Two conditions under which the PR interval may be transiently lengthened need to be recognized and should not be diagnosed as first-degree AV block: First, atrial premature complexes may be conducted slowly through the AV node (prolonged PR interval) or may be blocked within the AV node if the impulse arrives during the relative refractory period (the former) or during the absolute refractory period (the latter) of the AV node. Second, the sinus impulse occurring immediately following a ventricular premature complex may be conducted with the prolonged PR interval or may be blocked. This results from retrograde activation of the ventricular premature complex (VPC) to the AV node, rendering the AV node partially or totally refractory to the subsequent sinus impulse (concealed retrograde conduction to the AV node from a ventricular premature complex).

Diagnostic Options and Recommended Approach

No specific diagnostic studies other than the electrocardiogram and rhythm strip are required to establish the diagnosis. Regular atrial impulses are conducted with PR intervals greater than 0.20 second (Figure 15–16–1). In the presence of sinus arrhythmia, the PR interval may slightly fluctuate.

Therapeutic

Generally, for isolated first-degree AV block, no specific therapy is indicated irrespective of etiology. Therapy should be directed at the underlying disease process. First-degree AV block may be seen with therapeutic levels of digoxin (Lanoxin), although the development of first-degree AV block or an increasing PR interval should alert the clinician to the possibility of impending toxic levels. First-degree AV block is seen frequently in patients treated with flecainide (Tambocor) or amiodarone (Cordarone) and is *not* an indication to decrease dosage or stop therapy (Table 15–16–2).

FOLLOW-UP

In newly acquired first-degree AV block without identifiable cause, the patient should be followed for possible progression to higher degrees of AV block. Specifically, the patient should be told that there is a minor electrocardiographic abnormality that indicates that conduction of electrical impulses in the heart is slower than normal. The patient should be instructed to inform the physician of any episodes of fainting or lightheadedness. Follow-up is also dictated by the underlying disease process. In patients with newly acquired first-degree AV block without

obvious cause, a follow-up visit in 6 months would be appropriate, at which time the patient should be asked specifically about the symptoms listed above and a repeat electrocardiogram and rhythm strip should be performed.

DISCUSSION

Prevalence and Incidence

The true incidence and prevalence of first-degree AV block in the general population is unknown. In a selected population of approximately 122,000 healthy male U.S. Air Force flying personnel, mostly under the age of 45, the incidence of first-degree AV block was about 0.65% (Hiss and Lamb, 1962). In contrast, in the elderly population, the incidence of first-degree AV block ranges from 2% in an otherwise healthy ambulatory population to as high as 16% in centenarians. It should be emphasized that occurrence of first-degree AV block, sinus bradycardia, or Wenckebach AV block is occasionally noted in highly trained athletes (Viitasalo et al., 1982).

Related Basic Science

We review below the electrophysiology of impulse conduction in the heart. Electrical impulses normally arise from the spontaneously depolarizing pacemaker cells of the sinoatrial (SA) node. These impulses are conducted to the surrounding atrial myocardium to initiate atrial mechanical systole. Intraatrial conduction from the SA to the AV node is rapid, via specialized internodal (SA–AV) conduction pathways and/or via atrial myocardial cells. Conduction in the AV node is extremely slow (1–5 cm/s) and accounts for most of the delay between atrial activation and the onset of ventricular activation, which corresponds to the PR segment. Once an impulse has traversed the AV node, it enters the bundle of His, which bifurcates into the right and left bundles. The right bundle traverses as a long thin bundle along the right side of the interventricular septum, giving off a large branch across the right ventricular apex by way of the moderator band. The left bundle soon after its origin from the bundle of His fans out extensively along the left side of the interventricular septum. Although the left bundle does not anatomically bifurcate, it functions as if it were made of two separate fascicles (i.e., anterior and posterior fascicles) because of their different blood supplies (see Table 15–17–1). Conduction of an impulse through the Purkinje fibers of the His bundle system is fast (1–5 m/s). Thus, in bundle of His electrocardiography, the AH interval (impulse transmission from atrium to the bundle of His) is generally 60 to 125 milliseconds, and the HV interval (impulse transmission from the bundle of His to the ventricle) is 35 to 55 milliseconds. The PR interval corresponds to the sum of the AH and HV intervals.

In the case of first-degree AV block, the majority of the AV conduction delay represented as the lengthened PR interval is attributable to slow conduction through the AV node. The slow conduction within the AV node results from a combination of two factors: reduction in amplitude of the AV nodal action potential (or in slow channel current), and abnormal prolongation in the relative refractory period of the AV node. Uncommon causes of first-degree AV block not localized to the AV node have been documented in the His bundle and in symmetric conduction delays simultaneously in the right and left main bundles.

Natural History and Its Modification with Treatment

The natural history of first-degree AV block in acute myocardial infarction is of particular interest. In one series of 446 patients with acute myocardial infarction studied by Brown et al. (1969), 27 patients presented with or developed first-degree AV block. In 10 of these, this did not progress to more advanced heart block, in 8 there was progression to second-degree AV block, and in 9 complete heart block ultimately developed. Progression to higher degrees of AV block did not depend on the site of infarction.

Prevention

No specific preventive measures are available unless first-degree AV block is caused by drugs or metabolic abnormalities.

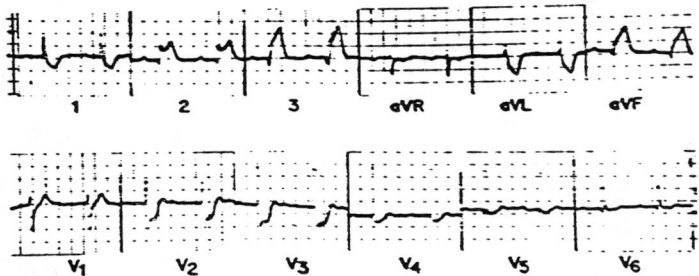

Figure 15–16–1. First-degree atrioventricular block in a patient with acute inferoposterior myocardial infarction. The PR interval is prolonged to 0.32 second in the presence of normal sinus rhythm at 66 beats/min. Evolving inferoposterior myocardial infarction is suggested by the ST-segment elevation and abnormal Q waves in leads 2, 3 and a V_F, and by ST depression and borderline prominent R wave in leads V_2 and V_3.

TABLE 15–16–2. DRUGS FOR ARRHYTHMIA AND ATRIOVENTRICULAR BLOCK

Generic name	Lidocaine	Quinidine	Procainamide	Moricizine

Product name	Xylocaine	Sulfate
		    Quinidex
		    Cin-Quin
		Gluconate
		    Duraquin
		    Quinaglute
			Procan SR
			
			Pronestyl
			Pronestyl-SR
				Ethmozine

Clinical indications	VD Some SVTs	VD SVTs	VD SVTs	VT, VF

Mechanism of action	↓ Purkinje excitability
	↑ VF threshold
	↓ APD (narrow QT)
	↓ TD
		Direct membrane effects and
		    indirect effects (atropine-like
		    effects and alpha-adrenergic
		    blockade)
		↓ Automatic rate of Purkinje
		↓ Conduction (↑ QRS width)
		↑ Refractory period (↑ QT)
		↓ Excitability (↑ QRS)
			Similar to quinidine,
			    though a weaker vagolytic
			    action and no alpha-
			    adrenergic blockade
			    (↑ QRS width, ↑ QT)
				↓ AP upstroke (↑ QRS width),
				    AV nodal and Purkinje conduction
				    (↑, PR) no change in JT

Metabolism and excretion	Hepatic	Hepatic and renal	Hepatic and renal	Hepatic and renal
Half-life	After a single IV dose, 10 min After sustained IV use, 2 h	After oral dose, 5 h	3 h NAPA longer half-life	2–6 h

Side effects*	Common in elderly or CHF
	CNS effects (drowsiness,
	    disorientation, slurred
	    speech, paresthesias,
	    convulsion)
		Frequent
		Cardiac (↑ QRS, ↑ QT,
		    depression of myocardial
		    contractility, syncope,
		    torsade)
		Cinchonism (tinnitus,
		    hearing loss, blurred vision)
			Drug induced lupus
			    (25–30%)
			Cardiovascular effects
			    similar to quinidine
			GI side effects
			Proarrhythmia
				Dizziness, nausea, headache, fatigue,
				    palpitations, dyspnea

Contraindications†		LVF ↑ QT	LVF ↑ QT	AV blocks (second or third degree)

IV dosage‡	A loading dose of 50–100
	    mg/2–3 min and this
	    dose may be repeated
	    in 5 min (max 300 mg in
	    1-h period); then, 1–4
	    mg/min
		Not recommended	25–100 mg/min q5min
			    until arrhythmia
			    suppression or side
			    effects (max 1 g);
			    maintenance 2–4 mg/min	

Oral dosage‡		Sulfate: 200–400 mg q6h
		
		Gluconate: 324 mg q8h
			250–1000 mg q3–6h (occ.
			    1–1.5 g q4–6h); also
			    time-release (Pronestyl
			    SR, Procan SR) 250–
			    1000 mg q6–8h
				200, 250, or 300 mg q8h

↑, increase or enhance; ↓, decrease or depress; AF, atrial fibrillation and flutter; APD, action potential duration; AV, atrioventricular; AVRT, atrioventricular reentrant tachycardia; AVNRT, atrioventricular nodal reentrant tachycardia; CNS, central nervous system; GI gastrointestinal; LVF, left ventricular failure; post-MI, post-myocardial infarction; SB, sinus bradycardia; SR, sinus rate; SSS, sick sinus syndrome; SVTs, supraventricular tachycardias; VD, ventricular dysrhythmia (VPCs, VT, VF); VF, ventricular fibrillation; VPCs, ventricular premature complexes; VTs, ventricular tachycardias; WPW, Wolff–Parkinson–White syndrome, including other preexcitation syndromes; TD, temporal dispersion; Torsade, Torsade de pointes; NAPA, N-acetylprocainamide; ↑ QT, prolonged QT.

Verapamil	Propranolol	Disopyramide	Bretylium tosylate	Adenosine
Calan, Isoptin, Verapamil HCl, Verelan	Inderal	Norpace	Bretylol	Adenocard
Termination of SVT ↓ Ventricular rate in SVT including AF	Same as for verapamil; digitoxic tachyarrhythmias; thyrotoxic tachyarrhythmias	VD SVTs	Life-threatening ventricular arrhythmias (VF, VT)	Termination and not prevention of AVNRT and AVRT
Slow Ca channel blocker (↑ PR, ↓ SR) Reduction in myocardial contractility and afterload	Beta-adrenergic receptor blocking (↓ SR, ↑ PR) ? Direct myocardial membrane (quinidine-like effects)	Similar to procainamide and quinidine: ↓ AP upstroke and ↑ APD (↑ QRS width, ↑ QT)	Chemical sympathectomy	↓ AV nodal conduction and sinus mode automaticity, ↓ peripheral arterial resistance
Renal	Hepatic	Renal	Renal	Vascular endothelial cells and erythrocytes
IV: 2–5 h PO: 3–7 h (first dose) 5–12 h (repeat doses)	IV: 2–3 h PO: 3–6 h	PO: 4–10 h (7 h)	IV: 8 h	< 10 s
Hypotension AV block	AV block, LVF, hypotension, bronchospasm	Anticholinergic activity (0.06% of atropine), urinary retention, negative inotropism, torsade	Postural hypotension	Facial flushing, dyspnea, chest pressure, asystole
Severe hypotension or cardiogenic shock or LVF, AV blocks, SSS, propranolol patients	Bronchial asthma, sinus bradycardia, AV blocks, LVF, cardiogenic shock	Urinary retention, cardiogenic shock, AV blocks, known hypersensitivity ↑ QT		AV blocks (second or third degree), SSS
5–10 mg over 1–2 min; may repeat 10 mg 15–30 min after first dose	A total of 0.05–0.1 mg/kg body weight at 0.25 mg/min		IV: 5–10 mg/kg body weight either rapidly or over 10 min; repeat q6h or constant infusion of 1–2 mg/min	Rapid bolus injection of 6 mg, followed by rapid flush; in 1–2 min, 12 mg may be given if the first dose is ineffective
80 mg tid or qid up to 120 mg qid	10–30 mg tid or qid	100–200 mg qid after initial loading dose of 300 mg		

*Most antiarrhythmics listed here have proarrhythmic side effects.

†Drugs are contraindicated when hypersensitivity to the drugs exist. Also, in the presence of AV blocks or bundle-branch block, most of these drugs are either contraindicated or should be used cautiously.

‡Maintenance dosage should be reduced in patients with impaired renal or hepatic function.

(continued)

TABLE 15–16–2. (*Continued*)

Generic name	Tocainide	Mexiletine	Flecainide	Propafenone
Product name	Tonocard	Mexitil	Tombocor	Rythmol
Clinical indications	Similar to lidocaine	VD	VT, VF, SVTs	VT, VF
Mechanism of action	Similar to lidocaine	Similar to lidocaine	↓ Conduction in all parts of heart (↑ PR, ↑ QRS width) Slight ↑ QT (no change in JT interval)	Similar to flecainide; also weakly beta-sympatholytic
Metabolism and excretion	Renal and hepatic	Mostly hepatic; some renal (10%)	Renal and hepatic	Hepatic and renal
Half-life	After oral dose, 13 h	After oral dose, 10–12 h	After oral dose, 20 h	2–10 h 10–32 h
Side effects*	Frequent CNS (lighheaded-ness, vertigo, tremor) GI (nausea, vomiting) Pulmonary fibrosis	GI (nausea, vomiting; heartburn), CNS (lighthead-edness, tremor, nervousness, coordination difficulties)	CNS (dizziness, visual disturbance) GI (nausea) Negative inotropism Proarrhythmia	Dizziness, unusual taste, nausea, vomiting, constipation, proarrhythmic
Contraindications†		Second- and third-degree AV blocks, cardiogenic shock	AV blocks, bifascicular blocks Post-MI VPCs	Bronchial asthma, LVF, AV block, SSS Post-MI VPCs
IV dosage‡	§	§	§	
Oral dosage‡	200–800 mg q8h	200–300 mg q8h May be tried with quinidine	100–200 mg q12h	150–300 mg q8h

‖Only for patients with SVT causing disabling symptoms and with no structural heart disease.
§Please note that this drug is only for oral dosages and *not* for IV dosages.

Cost Containment

Extensive evaluation of patients with isolated first-degree AV block is not warranted. Monitoring PR-interval prolongation in patients treated with digoxin can be a useful adjunct in guiding digoxin therapy and avoiding the morbidity and potential cost of hospitalization for digitalis intoxication.

REFERENCES

Brown RW, Hunt D, Sloman JG. The natural history of atrioventricular conduction defects in acute myocardial infarction. Am Heart J 1969;78:460.

Chou TC. Atrioventricular block: Concealed conduction. In: Chou TC, ed. Electrocardiography in clinical practice. Philadelphia: Saunders, 1991:411.

Davies MJ. Pathology of conducting tissue of the heart. London: Butterworth, 1971.

Hiss RG, Lamb LE. Electrocardiographic findings in 122,043 individuals. Circulation 1962;25:947.

Josephson ME, Seides SF. Atrioventricular conduction. In: Josephson ME. Seides SF, eds. Clinical cardiac electrophysiology. Philadelphia: Lea & Febiger, 1979:79.

Pick A, Langendorf R. Atrioventricular and intraventricular block. In: Pick A, Langendorf R, eds. Interpretation of complex arrhythmias. Philadelphia: Lea & Febiger, 1979:217.

Viitasalo MT, Kala R, Eisabo A. Ambulatory electrocardiographic recording in endurance athletes. Br Heart J 1982;47:213.

Wakida Y, Okamota Y, Iwa T, et al. Arrhythmias in centenarians. PACE 1994;17:2217.

Amiodarone	D,L-Sotalol	Atropine	Edrophonium	Digoxin
Cordarone	Betapace		Tensilon	Lanoxin
VD, SVTs, AF, WPW	VTs, VF	SB AV blocks	SVTs	SVTs, AF
↓ Conduction and ↑ refractoriness in all parts of heart (↑ PR, ↑QRS width, ↑ QT) ↓ SR	↑ Refractoriness in all parts of heart ↑ QT, ↓ SR, ↑ PR Beta-adrenergic receptor blocking	Muscarinic cholinergic blocking agents (↑ SR, ↓ PR)	Cholinergic (anticholinesterase)	Na, K-ATP use, indirect effects via autonomic system (↑ PR, ↓ SR)
Hepatic and renal	Renal, not metabolized		Renal	Renal and slight hepatic
25 (10–45) days	12 h		Effects appear within 60 s and last 10 min	1–7 d
Pulmonary fibrosis, photosensitivity, skin discoloration, abnormal liver function, hyperthyroid, hypothyroid, corneal deposits, torsade Proarrhythmia	Torsade, ↑ QT LVF Bronchospasm SB, AV block	Dryness of mouth, blurring of vision, difficulty in speech and swallowing, restlessness, hallucinations	Transient bradycardia, increased lacrimation, increased bronchial secretion, hypotension	GI (anorexia, nausea, vomiting), CNS (yellow vision), cardiac (AV blocks, arrhythmias)
↓ Pulmonary diffusion capacity, old age, post-MI VPCs ↑ QT §	Previous Torsade ↑ QT LVF Bronchial asthma SB, AV block ↑ QT §	0.5–1.0 mg q2h	Mechanical urinary or intestinal obstruction, bronchial asthma 5 mg; if not successful, an additional dose of 10 mg	AV blocks, hypokalemia 0.5 mg; then 0.25 mg q2–6h until a total dose of 1.0–1.5 mg
Loading with 600–1000 mg qd for 7–10 d; maintenance 100–400 mg qd	80–160 mg PO bid ↑ Dosing interval to 24–48 h in renal failure			Loading with 0.5–0.75 mg, followed by 0.25–0.50 mg q4–8h for a total dose of 1.0–1.75 mg; maintenance 0.125–0.5 mg qd

CHAPTER 15–17

Wenckebach Atrioventricular Block

Toshio Akiyama, M.D.

DEFINITION

Wenckebach atrioventricular (AV) block, also referred to as Mobitz type I AV block, is one of the two forms of second-degree AV block defined by intermittent failure of conduction of regular atrial impulses to the ventricles. In the Wenckebach phenomenon, conduction of atrial impulse to the ventricles lengthens progressively, finally culminating in nonconduction of the terminal atrial impulse. The other type of second-degree AV block, Mobitz type II second-degree AV block, is characterized by intermittent failure to conduct atrial impulses without preceding PR prolongation. Classic electrocardiographic features of Wenckebach second-degree AV block are as follows:

- There is a grouped beating pattern, terminated by a nonconducted P wave. The repeating unit is referred to as a Wenckebach period or cycle. In the Wenckebach period, the AV conduction ratio varies, but commonly it is 4:3 or 3:2, with the first number referring to the number of P waves and the second referring to the number of ventricular complexes.
- There is gradual PR prolongation on successive beats prior to the nonconducted P wave.
- The increment in PR lengthening is greatest between the first and second conducted beats of the Wenckebach period.
- There is RP–PR reciprocity, meaning that the shorter the interval between the preceding R wave and the P wave of the next beat, the longer is the following PR interval, and vice versa.
- There is progressive shortening of the RR interval through the Wenckebach period owing to progressive decreases in the absolute increment in AV conduction time. The longest RR interval, which contains a nonconducted P wave, is less than twice the shortest RR interval, which is usually the RR interval immediately before the nonconducted P wave.
- The QRS complex is usually narrow (normal intraventricular conduction) unless there is preexisting bundle-branch block.

An example of typical Wenckebach second-degree AV block is shown in Figure 15–17–1. Although the classic features of Wenckebach AV block are outlined above and illustrated in Figure 15–17–1, as many as two thirds of what appear to be cases of Wenckebach AV block and not Mobitz type II AV block may not have these "typical" features of Wenckebach AV block. Some of these are discussed under Plans, Diagnostic.

ETIOLOGY

Wenckebach AV block can occur as a result of most of the etiologies listed in Table 15–16–1. Wenckebach AV block most commonly is observed in acute inferior myocardial infarction, pharmacologic or toxic

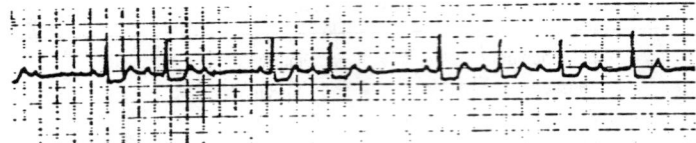

Figure 15–17–1. Wenckebach atrioventricular block recorded from a 68-year-old man with acute inferior myocardial infarction. In this monitor strip, sinus rate is relatively stable at 85 beats/min. There is intermittent failure of atrioventricular conduction preceded by gradual prolongation in the PR interval. The atrioventricular conduction ratio is 3:2 for the first two cycles and 5:4 for the last cycle (the last P wave falling on the T wave of the last QRS complex was not conducted).

dosage of various cardiac drugs (digitalis, beta blockers, calcium blockers, amiodarone), electrolyte disturbances, enhanced vagal tone, and a wide variety of acute febrile illnesses. The patient with this rhythm is usually asymptomatic. In most circumstances, this conduction disturbance is not associated with significant hemodynamic compromise and generally has a benign prognosis.

CRITERIA FOR DIAGNOSIS
Suggestive

If in a bradycardiac patient, group beating exists with occasional long pauses, the QRS complexes are narrowed, and there are no cannon a waves in the jugular vein, then Wenckebach AV block is usually the underlying mechanism. In the patient with acute inferior myocardial infarction, a pulse deficit occurring every few beats in the face of a relatively slow pulse rate and absent cannon a waves suggests the presence of Wenckebach AV block.

Definitive

Wenckebach second-degree AV block is diagnosed when on the electrocardiogram intermittent failure of regular atrial impulses occurs after progressive lengthening in the PR intervals as detailed under Definition.

CLINICAL MANIFESTATIONS
Subjective

Generally, the patient is asymptomatic from Wenckebach AV block per se. Symptoms such as lightheadedness, weakness, and syncope can occur if the ventricular response is very slow (usually below 45 beats/min) and cardiac output is reduced. These circumstances are unusual, although they can occur in the setting of acute inferior myocardial infarction, especially if the infarction is extensive (inferoposterior myocardial infarction with right ventricular extension).

Objective
Physical Examination

The first clue among physical findings is the presence by auscultation or palpation of the pulse of a grouped beating pattern. In addition, after the dropped beat, the first heart sound is loudest, with progressive diminution as the PR interval lengthens. A few unique cycle changes by auscultation occur in Wenckebach AV block: the first heart sound is the loudest for the first beat and then it becomes progressively fainter, and either the fourth heart sound becomes progressively louder or summation gallop appears toward the last beats of the cycle. Classically, Wenckebach described this pattern of AV conduction abnormality by examination of the *a, c,* and *v* waves in the jugular venous pulse. With typical Wenckebach conduction, a progressively longer *ac* interval would be expected, culminating in an *a* wave only, signaling a dropped ventricular beat. Although physical findings are useful, a surface electrocardiogram usually provides a rapid and definitive diagnosis.

Routine Laboratory Abnormalities

An electrocardiogram rhythm strip is sufficient to elicit the Wenckebach periodicity as outlined under Definition. Other routine laboratory test results are usually normal.

PLANS
Diagnostic
Differential Diagnosis

Differential diagnosis of Wenckebach AV block includes any group beating such as Mobitz type II AV block, intermittent sinoatrial exit block, frequent atrial premature complexes frequent ventricular premature complexes, and atrial fibrillation. Recognition of the Wenckebach periodicity in the presence of regular atrial rhythm separates Wenckebach AV block from these conditions with group beating.

Diagnostic Options and Recommended Approach

When the classic electrocardiographic features of Wenckebach AV block, as listed under Definition, are present, a definitive diagnosis is easily made. Unfortunately, atypical patterns of Wenckebach conduction may be the rule rather than the exception, especially with AV conduction ratios exceeding 4:3. In patterns of atypical Wenckebach conduction, there is an increase in the PR interval from one beat to any subsequent conducted beat prior to a nonconducted P wave. Beyond this broad definition, none of the other typical features of Wenckebach periods may be present. Specifically, the largest PR increment may not occur between the first and second conducted beats, and the longest PR interval may not be present in the last beat prior to failure of conduction. Prognosis of the patient with atypical Wenckebach AV conduction is not different from that with the typical pattern.

Diagnostic difficulty is encountered in discriminating Wenckebach AV block from Mobitz type II AV block if only a 2:1 conduction ratio is present or if there is an escape AV junctional rhythm. Electrocardiographic and clinical features that can be used to help make this important distinction are discussed in Chapter 15–18.

Finally, AV conduction block occurring in the presence of relatively rapid atrial rate (sinus tachycardia or supraventricular tachycardia) may be a normal physiologic response of the AV node. For instance, most healthy elderly patients develop Wenckebach AV block during rapid atrial pacing above 150 beats/min. These rhythms should not be misinterpreted as denoting the presence of pathologic AV block.

Therapeutic

Drugs known to prolong AV conduction time, such as digitalis, beta blockers, verapamil, and amiodarone should be discontinued or their doses should be reduced (see Table 15–16–2).

Wenckebach AV block usually does not require specific therapy. In fact, Wenckebach AV block should be treated only if there are symptoms or signs of reduced cardiac output. Wenckebach AV block is a conduction abnormality most often localized to the AV node. As such, AV nodal conduction can be enhanced and Wenckebach AV conduction can be abolished by an intravenous dose of atropine (Donnatal, 0.5 mg). An additional dose of 0.5 mg may be given if the initial dose is ineffective. Although not common, there may be a paradoxical worsening in AV conduction when sinus tachycardia occurs in response to atropine. Usually, in the setting of an acute inferior myocardial infarction, even if Wenckebach AV block may progress to complete heart block, it is associated with an adequate junctional escape rhythm (between 45 and 55 beats/min) and temporary transvenous pacing is not required. We do not recommend continued use of atropine beyond the first few hours because of the high incidence of side effects (disorientation, agitation, confusion) and loss of its efficacy with prolonged usage. In this situation, temporary transvenous ventricular pacing or temporary external pacing should be employed. Implantation of a permanent DDD pacemaker is indicated only if Wenckebach AV block with an extremely slow ventricular rate and a sign of depressed cardiac output persists beyond the first week of acute inferior myocardial infarction.

FOLLOW-UP

Generally, because Wenckebach AV block is transitory and asymptomatic, specific patient education is not required. If the patient is aware of palpitations or an irregular pulse, or notes an irregular rhythm on the monitor, he or she should be reassured that the abnormality is relatively common, usually transitory, and almost always benign. Even in the unusual cases where a temporary pacemaker is required, the patient should be reassured that few people require a permanent pacemaker for this condition.

Follow-up is determined by the underlying disease. In most cases, Wenckebach AV block is of very short duration; in the case of acute inferior myocardial infarction, it seldom persists past the first few days.

DISCUSSION

Prevalence and Incidence

The true incidence and prevalence of Wenckebach second-degree AV block in the general population are unknown. In a population of 122,043 healthy male U.S. Air Force personnel, the incidence was 0.3% (Hiss and Lamb, 1962). Wenckebach AV block or first-degree AV block along with sinus bradycardia is not uncommon among highly trained endurance athletes (long-distance runners, skiers, and basketball players). The incidence and natural history of this conduction abnormality, in the setting of acute inferior myocardial infarction, are of particular importance. In a large study of 884 patients with acute inferior infarctions reported in 1980 by Tans et al., approximately 11% developed Wenckebach second-degree AV block. In 59 of these patients it was preceded by first-degree AV block. In approximately half the patients, progression to third-degree AV block was noted with a median ventricular escape rate of 41 to 50 beats/min. Hospital mortality was significantly higher for those patients with second- or third-degree AV block (24 and 21%, respectively) than for those patients with no conduction abnormality or only first-degree AV block. These clinical findings are borne out in a number of other studies. It should be noted that death in patients with high-grade AV blocks (Wenckebach AV block and complete AV block) during acute inferior myocardial infarction is usually a consequence of their extensive myocardial infarctions and not of their high-grade AV blocks. As such, the high-grade AV blocks developing during acute myocardial infarction should be considered to be a marker for an extensive infarction.

Related Basic Science

The propensity for developing Wenckebach second-degree AV block in acute inferior myocardial infarction is readily understood by examining the blood supply of the specialized conduction system, as shown in Table 15–17–1, and by the pattern of innervation of the cardiac conduction system and ventricles. In 90% of patients, the AV nodal artery arises from the dominant right coronary artery. As a result, in inferior myocardial infarction with proximal occlusion of the right coronary artery, AV nodal ischemia occurs, although it generally does not progress to infarction. Another mechanism responsible for Wenckebach AV block in acute myocardial infarction is generally enhanced vagal tone, mediated by the Bezold–Jarisch reflex. Intracellular potassium and chemical mediators such as adenosine released from infarcting myocardial cells may also play a role in causing Wenckebach AV block in acute inferior myocardial infarction.

In a histologic study of 29 patients who died with acute myocardial infarction, in 21 of 24 with acute inferior infarction the proximal conduction system through the main bundles appeared normal or had only minimal focal necrosis (Sutton and Davies, 1968). In contrast, those with anterior infarction displayed necrosis of the distal bundle branches; this was also observed in 8 of 24 patients with acute inferior infarction. The His bundle and proximal main bundle branches more reliably receive a dual blood supply or are supplied solely be septal branches of the left anterior descending artery, and as a consequence, bundle-branch block or permanent AV block as a result of an inferior myocardial infarction is uncommon.

The electrophysiologic mechanisms responsible for Wenckebach second-degree AV block and Mobitz type II second-degree AV block have been poorly understood. A potential explanation was offered in 1979 by Pick and Langendorf, who proposed that these conduction disturbances are related to abnormal changes in the total duration of the refractory period, particularly in the duration of the relative refractory period of the cells at the site of block. In Wenckebach AV block, they propose that the relative refractory period may be prolonged, and thus as the first atrial impulse arrives at the anatomic site of conduction block, it falls in the relative refractory period of the previous beat with consequential decremental conduction and PR prolongation. On each successive beat, the atrial impulse occurs earlier in the relative refractory period and further PR prolongation occurs. Finally, an atrial impulse arrives during the absolute refractory period and fails to be conducted, terminating the Wenckebach period. In contrast, Mobitz type II AV block may represent a state of all-or-none conduction in the abnormal cells as a result of a very short or nonexistent relative refractory period. In this case, either the cells are completely refractory or completely recovered.

Natural History and Its Modification with Treatment

In the absence of acute inferior myocardial infarction or cardiac pump failure, Wenckebach AV block is usually a benign condition. Only when the ventricular rate becomes extremely slow (slower than 40–50 beats/min) or Wenckebach AV block develops in the presence of cardiac pump failure do symptoms or signs of reduced cardiac output appear.

Progression from Wenckebach AV block to third-degree AV block is not uncommon, especially during acute inferior myocardial infarction. Patients with acute inferior myocardial infarction developing high-degree AV block (including Wenckebach and third-degree AV blocks) have a higher mortality than those developing no high-degree AV block; however, deaths in these patients usually result from severe cardiac failure rather than from AV blocks. Wenckebach AV block following acute inferior myocardial infarction is replaced, most of the time before hospital discharge, by either normal AV conduction or first-degree AV block.

In relatively unusual patients with persistent Wenckebach AV block accompanied by decreased cardiac output, restoration of normal sequential AV contraction at a normal rate can be accomplished by implantation of a dual-chamber pacemaker, either a DDD or DDDR pacemaker.

Prevention

No specific measures are available for preventing this rhythm abnormality. In clinical practice, care should be taken to avoid drug-induced AV block, particularly that induced by digitalis intoxication, amiodarone (Cordarone), and concomitant use of digitalis, calcium channel blockers (especially verapamil), and beta blockers.

Cost Containment

As has already been emphasized, irrespective of the etiology, temporary or permanent pacing for Wenckebach AV block is rarely indicated. In the evaluation of patients with presyncope or syncope, detection of Wenckebach AV block alone is not sufficient to justify implantation of a permanent pacemaker unless symptoms are clearly associated with the Wenckebach periods.

TABLE 15–17–1. BLOOD SUPPLY OF THE SPECIALIZED CONDUCTING SYSTEM

Structure	Blood Supply
SA node	SA nodal artery: 55% RCA, 45% LCA
AV node	AV nodal artery: 90% RCA, 10% LCA
Bundle of His	Predominantly dual blood supply from AV nodal artery and first septal perforating branch of LAD
Proximal right bundle	AV nodal artery and septal branches in 50% and septal branches only in 40%
Anterior half of left bundle	AV nodal artery and septal branches in 40% and septal branches only in 50%
Posterior half of left bundle	AV nodal artery alone 50% and AV nodal artery and septal branches 40%

SA, sinoatrial; AV, atrioventricular; LAD, left anterior descending artery; LCA, left circumflex artery; RCA, right coronary artery.

REFERENCES

Berger PB, Ryan TJ. Inferior myocardial infarction: High-risk subgroups. Circulation 1990;81:401.

Crick SJ, Wharton J, Sheppard MN, et al. Innervation of the human conduction system: A quantitative immunohistochemical and histochemical study. Circulation 1994;89:1697.

Esente P, Giambartolomoi A, Gensini GG, Dator C. Coronary reperfusion and Bezold–Jarisch reflex (bradycardia and hypotension). Am J Cardiol 1983;52:221.

Hiss RG, Lamb LE. Electrocardiographic finding in 122,043 individuals. Circulation 1962;25:947.

Pick A, Langendorf R. Atrioventricular and intraventricular block. In: Pick A,

Langendorf R, eds. Interpretation of complex arrhythmias. Philadelphia: Lea & Febiger, 1979:217.

Sutton R, Davies M. The conduction system in acute myocardial infarction complicated by heart block. Circulation 1968;38:987.

Tans AC, Lie KI, Durrer D. Clinical setting and prognostic significance of high degree atrioventricular block in acute inferior myocardial infarction: A study of 144 patients. Am Heart J 1980;99:4.

Zeppilli P, Fenici R, Sassara M, et al. Wenckebach second degree AV block in top-ranking athletes: An old problem revisited. Am Heart J 1980;100:281.

CHAPTER 15–18

Mobitz Type II Atrioventricular Block

Toshio Akiyama, M.D.

DEFINITION

Mobitz Type II atrioventricular (AV) block can be diagnosed with certainty only when specific electrocardiographic abnormalities are evident. In contrast to Wenckebach second-degree AV block, Mobitz type II second-degree AV block is characterized by intermittent failure to conduct regularly occurring atrial impulses *without* PR prolongation in preceding beats. The site of Mobitz type II AV block is always infranodal, and as such it is almost always associated with the presence of hemiblock, bundle-branch block, or bifascicular block and a consequently widened conducted QRS complex.

PR prolongation is typically not present.

Patients with Mobitz type II AV block frequently and abruptly develop complete AV block and, thus, are at a high risk of experiencing syncope or dying suddenly without an effective therapy.

ETIOLOGY

Mobitz type II AV block is most commonly seen in extensive anterior myocardial infarctions. It also may be seen in patients with a history of Stokes–Adams attacks, where its presence indicates the potential for sudden development of hemodynamically significant complete heart block or ventricular standstill. In cases unassociated with ischemic heart disease, infiltrative damage to the AV junction and distal conduction system from a calcified mitral or aortic valve may occur and is sometimes referred to as Lev's disease. In Lenegre's disease, which occurs in old age, the AV conduction system develops degenerative and fibrotic changes surrounded by normal myocardium. Other uncommon causes are infiltrative diseases such as sarcoidosis or endocarditis complicated by abscess formation damaging the conducting system. Type II AV block is rarely observed with acute inferior infarction, electrolyte abnormalities, or as a result of pharmacologic therapy. In the presence of preexisting bundle-branch block or bifascicular block, electrolyte abnormalities (hyperkalemia) or antiarrhythmic drugs, which slow conduction in the His-Purkinje system, may cause type II second-degree AV block.

CRITERIA FOR DIAGNOSIS

Suggestive

Diagnosis of type II AV block should be considered whenever intermittent pulse deficits with a pause twice as long as a regular pulse interval and without cannon *a* waves occur, especially in a patient with acute anterior myocardial infarction, or when a patient with preexisting intraventricular conduction abnormalities presents with a Stokes–Adams attack. In the latter case, Mobitz type II conductions may appear intermittently leading to third-degree heart block, or third-degree heart block may occur abruptly.

Definitive

The diagnosis is secure if the following electrocardiographic criteria are met: First, in the presence of regular atrial rhythm, intermittent failure of AV conduction occurs without PR prolongation on preceding beats. Second, there is evidence of abnormal intraventricular conduction with a widened QRS complex. And third, the clinical setting is that of acute anterior myocardial infarction or a history consistent with Stokes–Adams attacks. The first criterion is most important among the three.

CLINICAL MANIFESTATIONS

Subjective

Patients with Mobitz type II AV block are frequently symptomatic not from Mobitz type II AV block but from its abrupt progression to third-degree AV block.

When third-degree AV block occurs, an escape rhythm originates from the distal conducting system, and its rate is in the range of 30 beats/min. Occasionally the onset of third-degree AV block is followed by ventricular standstill or ventricular fibrillation. Symptoms would include lightheadedness, syncope, shortness of breath, weakness, and angina.

Cardiac syncope (Stokes–Adams attacks) due to any severe bradyarrhythmia generally has no warning symptoms and is characterized by sudden collapse with loss of consciousness (syncope), which may occur with or be followed by seizure activity. It is important to remember that seizure activity may occur at the time of the attack, which may confuse the diagnosis; however, it typically occurs following some period of flaccid collapse.

Objective

Physical Examination

The physical finding of Mobitz type II AV block is intermittent skipped beats with a full compensatory pause; that is, a long pause is twice a regular pulse interval. Occasionally, the *a* wave in the jugular veins and the fourth heart sound are noted without being followed by the *c* and *v* waves or by the first and second heart sounds, respectively. Definitive diagnosis is made from the electrocardiogram.

Routine Laboratory Abnormalities

Except for the abnormality noted in the electrocardiogram there are no abnormalities in the routine laboratory tests. The electrocardiographic abnormalities are shown in Figure 15–18–1.

PLANS

Diagnostic

Differential Diagnosis

Differential diagnosis of Mobitz II second-degree AV block includes any conditions causing intermittent pauses: sinus arrhythmia, frequent atrial premature complexes, sinoatrial exit block, atrial fibrillation, frequent ventricular premature complexes, and Wenckebach AV block. Recognition of the electrocardiographic features as listed under Criteria

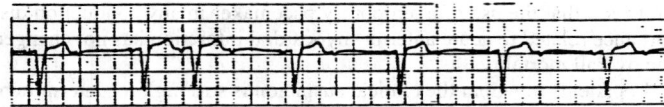

Figure 15–18–1. Mobitz Type II atrioventricular (AV) block (V_1 lead) recorded from a previously healthy woman with Adams–Stokes attacks of recent onset. The patient did not have any structural heart disease. In the face of borderline sinus tachycardia, there is intermittent failure of AV conduction at mostly 2:1 AV conduction ratio. As conducted QRS complexes are abnormally wide (0.13 second) and the PR intervals are normal (0.15 second), Mobitz type II AV block is a strong possibility. On further analysis, there is one cycle of 3:2 AV conduction ratio in the left part of the tracing, where two consecutive P waves are conducted with constant PR interval and the third P wave fails to be conducted. Thus diagnosis of Mobitz type II AV block is established. The underlying disease responsible for the AV block in this patient is probably Lenegre's disease.

for Diagnosis, Definitive, separates Mobitz II AV block from these abnormalities.

In patients with predominantly 2:1 AV conduction, the differentiation of Wenckebach from type II AV block may be difficult (see Figure 15–18–1). In this case, constant PR or gradually lengthening PR intervals cannot be used to discriminate between Wenckebach and Mobitz type II AV block because there is only one conducted PR interval in each cycle. The point to be emphasized is that not all 2:1 AV block is Mobitz type II block; in fact, as Wenckebach AV block occurs approximately 20 times more frequently than Mobitz type II block, statistically, most 2:1 AV block is of the Wenckebach variety. Table 15–18–1 summarizes the clinical and electrocardiographic features useful in differentiating the two types of second-degree AV block in the presence of predominantly 2:1 AV conduction.

Diagnostic Options

Several diagnostic options are available to aid the diagnosis of Mobitz type II second-degree AV block: a 12-lead electrocardiogram, a rhythm strip, a telemetric monitor, an ambulatory electrocardiogram, a loop monitor, and an invasive electrophysiologic test.

Recommended Approach

In the evaluation of a patient with a history consistent with Stokes–Adams attacks, hospital admission to a monitored bed is required. A 12-lead electrocardiogram is necessary to ascertain whether there is evidence of underlying intraventricular conduction abnormalities or of either acute or old myocardial infarction. If the diagnosis cannot be established during a few days of monitored observation, multiple 24-hour ambulatory recordings in a supervised setting may be warranted. Where the diagnosis still remains uncertain but the clinical history and baseline electrocardiographic abnormalities are strongly suggestive of syncope due to intermittent high-degree AV block but not due to primary cerebral disorders, invasive electrophysiologic study may be necessary to assess sinus nodal function, AV conduction, and arrhythmia.

TABLE 15–18–1. DIFFERENTIATION BETWEEN WENCKEBACH AND MOBITZ TYPE II BLOCK IN 2:1 ATRIOVENTRICULAR CONDUCTION

Characteristic	Wenckebach Block	Mobitz Type II Block
Frequency	Common	Uncommon
PR interval	Prolonged	Usually normal
QRS duration	Normal	Widened
Long rhythm strips	Typical Wenckebach periods may appear	Typical Mobitz II atrioventricular block may appear
Associated with site of acute infarction	Inferior	Anterior

Therapeutic

Therapeutic Options

Pharmacologic therapy is usually ineffective and unreliable in improving AV conduction in the distal His–Purkinje system, the site of Mobitz type II block. Pacemaker therapy is the mainstay of treatment.

Recommended Approach

The documentation of Mobitz type II block during acute anterior myocardial infarction is an indication for temporary pacing (or perhaps permanent pacing). If intermittent Mobitz type II block or complete heart block persists in this setting, a permanent pacemaker is required. The documentation of Mobitz type II block in evaluation of patient with clinical features consistent with Stokes–Adams attacks is also an indication for a permanent pacemaker. For most patients in whom cardiovascular function is normal and high-degree AV block occurs infrequently, a simple ventricular demand pacemaker (VVI pacemaker) is adequate. A dual-chamber pacemaker (DDD pacemaker) offers the advantages of providing physiologic sequential AV contraction and an increased ventricular rate in response to sinus tachycardia. This mode of cardiac pacing should be considered for the young, potentially physically active patient or for those patients with significantly impaired cardiac function in whom the atrial contribution to cardiac output is important. For the physically active patient unsuitable for DDD pacemaker implantation because of the presence of atrial tachycardias including atrial fibrillation, the use of a rate-responsive ventricular demand pacemaker (rate-responsive VVI pacemaker) should be considered. This pacemaker automatically increases its pacing rate in response to exercise.

FOLLOW-UP

Most patients who develop persistent Mobitz type II AV block require permanent pacemaker therapy. The patient should be reassured that the pacemaker therapy is extremely reliable in the prevention of syncope due to heart block. The reliability of pacemaker technology should be emphasized along with the ability of the pacemaker to eliminate the potentially lethal rhythm disturbances.

Regular follow-up, usually once or twice a year, is necessary to assess the pacemaker system. The pacemaker function should be followed at monthly or bimonthly intervals by transtelephonic monitoring. At the follow-up visit, the patient should be evaluated for any recurrence of presyncopal or syncopal episodes and physical examination of the pacemaker pocket should be done for evidence of tenderness, fluid accumulation, or infection. Then the pacemaker should be tested for pacing threshold and sensing function. Follow-up of patients with anterior myocardial infarction is generally dictated by their postinfarction status.

Patients also should be instructed that should there be any recurrence of symptoms similar to those requiring pacemaker implantation, the physician should be promptly contacted. The patient should be instructed by the physician to palpate the pulse and also to contact the physician if the pulse rate becomes slower than the programmed pacemaker rate.

DISCUSSION
Prevalence and Incidence

The incidence and prevalence of Mobitz type II block in the asymptomatic ambulatory population are unknown, but must be extremely small. The incidence of Mobitz type II block in acute myocardial infarction is 1 to 3%, occurring primarily in patients with extensive anterior myocardial infarction (Stock and Macken, 1968).

Second degree AV block and right bundle-branch block are commonly (around 10%) encountered in healthy centenarians, but are less common in healthy older persons between the ages of 63 and 95. These findings suggest that the conduction fibers degenerate with advancing age in very old persons.

Related Basic Science

The site of Mobitz type II block is generally distal to the bundle of His. This has been documented in invasive electrophysiologic studies showing an abnormally long HV conduction time and the preservation of impulse conduction to the level of the His bundle in the beat that failed to conduct to the ventricles (Josephson and Seides, 1979). Most frequently, all the main fascicles are diseased.

It is easy to understand why Mobitz type II AV block is most frequently encountered in acute anterior infarction. Anterior infarcts with extensive septal destruction accompany infarction of the left anterior fascicle and distal right bundle, which receive their predominant blood supply from septal perforating branches of the left anterior descending artery (Hudson, 1991). In contrast to the lesions of the AV node in inferior myocardial infarction, the damage to the fascicular structures in acute anterior myocardial infarction is frequently extensive and irreversible. Also, because of the extensive nature of the anterior myocardial infarction causing fascicular or bifascicular block, patients with these intraventricular conduction abnormalities have higher long-term mortality from left ventricular failure than do those without any intraventricular conduction abnormalities.

Natural History and Its Modification with Treatment

Unless Mobitz type II AV block occurs in the presence of hyperkalemia or antiarrhythmic therapy, it tends to persist or to be followed abruptly by third-degree AV block, ventricular standstill, or ventricular fibrillation. Thus, patients with persistent Mobitz type II AV block, before the era of permanent implantable pacemakers, used to experience frequent Stokes–Adams attacks and have an extremely poor long-term prognosis.

Though implantation of permanent pacemakers is a reliable and effective therapy for high-grade AV blocks (second- and third-degree AV blocks), the long-term prognosis of patients with high-grade AV blocks is dictated by their underlying structural heart diseases.

Prevention

No specific preventive measures are available. Efforts aimed at reducing the incidence of atherosclerotic coronary artery disease have a secondary preventive role.

Cost Containment

The use of temporary pacing in acute anterior infarction complicated by Mobitz type II block is widely accepted. It should be remembered, however, that the use of a temporary pacemaker in any conduction disturbance related to acute anterior myocardial infarction has not changed the overall mortality.

In patients in whom the clinical suspicion is still high for intermittent high-degree AV block but the diagnosis is not established by a combination of electrocardiographic monitoring and ambulatory electrocardiographic recordings, invasive electrophysiologic tests may be necessary. It is currently unknown whether this approach results in an overall benefit over the empiric approach using continuous monitoring and ambulatory electrocardiographic recordings. Indiscriminate use of permanent pacemakers in patients with syncope of unknown etiology is to be strongly discouraged because most of these patients do not have cardiac syncope, the cost of the procedure is high, and there is potential acute and long-term morbidity associated with a permanent pacemaker.

REFERENCES

Hudson REB. The conduction system: Anatomy, histology, and pathology in acquired heart disease. In: Silver MD, ed. Cardiovascular pathology. 2nd ed. New York: Churchill Livingstone, 1991:1367.

Josephson ME, Seides SF. Atrioventricular conduction. In: Josephson ME, Seides SF, eds. Clincal cardiac electrophysiology. Philadelphia: Lea & Febiger, 1979:217.

Kastor JA. Atrioventricular block. In: Kastor JA, ed. Arrhythmias. Philadelphia: Saunders, 1994:145.

Langendorf R, Cohen H, Gozo Eg Jr. Observations on second-degree atrioventricular block, including new criteria for the differential diagnosis between type I and type II block. Am J Cardiol 1972;29:111.

Pick A, Langendorf R. Atrioventricular and intraventricular block. In: Pick A, Langendorf R, eds. Interpretation of complex arrhythmias. Philadelphia: Lea & Febiger, 1979:217.

Sheinman MM, Remedios P, Cheitlin MD, et al. Effects of antiarrhythmic drugs on atrioventricular conduction in patients with acute myocardial infarction. Circulation 1980;62:20.

Stock RJ, Macken DL. Observations on heart block during continuous monitoring in myocardial infarction. Circulation 1968;38:993.

Wakida Y, Okamoto Y, Iwa T, et al. Arrhythmias in centenarians. PACE 1994;17:2217.

CHAPTER 15–19

Complete Atrioventricular Block

Toshio Akiyama, M.D.

DEFINITION

In complete atrioventricular (AV) block, the atria and ventricles beat independently (complete AV dissociation); electrocardiographically, the P waves and QRS complexes occur totally independently of each other. If the onset of complete AV block is followed by intermittent failure of idioventricular escape rhythm or by ventricular fibrillation, syncope or sudden death ensues. Although the P waves occur at a normal rate, wide and bizarre QRS complexes (QRS width ≥ 0.14 second) occur regularly at a rate of around 30 beats/min with a constantly changing PR interval if the site of heart block is distal to the bundle of His. If the site of heart block is within the AV junction (AV node and His bundle), then narrow and normal QRS complexes occur at a rate of around 45 beats/min (provided there is no preexisting bundle-branch block). Before diagnosis of complete AV heart block is made, however, presence of an abnormally slow dominant pacemaker (usually the sinus node) and/or tachycardia originating below the atria (usually ventricular tachycardia) must be excluded. As discussed under Plans, Diagnostic, complete AV dissociation is not synonymous with complete AV

heart block, and furthermore, complete AV block is only one of three causes of complete AV dissociation.

ETIOLOGY

Complete AV block may be classified into congenital, where the site of block is located usually within the AV junction, and acquired, where the site of block is located usually distal to the bundle of His. Complete heart block may be caused by any disorders listed in Table 15–16–1. In the adult, degenerative or idiopathic conduction system disease (including Lenegre's disease), ischemic heart disease, drug toxicity, calcific aortic and mitral valvular diseases, and Lev's disease (invasion of the infra-AV nodal conduction system from the surrounding fibrocalcific process) appear to be the most common causes. In ischemic heart disease, complete AV block occurs either from necrosis of bilateral bundles in acute anterior myocardial infarction or from enhanced vagal tone and/or ischemia of the AV junction in acute inferior myocardial infarction.

CRITERIA FOR DIAGNOSIS
Suggestive

The presence of complete AV block should be suspected if the patient presents with recent episodes of syncope or near syncope and has a slow but regular pulse (below 50 beats/min) and intermittently appearing large waves (cannon *a* waves) in the jugular venous pulse.

Definitive

When the P waves and QRS complexes are independent of each other on the electrocardiogram, complete AV dissociation is present. As already pointed out, however, complete AV dissociation is not synonymous with complete AV block. Complete AV dissociation can be caused by any one or a combination of three factors: slowing of the primary pacemaker (usually the sinus node), development of tachycardia below the atria, and complete AV block. Thus, in the patient with complete AV dissociation, the first two factors have to be excluded before complete AV block is diagnosed (Figure 15–19–1). If the site of complete AV block is located distal to the bundle of His, QRS complexes are wide (≥0.14 second) and slow, around 30 beats/min (range, 15–40 beats/min), and the T wave and ST segment are deviated opposite the QRS complex (see Figure 15–19–1). If, however, the site of complete AV block is within the AV junction, the escape rhythm originates usually from the AV junction just distal to the site of the block. The QRS complex is normal in the absence of preexisting bundle-branch block and its escape rate is around 45 beats/min (range, 30–55 beats/min). In the patient with atrial fibrillation, the diagnosis of complete AV block can still be made when QRS complexes occur regularly at a slow rate (usually below 50 beats/min). Occasionally, in the patient without clearly identifiable P waves, an esophageal electrocardiogram may become necessary to visualize the P waves. In patients suspected of developing complete AV block only sporadically, ambulatory electrocardiographic recordings are necessary for its demonstration.

CLINICAL MANIFESTATIONS
Subjective

Symptoms attributable to complete AV block vary widely. Patients with complete AV block but with an escape rate greater than 50 beats/min (especially children with congenital complete AV block) may be asymptomatic; however, when an extremely slow idioventricular escape rhythm (usually below 30 beats/min) or intermittent failure of the idioventricular rhythm develops, symptoms of cerebral ischemia and heart failure appear. The patient may suddenly collapse without warning symptoms and lose consciousness, sometimes followed by convulsions (Stokes–Adams attack or Margagni–Stokes–Adams attack), or the patient may develop only lightheadedness. Syncope or near syncope occurs more readily in standing or sitting positions than in the recumbent position and more readily in the presence of obstructive cerebral artery disease than in its absence. Other symptoms attributable to complete AV block include palpitations, feeling of forceful heartbeats, intermittent fullness in the neck, weakness, easy fatigability, re-duced exercise capacity, exertional dyspnea, and chest discomfort including angina pectoris.

Objective
Physical Examination

Unless an intermittent failure of idioventricular escape rhythm occurs, the patient may not appear acutely ill. The pulse is regular and slow (< 50 beats/min). Because of the constantly changing timing between atrial and ventricular contractions, cyclic changes may be noted: cannon *a* waves in the jugular vein as intermittent large waves occurring with simultaneous atrial and ventricular contractions; changing intensity of the first heart sound due to the changing PR interval (the first heart sound is louder with short PR intervals than with long PR intervals); the fourth heart sound appearing irregularly during the diastolic period, becoming loud as a summation gallop when atrial contractions fall during the early diastolic phase (rapid filling phase of the ventricles); and a slight variation in the amplitude of the arterial pulse. Although a slow and regular pulse in conjunction with these physical findings is highly suggestive of complete AV block, definitive diagnosis is made from the electrocardiogram.

Routine Laboratory Abnormalities

Except for the electrocardiogram (see Figure 15–19–1), the routine laboratory tests show no abnormalities.

Only a routine 12-lead electrocardiogram or a rhythm strip electrocardiogram is necessary for diagnosing complete AV block.

Occasionally, in the patient without clearly identifiable P waves, an esophageal electrocardiogram may become necessary to visualize the P waves. In patients suspected of developing complete AV block only sporadically, ambulatory electrocardiographic recordings or loop monitor electrocardiographic recordings are necessary for its demonstration. Please refer to Criteria for Diagnosis, Definitive.

PLANS
Diagnostic
Differential Diagnosis

Any conditions with a slow pulse rate and/or bradycardia need to be considered in the differential diagnosis of complete AV block. They include pulsus alternans, sinus bradycardia, sinus standstill with an escape rhythm, second-degree AV block of either type I or II, and frequent atrial or ventricular premature complexes accompanied by full compensatory pauses. A routine electrocardiographic recording is useful in separating complete AV block from these conditions.

Diagnostic Options and Recommended Approach

A routine 12-lead electrocardiogram, a monitor lead electrocardiogram, or an ambulatory electrocardiographic recording is sufficient in diagnosing complete AV block.

Therapeutic

Most adult patients with complete AV block require therapy, either temporarily or permanently, aimed at accelerating the heart rate. In rare patients this may not be required if the AV junctional escape rate in the presence of complete heart block within the AV junction is adequate both at rest and with exercise. In patients requiring therapy, the physician must therefore determine whether complete AV block is transient or permanent. If causative agents are identified, they should be removed. Until pacemaker therapy is established, atropine sulfate or isoproterenol (Isuprel) may be administered intravenously (see Table 15–16–2 and Chapters 15–8, 15–16, and 15–17). Extended use of these drugs beyond the first few hours should be avoided, and pacemaker therapy should be initiated instead. Usually, side effects from the extended use of these intravenous drugs outweigh complications of pacemaker therapy provided by experienced physicians. If complete AV block appears to be transient (as in drug-induced heart block), a temporary ventricular demand pacemaker should be employed. If, however, complete AV block appears to be permanent (as in heart block due to

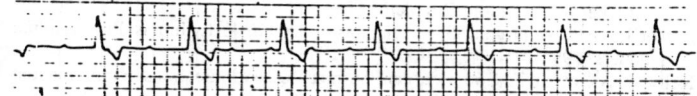

Figure 15–19–1. Complete atrioventricular (AV) block recorded on lead I from an 88-year-old man complaining of malaise of 2 days' duration. The patient previously had right bundle-branch block. In the presence of sinus arrhythmia at around 90 beats/min, wide QRS complexes of left bundle-branch block pattern (QRS width of 0.14 second) occur quite regularly at a rate of 41 beats/min. Thus, complete AV dissociation (complete dissociation between the sinus node and idioventricular escape focus) is present. Because the sinus rate is normal and is not slower than the idioventricular escape rate (which is obviously not tachycardic), complete AV dissociation in this case is caused by complete AV block. The electrocardiographic diagnosis is complete dissociation between the sinus node and the idioventricular escape focus caused by complete AV block.

degenerative conduction system disease) or might recur (as in heart block due to necrosis of bilateral bundles in anterior myocardial infarction), a permanent pacemaker should be promptly implanted rather than initial temporary pacemaker therapy followed later on by permanent pacemaker implantation. Except for chronically bedridden patients or patients with atrial fibrillation or frequent bouts of supraventricular tachycardia, a dual-chamber pacemaker (DDD pacemaker in particular) should be used to take advantage of the "atrial booster effect" and the increase in the ventricular rate in response to physiologic sinus tachycardia. For the latter patients with atrial fibrillation or frequent beats of supraventricular tachycardia, the use of a rate-responsive ventricular pacemaker (rate-responsive VVI pacemaker) should be considered.

FOLLOW-UP

The patient having persistent complete AV block should be told that a permanent pacemaker is required and that most of the troublesome symptoms caused by complete AV block usually disppear after successful pacemaker implantation. After pacemaker implantation, the physician should instruct the patient on how the pacemaker functions and how to monitor pacemaker function transtelephonically using an electrocardiogram signal transmitter. Furthermore, the patient, spouse, and family members should be taught how to take the pulse.

Patients with a permanent pacemaker for complete AV block but without underlying structural heart disease require follow-up in the pacemaker clinic once or twice a year. Patients with underlying structural heart disease other than degenerative conduction system disease, however, usually need to be followed for the underlying disease. Patients need to contact their physician promptly if symptoms suggestive of complete AV block recur or if their pulse rate drops well below the demand rate of a ventricular demand pacemaker or the lower rate of a dual-chamber pacemaker. The latter usually signifies a pacemaker malfunction or presence of frequent premature beats.

DISCUSSION
Prevalence and Incidence

The prevalence of complete AV block in the general population is not known. The incidence of complete AV block in patients with acute myocardial infarction is around 5%, with most cases occurring in patients with acute inferior myocardial infarction (about 10%). Among the complete heart block patients with acute inferior myocardial infarction studied by Tans et al. (1980), complete AV block was the initial conduction disturbance in slightly more than half, and progression from either first-degree AV block or Wenckebach AV block to complete AV block occurred in slightly less than half. Most patients had escape rates between 30 and 60 beats/min. The mean age of the patients with high-degree AV block (second- and third-degree AV blocks) was higher than that of patients without. The peak serum glutamic–oxaloacetic acid transaminase level was significantly higher, as was the hospital mortality rate, in patients with high-degree AV block than in those without. The cause of death in patients with high-degree AV block was primarily pump failure.

In contrast, complete AV block develops in slightly less than 5% of patients with acute anterior myocardial infarction. In this setting, complete AV block usually appears in patients who have first developed some form of intraventricular conduction defect (Mullins and Atkins, 1976). Classically, the infra-Hisian conduction system was divided into right and left bundles; however, as already discussed in Chapter 15–18, the left bundle behaves functionally as if it were made of two separate fascicles or divisions (anterior and posterior fascicles). Thus, it is not customary to consider the infra-Hisian conduction system as consisting of three fascicles (trifascicular concept): right bundle, left anterior fascicle, and left posterior fascicle. Conduction block in one of the fascicles of the left bundle is commonly referred to as a hemiblock. The incidence of various intraventricular conduction blocks varies between 1 and 5% in patients with acute anterior myocardial infarction. It is unusual for left anterior hemiblock or left posterior hemiblock alone to progress to complete AV block (< 3%). Progression to complete AV block from isolated right or left bundle-branch block is much higher than that from left anterior or posterior hemiblock (20 and 43%, respec-

tively). Equally high progression to complete AV block was noted for right bundle-branch block plus left anterior hemiblock (46%) and right bundle-branch block plus left posterior hemiblock (43%). In these patients developing intraventricular conduction abnormalities, there is usually good correlation between histologic changes (necrosis, fibrosis, and calcification) of the conduction system and electrocardiographic conduction abnormalities. Thus, it is not surprising that a few studies demonstrated that sudden death after hospital discharge is not infrequent in patients who have recovered from transient complete AV block developing in the presence of bifascicular block (commonly right bundle-branch block plus left anterior hemiblock). Although controversial, some studies have shown that prophylactic use of a permanent pacemaker in these patients reduced death rate as compared with no pacemaker therapy. It should be emphasized that patients with anterior myocardial infarction who develop intraventricular conduction disturbances or complete AV block have more extensive infarctions than those without. Therefore, these patients usually have a higher incidence of left ventricular failure and consequently a higher death rate (Mullins and Atkins, 1976). The issue of the value of the prophylactic use of a cardiac pacemaker in the setting of acute myocardial infarction complicated by new intraventricular conduction disturbances deserves a well-designed large-scale clinical study.

It is interesting that second degree AV block and right bundle-branch block, precursors of complete AV block were much more common in centenarians than in those between the ages of 63 and 95. These conduction disturbances appear to result from age-related degeneration of the conduction fibers as seen in Lenegre's disease.

Related Basic Science

Please refer to Prevalence and Incidence.

Natural History and Its Modification with Treatment

Before the era of implantable permanent pacemakers, patients frequently died following a Stokes–Adams attack. The vast majority of such patients, however, are now relieved of Stokes–Adams attacks with the use of a permanent pacemaker. Thus, the natural history of patients with complete AV block in the era of modern cardiac pacemakers is mostly influenced by the underlying disorder rather than by the complete AV block.

Prevention

No specific measures are available for preventing complete AV heart block. Efforts should be directed toward reducing the incidence of atherosclerotic coronary artery disease, rheumatic heart disease, and drug-induced complete AV block.

Cost Containment

In the vast majority of patients with complete AV block, the physician should be able to make crucial decisions (including whether a permanent pacemaker should be used) based on clinical information. Bundle of His electrocardiography is not necessary.

REFERENCES

Frye RL, Collins JJ, DeSanctis RW, et al. Guidelines for permanent cardiac pacemaker implantation. Circulation 1984;70:331A.

Kastor JA. Atrioventricular block. In: Kastor JA, ed. Arrhythmias. Philadelphia: Saunders, 1994:145.

Kelly P, Akiyama T. Common cardiac diseases as indications for permanent pacemakers. Compr Ther 1990;16:55.

Lev M, Kinare SG, Pick A. The pathogenesis of atrioventricular block in coronary disease. Circulation 1970;42:409.

Mullins CB, Atkins JM. Prognoses and management of ventricular conduction blocks in acute myocardial infarction. Mod Concepts Cardiovasc Dis 1976;45:129.

Tans AC, Lie KI, Durrer D. Clinical setting and prognostic significance of high-degree atrioventricular block in acute inferior myocardial infarction: "A study of 144 patients." Am Heart J 1980;99:4.

Wakida Y, Okamoto Y, Iwa T, et al. Arrhythmias in centenarians. PACE 1994;17:2217.

Ventricular Premature Complexes

Toshio Akiyama, M.D.

DEFINITION

Ventricular premature complexes (also referred to as ventricular premature beats, ventricular premature depolarizations, or ventricular premature extrasystoles) originate prematurely from the ventricles below the bundle of His and are the most common arrhythmia. Electrocardiographically, ventricular premature complexes (VPCs) are premature and consist of wide and bizarre QRS complexes (QRS width ≥0.14 second) and abnormal T waves and ST segments that are directed opposite the mean QRS force. Ventricular premature complexes are commonly accompanied by a full compensatory pause; that is, the interval between the two consecutive QRS complexes encompassing a ventricular premature complex is twice the regular cardiac cycle length.

Ventricular premature complexes may be classified into uniform ventricular premature complexes (monomorphic) or multiform ventricular premature complexes; ventricular premature complexes with fixed coupling intervals (the intervals between a sinus-induced QRS complex and subsequent ventricular premature complexes vary less than 0.04 second) or ventricular premature complexes with variable coupling intervals; and ventricular premature complexes with a full compensatory pause or interpolated ventricular premature complexes (the sinus P wave immediately following the ventricular premature complex is conducted to the ventricles, and thus the ventricular premature complex is interpolated between two successive P waves that are both conducted to the ventricles). When ventricular premature complexes occur regularly and frequently and alternate with a sinus-induced QRS on a beat-to-beat basis, they are called *ventricular bigeminy*. They are called *ventricular trigeminy* if a ventricular premature complex regularly follows two sinus-induced QRS complexes, and *ventricular quadrigeminy* if a ventricular premature complex regularly follows three sinus-induced QRS complexes. When three or more ventricular premature complexes appear in succession at a rate faster than 100 beats/min, the runs are called *ventricular tachycardia*. Ventricular premature complexes are also called *complex ventricular premature complexes* when they occur in bigeminal, multiform, or repetitive forms or with an R-on-T phenomenon (a ventricular premature complex falling on the T wave of a preceding sinus beat).

ETIOLOGY

Ventricular premature complexes occur in both health and disease, and their prevalence increases with age. Common underlying disorders are ischemic heart disease, hypertensive cardiovascular disease, valvular heart disease, cardiomyopathy, congenital heart disease, hypoxia, and digitalis toxicity. Less common underlying disorders are cor pulmonale, hypokalemia, hypomagnesemia, and myocarditis. Ventricular premature complexes also occur as a manifestation of proarrhythmic side effects of antiarrhythmic agents or digitalis glycosides, with the use of sympathomimetics (administered either intravenously, nasally, or bronchially) or with excessive use of caffeine, tobacco, or alcohol.

CRITERIA FOR DIAGNOSIS

Suggestive

When the patient presents with occasional pauses in the pulse (with the pauses about twice the regular pulse interval) and with large venous waves (cannon a waves) occurring during the pauses, ventricular premature complexes are statistically the most likely rhythm disturbance.

Definitive

The ventricular premature complexes are premature, occurring mostly prior to but occasionally shortly after a subsequent sinus P wave. The QRS complexes are wide (≥0.14 second) and differ grossly in configuration from those that are sinus induced; their T waves and ST segments are directed opposite the mean QRS force. Most ventricular premature complexes (>90%) have fixed coupling intervals, favoring reentry as their mechanism (see Figure 15–20–1). In contrast, in ventricular parasystole, coupling intervals vary widely and the parasystolic focus continues to discharge independently from the sinus node. The parasystolic focus captures the ventricles after the sinus-induced QRS complex only when the ventricles have fully recovered their excitability (Figure 15–20–2). A necessary substrate for ventricular parasystole is the presence of ectopic pacemaker cells in the ventricle that are protected from the depolarization impulse of the ventricles ("entrance block" in the face of intact impulse exit). It should be noted that animal studies showed some of the parasystolic rhythm occurring with the fixed coupling interval.

The sinus P wave commonly falls on the ST segment or T wave of a ventricular premature complex and fails to be conducted to the ventricles due to retrograde activation of the atrioventricular (AV) junction by the ventricular premature complex. The subsequent sinus P wave is finally conducted to the ventricles. This phenomenon of the interval between the two sinus-induced QRS complexes encompassing a ventricular premature complex and a nonconducted sinus P wave equaling twice the regular cardiac cycle length is called a *full compensatory pause* (see Figure 15–20–1). This phenomenon, however, is by no means pathognomonic of ventricular premature complexes, and it may occur with supraventricular premature beats. Under certain conditions, a ventricular premature complex may be sandwiched between two consecutively conducted sinus P waves (an *interpolated ventricular premature complex*). Interpolation of a ventricular premature complex is favored by a combination of two factors: relatively slow sinus rate and a relatively early ventricular premature complex. In this setting, a sinus impulse may fall far enough after a ventricular premature complex to allow the AV junction to recover sufficiently from the retrograde activation by the ventricular premature complex. Thus, this sinus impulse following the ventricular premature complex may be conducted to the ventricles, although it is commonly conducted with a prolonged PR interval due to incomplete recovery of the AV junction. This retrograde activation of the AV junction by a ventricular premature complex revealed only by the prolonged PR interval of the subsequent sinus P wave is called *concealed* retrograde conduction to the AV junction. In this setting of a relatively slow sinus rate and a relatively early ventricular premature complex, the ventricular premature complex impulse may be conducted retrogradely to the atria and may reset the sinus node. When a ventricular premature complex occurs relatively late and slightly after the subsequent sinus P wave, the resultant QRS complex may be intermediate in shape and width between the sinus-induced QRS complex and the QRS complex generated by the ventricular premature complex (a *fusion beat*). The presence of a fusion beat gives strong support for the diagnosis of ventricular premature complexes. It should be pointed out that intermittently occurring wide QRS complexes of preexcitation syndromes having short PR intervals are sometimes misinterpreted as ventricular premature complexes on a monitor strip or an ambulatory electrocardiographic recording. Careful analysis reveals a relatively constant and short PR interval, when abnormally wide QRS complexes occur, and a slow initial upstroke.

CLINICAL MANIFESTATIONS

Subjective

Symptoms attributable to ventricular premature complexes vary widely. Many patients are totally asymptomatic and are unaware of their presence. Some patients complain of palpitations, occasional fullness or discomfort in the neck, a feeling of skipped beats, occasional strong heartbeats, or a feeling of a "football turning around" in the

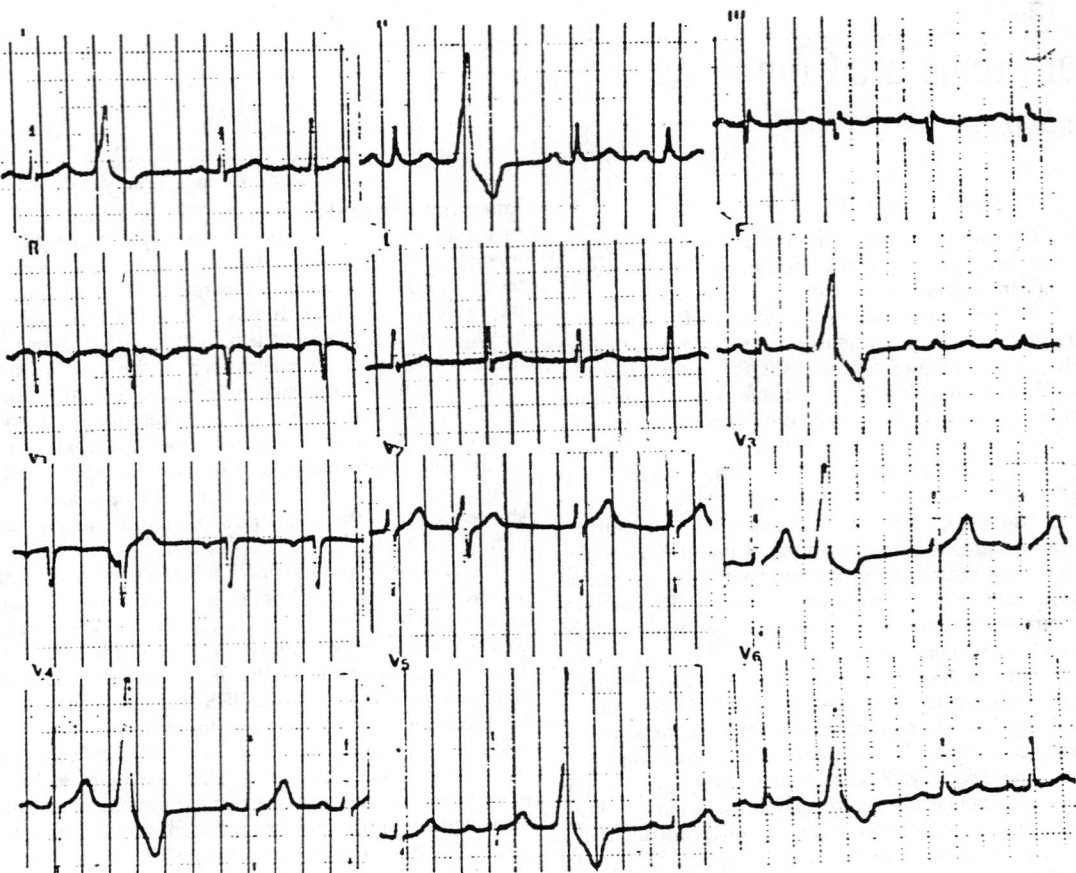

Figure 15–20–1. Frequent ventricular premature complexes recorded on a routine 12-lead electrocardiogram from a 66-year-old asymptomatic man having no structural heart disease. The ventricular premature complexes all have a fixed coupling interval of 0.48 second. Because of this relatively long coupling interval, the sinus P wave falls within the QRS complex of the ventricular premature complex and is blocked within the atrioventricular junction. Each of the ventricular premature complexes, therefore, has a full compensatory pause (see text).

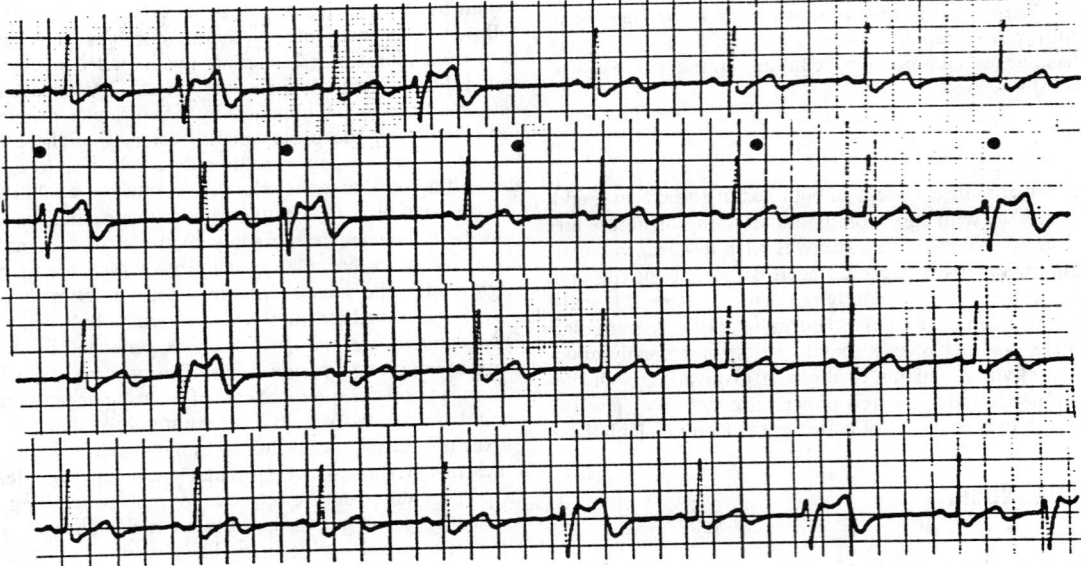

Figure 15–20–2. Ventricular parasystole recorded on a rhythm strip (four tracings are continuous) from a 29-year-old asymptomatic woman having no structural heart disease. Please note first that in contrast to the ventricular premature complexes having a fixed coupling interval as shown in Figure 15–20–1, the ventricular premature complexes in this patient have widely variable coupling intervals, ranging between 0.56 and 0.88 second. When two ventricular premature complexes appear relatively close to each other (this happens once each in the top and second tracings and twice in the bottom tracing), these interectopic intervals are fixed at 1.75 seconds despite the widely varying coupling intervals. Now, assume that a ventricular ectopic focus discharges every 1.75 seconds and is protected from the sinus impulses. Accordingly, the second strip is marked by a filled dot every 1.75 seconds starting from the first ventricular premature complex. The interval between the second and last ventricular premature complexes in the second strip is 5.20 seconds, which is very close to three times the basic cycle length of 1.75 seconds (1.75 × 3 = 5.25). Furthermore, it is obvious that in the second strip the third and fourth impulses failed to capture the ventricles because they fell during the absolute refractory periods of sinus-induced beats.

chest. When ventricular premature complexes occur frequently and reduce cardiac output in patients with severely compromised cardiac function, patients may complain of fatigue, weakness, dyspnea, or chest discomfort.

Objective
Physical Examination

Coincident with ventricular premature complexes, a variety of abnormal physical findings may be noted: pauses in the pulse generally lasting twice the regular pulse interval ("a full compensatory pause"), cannon *a* waves if ventricular and atrial contractions occur simultaneously, and a premature heart sound (either single or double) which may on occasion sound like a loud third or fourth heart sound. Furthermore, the arterial or apical impulses following the pauses may be stronger ("post-extrasystolic accentuation").

Routine Laboratory Abnormalities

The electrocardiogram reveals the abnormality. There are no other routine laboratory abnormalities except when the condition is related to hypokalemia.

PLANS
Diagnostic
Differential Diagnosis

Any premature beats with widened QRS complexes need to be included in the differential diagnosis of ventricular premature complexes: aberrantly conducted atrial premature complexes in patients with rate-dependent bundle-branch block; intermittently preexcited beats (having delta waves) in patients with preexcitation syndromes. Electrocardiographic findings favoring ventricular premature complexes over aberrantly conducted atrial premature complexes are: either no premature P wave in front of a wide QRS complex, or a PR interval too short to be conducted (i.e., a PR interval even shorter than a regular conducted PR interval). Aberrantly conducted atrial premature complexes are usually in the form of right bundle-branch block and much less commonly left bundle branch block. Although in intermittent preexcitation a QRS complex tends to be deformed for its initial portion in the form of a slowly ascending or descending delta wave and a terminal QRS complex tends to be inscribed swiftly, in a ventricular premature complex a QRS complex is inscribed slowly (a low *dV/dt*) throughout. Moreover, in intermittently preexcited beats, the PR intervals are not only shortened but also tend to be fixed.

Diagnostic Options and Recommended Approach

A routine 12-lead electrocardiogram or a rhythm strip is usually sufficient to diagnose ventricular premature complexes (Figure 15–20–1). Generally, patients having occasional pauses or ventricular premature complexes should be examined by the physician and should be screened for the presence of underlying structural heart disease, including history, physical examination, and a 12-lead electrocardiogram with a rhythm strip.

Therapeutic
Therapeutic Options

As detailed below, presence of frequent ventricular premature complexes in patients with structural heart disease signifies an increased risk of sudden arrhythmic death. A wide variety of therapeutic options are now available for these patients: beta blockers, antiarrhythmic drugs, radiofrequency ablation of ectopic ventricular foci, and surgical therapy with an implantable cardioverter defibrillator (see Table 15–16–2). Although it is rather tempting for physicians to suppress these ventricular premature complexes with antiarrhythmic agents, physicians must keep in mind that in two separate large clinical trials, pharmacologic suppression of the ventricular premature complexes with antiarrhythmic agents in post-myocardial infarction patients unexpectedly led to a higher mortality, both overall and sudden death, as compared with their matching placebo groups.

Recommended Approach

In general, therapy for patients with ventricular arrhythmias including ventricular premature complexes should be guided not only by the nature of ventricular arrhythmias but also by symptoms associated with the arrhythmias and by the degree of underlying structural heart disease. Patients without underlying structural heart disease having ventricular premature complexes, symptomatic or asymptomatic, should be reassured of their benign prognosis and do not require antiarrhythmic drug therapy. Ventricular parasystole is usually a benign condition and thus does not have to be treated (see Figure 15–20–2) unless its frequent occurrence results in impaired cardiac hemodynamics or it occurs in the presence of acute myocardial infarction, ischemia, or severe metabolic abnormalities (especially hypokalemia). As detailed below, patients with underlying structural heart disease (especially those following acute myocardial infarction) having frequent ventricular premature complexes (six or more per hour) or ventricular premature complex runs (two to more in a row) are at high risk for sudden cardiac death. For post-myocardial infarction patients with depressed cardiac function and frequent ventricular premature complexes, there is evidence that both reduced ventricular premature complexes and improved cardiac function occur with long-term use of captopril. Thus, in these patients the use of an angiotensin-converting enzyme inhibitor along with a beta blocker (see below) should be considered routine and essential unless contraindicated.

Although many antiarrhythmic drugs can effectively suppress ventricular premature complexes or runs in these patients, in the data from the Cardiac Arrhythmia Suppression Trial, encainide (Enkaid), flecainide (Tambocor), and moricizine (Ethmozine) all caused a significantly increased cardiac death rate (both sudden and nonsudden) as compared with matching placebo groups (CAST Investigators 1989, 1992). Physicians can no longer assume that class I antiarrhythmic drugs can be safely used in these patients. Furthermore, we cannot assume at this time that use of antiarrhythmic agents in these patients can reduce their cardiac mortality. In contrast, therapy with beta blockers has been shown to reduce cardiac death rate and suppress slightly the frequency of ventricular premature complexes in the patient with a history of myocardial infarction. Thus, at this time it appears prudent to treat patients having experienced myocardial infarction or other structural heart disease and having frequent ventricular premature complexes with beta blockers.

When the efficacy of drug therapy is guided by the results of ambulatory electrocardiographic recordings, the physician has to keep in mind that there is a great degree of spontaneous fluctuation in the frequency of ventricular premature complexes.

Currently no large-scale clinical studies are available that can guide us in determining which ventricular premature complexes during the acute phase of myocardial infarction should be treated and which drugs should be used. For patients with ventricular premature complexes during the acute phase of myocardial infarction, we recommend intravenous lidocaine infusion only for those patients with extremely frequent ventricular premature complexes, more than 3 per minute, or with frequent R-on-T ventricular premature complexes. As the prophylactic use in the hospital of lidocaine in all patients with acute myocardial infarction may even worsen mortality, the use of intravenous lidocaine infusion is usually limited to the first 24 hours of acute myocardial infarction (see Chapter 15–21). If ventricular premature contractions persist after the first 24 hours, lidocaine may be continued.

The need for long-term antiarrhythmic therapy in patients recovering from acute myocardial infarction should be guided by the results of 24-hour ambulatory electrocardiographic recording performed before hospital discharge. Patients having much more than six ventricular premature complexes per hour on average or runs of ventricular premature complexes should be considered for long-term therapy with beta blockers but not with antiarrhythmic agents as outlined above.

FOLLOW-UP

Reassurance is usually sufficient for patients without structural heart disease who have ventricular premature complexes. In contrast, patients with structural heart disease who have ventricular premature complexes should be told that long-term drug therapy with beta blockers and follow-up are necessary because of a slightly increased chance of sudden death. The physician should explain potential drug side effects. Patients should contact the physician if they experience symptoms suggestive of increased frequency of ventricular premature complexes or ventricular tachycardia or drug side effects.

Patients without structural heart disease who have ventricular premature complexes probably should be followed once a year, although they do not require drug therapy. Patients with underlying structural heart disease who have ventricular premature complexes should be followed once every 3 to 4 months. Frequency of follow-up in these patients is also influenced by the underlying disease.

DISCUSSION

Prevalence and Incidence

Ventricular premature complexes are the most common arrhythmia both in health and in disease. Ventricular premature complexes were found by routine office electrocardiogram in 0.8% of healthy aviators of the U.S. Air Force (Hiss and Lamb, 1962). In the epidemiologic study of 5129 persons aged 16 and over in Tecumseh, Michigan, ventricular premature complexes were detected by a routine 12-lead electrocardiogram in 3.5% and were more than twice as common as supraventricular premature complexes (Chiang et al., 1969). The prevalence of ventricular premature complexes increased with age, they were more common in men than in women, and they were found more in persons with coronary artery disease than in those without. Among persons over 30 years of age, the presence of ventricular premature complexes was correlated with an increased incidence of sudden death over a 6-year study period (Chiang et al., 1969).

Related Basic Science

In several follow-up studies of survivors of acute myocardial infarction, the relationship between the frequency and pattern of ventricular premature complexes and post-myocardial infarction sudden death was analyzed. In these studies, frequent and complex ventricular premature complexes have emerged as an independent risk factor for sudden cardiac death. Among 2035 patients in the placebo group of the Coronary Drug Project (survivors of myocardial infarction), 235 patients (11.5%) had one or more ventricular premature complexes in their resting baseline 12-lead electrocardiogram. During a 3-year follow-up period, deaths (including sudden coronary deaths) were about twice as frequent in those with any ventricular premature complexes (21.7%) as in those with none (11.4%). Excess long-term risk of death (including sudden death) was associated with the frequency of ventricular premature complexes, with ventricular premature complexes in pairs or runs, and probably with early-cycle ventricular premature complexes. The excess risk with ventricular premature complexes was considered to be independent of the risk associated with other electrocardiographic and clinical characteristics (Coronary Drug Project Research Group, 1973). In the subsequent follow-up study (average, 24.4 months) of 1739 men with prior myocardial infarction, Ruberman and associates (1977) used 1-hour ambulatory electrocardiographic recordings. The presence of complex ventricular premature complexes (R-on-T, runs of two or more, multiform, or bigeminal) in the monitoring hour was associated with a risk of sudden death three times that of the men free of complex ventricular premature complexes.

The ability of measures of heart function to predict mortality after myocardial infarction was most extensively studied by the Multicenter Postinfarction Research Group (Moss, 1984). In this study, most of the 866 patients enrolled after acute myocardial infarction underwent 24-hour ambulatory electrocardiographic recordings and determination of the resting radionuclide ventricular ejection fraction before hospital discharge. Cardiac mortality progressively increased as the ejection fraction fell below 0.40 and as the number of ventricular premature complexes exceeded one per hour. The following four factors were shown to be independent predictors of cardiac mortality: an ejection fraction below 0.40, ventricular premature complexes of 10 or more per hour, advanced New York Heart Association Functional Class before infarction, and rales heard in the upper two thirds of the lung fields while the patient was in the critical care unit. Furthermore, most of the ventricu-

lar arrhythmia risk prediction was contained in just two parameters: ventricular premature complexes runs and ventricular premature complexes frequency of three or more per hour. Not only in patients after myocardial infarction but also in patients with left ventricular hypertrophy, the presence of asymptomatic ventricular arrhythmias was associated with a statistically significant higher mortality.

The results of many antiarrhythmic drug studies on post-myocardial infarction patients with an endpoint of reducing mortality from sudden cardiac death have been disappointing. In the 20 clinical drug trials reviewed by Furberg (1983), favorable and unfavorable trends were equally common, and in none of the studies was a statistically significant favorable trend achieved. A pilot drug study (Cardiac Arrhythmia Pilot Study [CAST Investigators, 1989]) sponsored by the National Institutes of Health was followed by a full-scale drug study (Cardiac Arrhythmia Suppression Trial [CAST II Investigators, 1992]). This study was designed to test the VPC hypothesis that effective suppression of ventricular premature complexes in survivors of myocardial infarction would result in reduction of cardiac mortality, especially sudden cardiac arrhythmic death. In this study, encainide (Enkaid), flecainide (Tambocor), moricizine (Ethmozine), and their matching placebos were used on 1727 patients. Data on 1455 patients treated with encainide, flecainide, and their matching placebos indicated that during an average of 10 months of follow-up, the patients treated with encainide and flecainide had a significant increase in the sudden death rate and total mortality as compared with their placebo groups (56 events/730 patients versus 22 events/725 patients). Furthermore, the risk of the drugs continued to exist throughout the follow-up period, was remarkably consistent across all patient subgroups, and existed despite their continued efficacy in suppressing ventricular premature complexes.

During the late post-myocardial infarction period, however, therapy with encainide or flecainide was associated with a much steeper increase in death/cardiac arrest rate in the non-Q-wave infarction group than in the Q-wave infarction group. While in the same study (now called CAST I) no excess mortality occurred with the use of moricizine, in the subsequent CAST II study (comparing moricizine with placebo in 1374 patients), the moricizine group had a higher mortality, especially during the first 2 weeks. In the CAST I and II studies, though suppression of ventricular premature complexes was not related to age, older age was an independent predictor of serious side effects including death. Thus, suppression of ventricular premature complexes is not necessarily linked to improved survival. It has been long recognized that antiarrhythmic drugs all possess proarrhythmic side effects. A metaanalysis of six previous clinical trials on a total of 808 patients treated with quinidine or placebo for atrial fibrillation revealed a fourfold significant increase in total mortality in the quinidine group (2.7%) as compared with its placebo group (0.6%) (Coplen et al., 1990). Thus, it appears reasonable to assume at this time that serious side effects including sudden cardiac arrhythmic death are not unique for encainide, flecainide, and moricizine.

Natural History and Its Modification with Treatment

As discussed in detail under Related Basic Science, ventricular premature complexes are the most common arrhythmia. Although the presence of ventricular premature complexes in persons without organic heart disease does not appear to pose any serious threat, their presence in patients with organic heart disease (including coronary artery disease) signifies an increased risk of sudden cardiac death. On one hand, the suppression with antiarrhythmic agents of postinfarction ventricular premature complexes increases mortality. On the other hand, mortality and sudden cardiac death rate are reduced by the use of various beta blockers.

The natural course in the frequency of ventricular premature complexes after myocardial infarction has been examined in a few studies. Unexpectedly, the frequency of ventricular premature complexes becomes low one to a few weeks after acute myocardial infarction, and then it may gradually increase over the next several months. The clinical implication of this finding is currently unknown.

Prevention

No measures are currently available for preventing ventricular premature complexes in persons without structural heart disease. Coronary artery disease is the most common underlying substrate of ventricular premature complexes, and the prevention of coronary atherosclerosis should lead to the prevention of ventricular premature complexes; however, it should be emphasized that successful coronary artery bypass graft surgery appears to have no significant impact on the course of ventricular premature complexes.

Cost Containment

First, patients without structural heart disease usually do not require drug therapy, and unnecessary drug therapy should be avoided in these patients. Second, as indicated earlier, successful coronary artery bypass graft surgery generally does not improve ventricular premature complexes in patients with coronary artery disease. Thus, patients with ventricular premature complexes should not be sent for this surgery to treat ventricular arrhythmias. Third, prognostic information can be obtained from ambulatory electrocardiographic recordings, and invasive electrophysiologic tests are not indicated in patients suspected of having only ventricular premature complexes.

REFERENCES

Akiyama T, Pawitan Y, Campbell B, et al. Effects of advancing age on the efficacy and side effects of antiarrhythmic drugs in post-myocardial infarction patients with ventricular arrhythmias. J Am Geriatr Soc 1992;40:666.

Akiyama T, Pawitan R, Greenberg H, et al. Increased risk of death and cardiac arrest from encainide and flecainide in patients after non-Q wave acute myocardial infarction in the Cardiac Arrhythmia Suppression Trial. Am J Cardiol 1991;68:1551.

Bikkina M, Larson MG, Levy D. Asymptomatic ventricular arrhythmias and mortality risk in subjects with left ventricular hypertrophy. J Am Coll Cardiol 1993;22:1111.

CAST Investigators. Special Report. Preliminary report: Effect of encainide and flecainide on mortality in a randomized trial of arrhythmia suppression after myocardial infarction. N Engl J Med 1989;321:406.

CAST II Investigators. Effect of the antiarrhythmic agent moricizine on survival after myocardial infarction. New Engl J Med 1992;327:227.

Chiang BN, Perlman LV, Ostrander LD, et al. Relationship of premature systoles to coronary heart disease and sudden death in the Tecumseh epidemiologic study. Ann Int Med 1969;70:1159.

Coplen SE, Antman EM, Berlin JA, et al. Efficacy and safety of quindine therapy for maintenance of sinus rhythm after cardioversion: A meta-analysis of randomized control trials. Circulation 1990;81:1106.

Coronary Drug Project Research Group. Prognostic importance of premature beats following myocardial infarction: Experience in the Coronary Drug Project. JAMA 1973;223:1116.

Furberg CD. Effect of antiarrhythmic drugs on mortality after myocardial infarction. Am J Cardiol 1983;52:32C.

Hine LK, Laired NM, Hewitt P, et al. Meta-analytic evidence against prophylactic use of lidocaine in acute myocardial infarction. JAMA 1989;149:2694.

Hiss RG, Lamb LE. Electrocardiographic findings in 122,043 individuals. Circulation 1962;25:947.

Lichstein E, Morganroth J, Harrist R, Huble E, for BHAT Study Group. Effect of propranolol on ventricular arrhythmia: The beta-blocker heart attack trial experience. Circulation 1983;67:I–5.

Moss AJ. Update of post-infarction risk stratification: Physiologic variables. In: Kulbertus HE, Moss AJ, Schwartz PG, eds. Clinical aspects of life-threatening arrhythmias. New York: New York Academy of Science, 1984:280.

Ruberman W, Weinblatt E, Goldberg JD, et al. Ventricular premature beats and mortality after myocardial infarction. N Engl J Med 1977;297:750.

CHAPTER 15–21

Ventricular Tachycardia

Toshio Akiyama, M.D.

DEFINITION

Ventricular tachycardia (VT) is a rapid ectopic tachycardia originating below the bundle of His, frequently accompanied by a rapid hemodynamic deterioration, and occasionally followed by ventricular fibrillation. On the electrocardiogram, ventricular tachycardia consists of three or more consecutive beats of wide and bizzare QRS complexes (0.14 second or more) at a rate between 100 and 250 beats/min. When the rate is extremely fast (>200 beats/min) and the wide QRS complexes form continuous sinusoidal waves, the tachycardia is called *ventricular flutter*. Ventricular flutter usually degenerates rapidly into ventricular fibrillation, which consists of totally disorganized fibrillatory waveforms.

Ventricular tachycardia may be classified in many different ways. Ventricular tachycardia usually starts abruptly (paroxysmal ventricular tachycardia), but accelerated idioventricular rhythm (AIVR, slow ventricular tachycardia, or nonparoxysmal ventricular tachycardia) may start and end gradually. In accelerated idioventricular rhythm the rate is either at or slightly faster than sinus rate (50–100 beats/min). Ventricular tachycardia is arbitrarily called *sustained* (persistent) if it lasts for 10 or more beats (or 30 seconds or more in another definition) or *nonsustained* if it is shorter. Depending on its morphology, ventricular tachycardia may be divided into monomorphic (uniform) and polymorphic (pleomorphic, multiform). If short runs of monomorphic ventricular tachycardia recur continually and are interspersed with a few sinus-induced QRS complexes, it is called *repetitive monomorphic ventricular tachycardia*. Polymorphic ventricular tachycardia can be further classified into Torsade de pointes, bidirectional ventricular tachycardia, and polymorphic ventricular tachycardia. Torsade de pointe is a unique form of ventricular tachycardia that occurs in the presence of prolonged QT interval (prolonged QT syndrome). The tachycardia consists of a slowly shifting polarity from predominantly R wave to predominantly S wave, or vice versa, and usually terminates spontaneously. In bidirectional ventricular tachycardia, an upright QRS complex alternates on a beat-to-beat basis with downward QRS complex.

When ventricular tachycardia occurs in patients without structural heart disease or prolonged QT, it is called idiopathic ventricular tachycardia. Idiopathic ventricular tachycardia may originate from either the left or right ventricle. When it originates from the right ventricular outflow tract (a vertical or right axis and left bundle-branch block configuration), it is termed right ventricular outflow tract (RVOT) tachycardia.

ETIOLOGY

Ventricular tachycardia usually occurs in patients with heart disease. Common underlying heart disease include ischemic heart disease (acute myocardial infarction, ventricular aneurysm), cardiomyopathy, mitral valve prolapse, valvular heart disease, drug toxicity (antiarrhythmic drugs, tricyclic antidepressants, digitalis), prolonged QT syndrome, and metabolic disorders. Ventricular tachycardia may occur, although rarely, in apparently normal persons. Electrophysiologic mechanisms of ventricular tachycardia include reentry, early or delayed afterdepolarization, temporal dispersion, and phase 4 depolarization (automaticity).

CRITERIA FOR DIAGNOSIS
Suggestive

When the patient with structural heart disease, commonly ischemic heart disease, suddenly collapses or faints but still maintains a weak but palpable pulse, the patient must be assumed to be in ventricular tachycardia. The diagnosis of ventricular tachycardia can be made from the routine electrocardiogram with a high probability, but in some patients an esophageal or intracardiac electrocardiogram may be required for its diagnosis.

Definitive

Although the electrocardiogram is essential to diagnose ventricular tachycardia, there is no single criterion that can separate the rhythm from supraventricular tachycardia (SVT) with aberration. The wide and bizarre QRS complex is a result of the slow and abnormal sequence of ventricular activation, which, of course, can occur either with ventricular tachycardia or with aberrant conduction in the face of supraventricular tachycardia. In some patients, an esophageal or intracardiac electrocardiogram may be necessary for the differential diagnosis when the P waves cannot be detected on the body surface electrocardiogram. In general, the rate of ventricular tachycardia is greater than 100 beats/min except for accelerated idioventricular rhythm and is either extremely regular or only slightly irregular. Except for accelerated idioventricular rhythm, ventricular tachycardia starts and ends abruptly. The QRS complexes are wide and bizarre ($\geq$0.14 second), and the ST segment and T wave are directed away from the QRS complex (abnormal ST segment and T wave secondary to abnormal sequence of activation [Figure 15–21–1]). Features useful for the differential diagnosis between ventricular tachycardia and supraventricular tachycardia with aberration are listed in Table 15–21–1. It should be pointed out that none of these features is absolute, and therefore, in the differential diagnosis, as many of these features as possible should be used in conjunction with other clinical information. When the diagnosis is uncertain from a routine electrocardiogram or from an esophageal electrocardiogram, invasive electrophysiologic tests (intracardiac electrocardiographic recordings and programmed electric stimulation of the heart) may be required.

Torsade de pointe (torsion of the point) is a unique multiform tachycardia that occurs in the presence of a prolonged QT interval. Prolongation in the QT interval is frequently drug-induced (quinidine, procainamide, disopyramide, flecainide, amitriptyline, imipramine, amiodarone, sotalol), but it may be congenital, metabolic (hypokalemia or hypomagnesemia), or bradycardia dependent (idioventricular rhythm with third-degree atrioventricular block). The tachycardia typically starts following the beats concluding a long cycle length and thus having a grossly prolonged QT interval. It gradually transforms from a predominantly upright QRS complex into a predominantly downward QRS complex, or vice versa, and usually spontaneously terminates in less than half a minute (Figure 15–21–2).

CLINICAL MANIFESTATIONS

Subjective

Symptoms experienced by patients with ventricular tachycardia are variable and depend on the ventricular rate, underlying cardiovascular or pulmonary disorders, cerebrovascular status, and position of the patient. Patients may develop syncope, lightheadedness, or seizures, or they may complain of palpitations, weakness, dyspnea, or chest discomfort. Other patients may not even be aware that they have ventricular tachycardia.

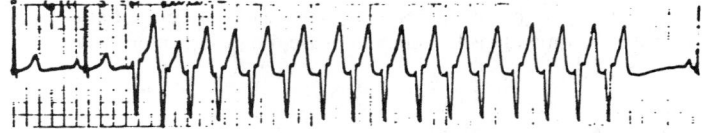

Figure 15–21–1. A 16-beat run of ventricular tachycardia recorded from a 57-year-old patient with acute inferoposterior myocardial infarction. This monitor strip shows a late ventricular premature complex precipitating ventricular tachycardia at the average rate of 117 beats/min. The rate of ventricular tachycardia varies slightly from beat to beat, and 1:1 retrograde conduction exists; that is, an inverted P wave closely follows each QRS complex.

15–21–1. DIFFERENTIAL DIAGNOSIS BY ELECTROCARDIOGRAM BETWEEN VENTRICULAR TACHYCARDIA AND SUPRAVENTRICULAR TACHYCARDIA WITH ABERRATION

Favors Ventricular Tachycardia	Favors Supraventricular Tachycardia with Aberration
Fusion beats	Tachycardia always starts with atrial premature complex
Occasional conduction of supraventricular impulse during tachycardia	Presistence of tachycardia despite intermittent absence of QRS due to AV block
Complete AV dissociation	Slowing or termination by vagal maneuvers
Retrograde AV block	Very short RP (0.1 second)
Rightward superior QRS axis	Typical right bundle-branch block (rsR' in V$_1$)
R in V$_1$ through V$_6$ without preexcitation	
QS in V$_1$ through V$_6$	
Left bundle-branch block configuration	
Right bundle-branch block but R or qR in V$_1$	

AV, atrioentricular.

Objective

Physical Examination

Physical findings also vary widely depending on the ventricular rate and underlying disorders. The patient may become unconscious, may develop seizure, or may appear anxious or agitated. The pulse is rapid and weak or unpalpable. The blood pressure may be low or unobtainable. Cannon a waves may appear either regularly in the presence of a 1:1 retrograde atrioventricular (AV) conduction or intermittently in the face of AV dissociation. The blood pressure may fluctuate depending

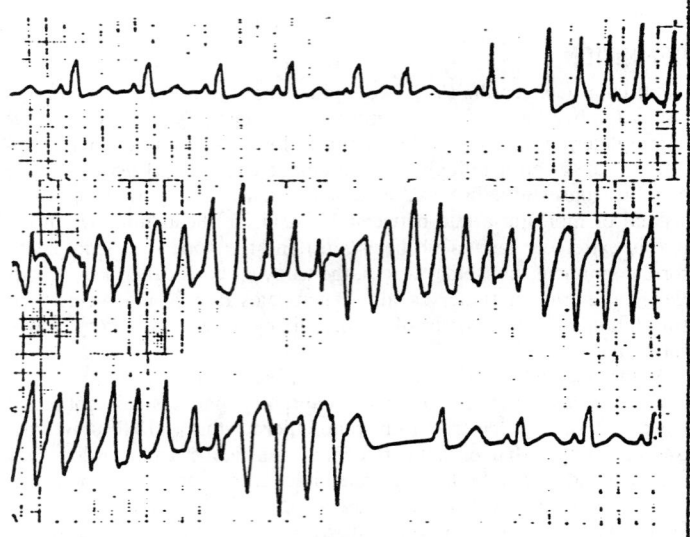

Figure 15–21–2. Torsade de pointes recorded from a 51-year-old woman taking thioridazine (Mellaril). In the monitor strips (continuous), the sixth QRS complex on the top tracing is premature and is conducted from an atrial premature complex, which deforms the T wave of the preceding QRS complex. This premature QRS complex is followed by a relatively long pause, which is concluded by a regular sinus impulse conducted with a QRS complex narrower than the previous six QRS complexes (thus, these wider QRS complexes appear to be a result of rate-dependent bundle-branch block). This relatively narrower QRS complex has a prolonged QTU interval (prominent U wave following T wave) because of the long preceding cycle length and precipitates a nonsustained multiform tachycardia in which a group of beats having predominantly upright QRS complexes gradually transforms into a group of beats having predominantly downward QRS complexes, and vice versa.

on the presence or absence of atrial booster effect if AV dissociation is present. If a relatively fast ventricular tachycardia occurs in the patient with significant cerebrovascular disease while in an upright position, the patient quickly develops signs of cerebral ischemia (such as syncope) or seizure. The patient with serious underlying cardiac disorders may rapidly develop signs of cardiac decompensation, such as hypotension, pulmonary edema, and oliguria. The heart sounds are generally muffled, and the intensity of the sounds may fluctuate in the presence of AV dissociation or retrograde AV Wenckeback block. If underlying cardiac disorders are present, their abnormal physical findings may be detected.

Routine Laboratory Abnormalities

The electrocardiogram reveals the abnormality. Other routine laboratory tests are usually normal but may reveal hypokalemia.

PLANS
Diagnostic
Differential Diagnosis

Although ventricular tachycardia and aberrantly conducted supraventricular tachycardia may look alike electrocardiographically, therapy for patients with ventricular tachycardia may significantly differ from that for patients with aberrantly conducted supraventricular tachycardia. Electrocardiographic clues useful in this differential diagnosis are listed in Table 15–21–1. Bradycardia-dependent QT prolongation and characteristic transformation of the QRS complexes separate Torsade de pointes from ventricular fibrillation (see Criteria for Diagnosis, Definitive).

Diagnostic Options

In addition to symptoms and physical findings, diagnostic tests useful in patients suspected of experiencing ventricular tachycardia are a routine 12-lead electrocardiogram (ECG); a rhythm strip; a telemetry ECG monitor; an ambulatory ECG recording; a loop monitor; a transesophageal ECG; a signal-averaged ECG; and a diagnostic electrophysiologic test.

Recommended Approach

The diagnosis of ventricular tachycardia can usually be made from routine electrocardiographic recordings such as a 12-lead ECG, a rhythm strip, and an ambulatory ECG. As discussed under Criteria for Diagnosis, recognition of P waves and their relationship to wide QRS complexes is essential in the differential diagnosis between ventricular tachycardia and aberrantly conducting supraventricular tachycardia. Thus, if P waves are not readily identifiable in patients with symptomatic wide QRS tachycardia, either transesophageal ECG or diagnostic electrophysiologic testing with intraatrial electrocardiographic recording becomes necessary. The latter is also indicated for patients with frequent and/or prolonged symptomatic bouts of wide QRS tachycardia so that specific therapy can be tailored to the mechanism and site of wide QRS tachycardia. Electrophysiologic testing is also indicated for patients with infrequent but symptomatic wide QRS tachycardias, which are seldom caught by ambulatory ECG recordings.

Therapeutic
Therapeutic Options

Multiple therapeutic options are now available for patients with ventricular tachycardia: no therapy, beta blockers, calcium blockers, antiarrhythmics, radiofrequency ablation of ventricular tachycardia foci, surgical excision of ventricular tachycardia foci, and implantation of an automatic implantable cardioverter defibrillator (see Table 15–16–2).

Recommended Approach

If a rapid clinical deterioration accompanies the onset of wide QRS complex tachycardia, direct-current countershock impulse should be promptly administered. If the patient is clinically stable, the physician should try to establish the diagnosis. Once the diagnosis of ventricular

tachycardia is established, the physician needs to decide whether the patient should be treated for ventricular tachycardia. Generally, patients with structural heart disease who have sustained or nonsustained ventricular tachycardia and patients without structural heart disease who have sustained ventricular tachycardia should be treated. Patients without structural heart disease who have nonsustained but symptomatic ventricular tachycardia also should be treated, but probably not as aggressively as the first two groups of patients. Patients without structural heart disease who have nonsustained and asymptomatic ventricular tachycardia probably do not need drug therapy, but they should be followed closely. Needless to say, it is important to correct or treat any metabolic abnormalities and underlying cardiac disorders as specific therapy for ventricular tachycardia is instituted.

In general, repetitive monomorphic ventricular tachycardia should be treated by antiarrhythmic drugs and not by direct-current countershock. Patients with accelerated idioventricular rhythm usually do not require therapy unless episodic loss of atrial booster effect results in cardiac failure or an increase in angina pectoris. In patients with Torsade de pointes, the initial step is to see whether there are any causative drugs or metabolic abnormalities. If present, these should be removed or corrected. Therapy of Torsade de pointes includes intravenous lidocaine (Xylocaine) and/or temporary ventricular demand pacing at a relatively fast rate (usually 80–100 beats/min). If the tachycardia recurs and prolonged QT intervals persist, a permanent ventricular demand pacemaker and/or oral propranolol may be tried. Recently, left stellate gangliectomy has been advocated, but its efficacy needs to be confirmed.

Patients who have relatively fast ventricular tachycardia but who are clinically stable should be treated first with lidocaine, with an initial bolus injection of 50 to 100 mg, followed by a continuous intravenous infusion at 1 to 4 mg/min. In this scheme, the blood lidocaine level may dip below the therapeutic blood level 15 to 30 minutes after the bolus injection. If resurgence of ventricular tachycardia occurs during that period, an additional bolus injection of 50 to 75 mg may be given. Lidocaine should be used cautiously in elderly patients or patients with severe structural heart diseases because its side effects, such as disorientation, agitation, and hypotension, are not uncommon in these patients. If lidocaine is ineffective, procainamide (Pronestyl) may be given intravenously (a total dose up to 1000 mg), with a bolus injection of 100 mg each over 2 to 3 minutes given every 5 minutes. Patients should be closely monitored during procainamide loading. If the QRS complex or QT interval widens by 25% or more of baseline, bundle-branch block develops, or hypotension occurs, procainamide loading should be stopped. If the initial response is favorable, procainamide may be continuously infused at 1 to 4 mg/min. We do not recommend parenteral use of quinidine because of the relatively narrow margin between its therapeutic and toxic levels. If sustained but clinically stable ventricular tachycardia does not respond to acute intravenous therapy, synchronized direct-current cardioversion in the presence of intravenously administered drugs should be tried. Usually the energy level required for successful cardioversion of ventricular tachycardia is relatively low, and we recommend an initial setting of 25 J (see Chapter 15–14). The "chest thump," striking the precordial wall with a fist, may on rare occasions terminate ventricular tachycardia and may be tried in life-threatening situations if a direct-current cardioverter unit is not immediately available. In patients with drug-resistant ventricular tachycardia, a temporary ventricular pacemaker may be used to terminate the ventricular tachycardia.

Prevention of recurring ventricular tachycardia is often very difficult. This is especially true in patients with infrequent attacks of ventricular tachycardia or with serious ventricular tachycardia resulting in syncope or rapid hemodynamic deterioration. In these patients complete suppression of inducible ventricular tachycardia with drugs during electrophysiologic tests correlates well with a long-term favorable prognosis.

In patients with relatively frequent episodes of ventricular tachycardia, the empiric antiarrhythmic drug therapy guided by the results of ambulatory electrocardiographic recordings and exercise stress tests appears to be as effective as that guided by the results of electrophysiologic tests.

Drugs currently used are amiodarone (Cordarone), sotalol (Betapace), quinidine sulfate (Quinidex), quinidine gluconate (Quinaglute), procainamide (Pronestyl, Pronestyl-SR, Procan SR), disopyramide

(Norpace), tocainide (Tonocard), flecainide (Tambocor), propafenone (Rythmol), and moricizine (Ethmozine) (see Table 15–16–2). When a first drug fails, it may be replaced by a second drug or a second drug may be added to the first. In some patients with idiopathic ventricular tachycardia, calcium channel blockers such as verapamil (Calan, Isoptin, Verelan) and various beta blockers may be also effective.

Patients with cardiac arrest due to ventricular tachycardia or with drug-resistant serious ventricular tachycardia should be considered for implantation of an automatic implantable cardioverter defibrillator (AICD), either nonthoracotomy pervenous or thoracotomy device, or for radiofrequency ablation of arrhythmia foci. The latter appears to provide favorable long-term results only for those with ventricular tachycardia without nonischemic heart disease or structural heart disease.

FOLLOW-UP

Patients with serious ventricular tachycardia should be told at the onset that prevention of tachycardia is of vital importance and that achieving this goal often takes many days. The patient should be reassured that serious attacks of ventricular tachycardia often can be brought under control with modern therapy, including new drugs, implantable defibrillators, and radiofrequency ablation. Once ventricular tachycardia is controlled, patients who had hemodynamically tolerable ventricular tachycardia may be seen two or three times a year. Patients who had hemodynamically poorly tolerated ventricular tachycardia who are treated with amiodarone or other drugs or AICDs may need more frequent follow-up, once every 3 to 4 months. Patients need to promptly contact their physician if symptoms suggestive of drug side effects or ventricular tachycardia recur.

DISCUSSION
Prevalence and Incidence

Ischemic heart disease is by far the most common substrate of ventricular tachycardia, either during acute myocardial infarction or during the post-myocardial infarction period. Ventricular tachycardia occurred in 2 to 31% during the critical care unit phase of acute myocardial infarction and in 11.6% in the pre-hospital discharge ambulatory electrocardiographic recordings (Bigger et al., 1981). The group with ventricular tachycardia in the prehospital discharge ambulatory electrocardiographic recordings had a 38.0% 1-year mortality rate as compared with a 11.6% rate for the group without ventricular tachycardia (Bigger et al, 1981). Although ventricular tachycardia had a significant association with many other postinfarction risk factors, including indices of left ventricular failure, it was shown to be an independent risk factor. In the post-hospital discharge phase (4–48 months), ventricular tachycardia occurred in 7.2% of patients. The mortality rate was slightly higher in the ventricular tachycardia group (16%) than in the group without ventricular tachycardia (8%).

Related Basic Science

Abbreviated and low-amplitude transmembrane action potentials have been recorded from ischemic ventricular myocardial cells. Mainly because of this low-amplitude action potential (which is, in turn, due to reduced fast sodium currents), impulse transmission in the ischemic myocardium is slow; sometimes its conduction velocity is depressed to that of AV nodal cells (1–5 cm/s) instead of the 50 to 100 cm/s of nonischemic myocardial cells. This delayed ischemic conduction and prolonged refractoriness along with unidirectional conduction block have been shown to be the essential factors that allow the reentry circuit to be established. Continuous reentry within the ventricle is considered to be the most common cause of ventricular tachycardia. This delayed myocardial conduction along potential reentry circuits can in some patients be disclosed as late potentials by body surface signal-averaged electrocardiographic recordings. Its clinical utility is currently one of the most intensively studied areas, and presence of abnormal signal-average electrocardiographic waves predicts subsequent arrhythmic events.

In addition to the previously well-recognized mechanisms of arrhyth-

mias such as reentry, automaticity (phase 4 depolarization), and temporal dispersion of repolarization, extensive observations have recently been made on early and delayed afterdepolarization (EAD and DAD). Both are unique cellular reactions of the Purkinje cells and M cells (myocardial cells located in the deep subepicardial and midmyocardial regions of the ventricle) in various pathologic states. Early afterdepolarizations and their triggered responses occur under the following conditions: hypokalemia, hypomagnesemia, bradycardia pause, and use of antiarrhythmic drugs such as quinidine, procainamide and sotalol. Torsade de pointes appears to be a clinical manifestation of early after-depolarization. Delayed afterdepolarizations and their triggered responses, on the other hand, tend to occur under the following conditions that lead to a marked rise in intracellular calcium: tachycardia, digitalis toxicity, use of catecholamines. Oscillatory release of calcium from the sarcoplasmic reticulum appears to be a cause of this phenomenon. This delayed afterdepolarization can be suppressed by calcium or sodium channel blockers. Its electrocardiographic correlates appear to be idiopathic ventricular tachycardia and accelerated AV nodal tachycardia.

Natural History and Its Modification with Treatment

Ventricular tachycardia is commonly encountered in patients with organic heart disease, especially ischemic heart disease. Among patients with organic heart disease, ventricular tachycardia tends to occur in those with impaired cardiac function. The presence of ventricular tachycardia in patients with organic heart disease signifies definitely poor short- and long-term prognoses, as outlined under Related Basic Science.

Prevention

Torsade de pointe caused by drugs or metabolic abnormalities and ventricular tachycardia resulting from proarrhythmic side effects can be prevented by removing their causes. Ischemic heart disease is the most common underlying disease of ventricular tachycardia, and therefore, prevention of coronary atherosclerosis should lead to reduction of the prevalence of ventricular tachycardia.

Cost Containment

Whether the use of invasive electrophysiologic tests results in cost savings as compared with the conventional approach guided by the ambulatory electrocardiogram and exercise stress testing is currently not known. A recent analysis suggests that use of the implantable defibrillator is cost effective as compared with pharmacologic therapy in patients with serious ventricular tachyarrhythmias.

REFERENCES

Anderson KP, DeCamilla J, Moss AJ. Clinical significance of ventricular tachycardia (three beats or longer) detected during ambulatory monitoring after myocardial infarction. Circulation 1978;57:890.

Antzelevitch C, Sicouri S. Clinical revelance of cardiac arrhythmias generated by after depolarizations. J Am Coll Cardiol 1994;23:259.

Bigger JT, Weld FM, Rolnitzky LM. Prevalence, characteristics and significance of ventricular tachycardia (three or more complexes) detected with ambulatory electrocardiographic recording in the late hospital phase of acute myocardial infarction. Am J Cardiol 1981;48:815.

Coggins DL, Lee RJ, Sweeney J, et al. Radiofrequency catheter ablation as a cure for idiopathic tachycardia of both left and right ventricular origin. J Am Coll Cardiol 1994;23:1333.

Dones P, El-Sherif N, Katz R, et al. Prognostic significance of signal-averaged electrocardiogram after thrombolytic therapy and/or angioplasty during acute myocardial infarction (CAST Substudy). Am J Cardiol 1994;74:216.

Kim CH, Daubert JP, Akiyama T. Antiarrhythmic agents in older patients. Current state of knowledge. Drugs Aging. 1994;4:(6):462.

Kuppermann M, Luce BR, McGovern B, et al. An analysis of the cost effectiveness of the implantable defibrillator. Circulation 1990;81:91.

Mason JW for the ESVEM Investigators. A comparison of electrophysiologic testing with Holter monitoring to predict antiarrhythmic-drug efficacy for ventricular tachyarrhythmic-drug efficacy for ventricular tachyarrhythmias. New Engl J Med 1993;329:445.

Wilber DJ, Garan H, Finkelstein D, et al. Out-of-hospital cardiac arrest: Use of electrophysiologic testing in the prediction of long-term outcome. N Engl J Med 1988;18:19.

Ventricular Fibrillation

Toshio Akiyama, M.D.

DEFINITION

Ventricular fibrillation is a chaotic, rapid ventricular rhythm without effective ventricular contraction. It is a lethal arrhythmia unless promptly defibrillated. On the electrocardiogram initially fine fibrillatory waves with no clearly discernible QRS complexes or T waves appear, and later on, coarse or undulating wider waveforms ensue. When the ventricular rate is greater than 200 beats/min and the wide QRS complexes form continuous sinusoidal waves, the tachycardia is called *ventricular flutter*. Ventricular flutter usually degenerates rapidly into ventricular fibrillation. Ventricular fibrillation is classified into primary and secondary ventricular fibrillation: primary if it occurs in the absence and secondary if it occurs in the presence of cardiac failure.

ETIOLOGY

Ischemic heart disease is by far the most common underlying heart disease of ventricular fibrillation, with its attacks occurring frequently during the first few hours of acute myocardial infarction. Its incidence declines subsequently, but it continues to be the most common cause of sudden death after hospital discharge in patients with myocardial infarction. Other diseases associated with ventricular fibrillation are cardiomyopathies and valvular heart diseases, including mitral valve prolapse and congenital heart diseases.

Less common causes of ventricular fibrillation include prolonged QT syndromes, severe hypokalemia, preexcitation syndromes with atrial fibrillation and a rapid ventricular response, proarrhythmic side effects of antiarrhythmic drugs, myocarditis, and electrical accidents, including accidental contact with alternating current or discharge of an electrical impulse during the vulnerable period of the ventricle (T wave).

CRITERIA FOR DIAGNOSIS

Suggestive

When patients with known structural heart disease suddenly collapse with no palpable pulse, they must be assumed to be in ventricular fibrillation and necessary emergency procedures should be initiated without delay. Clinicians must keep in mind that ventricular tachyarrhythmias, either ventricular fibrillation or tachycardia, underlie these cardiac arrests in patients with structural heart disease much more commonly than bradycardia or asystole.

Definitive

Either a routine 12-lead electrocardiogram (Figure 15–22–1) or a monitor lead is sufficient to establish the diagnosis of ventricular fibrillation. Initially, waveforms are rapid (faster than 300 beats/min) and fine without any identifiable QRS complex or T wave; later (in untreated pa-

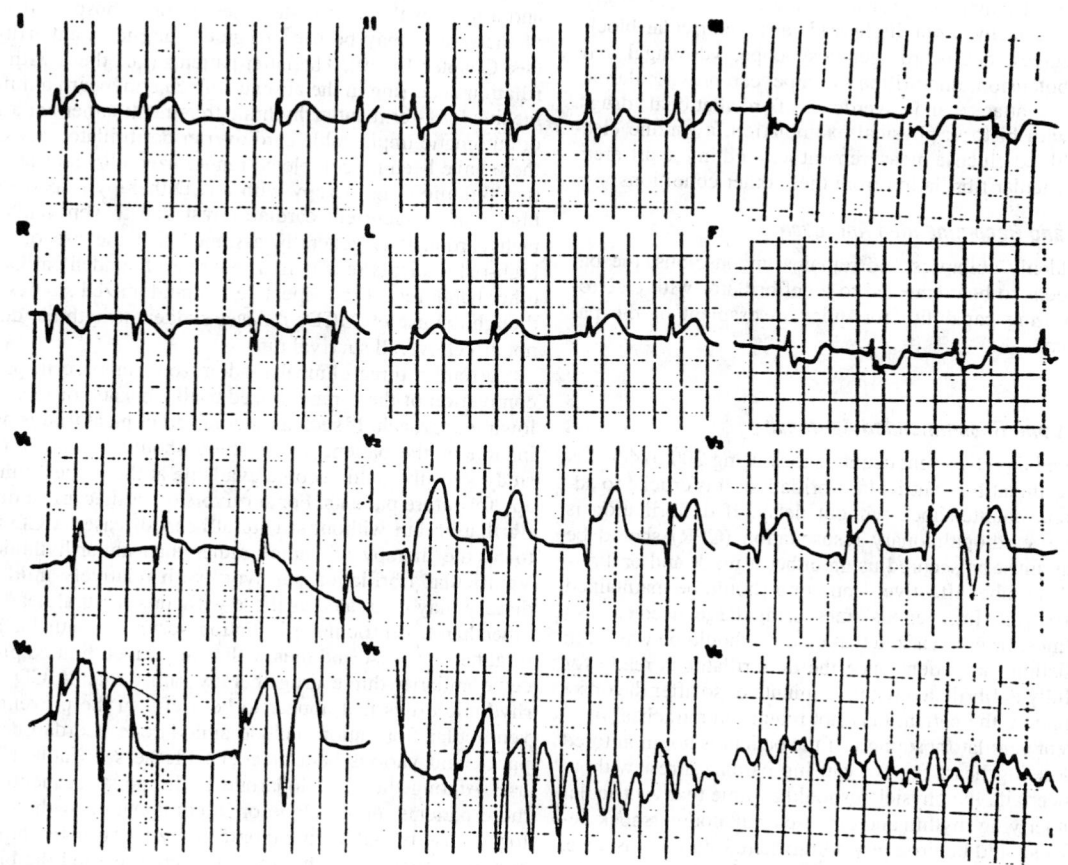

Figure 15–22–1. Ventricular fibrillation in a 47-year-old man developing during recording of a routine 12-lead electrocardiogram. Acute anterolateral myocardial infarction is easily diagnosed from the ST segment elevation, tall upright T wave, abnormal Q waves in leads V$_1$ to V$_5$, and ST segment elevation in leads I and aV$_L$. Frequent ventricular premature complexes falling on the T wave of preceding beats are recorded in leads V$_3$ to V$_5$ (R-on-T phenomenon). The R-on-T in lead V$_5$ finally culminated in a rapidly developing ventricular fibrillation (leads V$_5$ and V$_6$).

tients), the waves gradually transform into coarse, slowly undulating, low-amplitude waveforms. Frequently, periods of tall waveforms alternate with periods of small waveforms.

CLINICAL MANIFESTATIONS

Subjective

If ventricular fibrillation occurs in an upright patient with significant cerebrovascular disease, the patient becomes unconscious and collapses to the floor within a few seconds. If, however, ventricular fibrillation occurs in a supine patient without cerebrovascular disease, the patient may have such warning symptoms as faintness and gradually darkening sight and may be able to ask for help. Unless promptly resuscitated, the patient remains unconscious, may develop seizures, becomes apneic, and eventually dies.

Objective

Physical Examination

The patient quickly loses palpable pulses, becomes unconscious and apneic, and may develop seizures.

Routine Laboratory Abnormalities

The abnormality is identified in the electrocardiogram.

PLANS

Diagnostic

Differential Diagnosis

When a patient suddenly collapses and becomes unconscious, clinicians must assume ventricular fibrillation as its cause until proven to be otherwise. Its differential diagnosis includes both cardiac and noncardiac abnormalities: ventricular tachycardia, asystole or severe bradycardia, supraventricular tachycardia, high-grade atrioventricular blocks (second or third degree), neurocardiogenic syncope, vasovagal syncope, orthostatic hypotension, micturition syncope, cerebrovascular accident, hypoglycemic attack, and overdose of recreational drugs. Prompt evaluation with history, physical examination, a routine electrocardiogram, and blood glucose measurement will aid in the differential diagnosis of ventricular fibrillation from these other conditions.

Diagnostic Options and Recommended Approach

When a patient suddenly collapses and remains unconscious, the patient immediately needs to be connected to a defibrillator with electrocardiographic monitoring capability for quick assessment of the patient's cardiac rhythm.

Therapeutic

Therapeutic Options and Recommended Approach

Promptly administered direct-current countershock using 200 to 400 J is the only effective treatment for ventricular fibrillation. It is crucial to administer direct-current countershock without delay. If defibrillation is not readily available, cardiopulmonary resuscitation (CPR) should be initiated. The airway must be secured using either a mask and oral airway or an endotracheal tube; effective ventilation should be maintained with 100 percent oxygen. Intravenous lines using large needles also must be secured. It must be emphasized that no time should be wasted in electrically defibrillating the patient once the defibrillator is ready for use. When successfully defibrillated within a minute or so after the onset of ventricular fibrillation, the patient may not require intratracheal intubation and subsequent ventilatory support. If the patient is not monitored and his or her underlying heart rhythm causing cardiac arrest without palpable pulse is uncertain, the physician should assume that ventricular fibrillation is the underlying rhythm and direct-current countershock between 200 and 400 J should be promptly administered. In this instance, the physician is most likely dealing with ventricular fibrillation, ventricular tachycardia, or cardiac standstill. "Blindly" administered direct-current countershock, on the one hand, should be effective for ventricular fibrillation: it should not, on the other hand, result in serious complications in ventricular tachycardia or cardiac standstill. In the former, the

direct-current countershock impulse at 200 to 400 J will discharge all the cardiac cells simultaneously and should not cause ventricular fibrillation, even if the pulse falls in the vulnerable period. In cardiac standstill, again the direct-current countershock impulse simply activates (paces) all the cardiac cells simultaneously; it may even initiate heartbeats, but it should not cause any electrical complications. If, however, the patient's cardiac rhythm can be rapidly displayed, diagnosis should be established first while cardiopulmonary resuscitation is continued.

When ventricular fibrillation continues over a minute, sodium bicarbonate (44 mEq) should be given intravenously to correct for metabolic acidosis (which makes defibrillation difficult). Administration of additional sodium bicarbonate and adjustment in the ventilatory support should be guided by the results of periodically analyzed blood gases and pH. In the previously untreated patient, lidocaine (Xylocaine) at a dose of 50 to 100 mg should be given intravenously to facilitate defibrillation and/or to prevent recurrence of ventricular fibrillation. The initial bolus injection of lidocaine should be followed by a continuous infusion at 1 to 4 mg/min. If lidocaine is ineffective in preventing the recurrence of ventricular fibrillation, procainamide (see Chapter 15–21) or bretylium tosylate (Bretylol) may be administered intravenously. Bretylium is usually given intravenously at 5 to 10 mg/kg body weight every 6 to 8 hours, or it may be infused at 1 to 2 mg/min after the first dose. Its main side effect is postural hypotension.

Once the patient becomes stable, any underlying pathologic conditions, both cardiac and noncardiac, should be treated or corrected. Common underlying pathologic conditions include coronary artery disease, valvular heart disease, and severe metabolic abnormalities.

As discussed below, patients with ventricular fibrillation occurring in association with acute myocardial infarction are at a relatively low risk of recurrent ventricular fibrillation after hospital discharge; however, patients with ventricular fibrillation occurring in the absence of acute myocardial infarction are at a high risk of recurrence. Thus, the former patients should undergo ambulatory electrocardiographic recordings and a low-level exercise stress test prior to hospital discharge. Results of these tests may be used to guide long-term antiarrhythmic therapy (see Chapter 15–20). The latter patients (i.e., those with ventricular fibrillation occurring in the absence of acute myocardial infarction) should receive long-term antiarrhythmic treatment: either antiarrhythmic drugs or automatic implantable cardioverter defibrillators (AICDs). Although there have been no completed randomized clinical trials comparing antiarrhythmic drug therapy with AICD therapy in patients who are at a high risk of recurrent cardiac arrest due to ventricular fibrillation or tachycardia, it is generally assumed that the use of AICDs in these high-risk patients results in a low rate of sudden cardiac death. On the other hand, recent retrospective nonrandomized studies suggest that although the use of AICDs reduces sudden arrhythmic death rate, it may not affect overall survival rate.

Currently, three clinical randomized trials are in progress. Prior to completion of these randomized trials, this author recommends the following approach. If such a randomized clinical trial is available, participation of the patient in the study should be encouraged so that the study's result could become available at the earliest time to guide therapy for future patients. For survivors of cardiac arrest due to ventricular fibrillation but without structural heart disease, AICD therapy appears to be the therapy of choice rather than antiarrhythmic drug therapy. Ventricular fibrillation survivors with relatively mild structural heart disease may be treated as those without structural heart disease. On the other hand, ventricular fibrillation survivors with far advanced structural heart disease and thus with a very much limited prognosis may receive antiarrhythmic drug therapy rather than AICD therapy. Antiarrhythmic drugs that appear to be useful in the prevention of recurrent ventricular fibrillation include amiodarone (Cordarone), sotalol (Betapace), and various beta blockers. Please see Table 15–16–2 for their use. Among these, amiodarone is the most frequently prescribed for these patients, either alone or in combination with AICD therapy. As for the use of AICD, nonthoracotomy (pervenous implantation) is the preferred approach rather than thoracotomy, and the biphasic device is preferred to the monophasic device. Recent devices are additionally equipped with antitachycardia pacing capability, which may be used for ventricular tachycardia termination, and antibradycardia pacing capability.

If ventricular fibrillation occurs in the absence of acute myocardial infarction and if severe operable coronary artery disease exists, those patients should be considered for coronary artery bypass graft surgery. In a recent study (Kelly et al., 1990), this approach was shown to be protective against recurrence of ventricular fibrillation.

FOLLOW-UP

The patient developing ventricular fibrillation with acute myocardial infarction should be reassured that the prognosis after successful defibrillation is as good as for those with acute myocardial infarction who do not develop ventricular fibrillation. The patient who develops ventricular fibrillation in the absence of acute myocardial infarction should be told that ventricular fibrillation is likely to recur if untreated and that achieving the goal of minimizing the chance of recurrence may require up to 10 days of hospitalization. As many of the patient's immediate family members as possible should be trained in cardiopulmonary resuscitation. The patient and family members should be made aware of a recent finding: when bystanders initiated cardiopulmonary resuscitation, the percentage of patients who survived and returned home with little or no neurologic deficit was twice that of patients for whom cardiopulmonary resuscitation was not begun until arrival of the ambulance staff.

The frequency of follow-up for the patient who had ventricular fibrillation with acute myocardial infarction is influenced by the underlying coronary artery disease. The patient who had ventricular fibrillation in the absence of acute myocardial infarction or the patient with an automatic implantable cardioverter defibrillator requires frequent follow-up, once every 1 to 3 months, because ventricular fibrillation in these patients tends to recur. Patients need to contact the physician if they experience symptoms suggestive of drug side effects or palpitations suggestive of ventricular arrhythmias. As for resumption of driving, most states do not have any established guidelines for survivors of ventricular fibrillation cardiac arrest or for those treated with antiarrhythmic drugs or AICDs. This author recommends the following approach. No patients should be allowed to drive for a minimum of 6 months after ventricular fibrillation cardiac arrest. Patients who experience no recurrence of cardiac arrest or symptoms suggestive of ventricular tachyarrhythmias for a half to one year may gradually return to driving, initially short-distance supervised driving on quiet roads.

DISCUSSION
Prevalence and Incidence

Each year as many as 400,000 people are estimated to die suddenly of coronary heart disease in the United States. Most of these sudden deaths are presumed to be due to ventricular fibrillation or tachycardia. Ventricular fibrillation is a frequent complication during the first few hours of acute myocardial infarction, and its incidence among patients admitted to the coronary care unit on day 1 of acute myocardial infarction is up to 10%. From that time on, the incidence of ventricular fibrillation declines rapidly, but it continues to be the most frequent cause of sudden death in the post-myocardial infarction stage.

Related Basic Science

The ventricular activation sequence has been mapped during the first few seconds of ventricular fibrillation induced by coronary reperfusion in the dog (Ideker et al., 1991). Ventricular activation occurred in an orderly, rapidly repeating sequence in all hearts, each activation front arising near the border of the ischemic-reperfused region and passing across the nonischemic portion of the ventricles as a single and organized wavefront. As the arrhythmia progressed, the time between the appearance of successive activation fronts decreased, and at the same time, the time for each activation front to traverse the ventricles increased. This resulted in overlapping cycles in which a new activation front arose from the ischemic-reperfused region before the previous front terminated. The overlap between successive activation fronts increased as the arrhythmia continued and was the cause of disorganized waveforms of ventricular fibrillation on the body surface electrocardiogram. These ischemic-reperfused cells discharged extremely fast ini-

tially, and their excitation rate slowed to 235 beats/min during the first 5 minutes after the onset of ventricular fibrillation and 173 beats/min during the next 5 minutes (Akiyama, 1981). These cells had abbreviated and short transmembrane action potentials, significantly different from the wide and tall action potentials of normal ventricular cells.

Natural History and Its Modification with Treatment

In general, about 80% or more of patients suffering from out-of-hospital cardiac arrest do not survive to hospital. In a recent longitudinal study in Seattle, however, as many as 60% of patients having ventricular fibrillation on arrival of emergency paramedical staff were successfully defibrillated. About half of these survivors of ventricular fibrillation were discharged to home. About 75% of these survivors of ventricular fibrillation had coronary heart disease; however, only 19% of the patients had transmural myocardial infarctions (new Q waves on the electrocardiogram), and an additional 11% had enzyme evidence of acute myocardial infarction without new Q waves. Thus, 30% of ventricular fibrillations occurred in the presence of acute myocardial infarction and 70% occurred in its absence. Although patients with primary ventricular fibrillation, that is, ventricular fibrillation in the absence of cardiac failure or complicating acute myocardial infarction, have a much higher in-hospital mortality rate, they have about the same postdischarge mortality rate as those with secondary ventricular fibrillation.

In many electrophysiologic studies on patients with out-of-hospital cardiac arrest not associated with acute myocardial infarction, ventricular arrhythmias were electrically induced in more than 80%, with the incidence of ventricular fibrillation and ventricular tachycardia being more than 40% each. Furthermore, complete suppression of the inducibility of these serious ventricular arrhythmias with drugs appears to predict survival during the follow-up period.

In a study by Kelly et al. (1990), coronary artery bypass graft surgery was effective for prevention of ventricular fibrillation recurrence in all of 11 patients presenting with ventricular fibrillation in the absence of acute myocardial infarction and having severe operable coronary artery stenosis.

As discussed above, recent retrospective nonrandomized studies suggest that the use of AICDs reduces sudden arrhythmic death rate but not overall cardiac mortality rate, presumably due to continued exacerbation of the underlying structural heart diseases, which patients surviving ventricular fibrillation cardiac arrest frequently have. Currently, three prospective randomized studies comparing antiarrhythmic drug therapy with AICD therapy are underway: Antiarrhythmics Versus Implantable Defibrillator (AVID); Canadian Implantable Defibrillator Study (CIDS); Cardiac Arrest Study Hamburg (CASH).

Prevention

Ischemic heart disease is the most common underlying cause of ventricular fibrillation, and therefore, prevention of coronary atherosclerosis should lead to reductions in the prevalence of ventricular fibrillation.

Cost Containment

Electrophysiologic tests are not indicated for patients with ventricular fibrillation occurring during the acute phase of myocardial infarction. In contrast, electrophysiologic tests are necessary for patients with ventricular fibrillation occurring in the absence of acute myocardial infarction, as no other laboratory tests may be reliably used to guide antiarrhythmic therapy in these patients, who are at high risk for sudden death from recurrent ventricular fibrillation. In patients with recurrent ventricular fibrillation, use of the automatic implantable cardioverter defibrillator appears to be more cost effective than a purely pharmacologic approach using serial drugs. This issue is currently followed closely in the AVID study described above.

REFERENCES

Akiyama T. Survivors of arrhythmic cardiac arrest: antiarrhythmics vs. implantable cardioverter defibrillator. In: Toyama J. Recent progress in electropharmacology of the heart. Boca Raton, FL: CRC Press, 1996:179.

Akiyama T. Intracellular recording of in situ ventricular cells during ventricular fibrillation. Am J Physiol 1981;240:H465.

Brooks R, Garan H, Torchiana D, et al. Three-year outcome of a nonthoracotomy approach to cardioverter-debrillator implantation in 189 consecutive patients. Am J Cardiol 1994;74:1011.

Chiriboga D, Yarzebski J, Goldberg RJ, et al. Temporal trends (1975–1990) in the incidence and case-fatality rates of primary ventricular fibrillation complicating acute myocardial infarction: A community-wide perspective. Circulation 1994;89:998.

Cobb LA, Werner JA, Trobaugh GB. Sudden cardiac death: I. A decade's experience with out-of-hospital resuscitation. II. Outcome of resuscitation: Management and future directions. Mod Concepts Cardiovasc Dis 1980;49:31, 37.

Chone CW, Kim SQ, Fisher JD, et al. Comparison of defibrillator therapy and other therapeutic modalities for sustained ventricular tachycardia or ventricular fibrillation associated with coronary artery disease. Am J Cardiol 1994;73:1075.

Gilman JK, Jalal S, Naccarelli GV. Predicting and preventing sudden death from cardiac causes. Circulation 1994;90:1083.

Ideker RE, Tang ASL, Frazier DW, et al. Ventricular defibrillation: Basic concepts. In: El-Sherif N, Samet P, eds. Cardiac pacing and electrophysiology. Philadelphia: Saunders, 1991:713.

Kelly P, Ruskin JN, Vlahakes GJ, et al. Surgical coronary revascularization in survivors of prehospital cardiac arrest: Its effect on inducible ventricular arrhythmias and long-term survival. J Am Coll Cardiol 1990;15:267.

CHAPTER 15–23

Atrial Septal Defect, Secundum Type

Jerre F. Lutz, M.D., and Robert C. Schlant, M.D.

DEFINITION

An interatrial septal defect exists as an open communication in a position normally occupied by the completed interatrial septum. This is in contrast to the more common patient foramen ovale (found in approximately one third of adults), which exists as a flaplike structure and thus creates a potential space in the septum.

The major types of atrial septal defects are secundum, primum, and sinus venosus (Figure 15–23–1).

Ostium secundum defects occur in the midportion of the interatrial septum as a result of failure of the septum secundum to complete the interatrial septum during embryologic formation.

ETIOLOGY

There are two mendelian forms of atrial septal defect which exist as autosomal dominant traits, but in neither form has molecular analysis led to gene localization. The first form is associated with no other abnormalities; the gene is probably on chromosome 6p, near the HLA complex. The second form is associated with atrioventricular conduction delay and upper limb dysplasias; the gene locus is probably on chromosome 20q13.

In the vast majority of patients, no genetic inheritance is noted and the etiology for this malformation is unknown.

CRITERIA FOR DIAGNOSIS

Suggestive

Acyanotic patients with a midsystolic murmur over the upper left sternal border, fixed splitting of the second sound, a right intraventricular conduction delay on the electrocardiogram, and increased pulmonary flow and right ventricular hypertrophy on chest roentgenogram may be considered to have an atrial septal defect secundum type until proved otherwise.

Definitive

Although the presence of a secundum defect can be inferred from noninvasive tests, the diagnosis of a secundum atrial septal defect is dependent on evidence of interatrial shunting by angiography, by oxygen saturation determinations at cardiac catheterization, or by the ability to pass a catheter from the right atrium to the left atrium at the level of the fossa ovalis.

CLINICAL MANIFESTATIONS

Subjective

Some patients are asymptomatic, but dyspnea and fatigue on exertion are the most common complaints, particularly after age 20; three fourths of patients who reach adulthood with a significant left-to-right shunt with a ratio of pulmonary blood flow to systemic blood flow greater than 2:1 are symptomatic. With very large left-to-right shunts, dyspnea and orthopnea occur secondary to increased pulmonary flow and diminished pulmonary compliance.

Patients with secundum atrial defects who have progressed to pulmonary hypertension may have palpitations due to atrial arrhythmias (fibrillation, flutter, or paroxysmal atrial tachycardia), chest pain simulating angina, and hemoptysis; these are infrequent and occur predominantly after age 30. Paradoxical emboli with attendant neurologic symptoms occur predominantly with advanced pulmonary hypertension and right-to-left shunting. Syncope is uncommon unless there is severe pulmonary vascular disease and some right-to-left shunting.

Objective

Physical Examination

The general appearance of adults is usually normal, whereas children with secundum atrial septal defect often have a thin, delicate habitus. Cyanosis or clubbing is unusual. Hypoplasia or triphalangism of the thumbs (fingerlike), abrachia, or phocomelia suggests the Holt–Oram syndrome, which is often associated with a secundum atrial septal defect.

Carotid artery pulsations are normal or of small volume due to decreased forward output. Jugular venous pulses may be abnormal, depending on right atrial pressures and relative compliance of the right and left ventricles. The *v* wave may be larger than the *a* wave, resem-

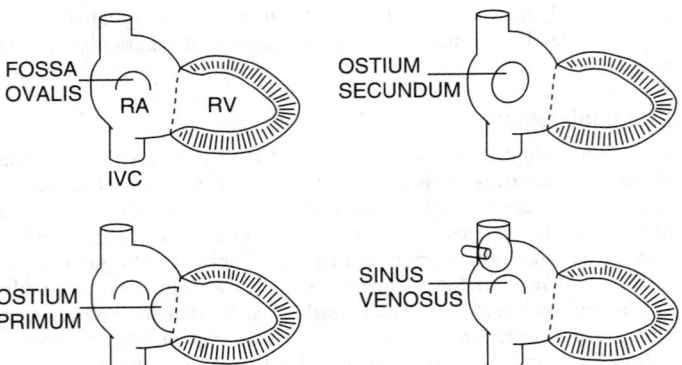

Figure 15–23–1. Schematic illustration of location of the normal fossa ovalis and of ostium secundum, ostium primum, and sinus venosus atrial septal defects. In the sinus venosus defect, note the relationship of the right superior pulmonary vein to the defect. SVC, superior vena cava; IVC, inferior vena cava; RA, right atrium; RV, right ventricle. *(Source: Perloff JK. Atrial septal defect. In: Perloff JK, ed. The clinical recognition of congenital heart disease. 2nd ed. Philadelphia: Saunders, 1994:295. Reproduced with permission of the author and publisher.)*

bling the normal left atrial tracing, whereas a large *a* wave suggests decreased right-ventricular compliance secondary to pulmonary hypertension. A large systolic regurgitant *r* wave can result from tricuspid regurgitation due to right ventricular dilation secondary to severe pulmonary hypertension.

Abnormal precordial movements would include a hyperdynamic right ventricular thrust along the left sternal border. The pulmonary artery and second heart sound vibrations may be palpable in the second left intercostal space. A systolic thrill over the pulmonary artery suggests concomitant pulmonary stenosis or a large intraatrial shunt. With pulmonary hypertension, the right ventricular lift tends to be more sustained.

Splitting of the first sound may be increased with a loud tricuspid component, as the tricuspid valve is held wide open at the beginning of systole by the increased flow. In the vast majority of patients with a significant shunt, the interval between the two components of the second sound is widely split, and the split varies little with respiration or the Valsalva maneuver. Delay of the pulmonic component of the second heart sound is a result of increased right ventricular output and, perhaps, to "hangout" due to the distensible pulmonary vascular bed. The abnormal splitting is less impressive in infants, perhaps due to increased impedance to left-to-right shunting or an increased capacity of the right ventricle to pump a volume load. Splitting of the second sound is less as the heart rate increases. In patients with fixed splitting of the second sound, the normal respiratory variations in right and left ventricular filling are ablated by reciprocal changes in left-to-right shunting; as a consequence, the stroke output from the right and left ventricles tends not to vary. Fixed splitting of S_2 may persist after successful closure of the atrial septum; the cause is unknown, but it may be related to conduction system abnormalities or to increased compliance of the pulmonary vasculature. Most healthy patients without an atrial septal defect but who have wide splitting of the second heart sound in the supine position usually have normal splitting while standing.

Patients with atrial septal defects and normal or mildly elevated pulmonary pressures have a midsystolic crescendo–decrescendo murmur, maximal in the left second or third interspace. The systolic murmur is due to increased (often torrential) flow across the pulmonic valve and is usually grade 3 or less unless there is concomitant pulmonic stenosis or a large shunt. The murmur may radiate to the apex or back. In newborn infants, however, reduced right ventricular compliance prevents significant left-to-right shunting and increased pulmonary blood flow. Apical holosystolic murmurs may be heard in patients with associated mitral regurgitation due to mitral valve prolapse.

Diastolic events can include an opening snap of the tricuspid valve and a middiastolic rumble due to increased flow across the tricuspid valve. A murmur of pulmonic valve regurgitation may be rarely noted in the absence of pulmonary hypertension; this is felt to be due to a dilated pulmonary trunk.

In patients with secundum-type atrial septal defects who have developed pulmonary vascular disease and pulmonary hypertension, the left-to-right shunt decreases, the systolic murmur across the pulmonary outflow tract becomes softer, and the tricuspid flow rumble disappears. A pulmonary ejection click with decreased loudness during inspiration may become more prominent, and the pulmonic component of S_2 increases in intensity. Fixed splitting of the second sound will persist as long as there is significant left-to-right shunting, but the degree of splitting tends to decrease as the amount of shunting decreases. A holosystolic murmur of tricuspid regurgitation loudest at the left sternal border and increasing with inspiration may appear, as may a Graham–Steell murmur of pulmonic valve regurgitation due to pulmonary hypertension. A fourth heart sound along the lower left sternal edge due to diminished right ventricular compliance is often found.

Routine Laboratory Abnormalities

The electrocardiogram (Figure 15–23–2) usually reveals normal sinus rhythm, with an increased incidence of atrial fibrillation, atrial flutter, and atrial tachycardia occurring with advanced disease in the fourth decade. The PR interval is frequently prolonged, but complete heart block is unusual. The P axis is nearly vertical in most patients with secundum atrial septal defects, but is nearly horizontal in patients with

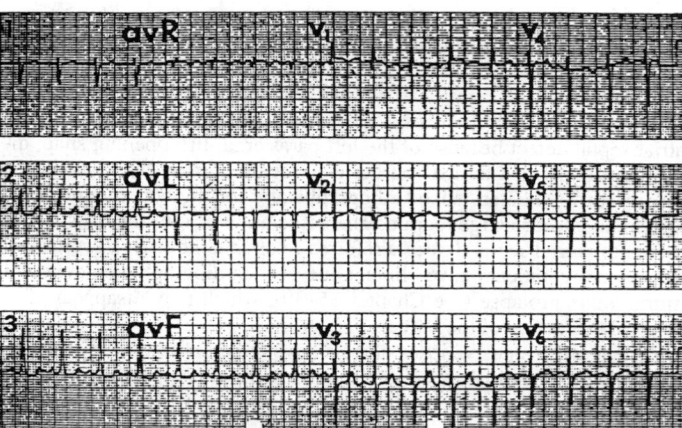

Figure 15–23–2. Electrocardiogram of a 29-year-old woman with a 4:1 secundum atrial septal defect (left-to-right shunt of 4:1) and mild pulmonary hypertension showing right axis deviation of the QRS complex and right intraventricular conduction delay.

sinus venosus defects. There is a slightly increased incidence of Wolff–Parkinson–White syndrome with secundum atrial septal defects. The QRS duration is usually normal, but there is right-axis deviation in more than half of patients. Patients with an atrial septal defect secundum may infrequently have a superiorly directed QRS axis resembling ostium primum atrial septal defects. This may be more frequent in those with associated mitral value prolapse. The QRS pattern in V_1 is usually RsR′, rSr′, or rsR′; no pattern correlates with the size of the shunt or pulmonary artery pressures; and an rSr′ can occur in some healthy patients. Only a small percentage of patients with secundum atrial septal defects have an rS in V_1 and they have small shunts and normal right ventricular pressures. With pulmonary hypertension and pressure overload of the right ventricle, a qR or rR may develop in V_1, and the T wave may shift more posteriorly.

Children and adults with a secundum atrial septal defect and a significant shunt will have an abnormal chest roentgenogram, whereas in an infant with a similar-size shunt the test can be normal (due to impedance to flow into the right ventricle). The typical roentgenogram shows an enlarged right atrium and ventricle, enlarged pulmonary trunk, increased pulmonary blood flow, and small aortic knob, left atrium, and left ventricle. Increased pulmonary flow is often readily detectable on chest x-ray when the pulmonary blood flow is twice systemic; if the pulmonic to systemic blood flow is less than 1.5:1, pulmonary flow is usually assessed as normal by most experienced clinicians. Flow diminishes as pulmonary vascular disease develops, and the left atrium may enlarge in adults with congestive heart failure that is usually associated with atrial fibrillation. Occasionally, one sees aneurysmally dilated pulmonary arteries with calcifications. Markedly pulsatile pulmonary arteries secondary to increased pulmonary blood flow may be seen on fluoroscopy.

Polycythemia may be secondary to arterial hypoxemia as a result of development of Eisenmenger's syndrome (see Chapter 15–27). Although the incidence of endocarditis is less than in primum defects, leukocytosis with a shift toward segmented and band neutrophils should raise the likelihood of an infection, especially in the patient with a large secundum atrial septal defect with a recent patch graft.

PLANS
Diagnostic
Differential Diagnosis

Differential diagnosis should include anomalous pulmonary venous connection. This is clinically similar but can be differentiated at the time of cardiac catheterization by the inability to cross the atrial septum with a cardiac catheter and by a difference in dye-dilution curves when dye is injected into the right and left pulmonary arteries. Anomalous pulmonary venous connection may be suggested by echocardiographic techniques. Anomalous pulmonary venous connection to the inferior vena cava (associated with a hypoplastic lung supplied by systemic circulation) may be seen on chest roentgenogram as a curvilinear, dense area parallel to the right heart border and extending to the diaphragm (scimitar sign). Mitral stenosis occasionally may be confused with an atrial septal defect because of the left parasternal lift, opening snap, diastolic rumble, and an rSr′ on the electrocardiogram, but it should be readily differentiated echocardiographically or by an enlarged left atrium on chest roentgenogram. The association of mitral stenosis with secundum atrial septal defect is referred to as Lutembacher's syndrome. Occasionally patients have clinical and echocardiographic evidence of mitral value prolapse (see Chapter 15–39), which may disappear after surgical correction of the defect.

Patients with sinus venosus defects have fixed splitting of S_2 and abnormal electrocardiograms less often than with a comparable-sized secundum-type defect.

Diagnostic Options

Although noninvasive evaluation of a patient with a secundum atrial septal defect can reveal the defect by two-dimensional echocardiography (either transthoracic or transesophageal) and determine the Q_p/Q_s as well as confirm the shunt at the interatrial level by Doppler techniques, cardiac catheterization is still recommended by most physicians to definitively demonstrate the anatomy, the degree of shunting as evidenced by oximetric measurements, and the pulmonary artery pressures prior to contemplated surgical intervention.

An M-mode echocardiogram reveals dilation of the right ventricle with paradoxical motion of the ventricular septum in 90% of patients with greater than 2:1 shunt. There is less sensitivity with smaller shunts.

At cardiac catheterization there may be normal or increased right atrial, right ventricular, and pulmonary artery pressures. An abnormal stepup in the oxygen saturations of intracardiac blood samples occurs in the right atrium. Left-to-right shunting at the atrial level can also be identified by a platinum-tipped catheter sensitive to changes in polarity from inhaled hydrogen gas or by dye injected into the pulmonary artery returning to the right atrium and left atrium almost simultaneously. There may be a systolic pressure difference between the right ventricle and the pulmonary artery of 20 mm Hg due only to the large flow across the pulmonary valve. Larger pressure differences are likely due to mild pulmonic stenosis.

Recommended Approach

Patients with small atrial defects do not develop large shunt volumes or pulmonary hypertension. This group of patients may be discovered on physical examination or, coincidentally, by echocardiography or cardiac catheterization. The prognosis is excellent and serial echocardiography over a lifetime should suffice.

Patients with large atrial septal defects and normal or moderately increased pulmonary pressures are candidates for surgical repair. Echocardiography combined with Doppler techniques can accurately delineate the intracardiac shunt and pulmonary artery pressures. Cardiac catheterization is indicated in patients with concomitant defects or a high likelihood of coronary artery disease in whom coronary arteriography should be performed prior to surgical repair.

Patients with large atrial septal defects and severe pulmonary hypertension should have cardiac catheterization to definitively delineate the diagnosis and to make sure *no* other form of therapy is indicated prior to consideration of lung transplant combined with closure of the defect.

Therapeutic

Therapeutic Options

Care should be taken in patients with secundum atrial septal defects who develop sore throats, as there may be an increased incidence of rheumatic heart disease and mitral stenosis. Bacterial endocarditis prophylaxis is currently not recommended by the American Heart Association for proven isolated secundum atrial septal defect, although some cardiologists do prescribe antibiotic prophylaxis. Prophylaxis is recommended if patients have a murmur compatible with concomitant mitral valve prolapse. No definite proof of effectiveness is available.

Surgery is currently recommended for patients with left-to-right shunting producing pulmonary blood flow that is 1.5:1 or greater than systemic blood flow. Surgical closure is recommended for patients with a $Q_p/Q_s \geq 1.5:1$ and pulmonary hypertension if systemic saturation exceeds 92% and total pulmonary resistance is acceptable. Patients with congestive heart failure and atrial fibrillation may be considered for surgical repair, although surgical mortality is increased. Patients with very severe pulmonary vascular disease and with a reversal of shunting or a predominant right-to-left shunt usually have irreversible pulmonary vascular disease and usually are not candidates for isolated closure of the atrial septal defect.

Although the surgical approach remains standard, transcatheter closure of atrial septal defects using a double-disk prosthesis advanced from the femoral vein has been successfully performed in some children and adults.

Recommended Approach

The operative morbidity and mortality of surgical techniques are so low that all patients who fulfill the above criteria should have surgery unless the defect is found at advanced age. Patients with large atrial septal defects and Eisenmenger's physiology should be considered for lung transplant combined with closure of the interatrial defect.

FOLLOW-UP

As arrhythmias may be poorly tolerated, palpitations should be reported to the physician for evaluation. Fever may be an indication of endocarditis in patients with concomitant mitral valve disease.

Evaluation of patients with secundum atrial septal defects who are not surgical candidates can be performed at yearly intervals with an electrocardiogram and chest roentgenogram. Patients may be seen every other year after surgical repair.

DISCUSSION

Prevalence and Incidence

Excluding bicuspid aortic valve and mitral valve prolapse, atrial septal defect is the most common congenital defect among adults.

Related Basic Science

Genetics

The postulated genetic transmission was previously described.

Anatomic Derangement

The most common defect in the intraatrial septum (70–80%) is the ostium secundum type that occurs in the region of the fossa ovalis secondary to failure of formation of the septum secundum (Figure 15–23–1). The sinus venosus defect (6–8%) is located superior to the fossa ovalis (Bedford, 1960). Ostium primum defects adjoin the endocardial cushion where the septum primum failed to form. The abnormal physiology present is determined by the magnitude of the shunt, resistance to pulmonary flow, and coexistent heart disease. There is little or no pressure difference between the right and left atria in a patient with an uncomplicated large secundum atrial septal defect. During diastole all four chambers communicate, and although the left atrium is less distensible than the right atrium, the major determinant of size and direction of shunt is the relative distensibility of the right ventricle versus the left ventricle. Thus, any disease processes that alter pulmonary artery, aortic, or left ventricular pressures may change the magnitude of shunting.

Natural History and Its Modification with Treatment

Spontaneous closure of an atrial septal defect may occur in up to half of patients less than 1 year of age but is rare thereafter.

The chance of developing pulmonary vascular disease with a secundum atrial septal defect is less than with a ventricular septal defect or patent ductus arteriosus. Among patients with significant atrial septal defects, most develop a pulmonary artery systolic pressure greater than 50 mm Hg, although relatively few develop increased pulmonary vascular resistance greater than 450 dyn·s·cm^{-5}. The incidence of pulmonary vascular disease and pulmonary hypertension is greater in children born at higher altitudes. After the fourth decade, atrial arrhythmias may significantly increase and further increase the degree of disability.

Endocarditis of the pulmonic valve secondary to flow or of the atrial septal defect is rare.

The life expectancy of patients with uncorrected atrial septal defects is diminished, although survival to adulthood is expected and many live to advanced age. Survival depends on the magnitude of the shunt and the degree of pulmonary vascular disease, although patients with significant pulmonary hypertension may reach age 40.

Death is usually secondary to congestive heart failure, pulmonary artery embolus or thrombosis, pulmonary infections, paradoxical brain abscess, or rupture of the pulmonary artery. Occasionally, infants die in congestive heart failure; some of these patients may have associated pulmonary vascular disease that may be primary. Patients with a patent foramen ovale may develop an atrial septal defect secondary to a marked increase in left atrial pressure by mitral valve disease. This results from stretching of the foramen ovale and an acquired left-to-right shunt.

Patients who undergo conventional repair have a low operative mortality and an excellent postoperative prognosis, which approaches 99 to 100% at 20 to 25 years following repair.

Prevention

Genetic counseling is indicated for those with familial predisposition.

Cost Containment

Serial echocardiograms are generally not indicated for follow-up of patients with secundum atrial septal defects. Cardiac catheterization should be used for quantitation of shunt flow and pulmonary artery resistance and to rule out associated lesions. Patients with suspected small shunts should be followed clinically unless there is a greater social reason, such as insurability, to pursue the diagnosis. Routine postoperative catheterization is not necessary.

REFERENCES

Bedford DE. The anatomical types of atrial septal defect: Their incidence and clinical diagnosis. Am J Cardiol 1960;6:568.

De Belder MA, Tourikis L, Griffith M, et al. Transesophageal contrast echocardiography and color flow mapping: Method of choice for the detection of shunts at the atrial level. Am Heart J 1992;124:1545.

Hamilton WT, Haffajee CE, Dalen JE, et al. Atrial septal defect secundum: Clinical profile with physiologic correlates in children and adults. In: Roberts WC, ed. Adult congenital heart disease. Philadelphia: Davis, 1987:395.

Horvath JK, Burke RP, Collins JJ, et al. Surgical treatment of adult atrial septal defect: Early and long-term results. J Am Coll Cardiol 1992;20:1156.

Nugent WE, Plauth WH Jr, Edwards JE, Williams WH. The pathology, pathophysiology, recognition and treatment of congenital heart disease. In: Schlant RC, Alexander RW, O'Rourke RA, et al., eds. Hurst's the heart. 8th ed. New York: McGraw-Hill, 1994:1773.

Pollick C, Sullivan H, Cujec B, et al. Doppler color flow imaging assessment of shunt size in atrial septal defects. Circulation 1988;78:522.

Rao PS, Wilson AD, Levy JM, et al. Role of "buttoned" double-disc device in the management of atrial septal defects. Am Heart J 1992;123:191.

St. John Sutton MG, Tajik AJ, McGoon DC. Atrial septal defect in patients ages 60 and older: Operative results and long-term postoperative follow-up. Circulation 1981;64:402.

CHAPTER 15–24

Atrial Septal Defect, Primum Type

Jerre F. Lutz, M.D., and Robert C. Schlant, M.D.

DEFINITION

An ostium primum atrial septal defect is the partial type of common atrioventricular (AV) canal or endocardial cushion defect. Interatrial shunting of blood occurs across the lower atrial septum at the region normally closed by the septum primum. Congenital clefts of the mitral and tricuspid valves producing valvular regurgitation also may be identified.

Two other types of endocardial cushion defects are described. The complete type of common AV canal is characterized by a single common (AV) valve and communication between all four intracardiac chambers. The term *left ventricular–right atrial communication* is used for a defect in the interventricular septum associated with a cleft in the septal leaflet of the tricuspid valve, allowing direct communication between the two chambers named. These lesions are identified by cardiac catheterization and angiography. Details of these conditions are not described in this chapter.

ETIOLOGY

In the partial type of AV canal, the endocardial cushions fuse centrally only. The upper part of the ventricular septum is closed by fibrous tissue. When the left side of the endocardial cushions do not fuse, the mitral valve is cleft.

Although half of children with Down syndrome (trisomy 21) have congenital heart disease (most often endocardial cushion defects), ostium primum defects are *not* usually associated with Down syndrome.

The etiology of this disorder is unknown.

CRITERIA FOR DIAGNOSIS
Suggestive

The diagnosis of ostium primum atrial septal defect is likely in an acyanotic patient with a midsystolic murmur at the upper left sternal border, an apical holosystolic murmur, increased pulmonary flow on chest roentgenogram, and an electrocardiogram revealing a mean QRS vector directed far to the left and anterior, indicating right bundle-branch block plus left anterior superior division block.

Definitive

Confirmation of the diagnosis may be made either by echocardiographic demonstration of a defect in the lower atrial septum, at cardiac catheterization from left ventricular angiography and evidence of interatrial shunting of blood, and occasionally by direct passage of a catheter across the defect.

CLINICAL MANIFESTATIONS
Subjective

Most cases of ostium primum defect occur sporadically, although occasionally a genetic predisposition, as in secundum atrial septal defect, may be evident. Symptoms are proportional to the size of the septal defect. In the absence of mitral regurgitation, symptoms parallel those of ostium secundum atrial septal defects.

Symptoms generally occur earlier (usually in childhood rather than infancy) and are more severe in patients with ostium primum plus mitral regurgitation than in those with a secundum atrial septal defect of similar size. Fatigue and dyspnea are common, as are recurrent respiratory infections. Symptoms are likely before age 20. Palpitations secondary to arrhythmias occur with increasing frequency with age.

Fever, malaise, and weight loss should suggest bacterial endocarditis, which is much more common in primum atrial septal defects or in complete endocardial cushion defects than in secundum atrial septal defects.

Objective

Physical Examination

Infants with a large primum atrial septal defect, especially one associated with significant mitral regurgitation, may present with congestive heart failure as evidenced by severe tachypnea, dyspnea, difficulty feeding, and an enlarged, tender liver.

Cyanosis at rest or provoked by crying or feeding is unusual with an uncomplicated ostium primum defect, but it is frequent in patients with complete atrioventricular canal. Both conditions are frequently associated with Down syndrome (mongolism and a variable degree of mental retardation), particularly complete atrioventricular canal.

The carotid upstroke and amplitude are usually normal, but the pulse pressure tends to be decreased with increased atrial shunting and mitral regurgitation.

Jugular venous pulses may be normal with small defects. A large regurgitant *r* or *v* wave may occur with a large atrial septal defect and significant mitral or tricuspid regurgitation, and this reflects the common atrial pressure pulse. The tricuspid regurgitation may be secondary to increased right ventricular pressures or a cleft tricuspid valve. A large *a* wave may be present with right ventricular hypertrophy and pulmonary hypertension.

Precordial movements in a patient with a large ostium primum defect and a cleft mitral valve will be similar to those in a patient with the secundum type of defect (a hyperdynamic right ventricle), but in addition, the left ventricular impulse is enlarged and displaced laterally if there is significant mitral regurgitation. With severe mitral regurgitation, an apical systolic thrill may be present. At times a thrill will be felt beneath or to the right of the sternum if significant flow occurs from left ventricle to left atrium and across the septal defect to the right atrium. If the ostium primum defect is small and the mitral regurgitation severe, the precordial examination resembles mitral regurgitation with a hyperdynamic left ventricular apex impulse, an apical thrill of mitral regurgitation, and a palpable rapid filling wave during diastole (S_3).

Auscultation of patients with primum atrial septal defect is similar to that of patients with secundum atrial septal defect. The S_1 is split with a loud tricuspid component, although this is less pronounced in patients with a long PR interval. Relatively fixed splitting of the second heart sound is usual, but this is slightly less frequent and less prominent than in patients with secundum atrial septal defect. The midsystolic murmur across the pulmonary outflow tract tends to be quite prominent; it is often harsh and loud because the left-to-right shunt is increased by mitral regurgitation. As with secundum atrial septal defect, the development of pulmonary vascular disease decreases the splitting of S_2 but increases the loudness of the pulmonic component. An opening snap of the tricuspid valve or flow rumble across the tricuspid valve due to increased flow may be heard along the lower left sternal edge.

An apical holosystolic blowing murmur of mitral regurgitation is frequently present. When mitral regurgitation is severe but the septal defect is small, the auscultatory findings are those of so-called pure mitral regurgitation with an apical holosystolic murmur, S_3 gallop, and apical diastolic flow rumble. In patients with both significant mitral regurgitation and a large atrial septal defect, there may be a diastolic flow rumble across the tricuspid valve. If no associated mitral or tricuspid valve abnormality is present, the auscultatory findings of a patient with an isolated ostium primum defect may be indistinguishable from those of a patient with a secundum atrial septal defect.

Patients with a congenital cleft in the tricuspid valve may have a holosystolic murmur along the lower left sternal border.

Routine Laboratory Abnormalities

The electrocardiogram of patients with ostium primum atrial septal defect is virtually diagnostic in the proper clinical setting. There may be a

left or right atrial abnormality. The duration of the QRS complex may be normal or prolonged. In either case, the mean QRS vector is usually directed to the left and anteriorly, signifying right ventricular conduction defect or right bundle-branch block plus left anterior division block. At times, as shown in Figure 15–24–1, the mean QRS vector is directed far to the left but is not anteriorly directed. There may be preexcitation of the ventricles (Figure 15–24–2).

The chest roentgenogram resembles secundum atrial septal defect with a small aorta, increased pulmonary flow, and enlarged pulmonary trunk. The right atrium and right ventricle tend to be larger than those in a patient with a secundum atrial septal defect and a comparable shunt. Unlike secundum atrial septal defect, the left atrium is often enlarged, particularly with moderate or marked mitral regurgitation. In the occasional patient with severe mitral regurgitation and small septal defect, the left atrium and ventricle are enlarged, whereas the pulmonary vasculature, right atrial size, and right ventricular size are normal unless pulmonary venous hypertension is present.

As pulmonary hypertension develops, arterial hypoxemia will occur as a result of increased right-to-left shunting (see Chapter 15–27). Polycythemia and clubbing are clues to this advanced stage of ostium primum defect. A leukocytosis, especially with a shift in the differential toward segmented and band forms, should raise the possibility of an infection such as bacterial endocarditis.

PLANS

Diagnostic

Differential Diagnosis

Combining clinical features with noninvasive testing usually separates patients with ostium primum defects from patients with ostium secundum defects or the complete form of AV canal defect.

Diagnostic Options

Noninvasive evaluation of the patient with an ostium primum atrial septal defect is very helpful for the following reasons: (1) the presence or absence of a complete atrial septum can be detected with a high degree of accuracy; (2) concomitant anatomic defects can be readily visualized; and (3) Doppler techniques allow detection of interatrial shunting as well as derivation of a Q_p/Q_s ratio by comparing flow in the aorta and pulmonary artery. Because of the ability to quantify shunts more accurately, measure pressures, and determine regurgitant flow across the atrioventricular valves, cardiac catheterization remains the most accurate method to establish the diagnosis and measure those anatomic and physiologic variables necessary to make a clinical decision regarding therapy.

At the time of cardiac catheterization, ostium primum septal defect must be distinguished from secundum defect, atrioventricular canal defect, and so-called pure mitral regurgitation.

Echocardiography in patients with a significant left-to-right shunt indicates right ventricular volume overload with paradoxical motion of the ventricular septum and an enlarged right ventricle. The anterior mitral valve leaflet may be anteriorly displaced with a decreased A wave,

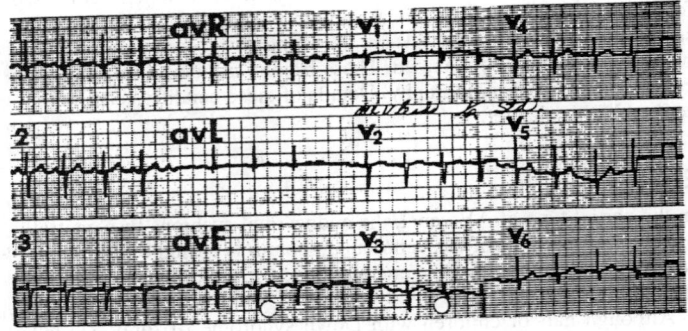

Figure 15–24–1. Electrocardiogram of a 15-year-old girl with an ostium primum defect. The mean QRS vector is directed far to the left, and slightly posteriorly. The mean QRS rector is more commonly directed to the left and anteriorly.

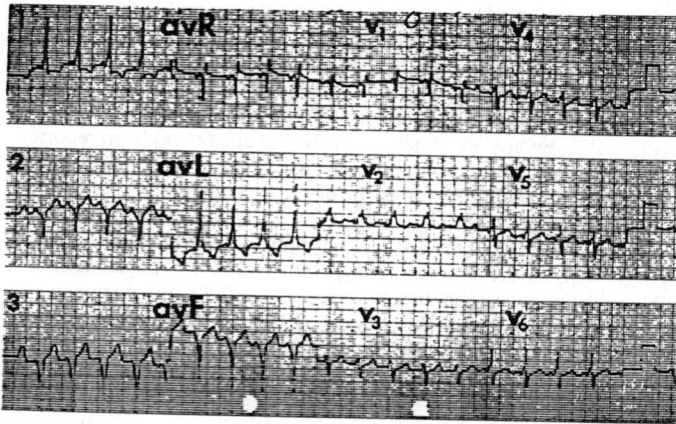

Figure 15–24–2. Electrocardiogram of the same patient as in Figure 15–24–1, showing conduction by way of a bypass tract indicating preexcitation of the ventricles (Wolff–Parkinson–White syndrome).

decreased amplitude of diastolic excursion, and diastolic apposition of the anterior mitral valve leaflet to the ventricular septum. The left atrium and ventricle may be dilated in patients with significant mitral regurgitation. Features that are present in patients with isolated primum atrial septal defect but are not found in atrioventricular (AV) canal defect include the following: (1) absence of definite mitral valve echoes crossing the interventricular septum; and (2) presence of septal echoes from apex to base, reflecting an intact ventricular septum.

The following findings are present at cardiac catheterization: (1) oxygen stepup at the atrial level, (2) low pass of the catheter across the atrial septum suggesting an ostium primum defect, (3) gooseneck deformity (Figure 15–24–3) of the left ventricular outflow tract due to

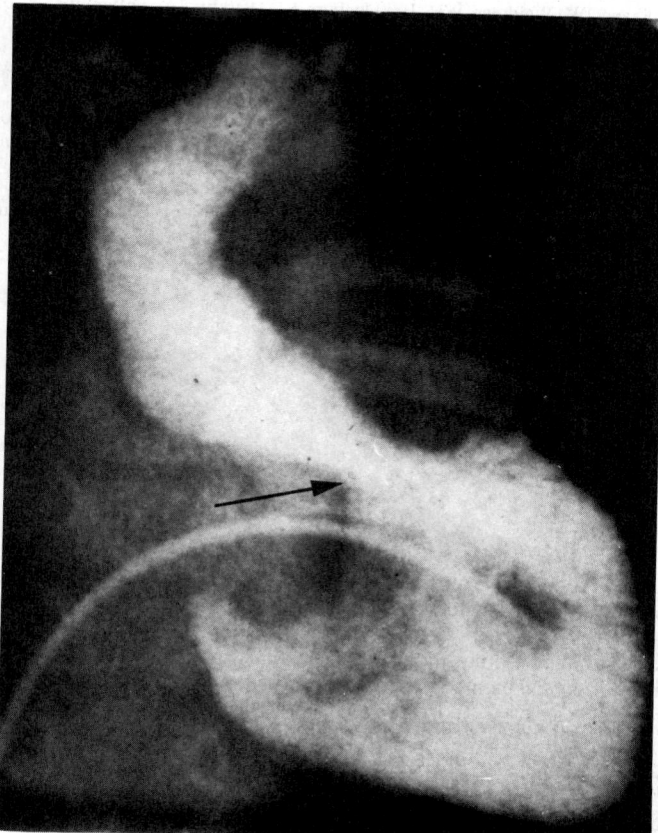

Figure 15–24–3. Left ventriculogram of a 3-year-old boy with an atrioventricular canal demonstrating the gooseneck deformity of the left ventricular outflow tract (arrow).

tethering of the anterior mitral valve leaflet to the ventricular septum, decreasing the size of the outflow tract, and (4) mitral regurgitation from left ventricle to left atrium and possibly to the right atrium.

Recommended Approach

Noninvasive procedures such as echo–Doppler and cardiac magnetic resonance imaging can accurately assess anatomy, pulmonary artery pressure, and direction of flow.

Cardiac catheterization is necessary in patients with additional complex congenital defects or those discovered at an advanced age who are surgical candidates and in whom coronary artery disease is a possibility.

Therapeutic

Therapeutic Options

Prophylaxis against endocarditis is indicated because of definite increased susceptibility to bacterial endocarditis. Congestive heart failure is treated with digitalis and diuretics. Arterial vasodilators to decrease afterload are also useful. With mild to moderate or no mitral regurgitation, indications for surgical correction are similar to those of secundum atrial septal defects. With severe mitral regurgitation, it is best to wait, when possible, until the patient can tolerate mitral valve replacement. Previously, surgery was performed at age 5 or 6 years unless congestive heart failure or growth retardation forced earlier surgery. Improved surgical techniques have allowed corrective surgery to be performed electively earlier in life.

Only a small percentage of patients who require surgery for primum atrial septal defect need mitral valve replacement. The overall perioperative mortality rate is considerably lower when the mitral regurgitation is moderate or less and valve replacement is not needed. Mortality is increased in symptomatic patients with pulmonary hypertension and increased pulmonary vascular resistance. Mild or moderate mitral regurgitation can often be improved with surgical mitral valvuloplasty. After surgery, more than three fourths of patients become asymptomatic and their heart sizes on chest roentgenograms become normal. The 15-year postoperative survival may approach 80% unless pulmonary hypertension is present. If the mean pulmonary pressure is greater than 30 mm Hg, however, this survival decreases to half.

Recommended Approach

Small defects can be managed medically and followed with serial echocardiography with concomitant Doppler interrogation.

Moderate to large defects should be managed similarly to patients with atrial septal defect secundum type. Surgical intervention is indicated in patients with left-to-right shunts greater than 1.5:1 and pulmonary hypertension secondary to increased flow. Mitral regurgitation may necessitate valve repair or replacement in the setting of significant but reversible pulmonary hypertension or evidence of declining left ventricular function.

Patients with large atrial septal defects (primum type) and severe pulmonary hypertension may be candidates for lung transplantation and closure of the atrial septal defect if the shunt was the dominant lesion and the mitral regurgitation minimal. Lung transplantation, closure of the atrial septal defect, and mitral repair or replacement would at this point constitute too great a surgical risk to hazard.

FOLLOW-UP

Fever may be a sign of endocarditis or of an upper respiratory infection and should be reported to the physician promptly. Any change in exercise tolerance or dyspnea also should be reported, as these symptoms may indicate progression of pulmonary hypertension or mitral regurgitation.

Recommendations are similar to those for patients with secundum atrial septal defects. Differences would include visits at 6-month intervals for patients with severe mitral regurgitation for noninvasive evaluation of ventricular function using either nuclear or echocardiographic techniques, and at yearly intervals in postoperative patients because of the increased incidence of complete heart block even after successful repair.

DISCUSSION
Prevalence and Incidence

Atrial septal defects are found in approximately 10% of children with congenital heart disease living beyond the first year (Nugent et al., 1994). Approximately 20% of interatrial communications are of the ostium primum type (Bedford, 1960).

Related Basic Science
Physiologic or Metabolic Derangement

The major determinant of the degree of shunting, as in secundum atrial septal defect, is the relative distensibility of the right and left ventricles. Mitral regurgitation increases the degree of left-to-right shunt. In a complete atrioventricular canal, the size of the ventricular septal defect is the greatest determinant of pulmonary arterial pressure.

If mitral mobility and chordal support are adequate, a cleft mitral valve can be competent; conversely, a partial cleft in the mitral leaflet can be associated with severe regurgitation.

Anatomic Derangement

The endocardial cushions fuse to form the mitral and tricuspid valves and the cornerstone of the atrial and ventricular septa. Ostium primum defects embryologically result when the septum primum fails to converge with the endocardial cushions. Variants of endocardial cushion defects include ostium primum atrial septal defect, some high ventricular septal defects, and clefts in the septal leaflet of the tricuspid valve or the anterior leaflet of the mitral valve. Any combination or isolated defect is possible. Ostium primum defects occur without ventricular septal defects, but these are associated with cleft mitral leaflet in the vast majority of cases and cleft tricuspid leaflet in half. Accessory chordae tendineae are important anatomic features of a cleft mitral leaflet and prevent flailing of the leaflet by attaching the margins of the cleft to the ventricular septum. These accessory chordae contribute to the characteristic gooseneck deformity of the left ventricular outflow tract seen on angiography.

Natural History and Its Modification with Treatment

Pulmonary hypertension and congestive heart failure occur earlier and are more common in patients with ostium primum defects than in those with secundum atrial septal defects.

Atrial tachyarrhythmias occur especially after age 30, but their occurrence does not seem to correlate well with the level of pulmonary hypertension or mitral regurgitation. Complete heart block may occur at any age, even after successful repair.

Bacterial endocarditis occurs not uncommonly in patients with ostium primum defects, but with modern therapy it rarely causes death.

Most patients with large ostium primum defects who are not treated surgically die by age 30, although survival to age 60 has been reported.

Partial defects without mitral regurgitation are expected to have the same excellent results described in ostium secundum atrial septal defects.

Hospital mortality rates are highest in infants with severe AV valve regurgitation, severe pulmonary hypertension, and hypoplastic left or right ventricle. Five-year survival greater than 90% following successful correction is reported (Berger et al., 1979) in patients with *complete AV canal defects.*

Prevention

Ostium primum atrial septal defect is a congenital lesion usually occurring sporadically; it is less often associated with trisomy 21 (Down syndrome).

Cost Containment

Recommendations are the same as those for secundum atrial septal defect.

REFERENCES

Abbruzzese PA, Napoleone A, Bini RM, et al. Late left atrioventricular valve insufficiency after repair of partial atrioventricular septal defects: Anatomic and surgical determinants. Ann Thorac Surg 1990;49:111.

Bedford DE. The anatomical types of atrial septal defect: Their incidence and clinical diagnosis. Am J Cardiol 1960;6:568.

Berger TJ, Blackstone EH, Kirklin JW, et al. Survival and probability of cure without and with operation in complete atrioventricular canal. Ann Thorac Surg 1979;27:104.

Blount SG, Balchum OJ, Gensini G. The persistent ostium primum atrial septal defect. Circulation 1956;13:499.

DuShane JW, Weidman WH, Brandenburg RD, Kirklin JW. Differentiation of interatrial communications by clinical methods. Circulation 1960;21:363.

McGoon DC, Puga F. Atrioventricular canal. Cardiovasc Clin 1981;1:311.

McMullan MH, McGoon DC, Wallace RB, et al. Surgical treatment of partial atrioventricular canal. Arch Surg 1973;197:705.

Nugent WE, Plauth WH Jr, Edwards JE, Williams WH. The pathology, pathophysiology, recognition and treatment of congenital heart disease. In: Schlant RC, Alexander RW, O'Rourke RA, et al., eds. Hurst's the heart. 8th ed. New York: McGraw-Hill, 1994:1761.

Silverman NH, Schmidt NH. The current role of Doppler echocardiography in the diagnosis of heart disease in children. Cardiol Clin 1989;7(2):265.

CHAPTER 15–25

Ventricular Septal Defect

Jerre F. Lutz, M.D., and Robert C. Schlant, M.D.

DEFINITION

Isolated ventricular septal defect is defined as a communication between the right and left ventricles (thus excluding endocardial cushion defects) or an incomplete ventricular septum (excluding single ventricle).

ETIOLOGY

Although ventricular septal defects can occur as a result of trauma or myocardial infarction, this chapter concentrates on congenital ventricular septal defects (VSDs). Congenital VSDs may occur as part of complex congenital abnormalities in patients with trisomy 13 or 18. The etiology of isolated VSDs is unknown.

Embryologically, muscular VSDs arise due to failure of completion of the ventricular septum. Perimembranous VSDs may be due to failure of fusion of the endocardial cushions of the upper border of the muscular ventricular septum and the conal septum. Supracristal VSDs form as a result of malalignment or failure of fusion of the truncal and conal septal.

CRITERIA FOR DIAGNOSIS
Suggestive

The diagnosis of VSD should be considered in a patient presenting with a holosystolic murmur near the lower left edge of the sternum, with or without other evidence of cardiac chamber enlargement.

Definitive

The diagnosis is proved either at cardiac catheterization by identifying the increased oxygen saturation in the right ventricle or by Doppler echocardiography demonstrating the flow of blood across the interventricular septum. Additional cardiac abnormalities and pulmonary hypertension may also be found at cardiac catheterization.

CLINICAL MANIFESTATIONS

Subjective

Infants with large VSDs may present with congestive heart failure manifested by severe dyspnea, tachypnea, and difficulty feeding; however, children with a small VSD (maladie de Roger) are usually asymptomatic.

The most common symptoms encountered in patients with moderate or VSDs are dyspnea, fatigue, and, occasionally, palpitations. Improvement of symptoms can occur as a result of spontaneous closure of the septal defect, increasing pulmonary resistance to pulmonary flow due to the development of reactive pulmonary hypertension, or the development of infundibular pulmonic stenosis. Hemoptysis suggests progression to Eisenmenger's syndrome (see Chapter 15–27).

Objective

Physical Examination

Infants with isolated VSDs usually have a normal birth weight. No murmur may be present at birth; however, a loud murmur may be heard a few days or weeks later with small or moderate defects. The infant's parents may also note a precordial thrill. The weight of a child with a large VSD is usually below the third percentile, although linear growth is preserved. Congestive heart failure is frequently seen at 6 to 12 weeks of age. An infant in congestive heart failure may be restless and irritable and have an increased respiratory rate of 80 to 100 per minute with grunting respirations. Flaring nostrils and intercostal retractions are common. A history of frequent respiratory infections or increased sweating is often present. Congestive failure is rare after the age of 8 to 12 months in infants with VSD unless there is concomitant anemia, endocarditis, or aortic regurgitation. Cerebral abscesses and thromboses are uncommon.

The signs of VSD with a predominant left-to-right shunt are summarized in Table 15–25–1. Patients with VSD who develop severe pulmonary vascular disease with right-to-left shunting or bidirectional shunting with predominant right-to-left shunting are classified as having Eisenmenger's syndrome (see Chapter 15–27).

The second sound is normally split, and splitting increases normally with inspiration in patients with a small or moderate VSD. Patients with a large left-to-right shunt usually have a left ventricular gallop (S_3) sound, a loud pulmonic component of the second sound (P_2), and accentuated splitting of the second heart sound; a fourth heart sound is rarely audible.

In infants who have spontaneous closure, the systolic murmur becomes shorter, softer, and higher-pitched. With a muscular VSD, the murmur can end in late systole when the defect is closed by contracting muscle. The systolic murmur of a supracristal VSD tends to radiate from the upper left sternal border to the neck. Inhalation of amyl nitrite may decrease the systolic murmur of a small VSD by decreasing systemic resistance and the volume of left-to-right shunt; in patients with vasoreactive pulmonary hypertension, however, amyl nitrite may also decrease the pulmonary vascular resistance and increase left-to-right shunting and the intensity of the murmur. An ejection sound is frequently audible in patients with aneurysm of the ventricular septum who may also have a systolic murmur from right ventricular outflow obstruction. Diastolic murmurs from aortic regurgitation are caused by nonsupport of the aortic valvular tissue. The murmur of pulmonary regurgitation signifies pulmonary hypertension.

Routine Laboratory Abnormalities

The electrocardiogram usually reveals a normal sinus rhythm and only rarely do arrhythmias such as atrial flutter, atrial or junctional tachycardia, and atrial fibrillation occur. The electrocardiogram remains normal

TABLE 15–25–1. VENTRICULAR SEPTAL DEFECT

Objective Parameter	Small	Moderate	Large
General	Normal	Normal	Frail, underweight; chest wall deformities
Venous pulses	Normal	Normal	Mean JVP elevated; large a and v waves
Arterial pulses	Normal	Brisk	Brisk with increasing LV contractility; decreased or alternans with heart failure
Precordium	Normal ± thrill 3rd, 4th inter-space or at base with supracristal VSD	PA palpable; LV but no RV thrust; thrill usual	PA palpable; LV and RV impulses palpable; thrill in half
Auscultation	Loud, harsh murmur, usually holosystolic from left sternal border to right of sternum	Murmur at left sternal border; S_3; diastolic rumble in two thirds	Murmur decreases as PA pressure increases; S_3 + rumble if pulmonary flow increased; rales
Electrocardiogram	Normal	Left ventricular hypertrophy	Biventricular hypertrophy; P waves enlarged if LA is increasing
Chest x-ray	Normal	PA, LV, and LA enlarged; aorta normal or small; pulmonary flow increased	PA and biventricular enlargement; flow increases until shunt equalizes
Size of defect	Less than 0.5 cm^2/m^2	0.5–1.0 cm^2/m^2	More than 1.0 cm^2/m^2
Q_p/Q_s	Less than 1.5:1	1.5:1 to 2:1 (occasionally greater)	More than 2:1 or 3:1
PA pressure	Normal	PA systolic less than half systemic	PA systolic greater than half systemic

JVP, jugular venous pulse; LV, left ventricle; RV, right ventricle; PA, pulmonary artery; VSD, ventricular septal defect; LA, left atrium

with a VSD, however, with a large defect, electrocardiogram indicates left ventricular enlargement initially, followed by combined left and right ventricular hypertrophy and, finally, right ventricular hypertrophy. Large R and S waves in leads V_2 to V_4 (the Katz–Wachtel phenomenon) indicate biventricular hypertrophy. Aneurysm of the ventricular septum is associated with an increased incidence of arrhythmias and conduction abnormalities.

The chest film of patient with a small VSD is normal; however, in those with moderate or large defects it usually shows enlargement of both ventricles and of the left atrium in association with increased pulmonary blood flow. A decreasing heart size may be seen either with spontaneous closure of the VSD in infancy or childhood or with the later development of infundibular pulmonic stenosis or Eisenmenger's syndrome, which decrease the volume of left-to-right shunt and pulmonary blood flow.

The main pulmonary artery and its branches may be larger than normal. When there is abrupt narrowing of the branches and right ventricular hypertrophy, pulmonary hypertension (Eisenmenger's syndrome) is usually present. Erythrocytosis occurs with the progressive systemic arterial hypoxemia seen with the development of Eisenmenger's syndrome. A leukocytosis, especially with a shift toward neutrophilic and band forms, is generally present in bacterial infections such as endocarditis.

PLANS
Diagnostic
Differential Diagnosis

Valvular pulmonic stenosis is distinguished from a small VSD by the location of the murmur and thrill, the presence of a murmur that increases with amyl nitrite inhalation, the presence of an ejection sound that decreases with inspiration, and a widely split second sound with a faint pulmonary component. The murmur of mitral regurgitation is also holosystolic, may be well heard at the left sternal border, and may be accompanied by an increased left atrial to aortic ratio on echocardiography; however, the presence or absence of increased pulmonary blood flow on chest film will differentiate the two. Left ventricular angiography and Doppler echocardiography are diagnostic in both instances. Hypertrophic cardiomyopathy is characterized by a murmur that increases with amyl nitrite inhalation, standing, or Valsalva maneuver; it also has a characteristic echocardiogram.

A ventricular septal defect with aortic regurgitation may require catheterization to distinguish it from aortic stenosis with regurgitation or from patent ductus arteriosus, although usually these can be readily distinguished clinically.

Diagnostic Options

Echocardiography may reveal dilation of both left and right ventricles and an increase in the ratio of left atrial to aortic diameter depending on the size of the left-to-right shunt. The defect in the ventricular septum can frequently be identified on two-dimensional echocardiography, but only occasionally on M-mode echocardiography unless the defect is very large. Aneurysms of the ventricular septum bulging into the right ventricular outflow tract also may be seen.

Doppler echocardiography can detect flow across a VSD with a high degree of sensitivity and specificity. The Q_p/Q_s has been measured by comparing flow across the mitral valve orifice (as flow in the pulmonary artery is nonlaminar in a VSD) compared with aortic flow and has demonstrated a good correlation with data derived at catheterization.

Cardiac catheterization is useful for the following purposes: (1) documentation of left-to-right shunting at the ventricular level by actual passage of the catheter across the defect, by measurement of oxygen saturation in blood samples from the right heart chambers, by the rapid (< 2–3 seconds) detection of inhaled hydrogen by a sensing catheter in the pulmonary artery, or by angiography; (2) measurement of ventricular, aortic, and pulmonary artery pressures and calculation of total pulmonary and pulmonary vascular resistances; and (3) detection of associated defects.

Recommended Approach

Noninvasive evaluation may suffice in the evaluation of patients who are felt to have small defects. Cardiac catheterization should be performed in patients with suspected large shunts, in patients in whom more complex lesions are suspected, and in patients in whom signs or symptoms suggest that surgical intervention is indicated.

Therapeutic
Therapeutic Options

Medical treatment includes prophylaxis against bacterial endocarditis for all patients with VSD and digitalis and diuretics when heart failure is present. Respiratory infections should be treated promptly.

Patients with small VSDs are managed medically. Surgical repair is recommended at an early age for those with a large defect, systolic pulmonary pressure greater than 50% of systemic arterial pressure, intractable congestive failure, or growth retardation. In general, pulmonary vascular resistance progressively increases in children with a large VSD and severe pulmonary hypertension unless they are operated on before the age of 3 years. A child who has congestive heart failure that is controlled with medication should have cardiac catheterization

early and again 6 months later. The defect should be surgically repaired if pulmonary artery pressure does not decrease significantly. Additional indications for closure of a significant VSD include the following: (1) a child over age 2 years with pulmonary artery hypertension and a 1.8:1 ratio of pulmonary to systemic blood flow; or (2) a child prior to entering school with a shunt greater than 1.4:1 and symptoms of congestive failure or cardiomegaly, even with nearly normal pulmonary pressures. A ventricular septal defect should be surgically corrected in an adult if the Q_p/Q_s is 1.4:1 or greater and severe pulmonary hypertension is not present. Patients with a VSD and infundibular pulmonic stenosis are managed similarly to those with tetralogy of Fallot. Patients with a small VSD and aortic regurgitation are followed as though aortic regurgitation were the only lesion.

In children less than 1 year of age with a large VSD and pulmonary hypertension, operative mortality for total correction is significant. Pulmonary artery banding is recommended for very small children requiring surgery for survival or for those with muscular or multiple VSDs, with complete repair planned for a later date.

Recommended Approach

Children with small defects can be treated medically. Patients with moderate defects should be treated as described above with cardiac catheterization reserved for strict indications prior to contemplated surgery or to define anatomy that is clinically obscure.

Patients with large defects and Eisenmenger's syndrome should be considered for lung transplant combined with closure of the intracardiac defect.

FOLLOW-UP

Fever should be promptly reported to the physician, as this may be indicative of bacterial endocarditis. Progressive dyspnea or fatigue and failure to gain weight may be indicative of the development or progression of pulmonary hypertension in a child with a significant VSD.

A child with a small or moderate defect should be seen every 2 months until the defect closes or the child reaches 8 months of age. Thereafter, visits at 4- to 6-month intervals should be made, at which time the physician should educate about prophylaxis against subacute bacterial endocarditis and watch for aortic or pulmonic valve regurgitation.

A child with a large VSD and congestive failure who is responsive to treatment should be very closely followed. The physician must watch for evidence of closure, congestive failure, or development of pulmonary hypertension. Catheterization should be performed early in most infants and should be repeated 6 months after the initial presentation.

After repair, the child should still be seen yearly for reinforcement and reassessment, as a small percentage of patients have small residual VSDs postoperatively. The incidence of conduction disturbances such as right bundle-branch block and left anterior hemiblock approaches 50%. Complete heart block rarely develops later.

DISCUSSION
Prevalence and Incidence

Next to bicuspid aortic valve and mitral valve prolapse, isolated congenital VSD is the most common defect among malformed hearts (20–30% of most series) and is thus the third most common congenital heart disease seen clinically. These defects may also arise secondary to trauma or to myocardial infarction with ischemic necrosis and subsequent septal rupture. This chapter deals only with congenital defects.

The risk of a child having a VSD is increased if one parent or a sibling is affected.

Although the incidence appears to be increasing, improved detection is the probable cause.

Related Basic Science
Physiologic Derangement

Physiologically, small VSDs are restrictive to flow between ventricles, and pulmonary arterial pressure is normal. The stepup in oxygen saturation of blood samples in the right ventricle due to left-to-right shunt may be minimal. Patients with a small VSD are at high risk for bacterial endocarditis. Such a small defect may contribute adversely to the course of an older patient who develops congestive heart failure due to systemic hypertension or atherosclerotic coronary heart disease.

In moderate-sized VSDs there is less restriction to flow and pulmonary pressures may be moderately increased, but accelerating pulmonary vascular resistance is unusual.

With VSDs, flow between ventricles is unrestricted and systolic pressures in both ventricles are equal. Flow is directed into the two great vessels depending on relative outflow tract resistances. With significant left-to-right shunting, there is a volume overload of the left ventricle and pressure and volume overload of the right ventricle until an increase in pulmonary vascular resistance decreases the left-to-right shunt volume (Eisenmenger's syndrome). If left atrial pressure increases with a large left-to-right shunt, the atrial septum may become stretched and may open a patent foramen ovale, permitting additional left-to-right shunting at the atrial level.

With a large VSD, congestive heart failure usually occurs at 4 to 12 weeks of age, when pulmonary vascular resistance normally decreases. In premature infants, congestive failure with pulmonary edema can occur at 2 to 4 weeks. Above sea level, so-called hypoxic banding due to increased pulmonary vascular resistance secondary to hypoxia may diminish the severity of congestive failure. In response to increased pulmonary pressure and flow, the pulmonary vascular resistance subsequently increases and decreases the amount of pulmonary congestion. Irreversible pulmonary vascular disease is unusual before the age of 3, but it increases significantly after the age of 12 years.

Spontaneous closure of a VSD may occur from the following: (1) apposition of the margins of the defect, (2) ingrowth of fibrous tissue, (3) endothelial proliferation, (4) tricuspid valve adherence to the defect, or (5) adherence of a prolapsed aortic cusp to the defect. Aneurysms of the ventricular septum, which are thought by some to occur occasionally with closure, may extend into the septal leaflet of the tricuspid valve or the right ventricular outflow tract.

Anatomic Derangement

The crista supraventricularis is a muscular ridge that separates the right ventricular body from the outflow tract. Anatomic types of VSDs are divided into supracristal and infracristal categories. Supracristal defects lie anterior to the crista supraventricularis and are closely related to pulmonic and aortic valves, thus accounting for the not infrequent finding of semilunar valve regurgitation due to nonsupport of the leaflets. Infracristal defects lie posterior to the crista supraventricularis and may be divided into membranous (three quarters of all ventricular septal defects) and muscular varieties. Membranous defects extend into the region normally closed by connective tissue arising from the crest of the muscular septum, superiorly from conotruncal tissues, and laterally from the endocardial cushions. A membranous VSD extends beneath the commissure joining the right and noncoronary aortic cusps with the atrioventricular bundle in the posterior and inferior rims of the defect. Muscular defects may be single (two thirds of defects) or multiple (one third of defects). The VSD of the atrioventricular commune type extends obliquely from the posteromedial commissure of the mitral valve across the outflow tract of the left ventricle and occupies the position of the VSD in the atrioventricular canal. Anatomic types are not distinguishable clinically.

Natural History and Its Modification with Treatment

Spontaneous closure of ventricular septal defects occurs in about 25 to 45% of defects present in the first month of life; it probably accounts for the fact that the incidence of VSD is three times greater in children than in adults. Small defects are more likely to close spontaneously. Spontaneous closure has been reported to occur even in the fifth decade of life, but most close by age 3 years (Alpert et al., 1979).

Aortic regurgitation, of which there is a low incidence in patients with supracristal VSDs, usually appears in the first decade of life and is often progressive. Infundibular pulmonic stenosis develops in approximately 5% of all large VSDs and may serve to protect the pulmonary circulation. Bacterial endocarditis is most common in the third and fourth decades and appears to be more likely with smaller septal defects. It has been estimated that there is a 13 to 30% incidence of bacterial endocarditis over the 70-year life span of a patient with a VSD (Weidman et al., 1977).

Twenty percent of all children with untreated large VSDs die by age 2 years, predominantly due to heart failure. The death rate is much lower thereafter. The development of Eisenmenger's syndrome is the next most severe complication of a large VSD.

In the second natural history study of congenital heart defects, 94% of the 516 patients managed surgically were New York Heart Association Class I. There was a 6% perioperative (30-day) mortality. Of the 483 survivors, only 55 died over the next 25 years. Many of the 55 died suddenly, suggesting an arrhythmic cause (Kidd et al., 1993).

Prevention

Ventricular septal defects can occur as part of Down syndrome or after maternal rubella infection in the first trimester of pregnancy. Genetic counseling is indicated if one potential parent or a previous child has a VSD. Otherwise, prevention centers around accurate assessment of the size of the defect and prevention of complications.

Cost Containment

The size of the VSD and pulmonary artery pressures can be estimated with a high degree of accuracy from physical examination, electrocardiogram, and chest roentgenogram. Cardiac catheterization is indicated for moderate to large defects when surgical intervention is a consideration or to document pulmonary artery pressures and association lesions. Once closure or reduction of the size of the septal defect has occurred, serial studies are of no value except to document or follow the size of a residual leak following surgical intervention.

REFERENCES

Alpert BS, Cook DH, Varghese PJ, et al. Spontaneous closure of small ventricular septal defects: 10 year follow-up. Pediatrics 1979;63:204.

Engle MA. Ventricular septal defect: Status report for the seventies. Cardiovasc Clin 1973;4:281.

Horowitz MD, Culpepper WS, Williams LC, et al. Pulmonary artery banding: Analysis of 25 years experience. Ann Thorac Surg 1989;48:444.

Kidd L, Driscoll DJ, Gersony Wm, et al. Second natural history study of congenital heart defects: Results of treatment of patient with ventricular septal defect. Circulation 1993;87(2, suppl.):I-38.

McNamara DG, Latson LA. Long-term follow-up of patients with malformations for which definitive surgical repair has been available for 25 years or more. Am J Cardiol 1982;50:560.

Vetter VL, Horowitz LN. Electrophysiologic residua and sequelae of surgery for congenital heart defects. Am J Cardiol 1982;50:588.

Weidman WH, Blount SG Jr, DuShane JW, et al. Clinical course in ventricular septal defect. Circulation 1977;56(suppl. 1):156.

CHAPTER 15–26

Patent Ductus Arteriosus

Jerre F. Lutz, M.D., and Robert C. Schlant, M.D.

DEFINITION

Patent ductus arteriosus is abnormal persistent patency of the ductus arteriosus, which connects the aorta and the pulmonary artery in fetal life.

ETIOLOGY

The ductus arteriosus is a normal structure that plays an integral role in the fetal circulation. Although all the factors that affect closure are not known, prolonged patency of the ductus arteriosus is more common in premature infants with birth asphyxia or respiratory distress syndrome. The incidence is also higher in newborns whose nonimmunized mothers were exposed to the rubella virus in the first trimester of pregnancy.

CRITERIA FOR DIAGNOSIS

Suggestive

Patent ductus arteriosus should be suspected in all patients with a continuous murmur in the second or third left intercostal space. Many patients also have radiographic evidence of increased pulmonary blood flow and left ventricular dilation.

Definitive

As demonstrated by echocardiography or at cardiac catheterization, patients with patent ductus arteriosus have evidence of shunting between the descending aorta and the pulmonary artery and/or angiographic visualization of this communication.

CLINICAL MANIFESTATIONS

Subjective

Symptoms generally vary with the size of the communication and age at presentation. In infants with a large patent ductus arteriosus, congestive heart failure frequently occurs at about 6 to 12 weeks of age and is associated with marked tachypnea, dyspnea, and inability to nurse. In late infancy or early childhood, patients usually present for evaluation of an asymptomatic murmur, vigorous precordial movements noted by the parents, or signs and symptoms of congestive heart failure. In patients with excess pulmonary flow and mild pulmonary hypertension, the most common symptoms are moderate effort dyspnea, orthopnea, and paroxysmal nocturnal dyspnea. As pulmonary hypertension increases further, pulmonary vascular resistance may increase and limit blood flow to the lungs; as a result, orthopnea and paroxysmal nocturnal dyspnea may decrease. Hoarseness can develop from compression of the recurrent laryngeal nerve by the enlarged pulmonary trunk. Hemoptysis can develop with severe pulmonary hypertension.

Fever and malaise often accompany lower respiratory infections or bacterial endocarditis, which occurs with increased frequency in patients with patent ductus arteriosus.

Objective

Physical Examination

Infants may present with aggravation of respiratory insufficiency due to hyaline membrane disease in a premature infant or congestive heart failure in the first weeks of life if the communication is large. Physical examination of these infants may reveal pulmonary congestion, tachypnea, and a murmur that may be continuous or may occur only during systole.

Children may be thin due to chronic congestive heart failure or numerous respiratory infections. Poor physical development, mental retardation, cataracts, and deafness are seen in patients with patent ductus arteriosus who had intrauterine rubella. Overlapping fingers, rocker-

bottom feet, and lax skin are seen in patients with trisomy 16 to 18 in association with patent ductus arteriosus.

Most patients with patent ductus arteriosus do not have clubbing or cyanosis of the extremities. Patients with patent ductus arteriosus and severe pulmonary vascular disease may have differential cyanosis and clubbing; these findings are more marked in the lower extremities than in the right arm, indicating pulmonary hypertension and a reversed shunt by way of the patent ductus arteriosus, one cause of Eisenmenger's syndrome. Accentuation of differential cyanosis in such patients may be brought out by exercise (increased right-to-left shunt) or by warm water (increased cutaneous blood flow).

The pulse pressure is increased in most patients with patent ductus arteriosus, with significant left-to-right shunting into the low-pressure pulmonary bed. Carotid pulsations have a rapid rise, single or bisferiens contour, and a rapid fall. The increased systolic pressure associated with a large left-to-right shunt lessens as congestive heart failure develops.

Jugular venous pulses can be normal if the ductus is small, but a large *a* wave may be seen with pulmonary hypertension, right ventricular hypertrophy, and diminished right ventricular compliance. In chronic congestive heart failure, the mean jugular venous pressure may be elevated.

Precordial movements include a systolic or continuous systolic thrill in the second left intercostal space and suprasternal notch and a sustained, laterally displaced apex impulse if the shunt is significant. Patients with pulmonary hypertension have a sustained parasternal lift.

The second sound may be paradoxically split with a large patent ductus arteriosus due both to early closure of the pulmonic valve and to prolonged left ventricular ejection caused by increased stroke volume of the left ventricle. The pulmonary component of the second heart sound is often accentuated, particularly in the presence of pulmonary hypertension.

The classic murmur of a patient with patent ductus arteriosus is a continuous "machinery" murmur at the second left intercostal space. The murmur peaks in late systole at about the time of the second heart sound and continues into diastole. Occasionally, there is an early systolic or late diastolic gap when pressures in the aorta and pulmonary artery equilibrate. The shape and length of the patent ductus arteriosus murmur vary with pressure difference between the aorta and pulmonary artery. The murmur varies from a soft, high-frequency systolic murmur in a small ductus with high flow to a loud machinery murmur with eddy sounds in late systole and early diastole in a large ductus with high flow. The murmur may vary or be intermittent due to changes in the pulmonary and systemic resistance or possibly angulation in a long, thin ductus or intermittent closure from anatomic flaps functioning as a valve at the aortic end of the ductus. With the development of pulmonary hypertension, the diastolic portion of the murmur may decrease or disappear prior to the systolic component. With severe pulmonary hypertension, there may be only a faint systolic murmur present despite some slight left-to-right shunting. Patients with pulmonary hypertension may have a pulmonary valve ejection click, a loud single or narrowly split S_2, or a diastolic murmur of pulmonary regurgitation. A third heart sound or a diastolic flow rumble across the mitral valve is occasionally heard in patients with a large left-to-right shunt. Very young infants with patent ductus arteriosus may have only a systolic murmur, but they may develop the diastolic component in association with the normal decrease in pulmonary vascular resistance in the first few months of life.

Routine Laboratory Abnormalities

The electrocardiogram is usually normal with a small ductus. Most patients with patent ductus arteriosus have a normal sinus rhythm, and atrial fibrillation usually occurs only late in association with severe left heart failure. The PR interval is prolonged in about one fifth of patients but may reverse after surgical correction of the ductus. The QRS axis is usually normal. When a significant left-to-right shunt is present for several years, there may be evidence of left ventricular hypertrophy. With the development of pulmonary hypertension, one may see biventricular hypertrophy and evidence of biatrial enlargement. Patients with severe pulmonary vascular disease and a predominant right-to-left shunt through the patent ductus arteriosus (a variety of the Eisenmenger's syndrome) may have only right ventricular hypertrophy.

The chest roentgenogram is normal with a small patent ductus. With significant left-to-right shunting there is increased pulmonary flow, enlarged pulmonary arteries, and an enlarged ascending aorta. With the development of severe pulmonary hypertension, all four chambers may enlarge; calcification may eventually develop in the ductus or the pulmonary arteries of older patients. With the development of severe pulmonary vascular disease, the pulmonary vasculature achieves a "pruned-tree" appearance with prominent proximal pulmonary vessels but cutoff, small, or indistinct distal vessels.

Polycythemia can occur as a result of arterial hypoxemia with development of Eisenmenger's syndrome. Leukocytosis, especially with a shift toward band and segmented neutrophils, may be seen with lower respiratory infections and bacterial endocarditis, which occurs with increased frequency in patients with patent ductus arteriosus.

PLANS
Diagnostic
Differential Diagnosis

In adults, the differential diagnosis is usually that of a continuous murmur. See Table 15–26–1.

Diagnostic Options

Cardiac catheterization is usually required to ensure that no concomitant congenital defect that would alter the approach or results of surgery is missed. Cardiac catheterization reveals evidence of shunting of blood from the descending aorta to the pulmonary artery. This may be demonstrated by measurement of the oxygen content of blood samples or by detecting inhaled hydrogen by way of a platinum-tipped catheter placed in the pulmonary artery. The patent ductus may also be crossed with a catheter or demonstrated angiographically with dye.

The combined use of echocardiographic and Doppler techniques can accurately demonstrate the presence of systolic and diastolic flow into the pulmonary artery, the Q_p/Q_s, and evidence of pulmonary hypension either by right ventricular enlargement (echo) or loss of diastolic flow into the pulmonary artery (Doppler).

In infants, a systolic murmur plus congestive heart failure and evidence of an enlarged left atrium and ventricle are compatible with either a ventricular septal defect or a patent ductus arteriosus, and catheterization may be required to establish the proper diagnosis.

Recommended Approach

In infants, echocardiography allows serial measurement of left atrial size and visualization of the ductus and directions of flow via color flow Doppler during pharmacologic manipulation of the ductus. Pulmonary pressure can be estimated by subtracting the Doppler gradient from the systemic systolic pressure.

In infants and children, if all clinical and echocardiographic findings are typical of an uncomplicated ductus arteriosus, catheterization is not necessary. If features are atypical or if there are other complicating anomalies, catheterization is indicated to define anatomy and pulmonary pressures.

Therapeutic
Therapeutic Options

Digitalis, diuretics, and water restriction are indicated for congestive heart failure. In preterm births and infants, pharmacologic intervention with a prostaglandin synthetase inhibitor (indomethacin), which may produce closure of a patent ductus arteriosus, may be beneficial, especially in the setting of respiratory distress syndrome or congestive heart failure.

If pharmacologic maneuvers are unsuccessful in these cases or if the shunt is sufficiently large to cause uncontrolled heart failure or pulmonary hypertension, early surgical intervention (usually triple ligation) is indicated. Otherwise, elective closure is recommended at 1 or 2 years of age. The presence of a patent ductus without severe pulmonary vascular disease is usually an indication for surgical closure. Surgical mortality is very low if pulmonary pressure is normal, but increases significantly with moderate or severe pulmonary hypertension. Surgical mortality approaches 50% with Eisenmenger's physiology (severe pulmonary vascular disease and development of right-to-left shunting); therefore, surgery is usually not indicated in such patients as pulmonary vascular resistance may not regress after ligation of the ductus.

Recommended Approach

In children with complex cyanotic heart disease or obstructive lesions of the left heart, prostaglandin infusion may be necessary to preserve ductal patency and vital flow via the ductus to the pulmonic or systemic circulations.

In infancy, intervention is indicated as early as the ductus is symptomatic. Newborn infants ventilated more than 72 hours who fail to improve should be evaluated for the presence of a patent ductus even in the absence of a murmur.

Asymptomatic patent ductus can be followed in infants up to 9 months of age. Beyond this point the ductus is unlikely to close spontaneously and surgical ligation is the treatment of choice.

The use of a double-umbrella device to achieve ductal closure without surgical closure is associated with a high success rate in selected individuals but remains an investigational technique. Lung transplantation and surgical closure of the ductus can potentially be offered to those patients who have progressed to Eisenmenger's physiology. If endocarditis develops in a patient with patent ductus arteriosus, 6 weeks of antibacterial therapy followed by surgical interruption is recommended.

FOLLOW-UP

Prior to closure, fever should be reported to the physician because of the possibility of infective endarteritis. Shortness of breath may indicate pulmonary hypertension or infection.

After closure of a patent ductus arteriosus, yearly visits for several years are indicated, with auscultation being the most reliable gauge of surgical effectiveness.

TABLE 15–26–1. DIFFERENTIAL DIAGNOSIS OF PATENT DUCTUS ARTERIOSUS

Diagnostic Possibility	Diagnostic Tests or Observations
Aorticopulmonary septal defect	Continuous murmur at base of heart; aortogram
Peripheral pulmonary artery stenosis	Continuous murmur in lung field; pulmonary angiogram
Coarctation of aorta	Continuous murmur over the back; lower extremity pulses; rib notching; aortogram
Pulmonary arteriovenous fistula	Usually right chest; normal heart size; murmur generally systolic; pulmonary arteriography
Anomalous origin of left coronary artery from pulmonary artery	Murmur lower than patent ductus arteriosus; abnormal electrocardiogram with evidence of lateral infarct; coronary angiography
Sinus of Valsalva rupture into right side of heart	Lower murmur, thrill; angiography
Ventricular septal defect and aortic regurgitation	Murmur lower; mitral valve flutter on echocardiogram
Coronary artery fistula	Murmur usually lower; chest x-ray often normal; coronary angiography

DISCUSSION
Prevalence and Incidence

Patent ductus arteriosus and ventricular septal defect are the two most frequent forms of congenital heart disease found in infants. The majority of both defects close within the first 2 years of life.

Females are more likely affected than males, except in the rubella syndrome, where sexes are equally affected.

Related Basic Science
Physiologic or Metabolic Derangement

Patent ductus arteriosus is the remnant of the left sixth aortic arch and is normally present in utero and at birth. At birth, there may be bidirectional shunting by way of the patent ductus. In the first few hours after birth, pulmonary vascular resistance decreases markedly, and left-to-right shunting may occur for 8 to 24 hours; functional closure then occurs. Episodes of crying may cause temporary increases in pulmonary artery pressure and momentary right-to-left shunting. Anatomic closure usually occurs at 2 to 3 weeks. Persistent patency is associated with (1) a larger ductus, (2) increased pulmonary vascular resistances, (3) hypoxia (maturation dependent), and (4) prostaglandin effect (maturation dependent). The development of pulmonary vascular disease is dependent on the size and length of the patent ductus, time, and individual susceptibility.

The ductus arteriosus often fails to close in premature infants, in children whose mothers developed rubella in the first trimester of their pregnancy, and in children born at high altitudes. There is seasonal variation, with increased incidence in children born in October through January; this correlates with a first trimester in late winter or early spring, the peak of the rubella season.

Anatomic Derangement

Associated congenital defects include coarctation of the aorta and ventricular septal defect.

Natural History and Its Modification with Treatment

The vast majority of patients with patent ductus arteriosus retain a predominant left-to-right shunt, and only a small percentage develop reversal of the shunt. Spontaneous closure of a patent ductus arteriosus after age 2 years may occur but is unlikely. Once a child reaches age 10, the chances of endocarditis are greater than that of heart failure. Prior to antibiotics, many patients with patent ductus arteriosus died as a result of infection, which usually occurred in the pulmonary artery opposite the "jet lesion."

In uncorrected patent ductus arteriosus, late causes of death are endocarditis, congestive heart failure, development of Eisenmenger's syndrome with severe pulmonary vascular disease, aneurysmal dilation of the ductus with rupture, and dissection of the ductus. Although patients are reported to live until age 90 with persistent patent ductus, once a patient with an uncorrected ductus reaches puberty, life expectancy is one half of normal.

Long-term results are excellent, with 25-year survival approaching 99 to 100%.

Prevention

Genetic counseling is indicated for families with a history of offspring with patent ductus arteriosus or trisomy 16 to 18. A female of child-bearing age ideally should have her rubella titer measured prior to conception and should receive rubella vaccine if immunity is not present. She should continue birth control for 3 months after vaccination. Endocarditis prophylaxis is recommended prior to and for 3 months following ductal ligation as long as there is no evidence of a murmur (see Chapter 8–12).

Cost Containment

Catheterization after closure to assess effectiveness is not indicated. Endocarditis prophylaxis should not be continued indefinitely after closure unless some other congenital or acquired defect dictates its frequent use. The low incidence of recanalization after triple ligation makes frequent follow-up visits unnecessary. If pulmonary hypertension and significant volume overload were not present prior to closure, serial electrocardiograms, chest roentgenograms, and echocardiograms are not indicated.

REFERENCES

Barst R, Gersony W. The pharmacologic treatment of patent ductus arteriosus: A review of the evidence. Drugs 1989;38:249.

Campbell N. Natural history of persistent ductus arteriosus. Br Heart J 1968;30:4.

Fisher RG, Moodie DS, Sterba R, et al. Patent ductus in adults-long-term follow-up: Nonsurgical versus surgical treatment. J Am Coll Cardiol 1986;8:280.

Heymann MA, Rudolph AM, Silverman NH. Closure of ductus arteriosus in premature infants by inhibition of prostaglandin synthesis. N Engl J Med 1976;295:530.

Keys A, Shapiro MJ. Patency of ductus arteriosus in adults. Am Heart J 1944;26:158.

Mavroudis C, Backer CL, Gevitz M. Forty-six years of patent ductus arteriosus division at Children's Memorial Hospital of Chicago. Ann Surg 1994; 220:402.

McNamara DG, Latson LA. Long-term follow-up of patients with malformations for which definitive surgical repair has been available for 25 years or more. Am J Cardiol 1982;50:560.

Swensson RE, Valdes-Cruz LM, Sahn DJ, et al. Real time Doppler color flows mapping for detection of patent ductus arteriosus. J Am Coll Cardiol 1986;8:1105.

CHAPTER 15–27

Eisenmenger's Syndrome

Jerre F. Lutz, M.D., and Robert C. Schlant, M.D.

DEFINITION

Eisenmenger's syndrome is an advanced form of congenital heart disease in which increased pulmonary blood flow via an intracardiac or extracardiac communication leads to severe reactive pulmonary vascular disease and hypertension with a resultant reversal of flow through the defect culminating in a right-to-left shunt with systemic oxygen desaturation and cyanosis.

ETIOLOGY

The most common underlying defects are ventricular septal defect, atrial septal defect, and patent ductus arteriosus. In the vast majority of patients the etiology of the underlying defect is unknown. Exceptions would include some familial autosomal dominant transmission in the Holt–Oram syndrome (atrial septal defect, secundum type); autosomal recessive familial transmission in the Ellis–Van Crevald syndrome (single atrium); trisomy 21 in children with Down syndrome (atrioventricular canal, ventricular septal defect); association with XO genotype in Turner's syndrome; and association with fetal exposure to the rubella virus in nonimmunized mothers (patent ductus arteriosus).

CRITERIA FOR DIAGNOSIS
Suggestive

Eisenmenger's syndrome should be suspected in patients with a left-to-right shunt who later develop cyanosis with signs of pulmonary hypertension and right ventricular hypertrophy. Echocardiography and magnetic resonance imaging can demonstrate intracardiac defects and right-to-left shunting and estimate pulmonary artery pressure.

Definitive

Eisenmenger's syndrome consists of the following: (1) one or more large communications between the systemic and pulmonic circuits with left-to-right shunting of blood initially, but subsequent development of either bidirectional shunting with right-to-left predominance or of pure right-to-left shunting, and (2) pulmonary vascular resistance greater than 800 dyn·s·cm^{-5}. When this disease process occurs in a patient with ventricular septal defect, it may properly be called Eisenmenger's disease or complex, as that is what Eisenmenger initially reported.

Cardiac catheterization is required to define the level of the defect by catheter pass, to definitively measure pulmonary pressures, and to eliminate the possibility of a correctable cardiac abnormality.

CLINICAL MANIFESTATIONS
Subjective

Most patients with Eisenmenger's syndrome develop progressive dyspnea, fatigue, palpitations, cyanosis, and edema in the second or third decade of life. Hemoptysis occurs in more than half of patients with Eisenmenger's syndrome who are older than 20 and usually indicates a very poor prognosis. Chest pain suggestive of angina pectoris and syncope may also occur.

Objective
Physical Examination

Cyanosis, clubbing, and polycythemia are usually mild or absent in children with Eisenmenger's physiology, whereas these signs are of greater severity and are uniformly present in adults. Differential cyanosis with cyanosis greater in the lower extremities than in the right arm suggests a patent ductus arteriosus as the cause of the syndrome.

The arterial pulse is normal or diminished in amplitude. Jugular venous pulsations are usually surprisingly normal. Large *a* waves in the neck veins are unusual.

A prominent right ventricular lift without thrill is the rule. The left ventricular impulse is usually unremarkable, but a palpable pulmonary artery and second heart sound are often present.

There is auscultatory evidence of pulmonary hypertension with a pulmonary ejection click, a loud pulmonic component of the second sound, and, occasionally, a diastolic murmur of pulmonic regurgitation. The second heart sound may give a clue as to the underlying communication. The second sound tends to be single with ventricular septal defect, split (fixed) with atrial septal defect or anomalous pulmonary veins, and normally split with normal respiratory variation and patent ductus arteriosus. As the left-to-right shunt decreases, the murmurs resulting from the original left-to-right shunt become minimal or disappear. Ventricular gallops are frequent, but atrial gallops are relatively unusual.

Routine Laboratory Abnormalities

The electrocardiogram usually reveals normal sinus rhythm. In some series, paroxysmal atrial tachycardia or flutter has been more frequent in patients who had an atrial septal defect as the underlying defect. Atrial fibrillation is relatively rare. A prominent P wave compatible with right atrial abnormality is found in nearly half of patients with Eisenmenger's syndrome. Right ventricular hypertrophy with right-axis

deviation of the mean QRS complex is usual; however, left-axis deviation can be seen in patients who develop Eisenmenger's syndrome as a complication of an endocardial cushion defect.

The chest roentgenogram reveals slightly enlarged heart size. The central pulmonary arteries are markedly dilated, whereas the peripheral pulmonary vessels notably lack prominence ("pruning"). Calcification of pulmonary arteries is highly suggestive of pulmonary hypertension. Calcification of a ductus arteriosus obviously favors patent ductus as the likely etiology. An enlarged right pulmonary artery greater than left pulmonary artery favors atrial septal defect rather than ventricular septal defect. A small or normal ascending aorta favors atrial or ventricular septal defects, whereas an enlarged aorta favors patent ductus arteriosus. An enlarged left atrium and left ventricle favor patent ductus or ventricular septal defect rather than atrial septal defect. A right aortic arch favors isolated ventricular septal defect.

As a result of arterial hypoxemia, an elevated hematocrit is almost uniformly present. An elevated uric acid level is not uncommon as a result of increased red cell production.

An elevated white blood cell count or a shift in the differential to more segmented neutrophils or band cells may be seen in the setting of a superimposed infection such as endocarditis.

PLANS
Diagnostic
Differential Diagnosis

Most patients have an established diagnosis of previous congenital heart disease. For those patients with end-stage Eisenmenger's syndrome with no antecedent cardiac history, the differential usually is limited to advanced primary pulmonary hypertension or pulmonary hypertension due to recurrent pulmonary emboli.

Diagnostic Options

Eisenmenger's disease or complex is a specific type of Eisenmenger's syndrome due to a large ventricular septal defect. About one third of the cases of Eisenmenger's syndrome are due to Eisenmenger's disease (ventricular septal defect). When the syndrome is considered likely, cardiac catheterization should be performed to exclude other diagnoses and to ensure that the pulmonary vascular resistance actually is irreversibly elevated and not surgically approachable.

Cardiac catheterization reveals the pulmonary artery pressure to be at systemic levels, with a calculated pulmonary vascular resistance of 800 dyn·s·cm^{-5} or more. Blood samples for oxygen saturation indicate shunts that are either exclusively right-to-left or bidirectional with right-to-left predominance. Shunting may occur at the level of the atria, ventricles, or patent ductus arteriosus. The left atrial and pulmonary capillary wedge pressures are not elevated in the absence of left ventricular, mitral valve, left atrial, or pulmonary venous disease. Angiography or passage of the catheter through a defect may detect the original site of the original left-to-right shunting.

Echocardiography usually reveals right ventricular enlargement and hypertrophy. Visualization of the intracardiac defect may be confirmatory in some cases where crossing of the shunt lesion was technically impossible at the time of catheterization.

Magnetic resonance imaging may demonstrate the intracardiac or extracardiac defect better than the other diagnostic methods. Magnetic resonance imaging also provides clinicians with the best method for determining right ventricular function, a pivotal piece of data when deciding whether heart–lung transplant or lung transplant combined with closure of the defect is best for the patient.

Recommended Approach

Noninvasive testing with echocardiography and magnetic resonance imaging should be performed in those patients in whom the diagnosis is in question and those in whom transplant is being contemplated.

If no shunts are detected, a ventilation–perfusion scan followed by cardiac catheterization should differentiate patients with primary pulmonary hypertension from those with pulmonary hypertension secondary to pulmonary emboli.

In those patients with an intracardiac or extracardiac shunt, cardiac catheterization is indicated to make the correct diagnosis definitively and to assess the correct timing of transplantation if indicated.

Therapeutic

Therapeutic Options

As no curative medical or corrective surgical therapy is available once severe pulmonary vascular disease develops, treatment must center on prevention of complications. Digitalis and diuretics are indicated for congestive heart failure. Antibiotics are useful as bacterial endocarditis prophylaxis and as therapy for cerebral abscesses. Phlebotomy or erythropheresis may be useful for an elevated hematocrit greater than 70%. Pregnancy is not advisable in patients with Eisenmenger's syndrome, as maternal mortality is increased (up to one third of patients) compared with a mortality of 1 or 2% in all patients with a left-to-right shunt. Maternal mortality is, unfortunately, not predictable by the prior severity of symptoms. The cause of death in pregnancy is often unknown, although pulmonary thromboembolism is often suspected. Heparin therapy is usually of greater risk than benefit in this situation. Pregnancy also frequently ends in spontaneous abortion or premature labor. Heart–lung transplant is possible (see below).

Recommended Approach

Medical therapy should be pursued as long as possible, because long-term results of heart–lung and lung transplantation are not as yet as good as those of cardiac transplantation. Supplemental oxygen therapy combined with phlebotomy can make enormous symptomatic differences in a patient's well-being. Encouragement to use oxygen all 24 hours of the day may be necessary for full benefit.

FOLLOW-UP

The patient should report any febrile illness as this may signal an episode of endocarditis. Arthritic symptoms may be an indication of gouty deposition. Headache or increased fatigue may be evidence of progressive polycythemia. Hemoptysis results most commonly from pulmonary hypertension and is a poor prognostic sign. Syncope and palpitations may occur as a result of arrhythmias and should be immediately reported to the physician.

As all therapeutic options fail, both patient and physician may need to increase frequencies of interaction if transplantation is judged to be in the patient's best interest.

DISCUSSION

Prevalence and Incidence

Patients with Eisenmenger's physiology now constitute only a few percent of all patients with congenital heart disease. As patients are detected at an earlier stage and receive definitive treatment sooner, the prevalence should continue to decrease.

Related Basic Science

Genetics

The role of mendelian inheritance in some patients has been discussed (see Etiology).

Physiologic or Metabolic Derangement

Although the left-to-right communication originally described was a ventricular septal defect, patients who have communications at atrial, ventricular, or aorticopulmonary levels may have similar clinical findings, natural history, and physiology once the progressive pulmonary vascular obstructive disease develops; therefore, all are included in the term Eisenmenger's syndrome or Eisenmenger's physiology. Severe

pulmonary vascular disease secondary to increased pulmonary blood flow from an atrial septal defect is unusual before age 20. When the pulmonary vascular resistance increases markedly, however, left-to-right shunting decreases and eventually the shunt reverses.

Anatomic Derangement

Pathologically, the changes present in the pulmonary vascular bed vary with age and the individual. The medial layer of the muscular arteries and the proximal portion of the arterioles are thickened. Nonspecific intimal fibrosis is first noted at the point at which small muscular arteries branch from large muscular arteries. This may be followed later by the development of "plexiform lesions," characterized by masses of endothelial cells within small arterial and arteriolar lumina. As pulmonary vascular obliteration progresses further, the larger vessels are also involved and calcified atheromata may form in the larger pulmonary vessels. Progression to a necrotizing vasculitis is uncommon. Secondary effects include hypertrophy of the right ventricle and dilation of the central pulmonary arteries. The left-sided structures that may have been originally enlarged (with ventricular septal defect or patent ductus arteriosus) may regress as blood flow to the left heart decreases.

Natural History and Its Modification with Treatment

The chances of surviving childhood with Eisenmenger's syndrome are good. Death usually occurs in the third or fourth decade, with sudden death in more than half of patients. Hemoptysis with sudden death, usually secondary to pulmonary thromboembolism, may occur in up to one third of patients. A few patients survive past age 50. The worst prognosis in Eisenmenger's syndrome occurs when it develops secondary to a ventricular septal defect. Transplantation results should dramatically improve both symptoms and prognosis in those patients who are expected to live less than 6 months without transplantation.

Prevention

The unquestioned single most important factor in prevention is early recognition and surgical treatment of the underlying congenital heart disease prior to development of irreversible pulmonary hypertension.

Cost Containment

Once the diagnosis is firmly established, serial cardiac catheterizations and echocardiograms are not indicated. Serial electrocardiograms and chest roentgenograms should be reserved for suspected arrhythmias or intrapulmonary complications.

REFERENCES

Aeba R, Griffith BP, Hardesty RL, et al. Isolated lung transplantation for patients with Eisenmenger's syndrome. Circulation 1993;88(5, pt. 2):II–452.

Brammell H, Vogel JHK, Pryor R, Blount SG. The Eisenmenger syndrome. Am J Cardiol 1971;28:679.

Dexter L. Pulmonary vascular disease in acquired and congenital heart disease. Arch Intern Med 1979;139:922.

Eisenmenger V. Die Angeboren defecte der Kammerscheidwand des Herzens. Klin Med 1897;32(Suppl.1):1.

Foster JM, Jones RM. The anaesthetic management of the Eisenmenger syndrome. Ann R Coll Surg Engl 1984;66:353.

Hoffman JIE, Rudolph AM, Heymann MA. Pulmonary vascular disease with congenital heart lesions: Pathologic features and causes. Circulation 1981;64:873.

Madden B, Radley-Smith R, Hodson M, et al. Medium-term results of heart and lung transplantation. J Heart Lung Transplant 1992;11(4, pt. 2):S241.

Nugent WE, Plauth WH Jr, Edwards JE, Williams WH. The pathology, abnormal physiology, recognition and treatment of congenital heart disease. In: Schlant RC, Alexander RW, O'Rourke RA, et al., eds. Hurst's the heart. 8th ed. New York: McGraw-Hill, 1994:1761.

Wood P. The Eisenmenger syndrome (2 parts). Br Med J 1958;2:701, 755.

Coarctation of the Aorta

Jerre F. Lutz, M.D., and Robert C. Schlant, M.D.

DEFINITION

Coarctation of the aorta is a congenital narrowing of the aorta, most frequently just distal to the left subclavian artery and ductus arteriosus or ligamentum arteriosum (Figure 15–28–1).

ETIOLOGY

Coarctation of the aorta arises embryologically as a malformation of the aortic arch system. Although coarctation of the aorta may arise as part of a congenital syndrome such as Edward's syndrome (trisomy 18), Patau's syndrome (trisomy 13), or Turner's syndrome, the etiology of the vast majority of cases is unknown.

CRITERIA FOR DIAGNOSIS

Suggestive

The anomaly is usually recognized when the blood pressure is found to be lower in the legs than in the arms of a patient with systemic arterial hypertension.

Definitive

The diagnosis is best confirmed at cardiac catheterization by demonstrating arteriographic narrowing of the distal aortic arch with a concomitant pressure gradient across this obstruction. Noninvasive techniques such as transesophageal echocardiography and magnetic resonance imaging can also identify the defect.

CLINICAL MANIFESTATIONS

Subjective

Coarctation of the aorta occurs predominantly in males. A child born to a parent with coarctation of the aorta has about a 2% risk of congenital heart disease; half of those affected have coarctation. Similar statistics are applicable when a sibling has been previously affected.

If coarctation is not so severe as to cause congestive heart failure within the first year of life, the clinical picture beyond the second year of life is one of good health, and growth and development are normal. In uncomplicated coarctation of the aorta, nonspecific symptoms of left ventricular dysfunction due to increased afterload are usually mild.

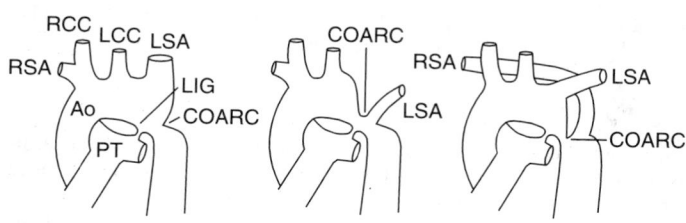

Figure 15–28–1. Illustrations of the typical variety of coarctation (COARC) of the aorta and two anatomic variations. **A.** In the typical variety, the coarctation is located immediately beyond the left subclavian artery (LSA), which is enlarged. The descending aorta is dilated distal to the coarctation. RSA, right subclavian artery; RCC and LCC, right and left common carotid arteries, respectively; LIG, ligamentum arteriosum; Ao, ascending aorta; PT, pulmonary trunk. **B.** The site of coarctation is just proximal to the left subclavian artery. The left subclavian is not dilated. **C.** The *right* subclavian artery arises anomalously below the coarctation. *(Source: Perloff JK. Clinical recognition of congenital heart disease. 4th ed. Philadelphia: Saunders, 1994:132. Reproduced with permission from the publisher and author.)*

Claudication may occur with running in a few patients and is more suggestive of abdominal coarctation. Many patients progress to young adulthood without symptoms.

Objective

Physical Examination

General inspection may reveal disproportionate development of the arms, chest, and shoulder girdle compared with the legs in some patients; otherwise, abnormalities are confined to the cardiovascular system.

Visible arterial pulsations, occasionally with a thrill, may be present in the suprasternal notch and carotid arteries. Pulsations in the radial arteries are strong, whereas those in the femoral arteries are diminished, delayed, or absent on simultaneous comparison. Systolic pressure is significantly higher in the arms than in the legs (the sine qua non of diagnosis), whereas the diastolic pressure is often less increased. It is important to measure the blood pressure in the arms and legs after the patient has exercised. The pulse pressure in the legs is reduced due to the damping effect of the coarctation an may not be measurable if the coarctation is severe. The upper extremity pressures are variable. One third of patients have little or no hypertension, one third have mild hypertension, and one third have severe hypertension. Severe hypertension is defined as systolic pressure above 150 mm Hg or diastolic pressure above 100 mm Hg. A systolic pressure difference between upper extremities suggests that the origin of the left subclavian artery is below the level of obstruction.

Examination of the venous system is unremarkable.

Precordial examination may reveal a forceful left ventricular apex impulse.

The aortic component of the second sound is often accentuated. An ejection click at the apex or left sternal border with or without a systolic ejection murmur in the aortic area suggests a bicuspid aortic valve or dilation of the ascending aorta. A bicuspid aortic valve occurs in more than one half of patients with coarctation of the aorta. The characteristic murmur that results from turbulent flow across the narrowed segment is systolic, midpitched, and blowing. It is usually heard in the interscapular area posteriorly, occasionally with radiation to the axilla and anterior precordium. Extension of the murmur into diastole suggests a higher grade of obstruction. A short middiastolic rumble at the apex without other evidence of mitral stenosis has been reported.

Routine Laboratory Abnormalities

The electrocardiogram in uncomplicated coarctation may be normal or may reveal left ventricular hypertrophy and left atrial abnormality. Early in life, the mean QRS vector may be directed rightward and a right atrial abnormality may be present.

The chest x-ray film usually shows left ventricular prominence and a diminished aortic knob. On overpenetrated chest film, a figure 3 configuration is evident, with the upper knob representing the aorta proximal to the narrowing, the indentation of the 3 due to the coarctation, and the lower knob due to poststenotic dilation. Notching of the inferior surfaces of the ribs by tortuous collateral vessels is seldom seen before age 8. Although it is commonly due to coarctation of the aorta, it is a nonspecific finding (Table 15–28–1).

PLANS

Diagnostic

Differential Diagnosis

The differential diagnosis of weak or absent femoral pulses in patients with congenital cardiovascular disease is given in Table 15–28–2.

TABLE 15–28–1. ETIOLOGIC CLASSIFICATION OF RIB NOTCHING

Arterial
    Aortic obstruction
        Coarctation of aortic arch
        Thrombosis of abdominal aorta
    Subclavian artery obstruction
        Blalock–Taussig operation
        "Pulseless disease"
    Widened arterial pulse pressure (?)
    Decreased pulmonary blood supply
        Tetralogy of Fallot
        Pulmonary atresia (pseudotruncus)
        Ebstein's malformation
        Pulmonary valve stenosis
        Unilateral absence of pulmonary artery
        Pulmonary emphysema
Venous
    Superior vena cava obstruction
Arteriovenous
    Pulmonary arteriovenous fistula
    Intercostal arteriovenous fistula
Neurogenic
    Intercostal neurinoma
Osseous
    Hyperparathyroidism
Idiopathic
Normal

Source: *Boone ML, Swenson BE, Felson B. Rib notching: Its many causes. Am J Roentgenol 1964;91:1075. Reproduced with permission of the American Roentgen Ray Society. © 1964 by Am Roentgen Ray Soc.*

Diagnostic Options

An important consideration is exclusion of concomitant congenital cardiac defects. In order of decreasing frequency, these anomalies include ventricular septal defect, atrial septal defect, aortic stenosis, mitral stenosis, mitral regurgitation, and transposition of the great vessels with a ventricular septal defect. Exclusion is accomplished by physical examination, the presence of electrocardiographic abnormalities, chest x-ray, echocardiogram, and cardiac catheterization and angiography (see individual chapters).

If a systolic pressure differential greater than 25 mm Hg exists between upper and lower extremities, catheterization is indicated. Aortography demonstrates the exact site and length of the coarctation, and intraaortic pressure measurements of gradient across the narrowing confirm the indirect measurements taken by blood pressure cuff on the extremities. Cardiac catheterization is indicated in patients with coarctation to assess the aortic valve because of the frequent coexistence of bicuspid aortic valve with either valvular stenosis or regurgitation. Angiography with large cut film is best for visualizing the size of the

TABLE 15–28–2. DIFFERENTIAL DIAGNOSIS OF COARCTATION OF THE AORTA

Diagnostic Possibility	Diagnostic Tests or Observations
Severe aortic stenosis	Arterial pulses decreased throughout body; echocardiogram can be normal or show flutter of anterior mitral valve leaflet with aortic regurgitation
Aortic atresia	Arterial pulses decreased throughout body; echocardiogram shows small aorta; only a small percent live past 1 month
Interrupted aortic arch	Decreased pulses in legs compared with arms; congestive heart failure and hypoperfused lower extremity increased as ductus closes; catheterization and angiography
Isolated coarctation of aorta	Decreased pulses in legs compared with arms; echocardiogram generally normal; catheterization and angiography

coarctation, the relative size of the aorta before and after coarctation, the distance from the coarctation to the left subclavian artery, the presence or absence of a patent ductus, and the number and size of collateral vessels. All are important in assessment for surgical repair.

Pseudocoarctation refers to a buckling of the aorta distal to ligamentum arteriosum, but without narrowing of the aortic lumen and without a pressure gradient at the site of buckling. This condition is seen in elderly patients with sclerosis of the aortic media.

Recommended Approach

Noninvasive techniques may suffice in younger patients in whom the coarctation is short and there are no associated congenital defects. Aortography and catheterization are recommended for older patients to demonstrate the site and length of the coarctation as well as any unusual features of the collateral circulation that may be important during proposed surgery.

Therapeutic

Therapeutic Options

Prior to surgical correction, bacterial endocarditis prophylaxis is indicated to prevent infection of either the coarctation site or the commonly associated bicuspid aortic valve. Prophylaxis is indicated after surgery when there is an associated aortic valve anomaly. Digitalis and diuretics are indicated for control of congestive heart failure. Antihypertensive agents may be required both prior to and occasionally after surgical correction.

After the diagnosis of coarctation of the aorta has been established, surgical repair is usually indicated. The optimum age for closure is prior to 6 years; at that age, vascular structures will have grown to such an extent that a single operation can be accomplished with optimal surgical anatomy. Operations performed prior to 1 year are complicated by a high rate of recoarctation, whereas patients repaired after 6 years of age have a high rate of persistent or recurrent hypertension. Medically unresponsive congestive heart failure in an infant with coarctation is an indication for early surgical repair, as is unresponsive hypertension, claudication, or cardiomegaly in a child less than 10 years of age. Operation should be undertaken if the condition is discovered during adult life, as some relief of hypertension has been accomplished even in the sixth decade.

Balloon angioplasty of both native coarctation and restenotic lesions can be successfully performed. The indication and value for this technique should be compared with the surgical results at the institution where the correction is planned.

The likelihood of correction of hypertension is inversely proportional to the age at which surgical repair is performed. The role of angioplasty of the coarctation site in the aorta has yet to be determined.

Recommended Approach

All symptomatic infants and any asymptomatic child should have coarctation repair prior to beginning school. This eliminates the high rate of recoarctation if repaired prior to age 6 and the high rate of persistent hypertension if repaired later in life.

FOLLOW-UP

Fever should be reported to the physician, as this may signal endocarditis in a patient with concomitant bicuspid aortic valve disease. Dyspnea and headache may result from poor blood pressure control.

The majority of postoperative care centers about detection and treatment of hypertension. On about the third to tenth postoperative day, necrotizing arteritis of the bowel (which may cause bowel necrosis) may occur, leading to increasing blood pressure, leukocytosis, and abdominal pain. The proper treatment is antihypertensive medication.

Immediately after surgery the patient should be seen at 2-week intervals for about three visits to check blood pressure and evaluate for surgical complications. Thereafter, the patient should have blood pressure checked every 6 months; more frequent visits are indicated only for blood pressure control. Recatheterization and reoperation should be considered for patients who show evidence of recurrent coarctation, manifest by a 30 mm Hg systolic gradient between upper and lower extremity pressures.

If surgery is done before age 20, about two thirds of patients become normotensive and most of the remainder have a decrease in blood pressure. Surgery performed at a later age is associated with less impressive results.

DISCUSSION

Prevalence and Incidence

Coarctation of the aorta accounts for about 8% of congenital heart disease in children, ranking only behind ventricular septal defect and patent ductus arteriosus in frequency.

Related Basic Science

Physiologic or Metabolic Derangement

Pathologically, the characteristic lesion of coarctation is a deformity of the media of the aorta that involves the anterior, superior, and posterior walls, thus creating an unfolding of the wall and causing the intraaortic lumen to be narrowed and eccentric. There may be poststenotic dilation of the aorta.

Physiologically, there is increased resistance to flow through the obstruction. Before birth, increased work is performed by both right and left ventricles against a higher pressure load in patients with either preductal or postductal coarctation. With preductal coarctation, the ductus arteriosus is more likely to remain open, and blood shunts from aorta to the pulmonary artery unless the ductus remains large and pulmonary vascular hypertension develops. When the pulmonary artery pressure exceeds the pressure in the aorta, the blood flow may reverse through the ductus to the aorta. This may be responsible for cyanosis of the toes compared with the fingers. In postductal coarctation the ductus is usually closed, and the majority of the pressure load falls on the left ventricle.

The proximal aortic and upper extremity systolic pressure and usually the diastolic pressure are increased in patients with coarctation of the aorta. The mechanism responsible for the hypertension is felt to be multifactorial, including mechanical resistance of the coarctation, decreased capacitance of vessels into which the left ventricle ejects, and, possibly, increased renin release due to diminished renal blood flow. Also, the frequently associated intracardiac defects may subject the ventricles to additional pressure or volume loads, which may produce ventricular failure.

Anatomic Derangement

The systolic pressure distal to the coarctation is lower than in the upper extremity, and the pulse pressure is narrowed due to the damping effect of the coarctation. With severe coarctation, survival depends on the development of collateral circulation distal to the coarctation. This occurs by way of the branches of the subclavian arteries, primarily the internal thoracic, scapular, and intercostal arteries (Figure 15–28–2). Sustained flow through the intercostal arteries is the cause of rib notching, a finding unusual before age 8.

Intracranial hemorrhage is a complication from coarctation due to the hypertension proximal to the coarctation, as well as associated aneurysms of arteries of the circle of Willis.

Fibroelastosis with or without associated aortic valve disease may be present. Patients with this disorder may have heart failure with only a slight rise in systemic blood pressure.

Left arm pain and weakness can result from involvement of the proximal left subclavian artery with the coarctation, and dysphagia can result from creation of a vascular ring around the esophagus by an aberrant right subclavian artery.

Natural History and Its Modification with Treatment

The patient with untreated coarctation has few symptoms through adolescence, but death occurs usually in the second or third decade of life from hypertension (cerebral hemorrhage or congestive heart failure) or from rupture of an aneurysm at the site of coarctation. The success of medical treatment in a surgically uncorrected coarctation is dependent

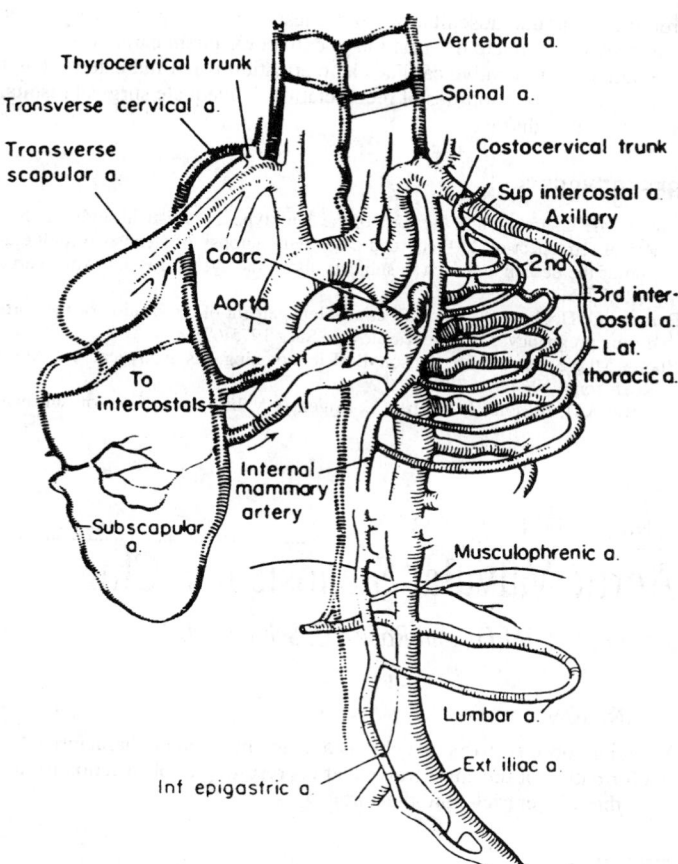

Figure 15–28–2. Diagrammatic portrayal of collateral circulation in coarctation of the aorta. *(Source: Edwards JE, Clagett OT, Drake RL, Christensen NA. The collateral circulation in coarctation of the aorta. Originally published in Mayo Clin Proc 1948;23:333. Figure amended by Edwards JE. Reproduced with permission from the author and publisher.)*

on the degree of blood pressure control. Even when the blood pressure is adequately treated, however, this does not totally protect the patient against rupture of the aorta.

Pregnancy is not precluded by coarctation of the aorta, but it does increase risk of rupture of the aorta, especially during the third trimester. Intracranial hemorrhage is more frequent, but congestive heart failure seldom develops unless there are associated intracardiac abnormalities. The incidence of toxemia of pregnancy appears to be less with coarctation of the aorta than with other causes of hypertension. The maternal mortality rate in uncorrected coarctation of the aorta is about 10%; the fetal mortality rate varies from 30 to 50% (Barash et al., 1975).

In Brouwer and colleagues' study, of 120 consecutive patients repaired between 1948 and 1966 and followed a mean of 32 years, nearly 97% were in New York Heart Association class I. The probability of survival 44 years later was 73%. Patients operated before age 10 had a 97% survival. By following guidelines of early repair, the probability of recoarctation is less than 3% and the probability of a normal blood pressure is about 80 to 85% (Brouwer et al., 1993).

Prevention

No preventive measures are known.

Cost Containment

Early recognition and therapy are of utmost importance. An initial echocardiogram to evaluate cardiac function and additional data to exclude associated abnormalities are indicated; thereafter serial chest x-rays together with physical examination usually suffice to follow the patient. Postoperatively, serial blood pressure measurements (all extremities), cardiac auscultation, and chest x-ray yearly or every other year provide adequate information to deliver excellent care.

Routine postoperative cardiac catheterization is not indicated, except to evaluate the possibilities of recoarctation, inadequate surgical results, or aortic valve disease.

REFERENCES

Abbott ME. Coarctation of the aorta of the adult type: A statistical study and historical retrospect of 200 recorded cases with autopsy of stenosis or obliteration of the descending arch in subjects above the age of 2 years. Am Heart J 1928;3:574.

Barash PG, Hobbins JC, Hook R, et al. Management of coarctation of the aorta during pregnancy. J Thorac Cardiovasc Surg 1975;69:781.

Boone ML, Swenson BE, Felson B. Rib notching: Its many causes. Am J Roentgenol 1964;91:1075.

Brouwer RM, Erasmus MF, Ebels T, Eijgelaar A. Influence of age on survival, late hypertension, and recoarctation in elective aortic coarctation repair. J Thorac Cardiovasc Surg 1993;108:525.

Edwards J, Clagett QT, Drake RL, Christensen NA. The collateral circulation in coarctation of the aorta. Proc Staff Meet Mayo Clin 1948;23:333.

George B, DiSessa TG, Williams SR, et al. Coarctation repair without catheterization in infants. Am Heart J 1987;114:1421.

McNamara DG, Latson LA. Long-term follow-up of patients with malformations for which definitive surgical repair has been available for 25 years or more. Am J Cardiol 1982;50:560.

Mendelsohn AM, Lloyd TR, Crowley DC, et al. Late follow-up of balloon angioplasty in children with native coarctation of the aorta. Am J Cardiol 1994;74:696.

Nugent WE, Plauth WH Jr, Edwards JE, Williams WH. The pathology, pathophysiology, recognition and treatment of congenital heart disease. In: Schlant RC, Alexander RW, O'Rourke RA, et al., eds. Hurst's the heart. 8th ed. New York: McGraw-Hill, 1994:1773.

CHAPTER 15–29

Aortic Valvular Stenosis in a Child

Jerre F. Lutz, M.D., and Robert C. Schlant, M.D.

DEFINITION

Valvular aortic stenosis in a chid is a congenital defect characterized by malformation of the aortic valve leaflets resulting in obstruction to flow from the left ventricle into the aorta.

ETIOLOGY

Aortic valve stenosis results embryologically from failure of development of an intercalated valve cushion or fusion of adjacent valve anlagen. The etiology is unknown. The abnormality is usually a *bicuspid* valve but unicuspid valve stenosis does occur.

CRITERIA FOR DIAGNOSIS

Suggestive

The presence of a systolic murmur at the right upper sternal border radiating to the neck, accompanied by evidence of pressure overload of the left ventricle on the electrocardiogram or echocardiogram, is highly suggestive of left ventricular outflow obstruction. Continuous-wave Doppler is a sensitive and reliable technique for estimating the gradient across a thickened aortic valve.

Noninvasive testing by echocardiography and magnetic resonance imaging will demonstrate pathologic features at the valvular level that should facilitate definition of the left ventricular outflow tract obstruction at the valvular, subvalvular, or supravalvular level.

Definitive

The definitive diagnosis of valvular aortic stenosis is made by demonstrating a pressure difference across the left ventricular outflow tract at the valvular level on cardiac catheterization or direct visualization of a narrowed aortic valve orifice.

CLINICAL MANIFESTATIONS

Subjective

Valvular aortic stenosis constitutes approximately 5% of congenital heart defects identified in children. Males are several times more frequently affected than females. A familial tendency has occasionally been reported.

Fatigue and dyspnea are usually the earliest symptoms. Episodes of inappropriate sweating are reported in children with aortic stenosis. Fatigue and dyspnea are twice as frequent in patients with severe obstruction as mild obstruction. Effort-induced lightheadedness or giddiness suggests significant obstruction. Syncope, especially effort induced, increases in frequency with severity of obstruction. Angina pectoris is seen with severe obstruction. Syncope or sudden death may occur with exertion or at rest. Sudden death may occur in children with recognized congenital aortic stenosis, but it is unusual without prior symptoms or electrocardiographic abnormalities. Some patients are completely asymptomatic despite severe obstruction. Arrhythmias are not so common in valvular aortic stenosis as in hypertrophic obstructive cardiomyopathy. The risk of endocarditis increases with age.

Objective

Physical Examination

A child with a bicuspid aortic valve may have no murmur, a systolic murmur, or the murmur of aortic regurgitation. Although the murmur in congenital aortic stenosis is usually present within 24 to 48 hours of birth, less than half of patients are diagnosed by age 1. Congenital aortic stenosis may present as unexplained congestive heart failure with or without a systolic outflow murmur during infancy. Growth and development are usually normal.

Left ventricular hypertrophy decreases distensibility of both the left and right ventricles, and the right atrium must contract harder against a less distensible right ventricle; thus, a large *a* wave in the jugular venous pulse is frequent.

The carotid artery pulsation is often prolonged with a slow and small rise and fall. This finding is less reliable in children than in adults with an equivalent obstruction. A bifid pulse suggests hypertrophic obstructive cardiomyopathy or combined aortic stenosis plus regurgitation.

The apical impulse may be normal or heaving and sustained. A thrill at the upper right sternal border (occasionally to the left) radiating to the supraclavicular space and to the carotids is usually present, particularly in those with severe obstruction. The absence of a thrill suggests that the gradient is less than 30 mm Hg or that the obstruction is subvalvular.

The first heart sound is normal. The aortic component of the second sound may be normal, and an ejection sound may be present with preserved doming motion of the leaflets. It is more likely to be heard at the apex than at the base. A paradoxically split second sound is rare, but may occur with severe obstruction to left ventricular outflow. Third and fourth heart sounds are frequent but of little assistance in assessing the severity of obstruction in smaller children. A fourth sound usually signifies significant obstruction in those between ages 12 and 40.

A crescendo–decresendo midsystolic murmur that is loudest at the right upper sternal border and that radiates to the apex and carotids is characteristic. The longer and louder the murmur, the more likely that obstruction is severe. The later that the peak intensity of the murmur occurs, the more likely that obstruction is severe. The murmur is often less harsh and higher-pitched at the apex. A diastolic murmur of aortic regurgitation is heard in about 15 to 20% of cases; it tends to be more frequent in those with mild rather than severe obstruction.

Routine Laboratory Abnormalities

Normal sinus rhythm is usual; however, premature atrial and ventricular complexes occur frequently under the age of 10. The electrocardiogram reveals a normal P axis, but evidence of a left atrial abnormality is present in one third of patients. Left ventricular hypertrophy with secondary ST-segment and T-wave changes is unusual with a small pressure difference across the valve. Left ventricular hypertrophy is usually present with moderate or severe obstruction, but a normal electrocardiogram can be present with severe obstruction. In a child less than 2 years old with severe obstruction, however, the electrocardiogram is virtually always abnormal. Small Q waves in leads III and aVF are common in congenital aortic stenosis; however, broad Q waves inferiorly and laterally suggest muscular subvalvular obstruction. Right ventricular hypertrophy is rarely seen even if the pulmonary artery pressure is elevated.

The chest roentgenogram may reveal no cardiomegaly or left ventricular prominence. Poststenotic dilation of the aorta is frequent, but this finding does not correlate with the degree of obstruction. Calcification of the aortic valve occurs, but usually not before midlife.

PLANS

Diagnostic

Differential Diagnosis

Valvular aortic stenosis must be differentiated from other forms of congenital left ventricular outflow obstruction.

Valvular aortic stenosis can be differentiated from aortic atresia on echocardiography by the presence of a normal-sized left ventricle and aortic root in a patient with aortic stenosis.

Hypertrophic obstructive cardiomyopathy can be identified by a systolic murmur at the lower left sternal border that increases in intensity during a Valsalva maneuver and with standing. Echocardiographically, these patients have systolic anterior motion of the mitral valve and asymmetric septal hypertrophy.

In discrete subvalvular stenosis, an ejection sound is unusual and aortic regurgitation is much more frequent. Poststenotic dilation on chest roentgenogram is less pronounced, and the membrane can often be visualized on two-dimensional echocardiography.

In supravalvular aortic stenosis, ejection sounds and aortic regurgitation are unusual, the systolic blood pressure is usually 15 mm Hg greater in the right arm than the left, and an "elfin" facies is common. There is often retardation of both growth and mental development.

All the conditions mentioned above can be identified at the time of cardiac catheterization.

Diagnostic Options and Recommended Approach

Noninvasive evaluation is appropriate for patients in whom the degree of aortic valvular stenosis is felt to be mild clinically. M-mode echocardiography may reveal an eccentric location of the closed aortic valve leaflets during diastole; however, a doming unicuspid valve may appear normal. Increased echoes from the aortic valve, increased left ventricular thickness, and left ventricular dilation may be present depending on the anatomy and degree and duration of obstruction. The ratio of left ventricular internal diameter at end systole to end-systolic thickness of the posterior left ventricular wall has been used to predict transaortic gradients with reasonably good results. Two-dimensional echocardiography is useful to visualize doming of the aortic valve and to delineate the number of cusps.

With experience, Doppler techniques can be used to accurately predict the transaortic valve gradient. Most clinicians, however, still rely on cardiac catheterization prior to surgical intervention.

Cardiac catheterization is indicated for symptomatic patients, for pa-

tients with a narrow pulse, and for those with cardiomegaly on chest roentgenogram. The essential data to be obtained are (1) cardiac output, (2) transaortic gradient, (3) left ventricular angiography, (4) aortography to evaluate aortic regurgitation, and (5) evaluation for concomitant defects. Critical aortic stenosis may be defined as a mean pressure difference across the aortic valve of 60 mm Hg, a 80 mm Hg peak-to-peak pressure difference, or a valve area of 0.5 cm^2/m^2. The significance of a gradient is determined by relating it to the cardiac output, as low output decreases the gradient. Thus, a gradient of 25 mm Hg can be quite significant (hemodynamically) if the output is low, whereas it would not be significant if the output was high.

Noninvasive testing should be used for initial evaluation as confirmation of clinical opinion and in long-term follow-up in assisting with timing of surgical intervention. Cardiac catheterization should be used if, after noninvasive testing, the diagnosis remains obscure and the data attained will make a difference in management. Invasive testing is also indicated prior to surgical intervention. Echocardiography is more valuable than catheterization in assisting a surgeon in deciding if commissurotomy or valve replacement is more likely to be successful.

Therapeutic

Therapeutic Options

Digitalis and diuretics are used for congestive failure. Prophylaxis against bacterial endocarditis is essential. Competitive sports and very heavy exertion should be restricted except in those with proven mild obstruction.

Syncope, angina, and heart failure are indications for valve replacement, as is the finding of cardiomegaly, even in an asymptomatic patient. Surgery should be done promptly in a patient with an 80 mm Hg pressure difference across the obstruction, whereas a patient with a 50 to 80 mm Hg gradient need not be considered a surgical candidate unless cardiac output is depressed and the calculated valve area is in the critical range. It should be emphasized that the pressure difference across the stenotic valve may increase markedly in only 3 to 5 years. In a few children, valvulotomy can be performed to avoid valve replacement. Eighty to ninety percent are symptomatically improved after valvulotomy, which can be performed with a low mortality rate. An increased mortality rate is seen in children with associated congenital defects who are less than 3 months of age and require surgery. Calcification and fibrosis can lead to restenosis 10 to 15 years after valvulotomy. Additional risks include sudden death, aortic regurgitation, persistent gradients, and bacterial endocarditis. Despite these serious potential complications, it is best to preserve the child's native valve as long as possible, as an ideal valve substitute for pediatric use is not available.

Although initial results are very promising, the role of percutaneous balloon angioplasty in valvular aortic stenosis is still uncertain.

FOLLOW-UP

Syncope, angina, or dyspnea should be considered indicative of significant aortic stenosis and reported promptly to the physician. Palpitations should be investigated, as dysrhythmias may be poorly tolerated by patients with significant aortic valve obstruction. Fever may be indicative of endocarditis and should be promptly reported.

Infants should be followed closely at 2- to 3-month intervals with chest roentgenogram and electrocardiogram. Beyond infancy, patients may be seen at 6-month intervals. After surgery, yearly examination with a chest roentgenogram and an electrocardiogram is recommended to watch for postoperative aortic regurgitation and a tendency to restenose 5 to 15 years after valvulotomy.

Echocardiography combined with Doppler techniques performed every 1 to 2 years should be sufficiently accurate to obviate periodic routine cardiac catheterization and facilitate correct timing of surgical intervention.

DISCUSSION

Prevalence and Incidence

Valvular aortic stenosis is present in about 5 to 7% of all patients who have congenital heart disease detected during childhood (Wagner et al.,

1977); however, bicuspid aortic valve, which rarely produces significant obstruction in infancy or childhood, is the second most common congenital defect found in adults, next to mitral valve prolapse. It may occur in about 2% of the population.

Related Basic Science

Genetics

Although some cases of familial transmission are reported, the vast majority are sporadic.

Anatomic Derangement

Pathologically, aortic outflow obstruction can be congenital or acquired. Congenital obstruction may be valvular, supravalvular, or subvalvular. Subvalvular obstruction can be produced by muscular hypertrophy of the ventricular septum or a discrete membrane that forms as a fibrous collar connecting with the anterior mitral leaflet. Supravalvular stenosis is usually either an hourglass deformity or a fibrous diaphragm, often with coronary ostial narrowing.

Aortic outflow tract obstruction occurs most commonly at the valvular level. Subvalvular and supravalvular stenosis occur much more infrequently. With valvular aortic stenosis the following anatomic variants are possible: (1) fusion of a tricuspid valve to form an acommissural domed valve (bicuspid valve), (2) unicommissural unicuspid valve, (3) hypoplastic annulus, (4) myxoid dysplasia, and (5) stenosis due to a quadricuspid valve. Congenital bicuspid aortic valve usually takes years to calcify and fibrose to a degree that produces critical obstruction. Associated patent ductus arteriosus or coarctation of the aorta may occur, but other cardiac defects are unusual.

Physiologic or Metabolic Derangement

Physiologically, the aortic obstruction places a progressive pressure load on the left ventricle and increases myocardial oxygen consumption. Generally, the left ventricle does not generate a systolic pressure greater than 250 mm Hg for a long period. Occasionally, with enlargement of the left atrium, the patent foramen ovale is opened and a left-to-right shunt is produced.

Natural History and Its Modification with Treatment

Half the infants with severe congenital aortic stenosis are hospitalized in the first week of life; the other half develop symptoms of congestive heart failure by age 6 months. During infancy, a child with moderate or severe obstruction may have increased symptoms with physiologic anemia. Complications of valvular aortic stenosis include endocardial fibroelastosis, mitral regurgitation secondary to left ventricular dilation, and, rarely, infarction of a papillary muscle. Rapid progression of valvular obstruction over a 2- to 3-year period may occur.

Infants with severe aortic stenosis have a poor prognosis due to the significant surgical mortality at this age; however, mortality within the first few years of life would be virtually universal in those patients presenting with symptoms due to severe aortic stenosis in the first weeks of life without surgical correction.

Balloon dilatation (valvoplasty or valvotomy) may prolong the life of some terminal patients, with about half surviving 3 years (Bu'Lock et al., 1993). Some patients may become surgical candidates after the procedure as they get older and their overall clinical situation improves. The outcome is definitely improved in those selected cases who are able to undergo surgical valvuloplasty and receive significant hemodynamic improvement.

Prevention

Genetic counseling is indicated in those few cases with familial incidence; otherwise, prevention involves close surveillance to avoid complications, and early intervention when progression is evident.

Cost Containment

An asymptomatic child with a systolic murmur but no thrill and with a normal chest roentgenogram and electrocardiogram does not require cardiac catheterization. The frequency of serial echocardiographic or Doppler studies should correlate with clinical, electrocardiographic, or roentgenographic evidence of progressive obstruction.

REFERENCES

Bu'Lock FA, Joffe HS, Jordan SC, Martin RP. Balloon dilatation (valvoplasty) as first-line treatment for severe stenosis of the aortic valve in early infancy: Medium term results and determinants of survival. Br Heart J 1993;70:546.

Hohn AR, Vah Praagh S, Moore AAD, Vlad P, Lambert EC. Aortic stenosis. Circulation 1965;32(suppl. 3):4.

Kelly TA, Rothbart RM, Cooper M, et al. Comparison of outcome of asymptomatic to symptomatic patients older than 20 years of age with valvular aortic stenosis. Am J Cardiol 1988;61:123.

Nugent EW, Plauth WH Jr, Edwards JE, Williams WH. The pathology, pathophysiology, recognition and treatment of congenital heart disease. In: Schlant RC, Alexander RW, O'Rourke RA, et al., eds. Hurst's the heart. 8th ed. New York: McGraw-Hill 1994:1761.

Ritter SB. Color Doppler assessment of congenital heart disease. In: Nanda NC, ed. Textbook of color Doppler echocardiography. Philadelphia: Lea & Febiger, 1989:229.

Wagner HR, Ellison RC, Keane JF, et al. Clinical course in aortic stenosis. In: Nadas AS, ed. Pulmonary stenosis, aortic stenosis, ventricular septal defect: clinical course and indirect assessment. Report from the Joint Study on the Natural History of Congenital Heart Defects. Circulation 1977;55(suppl. 1):20.

CHAPTER 15–30

Valvular Pulmonic Stenosis

Jerre F. Lutz, M.D., and Robert C. Schlant, M.D.

DEFINITION

Valvular pulmonic stenosis is characterized by morphologic changes in the valve tissue that cause obstruction to blood flow across the pulmonic valve.

ETIOLOGY

Although embryologically related to either a failure of development of an intercalated valve cushion or fusion of adjacent valve anlagen, the etiology of valvular pulmonic stenosis remains unknown. Acquired pulmonary valve stenosis can be caused by a carcinoid tumor (see Chapter 3–12).

CRITERIA FOR DIAGNOSIS

Suggestive

Valvular pulmonic stenosis is a relatively common form of congenital heart disease characterized by a systolic murmur loudest in the second left intercostal space, a decreased intensity of the pulmonic component of the second sound, electrocardiographic evidence of pressure overload of the right ventricle, and poststenotic dilation of the pulmonary artery on chest x-ray.

Definitive

The condition is confirmed by cardiac catheterization, which reveals a systolic pressure difference across the pulmonary valve and identifies no other cardiac lesions or identifies other associated cardiac abnormalities. Echocardiography, which demonstrates turbulent mosaic flow on color-flow mapping and a gradient on continuous-wave Doppler recordings, is reliably sensitive and specific.

CLINICAL MANIFESTATIONS
Subjective

Valvular pulmonic stenosis is of equal incidence in males and females. There is usually no familial tendency except with valvular pulmonic stenosis due to myxomatous dysplasia.

The severity of symptoms does not directly correlate with severity of obstruction, although there is a tendency. Although three fourths of patients with mild outflow obstruction are asymptomatic, one third with severe stenosis are also asymptomatic.

The most common complaints in symptomatic patients are exertional dyspnea and fatigue, the latter probably due to limited cardiac output. Symptoms present in childhood may decrease or disappear even without treatment. Orthopnea is very rare in pure valvular stenosis since the pulmonary vascular bed is protected. Effort-induced dizziness and syncope are rare, and when they do occur, the stenosis is usually severe. Chest pain compatible with angina may occur, usually with severe obstruction. Hemoptysis associated with peripheral pulmonic stenosis and rupture of distal thin-wall vessels does not occur with valvular pulmonic stenosis. Patients may sense the prominent *a* wave in the neck, especially with exercise.

Objective
Physical Examination

Children may present in the first year of life with a heart murmur with or without symptoms. Most patients with valvular pulmonic stenosis appear healthy, although growth retardation may occur if the condition is severe. Patients with pulmonic stenosis secondary to myxomatous dysplasia demonstrate decreased growth, a triangular face with hypertelorism, low-set ears, and a narrow chin (similar to Noonan's syndrome). When cardiac output is markedly decreased, peripheral cyanosis can be seen due to increased oxygen extraction. Cyanosis may also occur in severe obstruction with marked right ventricular hypertrophy if the right atrial pressure becomes elevated sufficiently to open a foramen ovale and produce a right-to-left shunt.

Jugular venous pulses may reveal an enlarged *a* wave if there is significant obstruction and decreased right ventricular compliance; however, this finding does not always correlate with severity of stenosis. Occasionally, presystolic hepatic pulsations can be felt. Tricuspid regurgitation may occur secondary to right ventricular pressure overload and may produce large regurgitant (*r*) waves in the jugular venous pulse. The carotid pulsation tends to be small if cardiac output is low. Chest asymmetry is present occasionally. With minimal stenosis, a right ventricular lift is absent or barely discernible; whereas with severe obstruction, the right ventricular impulse is more forceful and sustained. The parasternal lift extends up to the third intercostal space; whereas the parasternal lift is lower in patients with infundibular stenosis. A pulmonary artery impulse is rarely present. A precordial thrill is located in the left second or third interspace and may extend to the left side of the neck.

The first heart sound is normal. An early systolic ejection sound is present along the left sternal edge in the majority of patients with valvular pulmonic stenosis but is rare with infundibular or peripheral pulmonary stenosis. The interval between S_1 and ejection sound diminishes with increasing severity of obstruction, and the ejection sound may disappear with severe valvular stenosis. The ejection sound coincides with doming of the pulmonic valve, is best heard at the second left intercostal space, decreases in intensity with inspiration, and increases in intensity with expiration. An ejection sound is usually absent when valvular stenosis is associated with myxomatous dysplasia. As right ventricular ejection time increases due to valvular pulmonic stenosis, the pulmonic component of the second heart sound decreases in intensity with severe obstruction and may be delayed by as much as 0.14 second after the aortic component. The aortic component of the second sound may be covered by the systolic murmur in patients with severe pulmonary valve stenosis. The pulmonic closure sound may be faint in such patients and the entire second sound may be inaudible. A fourth heart sound is found more frequently in patients with severe stenosis and diminished right ventricular compliance. All patients with pulmonic stenosis have a spindle-shaped midsystolic murmur. In general, as the severity of pulmonic stenosis increases, the midsystolic outflow murmur across the pulmonic valve increases in intensity, lasts longer, and peaks later in systole. The holosystolic murmur of tricuspid regurgitation may occur if right ventricular dilation is present. The murmur of pulmonic valve regurgitation may be heard in some patients; it is fairly common after pulmonary valvotomy.

Routine Laboratory Abnormalities

In advanced disease, the electrocardiogram generally reveals normal sinus rhythm and only occasionally atrial fibrillation. Peaked P waves in the inferior leads are unusual with mild pulmonic stenosis, but occur in approximately half of patients with severe obstruction. In mild pulmonic stenosis, definite evidence of right ventricular hypertrophy is present in one third, but the evidence of hypertrophy increases to virtually all patients with severe obstruction. The axis of the QRS tends to move rightward and anterior with increasing severity. The T vector tends to move leftward, superiorly, and posteriorly.

On chest roentgenogram, only a small percentage of patients with mild valvular pulmonic stenosis have cardiomegaly; however, virtually all with severe pulmonary obstruction have cardiomegaly. The main pulmonary artery and the left pulmonary artery are usually enlarged from the poststenotic jet; however, the diameter of the right pulmonary artery is normal. Calcification of the valve rarely occurs except in older patients. The pulmonary vascular pattern is normal or decreased if cardiac output is diminished. If significant enlargement of the right ventricle or atrium is present on the chest film, severe obstruction is usually present. A right-sided arch should suggest infundibular rather than valvular stenosis.

Polycythemia may occur with severe pulmonic stenosis, elevated right atrial pressure, and right-to-left shunting via a patent foramen ovale. Leukocytosis is generally present with a bacterial infection, such as endocarditis.

PLANS
Diagnostic
Differential Diagnosis

Infundibular pulmonic stenosis is characterized by a systolic murmur that is loudest somewhat lower in the third and fourth intercostal spaces. Ejection sounds are rare, and there is no poststenotic dilation of the pulmonary trunk on chest roentgenogram, but there is often a right-sided aortic arch. M-mode echocardiography may reveal coarse systolic flutter of the anterior pulmonic valve leaflet, which is not seen with valvular stenosis.

Peripheral pulmonic stenosis may be associated with a systolic murmur heard diffusely over the chest and back. The murmur is systolic, but it may extend into diastole. Ejection sounds are rare. The chest roentgenogram may be normal or may show diffusely enlarged pulmonary arteries proximal to the multiple obstructions.

A ventricular septal defect can be confused with pulmonic stenosis, especially when an ejection sound is present due to aneurysm of the septum; the murmur is holosystolic and usually loudest in the fourth and fifth interspaces at the left sternal edge. A systolic thrill is common. The chest roentgenogram often shows left ventricular prominence and increased pulmonary flow (see Chapter 15–25).

An atrial septal defect may also be accompanied by an ejection click and midsystolic murmur, but the findings of increased pulmonary flow on chest roentgenogram, fixed splitting of S_2, and paradoxical septal motion on M-mode echocardiogram should allow differentiation (see Chapter 15–23).

Pulmonary valve stenosis due to a carcinoid tumor is an unusual cause of stenosis.

Diagnostic Options

In suspected mild pulmonic stenosis, noninvasive studies may suffice in establishing a diagnosis. An M-mode echocardiogram of patients with valvular pulmonic stenosis may be normal with mild outflow obstruction, but it usually reveals an enlarged *a* dip on the pulmonic valve in patients with moderate or severe valvular stenosis. Significant right ventricular enlargement or dilation also correlates with more severe obstruction. Doppler studies can be used to estimate the degree of obstruction across the pulmonic valve.

In patients with significant symptoms or in whom severe obstruction is suspected, cardiac catheterization is still the best method to confirm the diagnosis and rule out other intracardiac lesions. A slow pullback of the cardiac catheter from the distal pulmonary arteries (both sides to rule out concomitant peripheral pulmonic stenosis) with continuous pressure monitoring will reveal a systolic pressure difference at the level of the pulmonic valve. Further slow pullback across the right ventricular inflow allows evaluation of a concomitant infundibular obstruction. Oxygen saturations in all right heart chambers, as well as inferior and superior vena cava, should be measured to rule out associated shunt lesions. A right ventriculogram will show doming of the pulmonic valve and visualize the outflow tract and the pulmonary arteries, but the systolic pressure difference between the right ventricle and the pulmonary artery is the single most important piece of information. Severity is usually expressed in terms of the systolic pressure difference between the right ventricle and the pulmonary artery. Mild stenosis is defined as a pressure difference across the pulmonic valve of 50 mm Hg or less, whereas a pressure difference greater than 100 mm Hg is considered severe. The range 50 to 100 mm Hg is considered moderate. Evaluation of the pressure difference following exercise is indicated when the gradient is less than 60 mm Hg at rest.

Recommended Approach

Routine history and physical examination combined with noninvasive echocardiography are now capable of defining accurately the level and degree of pulmonic stenosis. Additional intracardiac defects such as atrial or ventricular septal defects should be identified by combined echo–Doppler techniques. Cardiac catheterization should be reserved until definitive procedures such as balloon valvuloplasty are being contemplated.

Therapeutic
Therapeutic Options

Bacterial endocarditis prophylaxis is recommended for all patients with pulmonic stenosis.

Surgery was indicated in children who have failure to thrive, cardiomegaly, cyanosis, and heart failure together with a pressure difference across the pulmonic valve of greater than 100 mm Hg. Fatigue, dyspnea, angina, and syncope were also indications for surgery in the presence of a significant pressure difference. A patient with a resting pressure difference greater than 60 to 75 mm Hg was scheduled for elective surgery, as it was likely that life expectancy was diminished. Surgery was also recommended for patients with a resting pressure difference less than 60 mm Hg and a markedly increased pressure difference across the pulmonic valve with exercise. After valvulotomy, pulmonic regurgitation was very common. Surgical mortality in children and older patients with less advanced disease was less than 1%, but approached 4% in older patients with severe long-standing obstruction, significant ventricular dilation, and tricuspid regurgitation.

Catheter balloon valvuloplasty has now become a common alternative treatment for relief of valvular and supravalvular stenosis. Although results with dysplastic valves are less impressive, attempts at catheter balloon valvuloplasty seem justified in all forms of pulmonic valvular stenosis of a severe degree. The procedure should be performed prior to development of irreversible ventricular dysfunction.

Catheter balloon angioplasty, although not without risk, has become the treatment of choice for distal pulmonary artery stenosis, unless other major cardiac surgical reconstruction is also required.

Recommended Approach

Surgery is now rarely indicated for isolated pulmonic valve stenosis, as catheter balloon valvuloplasty is virtually always successful in relieving clinically significant pulmonary valve obstruction. Surgical treatment is now reserved for valvuloplasty failures, a greater likelihood in dysplastic valves.

FOLLOW-UP

A fever should be reported to the physician, as there is an increased incidence of bacterial endocarditis in patients with valvular pulmonic stenosis both prior to and after surgical intervention.

Asymptomatic patients without cardiomegaly or right ventricular hypertrophy may be seen every 1 to 2 years with serial electrocardiograms and chest roentgenograms. Symptomatic patients with cardiomegaly or right ventricular hypertrophy should be seen at 6- to 12-month intervals and followed with electrocardiogram and chest roentgenogram until cardiac catheterization and/or surgery is performed. Patients who have not had surgery should continue under close observation, whereas those who have had surgery should be seen at yearly intervals if signs of right hypertrophy or cardiomegaly regress.

DISCUSSION
Prevalence and Incidence

The only congenital heart defects that occur with greater frequency are ventricular septal defect, patent ductus arteriosus, coarctation of the aorta, and bicuspid aortic valve. Pulmonic stenosis occurs in about one tenth of patients with congenital heart disease.

Related Basic Science
Physiologic or Metabolic Derangement

Subpulmonic obstruction may develop secondary to valvular pulmonic stenosis as an effect of right ventricular hypertrophy, placing an increased pressure overload on the right ventricle. The peak pressure difference across the pulmonary outflow tract may range from 160 to 240 mm Hg.

Anatomic Derangement

Valvular pulmonic stenosis is surprisingly constant in its anatomic appearance. The valve is domed-shaped with a narrow outlet at its apex. Three raphes may be present without separate leaflets. Occasionally, myxomatous dysplasia with thickened disorganized material leads to obstruction.

Congenital outflow obstruction of the right ventricle may be produced by valvular, subvalvular, and supravalvular pulmonic stenosis. Valvular pulmonic stenosis is often an isolated defect. Subvalvular pulmonic stenosis may exist as a membranous or muscular obstruction and is often associated with ventricular septal defect. Supravalvular obstruction may occur in the pulmonary trunk and in primary or multiple peripheral branches of the pulmonary artery. Single or multiple defects of a segmental, membranous, or diffuse nature may exist. Peripheral pulmonic stenosis is associated with atrial septal defects, patent ductus arteriosus, tetralogy of Fallot, and supravalvular aortic stenosis (with abnormal facies, abnormal dentition, hypercalcemia, and mental retardation).

Natural History and Its Modification with Treatment

Complications of valvular pulmonic stenosis include secondary infundibular pulmonic stenosis, the development of right-to-left shunts by way of a patent foramen ovale, tricuspid regurgitation, and endocarditis. Cerebral abscesses occur in adults but are rare in children.

Children who progress to cyanosis or heart failure in the first years of life have severe obstruction and require surgical intervention.

Mild gradients across the pulmonic valve usually do not progress in the first 20 years of life; thereafter, progression of mild disease is quite variable. Survival to adulthood is the rule, even when the murmur is heard in infancy. Calcification and fibrosis of the pulmonic valve increase with age. Although patients with valvular pulmonic stenosis may live to age 70, early studies revealed the average age of death without surgery to be approximately 30. Relief of obstruction by surgery or valvuloplasty obviously has a beneficial effect on longevity.

Prevention

Valvular pulmonic stenosis is generally a congenital defect occurring sporadically. Genetic counseling is indicated when the condition is secondary to myxomatous dysplasia.

Cost Containment

In an adult who has no cardiomegaly and is asymptomatic, minimal or no obstruction is likely, and cardiac catheterization or surgery is not indicated.

REFERENCES

Beekman RH, Rocchini AP, Rosenthal A. Therapeutic cardiac catheterization for pulmonary valve and pulmonary artery stenosis. Cardiol Clin 1989;7:331.

Fellows KE. Therapeutic catheter procedures in congenital heart disease: Current status and future prospects. Cardiovasc Interven Radiol 1984;7;170.

Kirklin JW, Connolly DC, Ellis FH Jr, et al. Problems in the diagnosis and surgical treatment of pulmonic stenosis with intact ventricular septum. Circulation 1953;8:849.

Levine OR, Blumenthal S. Pulmonic stenosis. Circulation 1965;32(suppl. 3):33.

McCrindle BW. Independent predictors of long-term results after balloon pulmonary valvuloplasty: Valvuloplasty and angioplasty of congenital anomalies (VACA) Registry Investigators. Circulation 1994;89:1751.

Nugent EW, Plauth Jr WH, Edwards JE, Williams WH. The pathology, pathophysiology, recognition and treatment of congenital heart disease. In: Schlant RC, Alexander RW, O'Rourke RA, et al., eds. Hurst's the heart. 8th ed. New York: McGraw-Hill, 1994:1797.

Scherlis L, Koenker RJ, Lee Y-C. Pulmonary stenosis. Circulation 1963;38:288.

Witsenburg M, Talsma M, Rohmer J, Hess J. Balloon valvuloplasty for valvular pulmonary stenosis in children over 6 months of age: Initial results and long-term follow-up. Eur Heart J 1993;14:1657.

CHAPTER 15–31

Tetralogy of Fallot

Jerre F. Lutz, M.D., and Robert C. Schlant, M.D.

DEFINITION

Tetralogy of Fallot is a combination of four defects that result from congenital heart disease. The defects include pulmonary infundibular stenosis, a ventricular septal defect with an overriding aorta, and right ventricular hypertrophy.

ETIOLOGY

A varying degree of anterior displacement of the conal septum leads to unequal partitioning of the conus. Thus, infundibular stenosis and a ventricular septal defect form. The etiology of this disorder remains obscure.

CRITERIA FOR DIAGNOSIS

Suggestive

Tetralogy of Fallot is the most likely diagnosis in a cyanotic infant, child, or adult who has right ventricular hypertrophy and evidence of diminished pulmonary blood flow on the chest x-ray film.

Definitive

The constellation of anatomic abnormalities seen in this disorder can be confirmed echocardiographically, angiographically, or pathologically.

CLINICAL MANIFESTATIONS

Subjective

Dyspnea that increases with feeding, crying, straining, or exertion is common; many patients also have significant exertional fatigue.

Between the ages of 18 months and 10 years, positional relief of cyanosis, dyspnea, and lightheadedness is common (this may take the form of squatting, sitting with legs folded beneath, standing with legs crossed, and in mother's arms flexing the legs against her body).

With increasing age, complications of uncorrected tetralogy are more likely. Fever, malaise, and weight loss suggest endocarditis. Chest pain, described as a bandlike constriction lasting minutes to hours, occurs not infrequently in adults with uncorrected tetralogy of Fallot and no coronary artery obstruction. Headache and mental confusion occasionally occur in patients with severe cyanosis and marked erythrocytosis.

Objective

Physical Examination

Patients usually present with cyanosis or for evaluation of a murmur. Older children may exhibit clubbing of the fingers and toes. If right ventricular outflow obstruction is severe, cyanosis may be present at birth; otherwise it usually appears by 6 months of age.

Hypoxic episodes, which are not proportional to the degree of obstruction, are common between the ages of 2 months and 2 years. They may be precipitated by tachyarrhythmias, infection, and exertion and may last minutes to hours. They tend to be more common in the morning than in the evening and in summer rather than winter. During an episode, the child is crying, irritable, and tachypneic. The blood pressure remains normal, although the systolic murmur and arterial oxygen saturation are diminished. Hypoxic episodes can culminate in syncope, seizures, or death.

Two to four percent of patients under 2 years of age with uncorrected tetralogy of Fallot develop endocarditis; some also have an antecedent infection, headache, signs of increased intracranial pressure, seizures, and focal neurologic defects from a cerebral abscess. With erythrocytosis there is increased incidence of pulmonary and cerebral thrombosis, especially in children under 2 years of age who have mild iron deficiency. Congestive heart failure secondary to uncomplicated tetralogy of Fallot is unusual. Precipitating factors include anemia, renal failure, hypertension, and endocarditis.

General examination may disclose the presence of growth retardation, mental retardation secondary to hypoxic episodes, cyanosis, and clubbing of the extremities. Abnormal development usually correlates with diminished pulmonary blood flow. Precordial asymmetry is minimal because the heart size is usually normal.

Examination of the jugular venous pulses and liver is usually normal, as heart failure is unusual. Elevated left jugular pulses alone suggest a persistent left superior vena cava. A large *a* wave can be seen in the neck veins of patients with tetralogy of Fallot, probably due to diminished right ventricular compliance.

Arterial pulsations are usually normal or increased. Systemic hypertension occurs with increased frequency.

Patients with a right aortic arch may have a pulsatile right sternoclavicular joint. Most have a palpable sternal or parasternal lift from right ventricular hypertrophy. A systolic thrill at the left sternal border is present in half of patients with tetralogy.

Most patients have a grade 3 or 4 spindle-shaped murmur that originates from the pulmonary outflow tract. The murmur ends before a loud single second sound, the aortic component of the second heart sound. A faint, delayed P_2 may be heard in patients with milder obstruction. As the degree of stenosis increases beyond a certain limit, the murmur may decrease in loudness. The murmur is also fainter during hypoxic episodes and after amyl nitrite inhalation, which produces a decrease in pulmonary blood flow; the murmur is made louder and longer by agents that produce systemic arterial vasoconstriction. Except in patients with pulmonary atresia, continuous murmurs due to a patent ductus or bronchial collaterals are unusual. Continuous murmurs can be heard after surgery designed to produce a systemic-pulmonic shunt. There may be ejection sounds that may lack respiratory variation in patients with more significant pulmonic obstruction or that are heard in patients with markedly increased systemic flow through dilated aorta. Gallop sounds are rarely heard.

Routine Laboratory Abnormalities

The electrocardiogram reveals right-axis deviation of the QRS complexes from +90° to +120°. Most patients have evidence of right ventricular hypertrophy with the mean QRS vector directed to the right and anteriorly. Therefore, there is a tall R wave in V_1 and V_2 and a deep S wave in V_5 or V_6. The T wave is upright in the anterior precordial leads (upright in V_1 approximately 50%) if right ventricular pressure does not exceed systemic pressure. Normal sinus rhythm is usually present with a normal PR interval. The Wolff–Parkinson–White syndrome is rarely seen, and enlarged P waves are present in only 10% of cases.

The chest roentgenogram may reveal a heart size within normal limits on anteroposterior view but retrosternal fullness on the lateral view that suggests right ventricular enlargement. Classically, the contour of the heart reveals an up-tilted apex *(coeur en sabot)*; this is due to right ventricular hypertrophy with a relatively small left ventricle and a concave pulmonary artery segment. Markedly dilated pulmonary arteries in the setting of tetralogy of Fallot suggest a concomitant absent pulmonic valve. Approximately one fourth of patients have an enlarged right-sided aortic arch; this tends to occur more frequently in patients with marked pulmonary outflow obstruction (or atresia). Unilateral rib notching may be seen following the surgical creation of a systemic-pulmonic shunt.

The degree of erythrocytosis roughly correlates with the extent of arterial hypoxemia and the amount of desaturated hemoglobin, but it is inversely proportional to the amount of pulmonary blood flow. Leukocytosis is generally seen in bacterial infections, such as endocarditis, or brain abscess.

PLANS
Diagnostic
Differential Diagnosis

The differential diagnosis includes all variants of cyanotic heart disease. Some patients with a small ventricular septal defect with pulmonic stenosis can have aortic overriding yet do not fulfill all the criteria for tetralogy. Differentiation is possible on echocardiography and angiography. The pentology of Fallot has the classic features of tetralogy of Fallot with the addition of an atrial septal defect. Pseudotruncus arteriosus is a form of tetralogy with severe pulmonary obstruction in which pulmonary blood flow occurs through bronchial arteries.

Diagnostic Options

Although the anatomic features of tetralogy of Fallot can be visualized by echocardiography and the Q_p/Q_s can be determined by Doppler techniques using a ratio of pulmonary artery to aortic blood flow, cardiac catheterization is the usual method to confirm the diagnosis of tetralogy and to eliminate the possibility of other intracardiac lesions.

Echocardiographic features in uncorrected tetralogy of Fallot include the following: (1) right ventricular size greater than or equal to left ventricular size, (2) decreased size of the right ventricular outflow tract, (3) presence of a ventricular septum that is often hypertrophic, (4) an aorta that is increased in size inversely proportional to the degree of pulmonic obstruction, and (5) continuity from the anterior mitral leaflet to the posterior aorta with discontinuity of the ventricular septum and the anterior aortic wall (unlike double-outlet right ventricle, where both are discontinuous).

Cardiac catheterization reveals normal right atrial pressure. As the ventricular septal defect is large, there is free communication of blood between the two ventricles, and the systolic pressure is equal in both ventricles and in the aorta. The right ventricular pressure tracing has a sharp upstroke, plateau, and a sharp downstroke, similar to the left ventricle. The pulmonary artery pressure in uncorrected tetralogy of Fallot is normal or reduced. There is a systolic pressure difference between the main right ventricular chamber and the right ventricular outflow chamber. Occasionally, there is an additional pressure difference between this infundibular chamber and the main pulmonary artery. Angiography reveals a narrowed pulmonary outflow tract and a large ventricular septal defect. Coronary angiography often reveals (1) a large conal branch of the right coronary, (2) the left anterior descending artery originating from the right coronary artery and passing in front of the pulmonary tract, or (3) all branches arising from a single orifice.

Recommended Approach

Two-dimensional echocardiography can delineate the anatomic components of tetralogy and associated defects.

Cardiac catheterization is necessary to define the continuity and size of the pulmonary arteries, as well as the size and position of the ventricular septal defect. Aortography or selective coronary arteriography should be done preoperatively to define anomalous coronary patterns that would complicate the surgical approach.

Therapeutic
Therapeutic Options

During infancy, medical treatment may include type E prostaglandins to preserve pulmonary blood flow by maintaining patency of the ductus arteriosus.

Hypoxic episodes are treated with oxygen, morphine, beta-adrenergic blocking drugs, and knee–chest position. Intravenous sodium bicarbonate is indicated if there is systemic acidosis. Cerebral abscesses are treated with surgical drainage and antibiotics. Cerebral thromboses are managed with oxygen, supportive care, and steroids for cerebral edema. Antibiotics are also useful for intercurrent infections and as prophylaxis for subacute bacterial endocarditis. Severe erythrocytosis is best treated with erythropheresis rather than phlebotomy, as significant hypovolemia increases chances of hypoxic episodes.

Early surgery is indicated for patients who have significant hypoxia at rest, erythrocytosis or hypoxic episodes. For children to be considered for total correction, they should be over 1 month of age and have a pulmonary artery larger than one third the size of the aorta. Total correction is usually indicated if children are under 2 years of age and the operative mortality in the hospital is less than 10%. If operative mortality is greater than 10%, treatment with propranolol or other beta blockers is indicated until age 2 years, when operative mortality is decreased. Elective surgery should be accomplished before the age of 4 or 5. In situations in which the risk of total correction is excessive, one may perform a Blalock–Taussig procedure, in which pulmonary blood flow is increased by anastomosing a subclavian artery to a pulmonary artery. For severe pulmonic atresia with small arteries, palliative surgery is indicated until the child matures, when it is possible to perform Rastelli's operation with the largest conduit possible.

Recommended Approach

Surgical repair rather than palliation is now preferred in most centers. Anatomic variables such as small pulmonary arteries pulmonary atresia, and coronary anomalies may make a palliative procedure favorable. Early correction should be performed in centers with an operative mortality of less than 10% in this group.

FOLLOW-UP

Fever may be indicative of endocarditis and should be promptly reported to the physician. Palpitations may be a warning of a serious underlying rhythm disturbance.

Corrective surgery carries a high incidence of right bundle-branch block. Residual significant ventricular septal defects, pulmonic outflow gradients over 40 mm Hg, and pulmonic regurgitation are not uncommon postoperatively. There is also an increased incidence of ventricular arrhythmias and sudden death. Follow-up visits should be at 3- to 6-month intervals with particular attention to the possibility of these complications.

DISCUSSION

Prevalence and Incidence

Tetralogy of Fallot, constituting 10% of all congenital heart disease, is the most likely diagnosis in a cyanotic patient with right ventricular hypertrophy and diminished pulmonary blood flow and is the most common cause of cyanotic heart disease over the age of 2.

Related Basic Science

Physiologic or Metabolic Derangement

The basic defect is the biventricular origin of the aorta above a large ventricular septal defect in association with obstruction to pulmonary blood flow that is usually due to stenosis of the infundibular region of the right ventricle. The pulmonary valve may be bicuspid or unicuspid, but although malformed, it rarely is the only site of obstruction to pulmonary blood flow. The overriding of the aorta probably has little physiologic effect, as the large ventricular septal defect allows mixing of the oxygenated and unoxygenated blood and the right and left ventricular and aortic systolic pressures are equal. With pulmonary outflow tract obstruction, shunting across the ventricular septal defect is bidirectional. As the obstruction to pulmonary blood flow increases, the right-to-left shunt across the ventricular septal defect into the aorta increases. Some patients with predominantly left-to-right shunting may have so-called acyanotic tetralogy of Fallot. If pulmonic atresia is present, survival depends on the presence of adequate pulmonary flow through either bronchial arteries or a patent ductus arteriosus. Congestive heart failure is unusual in uncomplicated cases, as there is little volume overload of the left ventricle and the right ventricle tolerates its pressure load reasonably well.

Infundibular pulmonic obstruction is very dynamic and is increased by drugs or maneuvers that increase right ventricular contractility or decrease right ventricular volume load. Crying decreases pulmonary blood flow by performing a Valsalva maneuver, breath holding, and by an increase in sympathetic activity to the heart, which increases the contractility of the right ventricular infundibulum. Squatting increases pulmonary blood flow and arterial saturation by increasing systemic vascular resistance. Hypercyanotic episodes are caused by increased infundibular obstruction, which markedly decreases pulmonary blood flow and increases right-to-left shunting. Beta blockers such as propranolol diminish infundibular obstruction and thereby increase pulmonary blood flow and oxygen saturation.

Anatomic Derangement

Tetralogy of Fallot arises as a consequence of underdevelopment of the pulmonary infundibulum. Abnormalities that are occasionally associated include (1) persistent left superior vena cava, (2) atrioventricular canal with tricuspid and mitral anomalies, (3) right aortic arch in one quarter, with incidence increasing with increasing severity of the pulmonary outflow tract obstruction, (4) multiple types of vascular rings, which may produce dysphagia, (5) coronary artery anomalies, and (6) semilunar valve regurgitation.

Natural History and Its Modification with Treatment

The right ventricular outflow obstruction can increase with age, accentuating the right-to-left shunting of blood and worsening the general-

ized cyanosis. Some patients with uncorrected tetralogy of Fallot have minor occlusive disease of the venous or arterial supply of the central nervous system at autopsy.

Adults with uncorrected tetralogy of Fallot have the following features: (1) large ventricular septal defect, (2) increased incidence of combined valvular and infundibular pulmonic stenosis, (3) greater frequency of congestive heart failure, (4) great frequency of oppressive chest discomfort, (5) normal or increased vascularity on chest roentgenogram due to collaterals, and (6) right bundle-branch block in more than half.

Approximately one third of the patients with untreated tetralogy of Fallot die by 1 year of age, half die by age 3, and three quarters by age 10. The average life expectancy without surgery is about 12 years, although patients occasionally survive until the sixth or seventh decade (Bertranaou et al., 1978).

In patients who survive (32-year actuarial survival) the perioperative period, long-term survival is excellent, above 90% in children repaired before age 12 (Murphy et al., 1993). The risk of late sudden death is small.

Patients repaired in adult life have a low operative and overall mortality. Right ventricular ejection fraction increases with time, whereas left ventricular ejection fraction declines slightly. The vast majority remain New York Heart Association functional class I. Exercise-induced arrhythmias decrease with time.

Prevention

There is increased incidence of congenital heart disease, including tetralogy of Fallot, in infants exposed to anticonvulsants in utero.

Cost Containment

Postoperatively, patients should be followed clinically and with periodic electrocardiograms and chest roentgenograms. Echocardiography every other year increases the possibility of early detection of postoperative complications. Serial catheterization is rarely needed. Periodic histories and electrocardiograms should detect frequent arrhythmias. Continuous ambulatory electrocardiographic monitoring and exercise testing should be used sparingly.

REFERENCES

Bertranaou EG, Blackstone EH, Hazlerig JB, et al. Life expectancy without surgery in tetralogy of Fallot. Am J Cardiol 1978;42:488.

Blalock A, Taussig HB. The surgical treatment of malformations of the heart in which there is pulmonary stenosis or pulmonary atresia. JAMA 1945;128:189.

Campbell RM, Dick M, Rosenthal A. Cardiac arrhythmias in children. Ann Rev Med 1984;35:397.

Garson AG, Gorry GA, McNamara DG, Cooley DA. Surgical decision in tetralogy of Fallot: Weighing risks and benefits with decision analysis. Am J Cardiol 1980;45:108.

McCord MC, Van Elk J, Blount SG Jr. Tetralogy of Fallot: Clinical and hemodynamic spectrum of combined pulmonary stenosis and ventricular septal defect. Circulation 1957;16:736.

Murphy JG, Gersh BJ, Mair DD, et al. Long-term outcome in patients undergoing surgical repair of tetralogy of Fallot. N Engl J Med 1993;329:593.

Waien SA, Liu PP, Ross BL, et al. Serial follow-up of adults with repaired tetralogy of fallot. J Am Coll Cardiol 1992;20:295.

Warnes CA. Tetralogy of Fallot and pulmonary atresial ventricular septal defect. Cardiol Clin 1993;11:643.

Transposition of the Great Vessels

Jerre F. Lutz, M.D., and Robert C. Schlant, M.D.

DEFINITION

In a patient with normally related great arteries, the aorta lies to the right of and posterior to the position of the pulmonary valve. *Transposition* refers to a reversal of the normal anteroposterior relationship of the great vessels at their origin from the ventricles so that the aorta is located anterior to the pulmonary artery.

In transposition of the great arteries (TGA), the aorta arises from the anatomic right ventricle and the pulmonary artery arises from the anatomic left ventricle. In transposition of the great vessels, when the aortic origin is to the right of the pulmonary origin, dextrotransposition (d-TGA) is present. When the reverse is present, levotransposition (l-TGA) is present. In complete transposition (d-TGA), the right atrium, the right ventricle, and the aorta are in sequence, whereas the left atrium, the left ventricle, and the pulmonary artery are in sequence. In congenitally corrected transposition (l-TGA), ventricular inversion in addition to transposition exists; thus, the right atrium, the morphologic left ventricle, and the pulmonary artery are in sequence; whereas the left atrium, the morphologic right ventricle, and the aorta are in sequence.

ETIOLOGY

Embryologically, transposition results from abnormalities of looping of the growing bulboventricular tube often combined with development of a straight rather than spiral infundibulotruncal septum.

Although levotransposition can be associated with partial trisomy of chromosome 7q and transposition can be associated with trisomy 18, the etiology of transposition in the vast majority of patients remains unknown.

CRITERIA FOR DIAGNOSIS

Suggestive

Complete transposition should be considered in a patient with cyanotic congenital heart disease. The presence or absence of pulmonary plethora on chest roentgenogram and chamber hypertrophy depends on the presence or absence of an associated ventricular septal defect and/or pulmonary outflow tract obstruction.

Corrected transposition should be considered in an acyanotic patient with an atrioventricular conduction disturbance on electrocardiogram and a narrow vascular pedicle on chest roentgenogram, with or without a holosystolic murmur.

Definitive

The ultimate diagnosis of transposition of the great vessels relies on either magnetic resonance imaging or angiographic evidence of abnormal anteroposterior relationship of the great vessels and abnormal intracardiac communications (Figure 15–32–1). Either method relies on concomitant morphologic characterization of the ventricular chamber from which the displaced vessels arise.

CLINICAL MANIFESTATIONS

Subjective

The majority of patients with complete transposition present during infancy with objective evidence of heart disease. Symptoms of dyspnea and fatigue from congestive heart failure are frequent; it is the most common cause of death in untreated complete transposition. In the presence of high pulmonary vascular resistance or pulmonic stenosis, the patient also may develop more marked dyspnea and chest pain from diminished pulmonary blood flow and systemic oxygen desaturation.

Patients with uncomplicated corrected transposition are usually asymptomatic, and any symptoms that occur are related to associated defects. For example, Stokes–Adams attacks with loss of consciousness may be due to associated heart block, whereas supraventricular tachyarrhythmias and symptoms of congestive heart failure may occur in patients with associated regurgitation or Ebstein's anomaly of the left-sided tricuspid valve.

Objective

Physical Examination

Complete transposition is uncommon in a first-born child. The birth weight is usually normal or increased; thereafter, growth and development are retarded. Cyanosis, which may occur or increase during feeding or crying, is often present from birth depending on anatomic and physiologic status. Patients with complete transposition rarely remain acyanotic throughout childhood unless pulmonary blood flow is increased. Congestive heart failure often develops in the neonatal period at 3 to 4 weeks of age, when the normal fall in pulmonary vascular resistance allows "flooding" of the pulmonary vascular bed. Recurrent respiratory infections are common and may aggravate or precipitate congestive heart failure. Hypoxic spells with transient loss of consciousness are seen occasionally, but squatting is uncommon.

Differential cyanosis with more pronounced cyanosis in the lower extremities than in the right hand may be seen when transposition and a patent ductus coexist. Varicosities of the scalp and upper extremities occasionally are seen in patients with transposition who have severe pulmonic stenosis or increased pulmonary vascular resistance.

Growth and development are usually normal in patients with corrected transposition unless there is a coexistant large ventricular septal defect and left-to-right shunt. The general appearance is usually normal. Cyanosis can be seen in corrected transposition with either significant pulmonic stenosis or increased pulmonary vascular resistance with a right-to-left shunt.

The findings on physical examination, electrocardiogram, and chest roentgenogram in patients with complete (d-TGA) and corrected (l-TGA) transposition are contrasted in Table 15–32–1.

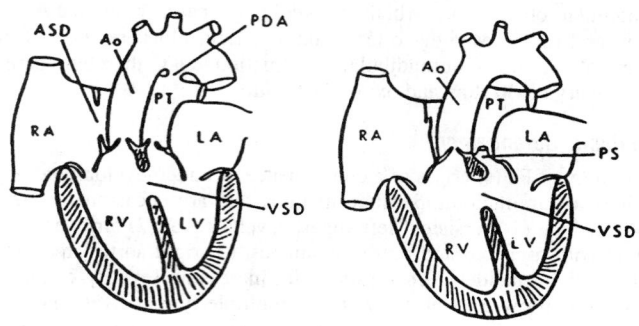

Figure 15–32–1. Schematic illustrations of complete transposition of the great vessels showing the relationships of the great vessels to each other, the principal types of communications that join the greater and lesser circulations, and the presence or absence of pulmonic stenosis. The aorta (Ao) is situated anterior and to the right of the pulmonary trunk (PT). Pulmonic stenosis is absent. Three types of communications, singly or in combination, join the two circulations, namely, atrial septal defect (ASD), ventricular septal defect (VSD), and patent ductus arteriosus (PDA). Pulmonic stenosis (PS) is present. A ventricular septal defect usually coexists. In addition, aortic blood may reach the pulmonary circulation by way of bronchial collaterals. RA, right atrium; LA, left atrium; RV, right ventricle; LV, left ventricle. *(Source: Perloff JD, ed. The clinical recognition of heart disease. 2d ed. Philadelphia: Saunders, 1978:664. Reproduced with permission of the publisher and author.)*

TABLE 15–32–1. FINDINGS IN PATIENTS WITH COMPLETE AND CORRECTED TRANSPOSITION

	Complete Transposition	Corrected Transposition
Arterial pulse	Bounding pulses with systemic circulation overload (severe PS or ↑ PVR)	Normal unless bradycardia with AV block
Jugular venous pulse	Normal until congestive heart failure, then elevated	Multiple *a* waves or cannon *a* waves with heart block
Precordium	Prominent RV impulse with severe PS; prominent LV impulse with large VSD	Apical impulse at left sternal border; systolic precordial lift with large left atrium
Auscultation	S_1 normal; S_2 loud single; pulmonary ES (no respiratory variation) with ↑ PVR and dilated pulmonary artery; aortic ES with severe PS, VSD, and dilated aorta	S_1 variable or soft; S_2 loud at second left intercostal space or split to right of sternum; ES even without PS or ↑ PVR Systolic flow murmur with angulated outflow tracts; holosystolic murmur with VSD or tricuspid regurgitation Diastolic flow rumble with large VSD Graham Steell with pulmonary hypertension
+ VSD	Systolic spindle-shaped murmur, grade 3 or less	
+ PS	Greater obstruction, less the murmur	
+ PDA	Systolic murmur often without diastolic component; S_3 or flow rumble with ↑ pulmonary flow; Graham Steell with pulmonary hypertension	
Electrocardiogram	*Large VSD, normal PVR:* biatrial abnormalities; right axis; combined ventricle hypertrophy; ↑ *PVR:* RVH (no left atrial abnormality or LVH as requires pressure plus volume overload) *Large VSD, severe PS:* right atrial abnormality; right axis, RVH	Three fourths with AV conduction disturbance; occasional atrial fibrillation, paroxysmal atrial tachycardia; Wolff–Parkinson–White syndrome with left-sided Ebstein's; reversed direction initial QRS with initial septal forces to left (qs in right chest, absent qs in left leads)
Chest x-ray	*Without PS and normal PVR:* ↑ flow, egg on side configuration; narrow vascular pedicle *With PS or ↑ PVR:* heart size smaller, and ↓ blood flow ↑ incidence right sided aortic arch only with concomitant VSD and PS	Narrow vascular pedicle; absent aortic convexity at upper right heart border; absent convex PA along left heart border; left heart border "humped" with apex off diaphragm secondary to prominent infundibulum of systemic ventricle

PA, pulmonary artery; PS, pulmonic stenosis; TR, tricuspid regurgitation; PVR, pulmonary vascular resistance; ES, ejection sound; PDA, patent ductus arteriosus; VSD, ventricular septal defect; AV, atrioventricular; RV, right ventricular; LV, left ventricular; RVH (LVH), right (left) ventricular hypertrophy.

Routine Laboratory Abnormalities

In addition to the electrocardiographic and roentgenographic abnormalities noted in Table 15–32–1, the degree of oxygen desaturation determines the extent of hypoxia noted on blood gases and the compensatory increase in hematocrit noted on a complete blood count.

PLANS

Differential Diagnosis

Complete transposition can usually be distinguished from the other forms of cyanotic congenital heart disease by history and physical examination, electrocardiogram, chest roentgenogram, echocardiogram, and angiography (Table 15–32–2).

Diagnostic Approach

Noninvasive testing, at times combined with invasive testing, is initially indicated to make sure all anatomic abnormalities are correctly identified in patients with cyanotic heart disease.

Results of M-mode echocardiography may be quite helpful in the diagnosis of complete transposition. The most prominent features are as follows: parallel aortic and pulmonary outflow tracts, with both semilunar valves visualized simultaneously; continuity between the ventricular septum and the anterior wall of the larger posterior vessel; continuity between the anterior mitral valve leaflet and the posterior wall of the larger posterior vessel; and identification of the pulmonary artery as the larger posterior vessel (the pulmonic valve closes later than the aortic valve as long as pulmonary vascular resistance is less than systemic vascular resistance). Problems may arise in the echocardiographic evaluation of patients with complete transposition, as 5 to 10% lack parallel outflow tracts. In addition, parallel outflow tracts can be seen in normal infants without congenital heart disease.

Angiography in complete transposition reveals the following: atrioventricular concordance (right atrium leads to the right ventricle, and left atrium to left ventricle); aorta at its origin transposed anteriorly to the pulmonary artery; and connection of the right ventricle to the aorta and left ventricle to the pulmonary artery. The pressures and oxygen saturations within the chambers of the heart depend on the associated intracardiac abnormalities.

Because of associated anomalies or complications, corrected trans-

position is often confused with large ventricular septal defect, ventricular septal defect with pulmonic stenosis, idiopathic mitral regurgitation, and isolated atrioventricular block. The diagnosis of corrected transposition can sometimes be suspected by the finding of reversed septal depolarization on electrocardiogram and chest roentgenogram. Otherwise, differentiation may require catheterization and angiography or autopsy.

Noninvasive testing combined with invasive testing is generally required to adequately evaluate the patients with suspected corrected transposition.

An adequate M-mode echocardiogram may be technically difficult to achieve in patients with corrected transposition. Because of altered anatomic connections and the direction of the ventricular septal plane, it may often appear normal; some observers have noted paradoxical motion of the ventricular septum.

Corrected transposition reveals the following angiographic abnormalities: atrioventricular discordance (right atrium leads to anatomic left ventricle, and the left atrium to the anatomic right ventricle); connection of the anatomic left ventricle to the pulmonary artery and the anatomic right ventricle to the aorta; and selective coronary angiograms that are mirror images of normal structures. The right ventricle is more globular with coarser trabeculations, whereas the left ventricle is more bullet-shaped with finer trabeculations.

Doppler echocardiography may correctly identify intracardiac shunts as well as the Q_p/Q_s by comparing aortic with pulmonary blood flow; however, cardiac catheterization remains the most accurate method of evaluating these patients with complex congenital heart disease.

Recommended Approach

The vast majority of cases of transposition are characterized using both noninvasive and invasive techniques during childhood. An occasional patient with isolated congenitally corrected transposition may present in adulthood. Electrocardiographic changes combined with altered features of the physical examination may suggest the diagnosis, which can be confirmed on magnetic resonance imaging.

Characterization of altered interrelationships of the great vessels combined with morphologic assessment of ventricular configuration may be adequate proof of the correct diagnosis. As long as no other intracardiac defects are recognized, cardiac catheterization may be superfluous.

TABLE 15–32–2. DIFFERENTIAL DIAGNOSIS OF TRANSPOSITION OF THE GREAT VESSELS

A. Cyanotic congenital heart disease with decreased pulmonary flow
  1. Defects in septation with stenotic lesions of pulmonary circulation
    a. Tetralogy of Fallot
      Echo: large RV, overriding Ao
      Cath: PS, VSD, overriding Ao
    b. Pulmonary atresia with atrial or ventricular septal defect
      Echo, Cath: atretic PA ± RV; patent ductus arteriosus present
    c. Pulmonic stenosis with PFO
      Echo: large a on PV
      Cath: gradient across PV with right-to-left shunt
    d. Tricuspid atresia with PFO
      Echo, Cath: atretic RV, absent TV
    e. Ebstein's anomaly with PFO
      Echo, Cath: atrialization of RV, delayed closure of TV
  2. Defects in septation with severe pulmonary vascular obstructive disease
    a. Complications of defects in septation with left-to-right shunts
      ↑↑ PVR, right-to-left shunt via defect
    b. Complications of transposition or common mixing chambers with increased pulmonary flow
      ↑↑ PVR with resultant shunt from pulmonic to systemic circuit (otherwise see below)
B. Cyanotic congenital heart disease with increased pulmonary flow
  1. Complete transposition of the great arteries
    Echo: parallel outflow tracts
    Cath: transposition; RV to Ao; LV to PA
  2. Common mixing chambers
    a. Conotruncal anomalies
      Truncus arteriosus
        Echo: single semilunar valve
        Cath: single outflow tract with truncal insufficiency
      Double-outlet RV
        Cath: both great arteries off RV
    b. Univentricular heart
      Echo, Cath: absent intraventricular septum
    c. Single atrium
      2D *Echo, Cath:* absent interatrial septum
    d. Total anomalous venous return
      Cath: venous return from pulmonary circuit to right atrium; otherwise, intracardiac connections normal

Echo, echocardiography; *Cath,* cardiac catheterization; PFO, patent foramen ovale; PVR, pulmonary vascular resistance; TV, tricuspid valve; PV, pulmonic valve; PA, pulmonary artery; Ao, aorta; RV, right ventricle; LV, left ventricle; ↑↑, markedly increased.

Therapeutic

Therapeutic Options

In patients with complete transposition, medical therapy includes digitalis and diuretics for heart failure, as well as inspired oxygen and truncal elevation during acute illness. Prostaglandin infusions to maintain patency of the ductus arteriosus may preserve pulmonary flow in a newborn until a surgical procedure can be accomplished. Bacterial endocarditis prophylaxis is recommended in all patients.

Most children with complete transposition require surgery to survive until adulthood. A child with complete transposition of the great arteries and an intact ventricular septum should have a Rashkind procedure (balloon atrial septostomy) at the first catheterization, a Blalock–Hanlen operation (atrial septectomy) if the Rashkind procedure is unsuccessful, and definitive correction by intraatrial transposition of venous return (Mustard's operation) between 4 and 12 months. Following balloon atrial septostomy and prostaglandin infusion, arterial switch repair to keep the ductus open and left ventricular pressure at systemic levels may be a preferable operation in expert hands.

In children with complete transposition of the great arteries and a large ventricular septal defect, early surgical repair with pulmonary banding is recommended prior to development of significant pulmonary vascular resistance. Infants with complete transposition of the great arteries, ventricular septal defect, and pulmonic stenosis require the creation of a systemic arterial shunt to the pulmonary artery until

after age 5, when Rastelli's operation (intracardiac tunnel from the left ventricle to pulmonary artery) is recommended. Arterial switch operations are becoming more surgically feasible even in more complex cases and, thus, have become the preferable definitive operation at an early age.

In an adult with corrected transposition, medical therapy consists of digitalis and diuretics for congestive heart failure and rigorous treatment of hypertension, as the anatomic right ventricle is exposed to the pressure overload. Bacterial endocarditis prophylaxis is recommended for all patients with mitral regurgitation or an intracardiac shunt.

In corrected transposition, the principal indications for surgery are severe mitral regurgitation or a significant ventricular septal defect plus pulmonic stenosis. Surgery in corrected transposition has a higher mortality than the same surgery in the absence of corrected transposition, often due to the occurrence of atrioventricular block.

Recommended Approach

Neonatal anatomic repair of complete transposition (d-TGA) by the arterial switch operation is now preferable. When the condition is discovered in older infants and childhood, preparation for an arterial switch must first be preceded by banding of the pulmonary artery and creation of a systemic arterial-to-pulmonary arterial shunt to prepare the left ventricle for systemic pressures.

Several weeks later, the band is removed, the shunt closed, and the arterial switch completed. Early and late survival rates approach the excellent results seen with neonatal repair.

Adults with congenitally corrected transposition should receive prompt closure of intracardiac defects if hemodynamically significant. Afterload reduction is indicated to protect the anatomic right ventricle from systemic pressures if elevated. Prophylactic use of afterload reduction in these patients should be considered, although a prospective double-blind trial to prove effectiveness is not available. This group of patients may require transplant if progressive congestive failure becomes a problem.

Cardiac transplantation may also be necessary in complete transposition following a Mustard repair if the anatomic right ventricle fails as a result of prolonged pumping against systemic pressures.

FOLLOW-UP

Patients with complete transposition should be closely followed at 1- to 2-month intervals until surgical intervention, and thereafter at 3- to 6-month intervals. Increasing cyanosis and evidence of progressive heart failure are the major warning signals.

Patients with corrected transposition should be seen at 6- to 12-month intervals, with therapy and management determined largely by the associated lesion (ventricular septal defect, pulmonic stenosis, mitral regurgitation) rather than by the primary underlying problem. In either disorder, fever may be indicative of endocarditis and should be promptly reported to the physician.

DISCUSSION

Prevalence and Incidence

Complete transposition of the great vessels is present in approximately 10% of children with recognized congenital heart disease. Patients with congenitally corrected transposition are unusual, constituting less than 1% of all recognized congenital heart disease.

Related Basic Science

Physiologic or Metabolic Derangement

Physiologically, with complete transposition, life is dependent on intracardiac or extracardiac communication between systemic and pulmonary circuits. Mixing of oxygenated and deoxygenated blood may occur by way of an atrial or ventricular septal defect, through a patent ductus arteriosus, or across large bronchial arteries. With corrected transposition, objective findings depend on the extent of concomitant lesions such as a ventricular septal defect and mitral regurgitation. If the anatomic right ventricle (systemic ventricle) is able to maintain itself against volume overloads from these lesions and additional insults in adult life, including hypertension and coronary atherosclerosis, survival well into adulthood can be expected.

Anatomic Derangement

The connections of the systemic, pulmonic, and coronary veins are normal; two ventricles are present. In complete transposition (d-TGA), due to the abnormal position of the great vessels, blood flows from the right atrium and right ventricle to the aorta, and blood from the lungs returns through the left atrium and left ventricle to the pulmonary artery (see Figure 15–32–1). In corrected transposition (l-TGA), blood flows from the right atrium through an anatomic left ventricle to the pulmonary artery, and blood returning from the lungs passes through the left atrium to an anatomic right ventricle to the aorta (Figure 15–32–2). A tricuspid atrioventricular valve is associated with the anatomic right ventricle, and the bicuspid mitral valve is associated with the anatomic left ventricle. Additional clinical findings are determined by variations in communications between the greater and lesser circulations, the presence or absence of valvular or subvalvular pulmonic stenosis, and other associated defects.

Although multiple variations of transposition are possible, complete transportation and corrected transposition account for the vast majority of cases. The atria can generally be identified by the position of the stomach bubble, as the right atrium lies on the same side as the liver and the left atrium lies on the same side as the stomach. The dextro-transposition refers to the position of the aorta to the right of the pulmonary artery and vice versa.

Natural History and Its Modification with Treatment

Complications in patients with complete transposition may include cerebrovascular accidents, brain abscesses, development of subvalvular pulmonic stenosis, and development of pulmonary vascular disease.

Longevity in complete transposition depends on the altered anatomy. Patients with intact atrial and ventricular septa have the shortest survival. Survival is also poor in patients with a large ventricular septal defect, which allows for development of severe reactive pulmonary vascular disease secondary to increased pressure flow. The best prognosis is with a large ventricular septal defect but limited pulmonary flow and pressure secondary to pulmonary outflow obstruction. Without surgical intervention, about half the infants with complete transposition die within the first month and almost all die within the first year of life.

Of 116 patients with TGA who underwent the Jatene operation, about 20% died in the immediate postoperative period. Another 5 patients died within 5 years. Of the survivors, about three quarters were anatomically normal at a mean of 8 years after surgery. Another 30% had mild dysfunction of no clinical significance, and another 26% had no recent examination (Jatene et al., 1992).

Most patients with corrected transposition should reach adult life. The natural history of congenital corrected transposition with associated defects parallels that of the associated lesion without corrected transposition. Surgical correction should benefit these patients to a similar extent as those patients who do not have underlying corrected transposition.

Prevention

Transpositions are types of congenital heart diseases and therefore not completely preventable at present. Bacterial endocarditis and brain abscesses are often preventable by appropriate prophylaxis. In complete transposition, prevention of severe pulmonary hypertension by early diagnosis and appropriate surgical intervention is imperative.

Cost Containment

Cardiac catheterization should be reserved for diagnostic purposes or when a surgical procedure (i.e., complete repair) is contemplated. Routine catheterization after a surgical procedure is not indicated.

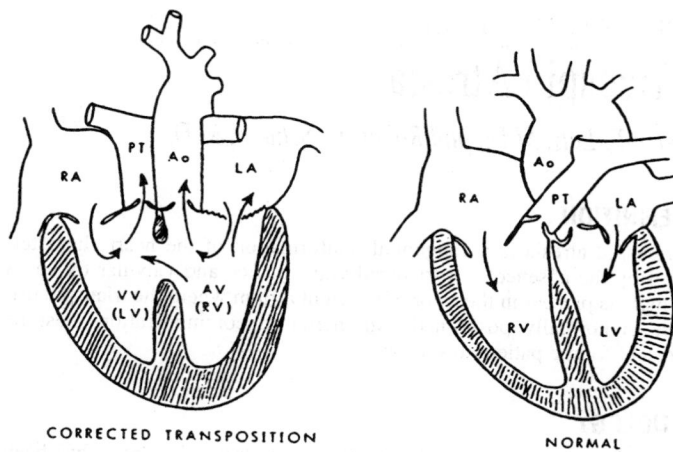

Figure 15–32–2. Schematic illustrations comparing congenitally corrected transposition of the great vessels with the normal heart. In corrected transposition, the aortic root is to the left of and anterior to the pulmonary trunk (PT); the two great vessels arise parallel to each other and do not cross as in the normal heart. The arrangement therefore resembles complete transposition. In corrected transposition, however, right atrial blood flows across an atrioventricular valve that is morphologically mitral into a venous ventricle (VV) that is morphologically left ventricle (LV) and then into the pulmonary trunk. Left atrial blood flows across an atrioventricular valve that is morphologically tricuspid into an atrial ventricle (AV) that is morphologically right ventricle (RV) and then into the aorta (Ao). The left atrioventricular valve is often malformed and incompetent (*reversed arrow*), and then there is often a defect in the ventricular septum. RA, right atrium; LA, left atrium. *(Source: Perloff JK, ed. The clinical recognition of heart disease. 4th ed. Philadelphia: Saunders, 1994:658. Reproduced with permission of the publisher and author.)*

Echocardiography is not diagnostic in corrected transposition but may be useful to follow associated lesions.

REFERENCES

Alexander JA, Knauf DG, Greene MA, et al. The changing strategies in operation for transposition of the great vessels. Ann Thorac Surg 1994;58:1278.

Fisher E, Paul MH. Transposition of the great arteries: Recognition and management in congenital heart disease. Cardiovasc Clin 1972;2:211.

Graham TP. Hemodynamic residua and sequelae following intraatrial repair of transposition of the great arteries: A review. Pediatr Cardiol 1982;2:203.

Hochreiter C, Snyder MS, Borer JS, Engle MA. Right and left ventricular performance 10 years after mustard repair of transposition of the great arteries. Am J Cardiol 1994;74:478.

Jatene FB, Bosisio IB, Jatene MB, et al. Late results (50 to 182 months) of the Jatene operation. European J Cardio-thoracic Surg 1992;6:575.

Masden RR, Franch RH. Isolated congenitally corrected transposition of the great arteries. In: Hurst JW, ed. Update III: The heart. New York: McGraw-Hill Book, 1980:59.

Oswal D, Ribeiro VG, Antunes J. Corrected transposition of the great arteries: Repair of regurgitant tricuspid, mitral, and pulmonic valves. J Heart Valve Dis 1993;2:478.

Soulen R, Donner RM, Capitanio M. Postoperative evaluation of complex congenital heart disease by magnetic resonance imaging. Radiographics 1987;7:975.

Tricuspid Atresia

Jerre F. Lutz, M.D., and Robert C. Schlant, M.D.

DEFINITION

Tricuspid atresia is a congenital malformation of the heart character-ized by the absence of a tricuspid valve orifice and valvular tissue. A dimple is present in the floor of the right atrium where the tricuspid ori-fice is normally positioned. An interatrial communication must be present for the patient to survive.

ETIOLOGY

The etiology is unknown. Embryologically, tricuspid atresia has been postulated to occur because of a malalignment of the interventricular septum with the atrioventricular canal such that the right arterioventric-ular orifice is obliterated.

CRITERIA FOR DIAGNOSIS

Suggestive

Tricuspid atresia should be suspected in a patient with cyanosis, a sin-gle first heart sound, and left ventricular hypertrophy or left-axis devia-tion on electrocardiogram.

Definitive

Although clinical features depend on the presence or absence of associ-ated cardiac defects (such as transposition of the great arteries, ventric-ular septal defect, and pulmonic stenosis), all patients have in common absence of the tricuspid valve orifice with an atretic right ventricular in-flow tract that can be demonstrated echocardiographically, angiograph-ically, or pathologically.

CLINICAL MANIFESTATIONS

Subjective

Dyspnea and fatigue are frequent symptoms when pulmonary blood flow is diminished, and chest pain is an occasional complaint.

Symptoms of congestive heart failure with dyspnea and tachypnea are frequent when pulmonary blood flow is normal or increased. There is also an increased incidence of respiratory infections. Once severe pulmonary vascular disease develops, symptoms are similar to those seen with diminished pulmonary blood flow.

Objective

Most patients with diminished pulmonary flow are cyanotic soon after birth; the condition is recognized in half these patients on the first day of life. Tachypnea, polycythemia, and hypoxic episodes are noted from an early age. Hypoxic spells are transient episodes of increased cyanosis, lethargy, dyspnea, and loss of consciousness. They may occur spontaneously or after crying or feeding. Clubbing and, less often, squatting occur at a later age.

If pulmonary blood flow is normal or increased, cyanosis is milder than in the group with decreased pulmonary blood flow, but signs of congestive heart failure with pulmonary congestion are frequent. Once severe reactive pulmonary vascular disease occurs, however, the sever-ity of cyanosis approximates that seen in tricuspid atresia with de-creased pulmonary flow. Growth retardation occurs in most patients.

Arterial pulsations are usually normal, but they may be diminished in amplitude in children with congestive heart failure. Jugular venous pulses often have an enlarged *a* wave with a blunted *y* descent if the in-teratrial communication is small. A large systolic venous wave suggests mitral regurgitation with transmission of the pressure wave across the atrial septal defect. Patients with tricuspid atresia have a prominent left ventricular impulse without a palpable right ventricular impulse. The

heart is generally not enlarged, although the left ventricular apex is eas-ily palpable and sustained.

The first heart sound is single, as there is no functioning tricuspid valve. An ejection sound is unusual, as the great vessels are not usually enlarged and flow is not usually increased. The second sound is single in patients with decreased pulmonary flow. Patients with an associated patent ductus arteriosus may have a systolic or, less often, a continuous murmur at the upper left sternal border. Continuous murmurs are also occasionally heard due to either collateral flow to the pulmonary arter-ies by way of bronchial collaterals (more often systolic only) or a surgi-cally created systemic-to-pulmonic shunt.

The right ventricle is hypoplastic in patients with tricuspid atresia with normally related great vessels and a small ventricular septal defect (the most common type). Pulmonary outflow across the ventricular sep-tal defect is always obstructed, and this is frequently associated with valvular pulmonic stenosis or atresia. If the degree of pulmonary out-flow obstruction is mild or moderate, there may be a spindle-shaped holosystolic murmur at the left sternal border, accompanied by a thrill. Patients with concomitant pulmonary atresia are severely cyanotic but may have no murmur. On chest roentgenogram the pulmonary blood flow is normal or decreased, the heart size is normal or mildly enlarged, and an enlarged right atrium is present. A right-sided aortic arch is rare.

In the unusual patients with tricuspid atresia who have normally re-lated great vessels and a large ventricular septal defect with no pul-monary outflow obstruction, there is increased pulmonary flow and an enlarged right ventricle despite the atretic right ventricular inflow tract. These patients are less cyanotic due to increased pulmonary flow. They have a hyperdynamic apical impulse together with a systolic thrill at the upper sternal border. The right ventricular outflow tract and the pul-monary artery are often palpable. The second sound is split. A long sys-tolic murmur at the left upper sternal border with a mitral flow rumble and a ventricular gallop at the apex are usually present. The chest roentgenogram reveals an enlarged heart and increased pulmonary blood flow. When reactive pulmonary vascular disease develops, the pulmonary vasculature may have a "pruned-tree" appearance.

Patients with tricuspid atresia and normally related great vessels usu-ally have normal sinus rhythm on electrocardiogram. In patients with a small ventricular septal defect, there is left ventricular hypertrophy or absence of the right ventricular dominance that is normal during in-fancy. Characteristically, the QRS vector is directed leftward, between 0° and −90° and posteriorly in most patients with normally related great vessels. The P waves are large, peaked, or bifid in most patients with tricuspid atresia without transposition. When tricuspid atresia is associ-ated with a large ventricular septal defect, there may be electrocardio-graphic evidence of biventricular hypertrophy.

In patients with tricuspid atresia in association with transposition of the great vessels, the aorta arises from the right ventricle and a large ventricular septal defect is usually present. Cyanosis is milder and there is splitting of the second heart sound and a holosystolic murmur and thrill at the sternal border with a diastolic apical rumble. The splitting of S_2 may be difficult to hear in some patients with some types of trans-position. Physical findings and radiographic evidence of pulmonary blood flow depend on the size of the ventricular septal defect and the pulmonary vascular resistance. If there is associated pulmonic stenosis, the systolic murmur decreases with increasing obstruction, and there is preferential shunting to the systemic circulation. Patients with a small ventricular septal defect may have relative subaortic stenosis and have the potential for mitral regurgitation secondary to left ventricular fail-ure.

Except for a narrowed vascular pedicle, the chest roentgenogram of patients with tricuspid atresia in association with transposition is simi-lar to that of patients with tricuspid atresia without transposition with the same relative pulmonary outflow obstruction. The electrocardio-grams are similar except the QRS vector is more likely normal (between 0 and +90). Right ventricular hypertrophy is more likely in patients with a large ventricular septal defect and absent pulmonic stenosis.

Some degree of hypoxemia and elevation of the hematocrit is uniformly present. A leukocytosis, especially with a shift toward band or segmented neutrophils, suggests a bacterial infection such as endocarditis.

PLANS
Diagnostic
Differential Diagnosis

Tricuspid atresia must be differentiated from pulmonary atresia with an intact septum and from other cyanotic congenital heart defects (see outline in Chapter 15–32). Patients with pulmonary atresia have a tricuspid valve on echocardiogram and a normal QRS axis on electrocardiogram. Patients with tetralogy of Fallot have right ventricular hypertrophy on electrocardiogram and a characteristic echocardiogram. Although the tricuspid valve is poorly developed in patients with congenital tricuspid stenosis and is virtually absent in those with congenitally unguarded tricuspid orifice, in each condition there is at least some type of communication, from right atrium to right ventricle.

Diagnostic Options

Echocardiography in patients with tricuspid atresia reveals no recordable tricuspid valve. The left atrium is larger than in patients with tetralogy of Fallot, the most common cyanotic congenital heart defect. The relative size of the cardiac chambers and the presence or absence of parallel outflow tracts depend on the associated defects.

Cardiac catheterization reveals the following: (1) right atrial pressure increased and greater than left atrial pressure, (2) an absent tricuspid valve with inability to pass a catheter from the right atrium to the right ventricle, (3) arterial desaturation even in acyanotic patients due to the obligatory right-to-left shunt at the atrial level, (4) similar oxygen content in blood samples from the left atrium, ventricles, and great vessels, (5) a triangular nonopacified area in the right ventricular inflow region, and (6) other hemodynamic and angiographic findings depending on the associated lesions.

Magnetic resonance imaging delineates all the above structural defects as well as the flow patterns within the heart.

Recommended Approach

Beginning with noninvasive techniques one should delineate any concomitant defects in a patient with tricuspid atresia. Cardiac catheterization should be performed prior to surgical palliation.

Therapeutic
Therapeutic Options

Medical treatment for actual or potential complications includes bacterial endocarditis prophylaxis and phlebotomy for very severe polycythemia. Digitalis and diuretics are indicated when congestive heart failure occurs. Beta blockade, oxygen, morphine, and the knee–chest position are useful in treatment of paroxysmal cyanotic spells. In hospitalized patients, care of intravenous lines is especially important because of the potential for paradoxical emboli. Type E prostaglandins may be useful for maintaining patency of the ductus arteriosus in infants who are dependent on it for pulmonary blood flow.

The goal of surgical treatment of children with diminished pulmonary flow is to increase both pulmonary perfusion and arterial oxygen saturation. If the mean right atrial pressure is less than 2 mm Hg greater than left atrial pressure and phasic pressure patterns are similar in the two atria, interatrial communication is usually adequate. If the pressure difference is greater, however, a Rashkind procedure (balloon septostomy) is indicated as the first procedure in an infant. If cyanotic episodes, severe hypoxemia, or acidosis persist, a Potts (descending aorta–left pulmonary artery anastomosis) or Waterston procedure (ascending aorta–right pulmonary artery anastomosis) is indicated for a child under 1 year of age, or a Blalock–Taussig operation (subclavian artery–pulmonary artery anastomosis) if the child is older. When the

child reaches age 10 to 12 years, definitive surgery such as Glenn's operation (anastomosis of the superior vena cava to the right pulmonary artery) or a more complex operation as described by Fontan using an atriopulmonary conduit with an interposed valve should be performed. Complications following this type of operation include dysrhythmias, systemic venous hypertension, deterioration of the valve in the interposed shunt, and low cardiac output.

Nearly two thirds of patients require surgery before 1 year of age. Operative mortality is increased in patients who are less than 6 months old.

The surgical therapy of patients with increased pulmonary flow includes pulmonary banding at an early age and definitive surgery at age 10 to 12.

Recommended Approach

Early intervention with surgical repair is becoming more common as surgical experience with the Fontan procedure increases. Surgery should be performed in centers with the greatest expertise.

FOLLOW-UP

Fever should be reported promptly to the physician, as endocarditis is a potential cause. Palpitations may be a signal of potentially lethal arrhythmias. Progressive dyspnea or cyanosis should also be reported so that the physician may search for reversible causes of either exaggerated or inadequate pulmonary blood flow.

Prior to surgery, most children should be seen weekly or monthly, with special attention to the degree of cyanosis and the development of heart failure or pulmonary hypertension. After a palliative procedure, children should be followed at 2- to 3-month intervals with serial chest roentgenograms, electrocardiograms, and hematocrits, watching closely for evidence of inadequacy of pulmonary flow or endocarditis. Patients with little cyanosis and fairly normal pulmonary flow may be followed twice a year or even annually.

After a Fontan procedure, long-term surveillance for arrhythmias and the development of congestive heart failure is of the utmost importance.

DISCUSSION
Prevalence and Incidence

Tricuspid atresia makes up only a small percentage of all congenital heart disease. The condition is found equally in both sexes.

Although the prevalence of these patients in an adult cardiologist's practice is low, the frequency is increasing due to the earlier age of intervention, and improved patients will become transplant candidates as they approach their young adult life.

Related Basic Science
Physiologic or Metabolic Derangement

The absent tricuspid valve orifice and atretic right ventricular inflow tract necessitate both interatrial communication and some other type of communication to provide at least some pulmonary blood flow. If a ventricular septal defect is not present, a patent ductus arteriosus or large bronchial collaterals are necessary to maintain adequate pulmonary flow to sustain life. The degree of arterial saturation is directly proportional to pulmonary blood flow.

Anatomic Derangement

Additional abnormalities that may be present include pulmonary outflow obstruction or transposition of the great vessels. The left ventricle must serve as the primary pump for both circuits. One fourth of patients with tricuspid atresia, dextrotransposition of the great arteries, and a large ventricular septal defect also have coarctation of the aorta and a patent ductus arteriosus.

Natural History and Its Modification with Treatment

Most patients with tricuspid atresia die from hypoxia, less often from endocarditis, brain abscess, cerebral thrombosis, or hemorrhage. Some patients with associated dextrotransposition of the great arteries die from congestive heart failure or the rapid development of markedly increased pulmonary vascular resistance.

The prognosis for all types of tricuspid atresia is poor, but it is best in patients with normal pulmonary blood flow and worst with decreased pulmonary flow. Of all patients with tricuspid atresia, half are dead at age 6 months, two thirds by 1 year, and about 90% by age 10. Even in those patients whose disease is recognized after infancy, one third who remain untreated die within 5 years. It is exceptional for patients to survive into the fourth decade without surgery (Nugent et al., 1994).

Prevention

The defect is probably not preventable; however, early recognition and appropriate management should prevent sequelae.

Cost Containment

In most patients, the physician can adequately assess the clinical situation from the history, physical examination, chest roentgenogram, and hematocrit. Occasionally, echocardiography is useful to follow pulmonary artery pressures. Cardiac catheterization should be reserved for diagnosis or for evaluation prior to a contemplated surgical procedure.

REFERENCES

Campbell M. Tricuspid atresia and its prognosis with and without surgical treatment. Br Heart J 1961;23:699.

Fontan F, Deville C, Quaegebeur J, et al. Repair of tricuspid atresia in 100 patients. J Thorac Cardiovasc Surg 1983;85:647.

Franklin RC, Spiegelhalter DJ, Sullivan ID, et al. Tricuspid atresia presenting in infancy: Survival and suitability for the Fontan operation. Circulation 1993;87:427.

Laschinger JC, Ringel RE, Brenner JI, McLaughlin JS. The extra cardiac total cavopulmonary connection for definitive conversion to the Fontan circulation: Summary of early experience and results. J Cardiac Surg 1993;8:524.

Nugent WE, Plauth WH Jr, Edwards JE, Williams WH. The pathology, pathophysiology, recognition and treatment of congenital heart disease. In: Schlant RC, Alexander RA, O'Rourke RA, et al., eds. Hurst's the heart. 8th ed. New York: McGraw-Hill, 1994:1773.

Taussig HB. The clinical and pathological findings in congenital malformations of the right ventricle associated with tricuspid atresia and hypoplasia. Bull Johns Hopkins Hosp 1936;59:435.

CHAPTER 15–34

Ebstein's Anomaly

Daniel Arensberg, M.D., and Robert C. Schlant, M.D.

DEFINITION

Ebstein's anomaly is an uncommon congenital malformation of the tricuspid apparatus of the heart that is characterized by the downward displacement of the tricuspid valve orifice into the right ventricle below the plane of the true atrioventricular junction.

ETIOLOGY

Ebstein's anomaly is congenital.

CRITERIA FOR DIAGNOSIS

Suggestive

Ebstein's anomaly can be suspected from the following findings: history of paroxysmal tachycardia; cyanosis; absent right ventricular impulse; widely split first heart sound, frequently together with third and fourth heart sounds; and murmur of tricuspid regurgitation on physical examination; tall P waves, prolonged PR interval, right bundle-branch block with Q waves in the inferior and right precordial leads, and occasionally preexcitation on the electrocardiogram; and large right atrium, prominent right ventricular outflow tract, inconspicuous aortic root and pulmonary trunk, and normal or decreased pulmonary flow on chest film. M-mode echocardiography demonstrates increased excursion of the anterior tricuspid leaflet and delayed closure of the tricuspid valve.

Definitive

The diagnosis can be established by two-dimensional echocardiography, which identifies the displaced septal tricuspid leaflet and mobile, elongated anterior tricuspid leaflet; atrialized right ventricle with distal functional right ventricle; and large right ventricular outflow tract.

CLINICAL MANIFESTATIONS

Subjective

About one third of patients have recognized heart disease at birth, and the majority are detected by 5 years of age. Others can be asymptomatic until adolescence or adulthood. Dyspnea, fatigue, and palpita-

tions are the most frequent presenting symptoms. About two thirds of patients develop dyspnea during the course of the illness. Palpitations occur in approximately one third of patients. Syncope due to cardiac arrhythmias can occur, and chest pain is often noted.

Objective

Physical Examination

The neonate may present with appreciable cyanosis and a loud murmur of tricuspid regurgitation, which may later diminish as pulmonary vascular resistance falls. Cyanosis is present in 60% of patients at the time of diagnosis, and another 20% will develop cyanosis later. Resting cyanosis is seen less frequently than that induced by effort, cold, or arrhythmias. Mild skeletal abnormalities are occasionally present.

The jugular venous pulse is usually normal despite tricuspid regurgitation because of the enlarged, compliant right atrium and the relatively weak right ventricle. A blunted x descent or regurgitant (R) wave during ventricular systole may be noted.

Carotid artery pulsations are usually normal, although they may be diminished due to the reduced cardiac output.

Precordial movement is generally absent despite marked cardiomegaly. Notably absent is a right ventricular lift. A systolic impulse in the third left intercostal space may be present due to enlargement of the infundibulum, but an impulse overlying the pulmonary trunk is routinely absent.

Auscultatory findings are prominent in newborns, children, and adults. In the neonate, the murmur of tricuspid regurgitation decreases with falling pulmonary vascular resistance and improved forward blood flow. The first heart sound is widely split with a loud, clicking second (tricuspid) component. Third and fourth heart sounds are frequently present. The components of the first heart sound are best heard between the apex and the left sternal border. The second heart sound may be single, as the pulmonic component is often faint and unusually widely split from the aortic component. A tricuspid valve opening snap may be audible. The medium frequency, scratchy holosystolic murmur of tricuspid regurgitation is usually best heard along the left sternal border, often radiating to the apex. This murmur is usually decrescendo and it may be heard only in early systole if the right atrial pressure is relatively low. The murmur of tricuspid regurgitation and the tricuspid component of the first heart sound rarely, if ever, increase with inspiration. A diastolic rumble is occasionally present due to tricuspid valve stenosis. Approximately 90% of patients have a systolic murmur, and about 50% have a diastolic murmur. The scratchy quality of the systolic murmur, wide splitting of the first heart sound, and the gallop sounds often make auscultation confusing, at times even mimicking the findings of pericarditis. At times, it may be difficult to distinguish between systole and diastole, particularly during tachycardia.

Routine Laboratory Abnormalities

The electrocardiogram can be very characteristic in Ebstein's anomaly. Giant P waves with voltages equal to the QRS complex may be seen. The PR interval is prolonged in about one quarter of patients, and the QRS conduction defect that is characteristic of the Wolff–Parkinson–White syndrome can be seen in about 10% of patients. A right intraventricular conduction delay or complicated right bundle-branch block is usually present. Cardiac dysrhythmias including atrial fibrillation, flutter, and atrial tachycardia are present intermittently or continuously in about one third of patients. A QR pattern with T inversion in leads V_1 to V_4, which is felt to be from the right ventricle shifting to the left, is uncommon but highly suggestive of Ebstein's anomaly.

On chest film the cardiac silhouette is usually enlarged, primarily because of the enlarged right atrium. Pulmonary blood flow is usually normal, but it may be decreased in patients with large right-to-left shunts. In a small percentage of patients, the chest x-ray is normal.

PLANS
Diagnostic
Differential Diagnosis

Because Ebstein's anomaly includes a wide spectrum of pathologic anatomy, the clinical findings may resemble pericarditis or cardiomyopathy. Two-dimensional echocardiography can easily differentiate most of these conditions. Congenital tricuspid regurgitation, which may be secondary to a dysplastic cardiomyopathy, can be distinguished from Ebstein's anomaly by two-dimensional echocardiography. Uhl's anomaly can be distinguished by an enlarged right ventricle with few trabeculae and a normally placed tricuspid valve.

Diagnostic Options and Recommended Approach

The condition should be diagnosed in many instances by physical examination, chest x-ray film, and electrocardiogram. Echocardiography is diagnostic.

Therapeutic

Digitalis and antiarrhythmic therapy may be required when the patient experiences congestive heart failure or arrhythmias. Endocarditis prophylaxis is recommended.

Indications for surgical intervention remain ill-defined. Patients with no or only mild symptoms should receive medical therapy. A progressive increase in heart size may be an indication for surgical intervention. Palliative surgical procedures such as systemic-to-pulmonary artery shunts or isolated repair of an atrial septal defect are generally not indicated in view of the high operative risk. Patients with congestive heart failure, cyanosis, associated cardiac anomalies, a cardiothoracic ratio in chest film greater than 0.65, and an established diagnosis in infancy have the greatest need for surgical intervention but the highest surgical risk. Tricuspid valve replacement or plication of the right ventricular inflow tract with tricuspid valve annuloplasty continue to be associated with high operative mortalities (approximately 25 and 70%).

Radiofrequency ablation techniques may be useful in selected patients with supraventricular arrhythmias, including those related to pre-excitation.

FOLLOW-UP

Infants and children must be seen frequently in view of their high mortality. In adolescents and adults, the frequency of clinical follow-up is a function of the wide range of pathologic anatomy. The more slowly progressive the illness, the less need for frequent evaluations. Annual electrocardiograms and chest films may be useful to define arrhythmias and early signs of congestive heart failure. Ambulatory electrocardiographic monitoring is indicated at periodic intervals in view of the high incidence of atrial and ventricular arrhythmias.

DISCUSSION
Prevalence

Ebstein's anomaly is rare, constituting less than 1% of all congenital heart disease. It is, however, being identified in more adults than it was formerly. It has been observed in elderly patients. Ebstein's anomaly occurs equally in males and females; familial occurrence is unusual.

Related Basic Science
Pathophysiology

The anatomic abnormality consists of displacement of the septal and posterior leaflets of the tricuspid valve from the atrioventricular annulus into the body of the right ventricle. This results in the atrialization of a portion of the right ventricle. The chordae tendineae attach abnormally to the right ventricle as well as to the papillary muscles and are frequently thickened with a mucoid type of connective tissue. The anterior tricuspid leaflet is normally attached to the annulus fibrosus but is enlarged, muscularized, and malaligned. The tricuspid valve leaflets are frequently fused and malformed. A thin-walled proximal chamber is created with poorly formed trabeculae. As a result of the atrialization of a portion of the right ventricle, the right atrium is usually massively dilated, whereas the residual right ventricle can be atrophic and hypocontractile. There is either an atrial septal defect or patent foramen ovale in 50 to 60% of patients.

Associated cardiovascular defects that are seen in combination with Ebstein's anomaly include coarctation of the aorta, ventricular septal defect, endocardial cushion defect, infundibular or valvular pulmonic stenosis, pulmonic atresia, and supravalvular mitral stenosis. Both diffuse and localized right and left ventricular contractile abnormalities have been reported.

The malformed tricuspid leaflets that allow tricuspid regurgitation and the small and often hypocontractile right ventricle contribute to the low cardiac output. Tricuspid regurgitation, which may range from mild to severe, is always present. Because of the large and compliant right atrium, the right atrial pressure is usually normal or mildly elevated. In most patients there is right-to-left shunting across the patent foramen ovale or secundum atrial septal defect, producing systemic hypoxemia and cyanosis. Associated abnormalities of the mitral valve and left ventricle are relatively frequent.

Natural History and Its Modification with Treatment

Nearly half the patients with Ebstein's anomaly die during the first year of life. Most of the surviving patients die by the second or third decade, with approximately 5% living beyond age 50 years. Sixty percent of adults with Ebstein's anomaly may have minimal disability. The later the onset of congestive heart failure and cyanosis, the better is the prognosis. Although congestive heart failure is a serious complication, patients can live 20 years after its onset. In addition to congestive heart failure, cardiac arrhythmias, brain abscess, endocarditis, and paradoxical emboli may occur. Sudden death occurs in about 20% of patients, presumably on the basis of arrhythmias. Corrective surgery may assist in the control of heart failure but may not control the cardiac arrhythmias.

Prevention

Ebstein's anomaly is a congenital defect, and the familial occurrence is 1%. An increased incidence of Ebstein's anomaly has been reported in the offspring of women receiving lithium carbonate (Eskalith) therapy during the first trimester of pregnancy. This antimanic agent should be avoided during pregnancy. An association between maternal rubella and Ebstein's anomaly also has been reported.

Cost Containment

The more severe the expression of Ebstein's malformation, the more frequent is the need for follow-up visits. Serial echocardiograms need not be performed once the diagnosis is established, unless endocarditis is suspected.

REFERENCES

Danielson GK, Driscoll DJ, Mair DD, et al. Operative treatment of Ebstein's anomaly. J Thorac Cardiovasc Surg 1992;104:1195.

Giuliani ER, Fuster V, Brandenburg RO, Mair DD. Ebstein's anomaly: The clinical features and natural history of Ebstein's anomaly of the tricuspid valve. Mayo Clin Proc 1979;54:163.

Kumar AE, Fyler DC, Miettinen OS, Nadas AS. Ebstein's anomaly: Clinical profile and natural history. Am J Cardiol 1971;28:84.

Nugent EW, Plauth WH Jr, Edwards JE, Williams WH. The pathology, pathophysiology, recognition, and treatment of congenital heart disease. In: Schlant RC, Alexander RW, O'Rourke RA, et al., eds. Hurst's the heart. 8th ed. New York: McGraw-Hill, 1994:176.

Radford DJ, Graff RF, Neilson GH. Diagnosis and natural history of Ebstein's anomaly. Br Heart J 1985;54:517.

Shina A, Seward JB, Edwards WD, et al. Two-dimensional echocardiographic spectrum of Ebstein's anomaly: Detailed anatomic assessment. J Am Coll Cardiol 1984;3:356.

Watson H. Natural history of Ebstein's anomaly of tricuspid valve in childhood and adolescence: An international co-operative study of 505 cases. Br Heart J 1974;36:417.

CHAPTER 15–35

Aortic Stenosis in the Adult

Douglas C. Morris, M.D.

DEFINITION

Aortic valve stenosis is obstruction of the propulsion of blood from the left ventricle. Generally, in the adult, the obstruction is valvular but may be subvalvular in the form of a discrete membrane or a hypertrophied septum.

ETIOLOGY

The most common cause of aortic stenosis is a calcified bicuspid aortic valve. These congenitally abnormal bicuspid valves undergo fibrosis, lipid deposition, and calcification presumably because of the abnormal mechanical stresses imposed on valvular tissue by its bicuspid configuration. These same processes presumably cause the aortic stenosis seen in tricuspid aortic valves at a much later age. These stenotic valves are referred to as aortic valve stenosis of the elderly. The congenital aortic valve, which is inherently stenotic, is a unicuspid, unicommissural valve. Such valves usually require surgical intervention by age 30. The aortic valve is rendered stenotic by rheumatic valvulitis either through extensive fusion of the commissures or by fusion of a single commissure with secondary calcium deposition.

CRITERIA FOR DIAGNOSIS

Suggestive

A diagnosis of severe aortic stenosis is suggested by a conglomeration of features indicating turbulence in the bloodstream as it exits the left ventricle, reduction of the amplitude of the pulse pressure in the aorta or the major arterial branches, development of left ventricular hypertrophy, and delayed emptying of the left ventricle.

The turbulence of the bloodstream is manifested by a systolic murmur, reduced pulse amplitude may be perceived by palpation of the carotids or by recording a narrowed pulse pressure with the sphygmotonometer, the left ventricle hypertrophy may be suggested by the electrocardiogram or palpation of the cardiac apex, and delayed emptying is heralded by delay in the aortic component of the second sound.

Definitive

The diagnosis is established by documenting hemodynamically significant obstruction to left ventricular outflow at the level of the aortic valve. Hemodynamically significant valvular aortic stenosis implies a reduction of the aortic orifice to one quarter its normal size, or an orifice area of less than 0.75 cm^2. In the setting of a normal cardiac output, a mean transaortic valve pressure difference of 50 mm Hg would be an acceptable documentation of this degree of reduction of orifice area. The transvalvular pressure difference can be established with echo–Doppler or cardiac catheterization.

CLINICAL MANIFESTATIONS

Subjective

The usual patient with aortic stenosis is middle-aged and male. This gender difference reflects the 4:1 male-to-female ratio for a bicuspid aortic valve. After age 70 the gender difference disappears. An occasional patient will give a past history of rheumatic fever. Often this diagnosis was erroneously made on basis of fever and a heart murmur in a young person.

Symptoms appear very late in the course of aortic stenosis; consequently, the absence of symptoms does not imply the absence of severe stenosis. Instead, the appearance of any one of a triad of symptoms (angina pectoris, syncope, or left ventricular failure) must be considered as an ominous reflection of critical stenosis. Each of these symptoms depends on the pathophysiologic consequences of left ventricular outflow obstruction and, as such, portends a life expectancy of less than 5 years.

Angina pectoris is the most common of the three symptoms, with a reported prevalence in symptomatic aortic stenosis of 50 to 70%. Of this group, approximately one half have no evidence of intrinsic disease of the coronary arteries. Syncope occurs much less often, with a reported prevalence of 15 to 30% of symptomatic patients. Left ventricular failure, usually manifest as exertional dyspnea in younger patients and nocturnal dyspnea in more sedentary persons, is associated with survival of only 2 to 3 years.

Objective

Physical Examination

The obstruction to left ventricular outflow is characteristically manifested by a narrowed pulse pressure secondary to depressed systolic pressure. A systolic arterial pressure greater than 200 mm Hg would be unusual in severe aortic stenosis. The obstructed outflow is also typically reflected by a slowly rising, small-amplitude carotid pulsation. Rigid atheromatous vessels may, however, obscure these expected changes in the arterial pressure contour.

The most common physical finding in a patient with aortic stenosis is a basal systolic murmur. This is typically a harsh, spindle-shaped murmur, intensified by inhalation with amyl nitrite or following a premature beat. In young adults, the murmur is preceded by an ejection sound. This high-pitched sound is usually loudest at the apex. In the elderly, the murmur of aortic stenosis frequently masquerades as a pure-

We thank Dr. Henry A. Liberman for his contribution to this chapter in the previous edition of this book.

frequency musical, cooing murmur that is loudest at the apex. A delay or absence of the aortic component of the second heart sound is usual in severe stenosis. An early diastolic basal murmur of aortic regurgitation is frequently present.

Routine Laboratory Abnormalities

Generally, a normal electrocardiogram denotes inconsequential stenosis, whereas the typical electrocardiogram in severe stenosis (at least 90% of the time) is the pattern of prominent QRS voltage with associated ST depression and T-wave inversion. In approximately 70% of cases of sudden death, this pattern is evidence.

Typical roentgenographic findings with aortic stenosis are a normal to slightly enlarged cardiac silhouette with convex bulging of the lower one third of the left cardiac border (Figure 15–35–1), poststenotic dilation of the ascending aorta (in 75–85%), and calcification of the aortic valve leaflets.

Examination of the blood and urine reveals no diagnostic information.

PLANS
Diagnostic

Differential Diagnosis

The differential diagnosis of aortic stenosis involves, first, the differential of left ventricular outflow obstruction and, second, the differential of the symptoms of angina, syncope, or heart failure. Most commonly, left ventricular outflow obstruction is secondary to valvular aortic stenosis, but hypertrophic obstructive cardiomyopathy and discrete membranous subaortic stenosis must be considered. A systolic ejection sound would exclude both of the latter possibilities and a diastolic regurgitant murmur is most unusual with a hypertrophic cardiomyopathy. Echocardiography firmly establishes the correct diagnosis.

Once the diagnosis of valvular aortic stenosis has been established, any associated symptoms (angina, dyspnea, or syncope) must be ascribed directly to the aortic stenosis or to coexisting diseases such as coronary atherosclerosis, left dysfunction, and conduction system disease.

Diagnostic Options

The presumptive diagnosis of aortic stenosis should arise from a careful history and physical examination. The electrocardiogram offers evidence as to the presence of left ventricle hypertrophy. The chest x-ray film demonstrates an increase in heart size and may provide evidence of valvular calcification, poststenotic dilation of the ascending aorta, left ventricular hypertrophy, or failure. Doppler echocardiography is the diagnostic test of choice for aortic stenosis. A complete examination defines the severity of the stenosis, left ventricular systolic function, and the presence or absence of coexisting valvular disease. Cardiac catheterization and coronary angiography may be needed to resolve discrepancies between clinical data and echocardiographic findings and to assess coronary artery anatomy.

Echocardiography can define the mobility of the aortic leaflets and denote the presence of calcium. Thickening, calcification, and decreased mobility of the leaflets are the characteristic echocardiographic features of valvular aortic stenosis. Left ventricular hypertrophy, an expected accompaniment of aortic stenosis, can also be defined in terms of its severity by echocardiography. Echo–Doppler techniques can estimate the systolic transvalvular gradient by determining the velocity of blood flow across the valve.

At cardiac catheterization, a 50 mm Hg or greater transvalvular pressure difference indicates critical stenosis. In the setting of diminished cardiac output, lesser pressure differences may be significant. Consequently, in patients with pressure differences less than 50 mm Hg, the effective valve orifice area must be calculated.

Recommended Approach

The symptomatic patient with physical findings compatible with aortic stenosis or the asymptomatic patient with the entire constellation of findings indicative of severe aortic stenosis should be initially evaluated with chest x-ray and electrocardiogram. Although the absence of left ventricular hypertrophy would be sufficient grounds for not obtaining further tests in a case of asymptomatic valvular aortic stenosis, this is not true for the symptomatic patient with possible aortic stenosis. In these patients, the workup should begin with echocardiography. Doppler echocardiography is now the diagnostic test of choice for

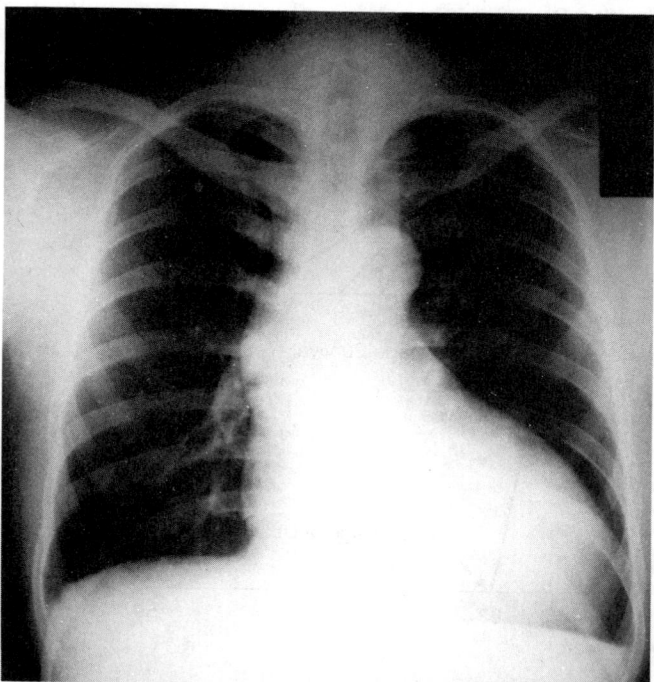
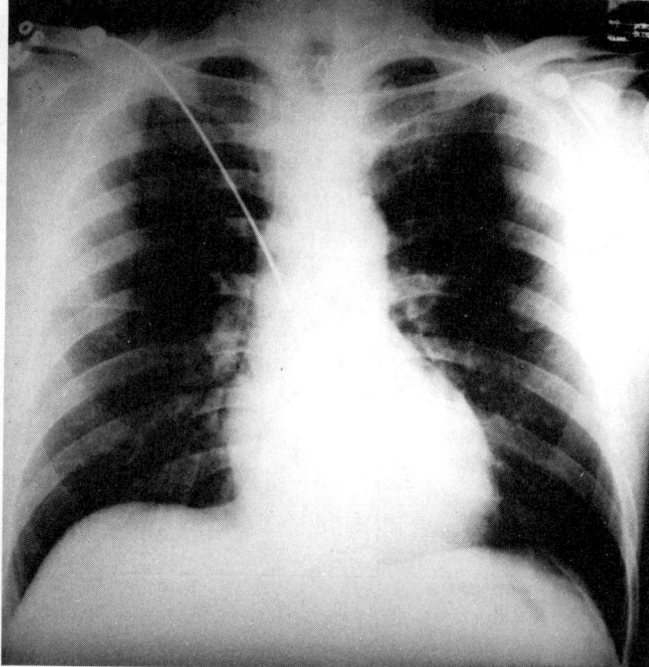

Figure 15–35–1. Comparison of posteroanterior chest x-ray films of a patient with aortic regurgitation *(left)* and a patient with aortic stenosis *(right)*.

symptomatic patients being considered for valve replacement. When the aortic jet velocity is greater than 4.0 m/s, the presence of severe aortic stenosis is confirmed. This approach assumes accurate Doppler echocardiographic data with careful attention to detail. In cases where the clinical findings are at variance with the echocardiographic findings, cardiac catheterization is helpful. Coronary angiography should be obtained in most patients prior to valve replacement.

Therapeutic

Therapeutic Options

There is no good medical therapy for severe aortic stenosis. The mechanical obstruction to left ventricular outflow is not altered by medical therapy. Symptoms warrant valve replacement surgery. Balloon valvuloplasty is a palliative procedure which should be limited to high-risk elderly patients with advanced symptoms.

Recommended Approach

Noncritical aortic stenosis warrants no therapy except bacterial endocarditis prophylaxis and careful follow-up. Although digitalis may offer a beneficial effect in isolated aortic stenosis with left ventricular failure, the physician must not delay aortic valve surgery in such patients in hopes of altering the course of the disease with digitalis. Severe symptomatic aortic stenosis requires urgent valve replacement. With present surgical techniques, valve replacement appears appropriate even in the face of significant left ventricular dysfunction. The threat of sudden death persuades many physicians (including ourselves) to consider valve replacement in the asymptomatic patient who has left ventricular hypertrophy with secondary ST–T wave changes.

FOLLOW-UP

The asymptomatic patient requires annual follow-up, which should be directed toward ferreting out any symptoms and detecting sequential electrocardiographic changes. The symptomatic patient needs aortic valve surgery with subsequent follow-up directed toward assessing the performance of the prosthetic valve.

The optimal timing of follow-up Doppler echocardiographic examination for asymptomatic aortic stenosis has not been defined. Once a baseline Doppler echocardiographic examination has established the diagnosis, probably the patient can be followed solely by clinical examination and electrocardiogram until symptoms develop.

DISCUSSION
Prevalence and Incidence

The bicuspid aortic valve is the most common congenital malformation of the heart, occurring in 1 to 2% of the general population. Bicuspid valves occur predominantly in males with a ratio of 4:1. The frequency of development of stenosis in the congenitally bicuspid valve is unknown. Less than 25% of the cases of isolated aortic stenosis (without mitral valve disease) are rheumatic in origin.

With our aging population, aortic stenosis is presently the most common valvular disease requiring valve replacement surgery.

Related Basic Science
Anatomic Derangement

The degenerative valvular changes producing aortic stenosis are not due to atherosclerosis. The primary change is an alteration of connective tissue with extracellular droplets of neutral fat occurring within the collagen. This fatty material serves as a precursor for calcium deposition. The thickening and alteration of the valvular collagen begin at the base of the cusps and extend toward the margins of the cusps. Usually the calcification is basal and entirely on the aortic side of the valve. These changes are the same as those that occur earlier in many bicuspid valves. The earlier degeneration of bicuspid valves is probably attributable to the abnormal mechanical stress imposed on the valvular tissue by its bicuspid arrangement.

Physiologic or Metabolic Derangement

The hemodynamic consequence of aortic stenosis is systolic overloading of the left ventricle due to increased impedance to left ventricular emptying. The compensatory response to systolic overload is augmentation of the contractile element mass by the development of concentric left ventricular hypertrophy. Unlike the case in the volume overload

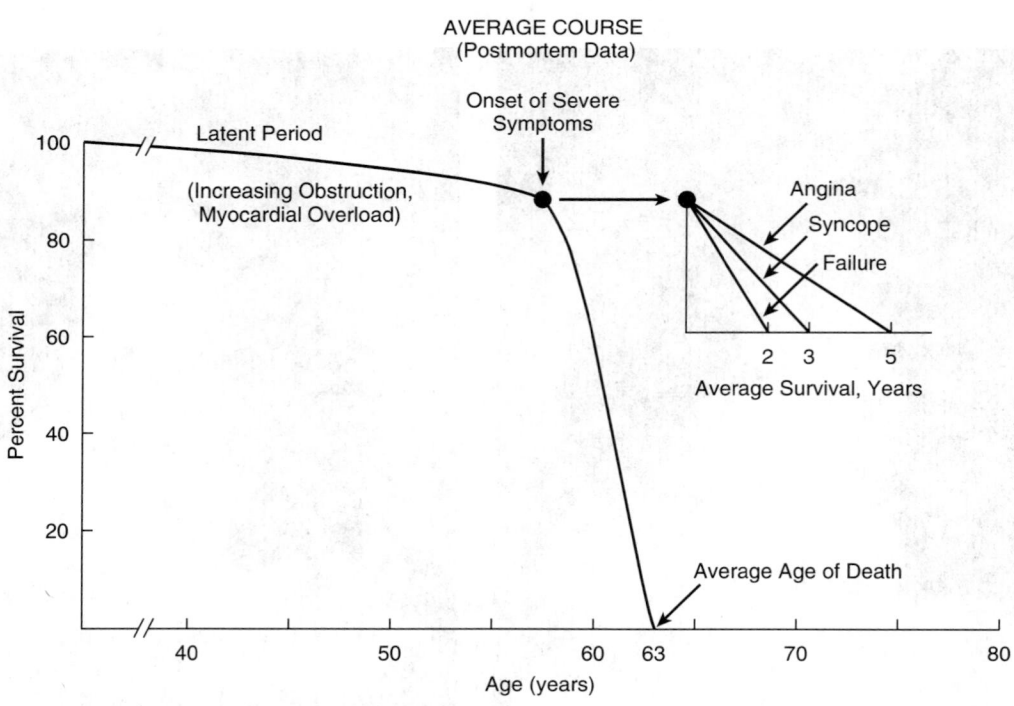

Figure 15–35–2. Natural history of adult patients with severe aortic stenosis. (*Source: Ross J Jr, Braunwald E. Aortic stenosis. Circulation 1968;38(suppl. 5):V61. Reproduced with permission of the author and by permission of the American Heart Association, Inc.*)

states (aortic or mitral regurgitation), left ventricular dilation is not a part of the compensatory mechanism in pressure overload lesions.

Natural History and Its Modification with Treatment

The natural history of aortic stenosis is depicted in Figure 15–35–2. During the asymptomatic period of this condition, the patient generally remains stable with only a small chance (3–5%) of sudden death. Conversely, once any one of the triad of symptoms of angina pectoris, congestive heart failure, or syncope develops, the prognosis is very poor, with a life expectancy of less than 5 years and a 15 to 20% incidence of sudden death. Following implantation of an aortic prosthetic valve, the actuarial survival at 5 years with various types of prosthetics is approximately 80%.

Prevention

Prevention of congenital bicuspid valve disease is at present not an option. Nevertheless, recognition that symptomatic aortic stenosis requires valve replacement will help to prevent many deaths from this disease. The incidence of aortic stenosis due to rheumatic fever can be reduced by prompt treatment of streptococcal infections.

Cost Containment

Inappropriate expense could be reduced with recognition of the relative lack of benefit and excess risk involved in attempting to treat this disease with drugs. Asymptomatic patients with aortic stenosis do not require medications for this condition. Their course can be monitored by regular inquiries about the appearance of angina pectoris, heart failure, or syncope and by sequential electrocardiograms screening for the development of ventricular hypertrophy. Follow-up echocardiograms are not required.

REFERENCES

Galan A, Zogbbi WA, Quinnes MA. Deterioration of severity of valvular aortic stenosis by Doppler echocardiography and relation of findings to clinical outcome and agreement with hemodynamic measurements determined at cardiac catheterization. Am J Cardiol 1991;67(11):1007.

Otto CM, Mickel MC, Kennedy JW, et al. Three-year sentence outcome after balloon aortic valvuloplasty: Insights into prognosis of valvular aortic stenosis. Circulation 1994;89:642.

Rapaport E, Rackley CE, Cohn LH: Aortic valvular disease. In: Schlant RC, Alexander RW, O'Rourke RA, et al., eds. Hurst's the heart. 8th ed. New York: McGraw-Hill, 1994:1457.

Roberts WC, Perloff JK, Costantino T. Severe valvular stenosis in patients over 65 years of age. Am J Cardiol 1971;27:496.

Ross J Jr, Braunwald E. Aortic stenosis. Circulation 1968;38:V61.

Selzer A. Changing aspects of the natural history of valvular aortic stenosis. N Engl J Med 1987;317:91.

CHAPTER 15–36

Aortic Valve Regurgitation

Douglas C. Morris, M.D.

DEFINITION

Aortic regurgitation is the return of a portion of the left ventricular stroke volume into the left ventricle as a consequence of incompetency of the aortic leaflets. The leaflet incompetence may be a direct result of leaflet damage or a result of aortic root dilation or dissection.

ETIOLOGY

Aortic regurgitation can be produced by diseases that affect primarily the aortic leaflets or by those that involve primarily the aortic root. Among the diseases affecting the leaflets are rheumatic valvulitis and infective endocarditis, which produce loss of valvular tissue mass by contracture or direct destruction of the leaflets, and myxomatous transformation, which primarily reduces the intrinsic rigidity of the valve. Aortic regurgitation may be observed in patients with systemic lupus erythematosus, Reiter's disease, rheumatoid arthritis, chronic ergot usage, and trauma. Processes involving mainly the aortic root include aortoannulo dysplasia, syphilis, ankylosing spondylitis, dissection of the aorta, osteogenesis imperfecta, and aneurysm of the sinus of Valsalva. Chronic systemic hypertension produces aortic regurgitation by dilating the aortic valve annulus.

CRITERIA FOR DIAGNOSIS

Suggestive

This condition should be suspected in the patient with a high-frequency diastolic decrescendo murmur and should be considered in any patient with a wide pulse pressure. The combination of these two findings is essentially diagnostic of significant aortic regurgitation. Other situations in which the careful physician searches diligently for evidence of aortic regurgitation are the following: (1) any patient with other stigmata of Marfan's syndrome, (2) any patient with dissection of the proximal aorta, and (3) any patient with infective endocarditis particularly if these conditions are associated with abrupt onset of left ventricular failure.

Definitive

A definitive diagnosis of aortic regurgitation can be made on the basis of the findings on physical examination. An early diastolic decrescendo murmur coupled with a wide peripheral pulse pressure and evidence of left ventricular enlargement is diagnostic of aortic regurgitation. In fact, in the absence of pulmonary hypertension or pulmonic stenosis, a diastolic decrescendo murmur should be attributed to aortic regurgitation.

A definitive diagnosis can also be made on basis of echocardiography (both M-mode and two-dimensional), Doppler echocardiography, and supravalvular aortography. The M-mode finding in aortic regurgitation is high-frequency fluttering of the anterior leaflet of the mitral valve. "Reverse doming" of the anterior leaflet of the mitral valve on the long-axis view is a manifestation of aortic regurgitation on two-dimensional imaging. These echocardiographic findings should always prompt a Doppler examination. Color flow Doppler and continuous-wave Doppler both establish the diagnosis of aortic regurgitation and provide an index of severity.

CLINICAL MANIFESTATIONS

Subjective

A review of the medical history may uncover a previous bout of rheumatic fever usually more than 10 years in the past. A history of preceding connective tissue disorder such as ankylosing spondylitis, systemic lupus erythematosus, Reiter's syndrome, or rheumatoid arthritis should be sought as a means of ascertaining a clue as to the etiology of the regurgitation. A history of long-standing severe systemic arterial hypertension would also be an important etiologic clue.

We thank Dr. Henry A. Liberman for his contribution to this chapter in the previous edition of this book.

The family history may give important contributory information by revealing a history of family members with the stigmata of Marfan's syndrome or with ankylosing spondylitis.

Objective

Physical Examination

The hallmark of aortic regurgitation is the high-frequency, decrescendo diastolic murmur. The contour of the murmur (reaching a maximum in early diastole and gradually diminishing thereafter) reflects the pattern of regurgitant flow. The point of maximal intensity of the murmur provides a clue to the pathologic process. Valvular lesions generally produce a murmur that is heard loudest along the left sternal border and at the apex; conditions associated with dilation of the aortic root are also usually loudest along the left sternal border, but not infrequently are louder along the right sternal border. Other auscultatory features of significant aortic regurgitation include a diamond-shaped systolic murmur (audible in at least three fourths of patients with moderate aortic regurgitation), a diastolic (S_3) gallop, and, in severe regurgitation, a diastolic rumble at the apex (Austin–Flint murmur).

The most striking physical findings in chronic severe aortic regurgitation are caused by the large left ventricular stroke volume and rapid diastolic runoff. The peripheral pulse rises abruptly on upstroke followed by a peripheral collapse. Most of the peripheral evidence of the condition is related to wide pulse pressure. The absence of a wide pulse pressure (greater than 50% of peak systolic pressure) or a diastolic blood pressure greater than 70 mm Hg usually excludes severe chronic aortic regurgitation, except in the very late stages when the murmur may lessen or disappear and the pulse pressure returns to normal.

The increased left ventricular volume and contractility should also be perceptible on physical examination as a displaced, diffuse, overacting apex impulse. A pulsus bisferiens is often found.

Routine Laboratory Abnormalities

The electrocardiogram in significant aortic regurgitation generally includes sinus rhythm, increased QRS amplitude, depressed ST segments, inverted T waves, and horizontal QRS axis. Occasionally, in the early stage of disease, increased QRS amplitude is accompanied by tall, peaked T waves and deep, narrow Q waves in the left precordial leads.

Significant chronic aortic regurgitation is manifest on the chest x-ray by dilation of the left ventricle (Figure 15–36–1). Marked dilation of the aortic root should suggest primary root disease or coexisting aortic stenosis. In acute aortic regurgitation, the left ventricle may be only slightly dilated, and the aorta is usually not dilated except in dissecting aneurysm with acute aortic regurgitation.

Examination of the blood and urine reveals no diagnostic abnormalities.

PLANS

Diagnostic

Differential Diagnosis

The differential diagnosis of an early diastolic murmur is between aortic regurgitation, pulmonic regurgitation, tricuspid stenosis, increased flow across the tricuspid valve, coronary arteriovenous fistula, and patent ductus arteriosus in which the systolic murmur is obscured. Practically speaking, this differential is rarely difficult because the infrequent occurrence of these conditions always makes aortic regurgitation the likely explanation. The other conditions should be considered in the absence of all of the following: a wide pulse pressure, other valvular disease, and echocardiographic manifestations of aortic regurgitation.

Diagnostic Options

Clinically significant aortic regurgitation is generally diagnosed by findings on the physical examination. Doppler echocardiography is a much more sensitive means of detecting aortic regurgitation. The physician should not be surprised or particularly concerned about Doppler evidence of aortic regurgitation in a patient with no physical findings of regurgitation.

The regurgitant jet impinges on the anterior leaflet of the mitral valve, which may be visualized on M-mode echocardiography by increased distance between the maximal anterior motion of the mitral valve and the interventricular septum (E-point separation) and high-

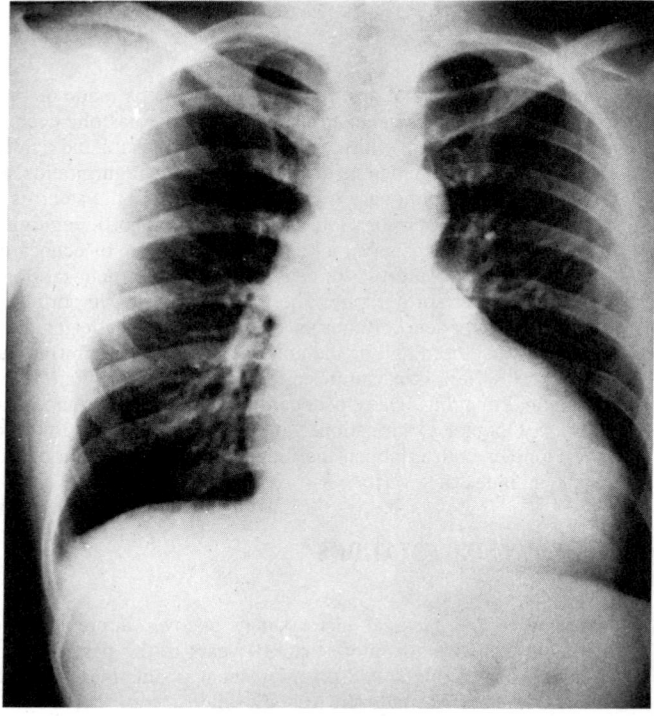
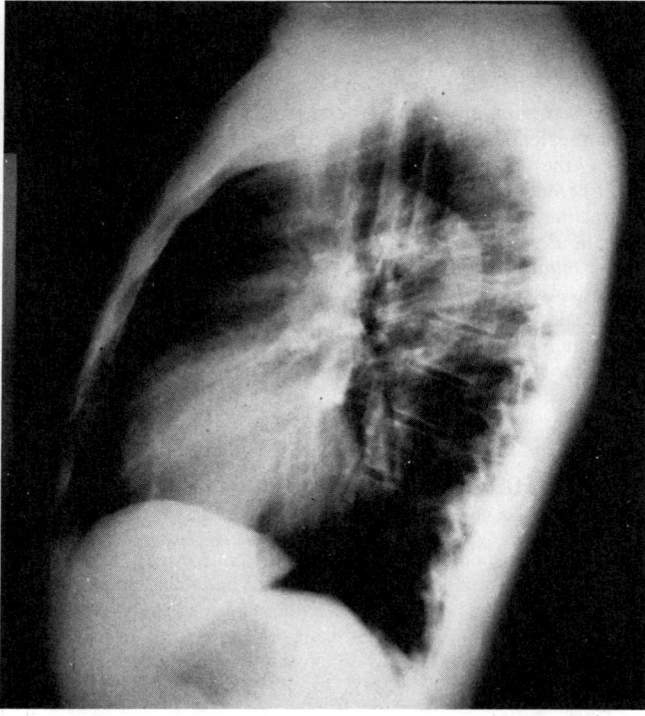

Figure 15–36–1. Chest x-ray of 36-year-old male with forme fruste of Marfan's syndrome and severe aortic regurgitation. A characteristic feature is a dilated left ventricle. Dilation of aortic root would suggest aortic root disease.

frequency fluttering of the anterior mitral valve leaflet. The chest x-ray film may give evidence of a volume overload lesion as manifest by left ventricular enlargement or evidence of aortic root disease as manifest by aortic root enlargement.

Recommended Approach

The diagnosis of aortic regurgitation is based on the findings on physical examination. A reasonably accurate assessment of the severity of the regurgitant flow and its hemodynamic consequences can be gleaned from the physical findings. The initial examination should also include an electrocardiogram and chest x-ray. The chest film is obtained primarily for ascertaining left ventricular size. Marked left ventricular enlargement or angina pectoris in patients with aortic regurgitation usually is an indication for cardiac catheterization. The electrocardiogram should show evidence of left ventricular hypertrophy in the presence of long-standing significant aortic regurgitation.

Although the echocardiogram in chronic aortic regurgitation may give a clue as to the etiology, the major benefit of echocardiography in this condition is to assess the dimensions of the left ventricular chamber. A left ventricular systolic dimension of 55 mm or greater in chronic aortic regurgitation warrants valve replacement. In acute aortic regurgitation, the echocardiogram is quite accurate in establishing or excluding the presence of proximal aortic dissection. Doppler echocardiography is not only quite sensitive and specific for establishing the presence of aortic regurgitation, but is also the best diagnostic technique for assessing severity, functional consequences, and associated abnormalities. Coronary arteriography may be needed to establish the status of the coronary arteries.

Therapeutic

Therapeutic Options

During the asymptomatic phase of the illness, the therapeutic options or, perhaps more appropriately, the therapeutic dilemma is between no treatment and the use of afterload reducers (arterial vasodilators). Once cardiac decompensation occurs, the therapeutic options are medical therapy with arterial vasodilators and aortic valve replacement.

Recommended Approach

Mild aortic regurgitation and asymptomatic severe aortic regurgitation with a normal heart size require only bacterial endocarditis prophylaxis. Although there is no unanimity of opinion, probably the patient with asymptomatic aortic regurgitation and mild cardiomegaly should be treated with digitalis. Cardiac decompensation with the development of left ventricular failure should be treated with digitalis, diuretics, and vasodilators. The use of vasodilators, such as ACE inhibitors or the second generation of calcium antagonists, is not definitely established to be of benefit but could be considered. In the presence of severe failure, medical therapy with arterial vasodilators (hydralazine, captopril, or intravenous sodium nitroprusside) may be lifesaving. Ideally, the aortic valve is replaced before clinical symptoms of heart failure develop.

The most difficult question for the physician is when to replace the aortic valve. There are no definite guidelines, but any of the patients who undergo cardiac catheterization based on the previously mentioned recommendations seem to be appropriate candidates for surgery if left ventricular function is not severely depressed (ejection fraction is less than 30%).

FOLLOW-UP

The asymptomatic patient with mild aortic regurgitation requires no more than an annual physical examination and, as long as the regurgitant flow is mild, requires an electrocardiogram and chest x-ray at the same frequency as the general population. Patients with moderate to severe aortic regurgitation require semiannual physical examinations and annual echocardiograms. Sequential echocardiography is used to evaluate changes in left ventricular size and systolic function and optimize the timing of valve replacement in the asymptomatic patient. Alternate approaches to follow-up in patients with chronic aortic regurgitation include rest and exercise, radionuclide ventriculography, magnetic resonance imaging, and cardiac catheterization.

DISCUSSION

Prevalence

Doppler echocardiography suggests that aortic regurgitation increases in prevalence with advancing age, and aortic regurgitation without auscultatory confirmation is present in the vast majority of persons over age 80. Aortic regurgitation is the third most common valvular abnormality requiring valve replacement, behind aortic stenosis and mitral regurgitation.

Related Basic Science

Anatomic Derangement

Aortic regurgitation is produced when the aortic leaflets are rendered incompetent either by a direct effect or indirectly by aortoannular dilations. The leaflets may be rendered incompetent by scarring and contracture by rheumatic valvulitis, by loss of intrinsic rigidity or valve substance with myxomatous transformation, or by destruction of valve tissue by infection. Dilation of the aortic annulus may occur with syphilis, ankylosing spondylitis, or Marfan's syndrome. The aortic annular support of the leaflets may be undermined with a dissection.

Physiologic or Metabolic Derangement

Volume overload of the left ventricle is the basic hemodynamic abnormality in the condition. The compensatory response of the left ventricle to this volume overload is dilation and development of eccentric hypertrophy. The left ventricle is able to eject the increased volume load by a combination of the Frank–Starling mechanism, by dilation and hypertrophy, and by some slippage of myocardial fibers. Ejection of the additional volume load is achieved primarily by an increase in the end-diastolic volume rather than by an increase in the proportion or fraction of the end-diastolic volume ejected. In the usual circumstances, the gradual increase in end-diastolic volume associated with chronic aortic regurgitation is not accompanied by an increase in end-diastolic pressure. This increased compliance of the left ventricle, so typical of chronic aortic regurgitation, does not develop with acute aortic regurgitation. This difference in myocardial compliance contributes to a large degree to the rapid clinical deterioration noted in acute severe aortic regurgitation.

Natural History and Its Modification with Treatment

Chronic aortic regurgitation is generally characterized by a prolonged course with little disability for many years. The 10-year mortality for patients with slight or moderate aortic regurgitation is little different from that of the normal population. With severe aortic regurgitation, the 10-year mortality approaches 50%. Once a patient has become symptomatic, there is a fairly rapid deterioration.

Aortic valve replacement prior to the development of left ventricular dysfunction and cardiomegaly results in excellent long-term survival.

Prevention

Rheumatic aortic regurgitation is largely preventable with prompt treatment of streptococcal infections. Syphilitic aortitis and some cases due to infective endocarditis are preventable by prompt treatment of the infection.

The goal is to prevent irreversible left ventricular dysfunction as a consequence of aortic regurgitation by the proper timing of surgical intervention. Even with the clues listed, it is not always possible to do this.

Cost Containment

With realization of the multiple etiologies of aortic regurgitation, the physician should refrain from routinely prescribing rheumatic fever prophylaxis to all patients unless there are clinical clues of rheumatic etiology. Recognition that hemodynamically significant chronic regurgitation must be accompanied by the peripheral manifestation of a widened pulse pressure should prevent the indiscriminate ordering of serial chest x-rays and electrocardiograms early in the course of this condition.

REFERENCES

Bonow RO, Lakatos E, Maran BJ, Epstein SE. Serial long-term assessment of the natural history of asymptomatic patients with chronic aortic regurgitation and normal left ventricular systolic function. Circulation 1991;84:1625.

Goldschlager N, Pfeifer J, Cohn K, et al. The natural history of aortic regurgitation: A clinical and hemodynamic study. Am J Med 1973;54:577.

Hann RT, Roman MJ, Mogtader AH, et al. Association of aortic dilation with regurgitant, stenotic and functionally normal bicuspid aortic valves. J Am Coll Cardiol 1992;19:282.

Rapaport E. Natural history of aortic and mitral valve disease. Am J Cardiol 1975;35:221.

Rapaport E, Rackley CE, Cohn LH. Aortic valvular disease. In: Schlant RC, Alexander RW, O'Rourke RA, et al., eds. Hurst's the heart. 8th ed. New York: McGraw-Hill, 1994:1457.

CHAPTER 15–37

Mitral Valve Stenosis

Douglas C. Morris, M.D.

DEFINITION

Mitral stenosis is an obstruction of blood flow from the left atrium into the left ventricle caused by the fibrosis and scarring of mitral apparatus or, rarely, the calcification of the mitral annulus.

ETIOLOGY

Mitral stenosis is almost always rheumatic in origin with rare exception. Other rare causes of obstruction of the mitral orifice are congenital mitral stenosis, left atrial myxoma, chronic ergot usage, and calcified mitral annulus in the setting of a small left ventricular chamber.

CRITERIA FOR DIAGNOSIS
Suggestive

The constellation of physical findings of an accentuated first heart sound, an opening snap, and an apical diastolic rumble heralds the presence of mitral stenosis. Atrial fibrillation is common. This constellation of findings should be sought in the middle-aged woman with dyspnea or easy fatigability, left atrial abnormality, inferior or rightward QRS vector on electrocardiogram, and left atrial and left atrial appendage enlargement on chest x-ray film.

Definitive

A definitive diagnosis of mitral stenosis can be established either by Doppler echocardiography or right and left heart catheterization. Both techniques can give accurate estimates of the diastolic gradient across the valve and mitral valve area. Although both techniques can identify other valve lesions and assess ventricular function, only cardiac catheterization can determine the response of pulmonary vascular pressure to exercise and determine the status of the coronary arteries.

CLINICAL MANIFESTATIONS
Subjective

The patient is usually 25 years of age or older. Women are more commonly affected than men.

The most common and earliest symptom of pure mitral stenosis is dyspnea. Initially, this is only exertional, but as the severity of the disease progresses, many patients develop this symptom at rest. Any factor that places increased demands on the heart, such as fever, emotional stress, and pregnancy, may also precipitate severe dyspnea and even frank pulmonary edema. Patients with severe mitral stenosis frequently experience orthopnea and paroxysmal nocturnal dyspnea. Patients with end-stage mitral stenosis complain primarily of fatigue.

Hemoptysis may occur in the course of this illness, usually at a time when a sudden rise in pulmonary venous pressure produces venous hemorrhage. As pulmonary vascular resistance rises, this occurrence is less likely.

Chest pain, indistinguishable in location and character from angina pectoris, is encountered in a few patients with mitral stenosis. Although there is a higher incidence of this pain in patients with more severe stenosis or higher pulmonary pressures, it is not confined to such patients.

Symptoms of systemic arterial emboli develop in 10 to 15% of patients with mitral stenosis and may be the presenting complaint. Two thirds to three fourths of these patients are in atrial fibrillation. A history of rheumatic fever is present in only half the patients with pure mitral stenosis.

Objective
Physical Examination

The general appearance of patients with mitral stenosis is usually unremarkable. A malar flush may be noted.

The peripheral pulses are normal except in those with severe obstruction, who generally manifest a pulse of decreased amplitude. The apical impulse is typically not displaced and may even be difficult to palpate unless the patient is in the left lateral decubitus position. A sustained parasternal lift is present with significant pulmonary hypertension and right ventricular hypertrophy. Distended neck veins reflect right ventricular failure with tricuspid regurgitation.

On auscultation, the principal signs of mitral stenosis include accentuation of the intensity of S_1, an opening snap of the mitral valve, and a low-pitched rumbling apical diastolic murmur. As severe mitral stenosis leads to pulmonary hypertension, the signs of the latter appear, including accentuation of the pulmonary component of the second heart sound, a pulmonic ejection sound, diastolic decrescendo murmur of pulmonic regurgitation, and a right atrial gallop.

Approximately one half of the patients with mitral stenosis, when first seen, have atrial fibrillation. The presence of this arrhythmia has little correlation with severity but does have some relation to duration of the condition.

Routine Laboratory Abnormalities

Common electrocardiographic features of mitral stenosis include left atrial enlargement and right ventricular hypertrophy secondary to pulmonary hypertension. Right-axis deviation of the mean QRS complex and an increased amplitude of the R wave in V_1 are the usual signs of right ventricular hypertrophy.

The typical radiologic findings in significant mitral stenosis are enlargement of the left atrium and left atrial appendage, pulmonary ve-

We thank Dr. Henry A. Liberman for his contribution to this chapter in the previous edition of this book.

nous hypertension, interstitial pulmonary edema (Kerley's B lines), and right ventricular enlargement. The presence of Kerley's B lines has good correlation with significant elevation of the pulmonary capillary wedge pressure. Calcium may be seen in the mitral valve.

Examination of the blood and urine reveals no diagnostic abnormalities.

PLANS
Diagnostic
Differential Diagnosis

The cardiac conditions that can occasionally be confused with mitral stenosis include atrial myxoma, primary pulmonary hypertension, and ostium secundum atrial septal defect. A left atrial myxoma can produce dyspnea in association with a diastolic rumble preceded by a tumor plop (misdiagnosed as an opening snap). An atrial septal defect can produce a similar chest x-ray film appearance coupled with a diastolic murmur secondary to flow across the tricuspid valve. Primary pulmonary hypertension can present with dyspnea and increased intensity of the pulmonic component to the second sound.

Diagnostic Options

The clinical suspicion of mitral stenosis can be confirmed by either M-mode or two-dimensional echocardiography, Doppler echocardiography, or combined right and left heart catheterization. All four techniques can also exclude atrial myxoma and ostium secundum atrial septal defect. Two-dimensional echocardiography by direct planimetry of the valve area, Doppler by the pressure half-time, and cardiac catheterization by recording the diastolic gradient across the valve can all reliably assess the severity of stenosis.

Recommended Approach

A careful physical examination should always suggest and can usually establish the diagnosis of mitral stenosis. Echocardiography serves to confirm the clinical impression and exclude rare causes of mitral orifice obstruction such as left atrial tumor.

Cardiac catheterization is reserved for symptomatic patients in whom surgical treatment or balloon valvuloplasty is contemplated. The hallmark of mitral stenosis on cardiac catheterization is a diastolic pressure difference across the mitral valve. The cardiac output must be measured simultaneously with the gradient to calculate the valve area. Severe mitral stenosis is present when the valve area is less than 1 cm^2. Cardiac catheterization is also performed in patients over 40 years of age to identify the presence of coronary atherosclerosis.

Patients under 40 years of age who have classic signs of pure mitral stenosis on physical examination, echocardiogram, and Doppler study may not require catheterization.

Therapeutic
Therapeutic Options

As there are no effective pharmacologic means of relieving the obstruction of the mitral valve, therapy in mitral stenosis should be directed toward the consequences of the stenosis. Fluid retention can be addressed by a controlled sodium diet and/or diuretics (loop diuretics or thiazides and related drugs). Ventricular rate control in the presence of atrial fibrillation can be achieved with digitalis, verapamil, diltiazem, or a beta blocker. Patients with atrial fibrillation should be anticoagulated with warfarin unless anticoagulation treatment is contraindicated.

The valvular obstruction can be addressed directly by balloon valvuloplasty, open commissurotory, or valve replacement.

Recommended Approach

Asymptomatic patients with mitral stenosis require no therapy except for endocarditis prophylaxis and some restriction in physical activity. Young patients who are exposed to streptococcal respiratory tract infections should receive rheumatic fever prophylaxis (see Chapter 15–48). Symptoms of pulmonary congestion frequently respond to sodium restriction and diuretic therapy.

Digitalis is not very useful in patients in sinus rhythm, but is necessary to control the ventricular rate in those with atrial fibrillation. A long-acting beta blocker or verapamil may also be added to control the ventricular rate. Quinidine or flecanide is helpful in maintaining sinus rhythm with recurrent paroxysms of atrial fibrillation, and electrical cardioversion is recommended when antiarrhythmics are not successful in restoring sinus rhythm. Oral anticoagulation (warfarin) is maintained in patients with atrial fibrillation, and it is generally recommended that patients receive anticoagulants for 3 to 4 weeks prior to cardioversion as well as 2 to 4 weeks after successful cardioversion.

Symptoms of pulmonary venous congestion unresponsive to medical therapy should prompt an evaluation for valvuloplasty or surgery. With the refinements in balloon valvuloplasty, it seems appropriate to consider valvuloplasty in any symptomatic patient who develops atrial fibrillation. There is also a trend to earlier intervention using balloon valvuloplasty in patients who have mitral stenosis.

FOLLOW-UP

Asymptomatic patients with mitral stenosis should be examined semiannually. The examiner should address heart rate and rhythm, evidence of pulmonary congestion and peripheral edema, and evidence for embolic events. Historical evidence of dyspnea, fatigue, or hemoptysis should be sought. The visit should also include a reminder about endocarditis prophylaxis. A chest x-ray or echocardiogram should be included every 1 to 2 years.

Once symptoms develop the patient should be evaluated by two-dimensional echocardiography. If echocardiography reveals a severely stenotic valve with pliable, minimally calcified leaflets, balloon valvuloplasty should be considered. The necessity for surgery, particularly in the presence of atrial fibrillation, may persuade the physician to try the restoration of sinus rhythm and diuretics initially.

DISCUSSION
Prevalence and Incidence

The prevalence of mitral stenosis is tied directly to the prevalence of rheumatic carditis. The past four decades have witnessed a dramatic decline in prevalence of both acute rheumatic fever and mitral stenosis. In some Western countries the decline in incidence over the last four to five decades has approached 90%, with half of this decline occurring prior to the widespread use of antibiotics. Nevertheless, acute rheumatic fever and rheumatic heart disease continue to be a major public health problem in the heavily populated developing countries.

Related Basic Science
Anatomic Derangement

Rheumatic valvulitis results in varying degrees of commissural fusion. Fibrosis and calcification of the cusps contribute to the obstruction by causing immobility of the cusps. Finally, chordal thickening and fusion restrict valve leaflet movement. These chordal changes accompanied by chordal shortening may also create subvalvular stenosis. The left atrium characteristically enlarges as the mitral valves becomes increasingly stenotic and the left atrial pressures rises.

Physiologic or Metabolic Derangement

Obstruction to flow across the mitral orifice increases the left atrial pressure and volume. As the left atrial pressure rises and, in turn, causes a rise in the pulmonary venous and capillary pressures, interstitial edema may ensue. Chronic elevation of left atrial and pulmonary venous pressure produces hyperplasia and hypertrophy of pulmonary arteries and, as consequence, pulmonary arterial hypertension. About 25 to 30% of patients develop marked disproportionate elevation of pulmonary vascular resistance. Generally, this pulmonary hypertension reverses after elimination of the mitral stenosis.

Natural History and Its Modification with Treatment

In the United States, acute rheumatic fever generally occurs in the early teenage years. Usually another decade elapses before a murmur is audible. Dyspnea develops over the ensuing 5 to 10 years. Symptoms usually worsen to the point that valve repair or replacement is required in the fourth or fifth decade of life. About 50% of the patients develop symptoms gradually, whereas the remainder experience a sudden deterioration in clinical condition. Atrial fibrillation, fever, emotional stress, and pregnancy can precipitate this deterioration.

Surgical commissurotomy is expected to delay valve replacement by 8 to 10 years. Results with balloon valvuloplasty have to date been somewhat shorter, in the range of 5 to 7 years.

Prevention

Prevention of mitral stenosis can be accomplished only with the eradication of rheumatic fever. Patients with mitral stenosis who are exposed to streptococcal respiratory tract infections should receive rheumatic fever prophylaxis to reduce the chances of recurrent carditis. Patients with mitral stenosis or those who have had mitral valve surgery should be instructed in endocarditis prophylaxis.

Cost Containment

The financial burden of care can be eased by avoiding expensive and unnecessary cardiac catheterizations.

REFERENCES

Carabello BA. Mitral valve disease. Curr Probl Cardiol 1993;18:423.
Chen C-R, Cheng TO, Chen Y-I, et al. Long-term results of percutaneous mitral valvuloplasty with the Inoue balloon catheter. Am J Cardiol 1992;70:1445.
Cohen DJ, Kuntz RE, Gordon SPF, et al. Predictors of long-term outcome after percutaneous mitral valvulotomy. N Engl J Med 1992;327:1329.
Gaasch WH, O'Rourke RA, Cohn LH, et al. Mitral valve disease. In: Schlant RC, Alexander RW, O'Rourke RA, et al., eds. Hurst's the heart. 8th ed. New York: McGraw-Hill, 1994:1483.
Selzer A, Cohn KE. Natural history of mitral stenosis: A review. Circulation 1972;46:227.

CHAPTER 15–38

Mitral Valve Regurgitation

Douglas C. Morris, M.D.

DEFINITION

Mitral regurgitation is ejection of a portion of the left ventricular stroke volume into the left atrium due to incompetence of the mitral valve apparatus.

ETIOLOGY

Although rheumatic valvulitis remains an important cause of mitral regurgitation, it is no longer the predominant cause. The most common cause of mitral regurgitation is mitral valve prolapse, but the regurgitation is usually trivial in this condition. Pure mitral regurgitation requiring valve replacement is most often secondary to myxomatous transformation and is frequently precipitated by rupture of chordae tendineae. Other less common etiologies of mitral regurgitation include papillary muscle ischemia due to coronary atherosclerotic heart disease, mitral annular calcification, infective endocarditis, idiopathic hypertrophic subaortic stenosis, a component of a congenital defect such as ostium primum atrial septal defect, and dilated cardiomyopathy.

CRITERIA FOR DIAGNOSIS
Suggestive

The possible presence of mitral regurgitation should be entertained with any systolic murmur. Although a holosystolic configuration with a fairly constant intensity, an apical location with radiation to the axilla, an associated diastolic rumble or third heart sound, and the presence of atrial fibrillation make mitral regurgitation the likely diagnosis, other locations and configurations of the mitral regurgitation murmur are common. The sudden worsening or appearance of a systolic murmur with radiation up and down the spine, particularly when associated with the development of dyspnea, is likely due to mitral regurgitation secondary to chordal rupture. The recording of prominent regurgitant waves on the pulmonary capillary pressure recordings suggests mitral regurgitation. The echocardiographic finding of an anatomically abnormal mitral valve in the presence of left atrial and left ventricular dilation also suggests mitral regurgitation.

Definitive

The presence and severity of mitral regurgitation can be established by contrast ventriculography or Doppler techniques (pulsed, continuous wave, or color flow). Combining echocardiography with Doppler techniques is the best means of defining the presence, severity, and consequences on cardiac size and function of mitral regurgitation as well as possibly defining the etiology.

CLINICAL MANIFESTATIONS
Subjective

During much of the course of chronic mitral regurgitation, the patient is asymptomatic. Slowly progressive dyspnea with effort is usually the first symptom. Patients with a large very compliant left atrium, however, may be limited by fatigue more than by dyspnea. Chest pain typical for angina pectoris is unusual with mitral regurgitation and should suggest the presence of an associated condition such as aortic valve disease or coronary atherosclerosis. Later in the course of the disease, palpitations are common and usually herald the onset of atrial fibrillation.

In contrast to this picture of a gradual appearance and worsening of symptoms typical of chronic mitral valve regurgitation, patients with acute mitral regurgitation present with the abrupt onset of dyspnea and pulmonary edema.

Objective
Physical Examination

The patient's general appearance is usually normal. Peripheral pulses are decreased in volume, but the upstroke is brisk. Jugular venous pressure is elevated in patients with right ventricular hypertrophy and right ventricular failure. The apical impulse typically associated with longstanding and significant mitral regurgitation is displaced laterally and inferiorly and is hyperdynamic. An early diastolic impulse (palpable S_3 or filling wave) may also be appreciated.

On auscultation, the heart sounds may be normal, but usually the first sound is diminished and the second sound is widely split with a loud pulmonary valve closure sound. The murmur, which is typical of severe chronic rheumatic mitral regurgitation, is holosystolic beginning with the first sound and extending through the aortic valve closure sound. It is heard best at the apex but radiates to the axilla and back. The murmur is described as blowing in quality and is usually grade 3 to 4 or louder, although there is not good correlation between loudness of the murmur

We thank Dr. Henry A. Liberman for his contribution to this chapter in the previous edition of this book.

and severity of mitral regurgitation. A diastolic rumble may be heard at the cardiac apex.

The murmur associated with nonrheumatic etiologies of mitral regurgitation may vary widely from this description. In these instances, it may occur only in late systole, have a spindle-shaped configuration, or radiate to the spine or base of the heart. When the murmur is heard up and down the spinal column and over the sacrum, one should consider rupture of the chordae tendineae as the cause. The listener should search for a systolic click along with a late systolic murmur, as this may identify mitral valve prolapse (see Chapter 15–39). In every circumstance, the murmur of mitral regurgitation should decrease in response to amyl nitrite inhalation. The intensity of the murmur of mitral regurgitation also shows little change with alterations in the cardiac cycle; this is helpful in differentiating it from the murmur of aortic stenosis, which also may be prominent at the apex.

The presence of a left ventricular atrial gallop (S_4) is rare in chronic mitral regurgitation, but is the usual finding in patients with acute mitral regurgitation and sinus rhythm. A left ventricular gallop (S_3) is present in both severe acute and chronic mitral regurgitation. As pulmonary hypertension develops, the intensity of P-2 increases and the murmurs of tricuspid and pulmonary regurgitation may appear.

Routine Laboratory Abnormalities

Approximately three fourths of the patients coming to valve replacement surgery for mitral regurgitation have atrial fibrillation. Those patients in sinus rhythm usually manifest signs of left atrial abnormality on the electrocardiogram. Electrocardiographic evidence of left ventricular hypertrophy is present in 50% of these patients.

The chest x-ray film reveals enlargement of the left ventricle and left atrium in chronic mitral regurgitation, but these chambers are normal in size in acute mitral regurgitation. The changes of pulmonary venous hypertension or pulmonary edema may be visible.

Examination of the blood and urine reveals no diagnostic abnormalities.

PLANS
Diagnostic
Differential Diagnosis

The differential diagnosis of the holosystolic murmur includes ventricular septal defect, hypertrophic obstructive cardiomyopathy, and tricuspid regurgitation in the presence of a significantly enlarged right ventricle. Particularly in the elderly patient, the auscultatory differentiation of an apical systolic murmur of aortic stenosis and mitral regurgitation can be difficult.

The differentiation of the etiology of mitral regurgitation usually rests with the echocardiogram, but can be aided by body habitus (tall, lanky habitus associated with myxomatous changes), past history (previous rheumatic fever), and symptoms (angina associated with papillary muscle dysfunction).

Diagnostic Options

The most cost-effective and appropriate means of making a reliable diagnosis of mitral regurgitation is the physical examination, particularly if it includes maneuvers such as auscultation of the heart with standing, squatting, Valsalva maneuver, hand grip, and amyl nitrite.

Although echocardiography cannot detect mitral regurgitation, the consequences of long-standing left atrial and left ventricular volume overload are evident. The etiology of the mitral regurgitation is usually apparent by visualization of a flail mitral leaflet, vegetations, leaflet fusion and calcification, mitral annular calcification, or systolic anterior motion of the anterior leaflet.

Doppler echocardiography combines the Doppler assessment of volume, timing, and dispersion of regurgitant flow with the echocardiographic findings.

Combined right and left cardiac catheterization and left-sided ventriculography provide semiquantitative assessment of the mitral regurgitation along with its hemodynamic consequences.

Recommended Approach

Characteristic findings on the physical examination are adequate for the diagnosis of mitral regurgitation. If the mitral regurgitation is assessed on the basis of physical findings and a lack of symptoms to be trivial, no further workup is indicated. If the severity of the regurgitation is uncertain or moderate or greater, Doppler echocardiography should be obtained. A patient with moderate or severe regurgitation should also have a baseline electrocardiogram and chest x-ray film.

The symptomatic patient, the patient with progressive increase in left ventricular size, or the patient with marked cardiomegaly should be evaluated by combined right- and left-sided heart catheterization and left-sided ventriculography. Cardiac catheterization gives no better assessment of chamber sizes or the severity of regurgitation than does Doppler echocardiography, but does more accurately evaluate the degree of pulmonary hypertension, diastolic functions of the left ventricle, and coronary disease. Transesophageal echocardiography is very helpful if valve repair is being contemplated.

Therapeutic
Therapeutic Options

Medical options for the treatment of mitral regurgitation include digitalis, diuretics, and afterload reduction. Surgical options include valve repair and valve replacement.

Recommended Approach

Symptomatic patients with chronic mitral regurgitation should be treated with digitalis, diuretics, and afterload reduction with angiotensin-converting enzyme inhibitors. If symptoms first appear or are exacerbated with the development of atrial fibrillation, cardioversion should be attempted.

Antibiotic endocarditis prophylaxis is recommended in all cases of mitral regurgitation, including patients with a prosthetic mitral valve (see Chapter 8–12). Rheumatic fever prophylaxis is indicated in children and young adults with evidence of a rheumatic etiology of their disease (see Chapter 15–48).

Patients with acute severe mitral regurgitation should be treated with afterload reduction by intravenous nitroprusside. An unsatisfactory response to nitroprusside would warrant aortic counterpulsation.

Surgical intervention is indicated in any patient with symptoms referable to the regurgitation and satisfactory left ventricular function (ejection fraction greater than 40%). Surgery is required emergently is acute severe mitral regurgitation.

FOLLOW-UP

Follow-up evaluations of the asymptomatic patient with significant mitral regurgitation can generally rest with biannual physical examination and symptom review coupled with an annual chest x-ray. Serial echocardiographic or Doppler studies are not required but can be substituted for the annual chest x-ray film. The appearance of symptoms or the sudden worsening of mild preexisting symptoms accompanied by a change in the objective data warrants cardiac catheterization.

DISCUSSION
Prevalence and Incidence

Mitral valve regurgitation is the most prevalent form of valvular heart disease. The most common form of mitral regurgitation is mitral valve prolapse, which occurs in approximately 5% of the adult population. The prevalence of the various etiologies of mitral regurgitation have changed through the years. Prior to 1970, rheumatic mitral regurgitation was the most common etiology leading to valve surgery, but more recently myxomatous transformation is the leading cause of mitral insufficiency requiring surgery.

Related Basic Science
Anatomic Derangement

The competence of the mitral valve depends on the anatomic and functional integrity of the five components of the mitral apparatus: the leaflets, the chordae tendineae, the papillary muscles, the ventricular wall surrounding the papillary muscles, and the annulus. The various etiologies of mitral regurgitation produce incompetence by adversely affecting one or more of these components. Myxomatous transformation affects the valvular stroma, resulting in a loss of rigidity and fragility to the leaflet structure as well as thinned, fragile, elongated chordae tendineae. Rheumatic valvulitis leads to fibrosis and contraction of the leaflets. Papillary muscle dysfunction is due to an ischemia-related contracture disorder of usually the posterior papillary muscle. Mitral annular calcification interferes with the systolic mitral orifice reduction.

Physiologic or Metabolic Derangement

The hemodynamic consequence of mitral regurgitation is volume overload of both the left atrium and left ventricle. As mitral regurgitation progresses, the left atrium dilates and becomes more compliant; therefore, left atrial pressures do not rise significantly and pulmonary congestion does not develop until late in the course of the disease. Initially, the pump function of the left ventricle remains well preserved because the systolic emptying into the left atrium serves as a low-pressure escape valve. The left ventricle also enlarges to accommodate a larger end-diastolic volume necessary to maintain an adequate forward output. Gradually, however, left ventricular contractility is compromised and left ventricular end-diastolic pressure rises, causing a passive increase in pulmonary venous and pulmonary arterial pressures.

Mitral regurgitation is a condition that progressively worsens. As the posterior leaflet is continuous with the left atrial endocardium, the posterior cusp functionally shortens as the left atrium enlarges. Second, dilation of the left ventricular cavity is accompanied by dilation of the mitral annulus. Finally, enlargement of the left ventricular cavity results in lateral displacement of the papillary muscle and abnormal traction on the chordae and leaflets.

Natural History and Its Modification with Treatment

Patients with mitral regurgitation generally follow a rather benign course until late in their illness. Symptoms usually begin with exertion

and gradually worsen over a decade. Abrupt changes in the course can usually be traced to the development of atrial fibrillation or to a sudden worsening in the incompetence of the mitral apparatus secondary to chordal rupture, papillary muscle rupture, or endocarditis. More than three fourths of the medically treated patients are alive 5 years after the diagnosis is made.

In patients with symptomatic mitral regurgitation, the long-term survival is improved with surgery. The 10-year surgical survival is also better with valve reconstruction than with prosthetic replacement.

Prevention

Prevention of rheumatic fever decreases the frequency of rheumatic mitral regurgitation. Prevention of endocarditis in patients with mild mitral regurgitation prevents further destruction of the mitral apparatus. In those patients whose valvular anatomy is amenable to reconstruction, perhaps earlier surgery will prevent deleterious effects on other components of the mitral apparatus, left atrium, and left ventricle.

Cost Containment

Savings can be achieved by eliminating routine serial use of procedures such as echocardiography in asymptomatic patients and by preventing complications with appropriate bacterial endocarditis prophylaxis.

REFERENCES

Carabello BA. Mitral valve disease. Curr Probl Cardiol 1993;18:423.
Cohn LH. Surgery for mitral regurgitation. JAMA 1988;260:2883.
Gaasch WH, O'Rourke RA, Cohn LH, et al. Mitral valve disease. In: Schlant RC, Alexander RW, O'Rourke RA, et al., eds. Hurst's the heart. 8th ed. New York: McGraw-Hill, 1994:1483.
Perloff JK, Roberts WC. The mitral apparatus: Functional anatomy of mitral regurgitation. Circulation 1972;46:227.
Woody CF, Baker PB, Kolibash AJ, et al. The floppy, myxomatous mitral valve, mitral valve prolapse, and mitral regurgitation. Prog Cardiovasc Dis 1991;33:397.

CHAPTER 15–39

Mitral Valve Prolapse

Joel M. Felner, M.D., and Robert C. Schlant, M.D.

DEFINITION

Mitral valve prolapse refers to the systolic billowing (ie, superior and posterior displacement) of one or both mitral valve leaflets into the left atrium with or without mitral regurgitation.

ETIOLOGY

Mitral valve prolapse is a common condition that includes a heterogenous group of patients with a wide spectrum of disease.

In the *primary idiopathic form,* the mitral valve is morphologically abnormal with myxomatous proliferation of the spongiosa portion of the leaflet. This form is inherited as an autosomal dominant trait with varying penetrance and has multiple causes, including various connective tissue disorders, such as Marfan's syndrome, as well as incompletely defined abnormalities of collagen synthesis.

In the *secondary acquired form,* the mitral valve is functionally abnormal without myxomatous transformation. This form occurs in patients with coronary artery disease, rheumatic valvulitis, and hypertrophic cardiomyopathy and is often associated with a low body mass index, distorted thoracic cavity, low intravascular volume, or other conditions that cause a small left ventricular size.

CRITERIA FOR DIAGNOSIS
Suggestive

The auscultatory identification of a systolic click(s) emanating from the mitral valve followed by a late systolic murmur is virtually pathognomonic for mitral valve prolapse (MVP). A completely normal auscultatory examination virtually excludes significant mitral valve prolapse.

Definitive

In the absence of the auscultatory signs of a systolic click and murmur, the diagnosis may be made by demonstrating prolapse of the mitral valve on either echocardiography or angiography.

CLINICAL MANIFESTATIONS
Subjective

Most patients with mitral valve prolapse are totally asymptomatic and are identified on routine examination. Most instances of the primary or idiopathic variety of mitral valve prolapse occur sporadically, but its familial occurrence has been documented. There is a preponderance of young females with this syndrome, who usually present between the ages 20 and 40 years, but it has been described in all ages and in both sexes. Chest discomfort, the most common symptom, is usually unrelated to exertion and not relieved by nitroglycerin. Palpitations are also a common presenting complaint. Vague, but occasionally disabling symptoms of dyspnea, fatigue, weakness, and dizziness may also be present; neuropsychiatric symptoms and syncope have also been described. Rarely, there may be an increased incidence of sudden death in the family, transient cerebral ischemic episodes and neurologic deficits, or symptoms or left-sided heart failure if mitral regurgitation is severe, or the individual may be aware of an intermittent systolic whoop or honk.

The chest pain or discomfort that occurs in approximately 20% of subjects is a particularly vexing clinical problem. It usually is either fleeting, sharp and stabbing, or atypical; it lasts from seconds to hours, is unrelated to exertion, and is poorly relieved by nitroglycerin. It varies from mild to disabling and in general is ill-defined, although occasionally it is substernal. Some patients may have pain that is typical of angina pectoris. The cause is unknown, but it may be musculoskeletal in origin and has been ascribed to ischemia secondary to excessive stretching of the papillary muscles. A major problem is distinguishing this atypical chest pain from that due to coronary artery disease, especially because ischemic heart disease may cause mitral valve prolapse or occur with it.

Palpitations have been noted in many of the reported patients with documented mitral valve prolapse and are almost certainly due to arrhythmias, most frequently premature ventricular contractions. Dyspnea and fatigue are also relatively common in patients with mitral valve prolapse. They are usually not associated with signs of heart failure or reduction of exercise tolerance, and are rarely progressive. No apparent cause for either symptom has been found. Dizziness and syncope are less common symptoms. They have a poor correlation with arrhythmias detected on ambulatory monitoring. Occasionally, the arrhythmias are present only during exertion or are much more frequent during exertion. Sudden death occurs very rarely and is presumably due to ventricular fibrillation.

Neuropsychiatric symptoms including anxiety, depression, psychoses, personality disorders, panic attacks, sleep disorders, migraine headaches, agoraphobia, and hyperventilation have been relatively prominent in some series of patients with mitral valve prolapse. It is not unusual for these symptoms to occur only when the patient is under considerable emotional stress. It now appears that many patients formally diagnosed as having some type of autonomic dysfunction, neurocirculatory asthenia, the effort syndrome, da Costa's syndrome, or soldier's heart probably had mitral valve prolapse.

Transient cerebral ischemic episodes, amaurosis fugax, and retinal artery occlusion have been reported and presumably are the result of cerebral emboli that originate in a cul-de-sac between the left atrial wall and the prolapsed mitral leaflet. There is increased stasis in this location that is necessary for thrombus formation, especially if atrial fibrillation is present.

Although the prevalence of symptoms in published series of patients with mitral valve prolapse has been as high as 75%, when patients with mitral valve prolapse are compared with a group of age-matched controls, the overall prevalence of symptomatology or of any particular symptom is the same in each group.

Occasional patients have a family history of mitral valve prolapse.

Objective

Physical Examination

The most frequent physical finding, and the hallmark of mitral valve prolapse, is an isolated midsystolic click. The click is a clear, crisp, high-frequency sound of short duration best heard at the apex and lower left sternal edge. It is clicking, snapping, or popping in character. The presence or absence of a click, its intensity, and its exact timing in systole can vary from beat to beat irrespective of the respiratory cycle. The click may be absent, single, or multiple, and it may occur in middle, late, or occasionally even early systole. On one examination a click may not be audible, whereas on reexamination there may be an isolated click, multiple clicks, and/or a systolic murmur. The click results from

sudden tensing of the mitral apparatus as the leaflets prolapse into the left atrium during systole.

The systolic click is often accompanied by an apical, mid- to late systolic murmur that is either initiated by, or begins just prior to, the click. The murmur may be the only auscultatory finding in some patients, and its timing often is inconstant. Its configuration is usually crescendo to the second heart sound, but a holosystolic murmur often obscuring the click is audible in up to 10% of patients. The murmur may be loud and musical or whooping or honking in character.

The most diagnostic of the auscultatory features of mitral valve prolapse is the variation in timing of the systolic click and murmur with changes in the patient's physical status, activity, and position. These systolic sounds are best heard with the diaphragm of the stethoscope, and their clarity can be enhanced by various physiologic and pharmacologic maneuvers (Table 15–39–1). The location in systole and the intensity of the click and/or murmur classically vary according to the size of the left ventricle at end diastole and the contractility of the left ventricle. This explains the observation of either no murmur or a soft, late systolic, apical murmur in a patient examined supine whose murmur becomes audible or longer and louder on sitting or standing. For these reasons, it is important to perform auscultation using several different patient positions, including left lateral, sitting, squatting, and standing.

The other aspects of the physical examination that are especially important in patients with mitral valve prolapse include the physical appearance and the apex impulse. Although the patient's general appearance is frequently normal, certain features should heighten the suspicion that mitral valve prolapse is present. Body habitus often is asthenic, and occasionally there is a high-arched palate, suggestive of Marfan's syndrome. Thoracic bony abnormalities are especially important and include loss of normal thoracic kyphosis (straight back), pectus excavatum, and scoliosis. In addition, patients with mitral valve prolapse may have unusual dermatoglyphic patterns in their fingerprints.

The apex impulse is usually normal. The apex impulse may be displaced, however, if the patient has a thoracic bony abnormality. Occasionally there may be a palpable midsystolic retraction producing a bifid apical impulse, especially if the patient is examined in the left lateral decubitus position. The midsystolic retraction may be difficult to palpate, but a prominent midsystolic dip on the apex cardiogram simultaneous with a systolic click can occasionally be recorded.

Systemic embolic events have been recognized increasingly in patients with mitral valve prolapse. In one study, 40% of patients under the age of 45 with cerebral ischemic episodes were found to have mitral valve prolapse, a much higher figure than the 4 to 6% reported in the general population. The emboli are usually small. Retinal occlusions with visual manifestations are most common, but cerebral and cerebellar infarcts with serious residual disability have occurred (Marks et al., 1989).

Routine Laboratory Abnormalities

Electrocardiographic changes associated with mitral valve prolapse can be seen on the resting electrocardiogram (ECG) or may only occur with

TABLE 15–39–1. EFFECTS OF PHYSIOLOGIC AND PHARMACOLOGIC MANEUVERS IN MITRAL VALVE PROLAPSE

Maneuver	Timing of the Click	Characteristics of the Murmur
Inspiration	Earlier in systole	Longer
Standing	Earlier in systole	Longer
Squatting	Later in systole	Shorter
Hand grip	Later in systole	Shorter
Valsalva (strain)	Earlier in systole	Longer
Valsalva (release)	Later in systole	Shorter
Amyl nitrite	Earlier in systole	Holosystolic, usually fainter
Propranolol	Later in systole	May become inaudible
Following a premature beat	Later in systole	Shorter

Adapted from Schlant RC, Felner JM, Miklozek CL, et al. Mitral valve prolapse. Dis Mon 1980;26(10):24. Reproduced with permission from the publisher and author.

exercise testing or during continuous ambulatory monitoring. Although the majority of patients have a normal resting ECG, there are several nonspecific abnormalities, the most characteristic of which is an inverted T wave in the inferolateral leads. Approximately one third of patients have arrhythmias detected on routine ECG, with premature ventricular complexes being the most common. Atrial tachycardia or fibrillation also may occur. Mitral valve prolapse is associated with an increased incidence of false-positive exercise tests.

Routine chest x-ray films are rarely of diagnostic value, as the cardiac silhouette is usually normal in size and contour in both the asymptomatic patient and the patient with mild mitral regurgitation. Thoracic bony abnormalities are commonly seen, and the spine may be relatively straight on lateral view.

PLANS
Diagnostic
Differential Diagnosis

The presence of a midsystolic click followed by a late systolic murmur is diagnostic of mitral valve prolapse, especially if these auscultatory signs vary appropriately with physiologic and/or pharmacologic maneuvers. Conditions that may be confused with mitral valve prolapse include patients with either an extra systolic sound (click) or an apical systolic murmur. Patients with a bicuspid aortic valve have an early systolic ejection sound that does not vary with hemodynamic maneuvers and is audible at the apex as well as the second right intercostal space. Other rare causes of nonejection clicks include ventricular aneurysms, cardiac tumors, and atrial septal aneurysms. Multiple systolic clicks may be confused with a single-component pericardial friction rub. Patients with apical systolic murmurs, most frequently those with mitral regurgitation, but occasionally those with aortic stenosis, whose murmur radiates to the apex as it frequently does in the elderly, may also be confused with patients with mitral valve prolapse. A variety of etiologies of mitral regurgitation including rheumatic heart disease, papillary muscle dysfunction (due either to dilated cardiomyopathy or to coronary artery disease), and mitral annular calcification must

be excluded. Occasionally, patients with ventricular septal defects whose systolic murmurs radiate to the apex must be excluded.

Diagnostic Options

If the systolic click and murmur are not present or are equivocal, echocardiography is the definitive diagnostic test. Identification of mitral valve prolapse on the M-mode echocardiogram requires the presence of systolic posterior bowing (displacement) of either mitral leaflet. This abnormal posterior motion may be either holosystolic ("hammocking") or, more commonly, middle to late systolic ("question mark on side"). Two-dimensional echocardiography is more accurate, as it visualizes more of the mitral apparatus than the M-mode study, including each of the scallops as well as the thickness and motion of the leaflets. Prolapse appears as a superior and somewhat posterior systolic displacement of the leaflet(s) above the level of the mitral ring toward the left atrium. Because of the saddle-shaped nature of the mitral apparatus, the parasternal long-axis view, and not the apical four-chamber view, is the image that is considered diagnostic. Nevertheless, careful scanning in multiple plans from all available echocardiographic views should be used (Figure 15–39–1). Associated echocardiographic signs include excessive leaflet thickness, leaflet redundancy, elongated chordae tendineae, and a dilated mitral annulus. In addition, the tricuspid valve prolapses in approximately 20% of cases. Although echocardiography is highly specific for the diagnosis, a negative echocardiogram does not rule out mitral valve prolapse, because the test can have a false-negative rate of 10 to 20%. The Doppler modality is used to determine the presence and estimate the degree of mitral regurgitation and supports the diagnosis when regurgitation is at least of a moderate degree. The combined use of M-mode, two-dimensional, and Doppler echocardiography has been shown to diagnose correctly more than 90% of patients with auscultatory evidence of mitral valve prolapse.

Recommended Approach

If the auscultatory data lead one to a definite diagnosis, the echocardiogram should not be performed solely to confirm the diagnosis, as mild mitral valve prolapse in the absence of dynamic auscultatory findings is not diagnostic. A complete echocardiographic study, however, will

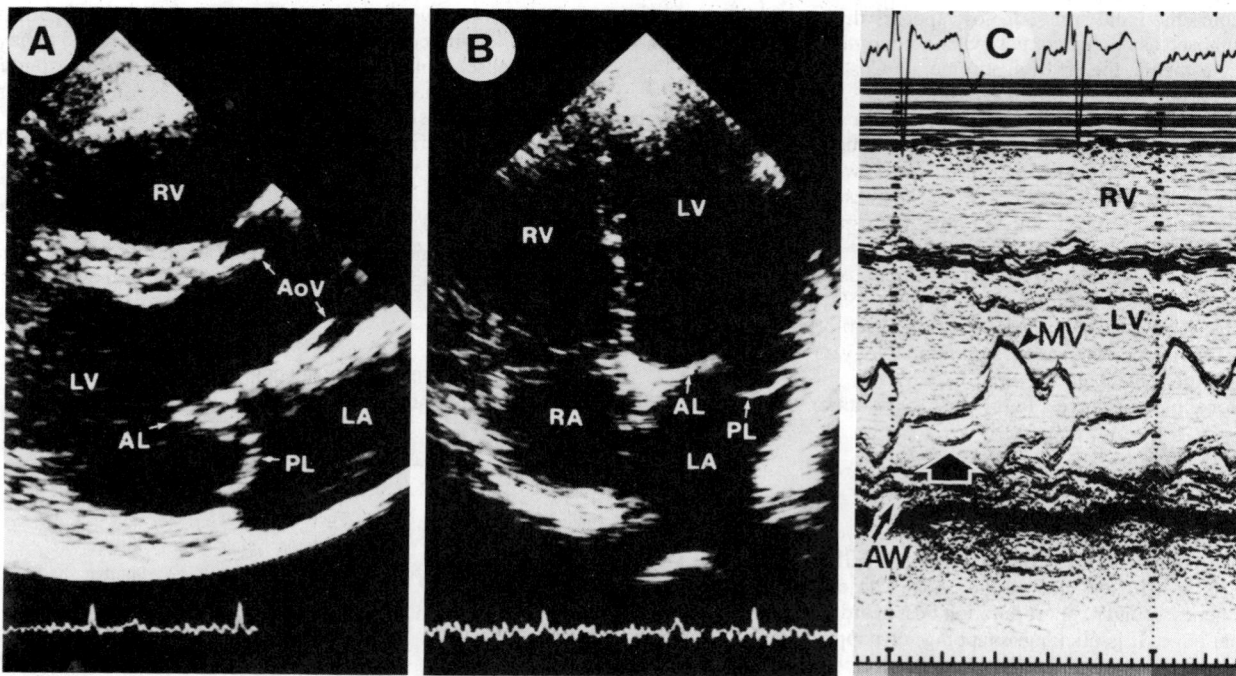

Figure 15–39–1. Echocardiogram from a 21-year-old woman with classic mitral valve prolapse. **A.** Two-dimensional parasternal long-axis view shows a slightly thickened posterior leaflet (PL) of the mitral valve bulging back (prolapsing) into the left atrium (LA). **B.** Two-dimensional apical four-chamber view also shows the posterior leaflet prolapsing into the left atrium. **C.** M-mode study shows that in early systole the mitral valve (MV) moves posteriorly (*arrow*) toward the left atrial wall (LAW) and finally coapts with the mitral valve at end systole. AL, anterior mitral leaflet; AoV, aortic valve; LV, left ventricle; RA, right atrium; RV, right ventricle.

help to evaluate leaflet morphology, estimate the degree of mitral regurgitation, identify associated tricuspid and aortic valve prolapse, determine left ventricular function, and estimate left atrial size. The occurrence of complications, especially infective endocarditis and moderate-to-severe mitral regurgitation, appears to be related to the presence of mitral leaflet thickening and redundancy as detected by echocardiography. There is thus a subgroup of patients with mitral valve prolapse and thickened (≥ 5 mm) leaflets who are at higher risk for complications that can be reliably identified by two-dimensional echocardiography. In selected patients, echocardiography is useful in following the course of mitral valve prolapse.

Therapeutic

Therapeutic Options

The asymptomatic patient with incidentally discovered mitral valve prolapse and a normal ECG, with or without prolapse detected by echocardiography, should be assured that this is a frequent finding in an otherwise normal individual that warrants no treatment and is almost always without consequence. Antibiotics should be given to patients with definite mitral prolapse detected by auscultation or echo–Doppler at the time of dental, gastrointestinal, genitourinary, or gynecologic procedures to help prevent the rare instance of infective endocarditis. Patients with minimal symptoms and a normal ECG should be reassured as to the generally excellent prognosis for life.

Symptomatic patients with disturbing palpitations or chest pain should be treated with a beta-adrenergic blocking agent. If the ECG is abnormal (ST–T changes, QT prolongation) or if arrhythmias are detected at the bedside, ambulatory ECG monitoring should be obtained. If the patient has symptoms on exercise, an exercise or stress ECG can be performed. Isolated T-wave abnormalities may normalize during or immediately after strenuous effort and ST–T segment changes suggestive of ischemia may be seen despite normal coronary arteriograms. In addition, during exercise, premature ventricular complexes may appear or increase in frequency. Ambulatory ECG monitoring, however, is a more sensitive method of detecting arrhythmias in patients with mitral valve prolapse. It may demonstrate premature ventricular complexes in many patients and even brief episodes of ventricular tachycardia in some. There is no relationship, however, between the presence of arrhythmias and the severity of prolapse.

The major complications of patients with mitral valve prolapse are the risk of developing infective endocarditis or progressive mitral regurgitation, and the very small, but real threat of sudden death. The latter seems to be greatest in the familiar form of mitral valve prolapse and in patients with the most severe grades of ventricular ectopy in association with T-wave inversion on the ECG. It would therefore seem reasonable to treat any dangerous arrhythmia detected. Although a beta-adrenergic blocking drug is the treatment of choice, quinidine or procainamide may be useful in selected cases. In a few patients, phenytoin (Dilantin) is useful. If the patient has sustained ventricular tachycardia, syncope with arrhythmias, or cardiac arrest with resuscitation, electrophysiologic studies to find an effective drug regimen are indicated. It is rare that such extreme measures are required. Patients with progressive, severe mitral regurgitation benefit from therapy with arterial vasodilators, diuretics, and digoxin. Ultimately, they may require valve replacement.

Recommended Approach

The primary responsibility of the physician in caring for an asymptomatic patient with idiopathic mitral valve prolapse is reassurance regarding the insignificance of the finding. The patient should be informed about the condition and the need for infective endocarditis prophylaxis (see Chapter 8–12) in a manner that does not precipitate anxiety and undue concern.

Symptomatic patients with mitral valve prolapse should be reassured as to the generally excellent prognosis for life. Patients with chest pain are treated with reassurance and a beta-adrenergic blocking agent. If palpitations and syncope are present, continuous ECG monitoring may be necessary; however, it is important to recognize that such patients may have these symptoms in the absence of arrhythmias.

FOLLOW-UP

The frequency of follow-up depends on the nature of the symptoms, the degree of mitral regurgitation, and the severity of arrhythmias. Patients with mitral valve prolapse should be followed periodically because there is some evidence that this may be a progressive disease, although most do not require frequent visits. Those with significant or progressive mitral regurgitation require semiannual to annual evaluation. In those requiring antiarrhythmic therapy, follow-up visits should be weekly until the arrhythmia is controlled or sufficiently reduced.

DISCUSSION

Prevalence

Mitral valve prolapse is perhaps the most common form of valve disease in the United States. It has a prevalence of 4 to 6% (range, 1–17%). Approximately 5% of routine autopsies have shown some redundancy of the mitral leaflets. There appears to be 2:1 female-to-male preponderance. Most instances of primary (idiopathic) mitral valve prolapse occur sporadically. The inheritance of the familial type appears to be autosomal dominant, with incomplete penetrance and reduced expressivity in the male and in the very young.

Related Basic Science

Genetics

The cause of the myxomatous transformation of the mitral valve is not known. The frequent association of mitral valve prolapse with joint laxity, musculoskeletal abnormalities, and distinctive anthropometric characteristics, as well as its presence in most cases of the Marfan and Ehlers–Danlos syndromes, suggests that this form of mitral valve prolapse may represent the cardiovascular manifestation of a generalized developmental disorder of connective tissue. This is based on the concept that because development of the mitral and tricuspid valves, septum secundum, thoracic vertebrae, ribs, and sternum occurs in the seventh week of embryonic life, there may be a common influence on growth patterns. Mild mitral valve prolapse may therefore simply be an anatomic variant and not a "disease" at all in otherwise normal young individuals. As mitral valve prolapse is associated with an array of psychiatric disorders, autonomic dysfunction, and elevation of plasma catecholamines, however, it has also been suggested that the valvular abnormality is part of a generalized neuroendocrine–cardiovascular abnormality. The secondary form of mitral valve prolapse occurs in some patients with secundum atrial septal defect. It also occurs occasionally in patients with rheumatic mitral valve disease and, rarely, in patients with coronary heart disease and papillary muscle dysfunction.

Anatomic Derangement

To understand the pathophysiologic mechanism that generates the click and late systolic murmur, the function of the mitral apparatus itself must be understood. Proper functioning of the mitral valve apparatus depends on the integrity of its components, including the leaflets, chordae tendineae, annulus, papillary muscles, and their supporting ventricular and atrial walls. During ventricular systole, the lack of support of any of these components allows a portion of the mitral leaflet to prolapse into an abnormal position in relation to the rest of the valve. When the leaflet is suddenly checked in movement, the resulting reverberation may generate a click. If there is sufficient prolapse, mitral regurgitation may occur. As the left ventricle continues to empty, the unsupported area of the mitral leaflet may extend further into the left atrium, progressively increasing the mitral regurgitation. In primary mitral valve prolapse, leaflet redundancy causes one or both leaflets to buckle posteriorly into the left atrium. In secondary mitral valve prolapse, ischemic heart disease, postinflammatory rheumatic carditis, and hypertrophic cardiomyopathy may cause posterior displacement of a normal-appearing mitral valve. Marked dehydration can induce mitral valve prolapse on echocardiography in some normal individuals.

Associated conditions include tricuspid valve prolapse and rarely aortic valve prolapse. Tricuspid valve prolapse can also occur as an isolated event. There is an increased incidence of secundum atrial septal defect and atrioventricular bypass tracts.

Several characteristic pathologic findings have been noted in the subset of patients with mitral valve prolapse who have died suddenly or who have required initial valve replacement. Grossly, the mitral valve leaflets are voluminous, thickened, and have an increased transparency. Either one or both leaflets may be affected; more commonly, the posterior leaflet alone is involved. The chordae tendineae are delicate, elongated, and attenuated. Microscopically, the most characteristic change is the marked mucopolysaccharide (myxomatous) proliferation of the spongiosa in the fibrosa layer of the mitral valve leaflets (cusps). This results in collagen dissolution and disruption with loss of leaflet support. The leaflets and chordae become weakened and cause the valve to prolapse or balloon into the left atrium during ventricular systole. Later, secondary fibrotic changes may occur in the leaflets, the chordae tendineae elongate, and fibrin deposits form on the atrial side of the mitral valve.

Physiologic or Metabolic Derangement

The timing of the click and the development of mitral regurgitation are dependent on the size of the left ventricle and on the velocity of emptying of the ventricle. Any maneuver that reduces left ventricular end-diastolic volume (e.g., standing or Valsalva strain phase) or increases the velocity of left ventricular contraction (e.g., amyl nitrite inhalation) causes the click to occur earlier and the systolic murmur to begin earlier. Maneuvers that increase ventricular diastolic volume or decrease contraction (e.g., squatting, hand grip, or beta blockade) cause the click and murmur to occur later in systole. Whether the systolic murmur becomes louder usually depends on the presence or absence of increased left ventricular systolic pressure. The occurrence of the click and murmur in mid- to late systole, when the majority of blood has been ejected from the ventricle, is evidence that the size of the left ventricular cavity and its relation to the length of the chordae tendineae play an important role in the pathophysiology of this condition. Therefore, in mitral valve prolapse, a geometric mismatch exists when the elongated chordae are in a relatively small left ventricular cavity as occurs in mid- to late systole when most of the ventricular volume has been ejected. That is why the click and murmur usually begin in the second half of systole.

Natural History and Its Modification with Treatment

Several retrospective natural history studies have shown that 60 to 80% of patients with mitral valve prolapse remain unchanged for the entire period of follow-up. In some studies there was no increase in deaths in an actuarial plot of patients with mitral valve prolapse compared with an age-matched population over a follow-up period of 10 to 40 years.

The prognosis for a patient with mitral valve prolapse depends to a large degree on whether the patient has the primary or secondary type. In the latter situation, the prognosis is determined largely by the particular condition or disease. In either case, however, the vast majority of patients never develop any of the serious complications, such as progressive mitral regurgitation, ruptured chordae tendineae, infective endocarditis, arrhythmias and sudden death, and thromboembolism with stroke.

Gradual progression of mitral regurgitation occurs in a small percentage of patients. In one natural history study over an 11-year period it occurred in 8% of patients, whereas it occurred in 3 to 19% in other studies. Most of these patients were men who had a "floppy valve" syndrome characterized by redundant valve leaflets and myxomatous transformation requiring valve surgery. In patients with mitral valve prolapse, ruptured chordae tendineae occurs spontaneously or as a result of infective endocarditis. The risk of endocarditis varies from 0 to 8%.

The most frequent complication of mitral valve prolapse is the occurrence of a cardiac arrhythmia, usually ventricular ectopy. The most important clinical problem however, is to identify those few patients (0–2% in long-term natural history studies) who are at greatest risk of sudden death. This has been accomplished mainly by continuous ECG monitoring. It appears that the patients at greatest risk are young or middle-aged women with a murmur, an abnormal ECG, multiple arrhythmias on ambulatory monitoring, and marked prolapse usually of both leaflets on the echocardiogram, and men over 50 years of age. In a few patients in whom arrhythmias were recorded during the time of sudden death, ventricular tachycardia deteriorating to ventricular fibrillation was responsible.

Thromboembolism, more specifically fibrin embolism, is a recently recognized complication of mitral valve prolapse. Several studies have linked cerebral and retinal ischemic events to mitral valve prolapse. The prevalence rate for cerebral infarction in patients with mitral valve prolapse is estimated to be four times greater than in the normal population, and platelet survival times may be abnormally short in patients with mitral valve prolapse and a history of stroke, compared with patients with mitral valve prolapse but without a history of stroke. Antiplatelet drugs (aspirin) or anticoagulants (warfarin) are indicated in those patients who have had a transient ischemic episode, stroke, and/or monocular amaurosis fugax in association with mitral valve prolapse.

Prevention

Mitral valve prolapse cannot currently be prevented, but many of the sequelae might be avoided by managing the condition as outlined. Most importantly, undue disability should be prevented by reassurance and proper education of the patient and family.

Cost Containment

Cost can be reduced by not routinely requesting an echocardiogram to confirm a well-documented clinical diagnosis and by not routinely prescribing a beta-adrenergic blocking agent for asymptomatic patients.

REFERENCES

Barlow JB, Pocock WA, Marchand P. The significance of late systolic murmurs. Am Heart J 1963;66:443.

Cheitlin MD, Byrd RC. Prolapsed mitral valve: The commonest valve disease? Curr Prob Cardiol 1984;8:1.

Felner JM. Determining the significance of mitral valve prolapse. In: Miller DD, ed. Clinical cardiac imaging. New York: McGraw-Hill, 1989:447.

Krivokapich J, Child JS, Dadourian BJ, Perloff JK. Reassessment of echocardiographic criteria for diagnosis of mitral valve prolapse. Am J Cardiol 1988;61:131.

Marks AR, Choong CY, Sanfilippo AJ, et al. Identification of high-risk and low-risk subgroups of patients with mitral-valve prolapse. N Engl J Med 1989;320:1031.

Nishimura R, McGoon MD, Shub C, et al. Echocardiographically documented mitral valve prolapse: Long-term follow-up of 237 patients. N Engl J Med 1985;313:1305.

Schlant RC, Felner JM, Miklozek CL, et al. Mitral valve prolapse. Dis Mon 1980;26:1.

Wooley CF, Baker PB, Kolibash AJ, et al. The floppy, myxomatous mitral valve, mitral valve prolapse, and mitral regurgitation. Prog Cardiovasc Dis 1991;33:397.

CHAPTER 15–40

Acquired Tricuspid Stenosis

Douglas C. Morris, M.D.

DEFINITION

Tricuspid stenosis is obstruction to diastolic flow across the tricuspid valve sufficient to cause an elevation in right atrial pressure.

ETIOLOGY

Tricuspid stenosis may be caused by rheumatic valvulitis, occasionally in Ebstein's anomaly, and congenital atresia.

CRITERIA FOR DIAGNOSIS
Suggestive

The following constellation of physical findings strongly suggests the diagnosis of tricuspid stenosis: a prominent *a* wave coupled with a small *v* wave in the deep jugular veins, absence of a right ventricular lift, and a low-pitched middiastolic or presystolic murmur near the lower end of the sternum. The murmur is accentuated during inspiration.

Definitive

Cardiac catheterization is generally needed to prove the presence of tricuspid stenosis. Documentation of a mean resting pressure difference across the tricuspid valve of 3 mm Hg or greater or a calculated valve orifice area of less than 1.5 cm^2 establishes the diagnosis of significant tricuspid stenosis.

CLINICAL MANIFESTATION
Subjective

The clinical presentation that is most suggestive of tricuspid stenosis is the patient who has severe mitral stenosis but relatively few symptoms. The symptoms most often attributed to tricuspid stenosis are easy fatigability and abdominal discomfort due to hepatomegaly or ascites; exertional dyspnea is an occasional complaint. Fluttering in the neck due to perception of the giant *a* wave and swelling secondary to peripheral edema may be observed.

Objective
Physical Examination

In patients with sinus rhythm, the most perceptible physical finding is a large *a* wave in the jugular venous pulsations. This large *a* wave can also reflect pulmonary hypertension or pulmonic stenosis, but these conditions can usually be excluded in the absence of a right ventricular lift. Although the auscultatory features of tricuspid stenosis are the most diagnostic physical findings, they are often obscured by the more apparent auscultatory features of the almost universally associated cardiac condition, mitral stenosis. Auscultatory features of tricuspid stenosis include splitting of the first heart sound secondary to delayed closure of the tricuspid component and a low-pitched middiastolic or presystolic murmur heard at the end of the sternum. The diastolic murmur typically increases in intensity during inspiration.

Routine Laboratory Abnormalities

Tall peaked P waves in the absence of right ventricular hypertrophy are the most characteristic electrocardiographic feature of isolated tricuspid stenosis. First-degree heart block and atrial fibrillation are also common. An electrocardiographic pattern that is more specific but not very sensitive for tricuspid stenosis is small QRS complexes of rsR' configuration in the right precordial leads coupled with P waves of amplitude greater than that of the QRS complex.

The roentgenographic pattern most characteristic of tricuspid stenosis is dilation of the right atrium without significant enlargement of the pulmonary arteries. There may be evidence of mitral stenosis including left atrial enlargement and pulmonary congestion.

PLANS
Diagnostic
Differential Diagnosis

The usual differential diagnosis of tricuspid stenosis includes mitral stenosis, right atrial myxoma, and increased flow across a normal tricuspid valve secondary to a large shunt from an atrial septal defect. Congenital tricuspid atresia and Ebstein's anomaly are discussed in Chapters 15–33 and 15–34.

Diagnostic Options

A definitive diagnosis of tricuspid stenosis must rest on the Doppler echocardiography findings or the hemodynamic findings from a simultaneous right atrial and right ventricular recording.

Stenosis of the tricuspid valve is manifested on echocardiogram by a pattern of motion identical to that described for mitral stenosis. If two tricuspid leaflets are visualized and both fulfill the criteria as outlined for mitral stenosis (see Chapter 15–37), the specificity of the findings is very high. Specificity is usually reduced, however, because of inability to visualize more than one tricuspid leaflet. Doppler echocardiography can give an estimate of the diastolic gradient across the valve. At cardiac catheterization, the diagnosis of tricuspid stenosis rests on finding a mean resting transvalvular pressure difference of 3 mm Hg or more and/or an effective orifice area of less than 1.5 cm^2. Angiography should be performed in selected patients to exclude a right atrial myxoma as the source of this obstruction.

Recommended Approach

As tricuspid stenosis occurs almost exclusively in the presence of mitral stenosis, all patients with mitral stenosis should be examined with this association in mind. Doppler echocardiography may detect and assess the gradient across the tricuspid valve. Any hint of the coexistence of tricuspid stenosis warrants the simultaneous measurement of right atrial and right ventricular pressures preferably with a double-lumen catheter and preferably at the same time at which the pressure difference across the mitral valve is measured. The small transvalvular pressure differences often associated with tricuspid stenosis may be difficult to measure accurately on pullback recordings.

Therapeutic
Therapeutic Options

Management of a patient with tricuspid stenosis is generally dictated by coexisting mitral stenosis. Treatment should include antibiotic prophylaxis for endocarditis. Treatment of tricuspid atresia and Ebstein's anomaly is discussed in Chapters 15–33 and 15–34.

Recommended Approach

Prior to surgical intervention for mitral stenosis, management is unaltered by the presence of tricuspid disease. At the time of surgery, moderately severe (1- to 1.5-cm^2 valve area) and severe (less than 1-cm^2 valve area) tricuspid stenosis should be corrected by commissurotomy or, if necessary, by valve replacement.

We thank Dr. Henry A. Liberman for his contribution to this chapter in the previous edition of this book.

FOLLOW-UP

The frequency of follow-up in tricuspid stenosis is generally dictated by the associated mitral valve disease. The physician, however, should avoid mistiming the frequency of follow-up visits, which can occur by underestimating the severity of mitral stenosis because of the coexistence of tricuspid stenosis.

DISCUSSION

Prevalence and Incidence

Rheumatic heart disease, and therefore rheumatic involvement of the tricuspid valve, is uncommon in the United States. Clinically recognized tricuspid stenosis is recognized in about 5% of patients with rheumatic heart disease. Rheumatic tricuspid stenosis never occurs in the absence of mitral stenosis.

Related Basic Science

Anatomic Derangement

Although rare instances of tricuspid stenosis secondary to carcinoid syndrome, fibroelastosis, endomyocardial fibrosis, systemic lupus erythematosus, and congenital heart disease have been reported, the condition is almost always secondary to rheumatic fever. Typically, the tricuspid valve leaflets show fusion of the free edges, which are thickened yet pliable. The chordae are infrequently severely deformed and calcification is rare.

Physiologic or Metabolic Derangement

The major hemodynamic alterations produced by tricuspid stenosis are a decrease in cardiac output and an increase in the right atrial pressures. Reduction of cardiac output in patients with tricuspid stenosis is typically greater than that with mitral stenosis.

Natural History and its Modification with Treatment

The natural history of tricuspid stenosis is determined primarily by the coexisting mitral stenosis. Unrecognized and uncorrected rheumatic tricuspid stenosis, however, can have a deleterious effect on the results of mitral valve surgery. In the carcinoid syndrome, cardiac failure due to tricuspid valve involvement is a cause of significant morbidity and mortality. There have been a few reports of tricuspid valve replacement in this situation.

Prevention

Prevention of most tricuspid stenosis is tied to prevention of acute rheumatic fever.

Cost Containment

Recognition of this condition in the patient with mitral stenosis and a diligent search for its existence can prevent the added cost and risk of repeated surgery in the patient who responds poorly to mitral valve surgery because of unrecognized tricuspid involvement.

REFERENCES

Kitcin A, Turner R. Diagnosis and treatment of tricuspid stenosis. Br Heart J 1964;26:354.

Perloff JK, Roberts WC. The mitral apparatus: Functional anatomy of mitral regurgitation. Circulation 1972;46:227.

Pearlman AS. Role of echocardiography in the diagnosis and evaluation of severity of mitral and tricuspid stenosis. Circulation 1991;84:1193.

Rackley CE, Wallace RB, Edwards JE, et al. Tricuspid and pulmonary valve disease. In: Schlant RC, Alexander RW, O'Rourke RA, et al., eds. Hurst's the heart. 8th ed. New York: McGraw-Hill, 1994:1519.

CHAPTER 15–41

Tricuspid Valve Regurgitation

Douglas C. Morris, M.D.

DEFINITION

Tricuspid valve regurgitation is ejection of a portion of the right ventricular stroke volume into the right atrium due to incompetence of the tricuspid apparatus.

ETIOLOGY

Isolated tricuspid valve regurgitation is extremely infrequent. The most common cause is infective endocarditis; other causes are usually associated with other cardiac lesions. These common conditions include rheumatic valvulitis, Ebstein's anomaly, atrioventricular cushion defects, carcinoid syndrome, and trauma.

Tricuspid valve regurgitation is more commonly caused by left ventricular disease, lung disease, and pulmonary hypertension. This condition is thought to develop because the weak anatomic support structure of the right ventricular papillary muscles and chordae tendineae cannot adequately anchor the leaflets as the right ventricle dilates in response to pulmonary hypertension. In addition, the tricuspid annulus actually dilates in some patients with long-standing tricuspid valve regurgitation. Functional tricuspid valve regurgitation may occur in patients with left-sided heart failure from any cause, mitral valve disease, or chronic or acute cor pulmonale.

CRITERIA FOR DIAGNOSIS

Suggestive

A diagnosis of tricuspid valve regurgitation can be made with reasonable certainty on documentation of any one of the following: (1) prominent systolic regurgitant venous pulsations in the internal jugular veins in the neck, (2) inspiratory augmentation of a holosystolic murmur heard best to the left of the lower sternum, (3) a pulsatile liver, (4) and an enlarged right atrium on chest x-ray film.

Definitive

A diagnosis of tricuspid valve regurgitation can be firmly established if all the previously mentioned physical findings are present; by documentation of regurgitation on Doppler echocardiography; or by a pressure curve in the right atrium resembling that of the right ventricle (obliteration of the normal systolic decline in right atrial pressure by a positive regurgitant wave).

CLINICAL MANIFESTATIONS

Subjective

The symptoms of tricuspid valve regurgitation are not distinctive, but usually include easily fatigability and exertional dyspnea. One rather distinctive, but actually quite uncommon, clinical course that should suggest the development of tricuspid valve regurgitation is sudden lessening of pulmonary congestion in the patient with long-standing left-sided heart (particularly mitral valve) disease.

We thank Dr. Henry A. Liberman for his contribution to this chapter in the previous edition of this book.

Objective

Physical Examination

No single physical finding is universally present in tricuspid valve regurgitation. Although a systolic murmur audible along the lower left sternal border is one of the earliest clinical features, it may be absent even in severe tricuspid valve regurgitation or may be obscured by the other cardiac murmurs. An inspiratory increase in this murmur (Carvallo's sign) establishes its tricuspid origin, but this finding is usually difficult to elicit, particularly in patients with atrial fibrillation. A positive systolic wave (regurgitant wave) in the jugular veins is a later manifestation than the murmur, but it may be difficult to see in some patients with markedly distended veins characteristic of the late stages of tricuspid valve regurgitation. An enlarged pulsatile liver is found only in severe disease.

Routine Laboratory Abnormalities

Atrial fibrillation is commonly present, with a prevalence greater than 75% in severe tricuspid valve regurgitation. There is also an increased prevalence of right bundle-branch block, in marked contrast to the much lower prevalence of right bundle-branch block in pure mitral valve disease.

Patients with tricuspid valve regurgitation usually have cardiomegaly on chest roentgenogram. In this setting, right atrial enlargement is suggested when the distance between the midline and right heart border is greater than 4 cm.

Examination of the blood and urine reveals no diagnostic abnormalities.

PLANS

Diagnostic

Differential Diagnosis

The major differential is between tricuspid valve and mitral valve regurgitation. The murmurs associated with these two conditions are similar in character and have overlapping auscultatory areas. A right atrial myxoma and ventricular septal defect should also be considered in the differential.

Diagnostic Options

Clinically significant tricuspid valve regurgitation can be diagnosed at the bedside. Other more sensitive techniques for diagnosing tricuspid valve regurgitation include echocardiographic microcavitation technique, radionuclide techniques, Doppler echocardiography, and right atrial pressure recordings.

Recommended Approach

The diagnosis of tricuspid valve regurgitation is based on the presence of any of the previously mentioned physical findings. Unless valvular surgery is contemplated, further diagnostic workup to confirm the diagnosis is unwarranted. It is worthwhile, however, to establish a cause for the tricuspid regurgitation. The existence of other rheumatic valvular disease suggests a rheumatic etiology. The presence of cyanosis, an ostium secundum atrial septal defect, and an electrocardiogram with giant P waves and right ventricular conduction delay suggests Ebstein's anomaly. The presence of paroxysmal flushing, diarrhea, and pulmonic stenosis suggests carcinoid syndrome. Evidence of blunt chest trauma and myocardial contusion suggests traumatic rupture of a chorda tendineae. Fever and recurrent pulmonary infiltrates in a drug addict suggest infective endocarditis of the tricuspid valve. Secondary or functional tricuspid valve regurgitation must be considered in those patients with chronic cor pulmonale or chronic left-sided heart failure from hypertensive heart disease, coronary disease, cardiomyopathy, or even aortic valve disease.

Direct evidence of tricuspid valve regurgitation can be obtained by color-flow echo–Doppler demonstrating regurgitation into the right atrium. The most reliable evidence of tricuspid valve regurgitation at cardiac catheterization is the finding of so-called ventricularization of the right atrial pressure curve. This ventricularization, or a prominent positive wave throughout systole, is the result of a loss of the normal x descent and the development of an early positive regurgitant (R) wave. Right ventricular angiography is relatively unreliable in establishing the diagnosis of mild tricuspid valve regurgitation because the catheter crosses the valve, and during injection there is frequent regurgitation of the catheter into the atrium and frequent stimulation of ventricular ectopy.

In the patient with impending surgery for left-sided valvular disease, it is important to establish whether the associated tricuspid valve regurgitation is secondary (functional) or organic. This distinction is difficult and at times impossible. Two helpful distinguishing features that suggest the regurgitation is organic are pulmonary artery systolic pressure below 60 mm Hg and a pressure difference between the right atrium and right ventricle during diastole.

Therapeutic

Therapeutic Options

The therapy for tricuspid valve regurgitation is usually treatment of the conditions leading to right-sided heart failure. The therapeutic options applicable directly to tricuspid valve regurgitation are limited to diuretics. The surgical options include annuloplasty, valve replacement, and tricuspid valve excision.

Recommended Approach

The hemodynamic burden imposed by tricuspid valve regurgitation is usually well tolerated. The usual approach is to use diuretics for patients with bothersome symptoms. Management in multivalvular disease is tricuspid annuloplasty; valve replacement is reserved for severe organic regurgitation. Occasionally, patients with drug addiction and infective endocarditis of the tricuspid valve require total excision of the valve.

FOLLOW-UP

The timing of the follow-up of the patient with multivalvular disease is determined by the severity of the disease of the left-sided valves that are involved. The presence of tricuspid valve regurgitation in such cases demands only that the physician more closely monitor liver size and function, abdominal girth, degree of dependent edema, and body weight. The same parameters should be monitored in isolated tricuspid valve regurgitation.

DISCUSSION

Prevalence

The most common form of tricuspid valve regurgitation is functional secondary to right-sided heart failure. The next most frequent entity is tricuspid valve prolapse. Tricuspid valve prolapse usually occurs in association with mitral valve prolapse and is present in about one third of these patients. As mitral valve prolapse occurs in approximately 6% of the population, the prevalence of tricuspid valve prolapse would be estimated to be 2 to 3%. Rheumatic involvement of the tricuspid valve is rare in the United States, but still occurs in areas where rheumatic fever is rampant.

Related Basic Science

Anatomic Derangement

Functional tricuspid valve regurgitation is generally ascribed to annular dilation secondary to right ventricular dilation. Rheumatic tricuspid valvulitis causes fibrosis contracture, thickening and fusion of the leaflets. Right ventricular infarction causes tricuspid valve regurgitation as a result of infarction and dysfunction of the papillary muscle and its free wall attachment. Carcinoid heart disease causes thickening of the leaflets and chordae, resulting in reduced mobility and separation of the leaflets.

Physiologic or Metabolic Derangement

With onset of tricuspid valve regurgitation there is a significant increase in both systolic and mean right atrial pressure that is reflected back into the systemic venous system. This elevation in systemic venous pressure is frequently sufficient to produce peripheral edema and ascites.

The hemodynamic burden of tricuspid valve regurgitation is generally relatively well tolerated. In general, the clinical course in patients with secondary tricuspid valve regurgitation appears to deteriorate more rapidly than in those with organic regurgitation. This difference most certainly reflects the associated pulmonary hypertension and right-sided heart failure secondary to severe disease of the left side of the heart.

Natural History and Its Modification with Treatment

The clinical course of a patient with tricuspid valve regurgitation depends on the underlying etiology. If tricuspid valve regurgitation is secondary to left-sided heart failure, the prognosis is relatively poor but depends on response to medical therapy and whether the left-sided valvular heart disease is amenable to surgery (see Chapters 15–37 and 15–38).

If tricuspid valve regurgitation is a secondary manifestation of cor pulmonale, the prognosis is poor but depends on the response to specific therapy such as bronchodilators (see Chapter 13–21).

The prognosis of patients with infective endocarditis of the tricuspid valve depends on the response to medical therapy and, if necessary, valve replacement. Overall, the natural history of infective endocarditis of the tricuspid valve is usually poor (see Chapter 8–12). Many patients with infective endocarditis of the tricuspid valve continue the abuse of intravenous drugs, from which they have recurrent complications.

Prevention

Functional tricuspid valve regurgitation can be prevented by appropriate management of the left-sided heart conditions that lead to pulmonary hypertension. This appropriate management would include proper timing of surgery for mitral and aortic valve disease. Control of infective endocarditis of the tricuspid valve is tied to control of intravenous drug use.

Cost Containment

Cost containment is related to the prevention of this condition as outlined above and to the recognition that the diagnosis of the condition can be reliably made at the bedside without expensive confirmatory tests.

REFERENCES

Edwards JE. The spectrum and clinical significance of tricuspid regurgitation. Pract Cardiol 1980;6:86.

Kay JH. Surgical treatment of tricuspid regurgitation. Ann Thorac Surg 1992;53:1132.

Pellegrini A, Columbo T, Donatelli E, et al. Evaluation and treatment of secondary tricuspid insufficiency. Eur J Cardiothorac Surg 1992;6:288.

Rackley CE, Wallace RB, Edwards JE, et al. Tricuspid and pulmonary valve disease. In: Schlant RC, Alexander RW, O'Rourke RA, et al., eds. Hurst's the heart. 8th ed. New York: McGraw-Hill, 1994:1519.

Wong M, Matsumura M, Kutsuzawa S, et al. The value of Doppler echocardiography in the treatment of tricuspid regurgitation in patients with mitral valve replacement. J Thorac Cardiovasc Surg 1990;99:1003.

CHAPTER 15–42

Infective Endocarditis (See Section 8, Chapter 12)

CHAPTER 15–43

Stable Angina Pectoris

David Waters, M.D.

DEFINITION

Angina pectoris is defined as a discomfort in the chest or an adjacent area, usually lasting from 1 to 10 minutes, caused by transient myocardial ischemia. Angina is classified as stable when the pattern of symptoms has not changed within the last 60 days.

ETIOLOGY

Transient myocardial ischemia develops when myocardial oxygen demand exceeds the supply delivered by coronary blood flow. Coronary atherosclerosis that has advanced enough to narrow severely the lumen of at least one coronary artery is the usual cause. The coronary narrowings limit the normal increase in blood flow required when stressors, most commonly physical activity, increase myocardial work and, thus, the need for increased blood supply. Rarely, myocardial ischemia can be caused by other types of coronary artery disease. Aortic valve disease and hypertrophic cardiomyopathy may also precipitate ischemia, because coronary perfusion pressure is reduced in comparison to the pressure load that burdens the left ventricle.

Myocardial ischemia is often silent, as discussed in Chapter 15–46. In some patients all episodes of myocardial ischemia are asymptomatic, and in others myocardial ischemia is always associated with angina.

Most patients have both symptomatic and silent episodes, with silent episodes the majority.

CRITERIA FOR DIAGNOSIS
Suggestive

The most important component of the diagnosis is the patient's description of the symptom. Angina is a discomfort and not a sharp pain; words commonly used to describe it include "tightness," "burning," "pressure," "squeezing," and "aching." Classically, angina is retrosternal in location and radiates to the arms or neck. The discomfort is sometimes located only in the arm, neck, jaw, back, or epigastrium. A pain in a small, circumscribed area that the patient points to is not angina. Typically, angina is provoked by physical exertion and relieved within a few minutes by rest or sublingual nitroglycerin. For many patients the angina threshold is relatively fixed and thus angina is predictable. Mental or emotional stress can also precipitate angina; cold or a copious meal often lowers the threshold at which exercise precipitates angina. Episodic chest pain that lasts longer than 15 minutes and has no clear relation to physical activity is probably not angina.

Chest pain is most likely to be angina in patients who are most likely to have coronary atherosclerosis. A high index of suspicion is appropriate in evaluating chest pain in patients already known to have coronary atherosclerosis: those with previous myocardial infarction or coronary bypass surgery, for example. At the other extreme, chest pain is un-

---

See Appendix 7, Exercise Stress Electrocardiogram, by J. David Talley, M.D.

likely to be angina in a premenopausal woman without coronary risk factors. Coronary disease manifests itself in women about a decade later than in men; the initial symptom of coronary disease in women is more often angina and less often myocardial infarction, compared with men.

Definitive

A definitive diagnosis of angina can be made when the history is typical and it would not be surprising for the patient to have coronary disease. In a 70-year-old with the characteristic symptoms and multiple risk factors for coronary atherosclerosis, the probability that coronary disease is the cause of the chest pain exceeds 90% and tests to confirm the diagnosis are not necessary; however, in a 50-year-old without multiple risk factors, in whom the symptoms of angina are not completely typical, the diagnosis is not certain. As discussed below under Plans, coronary arteriography should be performed in some such patients, both for diagnosis and to orient treatment. But if symptoms are minimal and probability of coronary disease is intermediate, an exercise test, often with a nuclear perfusion study, is indicated to confirm the diagnosis. A common and serious error is to diagnose and treat angina when the diagnosis is not definitive.

CLINICAL MANIFESTATIONS
Subjective

In addition to the features described above that are important for diagnosis, angina must be evaluated in terms of its severity and its impact on the patient's life. Many patients who are in fact quite restricted by their angina have only rare episodes, because they have curtailed their physical and social activities to avoid attacks. A degree of angina that might be acceptable to an inactive, elderly patient might be intolerable to a younger, more active individual. The Canadian Cardiovascular Society classification, listed in Table 15–43–1, is widely used to categorize the severity of stable angina. Stable angina is often the only symptom of coronary disease present in a patient; however, dyspnea on exertion may coexist, raising the possibility that left ventricular failure is also present, either chronically or transiently as a consquence of transient myocardial ischemia. Syncope in a patient with angina suggests severe aortic valve disease, hypertrophic cardiomyopathy, variant (Prinzmetal's) angina, or ventricular tachycardia as a consequence of previous infarction. Symptoms of ischemia in other vascular distributions, such as intermittent claudication and transient cerebral ischemic attacks, can sometimes be elicited from patients with angina.

The major coronary risk factors—cigarette smoking, diabetes, hyperlipidemia, hypertension, and family history of premature coronary disease—should be documented carefully, including their response to treatment. If the doctor does not pay careful attention to risk factors, it is unlikely the patient will. Controlling and eliminating these risk factors are the therapy that will have the greatest effect long term for most patients with stable angina.

Objective
Physical Examination

The physical examination of a patient with angina due to coronary disease may be entirely normal. Abnormalities caused by risk factors should be sought out and documented: obesity, hypertension, retinopathy, xanthelasma, and xanthoma. Vascular bruits are objective evidence of atherosclerosis outside the coronary circulation. The cardiac examination may be entirely normal. A sustained apical impulse indicating left ventricular hypertrophy, an anterior dyskinetic movement due to previous infarction, a ventricular gallop related to left ventricular dysfunction, or a paradoxically split second heart sound might be found in a patient with stable angina.

Routine Laboratory Abnormalities

The resting electrocardiogram is often normal but may reveal left ventricular hypertrophy or signs of previous infarction. ST and T-wave abnormalities may be due to ischemia, postischemic dysfunction, or ventricular hypertrophy, or may be unrelated to cardiac disease. Recording an electrocardiogram during a spontaneous episode of angina provides useful diagnostic and prognostic information: a normal tracing reduces the probability that the chest pain is due to myocardial ischemia, but by no means eliminates the possibility. Reversible ST depression during an angina episode confirms myocardial ischemia as the cause.

Routine laboratory tests may reveal evidence of diabetes or hyperlipidemia.

PLANS
Diagnostic
Differential Diagnosis

Some of the more common conditions that may cause chest pain and be considered in the differential diagnosis of stable angina are listed in Table 15–43–2. As discussed above, a definitive diagnosis of stable

TABLE 15–43–2. DIFFERENTIAL DIAGNOSIS OF CHEST PAIN

Cardiac causes
  Stable angina
    Coronary atherosclerosis
    Aortic valve disease
    Hypertrophic cardiomyopathy
    Syndrome X (myocardial ischemia with normal coronaries by arteriography)
  Unstable angina
    Coronary atherosclerosis
  Variant (Prinzmetal's) angina
    Coronary artery spasm ± atherosclerosis
  Myocardial infarction
  Dissecting aortic aneurysm
  Pericarditis

Gastrointestinal causes
  Esophageal reflux
  Esophageal spasm
  Hiatal hernia
  Esophageal motility disorders
  Peptic ulcer
  Biliary colic
  Pancreatitis

Pulmonary causes
  Pneumothorax
  Pulmonary embolus
  Pulmonary hypertension
  Pleurisy

Other causes
  Intercostal and costosternal pain (including Tietze's syndrome)
  Cervical radiculitis
  Herpes zoster
  Panic attacks
  Neurocirculatory asthenia

TABLE 15–43–1. CANADIAN CARDIOVASCULAR SOCIETY ANGINA CLASSIFICATION

I. Ordinary physical activity, such as walking and climbing stairs, does not cause angina. Angina results from strenuous or rapid or prolonged exertion at work or recreation.

II. Slight limitation of ordinary activity. Walking or climbing stairs rapidly, walking uphill, walking or stair climbing after meals, in cold, in wind, or when under emotional stress, or only during the few hours after awakening. Walking more than two blocks on the level and climbing more than one flight of ordinary stairs at a normal pace and under normal conditions.

III. Marked limitations of ordinary physical activity. Walking one or two blocks on the level and climbing more than one flight under normal conditions.

IV. Inability to carry on any physical activity without discomfort—anginal syndrome *may be* present at rest.

Modified from Campeau L. Circulation 1976;54:522. Letter to the editor. Reproduced with permission of the author and the American Heart Association.

angina can be made in many patients based on the history alone, and diagnostic testing is not needed to confirm the diagnosis. In most patients with stable angina, however, the problem must be resolved to a higher level: further testing is indicated to ascertain the best initial treatment.

Diagnostic Options

Stress Testing. A bewildering variety of stress test procedures are available to assess patients for myocardial ischemia. Any of the stressors listed in Table 15–43–3 can be combined with one or more of the methods of assessment. Treadmill exercise testing with electrocardiographic monitoring of the ST segment is most widely used; it is the least expensive and provides objective confirmation of the patient's functional capacity. Exercise testing provides limited diagnostic information in some settings, however. When the pretest likelihood that coronary disease is the cause of chest pain is very high, such as in a patient with typical angina and previous myocardial infarction, exercise testing may provide *prognostic* data, but adds no *diagnostic* information. When the pretest likelihood of coronary disease is very low, such as in a young patient with no risk factors and atypical pain, exercise testing is usually unhelpful because a false-positive result is more likely than a true-positive result.

For patients who cannot perform enough physical exercise to stress the heart adequately, pharmacologic testing with dipyridamole, dobutamine, or adenosine can be a useful alternative. When the ST-segment response to exercise is unreliable, for example, in patients with a left bundle-branch block, left ventricular hypertrophy, a pacemaker, or digitalis, other methods of assessing myocardial ischemia must be substituted. Nuclear perfusion imaging has a higher sensitivity and specificity than the ST segment does, and provides much additional information, albeit at a higher cost. The number, size, and severity of perfusion defects predict the risk of future coronary events. A normal maximal exercise perfusion study indicates that the risk of a future coronary event is extremely low, even if underlying coronary disease is present, and should usually obviate any need for coronary arteriography.

Stress testing in patients with only mild stable angina often reveals high-risk indicators. Patients who develop signs of myocardial ischemia at low heart rates or low workloads, a fall in blood pressure during exercise, marked (>2 mm) or prolonged (>5 min) ST depression, large or multiple perfusion defects, pulmonary uptake of radioisotope, left ventricular dilation or a marked fall in ejection fraction, or ventricular tachycardia related to ischemia are at increased risk and probably have severe coronary disease. Unless a compelling contraindication is present, they should undergo coronary arteriography even if their symptoms are not severe enough to warrant it, because coronary revascularization could improve their survival.

TABLE 15–43–3. CARDIAC STRESS TESTING METHODS

Stressors
  Exercise
    Treadmill
    Bicycle
  Dipyridamole (Persantin)
  Dobutamine (± atropine)
  Adenosine (Adenocard)
Assessment of myocardial ischemia
  Electrocardiogram
    ST-segment depression
  Nuclear perfusion imaging
    Agents: ^{201}Tl, ^{99m}Tc Sestamibi
    Modalities: planar, single photon emission computed tomography (SPECT)
    Endpoints: fixed defects, reversible defects, pulmonary uptake, transient left ventricular dilation
  Radioisotopic left ventriculography
  Echocardiography
Physiologic variables
  Chest pain and other symptoms
  Heart rate and blood pressure response
  Arrhythmias

Left Ventricular Function. An assessment of regional and global left ventricular function is helpful in patients with stable angina; this information can be provided by radioisotopic left ventriculography or echocardiography. Echocardiography also defines the sizes of the other cardiac chambers and detects valvular abnormalities with a high degree of accuracy. As ejection fraction decreases below 40%, mortality in patients with coronary disease begins to increase in an almost exponential fashion. An ejection fraction below 20% portends a poor prognosis. Occasionally, such a finding is a complete surprise in a patient with stable angina, because of a lack of symptoms or suggestive physical findings. Regional left ventricular dysfunction is usually irreversible and the consequence of previous infarction; however, myocardial hibernation may cause regional hypokinesis or akinesis. Recognizing this condition is important because restoring blood flow with coronary angioplasty or bypass surgery can dramatically ameliorate regional function. Improved ventricular function should improve survival and may eliminate symptoms of heart failure. Hibernating myocardium usually improves its systolic function in response to dobutamine stress echocardiography and takes up thallium during a rest injection.

Coronary Arteriography. The extent and severity of coronary disease can be defined only with coronary arteriography; however, this test should not be ordered without clear justification because it is expensive and is associated with a small but definite risk of serious complications. A normal coronary arteriogram is often very useful because it orients the diagnosis toward other causes of chest pain (Table 15–43–2). Typical angina with a normal coronary arteriogram in a patient with objective evidence of myocardial ischemia has been termed syndrome X. The extent and severity of coronary disease carry important prognostic and therapeutic implications. Taken together with an assessment of left ventricular function and myocardial ischemia, they determine which therapies are feasible and which is preferable.

Recommended Approach

The diagnostic approach to chest pain is somewhat controversial, with some authorities recommending widespread noninvasive testing to select patients for coronary arteriography, and others recommending coronary arteriography as the first step in most cases. It is widely agreed that patients with stable angina after a myocardial infarction or after bypass surgery or patients with an unacceptable degree of angina with medical treatment need a coronary arteriogram, unless there is a compelling contraindication. As the indications for coronary angioplasty have broadened, with improving success rates and fewer complications, the indications for coronary arteriography have also expanded, because in many cases angina can be safely and effectively eliminated without bypass surgery or continuous antianginal therapy.

Coronary arteriography is indicated in patients with high-risk features uncovered during stress testing, as outlined above. Patients with stable angina who need elective major noncoronary surgery often undergo coronary arteriography first so that high-risk lesions can be revascularized, to reduce the risk of perioperative coronary events. In otherwise healthy, nonelderly patients who develop stable angina, coronary arteriography with a view to angioplasty, if feasible, may be preferable to an initial trial of medical therapy, particularly if the outcome statistics of the local angioplasty physician are outstanding. Patients whose symptoms can be adequately controlled with medical therapy do not require coronary arteriography if the results of a stress test places them in a low-risk category.

Therapeutic

Therapeutic Options

Stable angina can be treated with medical therapy alone, with coronary angioplasty, or with coronary bypass surgery. A left main coronary artery diameter stenosis of 50% or greater is found in 10 to 15% of stable angina patients who undergo coronary arteriography. They should have bypass surgery to improve their otherwise poor survival. Survival will also be improved with surgery in patients with triple-vessel disease, particularly if left ventricular dysfunction or inducible ischemia is present. Patients with double-vessel disease that includes the left anterior descending coronary artery usually also obtain a survival benefit from surgery if left ventricular dysfunction or inducible ischemia is present. Some patients with double-vessel disease are excellent candidates for coronary angioplasty, but in general angioplasty becomes less attractive as the number of critical lesions increases, because each angioplasty site has a 30 to 40% chance of developing restenosis.

An angina episode can be relieved with sublingual nitroglycerin 0.4 mg. This drug should be kept in a closed, dark bottle to maintain potency, and should be replaced at 6-month intervals. Patients should be encouraged to take nitroglycerin prophylactically before performing physical activities that provoke angina. Nitroglycerin relieves angina by multiple mechanisms: reduced venous return, reduced afterload, and stenosis dilation with improved coronary flow to the ischemic segment. Side effects such as transient headache, palpitations, and dizziness are common and may limit the usefulness of the drug.

Three classes of drugs are used to prevent angina: long-acting nitrates, beta-adrenergic blocking agents, and calcium channel blockers. Long-acting nitrates are widely prescribed but their efficacy is limited in many patients due to bothersome side effects, particularly headache, at effective doses, and due to the rapid development of tolerance, necessitating intermittent dosing schedules. Beta blockers prevent angina by reducing heart rate, blood pressure, and myocardial contractility, the principal determinants of myocardial oxygen consumption. They reduce the risk of myocardial infarction by 25% in survivors of an infarct and probably in other coronary patients as well. In patients who do not tolerate a beta blocker, or for whom these drugs are contraindicated, the calcium channel blockers diltiazem (Cardizem, 180–360 mg/d) and verapamil (Isoptin, Calan, 120–360 mg/d) are excellent alternatives. The dihydropyridine calcium channel blockers nifedipine (Procardia, Adalat), nicardipine (Cardene), amlodipine (Norvasc), isradipine (Dynacirc), and felodipine (Plendil) are less effective as monotherapy to control stable angina, but are often helpful when used in combination with a beta blocker.

Recommended Approach

All patients with coronary atherosclerosis, including those with stable angina, should be treated with aspirin because it reduces the risk of myocardial infarction by one quarter to one half. A dose of 80 mg/d is probably sufficient, but it is more convenient to prescribe 160 or 325 mg/d, or 325 mg on alternate days. The control of risk factors, outlined below under Prevention, is the most important aspect of therapy for most patients; stopping smoking, controlling hypertension, and reducing low-density lipoprotein cholesterol levels below 100 mg/dL greatly reduce coronary events and even improve angina symptoms.

A patient with stable angina who has only one or two episodes per month and can perform normal physical activities may not require an antianginal drug other than nitroglycerin. Unless contraindicated, a beta blocker should be used first, for example, metoprolol (Lopressor) 50 mg twice daily, increasing to 100 mg three times daily if needed, or atenolol (Tenormin) 50 mg/d, increasing to 150 mg/d if needed. Heart rate is a useful indicator for dose titration; an optimal rate is between 40 and 60 beats per minute. If an additional drug is required to control symptoms, a long-acting nitrate such as isosorbide dinitrate (Isordil) 10 to 30 mg three times per day with an overnight drug-free period, or a dihydropyridine, such as sustained-release nifedipine (Procardia XL or Adalat CC) 60 to 90 mg/d, could be added. It is important to evaluate carefully the benefits and adverse effects of each antianginal drug prescribed; many patients with stable angina take three different antianginal drugs over many years, without any evidence of symptomatic benefit.

Comparatively little information exists on the treatment of syndrome X. The cause of this condition is thought to be an inadequate vasodilatory capacity of small vessels. Coronary events are rare in these patients but their angina is often difficult to control. Recent preliminary evidence suggests that postmenopausal women with syndrome X often improve with hormone replacement therapy, and calcium channel blockers have also been reported to reduce angina.

Coronary bypass surgery should be recommended for the category of patient where it will prolong life, as discussed above, and for patients whose level of angina is unacceptable with medical treatment. Surgery relieves angina in 90% of patients and can be performed with an opera-

tive risk of less than 2% in patients less than 70 years old without severe left ventricular dysfunction or other major complicating factor. The use of single or bilateral internal thoracic (mammary) arteries as bypass conduits enhances long-term outcome, for venous bypass grafts have an accelerated rate of closure after the first decade. The timing of surgery is important because reoperation becomes necessary in an increasingly large proportion of patients after 10 years. Reoperation carries a slightly higher risk and a somewhat less satisfactory outcome because complete revascularization is less likely. Using coronary angioplasty to treat single-vessel and sometimes more extensive disease, and reserving surgery for multivessel disease, is a useful strategy that allows surgery to be postponed for years in some patients.

FOLLOW-UP

Patients with stable angina should seek medical attention quickly if they experience a prolonged severe ischemic attack that does not respond to nitroglycerin, because they may be having a myocardial infarction. Any worsening in their angina pattern should also be promptly reported and should be treated as unstable angina. The patient should see his or her physician several times per year; control of risk factors and patient education should be the main focus of these visits. An electrocardiogram should be repeated, perhaps at yearly intervals, because approximately one quarter of myocardial infarctions are silent or unrecognized, but appear on the electrocardiogram. Many physicians repeat exercise tests at regular intervals, often with perfusion imaging, in patients with stable angina. The cost-effectiveness of this strategy is dubious when symptoms have not changed. Recurrent angina within 6 months of coronary angioplasty indicates restenosis. Coronary angiography will usually be repeated because repeat angioplasty is almost always feasible, and the restenosis rate after a repeat procedure is only slightly higher than after an initial one. Recurrent angina more than 6 months after angioplasty is almost always due to coronary progression at another site, and not due to restenosis. When angina recurs several years after bypass surgery, the grafts are usually diseased, and progression of coronary atherosclerosis is often present too. Coronary arteriography should be repeated unless there is an overweighing contraindication. Coronary disease progresses much more rapidly in diseased venous bypass grafts than in native arteries, and therefore coronary events are very frequent in patients dependent on diseased grafts. When angina recurs within the first year of bypass surgery, it may be more reasonable to begin with a stress perfusion test to evaluate the extent and severity of ischemia, as early reoperation may not be indicated or necessary. In some cases a graft with poor distal runoff has occluded, and in others a side branch occlusion proximal to a patent graft is the culprit.

DISCUSSION
Prevalence

Approximately 3 million individuals in the United States suffer from angina. The wide availability and success of coronary revascularization have produced a marked change in the characteristics of patients with chronic stable angina. In a recent survey of more than 5000 outpatients with this diagnosis (Pepine et al., 1994), the mean age of patients was 69 years, 53% were women, and more than 70% had at least one associated illness.

Related Basic Science

Coronary atherosclerosis develops over many years before it is severe enough to cause symptoms. Under normal conditions, myocardial oxygen extraction is already near maximal. Coronary blood flow can increase threefold to meet myocardial oxygen demand during exercise, but with coronary stenoses, this ability is curtailed. Coronary blood flow occurs primarily during diastole, and the subendocardium is most susceptible to ischemia because of intracavitary left ventricular pressure and the effects of systole. Coronary atherosclerosis is associated with dysfunctional endothelium that does not release nitric oxide to induce arterial dilation appropriately.

The major determinants of myocardial oxygen consumption are heart rate, myocardial contractility, and ventricular pressure. Myocardial ischemia develops when coronary blood flow (supply) does not meet myocardial oxygen consumption (demand). In many patients myocardial ischemia occurs reproducibly at a fixed level of exertion; however, in others, presumably due to fluctuating coronary tone, the ischemic threshold is variable.

Natural History and Its Modification with Treatment

Stable angina disappears spontaneously in some cases, presumably due to the development of collaterals, and may sometimes be "cured" by a myocardial infarction; however, stable angina usually persists and often worsens with time. Unstable angina and myocardial infarction often complicate the course of stable angina; however, some patients continue to have stable angina for 10 or 20 years with no untoward events. The severity of angina is not the best predictor of outcome. The extent and severity of coronary disease as assessed at arteriography, left ventricular function, and the presence, extent, and severity of inducible ischemia are the best predictors of outcome. Risk varies widely: an annual mortality rate of less than 2% would be expected in a young patient with single-vessel disease, normal ventricular function, and no inducible ischemia, whereas left main stenosis with severe left ventricular dysfunction and extensive ischemia would portend a mortality rate of 30% within the first year.

Coronary bypass surgery relieves angina in up to 90% of cases and improves survival when severe coronary disease is present, particularly if associated with left ventricular dysfunction; however, bypass graft attrition leads to a recurrence of symptoms after the first decade in most patients. Coronary angioplasty relieves angina but restenosis develops within 6 months in 30 to 40% of stenoses. There is no evidence that coronary angioplasty prolongs survival or that either angioplasty or bypass surgery reduces the risk of myocardial infarction.

Prevention

The goals of secondary prevention for all patients with coronary disease apply to patients with stable angina (see Chapter 15–1). For those who smoke cigarettes, stopping is the most important component of their treatment. The National Cholesterol Education Panel recommends that low-density lipoprotein cholesterol be reduced below 100 mg/dL in patients with atherosclerosis. It has been estimated that six of every seven patients with coronary disease require at least dietary counseling to attain this objective, and if low-density lipoprotein cholesterol remains above 130 mg/dL with diet alone, drug treatment is indicated. Diabetes and hypertension should be carefully controlled, and weight loss is important for obese patients. An exercise program is safe for stable angina patients if heart rate is kept below the ischemic threshold. Exercise improves well-being and aerobic performance, and leads to better control of risk factors. Patients with stable angina often benefit from a change in their lifestyle and the avoidance of stressful activities.

Target cholesterol levels are less stringent in subjects without atherosclerosis, and depend on age, sex, and other risk factors. Smoking cessation and control of hypertension and diabetes are important factors in primary prevention of atherosclerosis as well.

Cost Containment

The direct and indirect costs of cardiovascular disease in the United States exceed $150 billion per year, and the treatment of stable angina is a major component of this total. Yet inadequate data are available to provide detailed recommendations that will improve the cost effectiveness of patient management. Coronary bypass surgery costs more initially than either coronary angioplasty or medical therapy; however, the need for repeat procedures and rehospitalizations is much less in the early years after surgery, so that most or all of the additional initial expense is recouped.

The diagnostic evaluation of patients with stable angina is often inefficient and wasteful of both time and money. For example, noninvasive tests are often performed before coronary arteriography, even when the physician has decided to proceed to arteriography irrespective of the results of the preliminary tests. On the other hand, coronary arteriography is often performed in patients with a low risk of coronary disease, when a normal exercise perfusion study might have sufficed to eliminate the need for the angiogram.

Secondary prevention (preventing coronary events in patients known to have atherosclerosis) has been shown to be extremely cost effective for several interventions. Chronic aspirin therapy reduces coronary events by one quarter to one half, at almost no cost. Smoking cessation programs and treatment of hypercholesterolemia are very cost effective. The cost/benefit ratio for treating hypertension and diabetes in coronary patients is somewhat higher, but these interventions compare very favorably with other commonly applied medical interventions.

REFERENCES

Heller GV, Brown KA. Prognosis of acute and chronic coronary artery disease by myocardial perfusion imaging. Cardiol Clin 1994;12:271.

Landau, C, Lange RA, Hillis LD. Percutaneous transluminal coronary angioplasty. N Engl J Med 1994;330:981.

Pepine CJ, Abrams J, Marks RG, et al. Characteristics of a contemporary population with angina pectoris. Am J Cardiol 1994;74:226.

Schlant RC, Alexander RW. Diagnosis and management of chronic ischemic heart disease. In: Schlant RC, Alexander RW, O'Rourke RA, et al., eds. Hurst's the heart. 8th ed. New York: McGraw-Hill, 1994:1055.

Yusuf S, Zucker D, Peduzzi P, et al. Effect of coronary artery bypass graft surgery on survival: Overview of 10-year results from randomised trials by the Coronary Artery Bypass Graft Surgery Trialists Collaboration. Lancet 1994;344:563.

CHAPTER 15–44

Unstable Angina Pectoris

David Waters, M.D.

DEFINITION

Unstable Angina pectoris is defined as chest discomfort caused by myocardial ischemia occurring for the first time or with recent worsening. The worsening may include the appearance of angina at rest or myocardial ischemic pain that is only slowly or incompletely relieved by nitroglycerin. Characteristically, the angina threshold decreases abruptly, so that for the same level of physical activity, the patient now experiences more attacks. New-onset angina is categorized as unstable angina by most, but not all authorities. Classification systems for unstable angina have been proposed, but are not widely used.

ETIOLOGY

The appearance of unstable angina is a clinical marker that the underlying coronary atherosclerosis has progressed. In most cases, rupture of an atherosclerotic plaque with thrombus formation at the site of a preexisting lesion is the mechanism that accounts for coronary progression. This mechanism is also operative in most cases of myocardial infarction. Whether plaque rupture with thrombosis causes infarction, unstable angina or no symptoms at all depends on the site of the lesion and its severity and whether the jeopardized myocardium is served by collaterals. In a minority of cases, unstable angina is not caused by a worsening of the underlying coronary atherosclerosis, but by an increase in myocardial oxygen demand in a patient with stable coronary disease. Prolonged tachyarrhythmia, severe anemia, thyrotoxicosis, and pneumonia are examples of conditions that can cause unstable angina in susceptible patients. Identifying this subset of patients is important because treating the underlying cause will relieve their unstable angina.

In rare cases, the etiology of unstable angina is coronary spasm, with or without significant underlying coronary atherosclerosis. This topic is discussed in Chapter 15–45.

CRITERIA FOR DIAGNOSIS
Suggestive

The characteristics of angina are discussed under Criteria for Diagnosis in Chapter 15–43. The discomfort caused by unstable angina and that caused by stable angina are qualitatively similar, such that patients with stable angina who develop unstable angina will make the diagnosis themselves: they recognize both the origin of the discomfort and that its pattern has changed. The major diagnostic dilemma is posed by the patient without previous angina who presents with chest pain at rest compatible with myocardial ischemia, but with some atypical features. Dependent on age, sex, risk factors, and whether coronary disease is known to be present, the probability that unstable angina is the cause of chest pain may range from 10 to 70%. A definitive diagnosis is crucial, on the one hand, to avoid expensive treatment associated with a small risk of complications and, on the other, to avoid leaving untreated a patient at risk for developing myocardial infarction. The problem of "ruling out" myocardial ischemia as the cause of chest pain consumes many health care dollars.

Definitive

The diagnosis of unstable angina can be accepted as definitive in a patient with typical symptoms and with documented severe coronary atherosclerosis. When symptoms are typical and the patient has an age or risk factor profile that make coronary disease the probable cause, it is appropriate to proceed to coronary arteriography both to confirm the diagnosis and to orient therapy. Recording an electrocardiogram during chest discomfort in a patient with suspected unstable angina provides useful diagnostic and prognostic information. Reversible ST-segment depression during symptoms confirms that their etiology is myocardial ischemia. In patients with uninterpretable ST segments (due to left bundle-branch block, severe left ventricular hypertrophy, or paced rhythms, for example), a radioisotope injection during or soon after an episode of chest discomfort may reveal a reversible perfusion defect, confirming the diagnosis.

CLINICAL MANIFESTATIONS
Subjective

The patient with unstable angina seeks medical attention because of new or worsening symptoms. The frequency, severity, and duration of episodes of chest discomfort vary greatly from one patient to another. The clinical presentation of unstable angina and myocardial infarction overlap; however, symptoms lasting longer than 30 minutes are more likely to herald at least some myocardial necrosis. Nausea, sweating, dyspnea, and dizziness associated with chest discomfort are less common with unstable angina than with myocardial infarction. Partial or incomplete relief with nitroglycerin is characteristic of unstable angina.

Factors that may be causing unstable angina secondarily, such as severe anemia and thyrotoxicosis, should be sought out. Risk factors for coronary disease should be clearly documented. Noncardiac symptoms that may yield clues to a noncardiac cause of the chest pain should be investigated.

Objective
Physical Examination

The physical examination of a patient with unstable angina may be normal. Abnormalities caused by risk factors may be present: obesity, hypertension, retinopathy, xanthelasma, and xanthoma. Vascular bruits

are objective evidence of atherosclerosis outside the coronary circulation. The cardiac examination may be entirely normal or may reveal signs of previous myocardial damage, such as an anterior dyskinetic movement, or of left ventricular failure, such as a ventricular gallop. These signs may also develop transiently during episodes of myocardial ischemia.

Routine Laboratory Abnormalities

The resting electrocardiogram may be normal or may reveal left ventricular hypertrophy or signs of previous infarction. Baseline ST and T-wave abnormalities may be due to ischemia, postischemic dysfunction, or ventricular hypertrophy, or may even be unrelated to cardiac disease. Recording an electrocardiogram during an episode of chest pain in unstable angina usually reveals transient ST depression, unless the baseline electrocardiogram is already grossly abnormal or unless the ischemia is localized to an electrocardiographically silent area.

Cardiomegaly and pulmonary venous congestion are occasionally discovered on chest x-ray. Routine laboratory tests may reveal evidence of diabetes or hyperlipidemia.

PLANS
Diagnostic
Differential Diagnosis

The more common conditions that may cause chest pain and be considered in the differential diagnosis of unstable angina are similar to those listed for stable angina in Table 15–43–2. Esophageal and gastrointestinal disorders can easily masquerade as unstable angina. When the cause of chest discomfort is unclear, ruling out unstable angina is the priority because this condition requires urgent treatment.

Diagnostic Options

Cardiac Enzymes. Cardiac enzymes should be measured when the patient presents, and 8 and 16 hours later to rule out myocardial infarction. Minor elevations in the MB fraction of creatine kinase, or even of total creatine kinase, are often detected, dependent in part on the frequency at which these measurements are made. A more sensitive indicator of myocyte damage, elevated levels of cardiac troponin T, is found in approximately one third of unstable angina patients. This test is not yet available routinely, but may prove to be clinically useful because elevated levels correlate with increased risk. Technically, these abnormalities indicate that some myocardial necrosis has occurred, but for practical purposes, management does not change.

Coronary Arteriography. Most patients with unstable angina undergo coronary arteriography. The extent and severity of coronary disease can be defined only with this procedure, and in many cases, the results indicate which form of therapy is likely to produce the best outcome. When the cause of chest pain is uncertain, coronary arteriography often provides important diagnostic information; however, the demonstration that coronary atherosclerosis is present in a particular patient does not necessarily mean that it is the cause of symptoms. Approximately 10% of patients with unstable angina who undergo coronary arteriography have no significant coronary stenoses. Although a few of these patients may have coronary spasm or syndrome X as a cause of their symptoms, in most the chest pain is not of cardiac origin, and the results of the arteriogram orient the physician toward other diagnoses. Coronary arteriography should not be ordered as the initial test for patients with a low probability of coronary disease as the cause of their symptoms, because the test is expensive and is associated with a small but definite risk of serious complications.

Stress Testing. When the probability that chest pain is due to myocardial ischemia is high, stress testing is not indicated and coronary arteriography should be the initial diagnostic test. Irrespective of whether or not underlying coronary atherosclerosis is present, subjects with normal perfusion studies during maximal exercise have a 5-year prognosis that is as good as the normal population, and usually require no further cardiac investigation. Coronary arteriography is indicated for patients who develop signs of myocardial ischemia at a low workload or who have other high-risk features of their tests.

In some patients with coronary narrowings of intermediate severity, stress testing is useful to determine whether the stenosis is capable of causing myocardial ischemia. In some patients with more than one narrowing who are potentially candidates for coronary angioplasty, a stress nuclear perfusion study may be useful to clarify which stenosis is the culprit.

A minority of experts recommend that unstable angina patients whose symptoms are controlled on medical therapy undergo risk stratification with a stress test to select those who require coronary arteriography. Under this strategy, patients with a negative test are allocated to medical therapy. In the recently reported Thrombolysis in Myocardial Ischemia 3 (TIMI 3) Trial, this "conservative" treatment was compared with the more "aggressive" approach of performing early coronary arteriography on all patients and revascularizing all severe lesions with angioplasty or bypass surgery. At 6 weeks, no differences between the groups were seen for overall mortality or for other serious complications; however, the patients initially allocated to the conservative strategy spent more days in hospital. They were also often rehospitalized later for coronary arteriography, and by 1 year, their rate of revascularization was not much less than in the patients treated more aggressively.

Recommended Approach

Unless coronary arteriography is contraindicated, it should be performed soon after hospitalization in patients with definite unstable angina. If the diagnosis is uncertain but the pretest probability is *high*, coronary arteriography will also provide useful information. A stress test is not needed in such patients, and performing coronary arteriography instead usually leads to a more rapid and certain resolution of the problem. A stress test is usually a better option when the pretest probability is low. Patients who continue to have angina at rest after institution of medical therapy are at high risk for myocardial infarction and should undergo coronary arteriography urgently, with a view to urgent revascularization. Minor elevations of cardiac creatine kinase or its MB fraction should not affect this approach. Left ventriculography done at the time of coronary arteriography usually obviates the need for any other assessment of ventricular function.

Therapeutic

Therapeutic Options

The immediate goals of treatment in unstable angina are to control symptoms and to prevent myocardial infarction. Table 15–44–1 lists the commonly used treatments for unstable angina and how they affect these endpoints. Myocardial infarction occurs within 1 month in approximately 10% of unstable angina patients who are not treated with antithrombotic or antiplatelet drugs. Aspirin has been shown in several controlled trials to reduce by approximately half this risk of myocardial

TABLE 15–44–1. EFFECT OF TREATMENTS FOR UNSTABLE ANGINA ON THE GOALS OF CONTROLLING ANGINA AND PREVENTING MYOCARDIAL INFARCTION

	Control Angina	Prevent Infarction
Beta blockers	Yes	Possibly
Calcium channel blockers		
Dihydropyridines*	Poorly	No, possible ↑ risk
Diltiazem, verapamil	Yes	No
Nitrates	Yes	No
Aspirin	No	Yes, rate ↓ by half
Heparin	Probably	Yes, better than ASA
Thrombolytic therapy	No	No, probable ↑ risk
Coronary bypass surgery	Yes, 90% relief	No
Coronary angioplasty	Yes, if no restenosis	No

↑, Increased; ↓, decreased.
*When used alone. With a beta blocker, dihydropyridines can be useful to control angina.

infarction. In one controlled trial in unstable angina, heparin was significantly better than aspirin in preventing infarction, and in two of the three other trials that compared the treatments, a trend in favor of heparin was seen. Although the pathophysiology of myocardial infarction and that of unstable angina are usually the same, and thrombolytic therapy improves survival in acute infarction, it is of no benefit to unstable angina patients, and in fact probably increases their risk of developing myocardial infarction.

The three classes of antiischemic drugs—nitrates, beta-adrenergic blocking agents, and calcium channel blockers, are widely used in unstable angina to control symptoms. Nitroglycerin is usually administered intravenously as a continuous infusion beginning at 5 to 10 µg/min and increasing gradually until symptoms are controlled, side effects appear, or a maximum dose of 100 µg/min is reached. Beta blockers prevent angina by reducing heart rate, blood pressure, and myocardial contractility, the principal determinants of myocardial oxygen consumption. They are particularly useful in patients receiving intravenous nitroglycerin because they block the reflex increase in heart rate often induced by nitroglycerin. In patients whose symptoms persist, or in those for whom a beta blocker is contraindicated, diltiazem or verapamil should be used.

Studies comparing modern revascularization procedures with modern medical therapy in unstable angina are lacking, and practice patterns vary widely. A Veterans Administration Study performed in the early 1980s compared medical to surgical therapy in relatively low-risk unstable angina patients. Overall the rates of death and nonfatal myocardial infarction during the first 5 years of follow-up were similar; however, patients with triple-vessel disease had a much better outcome with surgery. Patients with single-vessel disease usually do well with angioplasty or medical treatment.

Recommended Approach

Almost all patients with unstable angina should be hospitalized immediately. Exceptions include those with mild symptoms who became unstable more than 2 weeks prior to being evaluated. Outpatient management must include close follow-up, with instructions to seek medical attention if symptoms worsen. The patient should understand how to use sublingual nitroglycerin to relieve angina attacks.

Aspirin should be given to all unstable patients; a dose of 160 or 325 mg/d is adequate and doses as low as 80 mg/d can be used if the risk of gastrointestinal bleeding or other serious side effects is high. A bolus of 5000 U of heparin should be administered intravenously, followed by a continuous infusion at 1000 U/h adjusted to maintain the partial thromboplastin time at 1.5 to 2 times control. Medical therapy should be initiated promptly because the risk of complications is highest in the first few days and because it is preferable to have symptoms controlled before coronary arteriography. Escalating oral doses of a beta blocker to lower the heart rate below 60 beats per minute should be prescribed, along with a continuous infusion of intravenous nitroglycerin. In patients who do not tolerate a beta blocker, or for whom these drugs are contraindicated, the calcium channel blockers diltiazem (Cardizem, 180–360 mg/d) and verapamil (Isoptin, Calan, 120–360 mg/d) are excellent alternatives. The dihydropyridine calcium channel blockers nifedipine (Procardia, Adalat), nicardipine (Cardene), amlodipine (Norvasc), isradipine (Dynacirc), and felodipine (Plendil) may increase risk when used as monotherapy in unstable angina, but may be helpful when used in combination with a beta blocker.

When the diagnosis of unstable angina is not definitive, medical treatment should be started in parallel with the diagnostic evaluation. The sensitivity of a stress test to detect myocardial ischemia may be impaired by antiischemic treatment and consideration should be given in stabilized patients to temporarily stopping these drugs before the test.

Intravenous heparin and nitroglycerin can be conveniently continued up to a revascularization procedure if it is scheduled early during the hospital course. For other patients, intravenous nitroglycerin can be discontinued when angina symptoms are controlled. Heparin is usually discontinued 2 to 3 days after the patient has stabilized. Aspirin should be begun before heparin is discontinued to prevent a reactivation of symptoms.

Unstable angina can be treated with medical therapy alone, with coronary angioplasty, or with coronary bypass surgery. A left main coronary artery diameter stenosis of 50% or greater is found in approximately 15% of unstable angina patients who undergo coronary arteriography. They should have bypass surgery to improve their otherwise poor survival. Survival is also improved with surgery in patients with triple-vessel disease or with double-vessel disease that includes the left anterior descending coronary artery. Some patients with double-vessel disease are excellent candidates for coronary angioplasty, but in general, angioplasty becomes less attractive as the number of critical lesions increases, because each angioplasty site has a 30 to 40% chance of developing restenosis. In approximately one quarter of unstable angina patients only one artery is narrowed by more than 50% of lumen diameter; most of these patients are excellent candidates for coronary angioplasty.

FOLLOW-UP

Patients whose symptoms are controlled on medical therapy or who have undergone successful coronary angioplasty can return to normal physical activity within 1 or 2 weeks. Patients who remain significantly limited by angina may need to be reassessed with a view to revascularization. Recurrent angina within 6 months of a successful angioplasty indicates restenosis and usually leads to a repeat angioplasty. The follow-up of unstable angina patients is similar in other respects to the management of other patients with chronic coronary disease.

DISCUSSION
Prevalence

In the United States, more than half a million patients are hospitalized with unstable angina each year. This number is roughly equal to the number hospitalized with acute myocardial infarction or with heart failure.

Related Basic Science

Plaque rupture is the pathophysiologic event that precipitates both unstable angina and myocardial infarction. The degree of narrowing of plaques that rupture is not necessarily severe, in the range of 30 to 70% diameter stenosis. Plaques containing large lipid pools with only thin fibrous caps are most at risk. The site of rupture is most often at the shoulder of the plaque, where stress is highest. Clusters of macrophages are often seen at these points.

Most plaque ruptures heal without causing symptoms, perhaps leaving a narrowing somewhat more severe than before. Plaque ruptures that expose larger areas of thrombogenic intramural debris to flowing blood in areas of high turbulence are most likely to provoke more extensive thrombosis. Risk factors, particularly smoking and hypercholesterolemia, increase thrombin deposition at the site of deep arterial injury, and aspirin and heparin reduce it. Thrombin deposition causes local coronary vasoconstriction that may contribute to the development of ischemia.

Natural History and Its Modification with Treatment

The natural history of unstable angina with medical therapy alone is quite variable. Patients with previous infarction or heart failure, those who became unstable while already taking multiple antianginal drugs, and those who continue to experience symptoms or have extensive ischemia on a stress test are more likely to fare poorly. Angina can be completely eliminated with medical therapy in about one third of cases and improved in most of the other two thirds; however, when the patient has stabilized, the underlying coronary lesion may still be unstable, and the increased risk of myocardial infarction only gradually declines over the ensuing year. Between hospital discharge and 1 year,

approximately 5 to 10% of unstable angina patients develop an infarction.

Coronary bypass surgery relieves angina in up to 90% of cases and improves survival when severe coronary disease is present, particularly if associated with left ventricular dysfunction; however, bypass graft attrition leads to a recurrence of symptoms after the first decade in most patients. Coronary angioplasty relieves angina, but restenosis develops within 6 months in 30 to 40% of stenoses. There is as yet no evidence that coronary angioplasty prolongs survival, or that either angioplasty or bypass surgery reduces the risk of myocardial infarction.

Prevention

For most patients, an episode of unstable angina is just one brief exacerbation in a pattern of symptomatic coronary disease stretching out over years, and the control of coronary risk factors is the component of treatment that has the greatest effect on long-term outcome in most cases. Smokers must stop. The National Cholesterol Education Panel recommends that low-density lipoprotein cholesterol be reduced below 100 mg/dL in patients with atherosclerosis. It has been estimated that six of every seven patients with coronary disease require at least dietary counseling to attain this objective, and if low-density lipoprotein cholesterol remains above 130 mg/dL with diet alone, drug treatment is indicated. The benefits of cholesterol lowering have recently been convincingly demonstrated in the Scandinavian Simvastatin Survival Study, where such treatment reduced both total mortality and coronary events by approximately 30% in coronary patients. Diabetes and hypertension should be carefully controlled, and weight loss is important for obese patients. An exercise program is safe after an episode of unstable angina has been stabilized, if heart rate is kept below the ischemic threshold.

Cost Containment

Although coronary bypass surgery is more expensive than coronary angioplasty, which in turn is more expensive than medical therapy alone, much of the initial cost advantage of the latter two options is subsequently lost due to rehospitalizations and more procedures in these groups. Comparisons between patients treated in the United States and in countries with more conservative treatment patterns such as Canada, however, indicate that equally good outcomes could be obtained after myocardial infarction with less coronary angiography and less revascularization. A similar pattern may exist for unstable angina, but this has not been documented.

Shorter hospitalizations for unstable angina are being advocated to cut costs. This strategy works best when early discharge does not lead to increased rehospitalization rates. Secondary prevention is very cost effective for interventions such as aspirin, smoking cessation, and cholesterol lowering.

REFERENCES

Braunwald E, Jones RH, Mark DB, et al. Diagnosing and managing unstable angina. Circulation 1994;90:613.

Fuster V, Badimon L, Badimon JJ, Chesebro JH. The pathogenesis of coronary artery disease and the acute coronary syndromes. N Engl J Med 1992;326:242,310.

Théroux P, Waters D. Diagnosis and management of patients with unstable angina. In: Schlant RC, Alexander RW, O'Rourke RA, et al. eds. Hurst's the heart. 8th ed. New York: McGraw-Hill, 1994:1083.

TIMI IIIB Investigators. Effects of tissue plasminogen activator and a comparison of early invasive and conservative strategies in unstable angina and non-Q-wave myocardial infarction: Results of the TIMI IIIB Trial. Circulation 1994;89:1545.

Waters D, Lam J, Théroux P. Newer concepts in the treatment of unstable angina pectoris. Am J Cardiol 1991;68:34C.

CHAPTER 15–45
....
Variant (Prinzmetal's)Angina
David Waters, M.D.

DEFINITION

In 1959 Prinzmetal et al. described a syndrome characterized by angina at rest associated with transient ST-segment elevation. Angina and the electrocardiographic changes are rapidly relieved by nitroglycerin, and in most cases exercise tolerance is well preserved.

ETIOLOGY

Variant or Prinzmetal's angina is caused by transient, severe coronary spasm that is usually focal and usually occurs at the site of an organic coronary narrowing. The underlying coronary atherosclerosis can vary from a subtotal occlusion to a very mild stenosis, and in some cases the coronary arteries are angiographically normal. Coronary artery spasm has also been demonstrated to cause angina at rest with only transient ST depression or pseudonormalization of abnormal T waves. Coronary spasm can be provoked by a variety of interventions, but despite intense speculation, the cause of spontaneous attacks is not known.

CRITERIA FOR DIAGNOSIS
Suggestive

Variant angina is uncommon, and although the classic features (described below) are distinctive, the presentation is usually not remarkable enough to be distinguished immediately from unstable angina.

Definitive

The demonstration of transient ST elevation during an episode of rest angina confirms the diagnosis. Patients with pseudonormalization of negative T waves during an attack often exhibit ST elevation during more intense episodes. Angina and ST elevation in response to a provocative test, as discussed below, also confirm the diagnosis.

CLINICAL MANIFESTATIONS
Subjective

Angina at rest occurs in all cases, and a cyclical pattern with most attacks occurring in the early morning hours is often noted. The location, severity, and other descriptors of the chest pain of variant and classic angina do not differ. Exertional angina coexists in slightly more than half of cases, but is often not a prominent feature and the ischemic threshold is extremely variable. Variant angina can occur during the recovery phase of myocardial infarction or in patients who have had coronary bypass surgery or recent angioplasty.

Most patients with variant angina are heavy cigarette smokers, but their age, gender, and risk factor profiles are otherwise similar to those of other coronary patients. Those with angiographically normal coronary arteries tend to be younger and more often women, and do not usually have multiple risk factors. One quarter of variant angina patients have a history of migraine headaches and one quarter have symptoms of Raynaud's phenomenon; 10% have both of these conditions. Syncope during rest angina, reported by up to one quarter of patients, is a useful diagnostic clue.

Objective
Physical Examination

Physical examination between attacks reveals no abnormalities caused by the syndrome. During an episode, signs of transient left ventricular dysfunction may appear.

Routine Laboratory Abnormalities

Laboratory tests, including cardiac enzymes, are normal. The electrocardiogram between attacks in a patient with active symptoms may re-veal postischemic T-wave changes (flattening or inversion). During an attack the electrocardiogram often shows remarkable ST elevation, often complicated by ventricular arrhythmias, or when the inferior leads are involved, advanced degrees of heart block.

PLANS
Diagnostic
Differential Diagnosis

The differential diagnosis of chest pain is discussed in Chapter 15–43, and Table 15–43–2 lists the major causes. When ST elevation is documented during myocardial ischemic pain at rest, variant angina and acute myocardial infarction are the only two diagnostic possibilities. An episode of variant angina is promptly relieved by nitroglycerin, with rapid normalization of the ST segment. In contrast, pain and ST elevation lasting longer than 30 minutes without relief from nitroglycerin signify myocardial infarction.

Diagnostic Options

The most important diagnostic procedure is to obtain a 12-lead electrocardiogram during an episode of chest pain at rest. In patients suspected of having variant angina, ambulatory electrocardiographic monitoring can be useful to confirm the diagnosis, particularly if attacks are infrequent. Exercise testing provokes angina with ST elevation in about one third of variant angina patients during an active phase of their disease.

Several different maneuvers have been used to induce attacks of variant angina or coronary spasm at the time of coronary arteriography. The cold pressor test, that is, immersing the patient's hand in ice water for 2 minutes, induces an attack in about 10% of cases, and hyperventilation provokes an attack in more than half of patients with active variant angina. Intracoronary acetylcholine has a much higher sensitivity, 90% in one large series, but cannot be used without a temporary pacemaker because of the high incidence of bradyarrhythmia and heart block after right coronary artery injection. Ergonovine, an ergot alkaloid that constricts vascular smooth muscle by stimulating both alpha-adrenergic and serotonergic receptors, normally causes coronary vasoconstriction but, in variant angina patients, induces a typical attack due to severe coronary spasm, often with transient occlusion of the involved vessel. Ergonovine is given intravenously, or in very low doses, directly into the coronary artery. The sensitivity of ergonovine testing is very high, such that a negative test in the absence of coronary vasodilators in a patient with recent chest pain effectively rules out variant angina as the cause.

Ergonovine has occasionally caused refractory coronary spasm resulting in death. Provocative testing for coronary spasm using any of these methods should be done only in carefully selected patients by experienced individuals prepared to deal with potential complications.

Recommended Approach

Patients with newly diagnosed variant angina have a high risk of developing myocardial infarction within 3 months and need coronary arteriography to define their risk and to select optimal treatment. Patients with chest pain at rest in whom variant angina is suspected usually undergo coronary arteriography too. Often the results of the angiogram indicate how the patient should be treated and the need to define a pathophysiologic cause for the angina disappears. For example, severe triple-vessel disease with rest angina is usually sufficient indication to proceed to coronary bypass surgery, whether or not variant angina and coronary spasm are superimposed on the underlying coronary atherosclerosis.

For some patients, a provocative test for coronary spasm can provide useful information for management after the results of the angiogram are available. If no significant coronary narrowings are present and the history is typical of variant angina, but an electrocardiogram has not been recorded during an episode of chest pain at rest, a provocative test might be helpful to establish or eliminate the diagnosis.

Therapeutic

Therapeutic Options

Calcium channel blockers completely prevent attacks in about 70% of variant angina patients when prescribed at adequate doses. For patients who need more than one drug, choosing agents with opposite effects on heart rate, for example, diltiazem with a long-acting nitrate or verapamil with a dihydropyridine calcium channel blocker, helps limit side effects. Beta blockers have been reported to lengthen attacks of variant angina without diminishing their frequency and should thus not be used in this syndrome.

In patients with multivessel disease, the short-term risk for myocardial infarction is high, and although no controlled studies have been done, coronary bypass surgery appears to decrease this risk. With adequate doses of vasodilators, coronary angioplasty can be performed safely at the site of a stenosis where spasm occurs; however, symptomatic spasm often recurs, and the rate of restenosis is very high. Some studies suggest that controlling spasm with calcium channel blockers after angioplasty reduces the rate of restenosis to usual levels.

Recommended Approach

Patients with variant angina should be instructed to take nitroglycerin promptly at the onset of an attack. This is more important than in other types of angina, because the myocardial ischemia during an attack of variant angina is worse, and is more frequently complicated by sudden death. A calcium channel blocker should be given at maximal or near-maximal doses, for example, diltiazem (Cardizem) or verapamil (Calan, Isoptin) 360 mg/d or nifedipine (Procardia, Adalat) 80 mg/d. Long-acting or sustained-release preparations should be used, particularly for dihydropyridines like nifedipine that have a short half-life. Long-acting nitrates can be added if necessary to control refractory symptoms, but are not a good first choice if used alone because of side effects and the development of tolerance. Approximately 20% of patients have symptoms not controlled by calcium channel blockers and nitrates alone. Although not approved for this indication in the United States, amiodarone, guanethidine, and clonidine have been reported to be effective in some such refractory patients.

Patients with multivessel disease should undergo bypass surgery, if feasible, to reduce their short-term risk of myocardial infarction. The role of coronary angioplasty in patients with single-vessel disease is unsettled; although the primary success rate is above 90%, coronary spasm usually recurs and the restenosis rate is high.

FOLLOW-UP

After bypass surgery or coronary angioplasty, medical therapy should be continued for at least several months. Variant angina tends to disappear over time in most cases. Calcium channel blockers can be safely tapered and discontinued in patients who have been entirely angina free for at least 1 year and who had no life-threatening arrhythmias during their attacks. In approximately three quarters of these patients, angina will not recur; however, the underlying coronary disease is still present, and they may later experience classic angina or myocardial infarction.

DISCUSSION

Prevalence and Incidence

Variant angina is common in Japan and other Far Eastern countries, but is quite rare in North America. Less than 1% of patients with myocardial ischemic pain admitted to hospital have documented variant angina. The condition is underdiagnosed because it is not considered in patients who have significant narrowings on their coronary angiogram. On the other hand, chest pain in patients with no significant coronary narrowings is often vaguely attributed to coronary spasm without confirmation of the diagnosis.

Related Basic Science

The cause of coronary spasm in variant angina is unknown; however, much recent research has improved our understanding of the problem. The frequency of variant angina attacks is not reduced by alpha-adrenergic blockade, serotonin receptor blockade, inhibition of thromboxane A_2 production, or administration of prostacyclin. Yet nitroglycerin and other nonspecific coronary vasodilators effectively prevent or relieve coronary spasm. The response of uninvolved coronary segments to vasoconstrictive stimuli in variant angina patients is normal, indicating that a generalized abnormality of coronary reactivity is not present. A central neural mechanism is unlikely to be involved because coronary spasm has been reported in the denervated transplanted heart.

Normal endothelium modulates coronary tone by releasing endothelium-derived relaxing factors (EDRFs), but this function is lost at sites of early atherosclerosis and is impaired by smoking and hypercholesterolemia. EDRFs inhibit platelet aggregation; aggregating platelets release vasoconstricting substances that can act unopposed in the absence of EDRFs. Abnormal endothelial function is probably a prerequisite for coronary spasm. Increased numbers of adventitial mast cells were found at autopsy at the site of coronary spasm in a patient with well-documented variant angina and were also seen in six patients with cocaine-related coronary spasm and thrombosis. Mast cells release histamine, prostaglandin D_2 and leukotrienes, all potential mediators of coronary spasm. The pathophysiologic consequences of coronary spasm are well understood. Severe spasm rapidly induces transmural ischemia, with ST elevation and bulging of the affected segment. If the ischemic zone is large, cardiac output and blood pressure may decrease. The risk of serious ventricular arrhythmias increases with the severity, extent, and duration of ischemia.

Natural History and Its Modification with Treatment

In a large series of variant angina patients, death or nonfatal myocardial infarction within 1 year occurred in 7% of patients with no coronary narrowings of 70% or greater, in 14% of those with single-vessel disease, and in 35% of those with multivessel disease (Walling et al., 1987). Calcium channel blockers have been reported to reduce the risk of serious complications, but this has usually been demonstrated only with historical comparisons. Coronary bypass surgery probably improves outcome in patients with multivessel disease. As noted above, symptoms disappear spontaneously in many patients and treatment can eventually be discontinued.

Prevention

At least some degree of coronary atherosclerosis is present in nearly all patients with variant angina, so that measures to prevent this underlying condition would be helpful. Heavy smoking is very common and may contribute to the pathophysiology through the mechanism of endothelial damage. Until more is known about the cause of variant angina, more specific prevention is difficult.

Cost Containment

The elimination of all angina attacks should be the goal of treatment for patients with variant angina, because otherwise most of them will lead restricted, nonproductive lives. Aggressive medical treatment and revascularization for patients with multivessel disease are probably more cost effective than the alternatives.

REFERENCES

Bertrand ME, Lablanche JM, Thieuleux FA, et al. Comparative results of percutaneous transluminal coronary angioplasty in patients with dynamic versus fixed coronary stenosis. J Am Coll Cardiol 1986;8:504.

Maseri A, Severi S, De Nes M, et al. "Variant" angina: One aspect of a continuous spectrum of vasospastic myocardial ischemia. Am J Cardiol 1978;42:1019.

Prinzmetal M, Kennamer R, Merliss R, et al. Angina pectoris: I. A variant form of angina pectoris. Am J Med 1959;27:375.

Walling A, Waters DD, Miller DD, et al. Long-term prognosis of patients with variant angina. Circulation 1987;76:990.

Waters DD, Bouchard A, Théroux P. Spontaneous remission is a frequent outcome of variant angina. J Am Coll Cardiol 1983;2:195.

CHAPTER 15–46

Silent Myocardial Ischemia

Peter F. Cohn, M.D.

DEFINITION

Silent myocardial ischemia (also referred to as silent ischemia) is defined as objective evidence of myocardial ischemia (by direct or indirect measurements of left ventricular function, perfusion, metabolism, or electrical activity) without chest pain or other anginal equivalents.

I proposed classification of patients with silent ischemia into three clinical types to help clarify the prevalence, detection, prognosis, and management of this syndrome (Cohn, 1988) Type I includes persons with ischemia who are asymptomatic, never having had any signs or symptoms of cardiovascular disease. Type 2 includes persons who are asymptomatic after a myocardial infarction but still show objective signs of active (but painless) ischemia. Type 3 consists of patients with both angina and silent ischemia.

ETIOLOGY

The most common cause of silent myocardial ischemia is coronary atherosclerosis, but cases have been reported in which the coronary arteriograms were normal and coronary vasospasm has been implicated as the etiology.

CRITERIA FOR DIAGNOSIS

Suggestive

There are several clues that make physicians consider the possibility of silent myocardial ischemia in the different clinical types. In totally asymptomatic individuals (type 1 persons), these clues are related to the presence of coronary risk factors (hypertension, diabetes mellitus, cigarette smoking, and hyperlipidemia), especially in men over the age of 40. Family history is not a factor in diagnosing silent myocardial ischemia per se, but because silent myocardial ischemia is part of the spectrum of coronary artery disease in general, any predisposition for the latter will of necessity suggest the presence of the former. In the other two clinical types, no specific clues are necessary, as silent myocardial ischemia is prevalent in patients with histories of myocardial infarction and/or angina.

Definitive

Definite diagnosis is usually made by the electrocardiographic demonstration of horizontal or downsloping ST-segment depression in the absence of symptoms in patients with coronary artery disease documented by radioisotopic procedures or coronary arteriography. These abnormalities are discussed more fully under Plans.

CLINICAL MANIFESTATIONS

Subjective

Symptoms are absent in type 1 individuals by definition. Again, by definition, symptoms are absent in type 2 patients (after the initial infarction if it is a symptomatic event) but are present in type 3 patients, who experience both silent ischemia and chest pain that may be either typical or atypical for classic angina patients.

Objective

Physical Examination

Abnormal physical findings related to the heart depend on whether the patient has had a prior myocardial infarction with resulting scar formation in the left ventricle, and the patient is being examined during an ischemic episode. If neither condition is present, then the cardiac examination is commonly normal; otherwise, third or fourth heart sounds may be heard. Abnormalities on the general physical examination can include systemic arterial hypertension and signs of hyperlipidemia such as xanthelasma.

Routine Laboratory Abnormalities

"Routine" laboratory tests are of little benefit in this syndrome, but they are, of course, helpful in suggesting the presence of coronary artery disease, especially those blood chemistries that document metabolic abnormalities associated with coronary atherosclerosis, such as diabetes mellitus and hyperlipidemia. The key laboratory tests are those that relate to direct or indirect evidence of myocardial ischemia and are described in the following section.

PLANS

Diagnostic

Differential Diagnosis

"Artifacts" in the exercise or ambulatory electrocardiogram represent the major differential: Is the patient truly ischemic or do the electrocardiographic findings reflect postural changes, electrolyte abnormalities, and so on?

Diagnostic Options

Clinicians can document silent ischemia by electrocardiography (stress test, Holter monitoring) and/or by some kind of imaging procedure (echocardiography, radionuclide scans). When to perform coronary angiography to confirm anatomic lesions depends on the clinical presentation; for example, a type 3 patient is much more likely to be referred for this procedure than a type 1 patient.

Recommended Approach

The exercise test is useful for detecting silent myocardial ischemia in patients who are asymptomatic postinfarction or who have angina, because the diagnosis of underlying coronary atherosclerotic heart disease is almost certain. In the general population, however, the exercise test must be used with more caution, and false-positive results are common. We recommend screening exercise tests to detect silent coronary artery disease only in selected patients. These are patients at high risk for developing coronary atherosclerotic heart disease because of two or more risk factors (elevated cholesterol levels, hypertension, diabetes, cigarette smoking) or family histories of premature coronary artery disease. Patients with diabetes are especially suitable for screening because visceral neuropathy could contribute to lack of pain from myocardial ischemia. Unless an exercise test is strongly positive (greater than 2-mm ST depression in stage I or II of the Bruce protocol), its results should be confirmed by a radionuclide procedure before an asymptomatic person either is labeled as having coronary atherosclerotic heart disease or is referred for coronary arteriography for anatomic definition. The decision to proceed to coronary arteriography is not obligatory. Many low-risk type 1 patients can be managed without this procedure.

The low-level exercise test after a myocardial infarction is still the most common way of detecting silent ischemia. Once detected, the frequency of ischemic episodes can be documented by ambulatory electrocardiographic (Holter) monitoring. There is a circadian variation in ischemic episodes recorded during daily life, with most occurring between 6 AM and noon. Holter monitoring can also be used when exercise testing is contraindicated. For the patient with type 2 silent ischemia, the decision to define coronary anatomy with arteriography is less controversial because, in addition to the presence of silent ischemia, an infarction has occurred. As noted earlier, exercise testing can also be used in patients with type 3 silent ischemia (angina), but Holter recordings are also helpful because they document out-of-hospital events.

Additional diagnostic tests can be either noninvasive or invasive. The noninvasive tests (radionuclide studies such as thallium stress tests or exercise echocardiography) are used in asymptomatic individuals who have abnormal electrocardiograms, but no other evidence of coronary artery disease. The gold standard for diagnosing coronary artery disease is still the coronary angiogram, an invasive procedure, but even when an exercise radionuclide test is abnormal, coronary arteriography is not always necessary; however, there will still be patients in all three clinical types in whom coronary arteriography is necessary to make the diagnosis.

Therapeutic

Therapeutic Options

Clinicians have at their disposal a variety of choices ranging from risk factor modification to antiischemic medications to coronary revascularization procedures. When to do what (and to whom) again depends on the clinical classification of the patient (type 1, 2, or 3).

Recommended Approach

For most patients with type 1 silent ischemia, management includes modification of coronary risk factors and avoidance of activities known to produce ischemia.

The cardioprotective effect seen with beta-blocker therapy after myocardial infarction suggests that there is a role for these agents in patients with type 2 silent myocardial ischemia. Prolongation of exercise time and amelioration of silent wall motion abnormalities occurring during exercise have been reported. A typical regimen would include atenolol (Tenormin) 50–100 mg once a day, or long-acting propranolol (Inderal LA) 80–240 mg once a day, or metoprolol (Lopressor) 50 mg twice a day.

In patients with angina and type 3 silent myocardial ischemia, the low heart rates seen during episodes of out-of-hospital silent ischemia may indicate a dominant vasospastic component, but supply-and-demand imbalance can also play a role. Thus, in type 3 patients, calcium antagonists, nitrates, and beta blockers all have been shown to reduce the number of ischemic episodes, both painful and silent. Combination therapy appears particularly beneficial. A typical regimen would include one of the beta blockers cited above and nifedipine (Procardia XL, 30–90 mg once daily) or diltiazem (Cardizem SR, 60–120 mg twice daily), plus nitroglycerin ointment or patch (doses vary with the type of preparation used) or isosorbide mononitrate (Ismo, 20 mg twice daily). When using the Holter monitor to document reduction in ischemic events and duration, one must consider the day-to-day variability of these events.

Surgical revascularization procedures for asymptomatic patients after infarction are best confined to patients with extensive disease (left main or triple-vessel disease) and left ventricular dysfunction. Data suggest that surgery improves longevity in such patients, especially if the exercise test shows ischemic changes. In patients with angina and silent ischemia, coronary angioplasty and coronary artery surgery are also therapeutic options, depending on the coronary anatomy.

FOLLOW-UP

Patients must report any new symptoms that occur. A change from an asymptomatic to a symptomatic state may be catastrophic; any forewarning is important (Thaulow et al., 1993).

On the physician's part, follow-up of symptomatic patients is usually guided by the symptoms: as angina increases, for example, more visits are scheduled. For the patient who continues to be asymptomatic, yearly visits with exercise tests are recommended.

DISCUSSION

Prevalence and Incidence

It appears that 2.5 to 10% of type 1 middle-aged men are asymptomatic but have active coronary artery disease. Figures for patients after infarction (type 2) can be calculated from the results of low-level exercise tests done after an acute infarction. About 70% of patients after infarction are suitable for such testing; that is, their course has not been com-

plicated by angina, severe heart failure, or high-grade ventricular arrhythmias. About 20% of these patients have silent ischemia. The prevalence of silent ischemia in patients with angina (type 3) is 40 to 50%, based on Holter data and exercise testing.

Related Basic Science

It has been theorized that differences in the amount of myocardium at jeopardy during painless and painful ischemia could account for the presence of symptoms during one ischemic episode but not another in patients with a history of angina. Some investigators have reported that painless episodes were generally shorter than symptomatic episodes and abnormalities of left ventricular function were not as marked. The overlap in these measurements was considerable, however, and the authors cautioned against extrapolating their results to individual patients; that is, one cannot predict the presence or absence of pain from the extent of left ventricular dysfunction. This conclusion was also reached in studies involving radionuclide ejection fraction measurements. Marked abnormalities in left ventricular function during exercise occurred just as readily without pain as with it.

Another explanation for lack of pain during myocardial ischemia that is particularly applicable to asymptomatic persons involves abnormalities in pain threshold or perception (Maseri et al., 1992). A generally defective perception of painful stimuli has been reported in some patients with silent ischemia. Whether the endorphin-mediated analgesic system plays an important role in silent ischemia is still unclear (Maseri et al., 1992).

Natural History and Its Modification with Treatment

Limited data are available concerning the prognosis with type 1, but yearly mortality is about 2% in individuals with triple-vessel disease. Progression of the angiographic lesions on repeat coronary angiography is also common. Sudden death has been associated with type 1 silent ischemia both directly and indirectly. About 50,000 of 250,000 sudden-death victims in this country per year have no history of heart disease, yet when autopsies are done, these apparently healthy persons have evidence of advanced atherosclerotic disease in their coronary arteries and scars in their myocardium.

Compared with type 1, prognosis appears worse with Type 2, especially when left ventricular dysfunction is present. This finding is most striking in patients with triple-vessel disease. The overall yearly mortality for patients with silent myocardial ischemia is about 5%. As expected, patients with triple-vessel disease have the highest mortality. Among patients with triple-vessel disease, there is a subgroup at even higher risk of cardiac death (approaching 10% per year) because of a combination of reduced exercise tolerance, severe ST depression, and marked fall in radionuclide-derived exercise ejection fraction.

Whether there is a difference in 5-year survival between patients with stable angina pectoris (type 3 patients) who have a positive, but painless, exercise test and patients with stable angina pectoris who have pain with a positive exercise test has not been conclusively determined.

Patients with unstable angina who have 60 minutes or more of silent ischemia per 24 hours of Holter monitoring are believed to have a significantly higher incidence of unfavorable clinical outcomes compared with patients with less silent ischemia or none at all.

The recent randomized multicenter Atenolol Silent Ischemia Study comparing atenolol with placebo has documented that beta blockade appears to influence short-term prognosis favorably (Pepine et al., 1994), whereas the multicenter Asymptomatic Cardia Ischemia Pilot (ACIP) Study demonstrated that revascularization procedures reduce daily life ischemia (most of which is silent) more effectively than medical treatment. The prognostic implications of the ACIP study are still uncertain, however (Knatterud et al., 1994).

Prevention

No specific preventive measures for silent myocardial ischemia are available; what is available are guidelines for reducing the incidence of coronary atherosclerotic heart disease through proper diet (e.g., low animal fat), cessation of smoking, control of hypertension, and regular exercise.

Cost Containment

Several antiischemic drugs are available in generic form, and this should help reduce the cost of medications. The most important aspect of cost containment, however, is the avoidance of procedures that are of little clinical value. For example, performing exercise electrocardiographic tests to look for silent myocardial ischemia in asymptomatic 30-year-old women is nearly useless. The prevalence of coronary artery disease is very low in such subjects, and the likelihood of a false-positive test result is high in this population.

REFERENCES

Cohn PF. Silent myocardial ischemia. Ann Intern Med 1988;109:312.

Knatterud GL, Bourassa MG, Pepine CJ, et al., for the ACIP Investigators. Ef-

fects of treatment strategies to suppress ischemia in patients with coronary artery disease: 12-week results of the Asymptomatic Cardiac Ischemia Pilot (ACIP) Study. J Am Coll Cardiol 1994;24:11.

Maseri A, Crea F, Kaski JC, Davies G. Mechanisms and significance of cardiac ischemia pain. Prog Cardiovasc Dis 1992;35:1.

Pepine CJ, Cohn PF, Deedwania PC, et al., for the ASIST Study Group. Effects of treatment on outcome in mildly symptomatic patients with ischemia during daily life: The Atenolol Silent Ischemia Study (ASIST). Circulation 1994;90:762.

Thaulow E, Erikssen J, Sandvik L, et al. Initial clinical presentation of cardiac disease in asymptomatic men with silent myocardial ischemia and angiographically documented coronary artery disease (the Oslo Ischemia Study). Am J Cardiol 1993;72:629.

CHAPTER 15–47

Myocardial Infarction

Michael E. Assey, M.D., and James F. Spann, Jr., M.D.

DEFINITION

Myocardial infarction is distinguished from other acute ischemic syndromes, such as unstable angina, by the presence of myocardial necrosis.

ETIOLOGY

Most patients who sustain a myocardial infarction have underlying coronary atherosclerosis, a ruptured plaque with overlying thrombus, and resultant coronary occlusion. Risk factors for myocardial infarction are those for atherosclerosis. They are age, male sex, a positive family history, cigarette smoking, hypertension, diabetes, and hyperlipidemia.

CRITERIA FOR DIAGNOSIS
Suggestive

Myocardial infarction may be completely silent and therefore unrecognized by patient or physician; however, the diagnosis is typically suspected by prolonged ischemic chest pain, often associated with dyspnea, diaphoresis, nausea, weakness, or syncope.

Definitive

The diagnosis is confirmed by electrocardiographic changes and/or elevated levels of cardiac enzymes in the peripheral blood. When electrocardiographic changes or enzyme results are equivocal, imaging techniques such as echocardiography and radionuclear studies are helpful in confirming the diagnosis.

CLINICAL MANIFESTATIONS
Subjective

Substernal chest pain ("pressure," "tightness") of variable intensity may radiate to the throat, jaws, arms, or back. It may be similar in quality to prior angina but more prolonged and less likely to respond to sublingual nitroglycerin. Associated symptoms include dyspnea, diaphoresis, nausea, weakness, and apprehension. Palpitations with dizziness or frank syncope may be due to arrhythmias or heart block which frequently accompany infarction. In women, the presentation may be atypical, with back pain frequently present. The elderly also have atypical presentations, with dyspnea being most prominent. This reflects preexisting left ventricular diastolic dysfunction, itself a manifestation of the aging process. Abdominal pain (reduced cardiac output superimposed on mesenteric arterial insufficiency), syncope, and a change in

mental status may be symptoms of myocardial infarction in the elderly. Completely silent, or at least unrecognized, myocardial infarction is more frequent in the elderly but may occur in all age groups. In the Framingham Heart Study, 25 to 30% of infarctions were diagnosed only by electrocardiographic changes on a biennial tracing.

Objective
Physical Examination

Anxiety and/or pain may produce tachycardia and hypertension. The patient is often pale and diaphoretic. Vasovagal reflexes may cause bradycardia and hypotension. A low blood pressure may be due to cardiac decompensation or diminished preload due to dehydration or drug therapy. Extracardiac signs of volume overload reflecting ventricular decompensation may appear, including neck vein distention, hepatomegaly, and peripheral or pulmonary edema (decreased breath sounds, rales, wheezes).

Cardiac examination typically shows an S_4 gallop unless there is atrial fibrillation. An S_3 gallop suggests ventricular failure or volume overload. A soft first heart sound may be due to reduced ventricular contractility, mitral insufficiency, or first degree atrioventricular block. Papillary muscle dysfunction may produce an apical systolic murmur of variable duration and intensity. Other systolic murmurs may be due to anatomic disruption of the mitral valve (papillary muscle or chordae) or a ventricular septal defect. Such mechanical complications usually occur during the first week. Pericardial rubs are frequent but often transitory in transmural myocardial infarction. The precordial impulse may be normal, may be displaced inferiorly and to the left (in the case of left ventricular dilation), or may reveal ectopic pulsations due to underlying ventricular dyskinesis.

Routine Laboratory Abnormalities

In addition to the cardiac enzyme changes noted below, routine laboratory abnormalities may occur. The erythrocyte sedimentation rate is elevated. Leukocytosis generally occurs, with the degree generally correlating with the size of the infarction. When the white blood count exceeds 16,000, another cause (such as infection) should be considered. Liver function tests are elevated in the patient in whom infarction, particularly right ventricular infarction, produces right-sided heart failure and passive hepatic congestion. If the patient is dehydrated, several nonspecific abnormalities may be noted on urinalysis including a high specific gravity.

PLANS
Diagnostic

Differential Diagnosis

There are many causes of chest pain that may mimic the pain of acute myocardial infarction. These include pericarditis, aortic dissection, and upper gastrointestinal problems such as esophageal spasm and/or reflux.

Diagnostic Options

Optimal management of the patient with an evolving myocardial infarction requires prompt and accurate diagnosis. Delay in seeking medical attention—or inaccurate diagnosis—places the patient at increased risk of death. Half of those who die from myocardial infarction do so before reaching the hospital. Delays may also limit the efficacy of thrombolytic therapy and other time-dependent interventions capable of limiting infarct size. Failure to recognize the early warning signs of myocardial infarction or denial of even classic symptoms may contribute to life-threatening delays.

The surface electrocardiogram may confirm an evolving infarction but in other cases may be normal or nondiagnostic. The electrocardiogram is less useful in patients with prior infarction patterns, repolarization changes due to ventricular hypertrophy, or underlying left bundle-branch block. In such cases, the use of two-dimensional echocardiography in the emergency room may facilitate the diagnosis. Electrocardiographic changes of a myocardial infarction include the development of pathologic Q waves, loss of normal R waves, or appearance of a pathologic R wave in lead V_1 (posterior wall infarction). Other changes include ST-segment elevation or depression and T-wave inversion, the magnitude and direction of which depend on the timing and evolution of the infarction. ST-segment elevation is typical in the early hours of Q-wave infarction. Patients with infarction who have only ST and T wave changes are said to have a non Q wave infarction.

Elevation of cardiac enzymes (creatine kinase MB band [CK-MB] and lactate dehydrogenase 1 [LDH_1]) confirm that necrosis has occurred. CK-MB isoenzyme levels begin to appear in the blood 3 to 12 hours after the onset of the infarction, peaking at 12 to 24 hours and remaining elevated for up to 3 days. Recurrent elevations would suggest reinfarction even in the absence of chest pain. LDH is made up of five isoenzymes, of which LDH_1 is most specific for myocardial necrosis. LDH_1 generally peaks between 48 and 72 hours after infarction, but may remain elevated for 7 to 10 days. Recently, new serum markers for acute myocardial infarction have been developed. These include CK-MB isoforms identifiable by immunoinhibition assays based on monoclonal anti-CK-MB antibodies. This allows myocardial infarction to be diagnosed earlier with a higher degree of sensitivity and specificity. Other serum markers for infarction include myoglobin and tropinins. Monoclonal antibodies against cardiac tropinin T have been developed without cross-reactivity to their skeletal muscle isoforms. Detectable levels may remain elevated for 14 days. Cardiac imaging by two-dimensional echocardiography and radionuclear studies have been used to diagnose infarction, when classic electrocardiographic and enzyme changes are not present.

Recommended Approach

The need to diagnose myocardial infarction quickly and accurately puts emphasis on history taking and electrocardiogram interpretation. Patients at high risk for acute myocardial infarction, for example, those with multiple atherosclerotic risk factors, should be managed as if an infarction has occurred, even when the electrocardiographic and enzyme changes are equivocal. This may require a change in conventional management, however, as thrombolytic therapy would generally not be given in the absence of a firm diagnosis. On occasion, early cardiac catheterization is recommended and will guide management when the diagnosis is uncertain.

Therapeutic

Therapeutic Options

The specific treatment of acute myocardial infarction varies with the mode of presentation. Although a small, uncomplicated inferior infarc-

tion might best be treated conservatively, large anterior infarctions require urgent intervention. An evolving myocardial infarction can be reduced in size by reperfusion (thrombolysis, angioplasty, bypass surgery) of the infarct vessel and by measures that reduce myocardial oxygen demand.

As a cardiac catheterization suite will not be immediately available to most infarct victims, intravenous thrombolytic therapy is frequently preferred for acute reperfusion of the occluded infarct artery. Streptokinase (Kabikinase, Streptase), tissue plasminogen activator (tPA, Activase), and anistreplase (anisoylated plasminogen streptokinase activator complex, Eminase) have been approved for such use. In placebo-controlled trials, each has reduced mortality and limited infarct size, particularly when used within the first 3 hours. Although tPA has a higher early reperfusion rate, neither the GISSI-2 (Gruppo Italiano per lo Studio della Streptochinasi nell'Infarcto Miocardico, 1986) nor the ISIS-3 (Third International Study of Infarct Survival, 1993) found a difference in mortality when tPA, streptokinase, and anistreplase were compared. The recent GUSTO Trial (Global Utilization of Streptokinase and Tissue Plasminogen Activator for Occluded Coronary Arteries [Gusto Investigators, 1993]), however, found better results with tPA. In that study, four different thrombolytic regimens were compared. An accelerated dose regimen for tPA was given. Following a 15-mg bolus, 0.75 mg/kg body weight was administered over 30 minutes (not to exceed 50 mg) and then 0.5 mg/kg was given over the next 60 minutes (not to exceed 35 mg). Aspirin was added to all four regimens, as was an intravenous beta blocker in those patients without a contraindication. A small but statistically significant mortality reduction was seen in patients receiving tPA as opposed to those given either of two streptokinase strategies. This large randomized study, including more than 40,000 patients, was the first to show a mortality benefit of one thrombolytic agent over another. The finding must be balanced by the much greater expense of tPA compared with streptokinase and an increased number of hemorrhagic strokes in the tPA group.

Streptokinase is given as a 1-hour infusion of 1.5 million U. Two to four hours following the infusion, or when the partial thromboplastin time (PTT) is two to three times the control value, a heparin infusion is started. A dose of 800 to 1200 U/h is usually needed to maintain a PTT two to three times control. The standard tPA regimen includes an initial bolus of 10 mg followed by a 50-mg infusion over the first hour. The remaining 40 mg is given at a rate of 20 mg/h. The "accelerated regimen," used for tPA in the GUSTO Trial, completes the total infusion in one half of the standard time. A 5000-U bolus of heparin is given along with the initial dose of tPA. A heparin infusion is administered to maintain the PTT at two to three times the control value. Anistreplase is given as a single intravenous bolus of 30 mg over 5 minutes. As with streptokinase, a heparin infusion is started when the PTT is approximately two to three times the control value. Hydrocortisone, 100 mg, is given as an intravenous bolus prior to either streptokinase or anistreplase. Aspirin (160–325 mg/d) is generally administered along with the thrombolytic agent and heparin. Aspirin alone, in one large international study (ISIS-2 Collaborative Group, 1992) significantly reduced mortality when administered as late as 24 hours after the onset of infarction.

Recommended Approach

Despite the proven efficacy of thrombolytic therapy, only one fourth of all patients are treated in this way. This is due to the relatively large number of contraindications and delays in seeking medical attention. In some centers, where an angioplasty suite is immediately available, patients are treated with angioplasty of the occluded vessel without prior thrombolysis. Indeed, this approach may open more vessels than any thrombolytic agent and would be applicable to those who fail thrombolysis or have a contraindication to thrombolytic therapy. Recent studies suggest that direct infarct angioplasty is preferable to thrombolytic therapy in evolving myocardial infarction. Angioplasty was more effective in restoring patency of the infarct vessel and in preventing reocclusion. Patients had a lower incidence of recurrent ischemia, reinfarction, and death. At this point, it remains controversial whether immediate angioplasty should be the standard of care for patients with evolving myocardial infarction. This option is limited to patients who live close to hospitals with angioplasty capability. The highest-risk patients might best be treated with immediate angioplasty. This would include those with cardiogenic shock or sustained hypotension, large anterior wall infarctions, and perhaps advanced age.

For patients receiving thrombolysis, catheterization and angioplasty of any residual lesion are usually delayed for 24 to 72 hours. Earlier intervention is associated with more complications (bleeding, urgent coronary bypass surgery) and no improvement in mortality or left ventricular function. In fact, the recently completed Thrombolysis in Myocardial Infarction (TIMI-IIB) Trial challenged the need for catheterization at all unless there was postinfarction ischemia (recurrent angina, positive stress test, etc.). There was extensive crossover, however, between the conservative and invasive groups in that study and more data are needed to determine optimal management.

Limiting myocardial oxygen demand complements the role of reperfusion techniques. Intravenous nitroglycerin decreases preload, reduces afterload at higher doses, relieves coronary artery spasm, and improves collateral flow. Infusion is usually started at 5 to 10 μg/min, adjusted to alleviate myocardial ischemia, normalize blood pressure, or reduce pretreatment systolic blood pressure by at least 10 mm Hg. Beta blockers can further reduce mortality and recurrent infarction and can be given late or early. The early administration of intravenous metoprolol (Lopressor), 5-mg bolus every 2 minutes × 3, or atenolol (Tenormin), 5 to 10 mg in a single bolus, reduces infarct size and improves prognosis. Beta blockers decrease myocardial oxygen demand by limiting heart rate, blood pressure, and contractility. They may also have antiplatelet effects and some have membrane-stabilizing activity which may prevent arrhythmias.

Routine treatment in the coronary care unit includes bed rest with appropriate sedation, nasal oxygen, and pain relief. Morphine sulfate is an effective analgesic and also decreases preload by venodilation. Meperidine (Demerol) is an alternative analgesic that has a vagolytic effect. It is preferred by some in inferior/posterior wall infarctions where bradycardia and hypotension are more frequent.

As warning arrhythmias are unreliable, many coronary care units use prophylactic lidocaine drips. Although meta-analysis of several trials has failed to prove mortality reduction, patients treated with prophylactic lidocaine are less likely to have ventricular fibrillation. When it is used, a loading dose of 200 mg is given simultaneously with the onset of a 2 to 3 mg/min infusion. Both loading and infusion doses should be reduced in patients with congestive heart failure and/or hepatic insufficiency.

Lipoprotein profile should be obtained at the appropriate time (see Chapter 15-1). We have been impressed by the number of young male smokers who present with a myocardial infarction and a normal total cholesterol. They often have very low high-density lipoprotein cholesterol levels, which at times require drug therapy. Aspirin remains a cornerstone of therapy for myocardial infarction. It should be administered along with thrombolytic therapy on presentation, with a dose of 2 grains chewable aspirin having been used in many large trials. Following the infarction, even if percutaneous transluminal coronary angioplasty or coronary bypass surgery is not needed, aspirin is continued for secondary prevention. The "best" dose of aspirin is unknown, but it appears that low doses (such as 81 mg/d) are adequate for aspirin's antiplatelet effect. Calcium channel blockers have limited usefulness in evolving myocardial infarction.

In non-Q-wave infarctions, diltiazem (Cardizem) and verapamil (Calan, Isoptin) can reduce recurrent infarction, postinfarction angina, and silent myocardial ischemia. These agents have intrinsic negative inotropic effects. They must be used with caution, if at all, in patients with left ventricular systolic dysfunction (left ventricular ejection fraction below 40%).

Angiotensin-converting enzyme inhibitors are being increasingly used in patients with acute myocardial infarction. The patient with a large anterior infarction who has an ejection fraction below 40% will benefit most. Enalapril (Vasotec) and captopril (Capoten) have been studied most closely, but the beneficial effect of angiotensin-converting enzyme inhibition following myocardial infarction is probably a class effect.

FOLLOW-UP

The patient and important family members should be updated regularly as to the patient's progress. When feasible, a pathophysiologic explanation of events and rationale for interventions should be offered. Non-Q-wave infarctions have a favorable early prognosis, but close follow-up is needed, usually including cardiac catheterization. Psychological support is important as the patient will be concerned about returning to work or recreational and sexual activities. If the patient has hyperlipidemia, siblings and children should have blood lipids measured as well.

Patients at increased risk for recurrent cardiac events can be identified. Techniques used include cardiac catheterization, exercise stress testing (generally at reduced workload), noninvasive imaging techniques, Holter monitoring, signal averaging of filtered electrocardiograms, and electrophysiologic testing. Those at greatest risk for recurrent cardiac events have sustained large infarctions with resulting low ejection fractions with residual myocardial ischemia and complex or sustained ventricular ectopy. Specific therapy depends on the presence and extent of each of these abnormalities.

DISCUSSION

Prevalence and Incidence

Myocardial infarction and its complications constitute the number one cause of death in the United States and other developed countries. In the United States alone, one million myocardial infarctions occur each year. Half of all myocardial infarction-related deaths occur outside of the hospital.

Related Basic Science

Acute myocardial infarction can occur in patients with normal coronary arteries. Examples include aortic stenosis, thyrotoxicosis, coronary artery spasm, and cocaine abuse. Most occur in individuals with atherosclerosis and are initiated by atherosclerotic plaque rupture. This produces a cascade of events culminating in thrombosis with occlusion of the coronary artery. The myocardium supplied by that occluded vessel is injured and, if reperfusion does not quickly occur, myocardial tissue necrosis occurs. Animal studies suggest that myocardial tissue viability is completely lost after 4 to 6 hours of coronary occlusion. In humans this interval is variable, influenced by the presence of collateral flow and intermittent obstruction ("winking") of the occluded artery. Coronary atherosclerotic plaques most likely to rupture are eccentric, lipid-laden, and covered by a thin fibrous plaque. At the site of rupture, macrophages (which have multiple atherogenic and plaque-destabilizing effects) are heavily infiltrated. Determining the triggers of plaque rupture represents an area of intensive medical research.

Natural History and Its Modification with Treatment

The natural history depends on the size of the infarction and what complications have occurred. In general, patients with normal postinfarction left ventricular ejection fraction, those with non-Q-wave myocardial infarctions, and young patients with initial infarctions have a good prognosis. The unexpectedly low (5–10%) 1-year mortality of the placebo groups in several recent thrombolytic trials is encouraging.

Prevention

As coronary atherosclerosis is the substratum for most cases of myocardial infarction, prevention can be realized only to the extent that coronary atherosclerosis can be controlled or mitigated. Early and aggressive risk factor modification is essential. Physicians should support the efforts of various volunteer organizations encouraging the general public to stop smoking, to reduce the amount of saturated fat in their diets, and to exercise regularly. At least half of the 500,000 myocardial infarction deaths occur early, often before hospitalization. Bypasser-initiated cardiopulmonary resuscitation may be lifesaving. Physicians should instruct their high-risk patients as to the early warning signs of myocardial infarction.

Cost Containment

The diagnosis and treatment of myocardial infarction and its complications are a major expense for the American health care system. More efficient use of coronary care beds is needed. To this end, more accurate and readily available serum markers to diagnose and exclude infarction are important. Patients with small infarctions can be mobilized sooner with obvious economic and psychological benefits. Recent studies suggest that patients with uncomplicated infarctions can be discharged after 7 days. Those successfully treated with thrombolysis and/or angioplasty should be able to return to work quicker and enjoy shorter lengths of recuperation. Enrollment in cardiac rehabilitation programs is often effective in returning the patient to an active lifestyle. If results of the TIMI-IIB Trial are confirmed, patients receiving thrombolytic therapy may not routinely require catheterization and angioplasty. This would save many millions of dollars, which could be used for research aimed at preventing this major epidemiologic problem.

REFERENCES

Feit F, Mueller HS, Braunwald E, et al. Thrombolysis in myocardial infarction (TIMI) phase II trial: Outcome comparison of a "conservative strategy" in community versus tertiary hospitals: The TIMI Research Group. J Am Coll Cardiol 1990;16:1529.

Gruppo Italiano per lo Studio della Streptochinasi nell'Infarcto Miocardico (GISSI). Effectiveness of intravenous thrombolytic treatment in acute myocardial infarction. Lancet 1986;1:397–402.

GUSTO Investigators. GUSTO Trials: An international randomized trial comparing four thrombolytic strategies for acute myocardial infarction. N Engl J Med 1993;329:673–682.

Lange RA, Hills LD. Immediate angioplasty for acute myocardial infarction. N Engl J Med 1993;328:726–729.

ISIS-2 Collaborative Group. Randomized trial of intravenous streptokinase, oral aspirin, both or neither among 17,187 cases of suspected acute myocardial infarction: 1515-2. Lancet 1988;2:349.

ISIS-3 (Third International Study of Infarct Survival) Collaborative Group. ISIS-3: A randomised comparison of streptokinase vs tissue plasminogen activator vs anistreplase and of aspirin plus heparin vs aspirin alone among 41,299 cases of suspected acute myocardial infarction. Lancet 1993;339:753–770.

Morris DC, Walter PF, Hurst JW. The recognition and treatment of myocardial infarction and its complications. In: Hurst JW, et al., eds. The heart. 7th ed. New York: McGraw-Hill, 1990:1054.

Yusuf S, Whittes J, Friedman L. Overview of results of randomized clinical trials in heart disease: 1. Treatments following myocardial infarction. JAMA 1988;260:2088.

CHAPTER 15–48

Acute Rheumatic Fever

Robert C. Schlant, M.D.

DEFINITION

Acute rheumatic fever (ARF) is an inflammatory syndrome that may involve many systems, particularly the joints, heart, brain, skin, and subcutaneous tissues.

ETIOLOGY

Virtually all attacks of ARF follow a streptococcal infection of the upper respiratory tract. On the other hand, most streptococcal infections are not followed by ARF. In epidemics of exudative pharyngitis due to group A streptococci, the attack rate appears to be 2 to 3%, whereas it is only 0.1 to 1% following sporadic cases of group A streptococcal infection. ARF appears to be a hypersensitivity response to a circulating antibody or a state of delayed hypersensitivity that is initiated by streptococcal membrane antigens. There appear to be "rheumatogenic strains" of *Streptococcus pyogenes*. Of the approximately 90 M serotypes of streptococci, about 8 are especially rheumatogenic (M-1, -3, -5, -6, -14, -18, -19, and -24). These have a common antigenic domain that is immunologically cross-reactive with human heart tissue. Most also have a mucoid colony form and produce pyrogenic exotoxins. Individuals with human leukocyte antigen (HLA) class II antigens (DR-4 in Caucasians and DR-2 in blacks) appear to be predisposed to the development of ARF. ARF is virtually unknown in children less than 2 years of age, who have only a feeble capacity for antibody formation.

CRITERIA FOR DIAGNOSIS

Suggestive

There is no single clinical manifestation that is pathognomonic for the diagnosis of ARF. In most patients, the syndrome begins 10 to 20 days following an infection of the pharynx with certain strains of streptococci. The presence of individual major and minor manifestations (Table 15–48–1) is suggestive. The occurrence of "growing pains," arthralgia, abdominal pain, or frequent nosebleeds is sometimes noted in children with ARF but these are so nonspecific as to be clinically of minimal value. It should be noted that in adults with acquired mitral stenosis, which is thought to be virtually always the consequence of ARF, a history of ARF is obtained in only 50 to 60% of patients.

Definitive

A definitive diagnosis of ARF can be made from the finding of Aschoff bodies in a microscopic study of myocardial tissue. Of note, these findings may persist for many years following the initial attack of ARF.

In general, the diagnosis of ARF is made on the combination of clinical and laboratory findings using the modified Jones criteria (see Table 15–48–1), as there is no single symptom, sign, or laboratory test that is pathognomonic or diagnostic of ARF. The current updated Jones crite-

TABLE 15–48–1. GUIDELINES FOR THE DIAGNOSIS OF INITIAL ATTACK OF RHEUMATIC FEVER (JONES CRITERIA, 1992 UPDATE)*

Major Manifestations
Carditis
Polyarthritis
Chorea
Erythema marginatum
Subcutaneous nodules

Minor Manifestations
Clinical findings
  Arthralgia
  Fever
Laboratory findings
  Elevated acute phase reactants
    Erythrocyte sedimentation rate
    C-reactive protein
  Prolonged PR interval

Supporting Evidence of Antecedent Group A Streptococcal Infection
Positive throat culture or rapid streptococcal antigen test
Elevated or rising streptococcal antibody titer

*If supported by evidence of preceding group A streptococcal infection, the presence of two major manifestations or of one major and two minor manifestations indicates a high probability of acute rheumatic fever.
Source: Special Writing Group of the Committee on Rheumatic Fever, Endocarditis, and Kawasaki Disease of the Council on Cardiovascular Disease in the Young of the American Heart Association. Guidelines for the diagnosis of rheumatic fever: Jones criteria, 1992 Update. JAMA 1992;268:2069. Reproduced with permission of the American Medical Association, copyright 1992.

ria are designed to establish the diagnosis of the initial attack of rheumatic fever, in contrast to former guidelines which also included recurrent rheumatic fever and previous rheumatic fever or rheumatic heart disease as major or minor manifestations. In general, there is a very high probability of an initial attack of ARF in the presence of either two major manifestations or one major and two minor manifestations (Table 15–48–1).

CLINICAL MANIFESTATIONS

Subjective

Patients usually have fever and malaise in association with migratory polyarthritis. Patients may have chest pain from pericarditis, symptoms of dyspnea and orthopnea from heart failure, or acute abdominal pain. These symptoms usually appear a week or 10 days after the "sore throat." Chorea may not make its appearance for some weeks after the original streptococcal infection.

Patients with ARF may have recurrences, particularly as adolescents or young adults.

There appears to be an increased susceptibility to ARF and rheumatic heart disease in some families although the molecular biology and genetics are not well established.

Objective

Physical Examination

Patients usually have generalized malaise and moderate fever.

Migratory polyarthritis with increased swelling, heat, and redness of several joints, particularly the hips, knees, ankles, elbows, and wrists, is the most common manifestation of ARF and is seen in perhaps 75% of patients. In most patients several joints are involved although the temporomandibular joint and small joints of the hands and feet are usually not involved in isolation. In most patients a joint is involved for about 1 or 2 weeks at a time while another joint becomes inflamed. In most patients with no treatment the arthritis usually lasts less than 3 weeks, although longer and more indolent instances are not infrequent. The joints are usually painful with severe tenderness, swelling, warmth, and redness. The prompt response of the arthritis to aspirin strongly supports the diagnosis of ARF.

Rheumatic carditis occurs in about 40 to 50% of patients with ARF and may involve the valves, myocardium, and/or pericardium. Thus, the patient may develop sharp precordial pain from acute pericarditis, symptoms of congestive heart failure with tachycardia and gallop rhythm from the myocarditis, and new murmurs from acute mitral and/or aortic valve regurgitation. Some patients with acute mitral valve regurgitation also have a short, low-pitched middiastolic murmur (Carey Coombs murmur) following the third heart sound. There may be evidence of congestive heart failure, with pulmonary rales, distended neck veins, hepatomegaly, and peripheral edema. Pericarditis, which clinically occurs in perhaps only 5 to 10% of patients with ARF may be manifested by a pericardial friction rub, but it rarely if ever proceeds to chronic constrictive pericarditis. It is virtually always present in patients who succumb to ARF.

Some patients have Syndenham's chorea, which is manifest by involuntary, abrupt grimaces and nonrepetitive purposeless limb movements. Occasionally, the children may also have emotional instability, cry or laugh inappropriately, and have slurred or halting speech for several weeks or months. Patients usually develop chorea several months following the responsible pharyngeal streptococcal infection.

Subcutaneous nodules usually occur weeks or months after the onset of ARF. They are painless, nontender firm nodules averaging about 3 mm in diameter. They are usually found over the elbows, knuckles, knees, vertebrae, and the back of the head.

Erythema marginatum may be present on the trunk or proximal extremities. It is characterized by macules that clear in the center, producing ovules, circles, or crescents.

Routine Laboratory Abnormalities

The erythrocyte sedimentation rate is virtually always elevated and is useful for following the activity of acute rheumatic fever. The white blood cell count is moderately elevated and the C-reactive protein is positive. The electrocardiogram often shows atrial tachycardia, at times with prolonged atrioventricular conduction and a long PR interval, and nonspecific ST changes. Atrioventricular junctional tachycardia may also occur. Patients with acute pericarditis may have diffuse ST-segment elevation or T-wave inversions. The chest film may show enlargement of the cardiac shadow and/or pulmonary congestion.

PLANS

Diagnostic

Differential Diagnosis

The differential diagnosis is extensive and includes rheumatoid arthritis, pyogenic arthritis, infective endocarditis, systemic lupus erythematosus, atrial myxoma, sickle cell crisis, tuberculosis, viral myocarditis, leukemia, dermatomyositis, flu, Lyme disease, serum sickness, drug reaction, and Reiter's disease.

Diagnostic Options

It is frequently important to rule out the various infections that can mimic ARF that are listed in the differential diagnosis. The clinical setting and the patient's characteristics usually differentiate many of the other conditions from ARF. It is important to determine whether the patient has had a recent streptococcal infection by obtaining repeated multiple streptococcal antibody determinations.

The plasma concentration of antibodies against one or more streptococcal extracellular products is regularly increased and its measurement forms an important part of the diagnosis. In approximately 80% of cases, the antistreptolysin O (ASO) titer is elevated to more than 333 U in children over 5 years of age and to more than 250 U in adults. In the 20% of patients in whom ASO titers are low, there is virtually always elevation of other antibodies indicating recent streptococcal infection. Thus, there may be elevations of anti-DNase B, antistreptokinase, or antihyaluronidase. The diagnosis of ARF is questionable in the absence of serologic evidence of a recent streptococcal infarction.

Recommended Approach

The patient should have a throat culture obtained, as about 25% of patients with ARF still harbor group A streptococcal bacteria. A complete blood count, erythrocyte sedimentation rate, 12-lead electrocardiogram, postero anterior and lateral chest films, and echocardiogram should be obtained. The ASO titer should be measured and followed every 1 to 2 weeks to obtain evidence of recent streptococcal infection. In the 20% of patients without diagnostic elevation or increasing levels of the ASO titer, it may be useful to perform one of the following other streptococcal antibody tests: anti-DNase B or, if available, the antistreptokinase (ASK) test, the antistreptohyaluronidase (ASH) test, the anti-NADase test, or the anti-group A carbohydrate test. Of these alternatives, the anti-DNase B is generally favored because of better reproducibility.

Echocardiography is useful to follow ventricular performance, pericardial effusion, or evidence of marked rheumatic valvulitis.

Therapeutic

After throat cultures have been obtained, patients should receive intramuscular benzathine penicillin G (1.2 million U for adults or 600,000 U for children). Restriction of activities is dependent on the extent of arthritis and the severity of the carditis. Suppressive therapy with aspirin or corticosteroids should not be initiated until a definite diagnosis of ARF has been established. Aspirin is very useful for the relief of the arthritis and frequently produces a dramatic improvement in 24 hours. A prompt and marked response of the arthritis to aspirin within 24 hours is also helpful in establishing the diagnosis. Aspirin is administered to children in a dose of 80 mg/kg per day for the first 2 weeks and 60 mg/kg per day for the following 6 weeks. Therapy should be adjusted to maintain a blood salicylate level of about 25 mg/dL. Corticosteroids are useful in patients in whom aspirin does not control the fever, discomfort, and tachycardia, particularly those who have evidence of heart failure. Unfortunately, there is no evidence that either corticosteroids or aspirin decreases the long-term valvular or myocardial damage. Corticosteroid therapy is begun with intravenous methylprednisolone 10 to 40 mg, followed by oral prednisone. Prednisone is usually begun in a dose of 40 to 60 mg/d, with an attempt to taper begun after 2 to 3 weeks. The dose is usually decreased at the rate of 5 mg every 2 to 3 days. If congestive heart failure occurs, it may also be necessary to use diuretics, angiotensin-converting enzyme inhibitors, and digoxin.

Patients with evidence of carditis should be hospitalized and observed carefully. Some patients have a smoldering form of carditis that may last for many months. In a rare patient with severe mitral or aortic valve regurgitation and smoldering rheumatic fever, it may be necessary to perform valve replacement, which occasionally appears to decrease the rheumatic activity. Chorea is treated by barbiturates, chlorpromazine (Thorazine), and haloperidol.

When the diagnosis of ARF is established or is highly likely, patients should be placed on prophylactic antibiotics to prevent recurrent streptococcal infection (see Prevention).

FOLLOW-UP

Following ARF, all patients should be on antibiotic prophylaxis to prevent rheumatic fever (see Prevention). Patients should be followed regularly for the detection and evaluation of valvular heart disease, which may develop to 10 to 20 years after the initial episode of rheumatic fever. Patients who have residual murmurs or who develop heart murmurs should be evaluated with periodic electrocardiograms, echocardiograms, and chest roentgenograms. Women with evidence of severe valvular heart disease should be counseled regarding the potential hazards of pregnancy.

DISCUSSION
Prevalence and Incidence

There is anecdotal evidence that the frequency and severity of ARF in the United States has decreased since the Civil War. There are firm data indicating that the incidence, prevalence, recurrence rate, and severity of rheumatic fever have been declining in both North America and Western Europe since the early years of the 20th century. This decline was particularly steep in the 1960s and 1970s. The reasons for the dramatic decline in the incidence of ARF in the United States and other highly developed countries are not clearly established. Some of the decrease may be related to improvements in living standards, but it is likely that changes in the streptococcal bacteria themselves are to a large degree responsible for the decrease. It is significant that the decline began before the antibiotic era and that there has been a mild resurgence of ARF since about 1984. These small outbreaks have been associated with the reemergence of strains of streptococci that exhibit M-protein types and the mucoid colonial form known to be associated with rheumatogenicity. Although ARF has decreased markedly in the Western World following World War II, the prevalence has remained elevated in areas such as India and Sri Lanka, where the prevalence is approximately 140 per 100,000 children between 5 and 19 years of age. The resurgence of ARF in the United States since about 1984 has been associated with a worldwide increase in severe and life-threatening streptococcal infections such as streptococcal necrotizing fasciitis and toxic streptococcus syndrome.

Related Basic Science
Genetics

Some families are thought to be more susceptible to ARF than others. In addition, the concordance rate for rheumatic fever is about seven times higher in monozygotic twin pairs than in dizygotic twin pairs.

Altered Molecular Biology

Streptococcal cell membranes have been shown to cross-react with myocardial sarcolemma. Thus, there may be an "autoimmune" reaction that results in the carditis seen in patients with ARF. A similar cross-reaction has been reported in the brain, with antibodies to the caudate nucleus reported in patients with Sydenham's chorea. There is some evidence of a marker on the surface of non-T lymphocytes in patients

with rheumatic fever or rheumatic heart disease. It is possible that these markers may assist in identifying individuals or families who process streptococcal antigens in an abnormal manner. The full pathogenic mechanisms responsible for ARF and rheumatic heart disease are only beginning to be understood. It is not known why ARF follows only streptococcal infection involving the upper respiratory tract.

Anatomic Derangement

Permanent joint deformity is unusual, although Jaccoud's deformity of metacarpophalangeal joints occasionally occurs. Chorea, which may last from several months to a year or more, is associated with an increased incidence of rheumatic heart disease 20 years later. Some patients who have no heart murmurs following their initial attack of ARF may develop murmurs after 10 to 20 years or longer, whereas in other patients who initially have the murmur of mitral valve regurgitation following ARF, the murmur may disappear or may be replaced by the murmur of mitral valve stenosis. In general, males appear to have more involvement of the aortic valve than women. In virtually all patients with rheumatic heart disease, the mitral valve is involved when it is thoroughly examined grossly and microscopically. ARF rarely, if ever, results in constrictive pericarditis.

Natural History and Its Modification with Treatment

Acute rheumatic fever can be virtually always prevented if the streptococcal infection of the respiratory tract is treated within 9 days with appropriate antibiotic therapy (penicillin). When patients have recurrent ARF, it tends to mimic previous attacks with similar patterns of arthritis and carditis. Although rheumatic heart disease may result from a single episode of ARF, it appears likely that recurrent episodes are associated with progressively greater valvular damage. In some areas of the world, significant valvular heart disease is encountered in young adolescents much more frequently than in the United States or Europe. Some patients who have no murmurs following their initial attack may develop them after many years, whereas many others who have mitral valve regurgitation may lose this murmur or it may be replaced by the murmur of mitral valve stenosis. Some studies have indicated that if a patient has an episode of ARF and there is no evidence of valvular disease with frequent thorough examinations, it is highly unlikely that the person will have permanent valvular heart disease. Treatment of ARF with either aspirin or corticosteroids does not decrease the long-term valvular or myocardial damage. It is uncertain whether ARF results in a permanent "myocardial factor" with myocardial damage due to perivascular microvascular scarring. Some patients with severe valvular heart disease resulting from ARF die of congestive heart failure unless this is treated by medical means and, in some instances, by valve replacement.

Prevention

Prompt treatment of streptococcal pharyngitis is very successful in the primary prevention of ARF. Successful therapy involves either penicillin or erythromycin. This therapy should be initiated within 9 or 10 days of the onset of symptoms at the latest. In epidemics, it is useful to treat all members of the group with intramuscular penicillin. Family members and other associates should have throat cultures to identify subclinical streptococcal infection or carrier states.

Recurrent episodes of ARF can be prevented with appropriate prophylaxis against streptococcal infection. Oral penicillin V (250 mg twice daily), sulfadiazine (1 g daily), and erythromycin (250 mg twice daily) are all effective. Intramuscular penicillin G benzathine (1.2 million U every 4 weeks) is probably the most effective method but is associated with moderate discomfort. Dosages should be modified for children weighing less than 60 pounds (27 kg). Prophylaxis should be continued for at least 20 years in patients who have had carditis and longer in high-risk individuals with valvular disease or in patients who have frequent exposures to possible streptococcal carriers. In patients with evidence of rheumatic heart disease, antibiotic-appropriate prophylaxis against bacterial endocarditis should be maintained for life.

Cost Containment

To establish the diagnosis of ARF, it is not necessary to obtain titers of all the antibodies to the preceding streptococcal infection. In most patients, an elevated or rising ASO titer is adequate. During follow-up, rheumatic activity can be followed by the erythrocyte sedimentation rate.

REFERENCES

Bisno AL. Group A streptococcal infections and acute rheumatic fever. N Engl J Med 1991;325:783.

Bland EF, Jones TD. Rheumatic fever and rheumatic heart disease: 20 year report on 1000 patients followed since childhood. Circulation 1951;4:836.

Dajani AS, Ayoub E, Bierman FZ, et al. Guidelines for the diagnosis of rheumatic fever: Jones criteria, 1992 update. JAMA 1992;268:2069.

Dajani AS, Bisno AL, Chung KJ, et al. Prevention of rheumatic fever: Commit-

tee on Rheumatic Fever, Endocarditis, and Kawasaki Disease of the Council on Cardiovascular Disease in the Young, the American Heart Association. Circulation 1988;78:1082.

Feinstein AR, Spagnuolo M. The clinical patterns of acute rheumatic fever: A reappraisal. Medicine 1962;41:279.

Kaplan EL. Acute rheumatic fever. In: Schlant RC, Alexander RW, O'Rourke RA, et al., eds. Hurst's the heart. 8th ed. New York: McGraw-Hill, 1994:1451.

Silber EN. Rheumatic fever and rheumatic heart disease. In: Sibler EN, ed. Heart disease. 2nd ed. New York: MacMillan, 1987:914.

Veasy LG, Weidmeier SE, Orsmond GS, et al. Resurgence of acute rheumatic fever in the intermountain area of the United States. N Engl J Med 1987;316:421.

CHAPTER 15–49

Myocarditis

Walter H. Abelmann, M.D.

DEFINITION

Myocarditis is an inflammatory disease of the heart muscle that may be acute, subacute, or chronic.

ETIOLOGY

Myocarditis may be caused by a specific infection (viruses or other organisms) or toxic agent or may be associated with a systemic illness such as a collagen–vascular or autoimmune disease. It may also be idiopathic.

CRITERIA FOR DIAGNOSIS

Suggestive

A frequent setting is the appearance of new cardiac abnormalities accompanying an acute infectious illness that is recognizable by its extracardiac manifestations. Myocarditis also should be suspected when there is new onset of heart failure, arrhythmia, or conduction disturbance in an individual not known to have heart disease.

Clues that should lead to the consideration of acute myocarditis include tachycardia out of proportion to the body temperature in any acute infectious illness, especially if accompanied by myalgias and tenderness of muscles; dyspnea, palpitation, gallop rhythms, or evidence of heart failure during or following an acute viral illness; and new electrocardiographic or echocardiographic abnormalities following an acute illness. Evidence of acute pericarditis should always lead the physician to question myocardial involvement. Chronic myocarditis should be suspected in any individual who presents with heart failure, idiopathic arrhythmias, or conduction disturbances of relatively recent onset.

Myocarditis is encountered primarily in childhood, adolescence, or young adulthood; it is not unusual in middle age, but it is relatively rare in the elderly. A presumptive diagnosis of myocarditis may be made when there is evidence of new or relatively recent onset of heart disease in the absence of evidence for coronary, valvular, congenital, hypertensive, or specific heart muscle disease.

Definitive

A definitive diagnosis requires histopathologic confirmation by means of myocardial biopsy.

CLINICAL MANIFESTATIONS

Subjective

In developed countries, the majority of cases of myocarditis are thought to be of viral etiology. The patient should be questioned as to recent viral illness or exposure thereto, exposure to birds (psittacosis), inges-

tion of poorly cooked pork (trichinosis), and travel (South American trypanosomiasis, Q fever). Myocarditis has been reported in individuals addicted to cocaine and in individuals with AIDS. Familial occurrence of myocarditis is rare.

The wide spectrum of presentation of myocarditis is given in Table 15–49–1. When myocarditis is focal, it may be entirely asymptomatic and remain undetected, or it may give rise to atrial or ventricular ectopic beats or rhythms, which may or may not be felt as palpitation. First- or second-degree heart block per se is usually asymptomatic, but complete heart block may lead to syncope or exertional dyspnea. When myocarditis is multifocal or diffuse, the systolic or pump function of the heart may become impaired, leading to exertional dyspnea, fatigue, and eventually congestive heart failure with pulmonary and/or peripheral edema and even anasarca. When the process is very severe and develops rapidly, it may result in cardiogenic shock with hypotension and vascular collapse. When a large focal region of myocardium is involved, symptoms and signs may simulate acute myocardial infarction secondary to ischemic heart disease.

Objective

Physical Examination

Physical findings range from ectopic rhythms to evidence of impaired ventricular function, such as S_3 and S_4 gallops, and evidence of cardiac enlargement. When dilation of the involved ventricle is severe, murmurs of mitral and/or tricuspid valve regurgitation may appear. Many infectious agents, such as Coxsackie viruses, may involve the pericardium as well as the myocardium, and pericardial pain, friction rub,

TABLE 15–49–1. SPECTRUM OF PRESENTATION OF MYOCARDITIS

Excessive fatigue
Chest pain
Unexplained sinus tachycardia
Acute pericarditis
S_3 and/or S_4 gallops
Abnormal electrocardiogram
Abnormal chest roentgenogram
Atrial or ventricular arrhythmias
Partial or complete heart block
Congestive heart failure
Cardiomyopathy of recent onset
Atypical myocardial infarction
Cardiogenic shock
Sudden death

and effusion may dominate the clinical picture, obscuring the frequently present simultaneous involvement of heart muscle.

Valuable clues to myocarditis may be derived from the involvement of other organ systems by the morbid process, for example, the lungs in *Mycoplasma,* the skin in exanthematous viral disease or herpes, the skeletal muscles (myalgia and muscle tenderness) in cardiomyotropic viruses, the liver in hepatitis, and the joints in acute rheumatic fever or Lyme disease.

Routine Laboratory Abnormalities

Like the physical findings, routine laboratory tests yield only nonspecific abnormalities.

The chest roentgenogram may be entirely normal or may reveal enlargement of one or both atria or one or both ventricles or even evidence of pulmonary congestion such as redistribution or frank pulmonary edema.

The electrocardiogram may be normal or reveal nonspecific ST–T wave changes, evidence of pericarditis, atrial or ventricular ectopy or arrhythmias, or any degree of heart block.

Urinalysis and blood chemistry are of value primarily because they may give clues to a systemic disease or infection. Cardiac enzymes may be abnormal early in the course of the illness.

PLANS
Diagnostic
Differential Diagnosis

The differential diagnosis includes noninflammatory cardiac toxicity secondary to ethanol, cocaine, anthracyclines, and other cardiotoxic agents or drugs, as well as new onset of congestive heart failure, arrhythmia, or disturbances of conduction, secondary to ischemic, valvular, or congenital heart disease, or cardiomyopathy.

Diagnostic Options

The only procedure that permits the diagnosis of myocarditis with complete certainty is cardiac biopsy. The preferred approach is transvenous or transarterial endomyocardial biopsy of the right ventricular septum or left ventricle, respectively. When a cellular infiltrate and myocardial necrosis can be demonstrated in the absence of coronary disease, a firm diagnosis of myocarditis may be made. Myocarditis may be focal or diffuse. The likelihood of missing the lesion by sampling error is decreased by taking multiple samples. In experienced hands, the procedure is quite safe. With rare exceptions, however, biopsy does not yield an etiologic diagnosis. The exceptions include detection of infiltration by eosinophils, or sarcoid lesions, of parasites such as *Toxoplasma* and trypanosomes. It must be kept in mind that with the acute form of myocarditis, the infiltrative process may be transient, and a delayed endomyocardial biopsy may yield only evidence of myofiber loss and replacement fibrosis, which are nondiagnostic. With regard to etiology, as viral myocarditis is thought to be the most frequent form of acute myocarditis in the West, efforts should be made to recover virus from throat washings, urine, stool, or myocardium during the acute illness. Acute and convalescent titers for neutralizing antibodies may be valuable if a fourfold rise or fall can be demonstrated; however, viral studies are not generally available, and results may be delayed.

Echocardiography and nuclear imaging, for example, by gated blood pool scanning, may be helpful in delineating the location and extent of ventricular dysfunction and ruling out other forms of heart disease. These tests are not diagnostic, but they are of value in monitoring the degree of dysfunction. The diagnostic value of gallium scans and antimyosin scans remains uncertain.

Recommended Approach

When a patient has developed new-onset cardiac abnormalities—be they arrhythmias, conduction disturbances, or heart failure—especially in young or middle age, it is recommended that an etiologic diagnosis be pursued, for prognostic as well as therapeutic reasons. If ischemic, valvular, congenital, and pulmonary heart disease can be ruled out, a cardiomyopathy is quite likely. Specific heart muscle disease must be

considered, of which myocarditis is one form. Myocardial biopsy may yield a definitive diagnosis and is used by some but not all cardiologists. This procedure also may lead to diagnosis of specific heart muscle disease such as hemochromatosis and amyloidosis.

Therapeutic

Treatment of myocarditis is symptomatic and nonspecific. During the acute phase of the illness, physical activity should be restricted to reduce cardiac work. Electrocardiographic monitoring is advisable to permit early detection of potentially life-threatening arrhythmias or conduction defects. Antiinflammatory drugs have not been proven effective, and steroids or other immunosuppressive drugs may exacerbate the myocardial lesions in the acute stage. Congestive heart failure may respond to digitalis glycosides, diuretics, vasodilators, and angiotensin-converting enzyme inhibitors, although caution is advised. The threshold for digitalis toxicity may be lowered, and heart failure may be converted into cardiogenic shock with excessive reduction of preload by diuresis or afterload by vasodilators. Atrial and ventricular premature beats are an indication for electrocardiographic monitoring; antiarrhythmic drugs, all of which also have negative inotropic properties, are not indicated. Supraventricular arrhythmias with rapid ventricular response, leading to heart failure, should generally be converted electrically. High-grade ventricular ectopy merits antiarrhythmic therapy as used in ischemic heart disease, although controlled studies are not available. High-grade heart block is an indication for transvenous pacing, which usually is required only on a temporary basis. Persistent high-grade congestive heart failure is often accompanied by thromboembolic complications; hence anticoagulant therapy is advised.

When congestive heart failure is intractable and progresses, or when cardiogenic shock is not responsive to medical therapy, intraaortic balloon pumping or even temporary external cardiac assist may be considered. Some cases of subacute and chronic myocarditis have been treated with a combination of corticosteroids and azathioprine or with cyclosporine. However, a recent controlled randomized trial does not support this approach (Mason, et al. 1995). Abstention from ethanol and avoidance of cardiotoxic drugs are recommended.

Chronic myocarditis presenting as intractable cardiomyopathy and unrelenting heart failure is one of the indications for consideration for cardiac transplantation. The surgical risk is relatively high, however, and the postoperative prognosis relatively poor.

FOLLOW-UP

Although the majority of patients with acute myocarditis go on to full clinical recovery, the process may continue subclinically or may recur. When the acute disease has resulted in significant heart failure, the likelihood of full recovery is decreased. Thus, all patients should be followed, initially at intervals of 1 to 3 months, and later, yearly. Tolerance of physical activity, exertion, and sports should be determined. S_3 and S_4 gallops should be carefully listened for, and heart size should be determined by chest roentgenogram, or, preferably, ventricular dimensions should be determined by echocardiogram.

Evaluation of ventricular function, including ejection fraction, by echocardiography or by radioventriculography at rest and during exercise is a valuable means of following ventricular function in patients who have manifested significant heart failure acutely.

DISCUSSION
Prevalence and Incidence

The true incidence of myocarditis is unknown; the great majority of cases are thought to be asymptomatic and subclinical. At autopsy, the prevalence of acute myocarditis ranges from 1.2 to 3.5%. Among patients with acute viral infections, myocardial involvement has been reported in 1 to 5%. Young males are most likely to be afflicted.

Related Basic Science

In the majority of cases of myocarditis in developed countries, the etiology remains unknown, although it is likely that most are initiated by viral infection. Coxsackie B virus, echovirus, influenza virus, and

Epstein–Barr virus are thought to be most frequently involved, but all pathogenic viruses may replicate in the heart. Based on experimental studies, these viruses are thought to replicate in cardiac tissue at most for 2 weeks, whereas the inflammatory infiltrate and necrosis of myofibers often can be demonstrated to persist for weeks to months. This has given rise to the infectious–immune theory of the pathogenesis of myocarditis; the inflammatory and necrotic process is initiated by a viral infection but maintained or enhanced by immune or autoimmune processes, which become the principal cause of subacute and chronic myocarditis. The inflammatory lesions and myofiber necrosis may ultimately lead to myofiber loss, interstitial and perivascular fibrosis, and hypertrophy of remaining myofibers, eventually resulting in cardiomyopathy, usually of the dilated type, indistinguishable from idiopathic dilated cardiomyopathy.

Much work with experimental models of myocarditis is supportive of the infectious–immune hypothesis of pathogenesis. The demonstration of virus-specific nucleotide sequences in the myocardium by means of in situ hybridization or polymerase chain reaction (PCR), however, is not necessarily diagnostic of viral myocarditis, as viral sequences have been detected in many control subjects. Experimental models have also yielded evidence of contributing myocardial damage by oxygen free radicals, cytokines, and microvascular involvement.

Natural History and Its Modification with Treatment

In the great majority of cases, acute myocarditis is a benign, self-limiting disease without clinically overt sequelae. Some patients, however, develop acute heart failure, shock, major arrhythmias, or conduction disturbances and thus are at risk of death. Follow-up of patients with these complications who have recovered has revealed that a significant number continue to have impaired pump function of the heart, decreased cardiac reserve, arrhythmias, or conduction disturbances, and some of these progress to chronic cardiomyopathy. It is also thought that this may happen in individuals whose initial myocarditis remained subclinical and undetected.

Prevention

To the extent that myocarditis is secondary to preventable infectious disease, it can be prevented. With the widespread use of vaccination,

myocarditis secondary to poliomyelitis, measles, rubella, mumps, and smallpox has all but disappeared, and myocarditis secondary to influenza has become rare. Similarly, myocardial involvement by trichinosis is rarely seen in developed countries. It may be hoped that control of infections with other cardiotropic viruses will become possible.

Cost Containment

Acute myocarditis, in general, remains undetected and undiagnosed. This form of cost containment may not be desirable. Alertness to cardiac involvement in the course of acute viral illness may lead to more careful auscultation, wider application of electrocardiography, and protection of an infected individual from excessive physical activity and life-threatening arrhythmias. Although echocardiography and nuclear imaging are clearly of value in the detection and quantitation of impaired cardiac function, the relative value of these studies in the follow-up of patients remains to be defined.

Patients with acute myocarditis and any degree of heart failure, arrhythmia, or conduction disturbance merit hospitalization and close monitoring to prevent life-threatening events and sudden death.

REFERENCES

Herskowitz A, Campbell S, Deckers J, et al. Demographic features and prevalence of idiopathic myocarditis in patients undergoing endomyocardial biopsy at the Johns Hopkins Hospital: A five year experience. Am J Cardiol 1993;71:982.

Kopecky SL, Gersh BV. Dilated cardiomyopathy and myocarditis: Natural history, etiology, clinical manifestations, and management. Curr Prob Cardiol 1987;12:569.

Mason JW, O'Connell JB, Herskowitz A. A clinical trial of immunosuppressive therapy for myocarditis. N Engl J Med 1995;333(5):269.

O'Connell JB, Mason JW. Diagnosing and treating active myocarditis. West J Med 1989;150:431.

O'Connell JB, Renlund DG. Myocarditis and specific myocardial diseases. In: Schlant RC, Alexander RW, O'Rourke RA, et al., eds. Hurst's the heart. 8th ed. New York: McGraw-Hill, 1994:1591.

Olinde KD, O'Connell JB. Inflammatory heart disease: Pathogenesis, clinical manifestation, and treatment of myocarditis. Annu Rev Med 1994;45:481.

Robinson JA, O'Connell JB, eds. Myocarditis: Precursor of cardiomyopathy. Lexington, MA: Heath, 1983:167.

CHAPTER 15–50

Hypertrophic Cardiomyopathy

Eric A. Peña, M.D., and J. Jeffrey Marshall, M.D.

DEFINITION

Hypertrophic cardiomyopathy (HCM) is present when there is primary myocardial hypertrophy with a nondilated ventricular cavity. By definition it occurs in the absence of intrinsic or systemic pathology known to induce ventricular hypertrophy (e.g., systemic hypertension, aortic stenosis, coarctation of the aorta).

ETIOLOGY

The etiology for this disease is unknown; however, in some patients, there appears to be a defect in the α and β subunits of the myosin heavy chain. The combination of several morphologic and physiologic characteristics serves to distinguish this heterogeneous patient population into an organized clinical spectrum. Morphologically the echocardiogram can localize the area of myocardium that is hypertrophied. Thus, there may be apical, midventricular, septal, or concentric hypertrophy. Physiologically, the echocardiogram can determine whether there is an outflow obstruction that generates a systolic, intracavitary gradient. Consequently, patients can be divided into those with obstruction and those without obstruction. Patients with obstruction can be further di-

vided into those with gradients at rest and those who only have a provokable gradient.

CRITERIA FOR DIAGNOSIS
Suggestive

The diagnosis of HCM is often suggested on the basis of a routine history and physical examination. A high index of suspicion must be maintained as the clues to the diagnosis are often subtle. Middle-aged patients with dyspnea and a systolic murmur should be considered patients with possible HCM. The clinical suspicion expands when objective evidence of left ventricular hypertrophy is found in the absence of a cause. Echocardiography has become the diagnostic procedure of choice both to confirm the diagnosis and to define the morphologic substrate of disease.

Definitive

The definitive diagnosis of HCM is made with two-dimensional Doppler echocardiography. In most patients with HCM, echocardiography demonstrates a pattern of hypertrophy that is most pronounced in the ventricular septum with extension into the anterolateral free wall. The posterior free wall is usually spared. These patients constitute the most notable morphologic subset among patients with HCM, and are characterized by marked hypertrophy of the basal ventricular septum. Narrowing of the left ventricular outflow tract between the ventricular septum and the anterior mitral leaflet produces a dynamic outflow obstruction at rest or with provocation. This variety of HCM is commonly referred to as idiopathic hypertrophic subaortic stenosis (IHSS) or hypertrophic obstructive cardiomyopathy. These patients constitute approximately 25% of patients with HCM (Maron et al., 1987). The echocardiographic criteria for a hypertrophied septum is a septum that is 1.3 to 1.5 times as thick as the posterior wall measured in diastole. The septum should be at least 15 mm thick, with the upper limits of normal being 11 mm.

Echocardiography has not only been useful in identifying this subset of patients, but has been instrumental in identifying systolic anterior motion of the mitral valve, which is believed to play a vital role in the pathogenesis of the obstructive physiology. Using Doppler interrogation of the blood flow velocity across this dynamic obstruction, one can estimate an accurate pressure gradient. Thus, Doppler echocardiography is very useful as a noninvasive index for quantifying the degree of obstruction that has prognostic implications. Echocardiography is also a reasonable test to identify the diastolic dysfunction common to all varieties of HCM.

An unusual form of HCM is that which is confined to the ventricular apex. These patients are most common in Japan where they may constitute up to 25% of all patients with HCM (Maron and Roberts, 1994). Patients with apical hypertrophic cardiomyopathy are further characterized by pronounced T-wave inversions in the mid-precordial leads, a "spade"-shaped deformity of the left ventricle on the ventriculogram, and a distinctively benign clinical course. Other morphologic abnormalities in the mitral valve, mitral apparatus, right ventricle, and atria may also be noted on echocardiography.

CLINICAL MANIFESTATIONS

Subjective

Hypertrophic cardiomyopathy is most often first recognized in patients during their thirties and forties. Dyspnea is the most common complaint reported by symptomatic patients with HCM. Angina pectoris is also very common and usually does not correlate with epicardial coronary artery disease. Fatigue, presyncope (often orthostatic), and syncope are also common. Most of these symptoms are exacerbated with exertion and with conditions or medications that decrease venous return or peripheral resistance (e.g., dehydration and nitrates or antihypertensives, respectively). An uncommon initial manifestation of this disease may be sudden death. The patient with sudden cardiac death is usually an older child or young adult. Although sudden death is most likely to occur while a patient is not performing heavy physical activity, unsuspected HCM is the most frequent finding at autopsy in young adults who die suddenly. Rarely, clusters of families with HCM and premature cardiac death have been reported. Such a history of malignant familial clustering denotes an ominous prognosis. Lastly, as more patients are discovered through echocardiography screening, it has been discovered that the majority of patients with HCM remain asymptomatic or mildly symptomatic.

Objective

Physical Examination

The physical examination in asymptomatic patients with HCM without a ventricular gradient can frequently be normal. On inspection, even moderately symptomatic patients may appear normal at rest. A bisferiens arterial pulse (two systolic peaks) can be noted in the obstructive variety of HCM. It may be precipitated or exacerbated by the Valsalva maneuver or inhalation of amyl nitrite. The apical impulse is usually abnormally forceful, enlarged, and laterally displaced. A prominent presystolic apical impulse may also be noted and corresponds to a prominent *a* wave in the neck vein pulsations. This is the product of a forceful atrial contraction and may result in a double apical beat. The more characteristic triple apical beat is less frequently recognized. This

occurs with the addition of a late systolic bulge that occurs as a practically empty ventricle performs near isometric contraction. Significant dynamic obstruction of the left ventricular outflow tract may result in a palpable thrill along the apex or lower left sternal border. Auscultation frequently uncovers a fourth heart sound, which is a hallmark of diastolic dysfunction. The first heart sound is normal or may be decreased if severe mitral valve regurgitation is present. The second heart sound is usually normally split, but patients with a significant outflow obstruction may have paradoxical splitting. Third heart sounds are common but do not necessarily suggest a poor prognosis. The typical systolic murmur associated with an outflow obstruction is frequently harsh in quality, with a crescendo/decrescendo pattern that is best appreciated between the apex and left sternal border. It radiates throughout the precordium and into the axilla, but poorly to the neck vessels. When pronounced gradients are present, concomitant mitral valve regurgitation may be present and produce a murmur with a more blowing quality toward the apex and axilla.

Differentiation of the murmur of hypertrophic cardiomyopathy from valvular aortic stenosis can readily be done at the bedside. The carotid pulse contour of significant valvular stenosis characteristically has a diminished amplitude and a delayed, slow rise (pulsus parvus et tardus). The carotid pulse contour in HCM is characterized by a brisk upstroke followed by a decline in midsystole then a second rise (pulsus bisferiens). In contrast to hypertrophic obstructive cardiomyopathy, the murmur of aortic valvular stenosis radiates well to the carotid arteries. Furthermore, bedside maneuvers that increase the murmur of hypertrophic obstructive cardiomyopathy, as opposed to valvular aortic stenosis, include squatting to standing and the Valsalva maneuver. Both murmurs may increase in loudness after the pause that follows a premature ventricular contraction.

Routine Laboratory Abnormalities

A normal electrocardiogram is found only in a minority of patients. The most common abnormalities are ST–T-wave changes followed by increased QRS voltage particularly in the mid-precordial leads. Abnormal Q waves are relatively common and often involve the inferior and/or lateral leads. This abnormality may be erroneously attributed to myocardial infarction. Atrial fibrillation will occur in 10 to 15% of the patients.

The findings on chest x-ray are variable. The left ventricular silhouette ranges from normal to enlarged and left atrial enlargement is common. Mitral annular calcification is infrequently noted.

PLANS

Diagnostic

Differential Diagnosis

Patients with systemic arterial hypertension who have systolic murmurs due to aortic valve disease may simulate patients with HCM. As one approaches the evaluation of HCM, it is important to be aware that echocardiographic demonstration of asymmetric left ventricular hypertrophy does not necessarily equate to the diagnosis of HCM. Other acquired and congenital defects can uncommonly present with asymmetric septal hypertrophy (i.e., hyperparathyroidism, neurofibromatosis, and pheochromocytoma). Long-standing hypertension in the elderly can result in severe concentric left ventricular hypertrophy. Furthermore, some elderly patients with ventricular septal hypertrophy may have dystrophic calcification of the mitral annulus and posterior mitral leaflets resulting in anterior displacement of the mitral apparatus facilitating an outflow gradient. These acquired conditions may mimic pathophysiologic features of primary HCM. Alternatively, patients with primary HCM may acquire systemic arterial hypertension.

Diagnostic Options

Patients with HCM who present with or develop symptoms of palpitations, chest pain, or dyspnea as well as those who have a strong family history of sudden death should obtain ambulatory (24 or 48 hours) electrocardiographic monitoring. Those patients who do not have arrhythmias on their ambulatory electrocardiographic monitoring can be reassured. Those who do have nonsustained ventricular tachycardia or other significant arrhythmias should be referred to a cardiologist or even to an academic center conducting clinical trials on these patients. New methods of electrophysiologic testing are being developed that may be capable of identifying a high-risk cohort in this subset of patients. Paroxysmal atrial fibrillation, other supraventricular tachycardias, and conduction system disease are also readily identified by electrocardiographic monitoring and can be treated accordingly. Patients who present with dyspnea or angina refractory to standard medical management should also be referred to a specialist for further cardiac workup and treatment, because as many as 20% of older patients with HCM may have atheromatous coronary artery disease (Wynne and Braunwald, 1992). Those patients with HCM who present with symptoms of impaired consciousness or prior cardiac arrest represent the patients at highest risk for subsequent cardiac events. These patients should be referred to a cardiologist or preferably a tertiary referral hospital with experience in electrophysiologic-guided therapy and implantation of automatic defibrillators.

Once a patient is diagnosed with HCM, current recommended practice is to screen family members with an echocardiogram. This has created a whole new cohort of patients who are asymptomatic and not categorized into previous natural history studies. Spirito et al. (1994) has recently described a series of 155 patients with no symptoms of heart failure or only mild symptoms. Of these, 88 patients (58%) remained asymptomatic during the follow-up period. None of these patients died despite the fact that 20 of the 88 patients had nonsustained ventricular tachycardia on ambulatory electrocardiogram. Based on this observation, it is our opinion that asymptomatic patients who are not otherwise at high risk for sudden death should receive infrequent follow-up with no other diagnostic tests. This should remain the standard until diagnostic modalities are developed that can identify a high-risk cohort of asymptomatic patients with nonsustained ventricular tachycardia. Once these modalities are studied prospectively and reasonable clinical trials show that we can positively impact the natural history of these asymptomatic patients, this position should be reconsidered.

An important caveat about echocardiographic screening of asymptomatic family members is that because morphologic expression may not be completed until adulthood, a single echocardiogram may not exclude HCM. Therefore, some family members may need to be rescreened prior to participation in competitive athletics or other high-risk endeavors.

Recommended Approach

The authors favor the following approach. The diagnosis can be made based on a careful history and physical examination. Finding the described murmur in a nonhypertensive patient with symptoms of dyspnea, chest pain, or presyncopal spells is strongly suggestive. Echocardiography then becomes a necessary confirmatory test to determine the location of the hypertrophy and the resting or provokable gradient for prognostic reasons (higher gradients portend a less favorable prognosis). If chest pain is present in men older than 40 and is exertional in nature, cardiac catheterization is recommended to rule out concomitant atherosclerotic heart disease. At catheterization, hemodynamic evaluation of the resting and provokable gradient can be made. If any historical clues suggest orthostasis or presyncope, a 24- or 48-hour Holter monitor should be obtained. If a history of frank syncope or a family history of sudden cardiac death is obtained, electrophysiologic testing is recommended.

Therapeutic

Various therapeutic modalities are available to patients with hypertrophic cardiomyopathy. Therapy should be individualized relative to predominant symptoms, pathophysiologic mechanisms, and the risk of sudden death. Despite the abundance of pharmacologic agents, electrophysiologic devices, and surgical interventions available, no properly controlled prospective clinical trials have been conducted to assess the relative efficacy of our therapeutic options.

Definitive therapeutic recommendations for asymptomatic patients identified by echocardiographic screening cannot be made at this time. These patients should be taught about their disease and alerted to symptoms that require follow-up. In general, most experts recommend avoidance of strenuous physical activity. Verapamil has been shown to significantly attenuate most myocardial perfusion abnormalities in exercise thallium stress tests of asymptomatic patients with HCM. As up to half of asymptomatic patients with HCM can develop reversible thallium perfusion defects during exercise, it may be reasonable to prescribe verapamil to those patients who remain physically active.

Medical therapy is recommended for patients who present with symptoms of dyspnea and angina. Beta blockers have been used extensively in the treatment of both obstructive and nonobstructive forms of HCM. They provide initial symptomatic improvement for one third to one half of symptomatic patients. Through their negative inotropic and chronotropic effects, beta blockers decrease oxygen consumption and may attenuate catecholamine-induced provocation of outflow gradient. They are less effective on the basal left ventricular outflow obstruction and do not consistently improve diastolic filling. Accordingly, symptoms of angina improve more consistently than dyspnea. Large doses are generally needed to be effective. Calcium channel blockers provide an increasingly attractive alternative to beta blockers. Oral verapamil is the most often used and best studied agent. Symptomatic improvement has been reported with up to 60% of patients refractory to beta-blocker therapy (Louie and Edwards, 1994). Beneficial effects include reversibility of exercise-induced perfusion abnormalities on thallium scans, reduction of basal left ventricular outflow tract obstruction, improvement of various parameters of diastolic dysfunction, and significant improvement in exercise tolerance. Doses up to 480 mg/d of verapamil are often required. Caution must be exercised in patients in whom the vasodilatory properties of verapamil predominate, in patients with conduction system disease, and in patients requiring antiarrhythmic agents (particularly quinidine). One must be careful not to precipitate pulmonary edema in susceptible patients. Disopyramide therapy may be effective in suppressing atrial and ventricular arrhythmias. In addition, the negative inotropic effects of disopyramide may be responsible for reducing the left ventricular outflow obstruction with a net effect of improving systolic function. These properties make disopyramide an attractive alternative for patients with significant arrhythmias responsive to type IA antiarrhythmic agents.

For those patients who reach the end stages of HCM with thinning of the ventricular walls and reduced ejection fraction, treatment should be as in idiopathic dilated cardiomyopathy. Angiotensin-converting enzyme inhibitors, digoxin, diuretics, nitrates, and hydralazine should be used accordingly. Refractory patients can be referred for cardiac transplantation.

For patients with hypertrophic obstructive cardiomyopathy who have refractory symptoms of angina and dyspnea despite maximal medical management, dual-chamber pacing is an attractive alternative to surgery. Pacing the right ventricle causes paradoxical movement of the interventricular septum. The net result is an increase in the size of the left ventricular outflow tract and a reduction in the velocity of blood ejected through the left ventricular outflow tract, resulting in less systolic anterior motion of the mitral valve and a significant reduction in the outflow gradient. Fananapazir et al. (1994) reported their experience with 84 patients with severe symptoms refractory to medications. At a mean follow-up of 2.3 years, symptoms were eliminated in 28 patients (33%), improved in 47 (56%), and remained unchanged in 7 (8%) others. Although a significant improvement was apparent at 6 weeks, they often became more pronounced over time. Despite a profoundly symptomatic high-risk population, there was a 97% cumulative 3-year survival. This compares favorably to surgical alternatives that carry an operative mortality of approximately 5% (range, 2–10%) and an 8 to 10% cumulative mortality for the same follow-up period. Furthermore, one would expect that implantation of dual-chamber pacing would be less operator dependent. Although longer follow-up of dual-chamber pacing is definitely necessary, it seems reasonable to attempt dual-chamber pacing prior to sending a patient to septal myotomy–myectomy.

Surgery is the best therapeutic option for those patients with hypertrophic obstructive cardiomyopathy who have symptoms of angina and dyspnea and are refractory to medications and pacing. This is also true of patients with severe mitral valve regurgitation (secondary to intrinsic mitral valve pathology) or who have outflow obstruction due predominantly to aberrant papillary muscles. Septal myotomy–myectomy (Morrow procedure) has been the operation of choice. Reported indications include intractable symptoms refractory to other treatment modalities and basal left ventricular outflow tract obstruction with a gradient equal to or greater than 50 mm Hg (some institutions operate for large provokable gradient). Septal myectomy has resulted in elimination or marked reductions of the subaortic pressure gradient in up to 95% of patients (Louie and Edwards, 1994). Significant improvement in symptoms has been described in 85% of patients at 5-year follow-up (Louie and Edwards, 1994). Mitral valve replacement is an alternative to septal myectomy and is preferred when there is a relatively thin septum, when the area of hypertrophy is inaccessible via a transaortic approach, and in cases of severe mitral valve regurgitation due to intrinsic valvular pathology. Studies from the National Institutes of Health suggest similar reductions in outflow gradients with mitral valve replacement compared with septal myectomy. In addition, suture plication of the anterior mitral leaflet in combination with septal myectomy may further reduce systolic anterior motion of the mitral valve and resultant gradient. Finally, patients with nonobstructive HCM and severe refractory symptoms should be considered for cardiac transplantation.

Patients who present with a history of cardiac arrest and syncope are at high risk for subsequent cardiac events. These patients should be referred for electrophysiologic testing and cardiac catheterization. An attempt should be made to identify the underlying mechanism of sudden cardiac death and to treat it accordingly. Patients with rapid atrioventricular conduction should receive electrophysiologic-guided ablation. Significant conduction system disease should be treated by dual-chamber pacing. Atrial fibrillation should be suppressed with antiarrhythmic agents (amiodarone if necessary). An attempt should be made to suppress inducible sustained ventricular tachycardia with antiarrhythmic agents, and if this fails an implantable cardioverter–defibrillator is suggested. Furthermore, many current recommendations include that all survivors of cardiac arrest receive an implantable cardioverter–defibrillator when a sustained ventricular arrhythmia is induced at electrophysiologic studies or when ischemia is believed to be the precipitating mechanism. Also noteworthy is that many authorities recommend that patients with a "malignant" family history for sudden death should receive the same aggressive evaluation and treatment protocol as patients with syncope.

The treatment of asymptomatic or mildly symptomatic patients with nonsustained ventricular tachycardia on ambulatory electrocardiogram is controversial. Some have advocated treating these patients with low-dose amiodarone. Others have reported adverse outcomes with such therapy. Although a definitive recommendation cannot be made at this time, it seems reasonable that patients who remain asymptomatic or mildly symptomatic (without symptoms of impaired consciousness) be treated with antiarrhythmic agents only in the context of clinical trials until satisfactory data resolve the issue. Atrial fibrillation should be treated with anticoagulation and cardioversion as soon as it presents. Patients with chronic atrial fibrillation refractory to both chemical and electrical cardioversion should have rate control with verapamil (or beta blocker) and chronic anticoagulation. A final recommendation is that all patients with HCM receive antibiotic prophylaxis for infectious endocarditis.

FOLLOW-UP

The follow-up for patients with HCM depends on the severity of disease. Asymptomatic patients who are discovered through routine echocardiographic screening as first-degree relatives should be followed infrequently. They should be educated about their disease and advised as to what symptoms require follow-up. They should be reminded about antibiotic prophylaxis for endocarditis. Patients who are screened as children or young adolescents and show no manifestations of disease should have at least one subsequent echocardiogram as young adults. All patients should be instructed to seek immediate attention for symptoms of impaired consciousness, increasing palpitations, or sudden deterioration of otherwise stable symptoms. Symptomatic patients require more frequent follow-up, particularly if they experience progression of their symptoms or side effects from their medications.

DISCUSSION

Prevalence and Incidence

The exact prevalence of HCM is unknown, but it has been estimated to occur in less than 0.2% of the population. HCM is thought to occur in a worldwide distribution and has been reported at necropsy of stillbirths as well as in geriatric populations. The genetics of HCM have been a topic of intense investigation during recent years. In more than half the cases, the disease appears to be genetically transmitted in an autosomal dominant fashion with variable penetrance and expression. In the majority of afflicted first-degree relatives, however, echocardiographic studies show a dissimilar pattern of segmental hypertrophy. In addition, several kindreds of patients with HCM have been found to carry mutations in the heavy myosin gene locus on chromosome 14.

Related Basic Science

Anatomic Derangement

The morphologic characteristics of HCM were discussed under Criteria for Diagnosis. Histologic sections of the involved tissue reveal cellular disarray forming whorls of bizarrely shaped myocytes at estranged angles to one another. In addition, the presence of abnormal intramural coronary arteries has been reported in up to 80% of autopsies of patients with HCM. These intramyocardial arteries are characterized by marked intimal and medial thickening and are frequently found in areas of focal myocardial fibrosis. This suggests that they may play a role in the pathogenesis of myocardial ischemia and/or infarction in the absence of epicardial coronary atherosclerosis. These histologic abnormalities may serve as the substrate for the physiologic derangements encountered in HCM.

Physiologic or Metabolic Derangement

The pathophysiologic features of HCM include diastolic dysfunction, ischemia, outflow obstruction, and electrophysiologic disturbances. The diastolic impairment results in diminished early diastolic filling and a disproportionate reliance on the late atrial contraction for the end-diastolic volume. This may result from an impaired cytosolic handling of calcium as well as a less distensible structural matrix of the involved myocardium. Myocardial ischemia in the absence of epicardial coronary atherosclerosis has been well documented by thallium-201 perfusion studies showing both fixed and reversible perfusion abnormalities. Some proposed mechanisms include inappropriate capillary density relative to the hypertrophied myocardium; diastolic collapse of intramyocardial arteries as a result of elevated end-diastolic pressures; intramyocardial coronary artery abnormalities; and increased myocardial oxygen requirements due to excessive wall tension in the face of a left ventricular outflow obstruction.

There is considerable controversy as to the mechanics of the left ventricular outflow obstruction. A commonly held view is that as the hyperdynamic ventricle expels blood through a narrowed ventricular outflow tract, a high-velocity jet is created that draws the anterior mitral valve toward the ventricular septum (Venturi effect), resulting in the dynamic outflow obstruction. In fact, the magnitude of the ventricular gradient has been shown to correlate directly with the duration of contact between the anterior leaflet of the mitral valve and the intraventricular septum.

Electrophysiologic findings in 230 "high-risk" patients have recently been reported by Fananapazir et al. (1994). Ambulatory electrocardiographic data showed nonsustained ventricular tachycardia in 115 patients (50%) and atrial fibrillation in 36 patients (11%). Electrophysiologic evaluation revealed a high incidence of sinoatrial dysfunction and His-Purkinje dysfunctions. Sustained ventricular tachycardia was induced in 82 patients (36%). Of the induced arrhythmias, sustained ventricular tachycardia was the most predictive for subsequent cardiac events. Historically, multiple studies have shown nonsustained ventricular tachycardia as a predictor of subsequent sudden death.

Supraventricular tachycardias (particularly atrial fibrillation) are poorly tolerated by patients with HCM. This occurs because ventricular diastole shortens with increasing ventricular response, decreasing the time to fill a "stiff" ventricle. In addition, the relative loss of the atrial contribution to ventricular loading is particularly deleterious in the setting of diastolic dysfunction. Finally, it is notable that accessory pathways are present in about 5% of patients with HCM.

Natural History and Its Modification with Treatment

The natural history in patients with HCM varies relative to the patient population being studied. Many early reports reflect selection bias from tertiary referral centers. In general, the clinical deterioration following diagnosis is slow. The presence of atrial fibrillation (or other supraventricular tachycardias) may lead to marked deterioration of symptoms and occurs in about 10% of patients. Approximately 10 to 15% of patients reach a final phase of disease characterized by thinning and fibrosis of the affected myocardium, depressed ejection fraction, and a clinical state more consistent with idiopathic dilated cardiomyopathy. Infective endocarditis may complicate HCM in about 5% of patients and antibiotic prophylaxis is recommended.

Throughout the clinical course of HCM, the risk of sudden cardiac death remains imminent. The risk of sudden cardiac death depends on the patient population being studied. It has been described to occur at a rate of 2 to 3% in adults and 4 to 6% in children (Louie and Edwards, 1994). Recent reports have shown that the annualized cardiac mortality may be as low as 1% in asymptomatic or mildly symptomatic patients. This number increased to only 1.4% per year if nonsustained ventricular tachycardia was noted on ambulatory electrocardiographic monitoring (Spirito et al., 1994). Historically, characteristics that have identified patients at high risk for sudden death include age less than 30 at diagnosis, a "malignant" family history, marked left ventricular hypertrophy, and nonsustained ventricular tachycardia on ambulatory electrocardiography. Syncope has been found to be the most ominous symptom complex.

The modification of the natural history with treatment is difficult to assess because double-blind, placebo-controlled trials with sufficient numbers of patients have not been conducted. It is unlikely that they will be conducted in the future, because it is unethical to refrain from treating abnormalities that are threatening to the patient based on the circumstantial evidence at hand. Fananapazir et al. (1994) have shown that with aggressive therapeutic management they were able to reduce the annual incidence of sudden death to 1.8% per year in the high-risk patient population. This is compared with a reported 6 to 10% annual incidence of sudden death in historical controls with similar clinical characteristics. Finally, although placebo-controlled trials are unlikely, we still need properly conducted prospective clinical trials to assess the relative efficacy of our therapeutic options.

Prevention

Short of genetic counseling, no other preventive measures are available at this time.

Cost Containment

With all the sophisticated diagnostic and therapeutic interventions available to patients with HCM, the cost of caring for these patients can be tremendous. Cost containment can be accomplished by avoiding routine diagnostic studies in the absence of symptoms or their progression. The various therapeutic and diagnostic modalities should be subjected to rigid outcome analysis to determine which are the most efficacious and cost effective.

REFERENCES

Fananapazir L, Cannon RO III, Tripodi D, et al. Long-term results of dual-chamber (DDD) pacing in obstructive hypertrophic cardiomyopathy: Evidence for progressive symptomatic and hemodynamic improvement and reduction of left ventricular hypertrophy. Circulation 1994;90:2731.

Fananapazir L, Chang AC, Epstein SE, et al. Prognostic determinants in hypertrophic cardiomyopathy: Prospective evaluation of a therapeutic strategy based on clinical, Holter, hemodynamic, and electrophysiologic findings. Circulation 1992;86:730.

Louie EK, Edwards LC. Hypertrophic cardiomyopathy. Prog Cardiovasc Dis 1994;34:275.

Maron BJ, Bonow RD, Cannon RO III, et al. Hypertrophic cardiomyopathy: Interrelations of clinical manifestations, pathophysiology, and therapy. N Engl J Med 1987;316:780.

Maron B, Roberts WC. Hypertrophic cardiomyopathy. In: Schlant RC, Alexander RW, O'Rourke RA, et al., eds. Hurst's the heart. 8th ed. New York: McGraw-Hill, 1994:1621.

McKenna WJ, Oakley CM, Krinkler DM, et al. Improved survival with amiodarone in patients with hypertrophic cardiomyopathy and ventricular tachycardia. Br Heart J 1985;53:412.

Spirito P, Rapezzi C, Autore C, et al. Prognosis of asymptomatic patients with hypertrophic cardiomyopathy and non-sustained ventricular tachycardia. Circulation 1994;90:2743.

Wynne, J, Braunwald, E. Hypertrophic cardiomyopathy. In Braunwald, E (Editor) Heart Disease A Textbook of Cardiovascular Medicine, 4th Ed., Philadelphia: W.B. Saunders, 1992:1404.

CHAPTER 15–51

Dilated Cardiomyopathy

Edward J. MacInerney, M.D., and J. Jeffrey Marshall, M.D.

DEFINITION

Dilated cardiomyopathy (DCM) is the term used to describe diseases of heart muscle that result in ventricular dilation and impaired myocardial contractility. This definition excludes the entities of restrictive or hypertrophic cardiomyopathy, and excludes myocardial dysfunction that results from disease or dysfunction of other cardiac structures, such as congenital heart disease, valvular disease, or coronary artery disease.

ETIOLOGY

Dilated cardiomyopathy can be subclassified on the basis of etiology into primary and secondary causes. Primary DCM, or idiopathic dilated cardiomyopathy, refers to a primary heart muscle disease of unknown cause(s) that results in impaired myocardial contractility and consequent ventricular dilation and systolic dysfunction. Secondary causes of DCM are often referred to as specific heart muscle diseases, and include a wide variety of diseases that result in impaired myocardial con-

tractility and ventricular dilation via a "final common pathway" of myocardial damage. These secondary causes of DCM are outlined in Table 15–51–1.

CRITERIA FOR DIAGNOSIS
Suggestive

The diagnosis of DCM should be considered in the differential diagnosis of any patient who presents with symptoms and/or signs of congestive heart failure. DCM should also be considered in the differential diagnosis of asymptomatic patients with unexplained cardiomegaly found incidentally by examination or chest x-ray.

Definitive

The diagnosis of DCM is established by the documentation of the presence of left ventricular dilation and impaired myocardial contractility in the absence of congenital, hypertensive, hypertrophic, ischemic, peri-

TABLE 15–51–1. CAUSES OF DILATED CARDIOMYOPATHY

Primary (Idiopathic)

Secondary
Infectious/inflammatory
  Infectious
    Viral (i.e., Coxsackie virus, HIV, cytomegalovirus)
    Bacterial (i.e., diphtheria)
    Parasitic (i.e., Chagas' disease, toxoplasmosis)
    Other (i.e., rickettsial, fungal, mycobacterial)
  Noninfectious
    Collagen–vascular disease (i.e., systemic lupus erythematosus, scleroderma, dermatomyositis)
    Hypersensitivity myocarditis (i.e., penicillin, phenytoin, isoniazid)
    Giant cell myocarditis
Toxins (i.e., ethanol, anthracyclines, cocaine, lead, cobalt)
Metabolic
  Endocrine (i.e., diabetes mellitus, pheochromocytoma, thyroid disease, acromegaly)
  Nutritional deficiencies (i.e., thiamine, selenium, carnitine)
  Electrolyte abnormalities (i.e., hypocalcemia, hypophosphatemia)
Neuromuscular (i.e., muscular dystrophy, myotonic dystrophy, Friedrich's ataxia)
Genetic/familial
Other
  Peripartum cardiomyopathy
  Tachycardia-induced cardiomyopathy
  Physical agents (i.e., hypothermia, radiation injury)

cardial, restrictive, or valvular heart disease. Once the diagnosis of DCM has been made, the definitive diagnosis of the etiology is then pursued. A specific etiologic diagnosis is often elusive, and a diagnosis of idiopathic dilated cardiomyopathy is assumed based on exclusion after the search for specific etiologies is exhausted.

CLINICAL MANIFESTATIONS
Subjective

The most common symptoms of DCM are those of congestive heart failure, although a proportion of patients may be asymptomatic for months or even years despite clinical evidence of ventricular dilation and systolic dysfunction. Initially, the symptoms of left-sided heart failure predominate, with the most common symptom at the time of presentation being dyspnea on exertion. Other symptoms of diminished cardiac output such as fatigue and weakness are also common, as are symptoms due to elevated left heart filling pressures such as orthopnea and paroxysmal nocturnal dyspnea. Symptoms of right-sided heart failure typically occur later, and if present usually signal advanced disease with a particularly poor prognosis. Such symptoms include edema, abdominal distention, nausea, anorexia, and right upper quadrant pain due to hepatic congestion. Chest pain may occur in up to one half of patients with DCM, and may be due to a variety of causes, including diminished vasodilator reserve of the coronary microvasculature and pulmonary emboli. It is important to exclude the presence of critical coronary artery stenosis in these patients with chest pain, because it is a potentially treatable form of systolic dysfunction, and it excludes the diagnosis of DCM. Palpitations may also be a common symptom at the time of presentation, and usually correlate with the presence of supraventricular and/or ventricular arrhythmias. Although ventricular arrhythmias are common in patients with DCM, it is rare for the initial symptom of DCM to be syncope or sudden death.

Objective

Physical Examination

The physical findings of patients with DCM may vary widely, ranging from subtle isolated findings, such as unexplained premature ectopy, to overt decompensated heart failure in extremis. In general, the degree to which physical findings are manifest is a reflection of the balance between the severity of left ventricular dysfunction and the adequacy of natural (and/or medical) compensatory mechanisms. The presence of

DCM may be evident in the general appearance of the patient as breathlessness, pallor, acrocyanosis, or the inability of the patient to lie recumbent on the examination table due to dyspnea. The blood pressure may reveal a narrowed pulse pressure (reflecting diminished stroke volume) and pulsus alternans with or without hypotension when severe left ventricular dysfunction is present. The peripheral pulses may be diminished, and a resting tachycardia may be present. Ectopy is not uncommon. Examination of the neck often reveals distention of the jugular veins, with prominence of the *a* and *v* waves, the latter suggesting tricuspid regurgitation when particularly prominent and associated with a rapid *y* descent. Palpation of the precordium reveals lateral displacement of the apical impulse correlating with the degree of the left ventricular dilation, and a right ventricular impulse is occasionally felt. A presystolic *a* wave is sometimes palpable in the apical impulse. Cardiac auscultation frequently reveals an S_4 gallop in those patients in sinus rhythm. The presence of an S_3 gallop is typical of more advanced or poorly compensated disease. Holosystolic murmurs of mitral and/or tricuspid valve regurgitation due to dilation of the valvular annuli are often present, although they rarely exceed grade II/VI in intensity. The pulmonary examination may reveal the presence of rales and evidence of pleural effusion. Wheezing due to bronchial hyperresponsiveness and dilation of the bronchial vessels is not uncommon, and may confound the distinction between cardiac disease and primary pulmonary disease. The abdominal examination may reveal ascites and hepatomegaly in the presence of elevated right-sided pressures, and the liver may be pulsatile when significant tricuspid valve regurgitation is present. Examination of the extremities may demonstrate the presence of peripheral edema, and cool extremities with poor capillary refill are often reflective of a low cardiac output state.

Routine Laboratory Abnormalities

There are no laboratory findings diagnostic of DCM, and in general the routinely ordered laboratory panels do not help to establish the diagnosis. On occasion, these tests do reveal ancillary data helpful in assessing the severity of the disease, such as abnormal liver function tests seen with hepatic congestion due to right-sided failure, or azotemia seen with renal hypoperfusion due to low forward cardiac output. The presence of hyponatremia usually heralds the presence of poorly compensated heart failure, and itself is a marker of a poor prognosis. It is rare that the chemistry panel reveals a secondary etiology of the DCM such as hypocalcemia or hypophosphatemia.

The electrocardiogram is seldom normal in patients with DCM. The abnormalities seen, however, are usually nonspecific and nondiagnostic. Sinus tachycardia is often found in the setting of poorly compensated heart failure. Atrial abnormalities are frequently found, particularly left atrial abnormality. Abnormalities of the ST segment and T wave are common, reflecting abnormal ventricular repolarization. Conduction abnormalities are also common and are manifest in a number of ways, including interventricular conduction delay, left bundle-branch block, and variable degrees of atrioventricular conduction block. Poor progression of the R wave in the precordial leads is often seen, and anterior Q waves mimicking old myocardial infarction may also be present. The entire spectrum of supraventricular and ventricular arrhythmias may be demonstrated, with nonsustained ventricular tachycardia evident on 24-hour ambulatory monitoring in approximately one half of all patients with DCM and with atrial fibrillation occurring in up to 20% of patients.

The chest x-ray of DCM demonstrates cardiomegaly. The enlarged cardiac silhouette is usually due to enlargement of the left ventricle, but biventricular enlargement may also be seen. If pulmonary venous hypertension is present, one may see cephalization of the pulmonary vasculature and evidence of interstitial and/or alveolar edema in advanced cases. When right-sided heart pressures are elevated, the azygous vein and superior vena cava may appear plethoric. Pleural effusions may be present in some patients.

PLANS
Diagnostic
Differential Diagnosis

A variety of cardiac diseases may mimic the clinical presentation of dilated cardiomyopathy, particularly those that present with heart failure.

These diseases include congenital, hypertensive, hypertrophic, ischemic, pericardial, restrictive, and valvular heart disease. These entities must be excluded before a diagnosis of DCM is made. Noncardiac diseases that may, in some ways, present with findings similar to heart failure and that must also be considered in the differential diagnosis include recurrent pulmonary emboli, volume overload, and primary pulmonary processes such as chronic obstructive pulmonary disease.

Diagnostic Options

The diagnostic approach to DCM should first confirm the presence of DCM while excluding its potential mimics. Once the diagnosis is established, a search for the etiology should be pursued, with the hope of discovering a potentially reversible or treatable cause of secondary DCM.

Additional laboratory studies are sometimes helpful in establishing the etiology depending on the clinical presentation. Screening thyroid function tests to rule out the possibility of occult hyper- or hypothyroidism are recommended in most patients. Some centers routinely perform an antinuclear antibody test as a screen for collagen–vascular disease. If risk factors are present, studies to rule out HIV should be performed. In the appropriate setting, a 24-hour urine sample for vanillyl-mandelic acid and metanephrine should be collected to evaluate the possibility of pheochromocytoma. Further laboratory studies, such as serum iron studies, should be ordered as dictated by the individual patient's presentation.

The most useful noninvasive diagnostic test used to establish the diagnosis of DCM is the echocardiogram. In most patients, the echocardiogram easily demonstrates the dilated left ventricular cavity and the impaired myocardial contractility required for the diagnosis of DCM. It also readily excludes many forms of concomitant cardiac disease previously mentioned. A left ventricle end-diastolic diameter of 6 cm or greater and an ejection fraction of 45% or less are general guidelines for establishing the diagnosis. The left ventricular systolic dysfunction is global in the majority of patients, although regional wall motion abnormalities are common despite the absence of significant coronary artery disease. The left ventricle wall thickness is typically normal. Biventricular or even four-chamber cardiac dilation may be present. Doppler interrogation may demonstrate the presence of mitral and tricuspid regurgitation, and may demonstrate evidence of concomitant impairment of diastolic function. Thrombus may occasionally be seen in the left ventricle apex.

Nuclear cardiology studies can be useful in the diagnostic workup. In particular, gated blood pool scintigraphy with technetium-99m, typically referred to as MUGA (multigated acquisition) or RVG (radionuclide ventriculogram), provides a quantitative assessment of systolic function. It also yields information regarding left ventricular volume and regional wall motion. Thallium-201 myocardial scintigraphy has been used to distinguish noninvasively between DCM and cardiac dysfunction due to ischemia. This modality unfortunately has proved unreliable in this regard, as patients with DCM often have abnormal scans indistinguishable from those found in ischemic heart disease. Nuclear scans using gallium-67, a marker of inflammation, and indium-111-labeled antimyosin antibodies, a marker of myocardial necrosis, may help identify a subset of patients with DCM most likely to have a positive endomyocardial biopsy demonstrating active myocarditis.

Cardiac catheterization is an invaluable tool used in establishing the diagnosis of DCM. In those patients with chest pain or in those patients with two or more risk factors for the development of coronary artery disease, coronary angiography is performed to rule out the presence of clinically significant coronary stenosis. In addition to defining the anatomic extent of atherosclerosis, cardiac catheterization is also useful for excluding other cardiac etiologies responsible for the patient's clinical presentation and for assessing the adequacy of natural and/or medical compensatory mechanisms in the patient with DCM. Measurement of the pressures and study of the phasic waveforms of the various cardiac chambers are helpful in understanding the underlying pathophysiology of DCM and help guide medical therapy in the individual patient. Typical findings in the patient with DCM undergoing catheterization include elevation of the left heart filling pressures, as reflected by elevated left ventricular end-diastolic pressure (LVEDP), elevated left

atrial pressure, and elevated pulmonary capillary wedge pressure (PCWP). Modest pulmonary artery hypertension is common, and in advanced cases of DCM there is also elevation of the right ventricular end-diastolic pressure (RVEDP) and the right atrial pressure. The coronary arteries are usually normal in their angiographic appearance, though impaired coronary flow reserve is usually demonstrated (if the catheterization laboratory is appropriately equipped to perform such measurements). Older patients may have incidental coronary atherosclerotic disease; however the presence of coronary stenosis of 50% or greater in one or more vessels should raise the suspicion of an ischemic etiology. Left ventriculography demonstrates many of the same features seen with echocardiography, including dilation of the left ventricle chamber, elevated left ventricle volumes, and diminished systolic function. Mitral valve regurgitation can be seen and its severity quantified, and thrombus within the left ventricle cavity can occasionally be demonstrated.

The role of endomyocardial biopsy as a routine part of the diagnostic workup of DCM is debatable. Although there is general agreement that biopsy may be beneficial in certain specific situations, including the detection and monitoring of myocarditis and the establishment of histologic diagnosis for some of the other secondary causes of DCM, the clinical role of routine biopsy for all patients with DCM has yet to be defined. This is in part due to the fact that it is estimated that only 10% of the general population with DCM will have a diagnosis established or confirmed by endomyocardial biopsy. In addition, even if the biopsy does reveal the etiology of the DCM, it is unusual that such information will alter the course of therapy. This is particularly true for myocarditis, where, at the time of this writing, there has been no consistent evidence that immunosuppressive therapy significantly alters the course of the disease.

Recommended Approach

A thorough history and physical examination constitute the essential foundation on which the rest of the workup of DCM is built. Routine laboratory panels, electrocardiogram, and chest x-ray are obtained and carefully reviewed. Additional, more specific, laboratory tests are ordered as dictated by the clinical presentation of the individual patient. An echocardiogram is performed in all patients to confirm or refute the clinical diagnosis and to quantitate the severity of left ventricle impairment. If two or more risk factors for coronary atherosclerosis are present, or if there still remains some question as to the diagnosis, left- and right-sided heart catheterization with coronary and left ventricular angiography is performed. Endomyocardial biopsy is reserved for the individual patient for whom, in the opinion of the consulting cardiologist, a histologic diagnosis is felt to be of integral importance in guiding further management (i.e., presumed connective tissue disease).

Therapeutic

Therapeutic Options

Therapy for DCM begins with supportive care. Changes in diet and lifestyle are important aspects in the management of these patients. Dietary restriction of salt (2 g sodium or 5 g NaCl daily) is necessary in patients with signs or symptoms of congestion. Fluid intake is restricted in those patients exhibiting hyponatremia. Overweight patients are encouraged to lose weight. Smoking cessation is obligatory. Ethanol use should be kept to a minimum or abandoned. Patients are to be instructed to get adequate rest and should have their activity restricted during periods of decompensation. When the patient's status is compensated, however, it is current practice to recommend regular moderate aerobic exercise at a level that does not provoke symptoms.

The only therapy (aside from cardiac transplantation) that has consistently been proven to prolong life in patients with DCM is vasodilator therapy (added to therapy with diuretics and digoxin) with either angiotensin-converting enzyme (ACE) inhibitors (captopril and enalapril), or the combination regimen of hydralazine and isosorbide dinitrate. The latter regimen is less efficacious than the former and should be reserved for those patients in whom ACE inhibitor therapy is either contraindicated or not tolerated. These agents reduce impedance to left ventricular outflow (i.e., reduce afterload) and thereby augment forward cardiac output and also reduce cardiac filling pressures. The

ACE inhibitors additionally counteract the state of abnormal neurohormonal activation that is often present in patients with DCM, and they also appear to decrease pathologic ventricular remodeling. Even asymptomatic patients with left ventricular dysfunction from coronary artery disease appear to benefit from ACE inhibitor therapy. The typical starting dose of captopril is 12.5 mg three times daily, and this is subsequently adjusted upward as tolerated to a target total dose of 150 mg daily. An equivalent dose of enalapril is 2.5 mg twice daily, adjusted as tolerated to a target total dose of 20 to 40 mg daily. Some initial hypotension is anticipated during the institution of these agents; however, this can be minimized by reducing or halting ongoing diuretic therapy prior to starting the ACE inhibitor. Azotemia and hyperkalemia are additional possible side effects of ACE inhibitor therapy. Patients therefore should have appropriate blood chemistry monitoring during the institution of these agents. Potassium supplementation, in those patients receiving concomitant diuretics, can typically be stopped or significantly reduced when ACE inhibitor therapy is instituted to prevent hyperkalemia. Persistent cough is another side effect of ACE inhibitor therapy which at times necessitates cessation of these agents. For those patients in whom ACE inhibitor therapy is either contraindicated or not tolerated, the combination regimen of isosorbide dinitrate (20–60 mg three or four times daily) and hydralazine (50–100 mg three times daily) is strongly considered. For those critically ill patients in the intensive care unit, the vasodilators of choice are intravenous sodium nitroprusside and intravenous nitroglycerin. An intravenous form of enalapril (enalaprilat) is also available.

Digitalis has long been considered a mainstay in the therapy of DCM. In addition to its action as a positive inotropic agent, some of the beneficial effect of digoxin is thought to be due to modulation of excessive neurohormonal activation. Its additional effect of controlling the ventricular rate makes its usefulness undisputed in those patients with DCM and concomitant atrial fibrillation. Although the long-term safety of digoxin has yet to be established in large prospective trials (currently underway), digoxin has been shown to decrease symptoms, increase exercise capacity, and increase ejection fraction in patients with DCM, even in those patients in sinus rhythm. The usual dose of digoxin is 0.25 mg daily, except in the elderly or in those patients with renal insufficiency, in whom the dose is individualized (usually 0.125 mg daily). Patients should be monitored for the development of signs and symptoms of digitalis toxicity such as arrhythmias, anorexia, gastrointestinal complaints, and visual disturbances. Serum electrolytes should be monitored to avoid diuretic-induced hypokalemia and hypomagnesemia, both of which appear to lower the threshold for digoxin-associated arrhythmias. Other oral inotropic agents, although theoretically appealing, have not shown beneficial effects in the long-term management of DCM. In fact, agents such as milrinone and flosequinon have proven to be detrimental to long-term survival when compared with placebo, despite their favorable subjective and hemodynamic effects. Research in this area is ongoing. In the intensive care unit, intravenous dobutamine, amrinone, and milrinone are frequently used positive inotropic agents.

Diuretics should be reserved for those patients with DCM who exhibit evidence of congestion, such as symptoms of orthopnea or paroxysmal nocturnal dyspnea, or physical signs such as elevated neck veins, rales, or peripheral edema. At the diminished glomerular filtration rates typically seen in patients exhibiting congestion, thiazide diuretics are not usually effective. Loop diuretics such as furosemide and bumetanide are therefore the logical agents of choice. A dosage regimen of furosemide 40 to 80 mg once or twice daily is effective for most patients. The diuretic regimen should be carefully titrated toward the therapeutic goal of relieving the evidence of congestion. Once this goal is achieved, an ideal "target" weight is thereby established, which allows the patient and the clinician to readily make further adjustments in the diuretic regimen as necessary. In the absence of concomitant ACE inhibitor use, supplemental potassium or the addition of a potassium-sparing diuretic is often necessary to maintain a normal serum potassium level. Such supplementation is often unnecessary if an ACE inhibitor is being used. For those patients who appear refractory to higher doses of furosemide, the addition of a more proximally acting diuretic such as metolazone (2.5–5 mg once daily, given 1 hour before the loop diuretic) is often beneficial. Extra caution must be used to avoid electrolyte disturbances and volume depletion in such patients.

Patients with DCM are at increased risk for systemic and pulmonary embolic events, although there is wide variation in the reported annual incidence, ranging from 1 to 12% per year. Although there are no controlled prospective clinical trials that demonstrate overall benefit, anticoagulants are widely used in the treatment of DCM. The patients with DCM who appear to be at increased risk for embolic events, and therefore theoretically benefit the most from anticoagulation, are those with severe left ventricular dysfunction (ejection fraction ≤ 20%), severely limiting symptoms (New York Heart Association class IV), echocardiographic evidence of mural thrombus, prior history of thromboembolism, or concomitant atrial fibrillation. Many physicians anticoagulate all such patients unless otherwise contraindicated. In general, all patients with a history of thromboembolism or atrial fibrillation should be anticoagulated. Those patients with DCM who do not meet these criteria should be assessed on an individual basis for consideration of anticoagulation depending on perceived risk and benefit. Current practice is to use daily doses to achieve a target therapeutic International Normalized Ratio (INR) of 2 to 3.

There is little evidence that antiarrhythmic agents prolong life or prevent sudden cardiac death in patients with DCM. In fact, almost all antiarrhythmic agents have the potential for adversely affecting the outcome of these patients due to their well-documented side effects of negative inotropy and potential for life-threatening proarrhythmia. The general approach to these patients should be aimed at correcting the exacerbating factors of arrhythmia, including correction of hypoxemia, electrolyte abnormalities, and acid–base disturbances, and treatment of clinically evident heart failure. Antiarrhythmic therapy is reserved for those patients who exhibit sustained ventricular tachycardia, syncope, or sudden death. Such patients are best managed in consultation with an electrophysiologist, and should be considered for invasive electrophysiologic testing. Insertion of an implantable defibrillator and administration of amiodarone are the two most widely used treatments for this group of patients.

The use of beta blockers for the treatment of DCM is not currently approved by the Food and Drug Administration and, therefore, remains investigational. Their use is based on evidence that the increased level of sympathetic tone seen in many patients with DCM has deleterious consequences over the long term. Proposed mechanisms of benefit of beta blockade include protection of the heart from circulating catecholamines, upregulation of myocardial beta receptors, improved diastolic performance, and possibly protection from sudden cardiac death. Patients with DCM treated with beta blockers have shown improvement in exercise capacity, New York Heart Association functional class, and ejection fraction. When instituted at low doses and carefully titrated up over weeks, these drugs are generally well tolerated. Ongoing studies appear to demonstrate a favorable survival trend, but until this benefit becomes well established, the routine use of these medications in this patient population cannot be recommended.

Cardiac transplantation should be considered for patients with DCM and severe heart failure. The current 5-year survival rate for transplantation approaches 80%, compared with only a 25 to 50% survival rate if no transplant is performed. The ideal candidate for transplant is a formerly vigorous patient less than 60 years of age in whom there are no contraindications, and in whom there has been persistent severe left ventricular dysfunction documented for longer than 6 months. A maximal oxygen uptake during exercise testing of less than 12 mL/kg/min helps to further identify those patients with a particularly poor prognosis and who might be considered to benefit most from transplantation. Current contraindications to transplant include active infection or systemic illness, fixed pulmonary hypertension (≥ 5 Wood units or 400 dyne·s·m^{-5}), recent cancer, active gastrointestinal bleeding, crossmatch incompatibility, and patient noncompliance. Diabetes mellitus is a relative contraindication.

Recommended Approach

Dietary and lifestyle changes are recommended for all patients, with emphasis on weight loss, smoking cessation, abstinence from alcohol, and regular moderate exercise. ACE inhibitors are first-line therapy in patients with DCM and are instituted in all patients unless otherwise contraindicated or not tolerated. This applies even to those patients who are asymptomatic despite evidence of systolic dysfunction by echocardiogram. Digoxin is often reserved for those patients who remain symptomatic despite ACE inhibitors and for those patients with a history of atrial fibrillation. Diuretics are given to those patients who exhibit symptoms or signs of congestive heart failure. Anticoagulation is instituted in those patients felt to be at significantly increased risk of thromboembolism as long as there is no contraindication. Transplantation is considered for appropriate candidates.

FOLLOW-UP

Follow-up is performed on an individualized basis, depending on the severity of cardiac decompensation, the intensity of the medical regimen, and the need to monitor relevant laboratory work. Well-informed, compliant patients with compensated disease on a stable medical regimen may be seen as infrequently as every 6 months. On the other hand, some patients require weekly outpatient visits and intensive home health ancillary services to survive outside of the hospital.

DISCUSSION
Prevalence and Incidence

The annual incidence of primary (idiopathic) DCM is estimated between 3 and 8 cases per 100,000 population, with approximately 20,000 new cases per year in the United States. The true incidence is probably underestimated, as many asymptomatic cases go unrecognized. The age-adjusted prevalence in the United States averages 36 cases per 100,000 population and accounts for approximately 10,000 deaths annually. Note that these figures apply only to primary (idiopathic) DCM, which makes up roughly one half of all patients with DCM.

Several factors are associated with increased risk for the development of DCM. They include pregnancy, hypertension, and chronic ethanol use. Cigarette smoking also appears to be associated with an increased risk for DCM, independent of its role as a risk factor for ischemic heart disease. Patients of any age may be affected, although the disease occurs more commonly in middle age. Men are affected more frequently than women.

Related Basic Science

The gross anatomic changes seen in DCM include overall increase in the cardiac mass, with concomitant dilation of the cardiac chambers, particularly the ventricles. Hypertrophy of the ventricular wall may be present, although the wall thickness-to-cavity diameter ratio is normal or decreased due to the marked cavitary dilation. Focal scarring of the ventricles is often seen. Intracardiac thrombi and mural endocardial plaques representing organized thrombus are present in more than 50% of hearts at autopsy.

Microscopic changes of DCM include hypertrophy of individual myocytes, with large, abnormally shaped nuclei. Interspersed myocyte atrophy, degeneration, and myofilament loss may also be seen. There are varying degrees of interstitial and perivascular fibrosis present, particularly in the subendocardium. Occasional small areas of focal inflammatory infiltrates, typically lymphocytic, are observed.

On a molecular level, there is ordinarily a significantly decreased number of β_1 receptors, a phenomenon believed due to "downregulation" secondary to chronic exposure to elevated levels of circulating catecholamines. There is also evidence of diminished β_2-receptor responsiveness, felt to be due to an "uncoupling" of the receptor from the normal intracellular signal transmission pathway. Also noted are abnormalities of calcium handling, of high-energy phosphate substrate, and of actin–myosin interactions.

No virus or other etiologic agent has been regularly identified in tissue from patients with DCM. The failure of polymerase chain reaction techniques to consistently demonstrate vial genomic sequences in patients with DCM draws the hypothesis of an initial viral insult into question. Immunologic abnormalities, such as the presence of circulating autoantibodies to cardiac antigens, evidence of diminished numbers of natural killer lymphocytes, and associations of some forms of DCM with specific HLA antigens, suggest an immune-mediated etiology for some patients. Additional patients appear to have a genetic predisposition to DCM, as approximately 20% of patients with primary DCM

have at least one first-degree relative with evidence of cardiomyopathy. The search for the etiologic agent(s) responsible for idiopathic DCM continues to be an area of intense research interest.

Natural History and Its Modification with Treatment

The course of DCM is usually one of progressive deterioration of ventricular function, resulting ultimately in death due to pump failure or arrhythmia. Although stabilization and sometimes spontaneous improvement occur in 20 to 50% of patients, the overall 5-year mortality is generally reported to be between 40 and 80%. This rate may decrease as patients are detected earlier and as treatment regimens improve. At this time, unfortunately, it is difficult to predict which individuals will spontaneously improve and which individuals will suffer progressive deterioration. Although there are factors that appear to be predictive of a poor prognosis when applied to populations of patients with DCM, in any individual patient the predictive accuracy of such factors is diminished considerably. Factors that have been shown to predict a bad outcome in patients with DCM include severe left ventricular impairment, severe symptoms (i.e., New York Heart Association class IV), complex ventricular ectopy, left bundle-branch block, S_3 gallop, hyponatremia, syncope, and elevated levels of circulating norepinephrine, renin, and atrial naturetic factor. As previously mentioned, a maximal oxygen uptake during exercise testing of less than 12 mL/kg/min (3.4 METs) is used to help identify those patients for consideration of transplantation. To date, the only interventions proven to decrease mortality significantly in patients with DCM are afterload reduction with ACE inhibitors (or hydralazine/isosorbide combination therapy) added to therapy with digoxin and diuretics and cardiac transplantation.

Prevention

There currently is no strategy for prevention of primary DCM, as no specific causal agent has yet to be identified. Prevention of secondary DCM is dependent on the specific culprit disease.

Cost Containment

The cost of the diagnostic workup for DCM pales in comparison to the cost incurred during the long-term management of these patients. This, however, is certainly no excuse for frivolous expenditure during the course of the diagnostic process. Each patient's workup should be individualized according to the clinical presentation and according to the incremental added value of each test obtained. For example, not every patient requires a coronary angiogram, and a majority of patients do not require endomyocardial biopsy. In the final analysis, however, the greatest potential for cost containment exists in the prevention of the significant cost associated with the substantial morbidity and mortality of this disease. Therapies that improve both quantity and quality of life in these patients ultimately lead to the greatest savings.

REFERENCES

Cohn JN, Sonnenblick EH. Diagnosis and treatment of heart failure. In Schlant RC, Alexander RW, O'Rourke RA, et al., eds. Hurst's the heart. 8th ed. New York: McGraw-Hill, 1994:557.

Dec GW, Fuster V. Idiopathic dilated cardiomyopathy. N Engl J Med 1994; 331:1564.

Gilbert, EM, Bristow MR. Idiopathic dilated cardiomyopathy. In Schlant RC, Alexander RW, O'Rourke RA, et al., eds. Hurst's the heart. 8th ed. New York: McGraw-Hill, 1994:1609.

Kasper EK, Agema WRP, Hutchins GM, et al. The causes of dilated cardiomyopathy: A clinicopathologic review of 673 consecutive cases. J Am Coll Cardiol 1994;23:586.

Keren A, Popp RL. Assignment of patients into the classification of cardiomyopathies. Circulation 1992;86:1622.

Mason JW. Endomyocardial biopsy and the causes of dilated cardiomyopathy. J Am Coll Cardiol 1994;23:591.

Mason JW. Classification of cardiomyopathy. In Schlant RC, Alexander RW, O'Rourke RA, et al., eds. Hurst's the heart. 8th ed. New York: McGraw-Hill, 1994:1585.

Wynne J, Braunwald E. The cardiomyopathies and myocarditides: Toxic, chemical, and physical damage to the heart. In Braunwald E, ed. Heart disease: A textbook of cardiovascular medicine. 4th ed. Philadelphia: Saunders, 1992:1394.

CHAPTER 15–52

Restrictive Cardiomyopathy

Edward J. MacInerney, M.D., and J. Jeffrey Marshall, M.D.

DEFINITION

Restrictive cardiomyopathy is a term used to describe the heart when it has been affected by disease processes that result primarily in the impairment of ventricular compliance. The diminished compliance, or increased rigidity, of the ventricular wall acts as an impediment to filling of the ventricular cavity in both early and late diastole. This results in impaired diastolic performance. Usually, the systolic function of the ventricle is not altered until late in the disease process. The alteration of ventricular compliance may result either from infiltration or deposition of substances into the myocardium or from fibrosis of the endocardium or endomyocardium. It excludes the diastolic dysfunction that commonly occurs from myocyte hypertrophy in hypertensive heart disease or hypertrophic cardiomyopathies.

ETIOLOGY

The disease processes that cause restrictive cardiomyopathy can generally be divided into two categories: those affecting the myocardium, and those affecting the endocardium or endomyocardium. Those diseases that affect the myocardium can further be subdivided into three groups: infiltrative processes (such as amyloidosis and sarcoidosis), inherited conditions of abnormal storage of biomolecules (such as those found in hemochromatosis or in the glycogen storage diseases), and noninfiltrative diseases (such as idiopathic restrictive cardiomyopathy) (Table 15–52–1).

CRITERIA FOR DIAGNOSIS

Suggestive

Restrictive cardiomyopathy should be considered in the differential diagnosis of those patients who present with progressive signs and symptoms of congestive heart failure in the absence of physical or radiologic evidence of cardiomegaly. Clinical suspicion of these disorders is further supported by the presence of abnormal jugular venous pulsations. The presence of prominent *x* and *y* descents (usually a more prominent *y* descent) should further alert the clinician to the possible diagnosis of restrictive cardiomyopathy.

Definitive

The definitive diagnosis of restrictive cardiomyopathy is usually quite challenging, because patients with constrictive pericarditis may present with many of the same clinical features. Because the treatment modalities and prognosis for these two entities are quite different, it is impera-

tive to make the correct diagnosis. Thus, an explicit diagnosis should include an echocardiogram that reveals thickened ventricular walls, with evidence of diastolic dysfunction and preserved systolic function and ventricular cavity size (biatrial enlargement may be present in the later stages of the disease); a right heart catheterization that depicts elevated central venous pressures with the classic "M" or "W" pattern in the right atrial pressure tracing; a left heart catheterization that reveals normal left ventricular systolic function with a small cavity size and no regional wall motion abnormalities; and, in many cases, a right ventricular biopsy that establishes the etiologic diagnosis.

CLINICAL MANIFESTATIONS

Subjective

The most common symptoms in patients with restrictive cardiomyopathies are usually related to congestive heart failure. The most prominent symptoms are complaints of dyspnea on exertion and fatigue. Symptoms typically associated with right-sided heart failure include increasing abdominal girth, peripheral edema, and right upper quadrant discomfort from hepatic congestion. In most patients, complaints of paroxysmal nocturnal dyspnea and orthopnea are usually absent. In those patients with restrictive cardiomyopathy due to infiltrative diseases, near syncope, syncope, or sudden cardiac death can be the initial presenting symptom. A minority of patients may have orthostatic hypotension as a prominent presenting symptom.

The past medical history is often noncontributory toward making the diagnosis, although in some instances, the history may suggest the etiology of the restrictive process. For example, a prior history of chronic inflammation might suggest a diagnosis of secondary amyloidosis.

The family history is, by and large, not suggestive of a restrictive cardiomyopathy except in inheritable infiltrative disorders such as hemochromatosis and glycogen storage diseases.

Objective

Physical Examination

The physical examination of the patient with a restrictive cardiomyopathy reflects the profound diastolic dysfunction that is characteristic of these conditions. The central venous pressure is usually elevated, resulting in distended jugular veins. To visualize the venous pulsations, it is often necessary to have the patient sit frankly upright or even stand. This maneuver brings the meniscus of the jugular venous column of blood out from under the angle of the jaw, where it may be obscured in the supine or partially recumbent position. Careful observation of the internal jugular venous waveforms is the most useful clue for suggesting restrictive cardiomyopathy as a possible diagnosis. In patients with restrictive cardiomyopathy, the *x* and *y* descents of the jugular venous waveform (the rapid, collapsing, inward movements of the jugular venous pulsations) are extremely exaggerated. Occasionally, the jugular venous pressure may increase on inspiration (Kussmaul sign), although this is usually more common in constrictive pericarditis. The apex impulse is usually palpable and not displaced in patients with restrictive cardiomyopathy. Cardiac auscultation often reveals a left ventricular S_3 gallop. A left ventricular S_4 may occasionally be present, although it is not as common as a ventricular gallop. Heart murmurs due to mitral and/or tricuspid valve regurgitation may be heard, especially in patients with endomyocardial fibrosis. A pericardial knock is absent. Signs of right-sided heart failure, including peripheral edema, hepatomegaly, ascites, and even anasarca, may be present.

Routine Laboratory Abnormalities

In general, the routinely ordered laboratory panels are not helpful in establishing the diagnosis of restrictive cardiomyopathy. On occasion,

TABLE 15–52–1. CLASSIFICATIONS OF CARDIOMYOPATHY

Myocardial Diseases
Diseases that infiltrate the myocardium
  Amyloid (primary and secondary)
  Sarcoidosis
Inherited diseases resulting from abnormal "storage" of biomolecules
  Hemochromatosis (excessive deposition of iron)
  Fabry's disease (excessive deposition of neutral glycolipids)
  Gaucher's disease (excessive deposition of cerebrosides)
  Numerous other inborn errors of metabolism
Noninfiltrative diseases
  Idiopathic

Endocardial or Endomyocardial Diseases
Endomyocardial fibrosis
Löffler's endocarditis (hypereosinophilic syndrome)
Radiation toxicity

certain abnormal blood chemistries may suggest a specific disease as a cause of restrictive cardiomyopathy. For example, abnormal liver function tests may suggest the presence of systemic infiltrative disease; however, passive hepatic congestion due to right-sided heart failure may also result in abnormal liver function tests. Patients with end-stage restrictive cardiomyopathy may develop renal failure secondary to a low-cardiac-output state with resulting elevation of blood urea nitrogen and creatinine, although these may suggest renal involvement due to a systemic infiltrative process.

The electrocardiogram is usually abnormal in patients with restrictive cardiomyopathy. Left or right bundle-branch block is common in patients with restrictive cardiomyopathies. Atrial fibrillation is often seen. In patients with restrictive cardiomyopathy from amyloidosis, generalized low-voltage and atrial arrhythmias are often present. High-degree heart block, or the occurrence of sustained ventricular tachycardia, should raise the suspicion of sarcoidosis as a possible etiology.

The cardiac silhouette on the chest x-ray film is usually normal. As the disease progresses, the cardiac silhouette enlarges and pleural effusions may develop. The chest x-ray film may also be helpful in the identification of sarcoidosis as an etiology of restrictive cardiomyopathy. Pericardial calcification indicates constrictive pericarditis as an alternative diagnosis.

PLANS
Diagnostic
Differential Diagnosis

The clinical entity that most closely masquerades as restrictive cardiomyopathy is constrictive pericarditis; however, the differential diagnosis should also include all causes of diastolic dysfunction and right-sided heart failure. The differential diagnosis therefore encompasses a myriad of disease states including, but not limited to, abnormal ventricular compliance due to ischemia or hypertension, hypertrophic cardiomyopathy, and heart muscle disease of any etiology (including ischemia, hypertension, ethanol, postpartum, viral, idiopathic, etc.). Noncardiac processes should also be included in the differential diagnosis, including severe chronic obstructive lung disease and recurrent pulmonary emboli.

Diagnostic Options

The diagnosis of restrictive cardiomyopathy should proceed on two parallel, but separate, tracks. The diagnosis of restrictive cardiomyopathy should be confirmed with diagnostic tests; then an etiologic diagnosis should be pursued.

A few blood tests are indicated. The possibility of hemochromatosis, a potentially treatable condition, as the responsible etiology should be investigated. Elevated plasma iron levels (≥ 200 µg/dL), elevated percentage saturation of serum transferrin (80–100%), low total iron binding capacity, and a markedly elevated serum ferritin (≥ 900 µg/dL) are all suggestive of hemochromatosis. An elevated absolute eosinophil count (≥ 1500/mm^3 for longer than 6 months) is compatible with Löffler's endocarditis.

Echocardiography is a useful starting point for the diagnostic workup. Two-dimensional echocardiography may reveal the following features of restrictive cardiomyopathy: thickened myocardial walls, dilated atria, and minimal thickening of valvular structures. Doppler interrogation of ventricular inflow may suggest diastolic dysfunction. This constellation of findings suggests the diagnosis of restrictive cardiomyopathy, regardless of the etiology, but is not generally regarded as diagnostic. There are, however, some echocardiographic findings that are essentially diagnostic of certain diseases that cause restrictive cardiomyopathy. For example, an echocardiogram that reveals a "speckled" appearance of the myocardial walls, four-chamber dilation, and a small pericardial effusion suggests cardiac amyloidosis. Specialized quantitation of the tissue density of this "speckled" pattern (i.e., tissue characterization) may be capable of diagnosing amyloid restrictive cardiomyopathy without the need for further studies. The restrictive cardiomyopathy from endomyocardial fibrosis (with or without eosinophillia) also has a distinctive echocardiographic appearance. The endocardium appears markedly thickened, and apical mural thrombi are

usually present. The posterior cusps of both the tricuspid and mitral valves may be thickened with significant mitral and tricuspid valve regurgitation.

Right and left heart cardiac catheterization is the gold standard for defining the hemodynamics of restrictive cardiomyopathy. The right atrial pressure tracings show the prominent x and y descents, with less prominent a and v waves creating a pressure waveform pattern that looks like an "M" or "W". The right atrial pressure usually falls with inspiration, but the presence of Kussmaul's sign (increase in right atrial pressure with inspiration) does not exclude the diagnosis of restrictive cardiomyopathy. The right ventricular diastolic pressure tracing shows a prominent dip and plateau pattern that resembles a "square root sign." In contrast to pericardial constriction, the right ventricular diastolic pressure is usually less than one third of the peak right ventricular systolic pressure. The pulmonary artery systolic pressure is usually greater than 45 mm Hg, again in contrast to pericardial constriction. Simultaneous right ventricular and left ventricular diastolic pressures are usually not equalized. The left ventricular diastolic pressure is usually greater than the right ventricular diastolic pressure (by more than 5 mm Hg), and this difference is exaggerated with exercise, as in normal patients. Coronary angiography is usually normal, unless concomitant atherosclerotic heart disease is present. Endomyocardial biopsy should be considered in patients when the diagnosis remains in question. In reality, this constitutes the majority of patients. There are data to support cardiac biopsy in most patients undergoing cardiac catheterization for the presumed diagnosis of restrictive cardiomyopathy.

Nuclear cardiology studies can be useful in the diagnostic workup of patients with suspected restrictive cardiomyopathy. Technetium-99m-pyrophosphate scintigraphy may be positive in patients with restrictive cardiomyopathy from infiltration of either amyloid substance or sarcoid granulomas. The time–activity curve, from a carefully obtained radionuclide angiogram, can demonstrate diastolic dysfunction, and in some cases, it can distinguish pericardial constriction from restrictive cardiomyopathy.

The ability of ultrafast cine computed tomography and magnetic resonance imaging to delineate pathologic thickening and calcification of the parietal pericardium makes these tests useful adjuncts in distinguishing restrictive cardiomyopathy from constrictive pericarditis. Typically, the pericardium is not involved by those processes that result in restrictive cardiomyopathy. The lack of significant pericardial thickening or calcification favors the diagnosis of restrictive cardiomyopathy.

When screening for etiologies of restrictive cardiomyopathy, obtaining a tissue diagnosis is strongly encouraged. The reasons for this are that patients deserve an accurate diagnosis to make a true estimate of prognosis, and the differentiation of restrictive cardiomyopathy from constrictive pericarditis may be extremely difficult and the latter may be successfully treated with surgery. Therefore, some form of biopsy should be considered. An exception to the consideration of biopsy might be made for those patients in whom the diagnosis of endomyocardial fibrosis is suspected. In these patients, cardiac biopsy may cause the dislodgment of mural thrombus, with resultant embolization. Another exception to cardiac biopsy would be those patients in whom a diagnosis can be otherwise established. For example, patients may have the diagnosis of hemochromatosis established by laboratory studies and/or liver biopsy. Likewise, the diagnosis of some forms of amyloidosis may be established by aspiration biopsy of abdominal fat. Sarcoidosis may be diagnosed by biopsy of other affected organs, including the conjunctiva, the lacrimal glands, or skin lesions. Of note, the patchy nature of granulomatous infiltration by cardiac sarcoid lowers the diagnostic yield of cardiac biopsy compared with other infiltrative diseases.

Recommended Approach

An echocardiogram should be the first test employed. If this is consistent with restrictive cardiomyopathy, a cardiac catheterization should be planned and performed to obtain the hemodynamic data outlined above. The only patients who should not undergo cardiac catheterization are those patients who have classic echo findings for amyloid-induced restrictive cardiomyopathy and a positive fat pad biopsy. We favor endomyocardial biopsy in all other patients. If cardiac catheterization does not distinguish restrictive cardiomyopathy from constrictive pericarditis, a cine computed tomography scan or magnetic resonance imaging should be performed to evaluate the pericardium. If the pericardium is thickened, the diagnosis of cardiac constriction is more likely.

Certainly, one of the most important principles to remember in the workup of restrictive cardiomyopathy is to distinguish it from constrictive pericarditis, as the treatment of these two entities may vary significantly.

Therapeutic

Therapeutic Options

In general, there is no specific medical therapy for the treatment of restrictive cardiomyopathy. Therapy is directed at providing the patient with relief from symptoms. One exception of note is that for some patients with restrictive cardiomyopathy due to hemochromatosis, regular phlebotomy of 250 to 500 mL of blood per week may result in near-total recovery. Calcium channel blockers may have a limited role in the early stages of the disease in an attempt to improve the diastolic function. Verapamil (90–240 mg/d), nifedipine (30–90 mg/d), and diltiazem (120–240 mg/d) can be used safely with some symptomatic improvement; however, results of therapy with calcium channel blockers are generally disappointing. Unfortunately, by the time most patients are diagnosed with restrictive cardiomyopathy, the disease is usually advanced and signs and symptoms of right-sided heart failure predominate. Therefore, these patients often need diuretics; however, the hemodynamics are such that elevated filling pressures are necessary to load stiff, noncompliant ventricles. Thus, there is a fine line separating appropriate diuresis from overdiuresis. Indeed, these patients are prone to hypotension even if low doses of diuretic are prescribed. When systolic function falls, digoxin may improve the symptoms of diminished cardiac output. Digoxin should be used very carefully in patients with cardiac amyloid. These patients are exquisitely sensitive to digoxin and are prone to developing digitalis toxicity.

In patients with restrictive cardiomyopathy from amyloid infiltration, treatment with alkylating agents has been tried with limited success. In patients with sarcoid-induced restrictive cardiomyopathy, treatment with steroids may have some therapeutic role. In patients who develop atrial fibrillation, control of the ventricular rate response is paramount because of the aforementioned hemodynamic considerations. The noncompliant ventricles need a long diastolic filling time to optimize ventricular loading. Thus, as the ventricular rate increases, effective loading decreases. Digoxin, beta blockers, and calcium channel blockers can be used in standard doses to control the ventricular response. If patients develop ventricular tachycardia, antiarrhythmic medications may be helpful. Frequently, however, the ventricular arrhythmias are refractory to medical therapy and occasionally an implantable cardioverter–defibrillator is indicated. In patients who develop heart block, pacemakers may be life prolonging. Notably, the pacing thresholds in patients with infiltrative diseases (particularly amyloid) are higher than those required in normal myocardium. Endomyocardial fibrosis can be treated with endocardial decortication, but the operative mortality approaches 1 in 4.

Cardiac transplantation is an option in patients with no evidence of systemic disease in whom the pulmonary artery pressure is only slightly elevated but intractable heart failure continues despite medical management.

Recommended Approach

In the early stages of the disease, treatment with calcium channel blockers or beta blockers may be marginally useful. Low doses of diuretics, carefully titrated over a period of weeks, may improve symptomatology. Instructing patients to weigh themselves every other day and self-titrate their furosemide or thiazide diuretic to a target "dry weight" seems to provide reasonable results. Phlebotomy and chelation therapy with desferroxamine constitute an effective treatment of the restrictive cardiomyopathy caused by hemochromatosis. In patients with sarcoid-induced restrictive cardiomyopathy and high-degree atrioventricular block, permanent pacing is usually indicated.

FOLLOW-UP

Follow-up is done on an individualized basis depending on the severity and rate of progression of the disease. Early in the disease more frequent follow-up is needed to titrate medications and to carefully discuss the prognosis with the patient.

DISCUSSION

Prevalence and Incidence

Fortunately, restrictive cardiomyopathy is a rare syndrome, and is the most infrequent type of cardiomyopathy in industrialized countries. Amyloidosis is the most common etiology of restrictive cardiomyopathy in Western cultures. In primary amyloidosis, restrictive cardiomyopathy is common and occurs in one third to one half of all patients. In secondary amyloid, restrictive cardiomyopathy is quite rare. Cardiac involvement in familial amyloidosis is unusual. Restrictive cardiomyopathy is an infrequent complication of sarcoidosis. Endomyocardial fibrosis, with or without eosinophilia, is more common in temperate climates.

Related Basic Science

The pathologic findings vary between the different diseases that cause restrictive cardiomyopathy. In amyloidosis, cardiac amyloid deposition is observed in at least three distinct pathologic patterns: a perivascular deposition of amyloid, a micronodular or pericellular infiltrative pattern, and a nodular pattern. It is suspected that these nodular patterns of amyloid infiltration produce the classic "speckled" pattern of tissue density sometimes seen in the ventricular walls on echocardiography. In cardiac sarcoidosis the pattern of granuloma distribution is distinctive. There appears to be a predilection for granuloma formation in the intraventricular septum and the left ventricular free wall. The septal location accounts for the high incidence of heart block, secondary to infiltration of the atrioventricular node. The lack of infiltration in the right ventricle accounts for the lower yield of diagnosis by right ventricular, endomyocardial biopsies.

Natural History and Its Modification with Treatment

The prognosis of restrictive cardiomyopathy is poor. Generally, the 5-year survival rates for patients with restrictive cardiomyopathy is 50% or less. Amyloid-induced restrictive cardiomyopathy has a particularly poor prognosis. Progressive heart failure, heart block, and arrhythmias are the sequelae that are most likely to cause morbidity and mortality. Occasionally, patients with idiopathic restrictive cardiomyopathy may live a decade following diagnosis; this is the exception rather than the rule.

As previously discussed, except for hemochromatosis, there are no specific therapies for restrictive cardiomyopathy that are effective.

Prevention

These diseases are not preventable. In hemochromatosis, patients who have routine phlebotomy typically do not develop restrictive cardiomyopathy.

Cost Containment

Even though the definitive diagnosis of restrictive cardiomyopathy depends on a number of technical studies, costs can be contained by following a reasonable workup. The best example of this is the patient with presumed restrictive cardiomyopathy from amyloid deposition. If the echo is strongly suggestive, and a fat pad biopsy confirms the diagnosis, the cardiac catheterization and computed tomography scans are not indicated. The other method to contain costs is to organize the cardiac catheterization protocol so as to optimize the hemodynamic data that can define restrictive cardiomyopathy and make a definitive diagnosis. Occasionally, unprepared or unsuspecting physicians perform a catheterization on a patient with suspected restrictive cardiomyopathy and the hemodynamic data are so disordered that no diagnosis can be made. This necessitates further studies that add unnecessary costs to the workup.

REFERENCES

Schoenfeld MH. The differentiation of restrictive cardiomyopathy from constrictive pericarditis. Cardiol Clin 1990;8:663.

Schoenfeld MH, Bowden RE, Abrams J, et al. Restrictive cardiomyopathy versus constrictive pericarditis: Role of endomyocardial biopsy in avoiding unnecessary thoracotomy. Circulation 1987;75:1012.

Shabetai R. Restrictive cardiomyopathy. In Schlant RC, Alexander RW, O'Rourke RA, et al., eds. Hurst's the heart. 8th ed. New York: McGraw-Hill, 1994:1637.

Wynne J, Braunwald E. The cardiomyopathies and myocarditis: Toxic, chemical, and physical damage to the heart. In Braunwald E, ed. The heart. 4th ed. Philadelphia: Saunders, 1992:1394.

CHAPTER 15–53

Athlete's Heart

George C. Haidet, M.D., and Jere H. Mitchell, M.D.

DEFINITION

Athlete's heart and athletic heart syndrome are terms used to describe normal anatomic and functional changes in the heart that result from chronic prolonged and/or intense exercise.

ETIOLOGY

In the 19th and early 20th centuries, endurance-trained athletes were noted to have slower heart rates and larger hearts than their sedentary counterparts. These findings were thought to be early signs of heart disease and were called the *athletic heart* because at the time it was felt that chronic exercise could eventually result in heart failure. Today, it is well recognized that the athlete's heart actually represents a very successful adaptation to extreme physiologic demands imposed by strenuous, repetitive exercise, and is not a disease.

CRITERIA FOR DIAGNOSIS

Suggestive

The athletic heart syndrome is usually discovered during routine physical examinations that are frequently required prior to participation in competitive athletics. In addition, athlete's heart can be diagnosed when a competitive athlete undergoes diagnostic workup for symptoms that may be cardiovascular in origin. In the course of diagnostic evaluations in highly conditioned asymptomatic and symptomatic athletes, findings suggestive of organic heart disease may be present. Some of these apparent abnormalities include an increase in heart size, extra cardiac sounds, and murmurs. Also, a wide variety of electrocardiographic changes may be seen. Most of these apparent abnormalities result from increases in heart size and mass, stroke volume, and parasympathetic tone, all normal consequences of chronic dynamic exercise training.

Definitive

Athlete's heart is most commonly seen in those who have a significant history of chronic participation in endurance-type dynamic exercise, and can also be seen in strength-trained competitive athletes. Other than vasovagal syncope, there are no associated symptoms that can occur as a consequence of athlete's heart. A third or fourth heart sound is often present on auscultation, as is a nonradiating systolic ejection murmur. The heart is often globular and can appear enlarged on chest x-ray film. The electrocardiogram frequently demonstrates sinus bradycardia with or without sinus arrhythmia. First-degree atrioventricular block can occur, as can other electrocardiographic findings including an increase in QRS amplitude, minor conduction abnormalities, and various ST-segment and T-wave changes. Although left ventricular wall thickness and cavity size may be somewhat increased on echo–Doppler cardiac evaluation, systolic and diastolic function are always normal.

CLINICAL MANIFESTATIONS

Subjective

The patient with the athletic heart syndrome usually has habitually performed strenuous physical activity. It is frequently possible to elicit a history of participation in endurance-type dynamic exercise that has been performed on a highly competitive level.

People with athlete's heart are usually asymptomatic; however, vasovagal syncope is not an uncommon finding in highly trained athletes, with symptoms occurring at rest but not during exertion. If symptoms such as chest pain or pressure, easy fatigability, dyspnea on exertion, or exertional presyncope or syncope are present, they are not due to the athletic heart syndrome and organic heart disease must be excluded. Such symptoms may be associated with conditions that may predispose the athlete to sudden death, including coronary artery diseases (atherosclerosis, congenital coronary artery anomalies); left ventricular hypertrophic cardiomyopathy with or without left ventricular outflow obstruction; fixed-subvalvular, valvular, and supravalvular aortic stenosis; dynamic hypertrophic cardiomyopathy; diseases responsible for ventricular dilation and/or dysfunction (aortic and/or mitral valve regurgitation, idiopathic cardiomyopathy, myocarditis, right ventricular dysplasia, shunt lesions); diseases of the aorta (aortic ectasia with Marfan's syndrome or other collagen vascular disease, coarctation); and arrhythmias (congenital prolonged QT syndrome, Wolff–Parkinson–White syndrome, right ventricular dysplasia, hypertrophic cardiomyopathy). Therefore, significant negative points in the history should include the absence of a history of heart murmur; rheumatic fever; congenital heart disease; high blood pressure; frequent joint dislocations and/or abnormal visual acuity with associated ectopic ocular lens; deafness or heart murmur in family members; or a family history of sudden death, cardiomyopathy, heart attack, coronary artery bypass graft surgery, or angioplasty in a family member before age 50.

Objective

Physical Examination

A slow pulse rate is the most common finding on physical examination. Extra heart sounds are frequently heard on auscultation. A third heart sound (S_3) has been heard in numerous studies in from one third to as many as all champion dynamic athletes. Below age 35 to 40, an audible S_3 is a function of rapid ventricular filling during early diastole and has no clinical significance. An increase in diastolic filling and thin chest wall probably combine to allow the normally inaudible (but easily recorded) fourth heart sound to be heard in one fourth to one half of endurance athletes. Systolic ejection-type murmurs are present in one third to one half of these athletes, presumably occurring secondary to nonlaminar flow across the pulmonic and/or aortic valves as the result of an increase in stroke volume. Finally, most elite endurance athletes also have a low percentage of body fat.

Routine Laboratory Abnormalities

Routine chest films often reveal a globular cardiac silhouette. Even though cardiothoracic ratios greater than 0.5 are found less than one fourth of the time, heart size is generally larger than that in sedentary controls. Previous studies have demonstrated a good correlation between maximal oxygen uptake, stroke volume, and heart size on chest x-ray film; all are increased in competitive endurance athletes.

A wide variety of electrocardiographic abnormalities have been observed in endurance athletes. Sinus bradycardia with a heart rate often less than 40 beats/minute is seen in the vast majority of competitive athletes and is commonly associated with marked sinus arrhythmia. As many as one fifth will have a wandering atrial pacemaker. The prevalence of ectopic atrial and junctional rhythms is less than 1 in 10. First-degree atrioventricular block (PR interval greater than 0.20 second) occurs as often as one third of the time, compared with less than 1% of the sedentary population. Second-degree atrioventricular Wenckebach block (Mobitz I) that resolves with exercise has a prevalence as high as 10% in some series, much higher than that reported in the general population (<1%).

In the age group under 40, the electrocardiographic diagnosis of ventricular hypertrophy is usually impaired by the normally higher QRS amplitudes seen in young adults. Likewise, it is also difficult to arrive at any reliable estimates of the prevalence of left and right ventricular hypertrophy by electrocardiographic criteria in most athletes; however, sequential voltage increases seem to develop during chronic exercise training, making increased QRS amplitude a very common finding in athletes. Additionally, minor conduction defects, usually in the form of incomplete right bundle-branch block, may occur in as many as one half of endurance athletes.

Numerous ST-segment and T-wave changes have been reported. Of these, the early repolarization pattern, which consists of ST-segment elevation with associated J-point elevation and peaked T waves, is most commonly observed. These changes usually revert to normal during exercise-induced sinus tachycardia. About 10% of the time, the juvenile pattern of T-wave inversions in leads V_1 to V_3 is found in younger, endurance athletes. Less commonly, anterolateral T-wave changes may be seen; however, these changes should not be confused with the deep, symmetric T-wave inversions and/or ST-segment depression often seen in the setting of hypertrophic cardiomyopathy or other pathologic conditions.

PLANS
Diagnostic

Differential Diagnosis

As athlete's heart is usually asymptomatic, competitive athletes who present with symptoms that are nonspecific or possibly cardiovascular in origin commonly undergo further evaluation to exclude structural heart disease. In the course of such a diagnostic evaluation, findings associated with athlete's heart must be differentiated from those associated with pathologic conditions responsible for ventricular enlargement such as aortic and/or mitral valvular regurgitation, dilated cardiomyopathy, myocarditis, and intracardiac shunts. Moreover, the physiologic hypertrophy that can be associated with athlete's heart must be differentiated from the left ventricular hypertrophy due to hypertrophic cardiomyopathy, fixed aortic (valvular, subvalvular, and supravalvular) stenosis, coarctation of the aorta, or hypertension (often secondary in younger athletes).

Although vasovagal syncope can occur as a consequence of intense endurance training, unexplained syncope in an athlete requires thorough evaluation because this symptom may or may not also occur due to structural heart disease and/or dysrhythmias. When syncope has occurred during exercise, cardiac pathology is especially suspect. Therefore, conditions such as fixed or dynamic aortic outflow tract obstruction, myocardial diseases (such as hypertrophic cardiomyopathy, right ventricular dysplasia, and myocarditis), preexcitation, and other structural and/or electrophysiologic conditions (including Wolff–Parkinson–White syndrome) that can be responsible for syncope must be carefully excluded.

Diagnostic Options

The diagnostic modalities most helpful in establishing the diagnosis of athlete's heart include the history and physical examination. The electrocardiogram and routine posteroanterior and lateral chest x-ray films can also be used to support this diagnosis. When an endurance- or strength-trained competitive athlete presents with symptoms and/or physical examination findings suggestive of organic heart disease, then other diagnostic options may need to be considered. Echocardiography,

usually combined with Doppler flow imaging, is often helpful in ruling out structural heart disease and/or in differentiating between organic heart disease and athlete's heart. Other diagnostic studies are usually used to exclude or screen for pathologic conditions that can occur in competitive athletes and are usually not required to establish the diagnosis of athlete's heart per se. For example, exercise electrocardiography can also be used to screen for coronary artery diseases and/or dysrhythmias in symptomatic athletes with normal physical examinations, normal electrocardiograms, and normal echo–Doppler studies. Likewise, cardiac event detection recorders can be used to diagnose dysrhythmias suggested by the appropriate history. Tilt-table testing is often positive in endurance athletes, but does not exclude other possible pathologic conditions that can also be responsible for syncope in these individuals. Therefore, it is always important to definitively exclude underlying structural heart disease in athletes with syncope using appropriate diagnostic modalities (discussed above). Finally, invasive electrophysiologic testing should also be considered as a diagnostic option to identify dysrhythmias in the athlete with syncope who also has cardiac disease or an abnormal baseline electrocardiogram, or when no other cause of syncope has been identified.

Recommended Approach

Further diagnostic studies are performed when the possibility of organic heart disease cannot be excluded on the basis of the subjective and objective information already discussed.

Characteristically, four-chamber cardiac enlargement with associated increased left ventricular thickness is seen on the echocardiogram in endurance athletes. Weight lifters and others who perform static exercise often have left ventricular hypertrophy by echocardiography, but without associated increases or decreases in chamber size. The heart mass to lean body mass ratio in weight lifters is normal, however, because of the degree of skeletal muscular hypertrophy these individuals generally develop. Most importantly, systolic function and diastolic function are both normal in endurance- and in strength-trained athletes, and a dynamic outflow tract gradient is not present or provokable in the normal athlete's heart.

Echocardiography combined with Doppler flow studies also can serve as an excellent method to screen for entities such as aortic valvular stenosis and subaortic and supraaortic obstruction in patients with symptoms and/or physical examination findings suggestive of any one of these abnormalities. Various causes of left and right ventricular dysfunction, including hypertrophic and ischemic cardiomyopathies, and right ventricular dysplasia that may be suspected on the basis of the history and/or physical examination, can also be detected by echocardiography and Doppler studies. In addition, both transthoracic and transesophageal echocardiography can be very sensitive techniques to evaluate aortic root dilation, as well as valvular dysfunction, which can be associated with Marfan's syndrome and other collagen–vascular diseases.

The exercise tolerance test in endurance athletes demonstrates normal blood pressure and electrocardiographic responses to exercise, as well as superior functional capacity. It is most commonly used to screen for the presence of coronary artery disease in competitive athletes over 30 years of age, especially participants with significant risk factors for developing atherosclerotic cardiovascular disease, including a family history of early myocardial infarction or sudden death. The exercise tolerance test is also recommended in those over 30 with complaints of chest pain who have had a normal physical examination, normal electrocardiogram, and normal echocardiogram. In the athlete under 30 years of age who complains of chest discomfort and has had a normal echocardiographic evaluation, the exercise tolerance test can be used to screen for the rare presence of a congenital coronary artery abnormality such as an aberrant coronary artery or intramyocardial bridging that could be responsible for exertional chest discomfort.

The 24-hour ambulatory ECG (Holter) monitor and/or a cardiac event detection monitor can be used to screen for significant arrhythmias when a history of palpitations or "racing heart" has been elicited, with the choice of diagnostic modality used based on the frequency of symptoms. These arrhythmia-detecting devices, as well as tilt-table testing, can also be used for diagnostic purposes when syncope or presyncope has occurred but the physical examination, baseline 12-lead electrocardiogram, and echocardiogram are within normal limits. Invasive electrophysiologic testing is usually reserved to identify dysrhythmias in those athletes with syncope, presyncope, palpitations, or "racing heart" in whom structural heart disease has been diagnosed in those with abnormal baseline electrocardiograms, and in other athletes when no other cause of syncope has been determined in the course of diagnostic evaluation.

Therapeutic

Because the athletic heart syndrome represents a normal adaptive response to chronic dynamic exercise and is not a disease state, no treatment is recommended or required. After appropriate evaluation has been completed and the diagnosis of athlete's heart has been confirmed, the most important thing to tell the patient is that he or she is normal and does not have heart disease. It should be emphasized that no special precautions are required, that the syndrome does not cause symptoms and is not progressive, and that chronic exercise will not result in heart disease. It should be pointed out that further medical evaluation is advised if symptoms such as chest pain, palpitations, syncope, or easy fatigability develop.

FOLLOW-UP

Asymptomatic patients without organic heart disease require only routine follow-up. Usually, those participating in competitive athletics from high school to professional levels should routinely have a medically supervised examination annually.

DISCUSSION
Prevalence and Incidence

Although it is clear that strenuous, prolonged endurance training is required for the development of athlete's heart, the exact prevalence and incidence of athlete's heart are unknown. This fact may reflect the fact that the vast majority of people with athlete's heart are asymptomatic and frequently are appropriately subjected to very limited medical evaluation and thus remain undiagnosed.

Related Basic Science

The major physiologic adaptations to chronic dynamic exercise have been described over the past two or three decades. This knowledge is largely responsible for our understanding of the athletic heart syndrome.

Dynamic exercise training results in significantly improved endurance (aerobic) exercise capacity. This improvement is directly proportional to the degree that maximal oxygen uptake (VO_2max) is increased. Maximal oxygen uptake is the maximal amount of oxygen that can be used by the body. It is largely dependent on two factors: the maximal amount of oxygen extraction that takes place in the various body tissues, especially in active skeletal muscle, and the maximal cardiac output. Most of the clinical features of athlete's heart can be attributed to the adaptive responses that improve maximal performance favorably in competitive athletes.

Cardiac output is the product of heart rate and stroke volume. Chronic endurance exercise training results in a relative slowing of the heart rate along with an increase in stroke volume at rest and during submaximal exercise. There is no resultant change in cardiac output and, as expected, no change in oxygen consumption at the same absolute submaximal levels of work before and after training. Although the exact mechanism is unknown, training-induced bradycardia appears to result from a combination of increased vagal tone and decreased sympathetic activation, as well as from other poorly delineated nonautonomic factors that decrease the intrinsic rate of the sinus node. Maximal heart rate, however, is unchanged.

The observed increase in maximal cardiac output associated with chronic dynamic exercise training is due to a significant increase in maximal stroke volume. Thus, stroke volume is augmented at rest and during all levels of exercise. Echocardiographic, nuclear, and magnetic resonance imaging techniques have demonstrated increases in left ventricular end-diastolic dimensions and volumes at rest and during exercise as a consequence of chronic endurance exercise training. Additionally, right ventricular and both atrial sizes are increased in endurance athletes; however, despite being increased, cardiac dimensions and volumes usually do not exceed the uppermost limits of the reported ranges for the normal adult population. Left ventricular free wall and septal thicknesses are also somewhat increased. These changes in volume and wall thickness in endurance-trained athletes result in an increase in absolute left ventricular mass, as well as in left ventricular mass normalized in relation to lean body mass. Moreover, systolic and diastolic ventricular function is always normal in athlete's heart. It is likely that the observed changes in left ventricular size are largely responsible for the improved cardiac function in endurance athletes. Such changes in left ventricular size and wall thickness appear to revert toward normal values in response to detraining in elite aerobic athletes.

In those who chronically perform static exercise, such as weight lifters, heart mass appears to be increased secondary to an increase in ventricular wall thickness. In these athletes, hypertrophy is usually not accompanied by an increase in left ventricular end-diastolic diameter, as occurs with endurance training. Also, the increased wall thickness seen in weight lifters does not result in a reduction in left ventricular cavity size, as occurs in certain types of hypertrophic cardiomyopathy. Abnormal systolic anterior motion of the mitral valve does not occur in power athletes as a result of training, even in cases where the apparent ratio of septal to left ventricular posterior wall thickness is greater than 1.3. This is a significant point of distinction between physiologic hypertrophy and idiopathic hypertrophic subaortic stenosis (hypertrophic obstructive cardiopathy). Moreover, a dynamic gradient in the left ventricular outflow tract is not present or provokable and diastolic function is normal by Doppler examination in the normal athlete's heart. The calculated left ventricular mass and left ventricular mass-to-volume ratio are both increased as a result of chronic weight training; however, cardiac mass in weight lifters is usually normal when corrected for lean body mass. It also should be noted that the physiologic hypertrophy that results from dynamic or static exercise training usually can be clearly distinguished from changes associated with severe chronic volume overload or pressure overload states. These disease states lead to chamber sizes and/or wall thicknesses that clearly fall outside accepted normal ranges and are accompanied by left ventricular dysfunction and/or other associated anatomic abnormalities responsible for volume and/or pressure overload.

Natural History and Its Modification with Treatment

Chronic dynamic and static exercise does not result in heart failure or other forms of heart disease. In addition, those who chronically exercise do not appear to be more prone to sudden death than their sedentary counterparts. As noted above, cardiac volume and wall thickness changes that occur with chronic exercise appear to revert toward normal when athletes become sedentary; however, the age of onset of activity as well as the number of years of exercise participation and genetic influences may be important factors in the determination of the effects of detraining on such changes. At this time, it has not been definitively established that exercise training improves coronary artery collateral blood flow or improves subendocardial myocardial blood flow, but epicardial coronary artery diameter appears to increase. Also, it is uncertain whether exercise has an effect on the development and progression of atherosclerosis independent of the beneficial effects produced by modification of known risks such as hypertension and hyperlipidemia. Finally, although the effect of habitually increased activity levels on the aging process and on longevity appears to be beneficial, further studies are required to support the limited observations currently published.

Prevention

Because habitually increased activity levels result in improved cardiovascular function and do not result in cardiovascular disease, preventive measures are unnecessary and possibly undesirable.

Cost Containment

The routine evaluation of most individuals can be limited to history and physical examination. Usually, a chest x-ray film and standard 12-lead electrocardiogram are obtained at least once in young adults to complete the adult database. Routine evaluations do not include echocardiography, ambulatory electrocardiographic monitoring, and electrocardiogram-monitored exercise tolerance testing; however, symptomatic individuals, as well as those with significant family histories or objective findings, may require further evaluation as previously discussed, pending the results of the physical examination, chest x-ray film, electrocardiogram, and the nature of the patient's history or complaints.

The most important and effective way to avoid ordering unnecessary tests and to control costs is to understand the physiologic adaptive responses to chronic exercise and the clinical manifestations of these responses, as well as to recognize those pathologic conditions occurring in young athletes that predispose those afflicted to significant potential cardiovascular morbidity and/or mortality.

REFERENCES

Maron BJ. The athlete's heart. Cardiol Clin 1992;10:197.

Maron BJ, Mitchell JH. Twenty-sixth Bethesda Conference: Recommendations for determining eligibility for competition in athletes with cardiovascular abnormalities. J Am Coll Cardiol 1994;24:845; Med Sci Sports Exerc 1994;10(suppl.):S223.

Maron BJ, Pelliccia A, Spataro A, Granata M. Reduction in left ventricular wall thickness after deconditioning in highly trained Olympic athletes. Br Heart J 1993;69:125.

Mitchell JH, Raven PB. Cardiovascular response and adaptation to exercise. In: Bouchard C, Shephard R, Stephens T, eds. Physical activity, fitness and health: International proceedings and consensus statement, Champaign, IL: Human Kinetics, 1994:286.

Urhansen A, Kindermann W. Echocardiographic findings in strength- and endurance-trained athletes. Sports Med 1992;13:270.

CHAPTER 15–54

Acute Pericarditis

David H. Spodick, M.D., D.Sc.

DEFINITION

Acute pericarditis is defined as inflammation—infectious, irritative, or immunopathic—of the pericardial sac.

ETIOLOGY

A vast number of etiologic agents and local and systemic disorders can produce acute pericarditis with inflammatory lesions that nearly always involve the subjacent myocardium with or without variable amounts of pericardial effusion. The absence of clinically significant amounts of fluid produces "clinically dry" acute pericarditis. Effusive pericarditis may occur with or without significant cardiac compression (cardiac tamponade).

The clinical setting of acute pericarditis is highly variable because there are nine very broad etiologic categories: idiopathic, infectious, immunopathic ("hypersensitivity"), extension from disease of contiguous organs, vasculitic (connective tissue disease), metabolic (mainly chronic or acute uremia), traumatic (direct and indirect), neoplastic, and diseases of uncertain origin (a large category including many syndromes). Thus, the usual clinical setting is either an infectious syndrome or pericarditis in the course (rarely the first manifestation) of diseases in every category of medicine. Idiopathic pericarditis syndrome is nearly always synonymous with viral pericarditis and is perhaps the most common clinical form.

CRITERIA FOR DIAGNOSIS

Suggestive

Acute "dry" pericarditis is nearly always suggested by pleuritic chest pain, usually central, and only rarely when a typical electrocardiogram or pericardial friction sound occurs in an asymptomatic patient.

Definitive

A definitive diagnosis of acute pericarditis is made by detecting a pericardial rub (friction sound), or by a typical stage 1 electrocardiogram, that is, nearly ubiquitous ST-segment elevations, PR-segment depressions, or both.

CLINICAL MANIFESTATIONS

Subjective

Patients may have nonspecific symptoms, such as fever, malaise, and cough; however, the definitive symptom is chest pain, nearly always pleuritic, that is exacerbated by inspiration and recumbency. The pain is nearly always located retrosternally, in the left precordium, or in both sites. It can radiate or occur simultaneously in all the areas typical of angina pectoris and, on occasion, can have a squeezing quality. Usually it is sharp, "nasty," and disabling. Frequently there is pain in one or both trapezius ridges (the patient should always be asked to point if he or she says the pain is in his or her "shoulder"). Trapezius ridge pain is almost pathognomonic for pericardial lesions; occasionally, it is the only pain locus. Odynophagia occurs rarely.

Family history, occupation, and environmental influences are nearly always irrelevant.

Objective

Physical Examination

The principal physical finding is the pericardial rub (friction sound), which usually is auscultated as a noise in three phases corresponding to ventricular systole, ventricular diastole, and atrial systole. Frequently only one or two components are audible, especially when rhythm disturbances (due to heart, not pericardial, disease) eliminate atrial systole. Rubs can be harsh, grating, scratching, or shuffling sounds that are nearly always best heard at the left midsternal to lower sternal border, although they may be detected anywhere around the cardiac perimeter. They are occasionally palpable, especially in patients with uremia. Many rubs, especially in the presence of increased pericardial fluid, are intensified by inspiration. Nonspecific findings include a variable degree of tachycardia (usually absent in uremic patients) and temperature elevation. If pericarditis is due to a generalized or adjacent disease process, evidence for that condition may also be present.

Routine Laboratory Abnormalities

Apart from "cardiomegaly" due to sufficient pericardial fluid, the chest x-ray film is usually within normal limits unless there is related or unrelated thoracic disease.

Electrocardiograms show ST-segment elevations in most leads without reciprocal ST-segment depressions (NB—depressions that always occur in lead aVR and usually in V_1 are not "reciprocal"). The PR segment may be depressed prior to or with ST segment elevation. This stage (stage 1) is by itself diagnostic if it is complete. Further evolution is either back to normal (or baseline) electrocardiogram or through three more stages: stage 2 involves flattening and beginning inversion of the T waves; stage 3 is a stage of ubiquitous T-wave inversion; and stage 4 is a final return to normal (which occasionally may not occur).

The hemogram may show leukocytosis with increased polymorphonuclear leukocytes or lymphocytes depending on etiology. Variable involvement of the subepicardial myocardium produces widely variable enzyme changes from normal to moderate and even high elevations in the levels of creatine kinase and lactate dehydrogenase and their isoenzymes. Although echocardiograms may show fluid, that is not in itself primary evidence of pericardial inflammation unless fibrin shreds are seen.

Urine analysis is not helpful.

PLANS

Diagnostic

Differential Diagnosis

Acute pericarditis must be separated from myocardial infarction (see Chapter 47).

Diagnostic Options

Suspicion of acute pericarditis calls for immediate recording of an electrocardiogram to attempt to detect stage 1, the presence of which is virtually 100% predictive. A negative electrocardiogram is not helpful in many cases of pericarditis, particularly in uremic pericarditis, where the electrocardiogram is virtually never altered, and during acute myocardial infarction, where (unlike Dressler's syndrome) pericarditis is restricted to and masked by the infarction itself. Moreover, electrocardiograms can also be negative with infectious pericarditis. When there is a definite pericardial rub, a stage 1 electrocardiographic change, or both, additional diagnostic tests are not needed except to search for an etiology.

Recommended Approach

As acute pericarditis has many causes, it is proper to consider preceding trauma, such as the trauma of cardiac surgery; neoplastic disease, such as carcinoma of the lung or breast; immunopathy, such as rheumatoid arthritis or rheumatic fever; collagen disease, such as lupus erythematosus; myocardial infarction; uremia; and bacterial and viral infections. The identification of these conditions is discussed in the chapters related to these conditions. As a rule, acute idiopathic pericarditis is thought to be present when none of the other causes is evident. It is most likely viral in origin. When pericarditis lasts longer than 2 weeks, it is wise to search for causes such as collagen disease and carcinoma.

Therapeutic

The treatment of acute, clinically "dry" pericarditis is aimed at managing pain, reducing inflammation (often accomplished simultaneously), and eliminating etiologic agents, if these are identifiable. The last must be adapted to the disease process and is not specific for pericarditis. Management of pain and inflammation depends primarily on nonsteroidal antiinflammatory agents. Excellent results are often obtained with ibuprofen (Motrin), 600 to 1000 mg every 6 hours for at least 4 days. Side effects occur in less than 10% of patients and include gastrointestinal distress, dizziness, rash, tinnitus, blood dyscrasias, fluid retention with edema, various allergic reactions, and renal failure in patients with preexisting renal disease. Ibuprofen has many fewer gastrointestinal side effects than aspirin, which may be used in common doses, or indomethacin (Indocin), 50 to 150 mg three times daily for at least 7 days. Indomethacin should be avoided whenever coronary disease is possible. The side effects of indomethacin are similar to those of ibuprofen. Failure with any of these agents should institute a trial-and-error search among other nonsteroidal antiinflammatory agents. If none of these is effective, or if the patient is extremely uncomfortable, prednisone (Sterapred), 60 mg daily orally, may be used but only as a last resort, and it should be progressively tapered following resolution of symptoms. Recently, colchicine, 1.0 mg b.i.d., has given promise as an effective agent, either as monotherapy or added to ANSAID.

FOLLOW-UP

Physicians should request at least a telephone follow-up within a month and should reevaluate the patient within 6 months if the patient is asymptomatic, to exclude subclinical evidence of pericardial effusion or constriction. If the patient has symptoms, an electrocardiogram and, if necessary, an echocardiogram should be performed in addition to a careful physical examination. Patients should be advised to report any recurrence of symptoms, appearance of edema, or distention of neck veins.

DISCUSSION

Prevalence and Incidence

The prevalence and incidence of acute idiopathic (presumably viral) or bacterial pericarditis fluctuates over the years and is probably related to particular strains of organisms. All forms of pericarditis, except those in the connective tissue disease group, have a 3:1 to 4:1 male-to-female predominance and tend to occur in younger people, except in defined chronic diseases.

Related Basic Science

Acute noneffusive pericarditis inflames the pericardium and, to a variable extent, the underlying myocardium (subepicardial myocarditis) without fundamental abnormalities in physiology. There are variable to absent changes in serum levels of cardiac enzymes depending on the presence and extent of the usually minor subepicardial myocarditis.

Natural History and Its Modification with Treatment

Most acute, clinically "dry" pericarditis is self-limited with or without appropriate treatment. Approximately 15 to 25% recur, particularly in patients initially treated with corticosteroid agents. Late pericardial effusion is extremely rare, and constrictive pericarditis is quite uncommon, except after severe attacks and in the relatively scarce tuberculous form. Constriction can occur from a few weeks to many years after the index attack, whereas recurrence usually begins within a period of months and may be limited to one or two or an indefinite succession of recurrences. Some patients are "hooked" on a corticosteroid agent and can only be weaned temporarily or cannot be weaned completely, resulting in attempts to use nonsteroidal antiinflammatory agents to help the patient discontinue the corticosteroid. In desperation, pericardiectomy may be attempted, but it is usually unsuccessful.

Morbidity varies widely with acute pericarditis. Except for destructive and resistant infections (e.g., some tuberculosis), the direct mortality is nil.

Prevention

No specific preventive measures are currently available. The onset of pericarditis remains unpredictable.

Cost Containment

Most patients can be treated at home and do not require hospital admission, particularly when there is an insignificant amount of pericardial fluid. Drug treatment is inexpensive, and aspirin often suffices; ibuprofen is preferred because of a lower gastrointestinal side-effect profile and a larger dose range.

It is not necessary to do routine echocardiograms if the stage 1 electrocardiogram is absolutely typical. Repeated electrocardiograms are not necessary unless the initial tracings are atypical or there is a complication.

REFERENCES

Spodick DH. Acute pericardial disease: Pericarditis, effusion, and tamponade. JCE Cardiol 1979;14:9.

Spodick DH. The normal and diseased pericardium: Current concepts of pericardial physiology, diagnosis and treatment. J Am Coll Cardiol 1983;1:240.

Spodick DH. Cardiac tamponade: A physiologic approach to diagnosis and treatment. J Cardiovasc Med 1983;8:1085.

Spodick DH. Frequency of arrhythmias in acute pericarditis determined by Holter monitoring. Am J Cardiol 1984;53:842.

Spodick DH. Pericarditis in systemic disease. Cardiol Clin 1990;8:704.

CHAPTER 15–55

Constrictive Pericarditis

David H. Spodick, M.D., D.Sc.

DEFINITION

Constrictive pericarditis is defined as compression of the heart by a contracting pericardial scar.

ETIOLOGY

When pericardial scarring and fibrosis contract over the cardiac surfaces to significantly restrict filling, the heart is constricted. The fibrotic process follows pericarditis (often unrecognized) and may entrap varying amounts of pericardial fluid or blood. Traditionally a chronic process (arbitrarily from one to many years in progress), it is now more often subacute, tending to begin within months of acute pericarditis. Occasionally, acute constriction follows the attack of acute pericarditis almost without interruption. Constriction may appear in varying clinical settings, such as gradually developing systemic venous congestion of "idiopathic" origin following diagnosed pericarditis, or in the course of conditions known to produce constriction with or without recognized antecedent acute pericarditis such as tuberculosis, Coxsackie virus infection, mediastinal radiation, and trauma, even remote trauma (including previous cardiac surgery).

CRITERIA FOR DIAGNOSIS
Suggestive

Peripheral edema and distended neck veins, especially with ascites (which often occurs without peripheral edema) in a patient without heart disease who has clear lungs and no dyspnea at rest suggest the diagnosis of constriction, particularly if there is a history of pericarditis.

Definitive

Because of the physiologic similarity of restrictive cardiomyopathies, a definite diagnosis is made from pericardial thickening (biopsy, magnetic resonance imaging) and by relief of the physiologic abnormalities after pericardiectomy; however, venous hypertension with distinct systolic and diastolic venous pulse collapse, plus an early third heart sound (sometimes of a "knocking" quality), strongly indicates the need for cardiac catheterization to demonstrate an early halt in ventricular filling and characteristic pressure curve configurations. Myocardial biopsy may be necessary.

CLINICAL MANIFESTATIONS
Subjective

Areas of endemic tuberculosis carry a relatively high risk of constrictive pericarditis, as does a history of acute pericarditis of any etiology other than acute rheumatic fever.

Exertional dyspnea, fatigue, abdominal distention and discomfort, palpitations, and dizziness (postural or exertional) are the most common complaints. Occasionally, patients have nonanginal chest pain. Nocturnal dyspnea and orthopnea are rare and perhaps related to other disorders.

The family history and occupation are usually irrelevant.

Objective
Physical Examination

Physical findings include edema, hepatomegaly, jugular venous distention, a loud abnormal third heart sound occurring soon after the aortic component of the second heart sound, ascites, and, in perhaps half the patients, a quiet precordium. Occasionally, the apex impulse demonstrates systolic retraction. Pulsus paradoxus may be noted, but probably only in occasional patients with residual pericardial fluid; it is rarely more than 10 mm Hg and is not due to constriction per se. In chronic cases, pleural effusions may be identified; severely constricted patients

have peripheral cyanosis and cold extremities. Rarely, a pericardial rub (which may be chronic) is detectable. The degree to which these are found and their detection, as in the case of ascites, depend on the rate at which constriction develops; chronic cases have more findings. Thus, atrial fibrillation occurs in perhaps a fifth to a quarter of chronic cases, as do other atrial arrhythmias. Kussmaul's sign—apparent inspiratory jugular venous swelling—is difficult to elicit and probably represents exaggerated jugular venous wave size rather than a true increase in venous pressure; ascites exaggerates this.

Routine Laboratory Abnormalities

Chest x-ray films show a normal to enlarged cardiac silhouette without distinctive features; a small "heart shadow" is not seen. Up to half the patients have pericardial calcification. Computed tomography scans show thickened pericardium.

Electrocardiograms are nonspecific, usually showing low-voltage with low to inverted T waves in a general distribution; acute and subacute constrictions have normal QRS axes and sometimes a left P-wave axis (i.e., less than $+30°$, P waves inverted in lead III). More chronic cases tend to have a vertical QRS axis and may have P-wave enlargement simulating "P mitrale" with a normal ($+40°$ to $+60°$) or vertical P-wave axis.

Urinalysis is nonspecific but may show excessive protein.

With chronicity, there may be an anemia, but the hemogram, like the blood chemistry, is not helpful.

PLANS
Diagnostic
Differential Diagnosis

The condition must be separated from restrictive cardiomyopathy.

Diagnostic Options

In most patients the diagnosis can be strongly suspected on the basis of history, physical examination, and noninvasive tests, including echo–Doppler studies and computed tomography. Cardiac catheterization has a high predictive value, demonstrating definite x and especially y collapses from the high pressure level in venous and atrial curves and a "square root" sign in the ventricles formed by a pressure dip in the beginning of diastole with a rapid rise to a pressure plateau occupying three quarters to one half of diastole. This establishes "restrictive dynamics." Most patients have an elevation of diastolic pressure in both the left and right ventricles. Diastolic pressures are often nearly equal unless there is underlying left or right ventricular disease. In most patients, the clinical and hemodynamic findings permit an accurate diagnosis. In a few patients, however, it is necessary to use pericardial biopsy (with the option to continue into a pericardiectomy) to establish the diagnosis. Myocardial biopsy (which can be done during the catheterization) may disclose some types of restrictive cardiomyopathy masquerading as constriction. Systolic function is normal in patients with constrictive pericarditis unless there is underlying left ventricular disease, in contrast to cardiomyopathies. Only rarely would one wish to defer surgical treatment and follow the course of constriction with further testing.

Recommended Approach

The testing described above is the recommended approach, in most instances.

Therapeutic

The definitive treatment is removal of as much of the pericardium as possible. Otherwise, the patient's condition may be optimized preoperatively by the use of digitalis and diuretics. Yet, the disorder is a mechanical one; although digitalis can control the ventricular rate in atrial fibrillation, it cannot relieve a normally functioning myocardium. Diuretics may relieve some symptoms (as these depend on systemic congestion), but this is only a temporizing measure. Doses must be adjusted to the patient's requirements with due attention, respectively, to digitalis excess and potassium loss.

The pericardium should be removed as completely as possible. In more chronic cases, this may be quite difficult owing to fibrosis and calcification penetrating the myocardium. Rather tedious dissection is required, and such patients will need cardiopulmonary bypass. Coronary disease (detected at catheterization) should probably be corrected at pericardiectomy unless there is extensive entrapment of the coronary arteries by the fibrous tissue. Angioplasty remains an option when obstructive coronary disease is also present.

FOLLOW-UP

Postoperative follow-up should be at 1 week to 10 days and thereafter at 3 months and 1 year (more often if suspicious symptoms return). At these times, the patient should be asked about any chest or generalized symptoms, and cardiovascular examination should be done to determine possible return of an abnormal third heart sound, changes in electrocardiogram, venous distention, or edema.

If the patient complains of chest pain, palpitations, undue fatigue, abdominal distention, or edema, an unscheduled visit should be arranged.

DISCUSSION
Prevalence and Incidence

Constrictive pericarditis is capricious in its occurrence after acute pericarditis and in its occurrence in patients without a known preceding history.

Related Basic Science

Constriction, like cardiac tamponade, restricts cardiac filling. Unlike cardiac tamponade, it does so after an initial, brief rapid-filling period. Thus, with a normally functioning heart (which is the rule), ventricular diastolic pressure first falls to zero (probably an artifact of fluid-filled catheters) or a few millimeters of mercury and then rises rapidly to an abrupt halt in early diastole. Early compensation is by tachycardia, so that in the presence of a low stroke volume the minute output is maintained, but there is progressively earlier restriction to the point where the heart cannot fill enough to produce a cardiac output that would satisfy the requirements of all organ systems, particularly during exercise. Later, with definitely inadequate resting output, there is obvious systemic congestion.

Natural History and its Modification with Treatment

In advanced countries, constrictive pericarditis is usually diagnosed relatively early. Thus, the patient generally has nondescript symptoms,

such as fatigue and exertional dyspnea, that he or she may not notice over long periods until they become critical (particularly in younger patients). In chronic constriction, the most important complication is atrial fibrillation (occasionally other atrial arrhythmias); these are being seen with decreasing frequency.

Untreated, the constriction ultimately leads to cardiac death due to low-output state, myocardial atrophy and fibrosis, and arrhythmias. Morbidity and mortality may also occur from allied conditions, such as tuberculosis and mediastinal radiation for malignancy.

In effusive–constrictive pericarditis, when a significant amount of fluid and constriction coexist (including constriction of only the epicardial layer of the pericardium), clinical and hemodynamic pictures between cardiac tamponade and constriction occur. Thus, a patient may have drainage of tamponading fluid only to reveal an underlying constricting syndrome.

In elastic constriction, occasional patients with fibrous tissue or with a tumor encircling the heart may show an intermediate syndrome in which there is no third heart sound (despite the absence of pericardial fluid), owing to a less rapid halt to filling. Some of these patients have a fourth heart sound. The pressure curves are otherwise characteristic of diastolic restriction.

Prevention

There are no preventive measures except mediastinal shielding during radiation. It has been demonstrated that both corticosteroid and nonsteroidal antiinflammatory treatment of acute pericarditis usually does not prevent constriction.

Cost Containment

The most important step in cost containment is to make the diagnosis as quickly as possible and to move on to pericardiectomy promptly.

Unless one is totally uncertain and therefore does not wish to elect biopsy or even catheterization, computed tomography (which usually shows a thickened pericardium) is unnecessary. The echocardiogram may be suggestive, showing various signs, but these have not yet been adequately distinguished from restrictive cardiomyopathy, except (tentatively) during respiratory maneuvers.

REFERENCES

Alio-Bosch J, Candell-Riera J, Monge-Rangel L, Soler-Soler J. Intrapericardial echocardiographic images and cardiac constriction. Am Heart J 1991; 121:207.

Fowler NO. Constrictive pericarditis. In: Fowler NO, ed. The pericardium in health and disease. Mt. Kisco, NY: Futura, 1985:301.

Roberts WL, Spray TL. Pericardial heart disease: A study of its causes, consequences, morphologic features. In: Spodick DH, ed. Pericardial diseases. Philadelphia: Davis, 1976:11.

Shabetai R. Constrictive pericarditis. In: Shabetai R, ed. The pericardium. New York: Grune & Stratton, 1981:154.

Spodick DH. Chronic and constrictive pericarditis. New York: Grune & Stratton, 1964.

CHAPTER 15–56

Acute Cardiac Tamponade

David H. Spodick, M.D., D.Sc.

DEFINITION

Cardiac tamponade represents the decompensated stage of cardiac compression due to intrapericardial accumulation of liquid, gas, or both. It may also be defined as any such cardiac compression, that is, compensated (by cardiocirculatory responses) or decompensated.

ETIOLOGY

Cardiac tamponade occurs during inflammatory or irritative pericardial effusions, during intrapericardial bleeding, or, rarely, during fistulas from hollow organs resulting from inflammatory, traumatic, or neoplastic diseases.

CRITERIA FOR DIAGNOSIS
Suggestive

The diagnosis of tamponade is suggested when a patient with known pericarditis, malignancy, blunt or sharp chest trauma, or any other illness known to be a potential cause of tamponade develops symptoms of shock, systemic congestion (with clear lung fields), or both.

Definitive

Diagnosis is based on reduced blood pressure, usually with pulsus paradoxus, characteristic neck vein abnormalities, and, excepting some rapidly bleeding wounds, an enlarged cardiopericardial outline demonstrated by any roentgenographic or imaging technique. Electrocardiographic QRS alternation and "swinging heart" on echocardiography are quasidiagnostic; the rare simultaneous electric alternation of both atrial and ventricular (P–QRS–T) complexes is virtually pathognomonic.

CLINICAL MANIFESTATIONS
Subjective

The family history is noncontributory. The past history is irrelevant, except for known etiologic diseases or processes, such as recent pericarditis, chest wounds, recent cardiopericardial manipulation (surgery, catheterization, pacing), known malignancy (especially in the lung), collagen or immunopathic conditions, uremia, bacterial infections, and radiation treatment.

Symptoms are nonspecific, unless there is pain from coexisting pericardial irritation (see Chapter 54), weakness, dizziness, hypotension, effort dyspnea, and sometimes air hunger.

Objective
Physical Examination

The most common physical finding is a systolic blood pressure much lower than the patient's customary level, varying down to shock levels (well under 100 mm Hg), usually with pulsus paradoxus (arbitrarily, a 10 mm Hg or greater drop in systolic blood pressure during normal inspiration). Diastolic blood pressure is normal or slightly elevated. Most patients have tachypnea. In patients with inflammatory or malignant disease, a pericardial rub is often present. Only about 50% of patients have muffled heart sounds. The jugular venous pulse shows a single (x) collapse from a distended, high level.

Routine Laboratory Abnormalities

Except for patients with very rapid intrapericardial bleeding, the chest x-ray shows an enlarged cardiopericardial silhouette, varying in appearance from that of nonspecific cardiomegaly to that of a large sac set down on a surface with complete loss of the normal arcuate contours. The electrocardiogram may be normal, may show changes consistent with pericarditis, may have reduced voltage (except the P waves), and often shows electric alternation at critical heart rates.

There are no specific changes on urinalysis, hemogram, or blood chemistry, although these may reflect any underlying etiologic disorder.

PLANS
Diagnostic
Differential Diagnosis

Diagnosis is usually made by a combination of the physical findings, especially the combination of elevated venous pressure and pulsus paradoxus.

Diagnostic Options and Recommended Approach

The echocardiogram shows both anterior and posterior pericardial fluid with evidence of tamponade, including diastolic collapse of the right ventricle and right atrium (and, in a few patients, the left atrium). Inspiratory decrease in left ventricular dimension and increase in right ventricular diastolic dimension are usually present. At critical heart rates (usually between 90 and 110 beats/min), swinging of the heart is seen, with oscillations covering two beats (often accompanied by electrical alternans in the electrocardiogram). These echocardiographic findings of tamponade have virtually 100% positive predictive value in the presence of clinical findings. A negative result with technically good echocardiograms (i.e., absence of fluid) is also virtually 100% predictive. Echocardiograms may be used to follow noncompressing pericardial effusions to monitor for any increase or decrease of fluid and early signs of cardiac compression, as well as to monitor patients after surgical or needle drainage of an effusion.

The diagnosis of tamponade is established if the systemic venous pressure returns to normal and pulsus paradoxus disappears after the pericardial fluid is removed.

Therapeutic
Therapeutic Options

The definitive treatment of cardiac tamponade is drainage of fluid as completely and as soon as possible. This may be done by needle pericardiocentesis or surgically if necessary. The latter may require a full thoracotomy, but more often it can be done through a subxiphoid approach, which has certain advantages: it is extrapleural and extraperitoneal; it permits digital and visual (broncho- or other endoscopic) examination and biopsy of the pericardium; it can be done under local anesthesia; and it even permits resection of a pericardial "window." Modern thoracoscopes allow drainage and resection under visualization from any reasonable chest wall point. While waiting for drainage equipment, "medical" measures may be taken, but these only temporize and in some patients have very little effect. Thus, an intravenous infusion of saline or blood may help maintain cardiac filling. Pressor agents may be used to maintain the blood pressure (but they need not have a marked inotropic effect, as the myocardium is functioning quite well). Norepinephrine (Levophed) is given by intravenous drip, 4 mL (4 mg) in 1000 mL 5% glucose via a plastic intravenous catheter, adjusting the rate of infusion to maintain a blood pressure of at least 100 mm Hg. Side effects include extravasation into the subcutaneous tissue, reflex bradycardia, headache, and, uncommonly in tamponade, hypertension.

Alternately, oxymetazoline (Neo-Synephrine) may be given intravenously, 10 mg diluted to 500 mL with glucose solution, with a comparable side-effect profile. If inotropic stimulation is desired, dobutamine (Dobutrex) may improve the stroke volume; intravenous infusion of 2.5 to 10 µg/kg per minute may be tried. Side effects include increased tachycardia, ventricular ectopic beats, nausea, headache, and angina. Any anticoagulants must be withdrawn or neutralized.

Recommended Approach

Failure of drainage by needle pericardiocentesis calls for prompt surgical drainage. Moreover, endoscopy and the subxiphoid surgical route are almost uncomplicated and rapidly gaining favor over the blind tap (even when done with echocardiographic monitoring). In acute stab or bullet wounds it is probably better to go directly to thoracotomy with or without prior emergent paracentesis.

FOLLOW-UP

When the emergency is over, it is necessary to search for the cause of the pericardial fluid and tamponade and, when possible, treat the cause.

DISCUSSION
Prevalence and Incidence

The prevalence and incidence of cardiac tamponade depend on the same factors as its etiologic spectrum. Traumatic tamponade, for example, is frequent in environments where there is considerable chest trauma and heart surgery. Infectious disease varies with seasonal and population factors. Thus, there is more tuberculous pericarditis in Third World countries than in Western countries. Heavy smokers are likely to have more carcinoma of the lung, a common cause of malignant tamponade.

Related Basic Science

Tamponade produces progressive restriction of ventricular filling from the beginning of diastole (the contribution of atrial collapse is not quite certain). The cardiac chambers are under continuous pericardial pressure that equals and even may exceed ventricular diastolic pressure. Compensation depends on several mechanisms. A powerful sympathetic response supports cardiac contractility and blood pressure. Venous hypertension with expansion of blood volume maintains cardiac filling. This fluctuates with inspiration (as it does normally), so that the right side of the heart fills more with inspiration, but left-sided filling decreases, yielding pulsus paradoxus. (Although inspiratory right-sided heart filling is less than normal, it increases the pressure in the tight pericardial sac and also shifts the ventricular septum to the left. Both reduce left ventricular compliance and filling. This is reversed in expiration.) Without relief, tamponade decompensates and ultimately decreases cardiac output to below the level that can sustain life. This point is reached sooner either with more rapid pericardial effusion or bleeding (as in hemorrhage) or with a stiffer pericardium (as in malignant infiltrations or due to previous pericarditis with scarring), or with both.

Natural History and Its Modification with Treatment

Tamponade occurs almost capriciously, being unpredictable from the onset of pericarditis. Occasionally it is the first sign of metastatic malignancy or connective tissue disease. Some conditions such as tuberculous pericarditis and, of course, cardiac wounds often provoke tamponade. Even in critical tamponade, sinus rhythm is the rule; however, tamponade is the only circumstance in which acute pericardial disease can cause significant arrhythmias in the apparent absence of heart disease, because the heart is now "diseased" as it is not in uncomplicated nontamponading pericarditis.

Prevention

Prevention is not possible unless treatment of acute pericarditis suppresses pericardial fluid production. Patients with acute pericarditis or thoracic metastases should be monitored, especially if there is already noncompressing pericardial fluid.

Cost Containment

Acute cardiac tamponade is an emergency situation over a relatively short period, so cost containment cannot be planned.

REFERENCES

Fowler NO. Cardiac tamponade. In: Fowler NO, ed. The pericardium in health and disease. Mt. Kisco, NY: Futura, 1985:247.

Reddy PS. Hemodynamics of cardiac tamponade in man. In: Reddy PS, Leon DF, Shaver JA, eds. Pericardial disease. New York: Raven Press, 1982:161.

Reydel B, Spodick DH. Frequency and significance of chamber collapses during cardiac tamponade. Am Heart J 1990;119;1160.

Shabetai R. The pathophysiology of cardiac tamponade and constriction. In: Spodick DH, ed. Pericardial diseases. Philadelphia: Davis, 1976:67.

Spodick DH. The normal and diseased pericardium: Current concepts of pericardial physiology, diagnosis and treatment. J Am Coll Cardiol. 1983;1:240.

Vaitkus PT, Herrmann HC, LeWinter MM. Treatment of malignant pericardial effusion. JAMA 1994;272:59.

CHAPTER 15–57

Pulmonary Embolism • Acute Cor Pulmonale

Nanette K. Wenger, M.D.

DEFINITION

Acute embolic occlusion of the pulmonary arterial circulation that results in pulmonary and right ventricular hypertension is termed acute cor pulmonale. This usually connotes at least 50 to 60% obstruction of the pulmonary circulation.

ETIOLOGY

Pulmonary embolism is a complication of venous thrombosis; dislodged clot traverses the right side of the heart and obstructs the pulmonary arterial bed. The clinical setting may be postoperative, postpartum, in patients with heart failure, with venous stasis, or with deep vein thrombosis. Old age, neoplasm, and obesity are additional risk factors. Pulmonary embolism can also occur from amniotic fluid, fat, or air.

CRITERIA FOR DIAGNOSIS

Suggestive

The condition can be suspected when there is sudden onset of dyspnea, chest pain, syncope, tachycardia, tachypnea, cyanosis, development of a right ventricular heave, right atrial and right ventricular gallops, and electrocardiographic or chest x-ray abnormalities (see Clinical Manifestations, Objective).

The diagnosis is further supported by a decrease in arterial PO_2 and $PaCO_2$, an abnormal alveolar–arterial oxygen gradient, and an abnormal radioisotope ventilation–perfusion lung scan. The antecedent venous thrombosis is identified by positive impedance plethysmography, duplex ultrasonography, or contrast venography.

Definitive

The diagnosis can be definitively established with pulmonary angiography, but the procedure is rarely indicated in clinical practice. A normal ventilation–perfusion lung scan usually excludes the need for pulmonary angiography. An abnormal scan in the proper clinical setting and a normal chest x-ray film are usually adequate information to diagnose pulmonary embolism. There are exceptions to this rule (see Plans, Diagnostic).

CLINICAL MANIFESTATIONS

Subjective

Dyspnea is the most frequent presenting symptom; sudden unexplained dyspnea in a patient with predisposing factors should be considered as pulmonary embolism until proven otherwise. Chest pain, often mimicking that of myocardial infarction, may reflect right ventricular ischemia; pleuritic pain is also encountered. Dizziness or syncope suggests massive embolic obstruction. Apprehension, restlessness, and cough are common, with hemoptysis and sweating less frequently described.

A history of deep vein thrombosis, recent surgery or immobilization, coagulation abnormalities, or oral contraceptive use may be contributory.

Objective

Physical Examination

Tachypnea and hyperventilation, often with shallow respirations, are characteristic, as is tachycardia, often with a weak pulse. Blood pressure is decreased, and the patient is sweaty and clammy. Mild temperature elevation may be present. Cyanosis may be evident. The jugular

We thank Dr. Robert C. Schlant for his contribution to this chapter in the previous edition of this book.

venous pressure is raised with a prominent *a* (presystolic) wave and a systolic wave if tricuspid valve regurgitation occurs. Atrial fibrillation may appear. A right ventricular left parasternal heave is often visible and palpable, the pulmonic component of the second heart sound is accentuated and delayed, and right ventricular (S_3 and S_4) gallops may be heard. Rales are a common but nonspecific finding; pleural and pericardial rubs are less frequent. Hepatic enlargement may ensue. Left ventricular failure with pulmonary edema may supervene in patients with underlying left ventricular disease.

Evidence of deep vein thrombosis reinforces the diagnosis and may define the source of the emboli, but the sensitivity of clinical diagnosis of deep vein thrombosis is as low as 30%.

Physical findings are often nonspecific with small to moderate pulmonary embolic obstruction of mild to moderate severity.

Routine Laboratory Abnormalities

About 20% of patients with angiographically documented pulmonary embolism have a normal PAO_2–PaO_2 tension difference. The chest x-ray film may be entirely normal in one fourth to one third of patients. Decreased vascular markings may be apparent in involved lung segments. The hemidiaphragm may be elevated on the side of embolic obstruction, and dilation of the main pulmonary artery, right ventricle and atrium, and azygos vein may be present. Some patients may have atelectasis, parenchymal infiltrates, or pleural effusion. A concurrent chest x-ray is required for the appropriate interpretation of the ventilation and perfusion scans.

Sinus tachycardia and nonspecific ST–T changes are the most frequent electrocardiographic abnormalities, present in more than 40% of patients. Other findings such as a P pulmonale (prominent, tall P wave in lead II), the S_1–Q_3–T_3 pattern, right bundle-branch block, and right-axis deviation are encountered in fewer than one third of patients. Changes of concomitant inferior and anterior ischemia may mimic myocardial infarction.

Neither the white blood cell count, serum enzyme or bilirubin levels, nor laboratory thrombotic indicators offer aid in diagnosing or excluding pulmonary embolism, although low plasma D-dimer levels have a high negative predictive value for pulmonary embolism.

PLANS
Diagnostic
Differential Diagnosis

No sign, symptom, or routine laboratory finding is diagnostically specifc for pulmonary embolism. A high index of suspicion is warranted for patients characterized as being at increased risk. Differentiation is often needed from myocardial infarction, pneumonia, pleurisy, pericarditis, pulmonary atelectasis, pneumothorax, and so on. The diagnostic algorithm in Figure 15–57–1 defines one suggested role of special procedures.

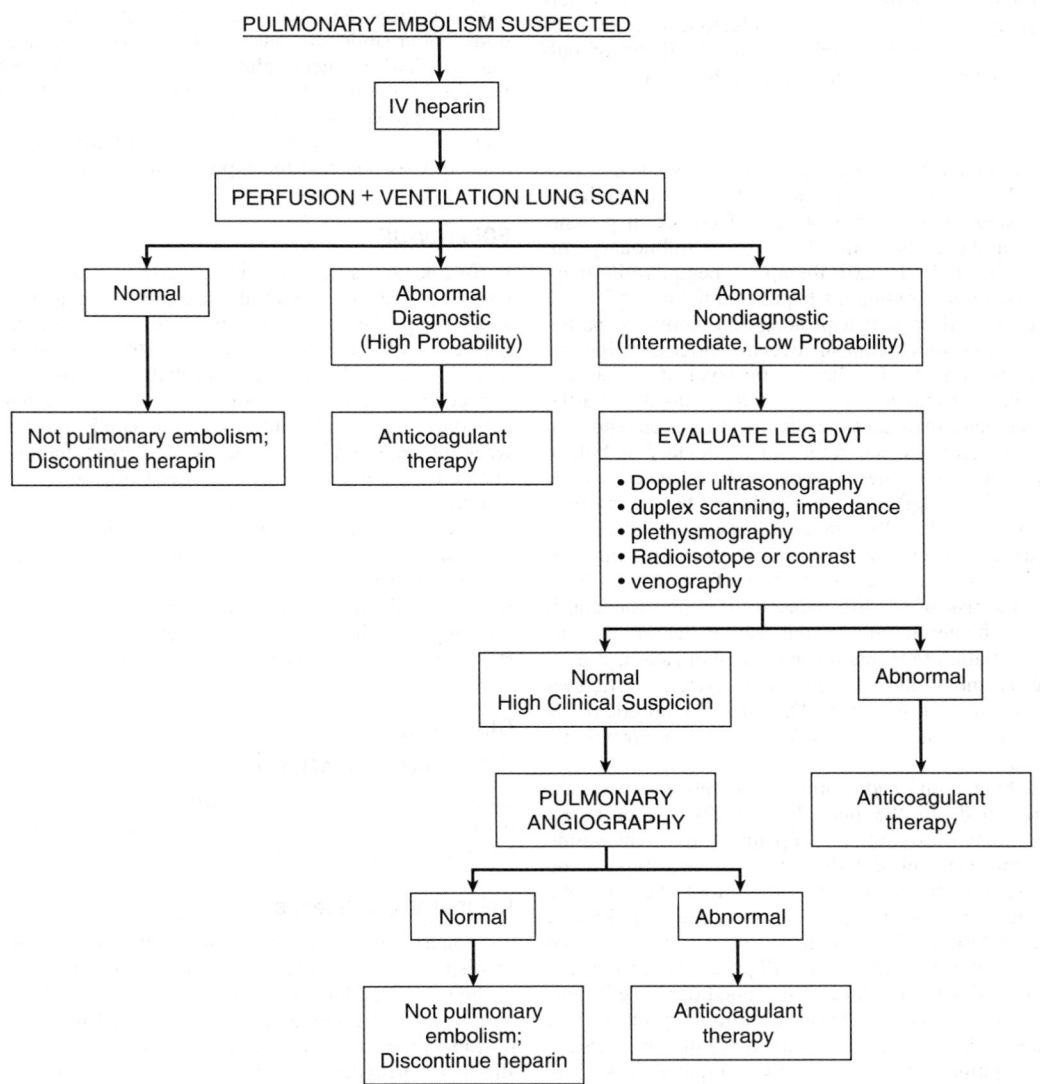

Figure 15–57–1. Diagnostic algorithm for pulmonary embolism.

Diagnostic Options

The arterial oxygen tension is usually but not always decreased below 90 mm Hg, with hyperventilation often concomitantly decreasing the $PaCO_2$. The alveolar–arterial oxygen gradient is generally abnormal, but a normal value does not exclude pulmonary embolism. Echocardiographic demonstration of right atrial, right ventricular, or proximal pulmonary arterial thrombi with signs of right ventricular overload permits initiation of therapy.

Radioisotopic ventilation–perfusion lung scanning is a sensitive screening procedure for embolic obstruction, with perfusion defects in the distribution of vascular segments having increased specificity when the chest roentgenogram is normal. A normal ventilation–perfusion lung scan virtually excludes significant pulmonary embolism, and subsequent pulmonary angiography is only rarely warranted (Stein et al., 1993). Test specificity is decreased in elderly patients who may have nonuniform perfusion in the absence of pulmonary embolization. Combined perfusion–ventilation scanning increases diagnostic specificity when normal ventilation is present in malperfused areas (PIOPED Investigators, 1990). Evidence of deep vein thrombosis in the legs by Doppler ultrasonography, duplex ultrasonography, impedance plethysmography, or radioisotope or contrast venography has a major impact on decision making in patients with suspected pulmonary embolism, may limit the need for pulmonary angiography, and determines the need for anticoagulation (Stein et al., 1993).

Pulmonary angiography is not needed for diagnosis in many cases, but it is warranted when the diagnosis remains equivocal in patients for whom anticoagulation may constitute a high risk or when surgical therapy (vena caval interruption or pulmonary embolectomy) seems indicated, as well as for patients with a high clinical likelihood of pulmonary embolism without noninvasive laboratory confirmation.

Therapeutic

Treatment is designed to manage the acute embolic episode and to prevent reembolization. Because of its rapid and predictable action, intravenous heparin anticoagulation is the treatment of choice in patients without specific contraindications. If the diagnosis of pulmonary embolism appears clinically likely, heparin therapy is begun while diagnostic studies are carried out. Continuous heparin infusion for 7 to 10 days is recommended in a dosage that prolongs the activated partial thromboplastin time to two times control levels; shorter-duration heparin therapy appears reasonable if a therapeutic level of warfarin is achieved (International Normalized Ratio [INR] 2.0–3.0). Partial thromboplastin levels greater than 2.5 times control values engender an excess of bleeding complications; recurrence of pulmonary embolism increases with values below 1.5 times control levels. In general, 10 U of heparin per pound (22 U/1 kg) of body weight per hour can effect this degree of anticoagulation, usually after an intranveous loading dose of 5000 IU. Others prefer starting with a fixed dose-sustaining infusion of 1200 to 1500 IU/h. Platelet counts should be performed at 3- to 4-day intervals to limit the risk of heparin-induced thrombocytopenia. It remains controversial whether low-molecular-weight heparin lessens bleeding risk. Anticoagulation prevents recurrent embolization; it does not dissolve existing thrombi, which depend on the systemic lytic system and on clot organization for resolution. Digitalis and diuretic drugs may be required to control right ventricular failure, and antiarrhythmic therapy may be needed.

Oxygen to combat hypoxemia and morphine for relief of pain and apprehension are indicated. In the hemodynamically compromised patient, hypotension may respond to dopamine or dobutamine (Dobutrex); isoproterenol (Isuprel) entails a risk of arrhythmia. If the patient is hypovolemic, volume expansion with colloid may improve cardiac output. Thrombolytic therapy with streptokinase (Kabikinase, Streptase), urokinase (Abbokinase), or recombinant tissue plasminogen activator (rt-PA) may be lifesaving in severely ill patients unresponsive to vasopressor therapy, inducing a rapid and sustained decrease in pulmonary hypertension in patients with massive pulmonary embolism; bleeding risk is greater with invasive than noninvasive diagnosis (Stein et al., 1994). Operative pulmonary embolectomy is an alternative therapy. Rarely, extraction of a large, centrally located embolus may be feasible by way of a transvenous embolectomy catheter. Thrombolytic

therapy with streptokinase, urokinase, or rt-PA offers advantage in patients with massive emboli, hemodynamic instability, and respiratory compromise by accelerating clot resolution and potentially lysing its source. Thrombolytic therapy should be administered by intravenous infusion; infusion in the pulmonary artery offers no advantage. Subsequent conventional anticoagulation is required, as thrombolytic therapy does not prevent future thrombus formation and it depletes the intrinsic fibrinolytic system.

Vena caval interruption by percutaneous insertion of a filter device in the infrarenal inferior vena cava is indicated to limit the likelihood of reembolization in patients with contraindications to anticoagulation or with failure of adequate anticoagulation to prevent recurrent embolization.

Long-term anticoagulation with warfarin (Coumadin) is designed to prevent recurrent embolization. Large loading doses of warfarin when therapy is initiated offer no benefit and increase the risk of bleeding. Heparin infusion should be continued until warfarin anticoagulation is adequate, prolonging the International Normalized Ratio (INR) to 2.0 to 3.0. Three to six months of therapy is usual, with indefinite anticoagulation recommended for patients with recurrent pulmonary embolism or persistent predisposing features.

Patients should be informed about alterable predisposing factors for pulmonary embolism, if any, and about the reasons for long-term anticoagulation. Patients receiving ambulatory warfarin must appreciate the need for periodic surveillance for adequacy of anticoagulation and for bleeding complications. They must be informed about both prescription and nonprescription drugs that may alter warfarin efficacy; common drugs enhancing anticoagulant effect include salicylates, indomethacin (Indocin), phenylbutazone (Butazolidin), clofibrate (Atromid-S), hydroxymethylglutaryl coenzyme A reductase inhibitors, bactrim, quinidine, chloral hydrate, and phenytoin (Dilantin); barbiturates, meprobamate, estrogens, oral contraceptive agents, thiazide diuretics, cholestyramine (Questran), rifampin (Rifadin), and most antacids may decrease the expected anticoagulant response to warfarin.

FOLLOW-UP

Perfusion lung scanning prior to hospital discharge establishes a new baseline, with an abnormal scan indicating that a subsequent study should be performed at 6 to 8 weeks to assess further resolution. Noninvasive tests for venous obstruction of the leg or isotope venography, if initially abnormal, should be repeated at discharge.

Frequency of prothrombin time testing varies with the precision of anticoagulant control, but is recommended at a minimum of 3- to 4-week intervals. Periodic urine and stool examination for clinically inapparent bleeding and hematocrit determinations should be performed routinely.

Assessment should be made at each visit for recurrent dyspnea, chest pain, palpitations, hemoptysis, syncope, or phlebitis. This information defines the need for repeating chest x-rays, perfusion lung scanning, and other diagnostic procedures. Patients must be questioned about bleeding complications; all medications should be reviewed and instructions about anticoagulant drugs repeated.

DISCUSSION
Prevalence and Incidence

Pulmonary embolism is estimated to affect more than half a million individuals annually, with mortality related to pulmonary embolism described to occur in 50,000 to 200,000 patients each year.

Related Basic Science

Pulmonary embolism is a complication of venous thrombosis. Features predisposing to thromboembolism include venous stasis, abnormalities of the venous endothelium, and a hypercoagulable state. It occurs commonly in the following settings: prolonged immobilization at bedrest; postoperative or postpartum; with thrombophlebitis, heart failure, stroke, or arrhythmias; extensive trauma, or orthopedic surgery especially to the lower extremities and pelvis; malignant neoplasms or debilitating diseases; major body burns; obesity; polycythemia and abnormalities of blood coagulation; and women taking oral contraceptive drugs. Most (>90%) thrombi resulting in pulmonary emboli originate in the deep veins of the calves of the legs and propagate proximally. Once venous thrombosis extends above the popliteal fossa, there is high risk of pulmonary embolism. Emboli are frequently fragmented within the right ventricle; obstruction of the pulmonary circulation reflects the preponderance of blood flow to the lower lobes. Mechanical arterial obstruction of more than 50% of the pulmonary circulation raises the proximal pulmonary arterial and right ventricular pressures; both the role and mechanism(s) of vasoconstriction remain controversial, although neurohumoral factors appear contributory. Because of dual circulation to the lung, extensive anastomotic connections between the pulmonary and bronchial circulations, and oxygen availability from the bronchi, pulmonary infarction is unusual; it is encountered when larger pulmonary arteries are obstructed or when systemic hypotension and/or pulmonary venous hypertension limit collateral flow.

Acute right ventricular hypertension results in ventricular dilation and often right ventricular failure with elevation of the right ventricular end-diastolic, right atrial, and systemic venous pressures. Bulging of the septum into the left ventricle may cause left ventricular underfilling and limit cardiac output. The decrease in cardiac output may be manifested clinically as syncope, hypotension, clinical shock, or sudden death. Coronary blood flow is initially increased but eventually may decrease if systemic blood pressure falls markedly. The severity of the hemodynamic consequences reflects both the severity of embolic occlusion and the cardiopulmonary status of the patient prior to embolization. Resolution of the pulmonary hypertension may relate to lessening of the pulmonary vasoconstriction, more distal movement of the obstructing emboli, partial revascularization distal to the embolus as the elevated pressure forces blood past the embolus, or opening up or dilation of vessels elsewhere in the lung; clot resolution by endogenous fibrinolysis occurs over days to weeks.

In one recent study, women under age 50 appeared to have a lower frequency of pulmonary embolism than comparably aged men; risk factors for pulmonary embolism were not different by sex, and, except for an increased risk of postoperative pulmonary embolism for women using oral contraceptives, estrogen use was not associated with an increased frequency of embolism (Quinn et al., 1992).

The current increased incidence of acute pulmonary embolism does not reflect solely improved diagnosis or increased use of estrogen-containing preparations. Older age, performance of more elaborate and extensive surgery (even in the elderly), and increased survival into old age of patients with significant cardiovascular disease and heart failure are contributory. Problems related to prosthetic heart valves and to hemoconcentration secondary to potent diuretic drugs may further increase incidence.

Natural History and Its Modification with Treatment

Two thirds of patients who die of an episode of pulmonary embolism do so within 1 hour of onset of symptoms, so application of thrombolytic therapy is unlikely to substantially limit acute mortality. The remainder continue to improve in the early days or weeks, with resolution of right ventricular hypertension and angiographic abnormalities common within 3 to 4 weeks. Lung scan abnormalities may persist in up to 40% of patients at 6 months, however. The more complete resolution of the obstructing embolus with thrombolytic therapy can preserve pulmonary vascular reserve capacity.

The natural history of undiagnosed (and therefore untreated) pulmonary embolism is one of recurrence in at least 40% of patients, with fatal massive emboli commonly preceded by a minor episode or episodes. Large, untreated pulmonary embolism may be fatal in 25 to 35% of patients. Nonfatal recurrent episodes commonly result in irreversible pulmonary hypertension and right ventricular failure (chronic cor pulmonale).

Adequate anticoagulation decreases the incidence of clinically detectable recurrent embolism and reduces death to less than 5%. Conventional anticoagulant therapy is associated with a favorable 1-year prognosis as well. Although long-term warfarin therapy entails a 2 to 6% annual risk of serious bleeding complications, occurrence of fatal bleeding is less than 1%.

Long-term prognosis varies considerably with the predisposing features and associated diseases. Prompt recognition of pulmonary embolism and meticulous acute and chronic management may favorably affect the outcome.

Prevention

Subcutaneous administration of low-dose heparin (5000 U every 8–12 hours) to patients at risk for thromboembolism undergoing elective major abdominal and thoracic surgery decreases venous thrombosis and pulmonary embolism. Usual contraindications to anticoagulation pertain. Surgical bleeding is not increased in patients with a normal baseline coagulation profile, adverse effects are minimal, and laboratory monitoring is not required as standard coagulation measurements remain normal. Therapy is begun preoperatively and continued until the patient is fully ambulatory (Prevention of venous thrombosis . . . , 1986). Comparable regimens are indicated for hospitalized patients with prolonged immobilization.

This therapy is not effective for hip surgery or abdominal prostatectomy; it has yet not been adequately evaluated for patients with myocardial infarction, heart failure, or other situations in which therapeutic anticoagulation is conventionally employed. The role of antiplatelet drugs remains controversial.

For patients at very high risk, for example, those requiring hip surgery, low-dose warfarin (INR 2.0–3.0 or prothrombin time 1.3–1.5 times control) and mechanical calf compression are recommended. Intermittent pneumatic leg compression is indicated for high-risk procedures where anticoagulation is contraindicated: neurosurgery, abdominal prostatectomy, major knee surgery (Prevention of venous thrombosis . . . , 1986).

The following ancillary measures designed to prevent or improve venous stasis are helpful: early ambulation, leg exercises, pneumatic leg compression, and elastic stockings.

Cost Containment

Radioisotopic ventilation–perfusion lung scanning and documentation of leg vein obstruction improve the accuracy of clinical diagnosis and avoid unnecessary anticoagulation. Ventilation scanning should be postponed until after the perfusion scan and should not be obtained if the perfusion scan is normal. A diagnostic strategy that includes clinical evaluation and both of these tests can decrease the percentage of patients who require pulmonary angiography. Prompt diagnosis permitting early institution of anticoagulation can decrease the morbidity of recurrent episodes and limit the morbidity of chronic cor pulmonale from thromboembolic pulmonary hypertension.

Preventive measures may avert pulmonary embolism.

REFERENCES

Carson JL, Kelley MA, Duff A, et al. The clinical course of pulmonary embolism. N Engl J Med 1992;326:1240.

Dudney TM, Elliott CG. Pulmonary embolism from amniotic fluid, fat, and air. Prog Cardiovasc Dis 1994;36:447.

Goldhaber SZ, Morpurgo M, for the WHO/ISFC Task Force on Pulmonary Embolism. Diagnosis, treatment, and prevention of pulmonary embolism: Report of the WHO/International Society and Federation of Cardiology Task Force. JAMA 1992;268:1727.

Hirsh J. Antithrombotic therapy in deep vein thrombosis and pulmonary embolism. Am Heart J 1992;123:1115.

Morpargo M, ed. Pulmonary embolism. New York: Marcel Dekker, 1994:1.

PIOPED Investigators. Value of the ventilation/perfusion scan in acute pulmonary embolism: Results of the Prospective Investigation of Pulmonary Embolism Diagnosis (PIOPED). JAMA 1990;263:2753.

Prevention of venous thrombosis and pulmonary embolism: NIH Consensus Development. JAMA 1986;256:744.

Quinn DA, Thompson BT, Terrin ML, et al. A prospective investigation of pulmonary embolism in women and men. JAMA 1992;268:1689.

Schwarz F, Stehr H, Zimmermann R, et al. Sustained improvement of pulmonary hemodynamics in patients at rest and during exercise after thrombolytic treatment of massive pulmonary embolism. Circulation 1985;71:117.

Stein PD, Hull RD, Raskob G. Risks for major bleeding from thrombolytic therapy in patients with acute pulmonary embolism: Consideration of noninvasive management. Ann Intern Med 1994;121:313.

Stein PD, Hull RD, Saltzman HA, Pineo G. Strategy for diagnosis of patients with suspected acute pulmonary embolism. Chest 1993;103:1553.

CHAPTER 15–58

Pulmonary Hypertension

Joseph S. Alpert, M.D.

DEFINITION

Pulmonary hypertension is defined as a mean pulmonary arterial blood pressure in excess of 20 mm Hg. Pulmonary systolic blood pressure in excess of 30 mm Hg also defines patients with pulmonary hypertension. There are three forms of pulmonary hypertension: (1) precapillary pulmonary hypertension is the result of increased pulmonary vascular resistance in the pulmonary arterioles and/or arteries; (2) passive pulmonary hypertension is caused by increased pulmonary venous pressure which is transmitted back to the arterial side of the pulmonary circulation; (3) reactive pulmonary hypertension is the result of increases in both pulmonary venous pressure and pulmonary arteriolar and/or arterial vascular resistance.

ETIOLOGY

Pulmonary hypertension is present when the mean pulmonary artery pressure exceeds 20 mm Hg.

Pulmonary hypertension is usually the result of cardiac or pulmonary disease, so-called secondary pulmonary hypertension. The only "pure" form of pulmonary hypertension is the uncommon disease, primary pulmonary hypertension, an idiopathic entity in which inexorable changes develop in the pulmonary vascular bed leading to progressively more severe pulmonary hypertension. In the majority of patients with pulmonary hypertension secondary to cardiac or pulmonary disease, the clinical manifestations of pulmonary hypertension are usually overshadowed by findings of the underlying cardiac or pulmonary disease. Moreover, the natural history, prognosis, and therapy of patients with secondary pulmonary hypertension depend on the underlying disease.

Most patients with primary pulmonary hypertension are discovered late in the course of the disease when symptoms of right ventricular function (fatigue, weakness, dyspnea, peripheral edema, increasing abdominal girth, and decreasing appetite) are noted. The earlier phase of this illness is almost invariably without symptoms. Occasionally, signs of right ventricular hypertrophy on the electrocardiogram suggest to the clinician that pulmonary hypertension might be present.

CRITERIA FOR DIAGNOSIS

Suggestive

The pulmonary component of the second heart sound, P_2, becomes louder than the aortic component, A_2. A parasternal right ventricular impulse or heave is present. Signs of right ventricular failure are noted: jaundice, jugular venous distention (large *a* or *v* wave present), a right ventricular S_3 and/or S_4 (louder on inspiration, softer on expiration), a murmur of tricuspid valve regurgitation, hepatomegaly, ascites, peripheral edema, and prominent superficial veins. Right ventricular hypertrophy on the electrocardiogram is observed. Enlarged pulmonary arteries and/or an enlarged right ventricle are seen on the chest x-ray film. Right ventricular dilation and/or hypertrophy are seen on an echocardiographic examination.

Objective

Estimated pulmonary arterial systolic pressure is in excess of 30 mm Hg by Doppler echocardiography. Directly measured pulmonary arterial mean pressure is in excess of 20 mm Hg. A definitive diagnosis of primary pulmonary hypertension is made *only* after all potential secondary causes of pulmonary hypertension have been excluded.

CLINICAL MANIFESTATIONS

Subjective

A variety of factors predisposing to various cardiac and pulmonary conditions are elicited in the history of patients with secondary pulmonary hypertension. For example, patients with congenital heart disease usually describe a murmur since childhood; patients with mitral stenosis often tell of earlier bouts of acute rheumatic fever; and patients with pulmonary disease may report on various industrial exposures or cigarette smoking.

Patients with primary pulmonary hypertension may rarely report a family predisposition to this entity. Ingestion of certain specific toxins (Jamaican bush tea, rapeseed oil, or the diet agent Aminorex) is rarely described.

Symptoms associated with secondary pulmonary hypertension are usually those of the underlying cardiac or pulmonary condition. For example, patients with mitral stenosis often describe dyspnea, hemoptysis, and rapid irregular heart beats. Patients with chronic obstructive pulmonary disease tell of dyspnea on exertion, cough, and sputum production. Late in the course of secondary pulmonary hypertension, right ventricular failure develops causing fatigue, weakness, peripheral edema, and increasing abdominal girth. As noted already, patients with primary pulmonary hypertension are usually asymptomatic until late in the course of the illness when long-standing, severe pulmonary hypertension results in right ventricular failure. At that time, patients may report exertional dyspnea, fatigue, weakness, effort syncope, palpitations, anorexia, and even anginal chest discomfort. Cough and/or hemoptysis are occasionally described.

Objective

Physical Examination

A variety of physical findings may be noted in patients with secondary pulmonary hypertension, depending on the underlying cardiac and pulmonary disease. Thus, the patient with congenital heart disease may manifest cyanosis and clubbing of nails; the patient with chronic left ventricular failure may have a loud third heart sound and pulmonary rales; and the patient with kyphoscoliotic pulmonary disease will demonstrate the characteristic skeletal abnormality of this condition.

Pulmonary hypertension itself leads to an increasingly loud pulmonary component of the second heart sound; signs of right ventricular dilation, hypertrophy, and failure; and eventually, the murmurs of tricuspid and pulmonic valve regurgitation (Table 15–58–1).

Routine Laboratory Abnormalities

The hematocrit may be increased when there is hypoxia due to a right-to-left intracardiac shunt or pulmonary disease.

The chest x-ray film may reveal pulmonary disease, a large main pulmonary artery, large pulmonary artery branches that taper abruptly, right ventricular hypertrophy, or deformity of the bony structures.

TABLE 15–58–1. PHYSICAL EXAMINATION FINDINGS RESULTING FROM SEVERE, CHRONIC PULMONARY HYPERTENSION

Increased loudness of pulmonic component (P_2) of S_2

Jugular venous distention with or without prominent *a* and/or *v* waves

Parasternal right ventricular impulse

Right ventricular S_3 and S_4 (louder on inspiration)

Pulmonic ejection click and systolic flow murmur

Murmurs of tricuspid and/or pulmonic valve regurgitation

Right ventricular decompensation
   Hepatomegaly
   Peripheral edema
   Ascites

Cyanosis (a late finding in very severe pulmonary hypertension)

The electrocardiogram may show a right atrial abnormality, right ventricular hypertrophy, and low voltage (in emphysematous patients).

PLANS
Diagnostic
Differential Diagnosis

The cause of the pulmonary arterial hypertension should be identified. It may be due to Eisenmenger's physiology, lung disease, left heart disease with heart failure, bony abnormality of the thorax, or primary pulmonary hypertension. The diagnostic procedures used to identify these diseases are listed in Table 15–58–2.

Diagnostic Options and Recommended Approach

Pulmonary hypertension is often suspected when the physical examination demonstrates a loud P_2, and right ventricular enlargement and/or pulmonary arterial enlargement are noted on the electrocardiogram or chest x-ray film. Confirmation of pulmonary hypertension and a quantitative estimate of its severity can be obtained from an echo–Doppler examination. If further confirmation and/or quantitation are felt to be necessary, pulmonary arterial pressure may be measured directly by cardiac catheterization. The simplest test, with excellent positive and negative predictive value, is the echo–Doppler study. This noninvasive test also enables the physician to follow the course of patients with chronic pulmonary hypertension. Serial studies demonstrate changes in pulmonary arterial pressure and the effect of such changes on right ventricular function.

Primary pulmonary hypertension is diagnosed only when all secondary causes of pulmonary hypertension (e.g., mitral stenosis, left ventricular failure, chronic obstructive pulmonary disease, pulmonary fibrosis, pulmonary embolism) have been excluded (Table 15–58–3).

Therapeutic

Secondary pulmonary hypertension resolves, at least in part, with successful management of the underlying cardiac or pulmonary condition. Thus, mitral valve replacement in a patient with mitral stenosis results in marked amelioration of pulmonary hypertension. Patients with acute or chronic pulmonary embolism may benefit from anticoagulant or thrombolytic therapy, embolectomy, or vena caval interruption (by ligation, plication, or insertion of an umbrella filter).

Unfortunately, the management of primary pulmonary hypertension is often unsatisfactory. Some patients respond to chronic anticoagulation with warfarin, while others respond to high-dose calcium channel blockade (nifedipine [Procardia] 20–40 mg four times daily, diltiazem [Cardizem] 120–240 mg three times daily). Systemic hypotension often limits the dose that can be employed. The vast majority of adult patients with this disorder are refractory to therapy. Right ventricular failure is managed with digoxin, diuretics, potassium replacement, and vasodilators (hydralazine, angiotensin-converting enzyme inhibitors, nitrates). Lung and heart–lung transplantation have been employed in highly selected patients with rather modest success. This latter form of therapy is still investigational.

FOLLOW-UP

Patients should be alert for signs or symptoms of heart failure, arrhythmia, or deep venous thrombosis, as these complications are potentially dangerous in both secondary and primary pulmonary hypertension. Moreover, effective medical and surgical therapy is often available for each of these complications depending on the etiology of the pulmonary hypertension.

Patients with mild secondary pulmonary hypertension whose underlying cardiac or pulmonary disease is not severe can be followed at 6- to 12-monthly intervals in the absence of changing symptoms. Such patients should be instructed to call their physician for an earlier appointment if symptoms of right ventricular failure, arrhythmia, or venous thromboembolism develop. In the absence of such symptoms, an electrocardiogram should be performed every 2 to 3 years. Some cardiologists obtain periodic echo–Doppler studies in these patients. More severe secondary pulmonary hypertension usually reflects a more advanced cardiac or pulmonary pathologic process. Such patients should be followed more closely (i.e., every 2–3 months or more frequently), depending on the severity of the illness. These individuals should be considered for appropriate medical and/or surgical therapy. Echocardiographic studies should be performed every 6 to 12 months.

Patients with primary pulmonary hypertension should be seen at least every 3 to 4 months (more often if pulmonary hypertension is severe). Patients awaiting heart–lung transplantation may need to be seen every 3 to 4 weeks.

DISCUSSION
Prevalence and Incidence

It is impossible to know exact demographic characteristics of pulmonary hypertension as no simple, portable, and inexpensive test (comparable to the systemic blood pressure cuff) exists for measuring pulmonary arterial pressure. Secondary pulmonary hypertension must be quite common, however, because it is found in some of the most com-

TABLE 15–58–3. SECONDARY CAUSES OF PULMONARY HYPERTENSION

Cardiac
    Mitral valve stenosis
    Mitral valve regurgitation
    Left ventricular failure from any etiology
    Congenital heart disease with Eisenmenger's reaction
    Cor triatriatum
Pulmonary
    Chronic obstructive pulmonary disease
    Central hypoventilation
    High-altitude hypoxemia
    Myasthenia gravis affecting respiratory muscles
    Cystic fibrosis
    Sarcoidosis
    Scleroderma
    Idiopathic interstitial fibrosis
    Extensive lung resection
    Extensive fibrothorax (trauma, tuberculosis)
    Kyphoscoliosis
    Pulmonary embolism
    Schistosomiasis
    Sickle cell disease
    Systemic lupus erythematosus and other
      collagen–vascular diseases
    Portal hypertension
    Bacterial sepsis

TABLE 15–58–2. LABORATORY FINDINGS RESULTING FROM SEVERE, CHRONIC PULMONARY HYPERTENSION

Electrocardiography	right ventricular hypertrophy and right atrial abnormality
Chest roentgenography	enlargement of the main pulmonary arteries, enlargement of the right ventricle and right atrium
Pulmonary function tests	abnormal diffusing capacity
Arterial blood gases	hypoxemia and hypocarbia (respiratory alkalosis, hyperventilation)
Echocardiography	right ventricular dilation and/or hypertrophy, right atrial enlargement, paradoxical interventricular septal motion, loss of *a* wave in the pulmonic-valve motion, enlargement of the pulmonary artery
Doppler echocardiography	tricuspid and pulmonic valvular regurgitation, elevated pulmonary arterial pressure (estimated)
Cardiac catheterization	elevated pulmonary arterial pressure and pulmonary vascular resistance, elevated right ventricular systolic and diastolic pressure, elevated right atrial pressure, dilated right ventricle and right atrium, tricuspid and pulmonic valve regurgitation, depressed cardiac output

mon cardiac and pulmonary diseases, for example, chronic obstructive pulmonary disease, pulmonary embolism, and left ventricular failure. As severe pulmonary hypertension (either primary or secondary) is associated with a poor prognosis, it is likely that most patients with these cardiac or pulmonary illnesses have more moderate degrees of pulmonary hypertension. Primary pulmonary hypertension is rather rare.

Related Basic Science

The resistance to blood flow across the *normal* pulmonary vascular bed is very low, one twelfth of the resistance across the systemic bed. Normal mean pulmonary arterial pressure is only 12 ± 2 mm Hg. As normal mean left atrial pressure is 6 ± 2 mm Hg, the pressure drop across the normal pulmonary circulation is only 6 mm Hg as opposed to a pressure drop of 80 to 100 mm Hg across the systemic circulation.

The low resistance of the pulmonary vascular bed is the result of the thin media of the precapillary pulmonary arterioles as compared with the more muscular media of the systemic arterioles. Consequently, the wall of the right ventricle is less than one half as thick as that of the left ventricle because of the low resistance and pressure of the pulmonary circulation.

Pulmonary hypertension develops if resistance to flow across the pulmonary bed increases. Such an increase occurs as a result of a variety of cardiac and pulmonary diseases that can affect the pulmonary circulation (see Table 15–58–3). Pulmonary hypertension is said to be present when mean pulmonary artery pressure exceeds 20 mm Hg.

Pulmonary hypertension can be divided into three classes based on the abnormal physiology (Table 15–58–4): precapillary, passive, and reactive.

In patients with precapillary pulmonary hypertension, the disease process involves the pulmonary circulation proximal to the pulmonary capillaries, that is, the pulmonary arteries or arterioles. Pulmonary arterial pressure is increased, but pulmonary capillary wedge and left atrial pressure remain normal. The result is a pressure drop from the pulmonary artery to the left atrium that exceeds 12 mm Hg.

Patients with precapillary pulmonary hypertension complain of dyspnea, but they do not experience orthopnea, paroxysmal nocturnal dyspnea, or pulmonary edema because their pulmonary venous pressure is normal. On physical examination such individuals often have an increased respiratory rate, but the lungs are usually clear. The chest x-ray film demonstrates right ventricular enlargement and prominent pulmonary arteries; the left ventricle is normal in size. Pulmonary venous redistribution and Kerley B lines are absent. The electrocardiogram usually demonstrates right ventricular hypertrophy and/or right-axis deviation.

Primary pulmonary hypertension is a form of precapillary pulmonary hypertension characterized by diffuse obliterative changes in the pulmonary arterioles. The etiology of the disease is unknown. Patients with primary pulmonary hypertension do not have intrinsic pulmonary or cardiac disease nor extrinsic causes of pulmonary vascular obstruction. Suggested etiologies include recurrent pulmonary vasoconstriction, pulmonary emboli, hypersensitivity, and various environmental stimuli.

TABLE 15–58–4. PATHOPHYSIOLOGIC CLASSIFICATION OF PULMONARY HYPERTENSION

	Precapillary	Passive	Reactive
Increased pulmonary arterial pressure	+ or ++	+	++
Left atrial pressure	normal	increased	increased
Pulmonary artery to left atrium pressure drop	>12 mm Hg	<12 mm Hg	>12 mm Hg
Examples	pulmonary embolism Chronic obstructive pulmonary disease	Left ventricular failure Mitral stenosis	Some patients with long-standing mitral valve disease

The diagnosis of primary pulmonary hypertension cannot be made without submitting the patient to an extensive evaluation including cardiac catheterization and pulmonary angiography to exclude all other cardiac or pulmonary causes of pulmonary hypertension. Some patients are too ill for one or both of these procedures, and in such individuals, the diagnosis remains tentative.

A variety of diseases result in elevation of pulmonary venous pressure. As pulmonary venous pressure increases, pulmonary arterial pressure must rise if forward pulmonary blood flow is to continue. This mandatory increase in pulmonary arterial pressure in response to increased pulmonary venous pressure is termed *passive pulmonary arterial hypertension*. The pressure drop across the pulmonary vascular bed remains normal, less than 12 mm Hg. Pulmonary venous pressure in these patients is usually 25 to 30 mm Hg at rest. Mean pulmonary arterial pressure at rest in these individuals with passive pulmonary venous hypertension is often 35 to 40 mm Hg. Increased pulmonary arterial pressure secondary to passive pulmonary venous hypertension increases the systolic workload of the right ventricle (increased afterload), eventually leading to right ventricular failure.

The primary clue to the diagnosis of passive pulmonary arterial hypertension is the presence of pulmonary venous hypertension, recognized by its symptoms of dyspnea, orthopnea, paroxysmal nocturnal dyspnea, and pulmonary edema. The chest x-ray film is also very helpful in recognizing pulmonary venous hypertension. Roentgenographic signs of pulmonary venous hypertension include prominence of upperlobe pulmonary veins, increased density of the central lung fields, and Kerley B lines. Common causes of passive pulmonary hypertension include left ventricular failure and mitral valve disease.

In certain patients with chronic pulmonary venous (passive) hypertension, pulmonary arterial pressure may rise out of proportion to the increased pulmonary venous pressure. The pressure drop from pulmonary artery to left atrium increases, and pulmonary arterial pressure may even reach systemic levels (so-called reactive pulmonary hypertension). This reaction to pulmonary venous hypertension is most likely to occur in patients with mitral valve disease, particularly mitral stenosis. It is probably the result of pulmonary arteriolar vasoconstriction added to passive, pulmonary venous hypertension.

Reactive pulmonary hypertension greatly increases the patient's disability. Right ventricular dilation and hypertrophy develop, and right ventricular failure often follows. Cardiac output decreases as does exercise tolerance. Most patients with reactive pulmonary hypertension are Class IV by the New York Heart Association criteria. The electrocardiogram demonstrates right ventricular hypertrophy, and the chest x-ray film reveals right ventricular enlargement and very prominent central pulmonary arteries. On physical examination, a parasternal (right ventricular) heave is present and the pulmonic component of S_2 is quite loud. Findings of right ventricular failure (distended neck veins, hepatomegaly, peripheral edema) are often present.

Natural History and Its Modification with Treatment

The natural history of secondary pulmonary hypertension is quite variable depending on the underlying etiology. Primary pulmonary hypertension has a poor prognosis as noted in Figure 15–58–1, taken from a long-term series of these patients (Fuster el al., 1984).

Prevention

No preventive measures are currently available for primary pulmonary hypertension. A variety of preventive measures exist for various forms of secondary pulmonary hypertension. For example, prophylactic, low-dose heparin therapy decreases the incidence of venous thromboembolism in patients at high risk. Smoking cessation programs may help decrease the incidence of chronic obstructive pulmonary disease. Many other preventive strategies exist for the various causes (Table 15–58–3) of secondary pulmonary hypertension.

Cost Containment

The evaluation of the patient with severe primary or secondary pulmonary hypertension is often expensive as many noninvasive and invasive tests may be employed, for example, cardiac echo–Doppler, pulmonary function testing, lung scanning, and cardiac catheterization. In

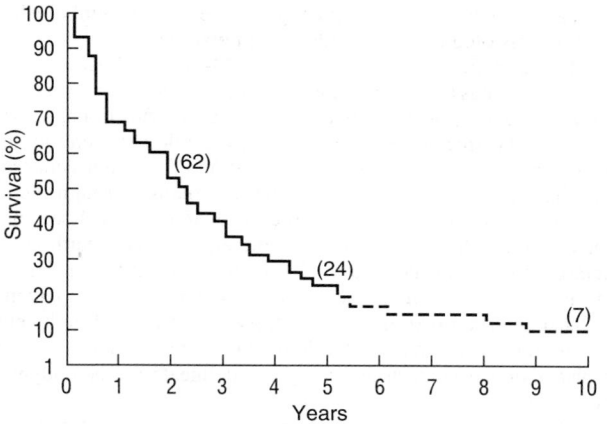

Figure 15–58–1. Ten-year survival curve for patients with primary pulmonary hypertension. The curve is derived from 115 patients who survived diagnostic cardiac catheterization at the Mayo Clinic. Parentheses enclose numbers of patients alive at 2, 5, and 10 years. *(Source: Fuster V, Steele PM, Edwards WD, et al. Primary pulmonary hypertension: Natural history and the importance of thrombosis. Circulation 1984; 70:580. Reproduced with permission from the author and the American Heart Association.*

phy scans and magnetic resonance imaging are rarely required. Cardiac catheterization is also expensive and should be reserved for patients with more severe pulmonary arterial hypertension in whom surgical intervention is being considered, for example, mitral valve replacement.

REFERENCES

Alpert JS, Irwin RS, Dalen JE. Pulmonary hypertension. Curr Probl Cardio vasc Dis 1981;5:1.

D'Alonzo GE, Barst RJ, Ayres SM, Bergofsky EH, et al. Survival in patients with primary pulmonary hypertension: Results from a National Prospective Registry. Ann Intern Med 1991;115:343.

Fuster V, Steele PM, Edwards WD, et al. Primary pulmonary hypertension: Natural history and the importance of thrombosis. Circulation 1984;70:580.

Rich S, Abenhaim L, eds. Primary pulmonary hypertension (Symposium). Chest 1994;105:1s.

Rich S, Brundage BH. High-dose calcium channel-blocking therapy for primary pulmonary hypertension: Evidence for long-term reduction in pulmonary arterial pressure and regression of right ventricular hypertrophy. Circulation 1987;76:135.

Round S, Hill NS. Pulmonary hypertensive diseases. Chest 1984;85:397.

Rubin LJ. Primary pulmonary hypertension. Chest 1993;104:236.

patients with milder degrees of pulmonary arterial hypertension, periodic electrocardiography and echo–Doppler studies may be the only tests required. Expensive noninvasive tests such as computed tomogra-

CHAPTER 15–59

Myxoma of the Heart

Nanette K. Wenger, M.D.

DEFINITION

A myxoma is a tumor of the heart. The overwhelming majority are benign, but a few present a wide spectrum of malignancy.

ETIOLOGY

Myxomas are true neoplasms, but uncertainty remains about their histogenesis. They likely originate from primitive multipotential mesenchymal cells.

CRITERIA FOR DIAGNOSIS

Suggestive

Atrial myxoma should be suspected with otherwise unexplained evidence of atrioventricular valve obstruction, pulmonary or peripheral emboli, and nonspecific constitutional symptoms (see below). Intermittent or postural-related symptoms or severe symptoms of recent onset should raise suspicion of a myxoma (Wenger, 1993).

Definitive

Diagnosis is made by echocardiographic demonstration of a mobile intracavitary atrial mass typically attached to the atrial septum and prolapsing through the atrioventricular valve. Histologic confirmation is obtained from the surgical specimen.

CLINICAL MANIFESTATIONS

Subjective

Atrial myxomas produce combinations of obstructive, embolic, and constitutional symptoms (St. John Sutton et al., 1980). Often the symptoms of atrioventricular valvular obstruction are of relatively recent onset. Left atrial myxomas initially cause acute paroxysmal dyspnea, often paradoxical, that is, exacerbated by sitting or standing and relieved by recumbency, and without relationship to physical effort; there may be postural hypotension. Progressive congestive cardiac failure is common and may progress to pulmonary edema. Occasional tumor entrapment in the mitral orifice may cause dizziness or syncope, at times with seizures, acute circulatory failure, or shock. Episodic bizarre behavior has been described. Right atrial myxomas produce progressive evidence of right-sided heart failure characterized by fatigue, dyspnea, and malaise, often with complaints of abdominal swelling and ankle edema; intermittent, posturally related exacerbations of episodic dyspnea and syncope also may occur; intermittent cyanosis may also be evident. Acute onset of tricuspid valve stenosis and/or rapid progression of right-sided heart failure, unresponsive to therapy, suggest right atrial tumor. Right and left atrial myxomas may cause pulmonary and arterial embolism, respectively; arterial embolism in a patient with sinus rhythm should raise suspicion of atrial myxoma. Cerebral embolism is a frequent presentation of left atrial myxoma (Knepper et al., 1988). Rarely, myxomatous embolism to a coronary artery may result in myocardial infarction. Constitutional symptoms are frequent and include fever, weight loss, fatigue, malaise, anorexia, sweating, and arthralgias. Raynaud's phenomenon and clubbing of the fingers are described.

Objective

Physical Examination

Physical findings vary with the location and mobility of the myxoma; heart rate, blood pressure, and auscultatory findings may vary with changes in position with mobile right- or left-sided myxomas.

Sinus rhythm with findings compatible with severe mitral valve stenosis should raise suspicion of left atrial myxoma. S_1 is delayed and accentuated, and is frequently widely split with the second component delayed. The delay in mitral valve closure corresponds to tumor expulsion from the ventricle through the mitral orifice to return to the left atrium. The pulmonic component of the second heart sound is delayed and increased as evidence of pulmonary hypertension. A "tumor plop," a prominent, low-pitched early diastolic sound, 0.05 to 0.12 second after S$_2$, may reflect the early diastolic entry of the tumor mass into the ventricle or the tensing of the tumor stalk at the end of its excursion into the ventricle. Alternatively, it may represent tumor impact on the ventricular wall (Keren et al., 1989). A diastolic murmur of mitral valvular obstruction is characteristic, and a systolic murmur of valvular regurgitation may be present if the tumor interferes with valve closure or if its "wrecking ball" action has damaged the valve. Endocardial sounds, reflecting tumor contact with atrial or ventricular endocardium, may mimic a friction rub. A notch felt on the upstroke of the cardiac apex impulse reflects ventricular decompression in early systole as the tumor returns to the atrium. The *a* wave in the jugular venous pulse becomes prominent when pulmonary hypertension is present.

With nonprolapsing left atrial myxomas, the apex impulse is normal, there is no "tumor plop," and systolic and diastolic murmurs are infrequent.

Mobile right atrial myxomas are characterized by elevation of the jugular venous pressure, often with a prominent *a* wave, and by prominent *c* and *v* waves in the jugular venous pulse due to sudden expulsion of the tumor from the ventricle in systole, with the rapid *y* descent reflecting atrial decompression in diastole. Systolic and diastolic murmurs are common and often have inspiratory accentuation. Some patients have a friction rub. With nonprolapsing right-sided myxomas, there may be evidence of systemic venous obstruction; the prominent *c* and *v* waves in the jugular venous pulse reflect the limitation of venous return, but the *y* descent is shallow because of diastolic obstruction to blood flow through the tricuspid valve. Pleural effusion, hepatomegaly, ascites, and peripheral edema occur.

An autosomal dominant heritable disorder consisting of cardiac and cutaneous myxomas, spotty pigmentation, and endocrine overactivity is also described (Carney and Toorkey, 1991).

Routine Laboratory Abnormalities

The routine laboratory examination of the blood and urine is usually normal. There may be slight hemolytic anemia and an elevated white blood count, and increased globulin level.

The electrocardiogram is typically normal because of the short time course of myxomatous valvular obstruction; occasionally, atrial (P-wave) abnormalities may be evident. Sinus rhythm is characteristic. The chest radiograph is often normal, and the heart is near normal in size unless protracted mitral valvular obstruction has caused pulmonary venous congestion or pulmonary hypertension; the atrium is not as enlarged as would be expected with severe atrioventricular valve stenosis. The lack of cardiac enlargement in a patient with significant heart failure should suggest atrial myxoma. Rarely, a right atrial myxoma is suspected by the calcification seen at fluoroscopy.

PLANS
Diagnostic
Differential Diagnosis

Characteristic positional variability of symptoms and physical findings suggests atrial myxoma, as does evidence of significant mitral or tricuspid valve stenosis in the presence of sinus rhythm and without cardiac enlargement. Absence of rheumatic fever further suggests the diagnosis, as does lack of correlation between severity of symptoms, physical findings, and roentgenologic examination. Intracardiac calcification, not in the area of the mitral valve but in an unusual location within the cardiac silhouette, suggests myxoma. Right atrial myxoma may mimic congenital heart disease, superior vena caval syndrome, or carcinoid tumor.

The protean manifestations of atrial myxomas may mimic a variety of other cardiovascular disorders. The constitutional manifestations, cardiac murmur, and emboli may suggest infective endocarditis, which must be excluded by blood cultures. The occurrence of emboli in the presence of sinus rhythm should suggest myxoma, particularly embolic

stroke in a young adult; large surgically removed arterial emboli should be examined histologically for evidence of myxoma.

The characteristics of atrial myxoma on M-mode echocardiography include a dense mass of tumor echoes behind the anterior mitral or tricuspid valve leaflet; a prolonged E-to-F slope of functional valvular stenosis; an echo-free space at the onset of diastole between the opening of the anterior mitral or tricuspid leaflet and the tumor echoes, reflecting the time needed for the myxoma to prolapse through the atrioventricular valve orifice; and the presence of tumor echoes in the respective atrium during systole. Two-dimensional echocardiography can demonstrate tumor movement, define the frequent tumor deformation as it prolapses through the atrioventricular valve, help identify nonprolapsing atrial myxomas, and identify the occasional multicentric tumor origin; the last can be better defined by transesophageal echocardiography. Doppler echocardiography can delineate the hemodynamic consequences.

Typically, atrial myxomas are large, mobile, intracavitary masses usually attached by a broad stalk to the interatrial septum near the fossa ovalis. Normal ventricular function and normal mitral or tricuspid valves essentially exclude the diagnosis of valvular vegetations or thrombi. Classic deformation of the tumor mass as it prolapses through the atrioventricular valve suggests that the mass is not firm, as is carcinoma; absence of other neoplasm is further suggested by lack of retrograde tumor extension into the pulmonary veins or tumor invasion of ventricular muscle or valvular tissue.

Diagnostic Options and Recommended Approach

Cardiac catheterization is done only if the echocardiogram is nondiagnostic, and coronary arteriography may be indicated to exclude concomitant coronary atherosclerosis. Because of the risk of dislodging an embolus from the friable tumor, contrast material should be injected into the chamber proximal to the suspected myxoma. Computed tomography and magnetic resonance imaging, as well as radionuclide-based scanning procedures, often enable fortuitous discovery of a myxoma.

Therapeutic

Prompt surgical excision is lifesaving and potentially curative and should be performed soon after diagnosis. Delay allows for tumor complications, most commonly embolic (St. John Sutton et al., 1980).

Cardiopulmonary bypass is required to allow tumor removal without embolization of the friable mass and to permit examination for multicentric origin. Intraoperative transesophageal echocardiography helps establish the site of tumor insertion. Wide resection of the tumor stalk is recommended to limit the risk of tumor recurrence. Rarely, valve replacement or annuloplasty may be necessary because of tumor damage to the atrioventricular valve.

The patient should be informed of the need for urgent surgery, as well as of the favorable prognosis. The need for postoperative surveillance should be defined (see below).

FOLLOW-UP

Despite the low incidence of these complications, follow-up examinations should search for intracardiac recurrence of the tumor or growth of a peripheral embolic fragment. Recurrence rates of 5 to 14% are reported and are more common with syndrome myxoma (McCarthy et al., 1986).

A postoperative two-dimensional echocardiogram should be obtained as a baseline study. Subsequent routine clinical examinations and annual or biennial echocardiographic examinations can detect growth of tumor, embolic fragments, or intracardiac tumor recurrences (Wenger, 1993).

DISCUSSION
Prevalence and Incidence

Myxomas are the most common cardiac tumors, accounting for 25% of all tumors and cysts of the heart and pericardium and for about half of all benign cardiac tumors.

Related Basic Science

The most widely accepted etiology of myxomas is that they arise from multipotential mesenchymal embryonic cell rests that have undergone neoplastic transformation (Lie, 1989). This benign sporadic neoplastic origin is more likely because myxomas differ significantly in location from thrombi (fossa ovalis versus atrial appendage) and have significantly different gross, ultrastructural, immunocytochemical, and tissue culture characteristics. DNA aneuploidy or elevated proliferative fraction seem associated with aggressive biologic behavior.

Antemortem diagnosis was infrequent prior to echocardiography. Left atrial myxomas are most common (75%), with most of the remainder located in the right atrium; biatrial tumors can occur. Ventricular myxomas are rare and are more common in younger patients. There may be simultaneous origin of myxomas in multiple cardiac chambers, and there is occasional familial occurrence; familial myxomas are more likely to be multiple and recurrent. Myxomas are rare in childhood and almost unknown in infancy.

Morphologically, myxomas are most commonly 6 or 8 cm in size, pedunculated, gelatinous, polypoid, friable, and attached to the atrial septum, usually near the fossa ovalis, by a broad base or stalk. Thrombi may be present on the tumor surface. Right atrial myxomas are generally larger and more solid than left atrial myxomas. Histologic examination shows myxomas, fibroblastic, and endothelial cells in an acid mucopolysaccharide matrix. Ninety percent of myxomas prolapse through the atrioventricular valve; the minority are sessile. Tumors may deform or damage the atrioventricular valve leaflet with resultant valvular regurgitation. Calcification is more common in right atrial myxomas.

Natural History and Its Modification with Treatment

The typical age of presentation is 30 to 60 years, with myxomas occurring slightly more commonly in women. Surgical removal has been undertaken in the ninth decade. Most patients are symptomatic, although occasionally myxomas may be a serendipitous finding at examination to evaluate a cardiac murmur. Tumor embolization is common, occurring in about half of patients. Occasionally tumors can rapidly increase in size, due to hemorrhage within the tumor. Sudden death is not uncommon and has been described in patients awaiting surgery (Wenger 1993).

Intracardiac recurrence has been reported after surgical removal, possibly representing incomplete primary tumor resection. Cerebral and systemic tumor emboli have been reported to penetrate arterial walls, resulting in aneurysmal dilation and rarely in late rupture. Postoperatively, there may be either local recurrence with subsequent embolization or peripheral growth of metastatic tumor fragments.

Prevention

At present, no preventive measures are available.

Cost Containment

Two-dimensional echocardiography is the most cost-effective procedure to confirm the diagnosis. Prompt surgery limits the morbidity associated with progressive obstructive symptoms and tumor embolization. Echocardiography also enables effective and inexpensive follow-up assessment, and should include family members when heritable myxoma is suspected.

REFERENCES

Carney JA, Toorkey BC. Myxoid fibroadenoma and allied conditions (myxomatosis) of the breast: A heritable disorder with special associations including cardiac and cutaneous myxomas. Am J Surg Pathol 1991;15:713.

Keren A, Chenzbruna A, Schuger L, et al. The etiology of tumor plop in a patient with huge right atrial myxoma. Chest 1989;95:1147.

Knepper LE, Biller J, Adams HP Jr, Bruno A. Neurologic manifestations of atrial myxoma: A 12-year experience and review. Stroke 1988;19:1435.

Lie JT. The identity and histogenesis of cardiac myxomas: A controversy put to rest. Arch Pathol Lab Med 1989;113:724.

McCarthy PM, Piehler JM, Schaff HV, et al. The significance of multiple, recurrent and "complex" cardiac myxomas. J Thorac Cardiovasc Surg 1986;91:389.

St. John Sutton MG, Mercier L-A, Guiliani ER, Lie JT. Atrial myxomas: A review of clinical experience of 40 patients. Mayo Clin Proc 1980;55:371.

Wenger NK. Tumors of the heart. In: Gravanis MB, ed. Cardiovascular disorders: Pathogenesis and pathophysiology. St. Louis, MO: Mosby-Year Book, 1993:270.

CHAPTER 15–60

Penetrating Injuries to the Heart

Panagiotis N. Symbas, M.D.

DEFINITION

Penetrating injuries to the heart are said to be present when there is evidence of heart disease that could logically be due to penetrating trauma.

ETIOLOGY

A penetrating wound of the heart may be due to a stab wound with a knife or ice pick or from a bullet or any other missile injury. The most frequently seen wounds are those from knife or bullet injury.

CRITERIA FOR DIAGNOSIS

The success of early diagnosis of penetrating wound of the heart is dependent on a high index of suspicion for the presence of such a wound. Penetrating injury to the heart should be suspected when a patient has sustained a stab or projectile wound of the neck, chest, upper abdomen, or, particularly, the precordium.

CLINICAL MANIFESTATIONS

Subjective

The clinical manifestations of wounds of the heart vary from no indication of the presence of such an injury to a moribund state. They depend on the site and the size of the cardiac wound and whether the pericardial wound remains open or becomes obliterated. When the cardiac wound seals shortly after the injury without significant bleeding into the pericardial or pleural space, the patient may have no manifestation from the cardiac injury. When the bleeding through the wound was significant before it sealed or when it is continuous and the pericardial wound remains open, allowing free drainage of intrapericardial blood into the pleural space, the clinical manifestations are those of hemorrhage and/or hemothorax. If, however, the pericardial wound becomes obliterated by blood clot, adjacent lung, or prepericardial fat, it can result in retention of the shed blood in the pericardial space. In such patients the cardiac wound usually is manifested by symptoms and signs of cardiac tamponade.

A large number of patients with penetrating cardiac trauma are in shock. The remaining patients may complain of weakness and/or shortness of breath. Some may be asymptomatic.

Objective

Physical Examination

The physical findings of a patient with penetrating cardiac injury depend on the pathophysiologic manifestation of the cardiac wound, bleeding in the pleural space, or cardiac tamponade. When blood shed through the cardiac wound drains into the pleural space, the patient may exhibit signs of blood loss, hypotension, tachycardia, feeble pulse or frank shock, and physical findings consistent with hemothorax, decreased breath sounds, and dullness to percussion. When the blood accumulates in the pericardial space and the patient develops cardiac tamponade, he or she may be in shock, with cold and moist skin and mild cyanosis of the lips and digits, and may be restless or even combative. The superficial neck veins may be distended with paradoxical filling during inspiration (Kussmaul's sign). The blood pressure may be unobtainable or below the normal level, there may be a paradox of 10 mm Hg or more during inspiration, and the pulse pressure is usually narrow. The pulse may be rapid and hypodynamic, the heart sounds may be distant and/or muffled, and the central venous pressure may be elevated. Occasionally, stigmata of neither cardiac tamponade nor bleeding are present, rather the patient has only a precordial penetrating wound.

Routine Laboratory Abnormalities

The electrocardiogram may show signs of fluid (blood) in the pericardium or cardiac damage.

PLANS

Diagnostic

The success of early diagnosis of penetrating wound of the heart is dependent on a high index of suspicion for the presence of such a wound. Penetrating injury to the heart should be suspected when a patient has sustained a stab or projectile wound of the neck, chest, upper abdomen, or, particularly, the precordium. The definitive diagnosis of penetrating cardiac injury is established by surgical exploration.

A central venous pressure line should be established as soon as possible, and a pressure above 12 cm of saline in a patient who is hypotensive or in shock strongly suggests the presence of cardiac tamponade. If time and the patient's condition permit, an electrocardiogram may be obtained and a chest x-ray film may be taken.

In stable patients with a precordial wound but no stigmata of cardiac tamponade or bleeding, echocardiography may be obtained to assess the presence or absence of cardiac injury.

Therapeutic

As soon as the diagnosis of penetrating wound of the heart is suspected or diagnosed, plans for immediate surgical repair of the wound should be made while vigorous measures are taken for the patient's hemodynamic improvement. Hemothorax found on chest x-ray film or on physical examination should be treated with tube thoracostomy. Blood evacuated from the pleural space may be autotransfused, and additional expansion of the circulating blood volume with crystalloids should be done if needed.

Patients presenting with signs and symptoms of cardiac tamponade should have the circulating blood volume expanded immediately, and drainage of the pericardial space attempted with pericardiocentesis or a pericardial window through a subxiphoid incision while appropriate arrangements for immediate thoracotomy are made. When immediate thoracotomy cannot be done, pericardiocentesis is performed with the patient in a semierect position and the needle inserted at the left substernal paraxiphoid area pointing toward the left shoulder.

Surgery is the only definitive treatment for penetrating cardiac injuries, and it should be done as soon as possible. Blood volume expanders, autotransfusion, pericardiocentesis, and, in general, all supportive measures are employed only to sustain the patient until surgical repair of the cardiac wound can be performed. The cardiac injury is exposed through an anterolateral submammary incision that can be extended if needed into the opposite side of the chest or to the neck or through a median sternotomy. After the chest is opened and the pericardium has been decompressed, the bleeding through the cardiac wound is digitally controlled and the wound is then repaired with pledgetted mattresses sutures. On extremely rare occasions, the magnitude of the injury is such that the wound edges cannot be approximated. In this circumstance the wound is best repaired after cardiopulmonary bypass is instituted, with or without a prosthesis. When injury to a small distal coronary artery is also found, it is best managed by ligation of the vessel near the area of injury. Injury of a larger, graftable coronary artery should be bypassed with saphenous vein or internal mammary artery graft after institution of cardiopulmonary bypass.

FOLLOW-UP

Once the cardiac wound is successfully treated, many patients are still not restored to their preinjury cardiac status. Rather, they may have a variety of residual or delayed posttraumatic lesions, for example, valvular lesions, shunts, ventricular aneurysm, retained missiles in the heart, a variety of electrocardiographic abnormalities, pericarditis, and infection. As a result, patients with cardiac injury should be followed closely for the development of any clinical manifestations from these residual cardiac lesions. If such manifestations do develop, the patients should undergo the appropriate diagnostic tests (echocardiography or cardiac catheterization). If indicated, the residual lesions should be repaired.

DISCUSSION
Prevalence and Incidence

The prevalence and incidence are not known but, in the light of reported violence, the condition must be common.

Related Basic Science

Penetrating wounds of the heart may be inflicted by knives, bullets, ice picks, or other projectiles, or, less frequently, from the inward displacement of rib or sternal fragments. The magnitude of the injury to the heart depends on the extent of the wound, the site, the direction in which the projectile entered the heart, and in the case of bullet wounds, the velocity and caliber of the missile. The state of the pericardial wound, as described earlier, also influences the clinical manifestation of this injury.

Natural History and Its Modification with Treatment

Very few patients with penetrating cardiac injury can be treated nonoperatively. In general, only those in whom the wounds seal quickly and who have no measurable bleeding into the pericardial or pleural spaces can be treated without surgery. Because the detection of who these patients are cannot be made accurately, and because many patients who seemingly appear to be doing well can rapidly deteriorate with disastrous results, all patients with penetrating cardiac wounds should be operated on as soon as possible.

The prognosis for patients with a penetrating wound is dependent on the preinjury cardiac status and the magnitude and site of the injury. As a general rule, because the vast majority of these patients have a normal heart prior to their injury, they subsequently have very few, if any, sequelae from the cardiac injury once their traumatic lesion is successfully repaired.

Prevention

The controversy of prevention of general trauma from bullet wounds applies also to bullet wounds of the heart, that is, restriction on the availability of guns. It appears, however, that correction of all the common denominators that may play a role in the precipitation of penetrating trauma, by education, by correction of socioeconomic factors, and, finally, by better control of guns, may lead to a reduction in the incidence of penetrating cardiac trauma.

Cost Containment

The use of autotransfusion and the judicious use of all the other diagnostic and therapeutic tests will lead to reasonable cost containment for the management of these victims.

REFERENCES

Symbas PN. Cardiothoracic trauma. Philadelphia: Saunders, 1989.
Symbas PN. Cardiothoracic trauma: Current problems in surgery. St. Louis, MO: Mosby-Year Book, 1991:28, 743.

CHAPTER 15–61

Blunt Injury to the Heart

Panagiotis N. Symbas, M.D.

DEFINITION

Blunt injury is defined as injury to the heart caused by trauma that does not penetrate the chest wall or heart.

ETIOLOGY

Blunt cardiac trauma may be caused by any form of such trauma to the thorax including that from contact sports, from falling of heavy objects, from compression between two moving objects, and most commonly from steering wheel injury.

CRITERIA FOR DIAGNOSIS

Injury to the heart should be suspected in all patients who have sustained significant blunt trauma, particularly to the thorax. Although vehicular accidents account for the vast majority of these lesions, significant force also can be generated during contact sports or altercations to result in such injuries.

CLINICAL MANIFESTATIONS
Subjective

The clinical manifestations of cardiac contusion vary according to the extent of injury and the interposing symptoms from other existing injuries. Many of the patients with cardiac contusion have no cardiac symptoms. The most common symptom in the symptomatic patient is chest pain, which is identical to the pain of myocardial infarction or ischemia but is not relieved by coronary vasodilating drugs. This pain may start immediately following or within a few hours of the injury. The patient also may complain of shortness of breath.

Patients who have sustained rupture of the heart may present in shock or may have varying complaints depending on whether the rupture involved the valvular structures, the interventricular septum, or the free wall of the heart. Patients with rupture of the free wall have symptoms and signs of cardiac tamponade, whereas those with rupture of the aortic, mitral, or tricuspid valves or ventricular septum may have symptoms of congestive heart failure, (i.e., dyspnea, orthopnea, fatigue, or palpitation), or they may be asymptomatic.

Objective
Physical Examination

Patients who sustained cardiac contusion may have no physical findings or may have findings consistent with myocardial ischemia or acute myocardial infarction (i.e., arrhythmias, diaphoresis, dyspnea, or hypotension). Myocardial contusion also may be accompanied by hemopericardium, which may manifest with signs of cardiac tamponade (i.e., distended superficial neck veins, peripheral cyanosis, increased central venous pressure, or hypotension), whereas patients with rupture of a cardiac valve or of the ventricular septum may present with a new and usually systolic cardiac murmur, dyspnea, orthopnea, palpitation, or shock.

Routine Laboratory Abnormalities

These patients should have an electrocardiogram on admission to the hospital. Occasionally, the electrocardiographic evidence of cardiac injury may not be apparent for 24 hours after the injury, or even more important, the electrocardiographic abnormality found may be due to other causes, for example, hypoxia, hypovolemia, hypokalemia, or head trauma. Therefore, another electrocardiogram should be obtained in the next 24 and 48 hours on all patients with suspected cardiac contusion. The electrocardiographic manifestations of cardiac contusion range from transient to long-range rhythm disturbances to changes similar to those of myocardial infarction. Also, blood should be drawn on admission and every 8 hours during the first 24 hours, for MB creatine kinase (MB-CK) determination.

PLANS
Diagnostic

Echocardiography can be used in establishing the diagnosis of cardiac contusion or rupture of the valves, septum, or free cardiac wall. When surgical repair of an intracardiac traumatic lesion is contemplated, echocardiography and cardiac catheterization should be performed to define the site of the injury and its hemodynamic significance.

Therapeutic

The treatment of patients with myocardial contusion is similar to the treatment of patients with myocardial infarction. Bed rest and antiarrhythmic drugs are used as necessary. Digitalis should be administered cautiously and only when atrial fibrillation or cardiac failure is present. Anticoagulants in the immediate postinjury period should be avoided, as they may precipitate intrapericardial or myocardial bleeding; coronary vasodilator drugs should not be used because they have little or no effect on the chest pain. In patients with global cardiac contusion and uncontrollable congestive heart failure, assisted circulation with intraaortic balloon counterpulsation or other assist devices may be used.

Patients with suspected rupture of the free cardiac wall should be operated on as soon as possible. Patients with rupture of the ventricular septum or cardiac valves are treated first with digitalis and diuretics as needed. Surgical repair of their lesions in the early postinjury period should be done only when their congestive heart failure cannot be controlled with medical therapy. Otherwise, the patients are appropriately assessed after they recover from the injury and the hemodynamically significant lesions are repaired electively.

FOLLOW-UP

The patient with blunt cardiac trauma should be followed carefully. In all patients with valvular injury, the hemodynamic status should be periodically assessed, and repair of the lesion should be undertaken when it becomes hemodynamically significant. Similarly, all patients with myocardial contusion should be followed closely for possible late rupture of the free wall or development of ventricular aneurysm.

DISCUSSION
Prevalence and Incidence

Before high-speed vehicular travel became available, blunt trauma to the heart was rare. The reported incidence of cardiac injury in vehicular accident victims ranges from 15 to 75%.

Related Basic Science

Circulatory derangements such as cardiac tamponade, blood loss, heart failure, and, particularly, arrhythmias are the most immediate threat to life shortly after blunt cardiac injury.

The extent of myocardial contusion can vary from small, discrete areas of damage to a global contusion, and it can be limited to small subepicardial hemorrhages or can extend to full-thickness myocardial damage or rupture.

Rupture of the ventricular septum or cardiac valves occurs as a result of compression of the heart between the sternum and spine, particularly during late diastole or early systole. The most common site of septal rupture is in the muscular septum near the apex, whereas the valvular injury may be limited to tear of the papillary muscle, chordae tendineae, or a valve leaflet or aortic cusps.

Natural History and Its Modification with Treatment

In the vast majority of patients with cardiac contusion who survive the initial insult from the blunt trauma, this form of injury leaves no measurable cardiac impairment. In patients with full-thickness myocardial contusion, however, rupture of the heart may occur immediately or within the first 2 postinjury weeks. In the remaining patients with such an extensive injury, healing of this area occurs with replacement of the destroyed myocardial fibers with scar tissue. After this process takes place, the injured area either remains relatively stable or, on rare occasions, may become aneurysmal.

A ruptured cardiac valve that is initially hemodynamically insignificant may remain unchanged or, in the follow-up period, may progressively impose greater load on the heart and require surgical correction.

Prevention

As many of the victims with blunt injury to the heart are thrust against the steering wheel or other parts of the vehicle, the use of seat belts and air bags and/or the development of other more protective devices will result in the reduction of such injuries.

Cost Containment

Judicious use of the various diagnostic tests such as electrocardiography, cardiac isoenzyme determinations, and echocardiography and careful assessment of the patient's clinical course will help in determining the appropriate length of monitoring and treatment of these patients. Cardiac catheterization should be used when indicated to define the site and hemodynamic significance of the injury prior to surgical repair.

REFERENCES

Symbas PN. Cardiothoracic trauma. Philadelphia: Saunders, 1989:I.
Symbas PN. Traumatic heart disease: Current problems in cardiology. Mosby-Year Book, 1991:XVI, 557.

CHAPTER 15–62

Cardiac Transplantation • Complications

Mark G. Perlroth, M.D., and John S. Schroeder, M.D.

COMPLICATIONS OF HEART TRANSPLANTATION

Adverse consequences of heart transplantation fall into two groups: those that affect primarily the engrafted heart and those that are the extracardiac consequences of the immunosuppressive drug regimen.

REJECTION

Definition

Rejection is defined by a biopsy showing perivascular lymphocytic infiltration, which may be focal or diffuse. With progressive increase in severity one sees interstitial hemorrhage, myocyte necrosis, and granulocytic infiltration.

Etiology

Rejection is caused primarily by cell-mediated immunity (although humoral factors may play a dominant role in some cases) of the host. HLA matching is not normally used for heart transplantation, as it is for kidney, pancreas, and bone marrow allografts.

Criteria for Diagnosis

See Definition.

Clinical Manifestations

Subjective. Patients with mild or moderate rejection are usually asymptomatic. Active cytomegalovirus infection, common among immunosuppressed patients, appears to predispose to rejection. A history of poor patient compliance should also raise the possibility of rejection and should be considered among adolescents, depressed individuals, or those who live alone. With more extensive moderate or severe rejection, patients may complain of fatigue and dyspnea.

Objective. Objective findings are few. The development of atrial or ventricular arrhythmias, particularly atrial flutter, is indicative of possible rejection. Arrhythmias may be difficult to control or to reverse successfully until the rejection has been eradicated. Unexplained tachycardia and the development of a new S_3 gallop have a similar import (although an S_4 sound is extremely common among otherwise normal heart transplant recipients). Pericarditis and pericardial effusions, sometimes accompanied by tamponade, have also been associated with rejection. Fever is rarely observed.

Plans

Diagnostic. The use of Doppler echocardiography has demonstrated that rejection is often heralded by changes in diastolic function that are more sensitive than the later decline in systolic function. The initial infiltrate and edema lead to a restrictive physiologic pattern with a reduced isovolumic relaxation time (IVRT) and shortened pressure half-time (PHT) for the left ventricle. The test is particularly useful if the patient serves as his or her own control and past measurements are available for comparison.

Diagnosis rests on confirmation by endomyocardial biopsy, which is performed weekly for the first month after transplantation, then biweekly for the next month, and then monthly for an additional 4 months. They are then scheduled at 3- to 4-month intervals and also constitute part of an annual catheterization.

Serologic studies and cardiac imaging by computed tomography and magnetic resonance imaging have not yet been shown to be accurate in the diagnosis of rejection.

Therapeutic. When suspicion of rejection is great and hemodynamic conditions are unstable, treatment is warranted even before final histologic results. For the first posttransplant rejection or for severe rejections at later times, treatment consists of 1.0 g of methylprednisolone (Solumedrol) intravenously for 3 consecutive days, with rebiopsy at 1 to 2 weeks.

For a subsequent episode of mild or moderate rejection, treatment can be carried out as an outpatient by raising prednisone dosage to 100 mg orally daily (in two divided doses of 50 mg) for 3 days and then tapering the dose by 10 mg every 2 days until the daily dose is 10 mg higher than at the time of rejection, after which it is tapered more slowly (e.g., 1–2 mg per week).

For rejection that is more severe, or recurrent and unresponsive to gram doses of corticosteroids, a course of OKT3 or other antilymphocyte globulin may be elected. Because these are foreign proteins, allergic reactions occur in up to one third of patients, and use of these agents is best guided by those with prior experience. It is given as 5 mg in 50 to 100 mL of diluent over 20 minutes. It is not effective if patients have high antibody titres (≥1:1000) in response to previous exposure (i.e., at the time of transplantation and/or prior therapy for rejection).

Preparation of the patient requires a central (e.g., jugular or subclavian) catheter and pretreatment with 0.5 g methylprednisolone, (Solu-Medrol), 50 mg diphenhydramine (Benadryl), and 100 mg ranitidine (Zantac) intravenously as well as acetaminophen (Tylenol), 300 mg by mouth, before each dose of OKT3. The methylprednisolone supplement can be discontinued after 3 days. In the event of hemodynamic collapse during OKT3 treatment, fluids, inotropes, and additional supportive therapy should be used in a critical care setting. OKT3 is usually given as a 10- to 14-day course after which biopsy is repeated.

Follow-up

If treatment is successful as shown by rebiopsy, the patient may return to his or her regular schedule of medications and surveillance. Failure to control rejection with a full course of OKT3 requires therapeutic tools available only to subspecialists (e.g., radiotherapy, plasmapheresis, other antilymphocyte globulins, or retransplantation).

Discussion

Prevalence and Incidence. During the first year after transplantation, 85 to 90% of patients suffer one or more bouts of rejection. The frequency of rejection diminishes considerably after that time.

Related Basic Science. See Etiology.

Natural History and Its Modification with Treatment. If untreated, acute rejection leads to death from acute heart failure or arrhythmia. Recurrent or refractory rejection leads to gradual myocardial dysfunction. Treatment is usually successful with resolution of histologic and clinical findings.

Prevention. Careful attention to patient compliance and to maintenance of therapeutic drug (cyclosporine) levels as well as routine surveillance biopsies constitute the major avenues of prophylaxis.

Cost Containment. Opportunities for cost containment are limited. Attention to prevention measures with avoidance of OKT3 rescue and hospitalization offers the major opportunity for limiting expenditures.

ACCELERATED GRAFT CORONARY ATHEROSCLEROSIS

Definition

A diffuse lesion involving intimal proliferation of graft vasculature is common. It affects primarily the coronary arterial tree, but has been identified to a lesser extent in coronary veins. Additionally there may be high-grade stenosis of proximal epicardial arteries.

Etiology

The etiology is unknown but is thought to be related to an ongoing subclinical rejection process causing chronic injury to the coronary endothelium, the interface between host and graft. There is no predilection for individuals whose initial cardiac failure was due to coronary disease rather than other cardiomyopathies, nor do lipid profiles reliably distinguish affected from unaffected individuals. Prior cytomegalovirus infection appears to heighten the risk of this complication and the mortality associated with it.

Criteria for Diagnosis

Suggestive. Routine electrocardiograms may demonstrate a myocardial infarction.

Definitive. Intravascular ultrasound will show lesions with great sensitivity. Coronary angiography is the usual standard to detect obstructive coronary disease.

Clinical Manifestations

Subjective. Because the donor heart is anatomically denervated, ischemic pain is very unusual. Patients suffer weakness or may develop congestive heart failure or sudden death from silent myocardial infarction. Nevertheless, occasional patients have complained of chest pain with ischemic features ameliorated by rest, angioplasty, or retransplantation.

Objective. Physical findings are nonspecific. Although the routine electrocardiogram may demonstrate a myocardial infarction, ischemic abnormalities are not regularly found by stress electrocardiography or radionuclide techniques, perhaps because of the diffuse and widespread nature of the lesions in the absence of infarction. Angiography may be performed at 4- to 6-month intervals instead of yearly, to document progression and to determine the time for retransplantation.

Plans

Diagnostic. See Criteria for Diagnosis.

Therapeutic. Isolated high-grade proximal single-vessel lesions have been treated with percutaneous transluminal coronary angioplasty (PTCA), but this is uncommon. The lesions are usually extensive and involve multiple small vessels, and therefore, bypass surgery is usually not considered useful. If there is no contraindication (such as severe physical and/or psychological debility, chronic infection, or malignancy), then retransplantation has been the usual therapy but yields only a 40 to 60% 1-year survival rate.

Follow-up

If patients are candidates for retransplantation, angiography is repeated at 4- to 6-month intervals, depending on severity, and patients are resubmitted for transplantation.

Discussion

Prevalence and Incidence. Coronary arteriography is abnormal in 10% of patients at 1 year and in approximately 50% at 5 years. Subclinical abnormalities in the vessel wall are still more frequent when assessed by intravascular ultrasound.

Related Basic Science. Although hyperlipidemia, diabetes mellitus, and hypertension are common among cardiac transplant recipients, they are not entirely sufficient to account for the development of an obliterative coronary arteriopathy at a rate of 10 to 20% per year in hearts that are usually from donors only 20 to 35 years old (Gao et al., 1988). Some degree of chronic low-grade rejection probably plays a major role (see Etiology).

Natural History and Its Modification with Treatment. Eventually, all heart transplant recipients show varying degrees of vasculopathy. Treatment has been limited to retransplantation or, more rarely, PTCA or coronary artery bypass grafting.

Prevention. Although management of hyperlipidemia and hypertension is desirable, it is likely that these are probably not the basic underlying factors. Cytomegalovirus infection and rejection are probably more important. If hypercholesterolemia is severe, lovastatin (Mevacor) may be used in low doses (i.e., 10–20 mg/d). Higher doses have occasionally been associated with rhabdomyolysis in the presence of cyclosporine. Recently the use of diltiazem has been shown to offer partial protection from the development of these lesions and it has been routinely added to the maintenance regimen for these patients.

Cost Containment. There are few opportunities for cost containment other than avoiding unnecessary testing.

IMMUNOSUPPRESSION

Immunosuppressive protocols are standard in the treatment of organ transplant recipients and are required indefinitely. Although x-ray treatment is employed in special cases, drug therapy is the rule. The typical regimen consists of corticosteroids (Prednisone), cytotoxic agents (usually Azathioprine [Imuran]), and a T-cell-specific agent (usually cyclosporine). Together they impair the ability of the host immune system to reject the allograft. The complications of immunosuppressive agents are discussed below.

Corticosteroids

Clinical Manifestations

Subjective. Fatigue, personality changes, blurring of vision (cataracts or hyperglycemia), joint pain (avascular necrosis), or back pain (vertebral collapse) may occur.

Objective. The characteristic cushingoid appearance, with a tendency to a ruddy, moon facies; acneiform eruptions over the thorax and face; fragile skin with ecchymoses over the hands, forearms, and shins; and livid striae on a protuberant abdomen are common. Extremities are usually thin. Posterior cataracts are seen on eye examination.

Hyperglycemia is common. Radiographs show osteoporosis and sometimes vertebral collapse. Bone scans and magnetic resonance imaging may be used to confirm the presence of avascular necrosis of bone, usually in the head of the femur.

Plans and Follow-up

If cataracts interfere with vision, surgical lens replacement may be employed. If arthritis becomes debilitating, joint replacement with a prosthesis has been used as needed. Because of adrenal cortical atrophy secondary to chronic exogenous corticosteroid administration, hydrocortisone 100 mg (or its equivalent) should be given every 8 hours in the event of medical stresses (e.g., general surgery, systemic infections, hemorrhage).

Discussion

Prevalence and Incidence. The prevalence of adverse effects is usually a function of dosage and duration of treatment. It is ubiquitous at daily doses of prednisone of 20 mg or larger.

Related Basic Science. The precise basis for these steroid-induced changes is not entirely clear.

Natural History and Its Modification with Treatment. The natural history is determined by the corticosteroid dosage and duration of treatment.

Prevention. The prevention of complications depends on keeping corticosteroid administration to a minimum, switching to alternate-day therapy, or discontinuing the drug, if possible. Exercise and a low-calorie diet are helpful in maintaining normal physique.

Cost Containment. Corticosteroids are relatively inexpensive.

Cyclosporine

Criteria for Diagnosis

Cyclosporine serum trough levels of 75 to 150 ng/mL (whole blood levels are usually three to five times higher) are considered the therapeutic range for chronic maintenance. Samples should be drawn immediately preceding administration of the drug. Serum levels of 400 ng/mL or higher are capable of causing acute (renal and/or hepatic) toxicity. Even when serum levels are maintained in the therapeutic zone, however, treatment is usually accompanied by chronic azotemia and hypertension.

Clinical Manifestations

Subjective. Some patients experience gastrointestinal distress or headache.

Objective. Tremor, hirsutism, and gingival hyperplasia have been reported. More serious complications include hyperlipidemia, renal tubular acidosis (type IV), and azotemia. When severe elevations of cyclosporine levels occur, acute renal failure and hyperbilirubinemia may ensue. These are reversible with temporary discontinuation of the drug.

Hypertension is nearly universal and its mechanism, other than that associated with renal dysfunction, is uncertain. Sympathetic neural activation, perhaps accentuated by cardiac denervation, may contribute to hypertension.

Plans

Diagnostic. Chronic administration causes a reduction in creatinine clearance and elevated blood urea nitrogen. Renal biopsies reveal varying degrees of interstitial fibrosis and glomerular sclerosis.

Therapeutic. Treatment of hypertension requires high-dose calcium channel blockers (which may require lowering the cyclosporine dosage). These agents have become the treatment of choice because of their effectiveness, because of a possible renal protective effect, and because of evidence that diltiazem appears to retard accelerated graft coronary artery disease. Supplementation with angiotensin-converting enzyme inhibitors, diuretics, hydralazine, prazosin, or beta blockers may be needed. If renal insufficiency is severe, cyclosporine may have to be markedly reduced or discontinued with augmentation of alternative immunosuppressive agents. A few patients have required chronic dialysis or renal transplantation.

Follow-up

Ongoing monitoring of renal and hepatic function as well as of cyclosporine levels is required. If oral medication must be discontinued for any reason, intravenous cyclosporine may be given as one third of the oral dose by a slow infusion of 4 to 8 hours' duration. Adequacy of treatment can be assessed by trough serum levels.

Discussion

Prevalence and Incidence. Mild to severe hypertension and azotemia occur in 90% or more of patients.

Related Basic Science. Cyclosporine is a cyclic peptide of fungal origin that attaches to cyclophilin, a cytoplasmic receptor protein. This complex in turn binds to calcineurin, the messenger compound responsible for nuclear initiation of interleukin-2 (IL-2) production. Without IL-2, clonal T-cell differentiation and proliferation cannot take place. Its benefits include a steroid-sparing effect and absence of bone marrow depression.

Prevention. Because of the many different assays available, individual institutions must develop in-house reference standards. In addition, patients should be kept well hydrated. The administration of nephrotoxic drugs (i.e., radiocontrast agents, antibiotics such as amphotericin B and aminoglycosides) should be minimized. Although serum creatinine levels usually stabilize after 1 year, 5 to 10% of patients develop more severe renal failure and require marked reduction or discontinuation of cyclosporine. A few have required kidney transplantation or dialysis.

Cyclosporine is metabolized exclusively by the liver, and hepatic failure interferes with excretion causing cyclosporine levels to rise, with the potential for acute renal failure. Certain medications that compete with cyclosporine for hepatic metabolism may have the same effect. Erythromycin, ketoconazole (Nizoral) (but not fluconazole), and calcium channel blockers are the best known of these. Conversely, some drugs such as rifampin (Rifadin) and barbiturates induce hepatic catabolic enzymes and augment cyclosporine elimination. If this effect is ignored, rejection may occur. In both cases (i.e., increased or decreased cyclosporine levels), close monitoring of trough serum levels provides the key to appropriate patient management. [More detailed information regarding drug interactions with cyclosporine may be obtained from the manufacturer (Sandoz).]

Cost Containment. Cyclosporine is expensive but newer immunosuppressants (such as FK-506) are unlikely to be less so. The drug interaction between cyclosporine and diltiazem (see above) results in cost savings of $3000 to $4000 per year, as lower doses of cyclosporine are required to maintain therapeutic drug levels.

Azathioprine

Etiology

Azathioprine is an antimetabolite agent that interferes with nucleotide synthesis and inhibits hematopoiesis and proliferation of lymphocytes.

Criteria for Diagnosis

Bone marrow depression with pancytopenia is the major signal of excess azathioprine. Hepatotoxicity occurs rarely. (Erythrocyte macrocytosis is common but can be safely ignored.)

Clinical Manifestations

Subjective. Malaise, sore throat, or easy bruising may be noted.

Objective. Anemia, thrombocytopenia, and leukopenia are signaled by pallor, ecchymoses, bleeding gums, and signs of infection, either local (oral, skin) or systemic (fever, chills, malaise). Hyperbilirubinemia and hepatic enzyme elevations (in the absence of evidence of viral etiology) accompany hepatitis.

Plans

Diagnostic. A search for renal dysfunction or concomitant administration of allopurinol (Zyloprim), either of which reduces elimination of azathioprine, may reveal the cause of (relative) overdosage. Both CMV infection and its treatment (with ganciclovir) may precipitate profound leukopenia.

Therapeutic. Azathioprine should be temporarily discontinued until hematologic indices return to normal.

Follow-up

A complete blood count, including a platelet count, should be obtained at each follow-up visit.

Discussion

Prevalence and Incidence. Severe pancytopenia is very infrequent in well-monitored patients. Hepatotoxicity requiring discontinuation of the drug is also very uncommon (<1%).

Related Basic Science. Azathioprine is a purine antagonist antimetabolite. It interferes with DNA and RNA synthesis. It suppresses (lymphocyte) cell-mediated rejection reactions.

Natural History and Its Modifications with Treatment. When pancytopenia is noted, a search for synergistic factors should follow. These factors include other drugs (e.g., allopurinol, ganciclovir, sulfonamides), and certain viral infections (cytomegalovirus). Withholding azathioprine and/or other offending drugs usually results in a return of blood counts to normal within 1 to 2 weeks. If granulocytopenia is severe (granulocytes < 1000/mm^3) granuloctye colony-stimulating factor may be administered.

Recovery from bone marrow depression usually takes place within 1 to 2 weeks.

INFECTIONS

Etiology

The immunosuppressed patient is vulnerable to a wide variety of common and unusual opportunistic infections, some of which are discussed below.

Criteria for Diagnosis

Customary diagnostic criteria for infection are used (see Chapter 8–32).

Clinical Manifestations

Manifestations depend on the site(s) of the infection, the timing of diagnosis, and the virulence of the etiologic agent.

Plans

Diagnostic. Specific etiologic diagnosis is essential, and routine as well as interventional techniques to obtain specimens for culture, staining, and histology should be used promptly and aggressively. In the immunocompromised patient, opportunistic infections are common and simultaneous infections with more than one organism may occur.

Therapeutic. The reader is referred to the chapters in Section 8 on infectious diseases for the discussion of treatment.

Follow-up

Careful follow-up is needed to assess the response to therapy. Resolution is determined by a change in physical signs, the attainment of negative cultures, and imaging techniques.

Discussion

Prevalence and Incidence. The frequency of the different infections encountered varies with the etiologic agent, the intensity of immunosuppression, and timing after transplantation. The risks are greatest during the first 6 months. Infection and rejection are the most common causes of death during the first year posttransplant.

Related Basic Science. Immunosuppression predisposes to infection with both common and opportunistic organisms. The approach to diagnosis and management of infections in immunosuppressed individuals is best sought elsewhere in specific articles or texts.

Natural History and Its Modification with Treatment. Serious infections are most likely to occur during the first postoperative year when rejection is most common and the patient is undergoing the most intense immunosuppression. Major viral infections include cytomegalovirus, herpes zoster–varicella, herpes simplex, and viral hepatitis.

Cytomegalovirus may be transmitted from the infected donor to the recipient. If it is the recipient's primary infection, it is likely to be more severe and disabling. The clinical picture consists of fever, pneumonia, hepatitis, and leukopenia. Retinitis or gastroenteritis (sometimes accompanied by hemorrhage) may occur. Diagnosis is made by viral culture of sputum, urine, and buffy coat. Endoscope biopsy of lung or gastric mucosa is often useful and prompt. A shell vial (immunofluorescence) test is also available as are immunoglobulin G and M antibody titers. Recently, polymerase chain reaction technology has made diagnosis faster and more specific. Treatment is available with intravenous ganciclovir (DHPG), which may cause bone marrow depression. Dose adjustment is necessary if renal insufficiency exists. The additional use of hyperimmune globulin is warranted for the treatment of a primary infection (i.e., in a previously seronegative subject) or in the case of cytomegalovirus pneumonia.

Herpetic infections other than gastroenteritis and pneumonia are usually evident clinically and can be confirmed by direct fluorescent antibody testing and culture. They respond to a 7- and 10-day course of intravenous acyclovir (Zovirax). Effective hydration should be maintained to avoid drug-induced cast formation and azotemia. Zoster can be quite painful and postzoster neuralgia may be highly refractory to therapy.

Prophylactic screening for hepatitis virus A and B infections is now highly effective, and transmission of the clinical disease is very rare. Tests for antibody to hepatitis C have only recently become available, but serologic conversion may take many months after infection. For these reasons, prophylaxis has not yet been equally effective for this agent. Progression of hepatitis B to hepatic insufficiency and hepatoma has been less in evidence since the introduction of cyclosporine.

Fungal infections have usually surfaced as pulmonary nodules first identified by chest x-ray, often before systemic symptoms. *Candida* and *Aspergillus* have been the most common organisms. Ketoconazole, fluconazole, and itraconazole have been used successfully for *Candida* (but require modification of cyclosporine dosage), whereas amphotericin B, administered by intravenous catheter, has been the drug of choice for aspergillus. Flucytosine is useful as adjunctive therapy but may cause bone marrow depression. When *Aspergillus* infection is extrapulmonary and widespread, treatment usually fails.

Nocardia infections are focal in lung or soft tissue and, although rare, are well controlled by sulfonamides or sulfamethoxazole–trimethoprim (Bactrim, Septra). Atypical mycobacterial infections often present as subcutaneous nodules and are relatively resistant to conventional antitubercular medications. Their indolent course has generally allowed treatment to be withheld with little in the way of adverse clinical effects.

Bacterial infections of all kinds occur in these patients. Staphylococcal and enterobacterial infections are frequent. Their incidence is lower since the advent of cyclosporine and the reduction of use of corticosteroids and azathioprine. Conventional antibiotic therapy, with attention to nephrotoxicity and interactions with cyclosporine, is generally effective. In addition, immunosuppressed patients are particularly vulnerable to *Legionella* pneumonia and *Listeria monocytogenes* meningitis. Both of the latter infections should be treated for 6 to 8 weeks because of the high likelihood of recurrence with treatment of shorter duration.

Infection with *Pneumocystis carinii* is also less prevalent since reduction in steroid doses and the addition of prophylactic trimethoprim–sulfamethoxazole, which is given as a double-strength tablet twice daily 3 days per week. *Pneumocystis carinii* pneumonia is typically marked by fever, cough, and dyspnea, and is accompanied by bilateral rales and mild cyanosis. Arterial PO_2 is reduced and chest x-ray films show bilateral infiltrates. Diagnosis is confirmed by bronchoalveolar lavage. The pneumonia usually responds to a 3-week course of intravenous trimethoprim–sulfamethoxazole. Trimethoprim raises serum creatinine levels by interfering with renal tubular excretion of creatinine, but glomerular filtration rate and overall renal function are unaffected.

Toxoplasmosis is rare and characteristically due to infection from the donor. It has commonly presented in the first few months after transplantation as an intracranial mass or masses signaled by progressive headache. Diagnosis has been by imaging (computed tomography or magnetic resonance imaging) studies of the brain, confirmed by rising antibody titers. Occasionally, microscopic *Toxoplasma* cysts have been found on cardiac biopsy. Toxoplasmosis should be treated with pyrimethamine (Daraprim, Fansidar) and sulfadiazine (Microsulfon) for 2 to 6 months.

Prevention. Attempts should be made to avoid transplantation from serologically positive donors (e.g., those with cytomegalovirus, toxoplasmosis, or viral hepatitis) to serologically negative recipients. HIV-positive donors are categorically refused. Prophylactic administration of ganciclovir or hyperimmune globulin to recipients who are serologically positive for cytomegalovirus or who are receiving an allograft from a cytomegalovirus-positive donor may reduce the frequency and severity of cytomegalovirus disease.

MALIGNANCY

Definition

Conventional definitions apply.

Etiology

Precise etiologies for malignancies are not well defined. Carcinomas of skin and cervix as well as posttransplant lymphomas may be partially caused by viruses.

Criteria for Diagnosis

The diagnosis requires biopsy confirmation. Fine-needle aspiration may be sufficient in some cases. The immunophenotyping of lymphoma may also be useful.

Clinical Manifestations

Manifestations of tumors do not differ from those in nontransplant patients. More specific to the transplant population is B-cell lymphoma. This malignancy condition differs from other lymphomas in several important ways and is also called posttransplant lymphoproliferative disorder (PTLD). Clinically it may manifest itself early (i.e., within 6 months posttransplant) or years later. It may resemble a mononucleosis-like illness with fever, pharyngitis, and diffuse lymphadenopathy. More often the patient is afebrile and the lesions (single or multiple) are found in extranodal sites such as the brain, testicle, lung, or liver because of local symptoms or serendipitously.

Plans

Diagnostic. Once lymphoma (PTLD) is diagnosed by biopsy, staging scans (computed tomography or magnetic resonance imaging) should be performed.

Therapeutic

Treatment differs from that for spontaneous lymphoma. Conventional multidrug cytotoxic regimens have helped occasionally, but have often led to rapid demise. Other regimens using interferon or monoclonal antibodies against B-cell surface markers have also been reported. Contemporary treatment calls for severe reduction of immunosuppressive therapy, radiation therapy or surgical resection of single tumors, and the empiric administration of acyclovir (Zovirax) (because of its in vitro effect on Epstein–Barr virus, a herpesvirus). Such a plan should be carried out under the supervision of experienced transplant physicians to ensure proper monitoring for rejection as well as tumor regression.

Discussion

Prevalence and Incidence. Malignancies are more common among transplant recipients than in control populations. This is particularly evident with respect to actinic keratoses and squamous cell carcinomas in sun-exposed areas of skin; however, Kaposi's sarcoma, cervical carcinoma, and other cancers are also more common, and physicians caring for transplant patients should maintain a high index of suspicion.

Posttransplant lymphoma (PTLD) occurs in 5 to 10% of heart transplant recipients. Its incidence is higher in children and cumulative with time.

Related Basic Science. Immunophenotyping reveals tissue usually composed of B lymphocytes, which may be polyclonal or monoclonal. Fifteen percent of PTLD tumors are of T-cell origin. Different tumor sites within the same patient may each be monoclonal but may differ from each other in immunoglobulin rearrangement, in contrast to "spontaneous" lymphomas which are identically monoclonal at all sites. The vast majority of affected individuals show evidence of Epstein–Barr virus infection by rise in antibody titers and/or identification of this virus genome within tumor tissue. These clinical and infective characteristics are compatible with the hypothesis that this is a virally driven mechanism whereby infected lymphocytes continue to proliferate in the absence of normal cellular immune-mediated control mechanisms.

Natural History and Its Modifications with Treatment. A number of patients with posttransplant lymphoma have been treated successfully with preservation of their graft function despite diminution of immunosuppressive therapy. Approximately 30% of patients survive PTLD.

Prevention. Routine prophylaxis against sun exposure and regular Papanicolau tests for cervical cancer are desirable. Presently there is no policy to restrict transplants from Epstein–Barr virus serologically positive donors.

REFERENCES

Billingham ME, Cary NRB, Hammond ME, et al. A working formulation for the standardizations of nomenclature in the diagnosis of heart and lung rejection: Heart rejection study group. J Heart Transplant 1990;9:587.

Gao SZ, Alderman EL, Schroeder JS, et al. Accelerated coronary vascular disease in the heart transplant patient: Coronary arteriographic findings. J Am Coll Cardiol 1988;12:334.

Garnnier JL, Berger F, Betuel H, et al. Epstein–Barr virus associated lymphoproliferative diseases (B-cell lymphoma) after transplantation. Nephrol Dial Transplant 1989;4:18.

Grattan MT, Moreno-Cabral CE, Starnes VA, et al. Cytomegalovirus infection is associated with cardiac allograft rejections and atherosclerosis. JAMA 1989;261:3561.

Hunt SA, Schroeder JS. Managing patients after cardiac transplantation. Hosp Pract 1989;24(10):83.

Kahan BD. Cyclosporine. N Engl J Med 1989;321:1725.

Scherrer U, Vissing SF, Morgan BJ, et al. Cyclosporine-induced sympathetic activation and hypertension after heart transplantation. N Engl J Med 1990;323:693.

Schreiber SL, Crabtree GR. The mechanism of action of cyclosporin A and FK506. Immunol Today 1992;13:136.

Schroeder JSS, Gao S-Z, Alderman EL, et al. A preliminary study of diltiazem in the prevention of coronary artery disease in heart-transplant recipients. N Engl J Med 1993;328:164.

CHAPTER 15–63

Infection in the Organ Transplant Recipient (See Section 8, Chapter 32)

CHAPTER 15–64

Arterial Embolism

Atef A. Salam, M.D.

DEFINITION

Arterial embolism is defined as lodgment of a thrombus or arteriosclerotic debris from a more central site in the arterial system to another more distal point causing acute obstruction of blood flow to an organ or limb.

ETIOLOGY

Clots in the heart represent a potential source of peripheral arterial embolism. Cardiac conditions associated with clot formation include myocardial infarction, atrial fibrillation, prosthetic valves, and infective endocarditis. Arterial embolism is usually due to dislodgment of blood clots from an aneurysmal cavity or fragmentation of atherosclerotic debris. The latter may occur spontaneously or as a complication of intraoperative clamping of the aorta during coronary bypass or aneurysm repair operations. Systemic embolization of portions of intracardiac tumors, particularly myxoma, may also occur. Metastatic tumors and foreign bodies may also produce arterial emboli. Patients with underlying peripheral vascular disease may have peripheral emboli; usually they originate from laminated thrombi within an aneurysmal sac or from ulcerated atherosclerotic plaques in a proximal location.

CRITERIA FOR DIAGNOSIS

Suggestive

Sudden onset of severe pain in the involved extremity followed by impaired sensation and motor function suggests the diagnosis of arterial embolism.

Definitive

Confirmatory findings on clinical examination include pallor, pulselessness, paresthesias, and paralysis (the four "P's").

CLINICAL MANIFESTATIONS

Subjective

Typical symptoms of peripheral embolism include pain of acute onset followed by numbness and eventual loss of motor function in the involved extremity. These symptoms are associated with coolness, pallor, and paresthesias distal to the site of arterial occlusion. The most common, and generally the first, symptom is pain. The pain is characteristically of acute onset, severe in degree, and continuous in duration. It persists until sensory dysfunction supervenes or the vascular supply is restored. Visceral arterial emboli are relatively uncommon, but if present, they may produce symptoms referable to the organ that becomes ischemic. Flank pain and hematuria may suggest renal emboli; severe abdominal pain with vomiting and diarrhea suggests acute mesenteric artery occlusion. A variety of neurologic manifestations, including abrupt hemiparesis and aphasia, may be seen in cases of emboli to the brachiocephalic system.

Objective

Physical Examination

The involved extremity is usually cool and pale with collapsed superficial veins and delayed or absent capillary refill. The most notable physical finding is the absence of pulses distal to the site of embolic occlusion. With more prolonged arterial obstruction, advanced findings of ischemia develop, such as hypesthesia, paresis, or paralysis, and, finally, rigor mortis of the involved extremity. Neglected early signs may result in the patient's reporting to the physician late with established gangrene of distal tissues. Other pertinent clinical findings include cardiac arrhythmias, murmurs of valvular heart disease, palpable arterial aneurysms, and changes consistent with chronic preexisting peripheral vascular disease. In most situations, an accurate diagnosis of peripheral arterial embolism can be made from the history and physical findings alone. If necessary, information can be obtained by noninvasive vascular tests and by angiography. The latter technique is especially vital to the prompt, accurate diagnosis of suspected visceral emboli.

The most frequent causes of a missed diagnosis of peripheral arterial embolism are failure to suspect the condition or an incomplete physical evaluation. On occasion, the physician can be misled by obstacles to the proper diagnosis. A common example is the patient with impaired sensorium due to heavy sedation or a neurologic disorder in which neither the pain nor loss of motor function would be readily apparent. Such might be the case in critically ill patients who have had a recent major operative procedure, particularly open heart surgery or aortic resection. It also might apply to patients who are hemodynamically unstable following a recent myocardial infarction. In these situations, arterial ischemia can be recognized only by careful routine evaluations of extremity circulation.

Routine Laboratory Abnormalities

There are no diagnostic routine laboratory abnormalities.

PLANS

Diagnostic

Differential Diagnosis

Acute ischemia due to arterial embolization also may be observed in the patient with long-standing peripheral atherosclerotic occlusive disease. Various degrees of either accentuation or masking of the usual symptom complex may be seen in these patients because of the tempering effect of the existing collateral circulation. In addition, arterial embolism may be difficult to recognize in the extremity affected with long-standing venous stasis disease. The vascular examination can be very difficult for an inexperienced observer in patients with the typical indurated, swollen postphlebitic limb. In such cases, the pain of acute ischemia is often misinterpreted as a manifestation of recurrent phlebitis unless a thorough arterial evaluation is performed.

Diagnostic Options and Recommended Approach

Peripheral arterial embolism may constitute a medical or surgical emergency. If the entire limb is ischemic, a "golden period" of 6 to 8 hours exists during which revascularization should be achieved. After that time, the likelihood of salvaging a fully functional limb declines rapidly. Because of the urgency of the situation, the diagnostic workup should be pertinent and kept to a minimum. Routine admission laboratory studies usually are not helpful in the diagnosis of acute arterial embolism. A chest x-ray film may show cardiac enlargement or a prosthetic valve in place. An electrocardiogram may confirm a cardiac arrhythmia or show evidence of a myocardial infarction or ventricular aneurysm. All of these tests may be negative in the patient who arrives promptly after the onset of symptoms. In neglected cases, however, metabolic acidosis, hyperkalemia, and myoglobinuria indicate underlying muscle necrosis and may herald the development of myonephropathy.

All patients should have a thorough cardiac evaluation to determine operative risk factors, and reasonable efforts should be made to optimize cardiovascular status. Preoperative noninvasive vascular laboratory studies are useful, if done expeditiously, to assess the severity of the underlying arterial insufficiency and to establish a baseline against which the postoperative status can be assessed. Doppler ultrasonic evaluation of the arterial system is extremely valuable in the diagnosis of acute ischemia. Absence of Doppler signals substantiates the clinical findings and confirms the diagnosis of acute arterial occlusion. In addition, the Doppler instrument can be used to follow segmental pressures in patients with arterial embolism in whom operation has been deferred because of progress toward spontaneous resolution. Angiography may be performed preoperatively in selected patients or intraoperatively depending on the clinical circumstances. In general, x-ray contrast studies are most useful for those patients with preexisting occlusive vascular disease to assist in the differential diagnosis between embolus and spontaneous thrombosis of a chronically diseased segment.

Therapeutic

Once the diagnosis of arterial embolism is made, the patient is immediately systemically heparinized to prevent distal propagation of thrombus while preparations are being made for urgent operation. Anticoagulation is frequently continued postoperatively because of the high risk of recurrent embolization. In certain circumstances, such as emboli originating from prosthetic valves or cardiac mural thrombi, patients are subsequently converted to chronic oral anticoagulants. The standard treatment of the patient with peripheral arterial embolism is surgical embolectomy. In most instances, the procedure can be done under local anesthesia using a balloon embolectomy catheter to extract clots from the involved arteries. A femoral arteriotomy is commonly used for unilateral occlusions due to obstruction of the iliofemoropopliteal segments. For an aortic bifurcation saddle embolus, the balloon extraction procedure is done via bilateral femoral approaches. The surgeon should exercise care to avoid residual thrombus material in the femoropopliteal or deep femoral systems. If there is any doubt concerning complete restoration of a patient arterial tree, completion angiography should be done intraoperatively and repeat embolectomy performed via secondary incisions if necessary. Fasciotomy must be considered for any limb that is tightly swollen or those with a prolonged period of muscle ischemia. A direct abdominal operative approach may be necessary for patients who fail to establish adequate flow by balloon catheter extraction or for those with visceral artery emboli. Postoperatively, the patient must be closely monitored for cardiac function and for complications of arterial ischemia, including both local and systemic changes. Aggressive fluid resuscitation and meticulous electrolyte and acid–base therapy are mandatory. It is important to minimize renal toxicity in patients with myoglobinuria. Osmotic diuretics are judiciously used to maintain high urine volume, to prevent renal insufficiency secondary to pigment deposition.

Fresh arterial clots can be lysed using thrombolytic agents such as urokinase. Because emboli usually originate from preformed and hence chronic clots, they are generally considered unsuitable for this form of treatment. There is also the risk of destabilizing a mural clot in the heart, leading to its fragmentation and further embolization. A brief trial of lytic therapy may be appropriate in patients in whom distinction cannot be made between embolism and acute thrombosis, provided that backup surgical intervention is not unduly delayed.

FOLLOW-UP

During the first 48 hours following embolectomy, the patient should be closely observed for evidence of recurrent arterial occlusion and for the development of postrevascularization compartment syndrome. Recurrence of ischemia is usually due to technical factors such as incomplete removal of thrombus, faulty closure of the arteriotomy, or balloon catheter injury causing intimal dissection. The treatment in all such instances is immediate reoperation as soon as the problem is detected, provided the patient's overall condition permits. Postembolectomy patients are at risk for developing compartment syndrome. The risk is higher in individuals who had prolonged ischemia before operation. In such cases, ischemic endothelial damage allows transudation of intracellular fluid into the extracellular space. In patients with rising compartment pressure and early sensory motor dysfunction, urgent fasciotomy is required to prevent the development of irreversible neuromuscular damage.

Another consequence of revascularization of an acutely ischemic extremity is a rise in the tissue concentration of oxygen free radicals. The damaging effect of these radicals on the cellular level has been documented in animal models. Certain pharmacologic agents have been shown to protect the animals against the harmful effects of the free radicals. The clinical significance of these findings, however, remains to be defined.

Long-term management of postembolectomy patients includes correction of any obvious sources for emboli, such as ventricular aneurysm, valvular heart diease, peripheral arterial aneurysm, or other probable sources (e.g., extensive ulcerative arterial plaques). Proper education and follow-up are mandatory in patients requiring anticoagulation. Extended care in patients with underlying peripheral vascular disease is required to detect progressive aneurysmal or occlusive disorders that may require treatment. Patients with atherosclerosis should have appropriate dietary counseling and careful attention to risk factor modification, if necessary with pharmacologic agents.

DISCUSSION
Prevalence and Incidence

Peripheral arterial embolization is a relatively common disorder that seems to be increasing in frequency, as noted by several recent reviews. This is probably due to a growing elderly population, extended survival of patients with cardiac disease, and the increased use of cardiac prostheses.

Generally, arterial embolization can be regarded as a manifestation of severe underlying cardiovascular disease. The heart is the source of the embolic material in more than 90% of patients. Atherosclerotic heart disease with its attendant complications of myocardial infarction, congestive heart failure, and ventricular aneurysm accounts for a large proportion of cardiac arterial emboli. Rheumatic heart disease with related valvular dysfunction, although less common than in years past, is still responsible for some peripheral emboli. Atrial fibrillation secondary to rheumatic or atherosclerotic heart disease is another common source of emboli from the heart. Other less frequent causes include atrial myxomas and bacterial endocarditis. The remaining instances of arterial embolism are usually attributable to contained material from an arterial aneurysm or ulcerative arterial plaque. Once emboli have been released from the heart, most of them proceed to the lower extremities, about one fifth of them enter the cerebral circulation, and a small percentage go to the upper extremities or visceral arteries.

Related Basic Science

Arterial emboli are propelled by the bloodstream until they are arrested at an arterial bifurcation where the lumen abruptly narrows. Local hypoxemia secondary to the arterial occlusion leads to accumulation of tissue metabolites, which stimulate vasodilation. If this compensatory circulatory change fails to meet resting tissue oxygen requirements, there is a resultant loss of cellular function. Evidence of tissue necrosis may be detected as early as 4 to 6 hours after total interruption of blood flow to a limb and much more rapidly following interruption to a metabolically active organ such as the kidney or liver. Neurogenic manifestations occur early because nerve cells are relatively sensitive to hypoxia. Although reversible at first, permanent nerve damage is to be expected if blood supply is not promptly restored. Pain associated with ischemia is presumably due to the accumulation of metabolic products during the early phases of arterial deprivation. With prolongation of ischemia and resultant neurologic damage, a causalgia pain may appear which can persist for some time after restoration of blood flow. A second important consideration is the absorption of toxic products of tissue breakdown, which is seen with prolonged and severe tissue ischemia and resultant cellular death. In addition to metabolic acidosis and hyperkalemia, derangements of renal function may occur secondary to myoglobinuria. Although the myonephropathic syndrome is uncommon, it can lead to renal insufficiency and loss of life if not appreciated early and treated aggressively.

Among the most serious threats to the limb itself is the propagation of thrombus throughout branches of the arterial tree distal to the site of occlusion. Unchecked, these secondary thrombi obstruct collateral vessels and intensify ischemia to the arterial bed. Moreover, extension of thrombus into the muscular branches may prevent successful embolectomy, as methods do not currently exist to reopen these multiple side channels successfully. Eventually, extensive venous thrombosis may occur as well, further diminishing the likelihood of successful limb salvage.

Natural History and Its Modification with Treatment

The natural clinical course of peripheral embolus depends on the location of the occlusion, the degree of completeness of luminal obliteration, the extent of secondary thrombosis, and the degree of spontaneous restoration of collateral circulation. In general, the outcome of an embolic event is most directly related to the duration of tissue ischemia before the embolus is removed and circulation restored. If catheter embolectomy is accomplished prior to the onset of significant tissue necrosis, within the first 8 to 12 hours, complete function recovery is to be expected in the great majority of patients. With more prolonged ischemia, the risk of permanent neurologic damage, myonecrosis, or limb loss steadily increases. Venous thromboembolism of the extremity involved with arterial embolism is probably more frequent than has been previously reported. Prevention of continued venous thrombosis is best accomplished with postoperative anticoagulation. Severe metabolic effects, including the myonephropathic syndrome, can be seen in prolonged arterial ischemia. Such changes have been observed in as many as 15% of patients following acute arterial occlusion.

The overall limb salvage rate varies among reported series but averages approximately 60%. The in-hospital mortality remains high at approximately 25%, due predominantly to the associated cardiovascular disease. Recent reported rates for amputation necessitated by arterial embolism are as high as 15%. Reembolization occurs in 5 to 10% of patients in long-term follow-up studies. The latter complication can be minimized by diligent anticoagulation and aggressive treatment of cardiac lesions.

Prevention

The most important preventive measures in the care of patients subject to peripheral arterial embolism are proper management of the cardiac condition known to be associated with this complication, including secondary risk factor modification, chronic anticoagulation therapy for the high-risk patient, and prompt recognition of the arterial embolism when it does occur. Patients with acute anterior myocardial infarction should have a two-dimensional echocardiogram and, if a mural thrombus is found, should be given warfarin (Coumadin) for at least 6 months. Patients with chronic atrial fibrillation should be anticoagulated. Advances in the care of cardiac patients may serve to decrease the incidence of embolic problems, although, at least at the present time, some surgical approaches that include the increased use of prosthetic material in the bloodstream seem to be associated with a higher risk of embolization.

Cost Containment

Costs for the care of this complication can best be minimized by its prophylaxis. Once embolism has occurred, timely recognition followed by rapid confirmation and appropriate treatment results in the best chance for limb salvage and the shortest possible hospital stay. Tissue loss, in addition to its functional and emotional impact, is associated with prolonged hospitalization and a high failure rate to rehabilitate the patient. Unfortunately, severe underlying cardiac disease can be responsible for a prolonged, expensive hospital stay for many of these patients; for a significant number, it is a terminal illness.

REFERENCES

Abbott WM, Maloney RD, McCabe CC, et al. Arterial embolism: A 44 year perspective. Am J Surg 1982;143:460.
DeMaioribus CA, Mills JL, Fugitani RM, et al. A reevaluation of intraarterial thrombolytic therapy for acute lower extremity ischemia. J Vasc Surg 1993;17:888.
Gordon RD, Fogarty TJ. Peripheral arterial embolism. In: Rutherford RB, ed. Vascular surgery. 2nd ed. Philadelphia: Saunders, 1984:449.
Kvilekval, et al. After the blue toe: Prognosis of noncardiac arterial embolization in the lower extremities. J Vasc Surg 1993;17:328.
McPhail NV, et al. Management of acute thromboembolic limb ischemia. Surgery 1983;93:381.

CHAPTER 15–65

Thoracic Aortic Aneurysm

Mark W. Moritz, M.D., and Robert B. Smith III, M.D.

DEFINITION

Thoracic aortic aneurysm is the condition of dilation of the aorta in the thorax to twice its ordinary diameter or greater. The ascending aorta, aortic arch, or descending aorta to the level of the diaphragm may be involved. These aneurysms may be fusiform, saccular, or dissecting in type.

ETIOLOGY

Aneurysms have several known etiologies, including atherosclerotic degeneration, Marfan's syndrome, aortic bacterial infection, aortitis due to Takayasu's disease or giant cell arteritis, and trauma. These degenerative, infectious, inflammatory, and injury processes cause mechanical weakening of the aortic wall. This then allows eventual enlargement by dilation or dissection of the involved portion, with thrombosis, embolization, tearing, and leakage ("rupture"). Idiopathic annuloectasia, particularly of the ascending thoracic aorta, also occurs and can reach aneurysmal size.

CRITERIA FOR DIAGNOSIS
Suggestive

The physician considering this diagnosis often suspects it in a patient who is otherwise known to have factors or conditions predisposing to aneurysmal disease. These include patients already known to have coronary or systemic atherosclerosis, defects of collagen metabolism (i.e., Marfan's syndrome), septic embolization (i.e., bacterial aortitis), or other known aneurysms. The patient with traumatic aneurysm of the thoracic aorta may present acutely after a major vehicular accident (automobile or aircraft) or penetrating wound. Chronic traumatic aneurysm is considered in patients with a remote history of major trauma.

All thoracic aneurysms can produce pain in the chest either substernally, intrascapularly, or radiating to the neck or arms. Change in voice (hoarseness) may be produced by compression of the left recurrent laryngeal nerve as it loops around the aortic arch. Compression of other intrathoracic structures may cause erosion, bleeding, and infection. The onset of either new back or chest pain or of compression of adjacent structures may indicate aneurysm expansion, dissection, or impending rupture. Deterioration of luminal plaque may cause embolization of atherosclerotic debris or thrombus to distal tissues, where pain and infarctions with neurologic or other focal symptoms suggest the diagnosis.

Definitive

The measurement of thoracic aortic diameter provides proof of enlargement, and quantification of the size of the vessel determines whether it is aneurysmal. Methods of measurement include x-ray (chest radiographs, computed tomography [CT] scans, or contrast aortography), magnetic resonance imaging (MRI), ultrasound (intravascular ultrasound [IVUS] or transesophageal echocardiography [TEE]), and direct measurement at operation.

CLINICAL MANIFESTATIONS

Subjective

Thoracic aortic aneurysms are seen in the atherosclerotic age group; most are asymptomatic at the time of diagnosis. When symptoms are present, chest and back pain are the most common, especially in those patients with dissecting aneurysms and large atherosclerotic aneurysms (greater than 6 cm in diameter). The discomfort may worsen with physical exertion. The pain is a deep ache in the substernal or lateral chest or back and radiates to the neck, shoulders, lumbar region, or epigastrium, depending on the site and extent of the aneurysm. Compression of adjacent mediastinal structures may cause dyspnea or cough from tracheal displacement, dysphagia, distention of jugular or upper extremity veins (by superior vena cava or innominate vein compression), or hoarseness due to recurrent laryngeal nerve compromise. Erosion into trachea, lung parenchyma, esophagus, pericardium, or vertebral bodies can cause hemoptysis, hematemesis, cardiac tamponade, or back pain. Embolism of laminated clot or atherosclerotic debris from the aneurysm's lumen may produce neurologic symptoms or infarction of peripheral tissues. Symptoms of congestive heart failure may occur due to aortic dilation and resultant aortic valve regurgitation.

A history of remote penetrating or deceleration injury to the chest may suggest trauma as the etiology for a known thoracic aortic aneurysm. Although presently rare, aneurysms due to syphilis or bacterial infection are associated with a history of lues or bacteremia.

Objective

Physical Examination

Physical findings specific for thoracic aortic aneurysm are usually absent. The large saccular syphilitic aneurysm that erodes through the anterior chest wall and presents as a pulsating, expansile mass in the anterior chest is rare. Indirect evidence of an aneurysm includes tracheal tug, brachiocephalic bruits, increased heart size, signs of cardiac failure, or the murmur of aortic valvular regurgitation. Brachiocephalic pulses may be reduced due to aneurysmal compression of branch artery origins. Vocal cord paralysis and hoarseness can develop from tension on the left recurrent laryngeal nerve. Other signs of atherosclerotic heart disease are often present. Patients with Marfan's syndrome as an underlying etiology present with either typical body habitus and findings of that condition or forme fruste.

Routine Laboratory Abnormalities

Hyperlipidemia and hyperglycemia may be discovered on the routine SMA.

Most thoracic aneurysms are first suspected on viewing posteroanterior and lateral chest radiographs, which are the most valuable screening test. Aneurysms involving primarily the proximal ascending aorta are often not visualized, but others can show calcification of the wall, which will allow delineation of the aortic diameter. Multiple projec-

tions assist in the examinations. Aortic root calcification, if present, may be a clue to luetic aortitis and aneurysm. Calcification in the aorta that is seen only in the ascending aorta is most often produced by leutic aortitis. Mediastinal widening, hemothorax, or displacement of intrathoracic structures may indicate expansion or rupture.

PLANS
Diagnostic
Differential Diagnosis

Aortic tortuosity, mediastinal mass (tumor, cyst, or abscess), and lung masses must be differentiated from thoracic aortic aneurysm. Any modality that demonstrates enlargement of the aorta to twice its normal diameter establishes the diagnosis.

Diagnostic Options

Although a widened mediastinal shadow on chest radiograph may indicate the presence of thoracic aortic aneurysm, it can be inaccurate, as visualization of the ascending and descending aorta can be obscured by the heart. Aortography, TEE, CT, IVUS, and MRI are all more sensitive and specific, yielding exact measurements of aortic size. Aortography, however, can distinguish only luminal characteristics and branch vessel relationships; the presence of intraluminal thrombus obscures measurement of actual size on aortography. IVUS requires catheterization via a femoral Seldinger technique. Although it provides detailed information and quantification of arterial wall anatomy, it lends itself to use only during aortography or during endovascular procedures.

Recommended Approach

Computed tomography and MRI are much less operator dependent than TEE, do not subject the patient to risks inherent in TEE probe insertion, and are widely available. As CT generally costs less than MRI at most sites, it is the recommended means to obtain the diagnosis. Aortography, however, provides essential information for planning surgical repair, and, when done with runoff views can demonstrate aneurysms elsewhere in the arterial system in more than 10% of patients. Before operation, contrast aortography or MRI angiography is indicated.

Therapeutic

Medical therapy may be used in patients at high risk for operative repair, those with generalized ectasia of the aorta which is not twice its normal diameter, and those with small aneurysms that do not meet criteria for elective repair. Control of hypertension and cessation of smoking are the mainstays of treatment. If the aneurysm is due to aortitis, treatment of the underlying process is also indicated. Optimal treatment is direct surgical repair. Interposition grafting with prosthetic material that is placed intraluminally and then wrapped with aortic wall is the standard therapy for fusiform aneurysms or extensive diffuse enlargement of the aorta. When more than one area of thoracic aorta is involved (ascending aorta, aortic arch, and descending aorta), operative exposure may require staged approaches via median sternotomy and lateral thoracotomy. Saccular aneurysms may be repaired by tangential excision with oversewing of the aneurysm base. As most thoracic aortic aneurysms are of atherosclerotic origin, all elective cases must be assessed for common coexisting risk factors, such as cardiac, renal, or cerebrovascular functional impairment, and appropriate treatment of these conditions accomplished preoperatively. Hypertension and diabetes mellitus should be controlled, and proper attention should be given to respiratory preparation. New or increasing pain, pleural effusion, periaortic hematoma, occlusion of major brachiocephalic aortic branches, and cardiac tamponade are all evidence of an acutely expanding or leaking thoracic aortic aneurysm and indicate the need for emergency repair.

Based on related anatomic structures and the possible need for special perfusion techniques to protect essential organs during aortic cross-clamping, the risks and results of surgical treatment vary depending on the aneurysm site and extent. Although short cross-clamp times and partial left heart bypass protect many organs from infarction or ischemic damage, paraplegia as a result of anterior spinal infarction is a significant complication in 15% of patients who have interposition grafts of the descending thoracic aorta for aneurysm. In these patients, the anterior spinal artery is dependent for adequate perfusion on the artery of Adamkewicz, which arises from an intercostal artery in the T10–L1 segment of the aorta. Attempts to include the appropriate segmental artery in the repair by implanting all intercostal arteries that backbleed into the prosthesis have not changed the incidence of paraplegia. The use of sophisticated arteriography techniques has made it possible to identify the specific intercostal artery to reimplant, lowering the paraplegia rate to 5% in some reports. Other techniques using partial bypass with segmental aneurysm reclamping and intercostal implantation, spinal cooling, and cerebrospinal fluid spinal decompression also show promise in decreasing the rate of paraplegia.

Recently a new method of interposition grafting by "endovascular" technique has been introduced. Prosthetic tube material is collapsed into a small cylindrical carrier and delivered to the aneurysm site via percutaneous or open catheter insertion through the common femoral artery. Once there, it is expanded into position proximally, then distally, and secured into position against the aortic wall by metallic expandable stents, thus excluding the aneurysm from blood flow and providing a new channel. Although several repairs of thoracic aortic aneurysms have been reported by this technique, its indications, complications, and durability have yet to be determined in larger numbers of patients.

FOLLOW-UP

Operated patients must be seen during the first 90 days for monitoring of healing and the occurrence of complications. Median sternotomy incisions are subject to infection, dehiscence, and instability. Thoracotomy incisions, in addition, cause more pain with possible associated chest wall splinting, atelectasis, pneumonia, and effusions.

Yearly visits are important to watch for signs and symptoms of new aneurysm formation in other locations, pseudoaneurysm formation at anastomotic sites, and progression of associated occlusive disease. As in the initial diagnostic workup, chest radiographs can be used for screening for thoracic aortic changes, but definitive assessment of a suspected aortic aneurysm is best done by CT, MRI, or TEE.

Control of hypertension, discontinuation of smoking, and proper ongoing treatment of chronic obstructive pulmonary disease are essential for both postoperative and medically treated, unoperated patients. Moreover, medically treated patients should be especially alert for new symptoms of aneurysm enlargement. Sudden onset of new chest or back pain is considered an urgent problem. Many patients with atherosclerotic disease should be placed on a dietary regimen and, if necessary, medications to lower the low-density lipoprotein cholesterol to below 100 mg/dL (2.6 mmol/dL).

DISCUSSION
Prevalence and Incidence

The actual prevalence and incidence of thoracic aortic aneurysm in the general population are unknown. Often, these aneurysms are discovered during workup for other causes, and there is no universal screening test available with which to develop a good estimate of their incidence. Most of the few studies in the literature examining the prevalence and rupture rates of thoracic aortic aneurysms were performed before modern noninvasive imaging techniques were available. The median age at diagnosis is 65 for men and 77 for women. Both sexes appear to be affected equally.

Related Basic Science
Anatomic Derangement

Three anatomic types of thoracic aortic aneurysm are recognized. First, a fusiform aneurysm consists of a circumferential dilation of the aorta, resulting from a diffuse weakness of a segment of aortic wall. Second, a saccular aneurysm is a localized, balloonlike dilation of the wall, beginning at a narrow neck on a small portion of the aorta. Fusiform and saccular aneurysms almost invariably contain laminated clot that may

obscure their true size on aortogram. Third, the dissecting aneurysm begins from an intimal tear with subintimal dissection of blood through the media, either prograde, antegrade, or both. Two channels are produced that conduct blood flow, often with a fenestration joining them distally. These are referred to as the "true lumen" and "false lumen," with the former being lined by intima and the latter by media. A blind-ended false lumen may thrombose if its enlargement is stopped, in which case medical management is optimized. An aneurysm may have mixed characteristics, but by the time the aorta has become aneurysmal, its original wall components are largely replaced by fibrous tissue. The most common site for thoracic aortic aneurysm is the ascending aorta (51%), followed by the descending position (38%), and the arch (1%). Autopsy studies have shown aortic dissection to be the most common cause (53%), followed by atherosclerosis (29%), aortitis (8%), cystic medial degeneration (6%), and syphilis (4%). Many patients have coexisting abdominal aortic aneurysm. Most atherosclerotic aneurysms occur in the descending aorta, just distal to the left subclavian artery.

Degenerative Etiology

Atherosclerotic degeneration of the aorta involves intimal deposition of lipid, which becomes plaque. With aging, plaque hemorrhage, calcification, ulceration, and superimposed thrombus formation occur. The media is eventually affected, and with medial destruction of the aortic wall, aneurysm formation follows. This process is accelerated by coexisting diabetes mellitus, hypercholesterolemia, hypertension, and smoking. Although the proximal descending aorta just distal to the left subclavian artery origin is preferentially affected, the ascending aorta and arch are involved more commonly in patients with diabetes mellitus and type II hyperlipidemia.

Cystic medial degeneration weakens elastic and smooth muscle fibers of the media, with resulting tortuosity, elongation, and fusiform dilation. There are also increased collagen fibers and mucoid ground substance. Marfan's syndrome causes degeneration of elastic fibers of the aortic media at a younger age. This process is often associated with aortic dissection and is most severe at the aortic root. Proximal aortic aneurysms that include the sinuses of Valsalva are a frequent presentation. Myxomatous degeneration of the aortic and mitral valves in Marfan's syndrome causes valvular incompetence, which contributes to heart failure.

Infection and Inflammation

Bacterial infection of the aorta usually occurs as a result of bloodborne inoculation into a previously damaged or atherosclerotic area of intima. Wall destruction then leads to aneurysm formation. These mycotic aneurysms are usually secondary to bacterial endocarditis, but may occur after bacteremia from noncardiac sources. Salmonella enteritis is a common cause. Although rare now, adjacent tuberculous lymph nodes may infect the aortic wall by direct spread, causing caseous necrosis and aneurysm formation. Syphilitic wall necrosis also produces mycotic aneurysms of the aorta. Takayasu's disease and giant cell arteritis also cause aortitis and weaken the wall structure, allowing aneurysms to form.

Trauma

Traumatic aortic aneurysms are usually due to transection occurring during closed chest trauma by deceleration injury in automobile or aviation accidents. Thus, they are more properly classified as pseudoaneurysms. Most often, the proximal descending aorta just distal to the left subclavian artery at the insertion of the ligamentum arteriosum is involved. Less often, the proximal ascending aorta is affected near the aortic root, and, rarely, the aneurysm occurs at the level of the diaphragm. Traumatic aneurysms may also follow direct penetrating injury at any location. When discovered acutely, traumatic aortic aneurysm requires emergency treatment. If the patient presents longer than 6 or 8 weeks after aortic trauma, however, the risk of acute rupture is small. These aneurysms enlarge slowly in their chronic phase and can be incidentally found decades after initial injury. Elective repair should be performed when the diagnosis is made.

Natural History and Its Modification with Treatment

Few studies have been performed to determine the natural history of thoracic aortic aneurysm since modern imaging techniques have been available. Five-year survival of untreated thoracic aortic aneurysms approaches 20%. Most deaths were due to rupture. The growth rate for thoracic aortic aneurysms 5 cm or larger in diameter is greater than for smaller ones: the 3-year cumulative survival is greater than 90% for aneurysms initially measured at less than 5 cm, and only 60% for the others. Experience has shown that the symptom-free patient with a small aneurysm, growing by 0.3 cm in diameter per year (the average amount), can be safely observed with serial studies every 6 to 12 months and operated when the longest transverse dimension reaches 6 cm. The operative mortality of repair varies between 5 and 25%, depending on the extent of the aneurysm, the comorbid factors present, and the experience of the surgical team.

Prevention

No preventive measures are currently available, except for treatment of underlying disorders when possible (e.g., atherosclerosis, infection, inflammation, Marfan's syndrome). Traumatic disruption of the aorta should be found and treated surgically at the time of injury to prevent aneurysm formation. Research is continuing into etiology, genetic basis, and possible prevention of aortic aneurysm pathogenesis.

Cost Containment

The most cost-effective and beneficial mode of therapy is early detection and repair to prevent death by rupture or complications of aneurysm enlargement. Currently, chest radiography and CT scans offer the best diagnostic capability at reasonable cost. The efficacy and cost of endovascular repair of selected cases remains to be established.

REFERENCES

Crawford ES, Coselli JS, Svensson MB, et al. Diffuse aneurysmal disease (chronic aortic dissection, Marfan and mega aorta syndromes) and multiple aneurysm. Ann Surg 1990;211:521.

Dapunt IE, Galla JD, Sadeghi AM, et al. The natural history of thoracic aortic aneurysms. J Thorac Cardiovasc Surg 1994;107:1323.

Goldstein SA, Mintz GS, Lindsay J Jr. Aorta: Comprehensive evaluation by echocardiography and transesophageal echocardiography. J Am Soc Echocardiogr 1993;6:634.

Money SR, Hollier LH. The management of thoracoabdominal aneurysms. In: Cameron JL, Balch CM, Langer B, et al. Advances in surgery. St. Louis: Mosby-Year Book 1994:285.

Piccione W Jr, Delaria GA, Najafi H. Descending thoracic aneurysms. In: Bergan JJ, Yao JST, eds. Aortic surgery. Philadelphia: Saunders, 1989:909.

Pressler V, McNamara JJ. Aneurysm of the thoracic aorta: Review of 260 cases. J Thorac Cardiovasc Surg 1985;89:50.

CHAPTER 15–66

Aortic Dissection

Joseph Lindsay, Jr., M.D.

DEFINITION

Longitudinal cleavage of the elastic lamina of the aortic media by a column of blood is the defining abnormality of aortic dissection (Figure 15–66–1). The "false channel" created by the plane of dissection communicates through one or more intimal tears with the "true" aortic lumen. One of these tears is almost always located near the proximal limit of the false channel. Aortic dissections should not be confused with aortic aneurysms, which consist of focal or diffuse dilation of all layers of the aortic wall.

ETIOLOGY

Hypertension with its attendant increase in wall stress is a central factor in the pathogenesis of this disorder. That is not to say that hypertension is the sole factor. Increased aortic wall stress may be unable to produce dissection unless the aortic media is susceptible because of a heritable or an acquired process.

It is clear that dissection is encountered with greater than expected frequency in patients known or suspected of having an abnormal aortic media, such as those with Marfan's syndrome. The same is true for those with coarctation of the aorta, anuloaortic ectasia, or bicuspid aortic valve.

On histologic examination, the aortic media in many patients with aortic dissection demonstrates fragmented, degenerated elastic fibers. Pools of mucopolysaccharide fill the areas vacated by the degenerated fibers. These lesions, so-called *cystic medial necrosis*, do not seem to be specific for any one process and indeed are found in the aortic wall of older individuals who have no overt aortic disease.

CRITERIA FOR DIAGNOSIS
Suggestive

The presenting clinical findings suggest the diagnosis of aortic dissection in nearly all instances. In fact, unless the initial examiners

promptly consider this possibility, the diagnosis may be delayed and the patient's chance for recovery compromised.

Sudden, severe pain in the trunk signals the onset of dissection in the great majority of instances. In those unusual cases in which the onset is painless, syncope is the most common initial manifestation. The characteristic patient is a hypertensive individual more than 50 years of age. In younger or normotensive patients, Marfan's syndrome, aortic coarctation, anuloaortic ectasia, or bicuspid aortic valve are frequent.

Once the possibility of aortic dissection has been considered, supporting physical findings such as diminished or absent arterial pulses or the murmur of aortic valve regurgitation are often easily identified.

Definitive

The diagnosis may be reliably confirmed by identifying the medial cleavage by means of transesophageal echocardiography, computed tomography, magnetic resonance imaging, or aortography.

CLINICAL MANIFESTATIONS
Subjective

Sudden, excruciating pain, presumably attributable to progression of the medial cleavage, announces the onset of aortic dissection in 90% of instances. Patients may describe the pain as "cutting," "ripping," or "tearing," but such vivid descriptors cannot always be elicited. Those afflicted most commonly locate the discomfort in the anterior chest, somewhat less frequently in the interscapular area, and less often still in the epigastrium or lumbar region. The propensity of the discomfort of aortic dissection to involve more than one of these locations, either simultaneously or sequentially, aids recognition. Even though pain in these sites initially may suggest more common processes (e.g., acute myocardial infarction or acute cholecystitis), the alert examiner must consider the possibility of aortic dissection when these possibilities are not immediately obvious.

A sudden neurologic episode heralds the onset of most instances of "painless" aortic dissection. Syncope, the most frequent neurologic

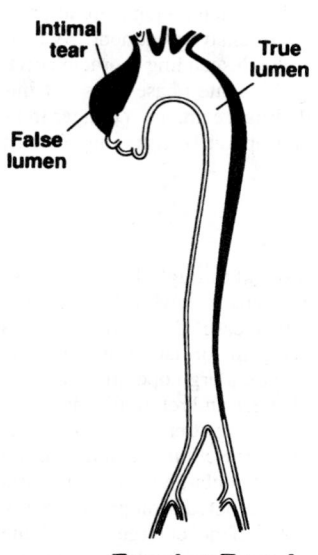

Type I or Type A or Proximal

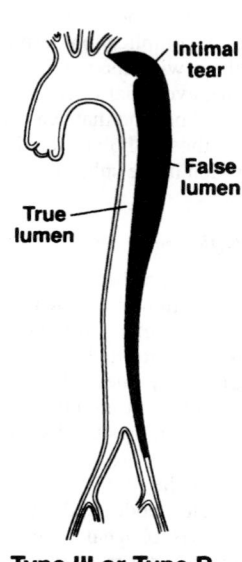

Type III or Type B or Distal

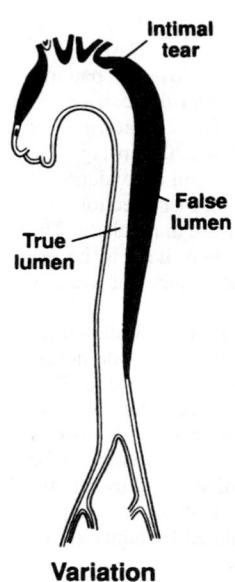

Variation

Figure 15–66–1. Artist's conception of the various anatomic patterns of aortic dissection. The most common variety, proximal dissection (type I of DeBakey), is shown on the left. The only other common variety, distal dissection (type III of DeBakey), is shown in the center, and an important, unusual variation is shown on the right. Depicted in each are the proximal ("entrance") tear and the false channel. Note that the true lumen is narrowed in all three instances. *(Source: Lindsay J Jr. Aortic Dissection. Heart Dis Stroke 1992;1:69. Reproduced with permission from the American Heart Association.)*

event, seems always to reflect external rupture, almost always of the ascending aorta into the pericardial space. Less frequently, focal neurologic signs reflect arterial occlusion of the cerebral or spinal circulation.

Rarely, investigation of patients with aortic regurgitation, with an arterial occlusion in a limb, or with an abnormal aortic silhouette on a chest x-ray film, to the surprise of the examining physician, discloses that an aortic dissection has produced the abnormality.

Objective

Physical Examination

Although none are diagnostic of aortic dissection, physical findings that greatly increase the probability of its presence can usually be detected on examination. The murmur of aortic valve regurgitation can be heard in about half of all patients with involvement of the ascending aorta. Loss or diminution of an arterial pulse is also frequent in that subgroup, so that only a small minority have neither of these two cardinal findings. In contrast, patients with dissection limited to the descending aorta often lack these confirmatory physical findings.

The vast majority of individuals with aortic dissection report a history of hypertension or have evidence of this process on physical examination (e.g., left ventricular hypertrophy or vascular changes in the optic fundi). Blood pressure elevation may be modest during the acute process, but extreme elevations are encountered, particularly in those with dissection limited to the descending aorta. Renal ischemia consequent to the dissection has been invoked to explain diastolic pressures of 140 to 160 mm Hg or more.

Twenty percent of patients with dissection involving the ascending aorta present with hypotension. Such a presentation requires immediate consideration of operative treatment, as external rupture almost always is responsible.

Routine Laboratory Abnormalities

Of all the routine diagnostic studies, only the chest x-ray film provides useful information. The aortic silhouette is frequently abnormal. On the other hand, when the possibility of aortic dissection has been raised by history and physical examination, a normal aortic shadow does not exclude the diagnosis.

PLANS

Diagnostic

Differential Diagnosis

Myocardial infarction must be differentiated from aortic dissection. The clinical features of dissection, including the location of the pain in the upper back, the development of a neurologic deficit, the development of aortic valve regurgitation, the development of unequal pulses, and an enlarged aorta on the chest x-ray film, serve to identify dissection. The electrocardiographic signs of infarction favor the diagnosis of myocardial infarction, but obstruction of the ostium of a coronary artery may rarely result from dissection.

Diagnostic Options

Transesophageal echocardiography is the most convenient, rapid, and most easily applied imaging modality. It can be performed in the emergency department or the intensive care unit. Its accuracy equals or exceeds that of any other imaging technique.

Computed tomography after intravenous injection of contrast material, probably the imaging technique most widely available, is also quite accurate in identifying the presence of aortic dissection.

More invasive than either of these two modalities, but not unduly risky in experienced hands, aortography can best be accomplished by means of a contrast injection through a catheter placed in the aorta. This procedure may be required to provide detailed information regarding the site of intimal tear, extent of medial dissection, and location of any obstructed branch vessels.

Magnetic resonance provides highly detailed images of the aorta and can be very valuable for the management of patients with aortic dissection; however, it is not as widely available and not as easily applied to very ill patients as the other three.

Recommended Approach

Transesophageal echocardiography is recommended as the best diagnostic tool to use in patients suspected of having dissection of the aorta.

Therapeutic

Therapeutic Options

Successful therapy of aortic dissection requires that progression of the medial cleavage be halted and that external rupture of the weakened aortic wall be prevented. Inasmuch as the aortic defect is structural, operative treatment represents the most effective long-term remedy. The preferred operation consists of resection of the segment of aorta containing the entry tear, closure of the false channel at the transected ends, and reapproximation of the ends either directly or by means of a graft.

Aggressive drug treatment designed to lower aortic pressure and to reduce its rate of rise is indicated prior to operative repair and, in selected patients, as an alternative to surgery. Such therapy retards the progression of the medial dissection and reduces the likelihood of external rupture.

Immediate intravenous drug therapy should be employed in patients who are not hypotensive. Sodium nitroprusside (Nipride) can be infused at an initial rate of 0.5 μg/kg per minute. The infusion rate is titrated to attain a systolic blood pressure of 100 to 120 mm Hg. The target blood pressure may need to be raised on detection of evidence of hypoperfusion of vital organs or lowered if the pain of dissection persists and adequate cerebral function and urine flow are maintained. The usually effective rate of 2 to 4 μg/kg per minute may have to be exceeded, but at rates above 10 μg/kg per minute the danger of cyanide toxicity is excessive.

In addition to lowering mean aortic pressure, drug therapy should reduce the rate of aortic pressure rise. Consequently, beta-adrenergic blocking drugs should be administered along with nitroprusside. Propranolol (Inderal) can be given intravenously in 0.5-mg increments at 1- to 5-minute intervals until the pulse rate slows or until a total dose of 1.5 mg per 10 kg of body weight has been reached. This dosing can be repeated at 4- to 6-hour intervals. Esmolol (Brevibloc), an intravenous, short-acting beta-adrenergic blocker, is an attractive alternative to propranolol because its effects may be rapidly modulated by adjusting its infusion rate.

Intravenous labetalol (Normodyne) has been reported to be an effective alternative to the nitroprusside and beta-adrenergic blockade, but as yet no large experience has been reported. An initial intravenous infusion of 20 mg over 2 minutes has been recommended. The hypotensive effects should be apparent in 10 minutes. If the response has not been adequate, additional boluses of 40 to 80 mg may be employed at 10-minute intervals up to a total dose of 300 mg. The half-life of labetalol is 5 to 8 hours. When the blood pressure has begun to rise after initial control, a slow infusion (initially 2 mg/min) may be employed, but because of the long half-life of the agent, the infusion should be interrupted once blood pressure has again been controlled. Intravenous therapy may be replaced by oral labetalol at an appropriate time.

For individuals who cannot be given beta-blocking drugs, trimethaphan camsylate (Arfonad), an intravenous ganglionic blocking agent, may be used in lieu of nitroprusside at an infusion rate of 1 to 2 mg/min. This agent is not as predictable in its antihypertensive effect as nitroprusside, especially after 24 to 48 hours when tachyphylaxis appears.

Hydralazine (Apresoline), diazoxide (Hyperstat), minoxidil (Loniten), and other direct vasodilator drugs cannot be recommended because of their potential for producing a reflex increase in the rate of rise of arterial pressure. Reports of the use of calcium channel-blocking agents and of angiotensin-converting enzyme inhibitors have appeared, but there is little experience with these agents during the acute illness.

Recommended Approach

Sudden, life-threatening complications, such as very severe hypertension, cardiac tamponade, massive hemorrhage, severe aortic valve regurgitation, or ischemic injury to the myocardium, central nervous system, or kidneys threaten patients with acute dissection. Thus, optimal management during the acute phase requires close surveillance of vascular pressures, urine flow, mental status, and neurologic signs in an intensive care unit. Pain relief may be difficult even with potent narcotics, but can usually be attained with drug therapy to reduce arterial pressure.

As has been stated, operative treatment must be considered in all patients with aortic dissection, but certain subgroups can be recognized whose clinical presentation dictates the timing of operation. At one extreme, surgery must be undertaken immediately in individuals who are hypotensive on admission, as they will have already had external rupture. On the other hand, operative treatment may never be an option in those with advanced age or associated cardiac, renal, or pulmonary disease, and may not be justified for those with severe neurologic injury from the dissection. In these inoperable individuals, antihypertensive therapy is continued indefinitely by converting to an oral drug regimen that avoids the direct vasodilators.

For patients whose dissection involves the ascending aorta, operative repair should be undertaken as soon as the patient can be stabilized and

appropriate diagnostic information compiled. Such patients are at great risk of a fatal complication despite antihypertensive treatment. By contrast, for those with dissection limited to the descending thoracic aorta, it is now believed that operation during the acute phase does not improve survival beyond that achieved with drug treatment. Younger individuals and those who are relatively good operative risks may benefit from operation in the subacute phase.

FOLLOW-UP

The patient who has been successfully brought through the acute phase of aortic dissection, either with operative repair or with drug therapy alone, requires lifelong follow-up. In either case, the aortic wall has been weakened and made subject to aneurysm formation and rupture. This is particularly true in those who did not undergo operation. Hypertension must be controlled to reduce wall stress and retard this process.

Once the patient has been stabilized as an outpatient on an appropriate antihypertensive regime, quarterly visits for clinical evaluation are optimal during the first year. Any suspicion of enlargement of the aorta on x-ray requires additional imaging with computed tomographic x-ray study or transesophageal echocardiography. If no enlargement of the aorta is evident after the first year, the time interval between examinations can be lengthened.

DISCUSSION
Prevalence and Incidence

Aortic dissection, encountered most commonly in hypertensive subjects in the sixth decade of life or later, is uncommon as compared with entities such as myocardial infarction from which it must be distinguished. Nevertheless, several are encountered each year in any busy emergency room.

Natural History and Its Modification with Treatment

The natural history of aortic dissection varies substantially depending on the extent of its aortic involvement (Figure 15–66–1). The most common pattern of involvement (type I of DeBakey) accounts for about two thirds of all dissections. The proximal limit of a type I dissection lies just above the aortic valve, and an intimal ("entrance") tear is typically located near its proximal end. The medial dissection often extends the entire length of the aorta. Type II of DeBakey, a subgroup of type I, includes patients whose dissection is limited to the ascending aorta. Without surgical correction and despite aggressive antihypertensive treatment, patients in these two categories experience a mortality of nearly 90% during the acute phase of their illness. With effective early operative repair the mortality, although still high, improves to about 25%. The only other common pattern, type III of DeBakey, includes about a quarter of all dissections. In this type the medial dissection is limited to the distal arch and descending aorta. The "entrance" tear characteristically lies just distal to the left subclavian artery. Even without modern therapy, type III carries a far more favorable prognosis than do those involving the ascending aorta; and with modern hypertensive therapy, acute survival approaches 75 to 80%. Late survival for any type after appropriate acute treatment is surprisingly good. Saccular aneurysm, rupture, and progression of aortic valve regurgitation may require additional treatment, but late mortality is often attributable to cerebrovascular disease or other complications of hypertension and not directly related to the dissection.

Prevention

The identification and control of hypertension almost certainly prevent the occurrence of many, perhaps most, dissections.

Cost Containment

The care of these very ill patients demands the most expensive and resource-intensive care. Unfortunately, even in the present cost-containment environment no specific suggestions can be offered for cost containment.

REFERENCES

Cigarrao JE, Isselbacher EM, DeSanctis RW, Eagle KA. Diagnostic imaging in the evaluation of suspected aortic dissection: Old directions and new standards. N Engl J Med 1993;328:35.

Crawford ES. The diagnosis and management of aortic dissection. JAMA 1990;264:2537.

DeBakey ME, Henly WS, Cooley DA, et al. Surgical management of dissecting aneurysm of the aorta. J Thorac Cardiovasc Surg 1965;49:130.

DeSanctis RW, Doroghazi RM, Austen WG, Buckley MJ. Aortic dissection. N Engl J Med 1987;317:1060.

Doroghazi RM, Slater EE, DeSanctis RW, et al. Long term survival of patients with treated aortic dissection. J Am Coll Cardiol 1984;3:1026.

Lindsay J Jr. Aortic dissection. In: Lindsay J Jr, ed. Diseases of the aorta. Philadelphia: Lea & Febiger, 1994:127.

Roberts WC. Aortic dissection, anatomy, consequences, and causes. Am Heart J 1981;101:195.

CHAPTER 15–67

Abdominal Aortic Aneurysm

Patrick M. Battey, M.D., and Robert B. Smith III, M.D.

DEFINITION

Aneurysmal disease of the abdominal aorta is defined by abnormal dilation of the abdominal aorta on physical examination or roentgenographic studies.

ETIOLOGY

Infrarenal aortic aneurysms are commonly (90%) due to aortic atherosclerosis. There is also degeneration of the elastic fibers in the arterial wall, causing their fracture and depletion of the muscular and collagen elements of the medial layer. Gradual dilation and expansion follow.

An increased incidence of aortic aneurysms in first-degree relatives of patients with abdominal aortic aneurysms suggests that aneurysm formation may be linked to hereditary changes in collagen and/or elastin metabolism.

Other rare causes of abdominal aortic aneurysms include syphilitic and bacterial infections (mycotic), trauma, previous aortic bypass surgery (anastomotic), and congenital abnormalities in the arterial wall seen with Ehlers–Danlos and Marfan's syndromes.

CRITERIA FOR DIAGNOSIS

Suggestive

An easily palpable pulsatile abdominal mass, usually located to the left of the midline, superior to the umbilicus, may suggest the presence of an abdominal aortic aneurysm. Calcification within the wall of an aneurysm may be apparent on abdominal x-ray films as a thin, opaque line. Lateral abdominal films may outline the calcified anterior wall of an aneurysm.

Definitive

In most cases, findings on physical examination and abdominal roentgenograms are sufficient for the diagnosis of abdominal aortic aneurysm. If body habitus makes abdominal palpation difficult and mural calcification is not visible on the x-ray films, additional studies may be needed. These are discussed under Diagnostic Options.

CLINICAL MANIFESTATIONS

Subjective

Abdominal aortic aneurysms are commonly present in men in their seventh or eighth decades as asymptomatic pulsatile abdominal masses. The majority of aneurysms are discovered by physical examination or radiologic evaluation for other reasons. There may be a family history of aneurysmal disease, and the patient usually gives a history of systemic arterial hypertension and tobacco use.

When symptomatic, a constant midepigastric or lumbar pain may be described. The pain may result from leakage of blood into the surrounding retroperitoneal tissue or rapid expansion of the aneurysm wall.

OBJECTIVE

Physical Examination

An abdominal aortic aneurysm larger than 5 cm in transverse diameter can be detected with reasonable certainty on physical examination in most individuals in the absence of abdominal obesity. With the patient supine and fully relaxed, attention is focused near or above the umbilicus at the level of the aortic bifurcation. Bimanual palpation may delineate the lateral walls of the aorta and provide an estimate of aortic width. Tenderness with careful palpation should be noted and may indicate rapid expansion. A thorough evaluation of carotid and extremity pulses should be included to establish the diagnosis of associated arterial occlusive disease.

Peripheral arterial embolization of thrombotic or atherosclerotic debris from the lumen of the aneurysm may result in discrete painful lesions on the tips of the toes ("trash foot") and may be the first manifestation of an abdominal aortic aneurysm. Limb-threatening ischemia may also be present.

Free rupture into the peritoneal cavity may present with profound hypotension and abdominal distention, which may mimic peritonitis from a perforated viscus.

Routine Laboratory Abnormalities

The routine laboratory tests are usually normal except for the abdominal x-ray film. There may be associated abnormalities such as hyperlipidemia.

PLANS

Diagnostic

Differential Diagnosis

The differential diagnosis of an asymptomatic pulsatile abdominal mass includes aortic aneurysm, hepatomegaly, and tumors of the stomach, intestine, or retroperitoneum transmitting the nearby aortic pulsation. An ectatic aorta in a thin individual may suggest abnormal aortic enlargement or may be accompanied by paramedian linear calcifications on abdominal x-ray films.

Pain from an expanding or leaking aortic aneurysm may be identical to any acute abdominal problem such as perforated peptic ulcer, pancreatitis, cholecystitis, appendicitis, diverticulitis, and renal colic.

Diagnostic Options

Abdominal ultrasound is reliable in the detection and measurement of the size of abdominal aortic aneurysms. Repeat sonographic examination may demonstrate rapid growth patterns, identifying those asymptomatic aneurysms that warrant surgical repair. Computed axial tomography (CT scan) is valuable when abdominal pain accompanies an abdominal aortic aneurysm. This study may reveal contained retroperitoneal leakage, irregularities within the outer calcified aneurysm wall, or a thick adventitial peel suggestive of the inflammatory variant of aortic aneurysms. Magnetic resonance imaging (MRI) is also very accurate in the evaluation of aneurysms of the abdominal aorta.

Aortography is frequently used in preoperative planning for aneurysm resection, but is not as useful in establishing the diagnosis. The contrast study may delineate the proximal extent of the aneurysm with particular concern for the proximity of the renal and mesenteric vessels, but an estimate of size may be misleading as the lumen of the aneurysm is frequently filled with laminated thrombus, concentrating the dye in the central lumen and obscuring the extent of aneurysmal dilation.

Recommended Approach

Abdominal ultrasound is the screening procedure of choice for an asymptomatic aortic aneurysm. It is safe, noninvasive, reproducible, and relatively inexpensive. In the presence of symptoms in a stable patient or a technically difficult ultrasound, a CT scan provides the anatomic detail.

Therapeutic

Therapeutic Options

Surgical resection and replacement by prosthetic graft are recommended for asymptomatic abdominal aortic aneurysms larger than 5 cm in the good-risk patient. Comorbid factors of previous myocardial infarction, angina pectoris, congestive heart failure, extreme obesity, and decreased renal or pulmonary function may argue for continued observation of an aneurysm between 5 and 6 cm in anteroposterior or transverse diameter. Transfemoral endovascular repair of aortic aneurysms uses intraarterial fixation of a prosthetic graft with stents or other devices and may prove to be an alternative to surgical resection in carefully selected individuals.

Preoperative evaluation prior to elective aneurysm repair should include evaluation of cardiac, cerebrovascular, or renal vascular impairment. Exercise stress testing, radionuclide cardiac imaging with pharmacologic stress testing (Persantine, dobutamine), or coronary angiography may identify patients at risk for perioperative myocardial infarction. Several reports have appeared recently that do not recommend the need for these tests in the preoperative evaluation of asymptomatic patients with abdominal aneurysms. In patients with a history of transient ischemic attacks or stroke, or in whom a carotid bruit is detected, direct carotid imaging with duplex scanning or carotid angiography may identify a critical stenosis in the extracranial carotid system. Renal artery bypass for preservation of renal function may be performed concomitantly with aneurysm repair if high-grade renal artery stenosis is demonstrated on preoperative aortography.

Recommended Approach

Aneurysm repair is the treatment of choice for aneurysms larger than 5 cm in the good-risk patient. In selected patients, coronary artery bypass and/or carotid endarterectomy may assume priority over elective aneurysmectomy. Observation is not warranted for any symptomatic aneurysm, regardless of size, as pain usually indicates impending rupture.

FOLLOW-UP

Semiannual follow-up visits are recommended for the patient with an asymptomatic abdominal aortic aneurysm less than 5 cm in diameter. Aneurysm size is determined at each visit with aortic ultrasound by noting the anteroposterior and transverse diameters. Repair is recommended at the onset of symptoms or if the aneurysm exceeds 5 cm. Patients with atherosclerosis should be treated to decrease vascular risk factors such as smoking, hyperlipidemia, and systemic arterial hypertension.

DISCUSSION

Prevalence and Incidence

Abdominal aortic aneurysms are found in approximately 2% of postmortem examinations. There is some suggestion from population-based epidemiologic studies that the overall incidence of aortic aneurysms may be increasing to the range of 1 per 100,000 person-years. Although the greatest increase is seen in the detection of small aneurysms, suggesting an increased awareness and earlier patient evaluation, increases have also been noted in complicated, symptomatic, and large aneurysms as well.

Related Basic Science

Although atherosclerosis contributes to the degeneration of aortic structural elements, hereditary factors and biochemical changes may play a dominant role in the etiology of abdominal aortic aneurysms in most patients. Both X-linked and autosomal dominant mechanisms of inheritance are postulated to explain an increased incidence of aneurysms in first-degree relatives of patients with aortic aneurysms, with X-linked variance as the most common type. Some imbalance between α-antitrypsin, a major inhibitor of elastase, and elastase may be an etiologic factor in aneurysm formation. Such an inherited abnormality in elastin metabolism may explain the definite familial clustering seen in some patients. An acquired imbalance may certainly be present in others. Smoking and hypertension are frequently found in the history of patients with aneurysm disease. Chronic lung disease may predispose to a more rapid growth rate of aneurysms, and one may postulate whether a defect in α-antitrypsin level is common to both conditions.

Natural History and Its Modification with Treatment

The best predictors of possible complications are size of aneurysm and presence of symptoms: Aneurysms greater than 7 cm have a risk of rupture within 3 years of greater than 50%. Associated coronary atherosclerotic heart disease and cerebrovascular disease combine for an expected 5-year mortality rate in this population subgroup of nearly 30%. With aneurysms greater than 6 cm in anteroposterior or transverse diameter, aneurysm rupture is the major cause of death.

Elective aneurysm repair may be accomplished with a mortality rate of less than 5%. Perioperative complications include myocardial infarction, hemorrhage, distal embolization, acute renal failure, and ischemic colitis. Long-term complications following repair (anastomotic aneurysm, graft infection, or thrombosis) are seen in less than 10% of cases. After rupture, the immediate surgical mortality exceeds 50%.

Prevention

The prevention of abdominal aortic aneurysms rests with control of underlying risk factors for atherosclerosis. Control of hypertension and avoidance of cigarette smoking may alleviate this risk. Once an aneurysm has formed, the major goal is to avoid rupture. The only effective treatment currently known to prevent rupture is graft replacement.

Cost Containment

Elective repair of large or symptomatic aneurysms provides the most cost-efficient mode of therapy as it removes the threat of rupture. With the small, asymptomatic aneurysm, regular follow-up with ultrasonography provides the safest and least expensive method of management.

REFERENCES

Bernstein EF, Chan EL. Abdominal aortic aneurysm in high risk patients: Outcome of selective management based on size and expansion rate. Ann Surg 1984;200:255.

Hollier LH, Taylor LM, Oshsner J. Recommended indications for operative repair of abdominal aortic aneurysms. J Vasc Surg 1992;15:1046.

Lindsay J Jr, DeBakey ME, Beale AC Jr. Diseases of the aorta. In: Hurst JW, ed. The heart. 7th ed. New York: McGraw-Hill, 1990:1408.

Szilagyi DE, Smith RF, DeRusso FJ, et al. Contribution of abdominal aortic aneurysmectomy to prolongation of life. Ann Surg 1966;164:678.

Thompson JE, Hollier LH, Patmon RD, Persson AV. Surgical management of abdominal aortic aneurysm. Ann Surg 1975;181:654.

Obstructive Atherosclerotic Disease of the Terminal Aorta and Its Immediate Branches

Joseph D. Ansley, M.D.

DEFINITION

Obstructive atherosclerotic disease of the terminal aorta and the iliac or femoral arteries is a condition characterized by progressive accumulation of atherosclerotic plaque, which partially or totally occludes the lumen of the arteries and results in reduction of blood flow to the pelvis, buttocks, thighs, or lower extremities. This reduction in blood flow causes clinical symptoms or physical changes when tissue perfusion in the areas supplied by these arteries is inadequate to meet metabolic demands.

ETIOLOGY

Atherosclerotic occlusive disease of the terminal aorta and its immediate branches is one of the several manifestations of generalized atherosclerosis. It occurs predominantly in the male population, especially in those with a history of long-term cigarette smoking; usually, it becomes symptomatic in the middle decades of life and later. Pathogenesis of the atheromatous plaque that progressively occludes the lumen of the aorta, iliac arteries, and femoral arteries is multifactorial, involving abnormalities in lipoprotein metabolism, injury to the endothelial layer of the arterial intima, platelet deposition, and smooth muscle cell proliferation. Hemodynamic stress related to hypertension, heart rate, and the relationship of flow velocity to vessel wall shear stress in the aortoiliac region are important factors in localization and thickness of the atheromatous plaque. The process begins as a minimally raised lesion on the endothelial surface known as a fatty streak and evolves into a fibrous plaque composed of lipids, smooth muscle cells, and connective tissue protruding into the lumen of the artery. As the atheromatous lesion progresses, there is further deposition of lipids and proliferation of smooth muscle cells and connective tissue, with areas of necrosis, ulceration, and calcification which eventually result in partial or total occlusion of the lumen. Common sites for development of atheromatous plaques are areas with increased turbulence of blood flow, associated with low and oscillating wall shear stress such as the aortic bifurcation, the common iliac artery bifurcation, and origins of the superficial femoral and profunda femoris arteries from the common femoral artery.

CRITERIA FOR DIAGNOSIS

The diagnosis of atherosclerotic occlusive disease of the terminal aorta and its branches is based on the clinical history and physical examination. A history of intermittent claudication involving the buttocks and thighs is usually present, or in the more advanced stages there may be a history of rest pain and/or ischemic tissue changes in the lower extremities indicating the threat of limb loss. In the male patient there may also be the additional history of impotence. On physical examination, there is a decrease or absence of arterial pulses at the femoral or more distal levels, and this is accompanied by a decrease in the segmental arterial pressures at the thigh, calf, and ankle levels.

CLINICAL MANIFESTATIONS

Subjective

Symptoms of atherosclerotic occlusive disease of the terminal aorta and its branches usually begin in the middle or later decades of life. This process occurs more frequently in men than in women by a ratio of approximately 4:1, although male preponderance has been decreasing over the past 20 to 30 years. Almost all patients with significant atherosclerotic occlusive disease have a long history of tobacco usage. As the atherosclerotic process is generalized, ischemic symptoms and physical changes may be bilateral; however, the degree of occlusion in the iliac or femoral arteries is often unequal, resulting in unilateral symptoms or physical findings. The diagnosis of obstructive atherosclerotic disease of the terminal aorta and its branches is suggested most often by a history of intermittent claudication with recurrent fatigue or pain in the buttocks, thighs, or legs with exercise that is relieved rapidly by resting in the standing position. After a short period of rest, walking can be resumed, but the symptoms recur predictably after a similar level of exertion is reached. The symptom of rest pain occurs at later stages when the degree of occlusion is more advanced and usually multisegmental. Typically, rest pain is experienced in the distal foot and is worsened by elevation of the leg and improved by placing the foot in a dependent position. In the man with internal iliac artery occlusion, impotence may be the initial or major complaint. When the arterial insufficiency is advanced, the patient also may describe coldness or numbness of the feet and poor ability to heal injuries to the limb or a history of nonhealing ulcerations and loss of motor function.

Objective

Physical Examination

Physical findings in atherosclerotic occlusive disease of the terminal aorta and its immediate branches are those of diminished or absent pulses in the femoral areas and distally, with or without changes of chronic ischemia in the legs. A palpable thrill or audible bruit may be present over the femoral artery, indicative of stenosis of the iliac or femoral vessels. The changes of chronic ischemia, when present, are noted most in the distal lower legs and feet with atrophic, dry, scaly skin; decreased hair growth; and thickened, dystrophic nails. Pallor of the skin may be noted in the feet. It is accentuated by elevation and improved by dependency, which may also bring out the finding of dependent rubor. Capillary refill after blanching the skin with gentle pressure is slow in the ischemic limb; comparison of refill time in both feet indicates which side is more severely involved. Decreased sensation in the feet may be noted with more advanced ischemia, but this finding must be differentiated from other neuropathies, especially in the diabetic patient. Pregangrenous skin changes or areas of frank necrosis on the toes or feet may be present with severe, neglected ischemia.

Routine Laboratory Abnormalities

Abnormalities of routine laboratory tests are not specific for atheromatous occlusive disease of the terminal aorta and its branches, but are indicators of frequently associated cardiac disease, hypertension, diabetes mellitus, hyperlipidemia, and chronic obstructive lung disease.

PLANS

Diagnostic

Differential Diagnosis

Coarctation of the aorta can cause diminished arterial pulsations in the legs. The blood pressure in the legs is less than it is in the arms. The classic murmurs and rib notching assist in the differential diagnosis (see Chapter 15–28).

Diagnostic Options and Recommended Approach

When atherosclerotic occlusive disease of the terminal aorta and its branches is suspected by the history or physical findings, noninvasive vascular laboratory studies should be performed to document the presence and hemodynamic significance of reduced arterial flow and tissue perfusion. Of the various types of noninvasive vascular studies available for evaluation of the lower extremities, the most frequently used and helpful is the Doppler determination of systolic arterial pressures at the thigh, calf, and ankle levels, with determination of the ankle systolic pressure-to-brachial systolic pressure index for both lower extremities. A normal ankle/brachial index is 1 or greater, indices of 0.7 to 0.5 are compatible with significant claudication, and indices of 0.3 or lower are compatible with rest pain and threatened limb loss. It should be noted that in some patients with calcified noncompressible arteries, particularly those with diabetes, the Doppler systolic arterial pressure may be artificially elevated. Thus, other forms of vascular laboratory evaluation using plethysmography and waveform analysis may be necessary for documentation. In patients with atheromatous occlusive disease of the terminal aorta and its branches who are not determined to be candidates for surgical revascularization or transluminal angioplasty, noninvasive vascular laboratory evaluation, along with clinical assessment, is useful for following progression of the occlusive process. The penile Doppler pressure index can be helpful in the workup of male patients with possible vasculogenic impotence. When the patient is felt to be a candidate for surgical revascularization or transluminal angioplasty because of disabling claudication or threatened limb loss, complete angiographic evaluation of the abdominal aorta, iliac arteries, femoral arteries, and distal runoff should be performed. Full evaluation of the aortoiliofemoral system is necessary to determine the site or sites of obstruction, adequacy of proximal inflow, distal runoff, and established collateral bed in order that an appropriate method for revascularization by surgery or angioplasty can be chosen. When an operation is contemplated, an appropriate evaluation of possible manifestations of cardiac, carotid, or renal atherosclerosis should be performed, in some instances including physiologic or invasive diagnostic studies. Elective aortofemoral revascularization should not be undertaken until the patient's risk factors have been optimized, including consideration of coronary bypass or angioplasty as a more urgent priority for some individuals.

Therapeutic

There is no specific drug therapy for the treatment of the atherosclerotic occlusive disease process in the terminal aorta and its branches. Various types of vasodilator drugs have been recommended in the past, but none has been proven to be effective in atheromatous occlusive disease, although some may have usefulness in vasospastic arterial disorders. Pentoxifylline (Trental) is effective in some patients for the treatment of mild to moderate intermittent claudication caused by chronic occlusive arterial disease of the lower extremities. Although its mode of action is not completely understood, it is felt to decrease the viscosity of blood and increase the deformability of red blood cells, resulting in improved tissue oxygenation. The usual dosage of pentoxifylline is 400 mg three times a day with meals, and the full effect may not be noted for 2 to 4 weeks. Reported side effects and drug interactions have been few. As much as a 50% increase in walking distance may be observed in the group of patients who respond to this medication. The most important aspect of medical therapy for patients with atherosclerotic occlusive disease is appropriate management of the frequently associated diseases: hypertension should be well controlled because of its potentiating effect on the progression of atherosclerosis; heart disease should be vigorously treated to maintain optimal cardiac function; hyperlipidemias and elevated cholesterol should be managed by dietary therapy, weight reduction, and drugs when indicated; and diabetes mellitus should be regulated by appropriate diet and medication. In addition to control of associated medical diseases, the single most important element of care is the cessation of tobacco usage by the patient with atheromatous occlusive disease. It is well known that both the progression of disease and the response to medical or surgical therapy are adversely affected by continuation of cigarette smoking.

Patients with disabling claudication or threatened limb loss from atherosclerotic occlusive disease should be considered candidates for surgical revascularization or transluminal balloon angioplasty, provided their associated disease status and operative risk factors do not contraindicate such interventions. The type of surgical procedure chosen depends on the location and extent of the occlusive process, as determined by clinical, hemodynamic, and angiographic evaluation. Endarterectomy may be used in selected patients with isolated segmental

stenosis or occlusion, but aortoiliac or aortofemoral bypass procedures using prosthetic graft material are used most commonly for terminal aortic or iliac occlusive disease. With correct selection of patients and appropriate management of comorbid conditions, operative mortality is less than 2% and successful revascularization is obtained in about 90 to 95% of patients. In patients with significant distal occlusive disease, concomitant or subsequent femoropopliteal or tibial bypasses may be necessary for adequate revascularization. Extraanatomic bypass procedures using axillofemoral or femorofemoral bypass can be performed in selected patients when intraabdominal procedures are contraindicated. Percutaneous transluminal arterial dilation of isolated occlusive lesions has become a safe and effective procedure to improve blood flow in the iliac and femoropopliteal arteries under favorable conditions. This procedure can be used as a primary procedure or in conjunction with surgical revascularization. Data accumulated to date indicate success rates approaching that of surgical revascularization for isolated stenoses, especially in the iliac artery. The more recent use of endovascular stents with angioplasty and the use of thrombolytic agents to remove associated thrombus to better visualize the atherosclerotic lesion have extended the indications for endovascular management to more complex lesions in some centers with experienced personnel. Complication rates are low in experienced hands, but if complications do occur, surgical intervention may be necessary for correction.

FOLLOW-UP

If the patient does not require immediate or urgent therapy when first seen, the frequency of patient follow-up can be determined by the severity of the atheromatous occlusive process. Initial visits should be more frequent to determine the rate of progression of disease and the effect of medical management instituted. When the process is determined to be stable and the patient is knowledgeable of the treatment plan and of the indications for early return, follow-up may be scheduled for once or twice a year; however, proper management of associated diseases may dictate more frequent visits. Lifelong periodic examinations are necessary to achieve optimal results after operation or endovascular management and to detect comorbid manifestations.

DISCUSSION
Prevalence and Incidence

There is some degree of atherosclerotic plaque formation in most of the population with aging but significant occlusive disease with claudication or threatened limb loss occurs in only a small percentage. The incidence does increase in the older age group and in those with atherosclerotic risk factors such as hypertension. Vascologenic impotence related to aortoiliac artery occlusive disease occurs in a small number of men, with neurogenic and psychological etiologies being more common.

Related Basic Science

The physiologic response to the reduction in arterial pressure that occurs distal to a critical stenosis or occlusion of a major vessel is the development of collateral circulation to supply the distal arterial bed. Despite enlargement of the collateral system, resistance to flow in the collaterals is always higher than that of the major artery it is replacing. Although circulation may be adequate to allow distal perfusion in the resting state, it may not suffice when the demand for perfusion is increased by exercise. At this point, intermittent claudication appears. In aortoiliac arterial occlusion, collaterals develop via the lumbar and mesenteric arteries through the pelvic vessels to communicate with branches of the common femoral artery. The adequacy of these collaterals is highly variable, however, and quite dependent on the rapidity of onset of the major vessel occlusion. The degree of ischemia in the distal lower extremities is also related to the status of the femoropopliteal and tibioperoneal arteries. With multiple levels of atherosclerotic occlusion, the degree of ischemia will be increased significantly, with a greater risk of ischemic gangrene and tissue or limb loss.

Natural History and Its Modification with Treatment

Atherosclerotic obstruction of the terminal aorta and its branches is usually progressive, but the rate is unpredictable. Depending on collateral blood flow and the degree of exertional activity, the symptoms and physical findings of ischemia may vary in a given patient. As the ischemia worsens, the patient may experience increasing claudication with eventual progression to rest pain or tissue necrosis and threatened limb loss. At that point, if revascularization is not carried out or is unsuccessful, amputation is almost certain. Death due directly to aortic, iliac, or femoral artery atherosclerotic occlusion is rare; rather, it is attributable most often to associated disease processes, primarily coronary atherosclerosis.

Prevention

Prevention of obstructive atherosclerotic disease of the terminal aorta and its branches is essentially the same as that for atherosclerosis in general. Proper diet and weight control with appropriate exercise are general measures for prevention. Control of hypertension, hyperlipidemia, and diabetes mellitus and, particularly, the avoidance of tobacco usage are specific goals. Medications that lower cholesterol levels decrease the risk of coronary artery disease and may also have a beneficial effect on aortoiliac occlusive disease, but further studies are needed to determine a specific benefit.

Cost Containment

Early recognition of the signs of atherosclerotic occlusive disease and proper education of the patient concerning preventive measures may delay progression of the disease and prevent potential complications that would require expensive hospitalization or loss of employment. In addition, prompt recognition of the need for operation or angioplasty, before extensive disability or tissue necrosis has occurred, should result in shorter, less complicated hospitalizations and earlier returns to work for the employed patient and less need for rehabilitation and long-term care services for all patients.

REFERENCES

Bassiouny HS, Zarins CK, Kadowaki MH, Glagov S. Hemodynamic stress and experimental aortoiliac atherosclerosis. J Vasc Surg 1994;19:426.

Fowl RJ, Kempazinski RF. Success rates and failure rates, and causes of failure for common arterial reconstructive procedures. Semin Vasc Surg 1994;7:132.

Hertzer NR, Beven EG, Young JR, et al. Coronary artery disease in peripheral vascular patients: A classification of 1000 coronary angiograms and results of surgical management. Ann Surg 1984;199:223.

Imparato AM, Kim GE, Davidson T, Crowley JC. Intermittent claudication: Its natural course. Surgery 1975;78:795.

Martin EC. Percutaneous therapy in the management of aortoiliac disease. Semin Vasc Surg 1994;7:17.

Perdue GD, Smith RB III, Veazey CR, Ansley JD. Revascularization for severe limb ischemia. Arch Surg 1980;115:168.

Seeger JM, Silverman SH, Flynn TC, et al. Lipid risk factors in patients requiring arterial reconstruction. J Vasc Surg 1989;10:418.

CHAPTER 15–69

Vasospastic Disorders

J. Timothy Fulenwider, M.D.

DEFINITION

Raynaud's syndrome (RS), livedo reticularis (LR), and acrocyanosis are vasospastic disorders involving primarily the extremities, with each characterized by unique color changes of the affected skin: RS is defined as periodic digital ischemia usually provoked by cold exposure or emotional excitement. LR is the violaceous, reticular, lacelike, geographic mottling of the extremity skin which may occasionally involve the trunk. LR has also been referred to as *cutis marmorata, livedo racemosa,* and *livedo annularis.* Acrocyanosis, the rarest of the vasospastic disorders, is the lifelong cyanotic discoloration of the fingers, hands, toes, and feet—rarely the face and ears—occurring in the absence of a central cyanosis or a peripheral arteriovenous shunt. All three clinical syndromes exist in primary and secondary forms; primary variants are usually harmless, whereas secondary disorders are often linked to serious medical conditions leading to ischemic gangrene, multiple amputations, or even death.

ETIOLOGY

Precise pathophysiologic mechanisms underlying these three primary vasospastic disorders are unknown despite extensive research efforts. Hypotheses to explain RS are explored under Related Basic Science in the Discussion. Conditions associated with secondary RS are listed in Table 15–69–1. The etiology of secondary LR is even more obscure; however, a benign form of LR is associated with amantadine therapy and resolves several weeks after the medication is discontinued. The constant small artery, arteriolar, and venular spasm of acrocyanosis may be related to elevated blood serotonin levels, a theory implicated by the association of acrocyanosis and autism (Asperger's syndrome), which is often related to elevated serotonin levels.

CRITERIA FOR DIAGNOSIS
Suggestive

The diagnosis of RS is made by history. The pathognomic episodic digital color changes involving the fingers (less frequently the toes, ear lobes, and tips of the nose and tongue) are diagnostic. Digital pallor during intense digital arteriospasm may involve one or all digits but rarely extends to the distal palmar skin crease. The variable period of pallor is followed by cyanosis and subsequently by intense rubor of reactive hyperemia. This classic triphasic color change is not observed by all patients. Some experience sequential pallor and cyanosis, whereas others note only pallor or cyanosis. The absence of the hyperemic phase does not preclude the diagnosis of RS. The diagnosis of LR is suggested by its typical cutaneous violaceous mottling of the extremities and trunk and favorable response to rewarming. Primary LR may rarely be associated with cutaneous ulceration of the leg, ankles, and feet. Acrocyanosis is obvious by visual inspection revealing persistent purple or blue discoloration of the fingers, hands, toes, and feet (occasionally the face and ears). This lifelong condition is worsened by cold exposure and incompletely relieved by rewarming.

Definitive

The clinical manifestations of these vasospastic disorders are so characteristic that definitive tests are usually not required to establish the di-

TABLE 15–69–1. CONDITIONS ASSOCIATED WITH SECONDARY RAYNAUD'S SYNDROME

Occupational or environmental trauma
  Pneumatic hammer
  Vibratory tool exposure (white finger syndrome)
  Hypothenar—hammer syndrome
  Cold injury frostbite
  Electric shock injury
Obstructive arteriopathy
  Arteriosclerosis obliterans
  Thromboangiitis obliterans (Buerger's disease)
  Peripheral arterial embolism
  Takayasu's arteritis
  Other arthritides (giant cell, syphilitic)
Neurologic disease
  Central or peripheral neuropathy
    (stroke, syringomyelia, poliomyelitis)
  Reflex sympathetic dystrophy
  Carpal tunnel syndrome
Endocrinopathy
  Myxedema
  Grave's disease
  Hypopituitarism
  Addison's disease
  Cushing's disease
Immunologic and connective tissue disease
  Scleroderma, CREST* syndrome
  Mixed connective tissue disease
  Systemic lupus erythematosus
  Rheumatoid arthritis
  Sjogren's syndrome
  Dermatomyositis
  Polymyositis
  Hepatitis B-associated polyarteritis nodosa
  Hypersensitivity angiitis
    Henoch–Schonlein purpura
    Polyarteritis nodosa
    Reiter's syndrome
Drugs
  Ergot alkaloids
  Methysergide
  Beta-adrenergic blockers
  Oral contraceptives
  Vinblastine
  Bleomycin
  Imipramine
  Bromocristine/bromocriptine
  Bromocriptine
  Clonidine
  Cyclosporine
  Amphetamines
  Dopamine
Miscellaneous conditions
  Paroxysmal hemoglobinuria
  Fabry's disease
  Primary pulmonary hypertension
  Pheochromocytoma
  Vinyl chloride disease
  Chronic renal failure
  Cryofibrinogenemia
  Cryoglobulinemia
  Cold hemagglutinin disease
  Hyperviscosity syndromes
  Malignant neoplasms
  Myeloproliferative disorders
  Lead poisoning
  Arsenic poisoning

*Calcinosis, Raynaud's phenomenon, esophageal dysmotility, sclerodactylia, and telangiectasia.

agnosis. Laboratory investigations are reserved to distinguish primary and secondary forms of these vasospastic states.

CLINICAL MANIFESTATIONS

Subjective

The vasospasm of RS may be accompanied by sensations of coldness, hypesthesia, paresthesias, and even pain depending on the duration of the attack. The reactive hyperemia phase may be associated with temporary throbbing discomfort. The clinical severity of RS is highly variable, and symptom patterns of individuals range from mild, infrequent episodes to daily, prolonged attacks of digital ischemia. The majority of RS patients present primarily with anxiety provoked by the digital color changes rather than symptoms produced by the attack. Historical facets of critical importance include recreational or occupational exposures (vibrating tools, typing, piano playing, chronic cold exposure), medications (ergot alkaloids, beta-adrenergic blockers, oral contraceptives, dopamine, bromocriptine, vinblastine, bleomycin), toxin exposures, endocrinopathies, malignant disorders, tobacco use, chronic renal failure, hepatitis B, electric shock, frostbite, neurologic disorders, blood dyscrasias, arterial occlusive disease, and connective tissue disorders.

Patients with primary LR usually complain only of the cutaneous cosmetic changes intensified by cold exposure. Rarely, coolness and numbness of the affected skin area are noted. In less than 0.5% of primary LR cases, especially during winter, medically recalcitrant, painful leg, ankle, or foot ulcers will occur and slowly resolve during warmer months. Secondary LR may be associated with a variety of disease states: connective tissue disorders, myeloproliferative disease, dysproteinemias, hyperviscosity syndromes, vasculitis, atheromatous microembolization syndrome, frostbite, and reflex sympathetic dystrophy (Table 15–69–2). Secondary LR patients occasionally suffer from ischemic ulcers, typically on the distal lateral leg and dorsum of the foot, in addition to the myriad of symptoms associated with their underlying disorders.

Acrocyanosis patients complain of the constant cyanotic hue and, rarely, coolness, edema, and hyperhidrosis of the hands and feet.

Objective

Physical Examination

The physical examination in primary RS patients is usually normal. The association of secondary RS with a variety of disease states warrants thorough physical examination with emphasis on the following: palpation and auscultation of all peripheral pulses, sclerodactyly, calcinosis cutis, open digital ulcers or pitted scars, dermatitis, petechiae, visceromegaly, lymphadenopathy, arthritis, and other evidence of connective tissue disease. Evidence of central or peripheral neuropathy should be noted, and maneuvers to detect carpal tunnel and thoracic outlet syndrome should be carried out. The Allen test should be performed to determine patency of the palmar arch. The peripheral pulses in primary RS, LR, and acrocyanosis are normal. Stigmata of connective tissue disease, cutaneous infarctions of atheromatous microembolization syndrome, and venous or arterial thrombosis may be seen in secondary LR. Lifelong persistence of digital cyanosis in the absence of a central cardiopulmonary cyanotic disorder or peripheral arteriovenous fistula is the hallmark of acrocyanosis.

Routine Laboratory Abnormalities

Primary forms of RS, LR, and acrocyanosis are not associated with routine laboratory abnormalities; however, secondary variants may demonstrate a wide range of abnormalities reflecting the pathology of the underlying systemic disorder.

TABLE 15–69–2. CONDITIONS ASSOCIATED WITH SECONDARY LIVEDO RETICULARIS

Connective tissue diseases
Cryoglobulinemia
Atheromatous microembolism
Hyperviscosity syndromes
Hypercoagulable states (anticardiolipin antibody, Sneddon's syndrome)
Amantadine

PLANS

Diagnostic

Differential Diagnosis

The history and morphologic features of RS and LR are so characteristic that these conditions are virtually unmistakable. The differential diagnosis of acrocyanosis must exclude central cyanotic cardiopulmonary conditions, peripheral arteriovenous fistulas, and the acral cyanosis occasionally seen in peripheral ischemic stages, hyperviscosity, and polycythemic syndromes.

Diagnostic Options

Diagnostic efforts must be directed toward distinguishing primary from secondary variants of these three vasospastic states. The performance of initial laboratory tests should be guided by the history and physical findings and aimed toward the detection of comorbid disease. Diagnostic options include routine laboratory investigations, erythrocyte sedimentation rate, specific tests for connective tissue or autoimmune disease, screening test for hypercoagulable states, noninvasive vascular examination, plain radiographs of the hands, chest, and cervical spine, and contrast arteriography.

Recommended Approach

A minimal laboratory evaluation should include complete blood count, erythrocyte sedimentation rate, chemistry profile, urinalysis, rheumatoid factor, antinuclear antibody, cold agglutinin assays, and hand x-rays. Should these tests fail to identify an underlying disease, in cases of high suspicion further laboratory testing is warranted as guided by conditions known to be associated with RS or LR (see Tables 15–69–1 and 15–69–2). Adjunctive laboratory testing includes the following: serum protein electrophoresis, anticentromere antibody, extractable nuclear antibody, anti-native DNA antibody, HEP-2 antinuclear antibody, cryoglobulins, complement levels, and hepatitis B screen. Occasionally, the diagnosis of RS is equivocal by history alone. Although ice water immersion of the hands may fail to provoke a typical vasospastic attack, confirmation of pathologic digital arteriospasm and an objective assessment of extremity arterial flow may be obtained in the noninvasive vascular laboratory. The combination of finger photoplethysmography (PPG) waveforms, digital blood pressures, and digital hypothermic challenge testing provides reliable information regarding patency of the digital arteries and susceptibility to cold. Patients with primary RS have digital artery pressures within 20 mm Hg of brachial artery systolic pressure and characteristic "double-peak" PPG waveforms. Segmental air plethysmography waveforms and segmental artery pressures of the extremity provide information of the status of the larger extremity arteries. The combination of Doppler ultrasound color flow mapping and duplex scanning may be used to directly interrogate the larger upper and lower extremity arteries for the presence of atherosclerosis, Takayasu's arteritis, ulnar artery aneurysms, thoracic outlet syndromes and arterial pseudoaneurysms following catheterization, and arteriovenous fistulas.

The evaluation of nailfold capillaries is a necessary office procedure performed best with a 10× microscope but satisfactorily with a magnifying lens or opthalmoscope. Normal nailfold capillaries are arranged in orderly hairpin loops aligned longitudinally. In scleroderma, mixed connective tissue disease, and dermatomyositis, the diminished numbers of capillaries appear ectatic and deformed with multiple avascular areas. In systemic lupus erythematosus, the capillary loops are tortuous and the subpapillary venous plexus is prominent. Normal nailfold capillaroscopy suggests the presence of primary RS; however, abnormal patterns suggest a secondary variant of RS. Extremity arteriography is reserved for potentially reconstructible arteriopathies as suggested by clinical and noninvasive vascular laboratory findings. Nonetheless, when arteriography is performed, the examination must include visualization from the aortic arch to the fingertips with magnification hand films.

Therapeutic

The therapeutic plans for RS are directed toward reducing the frequency and severity of vasospastic episodes. General measures such as minimizing cold exposure, use of mittens or hand warmers, discontinu-ation of tobacco in all forms, and avoidance of provocative medications are usually sufficient for 80 to 90% of primary RS patients. A simple explanation of the pathophysiology of RS and reassurance of its usually benign course are essential to allay fears of gangrene and digital loss. A small percentage of primary and the majority of secondary RS patients require pharmacologic therapy. Medication options have included calcium channel blockers (nifedipine, diltiazem, isradipine, felodipine), direct vasodilators (priscoline), alpha-adrenergic blocking agents (phenoxybenzamine, prazosin), sympatholytic agents (reserpine, methyldopa), serotonin antagonists (ketanserine), thomboxane synthetase inhibitors (dazoxiben), prostanoid infusions (prostaglandin E_1, iloprost), platelet release reaction inhibitors (aspirin), angiotensin-converting enzyme inhibitors (Capoten), topical nitrates, and rheologic agents (pentoxifylline). Of these, the calcium channel blocker nifedipine has proven most efficacious. Nifedipine causes direct vascular smooth muscle relaxation and may also improve digital artery flow through an antiplatelet effect or through postganglionic α_2-adrenoreceptor blockage. Therapy with nifedipine should begin with 10 mg orally three times daily or with 30 mg/d of the long-acting preparation and may be increased to 60 mg/d depending on patient response and tolerance. Approximately 50% of patients with primary RS report relief or improvement of symptoms with nifedipine, which may be tapered or discontinued during warmer seasons. Secondary RS patients respond less predictably. Approximately 15% of RS patients treated with nifedipine report intolerable side effects: headache, ankle edema, and lassitude. Patients intolerant to nifedipine may try prazosin (1–2 mg/d) or guanethidine (5–10 mg/d); however, both medications are also associated with significant side effects of orthostatic hypotension if not administered in slowly progressive dosages.

Highly motivated patients may respond to biofeedback, relaxation therapy, and Pavlovian conditioning; however, the role of these modalities in overall management of RS patients is unknown. Pharmacologic management of primary LR and acrocyanosis is usually unwarranted. Digital ischemic ulcerations should be managed by soap and water cleansing, conservative debridement, nifedipine, and antibiotics as necessary. With this regimen 85 to 90% of ischemic ulcers slowly heal and remain closed. The role of surgical sympathectomy for primary vasospastic disorders has disappeared with the emergence of improved medical regimens. In patients with severe digital ischemia, ulcerations, impending gangrene, and intolerable pain, cervicothoracic or selective digital sympathectomy may be considered. The success of surgical sympathectomy may be predicted by the response to bupivacaine stellate ganglion blocks or to epidural infusions of bupivacaine or fentanyl. Pain relief, digital perfusion, and skin temperatures should be followed. If regional blocks prove helpful, surgical sympathectomy may be considered, although the favorable response predictably lasts for only 3 to 6 months.

FOLLOW-UP

Long-term surveillance of patients with apparent primary RS is essential as the vasospastic disorder may antedate the clinical evolution of any underlying disorder by several years. With prospective evaluation, 50 to 60% of patients do not develop comorbid disease; however, almost 30% develop one of the connective tissue disorders, and 15 to 20% develop one of many underlying disease states (Table 15–69–1). Annual history and physical examination with antinuclear antibody and erythrocyte sedimentation rate testing are advisable. It is probably unwise to overinform patients of potential future medical developments, particularly because specific therapy for many of these disorders is lacking. The development of digital ulcerations warrants extensive investigation into the possibility of an underlying connective tissue disorder or other explanation of the severe ischemia.

DISCUSSION

Prevalence

The prevalence of RS varies with the definition used, methods of confirmation, and climate. The range of reported RS is 5 to 30% in the general population, realistically at the lower end of this spectrum. The prevalence of LR and acrocyanosis is unknown.

Related Basic Science

Physiologic or Metabolic Derangement

Induction of pathologic digital vasospasm producing primary RS is felt to be secondary to a "local vascular fault" with heightened digital artery reactivity to cooling. Presently, it is postulated that either increased numbers or sensitivity of postjunctional α_2-adrenoreceptors could result in episodic digital vasospasm. The theory of increased sympathetic nervous system activity proximal to the digits has been disproved. Similarly, increased concentrations of endogenously produced vasoconstrictor substances (serotonin, norepinephrine, angiotension II, thromboxane A_2, and endothelin-1) do not satisfactorily explain primary RS. The physiologic explanation for LR and the continuous arterial, arteriolar, and venular spasm in acrocyanosis is unknown.

Anatomic Derangement

Digital artery patency depends on the balance of forces creating arterial wall tension and intraarterial distending pressure. Fixed arterial obstructions resulting in diminished distal digital intraarterial pressure may cause secondary RS by allowing critical artery closure with normal local vasomotor and sympathetic efferent activity. This explanation most likely accounts for the majority of secondary RS episodes, although other humoral or rheologic factors may be involved.

Natural History and Its Modification with Treatment

Patients with primary RS, LR, and acrocyanosis have a favorable prognosis. Of those with primary RS, fewer than 20% become worse, whereas almost 40% remain stable and more than 35% improve. Ten percent of primary RS patients become asymptomatic. The risk of major tissue loss with primary RS is less than 0.5%. The natural history of primary LR and acrocyanosis is predictably benign. The natural history of secondary variants of these vasospastic conditions is highly unpredictable but is generally determined by the activity of the comorbid disease. Untreated secondary RS patients are likely to develop recurrent digital ulcers, which may result in major tissue loss; however, diligent management of these recalcitrant ischemic ulcers rarely results in major amputation. These data suggest that the natural history of secondary RS is favorably influenced by proper treatment. The influence of medical therapy on the primary vasospastic disorders is unknown.

Prevention

It is probable that most cases of primary and secondary vasospastic disorders are not preventable. The 40 to 50% incidence of RS in individuals operating vibratory equipment and in those processing food, with exposure to alternating hot and cold environments, suggests that wearing of proper thermal and vibratory insulating garments may lessen or eliminate episodic digital color changes.

Cost Containment

The physician is responsible for selective investigation and judicious pharmacotherapy of patients. Fewer than 20% of primary RS patients and probably no patients with primary LR and acrocyanosis will ever require drug therapy if the basic pathophysiology and benign course of these disorders are explained. Expensive laboratory and noninvasive vascular testing should be minimized, with more comprehensive evaluation pursued only if secondary vasospastic disorders are felt likely to be present.

REFERENCES

Coffman JD. The diagnosis of Raynaud's phenomenon. Clin Dermatol 1994;12:283.

Edwards JM, Porter JM. Raynaud's syndrome and small vessel arteriopathy. Semin Vasc Surg 1993;6:56.

Gerhard MD, Creager MA. Raynaud's phenomenon: Vasospastic disease and current therapy. Adv Vasc Surg 1994;2:245.

Porter JM, Friedman EI, Mills JL. Occlusive and vasospastic diseases involving distal upper extremity arteries: Raynaud's syndrome. In: Rutherford RB, editor-in-chief. Vascular surgery. 3rd ed, Philadelphia: Saunders, 1989:844.

Young JR. Vasospastic disorders. Cardiovasc Clin 1992;22:135.

CHAPTER 15–70

Thrombophlebitis of the Lower Extremity

Thomas F. Dodson, M.D.

DEFINITION

Thrombophlebitis is a descriptive term that means inflammation of a vein associated with a thrombus or clot.

ETIOLOGY

This common medical and surgical problem is typically found in patients who have one or more components of "Virchow's triad": stasis, damage to the lining of the vein, and hypercoagulability. Thrombophlebitis can occur in any age group and under a variety of conditions: the precipitating events can be as innocuous as a long plane flight or hitting one's leg against the dining room table, but the majority of patients have a comorbid condition that has initiated clot formation and inflammation of the venous system. Patients often notice either subtle or profound degrees of edema of the lower extremity, and evidence of inflammation and pain may or may not be demonstrable. Because physical findings are not sufficient to make the diagnosis in greater than 50% of patients, the physician called to "rule out" thrombophlebitis must depend on a number of objective tests.

CRITERIA FOR DIAGNOSIS

Suggestive

Although the swollen, tender leg is often suggestive of deep-vein thrombophlebitis, fewer than a third of patients with even a classic presentation turn out to have this condition. Knowledge of potential risk factors for deep-vein thrombosis (Table 15–70–1) increases the diagnostic accuracy of the careful clinician.

Definitive

Although currently five techniques are used to make the objective diagnosis of deep-vein thrombosis (Table 15–70–2), B-mode ultrasonography has the distinct advantage of being noninvasive, relatively inexpensive, and usable on an outpatient. It has the disadvantage of being insensitive with respect to clots in the calf musculature. Magnetic resonance venography should also be mentioned as a potential sixth diagnostic test. Although it is noninvasive, it is expensive, with limited availability at this time.

TABLE 15–70–1. RISK FACTORS FOR DEEP-VEIN THROMBOSIS

- Age > 40 years
- History of previous deep-vein thrombosis or pulmonary embolus
- Major surgery, particularly in the pelvis or lower extremities
- Cancer, particularly adenocarcinomas
- Obesity
- Trauma, particularly to the pelvis or lower extremities
- Heart disease, particularly myocardial infarction and congestive heart failure
- Stroke
- Fracture of leg or hip
- Prolonged immobilization, particularly paraplegia or quadriplegia
- Estrogen for hormone replacement therapy or oral contraceptives

CLINICAL MANIFESTATIONS
Subjective

The range of presentation of symptoms of thrombophlebitis is from asymptomatic to severe limb-threatening edema of the lower extremity. Either the superficial or the deep venous system can be involved by the process. When the superficial system is involved, the diagnosis is somewhat easier in that the skin overlying the vein is often erythematous, warm, and tender. This process often involves veins of the lesser or greater saphenous system and commonly affects varicosities of these superficial systems. The deep venous system, although of greater clinical significance, frequently belies even the careful diagnostician.

Objective
Physical Examination

Fortunately, the objective findings of superficial thrombophlebitis—a tender erythematous area overlying a palpable cord or clotted vein—are fairly common. It is important to remember that superficial thrombophlebitis and deep thrombophlebitis may coexist, and recent information would suggest that when superficial thrombophlebitis develops after previous surgery or when it is noted to extend *above* the knee, the risk of deep-vein pathology is greater. In these situations, heightened surveillance is recommended. Unfortunately, the objective findings of deep-vein thrombophlebitis are often lacking, subtle, or even frequently misleading. It has been noted that even the classic signs and symptoms of deep-vein thrombosis—muscle pain and tenderness, edema, and a positive Homans' sign (pain in the calf with dorsiflexion of the foot)—are found to occur in about equal frequency in patients *with* and *without* deep-vein thrombosis. These signs and symptoms should, however,

TABLE 15–70–2. DIAGNOSIS OF DEEP-VEIN THROMBOSIS

	Invasive	Cost*	Examiner Dependent	Detects Clots in Calf	Outpatient Procedure
Phlebography with intravenous contrast	Yes	$463	No	Yes	Yes
Phlebography with radio-nuclide	Yes	$419	No	No	Yes
Doppler velocity detector	No	$105	Yes	No	Yes
B-mode/ Doppler (duplex) ultrasonography	No	$430	Yes	Yes	Yes
Plethysmography	No	$184	No	No	Yes

*Emory University Hospital charge (including interpretation), January 1995.

stimulate the careful physician to perform some objective evaluation of the deep venous system.

Two severe forms of deep-vein thrombophlebitis deserve mention: phlegmasia alba dolens and phlegmasia cerulea dolens. These two entities are gradations of the same process, thrombosis of the iliofemoral venous system with subsequent massive edema of the extremity and variable amounts of pain and discomfort. In the former process, alba dolens, the limb often appears blanched or lacking in coloration. In the latter, more severe process, cerulea dolens, the leg is often bluish in color, skin changes may be evident with petechiae or bullae, and the arterial circulation is often diminished. In patients with alba dolens, some venous flow is maintained, whereas in patients with cerulea dolens, the total venous outflow is obstructed. This latter condition can obviously lead to loss of the limb or to loss of the patient, so early recognition and treatment are imperative.

Routine Laboratory Abnormalities

There are no diagnostic routine laboratory abnormalities.

PLANS
Diagnostic
Differential Diagnosis

The condition must be differentiated from cellulitis. Deep-vein thrombosis may lead to a compromise in the arterial circulation and, when that is the clinical picture, it must be differentiated from arterial occlusive disease.

Diagnostic Options and Recommended Approach

Ten or more objective tests can be performed to evaluate the patient with a swollen or painful extremity, and thus the combinations and permutations of venous diagnosis are legion. Thankfully, these tests can be categorized into three different techniques: (1) venous imaging or phlebography, (2) Doppler (duplex) ultrasonic scanning, and (3) plethysmography or measurement of venous volume change in the extremity.

Phlebography with intravenous contrast is the "gold standard" by which other tests are evaluated. It is, however, invasive, requires some special equipment, involves transport to the radiology suite, may be painful or can cause allergic reactions to the contrast material, and can even (in a small percentage of cases) cause thrombophlebitis. It is, on the other hand, highly sensitive and specific for the presence of clots in the veins of the lower extremity. Phlebography with technetium-labeled macroaggregates of albumin is another test in this category. This examination resembles conventional contrast phlebograms in that the radionuclide is injected into the dorsal vein of the foot, and its course is followed by means of a gamma camera. From a practical standpoint, its accuracy is highest in the thigh and pelvis and less so in the calf. In situations where calf vein thrombi are not critical to the decision making and where a concomitant lung scan is required, radionuclide phlebography may be the test of choice.

Use of the B-mode/Doppler (duplex) ultrasonic scanning device is changing the way in which patients suspected to have deep-vein thrombosis are evaluated. As opposed to phlebography, it is noninvasive, is not painful, cannot cause thrombophlebitis, and can be repeated at periodic intervals to assess progression of disease or adequacy of therapy. As every diagnostic test has a down side, duplex scanning is no different. The equipment is expensive, the evaluation requires time and expertise, and the accuracy of diagnosis is strongly dependent on observer diligence and experience. An early criticism of this technique was the difficulty in examining veins below the knee. It is now apparent that, with examiner persistence, anterior tibial, posterior tibial, and peroneal veins can be studied with regularity.

Another simpler technique that uses the Doppler device involves the 5-MHz Doppler velocity detector. It is ideal for a quick bedside determination of venous patency, is inexpensive, and has an accuracy of about 90% in experienced hands. The interpretation of venous flow depends on a number of factors: (1) the presence or absence of flow in the subject vein, (2) phasicity of flow with respiration, (3) augmentation or lack of augmentation with distal compression, and (4) degree of flow in the superficial veins. When an experienced examiner determines that the flow is phasic with respiration, augments with distal compression, and is equal in the superficial veins of both lower extremities, deep-vein thrombosis of that venous system can confidently be ruled out.

Plethysmography is based on the principle that venous thrombi cause decreased venous compliance and increased venous outflow resistance. The various types of plethysmographic techniques—impedance plethysmography, strain-gauge plethysmography, air plethysmography, and others—all measure volume changes in the lower extremity. The technique is noninvasive, requires relatively inexpensive equipment, and has standardized criteria by which to evaluate the possibility of deep-vein thrombosis. Its main drawback is its difficulty or inability to diagnose clots in the veins of the calf, and recent information has confirmed that serial compression ultrasonography is superior in the diagnosis of deep-vein thrombosis in symptomatic outpatients.

The algorithm to a diagnosis of thrombophlebitis of the lower extremity is a subject of some debate. Given the dictum of "Primum non nocere," it seems prudent to proceed first in a noninvasive manner and reserve invasive tests for equivocal results or urgent situations. Thus, Doppler (duplex) ultrasonic scanning is ideal as an initial study, and if this modality is not available, plethysmography is a logical second choice. If these techniques are not available or if their results are equivocal, then phlebography with intravenous contrast should be the examination of choice. Radionuclide phlebography could be considered in situations where the issue of calf-vein thrombi is not critical and a lung scan is part of the necessary evaluation (see Table 15–70–2).

Therapeutic

Patients with superficial thrombophlebitis generally have a benign course, and continued ambulation, warm packs, and nonsteroidal anti-inflammatory agents are the treatments of choice. As noted in the previous discussion, however, if the superficial phlebitis develops after a recent operation or if the process extends above the knee, the risk of development of simultaneous superficial and deep thrombophlebitis is enhanced. In these two conditions, appropriate diagnostic modalities should be used. Ligation of the offending superficial vein is rarely necessary, but it may be considered in progressive inflammation of the greater saphenous vein in the groin or of the lesser saphenous vein behind the knee.

Patients with deep-vein thrombophlebitis should be immediately anticoagulated with heparin. Contraindications to heparin therapy include any source of active bleeding; traumatic wounds of recent origin; severe hypertension; recent eye surgery; and central nervous system tumors, surgery, or hemorrhage. Relative contraindications include the elderly patient prone to falls and cancer patients undergoing chemotherapy. In the majority of these patients, intervention should be directed toward placement of an intraluminal device in the vena cava to thwart the passage of emboli to the heart and lungs. This can conveniently be done either by a cutdown and placement of a Greenfield filter device in the operating room or percutaneously in the radiology suite. This device obviates the need for immediate or long-term anticoagulation.

The initial loading dose of sodium heparin is approximately 5000 to 10,000 U, and then 1000 to 2000 U of heparin are given in a continuous drip each hour. This can be easily mixed by placing 25,000 U of sodium heparin in 250 mL of saline, producing a concentration of 100 U/mL. Thus, if 1000 U/h is selected as a continuous infusion, the patient can receive 10 mL/h by means of an infusion pump. Adequacy of anticoagulation is generally ensured by achieving twice the normal partial thromboplastin time (PTT); thus, if the normal PTT is 30 to 40 seconds, the aim of the anticoagulation regimen is 60 to 80 seconds. After anticoagulation has been started with sodium heparin, oral anticoagulation with warfarin (Coumadin) should be started as well. Warfarin is best regulated according to the International Normalized Ratio (INR), which has been developed to improve the uniformity of results. It is recommended that the INR be kept between 2.0 and 3.0 in patients with deep-vein thrombosis. The overall period in the hospital after the diagnosis of deep-vein thrombosis is about 5 to 7 days, and this should allow for at least 5 days of heparin therapy and the overlapping 4 to 5 days that it takes to establish the proper warfarin dose. Anticoagulation

with warfarin continues for approximately 6 months, and the patient is then weaned off the medication.

Complications of anticoagulation include gangrene of the skin and soft tissue necrosis with warfarin, thrombocytopenia with heparin, and bleeding secondary to both agents. Thankfully, the first two complications are rare, although patients on heparin should have daily platelet counts to monitor the possibility of heparin-induced thrombocytopenia. Although bleeding may occur in 10 to 20% of patients receiving heparin and/or warfarin, it is usually related to overanticoagulation and can be corrected by reducing the dose. If bleeding secondary to heparin or warfarin is life threatening, heparin can be reversed by intravenous administration of protamine (given slowly to reduce the risk of hypotension), and warfarin can be reversed by either vitamin K or the administration of fresh-frozen plasma. The latter is usually preferred so as to allow resumption of the anticoagulation after a brief interval.

Two other forms of therapy, fibrinolytic agents and operative removal of thrombi, should be mentioned briefly. Both streptokinase (Kabikinase) and urokinase (Abbokinase) have been used in a number of studies to dissolve the thrombi causing venous occlusion. Although they have the theoretical benefit of accelerating lysis of thrombi with preservation of venous valvular function, it is not clear from the literature that they are a significant advance in the treatment of deep-vein thrombosis. At present, heparin should be considered the treatment of choice, but as newer agents become available, clot lysis may be reconsidered as an initial modality of therapy. Venous thrombectomy, done in the operating room, remains a controversial procedure. No randomized, prospective study exists to determine the efficacy of this procedure, so a determination of its exact role in the management of deep-vein thrombosis is somewhat circumspect. At present, operative removal of clot along with a concomitant arteriovenous fistula would be considered only in patients who have iliofemoral thrombosis and who have not responded to conventional management. Thus, patients with phlegmasia cerulea dolens who are facing potential limb loss should be considered for operative intervention, as should a smaller group of patients with early iliofemoral thrombosis who have not responded to heparin and elevation.

FOLLOW-UP

After initial treatment with heparin, most patients are treated for approximately 6 months with oral anticoagulants. During that time, they should have blood drawn weekly for the first month to ensure that they are receiving an appropriate dose of warfarin. After that first month, if the level of anticoagulation has been consistent, the patient can be seen at monthly intervals to check a prothrombin time and to assess the extremity for any developing signs of chronic venous insufficiency. The major side effect of chronic anticoagulation is bleeding. Patients should be instructed to purchase a Medic-Alert bracelet that lists warfarin as one of their medications. They should be warned that even small injuries may cause problems with bleeding, and obviously dangerous occupations or hobbies should be avoided during the period of anticoagulation. A number of drugs potentiate anticoagulation with warfarin, and alcohol and salicylates are notable among them. After the warfarin has been discontinued, depending on the degree of lower extremity edema, the patient should be seen at periodic intervals to assess the potential for development of the postphlebitic syndrome. It is important to remember that if the ankle edema can be controlled, sequelae of the postphlebitic syndrome will rarely develop. Thus, before the patient is discharged from the hospital, he or she must be fitted with an elastic stocking designed to deliver at least 30 to 40 mm Hg external compression at the ankle. The majority of patients need such support only from the foot to the knee, but patients with iliofemoral thrombosis and thigh edema may need compression up to the thigh. Patients should be instructed to put the stocking on first thing in the morning before the edema becomes evident and to wear the stocking until bedtime. The foot of the bed should be raised 6 to 12 in. to aid in venous return, and the patient should be instructed to raise the leg above the level of the heart several times each day for 15 to 30 minutes at a time. Patients who have had deep-vein thrombosis should be cautioned about situations that lend themselves to recurrent thrombosis; for example, long trips by car or plane should be interrupted by frequent stops or leaving one's seat and walking briefly in the aisle. Occasionally, elderly patients are unable to wear elastic stockings due to weakness and inability to put on the hose. In these situations, intermittent compression devices may be used periodically to reduce the edema and lower the risk of chronic venous stasis. And finally, patients using oral contraceptive agents who have had an episode of deep-vein thrombosis are encouraged to change methods of birth control to lessen their risk of recurrent episodes. Evidence of persistent swelling, induration, and pigmentation suggests the need for greater compression and more frequent elevation in an attempt to avoid breakdown and ulceration of the lower extremity.

DISCUSSION

Prevalence and Incidence

Deep-vein thrombosis is a very common and frequently unrecognized health problem, and it has recently been stated that it is likely that more deaths occur each year from the complications of venous thromboembolism than from AIDS. About 1.5 million people are estimated to develop deep-vein thrombosis in the United States each year, although only about 250,000 patients are clinically detected. It has further been estimated that 6 to 7 million patients have evidence of chronic venous insufficiency, and nearly 500,000 patients have leg ulcerations.

Related Basic Science

Several categories of patients have a significantly increased risk of development of deep-vein thrombosis. Of 100 general surgery patients, about 30% develop deep-vein thrombosis when evaluated by screening techniques. Of this 30%, about 20 percent, or six patients, have extension of the clot into the deep veins of the knee or thigh. Of these six patients with proximal deep-vein thrombosis, one to three patients will have a pulmonary embolus. Other categories of patients at increased risk for the development of deep-vein thrombosis include patients older than 40 years (and, particularly, those older than 70 years) who have operations or are immobilized for 1 week or longer; patients with spinal cord injuries; patients with heart disease; patients with cancer of the breast, genitourinary system (particularly prostate), stomach, colon, and lung; patients with lower extremity trauma; and obese patients. In fact, a recent prospective study of trauma patients documented that 58% of patients with major trauma had deep-vein thrombosis (Geerts, et al., 1994). Spinal cord injury patients fared even less well: 81% were found to have deep-vein thrombosis. It can be seen that Virchow's observation in 1856 about the triad of stasis, endothelial injury, and hypercoagulability still rings true today.

Natural History and Its Modification with Treatment

Thrombosis in the lower extremities probably starts, in the majority of cases, in the calf and later propagates into the popliteal and femoral veins. As noted in postoperative patients, this propagation happens in only about 20% of patients with clots in the calf veins, but of that 20% of patients with proximal clot, up to one half are at risk for major problems, pulmonary emboli being most notable. Unfortunately, as stressed in this discussion, clinical signs and symptoms of clot in the deep veins of the lower extremity occur in less than 50% of patients.

Using duplex scanning, researchers have demonstrated that recanalization of occluded vessels occurs often soon after deep-vein thrombosis. In one study, at the end of 3 months, nearly one half of the patients showed recanalization in all previously blocked segments. Some recanalization was even noted as early as 1 week after the onset of deep-vein thrombosis. Thus, it was suggested that patients with edema early after onset of deep-vein thrombosis have residual occlusion, whereas later edema more closely correlates with valvular incompetence.

Prevention

Given that 90% of all pulmonary emboli come from deep-vein thrombi in the pelvis and lower extremities, and that greater than 60,000 people

die each year in the United States from pulmonary emboli, it can be seen that prevention is probably the key aspect of this medical problem. Fortunately, we have a number of very effective medical and surgical methods that have been shown to reduce the incidence of deep-vein thrombosis and the subsequent incidence of pulmonary emboli. First and foremost of these preventive measures is use of subcutaneous heparin. Data from 70 randomized trials in more than 16,000 patients collected by Collins and colleagues (1988) have shown that the perioperative use of subcutaneous heparin can prevent about one half of all pulmonary emboli and nearly two thirds of all cases of deep-vein thrombosis. Their information further demonstrated a marked reduction in deaths from pulmonary emboli in patients treated with perioperative subcutaneous heparin. Another high-risk group, patients undergoing total hip replacement, recently underwent a randomized trial, conducted by Hull and colleagues (1990a), comparing the effectiveness of sequential intermittent calf and thigh compression versus no prophylaxis. Deep-vein thrombosis, diagnosed by venography, was present in 42% of control patients and in only 24% of patients treated by intermittent compression. Other agents, with less persuasive data, include dextran, warfarin, and compressive stockings.

Cost Containment

This is one of the few areas in medicine where cost containment and cost effectiveness have been looked at in some detail. Clinical diagnosis has been shown to be "cost ineffective" with respect to deep-vein thrombosis. Thus, in keeping with today's emphasis on performing diagnostic tests outside of the hospital, it is important to have an objective test that can be performed as an outpatient. Fortunately, all of the tests listed in Table 15–70–2 can be used as outpatient examinations. It can easily be seen that making the correct diagnosis is the first step in cost containment. Prophylaxis against deep-vein thrombosis has also been studied in patients undergoing orthopedic surgery, and it has been estimated that between 60 and 121 lives could be saved per 10,000 patients, thus reducing the average cost of care between $20 and $180 per patient. Interestingly, all of the six prophylactic methods in this study were "cost saving." Finally, Hull and associates (1990b) have shown that a 5-day course of heparin is as effective as a 10-day course in treating deep-vein thrombosis. Estimates of the cost saving of this shorter approach have suggested that as much as $500 million (in 1986 dollars) could be saved in the United States each year.

REFERENCES

Clagett GP. Prevention of postoperative venous thromboembolism: An update. Am J Surg 1994;168:515.

Collins R, Scrimgeour A, Yusuf S, Peto R. Reduction in fatal pulmonary embolism and venous thrombosis by postoperative administration of subcutaneous heparin: Overview of results of randomized trials in general, orthopedic, and urologic surgery. N Engl J Med 1988;318:1162.

Coon WW, Willis PW III, Keller JB. Venous thromboembolism and other venous disease in the Tecumseh Community Health Study. Circulation 1973;48:839.

Geerts WH, Code KI, Jay RM, et al. A prospective study of venous thromboembolism after major trauma. N Engl J Med 1994;331:1601.

Hull RD, Raskob GE, Gent M, et al. Effectiveness of intermittent pneumatic leg compression for preventing deep vein thrombosis after total hip replacement. JAMA 1990a;263:2313.

Hull RD, Raskob GE, Rosenbloom D, et al. Heparin for 5 days as compared in the initial treatment of proximal venous thrombosis. N Engl J Med 1990b;322:1260.

Killewich LA, Bedford GR, Beach KW, Strandness DE Jr. Spontaneous lysis of deep venous thrombi: Rate and outcome. J Vasc Surg 1989;9:89.

Oster G, Tuden RL, Colditz GA. A cost-effectiveness analysis of prophylaxis against deep-vein thrombosis in major orthopedic surgery. JAMA 1987;257:203.

Weinmann EE, Salzman EW. Deep-vein thrombosis. N Engl J Med 1994;331:1630.

Varicose Veins

Thomas F. Dodson, M.D.

DEFINITION

The term *varicose* means dilated, and the majority of these dilated veins involve the greater saphenous system; a minority, about 15%, involve the lesser saphenous system.

ETIOLOGY

Varicose veins are among the most common afflictions of humankind. An important distinction to make, however, is in the probable etiology of the varicose veins: whether they are primary, either congenital or inherited with no apparent underlying etiology, or secondary, usually as a result of thrombosis of the deep venous system. Thus, the examiner should ask about occupation, amount of time spent on one's feet, history of trauma to the lower extremities, history of pregnancy, family history of varicose veins, and previous history of superficial or deep-vein thrombophlebitis. Interestingly, although theories of pathogenesis abound with respect to varicose veins, there is a strong family history of varicose veins in more than 75% of patients.

CRITERIA FOR DIAGNOSIS

Suggestive

Varicose veins are usually manifested by enlargement of veins in the greater and lesser saphenous vein systems. Therefore, observation, along with some degree of history, usually suffices to make the diagnosis, although in the large or obese extremity, palpation may be required to deduce the problem.

Definitive

Valvular competency and the presence or absence of venous insufficiency can be easily assessed by simple tests and by use of the bidirectional Doppler.

CLINICAL MANIFESTATION

Subjective

The patient's complaints about varicose veins run the gamut from concerns about appearance on the beach to severe heaviness, pain, and fatigue in the lower extremity at the end of the day. These latter symptoms are typically exacerbated by the day's progression and length of time on one's feet, and they are also typically somewhat ameliorated by a change in dependency to elevation.

Objective

Physical Examination

When one stands, about 300 to 800 mL of blood is transferred to the lower extremities. The result of this upright position is a column of blood whose greatest pressure is at the ankle, where it approximates 110 to 120 mm Hg. With movement and use of the "muscular pump" in the calf musculature, this hydrostatic pressure markedly drops as blood is forced up toward the heart and prevented from returning by competent valves in the venous system. It is thus easy to understand that dysfunction of the valves in any of the three venous systems in the lower extremity—superficial veins (greater and lesser saphenous), deep veins, and communicating veins or "perforators"—creates a column of blood that lends itself to greater problems over time. It is important, therefore, not only carefully to examine the lower extremity by observation and palpation, but also to assess the competency of the valves of the venous system to gain an understanding of the underlying pathophysiology.

Two simple and common tests to assess valvular competency are the Trendelenburg test and the Perthes test. In the former test, the patient, lying on the table, raises his or her leg from 30° to 45° and allows the blood to drain from the superficial veins. This should take place over about 10 to 15 seconds. A rubber tourniquet is then placed around the leg just below the knee to occlude the long and short saphenous veins. The patient then stands upright with the tourniquet in place, and the filling of the veins distal to the tourniquet is scrutinized. If there is sudden filling of the lower leg varicosities, then both the deep and communicating venous systems are incompetent. If the veins fill slowly but are full within 30 to 60 seconds, then the examiner can conclude that the deep veins are competent, but that some of the communicating veins are incompetent. In the case of simple varicosities, filling of the veins is quite slow, thereby indicating competency of both the deep and communicating systems. On release of the tourniquet, sudden increased dilation of the varicosities implies incompetence of the valves of the superficial venous system. The Perthes test is similarly easy to perform and frequently used. With the patient standing, a rubber tourniquet is placed around the thigh or the lower leg and then the patient raises and lowers on the balls of the feet. This exercise activates the muscles of the lower leg and causes blood to flow more readily from the veins of the superficial system to the veins of the deep venous system. If the communicating and deep systems have competent valves, blood largely disappears from the superficial varicosities. If the valves are incompetent, however, the varicosities remain distended despite the exertion.

As an adjunct to these examinations, one researcher has used the bidirectional Doppler to aid in the diagnosis of incompetent valves. He noted that the examination could be done easily, in a short period (less than 5 minutes in the majority of cases), and could be readily taught. In an examination of more than 200 limbs, all with "significant" varices, it was found that saphenofemoral incompetence was present in slightly more than 50% of limbs. Other factors to be sought by the careful examiner include the presence of eczema or dermatitis, increased pigmentation in the lower aspect of the leg, and presence and degree of ulceration with documentation of both size and depth.

Routine Laboratory Abnormalities

There are no routine laboratory abnormalities related to varicose veins.

PLANS

Diagnostic

Differential Diagnosis

The physical evidence of varicose veins permits a definite diagnosis.

Diagnostic Options and Recommended Approach

The diagnosis of varicose veins is largely clinical in nature. It may be necessary to use one of the noted examinations to ascertain the patency of the deep venous system and, thus, to differentiate between primary and secondary varicose veins, but this should ideally be done in a noninvasive manner. B-mode/Doppler (duplex) evaluation and plethysmography are particularly suited for this discrimination.

Therapeutic

Although Evans et al. (1973) documented 23 patients, primarily elderly women, who bled to death from ulcerations overlying large varicosities, varicose veins in general carry no risk to life or health. The majority of patients can be treated in a conservative, nonsurgical fashion, with the mainstay of therapy being graduated compression stockings fitted to the patient's limb. If edema on standing is a component of the patient's process, the stocking should be fitted early after rising, before onset of edema. For simple varicosities, compression at the ankle should be 20 to 30 mm Hg, with higher degrees of compression being reserved for either greater symptomatology or the complications of the postphlebitic state. Although graduated compression stockings are clearly efficacious in the treatment of varicose veins, patients are often resistant to their long-term use. Reasons given for such resistance include difficulty in pulling them on (particularly in elderly patients), unsightliness when wearing a skirt, increased heat in warm climates, and the need for frequent replacement due to loss of elasticity over time. Periodic elevation of the lower extremity several times a day is also an important adjunct to effective relief of the heaviness and fatigue often associated with varicose veins.

A minority of patients with varicose veins need some other form of therapy, either sclerotherapy or operation. It is important to be very clear about the indications for surgical intervention in this process: the venous segments that are to be removed must have incompetent valves; the veins must then be notably dilated or enlarged; and patients with obstruction of the deep venous system of the extremity should *not*, with few exceptions, undergo removal of the superficial system. With these caveats in mind, a small group of patients with intractable symptoms or a severe cosmetic burden come to operation. If both legs are significantly involved with varicosities, each leg should be done at a separate sitting. The classic operation is a "high ligation and stripping," and both greater and lesser saphenous systems can be removed by this technique if they are both involved with varicosities. Often there are several varicosities related to perforating veins that are not directly connected to the greater or lesser saphenous veins, and these varicosities can be removed by separate small transverse incisions. The length of time in the hospital can be reduced by same-day admission, and discharge of the patient can usually be expected by the second or third postoperative day. Lesser procedures involving either avulsion or ligation of multiple varicosities can be done under local anesthesia with small incisions and subcuticular closures. Patients in these circumstances, as noted by Goren and Yellin (1991), can be sent home the same day with instructions for leg elevation at home, limited activities for several days, and the necessity of external support for at least 1 month.

Sclerotherapy is usually reserved for patients with a limited number of varicosities or for patients with recurrent varicosities after a surgical procedure. Using a 25-gauge needle, one injects approximately 0.5 mL of 3% sodium tetradecyl sulfate (Sotradecol) into the varicosity, a cotton ball is immediately taped over the injected vein, and other veins are similarly injected. At the conclusion of the procedure, the leg is wrapped with an elastic bandage (Ace bandage), and the patient is instructed to walk for at least 30 minutes twice a day. The elastic bandage is kept in place for at least 2 to 3 weeks, at which time the patient is reexamined. Support hose for at least 1 month are recommended at the conclusion of this postsclerotherapy period.

FOLLOW-UP

Venous problems demand the same degree of long-term follow-up as arterial problems. Factors that can be altered over time include a change in the degree of compression at the ankle with respect to graduated compression stockings and an increase in the amount of time spent with the legs in an elevated position. Rarely, it may even be necessary to change occupation due to the necessity for sitting or standing for lengthy periods in one position and the subsequent exacerbation of chronic venous insufficiency. Patients who have undergone sclerotherapy or operation, after the initial 1- and 6-month visits, should be seen at yearly intervals to detect recurrence of varicosities or the appearance of new primary varicosities in unoperated areas. In general, the recurrence rate after operation should be less than 20%.

DISCUSSION

Prevalence and Incidence

In his review of varicose veins, Tolins (1983) noted that varicose veins were "as old as Hippocrates," that Galen had first proposed surgical treatment, and that Ambrose Pare in the 16th century first noted the association of varicose veins and leg ulcers. Varicose veins were first injected in 1835, and ligation and stripping were first used nearly 90 years ago. Between 12 and 20% of the adult population of the United States have varicose veins; thus, it is endemic within our population.

Related Basic Science

The etiology of varicose veins is a question still in dispute. Theories range from a lack of adaptation to the upright position to Haimovici's postulate of precapillary arteriovenous shunting. Regardless of the underlying cause, varicose veins are troublesome to a significant minority of the population, and with the aging or "graying" of the American population, more physicians will be confronted by patients with varicosities of the lower extremity.

Natural History and Its Modification with Treatment

With the development of varicosities in one lower extremity, the natural history is one of a gradual increase in the number or size of the varicosities over time. Interestingly, when only one leg has been affected, less than one third of patients develop varicosities in the opposite leg. Graded compression stockings and periodic elevation do not alter the underlying pathophysiology, but do slow or often halt the gradual deterioration noted in the untreated extremity. In the small group of patients who require either sclerotherapy or operation, the great majority have amelioration of their symptoms or their cosmetic burden. Patients must be instructed that varicose veins are primarily a cosmetic problem and unlikely to affect their overall life or health. It should also be noted that although 85% of patients undergoing operation have good to excellent results, about 5% of patients do not have salutary results after surgical intervention.

Prevention

Although the etiology of varicose veins is still debated, it would seem prudent to suggest graded compression stockings to individuals whose occupation requires lengthy periods of standing in one position. Other measures such as periodic movement to contract the muscles of the calves or elevation of the lower extremities may similarly be helpful. Patients with deep-vein thrombosis deserve especially close follow-up of extremities in an attempt to minimize the sequelae of occlusion of the deep venous system, commonly called the *postphlebitic syndrome*.

Cost Containment

By limiting surgical intervention to only those patients with severe varicosities, and by using sclerotherapy in other patients whose cosmetic burden is heavy or who have recurrent varicose veins, the costs of management of varicose veins can be diminished. Likewise, in patients who require operation, some limited procedures can be done on an outpatient basis, thereby reducing costs significantly. In the subgroup of patients who develop varicosities as a result of deep-vein thrombosis, close follow-up and careful attention to reduction of edema may also be effective in cost reduction.

REFERENCES

Bergan JJ. New developments in the surgical treatment of venous disease. Cardiovasc Surg 1993;1:624.

Evans GA, Evans DMD, Seal RME, Craven JL. Spontaneous fatal hemorrhage caused by varicose veins. Lancet 1973;2:1359.

Goren G, Yellin AE. Ambulatory stab evulsion phlebectomy for truncal varicose veins. Am J Surg 1991;162:166.

Gutman H, Zelikovski A, Haddad M, Reiss R. Clinical experience treating varicose veins in the aged. Am Surg 1989;55:625.

Haimovici H. Role of precapillary arteriovenous shunting in the pathogenesis of varicose veins and its therapeutic implications. Surgery 1987;101:515.

Large J. Doppler testing as an important conservation measure in the treatment of varicose veins. Aust NZ J Surg 1984;54:357.

Tolins SH. Treatment of varicose veins: An update. Am J Surg 1983;145:248.

Villavicencio JL. Excision of varicose veins. In: Ernst CB, Stanley JC, eds. Current therapy in vascular surgery. Philadelphia: Decker, 1991:967.

Weissberg D. Treatment of varicose veins by compression sclerotherapy. Surg Gynecol Obstet 1980;151:353.

Renal Disorders

Edmund Bourke, M.D.

CHAPTER 16–1

Oliguria

Brian N. Ling, M.D., and Michael Allon, M.D.

DEFINITION

Oliguria is defined as urine output of insufficient volume to remove excretory waste products (usually < 500 mL/day). Anuria, although implying the complete absence of urine, is clinically defined as a urine output of less than 50 to 100 mL/d.

ETIOLOGY

Oliguria can result from a reduction in renal blood flow or glomerular filtration rate, glomerular or tubular dysfunction, obstruction of urine flow, or leakage along the urinary tract.

CRITERIA FOR DIAGNOSIS
Suggestive

The patient notes a decrease in normal urinary frequency or volume. Voiding reflexes are normally stimulated when the bladder is filled with approximately 250 mL of urine; therefore, a 24-hour cessation would be significant. In the hospitalized patient, oliguria is usually detected by medical personnel when measuring daily or more frequent outputs and weights. Significant waste product accumulation can be asymptomatic and the physician may be alerted only after blood chemistries reveal an increase in blood urea nitrogen and serum creatinine.

Definitive

Importantly, in situations where renal functional compromise can be anticipated, 24 hours should not be permitted to elapse prior to intervening. Thus, a urine volume of 20 mL/h or less for 2 consecutive hours should prompt an evaluation.

CLINICAL MANIFESTATIONS
Subjective

Oliguria is not a familial or congenital disorder. Recent drug (e.g., nonsteroidal antiinflammatory drugs, diuretics, aminoglycosides, sulfonamides) or exogenous nephrotoxin exposure (e.g., ethylene glycol, carbon tetrachloride); surgery; infections; contrast dye; and underlying illnesses that may affect renal function (e.g., nephrotic syndrome, cirrhosis, congestive heart failure, peripheral vascular disease, prostatic hypertrophy) should be detailed.

The potential multisystem manifestations of oliguric waste product accumulation (uremia) are covered elsewhere (see Chapters 16–9 and 16–12).

Objective
Physical Examination

Prerenal failure due to true volume depletion may manifest with decreased skin turgor, flat neck veins, tachycardia, and orthostatic hypotension, whereas prerenal failure presenting with peripheral edema and/or ascites should raise the suspicion of impaired effective renal perfusion secondary to heart or liver failure, or nephrotic syndrome. Prostatic enlargement or an abdominal/pelvic mass may point to postrenal obstruction. Acute urinary retention must be one of the earliest exclusions by inspection, palpation, percussion, and catheterization of the bladder with quantitation of post-void residual. Hypertension and the presence of arterial bruits (especially abdominal bruits) should raise the possibility of prerenal vascular obstruction. Evidence of increased vascular capacitance and hyperventilation accompanying oliguria frequently precede a fall in blood pressure in impending septic shock.

Routine Laboratory Abnormalities

Most patients with acute oliguria demonstrate azotemia, an elevation in blood urea nitrogen and serum creatinine. The approximate day on which the blood urea nitrogen and serum creatinine began to rise can usually be ascertained for inpatients. This represents the onset of renal insult (e.g., ruptured aortic aneurysm) or the cumulative effect of some nephrotoxin (e.g., aminoglycoside-induced acute tubular necrosis [ATN]). Similarly, the time lag between the nephrotoxic insult and development of clinical signs is important (e.g., drug-induced acute interstitial nephritis [AIN]).

PLANS
Diagnostic
Differential Diagnosis

A conventional classification scheme for oliguria is divided into prerenal, intrarenal, and postrenal causes (Table 16–1–1). Although the mere presence of oliguria provides no specific information regarding its etiology (i.e., prerenal conditions, intrinsic renal disease, incomplete urinary tract obstruction), anuria is a much more uncommon presentation and narrows the differential considerably (asterisks in Table 16–1–1).

Diagnostic Options and Recommended Approach

Acute retention due to urethral obstruction from prostatic encroachment, strictures, and so on must be considered initially and postvoid residual volume ascertained. Once this has been excluded, a few "low-tech" laboratory tests will aid the physician in distinguishing the etiology of oliguria (Table 16–1–1).

An increase in blood urea nitrogen (BUN) that is out of proportion to the rise in serum creatinine (S_{Cr}) (BUN:S_{Cr} ratio > 20:1) usually accompanies prerenal conditions. Decreased effective arterial blood volume promotes proximal tubular reabsorption of both sodium and water and, with this, enhanced passive uptake of urea. Conversely, intrarenal disease demonstrates a more parallel increase in these two indices (BUN:S_{Cr} ratio = 10–15:1). Exceptions to these principles do occur: low BUN values are seen in hepatic failure or protein malnutrition despite decreased effective arterial blood volume; and high BUN:S_{Cr} ratio values due to recent meat intake, gastrointestinal tract bleeding, tetracycline, increased catabolism, and high-dose corticosteroids are seen even when the etiology is intrarenal. Although S_{Cr} increases steadily by approximately 0.5 mg/dL/d in oliguric intrarenal disease (e.g., ATN), prerenal causes usually feature a slower, more variable and fluctuating rise due to transient changes in renal perfusion.

Urinalysis is perhaps the easiest and most important discriminator of underlying renal disease. The benign urinary sediment usually seen in prerenal and postrenal oliguria reflects the lack of intrinsic structural kidney damage. Conversely, approximately 75% of ATN cases have a muddy sediment consisting of renal tubular epithelial cells and granular and epithelial cell casts. Red cells, white cells, and white cell casts are often seen in AIN. Hansen's stain of the urinary sediment demonstrates

TABLE 16–1–1. CAUSES OF OLIGURIA

Prerenal
Shock*
Volume depletion
Burns
"Third-space sequestration" (postsurgical, acute pancreatitis)
Congestive heart failure
Cirrhosis
Nephrotic syndrome
Hepatorenal syndrome
Bilateral renal vascular obstruction*
Periphery vasodilatation (increased capacitance, e.g., septicemia)
Nonsteroidal antiinflammatory drugs
Angiotensin converting enzyme inhibitors

Intrarenal
Acute tubular necrosis
Ischemic (as in prerenal) toxic (drugs, poisons) pigment (myoglobin, hemoglobin)
Acute glomerulonephritis*
Vasculitis*
Hemolytic uremic syndrome*
Cortical necrosis*
Preeclampsia
Papillary necrosis
Acute interstitial nephritis
Renal allograft rejection
Accelerated nephrosclerosis
Renal atheroembolic disease
Acute hyperuricemic nephropathy
Intratubular obstruction* (acyclovir, sulfonamides, methotrexate, dextran, hyperoxaluria, multiple myeloma)
End-stage renal disease (after initiation of dialysis*)

Postrenal
Bilateral ureteral obstruction* (or unilateral with single functioning kidney)
Bladder rupture*
Bladder catheter obstruction*
Urethral obstruction*

*Anuria not uncommon.

eosinophiluria in approximately 80% of cases of AIN. Acute glomerulonephritis will, in addition to white cells and red cells, demonstrate red cell casts and variable amounts of proteinuria. Dysmorphic red cells on phase-contrast microscopy are also indicative of glomerular pathology.

Urinary indices have been used mainly to distinguish prerenal disease from ATN, the two entities that account for approximately 75% of oliguric renal failure (see Chapter 16–9). Urinary osmolality (U_{Osm}) greater than 500 mOsm/kg, reflecting hypovolemic (appropriate) stimulation of water conservation by antidiuretic hormone, suggests prerenal oliguria. Conversely, an inability to concentrate urine ($U_{Osm} < 350$ mOsm/kg) indicates intrinsic renal damage (see Discussion). Urinary sodium concentration (U_{Na}) should be low (< 20 mEq/L) in pre­renal disease, reflecting proximal tubule sodium avidity, and high (> 40 mEq/L) with tubulointerstitial disease; however, urinary sodium concentration reflects not only renal sodium, but also water reabsorption. If water reabsorption is very low (e.g., nephrogenic diabetes insipidus due to AIN), the urinary sodium/H_2O ratio may be lowered and urinary sodium could decrease. Conversely, with the strong stimulus for water reabsorption in prerenal oliguria, urinary sodium concentration may approach 25 mEq/L in the absence of intrarenal disease. Because of this diagnostic overlap in urinary sodium values, several studies have demonstrated that the fractional excretion of sodium (FE_{Na}) is the most discriminatory test for distinguishing between prerenal disease ($FE_{Na} < 1\%$) and ATN ($FE_{Na} > 1\%$) (see Chapter 16–9 for calculation of FE_{Na}). Despite the accuracy of this test, there are numerous exceptions of which the physician must be aware (Table 16–1–2). Because of such exceptions, clinical judgment should supercede rigid interpretation of urinary indices.

Postrenal obstruction and prerenal obstruction should be considered in any patient presenting with oligoanuria. Exclusion of urinary retention by bladder catheterization focuses attention on supravesical causes of possible obstruction, either bilateral or unilateral, in a single functioning kidney. Renal ultrasound (or computed tomography) plus plain films of the abdomen are noninvasive radiographic modalities for assessing the presence of obstruction, mass lesions, and kidney size and number. Intravenous contrast dye should be avoided or minimized whenever possible, as preexisting renal insufficiency increases the risk of developing superimposed contrast-induced nephropathy. With our growing geriatric patient population and increased application of cardiovascular interventions (e.g., angioplasty, bypass, endarterectomies), the incidence of renovascular obstruction (e.g., atherosclerosis, dissection, thrombosis, embolism) as a cause of oligoanuria is increasing. Doppler renal ultrasound, computer tomography, magnetic resonance imaging, and renal nucleotide scans are potential radiologic modalities for assessing renovascular patency. Despite the risk of contrast, however, angiograms are still often needed to make the definitive diagnosis.

Therapeutic

General supportive care in the patient with oliguria requires close attention to fluid, electrolyte, and acid–base balance; nutrition; dosage adjustment for drugs metabolized by the kidney; uremic symptoms or signs; and, sometimes, institution of acute dialysis (see Chapter 16–9). Removal of potential nephrotoxic insults (e.g., drugs, infection, hyperuricemia, hypercalcemia, hypertension, crystalluria, light chains, autoantibodies) is an obvious goal in the treatment of intrarenal oliguria. Dietary manipulations (i.e., 0.6 g/kg/d high-biological-grade protein) will reduce the obligatory solute load to be excreted during the period of reduced urine output. Limiting protein intake decreases the load of urea, sulfates, phosphates, organic acids, and potassium, whereas the addition of carbohydrates and fats supplements calorie requirements and minimizes endogenous protein catabolism.

Reestablishing adequate renal perfusion is tailored to the underlying cause. Fluid resuscitation in true volume depletion; inotropic support, relief of coronary ischemia, and afterload reduction in congestive heart failure; or discontinuation of prostaglandin inhibitors (e.g., nonsteroidal antiinflammatory drugs) and diuretics in patients with decreased effective arterial blood volume should improve urine output in prerenal disease within 24 to 78 hours. Conversely, oliguric ATN does not respond to such interventions.

Much has been written about "conversion" of oliguric to nonoliguric (> 500 mL/d) ATN. Although increasing urine output with large doses of loop diuretics (e.g., furosemide 240 mg), osmotic diuretics (e.g., mannitol 25 g), or "renal dose" dopamine (< 3 μg/kg/min) often aids volume management in acute renal failure, it has not been shown to improve the prognosis for renal or patient survival. This is understandable, as diuretics in established oliguric ATN only increase natriuresis and diuresis in residual undamaged nephrons, but cannot stimulate formation of new functional nephron mass. If initially unresponsive to such large diuretic challenges, repeated dosing is discouraged as it only increases the risk of accumulated drug toxicity (e.g., ototoxicity from furosemide, fluid overload and oncotic renal failure from mannitol).

For obstructive uropathy above the level of the bladder neck (i.e., unrelieved by bladder catheterization), immediate consultation with radiology and urology colleagues is essential. Ultrasound, computer tomography, cystoscopy, and retrograde pyelograms direct the need for surgical or radiologic intervention to bypass or relieve the obstruction. The postobstructive diuresis following relief of the obstruction is usually "appropriate" to the patient's volume status, and fluid replacement beyond maintenance only perpetuates the high urinary flow. Rarely, in less than 5% of patients, the ensuing urine output is "inappropriate" due to tubular dysfunction causing severe volume depletion unless the fluid is replaced. Thus, the volume status must be monitored closely in patients with postobstructive diuresis. Similarly, high suspicion for renovascular occlusion (e.g., abrupt postoperative oligoanuria after aortic aneurysm repair or renal artery bypass surgery) should prompt immediate consultation with radiology and vascular surgery colleagues.

FOLLOW-UP

Outpatient management is dependent on the reversibility of the nephrologic insult and the degree of residual renal dysfunction at hospital discharge. Simple dehydration in a marathon runner during extreme heat, who responds to overnight fluid replacement, may require no follow-up. Chronic prerenal states (e.g., heart or liver failure) usually require careful attention to medications that influence blood pressure and intravascular volume status (e.g., antihypertensives, diuretics) and, therefore, renal perfusion. Oliguric renal failure, in a previously healthy individual, after a single reversible nephrotoxic insult (e.g., contrast-induced ATN) requires renal function follow-up for 1 to 2 months or until it returns to baseline (less commonly, recovery can take up to 3–6 months). On the other hand, many other intrarenal diseases (Table 16–1–1) require lifelong follow-up even after the acute oligoanuria resolves. Autoimmune vasculitis and glomerulonephritides (e.g., diffuse proliferative lupus nephritis and minimal change disease) may require

TABLE 16–1–2. MEDICAL CONDITIONS IN WHICH FE_{Na} MAY BE UNRELIABLE

$FE_{Na} < 1\%$ Despite Oliguric Intrarenal Disease
Underlying chronic prerenal disease (Table 1)
Hepatorenal syndrome
Sepsis
Nonsteroidal antiinflammatory drugs
Severe burns
Postcoronary artery bypass
Angiotensin-converting enzyme inhibitors with bilateral renal artery stenosis or unilateral renal artery stenosis with one functioning kidney
Acute glomerulonephritis
Vasculitis
Acute interstitial nephritis
Contrast- and pigment-induced acute tubular necrosis
Renal atheroemboli
Renal allograft rejection
Cyclosporine nephrotoxicity
Early obstructive uropathy

$FE_{Na} > 1\%$ Despite Oliguric Hypovolemia
Mineralocorticoid deficiency
Diuretic use within last 12–24 hours
Osmotic diuresis (mannitol, glycosuria)
Metabolic alkalosis with bicarbonaturia
Underlying chronic renal failure

close monitoring of serum creatinine, proteinuria, and urinary sediment during and after immunosuppressive therapy. After acute relief of obstructive uropathy, training in intermittent self-catheterization (e.g., neurogenic bladder) or nephrostomy care; or chemo/radiotherapy or resection for malignancy (e.g., transitional cell, prostatic cancer) and follow-up for possible recurrence of obstruction may be needed. Finally, some patients with acute oligoanuria do not resolve, but rather progress to end-stage renal disease (e.g., renal cortical necrosis, cholesterol emboli). These individuals require close follow-up of volume status, serum electrolytes, acid–base balance, drug dosage adjustments, and uremic symptoms and signs pending the need for renal replacement therapy (i.e., dialysis or kidney transplantation) (see Chapter 16–12).

DISCUSSION

Prevalence and Incidence

Given the multiple and varied pathologic processes that can present with oliguria (Table 16–1–1), specific prevalence and incidence statistics are not available.

Related Basic Science

Quantifying oliguria as less than 500 mL of urine output per day is based on the assumption that with consumption of an average mixed diet, renal excretion of nonvolatile waste products is approximately 720 mOsm/d. As maximal urinary concentrating ability is 1400 mOsm/kg, approximately 500 mL/d is required to excrete this osmolar load. The actual accumulated solute load (and, therefore, the output defining oliguria) varies with individual diet and metabolism. At physiologic extremes, as little as 10 mL/h maximumly concentrated urine maintains normal body composition on minimal solute and water intake. It is obvious that the minimum urinary volume in which this solute load is excreted is also determined by the concentrating ability of the kidney.

Normal urinary concentrating ability is dependent on maintenance of the countercurrent multiplier system in the renal medullary interstitium, the presence of antidiuretic hormone, and intact tubular responsiveness to antidiuretic hormone. The high solute gradient between the medullary interstitium and the renal tubular fluid is generated by NaCl transport via the Na^+–K^+–$2Cl^-$ cotransporter located in the water-impermeable, thick ascending loop of Henle. Antidiuretic hormone stimulates water channels in the cortical collecting tubule, allowing water reabsorption driven by this interstitial osmotic gradient. This water reclamation raises the fractional solute contribution and absolute urea concentration in the fluid delivered to the medullary collecting duct. Urea is then transported from the inner medullary collecting duct to the papillary interstitium down its chemical gradient.

When urine is maximally concentrated, urine volume is a function of the obligatory solute load to be excreted (the lower the solute load, the smaller the requisite urine output); however, if urinary concentrating ability is reduced, urine volume must increase to excrete the same amount of waste products. Importantly, maximum urinary osmolality progressively declines with age (i.e., "nonoliguric" > 500 mL of urine output per day may be required for an older patient to excrete his or her obligate solute load). Oliguria can result from disturbances in renal blood flow, glomerular filtration rate, tubular function, or urinary tract collecting system. The pathophysiology of prerenal, intrarenal, and postrenal acute renal failure is discussed elsewhere (see Chapter 16–9).

Natural History and Its Modification with Treatment

Oliguria may resolve in a few minutes to hours, as with rehydration in a patient with true volume depletion or bladder catheterization in a patient with prostatic obstruction. Severe, prolonged renal hypoperfusion can lead to ischemic ATN. Most cases of oliguria due to intrarenal disease (e.g., ATN, acute glomerulonephritis, AIN) last several days to a few weeks. One rare exception is the combination of interstitial nephritis and minimal change disease resulting from nonsteroidal anti-inflammatory drugs (NSAIDs). Although "NSAID nephropathy" usually presents with oliguria (67%) and renal failure (89%), often requiring acute dialysis (32%), approximately three quarters of patients regain renal function 3 months after discontinuing the drug. On the other hand, permanent oliguria and loss of renal function may occur in bilateral renal cortical necrosis and atheroembolic renal infarction. In some processes, such as obstructive uropathy and postinfectious glomerulonephritis, acute recovery of glomerular filtration rate occurs despite a significant loss of functioning renal mass. Over many years, the compensatory hyperfiltration/hyperperfusion of these remaining nephrons is thought to contribute to progressive renal failure secondary to hemodynamically mediated glomerulosclerosis.

Prevention

The causes of oligoanuria are generally not due to noncompliance, nor are they preventable by the patients. Possible exceptions are reversible prerenal conditions. Compliance with appropriate afterload reducers, inotropics, antiarrhythmics, and antianginal medications to maintain states of compensated congestive heart failure; adequate hydration (particularly in the debilitated elderly population without free access to fluids); and avoidance of hepatotoxins in cirrhotic patients (e.g., ethanol) and NSAIDs in patients with decreased effective arterial blood volume or chronic renal insufficiency are examples. Patients with a previous history of drug-induced AIN should be warned about the risk of hypersensitivity reactions with exposure to similar medications. Prophylaxis for patients at high risk for contrast-induced ATN (i.e., diabetics with renal insufficiency, multiple myeloma) includes adequate hydration, and possibly calcium channel blockers to reduce renal vasoconstriction. Recurrent renal stone formers may require special intervention (e.g., thiazides for hypercalciuria, allopurinol and urinary alkalinization for hyperuricemia) in addition to maintenance of high urinary flow rates to avoid urinary tract obstruction. Atherosclerosis risk factor intervention (e.g., smoking cessation, lipid-lowering and antihypertensive medications, blood sugar control, prudent diet) would be advisable for patients with renovascular ischemic disease/hypertension.

Cost Containment

As noted, only simple clinical assessment of the patient along with a few inexpensive laboratory screens are required in the initial diagnosis of oliguria. Unfortunately, oligoanuric renal failure often requires extensive therapeutic/supportive measures. The development of oliguria occurs most commonly in the setting of hospitalized patients. Therefore, education of our peers on avoidance of iatrogenic causes of oliguric renal failure (e.g., nephrotoxic drugs; diuretics, angiotensin-converting enzyme inhibitors, and NSAIDs in patients with decreased EABV; overly aggressive blood pressure control in hypertensive crisis) is a major cost containment strategy. Since prerenal causes of oliguria, if overlooked for too long, may progress to intrinsic acute tubular necrosis, a high index of suspicion with prompt intervention may avert the onset and very costly course of established acute renal failure.

REFERENCES

Eliahou HE. Oliguria and anuria. In: Massry SG, Glassock RJ, eds. Textbook of nephrology. 2nd ed. Baltimore: Williams and Wilkins, 1989:475.

Guyton AC. The mechanism for excreting excess solutes: The countercurrent mechanism for excreting a concentrated urine. In: Textbook of medical physiology. Philadelphia: Saunders, 1991:309.

Ling BN. Diuretic effects of "low dose" intravenous dopamine. In: Puschett JB, ed. Diuretics IV: Chemistry, pharmacology and clinical applications. Amsterdam: Elsevier Science, 1993:139.

Rose BD. Approach to the patient with renal disease. In: Rubenstein E, Federman DD, eds. Medicine. New York: Scientific American, 1994;10:III:1.

Sweny P. Is postoperative oliguria avoidable? Br J Anaesth 1991;67:137.

CHAPTER 16–2

Polyuria

Michael Allon, M.D., and Brian N. Ling, M.D.

DEFINITION

Polyuria is defined as a 24-hour urine volume exceeding 3 L.

ETIOLOGY

Polyuria may be caused by a large number of disorders (Table 16–2–1). They are most readily classified as nephrogenic, neurogenic (central diabetes insipidus), psychogenic, and osmogenic.

CRITERIA FOR DIAGNOSIS
Suggestive

Polyuria may be suspected in any patient complaining of frequency, nocturia, polydipsia, or excessive thirst. Some patients may express a strong preference for ice water. In patients in whom fluid intake is restricted, the first clue may be the development of hypernatremia or altered mental status.

Definitive

The diagnosis of polyuria is established definitively by measuring the volume of a 24-hour urine collection.

CLINICAL MANIFESTATIONS
Subjective

The most common symptoms offered by the patient are excessive thirst, frequent urination, and nocturia.

A family history of polyuria or excessive thirst may be present in a small number of patients with diabetes insipidus.

TABLE 16–2–1. DIFFERENTIAL DIAGNOSIS OF POLYURIA

Osmotic diuresis
Hyperglycemia
Mannitol
Radiocontrast media
Diuretics
Postobstructive diuresis
Excessive protein intake or catabolism
Salt-losing nephropathy
Paroxysmal atrial tachycardia
Psychogenic polydipsia
Neurotic
Psychotic (schizophrenic)
Central (neurogenic) diabetes insipidus
Infiltrative disease (e.g., sarcoidosis)
Infection (e.g., tuberculosis)
Neoplasm (primary or metastatic)
Head trauma or surgery
Drugs
Familial (autosomal dominant)
Idiopathic
Nephrogenic diabetes insipidus
Congenital (X-linked recessive)
Drugs (e.g., lithium, *cis*-platinum)
Tubulointerstitial disease (e.g., sickle cell anemia)
Electrolyte abnormalities: hypercalcemia, hypokalemia

Objective
Physical Examination

Physical findings are generally absent. If the patient has been fluid restricted, the physical examination will reveal evidence of extracellular volume depletion.

Routine Laboratory Abnormalities

Routine laboratory tests that should be obtained include complete blood count; serum electrolytes; urea nitrogen, creatinine, glucose, calcium, and osmolality; and 24-hour urine collection for volume, osmolality, sodium, and creatinine. These tests may provide an etiology for the polyuria (e.g., hypercalcemia, hypokalemia, or hyperglycemia) or evidence for dehydration or intravascular volume depletion (increased serum sodium or osmolality, increased hematocrit, increased urea nitrogen-to-creatinine ratio). On renal ultrasound, patients with profound polyuria may have dilation of the collecting system; this does not necessarily indicate postrenal obstruction.

PLANS
Diagnostic
Differential Diagnosis

The differential diagnosis is summarized in Table 16–2–1.

Diagnostic Options

Before embarking on a detailed diagnostic workup for the etiology of the polyuria (Table 16–2–1), biochemical tests should be ordered to exclude such causes as hyperglycemia, hypercalcemia, and hypokalemia. A clinical evaluation should be done to eliminate causes of osmotic diuresis (administration of mannitol, radiocontrast medium, or diuretics; diabetes mellitus; excessive protein intake or catabolism; paroxysmal atrial tachycardia). Urine electrolytes and osmolality, urine flow rate, and osmolar clearance rate should then be measured. If urine electrolytes, that is, $2[U_{Na}+U_K]$, account for the majority of the measured urinary osmolality, one needs to consider use of diuretics, tubulointerstitial renal disease, or increased excretion of organic anions (such as ketoacids) as contributing to the polyuria.

If these causes of polyuria have been ruled out, then a water diuresis is likely, and the next diagnostic step is a dehydration test. Fluid restriction is used to differentiate between primary polydipsia and diabetes insipidus (in other words, we are trying to distinguish between patients who drink because of excessive urinary water losses and patients who have large urine volumes because they drink water excessively). The patient is subjected to a monitored water deprivation for 16 hours, or until he or she loses 3 to 5% of body weight, whichever occurs first. After measuring the plasma and urine osmolality, the patient receives an injection of aqueous vasopressin, 5 U subcutaneously, and urine osmolality is rechecked after 2 hours (Table 16–2–2). A normal person increases the urine osmolality maximally (i.e., > 800 mOsm/kg) with dehydration, with no further increase following vasopressin. A normal response rules out diabetes insipidus and suggests the diagnosis of primary polydipsia; however, patients with primary polydipsia often have subnormal urinary concentration, due to medullary washout from a prolonged previous excess water ingestion. In patients with central (neurogenic) diabetes insipidus the urine osmolality rises very little with dehydration alone, but increases substantially after vasopressin administration. Patients with nephrogenic diabetes insipidus have a minimal increase in urine osmolality with dehydration and an increase of less than 10% following vasopressin.

The above tests are indirect, in that plasma vasopressin levels are not measured directly. The positive predictive value of these tests is 85%;

TABLE 16–2–2. LABORATORY TESTS FOR THE DIFFERENTIAL DIAGNOSIS OF POLYURIA*

Diagnosis	Urine Osmolality (mOsm/kg)	
	Water Deprivation	Vasopressin Administration
Central diabetes insipidus	<450	Increase >20%
Nephrogenic diabetes insipidus	<450	Increase <10%
Primary polydipsia	>600	Increase <10%
Normal response	>800	No further increase

*These tests are used after causes of osmotic diuresis have been ruled out. Note that these are representative values, and that there may be considerable overlap in these values among patients with the individual diagnosis. Therefore, Figure 16–2–1 is useful in enhancing the diagnostic accuracy.

the negative predictive value is 67% (calculated from data reported by Zerbe and Robertson, 1981). Unfortunately, the indirect tests outlined above do not always reliably establish the etiology of the polyuria. Diagnostic confusion is most likely to occur in distinguishing between partial neurogenic diabetes insipidus and primary polydipsia. Concurrent measurement of plasma osmolality, urine osmolality, and vasopressin concentration may be helpful in establishing a more definitive diagnosis (Figure 16–2–1). If the plasma vasopressin is undetectable when the plasma osmolality is elevated, complete central diabetes insipidus is present. If the plasma vasopressin levels are detectable but subnormal for the plasma osmolality, partial central diabetes insipidus is present. If the vasopressin concentration is normal relative to the plasma osmolality, the patient has either primary polydipsia or nephrogenic diabetes insipidus. To distinguish between the latter two diagnoses, it is necessary to examine the relationship between the plasma vasopressin and urine osmolality. Nephrogenic diabetes insipidus is diagnosed when the urine osmolality is inappropriately low for the plasma vasopressin concentration, whereas primary polydipsia is diagnosed when the urine osmolality is appropriate for the plasma vasopressin concentration. Although direct measurement of plasma vaso-

pressin enhances diagnostic accuracy in patients with polyuria, this biochemical test is not currently available in most clinical laboratories and, therefore, is not used routinely.

Recommended Approach

Initially, one checks serum glucose, potassium, and calcium, and urine electrolytes, to eliminate easily correctable causes of polyuria. If the patient is taking lithium, the drug is stopped. If the polyuria persists, a carefully supervised water deprivation test is performed to distinguish among primary polydipsia, central diabetes insipidus, and nephrogenic diabetes insipidus (Table 16–2–2). Measurements of plasma vasopressin are reserved for cases in which the diagnosis remains elusive despite measurements of urine osmolality.

Renal ultrasound patients with profound polyuria may have dilation of the collecting system; this does not necessarily indicate postrenal obstruction.

Therapeutic

Therapeutic Options

In polyuria due to an electrolyte disorder, correction of the underlying condition reverses the polyuria (e.g., insulin for hyperglycemia, potassium administration for hypokalemia). In patients with psychogenic polydipsia, fluid restriction corrects the polyuria. When drug-induced nephrogenic diabetes insipidus is suspected, consideration should be given to discontinuation of the offending drug. In patients with central diabetes insipidus the treatment involves exogenous replacement of vasopressin. This may be administered either as a subcutaneous injection of aqueous vasopressin 5 to 10 U subcutaneously every 3 to 6 hours, or as an intranasal spray of the long-acting vasopressin analog 1-desamino-8-D-arginine vasopressin (dDAVP) 10 to 20 μg every 8 to 12 hours. Vasopressin may rarely produce headaches, nausea, or nasal congestion. The nasal absorption of dDAVP may be erratic if there is nasal congestion. Occasionally, drugs such as chlorpropamide, clofibrate, and carbamazepine, which enhance the tubular sensitivity to vasopressin, may be effective for treatment of incomplete central dia-

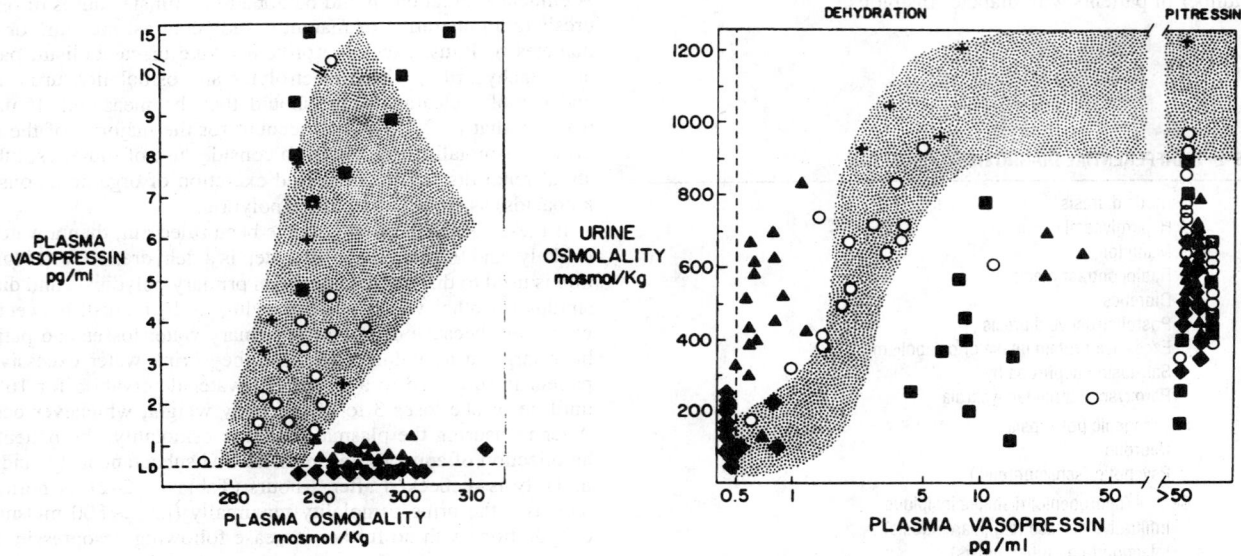

Figure 16–2–1. Left: Relationship of plasma vasopressin to concurrent plasma osmolality in patients with polyuria of diverse etiology. All measurements were made at the end of a standard dehydration test. The shaded area represents the range of normal. In patients with severe (diamonds) or partial (triangles) neurogenic diabetes insipidus, plasma vasopressin was almost always subnormal relative to plasma osmolality. In contrast, the values from patients with dipsogenic (circles) or nephrogenic (squares) diabetes insipidus were consistently above the normal range. **Right:** Relationship of urine osmolality to concurrent plasma vasopressin in patients with polyuria of diverse etiology. All measurements were made at the end of a standard dehydration test. The shaded area represents the range of normal. In patients with severe (diamonds) or partial (triangles) neurogenic diabetes insipidus, urine osmolality is normal or supranormal relative to plasma vasopressin when the latter is submaximal. In patients with nephrogenic diabetes insipidus (squares), urine osmolality is always subnormal for plasma vasopressin. In patients with dipsogenic diabetes insipidus (circles), the relationship is often normal but may be subnormal when plasma vasopressin is supramaximal due to blunting of concentrating capacity. *(Source: Robertson GL. Diagnosis of diabetes insipidus. In: Czernichow AP, Robinson A, eds. Diabetes insipidus. S. Karger, Basel, 1984. Reproduced with permission from the publisher and author.)*

betes insipidus. Several therapeutic options are available for the treatment of nephrogenic diabetes insipidus. Thiazide diuretics (e.g., hydrochlorothiazide, 50 mg daily), in conjunction with dietary sodium restriction (2 g/d), may be helpful. The most common adverse effects are intravascular volume depletion and hypokalemia. The administration of amiloride may decrease the polyuria due to lithium-induced nephrogenic diabetes insipidus. The usual dose is 10 mg twice daily. The most common side effect is hyperkalemia. Prostaglandin synthetase inhibitors (nonsteroidal antiinflammatory drugs) may also be effective in reducing urinary volume in some patients with nephrogenic diabetes insipidus. Indomethacin 50 mg three times daily is an effective regimen. Possible side effects may include gastrointestinal bleeding, hyperkalemia, and hemodynamically mediated acute renal failure in patients with decreased effective arterial blood volume.

Many cases of both central and nephrogenic diabetes insipidus are mild, manifested by moderate polyuria, and may not require any treatment.

An intact thirst mechanism is the major defense against dehydration in patients with diabetes insipidus. Fluid intake should never be restricted in such patients. When oral intake is not possible (e.g., patients fasted before surgery or a diagnostic procedure), hypotonic fluids should be administered intravenously, and volume status monitored closely.

A potentially life-threatening complication of diabetes insipidus is severe hypernatremia (see Chapter 17–1). Elderly patients are particularly susceptible to this complication because of inadequate water intake, due to decreased access to water or an impaired thirst mechanism. Treatment of these patients therefore requires careful attention to replacement of their free water deficit.

Recommended Approach

Central diabetes insipidus is treated with one or two daily doses of intranasal dDAVP, titrated according to urine output. Nephrogenic diabetes insipidus that is irreversible can be alleviated with thiazide diuretics in conjunction with dietary salt restriction; amiloride; or nonsteroidal antiinflammatory drugs, provided renal function is not impaired. Fluid intake should never be restricted. Psychogenic polydipsia requires psychiatric intervention.

FOLLOW-UP

The initial follow-up period involves individual titration of the drugs to achieve the desired reduction in urine output. It is helpful for the patient to keep a record of her or his drug administration schedule, frequency of urination, daily weights, and side effects. If there is no reduction in urine output, a follow-up visit is indicated to reevaluate the treatment regimen.

Initially, follow-up may be indicated every 2 weeks to optimize the drug regimen. In terms of symptoms, the desired objective is absence of nocturia and urinary frequency not exceeding every 2 to 3 hours during the day. In addition, it is useful to obtain a 24-hour urine collection to assess the urine volume and osmolality and a measurement of the serum electrolytes and osmolality. Once the patient is stabilized, follow-up at 3- to 6-month intervals is sufficient.

DISCUSSION
Prevalence

The prevalence of polyuria is highly variable, depending on the patient population studied. It is present in 10 to 30% of patients receiving chronic lithium therapy. It is also common in psychiatric patients not receiving lithium therapy (due to psychogenic polydipsia).

Related Basic Science
Genetics

There are rare cases of familial central diabetes insipidus exhibiting autosomal dominant inheritance. Similarly, there are rare cases of familial nephrogenic diabetes insipidus exhibiting X-linked recessive inheritance. The vast majority of cases of diabetes insipidus are acquired.

Altered Molecular Biology

X-linked nephrogenic diabetes insipidus has been associated with mutations in the V_2 vasopressin receptor, rendering it incapable of responding to vasopressin. Interestingly, such patients also have defective V_2 receptors in platelets and vascular smooth muscle. Recently, a mutation in the vasopressin gene has been identified in patients with familial central diabetes insipidus.

Physiologic or Metabolic Derangement

Urinary concentration occurs in the collecting duct of the renal tubule. The maximal concentrating ability depends on two factors: the presence of vasopressin (antidiuretic hormone), which increases the water permeability of this tubule segment, and the concentration gradient between the collecting duct and the medullary interstitium. The maximal interstitial tonicity is, in turn, dependent on the efficacy of the countercurrent concentrating mechanism in the loop of Henle (i.e., the ability of the ascending limb of Henle to reabsorb solute). Thus, impaired urinary concentration may arise due to three mechanisms: (1) an absolute or relative deficiency of vasopressin secretion by the pituitary gland, (2) a resistance of the collecting duct to the hydroosmotic effect of vasopressin, or (3) defective solute reabsorption by the loop of Henle.

Vasopressin secretion is normally stimulated by small increases in plasma osmolality. In patients with central (neurogenic) diabetes insipidus there is a complete or partial impairment of vasopressin secretion, resulting in impaired ability to concentrate the urine. The defect is easily corrected by the exogenous replacement of vasopressin. In nephrogenic diabetes insipidus, vasopressin is present in high concentrations, but the collecting duct does not respond appropriately to its hydroosmotic action. The action of vasopressin is mediated by cyclic AMP. Thus, the resistance to the biological action of the hormone may be due to impaired stimulation of cyclic AMP by vasopressin or a defective postreceptor event. The treatment of this condition is accomplished either by decreasing distal delivery of fluid to the collecting duct or by enhancing the biological effect of circulating vasopressin. Thiazide diuretics, in conjunction with dietary sodium restriction, produce volume depletion, and thereby increase proximal tubular reabsorption of water. As a result, less fluid is delivered to the collecting duct, resulting in a reduction of urine volume. Lithium inhibits vasopressin-mediated water reabsorption in the collecting duct, whereas amiloride antagonizes this inhibition. Amiloride also inhibits uptake and intracellular accumulation of lithium in the renal tubular cell. Thus, amiloride is useful in reducing the polyuria of patients with lithium-induced nephrogenic diabetes insipidus. Prostaglandins have been shown to antagonize the hydroosmotic effect of vasopressin, whereas prostaglandin synthetase inhibitors enhance the biological effect of the hormone. Thus, the resistance to the effect of vasopressin in nephrogenic diabetes insipidus can be partially overcome by the administration of nonsteroidal antiinflammatory drugs.

In normal circumstances, patients with diabetes insipidus do not develop significant dehydration or hypernatremia. A small increase in plasma osmolality stimulates the thirst mechanism, and the patient drinks an adequate amount of fluid to restore the deficit. Dehydration and hyperosmolality may develop in two circumstances: in patients who have an impaired thirst mechanism and in patients with limited access to water. The former is sometimes seen in stroke patients, whereas the latter may occur in babies or in adults with impaired level of consciousness. Hypernatremia may occasionally be iatrogenic in these patients, as a result of physician orders to withhold fluids prior to a surgical or radiologic procedure.

Anatomic Derangement

Some cases of nephrogenic diabetes insipidus are due to destruction of the renal medulla, resulting in defective urinary concentration. This is seen in chronic tubulointerstitial disease. The prototype is seen in patients with sickle cell disease.

Natural History and Its Modification with Treatment

Many cases of central diabetes insipidus due to trauma may be transient and resolve spontaneously within a few days to weeks. Lithium-induced nephrogenic diabetes insipidus may gradually improve within weeks to months of discontinuation of the drug or may be irreversible. Even permanent cases of diabetes insipidus are associated with low morbidity, as long as the patient has adequate fluid replacement. Complications such as dehydration and severe hypernatremia leading to coma occur only when there is inadequate fluid intake. Of course, if the diabetes insipidus is a manifestation of a systemic disorder, the patient is susceptible to the complications of the underlying disease.

Mortality from diabetes insipidus is rare, unless the patient develops profound dehydration, due to inadequate fluid replacement. The patient may, however, die from the underlying disease producing the diabetes insipidus.

Prevention

No preventive measures are currently available for most causes of polyuria. The focus of the physician should be to prevent future episodes of dehydration and hypernatremia by educating the patient about the importance of unrestricted fluid intake and medical compliance.

Cost Containment

The etiology of the polyuria can usually be rapidly diagnosed by examining the clinical context, obtaining simple biochemical tests, and where indicated, proceeding directly to a dehydration test, followed by a trial of vasopressin. The medications for treatment of central and nephrogenic diabetes insipidus are relatively inexpensive.

REFERENCES

Allen HM, Jackson RL, Winchester MD, et al. Indomethacin in the treatment of lithium-induced nephrogenic diabetes insipidus. Arch Intern Med 1989;149: 1123.

Bichet DG, Arthus MF, Lonergan M, et al. X-linked nephrogenic diabetes insipidus mutations in North America and the Hopewell hypothesis. J Clin Invest 1993;92:1262.

Boton R, Gaviria M, Batlle DC. Prevalence, pathogenesis, and treatment of renal dysfunction associated with chronic lithium therapy. Am J Kid Dis 1987;10:329.

Ito M, Mori Y, Oiso Y, Saito H. A single base substitution in the coding region for neurohypophysin II associated with familial central diabetes insipidus. J Clin Invest 1991;87:725.

Zerbe RL, Robertson GL. A comparison of vasopressin measurements with a standard indirect test in the differential diagnosis of polyuria. N Engl J Med 1981;305:1539.

CHAPTER 16–3

Edema

Vera Delaney, M.D., Ph.D., and Sheldon Adler, M.D.

DEFINITION

Edema is an excessive collection of fluid in the interstitial compartment. It can result from local causes or be part of a generalized condition. Unless otherwise specified, this chapter refers to generalized edema.

ETIOLOGY

Generalized edema is not a disease but a sign of an underlying disorder that is invariably associated with renal sodium retention. Underlying disorders include right-sided heart failure; congestive cardiac failure; renal disease; liver disease; other hypoalbuminemic states, including malnutrition, protein-losing enteropathy, and exfoliative dermatitis; and idiopathic or cyclic edema. Iatrogenic edema may also occur. Localized edema usually occurs secondary to inflammation or circulatory stasis in the venous system; less often it results from congenital or acquired obstruction of the lymphatic system.

CRITERIA FOR DIAGNOSIS

Suggestive

The diagnosis is suggested by swelling of tissues, localized or generalized, which indents on pressure and is usually more apparent in dependent areas.

Definitive

To definitively conclude that edema is generalized requires at least two of the following criteria: identification of an identifiable underlying cause; shift in edema when dependent areas are altered, for example, from pedal to lumbosacral and/or pulmonary areas on changing from prone to supine positions; gain in weight of at least 5 kg in a 70-kg patient; resolution following natriuresis; exclusion of local explanations.

CLINICAL MANIFESTATIONS

Subjective

Complaints of feeling swollen, heavy, and/or bloated are common. Shoes, clothes, underwear, and rings often become tight. The tissues around the eyes may become swollen, especially on awakening. Males may present with scrotal enlargement. Females may notice premenstrual accentuation of usual weight gain. Symptoms often relate to the underlying cause of the disorder. Edema resulting in pulmonary congestion causes orthopnea, dyspnea on exertion, and paroxysmal nocturnal dyspnea. Decreased urinary output, nocturia, and darkening and/or frothing of the urine may be recognizable features when proteinuria is a prominent accompaniment. The type and frequency of the various symptoms are determined by the underlying disease (Table 16–3–1). A past history of heart, lung, liver, or kidney disease may suggest the organ involved. Medications that may cause edema include, estrogens, other steroids, nonsteroidal antiinflammatory agents, calcium channel blockers, and vasodilators, especially minoxidil. A family history may be relevant in some forms of liver disease (e.g., α_1-antitrypsin deficiency), kidney disease (e.g., Alport's syndrome), lung disease (e.g., cystic fibrosis), and, rarely, heart disease (e.g., familial cardiomyopathy).

Objective

Physical Examination

Edema is commonly detected by compression of the skin against the bone (usually malleolus, tibia, or sacrum) for 10 seconds and noting the indentation or "pitting" produced. Anything in excess of a trace reflects alterations in Starling's forces and an underlying disease process. Gravitational forces enhance edema formation. Thus, it is most readily detectable in dependent parts of the body, that is, lower extremities in ambulatory patients and presacrally in supine or prone individuals.

TABLE 16–3–1. PRINCIPAL CAUSES OF GENERALIZED EDEMA

Cause	Subjective	Objective	Diagnostic Tests	Treatment	Mechanisms of Edema
Cardiovascular					
Congestive heart failure	Othopnea, dyspnea, paroxysmal nocturnal dyspnea, cough, nocturia	Cardiomegaly, neck vein distention, S_3, bibasilar rales, edema	Chest x-ray, ECG, decrease in spot urine sodium	Rest, 2-g Na diet, digitalis, before- and afterload reducers, diuretics prn	Increased venous hydrostatic pressure, decreased effective circulating volume, renal sodium retention
Cor pulmonale	Cough, dyspnea, fatigue	Parasternal heave, right-sided S_4, loud P_2 with paradoxical splitting, neck vein distention, tricuspid regurgitation, peripheral edema ± ascites	Decreased Po_2, chest x-ray, ECG, decrease in spot urine sodium	O_2, 2-g Na diet, antibiotics, bronchodilators, respiratory therapy, diuretics prn	As above
Constrictive pericarditis	Fatigue, dyspnea, chest pain	Pericardial knock, neck vein distention, peripheral edema ± ascites	Chest x-ray, ECG, echocardiogram, decrease in spot urine sodium, increase in urinary protein	Pericardiectomy	As above
Renal					
Nephrotic syndrome	Swelling, fatigue, orthostatic symptoms	Edema ± blood pressure elevation	> 3.5 g of urinary protein in 24 h, hypoalbuminemia, hypercholesterolemia, renal biopsy	2-g Na diet, specific treatment depends on cause, diuretics if necessary	Hypoalbuminemia with decreased plasma oncotic pressure, decreased effective circulating volume, renal sodium retention
Acute oliguric renal failure	Uremic symptoms, other symptoms depending on cause	Edema, increase in blood pressure, decrease in urine output	Oliguria, increasing BUN and creatinine levels, abnormal urinalysis	Decrease Na and H_2O intake, rule out obstruction and prerenal causes, specific treatment as per cause	Sodium retention, reduced water excretion, increased arterial hydrostatic pressure
Chronic renal insufficiency	Uremic symptoms	Nocturia, increase in blood pressure, edema	Elevated BUN and creatinine levels, abnormal urinalysis, small kidneys on ultrasonography or tomography	2-g Na diet, protein restriction, control of blood pressure, diuretics if necessary	Sodium retention, increased arterial hydrostatic pressure
Liver					
Hepatitis, acute and chronic Cirrhosis	Abdominal pain, fatigue ± fever, malaise, anorexia	Jaundice ± tender liver, spider nevi, ascites ± edema	Abnormal liver function tests, decreased serum albumin, liver biopsy, decrease in spot urine sodium	Avoid hepatic insults, rest, 2-g Na diet, diuretics if necessary	Hepatic venous obstruction, decreased plasma oncotic pressure, decreased effective circulating volume due to arteriovenous shunts, renal sodium retention
Protein-calorie malnutrition	Alcoholism, starvation, anorexia, malignancy, AIDS	Cachexia, bitemporal, thenar and suprascapular wasting, ascites ± edema	Hypoalbuminemia, decreased serum transferrin, decrease in spot urine sodium	Feeding: oral or parenteral	Decreased plasma oncotic pressure, decreased effective circulating volume, renal sodium retention
Idiopathic (cyclical) edema	Swelling, intermittent rapid weight gain, female, diuretic use, carbohydrate binges	Edema	Exaggerated renin–aldosterone increase and sodium retention with assumption of upright posture	2-g Na diet, low carbohydrate intake, avoid diuretics	Unknown, ? capillary permeability defect, ? resistance to atrial natriuretic factor
Edema of pregnancy	Swelling in third trimester	Peripheral edema	Exclude preeclampsia	Rest, 2-g Na diet	Increased venous hydrostatic pressure due to gravid uterus, increased vascular capacity with decreased effective plasma volume, sodium-retaining hormones, renal sodium retention
Drug-induced					
Steroid (e.g., progesterone, estrogen, prednisone)	Swelling, weight gain	Edema	Stop drug and observe	Stop drug	Mineralocorticoid-like activity, renal Na retention
Sympatholytic antihypertensive agents (e.g., methyldopa, clonidine, prazosin)	As above	As above	As above	As above	Renal Na retention

(continued)

16–3–1 *(Continued)*

Cause	Subjective	Objective	Diagnostic Tests	Treatment	Mechanisms of Edema
Vasodilators (e.g., minoxidil, diazoxide, hydralazine, diltiazem, nifedipine)	As above	As above	As above	As above	Marked renal Na retention
Nonsteroidal antiinflammatory agents (e.g., indomethacin, naprosyn, phenylbutazone, ibuprofen)	As above	As above	As above	As above	Decreased renal prostaglandin generation, renal Na retention

ECG, electrocardiogram; BUN, blood urea nitrogen.

Asymmetric and localized edema suggests local disease, whereas symmetric and generalized edema suggests a systemic etiology. Additional objective findings depend on the underlying disease (Table 16–3–1). Quantitation of the edema by the degree of pitting is unsatisfactory in view of the variable nature of edema distribution and differences in skin turgor depending on the age of the patient and because some forms of edema, such as lymphedema and chronic venous edema, often do not compress. Serial changes in body weight are a more satisfactory method of quantitating the degree of edema.

Routine Laboratory Abnormalities

Associated routine laboratory findings depend on the underlying pathologic process. Generalized edema usually indicates disease of either the heart, kidneys, or liver and may be reflected by abnormalities in the electrocardiogram, echocardiogram, chest radiograph, plasma biochemical screen, prothrombin time, and/or urinalysis.

PLANS
Diagnostic
Differential Diagnosis

This is dictated by the suspected etiology of the underlying disease (Table 16–3–1).

Diagnostic Options

Generalized edema may be the presenting feature of a diverse group of diseases (Table 16–3–1). Initial workup should focus on localizing the organ involved by physical examination, routine biochemical tests on plasma and urine, electrocardiogram, and routine radiographic procedures. Subsequent workup should then be steered toward elucidation of the precise pathologic defect within the affected organ. For example, the discovery of nephrotic range proteinuria points to the kidneys as the cause of generalized edema, but definition of the precise histopathologic defect requires a renal biopsy. The latter guides further treatment, overall prognosis, and risk of recurrence in a transplant. On the other hand, when clinical evaluation points to cardiac disease as the underlying cause of edema, further stratification into systolic or diastolic dysfunction by echocardiography guides subsequent therapy. A diagnosis of cor pulmonale as the cause of generalized edema needs more detailed studies to define the underlying defect to assess prognosis and direct subsequent therapy. These may involve pulmonary function tests, blood gas analyses, echocardiography, cardiac catheterization with measurement of central and intracardiac pressures, and/or lung biopsy. When liver disease is the cause of generalized edema, ultrasonography is a helpful screening test in the assessment of liver size and texture. Hepatitis serology and, occasionally, a liver biopsy may also be indicated. Iatrogenic edema is apparent from the history, but idiopathic edema, which is a disease of women, is diagnosed on the basis of exclusion.

Recommended Approach

This depends on the organ involved and the most likely underlying pathologic process. A brief outline of the approach to diagnosis is outlined in Table 16–3–1.

Therapeutic
Therapeutic Options

As all generalized edematous disorders ultimately represent excess sodium retention, they should be treated by dietary sodium restriction. In most cases sodium ingestion should not exceed 2 g daily. Bed rest favors redistribution of dependent edema into the vascular space. This increases the central blood volume which, in turn, improves renal blood flow and glomerular filtration rate and often results in a diuresis. Whenever possible, sodium-retaining drugs, such as nonsteroidal antiinflammatory agents, steroid preparations (birth control pills, androgens, prednisone), vasodilators (minoxidil, hydralazine), and calcium channel blockers (particularly nifedipine [Procardia] and nicardipine [Cardene]) should be stopped. Specific treatment is usually dictated by the underlying disease and should be implemented in an attempt to correct the primary defect, thereby improving renal hemodynamics sufficiently to abolish compensatory sodium retention. Despite these measures, additional therapy with diuretics is often necessary. The effective circulating plasma volume is usually reduced in edematous states, and diuretics may further reduce this volume. Thus, injudicious diuretic administration may be accompanied by many serious complications, including a decrease in cardiac output and hypotension, a fall in renal blood flow with a rise in the blood urea nitrogen: creatinine ratio (prerenal azotemia), and a variety of electrolyte and acid–base disorders. Other than pulmonary or laryngeal edema, excess fluid is not ordinarily life threatening. So, as a general rule, edema fluid should be removed slowly and weight loss should not exceed 1 kg in 24 hours. Diuretics should be discontinued or their dosage reduced when ankle edema becomes minimal and/or pulmonary congestion disappears.

When selecting a diuretic, it is wise to start with a thiazide or low doses of a loop diuretic such as furosemide (Lasix). If renal function is less than a third of normal (serum creatinine > 3.0 mg/dL or a glomerular filtration rate < 30 mL/min), thiazides become less effective and higher doses of loop diuretics are needed to promote diuresis. Addition of a distal blocker (amiloride [Midamor], triamterene [Dyrenium], spironolactone [Aldactone]) may promote more effective diuresis in certain clinical circumstances and may also prevent hypokalemia, a common problem when edema fluid is in the process of being mobilized. Distal blockers are contraindicated in patients with renal failure because these drugs may cause fatal hyperkalemia. They should also be used with caution in patients with severe congestive heart failure, because in this condition potassium excretion may also be reduced. Spironolactone is the initial diuretic of choice, however, in the treatment of cirrhosis with ascites because it induces natriuresis and minimizes hypokalemia. In these patients hypokalemia is a serious complication because it may precipitate hepatic encephalopathy. The role of diuretics in cirrhosis is to provide relief from increased intraabdominal tension and elevated diaphragms rather than total elimination of ascites. Strict dietary sodium restriction, bed rest, and spironolactone usually induce a weight loss of 2 to 3 kg per week. More rapid weight reduction in these patients can cause prerenal azotemia or even irreversible acute renal failure. Intravenous furosemide is the diuretic of choice for treating acute pulmonary edema. Separate from its diuretic effect, it increases venous capacitance, thereby reducing cardiac preload and improving cardiac function.

The use of diuretics is particularly controversial in the treatment of idiopathic (cyclical) edema of women. Indeed, it has been suggested that diuretic usage itself plays a role in the pathogenesis of this syndrome. Discontinuation of diuretics, replacement of potassium deficits, and strict enforcement of a low-sodium/low-carbohydrate diet usually promote spontaneous diuresis. An interim weight gain of 3 to 10 kg may occur, particularly if sodium intake remains high. Patients should be warned of this, supported through this uncomfortable period, and encouraged to withhold diuretic agents.

Refractory edema is present when the patient does not lose weight on twice the conventional dose of loop diuretics. Ingestion of excess salt (24-hour urinary sodium excretion > 100 mEq) and ingestion of sodium-retaining drugs must be ruled out. Hospitalization is often necessary for strict enforcement of bed rest, salt restriction, and intermittent intravenous administration of loop diuretics, with or without albumin infusion. The latter may help in the initiation of a diuresis in hypoalbuminemic patients.

There are three possible explanations for persistent, or refractory, edema:

- Proximal tubular sodium and water reabsorption is so intense that less sodium is delivered to the furosemide-sensitive site in the loop of Henle, resulting in resistance to loop diuretics. In this situation, administration of metolazone (Zaroxolyn), a diuretic with proximal and distal tubular actions, in a dose of 5 to 20 mg orally alone or 30 to 60 minutes prior to the initial dose of furosemide may initiate a diuresis.
- Avid salt and water reabsorption at the distal tubular level, usually accompanied by hyperaldosteronism, may nullify the effect of more proximal-acting loop diuretics. This situation is suggested by finding hypokalemia and/or a reversal of the normal urinary sodium:potassium ratio (4:1). Administration of a distally blocking agent in this situation often promotes diuresis. Occasionally, giving the loop diuretic intermittently, for example, every other day, enhances diuresis by lessening intravascular volume depletion.
- The diuretic fails to reach its renal site of action in sufficient quantity to be effective. Occasionally, bowel wall edema may cause malabsorption of orally administered diuretics. More commonly, resistance occurs when the glomerular filtration rate is reduced. In this situation, the renal tubular secretory pathway through which loop diuretics reach their site of action is saturated with other organic anions that accumulate in the plasma in renal failure. An increased diuretic dose (an approximate furosemide dosage is 40 times the plasma creatinine concentration in mg/dL) given as a single bolus intravenously may produce diuresis in these circumstances. Unfortunately, a small subgroup of patients with refractory edema do not respond to any of the preceding measures. Head-out total body water immersion, which redistributes body fluid and increases the central blood volume, may be tried. This technique improves renal hemodynamics and may promote diuresis. In rare circumstances, hemofiltration or dialysis may be necessary to remove resistant edema. For poorly understood reasons, this can restore subsequent diuretic responsiveness. These latter measures are invasive, expensive, and rarely necessary.

Recommended Approach

Implementation of nonpharmacologic measures is the safest form of therapy. These include bed rest, low-salt diet, and avoidance of sodium-retaining drugs if possible. Additional pharmacologic therapy is usually necessary. This should be directed primarily at improving the underlying pathogenetic defect rather than directed at the compensatory sodium retention. For example, improvement in cardiac output in congestive cardiac failure by the use of afterload reducers, especially converting-enzyme inhibitors, often promotes diuresis. Urinary protein may be decreased in patients with nephrotic syndrome, including diabetics, by the use of converting-enzyme inhibitors, thus reducing the need for diuretics and their attendant complications. Administration of oxygen may alleviate hypoxia-exacerbated pulmonary hypertension with right-sided heart failure and promote diuresis. Despite these measures, diuretics are often necessary. Low doses of short-acting diuretics, given on alternate days, if possible, occasionally in combination with

distal blocking agents with frequent monitoring of serum electrolytes, form the basis of prudent diuretic therapy.

FOLLOW-UP

The frequency of follow-up visits depends on the underlying cause, the response to therapy, and the compliance of the patient. Diuretics often cause electrolyte abnormalities, particularly when edema is being mobilized. Initially, therefore, at a minimum, weekly visits and biochemical profiles should be obtained until the patient is stabilized. This is particularly important in cirrhotics and digitalis-treated cardiac patients because diuretic-induced hypokalemia may produce life-threatening complications. Serial body weights, blood pressures obtained lying and standing, and plasma and, where indicated, urinary electrolyte determinations are crucial to the provision of rational therapy and follow-up care to patients with generalized edema irrespective of the cause.

DISCUSSION

Prevalence and Incidence

Most patients with severe heart, liver, pulmonary, or kidney disease become edematous at some stage in the course of their respective disease. The precise prevalence and incidence, however, are not available.

Related Basic Science

Edema, the accumulation of excess extravascular interstitial fluid, is initiated as a result of a breakdown in the normal balance of Starling forces across tissue capillary walls (Figure 16–3–1). Under normal conditions, fluid leaves the arteriolar end of the capillary to enter the interstitium because the hydrostatic pressure force (P_p) at this site exceeds the plasma colloid oncotic pressure (π_p). Fluid reenters the vascular tree at the venous end of the capillary because at this site the hydrostatic pressure force is reduced below that of the plasma oncotic pressure. Interstitial fluid is protein rich, containing proteins at approximately 50% of the circulating plasma concentration, and thus generates a significant oncotic pressure (π_i). Interstitial hydrostatic pressure (P_i) is subatmospheric at between −2 and −8 mm Hg. Thus, transcapillary fluid exchange (J_v) can be expressed mathematically as follows:

$$J_v = K[(P_p - P_i) - (\pi_p - \pi_i)]$$

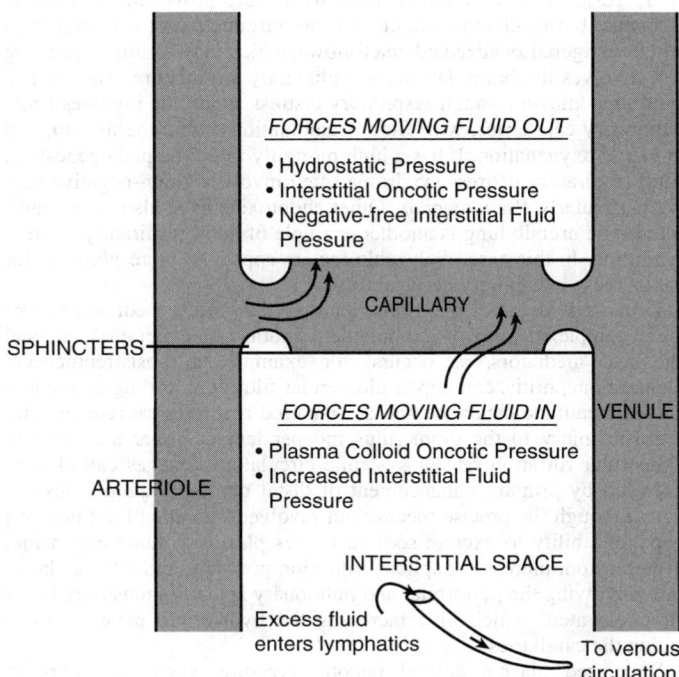

Figure 16–3–1. Starling forces governing transcapillary fluid exchange.

where K = hydraulic permeability of the capillary wall, P_p = plasma hydrostatic pressure, P_i = interstitial fluid hydrostatic pressure, π_p = plasma oncotic pressure, and π_i = interstitial oncotic pressure.

Nonreabsorbed interstitial fluid returns to the blood via the lymphatics. The main determinant of lymphatic flow is interstitial pressure, a small increase resulting in a large augmentation of lymph flow. The pressure in the terminal lymphatics is subatmospheric owing to a combination of an effective runoff system into the venous circulation, spontaneous myogenic contractions of the lymphatic vessels, and the presence of valves. Edema results when more fluid leaves the vascular compartment than can be sequestered by the venules and lymphatics. Thus, increased capillary permeability, lymphatic obstruction, decreased plasma colloid oncotic pressure, alterations in sphincter tone, and increased capillary hydrostatic pressure are the most important initiating factors in the pathogenesis of edematous states.

All edematous states induce compensatory renal sodium retention in an attempt to conserve plasma volume and blood pressure. Important afferent stimuli that signal the need for renal sodium rentention include volume and baroreceptors in the left side of the circulation, mainly the aortic arch, carotid sinus, and left ventricle; low-pressure volume receptors, located mainly in the atria; renal pressure receptors primarily in the juxtaglomerular apparatus, but also in other areas within the kidney including the ureteropelvic region; and hepatic receptors capable of initiating a renal response to changes in plasma sodium and osmolality.

These multiple afferents collectively sense a modest degree of intravascular volume depletion and initiate effectors that promote renal salt and water retention. These effectors include the sympathetic nervous system and hormones. The sympathetic nervous system increases peripheral and renal vascular resistance; alters intrarenal hemodynamics to produce a rise in filtration fraction that, in turn, promotes more avid sodium reabsorption at the proximal tubule; increases sodium reabsorption by a direct effect at the level of the renal tubular cell; and directly stimulates the juxtaglomerular apparatus to produce renin. Hormones include the renin–angiotensin–aldosterone system and antidiuretic hormone. The predominant action of the latter is water regulation, but it can also act as a vasoconstrictor, particularly in low-volume states. Other hormonal adaptations include an end-organ resistance to the action of atrial natriuretic factor and an increase in intrarenal vasodilatory prostaglandins.

Increased capillary permeability and changes in sphincter tone result from the release of chemical mediators, including histamine, leukotrienes, complement, and cytokines, particularly interleukin (IL)-2, IL-1, IL-3, IL-6, and tumor necrosis factor, provoked by trauma, ischemia, burns, chemical injury, or the introduction of a foreign protein or antigen. Localized edema follows, which may be life threatening if it involves the brain, larynx, or pulmonary vasculature. The clinical syndrome known as adult respiratory distress syndrome involves leaky pulmonary capillaries, with fluid accumulation within the alveoli, and impaired oxygenation. It has a high mortality rate. The pathogenesis of adult respiratory distress syndrome often involves Gram-negative sepsis, particularly *Pseudomonas*. Other endotoxins have also been implicated. The uremic lung is another example of adult respiratory distress syndrome. In this case, dialyzable factors appear to be responsible for the increase in capillary permeability.

Localized edema of the glomerular capillary walls mediated by immune complex deposition, complement fixation, and alterations in local chemical mediators, as occurs, for example, in poststreptococcal glomerulonephritis, can impair glomerular filtration, leading to a reduction in creatinine clearance and an impaired ability to excrete sodium. Intrinsic injury to the glomerulus independent of either a change in glomerular filtration rate or systemic circulatory changes can also be followed by primary enhancement of distal tubular sodium reabsorption, although the precise mechanism involved remains ill defined. An impaired ability to excrete sodium causes plasma volume expansion, hypertension, increased capillary filtration pressure, and edema classically involving the periorbital and pulmonary areas. Venous pressure is often elevated, which also increases the hydrostatic pressure force within the capillaries.

Decreased plasma colloid oncotic pressure, such as occurs in nephrotic syndrome, often causes generalized edema. A protective mechanism exists by which a drop in plasma oncotic pressure is, within

certain limits, attended by a corresponding fall in interstitial oncotic pressure so that the transcapillary oncotic pressure gradient remains constant and edema does not occur. This is due to augmented lymphatic removal of interstitial proteins, although the precise stimulus for this is unknown since neither interstitial volume nor pressure has been found to be elevated. When plasma oncotic pressure falls further, these compensatory mechanisms are exceeded, resulting in a fall in the transcapillary oncotic pressure gradient and a large rise in interstitial volume with the production of clinical edema. The pathogenesis of the increased glomerular permeability to albumin in nephrotic syndrome involves charge. Neutralization of the multiple negative charges within glomerular epithelial cells and basement membranes removes the electrostatic forces necessary to prevent a leak of albumin, with the production of "selective" proteinuria and hypoalbuminemia. This is typically seen in minimal-change disease. Interestingly, other cell membranes, namely, erythrocytes and platelets, show a similar electrostatic defect, suggesting that this disease may be associated with a generalized decrease in polyanion cell membrane residues. The precise pathogenesis of the latter is unknown, although platelet factor 4 has been shown to neutralize glomerular polyanions. With the development of edema, plasma volume contraction ensues with recruitment of various afferent and effector mechanisms as outlined above. This "underfilling" theory is supported by a measurable decrease in plasma volume in most children with minimal-change disease, unlike the situation in most adults with nephrotic syndrome, in whom, irrespective of the type of glomerulonephritis, plasma volume is usually normal or supranormal. The latter has led to the emergence of the "overflow" theory, which proposes that sodium retention is a direct consequence of glomerular injury rather than the sequel to reduced intravascular volume and, as such, contributes to edema formation.

Increased venous hydrostatic pressure forces (i.e., "backward failure") in conjunction with avid renal sodium and water retention are responsible for the edema of congestive heart failure. Renal sodium retention is activated by decreased effective circulating volume caused by impaired pumping of the heart. The latter constitutes the "forward failure" theory and leads to stimulation of the renin–angiotensin–aldosterone system and antidiuretic hormone release. Stimulation of low-pressure receptors in the right atrium also occurs. These ordinarily facilitate natriuresis but show a decreased response in chronic congestive failure, with destruction of the specialized nerve endings in the atrium in some experimental models. Furthermore, atrial natriuretic factor, elevated in some patients with congestive heart failure, is not associated with a significant natriuresis, suggesting, in addition, a resistance to its action at the level of the nephron. Alterations in natriuretic factors and prostaglandins appear to play a significant role in increasing renal sodium reabsorption in congestive heart failure.

The most widely accepted theory of edema formation in cirrhosis implicates increased hepatic venous outflow resistance with hyperfiltration across the sinusoid. Initially, increased hyperfiltration is effectively counteracted by increased lymphatic flow; however, when filtration exceeds the capacity for lymphatic return, ascites develops (weeping liver). At the same time, increased sinusoidal pressure is transmitted back to the portal and splanchnic beds, causing a further reduction in effective blood volume. Furthermore, systemic hemodynamics in patients with cirrhosis reflect widespread vasodilation with a decreased peripheral vascular resistance and an increased cardiac output. In large part this reflects shunting of blood flow through the generation of widespread arteriovenous fistulas. These shunts, perhaps endotoxin induced, contribute to the sense of the underfilled circulation and, thus, to renal sodium retention. Lastly, hypoalbuminemia resulting from progressive liver disease favors increased transcapillary flow. These mechanisms combine to produce a low effective circulating blood volume, thus explaining the commonly observed elevated levels of angiotensin, antidiuretic hormone, and norepinephrine. An alternative, but generally considered less likely, explanation is the "overflow theory," which suggests that edema is primarily the result of renal salt retention stimulated by hepatic injury rather than a decrease in effective plasma volume. As the accumulation of ascites occurs at the expense of the existing plasma volume, renal sodium-conserving mechanisms are activated, with further increases in total-body sodium and edema.

In summary, regardless of the underlying disorder, generalized edema develops only when there is both an alteration in local Starling forces and inappropriate sodium retention by the kidney.

Natural History and Its Modification with Treatment

This is determined by the underlying disease process (Table 16–3–1).

Prevention

Effective treatment of the underlying disease and strict dietary restriction of sodium intake can limit edema formation. Idiopathic (cyclical) edema of women may be ameliorated in many cases by avoiding carbohydrate binges and abuse of diuretics with strict adherence to a 2-g sodium diet. Drug- or chemical-induced edema can be minimized by avoidance of the offending agents.

Cost Containment

Strict adherence to a low-sodium diet is the safest and most inexpensive way of treating patients with edematous disorders. This may obviate the need for diuretics. When diuretics are necessary, frequent follow-up visits with body weights and plasma electrolytes are cost effective because they allow early detection and treatment of diuretic-induced complications, thereby preventing hospitalization. Once a stable pattern has been established, office visits and laboratory tests may be reduced and monitoring can be performed at home by daily weight tabulation.

REFERENCES

Delaney VB, Bourke E. The interrelationship of heart disease and kidney disease. In: Hurst JWH, Schlant RC, eds. The heart. 7th ed. New York: McGraw-Hill, 1990:1543.
Delaney VB, Bourke E. Diuretics. In: Hurst JWH, Schlant RC, eds. The heart. 7th ed. New York: McGraw-Hill, 1990:1767.
Moe GN, Xegault X, Skorecki KL. Control of extracellular fluid volume and pathophysiology of edema formation. In: Brenner BM, Rector FC, eds. The kidney. Philadelphia: Saunders, 1991:623.
Mees EJD. Fluid retention in renal disease: The genesis of renal edema. In: Cameron S, Davison AM, Grunfeld J-P, et al., eds. Oxford textbook of clinical nephrology. New York: Oxford University Press, 1992:262.
Schrier RW. Effective blood volume revisited: Pathogenesis of edematous disorders. In: Davison AM, ed. Proceedings of the Xth International Congress of Nephrology. London: Balliere Tindall, 1988:663.

CHAPTER 16–4

Proteinuria

Edmund Bourke, M.D.

DEFINITION

Proteinuria of clinical significance is the presence of greater than 150 mg protein in a 24-hour urine specimen in an adult (75 mg in children, 300 mg in adolescents).

ETIOLOGY

If other manifestations of renal dysfunction are uncovered, a renal etiology for the proteinuria can be assumed. Isolated proteinuria can be classified as renal or benign. Benign proteinuria (Table 16–4–1) can be a transient manifestation of extrarenal disease such as a febrile illness or congestive cardiac failure or can be due to a functional defect as in orthostatic proteinuria. The underlying renal syndromes that may be associated with proteinuria are summarized in Table 16–4–2.

CRITERIA FOR DIAGNOSIS

Suggestive

There are usually no clues to proteinuria. A possible clue is otherwise unexplained edema, but this is seen only when proteinuria is massive. Clues to the underlying renal syndromes that can be associated with proteinuria may be present (Table 16–4–2). Evidence of a systemic illness with a predilection for renal involvement may be noted.

TABLE 16–4–1. CAUSES OF "BENIGN" PROTEINURIA

Orthostatic
Exercise
Emotional stress
Exposure to cold
Prolonged lordotic posture
Norepinephrine excess
Fever
Congestive heart failure
Acute pulmonary edema
Head injury or cerebrovascular accident
Albumin infusion

Definitive

Qualitative tests usually suffice to define significant proteinuria. It is usually defined by a positive reaction to a dipstick that changes color roughly in proportion to protein concentration and is reported as between trace and 4+. A trace indicates protein in the range 5 to 20 mg/dL and can generally be regarded as clinically insignificant. As the dipstick reflects concentration rather than quantity, a false-negative result may occur in highly dilute urine. In cases of doubt or when quantitation is clinically relevant, a 24-hour urine collection is needed. Dipsticks do not detect the light chains of Bence Jones proteinuria. Highly alkaline urines (pH $\geq$ 8.0) may result in a false-positive dipstick for proteinuria, again requiring a 24-hour quantitation for confirmation.

CLINICAL MANIFESTATIONS

Subjective

Proteinuria causes no symptoms. When it is marked, the patient may note a tendency for the urine to foam and form bubbles in the commode.

Objective

Physical Examination

Massive proteinuria may result in the nephrotic syndrome (see Chapter 16–11). Otherwise there are no abnormal physical findings. Systemic manifestations of disease processes causing proteinuria are discussed in the appropriate sections.

Routine Laboratory Abnormalities

Careful microscopic examination of the urine sediment provides important clues to the significance of proteinuria (see Table 16–4–2). A benign sediment suggests a more indolent course and favorable outcome. An active sediment with red cells and red cell casts suggests an acute nephritic syndrome. Lipiduria manifested by oval fat bodies under polarized light is characteristic of the nephrotic syndrome. Leukocyturia results from urinary infections, but may also indicate other sources of inflammation, including interstitial nephritis (see Chapter 16–20).

An elevated serum creatinine level would indicate overall renal insufficiency as an accompaniment to the proteinuria. Other laboratory

TABLE 16–4–2. PROTEINURIA, CREATININE CLEARANCE, AND URINE SEDIMENT IN RENAL SYNDROMES

Syndrome	Usual Range of Urine Protein (g/24 h)	Creatinine Clearance	Likely Urine Sediment Abnormalities
Acute nephritis	0.3–3.0	N or ↓	RBCs, RBC casts
Nephrotic syndrome	> 3.5	N or ↓ or ↑	Oval fat bodies, fat droplets, casts
Acute renal failure	0–2.0	↓	Renal tubular cells, ±RBCs, RBC casts, "pigmented casts"
Chronic renal failure	0.5 to >3.5	↓	Casts
Urinary tract infection	<1.0	N or ↓	WBCs, bacteria, WBC casts
Tubular defects	<1.0	N	—
Hypertension	0.5–2.0*	N or ↓	—
Nephrolithiasis	<1.0	N	±RBCs
Isolated proteinuria	0.5 to 1.5	N	—

RBC, red blood cell; WBC, white blood cell.
*Proteinuria may be in the nephrotic range in malignant hypertension; under these conditions, RBCs may also be present on urinalysis.

abnormalities may be present as they relate to the underlying disease causing proteinuria.

PLANS
Diagnostic
Differential Diagnosis

Proteinuria may be present in virtually any disease affecting the kidneys or urinary tract, although it is usually absent to minimal in obstructive uropathy and uncomplicated urolithiasis. The cardinal features of the renal syndromes that may manifest proteinuria are summarized in Table 16–4–2 and further discussed in the individual chapters.

Diagnostic Options and Recommended Approach

Certain benign types of proteinuria should be confirmed or excluded before embarking on more detailed diagnostic plans. These, in contrast to the proteinuria of intrinsic renal disease, can be classified as functional proteinuria and the transient proteinuria commonly seen in the course of extrarenal disease (Table 16–4–1). Orthostatic proteinuria, not present when supine but occurring in the erect position, is a classic example of functional proteinuria. Also, heavy exercise, exposure to cold, assumption of an exaggerated lordotic position, and, very rarely, severe emotional stress can induce reversible proteinuria in certain individuals. Mild transient proteinuria is common in congestive heart failure, acute pulmonary edema, head injury, cerebrovascular accidents, febrile illnesses, and following albumin infusions. All the preceding may augment the proteinuria of intrinsic renal disease, and it is therefore essential to demonstrate complete resolution, not just reduction, of the proteinuria before ascribing such a benign etiology.

Persistent proteinuria calls for an accurate 24-hour urine collection to quantitate protein excretion and estimate glomerular filtration rate by creatinine clearance. When it is not feasible to obtain an accurately measured, timed urinary collection, one can get valuable information from a random urinary protein:creatinine ratio. It should normally be below 0.2. Values above 3.0 indicate nephrotic range proteinuria. A renal sonogram is also required to evaluate renal structure. For instance, two small, contracted kidneys indicate advanced chronic disease. These pieces of information, together with urinalysis and clinical evaluation of the patient, may point the physician to one of the established renal syndromes, such as the nephrotic syndrome, the acute nephritic syndrome, and chronic renal failure (see Table 16–4–2). The diagnostic plans for these are dealt with in the respective chapters. More often, however, proteinuria is an isolated abnormality or accompanied only by some urinary sediment changes.

Particularly in the first two decades of life, careful screening for orthostatic proteinuria is essential. This is simple in principle but requires attention to detail. True orthostatic proteinuria requires a negative test during recumbency, not merely a decrease, as can be seen in pathologic proteinuria. Urine voided during the first hour of recumbency should be discarded to avoid a false-positive result due to the urinary dead space. If the repeat specimen obtained from the recumbent patient is negative, orthostatic proteinuria can be confidently diagnosed. In the absence of any other evidence of renal disease, it carries an excellent prognosis and usually resolves, although it may persist for decades in some otherwise healthy individuals.

Although proteinuria is most often glomerular in origin, tubular proteinuria may be seen in tubulointerstitial disease. Urinary protein electrophoresis shows a qualitatively distinctive pattern in the latter conditions, with low-molecular-weight α_2- and β-globulins predominating over albumin. In addition to the hereditary and congenital tubular disorders, tubular proteinuria may indicate toxic or hypersensitivity-induced tubulointerstitial disease.

Factors requiring documentation that may less favorably influence the prognosis in proteinuria include other abnormalities on urinalysis such as microhematuria; other evidence of renal disease, including elevated blood pressure, decreased creatinine clearance, and renal radiologic abnormalities; and evidence of systemic diseases that may affect the kidney, such as diabetes mellitus and systemic lupus erythematosus. Evidence for systemic lupus or other vasculitides may be subtle and require immunologic screening, including antinuclear antibody and serum complement determinations.

A definitive investigation that requires consideration in otherwise unexplained proteinuria is renal biopsy. This is particularly so when proteinuria is in the nephrotic range, is accompanied by hematuria or other evidence of abnormal renal function, or is suspected as being a manifestation of a systemic disease such as lupus erythematosus. When the etiology is apparent, as in obvious diabetic nephropathy, or when advanced renal insufficiency is accompanied by bilateral small, contracted kidneys, renal biopsy is not warranted. In mild, isolated persistent proteinuria in the absence of other abnormalities, a role for renal biopsy is not yet established.

Therapeutic

Proteinuria is not treated; however, the disease that resulted in the proteinuria may require specific therapy. The consequences of massive proteinuria—edema, for example—may be treated as needed. In isolated persistent proteinuria in the absence of other abnormalities, watchful waiting is the most reasonable approach.

FOLLOW-UP

If a functional etiology (e.g., exercise proteinuria) or a transient cause (e.g., febrile illnesses) has been confidently diagnosed and the patient has been informed and reassured, no follow-up is needed. Should clinical evaluation bracket the proteinuria into one of the established renal syndromes, laboratory investigation reveal a specific disease state, or renal biopsy demonstrate a distinct histologic entity (e.g., membranous nephropathy, focal segmental glomerulosclerosis), the follow-up is dictated by the higher-order diagnosis. In the case of isolated persistent proteinuria, the patient should be seen initially at 3- to 6-month intervals, and blood pressure, urine microscopy, degree of proteinuria, and creatinine clearance should be monitored. When the condition is stable, follow-up can be extended to once or twice annually.

DISCUSSION

Prevalence and Incidence

Proteinuria has a prevalence of about 3%. It probably varies with age and other epidemiologic variables, but these have not yet been definitively established. The causes vary with age and other aspects of population selection. In screening young healthy college freshmen, proteinuria is noted in 5%, but the incidence of serious treatable disease among those found to have proteinuria is only about 1.5%.

Related Basic Science

The glomerulus is a selectively permeable membrane that permits the passage through its walls of molecules up to a certain size, including small proteins such as lysozymes (molecular weight [MW] = 14,000 daltons) or, when present, the light chains of Bence Jones proteins (MW = 22,000 daltons), but it excludes all but small quantities of albumin (MW = 68,000 daltons) and totally excludes the larger circulating globulins. Proteins escaping through the normal glomerular filter are largely reabsorbed by pinocytosis in the proximal tubule, accounting for the very small amount that reaches the final urine. In addition to size as a determinant of passing through the glomerular filter, shape and deformability also play a role, which explains why large amounts of the more streamlined hemoglobin molecule reach the urine during intravascular hemolysis, even though its molecular size is similar to that of albumin. The third component of glomerular permeability to protein is electric charge. Circulating albumin behaves as an anion, and the polyanions that form part of the structure of the glomerular membrane have a repellent action that impedes passage through its three membrane layers. Thus, the cell surface of the fenestrated endothelial lining layer is negatively charged, as are the polyanionic heparan sulfate proteoglycans in the interstices of type IV collagen, which constitutes the basement membrane, and also the anionic sialic acid residues in the coating of the foot processes, which abut the outside of the basement membrane. Inactivation of the glomerular polyanions appears to be the major cause of the selective proteinuria characterized by a preponderance of albumin seen in minimal-change glomerulopathy (lipoid nephrosis); however, increased glomerular porosity contributes to the nonselective proteinuria seen in such conditions as diabetic nephropathy, in which high-molecular-weight globulins also leak into the urine. Finally, altered renal hemodynamics has been proposed for the transient or intermittent proteinuria sometimes seen after exercise, in congestive heart failure, hypertension, fever, postural change, and the use of vasoactive agents such as norepinephrine and angiotensin and is seemingly related to reduction in renal blood flow. The precise mechanism is not yet known. Increased diffusive forces resulting from an elevated capillary pressure or filtration fraction may play a role. Importantly, the magnitude of the proteinuria has been reported to correlate with the rate of decline in renal function, at least in some nephropathies. Recently published data from experimental and clinical work suggest that angiotensin-converting enzyme inhibition reduces proteinuria and may slow the decline in glomerular filtration rate in diabetic nephropathy and membranous nephropathy. These beneficial effects appear to be related to lowering of angiotensin II levels, resulting in changes in intraglomerular pressures and glomerular permeability.

The following are the predominant types of clinically significant proteinuria:

- *Glomerular proteinuria:* This is the most common type, and the varied mechanisms are those outlined above.
- *Tubular proteinuria:* Impaired proximal tubular reabsorption may result in this form of proteinuria. Other markers of proximal tubular dysfunction, such as glycosuria, aminoaciduria, and renal tubular acidosis, usually accompany tubular proteinuria. It is distinguishable from glomerular proteinuria by the predominance of low-molecular-weight globulins in addition to the presence of albumin on urinary protein electrophoresis. Measurement of β_2-microglobulin is helpful in suspected cases.
- *Overflow proteinuria:* Immunoglobulin light chains, most commonly monclonal immunoglobulin G, hemoglobin, and myoglobin, appear in the urine when presented to the glomerulus in increased concentrations. These proteins may in turn induce nephrotoxic injury to the renal tubular cells, including an additional tubular proteinuria.
- *Increased secretion of Tamm-Horsfall protein and secretory immunoglobulin A in response to inflammation.* Tamm–Horsfall protein is synthesized and secreted predominantly in the ascending limb of Henle's loop. Its concentration is increased in conditions such as pyelonephritis and renal calculus disease, but it generally does not exceed 200 mg daily. Hyalin casts are composed of this protein, and it forms the matrix of granular casts, the granules themselves containing filtered plasma proteins.
- *Lysozymuria:* Lysozymuria is seen in proximal tubular disorders owing to impaired reabsorption and also as an overflow phenomenon in some cases of monocytic or myelomonocytic leukemia.

The principles underlying the dipstick and its limitations should be known to the physician. A test strip on the dipstick is impregnated with a pH sensitive indicator dye, bromphenol blue, together with a buffer to maintain it at pH 5. At this pH it has a yellow color and the buffer impregnated with it is strong enough to prevent a color change even in relatively alkaline urine for a short period. Based on the so-called protein error of indicator dyes, increasing concentrations of protein change the color of bromphenol blue from yellow to green to blue. This is the basis of the test. Markedly concentrated or diluted urines can give false-positive or false-negative results. So can some detergents used to clean urinals. The strongly alkaline urine resulting from urea-splitting bacteria may overwhelm the buffering capacity of the test strip and the resultant color change may falsely signify proteinuria. Finally, the dipsticks are only about one fifth as sensitive to globulins as to albumin. They underestimate tubular proteinuria and fail to detect light chains.

Natural History and Its Modification with Treatment

The most common setting where proteinuria is encountered is the routine screening of applicants for employment, life insurance, participation in athletics, or entrance into military service. The natural history has been most extensively studied in young men. Proteinuria detected under these conditions is constant in 5 to 10% of patients, orthostatic (reproducible recur on assuming the upright posture) in 15 to 20%, and transient or intermittent in 75%. Twenty-year follow-up confirms the generally favorable prognosis of orthostatic proteinuria. It undergoes resolution within 10 years in half the patients, and although it persists through 20 years in about 20% of patients, there is no increased incidence of hypertension or renal functional impairment. In a few patients orthostatic proteinuria becomes persistent. Currently available evidence indicates no untoward long-term sequelae of transient or intermittent proteinuria. Constant or persistent proteinuria, even as an isolated finding, is usually associated with definite structural or ultrastructural evidence of renal disease; however, it appears to run an indolent course at least in the short term. Although many patients will have developed an abnormal urinalysis and/or hypertension by 5 years of follow-up, renal failure is uncommon within this time frame. Major uncertainties still surround the long-term prognosis of isolated persistent proteinuria, although it is generally agreed that by 20 years there is a greater risk of developing end-stage renal disease than in the general population. In general, the risk increases with greater levels of proteinuria.

Where a specific disease entity is identified, the proteinuria carries the natural history of the disease that caused it.

Prevention

There are no preventive measures.

Cost Containment

The entire workup, with the possible exception of the need for renal biopsy, can be carried out on an outpatient basis.

REFERENCES

Avram MM, ed. Proteinuria. New York: Plenum Press, 1985.
Carlson JA, Harrington JT. The laboratory evaluation of renal function. In:

Schrier RW, Gottschalk CW, eds. Diseases of the kidney. 5th ed. Boston: Little, Brown, 1993:361.

Glassock RJ. Proteinuria. In: Massry SG, Glassock RJ, eds. Textbook of nephrology. 3rd ed. Baltimore: Williams & Wilkins, 1995:600.

Mallick NP, Short CD. The clinical approach to hematuria and proteinuria. In: Cameron S, Davison AM, Grunfeld JP, et al., eds. The Oxford textbook of clinical nephrology. Oxford: Oxford Medical, 1992:227.

Springenberg PD, Garrett LE, Thompson AL, et al. Fixed and reproducible orthostatic proteinuria: Results of a 20 year follow-up study. Ann Intern Med 1982;97:516.

Striegel J, Michael AF, Chavers BM. Asymptomatic proteinuria: Benign disorder or harbinger of disease. Postgrad Med 1988;83:287.

CHAPTER 16–5

Hematuria

Robert H. Barth, M.D., and Edmund Bourke, M.D.

DEFINITION

Hematuria is the presence of greater than normal numbers of red blood cells (RBCs) in the urine. A small number of erythrocytes are excreted in the urine of persons with no demonstrable pathology, at a rate of up to one to two million per day, or a concentration of about 1000/mL. Because of the imprecise nature of microscopic urinalysis, it is not easy to reliably convert excretion rates to RBCs per high-power field, and thus some controversy exists about what constitutes the upper limit of normal. Nonetheless, three or more RBCs per high-power field on examination of centrifuged urine sediment is an acceptably sensitive and specific definition of microscopic hematuria. Systemic viral illness, menstrual contamination, or strenuous exercise may transiently increase urinary RBCs, and in patients at low risk for urologic malignancy, further evaluation may be deferred unless the hematuria either is high grade (>100 RBCs per high-power field) or is present on at least two of three urinalyses.

More than about five million RBCs per milliliter—about two drops of venous blood per 10 mL—will result in gross hematuria, a reddish tinge to the naked eye. Any such episode should be considered significant and fully evaluated.

ETIOLOGY

The vast number of disorders that may lead to hematuria may be conceptually divided into four groups: (1) hematologic causes, such as coagulopathies, sickle trait, and hereditary telangiectasia; (2) primary or secondary glomerular diseases; (3) nonglomerular renal causes, such as papillary necrosis, renal cell carcinoma, arteriovenous malformations, and cystic diseases; and (4) urologic causes involving the renal pelvis, ureters, bladder, or urethra. The principal thrust of the workup is to identify life-threatening lesions, that is, malignancies, and less dangerous but potentially reversible conditions such as chronic or rapidly progressive glomerulonephritis, infection, calculous disease, and urinary tract obstruction.

CRITERIA FOR DIAGNOSIS

Suggestive

Hematuria may occur in the clinical setting of obvious systemic disease, or it may be an isolated finding on a routine screening urinalysis. In the case of the appearance of red urine, patients usually surmise the presence of blood and are strongly motivated to seek medical help, but hematuria may also result in orange, pink, brown, "smoky," "coke-colored," or almost black urine, depending on the degree of bleeding and the urinary pH. Visual inspection of the urine cannot, however, establish a diagnosis, as a number of other pigments derived from foods, medications, or endogenous metabolism can cause reddish discoloration of the urine, or pseudohematuria (Table 16–5–1).

Definitive

Dipstick testing for hematuria with ortho-tolidine-impregnated cellulose strips identifies two to five RBCs per high-power field with a sensitivity greater than 99% and can thus be used as an effective screening tool. The combination of dipstick and microscopic examinations of the urine can differentiate between true hematuria and pseudohematuria (Tables 16–5–1 and 16–5–2).

CLINICAL MANIFESTATIONS

Subjective

A family history of renal disease suggests hereditary renal diseases like Alport's syndrome, thin basement membrane nephropathy, and polycystic kidney disease. Deafness in young male relatives further suggests Alport's syndrome. Evidence of stone disease or sickle hemoglobinopathy in family members should be sought.

A thorough occupational history is extremely important, as work with industrial chemicals decades before may significantly increase the probability of urologic malignancy. Contact may occur with potent bladder carcinogens such as β-naphthylamine and benzidine or with suspected carcinogens such as polychlorinated biphenyls and creosote

TABLE 16–5–1. PSEUDOHEMATURIA

Mechanism	Cause
Endogenous Pigments	
Hemoglobinuria (glucose-6-phosphate dehydrogenase deficiency)	Nitrofurantoin, *para*-aminosalicylic acid, primaquine, sulfonamides
Myoglobinuria	Amphetamines, cocaine, colchicine, ε-aminocaproic acid, ethanol, phenylpropanolamine, pentamidine, theophylline, many sedatives
Other	Urates in high concentration, bilirubin, melanin, porphyrins
Exogenous Pigments	
Drugs	
Commonly cause red urine	Daunorubicin, doxorubicin; laxatives with cascara, phenolphthalein, or senna (in alkaline urine); phenazopyridine, rifampin
Rarely cause red or brown color	Aminosalicylic acid,* chloroquine, chlorzoxazone, deferoxamine mesylate, ibuprofen, levodopa, methyldopa,* metronidazole, nitrofurantoin, phenacetin, phenindione, phenothiazines, phensuximide, quinine sulfate, sulfonamides
Foods	Beets, blackberries, paprika, rhubarb
Dyes (in foods and cosmetics)	Rhodamine B, aniline dyes
Antiseptics	Povidone–iodine (may cause positive dipstick test), mercurochrome, phenols
Bacterial pigments	*Serratia marcescens* ("red diaper syndrome"); *Providencia* or *Klebsiella* spp. (purple urine in plastic drainage bags)

*Produce color on reaction with hypochlorites (in toilet bowl cleaners).

TABLE 16–5–2. PATTERNS OF ORTHO-TOLIDINE DIPSTICK TESTING AND MICROSCOPY

Dipstick	Microscopy	Cause
+	RBCs	True hematuria
+	No RBCs	Hemoglobinuria, myoglobinuria, bacteriuria
–	No RBCs	Drugs, exogenous pigments
–	RBCs	Nitrites (urinary infection)

RBC, red blood cell.

TABLE 16–5–3. RESULTS OF UROLOGIC EVALUATION OF 6504 ADULTS WITH MICROSCOPIC OR GROSS HEMATURIA

	Total		Asymptomatic Microhematuria		Gross Hematuria	
Number of reports	22		12		5	
Number of patients	6504		2944		1597	
No cause found	1729	(26.6)*	1370	(46.5)	173	(8.2)
Urinary tract infection	1703	(26.2)	538	(18.3)	484	(31.7)
Benign prostatic hypertrophy	821	(12.6)	365	(12.4)	230	(13.4)
Urolithiasis	590	(9.1)	224	(7.6)	161	(10.9)
Glomerulopathy	215	(3.3)	157	(5.3)	26	(1.9)
Carcinoma	656	(10.1)	165	(5.6)	341	(22.1)
Bladder/ureter/pelvis	502	(7.7)	120	(4.1)	254	(16.4)
Renal	93	(1.4)	21	(0.7)	56	(3.6)
Prostate	61	(0.9)	24	(0.8)	31	(2.1)
Renal cyst	260	(4.0)	248	(8.4)	5	(0.4)
Urethral polyps, strictures, etc.	188	(2.9)	72	(2.4)	58	(4.0)
Bladder abnormalities	119	(1.8)	73	(2.5)	5	(0.4)
Urinary tract obstruction	76	(1.2)	49	(1.7)	23	(1.7)
Trauma	49	(0.8)	0	(0.0)	25	(1.8)
Coagulopathy, anticoagulants	21	(0.3)	0	(0.0)	14	(1.0)
Polycystic kidney disease	15	(0.2)	3	(0.1)	6	(0.4)
Radiation cystitis	10	(0.2)	1	(0.0)	4	(0.3)
Sickle hemoglobinopathy	8	(0.1)	0	(0.0)	4	(0.3)
Papillary necrosis	7	(0.1)	1	(0.0)	3	(0.2)
Vesicoureteral reflux	4	(0.1)	3	(0.1)	0	(0.0)
Other	33	(0.5)	15	(0.5)	18	(1.1)

*Percentages are given in parentheses.

in a number of industries, including chemical and dye manufacture, aluminum smelting, dyeing of cloth, lumber processing, transformer manufacture, and occupations with exposure to tar, asphalt, or diesel exhaust. Hydrocarbons—hair sprays, paint solvents and paint removers, and dry cleaning and degreasing solvents—as well as the herbicide paraquat may precipitate several forms of glomerulonephritis, including anti-glomerular basement membrane disease. Smoking, analgesic abuse, and prior pelvic irradiation or therapy with cyclophosphamide or ifosfamide all increase the likelihood of urinary tract malignancy.

If gross hematuria is the presenting complaint, initial or terminal bleeding suggests a lower-tract origin, as does bright red urine. Flank pain may be associated with infection or a stone, but does not exclude malignancy or glomerulonephritis. Frequency, urgency, and suprapubic pain are suggestive of cystitis or urethritis, bacterial or otherwise, although gross hematuria itself may provoke these symptoms.

A past history of stones, infections, urinary tract catheterization, bleeding diathesis, rashes, arthralgias, tuberculosis exposure, diabetes mellitus, sickle cell disease, or travel to areas of endemic schistosomiasis should be investigated. If there is a relationship between a febrile illness and hematuria, the timing is important; a lag time of 10 days or so suggests postinfectious glomerulonephritis, whereas hematuria concomitant with or immediately following the infectious episode is more likely to be IgA nephropathy. Microscopic hematuria appears to be a common finding in diabetics with proteinuria greater than 500 mg/24 h, although many would consider persistent hematuria reason to suspect the presence of a complicating nondiabetic renal or urologic disease (Table 16–5–3).

Finally, a thorough drug history, including nonprescription medications and drugs of abuse, is important (Table 16–5–4). A number of foods, drugs, ingested dyes, or endogenous pigments may also impart a red or brown color to the urine which may be mistaken for hematuria. Causes of this pseudohematuria are listed in Table 16–5–1.

Hematuria may occur in patients on anticoagulant drug therapy, but experience has shown that anticoagulation alone should not be considered the sole etiology without further workup, as significant lesions of the kidney or urinary tract may be brought to light by the anticoagulant-induced bleeding.

Objective

Physical Examination

The physical examination should focus on a search for systemic illness such as vasculitis or endocarditis, and should include a thorough inspection of the skin and mucous membranes for bruises, petecchiae, or rash. Palpation of the prostate is essential, as prostatitis, benign hypertrophy, and prostatic carcinoma all may cause hematuria.

The presence of a Foley catheter is commonly thought to be sufficient explanation for hematuria. Nevertheless, several studies have demonstrated that catheter-induced hematuria almost never exceeds three RBCs per high-power field (Hockberger et al., 1987). Others have found that hematuria in intermittently or permanently catheterized patients is most frequently associated with the presence of urinary tract infection. Hematuria in a catheterized patient should not, therefore, be casually dismissed.

The most important initial examination is, of course, the urinalysis, which in addition to confirming the presence of RBCs in red or dipstick-positive urine can in many cases significantly focus diagnostic suspicion. The presence of RBC casts implies glomerular disease, as

does proteinuria, especially when quantitation reveals more than 500 mg per 24 hours. Pyuria suggests infection, although confirmation by urine culture is necessary and complete resolution of the hematuria with antibiotic therapy is a requirement before assuming that infection is the only cause. Sterile pyuria may indicate genitourinary tuberculosis, but more common causes today are chlamydial urethritis, analgesic nephropathy, and acute interstitial nephritis.

TABLE 16–5–4. DRUG-INDUCED HEMATURIA

Mechanism	Drug
Allergic interstitial nephritis	Beta-lactam antibiotics, sulfonamides, NSAIDs, rifampin, ciprofloxacin, allopurinol, cimetidine, phenytoin, many others
Anticoagulation	Warfarin, heparin, NSAIDs
Glomerulonephritis/ vasculitis	Hydralazine, hydrocarbons (including glue and paint sniffing), gold, penicillamine, amphetamines, NSAIDs, allopurinol, paraquat
Hemorrhagic cystitis	Cyclophosphamide, ifosfamide, mitotane, busulfan, penicillins (methicillin, ticarcillin, piperacillin, amoxicillin); danazol; cantharidin (Spanish Fly)
Loin pain–hematuria syndrome	Oral contraceptives
Papillary necrosis	Aspirin, phenacetin, NSAIDs
Retroperitoneal fibrosis	Methysergide
Thrombotic microangiopathy	Mitomycin C
Urolithiasis	Carbonic anhydrase inhibitors, triamterene, sulfonamides, vitamin D metabolites
Urothelial malignancy	Cyclophosphamide, phenacetin
Unknown	Tricyclic antidepressants, pentamidine

NSAID, nonsteroidal antiinflammatory drug.

Routine Laboratory Abnormalities

See discussion under Criteria for Diagnosis, Definitive. Initial laboratory evaluation should include complete blood count, serum urea nitrogen and creatinine, and urine culture in all patients and sickle cell screening in blacks. Further laboratory workup is dictated by history, physical, and urinalysis findings.

PLANS

Diagnostic

Differential Diagnosis

Table 16–5–3, based on pooled data from 22 published reports, shows the overall occurrence of different etiologies in patients presenting with hematuria, as well as the somewhat different distribution in patients with gross and asymptomatic microscopic hematuria. As can be readily appreciated, the prevalence of carcinoma is about 6% in patients with asymptomatic microscopic hematuria and almost fourfold greater in those with gross bleeding. It should be pointed out that the frequencies listed in the table reflect patients in whom hematuria is the primary finding, rather than part of a symptom complex or the manifestation of a previously diagnosed systemic illness such as systemic lupus erythematosus, hemophilia, or bacterial endocarditis—all of which may commonly cause hematuria.

Diagnostic Options

During the last decade, examination of the morphology of urinary erythrocytes has gained popularity as a method of differentiating glomerular from lower-tract hematuria. In glomerular bleeding, the RBCs appear smaller and "dysmorphic" or distorted and irregular in shape (Figure 16–5–1). Dysmorphic RBCs are most easily identified by phase-contrast microscopy, although oil immersion or even 450× light microscopy can be used, especially with a Wright-stained specimen. There is not a strong consensus on the minimum proportion of dysmorphic cells that reliably identifies hematuria as glomerular, the reported thresholds varying from 10–14 to 75–80%. A variation of this technique is determination of urinary RBC volume using an autoanalyzer; glomerular hematuria is characterized by RBCs markedly smaller than those in the patient's peripheral blood, often with a mean corpuscular volume less than 60 μm^3.

In both of these tests there may be considerable overlap between glomerular and nonglomerular patterns. The presence of urinary tract infection, for example, can cause excretion of dysmorphic "glomerular" RBCs, and dysmorphic forms have been reported in both exercise-induced hematuria and healthy controls. In patients with mild microscopic hematuria, autoanalyzer evaluation of cell volume is confounded by proteinaceous and cellular debris. Nevertheless, with these cautions, RBC morphology may be a quite useful initial test to differentiate glomerular from lower-tract bleeding, especially in combination with conventional urinalysis.

Several new methods have been proposed for the identification of glomerular hematuria based on patterns of urine protein excretion. Erythrocytes in hematuria of renal origin are reported to be coated with uromodulin, or Tamm–Horsfall mucoprotein, the protein secreted by renal tubular cells that forms the matrix of urinary casts. Immunocytochemical staining of RBCs using antisera to Tamm–Horsfall protein is said to reliably discriminate between renal and urologic hematuria. The test is not yet generally available but may in the future prove extremely useful. Similarly, bleeding in the lower urinary tract should result in a protein pattern similar to that of plasma, whereas glomerular hematuria should be associated with preferential excretion of lower-molecular-weight, filtrable proteins. Thus, the ratio of α_2-macroglobulin, a very large protein, to albumin should be reduced in glomerular hematuria, and in fact this measurement in a single urine sample is reported to differentiate quite clearly between renal and postrenal hematuria, as long as urine albumin concentration is at least 100 mg/dL.

Intravenous urography (IVU) is the initial radiologic procedure of choice for evaluation of hematuria. Renal ultrasound has somewhat greater sensitivity for small renal masses, but provides little or no information about the bladder and collecting system. In a patient at high risk for contrast nephropathy, however, an ultrasound might be done first, to be followed by an IVU if no lesion is detected. Renal computed tomography (CT) scanning is far more sensitive than the IVU at detection of masses smaller than 3 cm in diameter, and thus when clinical suspicion of malignancy is high but IVU and cystoscopy are negative, a CT scan might provide additional information.

Given their very low likelihood of carcinoma, asymptomatic patients under 30 years of age with negative IVU and urine cytology can probably be spared cystoscopy, almost certainly if there are glomerular RBCs and/or proteinuria. Once infection has been excluded as a cause of hematuria, all other patients should undergo cystoscopy. In patients with renal dysfunction, especially older patients at high risk for bladder neoplasms, cystoscopy might precede IVU.

Urine cytology is a useful adjunct to cystoscopy and IVU, and can provide a diagnosis when other tests are negative, particularly in carcinoma in situ. The sensitivity of the test for transitional cell carcinoma is about 65% when repeated three times, with a specificity greater than 90%. Cytology may be used as a follow-up test at intervals of 6 months to a year if the initial diagnostic workup is unrevealing.

Renal biopsy should be considered in three clinical settings: (1) other abnormalities in the urine sediment, particularly RBC casts or nephrotic range (> 3 g/24 h) proteinuria; (2) decreasing renal function or severe hypertension; (3) evidence of a systemic disease with a known predilection for renal involvement. In isolated hematuria a biopsy is rarely indicated, as it seldom reveals a condition that requires or responds to therapy. IgA nephropathy is found in 30 to 50% of cases; other common findings are nonspecific mesangial lesions, thin-basement-membrane disease, and normal anatomy.

Recommended Approach

The recommended approach to the workup of hematuria is outlined in Figure 16–5–2. An initial division of patients may be made based on

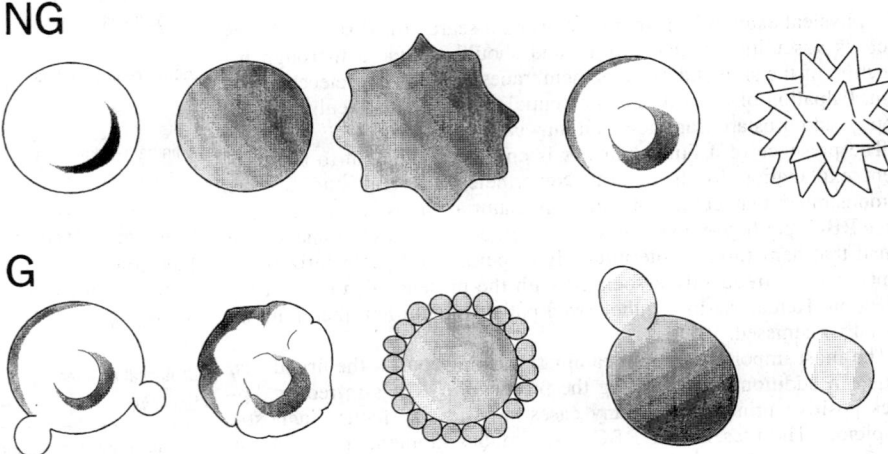

Figure 16–5–1. Red cell forms found in nonglomerular (*NG*) and glomerular (*G*) hematuria. *(Based on data from Tomita M, Kitamoto Y, Nakayama M, Sato T. A new morphological classification of urinary erythrocytes for differential diagnosis of glomerular hematuria. Clin Nephrol 1992;37:84.)*

HEMATURIA

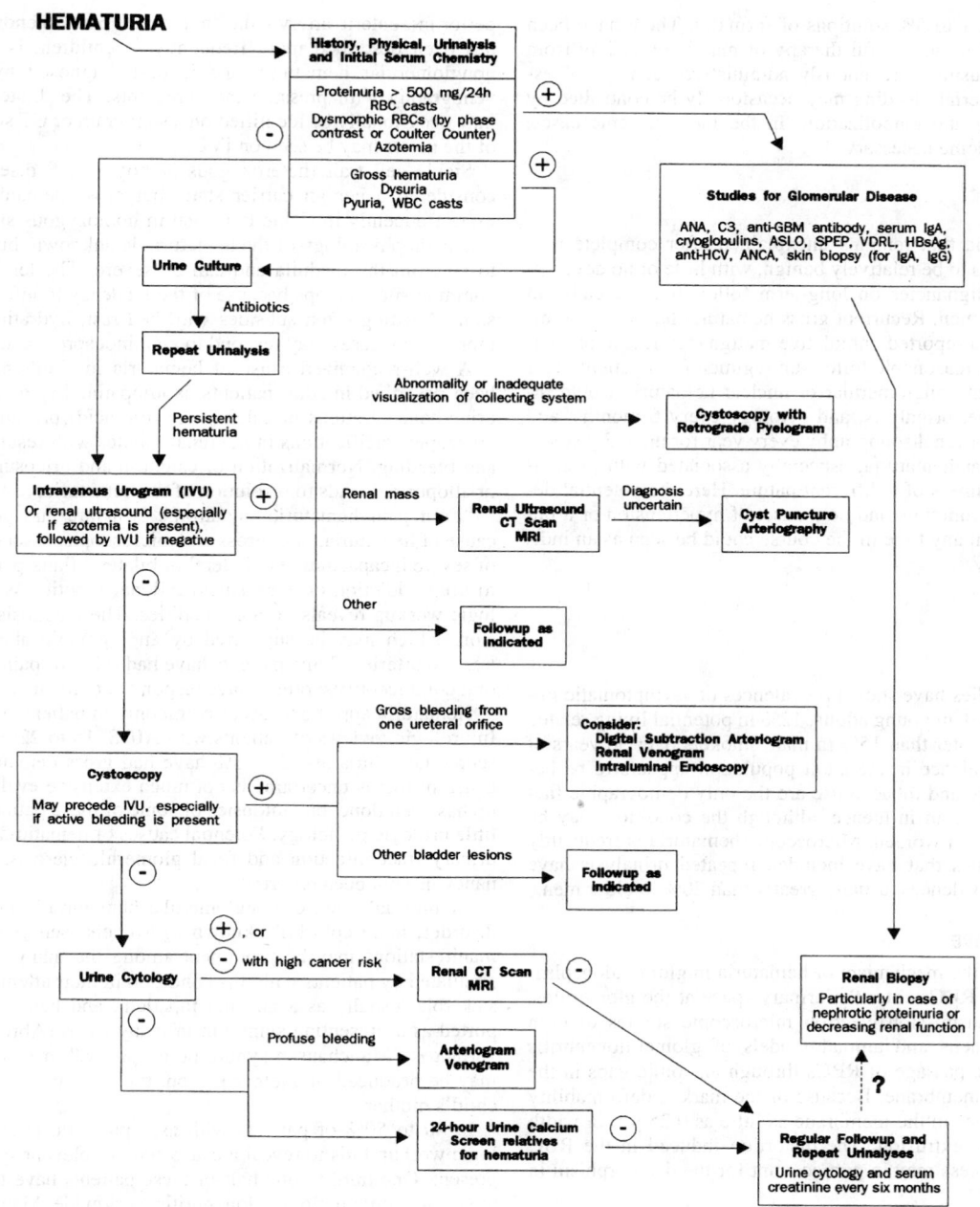

Figure 16–5–2. Algorithm for the laboratory and clinical evaluation of hematuria. *(Adapted from Sutton JM. Evaluation of hematuria in adults. JAMA 1990;263:2475. Reproduced with permission from the American Medical Association [Copyright 1990] and the author.)*

the presence or absence of evidence for glomerular origin of the hematuria. Nephrotic range proteinuria, RBC casts, and rapidly decreasing renal function are very strong indicators of glomerular hematuria and move the workup decisively in the direction of renal biopsy. The occurrence of urinary dysmorphic or microcytic RBCs, of 24-hour protein excretion of 500 mg to 3 g, or of stable azotemia is less definitive, but still orients the investigation toward renal pathology, especially if more than one of these features is present.

Urine culture should probably be performed in all instances of hematuria, but certainly in younger patients with gross hematuria, dysuria, pyuria, white blood cell casts, fever, or flank pain. Urinary tract infection is overwhelmingly the most common cause of hematuria in almost all clinical series, from young women to elderly residents of long-term care facilities.

It should be reemphasized that every episode of gross hematuria should be considered significant and fully evaluated, and that, especially in older men, microscopic hematuria in an asymptomatic patient may be the first and only indicator of serious pathology, most importantly carcinoma of the kidney or urinary tract (see Table 16–5–3).

Therapeutic

Management of hematuria is directed at the underlying illness. The exception is the patient with massive gross hematuria and significant blood loss. This degree of bleeding may occur in hemorrhagic cystitis, polycystic kidney disease, rupture of an arteriovenous malformation or aneurysm of an intrarenal artery, sickle trait, or after prostatectomy or renal biopsy, and may require blood replacement therapy. Bladder or prostate carcinoma may also cause serious bleeding, especially in the setting of a coagulopathy. ε-Aminocaproic acid, an inhibitor of plasminogen activation by urokinase, has been used successfully both orally and intravenously in bleeding from sickle trait, cystitis, polycystic kidneys, and renal biopsy. Life-threatening hematuria from hemorrhagic cystitis can be treated by irrigating the bladder with 1% alum solution or, if this fails, 1 to 5% solutions of formalin. There have been several recent reports of successful therapy of massive bleeding from hemorrhagic cystitis using intravenously administered conjugated estrogens. Intrarenal arterial bleeding may occasionally be controlled by selective angiography and embolization. In the most extreme cases, nephrectomy may become necessary.

FOLLOW-UP

Microscopic hematuria that remains unexplained after complete urologic evaluation seems to be relatively benign, with little or no development of urologic malignancies on long-term follow-up, especially in young men and in women. Recurrent gross hematuria has a more ominous prognosis, with a reported cumulative malignancy rate approaching 20% at 8 years. A reasonable follow-up regimen for a patient older than 40 with persistent nonglomerular or unclear hematuria would include serum creatinine, urinalysis, and cytology every 6 months, and cystoscopy and IVU or renal sonography every year for up to 3 years.

Clear-cut glomerular hematuria, especially associated with proteinuria, calls for watchfulness of a different nature. Here the potential deterioration is in renal function, and new onset of hypertension or a fall in glomerular filtration any time in the course could be seen as an indication for renal biopsy.

DISCUSSION

Prevalence

Population-based studies have shown prevalences of asymptomatic microhematuria of 2 to 5% in young adults, 12% in potential living related kidney donors, and greater than 15% in male smokers over 50 years of age. The overall prevalence in the adult population appears to be between 5 and 13%. Age and tobacco use are the only demographic factors that appear to have an influence, although the condition may be slightly more common in women. Microscopic hematuria is frequently intermittent, and studies that have included repeated urinalysis have found even higher prevalences, usually greater than 20% in older men.

Related Basic Science

Little is known about the mechanism of hematuria in glomerulonephritis. It is assumed that RBCs enter the urinary space at the glomerulus, and scanning and transmission electron microscopic studies of both human biopsy specimens and animal models of glomerulonephritis have demonstrated the passage of RBCs through anatomic gaps in the glomerular basement membrane. Because of the marked deformability of RBCs, discontinuities in the membrane as little as 0.25 μm in width suffice to permit their extrusion. The distortion induced in the RBC membrane by this process may in part account for the dysmorphism in glomerular hematuria.

Natural History and Its Modification with Treatment

As hematuria is caused by many different pathologic processes, it does not have a uniform natural history. A number of less frequently discussed causes of hematuria are explored in this section.

An increasingly common cause of hematuria is strenuous physical exercise. "Sports hematuria" has been described after running, football, boxing, swimming, and lacrosse in as many as 80% of examined athletes. The bleeding may be microscopic or gross, is frequently associated with proteinuria, and is usually asymptomatic. The mechanism has been controversial, and is probably multiple. Glomerular hematuria with dysmorphic RBCs occurs, and bladder lesions have been identified on cystoscopy, implying glomerular damage from vasoconstriction and hypoxia, as well as trauma to the lower urinary tract. The hematuria commonly clears with 24 to 48 hours of rest and needs no further investigation unless it persists beyond 72 hours or is associated with a history or laboratory evidence of parenchymal renal disease.

In unexplained gross hematuria, cystoscopy often reveals unilateral bleeding from the left ureter. Some of these patients have left renal vein hypertension, with consequent venous varices and apparent bleeding into the ureter and calyces. The elevated pressure is caused by compression of the left renal vein as it passes between the aorta and the su-

perior mesenteric artery—the "nutcracker phenomenon." The condition has been described more frequently in children, is characterized by nonglomerular hematuria, and is best diagnosed by selective renal venography with pressure measurements. The dilated left renal vein may occasionally be identified on a sonogram or CT scan, and notching of the ureter may be seen on IVU.

Sickle cell trait (heterozygous hemoglobin S disease) is generally considered a benign carrier state, but gross hematuria occurs much more frequently in sickle trait than in homozygous sickle cell anemia. The pathophysiology of the hematuria is unknown, but bleeding seems to be from the medulla and can be severe. The left side is the more common site, perhaps because of the tendency to left venous hypertension. Bleeding often subsides with bed rest, hydration, and diuretics; more severe cases may respond to ε-aminocaproic acid.

A well-recognized cause of hematuria in children, which has now been described in adult patients, is idiopathic hypercalciuria. The high urine concentrations of calcium (or uric acid) presumably lead to microscopic calcifications in the renal tubules with resultant microtrauma and bleeding. Normalization of calciuria and uricosuria with thiazides or allopurinol leads to resolution of the hematuria.

"Loin pain–hematuria" syndrome is a rare and poorly understood cause of hematuria, both gross and microscopic, associated with attacks of severe incapacitating unilateral or bilateral flank pain which can lead to drug addiction or even suicide. Renal function is normal and urologic workup reveals no abnormalities. The diagnosis is one of exclusion, which may be supported by angiographic abnormalities in intrarenal arteries. Some patients have had relief of pain on discontinuing oral contraceptives; others have responded to renal autotransplantation.

Hematuria appears to occur commonly in patients with HIV disease. In urologic reviews of patients with AIDS, 15 to 22% have had microscopic hematuria and 2 to 3% have had gross hematuria. The significance of this is uncertain, as not much extensive evaluation or followup has been done, but autopsies of some of these patients have revealed little urologic pathology. Potential causes of hematuria in AIDS include urinary tract infection and focal glomerulosclerosis. Urologic malignancy has not been reported.

An unusual cause of nonglomerular hematuria is a chronic factitious disorder, more colorfully known as Münchausen syndrome. Bleeding manifestations may be prominent among the many physical ailments simulated by patients with this condition in their attempts to assume the sick role, usually as a hospital inpatient, and hematuria has been reported as a presenting symptom in many cases (Abrol et al., 1990). A variant is "Münchausen syndrome by proxy," in which the hematuria may be produced in another person, typically in a young child by the child's mother.

In 40 to 50% of patients with asymptomatic microhematuria, urologic workup fails to reveal a cause and no relevant systemic disease is present. One third to one half of these patients have IgA nephropathy, the most common glomerulonephritis worldwide. Many of the rest have so-called benign familial hematuria (BFH), which probably represents a variety of pathologic lesions, including thin-basement-membrane disease. The prognosis is somewhat different: IgA nephropathy, although frequently having a benign course, may lead to end-stage renal failure in 15 to 20% of European and North American patients after 20 years of clinical disease; patients with BFH have been followed for up to 18 years with no deterioration of renal function.

Some differentiation between these entities is possible on clinical grounds. Both present with glomerular hematuria and normal renal function. Patients with IgA nephropathy frequently report episodes of gross hematuria, usually have greater than 500 mg protein/24 h, and demonstrate no familial occurrence. Hematuria in BFH is usually microscopic, proteinuria rarely exceeds 500 mg/24 h, and the urine sediment of first-degree relatives contains RBCs and RBC casts with an inheritance pattern consistent with autosomal dominant transmission.

Because IgA nephropathy can progress to end-stage renal disease, albeit in a minority of cases, attempts have been made to define the prognostic significance of clinical and histologic features. Hypertension, decreased creatinine clearance, proteinuria greater than 2 g/24 h, male sex, and biopsy evidence of glomerular sclerosis, severe mesangial proliferation, interstitial fibrosis, or glomerular crescents all are associated with a poorer outcome, although their predictive value in an individual case is weak. Episodes of gross hematuria appear to be a marker of a more benign variant of the disease. There is no effective therapy beyond control of blood pressure, careful follow-up, and reassurance, although a recent study has suggested that renal function may be stabilized by administration of fish oil (Donadio et al., 1994).

Prevention

Populations at high risk for urologic malignancy may be screened for microscopic hematuria. This includes men older than 50 and all persons with significant occupational exposures. Risk is increased in all groups by a smoking history. Dipstick screening of urine at home or in the workplace is a promising approach to early detection and treatment of urinary cancers.

The risk of hemorrhagic cystitis during therapy with the alkylating agents cyclophosphamide and ifosfamide may be reduced by hydration and maintenance of urine flow, but a specific preventive therapy is available. Mesna (sodium 2-mercaptoethanesulfonate) is a thiol compound that is rapidly oxidized in the plasma to its dimeric form, dimesna, which is converted back to mesna in the kidney by glutathione reductase. In the bladder, mesna protects against hemorrhagic cystitis by scavenging the toxic metabolite acrolein. It may be administered together with the alkylating agent and greatly reduces the incidence of urothelial toxicity.

Cost Containment

The very high prevalence of microscopic hematuria in asymptomatic adults leads to difficult questions about population screening and the extent of evaluation of affected individuals. The average cost of outpatient workup in a series of 1000 patients was $777 (Mariani et al., 1989); it is easy to calculate the astronomic costs that could result from full evaluation of 10% of the adult population. For this reason, and because of the infrequent occurrence of serious urologic disease in population-based studies of asymptomatic microscopic hematuria—less than 2% of positive patients—screening of urine for hematuria as part of periodic health examination is not recommended (Woolhandler et al., 1989). This philosophy does not apply to older men or to those with occupational exposure to urologic carcinogens, for whom regular screening can have important benefits.

The relatively low incidence of carcinoma in women and young men

has led some to recommend against full evaluation of hematuria in these groups. This is a hard position to support, but in a young woman one might be more easily persuaded away from urologic workup by moderate proteinuria or dysmorphic erythrocytes. Others have suggested abandoning the IVU in favor of sonography to reduce the cost and morbidity of workup. Sonography may in fact be more sensitive than an IVU for small renal masses, but these lesions are rare causes of hematuria and a sonogram yields little or no information about the ureters and bladder.

Most importantly, it is necessary to pause and reflect fully on the potential benefit to the patient before proceeding to costly and risk-laden examinations such as arteriography and renal biopsy.

REFERENCES

Abrol RP, Heck A, Gleckel L, Rosner F. Self-induced hematuria. J Natl Med Assoc. 1990;82:127.

Donadio JV Jr, Bergstralh EJ, Offord KP, et al. A controlled trial of fish oil in IgA nephropathy: Mayo Nephrology Collaborative Group. N Engl J Med 1994;331:1194.

Hockberger RS, Schwartz B, Connor J. Hematuria induced by urethral catheterization. Ann Emerg Med. 1987;16:550.

Ibels LS, Györy AZ. IgA nephropathy: Analysis of the natural history, important factors in the progression of renal disease, and a review of the literature. Medicine 1994;73:79.

Mariani AJ, Mariani MC, Macchioni C, et al. The significance of adult hematuria: 1000 hematuria evaluations including a risk–benefit and cost–effectiveness analysis. J Urol 1989;141:350.

Offringa M, Benbassat J. The value of urinary red cell shape in the diagnosis of glomerular and post-glomerular haematuria: a meta-analysis. Postgrad Med J 1992;68:648.

Shokeir AA, El-Diasty TA, Ghoneim MA. The nutcracker syndrome: New methods of diagnosis and treatment. Br J Urol 1994;74:139.

Sutton JM. Evaluation of hematuria in adults. JAMA 1990;263:2475.

Topham PS, Harper SJ, Furness PN, et al. Glomerular disease as a cause of isolated microscopic haematuria. Q J Med 1994;87:329.

Weisberg LS, Bloom PB, Simmons RL, Viner ED. Loin pain hematuria syndrome. Am J Nephrol 1993;13:229.

Woolhandler S, Pels RJ, Bor DH, et al. Dipstick urinalysis screening of asymptomatic adults for urinary tract disorders. I. Hematuria and proteinuria. JAMA. 1989;262:1214.

CHAPTER 16–6

Pyuria

Sithiporn Sastrasinh, M.D.

DEFINITION

Pyuria means pus in the urine. This is usually defined as 5 or more leukocytes per microscopic high-power field in centrifuged urine or as more than 10 leukocytes/mm^3 in uncentrifuged urine.

ETIOLOGY

Urinary tract infection is the most common cause of pyuria. Other diseases of the genitourinary tract that cause pyuria include genital infection, prostatitis, renal stones, papillary necrosis, polycystic kidney disease, and interstitial nephritis. One study reported that a large proportion of patients with malignant hypertension had pyuria. Many of these patients, however, had evidence of renal diseases, including pyelonephritis and renal stones. There were reports of pyuria in patients with acute glomerulonephritis. But the clinical picture of acute glomerulonephritis is dominated by hematuria and other clinical manifestations of acute nephritis rather than pyuria (see Chapter 16–18). With the exception of occasional eosinophiluria in patients with drug-induced acute interstitial nephritis, pyuria is usually not an important

factor in the diagnosis and management of patients with acute interstitial nephritis.

CRITERIA FOR DIAGNOSIS

Suggestive

A urine strip that detects leukocyte esterase activity is a useful screening test for pyuria. Examination of centrifuged urine with semiquantitative estimation of leukocytes per high-power field is widely used, but it is insensitive.

Definitive

A reliable and practical test for pyuria is to count the number of leukocytes in uncentrifuged urine with a hematocytometer (upper limit of normal, 10 leukocytes/mm^3). Two caveats about the tests for pyuria should be mentioned here. Neutropenic patients may not have pyuria even in the presence of urinary tract infection. Leukocytes disintegrate in alkaline urine pH. This may give a false-negative result for pyuria, especially in patients infected with urea-splitting organisms.

In drug-induced acute interstitial nephritis the excretion of eosinophils in the urine frequently increases. Eosinophiluria is a nonspecific finding. It is sometimes found in acute prostatitis, atheroembolic renal failure, glomerulonephritis, urinary tract infection, and schistosomiasis. Hansen's stain is better than Wright's stain for the detection of eosinophils in urine.

CLINICAL MANIFESTATIONS

Subjective

Pyuria per se is asymptomatic, but associated clinical manifestations are important as clues to the underlying cause. Patients with lower urinary tract infection may be asymptomatic or have complaints of frequency, urgency, dysuria, and suprapubic discomfort. Classically, patients with acute pyelonephritis complain of fever, chills, nausea, vomiting, and abdominal, back, and loin pain; however, many patients who are asymptomatic or who have symptoms of acute cystitis may actually have upper urinary tract infection. Patients with acute bacterial prostatitis have fever and chills, perineal or groin pain, dysuria, frequency, and difficulty in voiding. Complaints of perineal or groin pain, frequency, dysuria, and difficulty in voiding and a history of relapsing urinary tract infection are also common in patients with chronic bacterial prostatitis. Occasionally, patients with chronic bacterial prostatitis may be asymptomatic. Extrapulmonary tuberculosis most frequently involves the genitourinary tract. Renal involvement may not become apparent until long after the pulmonary lesion has ceased to be active. Although frequently asymptomatic in the early stages, patients with renal tuberculosis may complain of polyuria, nocturia, dysuria, gross hematuria, and flank pain. They may have constitutional symptoms related to tuberculosis, although this is not very frequent.

Diabetes mellitus, sickle cell nephropathy, and analgesic nephropathy are frequently associated with papillary necrosis. About half of the cases of papillary necrosis occur in patients with diabetes mellitus. It is a complication of late stages of the disease. Clinical manifestations of diabetic patients with papillary necrosis are diverse. They may be asymptomatic. They may notice gross hematuria or a papillary slough in the urine. They may have acute pyelonephritis with sepsis and oliguric acute renal failure. Papillary necrosis in analgesic nephropathy and sickle cell disease is usually insidious. Analgesic nephropathy is relatively rare in the United States, except in the Southeast. Patients with analgesic nephropathy have a history of analgesic–antipyretic consumption in large amounts, but this information may be difficult to obtain. Many patients with analgesic nephropathy have a history of emotional stress or psychiatric disorders. They may have a history of gastric ulcer and gastrointestinal blood loss because of long-term analgesic intake. Analgesic nephropathy causes a urinary concentrating defect with complaints of polyuria and nocturia. Recurrent gross hematuria, a positive family history, and episodes of sickle cell crises may be obtained from patients with sickle cell nephropathy. Polyuria and nocturia, secondary to a urinary concentrating defect, are also common in sickle cell nephropathy.

Renal stones may be asymptomatic or cause flank pain and hematuria during passage. The pain may radiate to the groin and genitalia. Many patients will have a past history of stones because recurrence is common in renal stone disease. There is a positive family history in about three quarters of patients with polycystic kidney disease.

Objective

Physical Examination

The physical examination may provide clues to the etiology of pyuria.

Acute Cystitis. There is no specific finding. Some patients may have suprapubic pain and tenderness.

Acute Pyelonephritis. Generally, the patient is acutely ill with high fever, rigors, and severe tenderness over the costovertebral angle.

Bacterial Prostatitis. These patients have fever with enlarged and tender prostates. Prostatic massage in the acute phase carries the risk of bacteremia. Acute epididymitis is an occasional accompaniment in acute bacterial prostatitis. Patients with chronic bacterial prostatitis may have a low-grade fever with an enlarged and tender prostate.

Diabetes Mellitus with Papillary Necrosis. These patients usually have other complications of long-standing diabetes, including diabetic retinopathy. Signs of acute pyelonephritis, sepsis, and oliguric acute renal failure may be the initial presentation of papillary necrosis in diabetics.

Sickle Cell Nephropathy. This diagnosis has usually been established by the time papillary necrosis occurs and signs of hemolytic anemia and other features of the disease may be evident.

Analgesic Nephropathy. Signs of premature aging have been reported in large series. Hypertension is also common in these patients.

Polycystic Kidney Disease. Hypertension is a common finding. The kidneys are enlarged with irregular surfaces. The liver may be palpable because of the cystic changes.

Routine Laboratory Abnormalities

Acute Cystitis. Urinalysis shows pyuria and occasionally hematuria. Chemical tests for the presence of bacteria may be positive. The finding of bacteria with Gram stain of the centrifuged urine has high sensitivity and specificity for the detection of significant bacteriuria ($\geq 1 \times 10^5$ organisms/mL).

Acute Pyelonephritis. Urinalysis shows bacteriuria, pyuria, and occasionally white blood cell casts. White blood cell casts are not specific and may be found in a variety of glomerular and interstitial diseases.

Renal Tuberculosis. "Sterile pyuria" is a classic finding. Urinalysis may show hematuria as well as pyuria. The chest radiograph may show an inactive or, more rarely, active pulmonary lesion.

Sickle Cell Disease. Patients have varying degrees of anemia. Sickle red blood cells may be evident on the peripheral blood smear. Urinalysis may show pyuria, hematuria, and proteinuria.

Analgesic Nephropathy. Anemia and occult blood in the stool may be encountered in patients who abuse analgesics and have gastrointestinal blood loss. Urinalysis shows pyuria, hematuria, and mild to moderate degrees of proteinuria. The patients have varying degrees of renal dysfunction.

PLANS

Diagnostic

Differential Diagnosis

Pyuria is a very useful parameter for the diagnosis of urinary tract infection. Pyuria is uncommon in asymptomatic and nonbacteriuric patients. When pyuria is found in asymptomatic females, contamination of the urine with vaginal secretions has to be ruled out. Pyuria is almost a universal finding in patients with significant bacteriuria. The majority of patients who have symptoms of lower urinary tract infection in the absence of significant bacteriuria (i.e., acute urethral syndrome) also have pyuria. Most of the patients with acute urethral syndrome and pyuria have either urinary tract infection with common uropathogens or genital infection. Rapid diuresis may be responsible for insignificant bacteriuria in patients with true urinary tract infection. The use of an early-morning specimen for urine culture avoids the problems of rapid diuresis with frequent voiding and may increase the finding of significant bacteriuria in patients with true urinary tract infection. Pyuria in patients who do not have significant bacteriuria also raises the possibilities of urinary tract infection with *Staphylococcus saprophyticus,* a bacterium with a relatively long generation time, or with fastidious bacteria such as *Ureaplasma urealyticum* and *Mycoplasma hominis.* A rarer cause of "sterile" pyuria is renal tuberculosis. Pyuria without significant bacteriuria is also found in sickle cell nephropathy and analgesic nephropathy. Although urinary tract infection is frequently associated with renal stones and polycystic kidney disease, pyuria may occur in these two conditions in the absence of infection.

Most of the patients with renal tuberculosis have a positive purified protein derivative (PPD) skin test. At least three to five urine specimens should be obtained for the culture of *Mycobacterium* species. Intravenous pyelogram (IVP) shows focal calyceal abnormalities in the early stage of renal tuberculosis. Some dilation of the renal pelvis may also occur early. In late stages of the disease, the IVP shows calcification, calyceal amputation, ureteral stricture, vesicoureteral reflux, and, possibly, a nonfunctioning kidney (autonephrectomy). Sickle cell preparation and hemoglobin electrophoresis are used to confirm the diagnosis of sickle cell disease. There may be evidence of papillary necrosis on the IVP in patients with sickle cell nephropathy. The diagnosis of analgesic nephropathy is based on history with the findings of "sterile" pyuria, hematuria, and renal papillary necrosis on the IVP. In patients with polycystic kidney disease, renal and hepatic cysts may be detected with either computed tomography (CT) scan or sonography. CT scan is slightly more sensitive than the sonogram for this purpose. Radiopaque stones are visualized on plain kidney/ureter/bladder (KUB) films. Renal ultrasound is a sensitive method to detect renal stones.

Diagnostic Options and Recommended Approach

Urine culture is the first step in the evaluation of pyuria. Patients must be carefully instructed about the collection of a clean-catch midstream urine specimen. The diagnosis of urinary tract infection is not difficult in symptomatic patients with pyuria and significant bacteriuria. In patients with pyuria and insignificant bacteriuria, true urinary tract infection with common uropathogens should be considered first. Genital infection with *Chlamydia trachomatis* or *Neisseria gonorrhoeae* or urinary tract infection with *Staphylococcus saprophyticus* or with fastidious bacteria should then be considered. After urinary tract and genital infection have been ruled out, the possibilities of renal tuberculosis, sickle cell nephropathy, analgesic nephropathy, polycystic kidney disease, and renal stones should be investigated.

Therapeutic

Therapeutic Options

In acute cystitis a single dose of the appropriate antimicrobial agent accomplishes results comparable to those of a longer course of treatment (7–14 days) with fewer side effects and better compliance. Asymptomatic bacteriuria during pregnancy should always be treated because it is associated with a high incidence of symptomatic infection, acute pyelonephritis, and, possibly, other morbidities in the mother and with increased fetal risk.

Recommended Approach

In symptomatic patients with pyuria a urine culture should be obtained, but treatment can be initiated before the result of urine culture is available. Clinical course, results of urine culture, and sensitivity test may dictate a subsequent change in antimicrobial agents. A single dose of amoxicillin 3 g orally or 2 double-strength tablets of trimethoprim–sulfamethoxazole orally (each tablet contains 160 mg trimethoprim and 800 mg sulfamethoxazole) or 400 mg trimethoprim orally can be used to treat uncomplicated acute cystitis. The reader is referred to Chapter 8–23 for more information about treatment and prophylaxis in patients with urinary tract infection.

Treatment of renal tuberculosis with antituberculous drugs usually lasts 18 to 24 months. Cessation of analgesic intake may stabilize or improve renal function in patients with analgesic nephropathy. There is no specific treatment for polycystic kidney disease or sickle cell nephropathy. Management of renal stones is discussed in Chapter 16–16.

FOLLOW-UP

Follow-up urine culture should be done 4 to 7 days after completion of the treatment for urinary tract infection. If pyuria persists despite negative urine cultures, further investigation for the cause of pyuria should

be considered. Otherwise, the follow-up of pyuria is the follow-up of the underlying conditions.

DISCUSSION

Prevalence and Incidence

Combined data from multiple studies on the association between pyuria and urinary tract infection showed that more than 90% of patients with symptomatic bacteriuria had pyuria. The prevalence of pyuria in patients who do not have bacterial urinary tract infection is low. Very few asymptomatic and abacteriuric patients had pyuria. This finding suggests that the incidence of pyuria is closely correlated with that of urinary tract infection. Cystitis is one of the most common bacterial infections. About one fifth of women between the ages of 24 and 64 have at least one episode of dysuria per year, mostly due to bacterial infection. With the exception of the infancy period, urinary tract infection is rare in men until they reach the fifth decade of life. As many as half of patients of both sexes who are chronically institutionalized have bacteriuria.

Related Basic Science

Pyuria is a host response to an inflammatory process in the genitourinary tract. The most reliable, but clinically impractical, test for pyuria is the measurement of leukocyte excretion in the urine over a fixed period (usually 3 hours). The number of leukocytes in uncentrifuged urine, counted in a hematocytometer, closely correlates with the leukocyte excretion rate. The estimation of cells per microscopic high-power field, although widely used, is poorly reproducible. It does not correlate well with the leukocyte excretion rate or with the leukocyte count in a hematocytometer.

Natural History and Its Modification with Treatment

Pyuria disappears after successful treatment for urinary tract infection, prostatitis, genital infection, and renal stones because the causative agents in these conditions can be eliminated. Pyuria persists in conditions that have no specific cures. Although renal function may stabilize or improve after the cessation of analgesic abuse, patients with analgesic nephropathy continue to have pyuria from chronic interstitial nephritis.

Prevention

Prevention must be aimed at the primary disease responsible for pyuria.

Cost Containment

Understanding the significance of pyuria helps clinicians to take care of patients in a cost-effective manner. The presence of sterile pyuria or the persistence of pyuria after urinary tract infection is eradicated should prompt a timely workup for other causes of pyuria. The recognition that pyuria can occur in the absence of infection in renal stone disease and polycystic kidney disease can prevent repetitious testing for urinary tract infection after an initial negative workup.

REFERENCES

Fairley KF. Urinalysis. In Schrier RW, Gottschalk CW, eds. Diseases of the kidney. 5th ed. Boston: Little, Brown, 1993:335.

Jenkins RD, Fenn JP, Matsen JM. Review of urine microscopy for bacteriuria. JAMA 1986;255:3397.

Schottstaedt MF, Sokolow M. The natural history and course of hypertension with papilledema (malignant hypertension). Am Heart J 1953;45:331.

Stamm WE. Measurement of pyuria and its relation to bacteriuria. Am J Med 1983;75(1B):53.

Stamm WE. Cystitis and urethritis. In Schrier RW, Gottschalk CW, eds. Diseases of the kidney. 5th ed. Boston: Little, Brown, 1993:1007.

CHAPTER 16–7
Hypertension (See Section 14)

CHAPTER 16–8
Pyelonephritis, Urinary Tract Infections (See Section 8, Chapter 23)

CHAPTER 16–9
Acute Renal Failure

Edmund Bourke, M.D., and Vera Delaney, M.D., Ph. D.

DEFINITION

Acute renal failure is an abrupt decline in glomerular filtration of such severity as to result in a progressive retention of nitrogenous wastes, for example, urea and creatinine. It may occur in a patient with previously normal renal function or be superimposed on preexistent but stable renal functional impairment.

ETIOLOGY

The etiology of acute renal failure is best classified as being due to prerenal, renal, or postrenal causes. Prerenal causes imply decreased renal perfusion, in turn a consequence of a decreased absolute circulatory volume, a decreased effective circulatory volume, or renal vasoconstriction. The term connotes a functional state that is at least potentially reversible. Renal parenchymal causes of acute renal failure include vascular, glomerular, interstitial, and tubular lesions, the last being the most common, namely, acute tubular necrosis. Acute tubular necrosis can result from toxic or ischemic insults. Ischemic acute tubular necrosis is most often a primary lesion, but it can also be secondary to a preexistent prerenal acute renal failure if it is of sufficient severity or duration. Postrenal acute renal failure implies an obstructing lesion that is at least potentially correctable. The obstruction can be intrarenal or extrarenal.

CRITERIA FOR DIAGNOSIS
Suggestive

Oliguria (see Chapter 16–1) should alert the clinician to the possibility of impending or existing acute renal failure. It is not specific enough to permit a definitive conclusion, however, and nonoliguric acute renal failure is now seen with increasing frequency.

Definitive

A rise in serum creatinine of 0.5 mg/dL per day or more can generally be taken as indicating acute renal failure. The initial rise may require exclusion of increased creatinine production from rhabdomyolysis, or inhibition of tubular secretion of creatinine by drugs such as cimetidine, trimethoprim, quinidine, or other organic cations. As the rise progresses over days the diagnosis becomes definitive. The rise in serum creatinine is accompanied by a rise in blood urea nitrogen (BUN) of approximately 10 mg/dL per day.

CLINICAL MANIFESTATIONS
Subjective

The predominant symptoms may be, in part, attributable to acute renal failure per se or, in part, to the underlying condition that caused it. Sometimes the patient notes oliguria or even anuria, the latter of which

is more definitive and strongly favors an obstructive etiology. The spectrum of symptoms of acute renal failure is the same as that for chronic renal failure (see Chapter 16–12). The severity of symptoms tends to parallel the rate of elevation of BUN and creatinine, which serve as markers for the accumulation of waste products responsible for the clinical features that constitute the uremic syndrome. For example, dyspnea; gastrointestinal symptoms such as nausea, vomiting, anorexia, and hiccups; as well as neurologic features such as headache, lassitude, impaired concentrating ability, and obtundation are usually the most prominent.

In some instances the clinical manifestations of the underlying condition leading to acute renal failure are more prominent. Features of hypotension, sepsis, liver failure, rhabdomyolysis, and vasculitis may lead the clinician to suspect the possibility of acute renal failure. Historical data concerning drugs or toxins known to be capable of inducing renal failure, including aminoglycoside antibiotics, radiocontrast media, and nonsteroidal antiinflammatory agents, may heighten the index of suspicion in appropriate circumstances.

Objective
Physical Examination

The physical findings in acute renal failure pertain both to its causes and its consequences. Signs of volume depletion including dry axillary skin and postural hypotension have obvious etiologic import. Decreased effective circulating volume may be suggested by the presence of severe congestive heart failure with features of fluid overload including a third heart sound and jugular venous distension; or hepatocellular decompensation manifested by jaundice, ascites, and asterixis; or the nephrotic syndrome manifested by massive proteinuria and edema. In critically ill patients it may not be easy to reliably determine the patient's effective circulating volume status clinically and measurement of pulmonary wedge pressure using a Swan–Ganz catheter may be indicated for a better evaluation. Livedo reticularis in the elderly should raise the strong suspicion of atheroembolic disease, which frequently results in acute renal failure. Muscle tenderness and pink urine suggest myoglobinuric acute renal failure from rhabdomyolysis. A cardiac bruit and peripheral evidence of bacterial endocarditis may indicate a cause of acute renal failure. Skin rashes are suggestive of a vasculitis including systemic lupus erythematosus or an allergic, most often drug-induced, acute interstitial nephritis.

In suspected acute renal failure acute urinary retention should be one of the earliest things to exclude by catheterization of the bladder and noting postvoid residual. Benign prostatic hypertrophy or carcinoma of the prostate may be evident on physical examination.

Clouding of consciousness, asterixis, delirium, myoclonus, seizure, and coma are progressive signs of uremic encephalopathy. A pericardial friction rub may indicate the presence of uremic pericarditis, a sign of advanced renal failure. Kussmaul's respiration points to severe uremic acidosis.

Routine Laboratory Abnormalities

The urinalysis is an indispensable part of the evaluation of patients with suspected acute renal failure. It is important not to discard the first specimen of urine obtained lest persistent oliguria cause a delay in the acquisition of essential information. A benign urine sediment in the face of acute renal failure suggests a prerenal or postrenal etiology. Microscopy of the urinary sediment may also help distinguish between renal parenchymal lesions due to different pathogenetic mechanisms. Renal tubular cells, coarsely granular casts, sometimes pigmented, and minimal proteinuria without prominent hematuria characterize acute tubular necrosis. Numerous pigmented casts are characteristic of pigment-associated acute tubular necrosis. Red cell casts or significant hematuria of glomerular origin (see Chapter 16–18), usually with moderate proteinuria, suggests an acute glomerular lesion. Prominent leukocyturia indicates inflammation in the parenchyma or collecting system. Prominent urinary eosinophils suggest acute interstitial nephritis or atheroembolic disease of the kidney.

Daily measurements of BUN and serum creatinine are axiomatic in the patient with acute renal failure to define its severity and course. BUN:serum creatinine ratios are useful as they generally approximate 10:1 in acute parenchymal renal failure. Ratios approximating 20:1 favor prerenal or sometimes postrenal causes or suggest a significant concomitant factor such as gastrointestinal bleeding, excessive tissue catabolism, or administration of steroids. Ratios significantly less than 10:1 may be seen when creatinine production is enhanced by rhabdomyolysis or when urea production is decreased by a low-protein diet or advanced liver disease or following dialysis, which removes the lower-molecular-weight urea more effectively than creatinine.

The routine biochemical screen (SMA 20) that reports the BUN and creatinine may reveal other abnormalities of etiologic or consequential importance in the acute renal failure setting. Hypercalcemia may present with nonoliguric acute renal failure. An unsuspected but substantial elevation of serum creatine phosphokinase may be the only clue to rhabdomyolysis-associated acute renal failure. Extreme hyperuricemia, especially in the setting of the injudicious use of chemotherapy without allopurinol, may present with acute renal failure. Abnormal liver functions tests require evaluation in the context of a variety of hepatorenal syndromes. Anemia is invariable.

Changes in plasma electrolytes are predictable as acute renal failure develops. The most prominent features initially are hyperkalemia, which can be life threatening, and hypobicarbonatemia due to an increased anion-gap metabolic acidosis. A rise in plasma phosphate and a fall in serum calcium concentrations are seen as the syndrome progresses.

Electrocardiographic changes of hyperkalemia or pericarditis may be present.

PLANS

Diagnostic

Differential Diagnosis

Prerenal acute renal failure (Table 16–9–1) is frequently called functional, as accurate and timely diagnosis permits its reversal by correcting the underlying abnormality when this is possible. Such is the rule when the cause is hypovolemia. If decreased effective circulating volume is a consequence of severe cardiac failure, improved renal perfusion will likely result from optimizing cardiac function. In prerenal azotemia of cardiac, hepatic, or renal origin, an iatrogenic component, such as the injudicious use of diuretics, angiotensin-converting enzyme (ACE) inhibitors, or cyclooxygenase inhibitors (nonsteroidal antiinflammatory drugs [NSAIDs]), often plays a precipitating role. When increased vascular capacitance is the cause of impaired renal perfusion, septicemia is the most likely culprit and progress to acute tubular necrosis is particularly likely if therapeutic intervention is not prompt. The afferent arteriolar vasoconstriction of NSAIDs is generally confined to the elderly or those with high-renin/high-angiotensin states, that is, where some degree of preexistent impairment of renal perfusion

TABLE 16–9–1. CAUSES OF PRERENAL FAILURE (INADEQUATE RENAL PERFUSION)

Hypotension	
Hypovolemia	
Gastrointestinal losses	Diarrhea, vomiting, gastrointestinal bleeding
Renal losses	Hyperglycemia, hypercalcemia, mineralocortical deficiency, diuretics, salt-loosing nephropathy
Third spacing	Pancreatitis, peritonitis, crush injury, retroperitoneal bleed
Cutaneous losses	Burns, excess sweating
Decreased effective circulating volume	Severe cardiac failure, cardiovascular shock, large pulmonary embolism, cirrhosis with ascites, nephrosis
Increased vascular capacitance	Sepsis, anaphylaxis, vasodilators
Afferent arteriolar vasoconstriction	Hepatorenal syndrome, nonsteroidal antiinflammatory drugs
Efferent arteriolar vasodilation	Angiotensin-converting enzyme inhibitors

is present. In this situation, inhibition of production of modulatory vasodilatory prostaglandins leaves unopposed the renovasoconstrictor action of increased angiotensin. The vasoconstriction of the hepatorenal syndrome, when severe enough to induce significant azotemia, can rarely be reversed except by liver transplantation. The efferent arteriolar vasodilation of ACE-inhibiting drugs can cause the glomerular filtration rate to fall sufficiently to induce azotemia only when there is a critical level of reduced perfusion through the afferent vasculature, as for instance in severe bilateral renal artery stenosis and in some instances of chronic renal failure or advanced congestive cardiac failure. Although not a prerequisite for the development of prerenal azotemia, hypotension is usually an early accompaniment when prerenal azotemia is a consequence of acute hypovolemia, acute cardiac decompensation, or the increased vascular capacitance of septic shock.

Acute parenchymal renal failure (Table 16–9–2) is classified into vascular, glomerular, tubular, and interstitial categories. The most common of these by far is tubular, acute tubular necrosis. Any of those conditions that can cause prerenal acute renal failure can, if of sufficient severity or duration, induce ischemic acute tubular necrosis. The patient may already have ischemic acute tubular necrosis on presentation or progress from a prerenal state when effective timely intervention has not been implemented. Toxic acute tubular necrosis is often distinguishable from the ischemic variety by careful history taking; however, it is not uncommon that nephrotoxic agents have been administered in the setting of impaired renal perfusion, making it impossible to determine which is causative and which is compounding. Rhabdomyolysis-

TABLE 16–9–2. CAUSES OF PARENCHYMAL ACUTE RENAL FAILURE

Vascular	Atheroembolic disease, vasculitis, bilateral renal artery stenosis, dissecting aneurysm
Glomerular	Acute proliferation and/or necrotizing glomerular nephritis, primary or secondary
Tubular	Acute tubular necrosis
Ischemic	Prerenal factors of greater severity and/or duration
Toxic	Aminoglycosides, amphotericin, radiocontrast materials, cis-platinum, other heavy metals, cyclosporine, carbon tetrachloride, mercuric chloride, copper sulfate, paraquat, leptospirosis
Pigment	Myoglobinuria, hemoglobinuria
Abruptio placentae	Cortical necrosis
Interstitial	Acute interstitial nephritis
	Drugs: penicillins, other antibiotics, other drugs
	Systemic infections: streptococcal, legionella, Hanta virus, etc.
	Idiopathic, transplant rejection, infiltrations

associated acute renal failure can occur in the setting of trauma and it is a major factor in the acute renal failure associated with the crush syndrome. Nontraumatic acute rhabdomyolysis is now diagnosed with increasing frequency. It is most commonly seen in association with alcohol and drug overdose, where the comatose patient lies motionless on a hard surface for a prolonged period with resultant patches of ischemic myonecrosis. Vasoconstriction of muscle vasculature associated with cocaine abuse is another cause of rhabdomyolysis increasingly recognized in urban settings. Incompatible blood transfusions are a rare occurrence today. Intravascular hemolysis can be substantial, however, in certain clinical settings. Ingestion of fava beans or certain drugs by patients with glucose-6-phosphatase deficiency can induce hemolysis that is severe enough to cause renal failure, not infrequently reported from India and other parts of the world. Falciparum malaria is another important cause of acute renal failure where hemolysis probably plays a significant contributory role. Finally, acute cortical necrosis, much less common than in the past, is still occasionally encountered, most often in association with abruptio placentae (concealed accidental hemorrhage) and less commonly with eclampsia and retained intrauterine death.

Atheroembolic disease of the kidney is an important cause of acute renal failure in the elderly (see Chapter 16–22). Acute allergic interstitial nephritis, most commonly due to an increasingly long list of drugs (see Chapter 16–20), is an important cause of acute renal failure to always consider, because it is not uncommon and usually reversible if appropriate remedial steps are taken. Though not yet reported in the United States, the Hanta virus group of agents are responsible for more than 100,000 cases of acute interstitial nephritis throughout the Eurasian continent, including Scandinavia, the Balkans, and Russia. Acute proliferative (crescentic) and/or necrotizing glomerulonephritis accounts for a relatively small percentage of patients with acute renal failure. It may represent a primary idiopathic glomerulopathy (see Chapter 16–18) or a secondary manifestation of severe forms of acute poststreptococcal glomerulonephritis, Goodpasture's syndrome, the hemolytic–uremic syndrome, lupus erythematosus, Wegener's granulomatosis, the nephropathy of bacterial endocarditis or intraabdominal abscess, or other immunologic disorders affecting the kidneys (see Chapter 8–12).

Postrenal causes of acute renal failure (Table 16–9–3) are divided into those in which the pathogenesis is to be found intrarenally and those in which it is to be found extrarenally. Myeloma cast precipitation can cause an intrarenal hydronephrosis which may manifest as acute renal failure. Multiple myeloma can cause renal damage by other mechanisms as well, including hypercalcemia and hyperuricemia. Intrarenal obstruction with uric acid crystals can complicate chemotherapy-induced tumor lysis in rapidly proliferating malignancies if the resultant overproduction of uric acid is not prevented by allopurinol. These intrarenal varieties of obstructive nephropathy do not result in dilation on renal sonography. Although dilation on sonography is seen in more than 90% of cases of extrarenal obstruction, nondilated obstructive nephropathy is occasionally encountered. If there is a suspicion of this, pyelography (intravenous, antegrade, or retrograde) may require consideration.

Diagnostic Options

The first step in the diagnostic evaluation of the patient with suspected acute renal failure is to search for a reversible cause. In the first instance this means confirming or excluding a pre- or postrenal etiology. The latter may be suspected from the history and physical examination, and in the great majority of instances of extraparenchymal obstruction, the issue can be resolved by a renal sonogram. Although several laboratory indices can aid in the distinction between prerenal and parenchymal renal failure, the former diagnosis cannot be established with confidence in the absence of clinical information supporting one of the mechanisms that can lead to impaired renal perfusion (Table 16–9–1). Occasionally, a transient period of hypotension that significantly decreases renal perfusion may have self-terminated by the time the patient presents, particularly following an acute cardiac event such as an episode of sustained ventricular tachycardia. A high index of clinical suspicion including support from the urinary indices listed in Table 16–9–4, helps uncover such an etiology. Although hypovolemia severe enough to induce azotemia is usually readily apparent on clinical assessment, in some instances, particularly in the elderly, doubt can exist regarding the patient's volume status following the initial clinical evaluation and a Swan–Ganz catheter placement may be indicated for pulmonary wedge pressure measurement. Because the causes of prerenal acute renal failure are the same as those of ischemic acute tubular necrosis and because acute tubular necrosis of whatever etiology is the most common cause of acute parenchymal renal failure, the differentiation of these two possibilities is frequently the major focus of initial evaluation. Although we now place the predominant emphasis on the clinical evaluation followed up by the judicious use of a fluid challenge or diuretic challenge to distinguish between these two possibilities, a number of indices have been proposed that for some 20 years have been emphasized by many nephrologists as very helpful (Table 16–9–4). Thus, it makes pathophysiologic sense that a patient with prerenal azotemia could achieve a higher urine concentration (osmolality) than in the case of acute tubular necrosis and the published literature supports this generalization. Similar pathophysiologic reasoning explains the tendency to greater urine:plasma creatinine and urea ratios in the prerenal situation compared with the established renal situation. Furthermore, the setting of prerenal azotemia would be predictably associated with avid sodium retention and a low fractional excretion of sodium, compared with acute tubular necrosis, whatever its etiology, since such a sodium gradient might not be achievable. The most widely used of these indices today is the fractional excretion of sodium (FE_{Na}), defined as

$$Fe_{Na} = \frac{U_{Na}}{P_{Na}} \div \frac{U_{Cr}}{P_{Cr}} \times 100$$

Also used is the renal failure index (RFI), defined as

$$RFI = U_{Na} \div \frac{U_{Cr}}{P_{Cr}}$$

In both of these instances, the FE_{Na} and the RFI, values less than 1 favor a prerenal etiology and values greater than 1 suggest acute tubular necrosis in the appropriate clinical setting. All these tests require only a single sample of blood and a spot sample of urine. There are a number

TABLE 16–9–3. CAUSES OF POSTRENAL ACUTE RENAL FAILURE (OBSTRUCTIVE NEPHROPATHY)

Intrarenal obstruction	Myeloma cast nephropathy
	Uric acid, methotrexate
	Acute oxalosis
Extrarenal obstruction	Papillary necrosis
	Ureteropelvic junction obstruction bilaterally
	Retroperitoneal fibrosis
	Ureteric calculi, strictures
	Malignant infiltration (prostatic cancer)
	Bladder outlet obstruction

TABLE 16–9–4. URINARY INDICES IN OLIGURIC ACUTE RENAL FAILURE

Index	Prerenal Status	Oliguric Acute Renal Failure
Urine osmolality, mOsm/kg H_2O	>500	<350
Urine sodium, mEq/L	< 20	>40
Urine:plasma urea nitrogen	>8	<3
Urine:plasma creatinine	>40	<20
Renal failure index	<1	>1
Fractional excretion of filtered sodium	<1	>1

Source: Miller TR, Anderson RJ, Linas SL, et al. Urinary diagnostic studies in acute renal failures. Ann Intern Med 1978;89:47. Reproduced with permission from the publisher.

of provisos, however. Patients with prerenal acute renal failure frequently have an FE_{Na} greater than 1 if there has been prior administration of diuretics or dopamine, an unintended fluid challenge, the presence of an osmotic load, or the superimposition of acute renal failure on preexistent chronic renal failure. On the other hand, an FE_{Na} less than 1 may be encountered in parenchymal acute renal failure associated with rhabdomyolysis, radiocontrast administration, established acute renal failure following severe burns, septicemia, and acute glomerulonephritis.

Meanwhile, as outlined under Routine Laboratory Abnormalities, a simple microscopic urinalysis is axiomatic.

If the preliminary clinical and laboratory evaluation has not pointed firmly to a pre- or postrenal etiology or to acute tubular necrosis of possible ischemic, toxic, or pigmentary origin, consideration must be given toward finding an alternative renal parenchymal lesion, a nondilated predominantly intraparenchymal obstruction, or one of the less common causes of toxin-induced acute tubular necrosis. In addition to the more common causes of toxic acute tubular necrosis such as aminoglycoside antibiotics, amphotericin, radiocontrast agents, and *cis*-platinum, a variety of other drugs, anesthetic agents, heavy metals, organic solvents, herbs, venoms, insecticides, and infections have been reported as occasional causes of tubular necrosis. Intrarenal obstruction due to urate crystals or methotrexate should be suspected in the appropriate clinical setting, and myeloma cast nephropathy should be picked up by screening all patients over 50 with undiagnosed acute renal failure for multiple myeloma.

The clinical and laboratory investigations leading to the diagnosis of atheroembolic renal disease (cholesterol emboli) and other vascular, glomerular, and interstitial diseases that may present with acute renal failure are dealt with in the respective chapters (16–18, 16–19, 16–20, 16–22, 16–24) and require confirmation or exclusion if one of the more common causes of acute renal failure has not been established. When the etiology of acute renal failure remains in doubt, renal biopsy requires consideration with a view to seeking a potentially reversible cause and to formulating a prognosis on which to base long-term plans.

Recommended Approach

Placement of a bladder catheter should be the initial step in all patients suspected of acute renal failure. If the patient is anuric, defined for clinical purposes as passing less than 100 mL of urine per 24 hours, the possibility of obstruction, acute necrotizing glomerulonephritis, or, occasionally, acute cortical necrosis requires focused attention with an urgent renal sonogram and a prompt search for clinical and laboratory features supportive of any of the secondary glomerulonephrites and, when appropriate, early consideration of renal biopsy to uncover a potentially immunosuppressible lesion (e.g., renal vasculitis). Meanwhile, it is important to obtain a meticulous history, study the medical record including intra- and perioperative records and medication records, and conduct a detailed physical examination (see Clinical Manifestations, Objective). The initial priority is to distinguish prerenal acute renal failure from ischemic acute tubular necrosis, which are the same with respect to causation but tend to differ with respect to the severity and/or duration of the underlying cause. The search for possible toxin- or pigment-induced acute tubular necrosis is incorporated into this initial evaluation. The FE_{Na} can be a helpful guide in conjunction with the clinical data and the urinalysis in pointing to prerenal acute renal failure (<1%) versus acute tubular necrosis (>1%) with the precautions referred to under Diagnostic Options. When prerenal acute renal failure is considered most likely or when there is a doubt, a fluid challenge is warranted. If the patient responds to a fluid challenge of 250 mL of normal saline with increased urine output, a prerenal etiology is highly likely. If the patient does not respond and the patient's state of hydration permits, a repeat fluid challenge (500 mL of normal saline) can be administered quickly but not further repeated in the absence of a response. If fluid overload precludes a fluid challenge, administration of an intravenous loop diuretic (e.g., Lassix 160–240 mg intravenously) should be tried. If the response to a fluid challenge or diuretic supports a prerenal etiology, corrective measures should be continued. If the clinical setting, for example, obvious aminoglycoside excess, or the laboratory data, for example, elevated creatine phosphokinase levels or

other features of rhabdomyolysis, or a failed response to a fluid challenge point toward acute tubular necrosis, the clinician should proceed to the management of acute parenchymal renal failure.

If the initial clinical and laboratory assessment do not confirm a pre- or postrenal etiology for acute renal failure and the more obvious causes of ischemic and toxin- and pigment-related acute tubular necrosis are not supported by the data, a search for vascular, glomerular, and interstitial causes of acute renal failure (see appropriate chapters), as well as the less common types of acute tubular necrosis (see Table 16–9–2), is required. If the subjective and objective clinical manifestations and appropriate laboratory investigations do not lead to a definitive conclusion, a renal biopsy is generally warranted to confirm or exclude possible steroid-responsive, immunosuppressible vascular, glomerular, or interstitial lesions and to formulate a prognosis for long-term planning.

Therapeutic

If clinical evaluation and/or the response to a fluid challenge or a high-dose intravenous loop diuretic indicate a prerenal etiology, the management focuses on correcting or improving the precipitating cause. This includes intravenous fluids, for example, normal saline and/or volume expanders preferably with albumin-containing solutions to correct hypotension or hypovolemia. Prompt broad-spectrum antibiotic coverage should be instituted in cases of suspected septicemia while awaiting blood cultures and sensitivities. Optimization of cardiac function is essential in severe cardiac failure or cardiogenic shock. Caution should be exercised in the use of diuretics, which may decrease intraarterial volume in patients with impaired effective circulation. NSAIDs should be withheld in patients whose renal perfusion is already threatened by angiotensin-mediated vasoconstriction. The use of ACE inhibitors, as afterload reducers, should be monitored, and if they are associated with a progressive rise in serum creatinine, they may have to be discontinued. If prerenal azotemia consequent to the injudicious use of diuretics with intravascular volume depletion has occurred in an edematous patient, gentle volume repletion will improve renal function and permit subsequent resumption of diuresis on a reduced or more intermittent scale.

The management of postrenal acute renal failure is carried out in conjunction with the urologist. Management involves decisions regarding definitive surgical correction versus such temporizing measures as nephrostomy tube placement. The possibility and complications of postobstructive diuresis require attention as outlined in Chapter 16–14.

If acute tubular necrosis has been diagnosed, treatment should be as for established acute parenchymal renal failure (see below) while trying to avoid all tubular toxins. This latter may not be easy, as infection is a major cause of morbidity and mortality in acute renal failure and the most or only effective antibiotic regimen may have a significant nephrotoxic profile. Because of the risk of infection in the acute renal failure setting, it is wisest not to compromise on choosing the most effective antibiotic regimen but to appropriately modify the dose or interval of administration, supported when possible by measurement of serum antibiotic concentrations, to minimize the toxic hazard.

If other diagnostic categories of acute parenchymal renal failure are entertained, attempts to confirm such a diagnosis may permit therapies specific to those individual etiologies to be instituted as defined under the appropriate chapter headings, for example, withholding a possible offending drug in acute allergic interstitial nephritis, use of high-dose steroids or cyclophosphamide in vasculitides and certain glomerulonephritides, plasmapheresis in Goodpasture's syndrome and essential mixed cryoglobulinemia, and avoidance of anticoagulants in cholesterol embolization.

Otherwise the management of established acute renal failure is basically supportive, aimed at minimizing abnormalities in the patient's internal milieu, optimizing his or her nutritional status, and monitoring for and correcting complications and consequences as they arise, including the timely use of dialytic intervention while awaiting the onset of spontaneous recovery.

Evidence generally supports the view that nonoliguric acute renal failure carries a better prognosis than oliguric acute renal failure. Based on this observation attempts are sometimes made to increase urine volume in oliguric acute renal failure patients by the repeated administration of high-dose loop diuretics, for example, 240 mg furosemide (Lasix) intravenously daily, or low-dose dopamine (e.g., 1–5 μg/kg/min). Although these measures frequently increase 24-hour urine volume to a variable degree, definitive proof is lacking that this alteration in urine volume alters the prognostic category. It is nonetheless possible that a nonoliguric state facilitates management, permitting less fluid restriction, reducing the tendency to fluid overload, and possibly mitigating electrolyte imbalances such as hyponatremia and hyperkalemia.

Daily weights are mandatory in the acute renal failure patient as an essential adjuvant to monitoring fluid balance. Fluid replacement in acute renal failure should include the previous day's urine volume and any other losses such as occurred through vomiting, nasogastric suction, or diarrhea plus the estimated insensible loss (about 500 mL per 24 hours in a 70-kg man). Daily protein intake should be restricted to 0.5 g/kg until dialysis becomes necessary. Meanwhile, a good caloric intake, 2000 calories per day or more, is needed to minimize endogenous catabolism. Once dialysis is instituted, protein intake can be liberalized to 1 g/kg per day. If the patient is unable to take adequate oral intake to keep up with nutritional requirements, parenteral nutrition should be implemented. Dialysis is indicated to correct and prevent severe hyponatremia, hyperkalemia, and metabolic acidosis. Although there is no agreed biochemical value(s) indicating when dialysis should be begun, it is a reasonable approach to plan to maintain the BUN below 100 mg/dL and the serum creatinine below 8 to 10 mg/dL. This generally necessitates hemodialysis about three times per week, although it could be less often in the nonoliguric patient and more often in the catabolic patient. This judgment is more often made on clinical than biochemical grounds, factors such as uremic pericarditis, uremic bleeding, pulmonary edema, and obtundation requiring urgent initiation or intensification of dialysis. Meanwhile, the institution of dialysis should not preclude conservative means to minimize hyperkalemia, metabolic acidosis, and hyperphosphatemia. Once it has been decided to institute dialytic therapy, the choice must be made whether to employ hemodialysis, continuous arteriovenous or venous–venous hemofiltration, or peritoneal dialysis. Peritoneal dialysis can be a gentler procedure in the hemodynamically unstable patient, where anticoagulants represent a serious hazard, or where vascular access is difficult to obtain. It requires less sophisticated equipment and personnel. Hemodialysis may be more desirable when there is intraabdominal disease or adhesions as from previous surgery, when the patient is catabolic, and when the patient is hemodynamically stable. Increasingly, continuous hemofiltration is replacing hemodialysis and peritoneal dialysis in the setting of the intensive care unit. With hemofiltration, the patient's blood flows through a very water-permeable extracorporeal biocompatible filter through which substantial but controlled "waste"-containing fluid is continuously removed accompanied by appropriate electrolyte replacement. The arteriovenous approach requires cannulation of a large artery (e.g., femoral) and is contraindicated where the circulation to the ipsilateral limb is compromised. In this instance, venous–venous hemofiltration is substituted. It requires a low-pressure pump to circulate the blood from a large-bore vein through the filter and back to another venous site. Hemofiltration is suitable for the unstable patient because of its clamp-controlled nature, and it is the best tolerated modality of substantial fluid removal. It requires heparinization.

In the patient with acute tubular necrosis the recovery (diuretic) phase can be anticipated within 2 weeks, although the skewed recovery curve does not exclude recovery as late as 2 months or more after the onset. During this phase polyuria may be prominent even while azotemia continues and the patient remains dialysis dependent for several more days. Accurate monitoring of intake and output and daily weights continues to be very important to anticipate and prevent volume depletion during the recovery phase. Once recovery is underway in acute tubular necrosis, a return of BUN and serum creatinine to within the normal range can be anticipated in the great majority of patients, especially those who are not elderly.

Although recovery and mortality are the two most likely outcomes of acute renal failure, some patients remain in renal failure requiring chronic maintenance dialysis therapy. In such instances, a pathogenesis other than acute tubular necrosis is more likely. If the patient is not showing evidence of recovery at the end of 1 month, therefore, it is ap-

propriate to reconsider the original diagnosis and reevaluate the patient including consideration of a renal biopsy.

FOLLOW-UP

Prerenal acute renal failure, once corrected, does not require a specific follow-up plan. The precipitating cause may require follow-up, taking account of the patient's proneness to a repeat renal perfusion impairment when the underlying cause is improperly addressed. Until the patient with acute tubular necrosis makes a complete recovery, intensive monitoring continues. After recovery has become complete, there is no need for specific follow-up. The same is true following recovery from a drug-induced acute interstitial nephritis. The follow-up of the less common other vascular or glomerular or obstructive etiologies is that of the intrinsic disease itself as dealt with in respective chapters (16–10, 16–14, 16–24, 16–25).

DISCUSSION
Prevalence and Incidence

Excluding patients with preexisting chronic renal failure, some 5% of nonelective medical or surgical hospitalizations are associated with a decline in renal function during admission and 20% of these patients develop frank acute renal failure. The majority of hospital-acquired acute renal failure patients are surgical admissions and the pathogenesis is frequently multifactorial involving, for instance, anesthesia, sepsis, nephrotoxic drugs, hypovolemia, and hypotension. Aortic aneurysmectomy, biliary tract surgery, and open-heart surgery are the most common predisposing surgical procedures. The prevalence of community-acquired acute renal failure, though less common, is not known and probably represents a different spectrum of etiologies, with acute glomerulonephritis being more likely than acute tubular necrosis. In the geriatric male patient, bladder outlet obstruction is sometimes overlooked until the patient has well-established acute azotemia.

Related Basic Science

Prerenal acute renal failure results when renal perfusion falls below a critical point. It can result from depletion of circulating volume, from increased vascular capacitance, or from a fault in the pumping effectiveness of the heart. It is reproducibly predictable when the mean blood pressure reaches 60 mm Hg, but may occur much earlier depending on a variety of factors not yet fully understood. When the causative factors are more gradual in onset, modifications may occur not only in the control of renal hemodynamics but also in systemic blood pressure regulation, with resultant preservation of homeostatic regulation at the expense of adaptive reserve. A quantitatively small additional physiologic stress at this "compensated" stage may have pathologic consequence because of the dramatically narrowed window of progression from circulatory compromise to prerenal acute renal failure.

The next stage in the process, assumed although not proven to reflect greater reduction in renal perfusion, is acute renal failure that does not reverse on correction of the underlying pathophysiology. The historical term used to describe this event, for want of an agreed better alternative, is *ischemic acute tubular necrosis*. This term has its shortcomings. Histologic confirmation is uncommon, as renal biopsies are generally not indicated today. Review of studies from several decades past, when renal biopsy material was more frequently obtained, often show poor correlation between the presence, distribution, and extent of tubular necrosis, on the one hand, and the pathophysiology and natural history of the syndrome, on the other. The same tends to apply to toxic acute tubular necrosis. Much of our understanding depends on animal models, especially in the rat, of acute renal failure produced by prerenal insults (ischemia), toxins, rhabdomyolysis, or combinations of these. Whatever the role of decreased renal blood flow in the initiation of acute tubular necrosis, it does not explain its progress, which continues as renal blood flow improves or even normalizes. The factors that seemed likely to play a role were all proposed before the end of the 1960s but have not yet been satisfactorily proven. Tubules, obstructed by casts composed of cellular debris from injured or necrotic renal tubular cells, markedly impede the flow of urine in some models. Back leakage of filtrate through damaged tubular epithelia or gaps along the length of the nephron, caused by the sloughing of necrosed cells from their moorings, has been shown to facilitate the return of filtrate to the circulation in other experimental studies. Although it cannot be measured in humans, animal models of acute renal failure have confirmed a decrease in the glomerular capillary ultrafiltration coefficient, and alterations in glomerular visceral epithelia on scanning electron microscopy are compatible with reduced glomerular permeability. Finally, the high incidence of acute tubular necrosis in septic shock, compared for instance with hemorrhagic shock, has pathophysiologic implications. With the onset of septic shock, severe renal vasoconstriction may relate to hemodynamic effects of endotoxins and endogenous cytokines, including tumor necrosis factor and leukotrienes. It is noteworthy that a somewhat different clinical setting of septicemia is encountered in intensive care units where renal involvement is only part of a syndrome of multiple organ failure and where the overall prognosis is very poor. In summary, despite ongoing work elegantly demonstrating a variety of factors at work in the pathogenesis of acute tubular necrosis, the precise etiology is still a matter of controversy and it seems likely that multiple factors are interacting to produce renal failure. Nor has the pathogenesis of acute renal failure in instances of other parenchymal renal diseases, including acute interstitial nephritis and rapidly progressive glomerulonephritis, been firmly established. It is particularly likely that human acute renal failure is usually multifactorial, with some or all of the above-described events playing a role.

Natural History and Its Modification with Treatment

Following its first clear definition as a syndrome during the "London Blitz" of World War II in 1941, the next couple of decades saw a fall in the mortality from acute renal failure from more than 90% to about 50% as proper management of fluid and electrolyte imbalance, the availability of antibiotics, and expertise in the use of dialytic techniques progressively improved. There has not been a significant improvement in the 50% overall mortality over the past 30 years. This is in part due to other advances keeping sicker patients alive who then develop acute renal failure, often in the setting of substantial comorbidity. It nonetheless emphasizes the unique importance of attempting to recognize and correct functional prerenal acute renal failure prior to its going on to acute parenchymal renal failure with its unavoidable mortality. The mortality is as high as 70% in surgical and posttraumatic patients, about 25% in medical patients, and 15% in obstetric patients. Three quarters of the deaths occur in the first week and are more often due to the underlying disease than to complications of the acute renal failure per se. Increasing age has been associated with increased mortality in some but not all studies. Nonoliguric acute renal failure has a better prognosis than oliguric acute renal failure, except when associated with burns. Anuric acute renal failure has a worse prognosis. The prognosis is significantly influenced by the number and severity of comorbid conditions. In the absence of comorbid conditions a mortality of 10% has been reported, rising to 75% if one or more other organs fail. Bad prognostic features include the need for mechanical ventilation, sepsis, cardiovascular complications, jaundice, and gastrointestinal bleeding. Infection is a major contributing factor to mortality, and attention to appropriate modifications in dosage and/or intervals of administration of potentially nephrotoxic antibiotics together with timely monitoring of serum antibiotic concentrations is very important. Recovery from acute tubular necrosis usually starts between 7 and 21 days after its onset in surviving patients. At 1 month from its onset, 30% of patients

are on the way to recovery without the need for dialysis, 60% have expired, and 10% are still dialysis dependent. Some of the latter remain indefinitely on chronic maintenance dialysis therapy; some have an overlooked nephrologic problem that may respond to different management strategies. The remainder die.

Prevention

As the mortality of established acute renal failure remains high despite major advances in the management of its complications, prevention is of great importance and hinges on an awareness and timely recognition of the clinical settings that predispose to it. The fact that prerenal azotemia accounts for 60% of hospitalized patients with an initial BUN above 50 mg/dL emphasizes the need for timely intervention to correct underlying causes and thereby avert the danger of acute tubular necrosis. Examples of important preventive measures include the following:

- Avoidance and prompt correction of hypovolemia and hypotension.
- Avoidance or caution in the use of NSAIDs in elderly patients or in those with predictably high-renin/high-angiotensin states, where inhibition of prostaglandin production permits unmodulated angiotensin-induced renal vasoconstriction.
- A high index of suspicion for and rapid treatment of sepsis.
- Modification of dosage and/or interval of administration and appropriate serum monitoring of nephrotoxic antibiotics in patients with subnormal glomerular filtration rates. This includes the age-related decline in glomerular filtration rate and concomitant nephrotoxic drug administration. Prompt discontinuation of offending drugs is warranted, if possible, when the serum creatinine rises.
- Adequate hydration prior to the administration of radiocontrast medium, especially in patients with diabetes, renal insufficiency, or multiple myeloma.

Cost Containment

Once established, the management of acute renal failure is costly and there are no specific measures for containment of these costs. The development of acute renal failure in hospital adds an average of 13 to 23 days to the length of stay. The benefits of cost containment lie in prevention. A carefully done retrospective study of 1756 patients receiving aminoglycosides revealed aminoglycoside-associated nephrotoxicity in 7% of patients (Humes and Messaur, 1989). The additional cost of treating this complication approximated $2500 per episode.

REFERENCES

Badr KF, Ichikawa I. Prerenal failure: A deleterious shift from renal compensation to decompensation. N Engl J Med 1988;319:623.

Better OS, Stein JH. Early management of shock and prophylaxis of acute renal failure in traumatic rhabdomyolysis. N Engl J Med 1990;322:825.

Brenner BM, Lazarus JM, eds. Acute renal failure. 2nd ed. New York: Churchill Livingstone, 1988.

Brezis M, Epstein FH. A closer look at radiocontrast induced nephropathy. N Engl J Med 1989;320:179.

Humes HD, Messaur JM. Acute renal failure and toxic nephropathy. Contr Nephrol 1989;5:283.

Parono C, Dunn MJ. The clinical significance of inhibition of renal prostaglandin synthesis. Kidney Int 1987;32:1.

Rainford DJ, Stevens PE. The investigative approach to the patient with acute renal failure. In: Cameron S, Davison AM, Grunfeld JP, et al., eds. Oxford textbook of clinical nephrology. Oxford: Oxford Medical, 1992:969.

CHAPTER 16-10

Acute Nephritic Syndrome

Douglas M. Landwehr, M.D., Ph.D.

DEFINITION

The acute nephritic syndrome (ANS) is an abrupt disturbance of renal function characterized by glomerular hematuria together with two or more of the following: oliguria, proteinuria, edema, azotemia, and recent-onset hypertension.

ETIOLOGY

Multiple diseases, both renal limited and systemic, cause the ANS. Although acute poststreptococcal glomerulonephritis is regarded as the prototype of the ANS, most episodes in temperate climates are caused by other diseases (Table 16-10-1).

CRITERIA FOR DIAGNOSIS

Suggestive

Acute nephritic syndrome should be considered in patients who present with hematuria and any evidence of acute renal dysfunction, such as edema, oliguria, hypertension, or reduced renal function.

Definitive

Acute nephritic syndrome may be diagnosed when hematuria is known to be of acute onset and of nephronal origin. The latter can be determined by demonstration of red blood cell casts in the urine or by presence of acanthocytes, dysmorphic red blood cells characteristic of glomerular bleeding. As hematuria and renal dysfunction may occur in chronic renal diseases, there must be evidence that these abnormalities are of recent onset. The diagnosis is defined by the presence of hematuria and two or more of the following: oliguria, proteinuria, edema, azotemia, and recent-onset hypertension.

CLINICAL MANIFESTATIONS

Subjective

Acute nephritic syndrome is associated with a wide variety of diseases, and a detailed history is necessary. Symptoms suggestive of recent streptococcal pharyngitis or impetigo should be specifically sought.

TABLE 16-10-1. MAJOR CAUSES OF THE ACUTE NEPHRITIC SYNDROME

Primary Renal Diseases
  Immunoglobulin A nephropathy
  Membranoproliferative glomerulonephritis
  Idiopathic rapidly progressive (crescentic) glomerulonephritis
  Idiopathic endocapillary glomerulonephritis

Secondary Renal Diseases
  Acute poststreptococcal glomerulonephritis
  Subacute bacterial endocarditis
  Infected ventriculoperitoneal shunt
  Glomerulonephritis with visceral abscess
  Glomerulonephritis with bacterial, viral, or parasitic infections

Multisystem Diseases
  Systemic lupus erythematosus
  Wegener's granulomatosis
  Goodpasture's syndrome
  Microscopic polyarteritis
  Mixed cryoglobulinemia
  Henoch–Schönlein purpura
  Hemolytic–uremic syndrome

Allergy
  Acute allergic tubulointerstitial nephritis

Nephritis typically follows pharyngitis after a latent period of 1 to 2 weeks; the latent period after skin infection is usually 3 to 6 weeks.

Findings associated with systemic vasculitis, such as skin rashes, arthralgia or arthritis, pulmonary lesions, and peripheral nerve deficits, should be sought. Rarely, ANS secondary to acute glomerulonephritis may be associated with illicit drug use or hydrocarbon exposure. Also, acute tubulointerstitial nephritis secondary to drug hypersensitivity may present with ANS. Finally, there is an increased familial incidence of acute poststreptococcal glomerulonephritis and glomerulonephritis associated with hereditary complement deficiency states. Accordingly, a detailed medication, occupational, environmental, and family history must be obtained.

Objective

Physical Examination

A complete physical examination is important in identifying complications associated with ANS and in recognizing systemic diseases that are associated with it. The majority of patients have hypertension. Evidence of circulatory congestion manifested by pulmonary and peripheral edema should be carefully evaluated, as serious morbidity and mortality may be associated with this frequent complication. Specific findings associated with systemic vasculitis, such as rashes, petechiae, joint abnormalities, and peripheral nerve dysfunction, must also be evaluated.

Routine Laboratory Abnormalities

Microscopic or gross hematuria is always present. Red blood cell casts confirm nephronal origin of hematuria and should be sought in the more concentrated, first-voided morning specimen. In the absence of red blood cell casts, dysmorphic red blood cells with surface blebs (acanthocytes) and granular casts, are indicative of glomerulonephritis. Proteinuria is usually detectable by dipstick and typically ranges between 0.5 and 1.5 g per 24 hours. Nephrotic range proteinuria greater than 3.5 g per 24 hours occurs rarely and is suggestive of membranoproliferative glomerulonephritis or systemic lupus erythematosus.

PLANS

Diagnostic

Differential Diagnosis

Etiologies of ANS are listed in Table 16-10-1. Although in the past, acute poststreptococcal glomerulonephritis (APSGN) has been the most common cause of ANS, the majority of patients now in temperate climates do not have clear evidence of recent streptococcal infection. Thus, other entities, often with less favorable prognoses, have become more frequent, and early etiologic diagnosis is especially important.

Diagnostic Options

Urine chemistries demonstrate a low fractional excretion of sodium (FE_{Na} < 1.0%). Although oligoanuria is infrequent, renal insufficiency is near universal. Renal imaging discloses normal to large-sized kidneys, a helpful finding in excluding renal atrophy of chronic renal disease.

Serologic diagnosis is critically important in ANS. Abnormalities of serum complement should be sought in the initial evaluation. Low C3 is expected in APSGN, membranoproliferative glomerulonephritis, lupus nephritis, subacute bacterial endocarditis, shunt nephritis, and essential cryoglobulinemia. Low C3 is transient in APSGN, and persistent depression for more than 6 to 8 weeks is strong evidence against this disorder. Other serologic tests are also important in establishing the etiology of ANS. Evidence of recent infection with group A (beta-hemolytic) streptococcus should also be sought in the initial evaluation. As cultures in patients with pharyngitis may be negative by the time patients present with ANS, measurement of serum antistreptococcal antibodies is necessary. The streptozyme test screens for antibodies directed against five streptococcal antigens and is more sensitive than tests for single antibodies.

Other serologic tests are especially important in identifying systemic diseases. These include anti-DNA (double-stranded) antibodies and antinuclear antibodies in systemic lupus erythematosus and anti-glomerular basement membrane antibodies in renal limited disease, as well as in nephritis associated with lung hemorrhage (Goodpasture's syndrome). Lastly, antineutrophil cytoplasmic antibodies are important in diagnosis of Wegener's granulomatosis, microscopic polyarteritis nodosum, and other related vasculitic syndromes.

In the absence of clear evidence of APSGN and especially when there is evidence of deteriorating renal function, renal biopsy should be considered early in the workup of ANS. This often provides definitive diagnosis and guides initial therapy necessary to prevent serious complications and severe, irreversible renal failure.

Recommended Approach

Initially, serologic studies to detect recent infection with group A beta-hemolytic streptococcus and serum complement should be obtained. Other serologic tests are also appropriate when there is evidence of a systemic disorder. If renal function is deteriorating, renal biopsy should be carried out if there is no serologic evidence of APSGN; however, early biopsy is not indicated when there is convincing serologic evidence of APSGN, as full recovery is expected and there is no specific therapy for the renal lesion.

Therapeutic

Initial therapy should be directed at preventing or controlling complications. Many patients have profound salt and water retention, and prompt restriction of dietary sodium and fluids and use of diuretics are important in preventing hypertension and circulatory congestion. Loop diuretics, such as furosemide 2 mg/kg, are effective, whereas other agents may not induce diuresis in these circumstances. Hypertension may be severe, especially in patients presenting with circulatory congestion and renal insufficiency. In addition to diuresis and salt restriction, antihypertensive medication may be necessary. Oral angiotensin-converting enzyme inhibitors, as well as calcium channel blockers, are efficacious, but the potential for serious hyperkalemia must be considered when using converting enzyme inhibitors in the presence of renal insufficiency. Occasionally, parenteral antihypertensive drugs, such as sodium nitroprusside, are needed. Finally, persistent oliguria with hyperkalemia, severe azotemia, or pulmonary edema may necessitate dialysis.

Specific therapy is indicated for several of the causes of ANS. All patients with APSGN who have evidence of active infection or colonization as determined by throat culture should receive oral penicillin G (125 mg every 6 hours). In case of penicillin allergy, erythromycin (250 mg every 6 hours) is an appropriate alternative. Although eradication of the bacterium probably does not affect outcome of established nephritis, it is important in preventing further spread of the nephritogenic strain and additional cases of APSGN. Antibiotic or surgical treatment of chronic infection associated with endocarditis and infected ventriculoperitoneal shunts generally results in resolution of other forms of infection-related ANS.

Renal limited and systemic vasculitic diseases associated with biopsy-proven crescentic glomerlonephritis require prompt treatment with antiinflammatory and immunosuppressant regimens. Cyclophosphamide and oral steroids are generally effective in preventing progressive renal injury and life-threatening involvement of other organ systems in Wegener's granulomatosis and microscopic polyarteritis. Anti-glomerular basement membrane antibody disease, with (Goodpasture's syndrome) and without lung involvement, is best treated with the addition of daily plasma exchange to rapidly reduce titers of circulating antibody. High-dose intravenous "pulse" steroid therapy, methylprednisolone 30 mg/kg to maximum of 3.0 g, daily for 3 days, followed by prednisone 2 mg/kg, tapered off over several months may also have a role in therapy of renal limited acute crescentic glomerulonephritis. Monthly "pulse" intravenous cyclophosphamide therapy may be less toxic than daily therapy and appears efficacious in diffuse proliferative lupus nephritis; however, it may be less effective than daily therapy in other disorders.

Patients being treated with immunosuppressive and cytotoxic therapy require close monitoring to avoid life-threatening infections and serious hemorrhagic complications. The addition of plasma exchange further increases the risk of deaths from infection.

FOLLOW-UP

Frequency and duration of follow-up depend on the etiology of ANS. Self-limiting diseases, such as APSGN, require daily to weekly monitoring during the initial phase of the illness; however, APSGN usually resolves within 1 to 2 weeks, complement levels normalize within 6 to 8 weeks, and microscopic hematuria disappears within 6 to 12 months. Once resolution of hypertension and renal insufficiency has occurred, patients should be seen at 3- to 6-month intervals. Although controversial, there is evidence that patients who have recovered from APSGN may be at increased risk for hypertension and renal insufficiency in the future. Thus, annual examination with close attention to blood pressure, urinalysis, and renal function tests is recommended.

Patients in whom ANS is a manifestation of some systemic disease need more frequent follow-up. Although quiescent for prolonged periods, systemic vasculitic diseases frequently recur with tapering or discontinuation of immunosuppressive therapy. Anti-glomerular basement membrane disease is self-limiting, however, and once antibody disappears from the serum, recurrence is very unlikely.

DISCUSSION
Prevalence and Incidence

Acute nephritic syndrome is now an uncommon disorder in developed countries, and this appears to be related to improved hygiene and decreasing rates of poststreptococcal and other infection-related glomerulonephritis. ANS, however, continues to be a common presentation of glomerular disease in many Third World countries.

The majority of cases of APSGN follow pharyngitic or skin infections with group A (beta-hemolytic) streptococcus. Children between the ages of 2 and 12 are most commonly affected, but APSGN may occur at any age. Males predominate with approximately a 2:1 ratio in serious cases, but both sexes are equally affected in mild episodes. In warmer areas, the disease most frequently follows secondarily infected skin lesions, especially scabies, and occurs more frequently in the summer. In colder climates, the disease occurs more frequently because of pharyngitic infection during the winter months. Cases may occur sporadically, or in epidemics, within close communities. The risk of developing ANS after infection varies with the streptococcal strain. Some "nephritogenic" strains with high attack rates for glomerulonephritis can be identified, although the basis for nephrogenicity has not been identified.

Related Basic Science

A genetic basis for susceptibility of APSGN is suggested by clustering of cases within affected families. Also, during the epidemics, familial incidence appears to be higher than the attack rate of the general population at risk. In other causes of ANS, such as anti-glomerular basement membrane disease, associations with specific HLA antigens also suggest an immunogenetic role in the pathogenesis.

The majority of causes of ANS involve antibody-mediated glomerular injury, although cellular immunity appears to play the dominant role in ANS of Wegener's granulomatosis and microscopic polyarteritis. Antigens may be native to the glomerulus, as with anti-glomerular basement membrane antibody disease, or they may be "planted" or deposited from the circulation, as is likely the case with postinfectious glomerulonephritis. Antibody–antigen complexes may be preformed in the circulation or formed in situ within the glomerular capillary wall after initial deposition of the antigen. Cationic charge appears to play a role in localization of these immune reactants within glomerular structures.

Inflammation that results in glomerular damage is mediated through activation of complement and infiltration with neutrophils and macrophages. In ANS, immune deposits localize within the subendothelial and mesangial areas, which are contiguous with the circulation through large endothelial fenestrae. This allows accessibility to circulating mediators of inflammation, and an intense inflammatory reaction can ensue. In other diseases, immune reactants are located deeper in the capillary wall and are not as accessible to circulating mediators. These disorders, which have little or no inflammatory reaction, are characterized by significant proteinuria, with little or no hematuria.

Natural History and Its Modification with Treatment

Mortality of ANS is generally low. Only 5 to 8 cases per 1000 of APSGN die as a result of complications of renal failure; however, outcome in systemic lupus erythematosus, systemic vasculitis, and Goodpasture's syndrome is less favorable, and the mortality rate is significant when diagnosis and specific therapy are delayed.

The risk for progression to end-stage renal failure with APSGN is very small in children, but becomes significantly worse with increasing age. In adults, approximately 5% have persistent proteinuria, hypertension, and reduced renal function. Some progress to end-stage renal failure. Histologic pattern of injury is also predictive of outcome. Cellular infiltration that is confined to the capillary loop, an endocapillary pattern, is predictive of complete healing, whereas infiltration and proliferation of cells within the mesangium and within Bowman's space are more likely to result in progressive scarring. Also, a "garland" pattern on immunofluorescent microscopy indicative of densely packed subepithelial deposits along the basement membrane carries a poorer prognosis. Finally, clinical findings of anuria, heavy proteinuria, and persistence of hypertension and/or reduced serum complement beyond 1 month are also associated with poor prognosis.

Recovery from other causes of ANS is less predictable. A majority of patients with rapidly progressive crescentic glomerulonephritis progress to end-stage renal failure if treatment is not initiated early. This is particularly true of patients with anti-glomerular basement membrane antibody disease and systemic vasculitis. Recovery from postinfectious glomerulonephritis other than APSGN is expected, except that which is associated with visceral abscesses, from which only 50% recover renal function despite successful eradication of infection.

Prevention

Although most forms of ANS cannot be prevented, APSGN and acute allergic interstitial nephritis are exceptions. Spread of "nephritogenic" strains of the streptococcus among susceptible close contacts results in clusters of APSGN. If carefully studied, 20 to 40% of siblings of index cases and other populations at risk, such as military recruits living in close quarters, develop evidence of glomerulonephritis. Accordingly, patients with APSGN and positive cultures should be treated with antibiotics to prevent spread of infection.

As drug allergies may cause acute allergic tubulointerstitial nephritis, it is important to evaluate any symptoms suggesting renal dysfunction in patients receiving medications. Maintenance drugs as well as those recently prescribed may cause ANS. Antibiotics and antiseizure agents are the drugs most commonly associated with ANS.

Cost Containment

Cost savings can be realized by prevention of end-stage renal disease and the associated expenses of chronic dialysis and transplantation. This requires early diagnosis and treatment, especially in patients with rapidly progressive glomerulonephritis. Patients suspected of having this disorder should be promptly referred for appropriate consultations. In general, only patients with significant renal failure or serious complications of ANS require hospitalization. Renal biopsy is not indicated when there are typical findings of APSGN.

REFERENCES

Cameron JS. Allergic interstitial nephritis: Clinical features and pathogenesis. Am J Med 1988;250:97.

Couser WG. Mechanisms of glomerular injury in immune-complex disease. Kidney Int 1985;28:569.

Falk RJ, Hogan S, Carey TS, et al. Clinical course of anti-neutrophil cytoplasmic autoantibody-associated glomerulonephritis and systemic vasculitis. Ann Intern Med 1990;113:656.

Madio MP, Harrington JT. The diagnosis of acute glomerulonephritis. N Engl J Med 1983;309:1299.

Rodriguez-Sturbe B. Epidemic poststreptococcal glomerulonephritis. Kidney Int 1984;25:129.

CHAPTER 16–11

Nephrotic Syndrome

George F. Schreiner, M.D., Ph.D.

DEFINITION

The nephrotic syndrome (nephrosis) consists of the clinical constellation of proteinuria, hypoproteinemia, hyperlipidemia, lipiduria, and edema. It is exclusively associated with the excessive loss of albumin into the urine, generally defined as exceeding 3.5 g of albumin per day. Renal disease of diverse etiologies may be associated with excessive albuminuria and thus with nephrosis. The glomerulopathies most commonly associated with the nephrotic syndrome are summarized in Table 16–11–1. They are classified as either primary, localized to the glomerulus with an undefined etiology, or secondary to known causes, which may be metabolic, immunologic, or toxic and either systemic or localized to the kidney. These are dealt with in more detail in Chapters 16–18, 16–19, and 16–20. Ongoing clinical advances may eventually render this standard classification obsolete. A significant percentage of cases of membranoproliferative glomerulonephritis, for example, are now known to be associated with hepatitis C infection.

ETIOLOGY

The clinical expression of the nephrotic syndrome is immediately attributable to the loss of albumin, immunoglobulins, and related serum proteins from the plasma and into the urine. This occurs in a variety of diseases affecting the renal glomerulus in which the glomerular basement membrane, the primary barrier to the diffusion of serum proteins into the urine, is damaged.

CRITERIA FOR DIAGNOSIS
Suggestive

The onset of edema with relatively rapid progression of its severity should make the physician suspect nephrosis, particularly in the absence of evidence of congestive heart failure. Periorbital edema may be the earliest expression of the nephrotic syndrome; but, with progression

TABLE 16–11–1. CAUSES OF THE NEPHROTIC SYNDROME

Primary Glomerular Diseases
  Minimal change disease
  Focal segmental glomerulosclerosis
  Membranous glomerulopathy
  Proliferative glomerulonephritis
  Membranoproliferative glomerulonephritis

Secondary Glomerular Diseases*
Infectious diseases
  Bacterial
  Viral (hepatitis, HIV)
  Protozoal
  Helminthic
Drugs, toxins, allergens
  Nonsteroidal antiinflammatory agents
  Penicillamine
  Gold salts
  Heroin
  Heavy metals (mercury)
  Bee stings, pollen, contact dermatitis
  Tumor-associated antigens
Collagen–vascular diseases (particularly systemic lupus erythematosus)
Diabetes mellitus
Amyloidosis
Light-chain nephropathy/cryoglobulinemia/myeloma
Chronic vesicoureteric reflux
Pregnancy
Familial
Obesity

*Secondary diseases may also show the glomerular lesions listed above.
A similar table was constructed by the late Dr. John Maher and appeared in the third edition of this book.

of nephrosis, dependent edema of the lower extremities and sacrum becomes more prominent. The voiding of foamy urine, sometimes accompanied by hematuria, strongly suggests a renal cause of edema.

Definitive

The most essential test for the nephrotic syndrome is the quantitation of protein in a 24-hour urine collection. The value for adult nephrotic patients is generally at least 3.5 g per day and may range as high as 20 g or more per day. The determination of hypoalbuminemia together with elevated serum cholesterol and triglycerides completes the diagnostic criteria for the nephrotic syndrome.

CLINICAL MANIFESTATIONS
Subjective

The patient typically presents with a complaint of persistent, worsening edema affecting the lower extremities and often the face. The patient may recollect an immediately preceding upper respiratory infection or allergic reaction to a bite or sting. Headaches and irritability commonly accompany the development of edema. Fatigue, depression, and malaise are often present, although obviously not diagnostic. The patient may present with a history of hematuria of recent onset or a change in urinary frequency or consistency, often noting the appearance of foam in the toilet after voiding, a consequence of the protein content of the urine.

As some of the causes of the nephrotic syndrome are characterized by relapses after therapy, clearly a previous history of nephrosis is essential to that diagnosis. Atopy can be associated with albuminuric glomerular disease. Thus, a history of allergy to pollen, foods, plants, bee stings, and housedust can be helpful. Finally, some forms of the nephrotic syndrome are precipitated by exposure to drugs, particularly the nonsteroidal antiinflammatory agents. A history of previous drug reactions and a detailing of current medications can quickly establish this diagnosis in certain instances.

Family history is rarely useful in the adult population; however, nephrotic children demonstrate an increased incidence of nephrosis among their siblings. Familial nephrotic syndromes typically have an infantile onset and a relatively poor prognosis.

Objective
Physical Examination

The clinical signs of the nephrotic syndrome are a function of the effects of losing particular serum proteins into the urine. Regardless of the etiology of the disorder increasing the glomerular loss of protein, the loss of those proteins evokes a stereotypical clinical response (Table 16–11–2). The loss of albumin, for example, decreases plasma oncotic pressure and thus causes peripheral edema. The patient characteristically presents with edema, often pitting, of the lower extremities. Facial edema can be present and can create the impression of pallor. The nail beds themselves may be white due to subungual edema, and the fingernails may demonstrate horizontal white lines. Diminished plasma oncotic pressure additionally evokes a hepatic response resulting in increased synthesis of lipoproteins, particularly very-low-density and low-density lipoproteins. The hyperlipidemia of the nephrotic syndrome results in the retina appearing wet on physical examination and confers a milky color to the retinal vasculature. The renal diseases underlying the nephrotic syndrome may result in hypertension, which is fairly common in adults with the nephrotic syndrome and less prominent in children.

The physical examination of the nephrotic syndrome may be positive for some of the complications of nephrosis. The immune depression arising from the loss of serum immunoglobulins and factor B can result in patients presenting with or developing cellulitis, peritonitis, or sepsis. The loss of antithrombin III and plasminogen activators produces a susceptibility to coagulation that may increase the risk in nephrotic patients for peripheral deep vein thromboses and subsequent pulmonary emboli. Acute renal vein thrombosis, whose incidence is increased in nephrosis, may present with flank pain and hematuria. Finally, diseases that underlie the nephrotic syndrome, such as diabetes and systemic lupus erythematosus, present with their own distinctive clinical findings in addition to those of nephrosis.

Routine Laboratory Abnormalities

The principal laboratory abnormalities center on the urinalysis (Table 16–11–3). On dipstick analysis, proteinuria is typically 3+ to 4+. A quantitative 24-hour urine analysis should demonstrate more than 3.5 g of protein excreted per day, although occasionally nephrotic patients with significant renal failure may excrete less than 3 g per day. As a result of the protein, urine specific gravity can be high, exceeding 1.025. Examination of the urinary sediment characteristically reveals hyaline casts and fatty vacuoles, or oval fat bodies, in the casts and desquamated epithelial cells. If the microscope is equipped with a polarized light filter, the fatty vacuoles appear doubly refractile, in the shape of Maltese crosses. Microscopic hematuria is common, particularly in the primary glomerular diseases.

Serum analyses invariably demonstrate decreases in total serum protein due to decreases in serum albumin, which is often less than 3 g/dL.

TABLE 16–11–2. CLINICAL CONSEQUENCES OF LOSS OF SERUM PROTEINS INTO THE URINE

Protein	Effect of Loss
Albumin	Decreased oncotic pressure Edema Hyperlipidemia
Immunoglobulin G	Immune depression
Factor β	Immune depression
Antithrombin III	Hypercoagulability
Plasminogen activator	Hypercoagulability
Vitamin D-binding protein	Vitamin D deficiency
Transferrin	Iron deficiency

TABLE 16–11–3. NEPHROTIC SYNDROME: LABORATORY FINDINGS

Urine
    Proteinuria (3.5 g/d)
    Oval fat bodies
    Microscopic hematuria

Blood
    ↓ Total serum proteins (4.5–6.0 g/dL)
    ↓ Albumin (1–3 g/dL)
    ↓ Serum immunoglobulins G and A
    ↑ Serum total cholesterol (250–1000 mg/dL)
    ↑ Triglycerides

Common Artifacts
    ↓ Serum Na^+
    ↓ Total serum Ca^{2+}
    ↓ Anion gap
    ↑ Erythrocyte sedimentation rate
    ↓ Total thyroxine

Patients present with variable decreases in gamma globulins, as determined by electrophoresis, with immunoglobulin G typically evincing the most severe decreases. Hyperlipidemia is part of the definition of the nephrotic syndrome. Serum cholesterol is elevated in rough proportion to the hypoalbuminemia; this is largely due to increases in very-low-density and low-density lipoproteins.

Serum creatinine and blood urea nitrogen are generally normal in the early stages of nephrosis; however, approximately 20% of patients with nephrosis do present with elevations of serum creatinine and blood urea nitrogen due to the aggressive nature of the glomerular disease producing the proteinuria. Focal segmental glomerulosclerosis and systemic lupus erythematosus are two examples where elevated serum creatinine levels may be noted on initial presentation.

It is extremely important to note that the altered serum protein composition in the nephrotic syndrome can produce significant artifacts that must be recognized to avoid inappropriate therapeutic maneuvers. For example, the loss of serum albumin may produce an increase in the erythrocyte sedimentation rate that is not reflective of an underlying inflammation. Similarly, the loss of albumin can result in a diminished anion gap due to the loss of the anionic albumin and a decrease in total serum calcium as a result of the diminished protein binding of calcium. The correct serum calcium can be calculated easily. Serum calcium is decreased a total of 0.8 mg/dL for every 1 g/dL decrease in serum albumin. In the setting of hypoalbuminemia, the level of ionized calcium is usually normal despite the decrease in total serum calcium. If the total serum calcium is depressed out of proportion to the degree of hypoalbuminemia, this may be due to the loss of vitamin D-binding proteins in the urine, resulting in the state of vitamin D deficiency, which is relatively uncommon. Loss of serum binding proteins results in a decrease in serum thyroxine (T_4) levels, which does not require therapy, as free T_4 is usually normal. In the presence of marked hyperlipidemia, the nonaqueous compartment of the plasma is increased. This may artifactually lower serum sodium expressed as equivalence per blood volume, depending on the analytic technique being used. This form of psuedohyponatremia can manifest as a modestly depressed serum sodium, in the range of 130 mEq/L. Because the concentration of sodium in the aqueous portion of the plasma is normal, this diminished measurement of serum sodium has no physiologic significance and requires no treatment.

PLANS

Diagnostic

The diagnostic evaluation of the edematous patient should be directed toward confirmation of the nephrotic state and elimination of nonrenal causes of edema, and determination of the specific glomerular disease producing the clinical complex of nephrosis. Quantitation of renal function and protein excretion is easily and inexpensively determined by the analysis of a 24-hour collection of urine. Although serum creatinine and blood urea nitrogen determinations are somewhat unreliable in the nephrotic state due to alterations in metabolic production of creatinine

(decreased due to diminished muscle mass) and urea (decreased due to diversion of nitrogen intake toward plasma protein synthesis), they are helpful when correlated with creatinine clearance and useful for evaluating changes in renal function from baseline. Determination of the laboratory findings of nephrosis (Table 16–11–2) is easy, reliable, and useful in that the findings improve as nephrosis responds to therapy.

The diagnosis of the nephrotic syndrome must be considered incomplete without determination of the associated glomerular disorder. Although this requires renal biopsy for definitive diagnosis, the diagnosis of many of the disorders noted in Table 16–11–1 can be confirmed or extended by clinical findings and available serum and urine assays. Diabetic glomerulosclerosis does not occur without diabetic retinopathy. Serum and urine electrophoresis is useful in diagnosing myeloma or light-chain disease. Antinuclear antibody assays, antineutrophil cytoplasmic antibody assays, determination of complement levels, and other tests are available for the diagnosis of a variety of autoimmune glomerular disorders. Hepatitis and HIV antigens or antibodies are easily quantitated. The range of disorders producing the nephrotic syndrome is too large for a complete listing here of distinguishing clinical findings and blood and urine tests for all the potential causes of the nephrotic syndrome. These are more comprehensively discussed in the chapters specifically addressing individual disorders. Nonetheless, the need to apply appropriate diagnostic tests aimed at determining the underlying renal disease must be recognized and employed when clinically indicated as one evaluates a patient whose nephrotic syndrome is not attributable to a previously determined etiology.

Differential Diagnosis

The differential diagnosis resides in those disease entities that reproduce part, but not all, of the spectrum of findings that constitute the nephrotic syndrome. First among these are causes of edema not associated with albuminuria. The most common causes are congestive heart failure and peripheral venous insufficiency. States combining hypoalbuminemia with edema include protein-losing enteropathies, malnutrition, and severe, exfoliative, generalized skin disorders. None of the above are associated with significant degrees of proteinuria. Neither are the various causes of essential hyperlipidemia, which can be associated with edema in the context of congestive heart failure. Once the diagnosis of the nephrotic syndrome is established, the underlying glomerulopathy (Table 16–11–1) must be determined by the use of renal biopsy and supporting serum and urine assays. The diagnostic approaches for specific glomerular disorders are discussed in more detail in Chapters 16–18 and 16–19.

Diagnostic Options

Quantitation of the protein in a 24-hour urine collection is essential, if the urine dipstick is at least 3+ to 4+. The presence of hematuria strongly supports a renal etiology of the edema. If a drug-induced induction of the nephrotic syndrome is suspected, then withdrawal of the offending agent, with subsequent resolution of the proteinuria, confers both diagnostic and therapeutic benefits. I believe that adult patients with the nephrotic syndrome and any abnormality in renal function or urinary sediment ought to undergo renal biopsy. Because the most common cause of nephrosis in children is the highly steroid-responsive entity of minimal change disease, most pediatricians give their patients a therapeutic trial of steroids without prior biopsy confirmation of the diagnosis. Some advocate a steroid trial before biopsy for adults with the nephrotic syndrome as well but with considerably less justification, given the very real hazards of corticosteroid therapy, which include hypertension, osteoporosis, protein catabolism, and immunosuppression.

Recommended Approach

Quantitate urine protein and obtain urine sediment. Measure serum albumin, total protein, total cholesterol, triglycerides, and electrolytes, including calcium. On ruling out other causes of edema and establishing the presence of the nephrotic syndrome, review the clinical and laboratory data to confirm or exclude a secondary glomerulopathy (Table 16–11–1). Common secondary causes such as diabetes, systemic lupus erythematosus, and drug-induced nephrosis are potential etiologies that are quickly assessable. Confirmation of a secondary glomerulopathy or diagnosis of a primary glomerulopathy still requires a histologic diagnosis, for which renal biopsy is essential. Histologic diagnosis is essential to establish both prognosis and therapeutic options in the adult nephrotic patient. Biopsy at first presentation is not so crucial in the pediatric population, as detailed above.

Therapeutic

Therapeutic Options

In treating the nephrotic syndrome, one must distinguish between treating the clinical disorders generic to the nephrotic syndrome and treating the renal disease underlying the nephrotic syndrome. Treatment of the former does not require a renal biopsy, but rather good, common clinical sense in diagnosing the deficiencies and replacing them. Not all kidney diseases are amenable to therapy; thus, a renal biopsy is essential before embarking on treatment of the underlying glomerular disease.

With respect to the therapy of the nephrotic syndrome itself, attention must be paid to symptomatic edema; generally this is what brought the patient to the physician in the first place. There is no unique feature recommending one diuretic over the other; however, it should be noted that in cases of severe edema, generally loop diuretics (furosemide, bumetanide) are required, often at two- to threefold normal dosages. One must be careful not to excessively diurese the patient. Severe intravascular volume depletion could exacerbate renal injury. Diuresis should be employed for significant symptomatology, not for cosmetic complaints. Significant edema is that which affects respiration, inhibits ambulation, or excessively distorts the skin, predisposing to ulcerations. Treatment of hypertension benefits the patient both with respect to coronary artery disease and with respect to the kidney, as poorly controlled hypertension accelerates the deterioration of renal function. Although choice of antihypertensive agent may be dictated by patient tolerance, it should be noted that angiotensin-converting enzyme inhibitors (fosinopril, enalapril, captopril) are effective in the nephrotic syndrome and confer the added benefit of decreasing albuminuria due to their unique effects on decreasing glomerular filtration pressure. Reducing albumin excretion may have a renal protective effect in chronic glomerular disease. In the setting of patients with marked decreases in serum immunoglobulin G, particularly after a demonstrated susceptibility to infection, pneumococcal vaccine is recommended as a prophylactic measure. The first sign of a possible infection in these patients should evoke a swift diagnostic and antibiotic response. In the precorticosteroid era, the most common infecting organisms in nephrotic patients were Gram-positive bacteria. Vitamin D supplementation should be considered for those patients who have a decrease in ionized calcium due to the loss of vitamin D-binding globulin into the urine. For the patient with iron deficiency due to loss of transferrin into the urine, iron replacement therapy should be considered. Although this recommendation may still be considered equivocal, many renal specialists advocate moderate protein restriction (0.8 g/kg/d) in the setting of preexisting renal insufficiency, as limiting the albumin synthesis by the liver correspondingly restricts the absolute amount of albumin lost into the urine. Eventual glomerular sclerosis correlates closely with the amount of albumin lost through the kidney.

There is increasing evidence that the severe hyperlipidemia of the nephrotic syndrome may carry the same implications for atherosclerotic disease as it does for the nonproteinuric patient. My practice is to treat the hyperlipidemia of nephrosis in the setting of prolonged proteinuria and hyperlipidemia, particularly when the patient has other risk factors for coronary atherosclerosis, including hypertension, diabetes, and family history. Of the various therapies that have been evaluated, the most clearly successful have been the hydroxymethylglutaryl-coenzyme A reductase inhibitors (lovastatin, simvastatin, pravastatin), which reliably decrease low-density-lipoprotein cholesterol 25 to 50% and triglycerides 25 to 40%. The fibrinates (gemfibrozil, fenofibrate) are not recommended because of equivocal effects on low-density-lipoprotein cholesterol levels and an increased susceptibility to myopathy, to which patients with renal disease are already prone. The bile acid sequestrants (cholestyramine, colestipol) are completely ineffective with respect to triglyceride levels and only mildly effective in decreasing low-density-lipoprotein cholesterol. That, coupled with their extensive gastrointestinal side effects, makes them generally untenable for long-term therapy of nephrotic range hyperlipidemia. There is no evidence that dietary restriction of fats confers any benefit.

It was previously noted that the nephrotic syndrome increases patients' susceptibility to thromboembolism. This can take the form of acute renal vein thrombosis, peripheral vein thrombosis, and pulmonary embolus. In the acute setting of a thromboembolism the patient may be started on convential heparin therapy but should be quickly converted to warfarin. One of the serum proteins lost into the urine is antithrombin III, which is the necessary cofactor for the anticoagulatory effect of heparin. Thus, heparin administration itself is only modestly effective in anticoagulation. Although warfarin is the preferred anticoagulant, it should be noted that doses must be monitored extremely carefully as warfarin is albumin bound. Nephrotic patients consequently may require much less warfarin than conventional patients and their levels of anticoagulation may fluctuate more markedly. In the acute emergency of renal vein thrombus and loss of renal function, anecdotal success has been reported with the use of thrombolytic agents such as streptokinase; this must still be regarded as an extreme measure for an extreme situation. Finally, there is some evidence that patients with chronic renal vein thrombosis, which is often asymptomatic, may experience an exacerbation of deterioration in renal function superimposed on that conferred by their underlying kidney disease. Some nephrologists place such patients on chronic warfarin therapy; this must be considered a judgment call at this time, however.

Only some of the numerous glomerulopathies capable of inducing the nephrotic syndrome are amenable to therapy specifically targeted at the underlying disorder. The most common specific glomerular causes of nephrosis are summarized by their incidence in the adult and pediatric populations in Table 16–11–4. Those diseases that frequently demonstrate clinical responsiveness to therapy are further denoted. The mainstay of the various therapeutic regimens consists of corticosteroids with supplementation as needed by cytotoxic agents such as cyclophosphamide, chlorambucil, and azathioprine. Therapies for the responsive glomerular diseases vary markedly with respect to dosage intensity and frequency and optimum combinations of immunosuppressant agents. Therefore, detailed discussion of therapeutic modalities is best left to specific discussions of the glomerular diseases in Chapters 16–18 and 16–19. Glomerular disorders unresponsive to immunosuppression only permit symptomatic therapy directed at the clinical expression of nephrosis and progressive renal insufficiency.

Recommended Approach

Diuresis should be reserved for significant symptomatology, with care not to overly deplete intravascular volume. Treatment of hyperlipidemia should be instituted in the setting of risk factors for coronary artery disease. Treatment of hypertension protects both the heart and kidneys. Attention must be paid to the possible complications of nephrosis, particularly infections and thrombus formation. When indicated, specific therapy should be initiated quickly and vigorously. Chil-

TABLE 16–11–4. CAUSES AND FREQUENCY OF THE NEPHROTIC SYNDROME

Relative Incidence in Children		Relative Incidence in Adults
76%	Minimal change disease*	8%
7%	Focal segmental sclerosis	21%
2%	Membranous glomerulonephritis*	20%
5%	Proliferative glomerulonephritis*	26%
<1%	Diabetes	5%
0	Amyloid	6%
4%	Systemic lupus erythematosus*	11%
5%	Henoch–Schönlein purpura*	0%
<1%	Congenital	0%
0	Drug/toxin/atopy associated*	3%

*Frequently responsive to immunosuppressive therapy.
Table constructed from data published by Cameron (1987) and Schnaper and Robson (1993).

dren with the nephrotic syndrome may undergo a therapeutic steroid challenge, with a biopsy only after failure to respond. Most adults should receive a renal biopsy before being started on a significant program of immunosuppression directed at the underlying kidney disease.

FOLLOW-UP

Close attention to the clinical response to diuretic, antihypertensive, and anticoagulatory therapies in nephrotic patients is essential due to altered pharmacokinetics associated with decreased serum binding proteins. Because excessive depletion of intravascular volume can amplify renal damage, the nephrotic patient undergoing diuresis should have monthly monitoring of edema, urinalysis, blood pressure, and renal function. This also permits surveillance for complications and monitoring for dietary compliance. Hyperlipidemia can be reevaluated every 3 to 6 months. Thrombotic complications require weekly overview until the anticoagulation status of the patient has stabilized.

When the patient is undergoing immunosuppressive treatment for the underlying disorder, the patient's protein excretion should be monitored serially, at least monthly, to detect remission. If remission occurs, corticosteroid dosage should be progressively and rapidly tapered with a view toward transition to alternate-day therapy followed by discontinuance, if clinically stable. During changes in immunosuppressive therapy, urine protein should be evaluated every 1 to 3 weeks. On attaining alternate-day corticosteroid therapy, evaluation can be spaced at monthly intervals. The addition of cytotoxic agents capable of suppressing bone marrow production of blood cells requires weekly attention to peripheral cell counts until the dosage is stabilized. The susceptibility of these patients to bone marrow failure and infection is very significant. Monthly visits are sufficient once the right combination of agents and their dosages are established. If the therapy is successful and the drugs are discontinued, the patient should be evaluated twice a year. Follow-up visits should focus on increases in proteinuria or hypertension, changes in the urinary sediment, or declines in renal function. Nephrotic patients in remission may relapse. Successful responses to a second round of therapy and preservation of renal function require early detection of relapse and rapid therapeutic intervention. Finally, the nature and frequency of follow-up visits will obviously be affected by the underlying disease; visits centered around diabetes, myeloma, or hepatitis B evoke quite different concerns and therapeutic monitoring.

DISCUSSION
Prevalence and Incidence

The prevalence of the nephrotic syndrome is difficult to estimate, as a wide cross section of renal disorders are associated with its occurrence. As can be seen in Table 16–11–4, minimal change disease accounts for three fourths of all cases of pediatric nephrotic syndrome; its prevalence is 15 cases per 100,000 children. Adults and children have markedly different profiles of renal disease associated with nephrosis. The incidence of the nephrotic syndrome in adults will vary with the incidence of the underlying renal disease in the population. It is worth noting that one of the fastest growing categories in both adults and children is focal segmental glomerulosclerosis. Although most cases are idiopathic, this morphology is also the expression of HIV-associated nephropathy, which frequently presents with nephrotic range proteinuria.

Related Basic Science

The symptoms of the nephrotic syndrome are directly attributable to the types of protein lost into the urine. The normal glomerulus has a basement membrane, lined by endothelial cells on the vascular side and epithelial cells on the urinary space side, that functions as a filtration barrier for medium- and large-molecular-weight serum proteins while permitting the passage of ions and solutes such as urea. The passage of serum proteins larger than molecular weight 40,000 (the approximate size of albumin) is blocked by a layer of matrix-associated anions, which repel serum proteins; the nature of the basement membrane as a porous gel; and the cellular processes of the epithelial cells. Damage to any one or all three of these components can allow increasingly larger

serum proteins to escape across the basement membrane and into the urine. Serum proteins of varying sizes up to and including molecular weight 150,000, which includes immuonglobulins, are variably present in the urine depending on the severity of the basement membrane damage; however, even badly damaged glomeruli do not generally allow proteins greater than molecular weight 300,000 to cross. Thus, molecules such as fibronectin, low-density lipoprotein, very-low-density lipoprotein, and immunoglobulin M stay within the circulation. The variation from patient to patient in the size of the serum proteins that escape into the urine accounts in part for some of the variable symptoms of the nephrotic syndrome. Damage can be immunologic as in immune complex glomerulonephritis, in which acute inflammation occurs in situ. It can also be metabolic, with glycosylation of basement membrane causing functional disruption, as is observed in diabetes. Finally, glomerular cells may be directly injured, as occurs with viral infections in the case of HIV nephropathy or with exposure to toxins such as heroin. The causes of the nephrotic syndrome cross the whole gamut of possible etiologies, with the final common pathway comprising increased protein filtration at the level of the glomerulus.

Natural History and Its Modification with Treatment

In the era before immunosuppression and symptomatic therapy, the nephrotic syndrome, in the absence of spontaneous remission, evolved along three distinct pathways. Patients experienced morbidity and mortality attributable to the complications of nephrosis. The loss of immunoglobulins increased susceptibility to infection, typically by Gram-positive organisms, resulting in severe, often fatal cases of cellulitis, peritonitis, and sepsis. The hypercoagulability induced thrombotic complications, including pulmonary emboli, in up to a third of persistently proteinuric patients. The second pathway reflected renal toxicity as a consequence of proteinuria itself, perhaps reflecting damage to the proximal tubules, which are the cells in the nephron that attempt to endocytose filtered albumin. It is well established that the longer and greater the proteinuria, the more rapidly the kidney develops glomerulosclerosis, regardless of the underlying etiology. The third pathway reflected the tendency to progressive renal failure as a function of the specific glomerulopathy underlying the nephrotic state. Thus, in the pretherapeutic era, patients with minimal change disease often experienced spontaneous remissions, whereas focal segmental glomerulosclerosis has always been characterized by relentless progression toward renal failure.

Careful attention to the complications of nephrosis and prompt therapy have markedly diminished the formerly significant morbidity associated with the nephrotic state. Many of the causes of the nephrotic syndrome are themselves amenable to therapy with corticosteroids and alkylating agents. Even in the cases of nephropathy not amenable to primary therapy, as is the case with diabetic nephropathy, the use of antihypertensives such as angiotensin-converting enzyme inhibitors seems to prolong the functional life of the kidney by decreasing the extent of albuminuria.

Prevention

Only a small fraction of cases of nephrosis are amenable to prevention. Avoidance of drugs or other allergens to which the patient has previously demonstrated renal sensitivity provides the only practical intervention.

Cost Containment

The diagnostic criteria for the nephrotic syndrome—excessive albuminuria, hyperlipidemia, and hypoalbuminemia—are readily established by serum and urine assays that are available and inexpensive. Renal imaging is rarely necessary, save for kidney localization to facilitate biopsy. The physician should treat significant symptomatology and eschew overly aggressive therapy directed at numbers rather than at the patient.

The prevention of chronic renal failure is the most cost-effective strategy. Renal replacement therapy, whether dialysis or transplantation, is associated with significant morbidity and mortality and is highly expensive. The diagnosis of the glomerular disease inducing the nephrotic syndrome should be made promptly and specific therapy initiated, if indicated. Posttherapeutic evaluations can be conducted using simple clinical parameters such as quantitative urinary protein measurements and determinations of serum creatinine. Preservation of renal function in therapeutically responsive glomerulopathies correlates with minimizing the extent and duration of proteinuria.

REFERENCES

Brater DC. Diuretic resistance: Mechanisms and therapeutic strategies. Cardiology 1994;84(suppl. 2):57.

Cameron JS. The nephrotic syndrome and its complications. Am J Kidney Dis 1987;10:157.

Glassock RJ. Therapy of iodiopathic nephrotic syndrome in adults: A conservative or aggressive therapeutic approach? Am J Nephrol 1993;13:422.

Harris RC, Ismail NI. Extrarenal complications of the nephrotic syndrome. Am J Kidney Dis 1994;23:477.

Kaysen GA. Nonrenal complications of the nephrotic syndrome. Annu Rev Med 1994;45:201.

Schnaper H, Robson A. Nephrotic syndrome: Minimal change disease, focal glomerulosclerosis, and related disorders. In: Schrier R, Gottschalk D, eds. Diseases of the kidney. Boston: Little, Brown, 1993:1731.

Wheeler DC, Bernard DB. Lipid abnormalities in the nephrotic syndrome: Causes, consequences, and treatment. Am J Kidney Dis 1994;23:331.

CHAPTER 16–12

Chronic Renal Failure

Eli A. Friedman, M.D.

DEFINITION

In health, the kidney performs multiple vital roles as an excretory organ, as a regulator of the volume, tonicity, and composition of the internal environment, and as an endocrine gland. Chronic renal failure (CRF) is the term applied to the syndrome of persistent impairment of renal function of such severity that the kidneys can no longer maintain a normal internal environment. Failure as an excretory organ is the most apparent feature initially so that persistently elevated serum levels of nitrogen-continuing metabolic end products of protein catabolism are prime indicators of kidney failure. Restricted capacity to regulate other aspects of homeostasis, including fluid, electrolyte, and acid–base balance, and of endocrine function, particularly regarding erythropoiesis and vitamin D metabolism, become increasingly manifest as the syndrome progresses toward end-stage renal disease. The multiplicity of signs and symptoms characteristic of CRF reflect the myriad contributions of the kidney in health to preservation of normal metabolism and endocrine balance.

ETIOLOGY

The multiple etiologies of CRF are summarized in Table 16–12–1. In those instances of acute renal failure where neither recovery nor death is the outcome, CRF usually of advanced degree is encountered, generally necessitating permanent renal replacement therapy within a short period as outlined in Chapter 16–13. The etiology of CRF is otherwise best classified (as in the case of acute renal failure) into prerenal (functional), intrinsic renal, and postrenal (obstructive) causes. Prerenal azotemia is generally reversible and hence encompassed within the syndrome of acute renal failure. Nonreversible persistent functional renal failure is, however, encountered in advanced cardiac failure, with ventricular ejection fractions approaching 10% or lower, and in advanced hepatic insufficiency, where cardiac or hepatic transplantation or, in a few select instances, dialysis may be indicated to correct the azotemia. The intrinsic renal diseases are discussed in the relevant chapters as is obstructive nephropathy. The four most common causes of CRF in the United States are diabetic nephropathy, hypertensive nephropathy, glomerulonephritis, and polycystic kidney disease in that order. Not uncommonly, clinical data do not permit a definitive etiology for CRF and reports forwarded to the End Stage Renal Disease Program represent only a "best guess." Even study of renal histology in an advanced chronically diseased shrunken kidney may not permit a precise pathologic diagnosis. Compounding variables increase this difficulty. Thus, diabetes is a common condition in which not all cases of CRF are necessarily due to diabetic nephropathy. Hypertension is not only a potential cause of CRF; it is also a frequent comorbid condition in CRF due to other etiologies so that it may be overdiagnosed as an etiology. It follows that when a search for a specific etiology of CRF is

thoroughly completed, identification of a specific kidney disease is never discerned in about 40% of patients.

CRITERIA FOR DIAGNOSIS

Suggestive

Chronic renal failure should be suspected in an adult manifesting otherwise unexplained lassitude, weight loss, anemia, digestive distress, and subtle changes in mental status including irritability and decreased concentrating ability. Features of fluid overload including dyspnea and edema, orange-yellow skin coloration, cold intolerance, pruritus, restless legs, and ankle edema are all consistent with worsening renal function. Uremia is on the short list of possible explanations of delirium and coma. Urine volume is nonetheless maintained in the "normal" range

TABLE 16–12–1. DIFFERENTIAL DIAGNOSIS OF CHRONIC RENAL FAILURE

Acute renal failure
Prerenal azotemia
    Salt depletion
    Addison's disease
    Congestive heart failure
    Advanced hepatic insufficiency
Intrinsic renal diseases
    Primary glomerulonephritides
    Secondary glomerulonephritides
    Infiltrative renal diseases
    Tubulointerstitial nephritides
    Hereditary renal diseases (glomerular and interstitial)
    Toxemia, preeclampsia of pregnancy
    Drug toxicity or hypersensitivity
    Vascular obstruction (atheromatous renal disease, nephrosclerosis)
Postrenal (obstructive renal diseases)
    Intrarenal tubular obstruction
        Light chains in multiple myeloma
        Uric acid
    Ureteric obstruction
        Calculi
        Retroperitoneal fibrosis
        Surgical ligation or severing
    Bladder obstructions
        Neurogenic
        Calculi
        Pelvic (prostate, cervix) tumor
        Prostatic hypertrophy

despite the loss of more than 95% of renal excretory capacity until the terminal stages.

Definitive

A persistent elevation of serum creatinine above the upper limit of normal for a patient's age, sex, and body size (muscle mass), accompanied by an elevation in blood urea nitrogen, indicates CRF. For a 70-kg man, a serum creatinine above 1.4 mg/dL can generally be taken as definitive evidence of failure of the kidneys to maintain a normal internal environment. Slightly lower or higher limits obtain in small elderly women and muscular heavy framed men, respectively (range, 1.1–1.7 mg/dL). In mild elevations in serum creatinine three alternative explanations require exclusion. Tubular creatinine secretion may be impaired by cimetidine, trimethoprim, and other pharmacologic agents without otherwise impairing renal function. Transient hypercreatininemia may accompany rhabdomyolysis due to increased production. In these situations, the blood urea nitrogen is not elevated. Individuals on a very-high-protein diet may have some elevation in serum creatinine and blood urea nitrogen concentrations. In such circumstances renal failure is best corroborated by demonstrating a substantial reduction in glomerular filtration rate (GFR). The normal GFR approximates 125 mL/min/1.73m^2. GFR should be reduced to 30 to 40% of normal to account for an elevated serum creatinine. GFR is most readily and reliably determined by measuring the clearance of [^{131}I]iothalamate or other suitable radionuclide, administered intravenously and then counted in plasma and urine. The endogenous creatinine clearance is less accurate, but is an adequate indicator of GFR except in drug-related impairment of creatinine secretion, where it will give a falsely low value for true GFR.

CLINICAL MANIFESTATIONS

Chronic renal failure may develop suddenly consequent to unremitting acute renal failure following traumatic loss of a solitary kidney; a vascular catastrophe (dissecting aortic aneurysm, atheroembolic disease); or cortical necrosis or exposure to a nephrotoxin like mercuric chloride. In these circumstances, renal functional reserve is at or approaching a stage of severity requiring renal replacement therapy for survival (see Chapter 16–13). More typically, the onset of CRF is gradual in onset and progression and clinically imperceptible. Over months to years, severe CRF induces a multitude of symptoms, physical signs, and abnormal laboratory values, which, in the aggregate, constitute the uremic syndrome that ultimately becomes life threatening. Importantly, because decades of renal parenchymal destruction may continue without clinical expression, as many as one half of adult end-stage renal disease (ESRD) patients do not admit to knowledge of antecedent CRF.

SUBJECTIVE

Although the extent of genetic predetermination of CRF is unknown, more than one in three ESRD patients has an inherited disease known to cause renal disease. Diabetes mellitus, clearly a genetic disorder, causes diffuse and nodular intercapillary glomerulosclerosis and the syndrome of diabetic nephropathy, which heads Medicare's lists of incident and prevalent causes of ESRD, accounting for about 35% of new cases of ESRD. Hypertensive nephropathy, the second most prevalent cause of ESRD in the United States, is also a disease with strong familial (genetic) overtones. Approximately 10% of Medicare-supported persons with ESRD have primary familial renal disease; polycystic kidney disease (8%) and Alport's syndrome (0.5%) are most prevalent. Additionally, realizing that the renal diagnosis listed in about 40% of ESRD patients is "soft," meaning inadequately substantiated, the proportion of patients with a genetic component to their CRF may exceed 50%.

Environmental factors including infectious agents (e.g., HIV, nephritogenic streptococci, hepatitis B, Hanta virus, leptospirosis, schistosomiasis), organic solvents, heavy metals (cadmium, lead, mercury), and self-administered toxins (analgesic abuse, heroin abuse) and medications (aminoglycoside antibiotics, cyclosporine, nonsteroidal anti-inflammatory drugs) may lead to irreversible renal injury with CRF.

The most common symptomatic renal disease is urinary tract infection in women. Second only to respiratory infections, urinary infection is a major cause of absence from work in adult women. Surprisingly, despite repeated symptomatic infections which alternate with silent bacteriuria, unless there are anatomic anomalies, calculous disease, or diabetes, renal insufficiency does not complicate urinary sepsis. Complaints resulting from urinary infection may, nonetheless, draw attention to the presence of previously unrecognized CRF. Urinary infection afflicts men at less than one-tenth the rate of women. In fact, it is reasonable to doubt urinary infection as an explanation for a renal syndrome in a man in the absence of anatomic abnormality, diabetes, or recent or current bladder catheterization.

Chronic renal failure may be minimally symptomatic throughout most of its course (Tables 16–12–2 and 16–12–3); discovery of azotemia is often a surprise without warning symptoms such as urinary bleeding, nephrotic syndrome, and urinary infection. The first symptom of lost renal function may be the realization of a subtle decreased capacity for concentration and discriminative thought. Patients who are unaware of the loss of two thirds of their renal function may complain of reduced "sex appeal" or drive or may report being passed over for corporate or military promotions. Symptoms and signs attributed to CRF generally parallel the progressive loss of renal function (Tables 16–12–2, 16–12–3, and 16–12–4). In slowly progressive CRF, adaptation may be remarkable to the extent that profound anemia, continuing acidosis, and reduced mentation are unappreciated and even denied when detected.

During progressive CRF, malaise and fatigue limit effort. Gradually, the patient withdraws from communal activity, adds clothing because of cold intolerance, and requires increased sleep. Peripheral neuropathy causes "restless legs," paresthesia, and, in advanced cases, foot drop and partial paraplegia. Pruritus, perhaps related to rising plasma levels of parathyroid hormone, worsens as renal function declines. Rarely, pruritus unresponsive to antihistamines or phenothiazine is disabling. Pain from renal bone disease may be accentuated by pathologic fractures, which in cervical vertebrae necessitate supportive neck collars. Gastrointestinal manifestations of reduced renal function begin with anorexia and intermittent mild nausea and progress to sometimes constant hiccoughs and repetitive retching. Late in the course of CRF, upper and lower gastrointestinal bleeding due to uremic gastritis and colitis, respectively, may preempt routine activity. The accompanying bleeding diathesis of uremia may compound this tendency. With reduction of GFR to about 5% of normal, the patient frequently complains of a constant sour metallic taste. Sleep is disrupted by reversal of diurnal pattern, with nocturnal insomnia resistant to sleep medications as a major problem. Nocturia, prompted by polyuria resulting from loss of urinary concentrating ability, may be the complaint that leads to detection of CRF.

Objective

Physical Examination

There is great individual variation in physical findings in CRF (Tables 16–12–3 and 16–12–4). When CRF is superimposed on a systemic disorder such as lupus erythematosus or diabetes mellitus, extensive morbidity from the systemic disease (myocardial failure, blindness, stroke, limb amputations) may overshadow renal failure. Indeed, the continuously rising "incidence" of nephropathy in diabetic persons may reflect the decision to refer patients with multiple comorbid conditions including CRF for ESRD care, whereas previously renal failure was sub-

TABLE 16–12–2. SYMPTOMS OF HIGH PREVALENCE IN CHRONIC RENAL FAILURE

General	Fatigue, lassitude, cold intolerance, irritability
Gastrointestinal	Anorexia, nausea, constipation, hiccoughs, vomiting, diarrhea from uremic colitis, gastrointestinal bleeding from uremic gastritis, colitis, metallic taste
Genitourinary	Polyuria, nocturia, decreased libido, impotence, gynecomastia
Cardiorespiratory	Dyspnea, air hunger
Neuroencephalopathic	Restless legs, paresthesia, headache, insomnia, decreased ability to concentrate, cognitive impairment
Musculoskeletal	Bone pain, fractures, proximal myopathy, joint pain
Cutaneous	Pruritus, increased pigmentation

TABLE 16–12–3. SYMPTOMS AND SIGNS OF AZOTEMIA ACCORDING TO RESIDUAL GLOMERULAR FILTRATION RATE (GFR)

Remaining Renal Function (GFR)	Symptoms and Signs
30–45 mL/min	Fatigue, muscle weakness, reduced libido, restless legs, anorexia, inability to concentrate, irritability, nocturia, mild anemia, decreased motor nerve conduction velocity
15–29 mL/min	Nausea, vomiting, hiccoughs, twitching and jerking of muscles, dyspnea, ecchymosis, pruritus, increasingly severe anemia, bone pain due to osteomalacia or osteitis fibrosa which may lead to fractures, motor neuropathy with foot drop, hypertension, volume overload or depletion, weight loss, reduced libido and potency, nocturia
5–14 mL/min	Sick most of the time with foul (metallic) taste, insomnia, vomiting, constant pruritus, weight loss, bleeding from gums and gastrointestinal tract and asterixis, loss of employment common, severe neuropathy, uriniferous breath, pericardial friction rub, urochrome skin pigmentation, profound muscle wasting
0–4 mL/min	Moribund; tachypneic, unable to walk or climb stairs; bleeding from gums, rectum, and into skin; advanced anemia; uremic frost

merged during more urgent treatment of heart or cerebrovascular disease. An isolated renal disease, like membranoproliferative glomerulonephritis, by contrast, totally governs an individual's health; morbidity derives entirely from the kidney disorder.

The term *uremic poisoning* aptly describes late CRF. Starting when GFR is reduced by about two thirds, CRF causes progressive intoxication. Late CRF may cause hypothermia. Kussmaul's breathing may be prominent due to severe acidemia. Hypertension is a ubiquitous finding in CRF. Hypertension is attributed to pathophysiologic changes in CRF in the majority of patients with ESRD. Reduced arterial elasticity caused by essential or malignant hypertension or diabetic macrovasculopathy induces hypertension before onset of ESRD. Many uremic patients are hypertensive because of expanded intravascular volume rather than intrinsic blood vessel disease. Whatever its etiology, hypertensive blood pressures require attention in all long-term management plans for CRF. Depending on the etiology of CRF, the patient may exhibit volume overload with pitting limb and periorbital edema with or without concomitant congestive cardiac failure (e.g., chronic glomerulonephritis, diabetic nephropathy), or dehydration with a super added prerenal component due to renal leakage of salt and water (e.g., interstitial nephritis). The absence of hypertension suggests the latter possibility and warrants judicious consideration of a more liberal sodium intake.

When decline in GFR occurs over many years (e.g., polycystic or hypertensive nephropathy, glomerulonephritis), an orange-yellow (urochrome) skin coloration develops. The skin in advanced uremia may be coated with powdered white urea left by evaporation of insensible water loss (uremic frost). Hanging skin folds in the extremities discol-

ored by multiple blotchy ecchymoses reflect loss of muscle and subcutaneous fat. Exocrine malfunction is characteristic of advanced CRF. Swelling of one or both parotid glands and acute and chronic pancreatitis are noted in about 5% of new ESRD patients.

Once the GFR falls below 5 mL/min, the uremic patient sleeps through the day but complains of insomnia unresponsive to commonly prescribed sleeping pills. Although the uremic patient's eyes are typically dull with pale conjunctivae, precipitation of calcium phosphate complexes in conjunctivae of patients with severe secondary hyperparathyroidism may cause bilateral eye redness: the "red eyes of uremia." Band keratopathy initially demonstrable by slit-lamp examination is clinically apparent in later stages. A fetid odor surrounds the patient whose expired breath smells like stale urine, and xerostomia may be noted. Cognitive impairment progresses to obtundation and/or delirium. Neurologic examination in the agonal uremic patient reveals an inability to follow simple instructions. The patient cannot repeat more than four slowly spoken numbers forward and three numbers backward (normal, seven and five numbers, respectively). Motor nerve neuropathy may lead to a slapping gait due to foot drop. Dorsiflexion of the fingers and toes prompts a jerky three to five times a second forward clonic motion of the hand or foot, with the fingers leading the hand (asterixis). As GFR approaches 2 mL/min, asterixis blends into whole-body shakes every few minutes. Coma and seizures are seen in preterminal stages.

Depending on family support and underlying personality, patients forced to confront the diagnosis of CRF may abruptly change behavior. Anger, hostility, disbelief, withdrawal, and flight are responses to learning of CRF. Forbearance and patience by the health care team facilitate adjustment to CRF.

Chest auscultation detects moist basilar rates in fluid-overloaded patients. A pericardial friction rub is an ominous sign in advanced CRF. Attributable to fibrinous pericarditis, it may be accompanied by a uremia-induced disordered coagulation and is thus a harbinger of hemopericardium and pericardial tamponade. Hemorrhage from erosive gastritis and colitis also result in deficient platelet factor 3 activity and reduced platelet binding of von Willebrand factor.

Routine Laboratory Abnormalities

The laboratory abnormalities associated with CRF are summarized in Table 16–12–5. Findings on urinalysis vary with the underlying renal diagnosis. Proteinuria may be minimal in interstitial disease and massive, that is, in the nephrotic range ($\geq$3.5 g/d), in some glomerular diseases. Examination of urine under polarized light may, in nephrosis, disclose doubly refractile fat bodies with a Maltese cross shape. An "active" sediment in which proteinuria is present along with red cells and red cell casts is found in rapidly progressive glomerular disorders. Nephrotic range proteinuria is a sign of extensive glomerular leakage as

TABLE 16–12–4. PHYSICAL FINDINGS OF HIGH PREVALENCE IN CHRONIC RENAL FAILURE

General	Emaciation
Cardiovascular	Hypertension, signs of fluid overload, pericardial friction rub, cardiac tamponade
Respiratory	Kussmaul's breathing, pleural friction rub
Cutaneous	Pallor, urochrome pigmentation, petechiae, ecchymosis, uremic frost
Oral	Xerostoma, parotid swelling
Neurologic	Lethargy, cognitive impairment, delirium, stupor, coma, myoclonus, seizures, paresis
Endocrinologic	Gynecomastia, galactorrhea, hypoglycemia, hyperparathyroidism

TABLE 16–12–5. BIOCHEMICAL AND HEMATOLOGIC SIGNS OF CHRONIC RENAL FAILURE

Elevated nitrogen-containing compounds	Urea, creatinine, uric acid, guanidines, amino acids, phenols, polyamines, indoles, hippuric acid, polypeptides, "middle molecules"
Hyperlipidemia	
Deficient hormones	Erythropoietin, estrogen, testosterone, growth hormone, triiodothyronine, thyroxine, aldosterone
High hormone levels (may be inactive form)	Reinin, parathyroid hormone, atrial naturetic peptide, prolactin, luteinizing hormone, follicle-stimulating hormone, insulin, glucagon
Electrolytes	Hyper- and hyponatremia, hyper- and hypokalemia, hypermagnesemia, hyperphosphatemia, hypocalcemia, deficient trace metals (zinc), excess trace metals (chromium, cooper)
Hematologic	Anemia, leukopenia and occasional thrombocytopenia, deficient platelet factors
Urinalysis	Proteinuria, cylindruria, isosthenuria
Nonspecific	Deficient carnitine, myoinositol

found in diabetic nephropathy, focal segmental glomerular sclerosis, membranous glomerulonephritis, and membranoproliferative glomerulonephritis. White cell casts suggest active urinary infection in the kidneys. Papillary necrosis is associated with sloughing of renal medulla into urine. Lupus nephritis and other collagen–vascular diseases produce an active sediment with a variety of casts including the broad renal failure cast generated by dilated hypertrophied tubules.

The electrocardiogram may indicate left ventricular hypertrophy in hypertensive renal disorders and may show confirmatory evidence of uremic pericarditis. Radiographs of the chest and thoracic sonography detect an enlarged heart, pericardial effusion, pulmonary congestion, or the "whiteout" of pulmonary hemorrhage in Goodpasture's syndrome. Bone radiographs of the spine may show alternating areas of rarefaction and sclerosis resulting from secondary hyperparathyroidism, the "rugger jersey" spine. Other bones may reveal cortical thinning due to hyperparathyroidism and/or vitamin D deficiency. Magnetic resonance imaging may afford more precise documentation though minimal advantage—at greater cost—over ultrasound and x-ray in detecting pulmonary hemorrhage and pericardial fluid or blood collections.

PLANS
Diagnostic
Differential Diagnosis

The differential diagnosis of CRF is summarized in Table 16–12–1. Occasionally, CRF is a sequel to acute renal failure that evolves into ESRD requiring renal replacement therapy for survival. More typically, CRF is gradual in onset and progresses over months to years. It is most readily classified as a consequence of prerenal, intrinsic renal, and postrenal causes.

Persistence of prerenal azotemia despite application of corrective measures may occur with advanced heart failure as evidenced by very low ventricular ejection fractions or severe hepatocellular decompensation as in a so-called hepatorenal syndrome. The prognosis is guarded and parallels that of the underlying condition. A third situation where chronic prerenal azotemia is likely to be misdiagnosed as intrinsic CRF is the nephrotic syndrome. The nephrotic syndrome with massive proteinuria resulting in marked hypoproteinemia is characterized by an expanded extracellular fluid volume, but may alternatively be associated with a contracted intravascular volume, either spontaneously or due to overzealous use of diuretics. On gentle expansion of plasma volume the azotemia disappears. That cardiac determined renal perfusion governs azotemia in congestive heart failure is evident from its disappearance on reestablishment of adequate cardiac function following cardiac transplantation in terminal heart disease. Vividly illustrating this point is the experience of the first long-term implantation of a total artificial heart during which the serum creatinine rose to 4 mg/dL when the heart rate was 80/min, then fell to 2 mg/dL when the rate was increased to 100/min (personal communication, Willem J. Kolff). Postrenal azotemia is also more often an acute process. When obstruction is significant but incomplete, its effects on renal function are, however, more gradual, progressing to CRF over time. Polyuria may be a prominent feature due to damage to the urinary concentrating process induced by backpressure. The possibility of obstruction always requires consideration, as its correction may arrest further deterioration or even result in partial recovery. Intrinsic renal disease is, nonetheless, by far the most common cause of CRF. Diabetic nephropathy, idiopathic glomerulonephritis, hypertensive nephrosclerosis, and polycystic kidney disease are the most common causes; however, investigation fails to pinpoint a precise etiopathogenesis in 4 of every 10 cases. A detailed search is nonetheless of crucial importance, as specific therapy may induce a remission or delay progress in many of the less common causes, thereby preventing the development of ESRD with its high costs for the patient's quality of life and for the economic issues involved in its management. The details of the investigations into the various groups of intrinsic renal disease are dealt with in the appropriate chapters in this section.

Diagnostic Options

In some series, approximately half the patients with CRF present for the first time with azotemia whose consequences are severe enough to require consideration for dialysis on presentation. In such instances it may not be initially clear as to whether one is dealing with acute renal failure or CRF and the initial appraisal should be directed toward resolving this issue. If the kidneys are normal or large, the search for a precise etiopathogenesis is more likely to be rewarding, as a reversible etiology may be uncovered. A renal biopsy may provide useful, sometimes unexpected information. Small kidneys are usually the consequence of gradual replacement of parenchymal structures by fibrosis, which is an irreversible process even if the initiating event were to be potentially reversible. Renal biopsy is less likely to help in management, and the approach should alter the focus to delaying or mitigating the consequences of established CRF.

Recommended Approach

An accurately estimated GFR is a useful basis for making decisions throughout the course of CRF. Both the blood urea nitrogen and the serum creatinine concentration are often employed as surrogates for more expensive and reliable estimates of GFR provided by the creatinine clearance or radionuclide determinations of GFR. Objection to use of the blood urea nitrogen for continuing assessment of GFR derives from its wide fluctuation with variations in dietary protein content, degree of hydration, and extent of endogenous protein catabolism. Especially during intervals of low urine flow rates, for example, prerenal and postrenal states, there is increased tubular reabsorption of filtered urea, adding a compounding variable to the rise in the blood urea nitrogen, thereby underestimating GFR. The serum creatinine level is more stable than the BUN though it also may be altered by changes in the amount of dietary protein, rising within hours of a meat meal. Importantly, certain drugs can result in elevations in serum creatinine concentration without affecting GFR. These are organic cations that block tubular secretion including cimetidine, trimethoprim, and quinidine. Falsely elevated laboratory values may be reported in patients with elevated blood keto acids or on flucytosine therapy. The upper limit of normal for serum creatinine in most automated laboratories is 1.4 mg/dL, but it varies with the age, sex, and size of the patient. Despite the foregoing reservations, inexpensive repetitive measurements of the serum creatinine level provide a reliable means for following most patients with CRF. That the serum creatinine is a durable clinical tool is evident from its nearly universal application in the long-term management of kidney transplant recipients.

Despite increases in blood urea nitrogen to more than 200 mg/dL, the serum creatinine level in prerenal azotemia is only rarely greater than 3 mg/dL, and when such a raised creatinine is due to cardiac or hepatic causes, the prognosis is poor. Features indicative of a chronic prerenal azotemic state are similar to those seen in acute prerenal azotemia. When the serum creatinine concentration reaches 4 mg/dL in CRF, the creatinine clearance is approximately 25 mL/min (Figure 16–12–1). A serum creatinine of 8 mg/dL or higher usually correlates with a creatinine clearance approaching 5 mL/min or lower and is reason for considering the initiation of renal replacement treatment. GFR declines with aging, decreasing approximately 10 mL per decade from the third to the eighth decade. Elderly patients with extensive muscle atrophy, however, may be in advanced renal failure with a serum creatinine as low as 3 to 4 mg/dL. Thus, although the serum creatinine concentration permits an educated guess at the GFR, resorting to the creatinine clearance is rational when there is a discrepancy between clinical findings and degree of renal reserve as estimated from the serum creatinine level.

The ratio of blood urea nitrogen to creatinine in health and in CRF is approximately 10:1. Prerenal azotemia, because of enhanced tubular reabsorption of filtered urea, is suggested by a higher blood urea nitrogen:creatinine ratio of 20:1 to 40:1. This is particularly important in CRF patients whose impaired regulation of sodium and volume status renders them at considerable increased risk of a superimposed prerenal component, which, if recognized, is correctable. A disproportionate elevation of serum creatinine in a patient with a raised blood urea nitrogen (e.g., a creatinine of 13 mg/dL with a blood urea nitrogen of 45 mg/dL) favors CRF with reduced generation of urea because of decreased dietary intake of protein due to anorexia or preference (vegetarian diet). Urea generation is also impaired in advanced liver disease and the oli-

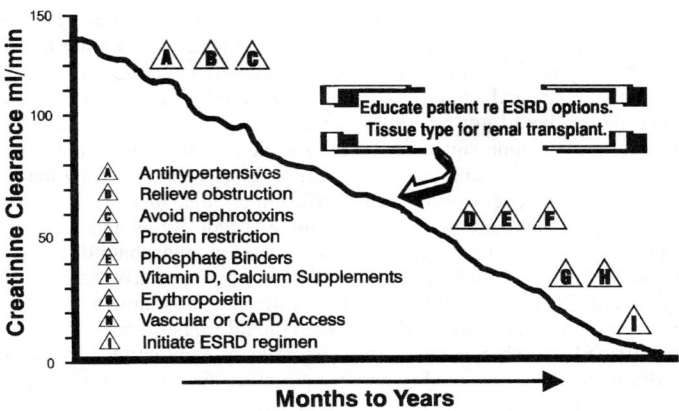

Figure 16–12–1. Major interventive measures in progressive renal disease are identified and listed according to the degree of renal insufficiency. At least half of the course of chronic renal failure is silent, meaning that clinical signs and symptoms are not evident until after preventive strategies would afford greatest benefit.

guria typical of the hepatorenal syndrome. Rhabdomyolysis is another cause of disproportionate innovation of serum creatinine.

Distinguishing CRF from acute parenchymal renal failure may not always be easy (Table 16–12–3), especially in patients too sick to proffer a detailed history. Review of the patient's earlier medical records may document the presence of azotemia months to years preceding the present evaluation, thereby affording a reliable means of achieving this goal. Lacking chart evidence of chronicity, determination of renal size by sonography is helpful, but to a limited extent. Generally, small kidneys indicate chronicity but normal or enlarged kidneys do not exclude a long-term renal disorder. Obstructive uropathy may present as CRF due to intrarenal intratubular obstruction, bilateral ureteric obstruction or unilateral obstruction in a single functioning kidney, or obstruction to the bladder outlet. Although complete urethral or ureteral obstruction causes anuria, partial obstruction may induce polyuria or alternating episodes of oliguria and polyuria—a pathognomonic sign of urinary obstruction. Cystopathy, a manifestation of autonomic neuropathy in long-standing diabetes, inhibits bladder emptying, simulating mechanical obstruction of the urinary tract. Discovery by bladder catheterization of a postvoiding urinary residual volume in excess of 50 mL is an indication for obtaining a cystometrogram to define bladder urodynamic function. Diabetic cystopathy is usually responsive to treatment with bethanechol. Prostatic obstruction is unlikely in the absence of a typical history of straining at urination, nocturia, dribbling, and the failure to find a significant postvoiding residual on bladder catheterization.

Ultrasound scanning of the bladder, ureters, and kidneys is the preferred diagnostic test (low cost and uninvasive) to exclude urinary obstruction. Ureteric obstruction, however, especially when due to periureteric retroperitoneal fibrosis, may be difficult to identify, occasionally failing to manifest dilated collecting systems on sonography. Cystoscopy with passage of ureteral catheters is the quickest route to both diagnosis and relief of obstruction. Alternatively, computed tomography or magnetic resonance imaging, as locally available, will detect a retroperitoneal mass, enlarged lymph nodes impinging on ureters, or unsuspected calculi. Magnetic resonance imaging, however, often fails to detect renal calculi.

Enlarged kidneys, in the presence of azotemia, are found in polycystic kidney disease. They may also be noted in amyloidosis, rapidly progressive glomerulonephritis (either primary or secondary), diabetic nephropathy, hydronephrosis, and infiltrative diseases of the kidney. Small kidneys and azotemia are noted in congenital dysgenesis, chronic interstitial nephritis, chronic glomerulonephritis (several histologic varieties), and hypertensive nephrosclerosis. A disparity in kidney size of more than 2 cm may be found in renovascular disease and renal tuberculosis; the more severely affected kidney is the small kidney in each instance. Normal-sized kidneys (approximately four vertebral lengths, which is usually 10–12 cm) are present in the majority of patients with CRF at the time of diagnosis. Included in this group of patients are those with remediable diseases. Especially important is exclusion of

drug-induced renal insufficiency. Recognition of a hypersensitivity reaction to a commonly prescribed nonsteroidal antiinflammatory agent, for example, prompts withdrawal of the drug, improvement in renal function, and avoidance of the tragedy of unwarranted ESRD. Computer programs (e.g., *Physicians Online, Physicians Desk Reference)* are broadly available to check all medications scheduled for the newly evaluated azotemic patient to determine whether drug toxicity is a greater risk in renal insufficiency. These programs can also be used to screen all medications previously taken by the patient to uncover unsuspected drug toxicity or hypersensitivity which may be reversible.

Isotopic renography using any of several available radiopharmaceuticals is a valuable means to establish a diagnosis of renovascular disease in patients with CRF. Renal scintigraphy employing o-[^{131}I]hippurate, after pretreatment with furosemide and the angiotensin-converting enzyme captopril, will detect renovascular hypertension due to unilateral renal disease, even in the presence of moderate azotemia (serum creatinine of 2–5 mg/dL). A positive test, indicating a renal artery stenosis of 60 to 90%, is present when blood pressure falls and the renal cortex retains the radiopharmaceutical at 20 minutes. The risk–benefit ratio of confirmatory selective renal angiography with potentially nephrotoxic contrast agents requires selectivity in its usage. Discovery of occluded renal artery segments prompts an attempt at renal angioplasty not only to improve blood pressure control but to restore renal function in selective cases of CRF due to renovascular disease.

Diabetic nephropathy may be discovered as the first sign of undiagnosed diabetes. When CRF results from diabetic nephropathy, proteinuria greater than 1 g/d (typically 2–10 g/d) is present and diabetic retinopathy (background and/or proliferative) on direct funduscopy or fluorescein angiography is uniformly present. In addition to the glomerulosclerosis of diabetes (see Chapter 16–21), diabetic persons risk a neurogenic bladder (cystopathy), with a functional obstruction to urine flow; bacterial and fungal infections of the kidney with destruction of renal parenchyma (papillary necrosis); and renal artery atherosclerosis and nephrosclerosis.

Diagnostic plans to define specific primary or secondary glomerulonephritides are essential and must include serum complement, antinuclear, anticytoplasmic, and antiglomerular basement membrane antibody tests, as well as cryoglobulin measurements. A systematic approach to glomerulonephritis is given in Chapters 16–18 and 16–19. Percutaneous renal biopsy may be helpful in confirming such a diagnosis and/or formulating a prognosis. It also permits direct culture of renal tissue for pathogens as well as polymerase chain reaction identification of viral DNA, which is evolving into the best means of specific diagnosis of some renal diseases. Whether the risk of the procedure (pain, bleeding, kidney loss, and rarely, death) is counterbalanced by the value of the information generated is debated by nephrologists. When performed under sonographic guidance, in kidneys of normal size, in a patient free of a coagulation defect, renal biopsy is remarkably safe and often yields an unsuspected diagnosis. In general, renal biopsy is indicated when either proteinuria (>1 g/d) or azotemia (serum creatinine >2.0 mg/dL) is unexplained and two normal- or large-sized kidneys are present. Another indication for renal biopsy is to guide therapy as in the use of cytotoxic drugs for lupus nephritis or membranous glomerulonephritis.

Renal insufficiency in a kidney transplant recipient poses special diagnostic problems considered in Chapter 16–26. The usual course in recipients of cadaver donor kidneys is that of gradual decline in GFR with a mean survival of the allograft of about 8 years. Recent evidence suggests that so-called "chronic rejection" may not be an immunologic reaction by the host against the allograft, but may reflect hemodynamic injury to the disproportionately small renal mass afforded by the transplant. Preliminary reports indicate that the larger the kidney size (number of nephrons) transplanted, the longer the survival of the allograft. Often, diagnosis of the cause of azotemia requires distinguishing allograft rejection from drug (e.g., cyclosporine) toxicity and less common infections (e.g., cytomegalovirus), obstructive lesions (e.g., ureteric stricture), renovascular disease, and recurrence in the kidney transplant of the renal disorder that caused renal failure prior to transplantation. Monitoring of kidney transplant recipients is usually effected by periodic measurements of the serum creatinine concentration. Definitive diagnosis of declining renal function entails radioisotope studies of GFR, sonography to exclude obstruction, fine-needle aspiration of the transplant to judge the type and intensity of rejection, and selective renal biopsy.

Therapeutic

Therapeutic Options

Four main objectives in treating CRF are detection of reversible contributors to CRF, slowing of the course of CRF by correcting perturbations that accelerate loss of remaining renal function, deletion of reversible consequences and complications of CRF that contribute to the associated ill health (e.g., osteodystrophy), and construction of a "life plan" to prepare the patient for the sometimes imperceptible transition to ESRD, thereby minimizing disruption of work, school, or home activities. Components of the life plan include actions based on key decisions, such as whether to have an intrafamilial renal transplant, the type of dialysis (peritoneal or hemodialysis) to be used, dialysis site (home or facility), and the point (creatinine level) at which uremia therapy should begin.

Recommended Approach

The first step is to search for any reversible contributors to the CRF. Potentially beneficial actions in CRF include cessation of renal damaging drugs (e.g., methysergide in retroperitoneal obstruction, nonsteroidal antiinflammatory drugs or analgesics in tubulointerstitial disorders, heroin abuse in glomerulonephritis); initiation of specific therapy to reverse renal insufficiency (e.g., steroids for lupus nephritis, cyclophosphamide for Wegener's granulomatosis, plasmapheresis for Goodpasture's syndrome or essential mixed cryoglobulinemia, melphalan for multiple myeloma or primary amyloidosis, bethanechol for a neurogenic bladder); and correction of superimposed prerenal insufficiency due to volume depletion or congestive heart failure. These reversible causes are summarized in Table 16–12–6.

In a small proportion of patients, about 3% in our experience, what was thought to be irreversible uremia improves inexplicably. These rare instances reflect either an incorrect initial diagnosis or insufficient understanding of the natural history of the renal disorder in question. Preparation of a life plan affords the means to prepare the patient for what may be decades of living with slowly progressive and intermittently symptomatic renal disease. Both maintenance hemodialysis and renal transplantation can extend life, in selected individuals, for more than 25 years. The patient should be informed fully to participate in all decisions pertaining to therapy.

The main components of therapy directed toward correction of the perturbations that may arise during the natural history of CRF are listed in Table 16–12–7. Prophylactic measures include cautious use of any drugs that may add nephrotoxicity to the underlying renal disorder. Some drugs should not be administered to patients with renal insufficiency and include nitrofurantoin, spironolactone, amiloride, triamterene, and metformin. Interstitial nephritis may be caused by many drugs including cyclosporine, captopril, cimetidine, methicillin, allopurinol, phenylhydantoin, and furosemide. Medications that require adjustment in dose according to GFR include cyclophosphamide, cimetidine, clofibrate, digoxin, and many antibiotics, particularly the aminoglycosides. Bladder catheterization, a significant risk variable for urinary infection, should be performed only when the information gained cannot be obtained by other means. Administration of radiographic contrast medium should be avoided, wherever possible, especially in CRF patients who are dehydrated or have marked hyperuricemia, diabetes, multiple myeloma, or abnormally high blood viscosity. Should the need for diagnosis based on radiocontrast medium override the risk of its nephrotoxicity, the best renoprotective strategy is to maintain hydration throughout infusion of the dye. Earlier studies indicating a protective benefit of mannitol-induced osmotic diuresis or furosemide administration show no advantage over a simple infusion of normal saline.

Measures advocated in the hope of reducing the rate of renal functional decline include normalization of hypertensive blood pressures, dietary protein restriction, and administration of intestinal phosphate binders. Rat models of chronic renal disease respond to blood pressure reduction by angiotensin-converting enzyme (ACE) inhibitors or calcium channel blockers, with a slowing of the rate of loss of GFR and a reduction in proteinuria. Glomerulosclerosis is also reduced in severity in hypertensive rats treated with antihypertensive drugs. Clinical trials in which loss of GFR has been prevented in diabetic nephropathy and essential hypertension indicate that the ACE inhibitors are applicable to human kidney disorders. There may be specific benefit to achieving blood pressure reduction by relaxation of the efferent glomerular arteriole by direct action of ACE inhibitors or as a secondary effect of calcium channel blockers, which retard entrance of calcium into vessel walls. Multicenter trials of captopril and enalapril, both ACE inhibitors, have shown an unquestioned delay in progression of diabetic nephropathy in both insulin-dependent and non-insulin-dependent diabetes. Hypertension resistant to various combinations of sequentially prescribed diuretics, beta blockers, vasodilators, ACE inhibitors, and calcium channel blockers usually responds to minoxidil in doses up to 75 mg/d. Bilateral nephrectomy is no longer performed as a method to control

TABLE 16–12–6. REVERSIBLE FORMS OF AZOTEMIA

Type	Examples	Remedy
Prerenal	Congestive heart failure	Compensate heart, heart transplant
	Advanced liver failure	Liver transplant
	Malignant hypertension	Reduce blood pressure
Postrenal	Urinary obstruction	Sonography, cystoscopy, surgical relief of tumor mass, extraction of calculi, nephrotomy, ureteric catheters, bladder catheter depending on level of blockage
Renal	Goodpasture's syndrome	Plasmapheresis
	Multiple myeloma, amyloid	Melphalan
	Wegener's granulomatosis	Plasmapheresis, cytotoxic drugs
	Lupus nephritis	Prednisone plus cyclophosphamide
	Membranous glomerulonephritis	Prednisone
	Drug toxicity or hypersensitivity	Withdraw drug (e.g., nonsteroidal antiinflammatory drug, trimethoprim, analgesic, aminoglycoside antibiotic); treat with prednisone for tubulo-interstitial hypersensitivity reaction (e.g., methicillin, sulfa drugs)

TABLE 16–12–7. THERAPY FOR CHRONIC RENAL FAILURE

- Discontinue injurious drugs (nonsteroidal antiinflammatory agents, aminoglycoside antibiotics)
- Detect and treat urinary infection. Relieve obstruction; remove calculi where possible. Avoid bladder catheters.
- Correct electrolyte imbalance. Minimize hypermagnesemia.
- Expand plasma volume if contracted.
- Control hypertension.
- Restrict dietary protein.
- Correct hyperlipidemia by diet modification and hypolipidemic drugs.
- Control hyperphosphatemia by dietary protein restriction and intraintestinal phosphate binders.
- Reduce hyperuricemia if >12 mg/dL by administering allopurinol (100 mg/d) if glomerular filtration rate >10 mL/min.
- Add oral bicarbonate for severe acidosis.
- Administer synthetic vitamin D and calcium supplements, checking for induced hypercalcemia.
- Administer erythropoietin (and iron as required to replete iron stores) to raise hematocrit above 32%.
- Avoid intravascular volume depletion by overuse of diuretics.
- Minimize exposure to radiocontrast media and maintain hydration if radiocontrast agents are necessary.

hypertension. Long-acting forms of antihypertensive drugs such as nifedipine-XL (calcium channel blocker) and lisinopril (ACE inhibitor) permit once-daily administration for the majority of azotemic patients with CRF.

Experimental studies suggest that a key mechanism underlying progressive renal damage in various kidney disorders is intraglomerular hypertension. Prevention of glomerular hypertension by dietary protein restriction or antihypertensive therapy with an ACE inhibitory drug is readily effected in rat models of renal disease. Restriction of dietary protein prolongs the life of rats (but not dogs) with reduced renal function. Advocates of a restricted protein diet in renal disease point to the transient increase in GFR (stressing the so-called renal functional reserve) that occurs in healthy subjects after a meat protein meal, likening this reaction to the glomerular hyperfiltration and subsequent glomerulosclerosis noted in rats after seven-eighths nephrectomy. These rats develop glomerulosclerosis on a normal protein diet, but have reduction in GFR to the basal level expected from the fractional remaining renal mass and preservation of glomerular integrity when fed a low-protein diet. Glomerular hypertension and hyperfiltration also occur in patients with diabetes, single or remnant kidneys, and various other acquired kidney disorders. Partially controlled trials in several kidney diseases found that dietary protein restriction (with or without addition of essential amino acids or their precursor α-keto derivatives) blunts progression of renal functional loss. Diseases presently thought to benefit from a low-protein diet include diabetic nephropathy, polycystic kidney disease, and various forms of glomerulonephritis. The final report of the National Institutes of Health-funded Modification of Diet in Renal Disease Study in 1994, however, is disappointing. In 840 patients with various chronic renal diseases whose GFR ranged from 25 to 55 mL/min and who were maintained on a low-protein diet (0.58 g/kg body weight) for a mean follow-up of 2.2 years, there was "no delay in the time to the occurrence of end-stage renal disease or death." Furthermore, among patients with more severe renal insufficiency (255 patients with a GFR of 13–24 mL/min), "a very-low-protein diet, as compared with a low-protein diet, did not significantly slow the progression of renal disease." Given trials completed thus far, the prudent physician may elect to discourage a high-protein diet while prescribing a moderately restricted protein diet (40–60 g/d), which is well tolerated by most patients.

Hyperphosphatemia, which becomes increasingly severe as the GFR declines below 25 mL/min, leads to reciprocal hypocalcemia and its consequence, the bone disease of hyperparathyroidism. Hyperphosphatemia sufficient to initiate parathyroid hyperplasia and excess secretion of parathormone first occurs when GFR is reduced by about 75%. Limitation in ingestion of dairy products, which are high in phosphate content, and use of intestinal phosphate-binding medications are appropriate to protect the skeleton of the azotemic individual with CRF. A total daily phosphate intake of 500 to 800 mg is generally acceptable with careful monitoring. Hyperphosphatemia may promote intrarenal calcium–phosphorus deposition, thereby hastening the progression of renal insufficiency. Gut binding of phosphate may be achieved by premeal feeding of calcium carbonate or acetate, aluminum hydroxide or carbonate, or magnesium hydroxide. Aluminum-based antacids in quantities sufficient to reduce serum phosphate concentration to normal may induce hypercalcemia and vitamin D-resistant bone disease. Aluminum toxicity is also associated with a syndrome of encephalopathy and anemia. Excess aluminum, when causing pathologic fractures or muscle and bone pain and weakness, can be removed from the body by binding the ion to deferoxamine, a relatively safe chelating agent. Avoidance of aluminum-containing antacids is possible in many individuals able to tolerate 4 to 12 g/d calcium carbonate taken before meals as a component of a regimen of supplemental synthetic vitamin D metabolites and dietary phosphorus restriction. Magnesium salts should be used with considerable caution as phosphate binders in CRF patients, and their usage requires frequent monitoring of serum magnesium. Once phosphate has been reduced to normal, hypocalcemia may also be treated by administration of 1,25-dihydroxyvitamin D_3. Benefits of treatment with 1,25-dihydroxyvitamin D_3 include prevention of renal bone disease, reversal of secondary hyperparathyroidism, and increased growth velocity in children. Initial concern that treatment with 1,25-dihydroxyvitamin D_3 might cause reduced renal

function has not been confirmed in later double-blind placebo-controlled trials.

Attention to the amount of dietary sodium and potassium is important as the GFR falls below 15 mL/min. At this level of renal reserve, some patients, especially those with interstitial nephritis or polycystic kidneys, lose large quantities of sodium, behaving as "salt wasters," not unlike that seen in Addison's disease. By contrast, individuals with glomerular disease retain salt and water, leading to anasarca and intravascular volume expansion. Both subsets of patients are acidotic, though the salt wasters often have more profound metabolic acidosis. A correct dietary salt prescription requires a process of trial and error termed *salt balancing*. Starting with a 40-g-protein, 2-g-salt diet, the patient is weighed daily (at home or in hospital). The salt waster's weight will decrease, necessitating supplementation with sodium bicarbonate pills (600 mg) given four times daily. With continued weight loss, the amount of sodium bicarbonate is raised by 2.4 g/d increments until a stable weight results. The salt retainer may have pulmonary congestion and peripheral edema with the initial 2-g salt prescription, in which case diuretics are added. Furosemide 80 to 240 mg twice daily plus metolazone 5 to 10 mg twice daily usually suffice to control salt balance so long as GFR is above 5 mL/min.

Dietary potassium restriction is usually not needed unless the daily urine output falls below 1 L or the patient is under treatment with drugs that impair potassium excretion, especially the ACE inhibitors. Unfortunately, in those hypertensive diabetics who appear most responsive in terms of normalizing blood pressure, the ACE inhibitors are also inordinately prone to induce dangerous hyperkalemia as a side effect. In the author's experience, approximately 10% of azotemic diabetic hypertensive patients experience an increase in serum potassium concentration above 6.0 mEq/L while otherwise tolerating enalapril. In these individuals, enalapril must be discontinued. Hyperkalemia below 6 mEq/L can usually be managed by reducing dietary citrus fruits, bananas, and potatoes. More severe potassium retention requires administration of a cation-exchange resin (e.g., sodium polystyrene sulfonate). Discontinuance of potassium-retaining drugs is a key step in management of hyperkalemia. Symptomatic anemia with a hematocrit below 30%, especially in geriatric patients or those with coronary artery disease, can be improved by treatment with recombinant erythropoietin. The exact indications for erythropoietin administration have not been defined in predialysis patients. Prior to starting erythropoietin, other causes of anemia should be excluded and the presence of adequate iron stores confirmed by measurement of serum ferritin and iron saturation. Erythropoietin is usually injected subcutaneously or intravenously, one to three times weekly, in individualized doses of 50 to 150 U/kg. A reasonable starting dose is 50 U/kg. The first response, a reticulocytosis, is noted in about 2 to 3 weeks, with a significant increase in hematocrit by 6 weeks. A reasonable target hematocrit is 35 to 39%. Maintenance doses of erythropoietin are given one to three times weekly. Repeat measurements of iron saturation should be obtained quarterly during treatment with erythropoietin. It is usual to have to administer supplemental iron either orally or intravenously to sustain the effect of erythropoietin. Recent reports suggest that hyperlipidemia may be an important mechanism underlying continuing renal damage in the nephrotic syndrome and CRF. Glomerulosclerosis is accelerated by ingestion of cholesterol in guinea pigs, rats, and rabbits and in rats with endogenous hyperlipidemia due to the nephrotic syndrome. Reducing the serum lipid level ameliorates the progression of renal disease in rats with a remnant kidney and with an induced nephrotic syndrome. Consensus opinion advocates treatment of hyperlipidemia in nephrotic and/or azotemic individuals. Hypertriglyceridemia and low levels of high-density lipoprotein are typical of uremia. In renal failure, the risk of coronary artery disease expressed as the ratio of total cholesterol to high-density-lipoprotein cholesterol is elevated. Treatment of these lipid abnormalities may be effected with a low-lipid diet, nicotinic acid, gemfibrozil, lovastatin (Mevacor), or probucol. Enthusiasm for the addition to the CRF treatment regimen of dietary fish oil supplements is derived from studies in Munich–Wistar rats subjected to five-sixths renal ablation and subsequently fed a 24% fish oil diet, which prevented glomerulosclerosis and abrogated dyslipidemia while reducing hypertension. In renal transplant recipients (individuals with only one functioning kidney), administration of 6 g of fish oil daily during the first postoperative year enhanced graft survival and lowered blood pressure. Caution in prescription of omega-3 fish oil supplements to predialysis patients has been advised because of an increase in serum lipid peroxidases measured as thiobarbituric acid reactants during their administration, a finding of unknown significance. For the present, the place of fish oil supplementation in the management of CRF is not defined.

FOLLOW-UP

The frequency of visits required for supervision of CRF is determined by the rate of deterioration of GFR, the activity of comorbid extrarenal disease, and the need of the patient and the patient's social support system for support from the medical care team. Comprehensive management of declining renal function necessitates an overall plan to normalize blood pressure, reduce hyperphosphatemia with phosphate binders and hyperparathyroidism with 1,25-dihydroxyvitamin D_3, control plasma lipids with diet and hypolipidemic drugs, and increase the hematocrit with recombinant erythropoietin. These measures carry risks of precipitating hypophosphatemia, hypercalcemia, and erythrocythemia. Key variables recorded at each visit should include patient weight, hematocrit, blood urea nitrogen, serum creatinine, serum electrolytes, serum phosphorus, and serum calcium. Inspection of the course of these data permits a grasp of whether the patient is stable, deteriorating, or improving. Decline in renal function over time is variable from patient to patient with the same renal disease. In polycystic kidney disease, for example, the interval between clinical expression of the first renal complaint (hypertension, hematuria, abdominal pain) and the need for ESRD therapy ranges from 5 to 30 or more years. Similarly, in diabetic nephropathy, some patients may deteriorate into ESRD within 2 years of onset of nephrotic range proteinuria, whereas others remain relatively stable for up to a decade. A plot of the reciprocal of the serum creatinine against time has been proposed as a method to estimate the future course of patients with established renal disease; however, application of powerful interventive measures, especially the use of ACE inhibitors for blood pressure control and a protein-restricted diet, often favorably alter the course of what previously was a linear and inexorable march toward ESRD. Nevertheless, graphing each patient's serum creatinine (or its reciprocal) is a simple means of assessing when to anticipate incapacitation because of ESRD.

A key objective of the health care team is the emotional fortification of the azotemic patient for the unavoidable coming disruption in lifestyle imposed by maintenance dialysis or a renal transplant. Depending on staffing and preferences at each institution, responsibility for instruction and support of the patient with CRF may be the assignment of a social worker, nurse educator, physician assistant, or lay patient advocate. The instructional curriculum should include an explanation of renal function and anatomy, the disease process, and the overall plan of therapy detailing the desired diet, target blood pressure, and prescribed exercise. Meetings with patients presently undergoing peritoneal dialysis and hemodialysis, as well as with renal transplant recipients, should be arranged to permit patient-to-patient interaction. Literature provided by patient-oriented organizations such as the National Kidney Foundation and American Kidney Fund is particularly helpful in communicating the basics of renal disease and ESRD therapy. Disease-specific foundations for diabetes (American Diabetes Association), systemic lupus erythematosus (Lupus Foundation), and polycystic kidney disease (PKD Foundation) will arrange for afflicted members to contact patients locally. Genetic counseling should be proffered to patients with inherited disorders including polycystic kidneys, Alport's syndrome, nephronopthisis, and diabetes. Self-help groups are extremely valuable in sustaining patient morale. Strong advocacy for individual patients as well as the cause of ESRD care in general has been the province of the American Association of Kidney Patients (and its predecessor organizations) for more than 20 years. There is no doubt that a fully informed patient, free to consult his or her own chart, becomes an effective ally to the health care team. One nephrologist who is also an ESRD patient instructed the author that the longest surviving patients are "givers of ulcers," rather than "getters of ulcers," a conclusion consistent with the author's position on the merit of patient activism.

Nephrologists in practice function as primary care physicians for ESRD patients because of their repetitive need for interventions unique to the specialty. Survival beyond a decade despite failed kidneys is no longer unique or unusual. Indeed, guiding patients with CRF to and through a program of dialysis supplemented with renal transplantation is a fulfilling component of renal medicine. The past 20 years have seen continuously improving ESRD management consequent to introduction of synthetic vitamin D metabolites for preemption of renal osteodystrophy; recombinant erythropoietin to overcome the anemia of uremia; and monoclonal antilymphocyte antibody, cyclosporine, and other highly effective immunosuppressive drugs to facilitate protracted allograft survival. Moreover, individual diseases are the subjects of specific protocols: intravenous chlorambucil and methylprednisolone for membranous glomerulonephritis, strict glucose regulation for diabetic nephropathy, and cyclosporine for focal segmental glomerulosclerosis. The frequency of repeat visits is determined by the slope of the curve of declining GFR; a break in slope suggests a superimposed complication such as a prerenal component, a urinary infection, drug toxicity or hypersensitivity, or uncontrolled hypertension. Stable normotensive patients with few symptoms can be seen at intervals of 2 to 4 months. Should hypertension be uncontrolled, GFR fall over several months by 10 mL/min or more, or residual GFR reach 20 mL/min, or less, monthly or biweekly visits may be necessary to establish regulation. Once GFR falls below 10 mL/min, and in symptomatic patients with higher residual function, weekly visits are needed. Decisions as to type of uremia therapy are best made prior to the time for its initiation. The months immediately preceding resort to uremia therapy offer time for exploration and discussion prior to selection of one of the available options when it is needed.

DISCUSSION
Prevalence and Incidence

Over the past quarter century, increasingly successful substitution for irreversibly failed kidneys by dialytic therapy and renal transplantation has focused attention on the uremic syndrome. In the United States, more than 250,000 individuals with so-called ESRD were registered in federal treatment programs in 1995. According to the U.S. Renal Data System 1994 report for calendar year 1991, approximately 198 per million Americans developed ESRD in 1991. The incidence rate in men (239/million) is greater than that in women (162/million) and is much higher in African-Americans (595/million) than in Asians (205/million) or whites (150/million). About 138,277 Americans are funded by Medicare while receiving dialytic therapy; an additional 50,468 have a functioning renal transplant.

Related Basic Science

Renal function is vital to life. There is very substantial renal reserve in the approximately 1 to 2.5 million nephrons present at birth. The number of nephrons in each individual varies directly with total renal mass. Of the total nephron endowment in both kidneys, it is estimated that about one half can be lost without substantive adverse consequence (Figure 16–12–2), which is the reason that living donor renal transplantation is possible. Further loss of one half of the remaining 50% of nephrons leaves about 25% of original renal mass, the usual starting point for recognition of symptomatic renal insufficiency. During decline in functioning renal mass, remaining nephrons undergo compensatory hypertrophy and hyperfunction. This means that when renal function is measured at 5% of normal, the actual remaining nephron population is not 5%, but, rather, that amount of nephrons that after hypertrophy and while hypersecreting simulates 5% of renal function.

The etiology of CRF is unknown in more than 40% of patients. It may be speculated that a substantive fraction of individuals who develop uremia without discernable cause have a genetic reason for their disease. The racial disparity in attack rate of ESRD is an often-cited example of how genetic factors contribute to renal failure. Critics of the genetic predisposition hypothesis argue that a higher rate of kidney disease in African-Americans, like other disorders, might reflect economic pressures and differences resulting from being poor rather than being genetically different. Alternatively, some argue that the high renal failure rate in African-Americans results from hypertension and diabetes,

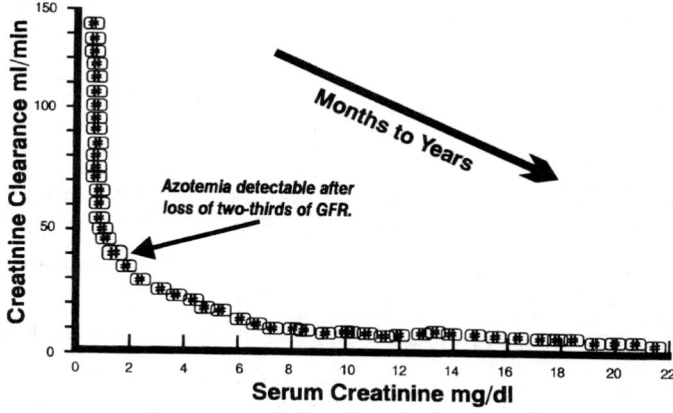

Figure 16–12–2. Relationship between serum creatinine concentration and glomerular filtration rate (GFR). More than 50% of renal excretory function can be lost without causing elevation in serum creatinine. Note that much more renal function is lost when the serum creatinine rises from 1.0 to 2.0 mg/dL than when the increase is from 10 to 20 mg/dL.

both disorders reflecting modification of lifestyle rather than genetic endowment. Similarly, the American Pima Indian has a 70% chance of contracting non-insulin-dependent diabetes (and the attendant risk of developing renal failure due to diabetic nephropathy) a genetic disease now ubiquitous in a population that has undergone drastically changed diet and habits. One hypothesis explaining renal functional decline in the absence of continuing injury is the remnant-kidney-hyperfiltration theory. Rats subjected to seven-eighths nephrectomy are unstable; their remaining nephrons enlarge, manifesting a supernormal GFR only to lose function as glomeruli become sclerotic. It is reasoned that imposing a normal kidney's excretory burden on a reduced renal mass will, by a mechanism yet to be understood, "burn out" remaining nephrons. In this perspective, the kidney (which has not evolved beyond the time when our ancestors ate meat only after a successful hunt) is overburdened by the high-protein American diet. Hypertension also injures the kidney. Partially nephrectomized rats fed a low-protein diet and/or treated with antihypertensive drugs have a slowed rate of GFR loss.

Natural History and Its Modification with Treatment

Chronic renal failure is nearly always progressive from its inception, but its rate of progression varies not only with etiology but also from patient to patient with the same etiology. Polycystic kidney disease usually takes decades to reach advanced azotemia, whereas diabetic nephropathy with nephrotic syndrome usually takes only 2 years. This interval may be reduced to weeks or months in the case of malignant hypertension, antiglomerular basement membrane disease, rapidly progressive glomerulonephritis, or HIV-associated nephropathy. On the other hand, some polycystic kidney disease patients may progress to ESRD within 2 years of presentation and some nephrotic diabetic individuals have not yet become dialysis dependent after two decades of observation. The best way to make a rough prediction of the rate of progression of renal impairment in an individual is by projecting from sequential measurements of GFR or by plotting sequential measurements of the serum creatinine. Moreover, deviations from the predicted rate of progression derived from such serial measurements may alert the clinician to the presence of a superimposed complication, which may be correctable. It may also permit evaluation of the effects of therapeutic interventions.

Extension of findings in the rat to the care of azotemic patients has prompted European and American studies suggesting that the progress of renal failure can be slowed. To incorporate the benefit of diet and blood pressure control, the natural history of renal disorders requires reevaluation. For diabetic patients, the impact of blood pressure regulation is extraordinary. In a Danish trial in insulin-dependent diabetes, the annual loss in GFR fell from 14 mL/min to about 1 mL/min after normotension was established—without ACE inhibitors or calcium channel blockers. Confirmation of the value of normotension was provided in a recently reported multicenter trial of treatment of insulin-depen-

dent diabetic adults with captopril, an ACE inhibitor, that showed a sharp reduction in the progression of diabetic nephropathy. Coupling enhanced glucose regulation with normalization of hypertensive blood pressure has greatly benefited diabetic patients by retarding the rate of renal functional decline while preventing progression of proliferative retinopathy.

Prevention

Of each 100 cases of CRF, fewer than 10 are preventable. Early recognition of extrarenal (e.g., prostatic hypertrophy) or intrarenal (e.g., sodium urate crystals in gout) obstruction permits its correction and avoidance of loss of GFR. Hypertensive nephropathy is probably fully avoidable with sufficient and sustained treatment. Powerful drugs including minoxidil, calcium channel blockers, and ACE inhibitors normalize hypertensive blood pressures in nearly all instances, thereby preempting what had previously been an inexorable decline to ESRD in malignant hypertension and systemic sclerosis. Restricted use of nephrotoxic analgesics and antibiotics avoids renal failure. In Australia, where toxic analgesics can be purchased without prescription, the proportion of ESRD patients with analgesic nephropathy exceeds 15%. The equivalent incidence is about 2% in the United States, where strict regulations remove nephrotoxic drugs from over-the-counter availability.

Elimination of environmental pollutants that have been linked to CRF (mercury in Minamata disease in Japan, lead-contaminated moonshine whiskey in the southern United States, aromatic hydrocarbons in automobile exhausts [shown to produce glomerulosclerosis in rats]) will prevent an unknown proportion of new cases of CRF. Large studies of the effect of strict metabolic regulation in insulin-dependent diabetes reported in Sweden and the United States have unequivocally shown that the onset of the renal disease in diabetic individuals is slowed by tight control of the plasma glucose level. For most patients with ESRD, however, any hope of prevention must await elucidation of the pathogenetic process responsible for renal damage—still an enigmatic issue despite a quarter century of successful treatment.

Cost Containment

The high cost of treatment of ESRD, nearly $8 billion in the United States in 1994, along with the expense of heart, liver, pancreas, lung, and bone marrow transplants, may exceed the limit of a health care system that consumes more than 13% of the gross national product. Presently, there is no national plan to determine limits (age, diagnosis, probability of benefit) to allocation of high-technology therapies. Linked directly to the question of who will be permitted dialysis or a renal transplant for ESRD are the funding criteria for treatment of CRF. Serious ethical issues pertain to restriction of uremia therapy to patient subsets most likely to benefit. In Great Britain, for example, individuals older than 55 years have been, for the most part, denied dialytic therapy as a component of expenditure limitation. At the other extreme, in the United States, no restrictions have been placed on the number of patients who may be enrolled for Medicare reimbursement for the cost of dialytic therapy. Senile, incontinent, nursing-home-restricted patients over the age of 90 are likely to be started on a regimen of maintenance hemodialysis though not comprehending what is happening at the time. Lacking critical supervision of who is to receive renal replacement therapy results in "all comers" being treated. Adding to the expense of ESRD programs are the add-on costs such as ambulance transportation to and from the dialysis facility and the salaries of guards who accompany prisoners for their dialyses. The amazing growth of application of recombinant erythropoietin, which is now administered to more than 80% of American dialysis patients, imparts more than $1 billion to the total ESRD expenditure. The growing use of erythropoietin to correct anemia in CRF prior to starting dialytic therapy will further increase the total bill for renal failure treatment.

Examination of differences in the regulation and governmental reimbursement for ESRD therapy in the United States, Europe, and Japan permits a window of understanding into the broader issues of macroallocation (institution and regimen) and microallocation (individual) of health resources when demand for treatment cannot be satisfied by the system. Not everyone can be funded for all organ transplants. Vegetative individuals in nursing homes ought not, the author believes, to be sustained by maintenance hemodialysis. Furthermore, growing successes in bionics and "spare parts" medicine will undoubtedly add to the demand for services forcing economists, politicians, and healthcare professionals to devise an orderly system of what amounts to rationing. Should physicians dissociate themselves from the reality of devising criteria for triage in high-technology medicine, the unhappy alternative of imposed regulations created to meet political expediency is unavoidable. In the United States, expansion of managed care organizations impinges on physician prerogatives in determining how, where, and who will manage a specific illness in an individual patient. The collapse in 1994 of efforts to "reform" the health care delivery system means that the American patchwork system will continue to govern access to ESRD therapy. On the bright side, renal failure is a shining example of conversion of a formerly universally fatal affliction to a universally treated disorder with a high rate of survival to an admittedly tenuous existence.

REFERENCES

Adamson JW, Eschbach JW. Treatment of the anemia of CRF with recombinant human erythropoietin. Annu Rev Med 1990;41:349.

Friedman EA. Death on hemodialysis: Preventable or inevitable? Dordrecht: Kluwer Academic, 1994.

Klahr S, Levey AS, Beck GJ, et al. The effects of dietary protein restriction and blood-pressure control on the progression of chronic renal disease: Modification of Diet in Renal Disease Study Group. N Engl J Med 1994;330:877.

Lewis EJ, Hunsicker LG, Bain RP, Rohde RD. The effect of angiotensin-converting-enzyme inhibition on diabetic nephropathy: The Collaborative Study Group. N Engl J Med 1993;329:1456.

Mitch WE, Price SR, May RC, et al. Metabolic consequences of uremia: Extending the concept of adaptive responses to protein metabolism. Am J Kidney Dis 1994;23:224.

Neuringer JR, Brenner BM. Hemodynamic theory of progressive renal disease: A 10-year update in brief review. Am J Kidney Dis 1993;22:98.

Schreiner GE, Maher JF. Uremia. Springfield, IL: CC Thomas, 1961.

Thomas DM, Coles GA, Williams JD. What does the renal reserve mean? Kidney Int 1994;45:411.

U.S. Renal Data System. USRDS 1994 Annual Data Report. Bethesda, MD: National Institutes of Health, National Institute of Diabetes and Digestive and Kidney Diseases, June 1994.

CHAPTER 16–13

End-Stage Renal Disease

A. Peter Lundin, M.D., and Barbara G. Delano, M.D.

DEFINITION

By definition, end-stage renal disease is the point at which the kidneys can no longer excrete sufficient toxic metabolites, electrolytes, and water to sustain life. Prior to this, numerous internal compensations and external adjustments in diet and control of high blood pressure may keep the individual patient in reasonably good health. Prior to the advent of maintenance dialysis and kidney transplantation, end-stage renal disease invariably resulted in death. A working definition of end-stage renal disease today is irreversible renal disease of such severity that renal replacement therapy is required for survival.

ETIOLOGY

Of 178,000 cases of end-stage renal disease reported to Medicare between 1988 and 1991, diabetes mellitus (33.8%) and hypertension (28.3%) accounted for the etiology in 62.1% (U.S. Renal Data System, 1994). Other causes for end-stage renal disease are those listed in Chapter 16–12 in the differential diagnosis for chronic renal failure. In many cases, however, the diagnosis is imprecise. The requirement to complete a form may allow only a "best guess" in the absence of a precise pathologic diagnosis. Hypertension is a frequent comorbid condition in chronic renal failure, being a consequence as well as a cause, and thus may be overdiagnosed as an etiology.

CRITERIA FOR DIAGNOSIS

Suggestive

Terminal renal failure may ensue within days of acute irreversible renal damage, such as acute cortical necrosis, or may follow a subacute course, but in most cases progression to end-stage renal disease is gradual and insidious. After years of functional loss, the onset of clinical features may be so subtle that they are often ignored by the patient or attributed to normal aging. The imperative for recognizing the point at which chronic renal failure has reached end stage derives from the need to determine when to begin life-saving therapies. This timing is not entirely precise, being influenced by how well the individual tolerates azotemia.

Definitive

The diagnosis of end-stage renal disease can only be made in a patient who has a marked and persistent elevation of serum creatinine with, in most cases, small kidneys and uremic symptoms. The need for dialysis or transplantation comes into consideration when serum creatinine exceeds 6 to 10 mg/dL or creatinine clearance falls to less than 5 to 10 mL/min. The precise value associated with the onset of symptoms may vary, depending on patient size and age, as well as type of disease. Creatinine production and appearance in the urine depend on muscle mass, which varies from person to person and is diminished with age and disease. Consequently, the same serum creatinine level, in an asymptomatic, younger, better muscled individual, may correspond to a lower clearance in an older, smaller person who could be uremic. Because of vagaries in creatinine excretion when renal failure is advanced, radionuclide measures of glomerular filtration rate may provide a more precise measure of kidney function. This is usually unnecessary, however, because the diagnosis of end-stage renal failure is a clinical one depending on symptoms and signs that improve with treatment.

CLINICAL MANIFESTATIONS

Subjective

Accumulation of toxic metabolites and disordering of fluid and electrolyte homeostasis will affect organ systems in the body. Symptoms indicating the need to start or intensify dialytic therapy include alterations of central nervous system function, particularly deficits in concentration and memory, often appearing to friends and family members as a change in personality. The patient may also complain of daytime drowsiness and somnolence and a reversal of the normal sleep pattern. Myoclonus may be experienced during waking hours. The skin becomes dry, contributing to the severe itching that may be so troubling to these patients. Slippage of academic grades or inability to keep up with work may result.

Loss of appetite and a bad or "metallic" taste in the mouth signal that end-stage renal disease is nearing. Some time can be gained by limiting protein in the diet, but the restriction may have to be so strict as to risk serious malnutrition, and earlier dialysis is to be preferred. Retention of salt and water may lead to orthopnea and paroxysmal nocturnal dyspnea, further interfering with sleep. Fluid retention, masking loss of real weight, may result in worsening hypertension.

Anemia and impairment of muscle activity by uremic toxins lead to a generalized weakness. The desire to engage in many of life's normal activities including sex may be lost. As end-stage renal disease and the time to discuss forms of replacement therapy approach, depression, anger, denial, and bargaining can all be present, interfering with appropriate adaptation if not properly channeled.

Attempts to carry the patient too long with dietary management before intervening with dialysis may lead to life-threatening uremic complications. Gastrointestinal symptoms such as nausea and vomiting are often the first indicator that dialysis is necessary.

Objective

Physical Examination

Prescribed protein restriction, as well as natural avoidance of meat due to uremia, could lead to a malnourished state marked by a loss of muscle mass, drop in serum albumin (in the absence of nephrotic syndrome), drop in total lymphocyte count (<1000), and the euthyroid sick state (low triiodothyronine and thyroxine, normal TSH).

As end-stage renal disease approaches, dietary restrictions may need to be so severe that, despite diuretics, even a small excess of sodium intake may cause edema and congestive heart failure. In most cases renal potassium excretory ability is sufficient to avoid hyperkalemia until the terminal stages of renal failure, but renal potassium excretion can be prematurely impaired by the use of angiotensin-converting enzyme inhibitors, nonsteroidal antiinflammatory agents, and potassium-sparing diuretics. Although patients with advanced renal disease may tolerate a somewhat higher potassium level than nonuremics, a hyperkalemic death from cardiac arrest is a well-established hazard.

Uremic pericarditis is probably caused by retained toxic by-products of protein catabolism. When complicated by uremic interference with platelet function, cardiac tamponade, marked by a severe drop in cardiac output and hence in blood pressure, can occur. Fever with an elevated white count may or may not be present. The outcome is fatal unless the hemorrhagic fluid is removed from the pericardial sac. Uremic pericarditis is a strong indication that dialysis is overdue or inadequate in application. Abnormal platelet function, marked by prolonged bleeding time, can also impair clotting at other sites of bleeding, such as stress ulcerations in the gastrointestinal tract. Uremia by itself does not precipitate bleeding but may exacerbate bleeding from other causes.

Prominent neurologic signs of end-stage renal disease include asterixis, myoclonus, peripheral motor and sensory neuropathy, and, terminally, seizures and coma; but presentation with depressed sensorium or coma early in the course of chronic renal failure or in an apparently well-dialyzed patient should cause one to look for coincidental causes of central nervous system dysfunction.

All of these late complications of uremia are prevented or ameliorated by prompt institution of efficient dialysis. If the physician waits too long to start dialysis, debilitating peripheral neuropathy may become irreversible, and malnutrition, pericardial tamponade, and hyperkalemia may be fatal. There is an increasing body of evidence to suggest that patients started on dialysis or treated with kidney transplantation prior to developing end-stage renal disease have significantly reduced morbidity with less interruption of lifestyle.

Routine Laboratory Abnormalities

The hematocrit may be abnormally low. Serum potassium may be normal or high. Serum urea nitrogen and creatinine levels are elevated. Serum albumin may be low and lymphocytopenia may develop. Hyperphosphatemia is a feature of end-stage renal disease that requires much attention while the patient is on dialysis. If left uncontrolled, it accentuates the severity of secondary hyperparathyroidism, renal osteodystrophy, and metastatic calcification.

PLANS

Differential Diagnosis

The differential diagnosis is the same as for chronic renal failure (see Chapter 16–12).

Diagnostic Options and Recommended Approach

Establishing a diagnosis of end-stage renal disease requires not only documentation of severity of renal failure but also exclusion of a reversible cause. A normal-sized kidney on sonogram should suggest a potentially correctable cause of azotemia. Reversible causes can be classified as prerenal, acute intrarenal, or postrenal. Malfunctioning kidneys are exquisitely sensitive to further impairment of renal perfusion that may result from iatrogenic causes, including inappropriate use of diuretics, angiotensin-converting enzyme inhibitors, and nonsteroidal analgesic drugs, or the superimposition of heart or liver failure. In the category of prerenal causes, the possibility of renal artery stenosis should also be considered in the proper setting, as its correction occasionally obviates the need for dialysis. The exclusion of a reversible renal parenchymal lesion first requires attention to the history of administration of nephrotoxic medications, drugs known to cause allergic interstitial nephritis, radiocontrast materials, or presence of a treatable systemic disease and may require a renal biopsy. Finally, it is important to recognize that patients with chronic parenchymal renal lesions are not immune to a superimposed obstructive lesion such as prostatic hypertrophy in elderly men or neurogenic bladder in patients with long-standing diabetes. Plans for exclusion of obstructive nephropathy are detailed in Chapter 16–14.

Therapeutic

Therapeutic Options

The majority of patients with end-stage renal disease have three therapeutic options: hemodialysis, peritoneal dialysis, and renal transplantation. The last, which is most often performed after an initial period on dialysis, is discussed in Chapter 16–26. A fourth choice, sometimes appropriate, is "death with dignity," mentioned below. The focus of this chapter is maintenance dialysis.

Recommended Approach

First comes the decision of when and what type of access to place: an arteriovenous fistula or graft for the hemodialysis patient or a peritoneal catheter for the peritoneal dialysis patient. An upper extremity fistula is the access of choice for the hemodialysis patient, providing the best opportunity for trouble-free dialysis. Patency of the veins in a prospective dialysis patient is so important for long-term survival that once it is apparent that a patient has progressive renal disease, every effort should be made to safeguard the veins in the nondominant arm by avoiding venipuncture in that limb. A fistula is created by surgically establishing a connection between an artery (usually radial) and a superficial vein with an anastomosis large enough to permit a blood flow of 400 to 500 mL/min, but not so large as to contribute to high-cardiac-output failure. About 8 weeks are necessary for the muscular wall of the vein to thicken, allowing repeated puncture with large-bore needles (15–16 gauge) without tearing. Synthetic grafts are required if the vessels are too small to permit an adequate anastomosis. However, they are more prone to infection, stenosis, and clotting.

Peritoneal catheters provide painless access for dialysis, but, in violating the skin barrier, leave the patient at risk of infection. They are made of a soft, flexible material such as Silastic to minimize trauma to skin and tissues on movement or when being manipulated. A single or double Dacron cuff is placed within the muscle and/or subcutaneously. If possible, hemodialysis grafts and peritoneal dialysis catheters should be placed at least 2 weeks before they are needed to allow time for healing of surrounding tissue, minimizing the risk of blood or fluid leakage and infection. For patients presenting with features of end-stage renal disease, dialysis may need to be started before an access can be readied for use. In such cases, access to the blood by puncturing the femoral vein or to the peritoneum by placing a temporary peritoneal catheter permits rapid and, at times, lifesaving treatment.

Dialysis is, in reality, a process of utmost simplicity, involving the diffusion of uremic toxins down a concentration gradient from the blood into a dialysis solution, with movement in the opposite direction of substances that are in low concentration in the blood of uremic patients such as bicarbonate. In addition, water and other small molecules can be convected by hydrostatic or osmotic pressure gradients across the dialysis membrane. Which molecules are removed depends on membrane permeability, greater in the case of the peritoneum and newer, highly permeable ("high-flux") dialyzers. Even today we remain unsure of which toxins need to be removed, although we do know, as demonstrated by the long survival of patients on hemodialysis (exceeding 30 years), that they can be adequately removed by this process. Major breakthroughs in providing hemodialysis have come from advances in hydraulics, electronics, and plastics. Fail-safe machines and more efficient, biocompatible dialyzers have led to short-time (3–4 hours), highly efficient dialysis treatments given three times per week. Hemodialysis may be performed in a hospital, free-standing center, or at home.

The majority of the almost 200,000 patients with end-stage renal disease in 1994 in the United States are currently being treated with maintenance hemodialysis. It is most often the initial therapy given to patients from which a possibly preferable alternative such as transplantation or peritoneal dialysis can be selected by the patient after he or she is stabilized. It may be inapplicable in situations where systemic blood pressure is so low as to preclude obtaining adequate blood flow for efficient treatment. There are also occasions when a patient is so close to inevitable death from other causes that dialysis treatment would be considered futile.

Adequacy of hemodialysis is most commonly measured by the efficiency of blood urea nitrogen removal. Two methods have been defined and standardized. These methods are based on urea as a marker for uremic toxicity of larger molecules. One method, referred to as urea kinetic modeling, is measured as a dimensionless Kt/V, where K stands for the clearance of blood urea nitrogen by the dialyzer, t for time of the dialysis treatment, and V for the volume of distribution of urea, which is equivalent to total body fluid space. The currently accepted value, based on evidence of good patient outcomes, is greater than 1.2. Another method, called the urea reduction ratio, is calculated from blood urea nitrogen levels drawn before and after the dialysis treatment. Reduction should be greater than 65% to correspond to a Kt/V above 1.2. Achieving these levels correlates positively with patient well-being and survival.

Complications specific to the hemodialysis treatment include excessive removal of fluid, causing cramps and hypotension; loss of blood in the dialyzer or related to venipuncture, exacerbating the anemia of renal disease; and long-term risks to bones, joints, and other organs attributable to suboptimal removal of larger molecules such as β_2-microglobulin or to the imperfect biocompatibility of dialyzers and blood tubing.

Availability of peritoneal dialysis allows flexibility in the management of patients with end-stage renal disease. The 1- to 2-m^2 peritoneal membrane, with its rich capillary bed, can be used as an endogenous dialysis membrane to remove uremic toxins and water from the body fluids of patients. The peritoneal membrane is less efficient than artificial hemodialysis membranes for removal of solutes; thus, peritoneal dialysis must be performed 24 hours per day. Simplified kinetic analysis predicts that approximately 10 L/day of volume exchange is required to maintain the average 70-kg, anephric patient at a blood urea nitrogen of approximately 80 mg/dL. In chronic ambulatory peritoneal dialysis (CAPD), the most common form of peritoneal treatment, this is achieved by instilling 1.5 to 3 L of a dialysis solution (dialysate) into the patient's abdomen via an indwelling catheter. The dialysate is drained by gravity after a dwell period that permits equilibration of solutes. Waste products such as urea and creatinine are removed via diffusion from the microcirculation of the peritoneum into the dialysate solution along concentration gradients. Bicarbonate precursors and other elements such as calcium can diffuse into the patient if their concentration is higher in the solution than in the patient's body. Larger molecules such as B_{12} are removed with increased efficiency compared with hemodialysis as a consequence of the prolonged dwell time and larger membrane pore size. Fluid removal or ultrafiltration is achieved using hyperosmolar solutions of glucose (1.5–4.25 g/dL) as an osmotic agent.

The basic treatment system consists of dialysate in polyvinyl chloride bags and a tubing transfer set to connect to the indwelling catheter. Continuous ambulatory peritoneal dialysis is a self-therapy performed by the patient at home. Three to five times a day, indwelling fluid is removed and discarded, after which fresh dialysate is infused.

Alternatives to continuous ambulatory peritoneal dialysis are forms of automated chronic peritoneal dialysis using cycling machines. Thus, in nightly peritoneal dialysis, patients are dialyzed at home during the night, further increasing their freedom of movement during the day and reducing the potentially contaminating disconnect procedures to two a day. Intermittent peritoneal dialysis in which patients receive a treatment of rapid, frequent short exchanges is used mostly for patients hospitalized with acute renal failure or patients with end-stage renal disease who are not suited for continuous ambulatory or cycled peritoneal dialysis and who cannot maintain satisfactory vascular access for hemodialysis. Advantages of peritoneal dialysis include more hemodynamic stability and better preservation of hematocrit, the latter being less important now that recombinant erythropoietin therapy is available. Contraindications to peritoneal dialysis include an "inadequate" peritoneal membrane due to adhesions from previous operations, systemic inflammatory diseases, previous peritoneal infections, and increased risk of peritonitis from the presence of a colostomy, ileostomy, or ileal conduit. Relative contraindications include chronic backache due to intervertebral disk disease, use of immunosuppressive drugs, and an uncooperative patient with severe psychological problems. Abdominal hernias should be repaired before commencing peritoneal dialysis and even then they may recur. Two liters of fluid in the abdomen of patients with severe chronic obstructive pulmonary disease may critically impair vital capacity. Peritonitis, the major complication of peritoneal dialysis, occurs with frequencies averaging from one to two episodes per patient per year, depending on the program and the techniques used. The major organisms are skin contaminants, coagulase-negative staphylococci (30–40%), and *Staphylococcus aureus* (20%). Infections with these bacteria can frequently be treated on an outpatient basis, with the patient adding appropriate antibiotics to the dialysate solution as instructed. More serious infections involving Gram-negative organisms and fungi require hospitalization for intensive treatment and frequently require removal and replacement of the peritoneal catheter. The presence of peritonitis with multiple Gram-negative organisms should alert one to the possibility of a ruptured viscus. Complications involving the peritoneal catheter, such as infection of the skin exit site or tunnel in which the catheter lies, are of considerable concern and, with persistence despite treatment, require removal of the catheter.

Other noninfectious complications of peritoneal dialysis include development of abdominal hernias and low back problems from weight and pressure of the fluid and hydrothorax and genital edema due to tracking of dialysate through the soft tissue planes.

Recently, attention has been paid to methods of determining the adequacy of peritoneal dialysis. Methods have been developed to derive an "index," Kt/V, analogous to that used in hemodialysis. Controversy exists as to its usefulness but a value of 1.9 is increasingly being accepted as a minimal standard for adequacy of peritoneal dialysis.

Technique survival for peritoneal dialysis is improving with time, now approximating 50% at 5 years. Patients move to hemodialysis or transplantation because of repeated episodes of peritonitis, catheter complications, or dysfunctional peritoneal membrane, or by choice.

The quality of extended life that follows both of these replacement therapies, hemodialysis and peritoneal dialysis, is punctuated by its own complications and consequences. Treatable complications including persistence of hypertension, renal bone disease, and anemia are also encompassed within the spectrum of dialysis patients with end-stage renal disease. Potentially preventable consequences include infection, access failure, and long-term results of bioincompatibility. Proper management of all patients on renal substitution therapy requires adequate dietary intake. An 80- to 100-g, high-quality protein, 2-g sodium, and 60-mEq potassium diet is usually satisfactory for the average 70-kg patient. Hemodialysis patients in particular must be urged to maintain sufficient caloric intake (about 30 kcal/kg body weight) to prevent muscle catabolism. Supplements of water-soluble vitamins replace losses in the dialysis fluid.

Hypertension in the dialysis population is most frequently due to fluid retention. Amounts of fluid too small to be detected by routine examination or felt by the patient may be sufficient to raise the blood pressure. Elimination of hypertension (reducing blood pressure to < 150/90 mm Hg) is possible in almost all dialysis patients but requires a great effort at persuasion, trust winning, and manipulation of antihypertensive agents to minimize side effects. The patient must come to believe that control of blood pressure is so vital to personal health that he or she will patiently undergo the cramps and relative hypotension frequently associated with convective fluid removal that precede blood pressure normalization in many patients.

Prevention of bone disease also requires patient cooperation. When properly used, calcium compounds as phosphate binders, oral and injectable forms of active vitamin D (1,25-dihydroxycholecalciferol), and chelators (deferroxamine), to remove aluminum taken previously as a phosphate binder, can at least slow the progression of renal osteodystrophy. Calcium compounds containing carbonate or acetate have replaced aluminum salts as phosphate binders because of the subsequently discovered complications of aluminum accumulation, such as osteomalacic bone disease. So-called "dialysis dementia," possibly due to aluminum accumulation in the brain, has been largely eliminated by removing aluminum from water used in dialysis by means of deionization and reverse osmosis. Deferroxamine, normally an iron chelator, is also effective in binding aluminum and, when given intravenously to the anephric dialysis patient, will remove chelated aluminum during the dialysis procedure. Vitamin D in its specifically active form has several functions including suppression of parathyroid hormone and facilitation of the absorption of ingested calcium.

A normochromic normocytic anemia is uniformly found in end-stage renal disease, although other forms of potentially treatable anemia, such as iron deficiency due to chronic blood loss, can also occur. Anemia can now be corrected in almost all dialysis patients by the use of recombinant human erythropoietin. Iron deficiency, not uncommon in dialysis patients, must first be corrected for the bone marrow to respond to the erythropoietin.

In long-term dialysis patients, carpal tunnel syndrome, arthropathy, and bone cysts have been identified in association with a type of amyloid containing β_2-microglobulin, found in increased amounts in the blood of dialysis patients.

Information derived from the National Cooperative Dialysis Study confirmed that the measuring of blood urea was a valid approach to monitoring dialysis, and established the "dialysis index" or Kt/V as the relevant parameter, with a desired minimum value of 1.0. Values of 0.8 or less were associated with substantial morbidity. Later studies have shown that increasing dialysis dose improves the survival of patients on hemodialysis, and today the acceptable minimum Kt/V is felt by most to be at least 1.2, and some have recommended higher values. An alternative approach to monitoring dialysis therapy is the measurement of the "urea reduction ratio," the difference between pre- and postdialysis blood urea nitrogen divided by the predialysis value, expressed as a percentage. Large outcome studies have shown that survival improves with increasing urea reduction ratio up to at least 65 to 70%, which roughly corresponds to a Kt/V of 1.25 to 1.4. As mentioned above, a similar approach is being developed for peritoneal dialysis, but outcome studies establishing the usefulness of urea modeling of this kind in that modality of treatment are not yet available.

With reliable access to blood or peritoneum, in the absence of other complicating medical conditions, dialysis has become so predictably successful that it is often requested when renal failure supervenes in patients who are otherwise in the terminal stages of life. Although kidney failure is not infrequent in the later stages of the course of failure of other organ systems, the hope that removing uremic toxins would benefit the dying patient may be a false one. Support of vital functions in the dying beyond reasonable hope of recovery is a complex controversy. At these times, a fourth option, death with dignity, should be cautiously but humanistically considered.

FOLLOW-UP

Neither dialysis nor transplantation is a cure for renal disease; therefore, lifelong medical follow-up is essential. Because of the limitations and burdens imposed by these treatments, patients often need help in attending to psychosocial needs. The new lifestyle of living with dialysis may alter relationships with spouse, family, and friends. Usual daily activities of school, work, homemaking, and retirement require adjustment.

Failure to thrive may be a problem in some dialysis patients who continue to look ill after starting on treatment or in whom the nonspecific signs and symptoms, seen before dialysis treatment, return, including weight loss and anorexia. Most often this is due to underdialysis as a result of a malfunctioning access (e.g., stenosis or recirculation), or a dialyzer that is inefficient, a time that is too short, or blood flow that is too low. Access inadequacy or ineffective dialysis may become unmasked when the patient has lost the last 3 to 6% of residual intrinsic renal function, leaving him or her dependent entirely on the dialysis for removal of uremic toxins. Loss of residual native kidney function is mostly a problem in larger patients on peritoneal dialysis for whom the replacement treatment is marginal at best.

In some patients, recurring or persistent signs and symptoms of failure to thrive signal the presence of another debilitating disease, such as cancer, chronic infection including cryptogenic tuberculosis, or failure of another vital organ such as the liver. Persistence of depression may also be an overlooked reason for failure to thrive and, if left untreated, can result in substantial morbidity and even mortality.

Home hemodialysis and peritoneal dialysis patients, like transplant patients, tend to overcome the dependency relationships of the in-center patients. Premorbid independent personalities, in fact, may be the reason for preferentially seeking these therapies. It is a laudable goal of patients with chronic medical problems to be involved in and take more control of their therapy. Adequate information and instruction are necessary along with a good basis for trust between patient and professional. Adequate dialysis, control of hypertension, and prevention of bone disease can be achieved only when the patient understands and willingly participates in the treatment plan. The peritoneal dialysis patient, in addition, must be alert for prevention and treatment of peritonitis.

DISCUSSION
Prevalence and Incidence

In 1991, the most recent year for which data are available from the U.S. Renal Data System, 188,745 patients with end-stage renal disease were receiving treatments for end-stage renal disease under Medicare. Of these, 138,277 were on dialysis (about 16% on peritoneal dialysis) and 50,468 had a functioning kidney transplant. An additional 10,686 individuals had dialysis paid for by other sources. Of the total patients, 65.8% were white, 30.8% were African-American, and the rest were Native Americans, Asians, or Pacific Islanders. Men constituted 54.4% and women 45.6%; 69.3% were younger than 65. The end-stage renal disease population continues to age and includes a larger number of patients with comorbid conditions. The number of new patients with end-stage renal disease started on treatment in 1991 was 50,640, with 33,233 deaths from the total population and 10,408 patients lost to follow-up

Related Basic Science

Patients with end-stage renal disease whose lives have been prolonged by dialysis have provided the opportunity to learn much about human physiology in the absence of kidneys. Two substances produced by the kidneys and deficient in renal failure are the active metabolite of vitamin D, 1,25-dihydroxycholecalciferol, and the stimulator of red blood cell proliferation, erythropoietin. A great amount has been learned about vitamin D and its metabolism and function, including its effect on bone, by the study of renal osteodystrophy in dialysis patients. Recombinant human erythropoietin was synthesized primarily to treat the anemia of chronic renal failure, which is due largely to a deficiency of this hormone.

Additionally important clinical knowledge has come from the study of end-stage renal disease complications and their treatments. Studies on heart and blood vessels in dialysis patients have been extensive. Heart disease and atherosclerosis are serious problems either as preexisting conditions or particularly if blood pressure is not brought under control. There are fewer data on the effects of absent kidney function and dialysis on the lungs and liver. Even the presumed nonfunctioning kidneys are not without activity. The development of an acquired form of multicystic disease is common with time, and a small percentage of these cysts undergo malignant transformation.

Natural History and Its Modification with Treatment

Although young and otherwise healthy patients can live 30 or more years on hemodialysis, most of those starting or remaining on dialysis are burdened with pre-end-stage renal disease, years of hypertension, diabetes, or other diseases and have a life expectancy less than that of others of their age and condition without renal failure. The adjusted 2-year survival of all end-stage renal disease patients in 1991 was 61.9%, with higher survival rates for younger patients without comorbid conditions. The mortality rate for all dialysis patients has improved over the past 3 years despite an aging, sicker population at risk.

As CAPD is a therapy of more recent vintage, survival with this treatment beyond 15 to 20 years is unknown, yet possible if one can tolerate the tedium of frequent (four times per day) exchanges of dialysis fluid and avoid recurrent peritoneal infections. As recently reported, three quarters of patients who start on CAPD are no longer receiving the therapy at the end of 3 years. Other outcomes include switching to hemodialysis, receiving a transplant, and death.

Prevention

Prevention of end-stage renal disease per se is the same as that for chronic renal failure (Chapter 16–12). Causes of morbidity and mortality in many dialysis patients are most amenable to prevention. Sixty percent of dialysis patients are said to die from cardiovascular causes. Uncontrolled hypertension, dietary indiscretion, and failure to reduce to dry weight can be responsible for many of the cardiovascular deaths, particularly if cardiovascular disease did not precede renal failure. Recurrent uremic features marked by malnutrition and pericarditis can only be due to access failure or underprescription leading to insufficient dialysis. Death from sepsis is often preventable if detected and treated early, and in frequently seen or carefully instructed patients, infection should be detectable quickly. In multiply exposed (at least 6 needle-sticks or 28 peritoneal fluid exchanges per week), infection-susceptible, dialysis patients, careful, aseptic technique is called for.

That leaves the severely noncompliant patient and those with known or subsequently discovered, untreatable mortal conditions to make up the greatest proportion of dialysis deaths.

Cost Containment

More than 150,000 patients receive some form of dialysis in the United States. The cost of maintaining this number of patients amounts to al-

most $6 billion per year, most of it paid by Medicare. To make dialysis and transplantation more cost effective, hindrances to employment must be overcome. These include excessive cost of employee insurance for those with preexisting medical conditions, time of day that the dialysis center is open (often daytime only), disincentives to give up disability payments, and unwillingness of employers to hire "the sick." Finally, dialysis and transplant patients who have no other disincentive to go back to work may have to overcome the reluctance to get back into life, a fear caused by having a chronic illness.

Despite 30+ years of successful dialysis treatments, per session costs (in actual, not inflated dollars) are little more today than at the start. This is because of efficiencies in manufacturing, less intensive staffing requirements, and reuse of expensive dialysis filters. Shorter treatment hours due to more efficient dialyzers have allowed greater utilization of facility hours and dialysis machines. After 3 years, successfully transplanted patients represent cost savings.

Prevention of morbidity in dialysis patients (if not of mortality) is also cost saving. Avoidance of rehospitalization with good first-time access surgery, efficient dialysis, and prevention of infection can save considerable amounts of money. Controlling blood pressure by bringing patients to dry weight can save in the cost of expensive antihypertensive medications and hospitalizations from cardiac complications. Educating patients in ways to care for themselves by preventing problems of noncompliance and detection of other treatable conditions may be the most important cost-saving measure of all.

REFERENCES

Drukker W. Haemodialysis: A historical review. In: Drukker W, Parsons FM, Maher JF, eds. Replacement of renal function by dialysis. The Hague: Martinus Nijhoff, 1978:3.

Hakim RM, Depner TA, Parker TF. Adequacy of hemodialysis. Am J Kidney Dis 1992;20:107.

Keshaviah PR. Adequacy of CAPD: A quantitative approach. Kidney Int 1992;42(suppl.38):s165.

Levinsky NG. The organization of medical care: Lessons from the Medicare End Stage Renal Disease Program. N Engl J Med 1993;329:1395.

U.S. Renal Data System. USRDS 1994 Annual Data Report. Bethesda, MD: National Institutes of Health, National Institute of Diabetes and Digestive and Kidney Diseases, 1994.

CHAPTER 16–14

Obstructive Nephropathy

Renee Garrick, M.D.

DEFINITION

Urinary tract obstruction occurs when the flow of urine is impeded by functional or structural changes intrinsic to or extrinsic to the kidney, ureter, urinary bladder, or urethra. The term *obstructive uropathy* refers to physical or functional changes of the urinary tract that impede the flow of urine. Hydronephrosis and calyectasis refer to dilation of the renal pelvis and calices. The term *obstructive nephropathy* refers to the structural and functional changes that occur within the kidney secondary to obstruction. Lower urinary tract obstruction occurs at, or distal to, the urinary bladder, whereas upper tract obstruction delineates pathology proximal to the ureterovesical junction. Obstruction can be intermittent, partial, or complete, and upper tract obstruction can be unilateral or bilateral.

ETIOLOGY

Both intrinsic and extrinsic abnormalities of the urinary tract can cause obstruction (Table 16–14–1). Intrinsic abnormalities can be intralumi-

nal or intramural. Intraluminal entities include stones, sloughed papilla, clots and fungus balls, and intrarenal obstruction due to acute deposition within the renal tubules. Intramural entities can be structural or functional. Examples of structural abnormalities include strictures, granulomas, tumors, and anatomic defects of the ureteropelvic and ureterovesical junctions. Functional abnormalities include ureterovesical reflux and abnormalities of bladder emptying, such as a neurogenic bladder and drug-induced urinary retention. Extrinsic obstruction can result from impingement by any of the structures with anatomic proximity to the urinary tract. These include retroperitoneal fibrosis and ureteral encasement by retroperitoneal tumors and adenopathy, both of which can cause painless nondilated obstructive uropathy.

Urinary calculi are more common in men and are the most common cause of upper tract obstruction. Disorders of the reproductive tract are, by far, the most common cause of external obstruction. Prostatic disease (hypertrophy and carcinoma) and cervical and uterine malignancies are responsible for the majority of cases. Pregnancy is also a common cause of ureteral obstruction, and the dilation typically resolves within 6 months of delivery.

TABLE 16–14–1. ETIOLOGY OF URINARY TRACT OBSTRUCTION

Intrinsic Obstruction	
Intrarenal	Acute deposition within tubular system
	Uric acid—tumor lysis syndrome
	Oxalate—enteric hyperoxaluria, ethylene glycol, fluoridated anesthetics
	Drugs—methotrexate, sulfonamides
Intraluminal	Stones—radiolucent or radiopaque
	Sloughed papilla—nonsteroidal antiinflammatory drugs, analgesics, sickle cell trait and disease, diabetes, pyelonephritis, amyloidosis
	Blood clots
	Fungus balls
Intramural	
Structural	Strictures—ureteral or urethral (congenital or acquired)
	Tumors and polyps—ureter, bladder, renal pelvis
	Anatomic defects—ureteropelvic or ureterovesical junction
	Urethral and ureteral valves, sphincter abnormalities
Functional	Ureterovesical reflux
	Adynamic ureters
	Urinary retention
	Drug induced—anticholinergics, alpha agonists, beta antagonists, morphine, codeine
	Neurogenic—upper motor neuron lesion (spastic bladder), lower motor neuron lesion (atonic bladder), sympathetic or parasympathetic disease
Extrinsic Obstruction	
Anatomic	
Abdominal	Ileum, left colon, duodenum
Pelvic	Prostatic hypertrophy and carcinoma
	Cysts and tumors of uterus, cervix, ovaries
	Endometriosis
	Pregnancy
	Urethral phimosis, meatal stenosis
Vascular	Aneurysms, anomalies, and thrombosis of mesenteric, iliac, pelvic, and abdominal aortic vasculature
Nondilated obstruction	
Retroperitoneal fibrosis	
	Idiopathic
	Drugs—ergotamine, hydralazine, beta blockers
	Radiation
Tumor encasement	Primary lymphoma, metastatic disease

CRITERIA FOR DIAGNOSIS
Suggestive

When accompanied by the appropriate constellation of subjective and objective clinical manifestations, a number of findings may suggest the diagnosis of urinary tract obstruction. The finding of a radiopaque calculus on a plain radiograph of the kidney, ureter, bladder (KUB) in a patient with flank pain, a dilated ureter by ultrasound, a palpable bladder, a change in urine volume (especially anuria), acute or chronic renal failure, and progressive renal insufficiency can all be clues to the diagnosis. If renal dysfunction is present in the setting of unilateral obstruction, the presence of only one functioning kidney should be considered.

Definitive

Abnormalities in serum creatinine, urea, and urinary volume are not necessary for the diagnosis of obstruction, as in the presence of two functioning kidneys, unilateral or partial obstruction may not alter these parameters. The presence of ureteral dilation alone is also not definitive, as prior obstruction may result in chronic dilation of the renal pelvis or ureter. Moreover, approximately 4% of patients present with *nondilated* obstructive uropathy. This can be seen with retroperitoneal fibrosis, intermittent or partial obstruction, or obstruction with coexisting volume depletion or severe renal insufficiency. Thus, definitive criteria for the diagnosis include functional evidence of impaired urine flow by nuclear scan or contrast urograms; the finding of ureteral or pelvic blockage by retrograde or antegrade pyelogram; the finding of

ureteral or pelvic dilation by ultrasound together with clinical symptoms and functional data; and the finding of improved renal function after the relief of obstruction by surgery or instrumentation.

CLINICAL MANIFESTATIONS
Subjective

Obstructive uropathy may be entirely asymptomatic, or it may present with azotemia or with life-threatening sepsis associated with an infection in an obstructed space. Chronic, slowly progressive dilation of the ureter is usually painless. The pain that accompanies acute obstruction results from the acute distention of the ureter, is often crescendo–decrescendo in quality, and typically radiates along the course of the ureter from the flank to the groin (typical renal colic). Patients with lower tract obstruction may have suprapubic pain. Fever may denote infection with obstruction, and gross hematuria may accompany either infection or stones. Patients may complain of nocturia (due to concentrating defects), fluctuating urine volumes, frequency, urgency, or other disorders of micturition. Symptoms of renal insufficiency including chronic fatigue, dyspepsia, and alterations in fluid balance may be present.

Relevant history includes a history of renal calculi, which can be both a cause and a consequence of obstruction, recurrent infections, pelvic diseases, and conditions or drugs associated with urinary retention, retroperitoneal masses, or retroperitoneal fibrosis.

Renal stone disease and vesicoureteric reflux are often familial, and reflux may be associated with other abnormalities such as bifid ureter, hypospadias, and ureteropelvic junction obstruction.

Objective
Physical Examination

Physical clues include a palpable bladder, prostatic hypertrophy, urethral, vaginal, cervical, or uterine pathology, and a palpable kidney. Signs of azotemia, including pallor, skin changes, volume expansion, or volume depletion (if salt wasting is present), are often present. Hypertension is frequent and may be due to volume expansion, which can occur in conjunction with obstruction, or it may be secondary to alterations in the renin–angiontensin axis.

Routine Laboratory Abnormalities

The urinalysis may be normal, show gross or microscopic hematuria, have rare white blood cells (in the absence of infection), contain abnormal struvite or cystine crystals, or reveal low-grade proteinuria (usually <2 g daily). Red blood cell casts are not present. Serum electrolytes may be normal or may reveal evidence of obstructive nephropathy such as hyperkalemia with a hyperchloremic renal tubular acidosis (type IV renal tubular acidosis). The glomerular filtration rate can be normal or may be markedly decreased; acute renal failure may be present. Urinary electrolytes do not provide a definitive diagnosis.

PLANS
Diagnostic
Differential Diagnosis

In patients with flank pain, abnormalities of neighboring anatomic structures and referred pain should be considered. Appendicitis, mesenteric adenitis, ectopic pregnancy and other abnormalities of the fallopian tube or ovaries, gallbladder disease, and abnormalities of the retroperitoneal vasculature (aneurysms) should be considered. In patients with renal insufficiency, other causes of acute and chronic renal disease including vascular, glomerular, and tubulointerstitial diseases should be considered.

Diagnostic Options

Routine blood and urinalysis studies alone are not sufficient for the definitive diagnosis of obstruction. Radiographic studies offer suggestive evidence. A plain radiograph of the kidney, ureter, and bladder (KUB) may show a radiopaque stone or enlarged kidneys. Ultrasound can detect obstruction with ureteral dilation with a sensitivity of approximately 90 to 95% and a specificity of approximately 75%. Ultrasound is less accurate when ureteral dilation is mild or absent. Thus, because ultrasound can fail to detect obstruction in up to 10% of cases, a negative ultrasound does not definitively exclude obstruction. As discussed above, a positive ultrasound should be linked with clinical or functional data for definitive diagnosis. Radiocontrast studies such as an intravenous pyelogram, antegrade and retrograde studies, and computed tomography with contrast offer functional data, as do nucleotide flow scans with DPTA or MAG-3. Intravenous pyelograms and nucleotide flow scans can be done prior to and after the administration of diuretics to determine if the ureter is patent, and to distinguish functional from anatomic obstructions. Occasionally a partial obstruction of uncertain functional significance is detected. In such cases, perfusion–pressure studies can be done by antegrade pyelography (Whitaker test) to evaluate if a gradient is present between the ureter and the bladder.

Recommended Approach

Following a complete history and physical examination, appropriate cultures, routine urinalysis, blood chemistries, and a complete blood count should be obtained. Depending on the clinical setting, transvaginal or transrectal ultrasounds, urodynamics, or cystoscopy may be required to determine the etiology of lower tract obstruction. For upper tract obstruction, a KUB should be obtained to evaluate renal size and to establish if radiopaque calculi are present. If renal function is normal, an intravenous peylogram should be performed next to establish if radiolucent stones are present and to ascertain the degree and location of obstruction. If renal function is abnormal, or if the patient is pregnant, an ultrasound should be done to determine if hydronephrosis is present. If the ultrasound is positive, and the clinical history suggests that the observed dilation is acute, then the diagnosis is secured. If, however, the history suggests that the obstruction is chronic, functional data can be obtained (in the nonpregnant patient) by radionucleotide scanning or by antegrade or retrograde pyelography. If obstruction is strongly suspected, and an intravenous pyelogram cannot be performed, and the ultrasound is negative or nondiagnostic, antegrade or retrograde pyelography should be performed.

Therapeutic

Therapeutic Options

Complete bilateral obstruction, unilateral obstruction of a solitary kidney, and complete or partial obstruction complicated by infection or renal insufficiency require urgent therapy. In these settings, acute therapy is directed at relieving obstruction, preserving renal function, normalizing blood pressure, correcting imbalances in fluids and electrolytes, treating infection, and providing relief of pain. In unilateral or partial obstruction where renal function is stable, such as is typical of stone disease, therapy is directed at relieving pain and monitoring for changes in renal function or infection. Appropriate definitive medical and surgical therapy is dictated by the etiology of the obstruction and whether it is anatomic or functional.

Recommended Approach

Lower Tract Obstruction. Urinary bladder catheterization is the acute therapy of lower tract obstruction. Chronic urinary retention secondary to prostatic disease may respond to therapy with α_1 blockers (terazosin, doxazosin) or the 5α-reductase inhibitor finasteride. Prostatic disease unresponsive to drug therapy and other causes of anatomic lower tract obstruction usually require surgery. Neurogenic bladder dysfunction may be addressed medically (intermittent catheterization, alpha blockers, cholinergic agents) or by surgical diversionary procedures, depending on the clinical setting.

Upper Tract Obstruction. When urgent therapy is required an antegrade or retrograde drainage procedure is appropriate. These procedures can be combined with contrast studies and, as such, can be simultaneously diagnostic and therapeutic. Hydration and intravenous pyelography occasionally induce passage of calculi or clots. In patients with chronic partial obstruction, it is sometimes difficult to assess if surgical intervention is needed to preserve renal function. The Whitaker test, diuresis

renography, and serial determinations of renal function may help to determine the best therapeutic approach. Occasionally, serial evaluation of renal function, before and after the temporary relief of obstruction by nephrostomy or stent placement, is needed before a definitive therapeutic plan can be made. In cases of obstruction from retroperitoneal fibrosis, any offending drugs should be discontinued and steroid therapy and/or surgical repair should be undertaken.

FOLLOW-UP

Acute follow-up after the relief of obstruction should focus on stabilizing extracellular volume and electrolyte status, monitoring renal function, and treating any underlying infectious complications. With a partial obstruction, follow-up should focus on serial determinations of renal function and monitoring for infection. Long-term follow-up is dictated largely by the site and exact etiology of the obstruction.

A postobstructive diuresis typically occurs following the relief of bilateral obstruction or unilateral obstruction of a solitary kidney. This diuresis may be mediated by underlying extracellular volume expansion induced by fluid administration in the setting of renal insufficiency, the osmotic effects of retained urea, and/or the effects of increased levels of atrial natriuretic peptide. Urinary and serum electrolytes and body weight must be monitored daily. The urinary electrolyte composition can be used as a guide for the electrolyte composition of replacement fluids, which should be formulated to normalize potassium, calcium, magnesium, phosphate, and sodium levels. Extracellular volume expansion is often present prior to the relief of obstruction. It is necessary to distinguish a sustained postobstructive diuresis from the physiologic correction of volume expansion and from overly vigorous fluid administration. This can be evaluated by reducing the replacement volume for 8 to 10 hours while monitoring blood pressure, urinary losses, and body weight.

DISCUSSION

Prevalence and Incidence

Obstruction is the most common urologic disease leading to end-stage renal failure. Between 1988 and 1991, obstruction accounted for 2% of new cases of end-stage renal disease. It is more common in men, largely due to prostatic disease and the higher rate of urinary calculi in men. Among hospital discharges in patients with kidney and urologic disorders, obstruction is typically the fourth most common diagnosis in men and the sixth most common in women.

Related Basic Science

A complete bilateral obstruction can permanently impair renal function within days, if left untreated, whereas an intermittent or chronic partial obstruction may have minimal untoward effects on renal function. Regardless of the etiology, the effects on renal function are dictated by the changes that occur in the renal parenchyma. In normal circumstances, ureteral peristalsis propels a bolus of urine from the renal pelvis to the bladder. With obstruction, the hydrostatic pressure within the ureter is increased and is transmitted in a retrograde fashion to the renal pelvis and tubule system. Marked dilation of the renal tubules can occur with subsequent medullary and cortical atrophy and interstitial inflammation and fibrosis. The interstitial changes are initially the most pronounced, but ultimately glomerular sclerosis occurs. The intratubular pressures are initially increased but return toward normal within 24 hours, even when bilateral obstruction persists. During the same time interval, renal blood flow, which initially is maintained or increased due to the effects of vasodilatory prostaglandins, begins to fall, due to the effects of the vasoconstrictors, angiotensin II, and thromboxane A_2. This reduction in renal blood flow, together with the altered hydrostatic pressure, causes a fall in the glomerular filtration rate. Drugs that further alter the balance between vasoconstrictor and vasodilatory hormones (nonsteroidal antiinflammatory drugs, salicylates) can lead to a further fall in glomerular filtration rate.

Thus, the mechanisms that contribute to the loss of renal function in obstruction inlude the physical disruption of medullary architecture, pressure atrophy, and alterations in renal blood flow, each of which contributes to cellular ischemia and necrosis.

The changes of obstructive nephropathy also affect other elements of renal function. Hyperkalemia may occur secondary to aldosterone resistance and this is often accompanied by a hyperchloremic non-anion gap acidosis (type IV renal tubular acidosis). A defect in concentrating ability occurs early, and is most likely secondary to altered tubular responsiveness to vasopressin and a distorted medullary architecture. The osmotic effects of retained urea may also contribute to the concentrating defect. Polycythemia may occasionally occur, due to increased erythropoietin synthesis. Patients with obstruction and urinary stasis are at increased risk for infection and urinary stones, including struvite stones.

Natural History and Its Modification with Treatment

Left untreated, complete obstruction of the upper or lower tract results in renal failure. Lesser degrees of obstruction have a less predictable effect on renal function. Low-grade, intermittent obstruction may have minimal effects or may evolve into a serious, even life-threatening condition, if infection intervenes. Appropriate diagnosis may reveal an underlying condition amenable to treatment, and appropriate therapy can preserve renal function and avoid the costs and complications of dialysis therapy.

Prevention

The diagnosis and correction of fetal urinary obstruction in utero constitute the most striking example of prevention of obstructive nephropathy. Intrarenal obstruction may be prevented by prophylactic therapy of tumor lysis syndrome, by maintaining adequate hydration when administering agents known to cause crystal deposition, and by avoiding the injudicious use of drugs associated with papillary necrosis. Upper tract obstruction may be prevented by the aggressive medical management of urinary calculi (see Chapter 16–16), the judicious use of drugs associated with retroperitoneal fibrosis, and by guarding against ureteral injury during surgical procedures.

Lower tract obstruction may be prevented by monitoring for prostate, cervical, and uterine disease, and other conditions associated with bladder outlet obstruction, and by the judicious use of drugs associated with urinary retention. Surgical correction of anatomic defects of the uteropelvic and ureterovesical junctions may also prevent recurrent obstruction.

Cost Containment

A carefully conceived evaluation and appropriate prevention are important cost containment means. Intravenous pyelograms, nucleotide scans, and ultrasounds are more readily available, and afford the same diagnostic information as do more costly studies such as computed tomography and magnetic resonance imaging. Prostatic disease must be evaluated, and drug therapy with costly agents such as finasteride must be carefully individualized. An appropriate differential diagnosis and prompt therapy are necessary to avoid permanent renal damage and the costs associated with disability and dialysis.

REFERENCES

Klahr S. Obstructive nephropathy: Pathophysiology and management. In: Schrier R, editor-in-chief. Renal and electrolyte disorders. 4th ed. Boston: Little, Brown, 1992:12.

Novick A. Urology for nephrologists. Semin Nephrol 1994;14:509.

Schlueter W, Batlle D. Chronic obstructive nephropathy. Semin Nephrol 1988;8:17.

Turka L, Rose B. Clinical aspects of urinary obstruction. In: Brenner B, Lazarus M, eds. Acute renal failure. 2nd ed. New York: Churchill Livingstone, 1988:16.

Yager W. Urinary tract obstruction. In: Brenner B, Rector F, eds. The kidney. 4th ed. Philadelphia: Saunders, 1991:36.

CHAPTER 16–15

Nephrocalcinosis

Edmund Bourke, M.D.

DEFINITION

Nephrocalcinosis is the deposition of calcium salts in the renal parenchyma. It is to be distinguished from nephrolithiasis (urolithiasis), in which the calcareous deposits are in the calyces or pelvis. In clinical practice, the term nephrocalcinosis is reserved for when the condition is detectable radiologically.

ETIOLOGY

Nephrocalcinosis is not a disease; it is a lesion that can result from a variety of diseases. The three most common settings in which it is encountered are hypercalcemic states such as hyperparathyroidism, distal (type 1) renal tubular acidosis, and structural anomalies, for example, medullary sponge kidney. A more detailed list is given in Table 16–15–1.

CRITERIA FOR DIAGNOSIS
Suggestive

In the presence of comorbid conditions that can result in nephrocalcinosis, a high index of suspicion is essential. Nephrocalcinosis can be a consequence of hypercalcemia and a cause or consequence of renal tubular acidosis (type 1). Investigation of these conditions requires that nephrocalcinosis be looked for. Nephrocalcinosis may coexist with urolithiasis, and discovery of the latter may lead to diagnosis of the former. Urinary infection and minor urinalysis abnormalities may be clues that lead to its detection. Occasionally, it is discovered in the course of workup of chronic renal failure.

Definitive

The definitive diagnosis is made by a plain radiograph of the abdomen.

CLINICAL MANIFESTATIONS
Subjective

Uncomplicated nephrocalcinosis is asymptomatic and may be discovered coincidentally when the abdomen or lumbar spine is x-rayed for unrelated reasons.

Nephrocalcinosis has no unique manifestations. Nocturia is frequently present due to a defect in the ability to concentrate the urine. If urolithiasis coexists, colic or hematuria may occur, as can symptoms of superimposed acute pyelonephritis.

A history of present or past exposure to potential toxic or iatrogenic causes is important. It should include a search for analgesic abuse or sickle cell disease, both of which may cause papillary necrosis and calcification. Therapy for glaucoma with the carbonic anhydrase inhibitor acetazolamide (Diamox) has been associated with nephrocalcinosis, as has hypervitaminosis D and prolonged steroid therapy. Hyperoxaluria-inducing causes include ethylene glycol poisoning, methoxyflurane anesthesia, inflammatory small bowel disease, and previous jejunoileal

TABLE 16–15–1. CAUSES OF NEPHROCALCINOSIS

Renal				Extrarenal			
Structural		Functional		Abnormal Calcium Homeostasis		Abnormal Oxalate Homeostasis	
Congenital or Hereditary	Acquired	Congenital or Hereditary	Acquired	Congenital or Hereditary	Acquired	Congenital or Hereditary	Acquired
Medullary sponge kidney	Cortical necrosis	Primary distal renal tubular acidosis	Secondary distal renal tubular acidosis:	Idiopathic hyper-calcemia of infancy	Hypercalcemic states, e.g., primary hyper-parathyroid-ism, sarcoido-sis, hyper-vitaminosis D	Primary hyperoxaluria	Enteric hyperoxaluria
Horseshoe kidney	Papillary necrosis		Immunologic, e.g., Sjögren's syndrome	Idiopathic hyper-calciuria			Ethylene glycol poisoning
	Renal tuberculosis		Toxic, e.g., amphotericin B				Methoxyflurane anesthesia
	Renal infarction		Acetazolamide				Pyridoxalate
	Autonephrec-tomy				Progressive bone mobilization, e.g., glucocor-ticoid excess		
	Transplant rejection						
	Calcification in cyst or tumor						

bypass for morbid obesity. Symptoms attributable to the underlying disease may predominate.

Objective

Physical Examination

Radiographic detection is the objective evidence of nephrocalcinosis. A plain radiograph of the abdomen with a kilovoltage less than 70 should be used. Oblique views or tomography may be needed to localize the calcification. Ultrasonography may fail to detect early nephrocalcinosis in adults, although it is more reliable in infants, in whom the relatively greater gaseous shadowing may obscure it on plain film. Computed tomography is a very sensitive detector of all types of nephrocalcinosis.

Routine Laboratory Abnormalities

The urinalysis may be entirely normal but minor abnormalities including mild proteinuria, a few red or white cells, and sometimes bacteri-uria may be seen. Although uncommon, prominent crystalluria is an important finding on microscopy. The detection of hypercalcemia or a low bicarbonate/high chloride value on routine blood chemistry screen-ing indicates disordered calcium metabolism or renal tubular acidosis as the likely underlying cause.

PLANS
Diagnostic

Differential Diagnosis

Nephrocalcinosis can have a renal cause or an extrarenal cause. Renal causes are due to either structural anomalies, for example, medullary sponge kidney, or functional defects, for example, congenital or ac-quired renal tubular acidosis. Extrarenal causes are attributable to either disorders of calcium metabolism or disorders of oxalate metabolism. A careful search for underlying causes should be made, as summarized in Table 16–15–1. For more detailed discussions of renal tubular acidosis, see Chapter 16–17, and of hypercalcemic states, see Chapter 9–36.

Diagnostic Options

Although formally emphasized, classifications of nephrocalcinosis as being metastatic or dystrophic or as being cortical, medullary, or papil-lary are less reliable than previously thought. Careful study of the plain radiograph of the kidney and an intravenous pyelogram nonetheless provide valuable information in defining the type of nephrocalcinosis and documenting its extent. If the clinical manifestations have not re-vealed an underlying explanation, for example, renal tubular acidosis, hypercalcemia, or analgesic abuse, a metabolic workup for hypercalci-uria or hyperoxaluria is required.

Recommended Approach

Review of the plain radiograph of the kidney and intravenous pyelo-gram is the first step. In cortical necrosis, the calcification is confined to the renal cortex and the finding of a double-line, or "tramway," ap-pearance is pathognomonic. Other types of dystrophic calcification may be strongly suggested by the initial radiologic evaluation, includ-ing calcification in a tumor or cyst, tuberculous calcification, AIDS-associated *Mycobacterium avium–intracellulare* infection involving the kidney, or a calcified infarct, lesions that are usually unilateral and may cause characteristic pyelographic deformities. The calcifications of papillary necrosis and medullary sponge kidneys are formed in the pap-illary region. Pyelographic appearances of papillary necrosis are fre-quently diagnostic. In medullary sponge kidneys, the renal outlines may be enlarged or asymmetric, and the pyelographic dye is character-istically seen in the dilated papillary collecting ducts or adjoining cystic outpouchings, wherein the microliths are actually formed and clustered. Moreover, the dye entering the dilated papillary lesions may obscure the calcifications. This is in contrast to renal tubular acidosis, in which the calcifications generally spread well into the cortex and medulla and are not entirely obscured by the contrast material. On many occasions, however, a definitive diagnosis does not emerge from the radiographic appearance of the nephrocalcinosis. Its extent, however, requires docu-mentation as a basis from which to judge subsequent progress, includ-ing the use of potential therapeutic intervention.

An accurate 24-hour urine collection for calcium is axiomatic. An excretion in excess of 4 mg/kg, or roughly 300 mg daily, indicates hy-percalciuria. It is present in the majority of patients with nephrocalci-nosis. Idiopathic hypercalciuria, an inherited disorder usually mani-fested by urolithiasis, occasionally results in nephrocalcinosis.

If these investigations have not indicated the cause, 24-hour urinary oxalate excretion should be measured.

The creatinine clearance should be determined to evaluate the extent of renal functional impairment at presentation and as a guideline for evaluating progress. Urine culture, including, where appropriate, cul-tures for *Mycobacterium* tuberculosis, is indicated.

Therapeutic

When possible, therapy should be directed toward the underlying cause (see Table 16–15–1). Avoidance of dehydration is advisable in condi-tions such as medullary sponge kidney to reduce the risk of stone for-mation. High doses of pyridoxine (Beesix) have dramatically reduced oxalate excretion in some cases of primary hyperoxaluria. Successful "cure" of primary hyperoxaluria and oxalosis has been reported follow-ing liver transplantation. In enteric hyperoxaluria, reduction of dietary oxalate, oral calcium supplements, and use of medium-chain triglyc-erides may reduce oxalate excretion to normal. Therapy for renal tubu-lar acidosis is discussed in Chapter 16–17. A cautionary note regarding alkali therapy in nephrocalcinosis is presented under Related Basic Science.

FOLLOW-UP

In some instances, removal of the causative agents results in substantial regression or even resolution of nephrocalcinosis. On other occasions, once established, it tends to persist or progress and remain a potential hazard for pyelonephritis, passage of stones, or a gradual decline in renal function. The likelihood of such progression cannot be predicted at the outset, requiring sequential renal functional measurements such as creatinine clearances at follow-up. Depending on renal functional status and the nature of the higher-order diagnosis, the patient should be followed up at intervals ranging from 3 months to annually to monitor renal function, evaluate the role of therapeutic maneuvers, and review periodic plain radiographs of the kidneys to assess alterations in the extent of nephrocalcinosis. Should the patient develop symptoms of urinary infection or passage of a kidney stone, he or she should inform the physician.

DISCUSSION

Prevalence

Radiologic detection is required to make the clinical diagnosis and is noted in about 0.1% of radiographs of the kidney. Histologic nephrocalcinosis is noted in about 10% of autopsies. The distinction is essentially arbitrary, as the same conditions can cause either the microscopic or the macroscopic picture.

Related Basic Science

Genetics

Medullary sponge kidney, the predominant structural renal abnormality characterized by nephrocalcinosis, is a congenital lesion although a familial incidence is occasionally encountered. Renal tubular acidosis can be genetically transmitted (see Chapter 16–17).

Pathophysiology

The predominant functional renal lesion associated with nephrocalcinosis is distal (type 1) renal tubular acidosis. Nephrocalcinosis does not occur in type 4 and is rare in type 2 (proximal) renal tubular acidosis except when associated with acetazolamide. This drug-induced renal tubular acidosis, unlike other forms of proximal renal tubular acidosis but similar to the distal variety, is associated with hypocitraturia, and a role for urinary citrate has been proposed in the inhibition of calcium crystal formation in urine. The major extrarenal cause of nephrocalcinosis is the presentation of excess quantities of calcium to the kidney. This may result from hypercalcemia, from situations in which calcium is being mobilized from the skeleton and leaked into the urine without concomitant hypercalcemia, and from idiopathic hypercalciuria. Less commonly, excessive absorption or production of oxalate with hyperoxaluria may result in nephrocalcinosis. Although any of the hypercalcemic states may theoretically produce nephrocalcinosis, one common cause of hypercalcemia in which this complication is strikingly rare is that associated with malignancy. The relatively short natural history is the presumed explanation. A hypercalcemic cause of nephrocalcinosis that has greatly declined over the past decade is the milk-alkali syndrome.

Many reviews include chronic glomerulonephritis and chronic pyelonephritis as causes of nephrocalcinosis. The evidence for such an etiology for radiologically apparent nephrocalcinosis, however, is not convincing. In patients with advanced renal failure from any cause, however, in whom the accompanying hyperphosphatemia is poorly controlled or even accentuated by an additional phosphate load, with calcium × phosphorus products consistently above 70, soft tissue calcification is known to result, including metastatic calcification of the kidney. This type of calcification is usually prominent in the blood vessels and is not confined to the kidney. It is nonetheless of current interest, as continued microscopic precipitation of calcium salts in the kidneys of chronic renal failure patients with resultant histologic nephrocalcinosis

may be a factor contributing to the rate of progressive decline in renal function seen in such patients.

Although distal (type 1) renal tubular acidosis is discussed in detail elsewhere, one point worth stressing here is the potential chicken and egg dilemma that may arise when it is associated with nephrocalcinosis. Nephrocalcinosis per se of diverse etiologies can impair tubular acidification mechanisms with resultant acquired distal renal tubular acidosis. It is sometimes seen in medullary sponge kidney. It is a likely explanation in some cases of hyperparathyroid-induced nephrocalcinosis that fail to regress following successful parathyroidectomy. A particularly difficult diagnostic situation in this regard is distinguishing nephrocalcinosis due to primary renal tubular acidosis with its associated hypercalciuria from renal tubular acidosis secondary to the nephrocalcinosis that occasionally complicates idiopathic hypercalciuria. The renal stones are predominantly calcium phosphate in the former and calcium oxalate in the latter. Hypokalemia favors the former. Such distinctions are therapeutically relevant. Although correction of primary distal renal tubular acidosis with alkali will likely diminish nephrocalcinosis, the role of such therapy in secondary distal renal tubular acidosis is far from clear. It is possible that alkalinization of the urine could enhance calcium precipitation in these circumstances.

Natural History and Its Modification with Treatment

The natural history depends on the cause, and the capacity to influence the natural history is related in part to the possibility of finding a reversible cause. Although medullary sponge kidney may present with dramatic radiologic appearances, progression to renal failure is particularly uncommon in this condition. There is ample experience to offer hope of substantial regression of nephrocalcinosis or even resolution following parathyroidectomy in primary hyperparathyroidism. Similar improvements have been reported over a period of months to years in treated primary distal renal tubular acidosis. The nephrocalcinosis of primary hyperoxaluria, once established, generally progresses to end-stage renal disease, although enteric hyperoxaluria-induced nephrocalcinosis may stop or regress following correction of its cause. Otherwise, untreatable diffuse nephrocalcinosis in general pursues a more indolent course, although gradual loss of renal function is the rule.

Prevention

In children, one of the most common causes of nephrocalcinosis is hereditary or primary sporadic distal renal tubular acidosis. The development of nephrocalcinosis can be entirely prevented if complete correction of acidosis is achieved and maintained. Similar treatment in adults with this condition, where some nephrocalcinosis is usually already apparent, will prevent further progression. Early recognition of other predisposing factors that will prevent the development of nephrocalcinosis has been aided by the routine availability of SMA screening procedures with detection of asymptomatic hypercalcemia.

Because of its generally asymptomatic nature and the fact that causative factors are not always readily recognized at an early stage, nephrocalcinosis may not be easily preventable.

Cost Containment

A carefully taken radiograph of the kidneys usually makes the diagnosis, and an intravenous pyelogram at the outset is generally needed to help define the etiology. There is little additional value to be gained from ultrasonography, computed tomography scan of the kidney, or retrograde pyelography. Magnetic resonance imaging does not detect nephrocalcinosis. The entire workup can be done on an outpatient basis. There is no need for routine follow-up intravenous pyelography.

REFERENCES

Boswell WD Jr. Radiology of the kidney. In: Massry SG, Glassrock RJ, eds. Textbook of nephrology. 3rd ed. Baltimore: Williams & Wilkins, 1995:1967.

Coe FL, Favus MJ. Nephrolithiasis. In: Brenner BM, Rector FC Jr, eds. The kidney. 4th ed. Philadelphia: Saunders, 1991:1728.

Goldman SM, Hartman DS. Medullary sponge kidney. In: Pollack HM, ed. Clinical urography. Philadelphia: Saunders, 1990:1167.

Santos F, Kaiser G, Chan JCM. Renal tubular acidosis. In: Suki WN, Massry

SG, eds. Therapy of renal disease and related disorders. Boston: Kluwer Academic, 1991:207.

Wrong O. Nephrocalcinosis. In: Cameron C, Davison AM, Grunfeld JP, et al.,

eds. Oxford textbook of clinical nephrology. Oxford: Oxford University Press, 1992:1882.

CHAPTER 16–16

Kidney Stones • A Medical Viewpoint

Jaime Uribarri, M.D., and Charles Y.C. Pak, M.D.

DEFINITION

Kidney stones, nephrolithiasis or urolithiasis, are concretions of different mineral salts which are formed within the urinary tract.

ETIOLOGY

Kidney stones may result from a variety of causes depending on the chemical composition and underlying physiologic–metabolic derangements of afflicted patients (Table 16–16–1).

CRITERIA FOR DIAGNOSIS

Suggestive

Sometimes, stones are never demonstrated but their presumptive diagnosis is made on the basis of the characteristic presentation of a patient with renal colic.

Definitive

Kidney stones are diagnosed by radiologic visualization or when they are passed in the urine or are surgically removed.

CLINICAL MANIFESTATIONS

Subjective

Kidney stones may produce hematuria or classic symptoms of renal colic, or they may be completely asymptomatic and be discovered incidentally during an abdominal x-ray examination.

Kidney colic occurs when a kidney stone enters the ureter. This causes sudden intense pain that is located in the costovertebral area and the left or right lower quadrant. The pain may radiate to the testicle or labial area.

Objective

Physical Examination

If the patient presents with renal colic, the physical examination may reveal some tenderness in the costovertebral area. If the stone is in the lower ureter, there may be some tenderness in the left or right lower quadrant of the abdomen. Frequently, stones may not produce any symptoms and may be discovered incidentally when an abdominal x-ray or sonogram is performed for some other reason.

Routine Laboratory Abnormalities

Examination of the urine reveals red cells. Routine laboratory tests may also give some clues for diseases that may be associated with kidney stone formation, for example, hypercalcemia in primary hyperparathyroidism and low serum bicarbonate in renal tubular acidosis.

PLANS

Diagnostic

Differential Diagnosis

The differential diagnosis of the patient presenting with clinical manifestations of kidney stones is discussed in Chapter 18–35.

The pain due to renal colic must be differentiated from the pain due to appendicitis, an abdominal aneurysm, and gallbladder disease (see chapters related to these subjects).

Diagnostic Options

The diagnostic options for the patient presenting with a kidney stone complication are discussed in Chapter 18–35. In this chapter we assume that the diagnosis of a kidney stone has already been made and our emphasis is on identifying underlying abnormalities that may explain kidney stone formation. From this perspective, the diagnostic options include stone analysis, whenever feasible, and a battery of blood and urinary tests to identify the common abnormalities associated with kidney stone formation.

Recommended Approach

Everyone who has formed at least one kidney stone should have a complete set of serum chemistries and a 24-hour urine collection obtained for measurement of calcium, uric acid, oxalate, and citrate. The stone, if recovered, should be analyzed, as knowledge of its composition allows the physician to focus attention on a more restricted number of underlying abnormalities as follows.

Cystine Stones. The presence of cystine stones indicates only one possible diagnosis: cystinuria. For the diagnosis of cystinuria a nonexpensive, qualitative urine screening test with nitroprusside can be used and, if positive, amino acid analysis by urine chromatography should follow.

Uric Acid Stones. Patients who form uric acid stones have either excessive urinary excretion of uric acid (hyperuricosuria) or a sustained low urine pH (<5.5). For diagnostic purposes, the patient requires a 24-hour

TABLE 16–16–1. CAUSES AND MECHANISMS OF KIDNEY STONES

Abnormality	Causes
Calcium stones	
Hypercalciuria	
Secondary	Primary hyperparathyroidism, sarcoidosis, etc.
Primary	Idiopathic
Absorptive	
Renal	
Resorptive	
Hyperuricosuria	Primary overproduction
	Purine gluttony
Hyperoxaluria	Dietary (high oxalate or oxalate precursor intake)
	Enteric hyperoxaluria
	Primary overproduction
Hypocitraturia	Renal tubular acidosis
	Chronic diarrhea
	Hypokalemia
	High-animal-protein diet, etc.
Infection stones	Urinary tract infection with urea-splitting organisms
Uric acid stones	
Low urine pH	
Hyperuricosuria	
Cystine stones	Cystinuria

urine collection for measurement of uric acid and serial measurements of urine pH.

Struvite Stones. These stones occur exclusively in urine infected with urea-splitting organisms. Pyuria, positive urine cultures for urea-splitting organisms such as *Proteus,* and high urine pH (<7.5) are the rule in these patients.

Calcium Stones. Most calcium-containing stones are made up predominantly of calcium oxalate. Stones composed predominantly of calcium phosphate tend to form in alkaline urine (or high normal pH) and, therefore, occur most frequently in urinary tract infection, distal renal tubular acidosis, and occasionally primary hyperparathyroidism.

Patients with recurrent calcium oxalate stones have one or a combination of the following abnormalities: hypercalciuria, hyperuricosuria, hyperoxaluria, and hypocitraturia. The diagnosis of each of these conditions requires the measurement of the specific compound in a 24-hour urine collection.

Therapeutic

Therapeutic Options

The therapeutic plan for the patient presenting acutely with a kidney stone complication is discussed in Chapter 18–35. Again, our emphasis in this chapter is on prevention of new stone formation or arresting the growth of already formed stones. Once the basic problem in the specific patient is identified, simple dietary manipulations and/or minimal drug therapy can afford long-term protection from recurrent stone formation in the majority of patients.

Recommended Approach

The recommended approach changes depending on the problem identified in the specific patient as follows.

Cystine Stones. Nonspecific therapy with increased water intake, urine alkalinization, and low-methionine diet is helpful, especially in patients with moderate cystinuria. Reduction of urinary cystine excretion may be obtained with penicillamine, which complexes cysteine, the monomeric form of cystine. Penicillamine controls stone formation effectively but its usefulness is limited by serious side effects, including proteinuria, dermatitis, and pancytopenia. α-Mercaptopropionylglycine (Thiola) shares with penicillamine similar biochemical and clinical activities, but its toxicity profile makes it preferable to penicillamine in the treatment of cystinuria.

Uric Acid Stones. Therapy in this group of patients is very effective. Oral potassium citrate seems to be particularly useful and should be given in doses sufficient to keep the urine pH around 6.5 at all times, usually 30 to 60 mEq of potassium citrate per day in divided doses. If hyperuricosuria is present, dietary purine restriction or allopurinol treatment is in order.

Struvite Stones. Treatment should emphasize control of infection with an antibiotic selected on the basis of urine cultures. Unfortunately, when a struvite stone is present, it is difficult to eradicate infection completely because the stone may harbor the organisms within its interstices. Even if sterilization of the urine can be achieved, reinfection could occur from organisms harbored by the stone; thus, surgical removal of the struvite stone is generally recommended. Good results in arresting growth or even causing dissolution of these stones have been reported with the use of urease inhibitors such as acetohydroxamic acid. Unfortunately, this drug may cause serious side effects: hemolytic anemia, thrombophlebitis, and nonspecific neurologic symptoms (disorientation, tremulousness, and headache).

Calcium Stones. The subdivision of patients with idiopathic *hypercalciuria* into those with absorptive and those with renal problems should allow for more specific therapy: cellulose phosphate (intestinal calcium binder) for those with intestinal hypercalciuria without bone disease and thiazide diuretics for those with renal leak. In practical terms, however, treatment with thiazides effectively reduces the rate of stone formation in most hypercalciuric patients. An alternative to thiazide therapy is oral phosphate supplements, which act by decreasing the intestinal absorption of calcium and by increasing the urinary excretion

of pyrophosphate and citrate (inhibitors of urinary crystallization of stone-forming calcium salts). Reduction of oral calcium intake is of partial value in patients with idiopathic hypercalciuria; it should always be accompanied by a parallel reduction in oxalate intake and should not be undertaken in the setting of bone loss. A practical approach gaining acceptance is the use of thiazides with potassium citrate in all patients with normocalcemic hypercalciuria.

Hyperuricosuria is treated by avoiding dietary purine excess, generally accomplished by a reduction in meat ingestion. If protein restriction reduces uric acid excretion to less than 600 mg daily, excessive purine intake is confirmed as the cause of hyperuricosuria and the patient is instructed to adhere to the restricted diet. Hyperuricosuria that persists after dietary purine restriction is treated with allopurinol (200–300 mg/d).

Stone formation in enteric hyperoxaluria, the most common form of hyperoxaluria, is multifactorial. The treatment should therefore be directed at correcting the various abnormalities including hyperoxaluria, hypocitraturia, hypomagnesuria, and low urine volume. Oral administration of large amounts of calcium has been recommended to diminish intestinal oxalate absorption; however, the concurrent increase in urinary calcium may negate the beneficial effect of this therapy.

Theoretically, at least, calcium given as the citrate salt may be indicated because it also provides an alkali load. Oral magnesium is beneficial but is limited by its tendency to cause diarrhea; magnesium citrate (5 mmol, two to four times daily) seems better tolerated than magnesium oxide and hydroxide. A liquid preparation of potassium citrate (40–60 mEq/d in three to four divided doses) may be useful in raising urinary citrate in these patients.

The combination of high doses of pyridoxine and magnesium or phosphate supplements has been shown to reduce the rate of stone formation in patients with primary hyperoxaluria.

All conditions accompanied by *hypocitraturia* may be effectively treated with oral administration of potassium citrate. At a rate of 30 to 60 mEq/d in divided doses, this treatment is generally well tolerated with only minimal gastrointestinal side effects.

FOLLOW-UP

Once the underlying metabolic abnormality had been identified, patients may be advised to follow some dietary changes and specific therapy started. Patients should be followed at regular intervals, initially every 3 months, then every 6 months, and later yearly to define the activity of stone disease and assess efficacy and side effects of therapy.

DISCUSSION

Prevalence

Renal stone disease (nephrolithiasis or urolithiasis) represents a worldwide problem of great socioeconomic impact. Although it is not usually fatal, renal stone disease causes significant morbidity due to renal colic, absenteeism from work, and hospitalization.

Data taken from combined reports of large numbers of stones sent for analysis show the following prevalence: calcium (oxalate and/or phosphate), 71%; struvite, 21%; uric acid, 5.5%; and cystine, 3.5%.

Calcium oxalate is the most common form of stones. Uric acid stones may be underrepresented in this series because these stones are usually small and passed spontaneously, and hence are seldom analyzed. By the same token, struvite stones may be overrepresented because these stones usually require surgical management and hence are more likely to be sent for analysis.

Related Basic Science

A great deal of information about mechanisms of renal stone formation has accumulated in the recent past. It is now clear that formation of stones is a manifestation of a variety of metabolic or physiologic disturbances including hypercalciuria, hyperuricosuria, hyperoxaluria, and hypocitraturia. In fact, a metabolic abnormality can be found in approximately 90% of patients evaluated for their renal stone disease. Many studies have shown that once the underlying derangements are identified, simple dietary manipulations and/or drug therapy may afford long-term protection from recurrent stone formation in the majority of patients.

Cystine Stones. Cystinuria is an autosomal recessive inherited disorder of cystine and dibasic amino acid transport affecting the epithelial cells of the renal tubules and gastrointestinal tract. The only known clinical manifestations of this condition are those due to renal stone formation, which is the result of the poor solubility of cystine. This disorder is characterized by recurrent nephrolithiasis with manifestations early in life and a family history of renal stones. Cystine stones are usually radiopaque because of the density of sulfur atoms.

Uric Acid Stones. As the pK of uric acid is 5.5, the greatest part of total urinary uric acid will be in the extremely insoluble undissociated form when urine pH is below 5.5. Many patients with uric acid stones have hyperuricosuria, but even with normal rate of uric acid excretion, stones may still form if the urine is persistently acidic. The reason for the sustained low urine pH in uric acid stone formers is unclear, occurring independently of excessive alkali loss or consumption of a diet rich in acid-ash content. Many of these patients have either primary gout or an early phase of primary gout before the onset of joint manifestations.

Struvite Stones. Triple phosphate stones (Ca, Mg, and NH_4 phosphate) occur in urine infected with urea-splitting organisms and are composed of struvite ($MgNH_4PO_4 \cdot 6H_2O$) and carbonate–apatite ($Ca_{10}(PO_4)6CO_3$).

Sterile urine is normally undersaturated with respect to struvite, but the combination of elevated ammonium concentration and high pH induces struvite supersaturation and crystallization. The experimental evidence suggests that struvite stones can be formed only in the presence of urea and urea-splitting organisms. Pharmacologic alkalinization of the urine, for example, with bicarbonate, results in supersaturation of calcium phosphate but not of struvite. Stone formation can be prevented by the inhibition of urease. Although struvite stones may form de novo from infection alone, they also occur as a complication of other causes of renal stones such as hypercalciuria.

These stones infrequently provoke colic; persistent or recurrent urinary tract infection is the usual presenting complaint. Struvite stones are radiopaque and sometimes may attain a large (staghorn) size.

Calcium Stones. In distal renal tubular acidosis (type 1), there are several risk factors for stone formation: hypercalciuria, persistently alkaline urine which increases urinary saturation of calcium phosphate by enhancing the dissociation of phosphate and raising the concentration of the divalent phosphate ion, and decreased urinary citrate excretion. This predisposition to stone formation is also seen in patients with incomplete distal renal tubular acidosis, that is, when blood pH is normal but urine pH cannot be brought below 5.5, but is not seen in patients with type 4 or 2 renal tubular acidosis.

Hypercalciuria is the most common underlying abnormality in patients with calcium oxalate stones. It is usually defined as urinary calcium excretion exceeding 250 mg/d in women and 300 mg/d in men eating an average diet (about 1 g of calcium intake). When dietary intake is reduced to 400 mg of calcium/d, the upper limit of normal for urinary calcium excretion is 200 mg/d. Several elements of the diet, other than calcium intake, also affect urinary calcium excretion: protein, sodium, phosphate, and acid content.

Many of the known conditions leading to hypercalcemia can produce hypercalciuria. The two most common causes of hypercalcemia are primary hyperparathyroidism and cancer. The first condition is often associated with renal stone formation, but patients with malignancy-induced hypercalcemia seldom develop renal stones, at least in part because the duration of life is too short once hypercalcemia develops.

Most patients with calcium oxalate stones are normocalcemic and have no obvious cause for increased calcium excretion, and they are said to have "idiopathic hypercalciuria." Idiopathic hypercalciuria may be the result of an enhanced intestinal absorption of calcium (absorptive hypercalciuria), increased bone resorption (resorptive hypercalciuria), or a primary inability of the renal tubules to reabsorb calcium (renal hypercalciuria). Fasting hypercalciuria with secondary hyperparathyroidism is the hallmark of patients with renal leak; fasting and postprandial hypercalciuria with suppressed parathyroid function should characterize resorptive hypercalciuria unrelated to primary hyperparathyroidism, although in clinical practice resorptive hypercalci-

uria leading to nephrolithiasis is almost always the result of primary hyperparathyroidism; normal or high normal fasting urinary calcium with postprandial hypercalciuria and secondary hypoparathyroidism define the subgroup of patients with absorptive hypercalciuria.

The primary abnormality in absorptive hypercalciuria is intestinal hyperabsorption of calcium. The exact cause of this abnormality is unknown. The etiology appears to be multifactorial, including vitamin D excess or upregulation or a vitamin D-independent mechanism. The disorder seems to have an autosomal dominant mode of inheritance. Absorptive hypercalciuria secondary to hypophosphatemia-induced stimulation of 1,25-dihydroxyvitamin D synthesis as the result of a primary renal leak of phosphate has also been described. A syndrome of primary 1,25-dihydroxyvitamin D overproduction has also been postulated and could account for both absorptive and fasting hypercalciuria with suppression of parathyroid hormone levels. A small number of patients with hypercalciuria have a biochemical presentation in keeping with a primary renal leak of calcium.

Hyperuricosuria is definitive if daily urinary uric acid exceeds 800 mg/d and borderline if it exceeds 600 mg/d. Hyperuricosuria may be secondary to excessive intake of purines or to endogenous overproduction of uric acid. Three well-studied enzymatic disorders of uric acid metabolism producing marked hyperuricosuria include hypoxanthine-guanine phophoribosyl transferase deficiency (Lesch–Nyhan syndrome), phosphoribosyl pyrophosphate synthetase overactivity and glucose-6-phosphatase deficiency (type I glycogen storage disease). In myeloproliferative disorders, leukemia, neoplasia, and hemolytic anemia, hyperuricemia and hyperuricosuria occur because of an increased rate of nucleic acid turnover. A high urinary uric acid can occur transiently when renal tubular handling of uric acid is impaired, for example, during early stages of volume expansion or following administration of uricosuric agents such as probenecid. In the steady state, however, normal urinary uric acid is restored because of the secondary decline in serum concentration and renal-filtered load of uric acid, even though renal tubular reabsorption of uric acid remains impaired.

The association of hyperuricosuria with uric acid stone formation is universally recognized. It is less commonly realized that hyperuricosuria is also associated with the formation of calcium oxalate stones, even in the absence of hypercalciuria or hyperoxaluria. Reduction of urinary excretion of uric acid by allopurinol leads to a reduction in the rate of formation of calcium oxalate stones. The mechanisms by which hyperuricosuria leads to calcium oxalate stone formation remain controversial, but the following scheme has been proposed: in the presence of hyperuricosuria and a urine pH greater than 5.5, either a colloidal or crystalline monosodium urate can form and initiate the formation of calcium stones by direct induction of heterogenous nucleation of calcium oxalate or adsorption of glycosaminoglycans, which are inhibitors of crystal aggregation or spontaneous nucleation of calcium oxalate.

Hyperuricosuria is second only to hypercalciuria as a cause of recurrent calcium oxalate stones and is usually attributed to high protein intake (purine load), rather than endogenous overproduction of uric acid.

Hyperoxaluria is defined as a daily urinary oxalate excretion exceeding 45 mg and has four major causes: excessive intake of oxalate or oxalate precursors, dietary calcium/oxalate imbalance, intestinal disease with steatorrhea, and primary hyperoxaluria.

Oxalate is present exclusively in vegetables and its intestinal absorption rate is markedly diminished in the presence of divalent cations such as calcium and magnesium. A given intake of oxalate is more likely to lead to hyperoxaluria if intestinal content of calcium is diminished. Thus, mild hyperoxaluria may be encountered in patients with intestinal hyperabsorption of calcium. Vitamin C is a natural precursor of oxalate, but controversy exists as to whether increased ingestion of vitamin C can significantly increase the urinary excretion of oxalate.

Hyperoxaluria with renal stone formation occurs in a variety of intestinal disorders. These patients all have steatorrhea and the colon, which is the major site of oxalate absorption, is always intact. It is generally believed that undigested fats undergo bacterial hydrolysis within the colon, leading to the local formation of fatty acids. The fatty acids would then form calcium soaps and the diminished availability of calcium within the lumen of the colon would enhance oxalate absorption. Bile salts and fatty acids also seem to increase the permeability of the intestinal mucosa to oxalate.

Primary hyperoxaluria is an inherited abnormality of oxalate metabolism. Two types have been described: type 1, the more common, also causes an accumulation of glyoxylate; type 2 also causes the accumulation of glycerate. Nephrolithiasis usually starts during the first decade (by the age of 4 years in 60%). The diagnosis of primary hyperoxaluria is based on the demonstration of hyperoxaluria that persists after dietary oxalate restriction, particularly when the patient is a child without gastrointestinal disease. Moreover, patients with primary hyperoxaluria usually excrete more than 100 mg/d urinary oxalate.

Citrate is an inhibitor of crystallization of stone-forming calcium salts. Several studies have described relative or absolute *hypocitraturia* in a significant number of calcium stone formers. Many reports have shown an encouraging decrease in the rate of stone formation with oral citrate supplements.

Hypocitraturia is defined as a 24-hour urinary citrate excretion of less than 320 mg. A well-known cause of hypocitraturia is systemic acidosis, which reduces urinary citrate excretion by enhancing renal tubular citrate reabsorption while impairing peritubular uptake and tubular synthesis of citrate. This mechanism accounts for the occurrence of hypocitraturia in distal renal tubular acidosis, chronic diarrheal states (from intestinal alkali loss), hypokalemia (from intracellular acidosis), thiazide therapy (from hypokalemia), and high-animal-protein diets (from high acid-ash content). In most patients with hypocitraturic calcium nephrolithiasis, however, the cause of low urinary citrate is unknown.

Natural History and Its Modification with Treatment

Nephrolithiasis is a chronic condition, which, if untreated, has a high tendency to recur. About one sixth of patients have a recurrence in 1 year, about one third of patients have a recurrence in 5 years, and about one half of patients have a recurrence in 10 years. Several studies have shown that dietary or pharmacologic intervention in these patients will significantly reduce their rate of stone formation.

The direct clinical consequences of stones include pain, bleeding, and urinary tract obstruction and infection. Loss of kidney function may occur because of kidney injury from infection and chronic obstruction, from damage during surgery, or from deliberate surgical removal of kidney.

Prevention

Prevention of stone recurrences by identifying and correcting the underlying abnormalities is of paramount importance. Prevention of renal stone formation is a particularly rewarding area of clinical medicine. Preventive measures are described in detail under Plans, Therapeutic.

Cost Containment

Prevention of kidney stone formation is the most effective cost containment action given the expense associated with the handling of the clinical consequences of stones. Cost containment can also be helped by restricting extensive metabolic workup only to those patients presenting with recurrent stone formation.

REFERENCES

Coe FL, Parks JH, Asplin JR. The pathogenesis and treatment of kidney stones. N Engl J Med 1992;327:1141.

Goldfarb S. Diet and nephrolithiasis. Annu Rev Med 1994;45:235.

Pak CYC. Citrate and renal calculi: New insights and future directions. Am J Kidney Dis 1991;17:420.

Pak CYC. Etiology and treatment of urolithiasis. Am J Kidney Dis 1991;18:624.

Uribarri J, Oh MS, Carroll HJ. The first kidney stone. Ann Intern Med 1991;111:1006.

CHAPTER 16–17

Renal Tubular Acidosis

Adrian Fine, M.D.

DEFINITION

The renal tubular acidoses are a group of disorders characterized by impaired renal acidification with resultant impairment of reabsorption or generation of bicarbonate by the kidney.

ETIOLOGY

Renal tubular acidosis may be primary or secondary to renal or adrenal disease. The renal diseases themselves may be primary or secondary (Table 16–17–1) and may affect the proximal or distal tubule, resulting in proximal or distal renal tubular acidosis, respectively. Renal tubular acidosis may be an isolated abnormality or may be part of a broader tubular defect including aminoaciduria. Geographical variation in incidence has been described.

CRITERIA FOR DIAGNOSIS
Suggestive

Renal tubular acidosis is commonly discovered by finding high or low plasma potassium levels and/or low plasma bicarbonate levels on routine biochemical screening. It may also be discovered in the course of investigating metabolic bone disease, renal calculus disease, nephrocalcinosis, or failure to thrive in early life.

The demonstration of hyperchloremic hypokalemic metabolic acidosis in the absence of gastrointestinal bicarbonate and potassium loss should lead to a high index of suspicion of renal tubular acidosis. Hyperkalemia, without obvious clinical explanation, may well be due to renal tubular acidosis (type 4).

The finding of a urine pH greater than 5.5 in an acidotic patient usually, though not invariably, confirms the diagnosis. Urine pH values, however, must be interpreted cautiously. For instance, urinary infection with urea-splitting organisms giving rise to a high urine pH must be ruled out. Other factors also may lead to misinterpretation of the urine pH; these are discussed under Related Basic Science.

As hyperchloremic (i.e., non-anion gap) acidosis is a hallmark feature of renal tubular acidosis, the presence of extra anions must be ruled out prior to diagnosis. Although the upper limit for plasma anion gap is 12, this will be reduced in hypoalbuminemia. For example, a patient with a serum albumin of 16 g/L would have an upper limit of normal for the anion gap of 6, and therefore, an anion gap of 12 would indeed be anion gap acidosis rather than hyperchloremic acidosis. It should be stressed that both hyperchloremic and anion gap acidosis may be found simultaneously in a patient, for example, diabetic ketosis + type 4 renal tubular acidosis.

Definitive

Proximal renal tubular acidosis, which is rare, is diagnosed by the demonstration of a large amount of bicarbonate in the urine when the blood bicarbonate is below normal. Distal renal tubular acidosis is diagnosed by the finding of less than expected urinary ammonia in the urine of a non-anion gap acidotic patient. This can be measured directly, but few laboratories do so. It is usually calculated indirectly by measuring the urinary anion gap. If the sum of urinary $Na^+ + K^+$ exceeds the urinary Cl^- in the presence of acidosis and in the absence of other urinary anions, then renal tubular acidosis exists.

TABLE 16–17–1

Proximal (Type 2)	Distal Hypokalemic (Type 1, Classic)	Distal Hyperkalemic (Type 4)
Primary defect (without associated disease)	Primary defects (without associated diseases)	Aldosterone deficiency
Idiopathic or sporadic	Idiopathic or sporadic	Primary
Genetically transmitted	Genetically transmitted	Diffuse adrenal disease
Secondary defects (drug/toxin-induced or	Secondary defects (associated with other diseases,	Addison's disease
associated with other diseases, systemic or	systemic or renal)	Various infectious, neoplastic, infiltrative, and
renal)	Genetically transmitted systemic diseases	traumatic diseases of the adrenal gland
Genetically transmitted systemic diseases	Marfan's syndrome	Specific impairment of aldosterone synthesis
Disorders in amino acid metabolism	Ehler–Danlos syndrome	Congenital biosynthetic defects
Cystinosis	Wilson's disease	Heparin-induced
Tyrosinemia	Hereditary elliptocytosis	Secondary
Disorders of carbohydrate metabolism	Sickle cell anemia*	Hyporeninemia
Hereditary fructose intolerance	Carbonic anhydrase B deficiency	Diabetic nephropathy
Galactosemia	Disorders of protein metabolism	Obstructive uropathy
Pyruvate carboxylase deficiency	Amyloidosis*	Tubulointerstitial diseases
Glycogen storage disease (Type I)	Hyperglobulinemia*	Aldosterone resistance
Miscellaneous	Multiple myeloma*	Tubular dysfunction
Wilson's disease	Drugs or toxins	Obstructive uropathy
Lowe's syndrome	Amphotericin B	Sickle cell nephropathy
Metachromatic leukodystrophy	Lithium carbonate	Amyloidosis
Medullary cystic disease	Analgesics*	Renal transplant: chronic rejection
Disorders of protein metabolism	Amiloride*	Diabetic nephropathy
Multiple myeloma*	Cyclamate	Lupus nephritis
Amyloidosis*	Toluene	Drug-related
Hyperglobulinemia*	Lead*	Angiotensin-converting enzyme inhibitors
Nephrotic syndrome	Acute drug-induced allergic interstitial	Amiloride
Drugs or toxins	nephritis*	Spironolactone
Outdated tetracyclines	Disorders causing nephrocalcinosis	Triamterene
Streptozotocin	Hyperparathyroidism	Cyclooxygenase inhibitors
Carbonic anhydrase inhibitors	Hyperthyroidism	Analgesics
Acetazolamide	Hypervitaminosis D	
Sulfamylon	Milk-alkali syndrome	
Methyl-5-chromone	Idiopathic hypercalciuria	
6-Mercaptopurine	Tubulointerstitial nephritis	
Glue sniffing	Immunologically mediated	
Heavy metals	Systemic lupus nephritis*	
Lead*	Renal transplantation rejection*	
Cadmium	Sjögren's syndrome*	
Mercury	Thyroiditis	
Copper (Wilson's disease)	Hyperglobulinemic states*	
Tubulointerstitial nephritis	Pulmonary fibrosis	
Immunologically mediated	Chronic active hepatitis	
Sjögren's syndrome	Primary biliary cirrhosis	
Lupus nephritis*	Cryoglobulinemia	
Renal transplantation rejection	Infiltrating diseases	
Miscellaneous	Leprosy	
Paroxysmal nocturnal hemoglobinuria	Sarcoidosis	
Osteopetrosis	Others	
Cyanotic congenital heart disease	Obstructive uropathy*	
York–Yendt syndrome	Hyperoxaluria	
Vitamin D deficiency	Edema-forming states	
	Miscellaneous	
	Empty cella syndrome	
	Fabry's disease*	
	Medullary sponge kidney*	

*These diseases may present as either proximal or distal renal tubular acidosis.
Source: Narins RG, et al., Metabolic acid–base disorders: Pathophysiology, classification, and treatment. In: Arieff AI, De Fronzo RA, eds. Fluid, electrolyte and acid–base disorders. New York: Churchill-Livingstone, 1985. Reproduced with permission from the publisher and author.

CLINICAL MANIFESTATIONS
Subjective

Commonly there are no symptoms attributable to renal tubular acidosis and the condition is recognized by routine electrolyte determination. This is especially likely to occur in hyperkalemic (type 4) renal tubular acidosis. Not infrequently in the other types of renal tubular acidosis, muscle weakness from accompanying hypokalemia may be found and can be profound. Other hypokalemic manifestations, such as polyuria and nocturia may occur. Sometimes, symptoms due to compli-

cations such as renal calculi and urinary infection are present. In others, vague arthralgias and muscle pains are present. In the infantile form of renal tubular acidosis, failure to thrive, nausea, and vomiting may be found. In children, bone pain and deformity may occur. When renal tubular acidosis is secondary to other diseases such as myeloma, liver disease, and collagen–vascular disease, the manifestations of those diseases may predominate. In patients without calculi, calcinosis, or a family history of renal tubular acidosis, one of the most common causes of renal tubular acidosis is mild chronic renal failure due to diabetes (type 4).

OBJECTIVE

Physical Examination

Usually, physical examination is unremarkable in adults with primary renal tubular acidosis, except for those with severe hypokalemia, in whom muscle weakness may be found. Abnormalities related to the underlying disorder may be found when the renal tubular dysfunction is secondary to underlying disease. Bone deformities may be found in children.

Routine Laboratory Abnormalities

Patients with classic distal renal tubular acidosis (type 1) are prone to renal calculi or nephrocalcinosis because of excess calciuria and low urinary citrate levels. The alkaline urine also predisposes to precipitation of calcium salts in the urinary tract. The serum calcium level is usually normal, and continuing calcium losses may lead to osteomalacia. Often these patients have a significant deficit in total body potassium and marked symptomatic hypokalemia may occur.

Patients with proximal renal tubular acidosis (type 2) may also manifest hypokalemia. This is more likely to occur during the onset of the disorder or with alkali therapy. They may have other defects of proximal tubular function (Fanconi's syndrome) characterized by glycosuria, hypophosphatemia, hypouricemia, and aminoaciduria. Although excess calciuria is found, nephrocalcinosis is not a feature of proximal renal tubular acidosis, presumably because of normal urinary citrate concentrations. An exception is the proximal renal tubular acidosis seen in patients treated for glaucoma with carbonic anhydrase inhibitors (e.g., acetazolamide [Diamox]), in whom urinary citrate is low.

Hyperkalemic distal renal tubular acidosis (type 4) is the most common form of renal tubular acidosis. Drugs are high on the list of causes (see Table 16–17–1). Otherwise it usually occurs in the presence of renal disease or occasionally with adrenal dysfunction. Tubulointerstitial disease, obstructive uropathy, and diabetic nephropathy are common causes. In the presence of intrinsic renal disease, a hallmark feature is the finding of hyperkalemia and acidosis that are disproportionately greater than expected for the degree of chronic renal failure.

These patients can acidify their urine but have a reduction in ammonium elimination. Unlike other forms of renal tubular acidosis, hyperkalemia is a consistent feature. Indeed, it is often hyperkalemia on routine blood chemistry screening that draws attention to this disorder, as normokalemia is otherwise the rule in chronic renal failure prior to the terminal stages.

Distal renal tubular acidosis can be diagnosed using routine biochemical values and a calculation of the urinary anion gap. This is described under Diagnostic Options.

PLANS

Diagnostic

Differential Diagnosis

Very few conditions give rise to hyperchloremic acidosis other than renal tubular acidosis and gastrointestinal bicarbonate loss. The latter is usually obvious from the history although surreptitious laxative abuse and bile salt binders should not be overlooked as occasional sources of intestinal bicarbonate loss. In diabetics, prior to making the diagnosis of hyperkalemic renal tubular acidosis (type 4), the blood glucose should be simultaneously checked as insulin deficiency is the most common cause of hyperkalemia in the diabetic with renal impairment. Patients who have had hypocapnia corrected may have a temporary (e.g., for a few days) hyperchloremic metabolic acidosis, as the reduced urinary ammonia from hypocapnia takes several days to be corrected.

Diagnostic Options

Diagnosis is confirmed by measurement of the urinary electrolytes, specifically the urinary anion gap (Figure 16–17–1). A word of explanation is necessary here. An invariable feature of all types of distal tubular acidosis is a reduction in the excretion of ammonium (NH_4^+). Most urinary NH_4^+ is excreted as $NH_4^+Cl^-$ and is not measured by routine laboratories. It has been shown that in acidosis, urinary Cl^- should equal the sum of $NA^+ + K^+ + NH_4^+$. Hence, quantitation of how much urinary Cl^- exceeds the sum of urinary $Na^+ + K^+$ give an indirect mea-

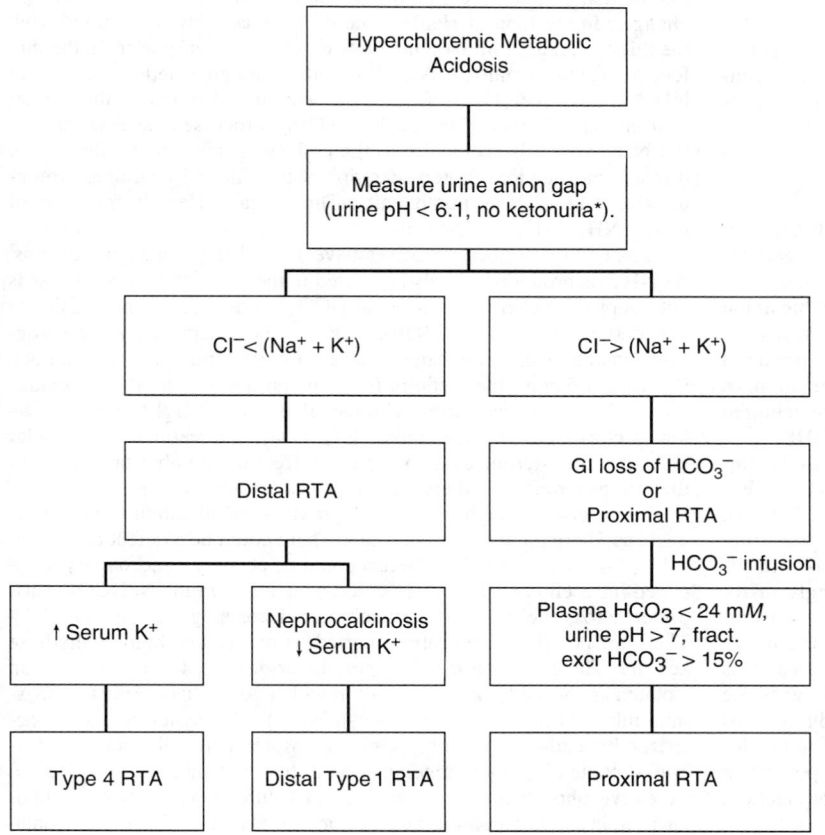

Figure 16–17–1 Diagnostic workup for a patient with hyperchloremic metabolic acidosis. *For the urine anion gap to be diagnostic the urine should have insignificant amounts of non-Cl⁻ anions (e.g., HCO_3^- or ketones).

sure of urinary NH_4^+. It has been determined that if the urinary Cl^- exceeds the sum of urinary $Na^+ + K^+$ in the presence of hyperchloremic metabolic acidosis, then that acidosis is not due to distal tubular acidosis; in other words, the kidney is producing appropriate amounts of NH_4^+. By contrast, when $Cl^- < Na^+ + K^+$ the acidosis is of renal origin, that is, renal tubular acidosis. The only exception to the validity of this simple test is when the urine contains significant amounts of other (i.e., non-Cl^-) anions; these are ketones and bicarbonate, as well as penicillins in large amounts. A raised plasma anion gap, ketonuria on routine urinalysis, or a urine pH above 6.1 should alert the physician to the first two possibilities.

Further characterization of the renal tubular acidosis can be determined by bicarbonate infusion. If significant amounts of bicarbonate appear in the urine (i.e., urine pH > 7.0) before the plasma bicarbonate reaches 24 mmol/L, then a proximal leak of bicarbonate exists; that is, proximal renal tubular acidosis. It should, however, be stressed that proximal renal tubular acidosis in adults is rare. If hyperkalemia accompanies the acidosis, then, provided no other cause of hyperkalemia is present, type 4 renal tubular acidosis is confirmed. The finding of nephrocalcinosis on radiograph confirms distal renal tubular acidosis. In individual patients it may be difficult to determine whether the nephrocalcinosis is a cause or a consequence of the renal tubular acidosis.

The above is a simplified but very useful approach to define the major types of renal tubular acidosis. In a more specialized setting, further testing such as the urine pCO_2 may be necessary, as there are many subgroups of both type 1 and 4 renal tubular acidosis. Plasma renin and aldosterone determinations are informative in type 4 where hypoaldosteronism, usually secondary to hyporeninemia, is the rule. The major diagnostic questions to be resolved, however, are whether the patient has proximal renal tubular acidosis (type 2) requiring large amounts of alkali replacement, classic distal renal tubular acidosis (type 1) requiring monitoring for nephrocalcinosis and prevention of hypokalemia, or type 4 renal tubular acidosis possibly requiring assessment of the renin–aldosterone axis and necessitating control of hyperkalemia. The above approach should amply define the vast majority of patients with renal tubular acidosis to such ends.

Recommended Approach

A spot urine for pH, Na^+, K^+, Cl^-, and plasma bicarbonate and potassium with the calculation of the urinary anion gap will diagnose accurately the vast majority of cases of distal tubular acidosis (Figure 16–17–1).

Therapeutic

In proximal renal tubular acidosis, very large amounts of HCO_3^- may be required (5–10 mEq/kg/d) because of the tubular leak of bicarbonate. Urinary potassium excretion increases in consequence, owing to the presentation of additional sodium with a poorly reabsorbable anion (HCO_3^-) to the distal nephron. Potassium supplements are usually required. Thiazide diuretics may be useful to induce increased proximal reabsorption of HCO_3^- due to extracellular fluid volume contraction. In distal renal tubular acidosis, smaller amounts of HCO_3^- are required (usually 1–2 mEq/kg/d). This is given in the form of $NaHCO_3$ or sodium citrate. In general, muscle aches and arthralgias may be improved with alkali therapy. Alkali therapy reduces urinary calcium excretion and new stone formation and probably lessens nephrocalcinosis. The accompanying bone disease is improved. Supplemental potassium salts are usually required and can be given in the form of potassium citrate. Sodium citrate and potassium citrate can be given singly or together (Shohl's solution). In type 4 renal tubular acidosis, administration of the mineralocorticoid fludrocortisone (Florinef, 0.1–0.2 mg/d) can improve both the hyperkalemia and the acidosis, but because of its sodium-retaining properties, it may cause fluid retention and aggravate hypertension. The addition of furosemide (Lasix) not only reduces these side effects, but also appears to potentiate the effect of mineralocorticoid on the acidosis. This may be partially due to the potassium loss induced by furosemide, as hyperkalemia inhibits NH_4^+ production, thereby contributing to the acidosis.

FOLLOW-UP

For patients who have presented with symptomatic hypokalemia, the serum potassium level should be monitored carefully after hospital discharge, approximately weekly until stable, and then every few months. Specifically, care should be taken to avoid the hypokalemia that could be induced or worsened by the overzealous correction of the acidosis without having adequately corrected the potassium deficit.

DISCUSSION

Related Basic Science

The most common renal disorder leading to renal acidosis is generalized loss of nephron mass, as seen in generalized chronic renal failure. The etiology of this acidosis has several components. Diminished renal mass is accompanied by diminished total NH_4^+ production. Renal interstitial damage may reduce the ability of NH_3/NH_4^+ to diffuse from its site of production (proximal tubule) to the distal nephron. Reduced renin production leading to hypoaldosteronism (type 4 renal tubular acidosis) may also complicate mild to moderate chronic renal failure. Retention of sulfate and other anions in advanced chronic renal failure produces anion gap acidosis.

When the renal elimination of acid is less than the intake and production of acid, mainly obtained from sulfur-containing amino acid catabolism, then renal acidosis exists. In the absence of generalized renal failure, this indicates renal tubular acidosis. Frank acidosis may be present, but in other patients, blood acid–based parameters and urine pH appear normal and the defect can be brought out only by acid loading. The acidosis can be due to a proximal tubular defect in bicarbonate reabsorption (type 2) or, more often, a distal (types 1 and 4) defect. Many possible defects can result in distal renal tubular acidosis. These include the inability to produce and maintain a sufficiently low urinary pH to trap and remove ammonium from the body, or impaired renal ammoniagenesis consequent to hyperkalemia or deficient transport of ammonium from its site of production to its site of excretion.

Major advances in our understanding of renal ammoniagenesis have recently been made. Ammonium (NH_4^+) and not ammonia (NH_3) is produced from the intracellular metabolism of glutamine in the proximal tubular cell and secreted into the lumen via the apical Na^+–H^+ exchanger. In the loop of Henle some NH_4^+ is actively transported from the thick ascending limb on the Na^+–K^+–$2Cl^-$ cotransporter. In the thin loop of Henle, ammonia is reabsorbed, although whether as NH_3 or NH_4^+ is unknown. Favoring the former is the alkalinity of the tubular fluid in that segment of the nephron. These processes increase interstitial NH_3, which is secreted into the collecting duct lumen, the site of urinary acidification. Proton secretion at this site is by luminal proton-translocating ATPase pump units. The overall effect is transport of NH_4^+ ($NH_3 + H^+$) into the urine.

The newly described processes have several important implications. As NH_4^+ is produced and also excreted in the urine, then this process is not coupled biochemically to renal HCO_3^- generation from H_2CO_3, as conventionally described. Rather, HCO_3^- is generated by the subsequent metabolism of the carbon skeleton of glutamine α-ketoglutarate. Diseases affecting the medulla (e.g., interstitial nephritis) may reduce urinary NH_4^+ by interfering with medullary NH_3/NH_4^+ transport. Various factors such as intracellular [H^+], Pco_2, extracellular/intracellular [K^+], and aldosterone availability may affect the number or affinity of these transporters and, thereby, renal NH_4^+ excretion.

The precise pathophysiology of proximal renal tubular acidosis is unclear. There are three possibilities. There could be a defect in the apical Na^+–H^+ antiporter. This defect could be primary or secondary to reduced intracellular [H^+]. There could be a defect in the $NaHCO_3$ transporter across the basolateral membrane, decreasing intracellular [H^+]. The third possibility, recently reported, is reduced carbonic anhydrase activity. The condition may be sporadic or genetic. It may occur as an isolated abnormality or in association with a generalized defect in proximal tubular function (Fanconi's syndrome). This syndrome is characterized by acidosis, normoglycemic glycosuria, and aminoaciduria. Hypophosphatemia, hypouricemia, and hypokalemia occur due to excessive phosphaturia, uricosuria, and kaluresis, respectively. Tubular proteinuria is common. Severe bone disease, rickets, or osteomalacia is the major consequence, in part attributed to a concomitant impairment of 1-α-hydroxylation of vitamin D. The syndrome can be hereditary, congenital, or acquired from such conditions as multiple myeloma (see Table 16–17–1).

It is important to note that during both the development and treatment of proximal renal tubular acidosis, large amounts of HCO_3^- and K^+ are lost in the urine, the latter due to the presentation of poorly absorbable anion to the distal nephron. During steady-state conditions, however (when the plasma HCO_3^- has stabilized at its reduced level), urinary pH and electrolytes can be normal for the degree of acidosis. It is only when HCO_3^- is administered that the renal HCO_3^- leak becomes apparent.

In distal (type 1) renal tubular acidosis, several pathophysiologic mechanisms occur. Backleak of H^+ may occur as a result of increased permeability of the distal membrane. This occurs with amphotericin administration and in the inherited form. Defective function of the H^+ pump can occur as a result of a decrease in the number of pump "units," as in interstitial renal disease, or as a result of aldosterone deficiency-induced failure to stimulate these units. In voltage-dependent renal tubular acidosis, insufficient distal sodium delivery occurs for K^+ and H^+ secretion. This can result from avid proximal sodium reabsorption states (e.g., cirrhosis of the liver) or from low mineralocorticoid bioactivity. The precise subgroup can usually be delineated by infusion of bicarbonate and measurement of the urine and blood P_{CO_2}. Bicarbonate administered to a normal person in sufficient quantities to exceed the proximal reabsorptive capacity of the kidney will result in large amounts of bicarbonate at the collecting duct, promoting maximal H^+ secretion. This gives rise to a urine–blood P_{CO_2} gradient greater than 25 mm Hg in normal individuals. A defective pump or voltage defect will result in an inability to obtain this value.

The wide usage of the urinary anion gap in the diagnostic workup of hyperchloremic metabolic acidosis has replaced the previous hallmark test, namely, the urinary pH. Indeed, the urine pH may give misleading information. For example, a pH below 5.0 could be found in distal renal tubular acidosis when reduction in NH_3 availability in the collecting duct exceeds the reduction in proton pumps. This H^+ will be secreted into a urine with less buffer, ensuring an apparently adequate pH response although renal tubular acidosis is present. On the other hand, the urinary pH may appear to be inappropriately high (i.e., > 5.0) in the metabolic acidosis of gastrointestinal bicarbonate loss, wrongly sug-

gesting a renal tubular acidosis as the cause. This is attributable to significant concomitant hypokalemia, as hypokalemia increases urinary NH_4^+ and thence urinary pH (by unclear mechanisms).

The increased secretion of K^+ in distal renal tubular acidosis (type 1) is related to the increased lumen negativity caused by decreased H^+ secretion as well as increased HCO_3^- in the lumen.

In some patients, normal acid–base parameters exist but distal tubular acidosis is detected after acid loading performed because of a suspicion of the condition due to recurrent calculi (incomplete renal tubular acidosis).

Natural History and Its Modification with Treatment

Relative stability can be obtained with appropriate therapy. In certain infantile forms, spontaneous improvement may occur.

Prevention

In hereditary forms, early recognition in related family members may prevent the development of clinically apparent disease with complicating nephrocalcinosis. Treatment of underlying systemic disorders may prevent this complication.

Cost Containment

The diagnostic workup and management can usually be completed in the ambulatory care setting, obviating the need for the more costly hospitalization. Costs are limited to 3- to 6-month office visits with testing of urine for infection, serum creatinine, and electrolyte determinations. Yearly bone radiology may be required for patients with bone disease.

REFERENCES

Caruana RJ, Buckalaw VM. The syndrome of distal renal tubular acidosis: Clinical and laboratory findings in 58 cases. Medicine 1988;67:84.

Halperin ML, Goldstein MB, Richardson RN, Stinebaugh BJ. Distal renal tubular acidosis syndromes: A pathophysiological approach. Am J Nephrol 1985;5:1.

Kamel KS, Ethier JH, Richardson RM, et al. Urine electrolytes and osmolality: When and how to use them. Am J Nephrol 1990;10:89.

Knepper MA, Packer R, Good DW. Ammonium transport in the kidney. Physiol Rev 1989;69:179.

Kurtzman NA. Disorders of distal acidification. Kidney Int 1990;38:720.

CHAPTER 16–18

Primary Glomerulonephritis

James V. Donadio, Jr., M.D.

DEFINITION

The primary glomerulonephritides are diseases of the glomerulus of unknown origin. Specific forms of glomerulonephritis are characterized by their histologic appearances.

ETIOLOGY

As implied in the definition, the etiology of the vast majority of primary glomerulonephritides is unknown. All studies of glomerulonephritis suggest that this group of disorders arise from activity of the immune system, itself the result of an interaction between a susceptible individual (the susceptibility being inherited in many patients) and an antigenic challenge, mostly from the environment. It is unknown whether glomerulonephritis results from over- or underactivity of immune reactions. There are examples of overactivity and underactivity in several forms of human glomerulonephritis. It is certain that the immune reaction is not appropriate when it leads to disease resulting from a perversion of a normal response to an antigenic challenge.

CRITERIA FOR DIAGNOSIS

Suggestive

Glomerulonephritis may be suspected by findings on urine microscopy of hematuria, cellular casts, and, in particular, red blood cell, leukocyte, and renal epithelial cell casts, and lipids with or without increased amounts of urine protein and reduced renal function. The primary nature of the glomerulopathy is determined by exclusion of known secondary causes by history, physical examination, and immunologic screening.

Definitive

A definitive diagnosis of primary glomerulonephritis can be made only by renal biopsy examination. Tissue examination by renal biopsy confirms the presence and the type of primary glomerular disease. Morphologic categories based on light, immunofluorescence, and electron microscopy can be used to classify most forms of human glomerulopathy. Unfortunately, one or more diseases may be present and expressed within a limited range of morphologic groupings that does not identify the specific disease or cause.

CLINICAL MANIFESTATIONS

Subjective

In primary glomerulonephritis, symptoms vary from none to a profound and acute illness. A patient may be entirely free of symptoms until renal failure is far advanced.

Objective

Physical Examination

Edema formation may be present due to large amounts of urine protein, resulting in the nephrotic syndrome, or there may be an acute nephritic syndrome characterized by gross hematuria, hypertension, azotemia, and edema. Chronic hypertension also may accompany glomerulonephritis in the asymptomatic or the proteinuric patient, in whom the high blood pressure is due to extracellular fluid volume expansion, parenchymal renal damage, or both.

Routine Laboratory Abnormalities

The first clue in making a proper diagnosis is careful urinalysis done on a first-morning, freshly voided urine sample. The physicochemical testing of the urine, reagent-strip sensitivity for proteinuria, hematuria, and glycosuria, has enabled clinicians to evaluate rapidly important chemical constituents. Urine sediment findings using unstained bright-field microscopy identify erythrocytes, leukocytes, and cellular casts, and, in particular, red blood cell casts, which are the most indicative of glomerular injury. Additional findings of dysmorphic or glomerular red blood cells also signify glomerular bleeding. Such renal (urinary) casts and dysmorphic red blood cells that accompany either macroscopic or microscopic hematuria also clearly indicate that bleeding in the urinary tract is glomerular in origin.

Qualitative proteinuria must be further assessed by 24-hour measurement of total urine protein. Also, adults who are first discovered to have proteinuria, especially in the nephrotic range (protein excretion of 3.5 g or more per 24 hours) should have screening for Bence Jones proteinuria with the sulfosalicyclic precipitation method and examination of monoclonal immunoglobulins by immunoelectrophoresis and immunodiffusion to exclude diagnoses such as amyloidosis, light-chain deposition disease, multiple myeloma, and Waldenström's macroglobulinemia. The presence of proteinuria and/or an abnormal urine sediment demands that renal function be measured, preferably by a clearance technique, to estimate the glomerular filtration rate. Severe azotemia, or even the requirement for dialysis, may be present at first examination in the most aggressive forms of glomerulonephritis.

A common clinical presentation of primary glomerulonephritis is the nephrotic syndrome. The nephrotic syndrome is a clinical entity characterized by several renal and extrarenal abnormalities, the most prominent of which are proteinuria exceeding 3.5 g per 24 hours, hypoalbuminemia, edema, hyperlipidemia, and hypercoagulability.

PLANS

Diagnostic

Differential Diagnosis

In clinical practice, the primary glomerulopathies may be subdivided in a differential diagnosis according to the clinicopathologic categories by which the vast majority of patients present themselves (Table 16–18–1).

Diagnostic Options

The overall diagnostic evaluation of a patient with presumed primary glomerulonephritis involves a three-pronged approach: exclude a secondary cause by clinical and laboratory investigations; look for historical and serologic features that would point to a particular subtype of primary glomerulonephritis; define the histologic pattern by light, immunofluorescence, and electron microscopy.

TABLE 16–18–1. DIFFERENTIAL DIAGNOSIS OF PRIMARY GLOMERULONEPHRITIS

Acute nephritic syndrome
  Acute poststreptococcal glomerulonephritis
  Non-poststreptococcal glomerulonephritis
Rapidly progressive glomerulonephritis
  Idiopathic: immune complex, anti-glomerular basement membrane associated and non-immune related
  Associated with systemic diseases that must be carefully excluded, e.g., Goodpasture's syndrome (glomerulonephritis and lung hemorrhage with anti-glomerular basement membrane and anti-alveolar basement membrane antibodies), lupus nephritis, vasculitides, etc.
Persistent urine abnormalities with minimal or no symptoms
  Immunoglobulin A nephropathy or Berger's disease (also commonly associated with gross hematuria)
  Nonnephrotic proteinuria secondary to many forms of glomerulopathy (identified on renal biopsy)
Nephrotic syndrome
  Minimal change glomerulopathy
  Focal glomerulosclerosis
  Immunoglobulin M nephropathy
  Membranous glomerulopathy
  Membranoproliferative (mesangiocapillary) glomerulonephritis, with three subtypes, i.e., types I, II, and III
  Other lesions associated with idiopathic nephrotic syndrome
    Focal proliferative glomerulonephritis
    Diffuse endocapillary glomerulonephritis
    Endocapillary and extracapillary proliferative glomerulonephritis
    Other unclassified lesions

Recommended Approach

The recommended approach to diagnosis depends on the clinical presentation. For example, in an acute nephritic syndrome, proliferative glomerulonephritis secondary to streptococcal and other infectious agents must be differentiated in the acute phase from the various diseases associated with rapidly progressive glomerulonephritis (also termed crescentic glomerulonephritis), from membranoproliferative glomerulonephritis, and from the diffuse form of glomerulonephritis associated with Henoch–Schönlein purpura. Serologic testing can be helpful.

Antistreptolysin O and antideoxyribonuclease B are exoenzymes that are good indicators of recent streptococcal infection when appropriate cultures may be negative. Antistreptolysin O titers greater than 200 U occur in up to 70% of patients with acute poststreptococcal glomerulonephritis. After the peak titer is attained within 3 to 5 weeks of infection, the titers decline to normal over the next several months. Antideoxyribonuclease B titers rise after streptococcal impetigo in more than 90% of patients. This serologic evidence of streptococcal infection is important in that the antistreptolysin O titers rise little, if any, after impetigo. Serial levels of twice the baseline are suggestive of recent infection. Elevated antistreptolysin O titers can be found in both poststreptococcal glomerulonephritis (70%) and membranoproliferative glomerulonephritis (20%). Antistreptolysin O titers may be normal in some cases of previously antibiotic-treated poststreptococcal and membranoproliferative glomerulonephritis.

In anti-glomerular basement membrane-associated nephritis, enzyme-linked immunoassay is the most common and sensitive method used to detect circulating anti-glomerular basement membrane antibodies. Circulating anti-glomerular basement membrane antibodies are detected in approximately 90% of patients with Goodpasture's syndrome and in 60% of patients with anti-glomerular basement membrane-associated rapidly progressive glomerulonephritis by the enzyme-linked immunoassay. By direct immunofluoresence of frozen kidney samples, anti-glomerular basement membrane antibodies are also demonstrated by a distinct linear fluorescence of glomerular capillary walls. Anti-glomerular basement membrane antibodies disappear from the circulation in approximately 8 months (range, 3–25 months) after initial detection. Immunofluorescence has the advantage of also detecting anti-nuclear and anti-tubular basement membrane antibodies, which are present in up to 20% of patients.

Measurement of complement levels, including CH_{50}, C3, and C4 are helpful screening tests. Low serum complement levels and a systemic illness implicate either systemic lupus erythematosus, cryoglobulinemia, the polyarteritis group, subacute bacterial endocarditis, or so-called shunt nephritis from infected ventriculoatrial shunts as the cause of an acute nephritis. Appropriate antinuclear antibody, cryoglobulin, rheumatoid factor, and bacterial culture testing should further narrow the differential diagnosis prior to renal biopsy. Acute nephritis, low complement levels, and no systemic symptoms suggest either post-streptococcal or membranoproliferative glomerulonephritis (type I or II most likely). Acute poststreptococcal glomerulonephritis is associated with low CH_{50} and C3 levels early in its course, with values returning to normal in less than 8 weeks. Membranoproliferative glomerulonephritis is associated with depressed C3 levels that are prolonged, especially in the type II variant. Also, an immunoglobulin (Ig) G autoantibody to C3 convertase, termed *C3 nephritic factor,* stabilizes the alternative pathway-converting enzyme and results in continuous C3 degradation. C3 nephritic factor is present in 20% of type I and more than 60% of type II cases of membranoproliferative glomerulonephritis.

Acute nephritis without detection of circulating anti-glomerular basement membrane antibodies, streptococcal exoenzymes, complement abnormalities, or systemic symptoms often can be attributed to idiopathic rapidly progressive glomerulonephritis of immune complex or non-immune complex types. Examination of renal tissue is the only way to define these entities.

Episodes of recurrent macroscopic hematuria associated with upper respiratory tract infections are common clinical manifestations of idiopathic IgA nephropathy. Rapid loss of renal function, however, is uncommon, and the hematuria usually disappears 48 to 72 hours following the infection. Serum IgA levels may be elevated in IgA nephropathy, but they are of no diagnostic aid otherwise.

Systemic lupus erythematosus, poststreptococcal glomerulonephritis, and anti-glomerular basement membrane-associated glomerulonephritis should be considered when serologic testing suggests such a diagnosis in a nephrotic patient. The differential diagnosis of idiopathic nephrotic syndrome must be made on examining renal biopsy specimens and is not appreciably narrowed by serologic testing; however, low serum complement levels, especially C3, may herald membranoproliferative glomerulonephritis.

Therapeutic

The treatment of primary glomerulonephritis remains controversial, largely unsatisfactory, and, where successful, empirical rather than logical. Minimal change glomerulopathy is the only primary glomerular disease that has a predictable response to corticosteroids. More than 90% of patients reduce their urine protein excretion to a normal level following use of corticosteroid drugs. The recommended approach is to treat a patient with minimal change glomerulopathy with prednisone 2 mg/kg/d (60 mg/m^2/d), up to a maximum of 80 mg, in a single daily dose. There is little merit in continuing daily therapy beyond 8 to 12 weeks when complete nephrotic remission is not achieved, as less than 10% of patients who are corticosteroid responsive clear their urine of protein during a second month of daily therapy. Between 30 and 50% of children and adults with minimal change glomerulopathy experience a relapse of the nephrotic syndrome within 3 years of their first episode. Repeated short courses of daily prednisone therapy may be required to maintain the urine free of protein. In steroid-responsive patients who experience frequent relapses of the nephrotic syndrome, and in whom prednisone therapy presents unacceptable side effects, the use of alternate-day prednisone and an oral alklyating agent (cyclophosphamide) in combination with prednisone has been useful. Also, cyclosporine has been shown to be effective in inducing or maintaining remission in patients with frequently relapsing or steroid-dependent nephrotic syndrome. The recommended dosage of cyclosporine is 150 mg/m^2/d in two oral doses. The dose may be adjusted to maintain trough whole blood levels between 100 and 200 ng/mL, but it should not exceed 200 mg/m^2.

The treatment of acute poststreptococcal glomerulonephritis is symptomatic. To control the possible spread of a streptococcal infection, penicillin or other antibiotics should be given to family members or contacts.

Although there is no direct evidence that such therapy will prevent or reduce the severity of poststreptococcal glomerulonephritis, many clinicians believe that the incidence of acute glomerulonephritis has declined appreciably since the advent of antibiotics. Immunosuppressive therapy has no role in the treatment of poststreptococcal glomerulonephritis.

Improvement in renal function with intravenous "pulse" methylprednisolone in immune complex- and non-immune complex-associated rapidly progressive glomerulonephritis has been reported. In the treatment of anti-glomerular basement membrane nephritis, neither plasmapheresis with immunosuppression nor "pulse" steroid treatment has been shown to have a favorable effect in patients with advanced renal failure (serum creatinine levels > 6–7 mg/dL); however, improvement of pulmonary hemorrhage and renal function (when less impaired) with plasma exchange plus immunosuppressive agents in anti-glomerular basement membrane disease is reported in the majority of patients so treated. Any of these aggressive forms of treatment are limited not only by the presence of advanced renal failure but also by additional risks, including advanced patient age, oligoanuria, and the degree of chronicity seen on renal biopsy samples.

In IgA nephropathy, until recently there has been no proven effective treatment; however, in a recently completed 2-year randomized, double-blind, placebo-controlled trial, fish oil (12 1-g capsules of menhaden oil containing the omega-3 fatty acids eicosapentaenoic acid [1.7 g] and docosahexaenoic acid [1 g]) was shown to effectively retard the rate of renal impairment in patients with progressive IgA nephropathy.

In membranous glomerulopathy, no beneficial effects were demonstrated in two completed randomized clinical trials of alternate-day prednisone therapy in adult nephrotic patients (Cattran et al., 1989; Cameron et al., 1990), failing to confirm results from an earlier study (Collaborative Study of the Adult Idiopathic Nephrotic Syndrome, 1979) in which renal function was stabilized. In another clinical trial (Ponticelli et al., 1992) in which an unusual regimen of methylprednisolone followed by oral chorambucil (Leukeran) therapy was used in monthly cycles for 6 months, proteinuria was reduced and renal function was preserved. A major concern in this trial is what appears to be a higher than expected progression rate in the control group, amplifying the difference in outcomes.

In membranoproliferative glomerulonephritis, current clinical reports show that more patients are surviving free of renal failure than was evident in past studies; however, the improvement cannot be attributed to a variety of treatments that were advocated, including alternate-day prednisone, combinations of prednisone and other immunosuppressive agents, nonsteroidal antiinflammatory drugs, and platelet inhibitors. The improved renal survival relates in part to a larger selection of patients biopsied soon after clinical onset, with life-table analysis portrayed in a longer clinical course.

Recent experimental and clinical studies have implied that enhanced glomerular capillary pressure is a major pathogenetic feature of progressive glomerular injury. The use of drugs such as angiotensin-converting enzyme inhibitors to reduce glomerular capillary pressure and membrane permeability may be useful in preserving glomerular function in a wide variety of heretofore progressive glomerulopathies. Such strategies of treatment are undergoing evaluation in controlled clinical trials.

FOLLOW-UP

The importance of follow-up examination is encompassed in the education of a patient with primary glomerular disease. Although treatment is largely controversial and unproven for each specific glomerulopathy, appropriate measures to slow renal progression can be taken, especially regarding secondary hypertension and the control of edema formation in patients with nephrosis.

Of course, when more aggressive forms of treatment are used, for example, corticosteroid and immunosuppressive drugs, frequent follow-up is needed to assess benefits and toxic side effects.

DISCUSSION
Prevalence and Incidence

Minimal change glomerulopathy generally occurs during early childhood, the majority of patients being between 1 and 6 years of age.

Acute poststreptococcal glomerulonephritis may occur sporadically or in epidemic form. The sporadic form is more common, it affects children more often than adults, and the peak age incidence is from 2 to 6 years. Approximately 5% of cases are found among children younger than 2 years, and 5 to 10% of patients with the disease are older than 40. The incidence of anti-glomerular basement membrane glomerulonephritis accounts for only 20% of all cases of rapidly progressive glomerulonephritis and probably represents fewer than 1% of all diagnostic renal biopsies. On the other hand, IgA nephropathy appears to be a ubiquitous disorder with a wide but irregular geographic distribution. It is very common in many countries, including those in southern Europe, Asia, and Australia; its incidence ranges from 20 to 25% of all primary glomerular disease in southern Europe and Australia to 30 to 40% in Japan and Singapore. In the United States, its incidence is 10 to 20% of all primary glomerular diseases. Membranous glomerulopathy is one of the most common causes of the nephrotic syndrome in adults and accounts for 10 to 25% of all cases and a somewhat higher proportion in patients over the age of 50. Membranoproliferative glomerulonephritis is uncommon, and although there are no epidemiologic studies, there are the clinical impressions from several areas of the world, including Australia, Europe, North America, and New Zealand, that the incidence of idiopathic membranoproliferative glomerulonephritis has declined in recent years.

Related Basic Science

Genetics

It is well known that some antigens coded for within the major histocompatibility complex and the area of genome coding for immunoglobulin synthesis are associated with the presence or progression of several forms of glomerulonephritis. DQ antigen B-chain polymorphisms have recently been associated with IgA nephropathy; however, substitution at the genomic level in susceptible individuals is only theoretically possible in the treatment of human glomerular disease.

Altered Molecular Biology

There are many potential mediators of glomerulosclerosis, the end result of progressive primary glomerulopathies. A central event in tissue repair is the release of cytokines (also known as growth factors) in response to injury, with a balance between mediators and modulators of glomerular injury currently being studied by techniques involving molecular programs of cascades of signal transductions within cells (autocrine activity) and between cells (paracrine activity).

Physiologic or Metabolic Derangement

Until recently, only two major primary immunopathogenetic mechanisms were generally considered to be important: the deposition of circulating immune complexes in glomeruli and the reaction of antibodies with antigenic components of the glomerular basement membrane. It is now recognized that immune complex deposits can be formed locally within glomeruli as a result of the combination of circulating antibodies with non-basement membrane autologous glomerular antigens or with antigens that have become trapped in glomeruli. There is mounting experimental evidence that disturbances of immune regulation and autoimmune mechanisms are responsible for the majority of human glomerulonephritis, including IgA nephropathy, membranous glomerulopathy, idiopathic crescentic glomerulonephritis, and membranoproliferative glomerulonephritis, in addition to the well-recognized autoimmune nature of anti-glomerular basement membrane-associated glomerulonephritis and lupus nephritis. Glomerular antibody deposition further mediates glomerular injury by way of inflammatory mediators, including the coagulation and complement systems, neutrophils, macrophages, growth factors, and platelets, and by noninflammatory lesions induced by glomerular antibody alone or in the terminal complement complex (C5b–9) that injures the glomerular epithelial cell and its surrounding integrity.

In those primary glomerular diseases that are presumed or known to be immune complex mediated, examination of frozen renal tissue by direct immunofluoresence shows glomerular deposits of immunoglobulins and complement that are irregular or granular and located variously in the glomerular capillary walls and in the mesiangium. Except for poststreptococcal glomerulonephritis, causes of the other glomerular diseases remain unknown, with one other exception. A large number of secondary associations and etiologies have been found in membranous glomerulopathy. These include infections (e.g., bacterial, viral, and protozoan), multisystemic diseases (e.g., lupus erythematosus, Sjögren's syndrome, and sarcoidosis), drugs (e.g., D-penicillamine, captopril, gold salts and all categories of nonsteroidal anti-inflammatory drugs [except aspirin]), some heavy metals, and a variety of solid tumors and lymphoproliferative malignancies, especially carcinomas. Although many in number, these secondary causes account for only about 10% of the cases of membranous glomerulopathy.

The cause of anti-glomerular basement membrane-associated disease is unknown. Both exogenous agents and autologous antigens have been implicated. Some patients have a flulike prodrome, but direct evidence for influenza or other viral infection is lacking in most cases. Exposure to hydrocarbons has been suggested as an initiating factor, but such exposure is not documented in the vast majority of cases. Antibodies are directed against constituents of glomerular basement membranes in a linear immunofluorescent pattern. About one half to two thirds of patients with circulating anti-glomerular basement membrane antibodies have Goodpasture's syndrome, defined simply as anti-glomerular basement membrane-mediated nephritis and lung hemorrhage.

Virtually all glomerular diseases are associated with increased glomerular capillary permeability to large plasma proteins. Recent studies have shown that the selectivity of proteinuria seen in some forms of human glomerular disease (e.g., minimal change glomerulopathy) is due to a loss of glomerular fixed-negative charges. There does not seem to be an increase in pore size, but rather a small decrease in both the size and number of pores. In more inflammatory or progressive glomerular diseases (e.g., rapidly progressive glomerulonephritis), greater structural damage occurs, accompanied by formation within the glomerular capillary walls of a second population of large protein-permeable pores. A size- and charge-independent flux of plasma proteins through these larger pores ensues. Whether the initial loss of fixed-negative charges by itself contributes to the subsequent structural changes remains to be determined.

Natural History and Its Modification with Treatment

The natural history of the chronic primary glomerular diseases is quite variable. By name, rapidly progressive glomerulonephritis from whatever cause is usually associated with a crescentic glomerulonephritis and a rapidly progressive course to terminal renal failure; however, the chronic glomerulopathies associated with nephrotic syndrome (e.g., membranous glomerulopathy and membranoproliferative glomerulonephritis) and those associated with microscopic hematuria (such as IgA nephropathy) are generally more indolent, with approximately 20 to 25% of patients progressing to end-stage renal disease over a 20-year period. Many patients with IgA nephropathy and membranous glomerulopathy remain stable for long periods or even show complete remission of their disease.

In poststreptococcal glomerulonephritis, the prognosis is usually favorable, especially in children. Less than 1% of pediatric patients die in the acute stages of the disease. The long-term evolution and prognosis, especially in adults, remain controversial because prospective studies on homogenous groups of patients are not available.

In minimal change glomerulopathy, the main feature is nephrotic syndrome that may show a relapsing course not associated with progressive renal insufficiency. When progressive renal failure occurs, focal glomerulosclerosis and the less frequent IgM nephropathy are the usual renal morphologic lesions responsible for progression. Patients with mild proteinuria do better than those who are nephrotic, as is the case with most of the other morphologically defined glomerulopathies.

Prevention

Prevention of the primary glomerulopathies is not possible at present.

Cost Containment

The majority of costs occur in the initial assessment of the patient with primary glomerular disease, and the procedure of greatest cost is renal biopsy. The costs of the procedure, including guidance with either television-monitored fluoroscopy or ultrasonography for kidney localization, and preparation and interpretation of the renal tissue for light, immunofluorescence, and electron microscopy, range from approximately $800 to $3000. Follow-up care and laboratory testing should be no more expensive than other medical practices that use routine laboratory tests.

REFERENCES

Bernard DB, Salant DJ. Clinical approach to the patient with proteinuria and the nephrotic syndrome. In: Jacobson HR, Striker GE, Klahr S, eds. The principles and practice of nephrology. St. Louis: Mosby, 1994:110.

Couser WG. Mediation of immune glomerular injury. J Am Soc Nephrol 1990;1:13.

Cameron JS, Healy MJR, Adu D. The Medical Research Council trial of short-term high-dose alternate day prednisolone in idiopathic membranous nephropathy in adults. Q J Med 1990;74:133.

Cattran DC, Delmore T, Roscoe J, et al. A randomized controlled trial of prednisone in patients with idiopathic membranous nephropathy. N Engl J Med 1989;320:210.

Collaborative Study of the Adult Idiopathic Nephrotic Syndrome: A controlled study of short-term prednisone treatment in adults with membranous nephropathy. N Engl J Med 1979;301:1301.

Davison AM. Steroid therapy in primary glomerulonephritis. Nephrol Dial Transplant 1990;suppl. 1:23.

Donadio JV, Bergstralh EJ, Offord KP, et al., for the Mayo Nephrology Collaborative Group. A controlled trial of fish oil in IgA nephropathy. N Engl J Med 1994;331:1194.

Guder WG, Baines AD, Itoh Y, Nilsson-Ehle P, eds. New markers of renal disease. Kidney Int 1994;46 (suppl. 47):51.

Ponticelli C, Zucchelli P, Passerini P, et al. Methylprednisolone plus chlorambucil as compared with methylprednisolone alone for the treatment of idiopathic membranous nephropathy. The Italian Idiopathic Membranous Nephropathy Treatment Study Group. N Engl J Med 1992;327(9):599.

CHAPTER 16–19

Glomerulonephritis Secondary to Systemic Diseases

James E. Balow, M.D., and Howard A. Austin III, M.D.

DEFINITION

Secondary glomerulonephritis is a heterogeneous condition in which kidney involvement represents one component of a more generalized systemic illness.

ETIOLOGY

The clinical settings in which secondary glomerulonephritis is likely to occur are highly diverse and characteristic for each systemic disease. As a rule, chronic, persistent, and debilitating illnesses tend to produce the greatest risk of secondary glomerulonephritis. The systemic diseases that are most likely to produce secondary glomerulonephritis are listed in Table 16–19–1. Immunologic factors are the most well-characterized nephritogenic mechanisms, but metabolic and hematologic disturbances are also important elements.

CRITERIA FOR DIAGNOSIS
Suggestive

Nocturia, altered urine volumes, hematuria, foamy urine, hypertension, and edema suggest one of the many forms of secondary glomerulonephritis.

Definitive

Cellular casts, proteinuria, and decreased filtration capacity are definite signs of glomerular injury. In some circumstances, glomerulonephritis may be the presenting manifestation of a systemic disease, and analysis of renal pathology may be useful in establishing the diagnosis of the underlying disorders listed in Table 16–19–1.

CLINICAL MANIFESTATIONS
Subjective

Family history is important for recognition of the metabolic and genetic categories of secondary glomerulonephritis. Weak genetic predisposition has been described for some of the rheumatic conditions. Environmental conditions and host susceptibility factors are obviously relevant for many of the infectious causes. Drug history should always be carefully scrutinized; secondary glomerulonephritis can result indirectly from drug-induced rheumatic diseases (e.g., systemic lupus erythematosus or vasculitis) or directly from drug-induced immunogenicity (e.g., gold, penicillamine, captopril).

Objective
Physical Examination

The extrarenal signs of systemic disorders are discussed in other chapters (see Table 16–19–1).

Routine Laboratory Abnormalities

Descriptions of the major renal manifestations are found under hematuria (see Chapter 16–5), proteinuria (see Chapter 16–4), acute nephritic syndrome (see Chapter 16–10), and nephrotic syndrome (see Chapter 16–11).

Laboratory assessment is critical for identifying early glomerular disease, which is frequently subclinical and overshadowed by extrarenal manifestations of the systemic diseases. Careful urinalysis is essential; the physician should personally analyze a fresh urine sample whenever glomerular disease is part of the differential diagnosis. The presence of hematuria is suggestive, but cellular casts are the clearest evidence of active glomerulonephritis. Broad and/or waxy casts indicate preexisting chronic nephritis.

Baseline estimates of renal function by blood urea nitrogen and creatinine levels are appropriate to establish the severity and subsequent rate of progression of glomerulonephritis. Expanded chemistry panels also may assist in the definition of the nephrotic syndrome and the metabolic consequences of uremia. Quantitative urinary protein excretion rate (alternatively, urine protein/creatinine ratio) is warranted in suspected secondary glomerulonephritis.

PLANS

The following discussion focuses on those disorders that are relatively common and those in which renal involvement usually affects the approach to management. Of the broad list of diseases in Table 16–19–1, diabetic nephropathy is described separately (see Chapter 16–21). Others are not further discussed because treatment is mostly ineffective (e.g., amyloidosis), dependent on removal of initiating factors (e.g., infections, malignancy, drugs), or unavailable (e.g., genetic disorders). Evaluation and management of the immunologically mediated rheumatic causes of secondary glomerulonephritis are described individually.

TABLE 16–19–1. SYSTEMIC DISEASES CAUSING SECONDARY GLOMERULONEPHRITIS

Rheumatic–Immunologic Diseases
Systemic lupus erythematosus
Polyarteritis (microscopic polyangiitis)
Wegener's granulomatosis
Systemic sclerosis (scleroderma)
Mixed connective tissue disease
Henoch–Schönlein purpura
Relapsing polychondritis
Behçet's disease
Sjögren's syndrome

Genetic–Metabolic Diseases
Diabetes mellitus
Amyloidosis
Alport's hereditary nephritis
Fabry's disease
Nail patella syndrome
Sickle cell disease

Hematologic–Oncologic Diseases
Multiple myeloma
Macroglobulinemia
Light-chain disease
Cryoglobulinemia
Thrombotic thrombocytopenia purpura
Hemolytic–uremic syndrome
Lymphomas, leukemias
Carcinomas

Infectious Diseases
Poststreptococcal
Endocarditis
Shunt infections
Occult abscesses
Syphilis, leprosy
Hepatitis B and C
Schistosomiasis
Malaria

Other Diseases
Drug-induced systemic lupus erythematosus, vasculitis
Drug-associated membranous nephropathy
Drug-induced interstitial nephritis
Nonsteroidal antiinflammatory drug-induced nephropathies
Serum sickness
Heroin nephropathy
HIV-associated nephropathies

Diagnostic

Differential Diagnosis

As evident from the categories of diseases causing secondary glomerulonephritis outlined in Table 16–19–1, the differential diagnosis is broad and overlapping. Specialized hematologic, immunologic, metabolic, and microbiologic tests are needed to define each type of systemic disease. Biopsy of affected tissues facilitates the diagnosis in certain instances. Renal biopsy is not always diagnostic, but it permits the definition of the type and severity of the kidney disease, assessment of prognosis, and formulation of therapeutic plans.

Diagnostic Options and Recommended Approach

Systemic Lupus Erythematosus. Systemic lupus erythematosus is defined by the presence of four or more of the American Rheumatism Association criteria (see Chapter 7–1). Debility from constitutional and ex-

trarenal manifestations dominates the management of early systemic lupus erythematosus; however, the physician should be cognizant of and instruct patients regarding the serious implications of renal involvement. Clinically, lupus nephritis spans nearly the entire spectrum of renal syndromes. Nephritic and nephrotic syndromes predominate. Azotemia may be insidious or rapidly progressive. Hypertension is prevalent and warrants aggressive management. On renal biopsy, high-grade proliferation, necrosis, cellular crescents, and extensive subendothelial immune complex deposits are considered indications for intensive therapy. Proliferative lupus nephritis carries the highest risk for progressive renal failure; however, the cardiovascular morbidity and mortality related to persistent nephrotic syndrome or hypertension are also grounds for intervention. Clinically, nephritic urinary sediment or rapidly progressive renal insufficiency are major indications for therapy. Isolated laboratory tests are rarely reliable predictors of an adverse course, although falling serum complement levels or rising anti-DNA antibody titers warrant intensified surveillance for evidence of progressive lupus nephritis.

Henoch–Schönlein Purpura. Henoch–Schönlein purpura is a vasculitic disease (more akin to lupus than polyarteritis) with characteristic features, including purpuric rash, arthritis, gastrointestinal hemorrhage, and glomerulonephritis. Transient and asymptomatic hematuria and proteinuria accompany the typically self-limited cases of Henoch–Schönlein purpura. Relapsing or chronic courses of systemic disease increase the likelihood of progressive nephritis. Hypertension, complicated nephrotic syndrome, persistently nephritic urinary sediment, and progressive azotemia reflect the proliferative glomerulonephritis that occurs in a minority of cases. Large percentages of glomerular crescents forebode an unfavorable prognosis and are important indications for treatment.

Polyarteritis. Polyarteritis is a vasculitic syndrome comprising constitutional symptoms (weight loss, fever, malaise, arthralgias, myalgias) and focal signs caused by inflammatory lesions in skin, peripheral nerves, gastrointestinal tract, or kidneys (see Chapter 7–8). Polyarteritis produces renal disease through inflammation and necrosis of medium-sized arteries (classic form) or glomeruli (microscopic form). Classic polyarteritis produces focal ischemia with consequences ranging from renovascular hypertension to infarctions. Microscopic polyangiitis (polyarteritis) produces the nephritic syndrome or rapidly progressive renal disease due to focal necrotizing and crescentic glomerulonephritis. Structural evidence of vasculitis is indicated by vascular irregularities and aneurysms on arteriography or by characteristic necrotizing inflammatory lesions in biopsy specimens. Aneurysms in the arterial bed of any viscera are both a diagnostic element and an indication for immunosuppressive therapy. Evidence of infarction or progressive azotemia warrants intervention. In microscopic polyangiitis, search for renal involement is critical because intensive treatment is warranted if there is any evidence of glomerulonephritis. Anti-neutrophil cytoplasmic antibodies (ANCA) provide useful serologic tests to support a diagnosis of renal vasculitis. In microscopic polyangiitis, a perinuclear pattern (P-ANCA), reflecting antibodies primarily against leukocyte myeloperoxidase, is characteristic.

Wegener's Granulomatosis. Wegener's granulomatosis is a vasculitic syndrome with specific components, including necrotizing vasculitis and granulomas of the upper and lower respiratory tracts and glomerulonephritis. Respiratory tract pathology is usually the key element in confirming diagnosis. Asymptomatic hematuria and active urinary sediment are signs of early focal proliferative glomerulonephritis. Escalation to necrotizing and crescentic glomerulonephritis is often accompanied by rapidly progressive renal insufficiency. Careful urinalysis and renal function tests are essential; virtually any sign of glomerulonephritis is taken as an indication for immunosuppressive therapy because of the high risk of rapid deterioration of renal function. ANCA serologic tests are quite sensitive in Wegener's granulomatosis; a cytoplasmic staining pattern (C-ANCA), reflecting antibodies primarily against leukocyte proteinase 3, is characteristic.

Systemic Sclerosis (Scleroderma). Scleroderma is characterized by progressive degeneration of connective tissue elements and sclerosing vasculopathy which leads to atrophy and secondary fibrosis of skin and major viscera. Low-grade proteinuria and renovascular hypertension are the usual signs of kidney disease in systemic sclerosis. Proliferative and mucoid arteriolopathy of the kidney may produce accelerated renal failure often in parallel with (but not necessarily due to) malignant hypertension.

Therapeutic

Corticosteroids are the mainstay of treatment of *lupus nephritis;* however, the threat of insidious long-term complications (e.g., avascular necrosis of bone, cataracts, and atherosclerosis) dictates that corticosteroid therapy should be used with restraint. This policy includes repeated trials of tapering dosage and administration on alternate days whenever possible. Initial therapy for major indications of active lupus nephritis includes prednisone (1.0 mg/kg/d, maintained for 4–6 weeks). Induction with intravenous pulse methylprednisolone (e.g., 1.0 g/m^2) for 3 days followed by maintenance prednisone is favored by some. If remission of renal disease is nearly complete, simply tapering to alternate-day prednisone over the subsequent month and establishing a maintenance dose targeted to be prednisone 10 to 20 mg every other day is acceptable. With incomplete renal response or unusually aggressive glomerulonephritis, most consultants would consider cyclophosphamide as the preferable adjunct to prednisone. Intermittent pulse cyclophosphamide (0.5–1.0 g/m^2) in single intravenous doses every 1 to 3 months is favored because of reduced long-term toxicity (e.g., bone marrow, gonadal, and bladder) compared with conventional daily oral cyclophosphamide. Plasma exchange has not proven efficacious in proliferative lupus nephritis. Cyclosporine has a limited role in treatment of lupus nephritis.

Immunosuppressive therapy is warranted in a minority of patients with *Henoch–Schönlein nephritis.* A trial of prednisone is usually initiated in patients with severe glomerulonephritis, although efficacy is controversial. There is growing opinion that cyclophosphamide is more effective than prednisone; however, experience is limited and uncontrolled for any form of treatment (including plasma exchange).

Polyarteritis of either the classic or microscopic form is initially treated with prednisone (1.0 mg/kg/d for 6–8 weeks). Pulse methylprednisolone (1.0 g/m^2) intravenously for 3 days is favored for patients with severe glomerulonephritis. Cyclophosphamide is warranted early for unusually severe and critical visceral involvement or later because of failure to maintain adequate control of disease activity after tapering of prednisone. Oral cyclophosphamide initiated at 2.0 mg/kg/d is favored. Some investigators prefer switching after 3–4 months from cyclophosphamide to azathioprine for long-term, maintenance treatment. Adjunctive plasma exchange may benefit some patients with very aggressive disease or those refractory to the standard therapy.

Prednisone (1.0 mg/kg/d) is indicated for therapy of *Wegener's granulomatosis* if debilitating constitutional symptoms, severe extrarenal distress, or glomerulonephritis is evident. Concomitantly, oral cyclophosphamide (2.0 mg/kg/d) should be instituted. Prednisone has a limited role in long-term therapy and is usually tapered to alternate-day dosage and subsequently discontinued after several weeks to months. Cyclophosphamide is continued until complete remission has been evident for at least 1 year. Intermittent pulse cyclophosphamide therapy is being actively investigated for treatment of several of the ANCA-positive glomerular diseases, as a technique to reduce the risk of long-term toxicity associated with prolonged daily cyclophosphamide treatment.

Although considered an immunologic disorder, *systemic sclerosis* does not appear to benefit from current forms of immunosuppressive treatment. At present, therapy is focused on interrupting the vicious cycle of renal vasculopathy, azotemia, and hypertension. Angiotensin-converting enzyme inhibition with appropriate drugs appears to be one of the most successful approaches to preservation of renal function in these patients. Other antihypertensives, including vasodilators, beta-adrenergic blockers, and diuretics, may be used as supplementary agents.

FOLLOW-UP

Monitoring of disease activity and the course of secondary glomerulonephritis must be highly individualized. Extrarenal disease commonly requires reassessment of severity and risk of permanent debilitation. The physician must estimate the severity and rate of progression of the renal disease and adjust follow-up accordingly, again emphasizing to the patient the need for scheduled follow-up because of the usual unreliability of clinical symptoms.

DISCUSSION
Prevalence and Incidence

The frequencies of disorders associated with secondary glomerulonephritis vary widely. For example, diabetic nephropathy is a common cause of nephrotic syndrome in the adult, lupus nephritis is moderately common in young women, but the majority of the disorders listed in Table 16–19–1 are quite rare.

Related Basic Science

The pathogenesis of glomerulonephritis is poorly defined for most forms that are secondary to systemic diseases. Circulating immune complexes are commonly observed in systemic diseases, but it is apparent that only a small fraction of immune complexes are nephritogenic. Deposits of immune complexes containing DNA, immunoglobulin G, immunoglobulin A, and/or complement components are seen in the mesangial, subendothelial, and subepithelial regions of the glomerular basement membrane in lupus nephritis. Similar patterns of immune complex deposits are seen with glomerulonephritis associated with Henoch–Schönlein purpura.

Circulating immune complexes and decreased reticuloendothelial clearance have been described in patients with polyarteritis and Wegener's granulomatosis; however, there is no evidence that glomerulonephritis associated with these diseases is due to renal deposits of immune complexes. Antibodies to neutrophilic cytoplasmic antigens (ANCA) are regularly present in patients with renal vasculitis. There is some evidence that these autoantibodies may activate neutrophils and enhance the potential for vascular injury by upregulating expression of cellular adhesion molecules, but their precise role in the vasculitic process is uncertain.

Natural History and Its Modification with Treatment

The prognosis of most of the secondary forms of glomerulonephritis seems to have steadily improved over the past several decades. Enhanced case recognition, improved ancillary care for hypertensive and infectious complications, better patient education, and improved follow-up have been substantial factors. Improved immunosuppressive therapy and judicious restraint in the use of corticosteroids have reduced iatrogenic complications.

Estimates of survival and maintenance of adequate renal function to avoid the need for dialysis or transplantation are commonly used as measures of outcome for secondary glomerulonephritis. Overall, the risk of developing end-stage renal failure at 5 years after the appearance of glomerular disease is approximately 20% for diffuse proliferative lupus nephritis. The risk is nearer 50% for microscopic polyangiitis and Wegener's granulomatosis, and even higher if renal involvement is present in systemic sclerosis. Specific features have been used to refine prognostic estimates of most of the rheumatic causes of secondary glomerulonephritis. Clinical evidence of rapidly progressive or crescentic glomerulonephritis, severe hypertension, complicated nephrotic syndrome, and a background of chronic atrophic and sclerosing renal pathology help to identify subsets of patients at higher risk of progressive renal disease in nearly all forms of secondary glomerulonephritis.

Prevention

Most forms of secondary glomerulonephritis are of unknown etiology and, therefore, are not preventable. Control of infectious diseases, particularly chronic bacterial and parasitic diseases, will prevent secondary glomerulonephritis. Careful monitoring of drugs with a known risk of inducing secondary glomerulonephritis may minimize the likelihood of severe renal disease.

Cost Containment

Costs for the definitive diagnosis of the primary systemic diseases vary greatly. Baseline data should be adequate to allow one to recognize activity and assess subsequent progression of the systemic disease. Standard renal function tests and often renal biopsy are warranted to assess glomerular disease and prognosis and to plan therapy. Careful urinalysis is frequently the most efficient and pragmatic means of monitoring the activity of glomerulonephritis. Routine, frequent serologic testing (e.g., anti-DNA, complement levels, ANCA) are not warranted; rather, they should be used selectively when there are questions about changes in disease activity. Immunosuppressive therapy with oral corticosteroids or cytotoxic drugs is comparatively inexpensive. Plasma exchange and cyclosporine therapy are extremely expensive; they are usually administered under experimental protocols.

REFERENCES

Balow JE, Austin HA, Boumpas DT. Immunologic renal diseases. In: Rich RR, Shearer WT, Strober W, et al., eds. Clinical immunology: Principles and practice. St. Louis: Mosby-Year Book, 1995.

Boumpas DT, Austin HA, Vaughan EM, et al. Severe lupus nephritis: Controlled trial of pulse methylprednisolone versus two different regimens of pulse cyclophosphamide. Lancet 1992;340:741.

Donohoe JF. Scleroderma and the kidney. Kidney Int 1992;41:462.

Goldstein AR, White RH, Akuse R, et al. Long-term follow-up of childhood Henoch–Schönlein nephritis. Lancet 1992;339:280.

Greenberg A, Cheung AK, Coffman TK, et al., eds. Primer on kidney diseases. National Kidney Foundation. San Diego: Academic Press, 1994.

Hoffman GS, Kerr GS, Leavitt RY, et al. Wegener granulomatosis: An analysis of 158 patients. Ann Intern Med 1992;116:488.

Kallenberg CG, Brouwer E, Weening JJ, et al. Anti-neutrophil cytoplasmic antibodies: Current diagnostic and pathophysiological potential. Kidney Int 1994;46:1.

CHAPTER 16–20

Tubulointerstitial Nephropathy

Edmund Bourke, M.D.

DEFINITION

Tubulointerstitial nephropathy is a clinicopathologic entity characterized by inflammation and/or fibrosis of the renal interstitial space with a variable degree of associated tubular damage. Although many renal diseases are accompanied by significant interstitial involvement, only those conditions in which it is the primary and predominant site of renal involvement are designated tubulointerstitial nephropathy.

ETIOLOGY

Tubulointerstitial nephropathy is best classified as acute or chronic. Acute tubulointerstitial nephropathy is generally regarded as a hypersensitivity reaction. It is most often attributable to a drug (Table 16–20–1). Occasionally it is attributable to a systemic infection. This is to be distinguished from bacterial invasion of the renal parenchyma, for which the term *acute pyelonephritis* is used and which is dealt with as a separate entity (see Chapter 8–23). The causes of chronic tubulointerstitial nephropathy are heterogeneous (Table 16–20–2). The term is best reserved for when tubulointerstitial disease is the primary event, although changes in the interstitium may also be secondary, as a consequence of vascular, glomerular, or obstructive renal disease.

CRITERIA FOR DIAGNOSIS

Suggestive

Acute allergic interstitial nephritis should be considered when an abrupt disturbance of renal function occurs in association with administration of a drug. The list of such drugs is sizable (Table 16–20–1) and

TABLE 16–20–1. CAUSES OF ACUTE INTERSTITIAL NEPHRITIS

Drugs	Beta-lactam antibiotics: penicillins, cephalosporins
	Rifampin, sulfonamides and other antibiotics
	Nonsteroidal antiinflammatory drugs
	Thiazides and other diuretics
	Other drugs: allopurinol, cimetidine, phenindione, diphenylhydantoin, carbamazepine, interferon, sulfinpyrazone
Infections	Streptococci, staphylococci, Legionnaires' disease, brucellosis, Rocky Mountain spotted fever, toxoplasmosis, leptospirosis, infectious mononucleosis, *Mycoplasma* pneumonia
Kidney transplant	
Idiopathic	

increasing. This hypersensitivity reaction is to be distinguished from direct nephrotoxicity. Fever, rash, and eosinphilia are important clues that recent-onset renal dysfunction may be part of such a hypersensitivity diathesis.

In the presence of a more insidious onset of renal dysfunction a drug- or toxin-induced chronic tubulointerstitial nephropathy also requires consideration, as does the presence of other factors known to be associated with damage to the tubulointerstitium (Table 16–20–2).

Definitive

Renal biopsy is the most reliable indicator of acute interstitial nephritis and of many cases of chronic tubulointerstitial nephropathy. In more advanced cases of chronic tubulointerstitial nephropathy, renal biopsy may be too nonspecific to permit a definitive diagnosis. This is particularly likely when the kidneys are shrunken. In these situations, evidence of the presence of or significant exposure to an established etiologic factor (Table 16–20–2), together with otherwise unexplained renal impairment, may permit sufficient certainty to make a definitive diagnosis. Specifically in the case of analgesic abuse, the radiologic demon-

TABLE 16–20–2. CHRONIC TUBULOINTERSTITIAL NEPHROPATHY

Primary, predominant	
Drugs	Analgesic abuse, mithramycin, streptozotocin, carmustine, methyl-CCNU, *cis*-platinum, amphotericin, cyclosporine, lithium, etc.
Heavy metals	Lead, cadmium, beryllium
Metabolic	Hypercalcemia, gouty nephropathy, chronic hypokalemia
Immunologic	Sjögren's syndrome, transplant rejection, sarcoid
Infective	Tuberculosis, malacoplakia
Infiltrative	Myeloma, lymphoma, leukemia, Waldenstrom's macroglobulinemia, xanthogranulomatous nephritis
Idiopathic	Familial, hereditary, endemic (Balkan), sporadic
Irradiation	
Unresolved acute interstitial nephritis	
Secondary to	
Glomerular disease	Focal glomerulosclerosis, membranoproliferative glomerulonephritis, lupus, Alport's syndrome, etc.
Obstruction	Reflux, other anatomic anomalies
Hereditary disease	Medullary cystic disease
Vascular disease	Nephrosclerosis, sickle cell hemoglobinopathy

stration of papillary necrosis is definitive evidence of analgesic nephropathy.

CLINICAL MANIFESTATIONS

Subjective

There is usually no pertinent family history. Very occasionally, a family history of renal tubular acidosis, sickle cell disease, or vesicoureteric reflux may point in this direction. Rarely, industrial exposure to nephrotoxins (e.g., cadmium, lead) may be evident. More often, evidence of exposure to one of the drugs known to be associated with tubulointerstitial disease (Tables 16–20–1 and 16–20–2) is obtainable.

In acute interstitial nephritis, a history of drug exposure is obtained in the majority of patients. Classically described with methicillin, other penicillins, and cephalosporins, other antibiotics and a host of other drugs have been implicated (Table 16–20–1) and the list continues to grow. Loin pain attributable to renal swelling may be experienced. The patient may complain of hematuria or symptoms attributable to azotemia. Renal colic or the passage of tissue (papillae) in the urine suggests analgesic nephropathy. Eliciting a positive history requires skillful clinical interviewing due to frequent denial of analgesic abuse by the patient. A history of keratoconjunctivitis sicca, xerostomia, arthralgias, photosensitivity, gout, tuberculosis, sarcoidosis, sickle cell disease, or previous abdominal irradiation may provide a diagnostic lead (Table 16–20–2). Polyuria and nocturia due to impaired renal concentrating ability are common to all tubulointerstitial nephropathies.

Objective

Physical Examination

Fever, skin rash, and eosinophilia in a patient presenting with renal dysfunction suggest the possibility of a drug-induced, hypersensitivity-related acute interstitial nephritis. They are present, however, in less than 50% of patients. The rash, usually maculopapular or petechial, due to a concomitant cutaneous vasculitis, is generally most prominent if not confined to the lower extremities. In such instances, the kidneys may be tender to palpation.

Rarely, the cyanotic discoloration of methemoglobinemia (phenacetin excess), tophi (gouty nephropathy), or features of the sicca syndrome point to the etiology of a chronic tubulointerstitial nephropathy. Hypertension is present in about 50% of patients.

Routine Laboratory Abnormalities

Proteinuria generally does not exceed 2+ on dipstick or 2 g per 24 hours. An exception is the nephrotic range proteinuria due to a concomitant glomerular lesion classically seen in acute interstitial nephritis due to nonsteroidal antiinflammatory agents. Variable degrees of leukocyturia and/or hematuria are common, and renal tubular cells are frequently seen. Eosinophiluria (Wright's strain or Hansen's stain of the urinary sediment) is a strong indicator of acute hypersensitivity interstitial nephritis, but a negative result does not exclude it. Significant bacteriuria may point to a primary pyelonephritis (see Chapter 8–23), but it is also a very common secondary phenomenon in other forms of tubulointerstitial disease. Sometimes, the urinalysis is extremely benign.

The presentation may be acute as is most commonly seen in acute hypersensitivity interstitial nephritis. It is thus part of the differential diagnosis of acute renal failure (see Chapter 16–9) or the acute nephritic syndrome (see Chapter 16–10). More insidious presentations, including asymptomatic urinary abnormalities and chronic renal insufficiency, characterize chronic tubulointerstitial disease.

Azotemia is, therefore, the rule in acute and a likely ultimate consequence in most untreated forms of chronic tubulointerstitial disease. Anemia out of proportion to the degree of azotemia is common in chronic tubulointerstitial disease. Renal tubular acidosis, sometimes with concomitant hyperkalemia (type 4 renal tubular acidosis), may be present. Hypercalcemia and moderate to severe hyperuricemia may be important etiologic findings. In the latter instance, the fact that secondary hyperuricemia is an accompaniment of chronic renal failure irrespective of etiology may make definitive identification of the rare

gouty nephropathy difficult. Tophi or renal histologic evidence may be necessary to make the distinction.

PLANS

Diagnostic

Differential Diagnosis

Acute interstitial nephritis can be a hypersensitivity reaction to a wide variety of drugs or, less often, to a systemic infection with a variety of microorganisms (Table 16–20–1). Not infrequently no etiologic factor is identified. Acute rejection of a kidney transplant is also an acute tubulointerstitial reaction addressed in Chapter 16–26.

Chronic tubulointerstitial nephropathy as a primary renal disease can be due to a wide variety of etiologies (Table 16–20–2), including exposure to drugs and toxins; metabolic, immunologic, infective, and infiltrative causes; radiation damage; unresolved acute interstitial nephritis; and idiopathic causes. In other diseases whose primary target lies elsewhere, for example, some glomerulopathies, obstructive nephropathy, and severe nephrosclerosis, secondary changes in the tubulointerstitium may be prominent and contribute significantly to the functional impairment. For classification purposes, however, these conditions are discussed under the heading of the primary diagnosis.

Diagnostic Options

Urinary protein electrophoresis generally reveals a pattern of tubular proteinuria (see Chapter 16–4). Impaired urinary concentrating capacity, acidification, and/or sodium conservation may be apparent when tubular dysfunction is prominent. Thus, impaired increase in urinary osmolality following vasopressin, renal tubular acidosis, or negative sodium balance may be demonstrable, particularly in the more chronic forms of the disease.

An immunologic screen, particularly when features of Sjogren's syndrome are suggested, should include rheumatoid factor, antinuclear antibodies, and immunoelectrophoresis. A monoclonal spike on plasma electrophoresis or light-chain proteinuria should be looked for in all patients over 50 to rule out myeloma kidney. A high index of suspicion is important in analgesic abuse nephropathy, and urine testing for analgesic metabolites may be required. Pyelography in such cases typically reveals clubbed calyces, medullary cavities, and the "ring sign," pathognomonic of papillary necrosis.

Blood lead levels are an unrealiable screen for lead nephropathy. Urinary coproporphyrin may be elevated and a 24-hour lead excretion following intravenous administration of the chelating agent EDTA may confirm excessive lead exposure.

Renal biopsy is the most definitive diagnostic step in acute interstitial nephritis. Infiltration of the renal cortical interstitium with mononuclear cells (polymorphonuclear cells in acute pyelonephritis), variable interstitial edema, and frequently scattered eosinopils are hallmarks of acute interstitial nephritis. Evidence of tubular damage is also generally apparent. In chronic tubulointerstitial nephropathy, the kidneys are often shrunken and the histologic features are no longer sufficiently diagnostic to distinguish it from other causes of small, contracted kidneys. In earlier cases, renal biopsy reveals increased fibrosis of the renal parenchymal interstitium with a modest mononuclear cell infiltration, dilated atrophied tubules, and periglomerular fibrosis. There is relative sparing of glomeruli, which may, however, reveal secondary glomerular sclerosis.

Recommended Approach

If acute interstitial nephritis is considered as a possible cause of renal dysfunction, all potential incriminating drugs should be withheld. If resolution of renal dysfunction follows discontinuation of the implicated drug, a cause-and-effect association is most likely and rechallenge should be assiduously avoided. If no such drug is identified but extrarenal infection is present, including streptococcal or staphylococcal sepsis and Legionnaire's disease (Table 16–20–1), an immunologic-type response to these agents can be considered likely if, again, resolution of renal dysfunction follows on their eradication. Renal dysfunction may not undergo spontaneous resolution following removal of the offending agent, be it drug or infection, however, and renal biopsy will be indicated for a confirmatory diagnosis.

If chronic interstitial nephritis is considered as a possible cause of renal dysfunction, potentially incriminating drugs should again be withdrawn, a history of possible exposure to toxins should be looked for, and clinical and immunologic evidence of Sjögren's syndrome or other autoimmune diseases investigated, including rheumatoid factor, antinuclear antibodies, and immunoelectrophoresis. A monoclonal spike requires consideration of myeloma kidney which should be considered in all patients over 50. Analgesic abuse may be denied by the patient, so a high index of suspicion is axiomatic.

Therapeutic

The importance of a detailed workup is underscored by the fact that in many instances therapeutic intervention, including removal of the offending agent, may result in arrest, regression, or even complete resolution of the renal dysfunction.

In acute interstitial nephritis due to drug hypersensitivity where discontinuity does not result in improvement of renal function within 1 week, it is customary to employ a trial of steroids, initially at a dose of 1 mg/kg/d for a couple of weeks. Although no controlled trials are yet available, anecdotal evidence suggests that partial or complete remission can be anticipated in most cases. When the lesion is an immunologic response to an extrarenal infection, eradication of the causative organism is the primary goal. The cautious use of steroids may play a contributory role in some such instances where renal functional improvement does not occur. Steroid therapy has also been beneficial in idiopathic acute interstitial nephritis and in granulomatous sarcoid nephritis and some acute forms of Sjögren's-associated interstitial nephritis. Specific cytotoxic therapy may play a beneficial role in myeloma kidney and other infiltrative disorders. Renal tuberculosis requires 18 months of therapy with two antituberculous agents.

In analgesic abuse nephropathy, when patients can be persuaded to refrain from such ingestion, progressively deteriorating renal function may be arrested and significant improvement in renal function is frequently observed. The timely recognition of excess heavy metal exposure may necessitate a change of occupation.

FOLLOW-UP

If complete resolution follows removal of the offending agent in acute interstitial nephritis, there is no need for long-term follow-up. Where steroids or chemotherapy has been embarked on, close follow-up, initially weekly or more often and then every few weeks, is generally required to monitor progress and prevent side effects. Chronic interstitial nephritis may progress to chronic renal failure, whereupon the frequency of follow-up is that for chronic renal failure in general (see Chapter 16–12). In cases of analgesic abuse nephropathy, follow-up at approximately 3- to 4-month intervals also serves to reinforce the need to remain off analgesics as far as possible. The superimposition of hypertension may accelerate the rate of progression of chronic tubulointerstitial nephropathy into end-stage renal disease. The disappearance of hypertension may indicate that negative sodium balance due to tubular dysfunction has supervened. This is not infrequently noted when significant bacteriuria occurs. It may add a significant prerenal component requiring liberalization of salt intake for a variable period and, thus, more frequent follow-up. Should the patient with analgesic abuse nephropathy experience colic or the passage of papillary-like material, he or she should notify the physician. Superimposed symptomatic pyelonephritis is another indication for contacting the physician. Symptoms suggestive of uremia also should prompt physician contact. Meanwhile, because of the ever-present possibility of developing renal failure at some stage, the diagnosis of chronic tubulointerstitial nephropathy is an indication for indefinite follow-up a few times a year.

DISCUSSION
Prevalence and Incidence

The real incidence of acute interstitial nephritis is unknown. It can only be definitively diagnosed in cases that warrant renal biopsy. In patients with acute renal failure who undergo renal biopsy, acute interstitial nephritis, often unsuspected, is found in about 10% of patients. This may be an underestimate of its incidence, however, as renal biopsy is performed only in selected cases of acute renal failure. The frequency with which chronic tubulointerstitial disease affects the kidney is also difficult to determine. When the disease is advanced it is often impossible to determine whether tubulointerstitial pathology is primary or secondary to glomerular or vascular disease. Statistics from end-stage renal disease patients suggest an overall incidence of about 20%; however, significant geographic differences are reported in the literature, in part due to significant geographic difference in analgesic abuse.

Related Basic Science

The diagnosis of tubulointerstitial nephropathy must be considered in any patient with either acute or chronic renal failure or asymptomatic urinary abnormalities of uncertain etiology. Bacterial infection of the kidney was formerly believed to be a major source and a cause of chronic renal failure due to repeated inflammation followed by fibrosis primarily of the tubulointerstitial space. Hence the term *chronic pyelonephritis*. It is now known that many other diseases can result in the same histologic picture. It has been further established that chronic urinary tract infections per se rarely lead to progressive impairment of renal function unless there is a primary underlying disease such as obstruction, vesicoureteric reflux, or diabetic nephropathy. It would appear that most of the previous reports of chronic renal failure attributed to chronic pyelonephritis were in effect other tubulointerstitial diseases, including the consequences of analgesic abuse in adults and vesicoureteric reflux in children or young adults. The significance of bacterial invasion of the kidney has now generally been relegated to a secondary role. It may nonetheless be important in drawing attention to an underlying renal disorder, in contributing to the symptomatology or natural history of the primary tubulointerstitial nephropathy, or as a source of urosepsis and potentially life-threatening septic shock. This potentially direct role of bacterial invasion of the kidney must be distinguished from an acute allergic tubulointerstitial reaction often accompanied by renal functional impairment, which may occur in the course of systemic infections. This is an immunologic reaction rather than a result of bacterial invasion of the kidney.

Although acute interstitial nephritis is generally believed to be an immunologic disorder, the precise mechanism has not been established. The initial reports of anti-tubular basement membrane antibodies in methicillin-induced acute interstitial nephritis are an inconsistent finding. Immune complexes in association with human tubulointerstitial disease have been observed in a few instances, particularly in patients with Sjögren's syndrome, but they are not a feature of the more common drug-induced cases. The frequent presence of eosinophilia and sometimes elevated serum immunoglobulin E levels suggest a possible contributory role for a reaginic (type 1) reaction in hypersensitivity-related interstitial nephritis. More recent studies using monoclonal antibodies indicate that the majority of infiltrating cells are T cells, particularly cytotoxic/suppressor T cells, and imply a major role for cell-mediated immunity in the pathogenesis of acute interstitial nephritis. In most cases of drug-related acute hypersensitivity nephritis, the onset is fairly sudden. It has been very gradual, however, in some instances of thiazide-related disease.

The most common primary chronic tubulointerstitial nephropathy in the adult in the Western world is analgesic abuse nephropathy. It requires prolonged ingestion of phenacetin-, acetaminophen-, or aspirin-containing compounds for several years to decades and a quantity generally in excess of 2 kg. In most studies of this disease, women outnumber men. Prevalence varies greatly, although it usually parallels the reported frequency of analgesic usage, and in various countries it accounts for between 5 and 20% of cases of chronic renal failure. The pathogenesis has not been established, but accumulation of the drugs or metabolites in the inner medulla due to the countercurrent multiplier action of the ascending limb of the loop of Henle with resultant toxic–metabolic effects has been implicated. Clinically, the features of the analgesic abuse may result in a syndrome characterized, in addition to renal disease, by anemia, upper gastrointestinal symptomatology, accelerated atherosclerosis, frequent psychiatric abnormalities, and the facial appearances of premature aging. Analgesic abuse has been much more frequently reported from Australia, South Africa, Canada, and Europe than from the United States, where it has been most often encountered in the Southeast.

Although marked proteinuria is not a classic feature of tubulointerstitial nephropathy, there are situations where it is encountered in both the acute and chronic settings. In some drug-induced acute interstitial nephritides, most notably following ingestion of some nonsteroidal antiinflammatory drugs, a concomitant glomerulopathy has accounted for a concomitant nephrotic range proteinuria. On the other hand, in chronic obstructive lesions, most notably in patients with vesicoureteric reflux, a focal and segmental glomerular sclerosis may develop that not only results in increased protein loss, but also contributes to the progressive decline in renal function. Furthermore, secondary interstitial inflammation may be prominent in a number of predominantly glomerular lesions (see Table 16–20–2). In some such primary glomerulonephritides, the extent of the tubulointerstitial involvement may be a better prognostic indicator than the primary lesion.

Natural History and Its Modification with Treatment

In most instances of acute interstitial nephritis, complete resolution follows withdrawal of the offending agent with or without a course of steroid therapy. In some such cases, however, the resolution is only partial due to healing by fibrosis. In chronic tubulointerstitial nephropathy, in which a correctable cause has not been identified in a timely manner, the natural history is generally one of progression to chronic renal failure and, ultimately, to end-stage renal disease, although the time course is remarkably variable from months to decades. In many instances, removal of the causative agent may lead to stable, although impaired, renal function. Among the possible exceptions where, once initiated, renal impairment may continue a downhill course despite drug withdrawal are some chemotherapeutic agents, including streptozotocin, mithramycin, methyl-CCNU, cyclosporin A, and, occasionally, *cis*-platinum.

Prevention

No indicator currently exists that will identify a patient prone to a particular drug-associated acute interstitial nephritis except a previous episode. The importance of avoiding such reexposure is axiomatic. The patient should be made aware of the specific causative agent and the family of drugs (e.g., ampicillin, a penicillin-related compound) so as to prevent inadvertent reexposure and to avoid other compounds from the same family of drugs when a satisfactory alternative is available. Proper dosage and methods of administration reduce the renal complications of the chemotherapeutic agents referred to above. In the case of cyclosporine, monitoring of plasma levels helps minimize renal toxicity. Moreover, the lower dosages now generally used have decreased the incidence of progressive tubulointerstitial nephropathy. Wider recognition in oncology has reduced the incidence of hypercalcemic and hyperuricemic nephropathy. Public education and the withdrawal of phenacetin from the market have helped reduce the incidence of analgesic nephropathy in Canada. Greater public health inspection of workplaces and imposition of regulatory requirements have helped reduce the incidence of chronic interstitial nephritis due to lead, cadmium, and other toxic exposures.

Cost Containment

Early recognition and treatment are esssential to avoid or postpone the extremely high cost of end-stage renal disease care.

REFERENCES

Eknoyan G. Tubulointerstitial nephritides. In: Massry SG, Glassock RJ, eds. Textbook of nephrology. 3rd ed. Baltimore: Williams & Wilkins, 1995:1036.

Molzahn M, Pommer W. Analgesic nephropathy. In: Cameron S, Davison AM, Grunfeld JP, et al., eds. The Oxford textbook of clinical nephrology. Oxford: Oxford Medical, 1992:803.

Neilson EG. The pathogenesis and therapy of interstitial nephritis. Kidney Int 1989;35:1257.

Sandler DP, Burr R, Weinberg C. Non-steroidal antiinflammatory drugs and the kidney. Ann Intern Med 1991;115:165.

Toto RD. Acute tubulointerstitial nephritis. Am J Med Sci 1990;299:392.

Diabetic Nephropathy

Francis Dumler, M.D., and Nathan W. Levin, M.D.

DEFINITION

Diabetic nephropathy is a long-term complication of diabetes mellitus characterized by specific glomerular lesions (diffuse and/or nodular diabetic glomerulosclerosis) that are clinically manifested as proteinuria, nephrotic syndrome, and relentless progression to end-stage renal failure.

ETIOLOGY

Diabetic nephropathy is a direct metabolic consequence of a state of insulin deficiency and hyperglycemia that is further modulated by additional genetic and environmental factors. Mechanisms involved in the genesis of diabetic nephropathy are not necessarily similar to those responsible for its progression.

CRITERIA FOR DIAGNOSIS
Suggestive

Clinical diabetic nephropathy is suspected by the presence of nocturia, dependent edema, hypertension, and proteinuria on routine urinalysis in patients with diabetes mellitus of several years' duration. About 60% of patients have clinical evidence of coexisting retinopathy or neuropathy. Once diabetic nephropathy is clinically recognizable as a nephrotic syndrome, it almost always progresses to end-stage renal failure.

Definitive

Pathologic examination of the kidney demonstrates the characteristic lesions of diabetic nephropathy, namely, thickening of the glomerular basement membrane, afferent and efferent arteriolar sclerosis, mesangial matrix expansion, and diffuse and/or nodular glomerulosclerosis.

CLINICAL MANIFESTATIONS
Subjective

The early stages of diabetic nephropathy are asymptomatic. As proteinuria and hypoalbuminemia become more severe, sodium and fluid retention occur, possibly in association with hypoalbuminemia and a decrease in effective intravascular volume. The patient may first note these changes as nocturia and dependent edema. As the nephrotic syndrome progresses in severity, anasarca may become apparent. Hypertension is usually well established at this point, and may cause headaches and symptoms and signs of congestive heart failure, including shortness of breath. As renal function worsens, uremic symptoms may become apparent, including asthenia, fatigue, lethargy, anorexia, nausea, and vomiting. Paresthesias, particularly in the lower extremities, visual symptoms, and episodes of gastroparesis may become more severe as uremia is superimposed on diabetic vasculopathy and neuropathy. Insulin or oral hypoglycemic agent requirements may decrease as renal failure worsens, particularly in type 2 patients, and hypoglycemic episodes may occur if doses are not reduced.

Objective

Physical Examination

Edema ranging from a trace to anasarca may be present, and hypertension usually develops over time. Physical findings of left ventricular hypertrophy may be apparent, as may findings of left- and right-sided congestive heart failure. Diabetic microvascular disease involving the retina, peripheral nerves, and skin may also be detected. As renal failure advances, pallor may become more noticeable and a pericardial friction rub may be heard at advanced stages of renal failure. Worsening of retinopathy and peripheral neuropathy may occur, and myoclonus and lethargy may become more obvious as uremia progresses.

Routine Laboratory Abnormalities

The earliest clue is found on routine urinalysis, which demonstrates significant proteinuria, usually in the absence of hematuria, when glomerular function is well preserved. A quantitative 24-hour urine collection documents nephrotic range proteinuria (>3.5 g/d) with the passage of time. Other laboratory features of the nephrotic syndrome (see Chapter 16–11) will become manifest. Laboratory features of chronic renal failure (see Chapter 16–12) are inevitably superimposed on the diabetic nephrotic syndrome within a few years.

PLANS

Diagnostic

Differential Diagnosis

The most important element for the diagnosis of diabetic nephropathy is the medical history. In the majority of cases, the history and physical examination are consistent with the natural course of diabetic nephropathy, making histologic confirmation unnecessary. It is therefore important to emphasize clinical features that suggest disease processes other than diabetic nephropathy (Table 16–21–1) to avoid diagnostic errors and to exclude other possible causes of nephrotic syndrome, such as membranoproliferative glomerulonephritis and focal segmental glomerulosclerosis in teenagers and young adults, and membranous nephropathy and amyloidosis in older patients.

In addition, the natural history of established diabetic nephropathy can be complicated by events that may result in superimposed acute loss of renal function. Diabetic patients are particularly at risk of developing acute renal dysfunction as a consequence of urinary tract obstruction and/or infection, and from use of radiocontrast agents and nonsteroidal antiinflammatory drugs. Angiotensin-converting enzyme

inhibitors also have the potential for causing loss of renal function in patients with significant micro/macrovascular renal disease (Table 16–21–2). Hyporeninemic hypoaldosteronism also occurs with greater frequency in patients with diabetic renal disease.

Diagnostic Options

The clinical characteristics of diabetic nephropathy are best presented in relation to its different stages, as shown in Table 16–21–3. Early in the course of diabetes an increase in glomerular filtration rate may be observed. This hyperfiltration is a result of diabetes-induced renal hemodyamic changes and the increased dietary protein intake related to the traditional diabetic diet. Incipient nephropathy is identified by increased rates of albumin excretion in the urine (microalbuminuria). Urinary albumin excretion rates greater than 20 to 30 µg/min are associated with a high risk for developing clinical diabetic nephropathy. Ambulatory blood pressure monitoring in patients with incipient nephropathy identifies a reduction in the expected decrease in systolic blood pressure normally observed during sleep.

Clinical nephropathy is characterized by detection of proteinuria on routine urinalysis. At this stage the duration of diabetes is at least 5 to 7 years in type 1 and 3 to 5 years in type 2 patients. Established hypertension is common (prevalence of 70 and 80% in types 1 and 2, respectively). In about 70% of type 1 diabetics, proliferative retinopathy is present; in type 2 diabetic patients the association between nephropathy and clinical retinopathy is less frequent. Approximately 1 to 2 years after the onset of the nephrotic phase, renal function begins to deteriorate and serum creatinine concentrations gradually increase. Because diabetic patients with renal failure tend to have a decreased muscle mass, significant reductions in creatinine clearance may be present with only modest increases in serum creatinine concentrations. It is important to measure creatinine clearances periodically in these patients and not solely rely on possibly misleading serum creatinine concentrations.

Recommended Approach

The diagnosis of diabetic nephropathy is mostly clinical, and is based on the presence of nephrotic range proteinuria within the time frame of the expected natural history of the disease when other apparent causes for nephrotic syndrome and decreased renal function are absent. If clinical parameters are not clear, or when there is strong suspicion for nondiabetic renal disease, a kidney biopsy is indicated for definitive diagnosis.

Therapeutic

Therapeutic Options

At present, the treatment of clinical diabetic nephropathy is aimed at minimizing the rate of loss of renal function, providing symptomatic improvement, and replacing renal function when end-stage renal failure is present. Two recent studies, however, have clearly demonstrated that strict metabolic control and the use of angiotensin-converting enzyme inhibitors independently decrease the risk of progression of diabetic nephropathy by approximately 50%. It is strongly recommended that patients with clinical evidence of nephropathy be placed on angiotensin-converting enzyme inhibitor therapy and that every effort be made to achieve the best possible blood glucose control.

TABLE 16–21–1. CLINICAL DATA SUGGESTIVE OF RENAL DISEASE OTHER THAN DIABETIC NEPHROPATHY

- Clinically significant nephropathy in type 1 patients with duration of diabetes less than 5–7 years
- Clinically significant nephropathy in type 2 patients with apparent duration of diabetes less than 3–5 years
- Presence of gross hematuria or persistent significant microscopic hematuria (particularly with erythrocyte casts) in the absence of a decrease in glomerular filtration rate
- Sudden unexplained deterioration in glomerular filtration rate
- Renal insufficiency in the absence of significant clinical proteinuria
- Absence of retinopathy in type 1 patients

TABLE 16–21–2. CAUSES OF ACUTE DETERIORATION OF RENAL FUNCTION IN PATIENTS WITH DIABETES MELLITUS

Obstructive uropathy
  Neurogenic bladder
  Prostatic hypertrophy (coincidental)
Acute pyelonephritis and acute papillary necrosis
Drug-induced
  Nonsteroidal antiinflammatory drugs
  Parenteral iodinated contrast agents
  Cholecystography agents
  Angiotensin-converting enzyme inhibitors
Severe uncontrolled hypertension

TABLE 16–21–3. CLINICAL STAGES IN THE DEVELOPMENT OF DIABETIC NEPHROPATHY

Stage	Clinical Stage	Major Clinical Features
1	Initial state	Glomerular hypertrophy Increased glomerular filtration rate
2	Early renal involvement	Thickened glomerular basement membrane Increased mesangial matrix Normal urinary albumin excretion
3	Incipient nephropathy	More prominent histologic changes Increased urinary albumin excretion Increased ambulatory blood pressure
4	Overt nephropathy	Proteinuria on routine urinalysis Edema and nephrotic syndrome Hypertension Normal/decreased glomerular filtration rate
5	End stage renal failure	Glomerular closure Relentless loss of glomerular filtration rate Significant hypertension Uremic syndrome

Hypertension is the most significant determinant of the rate of loss of renal function in diabetic nephropathy. Effective blood pressure control decreases the rate of progression of renal insufficiency. There is a linear correlation between loss of glomerular filtration rate and diastolic blood pressure that persists at values below 90 mm Hg, suggesting that therapeutic targets below this value may be desirable. In type 1 diabetes, the blood pressure goal should be the normal level for that particular age group. Only if unacceptable side effects result from aggressive control of blood pressure should one compromise with less than ideal blood pressure control (target value, <140/90 mm Hg). In type 2 diabetics, a more conservative approach may be warranted in view of the dangers of cerebral and myocardial ischemia, so that a reduction of blood pressure to about 140/90 mm Hg is quite acceptable. Weight reduction, moderate aerobic exercise, sodium intake of 100 mmol/d or less, cessation of smoking, and limitation of alcohol intake are all essential to blood pressure control and must not be overlooked.

Potassium-sparing diuretics should not be used in patients with diabetic renal insufficiency because insulin deficiency and hyporeninemic hypoaldosteronism are risk factors for hyperkalemia. Thiazide diuretics are suitable when serum creatinine concentrations are below 2 mg/dL. Above this level, loop diuretics (furosemide, ethacrynic acid, bumetanide, torsemide) are preferred. Metolazone, a quinazoline diuretic with properties similar to those of thiazide diuretics, is also effective in moderate to severe renal failure, and can be used with loop diuretics because of its additive effect.

Beta blockers have been used extensively in diabetic patients for blood pressure control. Patients should be warned that even selective beta blockers may mask symptoms of hypoglycemia, particularly tachycardia. Although selective β_1 blockers are preferred, there are no documented significant clinical advantages between beta blockers with nonselective, selective, sympathetic blocking, or hydrophilic properties. Their use may also be associated with development or worsening of hyperlipidemia.

Angiotensin-converting enzyme inhibitors and calcium channel blocking agents are very useful in controlling hypertension in diabetics. Angiotensin-converting enzyme inhibitors decrease microalbuminuria and clinical proteinuria in diabetic patients independent of their blood pressure effect. In addition, angiotensin-converting enzyme inhibitors decrease the rate of loss of renal function in patients with clinical nephropathy. Hyperkalemia, however, can be a significant problem when using these agents; particularly at risk are patients with renal failure, those with hyporeninemic hypoaldosteronism, and those taking potassium-sparing diuretics, potassium supplements, or nonsteroidal antiinflammatory drugs. A rapid decline in renal function is highly suggestive of bilateral renal artery stenosis, particularly in type 2 diabetics. Acute renal failure may occur, independent of renovascular disease, especially when other potential causes of acute renal failure are present, such as dehydration and/or use of nephrotoxic agents such as ra-

diopaque contrast agents, nonsteroidal antiinflammatory drugs, and aminoglycoside antibiotics. In contrast to angiotensin-converting enzyme inhibitors, use of calcium channel blockers is not associated with hyperkalemia or acute renal failure; however, only some calcium channel blockers (diltiazem, nitrendipine) have a beneficial effect on proteinuria, and a specific protective role in the progression of disease remains to be studied.

Orthostatic hypotension and impotence may occur more frequently in diabetic patients than in the general population when treated with any type of antihypertensive regimen. Commonly used antihypertensive drugs and their potential side effects in diabetic patients are summarized in Table 16–21–4.

An appropriate caloric and protein intake is necessary to maintain adequate nutrition, particularly when proteinuria is present; however, a high protein intake should be discouraged as it worsens proteinuria and may cause a more rapid loss of renal function. When the creatinine clearance has decreased to less that 20 mL/min, the diabetic diet should be modified to include a protein restriction of 0.5 to 0.75 g/kg/d and reductions in daily intake of sodium (2 g), potassium (1500 mg), and phosphate (750 mg). In addition, calcium carbonate should be used as needed to maintain normal serum concentrations of calcium and phosphorus at any level of renal insufficiency. When dialysis therapy is instituted, protein intake should be increased to 1 g/kg/d.

Definitive treatment for end-stage renal failure should be initiated at a creatinine clearance level of approximately 10 to 15 mL/min in younger patients (< 40 years of age) and at clearances of 5 to 10 mL/min in older patients. The four major modalities of therapy available at this stage are continuous ambulatory peritoneal dialysis, chronic maintenance hemodialysis, renal transplantation, and combined kidney/pancreas transplant.

For type 1 diabetics, the best choice is a living related renal transplant; other alternatives include cadaveric renal or combined kidney/pancreas transplantation, continuous ambulatory peritoneal dialysis, and hemodialysis in that order. Recent developments in surgical and preservation techniques have made cadaveric kidney/pancreas transplantation an established treatment option for type 1 diabetics. Both patient and graft survival rates are similar to those obtained with a cadaveric renal transplant alone. Combined cadaveric kidney/pancreas transplantation should be performed in patients with established diabetic nephropathy at a time when creatinine clearance is between 45 and 25 mL/min, as the rehabilitation potential is greater when done prior to the onset of uremia. Blood pressure control and improvements

TABLE 16–21–4. ANTIHYPERTENSIVE AGENTS COMMONLY USED IN THE TREATMENT OF PATIENTS WITH RENAL INSUFFICIENCY

Drug Type	Possible Side Effect of Relevance to Diabetes
Diuretics Loop diuretics Metolazone	Volume depletion, prerenal azotemia, impotence, hypokalemia
Amiloride, spironolactone, triamterene	Hyperkalemia
Sympathetic inhibitors	Orthostatic hypotension, impotence, drowsiness
Alpha-adrenergic agonists	Impotence, drowsiness, orthostatic hypotension
Alpha-adrenergic blockers	Orthostatic hypotension
Beta-adrenergic blockers	Cardiac failure, impotence, hyperkalemia, diminished symptoms of hypoglycemia
Vasodilators	Orthostatic hypotension, tachycardia, fluid retention (particularly with minoxidil)
Angiotensin-converting enzyme inhibitors	Hyperkalemia, orthostatic hypotension
Calcium channel blockers	Tachycardia, orthostatic hypotension

in autonomic and gastric function are better in recipients of combined kidney/pancreas than after kidney-alone transplantation. In addition, adequate glycemic control minimizes the likelihood of loss of renal function due to recurrence of diabetic nephropathy. In type 2 diabetes, renal transplantation may be associated with greater morbidity due to increased age, obesity, and coronary, cerebral, and peripheral vascular disease. In these older patients, transplantation may offer no greater advantage than continuous ambulatory peritoneal dialysis or hemodialysis; however, careful evaluation and correction of vascular disease pretransplant will allow patients the best possible chance following transplantation. The advantages and disadvantaged of these therapies for diabetic patients with end-stage renal disease are summarized in Table 16–21–5.

Recommended Approach

Therapy of diabetic nephropathy is aimed at optimizing preservation of renal function. This is best accomplished by a multifactorial approach that includes overall health measures (weight control, exercise, no smoking, avoidance of excessive alcohol intake), strict glycemic control, normalization of blood pressure and serum lipids, judicious dietary protein intake, and ongoing surveillance for early detection and correction of factors known to worsen renal function. When end-stage renal failure is reached, available options are individualized to provide the best possible state of health for as long as feasible while providing a quality of life that meets the patient's needs.

FOLLOW-UP

A careful follow-up plan is essential once the diagnosis of diabetic nephropathy is made. The purpose of this close supervision is dual: to minimize the rate of loss of renal function, and to plan the modality of treatment to be implemented at the time of end-stage renal disease. The patient should be routinely asked about symptoms that may relate to the urinary tract, particularly those ascribed to incomplete bladder emptying. Evaluation of bladder dysfunction due to neuropathy, benign prostatic hypertrophy with bladder outlet obstruction, and urinary tract infections should be pursued when symptoms arise and appropriate treatment plans implemented. Diabetic patients without bladder dysfunction do not have a higher incidence of urinary tract infections than the general population, but are at greater risk for acute papillary necrosis. Patients with diabetic nephropathy, particularly those in whom renal function is already decreased, are more likely to develop superimposed acute renal failure from the use of radiopaque contrast agents, nonsteroidal antiinflammatory drugs, and, possibly, angiotensin-converting enzyme inhibitors. Diabetic patients are also at risk of hyperkalemia when they are prescribed potassium-sparing agents, potassium supplements, or angiotensin-converting enzyme inhibitors. As end-stage renal failure therapy requires a multidisciplinary team approach, it is important that these patients be referred early to a nephrology center for planning of hemodialysis, chronic ambulatory peritoneal dialysis, and/or transplantation.

DISCUSSION

Prevalence

Diabetic nephropathy is the single most common cause of end-stage renal disease in industrialized countries and accounts for 30 to 40% of patients entering dialysis and transplantation programs in the United States. The overall prevalence of type 1 diabetes is 200 per 100,000, whereas that of type 2 is 1900 per 100,000. In type 1 diabetes, end-stage renal failure occurs in 30 to 40% of patients; in type 2 diabetes, the incidence is about 20%. The increased cardiovascular mortality seen in type 2 diabetics may account for the lower frequency of renal failure. The risk for developing renal insufficiency in patients with type 2 diabetes is two to four times greater in Asians, African-Americans, Hispanics, and American Indians than in whites. This race difference is not observed in type 1 diabetes.

Related Basic Science

The mechanisms responsible for the development of diabetic nephropathy are incompletely understood. A multifactorial pathogenetic process resulting as a consequence of and/or an adaptation to a state of insulin deficiency is currently advocated. These mechanisms include hemodynamic and metabolic factors. The most important hemodynamic changes involved in the pathogenesis of diabetic nephropathy are intraglomerular hypertension and hyperfiltration. Major diabetic-induced metabolic factors include glomerular hypertrophy, polyol and myoinositol pathway abnormalities, and nonenzymatic glycosylation. The increased glomerular filtration pressure may trigger cellular damage leading to glomerular sclerosis and renal insufficiency. A decrease in the glycosaminoglycan content of the glomerular basement membrane may result in loss of glomerular charge permselectivity which precedes or accompanies the formation of the functional glomerular macromolecular pathways responsible for the bulk of urinary protein loss.

Absolute or relative insulin deficiency increases the pentose phosphate pathway activity and results in a decreased NAD+/NADH ratio and enhances fructose formation. Fructose is the preferred substrate for nonenzymatic glycosylation of protein. The lower redox potential facilitates excessive crosslinkage (browning) of nonenzymatically glycosylated structural proteins (Maillard reaction). In addition, nonenzymatically glycosylated glomerular basement membrane collagen is less susceptible to degradation than native collagen. These metabolic changes produce a variety of intracellular metabolic abnormalities and glomerular dysfunction.

Natural History and Its Modification with Treatment

The earlier stages of type 1 diabetes are characterized by an increase in renal size and in glomerular filtration rate. Strict metabolic control results in normalization of glomerular filtration rate but not of renal size. Microalbuminuria is detected in about 60% of patients, and approximately one third progress to clinical nephropathy and end-stage renal failure.

In type 2 diabetes an increase in glomerular filtration rate and kidney size is not well documented, but is likely to occur in about 20% of patients. Microalbuminuria develops in approximately 30% of type 2 diabetic patients. As in type 1 diabetes, urinary albumin excretion rates greater than 20 to 30 µg/min predict progression to clinical diabetic nephropathy. The apparent period between the diagnosis of diabetes and the development of renal insufficiency may be shorter than in type 1 diabetes. This seemingly faster course may be related to the difficulty of defining precisely the time of onset of diabetes in type 2 patients. In addition, histologic lesions in type 2 diabetic patients are more heterogeneous, with glomerular ischemic lesions, arteriosclerosis, and nondiabetic glomerular changes superimposed on those of diabetic nephropathy. This lesion variability contributes in part to the differing rates of progression to end-stage renal disease in type 2 diabetic patients.

On reaching end-stage renal disease most patients with type 1 diabetes are treated by renal transplantation and/or continuous ambulatory peritoneal dialysis, whereas type 2 patients are usually treated with he-

TABLE 16–21–5. TREATMENT MODALITIES FOR END-STAGE RENAL FAILURE IN DIABETIC PATIENTS

Type	Pros	Cons
Kidney/pancreas transplant	Better survival Better control of uremia Correction of hyperglycemia Correction of anemia Best chance of rehabilitation	Greater perioperative morbidity Greater risk of infection Older patients excluded
Renal transplant	Better survival Better control of uremia Correction of anemia Better chance of rehabilitation	Greater risk of infection Worsening of hyperglycemia Greater morbidity in older patients
Chronic ambulatory peritoneal dialysis	Less cardiovascular stress Ambulatory/home setting	Recurrent peritonitis Less control of uremia
Hemodialysis	Easily used Frequent physician monitoring	Less control of uremia Less rehabilitation potential

modialysis. The 5-year survival rates for diabetic patients with end-stage renal disease are approximately 80% for living related transplant recipients, 50% for continuous ambulatory peritoneal dialysis patients, 50% for cadaveric renal transplant recipients, and 40% for hemodialysis patients. Regardless of therapeutic modality, survival rates are always lower than in nondiabetic patients. Atherosclerotic complications account for more than 50% of deaths in end-stage renal disease patients with diabetic nephropathy. Infectious complications are another major cause of death.

Prevention

There are no current practical methods for effectively avoiding the development or progression of diabetic nephropathy. The only proven approach for preventing diabetic nephropathy is a successful segmental pancreas transplant prior to the development of incipient nephropathy; however, pancreatic transplantation is not currently performed in relatively asymptomatic patients early in the natural history of their illness because of problems related to surgery and immunosuppression.

The Diabetes Control and Complications Trial (DCCT) has proven without doubt that strict metabolic control is associated with a 39% reduction in progression to microalbuminuria and a 54% reduction in progression to overt nephropathy in type 1 diabetic patients. Although the DCCT did not use renal histology as an endpoint, other studies have shown that tight control retards the progression of morphologic changes in patients with early diabetic nephropathy. Unfortunately, strict metabolic control is associated with a two- to three-fold increase in severe hypoglycemic episodes. No comparable studies have been done in type 2 diabetic patients.

Adequate treatment of hypertension is the most proven method for decreasing the rate of loss of renal function in diabetic patients. Experimental findings have suggested that angiotensin-converting enzyme inhibitors may confer a more specific protection because of their ability to decrease intraglomerular pressure. In type 1 diabetic patients with established nephropathy, captopril therapy is associated with a 50% reduction in the risk of progression to end-stage renal disease independent of blood pressure. This protective effect is particularly noticeable in patients with baseline serum creatinine concentrations greater than 2 mg/dL. Use of captopril in normotensive type 1 diabetic patients with microalbuminuria also retards the progression to clinical proteinuria. In type 2 diabetic patients, the use of enalapril over a 5-year period was also found to slow the rate of decline in renal function. There are no long-term studies assessing a specific protective effect of calcium channel blockers on the rate of progression of diabetic nephropathy.

The use of low-protein diets (0.6–0.7 g/kg/d) decreases glomerular proteinuria. The American Diabetes Association has changed its recommendation for daily dietary protein intake to 0.80 to 1.0 g/kg/d. Whether these interventions will translate into long-term prevention of the development and/or progression of diabetic renal disease remains to be proven.

Aldose reductase inhibitors have shown promise in the treatment of diabetic neuropathy, but their impact on nephropathy is less clear. Normalization of urinary albumin excretion has recently been reported with chronic use of tolrestat in type 1 diabetic patients with clinical proteinuria; however, both experimental and clinical studies are needed to define further the long-term renal effects of aldose reductase inhibition.

Cost Containment

End-stage renal failure therapy is expensive, time consuming, and inefficient. Good metabolic control and a normal blood pressure are substantially cheaper and more cost effective; however, because renal disease may be silent for a long time, it is difficult to emphasize the importance of healthy habits, periodic monitoring, and adequate treatment. In addition, these goals are difficult to realize because of compliance problems and a relative lack of awareness among patients and health care professionals.

REFERENCES

Cheung AHS, Sutherland DER, Gillingham KJ, et al. Simultaneous pancreas–kidney transplant versus kidney transplant alone in diabetic patients. Kidney Int 1992;41:924.

Diabetes Control and Complications Trial Research Group. The effect of intensive treatment of diabetes on the development and progression of long-term complications in insulin-dependent diabetes mellitus. N Engl J Med 1993;329:1977.

Lewis EJ, Hunsicker LG, Bain RP, Rohde RD. The effect of angiotensin-converting enzyme inhibition on diabetic nephropathy. N Engl J Med 1993;329:1456.

Schmidt RJ, Dumler F. Diabetic nephropathy: Diagnostic techniques and follow-up evaluation. In: Narins RG, Stein JH, eds. Contemporary issues in nephrology: Diagnostic techniques in renal disease, New York: Churchill Livingstone, 1992:119.

Stein PP, Black HR. Drug treatment of hypertension in patients with diabetes mellitus. Diabetes Care 1991;14:425.

CHAPTER 16–22

Atheroembolic Disease of the Kidney

Henry M. Yager, M.D., and John T. Harrington, M.D.

DEFINITION

Atheroembolic renal disease is defined as progressive renal insufficiency due to embolic obstruction of small and medium-sized renal arteries by atheromatous material.

ETIOLOGY

Atheroembolic renal disease can occur spontaneously, as a result of operative trauma in patients with severe atherosclerosis, following major vessel arteriography, and rarely following anticoagulation or use of thrombolytic agents.

CRITERIA FOR DIAGNOSIS
Suggestive

Most cases occur in male patients over the age of 60 with widespread, erosive atherosclerosis. Although small showers of renal artheroemboli occur relatively commonly spontaneously in elderly individuals, most patients who develop significant renal insufficiency have had direct aortic manipulation such as surgery, arteriography, or angioplasty. The diagnosis of atheroembolic renal disease is suggested by the development of renal failure within several days to 3 months of aortic manipulation, in association with embolic manifestations in many other organs, including skin, intestine, pancreas, spleen, eye, and central nervous system. Clinical manifestations rarely are diagnostic, but the finding of recurrent refractile crystals in the retinal vessels can help establish the diagnosis.

Definitive

Biopsy of skin, muscle, or kidney is necessary for definitive diagnosis.

CLINICAL MANIFESTATIONS
Subjective

Preexisting symptoms of vascular insufficiency such as angina, transient cerebral ischemic attacks, and claudication are common. Following embolization, symptoms depend on the distribution of affected organs. Painful toes, amaurosis fugax, myalgias, abdominal pain, or gastrointestinal bleeding may occur. Hematuria, flank pain, and diminished urine output are uncommon, but presenting symptoms may include uremic lethargy or nausea and vomiting. The disease is not familial.

Objective
Physical Examination

The physical examination, meticulously performed, usually reveals signs or hints of atheromatous embolization. Hypertension, hyperreninemic in origin, is usually present and accelerated hypertension can occur. Skin lesions include livedo reticularis, tender papules of the lower extremities, and tender, purple or gangrenous areas of multiple toes, often in the presence of palpable pedal pulses. Eye examination may reveal visual field defects or, as noted above, bright refractile emboli in the retinal arterioles (Hollenhorst plaques). Abdominal tenderness may result from embolization to spleen, pancreas, gallbladder, or intestines. Occult or gross blood may be present in the stool. Muscle tenderness and focal neurologic defects associated with spinal or cerebral embolization have been described.

Routine Laboratory Abnormalities

Laboratory findings are not specific. Blood urea nitrogen and serum creatinine concentration usually begin to rise within a day or so after the precipitating aortic insult. Their rise may progress inexorably to end-stage renal failure within 1 to 2 weeks, but more often follows a stuttering course lasting up to several months. In a minority of patients, probably in the range of 10 to 20%, renal function stabilizes at levels sufficient to avoid dialysis. Urinalysis may be normal or show mild proteinuria, pyuria, and microscopic hematuria and few granular casts. Cellular casts are not seen typically. Gross hematuria has been described infrequently. The common finding of normochromic normocytic anemia is probably a consequence of azotemia. Elevated erythrocyte sedimentation rate, greater than 100 mm/h in some cases, and transient eosinophilia (usually 6–18% of the total white blood cell count) are common findings. Hypocomplementemia may be present, as discussed below. Not surprisingly, ischemic electrocardiographic changes have been seen in patients with coronary artery embolization.

PLANS
Diagnostic

The diagnosis of atheroembolic renal disease should be considered in any patient over age 50 who develops progressive renal failure within 3 months of aortic surgery, angiography, angioplasty, intraaortic balloon pump placement, anticoagulation, or systemic thrombolytic therapy.

Differential Diagnosis

Differential diagnosis includes acute tubular necrosis secondary to radiographic contrast injection, hypotension, or aminoglycoside antibiotics; obstructive nephropathy; and drug-induced allergic interstitial nephritis. In patients with an elevated erythrocyte sedimentation rate, eosinophilia, hypocomplementemia, clinical evidence of involvement of multiple organ systems, systemic vasculitis, subacute bacterial endocarditis, and left atrial myxoma must be included in the differential di-

agnosis. Atheroembolic renal disease can coexist with arteriosclerotic renal artery stenosis.

The diagnosis of acute tubular necrosis is more likely if evidence for systemic emboli is lacking, urine sediment contains many "muddy brown" granular casts, and progressive improvement begins within 3 weeks of the insult. Complete anuria suggests lower urinary tract obstruction. The urine sediment in allergic interstitial nephritis usually has significant pyuria and leukocyte casts. Eosinophiluria, often seen in allergic interstitial nephritis, also has been described in a few cases of atheroembolic disease.

Diagnostic Options and Recommended Approach

Hypocomplementemia occurs in 30 to 40% of patients and can lead to an erroneous diagnosis of a primary immunologic disease. Experimental observations in rats and rabbits have demonstrated that atheromatous material can activate complement, supporting the importance of these clinical findings. Definitive diagnosis requires tissue biopsy (See Color Plate 16–22–1, after page 826). Biopsy of skin lesions of the toes or clinically uninvolved muscle of the leg often demonstrates the characteristic needle-shaped clefts in the arterial lumens, where cholesterol emboli were present prior to being dissolved by the process of tissue fixation. This finding provides strong evidence for atheroembolic disease in the kidney. We recommend kidney biopsy only when less invasive studies fail to yield a diagnosis, and a treatable lesion such as systemic vasculitis or allergic interstitial nephritis is strongly considered in the differential diagnosis. Although needle biopsy of the kidney may not always provide adequate tissue for a histologic diagnosis of atheromatous emboli, our experience and that of others suggest that when the disease causes severe renal failure, percutaneous renal biopsy has a high diagnostic yield and should be performed before open, surgical biopsy of the kidney.

Therapeutic
Therapeutic Options

No effective treatment has been identified. In uncontrolled trials using small numbers of patients, intrarenal low-molecular-weight dextran infusion, intravenous vasodilating agents and sympathetic blockers, and corticosteroids have been ineffective. As mentioned earlier, some investigators believe that anticoagulants and thrombolytic agents can actually cause atheromatous renal disease, and these agents are therefore contraindicated. Rare case reports indicate successful arteriographic identification and surgical resection of an isolated segment of eroded aorta, presumed to be the source of embolization. At best, such an approach can only prevent recurrent embolization, while running the high risk of exposing the aorta to two manipulations known to precipitate embolization.

Recommended Approach

Given the information just reviewed, we recommend conservative therapy. Dialysis may be required. The use of intermittent anticoagulation during hemodialysis treatments gives peritoneal dialysis a theoretical advantage in this disease; however, no studies have compared outcomes using these two modalities of therapy. A few patients requiring dialysis for up to several months recover enough renal function to discontinue dialysis. Many patients die within 1 to 2 years of disease caused by recurrent embolization.

FOLLOW-UP

In patients with stable renal insufficiency, follow-up at 1- to 3-month intervals is appropriate to monitor blood pressure and renal function and examine for new signs of atheromatous embolization. The history should focus on new symptoms described above under Clinical Manifestations. The physician also should attempt to identify or prevent acute, reversible causes of worsening renal function such as volume depletion, congestive heart failure, prostatic obstruction, and nephrotoxin exposure. The patient should be educated about the nature and prognosis of this disease. Hypertension should be controlled. Advice regarding dietary restriction of fluid, protein, sodium, and potassium should be tailored to the degree of azotemia and urinary excretion of water and electrolytes. Patients should avoid further arteriography and systemic anticoagulation.

DISCUSSION
Prevalence

The prevalence of systemic atheroembolism in unselected autopsies is less than 1% in patients over 60 years of age. Renal atheroemboli are found at autopsy in about 25% of patients with atherosclerosis and in about three quarters of patients following aortic aneurysmectomy. Yet only a small fraction of these individuals developed clinically significant renal failure. A review of the English literature, published by Lye et al. in 1993, found only 129 patients with "documented clinical evidence of renal involvement." We believe, however, that the incidence of this disease has increased in the past few decades, because of the increased performance of arterial catheterization in elderly patients.

Related Basic Science

Atheromatous debris is released from the aortic intima by mechanical trauma (e.g., arteriographic catheters or surgical clamps) or when anticoagulant or thrombolytic agents weaken the attachment of cholesterol crystals to the vessel wall. The tiny particles flow downstream until they lodge in intrarenal arteries measuring 150 to 200 nm in diameter; the biconvex or needle-shaped cholesterol crystals produce incomplete obstruction of the arterial lumen at this level. The embolus provokes an inflammatory response with intimal proliferation, infiltration of macrophages, formation of giant cells, and fibrosis, ultimately leading to total occlusion of the lumen. This process may explain the progression of renal failure over weeks to months in many patients. Biopsies demonstrate the characteristic shape of emboli, surrounded by varying stages of inflammatory response. Although formalin and paraffin fixation dissolves cholesterol, leaving empty clefts, no special tissue preparation is required, as the appearance of these empty clefts is pathognomonic of cholesterol crystals.

In animal experiments, cerebral embolization with pure preparations of each of the lipid moieties found in the atheromatous plaques was harmless, but combinations in proportions similar to those in advanced human atherosclerosis caused infarction. The aggregation of cholesterol crystals by oils such as cholesterol esters appears essential to the harmful potential of the emboli.

Natural History and Its Modification with Treatment

Stabilization or improvement of renal function occurs in only 10 to 20% of patients; the remaining patients require dialysis permanently. Despite dialysis, the mortality rate within 2 years of the onset of atheroembolic renal failure is extremely high, reaching 64% in the 1993 English literature review referred to earlier (Lye et al., 1993).

Death results from embolization, causing infarction in brain, heart, or gastrointestinal tract. Amputation of toes often is necessary early in the course of disease. No specific effective treatment is available.

Prevention

The devastating nature of atheroembolic disease and the lack of available treatment make prevention extremely important. It is reasonable to expect that the incidence of atheromatous embolization following angiography can be reduced by using soft, pliable catheters and minimizing catheter manipulation. More important is the careful selection of patients in the high-risk group to avoid unnecessary angiographic procedures.

During aortic surgery, clamps should be placed as far below the renal arteries as possible. In cases requiring an aortic clamp proximal to the renal arteries, the risk of renal embolization is reduced by gentle clamping of the renal arteries prior to release of the aortic clamp, followed by unclamping and flushing of the aorta before unclamping of the renal arteries.

When considering anticoagulation or thrombolytic therapy in patients with severe, generalized atherosclerosis, the risk of atheroembolic renal disease must be weighed against the potential benefits of therapy.

Cost Containment

In most cases the diagnosis can be based reliably on data obtained from the clinical setting, physical examination, and routine laboratory tests. Eosinophil count and erythrocyte sedimentation rate should be obtained routinely. Serum complement depression will support the diagnosis in some patients. Histologic diagnosis of atheromatous emboli in skin or muscle biopsies provides powerful confirmation of atheroembolic renal disease. Renal biopsy should be reserved for patients with atypical features such as significant hematuria, proteinuria, and cellular casts in the urine sediment.

REFERENCES

Cosio FG, Zager RA, Sharma HM. Atheroembolic renal disease causes hypocomplementaemia. Lance 1985;2:118.

Fine MJ, Kapoor W, Falanga V. Cholesterol crystal embolization: A review of 221 cases in the English literature. Angiology 1987;38:769.

Harrington JT, Sommers SC, Kassirer JP. Atheromatous emboli with progressive renal failure: Renal arteriography as the probable inciting factor. Ann Intern Med 1968;68:152.

Lye WC, Cheah JS, Sinniah R. Renal cholesterol embolic disease: Case report and review of the literature. Am J Nephrol 1993;13:489.

Meyrier A, Buchet P, Simon P, et al., Atheromatous renal disease. Am J Med 1988;85:139.

Smith MC, Ghose MK, Henry AR. The clinical spectrum of renal cholesterol embolization. Am J Med 1981;71:174.

CHAPTER 16–23

Renal Vein Thrombosis

Henry M. Yager, M.D., and John T. Harrington, M.D.

DEFINITION

Thrombosis of the main or branch renal veins defines the entity of renal vein thrombosis. Renal vein thrombosis (RVT) leads sequentially to clot propagation, progressively elevated venous pressure, interstitial edema, and reduction or, in some cases, total cessation of renal blood flow.

ETIOLOGY

Thrombosis of renal veins develops in clinical settings ranging from hypercoagulable states and severe hemoconcentration to mechanical

disorders causing partial or complete occlusion of renal veins. Sickle cell disease, papillary necrosis, pyelonephritis, and sepsis also have been associated with renal vein thrombosis (Table 16–23–1).

CRITERIA FOR DIAGNOSIS
Suggestive

Clinical manifestations may suggest an acute, severe renal problem but more often are absent. In adults, RVT most often is identified in patients with nephrotic syndrome, presenting with a pulmonary embolus or other thromboembolic event. Relatively few adults develop acute

TABLE 16–23–1 CAUSES OF RENAL VEIN THROMBOSIS

Depletion of the extracellular fluid volume*
   Vomiting
   Diarrhea
   Maternal hyperglycemia
Mechanical factors
   Compression of the inferior vena cava or renal hila by metastatic tumors or vascular malformations
   Extension of inferior vena cava thrombus into the renal veins
   Tumor invasion (usually a renal cell carcinoma) of the renal vein
   Trauma or surgery to the renal vein
Hypercoagulable states
   Nephrotic syndrome
   Oral contraceptives
   Pregnancy
   Systemic lupus erythematosus
   Antithrombin III deficiency
   Protein S or C deficiency
   Antiphospholipid syndrome
Miscellaneous associations
   Sickle cell disease
   Papillary necrosis
   Pyelonephritis
   Sepsis

*The usual setting for renal vein thrombosis in infants less than 1 month of age.

RVT associated with unilateral or bilateral flank pain, gross or microscopic hematuria, and acute renal insufficiency.

Definitive

Selective renal venography is the only reliable diagnostic test.

CLINICAL MANIFESTATIONS
Subjective

Any patient with the nephrotic syndrome or another predisposing clinical setting listed in Table 16–23–1 who presents with pleuritic chest pain, cough, dyspnea, and/or hemoptysis should be suspected of having RVT with pulmonary embolization. In acute RVT, sudden, severe abdominal, flank, or lumbar pain, gross hematuria, and diminished urine output, if thrombosis is bilateral, often occur.

Objective
Physical Examination

Most patients with acute RVT have abdominal or flank tenderness; low-grade fever is common. Rare physical findings include a palpable kidney, newly discovered left varicocele, or the appearance of dilated venous collaterals on the abdominal wall. Signs and symptoms of pulmonary embolism and infarction include dyspnea, tachypnea, hemoptysis, cyanosis, pleural friction rub, and increased intensity of pulmonic value closure. Bilateral lower extremity edema may result from associated thrombosis of the vena cava or, more commonly, from an underlying nephrotic syndrome.

Routine Laboratory Abnormalities

Laboratory findings are not specific. Gross or microscopic hematuria, leukocytosis, and azotemia are common in acute RVT. Azotemia, nephrotic range proteinuria, lipiduria, hypoalbuminemia, and elevated serum cholesterol may be found in either acute or chronic RVT. In patients with the nephrotic syndrome and associated RVT, proteinuria often exceeds 10 g/24 h, and serum albumin is often less than 2.0 g/dL. A sudden decrement in glomerular filtration rate in a nephrotic patient also may be a clue to the development of RVT.

The chest radiograph and electrocardiogram are usually normal, but may reveal signs associated with pulmonary embolism.

PLANS
Diagnostic
Differential Diagnosis

Acute RVT often presents with manifestations similar to those of a ureteral stone or acute renal artery thrombosis or embolus with infarction.

Diagnostic Options

If renal outlines are visualized on plain abdominal radiographs, unilateral or bilateral renal enlargement is usually seen. In patients undergoing renal biopsy for underlying renal disease, the histologic findings of glomerular congestion with erythrocytes and margination of leukocytes suggest the diagnosis of RVT. Among patients with the nephrotic syndrome, RVT is most often associated with membranous or membranoproliferative glomerulonephritis.

Selective renal venography is required for definitive diagnosis. The therapeutic implications of establishing or excluding a diagnosis of RVT usually are important enough to warrant the relatively low risk of this invasive study. Artificial filling defects in the renal veins are sometimes caused by streaming of contrast injected into the inferior vena cava. Selective renal vein catheterization, therefore, should be performed whenever the vena cavagram shows a patent vena cava and apparent filling defects in one or both renal veins.

Characteristic renal abnormalities have been described using intravenous pyelography, duplex Doppler ultrasonography, and, most recently, color flow Doppler imaging, computed tomography scanning, and magnetic resonance imaging. These modalities have not been compared systematically with respect to reliability. Acute RVT causes symmetric enlargement of the ipsilateral kidney as well as reduced function on dynamic imaging studies. Notching of the ureter by dilated collateral veins is a highly suggestive but infrequent finding on intravenous pyelography. Sonograms using duplex or color flow Doppler images and magnetic resonance imaging are capable of demonstrating thrombus within the inferior vena cava and/or renal veins, dilation of the renal vein proximal to the site of occlusion, and diminished or absent renal blood flow. Recent studies suggest that color flow Doppler represents blood flow more accurately than duplex Doppler. Renal arteriography may be indicated in patients with RVT associated with trauma or tumor because of the frequent association of renal artery thrombosis in these settings. Signs and symptoms suggesting pulmonary emboli should be investigated with a ventilation/perfusion lung scan or pulmonary arteriogram just as in patients without RVT.

Recommended Approach

We recommend an inferior vena cavagram with selective renal venography whenever the index of suspicion for RVT is high. In patients with suggestive findings such as the nephrotic syndrome with very heavy proteinuria and severe hypoalbuminemia, we perform color flow Doppler imaging.

Therapeutic
Therapeutic Options

Anticoagulation with standard regimens or intravenous heparin followed by oral warfarin is recommended for most cases of acute or chronic unilateral RVT. Hemorrhagic complications of anticoagulation occur frequently. Renal insufficiency increases the risk of hemorrhagic events.

Thrombolytic therapy has been used in patients with acute bilateral RVT and in unilateral RVT associated with clot propagation into the inferior vena cava. Streptokinase and urokinase have been administered systemically or infused directly into the renal vein. This therapy has not been shown to be superior to anticoagulation alone with regard to survival, kidney function, or proteinuria.

Prevention of recurrent thrombosis depends on identification and appropriate management of the underlying cause, for example, nephrotic syndrome, tumor, or oral contraceptive administration. If the underlying condition resolves, anticoagulation can be discontinued in 3 to 6 months. Otherwise, warfarin should be continued indefinitely.

When RVT is associated with venous occlusion by a resectable mass lesion, surgical thrombectomy should be performed at the time of resection. Thrombectomy also is indicated when anticoagulant or fibrinolytic therapy is contraindicated or ineffective. Strong radiographic evidence of hemorrhagic renal infarction contraindicates the use of these agents. Prevention of recurrent embolization after anticoagulant failure by catheter placement of an inferior vena cava filter may be useful.

Recommended Approach

We recommend intravenous heparin followed by oral warfarin in patients without a contraindication to anticoagulation. We reserve fibrinolytic therapy for patients with acute renal failure associated with RVT. When fibrinolytic therapy is given, we recommend intravenous streptokinase in a bolus of 250,000 U infused over 30 minutes, followed by continuous infusion of 100,000 U/h for 72 hours, to maintain the thrombin time (monitored every 12 hours) at two to three times control values. If streptokinase resistance is present, thrombin time measured 4 hours after initiating therapy will be less than 1.5 times control values. Streptokinase should then be discontinued and urokinase substituted. Standard doses of warfarin to keep the prothrombin time 1.5 to 2 times control values are started when the streptokinase infusion is discontinued.

FOLLOW-UP

Follow-up should focus on both the underlying condition and the regulation of warfarin therapy. We see nephrotic patients with a history of RVT every 2 to 4 months and monitor 24-hour urine protein excretion or random urine protein/creatinine ratio, hemogram, prothrombin time, INR, and blood urea nitrogen, serum creatinine, serum proteins, and serum cholesterol levels.

DISCUSSION
Prevalence

Renal vein thrombosis is found in less than 1% of autopsies on adult patients. In prospective studies of nephrotic patients, widely divergent prevalence rates of RVT (diagnosed by renal venography) have been reported. The average prevalence is about one third. Several selection factors may explain the variable findings among studies: inclusion of all nephrotic patients or only those with idiopathic nephrotic syndrome, as idiopathic membranous nephropathy has the highest incidence of RVT; selection of a group with severe hypoalbuminemia would overestimate the incidence of RVT in all nephrotic patients; studies selecting only nephrotic patients with symptoms suggesting acute RVT find a lower incidence of RVT in patients with the nephrotic syndrome than prospective studies of all nephrotic patients.

Related Basic Science

Hypercoagulable states, hemoconcentration, and venous stasis predispose to thrombosis of small renal veins with subsequent propagation into progressively larger veins, in some cases extending into the vena cava. In contrast, occlusion of the main renal veins by mechanical causes such as tumor and trauma causes thrombosis of these vessels with propagation into smaller veins. Regardless of the mechanism of thrombus formation, RVT leads sequentially to progressively elevated venous pressure, interstitial edema, and reduction or, in some cases, total cessation of renal blood flow.

Previously, it was believed that RVT was the cause of nephrotic syndrome. Several lines of evidence have reversed this concept, however:

- RVT has been reported in many patients without the nephrotic syndrome.
- Experimentally induced RVT in animals causes little proteinuria.
- In autopsy studies of patients with RVT, a history of nephrotic syndrome is present in only a small percentage.
- Renal biopsy of patients with nephrotic syndrome and RVT usually shows a specific glomerular lesion, most often membranous glomerulonephritis.

- RVT has been demonstrated to develop after the onset of nephrotic syndrome.

Patients with the nephrotic syndrome have been found to have abnormalities in all major functional classes of coagulation components. Factors V and VIII and fibrinogen are most consistently increased, apparently resulting from stimulation of hepatic synthesis of these proteins by decreased serum albumin concentration and/or decreased plasma oncotic pressure. Fibrinogen excess leads to increased fibrinogen–fibrin transition and increased plasma viscosity, which may be important in predisposing to RVT and other thromboembolic events. Deficiency of antithrombin III, a coagulation inhibitor with a molecular weight close to that of albumin, has been found in the serum of nephrotic patients in some but not all studies. Thrombocytosis and increased platelet aggregation with ADP and collagen also have been reported. Serum levels of β-thromboglobulin, a protein released by platelets on aggregation, are elevated in the nephrotic syndrome and return to normal with resolution of proteinuria. The pathogenetic significance of these abnormalities of coagulation in the development of RVT has not been well defined.

In addition to the abnormalities in coagulation, nephrotic patients, even patients with patent renal veins by venography, have persistently low plasma volumes and marked slowing of renal venous washout.

It has been suggested that immune-mediated glomerular injury may lead to systemic hypercoagulability. This phenomenon could explain the increased incidence of RVT in immune-mediated conditions, membranous and membranoproliferative glomerulonephritis, compared with the incidence in focal glomerulosclerosis and minimal change disease, in which immune complexes are absent.

Natural History and Its Modification with Treatment

Untreated acute RVT in a patient with inadequate collateral venous circulation rarely may cause hemorrhagic infarction of the kidney. Anticoagulation usually results in recanalization of the renal vein and rapid improvement in symptoms and renal function. Long-term prognosis depends on the underlying disorder. Chronic RVT in patients with the nephrotic syndrome is associated with a high risk of thromboembolic events, chiefly pulmonary emboli, which often are fatal. This risk is dramatically reduced by chronic warfarin anticoagulation. Anticoagulant therapy does not, however, alter the rate of decline in renal function compared with disease-matched nephrotic patients without RVT.

Prevention

As anticoagulation is associated with a high risk of bleeding complications, no safe method of prevention is available. A recent study employed a decision analysis model to evaluate prophylactic oral anticoagulation in nephrotic patients with membranous nephropathy. The authors concluded that the benefits of therapy outweighed risks. This finding rests on the assumptions of the study and needs testing in clinical trials. Some experts recommend venography to identify asymptomatic RVT in all patients with the nephrotic syndrome caused by membranous or membranoproliferative glomerulonephritis. This approach is not widely accepted because of the high degree of uncertainty about the true incidence of RVT in these conditions and the considerable risks of venography and anticoagulation. If a noninvasive imaging study such as ultrasonography using color flow Doppler proves to be highly accurate, its routine use in such patients would be appropriate.

Cost Containment

As discussed above we do not recommend routine screening of patients with membranous nephropathy for asymptomatic RVT.

If fibrinolytic therapy is employed, streptokinase is preferred to the far more expensive urokinase or tissue plasminogen activator (TPA).

REFERENCES

Crowley JP, Matarese RA, Quevedo SF, Garella SF. Fibrinolytic therapy for bilateral renal vein thrombosis. Arch Intern Med 1984;144:159.

Harris RC, Ismail N. Extrarenal complications of the nephrotic syndrome. Am J Kid Dis 1994;477:497.

Keating MA, Althausen AF. The clinical spectrum of renal vein thrombosis. J Urol 1985;133:938.

Llach F, Papper S, Massry SG. The clinical spectrum of renal vein thrombosis: Acute and chronic. Am J Med 1980;69:819.

Llach F. Hypercoagulability, renal vein thrombosis, and other thrombotic complications of nephrotic syndrome. Kidney Int 1985;28:429.

Rabelink TJ, Zwaginga JJ, Koomans HA, Sima JJ. Thrombosis and hemostasis in renal disease. Kidney Int 1994;46:287.

Sarasin RP, Schiefferli JA. Prophylactic oral anticoagulation in nephrotic patients with idiopathic membranous nephropathy. Kidney Int 1994;45:578.

CHAPTER 16–24

Renal Artery Embolism and Thrombosis

Henry M. Yager, M.D., and John T. Harrington, M.D.

DEFINITION

Renal artery embolism or thrombosis is defined as total or partial occlusion of the renal arteries from clot emboli that arise outside the kidney or from thrombosis arising within the renal arteries. Total occlusion causes infarction of the kidney or the affected portion; partial occlusion causes renal ischemia, which may present with a sudden elevation of blood pressure.

ETIOLOGY

Acute thrombotic or embolic occlusion of the main renal artery or its major branches results from a variety of etiologies. Thromboembolism from a cardiac chamber or valve, the most common cause of renal artery occlusion, results from the fact that 20 to 25% of the cardiac output is delivered to the kidneys. Patients with chronic atrial fibrillation, particularly those with associated mitral valve disease, are at high risk for development of renal artery emboli. Patients with a previous myocardial infarction and a mitral thrombus also are at risk of renal embolic disease. Prosthetic mitral or aortic valves also are susceptible to the development of thrombi that may embolize to the systemic circulation. Less commonly, in patients with subacute bacterial endocarditis of the aortic or mitral valve, bacterial vegetations may embolize to the kidneys. Left atrial myxoma and marantic endocarditis associated with advanced malignancy are unusual cardiac sources of renal artery emboli. Rarely, emboli of extracardiac origin (tumor, fat, or paradoxical emboli) occlude the renal arterial circulation.

Renal artery thrombosis usually results from mechanical injury of the vessel following blunt trauma, angiography, angioplasty, or arterial reconstructive surgery. Hypercoagulable states (antithrombin III deficiency, protein S or C deficiency, nephrotic syndrome, or systemic lupus erythematosus), atherosclerotic or dissecting aneurysms of the aorta, and arteritides (polyarteritis, Takayasu's disease, syphilis, and thromboangiitis obliterans) are rare causes of renal artery thrombosis.

CRITERIA FOR DIAGNOSIS

Suggestive

The diagnosis of renal artery occlusion is difficult. Difficulty arises because the disorder is uncommon and the presenting signs and symptoms may be nonspecific. Although the abrupt appearance of fever, flank pain, hematuria (either gross or microscopic), and anuria certainly suggests total renal artery occlusion, in patients with partial or segmental occlusion, few symptoms may be present and an erroneous diagnosis of renal colic, renal contusion, or musculoskeletal pain made.

Definitive

Definitive diagnosis requires radioisotope renography, renal arteriography, or contrast-enhanced computed tomography (CT) scanning.

CLINICAL MANIFESTATIONS

Subjective

A history of blunt trauma or flank, abdominal or lumbar pain is described by up to 75% of patients. Nausea and vomiting occur in approximately 50% of patients, and 20 to 30% have gross or microscopic hematuria. Of course, nepholithiasis and traumatic renal contusion, much more common renal disorders, often present with these same symptoms.

Objective

Physical Examination

Physical examination usually discloses flank tenderness in patients with total occlusion of a main renal artery. Abdominal tenderness and signs of peritoneal irritation also may be present. Fever, occasionally reaching 103°F, is common within the first 2 days of renal infarction. Evidence of extrarenal embolization, particularly focal central nervous system deficits, is frequently present. Although preexisting hypertension may be exacerbated, new-onset hypertension rarely occurs.

Routine Laboratory Abnormalities

Microscopic hematuria, pyuria, and variable degrees of proteinuria are found in approximately one third of cases. White blood cell count, usually elevated, averaged 20,000 cells/mm^3 in one series. Urine output remains normal except in cases of bilateral main renal artery occlusion, unilateral renal artery occlusion with acute tubular necrosis of the contralateral kidney, or renal artery occlusion in patients with a solitary functioning kidney. The arterial circulation of kidney transplants is particularly susceptible to external compression and occlusion, owing to the superficial location of the organ in the lower abdomen and the surgical arterial anastomosis. Blood urea nitrogen and serum creatinine concentrations may be normal or may rapidly rise, depending on the magnitude of renal ischemic damage.

Just as occurs with myocardial infarction, infarcted renal tissue releases intracellular enzymes into the circulation. Although a segmental infarct may not elevate serum enzyme levels above the normal range, sizable infarction causes serum glutamic–oxalic transaminase (SGOT), serum glutamic–pyruvic transaminase (SGPT), serum lactate dehydrogenase (LDH), and serum alkaline phosphatase to rise and fall in a characteristic temporal pattern. The SGOT level rises rapidly and returns to normal in 4 to 7 days; the SGPT rise parallels that of SGOT, but SGPT declines more slowly. LDH, the most frequently elevated enzyme, rises to levels four to five times normal within the first 2 days, then gradually declines over 2 weeks. Fractionation of LDH isoenzymes may help confirm the renal source of the enzyme. Mild elevations of alkaline phosphatase, present in 30 to 50% of cases, appear by days 3 to 5 and may not return to normal for 3 to 4 weeks. Increased urinary levels of LDH and alkaline phosphatase also help identify the kidney as the infarcted organ. Recently, some investigators have argued that a high likelihood of renal artery occlusion exists in patients with similar serum and urine concentrations of sodium, urea nitrogen and creatinine, and a fractional excretion of sodium that approaches 100%.

PLANS

Diagnostic

Differential Diagnosis

The differential diagnosis includes renal colic, renal contusion, and musculoskeletal pain in addition to renal artery embolism or thrombosis.

An intravenous pyelogram or radionuclide scan demonstrates absent or markedly reduced perfusion of the renal tissue supplied by the occluded artery. Contrast-enhanced CT scan is another sensitive method of demonstrating the absence of a nephrogram in devitalized renal segments and is particularly useful following blunt trauma because it provides information about other intraabdominal organs. CT scan of the involved kidney typically shows a thin rim of cortical enhancement in an otherwise unenhanced renal segment (rim sign). Some reports suggest that magnetic resonance aniography may prove to be the most valuable noninvasive imaging technique. Comparative studies are necessary to confirm this experience.

Recommended Approach

We believe that selective renal arteriography remains the most reliable diagnostic study in the evaluation of renal artery occlusion. Arteriography is recommended for patients who have acute renal failure (especially with anuria) and a contraindication to anticoagulation or abdominal trauma with a high likelihood of severe renal artery damage. Digital subtraction arteriography performed with low-dose radiographic contrast can provide reasonably high-resolution images with a low risk of contrast-induced acute renal failure. Evaluation of suspected or documented renal artery embolism should include a two-dimensional cardiac sonogram to identify mural thrombi, valvular vegetations, or atrial myxoma. At present, in patients with suspected occlusive renal artery disease, we recommend obtaining a radionuclide scan, then proceeding rapidly either to a contrast-enhanced CT scan in patients who are to be treated medically or to renal arteriography in patients who are to be treated surgically, by transcatheter embolectomy, or by intraarterial infusion of a thrombolytic agent.

Therapeutic

Therapeutic Options

The goal of management is prompt restoration of blood flow to the ischemic kidney or renal segment, thereby enhancing restoration of renal function. As most successful therapeutic efforts occur within 24 hours of arterial occlusion, rapid diagnosis and localization of the thrombus or embolus are critical. At present, however, the difficulties in making this diagnosis often result in the diagnosis being delayed for several days. Fortunately, return of renal function has been documented in a small number of patients treated surgically even up to 6 weeks after thrombosis. It is likely that these patients had gradual evolution of the occlusive process, allowing time for the development of collateral renal circulation. Controversy exists over the therapy of choice. Anticoagulation, intravenous or intraarterial fibrinolytic therapy, percutaneous transluminal angioplasty, clot extraction by percutaneous catheter, and surgical thrombectomy have all been proposed, but no prospective, comparative trials of efficacy and safety have been performed.

Recommended Approach

We prefer medical therapy, save in patients with traumatic renal artery thrombosis diagnosed within 3 to 6 hours. Anticoagulation with standard regimens of heparin and warfarin is effective in most cases of unilateral renal artery embolism. Although clinical data are accumulating supporting a more liberal use of fibrinolytic therapy, we currently reserve fibrinolytic agents for bilateral renal artery occlusion or arterial occlusion with a solitary functioning kidney. Streptokinase or urokinase can be administered by intravenous or selective intraarterial infusion. Arterial catheter insertion should be performed by an experienced physician, using care to minimize arterial trauma. We now use intraarterial streptokinase in a bolus of 20,000 IU in 20 mL 5% dextrose in water infused over 1 to 2 minutes, followed by 3000 IU/min for 2 hours. Arteriography is then repeated, and streptokinase is continued at a dose of 100,000 IU/h until clot lysis is complete, up to a maximum of 24 hours. Absence of clot lysis after 2 hours may indicate streptokinase resistance, demonstrated by failure to prolong the thrombin time above 1.5 times control values. Streptokinase should then be discontinued and urokinase substituted. During fibrinolytic therapy, thrombin time is measured every 12 hours and maintained at two to five times normal. Streptokinase is associated with serious hypersensitivity reactions in

approximately 0.1% of patients. This low incidence of reactions, coupled with the fact that urokinase is many times more expensive than streptokinase, accounts for our choice of streptokinase in these cost-conscious days. Heparin and warfarin are initiated in standard doses 3 to 4 hours after stopping fibrinolytic therapy, after thrombin time has fallen below two times control values. Warfarin should be continued as long as the patient remains at high risk for recurrent renal artery thrombosis or embolism.

Operative or percutaneous catheter clot removal is indicated in cases having extensive renal artery trauma, a contraindication to anticoagulant and fibrinolytic therapy, or failure of intraarterial streptokinase (or urokinase) to reestablish any renal blood flow after 2 hours. In a review of patients treated for renal artery embolism between 1970 and 1982, Nicholas and DeMuth (1984) found an 87% renal salvage rate and an operative mortality of 9%. Renal salvage with anticoagulation was not statistically different.

FOLLOW-UP

The patient should be advised that early treatment can restore kidney function and that long-term anticoagulation can be expected to prevent subsequent thromboembolic events. Bleeding risks and drug interactions of anticoagulants should be discussed. Patients taking warfarin should have prothrombin time monitored at least weekly until a stable therapeutic level is achieved, after which prothrombin time may be drawn at monthly intervals. Additional follow-up depends on the patient's general condition.

DISCUSSION
Prevalence

The prevalence of renal infarction at autopsy is less than 2% and a correct premortem diagnosis is rarely made. Underlying cardiac disease or arrhythmias were identified in 16 of 17 patients with renal artery embolism described by Lessman et al. (1978).

Related Basic Science

Whether sudden renal artery occlusion causes tissue ischemia or infarction depends on the cross-sectional area of the residual lumen, duration of occlusion, and extent of collateral circulation. In dogs with a postocclusion renal artery pressure of only 12 mm Hg, renal function and histology are preserved for up to 2 hours. The duration of ischemic tolerance for the human kidney is approximately 90 to 180 minutes. Thus, an optimum outcome requires institution of medical or surgical therapy within that period.

Patients with severe atherosclerotic stenosis of a renal artery may frequently sustain asymptomatic renal artery thrombosis, recognized incidentally on renal arteriography if at all. In these patients, the gradual reduction of renal blood flow prior to thrombosis stimulates the development of collateral circulation from lumbar arteries, which often preserves the viability of the kidney when renal artery thrombosis occurs. When severe renal failure results from bilateral renal artery occlusion of this type, surgery may restore adequate renal function even months after initiation of dialysis.

Natural History and Its Modification with Treatment

The natural history depends largely on that of the underlying condition (e.g., cardiac disease, trauma, or severe atherosclerosis). Recurrent thromboembolism to other vital organs such as brain or intestine is a common cause of death in patients with underlying cardiac disease who are not maintained on effective doses of warfarin. With early diagnosis and appropriate medical or surgical treatment as described above, renal failure is often prevented or reversed. Ischemic renal tissue may produce enough renin to cause persistent hypertension. The rate of immediate mortality in patients developing total renal failure from total renal artery occlusion has been reduced dramatically by the availability of dialysis.

Prevention

In patients with cardiac disease predisposing to intracardiac thrombosis formation, the incidence of systemic thromboembolism is markedly reduced by long-term warfarin anticoagulation. All patients with atrial fibrillation should be anticoagulated, unless there is a strong contraindication to chronic warfarin therapy.

Cost Containment

In deciding when to evaluate a patient for suspected renal artery thrombosis or embolism, the physician should attempt to identify an underlying condition (see above) causing increased risk. Evaluation then should proceed from less expensive imaging procedures (e.g., radionuclide scan) to more expensive procedures such as selective renal arteriography or CT. If fibrinolytic therapy is chosen, streptokinase is recommended over the far more expensive agent urokinase.

REFERENCES

Blum U, Billmann P, Krause T, et al. Effect of local low-dose thrombolysis on clinical outcome in acute embolic renal artery occlusion. Radiology 1993;189:549.

Lessman RK, Johnson SF, Coburn JW, Kaufman JJ. Renal artery embolism: Clinical features and long-term follow-up of 17 cases. Ann Intern Med 1978;89:477.

Liano F, Gamez C, Pacual J, et al. Use of urinary parameters in the diagnosis of total acute renal artery occlusion. Nepron 1994;66:170.

Lohse JR, Botham RJ, Waters RF. Traumatic bilateral renal artery thrombosis: Case report and review of the literature. J Urol 1982;127:522.

Nicholas GG, DeMuth WE. Treatment of renal artery embolism. Arch Surg 1984;119:522.

Salem TA, Lumsden AB, Martin LG. Local infusion of fibrinolytic agents for acute renal artery thromboembolism: Report of ten cases. Ann Vasc Surg 1993;7:21.

CHAPTER 16-25

Inherited Kidney Diseases

Vera Delaney, M.D., Ph.D., and Kenneth D. Gardner, Jr., M.D.

DEFINITION

Inherited kidney diseases are renal diseases that are transmitted in patterns that follow the Medelian theory.

ETIOLOGY

Inherited kidney diseases are due to genetic defects that are transmitted according to Mendelian laws of inheritance. Classic genetics uses the segregation pattern of the phenotype in families to suggest the diagnosis. This is now being replaced by molecular genetics, wherein the precise defect at the level of the genome is identified. This requires sophisticated molecular biological techniques and is still in its infancy.

CRITERIA FOR DIAGNOSIS

Suggestive

Kidney disease that runs in families suggests the diagnosis.

Definitive

The definitive diagnosis rests in finding the abnormal genetic sequence in affected family members and showing that this abnormality is responsible for the disease. This precision is not currently feasible for any significant hereditary kidney disease. Thus, at present, the definitive diagnosis is made by finding kidney diseases of similar phenotypic pattern within families, which are transmitted according to Mendelian laws of inheritance.

CLINICAL MANIFESTATIONS

Subjective

Hereditary kidney disease may involve the tubules, interstitium, or glomeruli and/or the urinary tract. Thus, the constellation of presenting symptoms is vast. Gross hematuria, loin pain, abdominal masses, fever, and/or sepsis secondary to complicating urinary tract infection or symptoms attributable to uremia are the most common presenting features. Renal insufficiency often presents with failure to thrive in the very young or growth retardation in the adolescent.

Hereditary nephritis or Alport's syndrome is clinically characterized by the occurrence of hematuria, often gross, frequently before the age of 5 years in males, often in association with bilateral hearing loss and accompanied in 15 to 40% of patients by ocular changes in the form of lens and retinal defects.

Bilateral flank masses (enlarged kidneys) at birth suggest congenital multicystic kidneys or recessive polycystic kidney disease. In later years, they are more likely to indicate autosomal dominant polycystic kidney disease. The latter may also present with hematuria, often gross, renal colic, or symptoms attributable to urinary tract infection. Fatigue, polyuria, nocturia, enuresis, and growth retardation are common presenting features of medullary cystic disease in children and adolescents.

Renal colic during the first two decades of life is typical of cystinuria, hypercalciuria, renal tubular acidosis, and oxalosis. Inherited renal tubular defects usually present during the first few years of life with failure to thrive, growth retardation, or rickets. Occasionally, the finding of hypertension, anemia, or bacteriuria leads to the diagnosis in an otherwise asymptomatic individual. Edema of the face and legs is a rare presenting feature of congenital nephrotic syndrome, hereditary nephritis, or hereditary disorders of a systemic nature such as diabetes mellitus and familial Mediterranean fever.

Obviously, family history is crucial to the diagnosis. The majority of these disorders are transmitted as autosomal recessive traits, affecting siblings within the same generation. Some, such as autosomal dominant polycystic kidney disease and vesicoureteral reflux, follow dominant patterns. A few, including hereditary nephritis, vitamin D-resistant rickets, nephrogenic diabetes insipidus, and Fabry's disease, are linked to the X chromosome. These tend to exhibit variable penetrance and expression in females, but manifest the full-blown disease in males. Some, such as Alport's syndrome and medullary cystic disease, express genetic heterogeneity, meaning that they exhibit interfamilial differences in their patterns of inheritance, associated conditions, ages at onset, or clinical severity.

Objective

Physical Examination

Normal or low blood pressure tends to accompany those heritable kidney disorders that involve the tubulointerstitium, for example, medullary cystic disease. An exception is autosomal dominant polycystic kidney disease, in which elevated blood pressure is common and may be the presenting manifestation.

Retardation of skeletal growth commonly reflects disordered metabolism. It may appear with advancing uremia, or it may reflect a specific metabolic defect, such as that found in Bartter's syndrome, Fanconi's syndrome, renal tubular acidosis, pseudohypoparathyroidism, vitamin D-dependent rickets, or vitamin D-resistant (hypophosphatemic) rickets.

Bilateral nerve deafness, detectable during the first decade of life, is a frequent accompaniment of hereditary nephritis. Ocular abnormalities involving the lens, cornea, or retina are seen less often. Eye defects are also found in Lowe's syndrome, galactosemia, and cystinosis, as well as in some families with recessively inherited medullary cystic disease (nephronopthisis).

Typical skin rashes are present in Hartnup disease, Fabry's disease, and the variant of systemic lupus erythematosus that is associated with a genetic deficiency of complement.

Routine Laboratory Abnormalities

Associated routine laboratory findings may include impaired renal function, as assessed by elevated serum blood urea nitrogen and creatinine, or impaired tubular function, as assessed by the findings of isosthenuria, glycosuria, persistent hypokalemia, hypomagnesemia, hypouricemia, hypobicarbonatemia, hypernatremia, hypocalcemia, or hypophosphatemia. Urinalysis is often abnormal, showing hematuria, proteinuria, and cellular casts in those patients with predominantly glomerular involvement, whereas those with tubulointerstitial disease often have unremarkable urinary sediments, usually of low specific gravity. Intermittent pyuria and bacteriuria are frequent in reflux nephropathy and may also complicate other forms of hereditary kidney disease.

PLANS
Diagnostic
Differential Diagnosis

The differential diagnosis of inherited kidney disease from congenital renal disease can be difficult on clinical grounds. Congenital disorders are due to genetic defects that occur during fetal development in utero and do not follow recognized patterns of genetic transmission. Congenital multicystic kidney, renal agenesis and dysplasia, and horseshoe kidney are examples of the latter; however, a few disorders seem to be inherited in some families but congenital in others. Medullary sponge kidney and renal dysplasia are examples of such "bridging" diseases.

Diagnostic Options

Once the presence of a hereditary renal disease is established, subsequent categorization into glomerular, tubular, or tubulointerstitial involvement should be based on routine laboratory findings, imaging techniques, renal histology, specific biochemical tests, and, finally, if available, DNA analysis in an attempt to define the defective area within the genome.

Ultrasonography is perhaps the most helpful imaging technique. It is increasingly available, noninvasive, and sensitive. It accurately depicts kidney size. It can detect cysts, as in polycystic disease, or reveal interstitial scarring in the form of increased echogenicity. The kidneys are more commonly symmetric (bilateral and diffuse) in heritable disease and asymmetric (unilateral and local) in congenital disease. Bilateral enlarged cystic kidneys characterize polycystic disease. Bilateral shrunken kidneys characterize medullary cystic disease and hereditary nephritis. The presence of cortical scars superimposed on shrunken kidneys suggests reflux nephropathy. An asymmetrically enlarged renal mass suggests congenital multicystic kidney. Intravenous urography, computed tomography scanning, and arteriography can be helpful in confirming obstruction, cysts, or tumors. Retrograde pyelography should be avoided in patients suspected as having renal cystic disease. Voiding cystoureterography is the procedure of choice for the staging of vesicoureteric reflux, but radionuclide cystography is also useful, especially in the neonate.

Renal biopsy is necessary to make a definitive diagnosis of hereditary nephritis and thin basement membrane disease. Direct examination of kidneys, for example, after nephrectomy or at autopsy, sometimes is required to demonstrate medullary cystic disease, because in this disease the kidneys are often too small at presentation for safe use of renal

biopsy. Among those heritable systemic disorders in which renal involvement occurs (diabetes mellitus, familial Mediterranean fever, Fabry's disease), renal biopsy may be required for diagnosis. Histologic staging is useful in planning therapy in complement-deficient lupus.

Biochemical analyses of stones, blood, and 24-hour urine samples help in diagnosing cystinuria, hypercalciuria, oxalosis, Hartnup disease, and Fanconi's syndrome. Cystinosis usually requires conjunctival, lymph node, or bone marrow biopsy to reveal characteristic deposits of cystine. Hypokalemia, inappropriate kaliuresis, and juxtaglomerular hyperplasia on renal biopsy are typical of Bartter's syndrome. Increased serum osmolality with isosmotic or hyposmotic urines and unresponsiveness to exogenous antidiuretic hormone are characteristic of nephrogenic diabetes insipidus. Hypophosphatemia, with inappropriate phosphaturia, is observed in vitamin D-resistant rickets. In contrast, most vitamin D-dependent rickets is characterized by hypocalcemia and absent 1,25-dihydroxyvitamin D. Pseudohypoparathyroidism gives rise to hypocalcemia, hyperphosphatemia, and increased plasma parathyroid hormone and is accompanied by a lack of phosphaturic response to exogenous parathyroid hormone. Renal tubular acidosis is suggested by the findings of hypokalemic hyperchloremic metabolic acidosis. The distal type of renal tubular acidosis is suggested by a first-voided morning pH greater than 5.5, whereas the proximal type is usually associated with a pH of 5.0 or less. Confirmatory tests involving the administration of ammonium chloride or sodium bicarbonate may be required to confirm the diagnosis (see Chapter 16–17).

More sophisticated biochemical tests and genetic analyses are available in research settings, which may be employed to better define the precise genetic and resultant biochemical anomalies.

Recommended Approach

A detailed family history, with special emphasis on consanguinity, early deaths, and miscarriages is of obvious importance in the workup of patients with possible hereditary disease. The biochemical defect should be defined as completely as possible with laboratory testing, imaging techniques, and renal biopsy, where indicated. Referral of the patient and family members to a research center should be considered for further, more sophisticated, testing employing advanced molecular biological technology in an attempt to define the precise genetic defect and, thus, aid genetic counseling.

Therapeutic

Therapy does not prevent the inexorable progression of renal failure in polycystic disease, medullary cystic disease, or hereditary nephritis. Treatment of salt wasting, bacteriuria, and hypertension may delay it. A diet low in protein (0.5 g/kg body weight) may slow deteriorating renal function in these, as in other, forms of chronic renal disease.

Prophylactic antibiotics and/or corrective surgery may be indicated in infants and preschoolers with vesicoureteric reflux in an attempt to prevent renal scarring, a prelude to the subsequent development of hypertension and/or renal failure. Liberal fluid intake, urinary alkalinization, and penicillamine increase the solubility of cystine and may prevent stone formation in cystinuria. Increased fluids, low-calcium diet, and thiazides decrease stone formation in idiopathic hypercalciuria. Oxalate deposition in oxalosis may be diminished in some patients by high-dose pyridoxine therapy. In others, enzyme replacement in the form of a liver transplant may be indicated in an attempt to prevent renal destruction and the subsequent development of oxalosis.

The treatment of Hartnup disease requires a balanced diet with nicotinamide supplements to prevent pellagra. Bartter's syndrome is treated with potassium chloride supplements and prostaglandin synthetase inhibitors (e.g., indomethacin); additional magnesium may also be necessary.

Fanconi's syndrome requires potassium and phosphate to replace renal losses. Supplementation with 1,25-dihydroxyvitamin D may also be necessary. Vitamin D-resistant rickets is treated with phosphate in large amounts (1–4 g/d) and 1-hydroxyvitamin D (0.5–1.0 µg every 12 hours). Vitamin D-dependent rickets is more amenable to therapy and merely requires 1,25-dihydroxyvitamin D (0.25–1.0 µg/d). Large amounts of calcium supplements and 1,25-dihydroxyvitamin D are necessary in pseudohypoparathyroidism.

Distal renal tubular acidosis calls for sodium bicarbonate (2–3 mg/kg/day) to correct the acidosis; potassium as the bicarbonate, citrate, gluconate, or acetate salt also may be necessary. Large doses of sodium bicarbonate (10–15 mg/kg/d) usually are required in proximal renal tubular acidosis. This amount of bicarbonate may aggravate urinary potassium wasting to the extent that potassium supplements may also be necessary. Addition of a thiazide diuretic (hydrochlorothiazide, 25–50 mg/d) may cause a tendency to contraction alkalosis, resulting in an improvement of the acidosis but a deterioration in the degree of hypokalemia.

Nephrogenic diabetes insipidus may benefit from thiazide therapy or prostaglandin inhibition. Both promote hyperabsorption of salt and water at the proximal tubular level, lessening polyuria. Replacement of urinary and insensible fluid losses with hypotonic fluids is vital to avoid dehydration.

FOLLOW-UP

The frequency and nature of follow-up visits depend on the disorder at hand. Polycystic disease and hereditary nephritis deserve semiannual observation so that complications may be detected as they arise. With the onset of renal failure, more frequent visits are required to ensure the timely treatment of metabolic abnormalities and to plan renal replacement therapy.

Patients with one of the metabolic stone diseases should be seen monthly until stabilized and at 6-month intervals thereafter. Children with renal tubular defects, particularly if growth is impaired, are best followed at least weekly until medical therapy is stabilized and improvement occurs. The frequency of visits can then be decreased.

Children with reflux need to be monitored at monthly intervals for infection, and more often if symptomatic. Voiding cystograms need to be repeated at least on an annual basis to plan future therapeutic strategies.

DISCUSSION
Prevalence

Inherited kidney disease is rare with the exception of autosomal dominant polycystic disease (see below).

Related Basic Science

Inherited kidney disease may be divided into the following seven subgroups.

Cystic Disease. Autosomal dominant polycystic kidney disease is the most common hereditary disease in the United States, more frequent than either sickle cell disease or cystic fibrosis, with a prevalence rate of 1:200 to 1:1000, and occurs in all races and nationalities. It accounts for 10% of end-stage kidney disease and an expenditure of more than $200 million per annum in the United States. The genetic defect has been localized to the short arm of chromosome 16 in the majority of patients studied so far (ADPKD-1). Recently, however, a number of families have been identified in whom the chromosomal abnormality is not on chromosome 16. These patients (ADPKD-2) have a slightly more benign course, although the course is, as in ADPKD-1, always progressive. In autosomal dominant polycystic kidney disease, progressive cystic dilation of some renal tubules leads to compression and destruction of adjacent nephrons and uremia, usually by the sixth decade. Hepatic cysts occur in 30 to 50% of patients, and Berry aneurysms involving the cerebral circulation are found in 10% of patients and rupture at a rate of 2% per year or less. Diverticular disease of the colon and cardiac valvular abnormalities are also seen with increased frequency in patients with this disease. This multiorgan involvement suggests a systemic defect rather than one restricted to the kidneys. Pathogenesis of the renal disease is unknown but may involve decreased compliance of basement membranes, malalignment of membrane-bound carrier proteins leading to abnormal fluid accumulation, and/or proliferation of tubular basement membrane with partial obstruction and distal dilation.

Polycystic disease in childhood is recessively inherited with a preva-

lence rate of 1:10,000 to 1:40,000. It is associated with varying degrees of hepatic fibrosis. The kidney dominates the picture in the neonate, with liver involvement becoming increasingly prominent as the child ages. Portal hypertension, not renal failure, may be the most significant disorder in affected adolescents or young adults.

Medullary cystic disease and nephronophthisis are the dominant and recessive forms of another heritable renal cystic disease. The former affects adults; the latter affects children and adolescents and is the most common cause of idiopathic renal failure during the teen years in some countries. It has been accompanied by retinal disease and hepatic fibrosis in several affected kindreds. Presentation is usually insidious, with fatigue, polyuria, polydipsia, growth retardation, relatively unremarkable urinary sediment, absence of hypertension, and bilaterally small, but smooth-surfaced kidneys. Because of the last effect, renal biopsy is rarely feasible, leading, perhaps, to underdiagnosis with only approximately 300 cases in the literature. Cysts are found at the corticomedullary junction or in the medulla in some 75% of kidneys with advanced disease and are small (<0.5 cm) and rarely detectable on ultrasound. Their role in the pathogenesis of the disease, which otherwise displays the histologic features typical of chronic interstitial nephritis, is unknown.

Hereditary Nephritis (Alport's Syndrome). Approximately 3% of children with chronic renal failure have hereditary nephritis. Males progress to end-stage disease unlike females who, in general, have milder disease. Hereditary nephritis is dominant in all kindreds. X-linked dominant inheritance appears more frequently than autosomal dominant, although both have been described. The gene frequency is about 1:5,000 in the United States, with approximately 15% of neonates with the disease having new mutations. It is a progressive glomerular disease characterized by a defective glomerular basement membrane, readily apparent on electron microscopic examination of involved glomeruli. The lamina densa is split and fragmented into multiple interlacing strands, often containing small electron-dense granules. The latter are diagnostic. These abnormalities presumably account for the hematuria and progressive renal failure that characterize the early and late (second to third decades) clinical courses, respectively, of the syndrome. Nerve deafness is frequent, but not a necessary accompaniment. Ocular (lenticular) and platelet abnormalities and/or polyneuropathy are less often associated. Pathogenesis may involve an abnormal persistence of fetal or neonatal basement membrane antigens or a defective component of type IV collagen, the predominant collagenous component of the glomerular basement membrane. Mutations, involving single base substitutions and/or deletions, have been mapped to the Xq22 chromosomal region in some, but not all, kindreds with hereditary nephritis.

A slightly different form of hereditary nephritis, called *thin basement membrane nephropathy,* is considered by some to be a forme fruste of Alport's syndrome. Like the latter, it may be associated with auditory and/or ocular problems and often presents with microscopic hematuria. Its inheritance is usually autosomal dominant and has a better prognosis for preservation of renal function than Alport's syndrome. Structurally it is also different, with a characteristic patchy moth-eaten appearance to the basement membrane and an apparently normal type IV collagen. The precise defect is unknown but is thought to reside in the subepithelial portion of the glomerular basement membrane.

Inherited Tubular Transport Defects. Impaired transport mechanisms along renal tubules lead to disease either because the body becomes deficient in an essential, but malabsorbed, substance (e.g., phosphate in vitamin-D resistant rickets) or because the malabsorbed material is relatively insoluble in urine (e.g., as is the case with cystine in cystinuria). Renal tubular and occasionally intestinal transport of the sulfur-containing amino acid cystine and the dibasic amino acids ornithine, arginine, and lysine are defective in this disorder. Clinical symptoms are due to the insoluble nature of cystine in an acid urine with the production of multiple calculi. The overall prevalence of cystinuria is approximately 1:7000 and its inheritance is autosomal recessive. The site of the tubular defect is, as yet, controversial, but is now thought to reside at the level of the brush border of the proximal tubule.

Inherited Deficiency of a Renal Hormone. Vitamin D-dependent rickets is due to an inherited deficiency of the enzyme that is necessary to hydroxylate 25-hydroxyvitamin D to its more active 1,25-dihydroxyvitamin D form. A clinically similar syndrome is due to an abnormality of the 1,25-dihydroxyvitamin D receptor, which can be distinguished from the former by a normal or elevated serum level of 1,25-dihydroxyvitamin D.

Inherited Defects of Hormonal Receptor Sites Within the Kidney. Pseudohypoparathyroidism and nephrogenic diabetes insipidus arise from increased end-organ resistance to the actions of parathyroid hormone and antidiuretic hormone, respectively. In most cases of pseudohypoparathyroidism, parathyroid hormone fails to activate adenyl cyclase due to a defect at the level of the stimulatory component of the receptor–adenyl cyclase complex. Similarly, in the majority of patients with nephrogenic diabetes insipidus, resistance to the V_2 actions of antidiuretic hormone resides in the failure of adenyl cyclase to generate cyclic AMP, and perhaps other intermediates, responsible for the phosphorylation of proteins, a prerequisite for microtubular formation and antidiuretic hormone-induced water absorption.

Hereditary Systemic Diseases with Major Renal Involvement. Sickle cell disease, diabetes mellitus, and familial Mediterranean fever are included in this category. All can be accompanied by the nephrotic syndrome. Galactosemia, Wilson's hepatolenticular degeneration, hereditary fructose intolerance, cystinosis, and Lowe's syndrome may underlie Fanconi's syndrome. Fabry's disease, due to a deficiency of a lysosomal enzyme α-galactosidase, manifests as an infiltrative disease involving glycosphingolipid in the kidneys and other organs. The former leads to progressive renal destruction in males and necessitates renal replacement in midlife. Primary oxaluria, or oxalosis, is a genetically transmitted disorder of glyoxalate metabolism causing renal failure secondary to calcium oxalate deposition in the kidney.

Congential Anomalies and Tumors of the Genitourinary Tract. These disorders include horseshoe kidney, multicystic kidney disease, unilateral hydronephrosis, renal dysplasia and agenesis, and hypernephroma. The last may occur bilaterally.

Vesicoureteral reflux is due to a congenital defect of either the length, diameter, musculature, or innervation of the submucosal segment of the ureter. It has a strong hereditary component. The gene frequency for this defect is about 1 in 600 and segregation analysis of affected families revealed that 45% of gene carriers will have reflux and/or reflux nephropathy as adults and 15% will have renal failure, as compared with 0.05% and 0.001%, respectively, of those who do not carry the gene. Early identification of this subgroup aided by the routine screening of family members, especially preschoolers, with the institution of therapy in the form of prophylactic antibiotics and/or corrective surgery where appropriate, may help prevent renal scarring and loss of function.

Natural History and Its Modification with Treatment

The evolution and severity of disease differ among the hereditary kidney diseases. Terminal renal failure typically presents in the sixth decade in autosomal dominant polycystic kidney disease, but is reached by the second to fourth decades in medullary cystic disease, nephronophthisis, and hereditary nephritis. Patients with Lowe's syndrome and cystinosis also have a poor prognosis, with death from terminal uremia or associated defects in the second decade. Oxalosis also progresses to renal failure in early life. Males with Fabry's disease become uremic by the fifth decade; accelerated vascular disease further increases morbidity and mortality.

In each of these diseases, strict control of blood pressure and early detection and treatment of secondary infection and other complications may decrease the rate of decline to terminal renal failure.

Morbidity from recurring renal colic may be diminished by treatment in renal tubular acidosis, cystinuria, and hypercalciuria. Prognosis for survival and preservation of renal function in the other inherited disorders is relatively good barring secondary complications.

Prevention

Birth control measures, in utero diagnosis with consideration of abortion in some situations, and gene replacement therapy offer the only promises for prevention and cure of those hereditary renal diseases that are progressive and ultimately fatal. Gradual progress is being made in the localization of the genetic defects within the chromosomes. The potential value of antenatal ultrasonography in the screening of family members with renal anomalies, especially vesicoureteric reflux, should be pointed out. In brief, a practical means for the prevention of these disorders does not exist at present.

Cost Containment

Careful history taking and repeated physical and laboratory examinations offer the most direct and inexpensive approaches to diagnosis and management. Ultrasonography probably offers the safest and least expensive avenue to diagnosis in those hereditary renal disorders that distort the architecture. It is more than 90% specific and sensitive in the diagnosis of autosomal dominant polycystic kidney disease in the over 20 age group but is less sensitive in younger age groups. Routine screening for cerebral aneurysms in patients with autosomal dominant polycystic kidney disease is not considered cost effective, save in the symptomatic at-risk and asymptomatic polycystic patients with a known intrafamilial predilection to intracranial aneurysms.

Ultrasound is also important in the evaluation of anatomic congenital anomalies of the urinary tract in utero. This is especially important in patients with a family history of renal agenesis or dysplasia, cystic kidney disease, obstructive uropathy with hydronephrosis, or vesicoureteral reflux and in those with oligohydramnios and/or elevated levels of α-fetoprotein. Fetuses with bilateral renal agenesis or cystic malformations have a very poor prognosis for survival and parents may chose to terminate the pregnancy. Fetal surgery may be indicated if bilateral hydronephrosis with renal functional impairment is present and early elective delivery is precluded by immature lungs and/or other problems. Success rate is approximately 40%, with a procedure-related death rate of about 5%. Bilateral obstructive uropathy with normal renal function in utero usually requires corrective surgery at term and is associated with a substantial improvement in renal function, especially if, at the time of surgery, the infant is less than 6 months old.

Kidney biopsy provides an opportunity for the definitive diagnosis of hereditary nephritis and should be performed in at least one member of any undiagnosed, but suspected, family. Biopsy of all affected siblings, however, is unwarranted unless a second disease process is suspected.

REFERENCES

Arthur RJ, Irving HC, Thomas DFM, Watters JK. Bilateral fetal uropathy: What is the outlook? Br Med J 1989;298:1419.

Bailey RR, Maling TMJ, Swainson CP. Vesicoureteric reflux and reflux nephropathy. In: Schrier RW, Gottschalk CW, eds. Diseases of the kidney. 5th ed. Boston: Little, Brown, 1993:689.

Delaney VB, Adler S, Bruns F, et al. Autosomal dominant polycystic kidney disease: Presentation, complications and prognosis. Am J Kidney Dis 1985;5:104.

Gardner KD. Medullary and miscellaneous renal cystic disorders. In: Schrier RW, Gottschalk CW, eds. Diseases of the kidney. 5th ed. Boston: Little, Brown, 1993:513.

Grünfeld J-P. Alport's syndrome. In: Cameron S, Davison AM, Grünfeld J-P, et al., eds. Oxford textbook of clinical nephrology. New York: Oxford University Press, 1992:2197.

Reeders ST. Molecular genetics of renal disorders. In: Cameron S, Davison AM, Grünfeld J-P, et al., eds. Oxford textbook of clinical nephrology. New York: Oxford University Press, 1992:2155.

CHAPTER 16–26

Dysfunction in the Transplanted Kidney

Vera Delaney, M.D., Ph.D., and Khalid Butt M.D.

DEFINITION

A well-functioning renal transplant has a glomerular filtration rate of 60 to 100 mL/min with the ability to maintain the milieu intérieur of the host within the normal range by the production of urine identical in composition to that produced by native kidneys. Dysfunction is present when the allograft fails to achieve or maintain this degree of function.

ETIOLOGY

The renal allograft is subject to similar prerenal, renal, and postrenal insults as affect native kidneys and, in general, responds in a similar manner. Rejection, acute and chronic, nephrotoxicity from some immunosuppressants, and obstruction due to compression by a pelvic collection of lymph are unique causes of renal dysfunction in the allograft recipient.

CRITERIA FOR DIAGNOSIS
Suggestive

Tenderness or swelling of the allograft, decreasing urine output, hematuria, frothy urine, edema, weight gain, and/or new-onset hypertension, alone or in combination, suggest allograft dysfunction.

Definitive

Retention of nitrogenous products, as reflected by an increase in blood urea nitrogen and creatinine, or a declining glomerular filtration rate, as measured by clearance of inulin, iothalamate, or, less preferably, creatinine, denotes allograft dysfunction. Pyuria, hematuria, eosinophiluria, and/or proteinuria in a patient with a functioning allograft and nonfunctioning native kidneys are also diagnostic of ongoing graft dysfunction. Hydronephrosis on ultrasound evaluation, the presence of transplant renal artery stenosis on arteriography, and/or abnormal allograft histology each give more specific answers as to the underlying cause of renal functional impairment.

CLINICAL MANIFESTATIONS
Subjective

Pain over the allograft, hematuria, a decrease in urine output, sudden and excessive weight gain, swelling either generalized or localized to the periorbital areas or lower extremities, or uremic symptoms suggest allograft dysfunction. Occasionally, symptoms are vague and nonspecific, consisting of malaise, fatigue, myalgia, arthralgia, and/or low-grade fever. Important past history includes the timing of the transplant, original disease, medication history, posttransplant complications, and date and results of the most recent laboratory evaluation. Family history is usually of relevance only in that a change in family circumstances, financial or otherwise, may be associated with noncompliance with immunosuppressants. This is particularly notable in adolescents.

Objective
Physical Examination

Fever (100–104°F), allograft tenderness or swelling, edema, pulmonary congestion, hypertension, and/or the stigmata of uremia may be present. A vascular bruit may be audible over the allograft.

Routine Laboratory Abnormalities

More commonly in the United States, allograft dysfunction is asymptomatic and picked up as a result of abnormalities on routine laboratory tests. The latter include a complete blood count, full biochemical profile, and urinalysis and trough blood levels of cyclosporine (Sandimmune) or tacrolimus (Prograf). An elevation of serum creatinine in excess of 15 to 20% of baseline, pyuria, hematuria, and/or the presence of proteinuria require further workup.

PLANS
Diagnostic
Differential Diagnosis

Prerenal causes of allograft dysfunction include advanced congestive heart failure, severe liver disease with ascites, and stenosis or obstruction of the renal artery supplying the allograft. Renal causes include acute tubular necrosis, rejection (acute and chronic), cyclosporine or tacrolimus nephrotoxicity, recurrence of the original glomerular disease, pyelonephritis, and drug-induced interstitial nephritis. Postrenal causes of allograft dysfunction usually reside at the ureter or bladder outlet. Blood clots, stones, strictures, and external compression by pelvic fluid collections, composed of blood (hematoma, seroma), urine (urinoma), or lymph (lymphocele), are common causes of ureteric obstruction. Bladder outlet obstruction is usually due to prostatic hypertrophy or urethral stricture, similar to the general population.

Diagnostic Options

A careful examination of the urine should be performed in all patients with allograft dysfunction. The presence of pyuria and/or bacteriuria demands a urine culture. The degree of proteinuria should be quantitated in a timed urine collection or by use of urine protein-to-creatinine ratio in a spot urine. Because most current transplant recipients take the nephrotoxic immunosuppressant cyclosporine, and because toxicity correlates to some extent with trough drug blood levels, the availability of the latter on a routine basis is clearly imperative when managing renal transplant recipients. The same applies to the smaller group of patients taking the equally nephrotoxic agent tacrolimus (Prograf). Ultrasonography is an extremely useful test in the evaluation of patients with allograft dysfunction. It is noninvasive, readily available, and, when combined with Doppler evaluation and performed by experienced personnel, can give useful diagnostic information. Hydronephrosis, hydroureter, bladder dilation, voiding ability, and extrarenal fluid collections are readily visualized. Parenchymal swelling, loss of corticomedullary junction, and/or dampening of the diastolic component of the intrarenal small arteries suggest acute rejection. Turbulence of flow in the renal arteries and poor intraparenchymal blood flow may point to renal artery stenosis. The latter usually needs confirmation by angiography. Scintigraphy, using the isotope MAG3, is also useful in evaluating transplant function, particularly when performed serially in the early posttransplant period. This agent is eliminated by a combination of tubular secretion and glomerular filtration and has excellent imaging properties. A baseline renal scan should be performed in all nondiuresing renal transplant recipients to confirm viability of the allograft. Complete occlusion of the vasculature results in no uptake of isotope. A decrease and/or delay in uptake suggests acute rejection, in contrast to the picture in acute tubular necrosis, wherein cortical retention and delayed excretion are prominent but uptake usually is preserved. Unfortunately, there is considerable overlap between these conditions, particularly since the advent of cyclosporine, which can by itself be associated with a decline in uptake and/or cortical retention as a manifestation of nephrotoxicity. Nevertheless, in the early postoperative period, MAG3 scintigraphy is useful, allowing semiquantitative evaluation of renal blood flow, tubular function, and the excretory system. Computer axial tomography is rarely used in the evaluation of renal allograft dysfunction, except in the evaluation of some deep-seated peritransplant fluid collections when aspiration is necessary for diagnostic purposes.

Magnetic resonance imaging, initially thought to be able to distinguish acute rejection from cyclosporine toxicity, is now rarely used.

Renal parenchymal causes of allograft dysfunction are best assessed, in the absence of a positive urine culture, by renal allograft biopsy. Automatic spring-loaded biopsy guns are now available that, when used with ultrasonographic localization, make this a relatively benign procedure that may be performed in an outpatient setting, provided monitoring is available for at least 4 hours postbiopsy. Examination of the tissue obtained by light microscopy and, occasionally, immunofluorescence and/or electron microscopy identifies rejection (acute and chronic), other interstitial nephritides, cyclosporine toxicity, and recurrence of the original glomerular disease. Potential reversibility of the underlying pathologic process may also be assessed. Fine-needle aspiration biopsies give information similar to that provided by core biopsies and are associated with less complications. Inconsistent results are obtained, however, if adequate samples are not obtained and examined by experienced personnel.

Serum electrolyte, acid–base, and calcium–phosphorus abnormalities are worked up in a manner similar to that used for nontransplant patients.

Recommended Approach

Allograft dysfunction in the early (0–90 days) posttransplant period must have an aggressive diagnostic workup aimed at excluding acute rejection as the underlying cause. Thus, the indication for renal transplant biopsy in this period merely requires a urine devoid of overt infection, a trough cyclosporine level less than 300 ng/mL, and an ultrasound showing no obstruction. Cyclosporine toxicity becomes a more likely cause of allograft dysfunction later posttransplant. When a reduction of cyclosporine dose may be undertaken as an initial diagnostic tool. If no improvement in renal function ensues within 24 to 72 hours, a renal biopsy should be performed, provided ongoing infection and obstruction have each been excluded. Nephrotic range proteinuria and/or glomerular hematuria also require a biopsy to identify the underlying pathology.

Allograft dysfunction with severe hypertension, particularly when accompanied by a bruit over the transplant, may indicate significant renal artery stenosis. Arteriography is the definitive test in this situation and is usually performed by puncture of the contralateral femoral artery and use of nonionic contrast medium. Appropriate angioplasty or stenting can usually be performed at the same sitting.

Ureteric obstruction, usually diagnosed initially by ultrasound, requires identification of the cause. Cystoscopic examination and an attempt at retrograde pyelography should be undertaken. The latter is often technically difficult and sometimes impossible. In this situation antegrade pyelography using a small-gauge needle with ultrasound guidance may be employed.

Recurrent urinary tract infections, particularly if accompanied by urosepsis, require a cystoscopy, detailed prostate examination, voiding cystography, and, occasionally, a computed tomography scan of the native kidneys in an attempt to identify the focus of infection.

Therapeutic

Prerenal causes of renal dysfunction require correction, if possible. Concomitant cardiac disease and/or liver disease in patients with a renal transplant, in general, require the same treatment as given to nontransplant patients. Converting enzyme inhibitors, as afterload reducers, particularly when used with aggressive diuretic therapy, may be associated with oligoanuria or an increase in serum creatinine. Although their use is not precluded in this circumstance, calcium channel blockers are probably a safer alternative.

Prerenal azotemia secondary to renal artery stenosis, particularly when associated with severe hypertension, requires correction. Converting enzyme inhibitors should be avoided in patients with tight stenoses in view of their tendency to cause oligoanuria often accompanied by dangerous hyperkalemia. The decision whether to perform angioplasty, stenting, or surgical correction depends on many factors, which include site, extent, type, and accessibility of the stenotic lesion and degree of atherosclerosis of the native blood vessels. Surgical backup should always be available for angioplastic procedures.

Renal transplant dysfunction secondary to acute tubular necrosis is common in recipients of cadaveric allografts in the early posttransplant period. It may be oliguric or nonoliguric. Supportive dialysis therapy is often necessary. Either peritoneal dialysis or hemodialysis may be employed. Usually the prior method of dialysis is continued, but occasionally use of the peritoneal route may have to be delayed for 48 to 72 hours if the peritoneum was breached during surgery. Attempts to convert oliguric to nonoliguric renal failure using high doses of furosemide, mannitol, and/or dopamine in low doses (2.5 – 4.0 μg/kg/min) are rarely successful and should, in general, be discontinued after 24 hours. Immunosuppression must be continued and should, if possible, be devoid of nephrotoxicity. Thus, antilymphocyte preparations (antiThymocyte Globulin [ATG] or OKT3), in conjunction with steroids and azathioprine, or mycophenolate mofetil (cellcept) are usually given without the addition of cyclosporine or tacrolimus until diuresis with improvement in allograft function is underway. Cyclosporine is then added at a daily dose of 8 to 12 mg/kg/d in an attempt to achieve a trough level of 300 to 450 ng/mL in the early posttransplant period. When therapeutic levels are achieved the antilymphocyte preparation is discontinued and the patient maintained on daily triple therapy consisting of prednisone (usually at 0.5 mg/kg), azathioprine (1–2 mg/kg) or mycophenolate mofetil (2 g/day) to maintain white blood cell count in excess of 4000, and cyclosporine (see above).

Acute rejection requires treatment with additional immunosuppressive therapy, aimed at the eradication of cytotoxic cells, mostly T lymphocytes. High-dose steroids (2–4 g methylprednisolone in divided doses over 2–3 days) and/or antilymphocyte preparations in the form of ATG (ATGAM, 10–15 mg/kg/d) or OKT3 (Orthoclone 3, 5–10 mg) are the currently available modalities of treatment. The presence of vascular involvement with severe endotheliatis and/or parenchymal hemorrhage or infarcts, in conjunction with a marked decrease in allograft perfusion on renal scintigraphy, usually indicates a poor prognosis for return of allograft function. In this situation, a viable therapeutic option is withdrawal of all immunosuppression with or without a transplant nephrectomy and return to dialysis.

Repeated bouts of acute rejection despite therapeutic levels of cyclosporine may occasionally be controlled by switching from cyclosporine to tacrolimus, which has, in general, a toxicity profile similar to that of cyclosporine. The recommended daily dose is 0.1 to 0.3 mg/kg to achieve trough therapeutic levels of 10 to 20 ng/mL.

Chronic rejection is currently not amenable to immunologic modification. It is nearly always accompanied by hypertension and proteinuria and often by hyperlipidemia. Aggressive management of blood pressure, with an aim to maintain systolic blood pressure at 140 or less, may slow the inexorable decline in renal function. Calcium channel blockers, in particular nifedipine (Procardia), are often effective in this clinical situation. Cardizem is usually ineffective, being a weaker antihypertensive agent. In addition, it interferes with the metabolism of both cyclosporine and tacrolimus, leading to increased blood levels and occasional aggravation of hypertension. Converting enzyme inhibitors are effective antihypertensive agents in renal allograft recipients, but may be associated with an initial increase in serum creatinine, hyperkalemia, and/or anemia. Institution of a low-protein diet has not been shown to alter the rate of decline of renal function in this patient subgroup, but protein intake in excess of 1 mg/kg/d is probably imprudent.

The original glomerular disease may recur in the allograft despite maintenance immunosuppressive therapy and is usually not amenable to additional immunosuppression. Elevation of cyclosporine or tacrolimus blood levels to supratherapeutic concentrations may rarely be associated with a diminution of proteinuria and a stabilization of renal function, albeit at a decreased level. For histologic recurrence of immunoglobulin A nephropathy with microscopic hematuria as the only clinical finding, no additional therapeutic intervention is usually necessary.

Treatment of allograft dysfunction secondary to cyclosporine and tacrolimus nephrotoxicity requires a reduction in their respective doses, which should result in an improvement in function within 48 to 72 hours.

Impairment in function in conjunction with pyuria, bacteriuria, and positive urine culture implies pyelonephritis and requires antibiotics. Definitive therapy requires identification of the organism and institution of an appropriate antimicrobial agent. Empiric therapy, pending cultures, with ciprofloxacin or trimethoprim–sulfamethoxazole is usually effective and well tolerated. Renal dysfunction secondary to drug-induced interstitial nephritis requires identification and discontinuation of the offending agent. Transplant patients are often maintained on furosemide and/or trimethoprim–sulfamethoxazole and, occasionally, allopurinol, all of which have been incriminated in the etiology of interstitial nephritis. Over-the-counter medications, which now include the prostaglandin synthetase inhibitors ibuprofen (Motrin, Advil) and naprosyn, may also be a cause of renal transplant dysfunction, causing interstitial nephritis and tubular dysfunction, and should be discontinued.

Renal calculi occur in renal transplant recipients and may obstruct the ureter or pelvicalyceal system or be a cause of recurrent urinary tract infections. They may be amenable to lithotripsy or basket removal via the ureteroscope or may occasionally require surgical removal. Workup and treatment of renal stones in a posttransplant patient should be undertaken in a manner similar to that used for other patients with stones, with the caution that allopurinol interferes with azathioprine metabolism, prolonging its half-life and leading to dangerous leukopenia if the dose of the latter is not reduced.

Ureteric stricture with obstruction may respond to a ureterotomy and temporary stent placement or may require direct surgical intervention with revision of the transplant ureter or diversion to the native ureter.

Lymphoceles are common posttransplant and may occasionally cause urinary tract obstruction. Percutaneous drainage is, in general, not recommended because of the high rate of recurrence and the increased tendency to infection. Internal drainage into the peritoneal cavity is the procedure of choice and may be accomplished by a laparoscopic or direct surgical approach.

Urine leaks or urinomas are more common in the early posttransplant period and best treated by direct surgical repair, usually with postrepair temporary stent replacement and/or prolonged bladder drainage via Foley catheter.

Bladder outlet obstruction, due either to prostatic enlargement or urethral stricture, is managed in the usual way with the exception that postinstrumentation antibiotics are usually continued for a longer period.

FOLLOW-UP

Patients with renal transplants need close follow-up for monitoring of transplant function, immunosuppressive medications, and infectious and metabolic complications. Initially, visits should be scheduled on a biweekly basis with laboratory evaluation at each visit. The latter should include at a minimum a full blood count, a biochemical screen to include blood urea nitrogen, creatinine, glucose, sodium, potassium, bicarbonate, calcium and phosphate, and a trough cyclosporine or tacrolimus blood level and a urinalysis. The presence of indwelling stents, pyuria, and/or bacteriuria necessitates a urine culture. In the early posttransplant period, focus of attention is placed on avoidance of rejection while gradually reducing immunosuppression to maintenance levels, which is usually achieved by 3 to 6 months. The incidence of acute rejection is highest in the first 3 months posttransplant, and any increase in blood urea nitrogen and creatinine, particularly when accompanied by fever, tenderness over the allograft, decrease in urinary output, or weight gain in excess of 1 kg overnight during this critical period, should be considered to be acute rejection until proven otherwise. Lymphoceles, urinomas, and ureteric strictures are also most common in the early posttransplant period. Thus, ultrasonographic evaluation, often on a repeated basis, is an indispensable component of the outpatient workup of transplant dysfunction.

Trough whole blood cyclosporine levels, as measured by TDX, should be maintained at between 200 and 450 ng/mL, with the higher levels in the first 3 months posttransplant. Tacrolimus levels, also monitored in the predose (trough) period, are usually maintained between 10 and 20 ng/ml. Exceptions to this rule abound, however. Patients with serious concomitant infections, severe and chronic renal allograft dysfunction with irreversible fibrosis, tubular atrophy, and vascular changes on biopsy may benefit from lower levels. Patients with well-matched kidneys who have never experienced rejection and who have

normal and stable allograft function since transplantation may also benefit from lower levels, particularly if accompanied by bothersome side effects.

Follow-up visits are usually biweekly until 6 weeks posttransplant, weekly until 3 months, every 2 weeks for 6 months, and monthly until 12 months posttransplant. Monthly laboratory evaluations should probably be undertaken for the lifetime of the allograft, with doctor visits at a minimum of three monthly. Vaccinations may lead to upregulation of the immune response and occasionally precipitate acute rejection. Thus, routine laboratory screening should be performed 2 to 3 weeks following all vaccinations.

In general, there is no restriction in work, exercise, or leisure activities posttransplant, although specific contraindications for individual patients may exist. A gradual increase in intensity of aerobic exercise is, however, prudent. Diet should usually be restricted in sodium to 2 to 4 g/d and protein to 1 g/kg/d.

DISCUSSION
Prevalence and Incidence

About 70% of cadaveric renal allograft recipients experience an episode of acute rejection usually in the first 90 days posttransplant. Chronic rejection is the leading cause of allograft loss after the first year and the most common cause of significant proteinuria. Graft loss due to recurrence of the original glomerular disease is rare, but can occur, particularly in aggressive focal glomerular sclerosis and membranoproliferative disease. Histologic recurrence is common in immunoglobulin A nephropathy, usually manifests itself as microscopic hematuria, but rarely causes allograft loss.

Technical problems with the vascular anastomoses are responsible for organ loss in approximately 2% of cases, whereas transplant renal artery stenosis is thought to occur in 5 to 10% of patients.

Urine leaks present in the early posttransplant period in 2 to 5% of patients. Ureteric strictures present later and also occur in 2 to 5% of recipients. Lymphoceles occur in 40% of patients but cause dysfunction in only 10%.

Cyclosporine nephrotoxicity probably causes intermittent dysfunction in all patients sometime during the lifetime of their allograft, the significance of which is undetermined.

Urinary tract infections are common posttransplant, but are usually confined to the lower urinary tract and cause recognizable dysfunction in approximately 15%.

Related Basic Science

Acute rejection is predominantly a T-cell response triggered by donor–recipient dissimilarity at the HLA-B and HLA-DR loci. Better matching at these loci reduces the incidence of acute rejection and favors longer allograft survival. Currently available immunosuppression is aimed at reducing the T-cell response. Cyclosporine and tacrolimus are the most specific immunosuppressants in that they decrease cytokine production, most notably that of interleukin 2, which plays a central role in T-cell activation and recruitment. Corticosteroids produce three main effects on the immune system in vivo. First, they blunt the synthesis and/or release of some lymphokines, monokines, and prostaglandins but do not affect primary antibody responses. Second, they inhibit the functional capabilities of lymphocytes and, to a lesser extent, those of monocytes in that proliferative responses, mediator production rates, and helper T-cell activities are all decreased. Third, they result in a transient alteration in leukocyte circulatory kinetics with a depletion of monocytes and a redistribution of CD4+ T lymphocytes into the spleen, lymph nodes, and bone marrow. Azathioprine is a nonspecific inhibitor of both DNA and RNA synthesis and as such inhibits most dividing cells, including B and T lymphocytes. Mycophenolate mofetil inhibits the de novo synthesis of purines. Since lymphocytes lack a salvage pathway for purine synthesis, it exerts a more profound effect on lymphocytes than on other cells.

The treatment of acute rejection requires additional immunosuppression in the form of antilymphocyte preparations, of which two are in current practice in the United States. Antithymocyte globulin is produced by injecting human thymocytes into horses and purifying and standardizing the antibody so produced. It is a potent immunosuppressant in humans, usually causing profound and immediate lymphopenia. OKT3 is a monoclonal antibody raised in mice against the T-3 cell receptor present on the surface of most mature T lymphocytes. It engages the T-cell receptor, causing initial activation with release of cytokines prior to causing a profound and often long-lasting T-cell depression. This cytokine release syndrome is responsible for the first-dose reaction observed in most patients treated with this medication and consists of a syndrome characterized clinically by fever, chills, headache, diarrhea, and, occasionally, severe bronchospasm.

Because of the nonspecific nature of present-day immunosuppression, microbial infections are common. The herpes group of infections are particularly troublesome posttransplant, particularly cytomegalovirus and Epstein–Barr virus. The latter has been implicated in the increased incidence of lymphomas observed in transplant recipients. Fortunately, specific antiviral agents are now available, although their benefit in lymphoma has still to be proven.

Natural History and Its Modification with Treatment

Survival of renal allografts has improved since the advent of cyclosporine. One-year allograft survival for living related recipients now approaches 90%, and that for recipients of cadaveric first kidney transplants, 85%. Subsequent allograft loss is mostly due to chronic rejection and does not appear to be influenced by antirejection medications. Aggressive control of blood pressure and minimal immunosuppression are probably prudent in this circumstance. Allograft survival at 5 years approaches 70% in living related recipients, with a dropoff to 50% at 15 years. The corresponding numbers for cadaveric transplant recipients are 50% at 5 years and 30% at 15 years. Maintenance of trough cyclosporine levels above 250 ng/mL may decrease this attrition rate.

Prevention

Allograft loss is usually due to rejection or patient death. The main causes of the latter are cardiovascular, infectious, or malignancy associated. Strict hypertension; glucose, lipid, and obesity control; and a graded exercise program may decrease cardiovascular deaths. Early diagnosis, prompt treatment, and decrease in immunosuppression, together with preemptive vaccination programs where possible, may prevent infection-related deaths. Constant surveillance for lymphomas and skin and cervical malignancies may allow early detection and treatment. Solid tumors are, in general, not increased over the general population. Thus, the general recommended methods of surveillance should be employed. Rejection is minimized by obtaining the best-matched allografts and by immunosuppression. Compliance with the latter is essential and needs to be constantly reinforced. To a limited extent, monthly laboratory tests that include a cyclosporine trough level may provide a checkup. Discussion with the patient, and occasionally the family, should be immediate and repeated if noncompliance is suspected. Many drugs interfere with cyclosporine and/or tacrolimus blood levels. For example, phenobarbital, dilantin, rifampin, and isoniazid markedly reduce blood levels and predispose the patient to underimmunosuppression and acute rejection. On the other hand, diltiazem, the antifungal agents, ketoaconazole, fluconazole and itraconazole, and erythromycin and analogs all increase cyclosporine blood levels and predispose to toxicity and overimmunosuppression. Maintenance of cyclosporine trough blood levels in the range of 200 to 250 ng/mL is, in general, desirable in the late posttransplant period.

Cost Containment

Renal transplantation is the cheapest form of end-stage renal disease replacement therapy, provided the allograft survives in excess of 1 year. It is still an expensive form of therapy, with drug costs alone of approximately $24,000 for the first year posttransplant. Subsequent drug therapy is usually less expensive at about $12,000 per year. The latter contrasts with approximately $36,000 and $32,000 for annual outpatient in-center hemodialysis and chronic ambulatory peritoneal dialysis, respectively.

REFERENCES

Briggs JD, Junor BJR. Long-term complications and results in the transplant patient. In: Cameron S, Davison AM, Grunfeld J-P, et al., eds. Oxford textbook of clinical nephrology. New York: Oxford University Press, 1992:1570.

Delaney VB, Whelchel JD, O'Brien DP, et al. Comparison of fine needle aspiration biopsy, Doppler ultrasound, and scintigraphy in the diagnosis of acute rejection in renal allograft recipients: Specificity, sensitivity, and cost analysis. Nephron 1993;63:263.

Doherty CC. Graft dysfunction and its differential diagnosis. In: McGeown MG, ed. Clinical management of renal transplantation. Norwell, MA: Kluwer Academic, 1992:243.

End Stage Renal Disease Program highlights: Payments. Washington, DC: ESRD Information Analysis Branch, Health Care Financing Administration, U.S. Dept of Health and Human Services, 1989.

Morris PJ. Transplant immunology. In: Cameron S, Davison AM, Grunfeld J-P, et al., eds. Oxford textbook of clinical nephrology. New York: Oxford University Press, 1992:1543.

Porter KA. Renal transplantation. In: Heptinstall RH, ed. Pathology of the kidney. Boston: Little, Brown, 1992:1799.

Abnormalities of the Inorganic Metabolism

Edmund Bourke, M.D.

CHAPTER 17–1

Hypernatremia

Man S. Oh, M.D., and Hugh J. Carroll, M.D.

DEFINITION

Hypernatremia is defined as an increase in serum (plasma) sodium concentration above 147 mEq/L.

ETIOLOGY

Hypernatremia is initially due either to water deficit or to sodium excess; however, because hypernatremia is natriuretic, in the presence of adequate renal function, even hypernatremia caused initially by sodium retention is later accompanied by water deficit. Causes of water deficit include excessive water loss, either renal or extrarenal, and reduced intake of water in the presence of normal ongoing losses. Because of the effectiveness of thirst as a defense against hypernatremia and the virtually unlimited capacity of the gastrointestinal tract to absorb water, hypernatremia will not develop unless a condition exists that interferes with normal intake of water, such as impaired thirst due to mental confusion, coma, or defective function of the thirst center, or inability to obtain or to drink water.

Of course, in the setting of impaired water intake, hypernatremia occurs more rapidly when water loss, renal or extrarenal, is abnormally increased (see Discussion).

CRITERIA FOR DIAGNOSIS

The sole criterion for the diagnosis of hypernatremia is documentation of high serum sodium by laboratory measurement.

CLINICAL MANIFESTATIONS

Subjective

Clinical manifestations of hypernatremia are due entirely to hypertonicity of the body fluid.

In the presence of an intact thirst mechanism in a conscious patient, a slight increase in serum sodium, for example, 2 to 3 mEq/L, above the usual baseline value elicits intense thirst. Thirst will be perceived by those patients who developed hypernatremia because of insufficient water intake due to inability to drink (e.g., esophageal obstruction) or to obtain water (e.g., mechanical restraint). The lack of thirst in the presence of hypernatremia in a mentally alert patient indicates a defect in the thirst mechanism, either in the hypothalamic osmoreceptor or in the cortical thirst center.

Objective

Physical Examination

Because hypernatremia is frequently associated with central nervous system diseases that limit voluntary water intake, it may sometimes be difficult to distinguish the effects of cell dehydration and hypovolemia from those of the underlying central nervous system disease. The most common objective sign of hypernatremia is lethargy, which may proceed to coma and convulsions. Muscular tremor and rigidity and hyperactive reflexes are also observed. Chronic hypernatremia may cause myotonic dystrophy.

With very acute and severe hypernatremia, the osmotic shift of water from the cells leads to abrupt dehydration and shrinkage of the brain, which results in tearing of the meningeal vessels and intracranial hemorrhage. Slowly developing hypernatremia is usually well tolerated because of the brain's ability to regulate its volume (see Discussion). Because hypernatremia is natriuretic, patients with hypernatremia tend to be dehydrated. Evidence of dehydration includes elevated blood urea nitrogen and serum creatinine levels. When reduced water intake is the cause of hypernatremia, urine is maximally concentrated; in other settings, urine is inappropriately dilute.

Routine Laboratory Abnormalities

The serum (plasma) concentration of sodium is above 147 mEq/L.

PLANS

Diagnostic

Differential Diagnosis

The differential diagnosis of hypernatremia is summarized in Table 17–1–1.

Diagnostic Options and Recommended Approach

Diagnosis of hypernatremia is confirmed by the measurement of serum sodium. Our approach to evaluation of the causes of hypernatremia begins with the measurement of urine osmolality. Hypernatremia caused by insufficient water intake is accompanied by a small volume of concentrated urine; urine osmolality is greater than 700 mOsm/L. When

TABLE 17–1–1. CAUSES OF HYPERNATREMIA ACCORDING TO BODY SODIUM CONTENT

Increased Total Body Sodium Content
- Osmoreceptor defect due hypothalamic disorders
- Defective cortical thirst center
- Acute diabetes insipidus treated with sodium-containing solutions
- Administration of hypertonic sodium bicarbonate during cardiac arrest or for treatment of lactic acidosis
- Dialysis accident
- Accidental absorption of excess sodium during hypertonic saline abortion
- Administration of sodium-containing solution to a patient with water deficit

Normal Total Body Sodium Content
- Acute diabetes insipidus without sodium intake and with inadequate water replacement
- Unattended patients who are comatose, too old, too young, or too sick
- No access to water

Decreased Total Body Sodium Content
- Osmotic diuresis
- Sweating
- Osmotic diarrhea
- Vomiting

renal water loss is the cause of hypernatremia, urine is inappropriately dilute, that is, less than 700 mOsm/L.

Urine osmolality less than 700 mOsm/L but greater than plasma osmolality in the presence of hypernatremia suggests "partial" diabetes insipidus, provided that three conditions are first ruled out: renal insufficiency, use of loop diuretics, osmotic diuresis.

Urine osmolality less than plasma osmolality in the presence of hypernatremia defines "complete" diabetes insipidus. Once the diagnosis of diabetes insipidus has been made, differentiation between the central and nephrogenic types is based on the response to vasopressin (see Chapter 9–42). A normal response, that is, substantial increase in urine osmolality following vasopressin administration, indicates central diabetes insipidus, and a poor or absent response suggests nephrogenic diabetes insipidus. When the baseline urine osmolality is greater than serum osmolality, an increase in urine osmolality by more than 15% is considered a normal response to vasopressin. If the baseline urine osmolality is below that of serum, a normal response is an increase by more than 50%. Aqueous pitressin 5 U intramuscularly or 2 U in 500 mL of saline infused at a rate of 1 mL/min is the test dose. Desmopressin (dDAVP) 2 μg subcutaneously may also be used. Urine specimens for the measurement of osmolality should be obtained for 3 hours at hourly intervals after the start of pitressin infusion, and the highest urine osmolality achieved be used to determine the response.

The diagnosis of osmotic diuresis is based entirely on the the rate of solute excretion. Osmotic diuresis is defined as polyuria with urine solute excretion greater than 60 mOsm/h or 1440 mOsm/d in an adult.

Therapeutic

In this section we discuss treatment of hypernatremia and, in addition, the treatment of diabetes insipidus, a disorder that can lead to hypernatremia when it occurs in patients who are unconscious or who have a concomitant thirst defect.

Treatment of Hypernatremia. Treatment of hypernatremia is aimed at restoring normal osmolality and volume of body fluids. When hypernatremia is accompanied by hemodynamic alteration due to volume depletion, the initial solution should be isotonic saline; the purpose is to restore the volume promptly without rapid reduction of serum sodium. The correction of hypernatremia can be achieved either by administration of water or by removal of sodium. Water is to be added when water deficit is the main cause of hypernatremia, and sodium is to be removed when excess sodium is the culprit. Removal of sodium without removal of water is possible only when the process is accomplished by dialysis. Removal of sodium through the kidney is always accompanied by removal of water. Net removal of sodium without changing water content can be achieved by removal of both sodium and water with a loop diuretic followed by administration of water as a dextrose solution.

The net increase in body water needed to correct hypernatremia can be accurately estimated from serum sodium concentration only when hypernatremia is due entirely to water loss. In most cases of chronic hypernatremia the total body sodium content is increased, because of retention of sodium secondary to volume depletion; hypernatremia is therefore caused by both water loss and sodium gain. Restoration of serum sodium to normal in this situation inevitably causes volume expansion and hence renal excretion of sodium. The quantity of water retained with correction of hypernatremia in a person who has retained salt is less than that predicted from the rise in serum sodium. The amount of water to be administered, however, can still be estimated from serum sodium concentration; urinary excretion of water by the subject who is recovering from hypernatremia has little effect on serum sodium concentration because in most instances the sum of urine sodium and potassium is quite similar to that of serum sodium and potassium. Urinary loss of water affects serum sodium only if the sum of the concentrations of urinary sodium and potassium is different from that of serum sodium and potassium. If the urinary value is greater than the serum value, urine output reduces serum sodium, and if it is less than the serum value, the effect is to increase serum sodium. The amount of water required to reduce serum sodium is calculated using the following formula

water required (L) = (dNa/desired serum Na) × TBW (L) =
(actual serum Na/desired serum Na − 1) × TBW (L)

where dNa is defined as actual serum Na − desired serum Na, and TBW is total body water.

Urinary electrolyte-free water excretion is calculated from the following equation

urinary electrolyte-free water excretion =
$$V - (U_{Na} + U_K) \times V/(S_{Na} + S_K)$$

where V is urine volume and U_{Na}, U_K, S_{Na}, and S_K are urine sodium, urine potassium, serum sodium, and serum potassium concentrations respectively. Urinary electrolyte-free water loss and insensible water loss (about 300–500 mL/24 h) should be added to the calculated water requirement. If the electrolyte-free water value is a positive number, the amount should be added to the calculated water requirement. If the value is negative, it should be subtracted from the calculated water requirement.

The speed of correction depends on the rate of development and the accompanying symptoms. Chronic hypernatremia is well tolerated, and rapid correction offers no advantage and may be harmful because it may cause brain edema. The rate of correction of chronic hypernatremia (defined as hypernatremia of more than 2 days' duration) should not exceed 0.7 mEq/L/h or about 10% of the serum sodium concentration per day. Hyperacute hypernatremia (< 12 hours) may be treated rapidly.

Treatment of Central Diabetes Insipidus. Patients with complete deficiency of vasopressin usually need hormonal replacement. Those with partial deficiency may be treated with the hormone or with agents that increase the rate of antidiuretic hormone (ADH) secretion or end-organ responsiveness to ADH. With either approach, salt restriction and diuretic therapy can help reduce the delivery of salt and hence of water to the site where dilute urine is made, and thereby reduce urine output.

- Desmopressin is an analog of ADH. Desmopressin intranasal or nasal spray is administered at the usual dose of 0.1 mL (10 µg) twice a day. The quantity used parenterally is 0.5 (2 µg) to 1 mL (4 µg) divided into two doses. The advantages of desmopressin are the prolonged effect, the ease of administration, and the lack of side effects. It is by far the most useful agent for chronic therapy.
- Lysine–vasopressin (Diapid, Lypressin), also an intranasal solution, has a half-life of 4 to 6 hours, and is given as 1 to 2 sprays four to five times a day.
- Aqueous pitressin is used only in acute situations; the usual dose is 2 U infused intravenously at a constant rate over 8 hours, 6 U over 24 hours, or 5 U subcutaneously every 3 to 4 hours.
- Pitressin tannate in oil has a prolonged effect (12–24 hours) and thus may be useful in treating hospitalized patients. The vial should be shaken well before use. One 5-U ampoule may be injected subcutaneously every 12 to 24 hours.
- Chlorpropamide can be used only for patients with central diabetes insipidus who have some residual ability to secrete ADH. Many patients with "complete" diabetes insipidus still have some ADH secretion and therefore respond to the drug. The usual dose is 50 to 500 mg. The advent of desmopressin has markedly reduced the popularity of this approach.
- Thiazide diuretics and a low-salt diet are also used. The usual dose of hydrochlorthiazide is 50 mg once a day. To prevent hypokalemia, potassium supplement or Moduretic (hydrochlorthiazide plus amiloride) and Dyazide or Maxzide (hydrochlorthiazide plus triamterene) may be used.

Use of pitressin analogs poses the danger of water overload if the medications are administered continually and without water restriction (in a sense, patients on continuous exogenous ADH therapy are in a state of inappropriate ADH secretion). The dosage should therefore be adjusted to allow awareness of thirst between doses or at least once a day; the onset of polyuria is a less reliable guide. The appearance of thirst would indicate that plasma osmolality has reached a high normal level, whereas polyuria could begin when plasma osmolality is still subnormal.

Thirst cannot be a guide for dosage in treating patients whose diabetes insipidus is due to an osmoreceptor disorder, because such patients have defective thirst as well as defective ADH secretion. In these cases water intake and medication dosage should be adjusted to maintain the daily weight within a narrow range, and serum sodium concentration should be checked regularly. A gross deviation in serum sodium concentration is always accompanied by a substantial change in body weight. For example, a 70-kg man with serum sodium concentration of 140 mEq/L would have to gain about 3 lb of weight as water to reduce serum sodium to 135 mEq/L. Chloropropamide occasionally improves thirst in patients with an osmoreceptor disorder and, therefore, may be a useful adjunct to therapy.

Treatment of Nephrogenic Diabetes Insipidus. The most effective way to ameliorate polyuria in this disorder is to reduce the volume of fluid delivered to the diluting segment of the nephron, and for this purpose, diuretics and a low-salt diet are used as suggested for treatment of central diabetes insipidus. Other methods have been tried with some success:

- Desmopressin in large doses: As the tubules are not totally unresponsive to ADH even in nephrogenic diabetes insipidus, a large dose of desmopressin may overcome the resistance, but the drug is very expensive. Only desmopressin may be administered in large doses, because unlike pitressin, it lacks a vasoconstrictive effect.
- Prostaglandin synthesis inhibitors, for example, indomethacin (25 or 50 mg twice or three times daily): These agents may enhance proximal reabsorption of sodium, or counteract the inhibitory effect of prostaglandins on ADH action.
- Removal of offending agents, for example, lithium and demeclocycline. Chlorpropamide is totally ineffective in nephrogenic diabetes insipidus.

FOLLOW-UP

Patients who have acute hypernatremia without a predisposing condition do not require follow-up. A patient who developed hypernatremia because of a defective thirst mechanism should be instructed to drink water at regular intervals, and serum sodium should be measured frequently as a follow-up. A patient with a defective osmoreceptor function treated with ADH requires water restriction and monitoring of serum sodium at regular intervals. Without water restriction these patients are in danger of developing hyponatremia.

DISCUSSION
Prevalence and Incidence

Hypernatremia is a fairly common electrolyte disorder in patients with impaired thirst perception usually due to mental confusion. The incidence is particularly high during summer months when skin water loss is greater. The exact prevalence and incidence are not known.

Related Basic Science

In the presence of adequate renal function, hypernatremia is always accompanied by water deficit. Total body sodium content depends on the clinical situation that led to hypernatremia. Body sodium content is normal when water is lost in the absence of sodium intake, as in the case of an unattended comatose patient or in acute diabetes insipidus treated with an insufficient amount of water. Body sodium content may be decreased when both salt and water are lost but water loss is greater than salt loss, for example, osmotic diuresis, osmotic diarrhea, sweating, and vomiting. In most cases of hypernatremia, especially in chronic hypernatremia, body sodium content is increased because of renal retention of sodium in response to volume depletion. Table 17–1–1 lists causes of hypernatremia according to body sodium content.

The pathogenesis of hypernatremia can be explained by four basic mechanisms: gain of sodium, as with the use of hypertonic saline; loss of water, as in diabetes insipidus; shift of water into cells, as in correction of hyperglycemia; and shift of sodium from cells in exchange for potassium, as when potassium is retained by a subject previously potassium depleted.

Signs and symptoms of hypernatremia result mainly from increased effective osmolality which leads to reduction in intracellular volume, especially the brain cell volume. Acute hypernatremia causes abrupt brain dehydration and shrinkage as water shifts into the extracellular fluid compartment. Because the brain, unlike other organs, is encased in a rigid structure, sudden shrinkage of the brain volume causes creation of negative pressure and leads to tearing of the meningeal vessels and intracranial hemorrhage. On the other hand, slowly developing hypernatremia is tolerated well because the brain can normalize its volume in chronic hypernatremia through volume-regulatory mechanisms. Volume-regulatory increase for the brain cells is accomplished by intracellular shift of sodium, potassium, and chloride, as well as by accumulation of organic solutes such as polyols (sorbitol and myoinositol), methylamines (betaine and glycerophosphorylcholine), and amino acids (taurine, glutamine, glutamic acid, aspartic acid). Normalization of the brain volume in chronic hypernatremia results in an increased solute content of the brain. If treatment of chronic hypernatremia suddenly lowers the osmolality of the extracellular fluid, the osmotic gradient will cause a shift of water into the brain, resulting in brain edema. The muscle cells, unlike the brain, do not have volume-regulatory mechanisms, and remain volume contracted in chronic hypernatremia; chronic volume contraction of muscle may lead to myotonic dystrophy.

Natural History and Its Modification with Treatment

The natural history of hypernatremia depends on the cause. When hypernatremia is due to such acute conditions as transient diabetes insipidus following head injury or in the postoperative state, hypernatremia will resolve as the acute condition improves. Chronic hypernatremia is always due to impaired water intake, either because of a defective thirst mechanism or because of concomitant medical conditions. The prognosis depends on the prognosis of the underlying condition that led to inadequate water intake.

Prevention

Prevention of hypernatremia may be accomplished by treating chronic conditions that may lead to hypernatremia, such as diabetes insipidus and thirst defect. Frequent monitoring of serum sodium concentration is essential for the follow-up care of patients who do not control their water intake for various reasons (e.g., they are comatose, confused, too sick, too old, or too young). If serum sodium measurement is not readily available, body weight can be monitored instead. For an average-size person, a clinically significant hypernatremia (e.g., increase greater than 10 mEq/L) would be accompanied by weight loss in excess of 5 lb.

Medical personnel who take care of patients with impaired water intake should be educated for the importance of maintaining water balance. They should also be instructed to watch for signs of hypernatremia, such as mental status changes. Patients who have defective thirst with or without concomitant diabetes insipidus should be instructed to drink water at regular intervals, and also be told about the meaning of a sudden weight reduction as a sign of water deficit. Patients who are treated with vasopressin chronically should be educated about the danger of hyponatremia and how to prevent it (see Plans, Therapeutic).

Cost Containment

Many unnecessary hospital admissions can be avoided by frequent monitoring of serum sodium concentrations of patients who cannot control their water intake and by education of the medical personnel responsible for care of these patients.

REFERENCES

Carroll HJ, Oh MS. Disturbances in body fluid osmolality. In: Carroll HJ, Oh MS. Water, electrolyte, and acid–base metabolism. Philadelphia: Lippincott, 1989.

Finberg L. Hypernatremic (hypertonic) dehydration in infants. N Engl J Med 1973;289:196.

Oh MS, Carroll HJ. Essential hypernatremia: Is there such a thing? Nephron, 1994;67:144.

Perez GO, Oster JR, Robertson GL. Severe hypernatremia with impaired thirst. Am J Nephrol 1989;9:421.

Trachtman H, Barbour R, Sturman JA, Finberg L. Taurine and osmoregulation: Taurine is a cerebral osmoprotective molecule in chronic hypernatremic dehydration. Pediat Res 1988;23:35.

CHAPTER 17–2

Hyponatremia

Hugh J. Carroll, M.D., and Man S. Oh, M.D.

DEFINITION

Hyponatremia is defined as decrease in serum (plasma) sodium concentration below the normal range, that is, 135 mEq/L. Generally, however, there is no particular concern unless serum sodium concentration falls below 130 mEq/L.

ETIOLOGY

Because the kidney is normally very effective in defense against hyponatremia through excretion of water, sustained hyponatremia is usually attributable to the inability of the kidney to excrete excess water. Hyponatremia may be due to grossly excessive water intake with slight impairment in ability to dilute urine or to the failure to excrete even normal amounts of water. In the latter case several pathophysiologic mechanisms may be responsible in a large variety of clinical settings (Table 17–2–1). The impaired water excretion in most instances is due either to inappropriate secretion of antidiuretic hormone (ADH) or to secretion of ADH in response to reduced effective arterial volume; in the latter case, ADH secretion is deemed appropriate even though serum sodium is low.

CRITERIA FOR DIAGNOSIS

With the exception that hyponatremia per se may worsen the effect of hypokalemia, low concentration of serum sodium ions in the plasma has no direct physiologic effect like low concentrations of plasma potassium, calcium, and magnesium. The feature that concerns us, because it causes all of the clinical manifestations of hyponatremia, is the cellular hyposmolality that usually accompanies hyponatremia. To certify the presence of hyponatremia with hyposmolality we must therefore exclude such phenomena as pseudohyponatremia, in which the concentration of sodium in the extracellular fluid may actually be normal, and hyponatremia associated with increased effective osmolality in cases where substances such as glucose and mannitol shift water to the extracellular fluid with resultant dilution of the extracellular sodium.

CLINICAL MANIFESTATIONS

Hyponatremia has predilection for certain clinical circumstances. Subjects taking thiazide diuretics may become depleted of sodium and potassium, and may also retain water if they ingest more than the aver-

TABLE 17–2–1. BASIC MECHANISMS IN PRODUCTION AND MAINTENANCE OF HYPONATREMIA

1. Excessive water intake: psychogenic polydipsia; iatrogenic
2. Shift of water from the cell: hyperglycemia, mannitol infusion
3. Shift of sodium into the cell: potassium loss
4. Loss of sodium through gastrointestinal tract, kidney, or skin
5. Retention of water
   a. Primary excessive ADH secretion or increased sensitivity to ADH
   b. Appropriate ADH secretion due to low effective arterial volume: sodium depletion or edematous states
   c. Reduced delivery of filtrate to the distal nephron (distal trickle effect): low effective arterial volume or renal vascular or inflammatory disease
   d. Advanced renal failure
   e. Inadequate solute excretion

ADH, antidiuretic hormone.

TABLE 17–2–2. CLINICAL CAUSES OF HYPONATREMIA

A. Pseudohyponatremia with normal effective osmolality: hyperlipidemia, hyperproteinemia
B. Hyponatremia with increased effective osmolality: hyperglycemia, mannitol retention
C. Hyponatremia with normal effective osmolality: gamma globulins, lithium, tris (hydroxymethyl) aminomethane
D. Hyponatremia with low effective osmolality
   1. Hyponatremia with low effective arterial volume
      a. Hyponatremia with edema (sodium excess): congestive heart failure, nephrotic syndrome, cirrhosis of the liver, idiopathic edema, hypoalbuminemic states
      b. Hyponatremia due to sodium depletion: renal or extrarenal salt wasting
   2. Hyponatremia with normal or expanded effective arterial volume
      a. Syndrome of inappropriate antidiuretic hormone secretion (Table 17–2–3)
      b. Water intoxication due to primary polydipsia
      c. Water overload in advanced renal failure
      d. Renal vascular disease and acute inflammation of the kidney
      e. Inadequate solute excretion with copious water intake

age amount of water. The elderly are more prone to hyponatremia than the young, and some evidence suggests that females develop symptomatic hyponatremia more readily than males. The chronically ill, particularly those with pulmonary diseases or malignancy, are prime candidates for hyponatremia. Patients with schizophrenia may ingest large amounts of water. Patients undergoing surgical operations often receive large amounts of water; a very familiar example is transurethral resection of the prostate, where large quantities of sodium-free fluid may be absorbed. Addison's disease and selective aldosterone deficiency may be found in a wide variety of clinical disorders; a recent addition of some importance to this category of diseases is AIDS.

Subjective

Although alteration in cell osmolality and, in the case of the brain, rapid expansion of volume can produce symptoms, these symptoms are commonly overshadowed by the symptoms of underlying diseases and by altered circulatory dynamics attributable to those diseases. Neurologic dysfunction due to hyponatremia presents with altered mental status, nausea, ataxia, and cramps.

Objective

Physical Examination

Severe brain swelling may be associated with convulsions, coma, and death. Again, the role of underlying diseases must be considered. It may not be possible, for example, to distinguish promptly convulsions due to hypoosmolality in a cirrhotic from other forms of metabolic encephalopathy, trauma, or intracerebral hemorrhage. Similarly, in a severely dehydrated patient with hyponatremia, alteration in central nervous system function may be due in part or entirely to cerebral underperfusion. Slowly developing hyponatremia may be attended by few or no symptoms or signs. It is not certain that significant structural damage or persistent neurologic deficit attends uncomplicated persistent hyponatremia, but there is little doubt that a devastating demyelinating syndrome may follow rapid elevation in serum sodium in the treatment of hyponatremia of more than brief duration.

Routine Laboratory Abnormalities

The serum (plasma) concentration of sodium is less than 135 mEq/L.

PLANS
Diagnostic

Differential Diagnosis

The differential diagnosis of hyponatremia is summarized in Table 17–2–2.

Diagnostic Options

Evaluation of patients with hyponatremia must include the following considerations: exclusion of pseudohyponatremia; exclusion of hy-

ponatremia associated with increased effective osmolality; differential diagnosis of hyponatremia with hyposmolality.

Diagnosis of Pseudohyponatremia. Pseudohyponatremia is caused by hyperlipidemia or hyperproteinemia; the presence of these conditions reduces the fraction of plasma water for a given quantity of plasma. Hyperlipidemia severe enough to cause pseudohyponatremia is almost always apparent from the lipemic appearance of the serum, but hyperproteinemia must be confirmed by measurement. Pseudohyponatremia due to elevated lipid or protein can be unmasked by showing that directly measured serum osmolality is significantly greater than the value calculated from serum sodium, urea, and glucose. An ion-specific electrode gives an accurate determination of serum sodium in the presence of hyperlipidemia or hyperproteinemia only when an undiluted specimen is used. The error in serum sodium concentration will obtain when the sample is diluted, whether the measurement is made by an ion-specific electrode or by flame photometry. The extent of reduction in serum sodium concentration due to lipid or protein can also be calculated from the concentrations of lipid and protein. Each gram per deciliter triglyceride results in a false reduction in serum sodium by about 1.7 mEq/L, and accumulation of 1 g/dL protein falsely reduces serum sodium by about 1 mEq/L.

Although low serum sodium with normal serum osmolality in the absence of hyperglycemia and azotemia strongly suggests pseudohyponatremia, it is important to note that by coincidence, true hyponatremia may be accompanied by accumulation of some other abnormal solutes (e.g., ethanol, ethylene glycol, methanol), and serum osmolality may therefore be normal. Reduction in serum sodium that does not affect serum osmolality can be seen with accumulation of exogenous cations such as lithium and tromethamine, and also when the excess globulin in the serum has an isoelectric point that makes the net charge of the protein positive at the pH range of the body fluids. The latter phenomenon is common in immunoglobulin G myeloma. In this condition reduction in serum sodium does not lead to hyposmolality because serum chloride rises. The hyponatremia of myeloma is therefore partly true hyponatremia and partly spurious hyponatremia.

Diagnosis of Hyponatremia Associated with Increased Effective Osmolality. Osmotically active solutes penetrate cells poorly, and hence they withdraw water from cells and expand the extracellular space with consequent reduction in serum sodium concentration. In the case of glucose, for example, every 100 mg/dL rise in concentration is accompanied by reduction in serum sodium by about 1.5 mEq/L. In some textbooks, this phenomenon is listed as pseudohyponatremia, but this designation is incorrect; the serum sodium concentration in this situation is actually low.

Hyponatremia with increased effective osmolality can be diagnosed only if the substances responsible for extracellular shift of water (e.g., glucose and mannitol) are identified by measurement (glucose) or history (mannitol).

Differential Diagnosis of Hyponatremia with Hyposmolality.

This condition, hereafter referred to as hyponatremia, is the major focus of our interest from the standpoint of management. Hyponatremia due to excessive water intake is usually obvious from a history of polydipsia and excretion of a large volume of urine. In an occasional instance the quantity of water ingested is not grossly excessive, but the quantity of solute excreted is so small that even maximal dilution of the urine (<100 mOsm/L) does not permit excretion of all the water ingested; water is therefore retained. Examples include the morose beer drinker who ingests little food (beer potomania) and the recluse who ingests little more than toast and drinks large amounts of tea. When impaired renal water excretion rather than excessive water intake is the cause of hyponatremia, urine volume is not large and urine is inappropriately concentrated. Appropriate urine osmolality in the presence of hyponatremia is defined operationally as a value less than 100 mOsm/L. The measurement of urine osmolality in the differential diagnosis of hyponatremia is usually unnecessary; the urine volume is a sufficient clue. At the usual rate of urinary solute excretion, more than 600 mOsm/d, a urine of volume of more than 6 L a day would be needed if the osmolality were less than 100 mOsm/L. Hence, if the urine volume is normal, it is overwhelmingly likely that its osmolality is inappropriately high.

A common misconception is that hyponatremia due to impaired urine dilution is always accompanied by very concentrated urine or at least urine osmolality in excess of serum osmolality; however, urine need not be highly concentrated to cause or maintain hyponatremia.

Impaired renal water excretion with inappropriately high urine osmolality occurs mainly through three mechanisms: advanced renal failure, inappropriate secretion of ADH (SIADH), reduction in effective arterial volume leading to appropriate ADH secretion and to renal underperfusion with reduced delivery of filtrate to the distal nephron. Advanced renal failure is easily ruled out by measurement of blood urea nitrogen and serum creatinine. ADH secretion is inappropriate in the presence of hyponatremia if effective osmolality is low and effective arterial volume is normal or increased. In contrast, ADH secretion is not considered inappropriate, despite hyponatremia, if effective arterial volume is reduced. As the vast majority of patients with hyposmolality and hyponatremia have either appropriate or inappropriate ADH secretion, the major diagnostic task in hyponatremia is differentiation between appropriate and inappropriate ADH secretion. The main distinguishing feature between the two is the status of effective arterial volume: increased in hyponatremic patients with SIADH and decreased when hyponatremia is associated with appropriate ADH secretion.

The physical signs of volume depletion such as low blood pressure, orthostatic hypotension, and tachycardia are not reliable signs of low effective arterial volume unless volume depletion is severe. Subjects with chronic illness frequently manifest systolic blood pressure of 100 mm Hg or less, and such subjects, particularly if they are hypokalemic, may have poor baroreceptor function and hence manifest orthostatic decrease in blood pressure. Signs of volume depletion such as dry mucous membranes, dry skin, and axillae are not as useful in hypotonic dehydration as they are in hypertonic dehydration. The kidney is usually the most sensitive monitor of effective arterial volume. Low effective arterial volume reduces glomerular filtration rate and enhances tubular reabsorption of sodium, urea, and uric acid. Blood urea nitrogen (BUN), serum creatinine, BUN/creatinine ratio, and serum urate tend to increase, and urinary sodium excretion tends to be reduced (usually less than 20 mEq/L). Plasma renin activity and aldosterone also tend to be increased. The following are the laboratory findings suggestive of normal or increased effective arterial volume:

- BUN < 10 mg/dL
- Serum creatinine < 1.0 mg/dL
- Serum uric acid < 3.5 mg/dL
- Urinary sodium > 20 mEq/L
- Low plasma renin activity
- BUN/serum creatinine ratio < 10

Recommended Approach

A useful scheme for the differential diagnosis of hyponatremia is shown in Figure 17–2–1.

Therapeutic

Rapid Versus Slow Treatment of Hyponatremia.

Two well-known dangers of severe symptomatic hyponatremia are uncontrolled seizure and brain edema leading to herniation. Both conditions are far more likely to occur with acute than with chronic hyponatremia. In the past, the only potential dangers of rapid correction of hyponatremia were thought to be vascular volume overload, which can be prevented by diuretics, and dehydration of the brain whose volume had already been normalized through the volume-regulatory mechanism. A far more serious danger is central pontine myelinolysis (CPM), a demyelinating disease involving primarily the central pons. In well-documented cases of CPM, the history of rapid correction of hyponatremia has been reported almost invariably. Chronicity of hyponatremia is an important factor for the development of CPM; the vast majority of reported cases of CPM have described rapid correction of hyponatremia that had been present for more than 48 hours. In CPM induced by rapid correction of hyponatremia, the correction was usually achieved by infusion of hypertonic saline, but serum sodium may also rise very rapidly, and CPM has occurred, with administration of isotonic saline.

In principle, rapid treatment of hyponatremia would be indicated if the danger of untreated or slowly treated hyponatremia is greater than the danger of rapid treatment. As the danger of central pontine myelinolysis with rapid treatment increases with increasing duration of hyponatremia, whereas the danger of untreated hyponatremia diminishes with increasing duration, rapid increase in serum sodium would be more beneficial and less dangerous in acute hyponatremia than in chronic hyponatremia. Thus, with symptomatic hyponatremia of clearly less than 48 hours' duration, rapid treatment probably would be indicated. Even then, there is no obvious advantage in normalizing serum sodium at once, and there may still be a danger of CPM.

In hyponatremia of more than 48 hours, which actually includes most cases of symptomatic hyponatremia, the danger of CPM resulting from rapid treatment outweighs the benefit of rapid treatment, in the absence of specific life-threatening manifestations of hyponatremia, such as intractable seizure and deepening coma. If hyponatremia has occurred in a patient over a period of several days, it is unlikely that severe brain edema is present. The only realistic danger of slow treatment of hyponatremia in such a patient would be the occurrence of uncontrollable seizure.

Review of the literature shows that patients with symptomatic hyponatremia that develops in the hospital or severe hyponatremia whose genesis has been observed to be rapid can tolerate a rapid rise in serum sodium. Such review also suggests that patients with symptomatic hyponatremia in whom the diagnosis is established on admission to the hospital have either adapted to hyponatremia and therefore can be treated slowly, or have advanced cerebral damage and are beyond help. In dealing with patients who are admitted to the hospital with symptomatic hyponatremia, it is best to limit the rate of increase in serum sodium to 8 mEq/L/d, but 5 to 6 mEq of this increase can be accomplished in 2 to 3 hours for patients with convulsions that do not respond to the conventional anticonvulsant therapy. For symptomatic hyponatremia that develops in the hospital, serum sodium may be increased at a rate of 1 to 2 mEq/L/h until it reaches or slightly exceeds 125 mEq/L. For hyperacute hyponatremia (< 12 hours), serum sodium may be increased as fast as 5 mEq/L/h.

Method of Rapid Correction of Hyponatremia.

Treatment of hyponatremia requires either addition of sodium or removal of water. Rapid removal of water is best accomplished by a loop diuretic (e.g., furosemide), plus hypertonic saline, 3 or 5% solution. The diuretic removes salt and water and administration of hypertonic saline returns salt to the body. The amount of sodium required to increase serum sodium to a desired level is calculated by the formula

$$\text{sodium required (mEq)} = d\text{Na} \times \text{TBW}$$

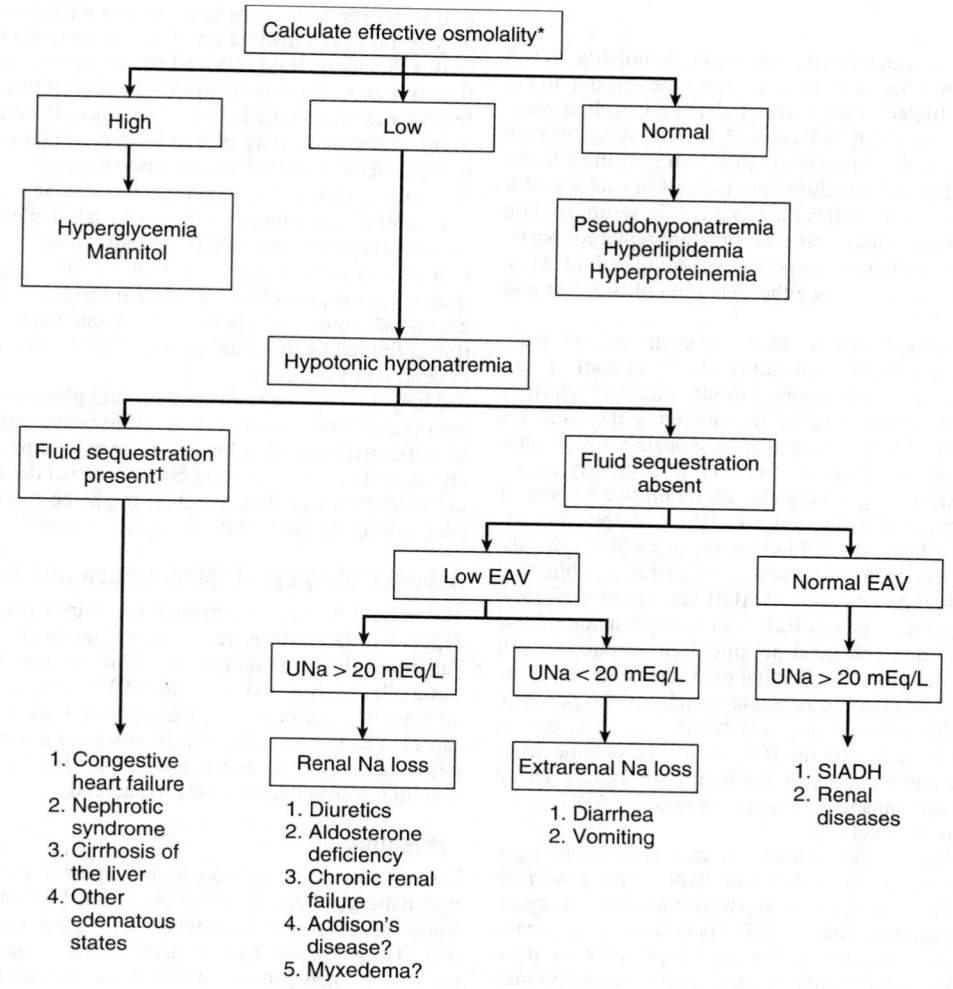

Figure 17–2–1. Differential diagnosis of hyponatremia. *Effective osmolality is calculated as measured serum osmolality minus osmolality due to ineffective osmoles (e.g., urea, alcohol). †Manifests as edema, ascites, or ileus. SIADH, syndrome of inappropriate antidiuretic hormone secretion; EAV, effective arterial volume. *(Source: Carroll HJ, Oh MS. Water, electrolyte, and acid–base metabolism. Philadelphia: Lippincott, 1989:122. Reproduced with permission from the publisher and author.)*

where dNa is defined as desired serum Na – actual serum Na, and TBW denotes total body water.

Osmotic diuretics such as mannitol can remove water if renal function is adequate, but the method is not as convenient or as predictable as when saline is used with a loop diuretic. Administration of urea has also been recommended as a means of treating hyponatremia through osmotic diuresis.

Slow Correction of Hyponatremia and Maintenance Therapy. Isotonic saline is commonly recommended for treatment of hyponatremia associated with volume depletion (hypotonic dehydration), with the expectation that restoration of volume will suppress the baroreceptor-stimulated ADH secretion and induce water diuresis. This treatment is appropriate when hyponatremia is chronic and the patient is suffering mainly from hypovolemia; however, administration of isotonic saline to a patient whose hypovolemia is more apparent than real may cause an unexpectedly rapid increase in serum sodium, especially if potassium chloride is given concomitantly, and the patient so treated is at risk of developing CPM. We recommend that alternate liters of normal saline and half-normal saline be given to treat hyponatremic dehydration and that serum sodium be checked at 6-hour intervals. If potassium chloride is administered concomitantly at 30 to 40 mEq/L, then half-normal saline should be the replacement fluid.

When slow correction of hyponatremia in a volume-expanded subject is desired, for example, for treatment of SIADH, water restriction is the best choice. If water restriction is unsuccessful, the next approach is to increase solute excretion. This can be achieved by increased salt and potassium intake, along with administration of a loop diuretic, which interferes with urine concentration. Urea has been tried for the same purpose.

Lithium and demeclocycline, both of which can cause nephrogenic diabetes insipidus, have been used with some success, but their untoward effects make them clearly inferior to salt and furosemide. The use of ADH antagonists is in an experimental stage.

FOLLOW-UP

Redevelopment of the circumstances that led to hyponatremia must be avoided. For example, schizophrenics who are known to have water drinking binges should be supervised closely and weighed daily in the hospital; frequent water withholding may be needed (in at least one instance the serum sodium rose with sufficient rapidity to cause CPM with only water restriction in a water-intoxicated schizophrenic). Patients with chronic diseases require outpatient supervision and care of their diseases with return visits for evaluation of, among other concerns, serum chemical profile.

DISCUSSION
Prevalence and Incidence

No precise data concerning prevalence and incidence can be obtained. If suffices to say that hyponatremia is the most common disorder of electrolyte and water metabolism encountered in clinical medicine.

Related Basic Science

Hyponatremia is usually associated with low serum osmolality. When hyponatremia results from acute shift of water from the cell due to accumulation of solutes restricted to the extracellular fluid, such as mannitol and glucose, serum osmolality is increased, and the symptoms are those of hyperosmolality. Loss of potassium may also contribute to the severity of hyponatremia as sodium shifts into the cell in exchange for potassium. This phenomenon underlies the rapid rise in serum sodium that may be seen when both sodium and potassium are replaced; potassium reenters the cell and sodium reenters the extracellular fluid. Most commonly, hyponatremia is caused by either retention of water or loss of sodium (Table 17–2–1).

Normally a slight reduction in serum sodium concentration, when accompanied by reduction in effective osmolality, results in marked suppression of ADH, which causes excretion of dilute urine and return of serum sodium to normal. Persistence of hyponatremia therefore requires an explanation. The basic mechanisms responsible for maintenance of hyponatremia are also listed in Table 17–2–1: grossly excessive water intake, impairment of renal water excretion due to lack of excreted solute, impairment of renal water excretion despite normal ADH control because of advanced renal failure, impairment of urine dilution by either appropriate or inappropriate ADH secretion, abnormal urine concentration without participation of ADH because of slow flow of urine in the collecting duct. The last factor needs explanation. If low glomerular filtration rate and enhanced proximal reabsorption of salt and water reduce urine flow to the collecting duct, the fluid may flow so slowly that urine may be concentrated substantially in the presence of little or no ADH. This phenomenon, the "distal trickle effect" is most commonly caused by reduction in effective arterial volume, as in congestive heart failure and cirrhosis of the liver with ascites. Distal trickle effect is usually accompanied by some increase in ADH secretion attributed to low effective volume.

When one has excluded pseudohyponatremia and hyponatremia due to mannitol or glucose excess, one is left with hyponatremia with reduced effective osmolality, the type of hyponatremia that can cause symptoms of cell overhydration. This condition is usually accompanied by a low measured serum osmolality, but in the presence of urea, ethanol, or other osmotically ineffective solutes, serum osmolality may not be reduced.

Hyponatremia may be accompanied by normal, increased, or decreased effective arterial volume. Causes of hyponatremia with increased effective arterial volume include primary polydipsia, advanced renal failure, and SIADH (Tables 17–2–2 and 17–2–3). Patients with hyponatremia accompanied by low effective arterial volume may be dehydrated or edematous; the former are salt depleted and the latter have excessive body sodium content. In the latter case, the kidney retains salt in response to low effective arterial volume and edema forma-

tion is the result. In some edematous subjects, salt and water retention may restore the effective arterial volume to normal and salt retention ceases. In others, fluid overload worsens progressively until salt restriction or diuretic therapy interrupts the unrelenting salt retention; low effective arterial volume is thus maintained. Patients who sequester fluid in the abdominal cavity or trap fluid in the dilated bowel may thereby reduce effective arterial volume and retain salt and water. If more water than salt is taken in, hyponatremia will develop.

Low effective arterial volume with salt depletion is caused by either renal or extrarenal salt loss. If the cause of salt loss is renal, renal excretion of salt is inappropriately high (> 20 mEq/L), whereas with extrarenal causes, the kidney would conserve salt. In both dehydrated and edematous subjects, hyponatremia is maintained because water excretion is limited by the distal trickle effect as well as by appropriately increased ADH secretion.

Many authors assign myxedema and glucocorticoid deficiency (e.g., hypopituitarism) to the category of hyponatremia with apparently normal effective arterial volume, but there is some evidence that effective arterial volume is reduced in both hormonal deficiency states, and thus, the mechanism of hyponatremia might be the same as that found in edema-forming states and salt depletion states.

Natural History and Its Modification with Treatment

The natural history of hyponatremia varies from benign to lethal and depends in large measure on the prognosis of the underlying disease. Patients with small cell carcinoma of the lung and SIADH may manifest a fall in serum sodium to about 130 mEq/L with no further fall and no symptoms of cell overhydration until the patient's death from the cancer. The term *resetting of the osmostat* describes this sort of behavior, which may be seen in many chronic debilitating diseases; treatment is neither warranted nor likely to succeed.

Prevention

Patients and their families can participate in the care and prevention of hyponatremia. Patients with SIADH must be instructed about excessive water ingestion and daily weighing to detect excess water accumulation. Those treated with thiazide diuretics and other culpable drugs must be warned against copious water intake; thiazide diuretics interfere with urinary dilution and hence with water excretion. Those who care for elderly patients must be given more precise instructions than "make sure he drinks plenty of water."

Schizophrenics may literally drink themselves to death. Patients who are unable to excrete water normally and who continue to receive salt-free water may die after intractable seizure and cardiopulmonary arrest. It is the physician's responsibility to guard against the occurrence of hyponatremia, to document its presence in timely fashion, and to deal with it without further hazard to the patient.

Cost Containment

No elaborate technologic structure is required for the management of hyponatremia per se; measurement of serum sodium is not expensive. The real savings come in prevention of neurologic catastrophe, whose short- and long-term management may be very expensive indeed.

TABLE 17–2–3. CAUSES OF INAPPROPRIATE ANTIDIURETIC HORMONE SECRETION

1. Tumors
2. Intrathoracic causes: virtually any pulmonary lesion
3. Central nervous system abnormalities: virtually any brain lesion
4. Surgical and emotional stress: emetic?
5. Endocrine causes: glucocorticoid deficiency, myxedema
6. Idiopathic
7. Drugs
   a. ADH analogs and oxytocin
   b. Drugs that increase ADH release directly: vincristine, vinblastine, cyclophosphamide, clofibrate, narcotics
   c. Drugs that stimulate ADH possibly in part through emetic stimulus: tricyclic antidepressants, tranylcypromine (Parnate), phenothiazines, haloperidol, cyclophosphamide, narcotics
   d. Drugs that enhance ADH effect on the kidney: chlorpropamide, tolbutamide, diuretics (especially thiazides), acetaminophen (Tylenol), nonsteroidal antiinflammatory drugs (indomethacin [Indocin], carbamazepine [Tegretol])

ADH, antidiuretic hormone.

REFERENCES

Carroll HJ, Oh MS. Disturbances in body fluid osmolality. In: Water, electrolyte, and acid–base metabolism. Philadelphia: Lippincott, 1989.

Oh MS, Kim HJ, Carroll HJ. Recommendations for treatment of symptomatic hypontremia. Nephron 1995;70:143.

Oh MS, Uribarri J, Barrido D, et al. Central pontine myelinolysis following isotonic saline. Am J Med Sci 1989;298:4.

Robertson GL, Berl T. Water metabolism. In: Brenner BM, Rector FC, eds. The kidney. Philadelphia: Saunders, 1986.

Sarnaik AP, Meert K, Hackbarth R, Fleischmann L. Management of hyponatremic seizures in children with hypertonic saline: A safe and effective strategy. Crit Care Med 1991;19:758.

Sterns RH. Severe symptomatic hyponatremia: Treatment and outcome. A study of 64 cases. Ann Intern Med 1987;107:656.

Weisberg LS. Pseudohyponatremia: A reappraisal. Am J Med 1989;86:315.

CHAPTER 17–3

Metabolic Acidosis

Mark D. Faber, M.D., and Robert G. Narins, M.D.

DEFINITION

Acidosis refers to the metabolic or respiratory process causing acid accumulation. Metabolic acidosis is characterized by a primary accumulation of fixed acids that titrate and thereby decrease serum bicarbonate concentration ($[HCO_3^-]$). This hypobicarbonatemia tends to reduce arterial (systemic) pH, causing acidemia (pH < 7.36). Respiration is stimulated by this low pH, causing hypocapnia, and this alkalinizing, compensatory response lessens the degree of acidemia.

ETIOLOGY

Metabolic acidosis can occur in three ways: net accumulation of fixed acid as a result of either renal underexcretion of normally produced acid (e.g., renal failure) or pathologic overproduction of acid (e.g., ketoacidosis); loss of bicarbonate or bicarbonate equivalents in the stool (e.g., diarrhea) or urine (e.g., renal tubular acidosis); or dilution of plasma bicarbonate by expansion of the extracellular space with bicarbonate-deficient fluid. Depending on the pathogenetic mechanism, metabolic acidoses may be further subclassified on the basis of the anion gap (i.e., normal and elevated anion gap variants) (see Differential Diagnosis below and Table 17–3–1).

CRITERIA FOR DIAGNOSIS
Suggestive

The presence of metabolic acidosis should be suspected when patients present with clinical disorders known to spawn this chemical abnormality (Table 17–3–1). It should also be considered when the various nonspecific manifestations of this disorder (see Clinical Manifestations) are present. Historical evidence of drug or toxin exposure, trauma, diabetes mellitus, renal insufficiency, diarrhea, or gartrointestinal disease should be sought.

Definitive

The definitive diagnosis of a simple metabolic acidosis requires demonstration of reduced serum bicarbonate levels, compensatory reduction in the partial pressure of carbon dioxide (PCO_2) proportional to the magnitude of hypobicarbonatemia (see below), and reduction in the arterial pH (< 7.36). An increased anion gap, in combination with the history and physical findings noted above, is useful not only in diagnosing metabolic acidosis but in establishing its specific cause. The normal anion gap acidoses are further subclassified on the basis of the serum potassium concentration (Table 17–3–1).

CLINICAL MANIFESTATIONS
Subjective

Metabolic acidosis causes a variety of symptoms the severity of which depends on the degree of acidemia and the rapidity of its onset. Severe acidemia may cause abdominal pain, vomiting, disorientation, stupor, seizures, and/or symptoms related to hypotension. Beyond these effects, metabolic acidosis causes no specific symptomatology aside from that associated with the underlying disorder.

Objective
Physical Examination

Kussmaul's respiration is the deep, labored breathing that reflects the compensatory increase in ventilation seen in the metabolic acidoses.

We thank Dr. Louis J. Riley, Jr., for his contribution to this chapter in the third edition of this book.

Acidemia also may cause peripheral vasodilation, resulting in hypotension, tachycardia, an increase in pulse pressure, and warm, flushed skin. Acidemia with a pH less than 7.20 depresses ventricular function. Advanced degrees of acidemia may be associated with depression of the respiratory center, venoconstriction, and congestive heart failure. Specific signs related to the underlying disorder also may be evident. These hemodynamic features constitute the main danger from acidemia.

Physical findings may aid in identifying the cause of a metabolic acidosis; for example, fever and hypotension may point to sepsis; retinal changes could yield clues to the presence of diabetic ketoacidosis or methanol intoxication (which causes retinal edema and papillitis). Patients with AIDS develop lactic acidosis and their eye grounds may reveal the changes characteristic of cytomegalovirus or *Candida* infections. Skin turgor, jugular veins and mucous membranes are indices of extracellular fluid volume depletion. The smell of ketones or urea could be the first clue to diabetic ketoacidosis or uremic acidosis. Such intraabdominal processes as cirrhosis, pancreatitis, and ischemic bowel may cause acidoses, making the abdominal examination an important part of the patient's evaluation.

Routine Laboratory Abnormalities

Simple metabolic acidosis by definition must include reduced serum bicarbonate concentration, appropriately reduced PCO_2, and systemic pH less than 7.36. Other electrolyte abnormalities might include a normal anion gap and hyperkalemia (especially in the case of mineral acidoses or hyperkalemic renal tubular acidosis) or hypokalemia which complicates diarrheal acidosis and the various forms of distal renal tubular aci-

TABLE 17–3–1. CAUSES OF METABOLIC ACIDOSIS

Elevated Anion Gap	Normal Anion Gap
Renal failure	Hypokalemic acidosis
Ketoacidosis	Renal tubular acidosis
Starvation	Proximal
Diabetes mellitus	Distal
Alcohol associated	Diarrhea
Type I glycogenosis I	Posthypocapnic acidosis
Defects in gluconeogenesis	Carbonic anhydrase inhibitors
Lactic acidosis	Acetazolamide
Tissue ischemia	Methazolamide
Diabetes mellitus	Dichlorphenamide
Hypoglycemia	Ureteral diversions
Hepatic failure	Ureterosigmoidostomy
Neoplasia	Ileal bladder
Biguanides	Ileal ureter
Congenital enzyme defects	Pancreatic transplantation to urinary bladder
Thiamine deficiency	Normal-hyperkalemic acidosis
D-lactic acidosis	Early renal failure including diabetic nephropathy
AIDS	Hydronephrosis
Toxins	Addition of hydrochloric acid
Methanol	Ammonium choride
Ethylene glycol	Arginine hydrochloride
Salicylates	Lysine hydrochloride
	Sulfur toxicity
	Toluene

Modified from Narins RG, Emmett M. Simple and mixed acid–base disorders: A practical approach. Medicine (Baltimore) 1980;59:161. Reproduced with permission from the publisher and author.

dosis. The anion gap is increased when titrated bicarbonate is replaced by those anions that are not usually measured (e.g., ketones, lactate).

Additional findings include leukocytosis (from decreased white blood cell margination) and hyperuricemia in organic acidosis (due to competitive inhibition of renal tubular uric acid secretion by lactate, ketones, etc.). Hypercalciuria may occur and acidemia causes a tendency toward hyperglycemia.

PLANS

Diagnostic

Differential Diagnosis

See Table 17–3–1. Metabolic acidoses occur in a variety of clinical settings. The serum electrolyte pattern resulting from the titration of bicarbonate with the offending acid allows for a practical classification of these acidoses based on the anion gap. Protons from the added acid destroy bicarbonate, which is then replaced by the acid anion. Hydrochloric acidoses (e.g., diarrhea) substitute the routinely measured chloride for serum bicarbonate, whereas all other acidoses exchange a usually unmeasured anion (e.g., acetoacetate, lactate) for the alkali. The normal difference between the serum sodium concentration (142 mEq/L) and the sum of the chloride and bicarbonate concentrations (105 + 25) is the anion gap, which reflects the unmeasured anions (albumin, sulfate, phosphate, organic anions) which normally counterbalance sodium's positive charge:

$$\text{anion gap} = Na^+ - (Cl^- + HCO_3^-)$$

The anion gap is normally 12 ± 2 mEq/L. Hydrochloric acidoses, by simultaneously lowering bicarbonate and raising chloride concentrations, leave the anion gap unchanged. All other acidoses lower bicarbonate without changing chloride concentration, thereby raising the anion gap. Thus, the acidoses are conveniently classified as having a normal or increased anion gap (Table 17–3–1).

Diabetes mellitus, alcoholic ketoacidosis, lactic acidosis, and starvation ketoacidosis are common examples of high anion gap acidoses caused by endogenous acid overproduction. The major sources of exogenous acid loads that also increase the anion gap are salicylate, methyl alcohol, and ethylene glycol. Finally, advanced renal failure allows endogenous acids to accumulate and thereby increases the anion gap.

Normal anion gap acidoses include those resulting from direct loss of bicarbonate or potential bicarbonate, those resulting from ingestion of hydrochloric acid or its equivalent, and those associated with dilution of the extracellular space with bicarbonate-poor fluid. Gastrointestinal loss of bicarbonate occurs in diarrhea, enterostomies, and ureteroenterostomies, whereas renal losses develop in the congenital and acquired forms of renal tubular acidosis. Arginine hydrochloride and ammonium chloride undergo hepatic conversion to urea and hydrochloric acid, thereby causing a hyperchloremic acidosis.

The osmolar gap is an important screening test for the presence of certain toxins. Low-molecular-weight toxins like ethylene glycol and methanol make significant contributions to the serum solute concentration, thereby causing the measured serum osmolality to increase. Routine calculations of serum osmolality, normally agreeing within 10 mOsm/L with measured values, include only sodium, its anions, and the osmolar contributions of glucose, urea, and ethanol (if present):

$$\text{calculated serum osmolality} = 2\,(Na^+)\ mEq/L$$
$$+ \frac{BUN\ mg\%}{2.8} + \frac{glucose\ mg\%}{18} + \frac{ethanol\ mg\%}{4.6}$$

When the measured osmolality exceeds the calculated value by more than 10 to 15 mOsm/L, some solute, unaccounted for by sodium and its anions, urea, glucose, or ethanol, must be present. This solute could be ethylene glycol or methanol.

Diagnostic Options and Recommended Approach

Determination of the arterial blood gas values (pH, PCO_2, [HCO_3^-]) along with simultaneous serum electrolyte values and calculations of the anion and osmolal gaps furnishes enough data to establish the diagnosis of metabolic acidosis and acidemia. The specific cause of a high anion gap variant is clarified by assessing the blood urea nitrogen and serum creatinine concentrations, ketonemia and ketonuria, lactatemia and, in suspected toxin exposure, screening of serum and urine for exposure to salicylate, methanol, and ethylene glycol. In addition, urinalysis may reveal calcium oxalate crystalluria ("envelope" or needle shaped variants) in cases of ethylene glycol poisoning. The clinical setting usually suggests the diagnosis in most cases of elevated anion gap acidosis. The osmolal gap is often useful in suggesting the presence of ethylene glycol or methanol. Hypokalemic hyperchloremic acidoses are usually due to diarrhea or rarely renal tubular acidosis, whereas the hyperkalemic hyperchloremic acidoses usually reflect a defect in the adrenal–renal axis (Table 17–3–1).

Therapeutic

Therapy of metabolic acidosis depends on the etiology, severity, and duration of the underlying cause and the resulting chemical changes. Attention must be directed at the underlying cause of acid overproduction or underexcretion as well as at the severity of associated acidemia. Most agree that acute, severe acidemia (pH <7.20, serum [HCO_3^-] < 10 mEq/L) demands alkali therapy. Estimates of the amount of alkali required to raise the serum bicarbonate concentration to more than 10 mEq/L and the pH to 7.20 are based on formulas that typically underestimate the volume of distribution of bicarbonate in acidemia.

Replacement is usually given slowly over several hours with clinical and laboratory (especially blood gas) monitoring as indicated. The rate of administration of alkali is adjusted to achieve and maintain a desired serum concentration. Clearly, if acid overproduction is ongoing, bicarbonate requirements will be that much greater. When large amounts of sodium bicarbonate are required, dangerous expansion of the extracellular fluid may result. Use of potent diuretics, or dialysis in the presence of renal failure, may be required.

Bicarbonate should be used sparingly, if at all, to treat the lactic acidosis of cardiopulmonary arrest. In this setting, the diminished cardiac output simultaneously impairs tissue perfusion and the return of venous blood to the lungs. Tissue hypoperfusion stimulates lactic acid overproduction, whereas sluggish pulmonary arterial flow allows the carbon dioxide derived from oxidative metabolism to accumulate in the venous circulation. The reduced load of carbon dioxide delivered to the lungs is effectively removed from mixed venous blood by mechanical ventilation. These events are reflected by the striking differences in the acid–base parameters of the two circulations. Similar degrees of mixed venous and arterial hypobicarbonatemia occur, but severe mixed venous acidemia due to hypercapnia contrasts with the eucapnic normal arterial blood gases. Bicarbonate infusion worsens this venous hypercapnia because in vivo acid titration converts administered bicarbonate to carbon dioxide and water. The clinical importance of this mixed venous hypercapnia is still debated. Therapy should be aimed at mechanical and pharmacologic improvement of the cardiac output in the hope of extinguishing lactic acid overproduction and increasing pulmonary venous blood flow.

Treatment of the chronic metabolic acidoses also varies with the severity and etiology of the underlying disorder. Patients with classic distal or type IV renal tubular acidosis or chronic diarrheal syndromes may be treated effectively with daily administration of sodium bicarbonate or Shohl's solution (sodium citrate). The latter is metabolized by various tissues to sodium bicarbonate. Daily doses should replace alkali deficits and ongoing losses. Once deficits have been replaced, patients with distal renal tubular acidosis usually require only 20 to 40 mEq/d alkali (1.5–3.0 g/d sodium bicarbonate or 20–40 mL/d Shohl's solution). Patients with proximal renal tubular acidosis may require much more bicarbonate, as much as 10 to 15 mEq/kg of body weight.

When hypokalemia coexists with metabolic acidosis the serum potassium concentration should be returned to approximately 3.5 mEq/L before or during correction of the acidosis. Without vigorous potassium administration alkali therapy could aggravate the hypokalemia and cause paralysis. Resulting loss of respiratory excursion may cause hypercapnia, which will precipitously lower blood pH to potentially fatal levels. Similarly, hypocalcemia associated with metabolic acidosis should be carefully followed because enhanced protein binding of calcium consequent to alkali therapy may result in tetany. Neuromuscular excitability, Chvostek's and Trousseau's signs, and prolongation of the QT interval on the electrocardiogram all serve as useful guidelines for initiating calcium therapy.

FOLLOW-UP

There is no set time frame for follow-up of the patient with metabolic acidosis. Patients with chronic stable metabolic acidosis receiving bicarbonate therapy may be seen as infrequently as every 3 to 6 months once an effective replacement regimen has been established. Patients with more labile underlying disorders, for example, diabetes mellitus, will almost certainly require more frequent, regular visits. In general, the presence and severity of coexisting diseases and patient compliance should be considered in making the decision as to when the patient should be seen in follow-up.

DISCUSSION
Prevalence and Incidence

Metabolic acidosis is a common condition. The exact prevalence and incidence are not known.

Related Basic Science

Intermediary metabolism in the adult produces 50 to 100 mEq of acid daily (1–1.5 mEq/kg of body weight per day) in the form of sulfuric acid, phosphoric acid, and various organic acids. Bicarbonate and other extracellular and cellular buffers prevent wide swings in systemic pH that might otherwise occur. In addition to this chemical buffering, the kidneys excrete the acid produced and simultaneously resynthesize the bicarbonate lost in buffering the daily acid load. Overproduction of acid, loss of buffer, and underexcretion of acid are the three mechanisms that can result in hypobicarbonatemia and acidemia, that is, metabolic acidosis. Reduction of the serum bicarbonate concentration defines an increase in the H^+ concentration or a decrease in pH:

$$[H^+] = 24 \times \frac{P_{CO_2}}{[HCO_3^-]}$$

This acidification of the extracellular fluid stimulates chemoreceptors located in the medullary respiratory center. The resulting increase in alveolar ventilation produces hypocapnia, which acts to return the pH (H^+ concentration) toward normal. The degree of ventilatory response is proportional to the degree of hypobicarbonatemia. This relationship is defined by the formula

$$\text{expected } P_{CO_2} = 1.5 \, (\text{measured } [HCO_3^-]) + 8 \pm 2$$

In this way, the P_{CO_2} that is appropriate for any given degree of metabolic acidosis can be precisely defined. This formula is applicable only in steady-state acidosis in which enough time has elapsed to allow for the maximal lowering of P_{CO_2}. Another quirk of the $[HCO_3^-]/P_{CO_2}$ relationship mandates that when the bicarbonate concentration is between 10 and 40 mEq/L, simply adding the number 15 to the measured $[HCO_3^-]$ value will define what the P_{CO_2} and last two digits of the pH

should be. (For example, in stable metabolic acidosis with a $[HCO_3^-]$ of 14 mEq/L, the P_{CO_2} should approximate 29 mm Hg and the pH 7.29.) If the measured P_{CO_2} is too high or too low for a given bicarbonate concentration, one may diagnose a mixed acid–base disorder.

Natural History and Its Modification with Treatment

The natural history of the metabolic acidoses is as diverse as the clinical scenarios in which they arise, because they are determined by the interplay of a number of factors: the nature, severity, and duration of the underlying disorder(s); comorbidity or the presence of concomitant disease(s); the timely administration of effective therapy.

For example, severe ongoing untreated metabolic acidemia predictably eventuates in death that is at least partly a result of the deleterious effects of acidemia on the cardiorespiratory and central nervous systems (see above). In contrast, the chronic untreated hyperchloremic metabolic acidosis of classical distal renal tubular acidosis is not associated with premature death, but it is likely to result in severe osteodystrophy and nephrocalcinosis. The sequelae of both these disturbances are obviated by effective therapy of the acidosis.

Prevention

Prevention of metabolic acidosis is probably best achieved through control of the underlying or predisposing disorders. Patient education with the goal of maximizing compliance with the therapeutic regimen is probably the most effective preventive measure. Patients with hyperkalemic metabolic acidosis associated with interstitial renal disease and early renal insufficiency often have impaired sodium conservation. They should be counseled to avoid salt restriction, which can lead to volume depletion, acute renal failure, and worsening of the hyperkalemia and acidosis.

Cost Containment

Acid–base disturbances that require hospitalization can be quite costly, particularly if the disturbance is severe enough to require intensive care facilities. Accordingly, the most effective cost-containing maneuver is proper care of the patient on an outpatient basis. This demands careful monitoring of high-risk patients, judicious attention to pharmacotherapy, and maintenance of control over underlying disorders.

REFERENCES

Cogan MG, Rector FC. Acid–base disorders. In: Brenner BM, Rector FC Jr, eds. The kidney. Philadelphia: Saunders, 1991:737.

Goodkin DA, Krishna GG, Narins RG. The role of the anion gap in detecting and managing mixed metabolic acid–base disorders. Clin Endocrinol Metab 1984;13:333.

Narins RG, Emmett M. Simple and mixed acid–base disorders: A practical approach. Medicine (Baltimore) 1980;59:161.

Narins RG, Krishna GG, Yee J, et al. The metabolic acidoses. In: Narins RG, ed. Clinical disorders of fluid and electrolyte metabolism. 5th ed. New York: McGraw-Hill, 1994:769.

Narins RG, Kupin W, Faber M, et al. Metabolic acid–base disturbances: Pathophysiology, diagnosis and therapy. In: Arieff AI, DeFronzo RA, eds. Fluid–electrolyte and acid–base disorders. New York: Churchill Livingstone, 1995.

CHAPTER 17–4

Metabolic Alkalosis

Mark D. Faber, M.D., and Robert G. Narins, M.D.

DEFINITION

Alkalosis is the term used to describe the metabolic or respiratory process that generates excess alkali. Whether or not the process (alkalosis) results in elevation of the systemic pH (alkalemia) depends on the severity of the alkalotic disturbance or the presence or absence of concurrent acidotic processes. Metabolic alkalosis is characterized by primary hyperbicarbonatemia leading to a reduction in the hydrogen ion concentration ($[H^+]$).

ETIOLOGY

Metabolic alkalosis occurs in a number of well-defined clinical settings (Table 17–4–1). The elevated serum bicarbonate concentration may be caused either by primary addition of new endogenous or exogenous bicarbonate to the extracellular fluid or by the loss of chloride-rich, bicarbonate-poor fluid from the extracellular space, increasing the concentration of the remaining bicarbonate ("contraction alkalosis").

CRITERIA FOR DIAGNOSIS
Suggestive

Situations associated with metabolic alkalosis are described in Table 17–4–1 and below (Differential Diagnosis). These circumstances should prompt a search for this disorder, especially in the presence of suggestive signs or symptoms such as neuromuscular irritability and deterioration in mental status (see Clinical Manifestations).

Definitive

The chemical diagnosis of metabolic alkalosis requires that the serum bicarbonate concentration ($[HCO_3^-]$) be increased; the partial pressure of carbon dioxide (PCO_2) should also increase by an amount dictated by the degree of hyperbicarbonatemia; the systemic (arterial) pH will be greater than normal, as required by the steady-state balance of the $[HCO_3^-]$ and PCO_2.

CLINICAL MANIFESTATIONS
Subjective

Symptoms of metabolic alkalosis may include mental confusion, obtundation, and neuromuscular irritability reflecting the direct effects of alkalemia on the central nervous system and the reduction in cerebral blood flow caused by alkalemia. Muscle cramping, circumoral and digital paresthesias, and frank tetany may also be symptomatic of alkalemia.

Symptoms of postural hypotension, lightheadedness, and dizziness may be the presenting features of alkalosis associated with significant volume depletion. Symptoms referable to the electrolyte abnormalities that frequently coexist with alkalosis may also be noted. Muscle weakness and fatigue may all be symptomatic clues to the existence of alkalemia. Finally, symptoms of the primary disorder resulting in alkalosis may be present (e.g., vomiting, diarrhea).

Objective
Physical Examination

Metabolic alkalosis may be associated with hypertension (e.g., Conn's syndrome), postural hypotension (e.g., vomiting and volume contraction), altered sensorium (somnolence, obtundation, coma), and hyperactive deep tendon reflexes. Chvostek's and Trousseau's signs may be present.

Routine Laboratory Abnormalities

Simple metabolic alkalosis, by definition, must include all of the following: an increased serum bicarbonate concentration; an increased PCO_2 (the PCO_2 rises by 0.7 mm Hg [range, 0.2–0.9 mm Hg] for each milliequivalent per liter increment in the serum bicarbonate concentration) and a reduction in hydrogen ion concentration (i.e., an increase in pH). Additional laboratory abnormalities often associated with metabolic alkalosis include hypokalemia, hypochloremia, hypophosphatemia, and a tendency toward hypoglycemia and hypocalcemia.

The electrocardiogram may reveal prominent U waves and a prolonged QT interval. Roentgenologic studies, the hemogram, and urinalysis are unlikely to be of any special diagnostic value.

PLANS
Diagnostic
Differential Diagnosis

See Table 17–4–1. Primary elevation of the serum bicarbonate concentration can result from creation of new extracellular endogenous or exogenous bicarbonate or from the increased concentration of existing bicarbonate through the loss of bicarbonate-free extracellular fluid. Fluid losses via the kidneys, gastrointestinal tract, or skin may cause contraction alkalosis. Edematous patients receiving diuretic therapy (other than acetazolamide [Diamox] and potassium-sparing diuretics) or suffering from emesis or gastric suction are likely candidates for this disturbance. Administration of exogenous alkali to patients whose kidneys retain bi-

TABLE 17–4–1. METABOLIC ALKALOSIS

Saline Responsive ($U_{Cl} < 10$ mEq/L)	Saline Unresponsive ($U_{Cl} > 10$ mEq/L)
Renal alkalosis	Normotensive
Diuretic therapy	Bartter's syndrome
Poorly reabsorbable anion therapy	Severe potassium depletion
Carbenicillin	Refeeding alkalosis
Penicillin	Hypercalcemia and hypoparathyroidism
Sulfate	Hypertensive
Phosphate	Endogenous mineralocorticoids
Posthypercapnia	Hyperaldosterone syndromes
Gastrointestinal alkalosis	Hyperreninism
Gastric alkalosis	Adrenal enzyme deficiency
Intestinal alkalosis	11-Hydroxylase
Chloride diarrhea	17-Hydroxylase
"Contraction alkalosis"	Liddle's syndrome
	Exogenous mineralocorticoids
	Licorice
	Carbenoxolone
	Chewing tobacco
	Exogenous alkali in renal failure patients
	$NaHCO_3$ (baking soda)
	Sodium citrate, lactate, gluconate, acetate
	Transfusions
	Antacids (Tums, Alka-Seltzer, Rolaids)
	Milk-alkali syndrome

U_{Cl} = urine chloride concentration.
Adapted from Narins RG, Jones ER, Stom MC, et al. Diagnostic strategies in disorders of fluid, electrolyte and acid–base homeostasis. Am J Med 1982;72:496. Reproduced with permission from the publisher and author.

We thank Dr. Louis J. Riley, Jr., for his contribution to this chapter in the third edition of this book.

carbonate can result in sustained hyperbicarbonatemia. These sources of exogenous bicarbonate include sodium bicarbonate or the salts of such strong acids as citric acid, lactic acid, and acetic acid. Oxidative conversion of citrate, lactate, or acetate to bicarbonate in the liver generates the alkali. This complication may develop in patients receiving massive blood transfusions (whole blood citrate, 17 mEq/L; packed red blood cell citrate, 5 mEq/unit), especially in the setting of hypovolemia (which is often coexistent).

Excessive ingestion of milk and absorbable antacids (most frequently calcium carbonate) can produce hypercalcemia, nephrocalcinosis, and renal failure in the milk–alkali syndrome. Many factors contribute to the maintenance of metabolic alkalosis in this disorder, including volume depletion (vomiting, polyuria) and hypercalcemia, which both decrease glomerular filtration of bicarbonate while increasing proximal renal bicarbonate reabsorption. This disease may become increasingly more common as the use of calcium carbonate and calcium citrate supplements to prevent osteoporosis becomes more widespread.

In fact, some degree of volume depletion is common to all aforementioned metabolic alkaloses. The metabolic alkalosis is generated by endogenous or exogenous means, but the maintenance of the hyperbicarbonatemia is effected by renal bicarbonate retention, and this is usually related to some degree of coexisting volume depletion. Metabolic alkalosis also may result from excess mineralocorticoid activity either from an endogenous source such as primary aldosteronism, accelerated hypertension, or certain adrenal enzyme deficiency states or from an exogenous source such as licorice or chewing tobacco. In summary, metabolic alkalosis should be suspected in clinical settings associated with volume loss from chronic diuretic administration or upper gastrointestinal losses or in states characterized by unprovoked hypokalemia caused by increased mineralocorticoid activity (Table 17–4–1).

Diagnostic Options and Recommended Approach

Determination of arterial pH, PCO_2, and $[HCO_3^-]$ values along with simultaneously drawn serum electrolyte values can establish the diagnosis of metabolic alkalosis and alkalemia. Knowledge of the blood urea nitrogen and serum creatinine concentrations may aid in determining the etiology of the disorder. Once the diagnosis of metabolic alkalosis has been established, determination of the urine chloride concentration (U_{Cl}) is most helpful (see Table 17–4–1). The metabolic alkaloses may be divided into two groups on the basis of the urine chloride concentration. If the urine chloride concentration is less than 10 mEq/L, the metabolic alkalosis is termed *saline responsive* and this suggests that the sustaining event is loss or deficiency of chloride-rich fluid. The renal retention of sodium, chloride, and water is assumed to reflect extracellular fluid volume contraction, which, in turn, stimulates renal conservation of volume. Diuretic-induced volume contraction results in sodium chloride diuresis despite hypovolemia, that is, as long as the diuretic effect continues. If the urine chloride concentration is more than 10 mEq/L, the metabolic alkalosis is termed *saline unresponsive*, and this suggests that a mechanism other than loss of chloride-rich fluid is etiologic.

Therapeutic

Metabolic alkaloses associated with a low urine chloride concentration (<10 mEq/L) are treated with volume replacement, usually in the form of physiologic saline solution. Replenishment of depleted sodium, chloride, and water stores and reexpansion of the extracellular fluid volume are required to enable the kidneys to excrete bicarbonate while retaining chloride, thereby reversing the hypochloremia. The magnitude of the salt and water deficit is assessed by clinical examination and laboratory findings. Discontinuation of diuretic therapy and replacement of associated potassium losses must, of course, also be carried out.

Supplemental potassium chloride administration or, in the edematous patient requiring ongoing diuretic therapy, the addition of potassium-sparing diuretics effectively reduces renal potassium and magnesium and hydrogen ion wasting. Intermittent therapy with acetazolamide may be especially effective in treating the metabolic alkalosis; how-

ever, this diuretic is strongly kaliuretic and will almost always require concomitant potassium chloride supplementation. Converting enzyme inhibition (e.g., captopril [Capoten], 12.5–150 mg/d in two or three divided doses, or enalapril [Vasotec], 2.5–20 mg/d) may be effective in mitigating diuretic-induced potassium losses in patients with hypertension and congestive heart failure. Therapy with an H_2 receptor antagonist (e.g., cimetidine [Tagamet] 300 mg two to four times a day, or ranitidine [Zantac] 150 mg twice a day) may prevent the development of gastric alkalosis in patients receiving nasogastric suctioning by blocking hydrogen ion secretion into the gastric lumen.

Patients with volume overload who have compensated chronic respiratory acidosis (primary hypercapnia and secondary hyperbicarbonatemia) are especially vulnerable to metabolic alkalosis as their pulmonary disease improves. Because their PCO_2 may decrease faster than their bicarbonate level, posthypercapnic metabolic alkalosis may result. The bicarbonaturic diuretic acetazolamide can be used to prevent or to treat an established alkalosis.

The saline-unresponsive alkaloses (urine chloride concentration >10 mEq/L) are best treated by decreasing the enhanced mineralocorticoid effects with spironolactone (Aldactone), amiloride (Midamor), or triamterene (Dyazide). In this setting, the degree of hyperbicarbonatemia is proportional to the degree of potassium depletion. Attenuation of potassium wasting with the aforementioned diuretics initiates corrective bicarbonaturia and chloride retention. Saline is usually contraindicated because its administration may augment urinary potassium losses, thereby aggravating the alkalosis. Large doses of spironolactone are usually required, because competition takes place for the aldosterone receptor site; approximately 400 to 600 mg/d is usually effective.

Licorice ingestion may cause a hypertensive, saline-unresponsive metabolic alkalosis. The active principle of licorice, glycyrrhizic acid, has been shown to inhibit the enzyme 11β-hydroxysteroid dehydrogenase, which catalyzes the conversion of cortisol (which binds to the mineralocorticoid receptor) to cortisone (which does not bind to the receptor). Inhibition of this enzyme causes cortisol to accumulate and bind to the "aldosterone" receptor, producing a clinical mineralocorticoid excess syndrome. Discontinuation of licorice ingestion is, of course, the best therapy.

When severe metabolic alkalosis and advanced renal failure coexist, reexpansion of the extracellular space often does not induce a bicarbonaturia. Removal of bicarbonate in this setting requires either titration with administered acid or withdrawal by dialysis. Endogenous acid production will slowly lower elevated bicarbonate levels, allowing asymptomatic patients to self-titrate their hyperbicarbonatemia. Symptomatic patients, however, require either acid therapy or dialysis. Hydrochloric acid (0.15 N[150 mEq H^+/L]) in distilled water or 5% dextrose in water, arginine hydrochloride (5% solution [250 mEq/L hydrochloride]), and ammonium chloride (0.9% solution [170 mEq/L ammonium and chloride]) can all be used. The latter two therapies should not be used in patients with liver or advanced renal disease. Hemodialysis, using either a normal or reduced bicarbonate bath concentration, rapidly lowers serum levels.

FOLLOW-UP

No set time frame for follow-up of the patient with metabolic alkalosis can be established a priori. The presence and severity of coexisting diseases, patient compliance, and the etiology of the metabolic alkalosis should all be considered when making the decision as to when the patient should be seen in follow-up.

DISCUSSION
Prevalence and Incidence

Metabolic alkalosis (simple or as part of a mixed disorder) is the most commonly encountered acid–base disturbance in hospitalized patients.

Related Basic Science

A review of simple acid–base physiology is a necessary prelude to a discussion of the pathophysiology of metabolic alkalosis. The interdependence of pH, [HCO$_3^-$], and [H$_2$CO$_3$] is expressed by the Henderson–Hasselbalch equation

$$pH = pK' + \log \frac{[HCO_3^-]}{P_{CO_2}}$$

where the constant (0.03 mmol/L/mm Hg) relates P$_{CO_2}$ (the partial pressure of carbon dioxide) to the concentration of dissolved CO$_2$ and H$_2$CO$_3$.

Rearrangement of the Henderson–Hasselbalch equation relates [H$^+$] in nanoequivalents per liter to P$_{CO_2}$ and [HCO$_3^-$] and has great clinical utility:

$$[H^+] = 24 \times \frac{P_{CO_2}}{[HCO_3^-]}$$

This equation emphasizes the interdependence of all three variables of the Henderson–Hasselbalch equation and allows quick calculation of any one variable given knowledge of the other two. It is important to note that acidity, that is, [H$^+$], is defined by the ratio of P$_{CO_2}$ to [HCO$_3^-$] and not by the absolute value of either one alone.

Metabolic alkalosis is characterized by a primary increase in the plasma bicarbonate concentration. A net gain of bicarbonate or loss of fixed acid from extracellular fluid decreases the P$_{CO_2}$/[HCO$_3^-$] ratio, thereby decreasing [H$^+$]. The resulting increase in arterial pH provokes a rise in the P$_{CO_2}$ by causing a compensatory decrease in alveolar ventilation, thereby returning the [H$^+$] toward, but not to, normal. This respiratory compensation for metabolic alkalosis causes the P$_{CO_2}$ to increase by 6 to 8 mm Hg for each 10 mEq/L increase in serum bicarbonate concentration.

Understanding the pathophysiology of metabolic alkalosis compels recognition of the fact that there are two phases in the establishment of the disorder: generation of the hyperbicarbonatemia, and renal retention of alkali. Factors that initiate metabolic alkalosis are listed in Table 17–4–1. Broadly, exogenous alkali administration and endogenous generation of alkali as a consequence of gastric or renal hydrogen ion secretion are the two major mechanisms of initiating a metabolic alkalosis.

If the initiating events were solely operative, one would expect that the normally functioning kidney, confronted with an excess of bicarbonate, would correct the abnormality by effecting a bicarbonate diuresis. In fact, this is true; that is to say, perpetuation of a metabolic alkalosis is essentially a renal event. The factors that sustain hyperbicarbonatemia are volume depletion (chloride depletion), hypokalemia, mineralocorticoid excess, hypercapnia, and renal failure. These factors in effect "reset" the kidney to retain excess bicarbonate; that is, they appear to raise the effective threshold for bicarbonate by one of three mechanisms: decreasing the glomerular filtration rate and by so doing keeping the filtered load of bicarbonate (filtered load = glomerular filtration rate × [HCO$_3^-$]) within the normal range, enhancing proximal bicarbonate reabsorption, or enhancing distal bicarbonate

reabsorption and synthesis. Effective treatment of metabolic alkalosis requires recognition of the factors augmenting renal bicarbonate reabsorption. Correction or eradication of these factors is necessary to allow a bicarbonaturic correction to occur.

Natural History and Its Modification with Treatment

Metabolic alkalosis is not characterized by a typical natural history. Indeed, the natural history of the chemical abnormality is a function of the nature, extent, and severity of the initiating disorder as well as the efficacy of treatment. Unless the underlying disorders are corrected and the renal factors associated with maintenance of the alkalemia are reversed, alkalemia will persist. Persistent severe metabolic alkalemia (pH >7.6) can have deleterious effects on the cardiovascular and central nervous systems with potentially fatal consequences (see above).

Prevention

Prevention of metabolic alkalosis requires knowledge of the potential causative agents and advice as to their judicious use. Patients with metabolic alkaloses on the basis of diuretic use or abuse must be educated about the potential deleterious consequences of overzealous self-administration and the importance of potassium supplementation. Additionally, informing patients of the common side effects of hypokalemia serves to heighten their awareness of this incipient disturbance. Occasionally, psychotherapy may be required for diuretic abusers and for surreptitious vomiters.

Cost Containment

Early recognition of the diagnosis of metabolic alkalosis is probably the most cost-effective maneuver, as this may allow outpatient therapy of this disorder. Failure to recognize progression of metabolic alkalosis may result in a serious disorder requiring hospitalization. Because most cases of metabolic alkalosis are likely to be associated with volume depletion, therapy usually entails the very inexpensive administration of fluid, sodium chloride, and potassium chloride and withdrawal of diuretics.

REFERENCES

Cogan MG, Rector FC Jr. Acid–base disorders. In: Brenner BM, Rector FC Jr, eds. The kidney. Philadelphia: Saunders, 1991:737.

Narins RG, Emmett M. Simple and mixed acid–base disorders: A practical approach. Medicine (Baltimore) 1980;59:161.

Narins RG, Kupin W, Faber M, et al. Metabolic acid–base disturbances: Pathophysiology, diagnosis and therapy. In: Arieff AI, DeFronzo RA, eds. Fluid–electrolyte and acid–base disorders. New York: Churchill Livingstone, 1995.

Narins RG, Stom MC, Beck TR. Metabolic and respiratory alkaloses. In: Martinez-Maldonado M, ed. Manual of renal therapeutics. New York: Plenum Press, 1983.

Sabatini S, Kurtzman NA. Metabolic alkalosis. In: Narins RG, ed. Clinical disorders of fluid and electrolyte metabolism. 5th ed. New York: McGraw-Hill, 1994:933.

CHAPTER 17–5

Respiratory Acidosis

André Gougoux, M.D., and Patrick Vinay, M.D.

DEFINITION

Respiratory acidosis or primary hypercapnia refers to an increase in carbon dioxide tension (P$_{CO_2}$ of 50 mm Hg or more) in the body fluids that decreases blood pH (acidemia less than pH 7.35) and is induced by alveolar hypoventilation. This excludes the secondary hypoventilation and hypercapnia produced by metabolic alkalosis.

ETIOLOGY

Acute or chronic respiratory acidosis occurs in four different categories of clinical situations, listed in Table 17–5–1: airway obstruction, restrictive disorders, neuromuscular disorders, and depression of the respiratory center in the central nervous system. The primary cause of respiratory acidosis is often obvious from history and physical examination.

TABLE 17–5–1. CAUSES OF RESPIRATORY ACIDOSIS

	Acute	Chronic
Airway obstruction	Foreign body Laryngospasm Bronchospasm	Chronic obstructive pulmonary disease
Restrictive disorders	Pneumothorax Hemothorax Respiratory distress syndrome	Fibrothorax Hydrothorax Interstitial fibrosis
Neuromuscular disorders	Guillain–Barré syndrome Severe hypokalemia Severe hypophosphatemia Drugs	Poliomyelitis Multiple sclerosis Amyotrophic lateral sclerosis

Respiratory center
depression
	Narcotics
	Sedatives
	General anesthesia
	Cerebral infarction
	Cerebral trauma
		Narcotics
		Sedatives
		Primary alveolar
		  hypoventilation
		Obesity–hypoven-
		  tilation syndrome

CRITERIA FOR DIAGNOSIS
Suggestive

In many patients, the diagnosis of acute respiratory acidosis is clinically suggested by the obvious hypoventilation. In patients with chronic pulmonary disease, characteristic clinical signs are usually evident.

Definitive

Because the physician cannot rely on physical examination alone to assess alveolar ventilation, a decreased arterial blood pH and an increased PCO_2 are required to confirm the diagnosis of respiratory acidosis. Both the clinical history and the magnitude of the compensatory rise in plasma bicarbonate concentration are needed to establish whether the respiratory acidosis is acute or chronic. In acute respiratory acidosis, plasma bicarbonate concentration is increased by only 1 mEq/L for every 10 mm Hg rise in PCO_2. In chronic respiratory acidosis, for each increment of 10 mm Hg in arterial PCO_2, plasma bicarbonate concentration increases by approximately 3.5 mEq/L; this compensation corrects more than half of the fall in arterial pH.

CLINICAL MANIFESTATIONS
Subjective

Because alveolar hypoventilation produces both hypoxemia and hypercapnia, it is often difficult to discriminate between their respective contributions to a specific clinical manifestation. Because the symptoms of hypercapnia correlate with the degree and rapidity of the rise in blood PCO_2, they are much more obvious in acute than in chronic respiratory acidosis. The effects of hypercapnia on the central nervous system account for most symptoms, especially in acute respiratory acidosis. For example, the carbon dioxide-induced cerebral vasodilation raises the intracranial pressure (pseudotumor cerebri) and probably accounts for the headache, usually more severe at night and on awakening. Anxiety, euphoria, and even a transient psychosis with hallucinations and delirium can be observed in patients with hypercapnia. Confusion, stupor, and coma can occur when blood PCO_2 exceeds 70 mm Hg (carbon dioxide narcosis).

Objective
Physical Examination

In acute respiratory acidosis, the physical examination may reveal asterixis, and, in severe cases, papilledema and occasionally focal neurologic signs. Peripheral vasodilation and warm skin are produced by the direct effect of hypercapnia on vascular smooth muscle. A rise in blood pressure can result from beta-adrenergic stimulation and increased cardiac output, whereas, with more severe hypercapnia, decreased myocardial contractility can induce hypotension. Several factors are involved in the generation of cardiac arrhythmias which frequently occur.

Signs resulting from the underlying chronic pulmonary disease, with or without cor pulmonale, are also observed in chronic respiratory acidosis.

Routine Laboratory Abnormalities

See Definition.

PLANS
Diagnostic
Differential Diagnosis

The primary hypoventilation inducing respiratory acidosis is clinically much more obvious than the small physiologic adaptive response to metabolic alkalosis. If blood pH is not measured, the low plasma chloride and high bicarbonate concentrations can be misinterpreted as metabolic alkalosis. The various central nervous system manifestations can be easily misinterpreted as delirium from other causes or an intracerebral space-occupying lesion.

Diagnostic Options

The plasma bicarbonate concentration is the most useful parameter allowing the distinction between acute and chronic respiratory acidosis and the identification of additional acid–base disorders.

Recommended Approach

Acute Respiratory Acidosis. Plasma bicarbonate concentration lies between 24 and 30 mEq/L, values outside this range indicating superimposed metabolic disorders. For example, a lower plasma bicarbonate represents a combined respiratory and metabolic (often lactic) acidosis. By contrast, a plasma bicarbonate higher than the anticipated value is observed when the respiratory acidosis is chronic or when a metabolic alkalosis (usually induced by vomiting or diuretics) is complicating the acute hypercapnia.

Chronic Respiratory Acidosis. Plasma bicarbonate concentration increases by approximately 3.5 mEq/L (with a range of 3.5 mEq/L in either direction) for each 10 mm Hg rise in arterial PCO_2. A lower plasma bicarbonate is observed when the respiratory acidosis is acute or when a metabolic acidosis is complicating the chronic respiratory acidosis. A higher plasma bicarbonate indicates that a metabolic alkalosis is superimposed on the chronic respiratory acidosis.

The underlying causes of acute and chronic respiratory acidosis are usually readily apparent once they are known (Table 17–5–1) but plans for their further definition are dealt with in the respective chapters.

Therapeutic
Therapeutic Options

Specific and nonspecific measures may be used in the treatment of respiratory acidosis. Prompt removal or treatment of the underlying pathologic state (Table 17–5–1) is usually easier in acute respiratory acidosis but most often impossible in chronic respiratory acidosis.

Recommended Approach

Acute Respiratory Acidosis. A patent airway must be restored as soon as possible and, if necessary, endotracheal intubation and mechanical ventilation should be performed. Oxygen must be administered immediately because hypoxemia rather than hypercapnia represents the major threat to survival. Alveolar ventilation should be improved to return the arterial PCO_2 to a normal value. Administration of sodium bicarbonate can be useful in two specific circumstances: first, to correct a severe metabolic acidosis superimposed on the acute respiratory acidosis, and second, to restore the responsiveness of the bronchial muscle to beta-adrenergic agonists in severe bronchospasm. Whenever possible, a more specific treatment of the underlying disorder must be achieved.

Chronic Respiratory Acidosis. The careful use of oxygen can improve the condition of many chronically hypercapnic patients, especially when their hypoxemia is severe. By contrast, the uncontrolled administration of oxygen can remove the essential hypoxemic stimulus to respiration in these patients partially insensitive to carbon dioxide. Attempts to correct the low pH by administration of sodium bicarbonate are useless because its rapid excretion in the urine prevents any significant rise in plasma bicarbonate concentration. When mechanical ventilation is instituted, arterial PCO_2 must be decreased in a stepwise fashion, over a few days, to avoid a complicating posthypercapnic metabolic alkalosis with its resulting neuromuscular irritability and cardiac arrhythmias. To remove its inhibitory effect on ventilation, this metabolic alkalosis should be corrected by the discontinuation of diuretic therapy when appropriate and the administration of adequate quantities of chloride. Several nonspecific measures can improve alveolar ventilation and help to return arterial PCO_2 within a normal range: appropriate antibiotics to treat the superimposed pulmonary infection, loop diuretics to reduce the pulmonary vascular congestion, and bronchodilators to decrease the airway resistance.

FOLLOW-UP

No follow-up is necessary for patients with acute respiratory acidosis when their underlying problem is resolved. In patients with chronic respiratory acidosis, a superimposed pulmonary infection is an indication for immediately contacting their physician for reevaluation. In these patients, the frequency of the follow-up visits, chest radiographs, and pulmonary function tests is dictated by the nature and the severity of the underlying disease.

DISCUSSION
Prevalence and Incidence

Acute or chronic respiratory acidosis is a relatively common disorder. Chronic respiratory acidosis is mostly found with chronic obstructive pulmonary disease, a condition more often affecting males than females and patients over 40 years of age.

Related Basic Science

Approximately 10 mmol of carbon dioxide per minute (or 15,000 mmol/d) is produced by the normal cellular metabolism and excreted by the lungs. On a theoretical basis, hypercapnia could therefore result from increased carbon dioxide production or decreased carbon dioxide excretion; however, accelerated carbon dioxide production does not usually induce hypercapnia because carbon dioxide is a strong stimulus to increase alveolar ventilation. When the normal metabolic production of carbon dioxide exceeds its reduced pulmonary excretion, the positive carbon dioxide balance increases blood PCO_2. Respiratory acidosis is partially corrected by the secondary physiologic rise in plasma bicarbonate concentration resulting from the acute titration of nonbicarbonate buffers and from the chronic renal compensation.

Acute Respiratory Acidosis. In the absence of any rise in plasma bicarbonate concentration when arterial PCO_2 is doubled from 40 to 80 mm Hg, arterial pH would decrease from 7.40 to 7.10 (Table 17–5–2). Blood and tissue protein buffers (including hemoglobin) are immediately titrated by the increased acidity of the body fluids. The dissociation of carbonic acid generates enough bicarbonate to increase its plasma concentration by 1 mEq/L for each 10 mm Hg acute rise in arterial PCO_2. This compensation is complete within 15 minutes and followed by an acute steady state of several hours during which no further changes in plasma acid–base parameters can be detected. In acute hypercapnia, a rise in plasma phosphate concentration and a much smaller one in plasma potassium concentration result from a shift of these ions from the cells to the extracellular fluid.

Chronic Respiratory Acidosis. The generation and retention of new bicarbonate by the kidneys produce a much larger increase in plasma bicarbonate concentration than in acute respiratory acidosis. For each 10 mm Hg rise in arterial PCO_2, the plasma bicarbonate concentration increases by approximately 3.5 mEq/L; this compensation corrects more than half of the fall in blood pH (Table 17–5–2). This rise in plasma bicarbonate is accompanied by a reciprocal fall in plasma chloride concentration resulting from its depressed renal reabsorption,

TABLE 17–5–2. EFFECT OF RESPIRATORY ACIDOSIS ON ARTERIAL ACID–BASE PARAMETERS

	PCO_2	$[HCO_3]$	pH
Normal	40	24	7.40
No compensation (theoretical)	80	24	7.10
Acute respiratory acidosis			
($\uparrow [HCO_3]$: 1 mEq/L/10 mm Hg PCO_2)	80	28	7.16
Chronic respiratory acidosis			
($\uparrow [HCO_3]$: 3.5 mEq/L/10 mm Hg PCO_2)	80	38	7.30
Chronic respiratory acidosis plus metabolic alkalosis	80	48	7.40

thereby maintaining electroneutrality; however, the physiologic rise in plasma bicarbonate concentration falls short of correcting completely the acidosis. The finding of a normal pH in these circumstances must represent a metabolic alkalosis superimposed on a chronic respiratory acidosis. This chronic renal compensation is complete within 3 to 5 days and followed by a new and long-term steady state.

Natural History and Its Modification with Treatment

Acute respiratory acidosis is usually a transient problem; however, brain and myocardium are very sensitive to the accompanying hypoxemia and may suffer permanent damage in the absence of adequate treatment. The natural history of chronic respiratory acidosis depends on the underlying condition, the most common cause being chronic obstructive pulmonary disease associated with chronic bronchitis and pulmonary emphysema. In many of these patients, the pulmonary function continues to deteriorate slowly and inexorably.

Prevention

Careful monitoring of patients with chronic respiratory acidosis represents probably the best preventive treatment. Early recognition and treatment of potentially reversible aggravating factors (e.g., pulmonary infection or airway obstruction) should help to prevent the acute exacerbations and delay the progression toward severe respiratory acidosis. In patients with chronic obstructive pulmonary disease, superimposed pulmonary infections remain the most frequent cause of respiratory decompensation. Because cigarette smoking is a major factor in the progression of chronic bronchitis and pulmonary emphysema, patients with this condition must be advised and helped to stop smoking. These patients should also avoid narcotics or sedatives, drugs known to depress respiratory center and ventilation.

Cost Containment

The diagnosis of respiratory acidosis can be obtained inexpensively from standard laboratory procedures. The treatment of acute respiratory acidosis is quite costly as intensive care facilities are frequently required. For chronic respiratory acidosis, the most effective maneuvers to reduce the cost of treatment remain regular follow-up on an outpatient basis and strict adherence to treatment of the underlying pulmonary condition.

REFERENCES

Brackett NC Jr, Cohen JJ, Schwartz WB. Carbon dioxide titration curve of normal man: Effect of increasing degrees of acute hypercapnia on acid–base equilibrium. N Engl J Med 1965;272:6.

Gennari FJ. Respiratory acidosis and alkalosis. In: Narins RG, ed. Maxwell and Kleeman's clinical disorders of fluid and electrolyte metabolism. New York: McGraw-Hill, 1994:957.

Madias NE, Cohen JJ. Respiratory alkalosis and acidosis. In: Seldin DW, Giebisch G, eds. The kidney: Physiology and pathophysiology. New York: Raven Press, 1992:2837.

Rose BD. Respiratory acidosis. In: Clinical physiology of acid–base and electrolyte disorders. New York: McGraw-Hill, 1994:604.

Weinberger SE, Schwartzstein RM, Weiss JW. Hypercapnia. N Engl J Med 1989;321:1223.

Respiratory Alkalosis

André Gougoux, M.D., and Patrick Vinay, M.D.

DEFINITION

Respiratory alkalosis or primary hypocapnia refers to a decrease in carbon dioxide tension (PCO_2 of 30 mm Hg or less) in the body fluids that increases blood pH (alkalemia pH above 7.45) and results from alveolar hyperventilation; this definition does not include the secondary hyperventilation and hypocapnia induced by metabolic acidosis.

ETIOLOGY

Table 17–6–1 lists the most commonly encountered clinical situations that produce respiratory alkalosis. Many of the listed causes can be associated with both acute and chronic respiratory alkalosis; however, acute respiratory alkalosis occurs characteristically with anxiety, mechanical hyperventilation, and in the seriously ill patient hospitalized in the intensive care unit. On the other hand, chronic respiratory alkalosis is more frequently encountered in persons living at high altitudes, in patients with lung disease characterized by diffusion defects or ventilation–perfusion imbalance, and in patients with central nervous system diseases and hepatic failure.

CRITERIA FOR DIAGNOSIS

Suggestive

Even if acute respiratory alkalosis may be suggested by a clinically evident hyperventilation, this diagnosis should not rely only on physical examination except where the underlying condition is obvious (e.g., panic attack). For example, hyperventilation may also represent the respiratory compensation to metabolic acidosis.

Definitive

An increased arterial blood pH and a decreased PCO_2 are required to confirm the diagnosis of respiratory alkalosis. Both the clinical history and the magnitude of the compensatory decrease in plasma bicarbonate concentration are needed to obtain an accurate diagnosis. In acute respiratory alkalosis, plasma bicarbonate concentration is decreased by 2 mEq/L for every 10 mm Hg fall in PCO_2. In chronic respiratory alkalosis, plasma bicarbonate concentration decreases by 4 mEq/L for every 10 mm Hg reduction in arterial PCO_2; this compensation corrects more than half of the rise in arterial pH.

TABLE 17–6–1. CAUSES OF RESPIRATORY ALKALOSIS

Mechanical hyperventilation
Stimulation of respiratory center
  Anxiety–hyperventilation syndrome
  Central nervous system diseases (brain stem)
    Cerebrovascular accident
    Inflammation
    Tumor
    Trauma
  Hypoxia
    High altitude
    Pulmonary diseases
  Chemical
    Ammonia (in hepatic failure)
    Bacterial toxins (in Gram-negative septicemia)
    Ethanol
    Progesterone (in pregnancy)
    Salicylates

CLINICAL MANIFESTATIONS

Subjective

The patient with a mild or a chronic respiratory alkalosis is most often asymptomatic. When the respiratory alkalosis is symptomatic, it is often not possible to discriminate between the effects of respiratory alkalosis and those of the underlying condition associated with this acid–base disorder; however, acute respiratory alkalosis itself produces an intense cerebral vasoconstriction decreasing cerebral blood flow by more than 50%. Lightheadedness, impaired mental functions, and confusion may result from this decreased cerebral perfusion. Syncope can even be observed if the cerebral vasoconstriction is severe enough. Tetany or generalized seizures can also occur. In the anxiety–hyperventilation syndrome, the patient may present peripheral paresthesias in the form of circumoral numbness and tingling in fingers and toes.

Objective

Physical Examination

Tachypnea or hyperpnea may be a clue reflecting the presence of hyperventilation and hypocapnia; however, this may not be obvious in many patients with chronic respiratory alkalosis if their hyperventilation results from slight increases in both the rate and depth of respiration. Because severe respiratory alkalosis increases irritability of the central and peripheral nervous systems, seizures, positive Chvostek and Trousseau signs, and overt tetany can be observed. In the presence of underlying coronary artery disease, respiratory alkalosis lowers the threshold for the development of both supraventricular and ventricular arrhythmias.

Routine Laboratory Abnormalities

See Definition.

PLANS

Diagnostic

Differential Diagnosis

Hyperventilation can be primary in respiratory alkalosis or represent a physiologic adaptive response to metabolic acidosis. When blood pH is not measured, the hyperchloremic hypobicarbonatemia can be easily misinterpreted as normal anion gap metabolic acidosis.

Diagnostic Options

The plasma bicarbonate concentration is especially useful to distinguish between acute and chronic respiratory alkalosis and to identify the presence of additional acid–base disorders.

Recommended Approach

Acute Respiratory Alkalosis. As a fall in plasma bicarbonate of 2 mEq/L should occur for every 10 mm Hg fall in PCO_2, plasma bicarbonate concentration is normally around 20 mEq/L if the arterial PCO_2 is 20 mm Hg. Results significantly above or below this value indicate superimposed metabolic disorders. For example, a lower plasma bicarbonate represents a metabolic acidosis (lactic acidosis, renal failure, or salicylate intoxication) superimposed on the acute respiratory alkalosis.

Chronic Respiratory Alkalosis. Plasma bicarbonate concentration decreases by 4 mEq/L for each 10 mm Hg fall in arterial PCO_2. A plasma bicarbonate higher than the anticipated value is observed when the respiratory alkalosis is acute or when a metabolic alkalosis (usually induced by diuretics or loss of gastric fluid) is complicating the chronic hypocapnia. A lower plasma bicarbonate indicates the presence of a metabolic acidosis superimposed on the chronic respiratory alkalosis.

Finally, in many patients, respiratory alkalosis provides an important diagnostic clue for the detection of an unsuspected underlying disease such as Gram-negative septicemia, hepatic failure, and various diseases involving the central nervous system.

Therapeutic

Therapeutic Options

It is usually not necessary to treat a mild respiratory alkalosis, except for the specific treatment of the underlying disorder. By contrast, a more severe alkalosis requires an immediate correction to prevent the potentially dramatic consequences of cardiac arrhythmias, tetany, and seizures.

Recommended Approach

When the hypocapnia results from *mechanical hyperventilation,* a normal PCO_2 can be obtained immediately by decreasing respiratory frequency and/or tidal volume. If the patient triggers the respirator, some dead space should be added to the tubing. This is particularly important in intensive care units when alkalosis increases the incidence of arrhythmias in patients with underlying coronary disease.

In the presence of abnormal *stimulation of the respiratory center,* the only satisfactory maneuver is, whenever possible, removal or specific treatment of the underlying disorder (Table 17–6–1). For example, if hyperventilation results from hypoxia, oxygen administration will correct both the underlying hypoxia and the respiratory alkalosis. The respiratory alkalosis associated with central nervous system diseases can be improved only by treating the underlying disorder whenever possible. In patients with the anxiety–hyperventilation syndrome, the attack can be terminated by reassurance in the first place, cautious consideration of the need for sedation, and/or increase in the PCO_2 of the inspired air by rebreathing into a closed system such as a paper bag. In other clinical conditions, attempts to increase the carbon dioxide content of the inspired air are not useful.

FOLLOW-UP

No follow-up is necessary in patients with acute respiratory alkalosis once the underlying problem has been resolved. In patients with chronic respiratory alkalosis, the follow-up is dictated by the underlying condition.

DISCUSSION

Prevalence and Incidence

Respiratory alkalosis probably represents the most common acid–base disorder, ranging from the critically ill patients treated in intensive care units to the less severe form frequently observed in the office of a primary care physician. The anxiety-induced hyperventilation syndrome is not an uncommon presentation in the emergency room and is recurrent in some individuals.

Related Basic Science

Approximately 10 mmol of carbon dioxide per minute (or 15,000 mmol/d) is produced by the normal metabolism and excreted through the lungs. Even if hypocapnia could theoretically result from either decreased carbon dioxide production or increased carbon dioxide excretion, in clinical practice it is only seen associated with alveolar hyperventilation. When the removal of carbon dioxide exceeds its rate of production, the negative carbon dioxide balance decreases blood PCO_2. Respiratory alkalosis is partly corrected, acutely by the secondary physiologic decrease in plasma bicarbonate concentration produced by the acute titration of nonbicarbonate buffers and chronically by renal compensatory mechanisms.

Acute Respiratory Alkalosis. In the absence of any fall in plasma bicarbonate concentration when arterial PCO_2 is acutely halved from 40 to 20 mm Hg, arterial pH would increase from 7.40 to 7.70 (Table 17–6–2). The decreased acidity of the body fluids acutely titrates the blood and tissue protein buffers (including hemoglobin). The release of hydrogen ions from these nonbicarbonate buffers consumes enough bi-

TABLE 17–6–2. EFFECT OF RESPIRATORY ALKALOSIS ON ARTERIAL ACID–BASE PARAMETERS

	PCO_2	$[HCO_3]$	pH
Normal	40	24	7.40
No compensation (theoretical)	20	24	7.70
Acute respiratory alkalosis			
($\downarrow [HCO_3]$: 2 mEq/L/10 mm Hg PCO_2)	20	20	7.62
Chronic respiratory alkalosis			
($\downarrow [HCO_3]$: 4 mEq/L/10 mm Hg PCO_2)	20	16	7.52
Chronic respiratory alkalosis plus metabolic acidosis	20	12	7.40

carbonate to decrease its plasma concentration by 2 mEq/L for each 10 mm Hg acute fall in arterial PCO_2. This acute compensation, complete within 15 minutes, is followed by an equilibrium state for a period of several hours during which no further changes in plasma acid–base parameters are detected. In acute hypocapnia, a fall in plasma phosphate concentration (and to a smaller degree in plasma potassium) can be accounted for by a shift of phosphate and potassium from extracellular fluid into the cells.

Chronic Respiratory Alkalosis. A further fall in plasma bicarbonate concentration results from the renal loss of bicarbonate and the decreased urinary excretion of ammonium and titratable acid. The plasma bicarbonate concentration decreases by 4 mEq/L for every 10 mm Hg reduction in arterial PCO_2, this fall correcting more than half of the rise in blood pH (Table 17–6–2). This fall in plasma bicarbonate concentration is accompanied by a reciprocal rise in plasma chloride concentration induced by its increased renal reabsorption; however the physiologic fall in plasma bicarbonate concentration does not return blood pH completely to normal. The finding of a normal pH in these circumstances must represent a metabolic acidosis superimposed on a chronic respiratory alkalosis. This renal adaptation, complete within 3 to 5 days, is followed by a new and long-term steady state.

Natural History and Its Modification with Treatment

The natural history may range from a very short-lived and completely reversible disorder in acute respiratory alkalosis to a much more prolonged state when associated with a chronic condition. In chronic respiratory alkalosis, the underlying condition stimulating the respiratory center rather than the acid–base disorder itself determines the prognosis. The death rate correlates in part with the severity of the acute or chronic respiratory alkalosis, potentially lethal consequences on the cardiovascular and central nervous systems being encountered when the blood pH exceeds 7.60.

Prevention

The iatrogenic respiratory alkalosis resulting from mechanical hyperventilation can be prevented by adjusting correctly the respiratory frequency and the tidal volume. This is particularly important if one considers that respiratory alkalosis remains the most common acid–base disorder observed in intensive care units. In the anxiety–hyperventilation syndrome, patient education and psychological counseling remain the best means of preventing recurrences; however, many disorders underlying respiratory alkalosis cannot be easily prevented.

Cost Containment

The diagnosis of respiratory alkalosis is obtained inexpensively from usual laboratory determinations. The cost of treatment is determined by the cause of respiratory alkalosis and can vary from the cost-free rebreathing into a paper bag in the anxiety–hyperventilation syndrome to the very expensive treatment of the seriously ill patient requiring intensive care facilities.

REFERENCES

Arbus GS, Hebert LA, Levesque PR, et al. Characterization and clinical application of the "significance band" for acute respiratory alkalosis. N Engl J Med 1969;280:117.

Gennari FJ. Respiratory acidosis and alkalosis. In: Narins RG, ed. Maxwell and Kleeman's clinical disorders of fluid and electrolyte metabolism. New York: McGraw-Hill, 1994:957.

Krapf R, Beeler I, Hertner D, et al. Chronic respiratory alkalosis: The effect of sustained hyperventilation on renal regulation of acid–base equilibrium. N Engl J Med 1991;324:1394.

Madias NE, Cohen JJ. Respiratory alkalosis and acidosis. In: Seldin DW, Giebisch G, eds. The kidney: Physiology and pathophysiology. New York: Raven Press, 1992:2837.

Rose BD. Respiratory alkalosis. In: Clinical physiology of acid–base and electrolyte disorders. New York: McGraw-Hill, 1994:629.

CHAPTER 17–7

Hypokalemia

Vera Delaney, M.D., Ph.D., and Harry G. Preuss, M.D.

DEFINITION

Hypokalemia is present when the serum potassium is less than 3.5 mEq/L (normal range, 3.5–5.0 mEq/L).

ETIOLOGY

Hypokalemia may be due to a redistribution in potassium from the extracellular to the intracellular compartment with no change in overall body potassium content. Causes of such shifts include alkalosis, hyperinsulinemia, and β_2-adrenergic stimulators. In the absence of such factors, the serum level roughly parallels changes in body potassium, each milliequivalent per liter decrement approximating a loss of 200 to 300 mEq. The most common clinical setting for potassium depletion accompanied by hypokalemia in the United States today is the elderly patient, usually female, on diuretics and/or laxatives with excess losses in the urine and/or stool.

CRITERIA FOR DIAGNOSIS

Suggestive

Symptoms associated with hypokalemia are nonspecific and thus of little diagnostic help.

Definitive

The definitive diagnosis of hypokalemia is made from laboratory screening. A serum level less than 3.5 mEq/L is diagnostic.

CLINICAL MANIFESTATIONS

Subjective

The symptoms, if any, are usually mild and nonspecific. Neuromuscular symptoms include weakness, particularly of proximal muscles, which in severe cases progresses to flaccid paralysis. Paresthesias, constipation, gastric atony, and, occasionally, tetany are also observed.

A detailed history is essential in the elucidation of possible causes. Iatrogenic causes are common in the United States. Diuretics, even the "potassium-sparing diuretics" such as dyazide and aldactazide, are at the top of the list. The use, and abuse, of diuretics in premenstrual women seeking weight control is often surreptitious. The same holds true for laxative abuse. Chronic diarrheal states, for example, ulcerative colitis and Crohn's disease, are apparent from the history. Less common causes of intestinal potassium loss include villus papilloma of the rectum and vasoactive intestinal polypeptide-producing tumors. Chronic vomiting may also be surreptitious (bulimia), and may require detailed and subtle history taking together with an index of suspicion. Other drugs that cause renal hypokalemia include the chemotherapeutic agents containing platinum (*cis*-platinum [Platinol], carboplatinum [Paraplatin]) and streptozocin (Zanosar), and antibiotics, particularly carbenicillin (Geopen) and amphotericin B (Fungizone). Redistribution hypokalemia follows use of the β_2-stimulating group of bronchodilators (e.g., albuterol, terbutaline), exposure to pesticides containing barium, and recent treatment of megaloblastic anemia with vitamin B_{12} or

folic acid, which may induce a transient, but often severe, fall in serum potassium.

Family history is important, particularly in the younger age groups, as such potassium-wasting nephropathies as Bartter's syndrome, Gittleman's syndrome, Liddle's syndrome, and renal tubular acidosis are autosomal recessive conditions. Periodic paralysis, caused by sudden intracellular shifts of potassium, is autosomal dominant.

Objective

Physical Examination

Signs of hypokalemia may be absent or consist of mild proximal muscle weakness with normal tendon reflexes and/or abdominal distention due to gastric atony or paralytic ileus.

Routine Laboratory Abnormalities

Routine laboratory abnormalities include electrocardiographic changes, which provide an insensitive indicator of potassium depletion. These include flat or inverted T waves, prominent U waves, depressed ST segments, and an increased incidence of supraventricular and/or ventricular ectopy. The last parallels to some extent the degree of potassium depletion. Hypokalemia sensitizes the myocardium to digitalis, predisposing to life-threatening arrhythmias at normal or even low plasma digoxin levels. The most frequent biochemical abnormality found in association with hypokalemia is metabolic alkalosis, reflecting, to some extent, the interchangeable roles of the cations hydrogen and potassium within the cell.

PLANS

Diagnostic

A single blood test gives the diagnosis of hypokalemia and its severity. Whether it represents a true potassium deficit or merely reflects transcellular shifts is based on clinical information, as measurement of total body potassium is not readily available.

Differential Diagnosis

The most common factors that promote potassium entry into cells include alkalosis or correction of acidosis (0.6 mEq/L drop in serum potassium for each 0.1-unit rise in extracellular pH); insulin, with or without glucose; and β_2 stimulators. Hypokalemia in these settings requires repeated monitoring, judicious potassium supplementation, but no further diagnostic workup.

The most common cause of hypokalemia and total body potassium depletion is diuretic use. Hypokalemia in the setting of hypertension is due mostly to diuretics or, occasionally, to primary hyperaldosteronism or renovascular hypertension. Diuretics are a particularly common cause of hypokalemia in the elderly, especially women whose dietary intake of potassium is frequently low. It may be assumed to be the cause if normokalemia was documented prior to initiation of diuretic therapy. Normalization of serum potassium following temporary cessation of diuretic therapy in this instance is diagnostic. Diarrheal states, as a result of either laxative use or underlying disease, should be documented and the degree of potassium wasting quantitated if possible.

Subsequent measures should be directed to decreasing potassium loss via this route prior to engaging on further workup.

Diagnostic Options

The small subgroup of patients in whom redistribution hypokalemia has been excluded and whose hypokalemia is persistent and unexplained after consideration of the above common possibilities needs further evaluation (see Recommended Approach).

Recommended Approach

The approach is outlined in Figure 17–7–1. The best screening test is the urinary potassium concentration. If a spot urinary test contains less than 20 mEq/L when the patient is hypokalemic, either inadequate dietary intake, malabsorption from the gastrointestinal tract, or excessive losses in the stool are causative.

If, however, a spot urinary potassium level exceeds 20 mEq/L, further subdivision based on plasma bicarbonate and systemic pH is helpful. Renal wasting with acidosis is due to either renal tubular acidosis (proximal or distal), diabetic ketoacidosis, or the therapeutic agents acetazolamide (Diamox) and amphotericin B.

When a urinary potassium level of more than 20 mEq/L coexists with alkalosis, urinary chloride is helpful. A low urinary chloride level (< 10 mEq/L) in this setting indicates either vomiting or gastric drainage, chronic diuretic use (last dose 2 or 3 days previously), or posthypercapnia losses. The last situation is observed when chronically hypercapnic patients are artificially ventilated with a sudden decrease in the partial pressure of carbon dioxide but maintenance of their previ-

ously acquired, high plasma bicarbonate level due to inadequate chloride replacement often coupled with concurrent diuretic-induced chloride depletion.

When hypokalemic metabolic alkalosis coexists with a high urinary chloride level, further subdivision should be based on blood pressure. Those with normal or low blood pressure are commonly diuretic users or, very rarely, have Bartter's syndrome. Those with high blood pressures who are not on diuretics need further analysis on the basis of the renin–aldosterone axis (Figure 17–7–1). These assays are expensive and need to be carried out under strictly defined conditions, as sodium intake, posture, time of day, and a variety of drugs can render interpretation useless. For further workup of these subgroups of hypertensive patients, see Chapters 14–1 through 14–9.

Therapeutic

Therapeutic Options

The treatment of hypokalemia associated with the use of drugs, including diuretics, laxatives, antibiotics, chemotherapeutic agents, and β_2 stimulators, ideally requires their cessation, reduction in dosage, or substitution. This is not always feasible. Potassium replacement should be judicious as hypokalemia may be transient. Irrespective of the cause, established hypokalemia with depletion of body stores requires potassium replacement and a decision regarding the type of potassium preparation, the route of replacement, and the quantity and speed of administration.

Ingestion of potassium-rich foods (dairy products, meats, fish, grains, potatoes and other vegetables, citrus fruits) is the most palatable

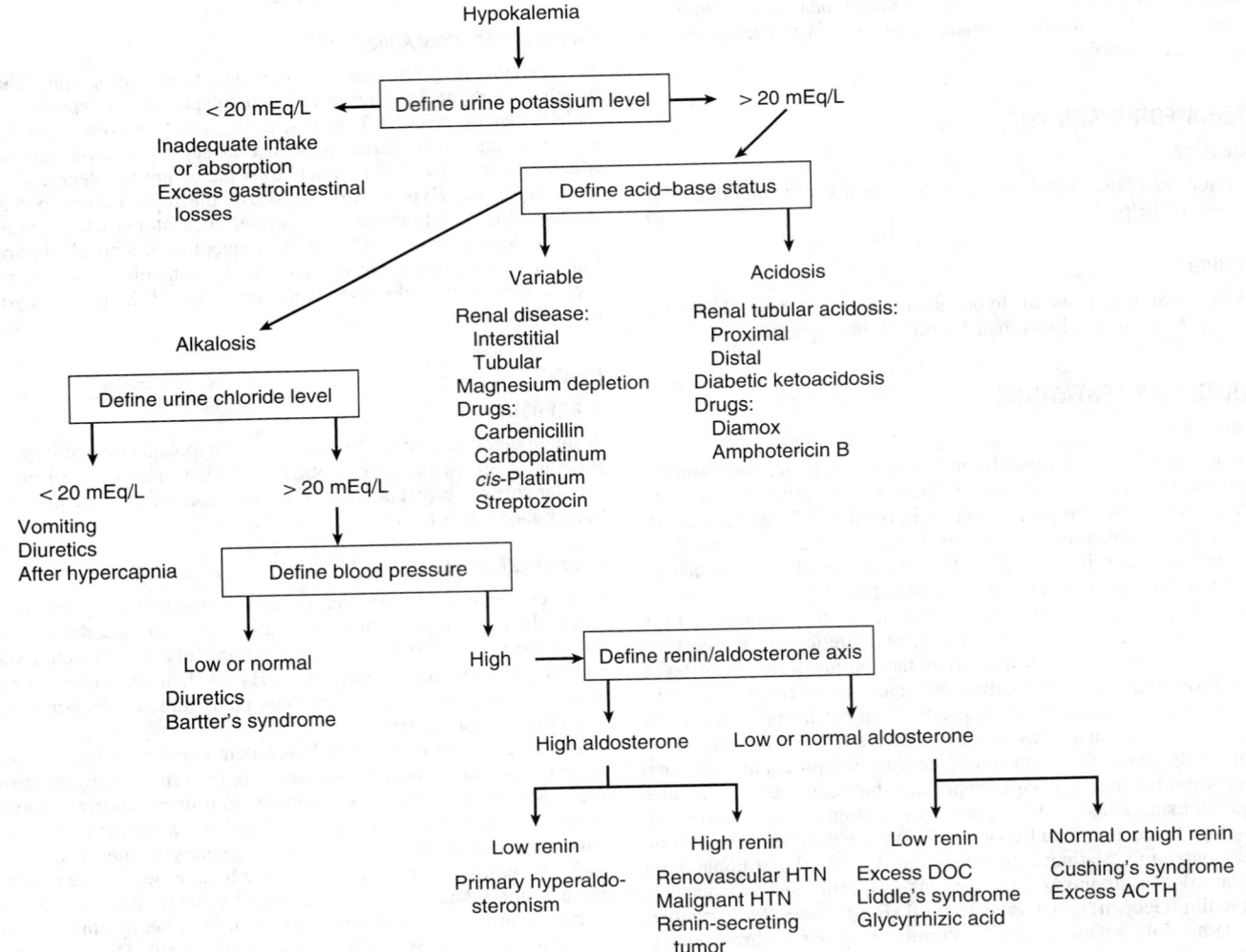

Figure 17–7–1. Workup of patients with unexplained persistent hypokalemia. HTN, hypertension; DOC, deoxycorticosterone; ACTH, adrenocorticotropic hormone.

method of increasing intake. Salt substitutes contain potassium chloride in high concentration (50 mEq per teaspoon) and are palatable and inexpensive. An array of pharmaceutical potassium preparations are available (Table 17–7–1). In general, liquid or powdered forms are more reliably absorbed than tablets, but are unpalatable, leading to poor compliance.

Patients with metabolic alkalosis who are chloride as well as potassium depleted require potassium chloride for effective correction of the potassium deficit. When metabolic acidosis coexists with potassium depletion, potassium bicarbonate or its metabolic precursors—gluconate, acetate, or citrate—are preferable. The hospitalized diabetic or alcoholic patient is often phosphate as well as potassium deficient. Thus, potassium phosphate may be the most rational form of supplementation. When the etiology of potassium depletion is unclear, potassium chloride is the best choice.

Replacement should be by the oral route if possible. Exceptions that may require intravenous administration include severe symptomatic potassium depletion with paralysis, arrhythmias, and/or an inability to tolerate oral supplements.

Because serum potassium is not a reliable indicator of body potassium stores and because the total extracellular content is only 65 mEq or 2% of total body stores, it is obvious that repeated serum monitoring is necessary as a guide to replacement therapy, particularly, in patients with renal insufficiency. Initial doses of 40 to 120 mEq/d, depending on the severity of the hypokalemia, generally suffice. Maintenance therapy is also variable but usually requires 20 to 60 mEq in divided doses per day. Intravenous fluids should not contain more than 40 mEq/L and potassium supplements should not, in general, be infused at a rate greater than 10 mEq/h. If more rapid administration is necessary, electrocardiographic monitoring in the setting of the intensive care unit is desirable. Parenteral potassium should be given in saline, not dextrose, because the latter stimulates insulin release, which may aggravate the hypokalemia by promoting intracellular shifts.

Recommended Approach

Dietary advice is particularly relevant to elderly patients who, in general, consume a low-potassium diet even when potassium-rich foods are available. Bananas (15 mEq each), instant tea (10 mEq/teaspoon), milk (14 mEq/cup), orange juice (14 mEq/glass), and salt substitutes (50 mEq/teaspoon) are palatable, cheap, and readily available in the United States. In hypertensive patients, cessation of diuretic therapy with substitution by another antihypertensive medication may be indicated until normokalemia is restored. Potassium supplementation with the liquid or powdered preparations is preferable in the acute setting, with a switch to the tablet form on a long-term basis. The microen-

capsulated preparation K-Dur comes in two concentrations and is, in general, free of gastrointestinal side effects. Sodium restriction in combination with potassium supplements is required in primary hyperaldosteronism. Alternatively, high doses of the aldosterone antagonist spironolactone (Aldactone) can be employed. Converting enzyme inhibitors, rather than diuretics, may be more appropriate and effective in the treatment of renovascular hypertension. Fluid retention, in association with cirrhosis, is best managed by sodium retention and institution of spironolactone as sole diuretic therapy.

FOLLOW-UP

Serial measurements of serum potassium are mandatory, as symptoms do not provide a reliable indicator of potassium depletion. A nadir of serum and whole-body potassium levels occurs approximately 4 weeks following institution of diuretic therapy. Thus, it is appropriate to repeat serum potassium determination after this interval and at approximately 6-month intervals once the patient is stable on diuretics, with or without potassium supplements. More frequent monitoring is necessary in the presence of heart failure, cirrhosis, and renal insufficiency. Importantly, addition of drugs known to decrease potassium excretion (see Chapter 17–8) warrant more frequent monitoring of serum potassium to avoid overshoot with iatrogenic hyperkalemia.

Patients in the intensive care setting who have hypokalemia requiring parenteral potassium replacement may need laboratory monitoring on a 4- to 8-hour basis, particularly if cardiac instability is a problem. Management of diabetic ketoacidosis may require large amounts of potassium supplements despite the frequently observed hyperkalemia at entry. Repeated monitoring may also be necessary in this situation.

DISCUSSION

Prevalence and Incidence

The prevalence of hypokalemia in the general population is unknown but appears to increase with age. Diuretic-induced hypokalemia is the most frequent cause, occurring in 20% of users. As more than 100 million prescriptions are issued for these medications on an annual basis within the United States, the incidence of potassium depletion and hypokalemia is probably quite high.

Related Basic Science

Potassium is predominantly an intracellular cation with a concentration of 150 mEq/L of cell water compared with 3.5 mEq/L of extracellular fluid. One of the most important physiologic functions of potassium is its effect on the generation and maintenance of the transmembrane electrical potential, alterations of which exert profound effects on cardiac and skeletal muscle. The electrical charge across the cell membrane is about 90 mV, with the interior of the cell negative to the exterior when the ratio of intracellular potassium to extracellular potassium is 30:1. The intracellular potassium is kept high and the intracellular sodium low by membrane-bound sodium–potassium ATPase, which pumps three sodium ions out of the cell in exchange for two potassium ions. It is the combination of this sodium pump carrying net positive charge out of the cell, the presence of nondiffusible complex multivalent anions within the cell, and the tendency for potassium to move down its concentration gradient that is responsible for the negative electrical potential within the cell interior. Potassium efflux is regulated by potassium channels. There is a relatively tight, although not understood, relationship between the activity of the ubiquitous sodium–potassium ATPase and the conductance of potassium through its channels. Thus, an increase in sodium–potassium ATPase is associated with an increase in potassium permeability, facilitating maintenance of physiologic intracellular concentrations.

Potassium homeostasis is maintained by two distinct mechanisms. The first keeps potassium in balance by matching potassium excretion with intake. The kidney is crucial to the former, conserving potassium when dietary intake is restricted, yet capable of excreting 1000 mEq per 24 hours when maximally adapted to a very high intake. Potassium conservation is slow and relatively inefficient as manifested by a total body deficit of approximately 250 mEq prior to achieving the minimum uri-

TABLE 17–7–1. SOME COMMONLY USED POTASSIUM SUPPLEMENTS AND THEIR COMPARATIVE WHOLESALE COSTS

Preparation	Ingredient	Wholesale Cost of 40 mEq (Cents)
Liquids		
Kaon-Cl	Potassium chloride	35
Kay Ciel Elixir	Potassium chloride, potassium gluconate	71
Kolyum	Potassium acetate, potassium citrate	70
Polycitra-K	Potassium citrate	65
Powders		
K-Lor	Potassium chloride	62
K-Lyte Cl	Potassium chloride	42
Kolyum	Potassium chloride, potassium gluconate	85
Neutraphos	Sodium, potassium, phosphate	51
Neutraphos K	Potassium, phosphate	30
Salt substitutes	Potassium chloride	4
Tablets		
Slow-K	Potassium chloride	65
Micro-K	Potassium chloride	60
Klotrix	Potassium chloride	60
K-Lyte	Potassium citrate, bicarbonate	80
K-Dur	Potassium chloride	70

nary potassium excretion of 15 to 20 mEq/24 h. Intestinal adaptation also occurs, particularly in renal failure and other potassium-retaining states, where an increase in stool potassium to 10 to 30% of daily intake may occur. Maximum adaptation is a slow process, taking 10 to 14 days, and requires aldosterone. The second homeostatic mechanism is rapid, occurring within minutes of a potassium load, and involves processes that shift potassium from the extracellular to the intracellular compartment, thus obviating repeated episodes of life-threatening hyperkalemia.

The renal handling of potassium involves reabsorption in the proximal nephron and ascending limb of the loop of Henle so that the filtrate reaching the distal tubule is extremely low in potassium. Urinary potassium is derived from a secretory process by the principal cells of the cortical collecting duct down electrochemical and concentration gradients. Factors that enhance secretion include increased intracellular potassium, increased sodium delivery to the distal secretory sites, increased tubular flow rate, increased delivery of nonreabsorbable anions (e.g., bicarbonate, sulfate, carbenicillin [Geopen]), and hyperaldosteronism. The renal response to a reduction in potassium intake involves decreased potassium secretion by the principal cells of the cortical collecting duct, consequent on reduced aldosterone levels. This occurs within 24 hours. A later response, less well understood, is aldosterone independent, takes place in the medullary collecting duct, and involves passive and, perhaps, active potassium reabsorption.

The potassium–aldosterone feedback loop is an important regulator of potassium balance. Intake of potassium raises the serum level, which, in turn, stimulates the adrenal cortex to synthesize and secrete aldosterone. The opposite holds true for decreased potassium intake. Aldosterone has two main effects on the principal cell of the cortical collecting tubule. The earliest result is an enhanced sodium permeability brought about by increasing the number of activated sodium channels in the luminal membrane, which, because of a coupling process, increases the activity of basolateral sodium–potassium ATPase. The latter results in a slight increase in intracellular potassium, which, in turn, favors urinary potassium secretion through luminal potassium channels down a favorable concentration gradient. A later (24–48 hours) effect of chronic hyperaldosteronism is an increase in the total number of sodium–potassium ATPase pumps, particularly striking within the basolateral membrane of the principal cells of the cortical collecting ducts, further enhancing urinary potassium excretion.

Insulin is important in potassium homeostasis. It lowers serum potassium in a dose-related manner, independent of glucose uptake, by stimulating sodium–potassium ATPase in skeletal muscle, liver, adipocytes, and other cells, thus promoting potassium movement into cells. This potassium-lowering effect is preserved in renal failure. Furthermore, hyperkalemia directly stimulates insulin release in vitro, suggesting a feedback control mechanism.

Catecholamines are also important in the disposal of excess potassium loads, an effect that appears to be mediated by the β_2-receptor subtypes. Epinephrine, in physiologic doses, enhances disposal of an intravenous potassium load and may be important in the modulation of exercise-induced efflux from skeletal muscles following exhaustive exercise. By the same mechanism, β_2 agonists are useful in lowering serum potassium. The mechanism involves activation of sodium–potassium ATPase through stimulation of adenyl cyclase. The alpha-adrenergic system, specifically alpha agonists, have the opposite effect, causing potassium to shift from the intracellular to the extracellular compartment. For this reason the alpha blocker prazosin may modulate the potassium-lowering effect of albuterol and other beta agonists.

The mechanism underlying the intracellular shift in familial hypokalemic paralysis is unknown. A sporadic form of this syndrome occurs in Asians in association with hyperthyroidism and appears to involve a hypersensitivity of beta-adrenergic receptors to circulating catecholamines, since it is reversed by propanolol. Barium poisoning blocks potassium channels and efflux from cells while influx continues normally.

Intracellular shifts of potassium occur in alkalemia, and independent of pH, an increase in serum bicarbonate concentration decreases serum potassium.

Diarrheal losses are an important cause of hypokalemia in less developed parts of the world due to a variety of enteric parasitic infections. They are usually accompanied by hyperchloremic metabolic acidosis.

The latter is due to concurrent stool bicarbonate loss. Diarrheal losses are usually less than 100 mEq/d because the potassium concentration of the stool appears to vary inversely with volume. Villous adenoma of the rectum and vasoactive intestinal peptide-secreting tumors are exceptions, capable of secreting large volumes of high-potassium fluid. Laxative abuse results in excessive fecal losses of potassium without concurrent losses of bicarbonate. Thus, normal acid–base status is usually preserved. Patients with ureterosigmoidostomies develop potassium depletion accompanied by hyperchloremic metabolic acidosis, consequent on reabsorption of ammonium chloride by the colon and ileum and secretion of potassium bicarbonate.

Vomiting, despite negligible amounts of potassium (6 mEq/L) in emesis, can cause profound potassium depletion. This is due to urinary losses secondary to volume contraction, hyperaldosteronism, and metabolic alkalosis due, in turn, to losses of large amounts of hydrochloric acid in the vomitus, with some contribution from poor intake.

Increased secretion of mineralocorticoid hormones causes potassium depletion only when it is accompanied by adequate distal delivery of sodium. A primary increase in mineralocorticoid production due to either endogenous production or exogenous administration produces hypokalemic metabolic alkalosis in association with hypertension. The severity of the former increases with increased sodium intake and decreases with a reduction in sodium intake. The diagnosis rests on finding increased levels of mineralocorticoids in association with suppressed plasma renin activity; however, because of the suppressive effect of hypokalemia per se on aldosterone production, levels of aldosterone may not be above the normal range.

Secondary hyperaldosteronism in association with hypertension also causes potassium depletion. Renal vascular hypertension and malignant hypertension are examples. Secondary aldosteronism due to decreased effective extracellular volume (e.g., congestive heart failure, active ascites formation) leads to increased proximal sodium reabsorption with reduction in delivery to the distal nephron and, thus, does not cause potassium depletion. If distal delivery of sodium is increased, however, through the use of diuretics or failure to adhere to a low-sodium diet, hypokalemia, often severe, may occur.

Potassium depletion is often a prominent component of distal renal tubular acidosis (type I). Its clinical manifestations, namely, weakness and flaccid paralysis, may be the presenting features of this disorder. In this situation renal potassium wasting is due to a combination of effects. Chronic acidosis decreases proximal sodium reabsorption with increased sodium delivery to distal potassium secretory sites, secondary hyperaldosteronism consequent on relative volume depletion, and accentuation of potassium secretion by the defect in proton transport in the distal nephron. Hypokalemia is usually less of a problem in untreated proximal tubular acidosis (type II). The latter is due to a defect in bicarbonate transport in the proximal tubule and needs large quantities of sodium bicarbonate for correction of the acidosis. It is the need for the latter therapy that results in hypokalemia, with the ensuing high rates of delivery of sodium bicarbonate favoring increased urinary potassium secretion at the distal nephron.

Bartter's syndrome is a familial potassium-losing nephropathy. The primary defect is not yet resolved but normal or low blood pressure, hypokalemic metabolic alkalosis, renal potassium and chloride wasting, hyperreninemia, hyperaldosteronism, and increased prostaglandin production are characteristic. Hypokalemia may be severe and difficult to manage. Potassium supplementation with potassium chloride, prostaglandin synthetase inhibitors, potassium-sparing diuretics, and converting enzyme inhibitors have each been tried with only modest, and often transient, improvement in the degree of hypokalemia.

Liddle's syndrome is a rare familial disorder characterized by hypertension, suppressed renin and aldosterone secretion, and hypokalemic metabolic alkalosis. The precise defect is unknown. Increased sensitivity to aldosterone does not appear to be etiopathogenic, as spironolactone does not lead to improvement. Instead, reduction in sodium intake and administration of triamterene or amiloride are effective at reducing renal potassium wasting.

Hypokalemia and potassium depletion can rarely result from ingestion of imported licorice or tobacco, both of which may contain glycyrrhizic acid, which has mineralocorticoid potentiating effects.

Two clinically important consequences of potassium depletion deserve mention. First, there may be increased susceptibility to rhabdomyolysis, which may be masked as the original cause due to efflux of potassium and which may contribute occasionally to acute myoglobinuric renal failure. Second, deterioration of mental status may occur in patients with hepatic cirrhosis due to increased blood ammonia consequent on hypokalemic stimulation of renal glutaminase activity.

Natural History and Its Modification with Treatment

Some patients with lifelong hypokalemia due, for example, to Bartter's syndrome may remain asymptomatic, and are detected on routine screening. Their life span does not appear to be shortened. Diuretic-induced hypokalemia is associated with increased ventricular and supraventricular ectopy, the significance of which remains controversial. An increased incidence of cerebrovascular events, exacerbation of hypertension, and renal dysfunction have been postulated to result from chronic potassium deficiency. Patients on digitalis who become hypokalemic run a risk of life-threatening arrhythmias and sudden death.

Prevention

Because diuretics are the most common cause of hypokalemia in the United States today, identification of the subgroups most at risk for this complication may aid prevention. Elderly women, particularly if edematous, on long-acting thiazides or loop diuretics are at increased risk. In this subgroup, a low-sodium, high-potassium diet, lower doses of shorter-acting diuretics, and addition or substitution, if necessary, of an alternate antihypertensive agent may diminish the problem. Premenstrual women taking diuretics for fluctuations of weight are at high risk for severe hypokalemia. Strict adherence to a low-sodium, low-carbohydrate diet often results in a spontaneous diuresis 10 to 14 days later as a form of escape phenomenon; however, up to 12 kg may be gained in the interval off diuretics, making compliance poor. Patients with cirrhosis who have ascites are at risk for the development of hypokalemia due to associated secondary hyperaldosteronism. Spironolactone in this subgroup may promote a diuresis and prevent hypokalemia. Patients on

diuretics and digitalis with normal renal function should receive prophylactic potassium supplements. The hypokalemia of primary hyperaldosteronism may be prevented by a low-salt diet in conjunction with spironolactone.

Surreptitious laxative abuse is a more common cause of hypokalemia than is generally recognized, particularly in women preoccupied by weight gain. Recognition of this behavior may aid prevention by encouraging the patient to seek counseling.

Cost Containment

The causes of hypokalemia are readily apparent in most patients and do not require further workup. Only patients with persistent, severe, unexplained hypokalemia off diuretics and laxatives require further investigation (Figure 17–7–1).

Potassium supplements (Table 17–7–1) are relatively expensive ($10 to $24 per month: 40 mEq per day). Salt substitutes which contain potassium chloride are cheaper and more palatable.

REFERENCES

Bigger JT. Diuretic therapy, hypertension and cardiac arrest. N Engl J Med 1994;330:1899.

Bourke E, Delaney V. Prevention of hypokalemia caused by diuretics. Heart Dis Stroke 1994;3:63.

Carroll HJ, Oh MS. Disorders of potassium metabolism. In: Carroll HJ, Oh MS, eds. Water, electrolyte and acid–base metabolism. 2nd ed. Philadelphia: Lippincott, 1989:167.

Field MJ, Giebisch GJ. Hormonal control of renal potassium excretion. Kidney Int 1985;27:379.

Knochel JP. Etiologies and management of potassium deficiency. Hosp Pract 1987;22:153.

Tannen RL. Hypo–hyperkalemia. In: Cameron S, Davison AM, Grunfeld J-P, et al., eds, Oxford textbook of clinical nephrology. New York: Oxford University Press, 1992;2:895.

CHAPTER 17–8

Hyperkalemia

Vera Delaney, M.D., Ph.D., and Harry G. Preuss, M.D.

DEFINITION

Hyperkalemia is defined as a serum potassium concentration greater than 5.0 mEq/L.

ETIOLOGY

When hyperkalemia is identified it is important to differentiate between pseudohyperkalemia, hyperkalemia due to a redistribution phenomenon, and an increase in total body potassium. Pseudohyperkalemia is usually due to in vitro breakdown of cells, erythrocytes or either leukocytes or platelets when present in marked excess. Hyperkalemia due to redistribution of potassium from the potassium-rich intracellular fluid (150 mEq/L) to the potassium-poor extracellular fluid (3.5 to 5.0 mEq/L) is most commonly due to acidemia or insulin deficiency. Potassium overload is frequently iatrogenic due to various combinations of oral potassium supplements and drugs that impair potassium excretion. Otherwise it is due to a renal tubular potassium secretory defect, hypofunction of the renin–aldosterone axis, or advanced renal insufficiency (Figure 17–8–1).

CRITERIA FOR DIAGNOSIS
Suggestive

The symptoms are generally too nonspecific to be of value as a diagnostic lead. Characteristic electrocardiographic changes (see Clinical

Manifestations) are strongly suggestive and aid in the exclusion of pseudohyperkalemia.

Definitive

The finding of a plasma potassium concentration greater than 5 mEq/L, in the absence of hemolysis, confirms the diagnosis of hyperkalemia. It is considered a medical emergency when it exceeds 6.5 mEq/L and pseudohyperkalemia is excluded.

CLINICAL MANIFESTATIONS
Subjective

The symptoms of hyperkalemia are predominantly neuromuscular and cardiac, the latter being a more serious threat to life. Neuromuscular symptoms include muscle weakness, particularly of the lower extremities, characteristically described by the patient as a heavy feeling in the legs. Rarely it progresses to flaccid paralysis. Cardiotoxicity, however, usually precedes these manifestations.

Past history may give clues as to the cause of hyperkalemia because its incidence is increased in patients with a history of renal disease, diabetes mellitus, recent difficulty in voiding, or intake of potassium supplements and/or drugs that decrease renal potassium excretion, such as prostaglandin synthetase inhibitors (nonsteroidal antiinflammatory agents), converting enzyme inhibitors, potassium-sparing diuretics,

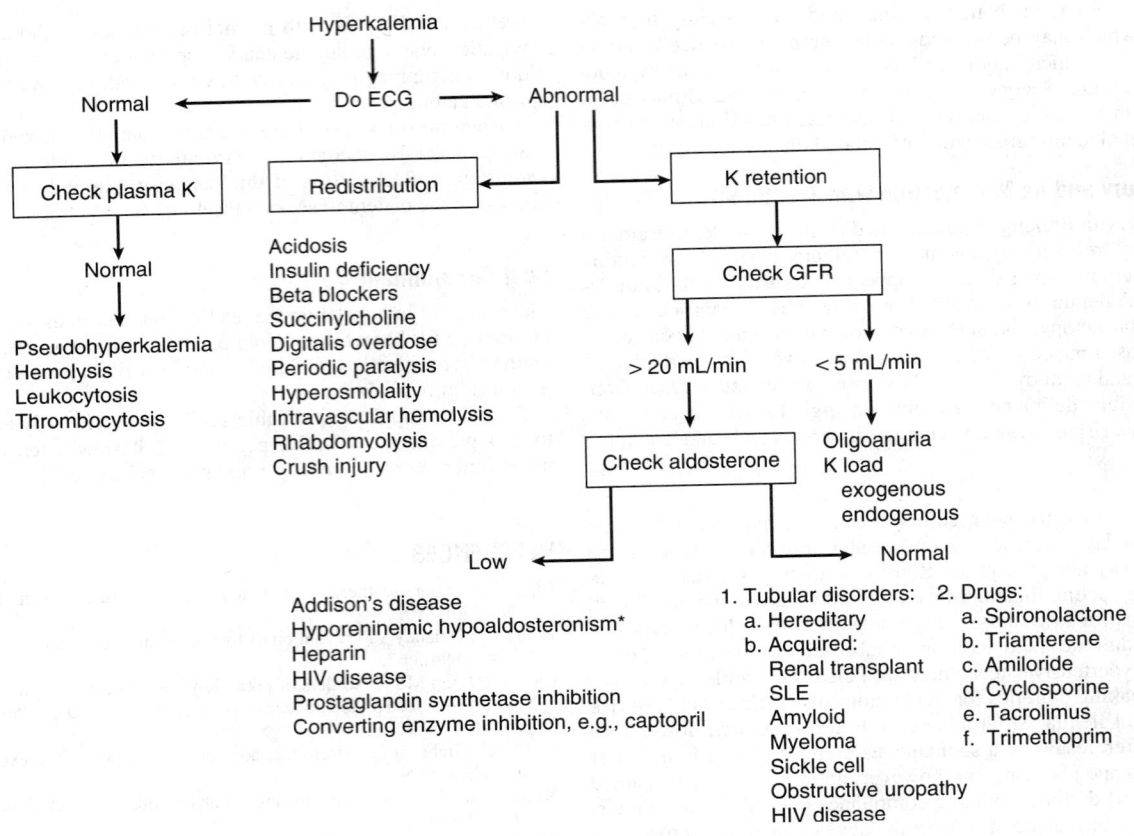

Figure 17–8–1. Scheme for the diagnostic workup of patients with hyperkalemia. *Often in association with diabetes mellitus and/or nephrosclerosis. SLE, systemic lupus erythematosus; ECG, electrocardiogram; GFR, glomerular filtration rate.

pentamidine or trimethoprim in large doses, and the immunosuppressants cyclosporine and tacrolimus. Very rarely a family history of profound, intermittent muscular weakness suggests familial hyperkalemic periodic paralysis, whereas hyperkalemia dating from childhood may suggest a congenital defect in mineralocorticoid synthesis.

Objective

Physical Examination

Detectable muscle weakness with normal tendon reflexes may be present, but is a nonspecific finding. By far the most important clinical manifestation of hyperkalemia is its effect on cardiac conduction, with its potential for cardiac arrest.

Routine Laboratory Abnormalities

Electrocardiographic changes are critical in assessing cardiotoxicity and correlate roughly with the severity of hyperkalemia. The first changes are peaking of the T waves and prolongation of the QT interval, occurring when the serum potassium concentration is about 6.0 mEq/L. Flattening of P waves, prolongation of the PR interval, and widening of the QRS complex with the development of a deep S wave occur at higher levels. As the serum potassium exceeds 8 mEq/L, a sine wave pattern develops and ventricular fibrillation follows.

PLANS

Diagnostic

Differential Diagnosis

Before initiating a workup of hyperkalemia, an electrocardiogram should be performed. If it is normal, this suggests pseudohyperkalemia, which can be confirmed by finding a normal plasma potassium concentration despite a high serum level. No further workup is necessary in

this instance. If the electrocardiogram shows changes compatible with hyperkalemia, then either redistribution or overload is causative. Acidosis, insulin deficiency, intravascular hemolysis or rhabdomyolysis, hyperosmolality, strenuous exercise in patients taking nonselective beta blockers, succinylcholine, massive digitalis overdose, and periodic paralysis of the hyperkalemic variety are causes of the former. Potassium overload is always due to a malfunctioning kidney, either intrinsic or related to drugs or hormones that act on the kidney. Thus, further subdivision may be based on the glomerular filtration rate. Oligoanuria or a glomerular filtration rate less than 5 mL/min when dietary intake is normal (approximately 1 mEq/kg/d) leads to potassium retention. This is often aggravated by excessive intake in the form of intravenous or oral potassium supplements, salt substitutes, blood transfusions (40 mEq/L), or increased endogenous production, such as hemolysis, tissue necrosis, gastrointestinal bleeding, and hypercatabolism. The capacity of the kidney and extrarenal sites to adapt to increased potassium loads is so great that if hyperkalemia occurs with a glomerular filtration rate in excess of 15 mL/min, aldosterone deficiency, an intrinsic renal tubular secretory defect, or iatrogenic causes should be sought. The finding of a low plasma aldosterone concentration when the patient is nonedematous, on a low-sodium diet, and off interfering drugs (e.g., spironolactone [Aldactone], converting enzyme inhibitors, or prostaglandin synthetase inhibitors [nonsteroidal antiinflammatory drugs]) will establish the latter diagnosis. Causes of a low aldosterone concentration include Addison's disease, congenital enzymatic defects of aldosterone production, HIV infection, prostaglandin synthetase inhibitors, converting enzyme inhibitors, heparin, and hyporeninemic hypoaldosteronism. The last is found commonly in association with diabetes mellitus and nephrosclerosis. Causes of a potassium renal tubular secretory defect include hereditary tubular defects, such as Gordon's syndrome, and acquired, usually interstitial, diseases such as occasionally observed in obstructive uropathy, sickle cell nephropathy, systemic lupus erythematosus, amyloidosis, and HIV disease. Drugs implicated as causative in the production of a secretory defect include spironolactone, triamterene, amiloride, trimethoprim in large doses, cyclosporine, and tacrolimus.

Diagnostic Options and Recommended Approach

These are outlined in Figure 17–8–1.

Therapeutic

Treatment of hyperkalemia is dictated by the level of the serum potassium and the electrocardiogram findings. If the electrocardiogram reflects changes of hyperkalemia other than peaked T waves, or if the serum potassium exceeds 6.5 mEq/L, urgent and aggressive treatment is indicated.

Therapeutic Options

Acute treatment of hyperkalemia (Table 17–8–1) has three aspects: to counteract the deleterious effect of hyperkalemia on membranes using intravenous calcium; to shift potassium into cells using glucose/insulin, β_2 stimulators, or sodium bicarbonate; and to remove potassium from the body using resin binders, laxatives, or dialysis. Potassium-exchange resins, usually Kayexalate, are very effective (0.5–1.0 mEq potassium removed per gram of resin). Kayexalate is a sodium-cycle cation resin that exchanges 1.5 mEq of sodium for each 1 mEq of potassium removed. Dialysis, although extremely effective, is rarely necessary to manage acute hyperkalemia. Massive release of potassium from extensive crush injuries, when combined with acute renal failure, may, however, need all the preceding measures, including dialysis, for effective control of life-threatening hyperkalemia.

Chronic hyperkalemia and more modest elevations of serum potassium may be managed in several ways, depending on the underlying pathogenesis. These include cessation of all potassium supplements, including salt substitutes, and restriction of potassium intake to 20 to 40 mEq/d; discontinuance of potassium-sparing diuretics (e.g., spironolactone, triamterene [Dyazide], or amiloride [Midamor]); avoidance of aldosterone-lowering drugs (e.g., prostaglandin synthetase inhibitors [nonsteroidal antiinflammatory drugs] or converting enzyme inhibitors); replacement of nonselective β blockers (e.g., propanolol, nadolol) with β_1 blockers (e.g., atenolol, metopropolol); avoidance of extreme volume contraction by the use of more liberal salt intake; augmentation of urinary flow and sodium delivery to the site of potassium secretion in the distal nephron by loop diuretics; correction of acidosis, if any, by sodium bicarbonate supplements; avoidance of severe hyperglycemia; decrease in gastrointestinal potassium absorption by daily Kayexalate or laxatives; and administration of fluorocortisone (Florinef), an exogenous mineralocorticoid, to patients with hypoaldosteronism. Large doses of this agent (0.4–1.0 mEq/d) may be necessary to restore normokalemia in conditions such as chronic renal insufficiency, suggesting resistance to its action at the level of the nephron.

Recommended Approach

Obviously all possible causative agents should be stopped. Intravenous calcium (10–20 mL of a 10% calcium gluconate solution given over 2–5 minutes) should be the initial emergent treatment for severe hyperkalemia. This acts immediately to improve cardiotoxicity; however, its effect is short-lived, lasting approximately 30 minutes. The goal of subsequent therapy is to move potassium from the extracellular fluid into the intracellular compartment. At the same time attempts to remove potassium from the body should be undertaken because, in general, these take longer to implement. The treatment of choice for promotion of transcellular shifts is insulin/glucose combination, given as an intravenous bolus of 50 mL of 50% dextrose with 10 U of regular insulin to nondiabetics. This should be followed by 10% dextrose infusion at a rate of 30 to 50 mL/h to prevent late-onset hypoglycemia. Diabetics may need larger amounts of insulin, with frequent blood sugar monitoring, to prevent hyperglycemia, which may aggravate the hyperkalemia. The potassium-lowering effect of insulin comes into play within 15 minutes, decreasing the concentration by approximately 1 mmol/L at 60 minutes and lasting 2 to 4 hours. This may be combined with albuterol, given as a nebulized solution of 20 mg in 4 mL of saline and inhaled over 10 minutes. Its potassium-lowering effect is quantitatively similar and additive to that of insulin/glucose. It acts within 30 minutes and lasts at least 2 hours. Sodium bicarbonate alone appears to be less effective than previously thought at reducing serum potassium acutely unless severe acidosis is also present.

Chronic hyperkalemia needs the institution of a low-potassium diet (40–60 mEq/d) and avoidance of medications that cause potassium retention. As underlying renal insufficiency is frequently present, often with hypertension, institution of a loop diuretic (furosemide 40–80 mg/d) is often helpful. Daily Kayexalate at a dose of 15 to 50 g, with or without sorbitol, is relatively well tolerated. Addition of the latter may be necessary to avoid constipation. In the treatment of chronic hyperkalemia secondary to hypoaldosteronism, particularly when renal insufficiency is also present, fluorocortisone may be tried but often needs to be given in large doses, leading to edema, congestive heart failure, and/or worsening hypertension. In this subgroup, the combination of a low-potassium diet, sodium bicarbonate to correct any concomitant acidosis, and loop diuretics may be more appropriate.

FOLLOW-UP

No follow-up is necessary in patients with acute hyperkalemia whose underlying problem is resolved. Patients with chronic hyperkalemia need continuous monitoring of serum potassium levels, the frequency depending on the type and stability of the underlying disease.

TABLE 17–8–1. TREATMENT OF ACUTE HYPERKALEMIA

Mechanism	Treatment	Onset of Action	Potassium Removed (mEq)
Reversal of membrane effects	Calcium gluconate (10–20 cc of a 10% solution) IV over 2 minutes. May repeat × 1 after 5 minutes	Immediately Lasts 30 minutes	0
Redistribution	Glucose (50 gm) over 5 minutes IV together with regular insulin (10 units) IV	15 to 30 minutes	0
	Albuterol 0.5 mg in 100 cc D_5W over 10–15 minutes or nebulized albuterol (10–20 mg) inhaled over 10 minutes	30 minutes Lasts 120–240 minutes	0
	Sodium bicarbonate (1 ampule; 44 mEq) IV over 5 minutes. May repeat × 1 after 15 minutes	15 to 30 minutes Lasts 240–360 minutes	0
Removal	Kayexalate		
	Oral: 50 gm in 100 cc 20% sorbitol. May repeat q 2 hours	120 minutes	1 mEq/g of resin
	Rectal: 100 gm in 200 cc H_2O by retention (30–45 minutes) enema. May repeat q 2 hours	60 minutes	0.5 mEq/g of resin
	Dialysis		
	Hemodialysis with potassium-free bath	Immediately	25 to 40 mEq/hr
	Peritoneal dialysis	Immediately	10 mEq/hr

DISCUSSION

Prevalence and Incidence

The prevalence of hyperkalemia in the general population is unknown but appears to increase with age. The incidence of severe hyperkalemia (serum potassium > 6.0 mEq/L) is 10% in patients maintained on chronic hemodialysis compared with 0.6% in patients on peritoneal dialysis.

Related Basic Science

The basic physiology and regulation of potassium homeostasis are outlined in Chapter 17–7.

Transcellular shifts of potassium from the cells occur in acidosis. In acidosis, hydrogen ions are taken up by cells from the extracellular fluid in exchange for intracellular potassium, thus explaining the tendency for serum potassium to rise in acidosis. Hyperkalemia is, however, less severe in organic and respiratory acidoses when compared with that produced by inorganic acids. This difference relates to the permeability of the accompanying anions. When acidosis is produced by inorganic acid (e.g., hydrochloric acid), most of the hydrogen ions entering the cell are exchanged for potassium, in contrast to organic acidoses (e.g., lactic acidosis). In this case, the anion is able to permeate the cell, thus minimizing potassium–hydrogen exchange and the degree of hyperkalemia. Independent of pH, serum bicarbonate concentration has an effect on serum potassium. With pH kept constant, a decrease in serum bicarbonate increases serum potassium.

Osmotic drag of potassium-rich intracellular fluid by high concentration of extracellular osmoles (e.g., hypernatremia, hyperglycemia, or mannitol) may result in hyperkalemia. Physical disruption of the cell barrier, as in crush injuries, hemolysis, and tissue necrosis, leads to hyperkalemia, as does inhibition of sodium–potassium–adenosine triphosphatase by massive overdose of digitalis. Familial hyperkalemic periodic paralysis is caused by an inherited defect of cell membranes, which leads to an intermittent and transient efflux of potassium-rich fluid. Succinylcholine (Anectine), an anesthetic agent, alters membrane permeability in some patients and may predispose to dangerous hyperkalemia.

Low-aldosterone states include Addison's disease and isolated hypoaldosteronism. The latter may result from specific congenital enzyme defects or from acquired diseases. By far the most common cause of aldosterone deficiency is a deficiency of renin. Hyporeninemic hypoaldosteronism is being observed with increased frequency in patients with chronic renal disease, particularly when the disease is caused by diabetic glomerulosclerosis or chronic interstitial disease. It is of variable pathogenesis. Hyporeninemia consequent on renal injury at the level of the juxtaglomerular apparatus with secondary hypoaldosteronism, failure to activate prorenin, a primary defect of aldosterone production at the level of the adrenal gland, and total-body sodium overload with secondary hyporeninemic hypoaldosteronism have each been described. The diagnosis is confirmed by finding low or undetectable aldosterone when the patient is nonedematous and consuming a low-sodium diet for the 3 to 5 days preceding the test.

Iatrogenic hypoaldosteronism is being recognized with increasing frequency. Vasodilatory prostaglandins are potent mediators of renin secretion. Prostaglandin synthetase inhibitors (e.g., indomethacin [Indocin], ibuprofen, naproxen) negate this stimulus, with resultant hypoaldosteronism and diminished potassium excretion. This is especially important in patients with decreased effective circulating volume (e.g., patients with cirrhosis and ascites, edematous patients with congestive heart failure), in which vasodilatory prostaglandins have an important role in modulating the vasoconstrictor effect of angiotensin, thus aiding the preservation of renal blood flow.

Impaired aldosterone secretion and hyperkalemia have also been observed following the administration of converting enzyme inhibitors. These agents inhibit the conversion of angiotensin I to angiotensin II. Because the latter stimulates aldosterone secretion in normal circumstances, its inhibition can result in hyporeninemic hypoaldosteronism with hyperkalemia.

Heparin interferes with aldosterone biosynthesis and has been occa-sionally associated with clinically important hyperkalemia, even when given in low doses (5000 U per 12 hours).

Patients with HIV disease have an increased tendency to hyperkalemia. This may be attributed to diverse defects at the level of both the adrenal gland and the renal tubule. Primary failure of the zona fasciculata, hyporeninemic hypoaldosteronism, and a distal tubular secretory defect of potassium have all been described. Pentamidine-induced acute renal dysfunction with life-threatening hyperkalemia has also been observed frequently in this population. Furthermore, administration of trimethoprim in high doses, as used in the treatment of *Pneumocystis* pneumonia, blocks the amiloride-sensitive luminal sodium channel in the distal nephron and may result in dangerous hyperkalemia.

An intrinsic defect at the level of the distal tubule with impairment of potassium secretion has been described in some forms of tubulointerstitial kidney disease, such as obstructive uropathy, diabetic glomerulosclerosis, systemic lupus erythematosus, sickle cell disease, renal allograft recipients, and amyloidosis. Aldosterone secretion is typically normal in this subgroup of patients. Impairment of renal ammoniagenesis, a voltage-dependent defect of hydrogen and/or potassium secretion, unresponsiveness to aldosterone, and abnormally functioning potassium channels are all possible mechanisms underlying the observed renal potassium retention.

Natural History and Its Modification with Treatment

Acute hyperkalemia is usually considered a transient problem; however, deaths from hyperkalemia may be underreported. It has recently been suggested that even mild elevation of serum potassium is an independent risk factor for mortality, even when controlling for age and other well-known risk factors. Anuric patients maintained on thrice-weekly hemodialysis have higher serum potassium levels than the normal population, but with dietary restriction some have remained alive since the early years of chronic maintenance hemodialysis, now in excess of 25 years. The subgroup with the highest predialysis serum potassium levels have, however, a higher mortality rate.

Prevention

Hyperkalemia secondary to acute renal failure may be prevented by early recognition and a timely decrease in potassium intake. Prevention of hyperkalemia in chronic renal failure requires dietary potassium restriction and avoidance of drugs known to cause hyperkalemia. The latter applies also to patients with normal renal function. In this regard it is of interest that two well-known nonsteroidal inflammatory drugs—ibuprofen (Advil) and naproxen sodium (Alleve)—are now available without prescription in the United States. Thus, specific questions as to the use of over-the-counter medications and warnings as to their possible ill effects are warranted, particularly in the elderly, a subgroup known to use many nonprescription medications and in whom the prevalence of hyperkalemia appears to be higher than in the general population.

Cost Containment

Frequent serum potassium determinations are necessary in patients predisposed to hyperkalemia, particularly when medications are being altered. These assays are relatively inexpensive as compared with the cost of a stay in the intensive care unit for treatment of life-threatening hyperkalemia.

REFERENCES

Allon M. Treatment and prevention of hyperkalemia in end-stage renal disease. Kidney Int 1993;43:1197

Bastl C, Hayslett JP. The cellular action of aldosterone in target epithelia. Kidney Int 1992;42:250.

Carroll HJ, Oh MS. Disorders of potassium metabolism. In: Carroll HJ, Oh MS, eds. Water, electrolyte and acid–base metabolism. 2nd ed. Philadelphia: Lippincott, 1989:167.

Kamel KS, Quaggin S, Scheich A, Halperin ML. Disorders of potassium homeostasis: An approach based on pathophysiology. Am J Kidney Dis 1994;24:597.

Tannen RL. Hypo–hyperkalemia. In: Cameron S, Davison AM, Grunfeld J-P, et al., eds. Oxford textbook of clinical nephrology. New York: Oxford University Press, 1992;2:895.

CHAPTER 17–9

Hypercalcemia and Hyperparathyroidism (See Section 9, Chapter 36)

CHAPTER 17–10

Hypocalcemia and Hypoparathyroidism (See Section 9, Chapter 38)

CHAPTER 17–11

Hypermagnesemia

Harry G. Preuss, M.D., and Vera Delaney, M.D., Ph.D.

DEFINITION

Hypermagnesemia is a serum magnesium level greater than 2.16 mEq/L (normal range, 1.7–2.16 mEq/L = 2.0–2.6 mg/dL).

ETIOLOGY

Normal kidneys have a remarkable ability to rid the body of excess magnesium, and hypermagnesemia rarely occurs unless renal compromise is present. The most common clinical setting for the development of hypermagnesemia is the patient with renal insufficiency given large amounts of magnesium in the form of antacids or cathartics.

CRITERIA FOR DIAGNOSIS

Suggestive

The diagnosis of hypermagnesemia should be considered in patients with renal insufficiency who are receiving magnesium-containing products and who are exhibiting new neurologic and/or cardiac manifestations.

Definitive

The definitive diagnosis of hypermagnesemia is based on a laboratory finding of a serum magnesium concentration greater than 2.16 mEq/L. Symptoms become usually apparent at values above 4 mEq/L and may require urgent treatment when serum magnesium exceeds 6 mEq/L.

CLINICAL MANIFESTATIONS

Subjective

Patients with hypermagnesemia are usually asymptomatic until the serum concentration exceed 4 mEq/L. Thereafter, progressive skeletal muscle weakness occurs, occasionally accompanied by flaccid paralysis and smooth muscle dysfunction in the form of nausea, vomiting, flushing, and sweating. Depression of the central nervous system with lethargy, drowsiness, confusion, and coma occurs when the serum level exceeds 6 mEq/L. A history of renal disease and consumption of magnesium-containing products is usually obtainable.

Objective

Physical Examination

Weakness, flaccidity, and hyporeflexia are characteristic. These clinical features precede involvement of the central nervous system as manifested by lethargy, drowsiness, confusion, coma, and respiratory depression. Hypotension, bradycardia, absent deep tendon reflexes, cardiac arrest, respiratory arrest, and coma occur with serum magnesium levels in excess of 8 mEq/L.

Routine Laboratory Abnormalities

Routine laboratory abnormalities may include an abnormal electrocardiogram, which may show bradycardia, prolongation of the QT interval, heart block, and asystole. Biochemical evidence of renal failure may also be present with elevations in blood urea nitrogen and creatinine levels.

PLANS

Diagnostic

Differential Diagnosis

The differential diagnosis of hypermagnesemia involves identification of the exogenous magnesium source. These include antacids (e.g., Maalox, Gelusil, Gaviscon, Mylanta), laxatives (e.g., Milk of Magnesia, magnesium citrate), enemas (e.g., magnesium sulfate [Epsom salts]), dialysis fluid, either in the form of hard water or magnesium-rich dialysate, and, finally, parenteral administration for the treatment of eclampsia. Use of some of these agents may be surreptitious or not considered as medications by the patient, as the majority are available without prescription. Use of over-the-counter medications is particularly common in the elderly, a subgroup with often unrecognized renal insufficiency. Renal insufficiency is virtually always an accompanying feature, the exceptions being the parenteral administration of magnesium sulfate for the treatment of eclampsia and the syndrome of familial hypocalciuric hypercalcemia.

Diagnostic Options

Diagnostic options are essentially confined to the finding of an elevated serum magnesium concentration. More laborious and expensive methodology, available to assess total-body magnesium balance (e.g., measurement of magnesium in erythrocytes, lymphocytes, myocytes, and/or bone), is of little relevance to the workup of the patient with hypermagnesemia.

Recommended Approach

Hypermagnesemia is extremely rare when renal function is normal; thus, in the absence of moderate renal failure, glomerular filtration rate should be measured, particularly in the elderly where the finding of a mildly elevated serum creatinine may signify severe underlying renal insufficiency. A detailed history from the patient and family members should include pointed questions as to possible exogenous sources of magnesium. In the absence of any of the above features, the rare syndrome of familial hypocalciuric hypercalcemia may be the explanation.

Therapeutic

Therapeutic Options

Most patients with hypermagnesemia with intact deep tendon reflexes require only removal of the causative, usually exogenous, magnesium source. Emergency treatment is indicated when respiratory depression or cardiac conduction defects occur. This consists of ventilatory and circulatory support and intravenous administration of 5 to 10 mEq calcium, which antagonizes the effect of hypermagnesemia. Glucose and insulin translocate magnesium intracellularly, but are rarely used clinically. The most effective and permanent method of magnesium removal is hemodialysis against a magnesium-free bath. This is rarely necessary when renal function is relatively normal. In the latter situation, volume expansion and loop diuretics enhance magnesium excretion. Neonatal hypermagnesemia may occasionally require exchange transfusions. The hypermagnesemia of familial hypocalciuric hypercalcemia rarely exceeds 4 mEq/L and does not require therapy per se.

Recommended Approach

All sources of exogenous magnesium must be removed and magnesium excretion promoted using volume expansion with 0.9% saline and loop diuretics (furosemide [Lasix] 40 mg intravenously), unless renal failure is acute or very advanced. Hemodialysis is indicated in the treatment of hypermagnesemia when life-threatening complications occur and/or when serum magnesium levels exceed 10 mEq/L. Hemodialysis should produce a safe serum level within 4 to 6 hours. This treatment usually takes several hours to implement. In the interim, monitoring in an intensive care setting with respiratory and circulatory support and intravenous administration of calcium gluconate (10–30 mL of a 10% calcium gluconate solution) should be undertaken. Glucose/insulin infusion adds little, and probably should not be employed.

FOLLOW-UP

Once the patient has been treated for the acute bout of symptomatic hypermagnesemia and warned of the dangers of exogenous magnesium sources, no further specific follow-up is necessary unless symptoms recur.

DISCUSSION

Prevalence and Incidence

The incidence in the general population is unknown. A recent study of more than 1000 specimens obtained from hospitalized patients found a serum magnesium in or above the upper range of normal in about 5%. Asymptomatic mild hypermagnesemia in the range 2.16 to 4 mEq/L is relatively common (occurring in one quarter to one half) among patients with end-stage renal disease when maintained on hemodialysis or peritoneal dialysis.

Related Basic Science

Magnesium is the second most abundant intracellular cation, with a cell concentration of 24 mEq/L, most of which is bound to nucleic acids and proteins. Free intracellular magnesium levels are thought to be approximately the same as serum levels (2 mEq/L), and subtle adaptive, poorly defined, mechanisms appear to exist that prevent wide fluctuations in cell magnesium levels when serum magnesium concentration is altered. This is important, as several key intracellular enzymes in intermediary metabolism, phosphorylation, transport, and protein and nucleic acid synthesis require magnesium for activation.

Magnesium appears to produce some of its effects by competing with calcium. For example, calcium binds to sites on the presynaptic neuron at sympathetic ganglia and at neuromuscular junctions, triggering the release of acetylcholine, which then initiates the appropriate response. Magnesium competes with calcium for the same sites but does not induce the release of acetylcholine. Thus, the contractility of smooth and skeletal muscle is reduced. The clinical effects of hyper-

magnesemia with flaccid paralysis of skeletal muscles, relaxation of the uterus, and hypotension are thus explained, as is the therapeutic efficacy of intravenous calcium in the treatment of hypermagnesemia. Magnesium is essential also in the maintenance of a low resting level of intracellular calcium by stimulating calcium sequestration within the sarcoplasmic reticulum and by competing for binding sites within the cell.

Magnesium exerts intracellular effects independent of calcium. It appears to facilitate the binding of other neurotransmitters to their receptors with the subsequent activation of G proteins and adenylate cyclase by magnesium-dependent phosphotransferases. It also blocks the movement of potassium through distinctive potassium channels, present in both cardiac and renal tubular cells, accounting for a magnesium–potassium interrelationship.

The renal handling of magnesium involves glomerular filtration and tubular reabsorption. The amount reabsorbed varies directly with serum magnesium levels, so that the fraction of filtered magnesium that is excreted increases sharply when serum magnesium rises. Thus, symptomatic hypermagnesemia is extremely rare when renal function is normal, requiring the intake of massive amounts of exogenous magnesium. An exception is the uncommon syndrome of idiopathic hypocalciuric hypercalcemia, in which hypermagnesemia (generally < 5 mEq/L) is usually an accompanying feature. When renal function is impaired, dangerous hypermagnesemia can follow routine doses of magnesium-containing antacids or laxatives. Extracellular volume contraction, hyperparathyroidism, hypothyroidism, and mineralocorticoid deficiency increase the amount of magnesium reabsorbed at the level of the renal tubule but rarely, if ever, cause symptomatic hypermagnesemia. For additional information on the basic science of magnesium, see Related Basic Science in Chapter 17–12.

Natural History and Its Modification with Treatment

Patients on long-term hemodialysis have persistent hypermagnesemia in the range 3 to 4 mEq/L for periods of 15 to 20 years and longer and remain asymptomatic. Renal osteodystrophy progresses with time on dialysis, but the role, if any, of magnesium in its etiopathogenesis is thought to be small.

Prevention

Patients with known renal insufficiency should not receive magnesium-containing gastrointestinal preparations. Elderly people, particularly women, with relatively mild elevations in serum creatinine concentrations often have unrecognized renal insufficiency due to decreased creatinine production consequent on the loss of muscle mass that usually occurs with aging. They are thus at risk for the development of symptomatic hypermagnesemia when given large magnesium loads and should be warned about the hazards of over-the-counter magnesium-containing preparations.

Cost Containment

No specific measures of cost containment have been identified for hypermagnesemia apart from avoidance of magnesium-containing preparations in patients with renal insufficiency.

REFERENCES

Iseri L, French JH. Magnesium: Nature's physiologic calcium blocker. Am Heart J 1984;108:188.

McLean RM. Magnesium and its therapeutic uses: A review. Am J Med 1994;96:63.

Quamme GA. Laboratory evaluation of magnesium status: Renal function and free intracellular concentration. In: Preuss HG, ed. Clinics in laboratory medicine: Renal function. Philadelphia: Saunders, 1993:209.

Seelig MS, Preuss HG. Magnesium metabolism and perturbations in the elderly. Geriatr Nephrol Urol 1994;4:101.

Whang R, Ryder KW. Frequency of hypomagnesemia and hypermagnesemia. JAMA 1990;263:3063.

CHAPTER 17–12

Hypomagnesemia

Vera Delaney, M.D., Ph.D., and Harry G. Preuss M.D.

DEFINITION

Hypomagnesemia is a serum magnesium concentration less than 1.7 mEq/L (normal range, 1.7–2.16 mEq/L = 2.0–2.6 mg/dL).

ETIOLOGY

The most common settings for the development of hypomagnesemia in the United States include chronic diarrheal or malabsorptive states, alcoholism, chronic diuretic use, prolonged parenteral nutrition with inadequate magnesium supplementation, and diabetes during or following ketoacidosis.

CRITERIA FOR DIAGNOSIS
Suggestive

Symptoms are, in general, vague and nonspecific and do not suggest the diagnosis. Tetany that is not attributable to a decreased ionized calcium concentration or that fails to respond to calcium therapy is most commonly due to hypomagnesemia.

Definitive

A serum magnesium concentration less than 1.7 mEq/L denotes hypomagnesemia and total-body magnesium deficiency. Interlaboratory differences of normal ranges occur due to a diversity of instruments and procedures used in the assay and loss of magnesium on storage, with some laboratories reporting a lower limit of 1.4 mEq/L. Total-body magnesium may, however, exist in the face of normomagnesemia. Measurement of urinary magnesium following a loading dose of intravenous magnesium (0.2 mEq/kg) gives a more accurate assessment of body stores. Retention of more than 20% of the administered dose suggests magnesium deficiency, even if the serum value is within the normal range. Other more elaborate and costly methodologies, such as measurements in erythrocytes, mononuclear cells, muscle, and bone using isotopes, ion-selective microelectrodes, fluorescent indicators, and nuclear magnetic resonance spectrometry, are available in specialized laboratories but, at present, offer little advantage.

CLINICAL MANIFESTATIONS
Subjective

Many patients with mild hypomagnesemia (1.4–1.7 mEq/L) are asymptomatic. Symptoms, when present, are mainly neuromuscular in type. Muscle weakness, tremors, cramps, restlessness, twitching, and convulsions may occur. Occasionally, psychiatric symptoms predominate with agitation, depression, psychosis, or organic brain syndrome. Cardiac symptoms occasionally present with palpitations and increased susceptibility to digitalis-associated arrhythmias. A history of chronic diarrhea, steatorrhea, parenteral alimentation without documentation of magnesium supplementation, chronic alcohol abuse, or use of the platinum group chemotherapeutic agents (*cis*-platinum, carboplatinum), amphotericin, or diuretics (thiazides or loop agents) may suggest the etiology. A family history of hypomagnesemia may suggest one of the hereditary magnesium-losing tubulopathies.

Objective
Physical Examination

Generalized muscle weakness, fasciculations, hyperreflexia, athetoid movements, and seizures (focal or generalized) may be present. Tetany or positive Trousseau's or Chvostek's signs may be elicited. Cardiac manifestations consist of arrhythmias, which are usually ventricular, with extrasystoles, tachycardia, atrial fibrillation, and supraventricular tachycardias.

Routine Laboratory Abnormalities

Torsade de pointes, a repetitive ventricular tachycardia with characteristic prolongation of the QT interval, is often successfully suppressed by magnesium therapy. Sensitivity to digitalis-induced arrhythmias is increased. Electrocardiographic changes also include prolongation of the PR and QT intervals and broad, flat T waves.

Laboratory findings often associated with hypomagnesemia are hypocalcemia and hypokalemia. Hypocalcemia is seen in about 30% of hypomagnesemic patients in the intensive care setting. This association is due to parathyroid dysfunction with both impaired release of the hormone and skeletal resistance to its action. It is characteristically refractory to calcium therapy unless magnesium is first repleted. Hypomagnesemia is found in about half of hospitalized patients with hypokalemia, and the presence of hypokalemia positively predicts hypomagnesemia. The associated hypokalemia is usually due to inappropriate renal potassium wasting from, for instance, diuretics or the platinum-containing chemotherapeutic agents. Its correction is facilitated by magnesium replacement.

PLANS
Diagnostic
Differential Diagnosis

Hypomagnesemia may result from one or more of three mechanisms: reduced magnesium input from the gastrointestinal tract, increased renal output, and redistribution of magnesium from the extracellular fluid to cells or bone.

Magnesium is ubiquitous in food and thus magnesium deficiency is rare in normal subjects. Protein-calorie malnutrition and prolonged magnesium-free total parenteral nutrition are causes of decreased intake. Malabsorption may be due to a defect in the carrier protein involved in the transport of magnesium in the small intestine as seen in primary infantile hypomagnesemia or chronic diarrheal states, particularly if accompanied by steatorrhea, as in Crohn's disease, sprue, coeliac disease, Whipple's disease, and short bowel syndrome. Magnesium deficiency is aggravated if further losses occur through fistula formation or continuous suctioning.

Some forms of hereditary renal tubular disorders are associated with magnesium deficiency. Bartter's syndrome is associated with hypomagnesemia and renal magnesium wasting in approximately 40% of patients. Gittleman's syndrome differs from Bartter's syndrome in that inappropriate renal magnesium wasting is the rule and it is accompanied by hypocalciuria, suggesting a defect at the level of the distal convoluted tubule. Acquired tubular or interstitial disease may also be associated with renal magnesium wasting and hypomagnesemia. These include postobstructive uropathy, diuretic phase of acute tubular necrosis, and, rarely, chronic interstitial nephritis.

A wide range of therapeutic agents have been implicated in the genesis of renal magnesium wasting syndromes. These include loop and thiazide diuretics; platinum-containing chemotherapeutic agents, with an incidence of hypomagnesemia of more than half; certain antibiotics, including amphotericin B, foscarnet (incidence of 70% in one study); aminoglycosides (incidence under 5%); and the immunosuppressants cyclosporine and tacrolimus.

Endocrine conditions may cause renal magnesium wasting. These include primary and secondary hyperaldosteronism and the syndrome of inappropriate antidiuretic hormone secretion (SIADH). Magnesium loss in these conditions is probably due to concomitant expansion of the extracellular fluid volume. Hypercalcemic states may be associated with hypomagnesemia due to competition between calcium and magnesium at the level of the thick ascending limb of the loop of Henle. Hyperthyroidism, by an unknown mechanism, is often accompanied by excessive urinary magnesium losses.

Transcellular shifts of magnesium into bone ("hungry bone syndrome") occur postparathyroidectomy for hyperparathyroidism, following vitamin D replacement therapy in severe osteomalacia, and in the development of diffuse osteoblastic metastases. Hypomagnesemia has been reported in 20% of patients with acute pancreatitis, probably as a result of magnesium deposition in areas of fat necrosis. Transfusion of large amounts of citrate-containing blood may be associated with hypomagnesemia.

Hypomagnesemia may complicate severe burns where it is caused by excessive losses through denuded skin. Transient mild hypomagnesemia may occur following surgical procedures, particularly cardiac surgery involving cardiopulmonary bypass, where the incidence of hypomagnesemia has been reported as high as 100% in one series. Mechanisms involved appear to be related to hemodilution by magnesium-free fluids, removal of magnesium by the bypass pump, catecholamine-induced intracellular magnesium shifts, and binding to free fatty acids.

Hypomagnesemia is common in diabetes mellitus; it has been observed in as many as 38% of outpatient insulin-dependent diabetics in one series and 55% of those with diabetic ketoacidosis (Elin, 1988). Mechanisms include an insulin-mediated intracellular shift and enhanced renal magnesium wasting due to a combination of glycosuria, ketoaciduria, and possibly hypophosphatemia.

Alcoholics are frequently hypomagnesemic and magnesium deficient. Multiple mechanisms are involved. These include poor intake, losses through diarrhea and vomiting, associated pancreatitis, alcohol-induced magnesuresis, and a reversible tubular defect present in about 21% of chronic alcoholics.

Diagnostic Options

The cause of hypomagnesemia is usually obvious (see Differential Diagnosis). If it is not apparent, then workup should proceed as outlined under Recommended Approach.

Recommended Approach

As renal tubular reabsorption is the major physiologic regulator of magnesium, measurement of urinary magnesium concentration provides crucial information in the workup of patients with hypomagnesemia. When nonrenal hypomagnesemia is present, urinary magnesium should be close to zero. If this is not so, a renal cause is likely. When magnesium deficiency is suspected but serum magnesium is within the normal range, urinary magnesium should be measured following a parenteral infusion as previously described. If greater than 20% of the loading dose is retained, magnesium deficiency is present and workup should proceed as described in Figure 17–12–1.

Therapeutic

Therapeutic Options

An attempt should be made to identify and ameliorate the underlying abnormality. Failing this, magnesium supplementation is necessary. The oral route is preferable. All magnesium salts induce diarrhea, but fortunately, the amount needed as supplementation (80–100 mEq) is usually below the cathartic dose (120 mEq). The amount of elemental magnesium in the different oral preparations varies greatly depending on the type of salt. Magnesium oxide (Mag Ox 400) contains 20 mEq magnesium per tablet and is inexpensive and relatively palatable. Magnesium chloride, in enteric-coated form, contains 5 mEq per pill, repairs both magnesium and chloride deficits, and is appropriate replacement in patients with alkalosis and in those with depressed gastric hydrochloric acid production.

Parenteral therapy may be necessary. Patients maintained on total parenteral nutrition need a daily dose of 10 to 15 mEq of magnesium to prevent deficiency. Magnesium is available as a sulfate derivative containing 4 mEq/mL of 50% magnesium sulfate solution. In emergencies associated with hypomagnesemia, parenteral administration of 16 to 24 mEq every 2 to 4 hours to a maximum dose of 50 mEq over the initial 8-hour period is followed by a continuous infusion of 1 to 2 mEq/kg

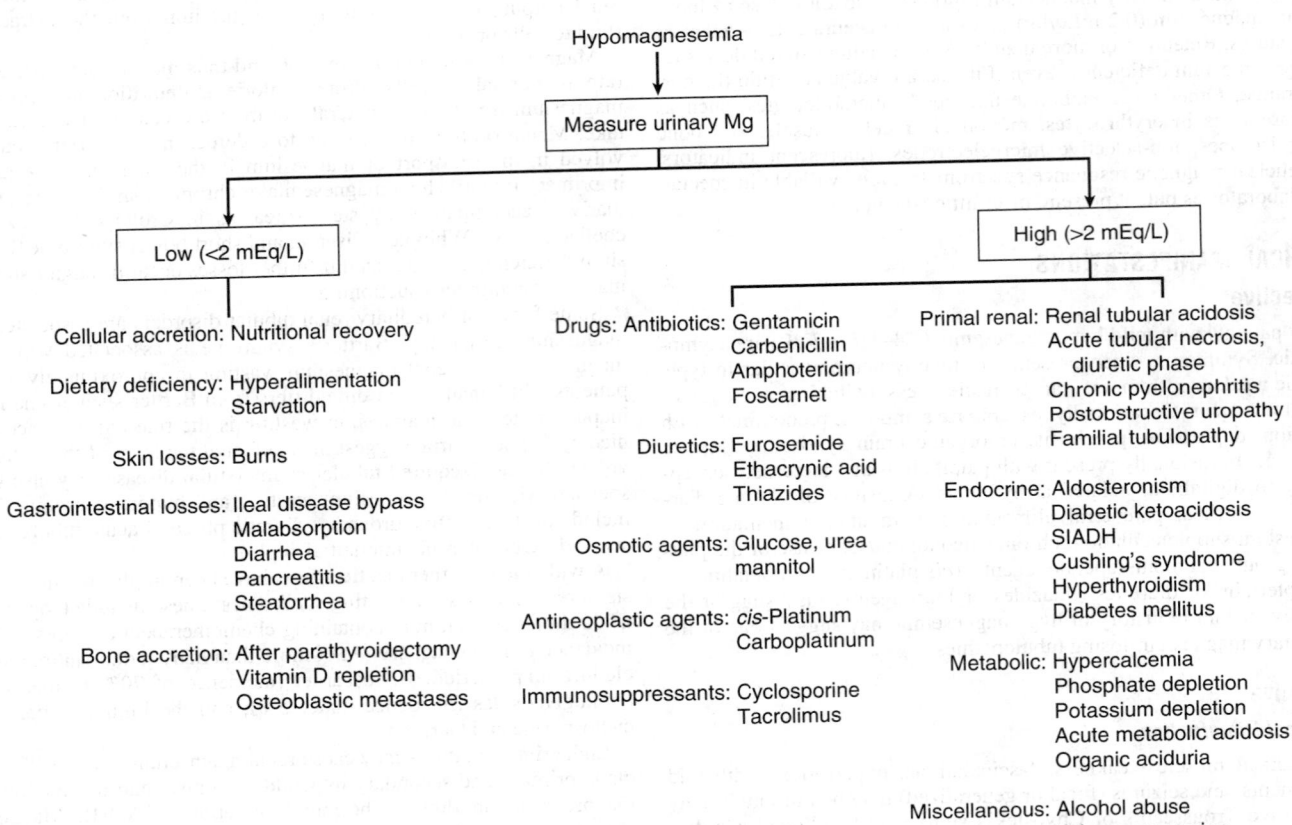

Figure 17–12–1. Diagnostic approach to hypomagnesemia. (SIADH, syndrome of inappropriate antidiuretic hormone secretion.)

over the subsequent 24 hours. When magnesium is given parenterally, frequent monitoring of patellar reflexes is helpful. With their disappearance, further magnesium supplements should be held until a current serum magnesium is available.

Recommended Approach

Magnesium oxide (Mag Ox 400) containing 20 mEq per tablet, given three to four times a day, is usually well tolerated. In severe deficiency with symptoms such as convulsions, parenteral dosing is indicated. Up to 24 mEq of elemental magnesium (3 g [6 mL] of 50% magnesium sulfate) should be given as a bolus in 100 mL of normal saline over 5 to 10 minutes, followed by a continuous infusion of 1 mEq/kg body weight magnesium over a 24-hour period. Monitoring of patellar reflexes and frequent monitoring of serum magnesium should accompany such infusions. Concomitant administration of calcium and potassium may be necessary, as associated loss of these cations is common in severe magnesium deficiency.

FOLLOW-UP

Patients with magnesium deficiency secondary to any of the predisposing causes are at risk for further episodes. Thus, they should have serum magnesium checked every 2 to 3 weeks while manipulation of medications is underway or should an additional diarrheal illness supervene. Insulin-requiring diabetics should have their serum magnesium measured during and following recovery from ketoacidosis. When serum magnesium is at a stable level, with or without supplements, testing may be reduced to once or twice a year.

DISCUSSION
Prevalence and Incidence

Hypomagnesemia is a common disorder found in about half of patients in an intensive care setting and in about 10% of patients in acute and chronic care facilities, respectively. The incidence of hypomagnesemia and magnesium depletion in the general population is unknown.

Related Basic Science

Magnesium is the second most abundant intracellular cation in humans, with a total-body magnesium level of 2000 mEq, more than 99% of which resides in the skeleton or intracellularly. The remainder is in the extracellular fluid at a concentration of 1.7 to 2.16 mEq/L, which is maintained within narrow limits. About 20% of serum magnesium is bound to albumin, but no adjustment is necessary for hypoalbuminemia. The remainder is ionized, with a small portion complexed to citrate, phosphate, and sulfate. Free intracellular magnesium is in equilibrium with serum magnesium and the bound intracellular component. Its concentration is maintained within a narrow range at the expense of both serum and bound intracellular magnesium and is regulated tightly by mechanisms that are, as yet, poorly defined.

Intracellular magnesium plays an essential role in energy storage, transfer, and utilization. Ubiquitous magnesium-requiring ATPases play a major role in the ultimate control of intracellular electrolytes, anaerobic metabolism, and oxidative phosphorylation. Magnesium plays an indirect role in protein synthesis by binding ribosomes to RNA and facilitating nucleic acid polymerization and degradation. It is also important in intracellular signaling processes, being required both by adenyl cyclase for the generation of the important intracellular second messenger, cyclic AMP, and for the regulation of intracellular free calcium. The latter is maintained by magnesium-stimulated uptake of calcium by sarcoplasmic reticulum and by calcium–magnesium competition for intracellular binding sites.

Magnesium is ubiquitous in food, apart from fat, and deficiency from inadequate dietary intake alone is uncommon. Green vegetables, seafood, and grains are particularly rich sources. The average daily intake is 25 to 30 mEq, 50% of which is absorbed from the gastrointestinal tract in normal circumstances. The minimum daily requirement to prevent negative balance is 10 mEq. Magnesium is absorbed in the small intestine, particularly the ileum. Its absorption varies with body magnesium status and dietary load and is thought to involve both a transcellular saturable process, mediated by facilitated diffusion, and an intercellular passive process, mediated by solvent drag and a favorable electrochemical gradient. Vitamin D and parathyroid hormone may have minor effects on magnesium absorption. Small fecal losses are obligatory, but diarrheal fluid may contain 5 to 10 mEq/L of magnesium and can thus be a source of magnesium deficiency.

The kidney is the major regulator of magnesium homeostasis. It is handled by glomerular filtration and reabsorption, mainly at the level of the thick ascending limb of the loop of Henle, where 60% of the filtered load is reabsorbed. The exact mechanism by which magnesium is transported across the tubular epithelium remains speculative, but is thought to be mainly passive. As the serum magnesium exceeds 2 mEq/L, a progressive increase in urinary magnesium occurs, which can reach 500 mEq per day. When the serum magnesium falls below 1.5 mEq/L, however, urinary magnesium approaches zero.

Various regulators, hormones, and medications affect overall magnesium balance by acting at the site of maximum reabsorption, namely, at the level of the loop of Henle. Salt reabsorption is a major controlling force. Factors that decrease salt reabsorption at this site, such as osmotic diuretics, loop diuretics, and extracellular fluid volume expansion, increase the fractional excretion of magnesium. Magnesium reabsorption is also dependent on tubular fluid flow rate: low flow rates promote reabsorption, whereas high flow rates promote excretion. Hypercalcemia and hypermagnesemia increase urinary magnesium by unknown mechanisms. Metabolic acidosis and, possibly, phosphate depletion also promote magnesium excretion. Hormones that enhance magnesium excretion include parathyroid hormone, antidiuretic hormone, glucagon, and calcitonin, whereas insulin appears to enhance magnesium tubular reabsorption.

Natural History and Its Modification with Treatment

The natural history of chronic hypomagnesemia uncomplicated by concurrent disease is unknown. Multiple studies suggest, but do not prove, a role for magnesium deficiency in the etiopathogenesis of ischemic heart disease, with or without symptomatic coronary spasm. In this regard, it is of interest that approximately 20% of healthy, young Americans consume less than the recommended daily allowance of magnesium.

Within a few days of experimental magnesium depletion, urinary magnesium falls to zero. Serum magnesium remains normal and the subjects remain symptom free until 4 to 6 weeks later, when the serum magnesium falls and symptoms occur. Symptoms are reversible with magnesium replacement.

Prevention

If oral intake is replaced by intravenous fluids for longer than 24 hours, supplemental magnesium should be given equaling the amount normally absorbed from the gastrointestinal tract on a daily basis (i.e., 10–15 mEq). Patients with chronic diarrhea, particularly those with disease of the ileum or those with steatorrhea, are at risk for magnesium deficiency and should be supplemented with oral magnesium to achieve a daily intake of 50 to 75 mEq. Because diarrhea is apt to be aggravated by oral magnesium preparations, parenteral magnesium supplementation may be necessary in this subgroup.

The development and treatment of diabetic ketoacidosis are frequently associated with a substantial magnesium deficit. As with potassium, serum magnesium is often increased at presentation, with a sudden and rapid drop on institution of fluid and insulin replacement. Thus, the prophylactic administration of 4 mEq magnesium to each liter of replacement fluid and frequent monitoring of serum levels are recommended.

Diuretic-induced hypomagnesemia is particularly important in heart failure. Its recognition, treatment, and prevention are critical in view of the increased susceptibility to arrhythmias caused by magnesium depletion, which are potentiated by digitalis. Magnesium-sparing diuretics (e.g., amiloride, triamterene) may reduce the magnesuric effect of the loop and thiazide diuretics and may be of use either as single agents or as combination therapy.

Alcohol abuse has been cited as the most common cause of symptomatic hypomagnesemia in the United States. Thus, if possible, all alcoholics should have frequent monitoring of serum magnesium and appropriate supplementation, if necessary. Hospitalized alcoholics are a particularly high-risk group for the development of symptomatic hypomagnesemia and should receive prophylactic parenteral supplements (4 mEq/L) if intravenous fluids are necessary.

Cost Containment

Frequent serum monitoring of high-risk patients is cost effective because early detection and treatment may prevent complications necessitating a costly admission to an acute hospital bed. The role of hypomagnesemia in the etiopathogenesis of ischemic heart disease and as treatment for cardiac arrhythmias is not yet clearly defined. Thus, routine prophylaxis with magnesium should be withheld until the outcomes of ongoing clinical trials become available.

REFERENCES

Al-Ghamdi SMG, Cameron EC, Sutton RAL. Magnesium deficiency: Pathophysiologic and clinical overview. Am J Kidney Dis 1994;24:737.
Elin RJ. Magnesium metabolism in health and disease. *Disease-a-Month* 1988;24:166.
McLean RM. Magnesium and its therapeutic uses: A review. Am J Med 1994;96:63.
Seelig MS, Preuss HG. Magnesium metabolism and perturbations in the elderly. Geriatr Nephrol Urol 1994;4:101.
Shils ME. Magnesium in health and disease. Annu Rev Nutr 1988;8:429.
Whang R. Magnesium deficiency: Pathogenesis, prevalence and clinical implications. Am J Med 1987;82:24.

CHAPTER 17-13

Hyperphosphatemia

Edmund Bourke, M.D., and Geoffrey M. Berlyne, M.D.

DEFINITION

Hyperphosphatemia is defined as a serum phosphate concentration greater than 4.7 mg/dL (1.5 mmol/L) in adults or greater than 6.2 mg/dL (2.0 mmol/L) in children.

ETIOLOGY

There are three clinical settings in which hyperphosphatemia develops (Table 17–13–1):

- Renal insufficiency: Acute or chronic renal insufficiency is by far the most common cause, accounting for more than 90% of cases in hospital practice.
- An increased phosphate load: This load has to be substantial to result in a sustained elevation in serum concentration unless it is superimposed on a significant reduction in glomerular filtration rate. An increased exogenous load is most often due to injudicious use of phosphate-containing laxatives or enemas in patients with renal dysfunction. The most common sources of an increased endogenous load are rhabdomyolysis and chemotherapy for certain malignancies.
- Increased tubular phosphate reabsorption: The absence of renal dysfunction or an identifiable phosphate load implies this etiology. The classic example is hypoparathyroidism.

CRITERIA FOR DIAGNOSIS

Suggestive

Anybody known to be suffering from acute or chronic renal failure can be assumed to be hyperphosphatemic unless specific measures are being undertaken to lower the serum phosphate.

Definitive

The laboratory measurement demonstrating the elevated value is the only definitive criterion for diagnosis. Hemolysis causes factitious hyperphosphatemia. Spurious elevations may also occur in the presence of hyperbilirubinemia and hyperlipidemia. Moreover, if methods that do not deproteinize prior to analysis are used (e.g., the Astra, New York autoanalyzer), hyperglobulinemic states may similarly result in falsely high values.

CLINICAL MANIFESTATIONS

Mild hyperphosphatemia as seen in acromegaly or hyperthyroidism has no apparent harmful effects. There are two major consequences of more severe degrees of hyperphosphatemia: hypocalcemia and metastatic calcification. The consequences of hyperphosphatemia are seen most commonly and most prominently in patients with renal failure. Thus, hyperphosphatemia contributes to the observed hypocalcemia seen in renal failure. The reciprocal drop in serum ionized calcium is due in part to inhibition of 1α-hydroxylation of 25-hydroxyvitamin D_3 in the kidney and in part to the formation and precipitation of calcium phosphate complexes. When the serum calcium:phosphate product exceeds 70, the rate of this precipitation accelerates with metastatic calcification.

TABLE 17–13–1. CAUSES OF HYPERPHOSPHATEMIA

Decreased glomerular filtration rate
  Acute and chronic renal failure
Increased tubular reabsorption
  Hypoparathyroidism
    Primary
    Secondary
      Radical neck surgery
      Thyroid surgery
  Pseudohypoparathyroidism
  Other endocrinopathies
    Acromegaly
    Hyperthyroidism
  Hyperphosphatemic tumoral calcinosis
  Therapy with diphosphonates
  Sickle cell anemia
  Volume depletion
Increased phosphate load
  Exogenous
    Oral
      Phosphate-containing laxatives
      Enemas (Fleet's)
      Vitamin D intoxication
    Intravenous
      Phosphate therapy for hypercalcemia
  Endogenous
    Cellular leak from catabolism, lactic acidosis, hypercapnia
    Rhabdomyolysis
      Traumatic
      Nontraumatic
    Chemotherapy for malignancies (lymphoblastic leukemia, etc.)
Factitious
  Hemolysis
  Hyperglobulinemia

Subjective

When a substantial increase in serum phosphate occurs acutely, such as following the administration of a phosphate enema (e.g., Fleet's) to a patient with renal failure, the reciprocal drop in serum calcium may be precipitous and the patient may complain of paresthesias or even frank tetany. Also, dizziness or complaints of fainting may indicate the hypotension of precipitous hypocalcemia. In a more chronic situation, the "red eye" or uremia, a symptom of conjunctival metastatic calcification may be a prominent feature in hyperphosphatemic renal failure patients. Uremic pruritus may also be partly a consequence of a similar pathogenesis.

Objective

Physical Examination

Although in renal failure patients with poorly controlled hyperphosphatemia the concomitant hypocalcemia may not be clinically manifest, two maneuvers may result in clear-cut physical signs: an additional phosphate load or overzealous correction of metabolic acidosis. The inadvertent administration of a phosphate load (e.g., Fleet's enema) can cause a dramatic further elevation in serum phosphate, depressing the ionized calcium to clinically dangerous levels. Metabolic acidosis as is found in renal failure decreases protein binding of calcium, increasing the ionized moiety despite low total calcium concentrations. Correction of this metabolic acidosis could reverse the adaptation with deleterious consequences. A positive Trousseau or Chvostek sign would be an early warning. Frank tetany represents a more advanced stage. If left uncorrected, tetany may progress to convulsions. Convulsions may also occur in hypocalcemic uremic patients with no previous symptoms. If the fall in serum calcium is brisk and substantial, as may follow a marked abrupt rise in serum phosphate, hypotension due to increased vascular capacitance occurs and can be profound. Death is a potential although underappreciated outcome.

Band keratopathy, readily visible on inspection of the eyes, is a manifestation of metastatic calcification in hyperphosphatemic renal failure patients. In less advanced situations, metabolic calcification can be apparent by slit-lamp examination of the eyes. Other evidence of metabolic calcification may be demonstrable radiologically in the arterial and arteriolar vessels. The syndrome of systemic calciphylaxis, a rarer presentation, is a rapidly progressive form of vascular occlusion and gangrene, particularly affecting the digits.

Finally, hyperphosphatemia is a potential and sometimes overlooked cause of an increased anion gap.

Routine Laboratory Abnormalities

See Definition.

PLANS

Diagnostic

Differential Diagnosis

If acute or chronic renal failure is present, hyperphosphatemia is almost axiomatic. It usually does not exceed a serum concentration of 10 mg/dL, however. A serum phosphate level of 12 mg/dL or more is the exception, even in advanced azotemia, and should be taken as presumptive evidence for an additional contributing factor such as rhabdomyolysis, with a release of phosphate from muscle; severe secondary hyperparathyroidism, with mobilization of bone phosphate; or phosphate-containing laxatives or enemas. About 2 g of elemental phosphorus may be required as an effective laxative, an exogenous load that the failing kidney may not readily dispose of. Equally important and potentially more life-threatening is the iatrogenic administration of a phosphate-containing enema to a renal failure patient either in preparation for a barium study or in the management of constipation. This maneuver has resulted in many fatalities.

In the presence of normal renal function, an increased phosphate load, whether exogenous or endogenous, must approach threefold the normal daily intake to induce a sustained elevation of the serum phosphate level. Apart from occasional surreptitious use of phosphate-containing laxatives or enemas, an increased exogenous load is readily apparent. The usual sources of an increased endogenous load are

rhabdomyolysis and chemotherapy for certain malignancies. Nontraumatic rhabdomyolysis may be ushered in unexpectedly following such diverse etiologies as a viral illness, cocaine abuse, or coma from alcohol or other drug overdose, accompanied by an elevated creatine kinase level, myoglobinuria, and, in some instances, acute renal failure, which further compounds the hyperphosphatemia. Clinical signs of rhabdomyolysis may be sparse: creatine kinase has a half-life of only 36 hours and myoglobin will not be detectable in urine if the glomerular filtration rate is low. The diagnosis may therefore be missed if not considered early in the course of the disease.

The tumor lysis syndrome is another important cause of hyperphosphatemia. As noted it is seen following chemotherapy for certain malignancies, particularly acute lymphoblastic leukemia. Blast cells have a much higher phosphate content than mature lymphocytes. Cytotoxic treatment of other forms of leukemia and lymphoma, including Burkitt's lymphoma, may also result in substantial hyperphosphatemia. This may be compounded if renal failure is permitted to develop from concomitant hyperuricemia. Prior to therapy myeloproliferative malignancies may be associated with hypophosphatemia because of cellular uptake by replicating cells. Yet acute hyperphosphatemia may follow the lysis induced by cytotoxic drugs once therapy is initiated.

In the absence of renal failure or an obvious phosphate load, hyperphosphatemia is due to increased tubular phosphate reabsorption (see Table 17–13–1). Hypoparathyroidism, although well recognized, has become a rather infrequent cause of hyperphosphatemia, accounting for less than 2% of cases. The decline in thyroidectomy in the United States in recent decades and the greater awareness of the need for parathyroid autotransplantation or appropriate vitamin D supplementation following block dissection of the neck for various malignancies contribute to the decreased incidence of secondary hypoparathyroidism. Hypocalcemia is an invariable accompaniment of both hypo- and pseudohypoparathyroidism. Short stature, round face, and short third and fourth metacarpals point to the latter condition. Vitamin D intoxication causes hyperphosphatemia, probably due to a combination of increased intestinal absorption and increased tubular reabsorption. Hypercalcemia is always concurrently present in this situation.

Diagnostic Options and Recommended Approach

The first step in the approach to the hyperphosphatemic patient is to document the presence or absence of renal failure. If the patient is azotemic, the cause of hyperphosphatemia has generally been discovered. If the serum phosphate level is very high (e.g., 12 mg/dL or higher even in advanced renal failure), a search for an increased load is warranted. An increased exogenous load should be apparent from the history alone. An increased endogenous load with or without renal failure is also frequently evident from the history, for example, iatrogenic as seen in the tumor lysis syndrome following chemotherapy. Serum creatine kinase and urinary myoglobin determinations are useful in pointing toward rhabdomyolysis as a potential etiology. Normal renal function and the absence of evidence of an increased phosphate load, exogenous or endogenous, point to increased tubular reabsorption. Hypervitaminosis D is always accompanied by hypercalcemia, and if hypercalcemia is present it dominates the diagnostic approach. If hypocalcemia is present it could be a consequence of hyperphosphatemia per se if the serum phosphate is markedly elevated. Otherwise, serum parathyroid hormone assays may help further define the problem. If both calcium and parathyroid hormone levels are low, hypoparathyroidism is the most likely. If the serum calcium is low but the parathyroid hormone level is high, parathyroid resistance (i.e., pseudohypoparathyroidism) is likely. If neither is low, hyperthyroidism, acromegaly, and sickle cell anemia, all of which are associated with increased tubular phosphate reabsorption, are possible explanations. When doubt remains as to whether an increased load or enhanced tubular reabsorption is operative in a patient with hyperphosphatemia, 24-hour urinary phosphate excretion is helpful, as it is increased in the former and normal in the latter condition.

Therapeutic

Therapeutic Options

Mild hyperphosphatemia does not require treatment. It requires a diagnosis that may in turn indicate the need for treatment.

Hyperphosphatemia from renal failure requires the avoidance of excess dietary phosphate. Other management strategies have become more challenging in recent years with the recognition that the oral phosphate binders most often used in the past, namely, aluminum gels, result in substantial untoward sequelae over time. Although gastrointestinal absorption of aluminum is small, its impaired elimination in renal failure leads to a progressive total-body accumulation. Its osseous precipitation impairs bone mineralization, resulting in a potentially severe vitamin D-resistant osteomalacia or in adynamic bone disease. Phosphate-binding magnesium salts present the potential hazard of dangerous hypermagnesemia. Calcium salts are now the preferred agent to bind phosphate in the intestine, but effective control of serum phosphate is sometimes not achievable at doses that do not simultaneously induce hypercalcemia. In patients with end-stage renal disease, dialysis, hemo- or peritoneal, plays an important role in keeping the serum phosphate concentration within an acceptable range.

Recommended Approach

Treatment of hyperphosphatemia should be initiated early in the course of chronic renal failure, and attempts made to keep the serum phosphate within or close to the normal range. Restriction on the ingestion of milk, cheese, and other dairy products is the first step. Calcium acetate (667 mg) binds phosphate in the intestine. The dose should be titrated based on serum phosphate and calcium determinations. Three tablets with meals and two with snacks constitute an average dose in moderate to severe renal failure. If the degree of hyperphosphatemia is inappropriate for the level of renal failure, a concomitant phosphate load should be sought. Phosphate-containing laxatives and enemas are contraindicated in renal failure. Severe secondary hyperparathyroidism is another cause of inappropriately elevated phosphate levels in chronic renal failure. Serum parathyroid hormone assays are helpful, and in severe cases subtotal parathyroidectomy requires consideration.

The increased phosphate load of the tumor lysis syndrome should be anticipated when chemotherapy is instituted for certain lympho- or myeloproliferative malignancies. Normal saline infusions coupled with diuretic therapy accelerate phosphate elimination, provided renal function is good.

Severe acute hyperphosphatemia most often is caused by exogenous or endogenous loads. Sudden elevation to 10 mg/dL or more in previously normophosphatemic patients or more marked elevations in patients whose serum phosphate levels are already above normal can induce life-threatening hypocalcemia. If renal function is normal, removing the cause results in a prompt decrease. If renal function is impaired, glucose and insulin administration induce a transcellular shift with a rapid, albeit temporary, decrease in serum phosphate concentration. Symptoms or signs of tetany mandate concomitant intravenous calcium administration. Hemodialysis is an effective serum phosphate-lowering technique but is rarely required.

FOLLOW-UP

The follow-up of hyperphosphatemia is essentially the follow-up of the causative disorder, for example, chronic renal failure, hypoparathyroidism or other endocrine causes, and Paget's disease treated with diphosphonates. In the case of chronic renal failure, serum phosphate determinations should be performed on a monthly basis.

DISCUSSION
Prevalence and Incidence

The prevalence of hyperphosphatemia in the community has not been established. A serum phosphate above 5 mg/dL is found in about 5% of hospital admissions.

Related Basic Science
Genetics

Hyperphosphatemic tumoral calcinosis is an uncommon autosomal recessive trait seen more commonly in African-Americans. There are genetic variants of hypo- and pseudohypoparathyroidism.

Physiologic or Metabolic Derangements

Although a decrease in glomerular filtration rate accounts for more than 90% of cases of hyperphosphatemia, it is not to be anticipated until the glomerular filtration rate falls to about one fifth of normal (25 mL/min). The progressive increase in fractional excretion of phosphate by residual nephrons as renal function deteriorates results in normo- or even hypophosphatemia in the early stages. This homeostatic adaptation is attributable in part to the secondary hyperparathyroidism that accompanies renal insufficiency. But parathyroidectomy does not abolish it, indicating other contributing factors. As the glomerular filtration rate declines below 25 mL/min, the serum phosphate begins to rise progressively, tending to level off in advanced renal failure at a concentration of about 10 mg/dL.

The established clinical consequences of hyperphosphatemia have been discussed. Extrapolation from experimental animal studies suggests the possibility that the hyperphosphatemia of renal disease may in turn contribute to the progression of the disease. The recent emphasis on non-immunologically mediated factors in the progression of chronic renal failure has included the concept that microscopic precipitation of calcium phosphate crystals in the renal parenchyma may contribute to progressive loss of nephrons and, thus, the downhill course toward end-stage renal disease. The implication of this concept, albeit not yet established in humans, is that rigid control of hyperphosphatemia might delay the inexorable decline in renal function that occurs over time. Alternatively, poorly controlled hyperphosphatemia in chronic renal failure may accelerate the natural history of the renal disease.

The hyperphosphatemia of chronic renal failure is complexly related to the secondary hyperparathyroidism and renal osteodystrophy seen in this condition. The initial effects of hyperphosphatemia have been ascribed in part to the formation and precipitation of calcium phosphate complexes with a small decrease in serum ionized calcium concentration. This, in turn, stimulates parathyroid hormone secretion with a resultant phosphaturia and a restoration of normophosphatemia, but at the expense of secondary hyperparathyroidism and renal osteodystrophy. The adaptation, therefore, constitutes a trade-off and has been termed the *trade-off hypothesis*. More recent in vitro studies imply that factors other than the simple physicochemical mechanism proposed in the trade-off hypothesis are necessary to induce azotemic secondary hyperparathyroidism. Likely contributing factors are impaired 1α-hydroxylation of 25-hydroxyvitamin D_3 and resistance to the calcemic action of parathyroid hormone in uremia. Paradoxically, in end-stage renal disease, when the renal tubules are no longer responsive to the phosphaturic action of parathyroid hormone, the secondary hyperparathyroidism may exacerbate the hyperphosphatemia via effects on phosphate release from bone.

Natural History and Its Modification with Treatment

Hyperphosphatemia due to an increased exogenous or endogenous load is generally intermittent and short-lived once the underlying cause is identified and corrected. Other forms of hyperphosphatemia such as those associated with hyperparathyroidism or acromegaly resolve when the basic disease is adequately treated. In disorders such as chronic renal failure, hypoparathyroidism, and tumoral calcinosis, the tendency to hyperphosphatemia persists indefinitely, although its manifestations can be minimized by appropriate therapeutic measures.

Prevention

In chronic renal failure, hyperphosphatemia can be prevented by minimizing the intake of high-phosphate food substances such as milk and dairy products and by administering phosphate-binding agents, particularly calcium acetate or calcium carbonate, in appropriate doses. The avoidance of phosphate-containing laxatives and enemas is axiomatic in these circumstances.

Cost Containment

Avoidance of high-phosphate foods, judicious use of calcium salts as phosphate binders, and periodic monitoring of serum phosphate levels are not costly. The osseous and extraosseous sequelae of poorly controlled hyperphosphatemia, most evident in the azotemic patient, may necessitate expensive hospitalizations for orthopedic or parathyroid surgery.

REFERENCES

Amiel C, Bailly C, Escoubet B, Friedlander G. Hypo- and hyperphosphatemia. In: Cameron S, Davison JM, Grunfeld J-P, et al., eds. Oxford textbook of clinical nephrology. Oxford: Oxford University Press, 1992:1782.

Bourke E, Yanagawa N. Assessment of hyperphosphatemia and hypophos-phatemia. In: Preuss HG, ed. Clinics in laboratory medicine. Philadelphia: Saunders, 1993;13:183.

Levine BS, Kleeman CR. Hypophosphatemia and hyperphosphatemia: Clinical and pathophysiologic states. In: Narins RG, ed. Clinical disorders of fluid and electrolyte metabolism. 5th ed. New York: McGraw-Hill, 1994:1045.

Massry SG. Hypophosphatemia and hyperphosphatemia. In: Massry SG, Glassock RJ, eds. Textbook of nephrology. 3rd ed. Baltimore: Williams & Wilkins, 1995:398.

CHAPTER 17–14

Hypophosphatemia

Edmund Bourke, M.D., and Geoffrey M. Berlyne, M.D.

DEFINITION

Hypophosphatemia is defined as a serum phosphate concentration of 2.5 mg/dL (0.8 mmol/L) or less in adults and 4.5 mg/dL (1.5 mmol/L) or less in children. Serum phosphate values below 1 mg/dL (0.3 mmol/L) constitute severe hypophosphatemia and an urgent need for correction.

ETIOLOGY

There are three clinical settings in which hypophosphatemia develops (Table 17–14–1):

- Low gastrointestinal input: This is most commonly seen in the patient ingesting excess quantities of phosphate-binding antacids.
- Excess urinary losses due to renal tubular disorders or, more often, to extrinsic phosphaturic stimuli such as hyperparathyroidism.
- Conditions associated with enhanced cellular replication or intracellular metabolism with increased demand for cellular phosphorus uptake and resultant transcellular shifts: This is classically seen in refeeding after severe malnutrition, during recovery from severe alcohol abuse, following treatment of diabetic ketoacidosis, or when total parenteral nutrition proceeds without recognition of the need for phosphorus replacement. Redistribution hypophosphatemia is also associated with respiratory alkalosis as a consequence of pH-sensitive intracellular glycolysis with resultant phosphorylation of metabolic intermediates.

More than one of the above etiologic mechanisms may coexist. Hypophosphatemia is frequently multifactoral in clinical practice.

CRITERIA FOR DIAGNOSIS

Suggestive

Mild to moderate hypophosphatemia does not result in clinical features. Severe hypophosphatemia may result in a wide spectrum of sequelae, but they are not specific enough to suggest hypophosphatemia except in settings where it is very much to be anticipated.

Definitive

The laboratory measurement demonstrating the low value is the only definitive criterion for diagnosis. Severe hypophosphatemia (< 0.5 mg/dL) causes hemolysis, which spuriously elevates the serum phosphate with the possibility of masking the underlying problem.

CLINICAL MANIFESTATIONS

Mild or even moderate hypophosphatemia is asymptomatic. The symptoms and signs do not generally develop until a serum phosphate concentration below 1 mg/dL is reached. The clinical manifestations are not due to hypophosphatemia per se, but rather are a consequence of intracellular inorganic phosphate depletion. The range of clinical manifestations identified is attributable to functional abnormalities in virtually every organ system. But florid clinical manifestations are less often encountered in the United States than was the case a few decades ago. With the incorporation of serum phosphate determinations into routine biochemical screens, severe hypophosphatemia is not being seen less

TABLE 17–14–1. CAUSES OF HYPOPHOSPHATEMIA

Inadequate gastrointestinal input
 Phosphate binders (aluminum hydroxide, magnesium oxide, calcium carbonate, calcium acetate)
 Low-phosphate diet, continuous vomiting, or nasogastric suction
 Malabsorptive states ± secondary hyperparathyroidism
 Vitamin D deficiency states ± secondary hyperparathyroidism
 Kwashiorkor
Excess losses
 Renal
  Intrinsic
   Isolated genetic or acquired hypophosphatemia
   Fanconi's syndrome: hereditary or acquired
   After renal transplantation
   Idiopathic hypercalciuria
  Phosphaturic agents, maneuvers
   Hyperparathyroidism (primary, secondary, ectopic)
   Acute volume expansion
   Recovery (diuretic) phase of acute renal failure
   Glycosuria
   Ketonuria
   Oncogenous hypophosphatemia
 Dialysis
  Hemodialysis
  Peritoneal dialysis
Transcellular shifts
 Carbohydrate load (oral or IV), fructose intolerance
 Humoral
  Insulin
  Epinephrine
 Alkalosis
  Respiratory
  Metabolic
 Rapidly replicating cells, e.g., hematologic malignancies
 Total parenteral nutrition
 Treatment of diabetic ketoacidosis
 Alcohol withdrawal
 Recovery from third-degree burns
 Refeeding after severe malnutrition
 "Hungry bones"
  Parathyroidectomy for secondary hyperparathyroidism
  Appropriate treatment of osteomalacia
 Miscellaneous
  Legionnaires' disease
  Theophylline overdose

frequently than in the past but is usually of shorter duration because therapy is instituted in a more timely fashion.

Subjective

The neurologic sequelae have been categorized most comprehensively in patients during prolonged parenteral nutrition. A multifaceted neuroencephalopathy or a peripheral neuropathy may predominate. The patient may complain of paresthesias and/or palsies. Malaise and apprehension may precede cognitive impairment. Marked muscle weakness is another presenting symptom, and myalgias may be prominent and cause considerable discomfort. Anorexia can be marked, sometimes making oral replacement therapy difficult.

Objective

Physical Examination

Delirium is a presenting feature. In the setting of the alcoholic it may aggravate hepatic encephalopathy or Wernicke's encephalopathy. Seizures and coma may follow in advanced cases. A variety of cranial and peripheral neuropathies have been described. Hyporeflexia is common. Abnormal nerve conduction and/or electromyographic abnormalities may be noted. An acute myopathy is seen most classically in the severely hypophosphatemic alcoholic patient either during withdrawal or refeeding. Full-blown rhabdomyolysis is also most classically seen in the hypophosphatemic alcoholic patient. Intravenous glucose administration may provoke rhabdomyolysis in these circumstances. Paradoxically, hypophosphatemia-induced rhabdomyolysis releases phosphate from muscle, causing a rise in serum phosphate, which may mask the underlying diagnosis. Cardiac muscle involvement and arrhythmias also occur in severe cases.

Routine Laboratory Abnormalities

See Definition. Radiologic manifestations of osteomalacia or vitamin D-resistant rickets are encountered in chronic phosphate depletion, such as the prolonged injudicious use of phosphate-binding antacids. Rarely, acute hemolysis may complicate a sustained serum phosphate concentration below 0.5 mg/dL. Also in severe cases, reduced red cell 2,3-diphosphoglycerate levels with impaired oxygen-carrying capacity may contribute to the central nervous system features.

PLANS

Diagnostic

Differential Diagnosis

Although it needs to be stressed that more than one mechanism is operative in many clinical conditions associated with hypophosphatemia, it nonetheless is convenient to classify it as due to inadequate input, excess losses, or transcellular shifts. Once hypophosphatemia is documented, it should be possible to limit the differential diagnostic possibilities by carefully reviewing the history, the physical examination, and routine laboratory studies. It is important not to overlook ingestion of phosphate-binding antacids or laxatives before embarking on more detailed studies. Rarely, a positive family history is found, as in familial X-linked hypophosphatemic rickets or some forms of the Fanconi syndrome.

Diagnostic Options

A urinary phosphate determination on a random sample of urine is very helpful clinically. If the concentration is below 4 mg/dL in the face of significant hypophosphatemia, renal losses can be excluded, implicating either inadequate gastrointestinal input or transcellular shifts. At higher urinary concentrations, a renal leak should be the focus of investigation. A 24-hour urinary phosphate determination is also useful. Values below 100 mg exclude a renal cause. Importantly, however, a primary gastrointestinal cause may be associated with a paradoxically elevated urinary phosphate. This is seen when secondary hyperparathyroidism complicates malabsorption of calcium and/or vitamin D. An elevated serum alkaline phosphatase is the rule in these circumstances. Parathormone and vitamin D metabolite assays help establish the diag-

nosis. In summary, therefore, although a low urinary phosphate excludes a renal etiology, high urinary phosphate need not exclude a gastrointestinal etiology because this can be the proximate cause of secondary hyperparathyroidism.

Recommended Approach

The physician should review the history, physical examination, and routine laboratory values, taking cognizance of the causative factors outlined in Table 17–14–1. In the more common clinical scenarios where hypophosphatemia is encountered, one or more etiologies usually becomes apparent or a high index of suspicion is aroused from these simple considerations alone. Readily overlooked are over-the-counter antacids that bind phosphate but that the patient may neglect to mention unless asked specifically. When hypercalcemia accompanies the hypophosphatemia, the hypercalcemia dominates the diagnostic approach. When the cause of hypophosphatemia is unclear, a urinary phosphate concentration below 4 mg/dL excludes a renal cause, helping to focus further diagnostic efforts. As outlined under Diagnostic Options, a high urinary phosphate may not exclude a gastrointestinal etiology because of possible secondary hyperparathyroidism. Hypocalcemia is the rule but not invariable in this situation. Biochemical tests of gastrointestinal absorptive function and radiologic examination are sometimes required to exclude occult malabsorption.

Therapeutic

Therapeutic Options

Mild hypophosphatemia requires no treatment. It requires a diagnosis, which may in turn indicate the need for treatment (e.g., hyperparathyroidism). In situations where severe forms of hypophosphatemia are to be anticipated, for example, treatment of diabetic ketoacidosis, the hospitalized alcoholic patient, or those undergoing total parenteral nutrition, careful monitoring of serum phosphate is indicated. Moderate hypophosphatemia, above 1 mg/dL, may resolve once the underlying mechanism is corrected. Failing that, oral phosphate supplementation suffices. Values below 1 mg/dL generally require phosphate replacement to prevent clinical sequelae. When clinical features are marked, intravenous therapy is indicated. Caution is required to avoid rebound hyperphosphatemia.

Recommended Approach

Moderate hypophosphatemia with values below 2.0 and above 1.0 mg/dL frequently require no more than monitoring while the underlying etiology is being corrected, followed by spontaneous resolution of the hypophosphatemia. Examples include the hypophosphatemia seen in hyperventilation and in most instances of diabetic ketoacidosis. Serum phosphate concentrations below 1 mg/dL, when an apparently transient cause is not present, require replacement therapy. If the patient tolerates oral intake this is the simplest and safest route to use. Skim milk is rich in phosphate (about 1 g/L) and is an efficient means of replacement. Fleet's phosphosoda 5 g (650 mg of elemental phosphorus) three times daily usually results in an adequate rise in serum phosphate within a few days. Anorexia from hypophosphatemia or diarrhea from high-dose oral replacement (> 2 g elemental phosphorus daily) may limit this approach. Moreover, when florid features of hypophosphatemia are present, parenteral therapy is always indicated. Because it is not possible to predict replacement needs from serum concentrations, the quantity needing replacement remains empiric. Potassium phosphate (K_2HPO_4) 9 mmol in half-normal saline over 12 hours is safe and efficacious if renal function is normal; this dose can be repeated as necessary. Serum phosphate, calcium, potassium, and, if indicated, magnesium levels should be monitored. In the event that calcium is needed to prevent tetany, it should not be added to the parenteral phosphate solution because precipitation may occur. Parenteral supplementation is normally discontinued when serum phosphate rises to 2.0 mg/dL.

FOLLOW-UP

Patients on long-term phosphate-binding antacids should be monitored for the development of hypophosphatemia a few times annually. Patients in whom hypophosphatemia has previously developed require more frequent monitoring. A phosphate-containing antacid (phosphogel) may be tried when renal function is adequate. In conditions such as acute pancreatitis with continuous nasogastric suction and no oral intake other than possible antacids, serum phosphate should be monitored on alternate days and parenteral replacement given as necessary until oral feeding is reinstated.

When metabolic bone disease ("hungry bones" syndrome) is being treated, frequent monitoring of serum phosphate is initially required, and thereafter, approximately monthly follow-up is indicated to monitor phosphate, calcium, magnesium, and alkaline phosphatase levels together with periodic bone radiology until remineralization is deemed adequate. Semiannual determinations are frequently indicated thereafter, as in the case of vitamin D deficiency that may follow gastric surgery.

When transient hypophosphatemia due to a nonrecurrent cause has been identified and corrected, no follow-up is required.

DISCUSSION
Prevalence and Incidence

Levels of plasma phosphate below 2 mg/dL have been reported in 2% of hospitalized patients and 10% of patients hospitalized with chronic alcoholism (Knochel, 1993). It should always be anticipated and looked for following the institution of therapy for certain common conditions leading to hospitalization: A nadir in serum phosphate is generally encountered within 24 hours of treatment of diabetic ketoacidosis, within 48 to 96 hours of treatment of alcoholism, and within 1 week to 10 days of total parenteral nutrition.

Related Basic Science
Genetics

Familial X-linked hypophosphatemic rickets is the most common inherited disorder of phosphate metabolism, being inherited as an X-linked dominant condition with variable expression, especially in females. The gene has been mapped to the distal part of the short arm of the X chromosome. Rarer genetic variants have also been described.

Physiologic or Metabolic Derangement

Hypophosphatemia is usually absent or minimal in malnourished individuals because of phosphate release into the circulation following starvation-induced cellular dissolution. It is common, however, in kwashiorkor. Additionally, malabsorption increases sensitivity to stimuli that shift phosphate into cells. Phosphate is absorbed in the jejunum, mediated in part by 1,25-dihydroxyvitamin D_3. The hypophosphatemia of malabsorptive states is only partly of gastrointestinal origin. Phosphaturia resulting from the secondary hyperparathyroidism of concomitant malabsorption of calcium and vitamin D may play the predominant role. A similar mechanism frequently applies in other states of abnormal vitamin D metabolism.

Renal hypophosphatemia can result from an intrinsic renal tubular reabsorptive defect or an agent or maneuver that decreases the tubular reabsorptive capacity. Hypophosphatemia caused by an intrinsic tubular defect may occur in isolation or as a manifestation of a more diffuse abnormality of proximal tubular function (the Fanconi syndrome). The Fanconi syndrome, in turn, may be a primary idiopathic defect or more often occurs as part of an inborn error of metabolism, for example, cystinosis. It also can occur as a secondary acquired phenomenon, as, for instance, a manifestation of multiple myeloma, amphotericin nephrotoxicity, or heavy metal poisoning.

The normal kidney can markedly enhance renal tubular phosphate reabsorption during phosphate deprivation. This may explain the infrequency of severe hypophosphatemia during such phosphaturic stimuli as hyperparathyroidism: The initial negative phosphate balance stimulates enhanced reabsorption at parathormone-independent transport sites.

Hypophosphatemia is common in the transplanted kidney and is variously attributable to persistence of the secondary hyperparathyroidism of preexisting uremic osteodystrophy or an increased skeletal uptake by

"hungry bones" during the remineralization phase that follows cessation of the stimulus to osteodystrophy. Occasionally, an isolated phosphate transport defect is encountered in the transplanted kidney.

The term *oncogenous phosphaturia* describes the hypophosphatemia reported with a variety of phacomatoses and other tumors, presumably due to a humoral agent elaborated by these tumors. Although much less common than tumor-associated hypercalcemia, resolution has been reported following removal of the causative lesion.

Hypophosphatemia due to transcellular shifts is the predominant category of hypophosphatemia seen in hospitalized patients and generally is attributable to enhanced phosphorylation of carbohydrates or synthesis of new protoplasm. Respiratory alkalosis of diverse etiologies is the single most common cause. It induces hypophosphatemia via increased intracellular pH which enhances the activity of the enzyme phosphofructokinase, stimulating glycolysis, and thereby binding phosphate in intracellular carbohydrate intermediates. This sequestration of inorganic phosphate results in its virtual disappearance from the urine. Anxiety and pain are among the most common causes of respiratory alkalosis, and this contributes significantly to the frequency of hypophosphatemia in hospitalized patients. The hypophosphatemia of respiratory alkalosis can be profound, with values of 0.5 mg/dL during severe hyperventilation. It is much less marked in metabolic alkalosis, which has a lesser effect on the intracellular pH. The hypophosphatemic effect of insulin is similarly mediated through increased formation of intracellular phosphorylated glycolytic intermediates. Significant hypophosphatemia is the rule during correction of diabetic ketoacidosis. These patients have already undergone a considerable negative balance due to acidosis- and osmotically induced phosphaturia. Insulin together with resolution of the acidosis results in a shift of phosphate back into cells.

Overzealous refeeding of starved individuals is a potential cause of life-threatening hypophosphatemia. The provision of nutrition, particularly carbohydrate, to the severely malnourished leads to regeneration of cells that have essentially undergone mitotic arrest, leading to sequestration of inorganic phosphate in organic forms within cell wall phospholipids, nucleoproteins, new protoplasm, and the glycolytic intermediates, as cell replication resumes. Inadequate supplementation with inorganic phosphate leads to progressive hypophosphatemia. Hypophosphatemia during total parenteral nutrition has a similar basis.

Whereas on the one hand hyperphosphatemia can occur during tumor lysis, the converse, hypophosphatemia, can occur during rapid cellular replication as in leukemia undergoing a blast crisis, Burkitt's lymphoma, and following vitamin B_{12} replacement in severe pernicious anemia, all attributable to enhanced uptake by the proliferating cells.

The "hungry bones" syndrome is seen following the initiation of appropriate therapy for severe metabolic bone disease, for example, vitamin D therapy for osteomalacia or parathyroidectomy for secondary hyperparathyroidism. Avid uptake of phosphate (as well as calcium and magnesium) accompanies the remineralization process. The hypophosphatemia can be prolonged and sometimes is a difficult management problem because the dose of oral phosphate required to maintain a satisfactory serum concentration causes gastrointestinal side effects.

The classic example of the multifactorial components that contribute to hypophosphatemia is that seen in the hospitalized alcoholic patient (Figure 17–4–1). Poor diet, phosphate-binding antacids to counteract alcoholic gastritis, and pancreatitis-induced malabsorption are among the features contributing to inadequate phosphate input. The phosphaturic action of ethanol per se, as well as that of the frequently accompanying organic acidoses and hyperglucagonemia, and the decreased tubular reabsorptive capacity for phosphate seen in alcoholic cirrhosis contribute to enhanced urinary losses. The hyperventilation and increased catecholamine release accompanying alcohol withdrawal stimulate transcellular phosphate shifts. Commonly administered intravenous glucose and bicarbonate accentuate these shifts. The anabolic state that accompanies recovery, with its combination of cellular regeneration and cellular replication, adds a further dimension to the sequestration of inorganic phosphate in organified intermediates and building blocks. Thus, by the end of the fourth day of hospitalization, a nadir in serum phosphate concentration will likely have been reached. Theophylline is another drug, overdose of which causes a clinical spectrum that includes severe hypophosphatemia of multifactorial origin.

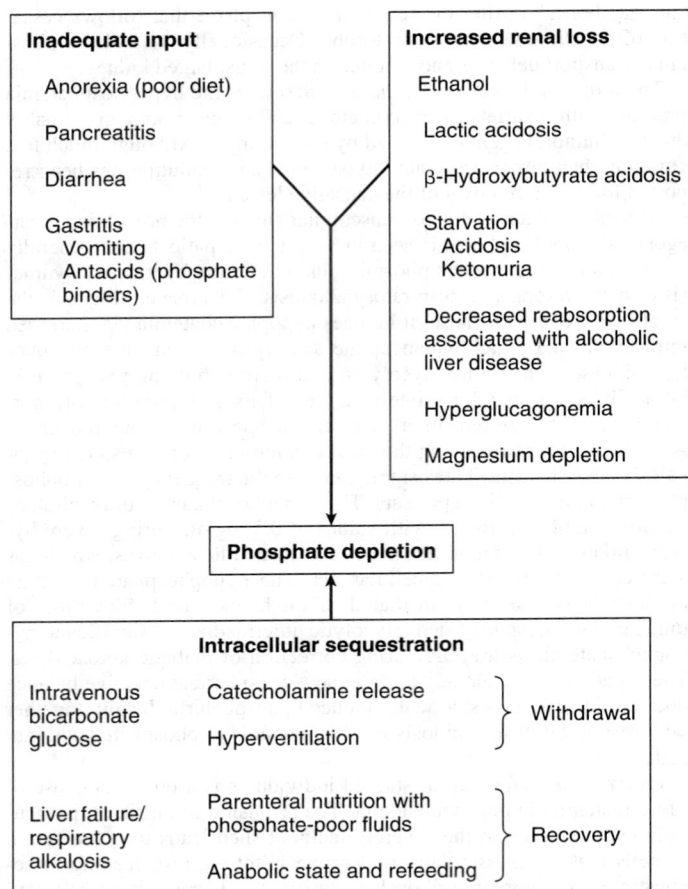

Figure 17–14–1. Phosphate depletion syndrome of alcoholism.

Natural History and Its Modification with Treatment

Acute hypophosphatemia is often self-limited, resolving spontaneously once the precipitating etiology is corrected, for example, acute hyperventilation, removal of a single parathyroid adenoma, and usually following therapy for diabetic ketoacidosis. When it is induced by unleashing the need for a markedly increased cellular phosphate uptake, as in those conditions encompassed by the term *refeeding the severely malnourished,* including the alcoholic, supplemental phosphate is frequently required and is always indicated if the serum concentration falls to consistently below 2 mg/dL, to prevent the development of clin-

ical sequelae, which can regularly be anticipated as the concentration falls below 1 mg/dL. In this situation, however, phosphate replacement restores normophosphatemia within a few to several days. More prolonged oral phosphate therapy may be required for the hypophosphatemia following chronic abuse of phosphate binders, especially in the occasional instance that results in frank osteomalacia. This is true in any chronic hypophosphatemic state associated with metabolic bone disease and its treatment. In these situations hypophosphatemia may persist for weeks to months during correction of the underlying defect due to continued skeletal uptake during the reparative process. If a renal tubular phosphate leak is severe and has resulted in rickets or osteomalacia, oral phosphate supplements several times daily may be required on an indefinite basis.

Prevention

Patients taking phosphate-binding antacids for a prolonged period should be aware that phosphate depletion is a possible side effect made more likely by significant increases in dosage, and periodic checkups are therefore warranted. Although hypophosphatemia per se is frequently not preventable, those conditions that can lead to symptomatic hypophosphatemia should be recognized and serum phosphate concentrations monitored with a view to early intervention. This especially applies to alcohol-abusing patients undergoing withdrawal or recovery, all patients receiving total parenteral nutrition, and during correction of metabolic bone disease. The timely and judicious introduction of supplemental phosphate orally or when necessary by the intravenous route should prevent symptomatic hypophosphatemia.

Cost Containment

Early detection and treatment of hypophosphatemia are inexpensive. Failure to detect and take corrective action may result in catastrophic consequences, the management of which is very expensive. These include acute complications such as rhabdomyolysis with acute renal failure and chronic complications such as osteomalacia and rickets.

REFERENCES

Amiel C, Bailly C, Escobout B, Friedlander G. Hypo- and hyperphosphatemia. In: Cameron S, Davison A, Grunfeld J-P, et al., eds. Oxford textbook of clinical nephrology. Oxford: Oxford University Press, 1992:1782.

Bourke E, Yanagawa N. Assessment of hyper- and hypophosphatemia. In: Preuss HG, ed. Clinics in laboratory medicine. Philadelphia: Saunders, 1993;13:183.

Knochel JP. The clinical and physiological implications of phosphorus deficiency. In: Seldin DW, Giebisch G, eds. The kidney: Physiology and pathophysiology. 2nd ed. New York: Raven Press, 1993:2533.

Massry SG. Hypo- and hyperphosphatemia. In: Massry SG, Glassock RG, eds. Textbook of nephrology. 3rd ed. Baltimore: Williams & Wilkins, 1995:398.

Tucker SB, Schimmel EN. Clinical nutrition cases: Postoperative hypophosphatemia: A multifactorial problem. Nutr Rev 1989;47:111.

Disorders of the Genitourinary System

Sam D. Graham, Jr., M.D.

CHAPTER 18–1

Dysuria

David P. O'Brien III, M.D.

DEFINITION

The present definition of *dysuria* is painful urination, although the derivation of the word *dysuria* implies altered urination.

ETIOLOGY

The etiology of dysuria may be inflammation, neoplasms, foreign bodies, stones, or obstruction.

CRITERIA FOR DIAGNOSIS
Suggestive

The symptoms suggest the diagnostic (see Definitive).

Definitive

Painful urination is diagnostic.

CLINICAL MANIFESTATIONS
Subjective

The patient describes a burning feeling with urination. In the male, it is frequently described as most acute in the region of the glans penis. In the female, the burning may be in the bladder or vaginal area. The intermittent or persistent nature of the complaint should be determined along with the diurnal or nocturnal nature. Pain may be described as occurring just before, during, or after voiding. Associated symptoms are frequency and/or urgency and sometimes chills or fever. A past history of urologic disease should be obtained, along with a history of antimicrobial agent intake. A family history of urologic disease should also be investigated.

Objective
Physical Examination

On physical examination, the patient should be evaluated for costovertebral angle tenderness, suprapubic tenderness, bladder distention, prostate size and/or tenderness in the male, and pelvic (bladder) tenderness in the female. A thorough testicular, epididymal, and spermatic cord examination is also essential. Vaginal irritation may be present in the female.

Routine Laboratory Abnormalities

Routine laboratory abnormalities may be apparent on the initial routine urinalysis. White blood cells may or may not be present.

PLANS
Diagnostic

Table 18–1–1 outlines the diagnoses and diagnostic options for dysuria. Dysuria may occur in both male and female patients with no other subjective or objective findings other than anxiety.

Therapeutic

Management of the symptom of dysuria depends on the etiology or primary diagnosis. Physicians should be alert to the possibility of prostatic carcinoma in men over 50. The rapid onset of symptoms with no prior history is subjective. When objective data are lacking, one may be left with the necessity of treating the symptom alone. A trial of urinary antispasmodic agents (e.g., hyoscyamine ([Cystospaz], flavoxate hydrochloride [Urispas]), anticholinergic agents, oxybutynin chloride (Ditropan), or dye-type compounds, such as phenazopyridine hydrochloride (Pyridium) may be instituted. Antibiotics such as nitrofurantoin (Macrodantin, Macrobid) or sulfa compounds also are used on a trial basis.

Reassurance of the anxious patient is very important. Sometimes just the recognition that some of the symptoms may be stress related is enough insight and reassurance for the patient.

FOLLOW-UP

Follow-up visits vary with the disease process. Repetitive testing urinalysis, urine culture, cystoscopy, and so on frequently are necessary.

DISCUSSION
Prevalence and Incidence

As is the case with symptoms of urinary frequency, the prevalence and incidence of the symptom of dysuria are indeterminate.

Related Basic Science

Dysuria may be caused by a variety of factors occurring singly or in combination. Dysuria develops in cases of inflammation of the mucosa of the lower urinary tract, whether the etiology is bacterial, mechanical, chemical, neoplastic, or foreign body. Mechanical trauma may occur in

TABLE 18–1–1. DYSURIA: DIAGNOSES AND DIAGNOSTIC OPTIONS

Diagnosis	Diagnostic Options
Inflammation	Urinary culture and sensitivity,
Cystitis	urinalysis, cystoscopy
Prostatitis	Urine culture and sensitivity,
Urethral syndrome	prostatic examination and secretions
Neoplasms	Cystoscopy, urinary cytology,
Bladder neoplasms	urinary flow cytometry
Foreign bodies	X-ray of kidney, ureters, and bladder; intravenous pyelograms cystoscopy
Stones	X-ray of kidney, ureters, and bladder; intravenous
Bladder	pyelograms; cystoscopy
Ureteral	
Obstruction	Bladder distention, catheterization, cystoscopy, urodynamics
Urinary retention	
Neurogenic	

conjunction with sexual intercourse, use of tampons, and so on. Chemical trauma may occur with local irritants such as soaps, particularly in the female. In women, the region of the trigone is the most sensitive area of the lower urinary tract and commonly is the site of origin of dysuria. Foreign body irritation of the bladder or urethral mucosa occurs with stones or catheters. Neoplastic lesions, particularly of the bladder or prostate and commonly in the early stages, may have dysuria as the only initial symptom. Carcinoma in situ of the bladder is notorious for this insidious presentation.

Natural History and Its Modification with Treatment

The natural history of dysuria and its modification with treatment vary with the disease entity involved.

Prevention

Prevention of dysuria follows the prevention of the specific disease.

Cost Containment

Prompt aggressive treatment of the individual disease process should contain costs effectively.

REFERENCES

Brooks D, Mandar A. Pathogenesis of the urethral syndrome in women and its diagnosis in general practice. Lancet 1972;2:893.
Greenfield S, Friedland G, Scifers S, et al. Protocol management of dysuria, urinary frequency, and vaginal discharge. Ann Intern Med 1974;81:452.
Lec F, Gray RD, McLeary TR, et al. Transrectal ultrasound in the diagnosis of prostate cancer: Location echogenicity, histopathology and staging. Prostate 1985;7:117.
Stamey TA. Urinary infections. Baltimore: Williams & Wilkins, 1972.
Waters WE, Elwood PC, Asscher SE, et al. Clinical significance of dysuria in women. Br Med J 1970;2:754.

CHAPTER 18–2

Urinary Retention

Niall T. M. Galloway, M.B., B. Ch., and R. E. S. El-Galley, M.B., B. Ch.

DEFINITION

Urinary retention refers to the inability to empty urine from the bladder. It may be acute retention, and an emergency, or it may be partial, clinically chronic retention. Residual urine more than 25% of the bladder capacity is regarded as significant.

ETIOLOGY

Obstruction to Urine Flow. Common causes are bladder neck stricture, enlarged prostate (benign or malignant), urethral stricture, a stone impacted in the urethra, and posterior urethral valve in children.

Neurogenic Bladder. Damage to the bladder nerve supply, either motor or sensory, can hinder normal bladder function. Damage can occur from spinal cord trauma, congenital anomalies, or disease states, such as diabetes mellitus and multiple sclerosis.

Iatrogenic Urinary Retention. Anticholinergic drugs (e.g., antihistamines, antiparkinsonian agents, antidepressants), and beta-adrenergic stimulants (e.g., nasal decongestants) can impede bladder emptying.

Postsurgical Urinary Retention. Anal, vaginal, perineal, or pelvic surgery due to pelvic pain can cause reflex sphincter spasm and result in urinary retention.

CRITERIA FOR DIAGNOSIS

Suggestive

Inability to empty the bladder with a feeling of not emptying completely in chronic retention or intense desire to urinate in acute retention suggests the diagnosis.

Definitive

Palpating the distended bladder in the suprapubic region defines the diagnosis. A urethral catheter drains a large volume of urine in acute retention. In chronic retention, the residual volume is more than 25% of the bladder capacity.

CLINICAL MANIFESTATIONS

Subjective

In acute urinary retention, lower abdominal pain is perceived as an intense desire to urinate and inability to do so. Pain may be absent or minimal with neurogenic bladder. Sometimes patients with bladder pain due to cystitis present with a picture similar to urinary retention, but clinical examination should differentiate between the two conditions. Patients with acute or chronic urinary retention might present with overflow incontinence.

In partial retention, there are symptoms of outflow obstruction in the form of increased frequency, urgency, hesitancy, straining, weak flow, interrupted showery stream, and feeling of not emptying the bladder completely.

Chronic retention, particularly in neurogenic bladder, might present with symptoms of recurrent urinary tract infections, bladder stones, or uremia.

Objective

Physical Examination

Signs of uremia (e.g., dry tongue, uremic smell) might be present. The temperature might be elevated in the presence of urinary tract infection.

The bladder might be identified by palpation and percussion in the suprapubic region. Percussion or pressure will accentuate the intense urge to urinate if bladder sensation is not diminished. Enlarged hydronephrotic kidneys might be palpated in chronic cases. The presence of a hernia might give a clue to chronic straining.

The tip of the penis should be examined for phimosis, external meatal stricture, or impacted stone. Palpation of the urethra might reveal an indurated patch (urethral stricture) or impacted stone.

Weak anal tone directs attention to the diagnosis of neurogenic bladder, and full neurologic assessment is required. The presence of hemorrhoids or rectal prolapse might be secondary to chronic straining. The prostate might be enlarged and smooth in the presence of benign prostatic hypertrophy. A firm or irregular prostate raises the suspicion of prostate cancer.

Routine Laboratory Abnormalities

The blood urea nitrogen may be elevated with chronic urinary obstruction. The blood glucose level may be elevated in patients with diabetes.

PLANS

Diagnostic

Passage of a 16-French (in adults) urethral catheter is both diagnostic and therapeutic. The residual volume is calculated in partial obstruction. Failure to pass this catheter might be due to urethral stricture, impacted stone in the urethra, or enlarged prostate obstructing the prostatic urethra.

In chronic retention, uroflowmetry shows an obstructed pattern. Serum creatinine, electrolytes, and blood urea should be tested to assess renal function. Urinanalysis, particularly specific gravity, is important to differentiate between anuria and retention. Ultrasound scan of the bladder helps in measuring postmicturition residual volume and can diagnose upper urinary tract dilation. Urethrography (both antigrade and retrograde) diagnoses urethral strictures. A micturating cystourethrogram is helpful in the diagnosis of posterior urethral valve in children. Cystoscopy might be needed for both diagnosis and therapy. Urodynamic studies are important when neuropathic etiology is suspected and to confirm the presence of obstruction.

Therapeutic

Acute urinary retention is a medical emergency. A 16-French urethral catheter should be passed gently with generous lubrication and without any force. It this fails, a coude-tip catheter might be better in negotiating its way through urethral strictures or a tortuous prostatic urethra. A catheter introducer can be helpful if the operator is experienced, but in unexperienced hands it can cause false passage with subsequent urethral stricture. It is better to abandon urethral catheterization if it proved to be difficult. Insertion of a suprapubic catheter under ultrasound guidance is a straightforward technique and less traumatic than difficult urethral catheterization. Blind suprapubic catheter insertion should be done only by an experienced surgeon and should not be done in the presence of previous pelvic surgery to avoid injuring other abdominal organs.

Any medications the patient is taking should be reviewed to make sure that she or he is not receiving drugs that inhibit bladder emptying. The definitive treatment for retention depends on the etiology.

FOLLOW-UP

The frequency of follow-up and observations to be made are determined by the cause and treatment of the urinary retention. Patients who are managed conservatively by permanent or intermittent catheterization should be watched carefully for the development of urinary infections, urinary stones, or upper urinary tract deterioration.

DISCUSSION
Incidence

Incidence is determined by the underlying cause.

Related Basic Science

It is important to remember that urine retention could be caused by medications received by the patient and the condition could be reversed by changing these drugs. Urethral stricture disease could develop from traumatic catheterization or instrumentation of the urethra. It can also be caused by gonorrheal urethritis, particularly if it is inadequately treated. A neuropathic element of the etiology should be suspected in elderly patients and in patients with spinal trauma, chronic back pain, diabetes, parkinsonism, or other neurologic history. Acute lumbar disk prolapse, particularly if the prolapse is central, can result in urinary retention. It should be treated emergently if permanent damage to the bladder nerve supply is to be avoided.

Natural History and Its Modification with Treatment

The natural history is determined by the underlying cause and its treatment (see appropriate chapters in this book).

Prevention

The prevention of urinary retention is determined by the preventability of the underlying cause. Gonorrheal stricture disease is properly considered preventable by early diagnosis and adequate treatment of gonorrhea, as well as by taking public health measures to reduce its incidence and prevalence. Traumatic instrumentation of the urethra should be avoided.

Cost Containment

Cost containment is determined by the cost required to treat the underlying cause.

REFERENCES

Gillenwater JY, Grayhack JT, Howards SS, Duckett JW. Adult and pediatric urology. 2nd ed. St. Louis: Mosby Year Book, 1991.
Smith DR. General Urology. Norwalk: Appleton & Lange, 1995.
Walsh PC, Retick AB, Samy TA, Vaughan ED. Campbell's urology. 6th ed. Philadelphia: Saunders, 1992.

CHAPTER 18–3

Urinary Incontinence

R. E. S. El-Galley, M.B., B. Ch., and Niall T. M. Galloway, M.B., B. Ch.

DEFINITION

Urinary incontinence is involuntary loss of urine that can be demonstrated objectively.

ETIOLOGY

Incontinence is a hygienic, social, and health problem. Urine loss usually occurs through the urethra. Extraurethral loss also occurs, for example, due to a fistula or, in the female, an ectopic ureter. Urethral leakage could be due to stress, urge, or overflow incontinence. Stress incontinence could be due to bladder or urethral displacement or intrin-

sic urethral weakness. Urge incontinence could be secondary to neurogenic disease or idiopathic. Overflow incontinence could be secondary to chronic obstruction to the bladder outlet or neurogenic bladder.

CRITERIA FOR DIAGNOSIS
Suggestive

Patients might complain from urine leaking with physical efforts (e.g., coughing or sneezing) or inability to hold the urine until they reach the bathroom.

Definitive

Urine leakage with coughing or sneezing is diagnostic of stress incontinence. The presence of a full bladder after voiding that leaks with suprapubic pressure would suggest overflow incontinence.

CLINICAL MANIFESTATIONS
Subjective

The patient may complain of leakage, but is often reluctant to admit wetting, and the physician must be alert to recognize the signs of staining, odor, or the use of pads for protection.

- Stress incontinence occurs with coughing, straining, or exertion. The magnitude of leakage is usually in drops rather than a flood. Stress incontinence is common in women, but may also occur in men after prostate surgery.
- Urge incontinence is leakage that occurs with a strong urge to void that cannot be resisted. Urge leakage involves a bladder contraction and is often a flood rather than just drops. Symptoms of urinary frequency, urgency, and nocturia are commonly present in patients who have urge leakage.
- Overflow incontinence may occur when an overfull bladder fails to drain because of obstruction or paralysis. Leakage of drops may occur with or without provocation by cough or movement and will occur by night as well as by day. Overflow incontinence may occur with or without urgency and with or without a bladder contraction.

Objective
Physical Examination

Stress Incontinence. The patient should be examined with a full bladder and provoked with coughing or straining in the erect position. In the adult woman, stress incontinence is common. Observation of the perineum may demonstrate excessive movement of the urethra and bladder base and simultaneous urinary leakage with coughing or straining. This leakage may be correctable by cephalad displacement of the bladder neck. There may be associated signs of cystocele, enterocele, or rectocele.

Urge Incontinence. Urge incontinence may be found in the absence of pelvic relaxation. Urge incontinence is more common in the elderly and in patients who have a neurologic deficit. In neurogenic disease, urge incontinence may be called reflex incontinence.

Overflow Incontinence. Overflow incontinence may also occur in patients with neurologic disease or hypothyroidism or in prostatic outflow obstruction. Examination of the abdomen after voiding may reveal a mass arising from the pelvis that is smooth to palpation and dull to percussion. Palpation or percussion may provoke leakage from the urethra. Digital rectal examination of the prostate should be done to distinguish benign prostatic hypertrophy from carcinoma of the prostate.

Routine Laboratory Abnormalities

There are no diagnostic routine abnormalities associated with urinary incontinence.

PLANS
Diagnostic
Differential Diagnosis

When the Criteria for Diagnosis are met, the condition can be diagnosed with certainty.

Diagnostic Options and Recommended Approach

Urinary leakage may be transient or persistent. In the elderly, temporary incontinence may be provoked by an episode of physical illness or debility. Provoking factors may include constipation, medication, disorientation, and confusion. Similarly, in women, weight gain or urinary infection may provoke leakage or exacerbate minor symptoms. It is important to consider and exclude these factors.

Demonstration of leakage on physical examination confirms the diagnosis of incontinence but may not clearly define the type of incontinence. Effective treatment is dependent on accurate diagnosis.

The patient should be asked to keep a record of voiding times and voided volumes (a bladder chart) for at least 2 full days and a night. The chart documents the time and number of episodes of leakage. Addition of the voided volumes in 24 hours reveals the total urine output. This should not exceed 2 L. If voided volumes are excessive, fluid restriction may be appropriate. The largest voided volume is the same as the functional bladder capacity. A normal capacity would be approximately 500 mL for men and 600 mL for women. A small functioning capacity (< 300 mL) would suggest an overactive bladder and urge incontinence. Stress incontinence is usually associated with a normal functional capacity.

If symptoms are moderate or severe and fail to respond to conservative treatment, urodynamic evaluation should be considered before proceeding with surgical treatment. Urodynamics is the study of bladder and urethral function by the measurement of volume pressures and flow.

Therapeutic
Nonsurgical Treatment

Stress Incontinence. Nonsurgical treatment is effective in many cases. Simple measures include moderation of excessive fluid intake, weight reduction, treatment of chronic cough, pelvic floor exercises (Kegel), use of intravaginal weights (Femine Cones), biofeedback, and pelvic floor stimulation. Postmenopausal women with estrogen deficiency benefit from systemic or vaginal estrogen.

Urge Incontinence. Timed voiding using a chart should be encouraged, and the voiding intervals slowly increased as tolerated. Anticholinergic medication may be used in conjunction with a timed voiding regimen. Effective agents include propantheline bromide (Spastil) 15 to 30 mg every 4 to 6 hours and oxybutynin chloride (Ditropan) 5 mg every 8 hours. The patient should be encouraged to start with a small dose and to slowly increase the medication as required to control symptoms without troublesome side effects.

Side effects include dry mouth, constipation, dyspepsia, and sometimes flushing. The patient should titrate his or her dosage as symptoms demand and reduce or stop the medication at intervals to confirm the need for medication.

Overflow Incontinence. Overflow incontinence may be improved by instituting a vigorous bowel program and/or intermittent catheterization.

Surgical Treatment

Genuine Stress Incontinence. Repositioning surgery is indicated if the major cause of leakage is displacement of the bladder base. This may be achieved by endoscopic needle suspension or by traditional open surgery, for example, Marshall–Marchetti–Krantz or Birch procedure. If the major cause of leakage is intrinsic urethral weakness, periurethral collagen injection is helpful. If this fails, rectus muscle sling procedure or artificial urinary sphincter placement would be indicated.

Urge Incontinence. Urge leakage is usually managed adequately with medication alone. If surgical treatment is required, the bladder may be enlarged by incorporating a segment of detubularized bowel into the bladder wall. This procedure is called *augmentation cystoplasty*. The use of a gut segment eliminates leakage due to bladder contractions, but this may be at the expense of voiding efficiency. Intermittent catheterization may be required after surgery.

Overflow Incontinence. Overflow incontinence due to outflow obstruction should be relieved by appropriate surgery, for example, transurethral prostatectomy. Urodynamic evaluation is usually necessary to determine the need for outflow surgery.

FOLLOW-UP

The need for follow-up depends on the severity of leakage and complexity of the treatment plan.

DISCUSSION
Prevalence and Incidence

The prevalence of significant urinary incontinence is on the order of 10% of the community. The prevalence is greater in women and in the elderly. Of those who do have significant incontinence, the majority fail to seek medical or nursing help.

Related Basic Science

The normal bladder is a low-pressure reservoir that stores urine that is constantly being produced by the kidneys. The bladder has two functions: to store and, at intervals, to empty. Bladder filling is largely passive. The bladder accommodates a large change in volume for only a small change in pressure (10 cm of water). Bladder muscle fibers are arranged in a loose latticework and move apart to accommodate filling. Stretching of muscle fibers occurs only as the bladder volume nears capacity. The normal outlet is closed by an involuntary passive mechanism and by an active sphincter mechanism that is controlled by volition. Normal voiding is initiated by the deliberate relaxation of the sphincter and pelvic floor muscles. Bladder contraction is initiated after sphincter relaxation and is sustained as the sphincter relaxation is sustained. When voiding is complete, a brief sphincter contraction is followed by bladder relaxation, and continence is maintained until the next voiding by passive continence mechanisms. Voluntary contraction of the sphincters and pelvic floor is not a requirement for resting continence but is an additional mechanism to complement the primary mechanisms during vigorous activity.

Stress urinary incontinence is due to a deficiency of the continence mechanism because of displacement, incompetence, or intrinsic urethral weakness. Urge incontinence is the result of an overactive bladder that contracts inappropriately during the storing phase. It is not uncommon for stress and urge leakage to occur together. Urodynamic evaluation has a critical role in selecting patients for appropriate surgical treatment.

Natural History and Its Modification with Treatment

Urinary incontinence is associated with significant morbidity. Personal, family, and social problems are common. For the elderly, it is often a continence problem that determines the need for residential rather than independent care. Medical problems associated with incontinence include urinary tract infection and skin problems, particularly dermatitis and bedsores.

Prevention

Postpartum pelvic floor exercises may have a role in reducing the incidence of postpartum incontinence. Urine output is proportional to the amount of fluid taken in. Excessive fluid intake worsens the symptoms of incontinence. Factors that exacerbate leakage should be discussed. Any medications used by the patient should be reviewed. For example, the patient with hypertension should be managed with a calcium channel blocking agent rather than a diuretic or sympathetic blockade. A simple bowel program to improve bowel function should always be considered before initiating bladder treatment.

Cost Containment

The physician should be ready to recognize and address continence problems. Provoking or exacerbating factors should be recognized and eliminated. Bladder charts should be used to recognize patients with excessive urine output. Nonsurgical methods should be used before proceeding with surgical treatment.

We should not encourage the use of pads and garments for protection. It is always possible to improve continence problems, and this can often be achieved by simple, inexpensive measures. Urodynamic evaluation should be reserved for patients who have failed on conservative measures and for whom surgical treatment would be appropriate.

REFERENCES

Bramble FJ. The treatment of urge incontinence by interocystoscopy. Br J Urol 1982:54:693.
Feneley RCL, Shepherd AM, Powell PH, et al. Urinary incontinence: Prevalence and needs. Br J Urol 1979:51:493.
Marshall VF, Marchetti AA. Krantz KE. The correction of stress incontinence of simple vesicourethral suspension. Surg Gynecol Obstet 1949:88:509.
McGuire EJ, Savastano JA. Stress incontinence and detrusor instability–urge incontinence. Neurourol Urodyam 1985:4:313.
Webster GD, Sihelnik SA, Stone AR. Female urinary incontinence: The incidence, identification and characteristics of detrusor instability. Neurourol Urodynam 1984:3:235.

CHAPTER 18–4

Urinary Frequency

David P. O'Brien III, M.D.

DEFINITION

Urinary frequency is a symptom complex in which the patient complains of abnormally frequent voiding of urine. The etiology of urinary frequency may be increased urine formation, diminished bladder capacity, incomplete bladder emptying, stress-related frequency, or frequency related to excess fluid intake.

CRITERIA FOR DIAGNOSIS
Suggestive

The patient's own symptoms of frequency of urination are often suggestive of urinary frequency.

Definitive

The definitive diagnosis of urinary frequency can be made only on the basis of a bladder chart, which documents both the times and volumes of urine voided over a standard period, such as 24 to 48 hours.

CLINICAL MANIFESTATIONS
Subjective

A diminished time between voidings of urine is the specific complaint. The duration of this complaint and the degree of frequency are important. That is, does it occur every day, every hour, every 2 hours? The intermittent or persistent nature of the complaint should be determined, along with its diurnal or nocturnal aspects. One should attempt to distinguish between the frequent voiding of small or large amounts and inquire whether pain, chills, or fever is associated.

Objective
Physical Examination

A time voiding record of the frequency and volume of urination documents the patient's voiding pattern and separates true frequency from polyuria. The patient should be examined for costovertebral angle pain, bladder distention, prostate size and/or tenderness in the male, and pelvic (bladder) tenderness in the female.

Routine Laboratory Abnormalities

Initial routine urinalysis should be performed for signs of infection, and the residual urine volume should be checked if bladder distention is suspected. The urine should be cultured if findings are present or in any patient in whom the persistent symptom is present even without urinary findings.

PLANS
Diagnostic

See Table 18–1–1. Stress-related episodes of urinary frequency are often diagnosed by exclusion. That is, when no objective data other than an anxious or emotionally stressed patient are available to the examiner, this diagnostic possibility should be considered.

Therapeutic
Therapeutic Options

Management of the symptoms of urinary frequency depends on the etiology or primary diagnosis (see Table 18–1–1). When objective data are lacking, one may have to treat the symptom alone. A trial of urinary antispasmodic agents (e.g., hyoscyamine [Cystospaz], flavoxate HCl [Urispas]), anticholinergic agents, and oxybutynin chloride (Ditropan) may be used. Treatment of depression or stress reactions also may be effective.

Recommended Approach

Again, the recommended approach for treatment of urinary frequency depends on the etiology or primary diagnosis.

FOLLOW-UP

Follow-up again varies with the disease process. Repetitive testing, urinalyses, residual urine volumes, and urodynamic evaluation are commonly necessary.

DISCUSSION
Prevalence and Incidence

The exact prevalence and incidence of urinary frequency are indeterminate. It is, however, one of the most common urinary symptoms.

Related Basic Science

Urinary frequency may be caused by a variety of factors occurring singly or in combination. Frequency may be caused by increased urine formation, diminished bladder capacity, incomplete bladder emptying, or bladder irritability. The pathophysiologic background entailed in specific entities may be found in the individual chapters related to those diagnoses.

Natural History and Its Modification with Treatment

The natural history of urinary frequency varies with the disease entities involved, as is modification of the natural history with treatment.

Prevention

Prevention of urinary frequency is determined by the preventability of the specific etiology.

Cost Containment

Prompt and aggressive treatment of the individual disease process should contain costs effectively.

REFERENCES

Fellner SK. Urinary tract infection. In: Walker HK, Hall WD, Hurst JW, eds. Clinical methods: The history, physical and laboratory examinations, 2nd ed. Boston: Butterworth, 1980:223.

Greenfield S, Friedland G, Scifers S, et al. Protocol management of dysuria, urinary frequency, and vaginal discharge. Ann Intern Med 1974;81:452.

Stamey TA. Urinary infections. Baltimore: Williams & Wilkins, 1972.

Steensberg J, Bartels ED, Bay-Nielson H, et al. Epidemiology of urinary tract disease in general practice. Br Med J 1969;4:390.

CHAPTER 18–5

Enuresis (Bedwetting)

Bruce H. Broecker, M.D.

DEFINITION

Enuresis is defined as the involuntary discharge of urine at night while asleep at an age by which control should be present. It may be classified as primary nocturnal enuresis, when it has always been present without any prolonged dry interval, or secondary nocturnal enuresis, when the onset has come after a prolonged period of nocturnal dryness (> 6 months).

ETIOLOGY

The etiology of primary enuresis is uncertain. It has been attributed to a micturitional delay, sleep disorder, and/or endocrinopathy. There is evidence for and against each of these proposed causes. Regardless of the precise cause, nocturnal enuresis is virtually always self-limited and has spontaneously resolved by late adolescence or sooner.

Secondary nocturnal enuresis may often be precipitated by emotional or psychological disturbances.

CRITERIA FOR DIAGNOSIS

Enuresis is the involuntary discharge of urine during sleep beyond an age when control of bladder function is normally expected. From this definition it can be concluded that urination during sleep is normal and expected during infancy, but as the child grows, it eventually ceases. The age at which this activity stops may vary; therefore, there is not an exact age at which "control of bladder function is normally expected." At 5 years of age, approximately 15% of normal children have frequent episodes of bedwetting. This decreases to approximately 5% by age 10 and 1% by age 15. The prevalence in adults is estimated to be 0.5%. Enuresis is commonly categorized as primary when it has always been present and secondary when there is an onset after a lengthy interval of dry nights.

CLINICAL MANIFESTATIONS
Subjective

Enuresis in most cases is a functional disorder but may occasionally indicate or be due to an underlying structural or neurologic abnormality. If the disorder is functional, bedwetting may be the only symptom or there may be associated daytime symptoms of bladder instability, such as urinary frequency, urgency, and/or incontinence. Dysuria, if present, may indicate the presence of a urinary tract infection. Many enuretic children have a family history of enuresis in one or both parents. Symptoms of encopresis, daytime urinary incontinence, gait disturbance, or limb weakness should arouse concern of a neurologic condition such as sacral agenesis, lipoma of the cord, or a tethered cord.

Objective

Physical Examination

A normal physical examination would be expected in a child with functional enuresis. A thorough examination is essential, however, to evaluate possible neurologic causes, and occasionally an unrelated structural abnormality is discovered in this manner. Children with enuresis due to a neurologic condition would be expected to have some abnormal findings on the neurologic examination such as abnormal perineal sensation, anal sphincter tone, or bulbocavernosus reflex activity.

Routine Laboratory Abnormalities

A urinalysis should always be done to screen for evidence of a urinary tract infection.

PLANS

Diagnostic

If historical and physical findings suggest a functional cause for the enuresis (i.e., the physical examination is entirely normal, the only symptom is bedwetting, and the urinalysis is normal), no further diagnostic studies are necessary. If for any reason there is concern about an underlying structural abnormality, a renal and bladder ultrasound is an excellent noninvasive screening study. If a neurologic cause is suspected, appropriate diagnostic studies to further evaluate this possibility would include lateral lumbosacral spine, urodynamic evaluation, and magnetic resonance imaging of the spine.

Therapeutic

Management of enuresis that is functional may require only reassurance of the parents and child of its eventual resolution (see Natural History and Its Modification with Treatment). Certainly, below the age of 5 or 6, this should be all that is done. It should be made clear to the parents that the child is unable to control this activity and that punishment is ineffective and inappropriate as a means to stop the bedwetting. Likewise, parents should not feel that their child's bedwetting is due to a lack of parenting skills on their part. In older children who may suffer embarrassment and emotional disturbance due to their bedwetting, one of several symptomatic therapies may be employed. Although the precise cause of enuresis is not clearly understood, it appears that all current therapies are directed primarily at a symptom rather than an underlying etiology. Successful or unsuccessful treatment of the symptom does not accelerate or retard the eventual spontaneous resolution of the disturbance. The currently accepted therapeutic approaches to enuresis include responsibility training, conditioning, and pharmacologic treatment. Responsibility training involves active involvement of the child in understanding the natural history of enuresis, documenting wet and dry nights, and changing bed linen coupled with positive reinforcement for desired behavior. Though improvement may be slow with this method, perhaps not much faster than spontaneous resolution, once a successful outcome has been achieved relapse is rare.

Conditioning involves the use of an alarm device. The most successful of these employ an electrode that clips to the pajamas in proximity to the urethral meatus. When this becomes damp an alarm is activated which awakens the child who then completes urination in the bathroom. In a short period the bladder becomes retrained or conditioned to hold urine all night. Success with alarm devices has been in the range of 60 to 70%, and again once success is achieved, relapse is rare.

The most common pharmacologic agents currently used are imipramine (Tofranil), propantheline (Probanthine), oxybutynin (Ditropan), and most recently desmopressin (DDAVP). The precise mechanism of action of imipramine for enuresis is not clear but is thought to be due to its anticholinergic action producing bladder relaxation and its central nervous system activity producing increased arousal. Success rates of 60 to 70% are achieved with this medication. Propantheline and oxybutynin are most successful when enuresis is accompanied by daytime symptoms of frequency and urgency. The most recent drug approved for use for enuresis is desmopressin, an antidiuretic hormone analog, which can be administered as a nasal spray. Success rates of 50 to 80% have been reported. In children who respond favorably, discontinuation of any of the above-mentioned medications before spontaneous resolution has occurred results in relapse. Overall, 75% of treated enuretic children improve on medication; however, in 25% the symptom does not respond to any current form of treatment.

Therapy of neurologic disorders or structural abnormalities associated with enuresis is covered in other chapters.

Parents and children should have their fears and concerns addressed. Many are concerned that renal or bladder function is seriously impaired. They should be reassured that functional enuresis is common, self-limited, and not an indication of serious renal or detrusor pathology. The parents also need to be made aware that enuresis is not deliberate and, therefore, punishment is not an appropriate response. Similarly, they should not feel that their child's enuresis represents a failure on their part.

FOLLOW-UP

If a child is being treated pharmacologically, follow-up should be every 1 to 3 months. Once a successful outcome has been achieved and the child is no longer on any form of treatment, routine follow-up is no longer necessary.

DISCUSSION

Prevalence and Incidence

See Criteria for Diagnosis.

Related Basic Science

The cause of enuresis is not fully understood. It has been attributed to a sleep disorder, maturational delay, and, most recently, an endocrinopathy. Evidence for all of these is divided and inconclusive.

Natural History and Its Modification with Treatment

The natural history of enuresis is spontaneous resolution in almost all cases by the age of 18.

Prevention

There is no known effective method of prevention.

Cost Containment

In those children in whom the history and physical examination suggest a functional disturbance, further diagnostic evaluation is an unnecessary expense without proven yield.

REFERENCES

Crawford JD, ed. Treatment of nocturnal enuresis. J Pediatr Suppl 1989;114(4, pt 2).

Koff SA. Enuresis. In: Walsh PC, Retik AB, Vaugh ED, Stamey TA, eds., Campbell's urology. 6th ed. Philadelphia: Saunders, 1992:1621.

Norgaards J, Rittiq S, Djurhuus J. Nocturnal enuresis: An approach to treatment based on pathogenesis. J Pediatr 1989:114:705.

Rushton HG. Nocturnal enuresis: Epidemiology, evaluation and currently available treatment options. J Pediatr 1989:114:696.

Hematuria (See Section 16, Chapter 5)

Pyuria (See Section 8, Chapters 23 and 24, and Section 16, Chapter 6)

Hematospermia

Michael A. Witt, M.D.

DEFINITION

Hematospermia is defined as the presence of blood in the seminal fluid.

ETIOLOGY

No known etiology exists for hematospermia. It is presumed to be due to inflammation of the seminal vesicles.

CRITERIA FOR DIAGNOSIS

Hematospermia can be diagnosed by the microscopic identification of red blood cells in the semen.

CLINICAL MANIFESTATIONS
Subjective

Hematospermia appears as either a bright red or brown coloration of the seminal fluid. Most patients report hematospermia in the absence of any other symptoms and at the time that it is first noted. It is not uncommon for the sexual partner to be the first to identify that hematospermia exists. The seminal fluid may have blood in the initial portion or the latter portion of the ejaculate, and this should be noted in the history. The patients are commonly in their fifth to sixth decade of life. The remainder of the history should encompass documentation of voiding dysfunction or hematuria. A past history of prostatitis or cystitis should be elicited.

Objective
Physical Examination

The physical examination should focus on the genitourinary tract. It should encompass abdominal, genital, and rectal examination. The examination is typically normal in all respects. It is difficult to palpate the seminal vesicles, and any abnormality on examination should warrant further evaluation.

Routine Laboratory Abnormalities

Red blood cells may be found in the urine.

PLANS
Diagnostic
Differential Diagnosis

The differential diagnosis lies between blood in the semen and abnormal pigmentation of the semen.

Diagnostic Options and Recommended Approach

If the patient is otherwise asymptomatic and has a completely normal genitourinary examination, it is wise to obtain a urinalysis for microscopic inspection and cytology, as well as an ejaculate, to confirm the presence of red blood cells in the semen. If these studies are all normal except for the presence of red blood cells in the semen, no other evaluation is indicated. If the digital rectal exam is abnormal, a serum prostate-specific antigen (PSA) test should be done, as should a transrectal ultrasound to examine the seminal vesicles. If urine cytology is abnormal, or if red blood cells are present in the urine, a workup for hematuria should be initiated.

The recommended approach is to follow patients with no identifiable malignancy to detect abnormalities that could not be identified initially.

Therapeutic

There is no specific treatment for hematospermia. If a urinary tract infection or prostatitis is suspected, then a course of antibiotics appropriate for prostatic pathogens and prostatic parenchymal penetration is indicated.

It is appropriate to counsel the patient that although this is a very disturbing finding, the likelihood of there being any significant pathology is very low. The patient should be made aware that this problem may recur, even in the absence of any significant findings on the formal evaluation.

FOLLOW-UP

If the examination is completely normal, the patient should be evaluated in 6 months or sooner if new symptoms appear.

DISCUSSION
Prevalence and Incidence

The incidence of hematospermia is not known. In young men, a rare congenital abnormality in the verumontanum or the prostate resulting in a friable polyp may produce hematospermia. Presumably, hematospermia arises from irritation of the seminal vesicles or prostate, which results in disruption of the microcirculation during ejaculation. Ejaculation is a vigorous process with intermittent strong peristaltic contractions that can easily rupture or denude granulation tissue or neovascularity resulting from inflammation or adenoma formation.

Natural History and Its Modification with Treatment

The condition typically resolves in 4 to 6 months but can recur.

Prevention

No method of prevention exists.

Cost Containment

Cost containment is achieved by limiting the examination of the patient to the tests described in this chapter.

REFERENCE

Worischeck JH, Parra RO. Chronic hematospermia: Assessment by transrectal ultrasound. Urology 1994;43:515.

CHAPTER 18–9
....

Pneumaturia and Fecaluria

R. E. S. El-Galley, M.B., B. Ch., and Niall T. M. Galloway, M.B., B. Ch.

DEFINITION

Pneumaturia is the passage of gas in the urine, and fecaluria is the passage of feces in the urine.

ETIOLOGY

Fecaluria is pathognomonic of an abnormal communication between the bowel and the urinary tract, usually a colovesical fistula. Pneumaturia is often due to a fistula, but can be the innocent result of instrumentation or catheterization of the lower urinary tract. Urinary infection with gas-forming organisms can also produce pneumaturia, especially in the diabetic patient.

CRITERIA FOR DIAGNOSIS
Suggestive

The patient might report the presence of air or feces in the urine. Irritative symptoms of frequency, urgency, dysuria, and stranguria might be present.

Definitive

The patient's complaint of passage of gas in the urine is diagnostic. Fecal material or stercobilin in a urine specimen collected from the urethra without contamination is diagnostic of fecaluria.

CLINICAL MANIFESTATIONS
Subjective

Air rises to the dome of the bladder and is therefore passed at the end of the urinary stream. There might be an audible fizzing sound as the flow of urine ceases.

Fecaluria produces a foul-smelling and turbid urine. Two thirds of patients have some lower abdominal symptoms attributable to underlying disease of the bowel. A past history of diverticular disease in the colon is common.

Objective
Physical Examination

The physical examination is often unremarkable, but there might be some degree of abdominal distention. The colon might be palpable, and there might be tenderness in the left iliac fossa or suprapubic area. Digital rectal examination might reveal a pelvic mass or induration, but it is often unremarkable.

Routine Laboratory Abnormalities

The urine may have a foul odor and a turbid appearance. Microscopic examination might reveal various organisms and white blood cells. There might be occult blood in the stools. A metabolic abnormality is rare, unless the fistula communicates between the bladder and the small bowel. When this condition is present, the metabolic abnormalities expected are, dehydration, metabolic acidosis, azotemia, and hyperkalemia.

PLANS
Diagnostic
Differential Diagnosis

Some patients go unrecognized with recurrent urinary tract infection for months or years before the fistula is diagnosed. The primary disease is usually of the bowel, diverticular disease, carcinoma, or Crohn's disease or, occasionally, trauma. In the past, tuberculosis and typhoid were

also important causes. The bladder is usually healthy, but disease of the bladder can give rise to a vesicocolic fistula, for example, direct spread of squamous cell carcinoma of the bladder into adjacent small bowel or large bowel.

Diagnostic Options and Recommended Approach

Sigmoidoscopy should be performed to obtain histologic diagnosis from a distal colonic lesion. The definitive investigation for suspected vesicocolic fistula, however, is a double-contrast barium enema. This is abnormal in almost all cases, and outlines the tract in about 50%. Cystoscopy is abnormal in 95% of cases of vesicocolic fistula. The classic finding is a "pseudotumor" on the left posterior bladder wall, but the fistulous opening itself is often obscured by surrounding edema. Biopsies should be taken to exclude the possibility of a bladder tumor or colonic neoplasm invading the bladder. Biopsy usually reveals only inflammatory changes at this site.

It is rarely necessary to carry investigations beyond barium enema and cystoscopy. In the event that both these tests are normal, a fistula more proximal in both the gastrointestinal and urinary tracts should be sought with an intravenous pyelogram and small bowel enema.

Therapeutic

Treatment is aimed at resection of the diseased segment of bowel and excision of the involved vesical tissue. This can generally be done as a single-stage elective procedure; however, a two-stage operation involving a proximal defunctioning colostomy is recommended in the presence of intestinal obstruction or overt sepsis or when the bowel has been subjected to previous radiotherapy. Provided the bowel is well prepared, the diseased segment can be excised, and a reanastomosis can be performed without tension. A defunctioning colostomy is unnecessary. Abnormal bladder tissue surrounding the fistula is excised, and the defect is closed. It is better to interpose the omentum between the bladder and the bowed anastomosis. The bladder should be drained with urethral and suprapubic catheters for 7 to 10 days postoperatively.

FOLLOW-UP

The frequency of follow-up depends on the nature and severity of the underlying disease. All patients should be seen within 6 weeks of surgery, when a physical examination and urine analysis should be done. Patients with benign conditions (diverticular disease or appendicitis) need only be reviewed thereafter if symptomatic. Those with colorectal or bladder cancer or Crohn's disease need long-term regular review with sigmoidoscopy, double-contrast barium enema, or cystoscopy, as appropriate for the condition.

DISCUSSION
Prevalence and Incidence

Vesicoenteric fistulas are rare. The incidence is higher in men than women (3:1) due to the interposition of the uterus and vagina.

Related Basic Science

A fistula between gastrointestinal and urinary tracts develops when an inflammatory or neoplastic process in one spreads to the contiguous surface of the other. The disease process weakens the walls of both organs, which eventually give way. Pressure within the gastrointestinal tract is greater than that within the urinary tract, which explains why gas or fecal material passes from the bowel into the bladder, rather than urine passing per rectum. The fistula persists while the pressure gradient across it exists, and fecal diversion via a defunctioning colostomy has no effect. The fistula opens in the dome of the bladder in 60% of cases and in the posterior wall in 30%.

Natural History and Its Modification with Treatment

Peumaturia is a symptom or sign that may indicate the presence of a fistula. The natural history is dependent on that of the underlying disease process. It is rarely a solitary symptom and is almost always preceded by more aggravating lower gastrointestinal tract symptoms. The results of surgery for uroenteric fistulas secondary to inflammatory conditions are good, but less favorable results can be expected in patients with radiation injury or advanced carcinoma.

Prevention

Prevention is determined by the ability to prevent the underlying disease. As diverticulitis, colorectal carcinoma, and bladder carcinoma are common causes of pneumonia due to fistula, attention should be directed at general health measures such as high-fiber diets and avoid-

ance of cigarette smoking. The early detection of an underlying disease process by screening for occult blood or microscopic hematuria is a controversial subject, but these may be useful in appropriate cases.

Cost Containment

Cost containment is achieved by avoiding unnecessary investigations to reach a diagnosis, by operating only after the acute phase of the disease has settled, and by limiting the overall hospital stay by using a one-stage operation when it is appropriate.

REFERENCES

Mileski WJ, Joehi RJ, Rege RV, Nahrwold DL. One stage resection and anastomosis in the management of colovesical fistula. Am J Surg 1987;153–57.
Pollard SG, MacFarlane R, Greatorex R, et al. Colovesical fistula. Ann R Coll Surg Engl 1987;69:1963.
Rao PN, Knox R, Barnard RJ, Schofield PF. Management of colovesical fistula. Br J Surg 1987;74:362.

CHAPTER 18–10

Impotence Due to Organic Causes

Michael A. Witt, M.D.

DEFINITION

Impotence can be defined as the inability to initiate or maintain a penile erection that is sufficiently rigid to achieve penetration and of adequate duration to obtain satisfaction.

ETIOLOGY

The etiology of impotence is organic or psychogenic. Organic etiologies include vascular, neurologic, hormonal, and pharmacologic causes.

CRITERIA FOR DIAGNOSIS

The diagnosis is made when the patient complains of the inability to obtain or retain an erection.

CLINICAL MANIFESTATIONS
Subjective

The patient complains of the inability to maintain or generate an erection. He often states that the erection is either too soft to penetrate or does not have appropriate durability for successful function. It is important to differentiate the difficulty of maintaining erection because of the presence of premature ejaculation from that due to aging.

In premature ejaculation a normal erection can be generated but, due to the onset of ejaculation prior to the patient's desire to do so, detumescence occurs. In addition, as a patient ages, erections become less frequent, the refractory period between ejaculations increases, and the orgasm is of shorter duration. Those patients complaining of these specific entities do not have impotence.

Objective

Physical Examination

The physical examination should focus predominantly on the genitalia and a thorough examination of the peripheral vasculature and the integrity of the lumbosacral neurologic output. It is important to assess the presence or absence of testicular atrophy and gynecomastia, which may suggest certain diseases.

Routine Laboratory Abnormalities

Routine laboratory testing may reveal glycosuria and hyperglycemia, strongly suggesting diabetes. The cholesterol level may be above the desirable range, suggesting an increased likelihood of atherosclerosis.

PLANS
Diagnostic

Differential Diagnosis

The possible causes of erectile dysfunction include psychogenic causes, neurologic causes, vascular causes, endocrine causes, and pharmacologic causes. The history and physical examination begin to narrow down one of these as responsible for the condition.

Diagnostic Options and Recommended Approach

If a psychogenic etiology is suspected because of the presence of normal erections in the absence of intercourse, then a psychosexual evaluation is initiated.

If pharmacologic etiology is suspected due to the initiation of antihypertensive agents, antidepressants, or beta blockers, then it is recommended to change or discontinue the medication, if possible, and observe if there is return of erectile ability.

If a neurologic etiology is suspected, an intracorporeal injection of a smooth muscle relaxant, either papaverine or prostaglandin, should be used to determine whether a normal erection is achievable.

If a vascular etiology is suspected, the same diagnostic maneuver is performed to determine if there is an arterial or venous abnormality.

For endocrine problems, the underlying endocrinopathy such as hypogonadism, hyperprolactinemia, or hypothyroidism should be treated. Following this, the patient's function should be reassessed. Once the appropriate etiology is identified, therapeutic maneuvers follow.

Therapeutic

The most common cause of erectile dysfunction tends to be vascular abnormalities producing arterial insufficiency or incomplete corporeal veno-occlusion. If this is a mild problem that is responsive to an intracorporeal injection of a pharmacologic agent, then this form of treatment would be appropriate. If the patient does not desire injection therapy, he should proceed with a vacuum erection device or a penile prosthesis.

If a neurologic abnormality is identified, then intracorporeal injection is the first line of treatment. If this is not acceptable, the patient can proceed with a vacuum erection device or a penile prosthesis.

When the problem is caused by a pharmacologic agent and the medication cannot be changed to achieve the appropriate response, the patient may use intracorporeal injections, a vacuum device, or a penile prosthesis.

For psychological causes, psychosexual therapy is indicated.

Endocrinoapathies should be corrected. For hyperprolactinemia due to a microadenoma, bromocriptine is indicated. If the patient has hypogonadism, testosterone can be administered to improve libido and sexual function. If thyroid function studies are abnormal, these should be corrected with appropriate medication. In a few cases, a pure arterial abnormality can account for erectile dysfunction. This tends to be in the younger patient who has sustained some sort of pelvic or perineal injury. In this case, a test intracorporeal injection will not be effective, and an arteriogram may be indicated. If a focal area of obstruction is identifiable, then arterial bypass surgery is indicated.

FOLLOW-UP

The patient should be seen in follow-up after a diagnosis has been made to discuss potential options for treatment. It is not uncommon for patients who have been started on intracorporeal injection therapy or a vacuum erection device to discontinue treatment. Thus, they should be followed on a biannual basis to modify or update treatment.

DISCUSSION
Prevalence and Incidence

Impotence affects approximately 10 million men in the United States.

Related Basic Science

The most common cause of erectile dysfunction tends to be damage to the microvasculature of the corpus cavernosum. As a result, there is ei-

ther altered inflow or incomplete corporeal veno-occlusion which is now thought to be a passive phenomenon. Recent studies have indicated that in men with impotence due to corporeal veno-occlusive dysfunction, the corpus cavernosum contains a larger amount of collagen. This may be due to atherosclerotic injury to the endothelium or prolonged low oxygen tension due to poor arterial inflow. As a result, the corpus becomes stiffer, impairing expansion and preventing retention of pressure and volume in the corpus. These current findings may explain the presence of nocturnal erections and also why, with the restoration of corporeal blood flow via intracorporeal injections, there is spontaneous function in 10 to 15% of patients. This is the potential basis for self-preventive therapy, in that with early diagnosis, early restoration of corporeal blood flow may reverse some of the intracorporeal changes causing impotence.

Natural History and Its Modification with Treatment

This difficult problem can be helped with the measures described under Plans, Therapeutic.

Prevention

Population studies have identified specific risk factors that predispose men to erectile dysfunction. These consist of smoking, vascular disease, and anger. Some of these are predominantly social habits, which can be modified, and men with these risk factors should be treated accordingly and counseled as to their risks regarding loss of sexual function.

Cost Containment

Early treatment is more likely to be successful and is the appropriate way to contain costs (see Related Basic Science).

REFERENCES

Moralis A, Seurage DHC, Marshall PG, et al. Nonhormonal pharmacologic treatment of organic impotence. Urology 1982;128:45.
Zorgniotti AW. LaFleurr's autoinjection of the corporis cavernosum with a vasoactive drug: Accommodation for vasculogenic impotence. Urology 1985;133:39.

CHAPTER 18–11

Premature Ejaculation

Michael A. Witt, M.D.

DEFINITION

Premature ejaculation is the inability to control ejaculation for a sufficient length of time during intravaginal containment to satisfy the male and female partner at least 50% of the time.

ETIOLOGY

Premature ejaculation is primarily sexual dysfunction and not a fertility problem. Organic causes are rarely implicated in premature ejaculation. The rare case of secondary onset of premature ejaculation indicates that a physical etiology may be present, and this must be pursued. Such things to be considered are multiple sclerosis and a tumor of the spinal cord. Some urologic conditions have also been implicated with premature ejaculation, such as benign prostatic hypertrophy and prostatitis, but these do not clearly cause the problem. Proposed psychological mechanisms include performance anxiety.

CRITERIA FOR DIAGNOSIS

The diagnosis is made if the patient reports the inability to delay the onset of ejaculation for his personal satisfaction up to 50% of the time.

CLINICAL MANIFESTATIONS
Subjective

The history is fairly straightforward, with the patient reporting the inability to control ejaculation. It is important in some patients who report with impotence to rule out the presence of premature ejaculation, which they may confuse with impotence.

The previous institution of medications or surgical endeavors should be queried, to rule out these possible contributing factors.

Objective
Physical Examination
Physical examination should focus on examination of the genitalia and a neurologic assessment of the lumbosacral dermatomes (see Etiology).

Routine Laboratory Abnormalities
There are no laboratory abnormalities.

PLANS
Diagnostic
Differential Diagnosis
The complaint is diagnostic. There is no differential diagnosis.

Diagnostic Options
The complaint is diagnostic.

Therapeutic
Management of premature ejaculation rests primarily on counseling and sex therapy. This therapy focuses the attention of the patient on the sensate feedback immediately prior to ejaculation, using this as the point at which to cease activity. This technique is commonly referred to as a squeeze technique. This type of therapy has proven successful.

Phenothiazines in low doses have also been reported to be helpful. Sympatholytics such as anafranil have been helpful in impeding the onset.

Some people have recommended the patient should apply a condom to decrease sensation in hopes of providing an opportunity to develop delayed onset of ejaculation.

The patient should specifically be counseled that this is a learned response. It is not uncommon for patients who have developed the ability to inhibit ejaculation, if there is a prolonged period of abstinence, to then redevelop the inability to inhibit ejaculation. It is important for them to monitor themselves quite closely. The patient needs to determine, first, how long he is able to inhibit ejaculation and, second, the duration of inhibition that he feels is appropriate. This, then, gives him a target for which he can strive. It does involve close cooperation with the sexual partner, and thus the partner should be incorporated into the therapy.

If initial sexual counseling or medical therapy is inappropriate, then intracorporeal injection therapy has also been helpful in maintaining the erection even after ejaculation, so that the patient may continue sexual activity to satisfy his sexual partner and in so doing develop the ability to inhibit his ejaculation.

FOLLOW-UP
Follow-up is needed to monitor performance and to shift the approach to therapy if the complaint continues.

DISCUSSION
Prevalence and Incidence
The prevalence and incidence are not known.

Related Basic Science
Little is known about the basic abnormality responsible for this condition.

Natural History and Its Modification with Treatment
The outcome with and without treatment is not known.

Prevention
There is no known method of prevention.

Cost Containment
The cost is not excessive except when the patient changes physicians or therapists.

REFERENCES
Masters WH, Johnson VE. Human sexual inadequacy. Boston: Little, Brown, 1970.

Schapiro B. Premature ejaculation: A review of 1130 cases. J Urol 1943;50:374.

CHAPTER 18–12

Retarded Ejaculation
Michael A. Witt, M.D.

DEFINITION
Retarded ejaculation can be defined as the inability to initiate an ejaculation at the time of orgasm or a lack of anterograde ejaculation at the time of orgasm.

ETIOLOGY
The etiology of retarded ejaculation can be either anatomic, related to surgical or congenital abnormalities, neuropathic, pharmacologic, or psychogenic.

CRITERIA FOR DIAGNOSIS
Retarded ejaculation is reported as the absence of antegrade ejaculation or the inability to achieve an ejaculation.

CLINICAL MANIFESTATIONS
Subjective
The patient typically reports the lack of antegrade ejaculation with orgasm or the absence of any ejaculation. Patients with retrograde ejaculation may also complain of cloudy urine after ejaculation.

Patients with both retrograde ejaculation and ejaculatory failure report abnormalities in ejaculation. It is important to focus historically on the past medical and surgical history. It is not uncommon for patients after a prostatectomy, Y–V plasty, or trauma to the posterior urethra, to have difficulties with ejaculation. Congenital states also exist, such as epispadias with exstrophy and posterior urethral valves. In addition, some specific conditions can produce neuropathic problems, such as a history of retroperitoneal lymph node dissection for testicular cancer, a sympathectomy, vascular surgery, colorectal surgery, diabetes, and spinal cord injury. A patient should also be queried about potential medications he is taking, because psychotropic agents, antidepressants, and antihypertensive agents have all been implicated in causing ejaculatory abnormalities. The concomitant finding of any significant psychiatric history is also significant, as the absence of ejaculation may be associated with these psychiatric disorders.

Objective
Physical Examination
The physical examination should focus on the genitalia as well as the abdomen and the neurologic assessment of the lumbosacral der-

matomes. This may reveal the presence or absence of scars or neurologic deficits, which may suggest the possible etiology.

Routine Laboratory Abnormalities

There are no routine laboratory abnormalities.

PLANS

Diagnostic

Differential Diagnosis

The differential diagnosis is limited to determining if the ejaculation is absent, antegrade, or retrograde.

Diagnostic Options and Recommended Approach

The only laboratory examination recommended is to have the patient achieve, or attempt to achieve, an orgasm with a full bladder and then to have the patient empty the bladder. The urine should be examined microscopically for the presence or absence of sperm. If sperm are present, and the patient does not have an antegrade ejaculate or has only a small antegrade ejaculate, then retrograde ejaculation can be diagnosed.

Therapeutic

Once the diagnosis of retrograde ejaculation has been made, it is useful to discontinue (if possible) any medication that might be causing the condition. If the condition is due to a neurologic or surgical abnormality, then a trial of sympathomimetic agents ranging from pseudoephedrine hydrochloride 60 mg four times daily to imipramine hydrochloride 25 mg twice daily is recommended. This approach may convert retrograde ejaculation to an antegrade ejaculation. If this is ineffective, no other therapy exists. If retrograde ejaculation is producing infertility, sperm retrieval with assisted reproductive techniques is recommended for the patient to initiate a pregnancy.

If no ejaculation exists, and it is presumed to be due to an anatomic or neurologic abnormality, then recovery of ejaculation may be achieved with sympathomimetic agents. If this fails, then a trial of vibratory or electroejaculation is indicated. In so doing, this will determine whether ejaculation can be achieved and whether sperm are present in the ejaculate.

If the absence of ejaculation is due strictly to the presence of a psychiatric abnormality, then this condition must be treated before the patient can proceed with more invasive therapeutic endeavors.

FOLLOW-UP

Follow-up is needed to determine the success of treatment and to change therapy if the prescribed approach is not achieving the desired effect.

DISCUSSION

Prevalence and Incidence

The prevalence and incidence are not known.

Related Basic Science

The anatomy is altered by transurethral prostatectomy or removal of the prostate. This causes retrograde ejaculation in the former and impotence in the latter. The exact mechanisms responsible for retarded ejaculation are not known.

Natural History and Its Modification with Treatment

The natural history is unknown and the results of treatment are unclear.

Prevention

There is no known method of prevention.

Cost Containment

The cost of care is not excessive except when the patient seeks the opinion of several professionals.

REFERENCE

Cunningham GR. Medical treatment of the subfertile male. In: Lipshild LI, Howard HS, eds. Infertility in the male. New York: Churchill Livingstone, 1983.

CHAPTER 18–13

Meatal Stenosis

Bruce H. Broecker, M.D.

DEFINITION

Meatal stenosis is an abnormally small urethral meatus causing partial obstruction and/or deflection of the urinary stream.

ETIOLOGY

The etiology of meatal stenosis is generally considered to be meatal irritation and inflammation caused by an abrasive, wet diaper. It almost never occurs in an uncircumcised infant due to the protection provided to the glans/meatus by the intact prepuce.

CRITERIA FOR DIAGNOSIS

The diagnosis of meatal stenosis requires the demonstration of a visibly small meatus *plus* a diminished caliber of the urinary stream. The patient must be both examined and observed voiding.

CLINICAL MANIFESTATIONS

Subjective

Although it is often the complaints of urinary frequency, urgency, and occasionally penile discomfort that bring the child to the attention of a urologist, these symptoms are equally common in boys with and without meatal stenosis and not clearly related to obstruction in all cases. Symptoms of a narrow or deflected urinary stream are clearly related to the stenosis.

Objective

Physical Examination

Observation of a small, sometimes pinpoint meatus and a thin, high-velocity urinary stream are the objective findings in a boy with meatal stenosis. The stream is often deflected laterally or dorsally. Occasionally, there may be associated meatal inflammation.

Routine Laboratory Abnormalities

There are no routine laboratory abnormalities. White cells may be observed in the urine when there is associated urinary tract infection.

PLANS
Diagnostic
Differential Diagnosis

When the criteria for diagnosis are met there is no differential diagnosis.

Parents and primary care physicians should be made aware that the symptoms of urinary frequency and urgency alone in children are more often due to a functional disorder (pediatric uninhibited bladder) than to meatal stenosis.

Diagnostic Options and Recommended Approach

Examination of the genitalia and observation of the urinary stream are the only diagnostic studies required for diagnosis. A urinalysis should be done to exclude an associated urinary tract infection.

Therapeutic

A meatotomy adequately corrects the problem. Associated meatal inflammation, if present, should be treated first using systemic and/or topical antibiotics. Meatotomy is performed by incising the ventral lip of the meatus until the meatus is of adequate caliber. This procedure generally requires a brief general anesthetic in children but may be performed with local anesthesia in adults.

FOLLOW-UP

It is critically important for the parents to separate the incised meatal lips several times per day for several weeks following the meatotomy to prevent restenosis. This may be done manually or by inserting the nozzle tip of a tube of antibiotic ointment into the meatus. Follow-up in the physician's office should be in several weeks to a month for reexamination.

DISCUSSION
Prevalence and Incidence

When the diagnosis of the condition is based on the observation of a narrow urinary stream it is a relatively infrequent disorder.

Related Basic Science

Meatal stenosis is rarely seen in uncircumcised males. The etiology is generally felt to be meatal inflammation followed by sclerosis from wet diapers. It is prone to overdiagnosis because of the frequency of irritative voiding symptoms in young boys and the frequent appearance of a small meatus.

Natural History and Its Modification with Treatment

Meatal stenosis tends to be progressive. Surgical intervention is curative.

Prevention

The use of local hygiene to minimize meatitis may help prevent the disorder. This includes the prompt removal of wet diapers.

Cost Containment

Local hygienic measures may prevent the condition. Avoidance of unnecessary meatotomy will reduce costs.

REFERENCES
Allen JS, Summer JL, Wikerson JE. Meatal calibration of newborn boys. J Urol 1972;107:498.

Elder JS. Congenital anomalies of the genitalia. In: Walsh PC, Retik AB, Stamey TA, Vaugh ED, eds. Campbell's urology. 6th ed. Philadelphia: Saunders, 1992:1920.

CHAPTER 18–14

Urethral Stricture

R. E. S. El-Galley, M.B., B. Ch., and Niall T. M. Galloway, M.B., B. Ch.

DEFINITION

Stricture of the urethra is an abnormal constriction or loss of elasticity of the urethral channel. It is more common in males.

ETIOLOGY

Urethral stricture can result form internal trauma during unskilled instrumentation of the urethra or external trauma (e.g., saddle injury, pelvic fractures). Gonococcal urethritis is the most common cause of inflammatory strictures. Congenital strictures are rare and affect the external urethral meatus.

CRITERIA FOR DIAGNOSIS
Suggestive

The patient may feel urethral distention and painful voiding and experience painful dribbling.

Definitive

Failure to pass a 16-French catheter into the bladder defines the diagnosis.

CLINICAL MANIFESTATIONS
Subjective

The patient might have a history of traumatic or infected catheterization, instrumentation, or perineal injury. Saddle injury can crush the bulbar urethra against the pubic bones, whereas anterior pelvic fractures might disrupt the prostatomembranous urethral junction. History of gonococcal urethritis is significant. Urethritis caused by *Chlamydia* or *Ureaplasma* has not been positively linked to the occurrence of strictures. Most urethral strictures are caused by external trauma. Symptoms vary according to the location, type, and severity of the stricture. Inflammatory strictures may be associated with chronic urethral discharge from inflamed periurethral glands. Primary symptoms are those of obstruction with decreased force and caliber of stream, hesitancy, intermittent stream, frequency, nocturia, sometimes dysuria, and recurrent urinary tract infection. The patient might experience sensation of urethral distention and uncomfortable or painful voiding. Postmicturition dribbling is common. Severe strictures might cause urinary retention and associated overflow incontinence with daytime and nighttime wetting. Epididymoorchitis, chronic bacterial prostatitis, periurethral abscess, and urethral fistula formation may occur in association with urethral stricture.

Objective

Physical Examination

Abdominal examination may reveal suprapubic distention and a firm rounded mass of the distended urinary bladder, which is always dull to percussion. There may be urinary incontinence and staining of the underclothes. A urethral discharge might be noted. Inspection of the urethral meatus might reveal meatal stenosis. The penile urethra and perineum should be carefully inspected. There may be a scar of old injury or surgery or signs of periurethral inflammation. The urethra should be palpated throughout its length from the navicular fossa to the bulbar urethra. This might reveal induration. The bulbar urethra should be palpated through the scrotal skin and posteriorly toward the perineal body. Examination is best done with the patient supine with knees flexed and hips flexed and abducted. Digital rectal examination of the prostate is important, particularly in older men in whom proximal obstruction by benign prostatic hypertrophy or carcinoma of the prostate may be missed.

Routine Laboratory Abnormalities

Urinanalysis, microscopy, and urine culture should be done. Urinary flow rate should be measured and gentle catheterization attempted for measurement of postvoid residual. Failure to pass a 16-French catheter because of urethral obstruction indicates the need for further objective evaluation.

PLANS

Diagnostic

Differential Diagnosis

The presence of urethral stricture can be identified as described under Criteria for Diagnosis. The cause of the stricture must be pursued.

Diagnostic Options and Recommended Approach

Urethrography demonstrates the location and severity of the stricture. It is important to use both retrograde and voiding cystourethrograms to determine the distal and proximal limits of the stricture, respectively. Multiple strictures may be present. Urethroscopy should be deferred until urethral imaging is complete. The evaluation of the anterior urethra by ultrasound has recently been reported. When the urethra is distended with saline, the normal spongiosum is easily compressed, whereas the areas of scarring maintain a rigid configuration. This technique complements conventional urethrography in determining stricture length and degree of fibrosis.

Measurement of urinary flow rate is not diagnostic but is a useful objective measure. Repeated flow rates provide evidence of successful treatment or give warning of recurrence.

Therapeutic

The choice of surgical treatment depends on the general condition of the patient, etiology, location, severity of the stricture, and presence or absence of complications. Treatments include dilation (simple stretching of the urethra with sounds), urethrotomy (cutting the stricture with cold or hot knife or laser), and urethroplasty (one- or two-stage surgical repair).

Urethral dilation is often the initial treatment. The purpose is to dilate the urethra gently without further traumatizing the urethra to avoid more scarring. Using local anesthetic lubricating jelly, the physician attempts to pass a 14-French coude-tip catheter. If this catheter passes easily, dilation can be started with 16- or 18-French dilators. Smaller dilators have sharp tips that can penetrate the urethra and cause a false passage. If the 14-French catheter does not pass, filiforms and followers showed be employed or a guidewire passed using a flexible cystoscope followed by passing dilators. The urethra should not be dilated more than 24 French, to avoid more damage. Dilation should start once or twice weekly, increasing the caliber each time by 1 or 2 French. When 24 French is reached, the interval between dilations is doubled each time to become once or twice per year. Recurrence of obstructive symptoms requiring shortening of this interval is evidence of a change in the character of the stricture, which will probably necessitate a change in its treatment.

Urethrotomy is appropriate for short strictures of the bulbar urethra. It can be done using a cold knife under general anesthesia with diathermy to control any bleeding. It should be done with optical urethrotome (under vision). Blind urethrotomy should be discouraged. The scar should be cut completely in length and thickness, usually at the 12-o'clock position; normal reddish urethral tissue should be seen in the depth of the wound. A Silastic Foley 18-French catheter should be left indwelling. The length of time the catheter remains ranges from a few days to a few weeks and depends on the size of the incision. Two or three urethrotomies might be needed. Recurrence of the obstructive symptoms is an indication for urethroplasty.

Surgical repair involves excision of the strictures and primary anastomotic repair or the use of vascularized flaps of penile skin or free grafts. Definitive repair is usually possible by means of a single-stage procedure rather than the multiple-stage procedures popular in the past. Because of the high cure rate of surgical repairs, up to 90%, the reconstructive ladder (starting with dilation, then urethrotomy, and finally urethroplasty for unsuccessful cases) has been outdated by many surgeons. Primary surgical repair has been advocated for most urethral strictures.

FOLLOW-UP

The frequency of follow-up depends on the method of treatment. Urethral dilation may require frequent visits for incremental dilation at intervals of 1 or 2 weeks, increasing to intervals on the order of every 6 months. Episodes of urinary tract infection should be investigated with urine culture and treated at the earliest opportunity. Problems with infection may indicate recurrence of stricture. Routine measurement of urinary flow rate at intervals of 3 months is appropriate for the first year; if the flow rate deteriorates, further investigation with retrograde urethrography would be indicated.

DISCUSSION

Prevalence

Urethral stricture disease is uncommon. The importance of the disease lies not in its prevalence but in the severity and chronicity of symptoms for the patient and the therapeutic challenge for the urologist.

Related Basic Science

The normal urethra consists of an epithelium (pseudostratified columnar) supported by a stroma rich in elastic tissue. These structures are enveloped in a surrounding tube of vascular erectile tissue (corpus spongiosum) that expands distally to form the head or glans penis. This structure allows for a wide-caliber channel for micturition, but small-caliber channel with erection and engorgement for efficient seminal emission. The urethra has numerous small glands, which predominate on the dorsal surface. Injury to the urethral epithelium or inflammatory change in urethral glands leads to destruction of the supportive tissues and replacement of the erectile tissue of the corpus spongiosum with fibrous tissue.

Natural History and Its Modification with Treatment

The presence of a stricture at any site may give rise to lower urinary tract obstruction, infection, or incontinence. For some patients, obstruction leads to decompensation and dilation of the lower urinary tract and may, in turn, cause hydronephrosis and azotemia. Urethral complications of stricture disease include periurethral abscess, necrotizing fasciitis, and urethral fistula formation. Severe complications are more commonly found in neuropathic patients who have a sensory deficit that involves the perineum and in diabetic patients.

Prevention

It is best to avoid urethral injury of gonococcal urethritis, but having occurred, it is best to recognize and institute early treatment of urethritis. The physician should always avoid unnecessary instrumentation of the urethra. When instrumentation is necessary, it should be gentle and with abundant lubrication. When passage of an instrument is not possible, the physician should desist and proceed immediately to urethrography and urethroscopy.

When a urethral catheter is used for bladder drainage, care must be taken not to inflate the balloon until it is in the bladder and urine has been returned. A small-caliber catheter should always be used, and it should be left in the bladder for as short a duration as possible.

Cost Containment

The cost of treatment can be diminished by early repair of urethral stricture instead of repeated dilation. Cystoscopy and dilation can be performed as an outpatient procedure in most patients, and this also reduces the cost of treatment.

REFERENCES

Gillenwater JY, Grayhack JT, Howards SS, Duckett JW. Adult and pediatric urology. 2nd ed. St. Louis: Mosby Year Book, 1991.
Smith DR. General urology. Norwalk: Appleton & Lange, 1995.
Walsh PC, Retick AB, Samy TA, Vaughan ED. Campbell's urology. 6th ed. Philadelphia: Saunders, 1992.

CHAPTER 18–15

Prostatitis

Harry S. Clarke, Jr., M.D., Ph.D.

DEFINITION

Prostatitis is a condition of inflammation of the prostate gland. The term *prostatitis*, however, has been used commonly in medical practice as a catchall to define any and all unexplained symptoms that arise from the prostate gland.

ETIOLOGY

Acute and chronic bacterial infections of the prostate are caused primarily by aerobic Gram-negative enteric bacteria. Of these the most frequent are *Escherichia coli*, *Proteus* species, *Klebsiella* species, and *Pseudomonas* species. Occasionally, Gram-positive enteric pathogens such as *Streptococcus fecalis* and *Enterococcus* are cultured and, rarely, *Staphylococcus aureus* has been found to be the offending agent.

CRITERIA FOR DIAGNOSIS
Suggestive

Acute bacterial prostatitis is relatively rare and usually presents with the rapid onset of dysuria, diurnal frequency, nocturia, and urgency. These symptoms of bacteriuria are sometimes associated with bladder outlet obstruction and low back pain as well as perineal pain due to the inflammation and swelling present in the prostate gland. Fever, chills, and general malaise are also common symptoms. The symptoms of chronic bacterial prostatitis and chronic nonbacterial prostatitis are remarkably similar. These patients also present with irritative voiding symptoms, such as urgency, diurnal frequency, and nocturia; ill-defined pelvic or perineal discomforts and pain with or just after ejaculation may also be present.

Definitive

The diagnosis of prostatitis is made by identifying inflammatory cells in the prostatic fluid (10 leukocytes/high-power field and 1 or 2 lipid-laden macrophages/high-power field indicate prostatic inflammation).

CLINICAL MANIFESTATIONS
Subjective

Acute Bacterial Prostatitis. The patient most often presents with the sudden onset of fever and chills, general malaise, and symptoms referable to a urinary tract infection including irritative voiding symptoms such as urgency, dysuria, diurnal frequency, and obstructive symptoms with occasional urinary retention.

Chronic Bacterial Prostatitis. Many men with chronic infection of the prostate are completely asymptomatic. Some, however, have perineal discomfort, low back pain, and dysuria. Fever, if present, tends to be low grade.

Chronic Nonbacterial Prostatitis. The features here are similar to those of the patient with chronic bacterial prostatitis, without the evidence of an antecedent urinary tract infection and no organism cultured. This entity may in fact be caused by infectious agents that we have been unable to culture.

Objective

Acute Bacterial Prostatitis. The patient more often than not presents with fever. The digital rectal examination is positive for a warm swollen prostate that is exquisitely painful on palpation. Prostatic massage should be avoided as this may precipitate bacteremia and sepsis.

Routine laboratory examination may reveal an elevated white blood count. The urinalysis is positive for pyuria, bacteriuria, and sometimes hematuria. The urine culture is also positive for the offending organism.

Chronic Bacterial Prostatitis. Fever, if present, tends to be low grade. Elevation of the white blood cell count may occur but is not the rule. There is often evidence of a relapsing urinary tract infection. Digital rectal examination does not provide consistently helpful information. Although the prostate may be enlarged or "boggy," it is usually not exquisitely tender as in acute prostatitis.

Routine laboratory examination may reveal bacteria in the urine.

Chronic Nonbacterial Prostatitis. There is no evidence of antecedent urinary tract infection, and bacteria in any significant numbers cannot be cultured. The findings on digital rectal examination are similar to those found in a group of age-matched controls and are not particularly helpful.

The urinalysis and other routine laboratory examination may reveal no abnormalities.

PLANS
Diagnostic
Differential Diagnosis

The therapy and response to treatment are different for each type of prostatitis. Consequently, the physician must be exact in diagnosis and specific in prescribing therapy. In addition, other conditions presenting with similar symptoms must be considered. These include pyelonephritis, bladder infection, prostate cancer, bladder cancer (especially carcinoma in situ), interstitial cystitis, prostatodynia, and prostatic abscess.

Diagnostic Options and Recommended Approach

If the midstream urine culture is positive, the hemogram shows an elevated white blood cell count with a left shift, and the digital rectal examination is positive for a warm tender prostate, with or without fever, the treatment is that for acute prostatitis. If the midstream urine is negative or the prostate is normal on digital rectal examination, bacterial localization cultures should be obtained and antibiotics prescribed to sterilize the urine. If the expressed prostatic secretions have greater than 10 white blood cells (WBC)/high-power field (HPF) and the culture is positive, treatment for chronic prostatitis is necessary. If the expressed prostatic secretions have greater than 10 WBC/HPF and the culture is negative, treatment for nonbacterial prostatitis is instituted. Finally, if the expressed prostatic secretions have fewer than 10 WBC/HPF and the culture is negative, treatment for prostatodynia is in order.

Therapeutic

Acute Bacterial Prostatitis. Hospitalization and parenteral antibiotic therapy are required for severe cases. Once cultures have been obtained, the patient is started on an aminoglycoside, gentamicin or tobramycin 3 to 5 mg/kg of body weight per day in three divided doses along with a semisynthetic penicillin such as Timentin 3.1 g every 6 hours. If obstructive symptoms are present, a suprapubic catheter should be placed to drain the bladder. Initial therapy with oral antibiotics can be employed in milder cases: trimethoprim–sulfamethoxazole (Bactrim DS, one double-strength tablet twice a day) or a fluoroquinolone such as ciprofloxacin (500 mg, one tablet twice a day) or floxin (400 mg, one tablet twice a day). The antibiotic regimen can be tailored to the culture and sensitivity results once they are available. The initial parenteral regimen should be continued until the patient has defervesced for 48 hours, the WBC count has normalized, and the voiding symptoms have abated. Oral therapy should then be continued for several weeks. The patient should be encouraged to increase oral hydration once converted to oral antibiotics, and follow-up should include repeat culture of the urine several weeks after completion of the antibiotic course to confirm eradication of the infecting organism.

Chronic Bacterial Prostatitis. Initial therapy should be with oral trimethoprim–Sulfamethoxazole (one double-strength tablet twice a day) for 4 to 6 weeks. A fluoroquin-o-lone such as ciprofloxacin (500 mg twice a day) or floxin (400 mg twice a day) may also be employed similarly for 4 to 6 weeks. Failure of therapy may indicate the need for a short course (3–5 days) of parenteral antibiotic therapy with an aminoglycoside (dosages as outlined for acute prostatitis above), followed by resumption of oral antibiotic therapy. The long duration required is due to the inability of the therapeutic agents to gain access to the area of infection. To facilitate this, sitz baths may be helpful and should be recommended to the patient. Also, alpha blockers (terazosin hydrochloride [Hytrin] 2–5 mg at bedtime) may be prescribed to relax the smooth muscle investiture of the prostate to allow increased blood flow and distribution of the antibiotics. Finally, a nonsteroidal antiinflammatory agent (ibuprofen [Motrin] 800 mg three times per day or naproxen [Naprosyn] 250 mg twice a day) will help reduce the prostatic inflammation and allow increased blood flow as well. The patient and physician must both be aware that treatment success may be short lived, as 30 to 50% of patients with chronic bacterial prostatitis relapse. In this situation it may be necessary to consider chronic prophylaxis for suppression (e.g., trimethoprim–sulfamethoxazole regular or double-strength tablet at bedtime). Some urologists perform radical transurethral resection of the prostate for severe refractory cases. The success rate for this is only about 30 to 40% at best, however. Current clinical investigations are underway to evaluate the use of finasteride (Proscar), a 5α-reductase inhibitor, for the adjuvant treatment, along with antimicrobial agents for chronic prostatitis. The rationale is based on this drug's ability to block the formation of dihydrotestosterone and, as a consequence, put the prostate gland into a state of senescence, allowing better distribution of the antibiotic.

Chronic Nonbacterial Prostatitis. An initial course of oral doxycycline 100 mg twice a day for 2 weeks should be tried as the offending agent may well be *Chlamydia* or *Ureaplasma*, which will not appear in routine bacterial cultures. A careful history of precipitating factors should be obtained. Some patients relate an association with long automobile rides or certain types of food as precipitating factors, which can be avoided. Treatment is otherwise largely symptomatic, with hot sitz baths, anticholinergic agents as needed (oxybutynin [Ditropan] 5 mg three times per day), and an alpha blocker as discussed above.

FOLLOW-UP

Once the course of therapy has been completed the urine culture should be repeated to ensure the infecting agent has been eradicated. Transrectal ultrasound may provide useful information with regard to identifying prostatic stones or prostatic abscesses, which may be a nidus for persistent or recurrent infection. Further evaluation with intravenous urogram and/or voiding cystogram and cystourethroscopy should be reserved for those patients whose history suggests underlying urinary tract disorders.

DISCUSSION
Prevalence and Incidence

It has been estimated that about 50% of men experience prostatic symptoms at some time during life. Acute bacterial prostatitis is, however, quite rare. The relative incidence of chronic prostatitis, either bacterial or nonbacterial, has not been well established. One large study reported 5% of patients had chronic bacterial prostatitis, 64% had nonbacterial prostatitis, and 31% had prostatodynia (Meares, 1986). This study confirms the findings of others, that acute prostatitis is a relatively uncommon cause of prostatitis.

Related Basic Science
Pathophysiology

The route of infection is thought to be an ascending pathogen from those colonizing the urethra in most instances. Hematogenous, lymphatic, and direct extension of infection has also been described, however. Vaginal cultures from partners of patients with prostatitis have been found to grow isolates of the same organisms, but no evidence to date has been presented to suggest sexual transmission of prostatitis.

Immunology

Bacterial infections of the prostate are usually associated with detectable antibody directed against the pathogen, found in both serum and prostatic fluid. This finding indicates ongoing or recent infection. With the advent of monoclonal antibodies, highly sensitive and specific assays are now available to detect pathogens that previously were impossible to culture, such as *Chlamydia* and *Mycoplasma.*

Natural History and Its Modification with Treatment
Acute Prostatitis. Without antibiotic therapy this entity may rapidly progress to generalized sepsis and has significant morbidity and mortality. Rapid recognition and institution of antibiotic therapy result in rapid resolution and significant reduction in morbidity.

Chronic Bacterial Prostatitis. The course is indolent, with gradually increasing symptoms which may escalate in severity without intervention with antibiotic therapy. The initiation of antibiotics is successful only 30 to 50% of the time, and a suppressive regimen may be required.

Nonbacterial Prostatitis. This entity follows a course similar to that of chronic bacterial prostatitis in some instances, because it is caused by an infectious agent that has not been identified; in others, initiation of therapy is aimed at ameliorating symptoms.

Prevention

There is at present no method for prevention of prostatitis, other than avoiding precipitating factors, particularly in allergic prostatitis. Chronic bacterial prostatitis flares may be prevented with continuous suppressive medication. Radical transurethral resection is of benefit in preventing further episodes in from 30 to 40% of patients.

Cost Containment

Historically, patients with symptoms of prostatitis would undergo a complete formal genitourinary workup, including intravenous urography, voiding cystourethrogram, and often cystourethroscopy. Review has shown that the yield on these studies has been extremely low and large savings have been achieved by limiting these studies to specific indications present in individual cases.

REFERENCES

Fowler JE Jr. Prostatitis. In: Gillenwater JY, Grayhack JT, Howards SS, Duckett JW, eds. Adult and pediatric urology. Chicago: Year Book Medical Publishers, 1987:1220.

Meares EM Jr. Prostatitis and related disorders. In: Walsh PC, Gittes RF, Perlmutter AD, Stamey TA, eds. Campbell's urology. Philadelphia: Saunders, 1986;868.

Stamey TA, Meares EM Jr, Winningham DG. Chronic bacterial prostatitis and diffusion of drugs into prostatic fluid. J Urol 1970;103:187.

Schultz RE. Lower urinary tract infections in men. In: Hanno PM, Wein AJ, eds. A clinical manual of urology. Norwalk: Appleton & Lange, 1987:133.

CHAPTER 18–16

Benign Prostatic Hyperplasia

Harry S. Clarke, Jr., M.D., Ph.D.

DEFINITION

Benign prostatic hyperplasia (BPH) is noncancerous enlargement of the prostate gland.

ETIOLOGY

Although the etiology of BPH remains poorly understood, two factors have consistently been demonstrated as risk factors for development of the disease: increasing age and the presence of androgens.

CRITERIA FOR DIAGNOSIS

Suggestive

Most patients seeking treatment for BPH do so because of bothersome symptoms that affect the quality of their lives. These include urinary hesitancy, urinary frequency, decreased force and caliber of the urinary stream, postvoid dribbling of urine, urinary incontinence, and, finally, a fear that these symptoms may signify the presence of prostate cancer.

Definitive

Four conditions are interrelated with the disease process of BPH: anatomic prostatic hyperplasia, presence of symptoms commonly referred to as prostatism, urodynamic presence of obstruction, and response of the bladder (detrusor) muscle to obstruction. Some patients have all four conditions and therefore are most likely to have the disease that physicians consider BPH. Other patients may have anatomic hyperplasia and urodynamic evidence of obstruction without symptoms of prostatism. This condition is termed *silent prostatism*. The findings on radiographs, specifically the large filling defect at the base of the bladder seen on intravenous urography, and a large prostate gland palpated on digital rectal examination do not correlate well with symptoms of BPH, and as such are not good clinical indicators of the disease. Conversely, a trabeculated thickened bladder wall, the presence of bladder stones, bladder diverticulae, and a high residual urine are strongly indicative of outflow obstruction, even in the absence of symptoms.

CLINICAL MANIFESTATIONS

Subjective

The classic complaints of a patient with outflow obstruction secondary to BPH are nocturia, frequency, urgency, hesitancy, decreased force and caliber of stream, prolonged voiding time, and postvoid dribbling. One or more of these symptoms may be responsible for a patient seeking treatment.

Objective

Physical Examination

The physical examination may show the presence of a palpable or percussable bladder. Digital rectal examination may detect an enlarged prostate and is vitally important to rule out induration or nodules, which may indicate the presence of malignancy; however, the absence of positive findings on physical examination does not rule out outflow obstruction due to BPH.

Routine Laboratory Abnormalities

Routine laboratory tests should include a complete blood count and a creatinine level to check for normal renal function. A urinalysis and urine culture should be performed to rule out other renal abnormalities, as well as infection, as a source of the patient's symptoms.

PLANS

Diagnostic

Differential Diagnosis

Symptoms similar to those of BPH can be caused by anatomic abnormalities of the bladder outlet and urethra, such as bladder neck contracture and urethral stricture. Neurogenic bladder dysfunction may produce atony of the bladder musculature, resulting in diminished intravesical voiding pressures and low flow rates. Diabetic neuropathy or direct injury to the spinal cord or pelvic plexus can result in an atonic neurogenic bladder. Medications such as tranquilizers, ganglionic blocking agents, and parasympatholytic drugs in the presence of a moderate degree of prostatism frequently result in acute urinary retention.

Diagnostic Options and Recommended Approach

A prostate-specific antigen (PSA) level should be ordered to detect malignancy in patients 50 years or older or at 40 years of age if there is a family history of prostate cancer.

Therapeutic

Therapeutic Options

Asymptomatic patients with prostate enlargement due to BPH rarely require treatment. In addition, the morbidity from the disease left to undergo its natural course is low. Less than 2% of patients experience damage to the upper tracts or go into urinary retention and require emergent drainage. Because of this a conservative approach to therapy is warranted. The physician, after determining the patient's level of discomfort and desire for intervention, may start the patient on a watchful waiting strategy and progress to medical management or surgical intervention using one of the therapies outlined below, depending on the patient's response to therapy.

Watchful Waiting. As stated above less than 2% of patients have significant complications from disease progression; therefore, if symptoms are not unacceptable to the patient, approach to management is rational. These patients should be reassessed for symptom severity, physical findings, routine laboratory testing, and optional diagnostic procedures as indicated in individual patients.

Medical Management. At present, two types of drugs are used to treat BPH. α_1-Adrenergic receptor blockers (terazosin hydrochloride) [Hytrin] titrated from 1 mg up to 5 mg over 1 to 2 weeks taken at bedtime). This acts to relax the smooth muscle investiture of the prostate and bladder neck to improve voiding. The second is finasteride, a 5α-reductase inhibitor, which blocks the conversion of testosterone to dihydrotestosterone, the steroid active in stimulating BPH (one tablet per day for life). The former acts rapidly and its effects are readily noted by the patient. The latter takes 3 to 6 months before its effects are noted (involution of the glandular portion of the prostate) and works in approximately one third of the patients treated. Both must be taken indefinitely to maintain their effects. There is no contraindication to prescribing both of these agents in concert, and they may be continued as long as there are no objectionable side effects.

Surgical Management. Of all treatment options, prostate surgery offers the best chance for symptomatic improvement; however surgery also has the highest rates of significant complications. Transurethral resection of the prostate (TURP) is the most commonly used surgical treatment for BPH. Transurethral incision of the prostate (TUIP) is limited to use in prostate glands of 30 g or less but is equivalent in efficacy to TURP. Open prostatectomy is reserved for patients with very large glands. The results of these three methods are similar, but the complication rates differ. Open prostatectomy has the greater incisional morbidity, whereas TUIP has the lowest risk and lowest rate of ejaculatory disturbance. Finally, the latest surgical therapy is laser ablation of the prostate. This is done using a side-firing Nd-YAG laser. Two techniques are currently being employed. The first uses deposition of energy at low wattage to induce necrosis and subsequent slough in approximately 6 weeks. The second uses higher energy to vaporize the prostatic tissue immediately. The former has the disadvantage of a long duration to improved voiding; the latter has an increased incidence of erectile dysfunction, secondary to damage to the neurovascular bundles by the higher energy. Neither of these techniques have follow-up data greater than 3 years' duration at present.

Recommended Approach

As stated above the treatment for BPH should be tailored to the patient's perception of this symptoms. Although a conservative approach is warranted surgery need not always be a treatment of last resort; that is, patients need not undergo other treatments for BPH before they can have surgery. Conversely, it is inappropriate to recommend surgery for a symptomatic patient on the grounds that progression is inevitable and that surgical risk will only increase with advancing age. BPH progresses slowly and classically the symptoms wax and wane and may disappear just as likely as they might increase with time.

FOLLOW-UP

The follow-up for medical or surgical management is similar to that outlined above for watchful waiting: symptom score, physical findings, routine laboratory tests, and additional tests as individually indicated.

DISCUSSION
Prevalence and Incidence

Benign prostatic hyperplasia is the most common benign neoplasm in the aging man. It has a high prevalence that increases progressively with age. The prevalence of histologically identifiable BPH for 60-year-old men is greater than 50%. By age 85, the prevalence is approximately 90%. About one half of men with microscopic evidence of BPH eventually have macroscopic enlargement of the gland, and approximately one half of these develop clinical symptoms of prostatism. The two risk factors for the development of BPH are increasing age and the presence of androgens.

Related Basic Science

Although age and androgens have long been known to be necessary for BPH, their exact mechanism is unknown. A large amount of research has evaluated the interactions between the stromal and glandular components and the implication of various growth factors and dietary factors. Despite extensive efforts, to date, no quantitative differences in steroid content or metabolism, enzyme activity, organic compounds, or metal ions has been documented between BPH tissue and either normal prostatic tissue or the peripheral prostate in a gland with BPH. No unique metabolic activity has been ascribed to BPH tissue.

Natural History and Its Modification with Treatment

The etiology of the disease remains poorly understood. Long-term outcome data regarding the natural history and treatment of BPH are lacking, and indicators for proper timing of treatment are sparse.

Prevention

No method of prevention short of castration or early initiation of finasteride is known for prevention of BPH, and neither of these is an acceptable alternative.

Cost Containment

The costs of therapy have been reduced considerably by reduction of costly imaging studies of the upper urinary tract, unless specifically indicated. The introduction of medical management with terazosin and/or finasteride is considerably less costly than surgery initially; however, the necessity for their continued lifelong use nullifies this cost difference in a short period.

REFERENCES

Barry MJ, Fowler FJ Jr, O'Leary MP, et al. The American Urological Association symptom index for benign prostatic hyperplasia. J Urol 1992;148:1549.

Drach GW, Steinbronn DV. Clinical evaluation of patients with prostatic obstruction: Correlation of flow rates with voided, residual or total bladder volume. J Urol 1986;135:737.

Grayhack JT, Kozlowski JM. Benign prostatic hyperplasia. In: Gillenwater JY, Grayhack JT, Howards SS, Duckett JW, eds. Adult and pediatric urology. Chicago: Year Book Medical Publishers, 1987:1062.

Lepor H, Knapp-Maloney G, Sunshine H. A dose titration study evaluating terazosin, a selective, once-a-day alpha-1-blocker for the treatment of symptomatic benign prostatic hyperplasia. J Urol 1990;144:1393.

McConnell JD. Medical management of benign prostatic hyperplasia with androgen suppression. Prostate (suppl.) 1990;3:49.

McConnell JD, and the Benign Prostatic Hyperplasia Guideline Panel. Benign prostatic hyperplasia: Diagnosis and treatment. AHCPR US Department of Health and Human Services. Rockville, MD Publication No. 94-0582, 1994:1.

CHAPTER 18–17

Carcinoma of the Prostate (See Section 3, Chapter 22)

CHAPTER 18–18

Lesions of the Penis

David P. O'Brien III, M.D.

DEFINITION

A penile lesion is defined as an abnormal growth, an ulceration, or a rash of the penis.

ETIOLOGY

A wide variety of lesions may occur on the penis. Because the penis is covered with skin, many of these lesions are routine skin diseases and are discussed elsewhere. Here we discuss those lesions that are peculiar to the penis. Lesions of the penis may be sexually transmitted diseases, infections and inflammations, parasitic, infiltrative, and neoplastic.

CRITERIA FOR DIAGNOSIS

The diagnosis of a penile lesion is made by inspection of the penis by the patient and physician. Its cause requires additional study.

CLINICAL MANIFESTATIONS

Subjective

As noted above a wide variety of lesions occur on the penis. It is important to establish the length of time that the lesion has been present. It is also important to determine whether the lesion was present previously and what therapy was used in the past. It is necessary to find out whether the lesion is painful and if there is a discharge from the lesion.

The sexual history is important and it is imperative to determine whether constitutional symptoms are present. The HIV status of the patient is also mandatory to determine.

Objective

Physical Examination

Examination of the penis and scrotum, inguinal areas, and rectum is necessary. Ulcerations, rashes, tumors, warts, growths, nodules, and so on should be noted. Retraction of the foreskin in the uncircumcised male may reveal unsuspected lesions. Many lesions may be diagnosed by inspection. Others need further study. Experience in inspection and observation is crucial.

Routine, Laboratory Abnormalities

There are no diagnostic laboratory abnormalities.

PLANS

Diagnostic

Table 18–18–1 outlines the diagnoses and diagnostic options for lesions of the penis. As most tumors of the penis go long periods before diagnosis, suspicion and early biopsy are required for adequate management.

Therapeutic

Syphilis. The following pharmacologic regimens are used:

- Benzathine penicillin G 2.4 million U intramuscularly as a single dose
- Aqueous procaine penicillin G 600,000 U intramuscularly daily for 15 days
- Tetracycline hydrochloride 500 mg orally four times a day for 15 days
- Erythromycin 500 mg orally three times a day for 15 days

The last two choices are for patients sensitive to penicillin.

Chancroid (Hemophilus ducreyi). Ceftriaxone (Rocephin) 250 mg intramuscularly is used. Oral antibiotics such as sulfisoxazole (4 g daily for 5 days) and tetracycline (2 g daily for 5 days), alone or in combination, are effective if intramuscular antibiotics are not available.

Herpes Progenitalis. Acyclovir (Zovirax) for initial infections is moderately effective to decrease the duration of infection and possibly the recurrence rate.

Lymphogranuloma Venereum. Oral antibiotics such as sulfisoxazole (4 g daily for 2–3 weeks) and tetracyline (2 g daily for 2–3 weeks) should be successful, but often they need to be repeated. Surgical intervention for abscess formation is sometimes necessary, and radical excision and grafting also have been done.

Balanitis. Balanitis may be caused by a variety of organisms or diseases, and treatment is directed toward the specific entity. Circumcision is mandatory in many chronically infected patients.

Scabies and Pediculosis Pubis. Both these parasitic diseases respond to therapy (Elimite) or Lindane (Kwell) lotion or shampoo.

Edema. Elevation and use of antihistamines and steroids may benefit the allergic type of edema, whereas only elevation may help edematous states of patients with generalized edema, ascites, and so forth.

Cysts and Angiomata. Cysts and angiomata of the penis are treated locally by fulguration and/or excision. They tend to be recurrent and multiple.

Condylomata Acuminata. Venereal warts, or condylomata acuminata, usually are located on the prepuce, the glans, or, occasionally, the penile shaft skin. Treatment is local, with podophyllin compounds, fulguration, or excision. Sometimes therapeutic and prophylactic circumcision is performed for condylomata occurring in the uncircumcised patient. Approximately 5% of patients may have associated intraurethral warts, and routine urethroscopy is indicated in those with lesions on the glans.

These lesions may all be associated with malignant change of the penis.

TABLE 18–18–1. LESIONS OF THE PENIS: DIAGNOSES AND DIAGNOSTIC OPTIONS

Diagnosis	Diagnostic Options
Sexually transmitted diseases	
Syphilis	Dark-field microscopy, rapid plasma reagin (RPR), fluorescent treponemal antibody (FTA)
Chancroid	Smear, culture (blood medium)
Lymphogranuloma venereum	Microinmmunofluorescence
Infections and inflammation	
Balanitis	Inspection, culture
Parasites	
Scabies	Inspection, microscopic
Pediculosis pubis	Inspection
Edema	Inspection
Benign tumors	Inspection and biopsy
Cysts	
Hemangioma	
Condylomas	
Malignancies or premalignancies	Inspection and biopsy
Erythroplasia of Queyrat	
Bowen's disease	
Buschke–Lowenstein tumor	
Balanitis xerotica obliterans	
Sarcomas	
Carcinomas	

Erythroplasia of Queyrat. This type of carcinoma in situ has a velvety red appearance. Treatment consists of local measures, circumcision, local excision, or topical chemicals in noninvasive cases, whereas more radical excisions, including penectomy, are indicated with invasive lesions.

Bowen's Disease. Bowen's disease is similar to erythroplasia of Queyrat, and therapeutic considerations are similar.

Buschke–Lowenstein Tumor (Giant Condylomata Acuminata). Surgical resection is advisable in most cases. Radiation and/or podophyllin is of little value.

Balanitis Xerotica Obliterans. Local excision is usually curative, for malignant degeneration is rare. Use of steroids topically or injected into the lesions has been successful.

Carcinoma in Situ. See Erythroplasia of Queyrat.

Sarcomas. Treatment of sarcomas of the penis normally begins with total penectomy and, rarely, lymph node dissection, as metastases usually occur by way of the bloodstream.

Carcinomas. Epidermoid carcinoma is the most common malignancy of the penis, and treatment varies with the site and extent of disease. Small tumors limited to the prepuce can be managed easily with circumcision. Partial penectomy (with amputation 2.0–2.5 cm proximal to the primary) is recommended for lesions of the glans or with corporeal invasion. Extensive lesions of the penis are treated with total penectomy and en bloc removal of the affected abdominal wall, scrotum, and so on.

Regional node (inguinal and iliac) dissection is recommended for clinically positive nodes, and some authors believe that nodes should be removed in all cases.

FOLLOW-UP

The need for and frequency of follow-up visits depend on the specific entity.

DISCUSSION
Prevalence and Incidence

Lesions of the penis are common. The exact prevalence and incidence are not known.

Related Basic Science

Syphilis. Syphilis is caused by the venereally transmitted spirochete *Treponema pallidum.* The chancre formed in the initial infection usually is located on the glans or prepuce and commonly is painless. Diagnosis is by dark-field examination of serum obtained from the chancre. The incubation period varies from 7 to 30 days.

Chancroid. Chancroid is caused by the venereally transmitted Gram-negative bacillus *Hemophilus ducreyi.* The chancre usually is painful and occurs typically on the prepuce or coronal sulcus. The incubation period is 1 to 7 days.

Herpes Progenitalis. Herpes progenitalis is caused by the venereally transmitted herpesvirus hominis, usually type II. It is typified by pruritic, tender groups of vesicles on an erythematous base lesion, occurring singly or in multiple areas.

Lymphogranuloma Venereum. Lymphogranuloma venereum is caused by the venereally transmitted *Chlamydia trachomatis.* Lesions begin on the genitals as vesicles on the penis. Incubation is 2 days to 3 weeks.

Balanitis. Balanitis may be caused by a variety of organisms or local inflammatory agents (drugs, tumors, etc.). The combination of being uncircumcised and having poor hygiene is an invitation for balanitis, especially in high-risk groups such as diabetics.

Scabies. Scabies is caused by the mite *Sarcoptes scabiei,* which is transmitted via close contact with an infected party or the bed clothes of an infected person.

Pediculosis Pubis. Pediculosis pubis is caused by the crab louse and is transmitted by close contact with an infected person.

Tumors. The cause of most tumorous lesions of the penis is not known. Condylomata acuminata are thought to be due to a venereally transmitted papovavirus.

Carcinomas. The cause of penile carcinoma is not known, although there is a relationship between the uncircumcised male and carcinoma, suggesting that there are carcinogenic properties to smegma. Males circumcised at birth rarely have carcinoma of the penis, which accounts for the rarity of this disease in Jews. The overall incidence of penile carcinoma in underdeveloped countries is consistent with the relationship to poor hygiene. Veneral diseases, trauma, and occupational exposures do not appear to play a role in the development of carcinoma.

Natural History and Its Modification with Treatment

Syphilis. Following the initial inoculation, the infection appears to be systemic as well as local. In the treated state, the chancre heals rapidly. If untreated, it also heals as the secondary stage develops.

Chancroid. The lesion of chancroid progresses over the penis if untreated and involves the regional (inguinal) lymph nodes. Fever and malaise are systemic symptoms.

Herpes Progenitalis. Herpes lesions resolve spontaneously but are notable for being recurrent, often at the same site. They are irritating at best, but they are not as debilitating in the male as in the female.

Lymphogranuloma Venereum. Lymphogranuloma venereum begins on the penis but may progress to involve the regional lymph nodes and/or the anorectal area. Advanced lymphogranuloma venereum produces marked enlargement of these areas with draining, open ulcers and sinus tracts.

Balanitis. In its mildest forms, balanitis is a mild inflammatory disease of the glans. With progression, however, phimosis may occur, and even gangrenous changes of the glans and entire penis may ensue. Regional lymph node involvement and systemic signs of infection occur in the advanced stages.

Scabies. The papular lesions of scabies usually resolve slowly with treatment. Secondary infection can occur, and marked excoriations from scratching and intense itching reactions are common.

Pediculosis Pubis. As with scabies, secondary infections may occur, and the intense itching and scratching produce excoriations.

Edema. The natural history of edematous states of the penis depends on the cause. Allergic phenomena resolve with time, even if untreated (see Chapter 18–23).

Tumors. Cysts and angiomas of the penis tend to be recurrent and multiple. Secondary infections of cysts are common, whereas local abrasion of angiomas produces minor hemorrhage.

Condylomata Acuminata. Frequently, venereal warts are recurrent and may be found in association with true carcinomas of the penis, which leads to suspicion of malignant degeneration or predilection of these patients for malignancy.

Erythroplasia of Queyrat and Bowen's Disease. Both progress to frank malignant tumors. Bowen's disease is associated with distant visceral carcinoma in 25% of patients. Metastases from either disease would be rare.

Buschke–Lowenstein Tumor. The Buschke–Lowenstein tumor differs from condylomata acuminata in that it tends to be more destructive, and even though it is histologically benign, it may compress and destroy tissue locally, growing to a large exophytic tumor. Malignant degeneration is thought to occur on occasion.

Sarcomas. Usually sarcomas of the penis are subcutaneous masses, of which 50% are malignant. Some recur locally after excision, whereas the malignant types metastasize via the bloodstream.

Carcinomas. Carcinomas of the penis begin as papillary growths under the foreskin. As the lesion increases in size, ulceration and infection may occur.

Both exophytic and endophytic lesions are known. If they are allowed to progress by neglect, invasion of the corpora ensues and destruction of the penis, including the urethra, can result. Inguinal lymph nodes are the common first site of metastases. Local recurrences and extension are the rule, but distant spread to the bones, liver, and lungs can occur.

The prognosis varies with the stage of the disease. Five-year cure rates with surgery are greater than 90% in early stages (limited to the penis and negative nodes), whereas 50% survival generally is found with positive nodes. Approximately 70% of unsuccessfully treated patients die within 3 years.

Prevention

Most of these diseases can be prevented by good hygiene. Many of the venereally transmitted problems could be avoided by meticulous hygiene, including condoms, or avoidance of infected individuals. The advantage of circumcision at birth in the prevention of some inflammatory and malignant disease of the penis has been suggested. In the uncircumcised, however, proper hygiene most likely would prevent these conditions.

Cost Containment

Rapid assessment, diagnosis (biopsy), and treatment usually contain costs in these diseases. Patient education regarding proper care and hygiene eliminates recurrent problems, thus containing costs. The use of condoms would obviate the occurrence of many of these lesions.

REFERENCES

Goette PK. Review of erythroplasia of Queyrat and its treatment. Urology 1976;8:311.

Johnson DE, Fuerst DE, Azala AG. Carcinoma of the penis. Urology 1973;1:404.

Persky L, Dekernion J. Carcinoma of the penis. Cancer 1976;26:130.

Skinner DG, Leadbetter WF, Kelly SB. The surgical management of squamous cell carcinoma of the penis. J Urol 1972;107:273.

Walsh PC, Gittes RF, Perlmutter AD, Stamey TA, eds. Campbell's urology. 6th ed. Philadelphia: Saunders, 1992.

CHAPTER 18–19

Phimosis

Bruce H. Broecker, M.D.

DEFINITION

Phimosis is the inability to retract the foreskin over the glans of the penis.

ETIOLOGY

Phimosis is physiologic and due to adhesions during infancy. Physiologic phimosis is normal and generally resolves over the first several years of life as the prepuce separates from the glans and the skin becomes more elastic. Pathologic phimosis occurs when the foreskin becomes scarred, inelastic, and permanently nonretractable. This is usually due to episodes of inflammation and infection in the foreskin or forcible retraction of the foreskin with subsequent scarring.

CRITERIA FOR DIAGNOSIS

Phimosis is the inability to retract the foreskin proximal to the coronal margin of the glans penis. Paraphimosis is the inability to return the retracted foreskin to its original anatomic position.

CLINICAL MANIFESTATIONS
Subjective

The patient or his parents note the inability to retract the foreskin (phimosis) or return it to its normal position (paraphimosis). There may be associated inflammation and/or infection of the foreskin or a history of such.

Objective
Physical Examination

The physician notes the inability to retract the foreskin or return it to its normal position. There may be inflammation of the foreskin (posthitis) and/or glans (balanitis).

Routine Laboratory Abnormalities

There are no diagnostic laboratory abnormalities.

PLANS
Diagnostic

The diagnosis is established by the physical examination.

Therapeutic

Phimosis during infancy is physiologic and needs no treatment unless associated with posthitis or balanitis. In older boys and adult men, circumcision eliminates the problem. If infection is present, appropriate local hygiene supplemented with topical and/or systemic antibiotics should be employed. Circumcision should not be performed until the inflammation has subsided. Paraphimosis can usually be reduced by firm, manual pressure supplemented, if necessary, with analgesics. Circumcision may then be performed, if desired, once edema and inflammation have resolved.

Parents, grandparents, nurses, and physicians should be made aware of the fact that phimosis is normally present in the newborn male and that this physiologic phimosis persists for several years. During this time it is not only unnecessary but meddlesome to retract the foreskin forcibly. In older patients, proper hygienic care of the foreskin should be taught.

FOLLOW-UP

Brief follow-up after circumcision will ensure that it has healed properly.

DISCUSSION
Prevalence and Incidence

The exact prevalence and incidence are not known. It is a common problem.

Related Basic Science

During gestation a fold of skin develops at the base of the glans that grows distally to envelop the glans. This foreskin is tightly adherent to the glans at birth and remains so for several years. Gradually it loosens and eventually allows retraction of the foreskin to expose the glans penis. The role of the foreskin is to protect the more sensitive epithelium of the glans. Pathologic phimosis usually develops as a result of fibrosis in the foreskin following episodes of posthitis or forcible retraction.

Natural History and Its Modification with Treatment

Physiologic phimosis, if not complicated by an episode of posthitis or forcible retraction, spontaneously resolves. Pathologic phimosis does not resolve and ultimately requires circumcision.

Prevention

Avoidance of forcible retraction of the foreskin of the penis of an infant with physiologic phimosis and proper hygiene in infants and older boys will help prevent pathologic phimosis.

Cost Containment

Measures that reduce pathologic phimosis minimize costs.

REFERENCES

American Academy of Pediatrics, Task Force on Circumcision. Report of the task force on circumcision. Pediatrics 1989;84:388.

Elder JS. Congenital anomalies of the genitalia. In: Walsh PC, Retik AB, Stamey TA, Vaugh ED, eds. Campbell's urology. 6th ed. Philadelphia: Saunders, 1992:1920.

Gairdner D. The fate of the foreskin: A study of circumcision. Br Med 1949;2:1433.

Wiswell TE. Decreased incidence of urinary tract infections in circumcised male infants. Pediatrics 1985;75:901.

CHAPTER 18–20

Priapism

David P. O'Brien III, M.D.

DEFINITION

Priapism is a persistent, painful penile erection that is unrelated to sexual desire.

ETIOLOGY

Etiologic factors related to priapism entail disorders of the following types: neurogenic, chemical and toxic infection (allergic and inflammatory), mechanical or traumatic, hematologic and oncologic, and idiopathic.

CRITERIA FOR DIAGNOSIS

The definitive diagnosis is made by the finding of a painful, persistent erection.

CLINICAL MANIFESTATIONS
Subjective

The patient's major complaint is usually a painful erection that may have been present for as long as 24 hours. Many patients relate a prior episode of priapism that resolved spontaneously. Approximately 50% of patients are unable to urinate. A past history of neurogenic disease, chemical or toxic infections, trauma, or hematologic disorders (especially sickle cell anemia) is important to discern. Some patients on injection therapy for erectile dysfunction may present with prolonged erections from this type of therapy.

Objective
Physical Examination

Examination of the penis reveals only that the corpora cavernosa are engorged. The corpus spongiosum is usually not involved. The bladder may be palpable because of retained urine. Other findings, physical or laboratory, may be related to a disease process in which the priapism is a secondary phenomenon (e.g., sickle cell anemia—see Chapter 12–7).

Routine Laboratory Abnormalities

Routine laboratory tests may all be normal.

PLANS
Diagnostic

Most diagnostic tests are related to a disease process in which priapism is a secondary problem. The causes of priapism are listed below. The reader should refer to the appropriate chapters elsewhere in the book for the individual topics.

Differential Diagnosis

Table 18–20–1 outlines the differential diagnosis of priapism.

Diagnostic Options and Recommended Approach

Diagnostic options vary with the differential diagnosis. As noted, 50% of these problems are idiopathic. The history should delineate those patients with sickle cell disease, neoplastic disorders, erectile dysfunction on injection therapy, and so on.

Therapeutic
Therapeutic Options

The initial management of priapism should consist of relief of pain with analgesics and local pain control with an ice bag to the penis. Urinary

TABLE 18–20–1. PRIAPISM: DIFFERENTIAL DIAGNOSIS

Neurogenic
  Psychic stimuli
  Direct central nervous system stimuli (multiple sclerosis, tabes, spinal cord injury, etc.)
  Reflux from local stimuli (phimosis, tumors, urethral stones, etc.)
Chemical and toxic infection, allergic and inflammatory
  Congenital syphilis
  Tetanus reaction
  Mumps
  Drug poisoning
  Carbon monoxide
  Hormones (testosterone)
  Hydralazine
  Trazodone hydrochloride
  Tularemia, periurethral abscess, appendicitis
  Local injection for erectile dysfunction (papaverine, Prostin, etc.)
Mechanical or traumatic
  Hemorrhage or hematoma from trauma (straddle injury, ruptured urethra, thrombophlebitis, thrombosis, ruptured aneurysm)
Hematologic and oncologic (25–40%)
  Leukemia (chronic myelocytic leukemia, chronic lymphocytic leukemia, chronic granulocytic leukemia)
  Sickle cell anemia
  Neoplasms (penile, urethral)
Idiopathic (50%)

retention, when present, can be solved with placement of a Foley catheter or with intermittent catheterization. Treatment of hematologic, neurogenic, or chemical precursors to the problem should be instituted. Irrigation of the penis with alpha-adrenergic agents such as ephedrine and ephedrine-like compounds may be effective in diminishing the erection. Often initial conservative therapy (analgesics, ice bag) results in detumescence of the penis. Optimal therapy of priapism, if these measures are not effective, may be the early construction of a venous shunt. A corporosaphenous shunt is an end-to-side anastomosis of the saphenous vein to one corpus cavernosum, which produces detumescence of the penis. A corpus spongiosum shunt is a shunt between either or both corpora cavernosa and the corpus spongiosum, which results in flaccidity of the penis, because the venous outflow of the corpus spongiosum is independent of that of the corpora cavernosa. The shunt may be created as a formal surgical "window," suturing the corpora cavernosa to the corpus spongiosum. An alternative and usually initially simple technique, the "glans stab" method, involves constructing a communication between the glans penis and the underlying corporeal bodies by a surgical knife or a large biopsy needle.

It is not uncommon to have an initial successful shunt rapidly thrombose, necessitating immediate construction of another shunt.

FOLLOW-UP

Early follow-up of the patient is for wound care in those undergoing surgical procedures (1–2 weeks). Later follow-up visits may be necessary to detect the early signs of other disease states that may be related. Patient education should be directed toward treating and preventing primary etiologic factors and impressing on the patient the need for this treatment. He should be advised of the necessity of seeking rapid treatment for future episodes of priapism. The patient also should be informed of the possibility of permanent impotence following any episode of priapism. The incidence of impotence is lower with early shunting.

DISCUSSION
Prevalence and Incidence

The prevalence and incidence of priapism are not truly known and are related to the prevalence and incidence of the individual etiologic disease.

Related Basic Science

The pathophysiology of erections and the derangement in priapism are complicated phenomena and are not fully understood. In the flaccid state, blood is shunted away from the fibroelastic tissue of the cavernous spaces in the corpora. With sexual stimuli, local or cerebral, valvelike and/or smooth muscles located in major arterial branches and the cavernous spaces allow an increase in arterial flow to the cavernous spaces and perhaps decrease the venous outflow. This results in turgidity of the penis. With detumescence, the process is reversed, and the normal elasticity of the corpora permits resumption of the flaccid state. In priapism, there is impaired venous outflow, which produces occlusion or blockage of venous outflow channels by sludging and stasis. Subsequent edema and arterial occlusion result in fibrosis of cavernous spaces and lead to impotence.

Natural History and Its Modification with Treatment

Priapism may occur between the ages of 7 and 80 years. The erectile capability of the penis after relief varies with the length of time the priapism has been present before initial treatment and the type of treatment received. Priapism may be recurrent, and it is common for patients to describe prior events with spontaneous regression. Recurrences also may occur after surgical shunting procedures. Clearly, these shunts do not remain open indefinitely.

Prevention

Priapism as an idiopathic occurrence cannot be prevented. Prevention, however, may be directed at the underlying etiologic factors noted under Differential Diagnosis.

Cost Containment

Rapid aggressive treatment of both the priapism and the etiologic disease would seem to contain costs. Initial irrigation of the penis with alpha-adrenergic agents and, if this fails, surgical management, rather than a prolonged conservative course, may also be cost effective.

REFERENCES
Becher LE, Mitchell AD. Priapism. Surg Clin North Am 1965;45:1523.
Falk D, Loos DC. Spongiocavernosum shunt in the surgical treatment of idiopathic persistent priapism. J Urol 1972;108:101.
Grace DA, Winter CC. Priapism: An appraisal of management of twenty-three patients. J Urol 1968;99:301.
Grayhack JT, McCullough W, O'Connor VJ Jr, Trippel O. Venous bypass to control priapism. Invest Urol 1964;1:509.
Hanri D, Spycher M, Bruhlmann W. Erection and priapism: A new physiologic concept. Urol Int 1983;38:138.
Sacher EC, Sagegh E, Frenselli F, et al. Cavernospongiosum shunt in the treatment of priapism. J Urol 1972;108:97.

CHAPTER 18–21

Peyronie's Disease

Michael A. Witt, M.D.

DEFINITION

Peyronie's disease is a tunical process resulting in pain, penile deformity, or erectile dysfunction.

ETIOLOGY

The etiology of Peyronie's disease remains unknown. It is suggested that there are some precipitating factors such as trauma and infection. There is also an increased incidence of Peyronie's disease in patients with Dupuytren's contracture. Whatever precipitates this inflammatory response, it results in subsequent fibrosis.

What initiates this inflammatory response and what determines the extent of tunical involvement remain unknown.

CRITERIA FOR DIAGNOSIS

The diagnosis of Peyronie's disease is initially made by the patient reporting historically that he has noted either penile pain or deformity that is resulting in either a cosmetic abnormality or a compromise in erectile function.

CLINICAL MANIFESTATIONS
Subjective

The patient typically reports the onset of penile pain with erection or a change in penile architecture consisting of constriction, tapering, shortening, or angulation, and possible loss of rigidity. In some incidences, there is a specific traumatic event, but in the majority of cases, no iatrogenic stimulus can be identified. The patient may report a family history of Peyronie's disease or a coincidental onset of Dupuytren's contracture.

Objective
Physical Examination

When the penis is flaccid, the physician may detect a thickening of the septum or the presence of a dorsal, ventral, or lateral plaque.

Routine Laboratory Abnormalities

There are no routine laboratory abnormalities.

PLANS
Diagnostic
Differential Diagnosis

The differential diagnosis includes a metastatic lesion to the penis such as melanoma, lymphoma, or renal cell cancer.

Diagnostic Options

Once the patient reports a history of Peyronie's disease, it is recommended to proceed with some assessment of underlying corporeal function as well as the degree of penile deformity.

Penile plaque can be measured and is suggestive of Peyronie's disease, but the penis must be examined in the erect state to determine the extent of the disease. This can be achieved by having the patient photograph his penis in the erect state from the dorsal and lateral aspects. It is also possible to administer an intracorporeal injection of prostaglandin E or papaverine to induce an erection or to subject the patient to dynamic fusion cavernosometry, in which insufflation of the penis occurs. All these maneuvers enable the examiner to determine the extent of the disease and the severity of the plaque.

If the patient reports a loss of rigidity or inability to maintain his erection, then color Doppler ultrasonography is useful as a noninvasive method of assessing underlying erectile dysfunction. This may help diagnose the presence of venogenic impotence, which is known to exist, as well as any arterial deficits, which may also occur. Knowing this is helpful in dictating therapy, because, if an arterial or venous component of erectile dysfunction exists, correcting the underlying plaque will only result in a straight penis that is not rigid enough to function.

Some investigators would recommend performing cavernosometric studies to identify the presence of venogenic impotence.

Biopsy of the plaque is not indicated.

Therapeutic

Any patient presenting with a history of Peyronie's disease should be observed up to a year to rule out the possibility of spontaneous resolution or continued progression. During this time it is recommended to treat the patient with vitamin E, as this medication has been shown to produce a better effect than placebo in double-blind trials.

Once the disease becomes stable, if the patient has underlying normal erectile activity, and the plaque is only causing minimal angular deformity, penile plication is the most effective form of treatment. If the plaque is so extensive that it is causing such severe deformity that plication is only going to render the penis shorter, or with greater con-

striction, then excision of the plaque is recommended. If a large defect exists at this point in time, then grafting is required, which may consist of a dermis, a vein patch, or tunical vaginalis.

If the patient has underlying corporeal veno-occlusive dysfunction or arterial insufficiency, then the recommendation is to proceed with correction of the deformity, excision of the plaque, and insertion of a penile prosthesis.

FOLLOW-UP

If conservative therapy is indicated, then the patient should be followed until he has had the disease for approximately 1 year. Once medical treatment is instituted, the patient should also be followed on a monthly basis, and if surgical treatment is performed, the patient is followed accordingly.

DISCUSSION
Prevalence and Incidence

The incidence of Peyronie's disease is found to range from approximately 0.05% in men aged 20 to 29 years to 0.06% in men 50 to 59 years of age. There is an increased incidence in men with rheumatoid arthritis and hypertension.

Related Basic Science

The pathophysiology of Peyronie's disease at the cellular level remains uncertain. Erectile dysfunction is common in Peyronie's disease, and impaired erection is best assessed by color duplex ultrasonography. Many patients with Peyronie's disease have some alteration of penile hemodynamics as assessed by formal cavernosometry. It is important to correlate investigation with the clinical picture in those patients with the vasculogenic defect and the lack of erection.

The penile plaque results from an inflammatory cell infiltrate, but what initiates this is still uncertain. There are some genetic and historical predisposing factors.

Natural History and Its Modification with Treatment

The condition may resolve without treatment. This is why a year should pass before any treatment is instituted. Treatment is not entirely satisfactory and the disease commonly continues.

Prevention

Prevention currently consists of counseling patients to avoid placing an undue amount of axial rigidity on the penis during sexual activity.

Cost Containment

Cost containment is best instituted by not initiating therapy until the patient has had the disease for approximately 1 year.

REFERENCES

Hinman F. Etiologic factors in Peyronie's disease. Urol Int 1980;35:407.

Schubert GE. Anatomy and pathophysiology of Peyronie's disease and congenital deviation of the penis. Urol Int 1991;47:231.

CHAPTER 18–22
Condyloma Acuminatum
Sam D. Graham, Jr., M.D.

DEFINITION

Condyloma acuminatum is also known as a venereal wart and presents as a verrucous growth on the external genitalia and within the lower genitourinary system.

ETIOLOGY

Human papillomavirus has been shown to be associated with condyloma acuminatum in men and women.

CRITERIA FOR DIAGNOSIS
Suggestive

The characteristic lesion is a hyperplastic, papillomatous, verrucal growth of the external genitalia or perianal region. Intraurethral and intraanal lesions are seen; intravesical lesions occur rarely and are associated with external lesions.

Definitive

The exophytic lesions are histologically characterized by keratinized papillomas, elongation of rete pegs, acanthosis, and cytoplasmic vacuolization (koilocytosis). Though there are more than 50 types of human papillomavirus, those associated with condyloma acuminatum are types 6 and 11, whereas types 6, 18, and 33 are associated with intraepithelial neoplasia and penile cancer.

CLINICAL MANIFESTATIONS
Subjective

External lesions are usually noted incidentally, whereas intraurethral and intraanal lesions may cause dysuria, itching, bleeding, or a discharge.

Objective
Physical Examination

Physical examination reveals a verrucal lesion that is soft, may be multiple, and involves the shaft or glans of the penis. Lesions within the distal urethra may appear as papillary growths at the meatus. Lesions may be less than 1 mm to several centimeters in diameter. Penetration into the deeper tissues is uncommon and is more indicative of a malignancy.

Routine Laboratory Abnormalities

There are no routine laboratory abnormalities.

PLANS
Diagnostic
Differential Diagnosis

Other lesions that can resemble condyloma acuminatum on the external genitalia include Buschke–Lowenstein giant condyloma, squamous carcinoma, Bowen's disease, papillary transitional cell carcinoma, and Goltz syndrome (familial angiofibroma).

Diagnostic Options and Recommended Approach

Flat or inverted papillomas can be identified by the use of topical 5% acetic acid. The condyloma can be seen as a white, small, flat lesion, at times requiring magnification for detection.

We thank Dr. Sam S. Ambrose for his contribution to this chapter in previous editions of this book.

A large, bleeding, or ulcerated condyloma should be biopsied to rule out a malignancy.

Therapeutic

Podophyllin 5 to 15% in tincture of benzoin should be applied to the lesion, avoiding the surrounding epithelium, and allowed to dry. The lesions should be washed 6 to 8 hours after the application. Multiple applications may be required at 4- to 6-week intervals to cause the lesion to completely disappear. Care should be taken to avoid application to the surrounding epithelium and to avoid large single doses and long repetitious doses.

Trichloroacetic acid should be applied locally with an applicator stick and allowed to remain for 4 to 6 days.

5-Fluorouracil cream 5% has shown efficacy in the treatment of intraurethral condyloma. Intralesional bleomycin has also been advocated.

For lesions that are resistant to topical therapy, the next level of therapy is usually *resection, electrodesiccation, laser ablation, or cryotherapy*. Total resection of the lesion is the treatment of choice in patients with Buschke–Lowenstein giant condyloma or in lesions undergoing malignant degeneration.

Sexual partners of the patient should be identified and evaluated for condyloma to reduce the chances of reinfection and recurrence.

FOLLOW-UP

Available methods of treatment are associated with a 40 to 60% recurrence rate. Regular surveillance and re-treatment of recurrences are essential to ensure a successful treatment outcome. Women with cervical human papillomavirus infection should be followed closely with routine Pap smears.

DISCUSSION
Prevalence and Incidence

The exact prevalence and incidence for this common disease are not known.

Related Basic Science

Human papillomavirus has been shown unequivocally to be associated with condyloma acuminatum and cervical dysplasia in men and women. Subtyping of the virus indicates that types 16 and 18 are associated with a high oncogenic potential, whereas types 6 and 11 are associated with condyloma only. Human papillomavirus can be carried by asymptomatic males and represent a reservoir to the female partners who are at risk for cervical carcinoma. Aggressive detection and treatment, although theoretically being the ideal, have unfortunately been associated with a high rate of recurrence. Though these viruses are associated with a variety of epithelial lesions, the exact role of the virus in the development of the lesions remains to be defined.

Natural History and Its Modification with Treatment

Untreated warts have been known to disappear spontaneously, presumably related to immunosurveillance. The incubation period from infection to development is highly variable.

Treatment is usually successful.

Prevention

Avoidance of contact, protected sex, and excellent local hygiene are the primary means of prevention. The public should be educated that condyloma acuminatum is a serious health problem that is sexually transmitted and carries significant oncogenic potential.

Cost Containment

Lesions could be prevented by adequate public education regarding the preventive measures to be taken, the seriousness of the disease, and improving local hygiene. Careful and complete treatment of the small lesions topically could reduce the costs of treatment of the sequelae of more advanced lesions.

Aggressive attempts at identification and eradication of human papillomavirus from the reservoir of aymptomatic patients are very costly and have not been shown to have a significant impact on the disease.

REFERENCES

Burns TNC, Lauvetz RJ, Kerr ES, Ross G Jr. Buschke Lowenstein giant condylomas: Pitfalls in management. Urology 1975;5:773.

Oriel JD. Natural history of genital warts. Br J Vener Dis 1971;47:1.

Powell LC Jr. Condyloma acuminatum: Recent advances in development, carcinogenesis, and treatment. Clin Obstet Gynecol 1978;21:1062.

Schneider A, Kirchmayr R, deVilliers EM, Gissman L. Subclinical human papilloma virus infections in male sexual partners of female carriers. J Urol 1988;140:1431.

Syrjanen KJ. Current concepts on human papilloma virus (HPV) infections in the genital tract and their relationship to intraepithelial neoplasia and squamous cell carcinoma. Obstet Gynecol Surv 1984;39:252.

CHAPTER 18–23

Scrotal Swelling and Pain

David P. O'Brien III, M.D.

DEFINITION

Scrotal swelling is defined as enlargement of the scrotum. Pain in the scrotal area is self-evident.

ETIOLOGY

The most common causes of this condition (testicular torsion, orchitis, epididymitis, hydrocele, and varicocele) are discussed completely in other chapters. The etiologies of this condition that are not discussed elsewhere are covered in this chapter. These may be divided into scrotal masses, conditions associated with scrotal trauma, and inflammatory or infectious conditions of the scrotum.

CRITERIA FOR DIAGNOSIS

The observation of swelling and/or pain in the scrotum makes this diagnosis.

This condition may occur in males of all ages. The patient's age and clinical setting are key factors in determining the specific etiology of this complaint and/or physical findings in an individual patient.

CLINICAL MANIFESTATIONS

Subjective

The duration of the complaint and rapidity of onset serve as clues in separating acute scrotal disease, such as testicular torsion, from more indolent problems, such as spermatocele. A history of scrotal trauma, especially blunt trauma, should be sought as even relatively minor blunt trauma can cause intratesticular or extratesticular bleeding or inflammation. Any prior similar episodes of scrotal pain or swelling should be discussed along with prior inguinal or scrotal surgery. Concurrent medical conditions that predispose a patient to infection, such as alcohol abuse, diabetes mellitus, and immunosuppressive therapy, are important in raising suspicion that intrascrotal or scrotal infection may be present.

Most patients find it difficult to localize scrotal pain. Pain from the epididymis and testicle is impossible for the patient to differentiate unless he is examined and tenderness is localized by palpation. Intrascrotal pain is often associated with radiation into the ipsilateral inguinal area of the flank, and the patient may complain of nausea if the pain is severe. The pain from the scrotal wall or skin may radiate into the ipsilateral inguinal area or proximal thigh.

Objective

Physical Examination

The physical examination should strive to categorize scrotal complaints into those arising from the scrotal wall or skin, the testes, and the adnexal structures. This examination should be carried out in the supine and standing positions. A careful and complete abdominal examination should be performed, as intraabdominal and retroperitoneal processes may yield scrotal pain as a manifestation. Rectal examination should be included as with a genitourinary evaluation.

The scrotal skin should be inspected for ecchymosis, edema, erythema, ulceration, or mass, especially fluctuance or crepitus. Although inflammatory processes within the scrotum may cause secondary inflammatory responses in the scrotal wall, a primary process within the skin or underlying muscular layer of the scrotum should be considered in the etiology of scrotal complaints.

The testis should be palpated for size and consistency, noting any irregularities on its normally smooth surface. Posttraumatic or inflammatory disorders are usually associated with tenderness, whereas testicular tumors usually cause a nontender mass. Inability to palpate the testis may indicate fluid (hydrocele) or blood (hematocele) within the tunica vaginalis. The ability to transilluminate the scrotum with a small bright light indicates the presence of fluid.

The testicular adnexal structures (epididymis, vas deferens, spermatic cord structures) should be examined next. The posterolateral groove that normally delineates the surface of the testis from the epididymis should be palpated and the consistency of the epididymis should be discerned, noting any masses, induration, or tenderness. A spermatocele manifests as a smooth, round transilluminating mass arising from the head of the epididymis. Epididymal cysts are palpably identical to spermatoceles, but they occur in the lower two thirds of the epididymis. The spermatic cords should be inspected and palpated for signs of a mass (cord hydrocele or tumor), abnormally dilated veins (varicocele), or inguinal hernia.

Routine Laboratory Abnormalities

A urinalysis should be obtained if trauma, infection, or inflammation is a suspected cause of scrotal swelling or pain. Microscopic hematuria, for example, may be a sign of significant trauma of the lower urinary tract, and pyuria may indicate infection.

PLANS

Diagnostic

Most scrotal problems are diagnosed after a careful history and physical examination. Scrotal ultrasonography is the best imaging study to confirm or clarify the findings of physical examination. This modality is commonly used to delineate an extratesticular mass from an intratesticular mass and to demonstrate the cystic or solid nature of any scrotal mass. An isotopic scan may be used to confirm testicular torsion. Urinalysis, urine culture, and sensitivity are indicated in inflammatory states.

It should be remembered that abdominal disorders, especially those arising within the retroperitoneum, may cause referred scrotal or testicular pain. Although patients with such disorders usually complain of abdominal or flank pain, abdominal aortic aneurysm, renal cell carcinoma, and renal stones are examples of problems that may cause referred scrotal pain alone. Appropriate imaging studies, therefore, should be performed if scrotal examination fails to yield a cause for scrotal pain.

If a testicular tumor is suspected, appropriate serum markers should be obtained.

Therapeutic

The choice of therapy is guided by the specific diagnosis. Scrotal masses that are not associated with trauma, discussed in this chapter, require therapy only for symptomatic relief. Spermatoceles rarely cause significant pain or tenderness. Scrotal spermatocelectomy, however, may be required if the size of the spermatocele causes discomfort or if repeated minor trauma, such as with exercise, causes pain or tenderness. An inguinal hernia requires repair for relief of pain and prevention of incarceration.

Posttraumatic scrotal masses require therapeutic surgical intervention when the diagnosis must be confirmed or when such intervention will reduce morbidity and shorten convalescence. A hematocele is usually explored through a scrotal approach to rule out testicular rupture or to repair a testicular rupture, evacuating the hematoma as part of the procedure. An intratesticular hematoma usually requires confirmation by an inguinal approach to the testis to rule out a testicular tumor. Serial examination and ultrasonography that show a gradual resolution of the hematoma are the only other appropriate diagnostic plans. If a hematoma is confined to the scrotal wall or skin and is not expanding, no surgical therapy is required. Scrotal support, rest, and analgesics are indicated as repeated examinations monitor the spontaneous resolution.

Infectious or inflammatory conditions of the scrotal wall and skin require specific therapy. A scrotal abscess requires immediate surgical drainage along with parenteral or oral antibiotic therapy. Small abscesses in the skin may be drained under local anesthesia. If the abscess is large or extension into the perineum or perianal tissue planes is suspected, the patient should be hospitalized for exploration in an operating suite under anesthesia. Aggressive and repeated debridement may be required if Fournier's gangrene is suspected, and all patients with scrotal infection should be observed closely for signs of progression to this sometimes deadly form of infection. Scrotal erysipelas, on the other hand, involves only the scrotal skin and subcutaneous tissues and requires scrotal support and antibiotic therapy specific to *Streptococcus,* the usual offending organism. Idiopathic scrotal edema is self-limiting and requires no specific therapy, although antihistamine therapy may make the patient more comfortable as the condition resolves.

FOLLOW-UP

The need for follow-up and the type of progress noted depend on the indications for therapeutic intervention, as outlined above.

DISCUSSION

Prevalence and Incidence

The most common causes of scrotal swelling and pain are discussed elsewhere in this book. These include testicular torsion, orchitis, epididymitis, hydrocele, and varicocele. The conditions discussed in this chapter are relatively uncommon.

Related Basic Science

A spermatocele is a cystic enlargement of the tubules of the rete testis, which transports spermatozoa from the upper pole of the testis into the head of the epididymis. The fluid within a spermatocele contains spermatozoa. There is no apparent cause, and fertility is not impaired.

Blunt trauma to the scrotum may cause bleeding within the testis (testicular hematoma), tunica vaginalis (hematocele), or the wall of the scrotum (scrotal hematoma). Rupture of small blood vessels within the seminiferous tubules or beneath the surface of the tunica albuginea yields bleeding that is usually confined, forming a hematoma, and perceived as a mass on examination. If the tunica albuginea of the testis is ruptured, bleeding and extrusion of the seminiferous tubules may occur into the extratesticular space lined by the tunica vaginalis. As this space fills with blood, an effective tamponade of the bleeding often occurs, and a hematocele is formed. A scrotal hematoma is formed by bleeding into the thick muscular (dartos) wall of the scrotum or into the subcutaneous space.

Infections of the scrotum may be relatively minor. Erysipelas, a streptococcal infection of the skin and subcutaneous tissues, is usually associated with preexisting skin abrasions or maceration. An abraded area is usually easily identified as a point of origin, and the border of the infection is well defined. The entire scrotum may become involved as the skin becomes erythematous, tense, and tender. Improved local hygiene and parenteral antibiotic therapy usually yield complete recovery. An area of abraded skin or inflamed sweat gland or hair follicle may develop a scrotal abscess. Debilitated patients, alcoholics, and diabetics are particularly prone to scrotal abscesses, which are usually caused by enteric organisms colonizing the scrotal skin from their anorectal origin. A scrotal abscess may also develop, however, secondary to extension of a periurethral abscess or anorectal abscess. These two problems should be remembered as surgical drainage is mandatory.

Fournier's gangrene is the potential disastrous sequela of minor scrotal infections. It is a rapidly progressive, necrotizing fasciitis, caused by a mixture of aerobic and anaerobic organisms. The scrotal skin initially becomes tender, tense, and pale due to ischemia. As areas of necrotic, dry skin form and enlarge, gas from gas-forming organisms often become entrapped beneath the skin, and crepitus is noted. Fluid resuscitation, the administration of parenteral antibiotics that provide adequate Gram-negative aerobic and anaerobic coverage, and aggressive surgical debridement may be lifesaving. Repeated debridement may be required as the process extends to adjacent fascial planes of the abdominal wall and upper extremity.

Idiopathic scrotal edema is a nonerythematous edema of the scrotum. It usually occurs in children with no apparent cause except as a possible manifestation of an allergy or variant of angioneurotic edema. This condition usually resolves spontaneously in 2 to 3 days.

Natural History and Its Modification with Treatment

The natural history is related to the specific problem. In general, the treatment for the conditions described in this chapter is successful.

Prevention

The only potentially preventable conditions discussed here are the scrotal infections; minor infections may be prevented by improved local hygiene, and more severe infections may be prevented by early recognition and treatment.

Cost Containment

Cost containment is directly related to the specific prompt attention for the problem.

REFERENCES

Cass AS. Testicular trauma. J Urol 1983;129:299.

Gibson TE. Idiopathic gangrene of the scrotum. J Urol 1930;23:125.

Jones RB, Hirschmann JV, Brown GS, Tremann JA. Fournier's syndrome: Necrotizing subcutaneous infection of the male genitalia. J Urol 1979;122:279.

Kaplan GW. Acute idiopathic scrotal edema. J Pediatr Surg 1977;12:647.

Testicular Torsion

W. Holt Sanders, M.D.

DEFINITION

Testicular torsion, a urologic emergency, is a condition in which the testis twists on the spermatic cord, and blood flow to the testis is thereby compromised, leading to ischemia and infarction.

ETIOLOGY

A narrow mesenteric attachment of the testis to the spermatic cord (the bell clapper deformity) is considered the primary predisposing factor.

CRITERIA FOR DIAGNOSIS
Suggestive

Acute-onset testicular pain in a young boy or adolescent is highly suggestive of torsion.

Definitive

Decreased perfusion on a technetium nuclear scan, decreased flow by Doppler ultrasound, and, finally, finding a twist of the spermatic cord on scrotal exploration provide definitive evidence that torsion has occurred.

CLINICAL MANIFESTATIONS
Subjective

The classic presentation of testicular torsion is the acute onset of unilateral testicular pain in a young boy or adolescent. The pain usually begins after very mild trauma (e.g., biking or playing soccer) but can occur during sleep. The pain may radiate into the ipsilateral groin and flank. Nausea and vomiting are frequent accompanying systemic symptoms, which are uncommon in other causes of acute scrotal pain. Although torsion is most common in young boys, as many as 25% of torsions occur in men older than 21.

Approximately 50% of the patients recall episodes of similar, although less severe, pain.

The family history is noncontributory.

Objective
Physical Examination

On physical examination, there is a tender scrotal mass, high in the hemiscrotum. There is frequently a reactive hydrocele around the testis, obscuring anatomic details. The scrotum can become edematous and erythematous. The cremaster reflex is frequently blunted on the side of the torsion. If the epididymis can be distinguished, it is neither tender nor enlarged. Fever is uncommon.

Routine Laboratory Abnormalities

Usually, the urinalysis reveals no red blood cells or white blood cells. No other laboratory tests contribute to the diagnosis.

PLANS
Diagnostic
Differential Diagnosis

Common conditions other than testicular torsion that cause unilateral scrotal pain include epididymitis and torsion of a testicular appendage. Strangulated hernia, hydrocele, testicular tumor, and idiopathic scrotal edema should also be considered in the differential diagnosis.

Epididymitis frequently presents with urethral discharge in association with testicular pain. It occurs more frequently in men older than 21. Elevating the scrotum tends to alleviate the pain to some extent. The epididymis is palpable, tender, and swollen. There are often white blood cells in the urinalysis, and fever is not uncommon.

The appendix testis, a remnant of the müllerian duct, or the appendix epididymis, a remnant of the wolffian duct, can twist on its stalk causing a small, painful nodule in the superior pole of the testis. Approximately 90% of males have an appendix testis; 30% have an appendix epididymis. Torsion of these structures closely mimics testicular torsion.

Diagnostic Options

Scrotal exploration is the gold standard for diagnosis of testicular torsion. If torsion is considered unlikely as a cause of a patient's testicular pain, it is reasonable to confirm adequate blood flow to the testis with either a technetium nuclear scan or a color Doppler ultrasound examination. The color Doppler examination requires an experienced ultrasonographer for reliable results. The two tests are of approximately equal accuracy, and the choice between the two depends on which test is available and which can be done more quickly.

Recommended Approach

If torsion is considered a likely possibility, no confirmatory studies are indicated, and immediate scrotal exploration should be performed. No other diagnostic study has an accuracy equal to surgery, and all diagnostic tests take time during which irreversible damage is occurring in the ischemic testis. Only if a patient is thought unlikely to have testicular torsion, and much more likely to have epididymitis or torsion of an appendage, should further evaluation with a nuclear scan or Doppler ultrasound be pursued.

Therapeutic
Therapeutic Options

Suspicion of testicular torsion requires immediate surgery. Detorsion of the ischemic testis is performed, and a decision is made concerning the viability of the testis. Failure of the testis to regain normal parenchymal color after detorsion signals testicular infarction, which is best treated by removing the testis. Orchiectomy lowers the morbidity of testicular infarction and decreases the time to convalescence. If the testis regains its pink color after detorsion, it is fixed to the surrounding scrotal tissue with a minimum of two nonabsorbable sutures. Because the anatomic abnormality that predisposed one testis to torsion is likely to be present in the contralateral testis, that testis is also secured to its surrounding scrotal tissues.

Recommended Approach

Immediate surgery is indicated (see discussion above).

FOLLOW-UP

As testicular torsion may recur despite orchidopexy, the patient should be counseled to call immediately should he experience similar symptoms. Subsequent problems with fertility and sexual function should be evaluated with semen analysis and appropriate hormonal studies. The testicular size should be documented at 6 months and 1 year after torsion to detect any testicular atrophy that may affect fertility.

DISCUSSION
Prevalence and Incidence

Although testicular torsion can occur at any age, it occurs most commonly in boys 12 to 18 years of age. The prevalence is estimated to be 1 in 4000 males less than 25 years of age.

Related Basic Science

Anatomic Derangement

The testis in adults is mobile within the layer called the tunica vaginalis. The mesenteric connection between the spermatic cord and testis is usually fairly wide. It has been proposed that a narrow mesenteric connection increases the risk of twisting of the testis within the tunica vaginalis. The cremasteric muscle, a continuation of the internal oblique muscle of the abdominal wall, contracts and draws the testis superiorly as it twists the spermatic cord. Venostasis occurs first, followed by thrombosis and cord edema, which lead to diminished arterial inflow with ischemia.

Natural History and Its Modification with Treatment

The likelihood of preserving testicular function is related directly to the amount of ischemia time. Approximately 80 to 100% of testes that undergo detorsion within 6 hours of onset of pain retain their full fertility and hormonal function. After 24 hours from onset of pain, almost no testes are salvagable.

Testicular torsion may reduce fertility. Even in patients for whom detorsion was performed within 4 hours of onset of pain and whose testicular size remained normal, abnormalities of semen are common. It has been suggested that patients treated for unilateral testicular torsion have bilateral testicular abnormalities. It is also possible that ischemia of one testis leads to an immunologic reaction to all testicular tissue. This controversy has not been resolved. In any case, approximately 50% of patients with unilateral torsion eventually develop poor semen quality or hormonal evidence of testicular dysfunction, findings that represent bilateral testicular damage.

Prevention

Once torsion has occurred, the most important preventive measure is orchidopexy on the contralateral testis.

Cost Containment

The most important principle is to proceed directly to scrotal exploration with orchidopexy in a patient in whom torsion is suspected. Further diagnostic tests in these circumstances waste precious time and money. Early detorsion may prevent later infertility and erectile dysfunction.

REFERENCES

Bartsch G, Mikuz G, Schachtner W, Janetschek G. Testicular torsion. In: Resnick MI, Kursh E, eds. Current therapy in genitourinary surgery. Philadelphia: B.C. Decker, 1987:381.

Caldamone A. Acute scrotal swelling in children. In: Resnick MI, Caldamone AA, Spirnak JP, eds. Decision making in urology. 2nd ed. Philadelphia: B.C. Decker, 1991:12.

Rajfer J. Congenital anomalies of the testis. In: Walsh PC, Retik AB, Stamey TA, Vaughan ED, eds. Campbell's urology. 6th ed. Philadelphia: Saunders, 1992:1543.

CHAPTER 18–25

Orchitis

R. E. S. El-Galley, M.B., B. Ch., and Niall T. M. Galloway, M.B., B. Ch.

DEFINITION

Orchitis is inflammation of the testis. It may occur as a result of hematogenous spread of various systemic infectious diseases. It is thought that orchitis without epididymitis originates in this manner.

ETIOLOGY

Mumps Orchitis. Mumps is the most common cause of orchitis. Epididymoorchitis, a fearful complication of mumps, is generally seen only in adolescent boys and young men. The factors that predispose to this complication are unknown. The onset is usually 3 to 4 days after the development of parotitis. Permanent testicular atrophy may develop within several months to several years of infection.

Bacterial Epididymoorchitis. Bacterial epididymoorchitis may be associated with systemic infections or inflammatory disease. Surgical procedures on the urethra or prostate (e.g., transurethral prostatectomy) may predispose to bacterial epididymoorchitis.

Tuberculous Orchitis. Tuberculous orchitis may result from hematogenous spread of tubercle bacilli from a pulmonary focus of infection or, more commonly, by direct extension from tuberculous epididymitis.

Syphilitic Orchitis. The testis may be involved in syphilis, manifesting gummas with large areas of necrosis.

Granulomatous Orchitis. Granulomatous orchitis, a nonspecific inflammatory process in the testis, occurs occasionally in middle-aged and older men. It may be caused by an autoimmune granulomatous response to spermatozoa.

CRITERIA FOR DIAGNOSIS

Suggestive

Mumps orchitis is preceded by a history of parotitis a few days earlier. There is high fever and acute scrotal pain and swelling.

Objective

The scrotum is very tender and swollen. The testis and epididymis are enlarged.

CLINICAL MANIFESTATIONS

Subjective

Mumps Orchitis. Orchitis, especially mumps, is rare prior to puberty. The onset of mumps orchitis is acute; it usually occurs about 3 to 4 days after the onset of parotitis. Unlike the findings in epididymitis, urinary symptoms characteristically are absent. Fever may reach 40°C (104°F), and prostration may be marked.

Bacterial Orchitis. Bacterial epididymoorchitis presents with severe scrotal pain of acute or gradual onset and may radiate along the spermatic cord and even reach the flank. There may be a history of urethral instrumentation, prostatic surgery, or urinary tract infection. Swelling is rapid and may cause the organs to double their size in the course of 3 to 4 hours. The temperature may reach 40°C (104°F). The patient may complain of systemic symptoms, such as malaise, nausea, and vomiting. Urethral discharge may be seen. Symptoms of cystitis or prostatitis, with cloudy urine, may accompany the painful scrotal swelling.

Tuberculous Orchitis. Tuberculous orchitis is nearly always secondary to infection of the epididymis, which in most cases is bloodborne. Usually it presents with scrotal mass and/or discharging sinus. The general symptoms of tuberculosis usually exist, such as malaise, loss of appetite, loss of weight, high fever, and sweating.

Objective
Physical Examination

The involved testis is diffusely enlarged, smooth, and tender. As the inflammation progresses, a tense hydrocele may obscure the ability to palpate the entire testis, and the scrotal skin may be edematous and erythematous. Sometimes it is difficult to palpate the epididymis separately due to the edema and inflammation. Tuberculous cases present with a firm irregular tender mass involving the testis and epididymis. A discharging sinus might be seen on the undersurface of the scrotum.

Routine Laboratory Abnormalities

Urinalysis is the most useful laboratory study. Pyuria might suggest epididymitis or other genitourinary infection as the primary etiology of the orchitis. Urine cultures and blood cultures might be needed to establish the diagnosis. Leukocytosis is present in most forms or orchitis, but lymphocytosis is common in mumps orchitis. When mumps is suspected, acute and convalescent serum viral titers may help to establish the diagnosis.

PLANS
Diagnostic
Differential Diagnosis

Torsion of the spermatic cord at times presents difficulty in the differential diagnosis. During the early stages of torsion, the epididymis is felt anterior to the testis. Absence of laboratory and physical findings suggesting an infectious disease tends to rule out orchitis. Scrotal ultrasound and nuclear imaging might help to differentiate between the two conditions. Sometimes exploration is necessary to exclude torsion.

Nonspecific granulomatous orchitis is easily confused with testicular tumors on the basis of clinical findings. The differentiation usually is made by the surgical pathologist following radical orchidectomy.

Diagnostic Options and Recommended Approach

The history and physical examination are usually sufficient to establish a diagnosis of orchitis. Urinalysis and complete blood count are essential in all patients. Blood cultures, urine culture, and viral titer for mumps are indicated when a specific diagnosis must be established. Scrotal ultrasonography may be required at the time of initial evaluation or later, if response to appropriate therapy for the initial diagnosis is poor. Scrotal scintigraphy might be useful to exclude spermatic cord torsion. Sometimes exploration might be necessary to confirm the diagnosis.

Therapeutic

Bed rest is necessary during the acute phase of orchitis. Local heat is helpful and may relieve the pain. Support to the organ affords comfort; a towel placed under the scrotum or the use of an athletic scrotal supporter may be helpful. Medication for relief of pain and fever is advised. Orchitis due to bacterial infection should be treated with appropriate antimicrobial drugs, but these drugs are useless against mumps orchitis. Infiltration of the ipsilateral cord with 20 mL of 1% lidocaine might help pain relief and resolution of the swelling. Needle aspiration of a tense scrotal hydrocele may relieve scrotal pain temporarily. In severe cases, incision of the tunica albuginea is indicated by some surgeons to relieve pain and avoid testicular necrosis due to the high pressure inside the tunica albuginea. The formation of testicular abscess or pyocele in the scrotum requires surgical drainage. Tuberculous orchitis is always secondary to epididymal tuberculosis and responds better to antituberculous medications after epididymectomy.

FOLLOW-UP

Mumps orchitis cases can be managed at home with follow-up visits to the physician every 2 to 3 days. The acute phase of mumps orchitis lasts for about a week. Rising temperature or increasing scrotal pain or size heralds the development of scrotal abscess. Hospital admission is indicated in these cases and surgical drainage might be required. Bacterial orchitis requires initial hospital admission to control the pain and temperature and daily examination to exclude the development of scrotal abscess. Tuberculous orchitis requires long-term therapy and follow-up.

DISCUSSION
Prevalence and Incidence

Mumps orchitis occurs in 20 to 35% of males with mumps and it is bilateral in 10% of cases. The prevalence of other causes is not known.

Related Basic Science

Mumps is the most common infectious cause of orchitis. It occurs only in postpubertal males. The testis is greatly enlarged and bluish. On section, because of the interstitial reaction and edema, the tubules do not extrude. Histologically, edema and dilation of the vessels are observed; neutrophils, lymphocytes, and macrophages are abundant; and tubular cells show varying degree of degeneration.

The testis involved by nonspecific orchitis is variably enlarged, congested, and tense; on section, small abscesses may be seen. Histologically, edema of the connective tissue and diffuse infiltration by neutrophils are characteristic. The seminiferous tubules may be involved and frank necrosis may be present.

Natural History and Its Modification with Treatment

Spermatogenesis is irreversibly damaged in about 30% of testes involved in mumps orchitis. Marked atrophy of the affected testis is the rule. If both testes are involved, permanent sterility may result, but androgenic function usually is maintained.

Prevention

Live attenuated mumps virus vaccine is highly effective in preventing parotitis and complicating orchitis; it is recommended for all susceptible persons over the age of 1 year. The incidence of mumps orchitis may possibly be reduced by the administration of mumps hyperimmune globulin 20 mL during the incubation period or very early stages of the disease. Administration of corticosteroids is suggested as prophylaxis against orchitis; however, its efficacy is controversial.

Cost Containment

Mumps vaccination should be generalized to help in the prevention of mumps and its complications.

REFERENCES

Gillenwater JY, Grayhack JT, Howards SS, Duckett JW. Adult and pediatric urology. 2nd ed. St. Louis: Mosby Year Book, 1991.

Smith DR. General urology. Norwalk: Appleton & Lange, 1995.

Walsh PC, Retick AB, Samy TA, Vaughan ED. Campbell's urology. 6th ed. Philadelphia: Saunders, 1992.

CHAPTER 18–26

Epididymitis

Thomas E. Keane, M.B., B. Ch., B.A.O.

DEFINITION

Epididymitis is inflammation of the epididymis.

ETIOLOGY

Epididymitis may result from an acute urinary tract infection with retrograde spread of infection along the vas deferens. There is a common embryologic derivation of the ureter, vas deferens, seminal vesicle, and epididymis, and in some cases, structural abnormalities of the termination of these organs in the trigone and posterior urethra may be present, predisposing these patients to retrograde inflammation of the vas deferens and epididymis. Indwelling urethral catheters may occasionally precipitate an attack of acute epididymitis, which in adults is usually secondary to retrograde spread of an infecting organism. Epididymitis is a more common cause of scrotal swelling in childhood than is usually believed. Gierup et al. (1975) reported 48 cases over a 25-year period, and more recently, Gislason and colleagues (1980) reviewed an additional 25 childhood cases seen over 5 years.

This condition may occur in boys who have urinary infections, commonly as a result of structural lesions of the urinary tract, or who undergo reconstructive surgery and who have indwelling urethral catheters. In an overview of four series of acute scrotal swellings occurring in boys, epididymitis was the underlying cause in 10 to 41% of cases. The peak incidence is usually in adolescence. (Leap, 1967; Kaplan and King, 1970; Moharib and Krahn, 1970; Bourne and Lee, 1975). In older boys epididymitis occurs as a cause of acute, painful scrotal swellings, often in the absence of demonstrable bacterial infection. Numerous studies including culture of direct epididymal aspirations have failed to demonstrate organisms in these incidences. Viral and atypical bacterial infections have been suggested as the cause of these conditions. Other unusual organisms that can precipitate an attack of epididymitis include *Salmonella* and *Hemophilus*. Such episodes usually occur in the absence of urinary tract infection, and in these circumstances direct hematogenous seeding may have been the cause. Purulent epididymitis or chronic epididymitis may occur requiring surgical exploration for diagnosis or drainage of the epididymal abscess. When such an acute scrotal swelling occurs in a child, adolescent, or man who is still within the usual age range for torsion of the testis, the weight is on the physician to rule out testicular torsion prior to making the diagnosis and undertaking subsequent treatment of epididymitis.

CRITERIA FOR DIAGNOSIS
Suggestive

Epididymitis is perhaps the most common intrascrotal inflammatory process, and although it is more common than is actually believed in childhood, with the peak incidence in adolescence, it remains primarily a disease of adults. More than 60% of the cases occur in men between the ages of 20 and 40 and frequently no underlying pathology is associated. Epididymitis in men occur following lower urinary tract surgery or inflammation, especially after transurethral prostatectomy or prostatitis. The condition usually presents as gradually worsening scrotal pain, tenderness, and swelling. Patients frequently associate a period of strenuous exertion with the development of the symptoms. It is frequently associated with a concomitant prostatitis or urethritis, and the patient may therefore also complain of voiding symptoms or a urethral discharge. Epididymitis may also be caused by other infectious agents including viruses, *Chlamydia*, and bacteria or it may occur secondary to an idiopathic inflammation of the epididymis.

Definitive

Epididymitis typically presents with scrotal pain and swelling which occur gradually, and physical examination indicates tenderness and in-

duration primarily of the epididymis. Secondary testicular involvement may occur, and primary orchitis in the absence of epididymitis is rare. This diagnosis is primarily a diagnosis of exclusion and is made when other causes of epididymal tenderness and induration that are associated with scrotal edema and erythema (particularly testicular tumor and testicular torsion) have been ruled out.

CLINICAL MANIFESTATIONS
Subjective

On questioning, patients frequently relate their episode of epididymitis as following a period of heavy lifting, strenuous exertion, or minor blunt trauma to the scrotum. Any association, however, can only be described as tenuous at best. The onset of scrotal pain associated with epididymitis is usually gradual. Radiation usually occurs to the ipsilateral inguinal region, the lower abdominal quadrant, or flank. Urgency, frequency, and dysuria are common, as many patients have an associated prostatitis or urethritis, in which case a urethral discharge is also present. When epididymitis is of bacterial origin, general malaise and fever usually accompany the scrotal pain and voiding symptoms. Nausea and vomiting are rare, and the presence of such symptoms is more suggestive of testicular torsion. Pain is exacerbated by standing or walking, and rest with elevation of the legs often provides dramatic relief. Elevation of the scrotum with a scrotal support also frequently provides relief.

Chronic epididymitis may be associated with a vague dull ache in the scrotum, which on examination reveals mild tenderness in the epididymal area. Frequently there is no history of a precipitating episode such as testicular trauma and no symptoms of urinary discomfort such as those seen with the acute episode, which oftentimes may have resulted in the chronic inflammatory process.

Objective
Physical Examination

On physical examination, the epididymis is enlarged and tender. The enlargement may be segmental or involve the entire epididymis. The involved area is usually firmer than normal and tender. Scrotal skin may show edema and erythema, and frequently palpation confirms the presence of an associated hydrocele, which may make the scrotal contents indistinct. The ipsilateral testis may be enlarged, tense, and tender if orchitis is associated with the epididymitis. As the condition progresses the intrascrotal contents may become indefinable, especially in the presence of a hydrocele. Epididymitis may be bilateral in approximately 10% of cases. Elevation of the scrotal contents frequently reduces the discomfort (Prehn's sign). Ultimately the intrascrotal contents may become fixed to the scrotal wall, in which case suppuration or abscess formation frequently follows.

In cases of chronic epididymitis, tenderness is usually minimal and the epididymis is totally or focally firm. Once again, testicular tumor must be ruled out, although frequently in such cases, the testis is palpably normal.

Routine Laboratory Abnormalities

Laboratory tests are dictated by the clinical condition. If the patient is afebrile and the suspected etiology is either traumatic or nonbacterial, a urinalysis is usually the only study required. A urinalysis showing pyuria suggests either chlamydial or bacterial infection of the prostate or urethra, where the primary source of infection may have occurred. Approximately 20% of cases are associated with a positive urine culture. If the patient is febrile and a bacterial etiology is suspected, then leukocytosis may be present, although an elevated white cell count may have many causes. Blood cultures are taken if bacteremia is suspected.

PLANS

Diagnostic

Acute and chronic epididymitis are usually diagnosed by history and physical examination alone. The presence of pyuria on urinalysis suggests a lower urinary tract infection, which may have been the etiology or the result of epididymitis.

Differential Diagnosis

Differential diagnosis includes hydrocele, testicular torsion, torsion of a testicular appendage, testicular tumor, spermatocele, and epididymal cyst, all of which are discussed in other chapters.

In cases that are unclear, further imaging studies include an isotopic flow study of the scrotum to differentiate testicular torsion. If a testicular tumor is suspected, especially in the presence of a large hydrocele, ultrasonography may be definitive.

Therapeutic

The treatment of epididymitis consists of measures primarily to relieve symptoms and reduce epididymal edema and possible resultant ischemia. Absolute bed rest should be instituted for 3 to 7 days, depending on the severity of the induration and tenderness. A scrotal support is recommended for all patients. This may vary from the use of an athletic support to a rolled towel placed between the thighs to elevate the scrotum. Strenuous exertion should be avoided for at least 2 weeks after the tenderness resolves. Occasionally, local anesthetic may be injected into the spermatic cord to provide temporary relief of severe scrotal pain.

Antiinflammatory agents such as ibuprofen and aspirin are recommended to relieve pain and reduce local inflammation. Such medications may be continued for 7 to 10 days.

When *Chlamydia* is the suspected causative organism, tetracycline, doxycycline, and minocycline are the most appropriate antibiotics. These medications are administered for a 14-day course.

Bacterial epididymitis is frequently caused by Gram-negative enteric organisms. In such cases, the most appropriate medications are the combination trimethoprim–sulfamethoxazole, ciprofloxacin, or cephalosporins. Depending on the severity of the condition, parenteral antibiotics may be required. Combination therapy is most appropriate until urine cultures are available with sensitivity data. If gonorrhea is the suspected cause, appropriate therapy for gonococcal urethritis may be insufficient; in such cases, a 7- to 10-day course of parenteral penicillin is more appropriate for gonococcal epididymitis. Surgical therapy is rarely indicated. Scrotal wall fixation suggests suppuration, impending abscess formation, or ischemia. In some patients in whom the viability of the testis seems threatened by the degree of epididymal or spermatic cord edema, epididymotomy has been used. Epididymectomy may be required if an abscess is diagnosed, and ultimately orchiectomy may be required in the presence of testicular ischemia or an associated testicular abscess. Epididymitis in the United States is rarely associated with infection due to fungi, exotic bacteria, parasites, or tuberculosis; however, such is not the case in many foreign countries, and such an etiology should be ruled out when epididymitis is seen in a person who has recently immigrated to this country. Such causes account for less than 1% of cases, and epididymectomy with associated treatment of the systemic disease is usually all that is required.

FOLLOW-UP

Mild cases of epididymitis are managed on an outpatient basis provided the patient agrees to report any signs of progression, such as worsening scrotal pain, swelling, erythema, fever, and chills. Any sudden increase in pain may represent secondary torsion, which can occur in acute epididymitis.

Follow-up visits with the physician should occur every 3 to 5 days during convalescence. Signs of progression to suppuration, abscess, or ischemia indicate the need for hospitalization and strict bed rest with parenteral antibiotics. Such measures may also be required if the patient fails to improve on the usual general measures and oral medications. Convalescence is slow and epididymal induration and tenderness

may persist for 3 to 6 weeks, although the patient should report a marked improvement within the first week of appropriate therapy.

DISCUSSION

Prevalence and Incidence

Epididymitis is uncommon prior to puberty in the absence of urinary tract abnormalities; however, as mentioned, this condition is more common in childhood than is usually believed. The prepubertal male child with epididymitis should undergo a complete imaging evaluation of the upper and lower urinary tracts to rule out any anatomic anomalies such as posterior urethral valves and ectopic ureter. Repeated episodes, even in adulthood, may indicate ureteral ectopia with insertion of the ectopic ureter into the seminal vesicle, bladder neck, or vas deferens.

Related Basic Science

The epididymis is a vermiform structure attached to the posterolateral aspect of the testis. After receiving mature nonmotile spermatozoa from the tubules of the rete testis within the upper pole of the testis, the primary functions of the epididymis are maturation and transport of spermatozoa to the vas deferens. This transport usually requires 1 to 2 days during which spermatozoa mature and become capable of moving spontaneously and fertilizing the ovum. With the prevalence of HIV-associated infections and the diminished resistance to infection that such patients have, such an etiology should be borne in mind in patients who demonstrate significant risk factors for HIV-associated illnesses.

In adult men under the age of 35, the most likely infectious etiology is *Chlamydia trachomatis* or gonorrhea. In such cases, infection has usually occurred through retrograde means by the vas deferens from the prostatic urethra, through lymphatic spread, or through hematogenous means. Such patients do not appear acutely ill and usually complain of urethritis and prostatitis symptoms. Chlamydial epididymitis is usually not associated with fever. In men over the age of 35, bacterial epididymitis is more common and usually caused by enteric Gram-negative pathogens. Once again, infection is usually through retrograde flow of the organisms via the vas deferens; however, in such cases these patients usually have fever and appear more ill.

Epididymitis following lower urinary tract surgery or instrumentation is most likely due to retrograde flow of pathogens to the epididymis. With the use of prophylactic antibiotics, the incidence of epididymitis following such instrumentation or surgery is low.

Chronic epididymitis is the residual inflammatory process from an acute episode. Recurrent acute epididymitis following appropriate therapy should prompt evaluation of the entire urinary tract for an abnormality or congenital anomaly. Chronic epididymitis may occur secondary to specific epididymal infections. Epididymitis has been associated with tuberculosis, syphilis, schistosomiasis, filariasis, and a variety of fungal infections. As mentioned, epididymectomy may have a role in such patients and control of systemic infection from these specific causes is mandatory.

Natural History and Its Modification with Treatment

General measures are equally important to medications in reducing the morbidity of epididymitis. Reducing epididymal edema and potential ischemia and subsequent scarring reduce the risk of epididymal obstruction. Such obstruction leads to infertility in some patients. Acute epididymitis responds to appropriate therapy within 7 to 10 days. The patient may resume light activity when epididymal induration has improved and tenderness has resolved. Persistent scrotal pain may last 3 to 6 weeks after the acute phase. A small number of patients progress to epididymal or testicular ischemia or infarction. Ipsilateral testicular atrophy may result in approximately 15% of patients with epididymitis from any cause.

Prevention

Prevention depends on reducing such risk factors as lower urinary tract infection and the potential for reflux of infecting organisms to the epididymis via the vas deferens. Patients with recurrent episodes should undergo a thorough urologic evaluation to rule out additional abnormalities or anomalies.

Cost Containment

The enforcement of general measures, particularly bed rest and scrotal support, during the first few days of acute epididymitis reduces the risk of prolonged morbidity from chronic epididymitis. Early surgical intervention when abscess or suppuration is suspected will shorten the course of this disease and further reduce the convalescence interval.

REFERENCES

Bourne HL, Lee RE. Torsion of the spermatic cord and testicular appendages. Urology 1975;5:73.

Gierup J, Von Hetenberg C, Osterman A. Acute non-specific epididymitis in boys. Scand J Urol Nephrol 1975;9:5.

Gislason T, Norona FX Jr, Gregory JG. Acute epididymitis in boys: A five year retrospective study. J Urol 1980;12:533.

Holmes KK, Berger RE, Alexander ER. Acute epididymitis: Etiology and therapy. Arch Androl 1979;3:309.

Kaplan GW, King LR. Acute scrotal swelling in children. J Urol 1970;104:219.

Leap LL. Torsion of the testis: Invitation to error. JAMA 1967;200:669.

Mikuz G, Damjanov I. Inflammations of the testis, epididymis, paratesticular membranes and scrotum. Pathol Ann 1982;17:101.

Moharib NH, Krahn HP. Acute scrotum in children with emphasis on torsion of the spermatic cord. J Urol 1970;104:601.

Vordermark JS, Favila MQ. Testicular necrosis: A preventable complication of epididymitis. J Urol 1982;128:1322.

Witherington R, Harper WM. The surgical management of acute bacterial epididymitis with emphasis on epididymectomy. J Urol 1982;128:722.

CHAPTER 18–27

Hydrocele

John A. Petros, M.D.

DEFINITION

A hydrocele is a collection of fluid within the intrascrotal tunica vaginalis.

ETIOLOGY

Hydroceles are of two main etiologies. The first etiology is a patent processus vaginalis, which allows peritoneal fluid to accumulate in the dependent scrotum. This is similar to an indirect hernia, except that no peritoneal structures (bowel, omentum, etc.) are contained in the hydrocele. This type of hydrocele is most commonly seen in childhood. The second is a reactive hydrocele, which is the result of fluid secreted by the tunica vaginalis itself in response to an inflammatory stimulus such as epididymitis, orchitis, or testicular tumor. This type of hydrocele is commonly seen in adulthood.

CRITERIA FOR DIAGNOSIS

Suggestive

The diagnosis of hydrocele is suggested when a smooth, nontender scrotal swelling is discovered. The testis may or may not be palpable, but if palpable, it is usually normal. Transillumination of the scrotum reveals a fluid-filled mass that transmits a red-orange light throughout the entire fluid mass. This is most readily seen by placing an otoscope underneath the scrotum applied directly to the skin and examining the anterior surface with the room lights out and the door closed. Communicating hydroceles with a patent processus vaginalis are usually reducible with manual pressure, much as a hernia would be. Reactive hydroceles with no patent processus vaginalis cannot be reduced.

Definitive

The definitive diagnosis of hydrocele is made with scrotal ultrasound, which shows a clear fluid surrounding the testes and distal spermatic cord structures in the absence of an inguinal hernia.

CLINICAL MANIFESTATIONS

Subjective

Hydroceles present as scrotal swelling, usually chronic though occasionally acute. They are usually painless, though a dull ache is frequently reported. If a sufficient size is achieved, the overlying scrotal skin may exhibit dermatitis. Patients usually report a gradual increase in size over a prolonged period. It is not unusual for patients to delay reporting the problem for several years. Children's parents may report that the size of the swelling varies throughout the day depending on position and crying, with diminution or disappearance after sleep.

Objective

Physical Examination

Scrotal swelling is the hallmark of hydrocele. It may appear unilateral or bilateral. In the presence of a small hydrocele, the testis is easily palpable, whereas large hydroceles make palpation of the testis impossible. Because testicular, epididymal, and spermatic cord pathology can induce hydrocele, it is important to evaluate these structures thoroughly. Transillumination should be performed (see Criteria for Diagnosis for technique). A fluid wave is usually present and percussive impacts are transmitted through the hydrocele.

Routine Laboratory Abnormalities

There are no routine laboratory studies indicated in the evaluation of a hydrocele. If the history or physical examination suggests inflammatory episodes such as epididymitis, orchitis, and urinary tract infection, then a urinalysis with microscopic examination and urine culture are indicated. If signs or symptoms suggest acute infection, a white blood cell count may be obtained.

PLANS

Diagnostic

Differential Diagnosis

The differential diagnosis includes hydrocele (communicating), hydrocele (noncommunicating), inguinal hernia, epididymoorchitis, hematocele, epididymal cyst/tumor, spermatocele, varicocele, testicular mass/tumor, idiopathic scrotal edema, hematoma, testicular torsion, and torsion of testicular appendage.

Diagnostic Options

The diagnostic options include bedside transillumination and scrotal ultrasound.

Recommended Approach

Following transillumination in the office, scrotal ultrasound should be obtained to make the diagnosis and rule out underlying testicular pathology. A thorough examination should rule out the presence of concomitant inguinal hernia.

Therapeutic

Therapeutic Options

The therapeutic options include observation, aspiration, sclerosis, and surgical repair.

Recommended Approach

Hydrocele is a benign process that does not damage the testes and requires no specific treatment if asymptomatic. Treatment may be applied if the hydrocele is considered unsightly by the patient or if it produces symptoms, such as ache or pain, dermatitis, and interference with normal activities. Hydroceles may be aspirated for acute relief, but ultimately recur after aspiration. Aspiration combined with sclerosis with tetracycline injection may be tried but can be associated with pain and recurrence. Surgical repair is the treatment of choice. Pediatric communicating hydroceles should be repaired through an inguinal incision that includes hernia repair. Adult reactive hydroceles should be approached through a scrotal incision unless definite hernia is also found, which would make the inguinal approach preferable.

FOLLOW-UP

Following surgical repair of hydrocele, the patient requires only routine follow-up at several weeks to examine the wound. Should hydrocele recur, repeat excision may be performed. Because aspiration and sclerosis are associated with significant recurrence rates, routine examination should be performed weeks to months following these procedures.

DISCUSSION

Prevalence

Hydroceles are very common in newborns, most of which resolve. Persistence after the age of 2 is rarely associated with spontaneous resolution. Reactive adult hydroceles are common, with up to 1 in 10 men demonstrating some fluid detectable by sonography. Only a small minority of these herald a significant underlying process such as tumor or attain a size or level of symptoms that requires intervention.

Basic Related Science

The testes are formed in the retroperitoneum of the developing fetus near the kidneys and descend during embryogenesis. The processus vaginalis forms as an outpouching of the peritoneum adjacent to the gubernaculum and progressively elongates through the inguinal canal. By the 12th week the testes lie adjacent to the inguinal ring. At approximately 7 months' gestation, the epididymis and testes descend into the scrotum, and a patent processus vaginalis is in continuity with the peritoneal cavity. This channel is obliterated with further development. Delays in this obliteration result in neonatal hydrocele or direct hernia.

Natural History and Its Modifications with Treatment

The natural history of hydrocele is either gradual enlargement or static size. Hydroceles are usually cured by definitive surgical repair.

Prevention

There is no means of prevention.

Cost Containment

Because of the benign course of hydroceles, no treatment is necessary unless symptoms develop. Once treatment is necessary, surgical repair is indicated as the first procedure.

REFERENCES

Kogan S. Cryptorchidism. In: Kelalis, King, Belman, eds. Clinical pediatric urology. 3rd ed. Philadelphia: Saunders, 1992:2.

Lowe FC, Brendler CB. Evaluation of the urologic patient: History, physical examination, and urinalysis. In: Campbell's urology. 6th ed. Philadelphia: Saunders, 1992:1.

Shokin AA, Eraky I, Hassan N, et al. Tetracycline sclerotherapy for testicular hydrocele in renal transplant recipients. Urology 1994;44(1):96–99.

Ziegler MM. Diagnosis of inguinal hernia and hydrocele. Pediatr Rev 1194;5(7):286–288.

CHAPTER 18–28

Varicocele

Michael A. Witt, M.D.

DEFINITION

A varicocele can be defined as a dilation of the pampiniform venous plexus in the region of the right or left spermatic cord.

ETIOLOGY

A varicocele is caused by the congenital absence of valves in the internal spermatic vein. This permits the retrograde flow of blood when the patient stands.

CRITERIA FOR DIAGNOSIS

Suggestive

The patient may detect "swelling" in the scrotum.

Definitive

The physician can identify the varicocele on physical examination.

CLINICAL MANIFESTATIONS

Subjective

Although varicoceles produce dilations in the pampiniform plexus, most patients are asymptomatic. Varicoceles are typically found on a routine physical examination for induction into the military service or prior to participation in sports. Sometimes the patient complains of a heaviness in the right or left hemiscrotum and a dull pain that is exacerbated by heavy lifting or is more pronounced at the end of the day. The pain may radiate into the right or left inguinal area or the medial side of the right or left thigh.

Objective

Physical Examination

The patient should be examined while completely relaxed in the supine and standing positions in a warm room. With the patient recumbent, there may be a bogginess in either the right or left spermatic cord but often the veins are not readily palpable. With the patient standing, the veins should fill and are either visible or palpable. If the veins are palpable, an abnormal fullness is noted superior to the testis. On palpation, there is a spongy tubular structure, which, if large, is readily identifiable. If small, it will be present within the cord and will increase in size when a Valsalva maneuver is performed. When the veins do not decompress in the recumbent position, obstruction should be suspected due to blockage in the vena cava or the left renal vein.

It is important, at the time of genital examination, to assess the consistency and size of the testis. It is not uncommon for the ipsilateral testis to be soft or atrophic due to a varicocele.

Routine Laboratory Abnormalities

There are no routine laboratory abnormalities.

PLANS
Diagnostic
Differential Diagnosis

The diagnosis of varicocele can be made by physical examination. No differential diagnosis exists.

Diagnostic Options and Recommended Approach

Other studies that have been used to diagnose varicocele are the Doppler stethoscope, duplex Doppler, venography, and nuclear scanning. These are not indicated in routine screening for varicocele, but sometimes can be helpful if there is only a suspicion of a varicocele on physical examination. The gold standard for the identification of a varicocele is venography, but this tends to be invasive and exposes the patient to contrast medium and radiation. As a result, this procedure is indicated only in individuals who have recurrent varicoceles after varicocele ligation.

Therapeutic

If a varicocele is present and the patient is symptomatic, surgical correction is offered. Surgical correction consists of occluding the internal spermatic vein at some point in its course from the vena cava or the left renal vein to the testis. This interrupts the retrograde blood flow that causes dilation of the veins and whatever symptoms the patient is experiencing.

If the patient complains of difficulty initiating a pregnancy, then a complete infertility workup is indicated. In this case, two semen analyses are usually obtained to demonstrate any abnormality in bulk seminal parameters. If an abnormality is noted and there are no other identifiable factors, surgical correction of the varicocele is indicated. By so doing, there is a 60% chance of improvement in seminal parameters, which translates into a 40% chance of initiating a pregnancy.

If the varicocele is due to caval or renal vein obstruction, the varicocele is indicative of a more serious problem and the etiology of either of these processes needs to be addressed.

If the patient is asymptomatic and is not attempting to initiate a pregnancy but the varicocele has been found incidentally specifically in the pediatric population, it is much more difficult to determine when inter-

vention is appropriate. If testicular atrophy is present, the case can be made for correcting the varicocele because the abnormality will probably become more pronounced with the passage of time.

FOLLOW-UP

If no testicular atrophy is associated with the varicocele, it is recommended to follow the patient on an annual basis after baseline studies have been obtained of seminal parameters and testicular volume. If either of these changes during follow-up, then intervention is indicated.

DISCUSSION
Prevalence and Incidence

Varicoceles occur in approximately 15% of all men. They are present at the time of puberty and are due to the absence of valves in the internal spermatic vein, resulting in retrograde flow when the patient is standing. Forty percent of all infertile men presenting for evaluation of male factor infertility have varicoceles. Sixty to seventy percent of varicoceles are unilateral and present on the left, and 30 to 35% are present bilaterally. In only 5% of cases is the varicocele located on the right.

Related Basic Science

The abnormal physiology related to varicoceles is poorly understood in situations where there is altered sperm production. The current theory is that there are alterations in the thermal regulatory mechanism. Scrotal temperatures in patients with varicoceles are elevated by approximately $0.2°C$. It is thought that this mild elevation in temperature alters sperm production and may lead to the demise of spermatogonia. Other theories regarding the alteration in spermatogenesis are reflux of adrenal or renal metabolites down the internal spermatic vein to the pampiniform plexus, elevated venous pressure and the drainage of the testis, germinal epithelial hypoxia due to venostasis, and disturbances in the hormonal axis associated with the varicocele.

Natural History and Its Modification with Treatment

Varicoceles are usually asymptomatic and develop shortly after puberty. Spontaneous resolution does not occur. Varicoceles may progress over time, sometimes rendering previously fertile men infertile.

Prevention

There are currently no preventive measures for varicoceles.

Cost Containment

The proper selection of patients who will benefit from surgical treatment is central to cost containment.

REFERENCES

Biggers RD. Soderdahl DW. The painful varicocele. Milit Med 1981;146:440.
Pryor JL, Howards SS. Varicocele. Urol Clin North Am 1987;14:499.
Turner TT. Varicocele: Still an enigma. J Urol 1983;129:695.

CHAPTER 18–29

Carcinoma of the Testis (See Section 3, Chapter 23)

Cystitis

W. Holt Sanders, M.D.

DEFINITION

Cystitis is an inflammation of the bladder mucosa, caused in the majority of cases by bacterial infection.

ETIOLOGY

Most infections occur when bacteria from the vagina, rectum, and perineum ascend the urethra to colonize the bladder.

CRITERIA FOR DIAGNOSIS

Suggestive

Irritative voiding symptoms associated with pyuria and bacteriuria in a bladder urine specimen are suggestive of cystitis.

Definitive

Although most bacteria incubating in the bladder reach colony counts of 10^5/mL, in symptomatic women, 10^2 or more colony-forming units per milliliter of a known urinary pathogen is sufficient to make the diagnosis of bacterial cystitis.

CLINICAL MANIFESTATIONS

Subjective

Symptoms of cystitis include dysuria, frequency, urgency, suprapubic discomfort, back pain, and a sensation of incomplete emptying. Although some patients have only one of these symptoms, many have the entire syndrome.

A history of congenital abnormalities of the urinary tract, stone disease, diabetes, or neurogenic bladder with incomplete emptying increases the risk of cystitis and makes complete resolution more difficult. Pregnant women are likely to have an associated pyelonephritis. In some women, recurrent urinary tract infections are related to intercourse.

Family history does not play a significant role in the evaluation of cystitis.

Objective

Physical Examination

The physical examination is usually remarkable only for suprapubic tenderness and for tenderness of the trigone during pelvic examination. Costovertebral angle tenderness frequently denotes pyelonephritis. It is controversial whether the presence of fever distinguishes cystitis from pyelonephritis.

Routine Laboratory Abnormalities

The urinalysis reveals pyuria and bacteriuria. The urine culture usually reveals 10^5 or more colony-forming units per milliliter.

PLANS

Diagnostic

Differential Diagnosis

The differential diagnosis for irritative voiding symptoms includes detrusor instability, interstitial cystitis, carcinoma in situ, and tuberculosis. Detrusor instability is characterized by urgency and less frequently by dysuria, and the urinalysis and culture are negative. Interstitial cystitis presents with suprapubic pain, urgency, and dysuria, but again, urinalysis is normal. The diagnosis of interstitial cystitis is suggested by a low functional bladder capacity and characteristic ulcers seen on cystoscopy. Carcinoma in situ usually is associated with an abnormal cytology. Tuberculosis of the urinary tract classically presents with sterile pyuria.

Diagnostic Options

Urine for culture can be obtained with a midstream clean catch, by urethral catheterization, or by suprapubic aspiration. The first is readily accepted by patients but likely to produce a contaminated specimen. Suprapubic aspiration, although neither painful nor dangerous, is unpleasant for the patient. Urethral catheterization combines ready acceptance with a low contamination rate.

Recommended Approach

A woman with dysuria, frequency, and pyuria on urinalysis should have a catheterized urine specimen collected for culture and sensitivity. Specimens obtained by clean catch are frequently contaminated with bacteria from the perineum and introitus. No further studies are necessary unless there is bacterial persistence at follow-up or recurrent urinary tract infections. A sterile urine culture in the face of pyuria should be followed by urine cultures for acid-fast bacilli. Irritative voiding symptoms without pyuria and with negative urine cultures should lead to evaluation for interstitial cystitis, detrusor instability, and carcinoma in situ.

Therapeutic

Therapeutic Options

In uncomplicated cystitis, complete eradication of bacteriuria can be accomplished with ampicillin, amoxicillin, a first-generation cephalosporin, fluoroquinolones, nitrofurantoin, or trimethoprim–sulfamethoxazole. A 3-day course of antibiotics is sufficient for cure in straightforward cases. A complicated urinary tract infection, that is, one occurring in a urinary tract with an anatomic or functional abnormality, requires 7 to 10 days of antibiotic therapy for cure.

Recommended Approach

A 3-day course of trimethoprim–sulfamethoxazole (160 mg of trimethoprim and 800 mg of sulfamethoxazole, one tablet twice daily) is excellent empiric therapy. If sensitivity testing of the cultured specimen shows poor susceptibility to trimethoprim–sulfamethoxazole, the therapeutic regimen should be adjusted appropriately. Persistent bacteriuria requires treatment for 14 days. More extended therapy of up to 6 weeks is not superior to the 14-day treatment. Persistent bacteriuria in women and any episode of cystitis in men should lead to an investigation of possible factors predisposing to urinary tract infections. This investigation should include an intravenous pyelogram, measurement of postvoid residual, and possibly cystoscopy.

Recurrent urinary tract infections are easily prevented with low-dose suppressive antibiotic prophylaxis. In patients who are reluctant to take antibiotics long term, self-administered single-dose therapy with trimethoprim–sulfamethoxazole at the onset of symptoms is a legitimate option. For women whose episodes of cystitis are temporally related to intercourse, single-dose prophylaxis after intercourse effectively prevents recurrent urinary tract infections.

FOLLOW-UP

All patients should have a follow-up urine culture to document complete elimination of bacteria from the urine. If the bacteria are only suppressed to low counts, the colonies will regrow and the urinary tract infection will be unresolved. The most common cause of unresolved bacteriuria is the presence of organisms that are resistant to the antibiotic therapy chosen initially. Positive repeat cultures guide the decision to consider a more appropriate antibiotic regimen. Other causes of unresolved bacteriuria include development of resistance in previously susceptible bacteria, azotemia, papillary necrosis, and staghorn calculi. Repeat cultures are also important in evaluating recurrent urinary tract infections. Recurrent urinary tract infections in women who initially achieve a negative urine culture are usually caused by reinfection by fecal bacteria and, only rarely, by bacterial persistence in an abnormal urinary tract.

DISCUSSION
Prevalence and Incidence

The incidence of bacteriuria rises from 1% in young girls to 4% in young adults, and continues to increase by 2% per decade of life. At least 20% of women over the age of 65 have bacteriuria. After the initial urinary tract infection, one fourth of women experience a recurrence within the next few years.

Related Basic Science

Susceptibility to urinary tract infections is caused by the presence of abnormally high counts of fecal flora on the vaginal and urethral mucosa, a phenomenon thought to be related to specific adherence between bacteria and epithelial cell receptors. Expression of these receptors is genetically mediated, and major histocompatability complex HLA-A3 has been associated with recurrent urinary tract infections. In addition, the presence of filamentous protein appendages, or pili, on bacterial cells is important in adhesion to epithelial cells. Two specific types of pili, called type 1 pili and P pili, have been associated with increased risk of developing recurrent urinary tract infections. These discoveries have been the basis for investigations of receptor blockade with indigenous bacteria and competitive inhibition with receptor analogs. Neither of these approaches has yet been applied in the clinical setting.

Natural History and Its Modification with Treatment

Between 60 and 80% of women with urinary tract infections who are treated with a placebo eventually experience spontaneous resolution of their bacteriuria, even though it may persist for several weeks. Prompt initiation of antimicrobial treatment decreases the course of the disease and diminishes its accompanying symptoms.

Prevention

Recurrent urinary tract infections can be prevented with low-dose, prophylactic antibiotics, which have little effect on normal bowel flora. Because of a better understanding that other disease states (such as interstitial cystitis and detrusor instability) can cause irritative voiding symptoms, it is now known that prophylactic suppression of bacteriuria is almost 100% effective in preventing recurrent urinary tract infections. The antibiotics most commonly used for suppression are trimethoprim–sulfamethoxazole, nitrofurantoin, cephalexin, and fluoroquinolones.

Cost Containment

The most important measures for cost containment include minimization of urethral catheterization, prompt initiation of appropriate antibiotics after onset of symptoms, and use of inexpensive yet effect antimicrobial drugs such as trimethoprim–sulfamethoxazole and nitrofurantoin.

REFERENCES

Schaeffer AJ. Cystitis in the adult female. In: Resnick MI, Caldamone AA, Spirnak JP, eds. Decision making in urology. 2nd ed. Philadelphia: B. C. Decker, 1991:52.
Schaeffer AJ. Infections of the urinary tract. In: Walsh PC, Retik AB, Stamey TA, Vaughan ED, eds. Campbell's urology. 6th ed. Philadelphia: Saunders, 1992:731.

CHAPTER 18–31

Carcinoma of the Bladder

Sam D. Graham, Jr., M.D.

DEFINITION

Carcinoma of the bladder is malignancy of the epithelial surface (urothelium) of the bladder.

ETIOLOGY

Most urothelial tumors have no known etiology. Transitional cell carcinomas are associated with exposure to certain organic chemicals (β-napthylamines, etc.), smoking, and deletions of tumor suppressor genes. Squamous cell carcinomas are associated with stones and chronic inflammations such as schistosomiasis.

CRITERIA FOR DIAGNOSIS
Suggestive

Hematuria (gross or microscopic) is the most common symptom associated with carcinoma of the bladder. Gross hematuria is usually total and painless and may be associated with clots. Other findings include vesical irritability, usually associated with invasion of the detrusor muscle, persistent urinary tract infections that do not clear under standard therapy, and, occasionally, findings of an exophytic filling defect on intravenous pyelogram.

Definitive

The diagnosis is made by transurethral biopsy of the tumor. Ancillary studies, including urinary cytology, are frequently positive.

CLINICAL MANIFESTATIONS
Subjective

Hematuria is the most common symptom of transitional cell carcinoma of the bladder. Usually, the hematuria is gross, total, and painless, and frequently it is dark. It may or may not be associated with clots. In addition, signs of vesical irritability such as frequency, urgency, and dysuria may accompany a bladder tumor, and these are usually asymptomatic of detrusor invasion. Symptoms of bladder outlet obstruction such as decreased force and caliber of stream, hesitancy, and straining to void are uncommon. Nonspecific symptoms such as weight loss, lower abdominal pain, hemoptysis, fevers, and obstipation may accompany bladder cancer.

Objective
Physical Examination

Physical examination in transitional cell carcinoma of the bladder is usually unremarkable unless there is either metastatic disease or a large, advanced local lesion. In large and invasive local lesions, the bimanual rectoabdominal examination may reveal induration of the bladder. Other positive findings may include nonspecific findings of pulmonary metastases or lymph node metastases.

Routine Laboratory Abnormalities

Laboratory studies of use include the urinalysis, which usually reveals red blood cells with or without pyuria and bacteriuria. Other laboratory studies that may be of use include serum chemistries, which may show nonspecific elevations of liver enzymes associated with metastatic disease. In addition, squamous differentiation of the tumor may produce ectopic parathormone, which in turn causes hypercalcemia. Hypercalcemia is also seen with metastatic disease to the bone, which is also usually associated with an elevated alkaline phosphatase level. Patients frequently are anemic due both to blood loss from the tumor and to the anemia of chronic disease. The remaining useful studies are radiologic, including chest x-ray for possible metastatic disease and intravenous pyelography.

PLANS
Diagnostic
Differential Diagnosis

The differential diagnosis for hematuria includes stones, infections, trauma, other tumors including renal cell carcinoma, arteriovenous malformations, and glomerulonephropathies. The differential diagnosis for vesical irritability includes inflammation, stones, neurologic dysfunction, and foreign bodies. The differential diagnosis for filling defects on radiography includes radiolucent stone, clot, fungus ball, and ureterocele.

Diagnostic Options

The diagnostic options include radiography (intravenous pyelogram and computed tomography) cystoscopy, biopsy of the bladder, urinary cytology, and urine culture.

Recommended Approach

Patients who are at risk for transitional cell carcinoma include any patient with gross painless hematuria regardless of age. Minimal studies that should be performed in such patients include urinary cytology, intravenous pyelography, and cystoscopy. Any patient with severe irritative symptoms also should be considered to be at high risk and should undergo these studies.

Therapeutic

Stage TAT1 Lesions. Low-grade tumors that are superficial (i.e., not invading the detrusor muscle) are usually managed by transurethral resection. These patients are followed every 3 months with repeat cystoscopies for 2 years and then every 6 months for 3 years. In addition to cystoscopy, cytologies and routine pyelography are performed. There is a slight increased incidence of upper tract tumors (5–10%) in patients with transitional cell carcinoma of the lower tract. This reflects the fact that transitional cell carcinoma is a field-change disease in which the entire urothelium is at risk for developing carcinoma. Patients who develop recurrent tumors are resected and may be treated with intravesical therapy, consisting of either thiotepa, mitomycin-C, doxorubicin, or bacille Calmette–Guérin (BCG).

Carcinoma in Situ. Carcinoma in situ is a grade III noninvasive transitional cell carcinoma with a high potential for developing later invasive disease. The diagnosis of carcinoma in situ is a bad omen and is usually treated very aggressively. Recent reports of success using long-term bacille Calmette–Guérin therapy in the treatment of carcinoma in situ have shown great promise. Other useful agents include intravesical mitomycin-C, intravesical interferon, and oral bropirimine. Failure to respond to these more conservative methods should prompt the clinician to proceed to radical cystectomy. Follow-up for these patients is the same as above.

Stage T2 and T3 Lesions (NO MO). Patients with tumor invading the detrusor muscle do not usually respond to conservative therapy. These pa-

tients should be managed aggressively, as invasion of the detrusor muscle connotes a 50% reduction in their expected survival. The treatment of choice is radical cystectomy combined with a prostatectomy in males and anterior vaginectomy and anterior pelvic exenteration in females. In addition, the lymph nodes are removed in both pelvic sidewalls. The preferred method of diversion is ileal conduit diversion; however, recently there has been interest in continent diversions, that is, the Koch pouch. Patients with deeply invasive lesions (A or T3b) should undergo external radiation therapy prior to radical cystectomy. It is only in this population of patients that a definite benefit for preoperative radiation therapy can be shown.

Stage TxN+M+. Patients with advanced disease are usually not candidates for radical cystectomy. This is so because they have systemic disease and the use of local therapy is not of benefit. Only in a small group of patients with minimal nodal disease (N1) is this therapy of any value. These patients usually have a poor prognosis. Recent advances in cisplatin-based chemotherapy have shown response rates between 35 and 70%. Radiation therapy is good for palliation of painful metastases. Hormonal therapy currently has no place in the treatment of carcinoma of the bladder.

Patients with Invasive Disease Who Are Not Surgical Candidates. Patients who are not surgical candidates have the option of external radiation therapy in combination with radiopotentiators such as cisplatin and arterial infusion. Radiation therapy to the bladder usually produces an approximate 20% with cure rate in stage T2 or stage T3a lesions. This should be contrasted with the 40 to 50% cure rate of surgery alone or with radiation therapy. Recent clinical trials of radiopotentiators such as cisplatin given weekly in addition to the radiation therapy have shown good success with no-evidence-of-disease rates as high as 50%. Another possibility would be arterial infusion of cisplatin. This has been tried in several clinical studies and has shown some success. The experience, however, is not large enough to make a meaningful statement.

Currently, several experimental modalities are available for carcinoma of the bladder. The first of these is neomydium-YAG laser therapy of bladder tumors. This modality has shown good success in the treatment of superficial recurrent lesions. This modality has the advantages of being accomplished on an outpatient basis without anesthesia and being able to treat larger areas of the bladder than are usually treatable with standard electrocautery. The disadvantage is that no tissue is procured, as with a standard transurethral resection of the bladder. Treatment of invasive lesions with the YAG laser has had mixed results. The YAG laser is therefore probably best used in very superficially invasive lesions; it is of questionable benefit in deeply invasive lesions. Trials with monoclonal antibody therapy of bladder carcinoma have not to date been instituted, so no meaningful statement can be made in this regard.

FOLLOW-UP

The follow-up for superficial disease requires the use of routine cystoscopy, cytologies, and pyelograms. Follow-up for the radical procedures includes serum chemistries, a complete blood count, and chest x-rays. In addition, loop cytologies may be indicated if pyelography reveals an abnormality. Periodic washing of the male urethra is important if the patient has not undergone previous urethrectomy.

The patient with carcinoma of the bladder should be aware of the reasons for the different diagnostic modalities necessary in his or her care. In addition, patients with superficial tumors should be made aware of the necessity to return on a regular basis for follow-up cystoscopy, as they have an approximately 50% chance of recurrence. There is also a 5 to 10% chance that such patients will develop invasive disease. It is important that they be followed up routinely. Patients who are to undergo radical cystectomy in combination with prostatectomy should be made aware of the long-term effects of the surgery, which are primarily impotence (which is virtually universal) and the necessity for urinary diversion. The use of qualified enterostomal therapists has greatly increased patient acceptance of the long-term consequences. Furthermore, advances in the use of urologic prosthetics have made the impotence much less of a problem. Females undergoing radical cystectomy may find the vagina to be stenotic and may require a secondary procedure if this is the case. Patients undergoing intravesical chemotherapy should be made aware of the vesical irritability associated with the therapy. In addition, thiotepa is associated with depressed platelet and white blood cell counts, and the patient should be advised of these possibilities.

DISCUSSION
Prevalence and Incidence

An increased incidence of squamous carcinoma of the bladder is commonly attributable to chronic infections. In Egypt, this is usually caused by schistosomiasis.

Related Basic Science

The first well-documented industrial exposure of humans to a carcinogen was that involving β-naphthylamines. These are common by-products of the aniline dye industry and are associated with an extraordinarily high incidence of carcinoma of the bladder. The latency period for action is several years. In addition, patients with altered tryptophan metabolism also appear to have a higher incidence of carcinoma of the bladder, because the by-products are similar in structure to the β-naphthylamines. The basic defect appears to be an absence of B_6-dependent enzyme activity, which is also blocked by nicotinic acid. This blockage of B_6 activity with relative B_6 deficiency is thought to be the motive action in carcinoma of the bladder in smokers. There is at least a three times higher incidence of carcinoma of the bladder in smokers. Other causative agents include cyclamates and saccharine, which combine with methyl N-nitrosurea to produce a powerful cocarcinogen.

The usual histology of carcinoma of the bladder in the United States is transitional cell carcinoma. This is graded I through III on the Broder grading scale. Typically, the tumors are papillary, although the high-grade tumors tend to be sessile. The higher-grade lesions tend to be more aggressive, tend to invade earlier, and are associated with a poor prognosis.

Recent advances in identification of subcellular markers such as cell surface ABO antigens, $β_2$-microglobulins, and DNA flow cytometry may yield promising methods of screening patients who are at high risk for developing recurrent and/or invasive disease.

Natural History and Its Modification with Treatment

The natural history of carcinoma of the bladder depends directly on the stage of the tumor. Patients with T1 lesions, for example, have a 90 to 95% life expectancy at 5 years. Patients with T2 lesions have approximately a 50% life expectancy, and patients with T3b lesions have an approximate 20% life expectancy. A small group of patients with T4 lesions (T4aN1) also can expect an approximate 20% survival. Patients with widespread disease currently have little likelihood of surviving 5 years.

Prevention

The patient must stop smoking. Furthermore, cessation of exposure to any of the aniline dyes or their by-products also will be of help. Attempts to use B_6 in patients with altered tryptophan metabolism have not proven to be successful.

Cost Containment

The cost containment in carcinoma of the bladder is primarily by judicious use of diagnostic modalities. An intravenous pyelogram is necessary to rule out upper tract disease. Cystoscopy is the primary method of diagnosis of carcinoma of the bladder. Urinary cytologies are an inexpensive method of follow-up as well as diagnosis of patients with no visible lesions. The primary staging modality is computed tomography scanning, which yields information on the pelvic lymph nodes as well as the liver and structures contiguous to the bladder. Arteriography and other invasive vascular procedures have no benefit or use in carcinoma of the bladder.

REFERENCES

Gittes RF. Tumors of the bladder. In: Harrison JH, Gittes RF, Perlmutter AD, et al., eds. Campbell's urology. 4th ed. Philadelphia: Saunders, 1979:1033.

Hicks RM, Chowaniec J. The importance of synergy between weak carcinogens in the induction of bladder cancer in experimental animals and humans. Cancer Res 1977;37:2943.

Jewett HJ. Cancer of the bladder: Diagnosis and staging. Cancer 1973;32:19072.

Marshall VF. The relation of the preoperative estimate to the pathologic demonstration of the extent of vesical neoplasms. J Urol 1952;68:714.

Utz DC, Hansh KA, Farrow CM. The plight of the patient with carcinoma in situ of the bladder. J Urol 1970;103:160.

Walton G, Graham S Jr, McCue P. Beta-2 microglobulins as a differentiation marker in bladder cancer. J Urol 1986;136:1197.

Weir JM, Duren JE Jr. Smoking and mortality: A prospective study. Cancer 1970;25:105.

CHAPTER 18–32

Carcinoma of the Kidney

Sam D. Graham, Jr., M.D.

DEFINITION

Renal cell carcinoma is a solid lesion of the parenchyma of the kidney. Transitional cell carcinoma is a lesion derived from the urothelium lining the collecting system.

ETIOLOGY

Most renal cell carcinomas are sporadic with no known etiology. There are familial occurrences of renal cell carcinoma especially in von Hippel–Landau disease. Recent evidence indicates that both the sporadic and familial forms may isolate to genetic alterations on the 3p chromosome.

Transitional cell carcinoma is associated with exposure to environmental toxins such as β-napthylamines, smoking, and phenacetin. Squamous dedifferentiation may be associated with chronic infections and stones.

CRITERIA FOR DIAGNOSIS
Suggestive

Symptoms include hematuria, pain, mass, or such nonspecific symptoms as weight loss. The increased usage of intravenous pyelograms, renal ultrasound, and computed tomography for both urologic and nonurologic reasons has been responsible for the discovery of the increased incidence of asymptomatic lesions.

Definitive

Histologic identification of renal cell carcinoma (parenchymal) or transitional cell carcinoma (collecting system) of the kidney confirms the diagnosis. Adenocarcinoma, renal cell carcinoma, and hypernephroma are synonymous, although renal cell carcinoma is the most correct nomenclature.

CLINICAL MANIFESTATIONS

Subjective

Renal Cell Carcinoma

Complaints are usually vague and nonspecific, if present at all. Approximately 45% of renal parenchymal tumors are discovered incidentally. Hematuria (50%) may be the most common subjective symptom. Abdominal pain, fever, and other constitutional symptoms such as weight loss, anorexia, weakness, nausea, and peripheral neuropathy may be present but are nonspecific.

Transitional Cell Carcinoma

Symptoms of transitional cell carcinoma include hematuria (gross, total, and dark), with or without clots, seen in over 50% of patients. Other symptoms may include flank pain, acute colic (due to clot obstruction), recurrent infections, and other nonspecific symptoms such as weight loss, nausea, and abdominal distention. These tumors are frequently silent until they are of significant size. As with renal cell carcinoma, transitional cell carcinoma of the collecting system may be found incidentally during radiologic studies for other suspected disease entities (e.g., urinary tract infections). As these tumors are of the lining of the collecting system, they are more likely to present at lower stages with gross hematuria than renal cell carcinoma.

Objective

Renal Cell Carcinoma

Physical Examination. Renal cell carcinoma is typically a "silent" tumor and may have no objective findings until it is advanced. Physical examination may reveal an abdominal mass (5%) or right-sided varicocele (rare).

Metastases of renal cell carcinoma are most common to the lungs (50%), with metastases to bone (30%), liver (30%), and brain (10%) being fairly common. Objective physical findings, therefore, may indicate advanced disease. Nonspecific findings of hepatomegaly, lymphadenopathy, or distant metastases (bone, lung, brain, skin, etc.) are found in 20 to 30% of patients on presentation.

Routine Laboratory Abnormalities. Red cells in the urine occur in 50% of patients, but this is a nonspecific finding. Anemia is common, but polycythemia (6–9%) occurs. Erythropoietin is elevated in up to 70% of patients. Derangement of liver function tests with elevations of serum glutamic–oxalacetic transaminase and lactate dehydrogenase and alterations of bromsulphalein (Stauffer's syndrome) may occur even without metastases. Hypercalcemia is usually due to bony metastases, although 5 to 10% is due to ectopic parathormone production.

Transitional Cell Carcinoma

Physical Examination. Physical examination in these patients usually is not helpful unless the disease is advanced.

Routine Laboratory Abnormalities. Laboratory studies of importance are urinalysis (up to 85% sensitive), urine cytologies (up to 100% specific), and x-rays (see below).

PLANS

Diagnostic

Renal Cell Carcinoma

Differential Diagnosis. Renal cell carcinoma is a mass lesion of the renal parenchyma. The differential diagnosis for a mass lesion of the kidney is as follows:

- Renal carcinoma
- Renal cyst
- Renal abscess
- Calyceal diverticulum
- Angiomyolipoma
- Adrenal mass
- Xanthogranulomatous pyelonephritis
- Hematoma
- Renal duplication

Diagnostic Options. An excretory urogram may reveal a mass lesion (85–95% accurate). A computed tomography (CT) scan of the abdomen is useful in the diagnosis and staging of the disease (95% accurate). Magnetic resonance imaging is usful in imaging tumor thrombi in the vena cava. A retrograde pyelogram may show a splaying of calyces (nonspecific finding). A sonogram may show a solid, cystic, or mixed pattern that is best for screening cysts.

Venacavagrams show the level of vena caval or renal vein involvement. Arteriograms show the vascular pattern of the lesion. A renal scan may show increased (or decreased) vascularity of lesion. Digital venous angiogram and cyst puncture are also employed.

Recommended Approach. The preoperative diagnosis of a renal cell carcinoma of the kidney is usually accomplished radiologically. More than 90% of renal masses on intravenous pyelogram are benign lesions, usually renal cysts. The secondary diagnostic tests attempt to aid the examiner in distinguishing between benign and malignant disease. There remain, however, a few clinical incidences in which surgical exploration is undertaken without a firm diagnosis.

The first radiologic study performed in any patient with hematuria should be bolus nephrotomography. This modality has up to 90% accuracy, and if done properly, it can accurately distinguish cystic from indeterminate lesions in most cases. Secondary studies should follow a logical sequence. If the lesion is highly suspicious of being cystic, a sonogram will confirm this. If, however, the lesion is indeterminate or the sonogram shows anything other than a simple cyst, the next study should be an abdominal CT scan. This modality demonstrates masses as small as 1 cm, shows the composition of the mass (solid, cystic, or fat), and, if the mass is a tumor, allows staging, as the perinephric fat, nodes, liver, and vena cava are also demonstrated. Depending on the results of the CT scan, other studies may or may not be required. If there is evidence of a tumor with renal vein or vena caval involvement (usually right-sided tumor), the next study would be a vena cavagram. Arteriography is not commonly performed unless either the diagnosis is not cleared on CT scan or there are extenuating circumstances (e.g., solitary kidney). Formal Seldinger-style arteriography has been replaced to a great extent by digital venous imaging, a less morbid procedure.

Bone scans are helpful in staging tumors, as are CT scans of the brain. Other useful studies are chest x-ray films and, occasionally, chest CT scans.

Staging of renal cell carcinoma of the kidney is classically the Robson method, although this is currently being replaced by the TNM system, which allows a more accurate definition of the tumor. These systems are outlined in Table 18–32–1.

Transitional Cell Carcinoma

Differential Diagnosis. Transitional cell carcinoma arises from the urothelium lining the collecting system and, thus, appears as a negative filling defect in contrast radiologic studies. The differential diagnosis of

TABLE 18–32–1. STAGING SYSTEMS

Tumor	Robson (1963)	TNM	Estimated 5-Year Survival (%)
Tumor confined to renal capsule	A		65
Small, minimal calyceal distortion		T1	
Large, calyceal distortion		T2	
Tumor invading perinephric fat	B	T3a	45
Tumor involving renal vein	C$_1$	T3b	55–60
Tumor involving inferior vena cava (below diaphragm)	C$_2$	T3c	45–55
Tumor involving lymph nodes	C$_3$	T1–3N1–4	20
Tumor with metastases	D		0–5
Neighboring structures		T4a	
Supradiaphragmatic vena cava		T4b	
Distant metastases		T1–4M1	

Table constructed from data in Robson CJ. Radical nephrectomy for renal cell carcinoma. J Urol 1963;89:37.

filling defects of the renal collecting system with appropriate diagnostic tests is as follows:

- Transitional cell carcinoma
- Nonopaque stone
- Ureteritis cystica
- Fibrous epithelioma
- Clots
- Papillary necrosis
- Fungus ball
- Venous impression on collecting system
- Varices of ureteral veins
- Extrinsic compression of ureter

Diagnostic Options. An intravenous pyelogram may show filling defects in the collecting system. A retrogram pyelogram may show negative filling defects. Urine cytology may be negative, suspicious, or positive for transitional cell carcinoma. Ureteroscopy allows direct visualization of lesions. A CT scan is useful in differentiating a tumor from stones; the results are useful for staging. A sonogram may distinguish a tumor from radiolucent stones. Brush biopsies are also employed.

Recommended Approach. Usually, contrast studies of the collecting system (intravenous pyelogram, retrograde pyelogram) are highly suspicious, showing an exophytic, intrinsic filling defect. Failure to completely opacify the collecting system with an intravenous pyelogram for hematuria requires a retrograde pyelogram.

Voided urine cytology is usually positive in high-grade tumors of the urothelium, but they do not localize the tumor. During retrograde pyelograms, urine should be collected from each ureter for cytology. In addition, barbotage of the renal pelvis with saline may increase the yield for cytology. Brush biopsies under radiologic control are also highly accurate. New technologic advances in optic systems now allow the physician to visualize directly ureteral and renal pelvic pathology with the ureterorenoscope.

Filling defects of the renal pelvis also can be differentiated by either sonograms or CT scans. These studies help identify stones (which are not discernible on pyelography) versus tumor. In addition, the CT scan is important for tumor staging. Angiograms and venograms have no place in the diagnosis of transitional cell carcinoma.

The staging system for transitional cell carcinoma of the upper tract is identical to the system for carcinoma of the bladder. Survival is directly related to the stage of disease.

Therapeutic

Renal Cell Carcinoma

Therapeutic Options. Therapeutic options include observation (not recommended), radiation therapy (not recommended for primary or most soft tissue lesions, but effective for symptomatic metastases), embolization (not useful except as palliation), chemotherapy (generally ineffective), nephrectomy, and immunotherapy.

Recommended Approach. Initial management of renal cell carcinoma of the kidney is radical nephrectomy, which includes en bloc removal of the kidney, perinephric fat, and lymph nodes contained within the retroperitoneal fascia (Gerota's fascia). Removal of the entire ureter to and including the ureteral orifice is recommended in transitional cell carcinoma, but is not necessary in renal cell carcinoma. Regional lymph node dissection is done primarily for its prognostic value. Bilateral tumors (1–2%) are treated with radical nephrectomy, partial nephrectomy, or a combination of the two. Palliative nephrectomy is sometimes necessary in patients with metastatic disease for bleeding, pain, or local symptoms or for treatment of patients with solitary metastatic disease, in which the metastatic lesion is also removed.

Currently, the optimal therapy for renal cell carcinoma of the kidney is surgical. Chemotherapy, radiation therapy, and hormonal therapy have poor response rates. Radiation does have a place in palliative therapy for painful metastases. Experimental therapies that have been tried include embolization of tumors with radioactive seeds and immunotherapy. The most promising therapy in renal cell carcinoma appears to be immunotherapy. A variety of modalities have been used including vaccines, monoclonal antibodies, interferon, and interleukin-2.

The results of the majority of these trials indicate limited response rates with variable toxicity. More recently, combinations of factors and the use of multiple factors generated by OKT-3 stimulation of lymphocytes (autolymphocyte therapy) have shown promise, with increased survival rates that are two to six times control rates.

Transitional Cell Carcinoma

Therapeutic Options. Surgical excision, intravenous chemotherapy, intracavitary chemotherapy, and endoscopic ablation are therapeutic options.

Recommended Approach. Classic management of transitional cell carcinoma of the renal pelvis and ureter is nephroureterectomy with total excision of the ureter and a cuff of the bladder around the ureteral orifice. Distal ureteral lesions that are of low grade may be treated by excision of the affected segment of ureter. Obviously, any therapy must be modified in patients with bilateral disease or tumor in a solitary renal unit. Alternative therapies with no large series showing their efficacy include neomydium–YAG laser fulguration through a ureterorenoscope, instillation of mitomycin-C through a ureteral stent, and intravenous chemotherapy concentrated by the kidney in an active form (e.g., cyclophosphamide [Cytoxan], cisplatin). All these modalities have had anecdotal success. Radiation therapy is usually associated with significant morbidity and low success.

Patients with metastatic transitional cell carcinoma are usually treated with a cisplatin-based chemotherapy similar to that for carcinoma of the bladder. Response rates of 40 to 50% have been reported. Occasionally, palliative nephrectomy is necessary to control bleeding, although this also may be controlled with embolization of the kidney or instillation of Formalin or silver nitrate.

FOLLOW-UP

Renal Cell Carcinoma

Once the diagnosis of renal cell carcinoma of the kidney has been established by nephrectomy and the extent of metastases ascertained by pathologic or radiologic means, a follow-up plan can be formulated. Patients with no evidence of metastatic renal cell carcinoma are usually seen 1 to 2 weeks following surgery, then every 3 months for 2 years, followed by 6- to 12-month follow-up visits. Observations to be made at each visit include physical examination of the surgical site, abdomen, chest, and lymph nodes; laboratory studies; and chest x-rays. Yearly bone and liver scans are advised by some authors. Late recurrences (≥ 5 years following nephrectomy) are not uncommon in this tumor.

Transitional Cell Carcinoma

Transitional cell carcinoma is usually a field-change disease, meaning that the entire urothelium is at risk for developing recurrent disease. Fifteen to twenty percent of these patients develop or have associated tumors of the bladder. Following nephroureterectomy, such patients should undergo periodic cystoscopy, cytology, and pyelography similar to the schedule for carcinoma of the bladder. In addition, as metastases are frequently pulmonary and/or hepatic, routine blood chemistries and chest x-rays should be performed.

DISCUSSION

Prevalence and Incidence

In 1995, approximately 30,000 cases of renal malignancy were diagnosed in the United States with a 2:1 male:female prevalence. The number of deaths for the same period is estimated to be about 11,000.

Related Basic Science

Renal Cell Carcinoma

Renal cell carcinomas have been shown to originate from the proximal tubule in the nephron. Three common cell types have been observed: clear cell (most common), granular cell, and spindle cell. Tumors may occur as one type or a combination of these cell types. Data on the etiology of renal cell carcinoma are sparse, but these tumors have been reproduced in golden hamsters in response to exogenous estrogen. Other etiologic agents include Thorotrast, adenoviruses, lead, and aflatoxin. A familial incidence is also noted, especially in von Hippel–Lindau disease (40–50% incidence) and certain chromosomal abnormalities.

Transitional Cell Carcinoma

The occurrence of transitional cell carcinomas has been directly related to aniline dyes, β-nephthylamines, and cigarette smoking. Other etiologies include phenacetin abuse, the suspected cause of the high incidence of upper tract urothelial tumors in the Balkan states. Histologic patterns generally reflect a papillary-type growth in the lower grades of malignancy. High-grade tumors may exhibit squamous differentiation. Tumors are frequently multiple, occurring in several parts of the urinary tract. In addition, the higher-grade tumors are associated with a higher incidence of invasion.

Natural History and Its Modification with Treatment

Renal Cell Carcinoma

Renal cell carcinoma accounts for approximately 85% of all renal cortical tumors and occurs twice as often in the male as in the female. The peak incidence is in the fifth to sixth decades. These tumors begin in the renal cortex and expand toward the renal capsule and medulla, compressing the parenchyma into a pseudocapsule. Hematuria connotes invasion of the collection system, usually seen in advanced tumors. Local extension occurs in the perirenal fat, whereas a metastatic tumor may involve regional periaortic lymph nodes, lung, liver, bone, or brain.

Transitional Cell Carcinoma

Transitional cell tumors of the renal pelvis are multifocal in origin and can occur in any portion of the transitional epithelium. They constitute approximately 85% of all urothelial tumors and are more common in men than women. Hematuria is far more common and may be associated with both large and small tumors. Invasion of the renal parenchyma or the muscularis indicates a poor prognosis. Follow-up of these tumors may reveal tumors in other portions of the urothelium. Once a tumor of the renal pelvis has been diagnosed, recurrent tumors have been diagnosed in the bladder or contralateral ureter of as many as 15 to 25% of patients.

Prevention

At present there is no proven method for the prevention of renal tumors, but a decrease in exposure to aniline dyes and smoking could reduce the incidence of transitional cell tumors significantly.

Renal Cell Carcinoma

Patients are informed of the malignant process involving the kidney parenchyma and the need for surgical removal. In addition, patients are instructed on the necessity for close and long-term follow-up, including, at a minimum, chest x-rays and serum chemistries in addition to physical examinations.

Transitional Cell Carcinoma

Patients are instructed that transitional cell carcinoma is a field-change disease involving the entire urothelium. They must be made aware of the necessity for repeated pyelograms, cystoscopies, and cytologies, in addition to routine chest x-rays and blood chemistries. The surgical options also should be explained to patients. In addition, patients should avoid phenacetins, smoking, and exposure to β-naphthylamines.

COST CONTAINMENT

Once the decision to operate has been made, based on a suspicious lesion indicated by intravenous pyelography and confirmed by CT scan, further radiographic studies (retrograde pyelography, ultrasound, nephrotomograms) are not necessary. Bone marrow examination almost never reveals intramedullary metastatic disease. Serial lactate dehydrogenase and other tumor-associated substances such as carcinoembryonic antigen are of unproven benefit.

REFERENCES

Ambrose SS, Lewis EL, O'Brien DP III, et al. Unsuspected renal tumors associated with renal cysts. J Urol 1977;117:704.

Batata MA, Grabstald H. Upper urinary tract urothelial tumors. Urol Clin North Am 1976;3:79.

Glenn JF. Renal tumors. In: Harrison JH, Gittes RF, Perlmutter AD, et al., eds. Campbell's urology. 4th ed. Philadelphia: Saunders, 1979:967.

Middleton RC. Surgery for metastatic renal cell carcinoma. J Urol 1967;97:973.

Robson CJ. Radical nephrectomy for renal cell carcinoma. J Urol 1963;89:37.

Skinner DG, Colvin RB, Vermillion DC, et al. Diagnosis and management of renal cell carcinoma: A clinical and pathological study of 309 cases. Cancer 1971;28:1165.

Skinner DG, DeKernion JB, eds. Genitourinary cancer. Philadelphia: Saunders, 1978.

CHAPTER 18–33

Hydronephrosis

John A. Petros, M.D.

DEFINITION

Hydronephrosis is increased volume of the intrarenal urinary collecting system including renal pelvis and calyces. It is always associated with dilation of these structures and may or may not be associated with dilation of the ureter (technically ureteronephrosis). When both ureteral dilation and renal dilation are present, the term *hydroureteronephrosis* is appropriate.

ETIOLOGY

The etiology of hydronephrosis is varied. It is commonly being diagnosed in utero due to the increasing use of sonography and, in these cases, may be transient and physiologic. When hydronephrosis persists in postnatal life, common etiologies include duplication of the renal collecting system, ureteropelvic junction (UPJ) obstruction, vesicoureteral reflux, ureterovesical junction (UVJ) obstruction, and urethral valves. Less common pediatric etiologies include ectopic ureter, ureteral valves, prune-belly syndrome, and neurogenic bladder. In the adult, hydronephrosis may commonly be due to acute obstruction from a urinary calculus, ureteral or bladder malignancies, chronic obstruction from ureteral stenosis (especially when previous ureteral instrumentation has occurred), vesicoureteral reflux, primary or secondary UPJ obstruction, neurogenic bladder, or presence of a urinary diversion such as ileal conduit. Less common etiologies include end-stage bladder outlet obstruction from benign prostatic hyperplasia, prostatic carcinoma, phimosis or meatal stenosis, retroperitoneal fibrosis or malignancy, colonic or uterine cancer, residual dilation that persists after relief of an acute obstruction, and iatrogenic ureteral ligation following hysterectomy or other pelvic procedures.

CRITERIA FOR DIAGNOSIS
Suggestive

An enlarged renal outline or displacement of bowel loops seen on plain abdominal film, a palpable flank mass, and symptoms of acute renal colic may suggest renal mass or obstruction.

Definitive

The definitive diagnosis of hydronephrosis depends on radiologic imaging. Ultrasound is the most accurate, followed by computed tomography (CT) scanning, intravenous urography, and retrograde pyelography. Mild degrees of hydronephrosis are recognized when the involved side is compared with the normal contralateral system, whereas more severe cases are easily diagnosed from inspection of the involved system alone. The intrarenal collecting system is normally not visualized on renal sonography, so any dilation or visualization constitutes hydronephrosis. If the renal pelvis is located outside the confines of the renal parenchyma (an anatomic variant known as extrarenal pelvis) some fluid collection may exist without actual hydronephrosis.

CLINICAL MANIFESTATIONS
Subjective

Because of the large number of different conditions that can lead to hydronephrosis, the relevant history and subjective data vary widely. In general, hydronephrosis may be due to obstructive or nonobstructive causes. Obstructive causes of hydronephrosis may cause a great deal of symptoms when the obstruction has occurred suddenly or relatively few symptoms when the obstruction has occurred gradually. In nonobstructive hydronephrosis or gradual chronic obstruction, the only symptoms may be those of mass effect, such as abdominal bloating and early satiety.

If acute flank pain is present it should be fully characterized, including onset, nature, duration, location and radiation to the groin, constant versus intermittent, previous episodes, and alleviating or exacerbating factors. Flank pain that is brought on by imbibition is a classic symptom of UPJ obstruction, though it cannot always be obtained in the history. Abdominal symptoms such as bloating, increased abdominal girth, and early satiety may be present in severe cases of long standing. Emesis is a symptom of ureteral obstruction. Patients may complain of chronic dull flank ache, which needs to be differentiated from back pain due to degenerative disease or nerve root compression. Lower urinary tract symptoms should be asked specifically, including irritative voiding symptoms of frequency, urgency, and nocturia, as well as obstructive symptoms such as decreased force of stream, hesitancy, sensation of incomplete emptying, and episodes of urinary retention. Suprapubic or perineal pain may suggest prostatic or bladder pathology, and gross hematuria similarly suggests uropathy.

A detailed past urologic history is necessary. Prior operations or procedures including retroperitoneal surgery (e.g., lymphadenectomy), renal surgery (e.g., nephrolithotomy, UPJ repair), pelvic surgery (e.g., hysterectomy, cystectomy, proctectomy), endoscopic manipulation (e.g., cystoscopy, ureteroscopy, ureteral stone basketing, ureteral stenting), and prostate, penile, or urethral surgery should be asked specifically. Past medical history that may be relevant to autoimmune disorders or methylsergide or LSD use may increase the chances of retroperitoneal fibrosis. Any history of malignancy is important, as mass effect on the kidney or ureter may produce hydronephrosis. A history or renal calculi and whether they passed spontaneously or were removed should be obtained. A history of hypertension may at times suggest hydronephrosis. Neurologic disorders that affect the innervation of the bladder may produce a neurogenic bladder with resultant hydronephrosis from either UVJ obstruction or vesicoureteral reflux. These include multiple sclerosis, Parkinson's disease, previous spinal surgery or trauma, alcoholic or diabetic neuropathy, and pelvic surgery such as low anterior resection or abdominoperineal resection.

Because many urologic disorders that may result in hydronephrosis have a (usually minor) familial component, the family history is important. Specifically, urolithiasis, benign prostatic hyperplasia, and prostate cancer all have inherited predisposing factors in some individuals.

Objective
Physical Examination

The following parts of the physical examination have particular relevance to the diagnosis of the myriad conditions that may produce hydronephrosis: vital signs, especially blood pressure; lymphadenopathy; cutaneous lesions suggestive of metastasis; chest examination, especially lung bases; abdominal examination, especially masses or tenderness in flank or suprapubic area or presence of a stoma; neurologic examination, especially lumbar and sacral segments; genital/pelvic examination to include search for phimosis or meatal stenosis, absence of uterine cervix, and so on; and rectal examination with attention to the size and consistency of the prostate.

Routine Laboratory Abnormalities

Two routine laboratory tests that may aid in the identification of the cause of hydronephrosis are the SMA-18 (including creatinine) and urinalysis with microscopic examination.

A patient with hydronephrosis may exhibit elevated creatinine level, hyperkalemia, and hypo- or hypernatremia if the underlying process is bilateral. Urinalysis may reveal proteinuria, hematuria, or the presence of infection.

PLANS
Diagnostic
Differential Diagnosis

The differential diagnosis includes obstructive hydronephrosis, hydronephrosis from reflux, renal cyst, solid renal mass, extrarenal pelvis, duplication anomaly, adrenal cyst, and transient hydronephrosis of the newborn.

Diagnostic Options

The diagnostic options include renal ultrasound, abdominal CT or magnetic resonance imaging (MRI), retrograde pyelogram, intravenous urogram, nuclear renogram, cystogram, contrast injection of ileal conduit ("loop-o-gram"), and percutaneous antegrade nephrostogram.

Recommended Approach

The most accurate test for diagnosing hydronephrosis is renal sonography. High-quality sonography is dependent on real-time interpretation by a skilled sonographer. Renal masses that can be accurately differentiated include hydronephrosis, solid renal mass, simple renal cyst, complex renal cyst, extrarenal pelvis, and duplication anomalies. Adrenal masses or cysts can usually, though not always, be differentiated from renal masses. If the anatomic diagnosis cannot be made with ultrasound, then abdominal CT or MRI should be used, though this is rarely necessary. Cystoscopy with retrograde pyelogram can also render an anatomic diagnosis. Once the diagnosis of hydronephrosis has been made, a renal function study should be performed to determine if the hydronephrosis is obstructive or nonobstructive and to determine the amount of renal function that has been lost. This would be either an intravenous urogram or nuclear renogram with furosemide administration. The furosemide renogram is more specific for ruling out obstruction and a normal half-life virtually rules out significant obstruction, whereas prolonged retention of radioisotope is suggestive but not diagnostic of obstruction. These studies may also suggest the level of obstruction, allowing the differential to be narrowed. Special consideration needs to be made in patients who have undergone urinary diversion with either an ileal loop or continent urinary diversion. It is normal to have bilateral mild to moderate hydroureteronephrosis in these patients. Symmetric, asymptomatic hydronephrosis, with normal blood urea nitrogen and creatinine, in the patient with a urinary diversion is normal and requires no further investigation. If ureteral stenosis or obstruction is suspected, then a loop-o-gram should be obtained. If bilateral reflux that promptly drains is observed, then obstruction is ruled out.

Therapeutic

Therapeutic Options

Because hydronephrosis can be due to so many different conditions, the therapeutic options depend on the exact etiology. Antenatal hydronephrosis frequently resolves spontaneously and may require no specific treatment at all. Acute renal colic and hydronephrosis from ureteral calculus require immediate symptomatic control with definitive treatment selection based on size, location, and type of stone, as well as degree of obstruction. Symptomatic UPJ obstructions may be treated by endoscopic dilation or incision or by an open pyeloplasty. Ureteral strictures may require a simple balloon dilation, ureteral reimplantation, transureteroureterostomy, ureteroileal interposition, renal autotransplantation, or nephrectomy depending on location and length of the stricture and remaining renal function. Vesicoureteral reflux may require no treatment if mild, asymptomatic, and not associated with infections or renal damage, whereas significant reflux in a neonate with recurrent pyelonephritis almost always requires ureteroneocystostomy, and reflux due to neurogenic bladder may be treated with anticholinergic agents, clean intermittent catheterization, urinary sphincterotomy, or urinary diversion depending on the cause and severity. Even hydronephrosis from bladder, prostatic, or ureteral malignancy can be treated with many modalities including expectant management in advanced carcinomatosis, temporizing percutaneous nephrostomy while radiation or chemotherapy take effect, and extirpative surgery if significant palliation or cure is possible.

Recommended Approach

When hydronephrosis is suspected, the anatomic diagnosis should be made as outlined above. Obstruction should be accurately ruled in or out, as should vesicoureteral reflux. If obstruction is present, the level of obstruction should be determined. Total and differential renal function should be determined. The presence or absence of concomitant urinary infection should be determined by culture. A thorough search for mass lesions and malignancy should be made for hydronephrosis in the appropriate age ranges. If acute relief of obstruction is required, either percutaneous nephrotomy or placement of a ureteral stent is highly effective in the short term. Definitive surgical repair can be done as the first step in elective situations (e.g., UPJ obstruction) or as a second step when emergency percutaneous diversion has been established (high-grade ureteral obstruction with proximal urinary infection).

FOLLOW-UP

Follow-up of hydronephrosis can almost always be done with serial renal ultrasounds, which are simple, accurate, and noninvasive. The intravenous urogram and nuclear renogram are appropriate tests for documenting renal function and the presence of recurrent obstruction. Frequency and duration of follow-up depend on the underlying condition and vary from a renal ultrasound every 3 to 6 months for 10 or 15 years in the child being managed expectantly with partial UPJ obstruction, to a single function test after definitive surgical repair.

DISCUSSION

Prevalence

Maternal ultrasound detects urologic anomalies in approximately 0.1% of fetuses examined, of which hydronephrosis is the most common diagnosis. The frequent causes of antenatal hydronephrosis in descending order of frequency are UPJ obstruction, posterior urethral valves, obstructing ectopic ureterocele, megaureter, and nonobstructive fetal hydronephrosis. Hydronephrosis in the adult is usually the result of acute obstruction from ureteral calculus, followed in order by malignant obstruction, nonmalignant mechanical obstruction such as strictures, neurogenic bladder, and reflux. Accordingly, the prevalence of hydronephrosis parallels the prevalence of these diseases.

Related Basic Science

Complete ureteral obstruction results in progressive dilation of the renal pelvis and calyces for several weeks. Parenchymal atrophy begins

at 4 to 8 weeks. The acute morphologic changes include flattened papillae and dilation of the distal nephron within the first few days. Progressive dilation and atrophy of the collecting and distal tubules ensue over the first 2 weeks. By the end of the fourth week, 50% of the renal medulla has been lost, cortical thinning is evident, and the distal nephron progressively dilates. The glomerulus first demonstrates histologic changes during the fifth week of obstruction.

Natural History and Its Modification with Treatment

Sudden, complete obstruction results in renal pelvis pressures of 20 to 70 mm Hg, which gradually fall over the following weeks. As pressure in the renal pelvis rises, there is initially an increase in renal blood flow due to vasodilation. By 90 minutes to 5 hours, the renal blood flow falls because of postglomerular vasoconstriction and increased intrapelvic pressure. Following this, vasoconstriction in the preglomerular vessels causes reduced renal blood flow and a gradual fall in pressure in the renal pelvis. Glomerular filtration and tubular function decrease. Lymphatic and venous backflow persist in chronic obstruction with turnover of urine within the renal pelvis.

The duration of obstruction determines the potential for recovery of renal function. Some function has been retained in obstruction lasting up to 69 days. The presence of infection greatly accelerates irreversible damage. Early intervention is warranted to prevent the steady decline in function seen in complete obstruction. Recovery following partial obstruction depends on duration and severity. The ability to concentrate urine is lost early, and the ability to dilute the urine is retained the longest.

Postobstructive diuresis may occur following the relief of obstruction, especially bilateral obstruction such as urethral obstruction. Initially a physiologic diuresis is observed that serves to rid the body of retained fluids and osmotic agents. Usually a pathologic diuresis does not ensue, but in the rare instances that it does it is due to a loss of the medullary osmotic gradient and resultant concentrating abilities.

Prevention

Hydronephrosis, obstruction, and their deleterious effects on renal function can be prevented by antenatal screening, by education of patients with urolithiasis about the signs and symptoms of ureteral obstruction, and by periodic imaging in patients with strictures or malignant factors predisposing to obstruction. Early diagnosis and relief of obstruction allow for maximal preservation of function. Concomitant infection constitutes a surgical emergency, with urgent relief of obstruction and antibiotics being the mainstays of acute management.

Cost Containment

Cost containment related to hydronephrosis may take many forms. In pediatric patients being followed for mild UPJ or UVJ obstruction, a simple sonogram on an annual basis suffices once more frequent studies have documented no significant change in severity of hydronephrosis. Endoscopic management of urethral and ureteral obstructions has generally lessened hospital length of stay and, in most instances, can be performed on an outpatient basis. The same is true for UPJ obstruction. Ureteral stents manufactured with an attached string allow for removal in the office without the need of cystoscopy. When obstruction has been of sufficient duration such that recovery of function is not expected, asymptomatic units do not need to be treated, and symptomatic units may be removed, preventing repeated interventions to save a minimally functioning kidney.

REFERENCES

Flashner SC, King LR. Ureteropelvic junction. In: Kelalis, King, Belman, eds. Clinical pediatric urology. 3rd ed. Philadelphia: Saunders, 1992:2.

Gillenwater JY. The pathophysiology of urinary tract obstruction. In: Campbell's urology. 6th ed. Philadelphia: Saunders, 1992:1.

Koff SA, Campbell KD. Nonoperative management of unilateral neonatal hydronephrosis: Natural history of poorly functioning kidneys. J Urol, 1994;152:593.

Mandell J, Peters CA, Retik AB. Current concepts in the perinatal diagnosis and management of hydronephrosis. Urol Clin North Am, 1990;17:247.

CHAPTER 18–34

Asymmetric Kidneys

Bruce H. Broecker, M.D., and Samuel S. Ambrose, M.D.

DEFINITION

Asymmetric kidneys implies inequality in the size, shape, position, function, or contour of the right and left kidneys.

ETIOLOGY

There are many causes for asymmetry of the two kidneys, some known and some unknown. The causes may be congenital (hypoplastic kidney, pelvic kidney, congenital hydronephrosis) or may be acquired (pyelonephritic atrophy, Wilms' tumor, renal vein thrombosis).

CRITERIA FOR DIAGNOSIS
Suggestive

There may be no symptoms, physical signs, or routine laboratory data that suggest the diagnosis. There may be nonspecific abnormalities such as dysuria, flank pain, and hematuria.

Definitive

Asymmetry of the kidneys is an imaging diagnosis. The diagnosis may be made on any one of several imaging modalities that give structural or functional information about the kidneys. The most common of these are sonography, computed tomography, intravenous urography, nuclear scintigraphy, magnetic resonance imaging, and arteriography. Asymmetry between the two kidneys may be present in size, position, function, or contour.

CLINICAL MANIFESTATIONS
Subjective

Symptoms related to asymmetry of the kidney may range from none at all to those indicative of primary renal pathology (dysuria, flank pain) to those with little apparent relationship to a nephrologic condition.

Objective

Findings related to asymmetry of the kidneys may range from none to those indicative of a primary renal condition (hematuria, flank mass) to those seemingly unrelated to any renal pathology.

PLANS
Diagnostic

Asymmetry of the kidneys is an imaging diagnosis. As such, an imaging study is always done when this diagnosis is made. In some cases the imaging study is done specifically to look for renal pathology, whereas in other cases, the finding is unexpected or "incidental" on a study obtained for other reasons (Table 18–34–1).

Therapeutic

Therapy is directed toward the cause of the renal asymmetry.

The significance of renal asymmetry varies from an incidental finding of no clinical importance to a potentially life-threatening finding. The patient and family should be appropriately educated as to its significance.

FOLLOW-UP

Appropriate follow-up is determined by the nature of the cause of the asymmetry and the treatment used to manage it.

TABLE 18–34–1. ASYMMETRIC KIDNEYS: DIAGNOSES AND DIAGNOSTIC OPTIONS

Diagnosis	Diagnostic Options
Asymmetry in size	Most of these conditions may be diagnosed with any or all of the commonly used imaging modalities (ultrasound, computed tomography scan, intravenous pyelogram, nuclear renal scan). Those for which a specific test(s) is most likely or necessary are so noted.
Unilateral small kidney	
Hypoplasia	
Atrophy	
Postobstructive	
Ischemic	
Inflammatory	
Unilateral large kidney	
With normal radiographic visualization	
Compensatory hypertrophy	
With abnormal radiographic visualization	
Renal vein thrombosis	Venogram, ultrasound, magnetic resonance imaging
Hydronephrosis	
Multicystic kidney	
Tumor (renal cell carcinoma, transitional cell carcinoma, Wilms' tumor)	
Trauma (contusion, edema)	
Inflammation/infection (pyelonephritis)	
Asymmetry in position	
Failure to ascend (ectopic kidney)	
Pelvic kidney	
Abnormal ascent	
Crossed renal ectopia	
Malrotated kidney	
Displaced after ascent (adjacent organomegaly or mass lesion)	
Unilateral decreased function (visualization)	
Obstructive	
Congenital (ureteropelvic junction obstruction, ureterovesical junction obstruction)	
Acquired (stones, strictures, tumors, etc.)	
Inflammatory	
Acute pyelonephritis	
Chronic pyelonephritis	
Xanthogranulomatous pyelonephritis	
Tuberculous pyelonephritis	
Ischemic	
Renal artery thrombosis	Arteriogram
Renal vein thrombosis	Venogram, ultrasound, magnetic resonance imaging
Arteriovenous fistula	Arteriogram
Tumor	
Trauma	
Cystic	
Asymmetry in contour	
Renal pseudotumor (column of Bertin)	
Renal mass	
Benign	
Cyst	
Abscess	

(continued)

TABLE 18–34–1. (*Continued*)

Diagnosis	Diagnostic Options
Adenoma	
Hamartoma	
Malignant	
Wilms' tumor	
Renal cell carcinoma	
Transitional cell carcinoma	
Renal scarring	
Chronic pyelonephritis	
Reflux nephropathy	
Ischemia	

DISCUSSION

Prevalence

The prevalence of asymmetric kidneys is unknown.

Related Basic Science

The kidneys are paired retroperitoneal organs lying close to the spinal column below the diaphragm. The longitudinal renal axis, when projected superiorly, intersects the thoracic spine. This axis may be altered by abdominal, retroperitoneal, adrenal, or renal pathology.

There is ordinarily bilateral symmetry between the two kidneys with regard to shape, size, blood supply, and pyelocalyceal pattern. The average kidney is between 11 and 15 cm (3.5 lumbar vertebrae) in length, 6 cm in width, and 3.5 cm in thickness. The right kidney may occasionally be smaller and lower than the left.

The embryologic development of the kidney consists of three stages, the last of which is the metanephros. The metanephros becomes mature renal parenchyma. The ureteral precursor, the metanephric bud, develops at a bend in the mesonephric duct (wolffian duct) close to the urogenital sinus. It elongates and meets the metanephric blastema, inducing nephrogenesis. The metanephric bud expands to form the collecting system and ureter, including the renal pelvis and calyces. The kidneys undergo their initial development in a pelvic location but ascend in a cephalic direction, rotating so that the ureter and pelvis assume a medial position as they rise.

Any distortion or interruption of the normal embryologic processes may result in renal asymmetry. The postnatal conditions of trauma, tumor, and inflammation may also lead to renal asymmetry.

Natural History and Its Modification with Treatment

The natural history of the asymmetric kidney is determined by the cause of the renal asymmetry.

Prevention

For most congenital causes of asymmetry there is no known method of prevention.

Cost Containment

Cost containment is determined primarily by the extent of the urologic evaluation.

REFERENCES

Meschan I. Analysis of roentgen signs in general radiology. Philadelphia: Saunders, 1983.
Reeder MM. Gamuts in radiology: Comprehensive lists of roentgenologic differential diagnosis. New York: Pergamon Press, 1975.
Teplick JG, Haskin ME. Surgical radiology: A complement in radiology and imaging to the Sabiston Davis–Christopher textbook of surgery. Philadelphia: Saunders, 1981.

CHAPTER 18–35

Urolithiasis as Viewed by a Urologist

Harry S. Clarke, Jr., M.D., Ph.D.

DEFINITION

Urolithiasis is the presence of concretions in the urinary tract. The majority are composed largely of calcium. They may be found in any portion of the urinary tract, from the renal parenchyma to the bladder in women, as well as the prostatic urethra in men.

ETIOLOGY

The three factors contributing to urolithiasis are anatomic, genetic, and environmental. Anatomic abnormalities of the urogenital system that result in poor drainage often lead to the formation of stones; often these are infectious in nature. The genetic factors include a long list of enzyme disorders that lead to cystinuria, oxalosis, renal tubular acidosis, and other more subtle chemical imbalances in renal metabolism. The environmental factors are largely related to climate. Areas with high humidity and high temperatures predispose the inhabitants to fluid loss through perspiration. This leads to a concentrated urine with high acidity. The other important environmental factor is diet. Individuals whose diet includes excesses of certain substances, such as oxalate, are predisposed to stone formation. Conversely, those whose diet is lacking in stone-inhibiting elements are also at increased risk of stone formation.

CRITERIA FOR DIAGNOSIS

Suggestive

Renal colic, the sudden onset of waves of severe flank pain that radiate to the groin, with or without nausea and vomiting, is the classic manifestation of a patient with an obstructing calculus. Nonobstructing stones, however, may go unnoticed as they often cause no symptoms.

Definitive

The pressure of calcification in a patient with symptoms suggestive of an obstructing stone may be seen on a radiograph, such as a kidney, ureter, and bladder film. The definitive test is the intravenous urogram. Care should be taken to ensure adequate renal function and hydration and the absence of pregnancy and allergy, prior to performing this test. In those patients who, for one of the above reasons, cannot undergo this examination, a renal ultrasound should be performed.

CLINICAL MANIFESTATIONS

Subjective

As stated, the patient with a nonobstructing calculus may be symptom free. The patient with obstruction may present with the classic symptoms of renal colic as outlined above. The passage of small stones may present with less dramatic, vague symptoms of a "dull" pain in the region of the flank or lower quadrant. Patients may also present with symptoms of infection or persistent hematuria.

Objective

Physical Examination

A thorough physical examination should be performed as an integral part of the workup for urolithiasis. In the emergency room, patients with renal colic can be distinguished from patients with other abdominal complaints, such as peritonitis and appendicitis, by their inability to find a comfortable position. The former is in constant motion; the latter remains perfectly still. The abdomen should be examined carefully; palpation of the flank often elicits pain due to the hydronephrosis of the acutely obstructed kidney. The patient may also have hypoactive bowel sounds due to a secondary ileus. Changes in voiding may range from irritative symptoms such as urgency and frequency to urinary retention, secondary to renal colic. Occasionally a man presents whose only symptom is testicular pain, which can be mistakenly ascribed to epididymitis or torsion. Diaphoresis, tachycardia, and tachypnea are frequently present. Pain may cause hypertension. Fever is usually not present unless there is infection.

Routine Laboratory Abnormalities

Urinalysis may show gross or microscopic hematuria, crystals, pyuria, or bacteriuria. Urinary pH should also be noted as patients with uric acid and cystine stones usually have acidic urine and those with struvite (infection) stones usually have alkaline urine. The white blood cell count is usually normal unless infection is present along with the obstructing stone.

PLANS

Diagnostic

Differential Diagnosis

The possible disorders that must be considered include pyelonephritis, cholecystitis, appendicitis, salpingitis, ovarian cyst, diverticulitis, and other bowel disorders, such as Crohn's disease and colitis, and peritonitis.

Diagnostic Options and Recommended Approach

A complete blood count, urinalysis, and serum creatinine should be obtained as initial screening laboratory tests. A kidney, ureter, and bladder film followed by an intravenous urogram in the patient without contraindication (as outlined above) should be obtained.

Intravenous urography demonstrates an opacity in 85 to 90% of cases, as only 10 to 15% of renal calculi are radiolucent. The other findings include a delayed nephrogram with hyperconcentration on the affected side, and dilation of the collecting system above the stone, which will usually be seen on later or delayed films. There are three areas of narrowing in the ureter where obstructing stones often lodge: the ureteropelvic junction, the pelvic inlet where the ureter crosses the vessels, and the ureterovesical junction. These areas should be examined carefully when analyzing the films. In patients allergic to contrast media, pregnant women, or patients with marginal renal function, renal ultrasound should be substituted for the intravenous urogram. Ultrasonography often shows hydronephrosis, along with acoustic shadowing beyond the hyperechoic image of the stone.

Therapeutic

The majority of stones causing acute renal colic are small. Depending on their size and location the clinician can counsel the patient on the likelihood of spontaneously passing the stone. Stones less than 5 mm in the lower portion of the ureter have an approximate 90% chance of passing spontaneously. Larger stones lodged higher in the system have a significantly lower chance of spontaneous passage; however, patients with a history of prior stones that passed spontaneously have a higher chance of passing larger stones without intervention. Initial manage-

ment of small distal stones in patients who are not having significant nausea and vomiting is expectant, with oral hydration and pain medication at home. Patients who are not able to keep fluids down, cannot be controlled with oral pain medications, or are febrile must be admitted to the hospital for management of their obstructing stone.

For those stones that fail expectant management the first line of therapeutic intervention is extracorporeal shock wave lithotripsy (ESWL). ESWL can be effectively performed on all stones with the exception of some cases where the stone is protected by the bony pelvis in the lower half of the ureter. Stones greater than 1.5 cm require placement of a stent prior to ESWL to prevent obstruction from the stone fragments generated by the lithotripsy. Stones impacted in the ureter may require stenting to create the fluid interface necessary for effective ESWL. Large staghorn calculi can sometimes be treated successfully with ESWL, but often multiple treatments are required. In some cases of large staghorn calculi, a combined approach using percutaneous lithotripsy followed by ESWL is used. This approach is successfully used today to treat 90% of all stones. Since the development of ESWL and newer percutaneous techniques, open surgical procedures such as open pyelolithotomy and anatrophic lithotomy are rarely performed. The patient with sepsis secondary to an obstructing stone must be managed by relief of the obstruction as expediently as possible. This can be done either by placement of a double J stent or by placement of a percutaneous nephrostomy tube. Once the obstruction is relieved and the infection cleared with antibiotics, the stone can be treated as outlined above. Often, after a stent has been in place for 4 to 6 weeks and removed, the stone passes spontaneously shortly thereafter.

For those stones that fail to pass and are not amenable to ESWL due to their location, cystoscopic stone basket extraction or ureteroscopic extraction can be undertaken. The effectiveness of the ureteroscopic approach is enhanced by the availability of ultrasonic, electrohydraulic, and laser lithotripsy, which can be operated under direct vision through the ureteroscope.

FOLLOW-UP

The patient who experiences a single or first episode of renal colic secondary to an obstructing stone that passes spontaneously should undergo a simplified or extensive evaluation based on his or her risk assessment. A history constituting increased risk includes a family history of stones; a history of bone/gastrointestinal disease; gout; chronic urinary tract infection; and nephrocalcinosis. Patients in the high-risk category should be referred to undergo a full metabolic workup. The simplified evaluation includes a history to assess for dietary aberrations, stone-provoking medications, fluid loss, and urinary tract infection. The laboratory tests include stone analysis, SMA-20, urinalysis and culture, and kidney, ureter, and bladder film. Dietary aberrations include low fluid intake; high calcium intake; high-oxalate diet; sodium excess; animal protein excess; and low citrus fruit intake. Some of the stone-provoking medications are acetazolamide; calcium channel blockers; vitamin C; triamterene; calcium/vitamin D; uricosuric agents; P-binding antacids; furosemide; and theophylline. The treatment should be tailored to correct the dietary abnormality and/or remove the offending medication, prevent infections, and increase hydration. Evaluation should also include follow-up films. A kidney, ureter, and bladder film is a minimum at yearly intervals to rule out recurrent stone formation. Patients who require intervention should have a follow-up intravenous pyelogram to assess for strictures which may form slowly, causing renal damage without the overt symptoms of obstruction.

DISCUSSION

Prevalence

The syndrome of idiopathic calcium urolithiasis accounts for 70 to 80% of stone disease in industrialized nations. Stone formation due to inherited enzyme disorders or renal tubular syndromes is found in fewer than 1% of patients. Primary hyperparathyroidism is the most common hypercalcemic state associated with urolithiasis and is responsible for stone formation in only 5% of patients.

Related Basic Science

Urinary tract stone formation involves the precipitation of a poorly soluble salt, usually in association with an organic matrix. Supersaturation of the precipitating phase must be present before crystallization can occur. The pathophysiologic factors leading to this in a particular individual are those mentioned earlier under Etiology.

Natural History and Its Modification with Treatment

The natural history of idiopathic calcium oxalate stone formation is such that an individual is unlikely to have a second attack for 10 to 20 years. Based on this, it is not productive to treat this patient with long-term medication or severe dietary restriction. A risk assessment and increased hydration constitute the appropriate approach, with education and reassurance of the patient. Recurrent stone formers or patients who require surgical intervention, in contrast, require a much more aggressive approach, including metabolic evaluation and institution of preventive therapy based on the findings.

Prevention

Increased hydration is the mainstay of stone prevention because it prevents supersaturation of the urine. The correction of dietary aberrations and removal of stone-provoking medications also are of great importance. Finally, prevention of infection and identification and treatment of enzyme disorders are vital to avoiding stones.

Cost Containment

The single most important factor in cost containment is identification of the cause of urinary tract stone formation and prevention of recurrence.

REFERENCES

Burns JR, Finlayson B. Why some people have stone disease and others do not. In: Roth RA, Finlayson B, eds. Stones: clinical management of urolithiasis. Baltimore: Williams & Wilkins, 1983:3.
Chaussy CG. Extracorporal shockwave treatment for kidney stone. In: Kaufman JJ, ed. Current urologic therapy. 2nd ed., Philadelphia: Saunders, 1986:164.
Jenkens AD. Calculus formation. In: Gillenwater JY, Grayhack JT, Howards SS, Duckett JW, eds. Adult and pediatric urology. Chicago: Yearbook Medical, 1987:355.
Pak CYC. Should patients with single renal stone occurrence undergo diagnostic evaluation? J Urol 1982;127:855.

CHAPTER 18–36

Epispadias and Exstrophy

David P. O'Brien III, M.D.

DEFINITION

Exstrophy describes the finding in a newborn of an exposed bladder mucosa on the lower abdomen while the penis is epispadiac. Epispadias alone describes the finding in a newborn of proximal and dorsal displacement of the urethral meatus.

ETIOLOGY

The exstrophy–epispadias complex encompasses numerous abnormalities of the hindgut of the embryo. Experimental study in the chick embryo has shown that this complex is most likely related to the persistent cloacal membrane in early embryologic life.

CRITERIA FOR DIAGNOSIS
Suggestive

There are no significant suggestive data.

Definitive

Definitive diagnosis of exstrophy is made by the physical examination (see below).

CLINICAL MANIFESTATIONS
Subjective

There are no pertinent subjective data.

Objective
Physical Examination

Physical examination of the male infant reveals the exstrophic bladder lying everted on the lower abdominal wall. The penis is spadelike, with the urethra exposed to the tip. The pubic bones are separated. In the female, the bladder is similar. The abdominal muscles and pubic bones are separated, as is the clitoris. Epispadias may be balanitic, penile, or penopubic (subsymphyseal in the female), indicating the progress of the disease proximally.

Routine Laboratory Abnormalities

Laboratory data are nonrevealing, whereas radiologic examination confirms separation of the symphysis in exstrophy and the most severe (proximate) forms of epispadias.

PLANS
Diagnostic
Differential Diagnosis

The physical examination is diagnostic.

Diagnostic Options and Recommended Approach

The urinary tract should be investigated fully, including urinalysis, urine culture and sensitivities, and a baseline chemical survey. A voiding cystourethrogram, sonography, and excretory urogram are mandatory, not only for initial evaluation, but also as a baseline for future reference.

Therapeutic

Therapeutic approaches may be conservative or aggressive.

The milder forms of epispadias (balanitic) usually require no treatment, whereas the most severe forms of epispadias and exstrophy require complicated reconstructive surgery. In patients with exstrophy, functional results (i.e., satisfactory bladder function with continence) may be difficult to obtain by closing the bladder and abdominal defects while reconstructing the bladder neck. Good results may occur by using a variety of urinary diversion procedures. Ureterosigmoidostomy, a commonly used diversion in the past, is not in vogue presently because of the long-term occurrence of neoplastic changes in the sigmoid. Intestinal conduits or continent diversions are commonplace today. In the severe forms of epispadias (with incontinence), penile and bladder neck reconstructions are required.

FOLLOW-UP

Frequency of follow-up varies with the severity of the problem. Mild anomalies need no future follow-up, unless related problems arise (e.g., urinary infection, voiding symptoms). Anomalies requiring surgery should be examined at frequent intervals initially (weekly to monthly). Barring complications, urinalysis, urine culture and sensitivities, radiographic studies, and evaluations of renal function may be done at short intervals until stable.

DISCUSSION
Prevalence and Incidence

The exstrophy–epispadias complex encompasses numerous abnormalities of the hindgut of the embryo. Classic exstrophy is the most common, occurring in 1 in every 40,000 to 50,000 live births. Epispadias occurs in approximately 1 in every 100,000 live births.

Related Basic Science

These anomalies are variations of midline-longitudinal abdominal wall defects created by an abnormally large or persistent cloacal membrane, which leaves the surrounding developing structures separated to varying degrees. The degree of the deformity depends on the degree of abnormality of the membrane.

Natural History and Its Modification with Treatment

The progress of disease in the exstrophy–epispadias complex depends on the severity of the initial deformity. Children with exstrophy or significant epispadias may need multiple surgical procedures for correction of the anomaly. Urologic, general, orthopedic, plastic surgical, and gynecologic procedures may be necessary. Untreated, these severe anomalies may result in incontinence, infection, and renal failure in some instances. With successful treatment, normal function and continence should ensue.

Prevention

At present, there is no proven method for the prevention of epispadias and exstrophy. The probable causes of these anomalies have been delineated (see Discussion), but methods of prevention, as in most congenital anomalies, have not been determined.

Cost Containment

Often, prompt aggressive treatment with an emphasis on a permanent form of management rather than temporizing with more transient regimens may diminish cost. These diseases require long and arduous follow-ups, including multiple surgical procedures. Therefore, too frequent testing (e.g., x-rays and urine cultures) may escalate costs and should be kept to the minimum necessary for good patient care.

REFERENCES

Ambrose SS. Epispadias and vesicoureteral reflux. South Med J 1970;63:1193.

Ambrose SS, O'Brien DP. Surgical embryology of the exstrophy–epispadias complex. Surg Clin North Am 1974;54:1379.

Lepor H, Jeffs RD. Primary bladder closure and bladder neck reconstruction in classical bladder exstrophy. J Urol 1983;130:1142.

Lepor H, Shapiro E. Jeffs RD. Urethral reconstruction in boys with classic bladder exstrophy. J Urol 1984;131:512.

Marshall VD, Muecke EC. Variations in exstrophy of the bladder. J Urol 1962;88:766.

Muecke EC. The role of the cloacal membrane in exstrophy: The first successful experimental study. J Urol 1964;92:659.

CHAPTER 18–37

Hypospadias

Bruce H. Broecker, M.D., and Samuel S. Ambrose, M.D.

DEFINITION

Hypospadias is a developmental anomaly characterized by a urethral meatus located on the ventral penile shaft rather than at the tip of the glans.

ETIOLOGY

Hypospadias may be part of a variety of syndromes, but most cases occur as isolated anomalies. The etiology, although long suspected to be hormonal in origin, remains unexplained.

CRITERIA FOR DIAGNOSIS

Hypospadias is present when the urethral meatus is located on the ventral side of the phallus in a position proximal to its normal position at the tip of the glans penis.

CLINICAL MANIFESTATIONS
Subjective

The initial discovery is generally made on the neonatal examination. Few symptoms related to hypospadias are experienced during infancy. The patient or his parents may note the abnormal location of the urethral meatus. Older boys may complain of difficulty directing their urinary stream and observe a curvature of the penis during erection.

Objective
Physical Examination

The extent of the urethral defect and position of the urethral meatus are apparent on physical examination. The foreskin (dorsal hood) is always incompletely developed, being deficient on the ventral surface. Ventral curvature of the phallus (chordee) is often present. If the urethral meatus is located proximal to the base of the phallus, the scrotum will be bifid. The incidence of additional genitourinary anomalies, including persistent müllerian remnants, is increased in the more severe degrees of hypospadias.

Routine Laboratory Abnormalities

There are no routine laboratory abnormalities.

PLANS
Diagnostic
Differential Diagnosis

There is no differential diagnosis when the diagnostic criteria are met.

Diagnostic Options and Recommended Approach

Mild hypospadias is more common and not associated with an increased incidence of other genitourinary anomalies. Physical examination and history are sufficient for evaluation.

More severe hypospadias should have additional evaluation with a renal/bladder ultrasound. Any degree of hypospadias that is associated with an undescended or nonpalpable gonad should have a full evaluation for intersex, including karyotype and hormonal evaluation.

Therapeutic

The goal of treatment is to reconstruct a phallus that is straight when erect and that has a urethral meatus located at the tip of the glans. There are numerous procedures to achieve these goals. Reconstruction can generally be achieved in one procedure, but occasionally with more severe hypospadias, a multistaged procedure is employed.

Parents should be informed that development of the urethra is incomplete but that full normal function as a male can be achieved with successful surgical reconstruction. If an intersex condition is present the implications of this should be discussed promptly and delicately with the parents by a team of physicians, including a geneticist, pediatric endocrinologist, neonatologist, and pediatric urologist. The diagnosis and management plans should then be determined as expeditiously as possible.

FOLLOW-UP

The frequency of follow-up is determined by the severity of the hypospadias and the treatment required.

DISCUSSION
Prevalence

Hypospadias is one of the most common congenital anomalies, occurring in 1 in every 200 to 250 live male births.

Related Basic Science

Mild hypospadias predominates. The urethra develops during the latter part of the first trimester of pregnancy. During this time the urethral folds fuse along the urethral plate on the ventral surface of the phallus. Premature cessation of this process results in an abnormally located urethral meatus. It is unknown what causes hypospadias. The process is influenced and directed by androgens, but in most cases the hormonal profile of infants with hypospadias appears to be normal. It has been proposed that abnormalities in the timing of hormonal surges in utero may be responsible, but this remains unproven. The occurrence of familial clusters of hypospadias suggest a possible hereditary factor in some cases.

Natural History and Its Modification with Treatment

If left uncorrected, hypospadias will remain unchanged. Surgical correction is usually successful when performed by an expert specializing in the correction of this condition.

Prevention

There is no known method of prevention of hypospadias.

Cost Containment

Hypospadias surgery is technically demanding surgery. Complications and, therefore, costs are reduced if it is performed by a surgeon who performs this type of surgery on a regular basis.

REFERENCES

Duckett JD. Hypospadias. In: Walsh PC, Retik AB, Stamey TA, Vaugh ED, eds. Campbell's urology. 6th ed. Philadelphia: Saunders, 1992:1893–1920.
Kallan B, Winberg J. Epidemiologic study of hypospadias in Sweden. Acta Paediatr Scand 1982;(suppl. 293):3.

CHAPTER 18–38

Undescended Testes (Cryptorchidism)

Bruce H. Broecker, M.D., and Samuel S. Ambrose, M.D.

DEFINITION

The definition of undescended testis is implicit in the term.

ETIOLOGY

The cause of testicular descent and its corollary testicular maldescent has been extensively studied for more than two centuries but remains unclear. It may be syndromatic, but in most cases it is an isolated abnormality. Hormonal and mechanical theories have predominated but failed to achieve consensus.

CRITERIA FOR DIAGNOSIS

A testis that cannot be palpated within or manually displaced into the scrotal sac is considered an undescended testis.

CLINICAL MANIFESTATIONS
Subjective

Undescended testes are generally asymptomatic; however, they may be subject to trauma, torsion, tumor formation, or infection and consequently may cause symptoms of pain or tenderness.

Objective
Physical Examination

Careful examination is essential to distinguish between a truly undescended testis and a retractile testis. Examination should be carried out in the supine, standing, and squatting positions. Gentle but firm downward pressure in the groin starting above the internal inguinal ring helps coax the frequently retracted prepubertal testis into the scrotal sac. If the testis cannot be displaced into the scrotal sac or if this can be done only with considerable pressure, and on release of this pressure it immediately "pops" back to its original position, it must be considered undescended.

Undescended testes may be found in several locations and are categorized as such: Intraabdominal testes are not palpable unless they intermittently descend into the inguinal canal; canalicular testes are located in the inguinal canal between the internal and external inguinal rings; and ectopic testes are in a location outside the normal path of descent, most commonly the femoral, perineal, or suprapubic area.

Cryptorchidism is bilateral in approximately 10% of cases. If a testis cannot be palpated it may be intraabdominal or absent. Undescended testes may be associated with one of several rare syndromes or genetic abnormalities. These include prune-belly, Noonan's, Klinefelter's, and Prader–Willi syndromes. If cryptorchidism is associated with any degree of hypospadias, it must be evaluated for a possible intersex condition.

Routine Laboratory Abnormalities

There are no laboratory abnormalities.

PLANS

Diagnostic

The diagnosis of a malpositioned or "absent" testis is based on the physical findings. Further diagnostic work is guided by the results of the physical examination (see below).

Table 18–38–1 outlines the possible diagnoses and corresponding tests or observations.

Therapeutic

Retractile testes require no treatment. Ectopic and canalicular undescended testes generally can be surgically relocated to the scrotal sac without difficulty. Intraabdominal testes are often difficult to place in the scrotal sac due to insufficient length of the internal spermatic vessels, the primary blood supply to the testes. The internal spermatic artery originates from the aorta on the right side and the renal artery on the left side. When the testes are located in an abdominal location, the artery may not have sufficient length to allow placement in the scrotal sac. If this situation is encountered in a child with a contralateral scrotally located and palpably normal testis, removal of the intraabdominal testis is generally recommended (see Natural History and Its Modification with Treatment). If both testes are located intraabdominally an attempt to place them in the scrotal sac is recommended. Usually this requires high ligation and division of the internal spermatic artery and vein and mobilization of the testis on a wide strip of peritoneum covering the vas deferens and its vasal artery (Fowler–Stephens orchiopexy). Prior to actual division of the internal spermatic artery, adequacy of collateral circulation is tested by clamping the internal spermatic artery and, after waiting several minutes, incising the tunica albuginea of the testis to inspect for bleeding. Generally, bilateral intraabdominal orchiopexy is done as a staged procedure due to a 30% incidence of testicular atrophy after division of the internal spermatic artery. Ligation of the internal spermatic artery as an initial step without mobilization of the testis has also been advocated. This presumably allows optimal development of collaterals prior to further mobilization of the testis.

Hormonal stimulation may be used therapeutically as well as diagnostically. Its popularity has tended to be higher in Europe than in the United States, and reports of its success differ substantially among various authors. Hormonal stimulation may be with pituitary gonadotropin—human chorionic gonadotropin—or with hypothalamic releasing hormones—luteinizing hormone-releasing hormone. The latter is not available in the United States in the nasal spray preparation recommended for treatment of cryptorchidism. Use of hormonal therapy is most popular when both testes are nonpalpable. In this situation, it is both diagnostic (a rise in serum testosterone after human chorionic gonadotropin stimulation confirms the presence of at least one intraabdominal testis) and potentially therapeutic. Even when human chorionic gonadotropin stimulation fails to result in complete and permanent descent of the testis, it may improve the chances of a subsequent successful orchiopexy by improving collateral blood supply and length of the internal spermatic vessels.

The recommended age of treatment is 18 to 24 months (see Natural History and Its Modification with Treatment).

The physician needs to discuss the issues involved in cryptorchidism (see Natural History and Its Modification with Treatment) with the parents. The patient, as he reaches puberty, should be taught self-examination.

FOLLOW-UP

Follow-up of patients with successfully treated cryptorchidism should include yearly examination through puberty for evaluation of testicular growth and position. Self-examination should be practiced by the patient throughout life to provide early detection of the infrequent malignancy.

DISCUSSION

Prevalence

The prevalence of cryptorchidism is less than 5% in full-term male infants. This prevalence rises to 30% in preterm infants. In preterm infants, the incidence can be further related to birth weight, being about 70% in those weighing less than 1800 g and 100% in those weighing less than 900 g. Many testes that are incompletely descended at birth spontaneously descend into the scrotum during the first 6 to 12 months of life. Consequently, the prevalence in boys at 1 year of age is about 1% and thereafter remains constant with little additional spontaneous descent. Cryptorchidism is bilateral in approximately 10% of affected children.

Related Basic Science

Undescended testes may be abnormal in ways other than position alone. Attachments between the epididymis and rete testis may be abnormal. There is commonly a patent processus vaginalis, though a clinically apparent inguinal hernia is uncommon. The increased incidence of malignancy in the cryptorchid testis is generally attributed to an intrinsic abnormality of the germinal epithelium.

Natural History and Its Modification with Treatment

Many incompletely descended testes spontaneously descend during the first year of life. Spontaneous descent after 1 year of age is rare. Those testes that remain in an abnormal position eventually demonstrate evidence of atrophy and hyalinization of the germinal epithelium. The earliest evidence of this gradual degenerative process may be found by electron microscopy around 24 months of age, hence the recommended age for treatment. The process is complete if the testis remains undescended until puberty. Placement of the testis in its normal intrascrotal location at an early age interrupts this degenerative process and preserves the integrity of the germinal epithelium.

Testicular malignancy occurs more often in an undescended testis than in a normally descended testis. The incidence is increased approximately 50-fold, with the greatest increase occurring in the intraabdominal testis. The predisposition appears to be intrinsic rather than strictly positional, and orchiopexy at any age may not alter the increased risk. The tumors continue to occur in the 20- to 40-year-old age group, as do tumors of the descended testis. They are highly curable tumors.

Prevention

There is no proven method of prevention of cryptorchidism. Early placement of the testis in an intrascrotal position reduces the adverse effects on the germinal epithelium. The only certain method to eliminate the increased risk of malignancy in the cryptorchid testis is orchiectomy.

TABLE 18–38–1. UNDESCENDED TESTES: DIAGNOSES AND DIAGNOSTIC OPTIONS

Diagnosis	Diagnostic Options
Retractile testis	Testis can be maneuvered into a normal scrotal position
Palpable undescended testis (unilateral or bilateral)	Testis is palpable in the inguinal canal but cannot be maneuvered into the scrotal sac
Ectopic testis	Testis is palpable in a location outside the normal path of descent
Nonpalpable testis	
Unilateral	Computed tomography scan, sonogram, laparoscopy
Bilateral	Gonadotropin stimulation test, computed tomography scan, sonogram, laparoscopy
Undescended testis with associated hypospadias	Evaluation for intersex Karyotype Endocrine studies

Cost Containment

Elimination of unnecessary treatment of retractile testes controls unnecessary expenditure of resources.

REFERENCES

Gibbons MD, Cromie WJ, Duckett JW. Management of the abdominal undescended testicle. J Urol 1979;122:76.

Hadziselimovic F, ed. Cryptorchidism management and implications. Berlin: Springer-Verlag, 1983.

Kogan SJ. Cryptorchidism. In: Kelalis PP, King LR, Belman AB, eds. Clinical pediatric urology. 3rd ed. Philadelphia: Saunders, 1992:1050.

Rajfer J. Congenital anomalies of the testis. In: Walsh PC, Retik AB, Stamey TA, Vaugh ED, eds. Campbell's urology. 6th ed. Philadelphia: Saunders, 1992:1543.

Scorer GC, Farrington GA. Congenital deformities of the testis and epididymis. London: Butterworths, 1971.

CHAPTER 18–39

The More Common Internal Urinary Anomalies

Bruce H. Broecker, M.D., and Samuel S. Ambrose, M.D.

DEFINITION

This group of conditions is defined by the shared characteristics of congenital anomalous development of the internal urinary tract (kidney, ureter, bladder). Although some are common, others are distinctly uncommon.

ETIOLOGY

There is no shared etiology for this group of conditions, and for most, the causation is unknown with the exception of vesicoureteral reflux, for which there is evidence of inheritance (approximately a 40% incidence in the siblings of children found to have vesicoureteral reflux), and polycystic kidney disease, which has either an autosomal dominant (adult form) or autosomal recessive (infantile form) mode of inheritance. The remaining anomalies appear as isolated, idiopathic anomalies.

CRITERIA FOR DIAGNOSIS

The criteria for diagnosis depend on the specific anomaly (see Clinical Manifestations and Plans, Diagnostic). The diagnosis requires a clear definition of structure and function by imaging studies (ultrasonography, computed tomography, excretory urography, voiding cystourethrography, nuclear scintigraphy, and magnetic resonance imaging), endoscopy, and surgical exploration, as well as a thorough understanding of embryology.

CLINICAL MANIFESTATIONS

Subjective

Symptoms indicative of an internal urinary anomaly may include flank or abdominal pain, hematuria, or voiding dysfunction; however, many of the anomalies may produce no symptoms.

Objective

Physical Examination

A palpable abdominal mass or fever due to a urinary tract infection may be the objective findings of a urinary tract anomaly. As with symptoms, however, there may be no objective findings.

Routine Laboratory Abnormalities

Routine laboratory abnormalities do not contribute to the diagnosis.

PLANS

Diagnostic

Table 18–39–1 outlines the diagnoses and diagnostic options.

Therapeutic

Many of the anomalies are curiosities without detrimental effects and require no treatment. If the anomaly causes symptoms such as pain, predisposes to urinary tract infection, or leads to deterioration of renal function, surgical correction is indicated when possible.

FOLLOW-UP

Follow-up varies according to the anomaly and its appropriate treatment.

DISCUSSION

Prevalence

Though each anomaly individually is uncommon, together their incidence is second only to cardiovascular defects among congenital anomalies.

Related Basic Science

The origin of most of these anomalies is a result of arrested or aberrant embryogenesis. The cause in most cases is unknown.

Natural History and Its Modification with Treatment

The natural history and its modification with treatment vary according to the individual anomaly.

Prevention

There is no known method of prevention.

Cost Containment

Measures for cost containment vary according to the specific anomaly.

REFERENCES

Bauer SB, Perlmutter AD, Retik AB. Anomalies of the upper urinary tract. In: Walsh PC, Retik AB, Stamey TA, Vaugh Ed, eds. Campbell's urology. 6th ed. Philadelphia: Saunders, 1992:1357.

Kelalis PP. Anomalies of the urinary tract. In: Kelalis PP, King LR, Belman AB, eds. Clinical pediatric urology. Philadelphia: Saunders, 1985.

Maizels M. Normal development of the urinary tract. In: Walsh PC, Retik AB, Stamey TA, Vaugh ED, eds. Campbell's urology. 6th ed. Philadelphia: Saunders, 1992:1301.

TABLE 18–39–1. MORE COMMON INTERNAL URINARY ANOMALIES: DIAGNOSES AND DIAGNOSTIC OPTIONS

Diagnosis	Diagnostic Options
Bilateral agenesis of kidneys	Incompatible with postnatal survival
Unilateral absence of a kidney	Usually an incidental finding; produces no symptoms or morbidity itself but absence of one kidney may alter the natural history of disease in the contralateral kidney; diagnosis is confirmed or discovered by imaging studies
Hypoplasia of the kidney	Generally an incidental finding; usually produces no symptoms but may be associated with hypertension; the congenital hypoplastic kidney is often dysplastic, poorly functioning, which may alter the natural history of disease in the contralateral kidney; the diagnosis is established when imaging studies demonstrate a small kidney (see Chapter 18–34)
Multicystic kidney	Generally asymptomatic but is rarely associated with hypertension, neoplasia, or infection; may present as a palpable mass in the neonate if large but more commonly discovered by antenatal obstetric ultrasonography; renal ultrasound and renal scintigraphy accurately diagnose this condition; controversy regarding management (surgical vs observation) (see Chapter 18–40)
Polycystic kidney	Two forms: autosomal dominant (most commonly seen in adults) and autosomal recessive (most commonly seen in children); renal ultrasound generally diagnostic; renal nuclear scintigraphy assesses degree of renal impairment (see Chapter 16–25)
Simple cyst of the kidney	Rare in children; generally peripelvic in location; renal ultrasound and/or computed tomography accurately demonstrate this anomaly

Ectopia of the kidney
  Simple
  Crossed
	
	Imaging evidence of an ipsilateral pelvic location
	Imaging evidence of contralateral position

Horseshoe kidney	Imaging evidence of fusion of the two kidneys
Anomalies of rotation of the kidney	Imaging evidence of incomplete rotation of the kidney
Anomalies of renal vasculature	Imaging evidence of accessory or aberrant vessels, aneurysm, or arteriovenous fistula
Diverticulum of the calyx	(See Chapter 18–33)
Hydrocalyx	(See Chapter 18–33)
Bifid pelvis	Imaging evidence of partial or complete division of the pelvis forming two major collecting systems at or above the ureteropelvic junction
Ureteropelvic junction abnormality	May be detected antenatally by ultrasound screening; may present asymptomatically in the neonate; older child may have flank pain or infection; renal ultrasound can be used to demonstrate the altered anatomy; renal nuclear scintigraphy assesses function; voiding cystometrogram necessary to exclude vesicoureteral reflux (see Chapter 18–33)
Duplication of ureter	Imaging evidence of partial or complete division of the ureter
Megaureter	May be discovered by antenatal obstetric ultrasound screening; may present asymptomatically in the neonate or with flank pain or infection in the older child; renal ultrasound demonstrates anatomy; renal nuclear scintigraphy assesses function; voiding cystometrogram necessary to exclude vesicoureteral reflux (see Chapter 18–33)
Ureterocele	May be discovered on antenatal obstetric ultrasound screening; may present asymptomatically in the neonate or with flank pain or infection in the older child; renal ultrasound demonstrates anatomy; renal unclear scintigraphy assesses function; voiding cystometrogram necessary to exclude vesicoureteral reflux (see Chapter 18–33)
Vesicoureteral reflux	Most common structural anomaly associated with childhood urinary tract infections; diagnosis established by voiding cystometrogram
Ectopic ureteral orifice	Urinary tract infection common; diagnosis made by imaging or endoscopic evidence of an abnormal location of the ureteral orifice; may be part of a duplex collecting system and associated with poor function in the corresponding renal segment
Retrocaval ureter	Imaging evidence of the ureter in a position posterior to the vena cava
Retroiliac ureter	Imaging evidence of the ureter in a position posterior to the iliac artery
Bladder exstrophy	(See Chapter 18–36)
Urachal sinus	Evidence on physical examination of a sinus at the umbilicus communicating with the bladder
Urachal cyst	Imaging evidence of a cystic structure between the umbilicus and the dome of the bladder
Urachal diverticulum	Imaging evidence of a diverticulum at the dome of the bladder
Posterior urethral valves	Most common cause of bilateral hydronephrosis in a male infant; may be associated with mild or severe renal impairment and often leads to urinary tract infection; diagnosis made by voiding cystourethrogram demonstrating valvular obstruction of the posterior urethra, usually after renal ultrasound has shown bilateral hydronephrosis; renal nuclear scintigraphy assesses degree of renal impairment

CHAPTER 18–40

Abdominal Mass in a Child

Bruce H. Broecker, M.D., and Samuel S. Ambrose, M.D.

DEFINITION

The definition of an abdominal mass is implicit in the term.

ETIOLOGY

The etiology of the many diagnoses included among abdominal masses in children are varied and in many cases unknown. Some are congenital (hydronephrosis, multicystic kidney); others are acquired (tumors).

CRITERIA FOR DIAGNOSIS

An abdominal mass is diagnosed by palpable or imaging evidence of an abnormal structure or mass or enlargement of a normal structure within the abdomen.

CLINICAL MANIFESTATIONS
Subjective

An abdominal mass is frequently asymptomatic and discovered by the parents while giving the child a bath or by the physician while doing a routine physical examination. Symptoms that may be related to an abdominal mass include flank and abdominal pain, fever due to urinary infection, hematuria, weight loss, lethargy, and anorexia.

Objective

Physical Examination

An abdominal mass is generally palpable. Its size, consistency, contour, position, and sensitivity are all important features that may give clues to its origin and nature. Careful examination of the genitalia and a bimanual pelvic examination with one finger in the rectum are necessary to complete a thorough physical examination of the mass. The patient's vital signs including height, weight, blood pressure, and temperature are also important features of the initial evaluation of an abdominal mass.

Routine Laboratory Abnormalities

The microscopic examination of the urine may reveal signs of urinary tract infection. Also see Table 18–40–1.

PLANS

Diagnostic

Differential Diagnosis

There is no differential diagnosis if the diagnostic criteria are met. Further diagnostic studies are designed to determine the cause of the mass.

Diagnostic Options and Recommended Approach

After a patient with an abdominal mass has had a thorough history and physical examination, imaging and biochemical evaluation further refine the diagnostic evaluation. Ultrasonography has become the preferred initial imaging study because it easily distinguishes between cystic and solid masses, and often identifies the organ of origin. It is readily available, noninvasive, quickly done, and relatively inexpensive

and eliminates the risk of allergic reaction to contrast medium. Occasionally, the abdominal/pelvic ultrasound enables the physician to determine the etiology of a mass. More commonly, however, the need for additional functional and structural information necessitates further imaging studies. The precise studies needed are dictated by the differential diagnosis at this point but could include one or more of the following: voiding cystourethrogram, computed tomography, intravenous urogram, nuclear renal scan, and magnetic resonance imaging. Rarely an arteriogram or venogram provides important information not revealed by the previously mentioned studies (Table 18–40–1).

Biochemical studies that may be useful or important in the evaluation of an abdominal mass include a complete blood count, serum creatinine, blood urea nitrogen, serum electrolytes, lactic dehydrogenase, serum and urine catecholamines, α-fetoprotein, and human chorionic gonadotropin.

Finally, although a diagnosis can almost always be made with relative certainty preoperatively, surgical exploration occasionally plays an important role in diagnosis as well as therapy.

Therapeutic

Therapy is specific to the particular lesion. In most cases surgical treatment is an important component of management. Obstructive lesions of the urinary or female genital tract require appropriate procedures to relieve the obstruction. Tumors require removal unless they have grown beyond the boundaries of safe or effective surgical resection. Some tumors (rhabdomyosarcoma, Wilms'), if not initially resectable, may become so after treatment with chemotherapy and/or radiotherapy. Renal vein thrombosis is most appropriately managed by hydration. Anticoagulant therapy and surgical thrombectomy, advocated by some, appear to carry more risk than benefit for the patient. Therapy of multicystic kidney merits special mention. It remains uncertain whether nephrectomy or observation is the preferred treatment. Reports of malignancy and hypertension occurring in and due to a multicystic kidney have led some to conclude that all such lesions should be removed at the age of 3 to 6 months, whereas the infrequency of these reports relative to the

TABLE 18–40–1. ABDOMINAL MASS IN A CHILD: DIAGNOSES AND DIAGNOSTIC OPTIONS

Diagnosis	Diagnostic Options
Hydronephrosis	Ultrasonography accurately identifies hydronephrosis; voiding cystourethrogram necessary to rule out reflux; nuclear scan helps determine the functional significance of the abnormality (see Chapter 18–33)
Multicystic kidney	Ultrasonography reveals characteristic cluster of cysts; renal nuclear scan reveals no function in affected kidney (see Chapter 18–39)
Polycystic kidneys	Ultrasonography reveals bilateral renal cysts; CT scan may complement the sonographic findings; family history generally positive for this diagnosis (see Chapter 16–25)
Renal vein thrombosis	Ultrasonography reveals enlarged kidney without collecting system dilation; renal scan reveals diminished or absent blood flow and poor to absent function; hematuria and thrombocytopenia are characteristic findings (see Chapter 16–23)
Solid tumor	Most common solid abdominal tumor in a child is a Wilms tumor arising from the kidney; less common childhood tumors include neuroblastoma, renal cell carcinoma, lymphoma, rhabdomyosarcoma, and ovarian tumors; diagnosis is established by renal sonography, which can define solid or cystic nature of mass, organ of origin, and patency of vena cava; CT scan or MRI may further define extent of spread (staging) and involvement of adjacent organs
Renal cyst	Ultrasound accurately demonstrates simple renal cysts
Neuroblastoma	Intraabdominal neuroblastoma arises from adrenal gland or sympathetic chain; second in frequency to Wilms' tumor as diagnosis for a solid abdominal tumor during childhood; prognosis for this tumor, unlike Wilms' tumor, remains poor; ultrasonography reveals extrarenal solid mass; CT scan further defines relationship of mass to adjacent structures; biochemical evaluation (serum and urine catecholamines) is often diagnostic
Lymphoma	Ultrasonography, CT scan, biopsy confirmation (see Chapter 12–23)
Distended bladder	Disappears after catheterizing for large volume of urine; imaging studies (ultrasound, voiding cystourethrogram) reveal etiology
Rhabdomyosarcoma	Rhabdomyosarcoma may arise in locations throughout the body but when presenting as an abdominal mass it generally arises from bladder neck, prostate, vagina, or uterus; diagnosis established by ultrasonography, CT/MRI, and biopsy
Hydrometrocolpos (in females)	Physical examination reveals obstructed vagina; ultrasound reveals cystic mass between bladder and rectum
Ovarian tumor	Ultrasonography reveals solid or cystic mass arising from ovary; CT scan defines relationship to adjacent structure; biposy confirms benign or malignant nature
Duplication of gastrointestinal tract	Suspected by imaging studies; may require laparotomy to confirm
Hepatic	Ultrasonography and CT scan reveal origin of mass in the liver
Spleen	Ultrasonography and CT scan reveal splenic enlargement, usually associated with leukemia or lymphoma

CT, computed tomography; MRI, magnetic resonance imaging.

frequency of the lesion have led others to conclude that periodic observation with removal only if there is evidence of a complication is the most appropriate management.

FOLLOW-UP

Follow-up is determined by the nature of the lesion and its subsequent therapy.

DISCUSSION

Prevalence and Incidence

The discovery of an abdominal mass in a child is a rare event. The exact prevalence and incidence are not known.

Related Basic Science

The majority of abdominal masses detected in a neonate are renal in origin, most commonly hydronephrosis and multicystic kidney, whereas half of those detected later in childhood are hematologic or lymphomatous in origin. Obstructive lesions are of significance because of their impact on renal function, which may vary from mild to severe (renal failure). Although children generally exhibit an impressive capacity to recover function after relief of obstruction, no studies obtained prior to that event are able to accurately predict the extent of that recovery.

Tumors in children, in general, respond well to the treatment modalities of surgery, chemotherapy, and/or radiotherapy. Their prognosis is often quite favorable with an excellent chance for cure.

Renal vein thrombosis occurs most commonly in neonates due to the combined effects of polycythemia and dehydration. These two factors lead to a sluggish circulation and hypercoagulability in the intrarenal circulation. Thrombosis begins in the small intrarenal venules and propagates proximally to the main renal vein. Vena caval thrombosis, though rare, may also occur. As the process resolves, it may leave a small shrunken kidney, which may cause hypertension. Bilateral renal vein thrombosis occurs less frequently and is associated with higher morbidity and mortality.

Natural History and Its Modification with Treatment

The natural history and its modification with treatment vary according to the specific lesion.

Prevention

There is no proven method of prevention of an abdominal mass in a child.

Cost Containment

Appropriate cost containment measures vary with the specific lesion.

REFERENCES

Kaplan GW, Brock WA. Abdominal masses. In: Kelalis PP, King LR, Belman AB, eds. Clinical pediatric urology. 2nd ed. Philadelphia: Saunders, 1985.
Mekiow MM, Uson AC. Palpable abdominal masses in infants and children: A report based on a review of 653 cases. J Urol 1959;81:705.
Raffensperger J, Abousleiman A. Abdominal masses in children under one year of age. Surgery 1968;63:514.
Woodard JR, Gosalbez R. Neonatal and perinatal emergencies. In: Walsh PC, Retik AB, Stamey TA, Vaugh ED, eds. Campbell's urology. 6th ed. Philadelphia: Saunders, 1992:1590.

CHAPTER 18–41

Male Infertility as Viewed by a Urologist

Michael A. Witt, M.D.

DEFINITION

Infertility is defined as unprotected intercourse for 1 year without conception. Most couples present to their physician prior to 12 months of timed intercourse because of the anxiety they experience and recent data that support that the earlier they are treated the better their likelihood is for initiating pregnancy.

ETIOLOGY

Male infertility can be caused by a host of different factors any of which can compromise sperm production or function.

CRITERIA FOR DIAGNOSIS

Inability to initiate a pregnancy after 1 year of unprotected intercourse is the criterion for diagnosis.

Subjective

In 20% of couples, the male factor is the sole cause for infertility, and in an additional 30% the male factor contributes to the couple's infertility. As a result, 50% of couples have a male factor contributing to the couple's difficulty initiating a pregnancy.

Patients will typically present concerned that they are unable to initiate a pregnancy for the first time or for a subsequent time. It is important to conduct a thorough history in order to identify specific risk factors that can produce known infertility abnormalities in the male.

The couple should be queried as to how long they have been attempting to initiate a pregnancy and what type of ovulation detection has been used. Often times the woman will be unaware as to when she ovulates. She should be instructed about maneuvers and measures that can be instituted to facilitate appropriate timing of intercourse for the couple. Basal body temperature monitoring is somewhat unreliable, and today what is currently accepted as first-line ovulation detection is the LH surge kit monitoring. In this fashion, couples are then aware of when the woman is ovulating and can time their intercourse accordingly. If a couple has not been doing this for at least three months, then it is important that this be instituted and the couple be reevaluated.

It is also important to take a thorough sexual history to rule out the presence of any erectile or ejaculatory abnormalities. It is not uncommon, due to the stresses placed in a couple who are struggling with initiating a pregnancy, for the male to suffer from premature ejaculation or some degree of impotence. This may compound the existing problem and make it very difficult for the couple to be successful in initiating a pregnancy. It is important to determine what types of lubrications are used because many are spermatotoxic. These spermatotoxic lubricants consist of Vaseline, Keri Lotion, and saliva. Nonspermatotoxic lubricants are now available over the counter, and the couple should be encouraged to use these.

The childhood history is also important to rule out the presence of posterior urethral valves, cryptorchidism, or testicular malignancy. In addition, it is important to rule out a previous history of testicular trauma or torsion and abnormalities in sexual development.

It is important to ascertain whether the patient is taking any medications. Those that have been implicated in altering sperm function are sulfasalazine and nitrofurantoin. In addition, excessive tobacco and alcohol use has been known to impair sperm production. There are chemotherapeutic agents that are known to produce severe alterations in sperm cell production.

One should also query the patient about exposure to gonadotoxins such as anabolic steroids or environmental agents that are known to devastate the testicular germinal epithelium.

A thorough medical history is also indicated because disease processes such as diabetes, which can produce neuropathy resulting in retrograde ejaculation or impotence, and cystic fibrosis, which can result in agenesis of the vas deferens, can produce known male factor infertility.

It is important to determine whether over the last 3 to 6 months the patient has experienced any high fever or debilitating systemic illnesses. Sperm production can be altered by either of these processes, and it takes approximately 74 days before the ejaculate reflects a rebound to normal levels of sperm production.

Objective

Physical Examination

In general, the physical examination should focus on secondary sexual characteristics to determine the presence or absence of normal sexual development. The absence of such features would be consistent with hypogonadism due to Klinefelter's syndrome or Kallman's syndrome.

The major portion of the examination should focus on the genitalia. It is important to assess the position of the meatus to determine whether deposition of the ejaculate is adequate. The testicular volume should be measured. As 80 to 90% of the testicular volume is composed of seminiferous tubules, abnormalities in testicular volume may translate into alterations in sperm production. The normal adult testis measures average 4.6 cm in length and 2.6 cm in width.

The peritesticular structures should be examined as well. Abnormalities in the epididymides may suggest scarring from previous infection or obstruction. The presence of a varicocele may also indicate a potential etiology of alterations in sperm production. Both vasa should be palpable, as 2% of infertile men have congenital absence of the vas deferens or seminal vesicles.

Routine Laboratory Abnormalities

There are no diagnostic routine laboratory abnormalities.

PLANS

Diagnostic

Differential Diagnosis

There is no differential diagnosis. The complaint itself is diagnostic.

Diagnostic Options and Recommended Approach

The essential laboratory evaluation of the infertile man is a semen analysis. It is important to recognize that a semen analysis is a test not of fertility but rather of sperm production. Two to three semen analyses over a 2- to 3-week period are recommended for initial assessment. Once these are obtained, the average seminal quality can be assessed. This is important because internal variability is often found, and thus the decision should not be made on a solitary semen analysis. Specimens should be collected by masturbation into a wide-mouth container after 2 to 3 days of sexual abstinence. It is also appropriate to obtain specimens in a seminal collection device after the same period of abstinence. Once a specimen is obtained, it should be analyzed within 1 hour of collection and kept at body temperature.

The semen analysis results can then be categorized as either normal or abnormal. Abnormal semen analysis can be due to abnormalities of an isolated seminal parameter, abnormalities of multiple seminal parameters, or azoospermia. The current criteria accepted by most clinicians as adequate for the semen analysis are a volume between 1.5 and 5 mL, density greater than 20 million/mL, motility greater than 60%, and forward progression greater than 2 on a scale of 0 to 4. The total motile fraction is probably a better indicator of overall seminal quality, and this should be greater than 50 million. There should also be no evidence of hyperviscosity, agglutination, or the presence of round cells. Sperm morphology based on World Health Organization criteria should have greater than 50% of normal forms.

Additional testing may also be indicated to assess hypothalamic–pituitary–gonadal axis dysfunction. This would result in assessing a serum follicle-stimulating hormone level, which can indirectly assess the presence or absence of normal testicular function. A testosterone level may be indicated if the patient complains of loss of libido or if there is a suspected hypogonadotropic abnormality. If the testosterone level is low, then luteinizing hormone and prolactin levels should be obtained.

Additional studies on the semen analysis that also may be indicated based on the history and physical examination include the presence or absence of white blood cells in the semen. The clinician may suspect this based on the history or physical examination or the presence of an increased number of round cells on the semen analysis. The presence or absence of antisperm antibodies can also be assessed, and typically this is indicated on the basis of history, if there is a suspicion of testicular trauma or infection, or on the semen analysis, if agglutination is present or decreased motility due to no other identifiable factors is found.

After the history, physical examination, and semen analysis, patients can be categorized as either having normal bulk seminal parameters, abnormality in one seminal parameter, abnormality in multiple seminal parameters, or azoospermia. Normal bulk seminal parameters would imply the presence of unevaluated female factors or an abnormality in sperm function. In this setting, sperm function testing is indicated in the form of sperm penetration assay, acrosome reaction, or strict Krueger morphology. If these are abnormal, then further evaluation of the man is indicated and assisted reproductive techniques may be required. If these are normal, then further evaluation of the female factor is pursued.

Isolated sperm parameter abnormalities can be abnormalities in either volume, count, motility, forward progression, viscosity, or morphology. The most common aberration is that of motility, which occurs 26% of the time. The least common aberration is that of morphology, which occurs 1% of the time. Sperm motility and forward progression depend on many factors including normal spermatogenesis, transport of the spermatozoa, and normal interrelationship between seminal vesicle and prostatic secretions. A general decrease in sperm motility has been termed *asthenospermia*. Sperm agglutination has been characterized as a decrease in sperm movement due to clumping and immobilization of spermatozoa.

Asthenospermia occurs if motility is less than 60% and can be due to any of the multiple factors mentioned. The seminal vesicles and prostate must function normally. These structures are not usually measured after infection, inflammation, and the possibility of hypoandrogenic state are excluded. Epididymal function remains a possible cause of impaired sperm movement. If sperm agglutination or immobilization exists, then immunopathology must be suspected. Antisperm antibodies can exist in serum, cervical mucus, or seminal fluid, and these antibodies can be quantified. Fertility is less likely in men demonstrating significantly elevated antisperm antibody titers in the plasma or with significant amounts of sperm-bound antibodies. Some patients have an abnormality only in sperm count, with numbers being less than 20 million/mL. After endocrine abnormalities have been excluded, a concentrate ejaculate may be placed directly into the uterus. This may improve fertility in men with this condition. Additionally, assisted reproductive techniques will then be helpful in these patients. In cases of a total ejaculate volume of less than 1 mL, retrograde ejaculation should be excluded as described previously. A large ejaculate volume greater than 5 mL may dilute the sperm density to the point where an ineffective sperm–cervical mucus interface is established. Mechanical concentration may be performed in such a specimen. Isolated abnormalities of sperm morphology are extremely rare. When present, this condition is generally transient, theoretically reflecting a limited and finally gonadal insult; however, electron microscopy has disclosed abnormalities in some patients' sperm with significant yet costly undetermined motility deficit.

Hyperviscosity is an infrequently encountered isolated deficit. It certainly should not be treated until confirmed as abnormal in a postcolloidal test in the presence of adequate cervical mucus. In hyperviscosity, sperm washing followed by intrauterine insemination has been reported to be effective.

When the seminal fluid analysis reveals abnormalities in sperm density, motility, and morphology, a transient nonspecific stress such as heat or environmental toxins should be considered. These conditions are rare, however, and consequently are most likely to be etiologic factors in a varicocele, which frequently causes the same combination of seminal deficits. Scrotal varicoceles are most commonly found in the subfertile man. Approximately 15 to 20% of men can be found to have scrotal varices; this proportion approaches 40 to 50% in subfertile men. Not all varicoceles require surgical correction; however, if there is scrotal discomfort secondary to the lesion, if the testis is felt through the scrotal varix and is found to be atrophic, and there is reasonable suspicion that it may be related to the varicocele, correction should be seriously considered. If the patient is azoospermic, which implies that there are no sperm, the ejaculate should be concentrated by centrifugation for 10 minutes at 1500 to 2000 RPM. The phallus should be inspected. It is not unusual to find sperm in a patient initially reported to be sterile. In this instance, total ductal occlusion has been painlessly disproved. In addition, absence of the vas should be ruled out.

The second step should be to obtain a serum follicle-stimulating hormone level. In all cases, azoospermia with an ejaculate volume less than 1 mL and a postejaculate urine specimen should be obtained to rule out the possibility of retrograde ejaculation. If the urine contains significant sperm, urinary alkalinization is achieved, and then an attempt is made to initiate antegrade ejaculations with medications. If this is not achieved, a voided catheter of the urine specimen should be centrifuged and artificial insemination should be performed with concentrated sperm. If the postejaculate urine does not contain spermatozoa, the seminal vesicles and the ejaculatory ducts should be examined by transrectal ultrasound. If ejaculatory duct obstruction is identified and normal spermatogenesis is found on testis biopsy, then a transurethral resection of the ejaculatory ducts should be performed.

A testicular biopsy should be performed in the azoospermic patient with a low-ejaculate volume but with no ejaculate duct obstruction identified by transrectal ultrasound. If no germinal elements are present, adoption and artificial insemination using donor sperm should be considered. Those patients with normal testes should undergo vasography. If both the testicular biopsy and vasogram findings are normal but diminution is absent, treatment with vibratory electroejaculation should be attempted. If vasography reveals ductal obstruction and the presence of normal testicular histology, a transurethral resection of the ejaculatory duct with microsurgical reconstruction of vasal or epididymal obstruction is indicated.

A serum follicle-stimulating hormone (FSH) level should be obtained in all azoospermic patients before any invasive studies. If the FSH level is greater than 2, no further evaluation should be performed with guarded prognosis. If the FSH is less than normal, then serum luteinizing hormone (LH) serum prolactin levels should be determined. When FSH and LH are both decreased or LH is inappropriately low with a normal testosterone level, the diagnosis of hypogonadotropic hypogonadism has to be considered and may be associated with deficiencies in other pituitary hormones, or as an isolated impairment of gonadotropin-releasing hormone secretion. Decreased levels of gonadotropins may also be secondary to a pituitary tumor with or without an increase in serum prolactin. If the prolactin level is elevated or if there is clinical evidence of a pituitary tumor, further evaluation of the pituitary gland is indicated. This should include evaluation of serum levels of adrenocorticotropic hormone and thyroid-stimulating hormone and computed tomography or nuclear magnetic resonance imaging. If there is no evidence of obstruction, further evaluation of the vas deferens can be completed with open scrotal exploration and vasography.

FOLLOW-UP

With respect to the treatment of infertility, patients are counseled to carry out certain general measures. Intercourse should be timed with ovulation. A frequency of every other day is appropriate during the time of ovulation.

The follow-up schedule is dictated by the physician and varies greatly with the etiology of infertility and treatment provided. It should, however, be remembered that spermatozoa are generated every 70 days. Any medical or surgical intervention, therefore, should be reassessed by obtaining a semen analysis in 3 to 6 months. Pregnancy is the ultimate outcome of intervention in the infertile male.

DISCUSSION
Related Basic Science

See comments in Diagnostic Options and Recommended Approach.

Natural History and Its Modification with Treatment

The natural history of male infertility depends on the exact etiology of the fertility problem. Most conditions are treatable and result in pregnancy rates of 50 to 60%.

Prevention

Although some causes of infertility are preventable, such as marijuana use and the use of anabolic steroids, the damage to the dermal epithelium by diseases and infections is variable and unpredictable.

Cost Containment

Other than a history and physical examination, the diagnosis of infertility in the male depends on analysis of the semen. Other diagnostic serum studies and imaging studies may be used to confirm or refute a suspected diagnosis. Cost containment is highly dependent on the specific cause of male infertility.

REFERENCES

Amelar RD, Dubin L, Walsh PC. Male infertility. Philadelphia: Saunders, 1977.
Vance ML, Thorner MO. Medical treatment of male infertility. Semin Urol 1984;2:115.

CHAPTER 18–42

Urinary Tract Infections as Viewed by a Urologist

Bruce H. Broecker, M.D.

DEFINITION

A urinary tract infection is colonization and organism growth in the urine. The organism is most commonly bacterial, but may also be fungal or viral. Discussion in this chapter is limited to bacterial infections. Urinary tract infections may be confined to the bladder alone (cystitis) or may also involve the kidney (pyelonephritis).

ETIOLOGY

The cause of many urinary tract infections remains obscure.

Structural abnormalities of the urinary tract when present increase the risk of acquiring an infection and increase the severity of that infection. Structural abnormalities include congenital obstruction, vesicoureteral reflux, and prostatic hypertrophy.

In the structurally normal urinary tract, chronic constipation, bowel colonization with virulent enteric bacteria, and intrinsic deficiencies in host defense mechanisms such as altered bacterial adherence are thought to play a role in the etiology of recurrent urinary tract infection.

Throughout most of life, women acquire urinary tract infections at a substantially greater rate than men (about 10 to 1). This is felt to be due to the urethra being considerably shorter in women than in men. Male neonates, however, are more susceptible to urinary tract infections than female neonates due to bacterial colonization underneath the prepuce. Elderly men acquire urinary tract infections almost as often as elderly women, largely as a result of prostatism with incomplete bladder emptying.

CRITERIA FOR DIAGNOSIS

Suggestive

A presumptive diagnosis of urinary tract infection is often made in patients with symptoms of urinary tract infection or by a urinalysis that shows bacteriuria and pyuria.

Definitive

The criteria for diagnosis of a bacterial urinary tract infection (UTI) is the growth of bacteria when a freshly collected specimen of urine is plated in standard culture medium. When there is growth of bacteria it is important, however, to distinguish between a true urinary tract infection and contamination of the specimen during collection. This distinction is generally made on the basis of the type of bacteria, the quantity of bacteria, and the method of collection. The growth of any type and any amount of bacteria in a specimen obtained by sterile catheterization or suprapubic aspiration should be considered significant. In a clean, midstream specimen, growth of fewer than 100,000 colonies/mL and/or organisms such as *Staphyloccus epidermidis* and *Lactobacillus* have been shown frequently to represent contamination when compared with the results of a sterilely aspirated specimen in the same patient.

CLINICAL MANIFESTATIONS

Subjective

Urinary tract infections may be asymptomatic or symptomatic. As many as 30% of patients with a culture-proven UTI have no symptoms of infection. This is more apt to occur with a recurrent rather than the initial infection. Those symptoms indicative of a bladder infection (cystitis) include frequency and urgency of urination, incontinence, burning during urinations (dysuria), suprapubic discomfort, and low back pain. Symptoms indicating renal infection (pyelonephritis) include fever and flank pain.

Objective

Physical Examination

There are no diagnostic physical findings that indicate a urinary tract infection.

Routine Laboratory Abnormalities

Inspection of the urine of a patient with a UTI may reveal it to be cloudy and malodorous, though this is not always the case. Microscopic inspection as noted may show hematuria, pyuria, and bacteriuria. Gross hematuria may occur (hemorrhagic cystitis), and pyelonephritis is generally accompanied by fever and flank tenderness.

PLANS

Diagnostic

The diagnosis of UTI is made by urinalysis and urine culture. Diagnostic radiography should be performed in some patients, as a UTI may be the presenting sign of an acquired or congenital structural abnormality. Radiographic studies that detect renal calculi (kidney, ureter, and bladder film), obstruction (renal ultrasound, intravenous pyelogram), and reflux (voiding cystourethrogram) are indicated in patients whose age, symptoms, or concurrent medical conditions would indicate an increased likelihood of one of these conditions. The young woman with a single episode of simple uncomplicated cystitis should not need diagnostic studies beyond a history, physical examination, and urine culture (Table 18–42–1).

TABLE 18–42–1. URINARY TRACT INFECTION: DIAGNOSES AND DIAGNOSTIC OPTIONS

Diagnosis	Diagnostic Options
Simple cystitis	
Adult	Urinalysis, urine culture
Child	Urinalysis, urine culture, renal/bladder ultrasound, ± VCUG
Complicated cystitis (i.e., recurrent, unresponsive)	Urine culture, renal ultrasound, ± VCUG
Pyelonephritis	Urine culture, renal/bladder ultrasound (early), VCUG (delayed)

VCUG, voiding cystourethrogram.

Therapeutic

Therapy of UTIs involves the use of appropriate antibiotics and, when present, the elimination of obstruction and/or foreign bodies such as urinary calculi. The choice of appropriate antibiotics may, in cases of simple cystitis, be an empiric one guided by the knowledge that in most cases of uncomplicated UTI, a wide range of antibiotics are highly effective. The physician treating a patient with a UTI enjoys the singular advantage that many antibiotics are concentrated and eliminated by the kidney in an active form, thus producing urinary antibiotic levels that may be considerably higher than the corresponding serum levels. When a more complicated infection is present (i.e., pyelonephritis, recurrent UTI, hospital-acquired UTI, or UTI acquired while on antibiotics), the choice of antibiotics should be guided by a urine culture and sensitivity. The duration of therapy should be guided by the severity of the infection. Courses as short as a single dose and as long as 14 days have been advocated. Most authorities, however, recommend treating a patient with an uncomplicated cystitis for 5 to 7 days and complicated infections for 10 to 14 days. The advantages of shorter courses of antibiotics include decreased cost and increased patient compliance; the disadvantage is primarily an increased relapse rate.

It is often desirable to document the eradication of the infection. With uncomplicated cases, this information may be provided by the resolution of symptoms and absence of pyuria and bacteriuria in the urine. With complicated cases, this documentation should include the absence of bacterial growth in a urine culture.

There are several situations in which the prophylactic use of antibiotics is advisable. Children with vesicoureteral reflux are often treated with prophylactic antibiotics if there are no immediate surgical indications. The rationale for this is the prevention of UTI until the child has had an opportunity to "outgrow" the vesicoureteral reflux. Children and adults who experience frequent recurrent UTIs may benefit from a brief (1–3 months) course of prophylactic antibiotics. In these patients, even this brief interval free of infection appears to allow restoration of normal bladder defense mechanisms and decrease the likelihood of subsequent recurrences.

Prompt diagnosis and treatment of UTI reduces the morbidity and possible renal damage. Patients/parents and primary care physicians should be aware of this and seek medical attention and obtain diagnostic tests, respectively, whenever there is any suspicion of the presence of a UTI. As the likelihood of structural abnormalities is highest in children presenting with UTI, all of these patients should have radiographic evaluation regardless of the severity of the infection.

FOLLOW-UP

Recurrence of UTI is common. A recurrence commonly occurs very quickly after resolution of a previous infection. Follow-up to ensure resolution and detect recurrence is extremely important (see Prevention).

DISCUSSION

Prevalence

Urinary tract infections are second in frequency only to upper respiratory infections. Urinary tract infections occur more frequently in women by a ratio of almost 10:1, except during the neonatal period when they are more prevalent among males.

Related Basic Science

The vast majority of UTIs are ascending infections, the source of which is the endemic enteric organisms of the lower intestinal tract. Specific causes of UTI may be found in some patients. Among these causes are foreign bodies, such as urinary calculi or indwelling urinary catheters, and obstruction in the urinary tract, such as prostatic hypertrophy or urethral stricture. Many patients, however, have no identifiable redisposing structural cause for their infection and the reason they became infected is unclear. Recurrence of infection is a common feature of UTIs. Recurrences are most apt to occur shortly after the preceding infection and are presumably due to alterations in the normal bladder defense mechanisms by the preceding infection. The most common causative agents are Escherichia coli, Enterococci, Pseudomonas aeruginosa, Klebsiella, and Proteus species.

Natural History and Its Modification with Treatment

There are many unanswered questions concerning the natural history of urinary UTIs: What is the incidence of renal scarring? What is the incidence of hypertension? What is the prevalence of subsequent symptomatic and asymptomatic bacteriuria? A number of long-term longitudinal studies have tried and are trying to answer these questions accurately. If there are structural abnormalities associated with the infection, the morbidity of the infection is generally increased and the outcome may depend as much on the presence and severity of the structural abnormality as on the presence of the infection. In those patients in whom there is no structural abnormality, the natural history is that there will often be recurring infections, but it appears they rarely cause significant renal damage.

Prevention

There is no certain way to prevent an initial UTI unless a structural abnormality has been identified prior to the infection and can be elimi-

nated. Recurrent UTIs may be prevented or minimized by the use of prophylactic antibiotics. The most useful antibiotics appear to be nitrofurantoin, trimethoprim, and sulfamethoxazole–trimethroprim combination.

The dosage employed is generally about one quarter of the therapeutic dose given on a once per day schedule. On a cost-effective basis, prophylactic antibiotics are indicated if patients have three or four UTIs in a 6- to 12-month period. Prophylaxis is generally employed for 3 to 6 months and then discontinued.

Cost Containment

Prompt recognition and treatment of UTI minimize morbidity and ultimately decrease costs. Shorter courses of therapy have been studied as a means to, among other advantages, decrease costs. Some as short as one dose or one day are advocated for lower tract infections. Although a shorter course of antibiotics may save money in the short term, it is not clear whether a resulting higher recurrence rate does not abrogate the initial savings. Until further studies are available most authorities recommend therapeutic courses of 5 to 7 days for lower UTIs and courses of 10 to 14 days for upper UTIs.

REFERENCES

Belman AB, Kramer S. Genitourinary infections. In: Kelalis PP, King LR, Belman AB, eds. Clinical pediatric urology. 2nd ed. Philadelphia: Saunders, 1985:235.

Gillenwater JY. The role of the urologist in urinary tract infections. Med Clin North Am 1991:75:287.

Herzog LW. Urinary tract infections and circumcision: A case–control study. Am J Dis Child 1989:143:348.

Infections and inflammations of the genitourinary tract, Section III. In: Walsh PC, Retik AB, Stamey TA, Vaugh ED, eds. Campbell's urology. 6th ed. Philadelphia: Saunders, 1992:729.

Kunin C, ed. Detection, prevention and management of urinary tract infections. 4th ed. Philadelphia: Lee & Febiger, 1987.

Smellie JM. Reflections on 30 years of treating children with urinary tract infections. J Urol 1991:146(pt 2):665.

CHAPTER 18–43

Urethritis (See Section 8, Chapter 24)

CHAPTER 18–44

Renal Transplantation

David P. O'Brien III, M.D., and John D. Whelchel, M.D.

DEFINITION

Renal transplantation is the procedure in which a donor kidney is surgically placed into an appropriate candidate.

ETIOLOGY

Renal transplantation is offered to carefully selected patients who have end-stage renal disease.

CRITERIA FOR DIAGNOSIS

Renal transplantation is one form of replacement therapy used in patients with irreversible renal failure (see Chapter 16–13). Dialysis (an alternative therapy for end-stage renal failure) has dramatically improved and prolonged the lives of those suffering from renal failure; however, most patients and physicians agree that a successful transplant offers a quality of life superior to that of dialysis. In selected

groups of patients, young adults, children, and diabetics, it is the preferred method of treatment. At all ages, patient rehabilitation is superior following successful renal transplantation. Because of the critical shortage of donor kidneys, however, the majority of patients choosing transplantation initially receive either hemodialysis or peritoneal dialysis treatments until a kidney becomes available. All patients with end-stage renal disease should be evaluated for renal transplantation (a Medicare requirement), although in most centers only approximately 35% of patients on dialysis are found to be medically suitable for renal transplantation.

CLINICAL MANIFESTATIONS
Subjective

Patients needing renal transplantation have the same complaints as those who present in renal failure (see Chapter 16–13), but there are also a group of patients who have been on dialysis for some time owing to the critical shortage of donor kidneys. In fact, the majority of patients choosing transplantation initially receive either hemodialysis or peritoneal dialysis treatments until a kidney becomes available.

Objective

The availability of an alternate therapy, dialysis, reduces the urgency of renal transplantation compared with patients in need of cardiac and liver transplantation, making comprehensive evaluations desirable to categorize patients into groups who may fare better with renal transplantation or may fare better with dialysis. The type of donor available (living or cadaver) also contributes to the recommended choice of therapy at many transplant centers. Patients with an available living renal donor must wait for the donor assessment (an inpatient process at our institution). The improved graft survival of living, related-donor renal transplants as compared with that of cadaver donor transplants has encouraged most centers to consider living related transplants whenever possible, while the limited availability of cadaver donor organs and the reported success with immune modifying techniques, specifically donor-specific blood transfusions, may also result in increased use of the live donor. As these donors are making a substantial sacrifice to help another person, they deserve the utmost consideration and care to support them through this experience. The potential risk to the living donor must be carefully determined prior to proceeding with donor nephrectomy, and great care must be taken in the selection as well as the operative and postoperative care of these living donors. It would be ideal, however, as immunosuppressive techniques are refined in the future to use only cadaver kidneys rather than exposing a healthy person to the risks (albeit minimal) of this major surgery.

At present, the most common etiologic factors requiring renal replacement therapy at our institution are glomerulonephritis (40%), diabetes mellitus (27%), and hypertension (25%), with the remainder being related to polycystic disease, immune disease, congenital disorder, and so on. It is also of interest to note that one group of patients awaiting transplantation whose numbers are growing rapidly are those with failed grafts who need second or third grafts: in the future, this group may account for the major percentage of pretransplant candidates.

PLANS

Diagnostic

Patients with the diagnosis of end-stage renal disease, or those who appear to be nearing end-stage, are evaluated extensively. In our center we have found that this is most expertly and expeditiously done on an inpatient basis. The patient is admitted for approximately 48 hours, during which the following studies are obtained:

- Routine vital signs
- Daily weights
- Renal failure diet with diabetic restrictions when necessary
- Laboratory studies: complete blood count with differential; SMA-18; HBsAG and HBsAb (anti-HBS), HIV, amylase, cytomegalovirus, Epstein–Barr virus, herpes simplex virus, and varicella–zoster virus titers; urine for urinalysis and culture and sensitivity; 24-hour urine for creatinine clearance if the patient is not already on dialysis; fasting lipid profile; and HLA tissue typing
- Electrocardiogram
- Radiologic studies: posteroanterior and lateral chest x-rays, hand x-rays (for renal osteodystrophy), panorex films for the oral surgeon, and renal ultrasonography.
- Consultations: dental, gynecology, psychiatry, social services, transplant nephrology, urology (Other specialists are consulted when deemed appropriate, e.g., cardiac, neurology, endocrine.)

Some people thought to have renal failure on the basis of one disease may have the diagnosis changed during the pretransplant evaluation if studies so indicate. It may also be necessary in some cases to review the original renal biopsies or perhaps perform the initial biopsy in some patients whose disease has not been well documented. This is of particu-

lar importance in patients thought to have diseases known to recur in the transplanted kidney.

As previously mentioned, the availability of dialysis reduces the urgency of renal transplantation. Thus, the above thorough evaluation becomes desirable to categorize patients into groups that may fare better with renal transplantation or those that may fare better with dialysis. Following these evaluations, recipients can be placed into one of three categories: (1) generally acceptable candidates, (2) less acceptable candidates, and (3) those in whom transplantation is usually not advisable. Generally acceptable candidates must have been diagnosed as having end-stage renal disease, should be in reasonably good health, be mentally competent, be compliant with their medical care, and desire a renal transplant. Candidates in this category of patients are usually between the ages of 5 and 60. Patients older than 60, however, may sometimes be excellent candidates, and renal transplantation is considered by most experienced pediatric transplant centers to be the ultimate therapeutic objective in children under the age of 5. Their small size does present different technical considerations from those encountered in older children and adults.

Evaluation of bladder function is vital prior to transplantation. Frequently this can be accomplished with only a thorough history. Further evaluation, including cystograms, urodynamics, and cystoscopy may be indicated in some patients. Reconstruction of the bladder, correction of urethral strictures, and bladder augmentation procedures may be necessary prior to transplantation. Routine sonography of the native kidneys has provided important information on many of our patients. Not only has the experience of others who have noted the development of acquired cystic disease in patients with renal failure been evident, but also management of several patients who have been found to have neoplasms of the native kidneys has been influenced dramatically, particularly if the neoplasms are found to be malignant. These patients are not candidates for transplantation and immunosuppression unless they have favorable histology and are disease free for an adequate period (years in most centers). Dental corrective procedures, usually for the neglected mouth, are necessary to remove sources of chronic infection that may have a devastating affect on the immunosuppressed patient, and whole-mouth extractions are not a significant price to pay for the patient if infection in the posttransplant period is to be avoided.

A thorough cardiac evaluation, especially in diabetics and individuals over the age of 40, should be performed on all potential recipients. This may include thallium stress studies and cardiac catheterization. The presence of significant cardiac disease may require surgical or medical intervention to prepare the patient for renal transplantation. One great advance in diminishing postoperative mortality in the renal patient has been the general acceptance that candidates with correctable cardiac disease undergo definitive therapy (e.g., coronary bypass or angioplasty) prior to transplantation. Candidates with metabolic disorders such as diabetes (27% of transplant patients at our institution), Alport's syndrome, cystinosis, gout, amyloidosis, and oxalosis may also be included in this category. Patients with inactive systemic lupus erythematosus are generally considered to be acceptable candidates. Patients with end-stage renal disease resulting from focal sclerosing glomerulonephritis, immunoglobulin A nephropathy, dense deposit disease, anti-glomerular basement membrane disorders, and oxalosis, among others, are at risk for the development of these diseases in the transplanted kidney. This should not, however, exclude the patient from consideration as an acceptable renal transplant candidate. Diabetic nephropathy also recurs in patients receiving renal transplants, but based on observations of diabetic transplant recipients, it apparently requires many years to lead to renal failure. Although there are reports of recurrence of systemic lupus renal lesions in the renal transplant, such cases are rare.

Less acceptable candidates (see list below) are candidates with the diagnosis of renal failure who might be advanced to the generally acceptable category with appropriate medical or surgical management:

- Serious medical problems that may be reversible, such as tuberculosis, liver dysfunction, and active systemic lupus erythematosus
- Organic neurologic disorders, psychiatric disorders, and drug addiction
- Severe peripheral vascular disease

- Current or prior malignancy (metastatic disease excluded)
- Moderately severe or severe cardiac disease, ischemic myocardial disease, congestive heart failure, valvular disease, and myopathies
- Chronic inflammatory or infectious disease such as Crohn's disease, eczema, hidradenitis, and infected dialysis access, among others
- Obesity or malnutrition to the extent that surgical risk is affected
- Chronic respiratory disease
- Uncorrected lower urinary tract abormalities

Conditions in which transplantation is usually not advisable are included in the following list:

- Active or chronic infections that cannot be eradicated
- Coagulation disorders such as hemophilia
- Extensive vascular disease or aortoiliac graft reconstruction
- Advanced age or general debilitation
- Severe mental disability
- Severe nonreversible respiratory disease
- Severe nonreversible cardiac disease
- Severe active vasculitis such as polyarteritis nodosa
- Metastatic carcinoma

The latter criteria are not all-inclusive and there are many other situations in which renal transplantation may not be advisable. Likewise, renal transplantation may be undertaken in patients in this category at a few specialized centers.

Therapeutic

Preparation prior to transplantation to include nephrectomy and splenectomy were once routinely carried out by many centers. Presently these procedures are more selectively applied. Severe hypertension, poor responses to drug therapy, persistent urinary tract infections, ureteric reflux with a history of infections, and polycystic kidney disease with infections, severe pain, or marked hematuria are frequent reasons for elective pretransplant nephrectomy. Nephrectomy for hypertension prior to tranplantation must be carefully weighed against the problems the patient will encounter if the transplant is lost (such as increased anemia and the greater need for transfusion). The use and efficacy of genetically engineered and produced erythropoietin have loosened some of our inhibitions regarding nephrectomy in the dialysis patient. The use of splenectomy, previously performed for a possible improvement in immunosuppressive drug tolerance, is now rarely recommended.

Of similar importance is the presence of significant vascular disease of the lower extremities or carotid arteries. Noninvasive vascular studies and arteriograms may be required to determine the extent of disease and need for surgical correction prior to transplantation. The presence of vascular disease does not automatically exclude an individual as a renal transplant candidate, especially if the condition can be corrected. Other disorders requiring consideration for preliminary surgical procedures include hyperparathyroidism, peptic ulcer disease, diverticulitis, and peripheral vascular disease.

Once the patient is identified as a potential transplant recipient he or she is placed on the cadaver donor waiting list and receives a kidney as an emergency procedure, or if a living donor is available, the transplant is scheduled and done as an elective procedure. Postoperatively, the patient is placed on an immunosuppressive regimen of steroids (usually prednisone), azathioprine (Imuran), and cyclosporine (Sandimmune). The exact dosages and combinations of medicines vary from center to center. Many centers use either a polyclonal antibody preparation (e.g., an antilymphocyte globulin) or a monoclonal antibody preparation such as OKT3 (Orthoclone) as an induction therapy prior to starting cyclosporine, which has some nephrotoxic properties especially in the kidney with acute tubular necrosis (however mild).

FOLLOW-UP

An important aspect of the recipient's evaluation and preparation is the provision of information about the risks and requirements of renal transplantation. An education program should be developed by the transplant center to include written and video materials in association with instruction interviews. Social service evaluation may have identified problems in the educational realm that need to be addressed. This education program should be initiated during the patient's medical evaluation and continued throughout the hospitalization for the transplantation itself and into the postoperative follow-up.

DISCUSSION

Prevalence and Incidence

More than 8 million Americans have renal disease. Each year thousands of these individuals develop renal failure and must consider either dialysis or transplantation to preserve their lives. In 1984 the lives of more than 65,000 Americans were being maintained by dialysis, and it was estimated that this population would increase to more than 90,000 by 1994. The figure is undoubtedly higher than that now. Not all dialysis patients are kidney transplant candidates; however, approximately 35% of new or continuing dialysis patients are medically suitable kidney transplant candidates. Thus, in 1984 more than 22,000 patients could have been considered as transplant candidates. In 1992, that number was more than 32,000.

Related Basic Science

Transplant kidneys are procured form either living or cadaver donors. The majority of transplant centers in the United States that perform more than 100 transplants yearly find that approximately 25 to 30% of their patients receive living donor kidneys and 70 to 75% receive cadaveric grafts. A few centers do not perform living related transplants. Thus, an active transplant center must be associated with or develop a productive cadaver procurement program.

Living related donor renal transplants have historically been 15 to 45% more successful than cadaveric transplants. In part, this increased success has been attributed to genetic similarity between the donor and recipient. The 1-year graft survival of renal transplants performed between related donor–recipient pairs that have genetically identical transplant antigens is almost 95%. The success of less well matched living related donor–recipient pairs has been 85 to 90% at 1-year follow-up. Both exceed the expected 1-year graft survival of 85% in cadaveric transplants; however, recent success with immune modifying techniques and the immunosuppressive drug cyclosporine has markedly improved the expected graft survival for the less well matched living donor and cadaveric transplants.

Types of Rejection

Hyperacute rejection is a process that occurs either immediately after the restoration of blood supply or within 24 hours of transplantation. Its occurrence indicates the presence in the recipient's blood of preformed circulating antibodies to the donor's tissue antigens. Destruction of the renal graft is virtually certain from intravascular thrombosis. Only infrequently (<5%) will the presence of these preformed recipient antibodies not be determined by a final recipient serum–donor lymphocyte crossmatch performed immediately prior to the planned transplant. Present immunosuppressive regimes have universally proven ineffective in inhibiting this type of rejection.

Acute rejection is a process usually occurring from 5 to 90 days following the transplant. Although uncommon with continuation of adequate immunosuppression, it may occur from months to years after transplantation, especially following viral infections. Clinically it is associated with acute inflammation of the transplant characterized by swelling and tenderness of the kidney, fever, and an abrupt deterioration of renal function.

Immunologically, the process may be primarily cellular, primarily humoral, or a mixture of both. Histologically, a heavy interstitial infiltration of mononuclear cells and "immunoblasts" with no significant vascular endothelial lesion is characteristic of a primary cellular mechanism. The presence of vascular inflammation with endothelial damage and minimal or no interstitial infiltration is characteristic of a primary humoral mechanism. The histologic picture may indicate both processes occurring, with neither considered as the major component of the rejection process.

With an increase in corticosteroids and/or the administration of biological immunosuppressive agents such as monoclonal antibodies, a favorable response is common in the treatment of acute rejection, especially with a primarily cell-mediated rejection.

Chronic rejection is a relatively slow process that results in the destruction of the renal transplant over months or years. Chronic renal vascular inflammation with narrowing of the vessel lumen is the histologic hallmark of this process. Deprived of blood, the renal parenchyma is destroyed and replaced by fibroblast. In general, this type of rejection is not responsive to presently known immunosuppressive regimes.

Evidence is now accumulating that patients who reject their first transplant within 3 months are more likely to reject a second transplant. Such patients may indeed be "hyperresponsive" and require careful consideration as to the degree of match and type of immunosuppressive regime needed to achieve a successful transplant.

Immunosuppression

Most programs use corticosteroids and azathioprine, drugs that depress the immune response. The protocols for the administration of these drugs vary considerably between transplant centers and it remains difficult to judge objectively the importance of these variances on ultimate kidney and patient survival. In general, azathioprine is administered at approximately 2.0 mg per kilogram of body weight. The corticosteroid prednisone is initially administered at a dose of 100 mg/d tapered to a maintenance dose of 10 to 30 mg/d. Rejection episodes are most commonly treated by increasing the oral dose of corticosteroid and/or administering three to four intravenous pulse doses of the corticosteroid Solu-Medrol.

Biological immunosuppressive agents, such as antilymphocyte globulin and specific monoclonal antibodies, are used by many transplant programs in initial immunosuppressive regimes or for the treatment of rejection episode. Antilymphocyte globulin, produced in animals against human lymphocytes or thymocytes, is administered in combination with the pharmaceutical immunosuppressive drugs. Although more selective in its inhibitory effect on the immune system than the pharmaceuticals, antilymphocyte globulin adversely affects other components of the hematopoietic system. The monoclonal antibody now used in the clinical setting is Ortho's OKT3. It appears to affect primarily human thymocytes. Both controlled and uncontrolled studies have suggested improved renal graft survival, and other studies have suggested no effect on graft survival with both antilymphocyte globulin and OKT3. Therefore, the exact role of these agents is yet to be determined. Both are potent immunosuppressive agents and neither can be used for a prolonged period. Once used, they can rarely be used again, as sensitization to these agents readily occurs.

In 1972, cyclosporine, a fungal metabolite, was found to have pronounced immunosuppressive properties. Cyclosporine inhibits the development of cytotoxic T lymphocytes while permitting the activation of suppressor T cells. Clinical studies indicate that the drug improves the expected allograft survival in renal transplantation by 10 to 30% over that of standard immunosuppressive drugs. Several studies have indicated that cyclosporine abrogates the effect of factors, for example, blood transfusions and matching, known to influence the outcome of transplantation under standard immunosuppression. Its use also has improved the success of repeat transplantation by 8 to 10% in patients with a previous history of early graft rejection over that achieved under standard immunosuppression. Other data, however, indicate that although cyclosporine improves the success of renal transplantation by a minimum of 10%, the influence of blood transfusions and matching remains evident within the comparison subgroups stratified for match and pretransplant transfusion. Troublesome side effects including renal and hepatic toxicity have been observed in many patients receiving cyclosporine. In general, nephrotoxicity has been the most limiting problem in its use. The serum creatinine levels in surviving grafts have generally been higher than those observed with standard therapy and usually average approximately 2 mg/dL at 1 year. This higher creatinine led to concern that continued deterioration of graft function would occur from chronic toxicity. Recently available data of 5-year follow-up of cyclosporine-treated transplant patients indicated that such deterioration was not observed. Although the value of this drug is yet to be

fully established, early experience indicates that it may be an important advance in the future of organ transplantation. The experience of those centers that have been using it for 8 or more years and the total U.S. experience suggest that it is now the immunosuppressive drug of choice for recipients of cadaveric transplants. Whether it will negate the need for blood transfusions and matching, as observed in several large single-center studies, or if these factors will continue to favorably influence the success of renal transplantation under cyclosporine, as observed in reported multicenter studies, remains to be seen. Promising new drugs such as FK506 and silacin are still in trials, and the final results are to be determined.

Natural History and Its Modification with Treatment

The expected 2-year graft survival with standard immunosuppressive therapy (azathioprine and prednisone) is more than 90% for HLA-identical living related donor transplants and up to 85% for one-haplotype living related donors. Recent personal observations indicate that donor-specific blood transfusions increase the expected 2-year graft survival in both HLA-identical living related donor transplants (98%) and one-haplotype living related donor transplants (90%). The latter observation is similar to that of many investigators for donor-specific blood transfusions in one-haplotype living related donor transplantation. Recipients of random and third-party blood transfusions followed by HLA-identical living related donor transplants have been reported to have success similar to that seen with donor-specific blood transfusions. After 2 years there is very little continuing graft loss in living related donor transplants, although some does occur because of chronic rejection.

Under standard immunosuppression, cadaveric donor 2-year graft survival is approximately 50%. A 2-year cadaver graft survival of greater than 90% has been observed in some series of fully matched recipients; however, such matches are difficult to obtain with the limited supply of cadaver kidneys and it is doubtful that this approach will offer a reasonable solution for the vast majority of patients awaiting cadaver transplantation until HLA identical xenografts become practical.

Prevention

Prevention of the need for renal transplantation implies prevention of end-stage renal disease as may be found in Chapter 16–13. In addition, as mentioned under Clinical Manifestations, Objective, prevention of the need for renal transplantation would also connote improvement in the present graft survival rates, which would, in effect, prevent the increasing numbers of patients awaiting second or third grafts.

Cost Containment

The majority of funding for renal transplant recipients is covered by both private insurance and federal funding provided through the Medicare End-Stage Renal Disease Program. Limited Medicaid Funding is available for indigent patients who do not qualify for Medicare coverage and are without private insurance. The average first-year cost for a patient receiving an initial transplant in the United States in 1978 was $27,000. The present cost is regulated by diagnosis-related groups allowance as outlined by Medicare and funding has been set at $17,000 for the transplant admission. Initial hospitalization following transplantation is usually limited to 2 to 3 weeks, with subsequent close follow-up in an outpatient clinic. Most transplant recipients require one or more admissions within the first posttransplant year for the treatment of a rejection episode or other potential complications. With the inclusion of these admissions, it is estimated that the average first-year cost of a successful transplant is approximately $30,000.

After the first year, stable transplant patients are usually followed on a 2- to 3-month basis, at which time the cost of medicine and laboratory tests is approximately $1500 per year. If cyclosporine A is used, the yearly cost increases to approximately $6000 per year. Medicare funding ceases after the patient completes the year with a functioning graft.

Prevention of end-stage renal disease is the only effective means of checking or diminishing the upward spiraling costs of renal transplantation. Improvement of immunosuppressive techniques, with subsequent reductions in rejection episodes and graft losses, would markedly reduce the overall costs of renal transplantation, as would the development of unlimited xenografts.

REFERENCES

End-Stage Renal Disease Network Coordinating Council. Program report 1984. Tampa, FL: National Forum of End-Stage Renal Disease Networks, 1985.

Kahan BD, Kerman RH, Wideman CA, et al. Impact of cyclosporine on renal transplantation practice at the University of Texas Medical School at Houston. Am J Kidney Dis 1985:5:288.

Najarian JS, Frey DJ. Renal transplantation in infants. Ann Surg 1990:212:353.

Nylander WA, Sutherland DER, Bentley RL, et al. Fifteen- to twenty-year follow-up of renal transplants performed in the 1960s. Transplant Proc 1985;17:104.

Ochiai T. A novel immunosuppressive agent FK506. Transplant Immunol Letter 1990;7:3.

Overview: Transplantation. In: Research needs in nephrology and urology. U.S. Dept. of Health, Education, and Welfare. Public Health Services, National Institutes of Health. Publication No. (NIH)78-14821978.

Salvatierra O, Vincenti F, Amend W, et al. Four year experience with donor-specific blood transfusions. Transplant Proc 1983;15:924.

Spees EK. Renal transplantation. II. Selection and preparation of the recipients. In: Chatterjee SN, ed. Organ transplantation. Boston: John Wright, 1982:221.

Sutherland DER. Living related donors should be used whenever possible. Transplant Proc 1985;17:1503.

Velosa JA, Anderson VE, Torres PP, et al. Long-term renal status of kidney donors: Calculated small risk of kidney donors. Transplant Proc 1985;17:100.

Whelchel JD. An overview of renal transplantation. Emory Univ J Med 1987;1(2):89.

Disorders of the Gastrointestinal System and the Liver

Eugene Straus, M.D.

CHAPTER 19–1

Abdominal Pain

Eugene Straus, M.D.

DEFINITION

The sensation of pain in the abdomen, as elsewhere, is most frequently the result of a process in which tissues are being damaged or distorted. Abdominal pain thus calls attention to pathophysiology, and familiarity with painful syndromes can lead the physician to correct diagnoses.

Discussion of the many illness that manifest abdominal pain and the description of their patterns of pain are left to specific chapters in this book. This chapter is limited to general approaches to the problem of abdominal pain and its management.

ETIOLOGY

Pain results from the activation of specific nerve endings on A delta and C afferent fibers by noxious mechanical stimulation and extremes of heat or cold. Certain endogenous and exogenous chemical substances may also affect pain receptors. The character of painful sensations relates to the type, location, and number of receptors, to the nature of the stimulus, and to cultural and individual factors.

Receptors on afferent sensory fibers in the gut are located in the muscular walls of the hollow viscera, in the capsules of solid organs, in the mesentery and parietal peritoneum, and in the adventitia of mesenteric blood vessels. Because of the location, number, and type of receptors in the abdomen, the viscera are relatively insensitive to cutting, tearing, or crushing.

Abdominal pain is caused primarily by stretching or tension in a hollow viscus, or of the capsule of a solid organ, or of the parietal peritoneum or mesentery. Inflammation and ischemia may also produce pain through the release of tissue hormones and the accumulation of metabolites.

CRITERIA FOR DIAGNOSIS
Suggestive

By its very nature pain is subjective and the physician is completely dependent on the patient's description of the sensations.

Definitive

As there are no definitive diagnostic criteria, the physician may be misled, as in the Munchausen syndrome, where the patient's fraudulent claims of abdominal pain may result in repeated abdominal surgery.

CLINICAL MANIFESTATIONS
Subjective

When pain arises from an abdominal viscus it is usually dull, poorly localized, and frequently felt around the midline as the organs have bilateral sensory afferents. Pain that arises from the parietal peritoneum is generally sharper, more intense, and better localized than visceral pain because each area of the peritoneum receives innervation from only one side of the nervous system. Parietal pain is frequently made worse by moving or coughing. Early in the course of appendicitis, for example, when the organ becomes obstructed and dilates, the pain is a dull, periumbilical, visceral type of sensation. Later, when inflammation reaches the parietal peritoneum, the pain is sharper, and located in the right lower quadrant.

Traction of the mesentery or posterior peritoneum has the dull, vague character of visceral pain. Pain felt in areas at a distance from the abdominal cavity, such as the skin, back, or shoulder, is referred because of the existence of common central pathways for afferent neurons coming from different locations.

In addition to anatomic and physiologic considerations, the perception of pain is influenced by cultural and psychological factors.

As a general rule, the more acute the painful condition, the more rapidly the physician should proceed with diagnostic and therapeutic approaches. Similarly, the severity of pain has some relationship to the severity of the etiologic process. Given the complexities of the subjective appreciation of pain, these guides may not always be easy to apply.

The physician should become familiar with the frequent characterizations of specific painful conditions such as the burning or gnawing pain of duodenal ulceration, the cramping pain of intestinal obstruction, and the squeezing pain of biliary colic. Meticulous attention to details of the history and physical examination serves the physician well.

Objective
Physical Examination

At present there are no objective methods for detecting or measuring pain. Nevertheless, relatively objective information can be obtained relating to the chronology of the pain, the circumstances that initiate, aggravate, or alleviate the pain, and associated events such as vomiting, diarrhea, and the appearance of bloody urine or jaundice. Objective physical findings, including alterations in the vital signs, distention of the abdomen, abnormal bowel sounds, tenderness, guarding, rigidity, and the perception of a mass, should be carefully described, documented, and given the greatest consideration. These findings, in association with specific conditions, are discussed in detail in appropriate chapters of this book.

Routine Laboratory Abnormalities

Routine laboratory abnormalities, such as the elevation of serum enzymes in pancreatitis, are described in specific chapters dealing with painful syndromes.

PLANS
Diagnostic
Differential Diagnosis

The list of conditions causing abdominal pain is extensive and includes entities resulting in generalized or local peritonitis, obstruction of hollow organs, hepatic capsule distention, ischemia and infarction, tumor necrosis, and ruptured ectopic pregnancy. The differential diagnosis of painful abdominal syndromes is considered in specific chapters dealing with these entities.

Diagnostic Options and Recommended Approach

So many disparate disorders manifest with abdominal pain that a single approach to diagnosis is not reasonable or possible. Nonetheless, the ultrasonic examination of the abdomen has the advantages of speed, non-invasiveness, efficacy, and low cost, making it a frequent choice in the initial evaluation of painful syndromes. This is especially true in right upper quadrant syndromes where the biliary tree is expected to be involved. Plain flat and upright radiographs of the abdomen are indicated when the clinician suspects intestinal obstruction. Computed axial tomography scans have advanced the diagnosis and management of pancreatitis and diverticulitis, among other disorders.

Endoscopic examinations should be withheld when the clinician suspects acute inflammatory disease such as diverticulitis, severe active colitis, ischemic bowel, and perforated organs.

It is frequently important to be sure that expert evaluation of the pelvis has been obtained in female patients. In the absence of any objective findings, diagnostic laparotomy is usually unproductive.

Therapeutic

In the best of circumstances a precise diagnosis leads to specific treatment; however, in some cases it is necessary to consider the diagnosis of an acute surgical abdomen without a precise cause being identified. Exploratory laparotomy may be indicated after ruling out acute myocardial infarction, pulmonary embolism, spontaneous pneumothorax, or other conditions that could contraindicate surgery. In this circumstance some exploratory surgical procedures fail to find any abnormality, and this outcome is acceptable in up to 20% of exploratory procedures, although studies indicate that hospital services can improve their approaches to exploratory laparotomy by carefully reviewing their experiences.

It is no longer acceptable to withhold analgesic medication from patients with acute pain in the belief that it would mask findings and prevent accurate diagnosis. After the initial examination the patient should be given analgesia but not to the extent of deep sedation. The comfort provided by this approach will facilitate repeated examination.

FOLLOW-UP

Patients with acute abdominal pain require frequent follow-up, often needing reexamination several times each hour until a diagnosis is established.

DISCUSSION
Prevalence and Incidence

The prevalence and incidence of conditions causing abdominal pain are discussed in chapters dealing with specific entities.

Related Basic Science

A delta fibers are found in muscle and skin and carry well-localized, sharp sensations caused by acute injury. C fibers are found in parietal peritoneum and viscera, as well as in muscle and periosteum, and they mediate dull, poorly localized sensations that tend to be longer lasting. The sensory afferents that convey abdominal pain are therefore primarily of the C type.

The visceral sensory afferent fibers that carry pain sensation centrally travel with the sympathetic nerves, except for those from the pelvic organs, which travel with the parasympathetics in the pelvic nerve.

Visceral afferents derived from the same dermatome mediate similar painful sensations. It is therefore hard to distinguish the pain of myocardial ischemia from the pain of esophageal inflammation, as both the heart and the esophagus are enervated by visceral afferents derived from dermatome T1–4. This is the basis of the problem of "noncardiac chest pain," and it is the explanation for the relative lack of precision in determining the origin of painful abdominal sensations.

Genetics

The genetics of conditions causing abdominal pain is discussed in chapters dealing with specific entities.

Physiologic or Metabolic Derangement

Physiologic or metabolic derangements relating to specific conditions are discussed in appropriate chapters.

Natural History and Its Modification with Treatment

The natural history and its modification with treatment of painful syndromes are discussed in specific chapters dealing with the disorders.

Prevention

Prevention of specific conditions is discussed in appropriate chapters.

Cost Containment

Cost containment in circumstances related to abdominal pain is dealt with in chapters dealing with specific conditions.

REFERENCES

Blacklock ARE, Gunn AA. The "acute abdomen" in the accident and emergency department. J R Coll Surg Edinb 1976;21:165.

Cope Z. The early diagnosis of the acute abdomen. London: Oxford University Press, 1963.

Piedrahita P, Butterfield WC. Abdominal exploration as a diagnostic procedure. Am J Surg 1976;131:181.

CHAPTER 19–2

Nausea and Vomiting

Eugene Straus, M.D.

DEFINITION

Vomiting is a protective mechanism through which material can be expelled from the proximal alimentary canal. The vomiting mechanism includes nausea, retching ("dry heaves"), and vomiting (emesis).

Nausea is a complex feeling of uneasiness, even disgust, that is related to the stomach and an expectation or desire to vomit. The stomach becomes flaccid with reduced tone and peristalsis, whereas the muscle tone in the duodenum and proximal jejunum tends to increase and duodenal contents may reflux into the stomach.

During retching, the mouth and glottis are closed and spasmodic inspiratory efforts of the diaphragm and chest are opposed by contractions of the abdominal muscles.

Vomiting takes place when the pylorus constricts, the cardia of the stomach rises into the chest, the abdominal muscles go into strong and sustained contraction, and the mouth opens to allow gastric contents to be forcefully expelled.

ETIOLOGY

Vomiting is a complex and stereotypical activity that is controlled from a "vomiting center" in the medulla. The vomiting center is adjacent to the medullary centers for the control of respiration, salivation, and defecation, and these functions are altered during the act of vomiting. Nonetheless, vomiting may occur as a part of a very wide range of conditions including pregnancy, motion sickness, gastritis, gastrointestinal obstruction, increased intracranial pressure, hepatitis, renal failure, radiation sickness, hyperthyroidism, drug toxicity, peritonitis, pancreatitis, cholecystitis, hypertensive crisis, and diabetic and other gastroparetic syndromes.

CRITERIA FOR DIAGNOSIS

Nausea is a sensation that is appreciated by the patient; it is therefore entirely subjective. Retching and vomiting are distinct acts that are entirely definitive.

CLINICAL MANIFESTATIONS
Subjective

Nausea and vomiting may occur in the absence of serious physical illness. Certain smells, tastes, or states of mind may cause nausea and vomiting in a susceptible individual. On the other hand, nausea and vomiting may be early or late manifestations of a great variety of conditions, some of which are listed above. The history is the physician's first and best guide to the significance of nausea and vomiting.

Special attention should be paid to the frequency or chronicity of vomiting, timing of vomiting with respect to the intake of food and drink, content of the vomitus, and relationship of vomiting to pain.

Chronic vomiting that occurs while eating or shortly thereafter is a common pattern in psychogenic vomiting, although nonobstructing peptic ulcer in the distal stomach may cause a similar pattern. Gastric outlet obstruction causes vomiting that generally occurs more than an hour after eating. Vomiting of material held in the stomach for 12 hours or more is suggestive of motor dysfunction of the stomach and is not suggestive of psychogenic vomiting. Nausea and vomiting in the morning before eating are seen in early pregnancy ("morning sickness"), but are also observed in alcoholic gastritis, uremic gastritis, and other conditions. Hyperemesis gravidarum (pernicious vomiting of pregnancy) refers to intractable vomiting in the first trimester that causes nutritional deficiency and fluid and electrolyte disturbances.

Vomiting of undigested food suggests that the material never got to the stomach. This can occur in achalasia or when food lodges in a large esophageal or pharyngeal (Zenker's) diverticulum. Blood or "coffee grounds" indicate hematemesis. Bile indicates that there is no obstruction between the stomach and the duodenum.

One cannot overemphasize the importance of a complete and well-considered history in the diagnosis of the cause of such common symptoms as nausea and vomiting.

Objective
Physical Examination

A careful physical examination is, of course, essential. As such a variety of disorders can cause nausea and vomiting, the physician must be alert to all evidence of disease. Findings of abdominal masses, distention, or tenderness may indicate obstruction or inflammatory disease. The character of the bowel sounds should be considered. A feculent odor suggests intestinal obstruction, but it may accompany a gastrocolic fistula. A succussion splash heard over the stomach is frequently found in gastric outlet obstruction and gastric atony.

Routine Laboratory Abnormalities

Persistent vomiting causes nutritional deficiency, as well as fluid and electrolyte imbalance. Losses of fluid, potassium, hydrochloric acid, and sodium result in dehydration, hypokalemia, alkalosis, and hyponatremia, respectively. Contraction of the extracellular fluid volume results in aldosterone release and increased loss of potassium in the urine. The most common routine laboratory abnormalities are therefore hypokalemia, hyponatremia, and an elevated serum bicarbonate.

PLANS
Diagnostic
Differential Diagnosis

The differential diagnosis includes the conditions mentioned under Clinical Manifestations.

Diagnostic Options and Recommended Approach

The cause of nausea and vomiting is generally apparent after the completion of the history and physical examination.

Other diagnostic tests are determined by the differential diagnosis.

Therapeutic
Therapeutic Options

In most cases the cause of nausea and vomiting can be treated. It is thus not generally necessary to use antiemetic drugs in patients with intestinal obstruction, diabetic ketoacidosis, cholecystitis, pancreatitis, and so on. There are, however, instances in which antiemetic drug therapy is indicated.

Recommended Approach

The anticholinergic belladonna alkaloid scopolamine provides effective prophylaxis of motion sickness. A single circular flat disk placed on a hairless surface behind one ear is designed to deliver 0.5 mg of scopolamine at a constant rate over a 3-day period. The single disk should be placed behind the ear at least 4 hours before the antiemetic effect is required. Dryness of the mouth and drowsiness are the most frequent side effects.

H_1-receptor antagonist antihistamines are effective in morning sickness, but some of these have been shown to be teratogenic in animals. Most women suffering from morning sickness respond well to reassurance and taking small meals during the early hours. In hyperemesis gravidarum, restoration of fluid and electrolyte imbalance is required.

Phenothiazines, especially prochlorperazine (Compazine), are effective in treating vomiting due to drugs including opiates, anesthetics, and cancer chemotherapeutic agents. They are also effective in vomiting caused by radiation and gastroenteritis. Compazine is available in tablets, in sustained-release capsules, in aqueous solution for injection, and as suppositories. To control severe nausea and vomiting the dose may have to be adjusted from the lowest recommended dosage. The oral dose should be begun at 5 mg three or four times daily. The rectal dosage is 25 mg twice daily. Dizziness, drowsiness, blurred vision, hypotension, skin rashes, amenorrhea, and extrapyramidal reactions may occur.

The dopaminergic antagonists metoclopramide and domperidone are effective in preventing vomiting caused by anesthetics, by cancer chemotherapeutic agents, and in diabetic and postvagotomy gastroparesis. An oral metoclopramide dose of 10 to 20 mg given before meals may be tried, but vomiting caused by chemotherapeutic agents such as cisplatin may require 2 mg/kg given intravenously.

Tetrahydrocannabinol (THC) is effective in the prevention of nausea and vomiting induced by cancer chemotherapy. It is administered at an initial dose of 5 mg/m^2, given 1 to 3 hours prior to the administration of chemotherapy, then every 2 to 4 hours after chemotherapy is given, for a total of four to six doses per day. Tetrahydrocannabinol is indicated only for treatment in relation to cancer chemotherapy.

FOLLOW-UP

Follow-up of patients with nausea and vomiting must be individualized and is determined primarily by the cause.

DISCUSSION

Prevalence and Incidence

No general statement can be made regarding the prevalence and incidence of nausea and vomiting. Virtually all patients taking certain chemotherapeutic agents or with proximal intestinal obstruction have some nausea and vomiting. On the other hand, nausea and vomiting in conditions like hepatitis are quite variable.

Related Basic Science

The classic studies of the central and peripheral mechanisms involved in vomiting have been done in cats and the conclusions extrapolated to humans. Electrical stimulation of the vomiting center in the dorsal portion of the lateral reticular formation of the medulla causes vomiting. If this area is destroyed, animals become refractory to chemically induced vomiting. Nevertheless, substances that induce vomiting do not stimulate the vomiting center directly; rather, the vomiting center coordinates the activities of adjacent centers to allow the complex pattern of responses involved in vomiting. Chemical stimuli reaching the circulation pass through a "blood–brain barrier"-free area in the floor of the fourth ventricle, the area postrema, adjacent to the vomiting center, and stimulate vomiting by acting on emetic chemoreceptors. This emetic chemoreceptor area is called the chemoreceptor trigger zone. Afferent neural impulses can reach the medullary vomiting center via the vagus and sympathetic nerves and stimulate vomiting without the involvement of the chemoreceptor trigger zone.

Genetics

Although rare genetic conditions of gastrointestinal dysmotility are associated with vomiting, these conditions are not within the scope of this chapter.

Physiologic or Metabolic Derangement

The physiologic and metabolic derangements caused by sustained nausea and vomiting include nutritional, fluid, and electrolyte deficiencies and have been discussed above. In addition to these, vomiting can cause injury to the stomach and esophagus. Mallory–Weiss tears at the esophagogastric junction caused by retching and vomiting can cause severe upper gastrointestinal bleeding. Deeper trauma may cause free perforation of the esophagus in what is known as Boerhaave's syndrome. Boerhaave's syndrome frequently requires emergency surgery and can be fatal. Chronic vomiting can cause loss of tooth enamel and cause dental caries. Aspiration pneumonia is a serious complication of vomiting and steps should be taken to avoid aspiration by limiting gastric contents, positioning patients, and possibly protecting the airway in patients who are at risk.

Natural History and Its Modification with Treatment

The natural history and its modification with treatment vary greatly depending on the cause of the nausea and vomiting.

Prevention

Nausea and vomiting can frequently be prevented by prompt treatment of the fundamental cause. In addition, use of the antiemetic agents mentioned above can prevent nausea and vomiting in the appropriate situations.

Cost Containment

Opportunities for cost containment are found in the prompt treatment of underlying conditions and in the judicious use of antiemetics so that the complications of vomiting can be avoided.

REFERENCES

Borison HL, Wang SC. Physiology and pharmacology of vomiting. Pharmacol Rev 1953;5:193.

Borison HL, Borison R, McCarthy LE. Role of the area postrema in vomiting and related functions. Fed Proc 1984;43:2955.

Malagelada JR, Camilleri M. Unexplained vomiting: A diagnostic challenge. Ann Intern Med 1984;101:211.

CHAPTER 19–3

Upper Gastrointestinal Bleeding

Eugene Straus, M.D.

DEFINITION

Bleeding into the gastrointestinal tract from a source located proximal to the ligament of Treitz is defined as upper gastrointestinal bleeding.

Hematemesis is bloody vomitus. When the blood is fresh it is bright red. Older blood emerging from the upper gastrointestinal tract is "coffee ground" in character.

Melena is stool that has become black, shiny, sticky, and foul-smelling from the degradation of blood which, in most cases, has entered the upper gastrointestinal tract (above the ligament of Treitz).

Hematemesis and melena are cardinal signs of acute upper gastrointestinal bleeding. They should be distinguished from hematochezia, which is the passage of bright red or maroon blood from the anus, and usually signifies acute bleeding in the lower gastrointestinal tract, most frequently from the colon.

Finally, it should be recognized that blood loss from the gastrointestinal tract is frequently occult. Occult blood loss can be detected only by testing the stool with a chemical reagent. Occult blood in the stool frequently indicates chronic bleeding located anywhere in the gastrointestinal tract.

ETIOLOGY

Hematemesis and melena are objective signs of acute bleeding from a source proximal to the ligament of Treitz. The practicing physician must be mindful that the bleeding patient may present without objective signs but with symptoms of blood loss including weakness, dizziness, dyspnea, angina pectoris, and shock.

There are many causes of upper gastrointestinal bleeding (Table 19–3–1). Details concerning the approach to these disorders can be found in other chapters. This chapter focuses on the general approach to the patient who is bleeding from the upper gastrointestinal tract.

CRITERIA FOR DIAGNOSIS

Suggestive

Hematemesis of fresh blood suggests loss of a large volume of blood into the upper gastrointestinal tract, whereas melena may occur when bleeding is occurring at a slower rate. When hematochezia results from an upper gastrointestinal source, it suggests a truly massive bleed.

These signs are not definitive of upper gastrointestinal bleeding because apparent hematemesis may, in fact, result from vomiting of swallowed blood from a nasopharyngeal or pulmonary source; melena may, in fact, be stool that has been turned black by ingested iron, or may result from slow transit of blood arising from a lower source; and hematochezia generally results from colonic bleeding. Other suggestive signs may include dizziness, palpitations, tachycardia, hypotension, dyspnea, and angina pectoris.

TABLE 19–3–1. CAUSES OF UPPER GASTROINTESTINAL BLEEDING

Cause	Associated Signs or Symptoms
Duodenal ulcer	Epigastric pain and tenderness
Gastric ulcer	Abdominal pain
Stress-related mucosal lesions	Serious illness
Cushing's ulcer	Central nervous system disease
Curling's ulcer	Major burn
Marginal ulcer	Prior gastric surgery
Gastritis	Alcohol, nonsteroidal antiinflammatory drugs, renal disease
Esophagitis	Heartburn
Barrett's ulcer	Heartburn
Mallory–Weiss tear	Vomiting
Esophageal or gastric varices	Liver disease
Hematobilia	Liver trauma
Gastric carcinoma	Abdominal pain
Dieulafoy's lesion	Massive bleed/inapparent source
Vascular anomalies	
Osler–Weber–Rendu syndrome	Hereditary telangiectasias
Angiodysplasias	Chronic renal failure

Definitive

When gastrointestinal bleeding is suspected, the physician should take immediate steps to ensure that the patient is hemodynamically stable even before confirming the diagnosis. When the patient is stabilized, coffee-ground vomitus and melena should be tested to confirm the presence of blood. Definitive diagnosis of upper gastrointestinal bleeding can be established with gastric aspiration. The physician must know that, occasionally, blood entering from a duodenal source may not reflux into the stomach and so the aspirate can be negative in the presence of an upper gastrointestinal bleed. The precise source of bleeding is best determined endoscopically. When this is not possible, barium x-rays, preferably double-contrast studies, may be employed. Occasionally, if bleeding is so massive that the endoscopist is unable to localize the source, angiography may be useful.

CLINICAL MANIFESTATIONS

Subjective

Symptoms and signs resulting from upper gastrointestinal bleeding are dependent on the rate and volume of the bleed, the patient's state of hydration, and the function of the cardiovascular and autonomic nervous systems. They range from little or no awareness of the episode to symptoms associated with shock and its consequences. Typically, weakness, dizziness, sweating, and anxiety are experienced as the patient progresses from hypotension to vascular collapse.

Objective

Physical Examination

Alterations in the patient's vital signs are the most direct indicators of the amount and rate of blood loss. Early in the course, or after some volume has been returned to the circulation, the only physical finding may be postural hypotension. At this stage the blood pressure is maintained in the supine position but falls when the patient sits up. As more volume is lost, tachycardia, vasoconstriction, and recumbent hypotension ensue. The patient may be sweating and appear pale; the extremities may feel cold. When the volume deficit has reached a liter or more, the systolic pressure may fall below 100 mm Hg or the postural drop may exceed 10 to 15 mm Hg.

Bowel sounds are frequently hyperactive as blood entering the upper gastrointestinal tract stimulates motor activity of the gut.

Routine Laboratory Abnormalities

A fall in the hematocrit is the test most frequently used to estimate the magnitude of blood loss. Although this is certainly a useful guide, sev-

eral caveats must be understood. If the bleeding is slow and chronic, the hematocrit does not fall until bone marrow iron stores are depleted. When this occurs the red cells are hypochromic and microcytic, and their mean corpuscular volume is low.

In acute bleeding, the fall in hematocrit reflects the extent of blood loss, but only after extracellular fluid enters the circulation to restore volume. Initially, the blood volume falls, but losses of plasma and red cell volumes are simultaneous and so the hematocrit does not change. It may take several hours for red cell-free fluid to dilute the blood enough to cause a fall in the hematocrit. After a major bleed, the process of redistribution of fluid into the vascular space may take 2 to 3 days. Only then does the hematocrit reach its lowest point, and the mean corpuscular volume is normal, unless there has been prior blood loss. The alteration of the hematocrit after a bleed is modified by the administration of fluids, including blood, and is diminished in patients who are dehydrated. The hematocrit is therefore a useful but imprecise guide to the restoration of the circulation.

The blood urea nitrogen level may be elevated out of proportion to the creatinine level if large volumes of blood (>1000 mL) enter the gut. This is caused by diminution of renal blood flow and absorption of plasma proteins.

PLANS

Diagnostic

Differential Diagnosis

The differential diagnosis includes bleeding from the nasopharynx, lung, and lower gastrointestinal tract.

Diagnostic Options and Recommended Approach

Examination of the nasopharynx and chest and the absence of obvious hemoptysis or signs of acute pulmonary disease are usually sufficient to rule out nasopharyngeal and pulmonary sources. The finding of blood in the gastric aspirate usually confirms upper gastrointestinal bleeding when bloody or melanotic stool is observed.

Therapeutic

The approach to management of patients bleeding from the upper gastrointestinal tract is determined by the rate of blood loss. Gastric aspiration and lavage provide a good indication of the extent of bleeding. The hemodynamically stable patient with chronic bleeding can be managed electively, whereas patients who are hemorrhaging acutely require urgent care.

In the patient who is bleeding acutely and has signs of hemodynamic instability, reliable venous access must be established immediately to facilitate resuscitation. Insertion of large-bore cannulas into two veins is recommended and infusion of normal saline or lactated Ringer's solution is started to restore vascular volume as rapidly as possible. The rate of infusion is limited by the condition of the patient's cardiopulmonary system. Monitoring of the central venous pressure or the pulmonary capillary wedge pressure may be advisable when the history or the physical examination indicates that rapid fluid administration may not be tolerated. The strategy is to improve oxygenation of tissues by allowing the remaining red cells to circulate. Oxygen should be administered by nasal cannula or face mask.

Gastric lavage should be performed using a 34- or 36-French orogastric tube. The smaller nasogastric tube should be removed prior to the lavage. Five hundred to one thousand milliliters of room-temperature tap water is instilled and then gently removed by suction and gravity drainage. This procedure is repeated until bleeding stops and the return is free of blood, or until it becomes evident that more vigorous measures are required. The use of iced fluids and levarterenol has not been shown to be more effective than tap water. In addition to giving an estimation of the rate of bleeding, lavage removes blood from the gastrointestinal tract, and this facilitates endoscopic examination and may prevent metabolic complications such as hepatic encephalopathy.

The physician must appreciate the fact that gastrointestinal bleeding from virtually any site is most frequently intermittent rather than constant. Regardless of diagnosis, as many as 90% of patients may stop bleeding temporarily during gastric lavage. Nevertheless, even if bleeding has apparently stopped, patients who have recently bled acutely should be admitted to an intensive care unit where vital signs, urine output, and cardiopulmonary parameters, including electrocardiogram, can be monitored. A flow sheet, as suggested in Figure 19–3–1, should be maintained to evaluate the patient's progress.

The decision to transfuse blood or blood products is of great importance and should be considered with care. Patients who are hemodynamically stable, are asymptomatic, and have hematocrits above 25% may not require transfusion. After appropriate diagnostic studies, such patients should receive iron supplements and observations should be made to ensure that the red cell mass is restored.

Indications for transfusion include continued acute bleeding, shock, a hematocrit below 25%, and symptoms and signs of poor tissue oxygenation. Consideration should also be given to the probability of further dilution of the red cell mass by continued vascular repletion and the ability of the patient to withstand a recurrence of bleeding. The transfusion requirement may be for red cells to improve tissue oxygenation, for plasma to allow coagulation at the bleeding site, or for both.

Patients who have stopped bleeding and have had volume replacement with cell-free fluid should received packed red cells. This conserves plasma and allows transfusion of a smaller volume.

Patients with preexisting deficiencies of coagulation factors, especially those with hepatic cirrhosis, frequently require fresh-frozen plasma. A unit of plasma may be given after every 2 or 3 units of packed red cells.

When patients are receiving very large volume transfusions (>10 units), platelet transfusion may be necessary.

Transfusion should generally be continued until the hematocrit is in the range of 30%.

FOLLOW-UP

Gastrointestinal bleeding from virtually any source is most frequently intermittent. When bleeding stops, it is therefore essential that the caregivers be mindful of the possibility of rebleeding. The risk of rebleeding is greatest in the first 48 hours after cessation of the initial episode. Patients should be monitored in an intensive care setting for at least this period. Subsequent follow-up is determined by the nature of the bleeding lesion and the condition of the patient.

DISCUSSION
Prevalence and Incidence

Accurate data concerning prevalence and incidence of upper gastrointestinal bleeding are not available. In the late 1970s it was estimated that in the United States, about 350,000 patients were admitted each year with acute upper gastrointestinal bleeding.

Related Basic Science

Hypovolemia and hypotension trigger reflexes that result in sympathetic stimulation. Alpha-adrenergic sympathetic receptor stimulation produces vasoconstriction in large vascular beds including the splanchnic, renal, muscular, and cutaneous areas. Renal ischemia may activate the renin–angiotensin system. Vasoconstriction, although initially helping to maintain arterial perfusion pressures, ultimately contributes to ischemia and can cause tissue damage. Increased alpha-adrenergic tone causes postcapillary venular constriction, in addition to precapillary arteriolar constriction. As shock progresses the arterioles relax but the venous constriction persists. Blood is trapped within the capillaries, hydrostatic pressure rises, and fluid is lost to the extravascular space. The result is increased hypovolemia, local hemoconcentration, sludging of blood in tissues, and capillary damage. This sequence may trigger diffuse intravascular coagulation. As the sequence progresses, pathways of oxidative metabolism are replaced by anaerobic metabolism and this may result in profound lactic acidosis.

Genetics

Hereditary hemorrhagic telangiectasia (Osler–Weber–Rendu syndrome) is transmitted as an autosomal dominant trait. Affected individuals characteristically have telangiectasias on the palms and soles, on the skin and buccal mucosa, and in the nail beds. Repeated epistaxis in childhood is the classic presentation and a family history is generally obtained. Chronic gastrointestinal bleeding is seen frequently as patients become older, usually in the fifth decade or later.

Physiologic or Metabolic Derangement

Physiologic and metabolic derangements are those caused by vascular collapse and hypovolemic shock. They include the mechanisms through which the body maintains circulation to vital organs and the damage that occurs when ischemia ensues. Acute tubular necrosis and renal failure, pulmonary failure due to "shock lung," "shock liver," and other syndromes, including lactic acidosis are discussed elsewhere in this book.

Natural History and Its Modification with Treatment

The majority of upper gastrointestinal bleeds stop spontaneously without treatment. Nonetheless, there is an overall mortality of about 10%, and patients over 60 years of age, with more serious chronic illness, have higher rates of mortality. In recent years the fraction of bleeding patients over the age of 60 has increased while the overall mortality has remained constant, suggesting that treatment has been successful in reducing mortality. This may be due to more timely and skillful support of the bleeding patient and the introduction and availability of techniques of achieving hemostasis through the endoscope.

Prevention

Reduction in the frequency of recurrent peptic ulceration, through treatment of *Helicobacter pylori* and/or maintenance suppression of acid se-

---

Patient's name: _____ Date: _____

MR #: _____ Admitting diagnosis: _____

Evidence of GI bleeding: _____

Suspected source: _____

Time: _____ BP: _____ P: _____ Hct: _____ BUN: _____

IV Fluids: _____

Remarks: _____

_____

_____

_____

_____

BP, blood pressure; P, pulse; Hct, hematocrit; BUN, blood urea nitrogen; IV Fluids, type and volume; Remarks, includes observations regarding continued bleeding, diagnostic and therapeutic measures, patient's mental status, and so on.

Figure 19–3–1. Suggested flow sheet for episodes of acute bleeding from the gastrointestinal tract.

cretion, should prevent a significant number of acute upper gastrointestinal bleeds. Similarly, understanding the important role of nonsteroidal antiinflammatory drugs in initiating and exacerbating bleeding lesions should allow physicians to use these drugs more judiciously and in conjunction with prophylactic agents to reduce the frequency of nonsteroidal antiinflammatory drug-related bleeds. Early and vigorous suppression of gastric acid secretion is effective in preventing stress-related upper gastrointestinal bleeding. Finally, successful treatment of chronic liver disease with antiviral, antiinflammatory, and other agents, including liver transplantation, may prevent the acute bleeding that complicates these disorders.

Cost Containment

Episodes of acute upper gastrointestinal bleeding require costly diagnostic and therapeutic responses including intensive care unit stay. Cost containment is offered by some of the preventive measures indicated above.

REFERENCES

Ebert RV, Stead EA, Gibson JG. Response of normal subjects to acute blood loss. Arch Intern Med 1941;68:578.

Luk GD, Bynum TE, Hendrix TR. Gastric aspiration in localization of gastrointestinal hemorrhage. JAMA 1979;241:576.

Luke RG, Lees W, Ruddick J. Appearances of the stools after the introduction of blood into the caecum. Gut 1964;5:77.

Schiff L, Stevens RJ, Shapiro N, Goodman S. Observations on the oral administration of citrated blood in man. Am J Med Sci 1942;303:409.

CHAPTER 19–4

Lower Gastrointestinal Bleeding

Michael Orenstein, M.D., and Arthur Boshnack, M.D.

DEFINITION

Lower gastrointestinal bleeding is defined as bleeding that originates distal to the ligament of Treitz. The source of the bleeding is usually a lesion of the colon or rectum, but bleeding occasionally may be localized to the small bowel.

ETIOLOGY

The four most common diseases accounting for the vast majority of lower gastrointestinal bleeding are diverticulosis, angiodysplasia, benign and malignant colonic neoplasms, and internal hemorrhoids. There are many other causes of lower gastrointestinal bleeding, some unusual and others quite rare. The severity of bleeding ranges from occult blood loss to massive hemorrhage or shock. Severe bleeding from the lower gastrointestinal tract is primarily a problem of the elderly; colonic diverticular disease and angiodysplasia are believed to be the source of hemorrhage in approximately two thirds of cases. Severe bleeding from the lower gastrointestinal tract is much less frequent in younger patients, but significant hemorrhage can occur from polyps, inflammatory bowel disease, and occasionally Meckel's diverticulum (Table 19–4–1).

Lower gastrointestinal bleeding in adults is usually mild and self-limited and can be evaluated on an outpatient basis. At times, however, hematochezia can be severe and ongoing, requiring hospitalization, resuscitation, and therapeutic intervention.

CRITERIA FOR DIAGNOSIS
Suggestive

Sudden passage of bright red blood, clots, or burgundy stools, with or without pain, calls attention to the onset of lower gastrointestinal hemorrhage. When patients also notice sudden weakness, syncope, and shortness of breath, severe hemorrhage should be suspected. Shock can be anticipated as blood loss approaches 40% of the blood volume. Chronic blood loss is detectable only by fecal occult blood testing, without additional clinical manifestations.

A history of diarrhea, with accompanying hematochezia, is suggestive of mucosal inflammatory disease. The patient may report anal pain during defecation, especially after passage of hard stools, suggesting an anal fissure or hemorrhoids. Repeated urgency to stool with hematochezia can be a symptom of tumor or other space-occupying lesions in the rectum or sigmoid colon.

Definitive

A history and physical examination should be performed which includes a digital rectal examination as well as observation of the blood on the examining finger. The spontaneous passage of frank blood, blood clots, maroon stool, or melena may suggest the nature of the bleeding.

Melena is sticky, black, foul-smelling stool resulting from bacterial degradation of hemoglobin. Melena suggests upper gastrointestinal bleeding but can originate from the small intestine or proximal colon if transit time is slow. Acute blood loss may produce melena for up to 7 days. After the stool color returns to normal, tests for occult blood may remain positive for over a week. Physical examination, in conjunction with appropriate utilization of both endoscopic and radiologic studies, should enable definitive diagnosis of the bleeding source in the vast majority of cases.

TABLE 19–4–1. CAUSES OF LOWER GASTROINTESTINAL BLEEDING

Common Causes	Uncommon Causes	Rare Causes
Diverticulosis	Solitary rectal ulcer syndrome	Hereditary hemorrhagic telangiectasia
Angiodysplasia	Stercoral ulcers	Thrombocytopenia
Inflammatory bowel disease	Endometriosis	Small bowel diverticula
Ischemic bowel disease	Uremic colitis	Dieulafoy's lesion of the colon and small intestine
	Radiation colitis	
Infectious colitis	Anticoagulants/coagulopathy	Small intestine ulceration
Hemorrhoids	Nonsteroidal antiinflammatory medications	Intussusception
Neoplasms	Colonic varices	Gastrointestinal bleeding in runners
Adenomas	Postpolypectomy bleeding	
Carcinomas	Vasculitis	
Kaposi's sarcomas	Mecke's diverticulum	
	Juvenile polyps	
	Aortoenteric fistula	

CLINICAL MANIFESTATIONS

Subjective

With the passage of appreciable amounts of blood in the stool, patients generally notify their physicians promptly. It can sometimes be difficult to determine the rapidity of bleeding on presentation, as bright red blood seen in a toilet bowl may lead one to overestimate the amount of blood loss. Hematochezia (bright red or maroon blood per rectum) usually arises from a colonic or rectal lesion, but with very rapid passage of blood, it may originate from the stomach or duodenum. Hematochezia due to upper gastrointestinal bleeding is generally accompanied by early signs of significant volume depletion. Lower gastrointestinal bleeding accompanied by abdominal pain suggests the possibility of inflammatory bowel disease, ischemic bowel disease, and/or infectious colitis, whereas painless bleeding is characteristic of diverticular disease, angiodysplasia, and most tumors. Bleeding accompanied by cramping and other symptoms of obstruction suggests distal colonic tumors, and the presence of pain in the lower rectum and anal canal makes anorectal disease, including prolapsed hemorrhoids, fissures, and fistula, more likely. A past history of peripheral vascular disease, trauma, inflammatory bowel disease, or previous pelvic radiation should be sought. Family history should attempt to elicit inflammatory bowel disease, polyposis syndromes, or connective tissue disorders.

Objective

Physical Examination

Patients with slow or intermittent bleeding may have a normal physical examination; however, as anemia worsens, they are noted to have generalized pallor but cardiovascular compromise is not noted. With an acute major hemorrhage, mild orthostatic symptoms can be noted on presentation, or patients can be found critically ill, with tachycardia, restlessness, cool skin, tachypnea, diaphoresis, and low urine output. In patients who are not in shock, blood pressure and pulse should be determined in both the supine and upright positions. A systolic blood pressure dropping to less than 90 mm Hg, in the upright position, correlates with roughly 25 to 50% blood volume loss. Postural changes of 10 mm Hg or more and/or heart rates above 120 beats per minute suggest volume losses of 20 to 25%. Younger patients may tolerate substantial losses of blood volume surprisingly well. Abdominal examination may reveal mild lower abdominal tenderness accompanied by abdominal distention and tympany. Bowel sounds are often hyperactive, but may be normal or hypoactive. Rebound tenderness would signify peritoneal irritation, but is not commonly associated with acute bleeding. Hemorrhoids, fissures, fistulas, or masses may be noted on examination of the perineum. Digital rectal examination may reveal a polyp or a mass.

Routine Laboratory Abnormalities

A mild anemia may be present. Chronic, intermittent blood loss may be accompanied by microcytosis with low ferritin levels and low transferrin saturation. With acute blood loss, prior to administration of fluids, initial hematocrit levels may not accurately reflect the degree of blood loss, as several hours are required for equilibration. Leukocytosis and thrombocytosis may develop within 6 hours of significant hemorrhage. Electrolyte abnormalities may reflect acidosis or renal failure. A blood urea nitrogen:creatinine ratio of greater than 25:1 is rare in lower intestinal bleeding and implies bleeding from the upper gastrointestinal tract. Abdominal radiographs are generally not helpful in defining the etiology of intestinal bleeding, although occasionally findings suggestive of bowel ischemia, such as thumbprinting, may be found on abdominal radiographs. The electrocardiogram shows tachycardia and should be examined for ischemic changes precipitated by blood loss.

PLANS

Diagnostic

Differential Diagnosis

The causes of lower gastrointestinal bleeding are outlined in Table 19–4–1.

Diagnostic Options

A definitive diagnosis can be made by performing a brief history and physical examination to direct appropriate utilization of endoscopic and radiologic studies. A useful approach to diagnosis considers patient age and the presence or absence of abdominal pain accompanying bleeding. In actively bleeding patients, a nasogastric tube is passed promptly to rule out upper gastrointestinal bleeding. Nasogastric aspiration is a critical part of the evaluation of patients with rectal bleeding because 10 to 15% of presumed severe lower intestinal bleeding actually originates in the upper gastrointestinal tract. The absence of blood and the presence of bile in the aspirate virtually exclude bleeding proximal to the ligament of Treitz.

A clear, nonbilious aspirate eliminates the possibility of active bleeding from the esophagus or stomach but, because of pyloric obstruction or spasm, cannot exclude the possibility of bleeding from a duodenal ulcer or aortoduodenal fistula. If upper gastrointestinal bleeding cannot be excluded, then upper endoscopy should be performed as early as possible. Flexible sigmoidoscopy and/or anoscopy should be the initial examinations performed in all patients with acute lower gastrointestinal bleeding. Anoscopy is used to examine the anus and anal canal for fissures and hemorrhoids. Sigmoidoscopy is used to examine for mucosal abnormalities and mass lesions in the rectum, sigmoid, and descending colon. Occasionally, it is possible to get above the bleeding site with sigmoidoscopy, confirming a distal colonic source. This is not always easy because blood from the distal colon frequently refluxes throughout the colon in an acute bleed. A flexible scope can be retroflexed to visualize sites in the rectal ampulla which may be difficult to see with rigid instruments. Stool cultures and specimens for fecal leukocytes can be obtained in the appropriate settings. The discovery of an anorectal lesion should not deter one from examining the remainder of the colon for additional bleeding sites.

Colonoscopy. If anoscopy/sigmoidoscopy has not yet identified a source and bleeding has ceased, or is suspected to be relatively slow, the procedure of choice is colonscopy. The bowel is cleansed with an oral isosmotic electrolyte solution to allow good visualization of the mucosal surface. If a bleeding lesion is identified, appropriate therapy can be undertaken. If colonoscopy is negative, upper tract endoscopy should be considered.

There has been reluctance by some physicians to perform colonoscopy in the setting of acute bleeding due to the belief that the presence of clotted blood and stool may make colonoscopic examination difficult and even dangerous. This reluctance has recently been challenged by investigators reporting that urgent colonoscopy was useful for detecting active bleeding sites in as many as 90% of cases. It is essential to avoid overdistention of bowel, as well as oversedation of the patient. The procedure is technically challenging and best performed by experienced endoscopists who are familiar with the use of a variety of transendoscopic devices. It can also be performed at the bedside, obviating the need for patient transport. The availability of isosmotic electrolyte solutions capable of rapidly purging the bowel has greatly enhanced the opportunity for performing urgent colonoscopy.

Scintigraphy. Patients with continued slow, but active intestinal bleeding should undergo scintigraphy, with injection of technetium-99m-labeled red blood cells. Although scintigraphy is not as precise as angiography in identifying the site of bleeding it is safer and more sensitive. Scintigraphy can reliably detect active bleeding at rates as low as 0.1 mL/min: with repeated scanning, bleeding sites are identifiable up to 24 hours later, although the false-positive cases increase with the duration of the test (Figure 19–4–1A,B). Bleeding sites in the hepatic and splenic flexures (see Color Plates 19–4–1C, D after page 1546) can sometimes be diagnosed specifically, because technetium is not readily cleared from these areas as is sulfur colloid. It is often used as a screening test prior to attempted angiography.

Angiography. Angiography is the most often used procedure with moderately severe to very severe active bleeding in a hemodynamically stable patient. Flush aortograms have not proven helpful; the initial study, therefore, should be selective superior mesenteric artery angiography. (It is performed first because this artery supplies the entire small bowel and right colon.) Fifty to eighty percent of diverticular bleeding and all

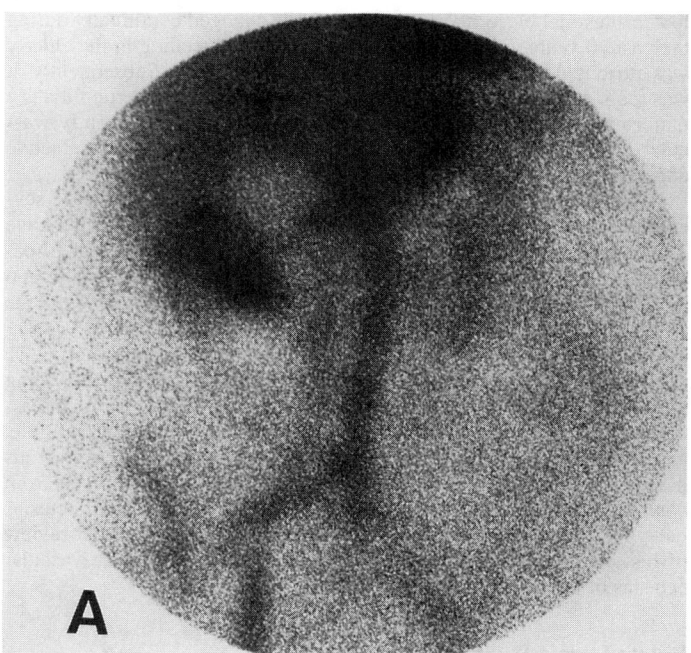 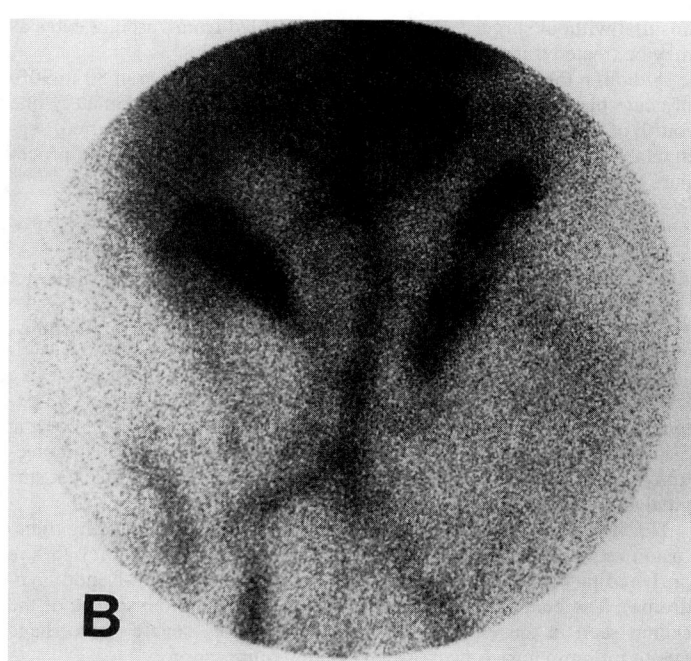

Figure 19–4–1. A,B. Technetium-99m-labeled red cell scan. Anterior views at 5 minutes (A) and 15 minutes (B), showing bleeding diverticulum localized to hepatic flexure.

bleeding from angiographically proved vascular ectasis occur in colon supplied by the superior mesenteric artery. If superior mesenteric angiography is negative, inferior mesenteric artery and celiac axis studies are performed next, in that order.

Exploratory Laparotomy. Patients in whom persistent bleeding occurs, but in whom a workup is unable to reveal a definitive bleeding site, are candidates for exploratory laparotomy with intraoperative small bowel endoscopy. Newer enteroscopes are being developed to more effectively examine the small intestine but are not available at most hospitals.

Barium Contrast Studies. Barium contrast studies of the colon and/or small intestine have a limited role in the management of active lower gastrointestinal bleeding and should not be done until it is apparent that active bleeding has stopped for at least 48 hours. Barium contrast studies may hinder subsequent performance of colonoscopy or angiography and are incapable of detecting vascular anomalies.

Enteroclysis. Enteroclysis instills barium via a tube passed into the duodenum. It is better at demonstrating intraluminal pathology than routine small bowel series but incapable of diagnosing angiodysplasias. Meckel's diverticulum should be considered in cases of painless massive rectal bleeding, especially in young patients. Enteroclysis provides more positive results than standard small bowel series. Approximately, 50 to 60% of Meckel's diverticula contain ectopic gastric mucosa, enabling detection via technetium-99m pertechnetate scan. The success of this method is limited during active bleeding. Angiography has also been used to visualize a bleeding Meckel's diverticulum.

Recommended Approaches

Colonoscopy is the preferred approach to diagnosis of lower intestinal bleeding in most situations. An attempt at colonoscopy should precede other diagnostic testing in almost all circumstances. If colonoscopy is technically not possible due to rapidity of bleeding, angiography is useful for diagnosis; however, success rates are lower for slow or intermittent bleeding. If neither procedure provides a diagnosis then upper endoscopy (to exclude upper tract pathology), small bowel enteroscopy, as well as exploratory laparotomy with intraoperative endoscopy, can be attempted to exclude small bowel lesions.

Nuclear studies have a limited role for specific diagnosis, in that a suspected area of bleeding will be inferred, but a specific lesion will not be identified.

Therapeutic

Therapeutic Options

Because most bleeding stops spontaneously supportive care is all that is required in most cases. Severe episodes mandate resuscitation with intravenous fluids and/or blood products, and a coagulation profile must be obtained and corrected promptly if necessary.

Colonoscopy is often the preferred approach to diagnosis and may enable treatment in many situations. Transendoscopic treatments include polypectomy, fulguration with bipolar electrode, heater probe or laser photocoagulation, and injection sclerotherapy. Lesions particularly amenable to transendoscopic treatment are polyps, vascular ectasia, radiation proctitis, and bleeding polyp stalks. There have been reports of successful cauterization of vessels within bleeding diverticula but this has not been generally feasible. Hemorrhoids rarely bleed severely enough to require therapy. If one elects treatment then dietary measures, cryodestruction, rubber band ligation, and thermal coagulation may be offered as in-office procedures. Surgical hemorrhoidectomy may be more consistently effective in eliminating the problem.

Selective Angiography with Vasopressin Infusion. When angiography shows extravasation of contrast, selective intraarterial vasopression infusion is initiated with an infusion of 0.2 to 0.4 U/min vasopressin for 24 hours, followed by gradual tapering. In 80% of cases, active bleeding from the right colon can be stopped at least temporarily by transcatheter infusion of vasopressin. Because tapering can be associated with rebleeding in up to 60% of patients, stabilization and preparation of the patient for colonoscopy or surgery should occur during vasopressin infusion. When bleeding is from the left colon, intravenous vasopressin appears as effective as an intraarterial infusion. Transcatheter embolization of ectasias has been reported, but should be employed only in desperate situations because of the danger of colonic infarction or delayed stricture formation.

In general, cases of lower intestinal bleeding are less frequently torrential than cases of upper gastrointestinal bleeding. If persistent severe bleeding occurs, emergency surgery is warranted. Because most diverticula do not bleed repeatedly, patients suspect of having had a lower intestinal hemorrhage from a diverticulum can be discharged from the hospital without surgery. Patients who have bled from vascular ectasias may be treated transendoscopically.

Although there is spontaneous cessation of hemorrhage in 80 to 90% of acute bleeding episodes, bleeding is recurrent in approximately one fourth of cases. If the bleeding site has been specifically identified, segmental resection of the involved small or large intestine is the procedure of choice in the following situations:

- Patients who require greater than 6 units of blood, fail a trial of vasopressin, or develop rebleeding during hospitalization
- When therapeutic endoscopists are not available, or ablation is not feasible because of the size or number of lesions
- When ectasias have been identified via colonoscopy or angiography, but endoscopic ablation has been unsuccessful

The presence of diverticula in the left colon should not alter the extent of resection. Even with a definitive diagnosis of right colonic bleeding, there is a 20% chance of rebleeding after right hemicolectomy. When a colonic bleeding site has not been localized, the best surgical approach is subtotal colectomy and ileoproctostomy.

Hormonal therapy (Enovid) appears to be effective in reducing transfusion requirements for angiodysplasias in patients with kidney failure or hereditary hemorrhagic telangiectasia (Osler–Weber–Rendu syndrome). The benefit of estrogens is less clear for angiodysplasia of the cecum seen in the elderly. Although uncommon, severe hemorrhage due to inflammatory bowel disease often requires surgery.

Recommended Approach

In patients with acute persistent lower intestinal bleeding, oral purging followed by an attempt at therapeutic colonoscopy with transendoscopic treatment is the preferred approach as a definitive diagnosis may be made in 70 to 90% of cases and many patients can be treated transendoscopically (see color plates 19–4–2 A and B).

Colonic neoplasms are treated with polypectomy or biopsy followed by surgery as warranted. Electrocoagulation with a BICAP probe or coagulation with a heater probe is well suited to treatment of bleeding vascular ectasias (Figure 19–4–2B). Laser photocoagulation with either Nd:YAG or argon lasers is quite effective although less convenient for intensive care units or emergency treatments. Patients with numerous vascular lesions may be stabilized and surgery may become elective rather than emergent. When hemorrhage is massive and colonoscopy is not feasible or is nondiagnostic, then angiography with vasopressin infusion becomes the next procedure for therapy of lower intestinal bleeding.

Surgery is reserved for lesions not treatable by endoscopic methods or persistently bleeding despite angiographic therapy.

FOLLOW-UP

Patients found to have specific disorders responsible for their initial bleeding episode (infectious colitis, inflammatory bowel disease, adenomatous polyps, hemorrhoids, colon cancer) are treated and followed up accordingly. In those treated transendoscopically for bleeding angiodysplasia and stabilized, interval endoscopic retreatment may be warranted unless severe anemia and persistent transfusion requirements make right hemicolectomy preferable.

All patients should be advised to have prompt reevaluation in the emergency department if recurrent episodes of hematochezia or melena are noted in conjunction with symptoms of weakness, palpitations, or syncope. Patients without previously identified bleeding sites should have angiography as the initial study to localize the site of bleeding. An exception to this approach might be prior inability to complete a full colonoscopy examination to rule out subtle abnormalities such as vascular ectasias, strong suspicion of worsening inflammatory bowel disease, or a new onset of ischemic colitis as the cause of recurrent bleeding.

DISCUSSION
Prevalence and Incidence

Diverticula, polyps, vascular ectasias, and hemorrhoids are often identified in the absence of active bleeding. Our conceptions of the causes of lower intestinal bleeding in the elderly have changed continually during the past 70 years. Initially, most lower intestinal bleeding in the elderly was attributed to neoplasms and, later, to diverticulitis. Subsequently, it was realized that diverticulosis without accompanying diverticulitis is a major cause of lower gastrointestinal hemorrhage. More recently, vascular ectasias were found to be the most frequent cause via selective angiography.

Diverticula are present in more than 50% of individuals by the seventh decade of life; less than 5% of those patients with diverticula have a major bleeding episode. Most cases of severe bleeding occur in patients over 60 years of age, and it appears that diverticular disease and arteriovenous malformation account for approximately two thirds of the major episodes of lower intestinal bleeding.

Vascular ectasias (angiodysplasia) are found in approximately 25% of asymptomatic elderly individuals, with two thirds of patients being over 70 years old. They are located predominantly in the cecum and ascending colon, are less than 5 mm in diameter, are frequently multiple, and are not associated with other vascular lesions of the skin or mucous membranes. In approximately 10 to 15% of subjects who bleed from vascular ectasias, the presentation is severe bleeding. Vascular ectasias have been reported in the small bowel and in the left colon, but review of histology showed changes different from those seen with vascular ectasias of the right colon.

Related Basic Science

In diverticular disease, bleeding occurs when a vasa recta artery penetrates obliquely through the colonic wall. Bleeding is more common from right-sided than left-sided diverticula; however, whether patients bleed from the right or left colon, bleeding ceases and does not recur in approximately 75 to 80% of cases. Bleeding from angiodysplasia is usually subacute and recurrent, although presentation with massive hemorrhage can occur.

An individual patient may have bright red blood, maroon stools, or even melena, on separate occasions. An association between bleeding ectasias and cardiac disease has been reported, with an approximate 25% incidence of aortic stenosis found in such patients. This association has been contradicted by others who report continued bleeding even after aortic valve surgery. Boley and co-workers have advanced a theory as to why angiodysplasias of the colon are seen predominantly in the cecum. They theorize that repeated episodes of colonic distention are associated with transient increases in both luminal pressure and size, resulting in multiple episodes of increased wall tension with obstruction of submucosal venous outflow, especially where these vessels pierce the muscle layers of the colon. Ultimately, the capillary rings dilate, the precapillary sphincters lose their competency, and a small arteriovenous communication forms, which is responsible for the characteristic "early filling vein" seen on angiography in patients with vascular ectasias.

Colonic ischemia is noted in elderly patients often without major vessel occlusion. Symptoms of colonic ischemia often include abdominal pain and bloody diarrhea. Chronic colonic ischemia may lead to stricture formation in approximately one fifth of cases.

Inflammatory bowel disease occurs predominantly in the young, but elderly patients can develop ulcerative colitis or Crohn's disease. These entities may be difficult to distinguish from ischemia, and sometimes both conditions may coexist. Infectious colitis can be difficult to distinguish from inflammatory bowel disease, particularly when caused by *Salmonella* or *Escherichia coli* 0157:H7. The latter agent, in particular, can present with severe hemorrhagic colitis, and endoscopic features may be indistinguishable from those of inflammatory bowel disease. Bleeding is also seen with chronic radiation injury, particularly after exposure to more than 4000 rad. This late manifestation of radiation therapy occurs 6 to 18 months after completion of therapy, and is due to tissue ischemia.

Chronic radiation injury causes a progressive obliterative endarteritis and leads to fibrosis, ulceration, and mucosal fissuring. Medical treatment of radiation proctocolitis, including oral sulfasalazine and both oral and topical steroids, was of inconsistent value. Endoscopic laser therapy, with both Nd:YAG and argon lasers, has been reported as useful in decreasing chronic bleeding and lessening the need for transfusions. Less common sites of bleeding include postpolypectomy stumps, colonic varices, and stercoral ulcers.

Other causes of hemorrhage include small bowel lesions and Meckel's diverticulum (seen on rare occasion in adults). When Meckel's diverticulum presents with bleeding, it is felt to be a consequence of peptic ulceration of intestinal mucosa adjacent to ectopic gastric mucosa present within the diverticulum. Bleeding tends to be fairly copious and the stools are intermediate in appearance between the bright red blood of colon lesions and melena most commonly seen with upper tract bleeding. The treatment of a bleeding Meckel's diverticulum is excision.

Natural History and Its Modification with Treatment

If a patient is resuscitated after a prolonged shock state there may be residual neurologic, cardiac, respiratory, or gastrointestinal dysfunction. Fortunately, however, most episodes stop spontaneously after mild bleeding. Emergency surgery places an elderly patient with massive bleeding at increased risk for complications or death. When no source of bleeding is found, it is essential that the patient return at the onset of a recurrent hemorrhage so that angiography can be done to localize the site of the bleeding lesion.

Emergency colonoscopy following oral purge has been increasingly advocated, allowing for a more effective and safer colonoscopy with a high degree of effectiveness at arriving at a prompt diagnosis. Sometimes the results of urgent colonoscopy with transendoscopic therapy obviate the need for emergency surgery or allow surgery to be done on an elective basis. When surgery is required urgent colonoscopy may assist surgeons in planning the procedure and shortening operative time. This results because extra surgical time is not required for a diagnosis, and the resection may become segmental or limited rather than radical or extensive.

Prevention

Although few preventive measures are available for bleeding lesions, electrocoagulation of arteriovenous malformations and endoscopic removal and/or ablation of polyps may reduce the frequency of acute hemorrhage. Increasing dietary fiber is advocated to decrease the rate of diverticulum formation, despite the lack of adequate clinical trials. The treatment of hemorrhoids responsible for bleeding using injection sclerotherapy, banding, and infrared coagulation has been advocated; however, efficacy of hemorrhoidal treatments remains to be established.

Cost Containment

Rapid evaluation and treatment of bleeding reduce the costs associated with intensive care unit monitoring and blood transfusions and lessen the need for emergency surgery. New avenues for potential endoscopic treatment of lower gastrointestinal bleeding lesions may offer an opportunity for improved outcomes and reduction in costs.

REFERENCES

Boley SJ, Sammartano RJ, Adams A, et al. On the nature and etiology of vascular ectasias of the colon: Degenerative lesions of aging. Gastroenterology 1977:72:650.

De Markless MP, Murphy JR. Acute lower gastrointestinal bleeding. Med Clin North Am 1993;77:1085.

Dusold R, Burke K, Carpenter W, et al. The accuracy of 99m technetium-labelled red cell scintigraphy in localizing gastrointestinal bleeding. Am J Gastroenterol 1994:89:345.

Jensen DM, Machicado GA. Management of severe lower gastrointestinal bleeding. In: Barkin J, O'Phelan CA, eds. Advanced therapeutic endoscopy. 2nd ed. New York: Raven Press, 1994:201.

Miller LS, Barbarevech C, Friedman L. Less frequent causes of lower gastrointestinal bleeding. Gastroenterol Clin North Am 1994;23:1:21.

Reinus JF, Brandt LJ. Vascular ectasias and diverticulosis: Common causes of lower intestinal bleeding. Gastroenterol Clin North Am 1994:23:1.

CHAPTER 19–5

Occult Gastrointestinal Bleeding

Arthur Boshnack, M.D., and Michael Orenstein, M.D.

DEFINITION

Occult gastrointestinal bleeding refers to the presence of gastrointestinal blood loss that is not apparent to the physician or the patient. Blood loss is detected as a result of stool testing for chemical evidence of blood or heme by laboratory techniques. Observation of iron deficiency anemia may also indicate blood loss into the digestive tract.

ETIOLOGY

The detection of occult gastrointestinal bleeding is characterized by blood loss into the digestive tract and detected when Hemoccult testing is performed as part of the rectal examination or occult blood screening of spontaneously passed stools. Usually, there are no specific symptoms referable to the gastrointestinal tract or to the bleeding itself, hence the word *occult*. The cause of occult gastrointestinal bleeding is important because it may indicate asymptomatic neoplasia in the absence of visible bleeding. The causes of *overt* gastrointestinal bleeding can also lead to occult gastrointestinal bleeding.

CRITERIA FOR DIAGNOSIS
Suggestive

Fecal occult blood testing has a role in early detection of large bowel cancers. Occult gastrointestinal bleeding may be detected by a positive fecal occult blood test or by observation of iron deficiency anemia due to gastrointestinal bleeding. The latter must be distinguished from hypochromic microcytic anemia due to nongastrointestinal hemorrhage, iron malabsorption, or inadequate iron ingestion. Anemias with similar morphologic abnormalities of red blood cells may be secondary to chronic disease, thalassemia, or sideroblastic anemia. These can be distinguished from iron deficiency anemia by measurement of total iron level, iron binding capacity, ferritin levels, and hemoglobin electrophoresis in the serum.

Definitive

Occult blood in the stool can be detected with or without iron deficiency anemia using a variety of fecal occult blood tests. Fecal blood loss in excess of 20 mL per day is needed to register consistently positive Hemoccult reactions. The most widely used test is the guaiac test. The current recommended screening procedure for colorectal neoplasia requires sample of three spontaneously passed stools twice, for a total of six potential reactions. The stool is collected by the patient and mailed to the physician. Some investigators advocate rehydration of the stool specimen to enhance sensitivity; however, rehydration of the stool specimen seems also to increase the rate of false-positive test results. Physician testing of the stool specimen obtained in the office on the gloved finger yields a specimen that has less predictive value than the six spontaneous specimens described above, but the compliance rate is inherently higher. The value of screening with digitally obtained specimens is the subject of some debate because of potential anorectal contamination, but is supported by most physicians and should be performed in the evaluation of patients with digestive symptoms or iron deficiency anemia.

CLINICAL MANIFESTATIONS

Subjective

Patients with occult gastrointestinal bleeding are often asymptomatic. Anorexia, weight loss, and abdominal pain, as well as changes in bowel habits, are suggestive of an advanced disease state such as gastrointestinal malignancy. Anemia could lead to symptoms such as weakness, anorexia, and exertional dyspnea. Increased physiologic blood loss is observed in long-distance runners. One must identify medications that may exacerbate gastrointestinal bleeding, such as coumadin and heparin. Physiologic blood loss does not appear to increase with anticoagulation therapy when the prothrombin time is controlled at usual therapeutic levels. If fecal occult blood loss is detected, pathologic explanation is usually identified in these patients. If prothrombin times are markedly elevated (> 2.5 times normal), clinical and occult bleeding may occur without a detectable abnormality.

Patients with family cancer syndrome, familial polyposis, first-degree relatives with colon cancer, or hereditary telangiectasias (Osler–Weber–Rendu syndrome) are at increased risk for occult gastrointestinal bleeding. Hemoccult-positive stool should not be attributed to supplemental iron or nonsteroidal drug therapy. It is recommended that patients stop using all nonsteroidal drugs prior to the screening for colorectal neoplasia. Ascorbic acid (vitamin C) taken orally can act as an antioxidant and produce a false-negative fecal occult blood test. A history of liver disease and portal hypertension should alert the physician to the possibility of esophageal and gastric varices, congestive gastropathy, or mesenteric varices. Abdominal pain may indicate mesenteric ischemia, peptic disease, or Crohn's disease. Amebic colitis can be found in homosexual men and from endemic areas in South America and Asia. *Strongyloides* is an occasional cause of chronic blood loss in other parts of the world.

Objective

Physical Examination

Except for the rectal examination the physical examination commonly reveals no abnormality. The rectal examination itself may reveal no abnormalities, but a sample of stool can be obtained and tested for blood.

Rectal examination may, of course, detect hemorrhoids, a polyp, or a mass suggestive of malignancy.

The vascular lesions of hereditary hemorrhagic telangiectasia are usually present on the face and oropharyngeal mucosa. Skin lesions of the blue rubber bleb syndrome and acquired telangiectasias of CREST (calcinosis, Raynaud's phenomenon, esophageal dysmotility, sclerodactylia, telangiectasia) syndrome are similarly located. Pigmented macular lesions of the lips, hands, and feet suggest chronic blood loss from Peutz–Jeghers hamartomas anywhere in the gut. Pigmented velvety plaques in the axilla or groin (acanthosis nigricans) may herald adenocarcinoma, most frequently in a hollow viscus. The presence of jaundice, spider nevi, or hepatosplenomegaly may suggest portal hypertension due to chronic liver disease. Aortic stenosis on auscultation increases the possibility of cecal angiodysplasias.

Routine Laboratory Abnormalities

It is important for the physician to realize that a positive Hemoccult test is as likely, or even more likely, to be due to bleeding from a colonic neoplasm than to be caused by consumption of red meat. There is a considerable risk of obtaining a false-negative test on the second occasion because of intermittent bleeding from a neoplasm or uneven distribution of blood in the stool sample. Discovery of iron deficiency anemia should prompt a workup for occult gastrointestinal blood loss and should not necessarily be attributed to dietary factors. Typically, iron deficiency anemia is characterized by low iron saturation (<12%), elevated total iron binding capacity, and low ferritin levels.

PLANS

Diagnostic

Differential Diagnosis

The goal of occult blood testing is to identify asymptomatic colorectal neoplasms (precarcinomatous polyps and malignancies). Hemoccult testing has a low sensitivity because the test is positive in only half of those with colorectal neoplasms. The specificity of the Hemoccult test for occult blood is fairly high when performed properly. Patients without gastrointestinal disease rarely have a positive test if one eliminates nonsteroidal antiinflammatory drug use and ingestion of meat fibers for 48 hours prior to testing. The predictive value of a positive Hemoccult test for colorectal cancer is between 5 and 10%. Benign colorectal neoplasms (polyps) are detected in approximately 20% of people with positive Hemoccult tests, depending on the intensity of subsequent investigation. Only about one third of patients with positive fecal occult blood testing found by routine screening programs have significant colorectal neoplasia. Most malignant neoplasms detected by colorectal screening programs using guaiac tests are found at an earlier Duke's stage than are observed in unscreened populations. Other neoplastic causes of occult bleeding include gastric cancer, mesenchymal tumors, lymphoma, and metastases to the gastrointestinal tract. A not uncommon cause of Hemoccult-positive stools is vascular abnormalities of the digestive tract. Angiodysplasias occur in 0.2 to 2% of adults over age 50. Other vascular abnormalities include hereditary hemorrhagic telangiectasia, portal hypertensive congestive gastropathy, watermelon stomach, and CREST syndrome. Inflammatory conditions such as Crohn's disease, ulcerative colitis, Meckel's diverticulum, celiac sprue, and eosinophilic gastroenteritis should be included in the differential diagnosis. The most common upper gastrointestinal cause of occult gastrointestinal bleeding in patients with iron deficiency is peptic ulceration. Tests for occult bleeding are less sensitive for bleeding from the upper gastrointestinal tract which may be diluted, digested, and degraded. Bleeding from the upper gastrointestinal tract is usually brisk, but because of the high prevalence of acid–peptic disease, some cases of occult bleeding and iron deficiency may develop. Benign mucosal erosions, include esophagitis (peptic reflux, Barrett's esophagus, pill esophagitis), gastritis including postgastrectomy, stomatitis, bile reflux gastritis, antral antritis, and nonsteroidal antiinflammatory drug-induced mucosal injury, are also to be considered. Less common causes are infections, including hookworm, *Ascaris,* amoeba, *Strongyloides,* and tuberculosis. Amyloidosis, blue rubber bleb syndrome, Whipple's disease, radiation-induced mucosal injury, and Henoch–Schönlein purpura are unusual causes of occult gastrointestinal bleeding.

Confounding nongastrointestinal causes include false positivity, that is, nonspecific test positivity which can be secondary to nasooropharyngeal bleeding, hemoptysis, and menstrual bleeding.

Diagnostic Options

Colonoscopy provides the best diagnostic test for colonic lesions (benign, malignant, and vascular) because direct endoscopic visualization enables the therapeutic options of biopsy, polypectomy, and cauterization. Flexible sigmoidoscopy with complementary air-contrast barium enema is an alternative, but endoscopy is more sensitive and specific than barium studies. If study of the lower gastrointestinal tract is negative, then upper endoscopy would be useful, even in the absence of any specific upper gastrointestinal symptoms. An upper gastrointestinal series again may miss some bleeding lesions more easily seen on endoscopy. If the upper and lower gastrointestinal tract workup is negative, evaluation of the small intestine by small bowel series has a 5% yield. Enteroclysis by double-contrast technique can increase the yield to 10%. This study occasionally reveals inflammatory bowel disease, small bowel tumors that would be more common than angiodysplasias in patients under 50 years old. Small bowel endoscopy (enteroscopy) has become the preferred method for evaluating the small bowel and should be considered in selected patients with repeated Hemoccult-positive stools or severe anemia. A radionuclide pertechnetate scan for detection of Meckel's diverticulum can be done. Angiography for evaluation of angiodysplasia is part of the diagnostic regimen but has a low yield. Nuclear bleeding scans and angiography are rarely used if the patient is not actively bleeding.

Recommended Approach

The patient with symptoms and gastrointestinal bleeding should undergo investigation directed toward those symptoms. For example, a patient who is identified as having peptic ulcer (by endoscopy) and compatible symptoms may not require colonoscopy.

In the absence of symptoms, evaluation of occult gastrointestinal bleeding should begin with an investigation of the lower gastrointestinal tract. Asymptomatic patients, particularly those who are elderly, should undergo colonoscopy, as they have an increased risk of colorectal neoplasia. If colonoscopy is negative, then esophagogastroduodenoscopy should be performed.

Barium enema and upper gastrointestinal series are less sensitive than endoscopy and do not offer the therapeutic options. Push enteroscopy offers therapeutic capability to the small bowel. A small bowel series should be considered if enteroscopy is not available.

Therapeutic

Therapeutic Options

In general, treatment of occult gastrointestinal bleeding must be tailored to the cause. If a polyp is found during the diagnostic workup, then endoscopic or surgical removal can be performed. Management of colon carcinoma is determined by the stage and clinical setting. Vascular lesions such as angiodysplasias may be amenable to endoscopic therapy (heater probe, bipolar electrode, or laser photocoagulation). Ulcer disease can be managed with antiulcer therapy with H_2-antagonists and/or antibiotics directed at *Helicobacter pylori* or, if symptoms persist, surgery. Nonsteroidal antiinflammatory drugs should be discontinued when possible. Exploratory surgery may be advocated in patients younger than 50 who have obscure bleeding in whom small bowel tumors and Meckel's diverticulum are most likely. The more widely used, push-type enteroscope can be advanced 80 to 120 cm beyond the ligament of Treitz and have therapeutic capability. The Sonde enteroscope, propelled through the intestine by peristalsis, has no biopsy or therapeutic capability. Hormonal therapy (Enovid) appears to be effective in reducing transfusion requirements for angiodysplasias in patients with kidney failure or Osler–Weber–Rendu syndrome.

If iron deficiency anemia is associated, treatment with iron is appropriate. Significant blood loss can be treated with blood transfusions.

Recommended Approach

Colonoscopy is the recommended approach for lower gastrointestinal lesions that are amenable to this technique. Colonic neoplasia is treated with colonoscopic polypectomy and biopsy. Fulguration with bipolar electrode, heater probe, or laser photocoagulation is effective for bleeding vascular lesions. Surgery is reserved for lesions not treatable by endoscopic therapy. Peptic ulcer disease is usually treated medically. Iron therapy and transfusions are recommended for patients with anemia in the appropriate clinical setting.

FOLLOW-UP

Follow-up of the patient with occult gastrointestinal bleeding must be tailored to the cause. If an adenomatous polyp or colonic neoplasm is identified, surveillance colonoscopy should be performed at regular intervals. Fecal occult blood testing should be performed annually in normal adults starting at age 50, and digital rectal examination yearly after age 40. Patients with a family history of familial polyposis or Gardner's syndrome, as well as family cancer syndrome, should begin testing at age 20. The annual fecal occult blood screening is performed in conjunction with flexible sigmoidoscopy in patients without risk factors who are age 50. Gastric ulcers require endoscopic follow-up until they are healed, whereas duodenal ulcers do not. Endoscopic therapy for esophageal varices and control of portal hypertension are the focus of treatment for patients with chronic liver disease and occult gastrointestinal bleeding. In a patient with occult blood loss without a clear etiology, periodic reevaluation is indicated if the occult blood loss continues. It is important to verify that the proper dietary and drug restrictions have been followed for 48 to 72 hours prior to the occult blood testing.

DISCUSSION

Prevalence and Incidence

The prevalence of occult gastrointestinal bleeding increases with increasing age, as does the prevalence of colorectal malignancy beginning at age 40.

The predictive value of a positive Hemoccult test for colorectal cancer is about 5 to 10%. Benign colorectal neoplasms are detected in approximately 20% of patients who undergo intensive evaluation. As mentioned earlier, about one third of patients with Hemoccult-positive stools have significant colorectal neoplasia.

Related Basic Science

Many commercial guaiac tests are available. This is based on the reaction that occurs when phenolic compound in the guaiac is oxidized to a blue quinone. The reaction is facilitated by hydrogen peroxide. The most commonly used test for occult blood testing performed at the time of physical examination is the Hemoccult II card (Smith–Kline Diagnostics, Sunnyvale, CA). Testing (often at home) of three consecutive stools, each with Hemoccult smears from two different areas of the stool, is the most commonly used method to increase sensitivity. A low sensitivity of 50 to 65% may be increased at the expense of decreased specificity by rehydration of the Hemoccult slides. Rehydration results in lysis of the red blood cells and dissolution of hemoglobin; however, rehydration of the stool specimen seems also to increase the rate of false-positive results. Elimination of meat in the diet for 48 hours prior to occult blood testing increases specificity. Uncooked peroxidase-rich plant food (raw turnips, radishes, or broccoli) sometimes produces false-positive results. This is of relatively minor importance.

Commercial immunochemical tests are now available that do not require a special diet and are not affected by medication. Most of these tests are more sensitive than the guaiac test. Immunochemical tests use antibodies against the globin moiety of human hemoglobin. The heme–porphyrin assay (Hemoquant) is a precise biochemical assay of heme and its porphyrin degradation products; however, if it is used as a screening test, patients would have to follow a strict no-red-meat diet and avoid aspirin and other nonsteroidal antiinflammatory drugs. Hemoquant is more expensive than guaiac and immunochemical tests. Hemoquant appears to be more sensitive than Hemoccult testing for occult blood in the stool. Normal fecal occult blood loss is less than 2 mL per day. Fecal blood loss greater than 20 mL per day is needed for regularly positive Hemoccult test. Hemoquant detects half this amount. At this point, Hemoquant is useful for investigation of unexplained iron deficiency anemia but may not be an appropriate method for routine screening of colorectal cancer.

Natural History and Its Modification with Treatment

The natural history of occult gastrointestinal bleeding generally follows the cause of the disease responsible for it. Mandel et al. (1993) demonstrated that annual fecal occult blood testing with rehdyration of the samples decreased 13-year cumulative mortality from colorectal cancer by 33%. Polyps can be detected before they become malignancies. Colorectal malignancies can be resected at an earlier, more manageable stage. This would then be associated with an improved patient survival.

Prevention

The prevention of occult gastrointestinal bleeding is related to the prevention of the underlying cause. As an example, aspirin-induced gastritis can be prevented by avoidance of aspirin ingestion. Adenomatous polyps are found more commonly than cancers in patients who have positive screening tests. The removal of these adenomas will, no doubt, increase the benefit of screening further by reducing the incidence and mortality of later colorectal cancer.

Cost Containment

The cost effectiveness of fecal occult testing is not established and should be weighed against the benefit of reduction in mortality from colorectal cancer. It is important for Hemoccult testing to be performed in the proper manner, with appropriate dietary and medication restrictions. In the diagnostic workup of a positive test for occult blood, colonoscopy and upper endoscopy are more sensitive and specific and may be more cost effective than barium studies. The endoscopic procedures allow for the use of therapeutic measures such as polypectomy and cautery to treat the underlying bleeding lesions. The current screening guidelines recommend that average-risk men and women over age 50 should undergo annual fecal occult blood testing and flexible sigmoidoscopy every 3 to 5 years.

REFERENCES

Eisner MS, Lewis JH. Diagnostic yield of a positive fecal occult blood test found on digital rectal examination: Does the finger count? *Arch Intern Med* 1991;151:2180.

Friedman LS, guest ed. Occult gastrointestinal bleeding. *Gastroenterol Clin North Am* 1994;23:53.

Mandel JS, Bond JH, Church TR, et al. Reducing mortality from colorectal cancer by screening for fecal occult blood. *N Engl J Med* 1993;328:1365.

Rockey DC, Cello JP. Evaluation of the gastrointestinal tract in patients with iron deficiency anemia. *N Engl J Med* 1993;329:1691.

Sugawa C. Gastrointestinal bleeding. Tokyo: Igaku-Shoin, 1992.

CHAPTER 19-6

Chronic Constipation

Hulya Levendoglu, M.D.

DEFINITION

Constipation is not an easily defined disorder. It is generally agreed that in men, more than two to three stools, and in women, three or four stools per week are normal. Stool frequency less than this number is considered constipation. Most patients and physicians in their definition of constipation also include the consistency of stool, ease of stool passage, and feeling of relief after defecation.

ETIOLOGY

Decreased colonic propulsive motor function due to drugs; metabolic, endocrine, psychogenic, and neuromuscular causes; and obstruction at the level of rectosigmoid colon and anal canal due to inflammation, neoplastic factors, and mucosal prolapse are the major etiologic factors. In rare instances failure of relaxation of anal sphincters and very high anal canal pressures are the reason for constipation. In most patients, however, the cause of constipation is not clearly elucidated.

CRITERIA FOR DIAGNOSIS

A commonly used definition for constipation is fewer than three spontaneous bowel movements per week; however, many patients who do not meet this criterion are clearly constipated. Some patients who have fewer than three bowel movements per week feel perfectly fine. Desiccated, hard, difficult-to-pass feces are most often included in the patients' complaints whether transit time in the colon is normal, accelerated, or delayed.

CLINICAL MANIFESTATIONS

Subjective

Patients with constipation complain of a decreased number of stools and difficult passage of hard stools. In slow transit constipation, symptoms are generally present for years and are initiated in early childhood. A family history of constipation is present in about half of the children referred for evaluation for constipation, which may be indicative of underlying genetic predisposition. In about 20% of these children identifiable psychological difficulties are found. Fecal soiling frequently accompanies constipation in this age group.

In young females symptoms generally start without any preceding event; however, in some patients abdominal and pelvic operations mark the onset of constipation. The interval between bowel movements steadily increases over several years until patients are unable to pass stools without the aid of laxatives.

In many elderly patients immobility is the causative factor. Elderly patients who are confined to bed rely on another person for defecation. If the urge to defecate passes, the rectum distends gradually and retains larger-than-normal volumes of stools. Consequently rectal stretch receptors loose their sensitivity, and the result is a diminution in the urge to defecate.

In a small group of patients, constipation may be caused by decreased colonic motor activity (colonic inertia) due to medications, endocrine and other metabolic factors, or neuromuscular disorders. Partial intestinal obstruction at the level of the sigmoid colon and anal canal from benign or malignant causes also may present with constipation. Symptoms of these associated conditions are present in addition to the constipation.

Constipation may be associated with abdominal pain and distention and may sometimes alternate with episodes of diarrhea. In these patients it is a part of the symptom complex irritable bowel syndrome. In such patients colonic transit is generally normal.

Constipation in a small group of patient is due to a disordered defecatory process. This may include failure of relaxation or paradoxical contraction of pelvic floor muscles, failure of relaxation of the internal anal sphincter, disturbed rectal sensory function requiring very large volumes for rectal distention to induce rectal sensation, increased pressure in the anal canal, or obstructing mucosal lesions. The following clinical conditions are associated with these factors: paradoxical contraction of the pelvic floor, descending perineum syndrome, Hirschsprung's disease, occult or complete rectal prolapse, rectocele, and solitary rectal ulcer syndrome.

Objective

Physical Examination

A digital rectal examination may reveal obstructing lesions, fissures, rectocele, or internally prolapsing mucosa. Presence or absence of stool helps in differentiating the cause of constipation. Muscular function can be assessed by asking the patient to squeeze and bear down (pseudodefecation). Anterior movement of the puborectalis with pseudodefecation indicates improper muscular coordination of the pelvic floor resulting in paradoxical contraction. Perianal sensation should be intact and the cutaneous external anal sphincter reflex (anal wink) should be evident. Intact reflex suggests that activation of the sigmoid colon by muscular activity of the pelvic floor is possible. A tender sigmoid colon may be felt in the left lower quadrant. Tympany may be noted throughout the colon.

Routine Laboratory Abnormalities

There are no diagnostic abnormalities in the routine laboratory examination.

PLANS

Diagnostic

A diagnostic workup is required in patients who have bowel movements once in 5 days or less if their symptoms persist longer than 18 months. A workup is also required if there is a recent change in bowel habits from normal to difficult evacuation. If the history is reliable, the plain radiograph of the abdomen generally shows large amounts of retained stool.

Routine blood tests should be obtained to detect any electrolyte abnormality (hypokalemia, hypo- and hypercalcemia, hypomagnesemia). Hypothyroidism should be ruled out. Systemic diseases should be considered and excluded. The patient's medication list should be reviewed, as many medications, including iron supplements, antihypertensive drugs, antidepressants, and pain medications, can cause constipation. When the diagnosis of idiopathic chronic constipation is considered, a radiopaque marker colonic transit study, anoscopy, anorectal manometry, rectal balloon expulsion test, defecography, and anal sphincter electromyography may be necessary to fully delineate the problem. Full-thickness rectal biopsy is necessary to exclude Hirschsprung's disease. Most patients require a barium enema and sigmoidoscopy to exclude obstructing lesions and to evaluate the colonic mucosa. Rectal biopsy during sigmoidoscopy may be necessary to rule out proctitis (ischemic or inflammatory) and solitary rectal ulcer syndrome.

A radiopaque marker study is a very useful diagnostic test although it is frequently underused. Abdominal films are taken after ingestion of a capsule containing a radiopaque marker. Eighty percent of the marker normally passes within 5 days and all of it is excreted by the seventh day. A wide distribution of marker suggests colonic hypomotility (colonic inertia), whereas accummulation of marker in the rectosigmoid implies an anorectal problem (i.e., outlet obstruction).

Anorectal manometry assesses baseline anal sphincter pressure, rectal sensation, and internal anal sphincter relaxation. It can also predict spinal cord or sacral nerve root injury. Both anal manometry and anal electromyography are excellent to show paradoxical pelvic floor contraction.

Defecography assesses defecation radiologically. The position of the anorectal angle can be assessed, and internal rectal prolapse, rectocele, and enterocele can be diagnosed. Normal individuals can expell a 50-cc balloon inserted into the rectum. In patients with pelvic floor dysfunction the 50-cc water-filled balloon cannot be evacuated spontaneously. Pulling with weight is needed on the opposite end to facilitate its passage.

Therapeutic

Symptomatic treatment of constipation starts with an exercise program to stimulate intestinal activity and to strengthen abdominal and pelvic muscles. Situps and straight-leg-raising exercises are helpful. Daily walks are to be encouraged. Adequate fluid and fiber intake is essential to fill the colon and stimulate motility. Bulk laxatives are helpful in addition to high-fiber diets especially in patients with small and hard stools. Generally, 10 to 20 g of fiber and 1.5 to 2.0 L of fluid are recommended daily; however, in patients with largely dilated colons and abdominal distention, the preceding regimen may increase gas, bloating, and abdominal distention. In such cases, bowel retraining is started to benefit from the gastroileocolic reflex. Patients are advised to attempt to defecate after a meal, especially after breakfast. For many individuals setting aside a daily toilet time is all that is needed to improve bowel function. If spontaneous defecation is not achieved, a glycerin or bisacodyl suppository is given to initiate evacuation. Meanwhile systemic causes of constipation should be eliminated or treated appropriately. Constipating medications should be discontinued or substituted.

If this regimen does not succeed, stool softeners (Colace, Docusate, Surfak) are started. Lactulose is an effective osmotic cathartic; one to two tablespoons daily produces its laxative effect in 24 to 48 hours. The other colonic stimulants (senna, cascara, and phenolphthalein) are not recommended for daily routine usage because they damage the myenteric plexus ganglion cells and further aggravate constipation. Oil retention enemas have the advantage of softening impactions for easy passage. Soap enemas should not be used because they are irritating and may cause severe colitis.

Patients with severe constipation not responding to medical treatment may be referred to surgery. When pelvic floor function is normal and colonic inertia is the cause of constipation, abdominal colectomy and ileorectal anastomosis have been successful in the majority of pa-

tients. Stool frequency increases and quality of life improves. Although this procedure is also recommended for idiopathic megacolon, some patients develop recurrent severe constipation due to megarectum. Ileoanal anastomosis is recommended for such patients. Patients with anatomic abnormalities such as rectal prolapse, rectocele, descending perineum syndrome, and posterior rectal hernia causing constipation require surgical correction of the anatomic defect. A pull-through operation is needed for treatment of Hirschsprung's disease. Patients with pelvic floor dysfunction but no anatomic abnormality are best treated with biofeedback training of the pelvic floor and relaxation exercises for pelvic floor muscles.

FOLLOW-UP

Follow-up examinations are essential to observe and document the progress. Frequency of follow-up depends on the type of problem. These visits are also important to define the severity of the problem and the need for further adjustments in the dosage and form of medications and also to plan the timing of surgery in selected group of patients.

DISCUSSION
Prevalence and Incidence

Four national surveys in the United States estimated that more than 4 million people complain of constipation (Everhart et al., 1984; Drossman et al., 1982; Sandler and Drossman, 1987; Connell et al., 1965). Therefore, the prevalence is estimated to be about 2%. Nearly half of patients older than 60 complain of reduced frequency of defecation; one fifth report straining, pain, and hard stool; and a third complain of both of these symptoms.

Related Basic Science

Constipation is a disorder of defecation. Understanding the factors that play a role in constipation requires knowledge of the physiology of defecation. The initial step in the normal defecation process is the delivery of stool to the rectum by colonic transit and sigmoid colon contraction. Rectal filling and increased rectal pressure cause internal anal sphincter relaxation (rectoanal inhibitory reflex) and automatic external anal sphincter/puborectalis contraction. If the time and place are not appropriate for defecation, increased external anal sphincter tone and pressure is maintained, which, in turn, inhibits sigmoid colon emptying. If defecation can socially proceed, voluntary external anal sphincter relaxation results in controlled defecation. Generation of an appropriate intrarectal pressure to overcome pressure produced by the anal canal is essential in this final stage of defecation. Any defect in each stage of this physiologic process results in constipation (Table 19–6–1).

Natural History and Its Modification with Treatment

It is likely that constipation due to recognizable factors such as drugs and hormones can be easily handled by elimination of these factors. Constipation dating back to childhood, however, is very difficult to manage. In some of these patients profound inhibition of colonic motility may be at the cerebral level; in some there is likely to be an abnormality of the enteric nervous system. A decreased number of argyrophilic neurons, morphologic abnormalities in the axons and nuclei of neurons, an increased serotonin level, a decreased vasoactive intestinal peptide level in the mucosa and muscular level of resected colon specimens from patients with severe idiopathic constipation have been reported. Although none of these findings are consistently present, these neural and neurochemical abnormalities are currently not known to change with treatment to alter the course of constipation. Some of these changes may be secondary to several years of constipation. Management should start as early as possible, as a majority of patients respond to lifestyle changes (exercise, a healthy diet, and proper defecation habit training).

Prevention

All patients should be assured that bowel habits vary from individual to individual and three to four bowel movements per week without difficulty or straining is normal. Most cases of constipation are treated with-

TABLE 19–6–1. CAUSES OF CONSTIPATION

Poor Delivery of Stool into Rectum
Colonic inertia
    Psychogenic (depression, laxative abuse)
    Metabolic (electrolyte abnormality, uremia, prophyria, diabetic neuropathy)
    Endocrine (hypothyroidism, hyperparathyroidism, pregnancy, carcinomatous
      pseudo-obstruction)
    Neuromuscular (parkinsonism, stroke, multiple sclerosis, myotonic dystrophy,
      scleroderma)
    Drugs (opiates, anticholinergics, antidepressants, antihypertensives,
      antiparkinsonism drugs)
Loss of spinal reflex (regulates sigmoid colon contraction in response to stimulation of
    pelvic floor)
    Spinal cord injury
    Sacral nerve root damage

Obstruction at the Level of Rectum and Anal Canal
    Neoplasms
    Proctitis
    Congenital and postoperative stenosis
    Rectal mucosal prolapse
    Rectocele
    Solitary rectal ulcer syndrome

High Anal Pressure, Failure of Relaxation of Internal and External Anal Sphincters
    Anal fissure
    Hirschsprung's disease
    Paradoxical contraction of pelvic floor
    Unusually sensitive anal canal—anismus

out the help of laxatives with a healthy proper diet, adequate fluid intake, and exercise. This approach is also important to prevent the development of constipation. Patients are advised to initiate bowel movements after meals and not to suppress the urge to defecate. Resistance results in diminished urges and chronic constipation. Appropriate use of public toilet facilities must be emphasized. Patients should also be instructed against the abuse of laxatives.

Cost Containment

Recognition of constipation as a problem at an early age and proper instructions for dietary and lifestyle changes will prevent dependence on laxatives in later years. Judicious use of high-fiber diets and of less costly fiber laxatives will contain costs. There are more than 700 different laxative preparations, and more than $250 million is spent yearly in treating constipation.

REFERENCES

Berman IR, Manning DH, Harris MS. Stream-lining the management of defecation disorders. Dis Colon Rectum 1990;33:778.
Connell AM, Hilton C, Irvine G. Variation of bowel habit in 2 population samples. Br Med J 1965;2:1095.
Drossman DA, Sandler RS, McKee DC, Lovitz AJ. Bowel patterns among subjects not seeking healthcare: Use of a questionnaire to identify a population with bowel dysfunction. Gastroenterology 1982;83:529.
Everhart JE, Go VL, Johannes RS, et al. A longitudinal survey of self-reported bowel habits in the United States. Dig Dis Sci 1984;34:1153.
Johanson JF, Sonnenberg A, Koch TR. Clinical epidemiology of chronic constipation. J Clin Gastroenterol 1980;11:525.
Read NW, Timms JM. Defecation and pathophysiology of constipation. Clin Gastroenterol 1986;15:937.
Sandler RS, Drossman DA. Bowel habits in young adults not seeking health care. Dig Dis Sci 1987;32:841.
Shouler P, Keighley MRB. Changes in colorectal function in severe idiopathic chronic constipation. Gastroenterology 1986;90:414.
Wald A, Hinds JP, Cavuano BJ. Psychological and physiological characteristics of patients with severe idiopathic constipation. Gastroenterology 1989;97:932.

CHAPTER 19–7

Irritable Bowel Syndrome

Hulya Levendoglu, M.D.

DEFINITION

Irritable bowel syndrome is a combination of chronic recurrent symptoms of abdominal pain and disturbed defecation not explained by structural or biochemical abnormalities of the bowel wall. It is a localized manifestation of functional gastrointestinal disorders.

ETIOLOGY

The etiology of irritable bowel syndrome is not known. Three mechanisms may be involved. First, it is possible that in these patients there may be a generalized alteration of the visceral receptors throughout the gut. Second, increased perception as an altered central processing of the signals may be present. Finally, there may be an imbalance in the autonomic nervous system. There is convincing evidence to support all three hypotheses.

CRITERIA FOR DIAGNOSIS
Suggestive

Irritable bowel syndrome is not a single, homogenous syndrome. Abdominal pain relieved by defecation and disturbed defecation should be present for at least 6 months to fulfill the criteria of irritable bowel syndrome complex.

Definitive

If the symptom complex is present longer than 2 years, the diagnosis is strengthened further. Six symptoms are found in this condition more than in any organic disease involving bowel: pain that eases after bowel movement, looser and more frequent stools at onset of pain, abdominal distention, diarrhea alternating with constipation, pellety stool or passage of mucus, and feeling of incomplete evacuation after defecation. Patients classified as having irritable bowel syndrome have a combination of two or more of these symptoms at least 25% of the time.

CLINICAL MANIFESTATIONS
Subjective

Irritable bowel syndrome is by definition a chronic condition, and waxes and wanes with exacerbations that may occur in response to stress. Most often, the diagnosis is made before the age of 50. Abdominal pain is often poorly localized but mostly to both lower quadrants. The character of pain is variable; it is described as a sensation of aching heavy fullness or stabbing or colicky. Pain occurs in bouts and is relieved by defecation or the passage of flatus. Most patients describe the exacerbation of pain in association with ingestion of food or stressful conditions. Disturbed defecation is described by patients as difficulty in passage of stool, straining during defecation, and inability to achieve complete evacuation. When diarrhea occurs it generally alternates with constipation; pure diarrhea is not included in the symptom complex of irritable bowel syndrome. In younger subjects diarrhea is associated with rectal urgency. Generally, the first bowel movement or the initial part of the first bowel movement is solid, which is followed by looser or liquid stools. Passage of mucus is common. It is often described as white or yellow streamy material. Rectal dissatisfaction or a feeling of incomplete evacuation after defecation is a common feature, but it is not associated with painful urge to defecate which is seen in severe proctitis of any form. A significant proportion—up to 20% of all patients with irritable bowel syndrome—may complain of fecal incontinence; the reason for fecal soiling is not clear. Abdominal distention and bloating may be very distressing to patients, especially if the distention is apparent visually. The quantity of abdominal gas was not found to be different than that in healthy individuals. Abdominal distention may be due to descent of the diaphragm and arching of the back. In addition, nocturia, urgency and frequency in micturition, back pain, fatigue, bad taste in the mouth, dyspareunia, and dysmenorrhea are reported to be more common complaints in patients with irritable bowel syndrome than in control subjects matched for age, sex, and social class.

Objective

Physical Examination

Patients look healthy on physical examination although they are generally tense and anxious. Evidence of autonomic lability such as elevated systolic blood pressure, rapid pulse, easy blushing, and sweaty palms may be present. The only physical finding is usually a tender palpable sigmoid colon. Extreme pain is generally produced during proctoscopy with air insufflation. Most patients admit occurrence of their first symptoms with an antecedent psychologic stress. Higher prevalences of depression, hypochondriasis, and somatization are found in these patients. Death in the family or loss of parent through divorce or separation before the age of 15, as well as sexual or physical abuse in childhood, is reported to occur in a larger percentage of these patients when compared with control patients with an organic diagnosis. Patients with irritable bowel syndrome also consult doctors more often for nongastrointestinal illnesses and undergo excessive numbers of surgical procedures such as hysterectomy and appendectomy.

Routine Laboratory Abnormalities

There are no diagnostic routine laboratory abnormalities.

PLANS

Diagnostic

Differential Diagnosis

Symptom complex, paucity of physical findings, and psychological profile of the patient help to diagnose irritable bowel syndrome. The symptoms of many inflammatory or infective diseases of the abdominal organs may be similar to the symptoms of irritable bowel syndrome. Diagnosis is made by exclusion of any organic gastrointestinal diseases.

Diagnostic Options and Recommended Approach

In many research studies a scoring system has been used for the diagnosis of irritable bowel syndrome that incorporates features from the history, physical examination, and some basic laboratory investigation. Onset in old age, steady progressive course, symptoms occurring at night interrupting sleep, presence of fever, and weight loss are features against the diagnosis of irritable bowel syndrome. Rectal bleeding not attributable to fissures or hemorrhoids also signifies organic disease, as does the finding of an inflammatory process by proctoscopy. There is no specific laboratory feature of this syndrome; however, the presence of leukocytosis and an elevated sedimentation rate argue against the diagnosis. Stool volume should be less than 200 mL per day; blood, pus, and fat should not be present in stool. Rectal biopsies are reported to show a significantly increased number of enterochromaffin cells, with scarce and even lacking adrenergic nerve axons by fluorescence histochemical study of rectal mucosa.

At a minimum, the workup should include a complete blood count with differential, erythrocyte sedimentation rate, and sigmoidoscopy; stool culture and stool examination for ova and parasites and for occult blood are usually performed. Especially in older patients a barium enema or colonoscopy may be indicated. The features of lactose intolerance can mimic those of irritable bowel syndrome; therefore, lactose intolerance must be ruled out with a simple breath hydrogen test. A thorough early evaluation convinces the patient that the disorder is real and helps to establish a confident therapeutic relationship and hence an effective treatment program.

Therapeutic

The goal of treatment is to modify the factors causing the exacerbation of symptoms and the patient's response to them. It is very important to educate the patient to the very real nature of the disorder in which the intestine is oversensitive to a variety of stimuli such as food, hormonal changes, and stress. Physicians should emphasize that the disorder is not solely organic or psychological, cure is not likely, the condition is not associated with malignancy, life is not shortened by this disorder, and there is no need for surgery.

Diet is the first approach to control or ease the symptoms; certain food items may be associated with gas production and exacerbation of symptoms. Food allergy is a consideration when abdominal symptoms are associated with a history of allergic reactions such as atopic dermatitis and asthma. Food intolerance is suggested with evidence of symptom occurrence with ingestion of lactose-containing foods, sorbitol intake, or fructose–sorbitol combinations. Fructose is a common constituent of fruits, berries, and plants, whereas significant amounts of sorbitol are present in peaches, apple juice, pears, plums, surgarless gums, dietetic jams, and chocolate. If a food item is identified as the cause, the patient should try to eliminate the offending food. Avoidance of large meals of high caloric content, poorly absorbed oligosaccharides, carbonated beverages, smoking, chewing gum, excessive fluid intake, and rapid eating may reduce the amount of gas swallowed or generated in the gut. Beanase enzyme, which assists in vivo digestion of oligosaccharides, is marketed with the trade name Beano. A few drops on a piece of bread consumed immediately prior to food intake significantly decreases the gas formation from ingested carbohydrates and, hence, reduces the frequency of flatulence. Its effect on bloating and fullness, however, is not that clear.

The use of fiber is recommended as there is some evidence that abdominal pain and constipation improve with ingestion of fiber. A diet containing 30 to 40 g of fiber is suggested; however, the average American diet contains less than half that. Either as bran or as psyllium, 15 to 20 g of fiber daily is recommended long term even when the symptoms are absent.

Anticholinergic and antispasmodic agents are the pharmacologic agents most frequently used to treat irritable bowel syndrome. They reduce the stimulated colonic motor activity. If the abdominal pain occurs in reponse to meals, dicyclomine hydrochloride (Bentyl) 10 to 20 mg three times or Donnatal 1 tablet three times usually relieves the symptoms.

In the diarrhea-predominant form of irritable bowel syndrome, opioid drugs such as loperamide 2 to 4 mg four times a day decrease intestinal motility, enhance fluid absorption by the gut, and increase anal sphincter pressure, thereby improving diarrhea, rectal urgency, and incontinence.

There is no role for narcotics in the treatment of irritable bowel syndrome. Peppermint oil has a relaxant effect on smooth muscle; this agent in capsule form may be of benefit as an antispasmodic agent.

Few data exist on the role of prokinetic drugs. In the constipation-predominant form of the disorder, however, dyspeptic symptoms may improve with administration of prokinetic drugs. Cisapride is now available and may be used at a dose of 10 to 20 mg four times a day.

Antidepressant drugs and anxiolytic agents have a role in the management of anxious, depressive patients with frequent panic attacks. Antianxiety agents should be used for brief periods for symptomatic relief, as the symptoms of irritable bowel syndrome are characteristically intermittent and recurrent. Patients may develop habituation or even addiction to some of these drugs. Chlordiazopoxide 10 mg three times daily, diazepam 2.5 to 5 mg three times daily, and buspirone 10 to 20 mg three times daily are the most common drugs used for this purpose. Patients with significant depressive syndrome require treatment with tricyclic antidepressants. The anticholinergic side effects of some of these agents may be an additional benefit. Amitriptyline (Elavil), imipraine (Tofranil), trazodone (Desyrel), and fluoxetine hydrochloride (Prozac) are started in small graded doses. Dosage is increased with consideration given to the significant variations in the metabolism of these agents and also to the response of the individual. Female patients with debilitating symptoms of intractable abdominal pain, daily nausea, distention, and altered bowel habits, particularly in the postovulatory phase of the menstrual cycle, respond to monthly injection of leuprolide (gonadotropin-releasing hormone analog).

Symptoms evoked by psychological factors may be effectively reduced by psychotherapy or hypnotherapy. A positive result to hypnotherapy is expected in almost all patients younger than 50 years of age. Behavioral treatment consisting of progressive muscle relaxation and thermal biofeedback, instruction in cognitive coping strategies, and education about irritable bowel syndrome resulted in a 50% or greater reduction in distress from the major symptoms by the end of 8 weeks of treatment.

FOLLOW-UP

Patients are encouraged to visit the physician periodically three to four times a year and whenever symptoms exacerbate. This course allows the physician to provide continued education and encourages a relationship based on patients' participation in the plan of care. Physicians can also offer insight into abnormal illness behavior and its relationship to psychological factors which are often rejected by the patient. Patients are encouraged to take more control of their progress, to develop self-initiated treatments to distract themselves from their own bodies, and to focus on developing hobbies and active productive work. Realistic expectations are set; behavioral treatment programs such as education, stress management, and biofeedback are offered; and patients are taught to engage in health-promoting behaviors in these follow-up visits.

DISCUSSION

Prevalence

The prevalence of irritable bowel syndrome in the nonclinical population is between 10 and 20%, but only 15% of these patients seek medical help. Worry about serious disease, anticancer propaganda, and the availability of free health care, as well as the severity of symptoms, lead those affected to consult a physician. In the medical setting, 25 to 50% of referrals to gastroenterologists are patients with irritable bowel syndrome.

Related Basic Science

Studies on this problem are concentrated in two areas: whether patients have a basic alteration in intestinal motility, and whether they have enhanced but qualitatively normal pain perception. There is no generalized increase in pain perception in patients with irritable bowel syndrome and somatic pain perception is not altered; however, the setpoint of visceral afferents is lowered, with a lower threshold for excitation. Referred pain, including that to the shoulder, back, and thigh, is reported to be more prevalent than in control subjects.

With respect to motility, the increase in colonic motor activity in response to stress, meals, and specific provocative stimuli (cholecystokinin, deoxycholic acid, and rectal balloon distention) is well known. Gastrocolonic motor responses reveal an early blunted but delayed and prolonged increase in motor activity in response to meals. Although stimulated motor activity shows these changes, basal colonic motility is normal. The basic electrical rhythm of colonic muscle shows an increase in frequency of 6 cycles/min as opposed to 3 cycles/min seen in normal subjects.

Although the abdominal pain and altered bowel habits associated with irritable bowel syndrome have been attributed to colonic dysfunction, the source of many of these symptoms may be the small intestine. Changes in migrating motor complex periodicity, specific motor patterns that are associated with abdominal pain, a shorter duration of postprandial fed motor pattern, and altered ileocecal transit time have been found in small bowel motility recordings. Inflation of a balloon in the esophagus, ileum, and rectosigmoid causes pain with smaller-than-control volumes of distention in this group of patients.

Natural History and Its Modification with Treatment

Irritable bowel syndrome is a chronic, usually lifelong condition with unpredictable periods of exacerbation and remissions. If symptom reduction is achieved with medical or nonmedical means, the long-term benefits are persistent; however, continued evaluation and implementation of behavioral methods are required. As in any other chronic illness, both the physician and the patient will be satisfied if the factors causing the behavior are identified and properly treated. As disease onset after age 50 is rare, the diagnosis should be made cautiously in this age group; an extensive workup should be performed to rule out organic disease.

Prevention

There are no specific recommendations that can be applied to prevention. Illness behavior is shaped by individuals' prior experience with the length, severity, and frequency of illnesses and stressful life events. Past psychological trauma and the attitudes and behavior of family, friends, culture and society are important determinants in the development of illness behavior. Adequate personality development helps to cope with these factors and may minimize their effect on the individual. Science will someday have a rational explanation for these conditions that we now call functional. This will be followed by better treatment and prevention.

Cost Containment

An extensive initial investigation of the patient's symptoms proves to the patient that organic disease is not present and eliminates the need for further tests. The investigation can be minimal if the symptoms are of long duration and patient is younger than 50. The stressed, the unloved, and the cancerphobic have very different needs in diagnosis and treatment. As only a minority of patients with irritable bowel syndrome seek health care, it is important to find out why the patient consults. For most, an explanation and reassurance are all needed. With adequate treatment consisting of a high-fiber diet, bulking agents, and antispasmodic agents, 85% of patients can become virtually symptom free in the short term, and about 67% remain symptom free in the long term.

REFERENCES

Drossman DA. Illness behaviour in the irritable bowel syndrome. Gastroenterol Int 1991;4:77.

Drossman DA, McKee DC, Sandler RS, et al. Psychosocial factors in the irritable bowel syndrome. Gastroenterology 1988;95:701.

Harvey RF, Manad EC, Brown AM. Prognosis in the irritable bowel syndrome: A 5 year prospective study. Lancet 1987;1:963.

Thompson WG. The irritable bowel: Progress report. Gut 1984;25:305.

Thompson WG, Dotevall G, Drossman DA, et al. Irritable bowel syndrome: Guidelines for the diagnosis. Gastroenterol Int 1989;2:92.

CHAPTER 19–8

Fecal Incontinence

Hulya Levendoglu, M.D.

DEFINITION

Fecal incontinence is defined as involuntary passage of liquid or solid stool or stool-stained mucus.

ETIOLOGY

The precise mechanism whereby the anal sphincter maintains fecal continence is not fully understood. When this mechanism fails, fecal incontinence occurs.

Criteria for Diagnosis

Symptoms may be intermittent and rare or may occur several times a day. Only leakage of mucus may be involved, or small or large amounts of liquid or solid stools may be lost. There may be very short warning times (<10 seconds) or no warning feeling at all. In certain patients, fecal incontinence occurs only when access to a toilet is not possible because of physical handicap or location. The problem is seen in every age group. Most often it is not voluntarily admitted unless it hinders an individual's mobility and independence. In children there is generally no apparent organic cause. Rarely, rectoanal agenesis and resultant surgery result in fecal incontinence. In the elderly, fecal impaction causing overflow incontinence and neurologic factors play a role. In adults, the prevalence of fecal incontinence increases with age. Idiopathic incontinence is more common in women.

CLINICAL MANIFESTATIONS

Subjective

Soiling in children often accompanies or follows constipation. This is also true in the very old with fecal impaction causing overflow incontinence. In children, fecal incontinence or mucus leakage may affect personality development. In severe cases, completion of school or professional training may be limited. On the other hand, incontinence may be a manifestation of antisocial behavior representing a voluntary statement of anger or hostility. Fecal incontinence secondary to impaction and neurogenic incontinence are equally common in the geriatric population. One fourth of nursing home residents suffer from it, most often in conjunction with urinary incontinence. Organic brain damage, confusion, and impaired mobility frequently accompany fecal incontinence in this group of patients. In young individuals the exact cause may not be apparent. Chronic diarrhea lasting more than 2 weeks may be associated with incontinence in nearly half of these patients, although less than half voluntarily admit the symptom to their physicians. Therefore, sensitive questioning of the patient, parents, or spouse is required. History taking should include questioning concerning prolonged diarrhea or constipation, physical and mental status of the patient, surgery and trauma to the perianal and rectal area including difficult vaginal deliveries, spinal cord disorders, injuries, systemic–neuromuscular and collagen–vascular diseases, and diabetes mellitus.

Objective

The presence of staining of the underclothes confirms the diagnosis. Visual inspection of the perianal area is usually normal, as incontinence generally results from decreased rectoanal sensation and dysfunction of the anal sphincters and pelvic floor muscles. Chemical dermatitis and scratch marks due to irritation of perianal skin from leaking mucus or stool may be present. Digital assessment of the strength of internal and external anal sphincters does not correlate with pressures obtained by anorectal manometry; however, squeeze and attempted defecation during examination give valuable information. Three muscle groups are differentiated with digital examination of the anal canal: internal anal sphincter tone is felt as the resting pressure of the anal canal when the examining finger is inside the anus; the external anal sphincter is located distal to the internal sphincter and is felt circumferentially on voluntary squeeze; the puborectalis is at the junction of the anus and rectum, when the examiner's fingertip faces toward the sacrum on contraction (squeeze) and moves toward the symphysis pubis. The cutaneous anal wink reflex in response to perianal pin scratch should also be checked. The findings on digital anorectal examination help in differentiating whether fecal incontinence is due to a direct loss of sphincter muscle function or to loss of its neurogenic innervation (Table 19–8–1).

PLANS

Diagnostic

Absent perineal cutaneous sensation, anal cutaneous reflex, and other neurologic findings in the gluteal region and legs strongly suggest a neurologic injury. In such cases examination with computed tomography scan or magnetic resonance imaging the lumbosacral spine is necessary. Anorectal manometry is important but not widely available. Anorectal manometry in fecal incontinence may demonstrate low basal and squeeze pressure, impaired and delayed rectal sensation, and low rectal compliance. Recently, electromyographic recording of anal muscles and the pelvic floor with a probe inserted into the anus was introduced. Electromyographic recording of less than 2 μV at rest with inability to raise the amplitude to 15 μV or higher on squeeze and a low endurance time of anal sphincter contraction have been reported in fecal incontinence not related to fecal impaction. Single-fiber electromyographic recordings are performed with a needle directly inserted into the sphincter muscle. With this test, increased fiber density in the external anal sphincter muscle has been found in all patients with fecal incontinence. In addition, increased duration of anal reflex latency is present. A combination of increased fiber density and prolonged anal reflex latency are consistent with damage to the nerves of the sphincter muscles. This, in turn, causes loss of functional muscle fibers from denervation. The saline incontinence test is markedly impaired. Anorectal radiology reveals a more obtuse anorectal angle in these patients, irrespective of wheither it was measured at rest, on squeezing, or on straining. Abnormal descent of the anorectal angle below the pubococcygeal line at rest, on straining, or on squeeze, is an additional radiographic finding.

Therapeutic

Patients who have incontinence of liquid stool require investigation. Many are eventually classified as having irritable bowel syndrome (see Chapter 19–7). in these patients, bulk laxatives absorb fluid from the

TABLE 19–8–1. FINDINGS IN DIGITAL EXAMINATION OF THE ANORECTAL REGION AND THEIR SIGNIFICANCE IN FECAL INCONTINENCE

Finding	Significance
Chemical dermatitis and scratch marks	Incontinence of liquid stool or mucus
Absent cutaneous anal reflex (wink)	Sacral nerve injury
Absent perineal cutaneous sensation	Sacral nerve root or suprasacral injury
Perineal descent	Weak pelvic floor; pudendal nerve injury
Deformity of anal canal	Traumatic, surgical, or obstetric injury
Short anal canal (<2.5 cm)	Loss of sphincter muscles
Low resting anal canal pressure	Sphincter muscle or nerve injury
Low squeeze pressure	Injury to puborectalis and external anal sphincter (nerve versus muscle)
No movement at pseudodefecation (strain)	Neurologic injury to puborectalis

lumen of the colon, preventing the accumulation of liquid stool in the rectum. Occasionally, bile acids entering the colon may be responsible for diarrhea and incontinence. Bile acids induce changes in anorectal motility, with smaller rectal volumes being required to produce a desire to defecate. Bile acid catharsis and incontinence should be considered in patients who have had radiation to pelvis, Crohn's disease, and a history of cholecystectomy. Cholestyramine is effective in controlling fecal incontinence in these circumstances. Generally, a single dose of 4 g before breakfast in patients with intact gallbladders, or 4 g at night in those who have undergone cholecystectomy, is required.

Ulcerative proctitis may cause rectal irritability and hypersensitivity of the rectum to fecal content. Treatment with glucocorticoids or 5-aminosalicylic enemas improves urgency and rectal compliance. Resting anal canal pressure is increased by administration of as little as 2 mg of loperamide. Whether this is important in maintaining continence has not been proven; however, beneficial effects have been observed in many patients.

Biofeedback training is useful in treating incontinence resulting from neurogenic or myogenic damage to anal sphincters. Anal manometry or electromyography with a probe inserted into anus can be used for biofeedback training. The aim is to lower the threshold for rectal sensation, to correct the delay in perception of volume in the rectum, and to improve the tone and electromyographic score of pelvic and anal muscles by squeezing exercises. This therapy is effective in about 75% of patients when they are able to carry out the instructions and perform the recommended exercises. Electrical stimulation of the external anal sphincter can improve the electromyographic and pressure response.

If fecal impaction is the cause of incontinence, bowel retraining for evacuation is necessary. Enemas and suppositories are used only when bowel retraining has failed. Psychotherapy is particularly helpful if an underlying social or psychological disorder is present.

Surgical treatment is required only in a minority of patients when there is extensive anatomic damage to sphincters. The aim is to decrease the size of the anal outlet, to increase the sphincter length, and to restore anorectal angulation. If rectal prolapse coexists, the prolapse should be repaired first, as this will restore continence in about half of patients. In cases of severe hypoplasia or agenesis of the sphincter muscle complex, gracilis muscle transposition may create a considerable improvement in continence in children.

FOLLOW-UP

Patients should be educated so that they understand the need for long-term commitment to management and care. Early follow-up is indicated especially in the beginning, so that social life can be maintained with minimal interruptions. For example, evacuations are done with suppositories before the patient leaves home for business or social events. Squeeze and relaxation exercises of the anal sphincter can be performed by the patient even during daily work to improve the strength of pelvic and anal muscles. Although a majority maintain continence for up to 2 years after biofeedback or rectal sensory training, in some patients training needs to be repeated intermittently to maintain continence.

DISCUSSION

Prevalence and Incidence

It is difficult to estimate the true prevalence and incidence of fecal incontinence, as 50 to 70% of affected individuals do not seek help. Approximately 1.5% of children and adults older than 65 suffer from fecal incontinence. Twenty percent of those with irritable bowel syndrome

and 10 to 50% of institutionalized persons (nursing home residents) have fecal incontinence. The estimated prevalence is 4.2 per 1000.

Related Basic Science

The maintenance of continence depends in a critical way on the anatomy of the pelvic floor. Although what constitutes continence is not entirely clear, continence depends on the sequential delivery of colonic contents to the rectum, rectal compliance and accommodation, internal anal sphincter responses, rectal sensation, and puborectalis and external anal sphincter responses. The internal anal sphincter normally contributes 70% to the resting tone of the anal canal; however, the actual role of anal canal pressure in preserving continence is unclear.

In incontinence the following mechanisms may be operating: (1) Large volumes of liquid stool may enter the rectum and overcome the pressure barrier (voluminous diarrhea, bile salt-induced diarrhea, irritable bowel syndromes). (2) Decreased rectal compliance may produce higher intrarectal pressures and overwhelm the sphincter pressure barrier (rectal ischemia, inflammatory bowel disease, radiation proctitis). (3) Impaired rectal sensation and perception may cause higher-than-normal thresholds for conscious perception of rectal distention (diabetes mellitus, stroke, dementia, etc.). (4) Internal anal sphincter muscle function may be impaired (diabetes mellitus, after dilation for hemorrhoids). (5) External anal sphincter and puborectalis muscle function may be impaired due to neurogenic or traumatic factors (perineal descent, pudendal nerve damage).

Natural History and Its Modification with Treatment

Patients with chronic fecal incontinence form childhood suffer most when inadequately managed. This results in loss of self-esteem, isolation, lack of social interaction, depression, and inability to achieve gainful employment. Education and psychological and intellectual stimulation are necessary to achieve meaningful interaction with physicians and others. Many benefit from treatment; however, success cannot be achieved if the patient's mental capacity is compromised (dementia, stroke), because extensive cooperation is needed for training.

Prevention

Better toilet training, avoidance of fecal impaction, proper episiotomies during vaginal deliveries, and a judicious approach to hemorrhoidal surgery will prevent fecal incontinence related to these causes.

Cost Containment

Bowel retraining and medical management of fecal impaction in children and in the elderly are simple methods for prevention and treatment of fecal incontinence. Rectal sensory training and biofeedback-assisted pelvic and anal muscle strengthening exercises provide the most rapid and dramatic improvement. Surgical treatment may be beneficial, although success cannot be guaranteed in patients with significant anatomic and structural defects.

REFERENCES

Bartolo DCC, Kamm MA, Kuijpers H, et al. Working party report: Defecation disorders. Am J Gastroenterol 1994;89:5154.

Cerulli MA, Nikoomanesh P, Schuster MM. Progress in biofeedback conditioning for fecal incontinence. Gastroenterology 1979;76:742.

Ihre T. Studies on anal function in continent and incontinent patients. Scand J Gastroenterol 1974;9(suppl. 25):5.

Miner PB. Fecal incontinence. Curr Ther Gastroenterol Liver Dis 1990;3:363.

Wald A, Tunuguntla AK. Anorectal sensorimotor dysfunction in fecal incontinence and diabetes mellitus. N Engl J Med 1984;310:1282.

Delayed Gastric Emptying

Ira W. Nierenberg, M.D.

DEFINITION

Delayed gastric emptying entails impaired transit of gastric contents into the small intestine and leads to gastric retention and stasis.

ETIOLOGY

Delayed gastric emptying may result from a gastric outlet obstruction (mechanical obstruction) or a gastrointestinal motility disorder. In the absence of mechanical obstruction, delayed gastric emptying is known as gastroparesis.

CRITERIA FOR DIAGNOSIS

Suggestive

Patients usually present with a variety of symptoms including nausea, vomiting (usually nonbilious), early satiety, abdominal pain, postprandial bloating, and weight loss, or they may give a history of peptic ulcer disease or one of the disorders associated with gastroparesis.

Definitive

An upper gastrointestinal series or upper endoscopy is necessary to rule out mechanical obstruction, and if endoscopy is elected, a small bowel series should also be done to rule out a partially obstructing lesion of the small bowel, especially in a patient with a previous history of abdominal surgery. Once this is done, the diagnosis of gastroparesis can be entertained.

Radioscintigraphy is the current gold standard to quantitate gastric emptying, and delayed gastric emptying with this study establishes the diagnosis.

CLINICAL MANIFESTATIONS

Subjective

The clinical manifestations may be acute (e.g., gastroenteritis) or chronic, range from asymptomatic to life threatening, and occur postprandially or in the fasting state. In addition to the above-mentioned symptoms, a detailed medical history as well as duration, severity, and whether symptoms occur postprandially, fasting, or only at a specific time of the day or month, is very important in helping to make a diagnosis of delayed gastric emptying and possibly ascertaining the underlying etiology. Important clues in the history include a history of peptic ulcer disease; prior gastric or abdominal surgery; a history of systemic diseases such as diabetes, collagen–vascular disease, amyloid disease, intrinsic myopathies or neuropathies (e.g., chronic idiopathic intestinal pseudo-obstruction), and metabolic or endocrine disorders; radiation; a history of central nervous system or psychiatric disorders (e.g., anorexia nervosa); and, most importantly, a detailed medication history (e.g., anticholinergic medications). Studies have shown a poor correlation between severity of symptoms and objective evidence of delayed gastric emptying. Patients with severe symptoms may have normal gastric emptying studies, whereas asymptomatic patients (e.g., diabetes) may demonstrate a marked delay in gastric emptying when studied by sensitive radionuclide techniques.

Objective

Physical Examination

The physical examination may be unrevealing or may reveal evidence of epigastric tenderness or bruit, distention, or a succession splash present more than 4 hours after a meal. In addition to the gastrointestinal findings, one should also look for evidence of orthostatic hypotension (evidence of possible autonomic neuropathy seen with certain systemic diseases), disorders of the lens of the eye or bladder dysfunction (seen with certain types of intestinal pseudo-obstruction), and possible evidence of a central nervous system lesion or peripheral neuropathy.

Routine Laboratory Abnormalities

No specific laboratory abnormalities are directly attributable to delayed gastric emptying. Hypokalemia, hypochloremic alkalosis, and elevation of the blood urea nitrogen level may occur secondary to vomiting and dehydration. Routine laboratory tests may help identify the underlying cause of delayed gastric emptying.

PLANS

Diagnostic

Differential Diagnosis

As mentioned above, delayed gastric emptying may occur in gastric outlet obstruction and gastroparesis. An upper gastrointestinal series and/or upper endoscopy should be done to rule out mechanical obstruction. Approximately 80% of gastric outlet obstruction is due to peptic ulcer disease (e.g., pyloric channel ulcer). Other causes include gastric carcinoma or lymphoma, pancreatic carcinoma or pancreatitis, annular pancreas, and postsurgical stenosis.

If mechanical obstruction is ruled out and the patient has a longstanding systemic disease such as diabetes, with upper gastrointestinal series showing residual food after overnight fast, gastric atony, or retention of barium sulfate, empiric therapy of gastroparesis can be undertaken but most patients require further studies. The differential diagnosis of gastroparesis is listed in Table 19–9–1.

Diagnostic Options

Thyroid function tests should be done. A human chorionic gonadotropin (B subunit) level should be determined in premenopausal women. An abdominal ultrasound is indicated if biliary tract or pancreatic disease is being considered. A computed tomography scan of the head may be indicated to rule out central nervous system disease if clinically suspected.

A number of techniques have been employed to quantitate the rate of gastric emptying and aid in the diagnosis of gastroparesis. Intubation tests such as the saline load test can be useful in patients with gastric outlet obstruction, but only measure gastric emptying of liquids and are insensitive in gastroparesis. A barium upper gastrointestinal series is also relatively insensitive as barium is a nonnutritive liquid that is not emptied in the same way as food. Barium burger meals have been tried, but the barium tends to dissociate from the hamburger.

Recommended Approach

Radioscintigraphy is the current gold standard. This noninvasive test uses two gamma-emitting radionuclides with different photon peak emissions, which enables both solid and liquid components of a meal to

TABLE 19–9–1. CAUSES OF GASTROPARESIS

Addison's disease	Hypothyroidism
Amyloid disease	Idiopathic
Anorexia nervosa	Immobilization
Atrophic gastritis	Ischemia
Central nervous system diseases	Medications
Collagen–vascular diseases	Pregnancy
Diabetes mellitus	Pseudo-obstruction
Electrolyte imbalance	Radiation
Gastroenteritis (viral)	Surgery

be imaged and quantitated simultaneously over time. Dual-labeled gastric emptying studies are done because solids and liquids empty differently from the stomach and at different rates. In gastroparesis, delayed solid emptying and normal liquid emptying can frequently be seen. Measuring gastric emptying of solids is felt to be more sensitive in detecting gastroparesis than measuring gastric emptying of liquids.

The patient ingests the radiolabeled meal, and then, using externally positioned gamma cameras, one can quantitate the emptying of each radiolabel from the stomach over time by taking images at regular intervals until 90% of each radiolabel has emptied from the stomach.

Debate exists as to how the results of gastric emptying studies should be expressed. One measure is the half-life, or the time it takes to empty 50% of the radiolabel from the stomach, but this is felt to be more useful for liquids than solids. Computerized methods of analysis with curve fitting have been developed and may be more representative of the entire gastric emptying curve, especially when dealing with emptying of solids. Regardless of how the results are analyzed, there are multiple factors other than disease that can influence gastric emptying, such as age, sex, smoking, drug or alcohol intake, and variations in the radiolabeled meal. Hence, these studies should only be done in a laboratory with established controls and standardized techniques. One must also remember that radioscintigraphic studies only indicate possible delays in gastric emptying, but do not indicate the underlying mechanism. This requires the use of complementary tests such as gastrointestinal manometry and electrogastrography, which are usually only available at selected tertiary referral centers. Work has been done using ultrasound and gastric impedance measurements to assess gastric emptying, but these techniques have their limitations and are not yet readily available.

Therapeutic

The management of gastric outlet obstruction includes intravenous hydration/nothing by mouth to correct fluid, electrolyte, and acid–base disturbances; gastric decompression via Ewald and then nasogastric tube; intravenous H_2-receptor antagonists; an attempt to determine benign versus malignant disease at the time of upper endoscopy via biopsies and brushings; and parenteral nutrition if indicated.

In the case of benign gastric outlet obstruction, in addition to the above measures, the patient should be followed with serial saline load tests. The saline load test entails instilling 750 mL of normal saline via nasogastric tube, clamping the tube, and waiting 30 minutes. More than 400 mL aspirated back at this time is indicative of gastric retention. Many patients respond to medical therapy and a liquid diet can be started. This is followed by gradual resumption of solid foods as tolerated. One must remember that patients can have a normal saline load test and still have difficulty emptying solid food. If no improvement is seen in 5 to 7 days, surgery or possibly endoscopic balloon dilation of the pylorus is necessary. Malignant gastric outlet obstruction is usually treated surgically after a period of medical therapy including gastric decompression.

The treatment of gastroparesis includes treatment of the underlying disease, if possible, dietary measures, and medical therapy. Surgical therapy is only rarely indicated.

Dietary advice is important. Small, frequent meals, as well as meals with increased liquid and soft solid content, should be consumed, as liquids usually empty more rapidly. Multivitamins and liquid calorie supplements should also be advised. High-fiber bulky solids should be avoided, as fiber delays gastric emptying and may contribute to the formation of bezoars. Hypertonic fluids and foods high in fat should be avoided because they also delay gastric emptying. Occasionally, only liquids are tolerated orally, and in very severe cases, feedings are via jejunostomy tube or rarely home total parenteral nutrition.

Metoclopramide (Reglan), a substituted benzamide, is the only prokinetic drug licensed in this country for the treatment of gastroparesis. It is a dopamine receptor antagonist with cholinomimetic activity and acts predominantly at the level of the upper gastrointestinal tract to coordinate motility. It contracts the lower esophageal sphincter, inhibits fundic receptive relaxation, accelerates gastric emptying by increasing the amplitude of antral contractions, relaxes the pylorus and duodenum, and increases jejunal peristalsis. Metoclopramide also has a prominent

central antiemetic and sedating effect, which may explain the poor correlation between improvement in symptoms and lack of improvement in gastric emptying as assessed by radionuclide studies. It can be given by the oral, intramuscular, or intravenous route depending on the severity of symptoms. The onset of action following an oral dose is 30 to 60 minutes, and its effect lasts 1 to 2 hours. The usual oral dose is 10 mg orally 30 minutes before meals and at bedtime. Approximately 80% of the drug is excreted unchanged in the urine. In severe gastroparesis, the intravenous route may be used until a symptomatic response permits oral use.

If symptomatic relief occurs, the drug should be discontinued, although this is often difficult due to the chronic nature of the illness. Approximately 20% of patients experience side effects while taking metoclopramide. The most common side effects include drowsiness, restlessness, and fatigue. Approximately 1% of patients experience extrapyramidal reactions that are rapidly reversed by diphenhydramine. The central nervous system side effects are secondary to the drug's ability to cross the blood–brain barrier. Prolactin can also be elevated and may result in galactorrhea, which usually ceases with withdrawal of the medication. Metoclopramide is absolutely contraindicated in mechanical obstruction of the gastrointestinal tract. There are other prokinetic drugs including domperidone, cisapride, and erythromycin, but these are not yet licensed for treatment of gastroparesis in this country. Antiemetics such as prochlorperazine (Compazine) and trimethobenzamide (Tigan) can be used to supplement the effect of metoclopramide (Reglan), if necessary. Surgery is usually reserved for jejunostomy tube placement and in the treatment of postvagotomy gastric stasis in patients (usually with a history of gastric outlet obstruction) who have undergone an antrectomy and vagotomy and fail to respond to medical therapy.

FOLLOW-UP

The patient should be seen on a regular basis by his or her physician. Any change in the patient's medical condition should be noted and treated accordingly. Dietary measures and drug therapy should again be reinforced and the patient encouraged to ask any new questions he or she may have about their medical condition.

DISCUSSION
Prevalence and Incidence

The prevalence and incidence of delayed gastric emptying vary depending on the underlying cause, the presence or absence of symptoms, and the method of diagnosis.

Related Basic Science

Gastric emptying is a fine-tuned process involving the interaction between gastric smooth muscle and the central, autonomic, and enteric nervous systems. This coordinated and programmed motor activity involves the entire gastropyloroduodenal segment and is under hormonal as well as nervous control. A defect at any of these levels can result in delayed gastric emptying.

Classically, the stomach has been divided into two functional areas. The proximal stomach (fundus, proximal body) relaxes with swallowing (receptive relaxation), and with food in the stomach (gastric accommodation), it (1) acts as a reservoir to accommodate large volumes of food or liquid, (2) produces tonic or sustained contractions that generate the gastroduodenal pressure gradient responsible for the gastric emptying of liquids, and plays a role in the transfer of solids from the proximal to the distal stomach. Liquid emptying occurs exponentially, or in other words, the emptying rate is highest initially when the gastric volume is greatest and decreases as the gastric volume decreases. The distal stomach (antrum, distal body) is involved in the trituration or grinding of solids. Peristaltic waves generated at a rate up to three per minute push the gastric contents distally but the pylorus functions as a sieve and only particles smaller than 1 mm become part of a liquid mixture called chyme, which is periodically spurted through the pylorus into the duodenum. Larger particles are retropelled, undergo further trituration, and eventually are propelled back toward the pylorus. This grinding of solids increases the surface area available for small intestinal enzymes to act on. Solid emptying is characterized by an initial lag phase in which very little solid empties from the stomach. This is felt to be the time it takes to grind solids small enough to pass through the pylorus. This is followed by a linear emptying phase. The consistency of the chyme also plays a role in gastric emptying. Hyperosmolar solutions, increased fat content, or caloric density and acidity can all delay gastric emptying after coming in contact with receptors on the duodenal mucosa by a feedback mechanism that is under neural and hormonal control. This enables digestion and absorption to proceed at an optimal rate.

Finally, gastric emptying occurs during both the fasting and fed states. A normal person ingests liquids, solids, and indigestible solids. Liquids and solids usually empty during the postprandial period (fed state) at different rates, whereas indigestible solids, sometimes 3 to 5 mm in size, empty in the interdigestive period (fasting state) during phase III of the migrating motor complex through a wide open pylorus. The migrating motor complex ("intestinal housekeeper") consists of periods of quiescence alternating with intense contractile activity. It moves in an orderly fashion down the gastrointestinal tract preventing stagnation and bacterial growth.

Gastric motility disturbances usually occur in the postprandial period, but can also occur in the interdigestive period. Delayed emptying of one component can occur without the others, but delayed gastric emptying of solids is more common than liquids and is usually associated with antral hypomotility. In diabetic gastroparesis, for example, many manometric abnormalities may play a role in the delayed gastric emptying such as weak antral contractions, gastric dysrythmias, pylorospasm, and intestinal dysmotility. Absence of phase III of the migrating motor complex can also be seen in diabetes and may contribute to the formation of bezoars.

Natural History and Its Modification with Treatment

Delayed gastric emptying can present acutely (e.g., gastroenteritis), but more commonly presents as a chronic process that waxes and wanes.

Patients with gastric outlet obstruction secondary to pyloric channel ulcer who respond to medical therapy should be treated with a full course of H_2-receptor antagonists or omeprazole (usually 8 weeks) and then switched to long-term maintenance therapy (half the full dose of H_2-receptor antagonist), to try and decrease the incidence of recurrence.

Gastroparesis usually responds to dietary and drug treatment, but there are patients refractory to all measures, some of whom require home total parenteral nutrition.

Prevention

At this time, there is no known way to prevent delayed gastric emptying from occurring.

Cost Containment

One must remember that there is a poor correlation between symptoms and objective evidence of delayed gastric emptying. A complete workup should be done but repeated studies should be avoided. It is hoped that advances will continue to be made to improve the identification and treatment of delayed gastric emptying.

REFERENCES

Feldman M, Schiller LR. Disorders of gastrointestinal motility associated with diabetes mellitus. Ann Intern Med 1983;98:378.

Goldstein H, Boyle JD. The saline load test: A bedside evaluation of gastric retention. Gastroenterology 1965;49:375.

Lin HC, Meyer JH. Disorders of gastric emptying. In: Yamada T, ed. Textbook of gastroenterology. Philadelphia: Lippincott, 1991:1213.

Malagelada J-R, Azpiroz F, Mearin F. Gastroduodenal motor function in health and disease. In: Sleisenger MH, Fordtran JS, ed. Gastrointestinal disease. 5th ed. Philadelphia: Saunders, 1993:486.

Reynolds JC, Putnam PE. Prokinetic agents. Gastroenterol Clin North Am 1992;21:567.

CHAPTER 19–10

Chronic Intestinal Pseudo-obstruction

Charles D. Gerson, M.D.

DEFINITION

Intestinal pseudo-obstruction is a condition wherein the small bowel, for all or part of its length, is chronically dilated in the absence of mechanical obstruction. The involved segment of small intestine lacks normal motility. In some patients, there may be motility disturbance of other parts of the gastrointestinal or other organs such as the urinary bladder.

ETIOLOGY

This syndrome occurs as a result of a disturbance in either neurologic or muscular control of peristalsis. Visceral neuropathies can be primary or secondary to other conditions, and visceral myopathies can also be primary or part of a more general disorder. Both may occur in familial patterns.

CRITERIA FOR DIAGNOSIS
Suggestive

Recurrent episodes of abdominal distention along with vomiting and marked reduction in passage of flatus or stool usually suggest the diagnosis of intestinal obstruction. The diagnosis of pseudo-obstruction is suggested if there is a history of prior workup and/or prior exploratory surgery without the finding of an obstructing lesion in the bowel or obstructing adhesions.

Definitive

The diagnosis is established by evaluating a patient with the clinical picture of obstruction, including a dilated small bowel on obstructive series, with careful barium study of the small intestine. The small bowel is usually dilated all the way to ileocecal valve without any cutoff or transition zone. In primary visceral neuropathy or myopathy, full-thickness biopsy of the small bowel demonstrates the pathologic basis for the syndrome.

CLINICAL MANIFESTATIONS
Subjective

Patients complain of abdominal bloating associated with a feeling of early satiety, nausea, and intermittent vomiting. They notice that passage of stool and flatus is markedly reduced during obstructive episodes. Because of inability to maintain normal intake, weight loss occurs, they feel dry, and also notice that urine output is decreased.

There is a history of recurring attacks of obstructive symptoms. Patients may feel well between episodes, though mild chronic abdominal distention may be noted. There may also be a history of wide fluctuations in weight, with marked weight loss during attacks. Occasionally, patients have had exploratory surgery for obstruction without definite diagnosis. Some patients may have been treated for ileitis without success.

In some patients, there is a family history suggesting an autosomal dominant or recessive mode of transmission. In severe cases, the onset is in childhood and may be associated with multiple neurologic or muscular defects.

Objective

Physical Examination

The most striking physical finding is abdominal distention; however, there are other findings, including abnormal vital signs. Blood pressure may be low and heart rate increased due to decreased intravascular volume. This may result in orthostatic changes in blood pressure. The patient appears weak and dehydrated and may show signs of marked wasting. An important physical finding is the succussion splash, which is usually heard over the upper half of the abdomen. Bowel sounds may be quiet, though there may be high-pitched rushes as well. There is usually no significant tenderness. Occasionally, dilated small bowel loops are visible on inspection of the abdominal wall.

If the pseudo-obstruction is secondary to a more generalized disorder such as scleroderma or hypothyroidism, the appearance of the patient may lead to the proper diagnosis.

Routine Laboratory Abnormalities

Abnormal laboratory data may reflect the consequences of vomiting, decreased fluid intake, and pooling of fluid in the small intestine and stomach. Thus, the patient may have elevated blood urea nitrogen and creatinine levels. Also, there may be hypochloremia and hypokalemia. In long-standing pseudo-obstruction, B_{12} deficiency can lead to megaloblastic anemia.

PLANS

Diagnostic

Differential Diagnosis

The most important differential is mechanical obstruction, due either to adhesions or to organic distal small bowel disease such as regional ileitis. Once it is clear that there is no distal obstruction, then the cause of pseudo-obstruction must be sought. This may be a primary visceral myopathy or neuropathy or a secondary manifestation of systemic disease. Table 19–10–1 lists such conditions.

TABLE 19–10–1. CAUSES OF INTESTINAL PSEUDO-OBSTRUCTION

Primary visceral myopathy
  Familial autosomal dominant or recessive
  Sporadic
Secondary visceral myopathy
  Scleroderma
  Hypothyroidism
  Amyloidosis
  Small intestinal diverticulosis
Primary visceral neuropathy
  Familial autosomal dominant or recessive
  Sporadic
Secondary visceral neuropathy
  Paraneoplastic syndrome
  Diabetes
  Chagas' disease
  Parkinson's
Drugs
  Opiates
  Tricyclics
  Phenothiazines

Diagnostic Options

Initially, obstructive series should document a dilated small bowel without distal cutoff. The colon may be dilated as well. Air–fluid levels may or may not be present. Eventually, barium study of the stomach and small bowel, motility studies, and even full-thickness biopsy of the small intestine are diagnostic options to consider.

Recommended Approach

On initial evaluation, obstructive series should be the first diagnostic procedure. After the patient has been stabilized, it is important to obtain an upper gastrointestinal radiograph with small bowel followthrough (Figure 19–10–1). This should be examined to see if dilation extends all the way to the ileocecal valve and also whether dilation involves only localized segments of the small bowel. In some patients, barium enema may show a motility disorder of the colon as well. Esophageal manometry may be abnormal and should be done if dysphagia is a complaint. It is important to look for a scleroderma-type motility pattern. Finally, if there is still a question of motility disorder versus organic obstruction, full-thickness biopsy of the small bowel should reveal muscular or neurologic abnormalities. Electron microscopy should be used. The biopsy can be obtained laparascopically.

Bacterial overgrowth is common in this condition and can be assesses by culture of aspirated fluid or with hydrogen breath analysis after administration of glucose.

Therapeutic

Patients with chronic symptoms seen in an ambulatory setting can be helped by antibiotics to treat bacterial overgrowth. It may be necessary to alternate various drugs such as ciprofloxacin, metronidazole, doxycycline, and tetracycline. Also, prokinetic drugs such as cisapride, taken before meals, can be helpful. There has also been some recent evidence that octreotide, a somatostatin analog that must be given parenterally, may also be effective in some patients.

In the acute situation, usually in a hospital setting, nasogastric drainage and intravenous feeding with correction of electrolyte disturbance are essential. H_2 antagonists protect against acid reflux into the esophagus. Again, antibiotics and promotility drugs may help.

In rare situations, the pseudo-obstruction occurs in localized seg-

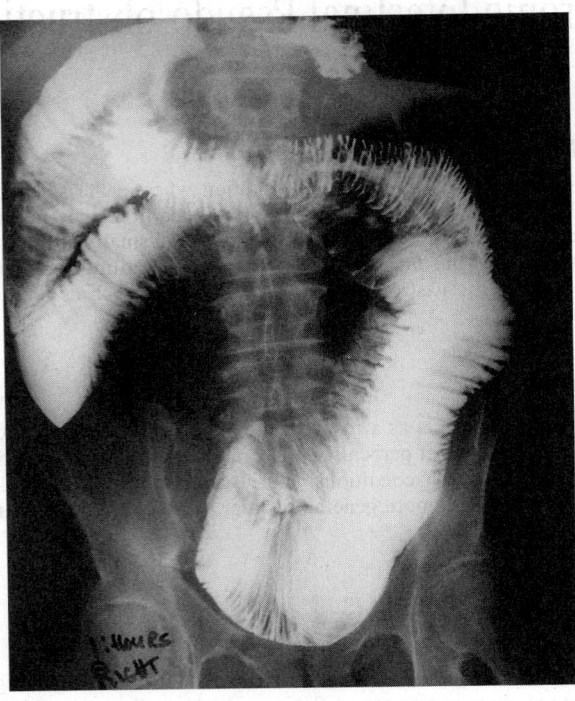

Figure 19–10–1. Barium study of the small intestine in a patient with intestinal pseudo-obstruction.

ments of intestine that can be surgically removed. In patients with diffuse disease, home hyperalimentation may be necessary in extreme circumstances.

FOLLOW-UP

These patients require regular follow-up. It may be necessary to make adjustments in antibiotic usage. It is also important to monitor nutritional status, which can fluctuate markedly.

DISCUSSION
Prevalence and Incidence

Chronic intestinal pseudo-obstruction is a rare condition. There are no data on prevalence and incidence in the adult population, though there does seem to be a female to male ratio of about 2:1.

Related Basic Science
Genetics

As indicated, there are dominant and recessive forms of both visceral myopathy and visceral neuropathy. Most patients with familial forms manifest the condition in childhood. Some of the neuropathies are associated with central nervous system disease as well.

Physiologic or Metabolic Derangement

Normally, peristalsis in the small intestine has varying patterns in fasting and fed states. In the fasting state, there is a migrating motor complex that sweeps through the small bowel about every 100 minutes. In the fed state, there is a change postprandially to an irregular phasic contractile activity that facilitates exposure of food to the mucosa and also propels contents distally. In pseudo-obstruction, migrating motor complexes are either of low amplitude or absent, in both myopathy and neuropathy. A meal may fail to induce the normal fed motility pattern or lead to a transient or disordered pattern.

As a result of impaired peristalsis, bacterial overgrowth ensues. This may lead to vitamin B_{12} malabsorption because of bacterial binding to B_{12} and also to impaired fat absorption. Bacteria can reduce and deconjugate intraluminal bile salts, leading to inadequate solubilization of fat.

Anatomic Derangement

In the visceral neuropathies, special silver staining technique may demonstrate abnormalities of the myenteric plexus affecting neurons, axons, and dendrites. In myopathy, the typical change is vacuolar degeneration of smooth muscle cells with replacement of muscle tissue by fibrosis of the muscularis propria.

Natural History and Its Modification with Treatment

The natural history depends on the severity of the condition. In some patients, proper treatment may be lifesaving, whereas in others, the syndrome is milder and is not life threatening. In either category, treatment can play a major role. The typical patient has a history of multiple hospitalizations for decompression and fluid and nutritional repletion. Administration of antibiotics and promotility drugs can prolong intervals between hospitalizations and also enable the patient to maintain a much better nutritional status.

Prevention

Prevention in this disease applies to preventing severe deterioration and weight loss, not to preventing the disease itself. It is, however, important to recognize that mechanical obstruction is not present, as many of these patients have a history of unnecessary exploratory surgery before the proper diagnosis is established.

Cost Containment

Like many patients with chronic illness, these patients may balk at taking antibiotics on a long-term basis or making regular follow-up visits to the doctor. In the long run, however, a close relationship between patient and physician is cost-saving, as it prevents acute deterioration which often leads to expensive hospitalizations.

REFERENCES

Anuras S, Shirazi S, Faulk D, Gardner G. Surgical treatment in familial visceral myopathy. Ann Surg 1979;189:306.

Camilleri M, Balm RK, Zinmeister AR. Determinants of response to a prokinetic agent in neuropathic chronic intestinal motility disorder. Dig Dis Sci 1992;37:10.

Schuffler M, Lowe M, Bill A. Studies of idiopathic intestinal pseudo-obstruction. I. Hereditary hollow visceral myopathy: Clinical and pathological studies. Gastroenterology 1977;73:327.

Stanghellini V, Camilleri M, Malagelada J. Chronic idiopathic pseudo-obstruction: Clinical and intestinal manometric findings. Gut 1987;5:28.

CHAPTER 19–11

Dysphagia

Vincent James Notar-Francesco, M.D.

DEFINITION

Dysphagia is the sensation that a bolus of food does not pass normally from the mouth to the stomach. The patient may report that the bolus "gets stuck" for a protracted period, goes down slowly, or passes in an abnormal fashion.

ETIOLOGY

Oropharyngeal dysphagia, or transfer dysphagia, refers to an inability to pass a bolus from the mouth to the esophagus. This is usually due to weakness or a lack of coordination between striated muscles of the mouth, pharynx, and upper esophageal sphincter. Although often a consequence of neuromuscular diseases, occasionally structural lesions of the mouth and pharynx are responsible. Rarely, motility disorders of the upper esophageal sphincter may lead to oropharyngeal dysphagia.

Esophageal dysphagia refers to an inability to pass a bolus through the body of the esophagus and into the stomach. In most cases, this is due to lesions protruding into the esophageal lumen. Sometimes it a consequence of a motility disorder of the esophagus.

CRITERIA FOR DIAGNOSIS
Suggestive

Complaints of difficulty initiating swallows, coughing with deglutition, bolus impaction, or delayed passage of a bolus strongly suggest the presence of dysphagia.

Definitive

The finding of an abnormality of the esophagus that is known to produce dysphagia on endoscopy, radiography, laryngoscopy, or esophageal manometry defines the diagnosis.

CLINICAL MANIFESTATIONS

Subjective

Oropharyngeal dysphagia is usually described as trouble beginning a swallow. There is difficulty in propelling the bolus either from the mouth into the oropharynx or from the pharynx into the proximal esophagus. The patient may report that food gets stuck in the mouth or neck. Very fine coordination of muscles of the oropharynx is required to pass liquid boluses into the esophagus without aspiration. Many patients may exhibit more difficulty with liquids, and coughing spells or aspiration during deglutition is frequently seen. In some cases, the bolus of food may pass cephalad into the nasopharynx, and rarely nasal regurgitation can occur. The duration of meals may increase as the patient uses a slow, deliberate method to swallow properly. Complaints of associated neurologic deficits such as hoarseness, dysarthria, drooling, and facial muscle and limb weakness are often present.

Esophageal dysphagia is usually described as food getting stuck in the chest or taking a long time to pass into the stomach. The reported level of obstruction is rarely useful as sensation can be referred either up or down the chest. Chronic, intermittent, nonprogressive dysphagia for solids only suggests a benign stricture typically due to esophageal webs or rings. Chronic dysphagia for solids initially with subsequent progression to liquids often implies the presence of an inflammatory or malignant stricture of the esophagus. Dysphagia that from its onset is to both solids and liquids may imply the presence of a motility disorder. Chronic, progressive dysphagia associated with the sensation of retained food in the chest and/or regurgitation of undigested food eaten hours before suggests achalasia. Intermittent, nonprogressive dysphagia for solids and liquids, especially if associated with chest pain, is typical of esophageal spasm. Patients with chronic dysphagia often learn to modify their diets and avoid foods that are more difficult to swallow, such as bread and meat. Some patients may develop strategies to relieve food impaction by changing posture or drinking water or carbonated beverages.

Objective

Physical Examination

Evidence of neuromuscular disease on physical examination in a patient with oropharyngeal dysphagia may suggest a specific etiology. There are no findings on physical examination specific for esophageal dysphagia except in patients with scleroderma who may have cutaneous or systemic signs of fibrosis.

Routine Laboratory Abnormalities

There are no routine laboratory abnormalities specific for dysphagia.

PLANS

Diagnostic

Differential Diagnosis

Oropharyngeal Dysphagia

NEUROLOGIC DISEASES. Control of swallowing is located in the swallow center of the brain stem, but this locus interacts with many subcortical and cortical areas of the brain. Dysphagia is most commonly associated with and most prolonged after bilateral brainstem *infarcts.* Infarcts of large areas of the cortex can also result in dysphagia, although eventual recovery of swallowing function is more likely.

Patients with bulbar *poliomyelitis* may develop weakness of the pharyngeal constrictor muscles resulting in mild dysphagia. Most learn to compensate for this weakness by eating small boluses and washing the food down with water. Dysphagia is now being reported in patients with postpolio syndrome.

When *amyotrophic lateral sclerosis,* a disease of motor neurons, involves the cranial nerves, severe and progressive dysphagia results. These patients experience marked difficulty with deglutition and frequently develop choking spells or frank aspiration.

Less than a quarter of patients with *Parkinson's disease* complain of dysphagia. Those who do report difficulty manipulating a bolus resting on the tongue and show poor coordination between contraction of the pharyngeal constrictors and relaxation of the upper esophageal sphincter. Treatment with medications for Parkinson's disease may ameliorate symptoms.

Dysphagia has also been reported in the following neurologic diseases: multiple sclerosis, Huntington's chorea, tabes dorsalis, cerebral palsy, brainstem tumors, and diabetes mellitus.

MUSCULAR DISEASES. About a third of patients with *myasthenia gravis* complain of dysphagia. Repetitive swallowing during a meal leads to a progressive weakness of the tongue and pharyngeal muscles, resulting in dysphagia. Meals are prolonged as patients must take frequent rests to rejuvenate muscle function. Medical treatment of myasthenia gravis improves deglutition.

Oropharyngeal dysphagia may also sometimes complicate the course of patients with the following disorders: muscular dystrophy, polymyositis, dermatomyositis, mixed connective tissue disease and metabolic myopathies.

STRUCTURAL LESIONS OF THE OROPHARYNX. Any process that obstructs the oropharynx can result in dysphagia. Inflammatory conditions such as pharyngitis, tonsillitis, and tonsillar abscess can transiently impair deglutition. Head and neck cancers can cause obstruction or infiltrate nerves that mediate swallowing. Extrinsic compression of the oropharynx from lymphadenopathy, thyroid enlargement, and Zenker's diverticulum are well-known causes of dysphagia.

CRICOPHARYNGEAL ACHALASIA. In this rare disorder, incomplete relaxation of the upper esophageal sphincter in conjunction with weakness of pharyngeal constrictors results in dysphagia. A cine cervical esophagram reveals an indentation of the column of barium at the cricopharyngeus, often called a cricopharyngeal bar. The proximal pharynx is often dilated and pharyngeal clearing of barium is delayed. Diagnosis is established by esophageal manometry, which reveals incomplete relaxation of the upper esophageal sphincter.

Esophageal Dysphagia

MOTILITY DISORDERS. *Achalasia* is a degenerative disorder of neurons of the myenteric plexus of the smooth muscle portion of the esophagus. This results in aperistalsis and incomplete relaxation of the lower esophageal sphincter. Patients experience chronic, progressive dysphagia for both solids and liquids. Delayed esophageal emptying results in stasis, esophageal distention, regurgitation, and weight loss. Diagnosis is made by manometry, which must reveal aperistalsis and may reveal hypertension and/or incomplete relaxation of the lower esophageal sphincter.

Those afflicted with *diffuse esophageal spasm* complain of attacks of chest pain and dysphagia that can present simultaneously, but usually occur separately. The dysphagia for liquids and solids is episodic, generally lasting from minutes to hours, and nonprogressive. Attacks are sometimes precipitated by eating rapidly, swallowing, and ingesting hot or cold liquids. Anxiety disorders and depression are frequently found in these patients and attacks of pain may be more frequent during periods of emotional stress. Diagnosis is made by manometry, which requires the presence of simultaneous, nonpropulsive contractions after greater than 10% of swallowed water boluses and intermittent normal peristalsis.

Scleroderma is a disorder characterized by fibrosis and vascular insufficiency leading to atrophy of the smooth muscles of the esophagus. Muscular atrophy is progressive and results in aperistalsis with a persistently open lower esophageal sphincter. Although these patients experience dysphagia, heartburn secondary to gastroesophageal reflux, is often the most prominent symptom.

BENIGN STRICTURES. Chronic gastroesophageal reflux may lead to the formation of a fibrotic stricture of the distal esophagus. Dysphagia usually begins with solids but eventually progresses to include liquids. A long history of heartburn or atypical chest pain is usually present. *Peptic strictures* of the proximal esophagus may occur in patients with Barrett's transformation.

A *mucosal ring (Schatzki's ring)* is a ring composed of mucosa that narrows the lumen at the gastroesophageal junction. Intermittent, nonprogressive dysphagia for solids only is usually seen when the lumen is reduced to less than 13 mm in diameter.

Webs are thin membranes of squamous mucosa that run transversely across the esophageal lumen and potentially obstruct the passage of solid boluses. Most frequent in the mid- to upper esophagus, they can cause intermittent, nonprogressive dysphagia for solids.

Radiation esophagitis and erosive esophagitis due to caustic ingestions can result in long strictures of the esophagus with marked dysphagia for both liquids and solids.

ESOPHAGEAL ULCERATION. Ulceration of the distal esophagus can occur as a complication of severe gastroesophageal reflux, Zollinger–Ellison syndrome, or medications such as tetracycline, potassium chloride, and quinidine. Typically these patients manifest chest pain and odynophagia in addition to dysphagia.

CANCER. Dysphagia for solids that progresses to include liquids in an elderly patient is strongly suspicious for malignancy. In addition to carcinoma of the esophagus, tumors of the lung and mediastinum may also produce dysphagia via extrinsic compression of the esophagus. Weight loss is a prominent symptom in most of these patients.

DYSPHAGIA LUSORIA. Dysphagia lusoria refers to difficulty swallowing as a consequence of extrinsic compression of the esophagus by anomalous vascular structures. Symptoms usually begin in childhood, although patients can occasionally first present as adults. Most commonly at fault are aberrations of the aorta, right subclavian, and left pulmonary arteries.

Diagnostic Options

Oropharyngeal Dysphagia. Oropharyngeal dysphagia is often apparent from the patient's complaints or history of neuromuscular disease. Careful examination of the mouth and pharynx supplemented by indirect laryngoscopy may exclude structural lesions. A video cervical and thoracic esophagram must always be performed to exclude structural lesions. An experienced radiologist can detect the presence of weakness or incoordination of the muscles of the oropharynx. The finding of compatible abnormalities, in a patient with known neuromuscular disease, ensures the diagnosis. In addition, the presence and severity of pulmonary aspiration of contrast can be documented in this way. If cricopharyngeal achalasia is suspected, an esophageal manometry should be performed to document incomplete relaxation of the upper esophageal sphincter. When a structural abnormality is noted, direct laryngoscopy, endoscopy, and/or bronchoscopy may then be employed to identify and biopsy the lesion. These procedures are also sometimes useful to rule out small structural lesions that may not be detectable by radiography.

Esophageal Dysphagia.

BARIUM SWALLOW WITH FLUOROSCOPY. This examination must be performed first in all patients with esophageal dysphagia to exclude diverticula and to delineate strictures. Most structural lesions of the esophagus will be evident on a well-performed study. In addition, an experienced radiologist can detect the presence of esophageal motility disorders on fluoroscopy. Achalasia, with its pattern of aperistalsis, esophageal dilation and narrowed column of barium at the lower esophageal sphincter, can be diagnosed with a high degree of specificity. Extrinsic compression is usually detectable, although an endoscopy may be required to exclude an esophageal etiology. Occasionally, esophageal webs, ulcers, or mild strictures may be radiographically silent and require endoscopy for diagnosis.

COMPUTED TOMOGRAPHY SCAN OF THE CHEST WITH CONTRAST. If extrinsic compression is suggested by a barium swallow and confirmed by endoscopy, a computed tomography scan should be performed to localize the lesion and direct further diagnostic modalities.

ESOPHAGOGASTROSCOPY. Endoscopy should be performed in every patient either to biopsy a known lesion or to exclude structural abnormalities that may have been missed by a barium swallow. All masses and any strictures must be biopsied to exclude malignancy. If a peptic stricture is present, biopsies to exclude Barrett's transformation distal to the stricture should be performed. Mucosal diseases such as esophagitis, Barrett's transformation, and ulcers may only be found at endoscopy.

ESOPHAGEAL MANOMETRY. If esophageal lesions have been excluded by radiography, an endoscopy and esophageal manometry study should be performed. A modified nasogastric tube containing pressure-sensing transducers at defined intervals is passed into the stomach and positioned so that simultaneous recordings can be taken from the lower esophageal sphincter and several points along the esophagus. In this way, one can measure the response of the esophageal body and sphincter to swallowed boluses of water. Esophageal manometry is the first test that should be employed in the workup of suspected motility disorders. Specific patterns have been identified for achalasia, diffuse esophageal spasm, and scleroderma (see Differential Diagnosis).

ANGIOGRAPHY. When extrinsic compression due to aberrant vascular structures is suggested, angiography of the aorta, aortic branches, and pulmonary arteries may be helpful.

Recommended Approach

In suspected oropharyngeal dysphagia, a cine cervical and thoracic esophagram should be performed to rule out structural lesions and/or document muscular contraction abnormalities. A history of neuromuscular disease with compatible findings on fluoroscopy is usually diagnostic. When structural lesions are found, endoscopy, indirect laryngoscopy, or bronchoscopy may be necessary to establish the cause. In esophageal dysphagia, a barium swallow must be performed first to exclude diverticula and to delineate the nature of esophageal strictures. Subsequently, esophagogastroscopy is performed to biopsy identified lesions or exclude mucosal disease. If both studies are normal then esophageal manometry is required to diagnose motility disorders.

Therapeutic

Therapeutic Options

A discussion of therapeutic options for all of the causes of dysphagia is beyond the scope of this chapter. Nonetheless a few brief comments can be made.

Oropharyngeal Dysphagia. Most neuromuscular diseases are difficult to treat and thus dysphagia does not improve. In many cases patients may learn to adapt their mode of deglutition to minimize symptoms. In severe cases, a feeding gastrostomy may be necessary to maintain nutrition. The dysphagia associated with disorders such as cortical cerebrovascular accidents, Parkinson's disease, and myasthenia gravis may improve with time or treatment.

Esophageal Dysphagia. Benign strictures of the esophagus usually respond to a course of forceful or pneumatic dilation. Aggressive acid suppression therapy may reduce the incidence of recurrent peptic strictures. In severe cases of radiation- or caustic ingestion-induced stricture that fails to respond to dilation, a surgical gastric pullup or colonic interposition may be required. Esophageal cancer is surgically resectable at the time of diagnosis in only a minority of cases. Chemotherapy and radiation therapy may palliate dysphagia for a time, but often do not provide a long-term solution. Esophageal dilation may alleviate symptoms in some patients, but the benefit is short-lived secondary to tumor growth. Endoscopic laser ablation of tumor, surgical resection, and endoscopically placed esophageal stents provide a more lasting palliation. In some cases, a surgically placed feeding gastrotomy is required if nutrition is to be maintained. Achalasia is best treated with endoscopic or surgical myotomy of the lower esophageal sphincter. Esophageal spastic disorders are difficult to treat, but may respond to nitrates, calcium channel blockers, or trazodone hydrochloride. There is no treatment for scleroderma esophagus, but aggressive therapy of gastroesophageal reflux in these patients prevents a host of complications.

Recommended Approach

The recommended approach depends on the etiology of the dysphagia. Please see appropriate chapters for recommendations based on the etiology of dysphagia.

FOLLOW-UP

No matter what the cause of dysphagia, patients must be followed closely for response to treatment. Treatment failures need to be evaluated to delineate the reasons for a poor outcome and treatment modified accordingly.

DISCUSSION
Prevalence and Incidence

The prevalence and incidence of dysphagia depend on the specific cause. Please see appropriate chapters for additional information.

Related Basic Science

Abnormalities of physiology, molecular biology, and anatomy are present to variable degrees in many etiologies of dysphagia. Please see specific chapters for derangements.

Natural History and Its Modification with Treatment

Neuromuscular disorders are, in general, poorly responsive to therapy and thus the dysphagia often does not improve. Notable exceptions are cortical cerebrovascular accidents, myasthenia gravis, and Parkinson's disease, which may improve with time or treatment. Dysphagia improves dramatically in patients with achalasia once a successful myotomy is obtained. Esophageal spasm is difficult to treat due to the lack of established therapeutic regimens. Most patients must undergo trials of several medications before settling on a drug that ameliorates their symptoms. The dysphagia of scleroderma responds in some cases to treatment with prokinetic agents. Benign strictures of the esophagus generally respond to a course of dilation. Long, severe strictures seen in radiation esophagitis or caustic ingestions may not respond to dilation and may eventually require surgical bypass. Esophageal malignancies are generally not resectable for cure at diagnosis and thus treatment is often aimed at palliation of dysphagia. The best long-term palliation results are achieved with laser ablation of tumor, esophageal stents, and surgical gastric pullup.

Prevention

Medical treatment of Parkinson's disease and myasthenia gravis can prevent recurrent dysphagia in these patients. Prompt diagnosis and aggressive treatment of gastroesophageal reflux can prevent the formation of peptic strictures. Avoidance of foods or behaviors that trigger attacks of dysphagia in patients with esophageal spasm may reduce the frequency of dysphagia.

Cost Containment

A careful history and physical examination can often differentiate between oropharyngeal and esophageal dysphagia. Significant savings can be incurred by thus avoiding an unnecessary workup. Aggressive therapy of reflux disease can reduce the incidence of one of the more common causes of dysphagia, peptic strictures.

REFERENCES

Castell DO. Approach to the patient with dysphagia. In: Yamada T, ed. Textbook of gastroenterology. Philadelphia: Lippincott, 1991:562.
Castell DO. Overview and symptom assessment. In: Castell DO, ed. The esophagus. Boston: Little, Brown, 1992:29.
Pope CE. Heartburn, dysphagia, and other esophageal symptoms. In: Sleisenger MH, Fordtran JS, eds. Gastrointestinal disease. Philadelphia: Saunders, 1989:200.
Ravich WJ. Esophageal dysphagia. In: Groher ME, ed. Dysphagia. Stoneham, MA: Butterworth-Heinemann, 1992:85.

CHAPTER 19–12

Achalasia

Vincent James Notar-Francesco, M.D.

DEFINITION

Achalasia is a motility disorder of smooth muscle in which there is a progressive loss of peristalsis of the esophageal body and failure of relaxation of the lower esophageal sphincter. This results in a reduced ability of the esophagus to propel food toward the stomach and an increased resistance to passage of the bolus past a tightly closed lower esophageal sphincter.

ETIOLOGY

Degeneration and loss of ganglion cells of the myenteric (Auerbach's) plexus in the distal two thirds of the esophagus have been described in achalasia. This loss appears to be progressive, as patients with the longest history of symptoms have the fewest remaining ganglion cells. The affected neurons appear to be postganglionic noncholinergic, nonadrenergic inhibitory nerve cells. Investigations have revealed that these fibers secrete vasoactive intestinal peptide (VIP). Most authorities believe that VIP, a potent smooth muscle relaxer, plays a role in both peristalsis of the esophageal body and relaxation of the lower esophageal sphincter. Because VIP-secreting neurons mediate the wave of smooth muscle relaxation that normally precedes peristalsis, their destruction may disrupt the swallowing mechanism and lead to aperistalsis. Selective impairment of inhibitory VIP-containing neurons with sparing of stimulatory cholinergic nerve fibers may explain the increased resting pressure and reluctant relaxation of the lower esophageal sphincter.

In some patients, degenerative changes have been noted in the vagal dorsal motor nucleus and in branches of the vagus nerve supplying the esophagus. At this time, the significance of these additional lesions is not well understood.

What triggers ganglion cell loss in patients with achalasia? Many believe that idiopathic achalasia is primarily a degenerative disease of neurons, whereas others maintain that the nerve cell damage is a consequence of infection by a yet unknown organism. The latter argument is supported by the fact that a protozoa, *Trypanosoma cruzi*, can cause the secondary achalasia seen in Chagas' disease.

CRITERIA FOR DIAGNOSIS
Suggestive

A history of chronic progressive dysphagia, often lasting years, for both solids and liquids associated with regurgitation of undigested food, sensation of retrosternal fullness, and weight loss strongly suggests the diagnosis. A barium swallow demonstrating aperistalsis and tapering of the column of contrast at the lower esophageal sphincter is highly suggestive.

Definitive

To confirm suspected cases of achalasia, the patient must undergo esophageal manometry testing. Aperistalsis of the smooth muscle portion of the esophagus is required for diagnosis. The presence of a hypertensive and/or incompletely relaxing lower esophageal sphincter, although not mandatory, generally ensures the diagnosis is correct.

CLINICAL MANIFESTATIONS
Subjective

Dysphagia for solids may precede that for liquids, but most patients complain of difficulty with both. Characteristically, the onset of dysphagia is gradual and has often been present for years before the patient presents. Most report that swallowed food "doesn't go down all the way," "takes a long time to go down," or "gets stuck in the middle of my chest." Many believe that their esophagus never completely empties after meals and are plagued by a chronic sense of retrosternal fullness. Patients in time develop strategies to improve esophageal emptying, such as ingesting carbonated beverages, Valsalva maneuvers, belching, and repetitive swallowing.

Regurgitation of undigested food is a common complaint. Typically, the regurgitated bolus represents food eaten many hours before and does not induce an "acid" taste in the mouth. Regurgitation of saliva or food retained within the esophagus may occur on recumbency and result in noctural coughing or choking spells. Occasionally, patients come to attention for complications of chronic aspiration such as pneumonia and chronic bronchitis.

One half of patients suffer from atypical chest pain. This is described as a retrosternal sensation of fullness that progresses during meals and may limit further consumption. Many patients report that they induce vomiting to relieve their chest pain. Some complain of heartburn, which predictably does not respond to H_2 antagonists and may be due to the products of bacterial fermentation of food retained within the esophagus.

Weight loss is a finding in the majority of patients and can often be used to gauge the duration or severity of their swallowing difficulty. In addition, weight gain after instituting therapy is an important clinical parameter of improved esophageal emptying.

A long duration of symptoms of dysphagia is usually present and in some patients may extend back to childhood. A history of residence in parts of South America where *Trypanosoma cruzi* is endemic, cardiac arrhythmias, congestive heart failure, or severe chronic constipation may be important clues to the possibility of underlying Chagas' disease. Malignancies can produce a disorder similar to achalasia, called pseudo-achalasia, as a result of either distal esophageal compression or infiltration of the myenteric plexus by malignant cells. Most of these cases are due to adenocarcinoma of the gastroesophageal junction; however, pseudo-achalasia in the setting of squamous cell carcinoma of the esophagus, lymphoma, and pancreatic cancer has been described. Lastly, diabetes mellitus with autonomic neuropathy or chronic intestinal pseudo-obstruction is rarely associated with a mild, generally asymptomatic, form of secondary achalasia.

Objective

Physical Examination

In general, there are no findings specific for idiopathic achalasia on examination. Many patients have lost weight and, in some cases, may appear emaciated. The presence of an irregular pulse or signs of congestive heart failure, especially right-sided, may suggest the presence of chronic Chagas' disease.

Routine Laboratory Abnormalities

There are no laboratory abnormalities that are specific for idiopathic achalasia.

PLANS
Diagnostic

Differential Diagnosis

Chagas' Disease. This condition is brought on by the bite of the reduviid bug, endemic to parts of South America, which transmits *Trypanosoma cruzi*. Chronic infection leads to degeneration of ganglion cells of the eosphagus, colon, heart, and other organs. Eventually a disorder ensues that is radiographically and manometrically indistinguishable from idiopathic achalasia. Congestive cardiomyopathy with marked rhythm disturbances and chronic constipation with megacolon are frequent features of this disease. In cases where chronic Chagas' disease is suspected, serology confirming the presence of antibodies to *T. cruzi* may help to establish the diagnosis.

Pseudochalasia. A number of malignancies can produce pseudo-achalasia by directly compressing the distal esophagus and/or infiltrating the

myenteric plexus. Adenocarcinoma of the gastroesophageal junction is the most common tumor reported, but cases of pseudo-achalasia have been described with squamous cell carcinoma, oat cell carcinoma, lymphoma, and pancreatic cancer. Pseudo-achalasia should be suspected in patients whose onset of dysphagia occurs after the fourth or fifth decade.

Secondary Achalasia. Some patients with diabetes mellitus and autonomic neuropathy may have similar manometric findings. Symptoms of dysphagia are generally mild in these patients. A similar condition has been reported in some patients with chronic idiopathic intestinal pseudo-obstruction. In rare cases of sarcoidosis and amyloidosis, infiltration of the esophageal wall may produce a condition mimicking achalasia.

Diffuse Esophageal Spasm. Those afflicted experience intermittent bouts of chest pain and/or dysphagia. The swallowing difficulty here is transient and does not progress. Therefore, these patients do not develop food impaction, regurgitation, or weight loss. Manometry reveals frequent nonpropulsive, simultaneous contractions intermixed with normal peristalsis.

Esophageal Strictures. Strictures of the esophagus as a consequence of tumors, gastroesophageal reflux, Barrett's esophagitis, caustic ingestion, esophageal rings, or webs may present with dysphagia.

Diagnostic Options

Chest X-ray. Chest films may demonstrate a widened mediastinum indicative of esophageal dilation. An air–fluid level in the mediastinum from swallowed air and retained food in the esophagus may be present. Absence of a gastric air bubble on an upright film has been described. These findings are suggestive but by no means specific for achalasia.

Barium Swallowing with Fluoroscopy. Under fluoroscopy, initial swallows of contrast reveal diminished or absent peristalsis of the distal two thirds of the esophagus. The contrast material may be seen to move randomly up and down as a consequence of weak nonperistaltic contractions. Very little contrast may pass into the stomach. When contrast is seen to pass through the lower esophageal sphincter, the stream is quite narrow, suggesting that the sphincter has not opened fully. On static films, the most constant finding is a smoothly tapering column of contrast at the level of the lower esophageal sphincter, which is commonly referred to as a *bird's beak*. This is highly suggestive of achalasia. Dilation of the distal esophagus is usually present and, in long-standing cases, may become tortuous giving it a sigmoid appearance. The severity of esophageal retention may be gauged by the amount of contrast material remaining in the esophagus and the amount of time required for esophageal emptying. In general, a positive barium swallow can suggest the diagnosis of achalasia with a high degree of specificity.

Esophagogastroscopy. Endoscopy must be performed in all patients to exclude other causes of dysphagia such as mucosal disease, peptic strictures, and malignancy. In achalasia, endoscopy may reveal a dilated esophagus, retained food, esophagitis, white plaques suggestive of infection with *Candida*, ulcerations, absent peristaltic waves, and a persistently closed sphincter. The lower esophageal sphincter often does not open despite insufflation of air and sometimes requires mild pressure to pass with the endoscope. Marked difficulty or inability to progress beyond the sphincter strongly suggests the presence of carcinoma at the gastroesophageal junction.

Esophageal Manometry. Esophageal manometry is required for a definitive diagnosis of achalasia. A modified nasogastric tube containing pressure-sensing transducers at defined intervals is passed into the stomach and positioned so that simultaneous recordings can be taken from several points along the esophageal body and the lower esophageal sphincter. In this way, the contractile response of the esophagus and sphincter to swallowed boluses of water can be measured. Of the four manometric features seen in achalasia (Table 19–12–1), aperistalsis of the smooth muscle portion of the esophagus is the only finding that is absolutely required for diagnosis. Incomplete or absent relaxation of the esophageal sphincter in response to a swallowed bolus is usually present. In early achalasia, lower esophageal sphincter relax-

TABLE 19–12–1. ESOPHAGEAL MANOMETRY FINDINGS IN ACHALASIA

Finding	Required	Frequency in Achalasia
Aperistalsis of distal esophagus*	Yes	All patients
Incomplete relaxation of lower esophageal sphincter†	No	Majority of patients
Hypertensive resting lower esophageal sphincter‡	No	Most patients
Elevated baseline intraesophageal pressure§	No	Many patients

*Aperistalsis refers to the absence of contractions that, when measured at several points along the esophagus, appear to be propagating distally.
†Incomplete relaxation of the lower esophageal sphincter refers to a sphincter that relaxes partially but not fully with swallows. Full relaxation requires a drop in the pressure of the sphincter to a level equivalent to that measured in the lumen of the stomach.
‡Hypertensive lower esophageal sphincter refers to an elevation beyond the normal range for the mean pressure, in mm Hg, measured at the sphincter at rest.
§Elevated intraesophageal pressure refers to an elevation of the pressure, in mm Hg, measured in the lumen of the esophagus at rest above that measured within the gastric lumen, which is taken as baseline.

ation may be complete but of abnormally short duration. Lower esophageal resting pressure is elevated above normal, that is, greater than 30 to 35 mm Hg, in more than two thirds of patients. In many cases the baseline intraesophageal pressure is elevated as a consequence of retained food and secretions.

Recommended Approach

The clinical history is often highly suggestive of achalasia especially if dysphagia has been present for years and there is a history of regurgitation of undigested food. On the strength of this information, a barium swallow should be obtained, which if positive is highly sensitive and specific for achalasia. An esophagogastroscopy must then be performed to rule out causes of pseudo-achalasia such as malignancy of the gastroesophageal junction. A definitive diagnosis requires the finding of aperistalsis on an esophageal manometry and must be performed prior to instituting therapy.

Therapeutic

Therapeutic Options

There is no therapy available that can reverse or prevent the progression of the neural lesions responsible for idiopathic achalasia. Therefore, the aim of treatment is to palliate dysphagia. All therapies are directed at alleviating the resistance posed by the lower esophageal sphincter.

Medical Therapy. A number of drugs known to relax the lower esophageal sphincter have been used to treat achalasia. These medications improve dysphagia by partially relieving the fixed obstruction at the sphincter, but do not affect the atonic esophageal body. The most commonly used preparations are isosorbide dinitrate 5 to 10 mg sublingually before meals and nifedipine 10 to 20 mg sublingually 30 minutes before meals. In general, these agents reduce lower esophageal sphincter resting pressure by one half during their therapeutic window. Less than half of patients treated in this manner show a good clinical response. For a number of reasons including poor response, tachyphylaxis, and limiting side effects, the use of these medications in the long-term management of achalasia remains controversial. They are most appropriately suited to mild cases where a good response has been obtained or in patients whose age, medical condition, or refusal makes invasive therapies impractical.

Pneumatic Dilation. Under endoscopic and fluoroscopic guidance a balloon-equipped catheter is passed into the stomach and centered across the lower esophageal sphincter. The balloon is then inflated to a prescribed pressure to stretch and tear the circular muscle that comprises the lower esophageal sphincter. Generally, a balloon of the smallest diameter (i.e., 3 cm) is tried first, and if that fails larger balloons up to 4 cm are employed at subsequent dilations. The procedure is successful in one half to two thirds of patients. Some patients may develop recur-

rent symptoms years later and require repeat pneumatic dilation. In the best hands, the risk of esophageal perforation is 5 to 10%. Therefore, after dilation it is imperative to evaluate the esophagus radiologically with water-soluble contrast medium to exclude this complication. Many small perforations can be managed conservatively with antibiotics and close observation, but some small perforations and all large perforations require surgical correction at which time a myotomy of the sphincter should be performed. The presence of an epiphrenic diverticulum or a large hiatal hernia is a relative contraindication to dilation because of the increased risk of perforation. H_2 antagonists and antireflux measures may need to be employed after successful rupture of the lower esophageal sphincter to prevent reflux esophagitis.

Surgical Myotomy. Through a transthoracic or transabdominal approach the esophagus is mobilized and the lower esophageal sphincter identified by palpation. A longitudinal myotomy extending several centimeters above and below the sphincter is performed. Some surgeons combine this procedure with a fundoplication to prevent gastroesophageal reflux. Fundoplication is not generally recommended because, in the absence of peristalsis, a tight wrap could result in recurrent dysphagia. Surgical myotomy is successful in the majority of patients. The incidence of subsequent gastroesophageal reflux is higher than that with pneumatic dilation, and therapy is more often required.

Recommended Approach

Medical therapy is best suited to those patients with mild symptoms without significant esophageal dilation who have demonstrated a prolonged good clinical response. In addition, medical therapy may be useful in those afflicted whose medical condition or refusal to undergo invasive therapy precludes myotomy. Because of the frequent failure of medical therapy in the long-term management of achalasia, most patients should be treated with pneumatic dilation or surgical myotomy. Although pneumatic dilation has a slightly lower success rate than surgical myotomy, its ease of performance, short hospital stay, reduced cost, and reduced recovery period make it the initial treatment of choice. Surgical myotomy should be reserved for those patients in whom pneumatic dilation is contraindicated or those who fail to respond to pneumatic dilation. Recently, endoscopic-guided injection of the lower esophageal sphincter with botulinum toxin has been successful in a small number of patients with achalasia. If found to be safe and efficacious, this may represent an important future therapeutic modality.

FOLLOW-UP

After the initial pneumatic dilation, patients should be followed to assess if there is an adequate reduction in symptoms of dysphagia and an increase in weight. When there is a question of adequacy of the endoscopic myotomy, a barium study can assess the patency of the lower esophageal sphincter and evaluate esophageal emptying. Occasionally, repeat esophageal manometry is indicated to measure the residual resting lower esophageal sphincter pressure. In those patients who have failed to respond, repeat pneumatic dilation can be performed with a larger-diameter balloon. Patients who do not respond to a second or third dilation should undergo surgical myotomy. After successful endoscopic or surgical myotomy, patients need to be monitored for the occurrence of symptomatic gastroesophageal reflux. If present, reflux should be treated aggressively to prevent esophagitis, esophageal ulceration, Barrett's transformation, and peptic strictures. The incidence of squamous cell carcinoma is increased in patients with achalasia possibly as a result of prolonged exposure of the mucosa to the products of bacterial action on retained food. Although no consensus is available, some physicians perform surveillance endoscopy in these patients.

DISCUSSION

Prevalence

The prevalence of achalasia is approximately 1 to 10 cases per 100,000 population. The disease appears to be more common in whites and there is no clear gender preference. Onset of achalasia in childhood is well known, but most patients present in their twenties to forties. Onset of achalasia in later life should raise concerns of pseudo-achalasia due to malignancy.

Related Basic Science

Physiologic or Metabolic Derangement

Degeneration of ganglia in the myenteric plexus of the esophagus of unknown etiology occurs, resulting in a loss of VIP-containing neurons. The decreased inhibitory neurologic input may result in loss of the wave of smooth muscle inhibition that precedes peristalsis and eventually causes aperistalsis. In addition, diminished inhibitory signals with preserved cholinergic stimulatory signals may lead to a hypertensive lower esophageal sphincter that fails to relax appropriately. Ultimately, dysphagia for solids and liquids results.

Anatomic Derangement

The lack of the propulsive force of peristalsis and the obstruction presented by a tightly closed lower esophageal sphincter lead to dilation of the esophagus.

Natural History and Its Modification with Treatment

Achalasia is a progressive disease for which no treatment is currently available that can retard or reverse its course. Medical therapy may alleviate symptoms transiently but does not generally provide a long-term solution. Most patients require pneumatic dilation or surgical myotomy. Those who are treated early, before marked esophageal dilation develops, may avoid complications of esophageal ulceration, esophageal candidiasis, pulmonary aspiration, and esophageal carcinoma. With successful myotomy, patients are able to gain weight and

lead a normal life. Some develop gastroesophageal reflux, especially after surgical myotomy, which responds to H_2 blockers and antireflux measures. In light of the increased risk of esophageal carcinoma, some gastroenterologists recommend endoscopic surveillance.

Prevention

The cause of idiopathic achalasia is not understood and therefore there are no specific recommendations for prevention. Prompt diagnosis and institution of therapy may prevent complications such as esophagitis, esophageal ulceration, pulmonary aspiration, and esophageal carcinoma. In achalasia secondary to Chagas' disease, efforts to eradicate the vector and prompt treatment of acute infection may greatly reduce the incidence of esophageal disease resulting from chronic infection.

Cost Containment

Costs can be reduced by performing pneumatic dilation whenever possible and reserving costly surgical myotomy for those cases that fail to respond.

REFERENCES

Cendes A, Braghetto I, Henriquez A, et al. Late results of prospective randomized study comparing forceful dilatation and esophagomyotomy in patients with achalasia of the esophagus. Gut 1989;30:299.

Katz PO. Achalasia. In: Castell DO, ed. Esophageal motility testing. New York: Elsevier, 1987:107.

Richter JE. Motility disorders of the esophagus. In: Yamada T, ed. Textbook of gastroenterology. Philadelphia: Lippincott, 1991:1083.

Wong RK, Maydonovitch CL. Achalasia. In: Castell DO, ed. The esophagus. Boston: Little, Brown, 1992:233.

CHAPTER 19–13

Diffuse Esophageal Spasm

Vincent James Notar-Francesco, M.D.

DEFINITION

Diffuse esophageal spasm (DES) is a motility disorder in which normal peristalsis is interrupted by intermittent simultaneous nonpropulsive contractions of the smooth muscle portion of the esophagus, resulting in dysphagia and chest pain. Diagnosis requires more than 10% simultaneous contractions following swallowed boluses of water and periods of normal peristalsis documented by esophageal manometry.

ETIOLOGY

Little is known about the etiology of DES. Mild abnormalities in afferent fibers of the vagus nerve suggest that the defect lies in the sensory pathway. When patients with DES undergo 24-hour ambulatory esophageal manometry, symptoms of pain and dysphagia often precede manometric changes. This supports the theory that attacks are triggered by an abnormality of the sensory pathway or central processing. In this schema, the abnormal manometric findings may be an epiphenomenon of a disorder whose genesis lies in aberrant sensation. Further evidence for central nervous system involvement comes from studies that indicate that stressful situations worsen symptoms and manometric abnormalities. Additionally, surveys of patients with DES have revealed a higher than expected incidence of psychiatric diagnoses, mostly anxiety disorders and depression.

On the other hand, some authorities have reported indirect evidence suggesting that the defect lies in impaired noncholinergic, nonadrenergic inhibitory neural mechanisms. In their view, diminished inhibitory input with sparing of excitatory signals leads to the high-amplitude, long-duration, nonperistaltic contractions seen in DES.

CRITERIA FOR DIAGNOSIS

Suggestive

A history of episodic chest pain and dysphagia that may occur together, but often occur separately. Pain is retrosternal in location and often mimics angina pectoris. Dysphagia is for both solids and liquids. Symptoms are often temporally related to stressful situations, ingestion of hot or cold liquids, and rapid eating. A barium swallow may reveal tertiary contractions defined as a series of simultaneous, nonperistaltic contraction waves which give the appearance of multiple indentations along the column of barium. Because DES is an episodic condition, these findings are not reliably present.

Definitive

Diagnosis rests on esophageal manometry testing. Manometric criteria required for diagnosis are greater than 10% simultaneous contractions and periods of normal peristalsis after swallowed boluses of water. Again, because of the intermittent nature of this disease, a normal manometry study does not exclude the diagnosis.

CLINICAL MANIFESTATIONS

Subjective

Most patients experience episodic attacks of chest pain and dysphagia, which may occur together or separately. Nearly all patients report chest pain described as a retrosternal pressure sensation of variable severity. It may radiate to the back, arms, and neck in a pattern indistinguishable from that of cardiac angina. To further confound things, the pain may even respond to nitroglycerin. The acute pain usually lasts from minutes to hours and is often followed by a residual dull discomfort. Swallowing is generally not impaired during these attacks. Retrosternal discomfort is occasionally related to meals or the ingestion of hot or cold liquids, but is not related to exertion. The etiology of the pain is poorly understood. Some feel that it is a consequence of strong, nonpropulsive contractions that these patients experience. Others, citing the reduced pain threshold with balloon distention of the esophagus seen in patients with DES, feel that chest pain is due to heightened esophageal sensitivity.

Dysphagia is present in two thirds of cases. The swallowing difficulty is generally of short duration and not progressive. Because dysphagia is neither severe nor chronic, patients do not usually manifest symptoms of food impaction, regurgitation, or weight loss. Impaction of a bolus is a very rare event in DES and, if present, should alert the physician to the possibility of other diagnoses. Dysphagia can occur at rest or be triggered by eating rapidly, swallowing large boluses of food, and ingesting hot, cold, or carbonated liquids. Symptoms are intermittent and vary from daily attacks to relatively infrequent bouts. Stressful situations, especially emotional stress, are reported by many patients to increase the frequency and severity of episodes.

A small number of patients may complain of pyrosis, which does not appear to be related to acid reflux as it is not reproduced by instillation of acid into the esophagus. Weight loss, regurgitation, and pulmonary aspiration are uncommon.

Surveys have noted a high incidence of pyschiatric disease, especially anxiety disorders and depression, in patients with DES. Many patients may also demonstrate a history of symptoms compatible with the diagnosis of irritable bowel syndrome.

Objective

Physical Examination

There are no findings on physical examination specific for DES.

Routine Laboratory Abnormalities

There are no abnormalities of routine laboratory tests suggestive of DES.

PLANS
Diagnostic

Differential Diagnosis

Coronary Artery Disease. The retrosternal pain of DES closely mimics that of angina pectoris and may even respond to nitroglycerin. Key differences are that pain in esophageal spasm is not related to exertion, often lasts for hours, and is usually followed by a residual dull sensation before resolving completely. Nonetheless, coronary artery disease should be excluded in all patients with appropriate cardiac testing.

Gastroesophageal Reflux. Heartburn is indistinguishable from the pain experienced by patients with DES, but dysphagia is generally not present. Reflux disease can often be separated on clinical grounds because it is provoked by large meals, postprandial recumbency, substances that reduce lower esophageal sphincter tone responds to antacids or H_2 blockers. In difficult cases, esophagoscopy or an upper gastrointestinal series may reveal esophagitis and/or hiatal hernia suggesting reflux. Twenty-four-hour intraesophageal pH monitoring provides the best way to document that episodes of pain are related to reflux of acid.

Nutcracker Esophagus. In this rare condition, patients experience episodic chest pain and, on manometry, are found to have extremely high amplitude peristaltic contractions. Strict diagnosis is made at manometry where these patients are shown to have normal peristalsis with contraction waves of very high amplitude, greater than 150 to 180 mm Hg. Frequent nonperistaltic simultaneous contractions are not seen in this disorder. Nutcracker esophagus remains a controversial entity as manometrically recorded high-amplitude contractions do not correlate with episodes of chest pain.

Achalasia. In general, the dysphagia seen in DES is not progressive and, therefore, does not lead to esophageal stasis, regurgitation, and weight loss. Because of this, achalasia can be excluded on clinical grounds in most cases. An esophageal manometric study in patients with achalasia reveals aperistalsis of the esophageal body, thus excluding DES.

Esophageal Disease. Lesions of the esophagus such as esophagitis, esophageal ulceration, and peptic or malignant strictures may present with dysphagia or chest pain. These entities are easily excluded by esophagoscopy or radiography.

Diagnostic Options

Barium Esophagram with Fluoroscopy. Barium studies may demonstrate findings typical of DES, even in patients who are not symptomatic at the time of the study. On fluoroscopy, the peristaltic wave is initially normal; however, as it reaches the smooth muscle portion of the esophagus, it becomes disrupted and appears as a series of nonpropulsive, segmental contractions. These tertiary contractions indent the column of barium at regular intervals and are caused by simultaneous contractions of the circular muscle. They delay transit of the bolus, which is seen to move randomly up and down in the lower esophagus. Radiologists have developed numerous descriptive names for tertiary contractions, including pseudodiverticula, rosary-bead appearance, and, in severe cases, corkscrew esophagus. Sometimes these contractions are so forceful that they obliterate the lumen. Intermixed with these simultaneous contractions are normal peristaltic waves. Tertiary contractions may occur in normal individuals but, when frequent, suggest an underlying motility disorder.

Esophagogastroscopy. Endoscopy has no role in diagnosing DES; however, it is frequently performed to rule out structural lesions of the esophagus.

Esophageal Manometry. A motility study is required for a definitive diagnosis of DES. A modified nasogastric tube containing pressure-sensing transducers at defined intervals is passed into the stomach and positioned so that simultaneous recordings can be taken from several points along the esophageal body and the lower esophageal sphincter. In this way, the contractile response of the esophagus and sphincter to swallowed boluses of water can be measured. Diagnosis of DES (Table 19–13–1) requires the finding of simultaneous contractions after greater than 10% of swallowed water boluses and the presence of periods of normal peristalsis. Simultaneous contractions refers to pressure waveforms measured at several points along the esophagus whose onset is simultaneous. They are by definition nonperistaltic and suggest that large

TABLE 19–13–1. ESOPHAGEAL MANOMETRY FINDINGS IN DIFFUSE ESOPHAGEAL SPASM (DES)

Finding	Required	Frequency in DES
Simultaneous contractions in >10% of swallowed boluses*	Yes	All patients
Intermittent normal peristalsis	Yes	All patients
Repetitive contractions with ≥3 peaks†	No	Some patients
Incomplete relaxation of lower esophageal sphincter‡	No	Few patients
Increased contraction duration§	No	Very few patients
High amplitude contractions‖	No	Very few patients

*Simultaneous contractions refers to contractions measured at several points along the esophagus whose onset is simultaneous. They are by definition nonperistaltic and suggest that large areas of the esophagus are contracting in unison.
†Repetitive contraction refers to a contraction waveform that has multiple peaks.
‡Incomplete relaxation of the lower esophageal sphincter refers to a sphincter that relaxes partially but not fully with swallows. Full relaxation requires a drop in the pressure of the sphincter to a level equivalent to that measured in the lumen of the stomach, which is taken as baseline.
§Contraction duration refers to the length of time in seconds of an individual esophageal contraction.
‖Contraction amplitude refers to the amount of pressure, in mm Hg, generated within the esophageal lumen by an individual esophageal contraction.

areas of the esophagus are contracting in unison. Less than a third of patients display contraction waves with multiple peaks (three or more peaks), which are called repetitive contractions. A few patients may demonstrate failure of the lower esophageal sphincter relaxation and/or esophageal contractions of increased pressure or duration. Because of the episodic nature of DES, a normal motility study does not exclude the diagnosis. Twenty-four-hour ambulatory esophageal manometry may assist in making a diagnosis in some patients. A manometry catheter is carefully positioned in the esophagus and connected to a recording device strapped to the patient's waist. The instrument has a button that the patient can depress when he or she develops symptoms. This action marks the onset of symptoms on the recording and allows for comparison of the temporal relationship between symptoms and changes in motility. Some catheters can also record intraesophageal pH, which can be used to exclude gastroesophageal reflux as a cause of symptoms. In this way, it can be confirmed that episodes of chest pain are related to motility changes. It should be pointed out that the patient does not need to be symptomatic at the time of a manometry study to have changes recorded that are consistent with DES. In fact, most patients who are diagnosed with DES are not symptomatic during the study.

Provocative Tests. Because of the intermittent nature of the disease, a number of methods have been developed to provoke attacks or manometric changes. Edrophonium chloride 80 μg/kg intravenously may reproduce the chest pain in a third of patients with DES. Unfortunately, manometry changes after edrophonium do not reliably predict the presence of the disease. Bethanechol has also been used with similar results, although its use has been limited by side effects. Chest pain can also be brought on in patients with DES by inflating a balloon-equipped catheter in the esophagus. Patients with DES develop chest pain much more frequently and at lower inflation volumes than control subjects. Interpretation of provocative tests is difficult because normal subjects may also develop symptoms. The studies may be more predictive of the presence of DES in patients who feel that the provoked symptoms closely mimic their usual pain.

Recommended Approach

Diffuse esophageal spasm is difficult to diagnose because of the lack of a definitive test and the episodic nature of symptoms and motility changes. The entity can be strongly suspected in a patient who has a chronic history of intermittent bouts of chest pain and dysphagia without evidence of progression to food impaction, regurgitation, or weight loss. In all patients, efforts to exclude coronary artery disease and gastroesophageal reflux must be undertaken first. In the workup of DES, a barium swallow is a good initial test to exclude structural lesions of the esophagus. It can strengthen the physician's suspicion if it reveals evidence of tertiary contractions. Esophagoscopy does not assist in diagnosis, but may be employed to rule out mucosal lesions. Esophageal manometry revealing frequent simultaneous contractions with intermittent normal peristalsis provides the strongest evidence for DES. When the above workup is not diagnostic, ambulatory 24-hour esophageal manometry should be considered. This test has the advantage of allowing the physician to correlate symptoms to changes in motility. When all else fails, the patient should be referred to a gastroenterologist familiar with the techiques of provocative testing. Accurate interpretation of provocative tests requires experience and judgment.

Therapeutic

Therapeutic Options

Antireflux Therapy. Gastroesophageal reflux may be difficult to separate from DES, especially in patients whose main manifestation is chest pain. If there is any suspicion that reflux is present, a trial of agresstive therapy with antacids and H_2 blockers should be initiated. If empiric therapy fails, then specific diagnostic and therapeutic strategies for DES may be contemplated.

Psychiatric Techniques. Trazodone hydrochloride 100 to 150 mg/d appears to alleviate symptoms in many patients, although no improvement in manometric findings has been noted. This medication may prove most useful in patients whose symptoms are exacerbated by stress. Scattered reports suggest that behavioral modification, stress reduction, and biofeedback techniques are beneficial for selected patients.

Nitrate Preparations. Isosorbide dinitrate 5 to 10 mg sublingually has been shown to improve symptoms and manometric abnormalities in a small number of patients. This agent is thought to act through its relaxant effect on smooth muscle. Unfortunately, most patients do not respond, and in those who do, the benefit is often short-lived.

Calcium Channel Blockers. Nifedipine and diltiazem have been found to be beneficial in anecdotal reports but larger series have failed to confirm this effect. Trials of nifedipine 10 to 20 mg orally three times daily or diltiazem 60 to 90 mg orally three times daily can be considered in individual patients who are not helped by other therapies.

Esophageal Dilation. Dilation with a large bougie has been used in the past; however, most authorities feel it is of little benefit and cannot be recommended. Pneumatic dilation appears to be successful in the subgroup of patients with DES who have mostly dysphagia and evidence of incomplete relaxation of the lower esophageal sphincter on manometry. Questions have arisen as to whether this group actually represents patients with early achalasia. In light of this, pneumatic dilation cannot be generally recommended for patients with DES. This is especially important considering the potential for esophageal perforation with this technique.

Surgical Myotomy. Long surgical myotomy extending from the lower esophageal sphincter up to the level of the aortic arch has been reported to be successful. Because of the invasiveness of this procedure, it is best reserved for the most severe cases where dysphagia is disabling and the diagnosis of DES is certain. Some authors insist that prior to contemplating surgery, the physician should document that attacks of pain are associated with abnormal changes in motility.

Recommended Approach

If reflux is suspected the patient should be treated aggressively with H_2 blockers and antireflux measures. In cases where there is no response, therapy directed at DES is warranted. Unfortunately, there is no standard treatment for DES and well-controlled studies evaluating potential therapies are lacking. For the patient with mild or infrequent attacks, sublingual nitroglycerin is a good choice. In those with more frequent attacks, long-acting nitroglycerin preparations, nifedipine, or diltiazem should be considered. The physician may have to experiment with trials of each of these medications to discover if any of them are beneficial in the patient. Those with evidence of psychiatric disease should be tried on trazodone hydrochloride in conjunction with psychotherapy and behavior modification. For those who fail to respond to trials of the above drugs, there are reports that the following agents are sometimes successful: diazepam 2 to 5 mg orally four times daily, doxepin 50 mg orally daily at bedtime, and hydralazine 25 to 50 mg orally three times daily. Pneumatic dilation should be reserved for those patients who fail medical therapy and have evidence of incomplete relaxation of the lower esophageal sphincter. This group may represent a very early stage of achalasia and thus have a better response to pneumatic dilation. Surgical myotomy is a very invasive therapy for a disease that is not progressive and generally episodic in nature. Only patients with a documented diagnosis of DES who have failed medical therapy and have unremitting symptoms should be considered for surgical therapy.

FOLLOW-UP

Diffuse esophageal spasm is not progressive; therefore, symptoms do not become more severe over time. Most patients require trials of several medications at various doses before settling on a drug that seems to control symptoms. If dysphagia becomes more persistent, the physician should be alert to the possibility of transition to achalasia. Approximately 1 in 20 patients initially diagnosed with DES eventually progress to achalasia.

DISCUSSION

Prevalence and Incidence

Esophageal spasm is a rare disorder whose prevalence and incidence remain unknown. The diagnosis is made in fewer than 1 in 10 patients referred for noncardiac chest pain. Most patients present in their forties and fifties and there is a slight female preponderance.

Related Basic Science

Physiologic or Metabolic Derangement

The etiology of the disorder remains obscure. A decreased esophgeal pain threshold coupled with abnormal central nervous system processing of sensory information may explain the symptomatology. Alternatively, diminished inhibitory neural input with spared excitatory input to the esophagus may result in the spastic contractions seen.

Anatomic Derangement

Thickening of the smooth muscle portion of the esophagus is sometimes seen at surgical myotomy in the most severe patients.

Natural History and Its Modification with Treatment

Diffuse esophageal spasm is not a progressive disease. Most patients have a steady frequency of symptoms for many years. There are few complications from the disorder, and it is rarely severe enough to interfere with the activities of daily living. The lack of medications that uniformly ameliorate symptoms means that many patients will continue to suffer attacks for a number of months to years before a successful therapeutic regimen is found.

Prevention

In many patients, bouts of chest pain and dysphagia are triggered by stressful situations, eating rapidly, swallowing large boluses of food, and ingesting hot, cold or carbonated liquids. Avoidance of known precipitants by the patient may reduce the frequency of attacks. Because undiagnosed or untreated psychiatric disease can affect the severity of DES, prompt therapy of anxiety disorders and depression may beneficially affect the course of esophageal spasm.

Cost Containment

Gastroesophageal reflux is by far the most common cause of noncardiac chest pain. A trial of aggressive therapy for reflux can reduce costs by obviating the need for further workup in patients with noncardiac chest pain. In those patients who do not respond to antireflux therapy, prompt referral to a gastroenterologist may save money by avoiding potential unnecessary testing.

REFERENCES

Clouse RE. Motor disorders. In: Sliesenger MH, Fordtran JS, eds. Gastrointestinal disease. Philadelphia: Saunders, 1989:559.

Katz PO. Disorders of increased esophageal contractility. In: Castell DO, ed. The esophagus. Boston: Little, Brown, 1992:261.

Kaye MD. Anomalies of peristalsis in idiopathic diffuse oesophageal spasm. Gut 1981;22:217.

Richter JE. Motility disorders of the esophagus. In: Yamada T, ed. Textbook of gastroenterology. Philadelphia: Lippincott, 1991:1083.

Reidel WL, Clouse RE. Variations in clinical presentations of patients with contraction abnormalities. Dig Dis Sci 1985;30:1065.

CHAPTER 19–14

Esophageal Causes of Chest Pain

Vincent James Notar-Francesco, M.D.

DEFINITION

Pain arising from the chest as a consequence of esophageal disease is the focus of this chapter.

ETIOLOGY

A great deal remains unknown about pain sensation in the esophagus. Despite this, there is indirect evidence for a number of possible mechanisms in the genesis of esophageal chest pain.

Mucosal Damage. Chronic gastroesophageal reflux produces inflammation and erosion of the esophageal lining. The damaged mucosa may become more permeable to hydrogen ions, which stimulate submucosal chemoreceptors causing pain. This pathogenesis is bolstered by the fact that instillation of hydrochloric acid into the esophageal lumen reproduces the pain experienced by patients with reflux. Esophageal distention due to refluxed material may also contribute to symptoms by stimulating mechanoreceptors in the esophageal wall. Other constituents of gastroesophageal reflux, such as pepsin and bile, may stimulate specific chemoreceptors.

Esophageal Dysmotility. Diffuse esophageal spasm, nutcracker esophagus, achalasia, and hypertensive lower esophageal sphincter are known to produce atypical chest pain. Simultaneous, nonperistaltic, high-amplitude, and/or long-duration contractions of the esophageal musculature present in these conditions may increase intraesophageal pressure. This results in activation of various mechanoreceptors leading to the perception of chest pain. Support for this pathogenesis comes from studies that report that balloon distention of the esophagus reproduces symptoms in many patients with motility disorders.

Esophageal Ischemia. There is some suggestion that esophageal ischemia may occur in spastic diseases of the esophagus. Contraction amplitudes in diffuse esophageal spasm and especially nutcracker esophagus are high enough to impair vascular perfusion transiently. Elevated intraesophageal pressure may adversely affect blood flow, resulting in mucosal ischemia and subjective pain.

Esophageal Hypersensitivity. There is considerable evidence that patients with spastic motor disorders of the esophagus may be more sensitive to changes within the esophagus. Balloon distention of the esophagus produces pain at lower inflation pressures in these patients than in healthy subjects. Increased sensitivity of esophageal pain receptors and abnormal central processing of sensory input have been touted as possible explanations.

CRITERIA FOR DIAGNOSIS

Suggestive

A history of episodic chest pain in a patient in whom coronary artery disease and painful chest wall syndromes have been excluded suggests the diagnosis. Esophageal origin of chest pain is likely if the discomfort lasts from 10 minutes to hours, radiates to the back, follows meals or swallowing, and occurs with recumbency. Patients with an esophageal cause of chest pain may have other gastrointestinal symptoms such as dysphagia, food impaction, regurgitation, pyrosis, and weight loss.

Definitive

Identification of an abnormality of the esophagus that is known to produce chest pain and resolution of symptoms with therapy directed at the esophageal abnormality define the diagnosis. The diagnosis is often achieved by the procedures discussed under Diagnostic Options.

CLINICAL MANIFESTATIONS
Subjective

Esophageal chest pain is usually described as a retrosternal pressure or burning sensation which may radiate to the arms, neck, or back. Because it mimics angina pectoris closely, coronary artery disease must always be excluded. Features that suggest an esophageal rather than cardiac origin of pain are duration of 30 minutes to hours, precipitation by meals or swallowing, onset while supine or asleep, radiation to the back or posterior neck, and lack of association with exertion. Many patients with chest pain of esophageal origin complain of other gastrointestinal symptoms such as regurgitation, dysphagia, bolus impaction, pyrosis, odynophagia, and weight loss. Some may report that specific foods trigger attacks. Relief of symptoms with antacids strongly suggests gastroesophageal reflux disease. Amelioration with nitroglycerin is not helpful in excluding cardiac disease because esophageal spastic disorders are often responsive to nitrates.

Any history of esophageal diseases known to produce chest pain should be sought. Prior therapy and response may assist in planning future diagnostic or treatment options. Because depression and anxiety disorders are found commonly in patients with esophageal spastic disorders, a thorough psychiatric history should be taken.

Objective
Physical Examination

There are no physical examination findings specific for any of these esophageal disorders. Weight loss may suggest significant dysphagia potentially due to achalasia, esophageal stricture, or malignancy.

Routine Laboratory Abnormalities

There are no routine laboratory abnormalities that are specific for esophageal disorders. Serum levels of high- and low-density lipoproteins are used to estimate the risk of underlying coronary disease.

PLANS
Diagnostic
Differential Diagnosis

Coronary Artery Disease. Coronary artery disease must be excluded in all patients prior to initiating a workup for esophageal causes of chest pain. Patients may, however, have both coronary artery disease and chest pain due to an esophageal cause.

Gastroesophageal Reflux. Reflux is by far the most common cause of esophageal pain. More than half of patients with noncardiac chest pain are eventually found to have reflux disease. Clinical features that suggest reflux are burning type of pain, sour taste in mouth, and pain occurring after meals or recumbency. Gastroesophageal reflux symptoms are often exacerbated by chocolate, coffee, alcohol, and cigarettes. Relief of pain with antacids is typically present.

Motility Disorders. Approximately one third of patients with noncardiac chest pain have abnormal esophageal motility. Of these patients, one half have manometric findings suggestive of nutcracker esophagus, 1 in 10 meet the criteria established for diffuse esophageal spasm, and a small number manifest findings consistent with achalasia or hypertensive lower esophageal sphincter. The rest have nonspecific abnormalities suggestive of a nonspecific esophageal motility disorder.

Nutcracker Esophagus. These patients suffer from episodic attacks of esophageal chest pain and/or dysphagia. Diagnosis is made at manometry, where normal peristaltic contractions of increased amplitude, greater than 150 or 180 mm Hg, are found. All other studies are usually normal. This existence of this disorder has recently come under attack because patients typically do not have chest pain during manometry studies despite the presence of very strong peristaltic contractions. In

addition, these patients often do not respond to medications that reduce the strength of esophageal contractions.

Diffuse Esophageal Spasm. Those afflicted present complaining of attacks of chest pain and/or dysphagia. Bouts are sometimes precipitated by swallowing and ingesting hot or cold liquids. Anxiety disorders and depression are frequently associated, and episodes of pain may be more frequent during periods of emotional stress. Diagnosis is made by esophageal manometry, which requires the presence of simultaneous contractions after greater than 10% of swallowed water boluses and intermittent normal peristalsis. Simultaneous contractions indicate that large areas of the esophagus are contracting in unison and are by definition nonpropulsive.

Hypertensive Lower Esophageal Sphincter. Patients present complaining of chest pain and dysphagia. Diagnosis rests on esophageal manometry, which reveals an elevated lower esophageal sphincter resting pressure of greater than 45 mm Hg. In a small number of cases, the sphincter does not relax completely. Normal peristalsis is always present.

Nonspecific Esophageal Motility Disorders. This "grab-bag" diagnosis is made in those who have abnormalities on esophageal manometry that do not meet the established criteria for any of the known motility disorders. Manometry reveals normal peristalsis in conjunction with any of the following findings: increased nontransmitted contractions (a swallowed bolus that is not followed by a peristaltic contraction), contractions of prolonged duration, multipeaked contractions (a contraction waveform that has more than three peaks), and increased spontaneous contractions (a peristaltic contraction that begins in the esophagus and is not initiated by a swallow). The clinical significance of the manometric findings in nonspecific esophageal motility disorders is poorly understood.

Achalasia. Those afflicted complain of progressive dysphagia, regurgitation, weight loss, and chest pain. Degeneration of neurons of the myenteric plexus in the esophagus results in aperistalsis and incomplete relaxation of the lower esophageal sphincter. Diagnosis is strongly suggested by barium studies, which reveal an atonic distal esophagus and a persistently closed lower esophageal sphincter. Diagnosis is confirmed by esophageal manometry, which must reveal aperistalsis. Incomplete relaxation of the lower esophageal sphincter, hypertension of the sphincter, and an elevated resting intraesophageal pressure are sometimes found.

Other Causes of Esophageal Chest Pain. A number of structural lesions of the esophagus can result in chest pain. Most of these abnormalities are readily diagnosed by radiography or endoscopy. The following disorders should be excluded in any workup of esophageal chest pain: infectious esophagitis, ulceration, peptic stricture, diverticula, and malignancies of the esophagus.

Diagnostic Options

Discussion of diagnostic tests is limited to those employed in evaluating esophageal motility disorders. For a discussion of diagnostic methods used in the diagnosis of gastrointestinal reflux or other causes of esophageal chest pain please see the appropriate chapters. Thorough testing to exclude coronary artery disease must be performed in all patients. The workup of esophageal causes of chest pain should always begin with a barium swallow with fluoroscopy and/or esophagoscopy to rule out structural lesions of the esophagus.

Esophageal Manometry. A modified nasogastric tube containing pressure-sensing transducers at defined intervals is passed into the stomach and positioned so that simultaneous recordings can be taken from the lower esophageal sphincter and several points along the esophagus. In this way, the response of the esophageal body and sphincter to swallowed boluses of water can be measured. Esophageal manometry is the first test that should be employed in the workup of suspected motility disorders. Specific patterns have been identified for achalasia, diffuse esophageal spasm, nutcracker esophagus, and hypertensive lower esophageal sphincter. Manometry may be normal in spastic esophageal motility disorders such as diffuse esophageal spasm, nutcracker esophagus, and hypertensive lower esophageal sphincter. Unfortunately, these conditions are episodic in terms of both symptoms and motility findings.

Provocative Tests. These studies attempt to provoke chest pain or motility changes in patients with esophageal spastic disorders. It is important to remember that these tests can elicit symptoms in normal subjects; therefore, producing chest pain alone is not helpful. If the patient experiences a pain that is identical to his or her usual symptoms, the test is considered positive. Although provocative tests can confirm the presence of esophageal chest pain, they cannot diagnose the specific disorder responsible. Therefore, results need to be interpreted carefully in conjunction with the patient's history and ancillary workup.

EDROPHONIUM CHLORIDE. Edrophonium chloride, a cholinesterase inhibitor, given in doses of 80 µg/kg intravenously produces an increase in the amplitude and duration of esophageal contractions. A positive test is one in which the patient's typical chest pain is reproduced. Manometry changes after edrophonium are variable and cannot be used to predict the presence of an esophageal disorder. Edrophonium is the best provocative test for spastic disorders of the esophagus because of its high sensitivity and low risk profile.

BETHANECHOL. Bethanechol, a cholinergic agonist, given in doses of 40 to 50 µg/kg subcutaneously increases the amplitude and duration of esophageal contractions. About one fourth of patients with esophageal spastic disorders manifest a positive response defined as reproduction of the patient's usual symptoms. Unfortunately, cholinergic side effects and the need for cardiac monitoring limit the usefulness of bethanechol.

INTRAESOPHAGEAL BALLOON DISTENTION. A balloon-equipped catheter is passed into the body of the esophagus and inflated slowly. Patients with spastic disorders of the esophagus develop chest pain at much lower inflation volumes than normal subjects. Reproduction of the patient's typical symptoms defines a positive study.

Twenty-four-hour Esophageal Manometry. A manometry catheter is carefully positioned in the esophagus and connected to a recording device strapped to the patient's waist. The instrument has a button that the patient can depress when he or she develops pain. This action marks the onset of symptoms on the recording and allows for comparison of the temporal relationship between symptoms and changes in motility. Some catheters also record intraesophageal pH, which can then be used to exclude gastroesophageal reflux. Interpretation of ambulatory manometry testing is difficult. Individual patients may have abnormal motility during some episodes of chest pain and not during others. In any case, continuous manometry is occasionally successful in diagnosing an esophageal cause of chest pain in patients with intermittent symptoms.

Recommended Approach

Myocardial ischemia must be ruled out in all patients with suspected esophageal chest pain. Radiography and/or esophagoscopy should then be performed to exclude structural lesions of the esophagus. If the patient's history or barium studies suggest gastroesophageal reflux, a trial of aggressive therapy with acid suppression should be tried. Those patients who fail to respond should undergo 24-hour intraesophageal pH monitoring to exclude reflux disease. If the above workup has been negative, then testing to evaluate for esophageal motility disorders is appropriate. An esophageal manometry study should be performed and will yield a diagnosis in perhaps one fourth of patients. If this study is negative, the patient should be referred to a gastroenterologist familiar with the techniques of ambulatory esophageal manometry and provocative testing.

Therapeutic

Therapeutic Options

Structural lesions of the esophagus and gastroesophageal reflux should receive therapy aimed at their cause. For details on treatment of these conditions please see the appropriate chapters. The discussion here is limited to the treatment of motility disorders resulting in chest pain.

Achalasia. A number of drugs that have been shown to relax the lower esophageal sphincter have been used to treat achalasia. The most com-

monly used preparations are isosorbide dinitrate 5 to 10 mg sublingually before meals and nifedipine 10 to 20 mg sublingually 30 minutes before meals. Less than one half of patients treated in this manner show a good clinical response and far fewer manifest sustained improvement. Because of the frequent failure of medical therapy in the long-term management of achalasia, most patients should be treated with pneumatic dilation or surgical myotomy. Although pneumatic dilation has a slightly lower success rate than surgical myotomy, its ease of performance, short hospital stay, reduced cost, and shortened recovery period make it the initial treatment of choice. Surgical myotomy should be reserved for those patients in whom pneumatic dilation is contraindicated or unsuccessful.

Esophageal Spasm. Diffuse esophageal spasm, nutcracker esophagus, and hypertensive lower esophageal sphincter are all considered spastic esophageal disorders. Most of what is known about the treatment of esophageal spasm comes from studies of patients with diffuse esophageal spasm. Similar treatments are often tried and sometimes beneficial in patients with nutcracker esophagus and hypertensive lower esophageal sphincter. Trazodone hydrochloride 100 to 150 mg/d appears to improve symptoms in many patients. This medication may prove most useful in those whose symptoms are exacerbated by stress. Isosorbide dinitrate 5 to 10 mg sublingually has been shown to improve pain and manometric abnormalities in a small number of patients. Unfortunately, many do not respond to this therapy and, in those who do, the benefit is often short-lived. Calcium channel blockers have been found to ameliorate attacks in case reports, but larger series have failed to confirm this. Trials of these medications, nifedipine 10 to 20 mg orally three times daily or diltiazem 60 to 90 mg orally three times daily, can be considered in individual patients who do not respond to other therapies. Pneumatic dilation appears to be successful in the subgroup of patients who have mostly dysphagia and evidence of incomplete relaxation of the lower esophageal sphincter at manometry. Questions have arisen as to whether this subgroup actually represents patients with early achalasia. In light of this, pneumatic dilation cannot be generally recommended for patients with spastic disorders. This is especially important considering the potential for esophageal perforation with this technique. Long surgical myotomy extending from the lower esophageal sphincter up to the level of the aortic arch has been reported to be successful in refractory cases. Because of the invasiveness of this procedure, it is best reserved for the most severe cases where dysphagia is a prominent symptom, medical management has failed, and the diagnosis is certain. Some authors insist that prior to contemplating surgery, the physician should document that attacks of pain are associated with abnormal changes in motility.

Nonspecific Esophageal Motility Disorder. Very little is known about this condition and specific recommendations for therapy cannot be made.

Recommended Approach

After coronary artery disease is excluded, gastroesophageal reflux is the most common cause of esophageal chest pain. A trial of aggressive empiric therapy for reflux should be undertaken. Those patients who fail to respond should be tested to exclude reflux disease. If gastroesophageal reflux is present, high-dose H_2 blockers and antireflux measures should be employed. The remaining patients should undergo testing for esophageal motility disorders. If a specific diagnosis is made, therapy directed at that etiology should be started. Isosorbide dinitrate and trazodone hydrochloride are the most efficacious agents for spastic esophageal disorders. In general, patients need to undergo trials of several medications before settling on one that proves beneficial.

FOLLOW-UP

Patients should be followed closely to ensure an adequate response to therapy. Those with gastroesophageal reflux may sometimes fail to respond to standard doses of H_2 blockers. In these cases, high-dose H_2 blockers or omeprazole may be required to alleviate symptoms. Patients with spastic disorders of the esophagus should keep logs of the frequency and severity of their attacks while on specific agents. This information may help the clinician to select the best therapy.

DISCUSSION
Prevalence and Incidence

Approximately one third of patients undergoing cardiac catheterization have normal coronary arteriograms. Many of these patients have an esophageal cause for their pain. Of patients with suspected esophageal chest pain, one half have gastroestophageal reflux and one fifth have an esophageal motility disorder. In the rest, diagnosis of a specific esophageal cause for their pain remains difficult.

Related Basic Science

A discussion of the etiology of all the disorders that can cause esophageal chest pain is beyond the scope of this chapter. Please see the appropriate chapters for details on specific diseases.

Natural History and Its Modification with Treatment

Gastroesophageal reflux generally responds well to aggressive therapy (see Chapter 19–16). Spastic disorders of the esophagus are difficult to treat as established therapeutic medical regimens are lacking (see Chapter 19–13). The patient is often forced to undergo trials of several medications before a good response is achieved. A significant number of patients do not respond to any of the known therapeutic agents. In these cases, referral to an expert in esophageal spastic disorders is warranted.

Prevention

Many patients learn that attacks of esophageal chest pain are brought on by specific behaviors. In reflux disease, avoidance of specific foods, large meals, and postprandial recumbency may reduce the frequency of symptoms. Episodes of chest pain may be reduced in spastic motility disorders by avoiding rapid eating, swallowing large boluses, or ingesting liquids of extreme temperature.

Cost Containment

Empiric therapy for reflux in patients with suspected esophageal chest pain reduces costs by avoiding unnecessary testing. A more extensive workup can then be reserved for those who fail to show a clinical response to antireflux therapy.

REFERENCES

Benjamin SB, Richter JE, Cordova CM. Prospective manometric evaluation with pharmacologic provocation of patients with suspected esophageal motility dysfunction. Gastroenterology 1983;84:893.

Just RJ, Castell DO. Chest pain of undetermined origin. In: Van Dam J, ed. Gastrointestinal endoscopy clinics of North America. Philadelphia: Saunders, 1994;4:731.

Richter JE. Motility disorders of the esophagus. In: Yamada T, ed Textbook of gastroenterology. Philadelphia: Lippincott, 1991:1083.

Richter JE. The esophagus and noncardiac chest pain. In: Castell DO, ed. The esophagus. Boston: Little, Brown, 1992:715.

CHAPTER 19–15

Scleroderma Esophagus

Vincent James Notar-Francesco, M.D.

DEFINITION

Scleroderma esophagus refers to esophageal involvement in progressive systemic sclerosis or in a more limited cutaneous variant called CREST (calcinosis, Raynaud's phenomenon, esophageal dysfunction, sclerodactyly, and telangiectasia). In either condition, smooth muscle atrophy and fibrosis occur in the distal two thirds of the esophagus. This leads to diminished or absent peristalsis, which causes dysphagia and a persistently open lower esophageal sphincter, which results in gastroesophageal reflux.

ETIOLOGY

The etiology of these disorders remains unknown although the presence of autoantibodies in the serum suggests an immune mechanism. Secondary to activation by unknown stimuli, fibroblasts deposit increased amounts of connective tissue in the lamina propria and submucosa. Intimal proliferation is common and results in luminal narrowing of arterioles and obliteration of capillaries. The resultant ischemia may hasten fibrosis and smooth muscle atrophy. In the esophagus, smooth muscle atrophy leads to decreased contractility. The reduced motility can progress to aperistalsis and subjective dysphagia. Muscular atrophy at the lower esophageal sphincter reduces tone and may result in a persistently open sphincter. In most patients, severe gastroesophageal reflux and its attendant complications ensue.

CRITERIA FOR DIAGNOSIS
Suggestive

A history of pyrosis or dysphagia in a patient with limited or systemic sclerosis strongly suggests the presence of scleroderma esophagus. Because most patients with esophageal involvement have Raynaud's phenomenon, the presence of this sign enhances the likelihood of esophageal involvement. A barium swallow revealing an atonic distal esophagus and a patulous lower esophageal sphincter nearly ensure the diagnosis.

Definitive

Diagnosis is confirmed by manometric findings of diminished or absent peristalsis and reduced or absent lower esophageal sphincter tone in a patient with limited or systemic sclerosis.

CLINICAL MANIFESTATIONS
Subjective

Pyrosis, that is, heartburn, is the most common symptom and is present in more than half of patients. Because of the persistently relaxed lower esophageal sphincter, reflux symptoms are markedly exacerbated by recumbency.

Dysphagia occurs in less than one half of patients. Those afflicted report that the swallowed bolus "does not go all the way down" or "takes a long time to go down." Dysphagia is generally for solids, but some patients may report symptoms with liquids. Most learn to take frequent sips of water during meals to assist in the passage of solids. Progressive dysphagia for solids and liquids may indicated progression of disease or herald the formation of a peptic esophageal stricture.

Weight loss can occur in cases with severe persistent dysphagia. This symptom should alert the physician to the possibility of esophageal adenocarcinoma, especially in those patients who have Barrett's transformation.

Odynophagia occurs in a small number of patients as a result of candidal infectious esophagitis.

Progression of systemic sclerosis in other organs does not reliably predict the presence or severity of esophageal involvement. Raynaud's phenomenon is the one finding that, if present, increases the likelihood of esophageal involvement.

Objective

Physical Examination

Physical examination reveals signs specific for systemic sclerosis. The skin may appear tight with loss of normal skin lines. The face may take on a taut appearance, limiting facial expression and oral aperture. Late in the disease, the skin appears atrophic and ischemic ulcers may become apparent on the extremities. Joints reveal evidence of arthritis with stiffness, decreased range of motion, crepitus, and, in some cases, flexion contractures. Lung examination is most often normal, but may reveal bibasilar rales and/or a pleural friction rub. A small number of patients manifest signs of cardiac involvement, such as pericardial friction rub and congestive heart failure.

Routine Laboratory Abnormalities

There are no routine laboratory abnormalities that are specific for scleroderma esophagus.

PLANS

Diagnostic

Differential Diagnosis

Mixed Connective Tissue Disease. This disorder represents a syndrome in which there are features of scleroderma, polymyositis, and systemic lupus erythematosus. Serology often reveals high titers of circulating antibodies to nuclear ribonucleoprotein. More than half of these patients have esophageal involvement with aperistalsis and a patulous lower esophageal sphincter. In some patients polymyositis may result in weakness of the striated muscle of the proximal esophagus, leading to aperistalsis of the entire esophagus. In addition, reduced tone of the upper esophageal sphincter and a chronic pulmonary aspiration have been reported.

Polymyositis and Dermatomyositis. Esophageal involvement in these disorders usually presents as weakness of the upper esophageal sphincter and aperistalsis of the striated muscle of the esophagus. Clinically, oropharyngeal dysphagia, proximal esophageal dysphagia, and aspiration are seen.

Gastroesophageal Reflux. Patients with severe reflux have been shown to have motility disturbances of the distal esophagus. At manometry these patients may have a decreased frequency of normal peristalsis after swallows, diminished amplitude of esophageal contractions, and decreased tone of the lower esophageal sphincter. Despite these manometric findings, most patients generally do not have clinically significant dysphagia.

Systemic Lupus Erythematosus. Esophageal involvement is infrequent in this condition. A minority of patients may display esophageal motor abnormalities similar to those seen in systemic sclerosis.

Rheumatoid Arthritis. Esophageal involvement is rare in rheumatoid arthritis. There are reports of patients with decreased contractility or aperistalsis of the distal esophagus. Dysphagia is generally mild or subclinical in these patients.

Diagnostic Options

Lateral Chest X-ray. Air in the esophagus without an air–fluid level is sometimes seen and is due to gastric air refluxed through a relaxed lower esophageal sphincter.

Barium Swallow with Fluoroscopy. Transit of the bolus through the oropharynx and proximal esophagus is normal. The distal esophagus may be normal in diameter with reduced peristaltic contractions, but more often it appears dilated and atonic. Esophageal emptying of a liquid bolus may be normal on standing, but when the patient is supine emptying time is prolonged. Contrast-coated solid boluses clearly demonstrate a reduction in esophageal motility. The lower esophageal sphincter is patulous and free gastroesophageal reflux is easily demonstrated. The study may actually reveal the formation of a common cavity comprising the stomach and the dilated distal esophagus. Mucosal

abnormalities suggesting esophagitis or ulceration of the distal esophagus may be present.

Esophagogastroscopy. Endoscopy should be performed to exclude mucosal disease such as esophagitis and ulceration which can be missed by radiography. Endoscopy may reveal gross evidence of aperistalsis and esophageal dilation. The lower esophageal sphincter is often patulous and free reflux of gastric contents may be noted. Biopsies to exclude Barrett's esophagus should be performed. Any suspicious lesions must be biopsied to exclude adenocarcinoma. In some patients a peptic stricture secondary to chronic gastroesophageal reflux may be evident.

Esophageal Manometry. The upper esophageal sphincter is of normal pressure and closed at rest. Normal peristalsis is present in the striated muscle portion of the esophagus. As the peristaltic wave travels distally it becomes weakened and disordered. In the lower esophagus, peristaltic contractions are of very low amplitude or absent. The lower esophageal sphincter is often difficult to locate due to the reduced or absent pressure gradient which normally signifies its location.

Radionuclide Esophageal Scintigraphy. Esophageal transit of a radiolabeled bolus of food is slowed in the distal esophagus due to defective peristalsis. This examination provides a noninvasive means to identify the peristaltic disorder seen in these patients.

Serology may be helpful in diagnosing systemic sclerosis or CREST. Antinuclear antibodies are present in the majority of cases of limited and systemic disease. More than half of patients with CREST manifest anti-centromere antibodies. Approximately a third of patients with systemic sclerosis have elevated antiscleroderma 70 antibodies.

Recommended Approach

Diagnosis of esophageal scleroderma is suspected in a patient with limited cutaneous or systemic sclerosis who complains of pyrosis and/or dysphagia. The presence of Raynaud's phenomenon increases the likelihood of esophageal involvement. As in all patients with dysphagia, a barium swallow must be obtained to rule out esophageal strictures, diverticula, or masses. The barium study can strongly suggest the presence of esophageal involvement if it reveals aperistalsis of the distal esophagus and a patulous lower esophageal sphincter. Endoscopy should then be performed to exclude mucosal abnormalities such as peptic esophagitis, Barrett's transformation, infectious esophagitis, and ulcer. Diagnosis rests on manometric findings of diminished or absent peristalsis and reduced lower esophageal sphincter tone.

Therapeutic

Therapeutic Options

Acid Reduction Therapy. Gastroesophageal reflux results in troubling pyrosis and may lead to complications such as esophagitis, esophageal ulcer, peptic stricture, and Barrett's transformation with its attendant increased risk of adenocarcinoma. Therefore, aggressive therapy for reflux must be instituted in all patients. Doses of H_2 blockers adequate to suppress acid reflux should be employed. In some cases, high doses of H_2 blockers or omeprazole may be necessary to suppress acid secretion. Antacids are a useful adjunctive therapy for breakthrough episodes of symptomatic reflux. Antireflux maneuvers such as avoidance of large meals, postprandial recumbency, and substances known to reduce lower esophageal sphincter pressure (i.e., chocolate, coffee, alcohol, and cigarettes) should be employed. Many medications can reduce lower esophageal sphincter pressure and exacerbate symptoms. Therefore, the following drugs should be avoided when possible: theophylline, anticholinergic agents, nitrates, benzodiazepines, and calcium channel blockers.

Metoclopramide. Metoclopramide has been shown to increase lower esophageal sphincter pressure and, in some patients, to augment esophageal contraction amplitude. Case reports suggest a reduction in symptomatic dysphagia with metoclopramide. Therefore, a trial of this agent should be considered in those patients with marked dysphagia or refractory reflux.

Cisapride. Improved esophageal emptying has not been demonstrated in case reports of patients on cisapride. At this time prospective studies are lacking in patients with scleroderma; thus, a trial of cisapride may be tried in those patients refractory to other therapies.

Surgical Fundoplication. Fundoplication is a useful method to control reflux in some patients. Because of the reduced ability of the esophagus to propel a bolus, fundoplication may exacerbate symptoms of dysphagia. Therefore, when fundoplication is performed, a relatively "loose" wrap should be placed to reduce the possibility of postoperative dysphagia. Fundoplication should be reserved for those patients with severe complicated gastroesophageal reflux who have failed to respond to aggressive medical therapy.

Recommended Approach

There is no therapy that can reverse the smooth muscle atrophy of scleroderma, and therefore, treatment is aimed at palliating symptoms. Gastroesophageal reflux must be treated aggressively in all patients using a combination of acid-reducing drugs and antireflux behavioral modifications. Prokinetic agents have not been universally successful in improving esophageal emptying. Trials with metoclopramide or cisapride can be tried in patients with severe dysphagia. Surgical fundoplication may worse dysphagia and should be reserved for those patients with severe refractory gastroesophageal reflux.

FOLLOW-UP

Patients on an acid reduction regimen should be followed closely to ensure an adequate clinical benefit. When the response to acid reduction is unclear, a 24-hour intraesophageal pH recording can document esophageal acid exposure. Many patients may require high doses of H_2 blockers or omeprazole to adequately control acid secretion. If dysphagia is problematic, trials of prokinetic agents can be considered. When the response of dysphagia to medical therapy is not clear, radionuclide esophageal scintigraphy provides a noninvasive way to assess esophageal emptying time. If Barrett's transformation of the esophagus is found on initial endoscopy, the patient should be entered into a program of surveillance endoscopy to screen for adenocarcinoma. Progressive or rapidly worsening dysphagia must be taken seriously as it may herald the presence of adenocarcinoma or peptic structure of the esophagus.

DISCUSSION
Prevalence

When looked for, evidence of esophageal involvement can be found in more than three quarters of patients with progressive systemic sclerosis or CREST. Clinically apparent esophageal disease is much less common and, perhaps, involves less than half of these patients.

Related Basic Science

Activated fibroblasts deposit increased amounts of connective tissue in the lamina propria and submucosa, resulting in fibrosis. Intimal proliferation of the vascular system leads to luminal narrowing of arterioles and obliteration of capillaries. Both ischemia and fibrosis are thought to result in smooth muscle atrophy. Weakened distal esophageal musculature leads to diminished contractile strength and aperistalsis. Reduced tone of the lower esophageal sphincter causes esophagitis secondary to gastroesophageal reflux.

Natural History and Its Modification with Treatment

Gastroesophageal reflux usually responds to aggressive antireflux therapy. If therapy is instituted early, complications such as esophagitis, ulcers, and peptic strictures can be avoided. Barrett's transformation of the esophageal mucosa is not reversible and these patients are at increased risk for esophageal adenocarcinoma. A program of screening with endoscopy may result in earlier detection and possibly improved prognosis for those patients who do develop adenocarcinoma.

Dysphagia usually progresses in these patients. Drinking water with meals may assist in the passage of solid food boluses. Addition of prokinetic agents may ameliorate dysphagia in some patients.

Prevention

Esophageal involvement in patients with scleroderma cannot be prevented, but the complications of chronic gastroesophageal reflux can be avoided with aggressive acid suppression therapy. Symptomatic dysphagia can be reduced by avoiding solid foods known to pass with difficulty and ingesting liquid with meals.

Cost Containment

Money can be saved by prompt diagnosis of esophageal involvement and institution of acid suppression. In this way, the complications of gastroesophageal reflux and their attendant costs can be avoided.

REFERENCES

Clemens PJ. Esophageal motility in progressive systemic sclerosis: Comparison of cineradiographic and manometric evaluation. Dig Dis Sci 1979;24:639.

Cohen S. The gastrointestinal manifestations of scleroderma: Pathogenesis and management. Gastroenterology 1980;79:1255.

Gulchin AE. Esophageal abnormalities in systemic diseases. In: Castell DO, ed. The esophagus. Boston: Little, Brown, 1992:367.

Richter JE. Motility disorders of the esophagus. In: Yamada T, ed. Textbook of Gastroenterology. Philadelphia: Lippincott, 1991:1083.

Scobey MW. Secondary motility disorders. In: Castell DO, Richter JE, eds. Esophageal motility testing. New York: Elsevier, 1987:163.

CHAPTER 19–16
Reflux Esophagitis

Harry A. Winters, M.D.

DEFINITION

Gastroesophageal reflux refers to the retrograde movement of gastric contents into the esophagus. It is not indicative of a pathologic process, as it occurs in normal, asymptomatic individuals. Gastroesophageal reflux disease, in contrast, implies pathologic reflux that is associated with clinical symptoms or esophageal mucosal alterations. Finally, reflux esophagitis refers to the gross or histologic changes of the mucosa in gastroesophageal reflux disease, whether or not it is associated with symptoms.

ETIOLOGY

Reflux esophagitis is caused by the reflux of gastroduodenal contents into the esophagus. It is probably the consequence of several factors in most patients, but the principal one may differ in individual cases. These factors can be divided into two categories. Factors that contribute to abnormal reflux include incompetence of the lower esophageal sphincter, possibly the presence of a hiatal hernia, abnormal esophageal motility, impaired esophageal clearance, and delayed gastric emptying. Factors that contribute to esophageal mucosal damage are the composition of the refluxed material and esophageal mucosal resistance.

CRITERIA FOR DIAGNOSIS

Suggestive

Heartburn and regurgitation are the hallmark symptoms of gastroesophageal reflux disease; however, reflux frequently occurs in the absence of any symptoms, and reflux symptoms often occur without esophagitis. Nevertheless, reflux esophagitis is likely when the symptoms are more severe or persistent. A barium swallow revealing marked, spontaneous reflux, a large hiatal hernia, or evidence of mucosal inflammation is suggestive of reflux esophagitis when symptoms of gastroesophageal reflux disease are present. Symptoms or radiologic evidence of a complication of reflux esophagitis are more supportive of the diagnosis.

Definitive

The finding of distal, small, shallow ulcerations or erosions, thickened folds, and luminal narrowing on a barium swallow or an endoscopy (Figure 19–16–1) confirms the diagnosis, in the absence of any findings that suggest other etiologies of esophagitis. Endoscopy with mucosal biopsies can differentiate reflux esophagitis from other etiologies, and histologically confirm esophagitis when there are minimal endoscopic findings. Endoscopic diagnosis of a reflux-associated complication such as Barrett's esophagus or a benign stricture or ulcer conclusively establishes the diagnosis.

CLINICAL MANIFESTATIONS

Subjective

Heartburn is typically described as a sensation of burning, acid, or heat in the retrosternal area that may extend from the epigastrium to the throat. It frequently occurs after meals, during strenuous activity involving bending or lifting, or when lying down. Certain foods such as citrus fruits and spicy, fried, or fatty foods can precipitate episodes of heartburn. Prompt relief occurs after the use of an antacid. Regurgitation is the passive return of bitter, acid, or sour liquid in the mouth, which the patient may "spit up." It is not forceful or associated with nausea as with vomiting, and the regurgitant material typically does not

contain undigested food. It usually occurs in the same settings as described for heartburn. Water brash, the sudden filling of the mouth with salty fluid, is a manifestation of reflux caused by hypersalivation rather than regurgitation. Odynophagia, which is pain on swallowing; dysphagia, particularly for solid food; and chronic, occult bleeding may occur with more severe, ulcerative reflux esophagitis. Reflux esophagitis may cause chest pain that is characteristic of angina. Extraesophageal involvement may be manifested by hoarseness, nocturnal coughing, or asthma.

A history including a complete list of medications, cigarette smoking, and the excessive use of alcohol may identify risk factors for reflux esophagitis or reasons for treatment failures.

Objective

Physical Examination

There are no findings on the physical examination related to reflux esophagitis.

Routine Laboratory Abnormalities

There are no routine laboratory studies that are useful in the investigation of reflux esophagitis; however, occult blood in the stool and iron deficiency anemia may be noted. A roentgenogram of the chest may reveal chronic changes such as fibrosis and aspiration that could be attributable to gastroesophageal reflux disease.

PLANS

Diagnostic

Differential Diagnosis

Odynophagia is more commonly associated with infectious causes of esophagitis such as *Candida,* herpes, and cytomegalovirus, but it can also occur with radiation esophagitis, ingestion of caustic substances, and pill esophagitis due to medications such as quinidine, potassium chloride, nonsteroidal antiinflammatory agents, and tetracycline. Progressive dysphagia is an indication of a benign peptic stricture or a malignancy, which may be an adenocarcinoma associated with Barrett's esophagus. Dysphagia for both solids and liquids occurs with esophageal motor disorders. In addition, heartburn and regurgitation may occur with achalasia, and chest pain with diffuse esophageal spasm. Esophageal dysmotility associated with certain collagen–vascular disorders like CREST (calcinosis, Raynaud's phenomenon, esophageal dysmotility, sclerodactylia, telangiectasia) syndrome or scleroderma can lead to severe reflux esophagitis. Dyspepsia is frequently confused or associated with heartburn, suggesting the possibility of peptic ulcer disease. Chest pain should lead to the consideration of coronary artery disease.

Diagnostic Options

A barium swallow combined with a fluoroscopic examination can demonstrate reflux, mucosal irregularities that are suggestive of reflux esophagitis, associated complications such as an ulcer or stricture, and gross motor function. Esophagoscopy can identify the same pathologic lesions as the barium swallow, but it can also detect milder degrees of esophagitis and allow the performance of mucosal biopsies for the histologic confirmation of esophagitis or to determine the etiology of the esophagitis. Esophageal pH monitoring, by means of a probe placed in the esophagus, can record luminal pH for a period of 24 hours. Its purpose is to quantify the number and the duration of reflux episodes and to correlate symptoms, which are recorded in a diary by the patient, with reflux episodes. Esophageal manometry provides data on the resting lower esophageal sphincter pressure and the presence of peristalsis. The Bernstein test involves alternately infusing hydrochloric acid and saline into the esophagus to attempt to reproduce the patient's symptoms with acid.

Recommended Approach

Diagnostic evaluation for reflux esophagitis is indicated when a therapeutic trial fails, recurrences occur after successful therapy, atypical

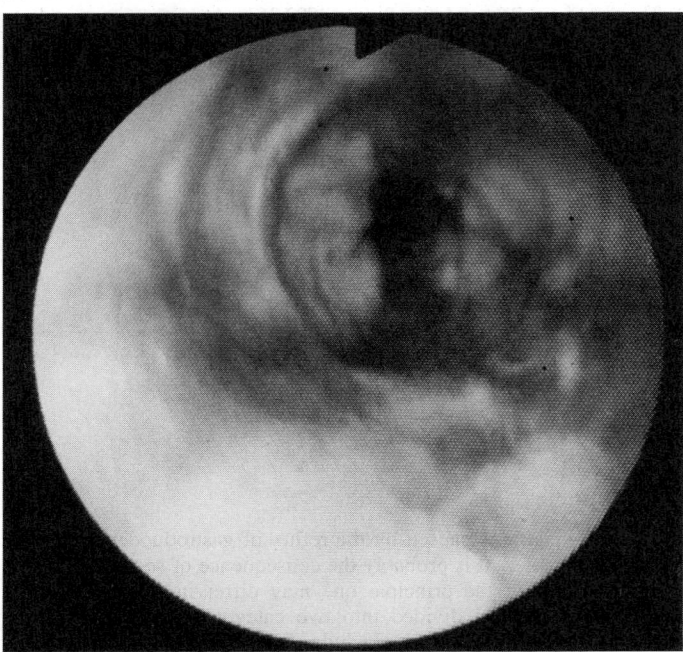

Figure 19–16–1. Endoscopic photograph of reflux esophagitis demonstrating shallow mucosal ulcerations.

symptoms are present, or an associated complication is suspected. Whether the initial procedure is an esophagoscopy or a barium swallow is dependent on the clinical setting and the differential diagnosis. The two studies are complementary; therefore, both may be necessary. The barium swallow would be appropriate to document gastroesophageal reflux or a hiatal hernia, for the evaluation of atypical symptoms, or when an esophageal motility disorder is suspected. Esophagoscopy should be the initial procedure when reflux or other types of esophagitis, Barrett's esophagus, a complication such as a stricture or an ulcer, or a malignancy is considered. Esophageal manometry is done when the clinical symptoms or the initial investigation suggests the possibility of an esophageal motility disorder and to document the presence of adequate peristalsis prior to antireflux surgery. Finally, 24-hour pH monitoring should be done when the initial investigation does not reveal evidence of reflux disease, for atypical symptoms including extraesophageal manifestations of gastroesophageal reflux disease, and to assess the adequacy of antireflux therapy.

Therapeutic

Therapeutic Options

Lifestyle changes that are aimed at diminishing reflux are the initial phase of therapy for reflux esophagitis. Factors that reduce lower esophageal sphincter pressure should be avoided. These include dietary fat, caffeine, alcohol, cigarette smoking, chocolate, and medications like theophylline, calcium channel blockers, and nitrates. These drugs may contribute to the problem for which they are given if gastroesophageal reflux disease is the actual underlying cause. Mechanical maneuvers include weight loss, avoiding gastric overdistention, abstaining from strenuous activity or lying down for up to 2 hours after eating, not wearing tight-fitting clothes, and raising the head of the bed on 6-in. blocks.

Antacids and alginic acid are useful adjuncts to therapy for occasional symptoms, but they are ineffective when used alone to treat reflux esophagitis. Therefore, when the symptoms are severe enough for the patient to seek medical attention, H_2-receptor antagonists should be used in addition to lifestyle modifications. Cimetidine (800 mg twice daily), ranitidine (300 mg twice daily), famotidine (40 mg twice daily), and nizatidine (300 mg twice daily) are equally effective and are well tolerated. Larger doses are required for successful therapy of reflux esophagitis than for peptic ulcer disease. A second class of drugs, the prokinetic agents, act by increasing lower esophageal sphincter pressure, esophageal clearance, or gastric emptying. This group includes bethanechol (10–25 mg four times daily), metoclopramide (5–10 mg four times daily), and cisapride (10–20 mg four times daily). Bethanechol and metoclopramide are no longer commonly used in the treatment of reflux esophagitis because of limited efficacy and somewhat intolerable or potentially serious side effects. Cisapride, the latest of these agents, appears to very effective in the treatment of reflux esophagitis, even when used alone, and it is much better tolerated. Omeprazole (20–40 mg daily) is the most effective treatment for reflux esophagitis and for the prevention of recurrence. It appears to be effective in cases that are refractory to therapy with H_2-receptor antagonists and in the management of the complications of reflux esophagitis. It is well tolerated, but its safety in long-term use is still being established. Histologic changes in the stomach have been demonstrated with long-term use of omeprazole. Therefore, its use is not recommended for longer than 8 to 12 weeks. H_2-receptor antagonists, cisapride, or a combination of the two may be necessary to maintain an adequate therapeutic effect when lifestyle changes alone fail. Surgical therapy may be required for definitive management of reflux esophagitis or its complications, with the exception of Barrett's esophagus. A fundoplication is the procedure of choice. Aperistalsis on manometry is a contraindication to surgery.

Benign esophageal strictures can be managed by dilation in combination with medical therapy. Dilation can be performed, after radiographic evaluation of the stricture, unguided by the peroral passage of mercury-filled dilators, by fluoroscopically guided passage of a dilator over a guidewire placed by endoscopy across the stricture, or by endoscopically guided dilation by means of a balloon catheter passed through the endoscope (Figure 19–16–2). Lifelong medical therapy may prevent stricture recurrence, but periodic dilation may be required.

Recommended Approach

Patients should be educated in the lifestyle modifications, which they will have to adhere to for life. Therefore, these instructions should be reinforced and compliance verified at each follow-up visit. Omeprazole at the larger dose is used for a period of 4 to 8 weeks. Then, maintenance therapy with an H_2-receptor antagonist at the full dose is continued. If symptoms recur, cisapride can be tried alone or in addition to the H_2-receptor antagonist. If the patient does well, discontinuation of the medication can be attempted, but if lifestyle modifications alone are ineffective, the lowest possible dose to maintain the desired effect should be continued. If either acute or maintenance therapy fails, other contributory factors should be considered such as Zollinger–Ellison syndrome and esophageal motility disorders. If there is no evidence of these conditions, antireflux surgery should be considered. Antireflux surgery may also be considered in young individuals who require lifelong therapy to achieve control of their disease. Finally, long-term therapy with omeprazole can be considered in selected patients, such as elderly patients or patients who are poor surgical candidates for other reasons, in whom standard medical therapy is ineffective. In this situation, informed consent should be obtained.

FOLLOW-UP

Routine follow-up of reflux esophagitis is not indicated; however, a repeat endoscopy may be required to document healing in more severe cases or when associated with a complication. Ulcers and strictures should be followed endoscopically for resolution.

DISCUSSION

Prevalence and Incidence

The prevalence and incidence of reflux esophagitis are unknown, but one quarter to one third of patients studied by endoscopy for symptoms of gastroesophageal reflux disease have evidence of reflux esophagitis.

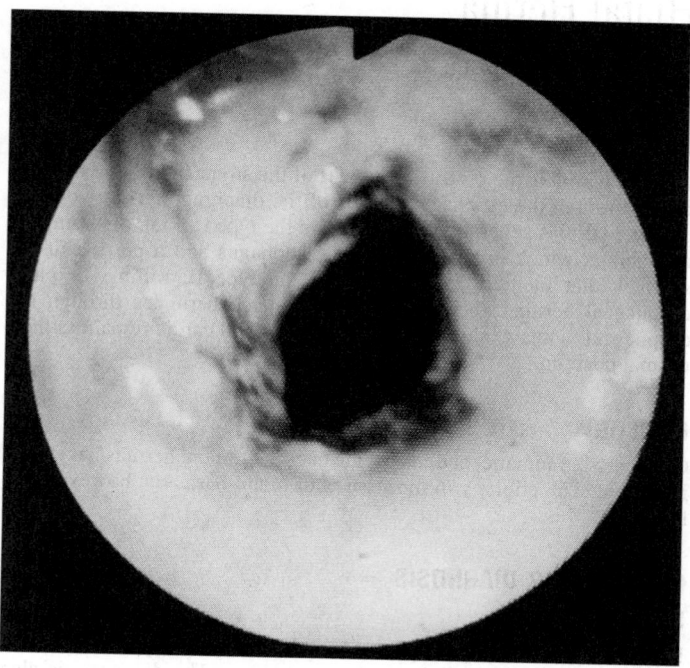

Figure 19–16–2. Endoscopic photograph of a benign peptic stricture following dilation with a transendoscopic balloon dilator. Disruption of the esophageal mucosa is apparent within the stricture as a result of the dilation.

Related Basic Science

The main determinant in the pathophysiology of gastroesophageal reflux disease has long been considered to be incompetency of the lower esophageal sphincter. Patients with symptomatic gastroesophageal reflux disease have lower resting lower esophageal sphincter pressures than asymptomatic refluxers. Furthermore, the lower the lower esophageal sphincter pressure, the more severe the reflux esophagitis. In addition, patients with reflux esophagitis have more frequent episodes of spontaneous and stress-related reflux caused by increases in intraabdominal pressure and relaxation of the lower esophageal sphincter.

Patients with reflux esophagitis have abnormal esophageal clearance. Primary peristalsis is the principal mechanism for esophageal clearance after an episode of reflux. Patients with reflux esophagitis have more prolonged esophageal clearance and require more swallows for clearance than do asymptomatic refluxers. In addition, swallowed saliva assists by neutralizing small amounts of refluxed gastric acid, and the rate of salivary secretion is increased by acid reflux. This reflex is impaired in some patients with reflux esophagitis.

On the basis of these possible etiologic factors, patients with reflux esophagitis have more frequent and prolonged episodes of nonphysiologic reflux. In addition, there appear to be local factors that may make the esophageal mucosa more sensitive to the refluxed material, and there are possibly cytoprotective mechanisms that are abnormal in reflux esophagitis.

Natural History and Its Modification with Treatment

The natural history of reflux esophagitis is unpredictable. The majority of patients respond well with lifestyle modifications and medical therapy. Patients with mild esophagitis may continue to do well with lifestyle modification alone; however, most patients with moderate to severe disease, those with complications, and those who cannot comply with the restricted lifestyle require lifelong medical therapy or antireflux surgery.

Prevention

The identification and elimination or reduction of risk factors, as described with lifestyle modifications, that contribute to the severity of gastroesophageal reflux disease may sufficiently reduce the degree of reflux to prevent the development of esophagitis.

Cost Containment

Diagnostic evaluation is reserved for patients who do not respond to an adequate course of therapy or whose symptoms rapidly recur after discontinuing medical treatment, as well as patients with atypical presentations or with associated complications. The evaluation may be limited to either a barium swallow or an endoscopy on the basis of a detailed medical history.

REFERENCES

Boyce HW, Jr. Hiatal hernia and peptic diseases of the esophagus. In: Sivak MV Jr, ed. Gastroenterologic endoscopy. Philadelphia: Saunders, 1987:401.

Hogan WJ, Dodds WJ. Gastroesophageal reflux disease (reflux esophagitis). In: Sleisenger MH, Fordtran JS, eds. Gastrointestinal disease. 4th ed. Philadelphia: Saunders, 1989:594.

Klinkenberg-Knol EC, Festen HPM, Jansen JBMJ, et al. Long-term treatment with omeprazole for refractory reflux esophagitis: Efficacy and safety. Ann Intern Med 1994;121:161.

Pope CE II. Acid-reflux disorders. N Engl J Med 1994;331:656.

Richter JE. Severe reflux esophagitis. Gastrointestinal Endoscopy Clin North Am 1994;4:677.

Skinner DB, Roth JLA, Sullivan BH, et al. Reflux esophagitis. In: Berk JE, ed. Bockus gastroenterology. 4th ed. Philadelphia: Saunders, 1985:717.

CHAPTER 19–17

Hiatal Hernia

Harry A. Winters, M.D.

DEFINITION

A hiatal hernia is the protrusion of part of the stomach into the thoracic cavity through the esophageal hiatus of the diaphragm. The two types of hiatal hernias generally recognized are the type I, axial, or sliding hiatal hernia, which involves the distal esophagus and a portion of the stomach that includes the cardia, and the type II, rolling, or paraesophageal hernia, where part of the stomach herniates through the esophageal hiatus while the distal esophagus and cardia remain in their normal position.

ETIOLOGY

Congenital, traumatic, and iatrogenic causes of hiatal hernias have been identified. The etiology in most cases of hiatal hernia is, however, unknown.

CRITERIA FOR DIAGNOSIS

Suggestive

Hiatal hernia is usually suspected when a patient complains of reflux symptoms such as heartburn and regurgitation. The diagnosis is also considered in patients with substernal chest or epigastric pain or discomfort, especially if it is precipitated or exacerbated by eating, drinking, or lying down.

Definitive

The sliding hiatal hernia is documented by visualization of the distal esophagus, gastroesophageal junction, and a variable length of stomach above the diaphragm on an upper gastrointestinal series or a barium swallow (Figure 19–17–1). When endoscopy is performed, the diagnosis of a sliding hiatal hernia may be made when the squamocolumnar junction is seen at least 2 cm proximal to the diaphragmatic hiatus, which appears as a circumferential, extrinsic compression. This is usually more apparent after entry into the stomach on a retroversion examination (Figure 19–17–2). With this view, the esophageal hiatus, which is usually widened, can be more readily appreciated. In the case of paraesophageal hernias, the barium swallow reveals herniation of a portion of the stomach through the diaphragm beside the esophagus. Very large paraesophageal hernias may have the appearance of an "upside-down stomach" (Figure 19–17–3). Endoscopic diagnosis of paraesophageal hernias may be more difficult because of distortion of the anatomy of the stomach or the inability to examine the entire stomach when torsion or a gastric volvulus is present.

CLINICAL MANIFESTATIONS

Subjective

Most patients with hiatal hernias diagnosed by an upper gastrointestinal series are asymptomatic. Symptoms that are frequently attributed to hi-

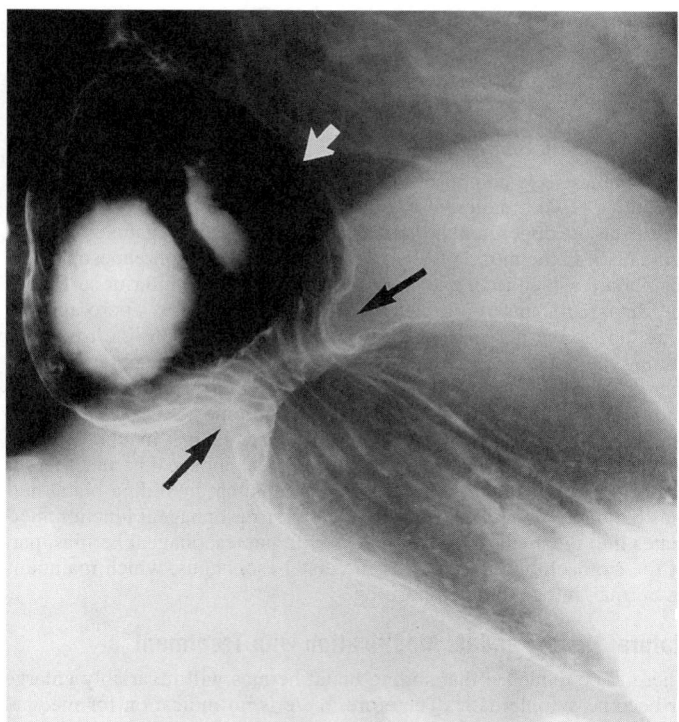

Figure 19–17–1. Large, sliding hiatal hernia (white arrow) demonstrated by upper gastrointestinal series (black arrows indicate the diaphragmatic hiatus). *(Courtesy of A. Samin, M.D.)*

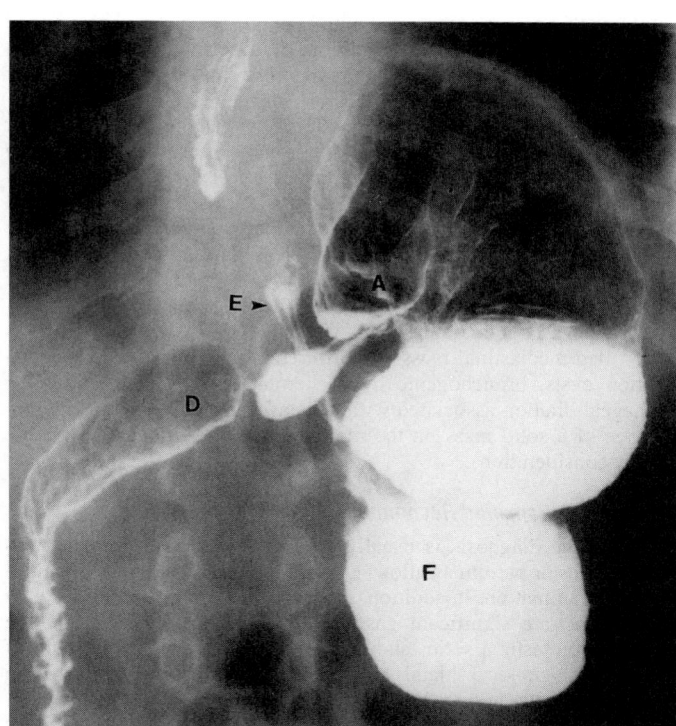

Figure 19–17–3. Paraesophageal hernia with a gastric volvulus demonstrated on upper gastrointestinal series. E, esophagus; A, antrum; F, fundus; D, duodenum. *(Courtesy of A. Samin, M.D.)*

atal hernias are usually nonspecific, and they cannot definitively be ascribed directly to the hernia, particularly when it is small. Nonetheless, the symptoms may initiate an investigation that establishes the diagnosis of the hiatal hernia. The symptoms that are frequently associated with hiatal hernias are more likely to be related to associated gastroesophageal reflux disease. These symptoms most commonly include heartburn, re-

gurgitation, a sensation of fullness or bloating, lower chest or upper abdominal pain or discomfort, and increased belching. Patients may also report feeling as though food sits in the region of the lower chest or epigastrium while eating. The symptoms may occur more commonly and with greatest intensity in the postprandial period, during strenuous activity or exertion, or while lying down. Large sliding hiatal hernias and paraesophageal hernias are also most commonly asymptomatic. When they become symptomatic, however, the symptoms are more clearly related to the hernia, especially when associated with complications. Dysphagia, early satiety, chest or epigastric pain, bleeding from gastric erosions or ulcers within the hernia pouch, and vomiting have been associated with large sliding hiatal and paraesophageal hernias.

Objective

Physical Examination

There are no findings on the physical examination associated with uncomplicated hiatal hernias. When a paraesophageal hiatal hernia is complicated by gastric volvulus and infarction, there may be fever or abdominal tenderness.

Routine Laboratory Abnormalities

There are no abnormalities on routine laboratory tests, unless a paraesophageal hernia is complicated by volvulus or infarction. In this case, there may be anemia due to bleeding, electrolyte abnormalities and metabolic alkalosis resulting from vomiting and dehydration, or leukocytosis and metabolic acidosis from infarction. Large hiatal hernias may be detected on routine chest or abdominal radiographs, which may demonstrate an air-filled structure or a solid density.

PLANS

Diagnostic

Differential Diagnosis

The diagnosis of a hiatal hernia is not difficult to establish by an upper gastrointestinal series or endoscopy; however, as discussed above, the

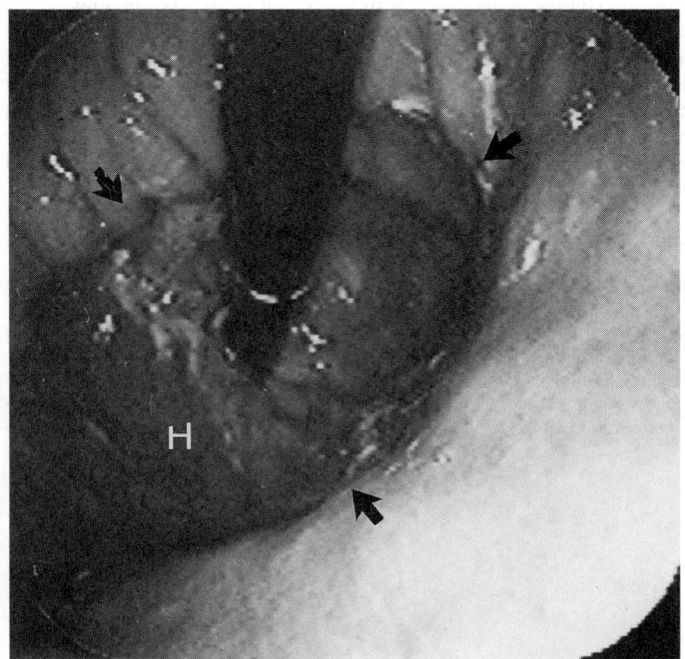

Figure 19–17–2. Endoscopic photograph of a large, sliding hiatal hernia (the letter "H" indicates the hernia pouch) on retroversion. The diaphragmatic hiatus (arrows) is very widened.

symptoms that may be associated with hiatal hernia are nonspecific and may be attributable to other conditions. Furthermore, because hiatal hernias are so common, they are frequently found in the presence of other conditions that may be responsible for the symptoms. Most commonly, the symptoms suggest the possibility of gastroesophageal reflux disease. When chest pain is present, coronary artery disease is often considered, and the possibility of a hiatal hernia is not considered until after a normal cardiac evaluation. When hiatal hernias are associated with dysphagia, motility disorders and carcinoma of the esophagus are also likely. The presence of vomiting, bleeding, and abdominal pain, which are more commonly associated with large hernias or gastric volvulus, raises the possibility of peptic ulcer disease or gastric carcinoma. When a large hiatal hernia is visualized on a chest radiograph as an air-filled mediastinal mass, the differential includes esophageal duplication cysts, bronchogenic cysts, herniation of the intestines, or esophageal dilation associated with achalasia. If the hernia has the appearance of a solid mass on the radiograph, then a malignancy is the primary consideration.

Diagnostic Options and Recommended Approach

The definitive diagnosis is usually established by an upper gastrointestinal series or barium swallow, especially when combined with fluoroscopic examination. In addition, the upper gastrointestinal series may also demonstrate significant gastroesophageal reflux. Therefore, the upper gastrointestinal series should be considered as the procedure of choice to diagnose a hiatal hernia. Although endoscopy can also demonstrate hiatal hernias, the sensitivity is probably less than that of an upper gastrointestinal series. Sliding hiatal hernias not detected by endoscopy, however, are unlikely to be clinically significant. Therefore, endoscopy is preferable if the symptoms suggest other, more significant conditions such as reflux esophagitis, peptic ulcer, and a malignancy. Large paraesophageal hernias can be diagnosed by endoscopy, but the upper gastrointestinal series may more clearly elucidate the anatomy, as discussed above.

Therapeutic

As most type I hiatal hernias are asymptomatic, no specific treatment is necessary when they are incidentally found. The relationship between pathologic gastroesophageal reflux and hiatal hernia is controversial. The current consensus is that hiatal hernia does not directly cause reflux disease; however, there are data that suggest that hiatal hernias affect lower esophageal sphincter pressures and that the effect is proportional to the size of the hiatal hernia. Nevertheless, if a sliding hiatal hernia is associated with symptoms that are consistent with gastroesophageal reflux disease, then the treatment is directed toward the reflux (see Chapter 19–16).

Type II, paraesophageal, hernias are also frequently asymptomatic, but the risk of serious complications is so great that surgical management is indicated even when they are asymptomatic. This is especially true if there is a large or an enlarging hernia. Fundoplication is the surgical procedure of choice.

FOLLOW-UP

Routine follow-up of type I hiatal hernias is not necessary; however, in the case of paraesophageal hernias, if surgery was not performed initially, repeat evaluation is indicated if symptoms develop or worsen. If enlargement or a complication of the hernia is evident on the upper gastrointestinal series, then surgery must be reconsidered.

DISCUSSION

Prevalence

Accurate data on the prevalence of sliding hiatal hernias are not available because of the lack of standardization of diagnostic criteria, which results in great variability in the diagnosis of hiatal hernias. Furthermore, the probability of diagnosing a hiatal hernia on an upper gastrointestinal series is directly related to the extent to which the radiologist attempts to demonstrate the hernia.

Related Basic Science

The diaphragm is composed of muscle fibers that arise from different structures. Two bundles of muscle fibers, termed *crura,* arise posteriorly from the upper lumbar vertebrae. The esophageal hiatus is a longitudinal slit in the muscle fibers of the right crus. The phrenoesophageal membrane, which is an extension of the fascia on the inferior surface of the diaphragm, inserts into the wall of the esophagus approximately 2 cm above the gastroesophageal junction. It is responsible for maintaining the position of the distal esophagus below the diaphragm. In either type I or II hiatal hernia, there is widening of the esophageal hiatus and relaxation of the phrenoesophageal membrane. With the sliding hiatal hernia, however, there is generalized laxity in the phrenoesophageal membrane, whereas with the paraesophageal hernia, there is a focal defect of the membrane. The result is that in sliding hiatal hernias the distal esophagus, including the gastroesophageal junction, herniates into the mediastinum, whereas with paraesophageal hernias, part of the stomach herniates beside the distal esophagus, which maintains its normal, intraabdominal position.

Natural History and Its Modification with Treatment

There is no evidence that sliding hiatal hernias will invariably enlarge or become symptomatic. Therefore, there is no indication for medical or surgical treatment of this type of hernia. Paraesophageal hernias, on the other hand, do predictably enlarge with the increasing risk of the development of gastric volvulus or infarction. Operative repair of paraesophageal hernias is effective and the risk of recurrence is small.

Prevention

No methods of prevention have been described in the development of hiatal hernias.

Cost Containment

As symptoms of gastroesophageal reflux disease occur frequently in the absence of hiatal hernias, and treatment is directed toward the reflux rather than the hiatal hernia, it is not necessary to perform any diagnostic studies to document a sliding hiatal hernia. When, however, a sliding hiatal hernia is considered in the differential diagnosis for more atypical symptoms (e.g., chest pain), or when a paraesophageal hernia is considered, then an upper gastrointestinal series would be the most cost-effective test. If an endoscopy had been performed initially and a hiatal hernia was not detected, it is not necessary to perform an upper gastrointestinal series to attempt to establish the diagnosis of a hiatal hernia.

REFERENCES

Boyce HW, Jr. Hiatal hernia and peptic diseases of the esophagus. In: Sivak MV Jr, ed. Gastroenterologic endoscopy. Philadelphia: Saunders, 1987:401.

Skinner DB. Hernias (hiatal, traumatic, and congenital). In: Berk JE, ed. Bockus gastroenterology. 4th ed. Philadelphia: Saunders, 1985:705.

Sloan S, Rademaker AW, Kahrilas PJ. Determinants of gastroesophageal junction incompetence: Hiatal hernia, lower esophageal sphincter, or both? Ann Intern Med 1992;117:977.

CHAPTER 19–18

Hiccups

Ira W. Nierenberg, M.D.

DEFINITION

A hiccup is an involuntary, intermittent, spasmodic contraction of the diaphragm resulting in a sudden inspiration that is abruptly terminated by closure of the glottis, resulting in a characteristic sound. Another medical term for hiccups is *singultus*.

ETIOLOGY

Most episodes of hiccups are self-limited. They can be persistent (lasting longer than 48 hours) or intractable (lasting longer than 1 month). Thus, hiccups can result in significant morbidity and, occasionally, may be a harbinger of a serious medical problem. The causes of hiccups are many, but can be divided into several groups: disorders affecting the central nervous system; disorders affecting the peripheral nerves, primarily the phrenic and vagus nerves; toxic–metabolic disorders affecting the central or peripheral nervous systems; psychogenic; and idiopathic.

CRITERIA FOR DIAGNOSIS

Suggestive

Hiccups are suggested by the characteristic sound they make.

Definitive

Fluoroscopy, electromyographic, and nerve conduction studies can help to definitively diagnose hiccups, but are usually not done routinely because the hiccup sound is so suggestive.

CLINICAL MANIFESTATIONS

Subjective

Patients usually seek medical attention when their hiccups have become persistent and incapacitating. The medical history is very important in ascertaining a possible underlying etiology, as are the duration and severity of the current episode. A history of recent surgery (usually within 4 days) is a common cause of hiccups and is felt to be due to hyperextension of the neck, general anesthesia, surgical manipulation, and gastric distention or ileus. The presence of hiccups during sleep suggests an organic cause, whereas hiccups that resolve during sleep and recur on awakening suggest a psychogenic or idiopathic cause. Many patients have had prior episodes of hiccups and a review of past treatments may help in current therapy.

Objective

Physical Examination

There are no physical findings directly attributable to hiccups. Physical examination may reveal evidence of a possible underlying etiology. Head and neck examination may reveal a foreign body or hair irritating the tympanic membrane, pharyngitis, laryngitis, or a neoplasm. Chest and abdominal examination may suggest pneumonia, pleuritis, pericarditis, or aortic aneurysm. Conditions associated with hepatomegaly, splenomegaly, or gastric distention may cause diaphragmatic irritation. Neurologic examination may reveal focal findings suggestive of a structural central nervous system lesion or a cerebrovascular accident.

Routine Laboratory Abnormalities

There are no laboratory abnormalities directly attributable to hiccups. Hypokalemia, hypochloremic alkalosis, and elevation of the blood urea nitrogen level may occur secondary to vomiting and dehydration.

PLANS

Diagnostic

Differential Diagnosis

Most episodes of hiccups are self-limited and are usually secondary to ingestion of food or alcohol, gastric distention (sometimes associated with gastroesophageal reflux), a sudden change in body or environmental temperature, or emotional factors. The differential diagnosis of persistent or intractable hiccups is listed in Table 19–18–1. Psychogenic or idiopathic hiccups is a diagnosis of exclusion after all possible organic causes have been ruled out.

Diagnostic Options and Recommended Approach

A blood alcohol level, chest x-ray film, and an electrocardiogram should be ordered on every patient undergoing a workup for hiccups. Head, chest, or abdominal computed axial tomography or magnetic resonance imaging scans, examination of the cerebrospinal fluid, and upper endoscopy or bronchoscopy should be done, as clinically indicated. Ambulatory 24-hour pH monitoring is now becoming more readily available and can be done to detect gastroesophageal reflux disease, as 10 to 40% of patients with hiccups secondary to gastroesophageal reflux disease deny any previous esophageal complaints.

Therapeutic

The treatment of hiccups includes treatment of the underlying disease, if possible; physical maneuvers; medical therapy; and surgical therapy.

Patients with self-limited hiccups should be advised to avoid excess alcohol intake, overeating, carbonated beverages, ingestion of very hot or cold food or beverages, cold showers, or emotional stress. No other therapy is usually necessary. Occasionally, physical maneuvers as described below need to be tried.

The treatment of persistent or intractable hiccups is much more difficult. If an underlying etiology is found, for example, a foreign body or hair irritating the tympanic membrane, removal may result in disappearance of the hiccups.

Physical maneuvers attempt to interrupt the hiccup reflex arc. These include swallowing a teaspoon of granulated sugar, breath holding, breathing into a paper bag, drinking from the wrong side of a glass, or traction on the tongue. More aggressive measures include irritation of the nasopharynx with a nasogastric tube and passage of the nasogastric tube into the stomach for gastric decompression. If these physical maneuvers fail, medical therapy is the next option, but it must be remembered that most of these medications have not been well studied in the treatment of persistent or intractable hiccups, even though they have gained widespread acceptance.

Chlorpromazine (Thorazine) is the most widely accepted agent for the treatment of persistent or intractable hiccups. It is predominantly a centrally acting psychotropic agent that also has sedative and antiemetic activity. It can be given by the intravenous, intramuscular, or oral route, but the intravenous route is considered the most effective. If the intravenous route is selected, the patient should be observed very closely for postural hypotension and sedation. The usual dosage is 25 to 50 mg diluted in 500 to 1000 mL of saline, infused slowly over 1 hour, and can be repeated up to three times at 6-hour intervals. If the hiccups resolve, chlorpromazine should be continued at a dose of 25 to 50 mg orally three or four times daily for 7 to 10 days. Chlorpromazine relieves hiccups in approximately 80% of patients.

Metoclopromide (Reglan) is the second medication of choice. It is a dopamine antagonist with cholinomimetic activity and is widely used to coordinate gastrointestinal motility. The usual dosage is 10 mg administered intravenously, over 1 to 2 minutes, and can be repeated at 4-hour intervals. If the medication is successful in terminating the hic-

TABLE 19–18–1. CAUSES OF HICCUPS, PERSISTENT OR INTRACTABLE

Central Nervous System
Infection (encephalitis, meningitis)
Multiple sclerosis
Neoplasm
Postsurgical
Trauma
Vascular disease

Peripheral Nervous System: Irritation of the Diaphragm
Neck
Laryngitis
Lymphadenopathy
Neoplasm
Pharyngitis
Postsurgical
Thyroid goiter
Tympanic membrane irritation

Chest
Aortic aneurysm
Esophagitis
Gastroesophageal reflux
Hiatal hernia
Lymphadenopathy
Mediastinitis
Myocardial infarction
Neoplasm
Pericarditis
Pleuritis
Pneumonia
Postsurgical

Abdomen
Aortic aneurysm
Gallbladder disease
Gastric distention
Gastritis
Hepatomegaly
Neoplasm
Peptic ulcer disease
Peritonitis
Postsurgical
Splenomegaly
Subphrenic abscess

Toxic–Metabolic
Alcohol
Diabetes
Electrolyte abnormality (hyponatremia, hypokalemia, hypocalcemia)
Medications
Uremia

Psychogenic
Anorexia nervosa
Excitement
Malingering
Stress
Idiopathic

cups, a maintenance dose of 10 mg orally four times a day for 7 days is recommended. Side effects include drowsiness, restlessness, and fatigue.

Other medications that have been reported to be effective include diphenylhydantoin (Dilantin), quinidine sulfate, haloperidol (Haldol), carbamazepam (Tegretol), valproic acid (Depakene), and phenobarbital.

If 24-hour pH monitoring indicates the presence of gastroesophageal reflux disease, patients should be treated with an H_2-receptor antagonist such as ranitidine (Zantac) 150 to 300 mg orally twice daily or famotidine (Pepcid) 20 to 40 mg orally twice daily. Proton pump inhibitors such as omeprazole (Prilosec) 20 mg orally once daily or lansoprazole (Prevacid) 30 mg orally once daily are used by some as an alternative therapy. If 24-hour pH monitoring is not available and no other cause for hiccups can be found, an 8-week empiric trial of H_2-receptor antagonists or proton pump inhibitors should be tried.

Surgical therapy is indicated only as a last resort when all else fails. This includes phrenic nerve blocking with anesthesia and phrenic nerve crushing or ligation. Surgical therapy is occasionally unsuccessful and may result in significant impairment of pulmonary function.

FOLLOW-UP

Patients with self-limited hiccups require only reassurance as to the benign nature of their condition. Patients with persistent or intractable hiccups should be seen frequently until their symptoms resolve and, it is hoped, an underlying etiology can be found. Persistent or intractable hiccups can be a very distressing condition so patients should be encouraged to ask any questions they may have to help put them at ease.

DISCUSSION
Prevalence and Incidence

Everyone has experienced self-limited hiccups at one time or another. Persistent and intractable hiccups occur much more frequently in men.

Related Basic Science

As mentioned above, a hiccup is an involuntary, intermittent spasmodic contraction of the diaphragm resulting in a sudden inspiration terminated by closure of the glottis. This glottic closure occurs approximately 35 milliseconds after the sudden inspiration, resulting in the characteristic sound. Fluoroscopic studies have shown that hiccups are usually confined to the left hemidiaphragm, but occasionally are bilateral. They serve no useful function and appear to be a primitive reflex.

The hiccup reflex arc consists of three parts: an afferent limb, a central connection, and an efferent limb. The afferent limb may be composed of the vagus nerve, the phrenic nerve, or sympathetic afferents arising from thoracic segments T6 to T12. The central connection has never been isolated to a specific anatomic location, but is felt to be located somewhere between cervical segments C3 and C5 and is also felt to involve an interaction among brainstem and midbrain areas. The efferent limb is primarily the phrenic nerve, but efferent nerves to the glottis and respiratory muscles are also involved.

Hiccups can be mediated at the level of the central or peripheral nervous system. Hiccups originating at the central nervous system level result from conditions that release the normal central inhibitory tone on the hiccups reflex arc. Peripheral nervous system-mediated hiccups are much more common and are usually associated with peripheral irritation of branches of the vagus or phrenic nerves. The vagus nerve has many branches including meningeal, auricular, pharyngeal, laryngeal, thoracic, and abdominal, any of which can be involved. The phrenic nerve can be irritated as it passes through the neck, through the mediastinum, or at the level of the diaphragm.

Toxic–metabolic disorders can involve either the central nervous system or peripheral nerves.

Natural History and Its Modification with Treatment

The natural history is dependent on the underlying etiology of the hiccups. Hiccups usually disappears if the underlying cause can be found and treated. Symptomatic therapy terminates most cases of hiccups, but recurrence may occur once the treatment is stopped.

Prevention

At this time, there is no known way to prevent hiccups from occurring.

Cost Containment

Even after an exhaustive workup of persistent or intractable hiccups, the etiology may not be found. Repeated tests should be avoided. Patients with self-limited hiccups do not require any other workup.

REFERENCES

Kolodzik PW, Eilers MA. Hiccups (singultus): Review and approach to management. Ann Emerg Med 1991;20:565.

Loft LM, Ward RZ. Hiccups: A case presentation and etiologic review. Arch Otolaryngol Head Neck Surg 1992;118:1115.
Shay SS, Myers RL, Johnson LF. Hiccups associated with reflux esophagitis. Gastroenterology 1984;87:204.
Wagner MS, Stapczynski JS. Persistent hiccups. Ann Emerg Med 1982;11:24.
Williamson BWA, Macintyre IMC. Management of intractable hiccups. Br Med J 1977;2:501.

CHAPTER 19–19

Barrett's Esophagus

Harry A. Winters, M.D.

DEFINITION

Barrett's esophagus refers to the replacement of the normal squamous epithelium of the esophagus with columnar epithelium. The significance of Barrett's esophagus is its propensity for the development of ulcers and bleeding, stricture formation, and, most seriously, adenocarcinoma of the esophagus.

ETIOLOGY

Columnar epithelium of the esophagus may be congenital in a small proportion of cases; however, it is well recognized that Barrett's epithelium is most commonly acquired as a result of severe, chronic gastroesophageal reflux.

CRITERIA FOR DIAGNOSIS
Suggestive

The diagnosis of Barrett's esophagus is usually considered in the presence of a long history of severe reflux symptoms. The index of suspicion is raised when reflux symptoms are associated with dysphagia, indicating the possibility of an esophageal stricture or malignancy, or with odynophagia or bleeding, which may be indications of Barrett's ulcer. In the presence of such symptoms, a barium swallow can suggest the diagnosis by demonstrating esophagitis, an esophageal stricture, or a large, deep ulcer, especially when these are located more proximally.

Definitive

The diagnosis of Barrett's esophagus can only be established by endoscopy with biopsies of the esophageal mucosa. On endoscopy, the squamocolumnar junction is displaced proximally, and there may be fingerlike projections of gastric mucosa extending proximally from the squamocolumnar junction (Figure 19–19–1). Biopsies, taken from 3 cm or more above the gastroesophageal junction, revealing columnar epithelium confirm the diagnosis. The application of Lugol's iodine solution to the mucosa during endoscopy can further aid in the diagnosis by staining the squamous mucosa so that it can be more readily distinguished from the columnar mucosa. Barrett's ulcers are larger, deeper, and more proximally located within the columnar mucosa than ulcers associated with reflux esophagitis (Figure 19–19–2).

CLINICAL MANIFESTATIONS
Subjective

When symptoms are present in the setting of Barrett's esophagus, they are usually attributable to the associated gastroesophageal reflux. Heartburn and regurgitation that have been present for a prolonged period may raise the concern of Barrett's esophagus, but the symptoms actually tend to be less pronounced than in reflux disease in the absence of Barrett's epithelium. Furthermore, the symptoms may be more fre-

quent earlier, and remit later as the squamous mucosa is replaced by the more resistant columnar epithelium. Symptoms that are associated with Barrett's related complications are more suggestive of the complication, but they are still too nonspecific to establish the diagnosis of Barrett's esophagus. Dysphagia for solid food is characteristic of a stricture or a carcinoma. Barrett's ulcers may cause odynophagia, persistent chest pain, or significant upper gastrointestinal bleeding. These symptoms do not commonly occur with reflux disease not associated with Barrett's esophagus. A history of esophageal motor disorders such as scleroderma, alcohol abuse, and cigarette smoking are more frequently associated with severe reflux disease and, therefore, Barrett's esophagus.

Objective
Physical Examination

The physical examination does not contribute to the evaluation of patients with Barrett's esophagus.

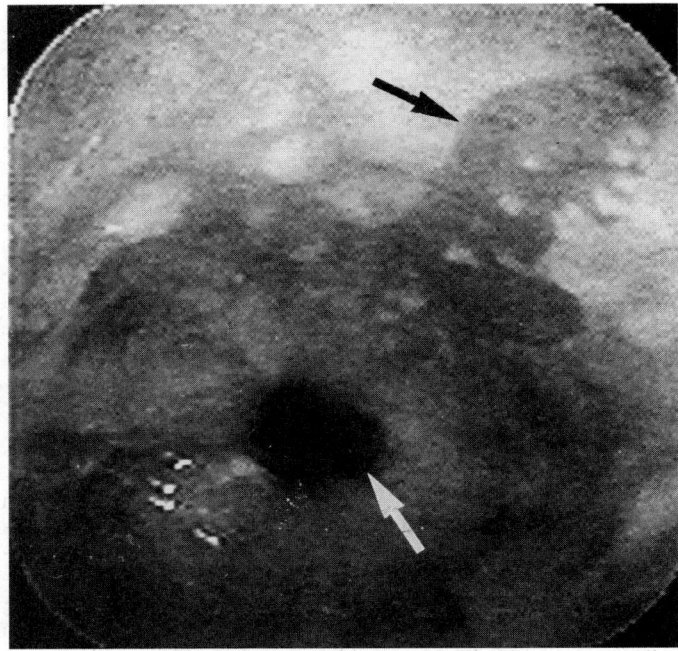

Figure 19–19–1. Endoscopic photograph from a patient with Barrett's esophagus demonstrating a fingerlike projection (black arrow) of gastric-type mucosa extending several centimeters proximal to the gastroesophageal junction (white arrow).

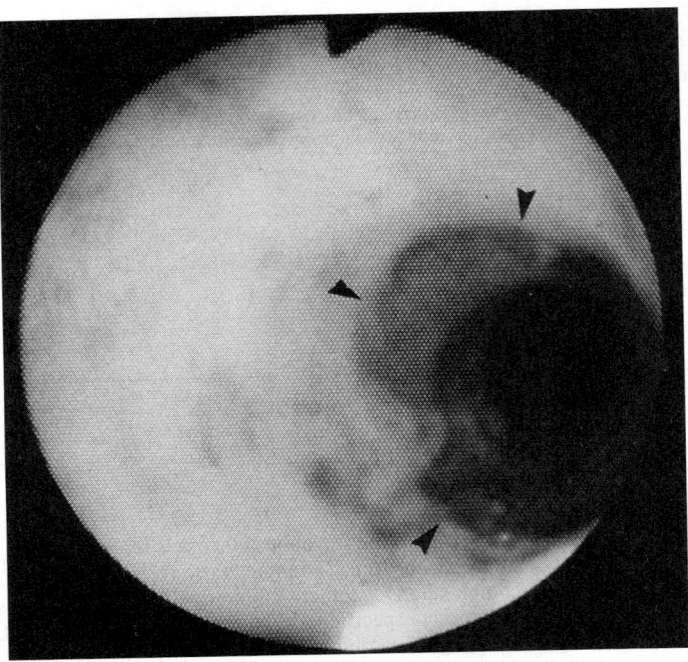

Figure 19–19–2. Endoscopic photograph of a large, circumferential Barrett's ulcer located in the proximal esophagus. Barrett's epithelium is visible adjacent to the ulcer border (arrowheads).

Routine Laboratory Abnormalities

There are no routine laboratory studies that are relevant to Barrett's esophagus.

PLANS

Diagnostic

Differential Diagnosis

Difficulty in establishing the diagnosis may be encountered when the location of the gastroesophageal junction is obscured, as with hiatal hernias, when reflux esophagitis is present, or when the distance between the gastroesophageal junction and the proximal extent of the columnar epithelium is less than 3 cm. The principal diagnosis in the differential is reflux esophagitis without Barrett's epithelium. When Barrett's esophagus is complicated by a stricture, the differential is again reflux esophagitis associated with a benign peptic stricture; however, dysphagia may also herald the presence of a Barrett's related adenocarcinoma of the esophagus, and both strictures and masses must be considered as the more common squamous cell carcinoma of the esophagus. Also, a distal stricture should be distinguished from a Schatzki ring. Finally, Barrett's ulcers would expand the differential to include various infections that involve the esophagus or esophageal mucosal damage caused by medications, radiation, or caustic ingestion. These are usually easy to differentiate by the history.

Diagnostic Options

The two accepted diagnostic modalities for establishing the diagnosis of Barrett's esophagus are the barium swallow and flexible esophagoscopy. The barium swallow is more sensitive than endoscopy in demonstrating gastroesophageal reflux, hiatal hernias, or Schatzki's ring. In addition to diagnosing an esophageal stricture, the barium swallow can give more specific details such as location, length, and the luminal diameter of the stricture. Finally, Barrett's ulcers, which have characteristic features that distinguish these from ulcers associated with reflux disease alone, can be well demonstrated on barium swallow. The radiologic examination, however, is neither sensitive nor specific for detecting Barrett's epithelium, especially in the absence of complications, or in distinguishing Barrett's from reflux or other varieties of

esophagitis. For this purpose, endoscopy must be performed. In addition to demonstrating strictures, ulcers, and masses, as can the barium swallow, endoscopy can document the gross appearance of Barrett's epithelium. Moreover, endoscopy affords the opportunity to obtain biopsies for histologic confirmation of Barrett's epithelium or the detection of dysplasia or carcinoma.

Recommended Approach

Esophagoscopy with biopsy should be the initial procedure to evaluate symptoms of gastroesophageal reflux if the diagnosis of Barrett's esophagus is being considered, especially if the history suggests the possibility of an associated complication. If a barium swallow was performed initially and had revealed evidence of reflux esophagitis, especially with those complications more commonly associated with Barrett's esophagus (i.e., ulcer or stricture), endoscopy should be performed to confirm the diagnosis of Barrett's esophagus. As Barrett's esophagus is a premalignant condition, the diagnosis must be considered in these situations.

Therapeutic

Therapeutic Options

Because Barrett's esophagus is usually diagnosed in the course of evaluation of symptoms of gastroesophageal reflux or its complications, treatment is directed toward the control of the reflux. Medical and surgical treatment of reflux is more completely discussed in Chapter 19–16. Lifestyle modifications, including diet, weight loss, and eating behavior, and H_2-receptor antagonists have been the mainstays of therapy for the management of the symptoms of reflux and its sequelae. More recently, omeprazole (Prilosec) has become available in the United States for the indication of reflux esophagitis. Cholinergic (bethanechol) and prokinetic (metoclopramide and cisapride) agents have also been used in combination with antisecretory agents in the management of refractory esophagitis. Barrett's esophagus is not, itself, an indication for antireflux surgery.

Treatment of reflux is probably not indicated when Barrett's esophagus is incidentally discovered in the absence of esophagitis or symptoms; however, the issues that must be considered when making this decision are whether antireflux therapy prevents progression of Barrett's epithelium or the development of adenocarcinoma or whether it promotes regression of Barrett's epithelium (see Natural History and Its Modification with Treatment).

Benign, esophageal strictures require dilation in addition to medical reflux therapy. Aggressive, lifelong medical therapy may prevent stricture recurrence, although periodic dilation may be required.

Recommended Approach

The recommended approach to the medical and surgical treatment of Barrett's esophagus is the same as that discussed in Chapter 19–16.

FOLLOW-UP

There are no clinical or laboratory data that are useful for following the status of Barrett's esophagus. As discussed above, the absence of symptoms does not correlate well with the degree of Barrett's epithelium; however, the goal of therapy remains the relief of reflux symptoms and the prevention of complications. Patients who respond well clinically to reflux therapy should be periodically reevaluated every 3 to 6 months for symptom recurrence or the development of new symptoms that may suggest the development of an esophageal stricture, ulcer, or malignancy. Patients who develop symptoms consistent with one of these complications should undergo an endoscopic examination with biopsy for the possibility of adenocarcinoma. As Barrett's esophagus is a premalignant disorder, routine surveillance for adenocarcinoma is required. What the most cost-effective schedule should be is controversial; however, endoscopy with biopsy to identify dysplasia is generally recommended on an annual or biannual basis. Patients in whom biopsy specimens reveal low-grade dysplasia associated with esophagitis should be aggressively treated for reflux, and the endoscopy should be repeated in 2 to 3 months. This will help differentiate neoplastic from metaplastic epithelium resulting from inflammation. If low-grade dysplasia persists, aggressive medical therapy should be continued, and endoscopy should be performed at more frequent intervals. If high-grade dysplasia is found on biopsy material, the finding should be confirmed by another experienced pathologist. If the finding is inconclusive, endoscopy should be repeated immediately with more numerous biopsies. Patients with definitive high-grade dysplasia should undergo resection of the portion of esophagus containing Barrett's epithelium because of a high risk of associated or subsequent adenocarcinoma.

DISCUSSION

Prevalence

The prevalence reported in the literature is largely dependent on the clinical circumstance in which the diagnosis was made. For example, the finding of Barrett's esophagus occurs in 5 to 20% of patients who undergo endoscopy for evaluation of gastroesophageal reflux; however, it is found in about 40% of patients with esophageal strictures.

The prevalence of Barrett's associated adenocarcinoma of the esophagus has not been well determined. Most available data, which generally indicate a prevalence of 10%, are derived from patients with Barrett's esophagus already with carcinoma at the time of the initial diagnosis. Most authors consider the risk to be increased by 30 to 40 times.

Related Basic Science

The columnar epithelium that is normally present in the fetal esophagus is eventually replaced by squamous epithelium. Islands of atopic columnar epithelium may persist and account for the small proportion of congenital cases of Barrett's esophagus. This is the most likely cause of Barrett's esophagus in children. The columnar epithelium in this situation is usually located more proximally than the acquired variety and is isolated from the normal squamocolumnar junction.

The more common acquired form of Barrett's esophagus is believed to represent a metaplastic, reparative response to damage of the squamous epithelium due to reflux esophagitis. Whether it is acid, pepsin, other agents, or a combination of agents that acts as the stimulus is unknown, but whatever the agent is, it tends to favor epithelialization by the more resistant columnar epithelium. Three types of columnar epithelial linings have been noted in Barrett's, either singularly or in combination. The specialized columnar epithelium, which is the most common type, has an appearance that is similar to that of intestinal mucosa. It has villi and crypts, and it contains columnar, goblet, and Paneth cells. The junctional epithelium resembles that of the gastric cardia. Finally, the gastric fundic-type epithelium contains pits and glands with chief and parietal cells that are capable of secreting pepsin and hydrochloric acid, respectively. The significance of these different epithelial forms with respect to the risk of adenocarcinoma is unknown.

Natural History and Its Modification with Treatment

In patients with reflux esophagitis and Barrett's esophagus, the squamocolumnar junction advances proximally, and the risk of ulcers and strictures is significantly increased without treatment. These events can be prevented, however, with adequate, aggressive medical antireflux therapy.

There have been conflicting data on whether or not regression of Barrett's epithelium occurs with effective antireflux therapy. Clearly, there is no evidence that therapy with H_2-receptor antagonists with or without cholinergic agents, which are effective in treating esophagitis or its sequelae, can cause regression of Barrett's epithelium. Whether the use of more potent antisecretory drugs (i.e., omeprazole) can cause regression remains to be determined. There are more data indicating regression of columnar epithelium after antireflux surgery, but the data are inconsistent and inconclusive. Therefore, the decision for an antireflux procedure for this indication cannot be advocated. Furthermore, regression of columnar epithelium has not been proven to reduce or eliminate the risk of the development of adenocarcinoma.

Current screening methods to identify dysplastic mucosa, which is a precursor of malignancy, may, in theory, prevent the subsequent development of carcinoma or identify carcinomas in an early stage that may have a better prognosis. Carcinoma, however, is frequently present when high-grade dysplasia is first detected. Furthermore, no data are available on whether current screening recommendations have a beneficial effect on survival.

Prevention

It has not been established that Barrett's esophagus can be prevented by vigorous antisecretory treatment of reflux esophagitis, but its complications, with the possible exception of carcinoma, can be prevented (see Discussion).

Cost Containment

As with gastroesophageal reflux disease, empiric treatment is considered to be the most cost-effective approach, and diagnostic studies are reserved for the situations or symptoms that are refractory to treatment or that recur after discontinuance of therapy. Because Barrett's esophagus is a pre-malignant condition, the diagnosis must be confirmed when it is suspected. For this purpose, endoscopy should be performed rather than a barium swallow, which is usually the first test performed for gastroesophageal reflux. Nevertheless, the major expense in the management of Barrett's esophagus is from the repeated endoscopies required for surveillance of carcinoma, and there is no consensus on the most cost-effective method of surveillance.

REFERENCES

Brand DL, Ylvisaker JT, Gelfand M, Pope CE. Regression of columnar esophageal (Barrett's) epithelium after anti-reflux surgery. N Engl J Med 1980;302:844.

Cameron AJ, Ott BJ, Payne WS. The incidence of adenocarcinoma in columnar-lined (Barrett's) esophagus. N Engl J Med 1985;313:857.

Falk GW. Barrett's esophagus. Gastrointest Endos Clin North Am 1994;4:773.

Hogan WJ, Dodds WJ. Gastroesophageal reflux disease (reflux esophagitis). In: Sleisenger MH, Fordtran JS, eds. Gastrointestinal disease. 4th ed. Philadelphia: Saunders, 1989:594.

Spechler SJ, Goyal RK. Barrett's esophagus. N Engl J Med 1986;315:362.

Esophageal Perforation

Neil M. Brodsky, M.D., and Harry A. Winters, M.D.

DEFINITION

Perforation of the esophagus refers to transmural or intramural disruption of the esophageal wall.

ETIOLOGY

Esophageal perforation may occur as a complication of medical instrumentation such as gastrointestinal endoscopy, esophageal dilation, and transesophageal echocardiography; in penetrating or blunt trauma of the chest; or following ingestion of a foreign body or caustic substance. Spontaneous esophageal perforation (Boerhhave's syndrome) may occur from forceful vomiting or childbirth. Less common causes of perforation are esophageal cancer and infections, particularly those associated with acquired immunodeficiency syndrome.

CRITERIA FOR DIAGNOSIS

Suggestive

The presence of neck, chest, or abdominal pain; fever; or signs of a pleural effusion or pneumothorax after esophageal instrumentation or other risk factors discussed above should always raise the suspicion of an esophageal perforation.

Definitive

The diagnosis of esophageal perforation is established by demonstrating an esophageal fistula or leak as discussed below.

CLINICAL MANIFESTATIONS

Subjective

The clinical presentation of an esophageal perforation is dependent on the etiology, duration, and site of the perforation. Patients with perforation in the hypopharynx or the cervical esophagus usually experience pain and stiffness in the neck, increased salivation, and odynophagia. The clinical manifestations of esophageal perforation distal to the cervical esophagus include dysphagia, odynophagia, shortness of breath, chest pain, and fever. Additionally, perforation of the esophagogastric segment may result in abdominal pain.

Objective

Physical Examination

Subcutaneous emphysema occurs in one half of patients with cervical perforation and less commonly in those with thoracic perforation. Hamman's sign, a respiratory crunching sound on chest auscultation, is a sign of pneumomediastinum. Fever, tachycardia, hypotension, sepsis, and shock occur frequently in patients with esophageal perforation, as do peritoneal signs in distal esophageal perforations. Signs of a pleural effusion occur in one half or more of patients with thoracic perforation, but in less than 10% of those with cervical perforation.

Routine Laboratory Abnormalities

Routine laboratory studies usually reveal leukocytosis and, possibly, hyperamylasemia. Roentgenograms of the chest may reveal mediastinal widening, pneumomediastinum, pneumothorax, pleural effusion, subcutaneous emphysema, or pneumoperitoneum.

PLANS

Diagnostic

Differential Diagnosis

Nonspontaneous perforations are usually not difficult to diagnose because of the characteristic setting in which they occur. In contrast, spontaneous esophageal perforation may mimic myocardial infarction, pulmonary embolus, dissecting aortic aneurysm, pneumothorax, pancreatitis, perforated peptic ulcer, incarcerated diaphragmatic hernia, or acute cholecystitis.

Diagnostic Options

Roentgenograms of the neck, chest, or abdomen may demonstrate any of the findings discussed above. Roentgenograms can be normal initially, but eventually become abnormal in the majority of cases. Subcutaneous emphysema becomes radiologically evident in approximately 1 hour, and pleural effusions after several hours. Roentgenograms performed with the ingestion of either water-soluble contrast or a barium sulfate suspension can detect 60% of cervical perforations and 90% or more of distal esophageal perforations. Radiography is also useful in the setting of foreign body ingestion.

Computed tomography of the chest can demonstrate a mediastinal abscess or an esophageal fistula, and it is particularly useful when the perforation site has sealed over.

Recommended Approach

Roentgenograms of the neck and chest should be obtained in patients when esophageal perforation is suspected or with a history of foreign body ingestion. The chest x-rays should be done in the erect position.

An esophagram with radiocontrast should be performed irrespective of the findings on routine roentgenograms, either to confirm or to identify the site of the perforation. A water-soluble iodinated compound such as diatrizoate meglumine (Gastrografin) should be used initially because of its relative safety and rapid absorption. If, however, the study does not demonstrate a leak, the examination should be repeated with barium sulfate, which better demonstrates small perforations.

If contrast radiographs do not confirm the presence of a perforation, computed tomography of the chest should be performed.

Therapeutic

Therapeutic Options

Medical management consists of oropharyngeal suction, parenteral alimentation, and broad-spectrum antibiotics. Surgical therapy includes drainage alone, drainage and primary closure, or drainage and diversion.

Recommended Approach

Perforations of the hypopharynx and cervical esophagus that are contained within the soft tissues of the neck can be managed medically, if recognized early. If mediastinal involvement is demonstrated, simple drainage in the neck is warranted with possible extension of drainage into the mediastinum.

Perforations in other locations have a higher mortality than cervical perforations and should be treated surgically.

FOLLOW-UP

If at any time after either conservative or surgical management the patient's clinical condition deteriorates, an esophagram and a chest computed tomography scan should be performed promptly.

DISCUSSION

Prevalence and Incidence

Esophageal perforation in flexible endoscopy occurs with a prevalence of one in a thousand procedures. The prevalence is much higher for rigid endoscopy and therapeutic procedures, in the range of 1 to 10%.

Related Basic Science

The area at greatest risk for transmural injury is the hypopharynx and cervical esophagus. Cervical perforations most often occur posteriorly where the esophageal wall is thin. Dissection through the retrosternal space allows spread of contamination to the mediastinum, but attachments of the esophagus to the prevertebral fascia may limit lateral spread. The next most common areas of instrumentation injury are narrow and fixed portions of the esophagus at the diaphragmatic hiatus and in proximity to the aortic arch and left main stem bronchus. Complete perforation of the thoracic esophagus results in an almost immediate exposure to both oral secretions and refluxed gastric contents, with a necrotizing inflammatory response. Within 8 to 12 hours both anaerobic and aerobic bacterial infection supervenes. The thin mediastinal pleura is usually ruptured by the inflammatory process, producing contamination of the pleural space and a pleural effusion. Intraabdominal esophageal perforations occur into the free peritoneal cavity and result in peritonitis. Progression to sepsis and shock occurs in hours.

Natural History and Its Modification with Treatment

The incidence of complications and mortality is dependent on the interval between the event and the initiation of treatment. Delay in treatment beyond 24 hours increases the risk of complications such as mediastinitis, empyema, peritonitis, and sepsis. Early recognition of the condition and prompt therapy can prevent these complications and decrease mortality.

Prevention

Esophageal perforation associated with fiberoptic endoscopy is extremely rare. Careful attention to proper endoscopic technique is critical to preventing this serious complication. More high-risk therapeutic procedures should be performed by experienced operators to minimize the occurrence of perforation.

Cost Containment

Cost containment is not applicable to esophageal perforation except for prompt recognition and initiation of appropriate treatment.

REFERENCES

Benjamin SB. Esophageal perforation. In: Haubrich WS, Schaffner F, Berk JE, eds. Bockus gastroenterology. 5th ed. Philadelphia: Saunders, 1995:497.
Dodds WJ, Steward ET, Vlymen WJ. Appropriate contrast media for evaluation of esophageal disruption. Radiology 1982;144:439.
Jones WG, Ginsberg RJ. Esophageal perforation: A continuing challenge. Ann Thorac Surg 1992;53:534.
Keeffe EB, Schrock TR. Complications of gastrointestinal endoscopy. In: Sleisenger MH, Fordtran JS, eds. Gastrointestinal disease. 5th ed. Philadelphia: Saunders, 1993:301.
Sawyer R, Phillips C, Vakil N. Short- and long-term outcome of esophageal perforation. Gastrointest Endosc 1995;41:130.

CHAPTER 19–21

Benign Tumors and Cysts of the Esophagus

Amiram Samin, M.D.

DEFINITION

Benign tumors and cysts of the esophagus are uncommon. Most of these lesions are asymptomatic, incidental findings on radiologic or endoscopic examination. The majority of these lesions are of nonepithelial origin, located within the esophageal wall deep to the mucosa (Figure 19–21–1). The malignant potential is very low.

ETIOLOGY

The etiology of benign tumors of the esophagus is not known. Most cysts of the esophagus are congenital. Several theories of causation of congenital cysts have been suggested but none is proven.

CLINICAL MANIFESTATIONS

Subjective

Most patients are asymptomatic. Large lesions may cause symptoms which depend on location within the esophagus.

Intraluminal lesions are usually polypoid and mobile. They may regurgitate into the mouth or may cause asphyxiation.

Intramural lesions may cause slowly progressive dysphagia or chest discomfort. Ulceration of overlying mucosa is very rare; therefore, bleeding is unusual.

Extramural lesions may encroach on the trachea or bronchi, presenting with cough or dyspnea.

Objective

Physical examination is nonrevealing. Rarely, a large pedunculated tumor may protrude into patient's mouth. Routine laboratory examination is of no value.

PLANS

Diagnostic

Differential Diagnosis

The most common intramural mass of the esophagus is leiomyoma. Lesions that resemble leiomyomas on radiologic and endoscopic examination include neurofibromas, lipomas, granular cell tumors, and duplication cysts.

Diagnostic Options

Barium swallow is often the initial study that discovers the unexpected, asymptomatic mass. Endoscopy is needed to confirm absence of mucosal involvement. Computed tomography of the chest or endoscopic ultrasound aids in assessing the size of the lesion as well as confirming location of the lesion and evaluating the mediastinum.

Recommended Approach

If an intramural lesion of the esophagus is first detected on barium swallow, endoscopy should follow. This confirms intactness of mucosa. Endoscopic biopsy is nondiagnostic because the tumor is located deep to the mucosa. Attempted biopsy of a submucosal lesion may lead to perforation. In addition, postbiopsy inflammatory changes complicate surgical enucleation of the mass.

Complementing endoscopy and providing valuable information is endoscopic ultrasound. The exact intramural location can be shown, as can the size and the solid or cystic nature of the lesion. If endoscopic ultrasound is not available, computed tomography of the chest is helpful in demonstrating soft tissue, fluid, or fat components of the lesion. The size of the mass can be determined and the remainder of the mediastinum evaluated.

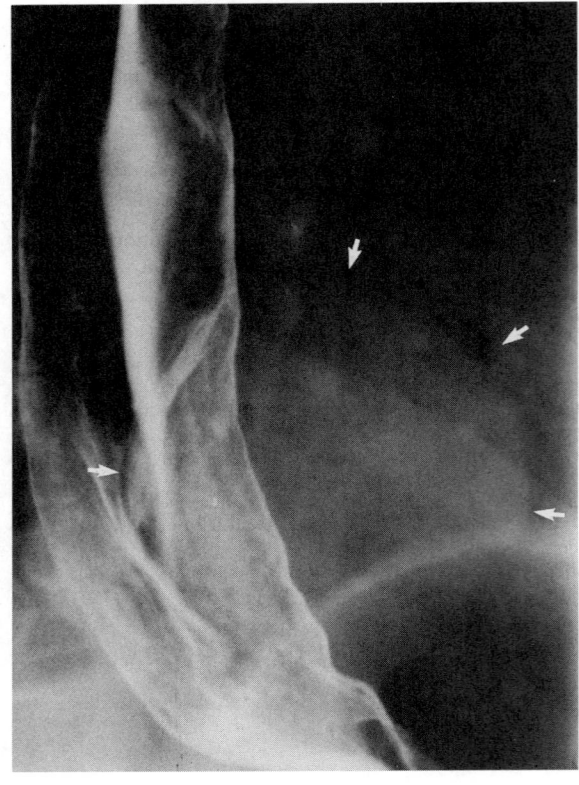
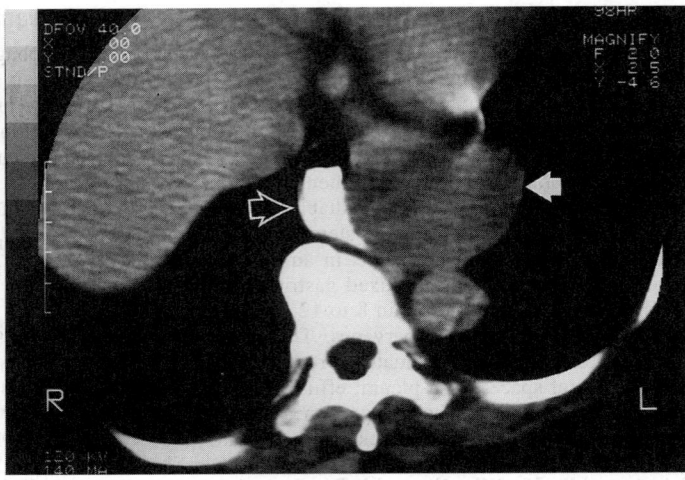

Figure 19-21-1. A. Double-contrast view of the distal esophagus. A large leiomyoma indents the esophageal wall. The overlying mucosa is intact. The lesion is outlined by arrows. **B.** Computed tomography scan through the center of the mass demonstrates the smooth interface with the esophagus (open arrow) and the large exophytic component of the leiomyoma (solid arrow).

Therapeutic

Therapeutic Options

Treatment options for intramural lesions include enucleation and esophageal resection. A number of patients have been treated by thoracoscopic enucleation with excellent results and minimal morbidity.

Mucosal abnormalities can be resected endoscopically or surgically.

Recommended Approach

Symptomatic lesions should be removed surgically. Thoracoscopic enucleation, when feasible, is preferred.

No general consensus exists as to the management of the asymptomatic mass. It seems that sharing the available information with the patient and presenting her or him with the option of long-term follow-up or surgical excision is the preferred approach.

FOLLOW-UP

Following removal of leiomyoma or cyst there is no need for long-term follow-up.

Asymptomatic lesions can be followed by barium swallow. Little or no increase in size has been described in up to 15 years of follow-up.

DISCUSSION

Prevalence and Incidence

Leiomyoma is the most common benign tumor of the esophagus; it represents three quarters of benign intramural esophageal tumors. Compared with malignant esophageal tumor, leiomyoma is rare. Esophageal carcinoma outnumbers leiomyoma 50:1. Duplication cyst is second to leiomyoma in frequency among benign esophageal mass lesions.

Related Basic Science

Most mesenchymal tumors of the esophagus are benign. Leiomyoma represent two thirds of these lesions. Ninety percent of leiomyomas arise in the mid- or distal esophagus. Most are solitary lesions ranging in size from 2 to 8 cm. Giant leiomyomas (up to 20 cm in length) have been described. Leiomyosarcoma is rare and usually has an irregular ul-

cerated surface as opposed to the smooth intact mucosa overlying leiomyomas.

Most epithelial tumors of the esophagus are malignant. The uncommon benign epithelial tumors include small papillomas. They are often multifocal and are not considered to be premalignant.

An inflammatory polyp is usually a small sessile polyp at the gastroesophageal junction. It is associated with reflux esophagitis. It consists of granulation tissue and disappears with effective treatment for esophagitis.

A fibrovascular polyp is a large pedunculated tumor that contains fibrous, vascular, and adipose tissue. It is covered by normal mucosa. The tumor most often arises in the proximal esophagus. This large mass may regurgitate into or even outside of the mouth. Asphyxia, due to aspiration of the mass into the airway, has been described. There is no malignant potential and this lesion is usually surgically removed.

The majority of esophageal cysts are congenital. Duplication cysts are located within the esophageal wall. The mucosal lining is variable. Most cysts do not communicate with the esophageal lumen. Some are associated with vertebral anomalies. Those cysts are called *neuroenteric cysts*. The appearance on barium swallow and endoscopy is similar to that of leiomyoma. Endoscopic ultrasound or computed tomography confirms the cystic nature of this lesion.

Less common are the acquired cysts known as retention cysts. These are caused by obstruction of mucous glands within the esophageal wall.

Natural History and Its Modification with Treatment

Small intramural benign mass lesions are usually asymptomatic. In long-term follow-up, no significant change in symptoms or size of the lesion was observed.

In asymptomatic patients, surgical removal of the lesion results in cure.

Prevention

Benign tumors of the esophagus cannot be prevented.

Cost Containment

During the initial evaluation, endoscopy and either endoscopic ultrasound or computed tomography of the chest are sufficient. When surgery is indicated, thoracoscopic enucleation cuts costs significantly due to short hospitalization (1 or 2 days) and faster recovery.

REFERENCES

Levine MS. Benign tumors. In: Levine MS, ed. Radiology of the esophagus. Philadelphia: Saunders, 1989.

Ming SC. Tumors of the esophagus and stomach. Washington DC: Armed Forces Institute of Pathology, 1973.

Postlethwait RW, Lowe JE. Benign tumors and cysts of the esophagus. In: Zuidema GD, ed. Shackelford's surgery of the alimentary tract. 3rd ed. Philadelphia: Saunders, 1991.

CHAPTER 19–22

Carcinoma of the Esophagus (See Section 3, Chapter 2)

CHAPTER 19–23

Infectious Esophagitis

Jean-Pierre Raufman, M.D.

DEFINITION

Infectious esophagitis occurs when infection of the esophagus with fungi, viruses or bacteria causes mucosal inflammation that may result in erosions, ulcers, or fistulas. Infectious esophagitis occurs most commonly as a complication of diabetes, corticosteroid or antibiotic use, cancer, or immunocompromise (e.g., organ transplant recipients and those infected with HIV). Some pathogens, like herpes simplex virus, can cause infectious esophagitis in otherwise healthy individuals.

ETIOLOGY

Infectious esophagitis is caused by infection of the esophagus with fungi (e.g., *Candida albicans* and other species, *Aspergillus* species, *Histoplasma capsulatum, Blastomyces dermatitides*); viruses (e.g., herpes simplex virus type 1, cytomegalovirus, and varicella zoster virus); or bacteria (e.g., *Mycobacterium tuberculosis, Actinomyces israelii, Streptococcus viridans, Lactobacillus acidophilus, Treponema pallidum*).

CRITERIA FOR DIAGNOSIS

Suggestive

Painful swallowing (odynophagia) and/or difficulty swallowing (dysphagia) are suggestive of infectious esophagitis, especially when these symptoms occur in a patient who has diabetes or cancer, uses corticosteroids or antibiotics, or is immunocompromised. These symptoms are frequently progressive and present for days to weeks by the time the patient seeks medical attention.

Definitive

At the very least, diagnosis of infectious esophagitis requires the presence of mucosal ulceration or other evidence of an infectious process on barium radiographs of the esophagus. Strict criteria require esophagoscopy with gross and histologic evidence of esophageal mucosal inflammation and identification of a pathogen by appropriate histologic or microbiological methods.

CLINICAL MANIFESTATIONS

Subjective

Odynophagia and/or dysphagia are the most common symptoms of infectious esophagitis. Odynophagia may be so severe that sitophobia, the fear of eating, results. Dysphagia, if present, is generally more severe following ingestion of solids rather than liquids. Severe dysphagia may indicate an esophageal stricture. Coughing of liquid or food after eating or recurrent pneumonia may indicate an esophagotracheal or esophagobronchial fistula.

The presence of diabetes, corticosteroid or antibiotic use, or immunocompromise (e.g., use of immunosuppressive agents for organ transplantation, cancer, or AIDS) indicates a patient at risk for infectious esophagitis. Cancer patients with leukemia or lymphoma are more susceptible to infectious esophagitis than those with solid tumors. A history of infectious esophagitis caused by a particular organism (e.g., *Candida albicans*) makes it likely that the patient's current complaints are due to reinfection with the same organism.

Objective

Physical Examination

Physical examination is helpful if oropharyngeal candidiasis (thrush) or mucocutaneous candidiasis is present. These findings, particularly in patients infected with HIV, suggest that the esophageal symptoms are caused by *Candida* esophagitis. Rales or other evidence of pulmonic pathology may indicate the presence of an esophagotracheal or esophagobronchial fistula with resultant pneumonia. Rarely, the presence of herpes zoster (shingles) involving a thoracic dermatome or disseminated zoster may indicate infectious esophagitis caused by varicella virus.

Routine Laboratory Abnormalities

Routine laboratory tests are not helpful for diagnosing infectious esophagitis or for identifying the microbe causing the infection. Nevertheless, some features, like leukopenia or lymphopenia, may indicate that the patient is immunocompromised.

PLANS

Diagnostic

Differential Diagnosis

The differential diagnosis includes reflux esophagitis, esophageal stricture, esophageal cancer, esophageal motility disorders including diffuse esophageal spasm and achalasia, ischemic heart disease, and mediastinal tumors.

Diagnostic Options

The three diagnostic options are clinical diagnosis, barium esophagram, and esophagoscopy.

Clinical Diagnosis. In some circumstances, the physician can make and act on a working clinical diagnosis. For example, in an HIV-infected patient with oropharyngeal candidiasis, the most likely cause of odynophagia or dysphagia is esophageal candidiasis. A patient with thoracic herpes zoster (shingles) may have concurrent esophageal involvement.

Barium Esophagram. A barium esophagram, particularly an air-contrast study, may demonstrate features that suggest a particular esophageal pathogen. Such findings include a "shaggy" appearance in esophageal candidiasis; circular "punched-out" ulcers with a "halo effect" in herpetic esophagitis; and longitudinal or stellate ulcers in cytomegalovirus infection. Such findings, however, are not pathognomonic.

Esophagoscopy. This represents the most sensitive and specific technique for diagnosing infectious esophagitis. On endoscopy, careful examination may reveal fungal plaques, ulcers, or other lesions that suggest a particular pathogen. Brushings and multiple biopsies of any lesions should be obtained for cytologic and histologic examination, respectively. Biopsy material should also be sent to the laboratory in appropriate transport media for fungal, bacterial, viral, and mycobacterial cultures.

Recommended Approach

Esophagoscopy is the most sensitive and specific method of identifying an esophageal pathogen. Although a barium esophagram may reveal pathology and suggest a diagnosis, this method is relatively nonspecific and commonly the radiologist requests endoscopic correlation. Nevertheless, because esophagotracheal or esophagobronchial fistulas are difficult to identify endoscopically, when these lesions are suspected, a barium esophagram may be helpful prior to endoscopy. Otherwise the clinician should proceed directly with esophagoscopy for the diagnosis of infectious esophagitis.

In patients infected with HIV, the most common esophageal pathogen is *Candida albicans*. This is particularly true if oropharyngeal candidiasis is present or the patient has a history of esophageal candidiasis. Figure 19–23–1 depicts a scheme for the evaluation and treatment of odynophagia or dysphagia in patients infected with HIV. In this setting, because of the high incidence of esophageal candidiasis, antifungal agents can be started without further diagnostic testing. Esophagoscopy is needed only if there is no symptomatic response to antifungal treatment within 7 to 10 days.

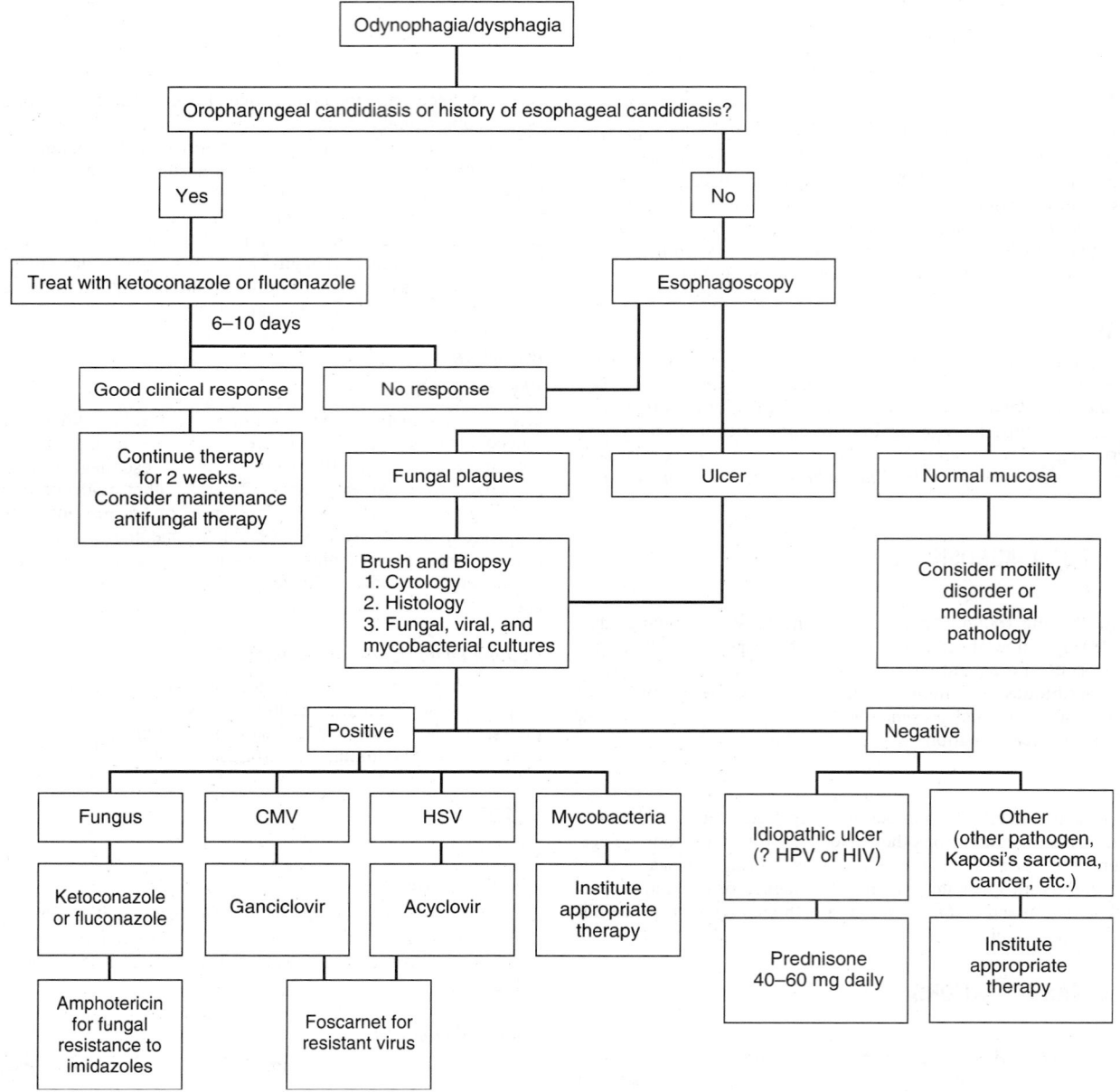

Figure 19–23–1. Proposed scheme for evaluation and treatment of odynophagia or dysphagia in persons infected with HIV. CMV, cytomegalovirus; HSV, herpes simplex virus; HPV, human papillomavirus.

Therapeutic

Therapeutic Options

In patients with severe symptoms, "swish and swallow" treatment with viscous xylocaine or cutaneous application of nitroglycerin ointment may be helpful while more specific antimicrobial therapy eradicates the infection. If possible, reversal of factors that predispose to infectious esophagitis (e.g., discontinuation of corticosteroid or antibiotic use) should be part of therapy.

Fungal Esophagitis. *Candida albicans* is the most common cause of fungal esophagitis. This organism is generally eradicated by oral treatment with imidazoles, such as fluconazole (100–200 mg/d) and ketoconazole (200–600 mg/d). Patients with AIDS commonly require the higher doses of these agents and may respond better to fluconazole than ketoconazole. Fungi resistant to fluconazole and ketoconazole have been reported and require intravenous therapy with amphotericin (10–50 mg/d). Amphotericin is generally the treatment of choice for fungal esophagitis caused by *Candida glabrata, Histoplasma capsulatum, Aspergillus* species, and *Blastomycosis* species.

Viral Esophagitis. Acyclovir (250 mg/m^2 intravenously every 8 hours or 200–400 mg orally five times daily for 2 weeks) is effective for reducing the symptoms of herpes simplex and varicella zoster virus esophagitis. Ganciclovir (5 mg/kg intravenously every 12 hours for 2 weeks) appears to be effective for cytomegalovirus esophagitis. Foscarnet (60 mg/kg intravenously every 8 hours for 2 weeks) is useful for treating strains of herpes simplex virus, varicella zoster virus, or cytomegalovirus that are resistant to acyclovir and ganciclovir. Idiopathic ulcers of the esophagus in patients infected with HIV may respond to therapy with prednisone (40–60 mg/d for at least 4 weeks).

Mycobacterial and Bacterial Esophagitis. Standard antituberculous therapy should be started as soon as mycobacterial esophagitis is diagnosed. Surgery or endoscopic stenting of the esophagus should be considered in patients with fistulas. If *Mycobacterium avium* is identified, treatment is more problematic. Combination therapy using several of the following drugs may be tried: isoniazid, rifampicin, ethambutol, amikacin, ciprofloxacin, clarithromycin, and rifabutin. Unfortunately, *M. avium* remains very resistant to therapy. Bacterial esophagitis (usually caused by Gram-positive organisms like *Streptococcus viridans* and *Staphylococcus aureus* responds to treatment with the combination of a broad-spectrum beta-lactam antibiotic and an aminoglycoside.

Recommended Approach

Treatment of infectious esophagitis should be directed at rapid relief of symptoms and eradication of the offending organism. Consequently, to alleviate esophageal symptoms, the patient should immediately be started on viscous xylocaine "swish and swallow." As soon as a likely pathogen is identified, appropriate therapy, as described above, should be instituted. As noted earlier (see Figure 19–23–1), empiric antifungal therapy is reasonable in many HIV-infected patients with symptoms of infectious esophagitis.

FOLLOW-UP

Further diagnostic evaluation depends on the patient's response to treatment. If symptoms resolve, no further diagnostic testing is needed. If, however, symptoms do not improve within a reasonable interval (7–10 days), and certainly if they worsen, repeat endoscopy must be performed to search for an overlooked pathogen and appropriate cultures obtained to detect resistance to the agents being used for treatment. In immunocompromised patients, particularly those infected with HIV, esophageal infection with more than one pathogen has been reported.

DISCUSSION

Prevalence

Primary esophageal infections are unusual in immunocompetent people. Infectious esophagitis may occur in up to 15% of patients with cancer. Currently, most cases of infectious esophagitis occur in patients who are immunocompromised because of infection with HIV or treatment to prevent transplant rejection. Infectious esophagitis has been reported in up to 25% of kidney transplant recipients, 50% of liver transplant recipients, and 75% of patients infected with HIV.

Related Basic Science

Physiologic or Metabolic Derangement

Suppression of leukocyte function and number by infection with HIV or the use of immunosuppressive agents (corticosteroids, cyclosporine, azathioprine, etc.) permits colonization and infection of the esophageal mucosa with *Candida* species. Progressive immunosuppression (e.g., CD4 lymphocyte counts below 200 cells/mm^3 in patients with AIDS) increases susceptibility to esophageal infection with cytomegalovirus and *Mycobacterium avium.*

Anatomic Derangement

Motility disorders of the esophagus that are associated with progressive systemic sclerosis, achalasia, and esophageal strictures, diverticula, and cancer cause stasis of esophageal contents, thereby predisposing to colonization with *Candida* species and subsequent fungal esophagitis.

Natural History and Its Modification with Treatment

In immunocompetent patients, most infections of the esophagus are self-limited. No studies have documented that acyclovir therapy for an immunocompetent person with herpes simplex virus esophagitis shortens the illness. Nevertheless, improvement of symptoms with acyclovir therapy has been reported. In immunocompromised patients, particularly those infected with HIV, the natural history of infectious esophagitis is devastating. Severe odynophagia leads to avoidance of eating. Consequent weight loss and malnutrition worsen the immune status, thereby setting the stage for other life-threatening opportunistic infections. Although few studies are available, there is much anecdotal evidence that vigorous treatment of esophageal infections, particularly those caused by fungi and viruses, improves these patients' quality of life.

Prevention

Efforts to avoid long-term therapy with antibiotics or corticosteroids, including steroid inhalers, will decrease the likelihood of developing an esophageal infection. In organ transplant recipients, screening of blood products for cytomegalovirus antibodies and removal of cytomegalovirus-containing leukocytes before infusion, antiviral prophylaxis with ganciclovir, and rapid treatment with ganciclovir when patients start excreting cytomegalovirus in the urine appear to decrease the risk of cytomegalovirus infections. In HIV-infected persons, aggressive treatment of oropharyngeal candidiasis and measures to improve the immune status of the patient should increase the risk of infectious esophagitis. Maintenance antifungal therapy following an episode of *Candida* esophagitis may be helpful in some HIV-infected persons, but studies documenting the efficacy of this approach have not yet been reported.

Cost Containment

Costs can be reduced by avoiding unnecessary testing. In HIV-infected patients, empiric therapy with antifungal agents may lead to resolution of symptoms. Esophagoscopy should be reserved for patients who do not respond to antifungal therapy within 7 to 10 days. In general, in any patient with symptoms suggestive of esophageal infection, esophagoscopy is the test of choice. Barium radiography of the esophagus, which is less sensitive and specific than esophagoscopy, should be reserved for patients in whom a stricture or fistula is suspected.

REFERENCES

Baehr PH, McDonald GB. Esophageal infections: Risk factors, presentation, diagnosis and treatment. Gastroenterology 1994;106:509.

Laine L. The natural history of esophageal candidiasis after successful treatment in patients with AIDS. Gastroenterology 1994;107:744.

Laine L, Dretler RH, Conteas C, et al. A prospective, randomized, double-blind trial of fluconazole vs. ketoconazole for *Candida* esophagitis. Ann Intern Med 1992;117:655.

Raufman JP. Esophageal infections. In: Yamada T, ed. Textbook of gastroenterology. Philadelphia: Lippincott, 1991:1143.

Shortsleeve MJ, Levine MS. Herpes esophagitis in otherwise healthy patients: Clinical and radiographic findings. Radiology 1992;182:859.

Tavitian A, Raufman JP, Rosenthal LE. Oral candidiasis is a marker for esophageal candidiasis in AIDS. Ann Intern Med 1986;104:54.

CHAPTER 19–24

Benign Tumors of the Stomach

Amiram Samin, M.D.

DEFINITION

Benign tumors of the stomach are uncommon. Some patients present with upper gastrointestinal bleeding or epigastric pain. The majority of these lesions are asymptomatic, discovered incidentally on endoscopic or radiologic examination. The malignant potential varies with the type of lesion.

ETIOLOGY

Most benign gastric tumors have no known etiology. There is an increased incidence of gastric polyps in patients with chronic atrophic gastritis. Certain polyposis syndromes involving the stomach are genetically transmitted.

CRITERIA FOR DIAGNOSIS
Suggestive

Most patients are asymptomatic. Some patients present with upper gastrointestinal bleeding, epigastric pain, or symptoms of intermittent gastric outlet obstruction.

Definitive

Definitive diagnosis can be made only by histologic examination.

CLINICAL MANIFESTATIONS
Subjective

Approximately 5% of patients present with symptoms that include gastrointestinal bleeding and epigastric pain. Intermittent gastric outlet obstruction caused by distal polypoid lesions may present as vomiting.

Objective
Physical Examination

Physical examination is nonrevealing in most patients. Rarely, an epigastric mass is felt. In patients with Peutz–Jeghers syndrome, mucosal pigmentation is found.

Routine Laboratory Abnormalities

Routine blood work may detect anemia, but is otherwise of no value.

PLANS
Diagnostic
Differential Diagnosis

Mucosal Lesions. Hyperplastic polyps represent up to 90% of gastric polyps. The typical lesion is smaller than 1 cm, sessile, and solitary. Much less common is an adenomatous polyp. It usually exceeds 2 cm in diameter and is most often in the antrum.

Many of the polyposis syndromes involve the stomach. These include familial polyposis coli, Peutz–Jeghers syndrome, and Cronkite–Canada syndrome.

Intramural Lesions. Leiomyoma is the most common mesenchymal tumor of the stomach. It is usually a solitary, submucosal lesion. Other less common lesions with a similar appearance include neurogenic tumors, lipomas, and fibromas.

Diagnostic Options

An upper gastrointestinal series readily detects mucosal polyps. Intramural lesions appear as smooth, rounded, and well-circumscribed filling defects. Central ulceration is frequently seen.

Endoscopy is superior to an upper gastrointestinal series in detecting small mucosal lesions, but intramural lesions could be missed on endoscopy because the overlying mucosa is often normal.

Lesions that are largely exophytic are best assessed by computed tomography scan or endoscopic ultrasound.

Recommended Approach

Following detection of mucosal polyp on an upper gastrointestinal series, endoscopy and biopsy are recommended. In intramural lesions with a central ulceration, endoscopy and biopsy may be diagnostic; however, when the overlying mucosa is intact, biopsy is usually nondiagnostic.

Endoscopic ultrasound assists in distinguishing a true intramural mass from a normal extrinsic impression or extramural mass. It also establishes the solid or cystic nature of the mass. Computed tomography can provide similar information.

Therapeutic
Therapeutic Options

Most mucosal polyps are treated by endoscopic polypectomy. Surgical resection is an option for large mucosal lesions as well as intramural lesions.

Recommended Approach

Whenever feasible, endoscopy and polypectomy are the preferred approach. Surgery should be reserved for adenomatous polyps larger than 2 cm that cannot be endoscopically removed, as well as mucosal lesions in which no definitive diagnosis can be made by endoscopic biopsy. The recommended approach for large or symptomatic intramural lesions is surgical removal.

FOLLOW-UP

Hyperplastic polyps are not premalignant lesions. In the absence of dysplasia of the gastric mucosa there is no need for long-term follow-up. Patients with adenomatous gastric polyps require annual endoscopic examination because of their increased risk of developing cancer. Patients with a small asymptomatic intramural lesion in which surgery is not advised can be followed annually by upper gastrointestinal series.

DISCUSSION
Prevalence and Incidence

Hyperplastic polyps account for up to 90% of gastric polyps. Lesions are multiple in 25% of patients. Adenomatous polyps account for 8 to 10% of gastric polyps. Leiomyomas constitute 60% of benign mes-

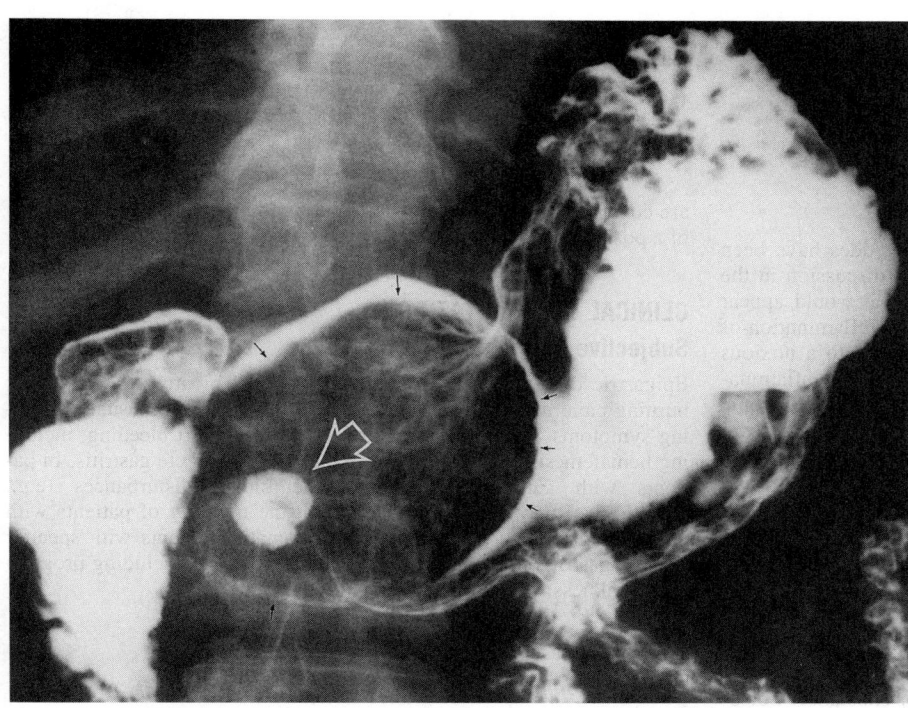

Figure 19–24–1. A large leiomyoma seen in the antrum. Please note the smooth margins of the lesion (black arrows). The collection of contrast at the center of the mass (open arrow) represents an ulcer.

enchymal gastric lesions. Two thirds of all leiomyomas of the gastrointestinal tract arise in the stomach.

Related Basic Science

Hyperplastic polyps are small, on average 5 to 10 mm in diameter, usually sessile and solitary lesions, distributed through the stomach. Chronic atrophic gastritis is seen in 70% of patients. Hyperplastic polyps are not premalignant; however, gastric carcinoma has been found in approximately 10 to 30% of patients with hyperplastic polyps in several large studies. This fact is most likely secondary to the high incidence of associated atrophic gastritis.

Adenomatous polyps usually adopt a tubulovillous pattern. Most are located in the antrum. One half are larger than 4 cm. Malignant transformation is related to the size of the polyps, usually seen in lesions larger than 2 cm. Cancer elsewhere in the stomach is found in one quarter to one half of the patients with adenomatous polyps. The majority of gastric smooth muscle tumors are benign. The prediction of malignant behavior of tumor by histology is inaccurate. The frequency of mitotic figures is a useful criterion. Another useful fact is tumor size. Tumors larger than 6 cm are more likely to be malignant. Metastatic disease has been identified in smaller, histologically benign-appearing leiomyomas.

Natural History and Its Modification with Treatment

Most hyperplastic polyps are smaller than 2 cm, although polyps up to 4 cm have been described. One third of hyperplastic polyps recur following polypectomy, usually elsewhere in the stomach. Gastric carcinoma may be present in 7 to 28% of patients with hyperplastic polyps. Most patients with hyperplastic polyps have chronic atrophic gastritis, and the high rate of gastric carcinoma is attributed to this fact. The natural history of gastric leiomyoma is not known.

Prevention

No preventive measures are known for benign tumors of the stomach.

Cost Containment

Patients with hyperplastic polyps in which a mucosal biopsy reveals no evidence of high-grade dysplasia should not be subjected to annual endoscopic follow-up. Intramural lesions that are not surgically removed are best evaluated by endoscopic ultrasound. If this is not available, follow-up can be performed by upper gastrointestinal series for intramural lesions and by computed tomography for exophytic lesions.

REFERENCES

Ming SC. Tumors of the esophagus and stomach. Washington, DC: Armed Forces Institute of Pathology, 1973.

Skandalakis JE, Gray SW, Brown BC, Mullins JD. Nonepithelial tumors of the stomach and duodenum. In: Nyhus LM, Wastell C, eds. Surgery of the stomach and duodenum. 4th ed. Boston/Toronto: Little, Brown, 1986.

White ME. Benign tumors of the stomach. In: Freeny PC, Stevenson GW, eds. Margulis and Burhenne's alimentary tract radiology. 5th ed. St Louis: Mosby 1994.

CHAPTER 19–25

Carcinoma of the Stomach (See Section 3, Chapter 8)

Acute and Chronic Gastritis

Gerald Fruchter, M.D.

DEFINITION

The classification and definition of the various gastritides have been confusing and thus have engendered a great deal of discussion in the literature. Merging recent discussion on the subject, it would appear that acute gastritis can aptly be described as an acute inflammation of the gastric mucosa representing the stomach's response to a noxious stimulus, be it a drug, pathogen, chemical, or ischemia. This inflammation can be detected either endoscopically or histologically. Chronic gastritis, on the other hand, is a diagnosis that requires histologic confirmation of a chronic inflammatory process in the gastric mucosa. Chronic gastritis is generally classified into specific (distinctive) and nonspecific entities, with the latter further divided into erosive and nonerosive forms.

ETIOLOGY

The causes of acute gastritis are multiple. Injury induced by drugs, primarily aspirin and other nonsteroidal antiinflammatory drugs, is a frequent offender. Alcohol is another common injurious substance. Corrosive agents, primarily strong acids, are capable of inducing significant gastric mucosal damage. Infectious causes include bacterial, viral, fungal, and parasitic agents. Cytomegalovirus, herpesvirus, syphilis, cryptosporidiosis, and tuberculosis are among the agents seen, particularly in immunocompromised hosts. Bacterial infection including gamma-hemolytic streptococci and *Clostridium* species can give rise to a fulminant phlegmonous gastritis. *Helicobacter pylori,* a Gram-negative spiral organism that generally causes a chronic gastritis, can give rise to an acute gastritis. Other insults, including radiation, physiologic stress, and duodenogastric reflux (of bile and pancreatic juice) can likewise cause an acute gastritis. The large majority (approximately 90%) of the chronic nonerosive nonspecific gastritides can be attributed to *H. pylori.* Autoimmune gastritis constitutes the remainder of this entity. Chronic erosive gastritis, also referred to as varioliform gastritis in view of the endoscopic appearance of thickened gastric folds with overlying erosive nodules, is another category of the nonspecific gastritides. This form may represent a subtype of the recently described entity of lymphocytic gastritis. The specific forms of chronic gastritis include sarcoidosis, Crohn's disease, and eosinophilic gastritis. Whether Menetrier's disease should be classified as a gastropathy or chronic gastritis remains a moot point.

CRITERIA FOR DIAGNOSIS

Suggestive

The symptoms and physical findings are discussed under Clinical Manifestations, Subjective. They are not diagnostic.

Definitive

The diagnosis of acute gastritis can be made endoscopically with the mucosal findings of erosions and/or mucosal hemorrhages. Frequently, though not always, biopsy reveals an acute inflammatory response consisting of polymorphonuclear leukocytes infiltrating the gastric mucosa. The diagnosis of chronic gastritis requires histologic confirmation of a chronic inflammatory reaction consisting of lymphocytes and plasma cells within the gastric mucosa. The identification of *H. pylori* organisms establishes the diagnosis of *H. pylori* chronic gastritis. Endoscopic findings correlate poorly with the histologic findings of chronic gastritis, and indeed, the endoscopy is frequently normal. The presence of chronic gastritis of the gastric body with relative antral sparing, the absence of *H. pylori,* a paucity of glandular elements (e.g., parietal cells), and the concomitant findings of hypochlorhydria or achlorhydria

are consistent with the diagnosis of autoimmune gastritis. The findings of a positive antiintrinsic factor antibody helps confirm the diagnosis.

CLINICAL MANIFESTATIONS

Subjective

Epigastric discomfort ranging from abdominal bloating to a sharp or burning pain, nausea, and occasionally vomiting are the usual presenting symptoms. Occult bleeding and sometimes overt bleeding, including hematemesis, may be present in patients with acute gastritis. In patients with autoimmune gastritis, neurologic disturbances (e.g., paresthesias) may occur. Of note is that the majority of patients with nonspecific chronic gastritis are asymptomatic. Patients with specific chronic gastritis may present in an array of fashions including progressive weakness, weight loss, and diarrhea.

Objective

Physical Examination

Physical findings are generally unremarkable. Mild epigastric tenderness may be present; an acute abdomen with peritoneal findings may accompany a severe corrosive gastritis or a phlegmonous gastritis. Guaiac-positive stools and/or melena are occasionally seen, particularly in the patient with an acute gastritis. For patients with autoimmune gastritis (especially those who have progressed to pernicious anemia), vitiligo, smooth tongue, and sensory deficits may be seen.

Routine Laboratory Abnormalities

Anemia, seen in a small proportion of patients with gastritis, is most vivid in patients with pernicious anemia who may have a profound macrocytic anemia. A subset of patients with specific chronic gastritis have hypoalbuminemia secondary to a protein-losing enteropathy.

Abdominal plain films generally are unremarkable; patients with phlegmonous gastritis may have gas dissecting into the gastric wall accounting for an emphysematous gastritis.

PLANS

Diagnostic

Differential Diagnosis

Though a double-contrast upper gastrointestinal series can potentially delineate gastric erosions and mucosal irregularity, gastroscopy with accompanying biopsy is more accurate in diagnosing acutely inflamed gastric mucosa (i.e., acute gastritis), which can manifest as erythematous mucosa, mucosal hemorrhages, and/or erosions. A history of ingestion of a potentially injurious substance (e.g., nonsteroidal antiinflammatory drugs or alcohol) heightens clinical suspicion of acute gastritis. Patients who present with corrosive substance ingestion should have an urgent endoscopy within 24 to 48 hours to assess for the presence of mucosal burns. Patients who are immunosuppressed and have persistent epigastric discomfort should be endoscoped and biopsied, with viral and fungal cultures made of suspected pathology, to exclude cytomegalovirus, herpes, cryptosporidia, and other opportunistic organisms. The entity of alkaline (bile) gastritis can be suspected in a patient with a prior gastroenterostomy who endoscopically has a beefy red gastric mucosa and presence of bile in the gastric pouch, though, by no means, are these findings conclusive. The quantitative analysis of intragastric bile acids over a select period and/or the use of hepato-iminodiacetic acid scintigraphic scanning to measure the amount of refluxed bile into the stomach can provide objective support for this diagnosis. The use of intragastric alkaline infusion as a provocative test (akin to the acid Bernstein test in testing for acid reflux disease) has been reported to aid in the diagnosis of alkaline gastritis.

Diagnostic Options and Recommended Approach

The diagnosis of chronic gastritis hinges on gastroscopic biopsy confirmation. Biopsies should be taken from both the body and antrum of the stomach. The presence of a chronic gastritis with histologic identification of *H. pylori* organisms establishes the diagnosis of an *H. pylori* chronic gastritis. Though the organisms are seen on hematoxylin and eosin staining, a Giemsa or silver (e.g., Warthin–Starry) stain facilitates identification of the organism. The results of the rapid urease test (Clo test) correlate excellently with histologic identification of *H. pylori*. By use of the unique urease properties of *H. pylori,* an antral biopsy specimen is placed in a commercially prepared gel. In the presence of *H. pylori,* ammonia is released and the yellow gel turns red as the gel alkalinizes. This reaction generally is initiated within 20 minutes; however, it may require up to 24 hours. Histology and the rapid urease test are about 95% accurate in diagnosing *H. pylori*. Culturing *H. pylori* is tedious and expensive and is not performed in the routine clinical setting. The diagnosis of *H. pylori* may be inferred by the presence of a positive carbon-radiolabeled urea breath test, though this test does not provide any assessment of the extent and severity of the presumed underlying chronic gastritis. Serologic testing for immunoglobulin G and A *H. pylori* antibodies via enzyme-linked immunosorbent assay is 90% accurate in establishing the presence of a prior *H. pylori* infection; however, a single determination has a limited role in diagnosing an ongoing chronic gastritis.

The presence of a chronic atrophic gastritis in the body of the stomach with relative antral sparing combined with *H. pylori* negativity is highly suggestive of an autoimmune chronic gastritis. The endoscopic appearance of flattening of the gastric folds, prominence of the submucosal vasculature due to mucosal thinning, mucosal friability, and a nonacidic gastric pH further increase the suspicion of an underlying chronic autoimmune gastritis. Serum intrinsic factor antibodies are present in about 50% of autoimmune gastritis and its presence is highly specific for this entity. Parietal cell antibodies, though present in 80% of patients with autoimmune gastritis, lack specificity and do not independently establish the diagnosis. An abnormal Schilling test reflective of inadequate intrinsic factor production and, consequently, diminished B_{12} intestinal absorption is seen in the advanced autoimmune chronic gastritis that is evolving into pernicious anemia.

Lymphocytic gastritis, an entity that is searching for its proper classification, is histologically diagnosed by the presence of an intraepithelial lymphocytic infiltrate with at least 30 lymphocytes noted per 100 epithelial cells. The endoscopic appearance is generally normal; alternatively it may present with prominent, thickened folds (hypertrophic lymphocytic gastritis) and overlying erosive nodules (varioloform gastritis). The hypertrophic form may endoscopically simulate Menetrier's disease and can likewise give rise to a protein-losing gastropathy. Pathologically, Menetrier's disease is distinguishable by its marked mucosal thickening consisting primarily of a foveolar (gastric pit) hyperplasia, a decrease in glandular elements, and only minimal inflammation. Indeed in view of the latter finding, some authors insist that Menetrier's be termed a gastropathy and not a gastritis. Eosinophilic gastritis is punctuated by a marked eosinophilic infiltrate of the gastric mucosa, a peripheral eosinophilia, and, usually, a concomitant enteritis. Other specific chronic gastritides (e.g., syphilitic, Crohn's, sarcoidosis, and tubercular gastritis) are diagnosed based on the particular pathology associated with these entities as discussed elsewhere in this textbook.

Therapeutic

Acute gastritis is usually transient in nature and resolves spontaneously. In addition to withdrawal of the noxious stimulus, a short course of intensive antacids often suffices; in its more severe form, a 2-week course of H_2 blockers may be warranted. Stress gastropathy, in particular, needs to be aggressively treated with administration of continuous intravenous H_2 blockers and maintenance of gastric pH above 5. Patients with corrosive injury to the gastric mucosa need intensive supportive care, including endotracheal intubation when applicable, as well as maintenance of intravascular volume. Steroids are no longer felt to

be effective and prophylactic antibiotics are not indicated. In patients presenting with findings of perforation, emergency surgery is undertaken.

Alkaline (bile) gastritis is usually refractory to medical therapy. Though various maneuvers are undertaken, either individually or in combination, including use of aluminum-containing antacids and cholestyramine to bind bile salts, sucralfate (Carafate), and/or H_2 blockers (to neutralize any superimposed acid mucosal injury), these invariably are unsuccessful. The use of cisapride (Propulsid) 10 mg 30 minutes before meals may be helpful, particularly when there is an associated delayed gastric emptying, not uncommonly present in patients status post gastroenterostomies. In patients with severe, persistent symptomatology and an objective diagnosis of a bile gastritis, a Roux-en-Y intestinal surgical reconstruction often provides relief. Patients with nonsteroidal antiinflammatory drug gastritis who require chronic nonsteroidal antiinflammatory drug therapy should be placed on misoprostol, a prostaglandin E analog (Cytotec), 200 µg four times daily, which significantly lowers the risk of developing a gastric ulcer.

As noted, the large majority of nonspecific nonerosive gastritis is due to *H. pylori*. The current consensus is that no treatment be given for this entity unless there is a coexisting or prior history of gastric or duodenal ulcer. If this condition is met, the preferred means of eradicating *H. pylori* consists of triple combination therapy with subsalicylate (Pepto-Bismol) 1 tablespoon or 2 tablets four times daily, tetracycline 500 mg four times daily, and metronidazole (Flagyl) 250 mg four times daily for a total of 2 weeks. Alternatively, omeprazole (Prilosec) 20 mg twice a day plus a 2-week course of amoxicillin 500 mg four times a day should be instituted. Patients with nonulcer dyspepsia and positive *H. pylori* represent a therapeutic dilemma. Though many, including the 1994 NIH Consensus Development Conference on *H. pylori* in Peptic Ulcer Disease, do not recommend treatment for this scenario, it appears reasonable that in the setting of persistent significant symptomatology, and an otherwise negative workup, triple combination therapy be instituted and the patient carefully assessed for clinical improvement.

Patients with autoimmune chronic gastritis are at risk of developing pernicious anemia and its attendant need for B_{12} replacement. Varioliform gastritis does not respond to H_2 blockers; some investigators recommend a short course of steroids. Eosinophilic gastritis is treated with a short course of steroids, 20 to 40 mg prednisone, for approximately 2 weeks. In a minority of patients, long-term low-dose steroids may be necessary.

FOLLOW-UP

Patients with acute corrosive gastritis need to be carefully followed up to determine whether any significant full-thickness injury has taken place. Though manifestation of such can be delayed, an upper gastrointestinal series performed 3 to 4 weeks after the initial insult can serve as a useful guide as to whether obstructive symptoms are likely to develop. Patients with symptomatic *H. pylori* chronic gastritis who were treated with combination therapy should undergo C_{13} or C_{14} urea breath testing 3 months after treatment to document eradication of the *H. pylori* organism. Alternatively, when breath tests are not readily available, quantitative immunoglobulin G and A *H. pylori* titers should be obtained 6 months after therapy. Successful eradication should reveal a significant dropoff in titers when compared with baseline serologies. Patients with chronic gastritis and associated gastric atrophy are at potential risk for developing dysplasia and gastric carcinoma. No clear recommendation for endoscopic surveillance exists currently, though it would appear prudent that patients with severe gastric atrophy and intestinal metaplasia, especially those with pernicious anemia, be entered into a surveillance program until further data are available. Inasmuch as 10% of patients with autoimmune chronic gastritis develop pernicious anemia, these patients should have annual monitoring of their hematocrit, periodic B_{12} determinations, and yearly clinical follow-up to detect any early, subtle manifestations of pernicious anemia.

DISCUSSION

Prevalence

Worldwide, more than 50% of the population is affected by *H. pylori* chronic gastritis. The prevalence increases with age, and in adults, the rise is about 1 to 2% per year. Higher rates are found in lower socioeconomic groups and underdeveloped countries. Long-standing *H. pylori*-related chronic gastritis is a significant risk factor, approximately 20% of patients developing peptic ulcer disease, with the risk of duodenal ulcer being greater than that of gastric ulcer.

Related Basic Science

The morphology of acute gastritis is characterized by a neutrophilic infiltrate in the gastric epithelial cell layer. With significant mucosal damage, erosions and/or hemorrhage develop. These pathologic changes generally revert to normal within a few weeks. Chronic gastritis requires the presence of a chronic inflammatory cell infiltrate composed mainly of lymphocytes and plasma cells. Frequently, especially in *H. pylori* chronic gastritis, polymorphs are interspersed within the chronic infiltrate, giving rise to the designation of chronic active gastritis. Nonerosive nonspecific chronic gastritis encompasses the entities of *H. pylori* gastritis and autoimmune gastritis. Both can give rise to a pangastritis; however, *H. pylori* preferentially favors the antrum, creating a chronic antral gastritis (formerly known as type B gastritis), and autoimmune gastritis involves the fundus and body of the stomach (formerly known as type A gastritis) with relative antral sparing.

The chronic inflammatory infiltrate may be confined to the surface epithelium and gastric pits (foveolar region) without damaging the underlying gastric glands, thus defining the process as a superficial chronic gastritis. In contradistinction to the persistent inflammation seen in panmucosal chronic gastritis, superficial chronic gastritis may recede spontaneously without any sequelae. Panmucosal chronic gastritis involves an inflammatory infiltrate of the full-thickness gastric mucosa. In the initial phase, gastric glands are intact; prolonged inflammation gives rise to chronic atrophic gastritis with glandular damage and variable degree of inflammatory cells, and intestinal metaplasia (replacement of inflamed gastric epithelium by an intestinal type of epithelium, ranging from goblet cells to intestinal-type absorptive cells) arises.

Helicobacter pylori organisms can be identified in approximately 90% of patients with chronic antral gastritis. The detection rate decreases with the development of atrophic gastritis, is unusual in the setting of gastric atrophy, and is virtually absent in intestinal metaplasia. That this pathologic process was initiated by *H. pylori* can be inferred by the presence of positive *H. pylori* serology. *Helicobacter pylori* is most commonly seen in the gastric mucus layer and adhering to the gastric epithelial surface and pits (Figure 19–26–1). Though the organism is identifiable on hematoxylin and eosin staining, it can better be appreciated by a Giemsa or silver (e.g., Warthin–Starry) stain. Though epithelial penetrance is uncommon and was thought not to take place, recent studies have documented that *H. pylori* is capable of epithelial invasion. Indeed, the depth of mucosal infiltration and the number of organisms appear to correlate with the degree of active inflammation as well as the amount of epithelial damage. Penetration may be facilitated by the spiral nature of the organism, its affinity for cell-associated receptors and basement membrane substances including laminin and collagen type IV, and *H. pylori* production of urease and various cytotoxins.

Autoimmune chronic gastritis is characterized by B-cell and, to a lesser extent, T-cell lymphoid infiltration of the gastric mucosa. By virtue of its dominance in the body of the stomach, the inflammation leads to progressive destruction of parietal cells, causing hypochlorhydria and culminating in achlorhydria. This phenomenon is associated with parietal cell antibodies in more than 80% of cases. Recent work has identified the canicular membrane H^+, K^+-ATPase, the proton pump of the gastric parietal cell, as the major parietal cell microsomal antigen. Parietal cell antibodies, however, are not specific and can be seen in 2 to 4% of healthy individuals, primarily the aged.

The presence of antiintrinsic factor antibody is highly specific for autoimmune gastritis and often heralds the development of pernicious anemia, which occurs in approximately 10% of patients with autoimmune gastritis. The relative sparing of the antrum in the face of hypochlorhydria/achlorhydria leads to the unopposed production of gastrin from antral G cells. This hypergastrinemia, in turn, can produce enterochromaffin-like (cell) hyperplasia which can eventuate in the for-

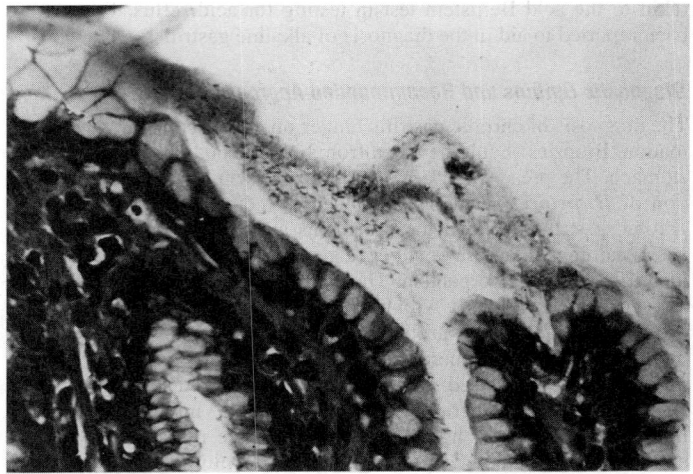

A

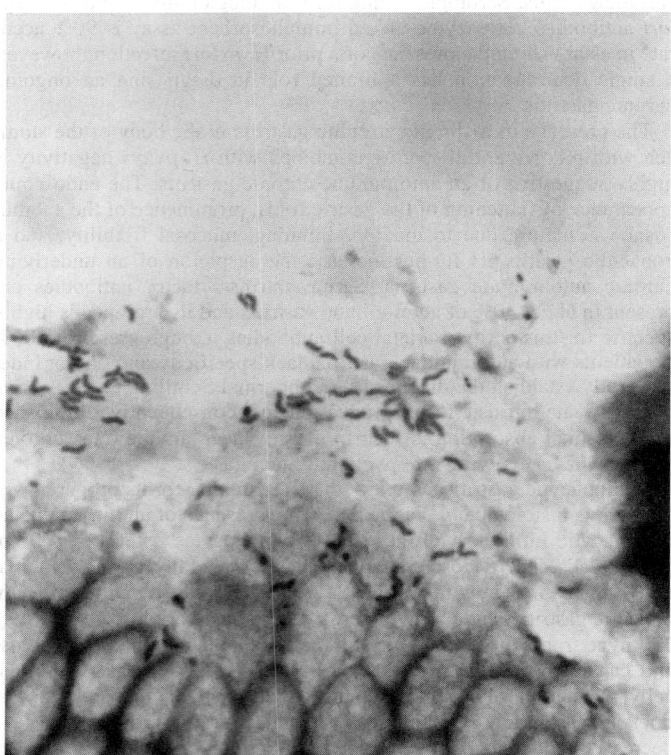

B

Figure 19–26–1. A. Multiple *Helicobacter pylori* organisms seen within the mucus layer overlying the gastric surface epithelium (Giemsa, ×100). **B.** High-power view of *Helicobacter pylori* organisms (Giemsa, ×400).

mation of gastric carcinoids. These tumors possess low-grade malignant potential and are seen in approximately 5% of patients with pernicious anemia.

Natural History and Its Modification with Treatment

The majority of acute gastritides spontaneously heal without any long-term sequelae. Exceptions include caustic gastritis, whereby the presence of a full-thickness burn eventuates in the development of a stricture, usually antral in location, that presents with symptoms and signs of a gastric outlet obstruction. Chronic nonspecific nonerosive gastritis tends to be lifelong, and especially when atrophic gastritis has developed, spontaneous healing is rare.

Autoimmune chronic gastritis represents about 5% of nonspecific nonerosive chronic gastritis. Long-term follow-up studies have shown that approximately 10% of patients with autoimmune gastritis progress to pernicious anemia. The best laboratory indicator that identifies patients with this risk is the presence of intrinsic factor antibody. Early recognition of autoimmune gastritis, even with a positive intrinsic factor antibody, may precede the development of pernicious anemia for years in view of the persistence of body vitamin B_{12} stores for more than 3 years. Gastric carcinoma associated with pernicious anemia has been recognized for many years. Studies estimate an approximately threefold increase in risk of gastric carcinoma in pernicious anemia patients above that observed in the general population. Carcinoid tumors have been found in approximately 5% of patients with pernicious anemia. These tumors act with low-grade biological virulence and the majority do not metastasize.

Inasmuch as autoimmune chronic gastritis is of low incidence, it does not contribute significantly to the overall incidence of gastric carcinoma. Of concern, and a subject that has received considerable attention in both the medical literature as well as the media, is the risk of developing gastric carcinoma as a long-term sequela of *H. pylori* chronic gastritis. In a subset of patients, *H. pylori* chronic gastritis advances to gastric atrophy and associated intestinal metaplasia. These patients are at risk of developing adenocarcinoma, though the actual incidence is not clear at this time. Additionally, a handful of cases of *H. pylori*-associated MALT (mucosa-associated lymphoid tissue) gastric lymphomas have been reported. The lymphoid reaction initially appears to be an immune response to the presence of *H. pylori*. Of major significance is the recent documentation of pathologic regression of the MALT lymphoma occurring after antibiotic eradication of the *H. pylori* infection. This provocative subject of *H. pylori*-linked neoplasms and its clinical consequences regarding follow-up and treatment of *H. pylori* chronic gastritis will surely be in the limelight in the ensuing years.

Prevention

Avoidance of agents potentially noxious to the gastric mucosa is the most effective prevention. Household cleansers that are corrosive substances should be placed out of reach of infants and children. The continued education of patients regarding the toxic effects of alcohol cannot be overstated. Chronic nonsteroidal antiinflammatory drug therapy should be undertaken only when necessary; prophylactic use of misoprostol (Cytotec) 200 µg four times daily in high-risk patients with a history of ulcer disease or the aged individual with comorbidity substantially reduces the incidence of nonsteroidal antiinflammatory drug gastropathy. Stress gastropathy is markedly diminished by the prophylactic use of continuous intravenous infusion of H_2 blockers in the intensive care setting.

Cost Containment

By use of the above-cited preventive measures, the incidence of gastritis with its attendant costs of hospitalization can be significantly lowered.

REFERENCES

Dooley CP, Cohen H, Fitzgibbons PL, et al. Prevalence of *Helicobacter pylori* infection and histologic gastritis in asymptomatic persons. N Engl J Med 1989;321:1562.

Robert ME, Weinstein W. *Helicobacter pylori*-associated gastric pathology. Gastroenterol Clin North Am 1993;22:59.

Sipponen P, Kekki M, Siurala M. The Sydney system: Epidemiology and natural history of chronic gastritis. J Gastroenterol Hepatol 1991;6:244.

Strickland RG. The Sydney system: Auto-immune gastritis. J Gastroenterol Hepatol 1991;6:238.

Vaira D, Holton J, Osborn J, et al. Endoscopy in dyspeptic patients: Is gastric mucosal biopsy useful? Am J Gastroenterol 1990;85:701.

CHAPTER 19–27

Stress Ulcer

Ira W. Nierenberg, M.D.

DEFINITION

Stress ulcers are acute gastric mucosal lesions occurring in critically ill patients that may result in acute upper gastrointestinal bleeding. They are usually superficial erosions but can develop into true ulcers.

ETIOLOGY

The exact mechanism is not known, but it is thought that gastric mucosal ischemia secondary to decreased gastric mucosal blood flow leads to an impairment in gastric mucosal protective mechanisms, resulting in an imbalance between aggressive and protective factors. Most patients do not hypersecrete acid, although some acid is felt to be necessary for stress ulcers to occur.

CRITERIA FOR DIAGNOSIS

Suggestive

Stress ulcer must be considered in all critically ill patients at increased risk, admitted with shock, sepsis, central nervous system trauma (Cushing's ulcer), multiple trauma, burns over greater than 35% of the body (Curling's ulcer), renal or liver failure, coagulopathy, and respiratory failure requiring prolonged mechanical ventilation. The greater the severity of the underlying illness, the greater the chance that stress ulcer and possibly bleeding will develop. Patients with uncomplicated cardiac disease are not at increased risk. Very frequently, stress ulcer disease is not considered unless patients have signs of upper gastrointestinal bleeding or a fall in hemoglobin and hematocrit.

Definitive

Upper endoscopy is the most sensitive means of detecting stress ulcer and identifying a specific site of bleeding.

CLINICAL MANIFESTATIONS

Subjective

Patients with stress ulcer are usually asymptomatic with respect to the gastrointestinal tract. If a critically ill patient complains of abdominal pain, one thing that must be considered among others is a perforation of a stress ulcer. A past history of peptic ulcer disease, chronic liver disease, or esophageal varices is also very important when dealing with a critically ill patient with gastrointestinal bleeding.

Objective

Physical Examination

Physical examination is usually unremarkable except for the possible presence of changes in pulse or blood pressure, hematemesis, melena, or hematochezia.

Routine Laboratory Abnormalities

A drop in hemoglobin and hematocrit may be noted (evidence of possible gastrointestinal bleeding). It must also be remembered that in acute upper gastrointestinal bleeding, the hemoglobin and hematocrit may remain relatively unchanged early on until equilibration has occurred and that the severity of bleeding may be underestimated. Blood urea nitrogen may also be elevated secondary to breakdown of red blood cells in the gastrointestinal tract and absorption of nitrogenous products. Unlike in renal failure, the creatinine level usually remains relatively unchanged.

PLANS
Diagnostic

Differential Diagnosis

The differential diagnosis is that of upper gastrointestinal bleeding. Occasionally, upper gastrointestinal bleeding in critically ill patients may be due to chronic duodenal or gastric ulcer disease. Stress ulcer and peptic ulcer are completely different entities. Patients with stress ulcer tend to be asymptomatic and lack a history of peptic ulcer disease. Stress ulcers are usually acute and multiple, occur in the proximal acid-secreting portion of the stomach, and are shallow and rarely perforate. The exception to this is Cushing's ulcer, which can be single and deep. Bleeding is usually from small superficial vessels and not massive. Hypersecretion of acid is rare and usually seen only in patients with Cushing's ulcer and sepsis. There is no association between stress ulcer and *Helicobacter pylori*. Peptic ulcers are usually chronic, symptomatic, single, and located in the distal non-acid-secreting portion of the stomach and duodenum. They can be deep, and bleeding is usually from a single larger vessel.

Diagnostic Options

Patients with signs of bleeding should be completely resuscitated before any further tests are done. This includes control of the airway, breathing, and circulation. Two large-bore intravenous lines (at least 18 gauge) should be placed in each antecubital fossa and in addition to routine laboratory tests, a prothrombin time, partial thromboplastin time, arterial blood gas, and type and hold should be ordered. Vital signs should be closely monitored. A nasogastric tube should then be passed to see if bleeding is active and contents of the stomach should be aspirated. If bleeding is intermittent, the nasogastric aspirate may be bilious. A clear nasogastric aspirate does not clear the duodenal bulb. Guaiac testing of gastric aspirate is useless and should not be done. Anteroposterior and lateral decubitus x-ray films should be made of the abdomen as clinically indicated. Barium upper gastrointestinal series should not be done in a bleeding patient because the presence of barium in the stomach may interfere with upper endoscopy or angiography if needed later.

Recommended Approach

In patients with overt gastrointestinal bleeding, upper endoscopy should be done to determine the etiology, as long as it is believed that the critically ill patient's medical condition can tolerate it. This is important because the prognostic and therapeutic considerations differ depending on the source. Hemodynamic status should be maximized, and vital signs and cardiac status should be closely monitored throughout the procedure.

Therapeutic

Therapeutic Options

The therapeutic options depend on whether a critically ill patient has signs of overt bleeding or not.

Recommended Approach

The treatment of uncomplicated stress ulcer disease includes the use of acid-neutralizing agents such as antacids or antisecretory agents such as H_2-receptor antagonists, although there are some studies supporting the use of sucralfate. The aim of this therapy is to prevent the progression of stress ulcer and decrease the incidence of bleeding. Even though most

patients do not hypersecrete gastric acid, and there are other factors that play a role in stress ulcer disease, it has been shown that neutralization of acid with antacids or inhibition of acid secretion with H_2-receptor antagonists markedly decreases the incidence of overt bleeding.

Prior to the introduction of H_2-receptor antagonists, antacids were the mainstay of treatment and are still used occasionally today. They are usually given via nasogastric tube every 2 hours with the dose titrated to keep the gastric pH above 4, although the optimal pH endpoint and the time this pH should be maintained are still unknown.

H_2-receptor antagonists are the most commonly used medicine for prophylaxis. They have been shown to be as efficacious as antacids in preventing overt bleeding, do not require as much nursing time to administer, and are associated with a decreased risk of aspiration. Of the currently available intravenous H_2-receptor antagonists (cimetidine, ranitidine, and famotidine), only cimetidine has received Food and Drug Administration approval for use in prevention of upper gastrointestinal bleeding in critically ill patients. Nevertheless, intravenous ranitidine and famotidine enjoy widespread in-hospital use as prophylactic therapy. H_2-receptor antagonists can be given as a bolus or as a continuous infusion. The recommended dose of cimetidine is 300 mg by intravenous piggyback every 6 hours or a continuous infusion at 50 mg/h. Patients with a creatinine clearance less than 30 mL/min should receive half the dose. Continuous infusion therapy is better able to consistently maintain an elevated gastric pH than is bolus therapy. Theoretically, one would think this would result in a further decrease in overt gastrointestinal bleeding, but this has not yet been conclusively shown.

Sucralfate 1 g via nasogastric tube every 6 hours has also been shown to be effective in decreasing the incidence of overt bleeding, probably by enhancing gastric mucosal defense. Treatment with sucralfate has been suggested to result in a lower incidence of aspiration pneumonia as compared with antacids and H_2-receptor antagonists, but further studies are necessary.

Most importantly, vigorous attention should be given to treating the underlying disease, maintaining ventilatory support, maximizing hemodynamic status, correcting any acid–base or electrolyte abnormality, and maintaining an adequate nutritional status.

Overt bleeding is usually self-limited, but if bleeding persists, it can be very difficult to treat because very frequently the bleeding is diffuse and not localized to one site as usually happens with bleeding peptic ulcers. Methods of treatment in addition to those described under prophylactic therapy that have been used with varying degrees of success include endoscopic therapy using electrocoagulation or laser photocoagulation, angiographic therapy using intraarterial infusion of vasopressin or selective arterial embolization of gastric vessels; and surgical therapy when all other treatment modalities fail.

FOLLOW-UP

Critically ill patients should be followed very closely by their physician. A complete physical examination and complete blood count should be performed daily. Any signs of gastrointestinal bleeding should be treated aggressively.

DISCUSSION
Prevalence and Incidence

Endoscopic studies have shown that stress ulcer disease is present in 75 to 100% of critically ill patients within 24 hours of admission to an intensive care unit. Approximately 15 to 20% of these patients, if not treated with prophylactic therapy, develop overt gastrointestinal bleeding usually within 2 weeks of the precipitating stress, but only 5 to 10% of patients who bleed require a blood transfusion. Prophylactic therapy with antacids or H_2-receptor antagonists lowers the incidence of overt bleeding to 3 to 5%. Mortality is significantly higher in patients who develop overt bleeding, but this is related primarily to the underlying disease.

Related Basic Science

Stress ulcer disease results from an impairment in gastric mucosal defense mechanisms, leading to an imbalance between aggressive and protective mechanisms.

Gastric acid is the most important aggressive factor, although pepsin and bile acids may also play a role. Most patients, as mentioned, do not hypersecrete acid, yet some acid appears to be necessary for stress ulcers to occur.

The protective mechanisms are contained in the gastric mucosal barrier which protects the stomach from potentially noxious agents such as just described. This barrier is not a single structure but rather is composed of several components. These include mucus–bicarbonate layer, the cell membrane of the surface epithelial cells and the tight junctions between the cells, gastric mucosal blood flow, gastric mucosal prostaglandin production, and epithelial cell renewal. The mucus–bicarbonate layer lies over the surface epithelium and is composed of a mucus gel. Contained within this gel is a pH gradient such that the pH at the cell surface is approximately 7.0 and the pH at the luminal surface is 2.0. The mucus layer slows hydrogen ion diffusion, allowing the bicarbonate to neutralize the acid. The cell membrane with its hydrophobic phospholipid layer and the tight junctions impede backdiffusion of hydrogen ion. Gastric mucosal blood flow brings oxygen, bicarbonate, and nutrients to the gastric epithelial cells and carries away hydrogen ions and other toxins. Gastric mucosal prostaglandins increase mucus and bicarbonate secretion, as well as increasing membrane phospholipid content and gastric mucosal blood flow. If the gastric epithelium is superficially damaged and the basement membrane and blood vessels are intact, it can be rapidly repaired by a process called restitution. This process does not involve cell division and repair occurs by neighboring cells migrating sideways under a protective cap of mucus and cell debris to cover over the defect. More extensive damage requires cell replication, a process called *regeneration*.

Decreased gastric mucosal blood flow resulting in gastric mucosal ischemia is felt to be the main event in the pathogenesis of stress ulcer. This results in damage to the surface epithelium, which leads to backdiffusion of acid. The degree of damage depends not only on how much acid backdiffuses but also on the ability of the gastric mucosa to neutralize the backdiffused acid. The decreased blood flow results not only in decreased delivery of oxygen, nutrients, and bicarbonate to the gastric surface cells but also in decreased removal of acids and toxins from this area.

Natural History and Its Modification with Treatment

The clinical course depends on the outcome of the underlying illness. In most patients, the greater the severity of the underlying illness, the more severe the damage to the gastroduodenal mucosa. Endoscopic studies have shown that as the underlying illness improves, so does the injury to the gastroduodenal mucosa. As the patient continues to recover and starts taking nutrition orally, intravenous medications can be switched to oral.

Prevention

Stress ulcer disease cannot be prevented, but progression of the lesions and the incidence of bleeding can be significantly reduced with vigorous treatment of the underlying illness and prophylactic therapy using H_2-receptor antagonists, antacids, or sucralfate.

Cost Containment

Even though the costs of prophylactic medical therapy can be high, the cost of a prolonged stay in the intensive care unit because of bleeding from stress ulcer can be even greater, including costs for nursing care, blood transfusion, diagnostic tests, and so on. Only patients at increased risk for stress ulcer should receive prophylactic therapy.

REFERENCES

Miller TA. Mechanisms of stress-related mucosal damage. Am J Med 1987;83 (suppl. 6A):8.

Ostro MJ, Russell JA, Soldin SJ, et al. Control of gastric pH with cimetidine: Boluses vs primed infusions. Gastroenterology 1985;89:532.

Robert A, Kauffman GL. Stress ulcers, erosions and gastric mucosal injury. In: Sleisenger MH, Fordtran JS, eds. Gastrointestinal disease. 4th ed. Philadelphia: Saunders, 1989:772.

Vorder Breugge WF, Peura DA. Stress-related mucosal damage: Review of drug therapy. J Clin Gastroenterol 1990;12 (suppl. 2):535.

Zuckerman DO, Shuman R. Therapeutic goals and treatment options for prevention of stress ulcer syndrome. Am J Med 1987;(suppl 6A):29.

CHAPTER 19–28

Gastric Ulcer

Gerald Fruchter, M.D.

DEFINITION

A gastric ulcer is a well-defined break in the gastric mucosal layer with penetration through the muscularis mucosa. It may be benign or malignant.

ETIOLOGY

Benign gastric ulcers develop as a result of an imbalance between aggressive factors and mucosal defense mechanisms. In 70 to 80% of patients with gastric ulcer, the Gram-negative curve-shaped *Helicobacter pylori* organism can be identified in the gastric mucosa and is felt to represent the causal agent responsible for formation of the gastric ulcer. In approximately 20% of gastric ulcers, nonsteroidal antiinflammatory drugs (NSAIDs) can be implicated as the offending agent. Stress-induced ulcers are generally multiple in nature and limited to seriously ill patients, typically in an intensive care setting. Patients with underlying immunodeficiency, particularly AIDS patients, are subject to opportunistic infections which can create gastric ulcers, with cytomegalovirus being the most likely organism. Tuberculous and syphilitic gastric ulcers are also being reported with increasing frequency. The hypersecretory state seen in Zollinger–Ellison syndrome very rarely presents with a solitary gastric ulcer.

Malignancy accounts for approximately 5% of gastric ulcers, with gastric adenocarcinoma being much more likely than lymphoma (see Chapter 3–8).

CRITERIA FOR DIAGNOSIS
Suggestive

The patient may complain of persistent epigastric pain. The pain may be relieved transiently by antacids. Weight loss is common. The patient may vomit blood or experience melena, but chronic blood loss and anemia are more common. Eating may, at times, make the pain worse.

Definitive

The diagnosis of gastric ulcer is established by radiographic and/or endoscopic visualization. Radiographically, a persistent collection of barium within an ulcer niche is sought. Endoscopically, a break in the continuity of the gastric mucosa with associated depth is indicative of a gastric ulcer. Though an upper gastrointestinal series alone can be diagnostic for a gastric ulcer, endoscopy with biopsy is warranted to exclude the possibility of a malignant gastric ulcer (see Chapter 3–8).

CLINICAL MANIFESTATIONS

Subjective

Abdominal pain is the characteristic presenting complaint of a patient with a gastric ulcer. The pain is typically burning in nature. It may also be described as a dull achiness, a bloating sensation, or a sharp pain. The location of the pain is generally epigastric or just to the left of the epigastrium, with subxyphoid pain being less likely. The intensity of the pain varies from minimal discomfort to a severe, incapacitating pain. The abdominal discomfort has generally been present for several weeks and tends to be daily in occurrence. An acute presentation with sharp abdominal pain or an abrupt worsening of a preexisting pain may herald a perforation. Persistent abdominal pain, especially when accompanied by radiation to the back, may signal a penetrating ulcer. Transient pain relief is usually achieved by antacids and food, though, in contrast to duodenal ulcer pain, eating may worsen the pain. Indeed, this phenomenon probably accounts for the 10- to 20-pound weight loss that may accompany the benign gastric ulcer and need not overly alarm the patient and clinician prior to the establishment of a definitive diagnosis. Vomiting, when present, tends to be intermittent in frequency. The presence of persistent postprandial vomiting requires the exclusion of a gastric outlet obstruction. Hematemesis and/or melena may be the cardinal presenting complaints. Careful questioning, however, frequently elicits a patient's acknowledgment of prior abdominal symptomatology. Occult gastrointestinal blood loss is more common than overt bleeding. Patients with giant gastric ulcers (>2 cm in diameter) have an increased complication rate and thus are more prone to present with evidence of bleeding, microcytic anemia, and signs of penetration. Malaise and progressive weakness are seen in patients with occult blood loss and failing hematocrit. Such a presentation is common in the geriatric patient population, where the absence of abdominal pain is frequent. These patients need to be carefully questioned regarding their usage of aspirin and other NSAIDS.

Objective

Physical Examination

Physical findings are generally unremarkable. Pallor may be noted in about 25% of patients due to anemia caused by occult gastrointestinal blood loss. Hemodynamic changes of tachycardia, hypotension, and/or orthostasis are generally limited to patients presenting with acute gastrointestinal bleeding or prolonged vomiting secondary to gastric outlet obstruction. Patients with a noncomplicated gastric ulcer may have mild epigastric tenderness with a soft abdomen. Significant abdominal tenderness may accompany a penetrating gastric ulcer. A rigid, tender abdomen with associated rebound is seen, though not invariably, with a perforated gastric ulcer. A confined, walled-off perforation can present with fever, abdominal pain, and leukocytosis without a surgical abdomen. A succussion splash may be present when the gastric outlet is obstructed.

Routine Laboratory Abnormalities

Anemia, when present, is generally low grade, though occasionally severe. In view of the intermittent nature of any accompanying occult bleeding, stool guaiac is frequently negative. A slight leukocytosis may be present; a significant leukocytosis should raise concern regarding a perforation, either free or confined. Patients with gastric outlet obstruction and associated vomiting frequently have electrolyte and fluid disturbances, including hypokalemia, metabolic alkalosis, and prerenal azotemia. Hyeramylasemia may be seen in both perforation and a penetrating posterior wall gastric ulcer; severe pancreatitis resulting from a penetrating gastric ulcer is unusual. Abdominal radiographs in a noncomplicated gastric ulcer are unremarkable. With a perforation, free air under the diaphragm is generally seen, though not predictably in a confined perforation.

PLANS

Diagnostic

Differential Diagnosis

The common presenting complaint of upper abdominal pain is nonspecific. The differential frequently includes the possibility of gastro-esophageal reflux disease, nonulcer dyspepsia, duodenal ulcer, and chronic cholecystitis. Patients with weight loss and/or evidence of occult gastrointestinal blood loss are suspect for having an underlying gastrointestinal malignancy, for example, gastric carcinoma. The history of chronic NSAID ingestion increases the suspicion of an underlying gastric ulcer. The concomitant presentation of a gastric ulcer with duodenal ulcers, esophagitis, prominent gastric folds, and/or excess gastric secretion requires the exclusion of a hypersecretory state such as Zollinger–Ellison syndrome. A fasting serum gastrin along with gastric secretory studies should be obtained.

Diagnostic Options and Recommended Approach

Although an upper gastrointestinal series is reliable in detecting a gastric ulcer and can be used as a screening test, the clinician who suspects significant pathology should have his patient proceed directly to an upper endoscopy. An upper endoscopy increases the diagnostic yield as well as enables performance of biopsies of any visualized gastric ulcer.

Multiple biopsies from the margins of the ulcer are required to exclude a malignancy. The inflammatory nature of a benign gastric ulcer serves to distinguish it from the infiltrative pattern of a malignant gastric ulcer. On upper gastrointestinal series, a benign gastric ulcer is characterized by the presence of an ulcer niche protruding beyond the expected contours of the stomach, symmetric folds radiating toward the ulcer, and a smooth, regular contour. The presence of Hampton's line, a thin radiolucent line traversing the neck of a gastric ulcer, though uncommon, is generally felt to be diagnostic for a benign ulcer. It represents intact, undermined gastric mucosa. A malignant gastric ulcer is often irregular in shape and generally does not protrude beyond the normal contour of the stomach. The margins are usually nodular and the region surrounding a malignant ulcer is frequently rigid and lacking in normal peristalsis (Figure 19–28–1). These discriminating features can also aid in the endoscopic diagnostic impression of a malignant versus a benign gastric ulcer.

The presence of a giant gastric ulcer increases the possibility of malignancy to approximately 20%. A negative endoscopic biopsy does not exclude the possibility of a gastric neoplasm. Complete ulcer healing needs to be documented and follow-up endoscopy is warranted after approximately 6 weeks.

Therapeutic

The treatment of carcinoma of the stomach is discussed in Chapter 3–8.

Standard benign gastric ulcer treatment has been directed toward the reduction of gastric acid secretion. To this end, standard treatment consists of H_2-blocker therapy. Two commonly employed regimens are cimetidine (Tagamet) 400 mg and ranitidine (Zantac) 150 mg twice daily. Healing rates with H_2 blockers range from 80 to 85% after a 6- to 8-week treatment course. The use of H^+, K^+-ATPase inhibitors ("proton pump" inhibitors) provides more complete acid suppression. Omeprazole (Prilosec) 20 to 40 mg daily provides somewhat faster healing, with 90% healing seen at 6 weeks. In addition, quicker symptomatic relief may be obtained with most patients pain-free within 2 weeks. Patients with giant gastric ulcer require therapy averaging about 3 months in duration. To hasten the healing of a giant gastric ulcer with its associated increased complications, it is reasonable to treat from the onset with omeprazole.

An alternate means of treatment is with sucralfate (Carafate) 1 g given before meals and at bedtime. Sucralfate heals gastric ulcers at a somewhat lower rate than H_2 blockers. An advantage is its minimal systemic absorption with its negligible adverse effects. The mechanism of action involves its binding to the proteinaceous base of an ulcer and providing a protective coating against bile, pepsin, and acid backdiffusion. It also has cytoprotective activity. Full-dose ulcer therapy with either of these modalities should be continued until documentation of ulcer healing with repeat endoscopy. In patients with documented *H. pylori* at the time of diagnosis of an active gastric ulcer, combination therapy with omeprazole 20 mg twice a day and a 2-week course of amoxicillin 500 mg four times a day eradicates *H. pylori* in approximately 80% of patients. If *H. pylori* eradication is not achieved, triple combination therapy consisting of bismuth subsalicylate (Pepto-Bismol) 1 tablespoon or 2 tablets four times daily, tetracycline 500 mg

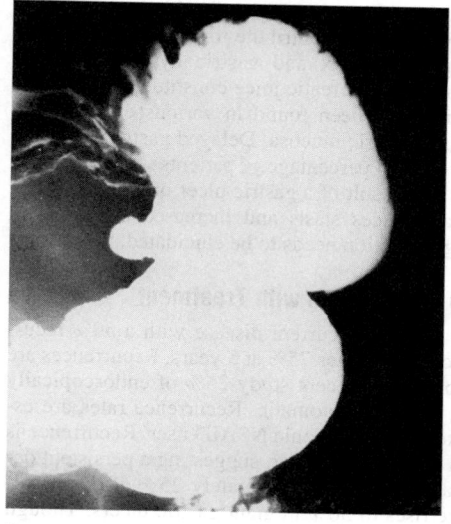

A

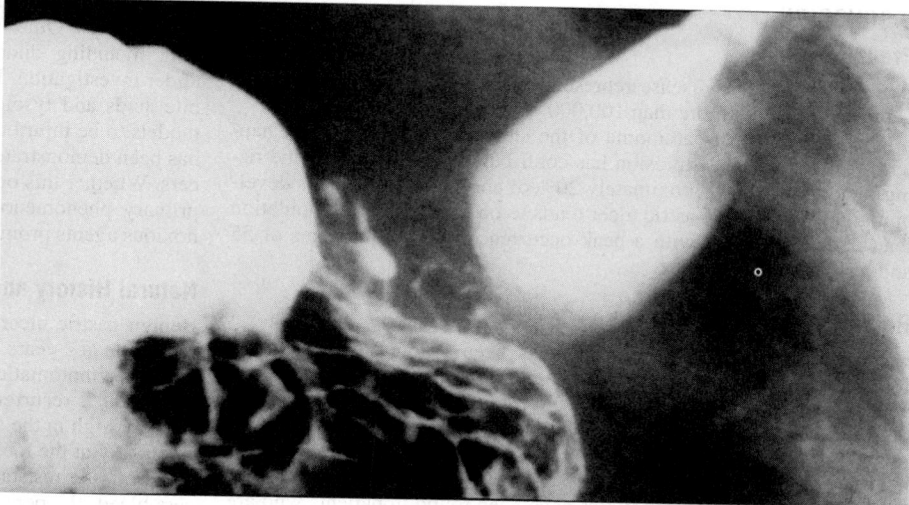

B

C

Figure 19–28–1. A. Benign lesser curvature gastric ulcer with smooth, round ulcer niche protruding beyond expected contour of stomach. **B.** Benign antral ulcer with symmetric folds radiating to ulcer niche. **C.** Malignant antral ulcer with irregular, nodular margin; ulcer does not protrude beyond expected contour of stomach.

four times daily, and metronidazole (Flagyl) 250 mg four times daily for a total of 2 weeks should be instituted. Successful treatment dramatically reduces the gastric ulcer recurrence rate from nearly 50 to 10% at 1 year. Thus, after successful eradication of *H. pylori* and healing of the index ulcer, H_2-blocker maintenance therapy need be employed only for patients who presented with complications of gastric ulcer. Maintenance therapy would be warranted after healing of *H. pylori*-negative ulcers. A regimen of 150 mg Zantac or 400 mg Tagamet at bedtime should be instituted. Ancillary measures in healing gastric ulcers involve the discontinuation of smoking and use of NSAIDs and alcohol. Though alcohol's causal relationship to ulcer formation is not clearly established, it would be prudent to discontinue its usage.

A nonhealing gastric ulcer may be secondary to an underlying neoplasm. Ulcers should be deemed refractory to medical treatment only if no further healing is demonstrated endoscopically after maximal medical therapy, including omeprazole, has been provided, and *H. pylori*-positive ulcers have been appropriately treated. As noted, benign giant gastric ulcer may take 3 to 4 months to heal.

Gastric ulcers that are truly refractory require surgical intervention. In addition to ulcer excision, a vagotomy and pyloroplasty versus a parietal cell vagotomy or antrectomy are performed. The nature of the surgery tends to be based on the preference and expertise of the individual surgeon. Bleeding gastric ulcers can generally be managed via

therapeutic endoscopy with either bicap, heater probe, or injection therapy. In the 10 to 20% of patients with uncontrolled bleeding or breakthrough bleeding, surgery is needed. Perforated gastric ulcers are treated with simple omental patch closure. In stable patients with a history of chronicity, the surgeon may elect to perform a partial gastrectomy. Gastric outlet obstruction that fails to respond to a 1-week course of no oral intake, nasogastric suction, and intravenous H_2 blockers requires surgical intervention generally consisting of an antrectomy and vagotomy.

FOLLOW-UP

All gastric ulcers should be followed until complete healing has been documented. A repeat endoscopy should be performed 6 weeks after the initial diagnosis. Incomplete healing with repeated negative biopsies would warrant a third endoscopy 4 to 6 weeks later. A nonhealing ulcer despite optimal medical management would necessitate surgery to exclude a malignant ulcer. In view of the high recurrence rate, patients who have had complete ulcer healing should be seen on a regular basis, two to three times yearly for 2 years and then annually, to monitor for any clinical evidence suggestive of recurrent disease.

The follow-up of patients with carcinoma of the stomach is discussed in Chapter 3–8.

DISCUSSION

Prevalence

Benign gastric ulcer disease represents a major health problem in the United States, with more than 100,000 patients hospitalized annually.

The prevalence of carcinoma of the stomach is discussed in Chapter 3–8. The NSAID explosion has contributed significantly to the rising incidence, with approximately 20% of chronic NSAID users developing gastric ulcers. Gastric ulcer tends to occur in an older population than duodenal ulcers, with a peak occurrence between the ages of 55 and 65.

Related Basic Science

For decades the prevailing dictum has been that gastric ulcers are formed as a result of an imbalance between the aggressive factors of acid and pepsin and gastric defensive forces. In particular, it was maintained that there was a weakening in the gastric mucosal defense inasmuch as gastric acid secretion in gastric ulcer patients is not greater than in control subjects, but rather shows a trend toward being lower. Furthermore, benign gastric ulcers have been found in patients who are achlorhydric. Though the injurious effect of acid to the gastric epithelium cannot be discounted, it now appears that gastric ulcers, as duodenal ulcers, are caused primarily by an infectious agent. *Helicobacter pylori* organisms are identifiable in the gastric antral mucosa in 70 to 80% of patients with gastric ulcer as opposed to approximately 50% of a control population. A causal relationship can be advocated in view of studies that have demonstrated that effective eradication of *H. pylori* not only brings about healing of refractory gastric ulcer, but, even more convincingly, significantly reduces the recurrence rate of gastric ulcer. The precise mechanism whereby *H. pylori* infection can create a gastric ulcer needs to be further elucidated. Postulated mechanisms center around *H. pylori*'s copious secretion of urease with the consequent formation of ammonia. The ammonia produced can be toxic to the gastric epithelial mucosa and induce gastric ulceration. *Helicobacter pylori* also releases enzymes (e.g., lipases, catalases), cytotoxins, as well as chemotactic factors and cytokines which cause mucosal injury and attract leukocytes to the damaged gastric epithelium. This, in turn, releases additional cytokines (e.g., interleukins and tumor necrosis factor) and produces superoxide radicals that further damage the gastric mucosa.

Twenty percent of gastric ulcers are attributed to the use of NSAIDs. The primary mode of action of NSAIDs is their cyclooxygenase inhibitory property which diminishes synthesis of gastric mucosal prostaglandins, especially E_2. This effectively lowers gastric mucosal cytoprotective properties by several mechanisms, including reduced mucus and bicarbonate secretion, diminished local blood flow, and altered cellular epithelial regeneration. These changes allow for increased mucosal permeability to hydrogen ions and consequent injury. NSAIDs, by inhibiting cyclooxygenase, divert the metabolism of arachidonic acid toward the lipoxygenase pathway with the subsequent formation of leukotrienes. These leukotrienes, especially B_4, enhance mucosal injury by their chemotactic properties, promoting increased vascular permeability as well as vasoconstriction.

Nonsteroidal antiinflammatory drugs can also cause direct damage by topical irritant effects. Most NSAIDs are acidic in nature and in gastric juice they are poorly ionized and lipophilic, allowing for their diffusion across the mucus and epithelial cell lining with accumulation in the mucosal cells. The intracellular drug concentration initiates metabolic dysfunction and ultimately predisposes to mucosal injury by altering cell permeability, allowing luminal aggressive factors to enter the mucosa. The concomitant decrease in prostaglandins hinders the reparative process. Other factors that may contribute to gastric ulcer formation, including duodenogastric reflux and gastric hypomotility, are under investigation. Biliary and pancreatic juice constituents, including bile acids and lysolecithin, have been found in various experimental models to be injurious to the gastric mucosa. Delayed gastric emptying has been demonstrated in a small percentage of patients with gastric ulcers. Whether this occurs as a result of a gastric ulcer or whether it is a primary phenomenon that induces stasis and increased contact with noxious agents promoting ulceration needs to be elucidated.

Natural History and Its Modification with Treatment

Benign gastric ulcer is a chronic, recurrent disease with a 50% recurrence rate at 2 years, which approaches 75% at 5 years. Recurrences are usually symptomatic, though in a recent study 25% of endoscopically documented recurrences were asymptomatic. Recurrence rates are especially high in the smoker and the chronic NSAID user. Recurrence is frequently at the location of the initial ulcer, suggesting a persistent defect in tissue resistance at that site. Approximately 25% of gastric ulcers bleed; the percentage rises to 50% in giant gastric ulcers. Though perforation is rare, penetration occurs in 10% of nongiant ulcers and in approximately 50% of giant gastric ulcers. Penetration can lead to the rare complication of a gastrocolic fistula.

Prevention

Patients should be educated regarding the negative impact of cigarette smoking and NSAID ingestion on gastric ulcer disease. Patients who require NSAIDs and have had previous ulcer disease or are aged with associated comorbidity should be placed on misoprostol (Cytotec), a synthetic prostaglandin E_1 analog at a dose of 200 μg four times daily. Such treatment can reduce ulcer development from 20% to approximately 2%. Diarrhea and abdominal cramps develop in 10 to 20% of individuals; however, a tolerance generally develops with subsidence of gastrointestinal symptoms. Those who remain intolerant can be placed on the lower dosage of 100 μg four times daily without losing significant efficacy.

Cost Containment

Identification and eradication of *H. pylori*-positive gastric ulcers will substantially diminish gastric ulcer recurrence and its attendant costs. Prophylactic use of misoprostol in high-risk chronic NSAID users should significantly lower gastric ulcer formation and related costs in this select group of patients who are particularly prone to develop complications of gastric ulcer.

REFERENCES

Borody TJ, Brandl S, Andrews P, et al. *Helicobacter pylori*-negative gastric ulcer. Am J Gastroenterol 1992;87:1403.

Graham DY, Lew GM, Klein PD, et al. Effect of treatment of *Helicobacter pylori* infection on the long-term recurrence of gastric or duodenal ulcer. Ann Intern Med 1992;116:705.

Graham DY, White RH, Moreland LW, et al. Duodenal and gastric ulcer prevention with misoprostol in arthritis patients taking NSAIDs. Ann Intern Med 1993;119:257.

Labenz J, Borsch G. Evidence for the essential role of *Helicobacter pylori* in gastric ulcer disease. Gut 1994;35:19.

Labenz J, Ruhl GH, Bertrams J, Borsch G. Medium- or high-dose omeprazole plus amoxicillin eradicates *Helicobacter pylori* in gastric ulcer disease. Am J Gastroenterol 1994;89:726.

CHAPTER 19–29

Duodenal Ulcer

Eugene Straus, M.D.

DEFINITION

A duodenal ulcer is a localized area in which the mucosal surface has been lost down to the level of the muscularis mucosa. The ulcer crater is surrounded by a rim of inflammatory cells and is generally covered by an inflammatory exudate. The crater may contain blood vessels which are visible at the surface.

The vast majority of duodenal ulcers are found in the first portion of the duodenum. When they are located more distally, it is highly suggestive of massive gastric hypersecretion.

ETIOLOGY

The etiology of duodenal ulceration is complex. Nonetheless, the old adage "no acid, no ulcer" has held true for duodenal ulceration, and so the etiologic importance of acid and pepsin is clear. This is underscored by the fact that inhibition of gastric acid secretion causes prompt healing of duodenal ulceration in more than 95% of cases. When sufficiently large groups of individuals are studied, patients with duodenal ulceration have higher mean maximum acid secretory rates, reflecting higher parietal cell masses, than control subjects. It is also clear that not all patients with marked hyperchlorhydria develop duodenal ulceration, whereas some patients with duodenal ulceration have minimal acid secretory rates. Acid-peptic activity is therefore a necessary but insufficient condition for the development of duodenal ulceration. It is currently believed that there are "aggressive" factors and "defensive" factors that play roles in determining the health of the duodenal mucosa.

Aggressive factors are those that mitigate toward damage of the tissue and include acid and pepsin, cigarette smoking, aspirin and other nonsteroidal antiinflammatory drugs (NSAIDs), and the presence of *Helicobacter pylori* in the antral mucosa. Despite the fact that alcoholic beverages stimulate acid secretion, there is no evidence that alcohol directly causes an increase in duodenal ulceration. Hepatic cirrhosis, regardless of the cause, is associated with an increased risk of duodenal ulcers. Although prolonged administration of high-dose corticosteroids has been thought to increase the risk of peptic ulcer, there are few data to support this view.

Defensive factors are thought to protect the mucosa from damage and these include prostaglandin, mucosal bicarbonate secretion, and duodenal mucus. There are data to suggest that some patients with duodenal ulceration have deficient tissue prostaglandin content, and even localized deficiency in duodenal bicarbonate secretion, but these have yet to be well established. In any case, the current thinking is that duodenal ulceration occurs when there is an imbalance in the normal array of aggressive and defensive factors: either an increase in aggressive forces, such as relatively excessive secretion of acid and pepsin and/or infection with *H. pylori,* or a decrease in defensive forces.

A central etiologic role is now being placed on the presence of *H. pylori,* a small, curved, motile, Gram-negative rod with great capacity for urease secretion. The organism is found in the stomachs of the great majority of patients with duodenal ulceration, living in the antrum below the mucous gel, with little ability to invade the mucosa. There is consensus that *H. pylori* is an important factor in the development of duodenal ulcers and that eradication of the organisms results in a reduced rate of recurrence. It should be understood that not all patients with duodenal ulceration harbor *H. pylori* and that the vast majority of those "infected" are free of disease. In most parts of the world at least half of all individuals over the age of 50 have *H. pylori* in their stomachs. In some places nearly 100% of the population carries the organism. Nevertheless, even though the ulcers are readily healed in the presence of *H. pylori,* there is consensus that the organisms should be eradicated with antibiotic treatment to prevent recurrence. In the light of the rapidly emerging problem of antibiotic-resistant bacteria, this author would be more confident if there were stronger data to indicate

that treatment is truly a "cure," as most maintain. This infection, which must be the most common bacterial infection of the human species, may reestablish itself over the course of some period, and the requirement for multiple courses of antibiotic treatment would certainly have to be considered with care. There is more to be learned about *H. pylori.*

CRITERIA FOR DIAGNOSIS

Suggestive

The primary symptom of duodenal ulcer is abdominal pain. The pain is usually epigastric, burning, relieved by taking food or antacids, and may awaken the patient in the early morning hours. The pain may be associated with epigastric tenderness. Other symptoms may include nausea and vomiting, diarrhea, and heartburn. Symptoms may persist for months and then subside. Activity is frequently greatest in spring and fall months.

It is important for the physician to understand that these symptoms, although characteristic, are not specific for duodenal ulceration. Nor is the typical pattern of pain a sensitive diagnostic indicator, as it is not unusual for patients to present with complications of duodenal ulceration without having had any prior symptoms. Complications of duodenal ulceration include bleeding, presenting with hematemesis, melena, or occult blood in the stool; obstruction, presenting with postprandial vomiting; and perforation, presenting with unrelenting abdominal pain.

Definitive

Definitive diagnosis is best made by direct visualization through gastrointestinal endoscopy, but can also be established by upper gastrointestinal barium x-ray examination.

CLINICAL MANIFESTATIONS

Subjective

The typical burning epigastric pain that occurs 1 to 3 hours after eating and is relieved by taking food and/or antacids, and that may awaken the patient in the early-morning hours, is characteristic, but neither a specific nor a sensitive diagnostic indicator. The patient may have no pain at all, or the pain may be more vague and hungerlike in nature. Significant numbers of patients do not relate their pain to a pattern relating to meals. Other nonspecific symptoms may include nausea and vomiting, heartburn, belching, bloating, and fatty food intolerance.

The physician should always be alert for symptoms of complications. Weakness, dizziness, and palpitations should suggest bleeding. Vomiting may indicate gastric outlet obstruction. A change in the character of pain, usually more severe, with greater radiation to the back, or more diffuse and over a greater area, and no longer relieved by antacids, suggests perforation.

Objective

Physical Examination

Uncomplicated duodenal ulceration results in nothing more than epigastric tenderness. When the diagnosis is being considered the physician should always search for evidence of complications. The stool should always be examined for evidence of occult bleeding. When vomiting has occurred, distention and a succession splash should be sought to diagnose gastric outlet obstruction. Symptoms consistent with perforation should initiate a careful search for peritoneal signs including involuntary guarding, rigidity, and rebound tenderness.

Routine Laboratory Abnormalities

There are no routine laboratory abnormalities associated with uncomplicated duodenal ulceration.

PLANS

Diagnostic

Differential Diagnosis

The differential diagnosis in patients presenting with epigastric pain is extensive and includes gastritis, gastric ulceration, gastric cancer, duodenitis, various infiltrative diseases of the stomach (syphilis, sarcoidosis, eosinophilic granuloma), Menetrier's disease, and the vague entity of nonulcer dyspepsia. Pancreatitis and cholecystitis are generally sufficiently distinct to be ruled out on clinical grounds.

Diagnostic Options and Recommended Approach

For many years the American College of Physicians has taken the position that patients presenting for the first time with symptoms consistent with uncomplicated duodenal ulceration should be treated with H_2-receptor blockers without further diagnostic testing. If treatment results in prompt and complete response, the treatment should be completed without subjecting the patient to endoscopic or radiographic testing. The rationale for this approach is based on the fact that the symptoms are very common and when all symptomatic patients are examined a major fraction are found not to have ulcers.

Patients with recurrent symptoms, with history of peptic ulceration, with evidence of a complication, and those who do not respond within a few days with complete remission of symptoms should be examined endoscopically or with double-contrast upper gastrointestinal x-rays.

Serum gastrin should be measured if ulcers are multiple, if they are distal to the first portion of the duodenum, if the patient has diarrhea or hypercalcemia, if the endoscopist finds large rugal folds or excessive secretions, if there is a family history of peptic ulcer disease, and prior to elective surgery for duodenal ulcer disease. See Chapter 19–30 for details.

Therapeutic

We are currently in a period of profound and rapid change in the approach to treatment of duodenal ulcers due to the emergence of *H. pylori* as a causative factor. Until recently, patients with presumed or proven duodenal ulcers received a therapeutic dose of an H_2 blocker (cimetidine 800 mg, ranitidine 300 mg, famotidine 40 mg) before going to bed for 8 weeks and this healed duodenal ulceration in more than 95% of cases. Patients with a history of recurrence or complication were kept on half of the therapeutic dose for maintenance. Nonetheless, there was a substantial recurrence while on maintenance therapy, especially in smokers, although complications while on maintenance was found to be uncommon. Currently the standard of care has shifted to the eradication of *H. pylori*. There are, however, more than a dozen regimens for eradication of *H. pylori* involving from 1 day to 2 weeks of treatment, and from one to three or more drugs. Most authorities agree that eradication of *H. pylori* results in rapid healing of duodenal ulcers and eliminates the problem of recurrence.

Table 19–29–1 lists 10 regimens along with their rates of eradication of *H. pylori*. Table 19–29–2 lists some pros and cons of various treatment options.

At this time the most commonly used treatment regimen is probably omeprazole 20 mg twice daily, along with amoxicillin 500 mg four times daily, taken for 2 weeks. This treatment is reported to result in an 83% eradication rate. Eradication is determined by repeat endoscopy and antral biopsy with culture of the tissue and/or detection of tissue urease in the CLO test.

Most authorities maintain that eradication of *H. pylori* is tantamount to cure of duodenal ulcer disease. They would thus not suggest any maintenance therapy. Nonetheless, this author does not believe that there are sufficient data to establish that an organism as prevalent as *H. pylori* will not return if given sufficient time. In addition, data on eradication rates have not been uniformly reproducible; most regimens have failure rates of 6 to 20%, and all patients will not have repeat biopsy to establish eradication. I therefore suggest that patients who have had complications be continued on maintenance H_2-blocker treatment for an indefinite period or until the question of the reinfection with *H. pylori* is more clearly defined.

Patients with duodenal ulceration should be encouraged to stop

TABLE 19–29–1. TREATMENT REGIMENS STUDIED FOR ERADICATION OF *H. PYLORI*

Regimen	Dose	Duration	Eradication Rate (%)
Two antimicrobials + antisecretory agent			
Metronidazole	500 mg 3 times/day	12 days	
Amoxillin	750 mg 3 times/day	12 days	89*
Ranitidine	300 mg at bedtime	6 weeks	
Clarithromycin	500 mg 3 times/day	10 days	
Amoxicillin	750 mg 3 times/day	10 days	86†
Ranitidine	300 mg at bedtime	6 weeks	
Metronidazole	400 mg 3 times/day	14 days	
Amoxicillin	500 mg 3 times/day	14 days	90‡
Omeparazole	40 mg/day	14 days	
Metronidazole	500 mg 2 times/day	14 days	
Clarithromycin	250 mg 2 times/day	14 days	88§
Omeprazole	20 mg 2 times/day	14 days	
Three antimicrobials			
Bismuth	#	14–15 days	
Metronidazole	0.6–1.5 g/day	14–15 days	89‖
Tetracycline	500 mg 4 times/day	14–14 days	
Bismuth	#	10–14 days	
Metronidazole	1.0–1.5 g/day	10–14 days	84¶
Amoxicillin	1.5–2.0 g/day	10–14 days	

*Hentschel E, Brandstatter G, Dragosics B, et al. Effect of ranitidine and amoxicillin plus metronidazole on the eradication of *Helicobacter pylori* and the recurrence of duodenal ulcer. N Eng J Med 1993;328:308–312.
†al-Assi MT, Genta RM, Karttunen TJ, Graham DY. Clarithromycin-amoxycillin therapy for *Helicobacter pylori* infection. Aliment Pharmacol Ther 1994;8:453–456.
‡Bell GD, Powell KU, Burridge SM, et al. Rapid eradication of *Helicobacter pylori* infection. Aliment Pharmacol Ther 1995;9:41–46.
§Yousif MM, el-Zimaity HM, al-Assi MT, Cole RA, Genta RM, Graham DY. Metronidazole, omeprazole, and clarithromycin: an effective combination therapy for *Helicobacter pylori* infection. Aliment Pharmacol Ther 1995;9:209–12.
‖Tytgat GNJ. Treatments that impact favorably upon the eradication of *Helicobacter pylori* and ulcer recurrence. Aliment Pharmacol Ther 1994;8:359–68.
¶Penston JG. *Helicobacter pylori* eradication—understandable caution but no excuse for inertia. Aliment Pharmacol Ther 1994;8:369–89.
#Bismuth subsalicylate (Pepto-Bismol) is available in the United States and is given as two 262 mg tablets 4 times/day. Tripotassium dicitrato busmuthate (De-Nol) is available elsewhere and is given in a dose of 120 mg 4 times/day.

TABLE 19–29–2. PROS AND CONS OF VARIOUS PROVEN TREATMENT OPTIONS

Therapy	Pro	Con
Bismuth, tetracycline, metronidazole	Safe, effective, inexpensive, validated	Side effects in 30%, inconvenient
Amoxicillin, metronidazole, ranitidine	Safe, effective, simple to add to patients already on H_2 blockers	Not well studied
Omeprazole, amoxicillin	Safe, effective, validated, convenient, twice a day	Expensive, variable reports of efficacy
Omeprazole, clarithromycin	Safe, effective, validated, convenient	Expensive, variable reports of efficacy
Omeprazole, clarithromycin, metronidazole	Safe, highly effective, short duration (7 d)	Not many data
Omeprazole, amoxicillin, metronidazole	Safe, highly effective	Not many data
Omeprazole, amoxicillin, clarithromycin	Effective (8 d)	Not many data

smoking, as this is associated with the development of ulcers and recurrence. They should also be restricted in their use of NSAIDs. Foods and beverages that stimulate acid secretion need not be restricted in patients on current treatment regimens.

Treatment of the complications of duodenal ulceration should be in the hands of gastroenterologists and general surgeons and is not within the scope of this chapter.

FOLLOW-UP

Patients who have responded to treatment for duodenal ulceration should be instructed about symptoms and signs of recurrence and should consult their physician if these occur. It is only necessary to perform repeat endoscopic or x-ray examinations in patients with complicated or unusual duodenal ulcers. These include giant ulcers and ulcers with visible vessels.

DISCUSSION
Prevalence and Incidence

The prevalence for peptic ulcers in the United States is about 2.0%. It is estimated that in the United States there are about 200,000 to 400,000 new cases of duodenal ulcer per year.

Related Basic Science

The balance of aggressive and defensive forces is at the center of our thinking with respect to the maintenance of a healthy duodenal mucosa. For many decades the focus of studies was on the aggressive factors, especially the secretion of acid and pepsinogen. The central finding was that duodenal ulcers do not develop in the absence of acid-peptic activity. It was also established that they could be healed by neutralizing gastric acid or inhibiting its secretion. Taken as a group, patients with duodenal ulcers were found to have higher rates of gastric acid secretion, and, somewhat paradoxically, to respond to provocations with greater release of gastrin. These observations have formed the basis of our approaches to treatment.

More recently, attention has been paid to defensive factors including mucus secretion, tissue prostaglandin content, and mucosal bicarbonate secretion. Nonetheless, the most recent emphasis on *H. pylori* has virtually swept away attention to other factors. *Helicobacter pylori,* of course, is an aggressive factor associated with ulceration, although, as mentioned above, the vast majority of people carrying this organism are well. The organism does not invade the mucosa and, in fact, is found in the antral mucosa rather than in the duodenum. It secretes urease and a variety of other substances, but the mechanism by which it encourages ulceration in the duodenum is not presently understood. Although it is clear that *H. pylori* is an aggressive factor whose elimination results in reduced recurrence, it is not yet well established that treatment produces permanent eradication of the organism. Because treatment of large segments of the population with broad-spectrum antibiotics is not without considerable risk, and because treatment with H_2 blockers is proven to be safe and effective, the future for research in this area should concentrate on the question of the permanence of the eradication of this nearly ubiquitous organism.

Genetics

Observations of familial aggregation, twin studies, associations with blood groups, HLA antigens, and secretor status have suggested that there may be genetic factors contributing to some patients' tendency to develop duodenal ulceration. For the most part, these factors have not been elucidated. On the other hand, there are some rare genetic syndromes in which duodenal ulceration is a prominent feature. These include multiple endocrine neoplasia type I, which is inherited in an autosomal dominant pattern and is characterized by adenomas in the pituitary, parathyroid, and pancreatic islet cell glandular tissues. Here the Zollinger–Ellison syndrome is a frequent manifestation. Systemic mastocytosis, also with a dominant pattern of inheritance, is associated with duodenal ulceration in nearly 50% of cases.

Physiologic or Metabolic Derangement

The most consistent physiologic derangement found in patients with duodenal ulceration is gastric acid secretion at rates that are higher than the mean for healthy people. It is not clear how this relates to the very frequent finding of *H. pylori* in association with duodenal ulcer. Patients with Zollinger–Ellison syndrome, with the highest rates of acid secretion and the most extensive duodenal ulceration, generally do not have *H. pylori* in their gastric mucosa.

Natural History and Its Modification with Treatment

Duodenal ulceration is a chronic disease with spontaneous remissions and exacerbations. There is a tendency to "burn out" as patients get older, although we know that *H. pylori* is more frequently found in older individuals. Nevertheless, most authorities now believe that treatment that eradicates *H. pylori* results in a permanent cure of the disease. This remains to be proven.

Prevention

Prevention of duodenal ulceration is best thought of as prevention of recurrence. This can be effected in a significant number of individuals by maintenance therapy with H_2 blockers, but proponents of *H. pylori* treatment maintain that eradication of the organism with antibiotics results in a permanent cure in the vast majority of cases.

Cost Containment

Cost containment can be achieved by treating initial symptoms without performing endoscopic and x-ray examinations as described above. As the natural history of duodenal ulceration is one of chronicity, with spontaneous remissions and exacerbations, prevention of recurrence and complications will contain costs. Clearly, if we now have the cure, eradication of *H. pylori* should go a long way to reduce the considerable costs of this disease.

REFERENCES

Elashoff JD, Grossman MI. Trends in hospital admissions and death rates for peptic ulcer in the United States from 1970 to 1978. Gastroenterology 1980;78:280.

Marshall BJ, Goodwin CS, Warren JR, et al. Long term healing of gastritis and low duodenal ulcer relapse after eradication of *Campylobacter pyloridis:* A prospective double-blind study. Gastroenterology 1987;92:1518.

Moore JG. Circadian rhythm of gastric acid secretion in man. Nature 1970;226:1261.

Zollinger–Ellison Syndrome

Eugene Straus, M.D.

DEFINITION

The term Zollinger–Ellison syndrome (ZES) refers to the pathophysiology resulting from hypergastrinemia caused by gastrin-secreting tumor(s). The most frequent manifestations are peptic ulceration and diarrhea.

ETIOLOGY

Zollinger–Ellison syndrome is caused by gastrin-secreting tumors which may be found in the pancreas or in the wall of the duodenum. Rarely, gastrin secretion may arise from tumors in the antral portion of the stomach, from ovarian cystadenomas, and from carcinoid tumors. In about 20% of patients with ZES the gastrinomas are part of the multiple endocrine neoplasia type I syndrome, and additional secretory neoplasias may be found within the parathyroid, pituitary, islets of Langerhans, and thyroid glands.

CRITERIA FOR DIAGNOSIS

Suggestive

Zollinger and Ellison (1955) described a clinical syndrome in the form of a triad including primary peptic ulceration in unusual locations, gastric hypersecretion of gigantic proportions, and identification of islet cell tumors of the pancreas. Nonetheless, now that serum gastrin measurements are readily available, none of these are generally identified in patients with ZES.

Although multiple gastrointestinal ulcerations and ulcers in unusual locations should immediately suggest the diagnosis of a hypersecretory state such as ZES, at least 75% of patients with ZES have a single ulceration in the first portion of the duodenum, indistinguishable from garden variety peptic ulcer disease. In fact, about 10% of patients with ZES have no demonstrable ulcer.

The most common presenting symptom is burning abdominal pain, which, although initially not different from that of ordinary peptic ulceration, may be more persistent and less responsive to medical treatment. Pain accompanied by a watery secretory diarrhea that is diminished by antisecretory medication (H_2 blockers or proton pump inhibitors) should be highly suggestive of ZES. The secretory diarrhea occurs in 20 to 50% of patients with the syndrome. It is not of the magnitude seen in the more rare Verner–Morrison syndrome, in which vasoactive intestinal peptide-secreting pancreatic tumors cause "pancreatic cholera," with massive losses of stool water leading to dehydration and hypokalemia. Occasionally, impaired digestion of fats may cause steatorrhea, but here the loss of fat in the stool is not as great as that observed in malabsorptive states.

Complications of peptic ulceration, especially perforation and obstruction, should suggest the diagnosis of ZES. The practicing physician should, however, be aware that gastric outlet obstruction in the absence of a gastrinoma may cause hypergastrinemia and hyperchlorhydria simply as a result of antral distention. Here, as in other situations, the use of the secretin test (see below) may be useful, although acid secretory rates and gastrin concentrations rapidly normalize if the obstruction is relieved by medical treatment.

Similarly, signs and symptoms of peptic ulceration in a hypercalcemic patient should cause the clinician to consider ZES. Here the physician must be aware of the fact that hypercalcemia of any cause may stimulate secretion of both gastrin and hydrochloric acid. The patient with primary hyperparathyroidism may have a duodenal ulcer along with hypergastrinemia and hyperchlorhydria, and this need not represent a multiple endocrine neoplasia type I syndrome with an associated gastrinoma. Again, the secretin test is required unless the parathyroid disease is cured and the circulating gastrin concentrations subsequently normalize.

Zollinger–Ellison syndrome should be ruled out prior to any elective surgery for peptic ulcer disease. The primary reason for this is the observation that the clinical manifestations of ZES may become more severe after the unsuspected patient has had one of the standard forms of gastric surgery. New ulcerations at or distal to the surgical anastomosis may occur within hours, and postoperative intestinal perforation is well known in this circumstance.

In summary, multiple peptic ulcerations and those found beyond the first portion of the duodenum, symptoms and signs of acid-peptic disease in association with diarrhea, complications, resistance to treatment, hypercalcemia, Cushing's syndrome and family or other history consistent with multiple endocrine neoplasia type I all should suggest the diagnosis of ZES.

Definitive

Locating the tumor and demonstrating that it contains gastrin provide the most definitive diagnosis, but this is not possible in the majority of cases because of the elusive nature of these neoplasms. A minority of patients may present with obvious tumor masses, usually metastatic lesions within the liver. Nonetheless, primary gastrinomas may be multiple, small (2 mm), and soft, making them hard to find on surgical exploration. Small primary tumors in the pancreas may not grow appreciably or metastasize for decades, and they often are not visualized by imaging techniques including sonography, computed axial tomography, magnetic resonance imaging, or angiography. Recently, we have been successful in finding duodenal gastrinomas using endoscopic ultrasound, but the sensitivity of this method has not been established.

Because patients most frequently present without demonstrable tumor masses, definitive diagnosis is generally made by satisfying pathophysiologic criteria. These include fasting hypergastrinemia, a basal acid output greater than 10 mEq/h, and the immediate release of gastrin into the circulation in response to an intravenous injection of secretin (positive secretin test).

CLINICAL MANIFESTATIONS

Subjective

Abdominal pain is the presenting complaint in more than 75% of patients. The pain does not differ from that seen in patients presenting with ordinary peptic ulceration, although it may occasionally be more severe, associated with heartburn, or unresponsive to standard medical treatment. It is generally epigastric, burning, and relieved by food, antacids, and medications that inhibit the secretion of gastric acid. A watery, secretory-type of diarrhea may accompany the pain in 20 to 50% of patients with ZES, and the typical pattern of pain associated with diarrhea should alert the practicing physician to the diagnosis. The pain and diarrhea are abolished if the patient takes sufficient doses of antisecretory medication.

Other symptoms may relate to complications of peptic ulceration such as bleeding (hematemesis and melena), gastric outlet obstruction (vomiting), and perforation (peritoneal irritation). The presence of additional hormonal excesses due to multiple endocrine neoplasia type I or secretion of multiple hormones from the primary and/or secondary gastrinomas will produce symptoms related to those hormones. In multiple endocrine neoplasia type I, parathyroid adenomas are the most frequent additional tumors followed by adrenocorticotropin-producing pituitary adenomas, insulinomas, thyroid adenomas. and pituitary prolactinomas. When Cushing's syndrome is caused by adrenocorticotropin secreted from the gastrinoma tissue rather than from a pituitary adenoma, in addition to the problems of controlling the consequences of adrenocorticotropin excess, the addition of adrenocorticotropin secretion heralds more rapid and aggressive growth of the gastrinomas.

Objective

Physical Examination

The most frequent abnormal physical finding is epigastric tenderness related to duodenal ulceration(s). If complications of peptic ulceration have occurred the physician may observe the abdominal distention and a succussion splash of an obstructed gastric outlet, the pallor and fecal blood resulting from bleeding ulcers, or the tenderness and peritoneal signs of a perforation. Again, these findings and those related to multiple hormonal excesses are infrequent as 75% of patients with ZES present with an uncomplicated duodenal ulcer.

When malignant gastrinomas metastasize they almost always involve the liver, which may then be palpable.

Although not part of the routine physical examination, gastrointestinal endoscopic examinations are almost always performed prior to the diagnosis of ZES. The observation of giant hypertrophic rugal folds and copious acid secretions should suggest the diagnosis, especially in a patient with peptic ulceration.

Routine Laboratory Abnormalities

The most frequent routine laboratory abnormalities are those caused by chronic blood loss, an iron deficiency anemia, with low hemoglobin, hematocrit, mean corpuscular volume, mean corpuscular hemoglobin concentration, serum iron, and ferritin. These need not be present as the patient may not have had any bleeding. Similarly, other complications such as obstruction with vomiting, or severe diarrhea, or hyperparathyroidism may result in abnormalities in routine laboratory tests.

PLANS

Diagnostic

In the clinical circumstances outlined above that suggest the diagnosis of ZES, the physician should obtain a fasting serum gastrin and a basal acid output. The gastrin determination is easily obtained, and it is important that the blood be drawn after a 12-hour fast; however, the basal acid output, although simple enough to perform, is nonetheless rarely done. At the very least the physician should determine the pH of the gastric contents following a fast of at least 6 to 12 hours. In patients with ZES the pH is below 2. If the patient is taking antisecretory medication and the physician is loathe to withdraw treatment because of the virulence of the ulcer diathesis, the pH of gastric contents should be determined just prior to a dose of medication.

The finding of fasting hypergastrinemia in the presence of a basal acid output greater than 10 MEq/h (normal, <5 MEq/h) is virtually diagnostic of ZES. Nonetheless, there are a number of caveats in the interpretation of these data and the physician should not make a definitive diagnosis in the absence of a positive secretin test or unequivocal evidence of a gastrin-containing tumor.

In ZES, fasting serum gastrin concentrations reflect the bulk of the gastrinoma mass. In our laboratory mean fasting gastrin concentrations are less than 50 pg/mL. In more than 100 patients with ZES we have seen only one case with fasting gastrin concentrations within the normal range (<100 pg/mL). When the fasting concentrations are relatively low (<300 pg/mL), we have not found large tumors. In the presence of very high fasting gastrin concentrations (> 5000 pg/mL), a substantial tumor mass is generally found.

The practicing physician must never interpret fasting serum gastrin concentrations in the absence of knowledge of gastric secretory capability. Although high fasting gastrin concentrations may occur in the presence of acid secretion in ZES, in hypercalcemic states, with insensitive acid-feedback inhibition, in renal failure, and with the very rare retained antrum syndrome, very high fasting gastrin levels may also accompany achlorhydric states such as pernicious anemia. Chronic antisecretory treatment with H_2 blockers and proton pump inhibitors also raises the fasting gastrin level.

Calcium is able to stimulate both gastrin release and gastric acid secretion, and therefore, hypercalcemic states such as primary hyperparathyroidism may be accompanied by hypergastrinemia and hyperchlorhydria in the absence of a gastrinoma.

In some individuals the gastrin-secreting cells (G cells) in the antral mucosa are insensitive to acid-feedback inhibition and gastric acidity fails to inhibit gastrin release (see Related Basic Science). These patients may have hypergastrinemia and hyperchlorhydria in the absence of a gastrinoma.

The secretin test is virtually always required to establish a diagnosis of ZES. When properly performed it has few false-positive or false-negative results and can be considered definitive. The patient with symptoms and signs consistent with ZES who has high levels of fasting serum gastrin and an elevated basal acid output should have a secretin test. It is best if this test is performed and interpreted by someone with experience in this area. After an overnight fast, five specimens of serum are taken at 5-minute intervals prior to an intravenous injection of secretin (2 CU/kg body weight). Postinjection samples are taken at 3, 5, 10, 20, and 30 minutes. If the preinjection baseline is flat, a postinjection rise of 200 pg/mL or more within 10 minutes should be considered indicative of a gastrinoma.

Therapeutic

All of the manifestations of acid-peptic disease and the secretory diarrhea that result from massive hypersecretion of gastric acid can be controlled with antisecretory medications. The treatment of choice for patients with suspected or documented ZES is an inhibitor of the H^+, K^+-ATPase, or proton pump, in the cell membranes of acid-secreting parietal cells. The substituted benzimidazole omeprazole is the current drug of choice. Patients may be started on doses of 20 mg given twice a day, but the dose should be adjusted on the basis of its effect on the basal acid output. The basal acid output, which can be in excess of 100 MEq/h in untreated patients, should be suppressed to less than 10 MEq/h when measured just prior to a dose of medication. Higher rates of unstimulated acid secretion are associated with peptic ulceration. Before the introduction of omeprazole, treatment with high-dose H_2 blockers was very effective. The greater potency of omeprazole, its longer duration of action, and fewer side effects make it superior to H_2 blockers, and patients clearly prefer this medication. Patients with ZES have taken this medication, even in high doses, for nearly two decades without ill effects. Surgical approaches to the control of gastric secretion in ZES should be considered only in patients who are unable to take medication.

The success that has been achieved with medical control of ZES has allowed greater attention to be focused on locating and removing primary gastrinomas. A careful endoscopic examination of the duodenum looking for the typical smooth mound with a central umbilication indicative of a submucosal mass should be accomplished soon after the diagnosis is considered. Primary gastrinomas in the wall of the duodenum are probably more frequent than the 10% estimated in the earlier experience. We have had some success in removing these endoscopically with the aid of endoscopic ultrasonography, but the role of this technique should be defined through more extensive experience, and it should not be attempted by any but the most experienced endoscopists.

When routine imaging techniques have failed to locate the gastrinoma(s), specialized methods such as transhepatic portal venous sampling have been tried with mixed results. The decision to perform a laparotomy to discover and remove gastrinomas should be made only by physicians and surgeons with extensive experience.

In patients with advanced disease, when hepatic metastases have caused massive hepatomegaly with pain and encroachment on vascular structures, liver transplantation can provide remarkable relief and many years of extended life. On the other hand, chemotherapy has not been successful.

FOLLOW-UP

Patients with ZES should be followed carefully, especially early in the course of their treatment, to be sure that medical suppression of acid secretion is adequate. Once this has been established, their disease may remain stable and without symptoms for many years. Fasting serum gastrin concentrations provide an excellent tumor marker and can be checked at 6-month or yearly intervals. There is no need to do frequent imaging of the abdomen. The physician should always be alert to signs of additional hormonal excesses.

DISCUSSION
Prevalence and Incidence
Precise data on the prevalence and incidence of ZES are not available.

Related Basic Science
William Beaumont, peering through a gastric fistula into the stomach of his reluctant patient Alexis St. Martin, noted that the organ was quiescent when it was not filled. In fact, normally there is little, if any, secretion entering the alimentary canal during interdigestive periods. In the fasting state the primary hormonal stimulants of secretion—gastrin, secretin, and cholecystokinin—circulate in concentrations that are too low to detect even by the most sensitive methods or in biologically inactive forms. When material is taken into the stomach, gastrin is immediately released into the bloodstream from the G cells of the antral mucosa and causes the parietal cells of the more proximal oxyntic mucosa to begin secreting hydrochloric acid. Acid entering the duodenum releases secretin, which immediately stimulates the secretion of water and bicarbonate from the pancreatic ductular epithelium. When the buffer capacity of the ingested meal is overcome and the pH in the gastric antrum falls to below 4, acid-feedback inhibition of the G-cell mass prevents further release of gastrin and concentrations in the circulation rapidly fall. When the stomach is empty again, there is no stimulus for gastrin release. For this reason the basal acid output is normally between 0 and 5 MEq/h, and only the first few centimeters of the duodenum are exposed to acid.

Genetics
Most cases of ZES are sporadic. Fewer than 20% of patients with gastrinomas have the multiple endocrine neoplasia type I syndrome, which is inherited as an autosomal dominant disorder with a high degree of penetrance but with considerable variability in its expression. About 90% of patients with multiple endocrine neoplasia type I have hyperparathyroidism and about half of these patients have ZES.

Physiologic or Metabolic Derangement
The gastrinomas that cause ZES constantly secrete gastrin into the circulation. This causes the parietal cell mass to constantly secrete hydrochloric acid. In addition, gastrin's trophic effects on the growth of the oxyntic gastric mucosa causes hyperplasia of the parietal cell mass. The result is constant secretion of acid at very high maximal rates. This most frequently causes peptic ulceration, sometimes in the more distal regions of the small intestine. Typically, *H. pylori* is not found in the tissues. The luminal contents, normally acidified only in the first few centimeters, may be acid down to the anus. This results in constant release of secretin with tremendous outpouring of water and bicarbonate from the exocrine pancreas. The high rates of gastric and pancreatic secretion may result in watery secretory diarrhea.

Natural History and Its Modification with Treatment
Medical treatment can completely abolish the symptoms and tissue damage due to acid secretory excess. In fewer than 50% of cases the primary gastrinomas can be located and removed, resulting in a cure. Most patients who succumb to the malignant effects of the tumor have hepatic metastases at the time of diagnosis. Nonetheless, malignant gastrinomas are slow growing and generally cause no symptoms for many years, even decades.

Prevention
Other then genetic counseling of patients with multiple endocrine neoplasia type I, there are no approaches to prevention.

Cost Containment
Early diagnosis can contain costs by preventing complications of acid-peptic disease with vigorous medical treatment.

REFERENCES
Isenberg JI, Walsh JH, Passaro E, et al. Unusual effect of secretin on serum gastrin, serum calcium, and gastric acid secretion in a patient with suspected Zollinger–Ellison syndrome. Gastroenterology 1972;62:626.

Straus E. Radioimmunoassay of gastrointestinal hormones. Gastroenterology 1978;74:141.

Straus EW, Raufman J-P, Samuel S, et al. Endoscopic cure of the Zollinger–Ellison syndrome. Gastrointest Endosc 1992;38:709.

Zollinger RM, Ellison EH. Primary peptic ulcerations of the jejunum associated with islet cell tumors of the pancreas. Ann Surg 1955;142:709.

CHAPTER 19–31

Postgastrectomy Syndromes
Jack Rudick, M.D.

DEFINITION
Postgastrectomy syndromes may occur in any patient undergoing gastric surgery. Severe symptoms occur only in a minority of patients and are related to the degree of disruption in gastric physiology. They are more commonly seen after total or subtotal gastrectomy and are less common after proximal gastric vagotomy. Disabling symptoms after gastric surgery are more common in younger patients, in females, and in patients with extensive gastrectomy, as well as those with personality problems.

ETIOLOGY
The majority of patients present with a mixed clinical picture and pure syndromes are rare; however, they usually have a dominant symptom. Table 19–31–1 classifies the long-term sequelae of ulcer surgery.

CRITERIA FOR DIAGNOSIS
Postgastrectomy syndromes may be defined as any unsatisfactory result occurring after surgical procedures on the stomach. The syndromes fall into various categories according to the symptomatology, although there may be significant overlap. Some symptoms are so constant and precise and can be related to definite mechanical features, such as a small reservoir, a faulty afferent loop, or a partly obstructed efferent loop. Other patterns are mixed and varying, resulting from more than one of these mechanical factors being operative at the same time. Another group, resulting from altered physiology, present with metabolic disturbance, such as malnutrition, anemia, or steatorrhea.

CLINICAL MANIFESTATIONS
Subjective
Evaluation of the postgastrectomy patient requires a careful history, as the symptoms may be compatible with multiple postgastrectomy syndromes. Nevertheless, most patients present with a predominant symptom. These are summarized in Table 19–31–2.

Pain. The type of pain is important. Alkaline reflux gastritis and marginal ulceration present with a burning type of pain, whereas afferent

TABLE 19–31–1. POSTGASTRECTOMY SYNDROMES

Nutritional consequences
    Weight loss
    Anemia
    Milk intolerance
    Bone disease
Dumping
Reactive hypoglycemia
Bile gastritis
Diarrhea
Small stomach syndrome
Mechanical complications
    Afferent/efferent loop obstruction
    Jejunogastric intussusception
    Bezoar
Other sequelae
    Cholelithiasis
    Carcinoma

loop syndrome presents with a colicky pain. Colicky pain may also accompany the dumping syndrome.

Patients with alkaline reflux gastritis obtain very little relief with vomiting, whereas afferent loop syndrome is completely relieved by projectile vomiting.

Nausea and Vomiting. The vomitus of alkaline reflux gastritis is typically bilious with undigested food, whereas that of afferent loop syndrome is classically bilious without food particles. In patients with delayed gastric emptying, there may be partially digested food from a previous meal.

Cardiovascular Symptoms. Lightheadedness, dizziness, syncope, and sweating are features of the dumping syndrome, and may also occur in afferent loop syndrome.

Relationships of Symptoms to Meals. In the early dumping syndrome, symptoms usually occur within 30 minutes of a meal, whereas in the late dumping syndrome, it occurs 1.5 to 3 hours later. Diarrhea accompanying the early dumping syndrome usually occurs shortly after a meal, whereas postvagotomy diarrhea occurs later after a meal or may be unrelated to meals. Ingestion of food may precipitate the symptoms, as in the dumping syndrome or afferent loop syndrome, or it may relieve the symptoms, indicating a marginal ulcer. Aggravation of symptoms by a meal may result in weight loss. The type of meal is important. Meals with high liquid and carbohydrate content aggravate dumping symptoms, whereas meals with high fat content may exacerbate delayed gastric emptying and afferent loop syndrome. Alkaline reflux gastritis patients have constant pain, whereas afferent loop syndrome and dumping syndrome patients are free of symptoms between meals.

Objective

Physical Examination

Unfortunately, a physical examination is not usually helpful in a diagnosis of postgastrectomy syndromes. Evidence of weight loss and malnutrition should be sought. In particular, signs of polyneuritis and vitamin deficiency of the skin and mucous membranes should be addressed. On occasion, patients with delayed gastric emptying may demonstrate a succussion splash from a dilated stomach.

Routine Laboratory Abnormalities

Nutritional Indices. In addition to weight measurement, the serum albumin and corrected calcium concentrations should be measured in all patients. Clinical vitamin deficiency is rare but many patients with severe symptoms may have low leukocyte counts and vitamin C levels.

Hematology. A complete blood count is necessary as anemia is common and the incidence increases with the duration of follow-up. Iron deficiency is the most common cause of the anemia. Macrocytic anemia is usually the result of vitamin B_{12} deficiency and, less commonly, combined B_{12} and folate deficiency. Investigation must therefore include serum iron, iron binding capacity, folate and B_{12} levels and preferably a Schilling test.

Alkaline Phosphate. Elevated alkaline phosphatase in the absence of liver disease may indicate some bone disease. Diminished dietary intake of calcium and vitamin D due to malabsorption after many years may occur. These biochemical changes predate the symptoms.

Routine Laboratory Abnormalities

Microcytic anemia due to iron deficiency may be present and macrocytic anemia due to B_{12} deficiency and/or folate deficiency may be present. The serum level of alkaline phosphatase may be elevated and the serum calcium may be low. Hypoglycemia may be identified.

PLANS

Diagnostic

Differential Diagnosis

Weight Loss. Weight loss is very common after gastric surgery and is more marked after total gastrectomy and Billroth II partial gastrectomy than after gastrectomy with gastroduodenal reconstruction. It is more common for patients to experience significant postprandial symptoms. Diminished dietary intake is the major factor and far outweighs other factors such as fat and nitrogen malabsorption and decreased intestinal transit time. Although mild steatorrhea is common and may affect 70% of patients, severe malabsorption is rare.

Anemia. Anemia is commonly seen after gastric surgery and its incidence increases with duration of follow-up. Regardless of the type of gastric surgery, iron deficiency accounts for the vast majority. Macro-

TABLE 19–31–2. POSTGASTRECTOMY SYMPTOMS

Syndrome	Pain	Vomiting	Other
Afferent loop	Postprandial cramping; relieved by vomiting	Postcibal; projectile; without food particles	Prominent malnutrition
Alkaline reflux gastritis	Continuous burning; aggravated by meals	Postcibal and other; with residual food	Malnutrition less pronounced
Diarrhea	None	None	Episodic diarrhea, with urgency; often unrelated to meals and may occur at night
Dumping Early	When present, usually described as cramping	Nausea and "fullness" may be present; vomiting rare	Prominent cardiovascular symptoms (weakness, fainting, palpitations, dizziness, with need to lie down); may be followed by cramping and diarrhea; usually precipitated by high-carbohydrate liquids and occurs within 30 min of meal
Late	None	None	Cardiovascular symptoms usually occurring 1.5–3 h postprandially; gastrointestinal symptoms usually absent

cytic anemia is usually the result of vitamin B_{12} deficiency and, less commonly, combined folate and B_{12} deficiency or folate deficiency alone. Especially in gastrectomized patients, anemia may result from a mixed deficiency of iron and vitamin B_{12} or folate. Iron deficiency may result from malabsorption of dietary iron, a loss of gastric juice factor capable of facilitating iron absorption, and diminished splitting of iron–protein complexes by the reduced pepsin activity of gastric juice. It may also result from complications such as reflux gastritis and recurrent ulcer. After total gastrectomy, vitamin B_{12} oral malabsorption is invariable, and unless replacement therapy is initiated, a megaloblastic anemia develops some 3 to 6 years later, when body vitamin B_{12} reserves are depleted. Although, vitamin B_{12} malabsorption is well documented after partial gastrectomy, frank megaloblastic anemia is rare. The main factor responsible for vitamin B_{12} malabsorption is the lack of acid environment, which normally facilitates the release of vitamin B_{12} bound to food. In patients with severe postgastric symptoms, vitamin B_{12} malabsorption may be the result of bacterial overgrowth or steatorrhea. Folate deficiency is usually encountered in patients after total and subtotal gastrectomy, and is due to inadequate dietary intake.

Bone Disease. Bone disease is found more commonly after total or Billroth II gastrectomy in elderly patients. There is a latent period of several years and a female preponderance. It more commonly presents as osteomalacia, but osteomalacia can occur together with osteoporosis. There may be diminished dietary intake of calcium and vitamin D or there may be malabsorption of these by bypassing the duodenum, which is the major site of calcium absorption. The biochemical (elevated alkaline phosphatase) and radiologic changes often predate the onset of symptoms. Symptoms generally include bone pain, weakness from associated myopathy, and development of stress fractures. Bone biopsy often shows features of osteomalacia.

Dumping Syndrome. The dumping syndrome comprises postprandial vasomotor and gastrointestinal symptoms. Vasomotor symptoms include dizziness, weakness, sweating, pallor, and palpitations and, when severe, compel the patient to lie down or precipitate syncope. They occur toward the end of the meal or within minutes thereafter and especially after high-carbohydrate meals and high-osmolality drinks. The symptoms are due to hypovolemia usually in association with a fall in peripheral resistance. Cardic output is diminished but there is increased renal and digital blood flow. The gastrointestinal symptoms occur later and include colicky abdominal pain, exaggerated bowel sounds, distention, and urge to defecate, sometimes associated with diarrhea. The symptoms do not usually persist beyond 1 hour after eating. Dumping is associated with rapid gastric emptying leading to hyperosmolar jejunal contents, abnormal transit, and intestinal luminal changes. The hyperosmolar bolus of gastric effluent leads to jejunoileal dilation and outpouring of fluid from the vascular compartment into the intestinal lumen, causing hypovolemia. Various hormones and gut peptides have been implicated in the vascular and gastrointestinal symptoms of the dumping syndrome, but their release may be coincidental and not the cause of symptoms.

Reactive Hypoglycemia. Reactive hypoglycemia is often known as late dumping and may be considered a variant of the dumping syndrome. The hypoglycemic symptoms occur 2 to 4 hours after a meal and include sweating, dizziness, tremor, and difficulty in concentration. Fainting and convulsions are rare and signify a profound fall in blood glucose. Characteristically, the symptoms are relieved by food and the diagnosis is established by a blood glucose estimation during an attack. It may be related to an increased sensitivity of insulin or an exaggeration of normal regulation of insulin secretion.

Delayed Gastric Emptying. The acute form of delayed gastric emptying occurs in the immediate postoperative period and is related to mechanical and inflammatory causes. The chronic type may occur with retrograde jejunogastric intussusception, hernia of the anastomosis, or stenosis of the anastomosis. A nonmechanical cause is chronic gastroparesis, which is a diagnosis by exclusion. There has recently been an increase in postsurgical gastroparesis following Roux-en-Y gastrojejunostomy. Patients usually present with intermittent vomiting and early satiety, which must be differentiated from dumping symptoms. The patients are relatively asymptomatic in the morning, but become progressively more symptomatic as the day progresses. Meals are ingested but are only partially emptied. Symptoms include anorexia, fullness, bloating, belching, hiccups, and abdominal pain.

Afferent Limb Syndrome. Afferent loop syndrome occurs in acute and chronic forms. The acute type is most frequent in the immediate postoperative period and is due to mechanical obstruction as a result of internal hernia, kinking of the afferent loop, stenosis of the anastomosis, bands or adhesions, or compression of the limb by mesentery or by the defect in the mesocolon. This is a closed loop obstruction and may be accompanied by acute pancreatitis. This is a surgical emergency.

The chronic form occurs secondary to partial obstruction, again from mechanical causes. Although this may not always be found at subsequent surgery, it characteristically presents with postprandial discomfort, relieved by vomiting of bile-stained fluid free of food particles.

Alkaline Reflux Gastritis. Alkaline reflux gastritis has become a common long-term problem requiring reoperation after gastric surgery. Symptoms include epigastric pain and vomiting. The pain is continuous and burning, not relieved by food or antacids, and aggravated by a meal. The vomiting is bilious, unpredictable, and nonprojectile and does not relieve the pain.

Retrograde reflux of duodenal contents including bile and pancreatic enzymes and intestinal secretion alters the mucosal barrier of the stomach and allows the backdiffusion of hydrogen iron. This causes varying grades of gastritis.

Alkaline Reflux Esophagitis. Although alkaline reflux esophagitis may coexist with alkaline reflux gastritis, it is relatively uncommon and occurs essentially in patients with total gastrectomy or a very high gastrectomy. The reflux of bile acids and trypsin results in a disruption of the esophageal mucosal barrier with significant histologic changes. The symptoms are similar to those of peptic esophagitis. The patient notes substernal burning distress postprandially, which is exacerbated by straining or the reclining position. In contrast to patients with peptic esophagitis, antacids do not relieve the symptoms, and symptoms are often present between meals.

Diagnostic Options and Recommended Approach

Upper Gastrointestinal Series. Liquid barium demonstrates the postsurgical anatomy and may demonstrate structural abnormalities. A mixture of barium and ground meat also gives information about emptying of the stomach.

Upper Gastrointestinal Endoscopy. Upper gastrointestinal endoscopy may confirm the diagnosis of marginal ulceration or mechanical obstruction and is essential for the diagnosis of alkaline reflux gastritis. Biopsies may also be obtained.

Radionuclide Emptying Studies. Measurement of liquid gastric emptying or test meals with radioisotopes should be performed in any patient with suspected delayed gastric emptying. Radionuclide biliary excretion studies such as hepato-iminodiacetic acid (HIDA) and scintigraphy can be helpful in confirming the diagnosis of afferent loop syndrome and alkaline reflux gastritis.

Other Tests. Even after all diagnostic modalities have been used, the diagnosis may still be in doubt and the "final test" may be a therapeutic trial of medical or dietary therapy. If the patient responds appropriately, the diagnosis is correct, whereas therapeutic failure suggests that the diagnosis was incorrect or incomplete.

Therapeutic

Chronic Delayed Gastric Emptying. The treatment consists of dietary measures and prokinetic agents. High-fiber and high-fat-content meals should be avoided and oral enzyme preparations may be necessary for recurrent bezoars. Erythromycin, cisapride, and bethanechol have given better results than metoclopramide. As a last resort, a near-total gastrectomy may become necessary.

Acute Afferent Loop Syndrome. Early surgery is necessary and the management depends on the condition of the afferent limb. Any herniation or mechanical obstruction should be carefully corrected and may require an enteroenterostomy or Roux-en-Y anastomosis.

Chronic Afferent Loop Syndrome. Again, the treatment is surgical and requires either reconstruction or decompression of the afferent limb.

Dumping Syndrome. Prevention is the best treatment of the postgastrectomy dumping syndrome. The mainstay of medical treatment is dietary manipulation. The diet should be low in carbohydrates and rich in an appropriate amount of fat. Only the solid part of the meal should be consumed and liquids should be taken an hour or later postprandially. When diet alone is ineffective, the addition of gel-forming carbohydrates may modify glucose absorption. Pectin may be of use. Somatostatin analogs have been shown to be very effective in many cases. Failure to respond to aggressive medical treatment or dietary manipulation may necessitate surgery. A variety of surgical procedures may be successful: conversion to Billroth I anastomosis, Roux-en-Y gastroenterostomy, enteroenterostomy, jejunal and colonic interpositions.

Late Hypoglycemic Dumping Symptom. Dietary manipulation is similar to that for the early vasomotor type. Carbohydrate intake should be restricted but can slowly be increased because the syndrome tends to abate with time.

Postvagotomy Diarrhea. Although alteration of bowel habit is common after vagotomy, severe diarrhea is very rare. Medical therapy includes dietary changes, especially meals with a low fluid content, frequent small feedings, and an increase in dietary fiber in an attempt to slow intestinal transit. Antibiotics may be used either to treat or to rule out bacterial overgrowth. Antidiarrheal agents may reduce the number of stools and transiently give relief. Only extremely rarely may surgery be necessary. A reversed jejunal interposition may be of value.

Alkaline Reflux Gastritis. Binding of bile acids with cholestyramine may be effective but this is questionable, because it binds primarily with the ionized bile salt and not with bile acids, which are usually considered the injurious agents.

Antacids such as aluminum hydroxide may be used to absorb bile salts. Gastric secretory inhibitors may be of value in preventing the backdiffusion of hydrogen ions through the damaged gastric mucosa. Use of cytoprotective agents, such as prostaglandin E analogs and sucralfate, may be of value. When the bile vomiting remains persistent, then surgery may become necessary. Various procedures have been used, but Roux-en-Y gastrojejunostomy has become the treatment of choice for alkaline reflux gastritis.

Alkaline Reflux Esophagitis. When intensive medical therapy has been unsuccessful, and surgery becomes necessary, a biliary diversion with a Roux-en-Y anastomosis should be performed.

FOLLOW-UP

The follow-up varies with the problem. The physician must be familiar with the complaints that follow gastrectomy and institute the appropriate treatment. Follow-up is essential to determine the success of management.

DISCUSSION
Prevalence and Incidence

Postgastrectomy syndromes are declining in frequency, and this trend should continue. The incidence of duodenal ulceration has decreased in Western countries over the past 40 years. Medical management, including H_2 blockers and proton pump inhibitors, reduces the need for elective surgery for duodenal ulceration. Fewer patients are refractory to medical therapy. Those patients requiring surgery can also be treated by more "physiologic" operations which do not require gastric resection. Avoidance of resection in patients with underlying psychological problems should also reduce the incidence of postgastrectomy problems.

Improved understanding of pathophysiology allows a more rational approach to the investigation and management of the problems. Dietary and medical management is the mainstay but surgical correction is often necessary; however, the emphasis has to be on the prevention of these syndromes.

Related Basic Science

All gastric surgical procedures produce fundamental alterations in the anatomy and physiology of the upper gastrointestinal tract. With a gastrojejunal reconstruction, food passes directly from a greatly reduced stomach reservoir into the upper jejunum in an almost totally undigested state, without any such mechanism as the pylorus to control the rate. After gastroduodenal reconstruction the reservoir is also reduced and food passes by its natural route via the duodenum and is therefore mixed with bile and pancreatic enzymes, but there is still no pyloric mechanism, so that food reaches the jejunum in a less well prepared state than normal.

Natural History and Its Modification with Treatment

Most postgastrectomy symptoms improve spontaneously with time, and only a hard core requires medical or surgical treatment. Simple dietary measures generally suffice in controlling most symptoms. Specific measures (both medical and surgical) have already been outlined.

Prevention

Prevention can be achieved by reducing the number of surgical procedures on the stomach. The incidence of peptic ulcer has decreased, and we now have more effective nonoperative management. Thus surgical procedures should be performed only when these measures have failed or when complications (e.g., hemorrhage, perforation, obstruction) have occurred. Lesser resections, with the emphasis on preservation of the gastric reservoir, should be advocated, and whenever feasible nonresection procedures should be performed. Metabolic complications can be prevented by appropriate dietary modification or supplementation.

Cost Containment

Establishment of the correct diagnosis by identifying the type of postgastrectomy syndrome and its proper treatment will decrease the cost of medical care. Gastrectomy is being done less often for the reasons cited above.

REFERENCES

Becker HD, Caspary WF. Postgastrectomy and postvagotomy syndromes. New York: Springer-Verlag, 1980:51.
Sawyers JL. Management of postgastrectomy syndromes. Am J Surg 1990:159:8.

CHAPTER 19–32

Acute Diarrhea

Veronica Prego, M.D.

DEFINITION

There is great variation in the bowel habits of healthy individuals, ranging from three movements a day to three a week. Therefore, acute diarrhea is best defined as a departure from the patient's bowel habit in which the stools become more frequent, more voluminous, or looser than usual for less than 1 month.

ETIOLOGY

Most acutely presenting cases are infectious in nature and usually occur after the ingestion of food or water contaminated with microbes (bacteria, viruses, parasites) or preformed bacterial toxins that overcome host defense mechanisms. Person-to-person transmission can occur through fecally contaminated hands or objects or by oroanal sex. Less common causes include fecal impaction, ischemia, enteral feedings, venereal proctitis (syphilis, gonorrhea, *Chlamydia,* and herpes simplex), acute presentation of Crohn's disease and ulcerative colitis, radiation injury, diverticulitis, and drugs. Almost any drug can be implicated including over-the-counter and alternative medications. Common offenders include Mg^{2+}-containing antacids, antibiotics, antineoplastics, prostaglandin analogs (misoprostol), laxatives, nonsteroidal antiinflammatory agents, alcohol, and caffeine-containing beverages. Diarrhea is a common extraintestinal manifestation of *Legionella* pneumonia. In addition, particularly in the elderly, diarrhea can be a nonspecific association of infectious processes outside the gastrointestinal tract, such as pneumonias, urinary tract infections, and pelvic inflammatory disease.

CRITERIA FOR DIAGNOSIS

Suggestive

The subjective perception that stools are larger, looser, or more frequent than usual for less than 1 month suggests the diagnosis.

Definitive

Objectively, diarrhea is present when the stool output exceeds 200 g/d on a typical Western (low-fiber) diet.

CLINICAL MANIFESTATIONS

Three major syndromes are defined according to their predominant symptom. Although overlapping, they can guide the physician to a specific diagnosis (Table 19–32–1).

Emetic Syndrome

Subjective

Abrupt onset of nausea, vomiting and abdominal pain occurs 1 to 6 hours after ingestion of food containing preformed toxins of *Staphylococcus aureus* or *Bacillus cereus.* Diarrhea often follows but may be absent. Symptoms spontaneously resolve within 24 hours. In *S. aureus* intoxication, patients commonly report having consumed foods high in protein, salt, and sugar, such as potato and macaroni salad, ham, and creams. For the *B. cereus*-emetic syndrome, the implicated food is usually fried rice. There is a high attack rate among other individuals who ate the tainted food.

Objective

Physical Examination. Fever is uncommon. The physical examination is normal. Stools are guaiac negative.

Routine Laboratory Abnormalities. There may be mild leukocytosis. Electrolytes are normal.

Noninflammatory Diarrhea

The cardinal feature is watery diarrhea without gross or microscopic blood or pus. In foodborne infections, symptoms develop 6 to 72 hours after ingestion when in vivo production of toxins begins.

Subjective

Norwalk Virus. Infection is linked to consumption of salads, undercooked shellfish, and contaminated municipal, well, or swimming water. Symptoms develop in 24 to 48 hours and are usually mild but can be life-threatening in the elderly. Affected patients complain of diarrhea, abdominal cramps, myalgias, and headaches; nausea and vomiting can be prominent. Fever is often present.

Clostridium perfringens. Watery diarrhea with severe abdominal pain develops 6 to 24 hours after ingestion of contaminated meat or poultry that has been allowed to sit for hours before consumption, such as in cafeterias and fast-food restaurants. Nausea and vomiting are uncommon. There is a high attack rate among similarly exposed people.

Bacillus cereus-Diarrheal Syndrome. Unlike the *B. cereus*-emetic syndrome in which preformed toxins are ingested, an incubation period of 6 to 24 hours reflects in vivo production of toxins. A variety of improperly refrigerated foods have been implicated. Clinical illness is characterized by watery diarrhea and cramps. Nausea and vomiting are uncommon.

Enterotoxigenic Escherichia coli. Patients give a history of recent travel to developing areas of the world, where enterotoxigenic *Escherichia coli* (ETEC) is endemic. Epigastric distress followed by watery diarrhea begins 24 to 72 hours after exposure to contaminated foods or beverages.

Vibrio cholerae. An afebrile illness begins 16 to 72 hours after visiting regions of South America, India, and Asia. Although mild cases occur, severe watery diarrhea of 1 L/h is characteristic.

Giardia. Patients develop diarrhea, bloating, and anorexia 1 to 3 weeks after exposure. There is a frequent history of travel to endemic areas of the world. Local cases are caused by drinking from natural water sources during camping or by person-to-person spread via fecal–oral route.

Drugs. Loose to watery diarrhea usually occurs shortly after the drug is started or the dose is increased. On occasion, diarrhea develops after years of using a fixed dose.

Fecal Impaction. Typically, patients are elderly, bedridden, or have a history of psychiatric illness. Medications are often contributory, particularly iron, antihypertensives, neuroleptics, tricyclic antidepressants, and narcotics. There is incontinence of pasty or watery stools that escape around the impacted fecal bolus. Vague lower abdominal pain may be present.

Enteral Feeding. Diarrhea develops in patients on enteral alimentation. Fever, abdominal pain, nausea, and vomiting are absent.

Objective

Physical Examination. In noninflammatory diarrheas, fever is uncommon except in Norwalk virus and ETEC infection. Patients may exhibit signs of dehydration. Abdominal tenderness is variable. In fecal impaction there may be abdominal distention and a firm left lower quadrant mass. Rectal examination reveals the impacted fecal bolus but its absence does not include the diagnosis, as in 20% of cases impaction occurs in the sigmoid and in 10% in the proximal colon. In cases of noninflammatory diarrhea, gross examination of the stool fails to reveal any blood, mucus, or pus. Fecal occult blood is negative.

Routine Laboratory Abnormalities. Leukocytosis is absent or mild. In severe cases there may be elevations of blood urea nitrogen, creatinine,

TABLE 19–32–1. ACUTE DIARRHEA SYNDROMES: EXPOSURE AND CLINICAL CHARACTERISTICS

Etiology	Exposure	Clinical Characteristics
Inflammatory Diarrhea*		
Nontyphoidal *Salmonella*	Poultry, beef, pork, eggs, travel	+ Chills + watery stools + dysentery in 10%
Shigella	Exposure to children, travel, male homosexuality, institutionalization	+ Watery stools + dysentery in 30% + Hemolytic uremic syndrome
Campylobacter	Milk, chicken, animals	+ 2-d prodrome (fever, myalgia, headache) then + watery diarrhea + abdominal pain + Occasional dysentery
Yersinia	Dairy, pork, beef	Pseudoappendicitis
Vibrio parahemolyticus	Seafood in summer months	+ Fever in 25% + explosive diarrhea + nausea + vomiting + abdominal pain
Enterohemorrhagic *Escherichia coli*	Meat, dairy in restaurants, institutions	+ Severe abdominal pain − fever + Bloody diarrhea − fecal leukocytes + Hemolytic uremic syndrome
Entamoeba histolytica	Travel, male homosexuality, daycare, institutionalization	From vague symptoms to fulminant colitis − Fecal leukocytes
Clostridium difficile	Antibiotic therapy	± Fever + Lower abdominal pain + tenesmus
Venereal proctitis	Anal intercourse	+ Tenesmus + rectal pain
Ischemia	History of cardiovascular disease ± documented hypotensive episode	+ Abdominal pain with paucity of abdominal signs; often bloody diarrhea, fever *follows*
Radiation enteritis/colitis	History of radiation	± Nausea and vomiting ± fever ± bleeding + Tenesmus (in radiation proctitis)
Inflammatory bowel disease (acute presentation)	History of inflammatory bowel disease, usually present	± Fever + Abdominal pain
Diverticulitis	Elderly	+ Fever + localized abdominal pain − Bleeding
Emetic Syndrome		
Staphylococcus aureus	Foods high in protein, salt, sugar	− Fever + Nausea + vomiting + abdominal pain
Bacillus cereus	Fried rice	
Noninflammatory diarrhea†		
Norwalk virus	Salads, shellfish, water	± Fever + headache + myalgia + Nausea + vomiting + abdominal pain
Clostridium perfringens	Meat, poultry	+ Severe abdominal pain − Fever − nausea − vomiting
Bacillus cereus-diarrheal syndrome	Improperly refrigerated foods	± Abdominal pain − Fever − nausea − vomiting
Enterotoxigenic *Escherichia coli*	Travel	± Fever + Abdominal pain
Cholera	Travel	− Fever + Severe watery diarrhea
Giardia	Travel, drinking from natural water sources, person to person	± Fever + Bloating
Drugs	Recently started or increasing dose	− Fever
Fecal impaction	Bedridden, elderly Drugs	− Fever + Incontinence + stool in rectum
Enteral feeding	Enteral feeding	− Fever − abdominal pain

*Stools contain gross/microscopic blood or pus. Fever and abdominal pain are prominent.
†Stools do not contain gross or microscopic blood or pus.

the blood urea nitrogen/creatinine ratio, as well as hypokalemia and acidosis.

Inflammatory Diarrhea

Inflammatory diarrheas are characterized by gross or microscopic blood, mucus, and pus in the stool that reflect damage to the intestinal mucosa caused by invasive microorganisms, ischemia, radiation, inflammatory bowel disease, or certain drugs such as antineoplastics. In general, fever and abdominal pain are prominent. The invasive pathogens listed below do not always cause typical inflammatory diarrhea, but may present with a noninflammatory picture.

Subjective

Nontyphoidal Salmonella. Illness develops 6 to 48 hours after ingestion of undercooked poultry, beef, pork, and eggs. Risk factors include prior antibiotic or antacid use, foreign travel, gastrectomy, diabetes, HIV infection, and lymphoma. Nausea and vomiting are followed by diarrhea, fever, chills, and periumbilical pain. Stools are usually not bloody, and may vary from small and frequent to profuse and watery. A small subset of patients present with classic dysentery: frequent passage of small stools that contain gross blood, mucus, and pus accompanied by painful defecation and tenesmus (sensation of incomplete evacuation).

Shigella. Transmission occurs by fecal-oral person-to-person spread and, less commonly, by ingestion of food contaminated with human feces, such as milk, ice cream, cheese, eggs, vegetables, and water. It is a disease of the pediatric age group; adult cases are linked to exposure to children, male homosexuality, and travel. Patients complain of fever, abdominal pain, and diarrhea. Stools are most commonly watery, but in the United States classic dysentery occurs in one third of the cases.

Campylobacter. Twelve to twenty-four hours after ingestion of under-cooked meats, particularly chicken, a prodrome of fever, myalgias, and headaches is quickly followed by watery, often bloody diarrhea and crampy abdominal pain. Dysentery is sometimes present.

Yersinia. In the United States, infection with *Yersinia enterocolitica* appears to be rare. Most cases have been traced to ingestion of dairy products or undercooked pork and beef. Diarrhea varies from loose to watery. Gross blood may be present. Some patients present with severe right lower quadrant pain mimicking acute appendicitis.

Vibrio parahemolyticus. Illness occurs 12 to 24 hours after ingestion of undercooked or poorly refrigerated seafood in the summer months. Patients develop explosive diarrhea accompanied by nausea, vomiting, and abdominal cramps. Fever and chills occur in 25% of cases.

Enterohemorrhagic **Escherichia coli.** Clinical illness develops 1 to 8 days after ingestion of contaminated meat or dairy products, usually in restaurants and institutions. Symptoms include bloody diarrhea and severe abdominal pain with remarkably little fever.

Entamoeba histolytica. Infection occurs after ingestion of fecally contaminated food or water, or because of poor hygiene and oroanal sexual practices. In the United States, travelers, male homosexuals, daycare workers, and institutionalized people are at higher risk. Patients can present with vague complaints of abdominal pain, bloating, and diarrhea (symptomatic noninvasive infection) or bloody stools, abdominal pain, and fever (dysentery). A few patients present severely ill and toxic, with marked abdominal pain (fulminant colitis).

Clostridium difficile *colitis.* Diarrhea develops during or up to 6 weeks after discontinuing antibiotic therapy. Stools are characteristically non-bloody.

Venereal Proctitis. Symptoms include tenesmus and rectal pain, with or without rectal discharge. A history of anal intercourse may be obtained.

Ischemic Colitis. Patients are elderly and have a history of cardiovascular disease. A hypotensive episode due to myocardial ischemia, arrhythmias, or surgery may or may not have been documented. Sudden, crampy abdominal pain is followed by loose to watery, often bloody diarrhea. Abdominal pain is absent in 25% of cases.

Radiation Injury. Diarrhea usually develops weeks after initiating radiation therapy. Fever is variable.

Acute Presentation of Inflammatory Bowel Disease. Occasionally, Crohn's disease and ulcerative colitis can present with an abrupt onset of diarrhea and abdominal pain that mimics acute infectious etiologies.

Diverticulitis. Elderly patients present with localized abdominal pain, most commonly to the left lower quandrant. Bleeding is absent.

Objective

Physical Examination. Fever is typical of most inflammatory diarrheas. The abdomen is tender; stools are frequently guaiac positive. In ischemic colitis there is a paucity of abdominal signs except for distention.

Routine Laboratory Abnormalities. Leukocytosis is present; in shigellosis there can be a leukemoid reaction. Hypokalemia, acidosis, and elevations of blood urea nitrogen and creatinine are found in severe diarrhea.

PLANS

Diagnostic

Differential Diagnosis

If nausea and vomiting followed by diarrhea develop within 6 hours of eating at a picnic or restaurant, ingestion of a preformed toxin is likely

(*S. aureus, B. cereus*-emetic syndrome). Diarrhea that develops between 6 and 72 hours after exposure suggests an organism that replicates in vivo before exerting its pathogenic effect. If fever is absent or low grade, and stools contain no gross or occult blood, a noninflammatory etiology is more likely, such as toxigenic bacteria (*C. perfringens, B. cereus*-diarrheal syndrome, ETEC, *Vibrio cholerae*), parasites (*Giardia*), and viruses (Norwalk, rotavirus). On the other hand, the presence of moderate or high fever and gross or microscopic blood in the stool suggests an inflammatory type of diarrhea caused by invasive microorganisms (nontyphoidal *Salmonella, Shigella, Campylobacter, Vibrio parahemolyticus, Yersinia,* enterohemorrhagic *E. coli* [EHEC], *Entamoeba histolytica, C. difficile*). Less commonly, a noninfectious etiology (radiation, inflammatory bowel disease, ischemia) is the explanation. Clinical signs and complications provide clues to the etiology: hemolytic–uremic syndrome in *Shigella* and EHEC; Reiter's syndrome in *Salmonella, Shigella, Yersinia,* and *Campylobacter* infection; appendicitis-like picture in *Yersinia, Salmonella,* and *Campylobacter* infection; thyroiditis, glomerulonephritis, and pericarditis in *Yersinia* infection. Pathogens frequently implicated in traveler's diarrhea include ETEC, *Salmonella,* and *Shigella;* parasites (*E. histolytica, Giardia, Strongyloides, Cryptosporidium*) are responsible for a minority of cases of traveler's diarrhea. Persistent diarrhea (> 2 weeks) may be attributable to parasites, *Shigella, Salmonella, C. difficile, Yersinia, Campylobacter,* and diverticulitis; it may also represent the onset of a chronic condition such as inflammatory bowel disease or radiation injury. Diarrhea accompanied by rectal pain and tenesmus (proctitis) may occur in dysentery (*Shigella, Campylobacter, Salmonella, E. histolytica*), *C. difficile* colitis, proctitis due to inflammatory bowel disease, radiation, and sexually transmitted diseases (syphilis, gonorrhea, *Chlamydia,* and herpes simplex). Venereal infection should be considered even when a history of anal intercourse is not available. Acute diarrhea that develops in the hospital is most commonly due to medications, enteral feedings, fecal impaction, ischemic colitis, or *C. difficile* colitis; other infectious etiologies are rare.

Diagnostic Options

Fecal Leukocytes. A thin smear of feces is placed on a glass slide, mixed with a few drops of methylene blue or Gram stain, and covered with a coverslip. Three or more leukocytes per high-power field in at least four fields constitutes a positive test and reflects underlying bowel inflammation. Fecal leukocytes may be absent in some cases of inflammatory diarrhea.

Stool Culture. Microbiology laboratories routinely culture stool for *Salmonella, Shigella,* and *Campylobacter;* if other pathogens are suspected, the laboratory should be notified. Cultures should be obtained early in the course of the disease when bacterial shedding is at its maximum. Specimens should be plated within 2 hours. If longer delays are expected, specimens should be refrigerated or placed in transport medium.

Stool for Ova and Parasites. Parasite shedding is intermittent, so three stool samples obtained 3 days apart may be needed. Limited viability requires immediate processing. The laboratory should be notified if a particular parasite is suspected.

Endoscopy. The intestinal mucosa may be visualized and specimens obtained for histologic examination and culture. Upper endoscopy permits aspiration of duodenal fluid for parasites (*Giardia, Strongyloides*).

Stool Immunoassay for C. difficile *Toxin.*

Recommended Approach

The first step is to check prescription, over-the-counter, and alternative medications taken by the patient and discontinue likely offending drugs. If an infectious etiology is suspected, the task of the clinician is to distinguish medically important from medically unimportant diarrhea. The vast majority of cases are mild and self-limited and do not warrant the use of antimicrobial agents; a search for specific pathogens is, therefore, of no benefit. Medically important cases of diarrhea require a diagnostic workup (Table 19–32–2). This judgment should be based on several factors: (1) severe clinical illness—severe diarrhea,

TABLE 19–32–2. INDICATIONS FOR DIAGNOSTIC WORKUP AND/OR EMPIRIC ANTIBIOTIC THERAPY IN ACUTE DIARRHEA

Diagnostic Workup Required	Clinical Characteristics	Empiric Antibiotics May Be Advisable
Yes	Severe clinical illness* Severe diarrhea High fever Bloody stools Severe abdominal pain Severe volume depletion Suspected bacteremia (rigors, toxicity) Suspected abdominal abscess Suspected perforation	Yes
Yes	Host's immuno- compromise* Very advanced age Cancer AIDS Corticosteroids Immunosuppressants	Yes
Yes	Persistent diarrhea* > 2 wk	No
Yes	Suspected pathogen requires antimicrobial therapy*	No
No	Traveler's diarrhea	Yes

*These clinical characteristics define acute diarrhea as "medically important."

high fever, bloody stools, severe abdominal pain, severe volume depletion, suspected bacteremia (rigors, toxic appearance), suspected intraabdominal abscess or perforation; (2) host's immunocompromise—very advanced age, cancer, AIDS, corticosteroid and immunosuppressive therapy; (3) persistent diarrhea (> 2 weeks); (4) suspected pathogen requires antimicrobial therapy. To develop a reasonable hypothesis regarding the likely pathogen the clinician must integrate the clinical picture with epidemiologic data, such as history of food ingestion, high attack rate among similarly exposed people, exposure to children, travel, and sexual activity. If the presentation corresponds to the emetic syndrome, spontaneous resolution can be expected in 24 hours; specific diagnosis is unnecessary. If onset of diarrhea is later than 6 hours after exposure, or a history of exposure is lacking, a diagnostic workup should be undertaken only if diarrhea is judged to be medically important. Examining the patient's stool can aid in the decision. A negative test for microscopic blood or pus (fecal leukocytes) characterizes noninflammatory diarrhea; when an infectious etiology is suspected, this finding supports the decision to withhold further workup as most pathogens in this category do not require antibiotic therapy. On the other hand, microscopic blood or pus is frequently present in inflammatory diarrhea; stool should be cultured because antimicrobial agents are recommended for some of the infectious agents in this category. When diarrhea persists longer than 2 weeks, stool specimens for ova and parasites should be submitted. In cases of proctitis, a flexible sigmoidoscopy is indicated unless a positive diagnosis has been made by stool culture or ova and parasites. If acute diarrhea develops in the hospital, a review of the patient's medication card is mandatory because it may reveal potentially offending drugs the physician was unaware of. Enteral feedings may need to be diluted. If fecal impaction is suspected and the rectal examination is negative, a plain film of the abdomen can detect impactions beyond the reach of the finger. In ischemic colitis, plain abdominal radiographs may show the characteristic "thumbprinting" of the colonic mucosa. A history of past antibiotic use (up to 6 weeks after discontinuation) raises the possibility of *C. difficile* colitis; antimicrobial agents should be immediately discontinued unless deemed essential; stool toxin for *C. difficile* should be obtained in moderate to severe cases or when stopping antibiotics is medically unsound. When diarrhea develops in hospitalized patients, other infectious etiologies are very rare. Stool culture and O&P are of little benefit and, therefore, not routinely recommended.

Therapeutic

Therapeutic Options

Fluid and Electrolyte Replacement. Volume repletion may be accomplished intravenously or orally by using oral rehydration solutions (ORS). In infectious diarrhea, the Na$^+$–glucose cotransporter in the intestinal cell remains intact allowing absorption of luminal Na$^+$ (and, therefore, Cl$^-$ and water) if coupled with glucose. The preservation of this important mechanism provides the rationale for using ORS that contain glucose or starch, water, and electrolytes (Na$^+$, K$^+$, Cl$^-$, and bicarbonate) to replenish losses due to diarrhea. A recommended homemade solution contains 3/4 teaspoon salt, 1 teaspoon baking powder, 4 tablespoons sugar, 1 cup orange juice, and 1 L clean water. Rice-based ORS can be prepared by replacing glucose with precooked instant rice cereal (Cream of Rice, Nabisco). Commercial preparations such as Pedialyte (Ross Laboratories) and ElderLyte (NutraMax Products) contain half the amount of sodium of the homemade solution given above.

Antidiarrheal Agents. Bismuth subsalicylate (Pepto-Bismol), in doses of 30 mL every 2 hours after each diarrheal bowel movement up to 4 doses in 24 hours, provides relief of diarrhea by direct antibacterial effect and possibly by binding toxins and stimulating Na$^+$ and water absorption. Kaolin and pectin (Kaopectate) are not recommended because they increase stool consistency without reducing stool volume. Opiate derivatives, such as loperamide (Imodium) and diphenoxylate with atropine (Lomotil), alleviate abdominal cramps and diarrhea by inhibiting intestinal motility. The recommended dose is 2 tablets initially, followed by 1 tablet after each diarrheal bowel movement up to 8 tablets a day, as needed, for 3 days. In adults, the sedative and addictive potential is minimal. Anecdotal reports have suggested that by slowing intestinal transit, these drugs may worsen infectious inflammatory diarrheas and inflammatory bowel disease.

Recommended Approach

The major morbidity and mortality of acute diarrhea result not from the septic state, but from loss of fluid and electrolytes. Therefore, the cornerstone of management is the prompt restoration of the fluid and electrolyte balance, which entails not only correcting preexisting deficits but keeping up with ongoing losses. Most cases are mild and can be managed at home by encouraging the patient to drink plenty of fluids, such as decaffeinated sugared beverages, strained juices, and broth. The electrolyte content of these liquids is inadequate to replenish losses in moderate to severe diarrhea. In such cases, the ORS described above are recommended. In elderly patients and in those with a history of congestive heart failure, the amount of salt in homemade ORS should be reduced by half. When diarrhea is severe, as well as when oral intake is not possible, admission to the hospital for intravenous fluid and electrolyte replacement may be necessary. In addition, hospitalization is recommended for patients with signs of toxicity and, occasionally, when serious underlying illness complicates the course. Patients should be advised to maintain oral nutrition as much as tolerated. Lactose-containing foods should be discouraged because there may be temporary lactase deficiency. Other foods to avoid include raw fruits, leafy vegetables, and caffeinated beverages. Bismuth subsalicylate is safe and effective. Opiate derivatives are best avoided in most cases of acute diarrhea. They are contraindicated in patients presenting with high fever and blood in the stool (inflammatory diarrheas). In the absence of these signs they can be used in mild cases of acute infectious diarrhea and with caution in traveler's diarrhea. Antibiotics are used far too liberally in the treatment of acute infectious diarrhea. In most instances, the illness is not responsive to antimicrobial agents because of viral etiology or its mild and self-limited nature. Inappropriate use of antibiotics exposes the patient to unwarranted toxicity, including the risk of pseudomembranous colitis, while promoting the emergence of resistant strains. Unfortunately, the etiology of acute diarrhea is often not clear at presentation. The physician must then rely on clinical and laboratory clues to decide whether or not to institute antimicrobial agents. Factors that favor the empiric use of antibiotics are summarized in Table

19–32–2 and include medically important cases of acute diarrhea as defined in Table 19–32–2 with the exception of persistent diarrhea (in this instance antibiotics may be indicated depending on the results of stool culture and parasitologic examination) and moderate to severe cases of traveler's diarrhea.

When empiric antibiotics are indicated, ciprofloxacin 500 mg orally twice daily is the drug of choice because it is active against most common bacterial pathogens, except for *C. difficile*. Trimethoprim—sulfamethoxazole in doses of 160 mg/800 mg (1 double-strength tablet) orally twice daily is a reasonable and cheaper alternative.

Table 19–32–3 lists the indications for antimicrobial therapy when the causative pathogen is known or strongly suspected. Antibiotics are not indicated in diarrheas caused by viruses, ingestion of preformed toxins (*S. aureus* and *B. cereus*), *B. cereus*-diarrheal syndrome, *Clostridium perfringens*, EHEC, *Vibrio parahemolyticus,* and prophylaxis for traveler's diarrhea, as well as in most cases of nontyphoidal salmonellosis, where they have been shown to prolong bacterial shedding without decreasing duration or severity of illness. It is well established that antimicrobial agents are useful in the treatment of *Shigella, Vibrio cholerae, Giardia,* and *Entamoeba histolytica* infection because they shorten duration of illness and decrease shedding. Between these two clear-cut extremes there is a third category in which antibiotics may be indicated only in special situations (Table 19–32–3).

Table 19–32–4 lists the antibiotic regimens recommended for specific pathogens.

TABLE 19–32–3. INDICATIONS FOR ANTIBIOTIC THERAPY IN ACUTE INFECTIOUS DIARRHEA

Antibiotics Not Indicated

Viruses

Emetic syndrome (*Staphylococcus aureus, Bacillus cereus*)

Bacillus cereus-diarrheal syndrome

Clostridium perfringens

Enterohemorrhagic *Escherichia coli*

Vibrio parahemolyticus

Prophylaxis for traveler's diarrhea

Most cases of nontyphoidal *Salmonella*

Antibiotics Indicated

Shigella

Vibrio cholerae

Giardia

Entamoeba histolytica

Antibiotics Indicated Only in Special Situations

Campylobacter	Early, moderate to severe dysentery
Yersinia	Severe, persistent or extraintestinal
Clostridium difficile	Moderate to severe infection or if offending antibiotic cannot be stopped
Traveler's diarrhea	Moderate to severe

Salmonella

  Patients who can poorly tolerate bacteremia

    Extreme ages of life: <3 months; >75 years

    AIDS

    Cancer, lymphoma, leukemia

    Corticosteroids, immunosuppressants

    Hemolytic anemia

    Vascular grafts

    Transplant recipients

    Prostheses

    Aneurysms

    Valvular heart disease

  Suspected bacteremia

    Toxic appearance

    Rigors

  Extraintestinal manifestations

    Osteomyelitis

    Reiter's syndrome

    Meningitis

TABLE 19–32–4. RECOMMENDED ANTIBIOTIC REGIMENS FOR ACUTE INFECTIOUS DIARRHEA

Pathogen	Recommended Antibiotic Regimen	
Shigella	**TMP–SMX***	160/800 mg PO q12h × 5 d
		10 mg/kg/d IV in 4 doses × 5 d
	Ciprofloxacin	500 mg PO q12h ×
		400 mg IV q12h × 5 d
Vibrio cholerae	**Tetracycline**	500 mg PO q6h × 2 d
	TMP–SMX	Dose as above
Giardia	Metronidazole	250 mg PO q6h × 5 d
Ameba	Metronidazole	750 mg PO q6h × 7–10 d
Campylobacter	Ciprofloxacin	Dose as above
	Erythromycin	500 mg PO/IV q6h × 5 d
Yersinia	**TMP–SMX**	Dose as above × 5–7 d
	Ciprofloxacin	Dose as above × 5–7 d
		for extraintestinal disease × 3 wk
Clostridium difficile	**Metronidazole**	250 mg PO q6h
	Vancomycin	125 mg PO q6h
Vomiting/ileus	Metronidazole	250 mg IV q6h
Fulminant colitis	Metronidazole plus	250 mg IV q6h
	Vancomycin plus/minus	500 mg via nasogastric tube q6h
	Vancomycin	500 mg IV q6h
Salmonella	**Amoxicillin**	1 g PO q6h × 5 d
	TMP–SMX	Dose as above
	Ciprofloxacin	Dose as above
Traveler's diarrhea	**TMP–SMX**	Dose as above
	Ciprofloxacin	Dose as above
Unknown pathogen	Ciprofloxacin	Dose as above, pending culture

TMP–SMX, trimethoprim–sulfamethoxazole.

*Drug of choice in boldface if more than one drug is recommended.

Treatment of perianal discomfort is a very important part of the management. Use of soaps and wiping after defecation worsen irritation and should be discouraged. Cleansing with warm water using a handheld shower or gentle patting with a damp cotton cloth is preferable. Witch hazel-moistened pads (Tucks) can also be used. Drying should be done by gentle patting with a soft cotton cloth. One percent hydrocortisone cream can be applied to the anus if burning is present. Beware that anal itching and burning can be secondary to anal candidiasis, especially in patients who received antibiotics, and should be treated with an antifungal cream, such as ketoconazole 2% cream, applied locally daily.

FOLLOW-UP

Mild diarrhea in immunocompetent hosts can be followed by telephonic contact in 1 to 2 days. Severe illness, especially in immunocompromised hosts, requires close follow-up. The most common threat of profuse diarrhea is hypovolemia, hypokalemia, and acidosis from loss of fluids, K^+, and bicarbonate in the stool. If bacteremia is present, sepsis and metastatic foci of infection, such as meningitis and osteomyelitis, may develop. Intraabdominal complications are infrequent but life-threatening and include abscess formation, perforation, and peritonitis. Extraintestinal manifestations may not be present initially but may develop later in the course. Reactive arthritis can be seen in *Salmonella, Shigella, Yersinia,* and *Campylobacter* diarrhea. Autoimmune phenomena, such as thyroiditis, pericarditis, and glomerulonephritis, can occur in *Yersinia* infection. Hemolytic–uremic syndrome can develop in diarrhea caused by *Shigella* and EHEC. The most common complication of traveler's diarrhea is a lousy vacation!

DISCUSSION
Prevalence and Incidence

Acute infectious diarrhea is responsible for 4 million deaths per year in the pediatric population worldwide. There are an estimated 12 million cases per year of foodborne infections in the United States alone. The most common etiology of acute infectious diarrhea is viral. *Salmonella* and *Campylobacter* infections account for the majority of bacterial cases in adults. The elderly account for 85% of fatalities; residents of nursing homes are particularly vulnerable.

Related Basic Science

Each day the intestine is presented with approximately 9 L of fluid composed of 2 L of oral intake and 7 L of digestive secretions. The small bowel is the principal site of reabsorption (8 L/d); the remainder is recovered by the colon. The intestine also has a fluid and electrolyte secretory function that is essential to provide an optimal medium for nutrient absorption and to maintain fluid and electrolyte homeostasis.

Noninflammatory diarrheas are caused primarily by noninvasive organisms. The main site of involvement is the small bowel, where most of the daily absorption of fluid takes place, explaining why diarrhea can be profuse. The pathogenic mechanisms are varied: production of enterotoxins (*Vibrio cholerae* and ETEC); intestinal villus blunting and mucosal inflammation (viruses); and adherence of pathogens to the intestinal mucosa inducing alterations that are poorly understood (*Giardia, Cryptosporidium*). The end results of these derangements are inhibition of absorption and stimulation of secretion of water and electrolytes by the intestinal cell. Inflammatory diarrhea is caused by invasive organisms that typically induce gross mucosal damage. The colon is preferentially involved, explaining the occurrence of dysentery in this category. These pathogens can also involve the small bowel, causing a syndrome of profuse watery diarrhea. Mucosal destruction reduces the absorptive intestinal surface, leading to decreased absorption of water and electrolytes. An intense inflammatory response is induced with release of mediators, such as prostaglandins and leukotrienes, that inhibit absorption and stimulate intestinal secretion and propulsive contractions. An exception is *C. difficile*, a noninvasive organism that causes inflammatory diarrhea and gross mucosal destruction by the production of enterotoxins.

Natural History and Its Modification with Treatment

The vast majority of cases of acute diarrhea are mild and self-limited, resolving spontaneously in a few days. Medically important cases also tend to be resolved by the host's natural immunity but may need fluid and electrolyte support until these mechanisms succeed. Antimicrobial agents shorten the duration and severity of cases due to *Shigella, Vibrio cholerae, Giardia, Entamoeba histolytica,* traveler's diarrhea, and in certain cases of *Campylobacter* and *Salmonella* infection.

Prevention

Prevention of foodborne infections includes strict adherence to safety regulations and inspection of foods and food handling facilities. Patients should be taught to avoid eating undercooked meats and not to contaminate raw foods, such as salads, by preparing them on the same surfaces or with utensils used to handle raw meats. Frequent hand washing should be encouraged, especially in the hospital setting. Hospitalized patients with infectious diarrhea should be placed on enteric precautions. Noninfectious etiologies are generally not preventable.

Cost Containment

Every year, acute infectious diarrhea costs billions of dollars in medical bills and lost productivity. Strict application of preventive measures listed above could have a major economic impact. It has been estimated that the cost of a positive stool culture is $1200, making this test among the most expensive in medical practice. This is due to the habit of routinely obtaining stool cultures for diarrhea even when the pretest likelihood is low. Stool cultures, ova and parasites, as well as the use of antibiotics should be limited to medically important cases of diarrhea when the suspected pathogens require antimicrobial therapy.

REFERENCES

Bishai WR, Sears CL. Food poisoning syndromes. Gastroenterol Clin North Am 1993;22:579.

Di John D, Levine MM. Treatment of diarrhea. Infect Dis Clin North Am 1988;2:719.

Fine KD, Krejs GJ, Fordtran JS. Diarrhea. In: Sleisenger MH, Fordtran JS, eds. *Gastrointestinal disease: Pathophysiology, diagnosis, management.* 5th ed. Philadelphia: Saunders, 1993:1043.

Park SI, Gianella RA. Approach to the adult patient with acute diarrhea. Gastroenterol Clin North Am 1993;22:483.

Siegel D, Edelstein P, Nachamkin I. Inappropriate testing for diarrheal diseases in the hospital. JAMA 1990;263:979.

CHAPTER 19–33

Chronic Diarrhea

Veronica Prego, M.D.

DEFINITION

There is great variation in the bowel habits of healthy individuals, ranging from three movements a day to three a week. Therefore, chronic diarrhea is best defined as a departure from the patient's bowel habit in which the stools become more frequent, more voluminous, or looser than usual for longer than 1 month.

ETIOLOGY

A pathophysiologic classification (Table 19–33–1) facilitates understanding of a bewildering list of etiologies (AIDS-related diarrhea is discussed in Chapter 8–76).

CRITERIA FOR DIAGNOSIS
Suggestive

A subjective perception that stools are larger, looser, or more frequent than usual suggests the diagnosis.

Definitive

Objectively, diarrhea is present when stool output exceeds 200 g/d on a typical Western (low-fiber) diet.

CLINICAL MANIFESTATIONS
Subjective

The physician should conduct a directed interview that attempts to categorize diarrhea into one of the following types (Table 19–33–2).

Small-volume Diarrhea. Stools are frequent, small, and dark in color; tenesmus (sensation of incomplete evacuation) is commonly present and reflects proctitis. If there is gross mucosal inflammation, stools may contain blood, mucus, and pus. Pain is frequent, and is located in the lower abdomen, the rectum, or the sacrum. These characteristics suggest left colonic and/or rectal involvement. Stool volume is small as most fluids have already been absorbed by the intact small bowel and right colon.

TABLE 19–33–1. PATHOPHYSIOLOGIC CLASSIFICATION OF CHRONIC DIARRHEA

Osmotic (Malabsorptive) Diarrhea	Poorly absorbable substances in the gut lumen attract water by exerting an osmotic pull.
Enzyme deficiency	
Carbohydrate malabsorption	Lactose intolerance secondary to intestinal lactase deficiency.
Generalized malabsorption	Sugar, protein, and fat are wasted.
Pancreatic exocrine insufficiency	Chronic alcoholic pancreatitis, cancer, surgical resection.
Small bowel disease leading to decreased brush border enzymes	Celiac and tropical sprue, radiation enteritis, diffuse Crohn's enteritis, short bowel syndrome.
Excessive ingestion of poorly absorbed carbohydrates	Sorbitol (chewing gum, candy, fruits), fructose (soft drinks, honey, dried and raw fruits), lactulose therapy.
Laxatives containing poorly absorbed anions	Saline purgatives.
Magnesium-induced diarrhea	Antacids, laxatives.
Secretory Diarrhea	Increased secretion of or reduction in the normal absorption of water and electrolytes.
Bile salt (choleretic) diarrhea	Malabsorbed bile salts spill into the colon, where they exert a cathartic effect.
Terminal ileal dysfunction	
Terminal ileum resection < 100 cm	
Terminal ileal inflammation	Crohn's disease, radiation injury, tuberculosis, lymphoma.
Postvagotomy and postcholecystectomy	
Fatty acid malabsorption	Unabsorbed fatty acids reach the colon, where they stimulate mucosal secretion. Fatty acid malabsorption may result from decreased intestinal bile due to biliary obstruction (cancer of the head of the pancreas, cholangiocarcinoma); cholestatic liver disease (primary biliary cirrhosis, primary sclerosing cholangitis); and as part of a generalized malabsorptive disorder.
Laxative abuse	Surreptitious use of phenolphthalein, bisacodyl, and anthraquinones.
Secretagogue-producing tumors	Rarely, diarrhea is mediated by a circulating secretagogue produced by a tumor. Examples include vasoactive intestinal polypeptide in pancreatic–cholera syndrome (VIPoma), calcitonin in medullary carcinoma of the thyroid, serotonin in carcinoid syndrome, and gastrin in Zollinger–Ellison syndrome.
Alteration of Bowel Integrity	Normal function depends on a structurally intact intestine.
Intestinal mucosal damage	Caused by inflammatory or infiltrative conditions including celiac and tropical sprue, radiation injury, Whipple's disease, Crohn's disease, ulcerative colitis, lymphoma, chronic intestinal ischemia, intestinal tuberculosis, eosinophilic gastroenteritis, amyloid, microscopic colitis, chronic or relapsing *Clostridium difficile* infection, and amebic colitis.
Intestinal anatomic derangement	
Stagnant loops leading to bacterial overgrowth	Fistulas, inflammation, small bowel diverticula, afferent loop in Billroth II gastrojejunostomy, and obstruction from strictures, adhesions, and neoplasms.
Short bowel syndrome	Generalized malabsorption occurs because of extensive small bowel resection.
Altered Motility	
Rapid transit	Postvagotomy, postgastrectomy diarrhea, and hyperthyroidism.
Slow intestinal transit with bacterial overgrowth	Primary intestinal hypomotility, diabetic autonomic neuropathy, scleroderma, amyloidosis, radiation injury, lymphoma, and intestinal pseudo-obstruction.
Dysmotility	Irritable bowel syndrome, painful diverticular disease.
Pseudodiarrhea	Incontinence from anal sphincter abnormalities may be perceived as diarrhea by patients.
Drugs	Almost any drug can be implicated including over-the-counter and alternative medications. Common offenders include Mg^{2+}-containing antacids, antibiotics, antineoplastics, prostaglandin analogs (misoprostol), laxatives, nonsteroidal antiinflammatory agents, alcohol, and caffeine-containing beverages.
Undetermined	*Giardia* and *Cryptosporidium* adhere to the small intestinal mucosa but the mechanism for diarrhea is unknown; colon cancer frequently presents with paradoxical diarrhea. Other causes include Addison's disease, diabetic autonomic neuropathy, and chronic idiopathic diarrhea.

Large-volume Diarrhea. Stools are often watery, profuse, and light in color. Tenesmus is absent. Pain, if present, is periumbilical or in the right lower quadrant. These features suggest small bowel or right colonic impairment; stool volume tends to be larger because these are the intestinal segments where most of the daily absorption of fluids takes place. In this category, if present, abdominal bloating and foul-smelling flatulence suggest bacterial fermentation of carbohydrates seen in malabsorption; stool characteristics are highly variable, ranging from loose to watery. The often repeated statement that malabsorptive feces are large, oily, and hard to flush is true only in a subset of patients.

Undetermined. Many cases of diarrhea escape anatomic classification because involvement is diffuse, or presentation is nonspecific or mild. Also, the subjective nature of the information can limit its utility: patients very troubled by their diarrhea may characterize it as profuse when the actual volume is small.

Objective

Physical examination

In severe cases patients may exhibit signs of dehydration. Feces obtained during rectal examination may contain frank or occult blood in inflammatory processes and neoplasia. Enterocutaneous fistulas and/or perianal pathology may be found in Crohn's disease; joint involvement in Whipple's, collagen–vascular, and inflammatory bowel diseases; peripheral neuropathy in diabetes, amyloidosis, and malabsorption (vitamin B deficiency); ocular involvement in inflammatory bowel disease; goiter in thyrotoxicosis; and vertebral collapse from osteopenia in calcium and vitamin D deficiency.

Routine Laboratory Abnormalities

Severe diarrhea may lead to hypokalemia, increased blood urea nitrogen/creatinine ratio, and acidosis. Anemia and leukocytosis may

TABLE 19–33–2. TYPES OF CHRONIC DIARRHEA AND THEIR CLINICAL CHARACTERISTICS

	Large-volume Diarrhea	Small-volume Diarrhea
Site of involvement	Small bowel, right colon	Left colon, rectum
Stool characteristics	Large, watery, light	Small, frequent, dark
Pain pattern	Periumbilical, right lower quadrant	Hypogastric, left lower quadrant, rectal, sacral
Tenesmus	No	Yes
Bloating, flatulence	Yes, if malabsorption present	No
Fecal and blood leukocytes	Frequently absent	Frequently present
Representative disorders	Malabsorption	Proctosigmoiditis
	Bile salt diarrhea	Ulcerative colitis
	Laxative abuse	Crohn's colitis
	Secretagogue tumors	Radiation injury
	Diseases that alter mucosal integrity	Clostridium difficile infection
	Bacterial overgrowth	Amebiasis
	Short bowel syndrome	
	Rapid transit	Rectosigmoid cancer

be present in chronic inflammatory conditions, chronic infections, and neoplasia. In generalized small bowel malabsorption, hypocalcemia, prolongation of the prothrombin time, hypoalbuminemia, and anemia may reflect fecal loss of calcium/vitamin D, vitamin K, protein, and folate/iron/B_{12}, respectively. Proteinuria may be present in diabetes and amyloidosis.

PLANS

Diagnostic

Differential Diagnosis

Irritable bowel syndrome should be suspected in otherwise healthy individuals with long-standing, ill-defined abdominal pain and diarrhea, often alternating with constipation. Stools can be small, loose, and mucoid or hard and pelletlike. Painful diverticular disease of the colon presents in older individuals with left lower quadrant pain with or without diarrhea.

Nocturnal diarrhea with fecal soiling suggests diabetic neuropathy or anal sphincter abnormalities. Incontinence often occurs when stools are liquid, particularly in the elderly. Nevertheless, it should alert the physician to consider anal sphincter abnormalities that may be misinterpreted by patients as diarrhea.

When diarrhea and weight loss associate, tuberculosis, Crohn's disease, ulcerative colitis, lymphoma, chronic pancreatitis, celiac sprue, tropical sprue, bacterial overgrowth secondary to bowel stasis, and thyrotoxicosis should be suspected. Tropical sprue should be considered if there is a history of having resided in a tropical area for at least 1 to 3 months; *Giardia* infection if there is a history of drinking from natural water sources or foreign travel to an endemic area. Fever may be present in tuberculosis, tropical sprue, Whipple's disease, lymphoma, ulcerative colitis, Crohn's disease, amebic colitis, diverticulitis, and thyrotoxicosis. Flushing is seen in carcinoid syndrome; peptic ulcer and diarrhea in Zollinger–Ellison syndrome; and fever, weight loss, and hyponatremia in Addison's disease.

Diagnostic Options

Table 19–33–3 lists tests commonly used in the diagnosis of diseases that cause diarrhea.

Fecal Leukocytes.
A thin smear of feces obtained during digital rectal examination is placed on a glass slide, mixed with a few drops of methylene blue or Gram stain, and covered with a coverslip. Three or more leukocytes per high-power field in at least four fields is positive and re-

TABLE 19–33–3. CAUSES OF CHRONIC DIARRHEA AND RECOMMENDED DIAGNOSTIC WORKUP*

Etiology	Diagnostic Workup
Osmotic (Malabsorptive) Diarrhea	
Enzyme deficiency	
Carbohydrate malabsorption	
Lactase deficiency	Dairy-free therapeutic trial Lactose–hydrogen breath test
Generalized malabsorption	Serum carotene, stool Sudan stain, 72-h fecal fat
Pancreatic insufficiency	Bentyromide test
Pancreatic resection	History
Pancreatic cancer	CT scan, ERCP
Alcoholic pancreatitis	Plain abdominal films, CT scan

SB mucosal disease
      (see diseases listed under
      Intestinal Mucosal Damage)
	Urine D-xylose

Excessive ingestion of poorly absorbed carbohydrates	
Sorbitol (chewing gum, candy, fruits)	Trial of low-sorbitol diet
Fructose (soft drinks, honey, fruits)	Trial of low-fructose diet
Lactulose therapy	Discontinue
Laxatives containing poorly absorbable anions	
Saline purgatives	Stool sulfate and phosphate levels
Magnesium-induced diarrhea	
Antacids, laxatives, food supplements	Stool Mg^{2+} levels
Secretory diarrhea	
Bile salt diarrhea	Trial of cholestyramine
Terminal ileal dysfunction	
Terminal ileal resection < 100 cm	History
Terminal ileal inflammation	
Crohn's disease	SB x-rays, BE with ileal reflux
Lymphoma	As above, CT scan, biopsy
Tuberculosis	As above, acid-fast stain and culture
Radiation injury	History, SB x-rays
Vagotomy and cholecystectomy	History
Fatty acid malabsorption	
Bile duct obstruction	Sonography, CT scan, ERCP or PTC
Pancreatic head cancer	
Cholangiocarcinoma	
Cholestatic liver disease	
Primary biliary cirrhosis	Liver biopsy
Primary sclerosing cholangitis	ERCP or PTC
As part of a generalized malabsorptive disorder	(see Osmotic Diarrhea)
Laxative abuse	
Phenolphthalein, bisacodyl, anthraquinones	Hospital room search, stool alkalinization, urine laxative screen by thin-layer chromatography
Secretagogue-secreting tumors	
VIPoma	Serum VIP
Medullary thyroid carcinoma	Serum calcitonin
Carcinoid	Urine 5-hydroxyindoleacetic acid
Zollinger–Ellison syndrome	Serum gastrin, secretin stimulation test
Alteration of Bowel Integrity	
Intestinal mucosal damage	
Chronic or relapsing *Clostridium difficile* colitis	History of recent antibiotics, stool toxin enzyme immunoassay
Celiac sprue	SB biopsy
Tropical sprue	Residence in tropics, SB biopsy
Radiation enteritis	History, SB x-rays, SB biopsy
Whipple's disease	SB biopsy with periodic acid–Schiff stain
Crohn's disease	SB x-rays, BE with ileal reflux, endoscopy with biopsy
Ulcerative colitis	BE, endoscopy with biopsy
Lymphoma	SB x-rays, CT scan, biopsy
Chronic intestinal ischemia	History, angiogram
Intestinal tuberculosis	Endoscopy with biopsy, acid-fast stain and culture
Eosinophilic gastroenteritis	Endoscopy and biopsy
Amyloidosis	Rectal valve biopsy, endoscopy and biopsy of involved areas

(continued)

TABLE 19–33–3. (*Continued*)

Etiology	Diagnostic Workup
Microscopic colitis	Colonic biopsy
Amebic colitis	Stool ova and parasites, colonic biopsy
Intestinal anatomical derangement	
Stagnant loops → bacterial overgrowth	[^{14}C]Xylose breath test, trial of antibiotics
Fistulas, strictures, adhesions, inflammation, neoplasms, diverticula, afferent loop syndrome	History, barium x-rays, CT scan, endoscopy and biopsy
Short bowel syndrome	History, SB x-rays
Altered Motility	
Rapid transit	
Postvagotomy, postgastrectomy	History
Hyperthyroidism	Thyroid function tests
Slow intestinal transit → bacterial overgrowth	[^{14}C]Xylose breath test, trial of antibiotics
Primary intestinal hypomotility	Exclusion diagnosis, SB x-rays, SB manometry, † SB scintigraphy†
Diabetic autonomic neuropathy	Evidence of autonomic neuropathy
Scleroderma	History, serum antibodies
Amyloidosis	Rectal valve biopsy, endoscopy and biopsy of involved areas
Radiation enteritis	History, SB x-rays, SB biopsy
Lymphoma	SB x-rays, CT scan, biopsy
Intestinal pseudoobstruction	Plain abdominal films
Dysmotility	
Irritable bowel syndrome	Diagnosis of exclusion
Colonic diverticular disease	History, BE
Pseudodiarrhea	
Incontinence secondary to anal sphincter abnormalities	History, anorectal manometry
Drugs	
Mg^{2+}-containing antacids, antibiotics, antineoplastics, prostaglandin analogs (misoprostol), laxatives, nonsteroidal antiinflammatory drugs, alcohol, caffeine-containing beverages	Discontinue
Undetermined	
Colon cancer	Colonoscopy
Giardia	Stool ova and parasites, stool enzyme-linked immunosorbent assay, for Giardia antigen
Cryptosporidium	Stool ova and parasites
Addison's disease	Morning serum cortisol levels
Diabetic autonomic neuropathy	Evidence of autonomic neuropathy, trial of clonidine
Chronic idiopathic diarrhea	Diagnosis of exclusion

ERCP, endoscopic retrograde cholangiopancreatography; CT, computed tomography; SB, small bowel; BE, barium enema; PTC, percutaneous transhepatic cholangiogram; VIP, vasoactive intestinal polypeptide.
*HIV-related diarrhea is reviewed in Chapter 8–76.
†Available only in specialized centers.

flects gross intestinal mucosal inflammation caused by infections, neoplasia, and inflammatory processes.

Stool Cultures. Infection with *Salmonella, Shigella, Yersinia,* and *Campylobacter* can be prolonged. If diarrhea is less than 3 months in duration, stool cultures should be obtained.

Stool Immunoassay for Clostridium difficile Toxin. Following antibiotic exposure, infection with *C. difficile* can become persistent or relapsing. Test results are available in 4 hours; sensitivity and specificity are 90 and 99%, respectively.

Stool for Ova and Parasites. Barium interferes with viability of parasites; stool for ova and parasites should be collected prior to barium studies. As viability is limited, immediate processing is crucial. Parasite shedding is intermittent, so three samples obtained 3 days apart may be needed. The laboratory should be notified if a particular parasite is suspected. Sensitivity for diagnosing *Giardia* and *Entamoeba histolytica* infection is 60 to 90%.

Stool Enzyme-Linked Immunosorbent Assay for Giardia Antigen. Sensitivity and specificity are 92 and 98%, respectively.

Stool Sudan Stain. The patient is instructed to ingest a high-fat diet for 3 days before the test. A stool smear is stained with Sudan III and examined under the microscope. The presence of numerous fat globules larger than red cells indicates steatorrhea. Unless the test is performed by an experienced observer, results can be unreliable.

Quantitative Fecal Fat Excretion. Stools are collected for 72 hours while the patient ingests a 100 g/d fat diet. Normal fat excretion is below 7 g/24 h; however, a recent study showed that when diarrhea was induced in healthy subjects, fecal fat excretion rose to 14 g/24 h as a consequence of rapid transit (secondary steatorrhea).

Urine D-Xylose. D-Xylose does not require pancreatic enzyme digestion before absorption by the small intestine. It is therefore used to distinguish between small bowel and pancreatic malabsorption. After ingestion of 25 g of D-xylose, the 5-hour urine excretion is measured. Results are low in small bowel malabsorption and normal in pancreatic insufficiency.

Bentyromide Test. After ingestion of bentyromide, the bond between its two molecules (nitroblue tetrazolium and *p*-aminobenzoic acid) is split by pancreatic chymotrypsin, allowing *p*-aminobenzoic acid to be absorbed. Low serum *p*-aminobenzoic acid levels reflect diminished absorption because of exocrine pancreatic insufficiency.

Lactose–Hydrogen Breath Test. Following milk ingestion, lactase-deficient individuals show elevated levels of breath hydrogen because of bacterial fermentation of undigested lactose.

[^{14}C]Xylose Breath Test. In bacterial overgrowth, ingested radiolabeled xylose is metabolized by bacteria, generating $^{14}CO_2$, which is measured in the breath.

24-Hour Stool Volume. Patients are instructed to collect all feces excreted during a 24-hour period into a preweighed container. As the severity of diarrhea varies from day to day, patients should be asked if the collection on that day was representative. Volumes above 200 g are considered abnormal.

Endoscopy. Endoscopy allows inspection of the digestive mucosa and obtaining samples for biopsy, culture, and parasitologic examination, including duodenal aspirate.

Barium X-rays. Upper gastrointestinal series, small bowel series, and barium enema are particularly useful in detecting fistulas, strictures, anatomic alterations secondary to surgery, and small bowel pathology beyond the reach of the endoscope. Enteroclysis provides the best definition of the small bowel mucosa. This procedure involves the administration under fluoroscopy of barium, cellulose, and air via a nasoduodenal tube.

Stool Alkalinization Assay. This assay is useful in detecting surreptitious use of certain laxatives by observing color changes after stool is alkalinized. Phenolphthalein and some anthraquinones turn red; bisacodyl turns blue.

Measurement of Stool Sulfate and Phosphate. Abnormally high levels are seen when sodium sulfate and sodium phosphate laxatives are being used.

Urine Laxative Screening by Thin-layer Chromatography. This test is useful in detecting anthraquinones, phenolphthalein, and bisacodyl.

Recommended Approach

Table 19–33–3 lists studies recommended for the diagnosis of specific diarrheal diseases.

Review medications, including prescription, over-the-counter, and alternative drugs, and discontinue any likely offending drugs.

Review the patient's diet for excessive ingestion of sorbitol and fructose. If present, a trial of a low-sorbitol or low-fructose diet should be recommended. Lactose intolerance is a very common cause of chronic diarrhea; a trial of a lactose-free diet is advisable before a diagnostic workup is undertaken (see below).

Follow epidemiologic clues. A history of travel or foreign residence as well as male homosexual activity indicates early evaluation for parasitic infection. HIV testing should be considered in patients with chronic diarrhea, especially if risk factors for HIV disease are present. Alcohol abuse should lead the physician to suspect alcoholic pancreatitis.

Attempt to classify diarrhea (small versus large volume or undetermined).

- Small volume: Stools are small and frequent, and there is tenesmus; lower abdominal or rectal pain is frequent. A directed search for diseases that involve the rectosigmoid colon is advised (Table 19–33–2). Workup may include stool samples for ova and parasites, barium enema, and sigmoidoscopy with biopsy.
- Large volume: Stools are large; there is no tenesmus or rectal pain. The investigation should be directed toward the small bowel and/or the right colon. Thyroid function tests should be routinely obtained.
- Undetermined: Stool volume is variable; tenesmus and rectal pain are absent. Investigation of both the small bowel and the colon may be necessary.

Follow historical clues (associated symptoms and conditions).

- Chronic diarrhea of short duration, particularly in elderly and middle-aged patients, should prompt an investigation for colon cancer by barium studies or colonoscopy.
- Bloating and foul-smelling flatulence suggest malabsorption. If patients are otherwise well and have no laboratory abnormalities, lactose intolerance is the most likely explanation; symptoms follow ingestion of dairy products, but this connection is missed by some patients. Avoidance of dairy products for 1 week should be recommended as a therapeutic trial. A lactose–hydrogen breath test can be used to confirm lactose intolerance. If diarrhea does not resolve, the physician should take a careful dietary history to establish compliance.
- In generalized malabsorption (steatorrhea) secondary to small bowel disease patients may exhibit weakness, weight loss, or hyperphagia with stable body weight. Laboratory abnormalities consistent with malabsorption may be present, such as anemia from iron and folate deficiency, prolonged prothrombin time, and vitamin deficiencies. The combination of a low serum carotene level and a positive stool Sudan stain can detect 85% of cases of steatorrhea. Seventy-two-hour fecal fat excretion should be obtained in difficult cases and, if necessary, as a confirmatory test for steatorrhea. A low urine D-xylose indicates small bowel disease as the cause of malabsorption.
- Weight loss with severe abdominal pain is seen in pancreatic exocrine insufficiency. The presence of steatorrhea should be evaluated by stool Sudan stain and fecal fat measurements. An abdominal computed tomographic scan should be done to evaluate for pancreatic pseudocysts, calcifications, inflammation, and ductal abnormalities. If the clinical presentation is atypical and the computed tomography scan normal, the bentyromide test may be useful. Weight loss and abdominal pain are also features of Crohn's disease and lymphoma. In colon cancer these symptoms are seen late in the course when metastatic disease has already developed.
- Disorders that promote bowel stasis, such as scleroderma, enteric fistulas, and primary intestinal hypomotility in the elderly, should lead the physician to suspect bacterial overgrowth. Patients present with steatorrhea and cobalamin and iron deficiency, but folic acid levels are normal; diagnosis can be made by [^{14}C]xylose breath test or by a therapeutic trial of antibiotics. A positive diagnosis is preferable to an empiric trial because of danger of inducing side effects and bacterial resistance.
- History of terminal ileal disease or resection, vagotomy, or cholecys-

tectomy raises the possibility of bile salt diarrhea. Diarrhea is mild (stool volume < 300 g/24 h), contains less than 20 g of fat/24 h, and occurs particularly after meals. Response to a trial of cholestyramine before meals supports this diagnosis.
- Suspected psychiatric illness heightens suspicion of surreptitious laxative abuse. Investigation includes hospital room search, stool alkalinization, urine laxative screening by thin-layer chromatography, and measurement of stool sulfate and phosphate.

Follow clues in the physical examination. Occult blood in the stool indicates gross damage to the intestinal mucosa, particularly the colon, caused by cancer and chronic inflammatory conditions, such as ulcerative colitis, radiation injury, and chronic infections. Inflammatory diseases of the colon more frequently give positive test results than those involving the small bowel. Endoscopy and barium studies are useful tests.

Measure the 24-hour stool volume. In puzzling cases, measuring the 24-hour stool volume can be helpful; very large volume diarrhea, usually in excess of 3 L/24 h, should raise the suspicion of vasoactive intestinal polypeptide tumor (VIPoma). Volumes below 200 g/24 h are normal and suggest intermittent, resolving, or illusory diarrhea, or incontinence because of anal sphincter disorders. Stool volume greater than 500 g is inconsistent with irritable bowel syndrome. The latter, although very common, is a diagnosis of exclusion; unless the clinical picture is long-standing and typical, the physician should avoid the temptation of attributing diarrhea to irritable bowel syndrome without further workup.

Therapeutic

Therapeutic Options

Opiate Derivatives. Loperamide (Imodium) and diphenoxylate with atropine (Lomotil) 1 tablet up to four times a day as needed alleviate abdominal cramps and diarrhea by inhibiting intestinal motility. In adults, the sedative and addictive potential is minimal.

Bulk-forming Agents. Psyllium (Metamucil) 1 tablespoon in 8 oz of water or juice, up to three times per day, as needed, relieves diarrhea by absorbing intestinal water. It also may be useful in alleviating incontinence by increasing stool bulk.

Cholestyramine. In doses of 4 g orally four times daily, cholestyramine is used for the treatment of bile acid-induced diarrhea because of its bile acid-binding properties.

Antibiotic Therapy. A 10-day course of ampicillin–clavulanic acid (Augmentin) 250 mg orally three times daily, cephalexin (Keflex) 250 mg orally four times daily, or metronidazole (Flagyl) 250 mg orally four times daily can be used for the treatment of bacterial overgrowth.

Somatostatin Analogs. These can be helpful in reducing diarrhea caused by secretagogue-producing tumors (carcinoid, VIPoma).

Recommended Approach

In mild to moderate dehydration, oral rehydration may suffice (for discussion, see Chapter 19–32). In severe cases, intravenous fluid and electrolyte replacement may be needed. Obviously, the best therapy for diarrhea is the treatment of the underlying disease, for example, gluten-free diet in celiac sprue, antibiotics in bacterial overgrowth, surgery and/or chemotherapy in neoplasia, pancreatic enzymes in pancreatic insufficiency. Irritable bowel syndrome is treated by reassuring the patient and with bulk-forming agents. In lactose intolerance all high-lactose dairy products should be removed from the diet. Milk pretreated with lactase drops (Lactaid) is available in supermarkets or can be prepared by the patient by adding 7 to 15 Lactaid drops per quart, depending on severity. Butter and small amounts of aged cheeses are permissible. Soft cheeses (ricotta, mozzarella, cream cheese) and ice cream should be avoided. Small portions of yogurt containing live cultures may be tolerated by many lactase-deficient people. Lactaid caplets are available but they are only moderately effective. A referral to a dietitian is helpful in educating the patient and ensuring compliance.

Incontinence caused by anorectal disorders can improve with bulk-forming agents or biofeedback. The treatment of fecal impaction consists of manual disimpaction followed by high colonic enemas twice daily.

When the etiology of diarrhea is unclear or when treatment of the underlying disease is unsatisfactory, symptomatic relief can be achieved by using bulk-forming agents or opiate derivatives. Bulk-forming agents are safe except in bowel obstruction and fecal impaction. Opiates should not be used if infection with invasive enteric pathogens, antibiotic-associated colitis, and severe inflammatory bowel disease are being considered because they may worsen diarrhea and precipitate toxic megacolon by slowing intestinal transit. Treatment of perianal discomfort is a very important part of the management. Use of soaps and wiping after defecation worsen irritation and should be discouraged. Cleansing with warm water using a hand-held shower or gentle patting with a damp cotton cloth is preferable. Witch hazel-moistened pads (Tucks) can also be used. Drying should be done by gentle patting with a soft cotton cloth. One percent hydrocortisone cream can be applied to the anus if burning is present. Beware that anal itching and burning can be secondary to anal candidiasis, especially in patients who received antibiotics, and should be treated with an antifungal cream, such as ketoconazole 2% cream, applied locally daily.

FOLLOW-UP

In lactose intolerance, symptomatic relief on a lactose-free diet is satisfactory. In cases of generalized malabsorption, in addition to clinical improvement, previously abnormal laboratory tests (serum carotene, prothrombin time) should be followed to normalization. Perforation can occur in inflammatory bowel disease, diverticulitis, ischemia, radiation injury, cancer, and lymphoma.

DISCUSSION

Prevalence and Incidence

Lactase deficiency is very common, affecting between 60 and 90% of Asians, blacks, Hispanics, and people of Mediterranean ancestry, and 25% of whites. Alcoholic pancreatitis ranks first among causes of malabsorption. Bacterial overgrowth secondary to motility abnormalities is probably the most common cause of malabsorption in the elderly. Secretagogue-producing tumors are rare. Celiac sprue is most common in childhood followed by a second peak between the ages of 20 and 40 years, but can occur at any age.

Related Basic Science

The reader is advised to complement this discussion with the pathophysiologic classification presented in Table 19–33–1.

Genetics

Lactase deficiency, although hereditary, may not become apparent until later in life. Undigested lactose cannot be absorbed, attracting fluid into the bowel lumen; fermentation of lactose by colonic bacteria produces excessive amounts of short-chain fatty acids, which also exert an osmotic effect.

Physiologic or Metabolic Derangement

Osmotic Diarrhea. Poorly absorbed solutes cause diarrhea by attracting fluid into the gut lumen. In pancreatic exocrine insufficiency maldigestion of sugar, fat, and protein occurs because of luminal deficiency of pancreatic enzymes. In diseases that affect the small bowel mucosa, global malabsorption ensues because of loss of intestinal absorptive surface with decreased intestinal brush border enzymes; in addition, colonic bacteria metabolize malabsorbed dietary lipids, producing hydroxy-fatty acids, which stimulate colonic mucosal secretion. Therefore, complex osmotic and secretory mechanisms are at play. In celiac sprue, atrophy of the intestinal villi results from ingestion of gluten, a protein found in wheat, barley, rye, and possibly oats.

Secretory Diarrhea. The primary defect is abnormal transport of ions across the intestinal mucosa, resulting in reduced absorption of or increased secretion of water and electrolytes.

BILE SALT DIARRHEA. The terminal ileum is the site where reabsorption of bile acids takes place (enterohepatic circulation). In terminal ileal dys-

function, malabsorbed bile salts spill into the colon where they stimulate mucosal secretion. Diarrhea is mild, with volumes of less than 300 g per 24 hours and containing less than 20 g of fat per 24 hours.

FATTY ACID MALABSORPTION. Fatty acid absorption requires solubilizing bile salts and an intact small bowel mucosa. In conditions that reduce the amount of intestinal bile (biliary obstruction from carcinoma of the head of the pancreas, primary biliary cirrhosis), fatty acids reach the colon and stimulate mucosal secretion. Stool volume is small, usually less than 400 g per 24 hours and contains more than 20 g of fat in 24 hours.

SECRETAGOGUE-PRODUCING TUMORS. In Zollinger–Ellison syndrome excessive gastrin production by the gastrinoma leads to gastric acid hypersecretion. The acidification of the intestinal milieu results in malabsorption by inactivation of digestive enzymes and by interference with bile salt micellar formation.

Alteration of Bowel Integrity.

INTESTINAL MUCOSAL DAMAGE. Injury to the intestinal mucosa can impair its ability to absorb water and nutrients. The small bowel is the site where most fluid absorption takes place, approximately 8 L/24 h, which explains why small bowel diarrhea is often profuse. In colitis (microscopic, ulcerative, Crohn's, amebic, radiation) the mucosa is incapable of reabsorbing the 1 L of effluent normally presented to the colon every day. When mucosal inflammation is present, inflammatory cells infiltrating the lamina propria release mediators (prostaglandins, cytokines, leukotrienes) that stimulate water and ion secretion.

INTESTINAL ANATOMIC DERANGEMENT. This can lead to stagnant bowel loops with secondary bacterial overgrowth. Malabsorption develops when bacteria compete with the host for nutrients, for example, fermenting carbohydrates, binding cobalamin, and by producing toxins that damage the intestinal mucosa. In addition, bacterial deconjugation of bile salts impairs absorption of fats by inhibiting micellar formation and stimulating mucosal secretion. Interestingly, megaloblastic anemia secondary to cobalamin deficiency resulting from bacterial binding is frequently found, whereas folate levels remain normal or even elevated because folate is synthesized by bacteria and absorbed by the host. Iron deficiency may coexist and pseudonormalize the mean corpuscular volume. Extensive small bowel resection causes malabsorption because of loss of absorptive surface (short bowel syndrome). Resection of less than 100 cm of terminal ileum is not sufficient to cause generalized malabsorption but leads to bile salt diarrhea because of malabsorption of bile salts. More extensive resections can result in global malabsorption. Postulated mechanisms for postgastrectomy and postvagotomy diarrhea include decreased contact time between luminal contents and the absorptive epithelium, poor mixing of digestive juices leading to malabsorption and hypersecretion, and bowel stasis with bacterial overgrowth.

Altered Motility.

RAPID TRANSIT. Diseases that stimulate intestinal contractility induce diarrhea by reducing contact time between the absorptive epithelium and the luminal contents.

SLOW TRANSIT. Intestinal hypomotility leads to diarrhea by promoting bacterial overgrowth.

DYSMOTILITY. Irritable bowel syndrome and colonic diverticular disease are discussed in Chapters 19–7 and 19–50.

Undetermined. In this category, the pathophysiologic mechanisms of diarrhea are poorly understood.

Natural History and Its Modification with Treatment

Resolution of diarrhea, associated symptoms, and laboratory abnormalities is expected when effective treatment of the underlying etiology is available. In the remaining cases, clinical improvement is usually obtained by symptomatic treatment.

Prevention

Avoiding excessive alcohol ingestion prevents most cases of exocrine pancreatic insufficiency. Periodic stool occult blood and flexible sigmoidoscopy have been shown to reduce mortality from colon cancer. The majority of causes of chronic diarrhea are not preventable.

Cost Containment

Stools cultures should not be a routine part of the workup of chronic diarrhea longer than 3 months in duration. An initial review of medications and dietary habits as well as a trial of a lactose-free diet may reveal the cause of diarrhea and avoid unnecessary testing.

REFERENCES

Donowitz M, Kokke F, Saidi R. Evaluation of patients with chronic diarrhea. N Engl J Med 1995;332:725.

Fine KD, Krejs GJ, Fordtran JS. Diarrhea. In: Sleisenger MH, Fordtran JS, eds. Gastrointestinal disease: Pathophysiology, diagnosis, management. 5th ed. Philadelphia: Saunders, 1993:1043.

Lynn RB, Friedman LS. The irritable bowel syndrome. N Engl J Med 1993;329:1940.

Powell DW. Approach to the patient with diarrhea. In: Yamada T, ed. Textbook of gastroenterology. Philadelphia: Lippincott, 1991:732.

CHAPTER 19–34

Traveler's Diarrhea

Stanley R. Yancovitz, M.D.

DEFINITION

Traveler's diarrhea is defined as acute profuse watery diarrhea occurring on travel to a new, usually tropical or semitropical environment.

ETIOLOGY

Approximately 50% of cases are due to enterotoxin-producing strains of *Escherichia coli.* A variety of other organisms produce the rest of the cases.

CRITERIA FOR DIAGNOSIS

Suggestive

Traveler's diarrhea is an acute self-limited diarrheal illness that occurs within days to weeks of arrival in a new tropical or semitropical environment. It is abrupt in onset and unaccompanied by prominent fever or blood, pus, or mucus in the stool.

Definitive

The definitive diagnosis requires demonstration of enterotoxin-producing strains of *E. coli* in the stool of patients with a compatible clinical syndrome with negative studies for other pathogens. These studies are performed only for research purposes and are not indicated or available for routine clinical practice.

CLINICAL MANIFESTATIONS

Subjective

Several days to weeks into a trip, patients develop crampy abdominal pain and malaise and then profuse watery diarrhea. There is low-grade or no fever. Stools are watery without blood pus or mucus.

Objective

Physical Examination

Patients are usually afebrile. They may show signs of dehydration if the diarrhea has not been adequately replaced with fluids. Abdominal examination reveals mild diffuse tenderness, especially during cramps. Bowel sounds are increased.

Routine Laboratory Tests

Complete blood count is normal. There is no eosinophilia. There may be evidence of dehydration with concentrated urine and an elevated blood urea nitrogen. There may be hypokalemia. The stool is negative for occult blood.

PLANS

Diagnostic

Differential Diagnosis

Invasive bacterial diarrheas commonly are accompanied by fever, toxicity, and blood, pus, or mucus in the stool. Mild cases of invasive bacterial diarrheas can mimic traveler's diarrhea. Parasitic infestations with *Entamoeba histolytica* or *Giardia lamblia* more commonly present after return from travel. *Giardia* results in more prolonged disease, commonly with weight loss. Amebiasis may cause fever, prominent abdominal pain, and blood in the stool. Eosinophilia suggests helminthic infection such as strongyloidiasis.

Parasitologic examination of the stool is necessary when these parasites are suspected. A variety of viruses such as the Norwalk agent and rotavirus may cause transient diarrhea in travelers. Some people develop diarrhea with ingestion of exotic foods or with the stress of travel.

Diagnostic Options

Stool cultures for bacterial or parasitologic causes of diarrhea can be performed. Research laboratories can document the presence of enterotoxin-producing organisms.

Recommended Approach

Patients can be educated to recognize traveler's diarrhea and instructed to seek medical evaluation when symptoms and signs of more invasive disease appear. Most cases of traveler's diarrhea can be managed without medical attention with supportive treatment or aborted with judicious use of empiric antibiotics, which patients can bring with them.

Therapeutic

Therapeutic Options

The most important feature of the treatment of watery diarrhea is adequate replacement of lost fluids and electrolytes. Patients should be instructed to drink adequate amounts of water, tea, or carbonated beverages. Bananas and oranges should be ingested to replace lost potassium. Commercial rehydration solutions are available but usually are not necessary. Abdominal cramps can be alleviated by loperamide (Imodium) 10 mg every 4 hours or diphenoxylate (Lomotil) 2 tabs every 4 hours. Bismuth subsalicylate (Pepto-Bismol) 30 mL every 4 hours for eight doses or empiric antibiotic therapy with trimethoprim–sulfamethoxazole 2 double-strength tablets every 12 hours or quinolones such as ciprofloxacin 500 mg every 12 hours along with loperamide can abbreviate the course of the diarrheal illness. Prophylactic antibiotic regimens can diminish the occurrence of traveler's diarrhea.

Recommended Approach

Patients should avoid prophylactic antibiotics as a rule. Careful attention to replacement of lost fluids and electrolytes is most important. Patients may begin bismuth subsalicylate or trimethoprim–sulfamethoxazole or ciprofloxacin with loperamide after the passage of three to five loose watery stools and continue the regimen for 3 days.

FOLLOW-UP

Patients who have continued diarrhea for more than 10 days or who have blood or pus in stool or who exhibit eosinophilia should have further evaluations for other pathogens.

DISCUSSION

Prevalence and Incidence

Traveler's diarrhea is extremely common. Studies have shown up to a 50% incidence in travelers who go from a temperate climate to the tropics for more than 2 weeks. Highest rates are currently seen in travelers to Mexico and Africa. Rates in descending order of incidence are seen in travel to the Middle East, southern Europe, India and Pakistan, South America, Australia, and North America.

Related Basic Science

Bacterial organisms produce diarrhea by a number of mechanisms. *Salmonella* and *Campylobacter* directly invade intestinal mucosa. *Shigella* invades colonic mucosa and elaborates a toxin that causes extensive local tissue necrosis in the bowel. *Vibrio cholerae* elaborates a potent enterotoxin that activates cellular cyclic AMP to cause a massive secretion of fluids and electrolytes. Patients can rapidly die of dehydration but have totally intact intestinal mucosa at postmortem examination. Enterotoxigenic *E. coli* elaborate similar but less potent enterotoxins which activate epithelial secretion. These toxins are initially subdivided

as to whether or not they are heat labile. Clinicians can readily distinguish invasive diarrheas from secretory ones by the clinical characteristics and examinations of the stool. Inflammatory bowel disease causes mucosal inflammation that may be clinically indistinguishable from invasive diarrheal disease.

Natural History and Its Modification with Treatment

Traveler's diarrhea is a self-limited illness. Approximately 80% of cases totally resolve within 1 week. The rest resolve in another week or so. Treatment with antibiotics can abbreviate the average duration of illness by 50%.

Prevention

Careful selection of food and beverages ingested can diminish the incidence of traveler's diarrhea to some extent. Prophylactic antibiotic regimens and prophylactic bismuth preparations diminish the incidence of traveler's diarrhea; however, extensive use of prophylactic regimens causes untoward reactions and increases the prevalence of antibiotic-resistant pathogens. Unless there are special circumstances, it seems best to avoid prophylactic regimens and manage the diarrhea when it occurs.

Cost Containment

Appropriate education and preparation of patients by their physicians prior to travel can prevent costly travel disruptions and unnecessary medical treatments. Avoidance of prophylactic antibiotic use eliminates the cost of managing untoward reactions.

REFERENCES

Dupont HL, Ericson CD. Prevention and treatment of travelers' diarrhea. N Engl J Med 1993;328:1821.
Ericson CD, Dupont HL. Traveler's diarrhea: Approaches to prevention and treatment. Clin Infect Dis 1993;16:616.
Steffen R, Rikernbach M, Wilhelm U, et al. Health problems after travel to developing countries. J Infect Dis 1987;156:84.

CHAPTER 19–35

Infectious Gastroenteritis (See Section 8, Chapter 17)

CHAPTER 19–36

Giardiasis

Stanley R. Yancovitz, M.D.

DEFINITION

Giardiasis is defined as abdominal symptoms and signs generally including prominent diarrhea due to infestation with *Giardia lamblia*.

ETIOLOGY

Giardia lamblia is a protozoan organism with cystic and trophozoite phases. Infection requires the ingestion of only a few cysts, which occurs when there is contamination of food or water supplies or close personal contact with infected individuals in daycare or during sexual activities.

CRITERIA FOR DIAGNOSIS
Suggestive

Prolonged diarrhea (generally > 1 week) in an individual who has likely been exposed to contaminated food or water or who may have had

close contact with an infected individual suggests the diagnosis. Fever and blood or pus in the stool are not present.

Definitive

The demonstration of typical facelike trophozoites or cysts of *G. lamblia* in stool or upper intestinal aspirates in symptomatic patients is diagnostic. Positive assays for *Giardia* antigens in the stool when performed at a reliable laboratory are also diagnostic.

CLINICAL MANIFESTATIONS
Subjective

Infected patients may experience abdominal pain, bloating, increased borborygmus, and flatulence. These sensations are commonly upper abdominal in location and may suggest consideration of gastritis or peptic ulcer disease. Profuse watery diarrhea that may be foul smelling but lacks blood, pus, or mucus generally but not always accompanies the abdominal discomfort.

The presence of any of the following exposures increases the likelihood of giardiasis:

- Recent travel to tropical areas
- Recent travel to Russia, especially St. Petersburg, where the water supply is known to be contaminated with *Giardia*
- Recent hiking, backpacking, or other outdoor activities where ingestion of untreated surface water may have occurred
- Exposure to daycare centers or to children who attend daycare centers
- Sexual activity, especially homosexual, with possibly infected persons

Objective

Physical Examination

Physical examination may reveal evidence of recent weight loss, abdominal distention with mild tenderness, and increased bowel sounds. Fever is absent or low grade.

Routine Laboratory Abnormalities

The stool is negative for occult blood, and on Gram stain no, or few, white blood cells are seen.

PLANS

Diagnostic

Differential Diagnosis

Viral diarrheal diseases generally subside in less than 1 week. Toxigenic bacterial diarrheas usually occur while a patient is still in a new environment, rather than when he or she returns. These infections subside in less than 1 week and do not result in substantial weight loss. Invasive bacterial diseases are accompanied by fever, and blood, pus, and mucus are found in the stool. Amebiasis commonly causes lower abdominal symptoms and occult or gross blood in stools. Amebiasis more commonly is accompanied by fever and amebas are found in the stool.

Diagnostic Options

Stool specimens can be sent for bacterial culture and examined for the presence of ova and parasites. Stool specimens can be sent for *Giardia* antigen detection. Duodenal aspirates can be obtained via the string test or by endoscopy for parasitologic examination. Duodenal biopsies can be performed.

Recommended Approach

Obtain stool for ova and parasite examination, bacterial culture, and *Giardia* antigen. With a consistent clinical picture, treat for *Giardia* even if stool studies are not positive, as *Giardia* may be difficult to find in the stool. Reserve endoscopy for cases in which the stool studies are negative and empiric therapy is ineffective.

Therapeutic

Proven therapeutic regimens include metronidazole 250 mg three times daily for 5 to 7 days and quinacrine 100 mg three times daily for 5 to 7 days. Quinacrine is currently very difficult or impossible to obtain.

Alternative therapies include furazolidone 100 mg four times daily for 7 to 10 days, paromomycin 25 to 30 mg/kg three times daily for 7 to 10 days, and tinidazole 2 g for one dose.

FOLLOW-UP

Relapses of giardiasis may occur. Patients should be instructed to return if symptoms reoccur. Failure to cure or multiple relapses should prompt consideration of reexposure, immunoglobulin A deficiency or other immunodeficiency.

DISCUSSION

Prevalence and Incidence

Giardia lamblia is the most commonly isolated parasite in the United States. Contributing to the prevalence are the hardy nature of the cysts and the ability of the organism to readily infect humans and many animal species which can then contaminate surface water.

Related Basic Science

The precise mechanism of diarrhea due to *Giardia* is not totally defined. Excystation and multiplication of trophozoites occur in the upper small intestine. The trophozoites adhere to the small intestinal mucosa. There is no evidence of toxin production and minimal mucosal inflammation. Small bowel biopsies reveal villus flattening, which may relate to disaccharidase deficiency and malabsorption. Local immunoglobulin A production in the gut appears to be an important host defense mechanism, which probably acts to prevent attachment of the trophozoites to the intestinal mucosa.

Natural History and Its Modification with Treatment

Many exposed individuals can successfully contain the parasite. Symptomatic individuals may suffer substantial discomfort and malnutrition, which can be aborted with appropriate antimicrobial treatment.

Prevention

Travelers and outdoor enthusiasts should take precautions to avoid untreated contaminated water. Daycare centers should enforce high levels of hygiene. Oral–anal contact should be avoided during sexual activities.

Cost Containment

Consideration of the diagnosis and appropriate empiric therapy should avoid some costly diagnostic workups.

REFERENCES

Birkhead G, Vogt RL. Epidemiologic surveillance for endemic Giardia lamblia infection in Vermont. The roles of waterborne and person-to-person transmission. Am J Epidemiol. 1989;129:762.

Char S, Cervallos AM, Yamson P, et al. Impaired IgA response to Giardia heat shock antigen in children with persistent giardiasis. Gut. 1993;34:38.

Craun GF. Waterborne giardiasis in the United States 1965–1984. Lancet. 1986;2:513.

Istre GP, Dunlop TS, Gaspard GB, et al. Waterborne giardiasis at a mountain resort; evidence for acquired immunity. Am J Public Health. 1984;74:602.

Nash TE, Herrington DA, Losonsky GA, et al. Experimental human infections with Giardia lamblia. J Infect Dis 1987;156:974.

CHAPTER 19–37

Amebiasis (See Section 8, Chapter 58)

CHAPTER 19–38

Malabsorption Syndromes

Steven F. Moss, M.B., B.S., M.D., and Peter R. Holt, M.D.

DEFINITION

Malabsorption syndromes are the clinical consequences of an inability to absorb through the small intestine into the bloodstream sufficient nutrients to maintain health, despite a normal oral intake. Malabsorption may be generalized, for all nutrients, or specific, where there is malabsorption of only one particular component of the diet.

ETIOLOGY

Absorbing nutrients into the bloodstream requires digestion of food in the lumen of the gut, uptake from the lumen into the gastrointestinal mucosa, biochemical transformation in the mucosa, and finally export of the nutrient into the portal circulation or the mesenteric lymphatics. Malabsorption may result from abnormality in any one or more of these mechanisms and it is useful conceptually to think of the cause of malabsorption as being abnormal digestion, abnormal mucosal uptake, or abnormal removal from the mucosa (Table 19–38–1).

CRITERIA FOR DIAGNOSIS

Suggestive

The diagnosis of generalized malabsorption is suggested by a patient with weight loss despite an adequate food intake, particularly if this is accompanied by a history suggestive of steatorrhea. Further supportive evidence includes a history of one of the known causes of malabsorption such as extensive intestinal resection or Crohn's disease. The suspicion of nutrient deficiency is sometimes first suggested by abnormalities in routine blood tests.

Definitive

There is no single test that is definitive for the diagnosis of malabsorption, as malabsorption may be limited to one of several different components of the diet; in that case, the definitive test for vitamin B_{12} malabsorption, for example, is quite different from that for lactose. By definition, determining whether there is generalized malabsorption requires at least two separate tests to confirm that there is malabsorption

of more than one nutrient, for example, proving that there is malabsorption of both fat (by the determination of increased fecal fat excretion) and carbohydrate (by an abnormal D-xylose test).

CLINICAL MANIFESTATIONS

Subjective

The clinical manifestations of malabsorption are due to a combination of increased fecal excretion of the nonabsorbed nutrients, colonic symptoms resulting from the bacterial degradation of malabsorbed substrate, and the symptoms and signs of nutrient deficiency. Malabsorption may present in several different ways, depending on whether the malabsorption is generalized or specific; however, weight loss and diarrhea, particularly steatorrhea, are common presenting symptoms. Typically, patients notice that they have lost weight over months to years; this may be despite eating normally, although longstanding malabsorption tends to lead to anorexia. Fat malabsorption gives rise to steatorrhea, the passage of fat-rich stools, which may be graphically described by patients with malabsorption. The classic description is of pale, bulky, and offensive-smelling, "silvery"-colored stools that tend to stick to, and float in, the toilet. Nocturnal diarrhea is a strong pointer to organic disease. Colicky abdominal pain, borborygmi, abdominal distention, and excessive flatus are consequences of unabsorbed macronutrients reaching the colon. These symptoms are most pronounced if carbohydrates are malabsorbed and are metabolized by colonic bacteria; steatorrhea in pancreatic disease may induce few abdominal symptoms.

Symptoms attributable to a lack of nutrients include muscle wasting, weakness, malaise, anemia due to malabsorption of any or all of the hematinics, and the consequences of other micronutrient deficiencies listed in Table 19–38–2.

The etiology of malabsorption may be apparent after taking the history; it is important to inquire specifically about medications and alcohol in patients with suspected malabsorption. Likewise, a history of previous gastrointestinal surgery and possible exposure to HIV are significant. Occasionally, a family history of lactase deficiency, Crohn's disease, or celiac disease may be elicited. Symptoms that started in childhood suggest a congenital defect.

Objective

Physical Examination

Physical examination often provides evidence of nutritional deficiency. Generalized malabsorption gives rise to evident weight loss, muscle wasting, and, in severe cases, finger clubbing, hyperpigmentation, edema, ascites, and hypotension. Some of the signs, and symptoms related to malabsorption of certain specific micronutrients are listed in Table 19–38–2.

Physical examination may also sometimes provide clues to the underlying cause of malabsorption, for example, a gastrectomy scar, evidence of perianal disease due to Crohn's disease, and skin changes of scleroderma or dermatitis herpetiformis, a condition that is associated with celiac disease. Finally, it should be remembered that examination of the stool is often extremely valuable as steatorrhea is virtually pathognomonic of fat malabsorption.

Routine Laboratory Abnormalities

Laboratory abnormalities are very common in patients with malabsorption. Anemia is a frequent finding and this may be micro-, normo-, or macrocytic, depending on whether there is a deficiency of folate, vitamin B_{12}, iron, or all three. A mixed deficiency may be suggested by a dimorphic picture and the blood film may also provide evidence of the functional hyposplenism that often accompanies generalized malabsorption. The serum calcium tends to be low and may be accompanied

---

TABLE 19–38–1. CAUSES OF MALABSORPTION

Maldigestion
  Enzyme deficiency or inactivation
    Pancreatic insufficiency
    Lactase deficiency
    Zollinger–Ellison syndrome
  Decreased micelle formation
    Impaired secretion of bile salts due to parenchymal liver disease, biliary obstruction or bile salt deficiency, e.g., terminal ileal resection or disease
  Rapid transit
    Postgastric surgery
Abnormal mucosal uptake
  Isolated defects, e.g., pernicious anemia, Hartnup disease
  Generalized small intestinal mucosal disease, deficiency or damage, e.g., Crohn's disease, celiac disease, small intestinal resection, AIDS enteropathy, giardiasis, bacterial overgrowth, amyloid, eosinophilic gastroenteritis, tropical sprue, Whipple's disease, radiation enteritis
Abnormal mucosal transport
  Into lymphatics
    Intestinal lymphangiectasia, lymphoma, etc.
  Into vasculature
    Intestinal ischemia
Drugs
  Colchicine, neomycin, methotrexate, laxatives, alcohol, cholestyramine

TABLE 19–38–2. CLINICAL MANIFESTATIONS OF MICRONUTRIENT DEFICIENCY

Vitamins	
A	Nightblindness, hyperkeratosis
B_{12}	Anemia, neuropathies, glossitis
Folate	Anemia, aphthous ulcers
C	Scurvy
D	Osteomalacia, proximal myopathy
E	Ataxia, muscle weakness
K	Coagulopathy, bruising
Minerals	
Potassium	Weakness, cardiac arrhythmias
Sodium	Hypotension, malaise
Calcium	Tetany, paresthesia
Iron	Anemia, glossitis, koilonychia
Magnesium	Tetany
Zinc	Acrodermatitis, poor wound healing

by an elevated alkaline phosphatase if there is bone disease. Other abnormalities include low serum albumin, hypomagnesemia, prolonged coagulation times due to vitamin K deficiency, and electrolyte abnormalities in severe cases.

PLANS
Diagnostic

Differential Diagnosis

In patients with weight loss and diarrhea, the main differential diagnoses are gastrointestinal malignancies and infectious diarrhea. Thyrotoxicosis and diabetes may each cause similar symptoms and, in addition, may also be associated with malabsorption, by several mechanisms. Patients with malabsorption but with only mild diarrhea as their main symptom may occasionally be labeled as having the irritable bowel syndrome; however, the discovery of any abnormal blood test excludes the latter diagnosis.

Diagnostic Options

Many investigations might be performed to establish whether or not there is malabsorption and to find the cause of the malabsorption. Useful first-line investigations include a complete blood count, urea, electrolytes, calcium, liver function tests, and the measurement of serum iron, vitamin B_{12}, and folate levels. A low serum folate suggests recent mucosal disease, as body folate stores are small. The red cell folate level is a more accurate indicator of long-term folate deficiency. The fasting plasma gastrin concentration should be measured if the Zollinger–Ellison syndrome is suspected. Stool microscopy may be helpful in excluding intestinal infections such as giardiasis and confirming fat malabsorption, particularly when the Sudan stain is used. A stool pH less than 5.5 is strongly suggestive of carbohydrate malabsorption and reflects the actions of colonic bacteria on unabsorbed carbohydrates. Plain abdominal radiographs may demonstrate pancreatic calcification (in around one third of cases of pancreatic exocrine insufficiency) or dilated bowel loops with fluid levels in intestinal obstruction.

A useful screening test for fat malabsorption, often used as a surrogate for generalized malabsorption, is the fecal fat excretion. This should be performed on stool specimens collected over a consecutive 72-hour period, while the patient is consuming a high-fat diet (at least 100 g fat daily), as a low fat intake may give a false-negative result. In practice, a complete collection is often difficult to obtain, even when the patient is in hospital. In contrast, the D-xylose test, which is a general indicator of proximal intestinal mucosal carbohydrate absorption, is much simpler to perform and is both sensitive and highly specific for mucosal malabsorption. After an overnight fast, the patient drinks 25 g D-xylose and the urine is collected for 5 hours and blood taken at 1 hour. Normal values are a urine output of at least 4 g D-xylose and a

serum level of at least 20 mg/dL. False-positive results may be due to bacterial overgrowth, in patients taking nonsteroidal antiinflammatory drugs and in delayed gastric emptying, whereas dehydration, renal insufficiency, or ascites may falsely reduce urinary xylose excretion.

The lactose–hydrogen breath test is a simple means to investigate for the specific malabsorption due to lactase deficiency (see Chapter 19–45), and an elevated fasting breath hydrogen reading is often found in the bacterial overgrowth syndrome.

The Schilling test, which measures vitamin B_{12} absorption, is the definitive test for pernicious anemia. In this condition there is malabsorption of radiolabeled vitamin B_{12} (part I Schilling test), which is corrected by the oral administration of intrinsic factor (part II Schilling test). If the part II Schilling test is also abnormal, then this may signify terminal ileal disease, for example, due to Crohn's disease or surgical resection or malabsorption in the terminal ileum due to bacterial overgrowth here. The part II Schilling test is also abnormal in pancreatic insufficiency, as pancreatic proteases are necessary to cleave vitamin B_{12} from "R proteins," which bind B_{12} in the intestine. In the case of bacterial overgrowth, repeating the part II Schilling test after oral antibiotics (sometimes referred to as the part III Schilling test) results in normal vitamin B_{12} absorption. Antibiotics also normalize an elevated fasting hydrogen breath test.

Another test of terminal ileal absorptive function is the SeHCAT test (^{75}Se-taurohomocholic acid). Reduced uptake of this radiolabeled bile salt analog together with a normal Schilling test indicates the rare defect of isolated bile salt malabsorption.

If malabsorption syndrome is established, but the cause remains unknown, the final diagnostic step is to determine whether the malabsorption is due to pancreatic exocrine insufficiency, liver disease or a deficiency of bile salts, or an intestinal mucosal disease such as celiac disease or Crohn's disease. Barium radiology of the small bowel often shows nonspecific changes such as mucosal edema and flocculation of barium in patients with malabsorption, but it may show diagnostic features in Crohn's disease or jejunal diverticulosis and is especially useful for detecting distal small intestinal disease which is relatively hidden from endoscopic examination. For definitive histologic diagnosis of the cause of most cases of malabsorption due to diffuse intestinal disease, however, multiple small intestinal biopsies are necessary, taken by a per oral biopsy capsule or through a conventional upper gastrointestinal endoscope or a longer version thereof.

To investigate whether malabsorption is due to pancreatic disease, it is necessary to assess pancreatic exocrine function. The earliest tests developed involved placing tubes into the duodenum, stimulating the pancreas, and measuring the activity of the aspirated pancreatic secretions. These tests are now rarely used, except in a research setting, as they are unpleasant for the patient and difficult to carry out accurately. Instead, "tubeless" tests of pancreatic function have been developed. In these tests the patient ingests a substrate that is dependent on pancreatic enzyme secretion for hydrolysis. Identifying the breakdown products, in blood or urine, following their absorption is evidence of pancreatic function. Currently available substrates include bentiromide (and measuring *p*-aminobenzoic acid excretion in urine) and pancreolauryl (fluorescein dilaurate is the substrate, fluorescein is excreted in the urine). An alternative test of exocrine pancreatic insufficiency is a therapeutic trial of pancreatic enzyme supplements. This may improve the patient's symptoms and steatorrhea, although it is not entirely satisfactory to treat without a diagnosis.

If a pancreatic cause of malabsorption is suspected, imaging the pancreas by ultrasound, computed tomography scanning, and/or endoscopic retrograde cholangiopancreatography are recommended, as changes of chronic pancreatitis or carcinoma may be found.

Recommended Approach

Although algorithms have been developed to try and simplify the approach to a patient with suspected malabsorption, they are often too unwieldy to be clinically useful. There are a wide range of causes of malabsorption and important clues as to etiology are often found on the history and physical examination; these should prevent all patients from undergoing an identical, exhaustive workup.

If a clinical suspicion of malabsorption is confirmed by blood tests and/or stool examination, then the 72-hour fecal fat excretion should be measured, to confirm fat malabsorption. The D-xylose test is often helpful too, because it is simple to perform and provides a good measure of intestinal mucosal function. Increased fecal fat excretion with a normal D-xylose test indicates that the patient very likely has pancreatic insufficiency. In this case imaging studies of the pancreas should be performed to try and determine the cause; tests of pancreatic function may not be necessary and a successful trial of pancreatic enzyme replacement therapy will confirm the diagnosis.

If malabsorption is not thought to be due to pancreatic disease, then capsule or endoscopic mucosal biopsy and barium radiology should be the next steps. At this point the cause of malabsorption is usually evident; if, following these examinations, bacterial overgrowth is suspected, this can be easily confirmed by breath tests (see Chapter 19–43) and a trial of treatment begun.

Therapeutic

Therapeutic Options

Treatment varies enormously, depending on the cause; however, the general principles of treatment are to correct the nutritional deficiencies and to treat the underlying cause of the malabsorption, wherever possible. Specific treatment of causes is dealt with in the appropriate chapters in this book. In severe cases of malabsorption immediate hospitalization is necessary, to replace fluids and electrolytes while further investigations are instituted. Occasionally, nonspecific nutritional treatment with readily absorbable nutrients is used when the diagnosis is unclear.

Recommended Approach

The correction of nutritional deficiencies may occur spontaneously once the cause of malabsorption is treated. For example, in early celiac disease, the introduction of a gluten-free diet may be the only treatment necessary; however, in most patients with malabsorption or where complete treatment of the underlying cause is not possible, it is necessary to administer the necessary macro- and micronutrients in a form that is readily available for metabolism. Sometimes this may even necessitate total parenteral nutrition, for example, in the short bowel syndrome following extensive intestinal resection.

Diarrhea due to malabsorption usually responds to reducing the intake of fat and carbohydrate. In general, a high-protein, low-fat diet is desirable as this is likely to minimize steatorrhea. As a substitute for fat, medium-chain triglycerides are a more readily absorbed form of lipid as they need little hydrolysis and do not require micelle formation. They may be especially beneficial in malabsorption due to lymphangiectasia, as they are absorbed into the portal circulation rather than the lymphatics. Milk products should be taken with caution because secondary lactase deficiency is very common in many intestinal mucosal diseases and intestinal lactase activity may take months to recover. If diarrhea continues to be a problem, standard antidiarrheal drugs may be tried. Cholestyramine in low doses may be useful in patients with terminal ileal disease or resection and who have diarrhea secondary to bile salt malabsorption. It is of limited benefit in extensive ileal disease, however, because cholestyramine further depletes the bile salt pool and steatorrhea may be worsened.

FOLLOW-UP

Follow-up varies according to the clinical state of the patient and should be modified according to the cause of malabsorption, for exam-

ple, celiac disease, Crohn's disease (for details, see other appropriate chapters in this book). In any patient with malabsorption, important parameters to follow serially in the clinic include weight; complete blood count; liver function tests; iron, folate, and vitamin B_{12} levels; and any previously abnormal laboratory test. Osteopenia is a common and severe complication of malabsorption, particularly in chronic mucosal disease and bile salt malabsorption. To avoid such osteopenia, supplemental vitamin D and calcium may be needed.

DISCUSSION

Prevalence and Incidence

The prevalence and incidence vary according to the prevalence and incidence of the underlying condition responsible for malabsorption.

Related Basic Science

Excessive absorption of dietary *oxalate* may lead to the formation of renal oxalate stones in the malabsorption syndrome. Normally, most dietary oxalate is not absorbed as it is complexed to calcium to form the highly insoluble calcium oxalate. In patients with malabsorption and steatorrhea, however, luminal calcium forms soaps with the unabsorbed fatty acids and oxalate is free to be absorbed. The absorption of oxalate is enhanced by diseases when there is damage to the colonic epithelium, for example, in Crohn's disease, due to bile salt malabsorption. Therefore, patients with steatorrhea and oxaluria should avoid foods rich in oxalate such as tea, cocoa, cola drinks, spinach, and rhubarb.

Natural History and Its Modification with Treatment

The natural history varies according to the underlying condition. For example, in celiac disease, the successful adoption of a gluten-free diet may lead to complete clinical recovery. In contrast, patients with malabsorption due to extensive intestinal resection may need to stay on total parenteral nutrition lifelong, with all its attendant complications.

Prevention

Prevention is not possible in most cases with the notable exceptions of alcohol abuse, peptic ulcer surgery, and some cases of AIDS.

Cost Containment

Careful history taking, physical examination (including examination of the stool), and attention to routine laboratory abnormalities should suggest the diagnosis of malabsorption at an early stage. This should lead to the minimum of diagnostic tests before starting appropriate therapy.

REFERENCES

Bo-Linn GW, Fordtran JS. Fecal fat concentrations in patients with steatorrhea. Gastroenterology 1984;87:319.
Craig RM, Atkinson AJ Jr. D-xylose testing: A review. Gastroenterology 1988;95:223.
Marotta RB, Floch MH. Dietary therapy for steatorrhea. Gastroenterol Clin North Am 1989;18:485.

CHAPTER 19–39

Celiac Disease

Steven F. Moss, M.B., B.S., M.D., and Peter R. Holt, M.D.

DEFINITION

Celiac disease (also known as celiac sprue or gluten-sensitive enteropathy) is a disease characterized by damage to the small intestine in response to certain dietary proteins, termed *glutens,* contained in wheat, barley, and rye. Damage to the intestinal absorptive surface leads in time to severe malabsorption affecting all nutrients, but both the clinical and histologic abnormalities are typically reversible on a diet free of these insoluble proteins.

ETIOLOGY

The toxic compound responsible for celiac disease is the gluten of these grains. In certain predisposed individuals, a T-cell-mediated hyperreactivity to gluten results in damage to the mucosal surface of the small intestine and a subsequent malabsorptive state.

CRITERIA FOR DIAGNOSIS

Suggestive

In childhood, celiac disease often presents as failure to thrive and with diarrhea, whereas in adults, the malabsorption of celiac disease is usually more insidious in onset. Thus, an unexplained iron deficiency anemia or micronutrient deficiency, for example, should lead to investigations to exclude malabsorption due to celiac disease. Celiac disease is an important cause of malabsorption in patients with family ties to northwest Europe, where celiac disease is relatively common, and especially if there is a family history of celiac disease. Around 10% of first-degree relatives of patients with celiac disease are themselves affected clinically and many more may have latent celiac disease. In addition patients with immunoglobulin (Ig) A deficiency have an increased incidence of celiac disease, and any patient with dermatitis herpetiformis should be considered to have celiac disease until proven otherwise.

Several autoantibodies have been identified in the serum of patients with celiac disease and this has led to the possibility of making the diagnosis by noninvasive means. These include antibodies against the α-gliadin component of wheat gluten, antiendomysial antibodies, and antireticulin antibodies. In general, the IgA antibodies have greater sensitivity and specificity than their IgG counterparts, and these antibodies have been used for screening purposes to identify individuals who may have latent celiac disease. Antigliadin antibodies have been found in some other inflammatory conditions, which tends to limit their usefulness, but antireticulin and antiendomysial antibodies appear more specific. Variations between laboratories exist, however, and although several studies have suggested that antibody testing may prove useful diagnostically, mucosal biopsy remains the definitive investigation.

Definitive

The definitive diagnosis of celiac disease requires the demonstration of the characteristic small intestinal abnormality and evidence that this resolves, either (ideally) histologically or clinically following the introduction of a gluten-free diet. In practice, a biopsy of the distal duodenum or proximal jejunum is needed, either by swallowing a spring-loaded capsule or by multiple endoscopic biopsies. In celiac disease, the histologic abnormalities are a loss of villus height and a compensatory crypt hyperplasia together with a mononuclear inflammatory cell infiltrate into the mucosa. Early changes include an increase in the number of intraepithelial lymphocytes. Although characteristic, this pathology is not entirely specific for celiac disease; similar changes may also be found in some other conditions so that it is essential to document an improvement on a gluten-free diet before celiac disease can be diagnosed with certainty. This can best be confirmed by repeating the biopsy after several months, although a clear demonstration of declining serum antibody levels together with clinical improvement may obviate the need for this.

CLINICAL MANIFESTATIONS

Subjective

Celiac disease may present at any age and affects both sexes equally. The original clinical descriptions of celiac disease were in infants who failed to thrive and had overt malabsorption and in middle-aged adults with gross weight loss and wasting. Such cases tend to be diagnosed relatively early today and it is now appreciated that there is a spectrum of clinical manifestations of gluten sensitivity from the latent or asymptomatic case through to the severe cases formerly described. This has been especially apparent with the use of noninvasive testing to screen relatives of clinically affected individuals.

In adults, around one third of the newly diagnosed cases have gastrointestinal symptoms suggesting malabsorption, including crampy abdominal pain, flatulence, diarrhea, and pale stools. It is common, however, for celiac disease to present nonspecifically with the effects of micronutrient malabsorption, particularly in the elderly. These symptoms include weight loss, lethargy, generalized weakness, and even bone pain as a result of osteopenia. Amenorrhea, neurologic symptoms, or even psychiatric presentations may bring the patient to medical attention.

Aphthous oral ulceration or glossitis may be the sole presenting feature of celiac disease, and it is therefore important to consider the diagnosis in a patient with recurrent oral ulcers, particularly if there is a family history of celiac disease.

Objective

Physical Examination

The abnormal physical signs of celiac disease are those of nutrient deficiency and they vary considerably across the celiac disease spectrum depending on the extent of intestinal damage. Adults with celiac disease commonly present with significant weight loss and they are below average in both weight and height, perhaps because the disease has been present without symptoms from a young age. The signs of severe anemia may be present; koilonychia and finger clubbing occur uncommonly (in 5–10%). Examination of the mouth may reveal oral ulceration and glossitis. Hypoplasia of the dental enamel has been described, especially in children. In severe cases, hypoproteinemia is accompanied by ascites and edema, and there may be signs of peripheral neuropathy or nutritional deficiencies in the central nervous system.

A minority of patients with celiac disease, fewer than 10%, have a skin lesion termed *dermatitis herpetiformis.* This pruritic papulovesicular rash on the extensor surfaces of the limbs and on the dorsum of the head and trunk is found only in patients with celiac disease. It may be the sole presenting feature of celiac disease; the intestinal mucosa is always abnormal when biopsied although the extent of involvement is variable. Of interest, the HLA associations with dermatitis herpetiformis are those found in celiac disease, and the skin lesions often respond to gluten withdrawal, implying that dermatitis herpetiformis is within the spectrum of clinical manifestations of gluten sensitivity.

Routine Laboratory Abnormalities

Mild to moderate anemia is frequent and is usually hypochromic and microcytic due to iron deficiency. Indeed, in areas where celiac disease is common the diagnosis is often considered in patients who present with anemia alone.

Chronic nutrient malabsorption together with diarrhea contributes to electrolyte abnormalities in untreated celiac disease. These include hypokalemia, hypomagnesemia, hyponatremia, hypocalcemia, and metabolic acidosis. Hypoalbuminemia due to both malabsorption and protein loss into the gut lumen is usual; hypoglobulinemia is more rare.

PLANS
Diagnostic
Differential Diagnosis

Unless the patient has dermatitis herpetiformis at presentation or a family history of celiac disease, in which case the diagnosis is relatively easy, the differential diagnosis is that of the patient with malabsorption. Investigations should be performed to document this (see Chapter 19–38). An abnormal D-xylose test is particularly helpful because it establishes that the malabsorption is due to a mucosal disease of the proximal small intestine.

Diagnostic Options

The diagnostic options include making a diagnosis on clinical grounds, perhaps with the measurement of serum antibodies, and then proceeding to a trial of gluten withdrawal, and making a formal diagnosis by intestinal mucosal biopsy before and after a gluten-free diet.

A low serum folate level despite an adequate intake is an important laboratory clue to early celiac disease. The blood film often shows evidence of folate or, more rarely, vitamin B_{12} deficiency or an associated hyposplenism. Abnormal blood coagulation from decreased vitamin K levels may be present and deficiencies of other vitamins and trace elements have also been described. The serum alkaline phosphatase is usually raised when there is osteomalacia.

Recommended Approach

We strongly recommend obtaining an intestinal biopsy, especially in view of the implications of making the diagnosis on future medical care (see Follow-up). It is quite common for patients to adhere to the relatively restrictive gluten-free diet for years when in retrospect they never did have celiac disease.

Biopsy may be performed with either a suction capsule passed into the jejunum by mouth or by multiple endoscopic pinch biopsies of the distal duodenum. Endoscopy also offers the opportunity to observe the duodenal mucosa directly; characteristic endoscopic signs have been described.

Therapeutic

The treatment of gluten-sensitive enteropathy is the avoidance of gluten, by dietary avoidance of products containing wheat, barley, rye, and usually oats. Most patients need to avoid gluten completely but some may be able to tolerate a small amount; however, avoiding gluten altogether is easier said than done. Despite scrupulous attention to the diet, gluten is sometimes inadvertently ingested in foods that contain no apparent cereal product. Fortunately, useful dietary advice may be obtained from self-help groups such as the Celiac Disease Foundation or the American Celiac Society. Failure to improve clinically within a few weeks on a gluten-free diet occurs in about one third of patients and is usually either because the patient is still ingesting gluten, which may be confirmed by the failure of serum antibodies to fall with time, or because the diagnosis is incorrect; for example, a lymphoma may have been missed. A third possibility is that the patient has a clinical type of sprue that is refractory to gluten withdrawal. This occurs in a minority of patients who, despite apparently avoiding all gluten, fail to improve. They often require steroid treatment and occasionally immunosuppression with cyclosporine or azathioprine. Finally, there may be a subset of patients who do not improve because they have an associated pancreatic insufficiency. Subclinical exocrine pancreatic insufficiency is fairly common in celiac disease, but overt disease is very rare.

Finally, it should be remembered that in patients who present with severe nutritional deficiencies it is necessary to replace calories, vitamins, minerals, and sometimes fluids and electrolytes rapidly, before the intestinal mucosa has begun to recover.

FOLLOW-UP

A repeat biopsy a few months after the institution of a gluten-free diet is advisable to ensure that the diagnosis is correct. The initial "flat" jejunal mucosa may have been due to a condition other than celiac disease, for example, tropical sprue, ulcerative jejunoileitis, diffuse lymphoma, and cow's milk protein intolerance. Some even advocate a third biopsy after rechallenging with gluten, as the diagnosis is so important to make. Alternatively, monitoring a fall in serum antibody levels has been used as a surrogate marker of histologic improvement.

Follow-up of the patient with celiac disease should be lifelong, as a number of diseases are associated with celiac disease, as are several well-defined potentially serious complications. Follow-up should include the periodic measurement of the complete blood count, electrolytes, liver function tests, and serum folate to screen for noncompliance or the development of a complication. In addition, calcium and vitamin D levels should be checked because of the complication of the development of osteopenia, especially in women. Osteopenia leading to osteoporosis and osteomalacia occurs in a substantial number of patients with celiac disease, despite adherence to a gluten-free diet. Supplementary calcium is therefore probably advisable for women of all ages, together with hormone replacement when necessary.

Other common associated abnormalities in celiac disease include pancreatic hypofunction, which is usually clinically unimportant, hyposplenism, and IgA deficiency, but there are a number of other conditions associated with celiac disease. These include diabetes mellitus, IgA nephropathy, inflammatory bowel disease, and immune-mediated liver disease.

The feared complication of celiac disease is the development of a gastrointestinal neoplasm. Overall the recorded incidence of malignancies in celiac disease (11–15%) is not dissimilar from that of the general population, and children with celiac disease who are diagnosed and treated lifelong appear not to be at increased risk. The increased incidence of carcinoma is due mainly to an 80-fold increased risk of developing adenocarcinoma of the small intestine; however, because this is an exceedingly rare tumor in the general population (around 1 case per 100,000 per year), it is still a rare cause of death in celiac disease patients, despite the increased relative risk. Carcinoma of the esophagus and pharynx is slightly more common in celiac disease patients.

Lymphoma is also relatively more common in patients with celiac disease: around twice that of the general population due to the increased incidence of small intestinal T-cell lymphomas. This may be an overestimate, however, because diffuse small intestinal lymphoma is notoriously difficult to distinguish from celiac disease and some patients thought to have celiac disease may turn out to have had a lymphoma all along. As uncontrolled studies suggest that adhering to a gluten-free diet lowers the incidence of developing a lymphoma, it is probably advisable for all celiac disease patients to avoid gluten completely, even though they may tolerate it without symptoms. In fact, a lifelong gluten-free diet is almost impossible to maintain and most patients continue to have some intestinal histologic abnormalities.

DISCUSSION
Prevalence

The distribution of celiac disease varies around the world. It is most prevalent in northwestern Europe, with a prevalence of 1 in 300 in western Ireland, but is much less common in non-Caucasians. The prevalence in U.S. Caucasians is around 1 per 5000.

Related Basic Science
Genetics

Celiac disease is closely associated with certain major histocompatibility complex haplotypes, in particular HLA-B8, -DR3, -DR7, -DQ2 and heterozygosity for HLA-DR5/-DR7. In different populations 80 to 100% of celiac disease patients are found to have one of these haplotypes, yet most individuals with these haplotypes do not go on to develop celiac disease. Precisely how a particular haplotype confers hyperreactivity to gluten remains unclear but is presumably related to the ability to present gluten antigens to the immune system in such a way as to chronically stimulate a T-cell response without the induction of tolerance.

Although the variation in HLA genetics explains most of the epidemiology of celiac disease, environmental factors may still be important, as monozygotic twins have a concordance rate of only 75%. The nongenetic elements may include the introduction of gluten into an infant's diet too early in life and exposure to an enteric virus (adenovirus 12) which may induce the production of antibodies that cross-react with gluten.

Molecular Biology

Recent studies have established that the toxic moiety of the wheat gluten responsible for immunogenicity is a short oligopeptide sequence common to several wheat glutens. This raises the possibility of manufacturing products from wheat that are deficient in only this toxin and are therefore safe for patients with celiac disease.

Anatomic Derangement

Celiac disease is a purely mucosal disease, usually starting in the duodenum and extending distally in more severe cases. There is a loss of villus height, which occurs within hours of gluten challenge, and a compensatory hyperplasia of the crypts so that the mucosal thickness is little changed. The crypt hyperplasia is due to an increase in the number of relatively undifferentiated enterocytes, however, so that the net effect is a loss of functional absorptive surface. Flattening of the mucosa is accompanied by an infiltrate of CD4-positive lymphocytes and IgA-secreting plasma cells in the lamina propria and an increase in the number of lymphocytes within the epithelium itself. These intraepithelial lymphocytes are mostly CD8-positive T cells which are capable of secreting cytokines. In celiac disease there is an increase in the population of T cells expressing the less common gamma/delta receptor and the enterocytes also carry evidence of immune activation by virtue of increased expression of major histocompatibility complex class II antigens. Interestingly, many of these changes, even including mucosal flattening, have been found in the family members of patients with celiac disease and also in individuals found to have celiac disease-related antibodies in screening studies. The incidence of such "latent" celiac disease is not established, but the discovery of asymptomatic patients has possible implications in the prevention of the conditions associated with celiac disease.

Natural History and Its Modification with Treatment

Untreated celiac disease may progress to a chronic debilitating state and even death from malnutrition or the development of an intestinal neoplasm. In contrast, treated celiac disease patients have a normal life expectancy. As discussed above, it is unclear which, if any, patients with latent celiac disease are at increased risk of developing the disease clinically or any of its complications.

Prevention

There is currently no proven preventive measure. In some parts of the world apparent declines in the incidence of celiac disease have accompanied changes in the way infants are fed, based on recommendations to delay the onset of feeding gluten. It remains to be established, however, whether this will prove to be an effective prophylactic method. Screening high-risk populations to identify latent celiac disease patients may ultimately prove beneficial, should early dietary intervention prevent the development of frank celiac disease or its complications.

Cost Containment

Cost could potentially be reduced by limiting the number of endoscopies and biopsies to make and confirm the diagnosis; however, this may merely result in an uncertain or wrong diagnosis, which is likely to prove far more expensive in the long term. The most important way to reduce costs is to think of the diagnosis early in a patient with suspected malabsorption and to biopsy the duodenum sooner rather than later.

REFERENCES

Goggins MG, Kelleher D. Celiac disease and other nutrient related injuries to the gastrointestinal tract. Am J Gastroenterol 1994;89(sppl.):S2.
Holmes GKT, Prior P, Lane MR, et al. Malignancy in celiac disease: Effect of a gluten free diet. Gut 1989;30:333.
Talley NJ, Valdovinos M, Petterson TM, et al. Epidemiology of celiac sprue: A community-based study. Am J Gastroenterol 1994;89:843.
Walters JRF. Bone mineral density in celiac disease. Gut 1994;35:150.

CHAPTER 19–40

Tropical Sprue

Steven F. Moss, M.B., B.S., M.D., and Peter R. Holt, M.D.

DEFINITION

Tropical sprue is a chronic malabsorptive condition due to jejunal mucosal damage occurring in those who live in or have traveled to the tropics.

ETIOLOGY

There is considerable debate about the precise etiology of tropical sprue. Travelers who develop tropical sprue commonly recall an acute onset of diarrhea consistent with an infective enteritis prior to their progressive chronic clinical course. This has led to the suggestion that the jejunal mucosal abnormality of tropical sprue is a postinfective enteropathy. Once the disease is established, however, the beneficial clinical response to broad-spectrum antibiotics in these patients implies that bacteria have a key role in the maintenance of the disease, but whether bacterial overgrowth is a primary or a secondary phemonemon is unclear. No specific bacteria have been consistently identified and it remains possible that other unidentified pathogens, such as enteric

viruses, may be important etiologic factors in areas where subclinical malabsorption is common.

CRITERIA FOR DIAGNOSIS
Suggestive

The diagnosis of tropical sprue should be entertained in any person living in or returning from the tropics with a history of diarrhea and clinical or biochemial evidence of malabsorption, particularly if there is megaloblastic anemia.

Definitive

Because subclinical malabsorption is common in the tropics, the diagnosis of tropical sprue depends not only on the laboratory findings but also on definite symptoms and signs of malabsorption. Biochemical evidence of malabsorption of at least two distinct substances (such as xylose and vitamin B_{12}) must be present, as evidence of a diffuse intestinal process, together with structural evidence of jejunal abnormality. In addition certain specific microbial pathogens of the gut, such as *Giardia*, should be excluded.

CLINICAL MANIFESTATIONS
Subjective

The clinical picture depends to some degree on the nutritional status of the patient before the illness develops. Thus, the disease is less severe in a previously well-nourished traveler. The typical symptoms are of an acute diarrheal illness, often with fever, malaise, and weakness, which lasts for a week or so. This is then followed by the development of a more chronic diarrhea, weight loss, and fatigue. The diarrhea is usually of large bulky, pale stools and is accompanied by borborygmi and the passage of flatus. Secondary lactose intolerance also occurs, due to loss of intestinal brush border lactase activity. The weight loss takes months to develop and is often severe. It is thought to be due to a combination of both nutrient malabsorption and anorexia from chronic ill health and it is often accompanied by anemia.

Objective
Physical Examination

In the early stages there are few abnormal signs except hyperactive bowel sounds. As the illness progresses there is evident weight loss and anemia. In severe cases, there may be fluid retention, hypotension, glossitis, and muscle wasting.

Routine Laboratory Investigations

There may be no laboratory abnormalities in the early stages. As the disease progresses megaloblastic anemia occurs due to a combination of folate and vitamin B_{12} deficiency. There may also be hypomagnesemia and hypocalcemia, though rarely of the degree seen in celiac disease. Serum albumin and globulin levels are usually low as a result of the malabsorption and a protein-losing enteropathy.

PLANS
Diagnostic
Differential Diagnosis

Tropical sprue is not the only cause of malabsorption seen in the tropics so that it is important to consider and exclude other potentially treatable disorders. Among these are chronic infections with intestinal tuberculosis, *Giardia*, *Cryptosporidium*, and other intestinal parasites, chronic liver disease, and tropical calcific pancreatitis.

Diagnostic Options

Simple investigations to confirm malabsorption include the D-xylose test, which is always abnormal in tropical sprue; the Schilling test (parts I and II) to confirm that there is vitamin B_{12} malabsorption that is not corrected with the addition of exogenous intrinsic factor; and the measurement of fecal fat excretion. In addition, several stools should be examined to ensure there are no parasites living in the gut. Barium radiology is not diagnostic but may be useful in excluding inflammatory intestinal disease or intestinal obstruction. The typical findings of thickening of the jejunal folds on a barium follow-through examination, together with flocculation of barium and slow gut transit, are seen in several intestinal mucosal disease processes. Jejunal biopsy, either through the endoscope or by a swallowed spring-loaded capsule, is very helpful in confirming the diagnosis; however, clear histologic changes in the jejunal mucosa (see below) may not occur until several months into the illness. The finding of a completely flat mucosa (subtotal villous atrophy) is most unusual and, if present, suggests celiac rather than tropical sprue.

Recommended Approach

In a traveler returning from the tropics with a history typical for tropical sprue and with no intestinal parasites found in the stool, a trial of treatment is warranted without further investigation. If, however, the patient then fails to make a rapid recovery, investigations into other causes of the diarrhea should be instigated rapidly.

Therapeutic
Therapeutic Options

Tropical sprue responds to a combination of antimicrobial therapy and folic acid. Folic acid may be important not only for correcting a folate-deficient anemia, but also for restoring normal enterocyte function. Giving folate alone, however, only partially corrects the loss of intestinal function.

Recommended Approach

Tetracycline is the drug of choice, in a dose of 250 mg four times daily, together with folic acid 5 mg per day. This treatment should be taken for several weeks, if not months, with the duration of treatment being decided by clinical features, as there are no trials on which to base recommendations. In patients with definite vitamin B_{12} malabsorption, daily followed by weekly intramuscular vitamin B_{12} injections are necessary.

In the severely malnourished patient, hospitalization and parenteral nutrition may be needed until there is a recovery of gut function.

FOLLOW-UP

Tropical sprue usually responds rapidly to treatment, especially in those travelers who return to temperate climes, so that it is not necessary to see these patients repeatedly in the office. In contrast, in some poorly nourished populations in the tropics the intestinal mucosa may never revert to normal, even after appropriate therapy. This has been taken as further evidence that it is the continuing microbial exposure that is responsible for tropical sprue. Intestinal lymphoma does not develop as a complication of tropical sprue, in contrast to the case in celiac disease.

DISCUSSION
Prevalence and Incidence

The true prevalence and incidence are unknown but severe cases are now not seen as commonly as they were 50 years ago. Tropical sprue is found throughout the central third of the globe, with the notable exceptions of sub-Saharan Africa and Jamaica. It is endemic in much of southern India. Indeed, the small intestinal mucosa of apparently healthy people in the tropics is often abnormal compared with residents of temperate climates, with evidence of increased inflammatory cells in the lamina propria and a more rapid turnover of epithelial cells. These microscopic abnormalities are often accompanied by biochemical evidence of mild malabsorption and appear to be a reaction to the luminal microflora of a tropical environment. These changes disappear spontaneously a few years after moving to a temperate zone.

Related Basic Science
Genetics

There is some evidence that the development of tropical sprue is linked to the patient's HLA haplotype, but this area warrants further study.

Physiologic or Metabolic Derangement

Tropical sprue was first described in travelers in the tropics more than a century ago. In recent years it has become apparent that similar but milder intestinal abnormalities and biochemical evidence of mild malabsorption occur commonly even in indigenous dwellers in many areas of the tropics. The clinical syndrome of tropical sprue may therefore represent only the end of a spectrum of intestinal abnormality found in those exposed to a tropical environment. Most evidence points to the primary abnormality in tropical sprue being luminal in origin, probably due to chronic microbial infection. The effect of this is increased proliferation throughout the intestinal epithelium, from the crypt stem cells right up to the mature cells at the villus tip. Whether the proliferative response is due to a direct effect on the stem cell or whether this represents a response to increased cell death at the villus tip is not known. Abnormalities of secretion of several gut hormones have been documented but they are also found in diarrhea of other etiologies, so that they probably represent the response to an increased fluid load in the lumen of the gut rather than the cause of tropical sprue. The jejunum is not the only part of the gut that is affected by tropical sprue; decreased gastric acid secretion is a common accompaniment, and in addition, the capacity of the colon to absorb the increased fluid secreted by the small intestine appears to be reduced.

Anatomic Derangement

The small intestinal abnormality found in tropical sprue is a flattening and broadening of the villi and a deepening of the intestinal crypts (crypt hyperplasia). The net result is a reduction in the normal villus:crypt height ratio. This is accompanied by an infiltrate of lymphocytes in the lamina propria, particularly of T cells bearing the gamma/delta receptor, as in celiac disease.

Natural History and Its Modification with Treatment

Tropical sprue had a fatality rate of 10 to 20% in the preantibiotic era. With modern antimicrobial therapy and correction of the associated vitamin deficiencies, a rapid return to health is to be expected. Nevertheless, recurrences occur in up to half of those treated for tropical sprue who continue to live in endemic areas.

Prevention

The increasingly widespread use of prophylactic antibiotics by travelers and their use early in the course of diarrhea may be an important factor in the apparent decline in the incidence of tropical sprue. Prompt recognition of the early stages of the illness by medical staff and the changing emphasis from antidiarrheal agents to rehydration and antibiotics may also prevent or limit the disease at an early stage, as has been shown in studies in military personnel.

Cost Containment

The degree to which a patient is investigated may vary from a trial of treatment to an extensive workup, and the extent of the investigation depends on the patient's history. In many cases costs may be contained by limiting the number of investigations performed when the history is typical of tropical sprue and other causes of malabsorption are unlikely.

REFERENCE

Mathan VI. Tropical sprue. Springer Semin Immunopathol 1990;12:231.

CHAPTER 19–41

Eosinophilic Gastroenteritis

Steven F. Moss, M.B., B.S., M.D., and Peter R. Holt, M.D.

DEFINITION

Eosinophilic gastroenteritis is a rare, chronic disorder characterized by a dense infiltrate of eosinophils within the wall of the gut in the absence of parasitic infection or systemic disease. It may affect any part of the gastrointestinal tract and therefore give rise to a wide range of symptoms, although the gastric antrum and the proximal small intestine are the sites most commonly affected. The disease may involve one or more of the layers of the gut wall and has traditionally been classified as being predominantly either mucosal, muscular, or serosal.

ETIOLOGY

The cause of eosinophilic gastroenteritis is not known; however, the frequent association of atopy and the occurrence of allergic diseases in individuals with eosinophilic gastroenteritis and its response to anti-allergic medications suggest that the condition may be a response to an oral allergen. Nevertheless, a true food allergy is rarely found in this condition. Eosinophilic gastroenteritis may not be the result of only one disease process, but may represent a common response to a range of different pathogenic mechanisms.

CRITERIA FOR DIAGNOSIS
Suggestive

The diagnosis of eosinophilic gastroenteritis should be considered in any individual with chronic abdominal symptoms and an unexplained eosinophilia. Sometimes the diagnosis is suggested by mucosal abnormality found during radiologic or endoscopic imaging of the gut. A wide variety of abnormalities have been described using various imaging techniques, although the findings are rather nonspecific; none is pathognomonic for eosinophilic gastroenteritis. The finding of a high eosinophil count in the ascitic fluid is strongly suggestive of the serosal form of eosinophilic gastroenteritis.

Definitive

Definitive diagnosis requires the demonstration of large quantities of eosinophils in a biopsy of the gut wall. This may be obtained either endoscopically or at operation. Typically, most of the eosinophils congregate in the submucosa but any layer of the gut may be involved, giving rise to ulceration and edematous, thickened bowel. In making the diagnosis it is essential to exclude infestation by gastrointestinal parasites as the cause for the eosinophilic infiltrate.

CLINICAL MANIFESTATIONS
Subjective

Eosinophilic gastroenteritis has been reported in all ages and racial groups, although it is most commonly found in middle-aged men. The symptoms are often vague and may be present for months to years. They vary according to both the site of involvement and the depth of the gut wall that is involved. For example, involvement of the muscular layer may lead to intestinal obstruction, whereas serosal disease is often accompanied by ascites.

Abdominal pain is almost always present and anorexia, nausea and vomiting, and diarrhea are found in around half those affected. Weight loss occurs in a fifth of cases; gastrointestinal bleeding and constipation are rare presenting complaints.

Approximately half the patients have a history of an allergic disorder or an apparent food intolerance, particularly patients subsequently found to have serosal disease.

Objective
Physical Examination

Physical examination is rarely helpful; occasionally there may be signs of malabsorption or ascites, the latter accompanying serosal disease.

Routine Laboratory Abnormalities

The peripheral blood usually contains increased numbers of eosinophils, about 2 to 10 times the normal number. The sedimentation rate is sometimes elevated and the serum albumin is low in around one third of cases, particularly in the mucosal form of the disease. Other routine laboratory tests tend to be normal.

PLANS

Diagnostic

Differential Diagnosis

Other major causes of eosinophilia include parasitic infection, drug reactions, and some systemic vasculitides and connective tissue diseases. An eosinophilic ascitic fluid may be caused by lymphoma, a vasculitic process, a ruptured hydatid cyst, or chronic peritoneal dialysis; however, the peripheral eosinophil count is often only mildly elevated so that the differential diagnosis includes a wide range of gastrointestinal diseases, including Crohn's disease and ulcerative jejunoileitis, lymphoma and gastric carcinoma, and Menetrier's disease. Occasionally, an inflammatory fibroid polyp (eosinophilic granuloma) may cause some diagnostic confusion for the pathologist. It should also be remembered that eosinophils constitute part of the cellular infiltrate whenever the gut is inflamed, particularly in Crohn's disease. In eosinophilic gastroenteritis, however, eosinophils are almost the only component of the infiltrate.

Diagnostic Options

Barium radiology and computed tomography scanning may be normal or may demonstrate nonspecific changes, the most common abnormality being an edematous area of gut wall due to mucosal disease. Other radiologic findings such as obstruction and stricturing, typically of the antrum and pylorus, suggest that there is involvement of the muscular layer.

Endoscopy provides the means to search directly for mucosal disease and to take biopsies. The abnormal endoscopic appearances that occur if there is mucosal disease include ulceration, edema, and erythema, but these abnormalities are nonspecific and require biopsy for definitive diagnosis.

Recommended Approach

In the past the diagnosis was often made after an inconclusive and extensive workup, eventually culminating in laparotomy. Barium radiology is often still useful to identify the region affected, particularly if it is the small intestine, as this area is relatively difficult to examine endoscopically; however, the increasing use of endoscopy and biopsy in the investigation of gastrointestinal symptoms has changed the way that the diagnosis is usually made. If the disease is suspected then multiple endoscopic biopsies should be taken, from the stomach and jejunum in particular. The finding of a dense eosinophilic infiltrate should then stimulate an active search to exclude parasitic infection. This is accomplished by searching for ova, cysts, and parasites in the stool and by duodenal biopsy and the aspiration of duodenal juice for culture.

Despite the advantages of making the diagnosis by endoscopy, a full-thickness surgical biopsy of the gut is sometimes still necessary, especially when the disease is confined to the deeper layers of the gut.

Therapeutic

Therapeutic Options

Despite the theoretical attraction of dietary manipulation, in practice it is extremely rare to induce a lasting response by avoiding specific foods. Fortunately, medical therapy is almost always successful. Surgery should be avoided as it is rarely necessary and seldom curative.

Recommended Approach

There are no randomized trials on which to base recommendations; however, oral steroids are the usual first-line treatment, producing a rapid response at doses of prednisolone of 20 to 40 mg/d. After 2 weeks the dose should be reduced and titrated against the clinical response. Some patients require continuous low-dose maintenance steroid therapy, whereas others have a complete response.

In patients with severe disease, immunosuppressive drugs such as azathioprine, cyclosporine, and cyclophosphamide have been used as steroid-sparing agents. In less severe cases or where there has been no response to steroids, there may be a role for oral sodium cromoglycate or ketotifen, drugs that are thought to reduce mast cell-mediated inflammation.

FOLLOW-UP

Eosinophilic gastroenteritis is often a long-lasting illness with relapses and remissions requiring careful alteration of therapy. In view of this and the side effects of therapy, the patient should be monitored closely.

DISCUSSION

Prevalence

Eosinophilic gastroenteritis is rare: only a few hundred cases have been reported in the world literature. It is likely that the increasing use of endoscopic biopsy will increase the number of diagnoses.

Related Basic Science

The hallmark of eosinophilic gastroenteritis is the large number of eosinophils that accumulate in the gut wall. Once activated, the eosinophil is capable of secreting a range of proinflammatory cytokines and cationic proteins which can cause tissue injury. Histochemical studies in eosinophilic gastroenteritis have demonstrated the presence of these products, which have been secreted by the degranulated eosinophil within the gut wall, implying that the eosinophils are indeed activated. Whether the accumulation of eosinophils is the primary abnormality or whether they congregate in the gut in response to another stimulus is unclear. One suggestion is that unknown oral allergens activate mast cells through crosslinking immunoglobulin E molecules on the cell membrane and that the activated tissue mast cell is responsible for the chemotaxis of circulating eosinophils into the gut. Conceivably, once the epithelial integrity is breached, this cycle continues unabated because the allergen now has greater access to primed mast cells.

Natural History and Its Modification with Treatment

The majority of patients treated with cromoglycate have a recurrence, whereas around half of the patients treated with steroids have an exacerbation of their disease after stopping treatment; on maintenance steroid therapy, this figure is reduced to 15%.

Patients with eosinophilic gastroenteritis do not have an increased risk of developing gastrointestinal neoplasms.

Prevention

There are no known preventive measures. In rare cases, avoiding specific food allergens may improve symptoms.

Cost Containment

Awareness of the diagnosis should lead to fewer investigations and early intervention.

REFERENCES

Klein NC, Hargrove RL, Sleisenger MH, Jeffries GH. Eosinophilic gastroenteritis. Medicine (Baltimore) 1970;49:299.

Naylor AR. Eosinophilic gastroenteritis. Scot Med J 1990;35:163.

Talley NJ, Shorter RG, Phillips SF, Zinsmeister AR. Eosinophilic gastroenteritis: A clinicopathological study of patients with disease of the mucosa, muscle layer, and subserosal tissues. Gut 1990;31:54.

Whipple's Disease

Steven F. Moss, M.B., B.S., M.D., and Peter R. Holt, M.D.

DEFINITION

Whipple's disease is a multisystemic disorder due to chronic infection by the bacterium *Tropheryma whippelii*. Infection almost always involves the small intestine, but other organ systems are commonly involved too so that patients with Whipple's disease may present with a wide spectrum of symptoms and signs. Although rare, Whipple's disease is an important diagnosis to make because simple antibacterial treatment can control and often cure this formerly fatal disease.

ETIOLOGY

Tropheryma whippelii is a Gram-positive bacterium belonging to the Actinomycete group of organisms. The bacteria survive inside macrophages for many years yet elicit little immune response from the host. Chronic, diffuse infection of the small intestine eventually gives rise to malabsorption, whereas infection of macrophages in other organs also occurs: the central nervous system, heart, and lungs are affected in about half of all cases of Whipple's disease.

CRITERIA FOR DIAGNOSIS

Suggestive

As Whipple's disease may present with a wide variety of symptoms and signs, it is important to consider this diagnosis early in any patient with clinical features of malabsorption or an obscure multisystem disorder. The combination of malabsorption with a seronegative arthropathy, fever, and lymphadenopathy is especially suggestive of Whipple's disease.

Definitive

As the bacterium responsible for causing Whipple's disease has never been successfully cultured, the diagnosis of Whipple's disease is currently made by finding the characteristic histologic abnormalities on biopsy of the affected organ, usually the small intestine as it is almost always involved and is relatively accessible. These changes consist of the accumulation of numerous "foamy" macrophages in the lamina propria (see Related Basic Science, Anatomic Derangement); however, similar histologic changes may occur in almost any other organ. With the identification of genetic sequences specific for *T. whippelii* it is likely that soon the definitive diagnosis of Whipple's disease will be much easier, by polymerase chain reaction amplification of the bacterial genome from tissue and perhaps even peripheral blood or cerebrospinal fluid.

CLINICAL MANIFESTATIONS

Subjective

Whipple's disease may present from infancy to old age and in any racial group, although it has most commonly been described in white, middle-aged men. The patient typically presents with a very long history of vague ill health, weight loss, and diarrhea due to chronic malabsorption. These symptoms have usually been present for years and are often preceded by severe and migratory polyarthralgias. Abdominal pain is present in about half the patients, as is a low-grade fever, which may be the most prominent presenting symptom. Sometimes patients with Whipple's disease report that they notice an improvement in their symptoms after receiving a short course of antibiotics for an unrelated infection, only to relapse several weeks later.

Other symptoms may also be present, depending on whether there is involvement of sites outside the intestine. Chronic cough and pleuritic pain signifying pulmonary infection by *T. whippelii* are experienced by about half the patients, and around 20% have a wide range of symptoms

due to involvement of the central nervous system, such as headaches, dementia, seizures, and symptoms of focal neurologic deficits. Cardiac symptoms are uncommon despite the heart being frequently affected.

Objective

Physical Examination

The physical signs are those of chronic malabsorption together with more specific signs related to the presence of extraintestinal involvement. Signs of malnutrition, including wasting, finger clubbing, peripheral edema, and hypotension, are almost always present. Mild abdominal tenderness is common, whereas hepatosplenomegaly and ascites are rare. Hyperpigmentation secondary to photosensitivity and palpable peripheral lymphadenopathy each occur in around half the patients. There may be evidence of a peripheral arthritis, with warm swollen and tender joints. Cardiac involvement can lead to signs of pericarditis or myocarditis with subsequent congestive cardiac failure. Endocarditis may result in valvular fibrosis, but when murmurs are heard they are more commonly secondary to anemia. Focal neurologic deficits or signs of dementia are present in around one third of patients, usually in association with disease elsewhere, and they may progress despite treatment. Ocular involvement occurs rarely.

Routine Laboratory Abnormalities

Laboratory abnormalities due to the chronic malabsorption are common and include electrolyte derangements, hypoalbuminemia, and elevated fecal fat excretion. The sedimentation rate is usually elevated and anemia due to iron and folate malabsorption is a very frequent finding. Leukocytosis occurs in the ill patients.

PLANS

Diagnostic

Differential Diagnosis

The differential diagnosis of Whipple's disease is wide and includes the causes of malabsorption (see Chapter 19–38). Other differential diagnoses include pyrexia of unknown origin, the connective tissue disorders (if arthralgia is prominent), and, occasionally, neurologic syndromes.

Diagnostic Options

A contrast study of the small bowel may show thickened folds and dilation in the upper small intestine, though this is not always present. Other radiologic investigations including computed tomography scanning and ultrasonography are nonspecific but may demonstrate abdominal lymphadenopathy.

Recommended Approach

Because these radiologic changes are nonspecific it is important to make a definitive diagnosis by an upper gastrointestinal endoscopy taking several biopsies of the duodenum or proximal jejunum, even if the gastrointestinal symptoms are not prominent. The intestinal biopsy should be stained with periodic acid–Schiff reagent, because making the diagnosis on routine hematoxylin and eosin-stained tissue alone is difficult unless the lesion is extensive. The intestinal biopsy is almost always diagnostic and it is rarely necessary to biopsy other organs.

Therapeutic

Therapeutic Options

The first case of Whipple's disease treated successfully with antibiotics was in 1952; before this the condition was uniformly fatal. Antibiotics are the only way to treat Whipple's disease.

Recommended Approach

Many different antibiotics have now been successfully used to treat Whipple's disease, but the choice of antibiotic is currently empiric and based on clinical observations as there have been no controlled therapeutic trials. In addition, as the organism has never been cultured, the selection of the antimicrobial agent cannot be based on in vitro sensitivity testing. Despite apparently adequate treatment, around one third of patients may have a clinical relapse and this is especially likely to occur in the central nervous system. For this reason it is probably best to treat Whipple's disease with drugs that readily cross the blood–brain barrier, and initiating therapy with parenteral penicillin and streptomycin is common practice. A recent retrospective study showed that trimethoprim–sulfamethoxazole (Bactrim) is superior to treatment with tetracycline. A dose of one double-strength tablet of trimethoprim–sulfamethoxazole twice daily is usual. Most authorities advise treating for at least 6 months and for up to 2 years. After this course of treatment an annual course of treatment is sometimes used, but whether such prolonged treatment is necessary is debatable; it is possible that a single course of 1 to 2 months may be sufficient. In addition to specific antibacterial therapy, it is important not to forget general nutritional support to replace macronutrients and micronutrients in the malnourished patient while clinical improvement is awaited.

FOLLOW-UP

Most symptoms rapidly improve within days to weeks, although laboratory abnormalities and the intestinal biopsy may take months or years to return to normal. The majority of patients are permanently cured. Because of the relatively frequent occurrence of relapses, patients should be seen in the office every few months and the complete blood count, serum electrolytes, and protein and folate levels measured on these occasions. A relapse may be diagnosed clinically and with the blood tests or, somewhat earlier, by intestinal biopsy. It is important to note that this can occur despite continuing antibiotics. A relapse in the central nervous system carries a poor prognosis, and it is thought that in many cases this may be due to ongoing scarring rather than active infection.

DISCUSSION
Prevalence and Incidence

The prevalence and incidence are unknown. Whipple's disease is rare and fewer than a thousand cases of Whipple's disease have been reported in the world literature.

Related Basic Science
Genetics

Although the disease was first described in 1907, the organism responsible for causing the disease has never been cultured; however, by using common bacterial 16 S ribosomal RNA primers and the polymerase chain reaction, a novel 16 S rRNA sequence has been amplified from the intestinal biopsies of patients with Whipple's disease. This sequence is specific for the bacteria found in Whipple's disease and has allowed these newly identified causative bacteria, now termed *T. whippelii*, to be classified phylogenetically. *Tropheryma whippelii* are related to the soil-living Actinobacteria in the Actinomycetes subdivision of the Gram-positive bacteria.

Physiologic or Metabolic Derangement

Chronic intracellular infection by *T. whippelii* is accompanied by a marked lack of inflammation. This has been suggested to be due to a specific defect of cellular immunity, but the data concerning in vitro lymphocyte responses and HLA associations are conflicting. There does not appear to be a generalized immune deficiency, despite some obvious similarity between the lack of inflammatory response seen in Whipple's disease and in the chronic intestinal *Mycobacterium avium–intracellulare* infection observed in some patients with AIDS.

Anatomic Derangement

The lamina propria of the small intestine is densely infiltrated with macrophages laden with *T. whippelii*, to the exclusion of most other inflammatory cells. These macrophages stain positively with the periodic acid–Schiff reagent and are resistant to diastase staining. Unlike *M. avium–intracellulare*, with which *T. whippelii* may be occasionally confused, they are not acid fast. This characteristic staining pattern is due to the presence of glycoproteins of numerous intracellular *T. whippelii*. The rod-shaped bacilli, measuring 1 to 2.5 µm by 0.25 µm, may be seen by electron microscopy and occasionally by high-resolution light microscopy.

In Whipple's disease there is often a loss of absorptive villus surface and the lymphatics are dilated and full of fat due to obstruction by enlarged mesenteric lymph nodes (hence the old name for Whipple's disease, intestinal lipodystrophy). Sarcoid-like noncaseating granulomata are occasionally seen in the intestine and other affected organs. The small intestine is usually diffusely involved, although occasionally these abnormalities may not be seen on biopsy due to patchy infection. Although most is known about the small intestine, similar accumulations of infected macrophages are found in other affected organs, such as the lymph nodes, pleura, central nervous system, and heart.

Natural History and Its Modification with Treatment

Before the era of antibiotics Whipple's disease was uniformly fatal. Now most patients are cured permanently by antibiotic therapy, although relapses do occur.

Prevention

There are no known preventive measures.

Cost Containment

Thinking of the diagnosis early in a patient with an often obscure disease decreases the cost to the patient, both financially and in health terms. In the future, polymerase chain reaction-based diagnostic tests may be cheaper than our current investigative techniques.

REFERENCES

Feurle GE, Marth T. An evaluation of antimicrobial treatment for Whipple's disease: Tetracycline versus trimethoprim–sulfamethoxazole. Dig Dis Sci 1994;39:1642.

Fleming JL, Wiesner RH, Shorter RG. Whipple's disease: Clinical, biochemical and histopathological features and assessment of treatment in 29 patients. Mayo Clin Proc 1988;63:539.

Keinath RD, Merrell DE, Vliestra R, Dobbins WO III. Antibiotic treatment and relapse in Whipple's disease: Long-term follow of 88 patients. Gastroenterology 1985;88:1867.

Relman DA, Schmidt TM, MacDermott RP, Falkow S. Identification of the uncultured bacillus of Whipple's disease. N Engl J Med 1992;327:293.

Wilson KH, Blitchington R, Frothingham R, Wilson JAP. Phylogeny of the Whipple's-disease-associated bacterium. Lancet 1991;338:474.

Bacterial Overgrowth Syndrome

Steven F. Moss, M.B., B.S., M.D., and Peter R. Holt, M.D.

DEFINITION

Bacterial overgrowth is defined by an increase in the numbers of bacteria in the upper small intestinal lumen to more than 10^5 to 10^6 per milliliter. This increased bacterial load may then interfere with the normal function of the gut and cause a variety of clinical effects known collectively as the bacterial overgrowth syndrome.

ETIOLOGY

The numbers of bacteria in the upper gut are kept relatively low by the antibacterial effect of gastric acid, the sweeping wave of intestinal motility that pushes the luminal contents aborally, the ileocecal valve, and intestinal bacteriostatic and immune mechanisms. Problems with any of these factors may lead to the bacterial overgrowth syndrome. Table 19–43–1 illustrates the more common causes.

CRITERIA FOR DIAGNOSIS

Suggestive

The diagnosis is suggested in any patient who has clinical and/or biochemical evidence of malabsorption and who is known to have one of the predisposing etiologic factors listed in Table 19–43–1. The reversal of malabsorption following a course of antibiotics is further supportive evidence that the malabsorption is accompanied by bacterial overgrowth. A number of breath tests are currently in use (see Plans, Diagnostic). Although none of them is perfect they may be very useful to confirm a clinical suspicion of bacterial overgrowth without invasive tests.

Definitive

The definitive diagnosis requires aspirating the intestinal contents and showing that the numbers of bacteria are higher than the normal range. A bacterial concentration greater than 10^5 to 10^6 organisms per milliliter is generally taken to be positive, but it should be emphasized that each laboratory needs to define its own normal ranges. There is no gold standard and the normal ranges that have been described are based on small numbers of individuals.

TABLE 19–43–1. CAUSES OF THE BACTERIAL OVERGROWTH SYNDROME

Decreased gastric acid secretion
   Chronic atrophic gastritis and pernicious anemia
   Antisecretory drugs, e.g., proton pump inhibitors
   Gastric surgery
Stagnant small intestinal contents
   Anatomic problems
      Jejunal diverticulosis, inflammatory strictures, neoplasms
      Iatrogenic (postoperative), e.g., construction of a blind loop, enteroenterostomy,
         Billroth II gastrectomy
   Decreased intestinal motility
      Neuropathic, e.g., diabetes mellitus, pseudo-obstruction
      Visceral myopathy
      Radiation enteropathy
      Stiff intestinal walls, e.g., scleroderma, amyloid
Increased coloileal reflux
   Jejunocolic fistula
   Resection of ileocecal valve
Other causes
   Decreased mucosal immunity
   Bile salt deficiency
   Pancreatic exocrine insufficiency
   ? Old age

CLINICAL MANIFESTATIONS

Subjective

The symptoms in patients with bacterial overgrowth may vary widely from almost none in an individual who has long-standing jejunal diverticulosis to a severely malnourished patient with Crohn's disease and multiple operations. In the latter case, many different factors are likely to contribute to the clinical presentation and bacterial overgrowth may be the least of them. Weight loss, watery diarrhea, nausea, and vomiting, however, are all common symptoms in the bacterial overgrowth syndrome. Patients may present with a symptom related to specific nutritional deficiency, such as anemia from folate or vitamin B_{12} deficiency, bruising due to vitamin K malabsorption, or muscle weakness caused by a lack of vitamin D. The past medical history may provide crucial information, particularly if there has been gastrointestinal surgery. Occasionally, the family history of a visceral neuropathy or myopathy will be found.

Objective

Physical Examination

The signs of bacterial overgrowth are those of the effects of malabsorption in general and again there is a wide spectrum of presentation. On examination, careful attention should be paid to abdominal surgical scars and evidence of systemic connective tissue disease or neuropathic processes which may be associated with intestinal dysmotility. This may provide valuable information about the cause of the bacterial overgrowth.

Routine Laboratory Abnormalities

Routine laboratory investigations often reveal the consequences of malabsorption. A macrocytic anemia is common and is usually due to vitamin B_{12} malabsorption, although folate deficiency may also contribute. Hypoproteinemia is often present and steatorrhea is common. A low serum cholesterol is almost universal.

PLANS

Diagnostic

Differential Diagnosis

The differential diagnosis of the bacterial overgrowth syndrome is that of the causes of malabsorption in general or specific nutritional deficiency states. Particular pointers to the malabsorption being due to the bacterial overgrowth syndrome are a past history of gastrointestinal surgery and one of the known predisposing factors.

Diagnostic Options

These include a battery of tests to establish that malabsorption is present and various investigations into the cause (see Chapter 19–38). An upper gastrointestinal series with small bowel follow-through is especially useful because it provides valuable information on anatomy and may also show abnormalities of motility. Several indirect tests have been devised to diagnose bacterial overgrowth noninvasively, and the variety of methods in use reflects the fact that none is perfect. The products of bacterial metabolism have been measured in the urine and blood, but although abnormalities have been described in the bacterial overgrowth syndrome, the assays are difficult to perform and are generally insensitive. In contrast, the breath tests are much simpler to perform and have a higher predictive value. The principle behind them is that a labeled bacterial substrate is swallowed and the split product is measured in the breath. When there is bacterial overgrowth in the small intestine the label is released in the breath to a greater degree and/or relatively earlier than normal (when it is metabolized by colonic bacteria). Substrates in use include [^{14}C] glycine glycocholate (a bile salt), D-[^{14}C]xylose, and (unlabeled) hydrogen in glucose or lactulose. Although these tubeless tests are simple for the patient to use, the interpretation of the result is often far from easy. For example, the elderly individual with hypochlorhydria may have an abnormal D-[^{14}C]xylose test without significant malabsorption.

Direct quantification of bacterial counts in the small intestine is achieved by aspirating juice from the jejunum through a sterile tube placed endoscopically or under x-ray control. The sample should be collected anaerobically and cultured on several different media; however, because of sampling variation, pockets of bacterial overgrowth may be missed, especially if they are in the distal small intestine.

An alternative approach is a trial of treatment. A rapid and complete clinical and biochemical response to a broad-spectrum antibiotic may be considered proof of the diagnosis. In practice, however, such clear-cut cases are the exception and Whipple's disease and even celiac disease may also respond to this maneuver.

Recommended Approach

The first question for the physician faced with a patient he or she suspects of having bacterial overgrowth is whether it is of clinical importance. If not, then why investigate? Intestinal diverticulosis is relatively common with old age and may not cause any harm. In addition, in the complicated Crohn's patient, for example, bacterial overgrowth may not be contributing to the patient's malabsorption substantially. If, however, bacterial overgrowth appears to be clinically important then, having established that there is malabsorption, the diagnostic approach may vary from an upper gastrointestinal series and a trial of treatment through to the use of breath tests and intestinal aspiration. In practice, the approach is likely to depend as much on the local expertise and resources available as the complexity of the individual clinical case. It may be reasonable to progress rapidly to a trial of treatment and reinvestigate if this is inconclusive.

Therapeutic

Therapeutic Options

The therapeutic options are to treat or not to treat. In addition, specific deficiencies such as that of vitamin B_{12} should be corrected. Parenteral therapy and even total parenteral nutrition may be needed. In many diseases associated with bacterial overgrowth syndrome a relatively elemental diet may be beneficial, as damage to the enterocytes may have resulted in an inability to digest or absorb complex molecules. In these cases a lactose-free diet with medium-chain, rather than long-chain triglycerides, may be necessary.

Recommended Approach

If it is deemed necessary to treat the bacterial overgrowth then the cause should be addressed. Sometimes this is simple to do; for example, in the elderly patient taking omeprazole, an alternative drug or no drug should be tried. Certain conditions, such as diverticulosis and a stricture or a blind loop, may be amenable to surgery; however, the mainstay of treatment is to suppress the bacterial growth by the use of broad-spectrum antibiotics. Treatment is almost always empiric because even if the bacteria are directly cultured, the resultant mixed growth does not suggest a simple choice of drug. There are no data from clinical trials to help. Oral tetracycline 250 mg four times daily for 1 to 2 weeks is commonly used, although anaerobes are resistant to this antibiotic and the response rate is only around 50%. Alternative drugs include amoxicillin–clavulanic acid (Augmentin) at a dose of 250 to 500 mg orally three times daily or a cephalosporin. Metronidazole and clindamycin, which are particularly effective against anaerobes, are disappointing when used as single agents. Initial treatment is generally for 1 to 2 weeks.

FOLLOW-UP

Although a clinical remission may be prolonged, unless the cause of the bacterial overgrowth is corrected it will recur. The patient should therefore remain under follow-up and the complete blood count and serum albumin and folate levels measured periodically to assess the response to treatment and the timing of relapses. There are a variety of ways to treat

recurrences, including a longer course of therapy (even up to a few months), recurrent short courses of 1 to 2 weeks, and cyclic treatment, for example, 1 of every 4 weeks. Again, good clinical trials are lacking. It is important not to neglect correcting the nutritional deficiencies that occur commonly in patients with bacterial overgrowth. Finally, prokinetic agents may have a place in management if the bacterial overgrowth is due to intestinal hypomotility, but this remains to be established.

DISCUSSION

Prevalence and Incidence

The prevalence and incidence of this condition are not known. Bacterial overgrowth is thought to increase with age, probably as a result of the increase in predisposing factors, particularly achlorhydria.

Related Basic Science

The fetal gut is sterile and becomes colonized by bacteria shortly after birth. Thereafter, large quantities of bacteria are found in the normal gut, with the highest concentration of bacteria in the colon (10^{10} to 10^{12} organisms/mL) and relatively fewer organisms in the upper intestinal tract (10^5–10^8/mL in the ileum, 0–10^4/mL in the jejunum). The ileocecal valve divides the heavily infected colon from the "cleaner" small intestine; however, a variety of conditions (see Etiology) may lead to great increases in the bacterial population of the small intestine.

Bacterial overgrowth interferes with the normal absorptive process by directly damaging the intestinal mucosa; indeed, a mucosal biopsy may be abnormal. In addition, bacterial overgrowth alters the normal contents of the intestine. The net effect of these processes is malabsorption of carbohydrate, protein, and fat.

Fat is not absorbed because the bacteria deconjugate luminal bile salts and this makes them rather insoluble. The deconjugated bile salts are therefore unable to participate in the formation of the micelles which are of critical importance for lipid absorption. As a result there is steatorrhea together with malabsorption of the fat-soluble vitamins. In addition, the unabsorbed fat may be metabolized by bacteria to unsaturated hydroxy fatty acids, which induce a secretory diarrhea.

Hypoproteinemia results from a combination of protein malabsorption, protein-losing enteropathy, and intraluminal breakdown of protein by the bacteria themselves. The increased numbers of proliferating bacteria convert the malabsorbed carbohydrates in the intestinal lumen into rapidly absorbed short-chain fatty acids. The malabsorption of vitamin B_{12} is rather paradoxical as cobalamin, like folic acid, is normally made by bacteria. In the bacterial overgrowth syndrome, however, the live bacteria appear to bind vitamin B_{12} excessively and prevent its absorption from the terminal ileum. In contrast, folate deficiency is rare in small bowel bacterial overgrowth.

Natural History and Its Modification with Treatment

The natural history depends on the cause. In general, however, the condition tends to remit and relapse and, without treatment, leads to progressive malnutrition.

Prevention

The incidence of bacterial overgrowth is expected to decrease with the decline of gastric surgery and may also be decreased by the judicious use of omeprazole. It is not clear whether repeated courses of prophylactic antibiotics are any better in preventing the complications of bacterial overgrowth than treating clinical exacerbations as they arise.

Cost Containment

Early recognition of the diagnosis in patients with one of the predisposing conditions is likely to lead to savings in diagnostic tests. Many of the tests to document bacterial overgrowth can often be omitted in favor of a trial of treatment.

REFERENCE

Saltzman JR, Kowdley KV, Pedrosa MC, et al. Bacterial overgrowth without clinical malabsorption in the elderly. Gastroenterology 1994;106:615.

Protein-Losing Enteropathy

Charles D. Gerson, M.D.

DEFINITION

In protein-losing enteropathy, protein is transported across the intestinal mucosal lining into the lumen with a resultant loss of protein in the stool, usually leading to hypoproteinemia.

ETIOLOGY

Protein can be lost from the gut in several ways. In conditions where the mucosa is inflamed, transmucosal protein leak can occur. Some intestinal diseases are associated with rapid turnover of mucosal cells. As the cells are shed, significant amounts of protein are lost into the lumen. Finally, protein may be leaked because of lymphatic obstruction.

CRITERIA FOR DIAGNOSIS

Suggestive

The combination of edema and diarrhea suggests protein loss through the gut.

Definitive

The finding of hypoalbuminemia is essential and most patients have signs of edema. In protein-losing enteropathy, there must be an underlying intestinal disorder that is known to be associated with protein leak. To be certain of this diagnosis, there should be confirmation with an α_1-antitrypsin clearance test.

CLINICAL MANIFESTATIONS

Subjective

In patients with inflammatory conditions, diarrhea is usually present, often accompanied by abdominal pain. Patients with malabsorption may complain of weight loss and diarrhea. In protein-losing enteropathy, edema usually occurs and may be the only notable symptom.

There may be a history of gradually increasing edema without any significant gastrointestinal symptoms. In other patients, the intestinal disorder may precede hypoproteinemia. Therefore, the patient may have a history of inflammatory bowel disease, malabsorption syndrome, or other disease entities associated with protein leak.

The family history may be relevant in intestinal lymphangiectasia, which can affect members of the same family, though the genetic transmission is not yet understood.

Objective

Physical Examination

Dependent edema is the most common physical finding. Rarely, the edema can be more generalized including ascites. Occasionally in intestinal lymphangiectasia, peripheral edema can be unilateral. Depending on the etiology, there may be signs of abdominal tenderness, distention, and weight loss.

Routine Laboratory Abnormalities

Hypoalbuminemia is the essential laboratory finding in this condition. Immunoglobulins are also depressed as is the lymphocyte count in patients with lymphatic obstruction. In patients with specific gastrointestinal diseases such as inflammatory bowel disease, laboratory tests reflect this, with findings such as anemia and an elevated sedimentation rate.

PLANS

Diagnostic

Differential Diagnosis

There are two aspects of the differential to consider: first, what are other causes of diarrhea and edema, and second, which entities cause protein loss from the gut.

Patients with severe malnutrition can develop hypoalbuminemia strictly on a nutritional basis. As there is usually a secondary reduction in immunocompetence, these patients are susceptible to infections. A common scenario in underdeveloped countries, especially in the pediatric age group, is malnutrition followed by hypoproteinemia followed by a fatal diarrheal illness, often in the setting of measles or other childhood diseases. A similar series of events could occur in patients with terminal cancer and profound malnutrition.

In patients with edema secondary to liver disease, albumin is low while globulin is usually high, so total protein is not depressed. Of course, the clinical setting and other laboratory tests should help establish the diagnosis of primary liver disease. Congestive heart failure is another possible etiology. Twenty-four-hour urinary protein can be measured to rule out nephrotic syndrome.

Protein-losing enteropathy has a number of causes, as listed in Table 19–44–1. Probably the most common cause is inflammatory bowel disease. In regional enteritis or Crohn's disease of the small bowel, a correlation exists between the length of diseased small bowel, protein leak from the gut, and serum albumin concentration. Colitis, whether ulcerative or granulomatous as in Crohn's colitis, also causes significant protein loss from the inflamed mucosa. Another inflammatory condition that can produce protein leak is radiation enteritis, usually when the ileum is involved.

The prototype condition associated with protein-losing enteropathy is intestinal lymphangiectasia. This rare condition usually begins in childhood, where lacteals in the small bowel lamina propria are markedly distended, resulting in their rupture into the lumen and loss of fat and protein. Other causes of lymphatic obstruction such as tuberculosis, lymphoma, and chronic congestive heart failure can have the same result.

Finally, there can be an element of protein loss in a setting of more widespread malabsorption, due to increased shedding of mucosal cells, such as celiac sprue. This has also been described in severe cases of bacterial overgrowth in the intestinal lumen.

Diagnostic Options

In suspected inflammatory bowel disease, evaluation of the colon by colonoscopy or barium enema can be done. Barium study of the small intestine may lead to the diagnosis. If a small intestinal mucosal disorder is suspected, small bowel biopsy via endoscopy should be consid-

TABLE 19–44–1. CAUSES OF PROTEIN-LOSING ENTEROPATHY

Inflammatory bowel disease
Radiation enteritis
Intestinal lymphangiectasia
Abdominal lymphoma
Intestinal tuberculosis
Congestive heart failure
Constrictive pericarditis
Chronic ischemic bowel disease
Celiac sprue
Bacterial overgrowth

ered. If documentation of protein leak is needed, often in a research setting, α_1-antitrypsin clearance is the most reliable current test.

Recommended Approach

First, blood testing for albumin and globulin measurement should be obtained. If these are low and diarrhea exists, evaluation for inflammatory bowel disease should be pursued. Colonoscopy and barium x-ray of the small bowel are indicated. In the absence of inflammatory bowel disease, primary liver disease, or obvious primary malnutrition, small bowel biopsy should be done.

Therapeutic

Therapeutic Options

In inflammatory bowel disease, treatment should be directed at the disease itself. Localized segments of diseased small bowel, as in radiation or regional enteritis, can be resected. Intestinal lymphangiectasia can be treated by dietary manipulation. Other etiologies such as sprue, lymphoma, and heart disease require treatment of the primary condition.

Recommended Approach

In inflammatory bowel disease, hypoalbuminemia is usually part of a larger symptom complex, so inflammatory bowel disease treatment should be addressed as the overall problem. There are, however, examples of patients with a highly localized segment of inflamed small bowel in whom protein loss and edema are the main manifestations. This is more likely to occur in an entity such as radiation enteritis, where surgical resection has been effective.

In intestinal lymphangiectasia, diet should be altered so that patients are ingesting a low-fat diet, supplemented by medium-chain triglycerides. Where protein loss is secondary to other conditions such as mucosal disease of lymphatic obstruction, treatment should focus on the primary condition.

FOLLOW-UP

Follow-up depends on the etiology. In conditions such as intestinal lymphangiectasia, patients can be followed at long intervals. In many of the diseases associated with protein loss from the gut, however, there are other clinical problems that require closer follow-up.

DISCUSSION

Prevalence and Incidence

With the number of conditions described above, it is difficult to cite meaningful statistics on prevalence and incidence. In addition, the presence of protein loss from the gut correlates with the severity of the disease, especially in the case of inflammatory bowel disease. The incidence of hypoalbuminemia has been documented in hospitalized patients with Crohn's disease where it can exceed 50%; however, this is not representative of a general population of patients with Crohn's disease.

Related Basic Science

Genetics

In intestinal lymphangiectasia, protein-losing enteropathy has affected multiple siblings in a family though most cases are sporadic. Therefore, there appears to be a genetic etiology, at least in part.

Physiologic or Metabolic Derangement

In normal circumstances, only about 10% of protein turnover in the body takes places via enteric losses. This is mostly due to shedding of intestinal mucosal cells. If the mucosa is inflamed, there appears to be an increased permeability to passage of protein into the lumen. This affects all protein, independent of molecular weight. In the lumen, the protein is digested back to amino acid subunits and partially reabsorbed. Hypoproteinemia results when the net loss exceeds the capacity for reabsorption, hepatic synthesis of albumin, and synthesis of immunoglobulins.

In lymphatic obstruction, the scenario is different because there is also loss of lymphocytes if lymphatics rupture into the intestinal lumen. Lymphocytopenia and impaired cellular immunity have been documented in this setting. Also, steatorrhea occurs because long-chain fatty acids are absorbed via the lymphatic system. That is why a low-fat diet and medium-chain triglyceride supplementation is effective. The medium-chain triglycerides can be absorbed via the portal venous system, bypassing the lymphatics.

Anatomic Derangement

In intestinal lymphangiectasia, there is a characteristic appearance on small bowel biopsy. Markedly dilated lymphatic channels or lacteals are seen in the lamina propria just below the mucosal cells.

Natural History and Its Modification with Treatment

The natural history depends on the etiology of the protein loss. In conditions like intestinal lymphangiectasia and sprue, the prognosis is generally fairly good when dietary treatment is effective. In inflammatory bowel disease, if effective medical or surgical treatment allows albumin to rise, edema resolves.

Prevention

Prevention depends on the etiology. In inflammatory bowel disease, prophylactic antiinflammatory treatment may prevent continual leaking of protein into the intestinal lumen. Radiation enteritis may be prevented by paying attention to radiation dosage and radiation field. The diagnosis of intestinal lymphangiectasia is often delayed leading to worsening edema while other diagnoses are pursued.

Cost Containment

Understanding that edema may be caused by protein loss in the intestine can lead to an appropriately directed evaluation and treatment, saving unnecessary costs.

REFERENCES

Beeken WL, Busch MJ, Sylwester DL. Intestinal protein loss in Crohn's disease. Gastroenterology 1972;62:207.

Florent C, L'Hirondel C, Dexmazures D, et al. Intestinal clearance of α_1-antitrypsin: A sensitive method for the detection of protein-losing enteropathy. Gastroenterology 1981;81:777.

King CE, Toskes PP. Protein-losing enteropathy in the human and experimental rat blind-loop syndrome. Gastroenterology 1981;80:504.

Mistilis SP, Skyring AP, Stephen DD. Intestinal lymphangiectasia: Mechanism of enteric loss of plasma protein and fat. Lancet 1965;1:77.

Strober W, Wochner RD, Carbone PP, Waldmann T. A. Intestinal lymphangiectasia: A protein-losing enteropathy with hypogammaglobulinemia, lymphocytopenia and impaired homograft rejection. J Clin Invest 1967;46:1643.

Lactase Deficiency

Steven F. Moss, M.B., B.S., M.D., and Peter R. Holt, M.D.

DEFINITION

Lactase phlorizin hydrolase is one of the digestive enzymes found in the brush border membrane of the small intestine. This enzyme splits the milk disaccharidase lactose, which cannot be absorbed directly, into its constituent monosaccharides, glucose and galactose, which are then rapidly absorbed. Lactase deficiency is a clinical syndrome caused by an absolute or relative lack of lactase, resulting in lactose malabsorption. Lactase deficiency is classified as primary—an isolated, usually acquired, deficiency of this enzyme alone—or, less commonly, secondary to disease of the small intestine.

ETIOLOGY

In all land mammals studied except humans, there is a fall in intestinal lactase activity after weaning, when milk is no longer an essential part of the diet. Humans are unique, however, because the drop in lactase activity after weaning is not uniform. In several parts of the world, particularly in northern Europe and the United States, where milk continues to be an important constituent of the diet, most of the Caucasian population retains high lactase activity into adulthood. In other regions such as Asia and Africa, however, acquired lactase deficiency is almost universal. Indeed, it is probable that primary lactase deficiency should be regarded as the norm, whereas the ability to tolerate lactose as an adult is probably due to an acquired genetic mutation that has conferred survival advantages in those populations that have domesticated dairy animals.

Secondary lactase deficiency may be caused by any disease that affects the small intestine, including resection. This usually occurs in association with a deficiency of other small intestinal brush border enzymes, although in these circumstances it is the deficiency of lactase that is the more important clinically.

CRITERIA FOR DIAGNOSIS
Suggestive

The acquisition of the typical symptoms of carbohydrate malabsorption in childhood or adolescence in response to milk products is highly suggestive of lactase deficiency, particularly in racially predisposed individuals. This diagnosis is further supported if the symptoms improve when a milk-free diet is followed for 3 to 5 days and recur on reinstitution of dietary milk. In these circumstances, further tests may not be considered necessary.

Definitive

Definitive diagnosis requires the demonstration of reduced small intestinal lactase activity by measurement of the specific enzyme activity in a small intestinal biopsy; however, this facility is rarely available outside research laboratories. Lactase activity may be more easily determined indirectly, by the oral lactose tolerance test or the lactose–hydrogen breath test.

CLINICAL MANIFESTATIONS
Subjective

The symptoms of lactase deficiency are abdominal bloating, borborygmi, flatulence, pain, and diarrhea following the ingestion of milk products. This symptom complex reflects a colonic response and may overlap to some extent with the irritable bowel syndrome, which can lead to diagnostic confusion. Generally, the severity of the symptoms is related directly to the amount of milk consumed; however, different individuals vary greatly in response to a standard amount of milk and this is partly due to differences in absolute intestinal enzyme activities (see

below) and partly because of a variation in sensitivity to colonic stimuli. The relationship between symptoms and the ingestion of milk may sometimes be difficult to prove, although patients have often noticed the association themselves by the time they seek medical advice. A family history of milk intolerance is common.

Primary lactase deficiency is an isolated defect and does not lead to generalized malabsorption, so that a history of weight loss is inconsistent with the diagnosis. A loss of weight accompanying the milk intolerance suggests a lactase deficiency secondary to small intestinal disease.

Objective
Physical Examination

Physical examination is normal and is important only in excluding malnutrition, mechanical intestinal obstruction, and rare conditions such as the carcinoid syndrome, which can also cause intermittent borborygmi.

Routine Laboratory Abnormalities

These tests are normal in primary lactase deficiency. In secondary lactase deficiency there may be laboratory abnormalities. These reflect the underlying small intestinal disease rather than the deficiency of lactase.

PLANS
Diagnostic
Differential Diagnosis

The diagnosis is normally apparent on taking the history, especially in the young in whom further tests may be unnecessary. The principal differential diagnosis is from the irritable bowel syndrome, but in older patients who have symptoms including a change in bowel habits, it is essential to exclude a colonic neoplasm before making the diagnosis of lactase deficiency.

Diagnostic Options

Lactase deficiency can be simply tested by the oral lactose tolerance test. In this test, 50 g of lactose is given by mouth after an overnight fast and the blood glucose measured serially over 2 hours. In an individual with lactase deficiency, the oral lactose load usually produces colonic symptoms accompanied by a failure of the blood glucose to rise by more than 20 mg/dL; however, false-positive results may occur due to abnormalities of gastric emptying and sometimes in diabetes. In addition, some cases are missed by this relatively insensitive test. For these reasons the noninvasive hydrogen breath test is generally preferred. In individuals with lactase deficiency, lactose is not absorbed in the small intestine. Instead, it reaches the colon where it is then metabolized by colonic bacteria and this results in an increased excretion of hydrogen in the breath. A rise of greater than 20 ppm after an oral lactose load is considered diagnostic, although occasionally false-negative results occur in patients colonized by strains of bacteria that do not excrete much hydrogen or following the use of enemas or antibiotics.

Recommended Approach

To some extent the degree to which an individual is investigated depends on the patient's race and diet. One should assume that black and Asian patients have lactase deficiency so that investigations are unnecessary, for example, in an Asian immigrant who adopts a high milk intake in adulthood and develops typical symptoms. If, however, there is any doubt about the diagnosis, an oral tolerance test and/or hydrogen breath test should be performed. This is particularly useful when it is unclear whether the patient has lactase deficiency or the irritable bowel syndrome; the treatment of these two conditions is very different.

Therapeutic
Therapeutic Options

Lactose intake should be reduced to a level that no longer causes symptoms. This may be achieved by reducing the intake of lactose-containing foods in the diet or by the chemical modification of milk and milk products. As a substitute for normal milk, low-lactose milks can be used; however, these are rather sweet and they may contain too much glucose for diabetics. Alternatively, β-galactosidase from microorganisms is available and this may be added to milk in the refrigerator to break down the lactose overnight. Ingesting tablets of β-galactosidase before drinking milk is another option.

Recommended Approach

First the patient must be reassured that he or she does not have a disease. Total avoidance of all milk-containing products is seldom necessary. Most people with lactase deficiency still have some intestinal lactase activity, albeit at a reduced level, and they can therefore tolerate some dietary lactose without symptoms, often up to two glasses of milk over the course of a day. The production of cheese and yogurt from milk leads to a reduction in lactose content so that, gram per gram, these dairy products are better tolerated than whole milk. Patients should be aware that lactose is often present in other foods and that this may not always be apparent.

FOLLOW-UP

Patients with lactase deficiency are at increased risk of developing osteoporosis because they are deprived of their main source of calcium. Therefore, dietary calcium supplements are advisable, especially in those at high risk for osteoporosis. Apart from osteoporosis, lactase deficiency is not associated with any other morbidity. Routine follow-up is unnecessary.

DISCUSSION
Prevalence

The prevalence of lactase deficiency varies enormously around the world from 1 to 3% in northwest Europe to almost 100% in Native Americans, native Australians, and most of Southeast Asia. It is also very common in Africans, Arabs, and those living around the Mediterranean. In the United States, the prevalence is around 15% in whites compared with approximately 70% in blacks. In areas where lactase deficiency is common, patients present at a relatively younger age. Thus, symptoms first occur in early childhood in the native Chinese, in the teens in African-Americans, and in adults in Greece. The geographic distribution of lactase deficiency is paralleled by the prevalence of milk drinking in these areas.

RELATED BASIC SCIENCE
Genetics

There is a rare form of congenital lactase deficiency that is autosomal recessive. The high frequency of the gene for the more common acquired lactase deficiency in many populations may be because this is the "normal" state. Persistent lactase activity in adulthood may have

occurred in some populations because it conferred some survival advantage, for example, by increasing calcium intake and therefore preventing osteomalacia where vitamin D and sunlight are in low supply. Retained lactase activity in adulthood should therefore be considered the result of a dominant mutation in the northern European population.

Altered Molecular Biology

Lactase deficiency is not an all-or-none condition. Many patients with lactase deficiency can tolerate milk in small quantities because they retain some intestinal lactase activity and a reduced amount of biochemically normal lactase. Whether the reduction of mature lactase protein is due to decreased lactase mRNA or altered translation or processing of the lactase protein has recently been addressed. It is apparent that even within the same lactase-deficient patient the enterocyte population is heterogenous. Some enterocytes have normal lactase activity, whereas others have reduced or absent activity due to a variety of lesions at the transcriptional, translational, and posttranslational levels.

Physiologic or Metabolic Derangement

Lactase deficiency results in a high osmotic load of undigested lactose leaving the small intestine, leading to salt and water retention in the colon. In addition the fermentation of lactose by colonic bacteria produces glucose, galactose, short-chain fatty acids, and hydrogen in the colon which also contribute to causing symptoms.

Natural History and Its Modification with Treatment

Primary lactase deficiency presents at different times during life in different populations. There is some evidence that the patient with lactase deficiency may develop some tolerance to lactose with continued milk consumption, perhaps because the elderly colon is less responsive or with time there is an increase in colonic lactase-producing bacteria. Most patients, however, must continue a reduced-lactose diet.

In secondary lactase deficiency, correction of the cause may restore lactase activity to normal but this is not always the case.

Prevention

Lactase deficiency is not preventable. Indeed, attempts to do so may be considered unphysiologic.

Cost Containment

The main area where costs may be reduced is in the diagnosis of lactase deficiency. It is often fairly simple to make a diagnosis on the basis of a typical history without the need for formal testing and once the diagnosis is made no further investigations are necessary. For treatment, simply reducing intake of lactose-containing foods and taking oral supplemental calcium as a substitute for the calcium normally derived from milk products are cheaper than attempting to chemically reduce the lactose content of milk.

REFERENCES

Gudmand-Høyer E. The clinical significance of disaccharide maldigestion. Am J Clin Nutr 1994;59(suppl.):735S.
Maiuri L, Rossi M, Raia V, et al. Mosaic regulation of lactase in human adult-type hypolactasia. Gastroenterology 1994;107:54.

Vascular Diseases of the Gastrointestinal Tract

Stephen M. Brenner, M.D.

DEFINITION

Vascular diseases of the gastrointestinal tract encompass those conditions that affect the major arterial and venous structure of the intestine. They are responsible for impaired arterial inflow or decreased venous outflow and may be acute or chronic.

ETIOLOGY

The clinical picture is due to embolic or thrombotic events or a nonocclusive ischemic event affecting the arterial supply of the gastrointestinal tract; primary vascular disorders, for example, vasculitides; or systemic conditions that predispose to coagulation disorders resulting in arterial or venous thromboses.

CRITERIA FOR DIAGNOSIS

Suggestive

Abdominal pain with or without gastrointestinal bleeding and unassociated with an organ-specific sign or symptom suggests the diagnosis.

Definitive

Definitive evidence of small bowel disease requires angiographic documentation of an acute or chronic intestinal ischemic process (Figure 19–46–1). Colonic involvement requires a clinical picture compatible with an acute ischemic injury, with endoscopic or radiologic and pathologic documentation supporting the diagnosis.

CLINICAL MANIFESTATIONS

Subjective

The disease states of ischemic origin are either acute or chronic. The clinical picture develops when the small bowel or colon is involved. The stomach is almost never involved in these processes. In acute arterial occlusion of the small intestine, the patient presents with periumbilical pain, constant in nature, perhaps associated with nausea, vomiting, or diarrhea. The clinical picture is usually associated with a known cardiac arrhythmia, usually atrial fibrillation, or a postmyocardial infarction by 3 to 10 days. Less likely are subacute bacterial endocarditis and acute bacterial endocarditis, as well as after an open heart procedure. There may be findings suggestive of emboli to other organs, for example, the skin, kidney, brain, or an extremity. In the patient with an acute thrombotic event the clinical picture is that of persistent abdominal pain without an explicable cause and remains a diagnosis of exclusion. In nonocclusive intestinal ischemia, the abdominal pain is preceded by the picture of hypotension or shock arising from any cause, for example, dehydration, sepsis, gastrointestinal bleeding, an acute myocardial infarction, or severe congestive heart failure, followed hours to days later by abdominal pain.

Acute ischemic colitis is a thrombotic disease of the elderly which begins as sudden crampy abdominal pain with bright red blood per rectum with or without diarrhea. The bleeding may be recurrent but is rarely massive.

Chronic small bowel intestinal ischemia is an uncommon clinical syndrome. It may manifest in one of three ways: a chronic syndrome of abdominal pain, so-called intestinal angina; a chronic diarrheal state with or without malabsorption; and occult gastrointestinal bleeding.

Chronic colonic ischemia usually presents as a nonbloody diarrheal condition or a syndrome of crampy abdominal pain due to partial colonic obstruction from a stricture.

In chronic intestinal angina, the patient usually has abdominal pain 20 to 30 minutes after a meal. The pain is usually more intense the larger the meal. Diminishing food intake may decrease the symptoms but would usually result in weight loss. It should be clearly noted that these patients are not anorectic but are afraid to eat.

Objective

Physical Examination

Early in the course of acute intestinal ischemia, the symptom of abdominal pain unassociated with any significant findings on physical examination of the abdomen is present. Conspicuous by their absence are abdominal tenderness, guarding, and rebound. There may be minimal distention; bowel sounds are usually normal. An irregular pulse may be present, but if the arrhythmia is paroxysmal, this may not be seen. If the patient presents later in the course of the disease, distention is more prominent, and with further compromise of blood flow, signs of peritonitis manifest.

In acute ischemic colitis, the abdomen may be minimally distended with varying degrees of tenderness over the affected segment of the colon involved. Localized peritoneal findings may be present if transmural infarction has occurred.

In chronic small intestinal ischemia, the physical examination is usually normal. There may be evidence of weight loss. An abdominal bruit may be present but is nonspecific.

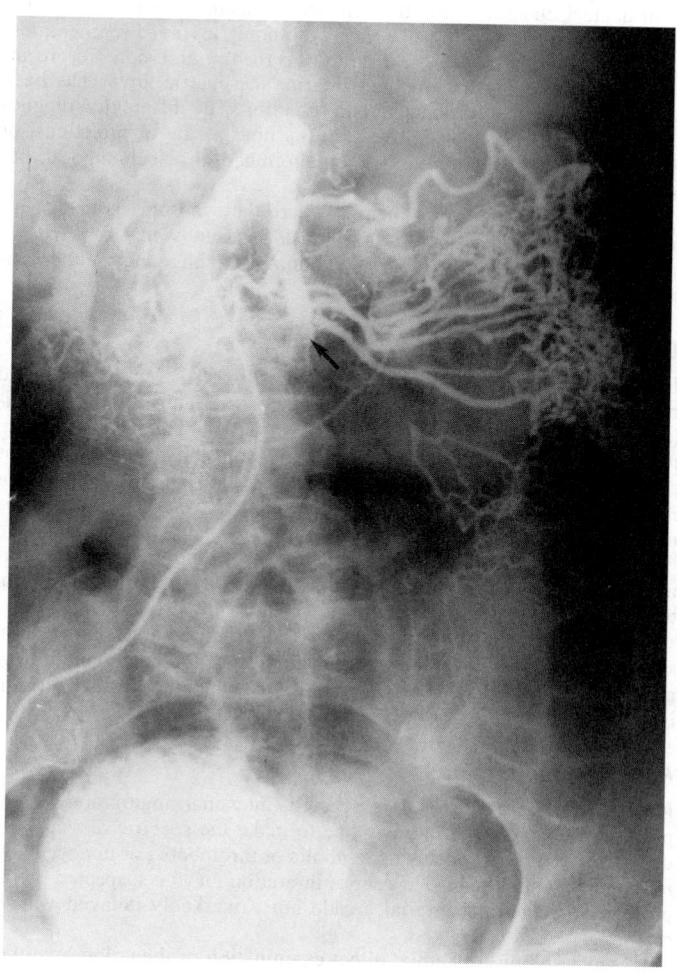

Figure 19–46–1. Angiogram of superior mesenteric artery, revealing a clot (arrow) in its proximal segment.

Routine Laboratory Abnormalities

In acute small intestinal ischemia, all blood chemistries are normal early in the course. The white blood count is normal to mildly increased, and the stool guaiac is negative. If emboli have occurred to the kidney, red blood cells are found in the urine and serum lactate dehydrogenase may be increased. Serum amylase is normal. As the disease progresses, fever, elevated white blood cell count, elevated serum amylase, and positive stool guaiacs occur as a result of bowel wall necrosis.

In acute colonic ischemia, all blood chemistries are usually normal as is the complete blood count. Repeated episodes of hematochezia may be responsible for a decrease in the hematocrit.

In chronic small bowel intestinal ischemia or chronic colonic ischemia, blood tests are usually all nonspecific and do not point to a specific diagnosis.

PLANS
Diagnostic

Differential Diagnosis

Early in the course of acute small bowel ischemia, the differential diagnosis includes other intraabdominal inflammatory conditions. The key factor in allowing the diagnosis to be entertained is the window period in which there is severe abdominal pain with the absence of any significant findings on physical examination of the abdomen, preventing a specific diagnosis, for example, of acute cholecystitis, acute diverticulitis, pancreatitis, renal calculus, or perforated viscus. Volvulus of the small bowel around its mesentery and resultant occlusion of the superior mesenteric artery are well known and are usually associated with the finding of an abdominal mass.

In acute ischemic colitis the affected segment is usually relatively short. The splenic flexure is the most commonly involved segment; less commonly the right colon and rarely the rectum and sigmoid are involved. The last occurs after the inferior mesenteric artery has been sacrificed following aortic aneurysm resection. The differential diagnosis is that of an acute ulcerative process, nonspecific or infectious, or that of an intussuscepting colonic lesion, mucosal or submucosal, benign or malignant.

In chronic small bowel ischemia, where the syndrome is that of intestinal angina, the differential diagnosis is usually that of a partial small bowel obstruction or an intraabdominal malignancy, either primary in the GI tract or the pancreas.

Diagnostic Options

In acute intestinal ischemia, a plain x-ray film of the abdomen should be obtained. Early in its course it will be normal; later it will reveal dilated centralized small bowel loops with or without edematous mucosa, giving an amorphous appearance to the loops of bowel as well as thumbprinting of the mucosa (Tomchik et al., 1970). A computed tomography scan of the abdomen may be suggestive of ischemia but is not diagnostic.

In acute colonic ischemia, a plain film of the abdomen may be normal or reveal edema of the colonic wall or the classic thumbprinting of the mucosa in the involved segment.

In chronic small intestinal ischemia, which is a diagnosis of exclusion, contrast studies of the gastrointestinal tract and computed tomography scanning of the abdomen are usually nondiagnostic in determining a specific etiology for the abdominal pain.

Recommended Approach

If acute arterial occlusion is suspected, intestinal angiography is the procedure of choice and allows one to make the specific diagnosis. It demonstrates arterial occlusion, embolic or thrombotic, or nonocclusive ischemia (Figure 19–46–1). Venous infarction may be suspected by the presence of a normal arterial arcade but a markedly delayed venous drainage.

In acute colonic ischemia, direct examination of the colon by either endoscopy, with or without biopsy, or a barium enema examination reveals the appropriate diagnosis. Endoscopically a short segment of disease is manifested by hemorrhagic mucosa with spotty submucosal masses, which are red-to-blue in color, suggesting the presence of hemorrhage. Biopsy confirms this. Barium enema shows the typical thumbprinting in the affected segment (Figure 19–46–2).

In chronic small bowel ischemia, the specific diagnosis is made by angiographic demonstration of occlusive diseases of the branches of the gastrointestinal tract.

Therapeutic

Therapeutic Options

In acute small bowel ischemia, the therapeutic options depend on the results of the superior mesenteric arteriogram.

In acute colonic ischemia, the treatment is predicated on the knowledge that it is almost always a self-limited disease that resolves without any sequelae.

In chronic ischemia of the small and large bowel, medical therapy or surgery may be necessary depending on the course in the individual patient.

Recommended Approach

In acute small bowel ischemia, if embolism or thrombosis is defined angiographically, embolectomy or thrombectomy and bypass are the procedures of choice (Boley et al., 1981). If spasm of the artery is defined with no clot or thrombus, then primary therapy with vasodilating agents such as papaverine, instilled directly into the superior mesenteric artery, is indicated (Ottinger and Austen, 1967). The latter with appropriate therapy of the underlying cause leading to shock or diminished perfusion may help to maintain and save small bowel integrity. It is

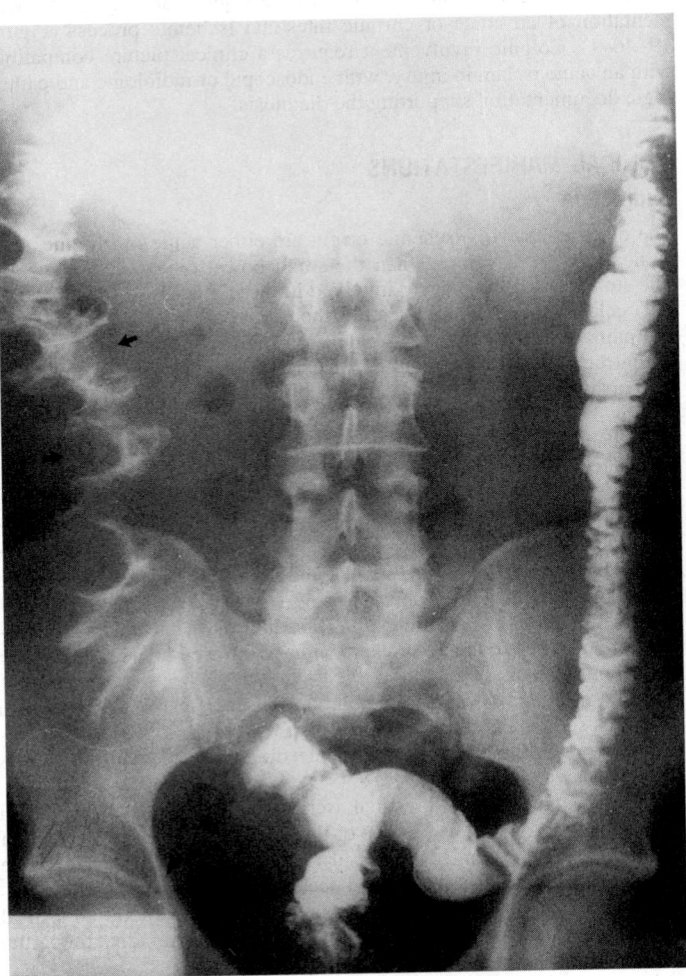

Figure 19–46–2. Barium enema examination revealing normal left colon and thumbprinting of the right colon (arrows) indicative of ischemic colitis.

generally suggested that following embolectomy or thrombectomy, a second-look procedure be performed 24 to 48 hours after the original surgery to assess small bowel viability, which may be very difficult to define clinically in the postoperative state. Gangrenous changes of the bowel may be spotty following reconstitution of the blood supply and segmental resection may be needed to sustain life.

In acute large bowel ischemia, which is usually self-limited, treatment should be conservative with bowel rest for 24 to 48 hours. Systemic antibiotics (cefoxitin 1 g intravenously every 8 hours or ampicillin 2 g intravenously every 4 hours and metronidazole 500 mg intravenously every 6 hours) or a nonabsorbable antibiotic (kanamycin 0.5 g by mouth twice a day or neomycin 1 g by mouth three times a day) in patients not so severely ill prevents secondary infection of the bowel wall. In almost all cases the acute event resolves rapidly and complete resolution occurs in 7 to 10 days. In 90 to 95% of patients, normal gut function ensues.

In chronic small bowel ischemia, reconstitution of the arterial circulation by transluminal angiography and dilation or bypass graft is indicated (Crawford et al., 1977).

FOLLOW-UP

Acute small bowel ischemia is associated with a mortality of 50 to 100% in various series. Rarely after appropriate therapy, in those people who survive, there may be long-term sequelae of the original insult. These include a localized stricture(s) or a chronic diarrheal state with or without malabsorption. Strictures may lead to partial or complete small bowel obstruction, for which surgical intervention may be necessary. The chronic diarrheal state may require therapy or may disappear after a variable period spontaneously.

In acute ischemic colitis, 90 to 95% of patients resolve completely within 7 to 10 days of onset of symptoms and no sequelae occur. The reconstitution of the arterial supply is preceded by a rapidly developing collateral circulation. In approximately 5 to 10% of patients who sustain acute ischemic injury to the colon, sequelae occur leading to a severe complication or a chronic state. If the acute process becomes transmural, it can result in perforation or gangrene with resultant peritonitis. This may necessitate laparotomy and segmental resection. A smaller percentage of patients progress to develop chronic strictures. These may be symptomatic and lead to partial or complete small bowel obstruction. They also may remain asymptomatic. Less commonly a chronic colitic state occurs due to a chronic ischemic injury of the affected segment.

DISCUSSION

Prevalence

Vascular diseases of the gastrointestinal tract are uncommon and represent no more than 1 to 2% of all gastrointestinal diseases.

Related Basic Science

Anatomic Derangement

Embolic disease of the superior mesenteric artery as a preferential site of embolism occurs because of the unique anatomic configuration of this vessel and its early branches. The inverted Y configuration favors the lodging of emboli at this site. Because of the location at the origin of the superior mesenteric artery, large segments of bowel are involved after embolization or thrombosis occurs, leading to significant mortality.

Physiologic or Metabolic Derangement

Localized arteritis of the vasculature of the gastrointestinal tract is seen in diseases such as polyarteritis nodosa, systemic lupus erythematosus, and scleroderma. Other manifestations of these diseases are almost universally present. Venous infarction of the small bowel may occur as a primary disorder or be part of other disease states, for example, a myeloproliferative disorder such as primary thrombocythemia or polycythemia vera. Antithrombin III deficiency, protein C disease, and anticardiolipin antibody are other conditions that may result in bowel infarction due to venous thrombosis.

Chronic intestinal ischemia is rare because of the unique vascular response to chronic arterial occlusion that occurs in the gastrointestinal tract. The three main vessels that supply the gastrointestinal tract from the aorta—the celiac axis, the superior mesenteric artery, and the inferior mesenteric artery—frequently extend collaterals to each other. Collateralization to the superior mesenteric artery may occur from the celiac axis via the pancreaticoduodenal or gastroduodenal artery. Retrograde filling of the superior mesenteric artery may occur from the inferior mesenteric artery as well. For this reason, the chronic ischemic syndrome does not occur unless two of the three vessels are involved with occlusive disease.

Natural History and Its Modification with Treatment

Acute ischemic disease of the small bowel is uniformly fatal if undiagnosed. A high index of suspicion with early diagnosis allows for survival. Acute ischemic colonic disease is almost always self-limited. Intervention as described decreases the progression of the transmural disease. The chronic disease states of intestinal ischemia are extremely uncommon. Diagnosis uniformly allows appropriate therapy to be instituted.

Prevention

More frequent use of anticoagulants in chronic arrhythmic states and postmyocardial infarction may well diminish the occurrence of embolic disease. Pharmacologic, dietary, and behavioral intervention may well over the course of years diminish the incidence of atherosclerotic disease and may diminish vascular disease of the gastrointestinal tract.

Cost Containment

Preventive measures will be the main instrument in diminishing the cost-intensive response to ischemic injury of the gastrointestinal tract. The availability of angiography in almost all centers now will allow physicians to move quickly in defining the presence of small bowel ischemic disease.

REFERENCES

Boley SJ, Feinstein FR, Sammartano R, et al. New concept in the management of emboli to the superior mesenteric artery. Surg Gynecol Obstet 1981;153:561.

Crawford ES, Morris CC Jr, Myhre HO, Roehm JO. Celiac axis, superior mesenteric artery and inferior mesenteric artery occlusion: Surgical considerations. Surgery 1977;82:856.

Ottinger LW, Austen WG. A study of 136 patients with mesenteric infarction. Surg Gynecol Obstet 1967;124:251.

Tomchik FS, Wittenberg J, Ottinger LW. The roentgenographic spectrum of small bowel infarction. Radiology 1970;96:249.

Short Gut Syndrome

Charles D. Gerson, M.D.

DEFINITION

The short gut syndrome refers to the condition of individuals who have lost most of their small intestine. The generally accepted concept of "short" is less than 5 ft of small bowel remaining beyond the ligament of Treitz. The importance of this definition is that it implies that there will be nutritional problems related to malabsorption because of the markedly shortened gut. These problems are mitigated if the colon is present, in which case 2 to 3 ft of small bowel may be enough to maintain nutritional sustenance.

ETIOLOGY

The basic cause of a shortened intestine is surgical resection. Surgical removal of most of the small bowel can occur in Crohn's disease, where it usually is the result of recurrent disease with multiple resections, finally leading to a short bowel. In contrast, massive resection can occur on an emergency basis as the result of a vascular event, usually mesenteric infarction. At one time, morbid obesity was treated with a jejunoileal bypass, purposely creating a short gut syndrome. On rare occasions, most of the small intestine may be resected because of neoplasm with multiple levels of obstruction. An example of iatrogenic short gut occurs if, after ulcer surgery, a gastroileostomy is inadvertently created instead of a gastrojejunostomy.

It is very important to include in the etiology whether the colon has been left in place and whether the ileocecal valve is intact. If the colon was removed along with most of the small bowel, then the patient is left with a jejunostomy. If the colon remains and jejunum is anastomosed to colon, fluid, electrolyte, and nutritional consequences are muted. It is the patient with Crohn's disease who is most likely to have lost the entire colon; mesenteric infarction can result in loss of the ascending colon.

CRITERIA FOR DIAGNOSIS

Suggestive

The patient may give a history of intestinal resection, diarrhea, and weight loss.

Definitive

A surgical report documenting the length of remaining small bowel after resection as less than 5 ft or a radiologic study with upper gastrointestinal series and small bowel follow-through demonstrating the length of the small bowel beyond the ligament of Treitz as less than 5 ft defines the diagnosis.

CLINICAL MANIFESTATIONS

Suggestive

The patient may have diarrhea, weight loss, and problems maintaining urine output and may feel dehydrated and debilitated.

The patient may have a past history of Crohn's disease or cardiac disease, especially cardiac arrhythmia such as atrial fibrillation.

The patient may have the history of a neoplasm that might cause obstruction of multiple segments of small intestine, such as intrinsic involvement with lymphoma or extrinsic involvement with desmoid or other mesenteric tumors.

The family history may indicate that some family members had Crohn's disease.

Objective

Physical Examination

The patient with a short bowel may show signs of malabsorption and dehydration. Aside from obvious wasting, there may be signs of specific nutrient deficiencies, as listed in Table 19–47–1.

On physical examination of the abdomen, there usually is a surgical scar and, possibly, a stoma. There also may be hyperactive bowel sounds and mild distention, as the remaining bowel compensates by dilation. In some of the conditions listed above, there may be tenderness, a mass, or an abdominal bruit.

Routine Laboratory Abnormalities

Malabsorption may be marked by a number of abnormalities in routinely obtained blood tests. Cholesterol may be strikingly low. In the patient with major fluid imbalance due to loss of alkaline intestinal secretions, there may be signs of metabolic acidosis. If there is deficiency of vitamin B_{12} or occasionally of folic acid or iron, anemia results; typically the anemia is macrocytic with an elevated red distribution width (RDW). Dehydration may also affect renal function with elevated creatinine, blood urea nitrogen (unless malnutrition is severe), and uric acid levels.

It is also important to be aware of the consequences of nutrient malabsorption because this may result in low blood levels of albumin, calcium, and magnesium and an abnormal prothrombin time.

PLANS

Diagnostic

Differential Diagnosis

Taking a careful history should lead to the proper diagnosis of short gut syndrome. Patients with profound malabsorption and dehydration associated with diarrhea and weight loss should be considered to have the following possible diagnoses, in addition to the short gut syndrome.

Intestinal Mucosal Disease. Although celiac sprue is the prototype, there are other conditions to consider such as inflammatory bowel disease without a short bowel, radiation enteritis, and AIDS enteropathy.

Secretory Diarrhea. Although secretory diarrhea usually does not cause significant malabsorption, diarrhea and dehydration can be severe. Vasoactive intestinal peptide-secreting pancreatic islet cell tumors and carcinoid syndrome are examples.

Diagnostic Options

Delineating the anatomy is first priority and this is best done via an upper gastrointestinal series with small bowel follow-through. If there is a question of tumor or infiltrative disease, computed tomography or upper endoscopy may be helpful.

TABLE 19–47–1. NUTRIENT DEFICIENCIES AND PHYSICAL FINDINGS

Nutrient	Physical Finding
Albumen	Edema
Calcium and vitamin D	Tetany, bone tenderness
Vitamin K	Ecchymoses
Vitamin B_{12}	Glossitis, pallor, neuropsychiatric syndromes
Zinc	Acrodermatitis
Vitamin A	Hyperkeratosis
Riboflavin	Cheilosis
Folic acid	Glossitis
Vitamin C	Perifollicular and gum hemorrhage
Niacin	Pellagra dermatitis

Recommended Approach

Reviewing surgical history, pathology reports, and barium study of the small intestine should indicate whether a patient has a short gut. Attention should then be paid to the consequences in terms of laboratory abnormalities and clinical assessment of nutritional status and dehydration.

Therapeutic

Therapeutic Options

Therapy can be directed at correcting abnormalities that have occurred as a result of a short gut. These can include anemia, electrolyte imbalance, nutritional deficiency, dehydration, and clinical malnutrition. Assessment of malnutrition can be validly determined by careful physical examination, especially in regard to weight loss.

Therapy can be given by the oral or parenteral route. In the early phase after surgery, parenteral needs are greater, though it is important to institute oral feedings as soon as possible because this may prevent mucosal atrophy and accelerate adaptation of the mucosa. If the patient seems dependent on parenteral fluids and calories for survival, hyperalimentation has to be continued after discharge. There is some evidence that intravenous administration of the amino acid glutamine may also prevent mucosal atrophy and enhance adaptation.

If the colon is present, parenteral needs are not as great. It has also been shown that a diet high in carbohydrates is appropriate in this setting. Carbohydrate that is not absorbed by the small bowel still provides a significant number of calories that can be absorbed by the colon after being converted to short-chain fatty acids.

Recommended Approach

Deficiencies must be corrected. Anemia may respond to iron, folate, or vitamin B_{12} repletion. Transfusion is usually not required. Calcium and vitamin D may be given orally or intravenously. Magnesium can be given intramuscularly if necessary. Profound weight loss and dehydration, often accompanied by hypokalemia, indicate that oral feeding will not suffice and intravenous supplementation is necessary. This may lead to consideration of a home hyperalimentation program.

If intestinal resection has occurred recently, this may be just a temporary measure while the remaining gut adapts to an increased need. In some patients, during the early postoperative phase, gastric acid hypersecretion may aggravate diarrhea. This problem responds to H_2 antagonists.

FOLLOW-UP

Because short gut syndrome is chronic, frequent follow-up is required, often at weekly or monthly intervals during the early phase. When patients are more stable, follow-up appointments can be at longer intervals. It is important to keep a record of weight and to follow blood count, electrolytes, calcium, magnesium, and renal function. If a patient is receiving home hyperalimentation, close collaboration must be established with the home nutrition service.

DISCUSSION

Prevalence and Incidence

Accurate population studies are not available concerning this aspect of the short gut syndrome. In areas where Crohn's disease is more prevalent, usually in urban settings, there is a correspondingly higher prevalence and incidence, but the numbers of patients with short gut remain small. There are some data concerning the use of home parenteral nutrition in the United Kingdom, where it is initiated in about two persons per million population per year. Home hyperalimentation figures in the United States would be less likely to represent short gut patients, as home hyperalimentation is also used for other conditions such as AIDS and cancer.

Related Basic Science

Anatomic Derangement

In the short gut syndrome, usually the ileum and most of the jejunum have been removed. In some patients, all or part of the colon has also

been removed. If not, the small intestine is anastomosed to colon, usually as a jejunocolic anastomosis with loss of the ileocecal valve. A variation may occur where the resection is from the ligament of Treitz to the distal ileum, leaving a short segment of ileum rather than jejunum.

After resection, the remaining small intestine undergoes anatomic change with hyperplasia of the mucosa. The ileum has a greater ability to do this than the jejunum. Absorptive capacity is also increased by dilation of the remaining gut.

Physiologic or Metabolic Derangement

Most nutrient absorption occurs in the small bowel. Therefore, massive resection has major consequences that can be explained in pathophysiologic terms.

First, what are the consequences of loss of the entire ileum? Table 19–47–2 lists the effects, which include vitamin B_{12} and bile salt loss. Bile salts normally are sent back to the liver via the enterohepatic circulation and thence to the duodenum. There, they solubilize intraluminal fat for transport across the intestinal mucosa. With depleted bile salts, fat malabsorption or steatorrhea occurs. Also with a limited ileal resection, bile salts in the colon provoke a watery diarrhea. Bile salt depletion may also lead to gallstone formation. Clearly, dehydration, hypokalemia, and metabolic acidosis can occur after resection. In addition to the debilitating effects of this, urine becomes more concentrated and kidney stones may occur. Another possible source of kidney stones is hyperoxaluria (see Chapter 19–48).

Early in the clinical course after massive small bowel surgery, patients may develop problems related to gastric acid hypersecretion with peptic ulcer or a lowered pH in the intestinal lumen. This is due to an increased release of gastrin in this setting, especially postprandially. This appears to be a relatively short-term problem.

Natural History and Its Modification with Treatment

Depending on length of remaining small bowel and continuity with the colon, the natural history of this disorder varies from sole reliance on oral feedings to total dependence on parenteral hyperalimentation. In many patients, there is a transition so that parenteral feeding is necessary in hospital or shortly after discharge but can be dispensed with thereafter.

In patients on home hyperalimentation, there is a risk of complications. Line sepsis is not uncommon, and a type of liver disease, cholestatic in nature, also may occur. Sometimes, reducing fat infusion can improve this. A majority of patients have a reduction in quality of life, though most are able to maintain employment. Survival figures indicate that patients with Crohn's disease and home hyperalimentation have an 80 to 90% survival after 2 years.

Prevention

The approach to surgical resection in Crohn's disease has changed over the years. Whereas previously there was an attempt to cure the patient with wide and repeated resections, it is now clear that this is ineffective and harmful in terms of nutritional needs. So it is recommended that small bowel resections be limited even if disease is left in place. Obstructing skip lesions can be treated with stricturoplasty and diffuse ileojejunitis may respond to immunosuppressive therapy.

Vascular emergencies that threaten the mesenteric circulation should

TABLE 19–47–2. CONSEQUENCES OF ILEAL DISEASE OR RESECTION

Vitamin B_{12} malabsorption
Bile salt malabsorption
Steatorrhea
Cholerrheic diarrhea
Fat-soluble vitamin depletion and hypocalcemia
Gallstones
Kidney stones
Hyperoxaluria
Gastric acid hypersecretion

be treated aggressively as there may be opportunity to remove a clot in the superior mesenteric artery or otherwise revascularize a compromised vessel.

Cost Containment

Because the major costs are related to parenteral hyperalimentation, attempts should be made to convert the patient to oral feedings with proper diet and treatment that may enhance intestinal adaptation. Patients should also be instructed carefully how to care for their intravenous access lines because prevention of line infection will also contain costs.

REFERENCES

Mughal M, Irving M. Home parenteral nutrition in the United Kingdom and Ireland. Lancet 1986;2:386.

Nordgaard I, Hansen BS, Mortensen PB. Colon as a digestive organ in patients with short bowel. Lancet 1994;343:373.

Powell-Tuck J. Management of gut failure: A physician's view. Lancet 1994;344:1061.

Straus E, Gerson CD, Yalow RS. Hypersecretion of gastrin associated with the short bowel syndrome. Gastroenterology 1974;66:175.

Woolf GM, Miller C, Kurian M, Jeejeebhoy KN. Nutritional absorption in the short bowel syndrome: Evaluation of fluid, calorie, and divalent cation requirements. Dig Dis Sci 1987;32:8.

CHAPTER 19–48

Enteric Hyperoxaluria

Charles D. Gerson, M.D.

DEFINITION

In certain disorders of the small intestine, an excess of ingested oxalate is transported down to the colon, where it is absorbed. This can result in an abnormally high excretion of oxalate in the urine, leading to kidney stones and, in some patients, kidney damage.

ETIOLOGY

Enteric hyperoxaluria occurs in association with malabsorption of fat, especially when an excess of intraluminal free fatty acids results. Because fatty acids bind to calcium, this leads to increased unbound oxalate, which is then absorbed by the colon and excreted in the urine.

CRITERIA FOR DIAGNOSIS

Suggestive

The condition should be considered in patients with kidney stones or disorders of the small intestine.

Definitive

The condition is likely to be present in patients with calcium oxalate kidney stones, increased urinary excretion of oxalate, or a small intestinal disease associated with steatorrhea.

CLINICAL MANIFESTATIONS

Subjective

The patient may experience renal colic, pass pink or red urine, or have bulky soft floating stools.

The patient may give a history of kidney stones, malabsorption syndrome, or intestinal resection.

Occasionally, there may be a family history of small intestinal disorders such as Crohn's disease and sprue.

Objective

Physical Examination

As two organ systems are involved, there may be physical signs of gastrointestinal or renal disease. Patients with sprue or other malabsorption syndromes may show signs of wasting or malnutrition. Because steatorrhea is the prime requisite, signs of vitamin D and calcium deficiency such as tetany and osteomalacia may be present. Decreased vitamin K can cause ecchymoses. In sprue, the patient often has some abdominal distention despite weight loss, because of small intestinal dilation. In patients with ileitis or intestinal resection, there may be evidence of prior abdominal surgery or tenderness in the right lower quadrant.

As patients usually present with renal colic, there may be tenderness over the costovertebral angle on the side with the stone.

Routine Laboratory Abnormalities

Passage of a kidney stone should cause hematuria, either grossly or on microscopic examination. In patients with steatorrhea, common findings in routine testing include a low serum cholesterol level. Malabsorption can also lead to anemia, often macrocytic, as well as low albumin and low calcium levels.

PLANS

Diagnostic

Differential Diagnosis

The differential diagnosis includes all conditions that lead to steatorrhea, especially with excess free fatty acids. This would include small bowel mucosal diseases such as celiac sprue, intestinal lymphangiectasia, and Whipple's disease. One should also consider inflammatory disease such as regional enteritis and radiation enteritis; surgical resection, especially of the ileum, and surgical bypass such as jejunoileal bypass for obesity; and motility disorders such as scleroderma and amyloidosis. Steatorrhea can also occur in conditions such as primary biliary cirrhosis and sclerosing cholangitis, where bile salt secretion into the duodenum is reduced.

Two caveats should be remembered. First, it is necessary for the colon to be present in a patient who has had intestinal resection. Second, pancreatic insufficiency leads to steatorrhea in the form of undigested triglycerides, not free fatty acids, so hyperoxaluria is not as common in this condition.

Diagnostic Options

Kidney stones can be identified and analyzed after passage. Urine concentration of oxalate can be determined. Finally, malabsorption and associated small intestinal disease can be sought.

Recommended Approach

To make the diagnosis of hyperoxaluria, passage of a kidney stone should be followed by its analysis for calcium oxalate, because some intestinal diseases are also associated with uric acid stones. Clearly it is important to evaluate the patient urologically, first looking for calcifications on plain radiographs. Further testing with sonography and dye studies depends on the clinical picture. Then the patient should submit a 24-hour urine specimen for oxalate measurement. Normal oxalate excretion in the urine should not exceed 40 mg per 24 hours.

If symptoms suggest possible malabsorption, then steatorrhea can be documented with a 72-hour stool collection, on a normal diet. In addition, small bowel barium study may indicate the specific disease present. If the disorder appears to be mucosal, then small intestinal biopsy should be performed endoscopically.

Therapeutic

Therapeutic Options

Therapy can be directed at improving a malabsorption syndrome or, if this is not possible, attempting to reduce oxalate absorption. Because fatty acids are responsible for binding calcium and freeing up oxalate, reduction of fat intake and increase of calcium intake may help increase the formation of insoluble calcium oxalate in the gut. In addition it is important to instruct the patient how to reduce oxalate in the diet. Foods with relatively high oxalate content are listed in Table 19–48–1. Cholestyramine also can be considered because it can increase oxalate binding.

It is also possible to reduce calcium availability in the renal system by administration of either citrate or sulfate, as these both bind to calcium in the urine.

Recommended Approach

Initially, the patient should be advised to increase fluid intake, to reduce fat in the diet, and also to go on a low-oxalate diet. If these measures do not succeed in lowering 24-hour urine oxalate, calcium supplementation can be instituted. Although supplementation of up to 2 g of calcium can be given, attention must be paid to possible excess calcium excretion in the urine. Finally, cholestyramine may help; however, this may increase steatorrhea in patients with extensive ileal resection who have a diminished bile salt pool.

If stones continue to form, citrate should be given orally in an attempt to bind urinary calcium. It is given as potassium citrate 500 mg three times per day.

FOLLOW-UP

Follow-up depends on the success of treatment and the subsequent clinical course with regard to kidney stones. If hyperoxaluria persists, renal colic is recurrent, or there are significant calcium deposits in the kidneys on radiographs, patients have to be followed regularly. If urinary oxalate is reduced, visits can be less frequent though dietary reenforcement is usually required.

DISCUSSION

Prevalence

Although accurate figures are not available, the highest frequency of enteral hyperoxaluria occurs in patients who have had a jejunoileal bypass procedure for obesity. That is one reason that this procedure has been largely abandoned. The other main cause of enteric hyperoxaluria is ileal resection.

It has been estimated that problems related to hyperoxaluria occur in about 10% of patients with free fatty acid steatorrhea.

Related Basic Science

Dietary oxalate is normally poorly absorbed because intraluminal calcium binds to most of the oxalate, making it unavailable for absorption. In conditions where there is an excess of fatty acids in the lumen because of malabsorption of fat, calcium binds to the fatty acids, making calcium soaps. This is most likely to occur when triglycerides have been digested by pancreatic enzyme to free fatty acids that then cannot

be absorbed because of inadequate solubilization by bile salts or because of mucosal disease. The reduced availability of calcium leaves an excess of oxalate in its free form. This results in an increase in absorption of ingested oxalate from a normal of 10% to about 40%.

Oxalate is then absorbed preferentially by the colon to a much greater degree than the small bowel. It diffuses passively across the colonic mucosa, and this permeability to oxalate is actually increased by the presence of fatty acids and deconjugated bile salts in the colonic lumen.

As oxalate is not highly metabolized, it is then excreted in the urine. Here it can bind to calcium to form insoluble calcium oxalate stones. This depends on oxalate concentration, calcium ion concentration, and the presence of other calcium-binding anions such as citrate and sulfate.

Natural History and Its Modification with Treatment

Passage of kidney stones in these patients is usually a sporadic process with increased frequency in warm weather when the urine may be more concentrated, similar to all kidney stones. Clearly, if oxalate excretion in the urine is reduced or returned to the normal range, kidney stone formation is much less likely to occur.

The main concern in regard to the natural history of this condition is deposition of oxalate in the kidney leading to uremia (Figure 19–48–1). This has been a problem in patients with jejunoileal bypass and also can occur in patients with Crohn's disease who have had ileal resection. It can lead to chronic dialysis treatment with all of its complications.

Prevention

It is important to quantitate urinary oxalate excretion in relation to treatment. Prevention can be achieved mainly by effective reduction in oxaluria by any of the means described under Plans, Therapeutic. Avoidance of unnecessary intestinal resection also prevents this problem.

TABLE 19–48–1. FOODS WITH HIGH OXALATE CONTENT

Tea	Chocolate
Coffee	Peanuts
Cola drinks	Cocoa
Spinach	Collard greens
Rhubarb	

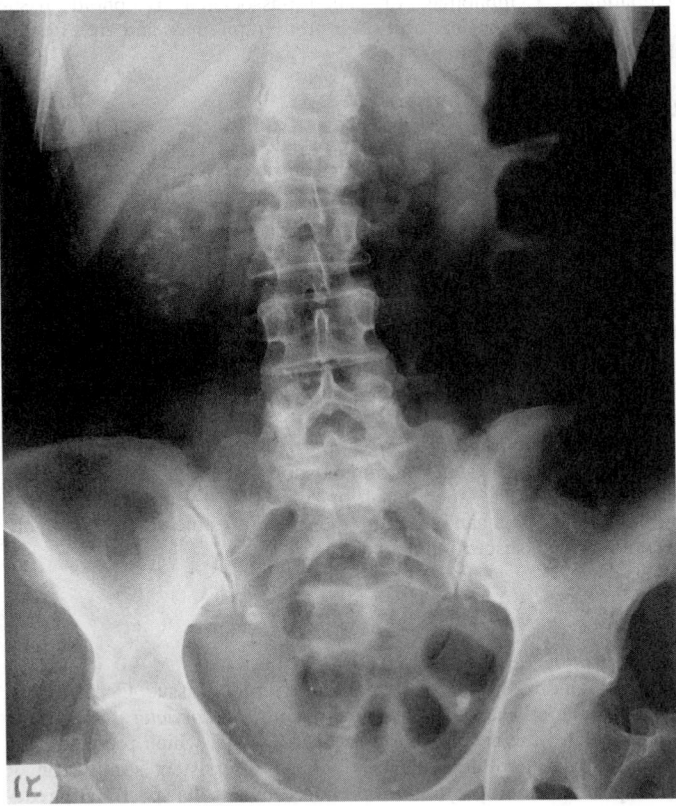

Figure 19–48–1. Calcium oxalate deposits in the kidney of a patient with enteric hyperoxaluria and renal failure.

Cost Containment

If dietary manipulation or other treatment is effective, then the frequency of acute renal colic or kidney damage will be reduced. As these complications may result in hospitalization or costly tests, this is the most effective way to contain costs.

REFERENCES

Anderson H, Jagenburg R. Fat-reduced diet in the treatment of hyperoxaluria in patients with ileopathy. Gut 1983;84:293.

Dobbins J, Binder H. Effect of bile salts and fatty acids on the colonic absorption of oxalate. Gastroenterology 1976;70:1096.

Dobbins J, Binder H. Importance of the colon in enteric hyperoxaluria. N Engl J Med 1977;296:298.

Earnest DL, Johnson G, Williams HE, Admirand WH. Hyperoxaluria in patients with ileal resection: An abnormality in dietary oxalate absorption. Gastroenterology 1973;66:1114.

Hylander E, Jarnum S, Nelsen K. Calcium treatment of enteric hyperoxaluria after jejuno-ileal bypass for morbid obesity. Scand J Gastroenterol 1980;15:349.

CHAPTER 19–49

Primary Gastrointestinal Lymphomas

William B. Solomon, M.D.

DEFINITION

Primary gastrointestinal lymphomas are neoplastic proliferations of lymphocytes that initially arise and cause symptoms within the gastrointestinal tract, and do not spread beyond the regional lymph nodes to peripheral lymph nodes, bone marrow, or liver and spleen. About 60% of primary gastrointestinal lymphomas arise in the stomach, 30% from the small intestine. The majority of primary gastrointestinal lymphomas are of B-cell origin; about 10% are derived from T cells.

There are three types of gastrointestinal lymphomas

Primary Gastric Lymphoma

The stomach is the most common site of primary extranodal lymphoma. Diffuse large cell type (B cell) accounts for two thirds of gastric lymphomas, most of which are intermediate and high-grade gastric lymphomas. Lymphomas of mucosa-associated lymphoid tissue (MALT) account for one third of gastric lymphomas, and are often indolent in their progression.

Lymphoma of the Small Intestine

In Western populations most are high-grade B-cell lymphomas. In Middle Eastern, African, and Mediterranean populations, B-cell small intestinal lymphomas associated with the production of alpha heavy-chain disease are more common than gastric lymphomas, and are often the end stage of immunoproliferative small intestinal disease (IPSID).

Epstein–Barr Virus-Induced Lymphomas of the Stomach and the Intestines

Epstein–Barr virus genomes are often found in gastric lymphoepithelioma or gastric adenocarcinoma with lymphoid stroma; the virus is likely to be an etiologic agent in these diseases. There is an increased risk of primary extranodal Epstein–Barr-associated lymphomas of the stomach (and other organs) in immunosuppressed individuals including AIDS patients. The sporadic form of Epstein–Barr virus-induced Burkitt's lymphoma can present in the small intestine often causing obstruction or intussusception.

ETIOLOGY

Gastric Lymphoma

The stomach does not normally contain lymphoid tissue. Chronic antigenic stimulation such as that occurring with *Helicobacter pylori* infection stimulates the accumulation of MALT cells, which produce lymphoid follicles (similar to Peyer's patches). Persistent stimulation of B-cell proliferation by cytokines produced by T cells specifically reactive to *H. pylori* may lead to the accumulation of genetic mutations within proliferating B cells, producing a clonal malignant proliferation of B cells—a lymphoma.

Small Intestinal Lymphoma

For the Mediterranean type of lymphoma, which is preceded by IPSID, it is likely that chronic antigenic stimulation of lymphocytes within Peyer's patches initiates the progression from polyclonal to monoclonal proliferation. A specific organism has not been implicated in this chronic antigenic stimulation; it is (presumably) orally ingested as the monoclonal B cells of the lymphoma often produce an IgA heavy chain.

CRITERIA FOR DIAGNOSIS

Suggestive

Lymphomas of the gastrointestinal tract develop insidiously. Manifestations of gastric lymphoma include symptoms of peptic ulcer disease including pain, change in appetite, and hematemesis. Lymphomas of the intestine may present with anorexia, persistent diarrhea, and weight loss. On occasion gastrointestinal lymphomas may present as acute surgical emergencies involving massive bleeding or obstruction or perforation of the stomach or intestine.

Persistence of symptoms such as diarrhea and unexplained weight loss in the absence of palpable adenopathy should raise the index of suspicion, particularly in patients who are immunosuppressed.

Definitive

The diagnosis of a gastrointestinal lymphoma is made on examination of the gastrointestinal mucosa usually obtained by endoscopic biopsy. There must be demonstration of a clonal population of B or T cells often by immunophenotype analysis. Concomitant with biopsy proof of lymphoma involving the gastrointestinal mucosa is exclusion via physical exam, examination, computed axial tomography scan, and bone marrow aspirate and biopsy of lymphomas involving peripheral nodes, bone marrow, spleen, or liver.

CLINICAL MANIFESTATIONS

Gastric Lymphoma

Subjective. There are no symptoms specific to primary gastric lymphoma. Virtually all patients give a history of epigastric pain that is indistinguishable from the pain of peptic ulcer disease. Other common symptoms include loss of appetite and nausea and vomiting. The initial symptom in many is upper gastrointestinal bleeding including hematemesis and/or melena. Some patients have B symptoms of lymphoma including night sweats, fatigue, and weight loss. Rarely, the initial presenting symptom can be the acute abdominal pain associated with gastric perforation.

Many patients give a history of chronic epigastric pain.

Objective.

PHYSICAL EXAMINATION. For proper planning of treatment, it is necessary to distinguish primary gastric lymphoma from the more common nodal lymphoma that also happens to involve the stomach. Particular attention should be paid to detection of enlarged peripheral lymph nodes as well as splenomegaly. Lymphomas involving the Waldeyer's ring of pharyngeal lymphoid tissues often involve the stomach too; therefore, careful examination of the tonsils and nasopharynx for evidence of lymphoma is required to rule out a lymphoma that requires treatment with systemic chemotherapy.

In addition to careful examination of nodal areas, it is also possible to palpate an epigastric mass in some individuals with primary gastric lymphoma.

Routine Laboratory Abnormalities. Many patients with primary gastric lymphoma are anemic secondary to chronic occult blood loss and, consequently, iron deficiency anemia. An elevated erythrocyte sedimentation rate is found in patients with weight loss, sweats, or itching.

Small Intestinal Lymphoma

Subjective. There are no symptoms that are specific to primary small intestinal lymphoma. The most common presenting symptom is abdominal pain often associated with partial small bowel obstruction. Common presenting signs include gastrointestinal bleeding and nausea and vomiting. Many patients complain of weight loss or diarrhea. It is of note that on average there is a 1-month delay between the onset of a patient's symptoms and a visit to the doctor; however, the time to diagnosis from initial doctor visit is on average 6 months.

In patients with intestinal lymphomas associated with chronic antigenic stimulation there is often a history of persistent diarrhea and weight loss at times accompanied by peripheral edema.

Objective.

PHYSICAL EXAMINATION. Patients with lymphomas associated with IPSID may have peripheral edema and finger clubbing. Patients with non-Hodgkin's lymphoma of the small bowel may have a palpable abdominal mass, signs of intestinal obstruction, or frank peritonitis secondary to perforation.

ROUTINE LABORATORY ABNORMALITIES. In patients with IPSID-related lymphomas, hypoalbuminemia is common.

PLANS
Diagnostic
Gastric Lymphoma

Differential Diagnosis. The presenting symptoms of primary gastric lymphoma are similar to those of peptic ulcer disease, chronic gastritis, and adenocarcinoma of the stomach.

Diagnostic Options. As almost all individuals with primary gastric lymphoma have symptoms and signs indistinguishable from those of peptic ulcer disease, they undergo gastroscopy. The endoscopic appearance of gastric ulcers caused by primary gastric lymphoma does not differentiate them from ulcers caused by gastric adenocarcinoma.

On occasion a "volcano ulcer" may be seen. This lesion is an ulcer raised above the surface of the gastric mucosa surrounded by raised margins of normal-appearing tissue. This type of ulcer is suggestive of gastric lymphoma, but is also found in ulcers caused by cancers that are metastatic to the stomach.

The diagnosis of gastric lymphoma is made by endoscopic brushings and biopsy of the visible gastric mucosal lesion.

About 85% of patients with primary gastric lymphoma have immunoglobulin G antibodies directed against *H. pylori*; however, 50 to 60% of all individuals have antibodies to *H. pylori*.

Recommended Approach. The diagnosis of primary gastric lymphoma is made by examination of tissue obtained at endoscopy. Under light microscopy, a characteristic invasion of gastric glands by small cleaved centrocytic lymphocytes and plasma cells is noted. At times, this appearance cannot be distinguished from that of florid *H. pylori* gastritis. Immunophenotype analysis is very useful in the diagnosis of primary gastric lymphoma. Identification of a monoclonal population of B cells using anti-kappa or anti-lambda light-chain antibodies is characteristic of lymphoma. Analysis of clonal rearrangements of immunoglobulin

gene DNA is useful to distinguish a polyclonal proliferation of lymphocytes as seen in lymphoproliferative gastritis from true lymphoma.

Once a diagnosis of primary gastric lymphoma is made by the pathologist, further staging tests are necessary. If endoscopic ultrasonography is available, it is used to assess the depth of invasion of the lymphoma (lymphomas often grow in the submucosa and can invade the mucosa as well as through the serosa) and the presence of enlarged perigastric lymph nodes. To determine the stage of the primary gastric lymphoma, workup should include computed axial tomography scans of the chest and abdomen, bone marrow aspirate and biopsy, and indirect laryngoscopy to rule out involvement of Waldeyer's ring of pharyngeal lymphoid tissues.

Small Intestinal Lymphoma

Differential Diagnosis. The presenting symptoms of primary small intestinal lymphoma are similar to those of infectious diarrhea syndromes, malabsorption syndromes, or acute abdominal crises such as obstruction and a perforated viscus.

Diagnosis Options. In patients with a long history of diarrhea and malabsorption the presence of a monoclonal alpha heavy chain is an indication for further evaluation. Small bowel contrast radiography can demonstrate evidence of a coarse and irregular nodular mucosal pattern; at times polypoid masses can be visualized. If the small bowel study is abnormal, multiple small bowel biopsies particularly of the duodenum can be taken (the area most frequently involved in alpha heavy-chain disease-related lymphoma). Investigation of the biopsy can distinguish a polyclonal lymphocytic infiltrate from a frank lymphoma (using the same technology as noted above for gastric lymphoma).

Elevated levels of serum immunoglobulin A or a monoclonal immunoglobulin A heavy chain (α-HCD) in serum or urine can be detected in almost all patients with IPSID-related intestinal lymphoma.

In many patients the only diagnostic option is surgery because of the emergent nature of the symptoms with which the patient presents.

Recommended Approach. Because of the varied presenting symptoms and signs of small intestinal lymphoma no single approach can be recommended; however, in patients with recurrent abdominal pain that is not responsive to a brief empiric trial of treatment, the diagnosis of small bowel lymphoma (or other neoplasm) should be considered and an upper gastrointestinal series with small bowel follow-through or high colonic enema (enteroclysis) ordered. These x-ray studies should be carefully reviewed because the abnormalities are often subtle.

Therapeutic
Gastric Lymphoma

Therapeutic Options. Therapy is based on the grade and stage of the lymphoma. Stage IE is gastric lymphoma confined to the stomach, IIE includes involvement of regional lymph nodes including perigastric and celiac axis, stage IIIE includes involvement of paraaortic and iliac nodes, and stage IVE includes disease that involves bone marrow, lung, and other organs.

For low-grade MALT lymphoma involving the stomach only (stage IE) without bleeding or perforation and with evidence of *H. pylori* infection, it is sometimes possible to induce regression of the lymphoma with vigorous antibiotic treatment; however, this treatment by itself has not been shown to produce a definitive cure. The therapeutic options for stage IE and IIE primary gastric lymphoma include subtotal gastrectomy and/or primary radiation therapy. For more advanced stages of gastric lymphoma, the treatment of choice is chemotherapy.

Recommended Approach. For low-grade stage IE and IIE gastric lymphomas, the treatment of choice is surgical resection (usually partial gastrectomy) followed by local radiation therapy or adjuvant chemotherapy. For high-grade gastric stage IE and IIE lymphomas, it is likely that radiation therapy followed by adjuvant chemotherapy is the preferred treatment. For more advanced stages the primary therapeutic modality is chemotherapy, though radiation therapy or surgery may be required to palliate bleeding or perforation of the stomach. Because of the complex therapeutic decisions and the small number of patients with primary gastric lymphoma, in the final analysis, all treatment decisions should be made on an individualized basis.

Small Intestinal Lymphoma

In patients with IPSID with polyclonal proliferation of lymphocytes, a treatment trial of tetracycline 2 g/d may result in a complete remission as demonstrated by decrease in the serum immunoglobulin A levels and reversal of the malabsorptive state. For patients with IPSID-related lymphoma, resection of bulky intestinal masses is recommended, followed by chemotherapy.

Patients with non-Hodgkin's lymphoma of the small intestine should undergo resection if the disease is stage IE or IIE (involving a segment of the small bowel and local lymph nodes), followed by adjuvant chemotherapy. For more advanced stages, systemic chemotherapy is required at the time of diagnosis.

FOLLOW-UP

Gastric Lymphoma

As many patients with primary gastric lymphoma relapse outside the area of original treatment, adjuvant chemotherapy should be considered in patients whose primary therapy was surgical. Aside from careful physical examination to detect enlarged nodes and splenomegaly, follow-up abdominal computed axial tomography scans (perhaps at yearly intervals) may be useful for detecting recurrence.

Small Intestinal Lymphoma

About 50% of patients with small intestinal lymphoma relapse within 5 years of treatment with combination chemotherapy, often outside the original area of disease. Follow-up should include physical examination to detect adenopathy, as well as abdominal computed axial tomography scans.

DISCUSSION

Prevalence

Gastric Lymphoma

Primary gastric lymphoma is the most common form of primary extranodal lymphoma; however, it is a rare disease probably accounting for about 1 to 3% of all primary gastric malignancies. In the era of AIDS it is likely that the incidence of Epstein–Barr virus-induced gastric lymphoepitheliomas will increase.

Small Intestinal Lymphoma

Primary small intestinal lymphoma is a rare disease. In some areas of the Middle East it is the most common primary extranodal lymphoma.

Related Basic Science

Malt lymphomas. For many primary gastrointestinal lymphomas of B-cell origin, infection with *H. pylori* or other organisms appears to be the primary etiologic event. MALT tissue can grow in culture when stimulated by cytokines derived from T cells that were specifically responsive to *H. pylori*. This may explain why eradication of *H. pylori* infection may reverse the early stages of MALT proliferation.

Epstein–Barr Virus-Associated Lymphomas. Infection of B lymphocytes with Epstein–Barr virus results in their immortalization. It appears that expression of the Epstein–Barr virus latent membrane protein or other Epstein–Barr virus-encoded proteins results in increased expression of the *Bcl-2* gene, which inhibits apoptosis of B lymphocytes. The dearth of cytotoxic T cells against Epstein–Barr virus-infected B cells in immunosuppressed individuals results in the failure of eradication of immortalized B cells, which can then acquire additional genetic changes that result in a malignant lymphoma.

Natural History and Its Modification with Treatment

Without treatment gastrointestinal lymphomas are almost always fatal due to either bleeding, perforation, or dissemination to other organs and the bone marrow. With treatment a substantial percentage of patients have a 5- or 10-year disease free survival.

Prevention

Because many gastrointestinal lymphomas are likely to be caused by chronic bacterial infections, treatment of chronic *H. pylori* infection or other bacteria may decrease the incidence of gastrointestinal lymphoma.

Cost Containment

The use of computed axial tomography scans for proper staging of gastrointestinal lymphomas will result in better staging of patients so that surgery will be performed only in patients with early-stage (IE and IIE) disease.

REFERENCES

Domizio P, Owen RA, Shepherd NA, et al. Primary lymphoma of the small intestine: A clinicopathological study of 119 cases. Am J Surg Pathol 1993;17:429.

Isaacson PG. Gastrointestinal lymphoma Hum Pathol 1994;25:1020.

Martin IG, Aldoori MI. Immunoproliferative small intestinal disease: Mediterranean lymphoma and α heavy chain disease. Br J Surg 1994;81:20.

Parsonnet J, Hansen S, Rodriguez L, et al. *Helicobacter pylori* infection and gastric lymphoma. N Engl J Med 1994;330:1267.

Strober W, James SP. The immunopathogenesis of gastrointestinal and hepatobiliary disease. JAMA 1992;268:2910.

CHAPTER 19–50

Diverticular Disease of the Colon

Stephen M. Brenner, M.D.

DEFINITION

Diverticular disease of the colon is present when there is a protrusion of the mucosa, without its mucosal coat, through the wall of the colon leading to single or multiple diverticula (Figure 19–50–1).

ETIOLOGY

Diverticulosis coli is asymptomatic, usually defined by either sigmoidoscopy, colonoscopy, or barium enema. Diverticulitis, which is an acquired condition, occurs when infection occurs within one or more diverticula leading to inflammation or hemorrhage.

CRITERIA FOR DIAGNOSIS

Suggestive

Acute diverticulitis is a disease of varying intensity. The patient presents with sudden pain, usually in the left lower quadrant or suprapubic region, which is usually constant with or without fever.

Definitive

The presence of an abdominal mass in the left lower quadrant or suprapubic area, associated with fever and varying signs of peritoneal irritation, strongly suggests diverticulitis.

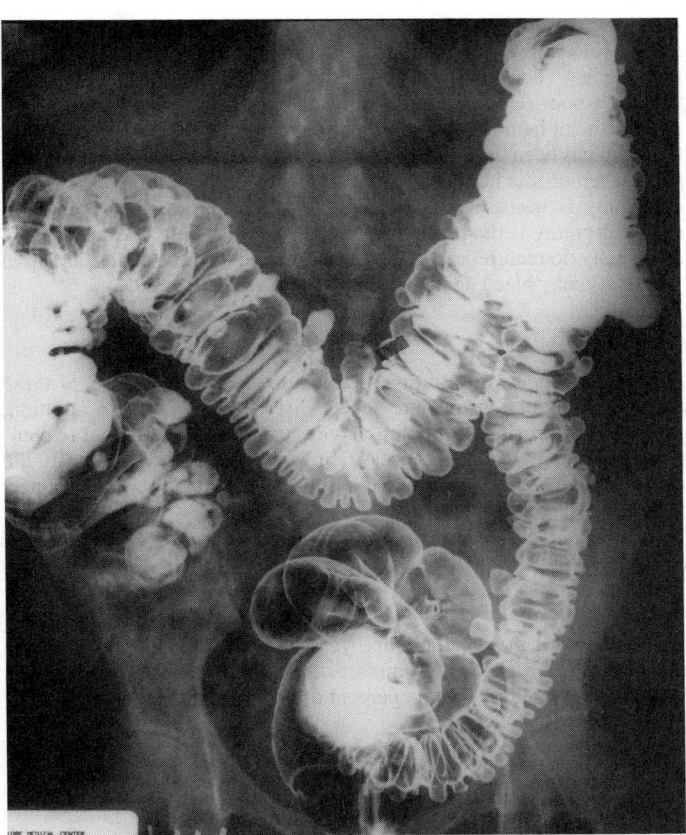

Figure 19–50–1. Barium enema demonstrating extensive diverticulosis of the entire colon.

CLINICAL MANIFESTATIONS

Subjective

The patient presents with relatively sudden onset of left lower quadrant or suprapubic pain, constant in nature with or without fever. There is usually no prodrome although some patients may have prior symptoms referable to a long history of spastic colon. In the more complicated case, fever and chills and nausea and vomiting develop. The patient may be constipated or may have mild diarrhea.

Objective

Physical Examination

Physical examination in the milder cases demonstrates only abdominal tenderness in the left lower quadrant or suprapubic area. Bowel sounds are usually normal in the milder cases. In more extensive disease, a palpable mass may be present and there may be voluntary guarding or rebound tenderness localized to the left lower quadrant. In most cases diverticulitis affects the left colon. Right-sided diverticulitis does occur with similar findings on the right side of the abdomen (Marcham and Li, 1992).

Routine Laboratory Abnormalities

In the milder cases, the routine laboratory tests are normal. There should be no blood in the stool. When more significant inflammation and infection are present, the white blood cell count is elevated and there is a shift to the left. Urinalysis may reveal white blood cells or red blood cells if the inflammatory process is contiguous with the bladder or ureter.

PLANS

Diagnostic

Differential Diagnosis

The differential diagnosis is mainly between a perforated or obstructing carcinoma of the colon and a mechanical process such as volvulus of the colon. In the female, a neoplastic or inflammatory process of the ovary or fallopian tube is to be considered. In most cases of right-sided diverticulitis, the patient is suspected of having acute appendicitis.

Diagnostic Options

An initial plain film of the abdomen with supine and upright films may be helpful in excluding a mechanical process such as volvulus or obstruction, as well as free air under the diaphragm. Barium enema should not be performed in the acute period (Cho et al., 1990).

Recommended Approach

The diagnostic procedure of choice is computed tomography of the abdomen and pelvis (Hachigian et al., 1992). Computed tomography of the abdomen and pelvis excludes an ovarian or fallopian tube etiology and, with diverticular disease, allows a classification of the process that will define the therapeutic options available. In mild uncomplicated diverticular disease, the computed tomography scan may be normal or reveal diverticula with a thickened wall and inflammation of the pericolic tissues and fat, the so-called phlegmonous inflammation. In the more complicated disease, a pericolic abscess or pelvic abscess may be defined.

Therapeutic

Therapeutic Options

The therapeutic options include the use of antibiotics and bowel rest combined with the specific indications for surgical intervention.

Recommended Approach

In the least severe process without any signs of inflammation, bowel rest with nothing by mouth or clear liquids, with or without the use of oral antibiotics, such as tetracycline 250 to 500 mg four times a day or ampicillin 500 mg four times a day with metronidazole 500 mg four times a day, is sufficient to control the disease. Most patients improve within 24 to 48 hours. In the patient in whom a palpable tender mass is present or in whom signs of peritoneal irritation are present, hospitalization is warranted and therapy instituted with bowel rest and systemic antibiotics. The antibiotics used should be directed toward eradication of the Gram-negative bacilli, enterococci, and anaerobic organisms resident in the colon. A combination of ampicillin 1.5 to 2 g every 4 hours intravenously, or intravenous vancomycin in the penicillin-allergic patient in doses dependent on the size of the patient and renal function, and metronidazole 500 mg every 6 hours intravenously and the use of an aminoglycoside (dose dependent on the size of the patient and renal function) is preferred. Cefoxitin 1 g every 8 hours intravenously with aminoglycoside may also be efficacious. In the patient with milder disease, therapy is usually successful and the antibiotics may be discontinued in 7 to 10 days and diet advanced accordingly. In the more severely ill patient who does not respond to antibiotics, it may be that the process had developed into a walled off abscess or an abscess was present initially and not appreciated. If the abscess develops and persists and does not abate with antibiotic therapy, percutaneous drainage, if feasible, using computed tomography or sonography is indicated (Stabile et al., 1990). If this is successful, surgical intervention may allow for a single-stage procedure. If signs of infection do not abate with percutaneous drainage, laparotomy is indicated. Diffuse peritonitis with or without free air is an indication for immediate surgical intervention. Evidence of bowel obstruction, either large or small bowel, in the presence of acute diverticulitis need not be an indication for early laparotomy. Treatment with antibiotics and nasogastric decompression with or without precutaneous drainage may allow for improvement of bowel obstruction. Fistula formation may occur acutely or chronically (Figure 19–50–2). The most frequent sites are to the bladder, vagina, adjacent loops of bowel, or skin. Surgical resection is indicated if bowel rest and

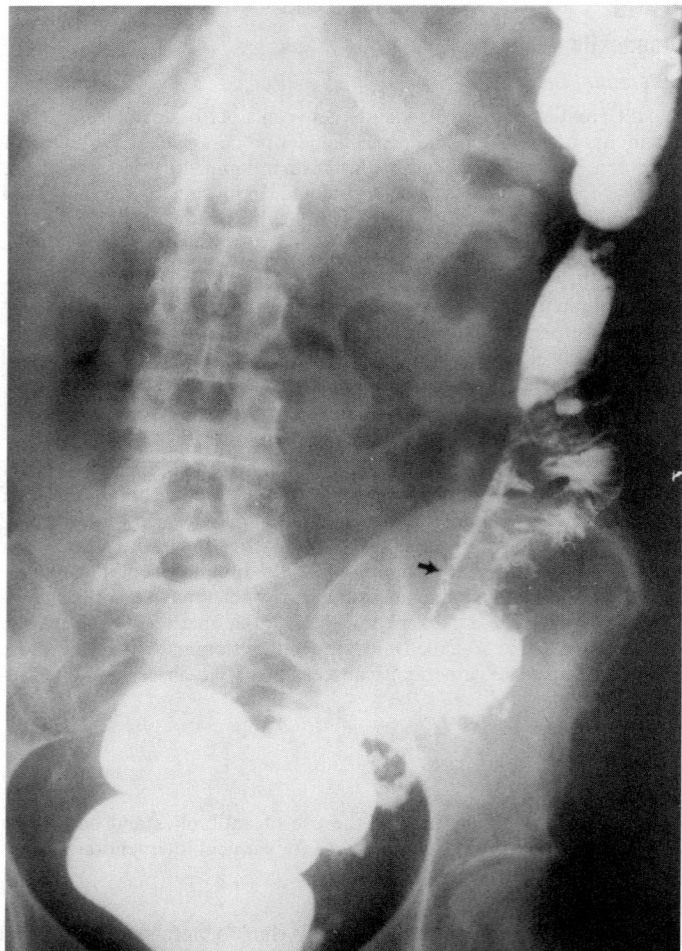

Figure 19–50–2. Barium enema demonstrating diverticulosis and a paracolic fistula (arrow).

antibiotics do not successfully allow reversal. Diverticulitis of the right colon is treated with antibiotics and usually surgically by right hemicolectomy.

Surgical intervention in acute diverticulitis has changed in the past decade, with most surgeons favoring a two-stage procedure rather than the previously employed three-stage procedure. In the uncomplicated stage of disease, surgery is not indicated. The presence of an abscess usually dictates surgical intervention. If percutaneous drainage is successful a single-stage resection and anastomosis may be preferred with acceptable morbidity and mortality. If smoldering infection continues with inadequate drainage, resection of the bowel and drainage of the abscess with proximal colostomy are usually performed. Reconstitution of bowel is performed at a later date after the sepsis is controlled. Generalized peritonitis calls for emergency laparotomy with resection of the perforated segment, proximal colostomy, and copious intraperitoneal lavage.

Acute hemorrhage may also occur from diverticulitis of the colon. This may occur because of the proximity of a medium-sized artery in the neck of the diverticulum to an area of inflammation. The bleeding is usually significant to massive and may result in shock. The bleeding is sudden and painless. Sigmoidoscopy is the procedure of choice to be sure a lower rectal or sigmoid source is not present. If bleeding is occurring higher up in the colon or in the small bowel, radionuclide imaging is indicated in an attempt to localize the site of hemorrhage. In most cases, the bleeding ceases spontaneously. If it does, colonoscopy should be performed to confirm that no other source of hemorrhage is present. This may be a neoplasm, benign or malignant, or an angiodysplastic lesion of the bowel. If bleeding does not stop, emergency colonoscopy may be attempted after colonic irrigation, and if a site is

identified, injection with saline or epinephrine may be attempted to stop the bleeding. Angiography, though less sensitive than radionuclide imaging, has been employed to identify the site of bleeding. In a patient deemed a poor risk for surgical intervention, if angiography does identify the site of hemorrhage, injection via the vessel of autologous clot or Gelfoam has been used in an attempt to stop the bleeding. On rare occasions when no site has been identified or if bleeding continues, subtotal colectomy is necessary. If right-sided colonic bleeding is identified, right colectomy is the procedure of choice. If bleeding does stop, there are usually no recurrences, although it is stated in some series that up to 10 to 25% may bleed again months to years later.

FOLLOW-UP

Repeated episodes of mild diverticulitis do occur. During any of these episodes, progression to more severe disease may occur. In addition, progressive fibrosis of the colon may occur, resulting in partial to complete colonic obstruction necessitating surgical intervention. In the chronic stage, fistulas may develop, also necessitating surgical intervention (Figure 19–50–3).

DISCUSSION
Prevalence

Sixty percent of the population 60 years or older have colonic diverticula. Of these, 20% become symptomatic and 10 to 20% of these require surgical intervention. Twenty percent of patients with acute diverticulitis are 40 years or younger.

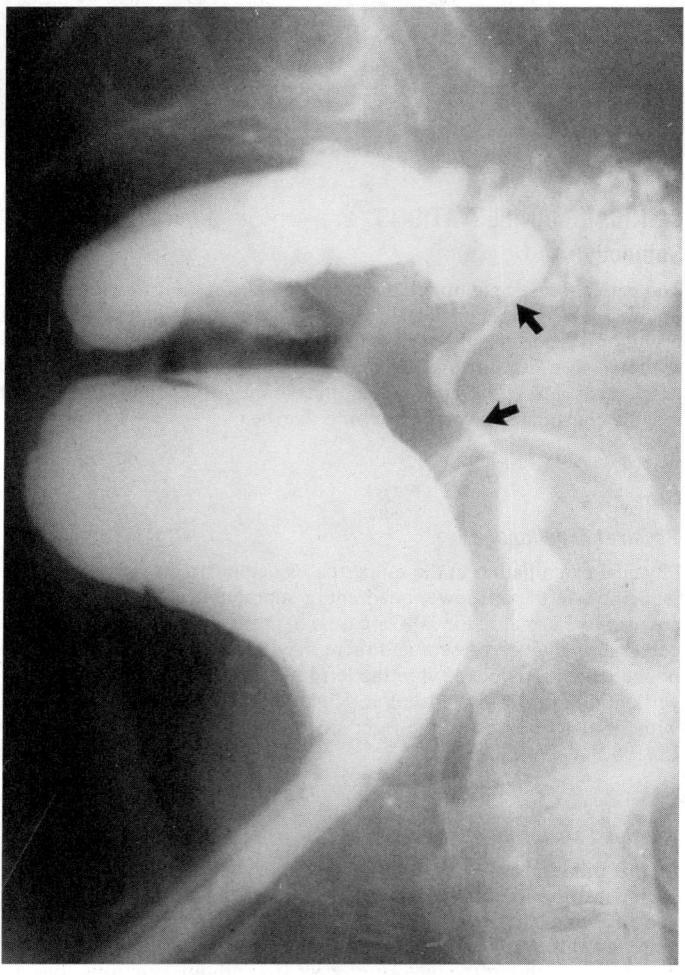

Figure 19–50–3. Barium enema demonstrating a colovaginal fistula (arrows).

Related Basic Science

The specific etiology of diverticulosis is speculative. Abnormal motor activity of the colon, increased intraluminal pressure, and loss of elasticity of the bowel have all been implicated.

Natural History and Its Modification with Treatment

Once acute diverticulitis has occurred, the recurrence rate is high. If perforation has occurred, the recurrence rate approximates 50% in some series. In uncomplicated cases, early intervention with appropriate antibiotics may allow for better treatment of the acute illness. Untreated, this disease is often fatal.

Prevention

Preventive steps are directed toward decreasing intraluminal pressure and avoiding trauma to the already developed diverticula. The mainstay of therapy is increased fiber in the diet in the form of either psyllium or methylcellulose or bran, combined with an adequate fluid intake of 7 to 8 oz of liquid per day as well as the avoidance of those food substances that may become lodged in the diverticula, such as nuts, large pits, and seeds or undigested pectins.

Cost Containment

Cost containment is directed at preventative measures and a change in direction of management with more extensive use of percutaneous modalities. This has allowed for a more shortened course of surgical intervention with the ability to provide surgical repair in either a primary or two-stage procedure.

REFERENCES

Cho KC, Morehouse HT, Altenmatu DD, Thornhill BA. Sigmoid diverticulitis: Diagnostic role of computerized tomography in comparison with barium enema studies. Radiology 1990;176:111.

Hachigian MP, Honickman S, Eisenthal TE, et al. Computerized tomography in the initial management of acute left-sided diverticulitis. Dis Colon Rectum 1992;35:1123.

Marcham NI, Li AK. Diverticulitis of the right colon: Experience from Hong Kong. Gut 1992;33:547.

Stabile BE, Puccio E, Vansonnenberg E, Neff C. Preoperative percutaneous drainage of diverticular abscesses. Am J Surg 1990;159:99.

CHAPTER 19–51

Radiation Enterocolitis

Stephen M. Brenner, M.D.

DEFINITION

Radiation enterocolitis is injury to the gastrointestinal tract that is caused by ionizing radiation.

ETIOLOGY

The tolerance to injury from radiation varies for different parts of the gastrointestinal tract, but is proportional in general to the total dose of radiation (Fletcher et al., 1958), and is dependent on the fractionation of the dose, the amount of gastrointestinal tract involved, and several other factors related to the host tissue. Although injury may occur with doses of 40 Gy (4000 rad), the incidence of intestinal injury increases with doses of 50 Gy or higher.

CRITERIA FOR DIAGNOSIS

Suggestive

Radiation injury to the intestine occurs in acute and chronic forms. The acute phase usually occurs after the institution of therapy, which may be external-beam therapy to the anterior abdominal wall or intracavitary therapy, as is used for carcinoma of the cervix. Gastrointestinal symptoms occurring during the course of or months to years following radiotherapy may be indicative of gastrointestinal damage by ionizing radiation.

Definitive

Definitive evidence of injury is the demonstration of damage to the gastrointestinal tract by either gastrointestinal endoscopy, roentgenographic evaluation, or pathologic evidence of radiation injury.

CLINICAL MANIFESTATIONS

The clinical manifestations of radiation injury to the gastrointestinal tract may occur in acute and chronic forms. The symptoms of the injury depend on the mode of administration of the radiation and the location of damage in the gastrointestinal tract.

Subjective

In the acute injury, if the small intestine is the major site of damage, colicky abdominal pain, mild nausea, vomiting, and diarrhea are the hallmark symptoms. Rectal involvement is manifested by tenesmus and diarrhea with or without the passage of bright red blood per rectum. The possibility of a delayed injury to the bowel is to be considered when the total radiotherapy exposure is 50 Gy or more. Radiation to the intestine may result in chronic damage that may manifest anywhere from 6 months to years after therapy has been completed. The clinical syndrome depends on the source of the radiation and the site-specific organ involved.

In general, the onset of symptoms is insidious. Rectal involvement usually results in tenesmus with some mucoid rectal discharge with or without the passage of bright red blood per rectum. If the sigmoid colon has been significantly damaged and the damage extends deeper than the mucosal surface, then the resultant fibrosis may be responsible for obstruction (Figure 19–51–1). The symptoms include crampy abdominal pain and increasing constipation leading to colonic obstruction. Perforation of the wall may occur secondary to severe fibrosis with colonic obstruction. If transmural inflammation occurs, formation of fistulas to the skin, bladder, vagina, and other loops of bowel may occur. The presenting symptoms may then be those of recurrent urinary infection or diarrhea or drainage of fecal material per vagina. Less commonly, more proximal segments of bowel are involved that may lead to skipped areas of colitis or pancolitis, similar to inflammatory bowel disease with resultant diarrhea.

Injury to the small intestine may occur independently or coexist with involvement of the colorectum (Shibata et al., 1982). The most frequent portion of the small bowel involved is the terminal ileum. The most frequent symptoms are those of partial or complete small bowel obstruction. Crampy abdominal pain, at first intermittent and mild, progresses over a variable period to persistent colic, nausea, and vomiting associated with weight loss. If small bowel obstruction is partial, diarrhea may supervene. Massive bleeding and perforation occur but are much less common. Formation of fistulas to the skin or other organs may likewise occur with small bowel involvement.

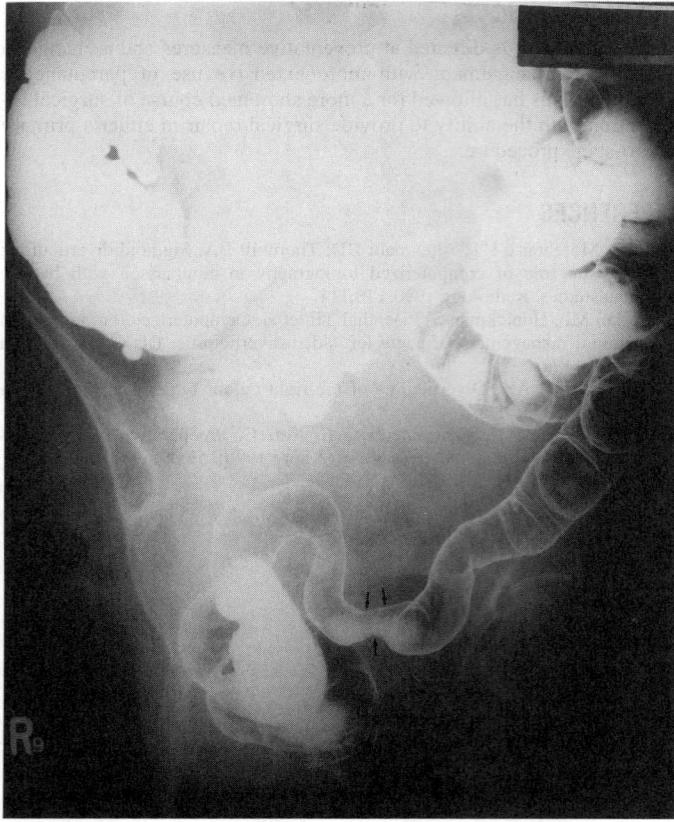

Figure 19–51–1. Barium enema demonstrating a narrowed sigmoid colon (arrows) with intact mucosa and no diverticula.

Objective

Physical Examination

In the acute radiation injury to the bowel, physical examination is usually not specific relative to the abdomen. Tenderness may be present over the area of bowel involvement. Bleeding may be present. In chronic radiation bowel disease, the physical examination varies according to the site of injury. In rectal disease, the examination is usually unrevealing except for pallor from a significant anemia. The rectal examination may reveal blood; rarely, a stricture is palpated. Physical examination in chronic small bowel disease usually shows some sign of weight loss and patients are pallid due to occurrence of anemia. A mass may be palpable in the right lower quadrant from matted bowel, simulating the occurrence of tumor. Blood may be detected in the stool. If diarrhea is present, dehydration may be present in addition to the findings associated with malabsorption, such as dependent edema and cachexia. Evidence of formation of fistulas to the skin or the vagina may be evident.

Routine Laboratory Abnormalities

Laboratory evaluation usually reveals an anemia with or without a vitamin B_{12} deficiency and a lowered serum albumin level, and may show a decrease in ionized calcium and magnesium levels and prolongation of the prothrombin time.

PLANS
Diagnostic

Differential Diagnosis

In acute radiation injury to the rectum, the major differential diagnoses are usually those of intercurrent infection leading to diarrhea with or without bleeding. In acute injury to the small intestine, bacterial or viral infection or a complication of the primary neoplasm is the most frequent condition assessed.

In chronic radiation injury to the rectum, the differential diagnosis includes recent infection or the occurrence of a metastatic or new primary neoplasm leading to bleeding or signs of obstruction. If the process has affected the small intestine, the differential diagnosis usually encompasses neoplasms, either metastases from originally diagnosed neoplasms or new tumors, and some superimposed mechanical process such as adhesive disease.

Diagnostic Options

Specific tests of malabsorption, for example, the D-xylose test, 72-hour fecal fat determination, or ^{14}C-labeled breath test, may be necessary to assess small bowel absorption and the presence of bacterial overgrowth.

These options include radiographic or endoscopic examination of the gastrointestinal tract associated with appropriate cultures.

Recommended Approach

In acute or chronic disease affecting the rectum, the procedure of choice is sigmoidoscopy. In acute radiation injury, a beefy red mucosa that traumatizes easily is seen diffusely. Appropriate cultures for ova and parasites and culture and sensitivities must be obtained. In chronic radiation injury, sigmoidoscopy reveals a pallid mucosa, with neovascularity and telangiectatic vessels. In more severe cases, diffuse ulceration may be seen. The process is usually not evenly distributed in the segment of bowel and is not circumferential in the piece of colon or rectum involved. Significant edema is not present; the bowel traumatizes easily. If no structure is present, the segment of involvement may be localized to a few centimeters of the rectum or may extend into the sigmoid colon. Biopsy may be taken to confirm the histologic nature of the radiation disease.

In chronic radiation small bowel disease, an obstructive series should be obtained to assess the radiologic expression of either partial or complete small bowel obstruction. If obstruction is present then decompression with nasoenteric intubation is indicated. If no evidence of obstruction is present, then direct radiographic evaluation of the small intestine is indicated. Evidence of fixation of the bowel, spiculation of the mucosa, and fistulas may be present (Figure 19–51–2).

Therapeutic
Therapeutic Options

In acute radiation disease, therapy is easily defined. The therapy must temporarily be stopped to allow the bowel injury to heal. In chronic ischemic injury, therapeutic options relate to the specific complications that occur in the area of injury.

Recommended Approach

In acute colonic disease, symptoms usually subside when therapy is stopped. If more extensive damage occurs with ulceration through the bowel wall, a localized perforation or hemorrhage may occur, in which case surgical intervention may be necessary. In milder cases, therapy is directed toward bowel rest and antidiarrheal therapy with medications, such as diphenoxylate hydrochloride 1.5 to 5 mg every 6 hours, and a low-fat diet. Cholestyramine, a resin that binds bowel salts intraluminally, has been efficacious if an ileal injury is suspected and is usually given in doses of 1 g two to four times per day.

Localized rectal or sigmoid disease of the mucosa without obstruction is primarily a disease of bleeding. Symptomatic therapy has not significantly altered the course of bleeding. Rectal steroids have been used with variable success, and the same may be said of short-chain fatty acids, both given in the form of rectal enemas. A low-residue diet and hydrophilic compounds to bulk up the stools such as methylcellulose or bran and mineral oil in doses of 1 to 4 oz per day are used to diminish trauma. This may sometimes decrease the bleeding. When bleeding is more extensive, laser ablation of the tiny ectatic vessels is used over several sessions and this may decrease the bleeding to a tolerable amount. When bleeding is more persistent and responsible for considerable blood loss and the necessity for frequent blood replace-

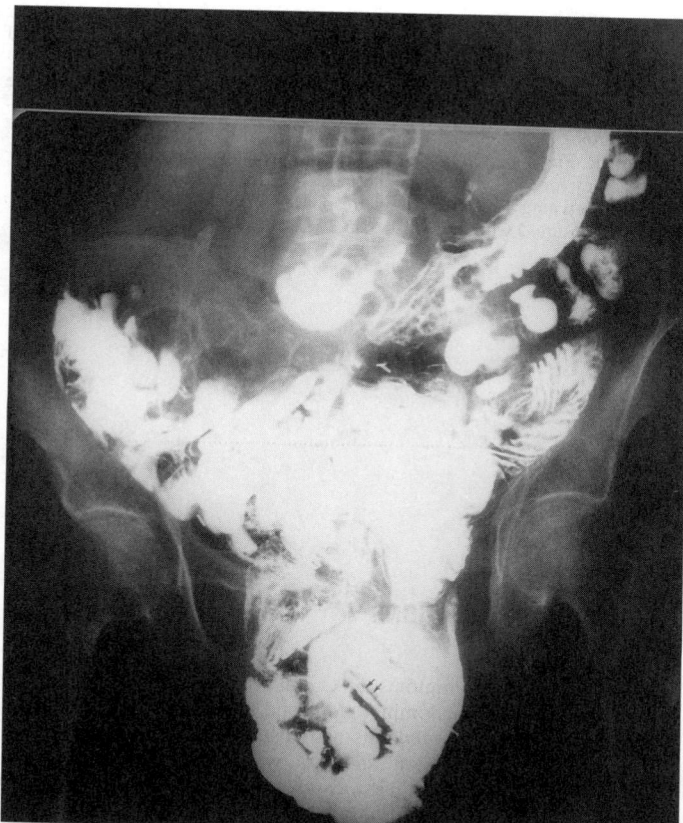

Figure 19–51–2. Small bowel series demonstrating spiculation of the mucosa, central fixation, and a linear enteroenteric fistula (arrows).

FOLLOW-UP

Radiation enterocolitis is an ongoing process. Treatment directed at one segment of the bowel may later be followed by subsequent disease in a separate segment. Careful follow-up for involvement of the same or subsequent loops of bowel is indicated to evaluate recurrence.

DISCUSSION
Prevalence

It has been estimated that upward of 50% of patients with a malignancy are eventually treated with radiotherapy. Of these patients, those who receive 40 to 50 Gy therapy are significantly at risk for radiation bowel disease. Of these patients, 5 to 15% have a resultant radiation enteritis or colitis (De Cosse et al., 1969).

Related Basic Science

The total dose delivered to the tissue remains the single most important factor of radiation injury. Also implicated are host factors that may enhance the radiation effect, such as body habitus (a thinner patient having a greater exposure) and the presence of diabetes mellitus, hypertension, or collagen–vascular disease, which may predispose to more significant injury. Prior surgery may fix one or more loops of bowel, allowing them to be more confined to the field of radiation with resultant damage.

With the development of megavoltage equipment and control of the factors governing the cutaneous response, skin toxicity is no longer a dose-limiting factor in radiotherapy. Those tissues with rapid cell turnover are those areas where radiation injury becomes most manifest. Mucous membrane damage is thus the most frequent tissue injury. The gastrointestinal tract epithelium is completely replaced within 3 to 5 days, which makes it one of the most rapidly reproduced tissues in the body. Cells in the mitotic phase are especially susceptible to radiation injury. Within 12 to 24 hours of radiation, injury can be seen with swelling, hyperemia, pyknosis, and death of cells. In the ensuing days, loss of crypt cells, shortening of the villi, and crypt dilation occur, accompanied by degenerative changes in the endothelial cells of the submucosa (MacDonald et al., 1964). Desquamation of the epithelial cells occurs. By the second to fourth week, infiltration of the lamina propria by inflammatory cells, plasma cells, or polys occurs, and focal erosions in a spotty fashion are the resultant injury. The erosions occur in a spotty fashion because of the high capacity for regeneration of the mucosa. A typical change in the mucosa of the rectum occurs with the development of crypt abscesses, which are composed mostly of eosinophils (Trier and Browning, 1966).

Following the acute injury and its repair after therapy has ended ensues a period during which the endothelial cells undergo edematous change and then detachment from the basement membrane and ultimate desquamation. Fibrin plugging leads to thrombosis. Recanalization may occur, but the result of this process is progressive ischemia to the affected segment of bowel. This may be accentuated by the host factors previously described. As a result, the submucosa becomes thickened and fibrotic with resultant obstruction, fistula formation, and perforation. Diarrhea with or without malabsorption may occur.

Natural History and Its Modification with Treatment

Because of the continued need for radiotherapy to control malignant disease, radiation-induced bowel disease will continue to be a challenge. Changes in dose fractionation, better delivery systems, utilization of three-dimensional portals, and more help to diminish tissue injury may lessen the injurious effects of radiation.

Prevention

Improved patient nutrition by hyperalimentation, either peripherally or centrally, or nutrient supplements may also help to prevent tissue injury. As we understand more about the nature of malignant cell changes, we may alter the need for extrinsic therapy in controlling malignant disease.

ment, it is occasionally more imperative to resort to surgical intervention. If bleeding is confined to the rectum, diverting colostomy has been used successfully. If the segment is higher up in the colon and the rectum and adjacent colon are found to be free of disease on biopsy, segmental resection may be employed. The same may be done with localized stricture of the colon.

If chronic small bowel disease is present with partial or complete obstruction, nasoenteric decompression is indicated. In small bowel disease without obstruction, small bowel x-ray defines the disease. Segmentation of the loops of bowel with effacement of the mucosa and spiculation of the bowel with superficial ulceration are hallmarks of radiation damage. Stricture formation may be present proximal to the obstruction. Fistulas to various sites may be demonstrated (Figure 19–51–2). Diffuse abnormality of the small bowel may be seen when generalized radiation has been used, with multiple segments of bowel showing involvement. Obstruction should be treated medically with decompression. Acute obstruction by food in a strictured area may be corrected by this means. If persistent obstruction is present and not medically correctable, surgical intervention is required. Bypass surgery is generally recommended because of the high complication rate that occurs when primary resection and anastomosis are attempted because of more diffuse radiation injury. Fistula formation is likewise treated by bypass, proximal to the loop involved. A direct surgical attack on the loop of bowel with a fistula is often associated with recurrent or new fistula formation. If bowel on either side of the fistula can be shown to be free of radiation damage, then a primary resection may be done if significant bowel can be restored. Malabsorption may be corrected by the use of antidiarrheal drugs such as diphenoxylate hydrochloride 2.5 to 5 mg four times a day to slow intestinal transit, a low-fat diet, and vitamin B_{12} replacement; antibiotic therapy with tetracycline 250 to 500 mg four times a day may be used to sterilize the bacterial overgrowth in a stagnant loop of bowel. Cholestyramine may decrease the effect of bile salt-induced diarrhea in doses of 1 to 4 g four times a day.

Cost Containment

As we define more precisely the genetic and environmental causes of malignancies, it is hoped we will learn how to modify therapy of these diseases. Until then, better understanding of radiation effects will allow us to decrease tissue injury and thus prevent the complications of therapy.

REFERENCES

De Cosse JJ, Rhodes RS, Wentz WB, et al. The natural history and management of radiation-induced injury to the gastrointestinal tract. Ann Surg 1969;170:369.

Fletcher GM, Brout C, Rutledge N. Clinical significance of rectal and bladder measurement of radiation therapy of carcinoma of the uterine cervix. Am J Roentgenol 1958;79:421.

MacDonald WC, Trier JS, Everett RB. Cell proliferation and migration in the stomach, duodenum, and the rectum of man: Radioautographic studies. Gastroenterology 1964;46:405.

Shibata HR, Freeman MB, Roman TN. Gastrointestinal complications after radiotherapy for carcinoma of the uterine cervix. Can J Surg 1982;25:1.

Trier JS, Browning TH. Morphologic responses of the human small intestine to x-ray exposure. J Clin Invest 1966;45:194.

CHAPTER 19–52

Crohn's Disease

David B. Sachar, M.D., and Jacob S. Walfish, M.D.

DEFINITION

Crohn's disease is a chronic idiopathic transmural inflammatory disease of the bowel. It may affect any part of the gastrointestinal tract from mouth to anus, but occurs most commonly in the distal ileum and colon. In the earlier medical literature, Crohn's disease was frequently referred to as "granulomatous" or "regional enteritis" or "ileitis." These designations, however, are now considered inaccurate, as granulomas and ileal involvement are not always present; hence the universal adoption of the time-honored, albeit nondescriptive eponym, Crohn's disease.

ETIOLOGY

The etiology of this idiopathic disease remains, by definition, unknown. Predisposing factors, etiologic theories, and pathogenetic mechanisms are discussed later in this chapter. The heterogeneous nature of the clinical course and manifestations of this disease, however, suggests that there may be more than one specific cause and, indeed, more than one discrete disease.

CRITERIA FOR DIAGNOSIS
Suggestive

Crohn's disease should be suspected in any patient, especially under the age of 35, who presents with more than 1 to 2 months of crampy lower abdominal pain, diarrhea, and weight loss. Low-grade fever, anemia, nonsymmetric arthritis, and other specific extraintestinal manifestations should increase the index of suspicion for this disease. The diagnosis is even more likely if a right lower quadrant mass or fullness is felt or if any history of perianal fistulous disease is obtained.

Definitive

Definitive diagnosis is made by barium contrast x-rays of the small bowel and/or colon, which show bowel wall thickening with luminal narrowing and separation of bowel loops, linear and transverse fissures, cobblestoning, and/or fistula formation. Crohn's colitis may also be diagnosed by colonoscopy, which will reveal discrete, punched-out linear and serpiginous ulcers and fissures with normal intervening mucosa. Skip areas, predominant right-sided disease, and rectal sparing further characterize "textbook" cases. Moreover, visualization and biopsy of the terminal ileum at colonoscopy may often provide further confirmation of the diagnosis. Endoscopic biopsies and surgical specimens of the bowel usually show inflammation that is nonspecific, but focality of lesions is suggestive, transmural inflammation and fissuring are characteristic, and epithelioid granulomas (present in up to 50% of cases) are virtually pathognomonic of Crohn's disease.

CLINICAL MANIFESTATIONS
Subjective

In early stages, the symptoms of Crohn's disease may be limited to mild and intermittent abdominal pains and altered bowel habits, indistinguishable from the complaints associated with irritable bowel syndrome; however, concomitant anorexia, weight loss, fever, anemia, or blood in the stool should quickly arouse suspicion of an inflammatory process. Not infrequently, inflammatory Crohn's disease presents less insidiously, mimicking acute appendicitis, with the sudden onset of right lower quadrant pain, tenderness, and fever. Meticulous history taking usually elicits an acknowledgment of chronic antecedent symptoms, but sometimes laparotomy or laparoscopy is still required to exclude acute appendicitis. If ileitis is found, differentiation between the acute self-limited infectious form and Crohn's disease is necessary as discussed later in this chapter.

The anatomic location of chronic inflammatory Crohn's disease can often be surmised by a careful history and physical examination. Persistent pain or a palpable tender mass in the right lower quadrant together with nonbloody diarrhea generally suggest terminal ileal disease, whereas colonic involvement may be manifested by more diffuse abdominal pain and by pus, mucus, and blood in the stool. Perianal lesions such as fistula and abscess, although more common in colonic disease, are seen in many cases of localized ileitis as well.

As the inflammation progresses, either of two broad patterns of clinical behavior may emerge, each attended by a different set of complications. The fibrostenotic pattern results in intermittent or chronic obstructive symptoms, initially due to reversible bowel wall edema and spasm, but evolving over several years to fixed scarring, luminal narrowing, and stricture formation. Postprandial pain and distention, which ultimately progress to acute episodes of frank intestinal obstruction, are the usual clinical hallmarks of this fibrostenotic pattern of disease.

The fistulizing form of Crohn's disease has somewhat different clinical manifestations. As the inflammatory process penetrates transmurally, sinus tracts traversing the serosa may result in intramesenteric abscesses causing spiking fevers with sweats and chills. Deeper penetration of sinus tracts into adjacent organs results in fistulous complications of manifold nature and consequence. For example, fistulas from the colon to the stomach or duodenum may cause foul-tasting eructation or even frank feculent vomiting. Dysuria, pneumaturia, and recurrent urinary tract infections may result from enterovesical fistulas. Feculent vaginal discharge may rarely be a sign of an enterovaginal fistula or, much more commonly, an indication of a rectovaginal fistula due to rectal ulceration penetrating the rectovaginal septum.

Enterocutaneous fistulas intermittently discharge pus or mucus often mixed with blood, gas bubbles, or slightly feculent fluid. They occur most commonly at the site of surgical scars from prior abdominal surgery or, in the absence of prior surgery, may drain at the umbilicus or track along the psoas muscle to present in the flank or groin.

In addition to its various local intestinal complications, such as inflammation, bleeding, obstruction, fistulization, and perforation, Crohn's disease may also exhibit many extraintestinal manifestations that may or may not parallel the activity of the intestinal disease. Inflammatory or immunologic complications outside the gastrointestinal tract most often affect the skin, joints, mouth, eyes, or bile ducts.

The principal skin manifestations are erythema nodosum, painful red bumps usually on the shins or thighs, and pyoderma gangrenosum, pustular lesions generally on the lower extremities or trunk, which ulcerate deeply with surrounding tissue necrosis. Peripheral arthritis tends to affect the larger joints (knees, ankles, hips, elbows, wrists) in an asymmetric distribution. The most common mouth lesion is aphthous stomatitis; the eyes are sometimes involved by episcleritis. All these findings are more common when colitis is present than when disease is confined to the small bowel, and they generally, though not always, tend to subside when the bowel disease is brought into remission.

In contrast, ankylosing spondylitis and sacroiliitis, which may cause hip and back pain and are diagnosed radiologically, follow a course independent of the bowel inflammation, as do the rarer complications of anterior uveitis and primary sclerosing cholangitis (the latter complication confined almost exclusively to cases of inflammatory colonic disease and discussed in more detail in Chapter 19–53).

In eliciting the past history, the physician should of course ask about any of the previously discussed extraintestinal manifestations, which may have developed before the bowel symptoms became clinically significant. Especially in children and adolescents, prominent extraintestinal symptoms may dominate the clinical picture. A history of unexplained growth failure and delayed pubertal development is common when Crohn's disease begins at a young age. Fevers of unknown origin, chronic anemia, recurrent peripheral arthritis, and perirectal fistulas are also common presenting signs in young people with undiagnosed Crohn's disease.

A dietary history is important in evaluation of the patient's nutritional status and in anticipating the need for caloric or nutrient supplements. Equally valuable is a careful inquiry into medication use, including prior treatment with steroids, antibiotics, and enema preparations, which may alter the clinical picture in addition to producing their own side effects. Nonsteroidal antiinflammatory agents can sometimes worsen symptoms or even precipitate a flare of Crohn's disease. Oral contraceptive use may rarely produce ileal or colonic inflammation mimicking Crohn's disease, so it should specifically be asked about in women. A smoking history may also be of value, as smoking has been associated with an increased risk of developing Crohn's disease and also an increased relapse rate in patients with established disease.

Environmental, toxic, and dietary factors, including neonatal bottle feeding and low fiber, high sugar intake have been extensively studied with only equivocal findings; the past history relating to these areas may be of research interest but is unlikely to be contributory to diagnosis or management.

A genetic component for inflammatory bowel disease is supported by the familial occurrence of both Crohn's disease and ulcerative colitis as well as by the predilection of these diseases for certain ethnic groups such as Ashkenazic Jews. Indeed, multiplex families are common and there is up to a 50% concordance for Crohn's disease among homozygous twins. In one study, 11.3% of patients with known inflammatory bowel disease had a positive family history of similar disease compared with only 4% in a control group. Therefore, a positive family history is certainly a risk factor for both Crohn's disease and ulcerative colitis. Other genetically determined diseases that have been associated with Crohn's disease include ankylosing spondylitis (especially with the HLA-B27 haplotype), tyrosine-positive albinism, Hermann–Pudlansky syndrome, and Turner syndrome.

Objective

Physical Examination

The most typical physical finding is abdominal tenderness, primarily in the right lower quadrant. A palpable mass in this area is highly charac-

teristic of distal ileitis. Besides the nonspecific physical signs of anemia or weight loss, the more specific joint, skin, mouth, and eye findings described above may also support the diagnosis of inflammatory bowel disease. Clubbing may be seen with extensive small bowel involvement. Less common but also reported are cutaneous vasculitis and cryoproteinemia, which may cause peripheral gangrene or skin necrosis, and "metastatic" Crohn's disease, which may appear as nodular, ulcerating skin lesions that reveal noncaseating granulomas on biopsy. Thorough examination of the perineum is particularly essential in suspected Crohn's disease, as giant skin tags ("elephant ears"), active perianal fistulas and abscesses, and scarring from old disease are found in many cases.

Routine Laboratory Abnormalities

Blood test abnormalities are nonspecific with regard to the diagnosis of Crohn's disease, but are helpful in assessing disease severity. Anemia may be due to blood loss, folate, and vitamin B_{12} malabsorption, or "chronic disease." Electrolyte abnormalities including hypokalemia and acidosis may be caused by severe diarrhea. Hypoalbuminemia may reflect gastrointestinal protein loss or severe malnutrition; other signs of malabsorption and malnutrition may include hypocholesterolemia, hypocalcemia, hypomagnesemia, and hypoprothrombinemia. Urinalysis and renal function tests are used to monitor urinary complications and the state of hydration.

Liver enzyme abnormalities are quite common and may reflect a variety of hepatic lesions ranging from fatty liver due to malnutrition, to "pericholangitis" and primary sclerosing cholangitis, seen for unknown reasons in certain patients with either Crohn's or ulcerative colitis and leading in rare cases to the late development of cholangiocarcinoma. Hepatic abscess due to portal spread of infection is rare but should be ruled out in cases of unexplained fever with or without abnormalities in liver function tests.

PLANS

Diagnostic

Differential Diagnosis

Whenever Crohn's disease of the terminal ileum is suspected, other intestinal and extraintestinal diseases that present in the right lower quadrant must also be considered. Of paramount importance is the exclusion of acute appendicitis in patients who present with acute right lower quadrant pain and tenderness. The principal distinguishing feature of acute appendicitis is the abrupt onset without any preexisting history of chronic bowel symptoms; however, even when symptoms are intermittent or more chronic, appendiceal disease may be present in the form of recurrent subacute appendicitis or appendiceal abscess. Imaging studies such as barium contrast x-rays, sonogram, and computed tomography are often helpful in such cases, but when these noninvasive tests are equivocal, laparoscopy or laparotomy may ultimately be necessary for definitive diagnosis. In such cases, the appendix should be removed if there is uncomplicated Crohn's disease without involvement of the cecum. Right-sided or cecal diverticulitis must also be considered, especially in the older patient presenting for the first time with acute right lower quadrant symptoms. Barium enema can be helpful in establishing this diagnosis.

Infectious diseases that produce localized inflammation in the right lower quadrant include ileocecal tuberculosis, amebiasis, anisakiasis, and *Yersinia* infection. Tuberculosis should be sought by chest x-ray; even if the x-ray is negative, a positive tuberculin skin test should still raise the index of suspicion. In such cases, endoscopic or laparoscopic biopsy and culture may be necessary. Although isolated amebic ileitis is a rare occurrence, amebic colitis can readily be mistaken for Crohn's disease when it is complicated by an ameboma in the ileocecal region. Amebiasis can be diagnosed by stool examination, serologic titers, or mucosal biopsy. Anisakiasis, a roundworm infestation usually due to ingestion of raw fish, and *Yersinia* infection, sometimes occurring as part of an epidemic, can both produce a syndrome of acute self-limited ileitis, but they do not progress to the chronic disease typical of Crohn's. In AIDS patients, *Mycobacterium avium–intracellulare* and cytomegalovirus may also cause a localized ileitis.

Among neoplastic diseases that can resemble Crohn's disease radiologically are carcinoma of the cecum, ileal carcinoid, lymphoma, and metastatic disease from breast, melanoma, stomach, pancreas, or especially ovary. Likewise, pelvic inflammatory disease, ectopic pregnancy, and direct extension of ovarian cysts and tumors can produce right lower quadrant inflammatory signs, so gynecologic consultation is often advisable. When these various neoplastic or gynecologic disorders cannot be definitely ruled out by noninvasive means, and there is no response to empiric therapy for Crohn's disease, open or laparoscopic exploration may, as with appendicitis, be necessary to establish a firm diagnosis.

Vascular disease can also mimic inflammatory bowel disease. Ischemic ileitis may occur in the older patient with vascular insufficiency or in women taking oral contraceptives. Systemic vasculitis may also affect the small bowel in such diseases as polyarteritis nodosa, systemic lupus erythematosus, and dermatomyositis.

Other miscellaneous disorders that can be confused with Crohn's disease are eosinophilic gastroenteritis, amyloidosis, and chronic nongranulomatous ulcerative jejunoileitis. The last condition has features of both Crohn's disease and sprue, but a malabsorption picture predominates, and granulomas, fistulas, and extraintestinal manifestations are absent.

In isolated Crohn's colitis, specific causes of acute colitis and chronic ulcerative colitis must be excluded. This differential diagnosis is discussed in Chapter 19–53.

Diagnostic Options

Barium contrast gastrointestinal x-rays are usually adequate to define the nature, distribution, and severity of the disease. In the absence of surgery, the anatomic site and extent of disease rarely change with time, although there may be progression of severity within the confines of the initial location.

Radiographic examination should be performed by radiologists experienced in gastrointestinal fluoroscopy to ensure that maximal information and quality films are obtained. An upper gastrointestinal series together with a small bowel series and spot films of the terminal ileum will most clearly show the extent of the ileal disease in addition to any involvement of the upper tract. In early cases, mucosal edema and ulceration are seen with thickening and distortion of the valvulae conniventes. Separation of barium-filled loops of bowel and mild luminal narrowing may be caused by edema of the bowel wall. Tracking of deep ulcerations, both transversely and longitudinally, results in the classic "cobblestone" appearance. A "string sign" caused most often by spasm or rarely by fibrotic stricturing is also a characteristic feature of ileitis. Enteroenteric fistulas and fistulas to adjacent organs can likewise be detected by barium study.

Although Crohn's disease of the colon may be diagnosed by colonoscopy, a barium enema examination may be the preferred initial diagnostic study because it has some advantages in demonstrating such features as fistulization and submucosal edema. Punched-out ulcers, linear and transverse fissures, and strictured segments, like those in the small bowel, are also seen in the colon. The lesions tend to be more prominent in the right colon and typically but not invariably spare the rectum. If barium refluxes on postevacuation films, terminal ileal disease may also be revealed, but in most cases of ileitis the ileocecal valve is tight and the terminal ileum is not visualized on barium enema.

In very early cases, when conventional radiographic diagnosis may be difficult, films obtained by double-contrast barium enema and small bowel enteroclysis may be more sensitive in showing superficial aphthous and linear ulcers, but these techniques are more difficult, expensive, and painful. Therefore, if single-contrast barium enema has proved suboptimal in evaluating a case of Crohn's disease of the colon, colonoscopy would be a logical next step. Indeed, the choice between barium enema and colonoscopy for initial diagnosis of Crohn's colitis may well be dictated by local and individual factors such as available expertise, relative cost, and patient preference. Where colonoscopy is perhaps of greatest value is in evaluating strictures or filling defects noted on barium enema and in distinguishing Crohn's disease from ulcerative colitis. Colonoscopy and biopsy are also useful when radiographs have not clarified the initial diagnosis or differential diagnosis

of suspected colitis or have not shown the cause of recurrent symptoms following ileocolic resection for established Crohn's disease. In these cases, the colonoscope may allow direct visualization and biopsy of the terminal ileum, as well as direct inspection of an ileocolic anastomosis. Colonoscopy and biopsy, moreover, are indispensable for cancer surveillance in long-standing, extensive Crohn's disease of the colon, whose cancer risk equals that of ulcerative colitis.

Upper endoscopy and biopsy are likewise of value in distinguishing peptic ulcer disease from gastroduodenal Crohn's disease when radiographs are nondiagnostic.

Other imaging modalities such as ultrasound and computed tomography scanning are not generally used as primary diagnostic modalities but may be very helpful in the evaluation of fistulas, abscesses, and hepatobiliary and renal complications.

Among the serum proteins used to gauge acute inflammation in the gut, C-reactive protein and orosomucoid, an α_1-glycoprotein, are most closely correlated with clinical disease activity. Erythrocyte sedimentation rate is useful in following the activity of Crohn's colitis but is less valuable when disease is limited to the small bowel.

Recommended Approach

In its classic presentation, with a typical chronic history and a tender right lower quadrant fullness or mass, a complete upper gastrointestinal and small bowel series lead to the diagnosis. Failure to obtain a complete small bowel series with adequate spot films of the terminal ileum often results in a missed diagnosis. In most cases, treatment can be begun once small bowel Crohn's disease is established, as the presence or absence of colonic disease generally does not affect the course of therapy initially. At some point afterward, presumably when the patient is better able to tolerate the preparation and procedure, barium enema or colonoscopy should be performed to evaluate colon disease.

In patients who present with more acute right lower quadrant pain, urgent laparoscopy or surgery may be necessary to exclude acute appendicitis. In such cases the diagnosis of ileitis is readily established by the characteristic gross appearance of thickened bowel and enlarged lymph nodes. If there is a question of ileocecal tuberculosis, *Yersinia* enteritis, or neoplasm at surgery, lymph node biopsy and cultures should be done. Biopsy of the bowel wall carries the risk of subsequent fistulization and should be avoided unless absolutely necessary for differential diagnosis. Ileal resection should usually not be performed when laparotomy reveals acute, uncomplicated, inflammatory disease of the terminal ileum, as surgical results tend to be poor in such cases and an opportunity is needed to see what medical therapy can accomplish.

When the patient presents with principally colitic symptoms of bloody diarrhea with mucus and pus, sigmoidoscopy should be the initial procedure, with further evaluation as outlined in Chapter 19–53.

Therapeutic

Therapeutic Options

Although not curative, the medical armamentarium for Crohn's disease now includes a wide variety of drugs, both old and new, that have been shown to be of benefit individually and in combination. Because of the known tendency for disease recurrence following surgical resection, aggressive efforts should be directed toward obtaining the maximal benefits achievable by medical therapy before resorting to surgery, unless specific complications mandate early surgical intervention. It is therefore imperative that the treating physician have a thorough knowledge of the agents available for the treatment of Crohn's disease, including their expected benefits, limitations, costs, and side effects.

Sulfasalazine, 5-aminosalicylic acid linked to sulfapyridine, is activated when bacterial azoreductase releases the salicylate moiety in the lower bowel. As would be expected, its greatest benefit has been demonstrated in patients with colitis or ileocolitis, although some modest benefit has been shown in ileitis as well. Sulfasalazine is used primarily in disease of mild to moderate severity and to maintain remission, although its efficacy for the latter indication is still not well established. The response to sulfasalazine is dose dependent as are many of its side effects, thus limiting its practical usefulness. The dose-related side effects include gastrointestinal intolerance such as anorexia, dyspepsia, nausea, vomiting, and headaches. An enteric-coated formulation can sometimes reduce the gastrointestinal side effects. Dose-related folate depletion is avoided by coadministration of folic acid supplements. Non-dose-related adverse reactions include allergic rashes, hemolytic anemia, agranulocytosis, and fibrosing alveolitis. Reversible infertility in men is also a common side effect of the sulfapyridine moiety.

Because many of the side effects of sulfasalazine are related to the sulfa moiety, newer drugs have been developed to allow delivery of the active ingredient, 5-aminosalicylate or mesalamine, to the affected areas. Olsalazine (Dipentum) is a 5-aminosalicylate dimer that is split by lower bowel bacteria according to the same pharmokinetic principles as sulfasalazine. Asacol is an acrylic resin-coated formulation of mesalamine, designed to release 5-aminosalicylate primarily in the distal ileum and colon at pH 7.0 or above, and Pentasa is a continuous-release ethyl cellulose microgranule preparation that delivers proportionally more 5-aminosalicylate to the small bowel. Although still under evaluation, these newer agents seem to be safe and effective in situations where sulfasalazine is indicated but restricted by its side effects. Pentasa, moreoover, has theoretical advantages for more proximal small bowel disease. Several mesalamine preparations also appear to have some efficacy in maintaining medically induced remissions and also in reducing or retarding the rate of postoperative recurrence of Crohn's disease, especially when initiated in high doses very early in remission or soon after surgery. On account of possible renal toxicity due to elevated blood levels of absorbed 5-aminosalicylate, renal function should be monitored occasionally when using these drugs on a long-term basis, especially in the very high doses favored by many experts. Mesalamine can also be given as enema and suppository preparations (Rowasa) for the topical treatment of rectosigmoid disease.

In view of their antiinflammatory effects, corticosteroids have long been prescribed with benefit for the treatment of inflammatory bowel disease in both the small and large bowel. Oral steroids can be used in the ambulatory setting, whereas intravenous steroids are used for sicker, hospitalized patients. The general principle in steroid use is to begin with a high dose and then taper gradually after a clinical effect is achieved. Although prolonged continuation of low-dose steroids often appears necessary to maintain remission in some patients, the decision to follow such a course must be carefully weighed against the side effects of long-term steroid administration including osteoporosis and osteonecrosis, glucose intolerance, cataract formation, fluid retention, muscle wasting, and electrolyte imbalance, particularly hypokalemia. Newer corticosteroid preparations such as budesonide that have maximal topical action within the bowel lumen with minimal systemic side effects are still under investigation for their role in long-term maintenance therapy, but efficacy for this purpose seems to be dissipated within 12 months of use. As a general rule, therefore, if sustained steroid treatment appears necessary to keep a case of Crohn's disease in remission, an alternative therapeutic approach should be sought, usually with immunomodulating therapy or surgery. The immunomodulating agents azathioprine (Imuran) and 6-mercaptopurine (6-MP, Purinethol), have now become accepted as safe and effective in the treatment of Crohn's disease when used for the proper indications. They appear to act through their antimetabolite effects on the lymphocytes that mediate the chronic inflammatory process. Unlike the mesalamine compounds and the corticosteroids, with which a response can be seen within a period of days to weeks, these agents must be administered for a period of 3 to 6 months before the response to treatment can be judged. When given for this length of time in adequate doses (1.5–2.5 mg/kg/d, unless leukopenia supervenes first), these drugs have 60 to 75% success rates in reducing or replacing steroid therapy, in healing internal and perianal fistulas, and in maintaining remissions without surgery. Side effects of the immunomodulators include early-onset allergic reactions, particularly fever and joint pains, in about 2% of patients, acute interstitial pancreatitis in another 3%, and later-onset drug-induced hepatitis occurring in perhaps 1% of patients. All of these allergic reactions represent absolute contraindications to the continued use of 6-mercaptopurine or azathioprine. Furthermore, all patients on these medications must be closely monitored for reversible, dose-dependent leukopenia and for infections. The theoretically increased risk of neoplasm related to long-term use of the

immunosuppressive agents has not been borne out in clinical experience.

Methotrexate is another antimetabolite that appears to be beneficial for acute therapy in Crohn's disease, although optimal dosages, routes of administration, and remission-maintaining capacity have not yet been established. By contrast, cyclosporine has proven to be disappointing in the treatment of Crohn's disease; except for rapid healing of fistulas, it has turned out to be of little value, especially in long-term use.

Broad-spectrum antibiotics should not be overlooked as useful agents in the management of Crohn's disease. In particular, metronidazole has been shown to be at least as effective as sulfasalazine in some patients. It is most helpful in healing of perineal disease, although relapse is common after its discontinuation and even during its administration. The limiting side effects of metronidazole are metallic taste, dyspepsia, and, most troublesome, paresthesias, which may occur in up to 50% of patients and may persist for long periods even after withdrawal of the drug. Alcohol ingestion is generally considered inadvisable while on metronidazole, although the highly publicized risk of a disulfiram-type interaction is in practice relatively uncommon. No carcinogenic or teratogenic effects in humans have been demonstrated.

Besides metronidazole, other broad-spectrum antibiotics such as cephalosporins and quinolones, particularly ciprofloxacin, can also be tried before resorting to corticosteroid usage after failure of 5-aminosalicylate compounds to induce or maintain remissions by themselves.

Recommended Approach

After a definitive diagnosis is made and the extent and severity of disease are determined, treatment must be individualized according to the pathophysiologic mechanisms responsible for the patient's presenting complaints. Is diarrhea due to active disease or malabsorption? Are pain and fever related to an abscess or to inflammation with obstruction? What is the patient's overall nutritional status and what specific nutrient deficits must be corrected? Simply attributing a patient's symptoms to "Crohn's disease" provides an insufficient basis to guide the proper choice of specific therapy.

While the workup is in progress, however, nonspecific measures can be instituted immediately. Diarrhea and cramps can be treated with anticholinergic agents, diphenoxylate, loperamide, codeine (ideally before meals), or deodorized opium tincture 10 to 15 drops four times daily in severe cases. As in the case of ulcerative colitis, antidiarrheal agents must be given with caution in cases of Crohn's colitis to avoid precipitating toxic megacolon. In nonobstructing cases, hydrophilic mucilloids such as methylcellulose and psyllium may also be useful in improving stool firmness, decreasing bowel frequency, and thus alleviating anal irritation, especially when perianal disease is present.

As patients want to feel they have some measure of control over their own disease and, faced with a digestive disorder, are afraid of eating the "wrong food," they often ask for dietary advice. Therefore, some dietary guidance is necessary, even though avoidance of specific foods rarely has much bearing on disease activity or outcome. In view of the wide prevalence of lactase deficiency, avoidance of milk can be suggested on a trial basis but should not be blindly prescribed in the absence of demonstrable benefit. Similarly, high-roughage raw fruits and vegetables may worsen obstructive or colitic symptoms and may therefore be eliminated initially. Otherwise, the importance of adequate nutrition cannot be overemphasized. Adequate caloric intake should be encouraged, guided by the patient's tolerance and tastes and monitored by weight and nutritional status.

Initial treatment of the inflammatory symptoms in patients with mild to moderate disease should be with 5-aminosalicylates and/or antibiotics. If sulfasalazine is prescribed, it should be started at a low dose (e.g., 0.5 g twice daily) and gradually increased over several days to 4 g/d in divided dosage. If allergy or intolerance supervenes, one of the newer mesalamine preparations can be substituted, using olsalazine (Dipentum) or Asacol for terminal ileal or colonic disease and Pentasa for more proximal small bowel involvement. Metronidazole or other broad-spectrum antibiotics, such as the cephalosporins and ciprofloxacin, may also be of benefit alone or together with the aminosalicylates, although controlled data to support their use are limited.

If these drugs do not achieve an adequate response, or if the patient has more severe disease with prominent systemic complaints, a short course of corticosteroid therapy may be warranted. Beginning with relatively high doses of prednisone of 40 to 60 mg daily often results in a rapid remission of symptoms. Tapering of the prednisone should begin after 1 to 2 weeks, with reduction of the dosage gradually by about 5 to 10 mg every week or so. When the prednisone dose is successfully reduced to about 20 to 25 mg/d, sulfasalazine or its newer analogs are generally added in the hope of maintaining remission as the steroids are tapered further, even though published studies have failed to demonstrate specific steroid-sparing effects with 5-aminosalicylate drugs. If 5-aminosalicylate treatment is to have any benefit at all in this situation, however, high doses in the 4 to 6 g/d range of active drug are probably required.

For severely ill patients with high fever, dehydration, vomiting, or intense abdominal pain, admission to the hospital for parenteral therapy and closer observation is necessary. In addition to supportive care with intravenous fluids and electrolytes, parenteral antibiotics such as metronidazole, cephalosporin, and ciprofloxacin should be administered. If there is no clinical response, intravenous steroids in the form of hydrocortisone 300 mg or methylprednisolone 48 to 60 mg daily by continuous drip can be added, but only after acute fistulization or abscess formation has been excluded, especially in the presence of high fever or marked leukocytosis. A favorable response should usually be seen within a few days, so that after 7 to 10 days of intravenous therapy, the regimen may be switched to the equivalent oral steroid dose. If the remission is maintained for another day or two, the patient may then be safely discharged with subsequent steroid tapering performed as described above.

The ultimate therapeutic goal should be complete elimination of the use of corticosteroids. An occasional patient seems both to need and to tolerate long-term continuation of prednisone at doses below 10 mg daily, but in the great majority of steroid-dependent cases, strong consideration should be given to the introduction of an antimetabolite, unless a short-segment ileocecal resection presents a swifter, safer, and surer alternative. Azathioprine or 6-mercaptopurine may be given in oral dosages ranging from 1.5 to 2.5 mg/kg/d or until modest leukopenia supervenes, with the full benefit often not seen until after 3 to 6 months of continued optimal-dose therapy. The precise roles, if any, for methotrexate, cyclosporine, T-cell apheresis, and multiple-drug antituberculosis regimens in the practical management of Crohn's disease are still under investigation, although the latest data on methotrexate are looking the most promising.

The value of "bowel rest" with total parenteral nutrition or with elemental or liquid polymeric diets has not been completely elucidated. It does appear, though, that bowel rest facilitated by total parenteral nutrition may accelerate closure of fistulas in conjunction with medical therapy. Total parenteral nutrition is also of value in maintaining nutrition in the preoperative patient, while defined enteral feedings have been useful as home therapy for children with growth failure and patients with short bowel syndrome.

For all the putative benefits of sophisticated medical management, the fact remains that surgery ultimately proves to be the treatment of choice for the vast majority of Crohn's disease patients. It is unfortunate, and sometimes tragic, that operative therapy has been labeled a "last resort." The object of treating Crohn's disease, after all, is not the avoidance of surgery; the principal goal is to make the patient well. Indeed, chronic short-segment obstructing disease and complicated fistulization are both primary indications for surgery without prolonged, fruitless, and meddlesome trials of medical therapy.

The most common procedure is ileocolic resection for chronically obstructing fibrostenotic disease of the terminal ileum. Although acute obstructive episodes in Crohn's disease almost always resolve with conservative management, repeated bouts and progressive bowel dilation due to fixed stenosis are invariably indications for elective surgery. In the case of widespread multiple strictures, strictureplasty has become an alternative to massive resection to stave off short bowel syndrome, but whenever limited resection appears safe and practicable, it is always the procedure of choice.

In contrast to simple stenotic obstruction, which always requires surgery, fistulizing Crohn's disease presents a more complex clinical spectrum. For example, uncomplicated ileoileal, ileocecal, or ileosigmoid fistulas may be discovered simply as incidental radiologic findings without clinical symptoms, not requiring any specific treatment for many years.

More troublesome though are enterovesical, enterocutaneous, and coloduodenal fistulas, which may respectively cause recurrent cystitis, skin irritation, or intractable vomiting and therefore usually require treatment. In such cases, medical therapy should first be attempted with oral or parenteral antibiotics, particularly metronidazole and/or ciprofloxacin.

If antibiotics fail, immunomodulators should be tried next, with the possible addition of total parenteral nutrition to expedite healing. Corticosteroids, however, are relatively contraindicated in the presence of fistulas and may promote suppurative complications. If medical therapy fails, or if fistulas are complicated by obstruction or abscess formation, resection of the diseased bowel becomes necessary. Rarer indications for emergent surgery are massive hemorrhage, toxic megacolon, and frank perforation.

FOLLOW-UP

Frequency of follow-up depends to a great extent on the degree of clinical disease activity and the type of therapy being administered. As a general rule, treatment is guided by patient symptomatology rather than by endoscopic or radiographic findings, and therefore routine endoscopies or x-rays are not indicated for stable patients. Patients in complete remission on sulfasalazine or its analogs should be seen two to three times a year with complete evaluation of nutritional status, hematologic, hepatic, and renal parameters, and urinalysis. When steroids or immunomodulators are used, more frequent follow-up is necessary, depending on the dosage and side effects.

The question of cancer surveillance in patients with long-standing Crohn's colitis is still a topic of debate, but mounting evidence suggests that the cancer risks in Crohn's colitis are equal to those in ulcerative colitis, given the same duration and anatomic extent of disease. There is therefore an increasing trend toward routine colonoscopic surveillance with biopsies to detect dysplasia, according to the same regimen adopted for ulcerative colitis, even though the cost–benefit ratio of this approach remains controversial even in the latter disease. Certainly, aggressive endoscopic examination of suspicious strictures or filling defects seen on radiographs is mandatory for any patient at risk for colorectal carcinoma. Also, refractory anal strictures merit thorough evaluation and biopsy on account of the increasing recognition of squamous carcinomas complicating these lesions.

Patients with active disease must be monitored closely with regard to response to therapy, development of malnutrition or isolated nutritional deficits, and possible intercurrent complications of disease. Iron, folate, potassium, or caloric supplements may be necessary. When surgery becomes a consideration, early surgical consultation is advisable so that preoperative evaluation and timing of surgery are optimal.

While attending to the multifaceted medical aspects of this disease, physicians must be equally sensitive to the physiological impact of both the disease and the treatment on the patients and their families. Anxiety, mood swings, and frank depression may all add to the patient's disability. The emotional effects of steroids play an especially prominent role in these regards, as may narcotic dependence in patients with chronic pain. As with all chronic diseases, patient education with regard to all aspects of diagnosis, treatment, and expectations is essential. Toward this end, patient support groups such as those sponsored by the Crohn's and Colitis Foundation of America (CCFA) can provide invaluable assistance in ongoing care.

DISCUSSION
Prevalence and Incidence

Epidemiologic evidence supports a steadily increasing incidence of Crohn's disease over the past 50 years. Although this trend may have leveled off somewhat in developed Western nations with northern European Caucasian populations, rates appear recently to be increasing in underdeveloped nations. Similarly, although the relative risk for Crohn's disease, as for ulcerative colitis, is higher in Jews, both diseases are occurring with increasing frequency among non-Jewish populations, including African-Americans and Hispanics. Males and females are nearly equally affected, with the peak incidence between ages 14 and 24 and the majority of cases beginning before age 30, although onset may be at any age.

Related Basic Science

Pathogenesis

Although the etiology of Crohn's disease has been the subject of intense research for over 60 years, the exact nature of this disease still remains an enigma. Multiple pathogenetic theories emphasizing genetic, microbial, immunologic, environmental, dietary, vascular, and psychosocial factors have been entertained; to date, however, none of them has been conclusively established. Nevertheless, epidemiologic and immunogenetic studies suggest that patients have an inherited predisposition to mount aberrant immunologic responses to one or more inciting agents. It remains to be seen whether these agents are ubiquitous and nonspecific like intestinal bacteria, whose peptidoglycan cell wall constituents may trigger unregulated immune activation in the gut of predisposed hosts, or whether they are particular organisms like mycobacteria or paramyxoviruses that initiate intestinal injury.

Pathology

The earliest macroscopic lesions are focal "aphthoid" ulcerations of the mucosa overlying lymphoid follicles. The inflammatory process then progresses to involve all layers of the intestinal wall, producing submucosal edema, lymphocytic infiltration, and ultimate fibrosis. Deep linear and longitudinal ulcerations result in the classic radiologic and endoscopic "cobblestone" appearance. Transmural extension of ulcers to the serosa culminate in deep sinus tracts, fistulas, and mesenteric abscesses.

Physiologic or Metabolic Derangement

Malabsorption with protein-calorie malnutrition, dehydration, and multiple nutrient deficiencies may result from loss of functional mucosal absorptive surface area. This loss may be due to extensive mucosal disease or to intestinal short-circuiting by enteric fistulas or, most commonly, by surgical resection. Bacterial overgrowth syndrome may develop from coloenteric fistulas or in stagnant segments proximal to strictures or in surgical blind loops. Extensive terminal ileal disease or resection may also lead to bile acid malabsorption with steatorrhea, deficiency of fat-soluble vitamins, and choleretic diarrhea due to the effects of unabsorbed bile salts on the colon. Vitamin B_{12} deficiency may also be seen in this setting.

Gallstones and kidney stones are other potential by-products of bile acid deficiency. Lithogenic bile is probably the cause of gallstone formation in 15 to 30% of patients with small bowel Crohn's disease. Excess enteric absorption of oxalate due to steatorrhea promotes oxalate kidney stone formation in 5 to 10% of patients. Other urinary complications of Crohn's disease include urinary tract infection from fistulization into the urinary tract, noncalculous hydronephrosis due to ureteral compression by retroperitoneal inflammation, and renal amyloidosis in long-standing disease complicated by chronic suppuration.

Natural History and Its Modification with Treatment

The role of medical therapy can be fully understood only in relation to the natural course of the disease in untreated patients. Surveys of placebo-controlled trials suggest that spontaneous remission occurs in approximately 30% of patients with mild to moderate Crohn's disease within 4 months. Only 20% remain well at 1 year and 10% at 2 years. If remission is induced by medical therapy, it will be retained on placebo in 50% after 1 year and 20% after 2 years. It is against these statistics that the efficacy of accepted and new treatments must be evaluated.

The long-term importance of surgery in the management of Crohn's

disease is reflected in the fact that approximately 70% of all patients undergo surgery at some point. The anatomic distribution and clinical "behavior" of the disease are the main factors determining the operative rates and indications. Up to 80 to 90% of patients with ileocolitis ultimately come to surgery, often for penetrating complications such as fistula and abscess. Chronic obstruction is the most common indication for surgery in patients with small bowel disease, whereas intractability, perianal disease, and toxic megacolon are the main reasons for surgery in Crohn's colitis.

Postoperative recurrence even after surgical resection of all gross disease ultimately occurs in the great majority of patients. Clinical recurrence of Crohn's disease after resection occurs in approximately 20% of patients by 2 years, 30% by 3 years, and 40 to 50% by 4 years. A patient undergoing initial resection for Crohn's disease has a 45% risk of requiring a second operation; however, only about 1 in 10 patients coming to first resection ever require a third procedure. Recurrence is less frequent after ileostomy than after an anastomotic procedure, especially if the initial disease spared the small bowel, but other factors that may influence or predict recurrence have not been fully elucidated. Despite the risk of recurrence, surgery is not only lifesaving when performed for acute complications, but has also been shown to improve the long-term quality of life for patients with medically intractable disease.

Prevention

As the etiology of Crohn's disease remains unknown, there are currently no known measures that can prevent this disease, although the prophylactic use of high-dose 5-aminosalicylate begun very soon after surgery may be effective in reducing the rate of postoperative recurrence.

Cost Containment

Cost containment depends on accurate recognition and characterization of the disease with appropriate high-quality radiologic and endoscopic examinations to the exclusion of unnecessary diagnostic tests. Once the diagnosis is established and treatment undertaken, x-rays and endoscopy should be selectively performed only when necessary for evaluating important changes in the clinical course or for guiding therapeutic decisions. With regular office and even telephone follow-up, with a few routine blood and urine tests, with avoidance of long-term steroid usage, and with home support services, hospitalization for complications may be kept at a minimum. As with most other chronic diseases, partnership between a well-informed patient and a sensitive, experienced physician provides the most efficient, economical, and satisfactory outcome.

REFERENCES

Caroline DF, Friedman AC. The radiology of inflammatory bowel disease. Med Clin North Am 1994;78:1353.

Carpani de Kaski M, Hodgson HJF. Rolling review: Inflammatory bowel disease. Aliment Pharmacol Ther 1994;7:567.

Kahng KU, Roslyn JJ. Surgical treatment of inflammatory bowel disease. Med Clin North Am 1994;78:1427.

Kornbluth A, George J, Sachar DB. Immunosuppressive drugs in Crohn's disease. Gastroenterologist 1994;2:239.

Lichtenstein GR. Medical therapies for inflammatory bowel disease. Curr Opin Gastroenterol 1994;10:390.

Meyers S. Medical therapy for Crohn's disease. Pract Gastroenterol 1994;18(7):9,18(8):11.

Quinn PG, Binion DG, Connors PJ. The role of endoscopy in inflammatory bowel disease. Med Clin North Am 1994;78:1331.

Sachar DB. Cancer in Crohn's disease: Dispelling the myths. Gut 1994;35:1507. Editorial.

Sachar DB. Maintenance therapy in ulcerative colitis and Crohn's disease. J Clin Gastroenterol 1995;20(2):117.

CHAPTER 19–53

Ulcerative Colitis

David B. Sachar, M.D., and Jacob S. Walfish, M.D.

DEFINITION

Ulcerative colitis is a chronic idiopathic, inflammatory, and ulcerative disorder of the colonic mucosa. The rectum is almost always affected with variable lengths of contiguous involvement of the colon proximally. Depending on the extent of disease, the terms *proctitis, proctosigmoiditis, left-sided colitis,* and *pancolitis* are applied to individual cases.

ETIOLOGY

By definition, the etiology is still unknown. Past theories, including infectious, allergic, environmental, and even psychosomatic causes, remain unproven. Predisposing factors and possible pathogenetic mechanisms are discussed later in this chapter.

CRITERIA FOR DIAGNOSIS

Suggestive

Ulcerative colitis should be suspected in any patient who has chronic bloody diarrhea with mucus and pus in the stool. When disease is limited to the rectum and sigmoid, tenesmus with mucus and blood may occur without diarrhea and even in association with constipation.

Definitive

Definitive diagnosis is made by sigmoidoscopic visualization of a diffusely granular and friable rectal mucosa together with the exclusion of other specific causes of acute and chronic colitis by stool examination and mucosal biopsies. Histologic features, although often supportive of the diagnosis of ulcerative colitis, are never pathognomonic in and of themselves.

CLINICAL MANIFESTATIONS

Subjective

The symptoms of ulcerative colitis vary with the extent and severity of disease, but usually include diarrhea with passage of mucus and blood. The initial presentation is occasionally acute and fulminant, with severe diarrhea, abdominal pain, high fever, and systemic toxicity. More commonly, however, there is a gradual onset of symptoms, with tenesmus, left lower quadrant cramps, and loose stools accompanied by blood, pus, and mucus. In the mildest cases of disease localized to the rectum (i.e., proctitis), the bowels may be normal or even constipated, with the only manifestations being rectal discharges loaded with mucus, red cells, and white cells, occurring with or between regular bowel movements.

Systemic symptoms, including malaise, fever, anemia, anorexia, and weight loss, often accompany more severe and extensive disease. Extracolonic complications that generally parallel disease activity include peripheral arthritis, pyoderma gangrenosum, erythema nodosum, and episcleritis. Ankylosing spondylitis, sacroiliitis, anterior uveitis, and sclerosing cholangitis are also associated with ulcerative colitis but follow a course independent of colitis activity.

A careful past history is of great value both in documenting prior episodes of active colitis or its extraintestinal manifestations, which would tend to support a diagnosis of chronic inflammatory bowel disease, and in excluding specific infectious, toxic, and iatrogenic causes. In particular, the physician should be wary of accepting a diagnosis of "colitis" that may have been made in the past, unless there is a clear history of rectal bleeding. Often patients report a diagnosis of "colitis" made on the basis of an altered bowel pattern, abdominal pain, and passage of nonbloody mucus. In fact, such patients have often been labeled with the misleading diagnosis of "mucous colitis" or "spastic colitis,"

reflecting an irritable bowel syndrome without the clinical, endoscopic, or histologic features of true ulcerative colitis.

A detailed travel, sexual, and medication history is essential to elicit the major risk factors for "acute self-limited colitis" or other infectious colitides. Many of the infectious agents that are responsible for "traveler's diarrhea" and "epidemic diarrhea," primarily enteropathogenic *Escherichia coli,* but also *Salmonella, Shigella, Campylobacter,* and *Entamoeba,* may also produce a clinical picture indistinguishable from a flare of acute ulcerative colitis. By the same token, a specific history of sexual practices and exposure to other HIV-related risk factors is mandatory, as a number of the organisms associated with the "gay bowel syndrome" and many of the opportunistic infections associated with AIDS may also lead to acute or chronic colitis. A history of concomitant or antecedent antibiotic use should always lead to suspicion of *Clostridium difficile* colitis. Other drugs that may result in a colitis attack include estrogens, nonsteroidal antiinflammatory drugs, gold salts, penicillamine, and anticancer chemotherapeutic agents. Prior pelvic radiation for neoplastic disease, especially prostatic, uterine, or cervical cancers, may be responsible for radiation colitis.

A detailed smoking history should also be obtained from all colitis patients. Ulcerative colitis occurs more often than expected by chance (and Crohn's disease less often) among nonsmokers and especially among people who have recently quit smoking. This observation suggests that some factor related to smoking, perhaps nicotine, may be protective against this disease.

Finally, in elderly patients, especially if there is a history of vascular disease, ischemic colitis must be considered. The differential diagnosis of this entity, and also differentiation of Crohn's from ulcerative colitis, is discussed later in this chapter.

About 15 to 20% of patients with inflammatory bowel disease have at least one affected family member, usually a first-degree relative. Indeed, the frequent occurrence of "multiplex" families (with many affected members from several generations) and the vast disparities in incidence among different ethnic groups also point to a strong role for genetic factors in both ulcerative colitis and Crohn's disease. On the other hand, the concordance rate for ulcerative colitis between monozygotic twins is only about 6%, no higher than between any other sibling pairs, whereas even Crohn's disease carries at least 50% discordance in expression between monozygotic twins. These observations, as well as the rapid shifts in incidence that occur among migrant populations, indicate that genetic predisposition can be only part of the story, with environmental factors playing an important role as well.

Finally, in terms of genetic counseling, it is useful to inform anxious patients that the chances of one parent with inflammatory bowel disease having similarly affected offspring is only about 8% for each child—higher than the general population, to be sure, but nowhere even approaching a range to discourage parenting for that reason alone.

Objective

Physical Examination

In patients who present initially with a short history and without toxicity, the general physical examination is usually unremarkable, except perhaps for some mild left lower quadrant tenderness. When the history is more chronic, however, pallor, lassitude, and signs of weight loss may be evident. In fulminant disease, there may be rapid progression to toxic colitis, with transmural extension of the ulcerative process producing a localized ileus and peritonitis. In such cases, the patient is acutely ill with fever, tachycardia, abdominal distention, diminished bowel sounds, and direct and rebound tenderness. These findings should lead to immediate hospitalization and prompt initiation of therapy as described below, to avert the dreaded and often fatal complication of colonic perforation.

Routine Laboratory Abnormalities

In cases extending beyond the rectum and lower sigmoid colon, laboratory studies often reveal the combined anemia of iron deficiency and chronic disease, while acute activity may be further reflected by elevations in the white blood cell count and erythrocyte sedimentation rate. A low albumin level and electrolyte abnormalities may indicate malnutrition and dehydration related to more chronic, severe, and extensive disease.

PLANS
Diagnostic
Differential Diagnosis

The differential diagnosis varies according to the duration of symptoms. In patients with an acute onset, short history, or affected contacts acute infectious colitis is the major consideration. Organisms that can produce this picture include *Salmonella, Shigella, Campylobacter, E. coli* 0157, and *Entamoeba histolytica. Clostridium difficile* colitis must be considered if there has been any recent use of antibiotics or cancer chemotherapy.

In severely immunocompromised patients, the spectrum of possible agents has to be broadened to include cytomegalovirus, herpes simplex virus, and *Mycobacterium avium–intracellulare.* Distal proctitis may also be a manifestation of sexually transmitted diseases such as gonorrhea, chlamydia, and lymphogranuloma venereum.

Ischemic colitis due to thromboembolic disease or a "low-flow state" must be considered in the older population, especially if there is a history of cardiovascular or peripheral vascular disease. In such cases, the colitis is usually segmental, often in the region of the splenic flexure, and abdominal pain is generally a more prominent symptom. The radiographic finding of colonic "thumbprinting," reflecting submucosal edema, is quite typical of ischemic colitis, although it can occasionally be seen in other forms of severe colitis as well.

Drug-induced colitis has been reported with nonsteroidal antiinflammatory drugs, gold salts, penicillamine, and oral contraceptives. Treatment with antibiotics within 2 months of onset of symptoms or recent cancer chemotherapy should always prompt consideration of *C. difficile* colitis, which may also develop in debilitated, elderly, or immunocompromised patients even in the absence of exposure to these drugs. Colon carcinoma must always be excluded as a cause of rectal bleeding, but it infrequently produces diarrhea and even less commonly presents with fever or purulent rectal discharge. Microscopic colitis and collagenous colitis may cause chronic diarrhea, but these idiopathic conditions are not associated with gross rectal bleeding and by definition are diagnosed on the basis of specific histologic findings in biopsies of macroscopically and radiologically normal mucosa.

Among cases of chronic colitis without a specific etiology, the major differential diagnosis is Crohn's disease. The presence of small bowel involvement, segmental colitis, rectal sparing, and perianal or intestinal fistulas are virtually diagnostic of Crohn's disease as opposed to ulcerative colitis. The consistent absence of bloody stool is also much more suggestive of Crohn's than ulcerative colitis. The histologic finding of epithelioid granulomas in mucosal biopsies is also pathognomonic of Crohn's disease, but it is encountered in only a minority of cases.

When there is pancolitis without any of the aforementioned findings, the differential diagnosis between Crohn's and ulcerative colitis may be more difficult; nonetheless, in nearly 90% of such cases the distinction can still be made on the basis of specific, albeit subtle, endoscopic, radiologic, and histologic features. Although roughly 10% of cases show certain features suggestive of both Crohn's and ulcerative colitis, hence being labeled "indeterminate," the initial medical treatment is rarely affected by this diagnostic distinction. It is only in the advanced stages of disease, when surgical intervention or experimental therapies may be under consideration, that the specific diagnosis may determine the management.

Recommended Approach

In the presence of a typical history, the diagnosis is confirmed by sigmoidoscopy. As emphasized above, specific causes for colitis must be excluded by stool studies and rectal biopsy. Initiation of therapy can usually be delayed until the results of these studies are back, unless the patient is seriously ill.

In patients with more severe symptoms, initial assessment should include plain films of the abdomen, which may help to judge the severity and proximal extent of the colitis by demonstrating loss of haustration, mucosal edema, and absence of formed stool in the diseased colon. In the most severe cases, the abdominal radiograph may show excessive accumulation of small and large bowel gas, which may presage the development of toxic megacolon. Barium enema or total colonoscopy to define precise proximal extent of disease is usually not necessary before initiation of therapy and may actually be hazardous in the presence of active disease because of the risk of perforation.

When performed at a later stage, the barium enema may show loss of haustration, mucosal edema, minute serrations, or in severe cases gross "collar-button" ulcerations. A shortened, rigid colon with atrophy and pseudopolyps may be seen in advanced stages. Minor abnormalities in a patulous terminal ileum noted on reflux of barium may be due to "backwash ileitis" and should not necessarily be interpreted as Crohn's disease. On the other hand, a severely deformed, rigid, stenotic, or fistulous terminal ileum clearly denotes Crohn's disease, other signs of which in the colon include segmental or asymmetric involvement, deep fissures or fistulas, strictures, and predominantly right-sided disease.

Therapeutic
Therapeutic Options

Medical therapy, although never curative, can usually induce and maintain remission for long periods. Aminosalicylates and corticosteroids in either oral or rectal formulations are the mainstays of therapy, with immunosuppressive agents reserved for refractory or steroid-dependent cases. The mechanisms of action and side effects of these drugs are discussed in Chapter 19–52.

Aminosalicylates. Many clinical trials and several meta-analyses show that sulfasalazine and the newer 5-aminosalicylate drugs, olsalazine and mesalazine, are all equally effective in a dose-dependent manner for treating mild to moderately active colitis as well as for maintaining remission. Sulfasalazine is by far the longest established and least expensive of the agents, but the nonsulfonamide preparations may be preferred for those patients who require but cannot tolerate higher doses of medication. Once remission has been achieved, aminosalicylate should be administered indefinitely, as its prophylactic effect extends over many years of steady use but is lost soon after the drug is discontinued.

Corticosteroids. The beneficial effect of cortisone in treating active ulcerative colitis was first demonstrated in 1955. Treatment with oral prednisone is usually begun at doses of 40 to 60 mg/d with gradual tapering after remission is achieved. When steroids are administered intravenously in hospitalized patients, hydrocortisone is given by continuous drip at 300 mg/d or methylprednisolone at 48 to 60 mg/d. Patients not recently treated with steroids may respond somewhat better to intravenous adrenocorticotropic hormone (ACTH) 120 U/d, but run the risk of adrenal hemorrhage on this therapy. In any event, the intravenous fluids should contain potassium supplements but should be kept free of sodium. Patients who are going to respond show clinical improvement within 7 to 10 days. Prolonged high-dose therapy beyond this period results in increasing adverse steroid side effects without significant incremental benefit. For these refractory patients, therefore, continued stalling with steroids or total parenteral nutrition is contraindicated; a prompt decision must be made to opt either for surgery or for intravenous cyclosporine, if not for some other potent experimental therapy under a research protocol. By the same token, steroids are ineffective for maintaining remissions and must therefore not be used on a long-term basis. Here also, chronically steroid-dependent patients must be offered alternative approaches to management, with either antimetabolites (6-mercaptopurine or azathioprine), experimental treatments, or surgery.

Surgery. Emergency colectomy is indicated for life-threatening complications such as massive hemorrhage, free perforation, and fulminating toxic colitis. The procedure of choice in these circumstances is usually subtotal colectomy and ileostomy with Hartman closure of the rectal stump, which may later be electively removed or reconnected via one of several newer procedures. An intact rectal stump should not be retained indefinitely on account of the risks of continued active disease and ultimate malignant degeneration.

Indications for elective surgery include clinically suspected carcinoma, epithelial dysplasia, symptomatic strictures, and, most commonly, intractable disease. Growth retardation may be an indication for surgery in children. Only in very rare instances do severe colitis-related extraintestinal manifestations (e.g., pyoderma gangrenosum, hemolytic anemia) provide indications for surgery.

Chronic ulcerative colitis is permanently cured by total proctocolectomy with traditional permanent ileostomy. Today, however, most surgeons and patients favor the newer sphincter-preserving procedures with an ileal pouch and ileoanal anastomosis. Although certainly more "physiologic" and aesthetically appealing, the newer procedures have their own problems, especially a steadily increasing incidence of "pouchitis," reaching at least 50% over the years. Although most cases of pouchitis are mild and readily responsive to antibiotic treatment, chronic refractory forms of this complication lead to ultimate failure of the anastomosis in more than 5% of cases. In those anastomotic procedures that preserve a narrow band of "transitional" mucosa, persistent inflammation and later carcinoma are theoretical, albeit only rarely observed, risks. Longer-term follow-up of these newer procedures is therefore awaited before their lifetime risks and benefits can be fully assessed.

Recommended Approach

Avoidance of gross dietary roughage like corn, nuts, and raw fruits and vegetables may help protect the inflamed and friable colonic mucosa. Restriction of dairy products may also decrease symptoms in lactose-intolerant patients but need not be continued unless clear benefit is noted. Otherwise, sweeping dietary limitations are pointless and counterproductive. On the contrary, adequate nutritional intake should be encouraged. Oral iron supplements for prevention or treatment of iron deficiency are also advisable if well tolerated.

Antidiarrheal agents such as loperamide, diphenoxylate, codeine, and tincture of opiate may be used with caution to control diarrhea in nontoxic patients, but should be avoided in the more severely ill lest toxic dilation be precipitated.

When disease is *limited to the rectosigmoid,* topical therapy is often effective in the form of steroid enemas or foam or 5-aminosalicylate enemas or suppositories. Applications once or twice daily are continued until the patient has been asymptomatic for 1 to 2 weeks, after which tapering doses of every other day for a few weeks and then every third day for a few more weeks should be given before complete discontinuation. In fact, patients who develop early relapse may benefit from long-term maintenance topical or oral 5-aminosalicylate therapy. Patients who find topical therapy per rectum unacceptable may be started on oral 5-aminosalicylate therapy, often with equally good results, but the doses may have to be as high as 4 to 6 g/d to be effective for distal disease. Occasionally, refractory proctitis may necessitate oral or intravenous steroid therapy to induce remission. Long-term therapy with oral steroids and even with steroid enemas should be avoided, however, on account of potential systemic steroid side effects.

The patient who is not systemically ill, but who has *mild or moderate disease* extending above the reach of enema applications, often responds to oral 5-aminosalicylate in the time-tested form of sulfasalazine or the newer nonsulfonamide 5-aminosalicylate preparations such as olsalzine (Dipentum) and mesalamine (Pentasa or Asacol). As upper gastrointestinal intolerance often occurs with sulfasalazine, this drug should be given with food and, if necessary, in the enteric-coated formulation. The initial dosage should be low (e.g., 0.5 g twice daily) with a gradual increase over several days to 3 to 4 g/d in divided dosage. This regimen, however, provides only 1.2 to 1.6 g/d active 5-aminosalicylate. Higher dosages of mesalamine or olsalazine (up to 4 g/d) may be given to patients who would not tolerate the doses of sulfasalazine required to reach these levels of active drug. The higher serum levels of 5-aminosalicylate that are achieved with high doses of these newer agents, though, require periodic monitoring of renal func-

tion. Also, a paradoxical exacerbation of colitis is in rare instances induced by mesalamine, in which case the drug must be permanently discontinued.

If there is no improvement with the aminosalicylates or if the response is incomplete, systemic corticosteroid therapy may have to be added in the form of oral prednisone or prednisolone. By the same token, steroids may have to be the initial treatment for more severe cases with systemic symptoms of anorexia, low-grade fever, and weight loss. A starting daily dose of 40 to 60 mg of prednisone or 32 to 48 mg of methylprednisolone frequently induces dramatic remission. After 1 to 2 weeks of well-established remission, the daily dose should be gradually tapered by 5 to 10 mg/wk. Although conventional doses of sulfasalazine have not been shown in clinical trials to have a steroid-sparing effect, sulfasalazine or its higher-dose analogs may still be added when the colitis remains controlled at a level of 20 mg of prednisone daily, with the theoretical objective of maintaining remission as prednisone is further tapered and ultimately discontinued.

Severe colitis manifested by more than 10 bloody bowel movements per day, high fever, severe abdominal pain, or dehydration requires hospitalization for parenteral therapy and close observation. Patients who have already received oral steroid therapy within 30 days of admission should be given hydrocortisone (300 mg/d) or methylprednisone (48–60 mg/d) by continuous intravenous infusion. If corticosteroids were not recently used, adrenocorticotropic hormone 120 U/d intravenously by continuous drip may be somewhat more effective but entails the risk of adrenal hemorrhage. Whichever form of parenteral therapy is used, it should be administered with supplementary potassium (about 40 mEq/L) in the intravenous vehicle but without any sodium except in rare cases with prominent dehydration. The parenteral corticosteroid therapy usually has to be given for 7 to 10 days while the physicians and consulting surgeons are closely monitoring the clinical response. Clinical indicators to be followed, besides temperature and vital signs, include the consistency, frequency, urgency, and gross blood content of bowel movements, preferably with a bedside stool chart; abdominal pain, tenderness, distention, and preservation of hepatic dullness; regular complete blood counts, erythrocyte sedimentation rates, serum electrolytes, and albumin levels; and periodic abdominal radiographs to watch for the early signs of small bowel or colonic ileus that may presage the development of toxic megacolon, as well as to rule out intramural bowel gas or even perforation, the typical physical signs of which may be masked by high-dose steroid therapy.

Other supportive measures may have to include blood transfusion, if continuing blood loss causes severe anemia. Antidiarrheal agents, antispasmodic agents, and narcotic analgesics should be avoided in the seriously ill or toxic hospitalized patient because of the very real risk of precipitating megacolon. In the absence of toxic dilation, ileus, or severe postprandial cramping, food intake should be encouraged so as not to deprive the colonic enterocytes of the short-chain fatty acids necessary for their metabolism and repair. Intravenous hyperalimentation may be of limited benefit for nutritional support in some cases, but "bowel rest" with total parenteral nutrition has absolutely no primary therapeutic value and often results in more mischief than benefit by inducing a false sense of security and encouraging delays in making vital decisions for more definitive therapy such as cyclosporine or surgery.

If remission is achieved within 7 to 10 days of intravenous steroid treatment, oral therapy may be initiated with prednisone 60 mg/d or prednisolone 48 mg/d. This dosage should be maintained for a week or so and then gradually tapered under medical supervision.

Toxic colitis is a grave emergency, as bowel perforation, hypercoagulable complications, or septic shock may rapidly supervene. In toxic colitis, the inflammatory process has become transmural, with paralysis of the colonic smooth muscle. Ileus with distention and thinning of the large bowel wall result, predisposing to bacteremia and microperforation. A paradoxical and often misleading decrease in bowel frequency may be noted, but the patient generally looks and feels sicker, usually with fever, tachycardia, increased abdominal distention and tenderness, and laboratory indications of increasing white blood cell count, erythrocyte sedimentation rate, and platelet count and decreasing hemoglobin and albumin levels.

Signs of toxic colitis or impending toxic megacolon mandate immediate intervention as follows:

- Discontinue all drugs that may inhibit bowel motility, especially narcotic analgesics and antidiarrheal agents.
- Place the patient on nothing-by-mouth status and pass a long intestinal tube on intermittent suction.
- Have the patient roll over in bed from the supine to the prone position every 2 to 3 hours to help redistribute colonic gas and prevent progressive distention. (Careful passage of a soft rectal tube may also be helpful in some cases but extreme caution must be taken to avoid bowel perforation.)
- Add broad-spectrum antibiotics to the intravenous corticosteroid regimen (e.g., metronidazole, ciprofloxacin, or a broad-spectrum cephalosporin with anaerobic coverage).
- Give aggressive intravenous fluid, electrolyte, and blood replacement as needed.

Surgical consultation should be obtained early in the course, and the patient must be followed vigilantly for signs of peritonitis or perforation. Loss of hepatic dullness on percussion over the liver may be the first clinical sign of free perforation, especially because high-dose steroids may suppress the usual local and systemic signs of these complications. Plain abdominal radiographs should be obtained daily or every other day to follow the degree of colonic distention and to detect free air. If definite improvement is not achieved by these medical measures within 24 to 48 hours, immediate surgery is required to prevent catastrophic bowel perforation and sepsis.

Until recently, surgery in the form of colectomy was considered the only alternative for patients who *failed to respond* to high-dose intravenous corticosteroids within 7 to 10 days or who could not be tapered to a nontoxic dosage of oral steroids without clinical relapse. Growing experience with immunomodulating agents suggests that this form of therapy may be of benefit in averting or at least significantly delaying the need for colectomy in selected patients.

The antimetabolites 6-mercaptopurine and azathioprine evidently have long-term steroid-sparing and remission-maintaining properties in ulcerative colitis, similar to those in Crohn's disease. Most recently, intravenous cyclosporine has been reported from one center to have dramatic efficacy in inducing rapid short-term remissions in more than 80% of patients with severe ulcerative colitis who had failed 10 to 14 days of high-dose intravenous corticosteroid therapy. Approximately two thirds of these salvaged patients can be kept in remission by oral cyclosporine for 6 months, by which time substitution of effective long-term therapy, usually with 6-mercaptopurine or azathioprine, is often able to sustain the remission throughout subsequent years. In other words, a "quick fix" with intravenous cyclosporine, followed by a transitional period with oral cyclosporine and ultimate long-term maintenance with oral antimetabolites, is able to prevent or at least defer colectomy in roughly half of patients with severe disease refractory even to high-dose intravenous corticosteroids. Over at least a few years of follow-up, these results can be achieved with only a moderate drug toxicity and with an acceptable quality of life, but it is far from proven that all these patients will be benefited in the long run by continuing to live their lives with colons afflicted by extensive colitis. Colectomy remains the "gold standard" of cure for patients with severe, extensive, intractable ulcerative colitis; cyclosporine should be considered only in the minority of cases for whom there are specific and compelling reasons not to operate.

Once remission is achieved, *long-term maintenance* on a 5-aminosalicylate drug is indicated to prevent relapse. In some patients, doses of sulfasalazine as low as 1 g/d turn out to be effective over many years, but most controlled studies suggest that statistically significant benefit requires doses in the range of 2 to 3 g/d. Although the temptation is strong to discontinue 5-aminosalicylate therapy completely after long-standing remission, experience has shown that the risk of relapse remains substantial ever after periods of complete remission as long as 3 years.

FOLLOW-UP

Patients can be evaluated on the basis of their clinical status: stool formation and frequency, urgency, abdominal discomfort, tenesmus, and rectal bleeding. Follow-up endoscopy to assess mucosal disease activity in patients who are clinically doing well is not generally indicated.

On the other hand, long-term follow-up of patients who remain in remission is advised primarily to monitor and prevent the risk of colorectal cancer. The risk of colon cancer is related directly to the extent and duration of disease, independent of clinical disease activity. Patients who have had more than 8 to 10 years of disease with involvement beyond the rectosigmoid bear a risk of developing colon cancer manyfold higher than age- and sex-matched populations. An initial *screening* colonoscopy is universally recommended for all such patients, as the yield of dysplasia or cancer on the first examination is in the range of 3%. There is some debate over the cost–benefit ratios of maintaining regular colonoscopic *surveillance* in this population once the initial screening has proved negative, but most authorities now agree, on the basis of several decades of worldwide experience, that cancer mortality might be averted in as many as 6% of a high-risk cohort under regular surveillance, thereby justifying the effort, especially in a relatively young patient population.

The usual protocol for patients with more than 8 to 10 years of ulcerative colitis is to perform colonoscopy every 1 to 2 years, preferably during periods of clinical remission, with multiple endoscopic biopsies taken throughout the colon. On review and confirmation by an experienced pathologist, the finding of definite mucosal dysplasia, whether scored "high grade" or "low grade," is a strong indication for colectomy. The likelihood of concomitant or imminent colerectal carcinoma in such patients may range from 30 to 80%, being highest when dysplasia is high grade or associated with a macroscopic lesion, but still carrying serious risk even in cases of definite low-grade dysplasia, whether or not the lesion appears to "regress" (probably due to sampling error) on subsequent examinations. It is essential to obtain corroborating pathologic review to confirm the unequivocal distinction between definite neoplastic dysplasia and regenerative atypia due to inflammation and repair, but it is unwise to wait for the repeated demonstration of dysplasia on subsequent examinations before recommending colectomy.

Pseudopolyps, which are inflammatory in nature, have no premalignant or other prognostic significance, but they may sometimes be difficult to distinguish grossly from adenomas or dysplasia-associated mass lesions. The endoscopist should therefore biopsy or preferably remove any polyp that appears suspicious, although the most informative protocol still requires multiple biopsies from endoscopically normal-appearing mucosa. Whether typical adenomas occurring in long-standing ulcerative colitis should be viewed differently from adenomas in the general population remains an issue of continuing uncertainty. Adenomas are least likely to be causes for alarm if they are found in older patients, if they have nondysplastic stalks that are completely excised, and if they can be shown to have arisen from contiguous mucosa that is itself free of both dysplasia and active colitis. In unexpectedly young patients, by contrast, or with sessile configurations or directly adjacent dysplastic or actively inflamed mucosa, adenomatous masses are perhaps most prudently regarded as colitis-related dysplastic lesions that warrant a recommendation for colectomy.

DISCUSSION
Prevalence and Incidence

The incidence of ulcerative colitis in developed Western countries has remained relatively constant over the past several decades, whereas Crohn's disease, at least until recently, has been rapidly increasing in both incidence and prevalence. Lately, though, ulcerative colitis has been appearing more frequently than before in Asia and in developing countries.

Other epidemiologic distinctions between ulcerative colitis and Crohn's disease include an apparently stronger genetic influence in the latter than in the former and opposite influences of smoking on the incidences of the two diseases, with current smokers carrying an increased relative risk of Crohn's disease and a low relative risk of ulcerative colitis. Otherwise, most demographic factors that have been studied appear to play similar roles in both conditions.

Related Basic Science

Sophisticated immunogenetic and immunopathologic studies have revealed several distinctions between ulcerative colitis and Crohn's disease. For example, the former may be characterized more by a TH_2 (humoral) pattern of immunologic reactions, whereas the latter may be associated more with a TH_1 (cellular) immunologic profile. Similarly, certain genetic markers like p-ANCA or HLA haplotype DR2 may be more frequent in ulcerative colitis, whereas Crohn's disease may be more often associated with anti-erythrocyte antibody 15 and HLA haplotypes DR1 and DQ5.

These subtle distinctions have not yet achieved levels of diagnostic or etiologic utility, but they are pointing in the directions of future study. Meanwhile, the very broad generalization still stands that both of the major categories of inflammatory bowel disease are characterized by inappropriately activated and insufficiently downregulated levels of mucosal immune response. Virtually all medical therapies for inflammatory bowel disease, old and new drugs alike, are therefore aimed in one way or another at restoring the normal balance to the immune response system in the gut.

By definition, the inflammatory process in ulcerative colitis involves predominantly the mucosa. The lamina propria shows nonspecific acute and chronic inflammation with epithelial invasion by neutrophils resulting in crypt abscesses. In severe disease, there is flattening of the surface epithelium with ulceration and some extension of the inflammation to the submucosa. In the most severe cases, which may result in toxic dilation, ulceration becomes transmural with inflammation and necrosis of the nerve and muscle layers.

There are no pathognomonic findings that allow the pathologist to definitively distinguish ulcerative colitis from acute infectious or self-limited colitis; however, the presence of distorted crypt architecture, separation and atrophy of crypts, "homing" of neutrophils preferentially to crypt epithelium, basal lymphoid aggregates, and chronic inflammatory infiltrate all support a clinical diagnosis of idiopathic ulcerative colitis.

Macroscopically, one finds hyperemia, edema, and granularity of the mucosal surface with loss of the normal vascular markings on endoscopic visualization. Friability is demonstrated by pinpoint hemorrhage that results from minimal trauma by a cotton swab or the endoscope tip. Increasing severity is marked by confluent ulceration and diffuse exudate. Inflammatory polyps (pseudopolyps) result from exuberant regeneration of the epithelium and have no prognostic significance. With long-standing chronic disease, the colon becomes atrophic, tubular, and shortened. Strictures, which occur less commonly than in Crohn's disease, must be considered potentially malignant until proven otherwise.

Natural History and Its Modification with Treatment

Complete recovery without relapse may occur in 10% of patients after an initial attack. Such cases present the possibility of an undetected specific pathogen, so that the need for cancer surveillance after 10 years remains unproven, especially if, in the interim, there has been complete histologic normalization of the colonic mucosa.

Most often, however, the disease has a chronic course with intermittent exacerbations and remissions. An additional 10 to 15% of patients have a "chronic continuous" course, whereas perhaps 5 to 10% present with an initial fulminant attack complicated by hemorrhage, perforation, or sepsis and toxemia requiring urgent colectomy.

Patients with localized ulcerative proctitis fare the best, as systemic complications and malignant degeneration are unlikely, and extension of the disease occurs in only 10 to 30% of cases. Nonetheless, refractory proctitis can be nearly disabling in the relentlessness of its symptoms of tenesmus, urgency, and incontinence. Moreover, when late proximal extension does occur, the disease tends to be particularly severe and aggressive.

In a recent Danish series of patients presenting with pancolitis, one third underwent colectomy within the first year, compared with fewer than 8% of those presenting with more localized disease. After the first year, the colectomy rate was about 1% per year regardless of the initial extent of disease.

With the occasional limited use of corticosteriods, with maintenance therapy using 5-aminosalicylate when possible and antimetabolites when necessary, with well-timed colectomy in cases of intractability or dysplasia, and with steady emotional support throughout, the length and quality of life for patients with ulcerative colitis can be essentially normal.

Prevention

There are currently no known measures for prevention of this disease. Maintaining a smoking habit clearly lowers the risk but obviously entails even worse health consequences of its own.

Cost Containment

Continuing aminosalicylate therapy for long-term maintenance of remission is the most cost-effective means of controlling this disease. It is unnecessary and wasteful to keep performing repeated endoscopies for patients in clinical remission who do not require cancer surveillance. Even patients who relapse mildly can generally be treated with a few office visits and more frequent telephone contacts. Colonoscopic surveillance for histologic dysplasia remains an imperfect method for cancer prevention; other techniques such as lavage or brushing cytology, flow cytometry, and assays for gene mutations or tumor antigen expression are still undergoing evaluation in research protocols.

REFERENCES

Binderow SR, Wexner SD. Current surgical therapy for mucosal ulcerative colitis. Dis Colon Rectum 1994;37:610.

Caroline DF, Friedman AC. The radiology of inflammatory bowel disease. Med Clin North Am 1994;78:1353.

Carpani de Kaski M, Hodgson HJF. Rolling review: Inflammatory bowel disease. Aliment Pharmacol Ther 1994;7:567.

Connell WR, Lennard-Jones JE, Williams CB, et al. Factors affecting the outcome of endoscopic surveillance for cancer in ulcerative colitis. Gastroenterology 1994;107:934.

Hanauer SB. Medical therapy of ulcerative colitis. Lancet 1993;342:412.

Lichtenstein GR. Medical therapies for inflammatory bowel disease. Curr Opin Gastroenterol 1994;10:390.

Quinn PG, Binion DG, Connors PJ. The role of endoscopy in inflammatory bowel disease. Med Clin North Am 1994;78:1331.

Sachar DB. Clinical and colonoscopic surveillance in ulcerative colitis: Are we saving colons or saving lives? Gastroenterology 1993;105:588. Editorial.

Sachar DB. Maintenance therapy in ulcerative colitis and Crohn's disease. J Clin Gastroenterol 1995;20:117.

CHAPTER 19–54

Appendicitis (See Section 8, Chapter 22)

CHAPTER 19–55

Peritonitis (See Section 8, Chapter 19)

CHAPTER 19–56

Fissure in Ano

Sidney M. Fierst, M.D., M.S.

DEFINITION

A fissure in ano is a linear ulcer in the anal canal extending from distal to the dentate line to the proximal margin of the anus.

ETIOLOGY

The primary factor in the development of a fissure is trauma, usually resulting from the passage of a large bulky stool.

Frequent bowel movements with tenesmus and bearing down produce increased intrarectal pressure against an incompletely relaxed sphincter, resulting in a mucosal tear.

CRITERIA FOR DIAGNOSIS

Suggestive

Anal pain and defecation with streaks of red blood on the stool in the presence of constipation or tenesmus suggest the diagnosis.

Definitive

Visual presence of a linear break in the anal skin and pain on spreading the buttocks define the diagnosis.

CLINICAL MANIFESTATIONS

Subjective

The patient with acute fissure presents with spasm of the anal sphincter and pain with defecation disproportionate to the size of the fissure. There may be a streak of blood on the stool or paper, but bleeding is minimal. There may be a double cycle to the pain. The pain occurs during defecation; this is followed by a period of relief and then recurrence of pain due to sphincteric spasm attributable to the overshoot phenomenon. Pain may be aggravated by walking. Because of the pain, the patient may voluntarily avoid bowel motion and become severely obstipated. This is particularly true in children.

Objective

Physical Examination

Inspection of the anus by gentle separation of the buttocks usually reveals the fissure. Digital examination is painful, and a lidocaine-soaked sponge applied to the anus aids in the examination. The well-lubricated finger is passed against the wall opposite the fissure. The sphincter tone is increased. A coexisting large hemorrhoid or hypertrophied papilla may hide the ulcer. Anuscopic examination should be performed but may be impossible without local anesthesia because of pain. Acute fissures are superficial. Sentinel piles are absent.

With chronic fissure, a triad of a sentinel pile, an anal ulcer, and a hypertrophied anal papilla are usually present. The chronic fissure has an indurated base as the result of repeated infection. The contiguous papilla becomes thickened and fibromatous. There is an edematous skin tag or condyloma. The chronic fissure extends down to the internal sphincter. This has a white appearance and the fibers run transversely. The sentinel pile is found at the external or internal end of the fissure. With severe prolonged fissures, sclerosis and stricture of the anal sphincter develop and anal stenosis results.

Routine Laboratory Abnormalities

There are no diagnostic laboratory abnormalities.

PLANS

Diagnostic

Differential Diagnosis

Anoscopy also demonstrates other associated conditions such as hemorrhoids and inflammatory bowel disease. In the patient with a fissure located off the midline, ulcerative colitis, Crohn's disease, carcinoma of the anus, syphilis, anal abrasions, and traumatic ulcers must be ruled out. Intersphincteric abscess may mimic a fissure if there is no external opening. It causes great pain and tenderness.

Diagnostic Options and Recommended Approach

See Clinical Manifestations, Objective.

Therapeutic

Acute Fissure Treatment. Elimination of constipation is most important. The aim is to avoid hard stools with a psyllium preparation and stool softeners such as sodium or calcium docusate. Warm baths relieve sphincter spasm. Analgesic ointments inserted into the anal canal as suppositories relieve pain. Attention to diet is very important. The patient should be instructed to take a high-fiber diet with adequate amounts of whole bran, fruits, and fibrous vegetables.

Injection of 1 mL of lidocaine followed by 0.5 mL of 1% sodium tetradecyl sulfate into the fissure has been suggested if the fissure fails to heal within 2 weeks (Antebi et al., 1985). Pain relief is immediate but there has been abscess formation in a few patients.

Chronic Fissures. Chronic fissures are fissures that do not heal within a month. The edges are indurated. Various operative treatments have been suggested. Excision of the fissure with or without sphincterectomy, anoplasty with sliding skin graft, and anal sphincter stretch all have advocates. Anal stretch is performed with intravenous anesthesia as a short-stay ambulatory procedure. The lubricated index finger of each hand is inserted into the anus and the sphincter is gently stretched for 2 minutes. A polyvinyl sponge pack is placed in the rectum to reduce hematoma formation. Analgesics are prescribed. The patient is instructed on the use of anal dilators; this is to be done for 30 minutes daily for the first week, twice weekly for 3 weeks, and twice monthly for 3 months. A psyllium preparation and stool softener are taken daily. This method should not be used in patients with large internal hemorrhoids.

The most popular surgical technique appears to be lateral subcutaneous internal sphincterectomy. The operation is performed under local anesthesia. Postoperative discomfort is of short duration and less time is lost from work. Fecal soiling is uncommon.

Fissures associated with Crohn's disease are often multiple and frequently painless. They have a violaceous coloring. Failure of the fissure to heal may be the first indication of this disease. Treatment of the underlying disease with metranidazole and 6-mercaptopurine may help control the disease and heal the fissure. Surgery should be avoided, if possible, until the disease is fully controlled, as fissures associated with Crohn's disease are resistant to healing.

FOLLOW-UP

The follow-up depends on the type of fissure and its severity. The follow-up for chronic fissures may be weekly for several weeks.

DISCUSSION
Prevalence

Anal fissure is very frequently found in constipated individuals.

Anal surgery, particularly for hemorrhoids and fistula in ano, may result in significant scarring and fixation of the anal skin and loss of elasticity from the formation of scar tissue. The resulting anal stenosis predisposes to tearing of the skin and ulceration.

Anterior fissures are more common in women. This may be attributed to perineal trauma and tethering of the anal submucosa during childbirth and subsequent loss of elasticity.

Related Basic Science

Studies have demonstrated that the chronic fissure developing after the acute tear results from increased tension within the internal sphincter (Hancock, 1977). Manometric studies show that the normal response to increased intrarectal pressure is relaxation of the internal anal sphincter. In patients with anal fissures, there is an overshoot phenomenon of increased pressure after the initial relaxation. When the anal fissure heals, this abnormal overshoot contraction disappears.

Natural History and Its Modification with Treatment

Acute fissures heal if promptly treated. Sitz baths, attention to promoting soft stools, and perineal cleanliness heal most acute fissures. Recurrences of the fissure with repeated healing result in scarring and chronicity with stenosis of external sphincters. This requires surgical management.

Prevention

Fissures in ano may be prevented by the prevention of constipation.

Cost Containment

Preventive measures decrease cost to the public at large. Individuals with fissures in ano should seek help promptly to receive treatment and prevent the development of a chronic fissure.

REFERENCES

Antebi E, Schwartz P, Gilon E. Sclerotherapy for the treatment of fissure in ano. Surg Gynecol Obstet 1985;160:204.
Hancock BD. The internal sphincter and anal fissure. Br J Surg 1977;64:92.
Hawley PR. The treatment of chronic fissure in ano: A trial of methods. Br J Surg 1969;56:915.
Nathman GJ, Schuster MM. Internal anal sphincter derangement with anal fissures. Gastroenterology 1974;67:216.

CHAPTER 19–57

Cryptitis and Papillitis

Sidney M. Fierst, M.D., M.S.

DEFINITION

Cryptitis is inflammation of the anal glands often resulting in abscess formation. Papillitis is inflammation of the anal ridges between glands.

ETIOLOGY

Foreign objects (i.e., stool, pinworm), inflammatory bowel disease and other diarrheal conditions, trauma, and anal intercourse may cause infection in the anal crypts. The anal papillae between the crypts become inflamed and fibrosed. Collagen deposition results in hypertrophy of the papillae.

CRITERIA FOR DIAGNOSIS
Suggestive

The patient presents with sharp pain aggravated by bowel motion. A dull ache in the anus or perianal pruritus may be present. There may be a history of poor bowel hygiene.

Definitive

Oozing from the anus and soiling of underclothes define the diagnosis.

CLINICAL MANIFESTATIONS
Subjective

Inflammation of the crypts causes sharp stabbing pain or dull ache in the anus. The pain is aggravated by bowel motion. There is very little bleeding. There may be purulent or serous discharge and pruritis may be a symptom. With hypertrophy of the papilla, there may be the sensation of a mass. There may be tenesmus.

Objective
Physical Examination

On spreading of the buttocks, pain is elicited. Inflamed papillae are seen. They may be hypertrophied and have collagen deposits, producing a polypoid mass. Prolapse of hypertrophied papillae may be confused with juvenile polyps or adenomas. Hypertrophied papillae are hyperkeratotic and the tips are white. The polyps are usually cherry red.

Routine Laboratory Abnormalities

There are no diagnostic routine laboratory abnormalities.

PLANS
Diagnostic

With anoscopy, edema and erythema are noted. On probing, the crypt purulent material is exuded. If suspected, especially in children, scraping for oxyuris (pinworm) should be done.

Therapeutic

Cryptitis is treated by incising the crypt with a hooked knife and painting the area with betadine or 10% phenol glycerine solution. Hypertrophied papillae can be snared and excised with electrocautery.

FOLLOW-UP

Advice should be given as to good bowel hygiene, a high-fiber diet, stool softeners, and warm baths twice daily.

DISCUSSION
Prevalence and Incidence

The prevalence and incidence are not known, but cryptitis and papillitis are two of the most frequent anal diseases encountered.

Related Basic Science

The pectinate line, the mucocutaneous junction derived embryologically from the joining of the endoderm and ectoderm at the cloacal membrane, is the site where squamous and glandular epithelium come together. The proximal ends of the anal epithelium form papillae between which are depressions, the anal crypts. These crypts contain the anal glands. The crypts are open superiorly so that debris, feces, and other foreign matter may enter and cause inflammation and abscesses. The contiguous papillae become secondarily inflamed, edematous, and enlarged. A polypoid mass may be produced by the collagen.

The anatomic arrangement of the anal glands and papillae and the lack of good cleansing of the anus after defecation predisposes to the development of cryptitis and papillitis.

Natural History and Its Modification with Treatment

With good bowel hygiene, daily bathing, and anal cleansing, the prognosis is good for cure. Recurrence is frequent.

Prevention

There is no known prevention except for good bowel hygiene.

Cost Containment

Costs can be diminished by seeking medical care early in the disease.

REFERENCES

De Los Rios Magrina E. Color atlas of ano rectal diseases. Translated by Galambos J. Philadelphia: Saunders, 1980:32.

Neiger A. Atlas of practical proctology. Bern: Hans Huber, 1973:37.

CHAPTER 19–58

Hemorrhoids

Sidney M. Fierst, M.D., M.S.

DEFINITION

Hemorrhoids are masses of venous, muscular, and connective tissue forming vascular cushions in the anal submucosa. Arteriovenous shunts are also present. Internal and external hemorrhoids are defined in relation to the dentate line. External hemorrhoids are located distal to the dentate line and are covered by squamous epithelium. Internal hemorrhoids are proximal and covered by columnar epithelium. Mixed hemorrhoids are those with elements of both internal and external hemorrhoids coexisting.

ETIOLOGY

Hemorrhoids are associated with increased intravascular pressure in the rectal veins. Cirrhosis of the liver, congestive heart failure, intraabdominal tumors, pregnancy, hard stools, chronic constipation, and straining at stool are factors contributing to the development of hemorrhoids.

CRITERIA FOR DIAGNOSIS

Suggestive

Patients present with painless passage of frank blood found on the surface of the stool, on the paper after defecation, or dripping into the bowl.

Definitive

Dilated vascular tissue can be observed or palpated.

CLINICAL MANIFESTATIONS

Subjective

Internal hemorrhoids present most often painless passage of frank blood at the end of defecation. The blood drips into the bowl or may squirt from a participating arteriovenous shunt. Blood is present on the toilet paper, on the surface of the stool, and in the water. Bleeding is intermittent.

External hemorrhoids are less likely to bleed than internal hemorrhoids. They are more symptomatic with pain, a palpable nodule, or skin tags. A general assessment of the patient is done to rule out a history of bleeding disorders, liver disease with portal hypertension, congestive heart failure, pregnancy, and intraabdominal tumors. Low-lying tumors, fistulas, and fissures are excluded by inspection. A family history of hemorrhoids, polyps, or colon cancer should be obtained. A low-fiber diet and constipation may be associated with hemorrhoids.

Objective

Physical Examination

Anoscopy is the definitive examination for diagnosing hemorrhoids, but proctoscopy or flexible sigmoidoscopy should be performed to visualize the rectum and lower colon to rule out coexisting tumors or inflammatory bowel disease. If anemia is present, total colonoscopy or barium enema should be performed. Also, patients over 50 should have colonoscopy or barium enema. Sigmoidoscopy is best performed in the knee–chest position with the buttocks spread. In debilitiated persons, the left lateral recumbent position can be used. The patient is asked to bear down, and the degree of prolapse is ascertained. The presence of hypertrophied papillae, condylomata, and perianal irritation can be noted. The sphincter is traversed with the well-lubricated gloved finger. Lidocaine jelly can be used to decrease the pain of the examination. The sphincter is dilated, noting its tone. Fissures, fistulas, herpes, thrombotic veins, and condylomata are evident. The hemorrhoids are seen as dilated veins with endoscopy (see Color Plate 19–58–1 after page 1546). Pain is rare with uncomplicated hemorrhoids. The complications are thrombosis and prolapse. Acute pain and mass usually represent a thrombosed vein. When both the internal and external plexuses thrombose, the pain is very severe. The mucosa becomes ischemic, ulcerates, and may become infected. The ulceration weeps, producing pruritis. With infection, periodic fever may occur. In some patients, the hemorrhoids prolapse and manual replacement is needed. When the prolapse is not reducible, strangulation of the tissue may result from the constricting pressure of the sphincter. Thrombosis, ulceration, gangrene, and sloughing of the tissue can result. Bleeding may occur. There is weeping of purulent or serous material, causing anal burning or itching. If infection with thrombophlebitis supervenes, fever is present.

Routine Laboratory Abnormalities

There are no diagnostic routine laboratory abnormalities. Blood, of course, may be found in the stool.

PLANS

Diagnostic

See Clinical Manifestations, Objective.

Therapeutic

To initiate effective therapy, staging (Table 19–58–1) is important to determine the nature of the treatment.

Treatment is aimed at curing symptoms. It should reduce pain and staining. Tissue should be fixated so as not to prolapse. Affected tissue should be destroyed or excised. The anal sphincter pressure should be reduced. For stage 1 hemorrhoids, medical treatment attempts to soften the stool and ease straining at defecation. Diet modification with increased fiber is advised. Fiber absorbs water and softens stool. The

TABLE 19–58–1. STAGING OF HEMORRHOIDS FOR TREATMENT

Stage	Symptoms	Findings
1	Painless bleeding, intermittent and sporadic	Variceal veins, no prolapse
2	Intermittent mass	Intermittent prolapse on bearing down, reduces after bowel motion spontaneously
3	Discomfort, soiling of underclothes	Recurrent prolapse, requires manual replacement
4	Bleeding Ulceration and infection Soiling—discharge Pruritus	Persistent prolapse Not reducible Ulcerations

branched-chain polysaccharides are acted on by colon bacteria to produce propionic and butyric acids, which result in mild laxation. Bulk stool softeners such as psyllium preparations and unprocessed bran can be used. Calcium or sodium docusate 200 mg twice daily can be supplementary.

Dilation Technique. Anal manometry has demonstrated a high resting pressure in patients with symptomatic hemorrhoids. Patients who have severe hemorrhoids with constricting bands can have manual dilation. Under light anesthesia, two fingers of the left hand are inserted and pulled upward. The index finger of the right hand is inserted simultaneously and pulled downward. The pressure should be minimal at the commissures. By a combination of gentle massage and rotation, up to three fingers of each hand are inserted. The three fingers of each hand inserted are rotated gently so that the anus and lower rectum are gradually enlarged. Too little dilation is better than too much. Care must be taken not to tear the commissures. Treatment can be repeated. A foam sponge is inserted into the anus after dilation to prevent bruising and hematoma. This procedure has been used for stage 3 hemorrhoids. It probably acts as partial "internal" sphincterotomy.

Therapy causing inflammation and scarring of the plexus and fixation to the underlying muscle is used for stage 1 and 2 and some stage 3 hemorrhoids.

Sclerotherapy. Sclerotherapy is a well-established treatment. With a 23-gauge needle inserted into the submucosa at the apex of the hemorrhoidal column, 1 to 2 mL 5% sodium morrhuate or 1% tetradecyl sulfate is injected. The submucosa is injected in a circular fashion so that the submucosal space around the hemorrhoid becomes inflamed and the mucosa becomes adherent to the muscularis, obliterating the plexus. Quinine urea has been used, but sodium morrhuate seems more effective as a sclerosing agent for stage 1 and 2 hemorrhoids. There have been some anaphylactic reactions to sodium morrhuate, so that adrenaline should be available. This is an office procedure and several veins can be injected at weekly intervals. The injection should be 1.5 to 2 cm above the dentate line so that pain is negligible.

Rubber Band Ligation. Rubber band ligation has become very popular. The special gun is loaded with a firm rubber band at the tip of the barrel. The hemorrhoid is grasped into the barrel. The trigger is pulled and the rubber band is forced onto the base of the tissue. The 1-mm diameter of the rubber band strangulates the tissue. The tissue sloughs in about 1 week. A fibrosing scar fixating the tissue results. This technique is excellent for elderly and debilitated patients. It can be performed without anesthesia in an outpatient setting. It can be used in stage 2 and selected stage 3 hemorrhoids. There may be a local ache and some tenesmus lasting for a few days. Precautions must be taken to band 1.5 to 2 cm above the pectinate lines to avoid postprocedure pain. There have been reports of bleeding after the sloughing that required suturing. Severe infection has also occurred.

Infrared Photocoagulation. Infrared photocoagulation involves destruction of tissue by creating a small burn. Long-term pain may occur if this is close to the anoderm. The photocoagulator must be applied at least 2 cm proximal to the pectinate line at several sites around the apex of the hemorrhoid. This is adequate for stage 1 or 2 hemorrhoids.

Cryotherapy. Cryotherapy causes tissue destruction by freezing using a special probe through which liquid nitrogen at −190°C is circulated. It is not possible to determine the extent of tissue damage at the time of treatment. A deep ulcer with muscle destruction or a superficial slough of the mucosa without obliteration and fixation of the hemorrhoid may result. Therefore, the results vary. There may be pain. This therapy is not recommended.

Bipolar and Direct Current Therapy. Bicap coagulation has been popular because it is simple to use as an outpatient procedure. The current is applied through a probe placed via the anoscope onto the mucosa at the apex of the hemorrhoid. The current set to the maximal tolerated level is continued for 5 to 10 minutes. It is best used for stage 1 and 2 hemorrhoids.

Laser. Neodynium–YAG lasers have been used. By retroflexing the fiberoptic sigmoidoscope, the apex of the hemorrhoid is visualized. A series of burns is made on the rosette of veins. The surface of the hemorrhoid may be burned superficially or vaporized. The hemorrhoid can also be excised with the laser. This technique requires expensive equipment and the complications of hemorrhage, abscess, and pain may occur in the postoperative period, as with the other types of obliterative treatment. It can, however, be used in stage 3 and 4 hemorrhoids and to cure prolapse.

Surgical Hemorrhoidectomy. Surgical hemorrhoidectomy should be considered after repeated failure of nonoperative treatment and for severely prolapsed hemorrhoids that require manual replacement. Surgical treatment is also required if there is associated pathology such as fissures, fistulas, and hypertrophied papillae. A thrombosed external hemorrhoid presents with a painful lump at the margin of the anus. Within the first 72 hours, the clot can be removed by using local anesthesia and making an elliptic incision in the skin overlying the clot and removing it. After 72 hours, sitz baths, stool softeners, and analgesics are suggested. Resolution of the clot takes time, often leaving a small fibrotic nodule.

Tissue destruction of hemorrhoids is obliterative therapy. These include cryotherapy with the freezing done by liquid nitrogen. Deep ulceration results that on healing obliterates the hemorrhoids. Neodynium–YAG laser ablation of hemorrhoids through the retroflexed sigmoidoscope requires skill in handling the laser. It may result in stricturing. Electrocautery of hemorrhoids also is an ablation technique. Ulceration is a complication. It can be done as an office procedure but care must be taken to burn at least 2 cm above the pectinate line. Surgical hemorrhoidectomy is a hospital procedure and is the therapy for type 4 prolapsed hemorrhoids. It has been demonstrated by anal manometry that patients with symptomatic hemorrhoids have a higher resting anal pressure. Sphincter pressure can be reduced by manual dilation of the anus. Some patients can be helped by gradual dilation of the sphincter; however, it does not appear effective when prolapse is present. The best treatment for stage 1 and 2 hemorrhoids, in our opinion, is sclerotherapy or banding. Surgical ablation is best for stages 3 and 4.

Complications. All procedures have complications. With sclerotherapy, deep ulcers may form. Pain should be minimal if the injection is 2 cm above the pectinate line. Infection may occur and there may be abscess. Rubber banding and electrocautery may have similar complications. These three procedures can be performed in outpatients.

FOLLOW-UP

Treatment is usually successful and little follow-up is needed.

DISCUSSION
Prevalence and Incidence

The exact prevalence and incidence are not known, but the condition is common.

Related Basic Science

The major venous return of the internal hemorrhoidal plexis is through the superior rectal veins, which drain into the inferior mesenteric vein and portal system. As these veins have no valves, increased intravascular pressure is readily transmitted, causing venous ectasia distally. The external hemorrhoidal plexus drains via the inferior hemorrhoidal veins into the internal iliac veins and into the systemic circulation via the inferior vena cava. Communication exists between the internal and external venous plexus.

Manometric studies of intraanal pressure have shown higher resting pressures in patients with hemorrhoids. It is therefore probable that a factor contributing to the formation is abnormal tone of the internal sphincter.

Natural History and Its Modification with Treatment

Mild hemorrhoids are tolerated and managed by medical means. Persistent and troublesome hemorrhoids may be corrected by one of several methods. Recurrences are uncommon.

Prevention

Adequate fiber intake and good bowel hygiene to prevent straining at stool may prevent hemorrhoids. In portal hypertension, however, the hemorrhoidal veins play a significant role in portosytemic shunting, similar to esophageal varices.

Cost Containment

The cost of treatment is small and the physician should choose the method of treatment that best suits the problem.

REFERENCES

Lau WY, Chow HP, Poon GP, Wong SH. Rubber band ligation of three primary hemorrhoids in a single session: A safe and effective procedure. Dis Colon Rectum 1982;25:336.

Lin JK. Anal manometric studies in hemorrhoids and anal fissures. Dis Colon Rectum 1989;32:839.

Shemesh ET, Kodner IJ, Fry RD, Neufeld DM. Severe complications of rubber band ligation of internal hemorrhoids. Dis Colon Rectum 1987;30:199.

CHAPTER 19–59

Fistula in Ano

Sidney M. Fierst, M.D., M.S.

DEFINITION

Fistula in ano is the track formed from a chronic abscessed anal gland dissecting through to form a communication between the anal canal and the perineal skin.

ETIOLOGY

The theory of the cryptoglandular origin of fistula in ano is attributed to Parks (1961). An episode of diarrhea may force liquid feces into the main duct of the anal gland, causing obstruction and suppuration. The trauma of hard stool, a foreign body, pinworm, tuberculosis, actinomycosis, pelvic inflammatory disease, postradiation lymphoma, and Crohn's disease are etiologic factors.

CRITERIA FOR DIAGNOSIS

Suggestive

Pain and swelling in the anal region with wetness and soiling or a history of Crohn's disease suggests the diagnosis.

Definitive

Visualization of a draining sinus opening in the buttocks or perineal region defines the diagnosis.

CLINICAL MANIFESTATIONS

Subjective

The patient may present with acute or chronic symptoms. In the acute phase, the abscess causes pain and swelling in the anal region. The pain occurs with sitting and is aggravated by motion, coughing, and straining. Fever, diarrhea, purulent anal discharge, and bleeding may be the presenting symptoms. The pain is generally throbbing, continuous, and aggravated by bowel motion. There may be the complaint of discharge on the skin with erosion, excoriation, and pruritis. The patient with a chronic fistula may present with discharge on the buttocks and pruritis, with pain being less prominent.

Objective

Physical Examination

The acute phase is marked by swelling, redness, and tenderness. Pus may be seen exuding from a crypt or sinus in the perineal skin. Rectal examination is very painful. A sense of a palpable tender mass suggests an intersphincteric abscess. An opening into the anal canal with pus exuding may be seen on anoscopy. There may be enlarged inguinal nodes.

In the chronic phase, the external opening is slightly elevated and red from granulation tissue. On pressure, purulent serosanguineous fluid may be expressed. The number of external openings and their relationship to the anal canal are observed. A posterior opening suggests the fistula originates from the dorsal midline crypt. If the opening is anterior, the track usually runs to the nearest crypt. Openings on both sides of the anus suggest a horseshoe-type fistula with an opening midline posteriorly. An external opening adjacent to the anal margin suggests an intersphincteric track. The further the external opening is from the anus, the greater the likelihood that the fistula is complicated by upper extension.

Palpating the skin between the anal canal and the fistulous opening may reveal the indurated cord of the track, indicating the direction to the opening in the anal canal. A ring of induration hugging the puborectalis sling in a horseshoe fashion indicates circumferential extension. A depression in the anal canal may be felt. This indicates the internal opening.

The external opening drains pus. Probing may be done very carefully with a blunt-type malleable probe. This should be done in the operating room. The danger of creating a false passage is very real. If the probe passes upward at an 80° angle to the skin or almost parallel to the anus, a high fistula or supralevator extension of a low fistula is likely. The probe passing at a 30° angle to the skin suggests a low fistula. Methylene blue injection is used to track complicated fistulas.

Routine Laboratory Abnormalities

There are no diagnostic routine laboratory abnormalities.

PLANS

Diagnostic

Differential Diagnosis

Radiologic examination should be performed if there is a history of recurrent fistulas. Both barium enema and small bowel studies may be indicated to rule out Crohn's disease. Further, in the differential diagnosis of fistula in ano, hidradenitis suppurativa, tuberculosis, actinomycosis, pilonidal sinus, and cloacal cardinoma must be considered.

Diagnostic Options and Recommended Approach

Anoscopy and sigmoidoscopy should be performed. It is important to rule out ulcerative colitis or Crohn's disease. The internal opening can be identified and the rectal or anal opening noted.

Therapeutic

In fistulas associated with Crohn's disease, fistulectomy often fails to heal. Incision and drainage of abscesses only temporize. Control of the underlying disease may often arrest the fistula so that surgical repair of the fistula can then be performed. Flagyl 250 mg thrice daily, azothiaprine 50 mg daily, and mesalamine 800 mg twice daily may also help produce remission of activity. There is little use for antibiotics in managing paraanal suppuration from other causes of fistula in ano.

The presence of a symptomatic fistula in ano is an indication for operation as spontaneous healing is rare. Neglected fistulas result in repeated abscesses, multiple openings, and complications.

The principles of surgery of the fistula involve identifying the primary opening and noting the relationship of the fistulous track to the puborectalis muscle. The division of the least amount of muscle in curing the fistula should be practiced.

FOLLOW-UP

The follow-up is designed to assess the healing process following surgery.

DISCUSSION

Prevalence and Incidence

The prevalence and incidence are not known. The condition is common in inflammatory bowel disease (Crohn's).

Related Basic Science

Fistula in ano may be the first manifestation of Crohn's disease in about 10% of these patients. It often occurs as the initial manifestation of cloacal carcinoma. It is classified as simple or complex. Simple fistulas are submucosal or subcutaneous, associated with a bridging fissure in the midline posteriorly. Complex fistulas arise from the anal gland abscess and may run upward, downward, or bidirectionally. A fistula may remain between the internal and external sphincter muscles as an intersphincteric abscess or point between the two sphincters as a perineal or low intersphincteric fistula. The barrier of the external sphincter may be penetrated and the fistula may extend laterally to enter the ischiorectal fossa. It may track distally to penetrate the skin some distance from the anus.

The track may extend upward in the intersphincteric space, perforating the levator ani muscle, resulting in a supralevator abscess lying adjacent to the rectal wall.

If the opening in the rectum is below the puborectalis muscle, it is considered a low fistula. A high fistula opens above the puborectalis intrarectally or extrarectally. Rarely, circumferential spread in the pararectal tissue above the puborectalis may occur. A stricture in the upper third of the rectum may result from the granulation tissue and fibrosis of the abscessed inflammatory tissue.

Natural History and Its Modification with Treatment

Fistula in ano usually requires surgical treatment. Surgical treatment is usually successful.

Prevention

There is no known method of prevention.

Cost Containment

Costs can be minimized by early definitive surgical treatment.

REFERENCES

Gordon PH, Nivatvonga S. Principles and practice of surgery for the colon, rectum and anus: Fistula in ano: Classification and treatment. St. Louis: Quality Medical, 1992: 234.
Parks AG. Pathogenesis and treatment of fistula in ano. Br Med J 1961;1:463.

CHAPTER 19–60

Pseudomembranous Colitis and Other Forms of Antibiotic-associated Diarrhea

Veronica Prego, M.D.

DEFINITION

Pseudomembranous colitis (PMC) is a severe form of antibiotic-associated diarrhea (AAD) characterized by the presence in the colonic mucosa of inflammatory plaques known as pseudomembranes. Colitis without pseudomembrane formation or even a normal mucosa can be found in milder forms of AAD.

ETIOLOGY

Clostridium difficile is responsible for almost 100% of cases of PMC, 50 to 70% of antibiotic-associated colitis without pseudomembranes, and 20% of cases of benign AAD. In most of the remaining cases the etiology remains obscure. In the early antibiotic era preceding the discovery of *C. difficile*, *Staphylococcus aureus* was thought to be the causative agent of PMC. Presently, this organism is only rarely linked to PMC.

Infection occurs in patients whose colonic flora has been altered by antibiotic therapy. Most commonly responsible are cephalosporins, amoxicillin, ampicillin, and clindamycin, but virtually any antimicrobial agent can be implicated regardless of the route of administration or the duration of therapy. Uncommonly, PMC has been described in the absence of antimicrobial use in ischemic colitis, leukemia, shock, burns, uremia, spinal fracture, abdominal and pelvic surgery, Hirschsprung's disease, and chemotherapy. The great majority of these cases are attributable to *C. difficile* infection. Recent antibiotic use is also a known risk factor for *Salmonella* infection. Controversial reports have described a syndrome attributed to *Candida* infection consisting of profuse diarrhea with normal colonic mucosal appearance in elderly, debilitated individuals on prolonged antibiotic therapy.

CRITERIA FOR DIAGNOSIS

Suggestive

Recent onset of diarrhea, with or without abdominal cramps and fever, and a history of current or recent antibiotic therapy (most commonly in the first week of use but up to 6 weeks after discontinuation) suggest the diagnosis.

Definitive

The diagnosis is defined by a positive stool assay for *C. difficile* toxin. Alternatively, endoscopic demonstration of colonic mucosal pseudomembranes in a patient with a suggestive history is virtually pathognomonic of PMC.

CLINICAL MANIFESTATIONS

The clinical manifestations of AAD span a wide spectrum that includes benign AAD, colitis without pseudomembranes, PMC, and fulminant colitis with toxic megacolon and perforation.

Mild Form
Subjective

The cardinal symptom is diarrhea, consisting of a few loose to watery movements a day without gross blood; mucus is frequently seen. Lower abdominal cramping is minimal or absent.

Objective

Physical Examination. Fever is typically absent or low grade. The blood pressure and pulse remain normal. The abdominal examination is normal or reveals minimal tenderness in the lower quadrants. In most cases, stools test negative for occult blood.

Routine Laboratory Abnormalities. Routine laboratory tests remain normal, except perhaps for mild leukocytosis.

Severe Form (Pseudomembranous Colitis)
Subjective

Frequent, watery stools with mucus but without visible blood are accompanied by fever and marked lower abdominal cramps. Tenesmus (sensation of incomplete evacuation) reflects underlying rectal inflammation. Anorexia, malaise, nausea, and vomiting are frequent complaints. Neutropenic cancer patients on chemotherapy may develop right lower quadrant pain with minimal or no diarrhea (typhlitis).

Objective

Physical Examination. Fever is present and may rise to 106°F. The abdomen is distended with pronounced tenderness, especially in the lower quadrants. Rarely, the patient's initial presentation may be an acute abdomen. Prior use of narcotic antidiarrheal agents may attenuate clinical manifestations. Stool tests positive for occult blood in 50% of the cases.

Routine Laboratory Abnormalities. Leukocytosis is present. Values commonly fluctuate between 10,000 and 20,000 but can rise to 60,000 white blood cells/mm^3. If dehydration is present, blood urea nitrogen, creatinine, and the blood urea nitrogen/creatinine ratio are elevated. Hypokalemia and acidosis may develop. Hypoalbuminemia reflecting stool protein losses is sometimes present.

PLANS
Diagnostic
Differential Diagnosis

It is important to consider other causes of colitis such as ischemic bowel disease, acute presentation of Crohn's disease and ulcerative colitis, gold-induced colitis, and infection with other intestinal pathogens such as *Salmonella, Shigella, Campylobacter, Yersinia,* enterotoxigenic strains of *Escherichia* coli, *Clostridium perfringens, Bacillus cereus, Vibrio, Entamoeba histolytica,* and *Giardia.* In older individuals, diarrhea accompanied by fever and abdominal pain may indicate acute diverticulitis. Gross blood in the stool is rare in *C. difficile* colitis and should lead the clinician to suspect other etiologies. In AIDS patients with diarrhea as well as in those presenting with an acute flare of inflammatory bowel disease, it is important to consider *C. difficile* as the etiology, if a history of antibiotic use is obtained.

Diagnostic Options

The key to diagnosing *C. difficile* infection is to demonstrate the presence of its toxins in the stool. The cytotoxin assay for toxin B is a tissue culture assay in which the patient's stool filtrate is incubated with fibroblasts in culture. Results are positive if cell rounding is induced and later neutralized by a specific toxin B antiserum. This test is the gold standard in the diagnosis of PMC because of its excellent sensitivity (95–100%) and specificity (100%). The disadvantages are expense, the need for specialized tissue culture facilities, and a delay of 2 to 3 days for results to become available. Many hospitals use outside laboratories, which causes further delays. Recently, enzyme immunoassays for toxins A and B were developed. Using specific monoclonal or polyclonal antibodies, they can detect the presence of toxins in the stool in 4 hours. They are less expensive and easier to perform. Their sensitivity is very good (90%) while maintaining excellent specificity (99–100%). The latex agglutination assay is often used because it is simple to perform and relatively inexpensive, but has poor sensitivity (50–60%) and lower specificity (95%).

Stool culture for *C. difficile* is not a clinically useful tool as 1 to 3% of adults are asymptomatic carriers. Moreover, in hospitalized adults who received antibiotics the carrier rate rises to 25%. Also, cultures detect nontoxicogenic as well toxicogenic strains, which further limits their utility. Fecal leukocytes are present in 50% of cases of *C. difficile* colitis.

Endoscopy and biopsy may be very useful. In patients with PMC, visualization of the rectal mucosa by limited flexible sigmoidoscopy or proctoscopy reveals 2- to 10-mm yellowish adherent plaques (pseudomembranes) with relative sparing of the intervening mucosa. Histologically, pseudomembranes are clumps of inflammatory cells, fibrin, and necrotic tissue in the colonic lumen accompanied by underlying mucosal inflammation. In colitis without pseudomembranes, the endoscopic abnormalities are limited to mucosal erythema and friability which corresponds to nonspecific colitis on microscopic examination. In benign AAD the mucosal appearance is normal.

Recommended Approach

In mild cases, simple withdrawal of the offending antibiotic may suffice, leading to the spontaneous resolution of symptoms. When the diagnosis is in doubt, when discontinuing antibiotics is not advisable, or in more severe cases, a specific diagnosis should be pursued (Table 19–60–1). The stool enzyme immunoassay for toxin A or B is a reasonable diagnostic choice because it provides a rapid answer while maintaining very good sensitivity and specificity. The stool cytotoxic tissue assay is more expensive and may be reserved for situations where clinical suspicion is strong but the enzyme immunoassay is negative. A negative stool toxin assay should prompt investigation for other enteric pathogens. In outpatients, stool culture and ova and parasites should be obtained. In patients who develop diarrhea in the hospital, however, only the parasitologic examination is recommended; stool cultures are not cost effective as infection with other enteric pathogens in this setting is rare. Endoscopy is probably unnecessary in typical presentations when a confirmatory stool toxin assay is available in a timely fashion. When delays are expected or when test results are negative despite strong clinical suspicion, endoscopic studies can be useful. In more severe forms of the disease, a limited flexible sigmoidoscopy or proctoscopy without bowel cleansing can identify characteristic rectal pseudomembranes and provide an immediate answer relatively inexpensively. In milder forms, the nonspecific appearance of the mucosa

TABLE 19–60–1. RECOMMENDED MANAGEMENT FOR *CLOSTRIDIUM DIFFICILE* INFECTION

Clinical Picture	Diagnostic Workup	Stop Offending Antibiotic	Anti-*Clostridium difficile* Antibiotics
Mild	No	Yes	No
Moderate	±	Yes	±
Severe	Yes	Yes	Yes
Immunocompromised host	Yes	Yes	Yes

makes endoscopy less useful. In patients with fulminant colitis with or without toxic megacolon, endoscopy should be avoided because of the risk of perforation. If a positive stool toxin assay is not immediately available, advancing a flexible instrument just beyond the anal canal to visualize the lower rectum using minimal air insufflation is safe and can be very helpful. Unfortunately, because some patients with fulminant colitis develop spontaneous perforation, even the most limited endoscopic study can have medicolegal consequences. Biopsy confirmation is often unnecessary and adds to the cost of the procedure. In 10% of patients lesions are confined to the proximal colon. Colonoscopy may be indicated if PMC is strongly suspected but the rectal mucosa appears normal. In patients presenting with abdominal distention, upright and supine plain films of the abdomen should be obtained to identify the intestinal segment involved and the degree of distention. Massive large bowel dilation indicates toxic megacolon due to fulminant colitis.

Therapeutic

Therapeutic Options

Metronidazole (250 mg orally four times daily) is highly active against *C. difficile* with a response rate of 98%. Resistant strains have rarely been reported. It is readily absorbed in the upper gastrointestinal tract but reaches high colonic concentrations by excretion across the inflamed bowel mucosa and into the bile. These mechanisms provide bactericidal colonic mucosal levels when metronidazole is administered intravenously as well. Side effects develop in 5% of patients and include nausea, vomiting, metallic taste in the mouth, and a disulfiram-like reaction to alcohol. Oral vancomycin (125 mg orally four times daily) is poorly absorbed and is excreted unchanged in the stool. Vancomycin and metronidazole have been shown to be equally effective. When vancomycin is given intravenously, however, colonic mucosal levels are unreliable. Resistance has not been reported. Side effects are negligible. The cost of a 10-day course of oral antibiotics is approximately $15 for metronidazole and $220 for vancomycin. Oral cholestyramine (4 g orally four times daily) is not active against *C. difficile* but binds to its toxins while allowing spontaneous restoration of the bowel flora. The response rate is 70%.

Recommended Approach

If clinically possible, the offending antibiotic should be immediately discontinued (Table 19–60–1). In uncomplicated mild to moderate cases, this simple measure usually leads to the spontaneous resolution of symptoms by allowing restoration of the bowel flora. In more severe or persistent cases, or when continued administration of the offending antibiotic is essential, antibiotic therapy aimed at the eradication of *C. difficile* should be instituted. Also, in elderly, debilitated individuals, in those with compounding medical conditions (cancer, AIDS, inflammatory bowel disease, etc.), and in those receiving chemotherapy, immunosuppressive agents, or corticosteroids, specific antimicrobial agents may be recommended. Oral metronidazole is the drug of choice because it is highly effective at a lower cost (Table 19–60–2). In patients who cannot tolerate metronidazole, oral vancomycin is a more expensive alternative. Bacitracin (25,000 U orally four times daily) should be considered a third-line drug because it is somewhat less effective and only moderately cheaper than vancomycin. Antimicrobial agents should be continued for 3 days after resolution of symptoms, usually for a total of 5 to 10 days. Shorter courses are preferable because they may be associated with lower relapse rates by allowing quicker restoration of the colonic flora. When patients cannot tolerate oral antibiotics (nausea, vomiting) or when ileus is present, intravenous metronidazole is effective. Routinely, vancomycin should not be used intravenously because colonic mucosal levels by this route are not reliable. Patients with fulminant colitis should receive intravenous metronidazole (250 mg every 6 hours) plus oral vancomycin via nasogastric tube (500 mg every 6 hours); some authors recommend adding intravenous vancomycin to this regimen, as bactericidal colonic concentrations are achieved by this route in some patients.

Rarely, a cecostomy or ileostomy may be placed to instill metronidazole and vancomycin directly into the colon. In patients with perforation and peritonitis or toxic megacolon, and in severely ill patients who deteriorate or fail to improve after 48 hours, emergency subtotal colectomy with temporary ileostomy may be lifesaving. Although scientific proof is lacking, several anecdotal reports have warned against the use of antidiarrheal agents that inhibit peristalsis, such as loperamide and diphenoxylate. Improvement of diarrhea occurs at the expense of retaining toxin-laden fecal fluid, which can lead to worsening of the clinical picture.

FOLLOW-UP

Hospitalized patients should be followed closely; depending on severity, the vital signs, clinical symptoms, and physical examination with particular attention to the abdomen should be followed at least three times daily. An input and output chart should be kept at the bedside; quantity and quality of diarrheal output, urine output, and vomitus as well as intravenous and oral fluid intake should be recorded every shift. Electrolytes should be monitored daily in severe cases. Stool toxin assay is not recommended as part of the follow-up evaluation. Nonhospitalized patients can be followed in a few days. They should be educated about their disease and encouraged to contact the physician sooner if their condition deteriorates.

Complications

If the patient deteriorates or fails to improve, any of the following may be responsible: perforation, peritonitis, toxic megacolon, noncompliance with medications, resistant strains, pathogens other than *C. difficile,* misdiagnosis or nonrecognition of coexisting conditions (diverticulitis, colon cancer, inflammatory bowel disease, ischemic bowel).

Perforation and Peritonitis. The abdominal examination reveals increasing tenderness with localization, rebound, and loss of bowel sounds. It is important to remember that classic peritoneal signs may be blunted in elderly, debilitated individuals as well as in those receiving steroids or narcotics. It is therefore advisable to keep a high index of suspicion in such cases. Paradoxical improvement of diarrhea can occur when severely ill patients develop ileus, peritonitis, or toxic megacolon. An immediate surgical consultation should be obtained. Upright and supine plain films of the abdomen may reveal free air. Abdominal computed tomography may show bowel thickening, pericolic fluid collection, and free air. A single-column Gastrografin enema administered under low pressure may reveal the site of perforation. If perforation is demonstrated or strongly suspected, an emergency subtotal colectomy with diverting ileostomy should be performed.

Toxic Megacolon. Marked, worsening distention of the abdomen with absent bowel sounds corresponds on plain films to a massively dilated colon. Treatment is subtotal colectomy with temporary diverting ileostomy.

Relapse

After initial improvement, 10 to 20% of patients who received antibiotics against *C. difficile* relapse, usually 3 to 10 days after discontinua-

TABLE 19–60–2. RECOMMENDED THERAPY AGAINST *CLOSTRIDIUM DIFFICILE* INFECTION

Drug of Choice:	Metronidazole 250 mg PO q6hr × 3d after resolution (~5–10d)	
Second line drug:	Vancomycin 125 mg PO q6h	
Third line Drug:	Bacitracin 25,000 U PO q6h	
Special Situations		**Treatment**
Nausea/vomiting/ileus	Metronidazole	250 mg IV q6h
Fulminant colitis	Metronidazole	250 mg IV q6h plus
	Vancomycin	500 mg via nasogastric tube q6h plus/minus
	Vancomycin	500 mg IV q6h
Relapse: mild to moderate	No antibiotics	
Relapse: severe or persistent	Repeat first course	

tion. If no specific antibiotics are used, the relapse rate is much lower. Multiple relapses are not uncommon. If relapse is mild, avoiding further antibiotic therapy is advisable to allow restoration of the colonic flora. In more severe, complicated, or persistent cases, re-treatment with antibiotics is recommended. There is no clear rationale for changing the initially successful antibiotic regimen. Response and relapse rates are 95 and 50%, respectively. The best strategy for treating multiple relapses is unknown. Reported modalities include a standard course of vancomycin or metronidazole for 10 days followed by one of these options: "pulse" vancomycin therapy (125 mg orally daily every 3 days for 3 weeks); slow tapering of vancomycin; cholestyramine for 4 weeks. Also, vancomycin 125 mg orally four times daily in conjunction with rifampin 600 mg orally twice daily for 1 week has been successfully. *Saccharomyces boulardii*, a nonpathogenic yeast, and *Lactobacillus* GG, although not commercially available, are promising novel therapies that appear to inhibit the growth of *C. difficile* while allowing reconstitution of the colonic flora.

DISCUSSION

Prevalence

In 1 to 3% of healthy adults *C. difficile* can be cultured from the stool but toxin assays remain negative. Fecal shedders are an important reservoir that keeps *C. difficile* in the environment. Fifty percent of healthy neonates are both fecal shedders and toxin producers. Presumably, immaturity of the colonic cell receptors prevents toxin binding and protects them from disease. Twenty-five percent of hospitalized patients without diarrhea receiving antibiotic therapy become colonized with *C. difficile*. The majority remain asymptomatic. In general, diarrhea develops in 3 to 10% of adults receiving antibiotic therapy. PMC develops in 1 to 3 per 100,000 outpatient courses of antibiotics, but the incidence rises to 1 per 100 to 1000 in inpatients. For unclear reasons, elderly people have the highest risk of developing *C. difficile*-associated disease.

Related Basic Science

In the setting of a bowel flora altered by antibiotic therapy, infection with *C. difficile* occurs by the fecal–oral route. Transmission most commonly occurs from person to person in places where environmental contamination with human feces is common, that is, hospitals and nursing homes. *Clostridium difficile* has been cultured from the hands of hospital personnel, toilets, bedpans, and floors. As 1 to 3% of patients are carriers, presumably the source of infection can be their own colonic flora. The mechanisms by which the intact colonic flora inhibits the growth of *C. difficile* are poorly understood. *Clostridium difficile* is not an invasive microorganism but causes colonic inflammation by the production of toxins. Toxicogenic strains produce toxins A and B. Preliminary data suggest that the human colon may be susceptible to both toxins. Animal studies have shown that after binding to its receptor, toxin A is internalized and elicits a marked inflammatory response with production of various mediators including leukotrienes, prostaglandins, interleukins, platelet-activating factor, and histamine. Destruction of the colonic mucosa follows, with the formation, in more severe cases, of exudative plaques of necrotic debris and inflammatory cells, known as pseudomembranes. Genetic typing of *C. difficile* indi-

cates that true relapse rather than reinfection is the most common mechanism for recurrent episodes, presumably due to germination of persistent spores.

Natural History and Its Modification with Treatment

The natural history in untreated patients is variable. Most patients have only mild complaints that resolve after discontinuation of the offending antibiotics. In more severe cases, protracted diarrhea is common. Institution of specific antimicrobial agents against *C. difficile* leads to the resolution of symptoms in 3 to 5 days. Approximately 98% of patients respond, and of these 10 to 20% relapse. After a second course of antibiotics, the response and relapse rates are similar. Multiple relapses are not uncommon. Avoiding antimicrobial agents directed against *C. difficile* markedly reduces the chances of relapse by allowing reconstitution of the colonic flora. In patients with AIDS and *C. difficile*-associated disease, clinical symptoms, response to treatment, and incidence of relapse are similar to those observed in non-immunocompromised hosts.

Prevention

Use of antibiotics should be judicious, particularly in the elderly who are prone to develop *C. difficile*-associated disease. Restricting clindamycin use in hospitalized patients has been shown to decrease the incidence of *C. difficile*-associated disease. Hospitalized patients suspected to have *C. difficile* diarrhea should be placed on enteric precautions. When coming in contact with these patients or their environment, use of vinyl gloves is recommended. Following exposure, hands should be washed with a bactericidal solution; rooms should be disinfected with a hypochlorite solution.

Treatment of asymptomatic carriers (fecal shedders) has not been successful.

Cost Containment

The stool enzyme immunoassay is cheaper than the cytotoxin assay while providing reasonable sensitivity and specificity. Patients with mild symptoms in whom the offending antibiotic can safely be stopped usually do not require diagnostic studies or specific antimicrobial agents against *C. difficile*. Oral metronidazole should be chosen over oral vancomycin because it is equally effective at a much lower cost.

REFERENCES

Bartlett J. Pseudomembranous enterocolitis and antibiotic-associated colitis. In: Sleisenger MH, Fordtran JS, eds. Gastrointestinal disease: Pathophysiology, diagnosis, management. 5th ed. Philadelphia: Saunders, 1993:1174.

Kelly CP, Pothoulakis C, LaMont JT. *Clostridium difficile* colitis. N Engl J Med 1994;330:257.

LaMont JT. Case records of the Massachusetts General Hospital: Weekly clinicopathological exercises. Case 6-1993: A 31-month old girl with fever, diarrhea, abdominal distention and edema. N Engl J Med 1994;330:420.

Pear SM, Williamson TH, Bettin KM, et al. Decrease in nosocomial *Clostridium difficile*-associated diarrhea by restricting clindamycin use. Ann Intern Med 1994;120:272.

Teasley DG, Olson MM, Gebhard RL, et al. Prospective randomized trial of metronidazole versus vancomycin for *Clostridium difficile*-associated diarrhoea and colitis. Lancet 1983;2:1043.

CHAPTER 19–61

Polyps of the Colon and Rectum

William B. Solomon, M.D.

DEFINITION

A colorectal polyp is a mass of cells that arises above the surface of the bowel mucosa and protrudes into the lumen of the bowel. Pedunculated polyps are attached to the bowel mucosa by a stalk. Sessile polyps

arise from the bowel mucosa as a mound of cells without a discrete stalk.

Hyperplastic Polyps. Hyperplastic polyps are small sessile polyps, usually less than 3 mm, most commonly found in the distal two thirds of the rectum. They are not due to clonal proliferation of cells, but to failure of mature colonic mucosal cells to detach from epithelium. A hyperplastic polyp has no potential for malignant transformation.

Inflammatory Polyps. Inflammatory polyps are usually small, frequently multiple, and most commonly found in patients with ulcerative colitis, but also in Crohn's disease and in infectious diseases such as amebic colitis. The colonic mucosa is infiltrated with macrophages and lymphocytes, causing fibrosis and distortion of the mucosal architecture.

Carcinoid (Polyps). Usually smaller than 2 cm in diameter, carcinoid polyps are found exclusively in the lower rectum. They are due to increased clonal proliferation of neuroendocrine cells in the rectal mucosa or submucosa. Carcinoid polyps greater than 2 cm in diameter can invade through the rectal wall and metastasize.

Adenomatous Polyps. Except in familial polyposis syndromes, adenomatous polyps are usually found in small numbers throughout the colon with a preponderance in the sigmoid and rectum. Either pedunculated or sessile, they very rarely may be flat. Adenomatous polyps vary in size from a few millimeters to a few centimeters. Gland morphology varies on a continuum from tubular to villous. Each polyp is due to clonal proliferation of cells throughout a single crypt of Lieberkuhn. Of all the types of colorectal polyps, only adenomatous polyps have the potential, over the course of a number years, to transform into invasive colorectal carcinomas. It is this propensity for *transition* from adenomatous polyp to adenocarcinoma that requires identification and removal of colorectal polyps.

Malignant Adenomatous Polyps. A malignant adenomatous polyp is an adenomatous polyp containing proliferating cells that have invaded through the muscularis mucosa of the colon into the submucosa of the colon. These proliferating cells have access to the lymphatics and veins of the submucosa, so that the polyp is considered to contain a carcinoma with immediate potential for spread to lymph nodes or other tissues.

ETIOLOGY

Inherited Mutations

Specific genetic mutations inherited via the germline DNA from either parent's gametes have been identified in the syndromes of familial adenomatous polyposis and hereditary nonpolyposis colon cancer syndromes. First-degree relatives of individuals with adenomatous polyps or colorectal carcinoma have an increased risk of developing adenomatous polyps and colorectal carcinoma; this increased risk may be secondary to as yet unidentified inherited genetic mutations.

Environmental Factors

There is a high prevalence of adenomatous polyps and colorectal carcinoma in populations that have increased consumption of total calories and calories derived from animal fat and meat, and decreased consumption of dietary fiber from grains, fruits, and vegetables in relation to total calories consumed.

CRITERIA FOR DIAGNOSIS

Suggestive

Most colorectal polyps are asymptomatic. The risk of having an adenomatous polyp varies from 100% in individuals who have inherited a mutant version of the familial adenomatous polyposis gene to approximately 30 to 40% for an individual over the age of 60 without family history of colorectal carcinoma.

Individuals with three first-degree relatives with colorectal carcinoma or one first-degree relative with colorectal carcinoma before the age of 30 should be considered to be members of a familial polyposis family or to have a hereditary nonpolyposis colorectal carcinoma syndrome (Lynch type I or II syndrome). They require genotyping and surveillance for detection of polyps, especially flat adenomas, and colorectal carcinomas (see Chapter 19–62).

Individuals with two first-degree relatives with colorectal carcinoma or with one first-degree relative with colorectal carcinoma before age 55 are likely to be at increased risk of developing adenomatous polyps and colorectal carcinoma and should be subject to surveillance.

Motivated individuals without increased risk factors for development of colorectal carcinoma may benefit from screening for adenomatous polyps to prevent transition to colorectal carcinoma.

Definitive

Colorectal polyps are readily visualized and biopsied during endoscopy. The type of polyp can then be determined by evaluation of histologic sections.

In patients who refuse sigmoidoscopy for screening or colonoscopy for surveillance/diagnosis, air-contrast barium enema is effective for identification of polyps greater than 1 cm in diameter. Air-contrast barium enema should also be performed in patients in whom colonoscopy did not result in adequate evaluation of the entire colon including the cecum.

CLINICAL MANIFESTATIONS

Subjective

The majority of individuals with colorectal polyps are asymptomatic. Patients may notice intermittent abdominal pain, diarrhea or constipation, abdominal distention, or bleeding from the rectum. Any of these symptoms are not specific manifestations of a colonic polyp.

Within 3 years of identification of a single adenomatous polyp, a patient has a 30 to 40% chance of developing a new adenomatous polyp. Patients with a prior diagnosis of several adenomatous polyps have more than a 50% chance of developing new adenomatous polyps within 3 years. Patients with a prior diagnosis of multiple adenomatous polyps, except those with a single tubular adenomatous polyp smaller than 1 cm, should be scheduled for future surveillance.

The familial adenomatous polyposis syndromes and hereditary nonpolyposis colorectal carcinoma syndromes are inherited in an autosomal dominant manner. First-degree relatives of individuals with adenomatous polyps and/or colorectal carcinoma are at increased risk for development of adenomatous polyps.

Objective

Physical Examination

In a minority of individuals with a rectal polyp there may be a palpable mass on rectal examination. Occasionally, rectal polyps may prolapse through the anus. At times polyps may cause intussusception of the colon with consequent symptoms of large bowel obstruction.

Intermittent bright red bleeding from large rectal or sigmoid polyps and occult bleeding from smaller polyps and right-sided colon polyps are the most common signs in patients who have a presenting sign of a polyp.

Routine Laboratory Abnormalities

The test for fecal occult blood may therefore be positive; however, development of a hypochromic microcytic anemia from iron deficiency secondary to persistent occult blood loss from colorectal polyps is rare. Therefore other causes of iron deficiency such as a frank adenocarcinoma of the bowel should be considered.

PLANS

Diagnostic

Differential Diagnosis

Individuals with Symptoms or Signs of a Colorectal Polyp. Individuals above the age of 40 who have symptoms or signs consistent with a colorectal polyp must undergo an immediate search for a polyp. The signs and symptoms of polyps can mimic those of colorectal carcinoma, diverticular disease, inflammatory bowel disease, or infectious bowel disorders.

Asymptomatic Individuals from Families with Familial Adenomatous Polyposis or Nonpolyposis Colorectal Carcinoma Syndromes. Please see Chapter 19–62.

Asymptomatic Individuals with Increased Risk of Sporadic Adenomatous Polyps or Colorectal Carcinoma. Please see the surveillance protocol detailed under Follow-up in this chapter.

Asymptomatic Individuals with Average Risk of Sporadic Adenomatous Polyps or Colorectal Carcinoma. Please see the screening protocol detailed under Follow-up in this chapter.

Diagnostic Options

In patients with symptoms or signs of a colorectal polyp, colonoscopy with biopsy has the advantage of yielding a histologic diagnosis as well as localizing the polyp or other pathology responsible for symptoms. Patients who refuse colonoscopy or are medically unable to undergo colonoscopy can have an air-contrast barium enema, which is useful for detection of polyps greater than 1 cm in diameter and for investigation of the cecal region of the colon.

Recommended Approach

Individuals with symptoms or signs of a colorectal polyp, such as rectal bleeding or a positive fecal occult blood test, should proceed directly to investigation of the entire colon via colonoscopy. If the entire colon to the cecum cannot be visualized during colonoscopy, then air-contrast barium enema is useful.

Therapeutic

Therapeutic Options

Colonoscopy is both a diagnostic and a therapeutic procedure for most colorectal polyps. Polyps that are 5 mm or less can be biopsied and then destroyed by heating. Polyps with stalks can be removed via endoscopic polypectomy and sent for histologic diagnosis. Large sessile polyps can be biopsied and often removed in pieces; however, some large sessile polyps may require surgical removal.

Additional therapy and follow-up of a colorectal polyp are contingent on the histology and malignant potential of the polyp.

Recommended Approach

Hyperplastic Polyps. If hyperplastic polyps are the sole polyp type identified during endoscopy, there does not appear to be an increased risk of colorectal carcinoma. Individuals with hyperplastic polyps can be placed in a screening protocol for colorectal carcinoma.

Inflammatory Polyps. Individuals with inflammatory polyps do not require removal of all inflammatory polyps. If the inflammatory polyps are a consequence of inflammatory bowel disease, then therapy should be directed against the underlying bowel disorder. Giant inflammatory polyps may require surgical removal, particularly if they are the cause of partial bowel obstruction or intussusception.

Carcinoid Polyps. If less than 2 cm in diameter, carcinoid polyps can be removed via colonoscopy. If greater than 2 cm in diameter, abdominal and pelvic computed axial tomography is needed for evaluation of invasiveness and distant spread. Rectal carcinoid tumors that are metastatic to the liver do not cause carcinoid syndrome. Most patients with rectal carcinoid tumors greater than 2 cm in diameter require surgery.

Adenomatous Polyps. The malignant potential of an adenomatous polyp determines its therapy and follow-up. The risk of the polyp being a malignant polyp is directly correlated with its size, shape, histology, and number. Size greater than 2 cm in diameter, sessile rather than pedunculated, and villous rather than tubular morphology of the adenomatous glands are all risk factors for malignant transformation.

The sine qua non of immediate malignant potential is invasion of the adenomatous cells through the muscularis mucosa into the submucosal lymphatics and veins. Pedunculated polyps rarely invade through the muscularis mucosa and invasion of cells into lymphatics and veins is rarer still, so endoscopic removal of pedunculated polyps is sufficient therapy. If, however, there is invasion of adenomatous cells through the muscularis mucosa of a sessile polyp, with identification of cells in the lymphatic or vascular system of the colonic submucosa, individuals who are good surgical risks may be referred to surgeons for segmental bowel resection. Surgery can determine if the entire sessile polyp has been removed and whether there has been spread to lymph nodes.

FOLLOW-UP

The schedule of follow-up examinations for identification of new polyps or polyps missed at the initial colonoscopy depends on the polyp type.

Individuals with a Malignant Adenomatous Polyp Removed Endoscopically. To ensure that the malignant polyp has been entirely removed, a follow-up colonoscopy should be performed at 3 months and at 1 year after the initial removal of the malignant polyp. If recurrence is found at the former site of the malignant polyp, then surgical resection is advised. If no recurrences are found, the patient can undergo colonoscopic surveillance every 3 to 5 years.

Surveillance Protocol for Individuals with Adenomatous Polyps Removed Endoscopically and Individuals with Risk Factors for Colorectal Carcinoma. The recurrent nature of adenomatous polyps, the rather long period of transition from adenomatous polyp to invasive colorectal carcinoma, and the likelihood that individuals from families who are at high risk for development of colorectal adenocarcinoma have adenomatous precursor lesions appearing 5 to 10 years prior to the development of invasive adenocarcinoma are all rationales for establishing a surveillance program.

For individuals with adenomatous polyps previously removed endoscopically, the initial follow-up colonoscopy can be performed at 3 years. If this colonoscopy is negative the surveillance interval may be increased to 5 years.

For high-risk individuals, yearly fecal occult blood testing (three tests done on 2 subsequent days) is likely to have greater specificity than in the general population and is recommended. The initial surveillance colonoscopy should be performed 5 years prior to the earliest age of onset of colon cancer in a family member, or when the fecal occult blood test is positive. A second surveillance colonoscopy can be performed 3 years after the first; if no polyps are found at either colonoscopy the surveillance interval can be increased to 5 years.

Screening Protocol for Individuals Without Prior Adenomatous Polyps or Without Increased Risk for Colorectal Adenocarcinoma. There are at least 160,000 new diagnoses of colorectal adenocarcinoma in the United States each year and 60,000 deaths each year from colorectal adenocarcinoma, representing a substantial morbidity and mortality to the population. Because of the long period of transition from adenomatous polyp to carcinoma, it is likely that detection and removal of polyps will lead to decreased death rates from colorectal carcinoma. That mass screening for adenomatous polyps and colorectal carcinoma leads to survival benefit, however, is not proven.

Screening for adenomatous polyps can be recommended to patients who are highly motivated to undergo screening procedures. Because the specificity of yearly fecal occult blood tests is low in the population without specific risk factors for development of colorectal cancer, yearly testing for occult blood cannot be recommended. A reasonable screening protocol should include a fecal occult blood test at age 50. If positive, that individual should proceed to a full colonoscopy for detection of polyps or other pathology. If negative, flexible sigmoidoscopy to 60 cm is recommended. If an adenomatous polyp is detected via the flexible sigmoidoscope, a full colonoscopy should be performed to detect polyps beyond the reach of the sigmoidoscope. Individuals who are found to have multiple adenomatous polyps at screening should then be placed on a surveillance protocol. Individuals without polyps at the initial screen may continue to have flexible sigmoidoscopy every 5 years.

DISCUSSION
Prevalence

In the United States, 25,000,000 individuals above the age of 40 have adenomatous polyps, for a prevalence rate of about 28% for all individuals above the age of 40. The prevalence of colonic polyps increases with each decade of life, so that in the sixth decade it is about 25%, in the seventh decade about 35%, and in the eighth decade 45%.

Related Basic Science

The development of adenomatous polyps and their transition to invasive adenocarcinomas with metastatic potential can be attributed to the progressive accumulation of mutations in genes that regulate the proliferation of cells within the crypts of Lieberkuhn.

Investigation of sporadic acquired adenomatous polyps has revealed that the earliest genetic change is likely to be point mutation of one of the two copies of the adenomatous polyposis coli (APC) gene. This is the same gene that is inherited as an autosomal dominant mutation in the familial adenomatous polyposis syndrome.

The point mutation in the APC gene causes the failure of expression of the APC protein encoded by the mutant allele of the APC gene. The level of APC protein in cells containing this mutant gene would then be 50% of the normal level. As it appears that the APC protein is involved in inhibition of colon cell proliferation, a decrease in its level may lead to increased proliferation of cells. A possible second event in the development of the adenomatous polyp could be mutation of the remaining normal copy of the APC gene, leading to the complete loss of all functional APC protein. Without any functional APC protein suppressing the proliferation of colon cells, the cells would gain a growth advantage over normal colon cells. Therefore, the APC gene is a tumor suppressor gene. Sporadic acquired adenomatous polyps have the same lack of functional APC protein as the cells in the myriad polyps found in familial adenomatous polyposis; however, in comparison to familial adenomatous polyposis syndrome, the likelihood of loss of both functional copies in the same cell is much lower. Therefore the number of adenomatous polyps is much smaller, and the age at which they occur is much older than in the familial adenomatous polyposis syndrome.

These proliferating cells within a crypt of Lieberkuhn can then acquire additional genetic mutations. It appears that a possible next step in the development of the adenomatous polyp and possibly a transition from the more well differentiated tubular form to villous form is point mutation in the Ki-*ras* oncogene. The Ki-*ras* gene mutation results in a change of function of the Ki-*ras* protein, the consequence being a change in cell morphology. As only one of the two copies of the Ki-*ras* gene must be mutated to result in increased cell proliferation and changed morphology, this type of mutation is a dominant mutation. The Ki-*ras* gene belongs to a family of *ras* genes, all of which have been shown to be activated to dominant oncogenes on point mutation.

If the sequence of genetic mutations is not interrupted by removal of the adenomatous polyp, then additional genetic mutations can occur which lead to the development of frank invasive adenocarcinoma. These additional mutations, which probably cause a frank transition to carcinoma, include mutation and loss of function of the p53 tumor suppressor gene and loss of a tumor suppressor gene on chromosome 18.

Natural History and Its Modification with Treatment

If adenomatous polyps are precursor lesions to colorectal carcinomas then removing adenomatous polyps ought to decrease the incidence of subsequent colorectal carcinoma. Prior to the era of colonoscopy, the evolution of colon polyps not surgically removed could be followed by barium enema. Within 10 years from the identification of a polyp, there was a 15% chance that a frank adenocarcinoma would develop at the site of the polyp.

Evidence for the effectiveness of intervening in this polyp-to-carcinoma transition stems from case–control studies. Removing rectosigmoid polyps via the rigid sigmoidoscope decreased the subsequent incidence of adenocarcinoma of the rectosigmoid to 30 to 40% of the incidence of a population that did not undergo rigid sigmoidoscopy.

Prevention

Some studies report that decreasing total caloric intake as well as decreasing the intake of saturated fats may decrease the development of new polyps. Supplemental dietary calcium 1200 mg/d may also decrease the incidence of new polyps.

The nonsteroidal antiinflammatory agent sulindac 150 mg orally twice a day has been shown to decrease the incidence of new adenomatous polyps in individuals with familial adenomatous polyposis. Individuals who take at least two aspirins per week also appear to have a decreased incidence of polyps and colorectal cancer.

Cost Containment

Screening the population at risk for adenomatous polyps and colorectal cancer would entail a large cost to the total health bill. It has been estimated that the annual cost for fecal occult blood testing and triennial sigmoidoscopy for all individuals over the age of 65 would be greater than $2.5 billion per year. The cost per year of life saved would be approximately $50,000, which is within the cost per year of life saved for renal dialysis patients. Savings can be obtained by increasing the interval between surveillance for polyps from 1 year to 3 years.

REFERENCES

Atkins WS, Morson BC, Cuzick J. Long-term risk of colorectal cancer after excision of rectosigmoid adenomas. N Engl J Med 1992;326:658.

Bond JH. Polyp guideline: Diagnosis, treatment, and surveillance for patients with nonfamilial colorectal polyps. Ann Intern Med 1993;119:836.

Fearon ER. Molecular genetic studies of the adenoma–carcinoma sequence. Adv Intern Med 1994;39:123.

Neugut AI, Garbowski GC, Lee WC, et al. Dietary risk factor for the incidence and recurrence of colorectal adenomatous polyps. Ann Intern Med 1993;118:91.

O'Brien M, Winawer SJ, Waye JD. Colorectal polyps. In: Winawer SJ, ed. Management of gastrointestinal disease. New York: Gower, 1992

Selby JV, Friedman GD, Quesenberry CP, Weiss NS. A case–control study of screening sigmoidoscopy and mortality from colorectal cancer. N Engl J Med 1992;326:653.

Winawer SJ, Zauber AG, O'Brien MJ, et al. The National Polyp Study: Design, methods, and characteristics of patients with newly diagnosed polyps. Cancer (Suppl.) 1992;70:1236.

CHAPTER 19–62

Hereditary Intestinal Polyposis Syndromes

William B. Solomon, M.D.

DEFINITION

Hereditary intestinal polyposis syndromes are characterized by the development of multiple intestinal polyps during the first two decades of life. The polyps may be neoplastic adenomatous polyps or nonneoplastic hamartomatous or inflammatory polyps. All of the intestinal polyposis syndromes are associated with an increased risk of the development of gastrointestinal malignancies. The risk varies depending on the histology of the predominant polyp found in each specific syndrome. Inherited polyposis syndromes are the cause of 1% of all colon cancers. (Hereditary nonpolyposis colon cancer accounts for 5 to 8% of all colon cancers.)

Adenomatous Polyposis Syndromes

Familial Adenomatous Polyposis. Familial adenomatous polyposis (FAP) is an autosomal dominant inherited disorder characterized by the development, by the second decade of life, of hundreds to thousands of adenomatous polyps primarily in the rectum and colon, but also in the stomach and small intestine. The subsequent development of colorectal adenocarcinoma approaches 100% in (untreated) individuals who have inherited a mutant allele of the adenomatous polyposis coli (APC) gene. Colorectal carcinoma is found during the fourth and fifth decades of life. There is also increased risk of other gastrointestinal malignancies, particularly adenocarcinoma of the duodenum (often in the ampulla of Vater region) and gastric and ileal adenocarcinomas.

Gardner's Syndrome. Gardner's syndrome is an autosomal dominant inherited disorder characterized by the development of adenomatous polyposis of the rectum and colon, as well as extracolonic manifestations including osteomas of the mandible, exostoses of the skull, sebaceous cysts and fibromas, and desmoid tumors of the retroperitoneum. The autosomal dominant mutation is in the APC gene. The extracolonic manifestations of Gardner's syndrome phenotype may be secondary to specific mutations in the APC gene encoding for a class of mutant APC proteins or to interaction of the mutant APC protein with other proteins encoded in particular genetic backgrounds.

Turcot's Syndrome. Turcot's syndrome is an inherited disorder characterized by the development of adenomatous polyposis as well as neuroepithelial tumors, especially medulloblastomas and infrequently astrocytomas. The majority of individuals with Turcot's syndrome have an autosomal dominant germline mutation of the APC gene; however, inherited autosomal dominant mutations in any of the genes (*hMLH1, hMSH2, hPMS1, hPMS2*) encoding for proteins involved in DNA nucleotide mismatch repair have been found in some families with the Turcot's syndrome phenotype, particularly in individuals with colon carcinomas and glioblastoma multiforme.

Additional genetic mutations involving the genesis of brain tumors in Turcot's syndrome have not been characterized as of yet.

Attenuated Adenomatous Polyposis Coli. A form of FAP characterized by fewer than 100 adenomatous polyps, attenuated adenomatous polyposis coli carries a high risk of development of colorectal cancer, usually during the sixth decade of life. Attenuated variants of FAP are caused by point mutations in the APC gene that limit the size of the truncated APC protein to fewer than 160 amino acids.

Nonadenomatous Polyposis Syndromes

Peutz–Jeghers Syndrome. Peutz–Jeghers syndrome is an autosomal dominant inherited disorder characterized by mucocutaneous hypermelanotic pigmentation of the oral/buccal mucosa and digits of the extremities, as well as multiple hamartomatous (disordered growth of mature tissues) polyps consisting of arborizing smooth muscle cells with overlying hyperplastic or adenomatous epithelium. Polyps are found from the stomach to the rectal dentate line. This syndrome is associated with increased risks of development of small and large bowel adenocarcinoma, pancreatic adenocarcinoma, and ovarian sex cord tumor and adenocarcinoma.

Juvenile Polyposis. Juvenile polyposis is an autosomal dominant disorder characterized by multiple intestinal polyps usually arising during the first decade of life. The polyps appear initially as inflammatory polyps that may undergo adenomatous change. It is associated with an increased risk for development of colorectal adenocarcinoma.

Cowden's Disease. Cowden's disease is a rare autosomal dominant disorder characterized by papillomas of the hard palate, keratoses of the skin, and multiple hamartomas of the gastrointestinal tract, thyroid, uterus, and breast. There is a high incidence of thyroid and breast cancer. Though the intestinal polyps are not neoplastic, there is likely to be an increased risk of gastrointestinal malignancy. Lhermitte–Duclos disease characterized by cerebellar hamartomas, seizures, and ataxia is often found in association with Cowden's disease.

ETIOLOGY

Adenomatous Polyposis Syndromes

Familial adenomatous polyposis, Gardner's and Turcot's syndromes are all caused by autosomal dominant germline mutations in one of the two APC gene alleles. About 25% of patients with FAP do not have a family history of FAP, indicating that these individuals received a new

spontaneous mutation in the APC gene. This spontaneous mutation occurs during gametogenesis of either a paternal or maternal germ cell.

Nonadenomatous Polyposis Syndromes

Peutz–Jeghers syndrome, juvenile polyposis, and Cowden's disease are each caused by autosomal dominant germline mutations of single genes, none of which have been identified to date.

CRITERIA FOR DIAGNOSIS
Adenomatous Polyposis Syndromes
Suggestive

As the FAP syndrome is inherited in an autosomal dominant manner, individuals who have a parent with a known diagnosis of FAP syndrome have one chance in two of inheriting the mutant APC gene. The earliest suggestion that a mutant allele has been inherited can be found by physical examination: the presence of congenital hypertrophy of the retinal pigment epithelium (CHRPE). This physical finding can be detected by indirect ophthalmoscopy, often in young infants, and precedes the development of adenomatous polyposis coli by many years. CHRPE is found in 70% of families with APC. Presence of CHRPE is correlated with mutations distal to exon 9 of the APC gene. The absence of CHRPE does not rule out inheritance of the mutant APC gene.

Definitive

Detection of multiple small adenomatous polyps developing during the second decade is via flexible sigmoidoscopy. Prior to the age of polyp development, a definitive diagnosis can be made in kindreds with FAP by molecular biological techniques including linkage analysis of genetic polymorphisms close to and within the APC gene and analysis of in vitro truncated protein translation products of in vitro transcribed APC mRNAs.

Nonadenomatous Polyposis Syndromes
Suggestive

Because the nonadenomatous polyposis syndromes are inherited in an autosomal dominant manner, individuals who have a parent with a known diagnosis of any of the nonadenomatous polyposis syndromes have one chance in two of inheriting the mutant gene.

Peutz–Jegher's Syndrome. The cutaneous manifestations develop during infancy and include melanotic hyperpigmentation of the buccal mucosa, lips, and, less commonly, digits and hard palate.

Juvenile Polyposis. Growth retardation during infancy, accompanied by anemia and rectal bleeding, is often present.

Cowden's Disease. The cutaneous manifestations of this disease may not be apparent until the second or third decade of life. Cowden's disease should be considered in individuals with thyroid goiters accompanied by multiple skin papules.

Definitive

Peutz–Jegher's Syndrome and Juvenile Polyposis. As the genetic mutation has not been identified as of yet, a definitive diagnosis can best be made by flexible sigmoidoscopy of colonoscopy with the identification of multiple small hamartomatous polyps.

Cowden's Disease. The constellation of cutaneous manifestations with thyroid or breast cancers is most compatible with this diagnosis.

CLINICAL MANIFESTATIONS
Adenomatous Polyposis Syndromes
Subjective

Most individuals with FAP are asymptomatic, save for extracolonic manifestations such as osteomas of the jaw or supernumerary teeth. Symptoms of rectal bleeding, intestinal obstruction, and abdominal pain are often indicative of the development of colonic adenocarcinoma.

The past history is not contributory.

About 75% of individuals with FAP have a family history of this syndrome. The other 25% of individuals have acquired spontaneous mutations that occurred in the germ cells of either parent. This group does not have a family history and will not be detected until they present with symptoms.

Objective

Physical Examination. As noted above, the earliest physical finding in FAP is CHRPE. This physical finding indicates that it is likely that an individual has inherited the mutant APC allele. Another early physical finding is osteoma of the mandible or other dental abnormalities.

Routine Laboratory Abnormalities. There are no routine laboratory abnormalities.

Nonadenomatous Polyposis Syndromes

Subjective

Rectal bleeding and abdominal pain are early presenting signs of Peutz–Jeughers syndrome and juvenile polyposis, and often occur during the first decade of life.

The past history is not contributory.

Individuals with a parent who has a nonadenomatous polyposis syndrome have a 50% risk of acquiring the autosomal dominant mutation causing the syndrome; however, there appears to be variable penetrance and expressivity of the autosomal dominant mutation in individuals who have inherited the mutation.

Objective

Physical examination. As noted above, cutaneous signs are often found in Peutz–Jeughers syndrome during the first decade of life. Areas of hyperpigmentation can be distinguished from common freckles. Freckles are not found within the buccal mucosa. Cutaneous physical findings are also prominent in Cowden's disease, particularly papillomas of the skin often appearing on the face.

Routine Laboratory Abnormalities. There are no routine laboratory abnormalities.

PLANS

Adenomatous Polyposis Syndromes

Diagnostic

Families with history of FAP or with newly diagnosed FAP should be enrolled in local or regional registries. Enrollment in a registry allows for early identification of first- and second-degree relatives who may be at risk for inheriting the mutant APC gene. Identification of individuals who have inherited the mutant APC gene allows for institution of flexible sigmoidoscopy during the second decade of life to confirm the diagnosis and then for prophylactic colectomy usually early in the third decade of life. Screening and treatment of FAP families has clearly demonstrated a reduced incidence of invasive colorectal cancer.

Screening of relatives at risk includes indirect ophthalmoscopy for detection of CHRPE and dental examination. Because the mutant gene responsible for FAP has been identified, genetic screening for inheritance of the mutant gene is now possible. The APC gene is quite large, producing a mRNA of 15 exons with marked variability in the location of mutations; therefore, direct sequence analysis of the APC gene or its mRNA is difficult. Screening for mutant APC genes is best accomplished by establishment of restriction fragment length polymorphism linkage analysis to the mutant gene within each family.

Therapeutic

Unless the colon is removed, the development of invasive colorectal adenocarcinoma is inevitable in individuals with FAP. Therapeutic decisions involve the timing and the extent of surgery. Because the onset of invasive colorectal adenocarcinoma usually occurs during the fourth decade of life, prophylactic surgery is most often performed during the third decade of life. The types of operations performed include procto-

colectomy with ileostomy and abdominal colectomy with an ileorectal anastomosis. Operations that retain the rectosigmoid colon require careful follow-up for detection of the development of cancer in the remaining rectal mucosa.

Nonadenomatous Polyposis Syndromes

Diagnostic

Children of an individual with Peutz–Jeughers syndrome may have a screening flexible sigmoidoscopy. If found to have hamartomatous polyps, they are at increased risk for development of intestinal obstruction or bleeding. Polyps can be removed at the time of sigmoidoscopy. Because of the increased risk of ovarian sex cord tumors, a gynecologic examination can also be performed at the time of initial evaluation.

Individuals found to have the typical cutaneous lesions of Cowden's disease are generally at increased risk for development of thyroid and breast cancer. Woman with Cowden's disease should receive frequent mammographic examinations starting during the fourth decade of life. Alternatively, Cowden's disease may be an indication for prophylactic bilateral mastectomy.

Therapeutic

Individuals with any of the hamartomatous polyp syndromes should have flexible sigmoidoscopy with removal of polyps. Individuals who develop intestinal obstruction secondary to intussusception require partial colectomies.

FOLLOW-UP

Adenomatous Polyposis Syndromes

Following removal of the colon, individuals with FAP still are at increased risk of the development of additional gastrointestinal malignancies. To detect premalignant lesions of the upper gastrointestinal tract, upper endoscopy is recommended for FAP patients who are in the fifth decade of life. No specific recommendations can be made about the frequency of this screening procedure.

Nonadenomatous Polyposis Syndromes

Recommendations for a specific follow-up protocol cannot be made. Attention to removal of polyps, particularly those that may have adenomatous changes (instead of hamartomatous) may result in decreased development of gastrointestinal malignancy.

DISCUSSION

Prevalence and Incidence

About 1 in 10,000 individuals have a mutant APC gene.

A few families with each nonadenomatous polyposis syndrome have been reported in the literature. Nonadenomatous polyposis syndromes are rare.

Related Basic Science

Karyotype analysis of an individual with FAP revealed deletion of a portion of chromosome 5. Researchers used this finding as a departure point for genetic linkage analysis and chromosome walking and then identified a gene on chromosome 5 called the APC gene. This gene demonstrates more than 100 different autosomal dominant mutations that cause FAP. This large gene encodes for a large protein of 2843 amino acids. The APC protein, localized to the cytoskeleton of cells, likely interacts with a group of proteins that are required for cell-to-cell contact. The loss of contact inhibition between cells, particularly at the bases of crypts of Lieberkuhn, may then lead to increased cellular proliferation within the crypts. Increased cellular proliferation may eventuate in the acquisition of additional genetic mutations, including loss of the other normal APC allele or activation of proto-oncogenes to oncogenes. With the acquisition of a sufficient number of genetic mutations the development of invasive colorectal adenocarcinoma is inevitable.

It is of interest that a mouse model of FAP exists. The FAP mouse has a mutation in its APC gene leading to the development of many adenomatous polyps in the colon. The number of polyps in the FAP mouse is determined not only by the mutation in the FAP gene but by additional mutations in other genes that may encode for proteins that interact with the APC protein.

Most importantly, acquired mutation of the FAP gene appears to be the initiating step in the development of sporadic adenocarcinoma of the colon, which represents more than 90% of all adenocarcinomas of the colon. The fact that individuals with germline mutations of APC universally develop cancer at a young age, whereas somatic mutation of APC genes leads to a relatively low incidence of subsequent colon cancer at an older age, is another example of the Knudson hypothesis.

Natural History and Its Modification with Treatment

Individuals with FAP who do not undergo prophylactic colectomy inevitably develop colon cancer during their thirties and die at a median age of 42. With the advent of screening of FAP kindreds the incidence of colon cancer has markedly diminished; many FAP patients may be able to live normal lifespans if treated surgically during their twenties.

Prevention

The use of nonsteroidal antiinflammatory drugs such as indomethacin and sulindac appears to decrease the rate of development of new adeno-matous polyps in FAP patients; however, there is no evidence that these drugs can prevent the development of invasive cancer in FAP patients. These drugs should be used only in the context of an experimental protocol.

Cost Containment

The use of genetic linkage analysis to identify carries of the APC gene will lead to further testing and follow-up of only those family members who are definitely at risk for FAP.

REFERENCES:

Giardiello FM, Hamilton SR, Krush AJ, et al. Treatment of colonic and rectal adenomas with sulindac in familial adenomatous polyposis. N Engl J Med 1993;328:1313.

Laughlin EH. Benign and malignant neoplasms in a family with Peutz–Jeughers syndrome: Study of three generations. South Med J 1991;84:1205.

Rhodes M, Bradburn DM. Overview of screening and management of familial adenomatous polyposis. Gut 1992;33:125.

Rustgi AK. Hereditary gastrointestinal polyposis and nonpolyposis syndromes. N Engl J Med 1994;331:1694.

Williard W, Borgen P, Tiwari R, et al. Cowden's disease: A case report with analyses at the molecular level. Cancer 1992;69:2969.

CHAPTER 19–63

Carcinoma of the Colon (See Section 3, Chapter 13)

CHAPTER 19–64

Carcinoma of the Rectum (See Section 3, Chapter 14)

CHAPTER 19–65

Familial Mediterranean Fever

Eugene Straus, M.D.

DEFINITION

Familial Mediterranean fever (FMF) is an autosomal recessive disorder characterized by recurrent and self-limited attacks of fever and abdominal pain in patients with the appropriate ethnic background. It may also be called recurrent familial polyserositis.

ETIOLOGY

The etiology of FMF is not known. Nevertheless, there is accumulating evidence to indicate that the gene for FMF is linked to the α-globin complex on chromosome 16p.

CRITERIA FOR DIAGNOSIS
Suggestive

The diagnosis of FMF is suggested by the recurrence of episodes of fever and abdominal pain lasting several days in a patient of Mediterranean descent. Although almost half of those diagnosed with FMF have no family history, the diagnosis is certainly suggested by the knowledge of the disease in a family member. In a minority of cases the febrile episodes may be associated with signs and symptoms of inflam-mation of serosal surfaces other than the peritoneum as described below.

Definitive

Familial Mediterranean fever poses a problem for the practicing physician because individual attacks of the disease mimic other disorders and there are no definitive diagnostic criteria.

CLINICAL MANIFESTATIONS
Subjective

The obscure etiology and pathophysiology of FMF and the lack of definitive diagnostic findings make an appreciation of the subjective clinical manifestations of paramount importance. This may be complicated by the fact that the clinical manifestations may vary, even between attacks in the same patient, and, as mentioned above, a family history may frequently be absent. Nonetheless, a pattern of febrile episodes lasting 1 or 2 days and associated with abdominal pain is most characteristic. The attacks usually begin during childhood or adolescence and typically occur once or twice a month.

Although abdominal symptoms of peritoneal inflammation are most common, pain relating to inflammation of other serosal surfaces can also occur. Pleuritic chest pain, transient arthritis involving a large joint or joints, and an erysipelas-like skin rash on the lower extremities are less constant but well-known features.

Before the pattern of recurring self-limited attacks is recognized, and especially in patients without a family history of FMF, there may be difficulty in arriving at the proper diagnosis. The fever and abdominal pain may mimic appendicitis, cholecystitis, pancreatitis, or intestinal obstruction. The arthritis involving one or more large joints may suggest oligoarthritic forms of juvenile rheumatoid arthritis.

Some of the uncommon presentations of FMF involve sterile inflammation of various serosal surfaces and include aseptic meningitis with or without convulsions responding to colchicine, pleuritis (usually unilateral) with pleural effusion, pericarditis with pericardial effusion, and acute scrotal pain.

In a typical attack the patient may experience mild abdominal discomfort for a day or two prior to the onset of fever and severe abdominal pain. The pain may begin in one area and then become generalized, frequently radiating to the back. The fever is often accompanied by chills. Nausea and vomiting are common.

Objective

Physical Examination

Fever is a constant finding during attacks. The abdominal pain, a manifestation of peritoneal inflammation, is frequently severe and associated with abdominal distention, rebound tenderness, involuntary guarding, and rigidity. These signs may be generalized or localized to a specific area of the abdomen. They generally reach their peak with minutes to a few hours of the onset of an attack. Signs of arthritis, including swelling, warmth, and pain over the affected joint or joints, are usually quite mild.

Routine Laboratory Abnormalities

Nonspecific abnormalities in the routine laboratory examination include a leukocytosis that averages 15,000 cells/μL but may be as high as 50,000.

Plain x-ray films of the abdomen may demonstrate air–fluid levels and edema in the small bowel. This may cause the physician to suspect mechanical obstruction and, along with the typical signs of peritoneal irritation, not infrequently results in surgical exploration before the diagnosis of FMF is established. Conversely, the diagnosis of acute surgical conditions of the abdomen may be challenging in patients with established FMF.

The finding of albuminuria, which may be associated with microscopic hematuria, may be ominous, for it can herald a clinical nephropathy resulting from the accumulation of amyloid fibrillar protein AA in the kidney.

The frequency of amyloidosis in FMF varies between ethnic groups, and most fortunately, the occurrence of this most serious aspect of the disease can be reduced by treatment. Nonetheless, in unusual cases the amyloid nephropathy is the first clinical sign of the disease.

PLANS

Diagnosis

Differential Diagnosis

The finding of fever and the symptoms and signs of an inflamed serosal surface (or multiple inflamed surfaces) frequently suggest an extensive list of differential diagnoses. Certainly the most common is acute appendicitis, and it is not surprising that as many as 75% of patients with FMF have been operated for that diagnosis, with a normal appendix usually found.

Other conditions commonly considered in the previously undiagnosed patient with FMF include acute pancreatitis, porphyria, cholecystitis, and intestinal obstruction. These and other serious abdominal conditions can usually be excluded by the absence of specific findings and by the rapid spontaneous resolution of symptoms and signs.

Diagnostic Options and Recommended Approach

The appropriate tests to rule out pancreatitis, porphyria, cholecystitis, and intestinal obstruction should be obtained. Appendicitis may be impossible to exclude.

The erythrocyte sedimentation rate and levels of acute-phase reactants such as fibrinogen and C-reactive protein may be elevated. The peritoneal, pleural, or joint fluids are sterile and contain a predominance of polymorphonuclear leukocytes.

Therapeutic

Low-fat diets (20 g) and colchicine (0.6 mg orally two to three times per day) have been observed to prevent attacks, although they do not alter symptoms when taken during attacks. By reducing the frequency of periodic inflammation, colchicine is thought to forestall the development of renal amyloidosis.

The high degree of efficacy and the safety of colchicine (1–2 mg/d) have been established in studies of hundreds of children followed for more than a decade. In general, complete remission of febrile attacks is achieved in about 65% of patients, with another 30% experiencing partial remission. In most large studies, amyloidosis has been prevented by the colchicine regimen, and doses of 1.5 mg/d have been shown to prevent amyloidosis of kidney transplants in FMF. Growth, development, and fertility have been normal in treated patients, and no abnormalities have been noted among babies born to mothers with FMF who took colchicine before or during pregnancy. These observations make early diagnosis and continuous treatment of FMF essential.

It has been suggested that patients with FMF undergo elective laparoscopic appendectomy because of the difficulty in determining the absence of the disease during an attack of abdominal pain.

FOLLOW-UP

Follow-up is important to adjust the dosage of colchicine, to ensure compliance with chronic colchicine treatment, and for genetic counseling.

DISCUSSION

Prevalence and Incidence

The highest prevalence and incidence rates occur among Armenians (highest gene frequency), non-Ashkenazi Jews, and Arabs, but the disease is well known among Turks and Italians. Occasional reports of cases in Japanese, Scandinavians, and others will probably be found to differ from FMF when genetic diagnosis is available.

Related Basic Science

Almost nothing is known about the pathophysiology of FMF. The active area of basic science relating to FMF concerns the identification of the gene.

Genetics

Studies from Israel, primarily among families of Sephardic Jews, indicate that FMF is inherited as an autosomal recessive disorder and that the gene is on the short arm of chromosome 16.

Physiologic or Metabolic Derangement

There have been suggestions of deficiencies of inhibitors of calcium, a role for tumor necrosis factor, and other speculations based on observed alterations of various factors, but these are either unconfirmed or could be the result rather than the cause of inflammation.

Natural History and Its Modification with Treatment

The natural history of FMF is benign. Patients who are correctly diagnosed and well managed can avoid complications and live relatively normal lives. They die of unrelated causes. Amyloidosis rarely occurs in the United States. This may relate to environmental or genetic factors, but the frequency of amyloidosis is falling in other parts of the world due to the use of colchicine.

Colchicine is important for the avoidance of additional complications such as depression and narcotic addiction. Alertness to the diagnosis avoids repeated abdominal surgery and unnecessary medical treatments and hospitalizations, which have their own complications.

Prevention

There is a high rate of consanguinity among parents of patients with FMF. Genetic counseling should be offered to those affected and especially to those in ethnic groups with a high gene frequency.

The prevention of attacks is discussed under Plans, Therapeutic.

Cost Containment

Cost containment is related primarily to making the diagnosis as rapidly as possible. This avoids the unnecessary hospitalizations, extensive workups, and treatments that can be repetitive and develop costs which are avoidable. In a similar fashion, good control with colchicine is achievable in the majority of cases and plays a role in cost containment.

REFERENCES

Shohat M, Bu X, Shohat T, Fischel-Ghodsian N, et al. The gene for familial Mediterranean fever in both Armenians and non-Ashkenazi Jews is linked to the alpha-globin complex on 16p: Evidence for locus homogeneity. Am J Hum Genet 1992;51:1349.
Zemer D, Livneh A, Danon YL, et al. Long-term colchicine treatment in children with familial Mediterranean fever. Arthritis Rheum 1991;34:973.

CHAPTER 19–66

Acute Pancreatitis

Jeremy S. Wilson, M.D., Romano C. Pirola, M.D., and Mark A. Korsten, M.D.

DEFINITION

Acute pancreatitis is a nonspecific term covering a variety of acute pancreatic pathologies including edema, interstitial inflammation, necrosis, and hemorrhage. The term *acute* implies functional and morphologic restitution to normal with resolution of the disease process.

ETIOLOGY

The associations of acute pancreatitis may be classified as common or uncommon.

Common associations are gallstones, alcohol abuse, and unknown causes.

Uncommon associations are hypertriglyceridemia; hyperparathyroidism; surgery (abdominal, nonabdominal); endoscopic retrograde cholangiopancreatography; trauma; drugs; infections (mumps, mycoplasma, Coxsackie virus, echovirus); connective tissue disorders with vasculitis; pancreas divisum; obstruction of the ampulla of Vater; pancreatic carcinoma; and penetrating duodenal ulcer.

With respect to drug-induced pancreatitis, some common agents with a definite association and some with a probable association are listed below:

Definite Association	Probable Association
Azathioprine	L-asparaginase
Thiazides	Chlorthalidone
Furosemide	Corticosteroids
Sulfonamides	Ethacrynic acid
Tetracyclines	Phenformin
Valproic acid	Procainamide
Estrogens	

CRITERIA FOR DIAGNOSIS

Suggestive

The diagnosis should be suspected in every patient with acute abdominal pain.

Definitive

The data required to make the definitive diagnosis generally include a compatible clinical picture, the presence of hyperamylasemia or hyperlipasemia, and corroborative evidence from abdominal ultrasonography or computed tomography (computed tomography is more reliable). Serum amylase remains the main laboratory test to confirm the diagnosis of acute pancreatitis. A serum amylase greater than three times the normal upper limit strongly supports the diagnosis of pancreatitis. The serum amylase returns to normal approximately 2 to 3 days after the onset of pancreatitis, and the test may therefore be falsely negative in a late presenting patient. In addition, the serum amylase may be normal throughout an attack of acute pancreatitis.

A normal serum amylase does not by itself exclude the diagnosis of acute pancreatitis. Other causes of hyperamylasemia may complicate interpretation of the test, particularly when they are associated with abdominal pain (Table 19–66–1). Problems with the sensitivity and specificity of serum amylase have prompted the search for a better diagnostic blood test for acute pancreatitis. Pancreatic isoamylase and serum lipase can now be measured in many laboratories. In acute pancreatitis, serum levels of these enzymes are elevated longer (up to 2 weeks for lipase) and are more specific for pancreatic disease. They therefore add to the sensitivity and specificity of the serum amylase determination.

CLINICAL MANIFESTATIONS

Subjective

The cardinal symptom of acute pancreatitis is abdominal pain, which may vary in intensity. It is generally localized to the epigastrium and periumbilical region and often radiates through to the back as well as to the lower abdomen, flanks, and chest. Nausea and vomiting are frequent accompaniments.

Objective

Physical Examination

Physical examination generally reveals a distressed patient. Low-grade fever, tachycardia, and hypotension may be present and shock is not uncommon. Examination of the abdomen reveals tenderness and guarding, but these signs may be unimpressive when compared with the severity of the pain and the general condition of the patient. Bowel sounds may be diminished or absent. Bluish discoloration around the

---

TABLE 19–66–1. NONPANCREATIC CAUSES OF HYPERAMYLASEMIA

Extraabdominal
Parotitis
Small cell pulmonary tumor
Macroamylasemia
Intraabdominal
Perforated viscus
Mesenteric infarction
Renal failure
Intestinal obstruction
Hepatitis
Biliary perforation

umbilicus (Cullen's sign) or in the flanks (Grey Turner's sign) are rarely seen but signify severe necrotizing pancreatitis.

Approximately 10 to 20% of patients with acute pancreatitis develop *pulmonary complications*. Clinically, basal rales and evidence of a pleural effusion are the most common signs. With severe pancreatitis, patients may develop hypoxemia and the adult respiratory distress syndrome. Erythematous skin nodules may be observed. These lesions result from subcutaneous fat necrosis and may mimic erythema nodosum.

Routine Laboratory Abnormalities

Blood Tests. Patients generally exhibit a leukocytosis. Prolonged vomiting may alter serum electrolytes. In severe cases there may be biochemical evidence of hypocalcemia, hypoxemia, hyperglycemia, renal insufficiency, and an increase in triglycerides.

Radiologic Tests. Chest radiographs may reveal basal atelectasis, pleural effusion (most commonly on the left side), or, in severe cases, evidence of full-blown adult respiratory distress syndrome.

PLANS
Diagnostic
Differential Diagnosis

The differential diagnosis of acute pancreatitis is extensive, including both intraabdominal causes (peptic ulcer, biliary disease, intestinal obstruction or perforation, mesenteric ischemia, and aortic dissection and aneurysm) and nonabdominal causes (pneumonia, myocardial infarction, vasculitis, and diabetic ketoacidosis). Alternate diagnoses must be systematically excluded by appropriate investigations if there is any doubt.

Diagnostic Options

Any suspected case of acute pancreatitis should undergo the following specific investigations: serum amylase, serum lipase (if available), plain abdominal radiograph (looking for a dilated loop of duodenum or "colon cut off" sign), chest radiograph, serum electrolytes and creatinine, blood gas analysis, liver function tests, serum triglycerides, blood glucose, abdominal ultrasonography, abdominal computed tomography (if the pancreas cannot be visualized by ultrasonography or if severe pancreatitis is suspected).

Recommended Approach

If there is a compatible clinical picture associated with hyperamylasemia and/or hyperlipasemia, a diagnosis of acute pancreatitis can be accepted. Careful attention should be paid to the differential diagnoses listed above. Particular care should be taken to exclude a perforated abdominal viscus or intestinal infarction. In these latter conditions, there are generally more pronounced signs of peritonitis. If there is doubt about the diagnosis and the patient appears clinically ill, a diagnostic laparotomy should be performed.

Therapeutic

The principles for the management of acute pancreatitis include hospital admission, "resting" the pancreas (see below), pain relief, monitoring for complications, and finding and treating the cause (see above).

Bed rest, intravenous fluids, and narcotic analgesia remain the cornerstones of treatment of acute pancreatitis. The patient is kept fasting to avoid stimulation of pancreatic secretion. Although resting the pancreas is conceptually attractive, the pancreas probably secretes very little when acutely inflamed. Randomized prospective clinical trials of nasogastric suction, atropine, glucagon, calcitonin, cimetidine, and somatostatin (all of which may reduce pancreatic secretion) have uniformly failed to show benefit in acute pancreatitis. Indeed, the overall mortality rate of 10% has remained constant over the years. Nonetheless, too early refeeding of a convalescent patient may cause a relapse of the disease.

Despite the considerable evidence that acute pancreatitis is an autodigestive disease, trials of enzyme inhibitors (particularly antiproteases) have been similarly disappointing.

Recent advances in the treatment of acute pancreatitis include early identification of patients with a worse prognosis using contrast-enhanced computed tomography and clinical parameters and early endoscopic retrograde cholangiopancreatography in gallstone pancreatitis.

Advances in intensive care mean that critically ill patients can be more successfully supported through their illness. It is thus important to recognize early the subgroup of patients with acute pancreatitis who are at risk of becoming critically ill. These patients may benefit from early transfer to an intensive care unit for close monitoring and early identification and treatment of complications which include cardiovascular collapse, respiratory distress, renal failure, and local complications such as pancreatic abscess, peripancreatic fluid collections, and pseudocysts (Table 19–66–2). Well-validated sets of criteria have been developed by a number of workers; an example is outlined in Table 19–66–3. Close observation, frequent examination, and attention to the biochemical indices listed in Table 19–66–3 increase the chance that critically ill patients will be identified before their condition deteriorates irretrievably.

Two well-controlled studies have shown that in patients with predicted severe gallstone pancreatitis, early endoscopic retrograde cholangiopancreatography and removal of common bile duct stones through an endoscopic sphincterotomy reduce morbidity and mortality.

Surgery for acute pancreatitis is indicated when there is an infected pancreatic necrosis or nonresolving pseudocyst. Surgery may also be performed if there is doubt about the diagnosis. Computed tomography scanning is the most reliable method of detecting necrotic tissue and fluid collections. Radiologically guided fine-needle aspiration is necessary to distinguish infected tissue from sterile necrosis. While sterile collections and necrotic tissue may resolve spontaneously, the mortality from infected pancreatic tissue (pancreatic abscess) approaches 100% without surgery. Surgery involves drainage of collections and debridement of devitalized and necrotic tissue. This reduces the mortality of patients with pancreatic abscess to approximately 30%. In patients too ill to undergo surgical exploration, consideration should be given to computed tomography-guided percutaneous aspiration of the abscess. There is also evidence that long-term peritoneal lavage may be a useful adjunct to surgical exploration.

FOLLOW-UP

On recovery from acute pancreatitis, the cause of the attack should be ascertained and treated. Gallstones can be diagnosed by ultrasonography, and if they are thought to be the cause of the attack, the patient should undergo a cholecystectomy. For alcoholic pancreatitis, abstinence is mandatory and the help of a specialized alcoholism treatment service may be necessary.

Serial determinations of serum calcium and triglycerides should be performed to exclude hypercalcemic disorders (such as hyperparathyroidism) and hypertriglyceridemia.

TABLE 19–66–2. COMPLICATIONS OF ACUTE PANCREATITIS

Local
Pancreatic abscess
Phlegmon
Pseudocyst
Ascites
Obstructive jaundice
Fat necrosis
Systemic
Respiratory failure
Circulatory collapse
Disseminated intravascular coagulopathy
Renal failure
Gastrointestinal hemorrhage
Metabolic derangement
Fat necrosis

TABLE 19–66–3. POOR PROGNOSTIC FEATURES IN ACUTE PANCREATITIS (WITHIN 48 HOURS OF DIAGNOSIS)

Age > 55
White cell count > 15×10^9/L
Blood sugar level > 10 mmol/L (in nondiabetic)
Urea > 16 mmol/L (after rehydration)
PaO_2 < 60 mm Hg
Serum calcium < 2.0 mmol/L
Lactate dehydrogenase > 600 IU/L
Aspartate or alanine transaminase > 100 IU/L
Albumin < 32 g/L

For those with unexplained acute pancreatitis (especially if recurrent), there should be repeated attempts to diagnose gallstone disease with repeated ultrasonography and possibly also oral cholecystography. A careful drug history must be taken. The bile should be examined for cholesterol crystals (which can cause pancreatitis). Finally, endoscopic retrograde cholangiopancreatography might be necessary to determine the cause (such as a pancreatic ductal stricture or tumor).

In acute pancreatitis, complete recovery of structure and function is the rule. In its early stages, alcoholic pancreatitis often presents as an "acute" process, although chronic changes (fibrosis, calcification) are probably present in the gland at the time of the first attack. In any event, the disease usually does progress to an overt chronic form and, therefore, individuals with alcoholic pancreatitis should be monitored for evidence of pancreatic exocrine and endocrine insufficiency (see Chapter 19–67).

DISCUSSION
Prevalence and Incidence

The incidence varies according to diagnostic criteria and geographic area but generally is between 15 and 30 per 100,000 and highest in elderly men.

Related Basic Science

Acute pancreatitis is thought to be an autodigestive phenomenon with inactive digestive enzyme precursors being prematurely transformed into their active forms within the pancreatic acinar cell. The mechanisms responsible for this phenomenon have not been well defined. Studies from animal models of experimental pancreatitis have suggested that the initial event is a blockage of exocytosis, followed by colocalization of digestive and lysosomal enzymes and subsequent activation of digestive enzymes.

Natural History and Its Modification with Treatment

If the patient survives an attack of acute pancreatitis, complete restitution of glandular structure and function is the rule. Treatment of the cause prevents further attacks.

Prevention

Adequate treatment of diseases that are known to be associated with pancreatitis will prevent attacks.

Cost Containment

The costs of the management of acute pancreatitis can be minimized by accurate diagnosis, identification, and treatment of the cause and avoidance of those (sometimes expensive) pharmacologic agents of no proven benefit. Costs relating to the management of severe cases exceed that of liver transplantation. Early identification of such cases may improve survival and shorten stay in intensive care units.

REFERENCES

Fink A. Pancreatitis in the 1990's: Diagnostic and therapeutic advances. Pancreas 1991;6:suppl. 1.

Glazer G, Ranson J. Acute pancreatitis: Experimental and clinical aspects of pathogenesis and management. London: Bailliere Tindall, 1988.

Go VL, Gardner JD, Brooks EP, et al. The Exocrine pancreas: Biology, pathobiology and diseases. New York: Raven Press, 1993.

Leach SD, Gorelick FS, Modlin IM, et al. New perspectives on acute pancreatitis. Scand J Gastroenterol 1992;27:suppl. 192.

Neoptolemos JP, Carr-Locke DL, London NJ, et al. Controlled trial of urgent endoscopic retrograde cholangiopancreatography and endoscopic sphincterotomy versus conservative treatment for acute pancreatitis due to gallstones. Lancet 1988;29:979.

CHAPTER 19–67

Chronic Pancreatitis

Mark A. Korsten, M.D., Paul S. Haber, M.B., B.S., B.Med. Sc., M.D., and Jeremy S. Wilson, M.D.

DEFINITION

Chronic pancreatitis is a persistent, often progressive, condition of the pancreas characterized by extensive fibrosis and calcification and associated with intractable pain, maldigestion, and diabetes mellitus.

ETIOLOGY

The vast majority of cases in Western societies are due to excessive consumption of alcohol. A relatively small number of patients have a hereditary form of the disorder. Chronic pancreatitis has also been linked to long-standing hypercalcemia. In developing countries, malnutrition is an important cause of the disorder.

CRITERIA FOR DIAGNOSIS
Suggestive

Chronic pancreatitis should be considered in an alcoholic patient who complains of intractable abdominal pain that radiates to the back and is accompanied by changes in bowel habits and/or weight loss.

Definitive

In advanced cases, a definite diagnosis can be established by the presence of pancreatic calcifications on a plain film of the abdomen (kidney/ureter/bladder) and neutral fat in the stool. Diagnostic certainty may be more elusive in earlier stages of the disorder. In the absence of obvious calcifications on the kidney/ureter/bladder film, abdominal ultrasonography and pancreatic function tests usually permit a definite diagnosis. Endoscopic retrograde cholangiopancreatography (ERCP) is necessary only as a last resort.

CLINICAL MANIFESTATIONS
Subjective

The patient's past history is characterized by a long period (10–15 years) of heavy drinking (usually > 100 g/d of ethanol). The onset of abdominal pain is usually slow and insidious. When the pain has an acute onset, it is often precipitated by an alcoholic binge, and often requires hospitalization. The abdominal pain is typically epigastric, may be associated with nausea and vomiting, and frequently radiates to the back. Symptoms indicative of pancreatic insufficiency may be present. Endocrine dysfunction (diabetes mellitus) is associated with polyuria and polydipsia. Exocrine insufficiency (inadequate amounts of digestive enzymes) results in symptoms of maldigestion (greasy, foul-smelling stool, diarrhea), fat-soluble vitamin deficiency (tetany, easy bruisibility, nightblindness), and malnutrition (weight loss and cachexia). An increasing abdominal girth may indicate the accumulation of pancreatic juice in the peritoneal cavity (pancreatic ascites) or an expanding pancreatic pseudocyst. Symptoms of coexisting alcoholic liver injury may be absent despite advanced alcohol-induced chronic pancreatitis.

Objective

Physical Examination

There may be no physical findings in patients with uncomplicated chronic pancreatitis other than mild epigastric discomfort on deep palpation. Despite severe and, at times, incapacitating pain, bowel sounds are usually present, and there is no abdominal rigidity or rebound tenderness. In the presence of a complicating pseudocyst or pancreatic neoplasm, however, an abdominal mass may be noted. Signs of an acute abdomen (fever, absent bowel signs, rebound tenderness, abdominal rigidity) appear when pseudocysts rupture, become infected, or erode a splanchnic vessel. In patients with pancreatic ascites, a fluid wave and shifting dullness may be present. In patients with extrahepatic biliary obstruction (the distal common bile duct traverses the head of the pancreas and can be strictured as a result of chronic pancreatitis), jaundice may be conspicuous. Right upper quadrant tenderness and high, spiking fevers indicate cholangitis. Nonspecific signs of weight loss, such as temporal and interosseous muscle wasting, are seen in patients with severe maldigestion. Positive Chvostek's and Trousseau's sign can be observed when vitamin D malabsorption leads to hypocalcemia. Ecchymoses on the skin and greasy stool on rectal examination also indicate the presence of clinically significant steatorrhea.

Routine Laboratory Abnormalities

The routine examination of the blood is normal except for hyperglycemia. The examination of the urine is normal except it may test positive for sugar. The chest radiograph is normal.

PLANS

Diagnostic

Differential Diagnosis

When confronted by an alcoholic patient with abdominal pain and a high serum amylase, the clinician must consider a number of conditions other than chronic pancreatitis. The differential diagnosis should include alcoholic gastritis, pancreatic cancer, peptic ulceration, and cholelithiasis. In women, tubal pregnancy is an additional consideration. The serum amylase is neither a sensitive nor a specific diagnostic marker of chronic pancreatitis. On the one hand, the specificity of serum amylase is limited because tissues other than the pancreas (e.g., intestines, biliary tree, fallopian tubes) are capable of releasing the enzyme. On the other hand, the serum amylase is of marginal sensitivity because its level may be low in advanced, "burned-out" chronic pancreatitis.

Diagnostic Options

There may be evidence of calcification in the pancreas in the abdominal radiograph and an increase in neutral fat in the stool. Further testing (ultrasonography, abdominal computed tomography, ERCP, and pancreatic function testing) may be required to exclude coexisting or complicating conditions (pancreatic cancer, pseudocysts, cholelithiasis) and to evaluate more fully a patient with vague complaints at an early, noncalcific stage of the disorder.

Recommended Approach

Ultrasonography is particularly helpful during an acute relapse of chronic pancreatitis and is probably an essential component of the diagnostic strategy. Specifically, ultrasonography permits visualization of the biliary tree and detection of calcifications and pseudocysts. The computed tomography scan is usually reserved for situations in which there is a need for detailed morphologic information (e.g., to assess for the presence of a tumor). ERCP is reserved for cases in which other modalities have failed to establish a definite diagnosis. In the future, however, it is likely that ERCP will be used more for therapeutic indications than for diagnostic ones (see below). Pancreatic function testing (the secretin test) is time consuming and invasive (fluoroscopy-assisted intubation of the duodenum is required), but it is still the diagnostic "gold standard" for chronic pancreatitis. A low bicarbonate concentration (<90 mEq/L) in the pancreatic juice is highly suggestive of chronic pancreatitis. It proves useful in distinguishing between maldigestion (pancreatic insufficiency, low HCO_3) and malabsorption (mucosal defects, normal HCO_3), as both may present with steatorrhea. To date, "tubeless" tests of pancreatic function (involving breath, urine, or stool collections) have proved too insensitive to be clinically useful.

Therapeutic

Therapeutic Options

No therapy exists to reverse the underlying fibrocalcific abnormalities of the pancreas. Thus, treatment is reserved for one or more of the numerous complications of chronic pancreatitis. These include intractable abdominal pain, diabetes mellitus, steatorrhea, pseudocysts, and biliary obstruction.

For intractable pain, the options include pancreatic enzyme administration, celiac axis ablation, surgical "decompression" of the pancreatic duct, and endoscopic stone removal. Clinical trials of pancreatic enzymes have not been uniformly successful and thus their use cannot be recommended for this indication. Celiac axis block provides pain relief but its effects are transient, lasting usually less than 6 months. Surgical approaches are effective in relieving pain; however, surgical intervention carries with it the risk of considerable morbidity (pancreatic function may deteriorate) and mortality. Endoscopic removal of pancreatic calculi (after extracorporeal shock wave lithotripsy) and endoscopic placement of pancreatic stents into a dominant stricture are newer modalities that have shown considerable promise. In the absence of long-term, randomized, placebo-controlled clinical trials, however, it would be premature to suggest their routine use to treat intractable pain in chronic pancreatitis.

Enlarging pseudocysts can be drained by the interventional radiologist, the therapeutic endoscopist, and, of course, the general surgeon. The interventional radiologist evacuates these cysts using computed tomography-guided needles passed percutaneously. The endoscopist creates a cystenteric fistula when there is an obvious indentation of the cyst on the stomach or duodenum. Alternatively, a stent can be passed through the papilla into the cyst if it communicates with the main pancreatic duct. The surgical approach is to establish a cystenteric anastomosis at open laparotomy. In terms of efficacy (especially recurrence rates), the surgical approach is highly effective and is the benchmark against which newer modalities are still judged.

Treatment of biliary strictures is based on the assumption that prolonged biliary obstruction may result in secondary biliary cirrhosis. Endoscopic intervention involves repeated placement of endoprostheses; the surgical approach achieves biliary diversion via a choledochoenterostomy.

Recommended Approach

Acute Management. The hospitalized patient with an acute relapse of chronic pancreatitis should be withdrawn from oral intake and given intravenous fluids and parenteral analgesia. A nasogastric tube is not indicated unless pain is accompanied by ileus. As the symptoms improve, oral feeding should be slowly increased. Empiric antibiotics (directed toward enteric organisms) should be administered when there is a strong suspicion of a pancreatic abscess. In patients who fail to respond, percutaneous drainage of pancreatic abscesses is recommended. Endoscopic placement of a nasobiliary stent is the procedure of choice if there are signs or symptoms of acute cholangitis.

Management of Long-term Complications. Chronic abdominal pain should be managed with nonnarcotic analgesic agents if at all possible. Celiac axis block may be useful in selected patients who are likely to remain abstinent. In such individuals, repeated blocks may obviate the need for surgery, as pancreatic pain tends to decrease with time in abstinent patients. Surgery (pancreaticojejunostomy or subtotal resection) is recommended in patients who require frequent celiac axis blocks for pain control. Endoscopic intervention should be limited to patients with contraindications for surgery. Only highly skilled endoscopists can reliably introduce pancreatic duct stents or safely remove pancreatic calculi.

Diabetes mellitus. Given the brittle nature of diabetes in patients with chronic pancreatitis, low doses of an oral hypoglycemic agent (glipizide 2.5–5 mg or glyburide 1.25–2.5 mg) should be initial therapy. The blood sugar should be monitored frequently and the dose of drug titrated accordingly. Management of diabetes is complicated by erratic absorption of carbohydrate. Thus, diabetic control is facilitated by optimal treatment of steatorrhea (see below). If insulin therapy is necessary, the patient must be advised about the possibility of hypoglycemia.

Steatorrhea. Initial management should consist of administration of enteric-coated (protects against acid inactivation) enzyme preparations with at least 16,000 U of lipase per capsule. By reducing the number of capsules necessary to prevent steatorrhea, patients are more likely to remain compliant. Should steatorrhea persist, gastric acid should be suppressed with an H_2-receptor antagonist such as ranitidine (150 mg twice daily) or cimetidine (300 mg four times daily). If these measures prove unsuccessful, total dietary fat is reduced (50–75 g/d) or medium-chain triglycerides are substituted.

Pseudocysts. In emergencies or in patients too ill for laparotomy, percutaneous computed tomography-guided decompression of pseudocysts should be carried out. Surgical decompression is indicated in elective situations.

Biliary Strictures. In acutely ill patients with acute cholangitis secondary to biliary obstruction, endoscopic placement of an endoprosthesis is recommended. Surgical diversion of bile via a choledochoenterostomy should be carried out electively in patients with signs and symptoms of chronic biliary obstruction. In patients too debilitated for surgery, biliary strictures can be managed by endoscopic stent placement, but numerous exchanges of occluded stents should be anticipated.

FOLLOW-UP

Patients with chronic pancreatitis should be seen every 2 to 3 months. At each visit, the following parameters should be assessed: quality and intensity of abdominal pain, if present; weight; abdominal examination; fasting blood sugar; serum amylase; serum bilirubin; serum alkaline phosphatase; blood alcohol concentration if the state of sobriety is in question. In patients with known pancreatic insufficiency, serum calcium and albumin determinations should be included. Changes in these parameters may reflect the development of complications such as a pseudocyst or pancreatic carcinoma (there is an increased risk of cancer in this setting). In patients already receiving therapy for the latter, the adequacy of replacement enzymes and the degree of compliance can be assessed. In patients known to have a new pseudocyst, repeat ultrasonography should be obtained every 3 months. Stable pseudocysts can usually be observed at 6-month intervals. Significant enlargement of a pseudocyst requires decompression (see Plans, Therapeutic, Recommended Approach).

DISCUSSION
Prevalence and Incidence

Chronic pancreatitis affects approximately 4.0 per 100,000 overall population, with a male-to-female ratio of 3:1. Among alcoholics, the prevalence is much higher.

Related Basic Science

By changing the composition of the pancreatic juice, ethanol consumption may cause protein and calcium to be precipitated within the pancreatic ducts. Proof for this hypothesis, however, is not yet convincing. Ethanol may also have effects at the subcellular level that increase the likelihood of premature activation of pancreatic enzymes and autodigestion. Recent evidence indicates that liberation of lipase may play a role in the pathogenesis of alcoholic pancreatitis.

Natural History and Its Modification with Treatment

The natural history of chronic pancreatitis involves exacerbations and remissions leading ultimately to chronic abdominal pain with exocrine and endocrine pancreatic failure. Drug addiction is a common association, possibly because of relentless pain or because of associated personality disorders. If the patient can remain abstinent, there is some evidence that the severity and frequency of painful episodes will decrease; however, chronic pancreatitis may be progressive in apparently abstinent patients. The 10-year mortality in chronic pancreatitis is about 25%, and this is not influenced by treatment.

Prevention

The clinical association between high levels of ethanol consumption and chronic pancreatitis is well established. Thus, efforts at prevention inevitably must be focused on prevention and treatment of alcoholism. Groups such as Alcoholics Anonymous provide the best form of therapy for both alcoholism and, indirectly, pancreatitis as well.

Cost Containment

Advanced cases of chronic pancreatitis can be diagnosed with a minimum of laboratory tests. If the kidney/ureter/bladder film demonstrates calcifications in the region of the pancreas, the diagnosis is established and little more is required. Ultrasonography and computed tomography are not required unless one suspects the complications noted above under **Diagnostic Options** as well as **Therapeutic**. Savings can also be generated by foregoing certain tests such as barium studies, angiography, and quantitative fecal fat determinations. Barium contrast studies are neither specific nor sensitive for diagnosing chronic pancreatitis. Angiography should be reserved for suspected cases of pancreatic hemorrhage from pseudoaneurysm. In the past, it was employed to differentiate chronic pancreatitis from pancreatic cancer; however, computed tomography-guided fine-needle aspiration is a more direct and reliable approach. Finally, except under metabolic ward conditions, collection of stool for 72 hours is rarely useful. Qualitative assessment of fecal fat by staining provides enough information to manage most patients.

REFERENCES

Cello JP, Wilcox CM. Endoscopic therapy for pancreatitis and its complications. Semin Gastrointest Dis 1991;2:177.

DiMagno EP. Early diagnosis of chronic pancreatitis and pancreatic cancer. Med Clin North Am 1988;72:979.

Korsten MA, Pirola RC, Lieber CS. Alcohol and the pancreas. In: Lieber CS, ed. Medical and nutritional complications of alcoholism. New York: Plenum Press, 1992:341.

Korsten MA, Wilson JS. Alcohol and the pancreas: Clinical aspects and mechanisms of injury. Alcohol Health Res World 1993;17:292.

Lowenfels AB, Maisonneuve P, Cavallini G, et al. Pancreatitis and the risk of pancreatic cancer. N Engl J Med 1993;328:1433.

CHAPTER 19—68

Cystic Fibrosis (See Section 13, Chapter 19)

CHAPTER 19—69

Carcinoma of the Pancreas (See Section 3, Chapter 10)

CHAPTER 19—70

Jaundice

David J. Clain, M.D.

DEFINITION

Jaundice is a yellow or orange discoloration of the skin, sclerae, and mucous membranes which may be reported by the patient (subjective) or observed by the physician (objective) and which is due to hyperbilirubinemia.

ETIOLOGY

Jaundice is due to hyperbilirubinemia, which has many causes. Serum bilirubin can be elevated because of overproduction (e.g., hemolysis), inability of the liver to process (e.g., inherited metabolic defect or cellular damage from hepatitis), or failure of excretion (e.g., biliary obstruction). See Table 19–70–1 and Related Basic Science for more detailed classification.

CRITERIA FOR DIAGNOSIS

Suggestive

The patient, relative, or friend may report the yellow discoloration of skin, sclerae, or mucous membranes, or the patient may have noted the onset of dark urine or pale stools. Many causes of jaundice are associated with generalized itching, which may be the chief complaint and first draw attention to the diagnosis. Slight jaundice when serum bilirubin is 2.5 to 3.0 mg/dL may be suspected by an experienced physician on focused examination.

Definitive

Marked hyperbilirubinemia is accompanied by obvious clinical jaundice. Mild to moderate jaundice may be missed in dim and or/yellow incandescent light. Jaundice is best seen in bright natural, fluorescent, or halogen light. Biochemically, jaundice is present when serum total bilirubin exceeds 1.2 mg/dL. Presence of bilirubin in the urine can be tested within 60 seconds by a dipstick and indicates that conjugated serum bilirubin is elevated.

CLINICAL MANIFESTATIONS

Subjective

Yellow bilirubin pigment in the skin or sclerae is common to all forms of jaundice. Some symptoms such as itching and dark urine are confined to conjugated hyperbilirubinemias. A knowledge of the classification of jaundice (Table 19–70–1) and of related basic science is essential to understand the significance of many symptoms. For example, pale stools may be caused by obstruction of the biliary tree (e.g., cancer of the pancreas) or by hepatocellular disease which damages the canicular membranes (e.g., cholestatic viral hepatitis). In unconjugated hyperbilirubinemia due to hemolysis, there is normal excretion of bilirubin and stools are normal or dark in color.

Table 19–70–2 summarizes the symptoms that may accompany different categories of jaundice. Nausea, loss of appetite, and fatigue may be present in many causes of acute hepatitis whether virus, alcohol, or drug induced. But a history of new sexual contacts, eating shellfish, injection drug use, travel to Third World countries, or dining with friends who have or later get jaundice is significant mainly for viral etiology.

Jaundice usually appears rapidly in acute hepatitis and is preceded by systemic symptoms. This contrasts with the gradual onset of jaundice, often with itching, in malignant biliary obstruction. Episodes of severe upper abdominal pain lasting several hours suggest colic due to gallstones in the common bile duct. Severe, persistent pain that is also felt in the back and may be relieved by leaning forward points to a pancreatic carcinoma. Aching pain over the liver may be seen in acute hepatitis, whether caused by viruses, drugs, or alcohol. Pain is a significant feature of the jaundice due to erythromycin toxicity, usually associated with the estolate salt.

High fever and shaking chills favor cholangitis due to common duct stones or stricture. The latter may by suggested by prior surgery on or around the bile ducts.

Family history is occasionally helpful. Many hemolytic anemias are inherited. Persistent light yellow jaundice is often hemolytic. There is a strong family incidence of gallstones. Young women with cholelithiasis often have close relatives with a similar history.

TABLE 19–70–1. CLINICAL CATEGORIES OF JAUNDICE

Category	Bilirubin	Examples
Hemolysis	Unconjugated	Sickle cell disease, thalassemia, drug-induced hemolysis
Disturbed bilirubin metabolism		Gilbert's disease Dubin–Johnson syndrome
Hepatocellular	Conjugated	Viral hepatitis Alcoholic hepatitis Drug-induced hepatitis Autoimmune liver disease Cirrhosis Infiltrations, infections
Cholestatic	Conjugated	Cholestatic virus or drug-induced hepatitis Primary biliary cirrhosis Alcoholic hepatitis Cancer of the pancreas, ampulla Sclerosing cholangitis Stones in the common bile duct

TABLE 19–70–2. DATA USED TO IDENTIFY THE THREE MAJOR CATEGORIES OF JAUNDICE

Data	Abnormal Bilirubin Metabolism	Hepatocellular Disease	Cholestasis (Obstruction)
Age	Young	Any	Any
Fever	No	Yes	Yes
Malaise	No	Yes	No
Anorexia	No	Yes	No
Nausea and vomiting	No	Yes	Yes
Epigastric pain	No	Rare	Yes
Pruritus	No	Yes	Yes
Physical findings			
Splenomegaly	Yes	Yes	No
Hepatomegaly	No	Yes	Yes
Tender liver	No	Yes	Yes
Palpable gallbladder	No	Yes	
Dilated abdominal veins	No	Yes	No
Ascites	No	Yes	Rare
Anemia	Yes	Yes	No
Laboratory tests			
Anemia	Yes	Yes	No
Leukocytosis	No	Yes	Yes
Leukopenia	No	Yes	No
Thrombocytopenia	No	Yes	No
Indirect bilirubin > 85% of total	Yes	Rare	Rare
AST Aspartate transaminase > 10 times normal	No	Yes	No
Serum alkaline phosphatase > 3 times normal	No	Yes	Yes
Serum albumin < 3 g/dL	No	Yes	No
Prothrombin time returns to normal in 24 h after 1 mg vitamin K_1	No	No	Yes
Unaffected by 10 mg vitamin K_1 daily × 3	No	Yes	No

Modified from Galambos JT. Jaundice. In: Hurst JW, ed. Medicine for the Practicing Physician. Boston/London: Butterworth-Heinemann, 1992:1396. Reproduced with permission from the author.

Objective

Physical Examination

There is a striking difference in the profile of jaundice at different ages. Drug reactions are rare in childhood; hepatitis A is common. Obstruction by cancer of the pancreas or bile duct is increasingly frequent over age 50. There is a low incidence of hepatitis A in the elderly. Hepatitis B is common in the age group 20 to 40 because of sexual activity.

Weight Loss. Weight loss may be substantial during any severe jaundice, probably due to loss of appetite and lack of bile salts. But loss of weight at the onset of jaundice often indicates an underlying malignancy.

Peripheral Features. In cirrhosis there are often multiple stigmata of chronic liver disease in addition to jaundice. These include vascular spiders in the upper half of the body, redness of the palms, and loss of axillary and pubic hair. Gynecomastia and testicular atrophy are often present in men. There are no special features on physical examination in acute viral hepatitis.

Abdomen. The signs of portal hypertension are dilated abdominal wall veins, splenomegaly, and ascites. The liver is usually of normal size or slightly enlarged in acute virus- or drug-induced hepatitis. Small livers that are impalpable and with reduced span on percussion are often cirrhotic, but are also seen in acute severe hepatitis. A very enlarged liver,

more than 4 cm below the right costal margin, is most often due to heart failure, alcoholic hepatitis, or metastases. Other causes are chronic biliary obstruction such as primary biliary cirrhosis, cysts, infiltrative disease, and Budd–Chiari syndrome. A tender liver is usually due to hepatitis, heart failure, tumor, or abscess. A firm liver, especially with a diffusely nodular surface, suggests cirrhosis. A very hard liver with an irregular edge is probably malignant.

An enlarged gallbladder that feels smooth and cystic or firm is usually due to common bile duct obstruction by pancreatic cancer.

Palpable splenomegaly is most often due to portal hypertension. Occasionally, the tip is felt in viral hepatitis, especially in children. An enlarged spleen is common in hemolytic anemias and in infectious mononucleosis. Rarely, splenic vein thrombosis in pancreatic cancer leads to an enlarged spleen.

Ascites associated with jaundice is very likely due to hepatocellular disease, most commonly cirrhosis and also severe alcoholic and viral hepatitis. Liver metastases or pancreatic cancer may be accompanied by peritoneal seeding and an exudative ascites. Rapid onset of ascites and jaundice can be caused by hepatic vein thrombosis.

Routine Laboratory Abnormalities

Urine. Bilirubin present by dipstick indicates conjugated hyperbilirubinemia. Urobilin is absent in cholestatic jaundice. Excess urobilin may be present in hemolysis, but is not specific.

Serum Biochemical Tests. The total bilirubin level confirms the presence and degree of jaundice. Direct and indirect bilirubin levels indicate conjugated and unconjugated portions, respectively, and are of value only in distinguishing pigment overload and metabolic defects from conjugated hyperbilirubinemias (Table 19–70–1).

The alkaline phosphatase level is markedly elevated, usually more than three times the upper limit of normal, in cholestatic jaundice.

A predominant abnormality in transaminases, more than 5 to 10 times the normal levels, is probably due to hepatitis.

The serum albumin level and prothrombin time after vitamin K injection reflect liver cell function and may be abnormal in severe, acute or chronic hepatocellular diseases.

Hematology. A polymorph leukocytosis may be present in cholangitis, alcoholic hepatitis, and, occasionally, severe viral hepatitis.

If an abnormal prothrombin time is corrected by injection of vitamin K_1, cholestasis is probable.

Reticulocytes are increased in hemolysis.

PLANS
Diagnostic
Differential Diagnosis

The clinical manifestations in jaundice often suggest a single, working diagnosis. Routine evaluation by an internist points to the correct diagnosis in about 75% of cases.

A sexually active young man with multiple partners who in 1 week develops fatigue, fever, anorexia, nausea, and dark urine, and is found to have jaundice, tender liver, bilirubinuria, an aspartate transaminase 10 times the normal level and an alkaline phosphatase level twice normal, almost certainly has acute viral hepatitis, probably due to hepatitis B virus.

A healthy college student who has occasionally noticed yellow eyes and has isolated elevation of unconjugated serum bilirubin likely has Gilbert's disease.

Cancer of the pancreas is suggested in a 60-year-old woman with recent weight loss, weeks of epigastric pain, gradually increasing jaundice, and an alkaline phosphatase level four times normal.

Each of the above vignettes represents a different category of jaundice. In the minority of cases, analysis of the subjective and objective findings does not achieve probability of a single, working diagnosis. A presumptive diagnosis can easily be confirmed without extensive tests. Table 19–70–1 outlines a classification of jaundice and Table 19–70–2 summarizes the chief distinguishing features. The options for additional testing in each category are listed below.

Diagnostic Options

Hemolysis or Disturbance of Bilirubin Metabolism. Fasting reduces serum unconjugated bilirubin in Gilbert's disease.

Reticulocyte counts, blood films, and Coombs' test distinguish hemolysis from nonhemolytic, usually familial unconjugated hyperbilirubinemias.

The bromsulphalein test shows a secondary rise of dye in serum in Dubin–Johnson syndrome.

Hepatocellular Disease.

DRUG- OR TOXIN-INDUCED HEPATITIS. The patient should be questioned again about prescriptions, over-the-counter medicines, herbal agents, mushrooms, and toxins.

ALCOHOLIC HEPATITIS. Family and acquaintances should be questioned if alcoholism is suspected but drinking is denied by the patient.

VIRAL HEPATITIS. In acute hepatitis, check hepatitis B surface antigen (HBsAg), immunoglobulin (Ig)M antibody to hepatitis B core antigen (anti-HBc IgM), IgM antibody to hepatitis A virus (anti-HAV IgM), and antibody to hepatitis C virus (anti-HCV). In travelers, the IgM antibody to hepatitis E virus is also checked. In chronic jaundice, HBsAg, total antibody to hepatitis B core antigen and anti-HCV are checked.

AUTOIMMUNE HEPATITIS. Antinuclear antibody, anti-smooth muscle antibody (ASMA), and liver, kidney, microsomal (LKM1) antibodies are checked.

PRIMARY BILIARY CIRRHOSIS. Antimitochondrial antibody is checked.

WILSON'S DISEASE. Ceruloplasmin, urine copper, and Kayser–Fleischer rings are checked.

OTHER TESTS. Liver biopsy establishes the pattern and severity of inflammation, infiltration, fibrosis, and cirrhosis and may define a diagnosis such as alcoholic hepatitis or primary biliary cirrhosis. Specific causes may be identified by special stains and immunohistochemistry.

Other tests include the α_1-antitrypsin, iron saturation, and ferritin.

Cholestasis. Sonography of the liver, gallbladder, and biliary tree is indicated if common duct stones or intrahepatic cholestasis is suspected.

Computed tomography of the liver, gallbladder, biliary tree, and pancreas is indicated if malignant obstruction is suspected. A dilated biliary tree (intra- and extrahepatic ducts) and mass lesions may be demonstrated.

Endoscopic retrograde cholangiopancreatography (ERCP) or percutaneous transhepatic cholangiography (PTC) is used to define the nature and level of obstruction.

Liver biopsy may define causes of intrahepatic cholestasis such as viruses, drugs, or infiltration.

Laparoscopy may identify tumors and facilitate liver biopsy.

Laparotomy is occasionally required to establish the cause of bile duct obstruction.

Biliary scintigraphy is rarely indicated for jaundice, except after liver and biliary surgery.

Pancreatic biopsy under computed tomography guidance may be helpful in suspected malignancy.

Recommended Approach

Detailed analysis of the symptoms, signs, and routine laboratory tests suggests a working diagnosis that can be confirmed by the appropriate tests, or the category of jaundice (Tables 19–70–1, 19–70–2) can be established and further investigated by choices from Diagnostic Options (Figure 19–70–1). Jaundice due to hemolysis or most familial disturbances of bilirubin metabolism is unconjugated and easily identified by serum chemistry and absence of bilirubin in the urine. Syndromes of familial conjugated hyperbilirubinemia such as Dubin–Johnson and Rotor syndromes are rare and recognized by the isolated abnormality of bilirubin in healthy subjects. The distinction between hepatocellular and cholestatic jaundice is not always clear-cut, not least because many causes of cholestasis are intrahepatic and essentially liver cell in origin. The history and physical examination alone may determine the category. Cholestatic jaundice can be arbitrarily defined by an aspartate transaminase level less than five times normal and an alkaline phosphatase level more than three times the upper limit of normal. Laboratory tests alone cannot distinguish intrahepatic cholestasis from large bile duct obstruction. Computed tomography or ultrasound establishes whether the biliary tree is dilated, indicating obstruction of major ducts. The absence of dilation points to an intrahepatic cause and is 95% ac-

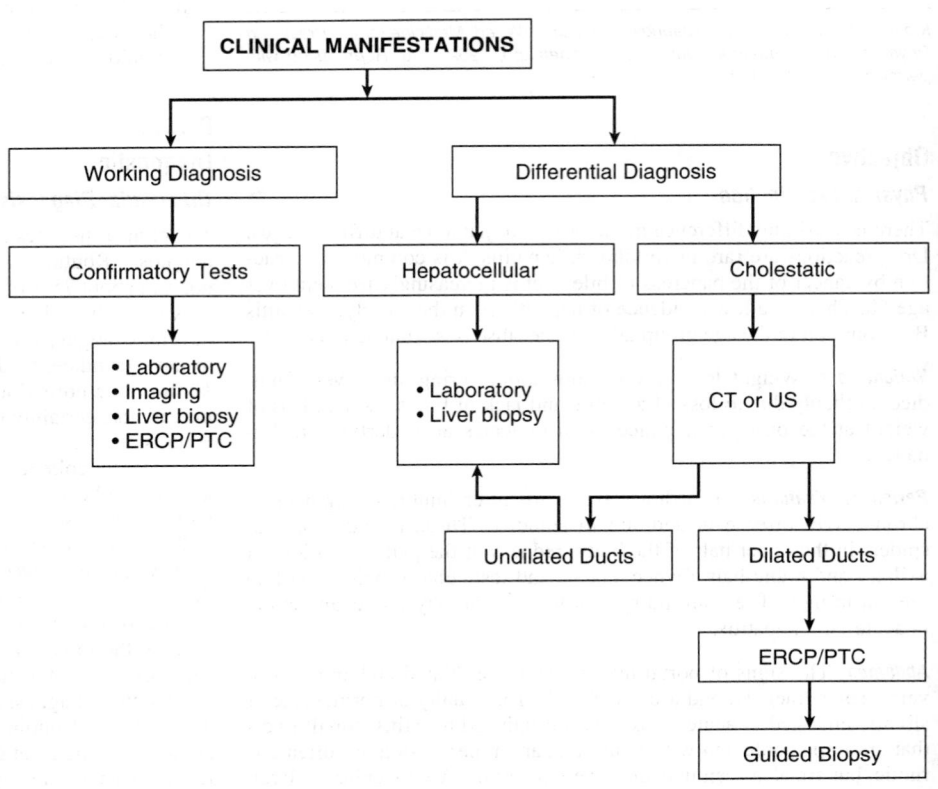

Figure 19–70–1. Diagnostic options in jaundice. CT, computed tomography; US, ultrasound; ERCP, endoscopic retrograde cholangiopancreatography; PTC, percutaneous transhepatic cholangiography.

curate if the bilirubin exceeds 10 mg. The etiology of bile duct dilation such as stone or tumor may be evident on imaging, but delineation of the nature and/or level of the lesion may require ERCP, PTC, or guided biopsy.

Intrahepatic cholestasis can be further investigated by detailed requestioning about cholestatic drugs, serologic tests such as antimitochondrial antibody (primary biliary cirrhosis) or IgM anti-HAV (cholestatic viral hepatitis), and liver biopsy. Rarely, a liver biopsy shows changes of duct obstruction although no dilated ducts are evident on imaging. This syndrome may be due to intrahepatic sclerosing cholangitis. A gallstone can cause intermittent obstruction of the common bile duct with fluctuating cholestasis without dilation. In addition, stones near the ampulla may be difficult to visualize on computed tomography or ultrasound.

Therapeutic

Treatment depends on the specific cause of jaundice (see appropriate chapters).

FOLLOW-UP

The frequency of observations and tests depends on the individual cause (see appropriate chapters).

DISCUSSION
Prevalence and Incidence

The incidence varies according to the cause of jaundice and is influenced by age, socioeconomic factors, and geography (see appropriate chapters).

Related Basic Science

Understanding the physiology of bilirubin metabolism clarifies the classification of jaundice and the clinical algorithms of diagnosis. Bilirubin arises from the breakdown of red cell heme and from myoglobin, respiratory enzymes, and immature cells in the spleen and bone marrow. This unconjugated pigment is tightly bound to albumin and therefore cannot be excreted by the kidney. Uptake by liver cells, transport to the endoplasmic reticulum, and conjugation by microsomal enzymes are separate steps that can be impaired by inherited defects or drugs and toxins. Any errors up to this stage of bilirubin metabolism result in unconjugated hyperbilirubinemia. Excretion across the canalicular membrane is by a specific transporter of organic anions. Pathology

at this level down through the ductules and interlobular and septal bile ducts into the major ducts causes cholestatic jaundice. Different causes such as viruses, drugs, primary biliary cirrhosis, and biliary atresia are operative at each level. Obstruction in small ducts is not evident on computed tomography or ultrasound and usually not on ERCP. Cholestasis prevents pigment from reaching the colon and interrupts the enterohepatic circulation so that stools are pale and urobilin is absent from the urine. The mechanism of jaundice in hepatocellular diseases such as viral hepatitis is multifactorial and cholestasis may be prominent.

Natural History and Its Modification with Treatment

The natural history depends on the cause of jaundice (see appropriate chapters).

Prevention

Prevention of jaundice depends on the individual causes (see appropriate chapters).

Cost Containment

By establishing a working diagnosis in the majority of cases, only a few confirmatory tests may be needed. Serologic tests should be focused on a specific problem. For example, in acute viral hepatitis it is necessary only to test HBsAg, IgM anti-HBC, IgM anti-HAV, and anti-HCV. Epidemiologic information may point to hepatitis A or B or C, and a single test may be appropriate. Imaging has defined goals but is often used without clear purpose. When indicated, either ultrasound or computed tomography is done, not both.

REFERENCES

Baron RL, Stanley RJ, Lee JKT et al. A prospective comparison of the evaluation of biliary obstruction using computed tomography and ultrasonography. Radiology 1982;145:91.

Camma C, Garofalo G, Almasio P et al. A performance evaluation of the expert system 'jaundice' in comparison with that of three hepatologists. J Hepatol 1991;13:279.

Chowdhury JR, Chowdhury NR. Conjugation and excretion of bilirubin. Semin Liver Dis 1983;3:11.

Fevery J, Vanstapel F, Blanckaert N. Bile pigment metabolism. Clin. Gastroenterol 1989;3:283.

Frank BB. Clinical evaluation of jaundice: A guideline of the Patient Care Committee of the American Gastroenterological Association. JAMA 1989;262:3031.

CHAPTER 19–71

Elevated Serum Alkaline Phosphatase Levels

David J. Clain, M.D.

DEFINITION

The abnormality can be defined as a serum alkaline phosphatase (SALP) level above the range of normal.

ETIOLOGY

Alkaline phosphatases are present in many organs and tissues. Under normal conditions, alkaline phosphatase in serum originates mainly from liver, bone, and intestine. Elevated levels of SALP are usually due to physiologic growth of bone, diseases of the liver and biliary system, and benign and malignant bone diseases. Uncommon causes include sepsis, ulcerative colitis, hyperthyroidism, and renal failure. Malignancies occasionally liberate an isoenzyme that resembles placental alkaline phosphatase.

CRITERIA FOR DIAGNOSIS

An elevation of the SALP level on routine blood tests is the only criterion needed for diagnosis.

CLINICAL MANIFESTATIONS
Subjective

The normal range of SALP differs in children, especially during periods of rapid bone growth and in the third trimester of pregnancy. These are physiologic variations. This chapter focuses on the significance of isolated elevation of SALP when there is no evidence of overt disease. It is not concerned with the value of abnormal SALP in specific situations such as the prediction of hepatic metastases in cancer patients or screening for osteodystrophy in patients on hemodialysis. In some cases of raised SALP levels, there are symptoms of the underlying cause. Jaundice and itching are often present in biliary obstruction. Abdominal pain is a common feature of cancer of the pancreas and chronic pancreatitis. There may be a cholestatic reaction to a drug. Sclerosing cholangitis can be silent but the underlying colitis may cause diarrhea, blood in the stools, or anemia. Back and bone pain occurs in Paget's disease, malignancy, and ostopenia.

The patient should be asked about previous liver disease or the use of hepatotoxic drugs. A past history of cancer is important.

Objective

Physical Examination

Physical examination may show signs of hepatobiliary disease, especially jaundice, xanthomata, scratch marks, and hepatomegaly.

Bones may be tender to palpation. Deformities of the skull and long bones may occur in Paget's disease.

Routine Laboratory Abnormalities

The cause of an elevated SALP may be evident from serum chemistry, which should include bilirubin, aspartate transaminase (AST), alanine transaminase (ALT), calcium, phosphorus, and creatinine.

PLANS

Diagnostic

Differential Diagnosis

Isolated elevations of SALP may be seen on routine screening of an apparently healthy population as well as in hospitalized patients. Most of these increases are due to the liver isoenzyme, but many persons will have no detectable evidence of hepatic disease. SALP elevations may be attributed to a specific cause, such as bile duct obstruction, infiltrative liver disease, heart failure, bone disease, or drugs such as dilantin (Table 19–71–1). In hospital, increases in SALP infrequently may be associated with sepsis, myocardial infarction, or ischemic damage to the intestine. Unexpected elevations in sick patients can be transient, and they return to normal with resolution of the acute illness.

Most of the abnormalities on screening healthy subjects are less than twice the upper limit of normal (ULN). The incidence of specific causes rises with the height of the SALP. When the SALP is more than twice the ULN, an associated disease is present about half the time. There is usually no detectable disease with slight increases, and levels 50% above normal have been found to have a significant cause in about one tenth of patients. In a study of 602 members of a health maintenance organization who had an elevated SALP on routine health screening, more than 90% had no active disease and no diagnosis emerged over a 2-year period of observation (Rubenstein et al., 1986). The normal range is widely known to be different for young, growing children. Few laboratories adjust values for older age groups, although

in the elderly, especially women, a normal upper limit is 30% higher than at age 40. Therefore, mild elevations of SALP over the age of 65 probably should be regarded as normal. The highest levels of SALP are due to cholestasis, malignant metastases, and diffuse granulomas of the liver. Table 19–70–1 lists the common causes in liver, bile ducts, and bone. They include cancer of the pancreas, chronic pancreatitis, primary biliary cirrhosis, gallstones, cirrhosis, and heart failure. In AIDS, marked elevations are often associated with *Mycobacterium avium* complex, drug reactions, sclerosing cholangitis, and, less commonly, with lymphoma.

Diagnostic Options

The diagnostic options include observation; γ-glutamyl transpeptidase and 5'-nucleotidase determinations; fractionation into isoenzymes of SALP; the antimitochondrial antibody test; bone x-rays and scans; liver ultrasound for dilated ducts; computed tomography of the abdomen for focal intrahepatic lesions and dilated ducts; endoscopic retrograde cholangiopancreatography (ERCP) to define the site and nature of the lesion; and thyroid function tests.

Recommended Approach

There is uncertain significance to an isolated level of SALP up to twice normal. Many abnormal values resolve within months. Others may have an obvious, extrahepatic cause. In most cases of marked increases, careful evaluation of symptoms, signs, and standard laboratory tests will indicate a hepatic, skeletal, or systemic etiology. Figure 19–71–1 is an algorithm that describes the choices in solving the problem of lone elevation of SALP. If there is no past history of a possible cause such as breast cancer or liver disease, or evidence of a probable cause (see Table 19–71–1) that requires appropriate investigation or confirmation, then further decisions should take into account height of the SALP, age of the patient, and presence or absence of significant acute illness. Moderate increases in sick, hospitalized patients often return to normal with resolution of the illness. Values above twice the upper limit of normal require further evaluation. But if the increase is less than twice the upper limit of normal, especially in older patients, a period of observation is advised because the yield of significant, treatable disease has been small in most prospective studies, provided that a detailed clinical evaluation has been normal. If repeated tests every 2 to 3 months are stable or decline, observation can continue. Rising values are an indication for further investigation.

When the SALP is more than twice the upper limit of normal in a middle-aged woman, asymptomatic or with pruritus, the antimitochondrial antibody level should be determined as a marker of primary biliary cirrhosis. If all other liver function tests are normal, a normal γ-glutamyl transpeptidase supports a source of SALP outside the liver, because γ-glutamyl transpeptidase is very sensitive to cholestasis and liver cell damage. An abnormal γ-glutamyl transpeptidase is misleading at times, however, because of nonspecific elevations in the presence of drugs, toxins, and systemic illnesses. A liver origin of SALP can be confirmed by an elevated 5'-nucleotidase level. The result of fractionation of isoenzymes is sometimes equivocal.

A different picture emerges when SALP is more than three times the upper limit of normal and especially when there is a clinical indication for the test. Elevation of SALP due to progressive biliary or liver disease is eventually accompanied by jaundice. The crucial decision point in the algorithm of elevated SALP is whether ultrasound shows dilated bile ducts. Dilation indicates obstruction of a major duct most often due to cancer of the head of the pancreas, gallstones, or chronic pancreatitis (Table 19–71–1). ERCP helps determine the site and nature of obstruction. Undilated ducts with a normal bilirubin do not exclude extrahepatic obstruction as the cause of a high SALP. The clinical findings indicate whether liver biopsy or ERCP is the next appropriate test.

In AIDS, when there is a high suspicion of a specific infection such as *Mycobacterium avium* complex, tuberculosis, or cytomegalovirus, it is reasonable to monitor SALP during a trial of therapy. Markedly abnormal and rising elevations in the absence of liver and bone disease raise the question of ectopic synthesis by cancer. A placental-type alkaline phosphatase can be shown by isoenzyme assay in some cases.

TABLE 19–71–1. DIFFERENTIAL DIAGNOSIS OF ELEVATED SERUM ALKALINE PHOSPHATASE (SALP)

Etiology	Comment
No SALP-associated disease	Most frequent if SALP < 2 × upper limit of normal
Liver	*Marked:* tumor metastases, granulomas space-occupying lesions, abscesses, amyloid, leukemias; in AIDS, *Mycobacterium avium* complex, lymphoma, drug toxicity
	Mild: cirrhosis, heart failure, alcohol, drugs
Biliary	Cancer of pancreas, ampulla, bile ducts; primary biliary cirrhosis; chronic pancreatitis; stone and strictures; sclerosing cholangitis
Bone	Metastatic cancer, Paget's disease, osteopenia, hyperparathyroidism, fractures
Other	Hyperthyroidism, renal failure, sepsis

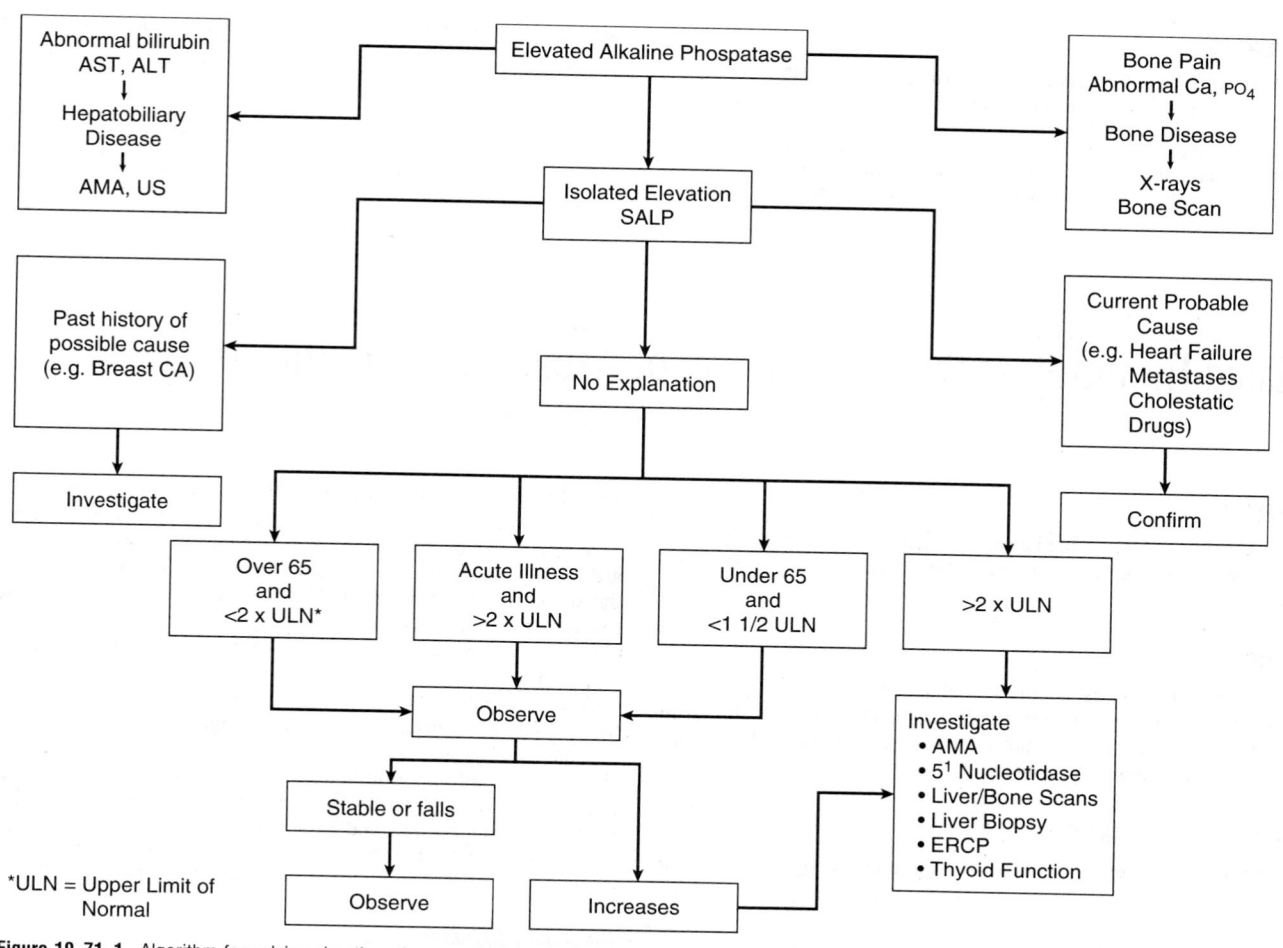

Figure 19–71–1. Algorithm for solving elevation of serum alkaline phosphatase. AST, aspartate transaminase; ALT, alanine transaminase; SALP, serum alkaline phosphatase; AMA, antimitochondrial antibody; US, ultrasound; Ca, cancer; ULN, upper limit of normal; ERCP, endoscopic retrograde cholangiopancreatography.

Therapeutic

Treatment depends on the specific cause of elevated SALP.

FOLLOW-UP

Observation of an unexplained elevation of SALP is discussed under Diagnostic, Recommended Approach.

DISCUSSION
Prevalence and Incidence

Elevations of SALP have been found in 5 to 10% of healthy individuals.

Related Basic Science

The alkaline phosphatases are a family of enzymes with differing properties and are present in a wide range of tissues. Alkaline phosphatase has been identified in human liver, bone, intestine, placenta, kidneys, leukocytes, and cancers. They are found mainly in plasma membranes. In the liver they are present in both sinusoidal and canalicular membranes. The exact function of alkaline phosphatase has not been identified. The mechanism of release of the enzyme into blood and body fluids is not well understood. There are many ways of measuring SALP based on a variety of substrates. Comparison of abnormal results generated by different methods is fraught with potential error even if expressed as a multiple of the upper limit of normal. Therefore, it is desirable in clinical practice to follow the progress of SALP in a single laboratory.

The circulating SALP in health is usually of the liver or bone type.

The intestinal fraction may be increased in subjects with blood groups O and B, especially after a fatty meal; however, this isoenzyme has no obvious role in lipid absorption or transport. Increase in intestinal alkaline phosphatase also has been reported in chronic hepatitis and cirrhosis. It has been suggested that fibroblasts in the liver synthesize the intestinal enzyme. Both bone and liver alkaline phosphatase may increase in metastatic cancer. A variety of tumors may produce ectopic isoenzymes that resemble placental alkaline phosphatase. The greatest increase in SALP is found in biliary obstruction. The mechanism was thought to be an overflow from liver cells into the plasma due to the blockage of excretion into the bile ducts. Experiments in bile duct-ligated rats have shown a marked increase in synthesis of alkaline phosphatase which is induced by retained bile acids. Translation of the mRNA is augmented by cholestasis.

Natural History and Its Modification with Treatment

The natural history depends on the cause of the abnormal SALP. Levels more than three times the upper limit of normal are often hepatobiliary in origin. A specific etiology will not become apparent in the majority of healthy subjects with elevation less than two times normal. Unexplained, lone elevations may resolve.

Prevention

There are no preventive measures.

Cost Containment

When there are minor elevations of SALP, observation rather than intensive tests is often the most appropriate initial management.

REFERENCES

Kaplan MM. Alkaline phosphatase. Gastroenterology 1972;62:452.

Penn R, Worthington DJ. Is serum gamma glutamyltransferase a misleading test? Br Med J 1983;286:531.

Rubenstein LV, Ward NC, Greenfield S. In pursuit of the abnormal serum alkaline phosphatase: A clinical dilemma. J Gen Intern Med 1986;1:38.

Seetharam S, Sussman NL, Komoda T, et al. The mechanism of elevated alka-

line phosphatase activity after bile duct ligation in the rat. Hepatology 1986;6:374.

Warnes TW, Hine P, Kay G. Intestinal alkaline phosphatase in the diagnosis of liver disease. Gut 1977;18:274.

Wolf PL. Clinical significance of an increased or decreased serum alkaline phosphatase level. Arch Pathol Lab Med 1978;102:497.

CHAPTER 19–72

Isolated Elevation of the Serum Level of Aspartate Transaminase

David J. Clain, M.D.

DEFINITION

The abnormality can be defined as an isolated elevation of the aspartate transaminase (AST, glutamic–oxaloacetic transaminase) level in the serum.

ETIOLOGY

Aspartate transaminase is an intracellular enzyme that is present in liver, heart, skeletal muscle, kidney, and brain. The source of the serum AST that normally circulates is not known. The level rises when tissues containing the enzyme are damaged.

CRITERIA FOR DIAGNOSIS

Elevation of AST in serum is all that is required to recognize the condition.

CLINICAL MANIFESTATIONS
Subjective

Isolated elevation of AST is usually an incidental finding on standard laboratory blood tests that are being done as a health screen, for life insurance examination, or during investigation of an unrelated clinical problem.

The patient should be asked the following questions: What is your intake of alcohol? Are you taking medicines? Do you use herbal and folk remedies? Is there liver disease in the family? Are you an intravenous drug user? Have you had a blood transfusion? Have you had joint pains, skin rash, or a thyroid disorder?

Objective
Physical Examination

There are usually no findings that relate to the elevation of AST. Occasionally, the presence of obesity, autoimmune changes (joint swelling, rash, thyroid enlargement), skin pigmentation, or Kayser–Fleischer rings provide a clue to etiology. Signs of liver, heart, or muscle disease are seldom evident.

Routine Laboratory Abnormalities

By definition, isolated elevation of AST indicates normality of other standard tests of liver and muscle diseases. A high blood glucose level may indicate diabetes as a cause of fatty liver.

PLANS
Diagnostic
Differential Diagnosis

Most isolated elevations of AST are mild or moderate, up to five times the upper limit of normal, and either transient or persistent. Persistent abnormalities of AST are often due to chronic viral hepatitis (B and C), fatty liver, alcohol use, hepatic drug reactions, autoimmune liver dis-

ease, heart failure, and, occasionally, inherited disorders such as hemochromatosis, α_1-antitrypsin deficiency, and Wilson's disease.

Marked rises in AST, more than 10 times the upper limit of normal, are usually acute and not isolated abnormalities and, therefore, are not the subject of this discussion. They include acute viral hepatitis, hepatotoxic drug reactions, acute bile duct obstruction by gallstones, ischemic injury, and, rarely, muscle damage due to rhabdomyolysis or myopathies.

A concurrent abnormality in alanine aminotransferase (ALT, glutamic–pyruvate transaminase) usually points to a liver source of AST because ALT is found predominantly in hepatocytes; however, extensive skeletal muscle injury as in rhabdomyolysis can also cause a marked rise in ALT. In this circumstance, the creatine phosphokinase level is extremely high and myoglobin is present in the urine. If the ratio of AST to ALT is high, greater than 2, alcoholic hepatitis should be strongly suspected but only if the total AST is less than 300.

Diagnostic Options

Diagnostic options include the following:

- Repeat AST and other liver function tests
- Repeat AST after abstention from alcohol
- Repeat AST after withdrawing hepatotoxic drugs for several weeks
- Repeat AST after weight loss and control of diabetes
- Hepatitis B surface antigen (HBsAg), antibody to hepatitis B core antigen, and antibody to hepatitis C virus (chronic viral hepatitis)
- Antinuclear and smooth muscle antibodies (autoimmune chronic liver disease
- Ferritin and transferrin saturation index (hemochromatosis)
- α_1-Antitrypsin
- Ceruloplasmin, urine copper, and Kayser–Fleischer rings (Wilson's disease)
- Liver biopsy (chronic hepatitis, fatty liver, iron and copper measurement)
- Liver ultrasound (fatty liver, cirrhosis)
- Computed tomography (suspected metastases)

Recommended Approach

Isolated elevation of AST is usually less than six times the upper limit of normal. The test should be repeated to confirm the abnormality. The clinical features should be reviewed with respect to a possible cause. If the ALT level is normal the γ-glutamyl transpeptidase level should be determined to exclude a liver origin. If the γ-glutamyl transpeptidase level is normal, the creatine phosphokinase level should be measured to detect muscle disease. If there is a working diagnosis such as fatty liver, alcoholic hepatitis, or drug reaction, the AST is repeated after treating or removing the cause. For fatty liver, this means weight reduction and treatment of diabetes.

If there are no clues to the etiology, markers for hepatitis viruses B and C, autoimmune chronic liver disease (antinuclear antibody and smooth muscle antibody) and inherited diseases should be checked. The patient should be asked again about prescription and over-the-counter medicines. Hemochromatosis is common and presents in men over 40, usually later in women. Wilson's disease is almost always diagnosed before age 35. Pulmonary disease is often present in α_1-antitrypsin deficiency. With liver cancer it is unlikely that an abnormal AST will be an isolated finding.

A liver sonogram may show diffusely increased echogenicity in fatty liver and in chronic hepatitis with scarring or cirrhosis. Liver biopsy is generally indicated in chronic viral and autoimmune hepatitis for confirmation and prognostic information before therapy. Liver biopsy may be helpful when the cause is unknown, and can define unexpected fatty liver or alcoholic hepatitis; however, biopsy is not recommended for minor elevations of AST if all diagnostic tests have been negative, as the outcome is unlikely to alter management. Liver biopsy to confirm a clinical diagnosis of fatty liver is controversial. Some authorities recommend biopsy. Others advise repeating the liver function tests after weight reduction and treatment of diabetes mellitus, if present.

Therapeutic

Treatment depends on the cause of the abnormal AST level.

FOLLOW-UP

Observations depend on the cause.

DISCUSSION
Prevalence and Incidence

The prevalence and incidence are unknown.

Related Basic Science

Aspartate transaminase is an enzyme present in liver, heart, skeletal muscle, kidney, and brain. In the liver it is present mainly in mitochondria but also in the cytosol, whereas ALT is entirely cytosolic. AST is present in serum with and without the cofactor pyridoxal 5-phosphate. The source of AST in the serum under normal conditions is not known. It is presumed that abnormal levels in disease are due to injury to cell membranes with leakage into the plasma. The concentration of the enzyme in the cell is many thousands of times higher than in serum. The height of the serum AST does not predict outcome, although there is a statistical correlation with extent of tissue injury. Ratios of mitochondrial and cytosolic AST, and of apo- and holoenzymes have not led to any formulas that are reliable in clinical diagnosis. The ratio of AST to ALT in the serum, however, has proved useful in supporting injury by alcohol. A ratio greater than 2 is only occasionally seen in other liver diseases. The ratio of serum levels is reflected in the hepatocytes. The cause of the lower ALT in liver cells appears to be due to pyridoxal 5′-phosphate deficiency. Spuriously low ALT levels have been reported in renal dialysis but are probably due to uremia. Therefore, the clinician should be cautious in interpreting normal or near-normal transaminases levels in patients with chronic renal failure who require dialysis.

Natural History And Its Modification with Treatment

The natural history depends on the cause of the elevated AST level.

Prevention

There are no preventive measures.

Cost Containment

An abnormal result should be confirmed by repeating the AST test before further tests. All information should be used to reach a single, working diagnosis if possible and to tailor confirmatory tests accordingly.

REFERENCES

De Ritis F, Coltorti M, Giusti G. Serum transaminase activities in liver disease. Lancet 1972;1:685.

Matloff DS, Selinger MJ, Kaplan MM. Hepatic transaminase activity in alcoholic liver disease. Gastroenterology 1980;78:1389.

McIntyre N. The limitations of conventional liver function tests. Semin Liver Dis 1983;3:265.

Patwardhan RV, Smith OJ, Farmelant MH. Serum transaminase levels and cholescintigraphic abnormalities in acute biliary tract obstruction. Arch Intern Med 1987;147:1249.

CHAPTER 19–73

Dubin–Johnson Syndrome

Curtis E. Scott, M.D.

DEFINITION

Dubin–Johnson syndrome is a benign hereditary metabolic disorder of bilirubin excretion associated with a predominance of conjugated hyperbilirubinemia.

ETIOLOGY

Although the direct cause of Dubin–Johnson syndrome is unknown, the disorder is found to be inherited in an autosomal recessive manner. The genetic defect appears to alter the function of an ATP-dependent transporter of conjugated non-bile acid organic anions at the level of the hepatic canaliculi. The exact nature of this transporter has not yet been elucidated.

CRITERIA FOR DIAGNOSIS
Suggestive

Jaundice in a patient with predominantly conjugated hyperbilirubinemia associated with the absence of other abnormal hepatic biochemical tests suggests Dubin–Johnson syndrome.

Definitive

Dubin–Johnson syndrome is characterized by icterus which may be intermittent. Patients are generally asymptomatic otherwise, but a few may complain of vague abdominal pain, weakness, nausea, or vomiting. Diagnostic factors include conjugated hyperbilirubinemia; increased ratio of urinary coproporphyrin I to coproporphyrin III despite normal total urinary coproporphyrin excretion; technetium-labeled hepato-iminodiacetic acid (HIDA, or its derivatives) showing a characteristic uptake and excretion pattern; demonstration of ineffective excretion of conjugated dyes (e.g., bromsulphalein) normally excreted in bile; and dark pigmentation of the liver seen on evaluation. There is not a sex preference and many different ethnic groups have been affected, including whites, blacks, Indians, Japanese, and Arabian Jews, who have the highest incidence identified.

CLINICAL MANIFESTATIONS
Subjective

Diagnosis of this syndrome may be made at any age but a majority of cases are identified by the third decade of life. Patients who are identified later in life may give a history of previous episodes of jaundice without sequelae, but some patients may have had mild scleral icterus without jaundice of the skin that may have gone unrecognized. Others may have neither identifiable icterus nor symptoms and are identified during the course of familial evaluation of an index case. Except for intermittent jaundice of fluctuating intensity, most patients are without symptoms. If symptoms are present, they may include vague right upper quadrant pain, malaise, anorexia, nausea, vomiting, and, rarely, diarrhea. It has been suggested that many of these symptoms may be related to the anxiety associated with a prolonged workup rather than a result of Dubin–Johnson syndrome (DJS). Dark urine and, less commonly, light stools may be recognized. Pruritis is notably absent. In some instances, patients with subclinical DJS develop jaundice during an intercurrent illness which persists following recovery from the illness. Pregnancy and the use of oral contraceptives can induce hyperbilirubinemia and unmask the syndrome in previously unrecognized susceptible women. A higher association with fetal loss has been observed in women affected with DJS. The reason for this is unknown.

Family history of a propositus may identify affected family members with previously noted intermittent icterus, but heterozygous members express no clinical abnormality and are identified only on further biochemical testing.

Objective

Physical Examination

With the exception of icterus, physical examination is usually normal in the majority of cases. A few patients demonstrate modest enlargement of the liver and/or associated right upper quadrant tenderness. Hepatosplenomegaly has been recognized.

Routine Laboratory Abnormalities

Abnormal laboratory findings are restricted primarily to elevation of serum bilirubin (in the range 2–5 mg/dL, but may be as high as 25 mg/dL), with a predominant conjugated fraction. Urinary bile and urobilinogen may also be elevated. Other hepatic biochemical tests, including aspartate transaminase, alanine transaminase, alkaline phosphatase, γ-glutamyl transpeptidase, albumin, and prothrombin time, are normal. Cholesterol level is also normal. There is no evidence of previous or ongoing hemolysis as evidenced by normal complete blood count, reticulocyte count, and red cell survival. Fasting and postprandial serum bile acid levels are normal.

PLANS

Diagnostic

Differential Diagnosis

Differential diagnosis includes extrahepatic biliary obstruction, acute and chronic hepatitis, Rotor's syndrome, and hepatic storage syndrome. Findings may sometimes suggest acute cholecystitis.

Diagnostic Options and Recommended Approach

Diagnosis of DJS should be considered in patients presenting with hyperbilirubinemia that is predominantly of the conjugated type. Identification of normal routine hepatic biochemical tests otherwise would support this consideration. Normal serum bile acids and alkaline phosphatase levels would help rule out true cholestasis, and ultrasonography showing normal bile ducts would help rule out extrahepatic bile duct obstruction.

The diagnosis of DJS has classically been based on two primary findings: First, there is characteristic elimination curve of bromsulphalein given intravenously in which serum levels are higher at 90 minutes than at 45 minutes. This is due to reflux of conjugated bromsulphalein from hepatocytes back into the plasma and results from a defective transporter at the level of the canaliculus causing selective ineffective excretion of conjugated substances. The T_m for bromsulphalein in affected patients is virtually zero. Unconjugated bromsulphalein and substances that do not require conjugation for excretion (e.g., dibromsulphalein, ^{125}-I-rose bengal, and indocyanine green) are not affected, and are freely eliminated. Second, the appearance of the liver at laparoscopy and liver biopsy show a distinctive feature of dark

pigmentation. Macroscopically, the liver has been described as ranging from green to dark gray to black. The biopsy specimen shows normal histologic architecture except for the intracellular deposition of course granular dark pigment in parenchymal cells located primarily in the perivenular area. Electron microscopic evaluation suggests that the accumulation of pigment represents a benign disorder of secondary lysosomal storage. The nature of the pigment has not been definitively elucidated, iron staining is negative, and on the basis of spectroscopic analysis, histochemical staining, and electron spin resonance studies, the determination has been made that it is not melanin as previously suggested. Recent studies indicate that the pigment may represent polymers of epinephrine metabolites.

A hallmark of DJS is the unusual ratio of urinary coproporphyrin I to coproporphyrin III. Coproporphyrins are the by-products of heme biosynthesis. Coproporphyrin III is formed by nonenzymatic oxidation of coproporphyrinogen III, an obligatory intermediate in the normal course of the heme synthesis pathway. Coproporphyrin III is excreted in urine and bile, as is coproporphyrin I, the product of spontaneous oxidation of coproporphyrinogen I in a dead-end branch in heme biosynthesis. In normal subjects, the ratio of urinary coproporphyrin III to coproporphyrin I is approximately 3–4 to 1. This ratio is reversed in Dubin–Johnson syndrome, with coproporphyrin I accounting for 80% or more despite normal levels of total coproporphyrin in a 24-hour urine collection. This differs from other conditions such as Rotor's syndrome, in which coproporphyrin I is increased, but is associated with a severalfold increase in total coproporphyrin levels and accounts for less than 80% of product. Patients who are heterozygous for DJS have an intermediate level of coproporphyrin I. Despite this characteristic finding, its molecular basis has not been satisfactorily explained. Selective impairment in biliary secretion (because coproporphyrin is anionic) has been suggested. The possibility of changes in the pathway of heme biosynthesis due to transport block has also been considered.

Cholescintigraphy with ^{99m}-Tc-labeled HIDA or its derivatives (DISIDA, PIPIDA, Disofenin) shows a characteristic image. These substances bind to the serum proteins and are transported through the hepatocyte by the same mechanism that transports organic anions like bilirubin. In DJS, uptake by the liver is good with rapid, intense, homogeneous visualization, but excretion is delayed and the bile ducts are not visualized at all. Very delayed opacification of the gallbladder may be obtained. Contrastingly, patients with Rotor's syndrome or with jaundice due to hepatocellular disease have no visualization of the liver, gallbladder, or bile ducts with administration of these agents, and there is not expression of radioactivity in the intestine with 24 hours of observation.

Oral cholecystography has also been used to assist in the diagnosis of DJS. The gallbladder fails to opacify even with supplemental doses of oral contrast; however, information obtained by this method may be limited by its pharmokodynamic requirements.

Thus, in the patient presenting with conjugated hyperbilirubinemia with or without jaundice or symptoms, a suspicion of biliary obstruction can be evaluated sonographically. The presence of jaundice, right upper quadrant pain, and an abnormal HIDA scan may also raise the suspicion of acute cholecystitis to the clinician. The patient with Dubin–Johnson syndrome, however, lacks the associated findings of leukocytosis, fever, nausea, or vomiting and has the notable absence of any other abnormal hepatic biochemical tests. The importance of this consideration is paramount in avoiding invasive and exploratory procedures in these patients. In addition, hepatitis is unlikely, as there is a lack of evidence of hepatocellular injury (i.e., normal transaminases) and HIDA scan shows normal homogeneous hepatic uptake. Other diagnostic considerations would include Rotor's syndrome and hepatic storage syndrome, which may be identical disorders, but differ from DJS as noted in Table 19–73–1. The diagnosis of DJS can be reasonably established using the 24-hour urine collection for coproporphyrins and cholescintigraphy (HIDA). For confirmation, laparoscopy and liver biopsy can be performed. Bromsulphalein has infrequently been associated with anaphylactoid reactions, which have rarely been fatal.

Therapeutic

As DJS is considered a benign disorder, no specific therapeutic intervention is required. Patients should be reassured about the lack of se-

TABLE 19–73–1. PRINCIPAL CHARACTERISTICS OF DUBIN–JOHNSON, ROTOR'S, AND HEPATIC STORAGE SYNDROMES

	Dubin–Johnson Syndrome	Rotor's Syndrome	Hepatic Storage Syndrome
Original description	1954	1948	1971
Appearance of liver	Grossly black	Normal	Normal
Histology of liver	Dark pigment, predominantly in centrilobular areas, otherwise normal	Normal; no increase in pigmentation	Normal, no increase in pigmentation
Serum bilirubin	Increased: usually between 2 and 5 mg/dL: occasionally as high as 25 mg/dL; predominantly direct-reacting ($\approx$ 60% of total)	Increased: usually between 2 and 5 mg/dL; occasionally as high as 25 mg/dL; predominantly direct-reacting ($\approx$ 60% of total)	Increased: usually reported between 3 and 7 mg/dL; predominantly direct-reacting
Routine liver function tests	Normal except for bilirubin	Normal except for bilirubin	Normal except for bilirubin
Oral cholecystogram	Usually does not visualize the gallbladder	Usually visualizes the gallbladder	Visualizes the gallbladder, although visualization may be delayed up to 20 h
Serum bile acids	Normal (usually)	Normal	Normal
45-Minute plasma BSP retention	Normal or moderately increased (usually $\leq$ 20%); secondary rise at 90–120 min	Increased (> 25%) owing to slow initial disappearance; no secondary increase	Increased (only reported value 36%); no secondary rise
BSP transport maximum (normal = 8.2 ± 1.5 [SD] mg/min)	Markedly reduced (0.9 ± 0.4 mg/min)	Minimally to moderately reduced; one series reported 4.4 ± 1.8 mg/min	Normal or slightly reduced (5.7–7 mg/min)
BSP storage capacity (normal = 61 ± 14 mg/mg/dL)	Normal	Reduced; values in one series were 7.7 ± 3.4 mg/mg/dL	Reduced; reported values 17–23 mg/mg/dL
Urinary coproporphyrin excretion	Normal or slightly increased total; > 80% as coporporphyrin I	Markedly increased total; increased proportion of coproporphyrin I but <80%	No data reported
Presumed defect	Impaired biliary excretion of conjugated organic anions	? Impaired biliary excretion; ? impaired storage capacity	? Impaired storage capacity
Age when hyperbilirubinemia first recognized	Variable (birth to age 70); usually by early adulthood (pregnancy, "pill")	Variable; usually in childhood	Few data
Symptoms	Nonspecific or absent	Nonspecific or absent	Nonspecific or absent
Physical findings	Jaundice, occasional hepatomegaly	Jaundice	Jaundice
Treatment	None; avoid estrogens	None	None
Progosis	Good	Good	Good
Incidence	Rare, but up to 1:1300 in Iranian Jews	Rare	Rare
Inheritance	Autosomal recessive in most kindreds	Autosomal recessive	Unknown

BSP, bromsulphalein

Source: Berk PD. Bilirubin metabolism and the hereditary hyperbilirubinemias. In: Berk JE, Haubrich WS, Kalser MH, et al., eds. Bockus gastroenterology. 4th ed. Philadelphia: Saunders, 1985:2762. Reproduced with permission.

quelae. Phenobarbital has been used in some cases to ameliorate bilirubin concentration, but this is not recommended for chronic use. Prognosis is excellent and life expectancy is normal. Invasive interventions and explorations should be avoided both during the evaluation, by considering DJS in the differential diagnosis of the jaundiced patient with conjugated hyperbilirubinemia, and once diagnosis is established. Women should be counseled to avoid oral contraceptives and other estrogen-containing compounds, as these may precipitate expression of the disorder.

FOLLOW-UP

No specific follow-up is required once the diagnosis is established; however, clinical judgment should be used in evaluating patients who develop worsening jaundice or symptoms to rule out development of other illnesses.

DISCUSSION
Prevalence and Incidence

In 1954, Dubin and Johnson and Spritz and Nelson independently described a benign disorder characterized by chronic or intermittent jaundice and a grossly pigmented liver. Many additional cases have since been described worldwide in many different ethnic groups and in both sexes. Although it is relatively uncommon globally, a higher frequency has been seen among Arabian Jews (1:1300), probably due to a greater degree of inbreeding. In this population, a coinheritance of factor VII

deficiency is sometimes associated, but this finding is not seen in any other groups with DJS.

Related Basic Science
Genetics

Inheritance follows an autosomal recessive pattern, with heterozygotes expressing an intermediate-range defect.

Physiologic or Metabolic Derangement

Recent studies suggest that in DJS, the inherited defect manifests as a disordered function of an ATP-dependent transporter at the level of the canaliculus. This transporter is responsible for the excretion into bile of conjugated non-bile acid organic anions such as conjugated bilirubin and bromsulphalein. Over time this impaired function causes the accumulation of conjugated products in hepatocytes and is recognized as pigment deposits on histologic evaluation of the liver. The nature of the pigment has been shown not to be melanin as was previously thought. Studies using animal models (Corriedale sheep and TR– and EHBR mutant rats) suggest that it is a lysosomal accumulation due to oxidation and polymerization of epinephrine glucuronide, an anionic metabolite of tyrosine, phenylalanine, and tryptophan degradation. These deposits do not affect the functioning of other organelles within the hepatocyte and, therefore, remain a benign presence throughout the life of the patient.

In the past, diagnosis required the performance of a laparoscopy, laparotomy, or liver biopsy; however, with the availability of noninvasive methods with typical findings, and the knowledge that this is a completely benign disorder, some have suggested approaching a diagnostic workup noninvasively with a 24-hour urine for coproporphyrin isomer I and III levels and cholescintigraphy (HIDA) studies. If these are not available or further confirmation is required, liver biopsy and laparoscopy may be performed. Laparotomy is never required.

Natural History and Its Modification with Treatment

The natural history of this disorder follows a benign path with excellent prognosis and normal life expectancy.

Prevention

No preventive measures are currently available.

Cost Containment

Cost containment is achievable if the evaluation follows a noninvasive approach. Initial evaluation comprises routine laboratory tests and sonography to rule out biliary obstruction. Twenty-four-hour urine for coproporphyrin and HIDA scan can achieve reasonable diagnostic certainty. If additional confirmation is necessary then a liver biopsy and

laparoscopy may be considered. Surgery is not required. An oral cholecystogram will not add to diagnostic yield.

REFERENCES

Berk PD. Bilirubin metabolism and the hereditary hyperbilirubinemias. In: Berk JE, Haubrich WS, Kalser MH, et al., eds. Bockus gastroenterology. 4th ed. Philadelphia: Saunders, 1985:2732.

Crawford JM, Gollan JL. Bilirubin metabolism and the pathophysiology of jaundice. In: Schiff L, Schiff ER, eds. Diseases of the liver. 7th ed. Philadelphia: Lippincott, 1993:42.

Dubin IN, Johnson FB. Chronic idiopathic jaundice with unidentified pigment in liver cells: A new clinicopathologic entity with a report of 12 cases. Medicine 1954;33:155.

Nishida T, Gatmaitan Z, Roy-Chowdry J, Arias IM. Two distinct mechanisms for bilirubin glucuronide transport by rat bile canalicular membrane vesicles: Demonstration of a defective ATP-dependent transport in rats(TR-) with inherited conjugated hyperbilirubinemia. J Clin Invest 1992;90:2130.

Pinos T, Constansa JM, Palacin A, Figueras C. A new diagnostic approach to the Dubin–Johnson syndrome. Am J Gastroenterol 1990;85:91.

Spritz H, Nelson RS. Persistent non-hemolytic hyperbilirubinemia associated with lipochrome-like pigment in the liver: Report of four cases. Ann Intern Med 1954;41:952.

CHAPTER 19–74

Gilbert's Syndrome

Simon S. Rabinowitz, M.D., Ph.D.

DEFINITION

Gilbert's syndrome, also known as constitutional hepatic dysfunction, consists of intermittent indirect hyperbilirubinemia in the absence of hemolysis or hepatic disease. Individuals with this condition are asymptomatic and have an excellent overall prognosis.

ETIOLOGY

The pathogenesis of Gilbert's syndrome is unknown and there is probably heterogeneity in the defects that cause the laboratory and clinical findings. All affected individuals, however, have a deficiency in uridine diphosphate (UDP) glucuronyl transferase, the enzyme responsible for conjugating bilirubin in hepatocytes prior to its secretion into the biliary system.

CRITERIA FOR DIAGNOSIS
Suggestive

Gilbert's syndrome usually presents either as an isolated, asymptomatic laboratory finding, as an elevation in the indirect, unconjugated, bilirubin fraction, or as mild jaundice associated with a viral illness. The physician should suspect this fairly common entity in the appropriate setting and limit the diagnostic evaluation to standard liver function tests, and an evaluation for hemolysis, complete blood count with peripheral smear, a haptoglobin, and a reticulocyte count. The patient should be reassured and told to have continued follow-up.

Definitive

If there are several successive documentations over 12 to 18 months of mildly elevated indirect bilirubin levels and still no evidence to suggest hemolysis or liver disease, then a definitive diagnosis is made.

CLINICAL MANIFESTATIONS
Subjective

Besides intercurrent viral illnesses, other conditions that cause a further elevation over the mildly elevated baseline indirect bilirubin level of Gilbert's syndrome include alcohol, fasting, and emotional stress. These transient periods of jaundice usually lead the patient to medical attention. Although it has been noted that a majority of patients with Gilbert's syndrome have other symptoms, particularly malaise and gastrointestinal discomfort, it is felt that these symptoms are not part of the syndrome. A recent history of a viral hepatitis would introduce doubt into the diagnosis, as indirect hyperbilirubinemia can follow this condition without being Gilbert's syndrome. Often, an elevated indirect bilirubin level is an incidental finding that is noted in the course of routine laboratory testing.

The majority of patients first present with jaundice after puberty, possibly related to increments in sex hormones. Children and infants with Gilbert's syndrome have been described and certain workers have hypothesized that some affected neonates have jaundice as an early manifestation, possibly related to maternal estrogen. The syndrome is widely believed to be autosomal dominant, although a recent publication suggests a different inheritance pattern (Schmid, 1995). However, a family history of other affected individuals, without regard to gender, should be sought.

Objective
Physical Examination

The patient's physical examination should be normal aside from mild jaundice. In particular there should not be any evidence of liver disease, splenomegaly, congestive heart failure, or thyrotoxicosis.

Routine Laboratory Abnormalities

An evaluation of the jaundice reveals that it is strictly unconjugated in the range 2 to 6 mg/dL. Transaminases, alkaline phosphatase, γ-glutamyl transpeptidase, albumin, and the coagulation profile should be normal. Screening tests for hemolysis (see above) should also be normal. More subtle investigations of hemolysis reveal a slight increase in erythrocyte turnover in up to 40% of patients and should not rule out Gilbert's syndrome.

PLANS
Diagnostic
Differential Diagnosis

After a thorough physical examination and the screening laboratory tests listed above, there should rarely be any confusion regarding the diagnosis. Two entities that may need to be considered are Crigler–Najjar type II and posthepatitis syndromes. The first is a rare autosomal recessive disease in which there is decreased activity of glucuronyl transferase, which can be stimulated by phenobarbital. Although the clinical and laboratory abnormalities are usually more marked, mild cases with bilirubin in the range of Gilbert's syndrome have been described. The absence of any affected parents, few affected relatives, any significant neurologic impairment, an onset at birth, and a level of bilirubin greater than 6 mg/dL suggest Crigler–Najjar.

After a viral hepatitis or even hepatic inflammation secondary to pancreatitis or cholecystitis there can be a prolonged elevated indirect bilirubin fraction in the absence of other abnormalities. The initial episode of viral hepatitis may be asymptomatic, so that a negative previous history does not rule out this possibility. A family history of multiple affected members is the strongest evidence that the physical and laboratory findings are due to Gilbert's syndrome. This type of posthepatitis syndrome also has an excellent prognosis. Therefore, serial determinations documenting a return to baseline values of serum bilirubin are the easiest way to distinguish this from Gilbert's syndrome. A liver biopsy will be normal histologically in both entities and should very rarely be necessary in evaluating the patient with Gilbert's syndrome.

Diagnostic Options and Recommended Approach

There are several diagnostic approaches that can help to confirm the diagnosis of Gilbert's syndrome in the unusual situation where the diagnosis is uncertain. The indirect bilirubin fraction is further elevated by fasting and by injection of nicotinic acid and is lowered to near-normal values by phenobarbital. The effects of these manipulations are similar in Gilbert's and Crigler–Najjar type II syndromes so that these manipulations should be used only to distinguish Gilbert's from other entities. Fasting usually entails limiting lipid calories to 400 daily for 3 to 5 days and intravenous phenobarbital dosage is approximately 160 to 180 mg/d. In both tests serial bilirubin determinations are made. During fasting a two- to threefold increase in bilirubin is noted in Gilbert's syndrome, whereas the serum bilirubin level normalizes after administration of phenobarbital. Nicotinic acid diminishes the survival time of circulating erythrocytes and therefore causes a greater load of bilirubin for excretion. Intravenous administration of 50 mg results in a threefold increase in serum bilirubin at 120 minutes (compared with a twofold increase at 90 minutes in control subjects), with continued delayed clearance at 5 hours. There are no prospective studies that compare the sensitivity and specificity of these tests in defining Gilbert's; however, the nicotinic acid challenge has been shown to be an effective way to distinguish between Gilbert's and posthepatitis syndromes.

Therapeutic

No therapy is necessary for Gilbert's syndrome because it is a completely benign condition. The astute clinician recognizes this condition early, curtails any lengthy diagnostic investigations, and reassures the patient.

FOLLOW-UP

At the time of initial presentation a presumed diagnosis can be made after a physical examination and routine blood work have ruled out the more important alternative explanations. Two to three repeat laboratory and physical examinations are usually made over the next 12 to 18 months. If similar findings are determined, then a definitive diagnosis is made. No further investigations are indicated or desirable unless evidence to suggest a different disease entity is uncovered.

DISCUSSION
Prevalence and Incidence

Because Gilbert's syndrome is an asymptomatic syndrome defined largely by a laboratory cutoff, there is some discrepancy in the literature as to what level of bilirubin is accepted as the upper limit of normal and what is considered Gilbert's syndrome. The argument has even been presented that Gilbert's syndrome is simply the upper end of a normal nongaussian population curve. As a result, there is some disagreement over the incidence of this entity; however, it is universally accepted as relatively common with an incidence of 3 to 7% usually quoted. It is more common in males than females, although again this may reflect the lower distribution of normal bilirubin in women than men.

Related Basic Science

The same problems that interfere with the determination of an accurate incidence for Gilbert's syndrome plague genetic analysis. A recent publication has characterized Gilbert's syndrome as an autosomal recessive (Schmid, 1995). Previously, the widely held view was that Gilbert's is an autosomal dominant condition with variable penetrance. An additional confounding variable is the recognition that Gilbert's syndrome may simply be a clinical phenotype that includes a heterogeneous population representing different genetic defects. Some investigators have hypothesized that Gilbert's represents a mutation in the same locus as Crigler–Najjar but this view is not widely held. Recently published data have demonstrated that some cases of Gilbert's syndrome are the result of a specific mutation in the promoter region of the UDP–glucuronyl transferase gene, which yields decreased enzyme synthesis (Schmid, 1995).

Physiologic or Metabolic, Anatomic, and Ultrastructural Derangement

Like all steady states, the serum concentration of bilirubin is influenced by its synthesis and excretion. Although some patients have a subtle increase in hemolysis parameters, Gilbert's syndrome is an impairment in bilirubin clearance. Kinetic studies have shown that bilirubin clearance is a multistep process that includes hepatocyte uptake, intracellular conjugation, and secretion into the biliary canaliculi. All patients with Gilbert's syndrome have decreased in vitro activity of the microsomal enzyme that conjugates bilirubin to glucuronic acid, hepatic UDP-glucuronyl transferase. The clearance of other organic anions that are excreted via the biliary system such as bromsulphalein and indocyanine green have been investigated in patients with Gilbert's syndrome. Bilirubin, bromsulphalein, and indocyanine green all compete for the same sites during the hepatocyte uptake stage, but bromsulphalein is conjugated differently than bilirubin and indocyanine green is secreted without intrahepatic modification. Although the majority of patients with Gilbert's have normal excretion of the other anions, some have delayed clearance based on abnormal uptake and others have delayed clearance based on an intracellular process. In all likelihood it will be shown that a variety of defects can lead to the same clinical presentation. Familial and genetic studies that individually analyze these various groups should be able to address these questions directly.

Another controversial aspect of Gilbert's syndrome is the role of the UDP-glucuronyl transferase defect in the pathogenesis. The amount of residual measurable enzyme activity in the in vitro assay would appear to still be an order of magnitude greater than the activity required to conjugate the expected bilirubin load. In addition, there is no correlation between in vitro enzyme activity and extent of hyperbilirubinemia. Finally, phenobarbital activity "corrects" the defect in Gilbert's syndrome yet does not influence enzyme in vitro activity. Based on the available data, the most likely explanation is that the in vitro assay is not an accurate reflection of the in vivo activity of this microsomal protein and that disturbances in the microenvironment by various impairments may all lead to the common phenotypic expression.

Natural History and Its Modification with Treatment

As stated above, Gilbert's syndrome is a benign condition with no morbidity or increased risk of mortality. As such, no attempts should be made to offer therapy to affected individuals.

Prevention

Gilbert's syndrome is an inherited condition that often does not manifest until after puberty. There is no need for the practitioner to make any attempts to alter its benign natural course.

Cost Containment

The diagnosis of Gilbert's syndrome should be made after a physical examination and the results of a few routine laboratory tests are ob-

tained. The general physician should be familiar enough with this common entity to realize that no additional imaging or invasive tests are necessary, and should be able to relieve any fears in the anxious, icteric patient.

REFERENCES

Israel JB, Arias IMA. Inheritable disorders of bilirubin metabolism. Adv Intern Med 1976;21:77.

Kirshenbaum G, Shames DM, Schmid R. An expanded model of bilirubin kinetics: Effect of feeding, fasting, and phenobarbital in Gilbert's syndrome. J Pharmacokinet Biopharm 1976;4:115.

Martin JF, Vierling JM, Wolkoff AW, et al. Abnormal hepatic transport of indocyanine green in Gilbert's syndrome. Gastroenterology 1976;70:385.

Odell GB, Childs B. Hereditary hyperbilirubinemias. Prog Med Genet 1980;4:103.

Schmid R. Gilbert's syndrome: A legitimate genetic anomaly? N Engl J Med 1995;333:1217.

CHAPTER 19–75

Acute Viral Hepatitis

David J. Clain, M.D.

DEFINITION

Viral hepatitis is an acute infection that causes diffuse inflammation of the liver and necrosis of hepatocytes, usually with malaise and jaundice.

ETIOLOGY

Clinical attacks of acute viral hepatitis in the United States are due mainly to virus A, B, or C. Hepatitis A is usually spread by fecal contamination of hands and runs a self-limited, rarely fatal course. Hepatitis B and C are parenterally transmitted and often become chronic. Hepatitis D occurs only in patients with hepatitis B. Hepatitis E is enterically spread and is not endemic to North America. These are the five types of hepatotrophic viruses. Epstein–Barr virus (infectious mononucleosis), cytomegalovirus, and herpes simplex virus are infections that occasionally involve the liver, preferentially or as part of a disseminated process. Several other common viruses spread to the liver on rare occasions.

CRITERIA FOR DIAGNOSIS

Suggestive

The mildest attacks of viral hepatitis are asymptomatic and are recognized only if transaminases are measured because of an epidemic, outbreak in an institution, or common-source exposure, such as contaminated food. Patients with anicteric hepatitis may have loss of appetite, general malaise, and nausea, but in the absence of jaundice, the significance of these symptoms may not be suspected unless there has been recent travel to an endemic area or there are close contacts with jaundice. Most often, viral hepatitis is suggested by the typical, febrile prodrome followed by dark urine, pale stool, and the rapid evolution of jaundice (see Clinical Manifestations).

Definitive

The presence of acute hepatitis is confirmed by a rise in transaminases more than 10 times the upper limit of normal. The history helps in excluding other causes of hepatitis such as drugs. Serology is essential for a definitive diagnosis of viral hepatitis. The presence of immunoglobulin (Ig)M antibody establishes recent infection with hepatitis A (anti-HAV IgM), hepatitis B (anti-HBc IgM) and hepatitis D (anti-D IgM). See a further discussion under Diagnostic Options. The second genera-

tion of tests for hepatitis C usually shows hepatitis C virus antibodies on clinical presentation. Hepatitis E has not been acquired in the United States. Travelers from developing countries can be tested for IgM antibodies to hepatitis E virus. Radiologic imaging and needle biopsy seldom contribute to the diagnosis of acute viral hepatitis.

CLINICAL MANIFESTATION

Subjective

In the typical, full-blown picture of acute viral hepatitis, patients have a gradual onset of malaise often with influenza-like body aches and fever, followed by gastrointestinal symptoms such as loss of appetite, distaste for food, and occasionally diarrhea. Fever is usually mild, sometimes high, rarely with shaking chills. The prodrome may last from days to weeks. Jaundice is preceded by dark urine and pale stools. The yellowness of skin and sclerae develops rapidly. Aching in the right upper quadrant is common. Nausea may be intense to the point of vomiting. Protracted vomiting is ominous and may herald a fulminant course. Less severe infection is common, especially in children with hepatitis A, and is described under Criteria for Diagnosis, Suggestive.

The epidemiology of viral hepatitis is often reflected in the history. Hepatitis A is common in crowded, unhygienic conditions, and often contracted by travelers or military personnel from a low-incidence area, visiting developing countries. An infected cook can cause an outbreak in a group of diners. Shellfish may be contaminated by sewage. Hepatitis B is most frequent in sexually active women and men, both straight and gay. Infected needles are common sources for hepatitis B and C. Hepatitis B has been associated with automatic finger-stick devices. Blood transfusion has been a very uncommon source since careful screening of donors, especially for hepatitis C, since 1990. Immunosuppression from chemotherapy, chronic dialysis for renal failure, or AIDS is a risk for the personnel providing care as well as the patients.

Objective

Physical Examination

There are no specific viral features. Acute hepatitis is accompanied by variable jaundice and tenderness of the liver. There is mild hepatomegaly, usually with a palpable edge. The spleen is sometimes enlarged. During the prodrome, angioedema, urticarial skin lesions, and joint swellings may occur due to circulating immune complexes usually associated with hepatitis B.

Routine Laboratory Abnormalities

Urine. Bilirubin and excess urobilin appear in the urine before clinical jaundice.

Feces. Stools become light in color at the onset of jaundice due to cholestasis. Recovery is heralded by the return of normal color.

Hematology. There is often a depression of the total white blood count, frequently with granulocytopenia and a relative lymphocytosis. Atypical lymphocytes may be seen. Leukocytosis is unusual and points either to another cause of jaundice, such as cholangitis or Weil's disease, or to very severe viral hepatitis with submassive necrosis.

Liver Function Tests. Serum transaminases are markedly increased, usually more than 10 times, often 20 times, normal at the onset of acute hepatitis. The alanine transaminase (ALT) level is generally higher than the asparate transaminase (AST) level. The height of the ALT does not predict outcome. Much lower levels are present later, even if jaundice persists; however, slightly abnormal values may persist for many months despite clearance of virus. ALT is valuable in screening asymptomatic contacts.

The total serum bilirubin is variable. Levels range from normal (anicteric hepatitis) to deep jaundice, occasionally exceeding 15 mg/dL. A high bilirubin predicts a longer course. The proportion of direct bilirubin has no clinical significance. The serum alkaline phosphatase is normal or mildly elevated, seldom exceeding three times normal unless the course is complicated by prolonged cholestasis. Serum albumin does not become abnormal unless the course is severe and prolonged, reflecting maintenance of synthetic function and the long half-life of albumin.

PLANS
Diagnostic
Differential Diagnosis

The diagnosis of acute viral hepatitis is determined easily once suspected. The differential diagnosis can be divided into three problems (Table 19–75–1).

Clinical Presentation with Jaundice and Abnormal Liver Function Tests Indicating Acute Hepatitis. Acute hepatitis due to hepatotrophic viruses (A to E) must be distinguished from other viruses such as infectious mononucleosis and cytomegalovirus; Weil's disease; and noninfectious jaundice

due to drugs, toxins, herbs, mushrooms, alcohol, ischemia, and acute passage of gallstones.

Anicteric Hepatitis with Nonspecific "Influenzal" and Digestive Symptoms. This may be mistaken for a range of viral disease or gastroenteritis. There are rare cases that present as aplastic anemia or acute renal failure. Urticaria, angioedema, and maculopapular rashes can appear during the prodrome, especially in hepatitis B.

Cholestatic Jaundice. Intrahepatic causes, such as drugs and sclerosing cholangitis, and major duct obstructions (e.g., by cancer, stones, strictures, and chronic pancreatitis) must be excluded (see Chapter 19–70).

Diagnostic Options
Viral Serology. See Table 19–75–2.

Radiology. Ultrasound distinguishes major bile duct obstruction from cholestatic hepatitis by the presence of dilated ducts.

Liver Biopsy. Liver biopsy is rarely indicated. It may be helpful in protracted, serologically negative, hepatitis and in the investigation of cholestatic jaundice (see Chapter 19–70).

Recommended Approach

Epidemiologic and symptomatic criteria suggest the diagnosis of acute viral hepatitis. They are supported by the findings of jaundice, tender hepatomegaly, and bilirubinuria. An elevated ALT confirms the presence of acute hepatitis. Under Clinical Manifestations, special subjective and objective features are described that point to specific viruses. Serologic tests are essential for diagnosis.

If the markers of acute viral hepatitis are absent, other causes, especially infectious mononucleosis and drug reactions, should be considered. The enzyme-linked immunosorbent assay (ELISA) for the antibody to hepatitis C virus is occasionally negative at first presentation. Non-A, non-B, and non-C hepatitis (hepatitis "F") accounts for a small percentage of posttransfusional hepatitis and of community-acquired infections, especially in older patients.

TABLE 19–75–1. DIFFERENTIAL DIAGNOSIS OF ACUTE VIRAL HEPATITIS: THREE COMMON CLINICAL PRESENTATIONS

Problem	Causes
Anicteric hepatitis	Viral hepatitis
	Other acute viral illness
	General infections
	Gastroenteritis
Acute Icteric Hepatitis	
Viral	
Primary hepatotrophic	A,B,C,D,E
Systemic	Infectious mononucleosis (Epstein–Barr virus)
	Cytomegalovirus
Bacterial	Weil's disease
Noninfectious	Drugs, toxins, herbs. mushrooms
	Gallstones
	Ischemia
	"Acute" autoimmune
Cholestatic jaundice	
Intrahepatic	Viral hepatitis
	Drugs
	Sclerosing cholangitis
Major bile ducts	Stones
	Strictures
	Cancer
	Pancreatitis
	Choledochal cyst

TABLE 19–75–2. VIRAL SEROLOGY

Test	Diagnosis
Hepatitis A	
IgM anti-HAV	Acute hepatitis A
Hepatitis B	
HBsAg	Acute hepatitis B or Chronic hepatitis B
IgM anti-HBc (high titer)	Acute hepatitis B
Hepatitis C	
Anti-HCV	Acute or chronic hepatitis C
Hepatitis D	
IgM anti-delta (with low-titer IgG)	Acute hepatitis D
IgM anti-delta (with high-titer IgG)	Chronic hepatitis D
Hepatitis E	
Anti-HEV IgM	Acute hepatitis E
Infectious mononucleosis	
Monospot test	Infectious mononucleosis
IgM to Epstein–Barr virus (Capsid)	Infectious mononucleosis
CMV	
Isolation of CMV from urine	CMV
IgM anti-CMV	CMV
Weil's disease	
Spirochetes on blood film	Weil's disease
IgM-specific enzyme-linked immunosorbent assay	

Ig, Immunoglobulin; anti-HAV, antibody to hepatitis A virus; HBsAg, hepatitis B surface antigen; anti-HBc, antibody to hepatitis B core antigen; HCV, hepatitis C virus; anti-delta, antibody to delta antigen; HEV, hepatitis E virus; CMV, cytomegalovirus.

Therapeutic

Therapeutic Options

There are no specific treatments for acute hepatitis types A to E. Cytomegalovirus hepatitis in immunosuppressed patients can be treated with intravenous ganciclovir.

Prophylaxis of susceptible contacts is discussed under Prevention.

A fulminant course requires emergency management in a specialized unit with access to transplantation.

Recommended Approach

Viral hepatitis is potentially fatal, may progress to submassive necrosis, and can relapse after recovery. Types B, C, and D ofen become chronic. There should be a serious approach to rest and good nutrition, although rigid confinement to bed and restricted diets have not been shown to reduce complications. The diet should be palatable and high in calories. Convalescence should continue until appetite has returned, fatigue has lifted, and bilirubin is near normal. Pain over the liver and extreme lack of energy on returning to work are common after hepatitis in adults. Patients should be strongly reassured if tests are satisfactory, especially after type A. Persistence of abnormalities may require liver biopsy, but only after 6 months of observation.

FOLLOW-UP

Uncomplicated viral hepatitis is generally treated at home. Clinical progress and liver function tests should be reviewed weekly until symptoms improve and bilirubin begins to decline. A fall in ALT has no prognostic significance. The development of prolonged cholestasis or relapse in convalescence will be obvious; however, a fulminant course may develop rapidly. Warning features are persistent vomiting, drowsiness, and a progressively increasing prothrombin time more than 4 seconds above control.

DISCUSSION

Prevalence and Incidence

Five viruses account for 95% of acute viral hepatitis in the United States. One third are hepatitis A, 40% hepatitis B, and 20% hepatitis C. Acute hepatitis D is rare, and is either a superinfection in a hepatitis B carrier or a coinfection with hepatitis B, usually in injection drug users. A few cases of hepatitis E have been reported in travelers returning from Africa, Asia, and Mexico.

Hygiene and socioeconomic factors strongly influence the prevalence of hepatitis A, which varies widely throughout the world. Antibody studies show a 100% exposure by the age of 10 in developing countries and as low as 10% in some Western nations. The overall prevalence in the U.S. population is 33%. Acquisition of acute hepatitis B is closely related to the prevalence of the chronic carrier state. In the United States, carriers constitute 0.3% of the population and the peak incidence is in the third decade. An estimated 200,000 new hepatitis B virus infections have occurred annually in the United States over the past 10 years. In some parts of Africa and Asia, carrier rates exceed 8% and new infection is most frequent in young children.

The prevalence of antibodies to hepatitis C is ±1% depending on age, socioeconomic status, and other factors. Chronic hepatitis C is present in 90% of asymptomatic blood donors with confirmed positive hepatitis C virus antibodies. An estimated 150,000 new cases of hepatitis C occur annually in the United States.

Related Basic Science

Hepatitis A

Hepatitis A virus (HAV) is an RNA virus that can be grown in human cell cultures. Propagation in diploid cells has provided material for vaccines. Vaccine-induced antibodies are different from natural antibody but highly protective. Virus replicates in the cytoplasm of hepatocytes, passes directly into bile, and is shed in the feces. Fecal virus declines after the appearance of clinical hepatitis. Viremia during the prodrome causes rare transmission by blood and needles. The IgM antibody to HAV appears early, is present before jaundice, and may persist for 9 months. The IgG antibody is long-standing and provides immunity against reinfection.

Hepatitis B

Hepatitis B virus (HBV) is a DNA virus and replicates by mechanisms similar to those of retroviruses. HBV is not directly cytopathic to hepatocytes. HBV peptides are expressed on the surface of the liver cell adjacent to HLA class 1 proteins. Cell necrosis occurs as a result of cytotoxic T cells, which recognize and attach to this complex. The genome of HBV has a circular form with overlapping reading frames that code for several polypeptides, including surface antigen and core antigen. A part of the core gene codes for hepatitis B e antigen (HBeAg), which correlates with replication, infectivity, and circulating HBV DNA. A single mutation of a stop codon leads to absence of HBeAg. Several mutations of the HBV genome have been described that may be important in modifying behavior of the virus with respect to fulminant hepatitis and the development of liver cell cancer.

Figure 19–75–1 shows the typical course of acute hepatitis B. Markers of infection—hepatitis B surface antigen (HBsAg), HBV DNA, and HBeAg—are present well before the rise in ALT and the appearance of IgM antibody to hepatitis B core antigen (anti-HBc). The loss of HBeAg usually predicts viral clearance and a self-limited infection. Conversely, persistence of HBeAg and HBsAg beyond 6 months indicates a carrier state with chronic infection. Clearance of virus is accompanied by a rise in antibody to HBsAg (anti-HBs), which is a neutralizing antibody providing immunity. There is no window between the disappearance of HBsAg and the appearance of anti-HBs using sensitive tests.

Hepatitis C

The genome of hepatitis C virus (HCV) has been cloned and sequenced although only tentatively identified by electron microscopy. The virus replicates in vitro in human T- and B-cell lines. Several HCV genotypes are recognized that vary in clinical severity and respond differently to therapy. Genotyping will be of great value in prognosis and management, but currently remains a research method. The immunoassays to detect antibodies to HCV (anti-HCV) employ a series of recombinant antigens. The second-generation enzyme-linked immunosorbent assay includes both structural and nonstructural proteins and is used as a diagnostic test and for screening blood donors. The recombinant immunoblot assay (RIBA) is a four-antigen confirmatory test. None of the antibodies detected by these tests has a protective value.

Hepatitis C virus RNA is the earliest marker of acute hepatitis C. The second-generation test for anti-HCV is more sensitive and specific than

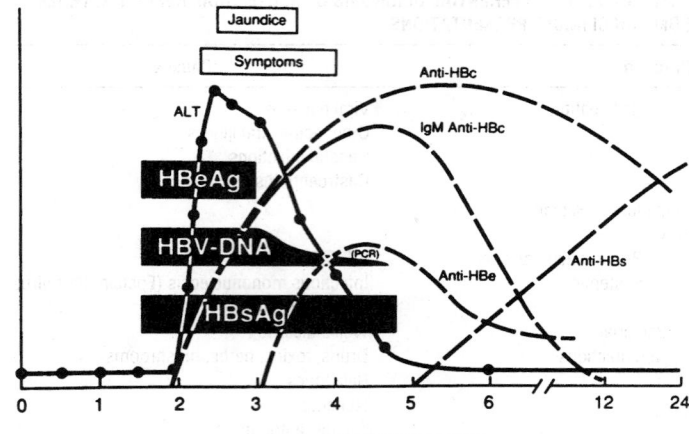

Figure 19–75–1. Course of acute hepatitis B. Initially, hepatitis B virus can be detected by blot hybridization but as the disease resolves only low levels detectable by polymerase chain reaction can be detected. ALT, alanine transaminase; HBsAg, hepatitis B surface antigen; HBeAg, hepatitis B e antigen; HBV-DNA, hepatitis B virus deoxyribonucleic acid; anti-HBc, antibody to hepatitis B core antigen; anti-HBe, antibody to HBeAg; anti-HBs, antibody to HBsAg; PCR, polymerase chain reaction. *(Source: From Hoofnagle JH, Bisceglie A. Serological diagnosis of acute and chronic viral hepatitis. Semin Liver Dis 1991;11:75. Reproduced with permission from the publisher and author.)*

the first, and is usually positive when ALT peaks. Anti-HCV remains positive after full resolution of an acute infection and also in chronic hepatitis. Return of ALT to normal is often misleading because transaminase levels may fluctuate widely over long periods. Recent studies of HCV RNA by the polymerase chain reaction indicate a much higher rate of chronicity, perhaps 80% after acute hepatitis C.

Hepatitis D

Hepatitis D virus (HDV) is a defective RNA virus that requires HBV for expression and infection. Figure 19–75–2 shows the typical course of acute delta hepatitis coinfection with HBV. HDV RNA and HBV RNA are present before the rise in ALT. Anti-HBs rises with clearance of viremia and antigenemia. There is no HDV equivalent of anti-HBs. IgM anti-HDV appears a few days or weeks after the onset.

Natural History and Its Modification with Treatment

Hepatitis A

Hepatitis A generally runs a benign course to full recovery. Rarely, hepatitis A may initiate autoimmune hepatitis in the presence of inherited immune dysfunction. The reponse to infection varies with age. Eighty percent of adults are jaundiced, but in young children 95% of cases go unrecognized. Fulminant disease with death is rare and occurs mainly in older patients. Unusual complications are a relapse of hepatitis during convalescence and the development of prolonged cholestasis. Cholestatic hepatitis may last from weeks to months and is often accompanied by pruritus, weight loss, and steatorrhea.

Hepatitis B

About 95% of adults recover completely from acute hepatitis B. From 1 to 10% develop chronic disease. In areas of high endemicity where infection of neonates and young children is common, 80% become chronic carriers, perpetuating a cycle of chronic infection. Hepatitis B is the most important cause of fulminant hepatitis. Intensive treatment has modified the outcome, but even with the improved survival of transplantation, the mortality exceeds 60%.

Hepatitis C

Hepatitis C is the most insidious of the viruses. Most acute infections, whether from contaminated needles, blood transfusion (now largely historic), or acquired in the community, are inapparent or mild. Virtually none has a protracted or severe, acute illness. A fulminant course is very rare; however, it is now apparent that in the majority of acute infections with type C, virus is not cleared, and a chronic course follows in about 80% of cases. About one fifth later develop cirrhosis, some

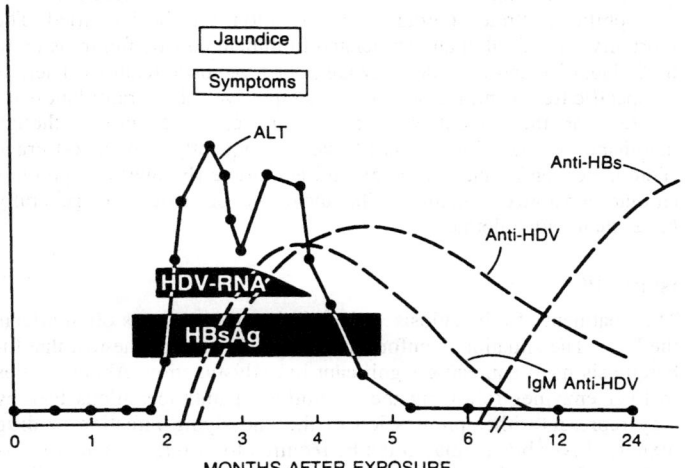

Figure 19–75–2. Course of acute delta hepatitis coinfection. ALT, alanine transaminase; HBsAg, hepatitis B surface antigen; HDV-RNA, hepatitis delta virus ribonucleic acid; anti-HDV, antibody to HDV; anti-HBs, antibody to HBsAg. *(Source: From Hoofnagle JH, Bisceglie A. Serological diagnosis of acute and chronic viral hepatitis. Semin Liver Dis 1991;11:79. Reproduced with permission from the publisher and author.)*

with decompensation of function that leads to liver transplantation. Hepatitis C in also an important cause of liver cell cancer.

There is now evidence that antiviral treatment of acute hepatitis C with interferon enhances clearance of the virus. As acute infections are seldom identified, this will have little impact on the overall incidence of chronicity. There are conflicting reports of the transmission of the virus sexually and from infected mothers to infants. Recent studies have shown the importance of a high viral titer in transmission in these low-risk situations. When titer is low, transmission is rare.

Hepatitis D

The hepatitis D virus is defective and is dependent on HBV for transmission. Infection of the two viruses may occur together (coinfection) and is often fulminant. Coinfection is usually self-limiting. Acquisition of HDV by a chronic carrier of HBV (superinfection) results in a severe exacerbation of hepatitis with an aggressive course. Hepatitis D is spread by blood products and needles, and community surveys show that antibodies are most frequent in injection drug users and hemophiliacs.

Hepatitis E

Hepatitis E is an enteric virus responsible for sporadic hepatitis and waterborne outbreaks in Asia, Mexico, and South America. No cases have arisen in the United States but there have been reports of infection in travelers and visitors. A fatality rate of 15 to 25% has been reported in pregnancy. Chronic infections do not occur.

Prevention

Hepatitis A

Prophylaxis with immune serum globulin should be recommended to all household and intimate contacts of patients with hepatitis A. Enteric infections are spread easily in schools and institutions for young children and the mentally handicapped. Outbreaks can be controlled by preventive doses of immune globulin. The dosage is 0.02 mL/kg, and immunity lasts about 3 months.

Active immunization with an inactivated hepatitis A vaccine (Havrix) has recently been approved and should be used for preexposure prophylaxis. Eighty to ninety-eight percent of vaccinees seroconvert by day 15. A booster should be given at 6 to 12 months. The vaccine is indicated for use in travelers to areas of high endemicity, military personnel going abroad, employees of daycare centers, and some institutional workers.

Hepatitis B

Sexual contacts of patients with acute hepatitis B should receive prophylaxis with a combination of hepatitis B immune globulin (HBIG) and hepatitis B vaccine. Vaccination for household and casual contacts is not recommended in the acute setting. Hepatitis B vaccine should be given to both intimate and household contacts of chronic carriers to prevent acute hepatitis. Two recombinant vaccines are available in the United States. The usual schedule is 20 μg in 1 mL at 0, 1, and 6 months. Universal vaccination of infants and of adolescents at age 11 is now recommended by the U.S. Public Health Service.

Hepatitis C

Anti-HCV antibody does not appear to be protective. Trials of immune serum globulin before transfusion have given conflicting results. Immune globulin prophylaxis is not recommended in the United States. No hepatitis C vaccine has been developed.

Hepatitis D

Hepatitis D is not pathogenic in the absence of hepatitis B. Therefore, hepatitis D can be prevented by immunizing against hepatitis B. There is no hepatitis D hyperimmune globulin or vaccine. Chronic carriers of hepatitis B can be protected against hepatitis D only by avoiding high-risk exposure, such as shared needles, and by practicing safe sex.

Cost Containment

Hepatitis A and hepatitis B are preventable by vaccination. The indications for vaccination are described in the section on Prevention. The public should also be informed about prevention by modifying behavior in high risk situations such as travel outside the United States, sexual contact with new partners, and use of drugs by injection. For serological diagnosis of acute viral hepatitis it is usually necessary only to test for hepatitis B surface antigen, IgM antibody to hepatitis B core, IgM antibody to hepatitis A virus, and hepatitis C virus antibody. Epidemiological information may point to hepatitis A, B, or C, and a single test may be appropriate in the first instance.

REFERENCES

Alter MJ, Margolis HS, Krawczynski K, et al. The natural history of community-acquired hepatitis C in the United States. N Engl J Med 1992;327:1899.

Centers for Disease Control and Prevention. Hepatitis E among US travelers, 1989–1992. MMWR 1993;42:1.
Centers for Disease Control. Public Health Service inter-agency guidelines for screening donors of blood, plasma, organs, tissues and semen for evidence of hepatitis B and hepatitis C. MMWR 1991;40(RR-4):1.
Gordon SG, Reddy KR, Schiff L, et al. Prolonged intrahepatic cholestasis secondary to acute hepatitis A. Ann Intern Med 1984;101:635.
Perrilo RP. Hepatitis B: Transmission and natural history. Gut 1994;34:S48.
Sjogren MH. Acute hepatitis A: An endangered species. Hepatology 1993;17:519.

CHAPTER 19–76

Drug-induced Hepatitis

Hillel Tobias, M.D., Ph.D., and Alex Sherman, M.D.

DEFINITION

Drug-induced hepatitis may be defined as the development of liver dysfunction secondary to the action of a drug or its metabolic products. The spectrum of drug-induced liver disease encompasses many patterns of injury including hepatocellular necrosis, cholestasis, fatty liver, hepatic fibrosis, "granulomatous hepatitis," vascular disorders, and hepatic tumors.

ETIOLOGY

Essentially all medications are potentially capable of producing some hepatic injury. Only a few, however, produce dysfunction with sufficient frequency and severity to be of clinical importance. A few of the prominent examples of drug-induced hepatitis are listed below to illustrate the range of clinical features that may be found.

ACETAMINOPHEN

Acetaminophen is a widely used and generally safe analgesic agent. Large doses of acetaminophen, however, can cause severe and potentially fatal hepatic toxicity. In Britain, acetaminophen is the most widely used agent for attempting suicide. Therapeutic doses may also cause significant hepatic toxicity, especially in patients who are metabolically susceptible. The clinical course of a patient with massive acetaminophen ingestion is characteristic. In the first several hours, the patient may develop nausea, vomiting, or diaphoresis. These initial symptoms are followed by a quiescent "latent" phase, lasting perhaps 24 hours, in which symptoms or signs of liver disease are absent. The latent period abruptly ends with the onset of acute hepatitis accompanied by nausea, vomiting, and right upper quadrant discomfort. Tender hepatomegaly is present. In severe cases, signs of liver failure, such as jaundice, asterixis, lethargy, and coma, are seen. Serum transaminases may be greatly elevated; aspartate and alanine transaminase values of 2000 to 7000 IU or greater are not uncommon. Elevations of serum bilirubin and prolongation of prothrombin time are seen in severe cases. Acute acetaminophen hepatic toxicity results in primarily centrilobular or diffuse hepatic necrosis.

Initially, acute acetaminophen overdose was associated with mortality of up to 25%. This figure has dropped, based both on increasing recognition of mild cases with good prognoses and the earlier recognition and more effective treatment of severe cases. Aggressive treatment of acetaminophen hepatitis must be started within 16 hours of ingestion and is based on the presumed mechanism of drug injury. N-Acetylcysteine (Mucomist), which increases hepatocyte stores of glutathione, is the agent of choice. Glutathione detoxifies toxic metabolic intermediates of acetaminophen. N-Acetylcysteine must be administered as early as possible, often before the diagnosis is secure. The diagnosis is based on a determination of a blood acetaminophen level and its position on a semilogarithmic plot of plasma concentration as a function of time from ingestion. With early treatment and supportive care, survival of acetaminophen overdose is greater than 90%. "Therapeutic" acetaminophen toxicity is also recognized; doses from 2 to 4 g/d may lead to hepatic injury, especially in patients with increased susceptibility, such as chronic alcoholics. Serum transaminase elevation in this latter group may be quite high, which is unusual for hepatitis due to alcohol alone.

Anesthetic Agents

Halothane, a previously widely used anesthetic agent, is a well-recognized hepatotoxin. Severe and fatal cases have been documented. Halothane hepatotoxicity is more common in women and in older and obese patients. The incidence of halothane hepatotoxicity is low, approximately 1 in 10,000 exposures. Increased risk among patients previously exposed and an association with fever and eosinophilia suggest an immunologically mediated mechanism. Halothane hepatitis may appear several days to 3 weeks after exposure. Fever usually heralds a bout of acute hepatitis with symptoms of nausea, vomiting, and anorexia. Subclinical illness may be manifested by elevations in serum transaminases. Many milder cases are subclinical and go unrecognized. Severe hepatotoxicity may produce symptoms, signs, or laboratory evidence of liver failure. Histologically, a pattern indistinguishable from that of acute viral hepatitis is seen. In some cases, necrosis (predominantly centrilobular) may be seen. Occasionally, significant esosinophilic infiltrate or granuloma formation may be identified. The mortality rate of halothane-associated fulminant hepatic failure is up to 80%. Jaundice and coagulopathy are poor prognostic features. There is no specific treatment; management is supportive. Liver transplant is indicated for the patient with fulminant hepatic failure. Although halothane is no longer used very frequently, methoxyflurane (Penthrane), enflurane (Ethrane), and isoflurane (Forane) can produce similar hepatotoxic pictures. The incidence of toxicity is generally lower than with halothane.

Isoniazid

The treatment of tuberculosis with antituberculous agents often affects the liver. The situation is unfortunately complicated by the fact that tuberculosis itself can cause significant liver dysfunction. Abnormalities in liver enzymes following the institution of antituberculous therapy may represent either progression of the underlying infection or drug toxicity. Liver biopsy may often be required to differentiate these possibilities. Isoniazid, the mainstay of tuberculosis treatment, is a well-established hepatotoxin. Two clinical patterns of isoniazid-associated hepatitis are encountered. The first is a mild, usually subclinical, and often transient elevation of serum transaminases occurring in about 10% of recipients of isoniazid. This usually disappears with continued treatment. The more important hepatotoxic pattern occurs in about 1%

of patients receiving the drug. This more severe reaction is age dependent: up to 2% of patients older than 50 receiving isoniazid may be affected. Isoniazid must be discontinued in these cases. Significant isoniazid-associated hepatitis usually develops within 2 months of beginning the medication. This results in an acute hepatitis-like injury. Clinical features resemble acute viral hepatitis. A broad range of severity is encountered. Severe cases may develop jaundice or overt liver failure. Histologic findings resemble those encountered with viral infection. Isoniazid administration may also cause a chronic hepatitis. There is no known treatment of isoniazid hepatitis besides discontinuance of the drug; treatment is entirely supportive. A mortality rate of 10% has been reported in jaundiced patients. Liver transplantation is necessary in very severe cases.

α-Methyldopa (Aldomet)

The older antihypertensive agent α-methyldopa can produce widespread hepatotoxicity, including acute and chronic hepatitis. Severity ranges from asymptomatic elevations of serum transaminases to massive hepatic necrosis and death from liver failure. Asymptomatic hepatitis is found in about 5% of patients on α-methyldopa therapy, beginning several weeks to months after the start of therapy. This subclinical toxicity may resolve despite continued administration of the drug. Overt clinical hepatitis occurs in less than 1% of patients and is more common in older, postmenopausal women. In most patients, complete recovery swiftly follows discontinuation of the drug. In up to 10%, massive hepatic necrosis resulting in liver failure ensues. Chronic liver disease from α-methyldopa may be indistinguishable from that due to other causes of chronic hepatitis. Discontinuation of the medication usually results in resolution of the chronic hepatitis, although recovery may be delayed. Cirrhosis has also been reported. Several features of α-methyldopa hepatotoxicity suggest an immune-mediated mechanism (i.e., the association of a positive Coombs' test and autoantibodies). This has not been definitely established. There is evidence of a role for a toxic drug metabolite in the generation of α-methyldopa hepatitis.

Phenytoin (Dilantin)

Phenytoin has been and remains the mainstay of anticonvulsant therapy. Almost all patients on phenytoin have elevated levels of alkaline phosphatase and γ-glutamyl transpeptidase, which persist as long as the drug is taken. Significant liver injury associated with the drug is infrequent but can lead to severe and fatal hepatitis. Women appear to be at a higher risk. An acute hepatitis may occur within 6 weeks of beginning the agent. Fever, rash, and lymphadenopathy are found in addition to typical symptoms of acute hepatitis. The generalized maculopapular rash may progress to exfoliation. Laboratory tests show marked elevation of serum transaminases, leukocytosis, and eosinophilia, as well as hyperbilirubinemia and prolongation of the prothrombin time in some cases. Signs of liver failure may ensue. The histologic picture is that of acute hepatocellular necrosis with eosinophilic infiltrate. Massive necrosis with centrilobular predominance occurs in severe cases. No specific treatment other than supportive treatment is available. Jaundiced patients with severe hepatitis have up to a 50% mortality rate. The mechanism of liver injury is complex; both immunologic and directly toxic mechanisms have been postulated. Liver transplantation is indicated in life-threatening cases.

Nitrofurantoin

The urinary antibiotic nitrofurantoin is a well-recognized cause of both acute and chronic hepatotoxicity. An acute hepatocellular hepatitis and an acute cholestatic pattern have been described. Of particular interest is the association of an illness resembling the syndrome of autoimmune chronic hepatitis. The chronic hepatitis generally develops in older women who have been taking the drug for months to years. Autoantibodies and hypergammaglobulinemia are present. Resolution after discontinuation of nitrofurantoin may be slow or incomplete; in some cases, cirrhosis has resulted. Some patients have been documented to carry the HLA-B8 antigen, which is also seen in the majority of patients with idiopathic autoimmune chronic hepatitis.

Tetracycline

Tetracycline causes predominantly microvesicular fatty liver, which may be fatal. Toxicity is strictly dose dependent. Doses greater than 2 g/d are potentially injurious. Pregnant patients and those with renal disease are at increased risk. Unlike other tetracyclines, doxycycline is metabolized exclusively in the liver and should be used cautiously in patients with liver disease. Minor degrees of transaminase elevations and minor fatty change may be seen in many patients on tetracycline. This is not clinically significant.

Methotrexate

Methotrexate is used in the treatment of severe psoriasis and rheumatic diseases. Patients usually receive the drug for prolonged periods, frequently many years. As with many agents, mildly elevated transaminase levels may occur transiently when therapy is begun. Sustained elevation is usually associated with the development of more serious potentially chronic liver disease. Liver lesions include hepatocellular necrosis, fatty liver, and fibrosis. Liver biopsy is essential to determine the extent of fibrosis. Early fibrosis may disappear after methotrexate is withdrawn. Continued methotrexate administration in the face of fibrosis leads to cirrhosis. Fibrosis may also be present in the face of normal liver function, hence the importance of liver biopsy in following these patients. Alcohol, diabetes, and obesity are increased risk factors.

Allopurinol

Allopurinol, widely used to treat hyperuricemia, may cause hepatotoxicity. The hepatic pathology may include granulomatous hepatitis, hepatocellular necrosis, and/or cholestasis. Clinically, abnormal liver function develops 1 to 6 weeks after starting therapy. Almost all patients are febrile and many have skin rashes. Mortality may be as high as 15%. Increased risk factors are advancing age, renal disease, and concurrent use of thiazide diuretics. The mechanism of liver injury is thought to be immunoallergic and corticosteroids appear to improve outcome in deteriorating cases, when the patient does not respond to drug withdrawal.

Estrogens

Estrogen replacement therapy and birth control pills may cause mild cholestasis in some patients. This rarely develops into jaundice. Prolonged administration is also associated with development of benign hepatic adenomas, which can bleed spontaneously intraabdominally.

Nonsteroidal Antiinflammatory Drugs

Aspirin, on prolonged administration to patients with connective tissue diseases, can cause mild to moderate hepatocellular liver dysfunction. Almost all nonsteroidal antiinflammatory drugs also cause hepatitis-like toxic injury to the liver. Sodium diclofenac (Voltaren) is potentially the most serious offender. Jaundice is not uncommon and fatal fulminant hepatitis has been reported.

Chlorpromazine

This antipsychotic agent generally produces a cholestatic pattern of hepatotoxicity. A few patients, however, develop a picture of hepatocellular necrosis; a mixed pattern may also result. The prognosis of chlorpromazine liver injury is generally good. Complete recovery within 12 months is the rule, but occasionally patients may develop a form of biliary cirrhosis.

CRITERIA FOR DIAGNOSIS
Suggestive

The consideration of drug-induced hepatitis is conceptually simple: any patient who develops clinical features of liver dysfunction and is receiving a medication should be suspected of having drug-induced toxicity. Consideration of a drug-mediated etiology is especially important in that treatment is direct—withdrawal of the offending agent; no other treatment will be effective as long as the offending drug is continued.

DEFINITIVE

There is generally no definite proof that a hepatotoxic reaction is due to the administration of a therapeutic agent. Circumstantial evidence, however, is often impressive and includes the onset of hepatic injury within weeks to months of beginning a new medication and the relatively rapid improvement of biochemical parameters once the agent is withdrawn. In unusual cases of drug-induced hepatitis, recovery may be delayed following discontinuation of the responsible medication; in such cases, liver biopsy may be required for diagnosis. In most such cases, however, hepatic histologic features are not specific and do not provide a definite diagnosis. Return of hepatic injury on rechallenge is the most conclusive test of drug-mediated toxicity, but should never be done, as the rechallenge liver injury may be severe and even fatal. Inadvertent rechallenge may be evaluated for a convincing cause–effect relationship between the drug and hepatic injury. Other causes of hepatocellular disease should be excluded; serologic evaluation for the presence of the hepatitis viruses is mandatory.

Clinical Manifestations

Subjective

Symptoms produced by drug-induced hepatitis are variable and depend on the severity of the toxicity and the particular agent involved. Asymptomatic subclinical illness may be a feature of mild hepatotoxicity. Signs and symptoms may be hepatocellular or cholestatic in nature depending on the offending agent. Overt clinical illness generally results in jaundice or symptoms of acute hepatitis with anorexia, nausea, vomiting, and right upper quadrant discomfort. More severe toxicity results in symptoms of liver failure including ascites, encephalopathy, and gastrointestinal hemorrhage. Symptoms associated with selective specific agents have been outlined above.

Women are more vulnerable to drug-induced hepatitis. Age may be a factor in certain toxicities. The incidence of halothane and isoniazid hepatitis increases with advancing age; conversely, hepatic reactions to aspirin and valproate occur more commonly in younger patients. Obesity increases the likelihood of halothane hepatitis, as does a history of previous exposure.

Genetically determined differences in the metabolism of toxic agents are important in the hepatic injury caused by certain medications. Genetic factors affecting susceptibility to halothane hepatitis have been proposed. The acetylation status of patients has been assumed to be important in the development of isoniazid injury. Chronic active hepatitis due to nitrofurantoin has been linked to the HLA-B8 genotype.

Objective

Physical Examination

Most cases of hepatic drug toxicity are recognized by laboratory tests and not physical findings; however, an enlarged tender liver may be apparent on physical examination in many patients with drug-mediated acute hepatitis. Jaundice, asterixis, ascites, lethargy, and coma are seen in severe toxicity. Fever, rash, and lymphadenopathy are distinctive features of phenytoin injury.

Routine Laboratory Abnormalities

Abnormalities of liver function may be hepatocellular or cholestatic in pattern. Elevation of serum transaminases is most commonly seen. The magnitude of this elevation is quite variable. Striking liver enzyme elevations are not uncommon. γ-Glutamyl transpeptidase and alkaline phosphatase elevations are most marked in phenothiazine hepatitis. Leukocytosis and eosinophilia are features of phenytoin hepatotoxicity. Elevation of serum transaminases for longer than 6 months defines chronic hepatitis as is seen in the nitrofurantoin-associated syndrome and chronic α-methyldopa or allopurinol hepatitis.

PLANS

Diagnostic

Differential Diagnosis

Drug-induced hepatitis often mimics acute viral disease. Alcoholic hepatitis and drug hepatitis may be confused, but serum transaminase elevations may be several orders of magnitude higher in drug-induced disease. Acetaminophen toxicity should be suspected in chronic alcoholic patients with unexpectedly high enzyme levels.

Diagnostic Options

Observation of response to withdrawal of the suspected hepatotoxin is usually the best diagnostic strategy. In a patient on multiple medications, it is often necessary to estimate the potential hepatotoxicities of several agents and withdraw those that are judged most likely to have contributed to the hepatitis. All drugs that are not critically necessary should be withdrawn. Resolution after withdrawal generally establishes the diagnosis of drug-induced hepatitis. A liver biopsy may be helpful, but is often difficult to interpret. Histologic features of viral hepatitis are often indistinguishable from those of drug-induced injury. Liver biopsy is indicated in patients whose recovery following discontinuation of the suspected hepatotoxin is delayed. Rechallenge provides the most definitive proof of drug-mediating hepatitis, but should not be tried because it places the patient at risk for fatal hepatotoxic reaction.

Recommended Approach

The administration of all suspected hepatotoxins must be stopped. Serologic markers for the hepatitis viruses are obtained, as are imaging studies to exclude focal lesions, infiltrates, and obstruction, especially in patients with cholestatic features. An improvement in serum transaminases is to be expected within 1 to 2 weeks of withdrawal of most hepatotoxic agents. Liver biopsy is reserved for cases of persistent live abnormalities despite the cessation of the suspected hepatotoxin.

Therapeutic

Therapeutic Options

In most cases of drug-induced hepatitis, no specific therapy is necessary or possible; resolution of liver injury rapidly follows discontinuation of the toxic agent. The treatment of acetaminophen toxicity is a significant exception. Treatment with N-acetylcysteine early in the course of toxicity is essential to avoid severe liver damage and improve overall mortality rate. Patients with severe hepatotoxicity and liver failure due to the action of any drug require intensive supportive care. An early referral to a center that has the capability for liver transplantation is indicated in cases of drug-induced hepatic failure. Liver transplantation is indicated in patients with progressive hepatic failure despite the discontinuation of the hepatotoxin.

Recommended Approach

Discontinuation of the offending agent is paramount; continuation of hepatotoxin will frustrate any other therapeutic efforts. The onset of deepening jaundice and liver failure are poor prognostic signs in most cases; their presence mandates an aggressive supportive approach and an expeditious referral to a liver transplantation center.

FOLLOW-UP

Most laboratory signs of liver dysfunction resolve within 3 months of cessation of the hepatotoxin. Once liver abnormalities resolve completely, no further follow-up is necessary. Recurring drug-induced damage without rechallenge does not occur. Chronic liver disease is not a usual feature of most drug-induced hepatitis; however, chronic hepatitis has been observed in some cases. If liver abnormalities do not resolve completely within several months, a liver biopsy should be performed for definite diagnosis.

DISCUSSION

Prevalence

Drug-related hepatic injury probably accounts for approximately 10% of cases of acute hepatitis; this figure may be 40% in patients over the age of 50. Drug-induced disease is a disproportionately prominent cause in patients with severe or chronic hepatic injury. One quarter of cases of permanent hepatic failure are due to hepatotoxins. From one quarter to two third of cases of chronic active hepatitis may be drug induced. In one study, 2% of jaundiced patients admitted to a general hospital had drug-related hepatic injury.

Related Basic Science

Drug-induced hepatotoxicity has traditionally been classified into predictable and unpredictable varieties. Predictable hepatotoxicity is generally dose related, can be reproduced in experimental animals, and is associated with a characteristic pattern of hepatocellular necrosis or cholestasis. Agents that cause predictable injury are thought to act through the intrinsic toxicity of the drug or its metabolites. Examples of these "direct hepatotoxins" include carbon tetrachloride and acetaminophen. Unpredictable or idiosyncratic reactions are more commonly encountered clinically. The hepatic lesion cannot be reproduced in experimental animals, nor is the toxicity dose related. A very small percentage (< 1%) of patients taking the drug develop hepatotoxicity. The presence of fever, rash, and eosinophilia in some cases of idiosyncratic reactions suggests a hypersensitivity-mediated mechanism (e.g., α-methyldopa hepatitis). In other instances, no evidence of drug allergy is apparent. Some drugs produce both dose-dependent and idiosyncratic toxicity (e.g., chlorpromazine). Much remains to be learned regarding the mechanism of most hepatic injuries.

The mechanism of acetaminophen hepatotoxicity has been the most extensively studied of the toxic reactions; the understanding of this molecular mechanism has led to an effective, rational mode of treatment. Acetaminophen is normally metabolized by glucuronidation or sulfation in the liver to a nontoxic metabolite. A small proportion of acetaminophen is converted by the cytochrome P450 enzyme system to a toxic metabolite; this toxic mediator can eventually bind to cell macromolecules, a process that can ultimately lead to cell death. The amount of acetaminophen substrate has a direct bearing on the amount of toxic metabolite produced; a massive quantity of acetaminophen will overwhelm normal metabolism and lead to toxin formation. The activity of the cytochrome P450 system is a determinant in this process; activation of the P450 metabolic pathway by stimulators such as alcohol and barbiturates results in the formation of more toxic metabolites.

The hepatocyte has a well-developed protective mechanism. Toxic metabolites produced by the cytochrome P450 system may bind to thiol groups on cell proteins. To "scavenge" these reactive metabolytes, a system involving glutathione is operative. The glutathione S-transferase enzymes facilitate binding of these toxins and prevent their covalent binding to critical cell macromolecules. When the glutathione within the hepatocyte is totally consumed, excess toxic metabolites accumulate. In the case of acetaminophen, massive ingestion leads to the accumulation of a toxic quinoneimine. Glutathione is used up and binding of the toxic product to macromolecules commences, leading to cell death. Replenishment of glutathione stores is a logical strategy for diminishing the hepatotoxicity of acetaminophen. Therapeutically administered N-acetylcysteine is taken up by the hepatocytes and the cysteine moiety drives glutathione synthesis. The glutathione produced detoxifies the reactive intermediate. Understanding of the acetaminophen hepatic toxicity mechanism also explains the particular susceptibility of the alcoholic to toxicity: ethanol stimulates the activity of the cytochrome P450 system and encourages production of the toxic metabolite with only modest acetaminophen intake.

Natural History and Its Modification with Treatment

The natural history of drug-induced hepatotoxicity is continued hepatitis until the hepatotoxic reaction is recognized and drug is withdrawn. This generally constitutes effective treatment and results in the rapid resolution of liver enzyme abnormalities. If no resolution has occurred within several months of drug withdrawal, alternative explanations may be considered. Adverse prognostic features include deepening jaundice, encephalopathy, and a prolonged prothrombin time. A dramatic improvement in prognosis is made possible by the performance of liver transplantation when progressive hepatic failure is evident. In some cases toxic drug injury may cause chronic hepatitis, permanent hepatic fibrosis, or cirrhosis when the drug is continued or even after it is discontinued.

PREVENTION

The awareness of the potential for hepatotoxicity of any medicinal agent is the key to the prevention of drug-induced liver injury. Heightened awareness of this entity also leads to early recognition of this adverse reaction when it occurs. The chronic alcoholic patient should be cautioned regarding the therapeutic use of acetaminophen. Repeated exposure to halothane should be avoided.

Cost Containment

Neither the diagnosis nor the therapy of drug-induced liver injury is expensive. Of absolute necessity is the serial determination of serum transaminases levels and other parameters of hepatic function and serologic tests to exclude viral hepatitis. Hepatic imaging is often useful, especially in patients with cholestatic features. Liver biopsy may be helpful in selected cases, when toxicity fails to disappear following withdrawal of the offending agent.

REFERENCES

Farrel GC. Drug-induced liver disease. New York: Churchill Livingstone, 1994.

Lee W. Drug–induced hepatotoxicity. N Engl J Med 1995;333:1118.

Maddrey WC. Toxic and drug induced hepatitis. In: Schiff L, Schiff ER, eds. Diseases of the liver. 7th ed. Philadelphia: Lippincott, 1993:707.

Ischemic Hepatitis

Alex Sherman, M.D., and Hillel Tobias, M.D., Ph.D.

DEFINITION

Ischemic hepatitis, also called "shock liver," is a distinctive clinical syndrome resulting from an acute decrease in hepatic perfusion. It is characterized by a transient, often marked, elevation in serum transaminase levels and centrilobular (zone 3) hepatocyte necrosis on liver biopsy.

ETIOLOGY

Ischemic hepatitis results from an acute decrease in hepatic blood flow and resultant hepatocyte hypoxia. Any condition that results in systemic hypotension may result in ischemic hepatitis. Cardiac causes are especially frequent and include acute myocardial infarction, congestive heart failure, cardiomyopathy, arrhythmias, constrictive pericarditis, and cardiac tamponade. Septic shock is a common noncardiogenic cause. Conditions that produce severe hypoxemia without hypotension, such as massive pulmonary emboli and severe pulmonary disease, may also result in hepatic ischemia. Hypovolemic shock, such as that resulting from acute blood loss or severe dehydration, is a well-recognized cause. Finally, the loss of intravascular fluid into "third spaces" with resulting hypotension, as in peritonitis and pancreatitis, may result in this syndrome.

CRITERIA FOR DIAGNOSIS

Suggestive

A rapid, marked elevation in serum transaminases in a clinical setting of acute hypoperfusion of the liver should raise the suspicion of ischemic hepatitis. The rapid normalization of "liver function tests" in the absence of further ischemic insult is further evidence of this syndrome. The lack of an alternative explanation for elevated liver enzymes is necessary for the diagnosis.

Definitive

Ischemic hepatitis is a distinctive clinical syndrome and its diagnosis can generally be made without a liver biopsy. In cases of diagnostic uncertainty, a liver biopsy provides a definitive diagnosis. Centrilobular (zone 3) hepatocellular necrosis is characteristic. Hemorrhage, sinusoidal dilation, and bile stasis may be seen. In more severe cases, midzonal hepatocellular necrosis may be seen as well. The reticulin framework of the hepatic lobule is preserved, even in areas of severe hepatocyte necrosis.

CLINICAL MANIFESTATIONS

Subjective

Symptoms related to the systemic cause of the hepatic ischemia generally dominate the clinical picture. Symptoms specific for hepatic disease, when present, are generally mild and nonspecific. Patients may complain of anorexia, nausea, vomiting, or right upper quadrant discomfort. Mild jaundice may be seen in 40% of patients. Rarely, fulminant hepatic failure is seen, with deep jaundice and encephalopathy.

The presence of systemic disorders that are capable of causing hepatic hypoperfusion or liver hypoxia is considered a prerequisite for this syndrome; however, the episode of "shock" producing the hepatic ischemia may be transient or inapparent. This accounts for cases of "shock liver" obstensibly without "shock"; up to 50 to 70% of cases of ischemic hepatitis reported in the literature are not associated with documented systemic hypotension. Conversely, severe systemic hypotension may occur without the development of hepatic ischemia; the liver is relatively resistant to ischemia due to its unique dual blood supply.

Objective

Physical Examination

Hepatomegaly, which may be tender, is seen in up to 95% of cases. Rarely, hepatic failure may result in asterixis, lethargy, or coma.

Routine Laboratory Abnormalities

Striking elevations in serum transaminase levels are the sine qua non of ischemic hepatitis. Transaminase levels rise suddenly, usually within 1 to 2 days of a recognized cause of hypoperfusion. Levels of the liver enzymes may rise up to 100 times normal, with values of 500 to 1000 IU/L or greater commonly seen. A dramatic decline in serum transaminase levels is also characteristic; they generally fall rapidly toward normal within 3 to 7 days of the onset of hepatitis. Elevations of serum lactate dehydrogenase may follow a similar time course. Serum bilirubin may be modestly elevated; typically, the total serum bilirubin value is less than 5 mg/dL. The serum alkaline phosphatase level is usually either normal or minimally elevated. Prolongation of the prothrombin time is commonly seen. Recovery of the serum bilirubin and prothrombin time may lag behind recovery in serum transaminase levels.

PLANS

Diagnostic

Differential Diagnosis

Ischemic hepatitis is a diagnosis of exclusion; other causes of acute hepatic necrosis need to be eliminated from consideration. In particular, viral hepatitis associated with hepatitis A virus (HAV), hepatitis B virus (HBV), and hepatitis C virus (HCV) should be excluded by appropriate serologic tests. Drug-induced hepatitis should be considered in all cases; medications suspected of contributing to hepatocyte necrosis should be discontinued if possible. The passage of a gallstone from the gallbladder into the duodenum may be associated with striking transient elevations in serum transaminase levels. Acute pancreatitis may also be associated with this sequence. Prominent right upper quadrant pain is usually associated with the passage of a gallstone. An abdominal ultrasound may show evidence of gallbladder or biliary tract inflammation and should be obtained in all cases of suspected ischemic hepatitis.

Cardiac failure can affect the liver in one of two ways. Ischemic hepatitis is the result of failure of "forward flow"; left-sided heart failure results in decreased hepatic perfusion. Right-sided heart failure, on the other hand, characteristically results in "backward flow" derangement, that is, passive congestion of the liver. The histopathology of hepatic congestion is distinctive. Central venous congestion is prominent. The hepatic sinusoids are dilated and congested; pressure necrosis and atrophy of perisinusoidal hepatocytes is seen. In long-standing passive congestion, hepatic fibrosis may ensue and eventually progress to a stage of chronic liver disease, so-called *cardiac cirrhosis*. The syndromes of ischemic hepatitis and passive congestion are generally distinct; however, they can coexist. Some authorities theorize that passive congestion may predispose to the development of ischemic hepatitis.

Diagnostic Options

The clinical picture generally suggests the proper diagnosis. As mentioned, viral, drug-induced, and gallstone-associated hepatitis need to be considered and ruled out. A hepatic imaging test should be performed in essentially all cases. Liver biopsy is rarely required.

Recommended Approach

Time generally clarifies the diagnosis of ischemic hepatitis. The temporal course of serum transaminase levels is striking in its onset and normalization. A dramatic recovery in transaminase values is generally apparent within a week of onset. Alternative explanations for hepatitis should be excluded. In cases of diagnostic uncertainty, or in the rare instance of fulminant hepatic failure, a liver biopsy should be obtained. In the case of hepatic failure, a liver transplantation must be considered.

Therapeutic

Therapeutic Options

No specific therapy for the hepatic derangements are possible or necessary. Correction of the underlying cause of the hepatic ischemia or hypoxia is all that is generally required. Normalization of serum transaminase levels occurs rapidly. Chronic liver disease is not a sequela. The rare case of fulminant ischemic hepatitis is treated as is any other case of hepatic failure. Supportive therapy includes treatment of ascites, encephalopathy, or esophageal variceal hemorrhage. Liver transplantation must be considered if fulminant hepatic failure is evident.

Recommended Approach

Once the diagnosis of ischemic hepatitis is made, the focus of management should be correction of underlying circulatory disturbance. Liver biopsy is rarely necessary.

FOLLOW-UP

Daily measurement of serum transaminase levels for the first 1 to 2 weeks after onset of liver abnormalities is optimal. As no chronic liver disease results, once liver chemistries normalize, no additional follow-up is necessary.

DISCUSSION

Prevalence

Despite the fact that cardiac failure, shock, and hypoxemia are relatively common clinical occurrences, "shock liver" is relatively rare. This is likely due to the fact that the liver is fortunate in having a dual blood supply; deprivation of one supply may lead to a compensatory increase in blood flow through the other vessel. Among patients with acute myocardial infarction, the prevalence of "shock liver" is less than 1%; the prevalence of elevated transaminase levels in patients with severe life-threatening hemorrhage has been reported to be less than 3%. The older population is particularly susceptible to ischemic hepatitis; this is due to the higher prevalence of cardiovascular and pulmonary predisposing conditions in the elderly.

Related Basic Science

Pathophysiology

The liver receives its blood via two sources: fully oxygenated, high-pressure systemic blood arrives via the high-resistance hepatic artery, and partially oxygenated, low-pressure blood is supplied by the low-resistance portal vein. In normal circumstances, the liver receives two thirds of its blood from the portal circulation; the hepatic artery supplies the remainder. There is a reciprocal relationship between the blood supplied by the hepatic artery and portal veins, such that the total hepatic blood flow tends to remain constant. When hepatic blood flow is reduced below 50% of normal, the liver has the ability to extract a greater percentage of oxygen from the blood so that total hepatic oxygen consumption is relatively preserved. The liver can extract an impressive 95% of the oxygen from its blood supply; this is perhaps due to the small diffusion distances from the hepatic sinusoids to the hepatocytes. The liver is thus unusually resistant to ischemia. The duration of the ischemic episode is important: hepatic necrosis is unusual if the

hepatic insult is less than 10 hours; with more than 24 hours of hepatic compromise, however, ischemic hepatitis is certain. Within 2 hours of hepatic hypoperfusion, reversible ultrastructural changes are detectable. Within 3 hours, irreversible changes, primarily in the centrilobular region, are apparent. These include dilation of sinusoids and narrowing of the hepatocytic cords. Physiologic alterations, including a shift to anaerobic metabolism, result in the loss of the ability of the cell membrane to maintain cell integrity. The hepatocyte contents leak out of the cell, producing the elevated serum transaminase levels that are clinically seen.

It is hypothesized that reperfusion plays a role in hepatic injury. Reoxygenation of previously ischemic tissue results in the formation of oxygen-derived free radicals. Lipid peroxidation of membrane components may follow with damage to cell membranes, causing cell necrosis, and damage to lysosomal enzymes, causing release of autolytic enzymes into the hepatocyte cytoplasm. The source of the free radicals is not entirely clear; xanthine oxidase, found in hepatocytes and endothelial cells, and NADPH oxidase, found in granulocytes and Kupffer cells, have been proposed as enzymatic sources of free radical formation.

Anatomic Derangement

Hepatocyte injury in ischemic hepatitis is predominantly centrilobular. This is a consequence of the direction of blood flow through the hepatic sinusoids, which proceeds from the portal tract (housing the portal venules and hepatic arterioles) to the central vein (containing the hepatic venule). Hepatocytes in zone 3 are the last to receive oxygenated blood, and in cases of ischemia, this region is the least oxygenated. Hepatocytes in this region are the most vulnerable to the effects of diminished perfusion and hypoxia.

Natural History and Its Modification with Treatment

The characteristic clinical course of ischemic hepatitis is not altered by treatment directed at the liver. Once the circulatory status is restored, regeneration of hepatocytes rapidly commences. Chronic liver disease does not occur. The prognosis of patients with ischemic hepatitis is often poor, with an approximately 60% mortality, due to the severity of the underlying circulatory compromise. The transient liver disorder has little effect on subsequent morbidity or mortality.

Prevention

Rapid and effective treatment of circulatory collapse prevents the development of ischemic hepatitis.

Cost Containment

In a patient with typical clinical and biochemical features, the diagnosis of ischemic hepatitis can be assumed without the need for a liver biopsy. Hepatitis viral serologies and hepatic imaging studies are generally required for a confident diagnosis and cannot be neglected.

REFERENCES

Bacon BR, Shobha JN, Granger DN. Ischemia, congestive failure, Budd-Chiari syndrome, and vaso-occlusive disease. In: Kaplowitz N, ed. Liver and biliary diseases. Baltimore: Williams & Wilkins, 1992:421.

Gish RG. Ischemic and congestive liver disease. In: Gitnick G, ed. Principles and practice of gastroenterology and hepatology. New York: Elsevier, 1988:1346.

Morali GA, Blends LM. The liver in cardiac diseases. In: Rustgi VK, Van Thiel DH, eds. The liver in systemic disease. New York: Raven Press, 1993:23.

Sherlock S. The liver in circulatory failure. In: Schiff L, Schiff ER, eds. Disease of the liver. 7th ed. Philadelphia: Lippincott, 1993:1431.

CHAPTER 19–78

Chronic Hepatitis

Alex Sherman, M.D., and Hillel Tobias, M.D., Ph.D.

DEFINITION

Chronic hepatitis (CH) is the presence of persistent liver inflammation and hepatocyte necrosis for a period of at least 6 months, manifested clinically by elevations in serum transaminase levels. CH has traditionally been classified into two major subgroups based on clinical and pathologic features. Chronic persistent hepatitis (CPH) has been histologically characterized by inflammatory infiltrates in the liver limited by the boundaries of the portal tract. It is characterized clinically by few or mild symptoms, mild elevations in serum transaminase levels, and a clinically benign course, with minimal tendency to progression. Chronic active hepatitis (CAH) has been characterized pathologically by the lesion of piecemeal necrosis: the extension of the inflammatory infiltrate beyond the confines of the portal tract into the hepatic lobule with necrosis of periportal hepatocytes. In more severe cases, the inflammation and necrosis extend across the hepatic lobule to an adjacent central vein or portal tract. This "bridging" distorts the hepatic architecture and is often accompanied by rapid deterioration in hepatic function, eventually resulting in cirrhosis and hepatic failure.

The traditional distinction between CPH and CAH has been called into question, principally because many patients with so-called CPH have been observed subsequently to develop histologic and clinical CAH. CH, according to the newer concepts, should be classified on the basis of grade, stage, and etiology. Histologic grade refers to the level of necroinflammatory activity (i.e., minimal, mild, moderate, or severe). Stage refers to the amount (i.e., mild, moderate, or severe) of fibrosis and whether cirrhosis is present. An etiologic diagnosis is essential and influences the clinical course, management, and prognosis of the patient with CH. The new terminology may supplant traditional concepts of CPH and CAH.

ETIOLOGY

Several different disease processes can result in the clinical and pathologic picture of CH. Recent advancements in serologic diagnoses, most notably identification of the hepatitis C virus (HCV) and the ready availability of hepatitis B serologies, have allowed clinicians to determine the cause of CH in the vast majority of cases.

In the United States, viral causes of CH predominate. Hepatitis B virus (HBV) and HCV are the agents that have been definitively associated with CH.

Chronic infection with HBV accounts for approximately one quarter of the cases of CH in the United States. HBV is spread parenterally or through sexual contact, but sporadic cases are recognized. Groups at high risk for HBV infection include institutionalized individuals, male homosexuals, intravenous drug users, and health care workers. Acute hepatitis B may develop into chronic hepatitis B in up to 10% of patients. Chronic hepatitis B may be characterized pathologically as either CPH or CAH. Infection with HCV accounts for the vast majority of cases previously referred to as "non-A, non-B hepatitis." This RNA virus is transmitted parenterally and is commonly contracted after blood or blood product transfusion. Unfortunately, up to 50% of hepatitis C acute infections go on to CH. High-risk groups for HCV infection are intravenous drug users and recipients of transfusions. A substantial percentage of HCV infection is sporadic, without an identifiable risk factor. As with HBV, either CPH or CAH may be seen pathologically.

Chronic hepatitis also occurs on an autoimmune basis, most frequently in young women in whom a variety of other autoimmune phenomena and serologic markers are present. Markers of viral infection are absent. Autoimmune CH may be classified on the basis of autoantibody pattern. Classic or type 1 autoimmune CH is the most common subgroup and is characterized by the presence of antinuclear antibody, smooth muscle antibody, and hypergammaglobulinemia. The term *lupoid hepatitis*, originally given to this group of patients because of

their serologic similarities to patients with systemic lupus erythematosus, has been discarded. Type 2 autoimmune CH, characterized by the presence of liver–kidney–microsomal antibody and the absence of antinuclear antibody and smooth muscle antibody, occurs in a younger age group and is more often associated with extrahepatic immunologic disorders. A third subgroup has been more recently described and features the presence of antibody to a liver-specific membrane lipoprotein. It has not been established that these subgroups of autoimmune CH correlate with distinct clinical, pathologic, or prognostic features.

Drug-induced CH has been well described. It should never be overlooked, as cessation of drug administration generally leads to a rapid clinical and pathologic resolution of CH. Drugs that have a definite association with CH include the laxative oxyphenisatin (not available in the United States but still in use worldwide), the antihypertensive agent, α-methyldopa, the urinary antiseptic nitrofurantoin, and dantrolene, a smooth muscle relaxant. The association with isoniazid, a mainstay of antitubercular treatment, is probable. Drug-induced CH may be clinically and pathologically indistinguishable from CH due to other causes.

Metabolic causes of CH are unusual but should be readily recognized. Wilson's disease, the genetic disorder of hepatic copper metabolism, results in the deposition of massive amounts of copper in the liver and results in a hepatic lesion of CH. Wilson's disease should be suspected in every young patient who manifests CH, especially if neurologic or psychiatric manifestations are present. Diagnosis involves detection of Kayser–Fleischer rings on slit-lamp examination of the eye, a low serum ceruloplasmin, and elevation of hepatic copper on liver biopsy. Specific treatment with a copper chelating agent (i.e., penicillamine) leads to dramatic clinical improvement, and may be lifesaving.

α_1-Antitrypsin deficiency is a genetic disorder characterized in homozygotes by reduced levels of the antiinflammatory α_1-globulin, resulting in CH and cirrhosis. Although the diagnosis is suggested by the findings of abnormally low levels of α_1-globulin on serum protein electrophoresis and the presence of periodic acid–Schiff-positive inclusions in the hepatocytes on liver biopsy, direct phenotyping makes the diagnosis more precisely. Heterozygotes with CH have been described. In a substantial number of patients with CH no definite etiology can be identified. These patients, with so-called "cryptogenic" CH, may have a viral infection with an as yet unidentified hepatitis virus (i.e., non-A, non-B, non-C hepatitis), may have an autoimmune disease that cannot be characterized by current immunologic markers, or may have been exposed to an unknown toxic agent. With advances in diagnostic techniques in recent years, the percentage of patients in whom no specific etiology is apparent has fallen. It is expected that future developments will eventually provide an etiologic explanation for all patients with CH.

CRITERIA FOR DIAGNOSIS
Suggestive

Chronic hepatitis is defined as the persistence of hepatic inflammation and hepatocyte necrosis for longer than 6 months, manifested clinically by elevations in the levels of serum transaminases. The diagnosis of chronic hepatitis is not based on symptoms; a substantial proportion of patients are asymptomatic. When symptoms occur, they are generally nonspecific (i.e., fatigue, malaise, and weakness).

Definitive

Liver histopathology is necessary to establish the diagnosis of CH. Classically, CPH is diagnosed when hepatic inflammation is limited to the portal tract, that is, portal "triaditis." CAH is diagnosed when the portal inflammation "spills over" into the hepatic lobule, leading to engulfment and destruction of individual hepatocytes. Severe CAH is characterized by "bridging necrosis" and fibrosis. Cirrhosis may be the end-stage pathologic lesion of CH. It is characterized by extensive fibrosis disrupting the normal lobular architecture of the liver and regenerating nodules of hepatocytes. Histologic CPH has been thought to be a more benign, less progressive liver disease than CAH and not likely to go on to end-stage liver disease. Recent studies, particularly with hepatitis C patients, have questioned the validity of this distinction. Furthermore, sampling error or an inadequate liver specimen may make the distinction between CPH and CAH difficult. A third pathologic entity, chronic lobular hepatitis, is characterized by focal inflammatory infiltrates within the hepatic lobule. Chronic lobular hepatitis generally corresponds clinically to resolving, protracted, or relapsing acute hepatitis.

When a diagnosis of CH is made, an attempt should be made to establish the etiology. Serologic markers for HBV and HCV should be obtained. Identification of any markers for autoimmune CH are mandatory. Medication history should be reviewed and drugs suspected of an association with CH should be stopped. Rechallenge with a drug suspected of causing CH is not necessary to make a diagnosis and may be fatal. Metabolic and genetic causes should be excluded.

CLINICAL MANIFESTATIONS
Subjective

The presence of symptoms is not necessary for the diagnosis of CH. Mild nonspecific symptoms such as malaise, fatigue, weakness, anorexia, and vague upper abdominal discomfort are encountered. The lack of symptomatology or mild symptoms are typical of CPH. Symptoms of CAH are generally more severe. Symptoms of liver failure (i.e., jaundice, gastrointestinal bleeding, increasing abdominal girth, and mental confusion) may occur with severe CH or late in the course of any patient with CH as cirrhosis evolves. Extrahepatic symptoms of vasculitis may suggest HBV-associated deposition of antigen–antibody complexes. Symptoms of an extrahepatic immunologic disorder suggest autoimmune CH.

The presence of risk factors for the acquisition of HBV and HCV should be identified. Geographic prevalence is especially relevant for HBV; rates are highest in patients from the Far East and Africa. HCV, unlike HBV, is distributed rather evenly worldwide. A past history of autoimmune phenomena may be elicited in patients with autoimmune CH. This form of CH has been described predominantly in women of northern European background. The patient with CH should be questioned closely regarding both prescription and nonprescription medications.

Cases of virus-induced CH may cluster within families or among close household or sexual contacts. This is especially true for the highly infective HBV. Prevalence rates of HCV among sexual contacts of patients with HCV are only slightly higher than in the general population. Autoimmune CH is seen in association with several HLA subtypes, particularly A1, B8, DR3, and DW3, and can be familial.

Objective
Physical Examination

The physical examination may be normal in many patients with early CH. Mild hepatic tenderness may be elicited and hepatomegaly may be seen. Stigmata of chronic liver disease are detected in late or severe CH, especially in the face of associated cirrhosis. These include jaundice, hepatomegaly, splenomegaly, spider angiomata, palmar erythema, ascites, and asterixis. These latter findings reflect the presence of portal hypertension and end-stage liver disease. The presence of Kayser–Fleischer rings on slit-lamp examination of the eyes is essentially diagnostic of Wilson's disease. In autoimmune CH, extrahepatic evidence of autoimmune disease may be evident, such as, arthritis, uveitis, and thyroiditis.

Routine Laboratory Abnormalities

By definition, elevation in serum transaminase levels is universal in CH. Elevation of the alanine transaminase level to a greater degree than the aspartate transaminase level is typical of viral CH. Elevation in the serum γ-glutamyl transpeptidase level generally parallels elevations in the transaminases. Elevation in the serum alkaline phosphatase level is not uncommon; however, the magnitude of this elevation is usually less than the transaminase elevation. Elevation in the serum alkaline phosphatase out of proportion to the elevation of the transaminases suggests cholestatic liver disease or a biliary tract disorder. Hypoalbuminemia and hypoprothrombinemia reflect disturbances in hepatic synthetic function and are seen late in the course of CH. Pancytopenia may occur in patients with portal hypertension, splenomegaly, and hypersplenism. Anemia may also reflect gastrointestinal bleeding in the patient with end-stage liver disease.

PLANS
Diagnostic
Differential Diagnosis

Conditions that result in chronic elevations in the serum transaminase levels should be considered in the differential diagnosis. Although hepatitis A virus infection is not a cause of chronic hepatitis, recovery from acute hepatitis A may rarely be protracted, resulting in elevations in transaminase levels for longer than 6 months. Rarely, relapsing hepatitis A may occur with a second or even multiple rebounds in enzyme levels after apparent complete recovery. Persistence of hepatitis A immunoglobulin M antibody aids in this diagnosis.

Primary biliary cirrhosis is an immunologically mediated liver disease affecting predominantly middle-aged or older women. Asymptomatic elevations in the serum alkaline phosphatase level and pruritus are typical presentations. The presence of antimitochondrial antibody is seen in 85 to 95%. The liver biopsy typically shows degeneration of interlobular bile ducts and hepatic granulomas. The predominance of cholestatic features generally allows distinction from CAH, but occasionally a patient is seen with transaminase elevations and the absence of antimitochondrial antibodies who is subsequently shown to have primary biliary cirrhosis on liver biopsy. Primary sclerosing cholangitis is a chronic inflammatory disorder of the intrahepatic and extrahepatic biliary tract that generally occurs in young men, frequently in association with inflammatory bowel disease. The patient presents with asymptomatic elevations in the alkaline phosphatase level or cholestatic symptoms. Occasionally, the "pericholangitis" seen on liver biopsy in patients with inflammatory bowel disease (representing the intrahepatic manifestation of the biliary inflammatory process) may be confused with CH. A cholangiogram (endoscopic retrograde cholangiopancreatography) establishes this diagnosis.

Alcoholic patients may have clinical and pathologic features that are typical of viral CH, rather than alcohol-related liver disease. This occurrence in an alcoholic is usually coincidental; the incidence of HBV and HCV infection in the alcoholic patient is substantially increased. The biochemical derangements of alcohol-related liver disease alone, however, generally have a characteristic pattern in which the aspartate transaminase level is at least two times greater than the alanine transaminase level. A history of heavy alcohol consumption should be elicited. Liver biopsy shows changes typical of alcoholic hepatitis which can usually be differentiated from viral CH. The cessation of alcohol consumption should lead to a clinical and biochemical resolution of alcoholic hepatitis, although biochemical abnormalities can last longer than 6 months.

Steatohepatitis may cause persistence of transaminase elevations in the obese or diabetic patient. Liver biopsy findings can be clearly distinguished from those of viral or autoimmune CH. Steatohepatitis may, however, persist as a chronic disease and go on to cirrhosis in some cases. Hemochromatosis is a metabolic disorder resulting in the heavy infiltration of the liver with iron, which may result in elevation of serum transaminase levels. Infiltration of other tissues and organs with iron may result in diabetes, endocrine abnormalities, arthritis, and cardiac dysfunction. Diagnosis is based on serum iron indices and the quantitative demonstration of hepatic iron overload.

Diagnostic Options

A patient with elevated levels of serum transaminases for longer than 6 months should be considered for a liver biopsy. The liver biopsy is essential to the etiologic diagnosis and staging of CH. In addition to establishing the presence of CH, a liver biopsy can assess for the presence of bridging necrosis and cirrhosis, which establishes the presence of severe liver disease.

Etiologic diagnosis of CH is important. Viral CH is diagnosed serologically. The presence of the hepatitis B surface antigen is strongly suggestive of HBV-associated CH. The presence of the hepatitis B e antigen indicates active HBV replication in the liver. The diagnosis of HCV infection is undergoing rapid refinements. The enzyme-linked immunosorbent assay for hepatitis C antibody has been superceded by the more sensitive recombinant immunoblot assay. A polymerase chain reaction assay is now commercially available to detect hepatitis C viremia. In practice, the finding of HCV antibody on first- or second-generation assay in a patient with CH is good evidence of HCV-associated CH. False-negative antibody tests occur, however, especially early in HCV infection, so that repeated testing may be necessary. The coexistence of HBV and HCV infection has been well described.

Recommended Approach

The patient with abnormal liver enzyme elevation suspected of having CH should be followed for at least 6 months to determine if the biochemical derangements are indeed chronic. During this time, medications suspected of causing CH should be withheld or replaced. Alcohol intake should be strictly forbidden. An etiologic diagnosis based on viral serologies, autoantibodies, and metabolic or genetic studies is searched for. Hepatic sonography to exclude the presence of biliary tract disease or focal hepatic lesions is recommended.

After 6 months of persistent serum transaminase elevations, liver biopsy should be performed. The demonstration of an etiologic diagnosis does not obviate the need for a liver biopsy. A pathologic diagnosis is important in staging and grading the severity of the CH, gauging the likelihood of progression, and determining if early cirrhosis is present.

Therapeutic

Therapeutic Options

Patients with the lesions of classic CPH were previously considered to have nonprogressive liver disease. This is no longer felt to be totally true. Patients with CH must be considered to have potentially progressive liver disease and are candidates for treatment. Although many therapies have been tried, the only established treatment for viral CH is the interferons. Interferons are a family of glycoproteins secreted by a variety of cell types that have antiviral, immunomodulatory, and antiproliferative effects. Recombinant interferon alfa given for at least 16 weeks results in sustained clearance from the serum of markers of viral replication, that is, hepatitis B e antigen and HBV DNA, in about 30% of patients. Doses of approximately 5 million units, 5 to 7 days a week, are required. In long-term follow-up, up to 40% of patients who responded to interferon eventually cleared hepatitis B surface antigen from their serum. The treatment of HCV CH with recombinant interferon alfa has also been the focus of numerous clinical trials. Various combinations of doses and durations have been tried. Three to five million units given three times a week for durations up to 6 months is the dosage most commonly used. Many hepatologists claim 12-month therapy yields better results. Responses, defined by normalization of serum transaminase levels during therapy, can be achieved in up to 70% of patients. Relapses once therapy is withdrawn, however, occur in up to 50% of respondents. The optimal dose and duration of interferon therapy for HCV CH have not been definitively established.

Interferon therapy is inconvenient; it must be given by subcutaneous injection. Side effects are frequent. A flulike syndrome, with fever, chills, myalgias, and arthralgias, is nearly universal, but subsides with continued treatment. Bone marrow suppression, thyroid abnormalities, and psychiatric disturbances, especially depression, may be encountered. Interferon administration is generally ineffective and may be dangerous in patients with end-stage liver disease. The stimulation of cellular immunity produced by interferon may result in the transient worsening of transaminase elevations. This may be poorly tolerated in patients with little hepatic reserve. Liver failure and death due to interferon administration in this setting have been reported.

In autoimmune CH, corticosteroids, alone or in combination with the immunosuppressive agent azathioprine, produce symptomatic improve-

ment, improve biochemical parameters and histologic appearances, and, most importantly, lead to increased survival. Untreated, 50% of patients with severe autoimmune CH may die within 5 years of diagnosis. The aim of therapy is remission of disease activity. Symptomatic and biochemical remission generally precedes histologic remission by approximately 6 months. The rate of histologic remission after 3 years of treatment is approximately 80%, with a 5-year survival of 87%.

Different therapeutic regimens have been tried in autoimmune CH. The addition of azathioprine to either prednisone or prednisolone allows reduction in corticosteroid dose, decreasing steroid-related side effects, such as hypertension, glucose intolerance, osteoporosis, psychiatric disturbances, aseptic necrosis of joints, and Cushing's syndrome (obesity, "buffalo hump," acne, and hirsutism). Theoretical risks of teratogenic side effects of immunosuppressive medications limit their use in pregnant women.

Drug-induced CH usually responds to withdrawal of the offending agent. Wilson's disease is treated with penicillamine or newer copper chelators.

Orthotopic liver transplantation is an effective treatment for end-stage liver disease of various etiologies. The patient with severe CH who has evidence of liver failure is a candidate for liver transplantation. Results of transplantation in patients with HBV have been disappointing because of the nearly universal recurrence of HBV in the transplanted liver. One-year survival rates in patients transplanted for HBV-associated end-stage liver diseases are only 50 to 60% compared with an approximately 85% 1-year survival in patients transplanted for other indications. Strategies to eliminate HBV recurrence in the transplanted liver with hepatitis B immunoglobulin (HBIG) or monoclonal antibody to hepatitis B surface antigen, have been developed. Transplantation is much more favorable in patients with HCV. Patients with severe autoimmune CH, unresponsive to medical therapy, are usually excellent candidates for liver transplantation. Liver transplantation is also indicated in patients with fulminant or severely progressive Wilson's disease.

Recommended Approach

Patients with virus-associated CH should be considered for treatment with interferon, in the dosages described above. Because side effects are almost universal and may be severe, treatment with interferon is best managed by a hepatologist. The goal in treatment of HBV disease is the disappearance of circulating hepatitis B e antigen, a marker of HBV replicative activity. Disappearance of hepatitis B surface antigen may also occur on long-term follow-up. The aim of therapy in HCV disease is the normalization of serum transaminase levels. Patients with severe autoimmune CAH require treatment with corticosteroids. The decision to initiate therapy in patients with mild to moderate autoimmune CAH should be individualized; a period of careful observation and reassessment may be a reasonable initial strategy. Many hepatologists feel even mild or moderate cases should be treated to prevent progression. The combination of prednisone and azathioprine has similar efficacy to corticosteroid-only regimens and a lower incidence of side effects. The goal of therapy is remission—symptomatic, biochemical, and histologic. When this has been achieved, withdrawal of treatment may be considered. Variable relapse rates have been reported, depending on the population studied. In all studies, however, relapse is quite common and re-treatment is usually required. Some hepatologists, therefore, keep patients on maintenance regimens. Liver transplantation should be considered in all patients with CH and end-stage liver disease.

FOLLOW-UP

Patients with CH should have periodic liver enzyme studies to assess the activity of hepatic inflammatory activity. The occurrence of end-stage liver disease in patients with CH may be indicated by the appearance of jaundice, ascites, severe upper gastrointestinal bleeding, hepatic encephalopathy, hypoalbuminemia, or encephalopathy. Liver transplantation should be considered at this point. The development of hepatocellular carcinoma is a devastating complication of CH, in patients with HBV. Evidence for HCV as a risk factor for hepatocellular carcinoma as well is rapidly accumulating. An increase in serum α-fetoprotein or the appearance of a hepatic mass on liver sonography may indicate hepatocellular carcinoma. Regular screening with serum α-fetoprotein and liver sonography is indicated. Hepatocellular carcinoma is rarely curable surgically and is poorly responsive to current chemotherapeutic or radiotherapeutic protocols, but patients with early small tumors often respond well to chemoembolization and liver transplantation.

DISCUSSION

Prevalence

The prevalence of chronic liver disease in the United States is estimated to be 2 cases per 100,000 persons. The frequency of the various etiologies of chronic liver disease vary geographically. The prevalence of HBV-related chronic liver disease is highest in regions of high endemicity. The prevalence of autoimmune CH varies with differences in HLA-B8 and -DR3 prevalence; these HLA markers are found most frequently in northern Europeans and their descendants.

Alcoholism is the most common cause of chronic liver disease in the United States, accounting for 50% of cases. Chronic viral causes account for 12% and autoimmune disorders account for 11 to 22% of cases. The incidence of autoimmune hepatitis in Western Europe is 0.69 cases per 100,000 persons per year; this figure is likely to be similar to the incidence in North America.

Related Basic Science

The mechanism of liver injury in chronic HBV infection is thought to be an immunologically mediated destruction of infected hepatocytes. HBV is not thought to be directly cytopathic; carrier states in which the HBV genome is integrated into the host genome and liver inflammatory activity is nonexistent have been well described. Recovery from acute HBV hepatitis requires the coordinated activity of the host immune system; chronic infection results from impairment in the host immune response to HBV. Destruction of hepatocytes infected with HBV is dependent on the ability of nonspecific killer and cytotoxic CD8-positive T cells to recognize viral antigens (hepatitis B core antigen) on the surface of the hepatocyte along with class 1 HLA glycoproteins. HLA expression by hepatocytes is greatly enhanced by endogenous alpha interferon in response to a viral infection. Patients with chronic HBV have decreased hepatocyte expression of HLA class 1 antigens. This may be due to a decrease in the synthesis or effectiveness of endogenous interferons. High titers of circulating antiviral antibodies may result in the masking of viral surface antigens, inhibiting cell-mediated cytotoxicity. Mutations may occur in the HBV genome, allowing it to escape immune-mediated elimination.

Hepatitis C virus is a single-stranded RNA virus of 10,000 nucleotides coding for approximately 3000 amino acids. The 100-3 antigen is used in the first-generation enzyme-linked immunosorbent assay to capture serum antibodies. The recombinant immunoblot assay measures the presence of serum antibodies to multiple viral antigens. The polymerase chain reaction allows the identification of minute quantities of HCV in serum. Many strains of HCV exist, with implications for diagnostic testing and vaccine development.

Hepatitis C virus, in contrast to HBV, is directly cytopathic. HCV infection of immunocompetent hosts is commonly found. Immune defects, however, can play a role in HCV liver disease, as evidenced by the fact that HCV disease in immunosuppressed patients with HIV may be accelerated.

Patients with autoimmune CH have a disturbed immunoregulatory response to the hepatocyte surface antigens. A defect in suppressor T cells results in the production of autoantibodies directed against these antigens. The cause of this abnormal production of autoantibodies is uncertain. The antigen to which the antibodies are produced is not precisely known, although liver membrane protein and liver-specific protein have been implicated. Antibody-dependent cell-mediated cytotoxicity is the mechanism for hepatocyte destruction.

Natural History and Its Modification with Treatment

The natural history of HBV infection varies considerably, based mainly on the severity of the hepatic inflammatory activity and the presence of cirrhosis. Patients with HBV-related CH may have prolonged asymptomatic survivals. Patients with severe CH may experience rapid progression through end-stage liver disease. Patients with HBV CH and cirrhosis at diagnosis have a 55% 5-year survival, compared with an 85% 5-year survival in those patients with HBV-related moderately severe CH without cirrhosis. Thus far, treatment with interferon has not been shown to improve survival rates in patients with severe HBV CH; however, long-term disappearance of the hepatitis B surface antigen from the serum after interferon treatment in a percentage of patients raises hopes that the burden of end-stage liver disease from HBV may be reduced. The natural history of HCV infection is also variable and dependent on the severity on the initial hepatic lesion. The clinical course is, in general, milder than that of HBV disease, and the time to development of cirrhosis is often longer, often 20 to 25 years. Studies of patients with posttransfusion hepatitis suggest an essentially normal longterm survival, although deaths due to hepatic causes are more frequently found in patients with chronic HCV. Interferon has so far not been clearly shown to influence mortality in HCV disease, although the approximately 25% long-term remission rate may improve the statistics.

Several series have shown that untreated severe autoimmune CAH is a rapidly progressive disorder with a high mortality rate. Treatment dramatically improves survival rates. In the Royal Free Hospital, London, trial (Kirk, et al., 1980), 62% of treated patients survived 10 years versus only 27% of the untreated group. In the Mayo Clinic study (Soloway, et al., 1972), only 6% of corticosteroid-treated patients died in 3.5 years, compared with 30% in a control group. Mortality in untreated patients is especially common within the first 5 years of diagnosis, suggesting that a spontaneous remission may occur in long-term follow-up in a minority of patients. The natural history of end-stage liver disease of all etiologies is dismal, with death commonly occurring from hepatic coma, esophageal variceal hemorrhage, or hepatorenal syndrome. This outlook is dramatically improved by a liver transplantation.

Prevention

The development of the recombinant HBV vaccine has the potential to dramatically reduce the worldwide prevalence of this pathogen. Its administration has been recommended to patients in high-risk groups, but immunization should be extended to the entire population. Pregnant women are routinely screened for the presence of hepatitis B surface antigen; hepatitis B immune globulin and hepatitis B vaccine are given perinatally to infants of hepatitis B surface antigen-positive mothers. Donor blood screening for HBV and HCV has essentially eliminated the occurrence of posttransfusion hepatitis due to these viruses. Patients with HBV and HCV infections should be counseled regarding sexual or parenteral transmission possibilities and appropriate precautions should be undertaken by them. The occurrence of acute HBV infection may be reduced in a patient with sexual or parenteral exposure to HBV by the administration of hepatitis B immune globulin. It is reasonable to administer immune globulin to patients with parenteral exposure to HCV. It is unclear what precautions, if any, sexual contacts of patients with HCV should undertake.

Cost Containment

The prevention of chronic HBV infection via vaccine is clearly cost effective; the relatively high cost of the vaccine, however, has prevented many patients in high-risk groups from receiving this intervention. Interferon treatment of chronic viral hepatitis is relatively expensive; however, there is no less expensive alternative at present. The cost of liver transplantation is extremely high; it should be used only in well-selected patients with end-stage liver disease. Whether this effective therapy can be withheld for cost considerations is more of an ethical question that has yet to be resolved.

REFERENCES

Boyer JL, Reuben A. Chronic hepatitis. In: Schiff L, Schiff ER, eds. Diseases of the liver. 7th ed. Philadelphia: Lippincott, 1993:587.

Czaja AJ. Clinical aspects of autoimmune hepatitis in North America. In: Nishioka M, Toda G, Zeniya M, eds. Autoimmune hepatitis, Amsterdam: Elsevier, 1994:27.

Desmet VJ, Gerber MA, Hoofnagle JH, et al. Classification of chronic hepatitis: diagnosis, grading, and staging. Hepatology 1994;19:1513.

Kirk AP, Jain S, Pocock S, et al. Late results of Royal Free Hospital controlled trial of prednisolone therapy in hepatitis B surface antigen-negative chronic active hepatitis. Gut 1980;21:78.

Sherlock S. Chronic hepatitis. In: Sherlock S, Dooley J, eds. Diseases of the liver and biliary system. 9th ed. Oxford: Blackwell, 1993:293.

Sheron N, Eddleston. Autoimmune chronic active hepatitis. In: McIntyre N, Benhamou JP, Bircher J, et al., eds. Oxford textbook of clinical hepatology. Oxford: Oxford University Press, 1991:758.

Soloway RD, Summerskill WH, Baggenstoss AH, et al. Clinical, biochemical, and histological remission of severe chronic active liver disease: a controlled study of treatments and early prognosis. Gastroenterology 1972;63:820.

CHAPTER 19–79

Hepatic Abnormalities in AIDS

Carroll B. Leevy, M.D.

DEFINITION

Hepatic abnormalities in AIDS are defined as the presence of clinical, laboratory, radiologic, and/or morphologic evidence of liver damage in a patient with AIDS.

ETIOLOGY

The presence of HIV-induced lesions of the liver; concurrent causes of liver injury due to intravenous drug abuse, alcoholism, risky sexual practices, tattoos, and so on; independent hepatic disorders due to infections, toxic injury, metabolic disorders, bile duct lesions, and vascular alteration; superimposition of infections of the liver due to immunodeficiency; or hepatotoxicity from drugs used in treatment of AIDS and its complications are considered hepatic abnormalities in AIDS.

CRITERIA FOR DIAGNOSIS

Suggestive

Progressive malaise and fatigue or evidence of fever, malnutrition, hepatomegaly, and/or jaundice at the initial evaluation or during follow-up of patients with AIDS suggests the diagnosis.

Definitive

See Table 19–79–1.

CLINICAL MANIFESTATIONS

Subjective

All patients with AIDS should be suspected of having hepatic abnormalities which contribute to malaise, myalgia, fever, weight loss, and other symptoms. Similarly, consideration should be given to HIV infection in patients with chronic viral hepatitis, alcoholic liver disease, or liver disease of unknown origin. A detailed past and family history usually allows documentation of the presence and cause of liver disease and AIDS. Maternal transmission, receipt of transfusions, and injections are responsible for these diseases in infants and young children. A history of prior association with patients with AIDS or hepatitis; intravenous drug abuse; alcoholism; receipt of transfusions, infections, or tattoos; aberrant sexual practices; surgical procedures; or previous medications are usually present in teenagers and adults with liver disease and AIDS.

Objective

Physical Examination

Patients with AIDS and liver disease may have lymphadenopathy, spider angiomata, jaundice, cutaneous manifestations of Kaposi's sarcoma, hepatomegaly, splenomegaly, abdominal masses, ascites, altered mental status, or evidence of bleeding tendency on physical examination.

Routine Laboratory Abnormalities

The routine laboratory test results do not reveal any diagnostic abnormalities.

PLANS

Diagnostic

Differential Diagnosis

Immunodeficiency in patients with liver disease may be due to the liver disease, HIV, or other conditions. Therefore, it is first necessary to determine if liver disease and AIDS are present. Once this is established hepatic abnormalities that respond to treatment should be identified. In addition, it is important to detect liver disease that is transmissible to others. Viral hepatitis is common in patients with a history of intravenous drug abuse, as well as risky sexual practices. Routine serology may not reveal the presence of hepatitis B surface antigen in patients with AIDS because of immune complexes. In these instances it is desirable to use the polymerase chain reaction to detect hepatitis B virus DNA and hepatitis C virus RNA. Special attention should be given to identifying other organisms, particularly *Mycobacterium tuberculosis* and *Mycobacterium avium–intracellular*. In selected patients with intercurrent infections, it may be helpful to serially evaluate CD4 and

TABLE 19–79–1. DEFINITIVE CRITERIA FOR DIAGNOSIS

Clinical
- Features of AIDS, including weight loss and infections involving the lungs, central nervous system, or other organs
- Hepatomegaly, jaundice, ascites, encephalopathy, or bleeding tendency
- Demonstration of features of infectious agents that produce liver injury (viruses, bacteria, fungi, parasites)
- Receipt of chemicals or drugs that produce liver damage

Laboratory
- Presence of serum HIV antibodies
- Abnormal liver function tests including increases in levels of transaminases and alkaline phosphatase, hyperbilirubinemia, and hypoalbuminemia
- Evidence of a genetic, autoimmune, or neoplastic disease
- Serologic evidence of hepatitis A, B, C, D, or E virus or other hepatic infection

Radiology/Imaging
- Liver or biliary abnormalities detected by ultrasonography, computed axial tomography, magnetic resonance imaging, or endoscopic retrograde cholangiopancreatography

Liver Biopsy
- Evidence of fatty metamorphosis, fibrosis, inflammation, necrosis, altered bile ducts, or neoplasia

CD8 cells and serum tumor necrosis factor and to perform other immunologic studies to assess the effectiveness of treatment regimens. Special diagnostic tests are needed to detect reversible pathophysiologic changes. The need to perform diagnostic and therapeutic measures designed to reduce morbidity and mortality from concurrent or secondary liver disease will increase with the ability to eliminate the HIV and correct immunodeficiency.

Diagnostic Options and Recommended Approach

The following diagnostic approach is necessary:

* Determine the presence of viral B or C hepatitis and other organisms or drugs that produce clinical and laboratory evidence of liver disease.
* Evaluate the cause of jaundice or cholestasis.
* Assess the cause and possible remedy for features of end-stage liver disease: ascites, bleeding varices, and encephalopathy.

Laboratory studies often reveal an anemia, bacteremia, bacteria, and sputum containing pathogenic organisms. The serum HIV and p24 antibody are positive and CD4 T-cell counts are decreased. Serology for hepatitis viruses A, B, and C, cytomegalovirus, and herpes simplex virus and studies for other viral bacterial, fungal, or parasitic infections may be positive. Radiologic studies often show infections involving other organs as well as the liver. Liver biopsy reveals evidence of a variety of hepatic lesions (Table 19–79–2).

An evaluation of renal function, neurologic status, and intestinal function is necessary in patients with tender hepatomegaly; fever of unknown origin; and evidence of liver failure, including fluid accumulation, mental changes, or intestinal bleeding. The presence of ascites on physical examination warrants a computed tomography (CT) scan and a diagnostic paracentesis to determine if bacterial or tuberculous peritonitis is present. The CT scan may show defects in the liver due to Kaposi's sarcoma or, less commonly, a lymphoma. Laparoscopy facilitates recognition of tuberculous peritonitis, as well as neoplasia.

A liver biopsy is desirable if there are no contraindications such as coagulopathy and lack of cooperation. In experience at the New Jersey Medical School Liver Center, this procedure has been invaluable in identifying the cause and severity of hepatic disease in AIDS. Laparoscopy or CT-guided biopsy has been valuable in identifying Kaposi's sarcoma or lymphoma. Special radiologic/imaging investigations are required in patients with cholangiopathy and AIDS. Such patients exhibit jaundice, fever, and right upper quadrant pain accompanied by an elevated serum alkaline phosphatase level and conjugated hyperbilirubinemia. Ultrasonography may demonstrate dilation of the intrahepatic and/or extrahepatic biliary tree. The etiology and anatomy involved are provided by endoscopic retrograde cholangiography (ERCP). Anatomic lesions include papillary stenosis, sclerosing cholangitis, and extrahepatic biliary strictures. It is often possible to identify the organism responsible for sclerosing cholangitis, including cytomegalovirus, *Cryptosporidium,* and Microsporidia (Table 19–79–3).

Therapeutic

The most important therapeutic modality in a patient with hepatic abnormalities associated with AIDS is elimination of the hepatotoxic drugs that are responsible for the liver damage encountered (Table 19–79–4). Drug toxicity should be suspected in patients with AIDS

TABLE 19–79–2. HEPATIC LESIONS IN AIDS

* Hepatitis
* Cirrhosis
* Cholestasis
* Fatty liver
* Nonviral infections
* Kaposi's sarcoma and lymphoma
* Peliosis

TABLE 19–79–3. COMMON HEPATOBILIARY INFECTIONS AND RELATED HISTOPATHOLOGY IN AIDS

Condition	Histopathology	Microbial Diagnosis
AIDS	Fatty metamorphosis	HIV in CD4 cells
Hepatitis B	Necrosis, inflammation	Hepatitis B virus DNA
Hepatitis C	Necrosis, inflammation, fatty metamorphosis	Hepatitis C virus RNA
Cytomegalovirus hepatitis	Granulomas, focal inflammation	Positive cDNA probe
Tuberculosis	Granuloma	*Mycobacterium tuberculosis, Mycobacterium avium-intracellulare*
Candidiasis	Necrosis, granuloma	Hyphae, PAS positive
Cryptococcosis	Granuloma	PAS positive
Histoplasmosis	Caseating granuloma	Gomori stain
Toxoplasmosis	Granuloma, necrosis	cDNA probe
Cryptosporidiosis	Periportal fibrosis	Oocytes
Microsporidia	Periportal fibrosis	Positive stain

PAS, periodic acid–Schiff reagent.

who receive symptomatic or supportive measures. Identification of the responsible drug may be difficult because of the large number of prescription and nonprescription agents taken by these patients. In addition, when antimicrobial agents, analgesics, or anticonvulsants are employed it is often necessary to substitute an alternative agent, which may also prove to be hepatotoxic. Management of pain in patients with liver disease and AIDS requires special attention because of both the untoward effects of analgesics on the liver and the potential for addiction.

The second important area in which treatment is indicated is man-

TABLE 19–79–4. DRUG-INDUCED HEPATOTOXICITY COMMONLY ENCOUNTERED IN PATIENTS WITH AIDS

Antimicrobial Agents

Amphotericin B
Itraconazole
Zidovudine
Isoniazid
Rifampin
Ethambutol
Pyrazinamide
Sulfides
Trimethoprim–sulfamethoxazole
Tetracycline
Carbenicillin
Ganciclovir
Acyclovir
Phosphonoformate
Thiabendazole
5-Fluorocytosine
Pentamidine
Sulfonamides
Oxacillin
Metronidazole
Erythromycin
Ketoconazole

Analgesics

Acetaminophen
Salicylates
Nonsteroidal analgesics

Anticonvulsants and Tranquilizers

Diphenylhydantoin
Chlorpromazine
Chlordiazepoxide
Diazepam

agement of cholangiopathy in patients with AIDS. At the time of ERCP papillotomy and placement of a biliary tree stent often allow relief of pain due to this condition. Ursodeoxycholic acid 300 mg three times per day changes the composition of excreted bile and may reduce jaundice and pruritus in patients with sclerosing cholangitis. A course of ganciclovir is helpful for management of cytomegalovirus during the immediate post-ERCP period.

Treatment of patients with liver failure and AIDS requires special measures. Although there may be a short-term response to standard treatment of encephalopathy, ascites, or bleeding varices, most patients rapidly progress downhill despite such therapy. Encephalopathy requires a decrease in protein intake supplemented by lactulose and/or a broad-spectrum antibiotic. Dietary sodium restriction, diuretics, paracentesis, and correction of hypoalbuminemia may control ascites. Bleeding from esophageal varices may stop spontaneously or require intravenous vasopressin (Pitressin) or somatostatin. Endoscopy with banding or sclerotherapy is often needed. With refractoriness to such therapy or the presence of bleeding gastric varices, prognosis is poor. Surgical shunts and transjugular intrahepatic portasystemic shunts used in non-AIDS patients are contraindicated. This is due to the complications of these procedures, as well as to the inability to control either HIV infection or immunodeficiency.

FOLLOW-UP

Patients with hepatic abnormalities and AIDS should receive supportive therapy continuously for both conditions. It is desirable to avoid alcohol, drugs, and other hepatotoxins; provide corrective measures for nutrient deficits and fluid accumulation; and treat intercurrent infections due to AIDS. As occurs with chronic hepatitis B or C, patients with AIDS and superimposed viral infections may not respond to available antiviral drugs.

DISCUSSION

Prevalence and Incidence

The prevalence and type of liver disease associated with AIDS vary with the population under study. Intravenous drug abusers have a high incidence of B and C hepatitis; alcoholics develop alcoholic hepatitis and cirrhosis; and homosexuals are more likely to have parasitic and other hepatic infections.

Related Basic Science

The basic science related to AIDS is discussed in Chapter 8–76. AIDS involves every body organ, but it is particularly devastating to the liver. HIV is readily demonstrable in liver CD4 cells, Kupffer cells, macrophages, and, occasionally, hepatocytes. The virus alters hepatic function; however, the major problem is the immunodeficiency, which facilitates replication of a variety of organisms that produce liver damage. The ability of the damaged liver to sequester or eliminate these organisms is diminished in AIDS, compounding the difficulty in control

of infections. In addition, immunosuppression allows an increase in replication of infective agents.

Natural History and Its Modification with Treatment

Patients with AIDS and overt liver disease have a poor prognosis. Quality of life may be modified by symptomatic measures for both AIDS and liver disease; however, outcome can only change when it becomes possible to modify the HIV infection and resulting immunodeficiency. Once this occurs, such patients will be identical to other patients with liver disease. At present, neither spontaneous subsidence of liver injury, elimination of agents responsible for liver disease, nor liver transplant survival are possible in the presence of AIDS. Thus, in subjects with end-stage liver disease, non-HIV-related liver disease, there is a rapid decline in hepatic function when AIDS develops posttransplant as a result of receipt of an HIV-infected donor liver or contaminated blood.

Prevention

Liver disease is preventable in patients with AIDS by avoiding hepatotoxic drugs or chemicals, abstaining from alcohol, and limiting exposure to infectious agents. Similarly, AIDS is preventable in patients with liver disease by discontinuing intravenous drug abuse, tattoos, and risky sexual practices. Mothers with AIDS should receive AZT to diminish the possibility their offspring will become HIV positive. The newborn of an HIV-positive mother should be vaccinated to prevent hepatitis B.

Cost Containment

Continuous education of the population to avoid intravenous drug abuse, alcoholism, and risky sexual practices is required to avoid liver disease and AIDS. The patient faced with these diseases should interrupt causative factors that contribute to infections and further disability. Such patients are best managed in an ambulatory or semiambulatory setting that allows treatment of both liver disease and AIDS. Hospital care should be limited to patients with end-stage liver disease in whom complications will respond to available measures.

REFERENCES

Leevy CM, Sherlock S, Tygstrup N, Zetterman R. Diseases of the liver and biliary tract, standardization of nomenclature, diagnostic criteria and prognosis. New York: International Informatics Group, Raven Press, 1994.

Leevy CB, Nurse H, Najendra K. Active viral B hepatitis in parenteral drug abusers with acquired immune deficiency syndrome (AIDS). J Assoc Acad Minor Phys 1989;1:18.

Levy JA. Pathogenesis of human immunodeficiency viral infection. Microbiol Rev 1993;57:183.

Pantaleo G, Grazios C, Fauci AS. New concept in the immunopathogenesis of human immunodeficiency virus infection, N Engl J Med 1993;328:327.

Scoazec JY, Felman G. Both macrophages and endothelial cells of the human hepatic sinusoids express the CD3 molecule, a receptor for the human immunodeficiency virus. Hepatology 1990;12:505.

CHAPTER 19–80

Cirrhosis

Hillel Tobias, M.D., Ph.D., and Alex Sherman, M.D.

DEFINITION

Cirrhosis is defined as a diffuse pathologic alteration in the structure of the liver, consisting of extensive fibrosis and regenerating hepatocyte nodules, such that the normal hepatic architecture is disrupted. Three major morphologic classifications of cirrhosis are recognized. These subgroups usually, but not always, mirror differences in etiology. In micronodular cirrhosis, nodules are uniform and less than 3 mm in di-

ameter. This form of cirrhosis is most commonly seen in chronic alcoholic patients. In macronodular cirrhosis, variations in the size of the nodules is seen, some of which are larger than 3 mm in diameter. This form of cirrhosis is seen following viral hepatitis ("posthepatitis") or following massive or submassive necrosis of hepatocytes ("postnecrotic"). Macronodular cirrhosis may also represent a later stage of micronodular cirrhosis. Finally, a mixed cirrhosis is seen, with both micro- and macronodules. The clinical relevance of these pathologic subtypes of cirrhosis is uncertain.

ETIOLOGY

Chronic, *excessive use of alcohol* is the predominant cause of cirrhosis in the United States, accounting for approximately 50% of the cases. Ingestion of alcohol also produces two forms of acute hepatic injury. The milder lesion, termed fatty liver, is characterized by the reversible fatty infiltration of the liver. Alcoholic hepatitis is a more serious liver disorder, characterized pathologically by a polymorphonuclear leukocyte cell infiltrate, pericentral hepatocyte necrosis, and the accumulation of alcoholic hyaline (Mallory bodies) within damaged hepatocytes. Alcoholic hepatitis has a 50% mortality rate in severe cases. Patients with alcoholic hepatitis are at high risk of developing alcoholic cirrhosis.

The development of alcoholic liver disease is not invariable in chronic alcoholics; only 50% of men who drink 200 to 300 g of alcohol daily for more than 20 years develop cirrhosis. Other factors apart from the alcohol itself apparently affect the development of cirrhosis.

Viral infections of the liver are next in importance as causes of cirrhosis in the United States. Ten percent of acute hepatitis B patients and 50% of acute hepatitis C patients develop chronic hepatitis. Liver biopsies in advanced chronic viral hepatitis show extension of the inflammatory infiltrate and hepatocyte necrosis beyond the portal tract ("piecemeal necrosis"), which leads to fibrous bridging; this may progress to cirrhosis after a variable period. Patients with hepatitis B virus are susceptible to infection with the hepatitis D virus, a defective RNA virus that can only replicate in hepatocytes infected by HBV. Infection with hepatitis D virus often results in the accelerated progression of liver disease and the frequent development of cirrhosis.

Metabolic disorders are rare causes of cirrhosis. Hemochromatosis, a genetic disorder resulting in the accumulation of hepatic iron, and Wilson's disease, a genetic defect resulting in the deposition of copper in the liver, are treatable causes of cirrhosis. α_1-Antitrypsin deficiency, the hereditary lack of an anti-α_1-globulin that controls the activities of trypsin and other proteases, results in the development of cirrhosis in childhood and more rarely in adults. Many other rare inherited disorders of metabolism may result in the development of cirrhosis. Chronic extrahepatic biliary obstruction may cause secondary biliary cirrhosis. Primary biliary cirrhosis is an immunologically mediated disorder, predominantly of middle-aged or older women, resulting in intrahepatic cholestasis and the eventual production of cirrhosis. Right-sided cardiac failure produces increased hepatic venous pressure, which may result in acute passive congestion of the liver. Severe long-standing cardiac failure may eventually result in the development of so-called "cardiac cirrhosis." Similarly, impedance to hepatic vein flow, as in veno-occlusive disease and hepatic vein thrombosis (Budd–Chiari syndrome), may also result in the development of cirrhosis. Several toxins and drugs have been reported to result in cirrhosis. The solvent carbon tetrachloride, an intrinsic hepatotoxin, produces predictable dose-related liver injury. Massive hepatic necrosis due to carbon tetrachloride has occasionally resulted in the development of postnecrotic cirrhosis. Methotrexate, an antimetabolite used in cancer chemotherapy and as a treatment for severe psoriasis, has caused hepatic fibrosis and cirrhosis.

Severe *autoimmune chronic active hepatitis* is associated with autoantibody production, occurs predominantly in young women, and can, if untreated, result in the development of cirrhosis. Intestinal bypass surgery for obesity has resulted in well-documented cases of cirrhosis. Indian childhood cirrhosis, occurring predominantly in India and Southeast Asia, results in severe liver disease in children. In approximately 10 to 15% of cases of cirrhosis in the United States, no etiology can be identified with certainty ("idiopathic or cryptogenic"). Many cases previously thought to be cryptogenic are now known to result from chronic hepatitis C virus infection.

CRITERIA FOR DIAGNOSIS
Suggestive

The presence of symptoms, signs, or biochemical evidence of liver disease is not a prerequisite for the diagnosis of cirrhosis. Patients with so-called "compensated cirrhosis" may have no objective clinical evidence of liver disease. Clinical evidence of hepatic decompensation, that is, jaundice, hepatic encephalopathy, or ascites, is good presumptive evidence of the presence of cirrhosis. Hypoalbuminemia and coagulopathy reflect failure of hepatic synthetic function and are especially strong indicators of cirrhosis. A hard nodular liver on physical examination or a nodular liver on hepatic imaging study is highly suggestive. The finding of esopheageal varices on upper endoscopic examination reflects portal hypertension, of which cirrhosis is by far the most common cause.

Definitive

Cirrhosis, is, by definition, a histopathologic condition and its definitive diagnosis requires a liver biopsy. All patients with suspected cirrhosis should have a liver biopsy, if clinical conditions permit. A liver biopsy not only establishes the presence of cirrhosis, but it may also provide an assessment of the activity of any associated hepatic inflammatory process. In addition, a liver biopsy can provide etiologic information.

CLINICAL MANIFESTATIONS
Subjective

The patient with cirrhosis may be asymptomatic. Symptoms of the hepatic inflammatory process, that is, hepatitis, may be prominent. These include fatigue, malaise, and, occasionally, upper abdominal discomfort. Most symptoms in patients with cirrhosis relate to one of several complications of liver failure. Ascites, the most common cirrhotic complication, is an accumulation of fluid within the peritoneal cavity, manifested by increased abdominal girth. Subtle neuropsychiatric symptoms, such as difficulty in concentration, irritability, and confusion, may result from mild hepatic encephalopathy. More severe encephalopathy may produce increasing lethargy and eventually coma. Thrombocytopenia and failure of hepatic synthesis of clotting factors may cause easy bruisability, hematemesis, melena, or hematochezia in the cirrhotic. Upper gastrointestinal bleeding is especially common, and usually results from the rupture of esophageal varices. Pedal edema reflects decreased intravascular oncotic pressure as a result of hypoalbuminemia.

A careful alcohol drinking history and description of other toxic or viral exposure is the most important historical information in the cirrhotic patient. The type of alcohol beverage ingested, the daily intake, and the total duration of alcohol use should be documented. Although no amount of alcohol intake is "safe," the intake of a substantial amount of alcohol for a long period is required for the development of cirrhosis. Men who drink 100 to 200 g of alcohol daily (4–8 drinks) for more than 5 years are at a high risk for the development of liver disease. Women are more sensitive to the intake of alcohol and may develop cirrhosis with lower total alcohol consumption than men. A history of alcoholic hepatitis is very common in patients with alcoholic cirrhosis.

Risk factors for viral hepatitis should be elicited. Groups that are at high risk for hepatitis B virus (HBV) infection include institutionalized patients, male homosexuals, intravenous drug users, health care workers, and immigrants from areas of high HBV endemicity. High-risk groups for hepatitis C virus carriage include intravenous drug users and recipients of transfusions.

A biliary cause of cirrhosis may be suggested by pruritis or episodic right upper quadrant pain, fever, and jaundice. A history of severe, prolonged cardiac failure and especially tricuspid insufficiency suggests "cardiac cirrhosis." Drug or toxin exposure should be identified. The presence of autoimmune phenomena may suggest autoimmune chronic liver disease. The presence of emphysema and cirrhosis in a young patient suggests α_1-antitrypsin deficiency. Neuropsychiatric disturbances in a young patient with cirrhosis should call Wilson's disease to mind. The presence of diabetes and endocrine disturbances in an older patient with cirrhosis calls for the investigation of hemochromatosis.

Family history may be helpful in the diagnosis of cirrhosis due to inherited disorders.

Objective

Physical Examination

In so-called "compensated cirrhosis" the physical examination may be normal. Liver size is variable: an enlarged, nodular, firm liver is most commonly encountered, but the liver may be normal in size or, in late stages, shrunken. The spleen is enlarged and palpable in up to 60% of cirrhotics. In decompensated cirrhosis, physical findings reflect derangements in hepatic physiology. Ascites is most commonly encountered as increased abdominal girth; bulging flanks and "fluid wave" signs are classically seen. Jaundice is often seen in late stages. Asterixis, or "liver flap," an asymmetric tremor on wrist extension, is seen in hepatic encephalopathy. Lethargy and coma are seen in later stages. Spider angiomata are seen on the skin. They are small vascular lesions consisting of a central arteriole with radiating small vessels resembling a spider's legs. Spider angiomata and palmar erythema are thought to result from derangements in estrogen metabolism by the liver. Liver-induced feminization may also produce gynecomastia and changes in body hair distribution.

Routine Laboratory Abnormalities

Abnormalities in hematologic parameters are common. Pancytopenia may result from hypersplenism. The hematocrit may be decreased, reflecting gastrointestinal bleeding. The most important indicators of hepatic synthetic function are the prothrombin time and serum albumin. Prolongation of the prothrombin time is a consequence of the failure of hepatic production of clotting factors. Albumin synthesis by the liver is depressed in cirrhosis and results in hypoalbuminemia. Hypergammaglobulinemia with an elevated serum total protein is common. Hyperbilirubinemia is generally a reflection of severe hepatic failure. Results of standard "liver function tests" are variable. Serum transaminases are elevated if hepatic inflammatory activity is ongoing. Elevation of the serum alkaline phosphatase level is common, perhaps reflecting compression of biliary ductules by the hepatic inflammatory or fibrotic process.

PLANS

Diagnostic

Differential Diagnosis

Cirrhosis is not the only cause of portal hypertension. So-called presinusoidal portal hypertension results from impairment to portal vein flow proximal to the hepatic sinusoids. Infestation of the portal venules with the parasite *Schistosoma mansoni* results in an intense fibrotic reaction ("pipestem fibrosis"), which results in impeded portal venous flow. These patients characteristically have evidence of severe portal hypertension with relatively well-preserved hepatic synthetic function. Portal or splenic vein thrombosis also produces presinusoidal portal hypertension. The extensive infiltration of the liver by metastatic tumor may produce pathophysiologic derangements that mimic cirrhosis. The emergence of hepatocellular carcinoma, often in the presence of established cirrhosis, may result in the deterioration of formerly compensated cirrhosis. Its presence is suggested by a focal mass on hepatic imaging study and an elevated serum α-fetoprotein level.

Encephalopathy is not specific to cirrhosis and may be found in uremia or other metabolic disorders. Ascites may be encountered in peritoneal carcinomatosis, nephrotic syndrome, or constrictive pericarditis. Jaundice may be seen in hemolytic states, biliary disease, acute hepatitis, and rare inherited disorders of bilirubin conjugation.

Diagnostic Options

Ascites may be obvious on physical examination; its presence should be confirmed by ultrasonography in questionable cases. A diagnostic sample of the ascitic fluid should be obtained by paracentesis in every patient with ascites. Fluid analysis may reveal the presence of spontaneous bacterial peritonitis, portal hypertension (determined by an increased serum:ascites albumin gradient), or peritoneal carcinomatosis (by cytologic examination). Upper gastrointestinal endoscopy documents the presence of esophageal varices. Hepatic imaging study should be performed in all patients to evaluate the morphology of the liver (i.e., size, contour, and texture), look for the presence of focal hepatic masses, and evaluate possible biliary or gallbladder disease. Intraabdominal collateral vessels resulting from portal hypertension are also recognized. Presence of hepatic encephalopathy is suggested by an alteration of mental status and confirmed by a elevation of serum ammonia. The electroencephalogram may show a characteristic slow wave pattern of hepatic encephalopathy.

Recommended Approach

Vigorous search for the etiology of the liver disease is mandatory. All medications suspected of contributing to the development of liver disease should be stopped. A hepatic imaging study should be performed. Ascitic fluid, if present, should be analyzed. The presence or absence of esophageal varices should be documented. Liver biopsy is recommended in all patients suspected of having cirrhosis in whom histologic confirmation has not been previously obtained. This invasive diagnostic test, which carries a small, but definite risk of bleeding, should be the last of the diagnostic efforts. Coagulation defects should be corrected prior to biopsy. Ascites is another relative contraindication to percutaneous liver biopsy. Transjugular biopsies via hepatic vein catheterization can be performed in patients with coagulopathy, but complications have been reported in up to 20% of patients. Skinny needle liver biopsy under hepatic imaging guidance may potentially decrease the risk of complications. The risks of liver biopsy may outweigh the benefits of a precise diagnosis in seriously ill patients with ascites and coagulopathy. In addition, the diagnosis of cirrhosis may be so strongly suggested by noninvasive studies that its documentation by liver biopsy is unnecessary. In these patients a presumptive diagnosis of cirrhosis may be made.

Therapeutic

Therapeutic Options

Cessation of alcohol intake is the most important therapeutic maneuver in patients with alcoholic cirrhosis. Survival is markedly improved in patients who abstain from alcohol intake, compared with those who continue to drink. Efforts to enroll the patient in a substance abuse program should be made if unassisted abstinence is impossible. If the patient with alcoholic cirrhosis cannot be made to stop drinking alcohol, the prognosis is poor, regardless of any other therapeutic efforts. Nutritional support is recommended as the majority of patients with alcoholic hepatitis and cirrhosis have evidence of protein-calorie malnutrition.

Treatment of chronic viral hepatitis with interferon in a patient with cirrhosis may be limited by exacerbation of hepatic inflammatory activity, which may produce hepatic decompensation. Interferon therapy is also less effective in patients with end-stage liver disease.

Some etiologies of cirrhosis can be treated specifically. Autoimmune chronic liver disease is treated with corticosteroids. Hemochromatosis is treated by phlebotomy or iron chelation. Wilson's disease is treated with penicillamine, a copper chelator.

In most instances the process of cirrhosis is irreversible; that is, the fibrosis and architectural distortion that define cirrhosis will not regress. Very few nonspecific agents have shown usefulness in checking the progression of the fibrotic process. Colchicine, an inhibitor of collagen synthesis, has been shown in a double-blind placebo-controlled trial to improve histologic appearances and survival in patients with cirrhosis. The effectiveness of colchicine is not universally accepted; its side effects, however, are minimal.

Given the lack of effective treatment for the fibrotic process itself, the therapy of cirrhosis mainly involves treatment of its complications. The treatment of cirrhotic ascites requires sodium restriction and diuretics. Sodium intake should be reduced to 2 g/d or less. The combination of a loop diuretic (i.e., furosemide) and an aldosterone antagonist (i.e., spironolactone) has been advocated by some as an optimal regimen. Desired weight loss is approximately 1 kg daily. Complications of diuretic therapy include azotemia, hyponatremia, and encephalopathy. The safety and efficacy of large-volume therapeutic paracentesis have been established. Intravenous infusion of albumin is believed to be a safeguard against hemodynamic instability following large-volume paracentesis. Peritoneovenous shunts designed to reinfuse the ascites into the systemic circulation via a one-way valve are ineffective. Transjugular intrahepatic portal systemic shunt (TIPS) is a new radiologic technique that has been shown to reduce ascites in some patients. The technique involves the placement of an expandable stent within the liver parenchyma which effectively produces a portal–systemic shunt. The precipitation of hepatic encephalopathy has been its primary drawback. Its place in the treatment of ascites remains to be established. The TIPS frequently occludes in 12 to 18 months.

Bleeding from esophageal varices is the most feared complication of cirrhosis. Mortality rates from an initial variceal bleed range from 40 to 70%. Rebleeding is frequent. The severity of the underlying liver disease is the most important determinant of survival in patients with variceal hemorrhage.

The management of patients with variceal bleeding is complex, and requires coordinated efforts by medical, surgical, and radiology specialists. Various modalities of treatment are briefly summarized here. Pharmacologic agents that decrease portal pressure (e.g., vasopressin, synthetic somatostatin, and nitroglycerin) are ineffective alone but are traditionally used in combination with other methods. Direct esophageal balloon tamponade (Blakemore tube) is generally ineffective and has a high complication rate. Esophageal sclerotherapy of varices, involving the direct injection of a sclerosant into the varices via endoscopic access, is the most well-established and widely used method of controlling acute variceal bleeding. A radiologic option is the percutaneous transhepatic embolization of varices involving occlusion of variceal vessels with a variety of injected substances. The recently introduced radiologic technique TIPS is very useful in the acute management of bleeding varices resistant to sclerotherapy. Surgical procedures previously used in the acute treatment of bleeding varices, for example, various portal–systemic shunts and nonshunt surgical options such as esophageal transection via a staple gun, devascularization of collateral feeding vessels, or splenectomy and/or splenic vein ligation, are subject to high mortality and complication rates and are no longer used extensively.

Onset of hepatic encephalopathy is often the result of a specific precipitating factor, such as gastrointestinal hemorrhage, diuretic overuse, sepsis, and narcotic or sedative use. Rapid identification and control of these precipitants are the most important steps in treating this syndrome. For the longer term, a protein-restricted diet is recommended to reduce the nitrogenous compounds thought to be important in the production of encephalopathy. The current mainstay of treatment of hepatic encephalopathy is lactulose. This nonabsorbed sugar moiety is metabolized by colonic bacteria to form organic acids. Acidification of the colonic lumen results in the formation of nonabsorbable ammonium ion from ammonia. Ammonium ion remains in the lumen of the gastrointestinal tract and is eliminated. Although other substances besides ammonia may contribute to encephalopathy, lactulose therapy is generally effective. Neomycin, a nonabsorbable antibiotic, has been used to reduce aerobic urease-splitting bacteria. The combination of lactulose and neomycin is commonly used; lactulose is metabolized mainly by anaerobic bacteria resistant to neomycin. A specific benzodiazepine antagonist, flumazenil, has shown some efficacy in the treatment of encephalopathy.

Recommended Approach

Alcohol should be strictly forbidden. Any other ingested toxic agents or drugs, for example, methotrexate, should be stopped. Any toxic exposures should be discontinued. Specific therapy for metabolic cirrhosis should be given as indicated. Cases of cirrhosis with ongoing viral hepatitis B or C may be helped by treatment with interferon alfa. Colchicine may be employed with relative impunity in most cases of cirrhosis to attempt to stop progression of scarring; however, its efficacy is uncertain. Development of complications of cirrhosis marks the development of decompensated disease. Successful management of these complications improves symptoms and survival; however, the underlying liver disease is generally unaffected. Beta blockers (e.g., propranolol [Inderal] 20–40 mg daily) decrease the risk of rebleeding in patients who survive an initial variceal bleed; they may also be used in patients with large varices who have not yet bled.

In patients with end-stage liver disease, evaluation for orthotopic liver transplantation should be undertaken. The introduction of the im-munosuppressive agent cyclosporine in 1979, as well as improvements in surgical technique and perioperative management, has led to dramatic improvements in survival rates after transplantation. One-year survival rates of approximately 85% are common, compared with dismal survival rates in patients with decompensated cirrhosis who are untransplanted. Alcoholic patients who continue to drink are not candidates for transplantation; those with alcoholic cirrhosis who are committed to abstinence may be transplanted. Although HBV has been considered a contraindication to transplantation in the past, due to its almost universal recurrence in the transplanted liver, 5-year survival rates of up to 80% or more have been reported by some.

FOLLOW-UP

Patients with compensated cirrhosis should be regularly evaluated for the development of complications. Those developing complications related to hepatic synthetic failure or portal hypertension should be referred, as early as possible, to a certified liver transplantation center.

DISCUSSION

Prevalence and Incidence

The prevalence of all types of chronic liver disease in the United States is estimated to be 2 cases per 100,000 persons. The prevalence of cirrhosis is likely to be underestimated due to the fact that many cases of compensated cirrhosis are clinically silent; up to 30 to 40% of cases of cirrhosis are discovered only at autopsy. Cirrhosis is the fifth leading cause of death in the United States in persons over 40 years of age, with a mortality rate of 14.8 per 100,000 persons. Alcoholic hepatitis and cirrhosis are the most important liver diseases in the United States, accounting for approximately 20,000 to 40,000 deaths annually.

Related Basic Science

The development of hepatic fibrosis is a common response to many forms of liver injury. The distortion of hepatic architecture by fibrosis is a sine qua non for the development of cirrhosis. Fibrosis results from the accumulation of extracellular matrix materials, including fibril-forming collagens (types I and III) in the subendothelial space of Disse. The key cell in the production of extracellular matrix constituents is the hepatic lipocyte or Ito cell. The activation of this cell, distinguished by large intracellular droplets containing vitamin A in the normal liver, is believed to be the initiating step of hepatic fibrosis. The process of lipocyte activation involves a morphologic change (including loss of intracellular retinoids), lipocyte proliferation, increased fibrogenesis, and the acquisition of smooth muscle-like features by the Ito cell. Increased expression of receptors for cytokines is apparent in the activated lipocyte. Platelet-derived growth factor is the most potent proliferative cytokine described and transforming growth factor β_1 is a powerful fibrogenic cytokine. Following activation, perpetuation of lipocyte activation is critical for continued deposition of extracellular matrix components. The stimulus for the initiation of Ito cell activation may involve hepatocyte necrosis or inflammatory mediators. Much remains to be learned. Progress in understanding the mechanism of hepatic fibrosis holds promise for more effective antifibrotic therapy.

Natural History and Its Modification with Treatment

Cirrhosis is an irreversible process. In certain instances, however, the cirrhotic process may be halted. In alcoholic cirrhosis, for example, the cessation of alcohol intake generally stops the progression of liver disease. Patients with well-compensated alcoholic cirrhosis who abstain from alcohol may have survival similar to that of age- and sex-matched control subjects. Patients with decompensated cirrhosis who continue to drink have a dismal short-term prognosis; if these patients stop drinking, their outlook is dramatically improved.

The decompensation of initially compensated cirrhosis is approximately 10% per year. Patients with decompensated cirrhosis have an approximately 20% 6-year survival. Child's classification based on jaundice, ascites, encephalopathy, serum albumin, and nutritional status provides a reasonable prognostic guide.

In the vast majority of patients with cirrhosis, no medical treatment alters the natural history of the disease. In end-stage liver disease, the performance of orthotopic liver transplantation radically alters the progressively downhill course and often leads to prolonged, relatively symptom-free survival.

Prevention

Alcoholic cirrhosis is a self-inflicted disease. It can be entirely prevented in the individual patient by the cessation of alcohol intake. Alcoholic patients may require professional support to overcome their addiction. Virus-associated cirrhosis may be prevented by the avoidance of sexual or percutaneous exposure to hepatitis B and C viruses. Postexposure prophylaxis may reduce the risk of infection after inadvertent exposure. The potential of the HBV vaccine to diminish the prevalence of worldwide HBV infection has yet to be exploited.

Cost Containment

Large-volume therapeutic paracentesis has been shown to significantly reduce length of hospital stay and reduce costs in patients hospitalized for ascites. The use of intravenous albumin infusion during large-volume paracentesis has been advocated. Albumin is very expensive and its utility in this setting should be definitively established before its use becomes routine. Less expensive plasma expanders may be as effective as albumin.

Liver transplantation is obviously an expensive intervention. It is, however, the only modality that improves survival in terminally ill patients with liver failure.

REFERENCES

Carrithers RL Jr. Alcoholic hepatitis and cirrhosis. In: Kaplowitz N, ed. Liver and biliary diseases, Baltimore: Williams & Wilkins, 1992:334.

Conn HO, Atterbury CE. Cirrhosis. In Schiff L, Schiff ER, eds. Diseases of the liver. 7th ed. Philadelphia: Lippincott, 1993:875.

Erlinger S, Benhamou JP. Cirrhosis: Clinical aspects. In: McIntyre N, Benhamou JP, Bircher J, et al., eds. Oxford textbook of clinical hepatology. Oxford: Oxford University Press, 1991:380.

Friedman SL. Seminars in medicine of the Beth Israel Hospital, Boston: The cellular basis of hepatic fibrosis: Mechanisms and treatment strategies. N Engl J Med 1993;328:1828.

Howard TK, Podesta LG, Sher LS, et al. Liver transplantation. In: Kaplowitz N, ed. Liver and biliary diseases. Baltimore: Williams & Wilkins, 1992:566.

Sherlock S. Hepatic cirrhosis. In: Sherlock S, Dooley J, eds. Diseases of the liver and biliary system. 9th ed. Oxford: Blackwell, 1993:357.

CHAPTER 19–81

Primary Biliary Cirrhosis

Nora Valeria Bergasa, M.D.

DEFINITION

Primary biliary cirrhosis (PBC) is a liver disease characterized by a chronic nonsuppurative destructive cholangitis that affects septal and the larger interlobular intrahepatic bile ducts; it tends to progress and to ultimately lead to biliary cirrhosis and liver failure (Kaplan, 1987).

ETIOLOGY

The etiology of PBC is unknown. It is referred to as an autoimmune disease. There is evidence suggesting an autoimmune pathophysiologic basis; however, at the time of this writing the interesting possibility that an infectious agent may be involved in the pathogenesis of the disease cannot be excluded.

CRITERIA FOR DIAGNOSIS

Suggestive

The classic presentation of PBC is in a middle-aged woman, who presents with pruritus, fatigue, and a hepatic biochemical profile suggestive of cholestasis. Also, patients can present with jaundice at the time of diagnosis. It is more common in women. Male patients present similarly. PBC is being increasingly recognized, particularly in asymptomatic patients.

Definitive

The definitive diagnosis of PBC is the presence of a "florid" bile duct lesion characterized by nonsuppurative destructive cholangitis in liver tissue and the presence of antimitochondrial antibody (AMA) in the serum of patients with PBC. There are AMA-negative PBC cases. Because PBC is a progressive liver disease and because of its patchy nature, there is an inevitable sampling error inherent in the evaluation of the liver specimens from these patients. The Scheuer classification of PBC consists of four histologic stages. This classification suggests, in the view of this writer, the dynamic nature of this illness. Stage I is characterized by the "florid" bile duct lesion of nonsuppurative destructive cholangitis (Figure 19–81–1). In the best cases, the attack of the biliary epithelium by mononuclear cells (lymphocytes) can be appreciated, with vacuolization and sloughing of bile duct basal membrane. Occasionally, granulomata in the nearby parenchyma can be seen. Stage II disease is characterized by bile ductular proliferation. In this situation, bile ductules with serpentine appearance appear in the periportal area. These biliary structures, as they proliferate, embrace the hepatocytes in the periportal region, giving them a rounded appearance, known as biliary piecemeal. Stage III is characterized by hepatic fibrosis of the biliary type. Bridges of collagen appear linking portal areas. Stage IV is characterized by biliary cirrhosis, which has been described as resembling a jigsaw puzzle. Histologic findings associated with PBC are cholangiolitis, characterized by the presence of polymorphonuclear leukocytes in the inflammatory infiltrate, and pseudoxanthomatous

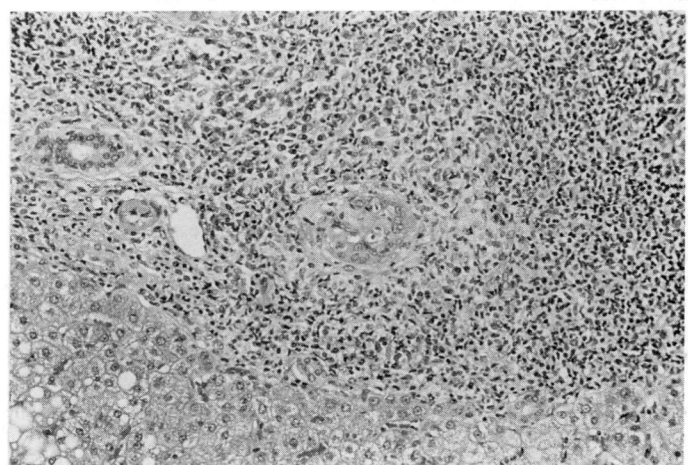

Figure 19–81–1. Liver biopsy from a patient with primary biliary cirrhosis. A dense mononuclear infiltrate surrounds an injured bile duct with a disappearing lumen. Another view of what appears to be the same duct is seen with vacuolization and the beginning of epithelial rupture. Bile ductules are seen at the periphery of the cellular infiltrate. Fat droplets are seen in periportal hepatocytes.

changes, a "bubbly" appearance of periportal hepatocytes resulting from cholate stasis (accumulation of bile acids). The histologic lesions result in the destruction of the intrahepatic bile ducts, leading to a decrease in their numbers or in their absence, a condition known as ductopenia.

The cellular infiltrate that characterizes nonsuppurative destructive cholangitis is composed of plasma cells, eosinophils, and T lymphocytes, the last representing the majority. Phenotypic immunologic studies have characterized these lymphocytes as being of the CD4+ and CD8+ types. It appears that the predominance of a particular phenotype may depend on the stage of the disease. The majority of the T lymphocytes found in PBC are T-cell alpha/beta receptor positive, with, a small percentage of cells being gamma/delta receptor positive. This latter receptor chain type has been implicated in the pathogenesis of autoimmunity and in formation of granulomata in diseases such as leprosy. The triggering factor and precise series of events that lead to bile duct injury and bile duct loss are unknown. It has been proposed that an unknown "antigen" is expressed on the surface of the biliary epithelial cell. This "antigen" is processed by periportal macrophages and specifically dendritic cells, which act as antigen presenting cells and present "it" to T cells for recognition. Antigen processing and presentation by antigen presenting cells result in secretion of interleukin (IL) 1, which activates CD4+ T cells. These "antigen"-stimulated T cells produce IL-2, which binds to IL-2 receptors on the surface of activated T cells. One of the effects of IL-2 is to induce the proliferation of "antigen"-activated CD4+ (and maybe CD8+) cells. Other cytokines are secreted by activated T cells, particularly interferon gamma, which induces the expression of HLA class II antigens on the biliary epithelial cells and tumor necrosis factor-α. The aberrant expression of HLA class II molecules enables the presentation of the "antigen" by the biliary epithelial cells, facilitating their inflammatory attack by lymphocytes. There is in vitro evidence suggesting that biliary epithelial cells can themselves be antigen presenting cells, thus facilitating their immunologic interactions by lymphocytes when foreign or self (if autoimmunity is responsible) antigens are being recognized. The secretion of inflammatory cytokines probably affects the endothelium of the peribiliary capillary plexus, contributing to the inflammatory events.

CLINICAL MANIFESTATION
Subjective

Primary biliary cirrhosis is characterized by a slowly progressive course. In symptomatic patients, the earliest and sometimes the only manifestations are pruritus and fatigue. Because pruritus can be the only symptom experienced by some patients with PBC, it is worth discussing some of its characteristics. Its recognition as a manifestation of a liver disease such as PBC may save the patient several trips to the dermatologist and/or allergist. The pruritus of PBC or the pruritus of cholestasis is of unknown etiology (see below). This form of pruritus can be mild, without interference with regular activities; moderate, prompting patients to seek therapeutic intervention; or severe and intractable, leading to sleep deprivation. The pruritus of cholestasis is not readily relieved by scratching; this characteristic stimulates the patients to scratch with abrasive objects such as forks, knives, and hair brushes. It can be generalized or localized to particular parts of the body, in particular the palms of the hands and the soles of the feet, where often the symptom is first perceived. The perception of the pruritus of cholestasis varies considerably among patients and it does not appear to correlate with serum biochemical parameters of liver disease. This form of pruritus can be persistent or intermittent. The perception of itch may be influenced by a variety of factors, such as changes in mood and distractions. It can be exacerbated by normal physiologic changes such as the premenstrual state in women; therefore, it is important to obtain this information during interview.

Fatigue can be subtle and, in general, patients state that they have to push themselves to do what they easily did in the past. Because PBC can be associated with thyroid disease, specifically hypothyroidism which is often subclinical, a systematic way to evaluate fatigue in a patient with possible PBC is comparable to the evaluation of patients with possible thyroid disease. Abdominal pain is a recognized symptom of

PBC; it tends to be dull, on the right side of the abdomen over the liver area. The "liver pain" is said to be due to "inflammation" and "stretching of Glisson's capsule." The cause is unknown but it may be related to the activation of hepatobiliary nerves by the inflammatory process. Bone pain secondary to osteoporosis is another symptom of patients with PBC and it can be debilitating. Osteoporosis can lead to fractures, often spontaneous, particularly involving trabecular bone (e.g., vertebral bodies). Loss of height may be subtle but apparent to the patient.

Primary biliary cirrhosis can be associated with other diseases, particularly those considered to be of autoimmune etiology. Nonhepatic disorders in patients with PBC have been reported in close to 70% of patients. Inability to produce tears, difficulties in wearing contact lenses, inability to eat a cracker without drinking fluids, and recent onset of dental caries are suggestive of Sjögren's syndrome, one of the most common syndromes associated with PBC. The CREST syndrome (calcinosis, Raynaud's phenomenon, esophageal dysmotility, sclerodactyly, and telangiectasias) can also be associated with PBC. It has also been associated with rheumatoid arthritis. Thus, joint pains, dysphagia, and pyrosis are among other symptoms that can be experienced by PBC patients. In addition, PBC has been reported in association with celiac disease, autoimmune thrombocytopenia, pancreatic insufficiency, lichen planus, systemic lupus erythematosus, pernicious anemia, ulcerative colitis, pulmonary fibrosis, cardiomyopathy, multiple myeloma, Grave's disease, and retroperitoneal fibrosis. The incidence of breast cancer has been reported to be significantly higher in women with PBC. Skin hyperpigmentation can be a presenting complaint of a patient. Although a sign, it is mentioned with symptoms because it is usually noted by the patients. The hyperpigmentation of PBC is generalized, starts insidiously, for example, when a patient becomes aware of its existence after the sun tan obtained during the summer persists for a long period of time and often does not go away. There is a higher incidence of cholelithiasis in PBC patients, which should be left alone when asymptomatic. The incidence of hepatocellular carcinoma may be increased in PBC.

The etiology of PBC is unknown and more often than not a past medical history is of no immediate help. On the other hand, there are medications known to precipitate cholestasis and there are cases of PBC that have been "unmasked" by the ingestion of a particular drug. In many instances, medication-induced cholestasis is reversible, but the occurrence of long-term drug-induced cholestasis with ductopenia is being increasingly recognized. Thus, in a patient presenting with symptoms of cholestasis (e.g., jaundice, pruritus, fatigue) a history of medication ingestion is very important, because it offers the opportunity for discontinuation of the drug and it may help elucidate some of the mechanisms that trigger this disease as well as other cholestatic syndromes. Estrogen-containing medications (e.g., contraceptives) can precipitate cholestasis, and a history of contraceptive use in female patients with PBC is not rare. This may only reflect that many women have taken contraceptives at one point in their lives. The classic drug that has been associated with a PBC-like syndrome is chlorpromazine.

Objective
Physical Examination

The physical manifestations of PBC range from a normal-appearing patient to a patient with advanced liver disease manifested by jaundice and ascites. The latter appears to be decreasing in incidence, perhaps because of increased access to medical care allowing for an earlier diagnosis or for unapparent reasons. PBC may be suspected in asymptomatic patients with stigmata of liver disease. Some of the signs can be seen in asymptomatic and symptomatic patients and, therefore, are considered together. On physical examination, cheilosis, spider angiomata, paper money skin, cutaneous xanthomata and xanthelasma secondary to the lipid-related abnormalities of PBC, Dupuytren's contractures (more common in alcoholic-related liver disease), palmar erythema, telangiectasias of buccal mucosa, and hyperpigmentation may be apparent. Patients who suffer from pruritus may have cutaneous excoriations and prurigo nodularis secondary to chronic scratching. Hepatomegaly may or may not be present; increased hepatic volume in PBC has been reported in stages I and II of the disease. Splenomegaly resulting from portal hypertension may be present. Xanthomatous neuropathy may be a symptom complex, as may carpal tunnel syndrome.

Routine Laboratory Abnormalities

The characteristic laboratory abnormality in patients with PBC is elevated serum activity of liver-associated enzymes, specifically, increased activity of serum alkaline phosphatase, γ-glutamyl transpeptidase, and 5'-nucleotidase. Alanine and aspartate transaminases are usually elevated, but to a lesser degree. Thrombocytopenia secondary to hypersplenism or to immune complex abnormalities may be present. Anemia and neutropenia may be present in advanced disease. Urine analysis may reveal an alkaline pH suggestive of renal tubular acidosis believed to be secondary to copper deposits in the distal renal tubules; also, bacteriuria, asymptomatic in many cases, is common in patients with PBC. Controversy on whether there is a higher incidence of urinary tract infections in patients with PBC exists. Serum bile acids are elevated (fasting and 2-hour postprandial levels are more accurate in reflecting cholestasis).

PLANS

Diagnostic

Differential Diagnosis

The differential diagnosis of PBC includes all the cholestatic disorders that are more common in adults. The differential diagnosis of PBC includes drug-induced cholestasis, granulomatous diseases (e.g., sarcoidosis), postcholescystectomy syndrome (e.g., biliary strictures), α_1-antitrypsin deficiency, hepatitis C, primary sclerosing cholangitis, Hodgkin's disease, and graft-versus-host disease after bone marrow transplantation. Hepatitis A can be complicated by prolonged cholestasis, but its serology is diagnostic. Recently, a form of cholangitis very similar to PBC has been described, and it has been termed *immunocholangitis*. This condition may well have an autoimmune basis.

Diagnostic Options

Serum immunoglobulins may be abnormal, in particular, PBC is characteristically associated with elevated levels of serum IgM although the disease can occur in patients with IgM deficiency. Approximately 90 to 95% of patients with PBC have AMA present in their serum, and this test is considered confirmatory for the disease (see below). This test should be requested when evaluating a patient for possible PBC. Antinuclear antibodies may also be present and the reported prevalence ranges from 0 to 46%. AMA-negative PBC also occurs, and the diagnosis is made when other signs, symptoms, laboratory abnormalities, and characteristic liver histology are present. The term *autoimmune cholangitis* has been cited to define a particular subgroup of these patients. A recent series of 20 patients described to have autoimmune cholangitis with no detectable AMA by immunoblotting and by enzyme-linked immunosorbent assay for M2 antigens and positive for antinuclear antibody did not report any distinctive clinical features compared with the 20 AMA-positive patients who served as the control group (Michieletti, et al.). Thus, subclassification of patients based on antibodies may not be helpful in terms of pathogenesis and prognosis; however, the nature of the "triggering factor" for the development of this disease(s) may be different or similar, in the face of specific patients' response (e.g., ability to develop antibodies versus lack of it). These differences remain to be elucidated. Antibodies to a nuclear core protein, gp200, appear in the serum of 10% of patients with PBC.

Recommended Approach

Asymptomatic patients with PBC may present to the physician for a routine "checkup." Routine laboratory blood work may reveal elevated serum activity of liver-associated enzymes (see above). PBC should be suspected in any patient with fatigue and/or pruritus, particularly in the absence of primary pruritic skin lesions. Abnormal liver-associated enzymes in the routine laboratory panel of a symptomatic patient, particularly when the laboratory picture suggests cholestasis, should trigger the initiation of a diagnostic workup for PBC. Asymptomatic patients with abnormal laboratory panels should be investigated in a similar

way. When the presentation of the disease is classic (as described above), the next available test that will confirm the suspicion of PBC is the presence of AMA. The commercial availability of M2 AMAs has reduced the incidence of false-positive results of the AMA test. Other causes of liver diseases should be excluded. Specifically, the possible existence of viral hepatitis B and C should be ruled out; in addition, serum levels of α_1-antitrypsin, ceruloplasmin, ferritin (in fasting state), and angiotensin-converting enzyme, and a serum VDRL should be obtained. It is recommended to check for the presence of antinuclear antibody and to request quantitation of total globulins and quantitative immunoelectrophoresis.

Once elevated activity of liver-associated enzymes has been documented on repeated testing, an expeditious workup is recommended. Because liver diseases may coexist, a comprehensive biochemical and serologic investigation, which has the advantage of being noninvasive, should be initiated. Liver sonogram is recommended to rule out biliary obstruction and for evaluation of the liver parenchyma; and, specifically, to rule out the presence of cysts (often benign) and hepatic hemangiomata, which may represent a problem when a blind procedure such as percutaneous liver biopsy is done.

If the patients have not been seen by a gastroenterologist or hepatologist during the laboratory workup, referral for case evaluation is in order at this stage. The decision to perform a liver biopsy should always be individualized, and it is not different in PBC. A cholestatic liver profile and a positive AMA in an elderly individual or one at high risk for bleeding is sufficient to make the diagnosis of PBC. Treatments for PBC are considered experimental at this point; thus, a liver biopsy is not crucial in every case. Alternatively, when evaluating a patient with a questionable diagnosis, a liver biopsy may be very helpful in confirming the diagnosis of PBC.

It is not imperative that all patients being investigated for possible PBC have the biliary tract (and pancreatic ducts) investigated by endoscopic retrograde cholangiopancreatography (ERCP). This should be done when the diagnosis is questionable (e.g., negative AMA, nondiagnostic liver biopsy). When the patients are male, in particular when AMA is negative, primary sclerosing cholangitis has to be considered, and in those cases, ERCP may be in order.

Once the diagnosis of PBC is confirmed, bone mineral density should be determined by noninvasive techniques such as dual-photon absorptiometry, dual-energy x-ray absorptiometry, and quantitative computed tomography scanning.

Therapeutic

Therapeutic Options

There is no curative treatment for PBC at this time or a treatment of choice. All drugs being used are considered experimental. Because of the immunologic association of PBC and the histologic resemblance of the PBC liver lesion to the lesion of graft-versus-host disease, most of the medications that have been tested for the treatment of PBC have been immunomodulators.

Several clinical studies of immunosuppressive drugs for PBC have been performed. The medications tested include azathioprine, cyclosporine, chlorambucil, and prednisone. None of these are recommended for routine treatment either because they have not proven to be beneficial or because of their toxicity. Because cholestasis is associated with copper accumulation in the liver, the cupruretic agent penicillamine was evaluated in a clinical trial, which did prove it to be of benefit for the treatment of the disease. Colchicine therapy has been associated with reduction of liver enzymes and, in one study, with improved survival. Its use in PBC continues to be studied; the major side effect to consider is polyneuropathy. Current attention is being given to ursodeoxycholic acid (Ursodiol, Actigal) and to the immunomodulator/anticancer drug methotrexate. Ursodeoxycholic acid is a hydrophilic bile acid that is less toxic to intrahepatic cells than hydrophobic bile acids. Its administration is associated with an increase in the ratio of ursodeoxycholic acid to taurocholic acid in plasma and in bile. The administration of this medication to patients with PBC is associated with a reduction in the serum activity of liver-associated enzymes, bilirubin, serum immunoglobulin M and AMA titers; thus, an immunologic action has been proposed. Its effect on symptoms is debatable. An unequivocally beneficial effect of ursodeoxycholic acid on the histologic lesion of PBC has not been demonstrated, and it has not been shown to improve the survival of patients with PBC who have received this treatment, although in one study, when a group of patients treated with ursodeoxycholic acid (13–15 mg/kg body weight per day in two divided doses) was compared with the placebo–treated control group of patients, the time to liver transplantation referral or death at 2 years was longer in the treated group. Determination of the effect of any drug on the survival of patients with PBC has been a difficult task because the natural history of PBC is characterized by its slow progress; thus, very large numbers of patients are needed to conclude if a drug alters survival. Methotrexate therapy has been reported to be associated with decreased serum activity of liver-associated enzymes, symptoms, and improvements on liver histology. Methotrexate therapy is associated with side effects, some of which can be serious (e.g., pneumonitis, questionable liver cirrhosis with its prolonged ingestion); thus, it should not be administered outside the context of clinical studies. Current proposed approaches to PBC suggest that successful therapy may require a combination of medications according to disease stages. If an immunologic phenomenon is what triggers the initial bile duct destruction, which is followed by cholestasis, fibrosis, and cirrhosis, the model of treatment that has been proposed is the administration of immunomodulators, anticholestatic/choleretics, and antifibrotics alone or in combination according to the stage of the disease. At the time of this writing, clinical trials are being conducted to evaluate the effect of ursodeoxycholic acid alone and in combination with methotrexate (National Institutes of Health, Clinical Research Information).

Recommended Approach

It is emphasized that the best way to approach the treatment of a patient with PBC is to identify centers that are conducting clinical trials where the patients can be referred for evaluation and possible entry into the trials. The most effective way to obtain this information is to call university hospitals or the National Institutes of Health. In cases of advancing PBC, suggested by increasing levels of serum bilirubin (see below) or well-established biliary cirrhosis near decompensation or in decompensation (e.g., ascites, episodes of hepatic encephalopathy), prompt referral to a center where liver transplantations are performed is the recommendation. It is preferable to have early evaluation to register the patient in the system rather than to have to make emergency decisions with regard to liver transplantation.

Because there are no specific therapies for PBC, often patients are treated according to their symptoms. It is recommended that patients eat a balanced diet. Vitamin supplements are not recommended unless a particular deficiency is documented by blood levels. In particular, the administration of vitamin A is not recommended because of the danger of toxicity. The general guidelines to prevent or treat postmenopausal osteoporosis are followed for patients with PBC. Physical activity and exercise as tolerated are recommended. If osteoporosis is diagnosed, advice from physical therapists is in order to formulate the best exercise plan for the patient. Calcium supplements in the range of 1.5 to 2 g/d are recommended. Because of the capability of estrogen to induce cholestasis, estrogen therapy has been avoided in cholestasis; however, therapy for osteoporosis with low-dose oral or transdermal estrogens is receiving consideration at present. If estrogens are indicated for gynecological indications, they can be administered with regular follow-up of liver profile. The role of calcitonin and biphosphonates has not been adequately studied in PBC. Steroids should be avoided because of their osteopenic effects.

Because the pruritus of cholestasis is of unknown etiology, its management has been empirical (Bergasa and Jones, 1991). The conventional management of this form of pruritus includes cholestyramine (Questran) and, more recently, colestipol. These are anion-binding resins that decrease the enterohepatic circulation of bile acids and bind a number of substances (anions) in the bowel. The mechanism of action of this type of drug in the management of this form of pruritus is unknown, but it is presumed that they bind the "pruritogenic substance(s)" that may be secreted in bile. The recommended dose of cholestyramine is 4 g before and after breakfast to increase the binding efficiency of the resin on the "pruritogenic substance" that has accumu-

lated in the gallbladder overnight. Four additional grams may be taken if necessary after each subsequent meal. It is important to take these resins at least 2 hours apart from the ingestion of any prescribed medications to ensure their absorption. The maximal recommended dose of cholestyramine is 16 g/d. Antihistamines do not appear to be helpful, and their sedative effect and the xerostomia associated with their ingestion tend to be unpleasant. Phenobarbital is a choleretic agent and it is also a sedative agent; thus, it is difficult for patients to deal with their regular activities under sedation. There are several clinical trials using subjective criteria that have shown that the antibiotic rifampicin (150 mg twice a day if bilirubin > 3 mg/dL and 300 mg twice a day if bilirubin < 3 g/dL) ameliorates this form of pruritus. A long-term study of the use of this drug in patients with PBC and pruritus reported lack of hepatic toxicity and good tolerability; however, it may be associated with hepatotoxicity and peripheral neuropathies. The mechanism of action of rifampicin or other enzyme inducers on this form of pruritus is unknown. More recently, the role of the endogenous opioid system in the pathogenesis of the pruritus of cholestasis has been studied. It has been shown by subjective and objective methodology that the administration of opiate antagonists (naloxone and nalmefene) significantly ameliorates pruritus and its behavioral manifestations such as scratching activity. These results strongly implicate the endogenous opioid system in the pathogenesis of the pruritus of cholestasis. Nalmefene is not commercially available at present; however, naloxone (0.4 mg intravenous bolus, followed by constant infusions 0.2–0.8 μg/kg/ min) can be used in emergency cases such as those involving a patient who is suicidal because she or he can no longer live with intractable pruritus. Hospitalization and consultation with a psychiatrist are recommended in these cases. Sometimes, changing the environment appears to have a beneficial effect on this condition. This form of pruritus may be so severe that it alone can be indication for liver transplantation.

FOLLOW-UP

The regularity of medical follow-up depends on the stage of the disease. Every 3 to 6 months may be adequate. If the patients are enrolled in clinical studies, those guidelines need to be followed.

DISCUSSION

Prevalence and Incidence

The reported prevalence of PBC from different countries in Europe ranges from 0.7 to 7.5 per 100,000 persons. The yearly incidence in the United Kingdom has been reported to be 5.8 per million population. Comparable studies in the United States have not been published. PBC is estimated to account for 0.6 to 2% of the deaths due to cirrhosis in the world. These numbers will change because PBC is being increasingly recognized in asymptomatic patients. This appears to be the result of routine periodical medical evaluations either sought by patients, mandated by insurance companies prior to the delivery of insurance policies, or initiated by physicians.

Related Basic Science

Genetics

Genetic predisposition may play a role in the development of PBC. PBC can occur in members of the same families, including twins; however, a well-defined genetic association has not been found. There appear to be limitations in the techniques that involve HLA genotyping; in addition, small sample size has been a problem in most of the studies. No association between PBC and HLA class I antigens has been shown to date. It has been proposed that HLA class II may play a role in the pathogenesis of PBC, particularly because the aberrant expression of HLA class II antigens occurs in the biliary epithelia of patients affected by PBC. The HLA class II associations with PBC that have been described include HLA-DR2 in Japan, HLA-DRw3 in Spain, HLA-DPB1*0301 in Germany, HLA-DRw8 in Germany and North America, and HLA-DR8 and the complement allele C4B2 in northern Europeans. A recent study has revised this last association and has confirmed that, HLA-DR8 is more common in the PBC-affected population and that it may confer susceptibility to develop PBC or, alternatively, that the susceptibility locus is located close to HLA-DR8. The lack of HLA-DR8 association in large numbers of PBC patients suggests that factors other than genetic susceptibility play a role in the pathogenesis of PBC.

Altered Molecular Biology

PBC is a disease of unknown etiology. Because of its association with autoimmune phenomena, an autoimmune basis for the disease has been postulated. The presence of autoantibodies in the serum of patients with PBC constitutes one of the most prominent laboratory features of this disease. The AMAs recognize proteins that are part of the 2-oxoacid dehydrogenase complex located in the inner membrane of the mitochondria, found in all nucleated cell types (Gershwin and Mackay, 1991). The dominant response of the antimitochondrial antibody is directed against the E2 component of the pyruvate dehydrogenase complex, dihydrolipoamide acetyltransferase (PDH-E2)—the major antigen—and of the branched-chain ketoacid dehydrogenase (BCKD-E2). The properties of the antibodies to 2-oxoacid dehydrogenase complex are interesting: (1) They may be present as immunoglobulin (Ig) M and IgG classes, with an important restriction to IgG3 subclass. This has been noticed in other autoimmune diseases. (2) These antibodies inhibit the activity of the enzyme to which they are directed (e.g., PDH *in vitro*). (3) There is no apparent cross-reactivity between the different antibodies and enzymes, suggesting immunologic specificity (Gershwin and Mackay, 1991). Monoclonal antibodies against PDH-E2 have been raised and they appear to react specifically with an antigen expressed on the luminal surface of biliary epithelial cells in liver tissue from patients with PBC. The significance of this finding is an active area of investigational interest.

Antibodies to the integral proteins of the nuclear membrane—the laminin B receptor—and antibodies to the nuclear pore protein gp210 have also been detected in the sera of patients with PBC. Antibody to gp210 has been reported to occur in 11% of patients with AMA-positive PBC and in approximately 21% of patients with AMA-negative PBC in one report. Patients with antibody to gp210 had a higher incidence of rheumatoid arthritis.

In summary, the use of molecular biology techniques and increasingly sophisticated methods to study the immune system has been crucial in the elucidation of the AMAs and other autoantibodies present in the serum of patients with PBC, however their role in the pathogenesis of PBC remains elusive.

Physiologic or Metabolic Derangement

Alterations in the endogenous opioid system have been described in cholestasis including that secondary to PBC (Bergasa and Jones, 1991). A well-described action of opiate drugs is the induction of pruritus, which is satisfactorily treated with the opiate antagonist naloxone. Patients with cholestasis suffer from pruritus, and this form of pruritus can be ameliorated significantly by the administration of opiate antagonist drugs (Sherlock and Dooley, 1991; Bergasa and Jones, 1991). In addition, patients with liver disease, primarily cholestatic, experience an abnormal reaction after the administration of opiate antagonists in the absence of exogenous ingestion of opiate drugs. These observations, which have been confirmed in clinical trials, suggest that altered neurotransmission/neuromodulation via the endogenous opioid system is a feature of liver disease and that endogenous opioids mediate the pruritus of cholestasis, at least in part. The origin of this alteration is unknown and includes increased availability of endogenous opioid ligands in the nervous system.

Metabolic bone disease is a major cause of morbidity in patients with PBC (and other cholestatic liver diseases) (Sherlock and Dooley, 1991). The most common form of bone disease in these patients is osteoporosis; osteomalacia is uncommon. Current evidence does not support the role of vitamin D deficiency, which can be a complication of cholestasis, in cholestatic osteopenia. The presence of circulating "osteoblast inhibitors" has been proposed but not demonstrated. Osteoporosis increases markedly after liver transplantation as a result of immunosuppression and lack of physical activity in the immediate postoperative period; however, there is long-term improvement in bone formation after liver transplantation in PBC patients.

Elevated basal metabolic rate was one of the first metabolic abnormalities described in PBC. Interestingly and unexplained to date, percutaneous biliary drainage decreases energy expenditure (Sherlock and Dooley, 1991).

Primary biliary cirrhosis is associated with accumulation of copper in the liver and other organs; this is an abnormality secondary to cholestasis. Plasma levels of copper and ceruloplasmin are elevated, as is the level of urinary copper (Sherlock and Dooley, 1991).

The skin hyperpigmentation of PBC is mediated by melanin, and probably secondary to increased activity or concentration of α-melancyte-stimulating hormone.

Serum lipids in PBC patients are elevated and the characteristics of these abnormalities are complex (Sherlock and Dooley, 1991). The majority of the circulating lipids are high-density lipoproteins. A recent study reported that high plasma lipid concentrations was not associated with an increased incidence of atherosclerosis in a PBC population when compared with a control population. It seems prudent to obtain a lipid profile in PBC patients and to follow the general guidelines of the American Heart Association. Clofibrate should not be used in PBC patients because its administration is associated with a parodoxical increase in serum cholesterol levels (Sherlock and Dooley, 1991).

Natural History and Its Modification with Treatment

Reports on the natural history of PBC have not been without controversy. It was initially reported that the survival of asymptomatic patients was similar to that of the normal population. More recently, decreased survival of asymptomatic PBC patients has been reported, precipitating arguments for the inclusion of asymptomatic patients in clinical trials of experimental treatments. The reported survival after the onset of symptoms ranges from 8 to 12 years depending on the series (Kaplan, 1987; Sherlock and Dooley, 1991). Thus, the consensus is that PBC, whether accompanied by symptoms or not, progresses and is associated with significant morbidity and mortality. In cases of hepatic decompensation, complications such as ascites, hepatic encephalopathy, and variceal bleeding develop. The plasma level of serum bilirubin is the best prognostic sign. A rising serum bilirubin augurs advancing disease and poor prognosis. Serum albumin, which appears to depend on both the rate of albumin synthesis and the plasma volume in chronic liver disease, may also be a useful marker in evaluating disease progression; however, appreciable changes in either serum bilirubin or serum albumin do not occur until the disease process of PBC has undergone substantial progression. A total serum bilirubin above normal suggests advanced disease. The need for serum biochemical markers of PBC and/or reliable liver function tests useful in the follow-up of PBC patients, including the asymptomatic phase, cannot be overemphasized. The limitation of routine serum biochemistry in monitoring progress in patients with PBC is illustrated by the occurrence of florid bile duct lesions characteristic of the disease in liver biopsies from some untreated patients who have normal values for serum bilirubin, transaminases, and alkaline phosphatase. There have been several attempts to design prognostic tools. The authors of the multicenter azathioprine trial developed a prognostic index to facilitate analysis of their data. A prognostic index for PBC has also been developed at the Mayo Clinic (Wiesner et al., 1992). The importance of clinical follow-up and continuity of care of one physician and her or his patient is, in the opinion of this writer, the gold standard.

Death and referral for liver transplantation constitute definitive endpoints for studies of the effects of immunosuppressive drugs on PBC. This is also a difficult issue. For example, the percentage of patients who underwent liver transplantation or died in the azathioprine trial was slightly less in the treated group than in the placebo group. Other trials had a small number of patients and survival studies could not be done. A clear example of the difficulties in assessing prognosis even in the context of clinical trials is depicted in the experience of the azathioprine trial. When the data were analyzed by use of the Kaplan–Meier method, the difference between treated and control groups was not significant; however, when the Cox regression model was used for data analysis, the difference between the two groups was highly significant.

Cirrhosis secondary to PBC is one of the major indications for liver transplantation in adult patients (Wiesner et al., 1992). Patients tend to do well after liver transplantation, and the 1-year survival is reported to be close to 70%. Retransplantation was necessary in 25% of the patients in one series (University of Pittsburgh) because of vanishing duct syndrome and cholestasis (Sherlock and Dooley, 1991). Liver transplantation is not without complications. Immunosuppressant therapy is associated with substantial morbidity (e.g., opportunistic infections, renal insufficiency, and hypertension). Thus, it is crucial to select the appropriate timing for liver transplantation: not too early and not too late because both extremes may negatively affect the quality of life of the patients (Sherlock and Dooley, 1991). It is prudent to identify resources available to patients (e.g., payment issues and center selection). Ample time should be allowed when possible for patients and their family members to consider their options and to receive support.

Early reports indicating that PBC recurs in the transplanted liver were controversial in part because the histologic lesion of rejection may have features in common with the PBC lesions(s); however, there is increasing evidence to suggest that PBC does recur in the transplanted liver (Balan et al., 1993).

Prevention

There are no prevention guidelines.

Cost Containment

As long as the pathogenesis of PBC is unknown and the therapy experimental, patients should be referred to centers where there is expertise in the management of PBC and where clinical trials are conducted. This plan allows for continuity of care by the referring physician. Therapy with medications that have not been shown to favorably modify the natural history of the disease leads to expense and deters from appropriate data acquisition. No shortcuts should be taken.

REFERENCES

Balan VK, Batts MK, Krom R, et al. Histological evidence for recurrence of primary biliary cirrhosis after liver transplantation. Hepatology 1993;18:1392.

Bergasa NV, Jones EA. Management of the pruritus of cholestasis: Potential role of opiate antagonists. Am J Gastroenterol 1991;86:1404.

Gershwin M, Mackay I. Primary biliary cirrhosis: Paradigm or paradox for autoimmunity. Gastroenterology 1991;100:822.

Kaplan MM. Primary biliary cirrhosis. N Engl J Med 1987;316:521.

Michieletti P, Wanless IR, Katz A, et al. Antimitochondrial antibody negative primary biliary cirrhosis: A distinct syndrome of autoimmune cholangitis. Gut 1994;35:260.

Sherlock S, Dooley J. Primary biliary cirrhosis. In: Diseases of the liver and biliary system. 9th ed. London: Blackwell, 1991:236.

Wiesner RH, Porayko MK, Dickson ER, et al. Selection and timing of liver transplantation in primary biliary cirrhosis and primary sclerosing cholangitis. Hepatology 1992;16:1290.

CHAPTER 19–82

Sclerosing Cholangitis

Nora Valeria Bergasa, M.D.

DEFINITION

Sclerosing cholangitis is a cholestatic syndrome that leads to fibrotic disappearance of intra- and/or extrahepatic bile ducts, biliary cirrhosis, and liver failure (Sherlock, 1987). Primary sclerosing cholangitis (PSC) is the term used when no precipitating factor is identified; it may or may not be associated with inflammatory bowel disease. Secondary sclerosing cholangitis is the term used when the precipitating factor of the condition is (are) known or deduced (see below) (Sherlock, 1987).

ETIOLOGY

The etiology of PSC is unknown (Lee and Kaplan, 1995). There is some evidence to suggest that it may have an autoimmune basis, including the presence of circulating immune complexes in the serum of patients with PSC and its association with diseases believed to be of autoimmune etiology (e.g., thyroiditis, arthritis). An infectious etiologic agent has not been excluded. PSC has been diagnosed in association with retroperitoneal fibrosis and mediastinal fibrosis. The syndrome of sclerosing cholangitis has been described in patients with histiocytosis X. In contrast to PSC, there are identified events that lead to secondary sclerosing cholangitis; these include bacterial or parasitic infections of the biliary tree; opportunistic infections in immunocompromised patients; hepatic artery infusions of chemotherapeutic agents (e.g., fluorodeoxyuridine [FUDR] for treatment of malignancies) the associated coagulative phenomena due to lupus anticoagulant; infusions of scolicidal solutions (formaldehyde, 20% sodium chloride) directly into hydatid cysts; and neoplasms of the biliary tract. The mechanisms by which these events lead to sclerosing cholangitis are unknown. Invasion of the biliary tract by pathogens and the effects of inflammation and its consequences are the reasons given to explain cholangitis in the first two cited examples. In the cases of patients with AIDS, polymicrobial cholangitis (e.g., *Cryptosporidium, Candida albicans, Klebsiella pneumoniae,* and cytomegalovirus) has been reported. The proposed basis for sclerosing cholangitis secondary to intraarterial infusions of FUDR is ischemia (Sherlock, 1987; and references therein). Caustic injury to the biliary epithelium secondary to the instillation of a scolicidal solution (20% sodium chloride, formaldehyde) into intrahepatic echinococcal cysts communicating with the biliary tree is the proposed mechanism for the development of sclerosing cholangitis in these circumstances; the development of sclerosing cholangitis in this situation is rapid. It was recommended that this practice be abandoned because of this complication.

CRITERIA FOR DIAGNOSIS
Suggestive

Because PSC is associated with inflammatory bowel disease in 70 to 80% of patients, cholestasis in this patient population suggests the diagnosis of PSC (Lee and Kaplan, 1995). It presents alone in a substantial number of patients; thus, it is included in the differential diagnosis of cholestatic liver disease. It is significantly more common in male than in female patients. It is most commonly diagnosed around the age of 30.

Definitive

The radiographic appearance of intra- and/or extrahepatic biliary strictures and sacculations demonstrated in cholangiography is diagnostic of sclerosing cholangitis (Figure 19–82–1). Four stages have been described histologically in PSC. In stage I disease, there is an inflammatory infiltrate composed of polymorphonuclear leukocytes and lymphocytes around the ducts, with vacuolation of the epithelium; the inflammatory infiltrate is less intense than that found in the lesion of nonsuppurative destructive cholangitis of primary biliary cirrhosis. The onionskin lesion is characteristic of sclerosing cholangitis; it consists of concentric layers of fibrotic tissue surrounding the bile duct. There is bile ductular proliferation. In stage II disease, the inflammatory infil-

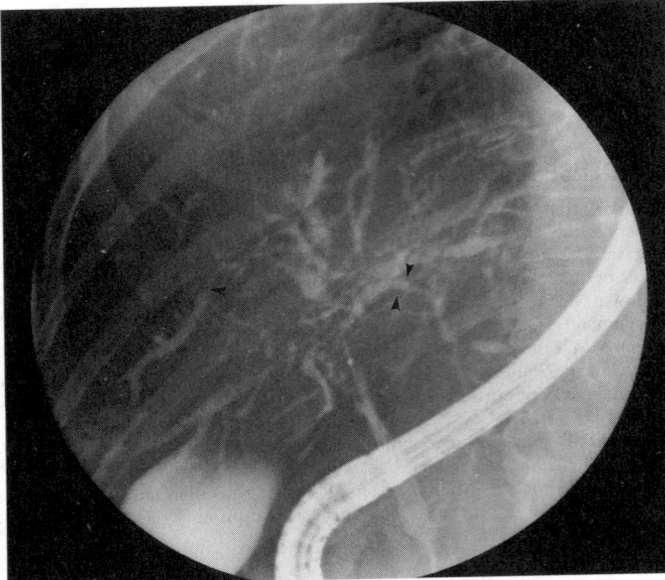

Figure 19–82–1. Endoscopic retrograde cholangiopancreatogram of a patient with primary sclerosing cholangitis showing strictures (arrowhead) and sacculations (double arrowhead) of intrahepatic bile ducts. *(Courtesy of Dr. William N. Katkov, Saint John's Hospital, Santa Monica, California.)*

trate and the fibrotic changes can be found outside the portal tracts; biliary piecemeal is a feature of this stage. Ductopenia is apparent (Figure 19–82–2). In stage III, portal-to-portal fibrosis is characteristic. Stage IV is characterized by biliary cirrhosis. Pseudoxanthomatous changes suggestive of cholestasis are usually found in the last three stages. PSC can be confined to the smallest branches of the intrahepatic bile ducts not readily seen in cholangiograms. In these cases the appearance of the biliary tree on cholangiogram may be normal; thus, only liver histology may be consistent with the diagnosis. The lesion that affects the smallest branches of the intrahepatic bile ducts has been termed *small-duct primary sclerosing cholangitis;* this lesion probably represents the same lesion usually referred to as pericholangitis characteristically found in patients with ulcerative colitis and abnormalities in the plasma activity of liver-associated enzymes. Abnormalities of the pancreatic duct consistent with chronic pancreatitis can also be observed in the pancreatogram.

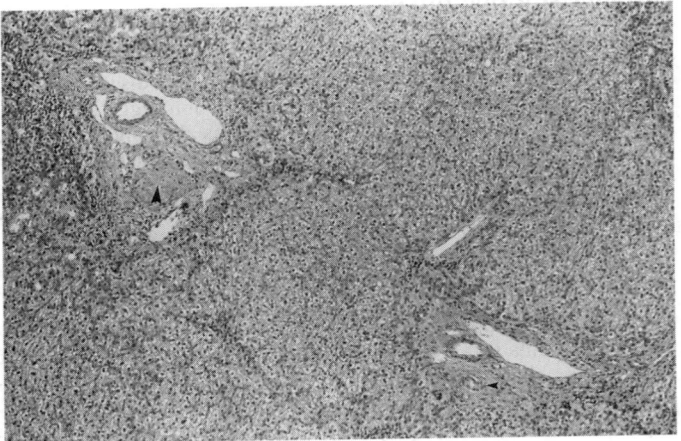

Figure 19–82–2. Liver biopsy of a patient with primary sclerosing cholangitis showing periportal fibrosis and absence of bile duct in a portal tract. The bile duct appears to have been replaced by a fibrous scar (arrowhead). Another portal tract shows fibrotic changes surrounding a bile duct with compromised lumen (smaller arrowhead). *(Courtesy of Dr. Lionel Rabin, M.D. Armed Forces Institutes of Pathology, Washington, DC.)*

CLINICAL MANIFESTATIONS

Subjective

In the case of PSC, the most common clinical manifestations are jaundice, pruritus, weight loss, right upper quadrant pain, and general malaise; jaundice may manifest alone or in combination with episodic cholangitis, which can be associated with fever and shaking chills. PSC can be asymptomatic. In cases of secondary sclerosing cholangitis, the symptoms are similar to those of PSC. Because PSC has been found in association with other disease entities such celiac disease, Hodgkin's lymphoma, and retroperitoneal and mediastinal fibrosis, among others, the dominating clinical presentation may be that of the associated disease.

As in other cholestatic syndromes, the pruritus of sclerosing cholangitis can be mild or severe, with sleep deprivation. It can be generalized or localized to certain areas of the body. It is described as a tingling, prickly sensation that may be briefly relieved by scratching or not at all. It is a very difficult symptom to treat and its etiology is unknown. Severe intractable pruritus can be an indication for liver transplantation.

Objective

The differential diagnosis of sclerosing cholangitis includes all cholestatic syndromes. PSC can present alone or, in a substantial number of patients, in association with inflammatory bowel disease, primarily ulcerative colitis, and less commonly Crohn's disease. PSC can be asymptomatic (Sherlock, 1987).

Physical Examination

Physical examination may be normal or compatible with cirrhosis. Dermatologic manifestations include palmar erythema, spider angiomata, and hyperpigmentation. In patients with ulcerative colitis, erythema gangrenosum and erythema nodosum may be found. Patients who suffer from pruritus may have cutaneous excoriations and prurigo nodularis. Also, in patients who have undergone proctocolectomy for ulcerative colitis, stomal varices secondary to portal hypertension may be appreciated. Jaundice, sometimes intermittent because of episodic cholangitis and/or new strictures, can be seen. Hepatomegaly, splenomegaly, and ascites may be found, as in other liver diseases.

Routine Laboratory Abnormalities

Cholestasis is the dominating biochemical feature; thus, elevated plasma activity of alkaline phosphatase is the characteristic laboratory abnormality. Modest elevations of the plasma activity of transaminases (alanine and aspartate) are common. Hyperbilirubinemia may be found depending on the stage of the liver disease, episodic cholangitis, or development of a benign dominant stricture or cholangiocarcinoma. The plasma activity of other enzymes characteristically elevated in cholestasis, such as γ-glutamyl transpeptidase and 5′-nucleotidase, may be elevated in the plasma of patients with PSC. Hypoalbuminemia and prolonged prothrombin time suggesting impaired liver function can be found; because PSC has been reported in association with celiac disease, these two abnormalities can potentially be observed in the context of good liver function but secondary to malabsorption. Also, hypoalbuminemia secondary to severe inflammatory bowel disease may be observed. Thrombocytopenia secondary to portal hypertension may be found in the complete blood count. Normocytic normochromic anemia secondary to cirrhosis may be observed; however, hypochromic microcytic anemia is not uncommon in patients who have PSC and who also suffer from inflammatory bowel disease because of chronic blood loss in their stool. Eosinophilia in the differential of the white blood cell count has been reported.

PLANS

Diagnostic

Differential Diagnosis

In the clinical history, information regarding possible causes of secondary sclerosing cholangitis should be explored (see above). The differential diagnosis of PSC includes all liver diseases associated with cholestasis. In general, cholestasis in a young male, in particular when inflammatory bowel disease is an accompanying disease, strongly suggests the presence of PSC. In contrast, in a middle-aged woman, the presence of cholestasis strongly suggests primary biliary cirrhosis. The differential diagnosis includes sarcoidosis, idiopathic adulthood ductopenia, and chronic active hepatitis. Apropos of the latter, an overlap syndrome with PSC has been described. Because cholestatic features of hepatitis C are being increasingly recognized, liver disease secondary to hepatitis C is included in the differential diagnosis of sclerosing cholangitis. Because secondary sclerosing cholangitis can result from traumatic cholecystectomies, history of cholescystectomy in a patient with cholestasis calls for the exclusion of this syndrome.

Diagnostic Options

Recently, antineutrophil cytoplasmic antibodies (p [perinuclear]-ANCA) have been detected in serum of approximately 80% of patients with PSC and should be obtained. Anti-smooth muscle antibody levels may be obtained because they have been found in approximately 10% of patients with PSC. In addition, elevated gamma globulins, IgG and IgM, may be substantially elevated in patients with PSC.

Recommended Approach

An expeditious workup of cholestatic liver disease should be initiated. Evaluation of the liver parenchyma and biliary system by sonogram and/or computed axial tomography is recommended. These tests may identify areas of dilation proximal to the biliary strictures. A serum antimitochondrial antibody (AMA) level should be obtained to rule out primary biliary cirrhosis. Hepatitis serology, particularly of hepatitis C, because it can be cholestatic, should be obtained. Other causes of liver disease should be ruled out by obtaining serum levels of α_1-antitrypsin, ferritin (in fasting state), ceruloplasmin, copper, and angiotensin-converting enzyme. Once cholestasis is confirmed, referral to a gastroenterologist and/or hepatologist is indicated. Cholangiographic studies of the biliary tract, preferably by the endoscopic method, are the diagnostic examination of choice (to minimize manipulations of the biliary tree that may result from this study when using the percutaneous transhepatic route). Liver biopsy does not necessarily have to be obtained to confirm the diagnosis if the cholangiogram is diagnostic; however, liver histology is useful in staging the disease (e.g., precirrhotic versus cirrhotic). If the cholangiogram is not diagnostic and cholestasis is unexplained, a liver biopsy may shed light on the nature of the underlying process.

Therapeutic

Therapeutic Options

No curative treatment for PSC has been identified. Because PSC is associated with some specific complications, the therapeutic options are divided into two categories, those aimed at the disease and those aimed at its complications.

Primary sclerosing cholangitis is rarer than primary biliary cirrhosis and therapies for primary biliary cirrhosis tend to be used as models for the treatment of PSC. D-Penicillamine, cyclosporine, corticosteroids, colchicine, azathioprine, ursodeoxycholic acid, and methotrexate have been evaluated in clinical studies. Cholestyramine and antibiotics have been evaluated also. None of these therapies are currently recommended for treatment and they are considered experimental (Wiesner, 1994). Ursodeoxycholic acid (Actigal) (13–15 mg/kg per day) has received a lot of attention as a therapeutic agent for cholestatic liver diseases, including PSC. This medication changes the composition of the bile acid pool to contain more hydrophilic bile acids, which are less toxic to the liver, and its toxicity appears to be minimal. No published controlled studies on its effects on secondary sclerosing cholangitis are available. Treatment of patients with PSC with ursodeoxycholic acid has been associated with a decrease in the plasma activity of liver-associated enzymes associated with cholestasis, equivocal effects on symptoms, and no effects on the progression of the disease. Because PSC is a slowly progressive liver disease, a large number of patients will need to be followed for a prolonged period of time on a particular

therapy. For this reason, data acquisition is difficult. The results of long-term controlled studies are awaited.

One of the most important complications of PSC is the development of cholangiocarcinoma. This is a difficult topic to discuss because of its presentation, prognosis, and lack of effective management. Patients with long-standing sclerosing cholangitis and ulcerative colitis appear to be at higher risk for developing this complication. The appearance of worsening cholestasis in a patient with stable PSC should trigger the investigation of cholangiocarcinoma. These tumors usually develop in the extrahepatic biliary structures, and characteristically appear like strictures, sometimes "bandlike" in the cholangiogram. They may look like benign strictures. It is recommended that an effort be made to obtain cytology by brushing the affected area during evaluation of the biliary tree during endoscopic cholangiography, although the diagnostic yield is not very high. Recently, levels of CA 19-9 have been reported to be elevated in the serum of patients with cholangiocarcinoma and PSC; final results on the study of this association are awaited with great interest because it may facilitate early tumor diagnosis. There is no radiotherapy or chemotherapy available for the treatment of this tumor. Patients with PSC and cholangiocarcinoma who have undergone liver transplantation, have had tumor recurrence in the graft. The prognosis of PSC complicated by cholangiocarcinoma is poor.

Benign dominant strictures are another complication of PSC. They can be difficult to differentiate from cholangiocarcinoma. They present with jaundice, fever, and cholangitis. Before and after the performance of diagnostic endoscopic retrograde cholangiopancreatography (ERCP), it is recommended that patients receive intravenous antibiotics because the biliary tract manipulations that accompany this procedure will most likely be associated with bacteremia. Brushings for cytology should be taken in an attempt to rule out cholangiocarcinoma. Mechanical dilation of dominant strictures is the favored therapeutic alternative. This technique consists of balloon dilation of the stricture, with retrieval of the sludge that tends to accumulate in the area. The approach (endoscopic versus transhepatic) depends on the location of the stricture; current data suggest that the endoscopic approach is preferable. When successful, dilation of the strictures has been associated with improvement of cholestasis of about 2 years' duration (Wiesner, 1994). Often, stents are placed in the biliary ducts to maintain patency of the duct lumen.

Bacterial cholangitis is one of the most common complications of sclerosing cholangitis. It may be secondary to sluggish bile flow that results from the strictures and sacculations that characterize the biliary tree in this syndrome. It presents with jaundice, fever, and chills and levels of liver-associated enzymes higher than what the patients tend to run when stable. Antibiotic treatment should be initiated promptly after appropriate blood cultures are taken. If this is a recurrent complication, long-term therapy with antibiotics with high access to the biliary tract and its organisms (e.g., ciprofloxacin [Cipro]) is recommended.

Cholelithiasis and choledocholithiasis occur in about a third of patients with PSC because of cholestasis and cirrhosis. When bacterial cholangitis is a complication, an ERC is recommended to try to elucidate the precipitating event: strictures(s) or stone(s).

Immunosuppressed patients such as those suffering from congenital or acquired immunodeficiency (e.g., AIDS) may develop secondary sclerosing cholangitis. The presumed mechanism is the invasion of the biliary tract by opportunistic organisms. Attempts should be made to identify the organisms involved, if any, by at least brushing the affected area, and treatment should be according to what is found. *Cryptosporidia,* cytomegalovirus, *Klebsiella,* and *Candida albicans* invasion of the biliary tree with radiographic appearance of sclerosing cholangitis has been reported in these patients (Sherlock, 1987); however, the pathogenesis of this condition is not known.

Intraarterial infusions of FUDR in the hepatic artery can result in sclerosing cholangitis. The management is difficult; palliation therapy by the placement of biliary stents or balloon dilation of dominant strictures to decrease bile stagnation can be undertaken.

Recommended Approach

Complications of sclerosing cholangitis, and specifically PSC, should be treated as they arise. As in all cases of diseases of unknown etiology without specific treatment, in the opinion of this author, referral of patients to centers where clinical trials are conducted or where a scientific interest in the disease exists is ideal. This allows the primary physician to be in touch with current developments and gives the patient and the investigators the opportunity to participate in clinical research. Because the disease is not common, one would think that the greater the number of referrals to academic centers, the more progress in understanding the disease will follow.

One of the most troublesome symptoms of cholestasis, pruritus, represents a real therapeutic challenge (Bergasa and Jones, 1993). Cholestyramine at doses up to 16 g/d is usually the first treatment to be given. Some patients appear to respond; some do not. Cholestyramine or colestipol should be administered immediately before and after breakfast (4 g each time) and, if needed, after lunch and dinner. Ingesting the drug after breakfast presumably facilitates the binding of the resin to the presumed "pruritogenic substance" that has accumulated in the gallbladder during the overnight fast. Phenobarbital and antihistamines are sedatives and do not appear to be very effective in treating this symptom, nor are they very well tolerated by the patients. Rifampicin has been evaluated for the treatment of the pruritus of cholestasis in several clinical trials, particularly in patients with primary biliary cirrhosis; at doses of 150 mg twice daily (if bilirubin > 3 mg/dL) and 300 mg twice daily (if bilirubin < 3 mg/dL), it has been reported to be well tolerated and associated with amelioration of pruritus. The mechanism of action is not known. More recently, opiate antagonists have been used. In emergency situations such as those involving a suicidal patient because of inability to live with pruritus any longer, intractable pruritus can be approached by hospitalizing the patient and administering the opiate antagonist naloxone (Narcan, 0.4 mg bolus intravenously and 0.2 μg/kg/min infusions in 500 mL of 5% dextrose/0.45 NaCl; up to 0.8 μg/kg/min has been administered and found to be well tolerated). Psychiatric evaluation in these suicidal patients is warranted.

Cholestasis can be associated with deficiency of fat-soluble vitamins. Pancreatic insufficiency contributes to this deficiency. Supplementation with vitamins is not recommended unless a particular deficiency has been documented by blood levels. This is particularly important when it comes to vitamin A because of its potential for liver toxicity.

Osteopenia secondary to osteoporosis can be a serious problem. Adequate exercise and calcium ingestion from 1.5 to 2 g/d are recommended. Baseline determination of bone density by noninvasive techniques offers the advantage of identifying patients who may be vulnerable to complications affecting the skeletal system (e.g., fractures). Current recommendations for the treatment of osteoporosis associated with menopause should be followed when managing female patients.

The recommended therapeutic approach to dominant strictures is balloon dilation. This can be performed endoscopically and transhepatically via the percutaneous route, depending on their location. Balloon dilation of the whole biliary tract, which is often involved in this disease, is not recommended.

The indications for biliary surgery in patients with PSC or its secondary counterpart are not clear. It is a real dilemma when the presence of a cholangiocarcinoma is being considered; in such cases a diagnostic laparotomy may be necessary and even in these circumstances the diagnosis may be difficult to make.

There are no controlled studies indicating that operations aimed at the diversion of bile flow in these patients should be performed to alleviate cholestasis, although they have been advocated. Surgical manipulations of the biliary tract complicate the operative procedure of liver transplantation if and when this becomes necessary.

The important question of proctocolectomy altering the progressive course of PSC has arisen. It has been recently concluded based on a clinical study that proctocolectomy in patients with PSC does not beneficially alter the course of the liver disease (Cangemi et al., 1989). Thus, proctocolectomy is not recommended with the hopeful aim of treating PSC; however, when patients with PSC meet criteria for proctocolectomy (e.g., development of colon cancer, intractability), there is no contraindication for performing the surgery.

Bleeding varices from portal hypertension, usually esophageal and less often gastric, are a complication common to all liver diseases; however, bleeding stomal varices in patients with PSC who have undergone colectomy is a dreadful complication and usually requires surgery to create portosystemic shunts or liver transplantation for management.

Liver transplantation has emerged as a surgical therapeutic alternative in advanced PSC. The 3-year survival has been reported to be 75 to 85% (Lee and Kaplan, 1995; Wiesner, 1994). Specific complications of liver transplantation for PSC have been described. Because of the frequent involvement of the choledocus by the disease, a choledocojejunostomy is usually the anastomotic technique used, and this appears to be associated with more postoperative complications than the duct-to-duct anastomosis technique. Recurrence of the primary disease in the transplanted liver is beginning to be reported.

FOLLOW-UP

The interval between medical visits depends on the severity of the disease. Frequent visualization of the biliary tree by endoscopic means is not recommended.

Liver transplantation has become part of the management of patients with advanced sclerosing cholangitis. Because the process may be quite traumatic for the patients and family, obtaining information on financial matters and choice of institutions where the surgery is performed, as well as emotional support, is important. Premature evaluation is not necessary; however, in cases where there is clear progression of disease, referral for an evaluation to get the patient "in the system" can facilitate things in the long run.

DISCUSSION

Prevalence and Incidence

This information is not known precisely. The incidence of PSC in patients with ulcerative colitis ranges from 2 to 8%. The estimated incidence of PSC extrapolated from the incidence of PSC has been reported to be 7 cases per 100,000 population (Wiesner, 1994). The incidence of secondary sclerosing cholangitis is also unknown but there are certain events that lead to this complication in a large percentage of patients (see above).

Related Basic Science

Genetics

Genetic susceptibility to PSC in affected patients is a topic of great interest. The human leukocyte antigens (HLA) B8, DR2, DR3, and DRw52A have been reported to be associated with PSC. Technical factors appear to complicate the results of the studies and the interpretation of these reports. It is possible that the differences reported in different world populations reflect true differences in genetic susceptibilities around the world. PSC has been reported in members of the same family, which always underscores the possibility of genetic susceptibility.

Immunologic Alterations

Circulating antineutrophil antibodies (ANCA) of the perinuclear type (p-ANCA) have been found in the serum of approximately 80% of patients with PSC, and with a similar incidence in patients with PSC and ulcerative colitis and ulcerative colitis alone. The specificity for PSC of these circulating antibodies is still questionable because they have been detected in the serum of patients with other liver diseases, although at much lower titers. No direct role of these antibodies in the pathogenesis of PSC has been identified. They seem to be useful as part of the noninvasive diagnostic plan. Other immunologic alterations in PSC are the presence of anticolon antibodies, immune complexes in bile, and augmented catabolism of one of the components of the complement system, C3. A decreased clearance of immune complexes has not been a uniform finding, although it has suggested an abnormality in the reticuloendothelial system of the affected patients.

The total number of circulating T cells, resulting from a decrease in CD8+ cells, has been reported to be decreased in patients with PSC. In addition, the enhanced expression of HLA class II by biliary epithelial cells suggests that in cholestasis, biliary epithelial cells may act as antigen presenting cells. It is not known whether this is a primary or secondary phenomenon and it is the focus of investigation. Immunologic studies of the biliary lesions in PSC suggest that the cells found are

CD4+ and CD8+. CD8+ cells have been reported to constitute the majority of cells found in the inflammatory infiltrate in the area of proliferating bile ducts and bile duct epithelium.

Physiologic or Metabolic Derangement

As are other cholestatic liver diseases, PSC is associated with copper accumulation in the liver and increased urinary copper.

Recently, increased opioidergic neurotransmission/neuromodulation has been described in patients with liver diseases primarily of the cholestatic type, such as sclerosing cholangitis. One symptom that appears to be related to this alteration is the pruritus associated with liver diseases, which can be ameliorated by treatment with opiate antagonist drugs (Bergasa and Jones, 1993).

Cutaneous hyperpigmentation is an interesting phenomenon of patients with cholestasis including PSC. The pigment is melanin. Increased melanin deposition in the skin appears to result, at least in part, from alterations in the availability and biological activity of α-melanocyte-stimulating hormone.

Osteopenia is a serious complication of cholestatic liver diseases such as sclerosing cholangitis. The underlying pathology is osteoporosis. The existence of circulating factor(s) that inhibits osteoblastic function has been proposed, but this factor(s) has not been identified.

Anatomic Derangement

The biliary tract is abnormal. The abnormalities can be visualized by contrast-requiring radiographic methods (e.g., endoscopic or transhepatic cholangiogram). The abnormalities consists of strictures and sacculations of the intra- and extrahepatic biliary tree, which give the characteristic radiographic picture (Figure 19–82–2). PSC with a normal cholangiogram has been described (see above).

Natural History and Its Modification with Treatment

Sclerosing cholangitis is a progressive liver disease that leads to biliary cirrhosis and, ultimately, liver failure. The survival of patients with symptomatic or asymptomatic PSC has been reported to be less than that of the control population, although this has not been a universal finding. Survival has been reported to range from 9 to 15 years after diagnosis (Schrumpf et al., 1994). To date, there are no treatments that halt the progress of the disease. There is an effort to develop prognostic indexes to aid in the prediction of survival and, in particular, to decide on the optimal time for liver transplantation. Different studies have identified different features that correlate with poor prognosis. These include hepatomegaly, splenomegaly, anemia, cirrhosis, female sex, and older age (Schrumpf et al., 1994; Wiesner, 1994; references therein). Increasing bilirubin levels have consistently correlated with poor prognosis because they indicate disease progression. Plasma levels of bilirubin consistently greater than 1.5 g/dL are indicative of advanced disease (Lee and Kaplan, 1995). Prognostic factors to aid in the identification of patients who will develop cholangiographic carcinoma have not been found; however, in one study, hyperbilirubinemia correlated with occurrence of this malignancy (Schrumpf, 1994).

Prevention

Primary sclerosing cholangitis is of unknown etiology and there are no preventive measures. Some cases of secondary sclerosing cholangitis can be prevented only by avoiding procedures that lead to complications that may result in the syndrome (see above). Specifically, cholecystectomies should be performed only when strictly indicated (i.e., symptomatic cholelithiasis). In the opinion of the author, one should not succumb to the enthusiasm of new procedures in the area of biliary tract surgery and they should be left for when they are fully approved and when performed by experienced surgeons.

Cost Containment

Expeditious diagnostic workup is necessary. Prompt referral to a gastroenterologist/hepatologist for diagnostic procedures, confirmation of diagnosis, and management advice is important. The author favors referral of patients to academic centers where clinical and basic research on sclerosing cholangitis is conducted.

REFERENCES

Bergasa NV, Jones EA. The pruritus of cholestasis. Semin Liver Dis. 1993;13:319.

Cangemi JR, Wiesner RH, Beaver SJ, et al. Effect of proctocolectomy for chronic ulcerative colitis on the natural history of primary sclerosing cholangitis. Gastroenterology 1989;96:790.

Lee Y-M, Kaplan MM. Primary sclerosing cholangitis. N Engl J Med. 1995;332:924.

Schrumpf E, Abdelnoor M, Fausa O, et al. Risk factors in primary sclerosing cholangitis. J Hepatol 1994;21:1061.

Sherlock S. The syndrome of disappearing intra-hepatic bile ducts. Lancet. 1987;2:493.

Wiesner RH. Current concepts in primary sclerosing cholangitis. Mayo Clin Proc 1994;969.

CHAPTER 19–83

Wilson's Disease

Irmin Sternlieb, M.D.

DEFINITION

Wilson's disease is an inherited disorder of copper metabolism transmitted in autosomal recessive fashion. It is characterized by the accumulation of excessive amounts of copper in the liver, central nervous system, kidneys, eyes, and other organs. Although the genetic defect is present from birth, clinically manifest pathologic changes do not appear before the age of 5 years and are sometimes delayed until the fifth decade, and very rarely even to the sixth decade. Fifty percent of symptomatic patients display abnormalities by the time they reach 15 years.

ETIOLOGY

The accumulation of toxic amounts of copper in the tissues is caused by a mutation of a normal gene, localized to chromosome 13 (13q14.3), that encodes a transmembrane copper-dependent P-type ATPase. The mutation disturbs both the biliary excretion of excess copper from hepatocytes and the incorporation of the metal into ceruloplasmin.

CRITERIA FOR DIAGNOSIS

Suggestive

The disease may start insidiously as unexplained transaminasemia or suddenly by mimicking acute hepatitis, infectious mononucleosis, fulminant hepatitis, chronic hepatitis, hemolytic jaundice, cirrhosis with all its complications, idiopathic thrombocytopenic purpura, deteriorating schoolwork, multiple sclerosis, "juvenile" parkinsonism, torsion dystonia, schizophrenia, depression and other affective disorders, vitamin D-resistant rickets, and acute glomerulonephritis.

A family history of unexplained liver or neurologic disease in a sibling or other relative should arouse the suspicion of Wilson's disease even in the absence of symptoms.

Definitive

A definite diagnosis of Wilson's disease can be established in the overwhelming majority of patients by examining the peripheries of the corneas, with the aid of a slit-lamp, for the presence of copper deposits in Descemet's membrane, the so-called Kayser–Fleischer ring, and by demonstrating an absence or deficiency of the serum copper protein ceruloplasmin. Additional support for the diagnosis may be obtained from measurements of urinary copper excretion (more than 100 μg per 24 hours) and from determinations of the hepatic copper concentration (in excess of 250 μg/g dry tissue). A radiocopper loading test may be helpful for the resolution of diagnostic dilemmas in the rare patients with low-normal serum ceruloplasmin concentrations (20–30 mg/dL) suspected to be suffering from Wilson's disease.

CLINICAL MANIFESTATIONS

Subjective

Lassitude, abdominal pain with or without swelling, jaundice, gastrointestinal bleeding, delayed puberty, and amenorrhea may be the complaints of patients with hepatic manifestations of Wilson's disease. Subjects with predominantly neurologic manifestations may first note a deterioration of schoolwork, behavioral abnormalities, worsening of handwriting, tremors of the head or extremities, clumsiness, drooling, difficulty in chewing and swallowing, slurred speech, loss of balance, stumbling, irritability, temper tantrums, withdrawal, or frank depression.

Objective

Physical Examination

The most important physical abnormality diagnostic of Wilson's disease is the Kayser–Fleischer ring. It consists of fine copper deposits in Descemet's membrane of the cornea demonstrable by slit-lamp examination. The rings are present in the majority of patients with hepatic manifestations and in all patients with neurologic Wilson's disease. They are, however, absent during the early stages of the disease.

Indications of liver disease that appear generally in late childhood and the second decade are nonspecific. They include some or most of the following: jaundice, hepatomegaly or reduced liver size, splenomegaly, ascites, edema, portal hypertension, esophageal varices, and spider angiomas. Gallstones also may be present. Some boys display gynecomastia. Spontaneous abortions occur in some women.

The involuntary movements that appear in patients with Wilson's disease during the second or third decade may result in mild to severe resting or intention tremors, diminished dexterity, unsteady gait, or choreiform movements. In other patients, rigidity of the mouth, arms, or legs, dysarthria, drooling, or dysphagia may cause the patient to be severely incapacitated.

Psychiatric abnormalities may herald the disease in 20 to 30% of patients. There may be an insidious deterioration of the quality of schoolwork, an inability to concentrate or read, memory loss, confusion, temper tantrums, paranoid delusions, manic–depressive disease, depression, schizophrenia, dementia, or impulsive, inappropriate, or antisocial behavior.

Gross or microscopic hematuria (suggesting glomerulonephritis in children), renal tubular acidosis, renal calculi, or nephrocalcinosis may be the first manifestation of Wilson's disease.

Routine Laboratory Abnormalities

Laboratory abnormalities detectable on routine tests are nonspecific. Leukopenia or profound thrombocytopenia may be the consequence of hypersplenism. Hypouricemia, a consequence of copper-induced renal tubular injury causing uricosuria, may be a clue to the diagnosis of Wilson's disease. Unexplained Coombs-negative hemolytic anemia with unconjugated hyperbilirubinemia is the hallmark of Wilsonian fulminant hepatitis. Unexplained persistent transaminasemia, hypoalbuminemia, or hypoprothrombinemia in a patient younger than 35 years with-

out evidence of viral hepatitis or exposure to toxins or alcohol should arouse the suspicion of Wilson's disease. The severity of liver dysfunction may vary depending on the stage of the disease. Routine biochemical tests may yield misleading normal results in adults with neurologic disease despite the presence of cirrhosis. Another pitfall in the assessment of the severity of the disease is often encountered in patients presenting with a clinical picture of fulminant hepatitis in whom the serum transaminase levels may be only modestly elevated and the serum alkaline phosphatase values may be inappropriately for an adolescent within the normal adult range.

PLANS

Diagnostic

Differential Diagnosis

Wilson's disease enters into the differential in young patients presenting with unexplained liver disease, after the exclusion of more common etiologies; Coombs-negative hemolytic anemia with jaundice; unexplained deterioration of schoolwork; multiple sclerosis; parkinsonism; and dysarthria.

Diagnostic Options and Recommended Approach

In the majority of patients suspected of Wilson's disease, two relatively simple tests—a slit-lamp examination of the corneas for Kayser–Fleischer rings performed by an experienced ophthalmologist and an assay of the concentration of ceruloplasmin in the serum—may provide all the information required to establish or exclude the diagnosis of Wilson's disease with certainty. The simultaneous presence of corneal Kayser–Fleischer rings and a serum ceruloplasmin concentration less than 20 mg/dL is characteristic of Wilson's disease. In many patients, however, confirmation of the diagnosis is more difficult: Kayser–Fleischer rings may not have formed in young patients; patients with active liver disease may exhibit a temporary rise in the ceruloplasmin concentration above 20 mg/dL and 5% of patients display low-normal concentrations (20–30 mg/dL) permanently; an acquired deficiency of ceruloplasmin may develop in patients with severely deficient hepatic synthetic function, whereas patients with long-standing cholestatic syndromes (e.g., biliary cirrhosis) occasionally exhibit Kayser–Fleischer rings (characteristically associated with elevated serum ceruloplasmin levels).

If there is a lack of congruence of the results of the slit-lamp examination and the measurement of the serum concentration of ceruloplasmin, a needle liver biopsy may resolve the diagnostic dilemma. Two specimens, one for quantitative copper determination and a second for light microscopic examination, should be obtained. A hepatic copper concentration in excess of 250 μg dry tissue, in the absence of histologic and functional evidence of cholestasis, Indian childhood cirrhosis, or idiopathic copper toxicosis, is indicative of Wilson's disease. Measurements of urinary copper showing an excretion of more than 100 μg per 24 hours (without any chelating agent) provide additional evidence supporting the diagnosis if precautions for the prevention of contamination of the collection with traces of copper are taken and the assay is performed in a reliable laboratory.

If biopsy is contraindicated because of clotting abnormalities, the diagnosis can usually be established or ruled out by a radiocopper loading test, which is of differential diagnostic value only in patients with normal concentrations of serum ceruloplasmin.

Wilson's disease should be suspected in all the siblings, even in the absence of symptoms, each having, a priori, one chance in four of having the disease. Genetic testing through haplotype analysis can be obtained, though its application is still limited to research centers. If the serum ceruloplasmin concentration is below 20 mg/dL or transaminase levels (aspartate and alanine) are elevated (above 40 IU/L), a liver biopsy is indicated. A hepatic copper concentration of more than 250 μg/g dry tissue in the presence of histologic abnormalities, ranging from fatty infiltration to cirrhosis, is diagnostic of Wilson's disease even if the individual appears healthy. A decreased concentration of serum ceruloplasmin in a healthy individual with a hepatic copper concentration less than 250 μg/g and normal histologic findings suggests that the subject is a heterozygous carrier of one abnormal Wilson's disease gene who will never develop the illness.

Ultrasound and magnetic resonance imaging studies of the liver do not contribute to the accuracy of the diagnosis. Imaging of the liver by isotope scanning following the injection of ^{99m}Tc-colloid may help evaluate the state of liver injury at the time of diagnosis if a biopsy cannot be obtained. Computed tomography and magnetic resonance imaging of the brain may help localize some of the anatomic changes that have occurred in the central nervous system. These tests may be the first to suggest the correct diagnosis, but they contribute little to predicting the clinical outcome.

Therapeutic

D-Penicillamine (Cuprimine, Depen) is effective in removing copper from the brain and liver of patients with Wilson's disease. Therapy is initiated at 1 g daily, given in divided oral doses of 0.25 g about half an hour before meals and before retiring. Sensitivity reactions to penicillamine may occur in the first few weeks of therapy, manifested by fever, maculopapular rash, lymphadenopathy, or, less frequently, leukopenia or thrombocytopenia. Patients should be appropriately monitored for these reactions, and if they occur, the drug should be temporarily withdrawn until the reaction subsides. Gradual reinstitution of D-penicillamine, starting with a daily dose of 0.25 g initially, and the temporary administration of 20 mg prednisone daily in progressively decreasing doses over several weeks may avoid a recurrent reaction. More serious reactions (proteinuria, nephrotic syndrome, lupus, pemphigus, myasthenia, and others), though rare, occur later, after months or years of therapy.

It is not uncommon for patients with neurologic manifestations to experience a worsening of their symptoms during the first few months of treatment before steady improvement occurs. In addition to clinical evaluation of the patient's status, periodic determinations of the 24-hour urinary excretion of copper while taking D-penicillamine provide a check on the quantitative effectiveness of therapy, as well as reassurance regarding the patient's compliance with the regimen.

If the response of the patient is inadequate after a few months on the initial dose of D-penicillamine, the dose may have to be doubled to 2 g daily or intramuscular injections of 3 mL BAL (British antilewisite [dimercaprol]) daily, or every other day, for several weeks may have to be administered. Water retention as a manifestation of hepatic insufficiency should be treated with salt restriction and diuretics (see Chapter 19–80) while attempting to improve the patient's nutritional status.

Dietary restrictions are minimal and consist merely of the avoidance of foods that are particularly high in copper content: chocolate, nuts, mushrooms, shellfish, liver, and broccoli.

In patients who are intolerant to penicillamine, triethylene tetramine (Syprine) is available as an alternative oral chelating agent. It is also given in an average dose of 1 g daily in divided dosage on an empty stomach. This drug is capable of maintaining patients in good clinical condition with hardly any side effects. Several groups of investigators are studying the role and effectiveness of zinc salts (150 mg zinc daily) as treatment for Wilson's disease.

Curative surgery for Wilson's disease requires liver transplantation. This procedure is indicated only in patients with Wilsonian fulminant hepatitis, in those with severe hepatic decompensation unresponsive to therapy, and in noncompliant patients who develop suddenly severe hepatic and renal decompensation generally not responsive to the usual forms of supportive therapy. Surgery for bleeding esophageal varices is rarely required and may be avoided if esophageal sclerotherapy or banding of the varices is effective.

FOLLOW-UP

Careful clinical and laboratory evaluation is required at weekly intervals during the first month of therapy, with progressively longer intervals over the following few months. Close questioning regarding the occurrence of fever and rashes, liable to appear during the first few weeks of penicillamine therapy, and close scrutiny regarding the appearance of leukopenia or thrombocytopenia are required. Urinalyses, with particular attention to proteinuria, should be obtained at intervals.

Checks for compliance with the regimen should consist of the documentation of clinical improvement, improved liver chemistries, a reduction in the amount of copper deposited in the corneas, follow-up of the level of non-ceruloplasmin serum copper (to be reduced to 10 µg/dL or less from an increased pretreatment level), and measurements of urinary copper excretion in 24-hour collections obtained in copper-free containers.

DISCUSSION
Prevalence and Incidence

The prevalence of Wilson's disease worldwide is estimated at about 1 in 30,000 individuals. The frequency of heterozygous carriers in the general population is 1 in 90.

Related Basic Science

The liver seems to be the primary organ affected by the accumulation of copper as a consequence of a defect in the function of a P-type ATPase resulting in a reduction in biliary copper excretion and a decrease in the incorporation of copper into ceruloplasmin. When the capacity of the liver to retain the excess copper is overwhelmed, release of the metal into the circulation and into other organs takes place. Only at this stage are increases in "free" nonceruloplasmin copper in the serum and urinary copper noticeable.

Natural History and Its Modification with Treatment

Most patients become symptomatic during late childhood, adolescence, or young adulthood. Symptoms do not appear before 5 years of age and are only rarely delayed until the fifth decade. Untreated, the disease is uniformly fatal. With appropriate treatment, symptomatic patients generally improve and asymptomatic patients continue to lead a normal life.

Prevention

Manifestations of Wilson's disease can be prevented, and normal longevity can be achieved in patients diagnosed while still asymptomatic who are treated prophylactically for life.

Cost Containment

Serum copper determinations are less sensitive for the diagnosis of Wilson's disease than are determinations of the oxidase activity of serum ceruloplasmin. Therefore, the former are superfluous for the screening of suspected patients. The measurement of urinary copper excretion following the administration of a loading dose of penicillamine is of little, if any, diagnostic value in adults.

REFERENCES

Brewer GJ, Yuzbasiyan-Gurkan V, Johnson V, et al. Treatment of Wilson's disease with zinc. XII. Dose regimen requirements. Am J Med Sci 1993;305:199.

Scheinberg IH, Sternlieb I. Wilson's disease. Philadelphia: Saunders, 1984.

Schilsky ML, Scheinberg IH, Sternlieb I. Hepatic transplantation for Wilson's disease: Indications and outcome. Hepatology 1994;19:583.

Sternlieb I. Perspectives on Wilson's disease. Hepatology 1990;12:1234.

Sternlieb I, Giblin D, Scheinberg IH. Wilson's disease. In: Marsden CD, Fahn S, eds. Movement disorders 2. Boston: Butterworths, 1987:288.

Sternlieb I, Scheinberg IH. Wilson's disease. In: Schiff L, Schiff ER, eds. Diseases of the liver. Philadelphia: Lippincott, 1993:659.

Ascites

David J. Clain, M.D.

DEFINITION

Ascites is the presence of an abnormal volume of fluid in the peritoneal cavity.

ETIOLOGY

About 80% of ascites is due to cirrhosis, in which portal hypertension has an important role in localizing fluid in the peritoneal cavity. Other causes of ascites with raised portal pressure are heart failure, severe viral or alcoholic hepatitis, and Budd–Chiari syndrome. Ascites with normal portal pressure is due to a variety of conditions, including peritoneal carcinoma, tuberculous peritonitis, pancreatic ascites, and nephrotic syndrome (Table 19–84–1).

CRITERIA FOR DIAGNOSIS
Suggestive

The patient or the physician observes diffuse swelling of the abdomen unrelated to obesity or pregnancy. The physician may elicit fluid dullness that shifts.

Definitive

In the presence of a large volume of ascites, shifting dullness on percussion and an obvious fluid thrill are virtually diagnostic. Rarely, a massive ovarian cyst is misleading. Paracentesis is confirmatory if the signs of fluid are distributed throughout the abdomen. Ultrasound definitively demonstrates 100 mL of intraperitoneal fluid.

CLINICAL MANIFESTATIONS
Subjective

The rate of swelling of the abdomen varies with the cause. An abrupt onset is unusual and may be due to hepatic vein thrombosis. In massive intraperitoneal hemorrhage, the abdominal expansion may be overshadowed by pain and symptoms of hypovolemia. Ascites may accumulate rapidly in hospital after variceal bleeding because of the sudden fall in albumin and hematocrit, plus the intravenous infusion of saline. Preexisting shortness of breath and ankle swelling draw attention to heart failure. Night sweats and known exposure raise the question of tuberculosis. Ascites may follow hemodialysis for end-stage renal disease.

As cirrhosis is by far the most common cause, there is frequently a history of liver disease or alcoholism. Recurrent ascites is common in alcoholics, because further bouts of drinking raise portal pressure due to steatohepatitis. Pancreatic ascites usually develops painlessly in the course of alcohol-induced chronic pancreatitis. It is important to inquire about previous treatment for breast, lung, or colon cancer.

Objective
Physical Examination

The classical maneuver to demonstrate intraperitoneal fluid is percussion of flank dullness that shifts on rolling the patient from side to side. Cystic ovarian tumors have a central distribution. Clinical examination has low sensitivity and specificity for small volumes of ascites. Gaseous distention of the bowel may obscure a moderate volume of ascites. Tense ascites often elevates the diaphragm with dullness at the base of the lungs. The umbilicus can be protuberant or herniated.

There are frequently signs of portal hypertension and chronic liver disease. Abnormal veins on the abdominal wall are often prominent, especially above the umbilicus. A fully formed caput medusae is rare. The liver is usually small in cirrhosis, but a hard left lobe may be felt or balloted in the epigastrium. Stigmata of liver disease include vascular spiders, palmar erythema, and gynecomastia in men. The liver is large and tender in heart failure, and may be hard and nodular in malignancy. Fever and abdominal tenderness may be present if there is spontaneous bacterial peritonitis. Florid signs of acute peritonitis such as rigidity and ileus are not seen. Examination should include palpation within the umbilicus for tumor nodules and behind the left clavicle for a "Virchow" lymph node. Anasarca in children suggests the nephrotic syndrome. Rarely, there will be lethargy, dry skin, and puffy eyes of myxedema.

Routine Laboratory Abnormalities

Urine. In cirrhotic ascites, urine is concentrated with low volume and high specific gravity.

Blood. Liver function tests are usually abnormal in ascites due to liver disease. Serum albumin is low, and frequently, prothrombin time and bilirubin are increased. Transaminase levels are high in viral and alcoholic hepatitis. Hyponatremia is common in cirrhotic ascites.

Radiology. Plain films show a diffuse, grainy increased density. Bowel loops are dilated, resembling an ileus. If ascites is infected with many different bacteria, an upright, plain film may show free air due to perforation.

PLANS
Diagnostic
Differential Diagnosis

The division of ascites into transudates and exudates based on total protein concentration in the peritoneal fluid has not stood the test of time. There are transudates with a high fluid protein such as cardiac ascites and exudates with a low fluid protein as in spontaneous bacterial peritonitis. The close correlation between portal hypertension and the serum–ascites albumin gradient provides a sound basis for classification into two groups (Table 19–84–1).

TABLE 19–84–1. DIFFERENTIAL DIAGNOSIS OF ASCITES

Serum–Ascites Albumin Gradient > 1.1 g	
Cirrhosis	Alcohol
	Hepatitis B and C
	Autoimmune
	Primary biliary
	Cryptogenic
Viral hepatitis	Fulminant
	Submassive necrosis
Congestive liver	Heart failure
	Constrictive pericarditis
	Hepatic vein thrombosis
Cancer	Primary liver cell
	Metastases
Other	Myxedema
Serum–Ascites Albumin Gradient < 1.1 g	
Malignancy	Cancer
	Mesothelioma
Infection	Tuberculous peritonitis
Renal	Nephrotic
	Hemodialysis
	Post transplant
Pancreatic	Duct/cyst disruption in chronic pancreatitis
Biliary	Gallbladder, duct or duodenal leak
Lymphatic (chylous)	Surgical section
	Malignant blockage

The difference between albumin in serum and ascitic fluid is more than 1.1 g in portal hypertension, and less than 1.1 g when portal pressure is normal. Most patients with a high gradient have cirrhosis or severe alcoholic hepatitis. Other causes of liver diseases are listed in Table 19–84–1. Heart failure is an important cause of ascites with a gradient above 1.1. Malignant disease of the peritoneum is the most frequent cause of ascites with a low albumin gradient. Additional causes with a normal portal pressure include leakage of bile or pancreatic juice, tuberculosis, and nephrotic syndrome. Ascites occurring with primary hepatocellular carcinoma is almost always due to underlying cirrhosis and, therefore, reflects portal hypertension with a high albumin gradient. Cytology is usually negative, but the ascites often contains blood.

Spontaneous bacterial peritonitis is frequently a complication of ascites in severe liver disease. Secondary bacterial peritonitis, which is uncommon, is due to perforation of bowel contents into existing ascites.

Diagnostic Options

The diagnostic options for all as well as selected patients with ascites are outlined in Table 19–84–2.

Recommended Approach

When the presence of ascites is established, three important elements aid in diagnosis. These are the history and physical examination, the serum–ascites albumin gradient, and a cell count of the peritoneal fluid. Eighty percent of patients with ascites have cirrhosis, which can often be determined by reviewing the clinical manifestations, especially a history of alcoholism, jaundice, dilated abdominal veins, and an abnormal liver. Ascites in liver disease is associated with portal hypertension and a high albumin gradient (Table 19–84–1, Figure 19–84–1). If the serum–ascites albumin difference is more than 1.1 g, and symptoms and signs are not conclusive for liver disease, a high total protein in the fluid often helps in distinguishing hepatic outflow obstruction due to heart failure, constrictive pericarditis, or hepatic vein thrombosis. Fluid total protein is usually less than 2.5 g in cirrhosis and more than 2.5 g in the congestive liver disorders. The protein level rises after diuresis in cirrhosis, which can be misleading if measured during treatment.

A low ascites–serum albumin gradient is found when portal pressure is normal (Table 19–84–1, Figure 19–84–1). Mostly, this is due to malignant infiltration of the peritoneum. There is usually a lymphocytosis in the fluid. Lactic dehydrogenase can be high in cancer or inflammation. Cytology, smears, and culture, as well as clinical criteria, distinguish cancer from tuberculosis. A lymphocytosis may also be found in chylous ascites. Triglycerides are above 200 mg/dL and often much higher with a milky appearance. Pancreatic ascites, which usually follows disruption of a duct in chronic pancreatitis, also has a low albumin gradient. Ascitic amylase is extremely high and irritates the peritoneum, causing increased polymorphonuclear and red cell counts.

In a small number of patients, full clinical evaluation, liver function tests, and analysis of the ascites do not provide a definite diagnosis. When cancer metastasizes both to liver and to peritoneum, the albumin difference may be equivocal or high. Sometimes there are two processes. Tuberculous peritonitis is common in decompensated cirrhosis because of diminished immune function. This can lead to lymphocytosis with a high albumin gradient due to the portal hypertension. Laparoscopy helps in these special cases, allowing for direct visualization and biopsy of both liver and peritoneum. Culture of ascitic fluid is mandatory in all patients with new-onset ascites and in all cirrhotics whose condition deteriorates. These are sick patients with obvious features of decompensated liver disease. Rarely, perforation of bowel in cirrhosis leads to a polymicrobial culture with a high total protein in the fluid.

Therapeutic

Therapeutic Options

The therapeutic options include treatment of the underlying cause, salt restriction, diuretics, paracentesis, transjugular intrahepatic portal–systemic shunt, and liver transplantation.

Recommended Approach

This discussion focuses on the treatment of ascites in cirrhosis. The mainstays of management are to restrict dietary sodium and to administer diuretics. But the cardinal rule is first to correct the underlying cause. The most frequent precipitating factors are steatohepatis due to alcohol and bleeding from varices. Systemic infection and a sodium binge can also contribute. Ascites is often iatrogenic. Normal saline is frequently infused into ill, often bleeding, cirrhotics with rapid accumulation of fluid. There is no mystique to treating cirrhotic ascites. Response to therapy is dictated by several factors which include a clear, precipitating cause, degree of portal hypertension, synthetic liver function, and spontaneous bacterial peritonitis. A Child's B patient who develops ascites after a controlled variceal hemorrhage usually responds promptly to salt restriction and diuretics. A sick patient with muscle wasting, jaundice, coagulopathy, and no precipitating cause is likely to be refractory to the most meticulous regimen. Resolution of ascites is not an end in itself. The goal is to make patients feel comfortable, although diuresis does appear to reduce the risk of spontaneous bacterial peritonitis; however, there is no evidence to show that vigorous treatment of ascites improves prognosis. Overzealous diuresis leads to serious electrolyte disorders and the hepatorenal syndrome.

The following steps are advised:

- Treat the precipitating cause.
- Assess the need for hospital admission (consider severity, alcohol detoxification, renal function, compliance with diet).
- Inoculate blood culture bottles with ascitic fluid at the bedside.
- If ascites is tense, remove 6 L by paracentesis to improve comfort and breathing.
- Establish baseline electrolytes and creatinine.
- Restrict fluid intake if the serum sodium is below 125 mEq/L.
- Twenty-four hour urine sodium output is the best guide to therapy but is seldom practical outside metabolic wards. Use if the patient is very compliant.
- Monitor body weight accurately, daily. This is simple and usually effective.
- Prescribe a combination of spironolactone 100 mg and furosemide 40 mg daily. Aim for a weight loss of 1 pound per day, 1.5 pounds if there is significant peripheral edema.
- If there is not adequate response in 3 days, double the dose to spironolactone 200 mg and furosemide 80 mg daily. The usual maximum doses are spironolactone 400 mg and furosemide 160 mg daily. Excessive diuresis leads to plasma volume contraction, rise in creati-

TABLE 19–84–2. DIAGNOSTIC OPTIONS FOR PATIENTS WITH ASCITES

All Patients

Total cell count (A)*

Differential count (A)

Inoculation of blood culture bottles at bedside (A)

Albumin (S, A)

Total protein (A)

Selected Patients

Test	Indication
Amylase	Pancreatic ascites
Lactic dehydrogenase	Infection or tumor
Tuberculosis smear and culture	Tuberculous peritonitis
Cytology	Malignancy
Triglycerides	Chylous ascites
Biliruin	Biliary or duodenal perforation
Serum α-fetoprotein	Primary hepatocellular carcinoma

Laparoscopy
  Peritoneal biopsy
  Liver biopsy
	Cancer or cirrhosis

Ultrasound or computed tomography of liver	Cancer or cirrhosis

*A, ascites; S, serum.

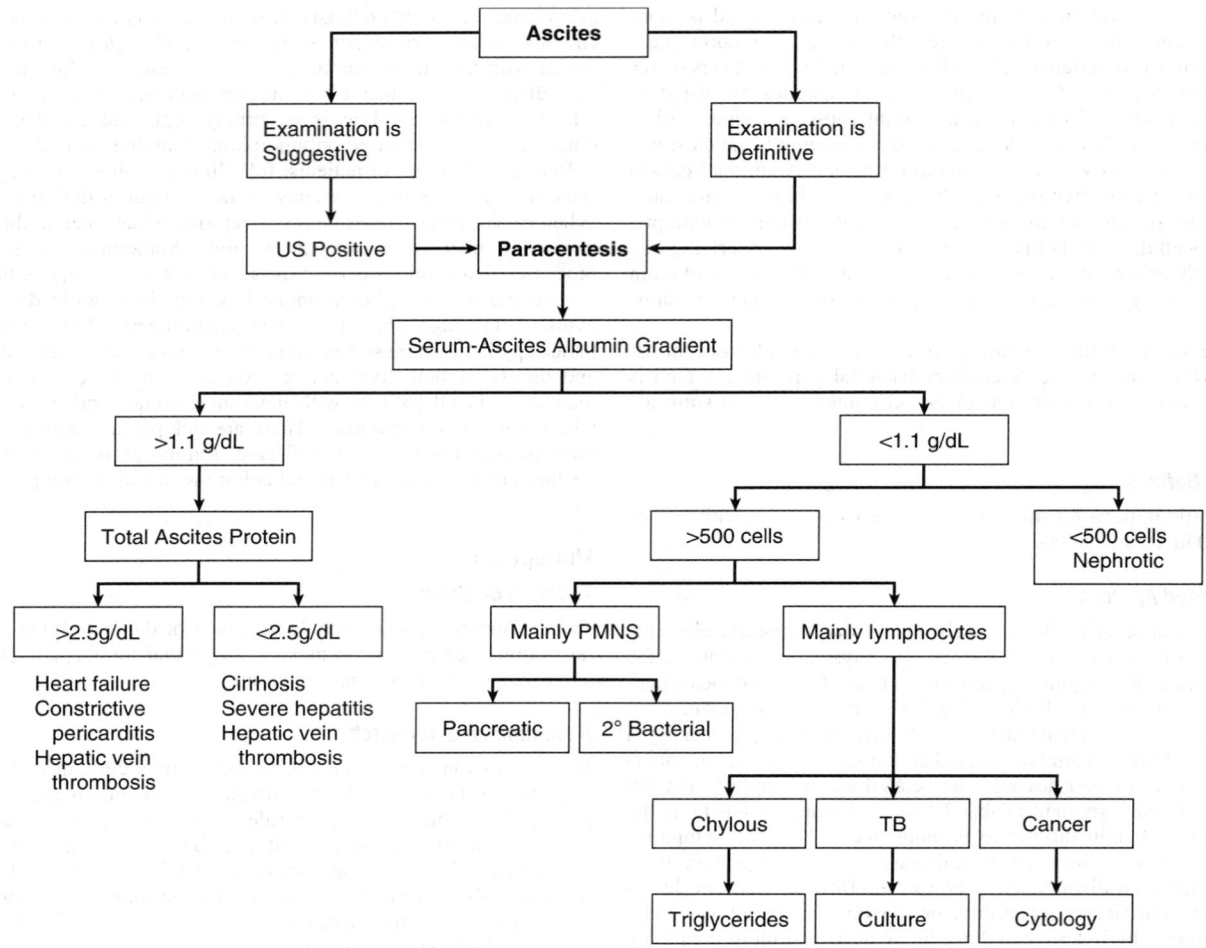

Figure 19–84–1. Algorithm for the diagnosis of ascites. US, ultrasound; PMNs, polymorphonuclear leukocytes; TB, tuberculosis.

nine, and electrolyte disorders such as hypochloremic acidosis and hypokalemic alkalosis.

Diuretics should be discontinued if potassium falls below 3.0 mEq/L. Lesser degrees of hypokalemia can be corrected by supplementary potassium. The development of electrolyte disturbance, azotemia, or encephalopathy during a controlled diuresis indicates a poor outcome. Truly refractory ascites is also a bad prognostic feature and can be defined as weight loss of less than 0.5 pound per day on maximal doses of diuretics with sodium restricted to 40 mEq/d and/or three or more episodes of tense ascites in 9 months despite adequate diuretic treatment and sodium restriction.

The options for treating refractory ascites are large-volume paracentesis, peritoneovenous (Le Veen) shunt, transjugular intrahepatic portosystemic stent shunt (TIPS), and liver transplantation.

Paracentesis. Total paracentesis of 5 to 20 L is safe and effective. There are fewer complications than with an intensive diuretic regimen which results in azotemia and electrolyte disorders. The loss of protein and complement is a disadvantage. Large-volume paracentesis should be reserved for diuretic-resistent patients. Expansion of plasma volume with albumin or dextran after paracentesis is controversial. Some studies have shown that large-volume paracentesis can be performed without an intravenous infusion. Many experts advise volume expansion if there is no peripheral edema.

Peritoneovenous Shunts. Peritoneovenous shunts and paracentesis are equally effective in relieving refractory ascites. Hospital admissions are less frequent after Le Veen shunt than with paracentesis. Neither method is completely satisfactory. Cirrhotics with refractory ascites are generally very ill and have a poor prognosis. Half will be dead in a

year. Complications of treatment are frequent and shunt occlusion is common. Current practice favors large-volume paracentesis. There has been recent experience with the treatment of ascites by placement of a TIPS. First observations were in patients treated for severe variceal bleeding in whom concomitant ascites was relieved. There has not been as yet a randomized comparison of large-volume paracentesis and TIPS for the management of refractory ascites.

The overall survival for cirrhotics who develop ascites is about 50% at 2 years; and for refractory ascites, about 50% at 1 year. After transplantation more than 75% are alive at 2 years. Therefore, the presence of ascites that is poorly responsive to treatment is a good indication for liver transplantation.

FOLLOW-UP

Complications are frequent with all methods of treating cirrhotic ascites. Electrolytes, renal function, and signs of portal–systemic encephalopathy should be carefully monitored. The appearance of asterixis and confusion can sometimes be reversed with lactulose and a low-protein diet while maintaining an adequate diuretic regimen. Frequently, side effects are the factors that limit therapy of ascites in chronic liver disease.

DISCUSSION
Prevalence and Incidence

The incidence of ascites varies greatly with different causes. About 80% of ascites is due to chronic liver disease. The incidence in cirrhosis varies with severity. Ascites is almost always present in Child grade C patients and never in grade A. The presence of ascites in addition to encephalopathy, levels of bilirubin and albumin, and prolonged prothrombin time is the basis of the Child–Turcotte (Pugh's modification) prognostic index.

Related Basic Science

In the traditional "underfill" theory of ascites formation, the initial events are increased hepatic lymph production and the transfer of fluid from the portal circulation due to hypoalbuminemia and high pressure. Sequestration of fluid in the peritoneal space leads to a contracted plasma volume, which causes intense sodium retention by the kidneys. There is, however, good experimental evidence to indicate that salt retention is the cause and not the result of ascites formation. The kidneys conserve sodium before the appearance of ascites in cirrhosis. The "overfill" theory proposes that renal salt retention leads to an expansion of plasma volume. The increased fluid is localized to the peritoneal space because of high portal pressure.

The current popular view is that there is a state of peripheral arterial vasodilation in cirrhosis which is sensed as a reduced intravascular volume. Sympathetic responses and the release of pressor agents such as renin, aldosterone, noradrenaline, and vasopressin lead to renal vasoconstriction and sodium and water retention.

Natural History and Its Modification with Treatment

There is no evidence that successful treatment of ascites alters the course of chronic liver disease. Patients with spontaneous bacterial peritonitis have a very poor prognosis and antibiotic therapy improves survival.

Prevention

Ascites is a complication of the diseases listed in Table 19–84–1 and may be prevented by early diagnosis and treatment of the various causes.

Cost Containment

Cost savings may be achieved by following the guidelines to diagnosis summarized in the algorithm in Figure 19–84–1, and applying the principles outlined in the recommended approach to therapy.

REFERENCES

Gines P, Arroyo V, Quintero E et al. Comparison of paracentesis and diuretics in the treatment of cirrhotics with tense ascites: Results of a randomized study. Gastroenterology 1987;93:234.

Pare P, Talbot J, Hoefs JC. Serum-ascites albumin concentration gradient: A physiological approach to the differential diagnosis of ascites. Gastroenterology 1983;85:240.

Perez-Ayuso RM, Arroyo V, Planus R, et al. Randomized comparative study of efficacy of furosemide versus spironolactone in non-azotemic cirrhosis with ascites: relationship between the diuretic response and the activity of the renin-aldosterone system. Gastroenterology 1983;84:961.

Runyon BA. Care of patients with ascites. N Engl J Med. 1994;339:337.

CHAPTER 19–85

Hepatic Encephalopathy

Curtis E. Scott, M.D.

DEFINITION

Hepatic encephalopathy (HE) is a syndrome of neuropsychiatric abnormalities that are associated with both chronic and acute liver disease.

ETIOLOGY

The most common form of HE is the portal–systemic encephalopathy (PSE) that is a consequence of portosystemic shunting resulting from chronic liver disease and portal hypertension, but may also occur with surgical portal–systemic anastomoses. Agents that precipitate or worsen PSE include azotemia, diuretics, analgesics, sedatives, gastrointestinal hemorrhage, dietary protein, diarrhea, vomiting, constipation, infection, and large-volume shifts of paracentesis.

Patients with acute (fulminant) hepatic failure due to viral hepatitis or drug and toxic hepatic injury also develop encephalopathy that can rapidly progress to coma, with high mortality if untreated.

CRITERIA FOR DIAGNOSIS

Suggestive

Hepatic encephalopathy is considered when there is a recent change in mental state following a precipitating event in a patient with cirrhosis.

Definitive

Such patients may demonstrate asterixis, an elevated plasma ammonia level, an abnormal electroencephalogram, and a slow response to trail-making and symbol recognition tests. Furthermore, responsiveness to therapy directed at this condition may help confirm the diagnosis.

CLINICAL MANIFESTATIONS

Subjective

Close relatives sometimes can provide a better assessment of changes occurring with the patient than that recognized by the patient himself. Changes in personality, speech, and attitude are noted. Interruption of nighttime sleep is recognized frequently with reversal of rhythm to daytime sleep that may be intermittent. Patients become lethargic, and may progress to confusion and even coma. Ability to perform intellectual and physical tasks progressively decreases. Patients develop subtle impairment of computation and shortened attention span and progress to amnesia of past events and complete disorientation.

Objective

Physical Examination

Examination of the patient uncovers progressive neuromuscular abnormalities. A metabolic tremor and asterixis are commonly present. Initially, subtle muscular incoordination and impaired handwriting may be elicited. There may be a progression to development of ataxia with hyperactive reflexes and slurred speech. In the precoma state, nystagmus, rigidity, clonus, and a present Babinski may be found. Decerebrate posturing may be seen in deep coma. Fetor hepaticus, a pungent sour odor, may be detected on the breath of encephalopathic patients.

Routine Laboratory Abnormalities

Laboratory analysis in patients with PSE may show a respiratory alkalosis due to toxin-induced stimulation of the respiratory center, elevated plasma urea and creatinine levels, and decreased serum potassium level. Evidence of decreased hepatic synthetic function may be demonstrated by an elevated prothrombin time and decreased serum albumin. Other hepatic biochemical tests may show variable results.

PLANS
Diagnostic
Differential Diagnosis

It is sometimes initially difficult to distinguish hepatic encephalopathy from other forms of delirium, but further assessment helps make the distinction. Other states that should be considered include carbon dioxide narcosis and uremic encephalopathy, which also present with asterixis; alcoholic withdrawal, where agitation and tremor are prominent, but asterixis is not conspicuous; hypoglycemia; Wernicke's encephalopathy; chronic meningeal infections such as tuberculosis and fungal infections; and subdural hematomas.

Diagnostic Options

Arterial plasma ammonia is increased by most precipitants that induce encephalopathy in cirrhotics; however, some, such as sedative-induced encephalopathy, may not have associated elevated ammonia levels. Other tests that are useful in identifying hepatic encephalopathy include the electroencephalogram, which shows slowing of frequency down to the delta range (2–3 cycles per second). This also is not a finding exclusive to hepatic encephalopathy, but helps make the diagnosis. The Reitan trail-making (number connection test) and symbol recognition tests may be used in early and subclinical encephalopathy. Elevated cerebrospinal fluid glutamine levels are sensitive but less practical.

Recommended Approach

An evaluation of the patient for HE should include a historical assessment of diuretic, analgesic, or sedative use, dietary intake, recent alcohol use, and the presence of vomiting, diarrhea, or constipation. Examination should assess the presence of orthostasis, asterixis, or other neurologic abnormality and stool for occult blood to rule out gastrointestinal bleeding. Routine blood tests are obtained with attention to serum blood urea nitrogen, creatinine, glucose, and potassium and complete blood count. Arterial serum ammonia and blood gases should be assessed. Infection should be ruled out with chest radiograph, urinalysis and culture, blood cultures, and diagnostic paracentesis if indicated.

If the diagnosis remains undetermined following the initial assessment, an evaluation of the differential diagnoses above should be pursued. If a lumbar puncture is performed, an elevation of levels of α-ketoglutarate and glutamine in the cerebrospinal fluid helps make the diagnosis.

Therapeutic
Therapeutic Options

Measures that may be useful in the treatment of HE include lactulose, lactitol (β-galactosidosorbitol), and nonabsorbable antibiotic agents such as neomycin, paromomycin, sulfasuxidine, and rifaximim. Metronidazole may also be beneficial. Correction of electrolyte abnormalities, shunt occlusion, branched-chain amino acid therapy, and use of L-dopa and bromocriptine have been suggested. Liver transplantation is considered in suitable candidates. Abdominal colectomy is a treatment of last resort.

Recommended Approach

The approach to therapy should at a minimum address the following three goals: control of factors that led to precipitant-induced encephalopathy; reduction of protein content of the diet; removal of the nitrogenous load from the intestine by increasing the frequency of bowel movements and reduction of the activity of intestinal flora by administering nonabsorbable carbohydrate or antibiotic.

If bleeding in the intestinal tract is responsible for the development of HE, this must be halted. If azotemia is the cause, aggressive treatment of prerenal factors is pursued. Where indicated, dialysis is performed. Diuretics are discontinued and electrolyte abnormalities cor-

rected. Infectious sources are identified and treated appropriately. If protein is found to be a precipitant, protein intake must be sharply reduced. Calories provided as glucose help avoid further protein degradation until the patient can be returned to regular dietary intake. Although studies have shown varying results, patients who are protein intolerant may benefit from a trial of a branched-chain amino acid diet, which may be less encephalogenic while improving nitrogen balance. Vegetable protein is preferred over animal protein for similar reasons.

Lactulose is the mainstay of therapy of HE, given in a dose of 15 to 30 mL two to four times per day, with the goal of two to three soft bowel movements per day. Lactulose enemas (300–500 mL in a total of 1-L volume) may also be used, particularly in comatose patients. Significant improvement occurs within 48 to 72 hours. If HE is suspected, this therapy should be initiated in parallel with the ongoing workup. Lactitol, a disaccharide analog of lactulose that can be prepared in powder form as well as syrup, is also effective. In patients who are lactase deficient, lactose has been shown to be effective.

Neomycin given enterally at 2 to 4 g/d in divided doses is effective in reducing aerobic urease-splitting bacterial flora that are responsible for production of ammonia absorbed through the gut. Although it is itself minimally absorbed, long-term use of neomycin may be associated with renal and auditory dysfunction. Neomycin given in combination with lactulose is also effective.

Metronidazole has been shown to be as effective as neomycin. Dose reduction may be necessary as hepatic metabolism is impaired. Therapy with L-dopa and bromocriptine has been suggested based on the hypothesis of a defective dopaminergic neurotransmission as occurs in other neurologic disorders such as Parkinson's disease. Controlled clinical trials, however, have not shown significant benefit.

Patients with chronic intractable encephalopathy who are no longer responsive to the medical therapeutic measures and who are suitable candidates for liver transplantation should be offered this therapy, as proven benefit has been documented following this procedure.

Approximately one third of cases of HE are nonnitrogenous in origin. Sedatives, depressants, and analgesics are among the most common offenders. Primary treatment in these cases consists of discontinuation of the offending drug.

FOLLOW-UP

Patient instruction in appropriate dietary intake is indicated and follow-up is focused on avoidance of precipitating factors.

DISCUSSION
Prevalence and Incidence

The most common type of HE is PSE, which occurs almost exclusively in patients with cirrhosis with portal hypertension and portal–systemic shunting. Approximately half of the cases of PSE occur in patients with surgical portal–systemic shunts, who constitute only about 5% of patients with cirrhosis. The other half occurs in patients with spontaneous portal–systemic shunting due to portal hypertension.

Related Basic Science

Hepatic encephalopathy may present as one of two major types. The most common, PSE, accompanies the development of portal–systemic shunting that arises either following portacaval anastomosis surgery during chronic liver disease or spontaneously following portal hypertension most often due to cirrhosis. Neuropathologically, PSE is characterized by astrocytic changes known as Alzheimer type II astrocytosis.

The second major type of HE is associated with acute or fulminant hepatic failure and is a clinical syndrome of rapid onset resulting from severe inflammatory and/or necrotic liver disease. Patients can progress to coma within hours to weeks. Massive brain edema frequently leads to increased intracranial pressure, resulting in brain herniation and death. Currently, the only proven beneficial therapy for these patients is liver transplantation.

A number of pathophysiologic mechanisms have been suggested for the development of HE. It is unclear whether the same mechanisms are applicable in both acute and chronic forms of HE, although this extrapolation has been made in most cases. Proposed hypotheses are based primarily on alteration or failure of neurotransmission systems and include ammonia neurotoxicity; effects of neuroactive and/or neurotoxic biogenic monamine metabolites; increased γ-aminobutyric acid (GABA)ergic tone due to increased bloodborne GABA or the presence of endogenous benzodiazopines that modulate GABAergic neurotransmission.

Arterial blood ammonia levels are frequently, but not always, elevated in patients with PSE. This is associated with an increased permeability of the blood–brain barrier, as well as a significant increase in the cerebral metabolic rate for ammonia. The apparent ease with which ammonia moves into the brain from the blood in patients with liver disease could account for the hypersensitivity of cirrhotic patients to ammoniagenic conditions such as high-protein diets and gastrointestinal bleeding, as well as for the presence of brain dysfunction in some patients with near-normal ammonia levels.

The absence of a cerebral urea cycle renders the brain almost entirely dependent on glutamine synthesis as a means of ammonia removal. Consequently, cerebrospinal fluid glutamine concentrations correlate well with the severity of neurologic impairment in patients with HE.

Neuroactive tryptophan metabolites such as serotonin, tryptamine, and quinolinic acid have been implicated in the pathogenesis of HE; however, available data show conflicting results. Therefore, their role in HE needs further elucidation.

Initial prospective consideration of a role for GABA in the development of HE has not held up to further scrutiny; however, an "endogenous" benzodiazopine effect has been identified that is marked by improvement in HE in patients given benzodiazopine receptor antagonists (e.g., flumazenil). Benzodiazopines exert their effect on central nervous system function by interacting with binding sites on the GABA–benzodiazopine–chloride ionophore receptor complex. Autopsied brain tissue from patients who died in fulminant hepatic failure has been shown by gas chromatography–mass spectrometry to contain increased amounts of diazepam and N,N-desmethyldiazepam. Although similar results could not be found using similar techniques in autopsied brain tissue from PSE patients, a clinical controlled trial of flumazenil in cirrhotic patients with HE revealed significant amelioration of neurologic function in more than one third of patients, none of whom had measurable levels of diazepam in blood. Other uncontrolled studies give even higher numbers.

Although other toxic substances such as mercaptans, phenols, and fatty acids, alone, do not have a primary role in causing HE, they otherwise appear to have synergism with ammonia in the development of HE.

Natural History and Its Modification with Treatment

Hepatic encephalopathy, if left untreated, can progress from mild disease to coma and death. Institution of appropriate therapy and maintenance can return many patients to preencephalopathic activity.

Prevention

Development of HE is not universal, but in fact may occur in about 50% of cirrhotic patients, and then may require a precipitating event. Predicting which patient will develop HE may be difficult. Prevention or prophylactic treatment is therefore impractical and may be cost ineffective. Close follow-up of the cirrhotic patient for early detection and therapy is the preferred method of management.

Cost Containment

Nonabsorbable carbohydrate therapy, lactulose, is quite effective for treatment of PSE and does not have the potential side effects associated with neomycin therapy. Combination lactulose and antibiotic therapy is usually not necessary, and should be reserved for cases in which single-agent therapy has not provided optimum results.

REFERENCES

Blei AT. Hepatic encephalopathy. In: Kaplowitz N, ed. Liver and biliary diseases. Baltimore: Williams & Wilkins, 1992:552.

Conn HO. Hepatic encephalopathy. In: Schiff L, Schiff ER, eds. Diseases of the liver. 7th ed. Philadelphia: Lippincott, 1993:1036.

Ede RJ, Williams R. Hepatic encephalopathy and cerebral edema. Semin Liver Dis 1986;6:107.

Mousseau DD. Butterworth RF. Current theories on the pathogenesis of hepatic encephalopathy. Proc Soc Exp Biol Med 1994;206:329.

Pomier-Layrargues G, Giguere JF, Lavoie J. Flumazenil in cirrhotic patients in hepatic coma: A randomized double-blind placebo-controlled crossover trial. Hepatology 1994;19:32.

CHAPTER 19–86

Spontaneous Bacterial Peritonitis

Stanley R. Yancovitz, M.D.

DEFINITION

Spontaneous bacterial peritonitis can be defined as bacterial peritonitis occurring in an individual with underlying cirrhosis or severe liver disease without the presence of an additional intraabdominal process such as appendicitis or cholecystitis.

ETIOLOGY

Bacteria involved are either enteric organisms such *Escherichia coli, Klebsiella,* and enterococcus or the respiratory organism *Streptococcus pneumoniae.*

CRITERIA FOR DIAGNOSIS
Suggestive

The occurrence in a patient with severe liver disease of a sudden increase in ascitic fluid with inflammatory changes in the absence of another acute abdominal process suggests the diagnosis.

Definitive

The demonstration of bacterial organisms in ascitic fluid by Gram stain and culture in the absence of other acute intraabdominal processes or an overt respiratory infection defines the diagnosis.

CLINICAL MANIFESTATIONS
Subjective

Patients with known or suspected chronic liver disease develop fever, chills, abdominal discomfort, and increase in abdominal girth.

Objective
Physical Examination

Fever may be present. Abdominal distention is present with ascites and abdominal tenderness. The patient commonly has other signs of chronic liver disease and may be obtunded or encephalopathic.

Routine Laboratory Abnormalities

Leukocytosis with leftward shift of the differential is commonly present. Leukopenia or normal total count with a left shift may be present. Ascitic fluid contains greater than 400 white blood cells/mm^3 and greater than 25% polymorphonuclear cells. The Gram stain is positive in approximately 40% of cases and culture positive in 90 to 95% of cases. Blood cultures are commonly positive.

PLANS

Diagnostic

Differential Diagnosis

Perforated viscus, pancreatitis, cholecystitis, alcoholic hepatitis, and all other acute abdominal events should be considered.

Diagnostic Options

Perform paracentesis with analysis of total cell count and differential, Gram stain, and culture. Also obtain blood cultures. If ascitic fluid appears to be loculated or not easily demonstrable, consider obtaining fluid under ultrasound guidance.

Consider plain films to rule out free air or other radiologic studies depending on the clinical picture.

Recommended Approach

If ascites is evident proceed to paracentesis. Obtain blood cultures and review ascitic fluid cell count differential and Gram stain. If Gram-positive cocci are present, begin ampicillin 2 g intravenously every 6 hours or ampicillin/sulbactam 3 g intravenously every 8 hours. If Gram-negative bacilli are present, begin cefotaxime 2 g intravenously every 8 hours or another third-generation cephalosporin. If no organisms are seen and the cell count or differential is abnormal, begin ampicillin/sulbactam. If the patient is allergic to penicillin, use a third-generation cephalosporin. If there is a history of immediate or life-threatening penicillin reactions, alternative antibiotics should be used.

FOLLOW-UP

Frequent clinical monitoring is indicated. Antibiotic adjustments should be made according to the results of blood and ascitic fluid cultures and sensitivity patterns. Failure of clinical improvement in 48 to 72 hours should prompt reconsideration of other pathologic processes. Recovery of fungal organisms suggests the presence of bowel perforation. Recovery of staphylococcal species suggests extraabdominal processes such as infective endocarditis, infected intravascular devices, and parenteral drug use.

DISCUSSION

Prevalence and Incidence

Spontaneous bacterial peritonitis complicates between 5 and 10% of patients with advanced alcoholic cirrhosis and ascites. It also occurs with acute and chronic viral hepatitis, nephrotic syndrome, malignant ascites, and congestive heart failure.

Related Basic Science

Normally few bacteria enter the portal circulation from the gut. Those that do are rapidly cleared by phagocytic cells in the liver. Any organisms that escape into the systematic circulation are phagocytosed by circulating polymorphonuclear cells or trapped in the spleen. This low-grade portal bacteremia may play a role in maintaining normal levels of circulating immunoglobins. Alcoholic cirrhotics with ascites have edematous bowels with frequent breaks in the integrity of the intestinal mucosa. Increased numbers of bacteria reach the systemic circulation where antiphagocytic factors and congested poorly functioning spleens allow bacteria to travel to ascitic fluid, which can then serve as an excellent culture medium. Alternatively, bacteria may reach ascitic fluid through lymphatic channels from the bowel. Erosions of umbilical hernias may allow skin bacteria to directly enter the peritoneal cavity. The ascitic fluid may also be infected as the result of a prior paracentesis because of entry into a loop of bowel or failure to maintain strict aseptic technique. *Streptococcus pneumoniae* is lysed on contact with bile. Therefore, it most likely originates from a respiratory source and travels to ascitic fluid via the bloodstream.

Natural History and Its Modification with Treatment

Untreated bacterial peritonitis in patients with cirrhosis is usually fatal. Prompt antibiotic treatment can be expected to eradicate spontaneous bacterial peritonitis in the vast majority of patients; however, patients may go on to succumb to their underlying liver disease despite successful antibiotic treatment. As the underlying pathophysiologic derangements persist infection may recur.

Prevention

Unnecessary paracentesis should be avoided. When ascitic fluid appears to be loculated or otherwise difficult to obtain, radiologic guidance should be used for paracentesis. Extraabdominal infections should be identified and treated promptly.

Cost Containment

Prompt diagnosis and treatment of spontaneous bacterial peritonitis should shorten hospital stays. Avoidance of unnecessary laparotomy and multiple radiologic studies can occur with prompt diagnosis and effective treatment.

REFERENCES

Conn HO, Fessel J. Spontaneous bacterial peritonitis in cirrhosis: Variations on a theme. Medicine 1971;50:161.

Conn HO. Spontaneous bacterial peritonitis, multiple revisitations. Gastroenterology 1976;70:455.

Runyon, BA, Hoefs JC. Spontaneous vs. secondary bacterial peritonitis: Differentiation by response of ascitic fluid neutrophil count to antimicrobial therapy. Arch Intern Med 1886;146:1563.

Wilcox CM, Dismukes WE. Spontaneous bacterial peritonitis: A review of pathogenesis, diagnosis and treatment. Medicine 1987;66:447.

CHAPTER 19–87

Bleeding Varices

Gerald Fruchter, M.D.

DEFINITION

Varices represent dilated, tortuous veins that are formed within the wall of the gastrointestinal tract invariably as the result of portal hypertension. The most common site of varices is the distal esophagus, where they are formed as the result of reversed blood flow from the portal vein to the coronary vein and into the esophageal venous plexus. Bleeding varices represent the clinical entity whereby the presence of gastrointestinal bleeding is attributed to a ruptured varix.

ETIOLOGY

Portal hypertension in the large majority of cases arises as a result of cirrhosis with its concomitant distortion of the intrahepatic vasculature causing resistance to portal venous flow. Alcoholic cirrhosis is the most common cause of portal hypertension in the United States. The second leading cause is postnecrotic cirrhosis induced by viral hepatitis, most commonly hepatitis C. In the Middle East, schistosomiasis with the development of periportal venule fibrosis is a common cause of portal hypertension and subsequent varices. Other causes of portal hypertension include portal venous and splenic vein obstruction and Budd–Chiari syndrome (hepatic vein obstruction). Infiltrative disease of the liver, for example, amyloidosis, can likewise give rise to portal hypertension.

CRITERIA FOR DIAGNOSIS
Suggestive

The endoscopic documentation of esophageal or gastric varices and exclusion of other pathology in the setting of an acute gastrointestinal bleed are highly suggestive of bleeding varices.

Definitive

The endoscopic visualization of bleeding from a varix or a stigma of recent bleeding, for example, an adherent clot overlying a varix, enables the clinician to make a definitive diagnosis of variceal bleeding.

CLINICAL MANIFESTATIONS
Subjective

Variceal bleeders invariably present with painless hematemesis as their cardinal complaint with or without accompanying melena and/or rectal bleeding. Gastric variceal bleeders frequently present in a similar fashion though they may only have melena. Colonic varices, particularly rectal varices, present with rectal bleeding. Associated features of significant acute blood loss (i.e., profound weakness, lightheadedness, and/or syncope) often accompany the bleed. A history of long-standing excessive alcohol intake, intravenous drug abuse, blood transfusions, and/or prior bouts of viral hepatitis may be elicited.

Objective
Physical Examination

The general appearance usually reveals pallor. Jaundice and generalized muscle wasting may be seen in the advanced cirrhotic or in the patient with superimposed alcoholic hepatitis. A resting tachycardia and/or the presence of orthostatic hypotension correspond to intravascular volume depletion of 20%. Findings of a thready, rapid pulse with a concomitant systolic blood pressure less than 90 mm Hg are indicative of 40% or greater blood loss. Other manifestations of shock include cold, clammy skin, agitation, and oliguria. Confusion, especially in the setting of lethargy, frequently signals the advent of hepatic encephalopathy. The latter may be precipitated by the bacterial breakdown of intestinal blood and the subsequent absorption of nitrogenous products. Asterixis is present in stages II and III of hepatic en-

cephalopathy. Other findings include physical evidence suggestive of portal hypertension, that is, ascites, dilated abdominal wall venous collaterals, and/or splenomegaly. An enlarged, nodular cirrhosis may be indicative of underlying alcoholic cirrhosis, whereby a shrunken, nodular liver accompanied by marked splenomegaly suggests postnecrotic (viral) cirrhosis. The presence of palmar erythema, gynecomastia, and/or spider angiomatas is highly suggestive of underlying chronic liver disease.

Routine Laboratory Abnormalities

Laboratory findings usually include an anemia; a normal hematocrit at presentation, however, should not instill a false sense of security inasmuch as equilibration may not take place for several hours. Platelet counts in the 50,000 to 100,000 range may be encountered due to either hypersplenism or acute marrow suppression related to excess alcohol intake. Coagulopathy, in the form of an increased prothrombin time/partial thromboplastin time would suggest hepatic decompensation. Liver function tests are frequently elevated and generally reflect an accompanying alcoholic hepatitis, chronic hepatitis, or advanced cirrhosis. Normal liver function tests do not eliminate the possibility of cirrhosis and variceal bleeding; indeed, the otherwise well-compensated cirrhotic may only have a reversal of albumin:globulin ratio as the sole laboratory abnormality. In the decompensated cirrhotic, electrolyte abnormalities are common, including hypokalemia, hyponatremia, and hypomagnesemia, as well as respiratory and metabolic alkalosis. A rising creatinine may be the result of prolonged hypotension and resultant acute tubular necrosis or may indicate impending hepatorenal syndrome.

PLANS
Diagnostic
Differential Diagnosis

Nasogastric aspiration and lavage determine the rate and extent of gastrointestinal hemorrhage as well as confirm its upper gastrointestinal location. Adequate lavage may require the use of a large-bore tube (Ewald) inserted via the mouth. The major diagnostic considerations include bleeding duodenal or gastric ulcer, Mallory–Weiss tear, and hemorrhagic gastritis.

Diagnostic Options and Recommended Approach

Gastroscopy represents the diagnostic procedure of choice and, considering the potentially exsanguinating nature of a variceal bleed, needs to be performed emergently. Gastroscopy is required even in the established cirrhotic with documented varices inasmuch as up to 50% of such patients may be bleeding from a nonvariceal source. Gastroscopy is diagnostic in nearly 90% of cases, although only in 50% of patients is variceal bleeding definitively diagnosed by either direct observation of bleeding from varices or finding of an adherent clot on a varix. In the remainder of patients, the diagnosis of variceal bleeding is inferred by the presence of ample varices and the lack of any other incriminating pathology. Rarely, gastroscopy is nondiagnostic, and in the face of ongoing, active upper gastrointestinal bleeding, a celiac and superior mesenteric angiography is needed to exclude arterial causes of bleeding and confirm the presence of varices on the venous phase of the study. In less than 10% of cases is contrast extravasation from varices demonstrated.

Therapeutic

Therapy of variceal bleeding can be divided into general supportive measures and specific measures aimed toward reduction and cessation of variceal bleeding. Active variceal bleeding requires intensive care monitoring. Proper positioning and oral pharyngeal sectioning help safeguard against aspiration of blood and gastric contents. Elective endotracheal intubation to protect the airway should be performed in the massive bleeder, especially prior to gastroscopic instrumentation and sedation. Fluid resuscitation should be initiated through two large-bore intravenous catheters while awaiting the availability of blood. Colloids are given to the patient in shock, and in dire circumstances, the massive bleeder may require the initiation of blood transfusion prior to the availability of crossmatch results. Whole blood infusions are given in the exsanguinating patient; the more stable patient can be given packed cells. Central venous pressure monitoring is warranted in the hemodynamically unstable patient and is helpful in avoiding overexpansion of the intravascular volume, which in turn can precipitate reexpansion of varices and recurrent bleeding. The goal of blood replacement is to achieve a stable hematocrit around 30. Ancillary fresh-frozen plasma transfusions are provided to patients with underlying coagulopathy in view of diminished clotting factors present in stored blood. One unit of fresh-frozen plasma is generally given for every 4 units of blood. The active variceal bleeder with platelet counts below 50,000 is in need of platelet transfusions.

Emergency gastroscopy is performed following initial attempts at hemodynamic stabilization. The endoscopist should be prepared to undertake intravariceal sclerotherapy in the active variceal bleeder. Using a retractable needle inserted through the suction port of the endoscope, the endoscopist injects 2 mL of sclerosing agent into the esophageal varices beginning at the esophogastric junction and advancing cephalad. The total amount of injections should preferably not exceed 20 cc. Sclerotherapy is successful in controlling from 70 to 90% of acute esophageal variceal bleeds. It can also be employed for gastric varices, particularly those located in the cardia, though the efficacy rate is lower. Patients who continue to bleed or rebleed are treated via pharmacologic intervention aimed at diminishing portal flow and, thus, portal pressure. Vasopressin (Pitressin), a splanchovasoconstrictor has been used for decades for this purpose and is given via a continuous intravenous infusion of 0.2 to 0.5 U/min over a 24-hour period with subsequent tapering and discontinuing over the ensuing 24-hour period. Vasopressin, however, is efficacious in controlling variceal bleeding in only 50 to 60% of cases. In addition, its systemic vasoconstrictive effects can induce myocardial ischemia and cerebral ischemia. Vasopressin is contraindicated in patients with unstable coronary artery disease and advanced cerebrovascular disease. Adding nitroglycerin to vasopressin, in either the intravenous, sublingual, or transdermal form, has been shown to counter the untoward systemic adverse effects of vasopressin and appears to enhance the efficacy of treatment via its effect on reducing portal venous resistance.

An alternative pharmacologic means of managing an acute variceal bleed is with somatostatin or its synthetic analog octreotide (Sandostatin). These agents reduce splanchnic blood flow while having little or no effect on systemic vascular resistance. Octreotide is the preferred agent inasmuch as its longer half-life of 90 minutes allows for both subcutaneous and intravenous administration and does not require the meticulous continuous infusion necessary for the administration of the extremely short-acting (2- to 3-minute half-life) somatostatin. Clinical trials of octreotide (using intravenous infusion of 25 to 50 μg/h) have reported that variceal bleeding was successfully controlled in 70 to 80% of patients with minimal side effects. Further randomized prospective trials are needed to establish octreotide's role in the management of variceal bleeding.

In patients who are hemodynamically unstable and where massive bleeding preempts the performance of endoscopic sclerotherapy, a Sengstaken–Blakemore tube is inserted for the purpose of compressing the coronary veins and short gastrics which anastomose with the periesophageal venous plexus. This tamponade effect is achieved by inflating the gastric balloon (approximately 250 cc) and applying tension against the fundus. Radiographic documentation of balloon location below the diaphragm should be obtained before complete insufflation. Tension is maintained by securing the external portion of the Blakemore tube either to a face mask or to a 1- to 2-pound weight by means of a pulley system slung from the top of the bed. Continued esophageal bleeding necessitates esophageal balloon inflation to a pressure of 40 mm Hg. To reduce the risk of esophageal necrosis/perforation, the

esophageal balloon should be deflated every 6 hours for 15 minutes and the balloon should not remain inflated beyond 24 hours. Esophageal balloon inflation requires concomitant placement of a nasogastric tube to lie within the esophagus to avoid aspiration. The Minnesota tube, a variant of the Blakemore, is equipped with an esophageal aspiration port to allow for continuous suctioning of esophageal contents. Inasmuch as the Blakemore or similar tubes can partially deflate and inadvertently migrate upward to compress the larynx, a pair of scissors must be available at the bedside to immediately cut the tubing and allow for complete balloon decompression if such a scenario develops. Overall efficacy in controlling hemorrhage is approximately 75%, yet the rebleeding rate within 3 days is high.

Patients who continue to bleed despite the above measures have limited viable options. Emergency portasystemic surgical shunting is associated with a prohibitive mortality rate approaching 40% and, as such, is performed in only a limited number of centers. Transhepatic variceal sclerosis performed under fluoroscopic guidance with selective sclerosant or Gelfoam embolization of peripheral varices has a high initial success rate; however, the rate of rebleeding is significant. Furthermore, patients who have failed the therapeutic measures noted above are usually Childs C cirrhotics who have moderate to severe coagulopathy and are thus at risk of developing subcapsular and intraperitoneal hemorrhage from iatrogenic trauma to the liver. A more promising radiologic procedure that is becoming increasingly available is the transjugular intrahepatic portosystemic shunt (TIPS). Following transjugular catheterization of the hepatic vein, portal decompression is achieved by creating a channel between the hepatic vein and portal vein with a needle puncture and then placing a metallic stent across the parenchymal shunt (Figure 19–87–1). The procedure is performed under fluoroscopic guidance and aided by a preprocedure sonography to identify and establish patency of the portal vein. Technical advances have al-

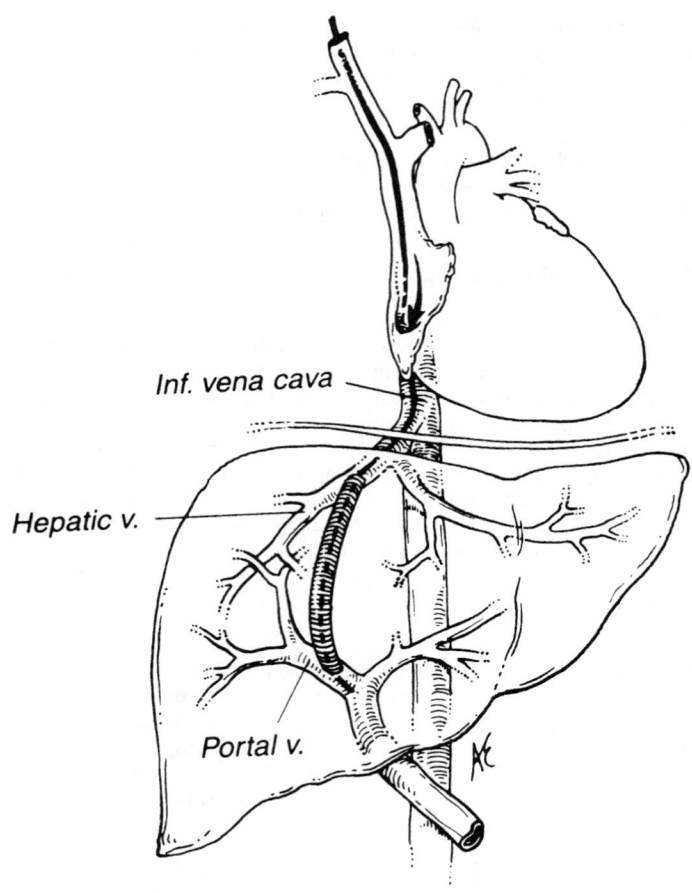

Figure 19–87–1. Transjugular intrahepatic portosystemic shunt (TIPS) demonstrating stent placement and the bridge created between the hepatic and portal veins.

Inf. vena cava

Hepatic v.

Portal v.

lowed successful expeditious placement of TIPS in more than 90% of patients with a low procedure-related morbidity. Control of active variceal bleeding is accomplished in 90% of patients. The major drawback of TIPS is the high postprocedure incidence of either new or worsening hepatic encephalopathy in approximately 25% of patients. The majority of these bouts are responsive to lactulose therapy. In addition, the shunts have a high occlusion/stenosis rate, approximating 15% at 1 year. Duplex sonography performed at 3-month intervals can diagnose shunt stenosis prior to recurrent variceal bleeding and allow for shunt dilation and/or repeat stent placement.

Successful treatment of the acute variceal bleeder brings the clinician and patient to the next therapeutic dilemma stage, that being, how to prevent the repeat variceal bleed. Strategies include endoscopic obliteration of varices, pharmacologic long-term intervention to reduce portal pressures, portosystemic shunting, and, the ultimate therapy, liver transplantation. Endoscopic obliteration of esophageal varices via sclerotherapy or with the innovative technique of rubber band ligation (Figure 19–87–2) lowers by approximately 50% the 1-year rebleeding rate from 50 to 25%. Successful treatment requires repeated sessions at frequent intervals (2–3 weeks) to obliterate the varices prior to recurrent bleeding. Gastric varices, with the exception of varices in the cardia, are not amenable to this therapy. Though there are fewer published data on the efficacy of endoscopic variceal ligation, it would appear that this technique is as efficacious as variceal sclerosis, may require fewer sessions for variceal obliteration, and has a better safety profile. Inasmuch as the ulcers resulting after tissue sloughing postligation therapy are shallower in nature than those formed postsclerotherapy, the incidence of ulcer bleeding is considerably less in the former. Furthermore, the incidence of mediastinitis, pleural effusions, and esophageal strictures is significantly lower in endoscopic variceal ligation as compared with variceal sclerotherapy.

Successful endoscopic obliteration of esophageal varices requires a cooperative and compliant patient. Patients not willing to undergo repeated sessions of therapeutic endoscopy or patients who had initially bled from noncardia gastric varices are candidates for long-term beta blocker therapy. The use of nonselective beta blockers at a dose titrated to reduce the resting heart rate to 25% of baseline has been shown to lower portal venous pressures primarily via its effect on lowering cardiac output and consequently portal flow reduction, as well as promoting splanchnic vasoconstriction by the blockade of β_2-adrenoreceptors in the splanchnic bed. Beta blockers have been shown to reduce the incidence of rebleeding by 40% when compared with randomized controls. Combination therapy with beta blockers and endoscopic variceal obliteration has been employed; however, it is premature to conclude that this therapy is additive in nature regarding clinical efficacy. Patients who fail medical management and have good hepatic reserve are candidates for surgical portosystemic shunting. In an effort to lower the incidence of postoperative hepatic encephalopathy and in anticipation of a potential future need for liver transplantation and its technical demands, a distal splenorenal shunt is preferable over a portacaval anastomosis. Whether the TIPS procedure can provide a nonsurgical means of long-term portal decompression remains to be determined. The limiting factor, for now, appears to be the high incidence of shunt stenosis/occlusion. An alternate surgical means of preventing further rebleeding is the stapled transesophageal transection wherein a mucosal ring of the distal esophagus is excised, and thus blood flow into the periesophageal venous plexus is interrupted. Short-term results have been quite satisfactory and hepatic encephalopathy is avoided inasmuch as no portosystemic shunt has been created; however, rebleeding rates are higher than after portal decompression. Lastly, patients with progressive hepatic insufficiency are candidates for liver transplants providing they have no other prohibitive medical illness that would significantly shorten their life expectancy. Being a liver transplant recipient would improve their overall 5-year survival from 20–30% to 65%. Alcoholic cirrhotics are now being transplanted in many centers provided that they have had several months of abstinence, are highly motivated, and have a psychosocial support system.

FOLLOW-UP

Patients who have had variceal bleeding require close lifelong clinical follow-up to continuously assess their chronic liver disease and monitor for evidence of hepatic decompensation. Patients who have undergone endoscopic variceal obliteration should be scoped at 6-month intervals to observe for any recurrent varices and, if present, to reinstitute variceal sclerotherapy or banding. Patients who have had a TIPS procedure or surgical portosystemic shunt should be closely observed for any evidence of hepatic encephalopathy. Duplex sonography performed at regular intervals can diagnose shunt occlusion at an early stage prior to recurrent variceal bleeding.

DISCUSSION
Prevalence and Incidence

Variceal bleeding accounts for 10% of upper gastrointestinal bleeding in the United States. Approximately 60% of cirrhotics develop varices. Bleeding varices occur in one third of patients with underlying varices and represent the most lethal complication of cirrhosis.

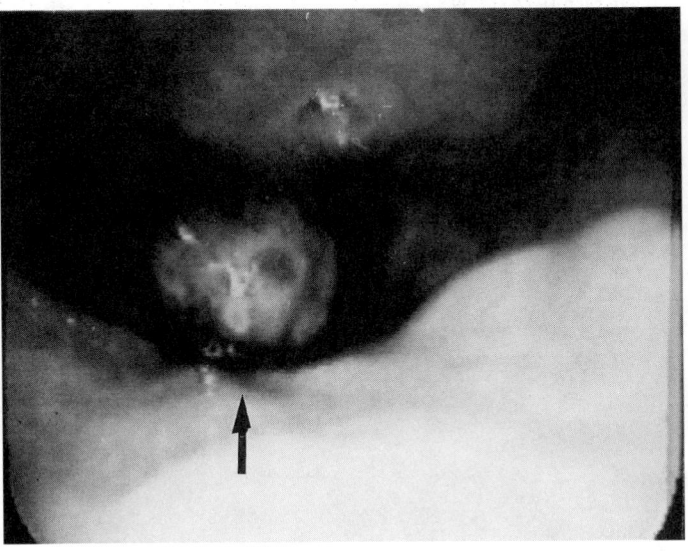
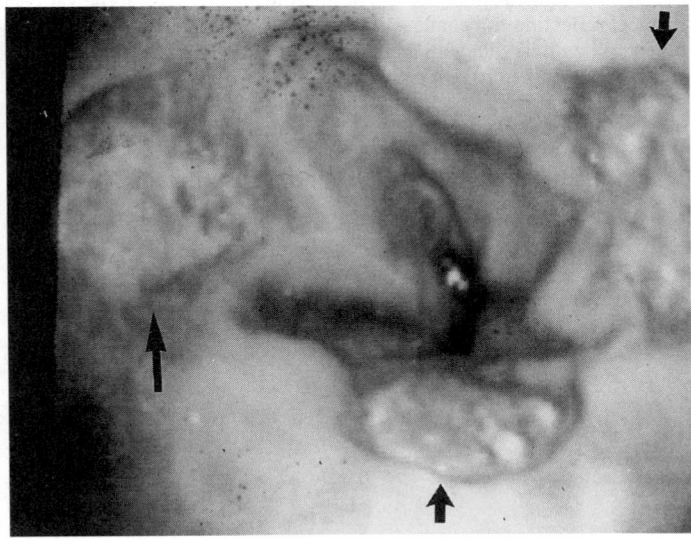

A   **B**

Figure 19–87–2. A. Endoscopic view of variceal ligation with band placement at base of varix (arrow) with resulting engorgement of varix. **B.** Endoscopic view 7 days after variceal ligation showing discrete ulcer formation (arrow) after tissue sloughing.

Related Basic Science

Varices develop when there is increased resistance to flow of blood through the portal venous system of the liver. This increased vascular resistance most commonly arises at the intrahepatic sinusoidal level as typified by cirrhosis. Prehepatic (e.g., portal or splenic vein thrombosis) or posthepatic (e.g., Budd–Chiari syndrome) block can also induce portal hypertension. Other factors contributing to portal hypertension are splanchnic hyperemia and expanded plasma volume. An increased portal venous inflow promoted by splanchnic vasodilation has been shown to exist in cirrhotics. Several humoral vasodilators have been identified, with the strongest evidence implicating glucagon. An expanded blood volume primarily due to avid renal sodium retention may cause further increases in portal pressure.

In an effort to decompress the portal venous system and normalize portal pressure, connections develop to neighboring low-pressure veins resulting in portosystemic collaterals. The gastroesophageal junction represents the most significant area of anastomosis between the portal and systemic circulations. Tributaries of the coronary vein (which feeds into the portal vein) form vascular channels with tributaries of the azygous vein (which drains into the superior vena cava). The increased blood flow at higher than usual venous pressures through the venous plexus in the proximal stomach and distal esophagus results in distended, tortuous veins termed *varices*. The superficial nature of the varices, particularly in the distal esophagus where the varices frequently course the lamina propria, accounts for the clinical scenario of gastrointestinal bleeding when a varix ruptures. Spontaneous portosystemic collaterals between the middle and superior hemorrhoidal veins (which drain into the inferior mesenteric vein) and the inferior hemorrhoidal vein (which drains into the inferior vena cava) give rise to rectal varices. Splenic vein obstruction with resultant elevation of pressure in the short gastric veins can give rise to solitary gastric varices. Chronic pancreatitis and pancreatic carcinoma are the two major causes of splenic vein occlusion.

A portal venous pressure of at least 12 mm Hg is required for the development of esophageal varices; however, of those patients who develop varices, only 30% experience a variceal bleed. This has led investigators to identify risk factors associated with future bleeding. It is now clearly recognized that varices rupture "from within"; the erosive theory attributing variceal bleeding to overlying esophagitis has been largely discounted. A strong correlation exists between the size of a varix and its propensity to rupture, which adheres to LaPlace's law that the larger the diameter, the greater the wall tension. Another strong predictor of bleeding is the presence of the red color sign on the surface of a varix. This sign, which encompasses the red wale (whip) mark, the small cherry red spot, and the larger hemocystic spot (blood blister), is evidence of dilated small vessels or microtelangiectasias on the variceal surface, reflecting the changes in varix wall structure and tension. The blue varix with its thin wall and presumably increased intravariceal tension also appears to have a greater tendency to bleed. The identification of high-risk varices is essential in selecting a subgroup of patients who may benefit from primary prevention of variceal bleeding.

Natural History and Its Modification with Treatment

Thirty percent of cirrhotics with known esophageal varices experience a variceal bleed. Mortality for variceal bleeding ranges from 30 to 50%.

The severity of the underlying liver disease, standardized by the use of the Childs–Pugh classification, is a major factor in determining mortality for a given bleed. Fifty percent of patients have a recurrent variceal bleed within 1 year and approximately 80% rebleed within 2 years.

Prevention

Patients with alcoholic liver disease should be counseled and referred to alcoholic rehabilitation units for the purpose of achieving abstinence and, thus, it is hoped, preventing progression of disease and its associated complications. Patients with chronic viral hepatitis C or B should be evaluated for interferon alpha therapy in an effort to avoid or slow their progression to cirrhosis. Whether patients with documented esophageal varices should receive treatment in an effort to prevent their initial bleed (primary prevention) has been addressed in a substantial number of randomized clinical trials. Beta blockers are warranted in patients with high-risk varices (see Related Basic Science) inasmuch as such therapy reduces the risk of developing a variceal bleed by 40 to 50% as compared with control subjects, with a minimum of adverse effects. Conflicting results have been obtained in the sclerotherapy trials, partially accountable by the heterogeneity of data. Though the majority of the studies have shown a reduction in the incidence of variceal bleeding, in view of key negative trials, including the multicenter Veterans Affairs Cooperative Group Study trial, which was prematurely terminated in view of the excess morbidity and mortality in the sclerotherapy arm, the overall efficacy of prophylactic sclerotherapy remains undetermined and hence cannot currently be recommended.

Cost Containment

Management of variceal bleeding requires an aggressive approach including intensive care unit utilization, and thus its attendant costs are high. Cost reduction can be achieved by lowering the incidence of recurrent bleeding as well as by primary prevention as elucidated above.

REFERENCES

Bosch J, Masti R, Kravetz D, et al. Effects of propranolol on azygos venous blood flow and hepatic and systemic hemodynamics in cirrhosis. Hepatology 1984;4:1200.

LaBerge JM, Ring EG, Gordon RL, et al. Creation of transjugular intrahepatic portosystemic shunts with the Wallstent endoprosthesis: Results in 100 patients. Radiology 1993;187:413.

Laine L, El-Newihi HM, Migikovsky B, et al. Endoscopic ligation compared with sclerotherapy for the treatment of bleeding esophageal varices. Ann Intern Med 1993;119:1.

Pagliaro L, D'Amico G, Sorensen TI, et al. Prevention of first bleeding in cirrhosis: A meta-analysis of randomized trials of nonsurgical treatment. Ann Intern Med 1992;117:59.

The Veterans Affairs Cooperative Variceal Sclerotherapy Group. Prophylactic sclerotherapy for esophageal varices in men with alcoholic liver disease. A randomized, single-blind, multicenter clinical trial. N Engl J Med 1991;324:1779.

Van Ruiswyk J, Byrd JC. Efficacy of prophylactic sclerotherapy for prevention of a first variceal hemorrhage. Gastroenterology 1992;102:587.

Hepatorenal Syndrome

Curtis E. Scott, M.D.

DEFINITION

Hepatorenal syndrome (HRS) is a functional acute renal failure that occurs in patients with liver disease in the absence of an identifiable source of renal injury.

ETIOLOGY

The precise pathogenesis of HRS remains obscure; however, several factors have been found to be associated with its development. Although the syndrome can develop in the absence of any precipitating event, a decreased effective arterial blood volume appears to be a key feature of the syndrome and may be precipitated by events such as gastrointestinal bleeding, vomiting, diarrhea, abdominal paracentesis, and aggressive diuretic therapy. Multiple neurohumoral mechanisms and vasoactive substances have been identified in association with the hemodynamic changes surrounding a decreased effective arterial blood volume, but none have been found to be singularly responsible for HRS. Mechanisms involved include changes in the renin–angiotensin–aldosterone system, the sympathetic nervous system, arachadonic acid metabolites, nitric oxide, endothelin, renal kallikrein, atrial natriuretic factor, and endotoxemia. Certain medications such as nonsteroidal anti-inflammatory drugs and demeclocycline can also precipitate HRS in patients with liver disease and ascites. Of note, HRS almost always develops while patients are in the hospital, which may suggest a larger role for the iatrogenic events mentioned.

CRITERIA FOR DIAGNOSIS

Suggestive

Hepatorenal syndrome typically occurs in patients with alcoholic cirrhosis and superimposed acute alcoholic hepatitis; however, it may be found in advanced cirrhosis, acute hepatic failure, and hepatic malignancy. A majority of patients also have ascites and may have a lower than usual blood pressure at the time of presentation. Following admission to the hospital, renal failure may develop with great rapidity, often occurring in patients with previously normal serum creatinine levels within a few days of onset of HRS.

Definitive

Patients with HRS develop oliguria with a rising serum creatinine in the range 2 to 5 mg/dL, but may vary depending on the severity of renal failure. The ratio of urine to plasma creatinine is greater than 30:1. Urine sodium excretion is markedly reduced, with urine sodium concentration less than 10 mmol/L. Urine osmolality is greater than serum osmolality. Urine sediment is normal with the absence of casts and debris, and challenge with plasma expanders in attempts to improve blood pressure and urine output often shows poor to no response.

CLINICAL MANIFESTATIONS

Subjective

Patients may complain of generalized malaise. Abdominal discomfort may be associated with tense ascites. Some degree of hepatic encephalopathy is present in many patients.

Objective

Physical Examination

Blood pressure with HRS is usually lower than normal for the patient, reflecting the presence of peripheral vasodilation and arteriovenous shunting. As a consequence, patients develop a hyperdynamic circulation with increased cardiac output and manifested by tachycardia and a bounding pulse. Jaundice is variable. Some patients may show stigmata of chronic liver disease, and ascites is often tense. Signs of hepatic encephalopathy and asterixis may be present.

Routine Laboratory Abnormalities

Elevated serum urea nitrogen and creatinine levels are the clinical markers used to identify the development of renal failure. One should keep in mind, however, that cirrhotic patients usually have a reduced synthesis of urea and creatinine, and the degree of renal failure may be more than is reflected by these elevations. Hyponatremia is found in many patients and hyperkalemia also occurs. Hepatic biochemical tests (aspartate and alanine transaminases, alkaline phosphatase, bilirubin, γ-glutamyl transpeptidase) may be abnormal in reflection of the degree of ongoing liver injury. Serum albumin is low and prothrombin time increases as hepatic synthetic function decreases. Urinalysis shows an absence of proteinuria, microhematuria, or sediment. Urine osmolality is increased above serum osmolality.

PLANS

Diagnostic

Differential Diagnosis

The most important differential diagnoses are prerenal azotemia and acute tubular necrosis. Myoglobinuric acute renal failure may also be considered. There are many similarities between prerenal azotemia and HRS, including oliguria, low urinary sodium, fractional extraction of sodium less than 1%, urine osmolality greater than serum osmolality, and normal urine sediment. Prerenal azotemia, however, responds to plasma expansion, whereas HRS usually does not. If plasma expansion leads to an increase in central venous pressure up to 10 cm water without any improvement in renal function, prerenal azotemia is unlikely. Acute tubular necrosis usually follows a major precipitating event such as sepsis, shock, or nephrotoxic drug use. It is characterized by high urinary sodium concentration greater than 30 mmol/L, fractional excretion of sodium greater than 1%, loss of urinary concentrating ability, urine-to-plasma creatinine ratio lower than 20, and a pathologic sediment with casts and debris. Response to plasma expansion is variable. In the setting of renal insufficiency, myoglobin is converted extensively to bilirubin. Myoglobinuric acute tubular necrosis may also be associated with a low urinary sodium concentration. Therefore, care should be taken to avoid misdiagnosing myoglobinuric acute tubular necrosis as HRS.

Diagnostic Options

The following data should be obtained: serum blood urea nitrogen and creatinine, serum bilirubin, serum osmolality, serum sodium, spot urine sodium, urine osmolality, urine creatinine, microscopic urinalysis, urine volume measurements.

Recommended Approach

The approach to the patient with acute renal failure and liver disease is first to exclude causes other than prerenal azotemia, acute tubular necrosis, and HRS, such as mechanical obstruction. Calculate the fractional excretion of sodium. If it is greater than 1%, acute tubular necrosis may be confirmed by the identification of a precipitating event, isotonic urine osmolality, and the presence of casts and debris on urine sediment evaluation. If it is less than 1%, central venous pressure should be measured. A low central venous pressure below 5 mm Hg is suggestive of prerenal azotemia and will be confirmed if renal function improves with improvement of central venous pressure following plasma expansion. If central venous pressure increases to greater than 10 mm Hg with no improvement in renal function, HRS would be the more likely diagnosis.

One should bear in mind in the evaluation of renal failure in patients with liver disease that the measurement of serum creatinine may be spuriously altered in some autoanalyzer measuring instruments by the presence of elevated bilirubin. Thus, a rise in creatinine may be masked in measurement, or conversely, a decrease in serum creatinine could be misinterpreted as improvement in renal function.

Therapeutic

Therapeutic Options

The mainstay of treatment of HRS is prevention of onset. Once established, it almost invariably progresses to a fatal outcome despite the therapeutic measures that are available. Therapeutic options include plasma expanders, vasoactive drugs such as prostaglandin analogs, peritoneovenous shunt (LeVeen shunt), portosystemic shunts, paracentesis, dialysis, and transplantation.

Plasma expansion with colloid agents may transiently improve hemodynamic status and increase urine output, but there is no predictor of the amount of volume expander that would be necessary for response. Furthermore, this maneuver does not alter the outcome of HRS.

Administration of vasodilator drugs to correct renal cortical ischemia also reduces systemic vascular resistance with worsening of renal perfusion. Vasodilatory prostaglandins have been tried in an attempt to correct the defective renal synthesis with little proven benefit. Alpha-adrenergic drugs, used in an attempt to restore effective arterial blood volume, have little effect in cirrhotic patients with impaired renal function. Octapressin, an antidiuretic hormone analog with reduced antidiuretic activity, improved renal function and hyperdynamic status in patients with HRS, but the long-term effects of the drug are unknown.

Studies investigating the effect of the LeVeen peritoneovenous shunt in patients with HRS show a trend toward improvement in serum creatinine, but no improvement in survival.

The beneficial effect of portosystemic shunts in HRS is unproven; some studies show reversal, whereas others do not. As patients with HRS do not usually tolerate major surgery, the role of the transjugular intrahepatic portosystemic shunt (TIPS) is considered. Benefit is suggested in one pilot study, but more extensive investigation is required.

Paracentesis might show transient improvement in renal function due to reduced intraperitoneal pressure, but ascites is recurrent, and paracentesis does not change survival.

Hemodialysis and peritoneal dialysis when used as primary therapy in HRS are ineffective and increase the risk of severe hypotension, infection, and hemorrhage. These procedures may be supportive, however, in patients with favorable prognosis of reversal of liver disease or candidates for liver transplantation.

Patients with HRS who undergo liver transplantation clearly demonstrate an improved glomerular filtration rate and renal function following transplantation. Analysis has shown survival comparable to that of transplanted patients without renal failure. Considering the poor prognosis of HRS, this therapeutic option should be considered in all HRS patients who are appropriate candidates.

Recommended Approach

Treatment of HRS is mainly supportive. Other likely diagnoses such as mechanical obstruction, prerenal azotemia, and acute tubular necrosis must always be ruled out first. Medications with potential adverse effects such as aminoglycosides, nonsteroidal antiinflammatory drugs, beta blockers, angiotensin-converting enzyme inhibitors, and calcium channel blockers should be discontinued. Overly vigorous diuresis should be avoided. General therapeutic considerations may be applied including sodium and fluid restriction, correction of acid–base disturbances, correction of anemia, and treatment of encephalopathy. The specific therapeutic options discussed above may be considered, but most are not proven to have significant beneficial effect. Patients who are suitable candidates for liver transplantation should be considered for this option.

FOLLOW-UP

With the onset of azotemia in HRS, survival is measured in weeks, and spontaneous recovery is uncommon. Those who regain renal function, for the most part, do so secondary to restoration of hepatic function. The few patients that achieve spontaneous hepatic regeneration, for example, in acute hepatic failure, have no long-term sequelae. In those with improved renal function following liver transplant, follow-up is centered around maintenance of the new graft.

DISCUSSION

Prevalence and Incidence

Hepatorenal syndrome occurs in about 5 to 10% of patients with decompensated cirrhosis and is associated with a 95% mortality within a few weeks of onset of azotemia.

Related Basic Science

Despite severe derangements of renal function in patients with HRS, renal pathologic abnormalities are minimal and inconsistent. Tubular functional integrity is maintained as manifested by unimpaired sodium resorptive capacity and concentrating ability. Furthermore, kidneys transplanted from patients with HRS are capable of resuming normal function in a recipient with normal hepatic function. Additionally, return of renal function occurs when patients with HRS successfully receive orthotopic liver transplantation. What then underlies the renal dysfunction seen in HRS?

Studies indicate that HRS is due to severe renal arterial vasoconstriction leading to marked decreases in renal plasma flow and glomerular filtration rate. Studies using xenon-133 washout techniques and others using renal angiograms in patients with HRS showed that there is significant renal cortical vasoconstriction and impairment of flow in HRS, with normalization of renal vasculature on postmortem angiography. A comprehensive explanation of the cause or causes of the sustained hypoperfusion and suppression of filtration is unavailable; however, several physiologic events, neurohumoral systems, and vasoactive substances have been implicated in the pathogenesis of vasoconstriction in HRS.

The triggering event for ascites formation in cirrhotic patients has traditionally centered on imbalance in the Starling forces of the hepatosplanchnic microcirculation associated with either decreased or increased plasma volume ("underfill" versus "overflow" theories). Recently, the focus of investigation has been on peripheral vasodilation as an early determinant of intravascular underfilling, causing decreased effective plasma volume leading to increased renal sodium and fluid retention. HRS, it is believed, constitutes an extreme extension of underfilling of the arterial circulation, with the most extreme elevations of vasoactive hormones and degree of renal vasoconstriction.

The renin–angiotension–aldosterone system appears to play a role in sustaining vasoconstriction in HRS. Cirrhotic patients with impaired renal function show marked elevations in plasma renin levels. Although plasma renin elevation here is partly attributable to decreased hepatic inactivation of renin, the major determinant is increased renin secretion by the kidney. Furthermore, studies using angiotension II infusion showed marked reductions in renal plasma flow and glomerular filtration rate. The role of possible depletion of renin substrate, α_2-globin, due to decreased hepatic synthesis, has also been considered. Infusion of renin substrate-rich fresh-frozen plasma was associated with increased creatinine clearance and urine output coincident with a significant rise in renin substrate and suppression of peripheral renin concentration. Discontinuation of the infusion led to a gradual decline in creatinine clearance, urine flow, and renin substrate concentration over subsequent days. Unfortunately, attempts to further define the role of the renin–angiotension–aldosterone system using antagonist agents have been associated with hemodynamic instability. Further study is required.

Sympathetic nervous system activity may be involved in the pathogenesis of HRS, but studies attempting to document this role have had conflicting results. Plasma norepinephrine concentration, an index of sympathetic nervous system activity, is high in patients with cirrhosis and ascites, the greatest levels being observed in those with HRS. Stimulation of sympathetic renal nerves causes afferent vasoconstriction and impairs renal plasma flow and glomerular filtration rate. But, administration of intrarenal alpha-adrenergic blockers did not consistently modify renal plasma flow, despite transient hypotension.

Urinary excretion of prostaglandin E_2 is reduced in patients with HRS due to reduced synthesis. 6-Ketoprostaglandin $F_{1\alpha}$ is also reduced. On the other hand, thromboxane B_2, the nonenzymatic derivative of the potent vasoconstrictor thromboxane A_2 is elevated. These findings led to the suggestion that an imbalance between vasoconstricting thromboxane A_2 and vasodilating prostaglandin E_2 may be of pathogenetic value; however, administration of thromboxane synthase inhibitor did not improve renal function in patients with HRS. The meaning of this result requires further clarification, as inhibition of thromboxane synthase may lead to the accumulation of prostaglandins G_2 and H_2, which mimic the renal effects of thromboxane A_2. Patients with HRS also have a higher urinary excretion of leukotriene E_4 of unknown pathogenetic relevance.

Recently, attention has focused on the role of nitric oxide as a mediator of both the hyperdynamic circulation and the renal failure of HRS. Nitric oxide, a vasodilator synthesized from L-arginine, accounts for the biological activity of endothelium-derived relaxing factor. An inducible enzyme, nitric oxide synthase, is induced in response to bacterial lipopolysaccharide endotoxin, and releases nitric oxide for many hours without further stimulation. In vitro studies show induction of nitric oxide synthase in both the endothelium and smooth muscle with progressive vascular relaxation and diminished responsiveness to vasoconstrictors. It is suggested that this mechanism underlies the peripheral dilation and consequent hyperdynamic circulation associated with cirrhosis and HRS, and that inhibition of nitric oxide synthesis should restore sensitivity to vasoconstrictors and reverse the hemodynamic abnormalities.

Endotoxemia in itself has been investigated as a causative agent in the renal failure of cirrhosis. Endotoxins are potent vasoconstrictors and are hypothesized to enter the systemic circulation through natural or surgical portosystemic shunts that bypass the hepatic Kupffer cells, the major site of removal from the circulation. Although endotoxemia is frequently observed in patients with chronic liver disease, attempts to correlate the occurrence of renal failure with the presence of endotoxemia have been conflicting. Therefore, its role in contributing to the development of renal failure remains unclear.

Other substances such as endothelin 1, endothelin 3, antidiuretic hormone, and atrial natriuretic factor are found to be elevated in patients with HRS, whereas the kallikrein–kinin system is depressed. Their role in the pathogenesis of HRS needs further clarification.

Natural History and Its Modification with Treatment

The development of HRS portends a poor prognosis, with a high mortality within several weeks of onset of azotemia. Spontaneous recovery of renal function is rare, and if it occurs, it is usually following improvement of liver function. This response reflects the functional nature of the renal disorder and is important in management choices made for these patients. Of the modalities currently available for management of HRS, most either lack significant sustained beneficial effect on renal function or are only supportive without prolongation of survival. Patients with HRS who are candidates for orthotopic liver transplantation, on the other hand, represent one group that has demonstrated improved renal function with improved survival, following transplantation.

Prevention

Prevention is the most important factor in the care of patients who are at risk for the development of HRS. Once the syndrome is established, it is very difficult to manage successfully. As previously mentioned, most cases occur during hospitalization; therefore, one should be vigilant to avoid known precipitating events such as excessive diuretic therapy, large-volume paracentesis without intravenous albumin volume replacement in patients with borderline hemodynamic status, severe gastrointestinal bleeding, and excessive diarrhea with lactulose therapy.

Cost Containment

As the exact pathogenesis of HRS is not established, therapy is essentially empiric. The rapidity of onset, very poor prognosis, and lack of soundly favorable therapeutic options make management difficult; however, it would be prudent to avoid therapeutic measures that lack proven benefit. Liver transplantation, the sole intervention to have emerged to this point with survival benefit, is expensive.

It is hoped that as the pathogenesis of HRS is established, more directed, less costly therapies will be developed.

REFERENCES

Epstein M. Hepatorenal syndrome. In: Epstein M, ed. The kidney in liver disease. 3rd ed. Baltimore: Williams & Wilkins, 1988:89.

Epstein M, Berk D, et al. Renal failure in the patient with cirrhosis. Am J Med 1970;49:175.

Gines A, Escorsell A, et al. Incidence, predictive factors, and prognosis of the hepatorenal syndrome in cirrhosis with ascites. Gastroenterology 1993;105:229.

Laffi G, La Villa G, et al. Pathogenesis and management of the hepatorenal syndrome. Semin Liver Dis 1994;14:71.

Moore K, Weldon J, et al. Plasma endothelin immunoreactivity in liver disease and the hepatorenal syndrome. N Engl J Med 1992;327:1774.

Vallance P, Moncado S. Hyperdynamic circulation in cirrhosis: A role for nitric oxide? Lancet 1991;337:776.

CHAPTER 19–89

Fulminant Hepatic Failure

Curtis E. Scott, M.D.

DEFINITION

Fulminant hepatic failure is a life-threatening condition induced by massive hepatocellular necrosis of an otherwise normal liver. It is recognized by arbitrary criteria first proposed by Trey and Davidson in 1970 as development of encephalopathy within 8 weeks of onset of symptoms. Bernuau et al. in 1986 advocated a definition wherein encephalopathy is found within 2 weeks of onset of jaundice.

ETIOLOGY

The list of causes of FHF is long and continues to grow. Table 19–89–1 lists agents that have been identified.

CRITERIA FOR DIAGNOSIS

Suggestive

Jaundice and mental status changes are findings that may be noted on presentation. A history of recent predisposing lifestyle activity or recent drug ingestion may be elicited.

Definitive

Diagnosis of FHF follows the generally accepted definition requiring the manifestation of signs of hepatic encephalopathy within 8 weeks of the onset of symptoms. Supporting data include the presence of markedly elevated serum transaminase levels and progressive signifi-

TABLE 19–89–1. ETIOLOGY OF FULMINANT HEPATIC FAILURE

Infectious	Metabolic
Hepatitis A, B, C, D, E, ?X	Wilson's disease
Herpes simplex virus 1 and 2	Fatty liver of pregnancy
Varicella–zoster virus	Reye's syndrome
Cytomegalovirus	**Miscellaneous**
Epstein–Barr virus	Autoimmune hepatitis
Adenovirus	Budd–Chiari syndrome
Drugs and Toxins	Hyperthermia
Acetaminophen	Massive malignant infiltration
Isoniazid–rifampin	Severe bacterial infection
Halothane	
Phenytoin	
Augmentin	
Nonsteroidal antiinflammatory drugs	
Valproic acid	
Tetracycline	
Nicotinic acid	
Amanita phalloides	

cant increases in prothrombin time and bilirubin. The underlying cause of FHF should be established if possible.

CLINICAL MANIFESTATIONS
Subjective

Patients may complain of general malaise. The onset of encephalopathy can be subtle and several grades are identified with the following associations.

- Grade I: change in sleep habits, altered mood, psychometric defects, slight asterixis
- Grade II: drowsy, inappropriate behavior, marked asterixis
- Grade III: stuporous but arousable, marked confusion; inarticulate speech
- Grade IV: comatose

The majority of patients presenting in FHF have no previous history of liver disease and many can be found to have an identifiable source of an acute onset of hepatic failure. Patients with Wilson's disease may also have FHF as a presenting event despite underlying chronic copper deposition.

There is usually no pertinent family history of liver disease in the relatives of the patient with FHF. Patients presenting with Wilson's disease may be an exception where familial evaluation should be pursued because this is known to be inherited as an autosomal recessive disorder.

Objective
Physical Examination

Findings on physical examination include jaundice, evidence of encephalopathy, and asterixis. Hepatomegaly and right upper quadrant tenderness may sometimes be present.

Routine Laboratory Abnormalities

Routine laboratory analysis demonstrates markedly elevated aspartate and alanine transaminase levels, with the alkaline phosphatase level less elevated. γ-Glutamyl transpeptidase, bilirubin, and prothrombin time are also elevated. Other abnormal findings include hypoalbuminemia, hypoglycemia, hyponatremia, hypokalemia, hyperkalemia, hypocalcemia, hypophosphatemia, and hypomagnesemia. Blood urea nitrogen and creatinine may be elevated. Metabolic and respiratory alkalosis occurs, as does metabolic acidosis, which is most common in acetaminophen-induced FHF. An elevated white blood cell count with left shift may be present in patients with infection. In patients with hemoly-

sis or bleeding, a drop in hemoglobin may reflect this activity, and a fall in platelet count may occur in patients with bleeding or disseminated intravascular coagulation (DIC). Elevated amylase is present in acute pancreatitis, which occurs in a significant number of patients with FHF. Urine may be dark in color with elevated urobilinogen.

PLANS
Diagnostic
Differential Diagnosis

Late-onset hepatic failure defines the development of encephalopathy 8 to 24 weeks following onset of jaundice and is associated with a high mortality. It tends to occur in older patients with the development of ascites, but is not associated with the development of cerebral edema. This is in contrast to FHF, which can occur at any age and is associated with cerebral edema but only rarely with ascites. Mortality from FHF is related to etiology.

In patients presenting with jaundice, biliary obstruction might be considered and ruled out sonographically. In a patient developing FHF, however, the degree of transaminase elevation is notably out of proportion to that which can be explained by obstruction alone. Furthermore, the rapid progression of evidence of hepatic dysfunction would signify the impending development of complete hepatic failure.

A recent change in mental status should prompt evaluation with computed tomography scan of the head to rule out an intracranial bleed or lesion. Patients with refractory encephalopathy should probably also have an electroencephalogram to rule out subclinical seizure activity.

Diagnostic Options

Diagnostic options are directed at assessment of the cause and degree of hepatic injury, cause of encephalopathy, identification of complications, and need for urgent orthotopic liver transplantation. The following approach may be considered.

Recommended Approach

Routine laboratory tests must be obtained including complete blood count, differential, platelets, SMAC-7, prothrombin time, partial thromboplastin time, aspartate and alanine transaminases, alkaline phosphatase, γ-glutamyl transpeptidase, total and direct bilirubin, albumin, and urinalysis. Additional laboratory tests should include hepatitis serologies for hepatitis A, B, C, D, and E, ceruloplasmin level in younger patients (< 35 years), amylase, arterial blood gas, fibrin degradation products, and blood and urine cultures. An HIV test should be done if status is unknown. A blood acetaminophen level is drawn for patients with unclear etiology or those with known ingestion. An abdominal ultrasound with Doppler is done to rule out hepatic lesion, biliary, or portal vein obstruction to flow. Chest x-ray rules out aspiration pneumonia and electrocardiogram rules out dysrhythmias. A factor V level may be obtained as a sensitive indicator of hepatic synthetic function. Serial levels can then be followed to chart progress. Percutaneous liver biopsy is associated with risk due to coagulopathy. If a review of liver pathology will alter management strategy, biopsy by the transjugular approach is relatively safe. In patients with encephalopathy, a computed tomography scan of the head should be obtained.

Results that should be obtained on high priority include serum glucose, potassium, ceruloplasmin, and copper; immunoglobulin M antibodies to hepatitis A virus and hepatitis B core antigen, as well as a hepatitis B surface antigen level; acetaminophen level, arterial pH, prothrombin time, and bilirubin level. These results help identify common causes, give prognostic information, and identify immediately supportable complications.

Therapeutic

The approach to management of these patients is moderated by an assessment of their prognostic features. Consequently, a determination of the patient's likelihood to survive without liver transplantation is crucial soon after initial presentation. If the patient is felt to be a candidate for liver transplantation, prompt transfer to a transplant center must be considered. Several factors have been assessed to be of value in determining the prognosis of patients with fulminant hepatic failure.

Non-acetaminophen-induced failure. A prothrombin time greater than 100 seconds, irrespective of the grade of encephalopathy, has a poor prognosis.

Any three of the following variables suggest criteria for liver transplantation: (1) The etiology is associated with causes such as non-A, non-B hepatitis and non-acetaminophen-induced FHF such as that caused by isoniazid or phenytoin. (2) Age less than 10 or greater than 40 is associated with greater mortality. (3) Development of encephalopathy more than 7 days following the onset of jaundice is associated with a worse prognosis. (4) Reduced survival is found among patients with a serum bilirubin greater than 18 mg/dL. (5) A prothrombin time longer than 50 seconds or an international normalized ratio (INR) greater than 3.5 denotes a poor prognosis.

Acetaminophen-induced Failure. An arterial pH of less than 7.30 is associated with a mortality of 85%. A prothrombin time longer than 100 seconds and a serum creatinine greater than 3.4 mg/dL in patients with stage 3 and 4 encephalopathy fit criteria for liver transplantation.

The preceding criteria used for identifying patients with poor likelihood of spontaneous recovery and, thus, greater likelihood to benefit from early liver transplant were adopted at the King's College Hospital, and are now widely accepted.

Therapeutic Options

Liver transplantation currently remains the gold standard for successful therapeutic intervention of FHF, with 1-year survival rates in the range 60 to 80% and continuing to improve.

In FHF due to acetaminophen overdose, acetylcysteine therapy may be initiated. Although previously felt to be of value only if given within 15 hours postingestion, recent investigations have suggested benefit if initiated up to 36 hours after ingestion. An enteral loading dose of 140 mg/kg is given, followed by 70 mg/kg every 4 hours for a total of 17 doses.

In patients with features of autoimmune etiology such as high-titer antinuclear antibody and elevated gamma globulin levels, many advocate a careful trial of systemic corticosteroids while awaiting urgent liver transplant.

Extracorporeal liver support using devises with biological hepatocyte activity has shown promise of benefit in early studies. Further development and testing of this system are in progress.

Although prostaglandin E$_1$ therapy showed initial promise, its effectiveness is not established.

Patients with Budd–Chiari syndrome may present acutely with FHF; however, dramatic improvement may follow portal vein decompression by emergency mesocaval or mesoatrial shunt procedures.

Plasmapheresis combined with high-performance hemodiafiltration may have a transient temporizing benefit but is yet experimental.

Charcoal hemoperfusion removes circulating toxins but does not replace hepatic homeostatic functioning. Hence, controlled trials have failed to show benefit.

Recommended Approach

The role of the primary clinician in management of these patients includes identification of FHF, establishment of an etiology, and assessment of the appropriateness of transfer to a transplant facility. Grade of encephalopathy and prognosis of the patient should be assessed. Based on King's College hospital criteria, if poor prognostic factors are identified, immediate transfer to a liver transplant center must be considered. Contacting the liver transplant center early once FHF is established is favored.

Patients should be closely monitored in the intensive care unit setting from the time of presentation. Candidates with grade III and IV encephalopathy should be at a center with liver transplant capability; however, for all patients awaiting definitive treatment with orthotopic liver transplantation or artificial liver support, the goal of patient care is the prevention of or the early identification and treatment of complicating events such as infection (sepsis, urinary infection, aspiration pneumonia); metabolic and electrolyte abnormalities; hypotension; renal failure; gastrointestinal bleeding; progressive encephalopathy; cerebral edema; and coagulopathy. If the patient is considered to have favorable prognostic features with less than grade II encephalopathy, close monitoring should also be instituted for early identification of decompensation or progression of failure.

In accomplishing this goal, frequent blood and urine cultures should be obtained and followed with appropriate management adjustments. Aspiration precautions should be taken. Blood glucose should be monitored for development of hypoglycemia. For serum glucose levels less than 100 mg/dL, 5 or 10% dextrose solutions should be initiated. If blood levels fall below 60 mg/dL, 50 mL of 50% dextrose should be given to follow with 10% dextrose infusion and hourly checks of serum levels. Hypokalemia should be corrected aggressively and hyponatremia, which is more commonly dilutional in these patients, should be treated with free water restriction as much as is possible. Swan–Ganz catheter monitoring should be instituted to guide volume management. Hypotension occurs frequently and can prove difficult to manage. The goal of adequate oxygen delivery and avoidance of tissue hypoxia is preferred over attempting to normalize systolic blood pressure. Aggressive inotropic drug use may worsen tissue hypoxia and should be avoided where possible in favor of adequate trial of colloids, crystalloid, and blood transfusions where appropriate. Identification and elimination of treatable causes of hypotension should be pursued.

With the development of renal failure mechanical causes should be ruled out. Loop diuretics may be used in combination with albumin infusion to enhance urinary output in patients with hypoalbuminemia. Sustained use of high-dose furosemide is not recommended. Low-dose dopamine may be helpful in maintaining renal perfusion. Where hemodynamic stability is preserved, hemodialysis or hemofiltration may be performed for the usual indications of marked elevation of blood urea nitrogen or creatinine, hyperkalemia, acid–base abnormality, and fluid overload. Continuous hemofiltration in combination with plasma exchange may also temporarily improve encephalopathy and coagulopathy. Aminoglycosides should be avoided where possible.

Prophylactic H$_2$-antagonist therapy or cytoprotective medications should be given for protection against stress-induced gastric mucosal injury. Gastric pH can be monitored via nasogastric tube.

The factors involved in causing hepatic encephalopathy in FHF have not been resolved but currently appear to be multifactorial, including ammonia, fatty acids, mercaptans, phenols, benzodiazopine agonists, and middle-molecular-weight substances. Medical therapeutic interventions are not universally beneficial and may be less so in patients with late-grade encephalopathy. Administration of lactulose and reduction of dietary protein may be beneficial in early encephalopathy, but evidence is lacking for the benefit of these therapies in grade III and IV encephalopathy. Sedative medications should be avoided in these patients. Benzodiazopine antagonists such as flumazenil have preliminarily shown ability to transiently reverse encephalopathy, but further study is needed before specific recommendations for general use can be made. Plasmapheresis may also transiently improve neurologic function, but does not affect outcome.

Seventy-five to eighty percent of patients with grade IV encephalopathy develop cerebral edema, which is the leading cause of death in patients with FHF. These patients should be managed at a center with a liver transplant unit. Effective, accurate detection and management of cerebral edema requires direct measurement of intracranial pressure using subdural transducer monitors. Computed tomography is not a sensitive method for detecting this problem. Adequate cerebral perfusion pressure must be maintained as must monitoring of cerebral oxygen consumption. Mannitol is the therapy of choice in boluses of 0.3 to 0.4 mg/kg while not exceeding plasma osmolarity of 310 to 320 mOsm. Patients with renal failure should undergo ultrafiltration 15 to 30 minutes following its administration, with removal of the equivalent of three dose volumes.

Coagulopathy may be treated by administration of intravenous vitamin K, although this often does not significantly improve prothrombin time. Fresh-frozen plasma and platelets should be administered to patients with bleeding. There is no proven benefit to prophylactic use of these agents except in patients undergoing invasive procedures. For this purpose, platelet counts should be greater than 50,000/μL. Furthermore, artificial correction of prothrombin time extinguishes its value as a prognostic indicator of hepatic function.

FOLLOW-UP

Patients who recover from FHF do so rapidly once regeneration begins. Once recovery is complete, they have no residual liver dysfunction and have a normal life expectancy. Patients who require liver transplantation need close follow-up of the new graft and lifelong management of immunosuppressive medications and their side effects.

DISCUSSION

Prevalence and Incidence

The causes of FHF show considerable geographic variation. The most common cause in the United States is viral hepatitis, whereas in the United Kingdom acetaminophen toxicity accounts for more than 50% of cases. Of the viral causes, non-A, non-B hepatitis and hepatitis B account for most cases. With the development of serologic markers for hepatitis C, this virus has been shown not to account for significant numbers of the non-A, non-B group. In fact, posttransfusion hepatitis C is only rarely associated with fulminant hepatitis and sporadic cases of fulminant failure due to presumed non-A, non-B hepatitis do not show serologic evidence of hepatitis C infection. A presumed non-A, non-B, non-C virus (hepatitis X) is considered to be responsible for a significant number of cases of FHF based on absence of serologic markers or hepatotoxic exposure. Hepatitis A accounts for less than 0.5% of cases of FHF. Hepatitis D was seen in as much as 30 to 40% of patients with FHF due to hepatitis B. FHF due to hepatitis E is seen most commonly in pregnant women in the third trimester. It has been found in epidemic proportions in India and Middle Eastern countries. In Western countries it is uncommon but increasing in occurrence.

Related Basic Science

As a major metabolic organ, the liver regulates the body's energy supply, secretes various essential compounds, and clears toxic substances by various methods including inactivation, excretion, and recycling. Catastrophic failure of a previously normal liver results in profound metabolic instability and disruption of these essential functions. If hepatic function is not restored, severe metabolic derangements occur, including hypoglycemia, hyponatremia, and hypokalemia. Hyponatremia is usually dilutional and can be severe, with serum sodium falling below 115 mEq/L in some cases. Hypokalemia requires aggressive correction to maintain adequate levels. Hyperkalemia may also be present in cases with hemolysis, for example, FHF due to Wilson's disease. Hypophosphatemia and hypomagnesemia accompany these derangements, as does hypocalcemia, which is aggravated by low serum albumin, a result of severely diminished hepatic synthetic function. Coagulopathy develops with progressively rising prothrombin time as coagulation factors are depleted. This can culminate in uncontrolled bleeding. Other complications such as sepsis follow with development of respiratory incompetence and cardiovascular collapse, leading to failure of dependent organs such as the brain and kidneys. Renal failure is frequently functional, that is, without parenchymal loss, and normal function is restored following liver transplantation; however, evaluation for causes such as prerenal azotemia, acute tubular necrosis, and drug-induced nephrotoxicity must be pursued. Early in the course of FHF, mixed metabolic and respiratory alkalosis can occur due to vomiting and increased respiratory drive. Later, acidosis develops due to renal failure, sepsis, and lactic acid accumulation.

Natural History and Its Modification with Treatment

Before the era of liver transplantation, the mortality rate of FHF ranged from 70 to 95% despite attempts at medical management. A few patients managed to survive with supportive treatment only. Surviving patients show complete recovery without any residual hepatic dysfunction; however, a majority of patients did not survive this event. In attempts to affect the outcome of this illness, several modalities have been tried, with only minimal effect on survival. These include exchange transfusion, plasmapheresis, charcoal hemoperfusion, hemodiafiltration, and bioartificial liver. With the successful application of liver transplantation in the mideighties, the survival rate has improved significantly and progressively.

Prevention

Prevention cannot be accomplished because it is not possible at this time to know which patients will develop FHF.

Cost Containment

Despite the success and noted importance of liver transplantation in FHF, it is an expensive procedure and requires lifelong management of patients and their immunosuppression. Therefore, it would be important to avoid transplanting patients who would recover spontaneously with supportive measures only. Identification of these patients is difficult. Criteria have been established in an attempt to identify patients with better prognostic features; however, the window of opportunity for successful transplantation may be missed with prolonged delay in determining transplant candidacy. The recently developed extracorporeal liver assist device shows promise and has potential to support essential biochemical and hepatocyte functions until either the native liver recovers or an appropriate donor is found for patients with irreversible failure. If this is accomplished, the number of unneeded transplants would be reduced and the opportunity for better candidate selection would enhance appropriate distribution of limited organs and aid in cost containment.

REFERENCES

Bernuau J, Rueff B, Benhamou JP. Fulminant and subfulminant hepatic failure: Definitions and causes. Semin Liver Dis 1986;6:97.

Munoz S. Difficult management problems in fulminant hepatic failure. Semin Liver Dis 1993;13:395.

O'Grady JG, Alexander GJM, Hayllar KM, et al. Early indicators of prognosis in fulminant hepatic failure. Gastroenterology 1989;97:439.

O'Grady JG, Portmann B, Williams R. Fulminant hepatic failure. In: Schiff L, Schiff ER, eds. Diseases of the liver. 7th ed. Philadelphia: Lippincott, 1993:1077.

Sussman NL, Gislason GT, Kelly JH. Extracorporeal liver support: Application to fulminant hepatic failure. J Clin Gastroenterol 1994;18:320.

Trey C, Davidson LS. The management of fulminant hepatic failure. In: Popper H, Shaffner, eds. Progress in liver disease. New York: Grune & Stratton, 1970:282.

Reye's Syndrome

Simon S. Rabinowitz, M.D., Ph.D.

DEFINITION

Reye's syndrome is an acute noninflammatory encephalopathy of childhood with microsteatosis of the liver and involvement of other viscera. The syndrome has a stereotypical progression of symptoms and signs, except during infancy. It results from a mitochondrial insult in the involved organs that follows a viral illness by 3 to 6 days.

ETIOLOGY

Although the etiology of Reye's syndrome remains elusive, multiple factors have been shown to be involved in its pathogenesis. Biochemical and ultrastructural studies have demonstrated mitochondrial dysfunction that accounts for the characteristic biochemical disturbances. Similar changes have been noted in neuronal mitochondria. The exact cause of the unrelenting intracranial hypertension and the rapid neurologic deterioration are unknown, but leading candidates include hyperammonemia, elevations of certain amino and fatty acids, hypoglycemia, hypoperfusion of brain parenchyma, and combinations of these.

Nearly two thirds of Reye's syndrome cases follow influenza infections, and clustering of cases have been noted during influenza outbreaks. The majority of the remaining cases are usually noted after chickenpox. *Although certain experts in this field have criticized the epidemiologic studies associating Reye's syndrome and salicylate use, the vast majority of data support this notion.* The lack of a suitable animal model has hindered the substantial number of investigators who have studied this syndrome.

CRITERIA FOR DIAGNOSIS

Suggestive

Because early recognition of Reye's syndrome and prompt institution of appropriate therapy dramatically decrease morbidity, it is essential for all physicians to be aware of this entity. Even though its incidence is falling, Reye's syndrome should be considered in any child with emesis and a worsening encephalopathy. Besides the fairly uniform progression of symptoms (Table 19–90–1), the antecedent influenza or varicella infection, and the history of salicylate use, there is also a typical pattern of laboratory disturbances. The most commonly encountered findings are hypoglycemia, hyperammonia, prolonged coagulation profile, and elevated transaminase levels. These findings in an anicteric child strongly suggest Reye's syndrome.

Definitive

Retrospective analysis of cases, even in experienced centers, has indicated that many children were incorrectly diagnosed as having Reye's syndrome. To standardize the recognition of this reportable syndrome, diagnostic criteria have been proposed.

Essential features, as defined by the Centers for Disease Control and Prevention include an acute, otherwise unexplained, noninflammatory (<9 leukocytes/mL of cerebrospinal fluid) encephalopathy of childhood that occurs several days after a viral illness, and liver involvement documented by a threefold elevation of either aspartate transaminase, alanine transaminase, or ammonia or by microvesicular steatosis on liver biopsy or autopsy.

CLINICAL MANIFESTATIONS

Subjective

The progression of clinical symptoms is so characteristic that the history alone should alert the physician to the possible diagnosis of Reye's syndrome. Three to seven days prior to the onset of emesis is a preceding illness, usually influenza during the winter months and varicella otherwise; however, other viral illnesses and perhaps even bacterial infections have been documented as antecedent events. Any salicylate therapy, even in over-the-counter medications, should be sought. Often the caretaker gives a history of a child improving and then developing lethargy and behavioral abnormalities, followed by pernicious emesis and agitated behavior. The agitated or delirium stage, characterized by other manifestations of sympathetic nervous system hyperactivity such as tachypnea, tachycardia, diaphoresis, and pupillary dilation, is often very transient. A child who requires several adults to restrain him or her and is verbally abusive is quite typical. The child then lapses into coma and requires aggressive intensive care unit management. The stages of coma are also fairly standard, with a progression from decorticate to decerebrate posturing accompanying diminished responsiveness to noxious stimuli.

In the United States the mean age is 7 to 10 years, whereas in the United Kingdom it is slightly lower. Reye's syndrome is well described in infancy, although the clinical signs and symptoms are not as typical as in the older child. The emesis may be less prominent and the onset of coma may be more sudden. On the other hand, about two dozen adults with Reye's syndrome have also been described in the literature. A history of previous Reye-like episodes and siblings with Reye's or of possible drug ingestion (see below) is less compatible with Reye's syndrome and suggests inherited disorders of fat metabolism or poisoning, respectively, which can both mimic Reye's syndrome.

Objective

Physical Examination

The most important physical findings are the behavioral changes. Because management decisions are based on the staging of the disease there is universal agreement on the importance of recognizing the condition of the patient at presentation and the development of sequelae. Two main systems are employed that share a number of common features. The staging that resulted from a consensus of experts convened

TABLE 19–90–1. CENTERS FOR DISEASE CONTROL AND PREVENTION STAGING OF REYE'S SYNDROME

Stage	Consciousness	Posture	Pain Response	Pupils	Doll's Eyes
1	Lethargic Follows commands	Normal	Purposeful	Brisk	Normal
2	Combative or stupor, inappropriate verbal	Normal	Purposeful or nonpurposeful	Sluggish	Conjugate deviation
3	Coma	Decorticate	Decorticate	Sluggish	Conjugate deviation
4	Coma	Decerebrate	Decerebrate	Sluggish	Absent or inconsistent
5	Coma	Flaccid	None	None	None

Source: From Dodge PR, Brown BS, Ector WL, et al. Diagnosis and treatment of Reye's syndrome. Consensus Conference. JAMA 1981;246:2441. Public Domain.

by the Centers for Disease Control and Prevention is presented in Table 19–90–1. A preliminary assessment should include a detailed neurologic examination with particular emphasis on the mental status in the earlier phases of the syndrome. Seizures may be present and suggest the need for aggressive management. Children will have tachypnea with a forceful expiratory phase that results in respiratory alkalosis.

Routine Laboratory Abnormalities

The routine laboratory test results reveal no diagnostic clues.

PLANS

Diagnostic

Differential Diagnosis

The differential diagnosis of Reye's syndrome can be divided into several categories (Table 19–90–2). The most important entities to consider are the metabolic conditions that affect medium-length fatty acid degradation such as medium-chain acyl coenzyme A dehydrogenase deficiency. These conditions often become clinically apparent after a viral syndrome or a prolonged fast, and, because of the similarity of their biochemical and histological profiles to those of Reye's syndrome, are often confused with it. A history of "recurrent" or "familial" Reye's syndrome should lead to a fibroblast biopsy, as serum determination of fatty acid metabolites may be unable to make a diagnosis. The cells can be grown in culture and then sent to a laboratory familiar with processing tissue for the specific enzyme activities. As these are autosomal recessive disorders, additional family members should be screened if a positive diagnosis is made.

If the history is at all compatible with a drug ingestion, including salicylate intoxication, then appropriate investigations should be performed. A positive result should prompt a social service referral to determine the circumstances behind the poisoning. Besides these two categories, a few other entities can be compatible with the histologic findings of microsteatosis of the liver.

Diagnostic Options and Recommended Approach

An initial evaluation should include the measurement of arterial blood gases, a full chemistry profile, an ammonia level, a coagulation profile, a complete blood count, an amylase, and, depending on the clinical suspicion, a salicylate level, a valproate level and a metabolic profile, which should include organic acids, amino acids, and a carnitine level. Blood gases, dextrostick, ammonia levels, liver profiles, electrolytes, and coagulation studies should be sequentially repeated to assist in the clinical management. If there is doubt about the diagnosis, then a liver biopsy should be obtained.

In almost all cases a detailed history, a complete physical examina-

TABLE 19–90–2. DIFFERENTIAL DIAGNOSIS OF REYE'S SYNDROME

Metabolic	Drugs/Poisons
Medium- and long-chain acyl coenzyme A dehydrogenase deficiency	Aspirin overdose
	Valproate overdose
Pyruvate carboxylase deficiency	Lead
Methylmalonic acidemia	Aflatoxin
Propionic acidemia	Methyl bromide
3-OH-3-methylglutaric aciduria	Isopropyl alcohol
2-Methyl-3-OH-butyric aciduria	Warfarin
Carnitine palmitoyl transferase deficiency	Pyrrolidine
	Margosa oil
Isovaleric acidemia	Jamaican vomiting sickness
Carnitine deficiency	Calcium hopantenate
Glutaric acidemia	Amiodarone
Ornithine transcarbamylase deficiency	Warfarin

tion, and the following laboratory tests permit the clinician to make a diagnosis of Reye's syndrome and confidently initiate appropriate therapy. An initial evaluation should include a blood gas, a full chemistry profile, an ammonia level, a coagulation profile, a CBC, an amylase, and depending on the clinical suspicion, a salicylate level, a valproate level, and a metabolic profile, which should include organic acids, amino acids, and a carnitine level. The blood gas, dextrostick, ammonia levels, liver profiles, electrolytes, and coagulation studies should be sequentially repeated to assist in the clinical management. If there is a high index of suspicion for meningitis then a lumbar puncture should be performed. However, there can be considerable morbidity and even brain herniation in the face of raised intracranial pressure. If a child presents in stage 1 or early stage 2, the diagnosis may not be so evident and it may be necessary to initiate therapy and observe the clinical progression. A liver biopsy is indicated if the diagnosis is in doubt, after correction of the coagulopathy with fresh-frozen plasma and vitamin K, to look for microsteatosis and mitochondrial abnormalities. Routine processing suggests the histologic findings in Reye's syndrome; however, lipid staining on frozen sections rather than formalin-fixed tissue and electron microscopy increase the diagnostic sensitivity. Ultrastructure of liver biopsies obtained in the early stages has shown expansion and dilation of the mitochondrial matrix with loss of dense bodies in some cells. Later there is universal involvement with pleomorphic and bizarre-shaped mitochondria. If there is a strong suspicion of an infectious encephalopathy then a small amount of spinal fluid should be removed for investigations including culture, in conjunction with a neurologist and possibly a neurosurgeon.

Therapeutic

All children with stage 2 Reye's syndrome should be managed by an interdisciplinary team in an intensive care unit setting. As the development of more serious symptoms is less likely with the prompt administration of high-glucose solutions, and long-term morbidity and mortality are diminished by controlling intracranial hypertension, an aggressive approach to the patient with Reye's syndrome is warranted.

If the child presents in stage 1 or 2, then a 10% dextrose solution should be administered via a central line at the rate of 1200 to 1800 mL/m^2/d. Perhaps supporting the central nervous system with adequate glucose in the face of depleted hepatic glycogen stores explains the benefits of this management strategy reported in a prospective study from Cincinnati. If the child presents in a more advanced stage or progresses in the hospital, he or she must be transferred to a pediatric intensive care unit to minimize brain swelling.

Although there are no prospective studies that separately evaluate clinical manipulations designed to prevent intracranial hypertension, a number of retrospective studies have demonstrated a marked improvement in outcome after attaining this goal. Once the child is in the intensive care unit an arterial catheter that will measure systemic pressure, a Foley catheter, a nasogastric tube, and an endotracheal tube are placed, in addition to the central venous catheter and a cooling blanket. Some intensivists also place a Swan–Ganz catheter at this time. Because the patient will experience elevated intracranial hypertension resulting from these procedures, a short-acting barbiturate, thiopental (4 mg/kg), and a muscle relaxant, succinylcholine (1 mg/kg), are administered while the procedures are performed. If indicated, a liver biopsy and lumbar puncture are also performed at this time.

Intracranial hypertension can be adequately controlled only if it is appreciated quickly by a monitoring device. The most common devices are an intraventricular cannula or a subarachnoid bolt placed through a burr hole. There have been no studies directly comparing these two approaches, so that the method with which the neurosurgeon is most comfortable with should be employed. The peak intracranial pressure should be maintained between 15 and 25 mm Hg. Initially, this should be done by elevating the child's head 20° to 30° and hyperventilating to maintain a pCO$_2$ of 20 to 27 Torr, which leads to cerebral vasoconstriction. If this measure alone is insufficient, then mannitol 0.25 g/kg should be given intravenously over a few minutes. The dose can be increased to 0.5 to 1 g/kg, administered over 15 to 20 minutes. A typical total daily dose is 4 to 6 g. Caution should be employed to prevent hyperosmolarity (>310 mOsm), which can lead to diuresis and a decrease in the cerebral perfusion pressure (mean arterial pressure − intracranial pressure) to below 50 mm Hg, which is also dangerous. By maintaining the blood glucose at 250 to 300 mg/dL), the amount of mannitol required is minimized. Once normal intracranial pressure has been maintained for 24 hours, intensive therapy is slowly withdrawn in the reverse order of its institution.

If the intracranial pressure cannot be adequately maintained by the above measures the prognosis is graver. The following management strategies have been employed, but few objective data are available to support their implementation and their use is somewhat more controversial. Most neurologists and intensivists who are faced with a child with frequent spikes of intracranial pressure unresponsive to mannitol and hyperventilation induce barbiturate coma (serum level of pentobarbital 30–50 mg/dL). This dose of pentobarbital commonly impairs cardiac output. The vast majority of children are controlled by combinations of the above. There are no available data that clearly support additional therapy, but other measures that have been tried include operative craniectomy and whole-blood exchange transfusion. There does not appear to be any role for steroids or peritoneal dialysis.

FOLLOW-UP

Fortunately, almost all children who survive Reye's syndrome ultimately have a full recovery. Sometimes, there is a prolonged period to achieve complete neurologic resolution. A few children have subtle neurologic sequelae that may impair long-term intellectual development. The child who leaves the intensive care unit and hospital after Reye's syndrome is not contagious and should be encouraged to return to school, even if a modified program is transiently required. Recurrences of Reye's syndrome is highly unusual and should prompt investigations for an alternative diagnosis.

DISCUSSION
Prevalence and Incidence

The incidence of Reye's syndrome has dramatically decreased since the early 1980s, coincident with the publicity surrounding its association with salicylate ingestion. In the United States, the peak incidence of reported cases was more than 500, and only 25 cases were reported in the last year reported, 1989. In Cincinnati a concerted effort was made to alert the community and health providers about the early manifestations of Reye's syndrome. In a prospective study from 1980 to 1981, the incidence of biopsy-proven cases was estimated to be 3 per 100,000 children, and that of probable cases to be 6 per 100,000. This is almost tenfold higher than in other epidemiologic studies. Although Reye's syndrome appears to be quite rare, a published report describing four recent cases at one center is a reminder that it still exists.

Related Basic Sciences
Genetics

At present there are no genetic markers for Reye's syndrome or for a predisposition to Reye's syndrome. The finding of a higher incidence in whites than blacks, however, suggests that an inherited predisposition at a molecular level exists.

Anatomic, Metabolic, or Physiologic, and Molecular Derangement

An overview of the accepted data on the pathogenesis of Reye's syndrome has been included above; however, a few recent exciting results and new hypotheses are worthy of mention. The majority of mitochondrial proteins are synthesized in the cytoplasm and coded for by nuclear DNA. They are then transported into the organelle and afterward assume their appropriate three-dimensional configuration and enzyme activity. Even though Reye's syndrome is associated with a substantial depression of enzyme activity, immunologically cross-reacting enzyme protein is present in the mitochondrial fraction. It has been suggested that a depletion of intramitochondrial ATP, which is required for the proper folding, is involved in Reye's syndrome. It may be that salicylates, in a time course that is similar to their effect on platelet dysfunction, may have a role in this depletion. Impaired mitochondrial beta oxidation of fatty acids has been suggested as the cause of the observed accumulation of unusual hepatic acyl coenzyme A intermediates. Because these compounds can themselves further compromise additional mitochondrial functions such as ureagenesis, gluconeogenesis, and fatty acid oxidation, it has been proposed that disruption of the beta oxidation pathway is the initiating event in Reye's syndrome.

Natural History and Its Modification with Treatment

Prior to the realization that raised intracranial pressure was the central feature in the pathogenesis of Reye's syndrome, the mortality rate was estimated to be 40% or greater. With the institution of a more aggressive approach, however, the mortality and morbidity rates have been reduced to less than half of the previous figures. In addition, the recognition of cases at earlier stages and the initiation of appropriate therapy have prevented the progression to more advanced stages and have also contributed to better outcomes.

Prevention

All health care providers who deal with children should routinely discuss the dangers of salicylate medication with parents and should remind them about the dangers of salicylates during influenza season and during the early stages of varicella. As alternative analgesics and antipyretics are readily available and economical, the importance of continuing this practice cannot be overemphasized.

Cost Containment

For any disease or condition that is preventable, the best way to contain costs is to use the measures that have resulted in its prevention. For Reye's syndrome, it is the realization that the illness is associated with aspirin therapy. Early recognition and initiation of therapy will minimize hospitalization and intensive care unit stay in the short term as well as long-term sequelae.

REFERENCES

Corkey BE, Hale DE, Glennon MC, et al. Relationship between unusual hepatic acyl coenzyme A profiles and the pathogenesis of Reye syndrome. J Clin Invest 1988;82:782.

DeVivo DC. Reye syndrome. Neuro Clin 1985;3:95.

Dodge PR, Brown BS, Ector WL, et al. Diagnosis and treatment of Reye's syndrome. Consensus Conference. JAMA 1981;246:2441.

Haller J. Intracranial pressure monitoring in Reye's syndromes. Hosp Pract 1980; Feb 15(2);101.

Partin JC. Reye's syndrome. In: Suchy FJ, ed. Liver disease in children. St. Louis: Mosby, 1994.

CHAPTER 19–91

Evaluation of Patients with Chronic Liver Disease

Albert D. Min, M.D., and Henry C. Bodenheimer, Jr., M.D.

DEFINITION

The term *chronic liver disease* connotes a disease process in the liver that has been present for at least 6 months and is likely to persist, whether it is congenital or acquired, and encompasses a very diverse group of disorders. Each disease may be distinguished from the others by features of etiology, natural history, therapeutic implications, and prognosis.

ETIOLOGY

The etiology of chronic liver disease may be classified into two major categories: hepatocellular and cholestatic disorders. Hepatocellular liver disease indicates parenchymal liver cell damage and encompasses chronic hepatitis due to viruses, alcohol, drugs, autoimmunity, nonalcoholic steatohepatitis, and genetic disorders of α_1-antitrypsin deficiency, hemochromatosis, and Wilson's disease. Chronic cholestatic liver disease is most commonly represented by primary biliary cirrhosis and primary sclerosing cholangitis.

CRITERIA FOR DIAGNOSIS
Suggestive

Clinical evidence of portal hypertension and stigmata of chronic liver disease on physical examination should raise one's suspicion for chronic liver disease. Persistent elevation of biochemical liver test results is also suggestive of chronic liver disease.

Definitive

A diagnosis of chronic liver disease can be established when a liver biopsy demonstrates histologic features characteristic of a particular chronic liver disease in conjunction with various viral or autoimmune serologic tests, quantitation of specific proteins (α_1-antitrypsin, ceruloplasmin, and ferritin), and a cholangiogram, when cholestasis is present.

CLINICAL MANIFESTATIONS
Subjective

Clinical features of chronic liver disease span a wide spectrum from the asymptomatic, otherwise healthy patient to the patient presenting with hepatocellular failure. The most common symptoms, however, are fatigue, anorexia, and pruritus of varying degrees. The history should include risk factors for acquiring viral hepatitis such as occupational hazard, transfusion of blood products, intravenous drug abuse, sexual behavior, birth place, or travel to endemic areas. Toxin exposure and a complete medication history should be sought. A family history of liver diseases is helpful in diseases such as hemochromatosis and Wilson's disease. Past medical or surgical history is warranted, as associated extrahepatic diseases may be characteristic of a particular liver disease such as sicca syndrome being associated with primary biliary cirrhosis. Patients with decompensated liver diseases may relate symptoms of encephalopathy, jaundice, fluid retention, or variceal bleeding.

Objective
Physical Examination

Scleral icterus is usually detected at total serum bilirubin levels above 3 mg/dL. Spider angiomata are common, particularly in the distribution of the superior vena cava. Palmar erythema is characterized by redness of the thenar and hypothenar eminences, with sparing of the center of the palm. Dupuytren's contracture involving the fourth and fifth fingers due to thickening of the palmar fascia is a nonspecific finding most commonly seen in patients with alcoholic liver disease. Gynecomastia,

testicular atrophy, and pectoral alopecia are also frequently present in addition to white nails and clubbing. Jaundice is an obvious sign, but xanthelasma, xanthomata, and calcinosis may also be seen in patients with cholestatic liver diseases. Xanthelasma occur around the eyes, usually on the inner canthal fold and the eyelid. Calcinosis typically occurs at pressure points such as the elbow and the ulnar surface of the forearm. Encephalopathy, ascites, peripheral edema, umbilical hernia, caput medusa, and muscle wasting are seen in patients with advanced disease.

Routine Laboratory Abnormalities

Rather than a single specific test, the pattern of several test results measured over a period can lead to establishing the diagnosis. Serum aminotransferase, formerly referred to as transaminase, activities are sensitive indicators of liver cell injury and hepatocellular necrosis. Alanine aminotransferase (ALT) and aspartate aminotransferase (AST) are two enzymes whose activities are measured most frequently in routine assessment of liver dysfunction. ALT is more specific for liver injury, whereas AST is less specific and found in liver, cardiac, and skeletal muscle, kidney, and brain. Aminotransferase activities are usually elevated in most liver disorders; however, in chronic liver disease the degree of elevation is less than in acute hepatitis, and levels rarely rise more than ten times above the upper limit of normal except during flares of chronic viral and autoimmune hepatitis. The AST/ALT ratio is of little diagnostic value except in the recognition of alcoholic liver disease, in which the AST/ALT ratio is often greater than 2. A prominent rise in alkaline phosphatase compared with aminotransferase activities suggests cholestasis. Associated elevation of γ-glutamyl transpeptidase activity can help to distinguish hepatobiliary alkaline phosphatase from that of other sources. These elevations, however, do not distinguish between intrahepatic and extrahepatic cholestasis. Unconjugated hyperbilirubinemia results from overproduction (e.g., hemolysis), impaired hepatic uptake, or inadequate conjugation as in Gilbert's syndrome. Conjugated hyperbilirubinemia results from impaired hepatic or biliary excretion of conjugated bilirubin. Detection of bilirubin (conjugated) on a urinalysis indicates the presence of hepatobiliary disease. Renal insufficiency further elevates the bilirubin level often out of proportion to other liver enzymes. Biosynthetic capacity of the liver is assessed by serum albumin and prothrombin time. Although serum albumin levels below 3 g/dL usually reflect severe liver damage, the awareness of other causes of hypoalbuminemia such as nephrotic syndrome, malabsorption, and malnutrition must be kept in mind. The hepatic synthesis of factors II, VII, IX, and X requires vitamin K. A prolongation of prothrombin time more than 4 seconds from control values not corrected by parenteral vitamin K administration suggests severe liver disease. Thrombocytopenia or leukopenia may be found on complete blood count due to hypersplenism of portal hypertension, and microcytic (due to chronic gastrointestinal blood loss) or macrocytic anemia (due to alcoholism) is not unusual.

PLANS
Diagnostic
Differential Diagnosis

The differential diagnosis of chronic liver disease should include hepatocellular diseases such as chronic viral hepatitis B, C, and D, alcoholic-related liver disease, autoimmune hepatitis, nonalcoholic steatohepatitis, hemochromatosis, α_1-antitrypsin deficiency, Wilson's disease, and drug toxicity and chronic cholestatic liver diseases such as primary biliary cirrhosis and primary sclerosing cholangitis. Extrahepatic biliary tract disease due to stones, stricture, or tumor may mimic chronic cholestatic liver disease.

Diagnostic Options

Serologic tests are useful as initial diagnostic measures, especially in patients with chronic hepatitis. Liver biopsy is often required to assess the degree of liver injury or fibrosis in addition to securing the diagnosis. Abdominal ultrasound with Doppler, computed tomography, and magnetic resonance imaging are frequently used to assess size of the liver and patency of hepatic vessels and to define mass lesions. Upper gastrointestinal endoscopy detects the presence of varices, whereas endoscopic retrograde cholangiopancreatography or percutaneous transhepatic cholangiography can differentiate between intrahepatic cholestasis and biliary tract diseases. Detection of hepatitis B surface antigen (HBsAg) in patients with suspected hepatitis and negative hepatitis B core antibody immunoglobulin M (HBcAb IgM) typically establishes the diagnosis of chronic hepatitis B. Antibody to hepatitis C virus (anti-HCV), in the setting of ongoing disease, suggests chronic infection with this virus. A supplemental recombinant immunoblot assay is now available to confirm the validity of anti-HCV test results. The ability to detect and quantify serum hepatitis C virus RNA remains investigational. Biochemical changes typically associated with nonalcoholic steatohepatitis are two- to fourfold increases in aminotransferase levels, with liver biopsy showing steatosis and, possibly, Mallory bodies. Serum protein electrophoresis can be a useful screening test for α_1-antitrypsin deficiency, and serum α_1-antitrypsin level and subsequent Pi typing should be determined in suspected patients. Wilson's disease is associated with low ceruloplasmin levels with elevated urinary copper excretion, and results in hepatic or neurologic dysfunction.

Recommended Approach

Once the clinical history, physical examination, or routine laboratory data suggest chronic liver disease, the practicing physician should assess the likelihood of hepatocellular or cholestatic disease. Chronic hepatocellular disease should be assessed with viral serologies (HBsAg and anti-HCV) and other diagnostic tests including autoantibodies, serum protein electrophoresis, ceruloplasmin, and iron studies among others. Evaluation of cholestatic liver disease warrants an abdominal ultrasound or endoscopic retrograde cholangiopancreatography to rule out biliary tract obstruction. Once structural abnormalities and primary sclerosing cholangitis are ruled out, antimitochondrial antibody, cholesterol, and immunoglobulin M should be assessed to diagnose primary biliary cirrhosis. In general, when the possibility of chronic liver disease is suspected, referral to a gastroenterologist or hepatologist is appropriate for further diagnostic tests including liver biopsy, prior to instituting therapy.

Therapeutic

Therapeutic Options

When deciding on therapy, one should consider etiology, duration of disease, and extent of histologic injury as seen on liver biopsy. Interferon alfa is the standard therapy for chronic viral hepatitis B and C. Several drugs such as other interferons, ribavirin, and lamivadine are currently being assessed. In autoimmune hepatitis, the utility of treatment with prednisone alone or in combination with azathioprine is well established. Patients with decompensated cirrhosis should be evaluated for liver transplantation. D-Penicillamine or trientine therapy in Wilson's disease removes the excess copper from the liver and other organs. Treatment for hemochromatosis includes phlebotomy and chelation therapy. Ursodeoxycholic acid improves biochemical liver test results in patients with primary biliary cirrhosis and primary sclerosing cholangitis, but does not halt histologic progression. The use of methotrexate is investigational in these disorders.

Recommended Approach

Patients with chronic hepatitis B who have evidence of viral replication with positive hepatitis B e antigen, hepatitis B virus DNA, and elevated aminotransferase activities are ideal candidates for interferon alfa therapy (5×10^6 U subcutaneously daily or 10×10^6 U every other day for 16 weeks). The recommended dose for chronic hepatitis C is 3×10^6 U every other day for 24 weeks, although modification of individual regimens may be beneficial. The major problem with this therapy is a high relapse rate once interferon is discontinued. In patients with autoim-

mune hepatitis, we recommend a combination of 10 mg prednisone and 50 mg azathioprine daily as the optimal therapeutic regimen that minimizes the side effects. In those patients who cannot tolerate azathioprine, 20 mg/d prednisone is a suitable alternative. If a patient develops decompensated liver disease, therapy is aimed at alleviating symptoms. These interventions may include intermittent use of diuretics for ascites, sclerotherapy or band ligation for esophageal variceal bleeding, and lactulose for encephalopathy. After evidence of a variceal bleed, patients not controlled with medical therapy who have good hepatic synthetic function should be considered for a portal decompressive procedure such as distal splenorenal shunt, whereas those with impaired synthetic function should be evaluated for liver transplantation.

FOLLOW-UP

The interval between follow-up visits is dependent on the etiology of the chronic liver disease, the therapy instituted, the clinical condition, and the severity of the liver injury. In patients with active disease this may be every 3 to 4 months. For patients receiving the interferon alfa, follow-up should be every 1 to 2 weeks for the first month and then monthly with careful monitoring of blood cell and platelet counts and liver tests.

DISCUSSION

Prevalence and Incidence

Chronic liver disease is common. Cirrhosis ranks as the seventh leading cause of death in the United States. Hepatocellular carcinoma is one of the leading causes of death in the world, especially in Asia and Africa, but its incidence is increasing in the West.

Related Basic Science

Portal venous inflow stems from splenic, superior mesenteric, and coronary veins, and ranges between 600 and 1200 mL/min. This flow is regulated by the vascular resistance of the splanchnic arteries. Much of portal vascular resistance occurs at the level of the hepatic sinusoids. The site of vascular resistance in cirrhosis has been localized by combined hepatic and portal vein pressure measurements. A higher portal venous pressure than hepatic venous wedge pressure, used as an estimate of sinusoidal pressure, is seen in nonalcoholic cirrhosis, and indicates the presence of presinusoidal resistance stemming from inflammatory activity or fibrotic changes in the portal triads. In alcoholic cirrhosis, however, the vascular resistance resides at the level of sinusoids as reflected by similar portal and hepatic venous wedge pressures. Portal hypertension in chronic liver disease, however, is the result of both increased portal vascular resistance and increased inflow. The increase in inflow reflects in part a number of generalized hemodynamic changes: peripheral vasodilation, an increase in cardiac output, and an increase in plasma volume. Furthermore, cirrhotic patients experience splanchnic vasodilation and a decrease in blood transit time from superior mesenteric artery to hepatic vein. These splanchnic changes in portal hypertension are in part thought to reflect a vascular defense mechanism involving nitric oxide in response to local tissue damage. The induction of nitric oxide synthase, as a consequence of the elevated circulating levels of endotoxins typically found in cirrhotic patients, produces the excessive formation of nitric oxide, resulting in a decreased response to vasoconstrictors.

Natural History and Its Modification with Treatment

The natural history for most chronic liver diseases involves a gradual, but often progressive course leading to cirrhosis and its sequelae, such as manifestations of portal hypertension and hepatocellular carcinoma. Much of therapy, such as use of diuretics for ascites, is aimed at treating the symptoms without changing the natural course of disease. For several diseases, including autoimmune hepatitis, viral hepatitis, hemochromatosis, and Wilson's disease, however, the disease course may be modified by effective medical therapy.

Prevention

Hepatitis B is a preventable disease, and vaccination is currently recommended for all newborns and for others who are at risk for acquiring hepatitis B. Encouraging abstinence or moderate use of alcohol to those who are predisposed to alcohol dependence may result in halting the progression to alcoholic liver disease.

Cost Containment

The efficient use of diagnostic tests and early institution of effective therapy lead to cost containment. Efforts should be made not to proceed with redundant imaging studies. The cost differential from sonogram to computed tomography or magnetic resonance imaging should be justified by the specificity of the expected data and its impact on therapeutic decisions. Effective therapy, such as interferon for chronic hepatitis B, which limits future medical costs, may yield significant financial benefits, especially if the need for liver transplantation can be avoided.

REFERENCES

Davis GL, Balart LA, Schiff ER, et al. Treatment of chronic hepatitis C with recombinant interferon alpha: A multicenter randomized, controlled trial. N Engl J Med 1989;321:1501.

Friedman SL. The cellular basis of hepatic fibrosis: Mechanisms and treatment strategies. N Engl J Med 1993;328:1828.

Haubrich WS, Schaffner F, Berk JE. Bockus gastroenterology. Philadelphia: Saunders, 1995: vol. 3.

Maddrey WC. Chronic viral hepatitis: Diagnosis and management. Hosp Pract 1994;29:71.

Sherlock S, Dooley James. Diseases of the liver and biliary system. Boston: Blackwell Scientific, 1993.

CHAPTER 19–92

Liver Transplantation

Leona Kim Schluger, M.D., and Henry C. Bodenheimer, Jr., M.D.

DEFINITION

Orthotopic liver transplantation is the removal of a patient's liver and replacement with another human liver. This operation is performed for the treatment of end-stage liver disease secondary to a wide variety of causes.

ETIOLOGY

The indications for liver transplantation can be broadly divided into acute and chronic liver disease. The most common causes of acute liver failure (fulminant and subfulminant) include viral hepatitis (A, B, and non-A, non-B, non-C hepatitis), drugs, and toxins. The chronic liver diseases can be subdivided into predominantly cholestatic, hepatocellular, or vascular in origin. The cholestatic disorders include primary sclerosing cholangitis, primary biliary cirrhosis, secondary biliary cirrhosis, and familial cholestatic syndromes. The hepatocellular disorders include chronic viral liver disease, chronic drug-induced liver disease, alcohol-related liver disease, hemochromatosis, Wilson's disease, α_1-antitrypsin deficiency, and autoimmune hepatitis. The vascular disorders include Budd–Chiari syndrome and veno-occlusive disease.

CRITERIA FOR DIAGNOSIS

Suggestive

Fulminant hepatic failure is defined as the rapid onset of severe hepatocellular dysfunction in the absence of previous liver disease occurring within 8 weeks of the onset of symptoms. Subfulminant hepatic failure is observed within 2 to 3 months of symptom onset.

Definitive

The majority of cases of acute liver failure, where diagnosis can be made, are caused by the hepatotropic viruses A, B, D, and E. Other common etiologies delineated by history include drug-induced liver failure secondary to acetaminophen, isoniazid, halogenated anesthetics, phenytoin, propylthiouracil, valproate, tetracycline, and sulfonamides. Ingestion of the poisonous mushroom *Amanita phalloides,* Wilson's disease, acute fatty liver of pregnancy, and autoimmune hepatitis can also present with the picture of acute liver failure. The etiology of each of these is suspected because of the clinical history or characteristic laboratory abnormality.

The vascular disorders of Budd–Chiari syndrome and veno-occlusive disorders usually present with the acute onset of ascites in the absence of previous chronic liver disease. Usually, these patients have an associated disorder to explain a hypercoagulable state such as a myeloproliferative disorder, tumor, paroxysmal nocturnal hemoglobinuria, pregnancy, or use of birth control pills.

The vast majority of patients who undergo orthotropic liver transplantation present with signs and symptoms of end-stage liver disease and complications from portal hypertension.

CLINICAL MANIFESTATIONS

Subjective

Patients with fulminant hepatic failure present with symptoms of increasing fatigue, nausea, malaise, and deterioration in mental status over an 8-week period. The onset of symptoms in patients with subfulminant hepatic failure is observed over 2 to 3 months. Patients with subfulminant hepatic failure, in contrast to those with fulminant hepatic failure, rarely develop cerebral edema.

Patients with chronic liver disease present with a gradual progressive debilitation characterized by weight loss, fatigue, or complications from cirrhosis. The criteria for patient selection for liver transplantation include the presence of refractory ascites, uncontrolled variceal bleeding, unmanageable encephalopathy, wasting, fatigue interfering with normal daily activities, hypoxemia secondary to liver disease, and the heptorenal syndrome (Fabry and Klion, 1992).

Objective

Physical Examination

Physical examination in patients with chronic liver disease reveals stigmata of cirrhosis including spider angiomata, palmar erythema, parotid gland enlargement, testicular atrophy, muscle wasting, ascites, and various stages of encephalopathy. Routine laboratory abnormalities include coagulopathy, hypoalbuminemia, hyperbilirubinemia, pancytopenia due to hypersplenism, and renal dysfunction secondary to the hepatorenal syndrome. Aminotransferase values do not accurately predict the severity of the pathology, but rather are indicators of an ongoing hepatocellular process in need of further evaluation. Aminotransferase activities may be normal even in the presence of cirrhosis.

The rapid progression of severe hepatocellular dysfunction in patients with acute liver failure manifests clinically with worsening jaundice, coagulopathy, acidosis, renal failure, and encephalopathy. The stages of encephalopathy are graded as stage I (personality changes), stage II (impending stupor), stage III (stupor), and stage IV (coma). Cerebral edema is seen in advanced stages and is a common cause of death in fulminant hepatic failure. Clinical signs of worsening cerebral edema include decerebrate rigidity, dysconjugate eye movements, and loss of pupillary reflexes, which do not always correlate with the degree of increased cerebral pressure.

Routine Laboratory Abnormalities

Investigators at King's College Hospital in London have developed a classification system predictive of the survival outcome of patients with acute liver failure (O'Grady et al., 1989). The classification is divided into acetaminophen poisoning and all other causes. Predictive of poor survival and probable need for early transplantation, in the acetaminophen cases, is an arterial pH below 3.0 or a prothrombin time longer than 100 seconds and serum creatinine greater than 3.4 mg/dL in patients with stage III or IV encephalopathy. Predictive of poor survival in the nonacetaminophen group is a prothrombin time longer than 100 seconds or a combination of any three of the following variables: age less than 10 years or greater than 40 years; etiology (non-A, non-B or halothane-induced hepatitis or idiosyncratic drug reaction); duration of jaundice before onset of encephalopathy longer than 7 days; prothrombin time longer than 50 seconds; serum bilirubin greater than 17.5 mg/dL (O'Grady et al., 1989). This categorization is useful, although prothrombin time is difficult to compare among institutions due to variable methods and reagents.

PLANS

Diagnostic

Differential Diagnosis

All patients who are undergoing consideration for liver transplantation, whether due to acute or chronic liver disease, are evaluated for the presence of several absolute contraindications to transplantation, which include HIV infection, extensive cardiopulmonary disease, extrahepatic malignancy, cholangiocarcinoma, uncontrolled alcohol or drug addiction, and active extrahepatobiliary sepsis.

Diagnostic Options

The diagnostic workup for patients presenting with acute liver failure begins with the historical assessment of exposure to toxins or hepatotoxic drugs or risk factors for the acquisition of viral infection. Serologic tests for the hepatotropic viruses, including markers for hepatitis A immunoglobulin M antibodies, hepatitis B surface antigen, hepatitis B core immunoglobulin M antibodies, hepatitis B virus DNA, and antibodies to the hepatitis D virus (delta agent), are obtained on all patients. Wilson's disease must be considered in any young patient presenting with acute liver failure. Suggestive diagnostic findings include low or low normal ceruloplasmin level, elevated 24-hour urinary copper, relatively low alkaline phosphatase levels, Coombs-negative hemolytic anemia, and the presence of Kayser–Fleischer rings on slit-lamp examination of the cornea.

The decision to transplant patients who present with acute liver failure is multifactorial and is partly based on the clinical course and pattern of laboratory test results, with particular emphasis on worsening coagulopathy, encephalopathy, and renal function.

The history, as in acute liver disease, plays a crucial part in the diagnosis of chronic liver disease. The presence of alcoholic liver disease is primarily based on history. Pathology, when available, can be consistent but not pathognomonic. For the genetic disorders such as hemochromatosis, Wilson's disease, and inherited metabolic disorders (primarily seen in the pediatric population), family history of liver disease or associated abnormalities is particularly important. Autoimmune markers are often present in patients with primary biliary cirrhosis (antimitochondrial antibodies) and autoimmune hepatitis (anti-smooth muscle antibodies, antinuclear antibodies, and anti-liver/kidney microsomal antibodies).

Recommended Approach

Proper timing of the referral for liver transplantation minimizes the morbidity and mortality due to both the late complications of end-stage liver disease and the surgery itself. The pretransplant evaluation includes both a medical and psychosocial assessment. The medical evaluation starts with diagnosis of the liver disease. Cholestatic liver disease predicts a more favorable surgical risk than hepatocellular disorders. The patients are evaluated for cardiac and pulmonary contraindications to transplantation. Each patient is seen in consultation by a social worker and a psychiatrist when indicated. Routine laboratory data include a complete blood count, electrolytes, liver tests (γ-glutamyl transpeptidase, alkaline phosphatase, bilirubin, alanine and aspartate transaminases, serum protein electrophoresis, and prothrombin time), α-fetoprotein, ferritin, serologic markers for hepatitis B and C, cytomegalovirus, herpes simplex virus, Epstein–Barr virus, varicella, and VDRL. Routine cancer screening as recommended by the American Cancer Society is performed on all transplant candidates. Imaging studies routinely obtained include an abdominal computed tomography scan with liver volume and an ultrasonography of the abdomen with duplex Doppler to assess the patency of the hepatic and portal veins. The presence of a hepatocellular carcinoma less than 5 cm and without invasion of the main portal vein is not a contraindication for liver transplantation. Transplantation of patients with tumors greater than 5 cm, in the absence of portal vein invasion, may also be considered.

Therapeutic

Therapeutic Options

The outcomes of patients who present with acute liver failure include death, recovery with aggressive supportive care and medical management in cases amenable to treatment (e.g., autoimmune hepatitis and acetaminophen toxicity), and recovery with liver transplantation. In cases of acetaminophen overdose, treatment with N-acetylcysteine should be instituted, with maximal effect seen if therapy is instituted within 24 hours of acetaminophen ingestion. All patients should be monitored in an intensive care setting with expeditious correction of metabolic derangements and attention to the possibility of infections with appropriate antibiotic coverage. Dialysis may be needed, but can be dangerous in patients with increased intracranial pressure. Continuous venovenous hemofiltration is an attractive alternative in patients in whom fluid balance is the main problem. Worsening cerebral edema as evidenced by progressive deterioration in the neurologic examination or elevation in monitored intracranial pressure should be managed with fluid restriction, mannitol, continuous venovenous hemofiltration, and induction of coma with pentobarbital as a last resort.

Recommended Approach

The treatment of patients with signs and symptoms of end-stage liver disease prior to liver transplantation involves the management of ascites, variceal bleeding, and encephalopathy. Patients with ascites should be placed on daily salt (500–750 mg of sodium) and fluid (1000 mL) restrictions. Protein restriction is not routinely necessary unless encephalopathy is an active problem. Patients are encouraged to maintain adequate protein and caloric intake. If dietary management for the control of ascites fails, diuretic therapy is added with intermittent use of furosemide (40–120 mg 3 or 4 days per week) and/or spironolactone (150–200 mg daily). If the use of diuretics is limited by electrolyte or renal function restrictions, therapeutic large-volume (5 L) paracentesis is an alternative option. Peritoneovenous shunts have efficacy in selected patients, but their use commonly leads to complications of thrombosis, disseminated intravascular coagulation, and infection.

Variceal hemorrhage is managed with sclerotherapy. When sclerotherapy fails to control variceal hemorrhage, transjugular intrahepatic portosystemic shunts may serve to temporize patients prior to transplantation and may also help to control ascites.

Encephalopathy is treated with lactulose 30 mL by mouth two or three times daily, titrated to induce two or three bowel movements per day and/or neomycin 500 mg to 1 g every 6 hours. Any acute episode of encephalopathy should alert the clinician to the presence of gastrointestinal bleeding, an occult infection, or the exaggerated effect of a sedative or analgesic medication.

When the medical management of end-stage liver disease is exhausted and the patient continues to deteriorate clinically, liver transplantation remains the only alternative. The surgical procedure can be broadly divided into three phases: removal of the liver, the anhepatic stage, and reperfusion of the implanted liver. Venovenous bypass is often used to relieve the venous hypertension and problems with bleeding frequently seen among patients with end-stage liver disease.

FOLLOW-UP

The follow-up of patients with chronic liver disease is guided by the recognition of irreversible liver damage. These patients need to be followed cautiously for clinical deterioration as manifested by refractory ascites, episodes of variceal bleeding, encephalopathy, fatigue, and muscle wasting. Progressive elevations in bilirubin and prothrombin time, an albumin level less than 2.5 mg/dL, and the onset of the hepatorenal syndrome are all poor prognostic factors indicating the need for liver transplantation in the near future.

Liver tests in the pretransplant setting are followed every 3 months or more often if needed. Abdominal sonography and α-fetoprotein are obtained every 6 months to look for the presence of tumor, particularly in patients with chronic viral hepatitis.

Patients are followed closely for the first 3 months after transplantation with particular emphasis on infectious complications and rejection. The common opportunistic infections encountered in the immunosuppressed state include those by viruses, fungi, and protozoa. Cytomegalovirus remains the most common viral infection, the mean interval to the development of disease occurring at approximately 6 weeks posttransplant. The incidence of cytomegalovirus disease has decreased with the prophylactic use of acyclovir (800 mg four times a day with normal renal function). The incidence of *Pneumocystis carinii* pneumonia has also decreased with the prophylactic use of trimethoprim–sulfamethoxazole (one single-strength tablet a day), inhaled pentamidine (4 mg/kg every month), and dapsone (1 mg/kg/d). The immunosuppressive agents used most frequently after transplantation include corticosteroids, azathioprine, cyclosporine, FK506, OKT3, and anti-lymphocyte globulin. The dosages of the immunosuppressive agents are adjusted according to the period after transplant, during episodes of rejection, and renal function. Cyclosporine, in conjunction with corticosteroids and/or azathioprine, has been the cornerstone of immunosuppressive therapy in liver transplantation. FK506, introduced earlier this year, appears promising both as rescue therapy for rejection and as primary immunosuppression. The major side effects of cyclosporine include renal dysfunction, neurologic disturbance, hypertension, hypercholesterolemia, and hypertrichosis. FK506 is a more powerful immunosuppressive agent than cyclosporine and does not cause hypertension, hypercholesterolemia, or hypertrichosis. FK506, however, has a similar spectrum of renal and neurologic complications. OKT3, anti-lymphocyte globulin, and corticosteroids are used for the treatment of acute rejection.

Recurrent disease in the liver allograft has been seen with primary biliary cirrhosis, primary sclerosing cholangitis, autoimmune hepatitis, and hepatitis B and C. For hepatitis B and C, severe recurrent disease has been observed leading to consideration of retransplantation (Sheiner et al., 1995; Crippin et al., 1994).

DISCUSSION
Prevalence and Incidence

The annual need for liver transplantation in 1982 for end-stage liver disease approached 15 per million population, but the current need is undoubtedly higher because of fewer restrictions on candidacy (Starzl et al., 1989). The number of liver transplantations performed is limited by the shortage of donors.

Related Basic Science

Advances in immunosuppression have changed transplantation from an experimental procedure into a therapeutic reality. The discovery of cyclosporine in 1972 made a major impact in the survival of patients after solid organ transplantations. Tacromilus, FK506, was approved for the treatment of rejection in liver transplantation in April 1994. It interacts with a lymphocyte-binding protein and the complex inhibits calcineurin, which in turn inhibits the transcription of interleukin-2, a major lymphokine involved in the pathogenesis of rejection. FK506 further decreases the severity and frequency of rejections after liver transplantation compared with cyclosporine.

Natural History and Its Modification with Treatment

Orthotopic liver transplantation was first performed by Dr. Thomas Starzl in 1963. Since then improvements in organ preservation, donor and recipient surgical techniques, and immunosuppressive therapy have all contributed in the utilization of liver transplantation as an acceptable form of management for end-stage liver disease due to a wide variety of causes. One-year survival following orthotopic liver transplant has risen from 30% in the early 1970s to approximately 80% currently.

Prevention

The progression of liver disease secondary to hepatitis B or C may be temporarily arrested by the use of interferon alfa 2b or other antiviral agents. The utility of ursodeoxycholic acid in halting the progression of cholestatic liver disease appears limited.

Cost Containment

The cost of liver transplantation ranges from $150,000 to $300,000 per procedure. A successful transplant obviates the need for medical care and expenses to be used in the management of progressive and chronic liver disease. The two most crucial criteria for successful liver transplantation are appropriate patient selection and timing. With the awareness that liver transplantation is available as a therapeutic approach to end-stage liver disease, it is hoped more patients will be referred to transplant centers appropriately early and the morbidity, mortality, and cost of the procedure will be minimized.

REFERENCES

Crippin J, Foster B, Carlen S, et al. Retransplantation in hepatitis B: A multicenter experience. Transplantation 1994;57:823.

Fabry TL, Klion FM. Guide to liver transplantation. New York: Igaku-Shoin, 1992:79.

O'Grady JG, Alexander GJM, Hayllar KM, et al. Early indicators of prognosis in fulminant hepatic failure. Gastroenterology 1989;97:4439.

Sheiner PA, Schwartz ME, Mor E, et al. Severe or multiple rejection episodes are associated with early recurrence of hepatitis C after orthotopic liver transplantation. Hepatology 1995;21:30.

Starzl TE, Demetris AJ, Van Thiel D. Liver transplantation. N Engl J Med 1989;321:1014.

CHAPTER 19–93

Gallstone Disease

Bruce W. Trotman, M.D., and Mark E. Jonas, M.D.

DEFINITION

Gallstone disease is the accumulation of concretions of various substances within the gallbladder and the physiologic complications caused by their presence.

ETIOLOGY

Cholesterol and pigment gallstones account for 80 and 20%, respectively, of the gallstones found at cholecystectomy in the United States. Various factors contribute to their formation (see below), but both have a similar clinical presentation as uncomplicated symptomatic gallstone disease.

CRITERIA FOR DIAGNOSIS
Suggestive

Typically, a patient complains of episodic right upper quadrant or epigastric pain that is steady and often associated with nausea and vomiting.

Definitive

The diagnosis is confirmed by the presence of gallstones on ultrasonography or, less commonly, oral cholecystography.

CLINICAL MANIFESTATIONS
Subjective

Multiple studies have established that most patients have asymptomatic gallstones. Approximately 1 to 2% of patients become symptomatic annually. When gallstones become symptomatic, the constellation of symptoms is known as *biliary colic*. Typically, patients describe episodic right upper quadrant or epigastric pain. The pain usually develops suddenly, steadily increases in intensity, and may last 30 minutes to several hours. Many patients also complain of pain referred to the right shoulder and scapula. Nausea and vomiting are also frequent. The pain is thought to be secondary to a stone occluding the cystic duct or neck of the gallbladder. Thus, gallbladder emptying is impaired, resulting in gallbladder distention and pain. Pain also results from contractions of the gallbladder and cystic duct around a stone. The pain resolves when the gallstone(s) is dislodged. If pain continues for several hours without abatement, complications of gallstone disease, such as acute cholecystitis and cholangitis, should be suspected.

Objective
Physical Examination

There are no particular findings on physical examination that suggest asymptomatic gallstone disease.

Routine Laboratory Abnormalities

Asymptomatic gallstones cannot be detected by any of the routine laboratory tests.

Icterus and an elevated alkaline phosphatase in a patient with fever, right upper quadrant pain, and leukocytosis are consistent with ascending cholangitis due to choledocholithiasis as opposed to acute cholecystitis.

PLANS
Diagnostic
Differential Diagnosis

The differential diagnosis in patients with biliary colic secondary to gallstone disease includes organs that when diseased can present with a similar pain pattern. As gallstone disease typically presents with right upper quadrant or epigastric pain, the other possible etiologies for pain in the same general region are extensive and include peptic ulcer disease, gastritis, reflux esophagitis, pancreatitis, renal disease, diverticulitis, pleurisy, nephrolithiasis, hepatitis, and myocardial ischemia. When symptoms are vague, it is essential to exclude life-threatening possibilities early in the hospitalization to ensure an optimal clinical outcome.

Diagnostic Options and Recommended Approach

History and radiographic imaging modalities are the primary methods used to diagnose gallbladder disease. Ultrasonography, oral cholecystography, and nuclear scintigraphy are methods of evaluating the gallbladder. Ultrasonography has become the method of choice because of its low cost and portability and the scope of information it provides. In the fasting patient, the sensitivity of ultrasonography for cholelithiasis approaches 98%. Ultrasonography can detect stones larger than 2 mm in diameter and provide structural information about the gallbladder such as wall thickness, anatomic anomalies, and the presence of tumor. It also provides information about choledocholithiasis and bile duct dilation. Classically, gallstones are recognized sonographically as intraluminal echogenic foci that cast acoustic shadows. Gallstones can be shown to move with gravity unless wedged in the gallbladder neck or cystic duct.

Oral cholecystography requires the ingestion of an iodinated contrast agent 1 day prior to the study. Once absorbed, the contrast agent is taken up by the liver, conjugated with glucuronic acid, and secreted into bile, where it is concentrated in the gallbladder. The contents of the gallbladder (stones, polyps) are then visualized. Limitations of this technique include poor gallbladder visualization secondary to poor absorption of the oral contrast agent by the gut, reabsorption of the contrast through an inflamed gallbladder wall, and liver dysfunction with impaired secretion of the contrast agent. Oral cholecystography is infrequently employed today. It is used in cases where ultrasonography results are equivocal or to evaluate gallbladder function.

Nuclear cholescintigraphy is used mainly in the setting of suspected acute cholecystitis to demonstrate nonvisualization of the gallbladder and to provide functional information about gallbladder contraction. It cannot provide anatomic information or identify gallstones. Abdominal plain films, although helpful in evaluating patients with abdominal pain, provide little information in gallstone disease, as only 10% of gallstones contain sufficient calcium to be detected.

Therapeutic

As both the age of the population and the use of abdominal imaging procedures increase, the incidence of asymptomatic gallstones will increase as well. Several studies using risk–benefit analysis have concluded that prophylactic cholecystectomy in asymptomatic patients with gallstones provides no benefit. Prophylactic treatment should be reserved only for certain select groups of patients.

Until this past decade, surgical cholecystectomy was the gold standard of treatment for symptomatic gallstone disease. Other surgical treatment options now include laparoscopic cholecystectomy. Nonsurgical options include oral dissolution therapy, extracorporeal shock wave lithotripsy, and contact dissolution therapy.

Elective open cholecystectomy in a patient without comorbid illness is age dependent and has an overall mortality of less than 1% in otherwise healthy patients (under age 65). It usually involves a 3- to 5-day hospital stay, followed by weeks of pain and disability primarily due to the abdominal incision at surgery. Therefore, surgeons have applied the laparoscopic technique to cholecystectomy. The first laparoscopic cholecystectomy was performed in 1988. In this operation, the gallbladder is removed via four small incisions in the abdominal wall, so the abdominal musculature is not incised. Although laparoscopic cholecystectomy is a new procedure, several studies have reported similar results with regard to conversion to open cholecystectomy (~5%) and complications (~5%). Most major complications involve bile duct injury and appear to occur early in the surgeons' experience with this novel procedure. Time, more surgical experience with this procedure, and more research are needed to better define the risks and benefits of this procedure as compared with traditional therapies.

Oral dissolution therapy employs bile acid preparations that when taken orally dissolve gallstones. The two bile acids currently available are chenodeoxycholic acid and ursodeoxycholic acid. Both increase cholesterol solubility of bile and dissolve cholesterol stones, but not pigment stones. Candidates for bile salt therapy should be those who have symptomatic gallstone disease who are either poor surgical risks or refuse surgery. Furthermore, selected patients should have radiolucent gallstones less than 10 mm in diameter in a functioning gallbladder. During treatment with ursodeoxycholic acid, stone size decreases approximately 1 mm per month. Success rates with bile salt therapy range between 30 and 60%. Once stones are dissolved successfully, they will recur at a rate of 10% per year for the first 5 years, then stabilize at 50% at 10 years. Fortunately, most recurrences result in asymptomatic gallstones, which can be treated. Other disadvantages of bile salt therapy include side effects, such as diarrhea with chenodeoxycholic acid, which can be avoided with ursodeoxycholic acid, and the cost of this treatment.

Extracorporeal shock wave lithotripsy (ESWL) employs focused high-amplitude sound waves to fragment stones. A functioning gallbladder is needed to ensure passage of stone fragments. ESWL is usually well tolerated with minimal side effects. Successful clearance is related to stones less than 2 cm in diameter that are not calcified. Combination with oral bile salt therapy markedly improves stone dissolution over time. This technique is still considered investigational in the United States and is limited to certain centers.

Lastly, methyl-*tert*-butyl ether (MTBE) is an excellent cholesterol solvent that has been used to dissolve gallstones. It remains liquid at body temperature and is introduced into the gallbladder via a percutaneous or retrograde nasobiliary catheter. Trials have shown that MTBE dissolves 95 to 100% of all radiolucent gallbladder stones regardless of stone size or number. This method was developed for patients at high risk and remains investigational, limited in its general use.

FOLLOW-UP

Patients with asymptomatic gallstones found radiographically need no particular scheduled follow-up because of their gallstones. Once silent gallstones become symptomatic, further workup is needed as outlined above. Oral bile acid therapy with ursodeoxycholic acid is preferred because it has no hepatotoxicity or potential for producing diarrhea. When on therapy for 9 to 12 months a repeat ultrasound or cholecystogram should be performed. Stone diameter should diminish by 1 mm per month. If at 12 months stone size is not appreciably reduced, therapy should be discontinued. If stones have dissolved, therapy should be continued for another 3 months.

DISCUSSION
Prevalence and Incidence

The prevalence and incidence of gallstones increase with age so that in America at age 75, 35% of women and 20% of men will have gallstones. Women have two to three times the incidence of gallstones when compared with men at any age. Stone incidence and composition vary widely around the world. For instance, it is rare for certain East African tribes to have gallstones, whereas the Pima Indians of the American Southwest have an 80% incidence of stones by age 65.

Related Basic Science

Gallstones form as the result of multiple physicochemical interactions within gallbladder bile. Cholesterol and pigment gallstone formation requires three stages: saturation, nucleation, and growth. Saturation of bile with cholesterol is required for cholesterol gallstone formation. When the solubilizing capacity of bile is exceeded, cholesterol precipi-

tates from bile as liquid crystals that act as nucleating foci for stone formation. Cholesterol solubilization is dependent on the interplay of two major substances: lecithin and bile salts. Lecithin and bile salts form mixed micelles that solubilize cholesterol. Factors that influence the proportion of biliary bile salts, lecithin, or cholesterol predispose to cholesterol gallstones. For instance, patients who have disease involving the ileum such as in Crohn's disease may have significant loss of the bile salt pool and, therefore, less bile salts in bile to solubilize cholesterol. In contrast, grossly obese patients merely secrete significantly more biliary cholesterol than nonobese subjects.

Pigment gallstones consist primarily of calcium salts of bilirubin and its polymers, phosphate, carbonate, and fatty acids. There are two major subtypes of pigment stones: black and brown stones. Both stone types contain calcium bilirubinate; however, the conditions leading to precipitation of calcium bilirubinate may differ. It has been suggested that brown pigment stones result from the hydrolysis of conjugated bilirubin to its unconjugated form, which is mediated by β-glucuronidase of bacterial origin. Recent reports strongly support this hypothesis: Bacteria have been identified in the interstices of brown stones and are uniformly cultured from bile. Furthermore, juxtapapillary duodenal diverticula are associated with bacterial β-glucuronidase activity and brown pigment common bile duct stones. Once stasis occurs, bacteria elaborate hydrolytic enzymes—β-glucuronidase, phospholipase A, and conjugated bile salt hydrolase—that react with conjugated bilirubin, biliary lecithins, and conjugated bile salts, respectively. This yields increased concentrations of unconjugated and monoconjugated bilirubin; free fatty acids and lysolecithin; and unconjugated bile salts. Furthermore, a decrease in effective bile salt micelles may promote cholesterol supersaturation and, thereby, coprecipitation of cholesterol with calcium bilirubinate and palmitate.

Black pigment stone disease is usually limited to the gallbladder and is not associated with bacterial infection. It is thus likely that abnormal hepatic bile composition or local gallbladder conditions contribute to black pigment stone formation. Because more than 99% of bilirubin in bile is conjugated, unconjugated bilirubin probably originates from nonenzymatic, nonbacterial hydrolysis of conjugated bilirubin. Furthermore, this occurs in a gallbladder that may have a mild degree of stasis. Defective acidification of gallbladder bile can result in an alkaline environment favoring formation of calcium phosphate and carbonate. In patients with chronic hemolytic anemia, a 10-fold increased secretion of total bilirubin in sickle cell patients is also associated with elevated residual gallbladder volumes indicating stasis. Consequently, persons with chronic hemolysis develop black pigment gallstones at a younger age than the general population. Black pigment stones in cirrhotics and chronic alcoholics may be due to a decreased secretion of bile salts that solubilize unconjugated bilirubin and buffer ionized calcium.

Other mechanisms promoting black pigment gallstone disease seem less likely: enhanced secretion of bilirubin photoisomers; presence of β-glucuronidase of cellular origin or a lack of its inhibitor; and enhanced concentrations of ionized calcium except in primary hyperparathyroidism.

Natural History and Its Modification with Treatment

Multiple studies over the last 80 years have tried to determine the natural history of both symptomatic and asymptomatic gallstones. With respect to asymptomatic gallstones found serendipitously, the rate to develop a manifestation of disease, that is, pain or biliary complications, seems to be greatest within the first several years of discovery of stones and declines with time. This generalization has been observed in several studies. The rate to develop biliary pain is around 2 to 4% during the first 5 years after discovery of stones and then decreases to 1% a year after that. In addition, it has also been noted that when gallstones manifest with symptoms, they present as typical biliary pain 90% of the time and as a biliary complication 10% of the time.

Research on the natural history of symptomatic stones suggests that 40 to 50% of patients have recurrent episodes of biliary pain within the first 2 years of their first presentation. A subgroup of patients (30%) had no recurrence of pain 10 years into the study follow-up. Furthermore, biliary pain is not a warning of more complicated disease. The rate of developing biliary complications in patients with symptomatic gallstones is 1 to 2% per year and remains steady over time.

Prevention

Several interesting studies have suggested that the prevention of gallstone disease can be achieved in certain clinical situations. Weight loss has been noted to be associated with symptomatic gallstone formation. Ursodeoxycholic acid, given at a dosage of 1200 mg/d, has been demonstrated to prevent gallstones in patients undergoing voluntary weight loss as compared with a similar group of patients receiving placebo. Similarly, other investigators have shown that cholecystokinin can be administered to patients on total parenteral nutrition to reduce pigment stone formation. Although these studies are very interesting, further research is needed to better define the role of these agents in the prevention of gallstones.

Cost Containment

Given that gallstone disease affects 10% of the American population, it is imperative that physicians distinguish symptomatic from asymptomatic patients. The mere presence of gallstones is not an indication for intervention. The patient, of course, should be informed of the presence of the gallbladder stones, but should be informed that the chances of requiring intervention are dictated by the development of symptoms. On the other hand, specific groups of patients, for example, obese patients undergoing weight reduction and those with hemolytic disease, may actually benefit from intervention.

REFERENCES

Johnston DE, Kaplan MM. Pathogenesis and treatment of gallstones. N Engl J Med 1993;328:412.

Ransahoff D, Gracie W. Treatment of gallstones. Ann Intern Med 1993;119:606.

Southern Surgeons Club. A prospective analysis of 1518 laparoscopic cholecystectomies. N Engl J Med 1991;324:1073.

Thistle JL, Cleary PA, Lachin JM, et al. The natural history of cholelithiasis: National Cooperative Gallstone Study. Ann Intern Med 1984;101:171.

Trotman BW. Pigment gallstone disease. Gastroenterol Clin North Am 1991;20:111.

CHAPTER 19-94

Acute Cholecystitis

Bruce W. Trotman, M.D., and Mark E. Jonas, M.D.

DEFINITION

Acute cholecystitis is the clinical manifestation of gallbladder inflammation.

ETIOLOGY

Most cases (95%) result from prolonged impaction of a gallstone in the cystic duct or gallbladder neck. It can rarely occur without gallstones—acalculous cholecystitis (<5%).

CRITERIA FOR DIAGNOSIS

Suggestive

The diagnosis of acute cholecystitis is confirmed by combining clinical signs and symptoms with radiologic imaging tests. Biliary pain (right upper quadrant, steady, nonparoxysmal) that has persisted for several hours to days, associated with fever, nausea, vomiting, and a leukocytosis, is most commonly acute cholecystitis.

Definitive

A positive ultrasound or biliary scintigraphy study confirms the diagnosis.

CLINICAL MANIFESTATIONS

Subjective

Right upper quadrant pain and fever with nausea relieved by vomiting may have etiologies other than acute cholecystitis. Hepatitis, appendicitis, pneumonia, and renal colic may have similar presentations and should be excluded to ensure the correct diagnosis. Occasionally, the early presentation of acute cholecystitis is missed because patients complain of epigastric discomfort only. As the inflammatory process continues, pain localizes to the right hypochondrium.

Rigors and a mild pain pattern suggest cholangitis.

Objective

Physical Examination

With continued inflammation, the gallbladder becomes edematous accompanied by peritoneal irritation and the classic physical findings of localized rebound and guarding. A positive Murphy's sign, inspiratory splinting during palpation in the right hypochondrium, is frequently present. Palpable gallbladders are found in 20 to 50% of patients with acute cholecystitis.

Routine Laboratory Abnormalities

Significant laboratory results usually include a leukocytosis with a left shift in 65% and hyperbilirubinemia in 10 to 15% of patients. Jaundice with an elevated alkaline phosphatase is more suggestive of choledocholithiasis and possible ascending cholangitis. Transaminase elevations are usually minimal with acute cholecystitis.

PLANS

Diagnostic

Differential Diagnosis

Given the number of organs within the right upper quadrant, other possible causes of pain and fever in this region should be considered prior to the diagnosis of acute cholecystitis. The differential diagnosis includes peptic ulcer disease (duodenal ulcer), hepatitis, cholangitis, nephrolithiasis, appendicitis, pleurisy, and torsion of the gallbladder. Radiologic imaging studies confirm the diagnosis of acute cholecystitis and eliminate other causes.

Diagnostic Options and Recommended Approach

Diagnostic confirmation of acute cholecystitis can be achieved by ultrasonography or biliary nuclear scintigraphy. Ultrasonography provides several benefits over biliary scintigraphy. It is quick and inexpensive and provides anatomic information about surrounding structures. For instance, it can help distinguish between cholelithiasis and choledocholithiasis and guide appropriate therapy. There is no radiation risk as in biliary scintigraphy. Although calculi seen in the gallbladder by ultrasonography support the diagnosis of cholecystitis, certain sonographic findings confirm the diagnosis. Particularly, visualization of an impacted stone at the gallbladder neck, dilation of the gallbladder with pericholecystic fluid, and a thickened gallbladder wall with a sonolucent layer within the wall strongly suggest acute cholecystitis. The specificity and sensitivity of ultrasonography to diagnose acute cholecystitis are 90 and 85%, respectively.

Biliary scintigraphy is a functional test. It employs the intravenous administration of technetium-99m-labeled radioisotopes (iminodiacetic acid compounds, HIDA). Technetium is metabolized by hepatocytes and then excreted into the biliary system. Visualization of the gallbladder with good filling of the biliary ducts and duodenum within 1 hour is considered a normal study. Nonvisualization of the gallbladder should not be declared until 4 hours has elapsed, as delayed filling of the gallbladder may occur. The sensitivity and specificity of biliary scintigraphy in the diagnosis of acute cholecystitis range between 94 and 100%.

Abdominal plain films are helpful in evaluating patients with right upper quadrant pain by excluding other disorders such as perforated gastric ulcer and pneumonia.

Acute acalculous cholecystitis, inflammation in the absence of gallstones or other mechanical obstruction, is a rare, but a life-threatening disease. It is often found in patients who are severely ill such as after trauma, burn injury, or sepsis. Its etiology remains unknown, but the diagnosis is confirmed by using ultrasonography or biliary scintigraphy.

Therapeutic

The optimal treatment for acute cholecystitis is surgical removal of the gallbladder. If the patient has other conditions, such as diabetes and heart failure, they should be treated prior to surgery. Fluid and electrolyte abnormalities should be corrected. Antibiotic administration has been shown to be beneficial in patients with acute cholecystitis who undergo cholecystectomy by reducing postoperative septic complications, particularly wound infections. Diabetic and elderly patients (>60 years old) also develop fewer postoperative septic complications when antibiotics are used perioperatively. A broad-spectrum antibiotic that covers Gram-negative and anaerobic bacteria should be used. A second- or third-generation cephalosporin or a ureidopenicillin with metronidazole is an appropriate choice.

Open cholecystectomy has been the gold standard procedure for gallbladder removal in acute cholecystitis. It is usually performed through a right subcostal incision and is associated with minimal morbidity, mortality, and complications (all <0.5%). First performed in 1988 for elective cholecystectomy, laparoscopic cholecystectomy is now becoming increasingly popular for uncomplicated acute cholecystitis. Several researchers have shown that as experience with this new technique is gained, complication rates decrease. This procedure is performed under general anesthesia via four small abdominal incisions (see Chapter 19–93). Compared with open cholecystectomy, patients undergoing laparoscopic cholecystectomy benefit from less hospitalization time and cost, decreased pain, and rapid return to work.

Patients with acute cholecystitis who have significant comorbid illness that makes surgery prohibitively risky can undergo percutaneous cholecystostomy. In this technique a drainage catheter is placed in the gallbladder by ultrasound guidance. Several studies have shown its effectiveness to drain and decompress the gallbladder in emergent situations. Cholecystostomy is often the only procedure possible in the critically ill with acute acalculous cholecystitis. Data on this group of patients remain limited.

Extracorporeal shock wave lithotripsy and gallstone dissolution therapy with oral bile acids or with methyl-*tert*-butyl ether via percutaneous cathether have no role in the treatment of acute cholecystitis.

DISCUSSION
Prevalence and Incidence

The incidence of acute cholecystitis is related to its most common cause, gallstones. Although 10% of the adult U.S. populace has gall-

stones, only a minority develop symptoms severe enough to require treatment (see Chapter 19–93). It is difficult to assess the true incidence of acute cholecystitis, as several studies have shown that clinical signs and symptoms do not correlate with findings on ultrasonography in a substantial number of cases. Studies that have followed patients with incidentally found gallstones noted a 1% per year incidence of severe events (acute cholecystitis, obstructive jaundice, or biliary pancreatitis). Most of these complications can be managed electively; however, emergent intervention may be necessary in a minority of symptomatic patients.

Related Basic Science

Once prolonged occlusion to gallbladder outflow has occurred, gallbladder inflammation soon follows. The mechanism that initiates inflammation remains unclear, with research suggesting several possible mediators (prostaglandins, lysolecithin). Several studies have shown that bacterial colonization is a secondary event related to duration of obstruction. As the inflammatory response continues, the gallbladder undergoes further changes including dilation, wall edema, and hypervascularization. If this continues, the possibility of developing a gangrenous gallbladder exists.

Natural History and Its Modification with Treatment

Although there are many patients who have recovered completely from an episode of acute cholecystitis without surgical intervention, experience over the years has shown that this disease should be treated surgically. There are no prospective, randomized, controlled trials proving surgical efficacy over conservative medical therapy in acute cholecystitis (nor should there be), but morbidity and mortality have been noted to be related most to age and coexisting medical illness.

Prevention

Prevention of acute cholecystitis is directly related to prevention of gallstones (see Chapter 19–93). Of patients known to have gallstones, approximately 1% per year become symptomatic and require surgical intervention.

Cost Containment

The major recent event in regard to acute cholecystectomy and cost containment is the increasing use of laparoscopic cholecystectomy. This technique eliminates an extensive abdominal incision and thereby allows patients to return home and to employment much sooner than open cholecystectomy.

REFERENCES

Kune GA, Gill GD. Cholecystitis. In: Schwartz SI, Ellis H, eds. Maingot's abdominal operations. 9th ed. Norwalk, CT: Appleton & Lange, 1989:1405.

Southern Surgeons Club. A prospective analysis of 1518 laparoscopic cholecystectomies. N Engl J Med 1991;324:1073.

Steimer CA. Surgical rates and operative mortality for open and laparoscopic cholecystectomy in Maryland. N Engl J Med 1994;330:403.

Zinner MJ, Roslyn JJ. Gallbladder and extrahepatic biliary system. In: Schwartz SI, Shire GT, Spencer FC, eds. Principles of surgery. 6th ed. New York: McGraw-Hill, 1994:1367.

Carcinoma of the Gallbladder

William B. Solomon, M.D.

DEFINITION

Carcinoma of the gallbladder is a rare gastrointestinal malignancy usually found in elderly women with a history of chronic cholecystitis. The vast majority of gallbladder cancers are adenocarcinomas; infrequently found are squamous cell, oat cell, and carcinoid cell cancers. Carcinoma of the gallbladder is usually diagnosed at the time of cholecystectomy for treatment of symptoms of cholecystitis.

ETIOLOGY

The etiology is unknown. Risk factors for carcinoma of the gallbladder include cholelithiasis, chronic cholecystitis, and, perhaps, exposure to carcinogens such as nitrosamines.

CRITERIA FOR DIAGNOSIS

Suggestive

The development of calcification of the gallbladder, the porcelain gallbladder, is the most common antecedent suggestion of gallbladder cancer. Thickening of the wall of the gallbladder is another antecedent finding. These observations are made at the time of sonography, usually in individuals who present with symptoms of cholecystitis or obstructive jaundice.

Definitive

The diagnosis is made at the time of surgery or by computed axial tomography scan showing a mass in the gallbladder with metastatic spread to the liver or intraperitoneally.

CLINICAL MANIFESTATIONS

Subjective

There are no symptoms specific to carcinoma of the gallbladder. Individuals may complain of the symptoms of cholecystitis, including nausea, vomiting, and anorexia.

Most individuals give a history of chronic cholecystitis.

In individuals with a family history of carcinoma of the gallbladder, the relative risk of carcinoma of the gallbladder is tenfold greater than that of the general public. Certain population groups, including Pima Indians, also have a greater relative risk.

Objective

Physical Examination

There are no physical findings specific for carcinoma of the gallbladder; however, abdominal mass or hepatomegaly is found in about 40% of individuals. Jaundice is also frequently found.

Routine Laboratory Abnormalities

There are no diagnostic routine laboratory abnormalities.

PLANS

Diagnostic

Differential Diagnosis

Diseases that can present with the same symptoms as carcinoma of the gallbladder include cholecystitis, hepatocellular carcinoma, pancreatic carcinoma, and other cancers within the biliary tree.

Diagnostic Options and Recommended Approaches

Sonography of the gallbladder followed by abdominal computed axial tomography scan can determine whether there is disease localized to the gallbladder or whether there is advanced metastatic disease to the liver or peritoneum that requires palliation. More than 90% of individuals with carcinoma of the gallbladder have an abnormal sonogram, including multiple gallstones, thickening of the gallbladder wall, and a polyploid mass within the gallbladder.

Therapeutic

Therapeutic Options

In patients who have disease localized to the mucosa of the gallbladder, as determined by sonography and computed axial tomography scan, cholecystectomy or cholecystectomy with wedge resection of the liver may offer the (rare) possibility of a cure. For individuals who present with obstructive jaundice, palliative stent placement or a biliary drainage procedure may give relief from pruritus.

Recommended Approach

Surgery is recommended for the small percentage of individuals with localized disease. Because there have been reports of iatrogenic spread of gallbladder cancer during laparoscopic cholecystectomy, laparoscopic removal is contraindicated in patients who preoperatively are suspected to have carcinoma of the gallbladder or at the time of laparoscopy appear to have carcinoma of the gallbladder.

The role of radiation therapy or chemotherapy for palliation of advanced gallbladder cancer is unclear and should be carried out only in the context of clinical trials.

FOLLOW-UP

Most patients with carcinoma of the gallbladder require palliation of chronic pain and/or obstructive jaundice.

DISCUSSION

Prevalence and Incidence

In the United States, approximately 500 cases of gallbladder cancer are diagnosed each year. The annual incidence rate of gallbladder cancer is estimated to be about 3 per 100,000 persons. The incidence increases with age, the mean age at diagnosis is 65 years, and the male-to-female ratio is 1:3.

Related Basic Science

Dominant activating mutations of the twelfth codon of the Ki-*ras* proto-oncogene have been found in about 40% of gallbladder cancers. In one published study, amplification of the c-*erb*2 (HER2/neu) proto-oncogene was found in 70% of 43 gallbladder cancers. Almost all gallbladder cancers appear to have mutations in the p53 tumor suppressor gene that result in the expression of mutant p53 proteins.

Natural History and Its Modification with Treatment

The prognosis of carcinoma of the gallbladder is dismal, with less than a 5% 5-year survival rate. Except for the rare early case cured by surgery, there are no data suggesting that any treatment alters this dismal prognosis.

Prevention

There is no method of prevention.

Cost Containment

Preoperative evaluation to identify those patients with limited-stage disease will prevent operations that have little prospect for cure.

REFERENCES

Abi-Rached B, Neugut AI. Diagnostic and management issues in gallbladder carcinoma. Oncology 1995;9:19.

Chijiiwa K, Tanaka M. Carcinoma of the gallbladder: An appraisal of surgical resection. Surgery 1994;115:751.

Rooholamini SA, Tehrani NS, Razavi MK, et al. Imaging of gallbladder carcinoma. Radiographics 1994;14:291.

Teh M, Wee A, Raju GC. An immunohistochemical study of p53 protein in gallbladder and extrahepatic bile duct/ampullary carcinomas. Cancer 1994;74:1542.

Neurological Disorders

Louis R. Caplan, M.D.

Peripheral Neuropathies

George D. Baquis, M.D.

DEFINITION

The generalized peripheral neuropathies are a diverse group of diseases affecting the motor, sensory, and autonomic nerves lying outside of the central nervous system. These conditions have variable clinical appearances and may be defined and classified based on temporal mode of onset, anatomic distribution of clinical abnormality, relative involvement of specific fiber types, association with predisposing diseases, and underlying pathophysiology.

ETIOLOGY

The peripheral neuropathies are not a single discrete entity, so clinicians often feel overwhelmed by the long list of causative diseases which necessarily reflect multiple etiologies. These include endocrine, metabolic, toxic, nutritional, inherited, infectious, paraneoplastic, inflammatory, and collagen–vascular diseases. A thoughtful systematic approach with careful follow-up results in a diagnosis for a majority of individuals.

CRITERIA FOR DIAGNOSIS

Suggestive

The diagnosis of a peripheral neuropathy should be considered when persistent symptoms of muscular weakness or atrophy, loss of sensation, paresthesias, muscular or skin surface pain, or autonomic insufficiency are described. A higher index of suspicion should be present when a disease or clinical condition exists that is known to frequently involve the peripheral nervous system. Occasionally, the presence of musculoskeletal deformity, such as a pes cavus foot deformity seen with hereditary motor and sensory neuropathies, may suggest the diagnosis in an otherwise asymptomatic patient. Clinical examination may show muscular weakness, loss of sensation, depressed or absent deep tendon reflexes, or signs of autonomic dysfunction.

Definitive

Although the diagnosis of a peripheral neuropathy may be based on clinical presentation and physical examination alone, additional confirmation is often needed. This often involves nerve conduction studies and electromyography. Laboratory studies can establish the diagnosis of a specific disease state. Less frequently, cerebrospinal fluid examination or nerve biopsy may be indicated. Genetic testing may confirm the presence of some inherited conditions.

CLINICAL MANIFESTATIONS

Subacute Progressive Distal Symmetric Polyneuropathy

Subjective

The earliest symptoms of a distal gradually progressive sensorimotor polyneuropathy consist of bilateral prickling or tingling involving the feet which gradually spreads up the lower legs. Eventually the hands become involved with spread to the arms. The sensations may be painful with a steady burning or paroxysmal sharp quality. Over months to years, the paresthesias and pain often subside and are replaced by loss of sensation. Fine finger dexterity may be impaired. Ambulation becomes unsteady and is described as if walking on sponges or cushions. Accompanying distal weakness is manifested by episodes of tripping and decreased hand grip. If the autonomic system is affected, symptoms of lightheadedness with standing, visual blurring with difficulty focusing, dry mouth, constipation or diarrhea, bladder voiding dysfunction, and impotence may be present. An abnormal pattern of sweating, with absence over the extremities and excessive diaphoresis over upper body areas, may be present.

Objective

Physical Examination. Examination shows predominantly distal muscular weakness that is more easily demonstrated in extensor than in flexor muscle groups. Wasting of intrinsic foot muscles and other distal muscles may be present. Cutaneous sensation to pin and cotton is decreased in a graded fashion from the toes or fingers proximally. When severe, the vertex of the head and midline anterior abdominal wall can be similarly affected. Hyperalgesia may be present to light touch. Gait imbalance and extremity ataxia are associated with loss of joint position and vibration sensation. Deep tendon reflexes are diminished distally with relative preservation proximally.

Routine Laboratory Examination. Routine testing is unrevealing for most of these diseases. Many are diagnosed based on the clinical recognition of associated underlying systemic disease. A megaloblastic anemia may occur with vitamin B$_{12}$ deficiency. Abnormal serum glucose, creatinine, and thyroid function studies may be present with specific conditions (Table 20–1–1).

Subacute Stepwise Progressive Asymmetric Neuropathy (Mononeuropathy Multiplex)

Subjective

Symptoms of stepwise sequential isolated peripheral nerve involvement result in a gradually accumulating neurologic deficit. Initial symptoms consist of acute weakness or paresthesias corresponding to the involved nerves. As multiple nerves become affected, incomplete recovery results in disease progression. Symptoms may then merge and appear similar to those of a severe generalized sensorimotor polyneuropathy.

Objective

Physical Examination. Weakness and altered sensation are detected in the distribution of involved nerves. Over time, coalescence of the sensory abnormalities and weakness results in the appearance of a generalized distal sensorimotor polyneuropathy. The presence of significant asymmetry of findings is a clue to this diagnosis.

Routine Laboratory Abnormalities. Routine laboratory testing may reveal an elevated glucose level (diabetes mellitus), elevated sedimentation rate (vasculitis), eosinophilia (Churg–Strauss vasculitis), or an abnormal urinary sediment with red cell casts (polyarteritis nodosa). (Table 20–1–2).

Acute Symmetric Motor Predominant Neuropathy

Subjective

Guillain–Barré syndrome presents with symptoms that include progressive muscular weakness classically affecting the legs first and then the arms. More than one half of patients describe an antecedent nonspecific illness prior to onset. Other symptoms include diplopia, difficulty swallowing, and progression of weakness to respiratory failure. Distal foot and hand tingling may be described. Muscular pain can be severe and is occasionally a prominent early symptom. Features of autonomic dysfunction include sinus tachycardia, cardiac arrhythmias, and neurogenic pulmonary edema. Symptoms can progress rapidly, and maximum deficit is usually reached by the fourth week.

Acute intermittent porphyria may present similarly, but is often preceded by acute abdominal pain and psychiatric disturbance. Arsenic or thallium poisoning may also present with acute muscular weakness preceded by nausea, vomiting, and abdominal pain.

Objective

Physical Examination. Examination shows weakness of proximal as well as distal muscles. Bifacial paresis may be present along with oropha-

TABLE 20–1–1. SUBACUTE SYMMETRIC DISTAL POLYNEUROPATHY

Diagnosis	Confirmatory Data
Nutritional deficiency	
Thiamine (B$_1$)	Erythrocyte transketolase level
Pyridoxine (B$_6$)	Clinical diagnosis
Cobalamin (B$_{12}$)	Vitamin B$_{12}$ level
Vitamin E	Viamin E level
Toxic	
Acrylamide	
Carbon disulfide	
Dimethylaminopropionitrile	
Ethylene oxide	Exposure history
Hexacarbons	
Trichloroethylene	
Organophosphorus esters	
Endocrine	
Diabetes mellitus	Glucose
Acromegaly	Growth hormone, somatomedin C
Hypothyroidism	Thyroid function tests
Metabolic	
Renal failure	Creatinine clearance
Acute intermittent porphyria	Urine porphobilinogen, δ-aminolevulinic acid
Infectious	
HIV	HIV testing
Lyme disease	Lyme serology
Connective tissue	
Scleroderma	Autoantibodies
Systemic lupus erythematosus	Autoantibodies
Sarcoidosis	Angiotensin-converting enzyme; nerve biopsy, chest x-ray
Amyloidosis	Nerve biopsy
Medication	
Almitrine	
Vinca alkaloids	
Isoniazid	Medication exposure
Nitrofurantoin	
Amiodarone	
Disulfiram	
Phenytoin	
Critical illness polyneuropathy	Clinical setting
Neoplasia	
Multiple myeloma	Serum and urine immunoelectrophoresis Bone marrow biopsy
Paraneoplastic	Evaluation for neoplasm
Inherited metabolic	
Hereditary motor and sensory neuropathies	Genetic testing, examination of family members
Refsum disease	Phytanic acid level
Adrenoleukodystrophy	Plasma very long chain fatty acids
Metachromatic leukodystrophy	Leukocyte arylfulfatase A

ryngeal weakness and ophthalmoparesis. Tendon reflexes are usually diminished or absent early in the disease course. With acute intermittent porphyria, the reflexes are generally lost in proportion to weakness. A distal symmetric pattern of sensory loss may be present that affects joint position sense and vibration more than pin prick and light touch.

Routine Laboratory Abnormalities. Routine testing is usually normal.

Subacute Symmetric Motor Predominant Neuropathy

Subjective

Chronic inflammatory demyelinating polyneuropathy evolves over months to years with symptoms of proximal as well as distal weakness predominating, often associated with distal paresthesias or sensory loss. Unsteadiness while standing and walking is common. Motor neuropathy with multifocal conduction block may present similarly, but early asymmetric upper extremity weakness or cramping prior to progressing to more generalized weakness may be a clue to this condition. Other diseases may also present similarly (Table 20–1–3).

TABLE 20–1–2. MONONEUROPATHY MULTIPLEX

Diagnosis	Laboratory Test
Diabetes mellitus	Glucose level
Vasculitis	
Polyarteritis nodosa	Erythrocyte sedimentation rate
Churg–Strauss	Erythrocyte sedimentation rate, complete blood count
Wegener's granulomatosis	Erythrocyte sedimentation rate, antineutrophil cytoplasmic antibody
Giant cell arteritis	Erythrocyte sedimentation rate, temporal artery biopsy, nerve biopsy
Peripheral nervous system (isolated)	Erythrocyte sedimentation rate, nerve biopsy
Rheumatoid arthritis	Rheumatoid factor
Systemic lupus erythematosus	Antinuclear antibodies
HIV infection (cytomegalovirus)	HIV testing, nerve biopsy
Leprosy	Skin biopsy or scrapings
Cryoglobulinemia	Cryoglobulins

Objective

Physical Examination. Weakness may be proximal as well as distal with disproportionate preservation of muscle bulk, suggesting the demyelinating character of most of these conditions. Tendon reflexes are depressed or absent. Palpable nerve enlargement may be present. The weakness of motor neuropathy with multifocal conduction block may conform to specific nerves rather than occurring diffusely. Distal sensory loss is often present.

Routine Laboratory Abnormalities. Routine testing is normal.

Symmetric Sensory Predominant Neuropathy

Subjective

Symptoms of sensory loss, paresthesias, gait imbalance, extremity incoordination, and pain predominate and can be disabling. Although a preponderance of sensory symptoms may be seen with a variety of systemic diseases (such as diabetes mellitus, HIV-associated, uremia, and nutritional deficiency diseases), and can represent an extreme of the spectrum of some of the conditions associated with subacutely progressive distal symmetric sensorimotor polyneuropathies (Table 20–1–1). Disproportionate sensory features, especially if proximal limb or truncal ataxia is present, should raise consideration of several less common entities (Table 20–1–4). Though most of these diseases progress suba-

TABLE 20–1–3. SUBACUTE MOTOR PREDOMINANT

Diagnosis	Test
Chronic inflammatory demyelinating polyneuropathy	Elevated cerebrospinal fluid protein; electromyography and nerve conduction study
Motor neuropathy with multifocal conduction block	Electromyographic and nerve conduction study; antiganglioside antibodies
Paraneoplastic	
Osteosclerotic myeloma	Serum and urine immune protein electrophoresis; bone x-ray survey; bone marrow biopsy
Waldenstrom's macroglobulinemia	Serum and urine immune protein electrophoresis; bone marrow biopsy
Lymphoma	Evaluation for neoplasm
Monoclonal gammopathy of undetermined significance	Serum and urine immune protein electrophoresis
HIV	HIV testing

TABLE 20–1–4. PREDOMINANTLY SENSORY NEUROPATHY

Diagnosis	Confirmatory Data
Idiopathic (inflammatory sensory ganglionopathy)	Sensory ganglion biopsy
Paraneoplastic	Antineuronal antinuclear antibodies (anti-Hu antibody); evaluation for neoplasm
Sjögren's syndrome	Antibodies to extractable nuclear antigens; clinical diagnosis
Pyridoxine toxicity	Excessive ingestion

Medications
  Cisplatin
  Misonidazole
  Metronidazole
	Medication exposure

cutely over months, idiopathic inflammatory sensory ganglionopathy may present acutely. Paraneoplastic sensory ganglionopathy may precede the diagnosis of cancer.

Objective

Physical Examination. Normal strength is present with variable loss of distal and proximal sensation. Loss of proprioceptive sensation is associated with limb, truncal, and gait ataxia that is accentuated by eye closure. Bruising and other signs of inadvertent extremity injury are sometimes present. Tendon reflexes are depressed or absent.

Routine Laboratory Abnormalities. Routine testing is normal.

Inherited Neuropathies

Subjective

The hereditary motor and sensory neuropathies, Charcot–Marie–Tooth syndrome, represent several distinct entities with different inheritance patterns and clinical features. They are an underdiagnosed cause of polyneuropathy which may present in older as well as younger individuals. Most are of insidious onset and generally come to medical attention because of foot disorders caused by skeletal deformity or because of difficulty running and walking. Symptoms of paresthesias or sensory loss are unusual. The hereditary sensory and autonomic neuropathies also are a heterogeneous group of conditions and are rare, usually presenting during infancy and childhood. Presenting symptoms include distal sensory loss with insensitivity to pain, painless foot ulcers, lancinating pain, neuropathic arthropathy, and loss of sweating.

Objective

Physical Examination. Pes cavus foot deformity with high arches and hammertoes are important clues to hereditary motor and sensory neuropathies that reflect the disease chronicity. Palpable hypertrophied nerves may be present. Distal muscles are atrophic and weak, and sensation is lost over the hands and feet in a graded fashion. The distal deep tendon reflexes are depressed or absent. Features of hereditary sensory and autonomic neuropathies include foot ulcers, loss of extremity sensation, joint arthropathy, and absent tendon reflexes. Absence of sweating and decreased pupillary light reactivity may accompany other autonomic features.

Routine Laboratory Abnormalities. Routine tests are normal.

PLANS

Diagnostic

Differential Diagnosis

Occasionally, spinal cord diseases such as transverse myelitis and cervical myelopathy secondary to degenerative arthritis may present with symptoms similar to those of a distal sensory neuropathy. The symptoms of tabes dorsalis can mimic those of a primarily sensory neuropathy. Myasthenia gravis, botulism, spinal muscular atrophy, poliomyelitis, polymyositis and other acute myopathies, transverse myelitis, and basilar artery thrombosis may all present with subacute or

acutely progressive weakness that must be differentiated from a predominantly motor neuropathy. Despite diverse etiologies, many of the polyneuropathies have similar clinical presentations. Distinction between these conditions is based on laboratory testing as well as clinical features.

Diagnostic Options

Electromyography provides essential diagnostic and prognostic information. It can distinguish demyelinative from axonal diseases, determine the anatomic sites and pattern of disease injury, and differentiate peripheral nerve from neuromuscular transmission, myopathic, and anterior horn cell diseases. The presence of multifocal conduction block and abnormal proximal temporal dispersion on motor nerve conduction study helps differentiate acquired from inherited demyelinating conditions. Additional laboratory tests may include thyroid function and other endocrine studies, vitamin levels, infectious disease serologies (i.e., VDRL, Lyme titer, HIV testing), serum or tissue for specific toxins, autoimmune antibody titers (antinuclear antibody, rheumatoid factor, antineutrophil cytoplasmic antibody, etc.), and serum and urine immune protein electrophoresis. Motor neuropathy with multifocal conduction block is only diagnosable by EMG and may be associated with antibodies to GM_1 or asialo-GM_1 gangliosides. Monoclonal protein-associated gammopathies may have antibodies directed against myelin-associated glycoprotein. Cerebrospinal fluid examination in Guillain–Barré syndrome and chronic inflammatory demyelinating polyneuropathy usually shows a protein elevation with fewer than 10 mononuclear cells per cubic millimeter of cerebrospinal fluid. Clinical conditions such as carcinomatous meningitis, HIV and other chronic infections, and other causes of chronic meningitis should be considered if more than 50 mononuclear cells are present. Nerve biopsy may be needed to establish the diagnoses of vasculitis, amyloidosis, sarcoidosis, and rare metabolic conditions such as a metachromatic leukodystrophy. Genetic testing is now commercially available for the evaluation of specific types of hereditary sensorimotor neuropathies.

Recommended Approach

A careful history and clinical examination are essential. Electromyography helps narrow the range of diagnostic possibilities. In the absence of abnormality on routine laboratory tests, the more focused laboratory studies may establish the diagnosis. Cerebrospinal fluid examination is helpful when an inflammatory demyelinating neuropathy is a consideration. As only a limited number of diseases are diagnosable by nerve biopsy, which requires a specialized laboratory for processing, biopsy should be pursued only when these conditions are a strong consideration and the diagnosis cannot be established by less invasive means.

Therapeutic

Therapeutic Options

The treatment of the neuropathies associated with systemic disease is that of the underlying disease condition. Known medication or toxic exposures should be eliminated when possible. Associated infections, such as Lyme disease, should be treated with antibiotics. Vasculitis and collagen–vascular disorder-associated neuropathies may respond to corticosteroid or other immunosuppressant therapy. Plasmapheresis for Guillain–Barré syndrome has been beneficial for treatment of moderate to severely ill patients when instituted during the first 2 weeks of illness. High-dose intravenous immune globulin may be beneficial, but its therapeutic role has not yet been well established. Improvements in chronic inflammatory demyelinating polyneuropathy have been demonstrated with both prednisone and plasmapheresis therapy, but long-term continuing therapy may be necessary. Although motor neuropathy with multifocal conduction block may respond to cyclophosphamide or intravenous immune globulin, therapeutic consensus regarding appropriate therapy has not been established. Peripheral neuropathy associated with monoclonal gammopathy may respond to immunosuppressive therapy with a variety of agents or to plasmapheresis. Carbamazepine (starting dose of 100 mg twice daily with gradual increase over 4–6 weeks to 400 mg three times daily) and the tricyclic antidepressants (starting dose of desipramine 10–25 mg with gradual increase to 200 mg over 6 weeks) may provide symptomatic relief of pain. Rehabilitative care, including nursing support and physical and occupational therapy, plays an important role in the recovery from all polyneuropathies.

Recommended Approach

The therapies for the immune-mediated and inflammatory neuropathies may be beneficial, but many have significant side and toxic effects. These need to be carefully considered and discussed with the patient prior to initiating treatment. (See above for approach to specific conditions.)

FOLLOW-UP

The neurologic examination is a useful indicator of response to therapy. Repeated electrodiagnostic studies are not usually indicated, but may be helpful in selected circumstances. Those patients receiving immunosuppressive therapy and those with acute syndromes need more frequent follow-up visits to monitor therapeutic response, as well as to follow the toxic and side effects of treatment.

DISCUSSION
Prevalence and Incidence

The prevalence and incidence vary with etiology and precise information is lacking for most conditions. Up to one half of patients with diabetes mellitus have a neuropathy depending on the criteria used for diagnosis. The reported incidence of Guillain–Barré syndrome varies between 0.6 and 2.4 cases per 100,000 population per year (Dyck e al., 1993).

Related Basic Science

Peripheral nerve disease generally reflects a combination of axonal injury and demyelination, with rapidity, degree, and recovery predicated on resolution of the underlying pathologic process. Recovery from axonal injury is protracted, reflecting slow regrowth of axons, at a rate of up to a few millimeters per day, over months to years. Demyelination may result in conduction block with a severe functional deficit, but with a potential to rapidly resolve over days to weeks. Nerve conduction study and electromyography may distinguish between these processes and provide useful prognostic information. The ultimate deficit reflects the location and extent of injury, with proximal and more severe axonal injury often associated with prolonged recovery. Diseases affecting larger fibers are associated with weakness, loss of vibration and joint position sensation, and ataxia. Alteration of pain and temperature sensation reflects dysfunction of smaller myelinated and unmyelinated axons. Paresthesias are a manifestation of ectopic spontaneous discharges of the sensory unit.

Pathologic and laboratory evidence supports lymphocyte- and macrophage-mediated demyelination in the pathogenesis for Guillain–Barré syndrome, but evidence for antibody- and complement-mediated injury also exists. Vasculitic neuropathies probably result from immune complex deposition in vessel walls leading to ischemic nerve infarction. The pathogenesis of diabetic polyneuropathies remains unclear. Theories include multifocal ischemic nerve injury, reduction of nerve growth factor, and increased polyol pathway metabolic activity with decreased nerve myoinositol content. Although a large percentage of patients with monoclonal gammopathy of undetermined significance have an immunoglobulin M antibody that binds to myelin-associated glycoprotein, the cause of monoclonal gammopathy-associated polyneuropathy is unknown.

Natural History and Its Modification with Treatment

Guillain–Barré syndrome usually resolves spontaneously, but recovery may be protracted. Therapy with plasmapheresis or intravenous immune globulin shortens the duration of recovery. Untreated chronic inflammatory demyelinating polyneuropathy has a gradually progressive or relapsing–remitting course. Treatment with prednisone or plasmapheresis alters this course, but the condition is often not cured with therapy. As such, long-term treatment is often needed. The course of diabetic distal symmetric sensorimotor polyneuropathy may be improved with tight glycemic control; however, tight control is often not beneficial once a severe sensorimotor neuropathy develops. Monoclonal gammopathy of undetermined significance may respond favorably to immunosuppressive treatment. Untreated, the course is usually slowly progressive. The peripheral neuropathy associated with multiple myeloma tends to gradually progress despite chemotherapy, but that associated with osteosclerotic myeloma may significantly improve with radiation therapy to solitary or restricted bone lesions. Those conditions associated with nutritional deficiency, toxin exposure, medications, and metabolic disease persist and worsen unless the specific underlying abnormality is treated. These conditions then stabilize and may slowly gradually improve. The polyneuropathy of renal failure may resolve with kidney transplantation. The sensorimotor polyneuropathy associated with critical illness in the intensive care unit is associated with a high mortality that reflects the severity of the underlying diseases. It gradually resolves with treatment of sepsis and multiorgan failure.

Prevention

Tight glycemic control in diabetes, attention to nutritional status of at-risk populations, and prevention of unnecessary toxic exposures can potentially prevent the occurrence of some polyneuropathies; most are not preventable.

Cost Containment

Failure of careful patient clinical assessment often results in the undirected ordering of multiple expensive unneeded tests. This is especially true with conditions such as the peripheral neuropathies, which can clinically appear similar but have multiple different etiologies and therapies. Identification of the underlying pathophysiology through careful electrodiagnostic testing narrows the range of possible diagnoses and helps direct further evaluation. The most cost-effective management is a thoughtfully directed evaluation, by a skilled neurologist.

REFERENCES

Asbury AK, Gilliatt RE. Peripheral nerve disorders: A practical approach. Boston: Butterworth, 1984.
Dyck PJ. Peripheral neuropathy: New concepts and treatments. Neurol Clin 1994;10(3).
Dyck PJ, Thomas PK, Griffen JW, et al. Peripheral neuropathy. 3rd ed. Philadelphia: Saunders, 1993.
Layzer RB. Neuromuscular manifestations of systemic disease. Philadelphia: Davis, 1985.
Ropper AH, Wijdicks EFM, Truax BT. Guillain–Barré syndrome. Philadelphia: Davis, 1991.

CHAPTER 20–2

Myopathies

Kenneth C. Gorson, M.D.

DEFINITION

A myopathy is a disorder that causes an anatomic or biochemical alteration of muscle.

ETIOLOGY

Myopathy can be broadly divided into hereditary and acquired disorders (Table 20–2–1). Hereditary myopathies include the muscular dystrophies, congenital, metabolic, and mitochrondrial myopathies, myotonic disorders, and periodic paralysis. Inflammatory diseases (polymyositis, dermatomyositis, inclusion-body myositis, sarcoidosis), infections (HIV, trichinosis), toxins and medications, and endocrine disorders constitute the causes of acquired myopathy.

CRITERIA FOR DIAGNOSIS

Suggestive

Myopathy most commonly present with bilateral proximal weakness. Sensation is typically preserved. An elevated creatinine kinase level frequently occurs in the inflammatory myopathies and muscular dystrophies, but is not diagnostic.

Definitive

An electromyogram and muscle biopsy are often necessary to establish the diagnosis. The electromyogram demonstrates "myopathic motor units"—small, short, polyphasic motor unit potentials with early recruitment. Fibrillation potentials and positive sharp waves (spontaneous depolarizations of muscle fibers) may occur in inflammatory myopathy. A muscle biopsy that shows characteristic myopathic changes (discussed later) is diagnostic.

CLINICAL MANIFESTATIONS

Subjective

Patients with myopathy characteristically present with proximal weakness. Weakness is usually bilateral and symmetric, and preferentially affects hip, pelvic, and shoulder girdle muscles. Fatigue is a very common complaint, and many patients have a tendency to confuse excessive fatigability with weakness. Cramps, stiffness, spasm, muscle pain, and changes in muscle size or volume are other presenting symptoms. Many patients complain of difficulty performing common daily activities, such as walking, running, climbing stairs, rising from a toilet or chair, and squatting. When the arms are affected, patients notice difficulty carrying objects, reaching for items on a shelf, combing the hair, or brushing the teeth. Although an occasional patient with polymyositis complains of pain, muscle pain is uncommon in most myopathies. Patients with myotonia, a symptom related to impaired muscle relaxation, may complain of excessive stiffness or impaired mobility.

The tempo of symptoms may be acute (viral myositis, periodic paralysis, electrolyte disturbance), subacute (polymyositis), chronic (Duchenne's dystrophy, endocrine myopathy, inclusion-body myositis), or episodic (periodic paralysis, glycogen storage disease, lipid myopathy). Weakness may be progressive (Duchenne's dystrophy) or static (most congenital myopathies).

Infantile hypotonia, weakness in early childhood, or delayed motor milestones suggest a congenital myopathy or muscular dystrophy. The patient or family members may recall difficulty "keeping up" with peers in routine physical activities. It is important to elicit a careful family history because many myopathies are inherited and accurate diagnosis is imperative for appropriate genetic counseling.

Duchenne's dystrophy is an X-linked recessive disorder that causes proximal weakness in early childhood. Weakness becomes apparent at the age of 3 or 4 as the boy begins to have difficulty running or climbing stairs. A lumbar lordosis with a waddling gait develops due to weakness of the illiopsoas and gluteal muscles. The course is inexorably progressive and most boys are confined to a wheelchair by age 12. Complications include joint contracture, tendon shortening, kyphoscoliosis with associated respiratory compromise, and cardiomyopathy. Becker's dystrophy has many of the features of Duchenne's dystrophy, but the course is milder and children remain ambulatory into the teenage years.

Facioscapulohumeral dystrophy (Landouzy–Dejerine dystrophy) is an autosomal dominant disorder that presents in the first or second decade with slowly progressive weakness of the face, biceps, triceps, and pectoral muscles. Patients may be aware of difficulty whistling or blowing up a balloon. The scapular fixators are also affected, and scapular winging is apparent with attempts at arm elevation or abduction. Leg weakness may develop as the disease progresses with preferential involvement of the hip flexors, quadriceps, and peroneal muscles, often asymmetrically. The disease can be quite variable within affected family members.

Myotonic dystrophy is an autosomal dominant dystrophy that affects several organ systems. The myotonia is painless and is rarely a cause of concern for the patient. Weakness usually begins in teenage life with slow and variably progressive distal hand and leg weakness. Neck muscles are thin and atrophic, producing the typical "swan neck" appearance. Facial weakness is common, and when associated with masseter and temporalis atrophy, produces a long, "hatchet" facies. Proximal muscles become weak over time and falling is a frequent problem in middle age. Cataracts, frontal balding, testicular atrophy and other endocrine abnormalities, sleep disturbances, cardiomyopathy with conduction defects, mental retardation, and cholecystitis are some of the other common manifestations of this disorder.

Limb–girdle dystrophy is a heterogenous group of muscle disorders with autosomal recessive and dominant inheritance patterns. Men and woman are equally affected. Pelvic girdle weakness is the initial symptom and usually begins in the third decade. Shoulder girdle and peroneal muscles may be affected over time, but facial muscles are spared. Occasionally, only one limb may be involved, or weakness is restricted to particular muscle groups, as in quadriceps myopathy. There is tremendous variability in symptom progression.

Exercise intolerance, fatigue, painful cramps, and myoglobinuria are common symptoms of the metabolic myopathies, such as myophosphorylase deficiency (McArdle's disease) and carnitine palmityl transferase deficiency. These myopathies are due to enzymatic deficiencies in muscle that preclude normal energy utilization. McArdle's disease is an autosomal recessive disorder that presents in teenage or young adult years as exercise intolerance. Muscle pain usually develops at the onset of strenuous activity and may be followed by painful muscle spasms. Many observe a "second wind" with resolution of symptoms if they slow down after the onset of pain. Continued activity may be associated with myoglobinuria. Patients are normal between episodes but may develop proximal weakness later in life. Acid maltase deficiency is an autosomal recessive glycogen storage disease with infantile and adult forms. Infants present with hypotonia and an enlarged tongue, heart, and liver. Adults develop insidious hip weakness, which may mimic limb–girdle dystrophy or polymyositis. Diaphragmatic weakness is common in the adult form and may cause respiratory failure.

Polymyositis and dermatomyositis may be idiopathic or associated with connective tissue disease, HIV infection, or carcinoma. One should inquire about the presence of constitutional symptoms, including weight loss, anorexia, malaise, fever, skin rashes, HIV risk factors, and a history of cancer. The onset of proximal weakness is usually insidious and progresses over weeks or months. Other symptoms include arthralgias, exercise-induced pain, neck flexor weakness, and dyspha-

TABLE 20–2–1. DIFFERENTIAL DIAGNOSIS OF MYOPATHY

Hereditary Myopathies
Muscular Dystrophies
Duchenne's
Becker's
Facioscapulohumeral
Limb–girdle
Scapuloperoneal
Oculopharyngeal
Ocular
Hereditary distal of Welander
Emery–Dreifuss
Congenital muscular dystrophy (Fukuyama type)

Congenital Myopathies
Central core
Nemaline rod
Centronuclear (myotubular)
Congenital fiber-type disproportion

Myotonic Disorders
Myotonic dystrophy (Steinert's disease)
Myotonia congenita (Thomsen's disease)
Paramyotonia congenita (von Eulenberg's disease)

Metabolic Myopathies
Glycogen storage disorders
Myophosphorylase deficiency
Phosphofructokinase deficiency
Acid maltase deficiency
Debrancher enzyme deficiency
Phosphoglycerate kinase deficiency
Phosphoglycerate mutase deficiency
Lactate dehydrogenase deficiency
Lipid storage disorders
Carnitine palmityl transferase deficiency
Carnitine deficiency
Myoadenylate deaminase deficiency
Mitochondrial disorders
Kearns–Sayre syndrome
Mitochondrial encephalopathy, myopathy, lactic acidosis, and strokelike episodes (MELAS)
Myoclonic epilepsy and ragged red fibers (MERRF)
Succinic dehydrogenase deficiency
Cytochrome C oxidase deficiency
Leigh's disease

Periodic Paralysis
Hypokalemic
Hyperkalemic
Thyrotoxic

Acquired Myopathies
Endocrine Myopathies
Thyroid disorders
Parathyroid disorders
Adrenal disorders
Pituitary disorders
Electrolyte disturbances

Inflammatory Myopathies
Polymyositis and Dermatomyositis
Idiopathic
Associated with connective tissue disorders
Associated with carcinoma
Associated with HIV
Inclusion-body myositis
Sarcoidosis
Postviral myositis (influenza B)
Toxoplasmosis
Cysticercosis
Trichinosis
Tuberculosis
Pyomyositis (Staphylococcus)

Toxic Myopathies (see Table 20–2–2)

Other Myopathic Conditions
Myopathy of chronic renal failure
Myopathy of critical illness
Vitamin D deficiency
Carcinomatous myopathy
Metastasis
Diabetic muscle infarction
Malignant hyperthermia
Neuroleptic malignant syndrome
Rhabdomyolysis
Muscle rupture and hemorrhage

---

gia, but other cranial nerves are typically spared. The inflammatory myopathy associated with HIV presents with painless proximal weakness early in the illness (the patient may not fulfill criteria for AIDS) and can be acute, subacute, or chronic. A history of a rash is suggestive of dermatomyositis.

The history should be reviewed for endocrine disorders and for exposure to toxins or medications know to cause myopathy (Table 20–2–2). Steroid myopathy is probably the most common medication-induced myopathy and is usually associated with long-term therapy. Weakness is painless and insidious, and affects predominantly proximal leg muscles. Symptoms may appear as early as 4 weeks or as late as 1 year after starting steroid therapy and are not dose dependent. Divided-dose regimens appear to be more toxic than single-dose or alternate-day therapy.

Objective

Physical Examination

Neurologic examination confirms weakness in proximal muscles (biceps, triceps, deltoids, infra/supraspinatus in the arms; illiopsoas, gluteii, hamstrings, and quadriceps in the legs) and possibly neck flexors. Ptosis, opthalmoparesis, or facial weakness may be present in some of the dystrophies and mitochondrial myopathies. Muscle atrophy is usually prominent at later stages and correlates with the severity of muscle weakness. Children with Duchenne's or Becker's dystrophy may demonstrate a paradoxical enlargement of the calf muscles related to replacement of muscle with connective tissue or fat (pseudohypertrophy). Reflexes are reduced or absent in proportion to the degree of limb weakness, but sensation is preserved. Patients with significant proximal hip and paraspinal muscle weakness may develop a characteristic waddling gait. In patients with mild symptoms, weakness may be detected only with functional testing; it may be necessary to observe the patient arise from a chair, noting whether there is a need to use the arms, climb stairs, or squat. Patients may have trouble arising from the floor unassisted (Gower's sign). Myotonia is demonstrated by percussion over a muscle or following vigorous voluntary muscle contraction. This produces a sustained contraction with delayed relaxation for several seconds and is characteristic of all myotonic disorders—myotonic dystrophy, myotonia congenita, and paramyotonia congenita (von Eulenberg's disease). This should be contrasted with myoedema, a ridge of muscle contraction produced after tapping a muscle, which is observed in patients with myxedema. Joint contractures may be prominent in Emery–Dreifuss dystrophy or end-stage Duchenne's dystrophy. In dermatomyositis, there is a purple rash over the eyelids (heliotrope) or in a butterfly distribution over the cheek and bridge of the nose. A rash may also develop over the extensor surfaces of the arms, the knuckles, or the pretibial region. There may be small hemorrhages or dilated capillary loops around the nail beds. Soft tissue calcification may occur as the disease progresses.

TABLE 20–2–2. MEDICATIONS AND TOXINS THAT INDUCE MYOPATHY

alcohol	lovastatin
aminocaproic acid	meperidine
amiodarone hydrochloride	mepivacaine
amphetamines	metoprolol
barbiturates	minoxidil
cimetidine	niacin
clofibrate	penicillamine
chloroquine, hydroxychloroquine	penicillin
cocaine	pentazocine
colchicine	perhexilene
corticosteroids	phencyclidine
cyclosporin A	phenylbutazone
diethyl ether	phenytoin
emetine	propranolol
enalapril	propylthiouracil
ethyl chloride	procainamide
ethylene	rifampin
etretinate	succinylcholine
gemfibrozil	sulfonamides
halothane	trichlorethylene
heroin	tryptophan
labetolol	vincristine
lidocaine	zidovudine (AZT)

Inclusion-body myositis is a slowly progressive adult-onset inflammatory myopathy that is often confused with polymyositis. Weakness and atrophy can be asymmetric. The quadriceps and finger flexes can be severely affected, and distal muscles are frequently affected as the disorder progresses.

Routine Laboratory Abnormalities

The creatinine kinase (CK) level is frequently elevated in myopathy and related to muscle fiber damage. The degree of elevation is variable, and a normal CK does not exclude myopathy as a diagnostic possibility. The CK may be elevated 10-fold or more in the muscular dystrophies, rhabdomyolysis, or polymyositis, but may be normal in steroid- or other medication-induced myopathy, endocrinopathies, inclusion-body myositis, or any chronic "end-stage" myopathy. The CK can be elevated for several hours after exercise in normal individuals. Lactate dehydrogenase and aspartate and alanine transaminase levels may also be elevated in patients with active muscle destruction (Table 20–2–3).

Because a myopathy may be the only clinical evidence of an endocrine or electrolyte disorder, calcium, magnesium, sodium, potassium, and phosphorus levels should be assessed. The sedimentation rate is frequently elevated in polymyositis and dermatomyositis.

PLANS
Diagnostic

Differential Diagnosis

The differential diagnosis of proximal weakness spans disorders of the neuromuscular junction, motor nerve, nerve root, motor neuron, and central nervous system (spinal cord and brain). The most common disorders that simulate myopathic weakness are myasthenia gravis, chronic inflammatory demyelinating polyneuropathy, polyradiculopathy from disk disease, lumbar stenosis, diabetes (diabetic amyotrophy), and progressive spinal muscular atrophy. Amyotrophic lateral sclerosis may rarely present with proximal weakness. Some of the less common disorders that present with proximal weakness include botulism, Eaton–Lambert myasthenic syndrome, porphyria, and arsenic intoxication. Spinal cord compression and parasagittal brain lesions (meningioma, bilateral watershed infarction, hydrocephalus) can cause proximal arm and leg weakness, but the presence of spasticity, hyperreflexia,

TABLE 20–2–3. EVALUATION OF PATIENTS WITH MYOPATHY

Laboratory Testing
Routine Studies
Sodium, potassium, calcium, magnesium, phosphorus
Creatine kinase, lactate dehydrogenase, alanine, and aspartate transaminase levels
Erythrocyte sedimentation rate
Blood urea nitrogen and creatinine levels
Thyroid function tests
Additional Studies
Serum parathyroid hormone, cortisol
24-Hour urine for 17-ketosteroids
Dexamethasone suppression test
Antinuclear antibody, rheumatoid factor, and complement levels; anti-Sjögren's syndrome antigen A and B, anti-DNA, anti-ribonucleoprotein, and anticentromere antibodies
Antineutrophil cytoplasmic antibody
Angiotensin-converting enzyme level
Anti-Jo-1 antibody
HIV titer
Serum and cerebrospinal fluid lactate
Urine porphyrin screen
Urine heavy metal screen
Urine for myoglobin
Toxin screen

Special Studies
Ischemic forearm exercise testing (metabolic myopathies)
Electromyographic and nerve conduction studies
Repetitive nerve stimulation
Muscle biopsy
Cardiac echo, Holter monitoring (some dystrophies)

and Babinski signs should direct the clinician to a central nervous system disorder. Table 20–2–1 lists the differential diagnosis of myopathy.

Diagnostic Options

Additional laboratory testing should include thyroid function tests, a parathyroid level in patients with an elevated serum calcium, and a cortisol level in patients suspected of having adrenal insufficiency. Cushing's disease should be excluded with a dexamethasone suppression test or 24-hour urine collection for 17-ketosteroids in selected patients. Evaluation for autoimmune disorders associated with poly/dermatomyositis should include antinuclear antibody, rheumatoid factor, complement levels, Sjögren's syndrome antigen A and B antibodies, anti-DNA, antiribonucleoprotein, anticentromere, and antineutrophil cytoplasmic antibodies, and an angiotensin-converting enzyme level. Anti-Jo-1 antibodies may be found in patients with polymyositis and interstitial lung disease. An HIV titer should be obtained if risk factors are present. In patients suspected of having a metabolic myopathy, ischemic forearm exercise testing helps establish the diagnosis by demonstrating a normal serum lactate during ischemic exercise. The presence of myoglobinuria may point to a glycogen or lipid storage myopathy. The serum or cerebrospinal fluid lactate may be elevated in mitochondrial myopathies. Urinary porphyrin, heavy metal, and toxin screen may be indicated in some instances.

Muscle biopsy is diagnostic of myopathy in clinically affected muscles and frequently suggests a specific etiology. Myopathic abnormalities include variation in muscle fiber size, internal nuclei, fiber splitting, moth-eaten fibers, and fibrosis. Endomysial inflammatory infiltrates associated with muscle fiber necrosis are characteristic of polymyositis. In dermatomyositis, the inflammatory infiltrates are perivascular and associated with perifascicular atrophy. Basophilic "rimmed" vacuoles and eosinophilic cytoplasmic inclusions are observed in inclusion-body myositis. "Ragged red fibers" (named for the characteristic staining with trichome) are observed in the mitochondrial myopathies and AZT myopathy. Prominent basophilic fibers and muscle fibrosis are common in Duchenne's dystrophy, and muscle dystrophin can be assayed to establish a definitive diagnosis. In myotonic dystrophy, there are numerous internal nuclei and "ring" fibers. The glycogen and lipid storage myopathies can be diagnosed with special enzyme staining. Type II fiber atrophy is frequently associated with steroid myopathy, but this finding is not specific and can be seen in any systemic illness that causes immobilization and disuse of the affected muscle.

Recommended Approach

Electromyography should be performed as part of the initial evaluation of myopathy. Motor neuron disease, polyradiculopathy, chronic inflammatory demyelinating polyneuropathy and other neuropathies, and myasthenia gravis can usually be differentiated from the electrophysiologic changes observed in myopathy. In particular, a normal response to repetitive nerve stimulation can help exclude myasthenia. In addition, the electromyogram is typically normal in polymyalgia rheumatica and other painful rheumatologic or orthopedic conditions, which may simulate myopathic weakness. Abnormal spontaneous activity (fibrillation potentials) is commonly observed in poly/dermatomyositis, facioscapulohumeral dystrophy, and some metabolic myopathies. The electrophysiologic hallmark of a myopathy is motor unit potentials that are small, short, and polyphasic in configuration.

A muscle biopsy should be obtained in patients in whom an electromyogram demonstrates a myopathy but a more definitive diagnosis cannot be established. This is particularly important in patients suspected of having poly/dermatomyositis because treatment may alter the course of the disease. Patients suspected of having a muscular dystrophy should have a muscle biopsy to establish a definitive diagnosis, allow for appropriate genetic counseling, and facilitate frank discussions regarding prognosis. Muscles that are moderately affected may yield the most diagnostic information, but severely affected muscles may show "end-stage" changes and should be avoided. The quadriceps are most commonly chosen.

Therapeutic

Therapeutic Options

Although there have been no well performed therapeutic trials in poly/dermatomyositis, immune modulating therapy is frequently employed. Corticosteroids are often the treatment of first choice, and azathioprine may be added for its steroid-sparing effects. Alternative immunosuppressant therapies include methotrexate, cyclophosphamide, cyclosporine, intravenous gamma globulin, and total lymphoid irradiation.

The treatment of HIV myopathy remains controversial and includes the use of nonsteroidal antiinflammatory agents, prednisone, plasma exchange, gamma globulin, and decreasing or discontinuing antiretroviral medications.

Recommended Approach

There is no specific therapy for Duchenne's or Becker's dystrophy. Physical therapy, night splints, and bracing are useful to prevent contractures and other complications of prolonged immobilization. Tendon release may also help delay contractures. Spinal surgery is increasingly used to minimize pulmonary complications and the extreme discomfort associated with progressive scoliosis. Recent trials have suggested that prednisone (0.75 mg/kg) may slow the progression of weakness, but side effects frequently prohibit long-term use. Cardiac conduction abnormalities are common in patients with Emery–Dreifuss and myotonic dystrophy and may require a cardiac pacemaker.

Treatment of the other muscular dystrophies is largely supportive. Ankle foot orthoses are beneficial in patients with foot drop. Dysphagia can be managed successfully with a pureed diet, but occasionally a gastrostomy tube is required. Myotonia can be diminished with phenytoin (100–300 mg/d), quinine (300–900 mg/d), procainamide (500–1500 mg/d), tocainamide (400–1200 mg/d), or acetazolamide (250–1000 mg/d), but the beneficial effects often wane after several months.

There is no effective therapy for the metabolic or mitochondrial myopathies. Patients with glycogen or lipid storage disorders should be instructed to avoid activities that precipitate myoglobinuria. Patients can

be taught to recognize the "second-wind" phenomenon and, with special training, can learn to slow down at the onset of symptoms and then resume activity in small increments.

Myopathies attributed to electrolyte or endocrine disorders improve with appropriate treatment of the underlying disorder. Medications or toxins known to induce myopathies (Table 20–2–2) should be discontinued. Weakness usually resolves when the offending agent is removed, but recovery may be prolonged.

Patients with polymyositis or dermatomyositis should be started on prednisone 80 to 100 mg/d in a single morning dose. This should be continued for several months until the weakness has resolved or improvement has plateaued for several weeks. The patient can be converted to alternate-day therapy over 2 to 3 months and then tapered slowly (5–10 mg/m). If weakness returns, the initial dose should be reinitiated. Patients need to be informed about the myriad side effects associated with the long-term administration of corticosteroids. The concomitant use of H_2-receptor blockers or antacids, vitamin D, and calcium should be considered. Because of associated side effects, it is reasonable to start azathioprine (50 mg/d, escalating the dose to a total of 1–2 mg/kg/d) with prednisone at the outset of therapy in older patients. If there is no response to steroids or side effects become prohibitive, a trial of intravenous gamma globulin (400 mg/kg/d for 5 days, followed by monthly "boosters" of 1000 mg/kg/d for 1–2 days) is warranted. If symptoms persist, successive trials of cyclophosphamide (2 mg/kg/d), methotrexate (2.5 mg three times daily for 3 weeks, then increasing by 2.5 mg/wk to a total of 25 mg/wk), and cyclosporine (5–10 mg/kg/d, monitoring trough levels at 100–250 ng/mL) should be offered, but the response is variable. Total lymphoid irradiation should be reserved for patients who are severely disabled and have failed all other therapeutic trials.

The myopathy associated with AIDS may be related to primary HIV infection or treatment with AZT. It is prudent to discontinue AZT for several weeks and observe for improvement; if weakness is severe, full recovery may not occur. If strength improves, AZT should be replaced with another antiretroviral agent. If the patient's strength worsens or fails to improve, AZT should be reinstituted along with a trial of prednisone (40–60 mg/d) or plasma exchange.

There is no proven effective therapy for inclusion-body myositis, and frequently the diagnosis is considered only after patients with "polymyositis" fail to respond to steroids. There are occasional patients who respond to steroids and an empiric trial is warranted in patients with significant disability. Intravenous gamma globulin has been reported to be helpful in some patients.

FOLLOW-UP

Changes in strength should be routinely recorded at follow-up visits so that response to therapy can be adequately assessed. Patients prescribed steroids for poly/dermatomyositis should be evaluated initially every 4 to 6 weeks. Although a rise in the CK may occur with a relapse, it is more important to follow the clinical response than to "chase" CK values. Improved function is often the best clinical parameter to follow. A steroid myopathy may develop after several months of therapy and differentiation from a relapse can be difficult. In steroid myopathy the neck flexors are usually spared and the CK level and electromyogram are normal. There are patients in whom differentiation is not possible and an arbitrary decision to raise or lower the steroid dosage needs to be made. The answer is usually evident in the next 1 to 2 months according to the change in the patient's clinical status.

Patients with an endocrine, medication, or toxic myopathy generally have a slower response to treatment and can be followed every 3 to 6 months. Similarly, the metabolic myopathies and muscular dystrophies are static or very slowly progressive and follow-up should be individualized accordingly.

DISCUSSION

Prevalence and Incidence

The most common myopathy is Duchenne's muscular dystrophy, with an incidence of 20 to 30 per 100,000 and a prevalence of 3 per 100,000 in liveborn males. Becker's dystrophy is approximately 5 to 10 times less frequent than Duchenne's dystrophy. The most common adult muscle disorder is myotonic dystrophy, with an incidence of 15 per 100,000 and a prevalence of 5 per 100,000; it is 3 to 5 times more common than facioscapulohumeral dystrophy. By contrast, polymyositis is a relatively uncommon disorder with an incidence of approximately 1 in 100,000. The frequency of the congenital, mitochrondrial, metabolic, endocrine, and toxic myopathies is unknown.

Related Basic Science

The pathogenesis of Duchenne's and Becker's dystrophies has been linked to the deficiency or alteration of the protein dystrophin. The dystrophin gene, one of the largest human genes, is located on the short arm of the X chromosome. There is an absolute deficiency of this protein in children afflicted with Duchenne's dystrophy, whereas in the Becker variant, the protein is present in normal quantities but is functionally altered. Dystrophin has been localized to the muscle membrane but its specific function is unknown.

The pathophysiology of the myotonic dystrophies has been attributed to abnormal excitability of the muscle membrane. In myotonic dystrophy there is altered phosphorylation of skeletal muscle ion channels, which has been linked to a protein kinase defect. This defective protein kinase may modulate proteins that occur in other tissues and may explain the frequent extramuscular manifestations of this disorder.

The metabolic myopathies can be divided into disorders of carbohydrate, lipid, and mitochondrial function. The glycogen storage disorders are due to enzyme deficiencies (myophosphorylase, phosphofructokinase, acid maltase, debrancher enzyme, lactase dehydrogenase, to name but a few) which disrupt the generation of ATP along different points in the Kreb cycle. This impairs glycogen use and produces exercise-related symptoms during strenuous or short-term activity. Carnitine palmityl transferase deficiency is the most common lipid storage myopathy. This enzyme effects the linkage of carnitine to long-chain fatty acids across the mitochondrial membrane. In carnitine palmityl transferase deficiency, fatty acids cannot be converted to acetyl coenzyme A to enter the Kreb cycle and thus are unable to release energy to muscle in the setting of sustained exercise.

The pathogenesis of the inflammatory myopathies is an autoimmune attack targeting muscle fibers or the microvasculature. In dermatomyositis, there is B-cell activation of the complement pathway initiated by antibodies bound to small blood vessels. Inflammatory cells infiltrate capillaries and produce ischemia, necrosis, and muscle fiber destruction characteristic of vasculitis. In contrast, the primary immune mechanism in polymyositis is mediated by cytotoxic T cells directed against the major histocompatibility complex on muscle fibers. The pathogenesis of HIV myositis in unknown, as the virus has not been isolated from muscle fibers, but patients may have inflammatory infiltrates on muscle biopsy. AZT myopathy is attributed to disruption of mitochondrial function. Muscle biopsy shows subsarcolemmal accumulations of mitochondria (ragged red fibers), which is characteristic of other mitochondrial myopathies.

Natural History and Its Modification with Treatment

The natural history of the myopathies is variable and related to the specific etiology of each disorder. Patients with Duchenne's dystrophy may live into the second or third decade, but ultimately succumb to complications of respiratory or cardiac failure. Patients with a metabolic myopathy or myotonic, facioscapulohumeral, or limb–girdle dystrophy may have a normal lifespan despite progressive weakness and variable disability. The prognosis of untreated polymyositis or dermatomyositis is poor, with mortality as high as 50%. Most patients experience significant clinical improvement with the administration of corticosteroids. Poor prognostic factors include associated malignancy, a fulminant course, cardiac or pulmonary involvement, and failure to respond to steroids.

Prevention

Prevention of the muscular dystrophies and the congenital, metabolic, and mitochondrial myopathies depends on appropriate genetic counseling. Early detection of an endocrine disorder and avoidance of medications associated with myopathy are important preventive measures. The diagnosis of HIV, malignancy, sarcoidosis, and connective tissue disorders associated with polymyositis may delay the development of further disability.

Cost Containment

Costs can be contained by ensuring that patients suspected of having a myopathy are evaluated by physicians with experience in the diagnosis and management of this disorder. Duplication of blood tests by the primary care physician and specialist should be avoided. Electrophysiologic testing unfortunately needs to be repeated in many patients because of an inadequate or incorrectly interpreted initial study; electromyograms and muscle biopsies should be performed and interpreted by qualified individuals with an expertise in neuromuscular disorders.

REFERENCES

Adams RD, Victor M. Principles of clinical myology: Diagnosis and classification of muscle diseases. In: Adams RD, Victor M, eds. Principles of neurology. 5th ed. New York: McGraw-Hill, 1993:1184.

Brooke MH. Disorders of skeletal muscle: In: Bradely WG, Daroff RB, Fenichel GM, Marsden CD, eds. Neurology in clinical practice, Boston: Butterworth-Heinmann, 1991:1843.

Dalakas MC. Clinical, immunopathologic, and therapeutic considerations of inflammatory myopathies. Clin Neuropharmacol 1992;15:327.

Kimura J. Myopathies. In: Kimura J, ed. Electrodiagnosis in diseases of nerve and muscle. 2nd ed. Philadelphia: Davis, 1989:535.

Mendell JR, Griggs RC. Inherited, metabolic, endocrine, and toxic myopathies. In: Isselbacher KJ, Braunwald E, Wilson JD, eds. Harrison's textbook of medicine. 13th ed. Boston: McGraw-Hill, 1994:2359.

Ptacek LJ, Johnson KJ, Griggs RC. Genetics and physiology of myotonic muscle disorders. N Engl J Med 1993;328:482.

CHAPTER 20–3

Myasthenia Gravis

David H. Weinberg, M.D.

DEFINITION

Myasthenia gravis (MG) is a disorder of neuromuscular junction function characterized by fatigable muscle weakness. The specific pattern of muscle involvement can often be a central feature of diagnosis.

ETIOLOGY

The antibody-mediated destruction of the nicotinic acetylcholine receptors found on the neuromuscular junction's postsynaptic membrane is the underlying pathophysiology of MG. The communication between normal nerve impulses and muscle fibers is impaired or lost, with weakness being the clinical correlate.

CRITERIA FOR DIAGNOSIS
Suggestive

The development of fatigable weakness sparing all sensory functions should raise the possibility of MG. The weakness can involve ocular, bulbar, truncal, and/or limb muscles, but involvement in extraocular or eyelid muscles is seen in about 50% of patients at the time of presentation and in close to 90% at some time during the course of the illness. Supportive data discovered during the workup can include improvement in the strength of a clearly weak muscle following edrophonium infusion and a decremental response of a single nerve on repetitive nerve stimulation.

Definitive

The presence of weakness (usually fatigable) without sensory abnormalities is necessary although not sufficient to make the diagnosis of MG. Elevated titers of acetylcholine receptor antibodies are strongly correlated with this disease. The rare false-positive tests are seen in other autoimmune disease, usually with high titers of other autoantibodies. Unfortunately, the sensitivity of this test in mild MG is not high, ranging from about 50 to 75% depending on the patient's symptoms and signs. Abnormal repetitive nerve stimulation in at least two nerves with an otherwise normal electrodiagnostic study is strong evidence of MG. An abnormal single-fiber electromyography test is of somewhat higher sensitivity and should be done if the acetylcholine receptor antibody test and the conventional electrodiagnostic tests (including repetitive nerve stimulation) are normal.

CLINICAL MANIFESTATIONS
Subjective

Weakness is the defining symptom of MG, although the patient may not identify it as such. For example, a patient may complain of double vision, difficulty swallowing, slurring of speech, or even a change in gait. Impairments in motor function potentially involve five regions: ocular, bulbar, respiratory, axial, and limb muscles. The major associated symptoms are outlined in Table 20–3–1. Identifying the fatigable nature of these complaints is a critical component of the interview process. It may be task specific (such as slurring of speech after a long phone conversation) or the cumulative effect of a day's activity (evening diplopia). Equally important is the absence of certain symptoms such as numbness, paresthesias, prominent pain, or cognitive problems.

The past history of patients who develop MG is usually unremarkable. Some patients have concurrent autoimmune disease, hyperthyroidism being the most common.

Myasthenia gravis is not an inherited disease; however, like many autoimmune diseases, the susceptibility for the development of the illness is influenced by the patient's HLA status, which is genetically transmitted. Often there is a family history of other autoimmune disorders, presumably from this association.

Objective
Physical Examination

The neuromuscular examination of patients with weakness is a critical step in the process of the diagnostic evaluation. The major muscle groups must be systematically studied for both weakness and fatigability. Equally important is a complete medical and neurologic examination focusing on the key elements in the differential diagnosis for the specific presenting complaints. For example, when the presenting complaint is diplopia, identifying proptosis, orbital engorgement, and pupillary changes will guide the diagnostician to the correct diagnosis of cavernous sinus thrombosis.

Several specific patterns of muscle involvement are worthy of mention. Ptosis and facial weakness are common concomitants. This combination of difficulty both opening and closing the eyes is very suggestive of MG. When fatigable ptosis can be demonstrated on sustained eye elevation, the diagnosis is secure. On occasion, bilateral ptosis is not evident when it is present. This is due to the symmetric bilateral central nervous system eyelid innervation that elevates the mildly weak side to a normal position. Forehead "wrinkling" at rest is a useful clue to excessive elevation drive that can be demonstrated by passively closing the ptotic eye and observing for lid depression on the "normal" side.

Ophthalmoplegia is also common. The combinations of involved eye muscles can occasionally simulate an ocular motor nerve palsy or a central nervous system abnormality (such as an intranuclear ophthalmoplegia). Red glass testing is at times necessary to objectify the symptom of diplopia and delineate the distribution of eye muscle weakness.

Some patients, particularly in the late-onset group, present with predominantly bulbar problems. The symptoms of dysarthria, dysphagia, and shortness of breath are difficult to objectify at the bedside. A rough vital capacity measure can be obtained by determining the highest number count a patient can generate on a single maximal breath. Each ten superficially corresponds with a liter of vital capacity. The use of accessory muscles can be another clue to diaphragmatic weakness. No function rivals respiratory insufficiency for rapid, potentially catastrophic deteriorations and careful intensive care unit monitoring is critical for safe management.

Axial muscle involvement is most often identified as weakness in neck flexors or, less often, extensors. Neck pain may be the only complaint.

The weakness of extremity muscles can be quite variable but they are infrequently the only muscles involved in generalized MG. It is important to distinguish the sense of malaise or "asthenia" from a true impairment of muscle power. MG patients usually describe the internal energy or drive to perform an action but without adequate muscle strength. Proximal muscles are more often involved than distal groups, although all can be weak or fatigable. Functional tests of stronger muscles, such as deep knee bends and kneeling, can be more effective than bedside strength determination.

Routine Laboratory Abnormalities

Routine laboratory tests are normal in MG. The specialty testing appropriate for the evaluations of these patients is discussed under Plans, Diagnostic.

PLANS
Diagnostic
Differential Diagnosis

The medical conditions to consider when a patient presents with weakness to large degree depend on the distribution of the involved muscles. When the cranial musculature is involved, intracranial mass lesions and botulism need to be considered. Hyperthyroid ophthalmopathy and progressive external ophthalmoplegia present with altered extraocular movements. The congenital myasthenic syndromes present with early-onset but static fatigable weakness. Drug-induced myasthenia is temporally associated with the use of specific agents. Other disorders occasionally confused with myasthenia gravis include idiopathic cranial neuropathies, Guillian–Barré syndrome, brainstem cerebrovascular disease, and polymyositis.

Diagnostic Options

The neurologic examination is the critical diagnostic first step in the diagnostic evaluation in MG patients. The patient's symptoms and signs

TABLE 20–3–1. DISTRIBUTION OF MUSCLE INVOLVEMENT

Ocular
Bulbar
Respiratory
Axial
Extremity

determine the relevant differential diagnosis and the direction of the testing. Appropriate diagnostic studies often include an edrophonium test, thyroid functions tests, acetylcholine receptor antibody and/or antistriational antibody levels, brainstem and orbital magnetic resonance imaging scans, chest computed tomography scan, nerve conduction studies, repetitive motor nerve stimulation, and single-fiber electromyography.

Recommended Approach

The diagnostic workup for MG is generally done in the outpatient setting, with the only exception being myasthenic crisis (which requires urgent hospitalization, usually to an intensive care unit setting). When the clinical findings are localized to a single region, the first step in testing is to exclude an anatomic lesion. This is most relevant with ocular MG, where lesions in the cavernous sinus, adjacent cranial roots, or brainstem have been reported to simulate this disorder. A magnetic resonance imaging scan of this region is the appropriate study. An edrophonium test is recommended only if there is a quantifiable and reproducible region of muscle weakness that can be monitored during the course of the test. A double-blind protocol with atropine premedication (0.4 mg intravenous push) is strongly recommended to minimize subjective impressions. Acetylcholine receptor antibody levels and thyroid function tests should be done at this time. If the edrophonium and acetylcholine receptor antibody tests are not clearly positive, nerve conduction studies with repetitive nerve stimulation testing are necessary. Single-fiber electromyography of an arm and/or face muscle is indicated if the diagnosis remains uncertain.

If MG is strongly suspected, a chest computed tomography scan should be done to exclude a thymoma, even in the pure ocular cases.

Additional tests that may be necessary based on specific symptoms or signs include pulmonary function tests and swallowing testing with videofluoroscopy.

Therapeutic

Therapeutic Options

Therapy for MG can be divided into four groups: symptomatic treatments (Table 20–3–2); immunosuppressive medications (Table 20–3–3); short-term immunosuppressant treatments; surgical thymectomy.

The *anticholinesterase drugs* improve strength by improving neuromuscular junction transmission without altering the autoimmune disorder. They are therefore useful only to lessen symptoms and are usually used in combination with another form of more substantive treatment. On higher doses, cholinergic excess can cause paradoxical weakness and be confused with an MG exacerbation.

Prednisone and azathioprine remain the main immunosuppressive medications for MG. The selection of the specific agent depends on the goals of therapy. High-dose daily corticosteroids are both effective and rapid in onset of action. The legion of both short- and long-term potential side effects with these drugs are well known. Additionally, high-dose daily corticosteroids can cause a transient, potentially severe exacerbation of weakness in about a quarter of patients during the first week of treatment. Fortunately, alternate-day prednisone is often effective, minimizing some toxicity.

Azathioprine is an effective drug but usually requires 3 to 12 months of use prior to the onset of a therapeutic benefit. It can be used alone in mild cases or added as a steroid-sparing drug to allow tapering to the minimal tolerated prednisone dose. The main complications involve bone marrow suppression and altered liver function.

TABLE 20–3–2. SYMPTOMATIC MEDICATIONS

Generic Name	Proprietary Name	Maximal Dose	Side Effects
Pyridostigmine bromide	Mestinon Mestinon Timespan	120 mg q3h 180 mg hs	Asthma, diarrhea, nausea, abdominal cramps, bronchial secretions, increasing weakness (overdose)
Neostigmine	Prostigmin	30 mg q3h	Same as above

Cyclosporine has only recently been introduced in the treatment of MG for refractory cases and those intolerant of corticosteroids. The major toxicity involves renal insufficiency and hypertension.

Short-term *immunosuppressant treatments* include plasma exchange and intravenous gamma globulin. Both promote rapid improvement in muscle weakness. Although these treatments are known to alter the function of the immune system, the actual mechanism of action is not clear. Their main indications in MG include myasthenic crisis, other less severe exacerbations, and preparation of a weak patient for thymectomy. Both are expensive and have a limited role in maintenance therapy for some difficult patients.

Thymectomy is felt to be the only therapy for MG that offers a significant chance for a drug-free remission. Additionally, the procedure is essential in those patients with thymomas for removal of the neoplasm. There is general agreement that the transsternal technique allows the most complete thymus resection. Maximal thymic tissue removal and early surgery appear to maximize the therapeutic benefits.

Recommended Approach

Ocular or Mild Generalized Myasthenia Gravis. For most patients with pure ocular or very mild generalized MG, symptomatic treatment alone is appropriate. Occasionally, the disabling symptom of diplopia justifies immunosuppressive drugs, but for the most part these medications are reserved for significant generalized MG. Thymectomy is reserved for those patients suspected of harboring a thymoma.

Generalized Myasthenia Gravis. There is general agreement that a surgical thymectomy is indicated as the initial substantive treatment for patients with significant *generalized MG* between puberty and about 50 years of age, as well as all patients with a thymoma. If the weakness is severe or respiratory insufficiency is present, the postoperative course can be very unstable and pretreatment with either plasma exchange or intravenous gamma globulin is recommended. Occasionally, preoperative prednisone is necessary but it would be preferable to avoid immunosuppressive treatments at this point in therapy. If a patient is already on prednisone or azathioprine, tapering trials should begin only when postoperative stability is ensured. In some cases, thymectomy is considered for patients over 50 years of age when excellent general health implies prolonged survival.

When thymectomy is deferred or ineffective, immunosuppressive treatments (Table 20–3–3) are often necessary. In the elderly with moderate or severe disease, one approach is to add both prednisone and azathioprine simultaneously. The prednisone is used for its rapid onset of therapeutic benefit and the azathioprine for its long-term effectiveness and steroid-sparing effect. The benefits of high-dose prednisone are often seen within about 2 weeks, whereas for azathioprine, they may be delayed 3 to 12 months. High-dose daily prednisone must be started on an inpatient basis because, as previously mentioned, some patients experience a transient but potentially severe exacerbation in the first week of therapy. If a delay in the therapeutic benefit can be tolerated, azathioprine alone or an alternate-day prednisone regimen is an excellent alternative for any age group.

Following thymectomy, major weakness is usually treated with the addition of high-dose steroids alone, as a slow steroid taper is more likely to be tolerated without a relapse. Azathioprine should be added when it is clear a steroid taper will not be possible. Cyclosporine and cyclophosphamide are reserved for the intractable cases that have not tolerated or benefited from the above regimens.

High-dose prednisone treatment begins with a dose of approximately 1 mg/kg. When clinical stability is achieved, patients often tolerate switching directly to 1.5 mg/kg every other day (up to a maximum of 100 mg every other day). The technique of steroid taper is critically important in the treatment of MG. One of the major management errors is an excessively rapid prednisone taper promoting relapses. An effective initial taper schedule is a 5-mg every-other-day drop every 2 to 4 weeks until 40-mg every-other-day dose is reached, followed by decreases of 2.5 mg every other day.

Late-onset Myasthenia Gravis. Patients with late-onset generalized MG often present with unstable bulbar disease. High-dose corticosteroids are often needed to prevent aspiration and/or respiratory insufficiency.

TABLE 20–3–3. IMMUNOSUPPRESSIVE MEDICATIONS

Generic Name	Proprietary Name	Side Effects	Recommended Monitoring	Drug Interactions
Prednisone		Weight gain, peptic ulcer disease, hypokalemia, osteoporosis, osteonecrosis of hip, myopathy, glucose intolerance, behavior change, cataracts, infections, pituitary suppression, reactivation of tuberculosis among others	Periodic glucose monitoring (urine or serum) + electrolytes; evaluate symptoms of others rapidly (i.e., infection, hip pain)	
Azathioprine	Imuran	Bone marrow suppression, hepatic dysfunction, idiosyncratic reactions, gastrointestinal upset, hematologic malignancies?, infections	Frequent: complete blood count with differential Infrequent: liver function tests	Allopurinol, rifampin, phenytoin, phenobarbital
Cyclosporine	Sandimmune	Nephropathy, hypertension, hirsutism, neurotoxicity, hepatic dysfunction, thromboembolism, infections, secondary malignancies?	Frequent: blood pressure, blood urea nitrogen/creatinine, liver function tests	Ketoconazole, verapamil, erythromycin, nicardipine, diltiazem, prednisolone, miconazole, danazol, itraconazole, drugs altering microsomal enzymes
Cyclophosphamide	Cytoxan	Bone marrow suppression, hepatic dysfunction, infections, gastrointestinal upset, acute hemorrhagic cystitis, infertility, secondary malignancies?, alopecia	Frequent: complete blood count with differential, urinalysis Infrequent: liver function tests	Allopurinol, rifampin, phenytoin, phenobarbital

It is important to hospitalize such patients for careful observation during the initiation of therapy. As outlined above, azathioprine is usually added to maximize the success of early prednisone tapering. The corticosteroid complication rate is very high with these patients and azathioprine is generally well tolerated. The use of plasma exchange and intravenous gamma globulin can be of benefit in severe decompensations but they have special risks in the elderly patient, especially when cardiovascular or renal compromise are present.

Myasthenic Crisis. Treatment for this life-threatening illness requires careful monitoring in an intensive care unit, often with ventilator support. Plasma exchange and intravenous gamma globulin are particularly effective in this setting due to their brief therapeutic latency. Unfortunately, the benefits are short lived (usually weeks), but the rapid stabilization allows other therapies to contribute (especially prednisone).

FOLLOW-UP

The frequency of monitoring depends on the intensity of the symptoms and treatments. An unstable patient may need to be seen weekly while another patient with few problems can be evaluated yearly. Each immunosuppressive medication discussed in the treatment of MG is included in Table 20–3–3 with a listing of the potential complications and recommended monitoring. High-dose prednisone requires particularly close supervision for complications such as diabetes, hypertension, infections, reactivation of tuberculosis, and osteoporosis.

DISCUSSION

Prevalence and Incidence

Myasthenia gravis has an overall incidence of about 4 cases per million and a prevalence of about 40 per million population. There are, however, two age groups with an increased incidence and a sex association. The first consists of young women with a peak incidence in the third decade, and the second is more heavily represented by men with a peak incidence in the seventh decade.

Related Basic Science

The autoimmune destruction of the acetylcholine receptors on the postsynaptic membrane is the etiology of MG. The process that initiates the aberrant immune response is unknown, but the thymus gland appears to be critical for both the autoimmune activation and the maintenance of the activated autoimmune state. Pathologically, the gland is usually abnormal with either thymic hyperplasia or a thymic neoplasm. The hyperplastic gland contains so-called "germinal centers" consisting of mature, activated lymphocytes specific for acetylcholine receptor epitopes. There is a developing consensus that myoid cells found in the interstitium of the thymus gland contain the acetylcholine receptors that serve as the antigen in the aberrant immune response.

The aberrant autoimmune response involves both the efferent and afferent limbs of the immune system. The activated B lymphocytes produce the receptor-specific antibodies, but the role of the helper T cells (CD4-positive cells) in the activation and amplification of the antigen-specific immune response appears critical. This latter process also requires the participation of the major histocompatibility complex class II molecules and antigen presenting cells.

The acetylcholine receptor antibodies are heterogeneous, recognizing many different epitopes of the large, multisubunit acetylcholine receptor. The majority bind to a region on the alpha subunit referred to as the "main immunologic region." The commercially available serum acetylcholine receptor antibody test is normal in 10 to 20% of patients with clear autoimmune MG. The immunologic abnormalities of this group are not different from those of the antibody-positive patients and antibody status does not alter treatment response.

Natural History and Its Modification with Treatment

The natural history of MG is not clearly delineated. The early studies were limited by the absence of a reliable diagnostic test, and the later studies were contaminated by inconsistent treatment programs. It is generally felt that the course of the illness tends to be defined in the first several years of illness. This is true both for the risk of developing generalized MG from a pure ocular onset and for the severity of relapses in established generalized MG.

Spontaneous remissions without treatment must be rare, as are drug-free remissions following immunosuppressive medication treatment alone. Thymectomy is felt to induce some drug-free remissions, although no controlled trials have been done and none are likely for the future.

Prevention

Early treatment may improve the chance of a drug-free remission but prevention is not possible.

Cost Containment

The appropriate workup and treatment of MG can be expensive; however, the cost of an incorrect diagnosis or unidentified thymoma is even greater. Patients with malaise and fatigue should not receive these studies or treatments; however, the outlined approach is cost effective for all patients with fatigable weakness. Single-fiber electromyography is not necessary for patients where the diagnosis is secure following other testing.

REFERENCES

Drachman DB. Myasthenia gravis. N Engl J Med 1994;330:1797.
Drachman DB, ed. Myasthenia gravis: Biology and treatment. Ann NY Acad Sci 1987;505:1.
Fink ME. Treatment of the critically ill patient with MG. In: Ropper AH, ed. Neurological and neurosurgical intensive care. 3rd ed. New York: Raven Press, 1993:351.
Penn AS, Richman DP, Ruff RL, Lennon VA, eds. Myasthenia gravis and related disorders. Ann NY Acad Sci 1993;681:1.
Sanders D, eds. Myasthenia gravis and myasthenic syndromes. Neurol Clin 1994;12(2).

CHAPTER 20-4

Cervical Root Disorders

C. Elizabeth Pringle, M.D.

DEFINITION

Cervical root disorders (or cervical radiculopathies) are the result of pathology affecting the first eight spinal roots (i.e., C1–8).

ETIOLOGY

Cervical radiculopathies in adults over 50 years of age are usually due to disk protrusions (herniations) causing nerve compression. Over the age of 50, the multiple degenerative changes associated with cervical spondylosis (osteophyte formation, thickening of the ligamentum flavum, facet hypertrophy, or subluxation) assume increasing importance. Less commonly, patients of any age may have traumatic avulsion of cervical roots, most often the result of forceful traction on the arm.

CRITERIA FOR DIAGNOSIS
Suggestive

The diagnosis is suggested by the clinical constellation as described under Clinical Manifestations, that is, radicular arm pain, lower motor neuron weakness in a myotomal pattern, decrease or loss of any deep tendon reflexes associated with the involved root, and dermatomal sensory symptoms. Arm pain and paresthesias may be affected by neck movements.

Definitive

The diagnosis may be confirmed radiologically and electrophysiologically (see Diagnostic Options).

CLINICAL MANIFESTATIONS
Subjective

The sensory symptoms of cervical radiculopathies include positive sensory symptoms (pain and paresthesias) and negative sensory symptoms (numbness). Because of the extensive overlap of cervical dermatomes, some sensory symptoms have poor localizing value; however, sensory symptoms involving certain "key" areas as outlined below may be quite localizing when they are present.

The pain of cervical root disorders is termed *radicular pain*. It characteristically radiates from the neck into the arm, roughly corresponding to a dermatomal pattern. It is characteristically severe and may be precipitated or worsened by neck movement. Compression of the fifth cervical root may cause pain in the interscapular region and along the lateral aspect of the arm to the elbow. The pain of a C-6 radiculopathy tends to extend into the lateral aspect of the arm and forearm and frequently, of more localizing value, into the thumb. Occasionally, the pain may also include the index finger. C-7 root pain may involve the posterior aspect of the forearm with radiation into the middle digits. C-8 root pain tends to involve the ulnar aspect of the forearm and the fourth and fifth digits.

The distribution of the numbness and paresthesias seen with various sorts of radiculopathies have dermatomal patterns similar to that described above for pain; however, they are in general of more localizing value than is pain, particularly when they involve the hand.

Although positive motor symptoms such as fasciculations and cramping may occur in cervical radiculopathies, the most common motor symptom is the negative symptom of arm weakness. The weakness is of a myotomal pattern; that is, it involves exclusively muscles innervated by a particular nerve root. Patients rarely localize arm weakness to specific muscles; therefore, specific patterns of weakness are discussed under Clinical Manifestations, Objective.

Disk protrusions may be precipitated by trauma or by the prolonged maintenance of an unusual posture of the head. Many patients, however, give no history of preceding trauma.

Degenerative disease of the cervical spine is so common in the general population that it is common to find a positive family history. No definite genetic link has been found, however.

Objective
Physical Examination

Twenty-five to thirty percent of patients with cervical radiculopathies have objective sensory loss in a dermatomal pattern; however, the borders are often indistinct, probably due to dermatomal overlap. Gentle downward pressure on the head or cautious lateral flexion toward the side of the lesion may reproduce the patient's pain (Spurling's sign) and, when present, can be helpful with localization.

Detailed strength testing of the individual muscles of the arm is very important in helping to localize cervical radiculopathies. Most muscles of the upper extremity are innervated by more than one cervical root; however, weakness of certain "key" muscles occurs frequently enough with radiculopathies at certain levels that they may be considered good clues to lesions of that root. For example, weakness or wasting of shoulder abduction, external rotation of the shoulder, or forearm flexion may occur with lesions of either the C-5 or C-6 root. Wasting or weakness of the forearm flexors, however, occurs more frequently with C-6 lesions. C-7 lesions are usually associated with weakness of forearm extension and extension of the wrist and fingers. C-8 root lesions tend to affect the finger and thumb flexors and, to a lesser extent, the intrinsic muscles of the hand (although the latter receive their predominant supply from the T-1 root).

The biceps and the brachioradialis reflexes tend to be diminished or lost with lesions of C-5 or C-6, as does the triceps reflex with lesions of C-7. The finger flexor reflex may be affected with C-8 lesions.

Routine Laboratory Abnormalities

There are no abnormalities of blood or urinalysis associated specifically with cervical radiculopathies.

PLANS
Diagnostic
Differential Diagnosis

There are numerous causes of neck pain, but few processes can mimic the full picture of radicular pain, dermatomal sensory changes, and myotomal weakness as described above; however, the cervical roots can be involved by processes other than disk herniations. Various inflammatory and neoplastic polyradiculopathies (e.g., Guillain–Barré syndrome, sarcoid, carcinomatous meningitis) can occasionally cause some confusion. Usually these processes involve more than one root and cause cerebrospinal fluid abnormalities, with or without meningeal signs. Infection of the dorsal root ganglion by varicella–zoster can cause pain, sensory loss, and occasionally weakness (so-called zoster amyotrophy), but usually the tell-tale skin lesions allow differentiation.

The myotomal weakness of motor neuron disease can be distinguished by the lack of radicular pain, by the absence of sensory changes, and usually by the mixture of upper and lower motor neuron signs.

Myofascial pain and occasionally fibromyalgia can cause seemingly radicular pain; however, although vague subjective sensory changes can accompany these syndromes, weakness and reflex loss should not occur and their presence should alert the physician to the possibility of underlying disk disease.

Lesions of the brachial plexus or of individual peripheral nerves can usually be distinguished on anatomic grounds (i.e., weakness involving muscles outside a single myotome, sensory symptoms outside a single dermatome).

Diagnostic Options

The importance of the history and the clinical examination cannot be overstated. In patients with appropriate clinical pictures, radiologic tests not only can confirm the diagnosis, but can also exclude other processes, as well as provide important anatomic information to the surgeon.

Plain cervical spine radiographs detect many of the changes of cervical spondylosis and degenerative disk disease, but often computed tomography (CT) or magnetic resonance imaging (MRI) of the cervical spine is necessary to detect disk herniations and to assess whether the cord or roots are compromised. MRI provides better visualization of the disk, cord, and soft tissues, but CT scan delineates bony structures better and is often more accessible. Myelography has been largely supplanted by CT and MRI, but occasionally is still done prior to CT scanning.

It is of utmost importance to use the history and clinical examination to guide the radiologist's attention to the appropriate level, and also to interpret any radiologic abnormalities in light of the clinical picture. For example, the finding of "disk bulges" (as distinct from disk herniations) on cervical MRI is very common and a causal role should not be assumed in a patient with vague symptoms.

Electromyography also has a role in the diagnosis of cervical radiculopathies. Standard nerve conduction studies should be normal (in the absence of coexistent disease), but needle electromyography can detect changes of denervation in muscles innervated by the affected root, even in the absence of detectable weakness. Needle examination of the paraspinal muscles is very important in localization on the proximodistal axis, as findings of denervation in the paraspinal muscles is proof positive that the lesion lies at the root level. Because of the extensive overlap of the myotomal supply of the paraspinal muscles, however, they are not by themselves localizing on a rostrocaudal (i.e., vertebral) level. That is, they require findings in other muscles to confidently localize the level.

Recommended Approach

A careful history and physical examination are the most important diagnostic maneuvers. In patients with the appropriate story or findings. radiologic examination should be obtained, either CT or MRI scan, depending on availability. In patients with appropriate history, physical findings, and radiologic findings of disk herniation, electromyography is not always necessary; however, electromyography may be helpful in directing the radiologic examination to the appropriate level as well as determining the significance of subtle radiologic abnormalities.

Therapeutic
Threapeutic Options

Cervical radiculopathies may be treated conservatively or interventionally, the decision depending on the severity of the symptoms and signs. Conservative measures include rest, analgesia, immobilization of the neck with a rigid cervical collar, nonsteroidal antiinflammatory agents, muscle relaxants, and, once the acutely painful stage is over, physiotherapy. The great majority of patients with cervical radiculopathies improve during weeks to months with conservative treatment. Nonsurgical interventions such as facet joint injections occasionally are helpful for pain relief, but are unlikely to change sensory or motor signs.

Surgical options should be undertaken only by experienced neurosurgeons or orthopaedic surgeons specializing in spinal surgery. Signs of coexisting cervical myelopathy are indications for surgical consultation. Surgical approaches can be anterior or posterior. The anterior approach (anterior discectomy with or without fusion) allows the surgeon to remove the disk without disturbing the posterior elements. The posterior approach (laminectomies with discectomy or osteophytectomy) is perhaps technically less demanding, but does not allow the surgeon access to the ventral spinal canal. Percutaneous lysis of disks using chymopapain injections has no role in the management of cervical root disorders.

Recommended Approach

As many as 70% of cervical radiculopathies improve with conservative therapy. Indications for surgery include severe intractable pain that is not improving, significant or progressive motor weakness, and signs of spinal cord compromise.

FOLLOW-UP

The frequency of follow-up varies from patient to patient and is dependent on the severity and acuity of the problems as well as on the therapeutic modalities employed.

DISCUSSION
Prevalence and Incidence

The true prevalence and incidence of cervical root disorders are difficult to determine, although they seem to be less common than lumbar root disorders. Cervical spondylosis, a frequent accompaniment of cervical radiculopathies, probably begins in the twenties or thirties and progresses with age.

As many as 70% of cervical radiculopathies involve the C-7 root, 20% involve C-6, and most of the remaining 10% are accounted for by C-5 and C-8 lesions. Clinically apparent radiculopathies involving the higher cervical roots are rare and usually occur in the setting of trauma, meningeal disease, or rheumatoid arthritis.

Related Basic Science

The vertebral bodies are separated from each other by intervertebral disks, fibrocartilaginous structures consisting of the gelatinous inner remnant of the notochord, the nucleus pulposus, and a tough outer fibrous ring, the anulus fibrosus. Disk herniations occur when tears in the annulus allow the soft nucleus pulposus to leak out and compress adjacent structures. Most herniations occur lateral to the posterior longitudinal ligament, resulting in compression of the spinal root as it passes through the intervertebral foramen. Less commonly, disk material may herniate more centrally, compressing the spinal cord itself and giving rise to signs of a cervical myelopathy. Such central herniations may be painless or accompanied by radicular pain, sometimes bilateral. Vertical herniation into the center of adjacent vertebral bodies may occur asymptomatically and give rise to Schmorl's nodes.

The symptoms and signs of cervical root disorders are probably the result of local damage (focal demyelination or axonal damage) to nerve fibers secondary to compression. Weakness, paresthesias, and reflex changes likely reflect damage to large myelinated fibers, whereas pain is probably the result of injury of unmyelinated or smaller myelinated fibers.

There are seven cervical vertebrae and eight pairs of cervical roots. Unlike the situation in the lower spinal segments, cervical spinal cord segments lie at approximately the same level as their corresponding vertebrae and cervical roots exit the neural foramina above the vertebral body with the same number. Thus, the C-6 root exits above the C-6 vertebra and is therefore jeopardized by a C5–6 disk herniation. The C-8 cervical root, having no correspondingly numbered vertebral body, exits below C-7 and above T-1.

Natural History and Its Modification with Treatment

The natural history of cervical root disorders is not well established. A significant number of cervical radiculopathies resolve or at least stabilize on their own within a few weeks, making evaluation of the role of a particular treatment difficult.

Prevention

Other than general methods of preventing trauma, there are no proven methods of preventing the occurrence of cervical root disorders.

Cost Containment

Significant cost containment can be achieved by avoiding duplication of imaging studies (e.g., most patients do not require both MRI and CT). Myelograms only rarely play a role and should be performed only after discussion with a radiologist as to whether useful information will be gained. Electromyography will show changes of denervation only 2 to 3 weeks after onset, so negative studies can be avoided by delaying needle studies a sufficient time to allow changes to develop. Not all patients require electromyography, as a typical history, examination, and radiologic visualization of a disk herniation at the appropriate level are enough to make the diagnosis. Electromyography is useful, however, when the history, findings, or radiology is equivocal or contradictory.

REFERENCES

Adams RD, Victor M. Principles of neurology. 5th ed. New York: McGraw-Hill, 1993:171.

Wilbourn AJ, Aminoff MJ. Radiculopathies. In: Brown WF, Bolton CF, eds. Clinical electromyography. 2nd ed. Boston: Butterworth-Heinemann, 1993:175.

CHAPTER 20–5

Lumbar Root Disorders

C. Elizabeth Pringle, M.D.

DEFINITION

Lumbar root disorders (or lumbar radiculopathies) are the result of pathologic processes involving the five lumbar roots (L1–5). Because of the frequency of involvement of the first sacral root by similar pathologic processes, S-1 radiculopathies are also included in this chapter.

ETIOLOGY

Most lumbosacral radiculopathies are the result of disk herniations and subsequent root compression. With increasing age, degenerative changes such as osteophyte formation and facet hypertrophy assume increasing importance. Less commonly, inflammatory, malignant, and ischemic lesions can cause polyradiculopathies (see Differential Diagnosis).

CRITERIA FOR DIAGNOSIS
Suggestive

The diagnosis is suggested by the clinical constellation as described below under Clinical Manifestations, that is, radicular leg pain, lower motor neuron weakness in a myotomal pattern, decrease or loss of reflexes associated with the involved root, and dermatomal sensory symptoms. In patients with disk disease, pain and paresthesias are often sensitive to change in position.

Definitive

The diagnosis may be confirmed radiologically and electrophysiologically (see Diagnostic Options).

CLINICAL MANIFESTATIONS
Subjective

The sensory symptoms of lumbar root disorders include positive symptoms (pain and paresthesiae) and negative symptoms (numbness). In general, sensory symptoms have greater localizing value in lumbar than in cervical root disorders.

Back pain can be the sole symptom of lumbar root disorders, but usually some leg pain is present. The general characteristics of the pain of root disorders (radicular pain) is described in Chapter 20–4. Compression of the L-1 root may cause pain in the inguinal region; L-2 lesions can cause pain over the upper anterior thigh, whereas those of L-3 cause pain over the lower anterior thigh and medial knee. L-4 lesions may cause pain of the knee or medial leg. L-5 pain typically radiates over the posterolateral thigh and leg into the great toe, whereas S-1 pain radiates down into the posterior calf into the lateral heel and foot.

The distribution of the numbness and paresthesias of lumbar root disorders is dermatomal in pattern and is similar to the distribution of pain described above. In general, however, sensory changes are of more localizing value than is pain.

The weakness of lumbar root disorders is lower motor neuron in nature and myotomal (i.e., confined to muscles innervated by a particular root) in pattern. Patients rarely localize weakness to specific muscles; therefore, specific patterns are discussed under Clinical Manifestations, Objective.

Disk protrusions may be precipitated by trauma or by the prolonged maintenance of an unusual posture. Many patients, however, give no history of preceding trauma.

Degenerative disk disease is so common in the general population that it is common to find lumbar root disorders in members of the same family. No definite genetic link has been found, however.

Objective
Physical Examination

Objective sensory loss may be present in a dermatomal pattern as described above, usually best defined distally. Many patients with lumbar root disorders (especially of lower roots) have diminished straight-leg raising. Detailed strength testing of individual muscles is important in localization, but as most muscles of the lower extremity are innervated by more than one root, patterns of muscle weakness must be looked for and combined with sensory and reflex findings to precisely localize the culprit root.

Lesions of L-1, L-2, or L-3 roots may cause weakness of hip flexion and adduction. In addition, L-1 lesions occasionally cause lower abdominal weakness, and L-3 lesions may cause weakness of knee extension. There is no reflex change associated with L-1 lesions, whereas L-2 lesions may depress the ipsilateral cremasteric and adductor reflexes, and L-3 lesions can depress the patellar reflex. L-4 weakness spares hip girdle muscles but weakens knee extension and ankle dorsiflexion. The patellar reflex is characteristically diminished. L-5 root lesions give rise to weakness of hip abduction, knee flexion, toe extension, ankle inversion, and eversion. Reflexes tend to be spared. S-1 radiculopathies characteristically weaken hip extension, knee flexion, plantar flexion, and toe flexion. The Achilles reflex is depressed or abolished.

Routine Laboratory Abnormalities

There are no abnormalities of blood or urinalysis associated specifically with lumbar root disorders.

PLANS
Diagnostic
Differential Diagnosis

Back pain is such a common symptom that it is important to remember that not all back pain is due to disk herniations and radiculopathies. Back strain, spondylitis, arachnoiditis, and spinal stenosis are other causes. The radicular quality of the pain as well as the neurologic findings help differentiate.

As in the cervical region, various inflammatory and neoplastic processes can occasionally involve the lumbar roots (Guillain–Barré syndrome, sarcoid, carcinomatous meningitis), but they tend to involve more than a single root (i.e., they are polyradiculopathies). Lumbosacral plexopathies (most often due to diabetes or mass lesions) involve more than one myotome/dermatome and lack electromyographic changes in the paraspinal muscles. Spinal stenosis causes "neurogenic claudication" (neurologic symptoms brought on by activity and relieved by rest) and findings are typically bilateral. Radiologic tests usually reveal multilevel narrowing of the spinal canal secondary to degenerative changes.

Diagnostic Options

The importance of the history and the clinical examination cannot be overstated. In patients with the appropriate clinical picture, radiologic tests not only can provide confirmation of the diagnosis, but can also rule out many other processes, as well as provide important anatomic information to the surgeon. Plain films of the lumbar spine detect many degenerative changes, as well as spondylolisthesis and scoliosis, but usually computed tomography (CT) or magnetic resonance imaging (MRI) of the region is necessary to detect disk herniations and to assess whether the roots are compromised. MRI provides better visualization of the disk, cord, and soft tissues, but CT delineates bony structures better and is often more accessible. Myelography has been largely supplanted by CT and MRI, but is occasionally still done in conjunction with CT. It is of the utmost importance to use the history and clinical examination to guide the radiologist's attention to the appropriate level, and also to interpret any radiologic findings in light of the clinical picture. For example, the finding of "disk bulges" (as distinct from disk herniations) on MRI scans is very common and a causal role should not be assumed in a patient with vague symptoms.

Electromyography also has a role in the diagnosis of lumbar radiculopathies. Standard nerve conduction studies should be normal (in the absence of coexistent disease), but needle electromyography can detect changes of denervation in muscles innervated by the culprit root, even in the absence of detectable weakness. Needle examination of the paraspinal muscles is especially important in localization on the proximodistal axis, as findings of denervation in the paraspinal muscles is proof positive that the lesion lies at the root level. Because of the extensive overlap of myotomal supply of the paraspinal muscles, however, they are not by themselves localizing on a rostrocaudal (i.e., vertebral) level. That is, they require findings in other muscles to confidently localize the level.

Recommended Approach

A careful history and physical examination are the most important diagnostic maneuvers. In patients with the appropriate story or findings, radiologic studies (either CT or MRI) should be obtained. In patients with appropriate history, physical signs, and radiologic findings of disk herniation at the appropriate level, electromyography is not always necessary; however, electromyography may be helpful in directing the radiologic examination to the appropriate level as well as determining the significance of subtle radiologic findings in patients with atypical presentations.

Therapeutic
Therapeutic Options

The treatment of low back pain is a complex area and is beyond the scope of this chapter. Treatment of lumbosacral radiculopathies can be conservative or surgical. Conservative treatment includes rest (complete bed rest is no longer felt to be necessary, but the patient should avoid activities that cause pain), antiinflammatory agents, muscle relaxants, and analgesics. Surgical procedures usually consist of laminotomy with simple discectomy. Recently, percutaneous techniques using suction or laser have been introduced, but their utility has yet to be established.

Recommended Approach

Surgery is urgently indicated in any patient with signs of conus medullaris involvement (sphincter impairment). In other patients, unless the neurologic deficit is severe, a 3-week trial of conservative measures should be undertaken. If symptoms and signs persist thereafter or if the deficit is severe, surgery is indicated. Surgery should be performed only by neurosurgeons or orthopaedists with experience in the field of spinal surgery.

Once the acute stage has passed, a graded program of exercise, ideally guided by a physiotherapist with expertise in the area, can be instituted. "Safe back techniques" for prevention of recurrence should also be emphasized (see Prevention).

FOLLOW-UP

The frequency of follow-up varies from patient to patient and is dependent on the severity and acuity of the problems as well as the therapeutic modalities employed.

DISCUSSION
Prevalence and Incidence

Low back pain is extremely common, it is estimated that three of every four people have an episode of significant low back pain at some time in their lives, and the prevalence at any given point in time is 10 to 20%. Not all low back pain is the result of lumbar root disorders, and in fact more often soft tissue injury is the culprit.

By far the most common roots to be involved are the L-5 and S-1 roots, which together account for more than 90% of lumbosacral radiculopathies. L-4 roots are the third most common, whereas L-3, L-2, and L-1 radiculopathies occur with decreasing frequency.

Related Basic Science

In the lumbosacral region, the nerve roots exit below the vertebral bodies with the same number; however, because the longitudinal growth of the bony spine with maturation greatly exceeds that of the spinal cord, the various lumbar spinal cord segments in the adult lie well rostral to their correspondingly numbered vertebral bodies. Thus, the lumbar nerve roots must travel caudally within the spinal canal (as the cauda equina) to reach their neural foramina. As a result, each lumbosacral nerve root must pass by several disks on its course to the neural foramen. Single-disk herniations in this region, therefore, can jeopardize several nerve roots.

Disk herniations occur when degenerative changes in the fibrous outer annulus fibrosus allow extrusion of the gelatinous inner nucleus pulposus. Disk herniations can be medial, lateral, or far lateral (Figure

20–5–1). The majority are lateral and result in compromise of the nerve root exiting at the level below the herniation (i.e., a lateral L4–5 herniation compresses the L-5 root). Medial disk herniations can compromise the root exiting two or more levels below (i.e., a medial L4–5 herniation may compress the S-1 and/or S-2 roots). Medial disk protrusions in the high lumbar region may compress the conus medullaris (the adult spinal cord usually ends at approximately the vertebral L-2 level). Far lateral disk herniations compress the root exiting at the same level as the herniation (i.e., a far lateral L4–5 disk herniation compromises the L-4 root).

Thus, a useful "rule of thumb" for both cervical and lumbar regions is that intervertebral disk herniations most often cause symptoms referable to the nerve root sharing the number of the lower vertebral body (i.e., a C5–6 herniation usually affects the C-6 root; an L5–S1 herniation most often affects the S-1 root).

Note should also be made that radiculopathies can be the result of degenerative changes other than disk herniations: facet joint hypertrophy can cause lateral recess stenosis and nerve root compromise.

Natural History and Its Modification with Treatment

The natural history of lumbar root disorders is not well established. Complete spontaneous remission probably occurs less often with lumbosacral radiculopathies than with cervical radiculopathies.

Prevention

"Safe back techniques" can reduce the incidence of back strain and herniated lumbar disks. All lifting should be done from a squatting or kneeling position with the feet apart. The load should be kept relatively close to the body and twisting movements should be avoided while lifting. General physical fitness also reduces the incidence of back strain and disk herniations by strengthening axial musculature.

Cost Containment

Principles similar to those discussed in Chapter 20–4 apply to lumbar root disorders with regard to duplication of tests. Avoiding the "failed back syndrome" and the disability associated with it is the aim of back surgeons throughout the world and is best done by careful preoperative evaluation.

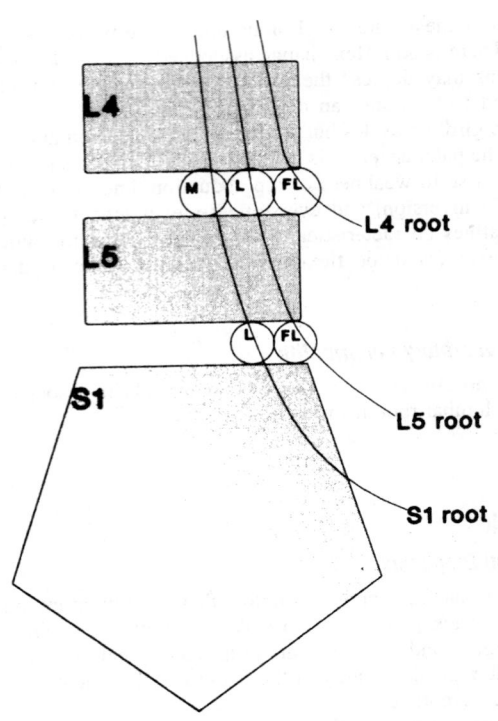

Figure 20–5–1. Lumbar disk herniations. M, medial disk herniation; L, lateral disk herniation; FL, far lateral disk herniation.

REFERENCES

Adams RD, Victor M. Principles of neurology. 5th ed. New York: McGraw Hill, 1993:171.

Wilbourn RD, Aminoff MJ. Radiculopathies. In: Brown WF, Bolton CF, eds. Clinical electromyography. 2nd ed. Boston: Butterworth-Heinemann, 1993:175.

CHAPTER 20–6

Motor Neuron Disorders

Dave Hollander, M.D.

DEFINITION

The motor neuron disorders (MNDs) are a group of diseases of the voluntary motor system. Motor neurons and their outflow tracts are affected, with the precise distribution of involvement determining the clinical presentation. The most common MND, amyotrophic lateral sclerosis, is the result of degeneration of upper motor neurons and lower motor neurons and the corticobulbar and corticospinal tracts. By contrast, pure lower motor neuron syndromes, such as spinal muscular atrophy, are restricted in involvement to the lower motor neurons.

ETIOLOGY

The etiology of the MNDs is, for the most part, unknown. Current research suggests that amyotrophic lateral sclerosis is the result of excitotoxic injury to motor neurons mediated by glutamate, the major central nervous system excitatory neurotransmitter. Some MNDs are inherited. In these cases, there presumably is a defect in a gene coding for an enzyme or structural protein.

CRITERIA FOR DIAGNOSIS

Suggestive

The presence of symptoms and signs indicative of upper and/or lower motor neuron dysfunction, in the absence of accompanying sensory, sphincter, and cognitive findings, suggests the presence of a MND. These symptoms and signs may involve bulbar or limb musculature, or both.

Definitive

The appropriate clinical presentation, together with electromyographic confirmation of the widespread nature of the denervative process, serves to make the definitive diagnosis. With amyotrophic lateral sclerosis, it is imperative to document the combination of both upper and lower motor neuron involvement. Often, amyotrophic lateral sclerosis initially presents with just lower or upper motor neuron findings. The diagnosis of amyotrophic lateral sclerosis may be suspected in such cases, but is not considered definite until dysfunction of both upper and lower motor neurons is present.

CLINICAL MANIFESTATIONS

Subjective

The hallmark of amyotrophic lateral sclerosis is progressive muscle wasting and weakness, which is a manifestation of the ongoing lower motor neuron degeneration. These symptoms may begin at any level of the neuraxis, often in an asymmetric fashion. The site of onset may involve limb or bulbar musculature. Patients may, for example, present initially with a foot drop or with slurring of speech. Rarely, dyspnea, due to respiratory muscle involvement, may be the presenting problem. With time, these symptoms generalize to involve all voluntary muscles. In the limbs, this results in progressive loss of function of the arms and legs. Muscles of the trunk and neck are affected, with resultant postural weakness. Bulbar symptoms include dysphagia and dysarthria. With progression, patients lose all ability to swallow solids and liquids, including their own saliva, and become anarthric. Aspiration is a real risk. Weakness of the diaphragm and other respiratory muscles leads to progressive difficulties with breathing. Ultimately, most patients die of respiratory failure. Other lower motor neuron symptoms include fasciculations and muscle cramps. Stiffness and loss of dexterity reflect upper motor neuron involvement, and may occur even before significant weakness has developed. Some patients manifest a pseudobulbar affect, characterized by emotional lability and inappropriate laughter or crying. Five to ten percent of cases of amyotrophic lateral sclerosis are inherited and have positive family histories. Most of these cases are transmitted in an autosomal dominant fashion.

Progressive muscular atrophy is a pure lower motor neuron syndrome that shares with amyotrophic lateral sclerosis the symptoms that are referable to lower motor neuron dysfunction. The limb muscles are predominantly affected, and bulbar and respiratory symptoms are much less common. The childhood spinal muscular atrophies are a group of autosomal lower motor neuron disorders. They have been classified on the basis of age of onset and severity of presentation, and include acute spinal muscular atrophy (Werdnig–Hoffmann disease, type 1) and chronic spinal muscular atrophy (Kugelberg–Welander syndrome, type 3). X-linked spinal and bulbar muscular atrophy (Kennedy's syndrome) features prominent bulbar symptoms and gynecomastia, in addition to the limb symptoms.

Objective

Physical Examination

The findings on examination parallel the distribution of the upper and lower motor neuron lesions. Lower motor neuron findings include muscle atrophy, fasciculations, and weakness, and upper motor neuron signs are spasticity and hyperreflexia. In amyotrophic lateral sclerosis, combinations of lower and upper motor neuron signs are present, involving limb and/or bulbar musculature. Babinski signs are decidedly uncommon, despite other evidence for pyramidal tract involvement.

In progressive muscular atrophy, the findings are purely lower motor neuron in manifestation. Patients with Kennedy's syndrome display prominent bulbar findings and gynecomastia, in addition to the limb muscle weakness and atrophy. Testicular atrophy may also be present.

Routine Laboratory Abnormalities

Complete blood counts, SMA, and urine analysis are normal in the MNDs.

PLANS

Diagnostic

Differential Diagnosis

Amyotrophic lateral sclerosis is distinguished from other MNDs by the presence of both upper and lower motor neuron symptoms and signs. In full-blown cases, with upper and lower motor neuron findings affecting both bulbar and limb musculature, the diagnosis is straightforward. Often, however, patients initially present with limited regional involvement, and may have only upper or lower motor neuron findings. At such times, their condition may be confused for other entities. In patients with generalized lower motor neuron presentations, the major dif-

ferential diagnostic consideration is progressive muscular atrophy or motor neuropathies. When the findings are restricted, such as in patients presenting with foot drop or wasting of intrinsic hand muscles, radiculopathies and focal neuropathies must be considered. Rare patients with focal, nonprogressive amyotrophy may present with atrophy restricted to one group of muscles. Findings limited to bulbar musculature may suggest brainstem lesions, including stroke, or myasthenia gravis. Pure upper motor neuron presentations may suggest stroke or primary lateral sclerosis, a rare disorder affecting the corticospinal pathways. Cervical spondylotic myelopathy is an important consideration in patients with no evidence for involvement above the foramen magnum. Such myelopathies may be associated with focal upper extremity wasting and weakness and, on occasion, with lower extremity fasciculations. This combination of upper and lower motor neuron findings makes the resemblance to amyotrophic lateral sclerosis all the greater.

Progressive muscular atrophy is most often confused for amyotrophic lateral sclerosis. The critical differentiating feature is the absence of upper motor neuron findings. Motor neuropathies, including multifocal conduction block neuropathy and GM_1-associated neuropathies, and the postpolio syndrome are other important entities to consider.

Diagnostic Options

Electromyographic studies serve to confirm the presence of a denervating process and establish its extent and characteristics. The diagnosis of amyotrophic lateral sclerosis requires the demonstration of widespread acute and chronic denervative changes in three limbs or two limbs and bulbar musculature. The electromyographic findings in progressive muscular atrophy are predominantly chronic in nature. Although some acute changes may be seen, these are much more limited and milder. Electromyographic studies are also important in evaluating many of the differential diagnostic considerations mentioned above. Muscle biopsy is another means of demonstrating denervation. Imaging studies of the brain and spinal cord are helpful in ruling out brain and spinal cord disease. Computed tomography (CT) and magnetic resonance imaging (MRI) may be used to evaluate for brain lesions, such as stroke. MRI is particularly useful for looking at the brainstem. Cervical spine MRI or myelography can demonstrate the presence of significant cervical spondylotic disease. Serum protein electropheresis and immunoelectropheresis screen for the presence of paraproteinemias occasionally associated with MNDs. Antiganglioside antibody levels, especially anti-GM_1 antibody levels, may be elevated in some cases.

Recommended Approach

Electromyographic studies are mandatory in all patients with suspected MNDs. In suspected amyotrophic lateral sclerosis patients, with both upper and lower motor neuron findings, such studies are often sufficient to confirm the diagnosis. It must be remembered that early in the course of disease, such studies may be negative or equivocal, particularly in patients presenting with predominantly bulbar or upper motor neuron features. In such patients, repeat studies in several months are usually revealing. Occasionally, muscle biopsies may be performed to demonstrate the presence of denervation in electromyogram-negative patients. Where the clinical picture still allows for consideration of brain or spinal cord disease, neuroimaging studies of the brain or spine should be obtained. Blood testing for paraproteinemias and antiganglioside antibody levels should be performed.

Therapeutic

At present, there is no effective treatment for amyotrophic lateral sclerosis. Nonetheless, there is a great deal that can be done from a symptomatic point of view. Gait-assistive devices, ranging from ankle–foot orthotics for patients with foot drop to walkers, are available and can help prolong a patient's ability to ambulate. The availability of electric wheelchairs may allow independence of movement for patients with even limited limb function. There are a wide array of speech-assistive devices for patients with dysarthria, ranging from simple alphabet boards to sophisticated menu-driven computers with voice synthesizers. Dysphagia may be managed early on by appropriate changes in food preparation, for example, pureeing food. In patients with more severe swallowing difficulties, gastrostomy may be performed. This allows for the complete, and easy, provision of the patient's nutritional needs, and greatly reduces the risk of aspiration pneumonia. Patients with difficulty swallowing saliva may benefit from anticholinergic agents, such as atropine and hyoscyamine. Suction devices are also useful. Early respiratory symptoms may be managed by the use of oxygen, delivered via nasal prongs. With progressive respiratory failure, patients have to decide whether or not they are willing to go on a ventilator. All patients should receive a Pneumovax and annual influenza vaccinations. Baclofen may be useful for treating spasticity. Valium may occasionally be added as well. Antidepressant medications, such as amitriptyline, may be helpful for depression, especially in patients with pseudobulbar affect. Psychosocial issues must not be neglected. Disease progression in amyotrophic lateral sclerosis places great burdens not only on the patient but on the family as well. The burden of patient management often exceeds the family's ability to cope. Timely referral to the appropriate social agencies is vital. In all these matters, the emotional support offered by the considerate and caring physician is of inestimable value.

Most cases of progressive muscular atrophy are of unknown etiology, and no specific therapy is available. On occasion, progressive muscular atrophy may be associated with an underlying paraproteinemia. In such cases, immunosuppressive therapy may be beneficial.

FOLLOW-UP

In those few MND patients with associated paraproteinemias, antibody levels may be followed. This is particularly useful in those patients who have had a clinical response to therapy. Rises in antibody titers may often herald a clinical relapse. Periodic measurement of respiratory function in amyotrophic lateral sclerosis patients, especially forced vital capacity, is useful in following respiratory function and anticipating developing respiratory failure.

DISCUSSION

Prevalence and Incidence

Motor neuron disorders know no geographic or racial boundaries. Amyotrophic lateral sclerosis, the most frequent of the MNDs, has an incidence of 1 to 2 per 100,000 and a prevalence of 4 to 6 per 100,000. Males are affected twice as often as females.

Related Basic Science

The gene for familial amyotrophic lateral sclerosis has been linked to chromosome 21. In a subset of patients with familial amyotrophic lateral sclerosis, a defect has been demonstrated in the gene coding for the enzyme Cu/Zn superoxide dismutase, which catalyzes the dismutation of the toxic superoxide anion to oxygen and hydrogen peroxide. This suggests a possible role for free radical-mediated injury in amyotrophic lateral sclerosis. Kennedy's syndrome has been linked to a mutation in

the androgen receptor gene, consisting of an expansion of CAG trinucleotide repeats. The spinal muscular atrophies have been mapped to chromosome 5q11.2–13.3, although the precise gene defect(s) is not yet known.

Natural History and Its Modification with Treatment

The natural history of amyotrophic lateral sclerosis is progressive muscle weakness, culminating in death, usually from respiratory failure. Fifty percent of patients die within 3 years, 80% by 5 years. No effective therapy is available to alter the inexorable progression of this disease. Patients placed on respirators and provided with nursing care may be maintained indefinitely, albeit in a totally dependent condition.

The natural history of progressive muscular atrophy is varied, with some patients having a slow and protracted course, and others a much more rapid and debilitating course. This variation is undoubtedly a reflection of the fact that progressive muscular atrophy is a heterogenic collection of MNDs rather than a unitary condition. Respiratory function is usually spared or only affected late in the course of the illness, thereby accounting for the far better prognosis of this condition as compared with amyotrophic lateral sclerosis.

Prevention

Until further insight into the causes of MNDs is obtained, little can be done to prevent their occurrence. Genetic counseling may be offered in cases of inherited MNDs.

Cost Containment

Routine laboratory investigations in MNDs are usually unrevealing. This includes standard hematology, biochemistry, and urine analysis screens, as well as thyroid profiles and vitamin B_{12} and folate measurements. MRI studies of the cervical spine or head are frequently ordered by physicians. The presence of bulbar symptoms obviates the need for cervical spine studies, as lesions in this region clearly cannot account for bulbar findings. The demonstration of widespread denervation on electromyograms likewise renders unnecessary imaging studies of the head, even in patients with bulbar symptoms.

REFERENCES

Plaitakis A. Glutamate dysfunction and selective motor neuron degeneration in amyotrophic lateral sclerosis: A hypothesis. Ann Neurol 1990;28:3.

Rosen DR, Siddique T, Patterson D, et al. Mutations in Cu/Zn superoxide dismutase gene are associated with familial amyotrophic lateral sclerosis. Nature 1993;362:59.

Rothstein JD, Martin LJ, Kuncl RW. Decreased glutamate transport by the brain and spinal cord in amyotrophic lateral sclerosis. N Engl J Med 1992;326:1464.

Rowland LP, ed. Amyotrophic lateral sclerosis and other motor neuron diseases. In: Advances in neurology. vol. 56. New York: Raven Press, 1991.

Tandan R, Bradley WG. Amyotrophic lateral sclerosis: Part 1. Clinical features, pathology, and ethical issues in management. Ann Neurol 1985;18:271.

CHAPTER 20–7

Huntington's Disease

Steven M. Hersch, M.D., Ph.D., Randi Jones, Ph.D., and Arthur Falek, Ph.D.

DEFINITION

Huntington's disease (HD) is an inherited, chronic progressive neurodegenerative disorder characterized by midlife onset, involuntary movements, cognitive decline, and emotional disturbance. HD was described in 1872 by George Huntington, a Long Island physician, who observed multiple generations of an HD family.

ETIOLOGY

Huntington's disease is caused by a mutant autosomal dominant gene localized to the short arm of chromosome 4. The gene, which was cloned in 1993, codes for a normal protein of unknown function termed *huntingtin*. In individuals with HD, a polymorphic trinucleotide repeat sequence (CAGn), near the 5′ end of the gene, is expanded beyond the normal repeat range, leading to translation of an expanded polyglutamine sequence in the protein. How the mutant protein leads to selective neuronal death in the central nervous system remains uncertain; however, some evidence suggests that cell death occurs by an excitotoxic mechanism.

CRITERIA FOR DIAGNOSIS
Suggestive

A *clinical* diagnosis of HD is strongly suggested by evidence of previous family history of the disease and the presence of involuntary movements. Affective disorder, personality change, and cognitive decline support the diagnosis, but are nonspecific unless the movement disorder is also present. In the absence of family history, this symptom complex is still most likely to be HD; however, the diagnostic certainty is not as great unless genetic testing confirms the presence of the HD mutation.

Definitive

A more definitive diagnosis of clinical disease is sometimes useful when there is no family history or when there are unusual clinical features. This can be achieved by confirmatory genetic testing. Furthermore, definitive presymptomatic testing (*genetic* diagnosis) allows individuals to make reproductive and other personal choices based on knowledge of whether the disease will manifest in the future. Genetic testing for HD is almost 100% sensitive and specific, and is performed by polymerase chain reaction analysis of the number of trinucleotide repeats present in each of the two copies an individual has of the HD gene. If both genes have fewer than 30 repeats, the HD mutation is not present. If one (heterozygote) or both (homozygote) genes have 38 or more repeats, the HD mutation is present and the disease will occur if the individual lives long enough. Individuals with repeat numbers in the middle range are rare and their risk status is uncertain. It is crucial to understand that a genetic diagnosis indicates whether the mutation is present, not whether the individual tested is symptomatic from the disease, a determination requiring a clinical examination.

CLINICAL MANIFESTATIONS
Subjective

The majority of individuals at risk for HD know of their risk, either from knowledge of the disease affecting family members or from presymptomatic genetic testing. This knowledge, hypervigilance about minor clumsiness and forgetfulness, the substantial incidence of depression in gene-negative as well as affected family members, and unavoidable comparisons at-risk individuals make between themselves and their affected family members commonly create great fear and anxiety about disease onset. Such "soft" signs should not tempt clinicians to make a diagnosis. Rather, more definitive motor and sometimes cognitive symptoms must be depended on. In the early stages of HD, the most common motor complaints of patients are jerkiness, clumsiness, incoordination, and restlessness; however, cognitive and behavioral changes, although not diagnostic of the disorder, frequently precede the motor complaint. Forgetfulness is the most common early cognitive complaint. Slowed planning and performance of domestic and occupational tasks may underlie many of the complaints family members and employers may have during pre- and early diagnostic stages. Emotional problems are common, but not inevitable, and may include depression, irritability, emotional lability, exaggeration of emotional responses, and impulsiveness.

Objective
Physical Examination

The most pathognomonic clinical feature of HD is the movement disorder. In the majority of affected individuals, chorea is the first motor abnormality to develop. Choreic movements frequently begin with periodic involuntary facial twitches, sniffing, or mild twitching of the distal extremities. As the disease progresses, the chorea becomes more generalized and has greater amplitude and frequency. Gait assumes a gliding,

dancelike form with increasing unsteadiness. Stress, excitement, and emotion exacerbate these symptoms, whereas in many cases the movement disorder disappears during sleep. After a few years of symptoms, the more sustained movements of dystonia appear within the background of chorea and gradually assume increasing prominence. In later stages, dystonia and rigidity are much more prominent than chorea, leading to a contracted, bedridden state. Some spasticity is also detected late with increased reflexes and upgoing toes being the most obvious signs. Speech is affected by vocal, oral–lingual, and diaphragmatic chorea, and later dystonia and rigidity. Patients eventually become unintelligible and develop great difficulty with swallowing. Clinicians frequently interpret lack of intelligibility as an aphasia; however, HD patients maintain excellent comprehension even when completely mute. Approximately 6 to 10% of patients with HD manifest minimal or no chorea and instead have progressive rigidity and bradykinesia. This rigid form of the disease (Westphal variant) is seen most frequently in patients with juvenile onset, defined as onset before age 20. Among those with juvenile onset, there is also an association with paternal transmission of the HD gene.

Although the movement disorder is usually the most dramatic evidence of HD at a clinical encounter, emotional and behavioral changes cause much more morbidity, especially in the first decade of the disease. Depression is most common, requiring treatment in 30 to 50% of all HD patients. Patients with HD, as well as family members at risk for the disease, are at an increased risk for suicide. Suicide in affected individuals is most frequent when the depression is severe and cognition intact. Poor impulse control, irritability, and heightened emotional responses to routine events are common problems causing much distress for patients, employers, and caregivers. Delusions, paranoia, obsessive–compulsive disorders, and frank psychosis also occur with some frequency.

Deterioration in cognitive functioning generally accompanies the onset of the disease, and as the disease progresses, this aspect of the disorder becomes increasingly incapacitating. In the initial stages, patients may show a pattern of focal cognitive impairment, while broad measures of intellectual functioning remain relatively unchanged. Neuropsychologic testing frequently reveals early disturbances in memory function and difficulty initiating a behavior, followed by a progressive deterioration of verbal and perceptual skills. Perceptual skills decline more rapidly than verbal skills in the early stages; knowledge of vocabulary is retained after other cognitive abilities have deteriorated. Productivity at work declines early due to a combination of motor dysfunction, slowed performance, distractability, and emotional problems. Signs of frontal system dysfunction, such as deficits in attention, organization, and sequencing abilities, may underlie many work-related difficulties. As the disease progresses, changes in broad measures of intellectual functioning become more apparent and debilitating.

Routine Laboratory Abnormalities

There are no routine laboratory abnormalities.

PLANS
Diagnostic
Differential Diagnosis

Several types of clinical and genetic diagnoses may exist in HD families. Based on clinical grounds, an individual may be unaffected, have possible HD based on "soft" signs, or have definite HD. Unaffected family members of unknown genetic status are "at risk" for HD. Individuals with an affected parent are at 50% risk, whereas those with an affected grandparent are at 25% risk. Genetic testing can alter these risks to nearly 100% (gene mutation positive) or nearly 0% (gene mutation negative). Genetic testing is thus creating a population of asymptomatic individuals at 100% risk who are awaiting the onset of clinical disease.

The clinical diagnosis of HD can be made without difficulty when chorea, psychiatric symptoms, and intellectual decline are exhibited by an individual with a family history of similar symptoms. This is especially true if family members are known to definitively have HD according to autopsy or genetic testing. In the absence of chorea or of positive family history, clinical differential diagnosis may be difficult, as a number of inherited and sporadic disorders may have some similar symptoms. Although there are many medical causes of chorea, very few illnesses besides HD also include such severe psychiatric and cognitive symptoms. Conditions with the greatest similarity to HD include neuroacanthocytosis, dentatorubral-pallidolysian atrophy, benign familial chorea, basal ganglia infarctions, Wilson's disease, and Joseph's disease. There are specific diagnostic strategies for differentiating each of these conditions from HD.

Diagnostic Options and Recommended Approach

For the clinical diagnosis of HD, further testing beyond the neurologic examination is seldom necessary in individuals with a known family history. If there is diagnostic uncertainty, either because of lack of family history or unusual symptoms, confirmatory genetic testing may be the most cost-effective supplementary test. If genetic testing does not identify the HD gene mutation, the differential diagnosis may be explored by judicious use of ancillary tests such as brain scans, neuropsychological testing, and special laboratory studies.

Restriction fragment length polymorphism studies initially identified a DNA marker on the upper arm of chromosome 4 that was genetically linked to the HD gene. This technology provided a laboratory presymptomatic test for HD; however, several affected and unaffected family members were required to be tested to determine which group the proband's restriction pattern most resembled, necessitating the cooperation of a number of family members before meaningful results could be obtained. Since there was a chance of recombination, the accuracy of the diagnosis was reduced to less than 90% as determined by studies in several large families. With the isolation of the HD gene in 1993, and the development of direct genetic testing using polymerase chain reaction analysis, the accuracy of the test result is now 98%. The new test does not require samples from family members, is technically much simpler, and is considerably less expensive.

Genetic testing is sometimes useful for confirming a diagnosis in a symptomatic individual; however, its main use is to provide genetic information for predicting whether or not the disease will occur in the future. This knowledge can be very useful for family and personal planning and prenatal testing can permit selection of a fetus free of the HD mutation; however, a positive genetic result may be devastating psychologically and may have adverse effects on employment, personal relationships, and insurability. It is thus crucial to consider the risks and benefits and to maintain confidentiality. Ethical issues frequently arise related to fetal testing, testing of minors, and testing of individuals whose results may lead to an unwanted genetic diagnosis in a parent. Presymptomatic testing is best performed by experienced centers using a multidisciplinary approach. The procedure recommended by national and international HD lay organizations and by most HD clinics for presymptomatic testing includes a neurologic examination, psychological or psychiatric evaluation, and pre- and posttest genetic counseling.

Therapeutic

Therapeutic Options

There are no medications or other treatments currently known to halt or slow progression of the disease; however, research has suggested that preserving neuronal metabolism and protecting neurons from excitotoxic damage may be promising strategies. Trials using potential neuroprotective agents have been initiated by the Huntington Study Group, a collaboration of North American HD clinics. A European consortium is investigating the use of transplantation techniques as an additional therapeutic strategy. As the gene product becomes better understood, therapeutic interventions based on it can be anticipated.

Although HD is a relentlessly progressive and debilitating disease, there are many therapeutic options that greatly aid affected individuals and their caregivers. Occupational therapy, physical therapy, and speech and swallowing therapy are often very helpful for improving motor function and communication. Controlling involuntary movements with medication is usually of only limited benefit and rarely worth the side effects these medicines cause. For example, dopamine blockers, such as haloperidol (0.5–12 mg/d) can suppress chorea with some effectiveness, although sedation, depression, rigidity, mental

dulling, and anticholinergic side effects generally outweigh the benefits of lessened chorea. In contrast, dopaminergic drugs like levodopa may be helpful for the rigid form of HD. Behavioral and psychiatric symptoms often benefit from psychotherapy and caregiver counseling. Frequently, medications are necessary. Serotonin reuptake inhibitors (fluoxetine or paroxetine, 10–40 mg/d), as well as secondary amine tricyclic antidepressants (nortriptyline 20–100 mg/d), are very effective and well-tolerated antidepressants in HD. Electroconvulsive therapy is an option for very severe psychotic depression. Irritability and violent outbursts can also be managed with serotonin reuptake inhibitors, carbamazepine (400–1600 mg/d in two or three doses), and neuroleptic agents, when necessary. Psychosis in HD can be very difficult to treat with conventional antipsychotic agents, sometimes necessitating the use of clozapine (25–200 mg/d). Obsessive–compulsive symptoms respond well to fluoxetine (40–60 mg/d) or clomipramine (75–250 mg/d). Anxiety can be treated with lorazepam (1–6 mg/d, divided), clonazepam (0.5–10 mg/d, divided), or buspirone (15–60 mg/d, in three doses).

Other aspects of patient care are often crucial. Employers are often sympathetic to workers with HD and, under a physician's guidance, can restructure their work, allowing continued employment. The care of a family member with HD is extremely demanding on care providers in the home. Provision of home services, day programs, respite care, and residential care must be integrated into medical planning. Patients with poor nutrition do poorly behaviorally and functionally. It is advisable to monitor weights and intervene when indicated with diet customization, dietary supplements, and, sometimes, a feeding gastrostomy.

Often individuals at risk for HD have witnessed the slow deterioration of an affected family member. For this reason, many at-risk individuals are intimately aware of the gradual progression of symptoms and may display a high degree of anxiety concerning their own potential for developing the disease. It is important to clarify to the at-risk individual that it is normal to feel restless, drop things or slip, and that observing these behaviors in themselves does not necessarily indicate the onset of HD. Periodic neurologic assessments, along with encouragement from the physician to lead as normal a life as possible, are very important in helping unaffected at-risk individuals live and cope effectively with their at-risk status.

The genetic nature of HD should be thoroughly explained to the patient at the time of initial diagnosis. It is important that he or she understand the autosomal dominant mode of inheritance of this disorder, in which each offspring of an affected individual has a 50% risk of developing the disease. Individuals at risk often contemplate the possibility of marriage and reproduction and may request counseling. This should be provided through referral to a genetic counselor who has worked in presymptomatic testing with HD families. Although the final decision regarding reproduction ultimately rests with the individual and spouse, the genetic counselor can be helpful in clarifying many of the crucial issues.

In addition to questions about reproduction, the individual at risk may also have questions related to the progression of the disease and the management of an affected parent or relative. Families should be encouraged to maintain their normal lifestyle for as long as possible; however, they should be aware that changes in the family arrangements are inevitable owing to the progressive nature of the disorder. Reversal of roles between spouses is especially problematic. Marital and family disruptions frequently occur when adolescent children or spouses who have been "protected" from knowledge of the disorder learn about it "accidentally" or after its onset. For this reason, patients with HD and at-risk individuals should be encouraged to be open with their immediate family members regarding their diagnosis or at-risk status. The need for appropriate referrals for individual and/or family counseling should be addressed in all HD families.

Recommended Approach

No single health care provider can easily meet the needs of an HD family alone. At different stages of the disease, the services of neurology, psychiatry, psychology, medical genetics, physical therapy, occupational therapy, speech pathology, and social services may assume importance. Regional multispecialty HD clinics exist that bring these disciplines together and can receive referrals, but an experienced primary care physician can also assemble such help as needed. The Huntington's Disease Society of America (212–242–1968) and other lay organizations are excellent resources for patient services, as well as for a large collection of written material, that may be of use to physicians, patients, and caregivers.

FOLLOW-UP

Owing to the progressive and hereditary nature of HD, medical follow-up of patients and their at-risk family members is advisable. Early recognition of symptoms may greatly influence decisions regarding education, profession, marriage, and reproduction. Patients with HD disease who are receiving medication require follow-up to adjust drug dosages to attain the best therapeutic effects. In cases where the diagnosis of HD is uncertain, follow-up evaluations may be helpful in making a differential diagnosis.

At-risk patients may periodically request a follow-up evaluation to confirm they are not showing early signs of the disease. Such diagnostic evaluations are frequently requested during times of depression or irritability for the individual, so the physician must be cautious not to confuse possible early signs of HD with symptoms of stress or as a result of factors external to HD.

DISCUSSION
Prevalence and Incidence

Huntington's disease occurs worldwide, in all races and ethnic groups. Its prevalence is 5 to 10 cases per 100,000, and its incidence has been estimated as 3 to 6 new cases per year for every million in population. About 35,000 individuals are affected in the United States. Another 175,000 Americans have a genetic risk for developing the disease. The average age of onset is about 37; however, the range is from infancy into the eighties.

Related Basic Science
Genetics

The clinical genetics of HD is that of autosomal dominance with complete penetrance. Fertility is not decreased as the average age of onset of the disease is beyond childbearing ages. HD demonstrates anticipation in the offspring of affected males who tend to develop the disease at a younger age than their fathers. As many as 1 to 3% of HD cases may be new mutations. Thus, there have been multiple founders. The HD gene was the first disease gene localized by the then new technique of linkage analysis using restriction fragment length polymorphisms. This discovery, in 1983, which depended on analyzing a unique large Venezuelan kindred, localized the HD gene to the short arm of chromosome 4. It was another 10 years before the precise gene and its mutation were discovered. The gene, which was cloned in 1993, codes for a large, highly conserved, normal protein ("huntingtin") containing about 3,000 amino acids. The nucleotide and amino acid sequences bear little resemblance to any known protein; however, its messenger RNA is expressed, with some regional variation, in most tissues of the body and in neurons and glia in the brain. In individuals with HD, a polymorphic trinucleotide repeat sequence (CAGn), near the 5′ end of the gene, is expanded beyond the normal repeat range, leading to translation of an expanded polyglutamine sequence in the protein. In the normal population the number of CAG repeats varies from 17 to 29. In individuals with HD there are more than 38 repeats. There is a correlation between the higher numbers of repeats (>60) and younger disease onset. With paternal inheritance, there is a greater probability for an offspring to have an increased number of repeats, whereas there is little probability of an increase with maternal inheritance. This underlies the genetic anticipation observed in the children of affected males. Other inherited diseases that have thus far been found to be linked to a trinucleotide repeat expansion include spinal bulbar muscular atrophy, fragile X, myotonic dystrophy, spinal cerebellar ataxia I, dentatorubral-pallidoluysian atrophy, and FRAXE mental retardation. How the mutant protein leads to selective neuronal death in the central nervous system remains uncertain; however, there is evidence that the mutation changes or increases the protein's function.

Physiologic or Metabolic Derangement

There has been increasing evidence from human studies, and from animal models of HD, that neuronal death occurs by glutamate-induced excitotoxicity. Glutamate, the most common excitatory amino acid neurotransmitter, is neurotoxic when a state of overexcitation occurs. It has been difficult, however, to demonstrate that there are increased levels of glutamate in HD, that there is an endogenous excitotoxin, or that glutamate receptors are causally altered. A recent hypothesis receiving growing support is that the HD mutation causes accumulating damage to cellular metabolic pathways, rendering neurons selectively vulnerable to excitotoxicity at physiologic levels of glutamate.

Anatomic Derangement

Neuropathologic studies of patients with HD show that at autopsy the brain is invariably reduced in size and weight as a result of widespread neuronal loss in the basal ganglia, cerebral cortex, and other regions. The striatum is affected earliest and most intensively, whereas cortical atrophy accounts for much of the loss in brain mass in the later stages. Within the striatum, the medium spiny projection neurons which contain γ-aminobutyric acid are lost, while interneuron populations containing somatostatin/neuropeptide Y and acetylcholine are preserved. Loss of the inhibitory striatal projections to the globus pallidus and substantia nigra are thought to be the anatomic basis of involuntary movements, impulsive behavior, and emotional dyscontrol. In the cerebral cortex, there is widespread loss of pyramidal cells, likely accounting for much of the dementia and spasticity that occur later in the disease.

Natural History and Its Modification with Treatment

Most patients first begin to show symptoms between the ages of 35 and 45, with death occurring within 15 to 25 years of onset. A small percentage of carriers (approximately 5%) have onset before the age of 20, and a similar number do not show symptoms until after age 60. Individuals who do not carry the gene cannot transmit it to future generations. Death is usually due to cardiopulmonary arrest, aspiration, or intercurrent infection in the setting of end-stage physical and mental debilitation. Survival and morbidity depend greatly on the quality of supportive care throughout the course of the disease. Key contributors to an optimal disease course are maintenance of physical and mental functioning, adequate treatment of affective disorders, minimization of antichoreic medication use, and provision of support for the caregivers. Attention should also be paid, in advance, to ensuring patient autonomy over her or his care and eventual death. Powers of attorney, living wills, and substituted judgments (medical custody) should be considered while the patient can still express his or her wishes.

Prevention

There is no known method for preventing or delaying the onset of HD in those individuals who inherit the mutant gene from an affected parent; however, the recent availability of the presymptomatic genetic test for HD provides the opportunity for preventing disease transmission to succeeding generations. Parents who are gene positive may choose not to reproduce. Furthermore, amniocentesis or chorionic villus sampling can be performed to determine whether a fetus will inherit the mutant gene. This provides parents with the opportunity to make a decision regarding aborting gene carriers early in pregnancy. Because in most gene carriers onset is in middle and later life, such testing raises many ethical questions that continue to be discussed among the community of clinicians who provide services to HD families.

Cost Containment

In most cases, the diagnosis of HD can be made on the basis of a positive family history in combination with presenting symptoms compatible with the clinical manifestations of the disorder. For such cases, extra studies such as brain scans, extensive laboratory studies, genetic testing, lumbar puncture, and neuropsychological testing are unnecessary. With a typical clinical presentation, but absence of a family history, confirmatory genetic testing can provide a definitive diagnosis when positive. If the genetic test is negative, a wide differential diagnosis must be considered and ancillary tests performed depending on the possible alternative etiologies.

REFERENCES

Beal MF, Hyman BT, Koroshetz W. Do defects in mitochondrial energy metabolism underlie the pathology of neurodegenerative diseases? Trends Neurosci 1993;16:125.

Folstein S. Huntington's disease: A disorder of families. Baltimore: Johns Hopkins Press, 1989.

Hersch S, Jones R, Koroshetz W, Quaid K. The neurogenetics genie: Testing for the Huntington's disease mutation. Neurology 1994;44:1369.

Huntington's Disease Collaborative Research Group. A novel gene containing a trinucleotide repeat that is expanded and unstable on Huntington's disease chromosomes. Cell 1993;72:971.

Ranen NG, Peyser CE, Folstein SE. A physician's guide to the management of Huntington's disease. New York: Huntington's Disease Society of America, 1993.

Wexler NS, Rose EA, Housman DE. Molecular approaches to hereditary disease of the nervous system: Huntington's disease as a paradigm. Annu Rev Neurosci 1991;14:503.

CHAPTER 20–8

Cerebellar Disorders

Claudia Jacob Chaves, M.D.

DEFINITION

The cerebellum is one of the three basic subdivisions of the brain, strategically located behind and below the cerebral hemispheres, overlying the fourth ventricle and brainstem. The cerebellum is responsible for the control of posture and gait, coordination of movements, and regulation of muscle tone. Disorders that affect the cerebellum are characterized by impairment of any or all of these functions.

ETIOLOGY

The cerebellum can be affected by several types of conditions including the following:

- Degenerative disease
- Demyelinating disease (multiple sclerosis)
- Vascular disease (cerebellar infarction, cerebellar hemorrhage)
- Cerebellar tumors
- Paraneoplastic cerebellar disorder
- Toxin (alcohol, medications)-induced disorders

CRITERIA FOR DIAGNOSIS
Suggestive

Cerebellar disease should be suspected in patients with gait ataxia, limb ataxia, tremor, and slurred or scanning speech. These signs are not pathognomonic for cerebellar disease, however, as damage to other structures such as the brainstem and spinal cord may produce similar findings. Also, lesions overlying the cerebellum, like meningiomas, shwannomas, and subdural hematomas, can produce cerebellar dysfunction through tissue compression or ischemia, with signs and symptoms similar to those caused by direct cerebellar involvement.

With structural lesions of the cerebellum, the patient's complaints and findings are more closely related to the site and rate of progression of the lesion than to the pathologic process itself, and lesions as different as infarction, hemorrhage, and infection may have similar findings.

Definitive

The definitive diagnosis of cerebellar disorders is usually by neuroimaging studies, especially magnetic resonance imaging (MRI). MRI has proved to be the most sensitive diagnostic neuroimaging technique for identification of lesions in the posterior fossa.

CLINICAL MANIFESTATIONS
Subjective

Most patients with cerebellar disease have a combination of four symptoms: gait instability, headache, nausea and vomiting, and dizziness.

Other symptoms, such as double vision, hearing disorders, and memory difficulty, can also occur and result from extension of the disease beyond the cerebellum. Patients with gait instability usually have difficulty in walking a straight line as if they have alcohol intoxication; they tend to lurch from side to side or to drift to the same side as the cerebellar lesion. Progressive gait unsteadiness is the most frequent complaint associated with degenerative disease. Headache, nausea, and vomiting are common with structural damage to the cerebellum, such as in tumors, hemorrhages, and infarctions. Headache usually is felt above or behind one eye or at the base of the skull, most frequently in the morning, and is secondary to irritation of meningeal nerve fibers, branches of the fifth nerve. Nausea and vomiting usually accompany the headache and probably arise from brainstem irritation. Dizziness can occur in patients with a variety of lesions, and can be described as vertigo, a feeling of instability when attempting to walk, or lightheadedness. Incoordination, altered speech, tremor, and other signs of cerebellar damage may be evident in patients with structural or degenerative disorders, but usually are not major complaints.

Objective
Physical Examination

Gait ataxia, limb dysmetria, dysarthria, tremor, nystagmus, and hypotonia are the most common signs of cerebellar disease. Cerebellar gait abnormalities include difficulty standing and walking; patients are able to maintain their balance only when their feet are widely separated. Limb dysmetria is one of the more obvious signs of incoordination seen with cerebellar disease and can be either hypermetric, falling beyond the target, or hypometric, falling short of the target. Slurred speech with inappropriate rhythms and emphasis is often seen with focal or diffuse cerebellar damage. Cerebellar tremor is characterized as being most marked at the end of the movement, when the patient attempts to achieve the greatest precision. The most common abnormality of eye movement is gaze-evoked nystagmus, with the amplitude of the fast component in both eyes greater when the gaze is directed toward the side of the cerebellar lesion. Hypotonia often appears in an individual limb or in part of a limb ipsilateral to the cerebellar hemisphere injury. It may appear with acute or chronic disease, with focal or diffuse damage. Usually it is associated with pendular tendon reflexes and impaired check and excessive rebound response of an outstretched limb.

Most of the cerebellar signs identified in humans can be attributable to damage to the midline (vermis) or lateral (hemispheres) zones of the cerebellum. The clinical signs resulting from midline cerebellar disease consist of gait ataxia and abnormalities of extraocular movements, whereas the signs of lateral cerebellar disease include limb dysmetria, dysarthria, kinetic tremor, and hypotonia.

Routine Laboratory Abnormalities

Routine laboratory tests are usually normal.

PLANS
Diagnostic
Differential Diagnosis

Degenerative Disease. Suspicion of cerebellar degenerative diseases usually arises when patients develop progressive gait difficulty or symmetric limb ataxia that evolves over the course of decades. The presence of tremor, clumsiness, or nystagmus in some members of the patient's family suggests a hereditary cerebellar degenerative disease, usually termed *hereditary ataxia.* Hereditary ataxias can have autosomal dominant or recessive patterns. The principal sites of the pathologic changes are the pons, spinal cord, and cerebellum. Friedreich's ataxia is the prototype of all forms of hereditary ataxia, and is characterized by age of onset before the end of puberty, progressive ataxia involving initially the lower limbs and then all four limbs, dysarthria, absence of deep tendon reflexes, and loss of vibration and position sense in the lower limbs. Pes cavus, kyphoscoliosis, and progressive cardiomyopathy are also constant features in this disorder. Most of the patients have an autosomal recessive inheritance.

Demyelinating Disease (Multiple Sclerosis). Multiple sclerosis lesions are commonly found in the cerebellum as well as in the afferent and efferent pathways of the cerebellar motor system. Most patients are between 10 and 50 years of age at onset of the disease. Any one or any combination of cerebellar signs can be seen in patients with multiple sclerosis, and they are qualitatively identical to those seen in other cerebellar disorders. The cerebellar signs, however, are usually associated with or follow the onset of other signs, such as optic neuritis, spinal cord attacks, and paresthetic attacks. Occasionally, the cerebellar dysfunction can occur as the first symptom of multiple sclerosis, but in these patients other neurologic deficits appear in the natural course of the disease. If not, it is prudent to consider other diagnoses.

Vascular Disease

CEREBELLAR INFARCTION. Cerebellar infarction should be suspected in patients who acutely develop difficulty with standing or walking, nausea and vomiting, dizziness or vertigo, slurred speech, and clumsiness. Headache, usually occipital or frontal, can also be present, making the distinction between infarct and hemorrhage difficult at times. Prior transient ischemic attacks in the same arterial territory, presence of risk factors for atherosclerosis, and potential cardiac embolic source are important factors that help with the assessment of this diagnosis.

CEREBELLAR HEMORRHAGE. Cerebellar hemorrhage usually develops over a period of several hours, and in the early phases of the disease complaints of occipital headache, vomiting, and dizziness are constant. Gait and limb ataxia, as well as ipsilateral gaze and facial palsies, are frequent; however, clinical signs of cerebellar involvement may be minimal or lacking initially. Within hours, the patient can become stuporous or comatose, sometimes with unanticipated suddenness, as the result of brainstem compression.

Cerebellar Tumors. The most common cerebellar tumors in children are medulloblastoma, ependymoma, and astrocytoma, whereas in adults, hemangioblastomas and metastatic disease are more common. The clinical picture is characterized by subacute development of signs and symptoms of increased intracranial pressure, including headache, nausea, vomiting, and papilledema. Gait and limb ataxia, diplopia, and other symptoms of bulbar dysfunction from brainstem compression may also be present at diagnosis. One fourth of the patients with hemangioblastoma also have retinal angiomas, pheochromocytomas, renal and pancreatic cysts and carcinoma, and epididymal cysts, which constitutes Von Hippel–Lindau disease, an autosomal dominant disease with variable expression.

Paraneoplastic Cerebellar Disorder. Paraneoplastic cerebellar dysfunction is probably the most common paraneoplastic syndrome affecting the central nervous system. It is common in patients with small cell lung carcinoma, Hodgkin's lymphoma, and carcinomas of the breast, ovary, and female genital tract. The onset of the symptoms is typically insidious, occurring over weeks to months, and patients usually have signs and symptoms reflecting diffuse dysfunction of the cerebellum, including vertigo, dysarthria, dysmetria of the limbs, and severe gait ataxia. Abnormalities of oculomotor function are common and include nystagmus, disruption of smooth pursuit movements, ocular dysmetria, and opsoclonus. The neurologic deficits generally worsen over a period of several weeks to months and then stabilize at a level of severe disability. Patients with paraneoplastic cerebellar degeneration often have cells in the spinal fluid and antibodies to Purkinje cells can be detected.

Toxin-induced Disorders

ALCOHOL. Chronic alcohol abuse associated with inadequate nutrition can affect the cerebellum and produce a syndrome characterized by a wide-based stance and gait, with legs primarily affected and the arms relatively spared. Speech disturbances and ocular motility abnormalities are less frequent signs. In most cases, the cerebellar syndrome evolves subacutely, over a period of several weeks or months, followed by periods of relative stability. Symptom progression is associated with continued ethanol consumption and poor nutrition.

MEDICATIONS. Some anticonvulsants and antineoplastic drugs can affect cerebellar function. Phenytoin, in high doses, can cause an acute, reversible vestibulo-ocular syndrome, with nystagmus and ataxia. Long-term phenytoin treatment can cause a persistent cerebellar syndrome. The relationship between serum phenytoin levels and the occurrence of this irreversible syndrome is unclear, but it seems that higher levels may increase the risk of the syndrome. Fluorouracil, cytosine arabinoside, and methotrexate are among the chemotherapeutic agents that cause cerebellar ataxia.

Diagnostic Options

Degenerative disorders, as a rule, do not present any specific finding on neuroimaging studies. Patients with Friedreich's ataxia can have slight cerebellar and spinal cord atrophy, best seen on MRI.

The diagnosis of multiple sclerosis can be substantiated by appropriate positive findings on MRI scans, evoked potentials, and analysis of cerebrospinal fluid proteins. MRI with and without gadolinium can demonstrate the presence of multiple disseminated lesions in white matter, progressive accumulation of lesions over time, as well as the presence of enhancing lesions that seem to correlate with the disease activity. Evoked potentials are valuable in detecting clinically silent or uncertain lesions, providing evidence of multiple lesions in early stages of multiple sclerosis. The analysis of the cerebrospinal fluid protein shows, in about 90% of patients, an increase in the proportion of gamma globulin and presence of oligoclonal bands. Myelin basic protein can also be present in the cerebrospinal fluid and indicates that the disease is active.

Cerebellar infarction and hemorrhage as well as cerebellar tumors can be detected by computed tomography (CT) or MRI of the head. MRI is in general more helpful than CT in detecting cerebellar infarcts and tumors. CT is reliable in detecting cerebellar hemorrhages, whereas MRI is particularly useful in detecting old hemorrhages, which can no longer be seen by CT scan after 4 to 5 weeks. Angiography, magnetic resonance angiography (MRA), ultrasound of the posterior circulation, and transesophageal echocardiogram are helpful in the elucidation of the stroke mechanism. Angiography is also used in patients with cerebellar hemorrhages, when there is suspicion of arteriovenous malformation.

Computed tomography and MRI of the head are generally completely normal in the first several months of paraneoplastic cerebellar degeneration, but eventually show diffuse atrophy of the cerebellum. Anti-Purkinje cell antibodies (so called anti-Yo) can be found in the sera of about half of these patients, and their presence strongly suggests an underlying breast or ovarian cancer.

The diagnosis of cerebellar toxicity secondary to alcohol abuse and medications is usually made by history, with imaging studies usually remarkable only for cerebellar atrophy.

Recommended Approach

In general, our recommendation when we suspect that the patient has cerebellar disease is to obtain an MRI of the head, because with this test one is able to identify precisely lesions characteristic of multiple sclerosis, different types of cerebellar tumors, cerebellar infarct, and hemorrhages. The presence of cerebellar atrophy or a normal test may represent cerebellar degenerative, paraneoplastic, or toxin-induced disease, and in those situations a careful personal and family history is essential. Once the cerebellar infarct is diagnosed, the mechanism of the stroke should be pursued with noninvasive studies of the vessels; we recommend magnetic resonance angiography and ultrasound studies of the posterior circulation, and if there is discrepancy between the two tests, we perform conventional angiography. The same principle applies to cerebellar hemorrhage; if there is any likelihood that the hemorrhage might be secondary to an arteriovenous malformation, we recommend conventional angiography.

Therapeutic

Therapeutic Options

No specific treatment is available for degenerative, paraneoplastic, or toxin-induced diseases. Significant neurologic improvement is distinctly unusual after successful treatment of the associated tumor and occurs occasionally after discontinuation of the toxic agent.

Acute attacks of multiple sclerosis can be treated with adrenocorticotropic hormone or corticosteroids; both drugs seem to help in the recovering process of the disease. Immunosuppressive agents such as azathioprine and cyclophosphamide have been used in the progressive form of this disease, whereas interferon-beta has been used to decrease the exacerbation rate of multiple sclerosis.

Surgical resection is the treatment of choice for all cerebellar tumors, excluding multiple metastases. Radiation therapy following surgery is used in the treatment of medulloblastomas, ependymomas, and single metastases. Whole-brain radiation therapy is the treatment of choice for multiple metastases. Chemotherapy can be used as an attempt to improve long-term survival in patients with recurrent medulloblastomas and ependymomas.

Cerebellar infarcts and hemorrhages can be treated medically or surgically, depending on the clinical picture. If the patient is alert and clinically stable, medical treatment alone is indicated; if deterioration of consciousness develops, surgical treatment is urgently required. The medical management for patients with cerebellar infarcts in the acute phase consists of maximizing the blood flow to the ischemic region and avoiding excessive reduction of blood pressure and hypovolemia. Surgery is usually indicated in the pseudotumoral form of cerebellar infarction; the severe cerebellar swelling may cause acute hydrocephalus, brainstem compression, and tonsillar herniation. Carefully controlling blood pressure, monitoring intracranial pressure and controlling it by the use of tissue dehydrating agents such as mannitol, limiting fluid intake, and hyperventilation (PCO_2 between 25 and 30 mm Hg) are the main steps in the medical management of cerebellar hemorrhages. Surgery is generally considered in patients with large cerebellar infarcts and hemorrhages with deterioration of the level of consciousness who do not respond to the clinical measures. Some centers also follow imaging parameters for directing management of cerebellar hemorrhage; hematomas larger than 3 cm are treated surgically.

Recommended Approach

Our recommendation for treatment of cerebellar tumors is similar to the one described above. Unfortunately, at this point no specific treatment is available for degenerative, paraneoplastic, and toxin-induced diseases involving the cerebellum.

We treat acute exacerbations of multiple sclerosis with corticosteroids. We recommend interferon-beta in patients who have had several exacerbations in a short period. Occasionally we use immunosuppressors, mainly in patients with severe progressive forms of disease.

Our recommendation in cerebellar infarcts is to treat according to the mechanism of the infarct. Patients with hemodynamic strokes should be maintained in strict recumbency and have their blood pressure carefully monitored, avoiding hypotension. We use heparin and warfarin for short periods, 3 to 6 weeks, in patients with recent occlusion of the vertebral artery in the neck or intracranially or of the basilar artery. When the lesion is a severe stenosis, anticoagulants are used for longer periods, until the vessel occludes or the artery recanalizes. Heparin followed by coumadin is also used for patients whose cerebellar infarct is caused by embolism from the heart. The doses of heparin and coumadin vary; we try to keep the partial thromboplastin time 1.5 to 2.0 times control levels and the international normalized ratio (INR) between 2.0 and 3.0, respectively. Aspirin 325 mg/d is used in nonstenotic irregular lesions.

Regarding cerebellar hemorrhages, we try to control the blood pressure, however avoiding excessive reductions. Elevation of the head of the bed, use of osmotic diuretics (mannitol or glycerol) or corticosteroids, and hyperventilation, keeping the PCO_2 between 25 and 30 mm Hg, are the measures we recommend to treat the edema associated with the hematoma. Monitoring of intracranial pressure is helpful in some instances, as it enables the clinician to use medical measures more precisely and helps with the decision on surgery.

FOLLOW-UP

Patients with suspected paraneoplasic cerebellar disorder in whom no tumor is initially found should have periodic clinical evaluations to detect and treat tumors, which may be discovered later.

Because of the high risk of recurrence, patients with medulloblastoma and ependymomas should be carefully followed for several years after the initial treatment. Any change in the neurologic examination should be investigated with neuroimaging studies, and chemotherapy should be started if recurrence of the tumor is confirmed.

The follow-up of patients with cerebellar infarcts should be done on a regular basis, with careful control of prothrombin time and international normalized ratio in patients on anticoagulants. In those patients with stenotic lesions, the vascular lesion should be monitored every 6 to 12 months, to identify the evolution of the lesion to complete occlusion or recanalization of the vessel. Cerebellar hemorrhages are in general associated with several complications in the acute phase of the disease; however, afterward, the outcome is usually good and follow-up can be done on a routine basis.

DISCUSSION

Prevalence and Incidence

The estimated prevalence of Friedreich's disease is about 1 per 100,000 population. The risk of developing multiple sclerosis varies with the latitude; the prevalence is 1 per 100,000 in equatorial areas, 6 to 14 per 100,000 in the southern United States and Europe, and 30 to 80 per 100,000 in Canada, northern Europe, and the northern United States. The incidence is higher in women than in men (1.7:1.0) and in whites than in blacks. Regarding cerebellar tumors, medulloblastoma accounts for about 25% of primary central nervous system tumors in the first two decades and less than 1% of adult brain tumors; astrocytoma and ependymoma account for 30 to 40% and 10% of childhood brain tumors, respectively; hemangioblastoma accounts for 1 to 2% of all intracranial tumors and about 8 to 12% of posterior fossa neoplasms. Paraneoplastic cerebellar disorders are uncommon. Cerebellar infarcts are more frequent than cerebellar hemorrhages, with cerebellar infarcts accounting for 1.5 to 4.2% of strokes in autopsy series. Cerebellar hemorrhages have been reported from 0.27 to 0.44% in autopsies series, and represent 5 to 13% of intracranial hemorrhages. Alcoholic cerebellar degeneration is a common disease.

Related Basic Science

The basic mechanism for degenerative disease is unknown. Extensive biochemical investigations in Friedreich's disease have shown no specific metabolic defect or marker. A single gene locus on chromosome 9 accounts for the classic form of this disease.

Multiple sclerosis is thought to be caused by an autoimmune attack against myelin, with involvement of both cellular and humoral mechanisms. Autoimmune reaction is also the mechanism proposed for paraneoplastic cerebellar disease, and the presence of antibodies against Purkinje cells is the strongest evidence for that.

Like other brain neoplasias, the etiology of brain tumors is unknown. Antecedent head injury, infection, metabolic and other systemic diseases, and exposure to toxins and radiation have all been invoked as causative factors; however, with the exception of radiation and possible viral infection, there is no conclusive evidence that any of them plays a part in the causation of cerebral neoplasms in humans.

Hypoperfusion secondary to hemodynamically significant narrowing of the vertebrobasilar arteries, as well as emboli, from the heart or from proximal intraarterial sites, is the main mechanism of cerebellar infarcts.

Cerebellar hemorrhage is considered to be, in 60 to 90% of patients, secondary to hypertension, with the remainder being attributed to vascular malformations, blood dyscrasias, or unknown mechanism. Anticoagulation and blood dyscrasias, as causes of cerebellar hemorrhage, have been more frequently reported recently, probably reflecting the current widespread use of anticoagulation in the management of strokes.

The mechanism postulated for the toxic effects of ethanol is a direct effect on the cerebellum cortex, mainly affecting the Purkinje cells of the anterior superior aspect of the cerebellum. Phenytoin also has a direct toxic effect on the cerebellar cortex, involving all the neurocellular elements.

Natural History and Its Modification with Treatment

The natural history of Freidreich's ataxia and paraneoplastic cerebellar degeneration is characterized by progressive deterioration during years and months, respectively.

Multiple sclerosis usually begins as a relapsing–remitting disease and evolves secondarily into a progressive neurologic illness. In about 10% of patients, however, the course of the disease is progressive from the beginning. Interferon beta seems to be, at this point, the only drug that interferes with the natural history of this disease, decreasing the number of exacerbations in patients with the relapsing–remitting form of the disease. Immunosuppressors have little benefit on the course of the chronic progressive form of multiple sclerosis.

Cerebellar tumors, if not treated, cause a progressive increase in intracranial pressure, followed by coma and death. The prognosis is good with treatment; however, medulloblastoma and ependymoma can recur, requiring further therapy.

In general, patients with cerebellar hemorrhages do better in the long term than patients with cerebellar infarcts of the same size. Both, however, have a higher incidence of strokes if risk factors are not treated.

The symptoms of alcoholic cerebellar degeneration progress with the maintenance of ethanol intake and poor nutrition. Occasionally, improvement can occur with discontinuation of the toxic agent.

Prevention

From all the cerebellar disorders discussed above, prevention is effective in decreasing the occurrence of cerebellar infarcts and hemorrhages, through the control of such risk factors as hypertension, diabetes, hypercholesterolemia, smoking, and cardiac embolic sources.

Cost Containment

Neuroimaging studies, especially MRI of the head, are indispensable for the diagnosis of cerebellar disease. Laboratory tests have not been very helpful so far and, therefore, are less crucial when cost containment is a consideration.

REFERENCES

Adams RD, Victor M. Principles of neurology. New York: McGraw-Hill, Inc., 1993.
Gilman S, Bloedel JR, Lechtenberg R. Disorders of the cerebellum. Philadelphia: Davis, 1981.
Kase CS. Cerebellar hemorrhage. In: Kase CS, Caplan LR, eds. Intracerebral hemorrhage. Newton, MA: Butterworth-Heinemann, 1994:425.
Lechtenberg R. Handbook of cerebellar disease. New York: Marcel Dekker, 1993.

CHAPTER 20–9

Stroke and Cerebrovascular Disease

Margaret E. O'Donoghue, M.D.

DEFINITION

Any acute vascular event occurring in the brain and causing brain damage may be classified as a stroke. Arterial and venous brain infarctions, intracerebral hemorrhage, and subarachnoid hemorrhage are all stroke syndromes. This chapter reviews arterial brain infarction and intracerebral hemorrhage, the two stroke syndromes most often encountered by practicing physicians.

ETIOLOGY

Brain infarctions may be caused by arterial thrombosis or embolism. Small vessel infarcts may result from hypertension-associated lipohyalinosis or atherothrombosis. Larger infarcts may occur as the result of cardiac embolism, artery-to-artery embolism, or local atherothrombosis.

Hypertension can cause damage to small blood vessels with weakening of the arterial wall and microaneurysm formation. It is in this setting that intracerebral hemorrhage is most commonly seen. Other causes include vascular malformations and amyloid angiopathy.

CRITERIA FOR DIAGNOSIS

Suggestive

Cerebral infarctions and intracerebral hemorrhages are suspected when a patient develops the sudden onset of a focal neurologic deficit. For a diagnosis of cerebral infarction to be entertained, the deficit should cor-

respond to a known vascular territory and be longer than an hour in duration. Symptoms of dysfunction in a particular vascular territory that last less than an hour are classified as transient ischemic attacks.

Definitive

To make a definitive diagnosis of a stroke syndrome, other causes of acute, focal neurologic deficits must be excluded. Brain imaging is very important in differentiating infarction from hemorrhage and in excluding subarachnoid and subdural hemorrhages and mass lesions such as tumors and abscesses.

CLINICAL MANIFESTATIONS
Subjective

Stroke patients often have a history of hypertension, smoking, diabetes, and coronary artery disease. Hyperlipidemia, clotting disorders, and valvular heart disease may also be present. The clinical pattern seen in cerebral infarction depends on the particular artery that is occluded. Thus, contralateral weakness or sensory loss, aphasia, and neglect syndromes favor infarcts in the regions supplied by the internal carotid artery and its branches, whereas hemianopia, diplopia, vertigo, and ataxia are indicators of infarction in the vertebrobasilar territory.

Lacunar strokes are infarcts no more than 1.5 cm in diameter that are related to occlusion of small vessels deep in the brain. Several distinct lacunar syndromes have been described. Pure motor strokes and ataxic hemiparesis can be seen in occlusion of the pontine perforating arteries or the lenticulostriate arteries supplying the internal capsule. The clumsy hand–dysarthria syndrome is also a pontine lacunar syndrome, whereas a pure sensory stroke suggests thalamic perforating artery occlusion.

Patients with intracerebral hemorrhage often have a history of hypertension. As in cerebral infarction, the symptoms and signs of intracerebral hemorrhage vary with the location and size of the bleed. Those related to hypertension most often occur in the putamen, pons, thalamus, and cerebellum. Putaminal and thalamic hemorrhages cause contralateral weakness by involving or compressing the internal capsule. Contralateral sensory loss is also found with thalamic hemorrhage. Symptoms of cerebellar hemorrhage include vertigo, imbalance, nausea, vomiting, and ataxia. Pontine hemorrhages usually result in coma with impaired eye movements and bilateral weakness or posturing; however, any hemorrhage that is large enough can produce raised intracranial pressure, altered consciousness, and even herniation.

Lobar hemorrhages are located in the subcortical white matter, most often in the posterior portion of the cerebrum. As with large infarcts, the localizing symptoms and signs are dependent on the lobe affected.

Objective

Physical Examination

Anterior circulation strokes (internal carotid, anterior and middle cerebral artery territories) commonly produce decreased gaze to the contralateral side, contralateral weakness and/or sensory loss, or contralateral visual field defects. Those occurring in the dominant (usually left) hemisphere often cause aphasia, whereas those on the nondominant side can result in visuospatial difficulties or neglect syndromes. Strokes occurring in the distribution of the vertebrobasilar system may produce contralateral sensory loss if the thalamus is affected and contralateral hemianopia if the occipital lobe is involved. Lesions in the brainstem produce a variety of findings such as cranial nerve dysfunction, contralateral weakness or sensory loss, ataxia, nystagmus, Horner's syndrome, and altered level of consciousness.

Routine Laboratory Abnormalities

Routine laboratory tests are most often normal in stroke patients. Hyponatremia may develop subacutely in large strokes from the inappropriate secretion of antidiuretic hormone. In patients with bleeding disorders, thrombocytopenia or a prolonged prothrombin time or partial thromboplastin time may be found. Conversely, patients with coagu-

lopathies may have thrombocytosis, polycythemia, or elevated partial thromboplastin time. Erythrocyte sedimentation rates may also be elevated in some vasculopathies associated with stroke. Finally, some embolic strokes occur in the setting of acute myocardial infarction or cardiac arrhythmia; all stroke victims should have an electrocardiogram performed.

PLANS
Diagnostic
Differential Diagnosis

The differential diagnosis of cerebral infarction or hemorrhage includes transient ischemic attack, seizure, tumor, migraine, subdural hematoma, and vestibular disorders.

Diagnostic Options

Brain imaging is the most important diagnostic test in cerebrovascular disease. Computed tomography is often the best initial test because of its ability to clearly show acute hemorrhage and its availability. Computed tomography scans may be negative in acute infarctions, however, and are limited in imaging the posterior fossa. Magnetic resonance imaging is superior in evaluating the brainstem and cerebellum and is more sensitive for very small infarcts. Magnetic resonance angiography provides a means of assessing extra- and intracranial blood vessels. In investigating the etiology of large vessel or embolic strokes, carotid Doppler ultrasonography and echocardiography are very important tools. Cerebral angiography becomes necessary when precise information is sought concerning areas of arterial stenosis, aneurysms, arteriovenous malformations, or vasculopathy. Finally, transcranial Doppler may be used to assess patterns of intracranial blood flow and to screen for intracranial occlusive lesions.

Recommended Approach

The recommended approach is outlined in Figure 20–9–1.

Therapeutic
Therapeutic Options

Several new strategies aimed at limiting the extent of neuronal damage in patients with brain infarction are currently being tested. Some therapies, such as thrombolysis and emergency endarterectomy or angio-

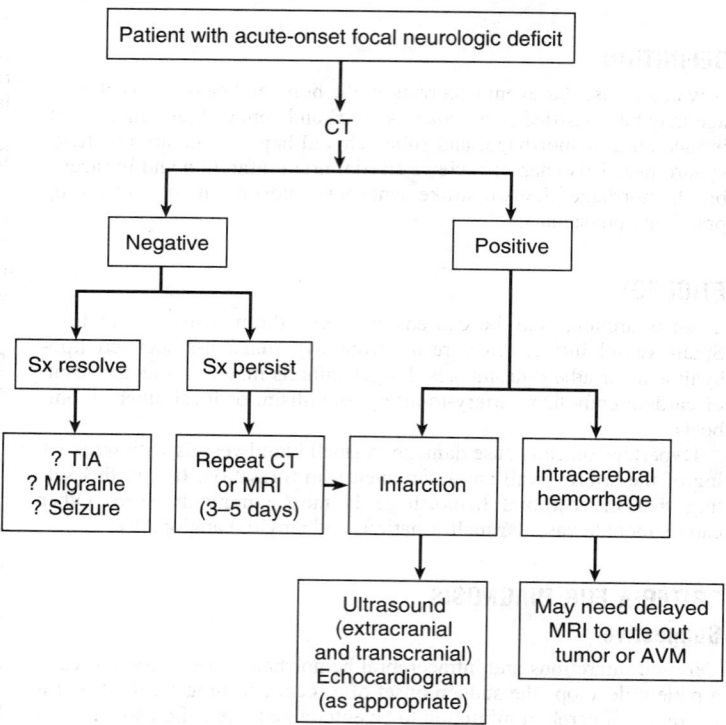

Figure 20–9–1. Recommended diagnostic approach in patients with possible stroke.

plasty, are designed to quickly restore blood flow. Other treatments attempt to limit secondary neuronal damage; N-methyl D-aspartate channel blockers, antioxidants, and free radical scavengers fall into this category. Currently such therapies are investigational and not available to all patients.

"Standard" therapy for stroke focuses on preventing additional ischemia or bleeding, and prophylaxing against the medical complications of stroke. Options for stroke prevention include the modification of risk factors, antiplatelet agents, anticoagulants, and endarterectomy. The proper use of these therapies is often controversial; one view is presented in the following section. Once the acute phase of stroke is past, rehabilitation with physical, occupational, and/or speech therapy is crucial.

Recommended Approach

Brain Infarction. As in any other medical emergency, respiratory and cardiovascular stability must be achieved first. Airway protection should be provided for patients with altered consciousness or the inability to handle oral secretions. Many patients with acute brain infarctions are hypertensive. In general, the elevated blood pressure is not as dangerous as overzealous treatment with antihypertensive medication. Because of the loss of cerebrovascular autoregulatory capacity in infarcted brain, decreasing mean arterial blood pressure causes decreased cerebral perfusion. Also, blood pressure tends to decrease spontaneously after the initial stage of stroke. Thus, the blood pressure should not be lowered unless it is exceedingly high (i.e., >210/120 or causing end-organ damage). If hypertension must be treated, a gentle and easily titratable regimen should be used. Labetalol, starting at a dose of 10 to 20 mg intravenously, is generally a safe choice. In terms of fluid management, only isotonic intravenous solutions should be used and normovolemia should be maintained. In large infarcts, increased intracranial pressure may develop and be life threatening. Mannitol (20% solution) should be given at a dose of 1 g/kg intravenously, followed by 0.25 g/kg every 4 hours as needed to produce a serum osmolarity of 295 to 310 mOsm/L. Hyperventilation to a pCO_2 of about 30 mm Hg also lowers intracranial pressure, but the effect is brief and rebound can occur. Occasionally, surgical removal of the infarcted tissue is attempted. This may be more successful in cerebellar versus supratentorial infarcts.

Treatment to prevent further ischemic events must be tailored to the particular stroke etiology. Patients with severe carotid stenosis ipsilateral to a partial internal carotid artery territory stroke should be referred for carotid endarterectomy. Anticoagulants may be used to prevent artery-to-artery embolism while awaiting surgery. In patients with cardiac embolism, long-term anticoagulation is generally appropriate unless the source of the embolus can be removed or there is a contraindication to anticoagulation. There is currently no evidence that anticoagulation is effective prophylaxis in small vessel disease or in cases of mild/moderate carotid stenosis. In these patients, antiplatelet agents such as aspirin and ticlopidine should be used. Because of the cost and side effect profile of ticlopidine, it is often reserved for those patients who fail aspirin therapy or cannot tolerate it.

Intracerebral Hemorrhage. Because of the risk of rebleeding, patients with intracerebral hematomas require control of blood pressure to near-normotensive levels (140–160/90). Often, the mass effect from the hematoma causes raised intracranial pressure, sometimes with threatened herniation. The treatment of intracranial hypertension is outlined above. Intracranial pressure monitoring is very helpful in managing such patients. Possible surgical evacuation of the hematoma should also be considered, though for hemorrhage outside the cerebellum the benefit of surgery is unproven.

When a vascular malformation underlies the hemorrhage, embolization, radiation, and surgical excision are available options. The choice of therapy depends on the size, location, and nature of the malformation.

In both brain infarction and hemorrhage, medical complications must be prevented. Aspiration precautions, such as elevating the head of the bed to at least 30° and placing a gastric feeding tube, may be necessary for patients unable to swallow effectively. Pneumatic compression boots, subcutaneous heparin, and low-molecular-weight heparinoids

have all been shown to lower the rate of deep venous thrombosis in patients with severe leg weakness. Such patients also require frequent repositioning to avoid skin breakdown.

FOLLOW-UP

After starting on prophylactic therapy, patients should undergo repeat neurologic examination at 1 month (to monitor progress with rehabilitation) and at 6- to 12-month intervals thereafter. The most common cause of death in patients with previous stroke is cardiac disease. Thus, careful monitoring of cardiac risk factors such as blood pressure and cholesterol is very important. In ambulatory patients with large vessel atherosclerosis, it is reasonable to obtain a cardiac stress test after recovery from stroke.

DISCUSSION

Prevalence and Incidence

Stroke is the leading cause of adult disability and the third leading cause of death in the United States. There are about 500,000 new cases of stroke per year in the United States.

Related Basic Science

Atherosclerosis of large and medium-sized arteries and lipohyalinosis or microatheromata of small arteries are the pathophysiologic substrate of atherothrombotic brain infarction. Cardioembolic strokes may originate from atrial thrombi in patients with atrial fibrillation or mural thrombi in recent myocardial infarction. Ulcerated atherosclerotic plaques in the aorta or extracranial cerebral vessels may also be nidi for platelet–fibrin aggregates or thrombi, which can embolize to the brain.

Once thrombosis or embolic occlusion of a cerebral artery occurs, blood flow to part of the brain may drop to zero, resulting in cell death. Surrounding the area of absent perfusion is brain that receives reduced flow. In areas of diminished perfusion, neuronal electrical activity ceases, but cell integrity may be temporarily maintained by functioning ion pumps. These surrounding areas of partially damaged brain are referred to as the ischemic penumbra, and may be salvageable. In addition to blood flow considerations, we also know that abnormally high levels of excitatory neurotransmitters are present in ischemic brain. Neurotransmitters such as glutamate may act on neuronal membrane receptors to cause calcium influx with subsequent intracellular enzyme activation, lipolysis, and free radical formation.

In many patients, intracerebral hemorrhage results from hypertensive damage to small arteries. Weakening of the arterial wall, sometimes with microaneurysm formation, has been proposed as the cause of bleeding. In cerebral amyloid angiopathy, the same amyloid found in Alzheimer's disease is deposited in the walls of cerebral arterioles, venules, and capillaries. The vessel walls become fragile and can rupture, causing lobar hemorrhage.

Natural History and Its Modification with Treatment

Over the past 20 years, stroke mortality has decreased significantly. The severity of the strokes also seems to be decreasing. Better treatment of hypertension is credited with much of this change, but improved intensive care is another factor in increasing survival. Overall, effective preventive treatments have the most impact on cerebrovascular disease.

Prevention

Modification of risk factors is the key to reducing stroke rates. Blood pressure control and smoking cessation, for example, significantly reduce the risk of stroke. Specific prophylactic treatments for patients with prior transient ischemic attacks or minor stroke are discussed under Plans, Therapeutic.

Cost Containment

The cost of the diagnostic evaluation of a stroke victim is best contained by focusing investigations on the most likely source of stroke. Thus, a 75-year-old man with a long-standing history of hypertension and a lacunar stroke is unlikely to benefit from echocardiography. Similarly, a patient with a posterior circulation infarct does not require a carotid Doppler study.

Perhaps the most important cost-saving factor, however, is the aggressive pursuit of the mechanism of stroke. Selecting the most appropriate prophylactic therapy reduces the risk of future strokes and disability. Prophylaxis against complications such as deep venous thrombosis and aspiration pneumonia is also very important. Aggressive rehabilitation programs decrease long-term costs by returning patients to more independent living situations.

As acute treatments become available, ultraearly stroke recognition and intervention will be critical to reducing the morbidity and mortality (and, thus, the cost) of stroke.

REFERENCES

Barnett HJM, Hachinski VC, eds. Cerebral ischemia: Treatment and prevention. Neurol Clin 1992;10:1.

Barnett HJM, Mohr JP, Stein BM, Yatsu FM, eds. Stroke: Pathophysiology, diagnosis, and management. 2nd ed. New York: Churchill Livingstone, 1992.

Caplan LR. Stroke: A clinical approach. 2nd ed. Boston: Butterworth-Heinemann, 1993.

Evans I, ed. Stroke octet from the *Lancet*. London: Lancet, 1992.

Zivin JA, Choi DW. Stroke therapy. Sci Am 1991;265:56.

CHAPTER 20–10

Primary Brain Tumors

Deborah O. Heros, M.D.

DEFINITION

Primary brain tumors represent a diverse group of tumors arising from the brain parenchyma, meningeal coverings, and ependymal lining of the ventricular system. The location and cell of origin determine the symptoms and tumor growth potential. The terms *benign* and *malignant* do not have the same significance as in medical oncology. A tumor with "benign" pathology may be incurable because it is infiltrating brain tissue or is not in a location that is amenable to surgical resection. Malignancy of systemic tumors usually refers to the metastatic potential. In general, primary brain tumors tend to recur locally and rarely metastasize outside of the central nervous system.

ETIOLOGY

In general, the etiology for primary brain tumors is unknown.

CRITERIA FOR DIAGNOSIS

Suggestive

A brain tumor should be suspected in patients presenting with atypical headaches or a change in headache pattern unresponsive to traditional therapy. Approximately 40% of patients with brain tumors describe headache. The headache may not respond to standard medication and often is severe on arising in the morning or awakens the patient from sleep. The patient may also experience nausea and vomiting. Cough, straining, or activities that may increase intracranial pressure increase the severity of the headache.

The location of the tumor determines the neurologic symptoms; therefore, the presenting neurologic symptoms vary widely. Approximately one third of the patients with a primary brain tumor experience either a focal or generalized seizure. A patient with a brain tumor may develop an alteration of mental status, behavior, or personality. A change in job performance, personality change, loss of interest in personal or social activities, or depression unresponsive to medical therapy may be the presenting symptom of a brain tumor. Focal neurologic symptoms and signs in the appropriate setting increase the suspicion of a brain tumor.

Definitive

A computed tomography (CT) or magnetic resonance imaging (MRI) scan is obtained if a brain tumor is clinically suspected. Identification of a suspicious mass lesion on the scan then prompts a definitive diagnosis obtained by biopsy.

CLINICAL MANIFESTATIONS

Subjective

The presenting symptoms are discussed above under Criteria for Diagnosis, Suggestive. Primary brain tumors most often occur in otherwise healthy people and therefore the past medical history is most often unremarkable. Although there is an increased incidence in cancer-prone families, in general, primary brain tumors are not familial.

Objective

Physical Examination

Papilledema is present in approximately one half of patients with brain tumors. Neurologic abnormalities are frequently seen on examination, depending on the location of the tumor. The neurologic examination may be relatively normal, especially if the tumor is located in the frontal lobes. A thorough general examination should be performed to identify a primary systemic malignancy.

Routine Laboratory Abnormalities

Routine laboratory testing is generally normal in patients with primary brain tumors. Systemic tumors with secondary metastatic tumors to the central nervous system may be identified by anemia, abnormal liver function studies, blood in the urine, or a mass on the chest radiograph.

PLANS

Diagnostic

Differential Diagnosis

An appropriate differential diagnosis is determined by the clinical presentation. An acute onset of symptoms may suggest a cerebrovascular accident or intracranial hemorrhage. An acute presentation from a hemorrhage secondary to a primary brain tumor is not common, but may be seen with metastatic brain tumors, especially melanoma, hypernephroma, choriocarcinoma, and, less commonly, tumors of lung or breast origin. An evolving process with focal neurologic symptoms, fever, and headache suggests an abscess. A change in mental status may occur with various metabolic derangements, meningoencephalitis, or neoplasms, either primary or metastatic. Seizures may occur with any of these disorders.

Benign intracranial hypertension or "pseudomotor cerebri" presents with headache, visual obscurations, and papilledema.

Diagnostic Options

A contrast-enhanced CT scan or MRI scan is the appropriate diagnostic study for patients presenting with mental status changes, seizures, or focal neurologic symptoms. Although either study may identify a tumor, the MRI scan is more sensitive, especially when performed with the paramagnetic contrast agent gadolinium DTPA. Confirmation by surgical biopsy is necessary for a definitive diagnosis. An unenhanced CT scan is obtained if the clinical presentation is acute to exclude the presence of a hemorrhage. The MRI scan may not identify an acute hemorrhage. A lumbar puncture may be performed to exclude an infectious process or leptomeningeal neoplasm, but is usually done after a neuroimaging study fails to identify a mass lesion, especially if the patient has focal neurologic signs or symptoms or evidence of increased intracranial pressure. Usually a scan is performed early in the course of the evaluation and obviates the need for angiography, skull x-rays, and electroencephalography.

Recommended Approach

A contrast-enhanced CT or MRI scan is obtained when a patient presents with unexplained or atypical headaches, signs of increased intracranial pressure, seizures, or focal neurologic complaints. The choice between the two imaging studies is made on the basis of availability, cost, allergies, or other contraindications to either study, and medical stability of the patient. The most sensitive study is the gadolinium DTPA-enhanced MRI scan.

Therapeutic

Therapeutic Options

Once a tumor is suspected, pathologic confirmation is necessary. A CT- or MRI-guided stereotactic biopsy is performed if the lesion is deep-seated or located in a surgically "eloquent" area, or the patient is elderly or medically unstable. If possible, a partial or subtotal resection for astrocytoma is generally performed. Reducing the tumor mass may acutely improve symptoms and possibly improve the survival by decreasing the tumor burden. An astrocytoma is an infiltrative process and is not surgically resectable or curable. Resection is often curative for a benign tumor such as meningioma and certain cases of ependymoma.

Radiation therapy often follows the surgical procedure for astrocytoma. Controversy does exist for radiation therapy of low-grade astrocytoma and oligodendroglioma, especially if a good resection can be performed. In general, chemotherapy has added minimal benefit to treatment of malignant astrocytoma. Younger patients may be somewhat more responsive to chemotherapy. The oligodendroglioma may be one subgroup of primary brain tumors that has been shown to be chemosensitive.

Primary central nervous system germ cell tumors are often very sensitive to radiation therapy. Medulloblastomas often require a multimodality treatment approach using radiation therapy and chemotherapy.

Once a mass is identified on the scan, dexamethasone may be initiated to treat symptoms acutely. The dose may vary (2–4 mg two or three times daily) depending on the size of the mass and the severity of the patient's symptoms. An anticonvulsant such as diphenylhydantoin or carbamazepine is often started prior to surgery.

Recommended Approach

Unfortunately, treatment options are limited for malignant astrocytoma and are outlined under Therapeutic Options.

FOLLOW-UP

The neurosurgeon is actively involved in the care of the brain tumor patient postoperatively. Radiation therapy is initiated about 2 weeks after surgery to allow for wound healing, and the radiation oncologist follows the patient for the 5- to 6-week duration of radiation therapy. A CT or MRI scan is obtained 6 to 8 weeks after completion of radiotherapy. Monitoring the patient with serial neurologic examinations and scans is appropriate at 4- to 6-month intervals. The patient may tolerate a tapering dose of dexamethasone during radiation therapy, but often dexamethasone is required for acute and subacute effects of the radiation therapy up to 2 to 4 months following completion of radiation ther-

apy. While the patient is on dexamethasone, glucose values should be monitored periodically. If appropriate, anticonvulsant levels should also be monitored.

An increase in neurologic deficit may be related to radiotherapy and may be divided into three recognized phases. Acute changes during radiation therapy may be related to cerebral edema and are responsive to dexamethasone. Subacute changes may occur for up to 4 months after completion of radiotherapy and are the result of demyelination, often responsive to dexamethasone. Chronic changes usually begin several months to a year after radiation therapy and include a generalized encephalopathy with progressive memory impairment and generalized neurologic dysfunction or a progressive process of radiation necrosis with localized development of a mass that is often indistinguishable from tumor recurrence. The generalized encephalopathy is not treatable. The symptoms related to radiation necrosis may be partially responsive to dexamethasone and surgical resection for reduction of the mass.

In patients who are long-term survivors of radiation therapy, pituitary function should be assessed periodically. Hypothyroidism and insufficient cortisol production are clinically treatable causes of decline in this group of patients. An early indication of pituitary and hypothalamic dysfunction related to radiation therapy is an elevation of the prolactin level. Complications from dexamethasone are common. Steroid myopathy may cause proximal leg weakness and may be easily mistaken for symptoms of "tumor progression." As a result of this error, the steroids may be incorrectly increased as an attempt to improve the situation. Hyperglycemia, weight gain, and steroid psychosis also occur.

Up to 30% of patients with malignant glioma may develop thromboembolic complications. Patients with primary brain tumors should be questioned and examined for signs and symptoms of deep venous thrombosis. A consensus on the treatment of deep venous thrombosis in patients with primary brain tumors has not been reached. Some clinicians prefer a filter or umbrella apparatus because of the concern for intracranial hemorrhage, whereas others recommend heparin and coumadin. In most studies addressing this issue, the risk of intracranial hemorrhage has not been found to be significant and anticoagulation appears to be a reasonably safe option.

The patients are also prone to seizures, toxicity from the anticonvulsant medications, and infections of the lung and urinary tract. Prompt recognition of the medical complications of this disease is important to optimize the quality of life for the glioma patient.

Unfortunately, tumor recurrence usually occurs within 6 to 12 months for patients with malignant glioma. Options for treatment of the tumor recurrence depend on the condition of the patient and the site of recurrence and may include reoperation, localized radiation therapy using the techniques of radiosurgery, and chemotherapy. Various combinations of chemotherapy are under investigation, although to date, no single agent or multiple-drug protocol has been found to be superior to a single-agent nitrosourea drug. Experimental treatments are available at various institutions. A national survey revealed a small percentage (7.67%) of patients potentially eligible for entry into treatment protocol actually participate in such therapy. Improved survival will come only through such investigations.

DISCUSSION

Prevalence and Incidence

Every year approximately 15,000 new cases of primary brain tumors are identified in the United States. The majority of primary brain tumors are astrocytomas. Men are slightly affected more often than women. The incidence of astrocytoma increases with age up to 65 years. "Childhood" tumors include germinomas, pineal tumors, medulloblastomas, and pilocytic astrocytomas.

Related Basic Science

Genetics

Epidemiologic studies have identified a possible association between brain tumors and various cancers in cancer-prone families, specifically cancers of breast, lung, and colon origin. The Li–Fraumeni syndrome consists of a familial association of breast cancer, sarcoma, brain tumors, and leukemia with a dominant inheritance pattern. The inherited neuroectodermal syndromes, tuberous sclerosis, and neurofibromatosis are associated with increased incidences of various primary brain tumors. Various syndromes characterized by adenomatous polyps in the gastrointestinal tract have been associated with an increased incidence of malignant gliomas.

Altered Molecular Biology

Various chromosomal abnormalities have been described in patients with primary brain tumors. The gene responsible for neurofibromatosis has recently been isolated. One form of neurofibromatosis is caused by a deletion on the long arm of chromosome 22 that has been associated with three central nervous system tumors (glioma, meningioma, and spinal neurofibroma). Abnormalities of chromosome 5Q have been associated with Turcot's syndrome, Gardner's syndrome, and familial polyposis. Various chromosomal abnormalities have been described in malignant astrocytoma, but no consistent abnormality has been identified.

Natural History and Its Modification with Treatment

The median survival for an untreated patient with a malignant glioma is 6 to 14 weeks. Standard radiation therapy techniques extend the median survival to approximately 36 weeks. Addition of the standard chemotherapy agent may extend the median survival slightly. For malignant glioma, a grade III glioma using the standard pathologic grading system carries a slightly better prognosis than a grade IV malignant glioma, also known as glioblastoma multiforme. The low-grade gliomas (grades I and II) have a better prognosis, but within 5 years,

50% of these tumors have recurred, and a 20% survival is expected at 10 years.

In general, primary brain tumors do not metastasize outside of the central nervous system. The recurrence is usually local, but may be multifocal. Certain tumors, usually if in proximity to the ventricles, have a propensity to seed the leptomeninges.

Prevention

No known preventive measures are available.

Cost Containment

Prompt recognition of medical complications and an understanding of the various potential effects of radiation therapy and chemotherapy may prevent unnecessary scanning and hospitalization.

Neuroimaging studies should be performed only when management decisions are to be made. Too often scans are done "just to see what the tumor looks like." Prompt initiation of home care and hospice reduces hospitalization as the disease progresses.

REFERENCES

Bondy M, Wiencke J, Wrensch M, Kyritsis A. Genetics of primary brain tumors: A review. Neuro-Oncology 1994;18:69.

Burger PC. Malignant astrocyte neoplasms: Classification, pathologic anatomy and response to treatment. Semin Oncol 1986;13(1):16.

Mahaley MS, Mettlin C, Natarajan N, et al. National survey of patterns of care for brain tumor patients. J Neurosurg 1989;71:826.

Shapiro WR, Shapiro JR. Principles of brain tumor chemotherapy. Semin Oncol 1986;13(1):56.

CHAPTER 20–11

Head Trauma

George F. Howard III, M.D.

DEFINITION

The term *head trauma* encompasses any mechanical injury to the scalp, the bones of the skull, or the brain and its covering. When the brain itself has been affected, the term *traumatic brain injury* is more appropriately used. This chapter deals mainly with the latter diagnosis.

ETIOLOGY

Head trauma is produced by a missile striking the head or by the head striking a relatively fixed object. Traumatic brain injury may also result from violent head motions without any direct impact against the skull, as in the acceleration and deceleration of a whiplash injury.

CRITERIA FOR DIAGNOSIS

Suggestive

Whenever there is a history of impact against the skull or violent movement of the head, the possibility of traumatic brain injury should be considered. Particularly in the elderly, seemingly trivial trauma may result in major neurologic consequences.

Definitive

In the appropriate clinical setting a wide variety of neurologic signs can serve to confirm the diagnosis of traumatic brain injury. These include altered level of arousal, memory impairment, seizures, and focal motor or sensory deficits. Abnormal findings on imaging studies of the brain are not required.

CLINICAL MANIFESTATIONS

Subjective

Immediately following head trauma conscious patients almost invariably report headache. Vertigo, nonrotational dizziness, nausea, and vomiting are other common symptoms. Confusion and amnesia suggest a more severe degree of injury. Less often one or more seizures may occur.

Weeks to months after traumatic brain injury, patients often continue to have headache, fatigue, dizziness, memory problems, difficulty concentrating, and irritability (the postconcussive syndrome). Following severe brain injuries, particularly when there has been direct cortical damage, partial or secondarily generalized seizures may develop.

Objective

Physical Examination

Acutely, direct examination of the head may reveal evidence of scalp, skull, or facial injuries. Abrasions, lacerations, hematomas, and depressions of the cranium should be sought. Ecchymoses beneath the eyes or behind the ears suggest a basilar skull fracture, as does bleeding in the ear canals. Level of responsiveness is paramount in assessing a patient's neurologic status. The Glasgow Coma Scale (GCS) is a widely used instrument for classifying and following the severity of a traumatic brain injury. Three parameters are measured: eye opening, verbal responsiveness, and motor responsiveness (see Table 20–11–1). A score of 3 to 15 can be obtained. The degree of injury is conventionally classified into one of three categories depending on the total score: mild (13–15), moderate (9–12), and severe (≤ 8).

TABLE 20–11–1. GLASGOW COMA SCALE

Eye opening	
Spontaneous	4
To speech	3
To pain	2
None	1
Best verbal response	
Orientated	5
Confused conversation	4
Inappropriate words	3
Incomprehensible sounds	2
None	1
Best motor response	
Obeys	6
Localizes pain	5
Withdraws from pain	4
Postures, flexing arms	3
Postures, extending arms	2
None	1

In conjunction with the Glasgow Coma Scale, a detailed neurologic examination helps define the nature and extent of a brain injury. Testing of eye movements, corneal reflexes, and pupillary reactions is essential to the determination of brainstem dysfunction in a comatose patient. Unilateral pupillary dilation is particularly important in the recognition of transtentorial herniation. In awake patients higher cortical functions need to be evaluated. The extent of amnesia should be documented. Focal sensory and motor defects should be sought.

After the initial period of recovery the neurologic examination may or may not reveal abnormalities. Following severe head injuries major cognitive deficits are likely. Spasticity often develops with persisting focal or widespread weakness and incoordination. Dysarthria and dysphagia are common. Following lesser degrees of injury such findings may be absent, even when subjective complaints are numerous. At times only subtle abnormalities can be elicited such as impaired ocular tracking, positional nystagmus, and difficulty with tandem gait. Mild deficits in concentration and information processing may be the only residuals.

Routine Laboratory Abnormalities

Routine laboratory analyses of blood and urine do not yield any important findings unless other organ systems have been involved.

PLANS
Diagnostic

Differential Diagnosis

Several types of intracranial bleeding are recognized, namely, subarachnoid hemorrhage, epidural hematoma, subdural hematoma, intracerebral hemorrhage, and parenchymal contusion. When the skull has been fractured there may be other types of pathology as well. Bone fragments or foreign bodies such as bullets may penetrate the brain and cause focal or widespread injury. If the sinuses have been violated, air may enter the subarachnoid space and ventricular system, causing pneumocephalus. With basilar skull fractures cerebrospinal fluid may leak into the ear canals or nasal passages (cerebrospinal fluid oto- and rhinorrhea).

Sometimes head trauma results only in microscopic injury to the brain, especially to the axons of the cerebral white matter. Substantial loss of neuronal function may occur without hemorrhage or obvious anatomic disruption.

The postconcussive syndrome is thought largely to be a manifestation of microscopic pathology; however, reactive depression and maladaptive coping behaviors can complicate the clinical picture. Infrequently hysteria, malingering, and compensation neurosis can enter into the differential diagnosis of a patient who fails to improve after seemingly minor head trauma.

Diagnostic Options

Routine radiographs are capable of demonstrating almost any fracture of the skull as well as metal fragments that may have lodged in the head. They are insensitive to abnormalities of the brain parenchyma. Both x-ray computed tomography (CT) and magnetic resonance imaging (MRI) are highly accurate in the diagnosis of hematomas and contusions; however, CT is superior in demonstrating fractures of the skull and subarachnoid hemorrhages. MRI has greater ability to show small anatomic lesions within the brain, but CT is less time consuming and requires less patient cooperation. Recent studies suggest that single-photon-emission computed tomography is highly sensitive for small areas of cerebral dysfunction following trauma. Electroencephalography is particularly useful when brain death is suspected on clinical grounds and supportive evidence is required. Electroencephalography is also important when an epileptic seizure is suspected as the cause of a patient's head injury. Especially in comatose patients, auditory and somatosensory evoked potential studies can help confirm the presence of brainstem dysfunction and may provide prognostic information.

Toxicologic studies on blood or urine can help identify patients with drug or alcohol problems that may have contributed to the occurrence of head trauma. Electrocardiographic monitoring may be important for elderly patients who have had an injury consequent to a fall, a situation in which syncope may have occurred.

When patients have prolonged posttraumatic symptomatology, further testing may be required to understand the cause. Otoneurologic studies (particularly electronystagmography) may serve to confirm the presence of vestibular dysfunction. Repeat imaging studies can demonstrate the development of hydrocephalus or cerebral atrophy. When paroxysmal symptoms occur, routine electroencephalography and prolonged electroencephalographic monitoring are most useful in confirming the presence of a seizure disorder. Detailed neuropsychological evaluation including a battery of standardized tests may disclose areas of persistent cognitive abnormalities.

Recommended Approach

Patients can be categorized into groups with low, moderate, and high risk of intracranial injury (Table 20–11–2). Those in the low-risk group

TABLE 20–11–2. RISK OF INTRACRANIAL INJURY BY CLINICAL DATA

Low
  Asymptomatic
  Headache
  Dizziness
  Scalp hematoma, laceration, contusion, or abrasion
  Absence of moderate or high-risk criteria
Moderate
  Change of consciousness at the time of injury or subsequently
  Progressive headache
  Alcohol or drug intoxication
  Unreliable or inadequate history of injury
  Age less than 2 years (unless injury very trivial)
  Posttraumatic seizure
  Vomiting
  Posttraumatic amnesia
  Multiple trauma
  Serious facial injury
  Signs of basilar skull fracture
  Possible skull penetration or depressed fracture
  Suspected physical child abuse
High
  Depressed level of consciousness not clearly due to alcohol, drugs, or other cause
    (e.g., metabolic and seizure disorders)
  Focal neurologic signs
  Decreasing level of consciousness
  Penetrating skull injury or palpable depressed fracture

Source: From Masters SJ, McClean PM, Arcarese JS, et al. Skull x-ray examinations after head trauma: Recommendations by a multidisciplinary panel and validation study. N Engl J Med 1987;316:84. Reproduced with permission from the publisher and author.

do not require immediate radiographic or imaging studies because there is almost no chance of finding a significant intracranial abnormality for which emergency treatment would be required. Patients in the high-risk group should have immediate CT imaging as they have a substantial chance of needing urgent neurosurgical treatment. Patients in the moderate-risk group may be observed for several hours before a final decision about imaging is made, but in any institution where CT is immediately available, early imaging is preferred. Routine skull radiography may be appropriate for patients in the moderate-risk category if CT imaging cannot be arranged without great inconvenience and cost of transportation. In such circumstances the finding of a skull fracture dictates that CT imaging should be obtained urgently despite logistical difficulties. In the postacute period of head injury management, any deterioration in level of responsiveness or the development of new focal findings should prompt repetition of CT imaging to exclude the possibilities of delayed hematoma formation, progressive edema, or hydrocephalus.

When posttraumatic symptoms persist beyond the initial period of recovery and CT imaging has been negative, alternative imaging modalities should be used to confirm the presence of brain damage. If MRI is normal, single-photon-emission CT should be obtained where available. When dizziness is a major symptom, evaluation should include audiometry, electronystagmography, and auditory evoked response testing to determine whether peripheral vestibulopathy or a perilymphatic fistula is likely.

Therapeutic

Therapeutic Options

The care of patients with a severe brain injury should be managed by a neurosurgeon or an intensivist with particular background in neurologic intensive care. Decisions may need to be made about the timing and appropriateness of neurosurgery as well as the need for intracranial pressure monitoring, topics that are beyond the scope of this chapter. Increased intracranial pressure may need to be reduced by hyperventilation, infusion of mannitol, anesthetic doses of pentobarbital, drainage of cerebrospinal fluid, or decompressive craniotomy. Intravenous phenytoin is usually administered prophylactically in patients with severe brain injuries to prevent seizures and their deleterious effect on intracranial pressure.

The approach to head injuries of mild and moderate severity is discussed immediately below.

Recommended Approach

Primary care physicians are sometimes called on to care for patients with mild or moderate brain injuries and no indication for surgical treatment. The most important step in the management of such cases is to ensure adequate monitoring of neurologic status. The nursing staff must be familiar with the Glasgow Coma Scale or some other standardized means of following the patient's condition. Antiemetics and sedatives are occasionally necessary, but their use should be kept to a minimum to avoid complicating assessment of neurologic status. Anticonvulsants are not required, as the risk of seizures is low in patients with closed head injuries and no intracranial bleeding. Corticosteroids have no proven value.

Patients with head injuries can be expected to have many neurologic symptoms even after discharge from the hospital. When headache occurs daily or continuously, narcotics and medications associated with rebound phenomena (such as those containing butalbital and caffeine) should be avoided. Nonsteroidal antiinflammatory drugs and the tricyclic antidepressants should be tried. If episodic, throbbing headaches are a major problem, antimigraine medications containing isometheptene or ergotamine can be tried during attacks. For frequent recurrences, migraine prophylactic medications such as beta blockers and calcium channel blockers are sometimes prescribed. Vertigo can be treated with scopolamine patches, promethazine 12.5 to 25 mg three times daily, or clonazepam 0.5 mg daily at bedtime, increasing to four times daily if necessary; however, side effects such as memory impairment, sedation, depression, and fatigue may be particularly bothersome in the face of brain injury.

Irritability, nervousness, and difficulty with concentration are com-

mon during the posttraumatic period. At times mood instability and lack of impulse control may be striking. Pharmacotherapy is largely empiric, and no medication should be continued unless its benefits are distinct. Stimulant drugs such as methylphenidate 5 mg three times daily and pemoline up to 75 mg daily may be tried to improve concentration and enhance attention. Sedative antidepressants are the best choice when mood disturbance and insomnia coexist. Benzodiazepine tranquilizers may be appropriate for simple nervousness, but they can worsen impulse control in patients with frontal lobe injury and produce depression. Valproate and carbamazepine may be useful as mood stabilizing agents. When severe behavioral outbursts occur, propranolol should be tried, as it does not have the severe side effects of the major tranquilizers.

If an anticonvulsant was administered prophylactically during the period of hospitalization, this should be tapered and discontinued within a few weeks unless the clinical data suggest a relatively high likelihood of late posttraumatic seizures developing. Patients who have had a penetrating wound to the brain or hemorrhage affecting the cerebral cortex are at particular risk for subsequent seizures, and for them continued treatment with an anticonvulsant is warranted. Valproate may be the best choice of anticonvulsant.

When a patient has difficulty returning to his or her prior level of function due to subtle abnormalities of information processing, concentration, and mood, steps should be taken to reduce the level of stress in the patient's life by limiting work hours and other demands for sustained mental effort. Support from the primary physician is essential, as family members and employers are sometimes critical and incapable of understanding the patient's disability. A head injury counselor should be found when adjustment problems are noted at home or on the job. A head injury support group may be appropriate.

FOLLOW-UP

After hospitalization for a head injury, patients should be seen frequently until symptoms have resolved or it is clear that a sound adjustment has been made. The level of a patient's disability may not be apparent until she or he attempts a return to work. Even when not receiving medications, patients should be seen for monitoring of symptoms, but laboratory and imaging studies are not required unless specific indications develop.

DISCUSSION

Prevalence

In the United States the yearly rate of traumatic brain injury is between 132 and 367 cases per 100,000 population depending on the community surveyed (Sorenson and Kraus, 1991). The highest risk of injury is in the age range 16 to 25 years, and men consistently outnumber women by 2:1 or more. The single greatest cause of brain injuries is motor vehicle accidents.

Related Basic Science

Subarachnoid hemorrhage results from tearing of small vessels on the surface of the brain. Its occurrence in the setting of head trauma does not imply an underlying aneurysm or arteriovenous malformation. Epidural hematomas most often arise when the middle meningeal artery is lacerated by a missile or a fracture of the temporal bone. High-pressure bleeding dissects the dura mater away from the inner surface of the skull, creating a localized clot. Subdural hematomas develop when bridging veins from the cortex to the dural sinuses are torn. Both types of hematoma may cause transtentorial herniation. When there is differential movement between the brain and the skull with direct impact on one against the other, intracerebral vessels may be disrupted. Brain contusions and hemorrhages result. Areas most likely to be affected are the temporal and frontal poles as well as the orbital surfaces of the frontal lobes. Contusions may occur directly under an area of impact and on the opposite side of the brain (coup and contrecoup injuries). Acceleration and deceleration of the head can exert shear forces on the brain, which can disrupt axonal functions without causing macroscopic evidence of damage. This may be a factor contributing to the persisting disability that can follow seemingly minor head injury. In diffuse axonal injury there may be severe clinical disability with normal anatomy on CT imaging.

Natural History and Its Modification with Treatment

With advanced life support systems and improvements in neurosurgery, some patients with severe head injuries are now saved, whereas previously they would have died. There is firm evidence that urgent evacuation of subdural and epidural hematomas reduces mortality, but it has been more difficult to demonstrate that intracranial pressure monitoring and measures to reduce intracranial pressure have had a major impact on outcome following brain injury. Patients presenting with a Glasgow Coma Scale score of 3 or 4 usually have an extremely poor prognosis, whereas those with scores greater than 8 have a high likelihood of good outcome. For patients with scores of 5 through 8 there is considerable uncertainty.

Prevention

Primary physicians can play an important role in head trauma prevention by asking patients about behaviors that may affect their risk of injury. An inquiry about drinking habits should be followed by an inquiry about whether the patient and his friends routinely designate a driver who will not drink when they go out together. Patients should be asked whether they use seat belts and insist that everyone in their car do so as well. Patients and their families should be encouraged to use protective

helmets when cycling. A physician may ask whether there is a firearm in a patient's home and whether it is adequately secured. In elderly patients and in anyone with a disorder that affects balance, the physician should carefully assess gait and recommend a physical therapy evaluation to maximize safety whenever instability is apparent. Care should be taken when prescribing sedatives and antihypertensive agents to the elderly to ensure that nighttime or postprandial orthostatic hypotension does not occur and lead to falling.

Cost Containment

Major savings can be achieved by not ordering skull radiographs and imaging studies in patients who are at low risk for brain injury (see Table 20–11–2).

REFERENCES

Cooper PR, ed. Head injury. 3rd ed. Baltimore: Williams & Wilkins, 1993.

Gualtieri CT. Pharmacotherapy and the neurobehavioral sequelae of traumatic brain injury. Brain Injury 1988;2:101.

Jennett B, Teasdale G. Aspects of coma after severe head injury. Lancet 1977;1:878.

Masters SJ, McClean PM, Arcarese JS, et al. Skull x-ray examination after head trauma: Recommendations by a multidisciplinary panel and validation study. N Engl J Med 1987;316:84.

Sorenson SB, Kraus JF. Occurrence, severity, and outcomes of brain injury. J Head Trauma Rehabil 1991;6:1.

CHAPTER 20–12

Spinal Cord Disorders

John R. Belden, M.D.

DEFINITION

This chapter considers disorders of the central nervous system that exclusively or predominantly affect the spinal cord (myelopathies). The inherited ataxias, degenerative/multisystem atrophy syndromes, and motor neuron disease involve the spinal cord but these topics are discussed in other chapters. Acute transverse myelopathy implies dysfunction of all spinal cord tracts, whereas Brown–Sequard syndrome is a lesion of one half of the cord, leading to ipsilateral motor and posterior column signs and contralateral loss of pain and temperature sensation. Spinal shock refers to an acute myelopathy (trauma, infarction, acute transverse myelopathy) where cord function suddenly ceases. A sensory level is present, voluntary control of bladder and bowel is lost, and the involved limbs are paralyzed, hypotonic, and areflexic. Myelitis refers to an inflammatory lesion causing intramedullary fiber tract dysfunction.

ETIOLOGY

Spinal cord disorders can be anatomically classified into extradural, intradural/extramedullary, and intramedullary lesions (Figure 20–12–1). Extradural disease typically involves the vertebrae and/or intervertebral disks and causes localized pain. Eventually, the spinal roots and cord may be involved with subsequent radicular pain and compressive cord signs and symptoms. Intradural/extramedullary disease doesn't involve bone (unless erosion through the dura has occurred) so localized bone pain is not present. Radiating pain from nerve root involvement occurs in these lesions. Intramedullary disease causes dysfunction of sensory, motor, and cerebellar fiber tracts with resulting signs and symptoms, but usually without bone or root pain.

Extradural disease consists of infections, tumors, disk herniations, cervical spondylosis, hematomas, and bony abnormalities that cause spinal elements to sublux and compress the spinal cord. At the craniocervical junction trauma, rheumatoid disease, Paget's disease, ankylosing spondylosis, platybasia, basilar invagination, achondroplasia, and mucopolysaccharidosis can cause spinal instability. Infections in the epidural space most commonly are bacterial (*Staphylococcus aureus,* Gram-negative organisms in intravenous drug users) with mycobacterial tuberculosis (Pott's disease) or atypical *Mycobacterium,* fungal, or parasitic causes less frequently seen. Any tumor of the vertebral body or the pedicle (metastatic carcinoma), if untreated or unresponsive to treatment, will compress the epidural space, the spinal cord, and exiting nerve roots.

Disk herniations most commonly do not impinge on neural structures. When they do, the exiting nerve roots are most commonly affected. Large central disk herniations (cervical most common, thoracic disks occurring in 1–2% of cases) can impinge on the cord and present with an acute or subacute myelopathy, with or without radiculopathy. Occasionally this occurs without spinal pain. Cervical spondylosis also presents with a usually slowly evolving myelopathy, often in addition to radicular pain and muscle weakness.

Intradural/extramedullary pathology is more limited in scope and is also less frequent. Subdural hematomas, meningiomas, neurofibromas, and schwannomas of nerve roots, sarcoidosis, lipomas, and chordomas are in this category. Meningeal carcinomatosis and chronic arachnoiditis (from oil-based myelogram dye [Panopaque], trauma, surgery, infections such as Lyme disease, bacterial/tuberculous/luetic organisms, injections of intrathecal steroids or anesthetics) are other examples. At times, these inflammatory conditions can obliterate small arteries, causing cord infarction.

Intramedullary disease is the most diverse. Tumors most commonly arise from primary neural elements. Ependymomas and astrocytomas are most common, with oligodendrogliomas, lipomas, dermoids, teratomas, epidermoids, hemangiomas, hemangioblastomas, and metastasis being less common. Intramedullary sarcoidosis and abscesses are rare. Both human immunodeficiency virus type 1 (vacuolar myelopathy) and human T-lymphotrophic virus type 3 (tropical spastic paraparesis) can cause a slowly progressive spastic paraparesis. Opportunis-

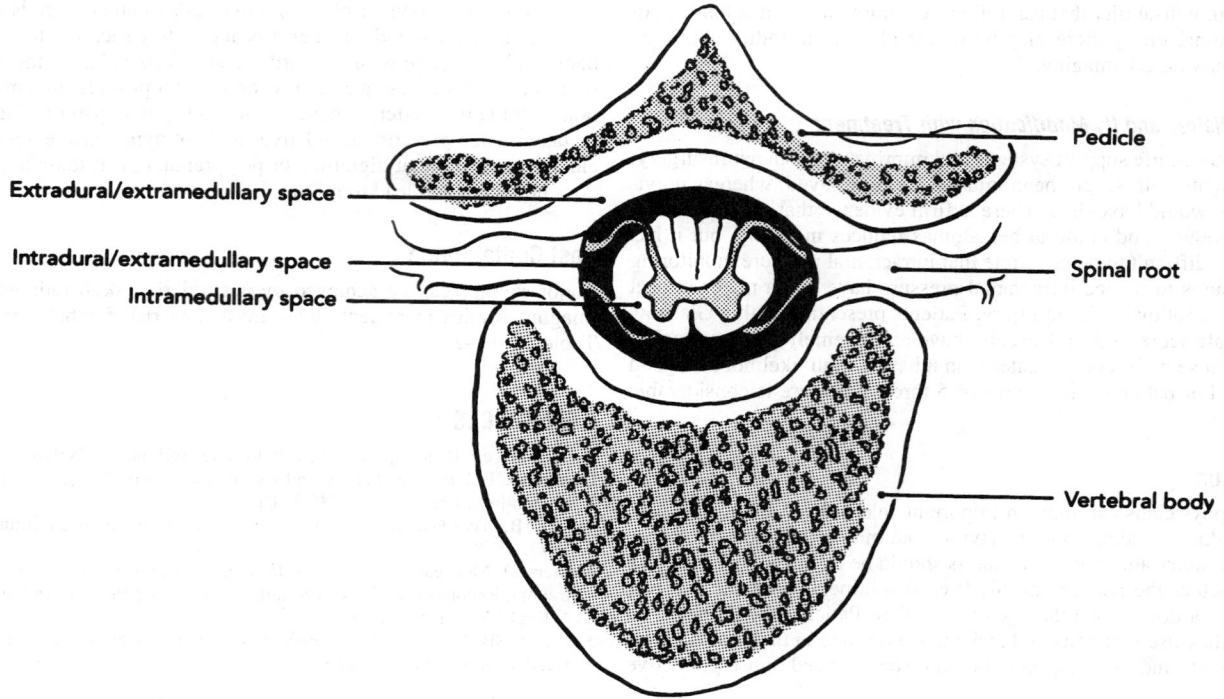

Figure 20–12–1. The spinal canal.

tic infections such as cytomegalovirus can involve the cord directly, causing a necrotizing or vacuolar myelopathy. Direct invasion can occur with herpes zoster, poliomyelitis (enterovirus), or *Mycoplasma pneumoniae*. Postviral autoimmune-mediated myelitis also occurs. Degenerative central nervous system diseases typically cause signs and symptoms referable to the cerebrum, cerebellum, and brainstem, but can be dominated by cord dysfunction in familial spastic paraparesis, adrenomyeloleukodystrophy, primary lateral sclerosis, and autonomic nervous system degenerative syndromes. Toxic and metabolic disorders affecting the cord in isolation are uncommon. Nitrous oxide abuse and vitamin B_{12} deficiency with subacute combined degeneration (dysfunction of the posterior columns and laterally situated motor and sensory tracts) are examples. Nitrous oxide abuse leads to hypermetabolism of B_{12} with subsequent cord degeneration. Low B_{12} levels are commonly found in older people, but their relation to central nervous system disease is often difficult to establish. Syringomyelia is a cyst within the spinal cord that usually communicates with the central spinal cord canal and causes segmental sensory and motor abnormalities in one or both arms. Most often it is due to an imbalance in spinal fluid dynamics due to craniocervical junction abnormalities such as the Arnold–Chiari malformation, but it can be associated with cord tumors or a delayed effect of compression or trauma. Lathyrism is a chronic myelopathy due to direct toxic effects of an excitatory neurotransmitter substance in grass peas eaten by Africans during famine. Clioquinol, used to treat diarrhea, caused a subacute myelopathy and optic neuropathy in Japan in the 1960s before it was withdrawn from usage. Neuroenteric cysts occasionally cause a compressive myelopathy from slow expansion and subsequent mass effect.

Myelitis from demyelinating disease (multiple sclerosis) usually develops during days to 1 to 2 weeks with ascending sensory symptoms with variable involvement of motor/cerebellar fibers and bladder and bowel function. Neuropathic pain, sometimes paroxysmal, into the extremities and trunk can be quite bothersome to patients. Recovery, complete or partial, is the rule, but severe disability from chronic myelopathy occurs in some multiple sclerosis patients.

Vascular disease occasionally affects the cord, usually in older individuals. Occlusion of branches from the aorta or vertebral arteries is thought to be the cause either from intrinsic vascular disease or as a complication of surgical procedures on the aorta. Rarely, fibrocartilagi-

nous emboli migrate across vascular channels and infarct the cord. Arteriovenous malformations and dural arteriovenous fistulas can acutely disrupt the cord or cause a slowly progressive myelopathy often with a fluctuating course. Decompression sickness in scuba divers ("the bends," or Caisson disease), intravenous drug use, systemic lupus erythematosus, sickle cell anemia, and coagulopathies are occasional causes. These disorders usually disrupt the thoracic portion of the spinal cord because of the tenuous collateral blood supply to this region. Acute epidural or subdural hematomas are rare and are usually limited to patients with trauma or bleeding disorders.

Delayed subacute and chronic myelopathies can develop many months to 1 to 2 years after radiation treatments when the port includes the spinal cord or days to months after electrical injury when current has passed through the cord. These are thought to be due to microvascular occlusive changes.

Congenital meningocele and meningomyeloceles cause paraplegia, obvious cutaneous stigmata, leg hypoplasia, and genitourinary abnormalities in a small number of newborns. Neural tube defects have been linked to maternal folate deficiency.

Acute transverse myelopathy is an abrupt loss of cord function across all fiber tracts. It is thought to be viral or autoimmune, rarely paraneoplastic. It presents with back and radicular pain with rapidly evolving, usually during hours, paraparesis, segmental sensory level, and bladder and bowel incontinence. Imaging studies are important to exclude spinal cord compression. Spinal fluid commonly indicates an inflammatory process, although the exact mechanism of the disease is usually not clearly delineated. Prognosis depends on the severity and duration of the neurologic deficit.

Trauma is a common cause of cord disease, especially in young people. The mechanism is a combination of dislocations and fractures of the spine with resulting cord injury. Most traumatic lesions occur at the first or second cervical level, fourth to fifth cervical level, or eleventh thoracic to second lumbar vertebrae. Occasionally, a trauma victim presents with a spinal shock picture, without penetrating injuries or spinal column dislocations. Rapid recovery ensues, giving rise to a diagnosis of spinal concussion. In small children, traumatic cord damage can occur without radiographic evidence of fracture/dislocation owing to the facet joints being in a sagittal plane, allowing hypermotility of the spine in hyperextension/flexion injuries.

CRITERIA FOR DIAGNOSIS
Suggestive

Bilateral symptoms of numbness, weakness, and incoordination suggest a cord lesion. A dermatomal sensory level or Lhermitte's sign (provocation of limb paresthesia with flexion/extension of the neck) is highly suggestive of cord disease. Bladder and bowel dysfunction is also an integral part of myelopathies.

Definitive

Objective findings on the neurologic examination to corroborate subjective symptoms secure the diagnosis of spinal cord disease. Imaging studies then give further anatomical verification. "Crossed sensory findings" (loss of posterior column function unilaterally with contralateral loss of spinothalamic function) or "suspended" sensory loss (loss of sensation over several dermatomes with normal sensation below) is a definitive and diagnostic sign of cord disease, with exceptions being diabetic thoracic radiculopathies, cutaneous herpes zoster, and discogenic radiculopathies. Remember that many spinal cord diseases do not have "positive" radiologic findings. Compressive or destructive processes are excluded by imaging studies, thereby securing the clinical diagnosis by eliminating "mimickers." Demyelinating lesions are not always seen on magnetic resonance imaging. A patient with the clinical picture of acute transverse myelitis who is medically treated must have a surgically treatable lesion promptly ruled out by the appropriate imaging study.

CLINICAL MANIFESTATIONS
Subjective

Extradural disease commonly presents with localized spinal pain. Unfortunately, this is an extremely common complaint in the general population. Spinal metastasis and abscesses present with steadily increasing pain, often quite severe, commonly without relief with bed rest. Spinal pain is followed by pain in a root distribution, then signs of spinal cord dysfunction, especially bladder and bowel dysfunction, weakness of the legs, and lower limb paresthesias. Intradural/extramedullary lesions also present with radiating sensory symptoms, usually without the spinal pain, or with compressive symptoms.

Pain or sensory symptoms in a uni- or multidermatomal distribution suggest discrete sensory tract dysfunction in intramedullary lesions. Involvement of nearby motor/cerebellar tracts leads to symptoms in the legs. Lamination in the motor tracts leads to early involvement of the more laterally placed feet and leg fibers in compressive, extramedullary lesions. Anterior horn cell involvement leads to segmental atrophy and weakness. Lesions of the lower spinal cord and lumbar and sacral roots in the filum terminale, cauda equina, and conus medullaris are usually associated with a great deal of pain and bladder/bowel signs and symptoms, along with the motor and sensory findings in the perineum and lower extremities.

Syringomyelia most often presents with segmental sensory symptoms secondary to destruction of crossing spinothalamic tracts as they pass by the enlarging central canal. Eventually, the posterior columns, autonomic fibers, and lateral corticospinal tract fibers are involved, giving rise to a "capelike" sensory loss over the shoulders and upper chest, a dissociated loss of pain and temperature/posterior column function, autonomic dysfunction, and pyramidal syndromes. Most commonly, the cavity involves the lower cervical and upper thoracic levels but the syrinx can extend rostrally to the brainstem or caudally into the midthoracic area.

Bladder and bowel dysfunction are common in patients with spinal cord disease. Supraspinal neural pathways are interrupted by most spinal cord disorders, leading to loss of voluntary control of the bladder and bowel. Reflex neural circuits in the lower cord, sacral nerve roots, and walls of the rectum/sphincter and bladder then predominate.

Past medical history is important to give information about the presence or absence of systemic neoplasia or infection. History of trauma, prior episodes of spinal pain, spinal surgery, radiation treatments, electrical injuries, radicular symptoms, and so on are important. Prior unexplained neurologic dysfunction can be important in the evaluation of myelitis as part of multiple sclerosis. Family history is important in hereditary degenerative syndromes. The presence of constitutional symptoms or dysfunction of other organs suggests that the myelopathy may be part of a systemic illness.

Objective
Physical Examination

The finding of a sensory level clearly implies a spinal cord lesion. Note that the actual level of the lesion may be several segments away from the level (see Related Basic Science, Anatomy). Crossed sensory findings ("dissociated" sensory loss) can only be caused by a spinal cord lesion. Corticospinal findings (weakness and spasticity, increased muscle stretch reflexes, extensor plantar responses) and ataxia are common and are usually symmetric in compressive lesions, but early are often asymmetric. The leg fibers are laterally placed and can be affected early in spinal cord compression. The arm fibers, especially the hands, are medially placed and can be preferentially affected in partial vascular insufficiency syndromes. The arm innervation lies in the border zone area between the anterior and posterior spinal arteries. This "central cord syndrome" is most commonly seen in neck and head retroflexion injuries. Bevor's sign, an upward movement of the umbilicus with tensing of abdominal muscles, owing to weakness of lower abdominal muscles and retained strength of upper abdominal muscles, is found in patients with lesions of approximately the T-10 level. Objective tenderness to palpation over vertebral bodies containing infection or tumor can also be an important physical examination finding.

Routine Laboratory Abnormalities

Routine laboratory testing is usually unrevealing in cord disease. Patients with acute infections or neoplastic conditions can have an elevated sedimentation rate or white count along with an anemia or platelet abnormalities.

PLANS
Diagnostic
Differential Diagnosis

The neurologic history and examination generate the differential diagnosis, in terms of whether the lesion is extradural, intradural/extramedullary or intramedullary.

Diagnostic Options

The neurologic examination should suggest anatomic levels that guide further studies such as magnetic resonance imaging, myelography, lumbar puncture, and neurophysiologic studies (e.g., electromyography and evoked potentials). The significance of low serum B_{12} levels can be elucidated by measuring serum methylmalonic acid levels, which are elevated in most cases of symptomatic B_{12} deficiency. Tumors, abscesses, disks, spondylosis, syringomyelia, and traumatic lesions all have characteristic imaging abnormalities. At times, magnetic resonance imaging can visualize discrete spinal cord demyelinating plaques.

Recommended Approach

Suspicion of spinal cord disease should prompt a thorough search for treatable causes, before irreversible damage is done. This usually involves at least magnetic resonance imaging to rule out compressive lesions. Management of trauma demands skills in spinal immobilization and access to neurosurgical care.

Therapeutic
Therapeutic Options

Any acute compression of the spinal cord needs prompt neurosurgical evaluation and often decompression. The exception to this is epidural compression from metastatic carcinoma, in which situation radiation therapy in most cases is optimal treatment. Surgery may be appropriate in some patients with metastases, especially when a tissue diagnosis is important. The pain from these lesions usually responds to high-dose steroids, usually dexamethasone 10 mg intravenously, followed by 6 mg intravenously every 6 hours. Cord trauma may be helped by high-dose methylprednisolone, 30 mg/kg bolus, followed by 5.4 mg/kg/h for 23 hours. Naloxone was not found effective in a recent trial. Recent studies show that GM_1 ganglioside may enhance recovery. Further clinical trials are in progress. Reduction of vertebral body subluxation and removal of herniated disk material are often helpful, although judgment is needed in case selection for surgery. On the scene of injury, spinal immobilization is mandatory. Antibiotic treatment of any spinal infection, after appropriate diagnostic and drainage measures, depends on the infecting organism. Vitamin B_{12} myelopathies are treated with 100 µg intramuscularly per month. Syringomyelia can be treated surgically when it is associated with an Arnold–Chiari malformation. In this day of frequent magnetic resonance imaging (indication neck pain without neurologic symptoms), syringomyelia can be uncovered before symptoms are prominent. Treatment of acute transverse myelopathy is of unclear benefit to the patient, but usually consists of a week or two of high-dose steroids. Tumors are treated with excision and radiation therapy when appropriate. Compressive lesions from bony abnormalities, spondylosis, disks, and so on, are treated with appropriate surgical procedures. Acute vascular infarction is untreatable.

In general, the prognosis of recovery in patients with severe deficits is poor, even if the disease is considered treatable; however, treatment when the neurologic deficit is mild can lead to excellent recovery.

Recommended Approach

Spinal cord disease is relatively uncommon in a primary care physician's practice. Neurologic evaluation is strongly recommended. Note that a lumbar puncture in the setting of spinal cord compression can lead to accelerated cord damage. If spinal cord compression is suspected, neurosurgical expertise must be immediately available to perform decompressive surgery.

FOLLOW-UP

The natural history of cord disease certainly depends on the cause. Repeated neurologic evaluations are important in confirming the disease and treating the underlying disease and any complications such as urinary tract infections, decubiti, spasticity, and pain syndromes. Evolution of the illness should conform to the expected natural history of the disease, and variation from this should prompt diagnostic reevaluation.

DISCUSSION
Prevalence and Incidence

Relatively few epidemiologic data have been collected about these diseases.

Related Basic Science
Anatomy

The adult spinal cord is approximately 45 cm long and 8 to 14 mm in diameter. The cervical and lumbar portions are wider, due to the in-creased number of cells in the gray matter with efferents into the limbs. At birth, the emerging roots correspond to the vertebral level, but with growth into adulthood, the tip of the cord is at the L1–2 level. Sensory nerves exit the cord posteriorly and the motor nerves anteriorly, each from a longitudinally running sulcus. A small central canal is present. The conus medullaris is the caudal end of the cord, and the filum terminale is the proximal portion of the sacral nerve roots.

The central H-shaped mass of gray (cell bodies) lies in the central portion of the cord, surrounded by longitudinally running tracts of fiber bundles (white matter) (see Figure 20–12–2 for details). The anterior portions of the gray matter contain the cell bodies for motor neurons (lateral corticospinal tract or pyramidal tract). The posterior portions contain cell bodies mediating sensation and pain (substantia gelatinosa). Cells of the autonomic nervous system lie intermediate to these cells (intermediolateral cell column and dorsal nucleus of Clarke) in the thoracic region. The columns of white matter in the posterior portion of the cord (fasciculus gracilis and cuneatus) carry information regarding position sense, joint movement, and two-point discrimination to the nucleus gracilis and cuneatus in the medulla oblongata. Pain and temperature impulses are carried in the lateral spinothalmic tract (pain and thermal sense) and anterior spinothalamic tract (light touch). Spinocerebellar tracts run laterally. The posterior column carries sensory information from ipsilateral afferents while pain and temperature afferents (second-order spinothalamic tracts) enter the cord, ascend one to five segments, then cross the cord near the central canal to ascend in the spinothalamic tracts. In the posterior columns, the leg fibers are situated more medially, and in the descending corticospinal tracts, leg fibers are more laterally placed (hand fibers medial).

The blood supply is from one medial anterior spinal artery and two posterior spinal arteries. The posterior spinal artery irrigates the posterior one third of the cord, and the anterior spinal artery irrigates the remainder of the cord. The border zone area encompasses the corticospinal tracts, explaining the unique clinical findings (central cord syndrome) of bibrachial paralysis/pareses, hands greater than shoulders, in partial vascular insufficiency syndromes (usually traumatic). The posterior spinal arteries originate from the vertebral or posterior inferior cerebellar arteries and the anterior spinal artery from branches of the intracranial vertebral arteries in the region of the foramen magnum. They then run longitudinally down the cord, with 7 to 10 arteries entering this anastomotic system from the aorta and its branches. The lower thoracic region (with the most tenuous irrigation) is supplied by the artery of Adamkiewicz, a branch of the abdominal aorta in the lower thoracic or upper lumbar area. The lumbar cord gets branches from the hypogastric and sacral arteries. The posterior spinal artery has a more generous set of feeding arteries throughout its course, and its territory is less likely to be infarcted than that of the anterior spinal artery.

Physiologic or Metabolic Derangement

The pathophysiology of cord ischemia is presumed to be similar to that of cerebral ischemia. Excess extracellular concentrations of excitatory amino acids, intracellular calcium release, and oxygen free radical release have been implicated in the cascade of neurochemical reactions

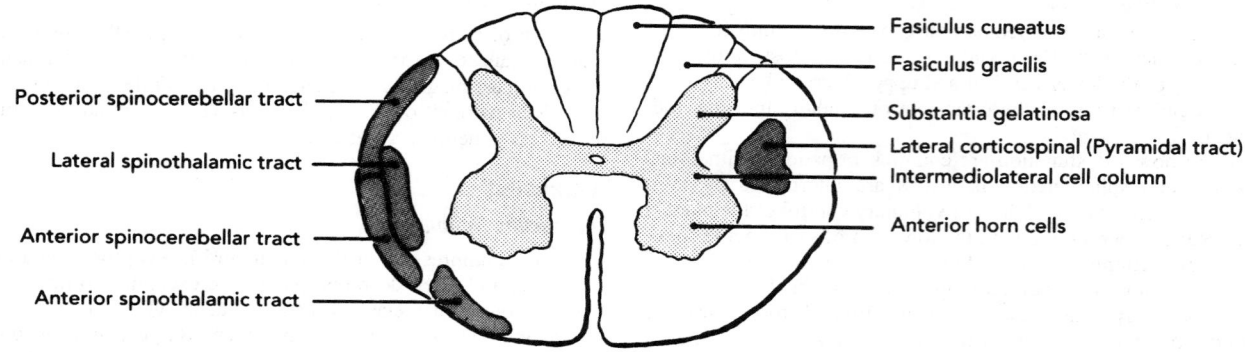

Figure 20–12–2. Spinal cord fiber tracts and nuclei.

that lead to cell death. Cord compressions (trauma, tumors, disks, spondylosis, infections, hematomas) are thought to damage neurons by both vascular compromise and direct compressive effects. Intrinsic infections damage the cord by direct invasion and by mass effect. Metabolic and toxic diseases likely to damage cell bodies and axons by biochemical disruption. The pathophysiologic disturbances in radiation and electrical injury myelopathies, familial syndromes, and other degenerative disorders are unknown.

Genetics

The molecular genetics of the inherited ataxias and familial spinal degeneration syndromes are beginning to be unraveled.

Natural History and Its Modification with Treatment

Only a few spinal disorders have been proven to be positively influenced by treatment. The treatment of cervical spondylosis surgically has been called into question (Rowland, 1992); however, any acute compressive lesion (save for metastatic cancer) needs immediate surgical attention. Infections need appropriate antibiotics and decompression. Attacks of demyelinating myelitis are likely shortened by a course of methylprednisolone 500 to 1000 mg/d for 5 days. Interferon beta may improve the natural history of multiple sclerosis, at least during the course of the 3-year study recently published. Surgical debulking of tumors likely improves outcome. Surgical treatment of a syrinx sometimes slows progression, although no randomized trials have been done. High-dose steroids in trauma improve outcome.

Prevention

No clear measures to prevent spinal cord disease are available, other than to avoid toxic exposures and maintain general good health to minimize vascular risk factors.

Cost Containment

No data are available to guide the neurologist in this important aspect of care. Because of the catastrophic nature (and hence expensive in terms of chronic care of the para- or quadraplegic) of missing a treatable cord lesion, one can assume that full diagnostic evaluation of potentially treatable disease is cost effective.

Plain computed tomography of the spine is helpful to rule out fractures and bone changes in neoplastic and infectious diseases. Computed tomography is cost ineffective in evaluation of other cord diseases because magnetic resonance imaging or contrast myelography would have to follow and the computed tomography scan would not add useful information.

In relapsing multiple sclerosis with repeated attacks of myelitis, repeat magnetic resonance imaging of the spine is not necessary if the clinical picture is typical of demyelinating disease. Cranial magnetic resonance imaging has a higher diagnostic yield than spinal cord imaging, even when the symptoms are spinal.

REFERENCES

Adams RD, Victor M, eds. Principles of neurology. 5th ed. New York: McGraw Hill, 1993.
Bracken MB, Shepard MJ, Collins WF, et al. At randomized, controlled trial of methylprednisolone or naloxone in the treatment of acute spinal-cord injury. N Engl J Med 1990;322:1405.
Byrne TN. Spinal cord compression from epidural metastasis. N Engl J Med 1992;327:614.
IFNB Multiple sclerosis study group. Interferon beta–lb is effective in relapsing and remitting multiple sclerosis. Neurol 1993;43:655.
Jeffery DR, Mandler RN, Davis LE. Transverse myelitis. Arch Neurol 1993;50:532.
Rowland LP. Surgical treatment of cervical spondylotic myelopathy: Time for a controlled trial. Neurology 1992;42:5.
Satran R. Spinal cord infarction. Stroke 1987;22:13.

CHAPTER 20–13

Visual Loss

Louis R. Caplan, M.D., and Judith A. Hinchey, M.D.

DEFINITION

Visual loss is the inability to see clearly in any part of visual space. This may involve a portion of one eye or both eyes, partially or totally. Visual loss in one eye is called *monocular blindness.* Losing a portion of the vision in either eye is called a *field defect.* If it involves a similar field in each eye, such as the left field of each eye, it is called a *homonymous visual field defect.* If it involves both temporal fields, it is a *bitemporal hemianopia.*

ETIOLOGY

Etiologies vary depending on whether the lesion is in the eye, optic nerve, optic chiasm, or brain. The most common causes are vascular disease, multiple sclerosis, and tumors (Table 20–13–1).

CRITERIA FOR DIAGNOSIS
Suggestive

The patient reports transient or persistent blurry vision or visual loss. Often, he or she cannot report if the visual loss is in both eyes or one.

Many field defects and slowly progressive monocular loss go unnoticed.

Definitive

The following define the diagnosis: loss of visual acuity; scotoma in either eye (visual field defect detectable by confrontation testing at the bedside); visual field defect detected by formal perimetry or tangent screen or automated field testing; abnormal appearance of retinal arteries, retina, or optic nerve on fundoscopy; afferent pupillary defect.

We first try to clarify if the problem is monocular or involves both eyes. We use this to help localize a process to the eye, optic nerve, optic chiasm, or optic radiations (postchiasm).

Monocular lesions are prechiasmatic (see Figure 20–13–1) due to either disease of the retinal vessels as in amaurosis fugax, central retinal artery occlusion, and temporal arteritis; disease of the optic nerve, as in optic neuritis or optic glioma, or an ocular problem, as in cataracts or glaucoma.

TABLE 20–13–1. ETIOLOGIES OF VISUAL LOSS

Monocular visual loss
Retina and eye
Retinal ischemia (transient monocular blindness, central retinal
    artery occlusion, central retinal branch artery occlusion)
    Glaucoma
    Macular degeneration
    Retinal diseases
Optic nerve
    Optic neuritis
    Optic nerve sheath meningioma
    Optic glioma
    Anterior ischemic optic neuropathy
Visual Loss, Both Eyes
Pituitary tumors
Multiple sclerosis
Homonymous Hemianopia or Quandrantanopia
Infarcts
Hemorrhage
Tumors
Inflammatory disease
Infectious disease

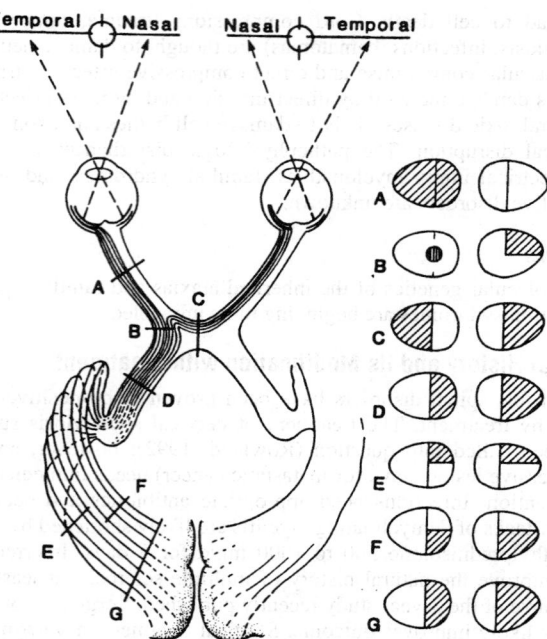

Figure 20–13–1. Diagram showing the effects on the fields of vision produced by lesions at various points along the optic pathway: **A.** Complete blindness in the left eye. **B.** The usual effect is a left junction scotoma in association with a right upper quadrantanopia. The latter results from interruption of the right retinal nasal fibers that project into the base of the left optic nerve (Wilbrand's knee). A left nasal hemianopia could occur from a lesion at this point but is exceedingly rare. **C.** Bitemporal hemianopia. **D.** Right homonymous hemianopia. **E, F.** Right superior and inferior quadrant hemianopia. **G.** Right homonymous hemianopia. *(Source: From Adams R, Victor M. Principles of neurology. 5th ed. New York: McGraw-Hill, 1993:212. Reproduced with permission from the publisher and author.)*

Retinal Diseases

TRANSIENT MONOCULAR BLINDNESS (AMAUROSIS FUGAX)
Clinical Manifestations

Subjective

Transient monocular blindness comes on abruptly, is painless, and involves the visual field of one eye either completely or partially. Often patients describe a shade coming down. This lasts minutes and resolves. The patient usually has risk factors for vascular disease and may have had episodes of transient arm numbness, weakness, or aphasia.

Objective

Physical Examination. The retina may be normal or emboli within arteries may be seen on ophthalmoscopic examination. A carotid bruit is often heard.

Routine Laboratory Abnormalities. Hyperlipidemia and hyperglycemia may be present.

Plans

Diagnostic

Differential Diagnosis. The most common cause of transient monocular blindness is carotid artery disease in the neck. Less often migraine and cardiac origin emboli produce TMB.

Diagnostic Options. Neuroimaging techniques have now greatly curtailed our need for more invasive tests. Ultrasound of the carotid arteries confirms the diagnosis. An adjunct study to define the degree of stenosis is magnetic resonance angiography (MRA). These two together often eliminate the need for standard dye angiography.

Recommended Approach. We are very aggressive with vascular disease and believe these patients need to be seen by a neurologist urgently. An event such as transient monocular blindness is a warning that the carotid artery may be diseased and the next event may be a stroke. Most of these patients undergo carotid ultrasound studies as soon as possible to confirm the diagnosis.

Therapeutic

Therapeutic Options A tight stenosis of the carotid artery that has caused transient monocular blindness is considered for surgical evaluation.

Other options include platelet inhibitors such as aspirin and ticlopidine. Still others may place the patient on anticoagulants (coumadin).

Recommended Approach. We recommend carotid endarterectomy to anyone with a symptomatic tight stenosis if he or she can tolerate the surgery. These patients are brought into the hospital and placed on heparin, unless otherwise contraindicated, and fluids are maintained. If surgery is not an option, then it is decided case by case whether aspirin or coumadin is indicated.

Follow-up

Acutely postsurgery, blood pressure is watched closely, as elevated blood pressure can result in further neurologic decline. After surgery we place most patients on aspirin.

Discussion

Prevalence and Incidence

Internal carotid artery atherosclerosis is thought to be the cause of transient monocular blindness in more than 50% of men over 50 years old. It is also estimated to occur in 40% of patients with symptomatic carotid artery disease.

Related Basic Science

Transient monocular blindness implies internal carotid artery occlusion or stenosis. Decreased blood is flowing to the ophthalmic artery, the first branch off the internal carotid artery.

Natural History and Its Modification with Treatment

It has been shown that patients with a symptomatic tight carotid stenosis, manifested by either transient monocular blindness or a hemispheric transient ischemic attack, are at a 26% risk of ipsilateral stroke within the next 2 years if treated medically. Surgical treatment with carotid endarterectomy lowers this risk to 9%. Even allowing for surgical risk, carotid endarterectomy was still found to be beneficial. The caveat is that surgery must be performed by skilled hands (perioperative risk of stroke and death should be less than 2%).

Prevention

Although transient monocular blindness cannot be prevented, a stroke may be prevented if transient monocular blindness is recognized early and treated quickly.

CENTRAL RETINAL ARTERY OCCLUSION
Clinical Manifestations
Subjective

Occlusion usually occurs abruptly, is painless, and much of the vision is lost and does not resolve quickly. Risk factors for stroke are usually present.

Objective

Physical Examination. Ophthalmoscopic examination shows obstruction in the central retinal artery or its branches by either calcium, white platelet–fibrin clots, cholesterol, or red clot. A pale disk is seen and may have a cherry red spot. A carotid bruit or an irregular heart rhythm may be heard.

Routine Laboratory Abnormalities. Hyperlidemia and hyperglycemia may be present.

Plans
Diagnostic

Differential Diagnosis. Central retinal artery occlusion is usually due to an embolic event from either the carotid artery or the heart. Less common causes are temporal arteritis, vasospasm, and in situ thrombosis.

Diagnostic Options. A fluorescein angiogram performed by an ophthalmologist may show a clot in the retinal artery. Patients should be evaluated for carotid artery and cardiac disease by ultrasound and echocardiogram. A sedimentation rate and hypercoagulable screen are done when clinically indicated.

Recommended Approach. The patient is usually evaluated for both cardiac and carotid disease. He or she is admitted to the hospital and placed on heparin unless otherwise contraindicated.

Therapeutic

Therapeutic Options. Anterior chamber paracentesis, digital massage, or carbon dioxide inhalation may help the occluded artery reperfuse. If carotid artery disease is the cause, then the options are similar to those outlined for transient monocular blindness. When cardiac disease is the cause, then anticoagulation for an arrhythmia, aneurysm, or clot is warranted. Surgical removal of an aneurysm may also be considered.

Recommended Approach. We admit patients to the hospital and begin heparin unless otherwise contraindicated. Ophthalmology may perform a paracentesis and place the patient on carbon dioxide. Cardiac and carotid evaluation ensues.

Follow-up

Monitoring visual acuity and visual fields during treatment is the best way to follow the clinical course.

Discussion
Prevalence and Incidence

Among older patients, carotid artery disease and temporal arteritis are the most common cause of central retinal artery occlusion. Central retinal artery occlusion occurs in 5 to 10% of patients with temporal arteritis. Young patients may often have cardiac disease.

Related Basic Science

The central retinal artery is a branch of the ophthalmic artery that supplies the retina. Its origin from the ophthalmic artery is variable, but it is at the region of the lamina cribrosa, where emboli or inflammatory processes result and cause central retinal artery occlusion. This produces a loss of the retinal circulation and visual loss.

Natural History and Its Modification with Treatment

If occlusion lasts for more than 1 hour, the retina becomes infarcted. Emergent treatment with digital massage, paracentesis or carbon dioxide inhalation may help the embolus migrate and help preserve vision.

Prevention

Often, central retinal artery occlusion is the presentation of cardiac or carotid disease. Controlling risk factors for these diseases is the only known prevention.

TEMPORAL ARTERITIS
Clinical Manifestations
Subjective

Temporal arteritis also causes sudden monocular visual loss. Clues to this diagnosis usually include advanced age of patient, headaches, malaise, fatigue, jaw claudication, and a low-grade fever.

Objective

Physical Examination. Scalp tenderness and a palpable, tender, nonpulsatile, cordlike superficial temporal artery define the diagnosis.

Routine Laboratory Abnormalities. Anemia, leukocytosis, and an elevated sedimentation rate are routine laboratory abnormalities.

Plans
Diagnostic

Differential Diagnosis. Retinal artery occlusion is the main differential.

Diagnostic Options. Temporal arteritis with impending visual loss is a medical emergency. The sedimentation rate should be determined and a temporal artery biopsy done to confirm the diagnosis. Angiography, especially looking at the external carotid artery, may be suggestive.

Therapeutic

A patient with temporal arteritis needs steroids even before the temporal artery biopsy is taken. The dosage is 60 to 80 mg/d, usually with rapid relief of the headache and systemic symptoms.

Follow-up

Steroids should be tapered slowly, watching the clinical symptoms and sedimentation rate.

Discussion
Prevalence and Incidence

Visual symptoms may occur in up to 40% of patients with temporal arteritis. Visual loss, complete or partial, occurs in 20% or less of patients. Occlusion of the central retinal artery occurs in 5 to 10%, and temporal arteritis accounts for 6 to 14% of the cases of anterior ischemic optic neuropathy.

Related Basic Science

The etiology of the disease is a granulomatous inflammation of the extracranial arteries: the external carotid, internal carotid, and vertebral arteries. Visual loss is felt to be due to ischemia of the anterior optic nerve, less often to the retina.

Natural History and Its Modification with Treatment

The ocular ischemia may not improve with steroids, but the systemic symptoms should resolve. Further eye ischemia should be prevented.

The opposite eye often becomes involved if steroids are not started immediately.

Prevention

Early diagnosis and treatment of temporal arteritis are the only way to prevent visual loss. Once visual loss occurs in one eye, the opposite eye may be affected within 48 hours unless treatment has begun.

MIGRAINE
Clinical Manifestations
Subjective

Migraine can also cause monocular visual loss but this usually results in a scotoma, lasting a few minutes due to retinal vessel "spasm." The patient may describe positive visual phenomena such as scintillations, which may be followed by a hemicranial headache. The individual is usually young and often has a family or personal history of migraine. Visual loss is most often temporary.

Objective

Physical Examination. Between migraine attacks the examination is normal. During an attack a small area (scotoma) of visual loss is found and retinal arteriolar vasoconstriction may be visible.

Routine Laboratory Abnormalities. There are no routine laboratory abnormalities.

Plans
Diagnostic

Differential Diagnosis. Retinal artery occlusion, transient monocular blindness, and causes of vasculitis such as collagen-vascular disease and sarcoidosis constitute the differential diagnosis.

Diagnostic Options. Patients with suspected migraine as the etiology of their visual loss still need an evaluation to exclude the possibility of an embolus, hypercoagulable state, or vasculitis. Given a good history for migraine and repeated benign events, there does not need to be repeated extensive evaluations.

Recommended Approach. The first episode of ocular migraine deserves a search for a cardiac or artery-to-artery embolic event. We would proceed with an MRA and an electrocardiogram and consider an echocardiogram. Also, we test for a hypercoagulable state.

Therapeutic

Therapeutic Options. Migraine patients need reassurance and consideration of prophylactic or abortive medications. Diamox or carbon dioxide may be given during a prolonged attack. Medications now used include verapamil, propranolol, nifedipine, and tricyclic antidepressants.

Recommended Approach. We use long-acting verapamil, another calcium channel blocker, as a preventive therapy.

Follow-up

Following visual acuity and visual fields is the best way to monitor treatment.

Discussion
Prevalence and Incidence

Retinal migraine is rare. It is considered a subgroup of complicated migraine that affects 1% of the population.

Related Basic Science

The etiology of ocular or retinal migraine is felt to be vasoconstriction of either the retinal or ciliary arteries.

Natural History and Its Modification with Treatment

Retinal migraine is generally considered a benign disease, although there have been several reports of permanent visual loss felt to be due

to ocular migraine. It is unclear if treatment with calcium channel blockers or beta blockers influences the course.

Optic Nerve

OPTIC NEURITIS
Clinical Manifestations
Suggestive

Optic neuritis causes monocular visual loss developing over hours to days, usually with pain on eye movement. A past history of similar attacks of visual loss or a history of other neurologic events, such as numbness, weakness, ataxia, and diplopia, lasting days to weeks suggests multiple sclerosis.

Objective

Physical Examination. On physical examination the visual acuity is decreased. There is a central area of reduced vision (central scotoma), and color differentiation, especially with red, is reduced in the affected eye. With the most common type, retrobulbar optic neuritis, the optic disk examination is normal. The pupil on the affected side has a reduced reaction to light.

Routine Laboratory Abnormalities. There are no routine laboratory abnormalities.

Plans
Diagnostic

Differential Diagnosis. Other causes of optic neuritis besides multiple sclerosis include sarcoidosis and systemic lupus erythematosus (Table 20–13–2).

Diagnostic Options and Recommended Approach. If a demyelinating disease is suspected, a search for other evidence of demyelinating disease by either magnetic resonance imaging (MRI) or evoked potentials is warranted. The spinal fluid may show a slight pleocytosis and monoclonal immunoglobulin bands in multiple sclerosis. MRI may show abnormalities of the optic nerve. A search for other causes of optic neuritis, by obtaining an angiotensin-converting enzyme level (sarcoid), or viral infection or tuberculosis (PPD test) may be warranted.

Therapeutic

Therapeutic Options. Management of optic neuritis is controversial. The literature supports the use of intravenous steroids but suggests that oral prednisone may be harmful. Most patients recover with or without steroids. Intravenous steroids seem to help hasten recovery.

Recommended Approach. If a spell of optic neuritis is affecting activities of daily living then it is reasonable to treat with outpatient intravenous steroids. If the visual loss is only mild, then no treatment may be warranted. Intravenous methylprednisolone 250 mg every 6 hours for 3 to 5 days, followed by an oral prednisone taper, has been the usual prescribed regimen. We advise tapering the dose over weeks and not as abruptly as is usually recommended.

Follow-up

These patients need to be followed either for recurrence or for other neurologic symptoms they may develop. The diagnosis of multiple

TABLE 20–13–2. CAUSES OF OPTIC NEURITIS

Multiple sclerosis
Viral infection
Postviral status
Sarcoidosis
Intraocular inflammation
Tuberculosis

sclerosis by definition requires evidence of two separate lesions in the central nervous system that are separated by time.

Discussion

Prevalence and Incidence

Optic neuritis occurs in a large percentage of patients with multiple sclerosis. It is said that 15 to 50% of patients who have monocular optic neuritis will at some time develop multiple sclerosis. This proportion is smaller in children. The occurrence of bilateral optic neuritis increases the risk of later developing multiple sclerosis severalfold.

Related Basic Science

Optic neuritis is caused by demyelination or inflammation of the optic nerve. The optic nerve supplies central vision and forms part of the pathway for color vision.

Natural History and Its Modification with Treatment

Visual loss due to optic neuritis usually resolves in a few weeks. Some patients are left with a small central scotoma, but the majority are not aware of the deficit. By 6 months there is no significant difference in visual recovery comparing treatment and untreated groups, although treatment with intravenous methylprednisolone may hasten recovery.

Prevention

There is no known method of prevention.

TUMORS
Clinical Manifestations

Subjective

Tumors usually present with slowly progressive visual loss. This may go unnoticed by the patient. The patient often does not have a headache but may develop proptosis.

Objective

Physical Examination. The ophthalmoscopic examination shows a pale optic disk and disk swelling. The vessels in the eye may have shunting. The affected eye may be proptotic.

Routine Laboratory Abnormalities. There are no routine laboratory abnormalities.

Plans

Diagnostic

Differential Diagnosis. Common tumors include optic glioma, meningioma, and carcinomatosis (Table 20–13–3).

Diagnostic Options. Detection depends on ultrasound or neuroradiology of the orbit and optic nerve by either computed tomography (CT) or MRI.

Recommended Approach. A CT scan with contrast or an MRI with gadolinium should be done to identify the etiology. Also, formal testing by an ophthalmologist should be performed to follow visual acuity. A surgeon should be consulted in the case of meningioma and glioma.

Therapeutic

Depending on etiology either surgery or chemotherapy is an option. Often surgery may not preserve vision but prevents further symptoms..

TABLE 20–13–3. TUMORS OF THE ORBIT OR OPTIC NERVE

Glioma
Meningioma
Metastases: lung, melanoma, lymphoma
Infiltrate lesions: sarcoidosis, leukemia, plasmacytoma

Follow-up

As most tumors are not fully resectable, follow-up by a neuro-opthalmologist should be continued at least yearly (or every few months) to detect any deterioration.

Discussion

See Chapters 3–36 and 20–10.

ANTERIOR ISCHEMIC OPTIC NEUROPATHY
Clinical Manifestations

Subjective

Older patients present with an acute field defect in one eye. Often the visual defect is altitudinal, involving an upper or lower half of vision in one eye. This is painless. Hypertension and diabetes are often present.

Objective

Physical Examination. There is visual loss, often altitudinal, on confrontational testing. In some patients the optic disk is pale and swollen and flame hemorrhages are often present. The pupil does not react as well to light. In some patients the fundus looks normal because the optic nerve infarction is further posterior.

Routine Laboratory Abnormalities. There are no routine laboratory abnormalities.

Plans

Diagnostic

Differential Diagnosis. Any acute loss of vision suggests a vascular etiology. The disk findings help separate this from other causes such as embolus, optic neuritis, temporal arteritis, and rapid expansion of a tumor. In latter conditions, the disks would appear normal.

Diagnostic Options. A careful examination by an ophthalmologist should reveal the ischemia to the optic nerve. The erythrocyte sedimentation rate should be determined as temporal arteritis can cause acute onset of visual loss.

Recommended Approach. We recommend an MRA looking for carotid stenosis.

Therapeutic

Underlying conditions, including diabetes and hypertension, should be treated.

Discussion

Prevalence and Incidence

Anterior ischemic optic neuropathy is one of the most common causes of visual loss in the elderly. Based on data from Missouri and Los Angeles, the incidence rates for nonarteritic anterior ischemic optic neuropathy are 0.54 per 100,000. The rate for the arteritic form was 0.09. The incidence rates for people 50 years of age and older were 2.3 and 0.36, respectively.

Related Basic Science

Anterior ischemic optic neuropathy is caused by ischemia to the optic nerve. It is generally felt to be due to small artery disease of the posterior ciliary arteries causing infarction of the optic nerve.

Natural History and Its Modification with Treatment

Involvement of the opposite eye is common. Unfortunately, controlling blood pressure and diabetes do not change the course of the disease.

Prevention

Ther are no known preventive measures once the disease has occurred. Preventing hypertension and diabetes and treating the arteritic forms quickly are the only forms of prevention.

Optic Chiasm

Clinical Manifestations

Chiasmatic lesions classically result in a bitemporal field defect, as the crossing fibers from each eye that supply vision to the temporal fields are affected (Figure 20–13–1C).

Subjective

Patients may say they have tunnel vision or have been bumping into objects.

Objective

Physical Examination. Findings on bedside confrontational testing show visual loss in both temporal fields.

Routine Laboratory Abnormalities. There are no routine laboratory abnormalities.

Plans

Diagnostic

Differential Diagnosis. The most common abnormality is a pituitary tumor, but any space-occupying abnormality in the suprasellar region can cause this condition (Table 20–13–4).

Diagnostic Options. Chiasmatic lesions are usually well visualized on neuroimaging. CT or MRI of the sellar region confirms the diagnosis. A referral to a neurologist or neurosurgeon would then be appropriate. Screening tests for secretion of growth hormone, prolactin, and adrenocorticotropic hormone are indicated.

Recommended Approach. We recommend an MRI with gadolinium with coronal cuts through the sellar region.

Therapeutic

Pituitary adenomas can be treated either medically or surgically. Medical agents include bromocriptine.

Follow-up

Following the visual fields and visual acuity helps assess treatment. This should be done in conjunction with an ophthalmologist.

Discussion

Prevalence and Incidence

The most common lesion causing bitemporal hemianopia is a pituitary adenoma. Of these, prolactinomas are most common. Somewhat less than 10% of brain tumors are pituitary adenomas.

Related Basic Science

Prolactin secretion causes galactorrhea. Bromocriptine is a prolactin inhibitor and is usually the treatment of choice for prolactin-secreting tumors.

Natural History and Its Modification with Treatment

Bilateral blindness may occur if left untreated. Prolactinomas respond well to bromocriptine, with improvement of the visual symptoms.

TABLE 20–13–4. CHIASM LESIONS ("SATCHMO")

Sarcoid
Adenoma (pituitary), **a**neurysm, **a**rachnoid cyst
Teratoma
Craniopharyngioma
Hamartoma, **h**ypothalamic glioma, **h**emorrhage
Meningioma, **m**alignant glioma
Other: chordoma, histiocytosis

POSTCHIASM (BRAIN)

Postchiasm lesions affect fibers from both eyes and cause homonymous hemianopias (Figure 20–13–1D–G). When visual loss in each eye is the same, the defect is called congruent. When the defect differs between the left and right eyes, the defect is incongruent. Most congruent lesions are due to pathology in the occipital lobe (Figure 20–13–1G).

Clinical Manifestations

Subjective

Cerebral infarctions and hemorrhages occur abruptly and cause a hemianopia or quadrantanopia. Cerebral infections or abscess may come on subacutely and tumors progress slowly. The overwhelming picture is that which accompanies the visual loss.

Objective

Physical Examination. On confrontation testing, the visual loss can be mapped out. If it is large, then the difference between congruent and incongruent may be detected. If small, then Amsler grid testing may need to be done. Associated symptoms of either aphasia, hemiparesis, hemisensory, or neglect should be examined.

Routine Laboratory Abnormalities. There are no diagnostic routine laboratory abnormalities.

Plans

Diagnostic

Differential Diagnosis. Acute-onset events are usually due to a vascular cause, cerebral infarction, or hemorrhage. Subacute causes include infections, abscesses, or inflammatory processes. Slowly progressive lesions are usually due to tumors.

Diagnostic Options. A CT or MRI scan can best visualize the cerebral hemispheres.

Recommended Approach. A CT scan is obtained for the acute onset of a hemianopia. Once an intracerebral bleed is excluded, cerebral infarction evaluation is performed. We order an MRI for more slowly developing hemianopias.

Therapeutic

Therapy depends on the diagnosis. As all postchiasm lesions are treated differently, we refer the reader to the individual chapters for therapeutic options and approach.

Follow-up

Follow-up depends on the specific diagnosis.

Discussion

Prevalence and Incidence

The prevalence and incidence depend on the etiology. Vascular disease is probably the most common cause of postchiasm visual defects.

Related Basic Science

Three different structures—the lateral geniculate body, the optic tract, and the optic radiations—may be affected. The lateral geniculate body and optic tract will generally give the same visual loss, a homonymous hemianopia (Figure 20–13–1D). Lesions that cause this include occlusion of the anterior choroidal artery. An associated symptom is an ipsilateral hemiparesis. The optic radiations split in the parietal and temporal lobes, with the fibers that supply vision in the superior half of the visual field traveling through the temporal lobe. The visual loss from a parietal or temporal lesion is a quadrantanopia (Figure 20–13–1E,F). Associated symptoms depend on which hemisphere is affected. A left hemisphere temporal lobe lesion is accompanied by aphasia. A right hemisphere temporal lobe lesion may be associated with behavioral changes. A lesion in either hemisphere may lead to visual hallucinations. A left hemisphere parietal lobe lesion is associated with a right hemisensory defect and aphasia. Lesions in the right parietal lobe are associated with a neglect syndrome, that is, the patient denies there is a problem with his or her left side. We have seen patients who are paralyzed on the left side and yet say there is nothing wrong. We can even show patients their left hand and they will not recognize it as being their own. They may also have trouble drawing the location of the bathroom in their house, as mapping and visual spatial skills are affected. After traversing through the parietal and temporal lobes, the optic radiation fibers come back together in the occipital lobe. Here it is easy to get all the fibers from both eyes, both lower and upper visual fields. Occipital lobe lesions commonly result in a congruent honomymous hemianopia (Figure 20–13–1G). The patients are usually aware of this difficulty even when the lesion is on the right side. An associated symptom is ipsilateral hemisensory loss.

Natural History and Its Modification with Treatment

The natural history depends on the etiology.

Prevention

Stroke, diabetes, and hypertension are common causes of visual loss of one form or another. Treating hypertension, diabetes, and the other stroke risk factors, hypercholesterolemia and smoking, is the best preventive measure.

COST CONTAINMENT

The most cost-effective way to evaluate eye visual loss is to know the anatomy of the nervous system. Diagnosis depends greatly on location of the lesion and tests should be tailored with this in mind. A neurologist or neuro-ophthalmologist should be consulted to minimize the number of tests and control costs.

REFERENCES

Adams R, Victor M. Principles of neurology. 5th ed. New York: McGraw-Hill, 1993.

Beck RW, Cleary PA, Anderson MM, et al. A random controlled trial of corticosteroids in the treatment of optic neuritis. N Engl J Med 1992;326:581.

Bernstein E, Amaurosis fugax. New York: Springer-Verlag, 1988.

Glaser, JS. Neuroophthamology. 2nd ed. Philadelphia: Lippincott, 1990.

Huston KA, Hunder GG, et al. Temporal arteritis: A 25 year epidemiologic, clinical, and pathologic study. Ann Intern Med 1978;88:162.

Johnson LN, Arnold AC. Incidence of nonarteritic and arteritic anterior ischemic optic neuropathy. J Neuroophthalmol 1994;14:38.

Johnson RF, Griffin JW. Current therapy in neurologic disease. 4th ed. St. Louis: Mosby Year Book, 1993.

North American Symptomatic Carotid Endarterectomy Trial Collaborators. Beneficial effect of carotid endarterectomy in symptomatic patients with high grade stenosis. N Engl J Med 1991;325:445.

CHAPTER 20–14

Eye Movement Abnormalities

Judith A. Hinchey, M.D., and Louis R. Caplan, M.D.

DEFINITION

The eyes are aligned so that an object is projected on the same part of the retina of each eye. If this does not occur, viewers note blurry vision or double vision. When it occurs in childhood, the patient learns to fixate with only one eye.

ETIOLOGY

The eyes may not move together if there is an abnormality of the eye muscles, the nerves, the nerve cells, or the brain that controls eye movements. Lesions of the eye muscles or nerves that innervate these muscles cause weakness of individual movements in one or both eyes. Brain lesions usually cause loss of motion of both eyes in one direction—gaze palsies to one or both sides or to up or down movement. Etiology depends on the structures involved. The most common myopathies are myasthenia gravis and thyroid disease. The nerves themselves can be damaged anywhere along their pathways by aneurysms, infections, tumors, trauma, raised intracranial pressure, and diabetes. The nerve cells may be affected by anything that causes dysfunction in the brainstem such as tumor, stroke, infection, hemorrhage, and demyelination. Of course, any condition that affects the gaze centers in the cerebral hemispheres and brainstem, such as stroke, tumor, infection, trauma, demyelination, and degenerative disease, may lead to a gaze palsy.

CRITERIA FOR DIAGNOSIS

Suggestive

The complaint of double vision or blurry vision suggests that the eyes are not always aligned together. The patient may say there are two objects, one on top of the other, side by side, or oblique. He or she may also be aware that the double vision occurs only looking in a certain direction. A gaze palsy usually does not produce double vision, as the eyes do not move separately. The patient may not even be aware of a gaze palsy, however, because associated neurologic abnormalities dominate the clinical picture.

Definitive

The following define the diagnosis:

- Observation of impaired eye movement
- Reproduction of double vision especially with a red glass examination (this is done by covering one eye with a red glass, which should make the two images stand out. The two objects appear farther apart as the eyes move toward the eye with the abnormal muscle function).
- Abnormalities on caloric testing

Eye Muscle Disorders

THYROID EYE DISEASE

See Chapter 9–18.

Clinical Manifestations

Subjective. Thyroid disease presents with insidious onset of muscle enlargement. Patients may notice exophthalmos. They may also have ophthalmoplegia and/or vertical diplopia.

Objective. Physical examination reveals the inability to move the eyes in some directions. It is especially difficult for the patient to gaze upward. Chemosis and conjunctivitis may be present. Lid lag is also a confirmatory sign: when the patient looks down, the eye lids may remain up and lag behind eye movement. Specifically, the pupils react normally, as these muscles are spared. The findings involve more than one nerve territory. The patient may have proptosis. Other findings such as coarse thick skin and a palpable goiter point to Graves' disease.

There are no specific routine laboratory abnormalities (see Chapter 9–18).

Differential Diagnosis

Other causes of ocular muscle weakness should be considered (Table 20–14–1), as well as retrobulbar tumors, cavernous sinus thrombosis, and other orbital lesions.

Diagnostic Options and Recommended Approach

Thyroid function tests should be checked, although often at presentation of eye findings the patient is euthyroid. An ultrasound of the orbit or computed tomography (CT)/magnetic resonance imaging (MRI) of the orbits shows enlarged muscles and excludes other abnormalities. A tensilon test for myasthenia gravis may be considered if the etiology is unclear.

We recommend obtaining either a CT or MRI first to exclude other causes of eye muscle dysfunction and order appropriate tests for hyperthyroidism (see Chapter 9–18).

Therapeutic Options and Recommended Approach

Maintaining a euthyroid state is recommended. This is generally considered a self-limited disease. If the optic nerve becomes compressed and visual acuity is affected, then more active treatment is required. When vision is affected, treatment with high-dose corticosteroids or surgical decompression may be required. An ophthalmologist should be consulted.

Follow-up

These patients should be followed looking for signs of optic nerve compression, that is, decreased visual acuity or a central scotoma. The thyroid function tests may need to be followed for months.

Prevalence and Incidence

Thyroid eye disease is the most common cause of diplopia in the middle-aged patient.

Related Basic Science

The pathophysiology of this disease is infiltration of the muscles by mucopolysaccharides and inflammatory cells with fibrosis of the muscles.

Natural History and Its Modification with Treatment
See Chapter 9–18.

MYASTHENIA GRAVIS
Clinical Manifestations

Subjective. Patients with myasthenia gravis may state that they have double vision or blurry vision. They furthermore say this usually occurs in the evening or after they have been reading. One key to the diagnosis is the fluctuation of the symptoms during the day. Myasthenia commonly presents with unilateral or bilateral ptosis.

Objective. The physical examination reveals ptosis on examination or ptosis that is brought out by having the patient look up for 1 minute. This may also cause diplopia with fatigue of the eye muscles. Again, the pupillary function is normal. On general physical examination, they may have proximal muscle fatigue when repeatedly exercised at the bedside.

TABLE 20–14–1. OCULAR MUSCLE ABNORMALITIES

Graves' disease
Myasthenia gravis
Progressive external ophthalmoplegia: Kearns–Sayre disease
Oculopharyngeal dystrophy
Myotonic dystrophy
Trichinosis

Differential Diagnosis

Drugs can induce eye muscle weakness and should be inquired about (i.e., neomycin, penicillamine). Care should be taken to exclude a cavernous sinus lesion or intraorbital lesion. Other causes of ocular muscle abnormalities are less common and are listed in Table 20–14–1.

Diagnostic Options and Recommended Approach

Myasthenia gravis studies include anti-acetylcholine receptor antibodies and an electromyogram. Many patients with pure ocular myasthenia do not have antibodies to the acetylcholine receptors, but this is worth checking. Also, a chest x-ray or CT scan should be done to look for a thymoma. A tensilon challenge test can be performed when there is readily identifiable weak muscle, that is, ptosis (lid levator).

Therapeutic Options and Recommended Approach

Treatments include mestinon (an antiacetylcholinesterase drug), immunosuppression with steroids or azathioprime, plasmaphresis, and thymectomy.

Mestinon may be tried first at 60 mg every 4 hours. This dosage should be adjusted based on the patient's symptoms. Many patients with pure ocular myasthenia do not respond to mestinon. These patients are generally older, and although corticosteroids are effective, long-term use has prohibitive side effects. Patients with generalized weakness should be evaluated for thymectomy as many have thymomas or thymic hyperplasia.

If these two methods do not work or the patient is in crisis, immunosuppressive therapy is instituted, with prednisone being considered the first-line drug. This often causes a temporary decrease in function, so patients should be hospitalized during initiation of treatment. If prednisone fails to control the symptoms or there is a contraindication to prednisone, then azathioprine is considered. Plasmaphresis is generally considered to control a crisis.

Follow-up

Patients should keep a daily and hourly log of their symptoms and when their medications are taken. The physician should adjust medication dosage and timing based on this log. Steroids should eventually be tapered to an alternate-day dosing.

Prevalence and Incidence

Ocular findings occur in 90% of patients with myasthenia gravis. At least 50% have ocular symptoms at onset, and in 15% of patients, the abnormalities remain purely ocular. The incidence of myasthenia is between 2 and 10 per 100,000 per year.

Related Basic Science

Myasthenia is a disorder of the neuromuscular junction. There are circulating antibodies to the acetylcholine receptor which are located at the nerve muscle junction (see Chapter 20–3).

Ocular Motor Nerve Dysfunction

Disease of nerves may be less common in general practice and are usually accompanied by other neurologic abnormalities that help localize the lesion.

SIXTH CRANIAL NERVE
Clinical Manifestations

Subjective. The patient notices horizontal double vision or blurry vision.

Objective. Cranial nerve 6 abducts or pulls the eye out laterally (Figure 20–14–1A). Inability to do this causes horizontal double vision, which is maximal when trying to look to the side. Inability to bury the conjunctiva laterally can easily be observed in the office.

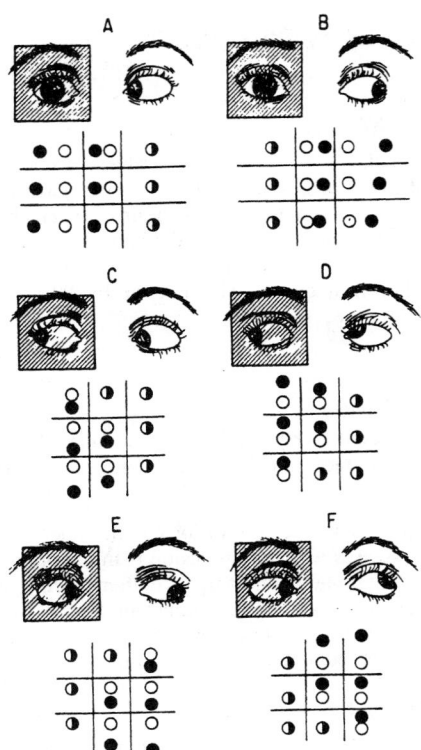

Figure 20–14–1. Diplopia fields with individual muscle paralysis. The dark glass is in front of the right eye, and the fields are projected as the patient sees the images. **A.** Paralysis of the right external rectus. Characteristic: right eye does not move to the right. Field: horizontal homonymous diplopia increasing on looking to the right. **B.** Paralysis of right internal rectus. Characteristic: right eye does not move to the left. Field: horizontal crossed diplopia increasing on looking to the left. **C.** Paralysis of right inferior rectus. Characteristic: right eye does not move downward when eyes are turned to the right. Field: vertical diplopia (image of right eye lowermost) increasing on looking to the right and down. **D.** Paralysis of right superior rectus. Characteristic: right eye does not move upward when eyes are turned to the right. Field: vertical diplopia (image of right eye uppermost) increasing on looking to the right and up. **E.** Paralysis of right superior oblique. Characteristic: right eye does not move downward when eyes are turned to the left. Field: vertical diplopia (image of right eye lowermost) increasing on looking to left and down. **F.** Paralysis of right inferior oblique. Characteristic: right eye does not move upward when eyes are turned to the left. Field: vertical diplopia (image of right eye uppermost) increasing on looking to left and up. *(Source: From Adams R, Victor M. Principles of Neurology, 5/e. New York: McGraw-Hill, 1993:235. Reproduced with permission.)*

Differential Diagnosis

The sixth nerve is most commonly involved in isolation by raised intracranial pressure, tumors, or infarction (diabetes).

THIRD CRANIAL NERVE
Clinical Manifestations

Subjective. Lesions of the third cranial nerve cause the patient to notice double vision, either horizontal or vertical, if the ptosis does not cover the eye.

Objective. At rest, the eyelid is ptotic, the pupil enlarged, and the eye down and out (Figure 20–14–1B,D,E). The double vision may be horizontal or vertical and will improve most when the patient is asked to look laterally toward the functioning sixth nerve/lateral rectus muscle.

Differential Diagnosis

The third cranial nerve is involved in isolation most commonly by aneurysms, tumor, temporal lobe herniation, infarction (diabetes—a painful, pupil-sparing condition), and migraine (ophthalmoplegic migraine).

FOURTH CRANIAL NERVE
Clinical Manifestations

Subjective. The trochlear nerve, or cranial nerve 4, supplies the superior oblique, which causes the eye to look down. Abnormalities cause vertical double vision which increases on downgaze and often is associated with a head tilt.

Objective. This may be a very subtle abnormality that is difficult to detect. The affected eye does not look down when the patient tries to look down and in (Figure 1E). Reproduction of double vision when asking the patient to look down and it may be more obvious. An associated head tilt may help in the diagnosis.

Differential Diagnosis

An isolated fourth nerve palsy is usually due to trauma.

Brainstem Disorders

Clinical Manifestations

The *abducens nerve* in the pons may be affected by stroke, tumors, or demyelination. The key to this diagnosis is that the surrounding ipsilateral facial fibers should be affected, causing a facial palsy and sometimes also a contralateral hemiparesis due to corticospinal tract involvement.

The *oculomotor nerve* in the midbrain is close to the fourth cranial nerve, the red nucleus, the corticospinal tract, and the cerebellar crossing fibers. Lesions here by tumors or strokes should cause either a contralateral hemiparesis, by damaging the descending corticospinal fibers, or an ataxia or tremor, by disrupting the cerebellar fibers. At its exit under the posterior cerebral artery and near the posterior communicating artery it is at risk for compression due to an aneurysm. This may grow slowly and anyone who presents with an isolated third nerve palsy involving the pupillary fibers should be evaluated for a berry aneurysm.

The *trochlear nerve* exits the midbrain from behind, after having crossed within the brainstem. Lesions involving the midbrain, including tumors, strokes, or infections, cause difficulty with upgaze and an ipsilateral or contralateral hemiparesis; *consciousness* may also be impaired.

Of course, any process that surrounds the brainstem may affect all three cranial nerves. Such processes include basilar meningitis from fungal infections, tuberculosis, syphilis, sarcoid, and meningeal carcinomatosis.

Diagnostic Options and Recommended Approach

An MRI best visualizes the brainstem. The evaluation depends on whether the lesion is a stroke, tumor, demyelinating lesion, or infection.

An MRI should be done first. If the differential still includes tumor, infection, or demyelinating disease, a lumbar puncture should be performed looking for infection, granulomatous disease, oligoclonal bands, and malignant cells.

Cavernous Sinus Disorders

DISORDERS OF CRANIAL NERVES 3, 4, AND 6
Clinical Manifestations

In the cavernous sinus all the ocular motor nerves are at risk due to carotid cavernous fistulas, infections that spread to the cavernous sinus, thrombosis, aneurysm, and inflammatory disease. The clue to this localization is that structures in the cavernous sinus; cranial nerves 3, 4, and 6; V1 and V2 of cranial nerve 5; and the carotid artery sympathetic fibers are affected without hemiparesis or hemisensory loss. Therefore, the patient has eye movement abnormalities and numbness of the face. As the abducens nerve is not encased in the wall of the cavernous sinus, as are the other cranial nerves, it may be involved as an early manifestation of cavernous sinus disease.

Diagnostic Options and Recommended Approach

Again, an MRI or CT scan with coronal cuts through the cavernous sinus can usually show the cranial nerves and the blood vessels within the cavernous sinus. If vascular malformation or aneurysm is considered, then magnetic resonance angiography (MRA) should be performed. Looking for signs of venous thrombosis either by the late phases on MRA or by magnetic resonance venography (MRV) would be warranted.

SUPERIOR ORBITAL FISSURE DISORDERS

Clinical Manifestations

In the superior orbital fissure, cranial nerves 3, 4, 6, and V1 are affected by the same processes, which may be a tumor or infection, and this may be difficult to differentiate from cavernous sinus disease. Lesions in this location more often produce proptosis.

Diagnostic Options and Recommended Approach

A CT scan or MRI with enhancement with special attention to the orbits should show the abnormality.

Therapeutic Options and Recommended Approach

Each disease—stroke, tumor, demyelinating disease, infection, or aneurysm—needs its own therapy (see specific chapters on these etiologies). Once a disease process has been localized, finding the etiology is much easier.

Related Basic Science

Abducens Nerve (CN6). Nerve cells are in the pons near the facial nerve fibers. The fibers exit the pons in the midline and enter the cavernous sinus after a long intracranial course, which makes it prone to many generalized cranial processes. It then enters the superior orbital fissure with cranial nerves 3 and 4 and the first division of 5. Cranial nerve 6 abducts or pulls the eye out laterally. Because of its long intracranial course, dysfunction of the sixth nerve may be the first objective sign of raised intracranial pressure. It is also why a sixth nerve palsy by itself is nonspecific. It may be due to a space-occupying tumor, infection, hydrocephalus, or any condition that produces global swelling intracranially.

Oculomotor Nerve (CN3). The nerve cells are in the midbrain, where the fibers exit between the posterior cerebral artery and the superior cerebellar artery. The nerve then enters the cavernous sinus with the other ocular motor nerves. It exits through the superior orbital fissure to supply most of the extraocular muscles. The oculomotor nerve, or cranial nerve 3, is the most complicated. It controls the pupillary constrictors, the lid levators, and most eye movements except looking out. It controls the superior rectus, which elevates the eye and turns it slightly inward; the medial rectus, which adducts; the inferior rectus, which depresses the eye and turns it slightly inward; and the inferior oblique, which turns the eye upward and outward.

Trochlear Nerve (CN4). These nerve cells arise from the dorsal half of the midbrain and exit from behind after crossing within the superior medullary velum. Like the other nerves, it then enters the cavernous sinus and the superior orbital fissure to supply the superior oblique muscle.

Cranial nerve 4 supplies the superior oblique, which causes the eye to look down when it is pulled in. It has a long course and therefore is at increased risk of traumatic injury.

Central Nervous System Lesions

HORIZONTAL GAZE PALSY

Horizontal gaze palsy is manifested by paralysis of both eyes in one or both horizontal directions. Voluntary and pursuit gaze is mediated by hemispheral centers, which report to the brainstem. The horizontal gaze centers are prefrontal and parietal, and the brainstem lateral gaze center is in the pontine tegmentum. Localizing the lesion to either brainstem or hemisphere aid in diagnosis. This is done by associated symptoms and caloric testing if necessary.

Brainstem

Clinical Manifestations

Subjective. The patient rarely reports a gaze palsy. Associated symptoms such as vertigo, facial weakness, and hemiparesis bring the patient into the office.

Objective. The patient is not able to look with either eye to one side. Caloric testing assesses whether the lesion is in the brainstem or hemisphere. No horizontal deviation of the eye after placing 30 mL of cold water in the ipsilateral ear implies brainstem dysfunction. Associated findings may include an ipsilateral seventh nerve palsy and a contralateral hemiparesis. The pupillary reflex is normal.

Differential Diagnosis

Stroke, tumor, infection, and demyelination are the most common causes of brainstem lateral gaze palsy.

Diagnostic Options and Recommended Approach

An MRI is best to visualize the brainstem.

Hemisphere

Clinical Manifestations

Subjective. The gaze palsy may be unnoticed. Almost all lesions are associated with a hemiparesis and other signs of unilateral cerebral dysfunction.

Objective. The patient is not able to look in one direction, either left or right. At rest the eyes may be deviated. Cold caloric testing should cause deviation in the opposite direction as the brainstem is functioning. Associated symptoms include a hemiparesis.

Differential Diagnosis

As eye deviation is a temporary event in most cases the differential includes acute processes such as ischemic and hemorrhagic strokes and seizures. Other causes such as tumors and abscess should be considered. Active seizures cause the eyes to be deviated toward the side of the hemiparesis, whereas stroke causes the opposite.

Diagnostic Options and Recommended Approach

A CT scan or MRI should be obtained, and an electroencephalogram is indicated if a seizure is suspected.

We recommend that a CT scan be obtained to diagnose an intracranial hemorrhage, infarction, or a reason for focal seizures such as a tumor.

Therapeutic Options and Recommended Approach

Treatment depends on the causative lesion. Strokes, hemorrhages, and seizures are treated differently.

Related Basic Science

Horizontal gaze palsies may be due to lesions in the frontal cortex, which contains the frontal eye fields; the parieto-occipital cortex, which also controls gaze; or the pons, which contains the parapontine reticular formation, which coordinates the third and sixth cranial nerves to move horizontally together (Figure 20–14–2). Localizing this lesion is usu-

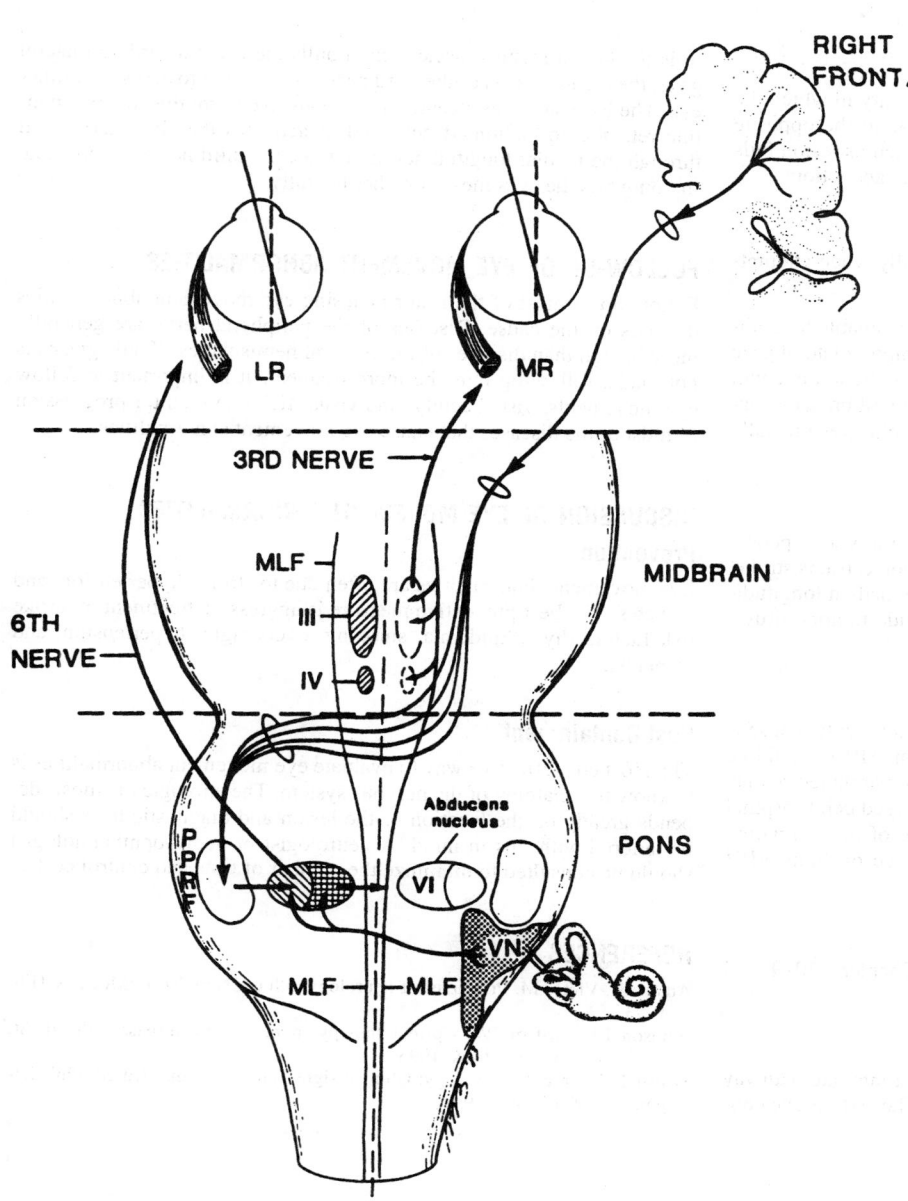

RIGHT FRONTAL

LR   MR

3RD NERVE

MLF

III

IV

MIDBRAIN

6TH NERVE

Abducens nucleus

PPRF   VI   PONS

VN

MLF   MLF

Figure 20–14–2. The supranuclear pathways subserving saccadic horizontal gaze to the left. Pathway originates in the right frontal cortex, descends in the internal capsule, decussates at the level of the rostral pons, and descends to synapse in the left pontine paramedian reticular formation (PPRF). Further connections with the ipsilateral sixth nerve nucleus and contralateral medial longitudinal fasciculus are also indicated. Cranial nerve nuclei III and IV are labeled on left; nucleus of VI and vestibular nuclei (VN) are labeled on right. LR, lateral rectus; MR, medial rectus; MLF, medial longitudinal fasciculus. *(Source: From Adams R, Victor M. Principles of Neurology, 5/e. New York: McGraw-Hill, 1993:227. Reproduced with permission.)*

ally straightforward as an isolated horizontal gaze paralysis is rare. If it involves the frontal eye fields, then there is an associated contralateral hemiparesis and the patient is "looking at the lesion" and away from the hemiparesis. The left frontal eye fields control gaze to the right. Lesions here are usually due to middle cerebral artery territory infarcts, but other causes such as tumors and postical state after a seizure show the same clinical findings. Lesions in the parieto-occipital lobe are accompanied by aphasia, hemineglect, sensory abnormalities, or a visual field defect. Again, the most common cause is a middle cerebral artery territory infarct or intracranial hemorrhage. A lesion in the pons causes the patient to be unable to look to the side of the lesion. Accompanying features are an ipsilateral facial palsy and a contralateral hemiparesis. In this scenario, the patient is looking at the hemiparesis, "away from the lesion," as he or she cannot look in that direction. Among the most common lesions in the pons that can cause this are stroke, tumor, infection, and demyelination.

Vertical Gaze Palsies

Clinical Manifestations

Subjective. The patient may note inability to look up or the need to tilt the head to see. When the etiology is a stroke, often the patient is not responsive.

Objective. Inability to move the eyes up or down either in response to command or by doll's eye maneuver can be demonstrated at the bedside.

Differential Diagnosis

Vertical gaze palsies are less common and are classically due to pineal tumors, which compress the dorsal midbrain where the vertical crossing fibers reside (Parinaud's syndrome). The vertical gaze area is at the midbrain diencephalon junction and lesions here such as infarct and hemorrhage may cause vertical gaze palsies along with alteration of consciousness. Many degenerative diseases of the nervous system cause dysfunction of vertical gaze, including progressive supranuclear palsy, parkinsonism, and vitamin B_{12} deficiency.

Diagnostic Options and Recommended Approach

Magnetic resonance imaging is the best technique to visualize the brainstem lesion.

Therapeutic Options and Recommended Approach

Therapy depends on the lesion. Please see Chapters 20–9 and 20–10.

INTERNUCLEAR OPHTHALMOPLEGIA

Internuclear ophthalmoplegia refers to a gaze abnormality in which the two eyes do not move conjugately on attempted gaze to the opposite side. The eye ipsilateral to a median longitudinal fasciculus lesion fails to adduct and the contralateral eye shows nystagmus in abduction.

Clinical Manifestations

Subjective. The patient notices double vision, especially when attempting lateral gaze.

Objective. Examination of the eyes shows the patient is unable to medially adduct the eye ipsilateral to the lesion when attempting lateral gaze to the opposite side. If the patient is trying to look left, the left eye will *ab*duct but the right eye will not *ad*duct. The left eye will have nystagmus. The patient should be able to converge (move both eyes medially together) (see Figure 20–13–1B in Chapter 20–13).

Differential Diagnosis

Most often, the cause of internuclear ophthalmoplegia in young people is multiple sclerosis. In older patients the most common cause is stroke. Any lesion in the brainstem tegmentum affecting the median longitudinal fasciculus can cause this syndrome. These include tumors, drugs, infection, and degenerative disease.

Diagnostic Options and Recommended Approach

Neuroimaging should be done, including an MRI. If a vascular cause is suspected then posterior circulation ultrasound and an MRA should be done. When demyelinating disease is suspected, a lumbar puncture may show a pleocytosis and oligoclonal bands with increased cerebrospinal fluid immunoglobulins. A search for other evidence of demyelinating disease by visual evoked potentials or other evidence on brain MRI may help in the diagnosis.

Therapeutic Options and Recommended Approach

Therapy depends on the diagnosis. Please see Chapters 20–9 and 20–27.

Related Basic Science

The third nerve and sixth nerves are connected by an intricate pathway so that the eyes are aligned when looking laterally. The sixth nerve controls the lateral rectus muscle, which pulls the eye outward. On lateral gaze, the medial rectus of the third nerve is activated to adduct the other eye. The brainstem has a center in the pons to control this, the parapontine reticular formation. If activated, it activates the sixth nerve, and through the medial longitudinal fasciculus, the third nerve is activated. In doing this the eyes move together laterally.

FOLLOW-UP OF EYE MOVEMENT ABNORMALITIES

Follow-up of most of the lesions causing eye movement abnormalities depends on the cause. Diseases of the peripheral nerve are generally more benign than diseases of the cerebral hemispheres. If a diagnosis is not made, follow-up must be more frequent. It is important to follow eye movements, visual acuity, and visual fields to monitor progression of most of the diseases that cause eye movement abnormalities.

DISCUSSION OF EYE MOVEMENT ABNORMALITIES
Prevention

Eye movement abnormalities are often due to stroke, hypertension, and diabetes. The best preventive measure is aggressive treatment of stroke risk factors (hyperlipidemia, smoking, overweight, hypertension, and diabetes).

Cost Containment

The most cost-effective way to evaluate eye movement abnormalities is to know the anatomy of the nervous system. The etiologic diagnosis depends greatly on the location of the lesion and diagnostic tests should be tailored with this in mind. A neurologist or neuro-ophthalmologist should be consulted to minimize the number of tests and control costs.

REFERENCES

Adams R, Victor M. Principles of neurology. 5th ed. New York: McGraw-Hill, 1993.
Johnson RF, Griffin JW. Current therapy in neurologic disease. 4th ed. St. Louis: Mosby Year Book, 1993.
Walsh T. Neuroophthalmology: Clinical signs and symptoms. 3rd ed. Philadelphia: Lea & Febiger, 1992.

CHAPTER 20–15

Neurogenic Orthostatic Hypotension

Paul F. Nassab, B.S.E., and David Paydarfar, M.D.

DEFINITION

Neurogenic orthostatic hypotension is a disorder of autonomic reflexes that results in a significant blood pressure drop in response to postural change from supine to upright position.

ETIOLOGY

Autonomic dysfunction as a cause of orthostatic hypotension can be classified according to diseases of the peripheral and central nervous systems. Table 20–15–1 outlines the causes of neurogenic orthostatic hypotension using this classification.

CRITERIA FOR DIAGNOSIS
Suggestive

A history of presyncopal symptoms (see Clinical Manifestations, Subjective) that develop within minutes of postural changes from supine to upright position is suggestive of orthostatic hypotension. Neurologic etiology of orthostatic hypotension should be considered when patients present with history of peripheral neuropathy or central nervous system disorders.

Definitive

The presence of orthostatic hypotension and clinical and laboratory signs of autonomic failure provide strong support for the diagnosis of neurogenic orthostatic hypotension. Definitive diagnosis, however, requires exclusion of cardiovascular, endocrine, iatrogenic, and other nonneurologic causes of orthostatic hypotension (see Plans, Diagnostic, Differential Diagnosis).

CLINICAL MANIFESTATIONS
Subjective

The patient with neurogenic orthostatic hypotension presents with a constellation of presyncopal symptoms caused by cerebral ischemia.

TABLE 20–15–1. ETIOLOGIES OF NEUROGENIC ORTHOSTATIC HYPOTENSION

Peripheral Neuropathies and Ganglionopathies

Pure autonomic neuropathies and ganglionopathies
  Postinfectious autonomic neuropathy
  Pure autonomic failure (Bradbury–Eggleston syndrome)
  Surgical thoracolumbar sympathectomy
  Chagas' disease

Polyneuropathies with autonomic fiber involvement
  Diabetic
  Amyloid (primary, familial)
  Hereditary
  Immune-mediated
  Acute intermittent porphyria
  Alcohol-relatd and nutritional neuropathies
  HIV-associated neuropathies
  Leprosy
  Drug- or toxin-associated neuropathy
    Vincristine
    Cisplatin
    Acrylamide
    Organic solvents
    Amiodarone
    Vacor (rodenticide)

Central Nervous System Disorders

Pure autonomic failure (multiple system atrophy)

Parkinson's disease

Syringobulbia

Multiple sclerosis

Wernicke's encephalopathy

Tumor, abscess, stroke involving brainstem or hypothalamus

Although the characteristic hypotensive episode usually occurs within a minute of postural shift, episodes may also result from prolonged standing. In either case, the patient complains of lightheadedness, faintness, generalized weakness, and visual blurring. Sweating or palpitation may be present if the underlying autonomic disorder spares these functions. Typically, sitting or lying down alleviates all of the presyncopal symptoms. If the hypotensive event results in syncope, consciousness is usually regained rapidly and without sequelae. The patient often identifies circumstances that aggravate or precipitate symptomatic hypotension, such as consumption of a large meal or alcohol, use of certain medications (Table 20–15–2), vigorous exercise, and exposure to excessive heat (e.g., sauna). All of these conditions lead to hemodynamic changes that require compensatory actions governed by autonomic reflexes.

Along with the presenting symptoms, details provided in the medical and family history may suggest that the hypotensive episodes are of neurogenic origin. For example, peripheral neuropathy is common in diabetic patients. Pain and temperature loss of the distal extremities are early symptoms of small fiber diabetic neuropathy. Autonomic small

TABLE 20–15–2. MEDICATIONS CONTRIBUTING TO ORTHOSTATIC HYPOTENSION

Class	Mechanism
Tricyclic antidepressants	Alpha-adrenergic blockade
Monoamine oxidase inhibitors	Inhibition of ganglionic transmission
Sympatholytics	Inhibition of storage/release of norepinephrine
Nitrates, Ca^{2+} channel blockers	Vasodilaton; decreased venous return
Diuretics	Volume depletion
Phenothiazines	Alpha-adrenergic blockade
Insulin	Vasodilation
Opiates	Depression of medullary vasomotor centers
Anti-Parkinson's medication	Uncertain
Alcohol	Central nervous system vasomotor depression and direct cutaneous vasodilation

fiber pathways also can be involved at an early stage, resulting in a variety of complaints: nausea, diarrhea, heat and cold intolerance, impotence, urinary retention or incontinence, and orthostatic hypotension. Autonomic symptoms in diabetic neuropathy are slowly progressive over many years. In contrast, acute panautonomic neuropathy presents with similar autonomic symptoms, including orthostatic hypotension, evolving over days to weeks. A family history of autonomic failure raises the possibility of amyloidosis and Riley–Day syndrome.

Chagas' disease should be considered in orthostatic patients with a history of habitation in the southern United States and most countries of Central and South America. The autonomic symptoms slowly progress, with prominent gastrointestinal dysmotility, including dysphagia, constipation, attacks of abdominal pain due to cholestasis, and ileus. The etiology of presyncopal symptoms in a patient suspected of Chagas' disease could also be due to destruction of cardiac conduction fibers leading to cardiac dysrhythmias.

The large overlap in autonomic symptoms for a wide range of diseases underscores the importance of obtaining a detailed history. Emphasis should be placed on natural history and risk factors associated with the disorders listed in Table 20–15–1.

Objective

Physical Examination

Careful measurements of blood pressure and pulse in the supine and standing positions are imperative in the diagnostic evaluation of the patient with a history of orthostatic symptoms. It is important to interview the patient while standing measurements are taken, specifically to determine if the patient's chief complaint can be provoked by the postural changes. If the patient is unable to stand, seated measurements should be attempted. Supine blood pressure and pulse rate are obtained after the patient has been recumbent for at least 5 minutes. Next, with appropriate safety precautions taken, blood pressure and pulse rate measurements are taken after standing. The arm should be outstretched and supported at the level of the right atrium. Measurements are made at 1, 2, and 5 minutes. No convention exists that correlates absolute pressure changes with a diagnosis of orthostatic hypotension, though most will agree that, in a middle-aged or younger individual, a fall in systolic pressure of 20 mm Hg or more and a decrease in diastolic pressure of 10 mm Hg or more constitute decreased orthostatic tolerance. People with normal autonomic function compensate to the gravitational stress within 1 minute. Absence of tachycardia in the presence of orthostatic hypotension is an important sign of autonomic reflex failure, specifically of the normal compensatory inhibition of cardiovagal tone.

Other signs suggestive of autonomic failure that can be observed reliably on routine examination include decreased or absent perspiration, abnormal pupillary responses to light, xerophthalmia, xerostomia, and dysphonia.

Neurologic deficits related to disease of the central or peripheral nervous system should be sought. Signs of peripheral neuropathy include diminished deep tendon reflexes, atrophy of muscle groups, and decreased perception of pain, cold or heat, vibration, and joint position. The neurologic examination should focus on identification of a recognizable clinical syndrome of autonomic failure.

A complete general physical examination must be performed, and important clues that would indicate nonneurogenic etiologies should be sought (Table 20–15–3). The presence of bilateral carotid bruits and orthostatic symptoms out of proportion to the degree of orthostatic hypotension raises the possibility of severe bilateral carotid stenosis.

Routine Laboratory Abnormalities

Routine laboratory testing of blood and urine does not provide data leading directly to the diagnosis of neurogenic orthostatic hypotension. Routine laboratory testing does, however, help to exclude medical causes included in the differential diagnosis (Table 20–15–3). Laboratory abnormalities indicative of hypovolemia include normal to increased serum sodium and blood urea nitrogen/creatinine ratio. Urine is highly concentrated and output is decreased. Urine production in diabetes insipidus is increased but is hypotonic. Patients with diabetes mellitus, on the other hand, produce urine that is hypertonic, with elevated glucose and, potentially, protein and low sodium.

TABLE 20–15–3. NONNEUROLOGIC CAUSES OF ORTHOSTATIC HYPOTENSION

States of Hypovolemia
Adrenal insufficiency (Addison's disease)
Age-related decrease in plasma volume (secondary to decreased sodium conservation)
Burns
Diabetes insipidus
Diabetes mellitus
Hemodialysis
Hemorrhage

Conditions associated with poor orthostatic tolerance without hypovolemia
Age-relaged decrease in vascular compliance
Exercise-induced vasodilation
Cardiac abnormalities
    Aortic stenosis
    Idiopathic hypertrophic subaortic stenosis
    Conduction block
Varicose veins
Tall and asthenic habitus
First- and third-trimester pregnancy
Anemia
Cerebrovascular disease

PLANS
Diagnostic
Differential Diagnosis

To establish the diagnosis of neurogenic orthostatic hypotension, other causes must be excluded. These can be broadly classified as hypovolemia, poor orthostatic tolerance, and pharmacologic side effects. Tables 20–15–2 and 20–15–3 summarize these differential diagnostic considerations, most of which can be excluded on routine evaluation comprising a complete history, physical examination, and laboratory examination. Even if signs of autonomic failure are identified, it is necessary to consider these etiologies as further exacerbating or unmasking hypotension in a more vulnerable patient.

Healthy elderly individuals are less tolerant to effects of medications and other hemodynamic stresses and, therefore, are more prone to orthostatic hypotension than are younger individuals. The cause of such age-related vulnerability is probably multifactorial, including decreased renal sodium conservation, decreased vascular compliance, and a decrease in parasympathetic, and possibly sympathetic, cardiovascular regulation.

Diangostic Options

Autonomic testing helps to localize disturbances in the circulatory reflex pathways. Table 20–15–4 provides a comprehensive list of diagnostic techniques. Most of these tests are best performed in a clinical autonomic laboratory in which each patient is evaluated with respect to a group of normal subjects.

An important test of cardiac parasympathetic function is the heart rate response to deep breathing. Heart rate normally increases during inspiration and decreases during expiration phase. This variation, called respiratory sinus arrhythmia, is a vagally mediated reflex with afferent fibers from the lung mechanoreceptors and efferent projections to the heart from medullary vagal motor neurons. The patient is instructed to take slow deep breaths with a respiratory period of 10 seconds. Heart rate is analyzed by determining the minimal R–R interval during inspiration and the maximal R–R interval during expiration. Strict criteria are used in autonomic laboratories to determine normal and abnormal responses. Significant reduction of heart rate variability with breathing is suggestive of vagal neuropathy. Isolated vagal dysfunction does not usually cause orthostatic hypotension because cardiac output is fairly constant over a broad range of heart rate (60–120 beats/min). Nevertheless, the presence of vagal dysfunction is often a marker of more widespread autonomic failure.

TABLE 20–15–4. DIAGNOSTIC OPTIONS IN NEUROGENIC ORTHOSTATIC HYPOTENSION

Test	A Test of/for
Clinical Autonomic Testing	
Heart rate response to deep breathing	Parasympathetic afferent/efferent
Heart rate response to postural change	Parasympathetic afferent/efferent
Heart rate response to Valsalva maneuver	Parasympathetic afferent/efferent
Blood pressure response to postural change	Parasympathetic afferent/ sympathetic efferent
Blood pressure response to Valsalva maneuver	Parasympathetic afferent/ sympathetic efferent
Blood pressure response to sustained hand grip	Sympathetic efferent
Heart rate response to atropine infusion	Parasympathetic efferent
Thermoregulatory sweat test	Somatic efferent/sympathetic efferent
Cold pressor test effects on blood pressure	Somatic afferent/sympathetic efferent
Laboratory Analysis	
Quantitative sudomotor axon reflex test	Sympathetic axonal reflex
Heart rate response to isoproterenol infusion	β_1-adrenergic receptor function
Blood pressure response to isoproterenol infusion	β_2-adrenergic receptor function
Supine and standing plasma catecholamine levels	Postganglionic sympathetic efferent integrity
Immune electrophoresis	Monoclonal proteins
Nerve biopsy	Neuronal degeneration; inflammation, amyloid
Electromyography nerve conduction	Somatic neuropathy

The normal blood pressure response to standing is a slight rise in diastolic pressure and little change in systolic pressure. Blood pressure is maintained by sympathetically mediated reflexes. Vasopressor sympathetic reflexes can be evaluated by measuring the blood pressure changes during the Valsalva maneuver. Initially, arterial pressure drops because of Valsalva-induced reduction in venous return. Consequently, a baroreceptor-mediated sympathetic vasoconstriction counteracts the decline in arterial pressure. In patients lacking the vasopressor response, Valsalva leads to arterial pressure that is significantly lower than in normal subjects. Sustained hand grip leads to a vasopressor-mediated rise in blood pressure, which is blunted in patients with sympathetic failure.

Serum catecholamine values are taken in the supine and standing positions and help to distinguish pre- and postganglionic lesions. For example, in pure autonomic failure the associated degeneration of postganglionic sympathetic fibers results in low resting norepinephrine levels. In multiple-system atrophy with autonomic failure, there is loss of preganglionic fibers and resting norepinephrine levels generally are normal. When patients with either of these diseases stand, plasma catecholamine levels remain unchanged, in contrast to the abrupt rise that occurs in individuals with normal autonomic function. Supine and standing catecholamine levels are also useful in diagnosing patients with orthostatic hypotension secondary to dopamine β-hydroxylase deficiency. Dopamine β-hydroxylase is the enzyme responsible for the conversion of dopamine to norepinephrine. Its deficiency results in low serum levels of norepinephrine and high levels of dopamine in both the supine and standing positions.

Protein electrophoresis of the serum and urine of individuals with amyloid disease reveals a monoclonal peak in about half of the cases. Immune electrophoresis of serum and urine is a more sensitive test, indicating excessive production of the monoclonal protein in about 90% of such patients. Diagnosis of amyloidosis can be confirmed by biopsy of abdominal adipose, rectal, or gingival tissue. Congo red stain and polarized light microscopy are required to demonstrate the green birefringence of amyloid.

Lumbar puncture is indicated in a patient who develops acute or subacute orthostatic hypotension and signs of generalized polyneuropathy. Increased cerebrospinal fluid protein with few leukocytes and electrophysiologic evidence of widespread demyelinating polyneuropathy confirm the clinical diagnosis of Guillain–Barré syndrome. Acute pan-autonomic neuropathy can present with similar features, but is characterized by profound generalized autonomic failure and relative sparing of somatic fibers.

Imaging studies of the central nervous system are not indicated for patients with pure autonomic failure and orthostatic hypotension. Imaging can be diagnostic when autonomic failure is associated with other central neurologic signs. For example, lesions of the brainstem (e.g., stroke, tumor, syrinx) can present with ataxia, cranial nerve dysfunction, and blood pressure lability, including orthostatic hypotension, and are best revealed by magnetic resonance imaging (MRI) of the brain. Autonomic failure accompanied by chronic progressive ataxia and rigidity is suggestive of multiple-system atrophy. Head MRI is not diagnostic but may show atrophy of the cerebellar cortex and the striatum.

Abnormal blood values seen in Addison's disease include decreased serum cortisol, low serum sodium and chloride, high serum potassium, increased hematocrit and adrenocorticotropic hormone levels, and a differential showing relative lymphocytosis with neutropenia and eosinophilia. The patient has decreased production of urine and low levels of 17-corticosteroids.

Recommended Approach

The clinical evaluation of neurogenic orthostatic hypotension should focus on identification of symptoms and signs that can be grouped into a recognizable syndrome of autonomic failure. Once this is accomplished, the laboratory evaluation can confirm the clinical diagnosis or suggest an alternative etiology. Therefore, the presence on neurologic evaluation of polyneuropathy, degenerative or focal central nervous system disease, or pure autonomic failure influences the clinical approach to the patient.

In autonomic syndromes without other neurologic signs, the major diagnostic considerations are acute pandysautonomia, pure autonomic failure, and early multiple-system atrophy. Acute pandysautonomia usually can be distinguished by rapid progression over several weeks followed by slow improvement over 6 to 12 months. Lumbar puncture early in the course of acute pandysautonomia can support the diagnosis by showing an elevated cerebrospinal fluid protein and few leukocytes. Pure autonomic failure is slowly progressive and can be clinically indistinguishable from early multiple-system atrophy. Laboratory evaluation (Table 20–15–4) can help differentiate between the preganglionic autonomic failure of multiple-system atrophy and the postganglionic failure of pure autonomic failure.

If autonomic failure presents with evidence of polyneuropathy, the clinical approach attempts to establish the etiology of polyneuropathy (see Chapter 20–1). The natural history, presence of systemic medical illness, and clinical and electrophysiologic features of the polyneuropathy further characterize the syndrome and guide subsequent laboratory testing.

Of central neurologic diseases that cause neurogenic orthostatic hypotension, the most common are multiple-system atrophy and Parkinson's disease, both of which have characteristic clinical features. Laboratory testing usually is not helpful in differentiating between the two. A link between other diseases affecting the central nervous system and neurogenic orthostatic hypotension should be regarded with caution; however, once other causes of orthostatic hypotension have been excluded, autonomic failure due to Wernicke's encephalopathy, multiple sclerosis, syringobulbia, and brainstem stroke can be diagnosed. MRI of the head is useful to demonstrate lesions involving central autonomic pathways.

Therapeutic

Therapeutic Options

The current therapeutic strategies are aimed at treating underlying disease processes and providing symptomatic relief through a combination of mechanical and pharmacologic strategies.

Examples of primary treatment include maintenance of euglycemia in patients with diabetic autonomic neuropathy, chemotherapy for myeloma-associated amyloid disease, and gamma globulin infusion or plasma exchange for Guillain–Barré syndrome. In patients with

dopamine β-hydroxylase deficiency, administration of dihydroxyphenylserine (L-DOPS) is highly effective in normalizing blood pressure regulation.

In most cases, the underlying cause of neurogenic orthostatic hypotension is irreversible. Symptomatic treatment reduces orthostatic hypotension by increasing plasma volume and venous return. Elastic waist-high stockings increase interstitial hydrostatic pressure and thus decrease venous pooling in the legs and splanchnic vessels. The major limitations of these stockings are patient discomfort and inconvenience. In addition, pooling is not completely prevented and patients with severe autonomic failure usually require additional interventions. Increases in salt intake to 150 to 250 mEq Na^+ per day can further increase plasma volume. During prolonged recumbence, the support stockings should be removed and the head should be elevated to at least 20°. These measures help prevent supine hypertension and decrease nocturnal diuresis associated with supine redistribution of fluids and minimize the disabling hypotensive state that many patients with autonomic failure experience when rising in the morning.

Symptomatic pharmacotherapy serves to achieve normovolemic or slightly hypervolemic states and may serve as an additional stimulus to the autonomic nervous system. Fludrocortisone acetate (Florinef) is the initial drug of choice. The therapeutic effects are due to sensitization of blood vessels to the effects of circulating catecholamines and expansion of blood volume through mineralcorticoid activity. The potential risks include fluid overload, congestive heart failure, supine hypertension, and hypokalemia. Patients without cardiac disease can be started on 0.1 mg each morning. If symptoms persist, the dose can be increased in 0.05- to 1-mg increments every 5 to 7 days, up to 0.3 mg twice a day.

Patients with severe diabetic autonomic neuropathy and renal disease are prone to severe symptomatic orthostatic hypotension because of the combination of autonomic failure and nephrogenic hypovolemia and anemia. Administration of erythropoietin can be highly effective in treating the anemia and may also lead to remarkable improvement in orthostatic hypotension (Hoeldtke and Streeton, 1993).

Sympathomimetic drugs (e.g., ephedrine, phenylpropanolamine) have been of limited value, mainly because most cause prominent side effects including tachycardia, nervousness, and tachyphylaxis. One exception is Midodrine (Gutron), a direct alpha-adrenergic agonist that reduces orthostasis by arteriolar and venous vasoconstriction without causing significant tachycardia and nervousness or other central nervous system side effects. This drug is currently undergoing investigational trials and is not yet approved by the Food and Drug Administration for general use. Clonidine at low doses (0.1–0.2 mg orally twice daily) can act as a pressor by its peripheral post-synaptic α_2-adrenegic agonist activity, but in our experience, variable presynaptic agonist activity leads to episodic worsening of hypotension. In patients with partial adrenergic failure, yohimbine (8 mg orally twice to three times daily) can enhance norepinephrine release by presynaptic α_2-adrenergic antagonist activity.

Indomethacin (25–50 mg orally three times daily) and caffeine (250 mg, 2 cups of coffee) can be effective in treating postprandial exacerbation of orthostatic hypotension.

Recommended Approach

Our approach is to advise all patients to avoid situations that exacerbate their hypotensive episodes such as large meals and alcohol, strenuous exercise, exposure to excessive heat, and use of certain medications. Conservative measures are initiated, such as elevating the head of the bed at night and liberalizing salt and fluid intake for appropriate patients. A regimen of moderate exercise helps to increase the activity of skeletal muscles that assist venous return. Examples of exercise that is well tolerated are walking and swimming. Highly motivated patients may opt to use elastic support stockings, although general compliance is low.

If the patient remains symptomatic, pharmacologic intervention is initiated. In most cases, low to moderate doses of fludrocortisone acetate result in adequate relief of symptoms with few side effects. In severe cases of orthostatic hypotension, higher doses of fludrocortisone or additional medication may be required, and appropriate selection of these options is determined mainly by anticipated side effects.

FOLLOW-UP

Appropriate follow-up is necessary to document the course of autonomic failure, the effectiveness of therapy, and the potential side effects of pharmacologic agents. The most common side effect of all forms of treatment is supine hypertension, which can lead to cerebrovascular and cardiac complications. Short-acting antihypertensive medication may be required to prevent severe supine hypertension at night. Hydralazine (25 mg) is a suitable choice and has the advantage of blunting the usual nocturnal natriuresis that so often exacerbates orthostasis the following morning.

DISCUSSION

Prevalence and Incidence

The prevalence and incidence of neurogenic orthostatic hypotension are not known. It generally is believed that diabetic dysautonomia accounts for the majority of cases. This is probably true given the estimated 1 to 5% prevalence of diabetes in the general population. Severe neurogenic orthostatic hypotension and other manifestations of autonomic failure are late complications of diabetes, developing after 10 or more years of poorly controlled hyperglycemia.

Multiple-system atrophy is a rare degenerative neurologic disorder with a prevalence of 10 per 100,000. Most eventually develop orthostatic hypotension and other signs of autonomic failure including vocal cord dysfunction, dysmotility of bowel and bladder, anhidrosis, impotence, and dysphagia.

Related Basic Science

On standing, approximately 400 to 700 mL of blood pools in the dependent capacitance vessels of the legs and splanchnic bed, decreasing both venous return and systolic blood pressure. The decreased venous return to the heart and decreased thoracic volume activate receptors in the vena cava, right atrium, aortic arch, and carotid sinus. Afferents from these baroreceptors travel through the vagus and glossopharyngeal nerves and synapse in the nucleus tractus solitarius, which, in turn, projects to other vagal and brainstem nuclei. The net result is a decrease in parasympathetic and an increase in sympathetic efferent activity. Parasympathetic responses exit the brain via the vagus nerve and synapse in respective visceral plexi. Sympathetic efferents descend and synapse in the intermediolateral cell column of the spinal cord, which projects to the sympathetic ganglia.

There is normally continuous vagal efferent activity that hyperpolarizes the sinoatrial and atrioventricular nodes. Activation of the baroresponse reduces vagal tone, thereby causing the reflexive tachycardia associated with the acute orthostatic stress. Increased sympathetic activity stimulates the release of norepinephrine from sympathetic efferent terminals in vascular smooth muscle and the release of epinephrine from the adrenal medulla. The result of this reflex activity is to increase cardiac output and arterial pulse pressure. Sympathetic stimulation of cells in several structures of the nephron leads to the release of renin, activating the renin–angiotensin–aldosterone cascade, and also directly stimulates the reabsorption of Na^+. Both mechanisms function to increase plasma volume in the long term.

Natural History and Its Modification with Treatment

The natural history of neurogenic orthostatic hypotension follows the course of the primary neurologic pathology. In general, neurogenic orthostatic hypotension due to multiple-system atrophy and Parkinson's disease is more severe and recalcitrant to treatment than is orthostasis associated with pure autonomic failure, which is manageable with nightly elevation of the head, daily use of elastic stockings, and low-dose fludrocortisone.

In cases of small fiber neuropathy, orthostatic hypotension occurs after substantial damage to peripheral sympathetic and parasympathetic nerves. In diabetes, an added complication is the hypotensive effect of insulin through its vasodilatory effects on the splanchnic vessels. Treatment centered around increasing vasoconstriction around mealtime has been equivocal. Best results have been attained with the administration of indomethacin.

In contrast to neuronal damage associated with primary autonomic failure syndromes and with the chronic small fiber neuropathies, patients with acute pandysautonomia usually recover some autonomic function in the years following the illness, but many continue to have symptomatic orthostatic hypotension.

Prevention

Some of the acquired peripheral autonomic neuropathies, notably those caused by diabetes, HIV, toxins, and alcohol/nutritional deficiency, can be prevented; however, preventive measures have not been identified for most of the diseases that cause dysautonomia.

Cost Containment

The most cost-effective step in the assessment of neurogenic orthostatic hypotension is characterization of a well-defined syndrome of autonomic failure. This can be achieved only by a careful history and physical examination. Laboratory testing is useful to exclude nonneurogenic orthostatic hypotension and to arrive at specific diagnoses once the autonomic syndrome has been defined. Only selected cases require extensive autonomic testing or imaging studies of the central nervous system.

REFERENCES

Fealey RD, Robertson D. Management of orthostatic hypotension. In: Low PA, ed. *Clinical autonomic disorders.* Boston: Little, Brown, 1993.

Hoeldtke RD, Streeten DHP. Treatment of orthostatic hypotension with erythropoietin. N Engl J Med 1993;329:611.

Wieling W. Standing, orthostatic stress, and autonomic function. In: Bannister R, ed. Autonomic failure: A textbook of clinical disorders of the autonomic nervous system. New York: Oxford University Press, 1988.

CHAPTER 20–16

Seizures

Teresa A. Tran, M.D.

DEFINITION

A seizure represents a single clinical event that results from hypersynchronous neuronal discharges that are self-limiting, producing transient impairment of brain function. Epilepsy refers to chronic recurrent seizures. Thus, an isolated episode of abnormal brain function constitutes a single seizure, but does not necessarily imply that the patient has epilepsy, unless he or she goes on to have recurrent episodes of similar spells. Clinical manifestations of the epilepsies are diverse and are dependent on the cause of the seizure, site of origin, and extent of the spread in the brain.

ETIOLOGY

The likely etiology of symptomatic seizures depends on the age of the patient and the type of seizure. In young infants, perinatal anoxia or ischemia, intracranial birth trauma, metabolic disturbances (i.e., hypoglycemia, hypocalcemia, hypomagnesemia), congenital malformations of the brain, and infections are some of the common causes. Common intrauterine infections responsible for chronic seizures include toxoplasmosis, cytomegalovirus, rubella, herpes, and syphilis. Some of the inheritable metabolic disorders and neurocutaneous syndromes have seizures as a secondary clinical manifestation (Table 20–16–1).

In young children, trauma and infections are the most common causes of the symptomatic epilepsies. Approximately 2 to 5% of young children develop seizures associated with high fever (febrile seizures). Febrile seizures usually occur in the early phases of a febrile illness in children between the ages of 3 months and 5 years. The fever is caused by systemic infections, and must be distinguished from fever caused by meningitis or encephalitis, which can also give rise to seizures. Uncomplicated febrile seizures, defined as brief, generalized tonic–clonic seizures, not associated with any focal neurologic deficits, are less likely to result in neurologic impairment or lead to chronic epilepsy. Interictal electroencephalogram (EEG) is normal. The mainstay of treatment is to treat the fever aggressively in children prone to febrile convulsions. There is no basis for treating these patients with chronic anticonvulsant medications unless the seizures are prolonged, are focal in onset, or are associated with focal neurologic deficits.

In adolescents and young adults, head trauma is a major cause of epilepsy. Epilepsy can be caused by any kind of serious head injury, with the likelihood of developing recurrent seizures being proportional to the extent of brain damage. Seizures that occur immediately or within the first 24 hours of injury are not associated with a poor prognosis, whereas seizures occurring after the first day and within the first 2 weeks indicate a higher likelihood of developing epilepsy. Most recurring seizures occur within 2 years of trauma.

Between the ages of 30 and 50 years, the most common cause is brain tumor. Approximately one third of brain tumors present with a first-time focal seizure. Slow-growing tumors such as meningiomas and low-grade gliomas are more likely to cause chronic epilepsy than malignant tumors such as gliobastoma multiforme and metastatic tumors. Mass lesions such as vascular malformations and abscesses involving the neocortex also cause seizures.

Above the age of 50, cerebrovascular disease is the most common cause of focal or generalized seizures. Acute reactive seizures are more likely to occur in the setting of an embolic or hemorrhagic stroke. Thrombotic strokes are more likely to cause late seizures. Seizures can also result from "silent" strokes in elderly patients who have no other apparent cause for seizures.

Central nervous system infections, such as meningitis, encephalitis, and granulomatous diseases, can cause acute reactive seizures in pa-

---

TABLE 20–16–1. INTERNATIONAL CLASSIFICATION OF EPILEPSIES AND EPILEPTIC SYNDROMES

I. Localization-related (focal, local, partial) epilepsies and syndromes
   A. Idiopathic with age-related onset
     1. Benign childhood epilepsy with centrotemporal spike
     2. Childhood epilepsy with occipital paroxysms
   B. Symptomatic
     1. Frontal lobe epilepsies
       a. Supplementary motor
       b. Cingulate
       c. Anterior (polar) frontal region
       d. Orbitofrontal
       e. Dorsolateral
     2. Epilepsies of the motor cortex
     3. Temporal lobe epilepsies
       a. Hippocampal (mesiobasal, limbic, or primary rhinencephalic psychomotor) epilepsy
       b. Amygdalar (anterior polar-amygdalar)
       c. Opercular (insular)
     4. Parietal lobe epilepsies
     5. Occipital lobe epilepsies

II. Generalized epilepsies and syndromes
   A. Idiopathic, with age-related onset, listed in order of age
     1. Benign neonatal familial convulsions
     2. Benign neonatal convulsions
     3. Benign myoclonic epilepsy in infancy
     4. Childhood absence epilepsy (pyknolepsy)
     5. Juvenile absence epilepsy
     6. Juvenile myoclonic epilepsy (impulsive petit mal)
     7. Epilepsy with grand mal seizures on awakening
       (Other generalized idiopathic epilepsies, if they do not belong to one of the above syndromes, can still be classified as generalized idiopathic epilepsies.)
   B. Idiopathic and/or symptomatic, in order of age of appearance
     1. West syndrome (infantile spasms, Blitz–Nick–Salaam Krampfe)
     2. Lennox–Gastaut syndrome
     3. Epilepsy with myoclonic–astatic seizures
     4. Epilepsy with myoclonic absences
   C. Symptomatic
     1. Nonspecific etiology
       a. Early myoclonic encephalopathy
     2. Specific syndromes
       a. Malformations
         i. Aicardi's syndrome
         ii. Lissencephaly–Pachygyria
         iii. Neurophakomatoses (tuberous sclerosis, Sturge–Weber Syndrome)

       b. Proven or suspected inborn error of metabolism
         i. Neonate
          • Nonketotic hyperglycemia
          • D-Glyceric acidemia
         ii. Infant
          • Phenylketonuria
          • Phenylketonuria variant (biopterins deficiency)
          • Tay–Sachs disease
          • Sandhoff's disease
          • Santavuori–Haltia–Hagberg disease (infantile ceroid lipofuscinosis)
          • Pyridoxine deficiency
         iii. Child
          • Jansky–Bielschowsky disease (late infantile ceroid lipofuscinosis)
          • Infantile Huntington's disease
         iv. Child and adolescent
          • Juvenile Gaucher's disease
          • Spielmeyer–Vogt–Sjögren disease (juvenile ceroid lipofuscinosis)
          • Lafora's disease
          • Progressive myoclonic epilepsy (Lundborg type)
          • Ramsay–Hunt syndrome
          • Sialidosis (cherry red spot myoclonus)
         v. Adult
          • Kufs' disease

III. Epilepsies and syndromes undetermined as to whether they are focal or generalized
   A. With both generalized and focal seizures
     1. Neonatal seizures
     2. Severe myoclonic epilepsy in infancy
     3. Epilepsy with continuous spike waves during slow-wave sleep
     4. Acquired epileptic aphasia (Landau–Klefner syndrome)
   B. Without unequivocal generalized or focal features
     (This heading covers all cases where clinical and electroencephalographic findings do not permit classification as clearly generalized or localization related, such as in many cases of sleep grand mal.)

IV. Special syndromes
   A. Situation-related seizures
     1. Febrile convulsions
     2. Seizures related to other identifiable situations such as stress, hormonal changes, drugs, alcohol, and sleep deprivation
   B. Isolated, apparently unprovoked epileptic events
   C. Epilepsies characterized by specific modes of seizure precipitation
   D. Chronic progressive epilepsia partialis continua of childhood

---

Source: From the Commission on Classification and Terminology of the International League Against Epilepsy. Proposal for classification of epilepsies and epileptic syndromes. Epilepsia 1985;26:270. Reproduced with permission from the author and publisher.

tients of any age group. The residual brain injury from these infections can then give rise to chronic recurrent seizures. AIDS needs to be considered in high-risk individuals. Seizures in this population of patients are usually mediated by primary central nervous system lymphoma and opportunistic infections, such as toxoplasmosis, cytomegalovirus, herpes, and syphilis; however, HIV, the causative agent in AIDS, can also have direct effect on the cerebrum and be the primary cause of seizures.

CRITERIA FOR DIAGNOSIS
Suggestive

The diagnosis of epilepsy requires a working knowledge of the symptoms of the different seizure types. It cannot be emphasized enough that a detailed history from both the patient and witnesses is crucial to accurate diagnosis. The taking of a detailed history requires a careful listing of the symptoms that occur during the seizure. Such a list allows establishment of the diagnosis and classification of the seizure type. The general physical and neurologic examinations are important to help establish or rule out underlying diseases that may have seizures as a secondary manifestation.

Definitive

The laboratory hallmark of epilepsy is abnormal electrical discharges recorded on the electroencephalogram during a seizure. Although an interictal EEG can be normal in as many as 50 to 60% of patients with a confirmed diagnosis of seizures, the combination of an abnormal EEG in association with a compatible clinical history is diagnostic. All patients suspected of having epilepsy should have an EEG.

CLINICAL MANIFESTATIONS
Classification of Epileptic Seizures

The epilepsies are a heterogeneous group of symptom complexes, most of them empirically determined, whose only common denominator is the recurrence of seizures caused by abnormal neuronal discharges. Proper classification of the kinds of seizures is important for an appropriate diagnostic evaluation, prognosis, and selection of therapy. The current classification of epileptic seizures (Table 20–16–2) emphasizes the clinical seizure type and ictal and interictal EEG pattern. The major underlying premise of the seizure classification is that partial or focal seizures start in one area of the cortex or in one cerebral hemisphere, and generalized seizures involve both cerebral hemispheres.

Classification of seizures is extremely useful in the diagnosis and treatment of patients; however, it is restricted in providing information about prognosis and long-term therapeutic decisions. A more useful approach is to use seizure type and other information to classify patients into meaningful patterns representing epileptic syndromes or diseases. Classification of the epilepsies (Table 20–16–1) takes into account clinical semiology, interictal and ictal electrographic patterns, as well as age of onset, etiology, anatomic and physiologic abnormalities, neurologic and psychiatric findings, and imaging studies. Similar to the seizure classification system, the epilepsies are divided into localized and nonlocalized epilepsies. Each category is further divided into "idiopathic" (or primary) and "symptomatic" (or secondary). The idiopathic epilepsies have no known etiology, whereas the symptomatic epilepsies are caused by specific underlying central nervous system diseases or abnormalities.

Subjective and Objective

Discussion of the different clinical manifestations of epileptic seizures follows the outline of the seizure classification system. The different epileptic syndromes are not discussed in this section, as it is beyond the scope of this chapter.

Partial Seizures

Partial seizures begin with the activation of neurons in one area of the cortex. The specific clinical symptoms depend on the area of cortex involved. Partial seizures are classified as "simple" if the patient maintains consciousness during a seizure, and "complex" if there is alter-

TABLE 20–16–2. CLASSIFICATION OF EPILEPTIC SEIZURES

I. Partial (focal, local) seizures
  A. Simple partial seizures
    1. With motor signs
      a. Focal motor without march
      b. Focal motor with march (jacksonian)
      c. Versive
      d. Postural
      e. Phonatory (vocalization or arrest of speech)
    2. With somatosensory or special sensory signs (simple hallucinations, e.g., tingling, flashes, buzzing)
      a. Somatosensory
      b. Visual
      c. Auditory
      d. Olfactory
      e. Gustatory
      f. Vertiginous
    3. With autonomic symptoms or signs (including epigastric sensation, pallor, sweating, flushing, piloerection, and pupillary dilation)
    4. With psychic symptoms (disturbance of higher cerebral function)
      a. Dysphasic
      b. Dysmnesic (e.g., deja vu)
      c. Cognitive (e.g., dreamy states, distortions of time sense)
      d. Affective (e.g., fear, anger)
      e. Illusions (e.g., macropsia, micropsia)
      f. Structured hallucinations (e.g., music, scenes)
  B. Complex partial seizures
    1. Simple partial onset followed by impairment of consciousness
      a. With simple partial features (A.1–A.4) followed by impaired consciousness
      b. With automatisms
    2. With impairment of consciousness at onset
      a. With impairment of consciousness only
      b. With automatisms
  C. Partial seizures evolving to secondarily generalized seizures
    1. Simple partial seizures evolving to generalized seizures
    2. Complex partial seizures evolving to generalized seizures
    3. Simple partial seizures evolving to complex partial seizures evolving to generalized seizures
II. Generalized seizures (convulsive or nonconvulsive)
  A. 1. Absence seizures
      a. Impairment of consciousness only
      b. With mild clonic components
      c. With atonic components
      d. With tonic components
      e. With automatisms
      f. with autonomic components
    2. Atypical absence
      a. Changes in tone that are more pronounced than in A.1
      b. Onset and/or cessation that is not abrupt
  B. Myoclonic seizures
  C. Clonic seizures
  D. Tonic seizures
  E. Tonic–clonic seizures
  F. Atonic seizures (astatic)
    (Combinations of B–F may occur.)
III. Unclassified
  All seizures that cannot be classified because of inadequate or incomplete data and some that defy classification in hitherto described categories. This includes some neonatal seizures (e.g., rhythmic eye movements, chewing, and swimming movements).

Source: From the Commission on Classification and Terminology of the International League Against Epilepsy. Proposal for revised clinical and electroencephalographic classification of epileptic seizures. Epilepsia 1981;22:493. Reproduced with permission from the author and publisher.

ation in consciousness or awareness of the surrounding environment. Simple partial seizures may spread to contiguous brain areas and become complex partial seizures. Both simple partial and complex partial seizures can spread to become secondarily generalized tonic–clonic seizures.

Simple Partial Seizures. Simple partial seizures can occur with motor, sensory, autonomic, or psychic symptoms. Motor signs consist of recurrent contractions of the muscles of one part of the body (e.g., finger, hand, arm, face), which may remain confined to that area or may spread from the affected area to involve contiguous ipsilateral body parts (Jacksonian march). The ictal EEG demonstrates regularly occurring spike discharges in the appropriate area of the contralateral motor cortex. Interictal EEG may demonstrate irregular focal spikes or sharp waves localized to the cortical area involved in the seizure. Sensory seizures consist of paresthesias, vertiginous feelings, or simple auditory or visual hallucinations, with epileptiform discharges arising from the corresponding contralateral sensory cortex on EEG. Autonomic symptoms may also be observed during a simple partial seizure.

Commonly experienced psychic symptoms in a simple partial seizure include disturbed cognitive function, abnormal affect, illusions, dysphasia, amnesic syndromes, and structured hallucinations. Déjà vu describes a sense of familiarity, as if the present new situation has been previously experienced. Some patients experience a previous event very rapidly as if in a panoramic vision and may describe seeing a whole series of events as if they returned to a previous time in their life. Cognitive symptoms include distortions of time, reality, or place. The patients may be in a dreamlike state, with feelings of detachment or depersonalization. Depersonalization is the sensation of feeling outside of one's own body and observing it. Affective symptoms may be characterized as fear, displeasure, rage, anger, irritability, eroticism, or pleasure. Fear is the most common symptom and is associated with pupillary dilation, flushing, hypertension, palpitations, and other autonomic responses. These psychic symptoms are usually associated with spike discharges arising from the medial temporal lobe and limbic system on EEG. Visual illusions include monocular diplopia, macropsia, and micropsia. Auditory disturbances include increased sensitivity to sound or the perception that sounds become very faint. The sensory illusions correspond to abnormal EEG discharges in the primary visual cortex and Heschl's gyrus. Structured hallucinations are forms of somatosensory, visual, auditory, olfactory, or gustatory perceptions that make the patient think the actual event did occur. These hallucinations are derived from seizures arising from the primary receptor area of the cortex.

Many patients with complex partial seizures have psychic symptoms before full development of complex partial seizures. As a consequence, psychic symptoms were previously interpreted as warning signs and were referred to as auras. Today, it is well established that auras are simple partial seizures. Although psychic symptoms commonly occur before development of a complex partial seizure, any symptom that occurs as a simple partial seizure may precede a complex partial seizure.

Complex Partial Seizures. Because of the frequent association of complex partial seizures with psychic symptoms and with pathology in the temporal lobe, these seizures were previously referred to as psychomotor seizures or temporal lobe epilepsy. It is now recognized that complex partial seizures do not always originate in the temporal lobe, but may also arise from the frontal, parietal, or occipital lobes. They may or may not be preceded by a simple partial seizure (aura). Automatisms, characteristic features of complex partial seizures, are highly integrated, complex behavioral acts that occur during seizures for which the patient has no recollection afterward. Five types of automatism have been described. Alimentary automatism is the most common form and consists of chewing, lip smacking, increased salivation, or borborygmi. Mimetic automatism consists of facial movement producing expressions of fear, discomfort, crying, or laughter. Gestural automatism consists of repetitive hand movement or shuffling of feet. These movements may or may not be purposeful. Rarer forms of automatism include ambulation and vocalization. Vocalization may either produce well-formed words and phrases or nonsensical syllables. Perseverative speech is commonly seen and may sometimes reflect a previously learned expression.

Generalized Seizures

Generalized seizures refer to those whose onset involves both hemispheres. Most such seizures are associated with loss of consciousness at the onset. Generalized seizures can be either convulsive or nonconvulsive.

Absence Seizures. Absence seizures represent both a seizure type and an epileptic syndrome. Typical absence seizures are very brief, lasting less than 10 seconds, and are of sudden onset, associated with decreased responsiveness or altered consciousness without significant warning or postictal symptoms. Absence seizures may be associated with other symptoms, particularly automatism (chewing, lip smacking, fumbling with the fingers, or vocalizations), clonic movements (eyelid flutter, or fine movement of the corner of the mouth, extremities, or arms), atonic and tonic symptoms, and myoclonus. Absence seizures are the principal manifestations of childhood absence epilepsy and are one of the seizure types in juvenile myoclonic epilepsy. Typical absence seizures have a good prognosis, with most patients responding well to anticonvulsant medication. Ictal EEG shows the characteristic generalized symmetric and regular 3-Hz spike–wave complexes. Background activity is normal during an interictal EEG.

Atypical Absence Seizures. Atypical absence seizures must be differentiated from typical absences, as they have different diagnostic and prognostic implications. They are typically seen in patients with symptomatic epilepsy who have diffuse or multifocal structural brain lesions. They are one of the hallmark seizure types associated with the Lennox–Gastaut syndrome, which is characterized by mental retardation, multiple generalized seizure types, and slow spike–wave complexes on EEG. The seizures are usually refractory to medical therapy. Clinically, atypical absences are almost always associated with motor symptoms, particularly alteration in muscle tone, which may be much more dramatic than that observed in typical absences. The seizures last longer than 10 seconds. Onset and cessation are usually not abrupt as in a typical absence, and they are invariably associated with some degree of postictal confusion.

Ictal EEG is more heterogeneous than typical absence, and may include irregular spike and slow wave complexes, fast activity, or other paroxysmal activity. The abnormalities are bilateral, but are often asymmetric and irregular. Interictal EEG usually has an abnormal background, with frequent paroxysmal activity, such as spikes or spike–slow wave complexes that are irregular and asymmetric.

Myoclonic Seizures. Myoclonic seizures are bilaterally synchronous jerks that may occur singly or repeated in trains. Muscle masses involved can be restricted to the periocular or facial muscles, or be extensive, involving arms and legs, with falling or retropulsion. Myoclonic seizures can be provoked by simple sensory stimulation, particularly photic stimulation. Patients remain alert during the seizures, although repeated events at one to five per second that last for minutes or hours (myoclonic status, myoclonic storm) can be associated with some mental impairment. Myoclonic seizures occur in both primary and secondary generalized epilepsies. They may be associated features of absences or atonic seizures, and are the principal abnormality in juvenile myoclonic epilepsy.

The EEG shows bilaterally synchronous spike–wave discharges during myoclonic seizures, but the temporal relationship between EEG paroxysms and muscle jerks is not always fixed. Polyspikes can occur at double or triple the frequency of myoclonic jerks, usually at the beginning of a repeated train of myoclonus.

Tonic, Clonic, and Tonic–Clonic (Grand Mal) Convulsions. Convulsive seizures can take the classic form of a tonic–clonic grand mal convulsion or have only clonic or tonic components. Clonic seizures begin in early childhood and can resemble massive bilateral epileptic myoclonus, although the motor features may be less symmetric, and there is loss of consciousness. The seizures are followed by a period of postictal confusion.

Tonic seizures are most common in childhood, but can occur at any age. Tonic spasms of truncal and facial muscles occur, often with associated flexion of the upper extremities and flexion or extension of the lower extremities. Consciousness is impaired. Brief tonic seizures are grouped with absences, myoclonic seizures, and atonic seizures. More prolonged tonic seizures are regarded as convulsions, are accompanied by autonomic changes such as pupillary dilation, tachycardia, apnea, cyanosis, salivation, and urinary incontinence, and are followed by a period of postictal confusion.

Tonic–clonic or grand mal seizures are the most common convulsive seizure type. The seizure begins suddenly, without warning. Occasionally, the tonic phase is immediately preceded by one or more brief myoclonic jerks, giving rise to a clonic–tonic–clonic ictal pattern. Typically, there is a cry as the tonic spasm occurs in truncal muscles, followed by a predictable series of motor and autonomic phenomena. Tonic spasms rapidly involve all muscles. The resultant rigidity is eventually interrupted by brief intermittent muscle relaxation, which creates the clonic phase. The periods of relaxation become longer and closer together, causing the clonic movements to decrease in frequency and duration until they cease completely. The ictal episode usually lasts a minute or less, and a second tonic phase occasionally occurs. Postictal muscular flaccidity and coma last for a variable period. Patients often fall into a deep sleep and can awaken minutes or hours later. They may initially be disoriented as consciousness is slowly regained and frequently have a headache and fatigue.

Generalized tonic–clonic seizures are the predominant seizure type in approximately 10% of most persons with chronic epilepsy and most persons who have acute reactive seizures. Focal behavioral or EEG features seen at onset or postictally indicate a partial seizure that has secondarily generalized. Tonic and clonic seizures occur in either primary or secondary generalized epilepsies, but are more common with the secondary types.

The EEG correlate of the tonic phase of a tonic–clonic seizure consists of a buildup of generalized low-voltage fast activity. This typically evolves into a high-amplitude generalized polyspike or polyspike-and-wave discharge. The alternating periods of muscular relaxation and contractions during the clonic phase correspond to the alternating periods of EEG suppression and high-amplitude polyspike or polyspike–wave discharges on EEG, respectively. Postictally, the EEG shows diffuse slowing.

Generalized tonic and clonic seizures have EEG patterns that correspond to the tonic and clonic phases of a generalized tonic–clonic seizure, respectively. As with epileptic myoclonus, EEG discharges and motor manifestations of clonic seizures may not be absolutely time locked.

Atonic Seizures (Drop Attacks). Atonic seizures consist of a sudden loss of muscle tone. In some epileptics, this may be preceded by one or more generalized clonic jerks (myoclonic–astatic seizures). In mild cases, only the head drops. In the more severe form, the person suddenly collapses to the ground. The attacks are usually brief and are associated with impaired consciousness. Less commonly, atonic seizures can be prolonged, with the patient remaining unconscious and flaccid for 1 or more minutes. The ictal EEG can show polyspike–wave discharges or a suppression of electrical activity (electrodecremental response).

Atonic seizures commonly occur with the secondary generalized epilepsies and are a major cause of disability in the Lennox–Gastaut syndrome. Frequent falls often result in injury. Drop attacks can be extremely difficult to treat medically, but respond better than any other generalized seizure type to corpus callosotomy.

Infantile Spasms

Infantile spasms are both a seizure type and an epilepsy syndrome. The incidence is 1 per 2000 to 5000 live births. The spasms have been described previously as infantile myoclonic epilepsy, massive myoclonic jerks, salaam seizures, jackknife convulsions, and flexor spasms. The spasms are brief, lasting from 1 to 5 seconds, although they may occasionally last up to 1 minute. They occur in clusters of 10 or more spasms and may occur several times a day. There is considerable variation from patient to patient in the frequency and intensity of the spasms. The myoclonic movements associated with these seizures may be extensor, flexor, or a mixture of the two, with the mixed type being the most common and the extensor type being the least common. In flexor spasms, the neck is usually flexed at the same time as the trunk. There is usually abduction of the legs and flexion and abduction of the arms.

In extensor spasms, the leg extension is constant, and arm extension is more variable. The arms are more usually abducted and thrust forward. Extension of the trunk and neck may occur as well.

Hypsarrythmia is the characteristic EEG pattern of infantile spasms. It consists of continuous high-amplitude, irregular, and asynchronous sharp and slow waves occurring in a chaotic fashion. The electrographic correlate of the spasm is usually a high-amplitude frontally predominant delta wave, followed by a brief cessation of activity (electrodecremental response).

PLANS

Diagnostic

Differential Diagnosis

Partial seizures should be differentiated from other paroxysmal spells that cause focal symptoms. Migraines can sometimes be preceded by focal symptoms, such as visual scotomas, or focal sensory or motor deficits. Patients may describe numbness, tingling, or even weakness, which involves the lips, face, and arm in a migratory fashion. Some patients may also have transient aphasia. Unlike partial seizures, which are usually brief, lasting for seconds only, premonitory symptoms to a migraine attack are longer and can last as long as 15 minutes. As the symptoms subside, they are followed by a unilateral throbbing headache which may last hours and sometimes days. Transient ischemic attacks can also present with paroxysmal focal neurologic deficits. Unlike partial seizures, the onset of symptoms tends to be sudden rather than in a migratory fashion. Although transient ischemic attacks may last anywhere from a few seconds up to 24 hours, most of them last 2 to 15 minutes only. Presyncopal attacks and syncope with autonomic manifestations can also mimic partial seizures and drop attacks.

Given the extensive psychic phenomenon in complex partial seizures, it is not surprising that complex partial seizures may sometime be misdiagnosed as psychosis. The consistency of the symptoms from seizure to seizure and abnormal EEG findings help confirm the diagnosis of seizures. Hysterical seizures or pseudoseizures pose a special problem because they often coexist with complex partial seizures. The use of video EEG telemetry may be very helpful in differentiating between syncope, pseudoseizures, and epileptic seizures in these situations.

There are many clinical similarities between complex partial seizures and absence seizures. Distinction between these two seizure types is important, as they have different therapeutic and prognostic implications.

Diagnostic Options and Recommended Approach

A detailed history and thorough physical and neurologic examination should be obtained in every patient presenting with an acute seizure. Laboratory studies that should be done in the acute setting include blood gas, metabolic screens (glucose, liver function tests, blood urea nitrogen, creatinine) electrolytes (sodium, calcium, magnesium), anticonvulsant drug level, and toxicology screen. The number one cause of seizures in known epileptics is noncompliance. An EEG should be performed on all patients with an epileptic seizure. Findings on EEG not only confirm the diagnosis, but also help classify the specific seizure disorder and suggest treatment and prognosis. In instances where the nature of the clinical spells is not straightforward, and the diagnosis of epileptic seizure is questionable, the patient may be admitted to the hospital for long-term continuous audiovisual EEG telemetry, for better characterization of the clinical spells. Head computed tomography and magnetic resonance imaging scans may provide additional information on underlying causes, particularly in cases involving structural lesions. A lumbar puncture should be performed when infection is suspected.

Therapeutic

Medical Therapy. Anticonvulsant drugs remain the mainstay of medical therapy for patients with chronic recurrent seizures. Table 20–16–3 summarizes the common anticonvulsant medications used in treatment of partial seizures, generalized tonic–clonic seizures, absence seizures,

TABLE 20–16–3. COMMONLY USED ANTICONVULSANT MEDICATIONS

Drug (Trade Name)	Principal Uses	Maintenance Dose	Route
Phenytoin (Dilantin)	PS, GTC	5 mg/kg/d	PO, IV
Carbamazepine (Tegretol)	PS,GTC	7–15 mg/kg/d, divided into 2–3 doses	PO
Phenobarbital (Luminal)	PS,GTC	1–5 mg/kg/d	PO, IV, IM
Primidone (Mysoline)	PS,GTC	10–25 mg/kg/d, divided into 2–3 doses	PO
Valproic acid (Depakote/Depakene)	GTC, ABS, MYO, PS	15–60 mg/kg/d, divided into 3 doses	PO
Ethosuximide (Zarontin)	ABS	Up to 20 mg/kg/d, divided into 2–3 doses	PO
Felbamate* (Felbatol)	PS	Adults: 1200–3600 mg/d, divided into 3–4 doses Children: 15 mg/kg/d	PO
Gabapentin[†] (Neurontin)	PS	900–1800 mg/d, divided into 3 doses	PO
Lamotrigine[‡] (Lamictal)	PS	300–500 mg/d, divided into 2 doses With valproic acid: 100–150 mg/d, divided into 2 doses	PO

PS, partial seizures; GTC, generalized tonic–clonic seizures; MYO, myoclonic seizures; ABS, absence seizures.

*As of 1993, felbamate has been approved by the Food and Drug Administration for use as monotherapy or as adjunctive therapy in adults with partial seizures, and as adjunctive therapy only in children with the Lennox–Gastaut syndrome.

[†]As of 1994, gabapentin has been approved by the Food and Drug Administration for use as adjunctive therapy in adults with partial seizures with or without secondary generalized tonic–clonic seizures.

[‡]As of 1994, lamotrigine has been approved by the Food and Drug Administration for use as adjunctive therapy in adults with partial seizures.

and myoclonic seizures. In general, carbamazepine, phenytoin, and phenobarbital are equally effective in treating partial seizures; however, carbamazepine and phenytoin are usually preferred over phenobarbital due to the latter's sedating effect. These medications are also equally effective in treating generalized tonic–clonic seizures.

More recently, new antiepileptic drugs have been approved by the Food and Drug Administration (FDA) primarily for the treatment of partial seizures. Both gabapentin and lamotrigine have been approved for use as adjunctive therapy in adults with partial seizures (with or without secondary generalized tonic–clonic seizures) only. Clinical trials are currently underway to investigate their effectiveness as monotherapy agents and safety in children. Felbamate may be used either as monotherapy or as adjunctive therapy in adults with partial seizures, with or without secondary generalized tonic–clonic seizures. It may also be used as adjunctive therapy in children older than 2 years old with the Lennox–Gastaut syndrome. Felbamate can be associated with aplastic anemia and hepatitis. Thus, blood counts and liver enzymes should be monitored closely if it is used.

Valproic acid is generally the drug of choice in treating the different types of generalized seizures. It is particularly effective against primary and secondary generalized tonic–clonic seizures, absence seizures, and myoclonic seizures. Although ethosuximide and valproic acid are equally effective against absence seizures, valproic acid is usually preferred in patients who also have generalized tonic–clonic seizures. Adrenocorticotropic hormone continues to be the drug of choice in children recently diagnosed with infantile spasms. For children who fail to respond to one or two courses of adrenocorticotropic hormone, valproic acid may be considered for long-term therapy.

Surgical Therapy. Seizures that are due to structural lesions of the brain may be controlled or cured by resection of the lesion. There remains a small group of patients with partial seizures that are not related to central nervous system lesions and are refractory to medical therapy. In selected patients, the seizure focus may be localized to a discrete cortical area by long-term video EEG telemetry, head magnetic resonance imaging scan, and neuropsychological evaluation. These patients may be amenable to focal cortical resection for seizure control. Most of these patients have complex partial seizures localized to the temporal lobe.

Patients with intractable seizures associated with more diffuse disease involving an entire hemisphere may benefit from functional hemispherectomy. These patients have more extensive neurologic impairment, with hemiplegia, varying degree of hemianopia, and severe partial seizures with frequent secondary generalized tonic–clonic seizures.

There remains a population of medically intractable epileptics who have diffuse involvement of both hemispheres, and their seizures cannot be helped by focal resection or hemispherectomy. It is often this group of patients who require some form of surgical intervention, as their seizures are frequently generalized, rendering them physically debilitated. Corpus callosotomy has become increasingly popular over the last few decades for this group of patients. Its intent is not to suppress seizures altogether, but to stop generalization of seizure activity, thereby preventing falls and injuries.

FOLLOW-UP

Patients who are initially diagnosed with epileptic seizures and are placed on anticonvulsant medications should be followed closely for seizure activity, responsiveness to medication, and side effects from the medication. Anticonvulsant blood levels and blood tests to monitor potential hemotologic and hepatic side effects of medications should be done routinely until the patient's seizures are brought under control. The current practice of medical therapy is to exhaust patients on one drug at a time (monotherapy) before resorting to multiple drugs (polytherapy). It is felt that monotherapy alleviates the problem of drug interactions. Thus, it allows maximal pharmacologic effectiveness of one drug and minimizes potential side effects of multiple drugs. Once seizures are under good control, follow-up may be on a yearly basis.

DISCUSSION

Prevalence and Incidence

It is estimated that approximately 1.5 million individuals have active epilepsy in the United States (Hauser and Hesdorffer, 1990). Anywhere from 70,000 to 128,000 new cases of epilepsy are reported each year.

Related Basic Science

Everyone has the potential of having a seizure, with individual seizure thresholds being the primary determinant of one's susceptibility. Seizure thresholds are predetermined by genetic makeup. Its inheritance pattern is complicated and is suspected to be polygenic. Seizure thresholds are also influenced by external factors. Fever, stress, sleep deprivation, medications (particularly neuroleptics and antidepressants), and drug withdrawal (particularly barbiturate and alcohol withdrawal) are common provoking factors. Metabolic disturbances and electrolyte imbalance such as uremia, hepatic encephalopathy, hypo- or hypernatremia, hypo- or hyperglycemia, and hypo- or hypercalcemia can also cause acute reactive seizures, even in individuals with no underlying seizure disorder.

There is a high concordance for epilepsy in identical twins, suggesting that there may be some genetic basis for the idiopathic epilepsies. A history of epilepsy can be elicited in as many as 8 to 10% of first-degree relatives of these patients. Furthermore, as many as 50% of these first-degree relatives have an abnormal EEG in the absence of a seizure disorder. Although there is evidence for increased tendencies of seizures in relatives of patients with epilepsy, no single genetic trait can account for the vast heterogeneity of the epilepsies. Active research is currently underway to try and isolate specific genetic markers associated with increased seizure frequency.

Natural History and Its Modification with Treatment

The development of anticonvulsant medications over the last 100 years has greatly improved the prognosis of seizures. Compared with the low remission rate of less than 30% in the early 1900s, the overall prognosis of epilepsy has improved significantly one century later, with cure rates ranging from 50 to 80%. Patients with generalized idiopathic epilepsy consistently respond well to medical treatment. On the other hand, some 20% of patients with partial seizures are medically intractable. Among this group, approximately 15 to 20% are helped by surgery. Among those patients who have local surgical excision of epileptic tissue, the best outcome is observed among those undergoing temporal lobectomies, with approximately 80% of patients achieving a seizure-free status. Surgical outcome from extratemporal resection has been disappointing, with cure rates ranging from 20 to 30%. Good results of temporal lobectomy are because most seizures originating from the temporal lobe are associated with a specific pathology, hippocampal sclerosis. Its disease process has been well studied, and its seizure focus can be easily localized by EEG telemetry, head magnetic resonance imaging, and neuropsychological testing. Extratemporal seizures not associated with a structural lesion, on the other hand, are usually poorly localized by these methods. Approximately 75% of patients undergoing functional hemispherectomy achieve a seizure-free state. Corpus callosotomy decreases the incidence of generalized seizures, particularly atonic, tonic, and generalized tonic–clonic seizures, in 50 to 70% of patients; however, most patients continue to have frequent partial seizures, in the form of auras or motor or sensory symptoms. Although medical management continues to be difficult in some of these patients, the advantage gained from callosotomy is that patients can now secure themselves, prior to generalization of seizures. Thus, bodily injury is reduced significantly.

Prevention

There is no primary prevention of epilepsy. For patients with epilepsy, seizures may be minimized or prevented by avoiding provoking factors,

discussed earlier. The most common cause of seizures in epileptics is subtherapeutic anticonvulsant drug levels. The importance of drug compliance cannot be emphasized enough with patients. Any systemic illnesses, including fever, infections, metabolic diseases, and electrolyte imbalances, can lower seizure threshold and precipitate seizures. Thus, these medical conditions must be treated aggressively to control seizure occurrence. External factors known to cause seizures should be avoided when possible. These include drugs and medications, particularly alcohol and neuroleptics, and acute withdrawal from sedative drugs such as barbiturates and benzodiazepines. Patients with epilepsy should be advised to maintain a healthy, well-balanced diet and keep regular sleep habits.

Cost Containment

Few studies have considered cost containment of the diagnostic approach and management of seizures. One recent study (Landfish et al., 1992) analyzed 56 new-onset seizures evaluated in a pediatric emergency room. The majority of patients were less than 2 years old. The most common seizure type was febrile convulsions (71%), followed by idiopathic seizures (21%). Significant laboratory abnormalities were found in only 4 patients. This study found screening laboratory tests, including head computed tomography scans, not very helpful. Instead, a thorough history including specific details regarding the seizure and a complete physical and neurologic examination was found to be adequate in making the diagnosis, and should eliminate the need for major laboratory and radiologic tests in the emergency room.

REFERENCES

Commission on Classification and Terminology of the International League Against Epilepsy. Proposal for revised clinical and electroencephalographic classification of epileptic seizures. Epilepsia 1981;22:489.

Commission on Classification and Terminology of the International League Against Epilepsy. Proposal for classification of epilepsies and epileptic syndromes. Epilepsia 1985;26:268.

Engel J. Seizures and epilepsy. Philadelphia: Davis, 1989.

Hauser WA, Hesdorffer DC. Epilepsy: Frequency, causes and consequences. New York: Epilepsy Foundation of America, 1990.

Landfish N, Gieron-Korthals M, Weibley RE, Panzarino V. New onset childhood seizures: Emergency department experience. J Fla Med Assoc 1992;79:697.

Primrose DC, Ojemann GA. Outcome of resective surgery for temporal lobe epilepsy. In: Luders HO, ed. Epilepsy surgery. New York: Raven Press, 1991;601.

Rasmussen T. Hemispherectomy for seizures revisited. Can J Neurol Sci 1983;10:71.

Van Ness PC. Surgical outcome for neocortical (extrahippocampal) focal epilepsy. In: Luders HO, ed. Epilepsy surgery. New York: Raven Press, 1991:613.

Wyllie E. Corpus callosotomy: Outcome with respect to seizures. In: Luders HO, ed. Epilepsy surgery. New York: Raven Press, 1991:633.

CHAPTER 20–17

Stupor and Coma

A. Bernard Pleet, M.D.

DEFINITION

Consciousness is the awareness of self and of the environment. Stupor and coma represent pathologic alterations in that awareness. The stuporous patient appears to be asleep, most often with eyes closed. She or he shows arousal and an appropriate reaction to either vocal or to painful stimuli, but arousal continues only as long as the stimulus. Comatose patients have no appropriate reaction to external stimuli.

ETIOLOGY

Although the specific causes of stupor and coma are many, they are conveniently considered in three categories:

- Structural disease of the cerebral hemispheres and subcortical structures that secondarily compromise midline thalamic and hypothalamic activating structures, or structural infratentorial disease that compromises the reticular activating system of the upper brainstem
- Toxic, metabolic, infectious, and inflammatory insults to the cerebral hemispheres and the brainstem, involving the reticular activating system
- Psychogenic unresponsiveness

CRITERIA FOR DIAGNOSIS

Suggestive

The patient appears to be asleep and does not sustain arousal.

Definitive

The patient fails to respond appropriately to vocal commands or to painful stimuli. The latter can include firm pressure over the mastoid or styloid process, a knuckle pressed into the sternal angle, or a pencil placed between the last two toes and squeezed.

CLINICAL MANIFESTATIONS

Subjective

Historic data may prove key to the diagnosis. A history of hypertension with sudden headache, vomiting, and loss of consciousness can point to an intracerebral hemorrhage. In a young person sudden headache and a convulsion can indicate a subarachnoid hemorrhage. A history of hepatic cirrhosis and increasing lethargy and confusion suggest hepatic encephalopathy. Prolonged unconsciousness in a patient with epilepsy may indicate ongoing seizures or a postictal state. A history of a febrile illness with headaches suggests a meningoencephalitis. A similar presentation with aphasia suggests herpes simplex encephalitis. Fluctuating consciousness suggests a metabolic encephalopathy. One must always consider illicit drug use.

Objective

Physical Examination

Stupor and coma are not diagnoses, but are a "shorthand" for abnormal levels of consciousness. Having determined that the patient fails to arouse to vocal or painful stimuli, a general physical examination should precede the neurologic assessment.

The blood pressure, pulse, respiratory rate, and temperature should be recorded. Hypertension and a slow pulse suggest increased intracranial pressure. Hypotension may necessitate emergency resuscitative measures. An irregular pulse rate indicates atrial fibrillation with the possibility of a cerebral embolus. A paradoxical pulse points to cardiac tamponade. An elevated temperature may be the first clue to a systemic inflammatory response syndrome.

The adequacy of ventilation can be determined by ear or fingertip oximetry. Deep sighing respirations suggest systemic acidosis (Kussmaul). Slow shallow respirations may indicate sedative or hypnotic overdose. Cyclical changes in the depth of respiration (Cheyne–Stokes) are seen with cerebral and upper brainstem dysfunction and with a low cardiac output. Rapid respirations are seen with sepsis and structural damage to the mesencephalon. Irregular respirations are found with damage to the lower brainstem.

Breath odor is "fruity" with ketoanemia and "mousy" with advanced liver diease. The odor of alcohol can be obvious.

The patient should be inspected for evidence of trauma; bruising over the mastoid process or around the eyes or blood behind the tympanic membrane suggests a basal skull fracture. The skin of the antecubital fossae, the inguinal region, the areas between the toes, and the dorsum of the penis should be inspected for needle punctures. The color of the skin and mucosa should be noted: cyanosis of the lips or nail beds betokens hypoxia; a "cherry red" discoloration suggests cyanide poisoning. Spider angiomas, a caput medusa, and scleral and skin icterus may provide clues to hepatic encephalopathy. The degree of moisture in the axillae and groin as well as the oral mucosa should be estimated for evidence of dehydration. "Uremic frost" can be found with chronic renal failure. Bullae and vesicles may be seen over pressure points with barbiturate coma. Petechiae suggest a blood dyscrasia or a rickettsial or meningococcal infection.

Flexion of the neck can reveal resistance ("stiffness"), seen with meningitis and subarachnoid hemorrhage. Neck resistance can also be seen with parkinsonism, with diffuse bilateral cortical injury (paratonia), with advanced osteoarthritis, and with rheumatoid spondylitis.

Percussion of the chest and auscultation of the lungs provide confirmation of the adequacy of air exchange and may demonstrate characteristic changes with pneumonia, pulmonary edema, and pleural effusion. Auscultation of the carotid arteries may reveal a bruit, which correlates with cerebral infarction. Auscultation of the heart may demonstrate the gallop rhythm of heart failure or the paradoxical split of the second heart sound of a left bundle-branch block, suggesting an acute myocardial infarction. Palpation and auscultation of the abdomen may afford clues to an intra-abdominal catastrophe such as mesenteric vascular occlusion, bowel volvulus, or ruptured abdominal aortic aneurysm.

The neurologic assessment begins with noting the posture of the patient. Fingers tightly clasped around the thumbs ("cortical fisting") are seen with hypoxic encephalopathy. Abnormal motor responses, either decerebrate or decorticate, are more often seen in the context of primary injury to the brain or brainstem rather than as a consequence of a systemic illness. External rotation of a lower extremity suggests a hemiparesis or a hip fracture. Lack of spontaneous movement on one side may be seen with a hemiparesis.

Persistent deviation of the eyes to one side suggests injury to a frontal lobe (the eyes "look at" the injured hemisphere) or damage to the brainstem (the eyes "look away" from the lesion). Pupils that fail to constrict to a bright light denote structural damage to the brainstem. Small (1–2 mm) and unreactive pupils are seen with pontine lesions; midposition (4–6 mm) and unreactive pupils are seen with midbrain lesions; large (7–8 mm) and fixed pupils are seen with injury to the tectum; a unilateral dilated (8–9 mm) pupil is seen with third cranial nerve compression. Medications such as glutethemide and belladonna alkaloids can produce transiently large fixed pupils, as can hypoxia. Small but reactive pupils are usually due to metabolic depression or dysfunction of the upper brainstem. Examination of the fundus may demonstrate papilledema, indicating increased intracranial pressure, or subhyaloid hemorrhage from subarachnoid hemorrhage. Once the eyelids are released, absence of tone on both sides (the eyelids close slowly) is consistent with an impaired level of consciousness (and excludes psychogenic unresponsiveness). If tone is abnormal on only one side, it suggests a lesion of the opposite cerebral hemisphere or brainstem. Absence of both corneal reflexes is confirmatory for impaired consciousness, but absence of only one side tends to suggest unilateral impaired sensibility or motor function and is suggestive of an opposite hemispheric or ipsilateral brainstem lesion. When the head is rotated sharply to the side, deviation of both eyes to the opposite direction establishes an intact brainstem (the oculocephalic reflex). If only one deviates there is impairment of brainstem function. If neither eye moves, there may be impairment of the lower brainstem, or the stimulus may be insufficient to overcome metabolic suppression, in which case cold (iced) water is instilled into each ear in sequence, with the head elevated to 30° from the horizontal (oculovestibular reflex). The tympanic membranes are first visualized to exclude perforation or cerumen blockage. When both eyes conjugately deviate, the brainstem is intact. Failure of bilateral conjugate deviation suggests brainstem dysfunction. In psychogenic unresponsiveness the oculovestibular reflex induces nystagmus and often vomiting.

Muscle tone is tested by moving a limb at a large joint. Tone may be either increased or decreased on the side opposite a brainstem or cerebral injury, but noting an asymmetry in tone is important, even if the "abnormal" side cannot be defined with confidence.

Finally, the deep tendon reflexes are tested. Complete absence may simply be compatible with metabolic or hypoxic depression. Asymmetries of the reflexes suggest hemispheric or brainstem abnormality on the side opposite the more brisk of the reflexes. A Babinski sign on the same side as the brisk reflexes is confirmatory.

Routine Laboratory Abnormalities

Laboratory abnormalities depend on the etiology. If stupor or coma is due to a primary injury to the brain or brainstem, laboratory studies are normal. Metabolic, toxic, and infectious causes of stupor and coma give rise to laboratory abnormalities that reflect the nature of the disease.

PLANS
Diagnostic
Differential Diagnosis

The more common causes of stupor and coma are outlined in Table 20–17–1.

TABLE 20–17–1. DIFFERENTIAL DIAGNOSIS OF STUPOR AND COMA

Structural Brain Disease or Brainstem Disease
Supratentorial
  Cerebral hemorrhage or infarction
  Subdural hematoma
  Brain tumor (primary [glioma] or metastatic)
Infratentorial
  Brainstem hemorrhage or infarction
  Cerebellar hemorrhage or infarction
  Brainstem (rare) or cerebellar tumor (primary [glioma] or metastatic)

Metabolic and Diffuse Lesions
Drugs and poisons
Infections
  Meningitis
  Encephalitis
  Sepsis and sepsis syndrome
Head trauma and postictal states
Hypoxia and ischemia
Hypoglycemia
Electrolyte imbalance
Organ failure or deficiency
Nutritional deficiency
Psychogenic Unresponsiveness

Modified from Plum F. Sustained impairments of consciousness. In: Wyngaarden JB, Smith LH, Bennett JC (eds), Cecil Textbook of Medicine, 19th ed., Philadelphia: WB Saunders 1992:2049. Reproduced with permission.

Diagnostic Options and Recommended Approach

Structural disease of the brain or brainstem is suspected in part by the history, but is confirmed by lateralizing or localizing findings including papilledema, a hemiparesis, and abnormalities of eye movements or pupillary responsiveness.

A computed tomographic (CT) scan of the head, without contrast enhancement, identifies almost all supratentorial structural causes of stupor and coma. Acute ischemic hemispheric infarctions are occasionally "CT scan negative" during the first 24 hours, but within 48 to 72 hours show the characteristic changes of stroke. Most infratentorial structural lesions are also detected by CT head scanning, but when negative, a follow-up magnetic resonance imaging (MRI) scan proves more sensitive and detects most infratentorial structural lesions capable of causing stupor or coma.

Spiral CT scanning with three-dimensional reconstructions are useful for fractures of facial bones and may allow better visualization of basilar skull fractures. The technique is faster than usual CT scanning techniques, but is sensitive to patient movement and may not be practical when the patient is restless.

When there is no history nor physical sign of trauma, when the neurologic examination discloses no localizing or lateralizing signs, and when there is no evidence for seizures, one must entertain toxic, infectious, and metabolic causes for an encephalopathy. An electrocardiogram should be obtained as fingerstick blood is being examined for glucose. If a rapid bedside determination for glucose is not available, 50 mL of a 50% solution of dextrose in water may be given intravenously. Venous blood should be examined for electrolytes (Na, K, Cl, CO_2, Ca, and PO_4), urea, creatinine, osmolality, and liver function abnormalities (serum alanine and aspartate transaminases and bilirubin). Ammonia may be deferred unless there is clinical or laboratory evidence of liver disease. Blood should be analyzed for anticonvulsant levels (phenytoin, carabamazepine, and valproic acid) if there is any indication of a seizure.

Arterial blood should be examined for color and for pH, pCO_2, HCO_3, and HbCO. Where the cause of stupor and coma is not obvious, examination of the spinal fluid is necessary. If meningitis is suspected, the lumbar puncture should not be delayed pending a head CT scan. So long as there is no papilledema, the procedure can be carried out safely with a 22-gauge needle. Spinal fluid pressure should be measured and the fluid examined for cells, glucose, and protein and sent for culture and a Gram stain. If there is evidence of a bacterial meningitis, antibiotics should be started immediately after obtaining blood cultures and the cerebrospinal fluid, and should not await laboratory confirmation.

Blood should always be obtained for later examination for sedative and hypnotic drugs, a coagulation profile, thyroid and adrenal function, and viral titers. Urine should be obtained for later examination for drugs and for culture. An extra tube of cerebrospinal fluid is useful for viral and fungal titers if later indicated.

Even when there are no focal or lateralizing findings, the head CT scan remains a useful exclusionary tool, but it may be obtained after the appropriate laboratory studies have been obtained. Often those studies may obviate the need for imaging, as in the case of diabetic ketoacidosis, nonketotic hyerosmolar coma, and other disorders.

If the laboratory studies do not reveal an etiology for coma, an electroencephalogram is useful. In the case of psychogenic unresponsiveness it will be normal and reactive to external stimuli; it may reveal the presence of seizure discharges; in metabolic encephalopathies, particularly due to liver failure, there may be characteristic frontal triphasic waves.

Therapeutic

Identification of the cause of the altered level of consciousness often defines a treatment plan. Careful attention must be paid to adequate ventilation and oxygenation and circulatory support. In the case of an undiagnosed toxic or metabolic encephalopathy, if a blood glucose is not immediately available, 25 g of glucose (50 mL of a 50% solution) should be given intravenously with 50 mg of thiamine. If there is any possibility of narcotic overdose, 0.4 mg of naloxone may be administered intravenously, and if there is improvement, it may be repeated every 5 minutes until consciousness returns.

FOLLOW-UP

Stuporous and comatose patients should be followed in an intensive care setting until consciousness has returned. Once awake, medical or surgical follow-up depends on the condition that caused the altered state of consciousness.

DISCUSSION
Prevalence and Incidence

Considering the frequent occurrence of head trauma and alcohol and drug abuse, stupor and coma are common causes for admission to an emergency department.

Related Basic Science

In many cases of supratentorial or infratentorial mass lesions, failure to treat the underlying disorder results in a progressive rostral-to-caudal deterioration of brainstem function with a progressively changing neurologic examination. Pupils may start as pinpoint with Cheyne–Stokes respirations (diencephalic dysfunction) and progress to midposition fixed pupils and hyperventilation (midbrain dysfunction). Periodic neurologic examination documents the level of brainstem impairment and maps improvement or worsening.

Natural History and Its Modification with Treatment

Many causes of stupor and coma are treatable and reversible. Prompt identification of the cause of the altered level of consciousness often leads to a favorable outcome.

Prevention

Prevention of stupor and coma depends on prevention of the underlying disorder.

Cost Containment

It is important to discern neurologic abnormalities that suggest structural disorders of the brain or brainstem. Appropriate imaging rather than extensive biochemical screening is most cost efficient. Identification of toxic or metabolic encephalopathies allows specific early treatment and the avoidance of costly imaging.

REFERENCES

Massey EW, Pleet AB, Scherockman BI. Diagnostic tests in neurology: A photographic guide to bedside techniques. Chicago: Year Book Medical, 1985.

Plum F. Sustained impairments of consciousness. In: Wyngaarden JB, Smith LH Jr, Bennett JC, eds. Cecil: Textbook of medicine. 19th ed. Philadelphia: Saunders, 1992;2:2049.

Plum F, Posner JB. The diagnosis of stupor and coma. Contemporary Neurology Series No. 19. 3rd ed. Philadelphia: Davis, 1980.

CHAPTER 20–18

Acute Confusional States

Daniel H. Jacobs, M.D.

DEFINITION

The hallmark of acute confusional states is impairment in attention and/or arousal or acute changes in perception or other higher-order behaviors. An acute confusional state should be contrasted with delirium, which is defined as an impairment of attention or arousal. Therefore, an acute confusional state encompasses a wider range of patients than delirium, including patients who have serious neurologic illness yet who do not meet the criteria for delirium.

ETIOLOGY

The neurologic localization of acute confusional states includes both focal neurologic disorders and diffuse neurologic disorders. The spectrum of confusional states also includes a large number of systemic or medical disorders and ingestions that secondarily affect the central nervous system. The delineation of specific diagnostic entities from similar phenotypic disorders requires meticulous consideration of a vast differential diagnosis (Table 20–18–1). Of course, patients without confusion per se may complain of changes in mental status requiring just as aggressive an evaluation; for example, sleepiness can be the sole manifestation of a toxic ingestion or of an acute intracerebral hematoma. A systematic, rational approach can usually uncover the cause of an acute confusional state.

CRITERIA FOR DIAGNOSIS

A confusional state is a syndrome rather than a diagnostic entity. Generally it requires impaired or fluctuating attention, alertness, or arousal or other acute deficits of a higher-level behavior.

CLINICAL MANIFESTATIONS
Subjective

The history should necessarily include information from reliable relatives or persons who know the patient well and who can describe the temporal course and acuteness of the mental status changes. The history should include the context of the onset of the disorder (was the onset in the intensive care unit, postsurgical, in a nursing home, or in a patient's own home) and a history of systemic diseases the patient may have (e.g., diabetes, chronic pulmonary disease, epilepsy), as well as medications the patient is taking. A history of ingestions and nonprescription medicines should be especially elicited. A family history may be important to establish the diagnosis of systemic disorders (e.g., porphyria, bipolar affective disorder). The history regarding whether or not the patient is agitated or sedate can be helpful. From a relatively small number of details, a working hypothesis can be formulated and tested objectively.

Objective
Physical Examination

The physical examination should include a thorough systemic examination to look for clues to systemic diseases and/or ingestions. The initial part of the neurologic evaluation should be directed at excluding nonconfusional states that might be missed, such as Wernicke's aphasia (see Chapter 20–21), the locked-in syndrome (vertical eye movements remain intact), and akinetic mutism. Additionally, signs of treatable neurologic emergencies must be sought, such as disorders of eye movements (sign of Wernicke's encephalopathy), stiff neck and fever

TABLE 20–18–1. CAUSES OF ACUTE CONFUSIONAL STATES

I. Neurologic Causes
  A. Diffuse neurologic disease
    1. Seizures- postictal state; spike-wave stupor; absence epilepsy
    2. Infection- herpes virus, other viral, bacterial, fungal, cryptococcal retroviral
  B. Focal neurologic disease
Medical causes
  Systemic diseases
    Porphyria
    Lupus
  Uremic states
    Dialysis dementia
    Dialysis dysequilibrium
  Liver disease
    Acute hepatic encephalopathy
    Hepatic degeneration
  Pulmonary diseases
    Hypoxic
  Endocrine disorders
    Thyroid (hyperthyroidism, hypothyroidism, euthyroid Hashimoto's encephalopathy)
    Adrenal disease (hypo or hypercortisolism)
  Toxic
    Prescription and over-the-counter medications
    Street drugs
    Alcohol
    Poisonings
Nonacute confusional states misdiagnosed as acute confusional states
  Aphasia (especially Wernicke's aphasia)
  Locked-in state
  Affective disorder (unipolar or bipolar)
  Catatonia (drug-induced or associated with affective state)
  Hysteria or malingering
  Chronic confusional state (i.e., dementia)

(meningitis or subarachnoid hemorrhage), or subtle eye or limb movements (indicative of a seizure).

Picking at the bedclothes is a sign of either an acute confusional state (carphologia, per Hippocrates) or of seizures. Postictal states also are common causes of transient acute confusion and should be considered if the patient's mental state clears during the evaluation. If the patient is not sufficiently attentive to cooperate with a full neurologic examination, subtle findings that indicate focal disease, such as a failure to respond to a threat in a visual field (indicative of a field cut) or limited movement of one side (indicative of a hemiparesis) or limited response to pain, should be sought. Although focal findings by themselves do not exclude metabolic disease such as diabetes, any patient with acute confusion and focal findings needs to have a focal brain lesion excluded by neuroimaging studies.

A full mental status examination may be limited or uninterpretable due to changes in attention and arousal; however, certain basic assessments can always be made. First is the assessment of the patient's spontaneous activities. Is he alert, or sleepy but arousable to a normal state, or arousable only to a lethargic state? Is she hyper- or hypoactive? Does he appear to be or admit to hallucinating? If so, do the hallucinations appear to be bothersome or frightening to the patient? Patients with Alzheimer's disease, for instance, commonly have hallucinations of "phantom boarders," but may either recognize their hallucinations as abnormal or not be bothered by the "little men in the kitchen." In such instances, the presence of the hallucinations remains of diagnostic importance, but there is no urgency to administer toxic drugs that will mask the mental status and prevent the benefits of serial examinations.

The patients do not necessarily have to be taken at their word regarding their history, as the ability to self-monitor may be an important diagnostic point. Patients with right-hemisphere brain strokes, for example, are notorious not only for denying or minimizing their neurologic deficits, but for presenting for care days or weeks after the onset of their brain injury. Patients with right-hemisphere lesions also are more likely to have hemispatial inattention, usually on the left side, rather than global attentional problems as are seen in most toxic and metabolic encephalopathies. Conversely, patients with transient global am-

nesia (TGA), a benign condition, do not have inattention at all and may perform at exceedingly elevated levels (e.g., in one reported case, performing surgery) yet repetitively ask "Where am I," indicating that they recognize that an acute deficit is present and that they are profoundly bothered by it.

If possible, a formal mental status examination should be performed to assist in localization and diagnosis. The first tests should be ones of attention and arousal, such as forward and reverse digit span or spelling "world" forward and backward. If these tests are abnormal, the remainder of the mental status examination (see Appendix 8, "Mental Assessment") may be less meaningful as abnormalities could be attributable to attentional problems. The clinical response should be observed to the administration of 100 mg of thiamine intramuscularly and boluses of glucose, naloxone, and flunarizil, which should be given consecutively in acutely confused patients, to treat a possible Wernicke's encephalopathy, hypoglycemia, or overdoses of narcotics or benzodiazepines, respectively.

Routine Laboratory Abnormalities

The laboratory is crucial in the emergent and routine evaluation of mental status changes. In an emergency setting, abnormalities of serum levels of sodium, calcium, phosphorus, magnesium, and glucose, as well as uremia need to be excluded. Liver function tests should be checked (including an ammonia if the patient has asterixis). A complete blood count and differential to evaluate for an infection, a chest radiograph to look for heart failure and pneumonia an electrocardiogram to look for silent infarction and cardiac arrhythmia, coagulation studies (prothrombin time and partial thromboplastin time), and urinalysis (to look for evidence of either urosepsis or renal disease) should be done.

PLANS

Diagnostic

Differential Diagnosis

Despite an imposing number of differential diagnoses, the data base can point strongly to certain items that ought to get priority in the thinking. In the emergency setting, items that should get particular priority are either those that seem particularly likely or those that, because of their treatability, cannot afford to be missed. Among the neurologic conditions in the latter category are bacterial meningitis, which may lack typical febrile or meningeal signs in an elderly or immunocompromised patient; most metabolic and toxic disorders, which are summarized in the recommended laboratory evaluation described above; subtle status epilepticus (either "spike–wave stupor" or absence status, which have different treatments); and herpes simplex encephalitis. Herpes is the most common viral encephalitis, can occur at any time of the year, and may present with combinations of symptoms including fever, headache, behavioral abnormalities, lethargy, and seizures. In contrast to herpesvirus, arboviral encephalitides occur in the late summer or fall and do not have specific treatments.

In the emergency room, street drugs and alcohol withdrawal should be strongly considered in agitated patients with confusion; even if a patient is not intoxicated, she or he may be at risk for withdrawal syndromes including delirium tremens, which can be fatal if not treated. Alcohol can also indirectly cause confusional states, including alcoholic dementia, Korsakoff's amnesia, alcoholic blackouts, and seizures.

Systemic infections (urinary tract infections or pneumonia); metabolic disturbances related to chronic cardiac, pulmonary, hepatic, or other systemic disease; and toxic effects of prescribed medications are frequently the cause of altered mental status in frail patients without focal neurologic signs. Postoperative patients especially susceptible to confusional states are those undergoing orthopedic procedures who may be susceptible to fat emboli. Patients undergoing open heart procedures have a high incidence of confusional states, as much as 30%. Ophthalmologic (associated sensory deprivation) and urologic (i.e., prostate [associated water intoxication]) procedures also are common culprits, as are as-needed medications such as all benzodiazepines and other sedative medications, nonsteroidal medications, haloperidol, antihistaminergic medications. Prolonged stays in the intensive care unit may be culpable.

An amnestic state after treatment for an anterior communicating artery aneurysmal bleed can present acutely and is sometimes related to infarction in the basal forebrain. It presents with acute agitation and confusion. The deficit is usually permanent, although patients become less agitated over time. Caudate infarctions can produce acute agitation, but rarely true aphasia or memory loss unless the lesion is extensive. Thalamic infarcts can cause agitated amnestic states if strategically located to involve components of both the Papez circuit (mammillary bodies, mamillothalamic tract, or anterior nucleus) as well as components of the basolateral circuit (dorsomedial nucleus, intralaminar nuclei).

Confusion in epileptics can occur due to an ictal state, a postictal state, a side effect of antiepileptic drugs, or hippocampal atrophy that is either the cause or a chronic effect of epilepsy. Confusion can occur as a typical aura of a migraine, but should resolve with the migraine. Patients with chronic head injury may experience memory loss, but fluctuating deficits should not occur. In acute head injury, fluctuating deficits should prompt an investigation for acute epidural or subdural hematoma or delayed intracerebral hematoma, as these are potentially lethal yet sometimes treatable conditions.

The differential diagnosis of acute confusional states potentially encompasses most of the conditions listed in Chapter 20–19, and readers are referred to that Chapter for a fuller discussion of those conditions.

Diagnostic Options and Recommended Approach

To complete the emergency workup for treatable toxic and metabolic problems causing confusion, a urine and/or serum drug screen and, if appropriate, antiepileptic drug levels should be ordered. An arterial blood gas determination should be made to identify hypoxemia. Although an uncommon cause of changes in mental state, porphyria can be relatively easily diagnosed by measuring porphobilinogen and δ-aminolevulinic acid in the urine; this condition might be suspected in a patient who has been exposed to paints or solvents, or who has abdominal pain, or who has reactions to antiepileptic drugs, especially barbiturates but also phenytoin, carbamazepine, and valproic acid. Intoxications with the heavy metals lead, mercury, and arsenic can be considered in susceptible patients.

If after the above evaluation, no adequate explanation of the patient's confusional state exists, or if it only partially or unsatisfactorily explains the deficits that exist (e.g., a confused patient with a sodium level of 115 may have a syndrome of inappropriate antidiuretic hormone secretion, but also an underlying central nervous system disease), additional neurologic laboratory studies should be obtained. These can include, where appropriate, computed tomography or magnetic resonance imaging (MRI) of the brain, an electroencephalogram (EEG), and a lumbar puncture. The computed tomography scan should be ordered acutely to rule out the presence of an intracerebral bleed, which can be missed on the MRI, to look at the bony structures at the base of the skull if a fracture is considered, or if an MRI is not available emergently. The MRI offers more anatomic detail and is a better test in most subacute evaluations. The EEG can be extraordinarily helpful in the emergency setting to document the presence of either subtle seizures or encephalopathy. The EEG is also a crucial laboratory test in suspected herpes encephalitis, as it may show periodic lateralizing epileptiform discharges. The EEG can be exceptionally helpful if it is normal, to support a clinical diagnosis of either acute mania, hysteria, or malingering.

The lumbar puncture can show evidence of recent subarachnoid hemorrhage or infection or inflammation. It should not be performed in the presence of increased intracranial pressure, and if bacterial meningitis is strongly suspected, treatment should not be withheld pending laboratory confirmation of the cerebrospinal fluid (CSF) analysis. A low glucose can be seen in the CSF in bacterial, tuberculous, or fungal infection and in some inflammatory conditions. The lumbar puncture also can show evidence of demyelinating disease, neurosyphilis, cryptococcal meningitis (in patients with or without immunosuppressive illnesses), tuberculous disease, carcinomatous meningitis, and viral or fungal meningitis. Multiple taps may be necessary to make a diagnosis.

In difficult cases, subtle or seemingly odd laboratory findings can be helpful and even lifesaving. Histoplasmosis is an uncommon cause of

meningitis or abscesses in patients living in the Mississippi and Ohio river valleys; if the cerebrospinal fluid is negative it can be diagnosed in the urinary sediment. Eosinophilia in the spinal fluid can be a clue to the presence of *Aspergillus* infection or parasitic infection, although it is not specific. I have seen one case of an infant with a cerebrospinal fluid glucose of 20, elevated protein, and 200 cells, which were reported to be monocytes. The patient was treated with antibiotics and died. Had a wet smear been done, a diagnosis of amebic meningoencephalitis could have been made, rather than cerebrospinal fluid monocytosis, and the patient could have been appropriately treated.

In patients who, after evaluation, are thought to have a confusional state but not an acute confusional state, additional laboratory studies can be considered (see Chapter 20–19).

Therapeutic

The therapy and follow-up of the acute confusional state depend entirely on the underlying cause. Often, relatively simple measures such as withdrawing a medication or treating a urinary infection or abnormality of the electrolyte levels can have salutary effects. Although there is a certain push in many clinical situations to "treat" confusional states with various sedative medications, treatment can often mask the neurologic examination and should be limited to situations in which treatment is absolutely necessary. It is much better to find an underlying etiology or suspected etiology of the confusional state, and monitor the clinical examination.

Systemic toxic, metabolic, and infectious conditions are treatable depending on the underlying cause. Herpesvirus encephalitis is treatable with intravenous acyclovir and management of the increased intracranial pressure in a monitored unit. Seizures may be treated with antiepileptic drugs. Absence status, which can occur in elderly patients with no history of epilepsy, is treatable with diazepam intravenously followed by valproate. Nonconvulsive complex partial status epilepticus is treatable with phenytoin, valproate, or benzodiazepines. Subarachnoid hemorrhage needs to be further investigated with angiography to determine if the bleed is aneurysmal and whether emergency surgery can be performed. Bipolar affective disorders can be treated with psychotropic medications including lithium, carbamazepine, valproate, and antipsychotic medications.

FOLLOW-UP

The follow-up depends on the specific etiology. If an etiology is suspected yet treatment (e.g., withdrawal of a medication) fails to result in improvement, it is essential to persevere with a diagnostic workup systematically and to test additional hypotheses.

DISCUSSION
Prevalence

Acute confusional states are extremely common in virtually all clinical settings (outpatient, inpatient, and emergency). In one study, acute confusion occurred in 10 to 30% of those on medical or surgical wards and as many as 80% of those on geriatric wards.

Related Basic Science

Attention and arousal are mediated through the reticular activating system, a neurologic system that projects diffusely through the brainstem and thalamus, and cortex. At the cortical level, the right hemisphere is dominant for attention. The reticular activating system can be affected not only by toxic, metabolic, and infectious states, but also by mass lesions producing diffusely increased intracranial pressure. Confusional states may also be produced by focal cortical lesions involving the heteromodal association cortex in the temporal, frontal, or parietal lobes. Amnestic states signify disease of the temporal lobes, thalamus, or basal forebrain. Patients with diseased brains, or the elderly, may have a lower threshold for the development of the confused state.

Natural History and Its Modification with Treatment

The natural history depends on the diagnosis. Clearly, some patients with toxic, metabolic, and infectious causes of confusional states get better fairly quickly, and some patients with vascular or traumatic causes of confusional states may improve over a somewhat longer course. Patients with degenerative disease may deteriorate, but the diagnosis is one of exclusion.

Prevention

The prevention of acute confusional states depends on the prevention of specific diseases causing the confusional states. A prudent and rational approach to prescribing medication in elderly patients, based on the knowledge that their brains, as the rest of their bodies, becomes more fragile over time, would be one way to prevent confusional states from developing.

Cost Containment

Although the cost of performing a series of diagnostic tests is high, the financial and human cost of failing to diagnose a treatable neurologic

illness is so great as to suggest that every patient with an acute confusional state should be promptly worked up until a satisfactory cause of the state has been established or the patient improves. A delay in diagnosis and treatment would ultimately be much more expensive than the cost of a systematic and thorough evaluation on the patient's presentation.

REFERENCES

Heilman KM, Valenstein EV. Clinical neuropsychology. 3rd ed. New York: Oxford University Press, 1993.

Plum F, Posner JB. The diagnosis of stupor and coma. 3rd ed. Philadelphia: Davis, 1980.

CHAPTER 20–19

Loss of Cognitive Function

Daniel H. Jacobs, M.D.

DEFINITION

Loss of cognitive function is a descriptive term without a precise definition that includes a wider grouping of patients than does the term *dementia*. Because patients who do not meet published criteria for dementia may still have neurologic disease, and because their deficits in language, memory, praxis, attention, or executive skills may have localizing value, we prefer the broader term. In this chapter we consider patients with more or less stable deficits in cognitive function, whereas patients with acute presentations of confusion or cognitive loss are discussed in Chapter 20–18, although some of those patients are eventually found to have loss of cognitive function.

ETIOLOGY

Loss of cognitive function can occur due to toxic, metabolic, infectious, traumatic, neoplastic, epileptic, vascular, or degenerative processes. Very often the clinical setting seems to point to one process or to another, but because a definitive anatomic diagnosis is frequently absent, all possible processes should be kept in mind while evaluating patients.

CRITERIA FOR DIAGNOSIS

The diagnosis of loss of cognitive function can best be made on the basis of serial physical and neurologic examinations and/or neuropsychological evaluations. Practically, the diagnosis depends on taking a careful clinical history from the patient and/or relatives and friends about the premorbid level of function, as well as making a rational assessment of the patient's ability to perform normally on tests of higher cortical function. Considerations that should be taken into account when looking at neuropsychological data include the patient's educational attainments, past job performance, and native language. Language-based tests of memory may be invalid if the patient has aphasia, and most tests of specific aspects of higher cortical function are invalid in the presence of severe attentional deficits.

CLINICAL MANIFESTATIONS

Subjective

See Criteria for Diagnosis.

Objective

Physical Examination

In addition to systemic physical examinations including the neurologic examinations, patients with cognitive loss should have detailed testing of their higher cortical functions and, if any question remains afterward regarding the presence of abnormalities, formal neuropsychological testing. The physical and elemental neurologic examinations are as in other neurologic conditions, but the mental status test should be more detailed. Some of the major components of a detailed mental status test are listed in Appendix 8. The elemental neurologic examination should be directed, in part, toward "neighborhood signs" and associated findings such as field cuts, pronator drift, Babinski signs, or a gait disorder.

The mental status assessment should, at the very least, attempt to delineate the nature of the abnormalities of higher cortical function and to assist in localization. Are the findings localized within the cortex, for example, to angular gyrus or to the orbitofrontal lobes or, more broadly, to either the left or right hemispheres, or are they global in nature? Does the patient have the features of a frontal–subcortical dementia? These would include poor recall, poor performance on semantic category or letter fluency tasks (FAS test), impaired response inhibition, and impaired executive performance on tests such as the Wisconsin Card Sorting test, but would not include anomia, other features of aphasia, apraxia, agnosia, neglect, or other features that localize away from the frontal lobes. The concept of frontosubcortical dementias is difficult to sustain anatomically, but is widely used descriptively to differentiate the type of deficits seen in some patients with Parkinson's disease, progressive supranuclear palsy, multiple sclerosis, AIDS, and other so-called "subcortical" diseases from those seen in so-called "cortical" dementias such as Alzheimer's disease and Pick's disease.

Routine Laboratory Abnormalities

The routine laboratory tests are usually negative.

PLANS

Diagnostic

Differential Diagnosis

Degenerative disease in an elderly person remains a diagnosis of exclusion. The National Institute of Neurological and Communicative Disorders and Stroke criteria for Alzheimer's disease are given in Table 20–19–1. If the laboratory evaluation suggested above is completed and

TABLE 20–19–1. NINCDS–ADRDA CRITERIA FOR THE CLINICAL DIAGNOSIS OF ALZHEIMER'S DISEASE

1. The criteria for the diagnosis of probably Alzheimer's disease include:
   a. Dementia established by the clinical examination and documented by the MiniMental test, the Blessed Dementia Scale, or some similar examination and confirmed by neuropsychological tests
   b. Deficits in two or more areas of cognition
   c. Progressive worsening of memory and other cognitive functions
   d. No disturbance of consciousness
   e. Onset between ages 40 and 90, usually after 65
   f. Absence of systemic disorders that could themselves account for the progressive deficits in memory and cognition

2. The diagnosis of probable Alzheimer's disease is supported by:
   a. Progressive deterioration of specific cognitive functions such as language (aphasia), motor skills (apraxia), and perception (agnosia)
   b. Impaired activities of daily living and altered patterns of behavior
   c. A family history of similar disorders, particularly if confirmed neuropathologically
   d. Laboratory results including a normal lumbar puncture when evaluated by normal techniques, a normal or nonspecific pattern of abnormality on electroencephalogram, and evidence of atrophy on neuroimaging scans with evidence of progression on serial scans

3. Other clinical features consistent with the diagnosis of probable Alzheimer's disease, after exclusion of other causes of dementia, include:
   a. Plateaus in the course of the progression of the illness
   b. Associated symptoms of depression; insomnia; incontinence; delusions; hallucinations; catastrophic verbal, emotional, or physical outbursts; sexual disorders; weight loss; other neurologic abnormalities in some patients with more advanced disease including increased muscle tone, myoclonus, or gait disorder
   c. Seizures in advanced disease
   d. Normal neuroimaging for age

4. Features that make the diagnosis of probable Alzheimer's disease uncertain or unlikely include:
   a. Sudden, apoplectic onset
   b. Focal neurologic findings such as hemiparesis, sensory loss, visual field deficits, and incoordination early in the illness
   c. Seizures or gait disturbance at the onset or very early in the illness

5. Clinical diagnosis of possible Alzheimer's disease:
   a. May be made on the basis of the dementia syndrome, in the absence of other neurologic, psychiatric, or systemic disorders sufficient to cause dementia, and in the presence of variations in the onset, in the presentation, or in the clinical course
   b. May be made in the presence of a second systemic or brain disorder sufficient to produce dementia, which is not considered to be the cause of the dementia
   c. Should be used in research studies when a single, gradually progressive severe cognitive deficit is identified in the absence of other identifiable causes

6. Criteria for diagnosis of definite Alzheimer's disease are:
   a. The clinical criteria for probable Alzheimer's disease
   b. Histopathologic evidence obtained from an autopsy or biopsy

7. Classification of Alzheimer's disease for research purposes should specify features that may differentiate subtypes of the disorder, such as:
   a. Familial occurrence
   b. Onset before age 65
   c. Presence of trisomy 21
   d. Coexistence of other relevant conditions such as Parkinson's disease

NINCDS–ADRDA, National Institute of Neurological and Communicative Disorders and Stroke–Alzheimer's Disease and Related Disorders Association
Source: From McKhann G, Drachman D, Folstein M, et al. Clinical diagnosis of Alzheimer's disease: Report of the NINCVDS–ADRDA work group under the auspices of Department of Health and Human Services Task Force on Alzheimer's Disease. Neurology 1984;34:940. Reproduced with permission from the publisher.

no treatable form of memory loss is found, and if the patient meets the clinical criteria for Alzheimer's disease (i.e., both memory loss and cognitive deficits such as anomia and apraxia), then a clinical diagnosis of probable Alzheimer's disease can be made.

Alzheimer's generally presents with difficulty in new learning, but also can mimic focal neurologic disease with a single prominent neu-ropsychologic deficit, such as aphasia, Balint's syndrome (defined by a triad of optic ataxia, ocular apraxia, and simultanagnosia), or features of an angular gyrus syndrome (right–left disorientation, acalculia, alexia with agraphia, and finger agnosia). In such circumstances, after evaluation, the differential diagnosis should be expanded to consider other degenerative dementias such as Pick's disease and progressive subcortical gliosis. In the setting of frontotemporal atrophy and predominant deficit of language and/or behavior changes, Pick's disease is very likely. In patients with extrapyramidal symptoms and a frontosubcortical dementia, Lewy body disease should be considered. In patients who present with unilateral apraxia, magnetic dyspraxia (a syndrome in which the extremities are drawn, magnetlike, toward presented stimuli), cortical sensory deficits, and myoclonus but otherwise normal mentation, the likely diagnosis is corticobasal–ganglionic degeneration (Rebeiz' syndrome).

Wernicke–Korsakoff syndrome presents in patients with nutritional deficiency or heavy alcohol use. The clinical presentation is one of an amnestic dementia in which the patient has a striking ability to confabulate parts of her or his history and has no "cognitive deficits," nor deficits of subcognitive procedural skills such as mirror reading and rotor pursuit motor learning. In contrast, patients with Huntington's disease or Parkinson's disease have marked abnormalities on procedural memory tasks.

Patients with Parkinson's disease are frequently demented and depressed. The differential in these patients, after exclusion of coexisting remote infections or other metabolic abnormalities, includes medication toxicity from virtually any antiparkinsonian medicine but especially anticholinergic drugs, even relatively mild ones such as diphenhydramine. Levodopa frequently causes, in addition to confusion, formed visual hallucinations. After excluding toxic and metabolic causes of memory loss, many parkinsonian patients have either coexisting Alzheimer's disease, Lewy body disease with dementia, or a frontosubcortical dementia related to Parkinson's disease.

Normal pressure hydrocephalus is characterized by a clinical triad of dementia, usually of the frontosubcortical type, gait apraxia, and incontinence, with a finding of enlarged ventricles on neuroimaging. Although all these features need not be present, a gait disorder is the sine qua non of the triad without which the diagnosis cannot be made, no matter how enlarged the ventricles. The pathophysiology may involve the loss of the ability to reabsorb cerebrospinal fluid at the arachnoid villus consequent to recent or old meningitic infection; hence the purpose of a lumbar puncture in these patients, in part, is to exclude chronic meningitis as well as to establish the diagnosis by noting clinical improvement when the tap is performed. Normal pressure hydrocephalus always emerges in a discussion of the "treatable dementias," yet the treatment, placement of a ventricular shunt, is as likely to place the patient at risk for shunt-related complications, such as subdural hematomas and infection, as it is to result in sustained benefit.

Consequently, the selection of patients likely to benefit from a shunt is a challenging and complex venture. Poor-risk shunt candidates may include those with moderate or severe cerebral atrophy, alcoholism, or anomia or apraxia. The sequence and duration of symptoms are also important. Patients who have had dementia less than 6 months or who developed dementia following gait apraxia are much better candidates than those who developed their dementias before their gait apraxias. The strong association between the disorder and hypertension provides both another useful historical marker of the disease and a clue regarding its pathophysiology, as it suggests that cerebral autoregulation is impaired in these patients and that treatment of the hypertension is potentially important.

Head injury, if severe enough to cause a visible lesion on neuroimaging, frequently produces impairment in memory. Deficits are typically seen on response inhibition tasks, due to orbitofrontal lesions, and memory, presumably due to temporal lobe contrecoup injuries. Patients may have severe emotional response inhibition problems that are incapacitating. Occasionally, patients with right orbitofrontal injuries may perform at ceiling level on all neuropsychological tests, yet be devastated in terms of social behavior, and lose the ability to plan, exercise judgment, or stay out of trouble with the law. These patients with acquired sociopathy may have intelligence quotients in the 130s and yet be unable to hold a job due to their head injuries. Patients with so-called "mild head trauma," who have no neuroimaging findings and who have brief periods of unconsciousness ranging from minutes to hours, may have persistent headaches, dizziness, and memory loss that seems out of proportion to their injuries; usually, counseling these patients that they will likely improve gradually and can be treated symptomatically is helpful to them.

The younger patient (i.e., < 60) with loss of cognitive function is a particular vexing challenge. Alzheimer's disease can present in younger patients, sometimes in those patients with a family history of early Alzheimer's disease, but is less common in such patients and very rare below age 50 unless the patient has Down syndrome. HIV is an increasing cause of loss of cognitive function and should be kept in mind in patients in whom the clinical findings are not otherwise easily explained. Patients with HIV-related dementia typically present with a triad of cognitive symptoms (forgetfulness), motor symptoms (loss of balance and leg weakness), and behavioral symptoms (apathy and social withdrawal, followed by psychomotor slowing); however, most patients with HIV-related dementia are already known to have AIDS-defining infections. The field of metabolic disorders presenting with loss of cognitive function in adults has vexed those physicians who felt such diseases were confined to pediatric neurology; the presentations of these disorders are summarized by Coker (1991).

In a younger patient with a movement disorder, Huntington's disease and Wilson's disease can be considered. Huntington's disease presents most often from the second to fourth decades of life, as an autosomal dominant disorder with complete penetrance. Clinically, chorea, dementia, and personality changes are seen. The differential would likely include Sydenham's chorea, lupus, thyroid disease, tardive dyskinesia, and, if a peripheral neuropathy is present, neuroacanthocytosis. In patients with suspected Huntington's disease who do not wish to receive genetic testing, it is important to determine both the inheritance and whether one or more family members has had clinically definite or anatomically proven disease. If not, the patient's diagnosis should be approached with an inquisitive mind. In a patient with combinations of hepatic disease or nausea, prominent emotional symptoms, cognitive loss, or dysarthria, excluding Wilson's disease would be mandatory, as the cognitive loss is entirely preventable, and patients with Wilson's disease who are properly treated are capable of leading normal lives. Wilson's disease is an inherited autosomal recessive trait.

Dignostic Options and Recommended Approach

Treatable causes of dementia should be sought and excluded with appropriate laboratory tests. All patients require a quality neuroimaging study of the brain, either computed tomography or magnetic resonance imaging, to exclude a treatable mass lesion such as a meningioma or a subdural hematoma, as well as to assess the degree and pattern of atrophy, ischemic gliosis, and other pertinent findings. All patients should have hyper- and hypothyroidism excluded with sensitive tests of thyroid function, vasculitis screened with measurement of an antinuclear antibody and sedimentation rate, and neurosyphilis excluded with a free treponemal antibody test, which has less false-negative results than an RPR or a VDRL. Levels of electrolytes (sodium, potassium, chloride, bicarbonate, glucose, urea nitrogen, creatinine, calcium, magnesium, phosphorus), a complete blood count, and vitamin B_{12} and folate levels should be checked. An electroencephalogram (EEG) can exclude subclinical seizures, either spike–wave stupor or absence status (two forms of nonconvulsive status epilepticus that have different treatments), and can confirm or exclude the presence of periodic discharges that are seen in up to 90% of patients with Creutzfeldt–Jacob disease. Occasionally, Hashimoto's encephalopathy can present with normal standard thyroid function tests and is diagnosable through tests for antimicrosomal and antithyroglobulin antibodies (titers > 1:1000); the importance of testing for this syndrome is that it can be treated with corticosteroids with reversal of the dementia.

The remainder of the laboratory workup can be tailored to the individual patient. Lumbar puncture is indicated only for some patients with unexplained neurologic signs, such as an upgoing toe and memory loss, that might be explainable by vasculitis or a chronic meningitis. In patients with suspected progressive supranuclear palsy, a lumbar puncture can show a cerebrospinal fluid pleocytosis that is an indication for

a small bowel biopsy to exclude central nervous system Whipple's disease. Patients with a frontosubcortical dementia but no other explanation for the memory loss (such as extensive small vessel vascular disease or Parkinson's disease) should have a spinal tap to exclude a subacute or chronic central nervous system infection such as cryptococcal meningitis (present in patients with and without immunodeficiency). Patients with suspected central nervous system vasculitis often have a lymphocytosis in the cerebrospinal fluid, but may require a brain and meningeal biopsy for diagnosis.

In suspected Wilson's disease, the diagnosis can be made through measurement of serum ceruloplasmin, measurement of urine copper, ophthalmologic examination for Kayser–Fleischer rings, and, in some cases, liver biopsy.

In the evaluation of normal pressure hydrocephalus, neuropsychological testing and assessment of gait (with a video camera) before and after a lumbar puncture can be helpful. Other diagnostic tests that are sometimes useful include magnetic resonance imaging (which can show enlarged ventricles and decreased transependymal flow), single-photon-emission computed tomography (may show reduced flow in the frontosubcortical areas bilaterally but not decreased bitemporoparietally as would be seen in Alzheimer's disease), and continuous cerebrospinal fluid pressure monitoring. The last test is highly invasive and carries the risk of inducing a central nervous system infection. Cisternography adds little to clinical management.

Therapeutic

Only one pharmaceutical agent, Tacrine, has been approved by the Food and Drug Administration for use in Alzheimer's disease. Tacrine is a reversible acetylcholinesterase inhibitor that has been studied extensively in at least five large clinical trials in several thousand patients. Two of the studies showed no benefit, two showed a modest benefit, and one showed a modest benefit only if very high doses, 120 to 160 mg/d, are given. The potential mild benefit in some patients must be considered against the high cost and adverse effects of the drug. Tacrine causes reversible elevations of liver function tests as well as nausea. Liver enzymes (alanine and aspartate transaminases) must be monitored weekly for the first 16 weeks on the drug, and in some of the published studies almost half the enrolled subjects dropped out. I typically inform patients that Tacrine exists, has a high cost and side effect profile, and I would be willing to prescribe it if they were willing to comply with the weekly laboratory tests. An alternative to Tacrine is thiamine, in doses of 5 g/d. Thiamine acts at least partly as a cholinergic drug, promoting acetylcholine uptake and inhibiting degradation, and has been shown to reverse scopolamine-induced deficits in humans and animals. The efficacy is mild, as is that of Tacrine, but unlike Tacrine, the drug is cheap and does not require weekly liver function monitoring.

Once the diagnosis of Alzheimer's disease has been made, the mainstay of treatment is discussing with the patient and caregiver the multitude of psychological and social issues that either have come forth or will do so in the period after diagnosis. These include such issues as driving (most patients with Alzheimer's disease are not safe drivers), spousal powers of attorney, living wills, and a support framework for the caregiver. The latter may include Alzheimer's support groups, adult daycare programs, skilled nursing, home health aides, and Meals on Wheels. It also may need to include psychological support for the caregiver who may be unaccustomed to dealing with problem behaviors in his or her spouse or who may feel overwhelmed at assuming responsibilities in the household that theretofore were not hers or his. An excellent reference for caregivers is the book *The Thirty-Six Hour Day*, (Mace and Rabins, 1981) available in most bookstores.

Although a low-dose antipsychotic agent is frequently administered to demented patients, the medicine further blunts frontal lobe function and personality and should be reserved for cases in which the patients' behaviors present a danger to themselves or to others. The presence of hallucinations or delusions is not by itself an indication for administering medication. Significantly, delusions do respond to Tacrine. Antidepressant trials may be indicated in patients who have a depression secondary to their dementia or in whom pseudodementia is suspected. Again, a caveat should be administered: patients with abnormal brain function may be unable to tolerate even those mildly anticholinergic drugs that have a low side effect profile, such as nortriptyline and desipramine. If the patients appear to do worse on such drugs, they need to be withdrawn. Selective serotonin uptake inhibitors may be a better choice. Sleep problems can be managed by counseling regarding sleep hygeine (avoid daytime naps, excessive fluid consumption in evenings). If sedatives are absolutely needed, temazepam in low doses can be tried, as temazepam lacks anticholinergic effects and has less rebound or carryover effects than other benzodiazepines.

Patients with amnestic dementias who do not have sufficient cognitive deficits to qualify for a diagnosis of Alzheimer's disease, especially those who have a history of heavy alcohol use, should be given thiamine intramuscularly as a potential treatment for Wernicke's encephalopathy.

Wilson's disease is treated with D-penicillamine, which lowers the levels of copper that accumulate and cause toxicity otherwise.

FOLLOW-UP

Patients with Alzheimer's disease and their caregivers frequently need follow-up to manage psychosocial aspects of the disease. Many of the same issues discussed above need to be readdressed as the patients' symptomatologies worsen.

DISCUSSION

Prevalence and Incidence

Dementia is a major cause of disability in developed countries and is becoming increasingly common as our population ages. The prevalence of dementia rises from 1% at age 65 to more than 25% at age 85. The majority (60–80%) of cases are due to Alzheimer's disease and the remainder to a mixture of causes. Incidence studies are more rarely performed and data harder to find.

Related Basic Science

Genetics

Alzheimer's disease in some cases is familial and may be inherited as an autosomal dominant gene, which may not be expressed until late in life. There are a number of different genetic abnormalities that can present similarly phenotypically. They are usually described on chromosomes 21 and 19. Pick's disease may be inherited as an autosomal dominant trait. Familial slow viruses (Creutzfeldt–Jacob disease and Gerstmann–Straussler syndrome) are related to specific mutations on chromosome 20. The gene for Huntington's disease (autosomal dominant) has been localized to the short arm of chromosome 5. Wilson's disease is an autosomal recessive disease related to changes on chromosome 13.

Histopathology

The histopathologic hallmarks of Alzheimer's disease include the presence of neurofibrillary tangles, amyloid plaques, and granulovacular degenerations. As these changes are sometimes found in nondemented elderly patients, the location and number of pathologic changes is important. Plaques occurring in the outflow tracts of the hippocampal formation (layers 2 and 4 of the entorhinal cortex) isolate the hippocampus from higher-order association cortices and contribute to memory loss. Cholinergic deafferentation occurs but is not specific to Alzheimer's disease.

On the molecular level, the formation of amyloid protein is related to altered cleavage of the precursor protein to beta amyloid. The gene for amyloid precursor protein has been cloned and localized to chromosome 21. Several different mutations have been linked to the abnormal

formation of beta amyloid in Alzheimer's disease, and in other families the abnormality has been linked to chromosome 19.

Wernicke–Korsakoff syndrome is associated with pathology of the dorsomedial nucleus of the thalamus, the cholinergic neurons of the basal forebrain, and the mammillary bodies. Parkinson's disease is associated not only with loss of dopaminergic neurons in the substantia nigra, but also loss elsewhere in the brain of cholinergic, noradrenergic, and serotenergic neurons and independent cortical atrophy.

The pathogenesis of HIV dementia is not entirely understood but probably is due to a release of cytotoxic cytokines or blockage of neuronal growth factor receptors rather than direct HIV destruction of neural tissue. As patients with HIV are susceptible to innumerable secondary diffuse and focal central nervous system infections, ranging from cytomegalovirus encephalitis to cryptococcosis to lymphoma, and as some of the secondary infections have specific treatments, each patient with HIV and cognitive loss deserves a full evaluation for treatable causes of cognitive loss, including a lumbar puncture, if lumbar puncture is not contraindicated medically.

Natural History and Its Modification with Treatment

The proportion of cases in which reversible causes of dementia are found after investigation ranges from 10 to 30%, although the number of treatable dementias is higher. In Alzheimer's disease, the lifespan may be significantly shortened, yet patients with Alzheimer's disease may live a mean of 6.0 to 6.9 years after diagnosis and a range that is much longer. In part that reflects our ability to treat the intercurrent problems of very demented patients, such as frequent urinary tract infections and pneumonias. No form of treatment currently available has been shown to affect the prognosis. Wernicke's encephalopathy and Wilson's disease can be helped with specific treatments. Some of the metabolic and biochemical disorders, such as cerebrotendinous xanthomatosis (Coker, 1991), although rare, are important to diagnose as they have specific treatments that effectively prevent progressive disease.

Prevention

At present, there are no known ways to prevent Alzheimer's disease in susceptible individuals. There has been an explosion of knowledge concerning the basic and clinical science of the disease, and in the future, early diagnosis may lead to treatment trials that are designed to prevent the expression of the disease.

Cost Containment

The average annual cost of nursing home care is exorbitant. A broad-based supportive approach to the clinical care of patients with dementia that focuses on the caregiver and is tailored to help caregivers manage specific behavioral problems that arise with appropriate specific treatments may be the best way to forestall nursing home placements and to contain costs in these patients.

REFERENCES

Alzheimer's Association (national); 70 East Lake Street, Suite 600, Chicago, Illinois, 60601–5997, (312) 853–3060.

Coker SB. The diagnosis of childhood neurodegenerative disorders presenting as dementia in adults. Neurology 1991;41:794.

Mace NL, Rabins PV. The 36-hour day: A family guide to caring for persons with Alzheimer's disease, related dementing illnesses and memory loss in later life. Baltimore: Johns Hopkins University Press, 1981.

McKhann G, Drachman D, Folstein M, et al. Clinical diagnosis of Alzheimer's disease: Report of the NINCDS–ADRDA work group under the auspices of the Department of Health and Human Services Task Force on Alzheimer's Disease. Neurology 1984;34:939.

CHAPTER 20–20

Neuroendocrine Disorders as Viewed by a Neurologist

A. Bernard Pleet, M.D.

Neuroendocrine disorders can be defined as abnormalities of the hypothalamus and its neurosecretory cells, the pituitary gland, and the endocrine glands including the parathyroid and thyroid glands, the adrenal glands, and the insulin-secreting cells of the pancreas. In this chapter, we concern ourselves only with those disturbances that result in neurologic abnormalities.

Disorders of Hypothalamic Function

DIABETES INSIPIDUS

Definition

A deficiency of antidiuretic hormone (vasopressin) leads to excessive thirst, polydipsia, and polyuria (with a low specific gravity), which defines the syndrome of diabetes insipidus.

Etiology

Brain tumors cause diabetes insipidus in 30% of patients. In men it is usually due to pituitary metastases from carcinoma of the lung; in women, from pituitary metastases from carcinoma of the breast. Idiopathic disease makes up another 30% of cases. Head trauma accounts for 20%, and less common causes include sarcoidosis, histiocytosis, and surgical injury to the pituitary gland or stalk.

Criteria for Diagnosis

Suggestive

Excessive thirst and the production of 3 to 4 or more L of dilute urine per day should suggest the possibility of diabetes insipidus.

Definitive

A hyposmolal urine of 50 to 150 mOsm/L is sufficient to recommend further diagnostic testing.

Clinical Manifestations

Subjective

In patients whose abilities to slake their thirst is unimpaired there are no complaints save thirst, excessive drinking, and frequent urination. In those whose level of consciousness is impaired for other reasons, such as the appearance of intercurrent illnesses or when undergoing operative procedures under general anesthesia, the appearance of hypernatremia may be the first indication of diabetes insipidus. Once hypernatremia makes its appearance, patients complain of lethargy, anorexia, depression, and muscle cramps.

Objective

Physical Examination. Patients who indulge their thirst have no abnormalities on physical examination. When the ability to drink is interfered with, and when hypernatremia occurs, the subject may exhibit paranoia, irritability, muscle weakness and tenderness (or even paralysis), ataxia, and fever. With advancing dehydration the eyes appear sunken, mucous membranes become dry and cracked, moisture disappears from the axillae and inguinal regions, the skin "tents" when pinched, and pressure over a bony prominence results in "fingerprinting." When the sodium concentration approaches 180 mEq/L, confusion, stupor, coma, and death may supervene.

Routine Laboratory Abnormalities. In the absence of dehydration and hypernatremia, the routine laboratory studies are normal although the urine demonstrates a low specific gravity (≤ 1.005). When dehydration occurs there is a rise in the serum sodium concentration, a rise in the hematocrit, an elevation of the blood urea nitrogen (with a normal creatinine concentration), and the urine is dilute.

Plans

Dignostic

Differential Diagnosis. To be considered are diabetes mellitus, psychogenic polydipsia, use of drugs and medications (lithium, phenothiazines, anticholinergics), chronic renal disease, nephrogenic diabetes insipidus (including familial and acquired), primary aldosteronism, and hypercalcemia (either from a malignancy or from hyperparathyroidism).

Diagnostic Options and Recommended Approach. A 24-hour urine specimen is collected for volume and osmolality. If the volume is high (>3 L/24 hours) and the osmolality low (50–150 mOsm/L), 5 U of vasopression is administered parenterally and the osmolality rechecked. Doubling of the urine osmolality is diagnostic for diabetes insipidus; no response suggests nephrogenic diabetes insipidus. The dehydration test assists in distinguishing between psychogenic polydipsia and diabetes insipidus. Following the plateau phase of urine osmolality, 5 U of vasopression is administered parenterally. Plasma osmolality (pOsm) and urine osmolality (uOsm) are measured simultaneously. With psychogenic polydipsia the uOsm/pOsm ration remains constant or increases during dehydration; with diabetes insipidus, the ratio decreases due to an abrupt rise in uOsm.

Therapeutic

Therapeutic Options. When there is a complete deficiency of antidiuretic hormone, it must be replaced. This may be accomplished by the administration of parenteral vasopressin, with the frequent administration of an aqueous solution (every 3–6 hours), or by the use of a longer-acting preparation of vasopressin tannate in oil (every 24–72 hours). Where the lesion is incomplete (as following head trauma), administration of oral nonhormonal agents such as carbamazepine and chlorpropamide, which stimulate antidiuretic hormone secretion, is appropriate. For nephrogenic diabetes insipidus, hydrochlorothiazide and chlorthalidone are often effective. Magnetic resonance imaging of the hypothalamic and pituitary region is necessary to exclude a structural lesion that may be responsible for the deficiency.

Recommended Approach. When there is reason to suspect there may be residual antidiuretic hormone release (as is often the case following head trauma, localized pituitary lesions, and with idiopathic diabetes insipidus), chlorthalidone in a single daily dose of 200 to 500 mg may be sufficient. Carbamazepine as 200 mg two to three times a day may be added, as may clofibrate as 500 mg four times a day. If these agents are ineffective, antidiuretic hormone must be substituted. In patients who are able to drink freely, nasal insufflation of desmopressin as 10 to 20 µg every 12 to 24 hours is reliable. Alternatively, vasopressin tannate in oil in a dose of 2.5 to 5 U every 24 to 72 hours by intramuscular injection may be used. Aqueous vasopressin as 5 to 10 U subcutaneously every 3 to 6 hours is reserved for those with an altered level of consciousness and a changing clinical situation. Patients with nephrogenic diabetes insipidus may be treated with hydrochlorothiazide as 50 to 100 mg/d or with chorthalidone in a single daily dose of 50 mg.

Follow-up

Patients who are awake and alert may be followed by their degree of clinical comfort and with occasional monitoring of their 24-hour urine volumes. The unconscious patient requires monitoring of fluid volumes (both intake and output), serum sodium concentration, and careful attention to central venous pressure. All patients should carry some form of identification, be it a card in their wallet or a medical alert bracelet or necklace stating the diagnosis, medication, dose, and frequency of dosing.

Discussion

Prevalence and Incidence

Diabetes insipidus occurs in less than 1% of women with breast cancer and 7% of cases of men with lung cancer. It is seen most commonly in its idiopathic form (30–40% of cases) and following head trauma.

Related Basic Science

Antidiuretic hormone is a product of the supraopticoneurohypophyseal system, arising in magnocellular cells of the supraoptic and paraventricular nuclei and conveyed to the neurohypophysis and the median eminence from which it is released into the systemic circulation. It interacts with thirst, drinking behavior, and atrial natriuretic factor to regulate body water and osmolality. The supraopticoneurohypophyseal system is remarkably vulnerable and many intracranial processes may produce antidiuretic hormone insufficiency. In contrast, irreversible diabetes insipidus requires a loss of at least 90% of vasopressin-secreting cells, something that occurs only with direct hypothalamic injury. It is usually seen with tumors, the most common of which is an infiltrating dysgerminoma. Intrasellar lesions often produce subclinical deficiencies of antidiuretic hormone, and a degree of diabetes insipidus may be seen when a neoplasm destroys the posterior pituitary. In women this is most commonly a metastatic breast carcinoma, and in men, a metastatic lung cancer. Chronic granulomatous disease such as sarcoidosis and tuberculosis can result in a similar abnormality. Diabetes insipidus may follow trauma. It occurs after surgery on the posterior pituitary or on the pituitary stalk. Thirty percent of cases are idiopathic. Nephrogenic diabetes insipidus arises when the renal tubules fail to respond to antidiuretic hormone and may occur as an hereditary familial disorder or may be acquired from hypercalcemia (as in cancer or hyperparathyroidism), from hypokalemic nephropathy, or from renal amyloidosis, and it is seen in the context of acute relief of urinary obstruction. Rarely, antibodies to antidiuretic hormone may be part of an autoimmune disease.

Natural History and Its Modification with Treatment

Many cases of diabetes insipidus are subclinical, and so long as the patient is able to drink, dehydration and hypernatremia do not occur. Many cases, especially those following head trauma, are transient and improve so long as the patient is supported during the acute phase. In other cases in which there is a defined structural etiologic cause (such as metastatic cancer) the prognosis is dependent on the underlying illness rather than diabetes insipidus. So long as diabetes insipidus is recognized, and treated to prevent dehydration, a normal lifespan is possible but the natural history of the disorder may not be modifiable.

Prevention

Diabetes insipidus is not usually preventable. The prevention of bronchogenic carcinoma by avoiding tobacco would eliminate diabetes insipidus due to this cause.

Cost Containment

The diagnosis of diabetes insipidus should be established by laboratory means before using expensive techniques of imaging the hypothalamus and pituitary.

SYNDROME OF INAPPROPRIATE SECRETION OF ANTIDIURETIC HORMONE

Definition

Elevated or continued secretion of antidiuretic hormone in the context of evolving hyponatremia, plasma hyposmolality, normal renal excretion of sodium, and an inappropriately high urine osmolality, without evidence for depletion of body water, defines the syndrome of inappropriate secretion of antidiuretic hormone (SIADH).

Etiology

Parasellar neoplasms may cause excessive vasopressin release by direct compression or irritation of the hypothalamus. More often the disorder accompanies neoplastic disorders and is due to antidiuretic hormone elaboration by the tumor. Common neoplasms include bronchogenic carcinoma (80% of cases), pancreatic carcinoma, thymoma, malignant lymphoma including Hodgkin's disease, and malignant tumors of the gastrointestinal tract. A number of nonmalignant diseases are associated with this syndrome, including chronic lung disease such as tuberculosis and pleural empyema, stroke, and tetanus. It may also be seen as a neurotoxic complication of treatment with vincristine and as a consequence of the effect of the metabolites of cyclophosphamide on the kidney. It can be found following head trauma, during the course of subarachnoid hemorrhage, with encephalitis, and with meningitis. It can be due to the use of medications including carbamazepine, tricyclic antidepressants, and clofibrate, presumably by stimulating release of antidiuretic hormone. Other drugs such as vincristine and cyclophosphamide are directly toxic to neurohypophyseal tissue. SIADH is also seen with porphyria.

Criteria for Diagnosis

Suggestive

The presence of unexplained hyponatremia should alert the clinician to the possibility of SIADH.

Definitive

If hyponatremia is accompanied by an elevated urine osmolality, if the patient is not using diuretics, if there is no chronic renal disease, and if there are no stigmata of Addison's disease, the diagnosis of SIADH is likely.

Clinical Manifestations

Subjective

Unless hyponatremia is severe (<120–125 mEq/L), the patient is asymptomatic. As the serum sodium falls to this range, weight gain supervenes and weakness, lethargy, and nausea develop. As brain swelling evolves, seizures occur.

Objective

Physical Examination. When the serum sodium concentration is between 125 and 130 mEq/L the physical examinations is normal. Below 125 mEq/L, the patient may appear lethargic and confused but the elemental neurologic examination remains normal. When seizures occur the patient may demonstrate Babinski signs in the postictal phase. Peripheral edema is not found.

Routine Laboratory Abnormalities. There is hyponatremia with a serum sodium less than 130 mEq/L, serum hyposmolarity (<275 mOsm/L), and an increased urinary sodium (>30 mEq/L) associated with a relatively high urine osmolality. If measured, the plasma antidiuretic hormone level may be normal, but during dehydration it does not vary with changing osmolality.

Plan

Diagnostic

Differential Diagnosis. Hyponatremia may be noted with Addison's disease, chronic renal disease, and the use of diuretic medications. Sodium may also be lost in the course of protracted vomiting, with severe diarrhea, and occasionally with sweating.

Diagnostic Options. The diagnosis is established by measuring both plasma and urine osmolalities to confirm an inappropriate elevation of the latter in the face of hyponatremia and a low plasma osmolality. The history should ascertain the use of medications associated with this syndrome. Addison's disease can be excluded by the lack of abnormal skin pigmentation and a normal to low serum potassium. If doubt persists an 8:00 AM serum cortisol in the normal range and a normal adrenocorticotropic hormone level are useful. Vasopressin can be assayed in the unusual circumstance. A source for the high level of antidiuretic hormone should be sought. The evaluation should include chest roentgenography and computed tomography (CT) imaging if necessary. A head CT scan may be of some use. If signs or symptoms indicate an encephalitic or meningitic process, a lumbar puncture with examination of the cerebrospinal fluid may be helpful.

Recommended Approach. Measurement of the serum and urine osmolalities and serum and urine sodium concentrations, as well as serum electrolyte levels, should be sufficient to establish the diagnosis. An appropriate search for a cause for hypersecretion includes chest roentgenography and CT, a CT examination of the head, and an examination of the stool for occult blood. Further evaluation is guided by the results of these studies.

Therapeutic

Therapeutic Options. Fluid balance must be corrected by restricting fluid ingestion. Demeclocycline and lithium may prove clinically useful by antagonizing the effect of antidiuretic hormone at the level of the renal tubules.

Recommended Approach. When fluids are restricted to 800 to 1000 mL/d the serum sodium gradually increases toward normal. The result of treatment should be to restore a feeling of normalcy to the patient rather than striving for a normal serum sodium concentration. Demeclocycline in a dose of 600 to 1200 mg/d may be helpful, but it should not be used in the presence of liver disease, and it has caused acute renal failure. Lithium is no longer used because of adverse reactions in the treatment of hyponatremia. In the case of a dangerously low serum sodium (<110 mEq/L), or when the hyponatremia has caused disturbances in mentation or seizures, more rapid correction is needed to restore the sodium to an intermediate value (120–125 mEq/L). Three or five percent saline may be infused at the rate of 3 mL/kg of body weight per hour. Too rapid a correction may lead to central pontine myelinolysis. If possible, the source of the excessive antidiuretic hormone secretion should be identified and treated.

Follow-up

The patient may be followed by periodic evaluation of the serum sodium and monitoring the sense of well-being. Other follow-up is dependent on the cause of the SIADH.

Discussion

Prevalence and Incidence

The syndrome of inappropriate secretion of antidiuretic hormone is common.

Related Basic Science

Although not presently of demonstrated human clinical relevance, antidiuretic hormone has significant effects on memory in experimental model systems. It enhances both storage and retrieval of memory by its action on the limbic system. Memory testing in humans, in whom serum osmolality has improved with fluid restriction but in whom antidiuretic hormone remains elevated, would be instructive.

Natural History and Its Modification with Treatment

The prognosis of this disorder depends on the etiology and no general statement will suffice. When occurring in the context of a nonmalignant pulmonary or cerebral process, SIADH tends to improve gradually, necessitating a constant revision of therapy.

Prevention

This syndrome cannot be prevented.

Cost Containment

Rapid correction of a low sodium level, especially with hypertonic saline solutions, can cause central pontine myelinolysis, which requires intensive treatment and has a poor outcome.

Disorders of the Pituitary Gland

Signs and symptoms of dysfunction of the pituitary gland are due to disturbances from abnormalities of its hormone secretion and indirectly either from changes in the target organs and their secretions or from mechanical pressure on structures contiguous to the pituitary gland, their blood supplies, or both. It should be noted that the signs and symptoms of hormonal imbalance, although often involving the central nervous system, are far more striking in their systemic manifestations than in their central nervous system effects.

ACROMEGALY

Definition

Acromegaly results from the excessive secretion of growth hormone. There is resultant bony and soft tissue overgrowth in adults. In children the excessive secretion of growth hormone results in gigantism.

Etiology

Most commonly, acromegaly is a consequence of a pituitary tumor of the somatotroph series, although it may also be due to gangliocytomas of the hypothalamus that secrete growth hormone-releasing factor.

Criteria for Diagnosis

Suggestive

The disorder is suspected when there is overgrowth of the soft tissues of the hands and feet causing a change in ring or shoe size. There is coarsening of the facial features often noted by relatives and acquaintances, and in many cases there are complaints of headache (50%) and disturbances in vision (14–49%).

Definitive

The diagnosis is established when growth hormone levels remain elevated following an oral carbohydrate challenge. Because growth hormone levels are pulsatile, it is useful to measure blood levels of somatomedin C (also known as insulin-like growth factor I), a protein produced by the liver in response to the effects of growth hormone, for confirmation. If abnormal, imaging of the pituitary gland and hypothalamus by magnetic resonance imaging (MRI) is indicated.

Clinical Manifestations

Subjective

Patients with acromegaly complain of headache (50%). Less common complaints include loss of libido, impotence, and amenorrhea (when prolactin levels are elevated, either due to interruption of pituitary stalk dopaminergic pathways, with hypothalamic tumors, or due to cosecretion of prolactin from neoplastic cells). Patients may note an increase in ring or shoe size, and acquaintances may note a coarsening of facial features. Many patients complain of excessive sweating (60–80%). There is often numbness and paresthesias of the hands from median and ulnar compressive neuropathies, and proximal limb weakness from myopathy is not rare. Excessive drowsiness and sleepiness as well as a depressed mood may occur.

Objective

Physical Examination. Changes in facial appearance may be detected if early pictures of the patient, such as those on a driver's license, are available for scrutiny. Hypertension is found in as many as 30% of patients, and a gallop rhythm or displaced cardiac apex may be due to underlying hypertrophic cardiomyopathy, which is found in up to 50% of patients. Proximal muscle weakness may be prominent, as may be depressed deep tendon reflexes from a diffuse polyneuropathy. Sensory and motor abnormalities may be detected in the distributions of the ulnar and median nerves, and there may be Phelan and Tinel signs at the wrists as well as Tinel signs at the olecranon grooves.

Routine Laboratory Abnormalities. An elevated blood glucose level is common, as impaired glucose tolerance occurs in up to half of patients with acromegaly. Routine chest roentgenograms may reveal cardiomegaly and the bony changes of osteoporosis. Incidental roentgenograms of the hands may disclose "tufting" and "arrowhead" deformities of the distal phalanxes, and roentgenograms of the feet may show soft tissue thickening of the heel pads.

Plan

Diagnostic

Differential Diagnosis. One must distinguish between hypothalamic and pituitary acromegaly (usually accomplished by MRI). Rarely, tumors secreting growth hormone-releasing factor occur in the lung and in the thyroid gland. Ectopic growth hormone-secreting tumors are extremely rare. Acromegaly may occur in the context of the syndrome of multiple endocrine neoplasia, and one must be alert for the coexistence of panhypopituitarism due to glandular destruction by a pituitary tumor.

Diagnostic Options. Screening with a basal growth hormone determination at 8:00 AM may be helpful, but false normal results are common due to the pulsatile nature of growth hormone release. Measurement of growth hormone levels at 1 and 2 hours following an oral glucose challenge are necessary, and measurement of somatomedin C is confirmatory. MRI is much preferred over CT scanning. Routine skull radiographs are no longer used.

Electromyographic and nerve conduction velocity testing confirms a polyneuropathy and changes of the carpal tunnel syndrome as well as ulnar entrapment neuropathy.

Recommended Approach. Blood should be obtained for a somatomedin C level and then the patient presented with an oral glucose load of 100 g, with growth hormone levels obtained 60 and 120 minutes after glucose ingestion. If growth hormone levels greater than 2 ng/mL in males or 5 ng/mL in females are detected in either time interval, MRI of the hypothalamus and pituitary gland is obtained. Visual fields are quantitatively measured, and in the case of a pituitary or hypothalamic tumor, levels of other pituitary hormones including thyroid-stimulating hormone, follicle-stimulating hormone, luteinizing hormone, testosterone (in males), adrenocorticotropic hormone, and prolactin are determined. Determination of serum electrolytes and serum and urine osmoalties serves to confirm the adequate secretion of antidiuretic hormone.

Therapeutics

Therapeutic Options. The goal of treatment is to obtain normal growth hormone levels. Modalities for treatment include pharmacotherapy, surgery, and radiation. Pharmocotherapeutic modalities include dopamine agonists and somatostatin. Some adenomas of the pituitary gland, especially those that secrete both growth hormone and prolactin, contain dopamine receptors. Blockade of these receptors by agonists such as bromocriptine leads to a decrease in growth hormone secretion in as many as 70% of the tumors; however, growth hormone levels are reduced to less than 5 ng/mL in only 10 to 20% of the tumors, and the tumor mass is reduced little, if at all. Treatment is begun with 1.25 mg of bromocriptine per day and increased every other week to a total daily dose of 40 mg per day in three divided doses. Side effects include nausea, hypotension, and psychiatric symptoms including hallucinations. Octreotide is a long-acting somatostatin analog that can reduce tumor mass by 30 to 40%. Growth hormone levels are reduced to below 5 ng/mL in 80 to 90% of microadenomas and in 50% of macroadenomas. Somatostatin is given subcutaneously three times daily in an average dose of 100 mg (range, 50–250 mg). When given prior to surgery, octreotide results in more complete tumor removal due to a reduction in tumor mass. Surgical removal of the tumor can be employed as a primary treatment modality, especially when there are mass effects such as visual compromise. Pituitary apoplexy (hemorrhagic infarction of the tumor) is considered a surgical emergency. The surgical approach may be transsphenoidal, which gives good visualization of the sellar contents and less chance of damage to cranial nerves or the frontal lobes, or it may be transcranial, which provides better access when the tumor is parasellar or suprasellar, when it invades the subfrontal or retrochiasmal regions, or when the tumor is invasive or malignant. Radiation therapy may be used as a primary treatment modality, or when growth hormone levels continue to exceed 5 ng/mL 3 months after

surgery, or when pharmacotherapy is either ineffective or poorly tolerated. Radiation options include conventional high-voltage radiation; heavy-particle therapy using alpha particles or protons; and transsphenoidal implantation of a radionuclide. The transsphenoidal approach is most useful for intrasellar adenomas and the proton beam for well-defined intrasellar adenomas without significant extension.

Recommended Approach. Whenever possible, growth hormone-producing pituitary tumors should be removed surgically and preferably by the transsphenoidal route. In advance of surgery, medical management should be initiated and maintained for about 3 months with octreotide. If octreotide is not tolerated, or is ineffective, bromocriptine may be substituted. If growth hormone levels remain above 5 ng/mL 3 or 4 months after surgery, octreotide or bromocriptine should be reinstituted. Only if elevated growth hormone levels persist after 3 to 4 months of medical management should radiation therapy be considered. During radiation, pharmacotherapy is continued but it is stopped for 4 weeks every year to see if and when radiation has been effective. Radiation as a primary therapeutic choice is recommended only if the patient is not an operable candidate and pharmacotherapy has proven ineffective or is not tolerated.

Follow-up

Each patient should have a neurologic examination that includes visual acuity and visual fields every year. This should be accompanied by an endocrinologic assessment that includes the pituitary hormones.

Discussion

Prevalence and Incidence

Acromegaly occurs with an incidence of 5.3 per 100,000 per year. It occurs in the fourth and fifth decades. It is estimated that 6 years elapse between the onset of symptoms and the definitive diagnosis.

Related Basic Science

The tumors secreting growth hormone are somatotrophs, often secrete both prolactin and growth hormone, and often contain cell surface receptors for dopamine. The tumors are usually intensely eosinophilic staining and were classified as eosinophilic adenomas, although those without sufficient granules to stain were classified as chromophobe adenomas.

Natural History and Its Modification with Treatment

The life expectancy of a patient with untreated acromegaly is about 50 years, most dying from a hypertrophic cardiomyopathy and malignant ventricular arrythmias. Osteoporosis with fractures and painful arthropathies are frequent complications. Although glucose intolerance is common, very few develop ketoacidosis or other significant complications of diabetes mellitus. The tumor itself may compromise both visual acuity and visual fields, leading to significant visual loss and disability. When acromegaly is adequately treated, life expectancy returns to normal and the other complications remit.

Prevention

Acromegaly cannot be prevented.

Cost Containment

Skull roentgenography with imaging of the sella turcica is no longer performed. MRI is superior to CT scanning.

CUSHING'S DISEASE AND CUSHING'S SYNDROME

Definition

Both Cushing's disease and Cushing's syndrome are defined by hypercortisolism. Cushing's disease is caused by excessive adrenocorticotropic hormone (ACTH) secretion from a pituitary adenoma. All other causes of hypercortisolism represent Cushing's syndrome.

Etiology

The vast majority of cases of hypercortisolism represent Cushing's disease and are due to a pituitary adenoma that secretes ACTH. Most cases of Cushing's syndrome are due to the medicinal use of glucocorticoids. In perhaps 15% of cases, the hypercortisolism of Cushing's syndrome is due either to a tumor of the adrenal gland that secretes cortisol autonomously or to ectopic ACTH production by a remote neoplasm, which is usually both malignant and metastatic. Very rarely, Cushing's syndrome may be due to excessive release of corticotropin-releasing factor from a hypothalamic or ectopic tumor.

Criteria for Diagnosis

Subjective

Features that alert the clinician to a diagnosis of Cushing's disease include a change in body habitus with obesity of the upper third of the body, sparing the arms and the legs ("truncal" obesity); thinning of the skin with easy bruising; a purplish discoloration to abdominal striae; facial plethora; and increased fat over the upper thoracic dorsal spine ("buffalo or dowager's hump"). Hypertension, glucose intolerance, and leg weakness increase the index of suspicion.

Definitive

The diagnosis is established by the determination of elevated 24-hour urinary free cortisol levels greater than 150 μg/24 h. When hypercortisolism is due to a pituitary adenoma or ectopic production of ACTH by a tumor, the blood ACTH level exceeds 400 pg/mL. When the ACTH level is low, cortisol production is most likely due to a tumor of the adrenal gland. Visualization of a pituitary adenoma by MRI or an adrenal tumor by gadolinium-enhanced MRI or discovery of a malignant or metastatic tumor is then confirmatory.

Clinical Manifestations

Subjective

Patients note a change in their bodily appearance with obesity. They are seldom aware of the truncal and facial predilection for the fat deposition, but women in particular are aware of a dorsal deposition of fat ("dowager's hump"). Common complaints include easy bruising and leg weakness (especially when climbing stairs or arising from the toilet). Lassitude, depression, manic outbursts, and sleep disturbances are common. Women of childbearing years may develop amenorrhea. Men admit to impotence when specifically questioned. Pedal edema, exertional dyspnea, orthopnea, and paroxysmal nocturnal dyspnea may announce heart failure.

Objective

Physical Examination. Truncal obesity, increased facial fat ("moon" facies), and dowager's hump are present in more than 90% of patients. Skin atrophy with abnormal pigmentation of pressure points (over the elbows, knees, ischial tuberosities and where the buccal mucosa contacts the teeth, as well as hyperpigmentation and a purple discoloration of abdominal striae) is present in 80% of patients. Hirsutism and acne are common. An elevated blood pressure is found in more than 80% of cases. Pedal edema is not uncommon. Proximal myopathic weakness of the upper and lower extremities can often be detected. The examiner should have the patient arise from a chair without using the hands; inability to comply suggests proximal muscle weakness of the pelvic girdle. The physical findings with the greatest discriminatory value are obesity, hirsutism, menstrual irregularity, hypertension, diabetes mellitus, ecchymoses, and muscle weakness.

Routine Laboratory Abnormalities. Fasting hyperglycemia, glycosuria, impaired glucose tolerance, and hypokalemic alkalosis may be present. Occasionally there is hypernatremia. Roentgenograms may demonstrate osteoporosis and pathologic fractures.

Plans

Diagnostic

Differential Diagnosis. Considerations include exogenous ingestion of cortisol or other steroids, ectopic production of ACTH from primary and metastatic malignant tumors; and cortisol production from an adrenal tumor. Depression and other emotional states, anorexia nervosa, chronic illness, and alcoholism can cause an abnormal dexamethasone suppression test. Alcoholics may also mimic the features of Cushing's disease because of hypertension, facial plethora, glucose intolerance, ecchymoses, and proximal muscle weakness.

Diagnostic Options. Blood cortisol levels obtained at 8:00 AM and 4:00 PM normally show the afternoon value to be half or less than that of the morning value, a pattern often lost in Cushing's disease. A low-dose dexamethasone suppression test may be employed for screening purposes: 1 mg of dexamethasone taken at midnight normally results in a blood cortisol level at 8:00 AM the following morning that is less than 5 μg/mL or half the baseline value. Patients with Cushing's disease fail to show this suppression. The 24-hour urinary excretion of free cortisol is elevated in Cushing's disease. A normal value is less than 75 μg/24 h; borderline values are 75 to 150 μg/24 h; diagnostic levels exceed 150 μg/24 h. A blood ACTH level in excess of 400 pg/mL indicates ACTH secretion by a pituitary adenoma or ectopic production of ACTH by a primary malignant or metastatic tumor. A high-dose dexamethasone suppression test may be performed when the low-dose test is abnormal and the urinary free cortisol level is elevated: 8 mg of dexamethasone is given at midnight and ACTH and blood cortisol levels are measured the following morning. In cases of small (< 5 mm) pituitary tumors, recourse may be had to catheter sampling of the petrosal sinuses and to sampling of other suspected body sites for ACTH determination in the case of an ectopic tumor. A pituitary adenoma may be imaged by either CT or MRI. An adrenal cortical tumor may be imaged by CT, by MRI, or by abdominal ultrasound. Adrenal scanning may also be employed.

Recommended Approach. In cases of suspected Cushing's disease or syndrome, a 24-hour urine is collected for free cortisol and an 8:00 AM blood specimen obtained for baseline cortisol. A low-dose dexamethasone test is performed: 1 mg of dexamethasone is ingested between 11:00 PM and midnight and a blood cortisol level obtained at 8:00 AM. If the urinary cortisol is normal and the suppressed blood cortisol is less than half the baseline or below 5 μg/mL, Cushing's disease and syndrome are excluded. When abnormal, blood is obtained for an ACTH level and a high-dose dexamethasone suppression test is employed: 8 mg of dexamethasone is ingested between 11:00 PM and midnight and blood for cortisol is obtained at 8:00 AM. If ACTH is not detectable and cortisol is not suppressed, an adrenal tumor is present; if ACTH is elevated and there is no suppression, ACTH is being produced from an ectopic site; if ACTH is normal or elevated and cortisol is suppressed to less than half the baseline, Cushing's disease is present. In the case of the latter, the pituitary gland is visualized by MRI with gadolinium contrast enhancement. Where a pituitary tumor is not visualized because of small size (about 50% of cases), selective catheterization of the inferior petrosal sinuses for ACTH levels is needed to confirm a pituitary etiology. In the case of an adrenal tumor, any of the visualization methods is sufficient (CT, MRI, or ultrasound). On occasion, radionuclide scanning of the adrenal gland may be useful. In the case of ectopic secretion of ACTH, appropriate radiographic, CT, MRI and ultrasound imaging must all be applied to the search for a tumor, and when found, venous sampling for ACTH secretion is indicated.

Therapeutic

Therapeutic Options. The goal of therapy is to reduce the level of cortisol to normal. Treatment modalities include surgery, heavy-particle radiation, and chemotherapy. For an ACTH-secreting pituitary adenoma, the surgical procedure of choice is a transsphenoidal adenoma removal. Bilateral adrenalectomy may be indicated if the pituitary tumor cannot be removed, if the source of ACTH production cannot be found, or production from a widespread metastatic tumor makes direct surgical removal improbable. Primary heavy-particle radiation is reserved for those patients who are not surgical candidates or who refuse surgery. It is less effective than surgery, giving good results in 50 to 80%, as contrasted with transsphenoidal tumor removal with a 90% success rate. Conventional radiation is effective in only 15 to 25% of cases, and once used, it precludes the use of heavy particles. Medical management is limited and is usually restricted to the preoperative phase or when the source of ACTH is unknown or cannot be surgically removed.

Bromocriptine has the least side effects but is least active. Reserpine, cyproheptadine, and valproic acid may reduce ACTH production but are not often very effective. Drugs that inhibit cortisol secretion may be used when other treatments are not successful. Ketoconazole given as 400 to 500 mg twice a day is often effective, but is toxic to the liver. Metyrapone given as 2 g/d and aminoglutethemide as 1 g/d, each divided into four equal doses, may be useful but have gastrointestinal side effects and result in excessive ACTH levels, which eventually overcome enzyme inhibition, making them ineffective for long-term use. Mitotane used in doses of 3 to 6 g/d can also be given.

Recommended Approach. When Cushing's disease or syndrome is due to ACTH overproduction, the source of the hormone should be surgically extirpated whenever possible. In the case of a pituitary adenoma, transsphenoidal removal is the method of choice. There is often immediate transient suppression of pituitary function, which will return to normal. Hydrocortisone is given as 100 mg intravenously every 8 hours on the day of surgery and for 2 to 3 days after. The dose is then reduced to 15 mg/m^2 for the next week or two. A morning dose of hydrocortisone is then witheld and an 8:00 AM blood cortisol level is measured; hydrocortisone is then given. If the blood level is greater than 12.5 µg/mL, the hydrocortisone can safely be discontinued. When a pituitary adenoma cannot be surgically removed, radiotherapy is indicated. If the source of ACTH cannot be located, or is too diffuse to be affected by radiation, pharmacotherapy may be attempted and, if ineffective, chemical or surgical adrenalectomy can be considered. Cortisol-secreting adrenal adenomas and carcinomas should be removed surgically whenever possible. Adrenalectomy may result in a secondary basophilic pituitary adenoma with ACTH overproduction (Nelson's syndrome) which causes skin hyperpigmentation. The adenoma can undergo malignant degeneration. Such tumors may be removed by transsphenoidal hypophysectomy or by radiation.

Follow-up

Patients having undergone a successful transsphenoidal tumor removal have a significant incidence of tumor recurrence over the next 3 to 4 years, and yearly reevaluation is indicated with both MRI and 24-hour urinary free cortisol determinations. For Cushing's syndrome, the extent of follow-up in large measure is determined by the nature of the etiology.

Discussion

Prevalence and Incidence

Cushing's disease is more common in women than in men (female:male ratio 8:1) although rarely it occurs in infants and children. In women it occurs predominantly from ages 20 to 40. Cushing's disease accounts for 60% of cases of hypercortisolism. Spontaneous Cushing's syndrome is a rare disorder, whereas iatrogenic Cushing's syndrome, due to administration of glucocorticoids, is common.

Related Basic Science

Significantly increased skin pigmentation is most commonly noted in Cushing's syndrome due to ACTH-producing extrapituitary neoplasms, although it is sometimes noted with Cushing's disease as well. In patients with pituitary adenomas one most commonly observes the peculiar pattern of fat distribution previously described. With extrapituitary ACTH-secreting tumors, the cushingoid fat distribution rarely if ever occurs, perhaps owing to the shortened survival time of this group.

Natural History and Its Modification with Treatment

In those with untreated Cushing's disease, life expectancy is shortened due to hypertension-induced cardiovascular disease, congestive heart failure, the complications of diabetes mellitus, and a propensity to thromboembolic disease. The quality of life is impaired by psychiatric abnormalities, asthenia, and proximal muscle weakness. Patients with adrenal cortical adenomas have basically the same outlook as those with pituitary adenomas. Patients with metastatic malignant tumors producing ACTH have a very short life expectancy.

Prevention

Cushing's disease cannot be prevented. ACTH-producing lung carcinomas may possibly be avoided by smoking cessation, and perhaps by avoidance of radon gas and other carcinogens. Other causes of Cushing's syndrome cannot be prevented.

Cost Containment

The low-dose dexamethasone suppression test should always be the starting point in the evaluation of Cushing's disease.

HYPERPROLACTINEMIA

Definition

Hyperprolactinemia is defined as an elevation of the prolactin level above 25 ng/mL in women of childbearing years and above 20 ng/mL in men and postmenopausal women.

Etiology

In most instances hyperprolactinemia is the result of a prolactin-secreting microadenoma or macroadenoma of the pituitary. It is also cosecreted with growth hormone and ACTH in some tumors. Nonsecreting adenomas of the pituitary gland or hypothalamus may cause elevations in prolactin due to interference with dopaminergic inhibitory mechanisms.

Criteria for Diagnosis

Suggestive

Although often asymptomatic, women may experience irregular menses, amenorrhea, and anovulatory sterility. Men may note impotence and azospermia. Both sexes may experience gynecomastia, galactorrhea, and headaches.

Definitive

By definition, hyperprolactinemia is suspected when the prolactin level exceeds 20 to 25 ng/mL. Prolactinomas are found only when the prolactin level exceeds 150 ng/mL.

Clinical Manifestations

Subjective

Headaches are very common, occurring in about 60% of male and female patients. Amenorrhea is often noted in women when the prolactin level exceeds 40 ng/mL, and is routinely present when the level exceeds 100 ng/mL. In both men and women there may be a decrease in libido, and impotence occurs in up to 8% of men. Gynecomastia and galactorrhea are common in women, but occur in only about 13% of men.

Objective

Physical Examination. The physical examination may be entirely normal, but occasionally gynecomastia, which is more readily detected in men than in women, may be noted. Palpation of the breasts may express milk in either sex. Hirsutism may be evident but difficult to assess. On occasion there may be a visual field defect to confrontation as the result of the pressure of a large pituitary tumor on the optic chiasm.

Routine Laboratory Abnormalities. There are no routine laboratory abnormalities. Roentgenograms, obtained for other reasons, may show osteoporosis.

Plans

Diagnostic

Differential Diagnosis. Elevations of prolactin are found in hypothyroidism, with adrenal insufficiency, in chronic renal disease with dialysis, and with polycystic kidney disease. Hyperprolactinemia is found in association with the use of a number of psychotropic medications including dopamine antagonists, antidepressants, lithium, valproic acid, buspirone, carbamazepine and even the benzodiazepines. Other drugs such as verapamil and H_2-receptor-blocking agents may cause prolactin elevations. Prolactin levels are elevated soon after a generalized tonic–clonic convulsion, returning to normal within 45 minutes to an hour.

Diagnostic Options and Recommended Approach. Blood should be drawn through an indwelling catheter for a prolactin level. If infertility is being evaluated, a nocturnal sample may be worthwhile for identification of nocturnal hyperprolactinemia.

Skull roentgenograms, rarely indicated, may show enlargement of the sella turcica or suprasellar calcifications in the event of the rare craniopharyngioma causing interference with hypothalamic function. When prolactin levels are elevated, MRI of the pituitary gland, pituitary stalk, and hypothalamus are indicated.

Therapeutic

Therapeutic Options. Hyperprolactinemia is often asymptomatic. Symptoms arise as a result of the mass effect of the tumor or are due to the physiologic effects of the hormone. If the hormone elevation is due to a tumor other than a prolactin-secreting microadenoma or macroadenoma, treatment depends on the nature of the tumor. When the elevation is due to a prolactin-secreting adenoma, or no definite tumor or identifiable etiology is discerned, treatment depends on whether or not symptoms are present. When asymptomatic, both from a mass and hormonal point of view, no treatment is required. One may elect to follow the patient with serial MRI and prolactin levels. When symptomatic, treatment options include surgical extirpation of the tumor, usually through a transsphenoidal approach; conventional radiation; and pharmacotherapy employing dopamine agonists such as bromocriptine and pergolide.

Recommended Approach. When hyperprolactinemia either is due to a prolactin-secreting adenoma (prolactinoma) or no definite cause can be determined, and is asymptomatic, no treatment is indicated. Prolactin levels should be followed at 6-month intervals and MRI is useful every 2 to 4 years to allow detection of tumor progression. When symptomatic for any reason, the treatment of choice is a dopamine agonist such as bromocriptine or pergolide. These agents not only lower prolactin levels, but lead to tumor shrinkage in a substantial number of patients. Bromocriptine is given twice daily and is begun as 1.25 mg once a day and increased by 1.25 mg every month until the prolactin level falls below 20 ng/mL. This usually requires about 2.5 mg twice daily. Bromocriptine may be given in doses of up to 30 to 45 mg/d if needed and tolerated. Pergolide is usually administered three times a day and is begun as a single dose of 0.05 mg for the first 2 days and then may be increased by 0.1 to 0.15 mg every third day for the next 12 days. It may then be increased by 0.25 mg every third day until the prolactin level falls below 20 ng/mL. Pergolide may be used in dosages up to 5 mg/d in three divided doses. Either medication may be discontinued during pregnancy as tumoral enlargement is rare. Surgery and radiation are reserved for those symptomatic patients in whom medical management does not afford relief.

Follow-up

Prolactin levels should be obtained twice yearly and an MRI of the pituitary gland obtained every 2 years initially and every 4 years if both the tumor size and prolactin levels are stable, whether or not the patient is under active treatment.

Discussion

Prevalence and Incidence

Hyperprolactinemia is the most common cause of pituitary hyperfunction. It is present in up to 25% of infertile women. It occurs in 60 to 80% of all cases of pituitary gland tumors.

Related Basic Science

Prolactin is a peptide that is continuously secreted from the anterior pituitary gland with a pulsatile or ultradian rhythm dependent on neural influences, sleep, and the protein content of meals. It circulates in both a glycosylated as well as a nonglycoslylated form, as a monomer or a polymer, and a small amount may be antibody bound. Stimulation of increased amplitude of secretory pulses of prolactin is also caused by thyroid-releasing hormone, by vasoactive intestinal polypeptide, by go-

nadotropin-releasing hormone, by serotoninergic and opioidergic pathways, and, possibly, by galanin. Secretion of prolactin is under tonic inhibitory control by dopamine secreted by cells of the tuberoinfundibular system and released into the hypophyseal portal system. Some inhibitory influence is exerted by γ-aminobutyric acid (GABA) and perhaps by endothelins. Excessive prolactin secretion may occur with any lesion capable of affecting the tuberoinfundibular dopaminergic cells or by lesions that compress the pituitary gland or pituitary stalk and interfere with the impingement of dopamine on the pituitary gland. It may result from functional derangements of neurotransmitters as described above, and it may result from a prolactin-secreting pituitary tumor. Hyperprolactinemia is found in 70% of patients with nonfunctioning pituitary tumors. It is also cosecreted with both growth hormone and ACTH and is therefore often found in association with both acromegaly and Cushing's disease. Almost 30% of pituitary adenomas are true prolactinomas.

Natural History and Its Modification with Treatment

Primary prolactinomas, whether micro- or macroadenomas, are generally benign and tend not to progress. When asymptomatic, they may be followed by clinical and laboratory methods. When symptomatic, they usually respond promptly to dopamine agonists, demonstrating both a lowering of prolactin levels to normal and a shrinkage of tumor bulk in the majority of cases.

Prevention

Hyperprolactinemia cannot be prevented, although the medications known to elevate prolactin levels can be avoided. Often that is neither feasible nor necessary.

Cost Containment

Knowledge of the basically benign nature of most cases of hyperprolactinemia allows for a conservative approach in most cases. Where asymptomatic, simple serial laboratory and radiographic evaluation is all that is needed. Where treatment is needed, relatively inexpensive medical management suffices, avoiding costly and sometimes dangerous surgery or radiation therapy.

HYPOPITUITARISM

Definition

Hypopituitarism is a condition whereby there is a deficiency of all of the hormones of the pituitary gland, which include thyroid-stimulating hormone (TSH), growth hormone, ACTH, follicle-stimulating hormone (FSH), luteinizing hormone (LH), prolactin, oxytocin, and vasopressin. As a result of the loss of these hormones, there are deficiencies of triiodothyronine (T_3), thyroxine (T_4), cortisol, and testosterone.

Etiology

Those conditions leading to pituitary deficiency are the same as those causing hypothalamic dysfunction. With the latter, the damage is bilateral and can be assumed when, in addition to endocrine disturbances, there are symptoms of obesity (suggesting altered food intake), impaired thermoregulation, alterations in affect and arousal (apathy and rage), and alterations in memory. Among the causes are inflammatory and neoplastic disease such as meningoencephalitis, Hand–Schüller–Christian disease, toxoplasmosis, syphilis, tuberculosis, sarcoidosis, dysgerminomas, teratomas, choriocarcinomas, and metastatic malignancies. On rare occasion, lymphocytic adenohypophysitis may be the result of an autoimmune disorder. Both intrasellar and parasellar tumors can be responsible, including secreting and nonsecreting pituitary adenomas and craniopharyngiomas. Miscellaneous causes include pituitary gland infarction, carotid artery aneurysms, and subarachnoid hemorrhage.

Criteria for Diagnosis

Subjective

Most patients are aware of a general feeling of apathy with decreased interest and energy. Weight loss is usually prominent and abdominal pain or discomfort is frequent.

Definitive

There are demonstrable deficiencies of multiple hormones. Plasma growth hormone may be low, Somatomedin C is low, and growth hormone fails to elevate in response to a hypoglycemic challenge provoked by intravenous insulin or oral levodopa. T_4, T_3, and TSH levels are low. FSH, LH, and testosterone levels are depressed. FSH and prolactin fail to rise with administration of intravenous thyrotropin-releasing hormone. Morning serum cortisol levels are low and are less than twice the evening values; 24 hours urinary free cortisol levels are low. Urine and plasma osmolality may be low consequent to antidiuretic hormone deficiency. Radiographic imaging usually shows the responsible lesion in the sella, parasellar region, or hypothalamus.

Clinical Manifestations

Subjective

Depending on the etiology of the disorder, there may be symptoms due to local manifestations, such as headache, impaired visual acuity, and diplopia. The patient may be aware of polydipsia and polyuria and is usually aware of a lack of energy, alterations in mood and affect, weight loss, and impaired libido and sexual ability. Postpartum women may stop lactating, an indication of prolactin deficiency, perhaps due to postpartum pituitary infarction (Sheehan's syndrome).

Objective

Physical Examination. Examination of the eye grounds may disclose papilledema in the case of intracranial neoplasms and there may be impairment of ocular motility and balance. Visual acuity may be impaired and confrontation visual fields may demonstrate a defect. There may be difficulty in concentration, and there may be difficulty with recent memory. "Punched out" lesions of retinal sarcoidosis may be present. There is often evidence of recent weight loss (extra holes punched in a belt, loose shirt collar, rings, and watch band). The patients usually appear pale owing to a loss of skin pigmentation, the skin may have a "waxy" appearance, and there is loss of axillary and pubic hair, although testicular and penis size are normal. The pulse rate is usually slow and the blood pressure is often low normal and demonstrates an orthostatic fall. Periorbital and perioral wrinkling is common.

Routine Laboratory Abnormalities. A moderate normochromic normocytic anemia is common, although on occasion it may be either hypochromic or macrocytic. Urine specific gravity or osmolality is often low. If sarcoidosis is the cause of the syndrome, the serum calcium may be modestly elevated. Chest radiography may demonstrate lymph node enlargement and interstitial changes in the presence of sarcoidosis, and may reveal cavity lesions in the case of tuberculosis. A primary or metastatic lung tumor may be detected, and the ribs may show the lesions of eosinophilic granuloma. The electrocardiogram is often of low voltage and substantiates bradycardia.

Plans

Diagnostic

Differential Diagnosis. Chronic malnutrition and liver disease may produce weakness, lethargy, cold intolerance, and a decrease in libido, suggesting hypopituitarism. Anorexia nervosa may also simulate this disorder. Primary failure of individual endocrine glands must also be considered, such as primary gonadal failure or primary adrenal insufficiency.

Diagnostic Options. Three avenues of approach are available for the assessment of suspected hypopituitarism.

1. Measurement of static levels of pituitary hormones or those of their target organs:
   - Plasma growth hormone and somatomedin C
   - Serum prolactin
   - TSH, T_3, T_4, and free T_4
   - FSH, LH, and testosterone
   - 24-hour free urine cortisol excretion, plasma cortisol at 8:00 AM and 4:00 PM (the morning value is usually double that of the evening), and serum ACTH
   - Serum and urine sodium and osmolality

2. Measurement of stimulated levels of pituitary hormones or those of their target organs:
   - Plasma growth hormone before and 30, 60, and 120 minutes after stimulation by insulin 0.1 U/kg intravenously or levodopa 10 mg/kg orally
   - Serum prolactin levels before and 20 minutes after administration of thyrotorpin-releasing hormone 250 µg intravenously
   - Serum FSH before and after intravenous thyrotropin-releasing hormone
   - ACTH response during insulin-induced hypoglycemia, obtained at the same time as the plasma growth hormone
   - Functional testing for antidiuretic hormone deficiency as has been described previously

3. Imaging procedures for the pituitary gland and hypothalamus to discern the structural abnormality causing the hormonal deficiencies. (Modalities include skull roentgenography with tomography of the sella turcica, contrast-enhanced CT scanning, and MRI with gadolinium contrast enhancement.)

Recommended Approach. For adequate assessment of hypopituitarism, all three methods are used. Basal values for all hormones are assessed as indicated above, usually at the time of a stimulation test where available for the appropriate hormone. Routine skull roentgenography and tomography of the sella turcica are rarely used, and MRI with gadolinium enhancement is the preferred imaging modality.

Therapeutic

Therapeutic Options. Wherever possible, the etiology of the disorder is treated. That may include surgery, medical therapy, or radiation of a tumor, immunosuppresion of an inflammatory disorder, or specific antibacterial treatment for infections such as tuberculosis. Thyroid hormone and adrenal corticosteroids must be replaced on a daily basis. Treatment with sex hormones is situation dependent. Diabetes insipidus can be managed as discussed earlier.

Recommended Approach. Female hypogonadism should be treated with the simultaneous administration of an estrogenic preparation such as conjugated equine estrogens 0.6 mg daily in association with a progestational agent to suppress endometrial hyperplasia and reduce the risk of endometrial carcinoma. Estrogen therapy is necessary to prevent osteoporosis and atrophy of the vaginal mucosa. Treatment with estrogen and a progestational agent does not improve libido, and a low dose of an androgen may be added if needed. If fertility is the goal, ovulation may be induced by the pulsatile pump administration of gonadotropins; human menopausal gonadotropins and human chorionic gonadotropins, as well as LH-releasing hormone, are available, but should be administered by a specialist in problems of fertility. Male hypogonadism may be treated with testosterone enanthate given intramuscularly in a dose of 100 to 200 mg every 1 to 3 weeks. This improves libido and preserves secondary sexual characteristics, but does not improve fertility. Spermatogenesis may be induced by the administration of gonadotropins, as discussed above. Where needed, adrenal corticosteroid replacement should precede replacement with thyroid hormone, as the latter increases metabolism of the steroid hormones and might precipitate adrenal insufficiency. Replacement may proceed with hydrocortisone, 15 to 20 mg in the morning and 5 to 10 mg at 4 to 6 PM. Cortisone acetate may be substituted for hydrocortisone in doses of 25 mg in the morning and 12.5 mg in the evening. The dose may be doubled or tripled during superimposed illnesses ("stress" doses). Mineralocorticoid production is relatively free of dependency on ACTH and need not be replaced in most instances. Thyroid hormone is introduced as levothyroxine beginning with 0.125 mg per day, with increases dependent on the T_4 level. Growth hormone is used for the correction of linear growth and is therefore of use only in childhood and adolescence.

Follow-up

Most patients require a lifetime of treatment. Diabetes insipidus is managed by periodic documentation of urine production. Periodic measurement of the blood pressure and serum sodium and potassium levels (about 3-month intervals) is usually sufficient to assess the adequacy of adrenal corticosteroid administration. Blood T$_4$ levels should be measured every 3 to 6 months.

Discussion

Prevalence and Incidence

Panhypopituitarism is rare and, in general, is an uncommon complication of a number of disorders, all of which have their own incidence and prevalence.

Related Basic Science

In cases of acute hypopituitarism, as might be true with acute postpartum pituitary necrosis (Sheehan's syndrome), a major concern is the development of acute adrenal insufficiency. Treatment is immediately begun with an intravenous bolus of 100 mg of hydrocortisone followed by a continuous intravenous infusion of 5 mg/h. After 24 hours, the dose is reduced to 2.5 mg/h. At the end of 24 hours, maintenance is begun with either oral hydrocortisone or cortisone in doses as described above.

Natural History and Its Modification with Treatment

The course of panhypopituitarism is dependent on two independent factors. The first is the nature and severity of the hormonal deficiencies. ACTH deficiency leading to secondary adrenal insufficiency may prove acutely life threatening or may be so at the first occurrence of an unrelated illness or stress, such as pneumonia. Antidiuretic hormone deficiency may become life threatening when drinking behavior is altered, such as following head trauma or during the course of surgical procedures. Estrogen deficiency may lead to long-term osteoporosis and pathologic fractures, and thyroid deficiency to cardiovascular disease because of abnormalities of lipid metabolism. All of these effects are favorably modified by hormone replacement. The second factor is the etiology of the hormone deficiency. When it is caused by a lung carcinoma metastatic to the sella turcica, the prognosis becomes that of the tumor rather than of the hormonal deficiency. Thus, the availability of effective treatment for the etiologic agent determines the long-term prognosis.

Prevention

Depending on the etiology, panhypopituitarism may be preventable by treating the underlying disease, such as pulmonary tuberculosis. In most cases, the underlying disease either is not recognized or cannot be prevented (such as pituitary adenomas and craniopharyngiomas).

Cost Containment

Hormone replacement and periodic follow-up are relatively inexpensive. Emergency treatment of adrenal insufficiency (when not recognized or previously inadequately treated and followed) is very expensive, as are the long-term consequences of osteoporosis and cardiovascular disease.

Disorders of the Endocrine Glands

See Section 9.

REFERENCES

Endocrine and reproductive diseases. In: Wyngaarden JB, Smith LH Jr, Bennett JC, eds. *Cecil Textbook of Medicine.* 19th ed. Philadelphia: Saunders, vol. 2, XVI, p. 1195.

Martin JB, Reichlin S, eds. Clinical endocrinology. 2nd ed. Philadelphia: Davis, 1987.

Pleet AB, Saphir DJ. Neurologic aspects of endocrine disturbances. In: Joynt, RJ ed. Clinical neurology. Philadelphia: Lippincott, 1992; vol. 4, ch. 62, p. 1.

CHAPTER 20–21

Aphasia and Related Disorders

Daniel H. Jacobs, M.D.

DEFINITION

Aphasia is an acquired disorder of previously intact language ability secondary to brain damage. As defined here, aphasia does not include developmental disorders of language, nor speech disorders limited to a defect in the motoric apparatuses of speech (dysarthria). Related disorders include alexias (disorders of reading), agraphias (disorders of writing), and apraxias (disorders of performing skilled movements). The related disorders may coexist with an aphasic syndrome or occur independently.

ETIOLOGY

Aphasias and related disorders can occur after almost any type of brain injury in either hemisphere affecting cortex or subcortex devoted to language, reading, writing, or praxis. Most brain injuries causing aphasias and related disorders, however, involve the left cerebral hemisphere. Language functions lateralize to the left hemisphere in 96 to 99% of right handers and 60% of left handers; of the remaining left handers, half have mixed dominance and half have right-hemisphere dominance. Most aphasias and related disorders are due to stroke, head injury, cerebral tumors, or degenerative diseases.

CRITERIA FOR DIAGNOSIS

A careful assessment of language functions together with "neighborhood signs" that are found in a thorough neurologic examination (neurologic signs that occur due to injury to fiber tracts lying in proximity to parts of the language cortex) are important to the localization of neurologic injury and the diagnosis of aphasic syndromes. The diagnosis is based on clinical findings that are listed below (see Clinical Manifestations). The diagnosis also is based on excluding syndromes that could potentially be misinterpreted as an aphasia or related syndrome. Mutism, attentional disorders, perceptual abnormalities (i.e., elemental hearing or visual impairment), psychiatric illnesses, and the locked-in state need to be considered. Acquired alexia may be difficult to differentiate from developmental dyslexias. Apraxia is excluded if the deficit in performing skilled movements is attributable to weakness, akinesia, deafferentation (sensory loss), abnormal tone or posture, movement disorders, intellectual deterioration, lack of comprehension, or uncooperativeness.

CLINICAL MANIFESTATIONS

Subjective

Patients may or may not be aware of or be able to describe their deficits, yet that in no way minimizes the clinical importance of finding those deficits. Patients with Wernicke's aphasia (below), for example, may be agitated to the point of being disruptive to a hospital ward, in part because they are unaware of their deficit. They may be misdiagnosed as having an attentional or toxic–metabolic disturbance.

Objective

Physical Examination

Adequate assessment of language requires careful and systematic evaluation of the patient's higher cortical functions. First is the assessment of the patient's spontaneous speech. Is it fluent or effortful and/or nonfluent? Is there jargon speech? Are there word-finding hesitations or circumlocutions seemingly based on the inability to find a needed word? Are sentences abnormally shortened or telegraphed with the omission of functor words (articles)? Does each utterance contain at least four or five words? Is the patient either mute or productive of less than a normal amount of spontaneous speech (i.e., excessively short answers to questions). Does the patient's spontaneous speech deteriorate precipitously after 30 to 60 seconds? Does the patient's speech contain grammatically complex productions? Does the speech convey meaning? Is the patient capable of narrative, that is, producing several relatively complex sentences connected in meaning?

Much communication is related to the tone, emphasis, gestures, prosody, and facial expressions of the speaker. Are these nonlinguistic aspects of speech normal, including tone, accent, rhythm, facial affective expression, pragmatics (knowing when to yield the floor), articulation, and rate? If the patient's spontaneous speech is abnormal in one or more respects, can the patient produce either song or overlearned expressions, such as the Pledge of Allegiance? Each of these questions bears both on diagnosis and on rehabilitation.

Directed language assessment should include assessments of verbal fluency (e.g., tell me words that begin with the letters F,A,S in 1 minute) and semantic category fluency (number of animals or fruits in 1 minute). A patient can be asked to describe a complex scene (e.g., the Cookie Theft Picture) or to describe how to perform procedural tasks (e.g., changing a tire). These tasks give an idea of whether a patient has a normal or abnormal amount of spontaneous speech. Repetition of sentences with a large number of functors (e.g., "no ifs, ands, or buts") and multiple clauses (e.g., "The orchestra played and the audience applauded") should be assessed. Auditory comprehension of sentences with one- and two-step commands (or even more complex grammatical contrivances) should be tested, and if abnormal, visual comprehension of written sentences should be undertaken (a dissociation would be expected in pure word deafness, a modality-specific disorder of phonologic decoding of language).

Confrontation naming should be assessed by asking the patient to name objects and then increasingly difficult parts of objects and, if un-able to name, to describe the use of the object or to write the name. If the patient is anomic, what are her or his error types? Does he or she substitute an ordinal category name for an exemplar (e.g., bird for pelican), a sign of semantic degradation as might be seen in Alzheimer's disease? Does the patient use the wrong words (paraphasic errors) or use nonwords? Paraphasic errors can be phonemically similar (sime for dime) or semantically similar (nickel for dime). Are there errors signifying visual misidentifications (e.g., calling a pencil a candle)? Does rotating or moving a real object or providing an auditory cue (e.g., jingling keys) help with the production of the name, as it would in an anomia restricted to visual stimuli (optic aphasia)?

Next, reading, writing, and spelling should be systematically tested. Written language may be preserved despite mutism or excessively succinct dysprosodic speech (aphemia), a disorder that may localize to inferior frontal cortices. Patients with aphasic syndromes may be able to read aloud, to read silently with comprehension, or even to spell aloud. If the patient cannot read but is not aphasic, it is essential to look for so-called neighborhood signs. In pure alexia (alexia without agraphia, Dejerine's syndrome), patients can write but cannot read what they have written; they most often also have color anomia and a contralateral superior quadrantoanopsia, and the lesion is localized to the visual cortices in the territory of the posterior cerebral artery on the left side. In alexia with agraphia, they may have signs of Gerstmann's syndrome, including finger agnosia, right–left confusion, and acalculia, and the lesion is localized to or around the angular gyrus. Alexia also may localize to Broca's area. Hemialexia may occur due to a neglect syndrome that is related to right-hemisphere damage. Agraphia, in turn, can be due either to a language disorder (aphasic agraphia) or to a loss of the knowledge of how to write (apractic agraphia). Spelling of regular words and nonwords that can be spelled through the phonologic system and spelling of irregular words that can be spelled only through stored representations of the words themselves (the lexical system, e.g., including words such as "yacht," "island," and "colonel") should both be checked; spelling can be impaired due to a deficit of either the phonologic or the lexical system.

The assessment of praxis should include tests of buccofacial praxis (e.g., show me how to blow a kiss, lick a lollipop, brush your teeth) and ideomotor limb praxis (show me how to hammer a nail, cut with scissors, turn a key in a lock). Buccofacial apraxia may represent a loss of the ability to program movements of the mouth, lips, tongue, and pharynx and often, but not always, coexists with nonfluent aphasia or aphemia. Buccofacial apraxia localizes to the inferior frontal cortices. The representations of limb apraxia are stored in the left inferior parietal lobule, and translated into innervatory patterns in the premotor cortices, including the supplementary motor areas. Therefore, limb apraxia is dissociable from buccofacial apraxia anatomically as well as functionally. Occasionally, patients may have apraxia restricted to the left hand in the presence of a tumor or infarct of the corpus callosum; only rarely does a surgical callosal resection produce this deficit.

The classic classification of aphasias is given in Table 20–21–1. The classic descriptions have been criticized within the psychological literature, but within the medical literature remain widely used as they allow physicians to communicate with one another regarding the nature and localization of their patients' deficits. In *Broca's aphasia*, damage to the inferior left frontal gyrus and underlying white matter causes agrammatism, effortful nonfluent speech, and an inability to repeat or

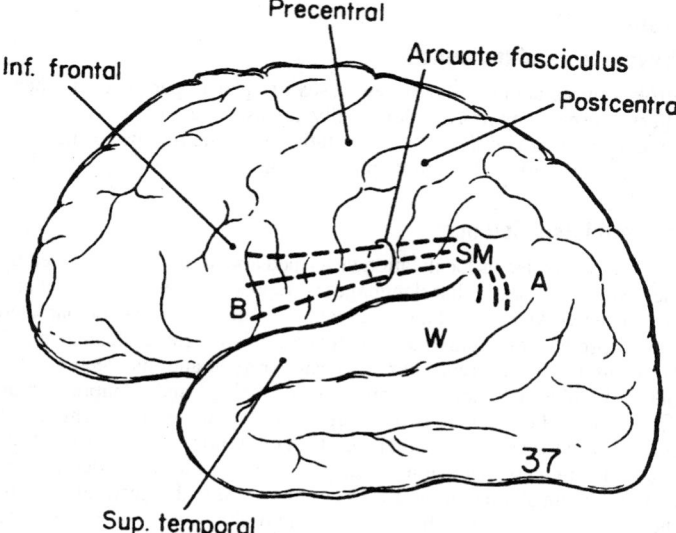

Figure 20–21–1. Anatomy of aphasia. A = angular gyrus; B = Broca's area; SM = supramarginal gyrus; W = Wernicke's area; 37 = Brodmann area 37. *(Source: From Benson DEF, Geschwind N. Aphasia and related disorders: A clinical approach. In: Mesulam MM, ed. Principles of behavioral neurology. Philadelphia: Davis, 1985:200. Reproduced with permission from the publisher and author.)*

TABLE 20–21–1. CLASSIC DEFINITIONS OF APHASIC SYNDROMES

Syndrome	Fluent	Repeats	Names	Comprehends
Broca's	No	No	Poor	Yes
Wernicke's	Yes	No	Poor	No
Conduction	Yes	No	Poor	Yes
Transcortical motor	No	Yes	No	Yes
Transcortical sensory	Yes	Yes	No	No
Transcortical mixed	No	Yes	No	No
Global	No	No	No	No
Thalamic	Usual	Usual	Poor	±

to name. Distortion, addition, or elimination or phonemes (phonemic disintegration) is common. If the lesion is restricted to Broca's area, a mild transient aphasia or aphemia (see above) occurs. Neighborhood signs include buccofacial apraxia and right arm and face weakness. The subcortical component of Broca's aphasia includes the caudate and putamen together with underlying white matter tracts.

Although cases of *subcortical aphasia* without lesions of Broca's area are described, current evidence suggests that such lesions are often associated with decreased metabolic function in the classic Broca area. Moreover, putamenal or caudate lesions without involvement of the surrounding white matter tracts probably do not cause aphasia. The putamen may be important for the production of overlearned so-called "automatic" speech segments. A recent case described an Orthodox Jew with stroke in the neostriatum who, though not aphasic in the classic sense, was no longer able to say prayers he had recited three times daily for his whole life.

Wernicke's aphasia occurs most commonly due to a lesion of the left superior temporal gyrus. Wernicke's area is thought to be crucial for phonologic decoding of words and for word selection during speech, rather than for auditory comprehension per se. Comprehension involves the connection of words already decoded to meaning, a step that involves additional cortical components. Misselection of phonemes causes paraphasic errors in speech output and difficulty in naming and repetition, but does not affect fluency. Although in most cases auditory language and visual language are both affected, some patients with Wernicke's aphasia have preserved reading; such patients need to be carefully evaluated to exclude pure word deafness.

Conduction aphasia can occur with lesions of the supramarginal gyrus, with or without extension to the subjacent white matter beneath the insula, or with lesions in the left primary auditory cortex, insula, and underlying white matter. Therefore, the lesion can be indistinguishable from lesions causing Wernicke's aphasia. As in Wernicke's and Broca's aphasias, patients with conduction aphasia cannot repeat or name, but are more likely than patients with Wernicke's aphasia to have normal comprehension for complex auditory and written material. The original description of conduction aphasia as a disconnection of the tracts connecting Wernicke's and Broca's areas is not supported by all evidence; however, alternative formulations also remain unproved.

In *global aphasia*, patients lose the ability to produce speech, to comprehend speech, to name, and to repeat. Grammar is defective as well. If global aphasia is accompanied by a hemiplegia, the lesion is an infarct of the middle cerebral artery. Less commonly, global aphasia occurs without hemiplegia, and suggests double lesions, one in the anterior and one in the posterior language areas. That has implications for etiology, as tandem lesions are most likely due to embolic stroke or tumors, each of which has important treatment implications.

Transcortical aphasias are characterized by intact repetition. In transcortical motor aphasia, the lesion is anterior or superior to Broca's area (anterior arterial watershed area) or in the dominant medial frontal lobe structures (supplementary motor area and cingulate gyrus). Patients may have decreased spontaneous verbal output and difficulty naming. Transcortical sensory aphasia is a fluent aphasia with impaired comprehension, naming, reading, and writing. The lesion is in the parietal cortex posterior to Wernicke's area (often the posterior watershed area). Transcortical sensory aphasia also is relatively frequent in Alzheimer's disease. Mixed transcortical aphasia is characterized by echolalia, that is, impairment of all aspects of speech except repetition. Formerly, it was called isolation of the speech area, and may be caused by combined watershed infarcts of the anterior and posterior border zones.

Thalamic aphasia may be confused with transcortical aphasias because the speech is fluent, repetition is intact, and anomia and paraphasic errors are present. In thalamic aphasia, however, neologisms and logorrhea are more common, attentional disturbances are more apt to occur, and, unlike the transcortical sensory aphasias, speech is likely to convey meaning.

Routine Laboratory Abnormalities

There are no specific routine abnormalities.

PLANS
Diagnostic

After the history is obtained and the neurologic findings from the examination are localized, a neuroimaging study is performed, and the results of both are considered together to establish a likely diagnosis. Among the questions to consider when reviewing the neuroimaging study of a patient presenting with an acute onset of an aphasia are: Does the lesion conform to a known vascular territory? Does it seem to explain the deficits? If the anwer to either question is no, one must first and foremost reconsider the diagnosis (is it stroke, tumor, epilepsy, or something else) and plan an appropriate evaluation. A lesion that seems excessively large to explain the clinical findings may be due to a subacute tumor rather than to an acute infarct.

Therapeutic

Speech, occupational, and physical therapies are widely used, but the scientific basis of the therapies are poorly grounded. Nonetheless, despite differences in techniques, many aphasic patients benefit from speech therapy, because of the serial functional assessments that are made and the rational compensatory strategies that can be designed by a good therapist who understands the neurologic basis of the deficit. In selected patients, melodic intonation therapy, visual communication strategies, and syntax training for agrammatism may be appropriate. Consequently, it is important that neurologists become more involved with aphasia treatment than they have been heretofore to match such treatments with appropriate neurologic deficits. An additional element that cannot be overemphasized is the psychological support given by the therapist, as well as the recognition of associated problems such as depression.

Pharmacologic treatments have been attempted in aphasia, but as yet are of unproved benefit.

FOLLOW-UP

The follow-up depends on the nature of the underlying neurologic problem (i.e., management of the stroke, head injury, degenerative disease). Some patients may be at risk for deteriorating functionally, and those patients should be identified. Other patients may have a need for outpatient treatment that is not recognized or met. Because patients may progress from one level of aphasia to another, they should be assessed serially and the therapy plan should be periodically updated.

DISCUSSION
Prevalence and Incidence

Stroke causes about 100,000 new cases of aphasia per year, and head injury causes many more. Additionally, aphasia is a common accompaniment of aging and dementia, but statistics on the number of new dementia cases with and without aphasia are not available.

Related Basic Science

The pragmatic use of localization described above must be tempered by the evolving notion that language is represented by bihemispheric neural networks rather than localizable "centers," so that demarcated lesions produce qualitative deficits that are relative rather than absolute. For example, similar types of paraphasic errors or anomias seen in a variety of aphasia syndromes are not localizing, and comprehension deficits may be seen in Broca's aphasia. Moreover, the right hemisphere is increasingly acknowledge to have a normal role in most aspects of language. The right hemisphere is capable of producing and comprehending prosodic and facial affective signals, gestural signals, the pragmatics of speech (when to yield the floor), narrative, and humor. The right hemisphere can also read single words or phrases. It appears less able to participate in grammar and syntax than in other aspects of language.

The above is important for understanding recovery. Not only is rescue of the "ischemic penumbra," reabsorption of hemorrhage, axonal regrowth, and reorganization important for recovery, but so are processes occurring in uninvolved parts of cerebral cortex, including the opposite hemisphere.

Natural History and Its Modification with Treatment

The prognosis of aphasic syndromes depends on the nature and etiology of the syndrome. In Alzheimer's disease, for example, an evolution from anomic to transcortical sensory to Wernicke's to global aphasia is relatively common. After a stroke, a patient may evolve from Wernicke's to a conduction to an anomic aphasia, or from Broca's to a transcortical motor to an anomic aphasia. Age is an exceptionally important factor in determining the prognosis (inversely related), as is the type of lesion (head injury, ischemic stroke, or bleed), size of lesion, and severity of initial deficit. A small deficit associated with some amount of early recovery, for example, Wernicke's aphasia due to an embolus, is more likely to continue to recover than a large initial deficit with no early recovery, such as a global aphasia due to a major vessel occlusion. Even patients with severe deficits may recover single word comprehension. Most recovery occurs in the first 3 to 6 months after the initial injury. Left handers or right handers with anomalous lateralization may recover better than pure right handers. Patients who receive speech therapy have better recoveries.

Prevention

Prevention of aphasic and related syndromes can be accomplished only by prevention of the underlying conditions, such as stroke and head injury, and is discussed in other chapters.

Cost Containment

Identifying and treating behavioral deficits may be important for the quality of life of patients with neurologic injuries. Identifying such deficits is essential to planning a rational rehabilitation strategy and toward maintaining the individual as someone capable of living independently or with less care than would otherwise be required. Apraxia, even more than aphasia, interferes with activities of daily living and may prevent the patient from living independently. Consequently, it has extensive implications for long-term cost containment and diagnosis, and treatment of the deficit is important.

REFERENCES

Alexander MP, Benson DF, Stuss DT. Frontal lobes and language. Brain Lang 1989;37:656.

Basso A, Capitani E, Vignolo L. Influence of rehabilitation on language skills in aphasic patients: A controlled study. Arch Neurol 1979;36:190.

Heilman KM, Valenstein E. Clinical neuropsychology. 3rd ed. New York/Oxford: Oxford University Press, 1993.

Kurtzke J. The current neurologic burden of illness and injury in the United States. Neurology 1982;32:1207.

Luria AR, Hutton JT. A modern assessment of the basic forms of aphasia. Brain Lang 1977;4:129.

CHAPTER 20–22

Dizziness

Richard E. Toran, M.D.

DEFINITION

When a person experiences the sensation that his or her relationship to the environment is different than usual, he or she most often uses the words *dizziness, unsteadiness,* and *lightheadedness* to describe the experience. More utilitarian in coming to terms with the pathophysiology of these disorders is the word *disequilibrium,* which is inclusive of all these complaints.

ETIOLOGY

The multiple causes of dizziness are best understood by a careful, orderly consideration of the systems that ordinarily provide us with a sense of equilibrium: cerebral hemispheres, labyrinthine system, sensory system (exteroceptive), sensory system (proprioceptive), motor system, and cerebellar system.

CLINICAL MANIFESTATIONS

Subjective

The first task is in separating out the *vertiginous* (spinning, turning) presentation from the others. If vertiginous, this allows one to conclude that the disorder is in the labyrinthine system or connections thereof. The next task is a declaration of whether the labyrinthine dysfunction is peripheral (aural) or central (brain). Other aural symptoms referable to cochlear dysfunction such as tinnitus, hearing loss, fullness, and/or previous ear disease help to indict the end organ as causal, but their absence does not exonerate the ear as the culprit. Also, one must remember in eliciting the history that there are disorders between the end organ and the brain, such as acoustic neuroma, which can include vertigo, although this symptom is almost always anteceded by hearing loss and tinnitus. Another such entity is vestibular neuronitis, which is analogous to Bell's palsy, a neuronitis of the facial nerve. Conversely, other symptoms referable to the central nervous system such as diplopia, dysarthria, and lateralized sensory or motor complaints indict a central cause, often involving the brainstem.

If the condition is nonvertiginous, then a careful history and physical examination with attention to all of the usual attributes of hemispheric, sensory, motor, and cerebellar functions are required.

Objective

Physical Examination

Most important is nystagmus, which is simply a movement disorder of the eyes. Spontaneous nystagmus, in the vertical plane, in the primary position, upward or downward gaze, is usually central in origin. Horizontal nystagmus may be either central or peripheral in origin. If pendular (equal velocity left and right) and accentuated by lateral gaze, it is of cerebellar origin. If characterized by a fast and a slow component, it is the latter that tells of ipsilateral vestibular hypofunction (damage) or contralateral vestibular hyperfunction (irritative), and these findings need to be related to the remainder of the history and physical examination regarding lateralized symptoms or signs. If vertigo and nystagmus are not present at the time of examination, then one needs to try and precipitate these by the Nylen–Bárány maneuver (Figure 20–22–1).

Routine Laboratory Abnormalities

There are no routine laboratory abnormalities.

PLANS

Diagnostic

Differential Diagnosis

In eliciting the history and performing the physical examination, one listens with an ear toward, and performs the physical examination with

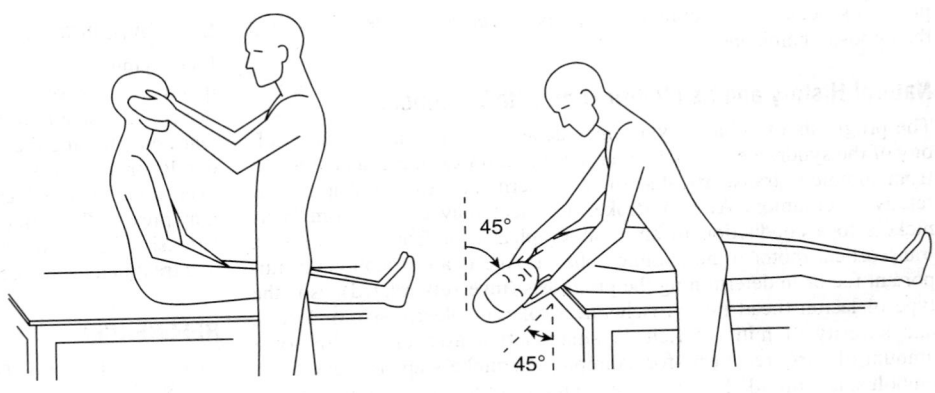

Figure 20–22–1. The Nylen–Bárány maneuver for positional vertigo and nystagmus. The patient is moved abruptly from a seated (A) to a supine (B) position, with his or her head hanging 45° below the horizontal and rotated 45° to one side. He or she is observed for the development of nystagmus and vertigo. *(Source: Modified from Drachman DA, Hart CW. An approach to the dizzy patient. Neurology 1972;22:325. Reproduced with permission.)*

the hope of, being able to assign the complaint to either hemispheres, sensory exteroceptive (vision, hearing, peripheral sensation), sensory enteroceptive (proprioception), motor (weakness), cerebellar (incoordination), or some combination thereof. Once the complaint is localized, one is faced with an even longer list of possible etiologies. This approach is better understood by way of some examples.

Aging. The nervous system distinguishes itself by its lack of regenerative capacity. There is a steady loss of neurons that begins in one's twenties. As there is considerable neuronal reserve, these losses are usually not reflected in any major loss of function. With increasing age, the associated subtleties of these losses become more apparent, none more so than the decrease in agility and balance. This fact is exemplified by the likelihood of an elderly person seeking the reassurance of a cane. Frequently, the elderly patient who complains of dizziness, nonvertiginous, not lightheadedness, is relating his or her sense of unsteadiness, and the physical examination reveals no other specific cause beyond age. More often, history and physical examination reveal common, clearly discernible, and contributory causes such as degenerative arthritis, visual difficulties, and/or hearing loss. Less common, but important, are peripheral neuropathy and spondylitic radiculopathy or myelopathy. Hypertension, and its liability for associated cerebral lacunes, may also be a contributory factor. The challenge is separating the conditions that might be amenable to treatment, such as toxin-induced conditions (alcohol, polypharmacy), orthostatic hypotension, Parkinson's disease, subdural hematoma, and hydrocephalus. This requires a familiarity with each and the ability, by way of the history and physical examination, to declare their probability and to decide on the wisdom of their pursuit.

Parkinson's Disease. Parkinson's disease is a classic example of dysfunction limited to a specific population of neurons. Loss of neurons in the nigrostriatal pathway is characterized by tremor, cogwheel rigidity, akinesia, and impairment of righting reflexes. Usually idiopathic, it is sometimes postencephalitic, caused by drugs, or arteriosclerotic. Its response to dopaminergic agents can be dramatic, usually in direct proportion to whether the nervous system's dysfunction is restricted to that population of neurons. Sometimes, parkinsonian symptoms and signs are found in patients with a less discrete loss of neurons, as in Alzheimer's or multiinfarct dementia, and their response to medication is often less gratifying. Akinesia and impairment of righting reflexes can occur without obvious tremor or rigidity, and be quite responsive to dopaminergic treatment. Therefore, careful attention to examination of the extrapyramidal motor system is required.

Diabetes. The permutations and combinations of ways that diabetes can affect the nervous system are considerable. Common is neuropathy, which may have a predilection for large fibers, causing a deficit in proprioception with considerable disequilibrium. Diabetes seems to bring the brunt of the atherosclerotic process to the small vessels and, with it, ischemic mononeuropathies (motor and sensory, exteroceptive and proprioceptive), retinopathy (exteroceptive sensory), and multiple cerebral lacunes (hemispheres). Diabetes can have a predilection for muscle, causing amyotrophy (motor) with proximal weakness and disequilib-

rium. Clearly, in the diabetic complaining of dizziness, the physical examination is key.

Cancer. Cancer, the second most common cause of morbidity and mortality, is sure to include disequilibrium, as inanition attends the disease. More difficult is when it is a presenting feature of the disease. This happens most often when cerebral or spinal metastasis occurs early, and rarely, with the paraneoplastic syndromes. Usually, but not always, metastases declare themselves by ominous headaches or back pain and/or focal findings on neurologic examination. If neither is present, then the only clues may be the inappropriateness of the disequilibrium, visceromegaly, adenopathy, or the ecology of the complaint. If suspect, periodic follow-up is key, and this is usually very helpful in choosing the appropriate imaging. Certain neurologic presentations, albeit rare, may raise considerable suspicion regarding occult malignancy. Cerebellar ataxia, pure sensory small fiber neuropathy, or opsoclonus–myoclonus rarely can be the presenting feature of tumor, most often with tumors of the lung, breast, uterus, ovary, or neural crest.

Thyroid Disease. Experienced clinicians develop considerable respect for the misleading presentations of thyroid disease, both hyper- and hypofunction. Understandably, the results of either are multisystemic, and the nervous system is usually involved. Weakness and unsteadiness can attend either, and may or may not be associated with tremor, reflex changes, weakness, eye signs, or affective disorder. A very high index of suspicion is required and, when present, can often be resolved only by appropriate diagnostic tests.

Toxins. All the systems that subserve equilibrium are susceptible to the effects of toxins. The most common toxin is alcohol. Acute intoxication almost always leads to vertigo, often severe and including nausea and/or vomiting. Chronic abuse of alcohol brings with it the nutritional deficiency and other organ dysfunction that, in turn, adversely affect all of the systems that subserve equilibrium, with neuropathy, cerebellar ataxia, myopathy, and encephalopathy. Also common, especially among the elderly, are the effects of polypharmacy. With aging, the ability to both inactivate and excrete drugs decreases substantially. The increased number of visits to physicians as one ages often results in an accumulation of a large number of medications. The combinations of medications often lead to uncertainty regarding their efficacy and the possibility of an overall soporific effect, with imbalance. A keen awareness to minimizing the number of medications is essential to the care of the elderly. The rate at which one metabolizes drugs also becomes very important in the inpatient setting when aminoglycosides are used. These can be very toxic to the labyrinth and require careful monitoring of blood levels.

Diagnostic Options and Recommended Approach

Occasionally, the finer nuances of nystagmus such as direction changing, latency of onset, and fatigability are better determined by electronystagmography, which is a quantitative assessment. With electronystagmography, electrodes are placed on the face, about the eye. Whereas the eye acts as a dipole, eye movements can be recorded, and the results of both positional and caloric stimulation can be assessed. Other quantitative methods for this system include a variety of hearing test batteries and evoked potentials. Rarely are these necessary to determine the cause of dizziness.

Therapeutic

Despite so many etiologies of disequilibrium, there are some common denominators of treatment such as removal of the inciting cause, replacement of a missing substrate, antibiotic agents, antiinflammatory agents, and attempts at alleviating the symptoms (symptomatic). The most common cause, labyrinthine peripheral, is often self-limited and benign. Antivertiginous medications, such as meclizine are often prescribed and of some help, although clinical studies have shown them to be only minimally more effective than placebo. The usual dosage is 25 to 100 mg daily, in divided doses, using 12.5- and 25-mg tablets. Ménière's disease, analogous to glaucoma (i.e., an elevated pressure in a closed system), has not enjoyed the same response to medicinal or surgical treatment as has glaucoma. If the vertiginous component of Ménière's disease becomes disabling, one may have to resort to advising ablative therapy, either surgical (section of vestibular nerve) or medical (microneedle insertion of labyrinth with instillation of aminoglycoside). Some patients with recurrent peripheral vestibular vertigo benefit from a variety of exercises, which include eye movements, neck movements, and assumption of the standing position and walking.

FOLLOW-UP

There are multiple causes of dizziness (see Etiology and Table 20–22–1). The type of follow-up varies with the cause of the dizziness and is supported under Etiology.

DISCUSSION

Prevalence and Incidence

Dizziness is a common experience, and patients who suffer severe or recurrent episodes are likely to seek the help of their physician. Studies of dizzy patients vary in their conclusions about the incidence within the various diagnostic categories, but all are agreed that dysfunction of the vestibular system is most common. There is also agreement that benign positional vertigo is the most frequent vestibular disorder, but the variations in the other categories of vestibular causes serve as testimony to our lack of precision in fathoming vestibular dysfunction. Second to vestibular disorders are hemispheric dysfunctions, and the most common of these is psychiatric. Often, if not the sole cause, psycholog-

TABLE 20–22–1. CAUSES OF DIZZINESSS (ACCORDING TO SYSTEMS WHOSE FUNCTION IS ESSENTIAL TO EQUILIBRIUM)

Cerebral hemispheres		30–40%
Psychiatric		
Hypoperfusion		
Cardiac dysrhythmia		
Orthostasis		
Hyperventilation		
Other neurologic disorders		
Other medical disorders		
Labyrinthine		40–50%
Benign positional vertigo		
Meniere's disease		
Vestibular neuronitis		
Recurrent vestibulopathy		
Others		
Sensory—exteroceptive		
Visual loss	Multiple	
Hearing loss	sensory	20–30%
	deficit	
Sensory—proprioceptive		
Neuropathy		
Myelopathy		
Motor		0–5%
Cerebellar		0–5%

ical factors are a major contributor. When the psychiatric cause manifests as hyperventilation, it brings to the fore cerebral hypoperfusion, also caused by such conditions as cardiac dysrhythmia and orthostasis. Also, there is a long list of both neurologic and medical disorders that may affect the hemispheres. Table 20–22–1 represents a likely distribution of patients, according to the systems whose function is essential to equilibrium.

Related Basic Science

The *hemispheres* and the consciousness they afford allow for the report of "I'm dizzy." The hemispheres are endpoints for reception and integration of all the information from all the other systems that subserve equilibrium, and serve as the repository (memory) of this information. It is when the hemsipheres recognize the incoming information as "different" or "imbalanced," compared with previous experience, that these symptoms occur. Thus, any condition that affects the cerebral hemispheres in a diffuse or focal manner may result in disequilibrium. Psychiatric disorders are a common cause of such complaints. Cerebral hypoperfusion and hypoglycemia with deficiencies of oxygen and/or glucose may cause dizziness or lightheadedness. Many toxins may affect the hemispheres and can cause dizziness. The neuronal loss associated with aging brings with it a sense of imbalance compared with one's youth. Structural disorders of the hemispheres usually declare themselves by focal symptoms or signs, but often include complaints of disequilibrium. Imbalance may be the first symptom of hydrocephalus. Disorders of the deeper portions of the hemispheres (basal ganglia), such as Parkinson's disease, frequently include such complaints.

The *labyrinthine system* serves as the body's inertial guidance system. This system obeys Newton's first law: For every action there is an equal and opposite reaction. Any movement of the body (head) through space results in a motion (reaction) of the fluid in the vestibular portion of the middle ear, with saccule, utricle, and semicircular canals being the sensors of this movement. Whereas the semicircular canals measure rotational movements, their dysfunction results in a similar sensation called *vertigo,* which is the sensation of turning or spinning. The saccule and utricle measure linear movements and their dysfunction can include complaints of lightheadedness or unusual sensations such as falling, rising, or being propelled in any direction. The common disorders of this most peripheral part of the labyrinthine system are often related to two common pathophysiologies of fluid-containing systems: crystallization of solute with stone formation and disparity of rates of production and resorption, the latter usually resulting in increased pressure. An example of stone formation is benign positional vertigo, a common disorder, more frequent in the elderly, characterized by the acute onset of severe vertigo precipitated by a change in position, often occurring at night. The cause is thought to be microlithiasis within the vestibular fluid, although a similar syndrome can occur after trauma and from a number of miscellaneous causes. If these "stones" impact on the cupola of a semicircular canal they provide a stimulus quite different from that caused by the motion of fluid. An example of increased pressure is Ménière's disease. As the fluid in the vestibular portion of the labyrinth is in communication with the fluid in the cochlear portion, increased pressure may adversely impact on both balance and hearing, and accounts for the symptom tetrad of Ménière's disease: tinnitus, hearing loss, vertigo, and a sense of fullness of the ears. Toxins, such as aminoglycosides, are another common, identifiable cause of labyrinthine dysfunction. Frequently, peripheral labyrinthine disorders are of uncertain cause, self-limited, and benign. Often, they are mislabeled as *labyrinthitis.*

Although the labyrinthine system is rightly a *sensory–exteroceptive system,* it is afforded the aforementioned separate consideration, because of its prominence in the hierarchy of equilibrium systems. Vision, hearing, and tactile sensation are the other exteroceptive mechanisms. The degree of disequilibrium caused by the loss of vision, hearing, or tactile sensation is proportional to the degree, acuteness, and combination of such losses. Most common is the multiple sensory deficit syndrome seen in the elderly who have partial losses of all three; however, subtle changes in one, such as a new pair or eyeglasses or a blocked ear, can induce a short-lived sense of disequilibrium.

The *sensory–proprioceptive system* is characterized by posterior columns of spinal cord, large fibers of nerves, and their position receptors in muscles, tendons, and joints. They serve the very important role of relaying information to the brain as to where one part of the body is in reference to another. Key is the relationship of the head to the rest of the body. Whereas all of the sensory–exteroceptive systems reside in the head, it is essential that the hemispheres be able to relate that information to the position of the rest of the body. It is the neck that governs this relationship; thus, the neck is richly innervated with position sense receptors. This relationship becomes most apparent in those suffering from "whiplash," who suffer from vague but significant disequilibrium for a period of weeks. Other diseases—deficiency (vitamin), inflammatory (tabes), metabolic (diabetes), and structural (spinal cord compression)—can interfere with this system and present as disequilibrium.

Malfunction of the pyramidal *motor system,* weakness, is an uncommon cause of the complaint of disequilibrium. When weakness is mild, involves the lower extremities, and is moderately acute, proximal, and fairly symmetric, patients do present complaining of dysequilibrium rather than weakness. Diseases of nerves (Guillain–Barré syndrome), myoneural junctions (myasthenia), and muscles (proximal myopathy) can be the cause. Whereas the complaint is not weakness, the physical examination usually provides the answer. Malfunction of the extrapyramidal motor system (Parkinson's disease) often includes disequilibrium.

The *cerebellar system* plays a major role in the coordination of all the aforementioned sensory inputs and motor system, and is the repository for the "memory" of the many functions we take for granted, such as walking. Disruption of cerebellar function interferes in a major way with ambulation and balance. Most patients with cerebellar lesions describe the disequilibrium as being in their feet; in contrast, patients with vestibular lesions say their head feels dizzy. Given the close relationship between the vestibular system and the cerebellum, dizziness (vertigo) is a frequent accompaniment of cerebellar dysfunction. Most important is the acute disorder of cerebellar parenchymal hemorrhage. Rarely, this entity presents with isolated vertigo. More often, the presentation is headache, vertigo, and difficulty with gait without other obvious abnormalities. The more severe cases present with obvious brainstem signs or are lethal at onset. It is the lethal potential of this disorder that obligates its consideration in every patient complaining of the acute onset of vertigo. In less acute disorders of the cerebellum, be they inflammatory (postvaricella), structural (tumor), deficiency (alcohol), degenerative (idiopathic), or hereditary (Friedreich's) diseases, one relies on the physical examination and the ecology of the disorder to determine causality.

Natural History and Its Modification with Treatment

Please see Plans, Therapeutic, under which the common denominators of treatment for multiple causes of dizziness are discussed.

Prevention

Given the very wide array of causes of disequilibrium, prevention is an equally broad topic, but applicable to all are the basic health issues of appropriate body weight; diet; exercise; sleep habits; time allocations to family, work, and play; and avoidance of toxins and substance abuse.

Cost Containment

In analyzing what we do to control costs it is helpful to look at the common denominators of what we do, and then see if costs can be reduced without compromising quality (see Cost Containment in Chapter 20–27). Usually the history and physical examination are all that are required in caring for patients who complain of dizziness. Rarely, more detailed evaluation may be required, such as hearing test batteries, evoked potentials, electronystagmography, cerebral imaging via computed tomography scan or magnetic resonance imaging, ultrasound evaluation of cerebral vasculature, magnetic resonance angiography, contrast arteriography, and searches for toxins, deficiency states or inflammatory diseases. The cost of such pursuits is often considerable, and the discretion used in minimizing the number of steps in a diagnostic pursuit should be that of the physician with the most experience. Thus, if a primary care physician concludes that a patient with dizziness needs further evaluation, it is most cost effective to first refer the patient to the appropriate subspecialist. In the interest of optimal and cost-effective care, primary care physicians will have to choose their consultants carefully, avoiding those who overuse technologies or treatments. Consultants are obliged to devise and teach paths to wellness with the least number of tests and best treatment.

CHAPTER 20–23

Parkinson's Disease and Other Extrapyramidal Disorders

John T. Murphy, M.D., Ph.D.

Disorders of the extrapyramidal system are those that involve primarily basal ganglia structures. By definition and convention, two other central systems intimately involved in movement production, namely, the corticospinal (pyramidal) tracts and cerebellum, are excluded. In certain conditions, all three control systems are involved; however, weakness and incoordination (representing corticospinal tract and cerebellar dysfunctions respectively) are typically not major manifestations of extrapyramidal disorders. Involuntary decrease and increase in production of movement, termed *hypokinesia* (bradykinesia) and *hyperkinesia,* respectively, are prominent features. Current classification schemes emphasize this polarity.

Idiopathic Parkinson's Disease and Other Hypokinetic Disorders

DEFINITION

Parkinsonism is a condition in which movement is functionally disordered because of difficulty with initiation and/or slowness. The reduced movement production is in some cases combined with tremor.

ETIOLOGY

The cause of idiopathic Parkinson's disease is unknown. A variety of factors have been suggested, including toxic effects on neurons from oxidative reactions by free radicals, exposure to environmental toxins such as industrial chemicals or pesticides and herbicides, and genetic factors.

CRITERIA FOR DIAGNOSIS
Suggestive

Poverty of movement and resting tremor should lead to consideration of the diagnosis.

Definitive

The diagnosis is made on clinical grounds. Either or both resting tremor and bradykinesia constitute hallmarks. A beneficial symptomatic response to levodopa therapy, particularly with respect to bradykinesia and rigidity, is now considered essential to the diagnosis. Failure to respond should lead to consideration of other conditions described under Differential Diagnosis.

CLINICAL MANIFESTATIONS

Subjective

In the early stages, most patients present with a resting tremor usually in the frequency range 4 to 7 Hz, most commonly about 5 Hz, or very mild bradykinesia together with a particular type of hypertonia termed *cogwheel rigidity*. Often, only one of these two symptoms is present, and early presentation especially in young patients is typically unilateral. Personal history may reveal exposure to industrial chemicals or pesticides/herbicides, especially in patients whose age of onset is below 50. A positive family history suggesting a mendelian autosomal dominant pattern of inheritance has been described but is rare.

Objective

Physical Examination

Fluctuating 5-Hz resting tremor, bradykinesia, impaired postural reflexes, postural instability, and a shuffling gait disturbance with a tendency toward propulsion or retropulsion (gait festination) are the predominant clinical findings. Cogwheel rigidity is present on testing of muscle tone. A characteristic expressionless facies (hypomimia) is often present. Mental status testing reveals evidence of dementia in more than half of all patients above age 60.

Routine Laboratory Abnormalities

There are no routine laboratory abnormalities.

PLANS

Diagnostic

Differential Diagnosis

Secondary parkinsonism is most commonly due to drugs, especially psychotropic agents. A multiinfarct state should be considered in older-onset patients. Several clinical constellations may be grouped together under the term *parkinsonism-plus syndromes*. These include multiple system atrophy syndromes including striatonigral degeneration, Shy–Drager syndrome manifesting as autonomic insufficiency, and olivopontocerebellar atrophy (OPCA). Other parkinsonism-plus syndromes include progressive supranuclear palsy, which often includes impaired downward gaze as well as axial dystonia and extensor posture of the neck, and cortical basal ganglionic degeneration, which is highlighted by its asymmetric presentation, associated dystonic postures, mixed postural and action tremors, as well as stimulus-sensitive myoclonus, alien limb phenomena, and oculomotor dysfunction. The last symptom is often a dyspraxia of gaze. A variety of rare heredodegenerative diseases may include parkinsonism. Neuroacanthocytosis and Huntington's and Wilson's diseases are the most frequently occurring of these. A number of gait disorders exist in the elderly that may be misdiagnosed as Parkinson's disease. These include many subgroups that have been termed *senile gait disturbance*. The gait disturbance of normal-pressure hydrocephalus may be mistaken for parkinsonism. Failure to respond to levodopa may be suggestive of a parkinsonism-plus or heredodegenerative condition. Juvenile Parkinson's disease (below age 21) may present as dystonia.

Diagnostic Options

Magnetic resonance imaging may be helpful in certain circumstances. If Wilson's disease (hepatolenticular degeneration) is suspected in a young patient, slit-lamp examination and biochemical tests of copper metabolism and storage may be useful. Computed tomography head scan, electroencephalography, and single-photon-emission computed tomography are usually of no value. The use of positron-emission tomography is at present confined to research studies.

Recommended Approach

The clinical assessment, including a history of medication use, tests for orthostatic blood pressure change, examination of conjugate eye movements, and the general neurologic examination, should serve to reduce the likelihood of a symptomatic or parkinsonism-plus syndrome. In patients below the age of 21, screening tests of copper metabolism and slit-lamp examination may be considered. A fresh blood smear and creatine phosphokinase level are used to assess neuroacanthocytosis. Magnetic resonance imaging is recommended if multiple system atrophy is suspected on clinical grounds. It also serves to evaluate the possibility of vascular parkinsonism, Huntington's disease, progressive supranuclear palsy, and neuroacanthocytosis.

Therapeutic

Therapeutic Options

Replacement of deficient dopamine in brain with dopamine precursors or agonists, the monoamine oxidase B inhibitor selegiline, and anticholinergic medications are the most important therapeutic options. Transplantation of adrenal medulla or of fetal midbrain cells into the striatum is an investigative therapy. Ventrolateral thalamotomy may occasionally be used in patients with severe tremor unresponsive to drug treatment or in other patients with severe levodopa-induced dyskinesias. This surgical treatment may lead to complications, however, including permanent hemiparesis, dysphasia, or dysarthria. Stereotactic lesioning of the subthalamic nucleus or posteroventrolateral glomus pallidus internus is also the subject of recent study, with reported benefit in rigidity, tremor, bradykinesia, and dyskinesias. A low-protein diet may be helpful for motor fluctuations.

Recommended Approach

Patients with resting tremor as the predominant symptom may be started on a low dose of an anticholinergic agent such as benztropine 2 mg orally once daily up to three times daily, as needed. When rigidity and bradykinesia become disabling, initiation of dopaminergic therapy usually with a levodopa–carbidopa (Sinemet) or levodopa–benzazeride (Prolopa) preparation is recommended. The comedication blocks peripheral dopaminergic effects including nausea, hypotension, and cardiac arrhythmias. The drug should be given at a low dose initially, that is, 100/25 or 50/12.5 mg orally once daily, increasing to twice daily over 1 week or several days if well tolerated. Thereafter, very slow increments in dosage over a period of months or years is usually required. The maximum recommended adult dose for most patients is 4 to 6 tablets daily. A 200/50 mg controlled-release levodopa–carbidopa preparation may be used less frequently with the possible benefit of reduced motor fluctuations. Patients with severe or rapidly progressive disease may require higher doses; however, high doses eventually lead to dykinesias, motor fluctuation, or other unwanted side effects in most patients. A dopamine agonist such as bromocriptine can be added as necessary when further benefit is not achieved with additional increments of the levodopa preparation. Initial doses of bromocriptine are 1.25 mg orally once daily, increasing to three times daily over 1 to 2 weeks if well tolerated. Further increments, usually up to 3 to 4 tablets daily, can then be made again over a period of months to years. This dual-therapy approach appears to have a better risk–benefit profile than does the use of high-dose levodopa or bromocriptine preparations alone. Serious pulmonary or retroperitoneal fibrosis has been reported with long-term bromocriptine use.

Selegiline has a weak dopaminergic effect, which will produce symptomatic benefit. The possibility of a protective effect due to antioxidant mechanisms has been considered, but remains uncertain. Another available dopamine agonist is pergolide. Antidepressant medications can be used when depression is significant, although nonselective monoamine oxidase inhibitors are contraindicated in levodopa-treated patients because of the risk of hypertensive crisis. Orthostatic hypotension, if present, may be treated in the usual fashion with an increase of salt intake, support hose, and, if necessary, administration of fludrocortisone. Cisapride may be useful for constipation, and regular exercise is recommended for all patients.

FOLLOW-UP

The primary follow-up should be clinical. Initially, patients should be reevaluated at 3-month intervals or more frequently if specific clinical problems are anticipated. Once a stable clinical path in response to treatment has been established, the follow-up interval may be increased to 6 months to 1 year. Problems with response including on/off motor fluctuations, end-of-dose akinesias, dyskinesias, and psychiatric side effects of the dopamine therapy including confusion and hallucinations require more frequent follow-up.

DISCUSSION
Prevalence and Incidence

Prevalence rates are about 200 per 100,000 population, whereas incidence rates are about 20 per 100,000. These are age specific, with peak incidence rates at about age 75. Patients who developed parkinsonism following the influenza pandemic after World War I were typically of younger age at onset. As the number of these patients has gradually lessened due to death, the peak age incidence has increased accordingly.

Related Basic Science
Pathology

Degenerative changes in the zona compacta of the substantia nigra are found in primary Parkinson's disease. Cytoplasmic inclusion bodies consisting of an eosinophilic core surrounded by a clear halo (Lewy body) are typically present. Similar abnormalities are at times seen in the locus ceruleus and dorsal motor nucleus of the vagus nerve, as well as in the substantia innominata and intermediolateral cell column of the spinal cord.

Biochemistry

Reduction of dopaminergic neurons in the substantia nigra leads to reduction of dopamine in the striatum.

Natural History and Its Modification with Treatment

Parkinson's disease is typically progressive if left untreated, although at a variable rate. Modern treatment with dopaminergic replacement has had significant impact in terms of morbidity and longevity. It is unknown as yet whether treatment with selegiline or other putative protective agents might produce a significant long-term delay in progression.

Cost Containment

Routine use of computed tomography, electroencephalography, and single-photon-emission computed tomography is not recommended. The use of controlled-release dopaminergic preparations is reported to lead to reduced motor fluctuations. The cost–benefit ratio of this approach should be evaluated carefully in individual patients. In many cases a similar benefit may be achieved with more frequent lower doses of less costly preparations.

Hyperkinetic Disorders

DEFINITION

Hyperkinetic disorders are those in which the production of movement, both voluntary and involuntary, is excessive in relation to the functional objective of the person. The movements may be regular, as in various forms of tremor, or irregular, as in choreoathetosis, myoclonus, and various tics. Frequency and amplitude of the movements may also vary. These abnormal movements may occur spontaneously, in the context of attempted voluntary movement, or in response to reflex stimulation.

ETIOLOGY

Hyperkinetic movements may occur as a component of a wide variety of neurologic conditions. *Huntington's disease,* manifest by choreic (rapid, dancing) movements, is genetically transmitted in autosomal dominant fashion. It is due to extra copies of the cytidine–adenine–guanidine trinucleotide located near the end of the short arm of chromosome 4. Other irregular movements may be acquired. *Athetosis* is a

continuous, slow, and writhing type of movement that occurs most commonly as a result of injury of basal ganglia structures in early life. *Hemiballism* represents large-amplitude, very rapid choreiform movement of a limb usually due to infarction in the contralateral subthalamic nucleus. Other structural abnormalities or rarely metabolic states may also produce this disorder.

Dystonia is a condition in which inadequate separation of agonist and antagonist muscular contractions leads to sustained twisting and repetitive movements with distorted postures occurring spontaneously or with attempts to move voluntarily. It may be idiopathic or symptomatic. Inheritance of classic idiopathic tortion dystonia is now believed to be of autosomal dominant type in both Ashkenazi Jews and non-Jewish families. The long arm of chromosome 9 has been implicated for this type. Heterogeneity of this condition is indicated by the fact that another type, dopa-responsive dystonia, is located on chromosome 14Q. A variety of structural lesions including infarctions, prior head trauma, encephalitis, drug exposure, and anoxia may lead to symptomatic dystonia. Many focal or segmental dystonias are idiopathic.

Tourette's syndrome, which includes tics or other involuntary movements, is believed to result from an autosomal dominant gene that affects males more than females. Studies of genetic linkage are underway in an attempt to confirm this hypothesis. *Hemifacial spasm* may occur as a result of irritation of the seventh cranial nerve or its fibers of exit from the brainstem due to compression or in some cases demyelinating disease. *Myoclonus,* which represents a very brief muscular contraction of sudden onset, may occur as a consequence of a variety of acquired disorders affecting the cerebral cortex or brainstem. Action myoclonus, which occurs with voluntary movement, often results from cerebral hypoxia or, more rarely, degenerative disorders. *Essential tremor* is an autosomal dominant disorder with kinetic and postural components. Drugs, notably neuroleptic agents, metoclopramide, and some calcium channel blocking agents, may produce a variety of hyperkinetic as well as hypokinetic movement disorders. *Wilson's disease* is caused by a gene linked to markers on chromosome 13 and transmitted by autosomal dominance. Pathophysiologic changes in the brain, liver, and cornea results from deposition of copper due to reduced combination with ceruloplasmin and impairment of biliary excretion.

CRITERIA FOR DIAGNOSIS
Suggestive

The presence of movements that do not have a functional purpose and that appear to occur involuntarily should lead to consideration of these diagnoses.

Definitive

The diagnosis is usually made on the basis of clinical data including symptoms, family history, and physical signs. Specific genetic studies may be helpful, particularly with respect to Huntington's disease. Imaging studies including computed tomography of the head and magnetic resonance imaging may provide helpful information regarding etiology or classification.

CLINICAL MANIFESTATIONS
Subjective

Patients with Huntington's disease usually have a positive family history and symptoms of chorea, impaired cognition, and psychiatric or behavioral problems. Juvenile Huntington's disease occurring before age 20 may be associated with parkinsonism, seizures, and an unsteady gait in addition. Postinfectious (Sydenham's) chorea is now rare. A history of the particular movement disorder is present in the other hyperkinetic disorders. Family history is usually positive in essential tremor and in some cases of dystonia.

Objective
Physical Examination

Characterizations of chorea, athetosis, dystonia, tics, myoclonus, and tremor have been provided above. Classification of the abnormal movement is provided by analysis of frequency and circumstances of onset, as well as by amplitude, frequency, and spatial analysis of the movement. Abnormalities in the mental status examination may be present in Huntington's and Wilson's diseases in particular. Many older patients with Huntington's disease may eventually exhibit rigidity and bradykinesia. Forced verbal utterances are associated with Tourette's syndrome. Note is made that childhood-onset Wilson's disease may present as dystonia and parkinsonism, whereas tremor and psychiatric symptoms may predominate in older patients.

Routine Laboratory Abnormalities

Peripheral blood smear may reveal acanthocytes in cases of chorea caused by neuroacanthocytosis. Some patients with Wilson's disease may show evidence of hemolytic anemia and/or abnormal renal or liver functions.

PLANS
Diagnostic
Differential Diagnosis

The differential diagnosis of any particular hyperkinetic disorder, in general, includes each of the others. Clinical distinctions in many cases are straightforward and in others blurred. A primary psychiatric disorder with habitual or attention-gathering production of excess movement should be included in the differential diagnosis. Absence of sterotypy may provide a clue in many cases; however, some tic disorders with a psychiatric basis may be sterotypic. Dystonia may predominate in juvenile Parkinson's disease.

Diagnostic Options

Genetic testing is available for Huntington's disease. Magnetic resonance imaging and computed tomography of the head may be considered in several of these disorders. Slit-lamp examination looking for deposition of copper in the cornea, determination of plasma ceruloplasmin and copper levels, and analysis of 24-hour urine excretion of copper are available in cases of suspected Wilson's disease. Neuropsychological testing may be considered when dementia is associated with a hyperkinetic movement disorder.

Recommended Approach

Genetic testing is recommended in Huntington's disease if the patient and family members desire this. Copper studies and slit-lamp examination are recommended in cases of suspected Wilson's disease. Computed tomography of the head and magnetic resonance imaging are recommended in all cases in which a hyperkinetic movement disorder is associated with dementia or disturbances of consciousness, as well as in those cases in which multiple infarcts may be present.

Therapeutic
Therapeutic Options

Botulinum toxin injections provide localized neuromuscular blockade. Options for systemic pharmacologic treatment include anticholinergic agents, dopaminergic agents, baclofen, benzodiazepines, tegretol, and antidopaminergic agents. Surgery is an option in very selected cases.

Recommended Approach

Neuroleptic agents such as haloperidol are useful for chorea and tics. Because these may produce tardive dyskinesias or secondary parkinsonism, their use should be limited to very late stages of Huntington's disease. In most cases of Tourette's syndrome, these agents should not be used. Clozapine may produce less in the way of extrapyramidal side effects and is recommended if not prohibited by cost. Monoamine oxidase inhibitors such as reserpine are recommended only as a secondary agent in the event that a neuroleptic agent has produced tardive dyskinesias. These, however, may produce depression and parkinsonism. Benzodiazepines are recommended when chorea and anxiety are not adequately controlled by the above means.

Botulinum toxin injections are recommended as primary treatment for focal dystonias including blepharospasm, adductor laryngeal dystonia, torticollis, and oromandibular dystonia. Their effectiveness in focal limb dystonias such as writer's cramp is less predictable. Gradually increasing doses of anticholinergic agents are recommended as primary treatment for generalized dystonias. The peripheral side effects of dry mouth and nausea can be eased by pyridostigmine bromide and those of blurred vision by pilocarpine eyedrops. Levodopa should be tried in all cases of childhood-onset dystonia, as about one fifth of cases respond. Benzodiazepines, carbamazepine, and baclofen are of limited efficacy in dystonia and are not recommended as primary treatments.

The recommended approach to control of hemifacial spasm is the use of tegretol or, alternatively, dilantin. Botulinum toxin injections are an appropriate second line of treatment. Myoclonus should be treated with clonazepam or valproic acid as the primary agent. Add-on medications that are useful include tegretol and primidone. Dopaminergic agents such as sinemet are useful for restless legs. Benzodiazepines are recommended as a second-line agent. Essential tremor is best treated with low to moderate doses of a beta-adrenergic blocking agent such as propranolol (Inderal). Primidone may be used if propranolol is ineffective or contraindicated for medical reasons.

Drug-induced movement disorders such as tardive dyskinesia should be treated with gradual withdrawal of the offending agent. Reinstitution of the agent at lower doses may be required, with attempts at further withdrawal after the patient is stabilized. Clozapine may be particularly helpful in these circumstances.

Wilson's disease should be treated with penicillamine as a copper chelating agent. Levodopa, anticholinergic agents, and botulinum toxin injections are adjunctive treatments that can be used. If the use of penicillamine is limited by complications, alternatives including triethylene tetramine and zinc sulfate may be considered. Liver transplant is a treatment of last resort. A low-copper diet helps to reverse the neurologic and hepatic symptoms of Wilson's disease if instituted early in the course.

FOLLOW-UP

Frequency of clinical follow-up should be individualized to the patient's needs. The only routine laboratory follow-up that may be helpful would be copper studies in Wilson's disease.

DISCUSSION
Prevalence

The prevalence of Huntington's disease is estimated to be about 10 per 100,000. There is a much higher prevalence in certain localized geographic regions such as Lake Maracaibo, Venezuela. Prevalence of generalized idiopathic tortion dystonia has been estimated to range from about 3 to 7 per 100,000, depending on the populations studied. Focal dystonias are estimated to have a 5- to 10-fold higher prevalence. The gene prevalence in Wilson's disease is estimated to be about 1%, whereas the disease prevalence is about 3 per 100,000.

Related Basic Science

Genetics are discussed above. The trinucleotide cytidine–adenine–guanidine repeat code is believed to cause an overexpression of the normal gene, which produces an as yet unidentified protein that has been called *Huntingtin*. The chorea that results appears to be correlated with loss of the medium-size spinal striatal neurons which project to the globus pallidus externus. In contrast, rigid/akinetic manifestations may correlate with loss of those striatal neurons that project to the globus pallidus internus. A decrease in γ-aminobutyric acid and enkephalin levels has been observed. N-Methyl-D-aspartate receptors are reduced in the putamen. This agent and glutamate have been proposed as excitotoxins that could produce neuronal degeneration.

The pathophysiology of dystonia is poorly understood. The basis for the simultaneous contraction of agonist and antagonist muscles during attempted voluntary movements that occurs in this condition is unknown. Hyperactivity of dopaminergic neuron systems may underlie some tic disorders including Tourette's syndrome. No structural or pathologic correlates have as yet been identified in this condition. In

Wilson's disease, positron-emission tomography studies have shown damage to nigrostriatal dopaminergic neurons, which correlates with alterations in signal intensity on T_2-weighted magnetic resonance images. Pathologic changes are diffusely distributed throughout brain in Wilson's disease. Copper concentration is usually increased by a factor of at least 10 in brain, especially in the striatum.

Natural History and Its Modification with Treatment

Relentless progression is the norm in Huntington's disease, with treatments providing only symptomatic benefit. The course of Wilson's disease is markedly altered and at times reversed with a low-copper diet and provision of a copper chelating agent. Botulinum toxin provides very effective symptomatic control in the focal dystonias. Anticholinergic agents provide partial relief and reduction of disability in the generalized dystonias. Hemifacial spasm and essential tremor are usually effectively controlled by the recommended treatments. Control of myoclonus by drug treatment is variable. Tardive dyskinesia and secondary parkinsonism may be reversed by withdrawal of offending drug; however, in some cases the process is irreversible.

Prevention

Genetic counseling is of paramount importance with respect to Huntington's and Wilson's disease and hereditary dystonia. Premature or excess use of psychotropic drugs is a major cause of extrapyramidal movement disorders and should be discouraged.

Cost Containment

Development and use of agents such as clozapine that may produce no or fewer extrapyramidal side effects may provide significant cost benefits in relation to development of drug-induced extrapyramidal syndromes.

REFERENCES

American Academy of Neurology, Therapeutics and Technology Assessment Subcommittee. Assessment: The clinical usefulness of botulinum toxin-A in treating neurologic disorders. Neurology 1990;40:1332.

Gusella JF, MacDonald ME, Ambrose CM, et al. Molecular genetics of Huntington's disease. Arch Neurol 1993;50:1157.

Hughes AJ, Daniel SE, Kilford L, et al. Accuracy of clinical diagnosis of idiopathic Parkinson's disease: A clinicopathological study of 100 cases. J Neurol Neurosurg Psychiatry 1992;55:181.

Riley DE, Lang AE, Lewis A, et al. Cortical-basal ganglionic degeneration. Neurology 1990;40:1203.

Rinne UK. Early combination of bromocriptine and levodopa in the treatment of Parkinson's disease: A 5-year follow-up. Neurology 1987; 37:826.

CHAPTER 20–24

Tremor

Michael T. Hayes, M.D.

DEFINITION

Tremor is defined as a rhythmic, mechanical oscillation of a body part. There are two main categories of tremor. Rest tremor, or tremor with the limb in a state of repose, is tremor that occurs in the absence of any voluntary movement. Action tremor includes two subclasses, postural tremor and movement tremor. Postural tremor occurs when the limb is held, unsupported, in a fixed position. Movement tremor may occur at any stage of a purposeful movement. The therapeutic approach to any tremor is based on this categorization.

Physiologic tremor is not a disorder. It is the minute tremor we all exhibit. It may be enhanced by a number of metabolic derangements or emotional factors.

ETIOLOGY

Rest tremor, most commonly noted in Parkinson's disease, is of unknown etiology. Central mechanisms appear to play the most important role, but these mechanisms have yet to be defined. It has been shown that rest tremor is unaffected by deafferenting muscle, suggesting that proprioceptive mechanisms are not of much importance in this tremor. The finding of neurons in the basal ganglia that fire at the same frequency as resting tremor and the demonstration that surgical lesioning of the ventrolateral thalamus may abolish resting tremor give more credence to the suggestion that it is of central origin.

Essential tremor includes benign essential tremor and familial tremor. These tremors, affected by all the same factors that enhance the physiologic tremor we all exhibit, are a combination of motor neuron firing, synchronization around peripheral reflexes from muscle spindle feedback, and supraspinal and pharmacologic influences. Essential tremor is more noticeable and may be in part due to synchronous motor unit discharges from central oscillators.

Movement tremor is due to lesions in the thalamodentate connections and injuries around the red nucleus or some of the neocerebellar nuclei. These lesions may be seen in cerebellar strokes, bleeds, or masses, in degenerative diseases of the cerebellum, or, particularly in the brainstem, with lesions of multiple sclerosis.

CRITERIA FOR DIAGNOSIS
Suggestive

Rest tremor is seen in Parkinson's disease or in parkinsonian conditions, degenerative or drug induced. Symptoms of parkinsonism associated with tremor generally suggest that the tremor is a rest tremor.

Essential or familial tremor is generally a condition manifested solely by the presence of a tremor. Therefore, suggestive evidence of a tremor being an essential tremor is the absence of other neurologic signs.

Movement tremors are, as already noted, seen with lesions to the cerebellum and brainstem. Aside from the nature of the tremor itself, the presence of ataxia, truncal or appendicular, suggests that a tremor is of this variety.

Definitive

The *resting tremor* is seen in an attitude of repose. It disappears when the limb makes a purposeful movement. It is usually an "alternating" tremor, meaning that the agonist and antagonist muscle groups moving the limb fire alternately instead of synchronously. The frequency of the tremor is about 4 to 5 Hz. The presence of the tremor with other parkinsonian signs is typical whether due to Parkinson's disease, to other degenerative diseases with parkinsonian features, or to drug-induced parkinsonism.

Essential or familial tremor is a 5- to 10-Hz tremor that is usually symmetric and is initially noted in the upper extremity, although it may spread to the head and less frequently to the legs. It is a synchronous tremor with antagonist and agonist muscles firing together rather than alternately. The tremor is produced as the force of contraction varies between antagonist and agonist muscles.

Movement tremor, or those tremors associated with the cerebellum or cerebellar brainstem connections, are large-amplitude 2- to 4-Hz tremors that are usually exaggerated at the end of a voluntary movement, such as is observed in finger-to-nose testing. These tremors are rhythmic and can be distinguished from dysmetric and ataxic movements associated with these conditions.

CLINICAL MANIFESTATIONS

Subjective

In all forms of tremor, the complaint of tremor by the patient or family member is what brings it to medical attention. Some complaints go along with specific forms of tremor.

In rest tremor, complaints associated with parkinsonism are common. Tremor associated with bradykinesia and akinesia or occurring after starting a drug known to cause parkinsonism, such as haloperidol or metoclopramide, is suggestive of drug-induced parkinsonian tremor. In true Parkinson's disease, the tremor frequently starts unilaterally, which is unusual in other diseases associated with tremor.

Familial tremor is defined by the presence of an appropriate tremor and a family history of tremor. This is the sole distinguishing factor between familial tremor and essential tremor. Both typically start with shaking of the hands when specific tasks such as writing and drinking from a cup are undertaken. Often the tremor spreads to the chin or head or causes a quavering of the voice. Difficulty doing tasks requiring fine-motor movements is a common complaint. An important point in taking a history for essential or familial tremor is whether the tremor is affected by the ingestion of ethanol. Frequently, essential or familial tremor is significantly reduced when even small amounts of ethanol are consumed. It is important to ask about the use of adrenergic drugs such as theophylline and albuterol or use of thyroid replacement medications, which may enhance a physiologic tremor.

Generally, cerebellar or movement tremors appear with other neurologic diseases causing cerebellar or brainstem lesions. The history of tremor associated with ataxia, vertigo, and vomiting or other brainstem signs such as dysarthria and diplopia suggests this type of tremor. In slow-growing cerebellar tumors or in cerebellar degeneration of any nature, the tremor may be the predominant complaint, but it is usually paired with complaints of imbalance or dysarthria.

Objective

Physical Examination

The physical findings of resting tremor consist of the presence of a 4- to 5-Hz tremor that occurs when the affected limb is in a state of repose. As is seen with parkinsonian syndromes, other physical findings that might be expected are those associated with parkinsonism, such as hypomimia (reduced facial expression), increased tone in the limbs (often cogwheel rigidity), decreased rate of eye blink, bradykinesia, retropulsion, and a parkinsonian gait with short, shuffling steps, a stooped posture, and decreased arm swing.

The physical findings of essential or familial tremor are the presence of a 5- to 10-Hz, usually symmetric, tremor seen with voluntary movement and the absence of other neurologic symptoms or metabolic abnormalities. It is important to distinguish an essential or familial tremor from an enhanced physiologic tremor.

In movement tremors one should observe a coarse 2- to 4-Hz tremor that is induced with purposeful movement. The most significant tremor usually occurs at the end of the movement, as the limb approaches its target. In more severe cases the head may also shake when the arm is used. Tremor in the legs may occur when attempting to walk and may become so severe as to make ambulation, even with assistive devices, impossible. These symptoms are usually accompanied by ataxia, truncal or appendicular, and may be accompanied by dysarthria or other signs associated with brainstem pathology such as dysarthria and diplopia. Vertigo is usually seen early in these syndromes as well. Sometimes these symptoms may be seen with toxic levels of phenytoin, alcohol, or sedative drugs or with hypothyroidism, and these causes should be ruled out. Except in cases of cerebellar degeneration, a discreet structural lesion of the cerebellum or brainstem is responsible for the majority of these tremors, and evaluating these areas with neuroimaging (especially magnetic resonance imaging) is the most efficient way of making a diagnosis.

Routine Laboratory Abnormalities

A laboratory workup is not usually necessary in parkinsonism, but if other symptoms such as dementia, dystonia, or muscle spasms are present, especially in a young person, a diagnosis of Wilson's disease should be entertained, serum copper and ceruloplasmin levels should be determined, and, if necessary, a slit-lamp examination should be done.

Thyroid function tests should always be checked if essential or familial tremor is suspected. If there is a suggestive history, a pheochromocytoma should be looked for with a 24-hour urine sample tested for abnormal amounts of catecholamines, metanephrine, and vanillylmandelic acid.

PLANS

Diagnostic

Differential Diagnosis

The differential diagnosis of a specific tremor includes disorders with tremor as a primary characteristic, tremors caused by metabolic disorders, drug-induced tremors, withdrawal and emotional states associated with tremulousness, and disorders that may be mistaken for tremors (Table 20–24–1).

Diagnostic Options

A number of diagnostic tools are available for evaluating tremor. If an anatomic lesion is suspected, neuroimaging techniques such as computed axial tomography and magnetic resonance imaging are useful. As lesions are generally in the basal ganglia, brainstem, or cerebellum, magnetic resonance imaging is usually superior unless an acute bleed is suspected.

Metabolic causes of tremor may be evaluated with thyroid function tests and 24-hour urine collection for catecholamines, vanillylmandelic acid, and metanephrine.

When appropriate, serum screens for anticonvulsants, tricyclic antidepressants, theophylline, heavy metals, lithium, and amphetamines can be obtained.

In cases where the nature of the tremor is unclear, tremor analysis may be helpful. Tremor analysis involves measuring electromyographic activity from agonist and antagonist muscles in an affected limb. Accelerometers are also placed on the limb to assess the frequency and amplitude of the tremor. The tremor may then be categorized in terms of frequency, whether it is an alternating or synchronous tremor, and even how it is affected by specific drugs.

TABLE 20–24–1. DIFFERENTIAL DIAGNOSIS OF TREMOR

Disorders with tremor as a primary component
  Rest tremor (parkinsonism)
  Essential or familial tremor
  Movement tremor (lesions of the cerebellum or brainstem)
Metabolic disorders inducing tremor
  Hyper- or hypothyroidism
  Pheochromocytoma
  Fever
  Hypoglycemia
Drug-induced tremor
  Adrenergic drugs (theophylline, epinephrine, terbutaline, metaproterenol)
  Dopaminergic drugs (levodopa, amphetamine)
  Psychotropic drugs (neuroleptic agents, lithium, tricyclic antidepressants)
  Anticonvulsants (phenytoin, valproate)
  Hormones (corticosteroids, thyroxine)
Heavy metal intoxication
Withdrawal states (alcohol, opiates, benzodiazepines)
Movement disorders mistaken for tremor
  Myoclonus
  Clonus
  Asterixis
  Dystonia
Emotional states (anxiety, anger)
Hysterical tremor

Recommended Approach

Once a tremor is categorized (if this is difficult, tremor analysis may be helpful) the diagnostic workup can be more focused.

In patients exhibiting rest tremor, other features of parkinsonism should be sought. If these are found, clinical evidence separating Parkinson's disease from other parkinsonian syndromes such as progressive supranuclear palsy (with its eye movement abnormalities), Shy–Drager syndrome (with autonomic insufficiency), striatonigral degeneration, parkinsonism associated with use of neuroleptic agents, and Wilson's disease. If Wilson's disease (an abnormality of copper metabolism in which copper is deposited in various organs including the brain) is suspected, serum copper and ceruloplasmin levels are determined. No further laboratory evaluation is necessary. Neuroimaging may be helpful if a structural lesion of the basal ganglia or normal-pressure hydrocephalus (which may mimic Parkinson's disease early in its course) is suspected.

In patients with what clinically appears to be familial or essential tremor, the most important point of the workup is ruling out an enhanced physiologic tremor. Patients must be asked about the use of drugs that induce tremor or possible exposure to heavy metals. Appropriate tests for drug levels (theophylline, phenytoin, or lithium, for instance) should be done and a heavy metal screen ordered if deemed a possibility. The workup should always include thyroid function tests. If sweating, tachycardia, or weight loss is part of the illness, pheochromocytoma should be considered and a 24-hour urine collected for urine catecholamines, vanillylmandelic acid, and metanephrine. If a neuropathy is suspected, electromyography may be helpful. When other types of tremors have been ruled out, the distinction between familial and essential tremor rests on the presence or absence of a family history of tremor.

If movement tremor is suspected, careful neurologic examination to detect evidence of brainstem or cerebellar pathology is performed. Nystagmus, truncal or appendicular ataxia, dysmetria, diplopia, dysarthria, and complaints of true vertigo are noted with lesions in these areas. History of use of phenytoin should be specifically obtained and levels tested if phenytoin intoxication is a possibility. The most useful test in determining the nature of the illness is magnetic resonance imaging. Stroke, tumor, cerebellar degeneration, and especially multiple sclerosis can cause these syndromes. Computed axial tomography is preferable only if a high suspicion of a cerebellar bleed exists. If lesions consistent with multiple sclerosis are noted, it would be prudent to order Lyme titers and sedimentation rates to help rule out Lyme disease and arthritis as possible causes of suspicious lesions. Usually, no further workup is needed in the evaluation of these kinds of tremors.

Therapeutic

Therapeutic Options

A number of drugs are available to treat different kinds of tremors (Table 20–24–2). Occasionally, weights for the wrists or legs are effective in helping patients with cerebellar or brainstem lesions. Rarely, surgical lesioning of the thalamus is helpful in patients with severe rest or movement tremors.

Recommended Approach

The therapeutic approach taken toward a tremor, again, depends on its categorization.

In rest tremor associated with Parkinson's disease, it must first be clinically determined whether the tremor or the other symptoms of the disease are most limiting to the patient. If bradykinesia is a salient part of the disease, then the tremor is treated with the rest of the symptoms and with the same drugs. Tremor may respond to levodopa, bromocriptine, or pergolide, but it is the least predictable in terms of a clinical response to these drugs. If the tremor does not respond or is the only clinically bothersome aspect of the disease (as happens not infrequently), then trihexyphenidyl hydrochloride (Artane) or benztropine mesylate (Cogentin) may be used alone or in conjunction with other drugs. Another useful drug for rest tremor is ethopropazine hydrochloride, which is often better tolerated than trihexyphenidyl hydrochloride, especially in older patients. In some patients with severe and intractable tremor,

TABLE 20–24–2. DRUGS USED IN THE TREATMENT OF TREMOR

Rest tremor
  Carbidopa/levodopa
  Anticholinergic agents
    Trihexyphenidyl hydrochloride (Artane)
    Benztropine mesylate (Cogentin)
  Ethopropazine hydrochloride
  Dopamine agonists
    Bromocriptine
    Pergolide
    Lisuride
  Amantadine
  Clozapine
Essential or familial tremor
  Beta blockers
  Primidone (Mysoline)
  Phenobarbital
  Benzodiazepines
  Amantadine
  Methazolamide
Cerebellar or rubral tremor
  Carbamazepine
  Valproate
  Clonazepam
  Carbidopa (with or without levodopa)
  Isoniazid
  Lithium

clozapine has been effective; however, its tendency to cause leukopenia and the close monitoring required (weekly white blood counts) make it less convenient to use. In particularly resistant and debilitating cases, stereotactic lesioning of the thalamus may markedly improve tremor. This option is most attractive in unilateral parkinsonian tremor, as the morbidity of the procedure is considerably less if performed unilaterally.

In essential or familial tremor, the drugs of choice are beta blockers. We favor long-acting propranolol. The beta blockers are generally well tolerated and are particularly effective, although high doses (280–320 mg of Inderal) are sometimes needed for maximum effect. Patients with chronic obstructive pulmonary disease or asthma may not tolerate propranolol. Metaprolol, a selective β_1-agonist, may be tried in these patients. One must keep in mind that all so-called selective drugs are only relatively selective, and high doses of metaprolol may have β_2-agonist properties. Primidone (Mysoline) is also a potentially effective drug. Some studies have suggested that it is more effective than propranolol. Treatment is instituted at 50 or even 25 mg/d and slowly increased. Primidone is significantly more sedating than propranolol and patients who must drive or use machinery may not be suitable candidates for it. In a few patients there are severe side effects, with marked sedation, confusion, and even delusional behavior with even the smallest doses. Clonazepam may be somewhat effective for essential (or for almost any kind of) tremor. As all tremors are exacerbated by anxiety, it may be the anxiotic properties of clonazepam that result in the improvement. A number of other drugs such as amantadine, methazolamide, and trazadone have been reported to reduce tremor and might be used on a trial basis with individual patients, but they are considerably less effective than the drugs mentioned above.

Tremors due to lesions of the cerebellum and brainstem are often very resistant to treatment. First-line drugs for treating these tremors include valproate and clonazepam. These two drugs often act synergistically with each other and are much more effective in combination. We have had significant success with carbamazepine alone in a number of patients with rubral tremor associated with multiple sclerosis and closed head injury. Patients are started on 400 to 600 mg/d, and the dosage is slowly increased. Hand function has been significantly improved in a number of patients treated this way, and we have frequently used carbamazepine as a first-line drug. Carbidopa/levodopa can also be effective, and sometimes carbidopa alone in doses of 100 to 200 mg/d is more effective than the combination. Lithium and isoniazid may occasionally be effective, but we have not found them particularly effective. Stereotactic thalamotomy may also be employed in severe and refractory cerebellar and brainstem tremors, but as the tremor is generally bilateral, morbidity is increased unless only one side is done. Also, these tremors are due to, often significant, lesions of the central nervous system, making outcome less predictable. Thus, thalamotomy should be a last resort and only in patients with debilitating tremors.

FOLLOW-UP

Evaluation of therapy in patients with any form of tremor is focused on improvements in functions such as writing, buttoning, using a cup or utensils, and reducing self-consciousness in social situations. Noting the amplitude of the tremor (i.e., 1- to 2-in. excursions) and following handwriting samples and drawings of figures like Archimedes' spiral are more objective assessments. The goal of therapy is not to obliterate the tremor completely, but to return as much such function to the patient as possible. When the patient does not feel limited by the tremor, treatment is adequate.

DISCUSSION
Prevalence and Incidence

Rest tremor is seen in about 90% of patients with Parkinson's disease. The prevalence of Parkinson's disease is estimated at 80 to 180 per 100,000.

Few epidemiologic studies have been done on essential tremor, but the prevalence is estimated at 0.5 to 5% of the population over 40 years of age.

No significant studies of the prevalence of cerebellar or brainstem tremors have been done.

Related Basic Science

The tremor that has a genetic predisposition is, of course, familial tremor. Several types of familial tremor have been observed. Some involve the arms alone or the chin alone. Some families have a predictable frequency to their tremor. Most are autosomal dominant.

Natural History and Its Modification with Treatment

Resting tremor is associated most closely in Parkinson's disease, a progressive disease. Treatment of the tremor affords relief from a trouble-some symptom, but does not alter the course of the disease. The only medication that appears to slow the progress of the disease (and thus, the worsening of all symptoms) is selegiline hydrochloride (Eldepryl). It is probably reasonable to treat all patients who tolerate the drug.

Essential or familial tremor is also a progressive disease that tends to slowly worsen over years or decades. Pharmacologic treatment of the tremor reduces symptoms but does not alter the course.

With the exceptions of progressive forms of multiple sclerosis and cerebellar degeneration, lesions inducing cerebellar or brainstem tremors are static. If effective treatment is obtained no changes will be necessary over time.

Prevention

Unfortunately, most causes of tremor cannot be prevented. As mentioned above, symptoms of Parkinson's disease may be stayed for a while with the use of selegiline. The dearth of knowledge as to how tremors are actually generated limits efforts to affect them beyond responding to symptoms. As the nature of tremors is better understood, preventive strategies may evolve.

Cost Containment

The greatest cost of tremor disorders comes with their attendant loss of manual function in working situations and in the human cost of a cosmetically troubling condition that can result in isolation and even depression. Prompt categorization of the tremor and diligent attempts to reduce tremor are cost effective in that they help patients retain function. The effect of tremor on an individual should not be underestimated.

REFERENCES

Adams R, Victor M. Principles of neurology. 5th ed. New York: McGraw-Hill, 1993.
Jancovic J, Tolousa E, eds. Parkinson's disease and movement disorders. 2nd ed. Baltimore: Williams & Wilkins, 1993.
Marsden D, Fahn S, eds. Movement disorders 3. Oxford: Butterworth-Heineman, 1994.
Weiner W, Lang A. Movement disorders: A comprehensive survey. New York: Futura, 1989.

CHAPTER 20–25

Abnormalities of Gait

George D. Baquis, M.D., and A. Bernard Pleet, M.D.

DEFINITION

Neurologic disorders of gait are a group of conditions that affect independent voluntary biped stance and ambulation. These conditions interfere with normal posture, balance, walking, and running, and contribute to an increased risk of falls.

ETIOLOGY

As normal gait requires the coordinated activity of many central and peripheral nervous system structures, the abnormalities reflect a diverse group of diseases. Characteristic disturbances are associated with myopathies, peripheral neuropathies, myelopathies, diseases affecting vestibulocerebellar function, basal ganglia disorders, diseases resulting in hydrocephalus, injury to subcortical white matter, and those conditions characterized by cortical hemispheric dysfunction.

CRITERIA FOR DIAGNOSIS
Suggestive

Gait disorders are usually a reflection of an underlying disease and should be considered whenever symptoms of abnormal posture, decreased speed of ambulation, disordered balance, tripping, stumbling, or frequent falling are described.

Definitive

The diagnosis is established through clinical observation of the patient's pattern of standing and walking. The underlying etiology is determined through clinical investigation of the multiple possible underlying conditions. This may require blood studies, nervous system imaging, electrophysiologic studies, genetic analysis, cerebrospinal fluid examination, and examination of other specific tissues and structures. Occasionally, a definitive diagnosis can be determined only through the response to therapy (e.g., the response of normal-pressure hydrocephalus to shunting).

CLINICAL MANIFESTATIONS
Subjective

Symptoms of gait dysfunction vary with the underlying disease. The proximal muscle weakness of myopathies results in difficulty arising from a chair or from the toilet and walking up inclines or steps. Aching of axial muscles can result from abnormalities of trunk, pelvic, or shoulder posture.

The weakness of distal polyneuropathies results in tripping, stumbling, or episodic falls. Occasionally, polyradiculoneuropathies such as Guillain–Barré syndrome may present with symptoms of "rubbery legs" or knee buckling. Unilateral knee buckling suggests weakness of the quadriceps femoris muscle.

The ataxic patient describes imbalance and unsteadiness that is accentuated by changing direction, ambulating in dimly lighted or darkened surroundings, or ambulating on rough surfaces. Patients prefer to walk with someone who steadies them and easily fall when changing course or position. Walking downstairs is especially difficult. Those with acute vestibular or labyrinthine dysfunction describe tilting, spinning, or oscillopsia ("dancing vision") in conjunction with disturbances of balance. They often feel particularly insecure when in a moving car, the appearance of the moving surroundings inducing sensations of visual disorientation.

Slowness of walking and "weakness" are common symptoms and complaints in patients with extrapyramidal disease. Typically, these patients describe falling backward on attempting to stand, have difficulty in initiating stepping, and have episodes of tripping associated with falling forward. They may also feel that their legs are about to buckle beneath them, although overt muscular weakness is absent.

Symptoms of spasticity include unilateral or bilateral leg stiffness, slowness of ambulation, and episodes of tripping associated with forward falls.

As symptoms of gait dysfunction are often nonspecific, associated symptoms provide important diagnostic clues. Decline of cognition, change in behavior, and sphincter incontinence suggest hemispheric disease. Distal extremity tingling or loss of sensation suggests peripheral nerve disease, but may occasionally be an early symptom of a myelopathy. A past history of optic neuritis in association with symptoms of spasticity and ataxia suggests multiple sclerosis. Somnolence may occur in the setting of hydrocephalus or expanding hemispheric space-occupying lesions. Isolated unilateral symptoms may occur with hemispheric or peripheral nervous system disease, but are less common with myelopathies. Radiculopathies and plexopathies are often painful and asymmetric. A number of inherited conditions may present with primarily gait dysfunction, including the muscular dystrophies, spinal muscular atrophy, the hereditary motor and sensory polyneuropathies (Charcot–Marie–Tooth disease), hereditary cerebellar ataxias, and familial spastic paraplegia. The medical history may reveal head trauma (subdural hematoma), focal neurologic dysfunction (stroke, multiple sclerosis), polyradiculopathy, mono- or polyneuropathy, or cancer.

Objective
Physical Examination

Myopathies are associated with a waddling gait, proximal muscle atrophy and weakness, and depressed proximal deep tendon reflexes proportionate to the loss of strength. Generalized sensorimotor polyneuropathies are associated with distal sensory loss, distal muscular atrophy and weakness, depressed distal deep tendon reflexes, and a foot-slapping gait. Polyradiculoneuropathies such as Guillain–Barré syndrome may occasionally present as primarily a gait disturbance, and the early absence of proximal and distal deep tendon reflexes is an important clue. Focal atrophy and weakness of a single extremity suggest either a mononeuropathy, plexopathy, or radiculopathy. Disproportionate weakness of foot extensor or dorsiflexor muscles can result in a foot drop. This can be seen in the context of an L-5 radiculopathy, lower lumbar plexopathy, or peroneal nerve injury, or, when bilateral, can be

secondary to a peripheral neuropathy. Abnormal posture in association with scoliosis and hammer toes is seen with hereditary motor and sensory neuropathies.

Ataxic gaits are broad-based and unsteady with an inability to correct for abrupt changes in direction. The intermalleolar distance varies as the patient weaves while walking and clutches at his or her surroundings. Sensory ataxia is associated with loss of proprioceptive modalities and the patient hesitantly taps the floor before placing the foot forward to walk. Midline vermian cerebellar disease is associated with a staggering, "drunken sailor" quality. Eye closure while standing increases sway and may be associated with falling (Romberg's sign).

The spastic gait is manifested by a slowness with short steps, a stiff-legged appearance, and the legs are held closely together. The hip circumducts, toes may scrape the floor while walking, and the knees may either rub or cross each other as the legs adduct while the patient ambulates.

Extrapyramidal gait patterns are characterized by slowness, short steps, acceleration of the rate of stepping (festination), a stooped posture, episodes of freezing while walking, and an inability to compensate for sudden changes in position which results in frequent falls. Arm swing is diminished. Rather than pivoting while turning, the patient takes several short steps (turns en bloc). Bumping into objects is common because the patient fails to turn the head in anticipation of changing directions. The patient is unable to lean sufficiently far forward when attempting to stand from a chair, with a tendency to retropulsion. Some patients are unable to lift or move their feet while standing, although they can easily move them while sitting or lying. These patients have a great deal of difficulty changing position in bed, leading to impaired sleeping and resting.

Patients with disease of the deep white matter and with hydrocephalus bear some resemblance to those with Parkinson's disease, but can be differentiated because they walk on a wider base, may appear ataxic, and do not festinate. Abnormal associated behavioral and cognitive features suggest hemispheric disease, and they may be incontinent.

Dystonias result in abnormal positioning of the shoulders, hips, trunk, and extremities.

Psychiatric gait disorders are often associated with bizarre postures, abnormal movements, and unusual behaviors. They may be difficult to distinguish from neurologic disease. Features we have found suggestive of a psychiatric disturbance include dragging of the feet with failure to lift them while walking; severe side-to-side hip and arm sway while tandem walking (heel to toe) without the need for corrective shifts of ankle–foot position and without falling; and the ability to tandem walk or to hop on one foot without falling, despite apparent severe ataxia and imbalance.

Patients with multiple sclerosis often exhibit a pecular gait, best described as "jiggling," which is the result of both spasticity and ataxia.

Routine Laboratory Abnormalities

Routine laboratory testing is usually normal unless there is an underlying systemic disease.

PLANS
Diagnostic
Differential Diagnosis

The differential diagnosis varies depending on the underlying type of gait disturbance. The differential diagnosis of peripheral neuropathies and myopathies is broad and includes both acquired and inherited conditions. The myelopathies produce spastic or spastic–ataxic gait patterns and can be due to extrinsic compressive lesions (cervical spondylosis with spinal stenosis, cervical disk herniation, tumors), vascular malformations, intrinsic structural spinal cord disease (syringomyelia, tumors), demyelinating disease (multiple sclerosis, transverse myelitis, Devic's syndrome), infections (syphilis, HIV), metabolic disorders (vitamin B_{12} deficiency), and traumatic and inherited conditions (familial spastic paraplegia, Friedreich's ataxia).

Parasagittal tumors, foramen magnum tumors, and bilateral strokes may present with a spastic gait.

The acquired cerebellar ataxias include toxic (alcohol, medications), neoplastic (primary and metastatic), paraneoplastic, mitochondrial (Kearns–Sayer syndrome), and miscellaneous inherited disorders. Ataxia after mild head trauma may occur in the setting of congenital cerebellar malformations, such as the Arnold–Chiari malformation.

Extrapyramidal patterns are seen with Parkinson's disease, progressive supranuclear palsy, striatonigral degeneration, and other degenerative basal ganglia diseases. A similar pattern may be seen with frontal lobe disease (neoplasm, subdural hematoma, traumatic contusion, stroke), Binswanger's disease, and normal-pressure hydrocephalus.

Many diseases present with clinical patterns of multisystem disease. These include amyotrophic lateral sclerosis (spasticity and atrophic muscular weakness), multiple sclerosis, stroke syndromes, and metastatic disease.

Normal aging is also associated with a change in gait pattern, with features that may include difficulty with tandem walking, slowness, poor truncal stability, short steps, and loss of associated arm movements.

Diagnostic Options

The options for evaluation of peripheral nervous system disease include electromyography and nerve conduction studies, along with other tests that are outlined in Chapter 20–1.

In the setting of a myelopathy, cervical spine radiographs may demonstrate cervical spondylosis or spondylolisthesis. Magnetic resonance imaging of the spinal cord is the procedure of choice for demonstrating disk herniation, neoplasms, and intrinsic spinal cord disease.

Brain computed axial tomography may reveal tumors, strokes, subdural or epidural hematomas, or hydrocephalus. Brain magnetic resonance imaging is more sensitive for detection of demyelinating lesions, small strokes, and structural disease of the cerebellum and other posterior fossa structures.

Cerebrospinal fluid examination may be indicated for assessment of multiple sclerosis and transverse myelitis and for the diagnosis of infections, as well as for the measurement of opening pressure (normal-pressure hydrocephalus).

Recommended Approach

Historical data provide useful clues about the temporal profile. It is the associated features of cognitive or behavioral change, visual or auditory impairment, sphincter incontinence, back pain, abnormalities of symmetry, alterations of sensation, and manner of falling that provide information about disease pathogenesis. Ultimately, gait must be observed carefully over a sufficient distance to facilitate adequate description. Associated neurologic findings need to be elicited to direct the laboratory evaluation to the brain, spinal cord, or peripheral nervous system. Appropriate imaging or directed diagnostic testing may then be pursued.

Therapeutic

Therapeutic Options

Offending toxins (alcohol) should be eliminated and medication side effects (e.g., phenytoin) identified. Specific metabolic disorders (vitamin B_{12} deficiency) and infections (HIV, syphilis) should be treated. Tumors, subdural hematomas, and cervical spondylosis or disk herniation with spinal cord compression require neurosurgical evaluation. Treatment of stroke syndromes requires identification of the underlying pathogenesis, as well as evaluation of risk factors. The syndrome of normal-pressure hydrocephalus may improve with ventriculoperitoneal shunting, although not all patients improve and consensus is lacking regarding which criteria are most predictive of a beneficial response to treatment.

Recommended Approach

Identification of the underlying cause of a gait disturbance is essential for appropriate treatment. All patients with gait disorders benefit from careful physical and occupational therapy assessments. A cane, walker, or appropriate bracing-orthotic device may prevent falls. A wheelchair may be necessary when safe ambulation is no longer possible.

FOLLOW-UP

Response to therapy is best assessed through clinical observation of gait and through the patient's description of change and the patient's functional capacity. The need for additional testing depends on the disease process.

DISCUSSION

Prevalence and Incidence

The prevalence and incidence of gait disturbances are not known. The most common causes in the elderly include myelopathy, multiple cerebral infarctions, sensory disorders, Parkinson's disease, and the side effects of medications.

Related Basic Science

Walking is a complex activity that is performed automatically, with many components that are difficult to analyze individually through simple observation. Proprioceptive, visual, and vestibular information must be integrated, and postural reflexes play a role in balance. Readily observed features include rate, rhythmicity, velocity, stride length, and joint motion. Gait laboratory investigational studies focus on quantitative assessment of these characteristics using techniques that include video, computer-assisted, and dynamic electromyographic recordings.

Natural History and Its Modification with Treatment

Early identification and treatment of neoplasms, subdural hematomas, and spinal cord compressive lesions result in stabilization with the potential for improvement. Identification of stroke risk factors and treatment of causes may prevent further events. The goal is to intervene prior to the accumulation of significant deficits, as there is no therapy that will facilitate more complete recovery once central nervous system injury has occurred. Parkinson's disease, Alzheimer's disease, amyotrophic lateral sclerosis, and the inherited cerebellar disease are progressive and incurable. Medical therapy of Parkinson's disease alleviates clinical disability and improves quality of life. Although shunting for normal-pressure hydrocephalus may result in improvement, not all patients benefit. The disease gradually progresses over months to years when untreated. Relapsing and remitting multiple sclerosis may benefit from interferon beta treatment, and chronic progressive multiple sclerosis may temporarily stabilize with cyclophosphamide and adrenal corticosteroid therapy. The myelopathy of vitamin B_{12} deficiency stabilizes with treatment and may gradually improve over months. The prognosis for disorders of the peripheral nervous system and for those disorders associated with systemic disease and cancer is that of the underlying disease.

Prevention

Most of these conditions are not preventable. Identification of those conditions that are treatable may allow for early intervention and prevent the accumulation of further disability.

Cost Containment

Identification of gait disorders in the elderly may prevent falls. As falling is associated with significant morbidity from fractures and other physical injuries, early intervention has the potential to impact on hospital and other medical costs.

REFERENCES

Fisher CM. Hydrocephalus as a cause of disturbances of gait in the elderly. Neurology 1982;32:1358.

Haerer AF. Dejong's the neurologic examination. 5th ed. Philadelphia: Lippincott, 1992.

Jankovic J, Tolosa E, eds. Parkinson's disease and movement disorders. Baltimore: Williams & Wilkins, 1993.

Koller WC, Glatt SL, Fox JH. Senile gait, a distinct neurologic entity. Clin Geriatr Med 1985;3:661.

Sudarsky L, Ronthal M. Gait disorders among elderly patients: A survey study of 50 patients. Arch Neurol 1983;40:740.

Thompson PD, Marsden CD. Gait disorder of subcortical arteriosclerotic encephalopathy: Binswanger's disease. Movement Disorders 1987;2:1.

Tinetti ME, Williams TF, Mayewski R. Fall risk index for elderly patients based on number of chronic disabilities. Am J Med 1986;80:429.

CHAPTER 20–26

Insomnia and Hypersomnia

Bruce L. Ehrenberg, M.D.

DEFINITION

Insomnia

Nearly everyone has occasional sleeplessness, but insomnia is a self-perceived inadequacy of sleep quantity (or sometimes of sleep quality) occurring chronically or in recurrent bouts. As some normal healthy individuals have very short sleep times, insomnia further implies some dissatisfaction with daytime alertness, performance, or mood. Insomnia can be subdivided into three types: trouble with sleep initiation, poor sleep maintenance, and early-morning awakening; there are numerous causes for each type.

Hypersomnia

Excessive daytime sleepiness is subjectively perceived but also can be objectively measured. If chronic or recurrent, excessive daytime sleepiness should lead to a search for one of the several causes of hypersomnia. Most such disorders involve disordered, nonrestorative sleep, although excessive daytime sleepiness can occur with a normal sleep pattern.

ETIOLOGY

Insomnia is most often caused by a psychiatric disorder or in conjunction with the abuse of drugs or alcohol, but in about a third of cases is caused by a medical or neurologic illness that either directly or indirectly impacts sleep quality and quantity.

Hypersomnia is usually caused by a neurologic or medical disorder detracting from sleep quality, but occasionally there is an additional primary disturbance of daytime waking mechanisms, and rarely, the latter occurs alone.

Further, disturbances of circadian rhythm can be a primary cause or an aggravating factor in several types of hypersomnia and insomnia.

CRITERIA FOR DIAGNOSIS

Suggestive

Patients who, despite their best efforts, obtain less than 6 to 7 hours of sleep per night and do not feel fully rested make up the vast majority of insomnia patients. If the insomnia is due to psychiatric problems, there will be strongly positive answers to most of the following questions: Do you have trouble getting to sleep at night? Do you feel depressed or have racing thoughts at bedtime? Do you have frequent nightmares or intense dreams? Do you have major social problems? Do you have a family history of psychiatric illness?

Medical/neurologic insomnia and, more often, hypersomnia are caused by disorders that directly impact sleep quality: periodic limb movement disorder of sleep (PLMS), restless legs syndrome (RLS), or obstructive sleep apnea. Narcolepsy is a disorder caused by both a deficit in quality of nocturnal sleep and an idiopathic excess of daytime sleep pressure, particularly for rapid eye movement sleep. In addition, any medical or neurologic condition that causes discomfort of any kind can indirectly affect sleep and lead to insomnia or hypersomnia: chronic lung diseases or asthma with nocturnal respiratory distress, chronic anginal pains or congestive heart failure with paroxysmal nocturnal dyspnea, gastroesophageal reflux or other intestinal pain disorders with nocturnal manifestations, arthritis with chronic joint pain, osteoporotic or neoplasm-related bone pain, polyuria of any cause, hyperthyroidism, advanced pregnancy, nocturnal migraine headache, Parkinson's disease with rigidity and chronic muscle pains, neuromuscular disorders with painful spasms or chronic respiratory insufficiency, painful peripheral neuropathies or nerve root irritations, or the rare prion-related fatal familial insomnia.

A careful sleep history and general medical/neurologic history and review of systems delineate the underlying problem in most cases. Patients with obstructive sleep apnea are not always aware of their loud snoring, but a bed partner will usually give a strong history. Patients with RLS complain of restless legs in the evening, especially when lying down for bed, and this may prevent them from getting to sleep. During sleep, however, the RLS patients as well as those with PLMS usually are not aware of their repetitive limb (mostly leg) movements, and less than half of their bed partners have noticed this tendency. Although each of the above disorders can be associated with either insomnia or hypersomnia, with advancing age patients are increasingly likely to have hypersomnia.

Definitive

The definitive diagnosis of any case of insomnia may require an overnight in-laboratory polysomnogram, as about 50% of cases may be misdiagnosed if one relies on the history alone. Most of the missed diagnoses involve unsuspected sleep apnea or PLMS but occasionally are due to sleep misperception syndrome, where the patient's sleep complaints are not verified and the polysomnogram is entirely normal. In the diagnosis of severe hypersomnia, nearly all cases should have a polysomnogram done, followed by a multiple sleep latency test the next day, to confirm the degree of daytime sleepiness present.

CLINICAL MANIFESTATIONS

Subjective

Patients with insomnia are aware that the quantity and/or quality of their sleep are deficient, and although they do not have daytime sleepiness, they are usually unsatisfied with some part of their daytime functioning. Some studies of cognitive and memory functions show mild deficits in these patients, but the majority of subjective complaints may be difficult to verify with routine testing. Many patients with insomnia due to psychiatric problems have anxiety at bedtime that keeps them up, and they may become frustrated with their inability to relax and fall asleep within a reasonable time. This may become a self-fulfilling prophecy in so-called "psychophysiologic" insomnia.

On the other hand, patients with hypersomnia may have moderate to severe daytime problems related to lack of alertness. These may include falling asleep while driving or at other inappropriate times, episodes of performing tasks and then not remembering having done so later, and difficulty with concentration or learning of new material. Furthermore, the physical effects of sleep deprivation may include exacerbations of epileptic seizures or migraine headaches, hypertension (in sleep apnea), myalgias (see fibromyalgia and chronic fatigue syndromes), and other stress-related physical problems.

Patients with either insomnia or hypersomnia may develop depression, which can be secondary to their sleep disorder-related quality-of-life problems. Often the depression is the cause of the sleep disorder, especially bipolar depression, where the insomnia and hypersomnia episodes can be extreme.

The past history can help pinpoint when the sleep problem started; this helps to gauge chronicity and also may help relate changes in sleep patterns to major life events. For example, middle-aged women with RLS/PLMS may have first noted problems during pregnancy, older women with sleep apnea may date the onset of snoring to menopause, and men with depression-related insomnia may have started having sleep problems after losing a spouse. A complete history of major illnesses is necessary to diagnose any of the secondary sleep problems that relate to medical/neurologic diseases.

The family history is sometimes helpful in making the diagnosis of the uncommon idiopathic insomnia and is often helpful in diagnosing RLS or PLMS, but is less useful in other disorders, except as regards associated diagnoses such as alcoholism and depression.

Objective

Physical Examination

The physical examination is normal in most patients with primary sleep disorders except that a large proportion of obstructive sleep apnea patients are obese and have hypertension. Routine laboratory studies are also usually normal, although there may be secondary polycythemia in about 5% of obstructive sleep apnea patients and anemia in a similar proportion of RLS patients.

Routine Laboratory Abnormalities

Patients with sleep disorders associated with a medical or neurologic condition will have the stigmata and laboratory findings of the associated diseases.

PLANS

Diagnostic

Differential Diagnosis and Diagnostic Options

The rather long list of differential diagnoses in Table 20–26–1 is easier to use if one understands that most patients presenting with a primary sleep problem requiring medical treatment have one of the major entities named under "intrinsic sleep disorders." Many of the other disorders can be alleviated by simple commonsense suggestions, reassurance or counseling, or lifestyle changes, and still others require psychotherapy or treatment of the underlying medical/neurologic disease. Not listed in the table are medical disorders causing fatigue that can simulate hypersomnia, such as Addison's disease, diabetes, hemochromatosis, hypothyroidism, uremia, and also diseases causing ac-

TABLE 20–26–1. INTERNATIONAL CLASSIFICATION OF SLEEP DISORDERS

I. DYSSOMNIAS

A. Intrinsic Sleep Disorders
  1. Psychophysiologic insomnia
  2. Sleep state misperception
  3. Idiopathic insomnia
  4. Narcolepsy
  5. Recurrent hypersomnia (Kleine–Levin syndrome)
  6. Idiopathic hypersomnia
  7. Posttraumatic hypersomnia
  8. Obstructive sleep apnea syndrome
  9. Central sleep apnea syndrome
  10. Central alveolar hypoventilation syndrome
  11. Periodic limb movement disorder
  12. Restless legs syndrome

B. Extrinsic Sleep Disorders
  1. Inadequate sleep hygiene
  2. Environmental sleep disorder
  3. Altitude insomnia
  4. Adjustment sleep disorder
  5. Insufficient sleep syndrome
  6. Limit-setting sleep disorder
  7. Sleep-onset association disorder
  8. Food allergy insomnia
  9. Nocturnal eating (drinking) syndrome
  10. Hypnotic-dependent sleep disorder
  11. Stimulant-dependent sleep disorder
  12. Alcohol-dependent sleep disorder
  13. Toxin-induced sleep disorder

C. Circadian Rhythm Sleep Disorders
  1. Time zone change (jet lag) syndrome
  2. Shift work sleep disorder
  3. Irregular sleep–wake pattern
  4. Delayed sleep phase syndrome
  5. Advanced sleep phase syndrome
  6. Non-24-hour sleep–wake disorder

II. PARASOMNIAS

A. Arousal Disorders
  1. Confusional arousals (sleep drunkenness)
  2. Sleepwalking (somnambulism)
  3. Sleep terrors (pavor nocturnis)

B. Sleep–Wake Transition Disorders
  1. Rhythmic movement disorder ("headbanging")
  2. Sleep starts
  3. Sleep talking
  4. Nocturnal leg cramps

C. Parasomnias Usually Associated with REM Sleep
  1. Nightmares
  2. Sleep paralysis
  3. Impaired sleep-related penile erections
  4. Sleep-related painful erections
  5. REM sleep-related sinus arrest
  6. REM sleep behavior disorder

D. Other Parasomnias
  1. Sleep bruxism
  2. Sleep enuresis
  3. Sleep-related abnormal swallowing syndrome
  4. Nocturnal paroxysmal dystonia
  5. Sudden unexplained nocturnal death syndrome
  6. Primary snoring
  7. Infant sleep apnea
  8. Congenital central hypoventilation syndrome
  9. Sudden infant death syndrome
  10. Benign neonatal sleep myoclonus

III. SLEEP DISORDERS ASSOCIATED WITH MEDICAL/PSYCHIATRIC DISORDERS

A. Associated with Mental Disorders
  1. Psychoses
  2. Mood disorders
  3. Anxiety disorders
  4. Panic disorder
  5. Alcoholism

B. Associated with Neurologic Disorders
  1. Cerebral degenerative disorders
  2. Dementia
  3. Parkinsonism
  4. Fatal familial insomnia
  5. Sleep-related epilepsy
  6. Electrical status epilepticus of sleep
  7. Sleep-related headaches

C. Associated with Other Medical Disorders
  1. Sleeping sickness
  2. Nocturnal cardiac ischemia
  3. Chronic obstructive pulmonary disease
  4. Sleep-related asthma
  5. Sleep-related gastroesophageal reflux
  6. Peptic ulcer disease
  7. Fibrositis syndrome

IV. PROPOSED SLEEP DISORDERS

  1. Short sleeper
  2. Long sleeper
  3. Subwakefulness syndrome
  4. Fragmentary myoclonus
  5. Sleep hyperhidrosis
  6. Menstrual-associated sleep disorder
  7. Pregnancy-associated sleep disorder
  8. Terrifying hypnagogic hallucinations
  9. Sleep-related neurogenic tachypnea
  10. Sleep-related laryngospasm
  11. Sleep–choking syndrome

REM, rapid eye movement.

Source: Slightly modified from Diagnostic Classification Steering Committee, Thorpy MJ, Chairman. International classification of sleep disorders: Diagnostic and coding manual. Rochester, MN: American Sleep Disorders Association, 1990. Reproduced with permission.

tivation and insomnia, such as hyperthyroidism. A complete blood count, creatinine, electrolytes, erythrocyte sedimentation rate, glucose, transaminases, and thyroid-stimulating hormone along with the medical history should help rule out most of these disorders. When undisclosed drug use is suspected, a toxicology screen may be useful.

The diagnostic test options are otherwise limited to the electroencephalographic studies of sleep: the polysomnogram and the multiple sleep latency test.

Recommended Approach

A polysomnogram is necessary to diagnose the major common sleep disorders: obstructive sleep apnea, PLMS/RLS, and most of the parasomnias. A multiple sleep latency test is needed to diagnose narcolepsy, and is important in all other cases of severe hypersomnia, especially where revocation of a driver's license may be at issue. Many of the remaining sleep disorders can be diagnosed from the history of sleep patterns and any associated nocturnal factors affecting sleep; a 7- to 14-day sleep log showing the patient's habitual bedtimes and wakeup times, as well as daily medication, alcohol, and caffeine use at home, is essential in most undiagnosed cases, and should also be done before a polysomnogram or multiple sleep latency test to establish the context in which these tests are accomplished.

Therapeutic

Therapeutic Options

The treatment varies according to the type of sleep disorder. Obstructive sleep apnea can be treated in a variety of ways to relieve the obstruction, or with medication in mild cases (see Chapter 13–1). The treatment of PLMS/RLS usually involves levodopa, benzodiazepines, opiates, or valproate. The treatment of circadian disorders includes bright light therapy and efforts to regularize bedtimes and wakeup times. Parasomnias often do not need a specific treatment, but occasionally a benzodiazepine (e.g., clonazepam 0.5 mg at bedtime) or an antidepressant such as imipramine 25 mg at bedtime may be useful. For most cases of severe intractable insomnia, benzodiazepines and the older barbiturates may be initially effective but there is great potential for the development of tolerance, so alternatives have been sought; these include antihistamines (H$_1$ blockers) such as diphenhydramine, sedating antidpressants such as trazodone, and clonidine, a sedating antihypertensive agent. If only a benzodiazepine or related drug is found helpful, it is preferable to use one of the short-acting varieties, triazolam or zolpidem, in low doses. In many cases it is possible to overcome sleep problems with simple commonsense suggestions. For example, good sleep hygiene requires that distractions be removed from the bedroom and that a regular habitual bedtime be established. In addition, if sleep is not achieved within 30 minutes, it is best to go to another room and read or watch TV until drowsy. Many patients, however, cannot suppress "internal" distractions resulting from life stresses, and some may need psychotherapy with or without additional medications aimed at underlying affective or psychotic disorders. Behavioral therapies such as biofeedback and sleep restriction are also used.

Recommended Approach

It is best to remain flexible and be prepared to use a variety of different medications for sleep problems until a workable regimen is found. This may sometimes involve using more than one medication in rotation on alternate nights, to avoid tolerance. It is also important to use caution with medications that are known to exacerbate a sleep disorder, such as benzodiazepines in sleep apnea and tricyclic antidepressants (e.g., amitriptyline) and serotonin reuptake inhibitors (e.g., fluoxetine) in PLMS/RLS.

FOLLOW-UP

It is important to keep close contact with patients just starting therapy, especially with those on nasal continuous positive airway pressure for sleep apnea, because there is a high rate of noncompliance, and these patients are at highest risk for death due to daytime accidents caused by drowsiness or for nocturnal cardiac arrest due to arrhythmias. In cases where severe daytime sleepiness has limited a patient's driving privileges, it is helpful to repeat the multiple sleep latency test after effective therapy has been established, to provide documentation of alertness. If a patient has not improved as much as expected, a follow-up polysomnogram may also be needed. This is sometimes true in patients with sleep apnea where, after nasal continuous positive airway pressure therapy has begun, underlying PLMS emerges and continues to disrupt sleep as had the apneas, thus requiring additional medications (this is usually evident at the time of the first follow-up polysomnogram when continuous positive airway pressure titration is carried out). Conversely, some patients who appear to have classic PLMS may actually have a subtle form of sleep apnea (called upper airway resistance syndrome) and may therefore respond to continuous positive airway pressure but not to medications aimed at the PLMS.

DISCUSSION
Prevalence and Incidence

Sleep disorders as a whole are extremely common, almost universal. Of the major "primary" sleep disorders, the severe or persistent insomnias are said to affect 10 to 20% of the population, and the hypersomnias may affect another 5%. Up to 50% of the population may have had insomnia at some point in their lives. There is also a marked tendency for hypersomnia due to sleep apnea and the PLMS/RLS to increase with advancing age. Stability of the circadian sleep–wake pattern may also deteriorate with age.

Related Basic Science

The DR2 locus in the HLA region of chromosome 6 is under study in familial cases of narcolepsy. Similarly, there are ongoing studies to look for a chromosomal marker in large families found to have an autosomal dominant form of RLS. Also, a tendency to early-age onset of PLMS or sleep apnea may be inherited, but the genetic factors involved are unknown. A circadian pacemaker, thought to be associated with the suprachiasmatic nucleus in the hypothalamus, is affected by γ-aminobutyric acid and other neurotransmitters, offering possible future hope of improved control of sleep–wake cycling. The close relationship between the cytokines that control the immune system and the major sleep–wake mechanisms in the brain provides avenues for better understanding the physiologic functions of sleep. Memory and learning functions have also been found affected by rapid-eye-movement sleep deprivation.

Natural History and Its Modification with Treatment

Sleep apnea may progress with age, but usually weight gain is a concomitant factor that is also probably a contributing factor. Treatment of sleep apnea may forestall progression, especially if significant weight loss is accomplished. RLS/PLMS and narcolepsy tend to progress with age, and although medical treatment does not appear to alter the course, the long-term effects of exercise and diet have not been adequately assessed as yet. Insomnias not caused by easily treatable conditions tend to resist all treatment, but usually do not worsen with time, except that it is "normal" for the amount of sleep, especially deep sleep, to decline with advancing age.

Prevention

Avoiding middle-age weight gain may prevent many cases of sleep apnea, and maintaining a lifelong regimen of vigorous exercise may help delay the onset of RLS or PLMS, but no long-term studies have been done to prove that such suggestions will routinely succeed. The genetically determined disorders may yield to specific therapies once the chromosomal loci (and their functions) have been determined. For now, the major thrust should be to increase public and professional awareness of sleep disorders and their consequences, as many of the secondary effects of sleep disorders may thereby be prevented.

Cost Containment

A self-administered 175-item sleep disorders questionnaire (the "SDQ" of Douglass et al., 1994) gives each patient a percentile ranking in four categories: sleep apnea, periodic limb movements, narcolepsy, and psychiatric-related sleep disorder. These categories have been validated against a large group of patients, each of whom was diagnosed by polysomography. As the use of such questionnaires becomes more refined, a decision tree may be developed that reduces unnecessary laboratory testing. Nevertheless, the polysomnogram remains the "gold standard" for a sleep disorders diagnosis.

As polysomnograms are costly, there have been efforts to produce less expensive technologies, such as ambulatory sleep apnea monitors with built-in oximeters to record oxyhemoglobin saturations continuously. Although these units can help diagnose moderate and severe sleep apnea in straightforward cases, they often provide few or no data for diagnosing other sleep disorders (still leaving one with the need for a polysomnogram). Likewise, a simple movement monitor may only provide confirmation that the patient has unsound sleep. More advanced ambulatory systems now becoming available have the ability to record 16 to 32 channels of electroencephalographic and polygraphic data, thus duplicating the polysomnogram in the patient's home without having a technologist remain on duty overnight to monitor the study as

is done in the hospital laboratory. Until computerized interpretation capabilities fully mature, however, the large amount of data obtained still require a time-consuming and labor-intensive analysis before a full interpretation can be given, and the data quality is limited by the lack of technologist support during the recording.

REFERENCES

Diagnostic Classification Steering Committee, Thorpy MJ, Chairman. International classification of sleep disorders: Diagnostic and coding manual. Rochester, MN: American Sleep Disorders Association, 1990.

Douglass AB, Bornstein R, Nino-Murcia G, et al. The sleep disorders questionnaire I: Creation and multivariate structure of SDQ. Sleep 1994;17:160.

Guilleminault C, ed. Sleeping and waking disorders: Indications and techniques. Menlo Park, CA: Addison-Wesley, 1982.

Guilleminault C, Lugaresi E, eds. Sleep/wake disorders: Natural history, epidemiology, and long-term evolution. New York: Raven Press, 1983.

Kryger MH, Roth T, Dement WC, eds. Principles and practice of sleep medicine. 2nd ed. Philadelphia: Saunders, 1994.

Thorpy MJ, ed. Handbook of sleep disorders. New York: Marcel Dekker, 1990.

CHAPTER 20–27

Multiple Sclerosis

Richard E. Toran, M.D.

DEFINITION

Multiple sclerosis is the most common chronic disease of the nervous system afflicting the young. It is an inflammatory disease limited to the central nervous system; it is restricted to white matter.

ETIOLOGY

Multiple sclerosis is considered to be an autoimmune disease. In multiple sclerosis, white matter inflammation interferes with neuronal message transmission and the area of the central nervous system involved determines the symptoms and/or signs. Often, when the inflammation subsides, the symptoms and signs resolve; however, the inflammation can be so vigorous and necrotizing that it damages the adjacent axons. Then, subsequent scarring (sclerosis) leads to permanent dysfunction. Because this pathophysiologic process tends to be recurrent (multiple), or gradually progressive, the multiple areas of inflammation take their toll on overall functioning. Much of the central nervous system's function is elemental motor, sensory, or coordination, and alterations in these account for the majority of symptoms and signs in multiple sclerosis. Any function of the central nervous system, however, may be disrupted.

CRITERIA FOR DIAGNOSIS

Suggestive

With the potential for an infinite array of symptoms and signs, diagnosis is often a considerable challenge. Diagnostic schemas/criteria have evolved. Central to all is the requirement that the neurologic dysfunction *not* be a monophasic illness; that is, there are two neurologic events, separate in time (by at least a month) and separate in their location within the central nervous system. These simple clinical criteria have proven themselves 75% accurate.

Definitive

We have been able to improve the accuracy of diagnosis with three additional indicators. In order of their discovery, they are cerebrospinal fluid, evoked potentials, and magnetic resonance imaging.

Cerebrospinal Fluid

The cerebrospinal fluid may reveal evidence of inflammation with excess white cells and/or elevated protein. A closer look at the proteinaceous evidence of this inflammation reveals a prevalence of gamma-globulin, and it tends to be specific for particular clones of white cells, that is, oligoclonal. Present in 90% of patients, they are the most sensitive indicator in cerebrospinal fluid. This finding, however, is not specific, and these white cells are found in other inflammatory diseases capable of mimicking the disease, such as Sjögren's syndrome, syphilis, and Lyme disease.

Evoked Potentials

Evoked potentials are a quantitative, neurophysiologic means of demonstrating the interruption of the message-carrying capacity of axons whose myelin is inflamed. Whereas myelin speeds transmission, these tests show a slowing transmission. Measurement of central nervous system conduction times was, for a long time, precluded by the considerable electroencephalographic activity of the resting cerebral cortex, rendering the response to any applied stimulus "lost" in all this electroencephalographic activity. Computer averaging, however, "erases" this background activity, and in conjunction with looking for the expected response at the appropriate time, we are now able to measure the latency. The pathways tested are either visual, auditory, or posterior columns of spinal cord. Their utility in in demonstrating abnormality in an area not necessarily having had symptoms or signs, that is, satisfying the criteria for multiplicity of lesions, but overall evoked potentials sensitivity is less than that of cerebrospinal fluid oligoclonal bands. Although the abnormalities are specific for location they are not specific for the pathophysiologic process.

Magnetic Resonance Imaging

Magnetic resonance imaging of the central nervous system usually allows us to see the evidence of multiple areas of inflammation. This most recent method has proven itself to be our most sensitive diagnostic tool, but it too suffers from lack of specificity, with a large number of other diseases having similar changes. Remote episodes of inflammation may resolve clinically, but they usually show a persistent abnormality on magnetic resonance imaging. Concurrent administration of gadolinium shows enhancement of acute lesions, demonstrating the disruption of the blood–brain barrier that occurs with acute inflammation. Examples of the high degree of sensitivity of magnetic resonance imaging are given here:

- Magnetic resonance images have shown anywhere from 4 to 10 times as many lesions as a patient has had clinical episodes.
- Patients with a monophasic central nervous system event localized to white matter who have multiple lesions on magnetic resonance imaging have a 60% likelihood of progressing to multiple sclerosis within 5 years, whereas the absence of such findings is associated with only a 5% likelihood.
- Monozygotic twins have a concordance rate for symptomatic multiple sclerosis of approximately one third; however, magnetic resonance images, including unaffected twins, are likely to be abnormal in one half, suggesting that asymptomatic cases of the disease exist.

CLINICAL MANIFESTATIONS
Obvious and Dramatic
Optic Neuropathy

Subjective. When the inflammation occurs in the portion of the brain that has outreached to the eye, optic neuritis, it is likely to be symptomatic given our keen awareness of vision. Unilateral blurring or diminution of vision not ocular in origin places the problem in the optic nerve. The visual disturbance varies according to the severity and extent of the lesion, often being patchy (scotomata) and sometimes so subtle as to impair only color discrimination, although total blindness can occur. Pain is a common accompaniment.

Objective. The involved eye's pupillary response to light is often diminished, proven by providing the same light stimulus to the uninvolved eye, which elicits a normal, brisker response in the affected eye, than did the direct light stimulus (Marcus–Gunn pupil). Often, the inflammation is a distance behind the optic papilla, accounting for the clinical caveat regarding fundoscopy: "The doctor sees nothing and the patient sees nothing." If optic neuritis is the first neurologic event, the probability of multiple sclerosis can be predicted using sex and age as determinants. If the patient is female and young, the odds of developing multiple sclerosis approach 90%. Other causes of optic neuropathy include other causes of inflammation, structural disorders, and ischemic disease.

There are no routine laboratory abnormalities.

Inflammation of the Spinal Cord

Subjective. When the inflammation occurs in the spinal cord and is so extensive as to involve an entire cross-sectional area of the spinal cord (transverse myelitis), all function caudal to the most rostral extent of the lesion is lost.

Objective. Paraplegia or quadriplegia develops. The classic example of less severe transverse myelitis would be a predilection for one half of the spinal cord as in the Brown–Séquard syndrome or variations thereof. If transverse myelitis is the first neurologic event, the likelihood of multiple sclerosis can be predicted with less certainty than optic neuritis, but is probably at least one third. Other causes of myelopathy include other causes of inflammation, as well as structural and ischemic disease.

There are no routine laboratory abnormalities.

Less Obvious: Numbness

Subjective. A common presentation is the complaint of numbness, of variable distributions. Although very disturbing to the patient, this seldom leads to any loss of function.

Objective. There may be a loss in sensation. The physical findings are not dramatic and often improve. The same subtleties can occur if smaller lesions occur in corticospinal tracts or cerebellar connections, with mild motor or coordination problems of variable distribution. Sometimes, associated reflex changes or extensor plantar responses

occur, or there is evidence of incoordination. When numbness, weakness, or incoordination is the first neurologic event, the likelihood of multiple sclerosis cannot be predicted with any certainty. Other causes of such complaints and findings include other causes of inflammation and structural and ischemic disease.

There are no routine laboratory abnormalities.

Puzzling: Paresthesias with Normal Physical Examination

Subjective. Retrospectively, the most common presentation of multiple sclerosis is almost certainly paresthesias (i.e., uncomfortable sensations) without any physical findings. Words such as tingling, numbness, sensitive, and tightness are used to convey the discomfort. Given the ubiquity of such complaints referable to the extremities and head, these complaints attain specificity, albeit minimal, only when they involve the trunk.

Objective. The lack of associated physical findings makes the complaint puzzling.

There are no routine laboratory abnormalities.

Misleading: Findings Possibly Suggesting Another Condition

Although restricted to the central nervous system, sometimes the inflammation can occur at the site of a nerve's entry into the central nervous system, and thus the disturbance mimics a mononeuropathy. Examples are tic doloreux (trigeminal nerve) and radiculopathic complaints, such as sciatica. Any nerve can be involved, however, and thus, any mononeuropathic presentation can occur, such as diplopia, deafness, vertigo, and hoarseness. All mononeuropathic presentations must include consideration of a central nervous system cause, such as multiple sclerosis.

There are no routine laboratory abnormalities.

The Rare Presentation

Whereas inflammation can occur anywhere in the central nervous system where axons are myelinated, unusual presentations do occur, such as isolated urinary retention, aphasia, hypothermia, hiccups, and vomiting.

There are no routine laboratory abnormalities.

PLANS
Diagnostic

See Criteria for Diagnosis. It is the lack of specificity of all of these diagnostic tools that leads to the diagnostic categories of suggestive and definitive and requires a consideration of both clinical and laboratory information. Criteria that are sensitive but not specific need to be multiple and, if concordant, compensate for the lack of specificity they afford; however, the practical approach to this disease acknowledges that time becomes a powerful diagnostic tool, and restricting one's attention to the clinical course along with magnetic resonance imaging has the advantage of avoiding the invasiveness of lumbar puncture and the cost of evoked potentials. This is an acceptable approach with a disease for which there is no evidence that treatment, in the face of uncertain diagnosis, offers any benefit.

Therapeutic
Treatment of the Primary Disease

Most difficult for multiple sclerosis patients is the uncertainty. What will their clinical course be? How will their illness affect their family? Will they be able to work? Are the current treatments helpful? Will there be a meaningful treatment in their lifetime? Anytime they do not feel well, is it the multiple sclerosis or something else? Obviously, the mainstay of treatment is addressing these issues with support and education. This is often accomplished with the greatest success by multiple sclerosis centers, which afford "one-stop shopping" with the opportunity for patients to relate to peers, psychologists, psychiatrists, social workers, occupational and physical therapists, nurses, neurologists, urologists, and, when necessary, other medical subspecialists and attorneys expert in the problems of those with chronic illness.

This paradigm of the inflammatory response allows for an understanding of 14 potential treatments. Figure 20–27–1 depicts the locus of action of immunosuppression. Numbers 1 through 7 (Figure 20–27–1) are selectively immunosuppressive. All except interferon beta are experimental.

- Anti-vla-4 monoclonal antibodies inhibit the adhesion of white blood cells to the walls of the blood vessels at the site of invasion, preventing them from reaching the target.
- If infectious, and the agent could be determined, then vaccination in the classic manner could be tried.
- If myelin is the antigen, then maybe, by oral feeding of substantial amounts of bovine myelin, we can "downregulate" the immune response.
- If what is presented at the cell surface and perpetuates the immune response is similar to myelin, then maybe a segment of that molecular structure (COP-1) might displace the antigen and thereby decrease the inflammatory reaction.
- Whereas the lymphocytes responding to the presented antigen are CD4 lymphocytes, then maybe anti-CD4 monoclonal antibodies could decrease the inflammatory response.
- If one of the ultimate mediators of dissolution of myelin is tumor necrosis factor, then anti-tumor necrosis factor monoclonal antibodies could decrease the inflammatory response.
- Interferons are so named because of their inhibition of viral replication, yet a trial of interferon gamma for multiple sclerosis actually increased the inflammatory response. Interferon beta, however, has been demonstrated to decrease the inflammation of multiple sclerosis.

The following methods are nonselective (global) methods of immunosuppression: cyclophosphamide, azothioprine, cyclosporine, lympatic irradiation, plasmapheresis, immunoglobulin, corticosteroids.

Treatment of Associated Problems

The most common problems associated with multiple sclerosis are psychiatric. By being multidisciplinary and involving a peer group, multiple sclerosis centers can serve a major role in the management of these problems. Anxiolytic and/or antidepressant medications are occasionally required.

Spasms and spasticity are other common and troubling sequelae of this disease. Spasms, more frequent at night, often respond to a benzodiazepine at bedtime and, if severe, three to four times daily, 5 to 20 mg each dose. Spasticity is often treated with baclofen three to four times daily, 5 to 20 mg each dose. Maintenance physical therapy programs may help in the treatment of both.

Bladder dysfunction can be characterized as failure to store, failure to empty, or dyssynergia (incoordination between contraction of bladder wall and bladder neck). Failure to store is treated with anticholinergic agents such as propantheline bromide (Pro-Banthine) four times daily, 7.5 to 30 mg each dose, or oxybutynin chloride (Ditropan), four times daily, 5 mg each dose. Failure to empty is treated by the Credé maneuver or intermittent catheterization. Dyssynergia often requires combination therapy, including alpha blockers such as phenoxybenzamine hydrochloride (Dibenzyline) two to four times daily, 10 to 30 mg each dose. Symptomatic bacterial infection requires specific antimicrobial treatment. For antisepsis, vitamin C is often used four times daily, 500 to 1000 mg each dose.

Fatigue is common. Sometimes helpful is amantadine two times daily, 100 mg each dose.

Tremor, often of the cerebellar type, is especially refractory to treatment. Sometimes, if there is an epinephrine component, it responds to beta blockers.

FOLLOW-UP

Follow-up varies according to the initial assessment of the patient. When the diagnosis is definite from the outset, the physician should follow the patient in an effort to identify treatable complications and determine the value of any treatment that has been initiated. When the diagnosis is in doubt or has not been definitely established, the follow-up examination is designed to search for other diagnostic clues that will assist in ruling in or out the diagnosis of multiple sclerosis or identifying some other neurologic disease. The frequency of visits to the doctor varies according to the initial concerns of the physician and patient.

DISCUSSION

Prevalence and Incidence

Although one of the more intriguing features of this disease has been the variation in incidence/prevalence according to geographic distribution, the likelihood of a primary care physician encountering such a patient is small, approximately 1 case per 1000 patients.

Related Basic Science

Current and potential treatments for this disease are best understood in the context of our understanding of the pathophysiology of the inflammatory response (Figure 20–27–2). Inflammation is the body's defensive response to what is perceived as foreign invasion. Inflammation is characterized by the marshalling of white blood cells at the site of invasion. Further characterization of inflammation reveals two different, but

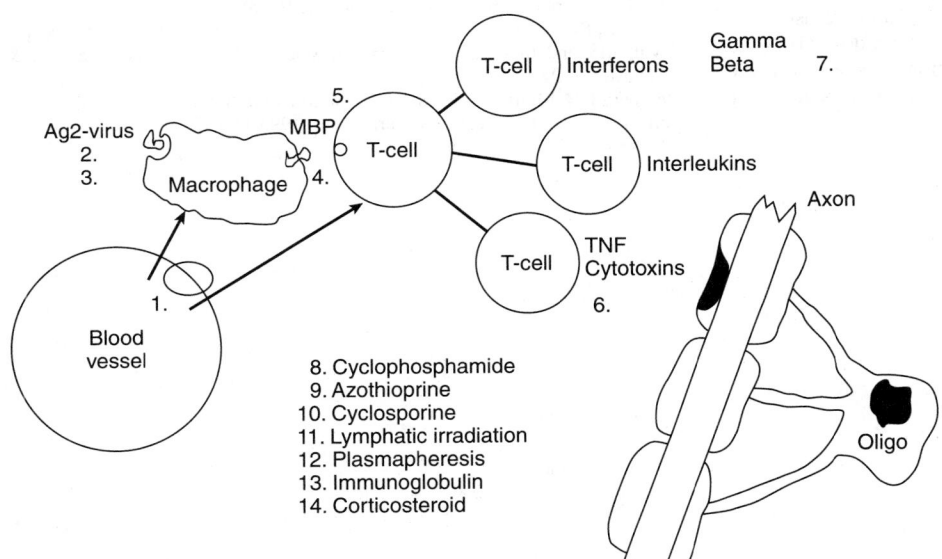

Figure 20–27–1. Site of action of immunosuppressive agents. AG = antigen. The numbers in the diagram refer to selective immunosuppressive therapy and the postulated site of action (see text). The numbers 8 through 14 are global immunosuppressive agents. ■ = destruction of myelin.

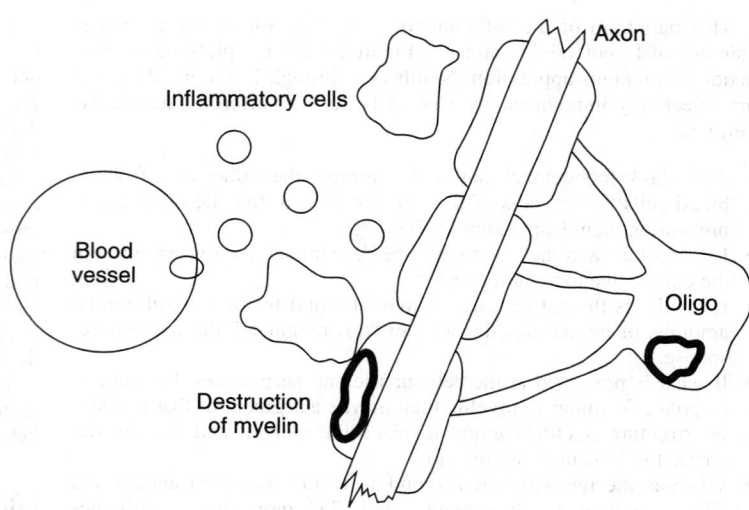

Figure 20–27–2. Schematic diagram of the pathophysiology of the inflammatory response.

related, defensive strategies of humoral and cell-mediated response. The humoral response is initiated by white blood cells which produce antibodies, of various classes (IgG, IgA, IgM, IgD, IgE), that recognize the invader within the intercellular fluids. These antibodies are often aided by complement. The cell-mediated response is a more complex scenario, and comes into play for those foreign invaders that escaped recognition in the intercellular fluids and have already gained access to the cytosol within cells. For these now intracellular invaders to be recognized, they must be brought to the cell wall and then presented to the outside surface of the cell, to be recognized by those white blood cells (lymphocytes) capable of eradicating the invader. The manner of presentation and eradication is complex but involves the major histocompatibility complex and substances called cytokines. Some cytokines initiate a direct attack (tumor necrosis factor) and others are indirect (interferons) or modulatory (interleukins). Still uncertain in multiple sclerosis is the exact nature of the antigen that is being presented. Is it a segment of myelin? Is it a segment of an infectious organism that mimics myelin?

Natural History and Its Modification with Treatment

Interferon beta is the only treatment demonstrated to alter the natural history of multiple sclerosis. Drawbacks are every-other-day injections and substantial side effects, flulike, resolving over weeks. Ambulatory patients with exacerbating remitting disease have the burden of their disease decreased by one third after 5 years of treatment, with both clinical events and magnetic resonance imaging as endpoints. Corticosteroids are the only other widely accepted therapy, and are used only for acute attacks, intravenously for 3 to 5 days, at high dose (1000 mg daily), sometimes with subsequent oral medication, tapered over several days. The brevity of this therapy avoids the long-term side effects of steroids.

Prevention

The disease cannot be prevented at this time.

Cost Containment

If, based on history and/or physical examination, a primary care physician suspects multiple sclerosis, the patient should first be referred to a neurologist. A magnetic resonance image should *not* be the initial response. Neurologists, expert in separating out monophasic neurologic illness, somatoform disorder, fibromyalgia, and chronic fatigue syndrome and sensitive to the sometimes unwanted information provided by an untimely magnetic resonance image, will effect a substantial decrease in health care costs by decreasing the number of magnetic resonance images. Also, neurologists, having seen large numbers of multiple sclerosis patients, are better able to help patients deal with the major problem of their illness, which is the uncertain future. Neurologists should avoid cerebrospinal fluid examination and evoked potentials whenever possible and, rarely, if ever, do electromyography and nerve conduction studies. When timely, a multiple sclerosis center provides optimal care, "one-stop shopping," at the lowest cost.

REFERENCES

Goodman A, McFarlin DE. Multiple sclerosis. Curr Neurol 1987;7:91.
Rolak L. Multiple sclerosis. Curr Neurol 1989;9:109.
Rosner LJ, Ross S. Multiple sclerosis: New hope and practical advice for people with MS and their families. First Fireside Edition. New York: Simon & Schuster, 1992.
Silberberg DH. Multiple sclerosis. Curr Neurol 1988;8:79.
Wolinsky JS. Multiple sclerosis. Curr Neurol 1993;13:167.

Headaches

W. Brem Mayer, Jr., M.D.

DEFINITION

Pain or discomfort in the upper half of the head constitutes headache.

ETIOLOGY

The etiologies of headache are diverse. Headache can be caused by systemic illnesses such as malignant hypertension, temporal arteritis, and influenza; infections in the meninges, sinuses, and brain; intracranial masses and hemorrhages; toxins such as carbon monoxide and alcohol; and the most common causes, muscle contraction from stress and/or vasodilation as in migraine.

CRITERIA FOR DIAGNOSIS

The Headache Classification Committee of the International Headache Society recently published an extensive new classification that outlines the diagnostic criteria for most headaches. Some names have been changed. Common migraine has become migraine without aura, classic migraine has become migraine with aura, and tension or muscle contraction headaches have become tension-type headaches.

Diagnostic clues and criteria for diagnosis of specific types of headaches are covered under Plans.

CLINICAL MANIFESTATIONS

Subjective

Headache is a very frequent complaint, occurring at all ages and having numerous causes and varying significance. Headaches are brought to the physician's attention because of their severity, their frequency, their interference with the patient's life, or their recent onset and persistence.

In a patient with headaches, most of the useful diagnostic and therapeutic information is derived from the history. If the physician does not have a good idea about the etiology of the headache before beginning the physical examination, it is unlikely he or she will arrive at diagnosis. Therefore, a meticulous and thorough collection of historical data concerning the headache is of utmost importance. The physician should not rush through it to get to the physical examination. The patient should be given the opportunity to tell all the facts he or she feels are important. Then the physician can direct his or her inquiries toward the descriptive and temporal characteristics of the headache, the precipitating causes, and associated symptoms. By the end of the interview, the following points need to have been covered (see Table 20–28–1):

- *Location of headache:* hemicranial or bilateral at onset; if hemicranial, does it change from side to side during the headache or from headache to headache; frontal or occipital; radiate into neck or eyes.
- *Character of headache:* throbbing or pounding; viselike, bandlike, or expanding; made worse by light, noise, position.
- *Profile:* abruptness of onset, rate of spread, duration; if recurrent, age at onset, frequency; time of day they occur, early morning, late afternoon, awaken at night.
- *Associated symptoms:* aura such as visual disturbance, numbness, weakness, aphasia; nausea and vomiting; muscle tension; fever; stiff neck; pain on chewing; diplopia, progressive neurologic deficit, incoordination, memory loss.
- *Precipitating factors:* food or drink, particularly alcohol, caffeine, or monosodium glutamate; menstrual period; tension or stress; oversleeping; cough; exercise; intercourse; trauma.
- *Response to headache:* amount of time missed from work and interference with plans; have to be in dark room; require medications; emergency room visits; live in dread of headache.
- *Medical history:* drugs taken for acute attacks and prophylaxis; hospitalizations; past diagnostic tests; physicians seen.

- *Women:* any relationship to birth control pills and other estrogens; effect of menopause, menses, or pregnancy.
- *Family history.*
- *Personality and life stresses:* perfectionist, worrier; family discord, financial problems; job requirements and satisfaction, workload; depression.

Objective

Physical Examination

Most of the patients seen with headaches have normal physical examinations, as most headaches are due to migraine, tension, or a combination of the two. There are, however, certain portions of the physical examination that need special emphasis. Examination of the optic disk for papilledema is one of these. Early disk swelling begins in the superior and inferior quadrants of the disk and may give the disk a reddish hue. Venous pulsations can be seen where the veins enter the disk cup and, if present, strongly suggest normal intracranial pressure. Their absence does not suggest increased intracranial pressure, but swelling and tortuosity of the veins do. Fundoscopic evaluation may reveal subhyaloid hemorrhage, optic atrophy, grade 4 hypertensive changes, or Roth's spots as clues to other specific etiologies of the headache. The neuro-ophthalmologic examination may reveal other diagnostically helpful physical findings that have been unnoticed by the patient: hemianopsia, unilateral visual loss, Horner's syndrome, or nystagmus. The remainder of the neurologic examination requires careful scrutiny also.

Head and neck structures often give rise to pain. The oral cavity can be evaluated for dental abcesses by pressing on the teeth with a tongue blade. An ear, nose, and throat evaluation, at times with blind biopsies, is necessary to exclude adequately occult carcinoma in the nasopharynx. If sinus disease is suspected, the sinuses should be percussed for tenderness. Headache with onset after the age of 50 may be due to temporal arteritis, and the size, thickness, tenderness, and pulsation of the temporal artery and other extracranial arteries should be determined.

Fairly consistent clinical patterns can be seen in migraine, cluster headache, temporal arteritis, increased intracranial headache, headache due to meningeal irritation, and tension or muscle contraction headaches. Selected diagnostic characteristics of some of these

TABLE 20–28–1. HEADACHE CHARACTERISTICS

	Migraine	Cluster	Tension	Arteritis	Neoplasm
Unilateral	+++	++++	++	++	++
Bilateral	++	0	+++	+++	+++
Throbbing	+++	++	+	++	++
Viselike	+	+	+++	+	+
Early morning	+++	+	+	++	+++
Awaken at night	++	+++	++	++	+
Aura	++	0	0	0	0
Pain on chewing	0	0	0	++*	0
Progressive neurologic disturbance	0	0	0	0	+++
Brought on by ethyl alcohol	+++	+++	0	0	0
Brought on by exercise, intercourse	++	0	0	0	+
Family history	+++	0	0	0	0
Age > 50	+	++	+	++++	++

++++, always; +++, usually; ++, commonly; +, rarely; 0, hardly ever.
*Also seen with temporomandibular joint dysfunction.

headache types are presented followed by general diagnostic considerations and plans.

Routine Laboratory Abnormalities

Except for the abnormalities found in headaches due to infections, there are usually no abnormal routine laboratory abnormalities.

PLANS
Diagnostic

The history usually identifies quickly the typical headache: migraine with aura, migraine without aura, tension-type heaches, and so on. If the history does not fit a customary pattern, then structural disease must be considered. Headaches of recent onset that are persistent and not eased by over-the-counter medications suggest increased intracranial pressure. Additional symptoms such as new seizures, diplopia, memory disturbance, and incoordination warrant additional diagnostic testing. Papilledema, a stiff neck, fever, and persistent neurologic deficit are also indicative of a mass lesion or intracranial infection. The sudden onset of a headache the like of which has been unimaginable previously poses little diagnostic problem: subarachnoid hemorrhage is the most common cause.

The additional testing required should be directed by the clinical impressions after the history taking and physical examination. If migraine, tension, or cluster headaches are suspected, the diagnostic workup does not have to go further unless it appears the patient needs further testing for reassurance. Of the tests done in an internist's office, a complete blood count, SMA-18 determination, chest radiograph an an erythrocyte sedimentation rate in patients over 50 may point to a systemic disease as a cause for the headache. If a mass lesion is suspected, a computed tomography (CT) scan of the head should be done without and with contrast. This should show up any mass large enough to cause headaches. Some small lesions, particularly in the pituitary region, may cause headaches and can be seen better with magnetic resonance imaging. In a subarachnoid hemorrhage, the CT scan often shows blood in the subarachnoid spaces, and when it does, a lumbar puncture is not required or indicated. If the amount of blood in the subarachnoid space is too small to be seen on a CT scan, a lumbar puncture is necessary to establish the diagnosis. The only time a lumbar puncture should be done without a preceding CT scan in a patient with headache is when acute bacterial meningitis is suspected. An electroencephalogram is not usually helpful in the evaluation of patients with headaches.

Migraine. The onset of the headache is typically not abrupt, but rather a gradual increase over an hour, starting with a dull headache. It may occur at any time of day, sometimes awakening the patient from sleep, but most often being present when the patient awakens in the morning. The usual age of onset is in the late teens or early twenties, but it may begin in childhood or old age. An aura occurs in some migraine headaches; visual phenomena are the most common, and they tend to be a combination of positive phenomena, such as bright lights, zigzag lines (referred to as fortification scotomata), and wavy lines (like heat rising from the road), and negative phenomena, such as decreased vision. The visual disturbance may involve the entire visual field of both eyes, but it can be hemianopic, either homonymous or bitemporal. Additional prodromata may include aphasia, hemianesthesia, and hemiparesis. These neurologic symptoms usually precede the headache by 10 to 20 minutes and clear with its onset, but they can occur during the headache and persist. Occasionally, the aura occurs without a headache, and this is referred to as a "migraine equivalent."

The headache is unilateral in 66% of patients, always on the same side in 20%, and bilateral in 33% (Lance, 1981). The pain is usually frontal and temporal, but it may radiate into the face or the neck and shoulders posteriorly. The pain is initially dull and crescendos into a severe, throbbing, pulsatile pain. Nausea and vomiting are frequent, and the victim is often driven to bed in a dark room until time, vomiting, or sleep relieves the symptoms. The duration varies from several hours to 3 days. These headaches often severely interfere with the patient's life, and their occurrence is viewed with a dread that can lead to analgesic abuse.

The frequency varies from one or two per decade to one or two per week. Patients that fall in the latter category are the ones who are most desperate.

There is often a family history of migraine. It is more common in women. The use of estrogen products for birth control and menopause can precipitate or aggravate the problem, and pregnancy tends to alleviate the attacks. Some migraineurs can have the attacks precipitated by food, drink, or certain activities: wine (particularly red), monosodium glutamate, chocolate, exercise, orgasm, relaxation after stress, sleeping late on weekends, menstruation, and stress. Many patients are perfectionists and worriers.

Migraine is a common form of headache in children. The characteristics are generally similar to those of adult migraine. However, in children, cyclical vomiting and periodic abdominal pain may be related to the migraine syndrome.

There is an increased incidence of motion sickness and positional vertigo in migraine sufferers. Some patients "grow out" of their migraine during their fourth or fifth decade.

Cluster Headache (Histamine Cephalagia, Horton's Headache). Like migraine, cluster headache is considered a vascular headache, but its treatment is not the same, and it must be differentiated from migraine. It involves men in a ratio of up to 7:1. Seventy percent of the patients begin having attacks between 15 and 40 years of age, but individuals in their sixties have had onset of this type of headache.

There is no recognized prodrome to an attack. Onset is typically abrupt, often awakening the patient from sleep and reaching a peak in 2 to 10 minutes. The pain is in and around one eye, radiating to contiguous areas such as the temple, maxilla, and nose. It is unilateral, affecting the same side during successive bouts. The pain is extraordinarily severe and is of a constant, burning, piercing, or tearing quality. The headaches usually last 30 minutes to an hour, and the patient may have three in a day. In 80% of patients, the attacks occur in clusters that last 4 to 8 weeks. During the clusters, the headaches occur on a daily basis and are often brought on by alcohol. The headache causes the patient to pace the floor; nausea is less common than with migraine. Associated features of the affected eye include lacrimation, injected conjunctivae, ptosis and miosis, and a blocked or runny nostril. The author has observed a larger proportion than expected of self-employed or unusually independent individuals in the group of people with cluster headaches.

The clusters of headaches are usually separated by months or years of pain-free intervals. About 20% of patients have "chronic" clusters. The headaches have the same clinical characteristics that recur without remission. A third variety, chronic paroxysmal hemicrania, has been described in a small number of patients with a preponderance of women. The headache is like cluster, but it is shorter in duration, more frequent, and occurs on a background of a constant dull headache. It is distinguished by its response to indomethacin (Indocin) (Sjaastad, 1986).

Migraine-like Headache. Headaches typical of migraine can be associated with arteriovenous malformations or slow-growing tumors such as meningiomas and low-grade gliomas. The headaches occur on the same side as the lesion, and with arteriovenous malformations, a bruit may be heard on auscultation with the bell of a stethoscope over the eye or head. The failure of the headache to ever change sides and the onset of a seizure disorder are clues that one may not be dealing with ordinary migraine.

Temporal Arteritis (Giant Cell Arteritis). New-onset headache in anyone over the age of 50 should bring temporal arteritis to mind. The onset of headache is characteristically gradual, peaking over a few hours, although it can be explosive. The pain may be unilateral or bilateral. It is often temporal, but it may be anywhere over the head. Scalp tenderness is often present. The patient may have a depressed appearance because of the persistence of the headache and other systemic symptoms.

Age of onset is almost always over 50 and usually close to 70. A few scattered reports of patients under 50 have been confirmed. Headache occurs at one time or another in 85% of patients. Other findings that occur in large numbers of patients include erythrocyte sedimentation rate over 50 mm/h (95%), temporal artery tenderness (70%), jaw claudication with chewing (65%), brachiocephalic bruits (50%), thickened or nodular temporal artery (45%), pulseless temporal artery (40%), visual symptoms (40%), and symptoms of polymyalgia rheumatica (40%). The neuro-opthalmologic complications of temporal arteritis and its association with polymyalgia rheumatica are discussed in Chapter 6–16 and are presented in detail in Chapter 7–11. It should be remembered that visual loss due to optic nerve infarction can be abrupt and permanent. Once the diagnosis is seriously entertained, treatment with cortisone should be undertaken with haste.

Intracranial Neoplasm. Intracranial neoplasms are found in a small fraction of patients with headaches. But the importance of considering a tumor in the differential diagnosis of headache is brought home by the finding that about two thirds of patients with brain tumors complain of headache. One fifth of tumor patients have headache on arising that diminishes during the day. Onset during sleep occurs in about one tenth. The location of the headache may be ipsilateral to the tumor initially, but it becomes generalized with time. The pain is described as a dull ache. Aggravating and precipitating factors include Valsalva maneuvers such as coughing, sneezing, straining at stool, and bending over. Frequency and duration are variable, depending on the location and size of the tumor. Slow-growing tumors can be associated with intermittent headaches that have lasted for years, but this is extremely rare. Posterior fossa tumors that have obstructed the flow of spinal fluid or rapidly expanding masses cause daily headaches that have their onset in the recent past. Colloid cysts of the third ventricle may give a history of explosive paroxysmal headaches that last minutes to several hours and can be brought on or alleviated by sudden changes in position. This is so because they produce position-dependent intermittent obstruction. This classic history occurs in only 20% of patients with colloid cysts. Making the diagnosis of an intracranial neoplasm creates no difficulty when papilledema or neurologic deficits are present. Unfortunately, these signs are not present early in the course of many tumors.

Chronic Subdural Hematoma. Subdural hematomas cause headaches that are similar to those seen with brain tumors. Their onset can be measured in weeks or months, and they are daily, usually not responding to over-the-counter medications. A history of trauma, a recent fall, or an automobile accident may be obtained, but the inciting incident cannot always be recalled. Alcoholics, patients on dialysis or anticoagulants, the elderly, and others subject to frequent falls are particularly susceptible to subdural hematomas.

Cerebrovascular Disease. Cerebrovasular disease is a major cause of headache, usually presenting little diagnostic difficulty. The headache associated with subarachnoid hemorrhage has an abrupt and devastating onset and is associated in most cases with a stiff neck and vomiting. The suddenness of onset of a headache unlike any previous headache in a patient without focal neurologic signs is usually the key to diagnosis. In a similar vein, the diagnosis of headache associated with hypertensive intracerebral hemorrhage usually offers few diagnostic challenges: the sudden onset of excruciating headache associated with an alteration in the level of consciousness and focal neurologic deficits.

Infections. Infections such as meningitis and encephalitis are often associated with headache. The severity of the headache and the acuteness of the infection are directly proportional. A bacterial meningitis gives an abrupt headache associated with a high fever, a viral meningitis gives a less severe headache that may develop over several days while the temperature usually stays below 102°F, and a fungal meningitis gives a more chronic picture and may not have any fever. A brain abscess gives a headache history similar to that seen with a rapidly expanding tumor.

Tension-type Headaches. Tension-type headache (muscle contraction) is perhaps the most common of all headaches. About 75% of such headaches occur in women, as is the case with migraine headache. Forty percent of patients have the onset of symptoms by the age of 20. Onset after age 50 is rare except in obviously depressed patients.

As a consequence, many patients who present to a physician complain of years of headache. In most patients, the headache is bilateral (90%). The pain is often in the back of the head and neck, extending into the temples, with a concomitant increase in contraction of the muscles of the neck and scalp. The pain is described as dull and aching, heavy, tight, or throbbing. It may be bandlike. Specific stress is tempo-

rally associated with headache in a few patients, but a clear-cut relationship may not be present. A frequent story is that the headaches have recurred day after day, year after year. They may begin in the morning, but they usually occur in the midafternoon. There are no distinctive associated phenomena, but on physical examination, one may find increased tenderness in the pericranial muscles.

A curious feature is shared findings between migraine and tension-type headache groups. A number of studies have reported the same incidence of women (75%), about the same number complain of throbbing headaches, and both groups have increased contractions of neck muscles. But significant differences also exist: premonitory symptoms are rare in tension headaches; frequency is less in migraine headaches; unilateral location is more common in migraine patients. Many patients are felt to have a combination of migraine and tension-type headache. This is referred to as a *mixed headache.*

Rebound Headache. Frequently, patients with tension, migraine, or mixed headaches progress from intermittent headaches with pain-free intervals to daily headaches with superimposed severe attacks. When this occurs, a history of chronic daily analgesic abuse usually can be elicited. The medications can include the medications well recognized from abuse such as narcotics, those that contain butalbital (Fiorinal) and propoxyphene (Darvocet) but also include aspirin and acetaminophen. If the patient with daily headaches is taking the medications on a daily basis in large amounts, this condition should be considered. Stopping the regular use of the analgesic in question will usually cause the daily headaches to abate. This course of action should be followed despite the patient's resistance.

Other Causes. Other causes must be considered in the differential diagnosis of headache. The cranial nerves carrying sensation from the head include V, VII, IX, and X, as well as the upper two or three cervical nerves. As some of these nerves supply intracranial pain-sensitive structures, as well as extracranial structures, it follows that headache can be due to local and distant disorders, that is, local pain and referred pain. A wide variety of inflammatory, neoplastic, traumatic, and idiopathic disorders can involve these nerves. Some associated disorders and syndromes with these nerves include trigeminal and glossopharyngeal neuralgias, Raeder's paratrigeminal neuralgia (painful Horner's), atypical facial pain, and temporomandibular joint dysfunction (Costigen's syndrome) (Guralnick et al., 1978). Infections and neoplasms in and around the sinuses and nasopharynx can cause headache. Dental pain usually begins locally but can spread to be hemicranial and can give ticlike symptoms.

Some patients who have closed head trauma develop posttraumatic headaches that can last many months. The trauma is usually severe enough to cause hospitalization, and the patients complain of vertigo, inability to concentrate, and poor memory. Headaches that are similar may occur after trivial head trauma. In these patients, the relationship to secondary gain and litigation needs to be explored.

Headaches occur in a variety of other conditions. Ice cream headache occurs when cold substances come into contact with the palate, and coital headaches occur at climax. These are both vascular headaches. Headaches occur following lumbar puncture 20% of the time and are due to leakage of cerebrospinal fluid from the subarachnoid space. The larger the bore of the needle used, the more likely the headaches are to occur. They characteristically are worse in sitting or standing positions and improve markedly on lying down.

Cough headache is a paroxysmal headache that occurs with coughing, sneezing, or any Valsalva maneuver. They are brief, severe, and often associated with lesions in the regions of the foramen magnum, such as the Arnold–Chiari malformation. Magnetic resonance imaging is the best way to evaluate this area (Ekbom, 1986).

Therapeutic

The therapy of headaches can be quite difficult. Many patients make the rounds of all nearby physicians and emergency rooms, and can wind up as drug abusers. Patients with chronic headaches of many years' duration often approach each new physician with immense hostility. An important principle in all patients with chronic headache is to get a list of all medications, maneuvers, and consultations that have occurred previously. The patient and physician then need to approach the chronic headache with the expectation of a trial-and-error course of therapy; first one drug or maneuver and then another is tried. The physician must possess in full measure empathy, understanding, and patience. These last attributes on the part of the primary physician may well be more beneficial than formal psychotherapy.

Avoiding dependence-generating drugs in patients who have chronic headaches is of the utmost importance. Drug dependency increases the frequency of the headaches and keeps the prophylactic medications from being effective. Narcotic medications as well as restricted medications, such as propoxyphene (Darvon) and those that contain butalbital (Fiorinal), should be closely monitored. They should be supplied by only one physician. (Please see Diagnostic, Rebound Headache).

Mild migraine attacks may be aborted acutely by simple analgesics. Various analgesics and combinations with antiemetics and sedatives can be tried. Nonsteroidal medications in large doses such as ibuprofen 800 mg (Motrin) are often effective and are less apt to cause rebound headaches. More severe attacks usually need an ergot preparation. The initial dose should be taken as soon as possible after the onset of headache, be adequate for that patient, and be below the level that produces nausea in that patient. Ergotamine suppositories (e.g., Cafergot) are probably the most effective practical form of the drug, followed by sublingual preparations. There is a large variety of preparations on the market. Contraindications include peripheral vascular disease, hypertension, pregnancy, coronary atherosclerosis, renal failure, and hepatic failure. Isometheptene (Isocom, Midrin) is less effective than ergotamine but has fewer reactions and contraindications.

Many patients with migraine do not respond to oral medications. Sumatriptan (Imitrex) can be injected subcutaneously and aborts about four fifths of the headaches. It is a 5-hydroxytryptamine agonist and causes vasoconstriction, which eases the headache. The first dose should be given under medical supervision; it can then be self-administered at home with a reusable injector. It can be repeated in 4 hours if the headache returns. Sumatriptan can cause coronary vasospasm and should not be used in patients at high risk for coronary artery disease. Sumatriptan is now available as an oral preparation. It may be a little less effective than the injection.

If the above-mentioned measures do not relieve the headache, the patient may need to go to the emergency room for treatment. Again, avoidance of narcotics is best, though not always possible. Prochlorperazine (Compazine) administered intravenously has been found to work as well as intramuscular narcotics, as has intravenous dihydroergotamine (D.H.E. 45). Prolonged migraine—status migrainosus—can sometimes be managed by hospitalization and administration of intravenous dyhydroergotamine.

Migraine-preventive measures should start with an identification of triggering factors, such as birth control pills and foods. Further therapy may not be necessary in a patient who has infrequent attacks. If prophylactic measures are indicated, there are a number of drugs to be considered: methysergide (Sansert), amitriptyline (Elavil), propranolol (Inderal), verapamil (Calan), and valproic acid (Depakote). The effectiveness of each is less than 70%. Methysergide may be the most effective, but it has the most serious potential side effect: retroperitoneal fibrosis. Consequently, it is prudent to try propranolol, amitriptyline, and verapamil in sequence, allowing a trial period of one to several months for each drug. With this approach, there should be a reduction in the severity and frequency of the headaches in 80 to 90% of patients.

If the preceding array of medications has been tried unsuccessfully, then methysergide or phenelzine (Nardil) should be tried (Table 20–28–2).

Cluster headaches may be treated acutely with ergotamine tartrate aerosol or other ergotamine preparations, inhalation of 100% oxygen for 5 to 10 minutes, or inhalation of a topical anesthetic up the ipsilateral nostril by means of a dropper or spray. Butorphenol tartrate nasal spray (Stadol) can be used but it has addictive potential. Sumatriptan can also be used with some benefit. Prophylactic therapy is basically similar to that for migraine, except steroids and lithium carbonate (Eskalih) have been reported to be useful. Lithium is said to be quite effective in patients with chronic cluster headaches and also helps in some patients with intermittent cluster headaches. Calcium channel blockers are beneficial in prevention of cyclical cluster headaches.

TABLE 20–28–2. PREVENTIVE MEDICATIONS FOR MIGRAINE

Drug	Daily Dose Range	Common or Serious Side Effects
Propranolol (Inderal)	40–320 mg	Postural hypotension, depression, tiredness, insomnia
Amitriptyline (Elavil)	10–175 mg	Postural hypotension, dry mouth, urinary retention, sedation, increased appetite
Verapamil (Calan)	240–480 mg	Hypotension, constipation
Cyproheptadine (Periactin)	12–32 mg	Sedation, increased appetite
Valproic acid (Depakote)	750–1500 mg	Weight gain, alopecia, tremor
Fluoxetine hydrochloride (Prozac)	10–40 mg	Anxiety, nausea, diarrhea
Methysergide (Sansert)	2–8 µg	Nausea, cramps, insomnia, weight gain, edema, retroperitoneal fibrosis
Phenelzine (Nardil)	15–75 µg	Insomnia, constipation, hypotension, hypertensive crisis with certain foods

Tension-type headaches are treated acutely with analgesics, the weaker the better. Some of these patients become drug abusers; great care must be exercised by the physician. The best prophylactic drugs are antidepressants. Of the tricyclic antidepressants, amitriptyline (Elavil) seems to be the most successful and fluoxetine hydrochloride (Prozac) has been helpful also. Biofeedback and other methods of stress management are useful.

Headaches caused by inflammation, masses, and other organic causes are approached by treatment of the underlying lesion. Analgesics are used to ameliorate the headache while this is occurring.

If temporal arteritis is strongly suspected, an erythrocyte sedimentation rate should be determined right away. If it is elevated above 40 mm/h, prednisone should be begun at 60 mg/d and a temporal artery biopsy should be done within 48 hours. A 4-cm length of artery should be obtained, and if negative, the opposite side should be biopsied.

Post-lumbar puncture headaches can be treated with epidural blood patches. About 10 mL of the patient's blood is injected in the lumbar epidural space and the headache dramatically and immediately abates in 80% of the patients. The services of an anesthesiologist are often required.

FOLLOW-UP

The follow-up of a headache is determined by its severity and the physician's estimate of the likelihood that an organic lesion is the cause.

DISCUSSION
Prevalence and Incidence

Headache is common. The exact prevalence and incidence are not known.

Related Basic Science

Intracranial pain-sensitive structures include the main trunks of all the dural arteries, the dural floor of the anterior and posterior fossae, the superior surface of the tentorium cerebelli, the dural sinuses and the proximal parts of most of the tributary veins, the proximal parts of the major intracranial arteries, cranial nerves V, IX, and X, and the upper cervical nerves. If a line is drawn coronally joining the two ears, the fifth cranial nerve carries pain that projects in front of this line, supplying intracranial structures on or above the tentorium cerebelli. The ninth and tenth cranial nerves and the upper three cervical nerves carry pain from structures below the tentorium; the pain is projected behind the coronal line just described.

Organic causes such as masses and meningitis produce headache by traction on or inflammation of the structures described above. Migraine prodrome is associated with a decrease in cerebral blood flow, whereas the headache phase is associated with increased cerebral and extracranial blood flow, although not all reports support these generalizations. The vasoconstrictive phase is felt to produce focal cerebral ischemia, accounting for focal neurologic signs, whereas vasodilation produces the pain. Vasoactive substances that are postulated to play a role in the vasodilation include histamines, serotonin, and prostaglandins. Platelet aggregability and adherence increase at various phases during a migraine episode. These changes are felt to be related to changes in serotonin concentration that occur during the episode. The roles of sex hormones and monoamine oxidase have been investigated. There is currently no unifying concept that explains the alterations that are known to occur, although progress is being made.

Natural History and Its Modification with Treatment

The natural history of headaches varies depending on the cause. Migraine headaches usually begin in the second or third decade and abate around menopause in women. Pregnancy tends to make them better and estrogens can make them worse or bring them back after menopause. Cluster headaches often persist into late life. Tension-type headaches may wax and wane depending on the amount of stress or depression in the patient's life. Temporal arteritis may clear after 6 months to a year, though some patients require steroids for a much longer period.

Prevention

Prevention for migraine and cluster headaches has been described above. The use of a small-gauge needle in performing lumbar punctures will decrease the number of post-lumbar puncture headaches. Keeping the patient prone for 6 to 24 hours probably does nothing to reduce the number and severity. Preventive measures for the other varieties of headache are unknown or relate to the underlying cause.

Cost Containment

A systematic approach to sequential trials of therapy, coupled with support from the physican, goes far toward diminishing headache episodes and encouraging the patient to continue working despite the pain. Generic medications, when available, are as good as the brand names. Sumatriptan injections are expensive, about $32 a shot, but if they get the patient back to work and prevent emergency room visits, they are a bargain.

REFERENCES

Dalessio, Donald J, Siberstein S, eds. Wolff's headaches and other head pains. New York: Oxford Press, 1993.

Diamond S, Millstein E. Current concepts of migraine therapy. J Clin Pharmacol 1988;28:193.

Ekbom K. Cough headache. In: Rose FC, ed. Headache: Handbook of clinical neurology. Amsterdam. Elsevier, 1986;4(48):376.

Guralnick W, Kahan LB, Merrill RG. Temporomandibular-joint afflictions. N Engl J Med 1978;299:123.

Headache Classification Committee of the International Headache Society. Classification and diagnostic criteria for headache disorders, cranial neuralgias and facial pain. Cephalgia 1988;8:9.

Hering R, Steiner TJ. Abrupt outpatient withdrawal of medication in analgesic-abusing migraineurs. Lancet 1991;337:1442.

Jones J, Sklar D, Dougherty J, White W. Randomized double-blind trial of intravenous prochlorperazine for the treatment of acute headache. JAMA 1989;261:1174.

Lance JW. Headache. Ann Neurol 1981;10:1.

Raskin NH. Headache. New York, Edinburgh, London, Melbourne:Churchill Livingstone, 1988.

Sjaastad O. Chronic paroxysmal hemicrania (CPH). In: Rose FC, ed. Headache: Handbook of clinical neurology. Amsterdam: Elsevier, 1986;4:257.

CHAPTER 20–29
Bacterial and Viral Infections of the Nervous System (See Section 8, Chapter 82)

CHAPTER 20–30
Carcinomatous Meningitis (See Section 3, Chapter 40)

CHAPTER 20–31
Encephalitis (See Section 8, Chapter 11)

CHAPTER 21–1

Sensorineural Hearing Loss

John S. Turner, Jr., M.D.

DEFINITION

Hearing loss related to a disorder in the cochlea or its neural connections with the brainstem and auditory cortex is designated *sensorineural.*

ETIOLOGY

Sensorineural hearing loss may have either genetic or nongenetic causes.

CRITERIA FOR DIAGNOSIS

Suggestive

A patient with sensorineural hearing loss usually gives no history of ear infection, and the ear canal, eardrum, and middle ear are normal in structure and function.

Definitive

Sensorineural hearing loss can be diagnosed in most cases when air conduction is greater than bone conduction and the Weber test does not refer, or else it refers to the better-hearing ear.

Highly specific audiometric tests often must be correlated with neuroradiologic studies for proper diagnosis.

CLINICAL MANIFESTATIONS

Subjective

The hearing loss may be sudden or insidious. Sudden loss is almost always unilateral except in trauma- or drug-induced deafness or generalized central nervous system disease. Insidious loss is far more common and may be manifest by the patient's asking others to repeat, by the statement that others are "mumbling," or by the statement "I hear but don't understand." The patient speaks with a louder voice than is normally used in quiet conversation. Tinnitus accompanies sensorineural hearing loss in almost all cases. Vertigo and ear fullness are common complaints.

The patient may mention parents and grandparents with hearing loss.

Objective

Physical Examination

Virtually no signs except poor communication are present. Congenital anomalies or signs of trauma or generalized neurologic involvement may give a clue to the diagnosis. The patient may already use a hearing aid as self-treatment. The patient asks the examiner to repeat statements often during the interview. The hand may be cupped behind the ear. The patient often watches the speaker's face intently to gain clues from facial expression and lip movement. Inappropriate answers may be forthcoming from the patient because of discrimination loss for similar-sounding words.

Routine Laboratory Abnormalities

The examinations of the blood and urine reveal no specific abnormalities related to hearing loss, except in drug toxicity or in certain hereditary syndromes such as Alport's syndrome and hyperlipidemia. Diseases such as those listed under Plans may be identified.

PLANS

Diagnostic

Differential Diagnosis

An immediate classification of causes as genetic and nongenetic should be considered. A careful examination of the ear and related structures is also essential. Tuning fork testing in a quiet area with 256 and 512 forks permits a sensorineural hearing loss to be differentiated from a conductive loss.

Diagnostic Options

Unless the diagnosis is obvious, a fasting metabolic analysis should be done to exclude disorders such as hyperlipidemia, diabetes, and renal disease. Knowledge of the patient's general health is essential, as sensorineural hearing loss is commonly seen with renal disease, diabetes, gout, hypothyroidism, hypertension, multiple sclerosis, and aspirin toxicity from arthritis treatment. The common use of furosemide (Lasix) in cardiac disease has led to the development of severe sensorineural deafness in many older individuals. A careful history of diuretic use must be taken in all cardiac and renal patients.

Recommended Approach

Complete audiometric testing performed by a graduate audiologist is the next step. Proper audiologic testing includes air, bone, speech, and impedance testing. More specific tests may be recommended by the consulting otolaryngologist depending on these basic studies. Evoked response audiometry and performance intensity with phonetically balanced words are currently very helpful in diagnosis. Neuroradiologic tests such as computed tomography, magnetic resonance imaging, and angiography are final steps in the differentiation of cochlear from retrocochlear problems.

Therapeutic

Therapeutic Options

No effective medical or surgical treatment is known for sensorineural hearing loss as a general rule. When an exact cause can be determined, then a few treatment methods are available.

Fluctuant hearing loss associated with elevated levels of lipoproteins may be improved with a low-fat diet. Viral infections may occasionally improve with cortisone, and luetic deafness may respond to continued penicillin and steroid therapy, at least temporarily. Fluctuant hearing loss from Ménière's disease has been treated by various forms of endolymphatic shunt surgery. Hearing is preserved in only 60% of these patients, however, and these methods offer only minimal benefit. Vasodilator therapy with carbon dioxide inhalation, cyclandelate (Cyclan), or intravenous histamine is often tried, but no conclusive, controlled studies are available.

Barotrauma from scuba diving, weight lifting, or a hard sneeze with round window rupture is an indication for emergency surgery to close the leak. Again, the history is paramount along with a high index of suspicion.

Treatment of sudden acute sensorineural hearing loss remains empiric. The diagnosis may offer the therapist some guidance: hearing loss associated with inflammation may require cortisone therapy; probable vasospasm in hypertension or diabetes may need vasodilator therapy as described above; and syphilitic sudden loss may respond to penicillin and steroids. Any potentially ototoxic drugs should be stopped immediately.

Sensorineural hearing loss associated with otosclerosis has been treated for more than 30 years with fluoride therapy. Many anecdotal accounts of results with this treatment have been reported. The reader is referred to the writings of Shambaugh (1980) on this subject.

Recommended Approach

The most effective management of sensorineural hearing loss is a properly prescribed and fitted hearing aid. These appliances are very effective when prescription is accurate for the individual's hearing loss and when patient compliance with proper usage is good. These patients should never go directly to a hearing aid dealer, but should have a "hearing aid evaluation" performed by a graduate audiologist. This may be available privately or at a speech and hearing center.

Cochlear implants have shown dramatic improvement in patients with cochlear disease who have remaining good eighth nerve function. This implant is indicated only for total deafness unresponsive to hearing aid use.

The patient should be encouraged that almost all sensorineural hearing loss can be helped with correct methods of management. Careful adherence to specific regimens should be advised because early therapy in fluctuant or acute sensorineural hearing loss offers the best chance of help. If a hearing aid is necessary, the patient must be encouraged to wear it at all times. Adaptation to a hearing aid usually takes from 2 to 6 months.

FOLLOW-UP

All patients with unilateral hearing loss should be reevaluated at 6-month intervals or more frequently if any fluctuation or new symptoms develop. In patients with symmetric, bilateral loss, hearing tests should be repeated at 2- to 5-year intervals.

DISCUSSION

Prevalence and Incidence

Hearing loss is the most common disability that affects our population of more than 200 million. The incidence is generally about 66 per 1000. Significantly, only about 2 in 1000 develop their loss before the age of 19 years. It is estimated that 40 to 50% of all forms of deafness are due to genetic predisposition; in most cases the impairment is developed later in life. Eight genetic syndromes account for 27 of the 66 who have a significant hearing loss among each 1000 persons.

Related Basic Science

The importance of the estimates stated above suggests that a classification of progressive sensorineural hearing loss should incorporate two categories: genetic and nongenetic.

Genetic

In dominant sensorineural hearing loss, the gene is fully expressed in a heterozygote combination. When one parent carries the affected gene, the chance of the offspring being affected is 50%. It is important to note that in all these syndromes the hearing loss is not present at birth but appears later in life. The family history is strongly positive.

- Hyperlipoproteinemia (familial hypercholesterolemia), 10 in 100: Hyperlipoproteinemia causes a sensorineural loss that may be progressive, fluctuating, or sudden; hypersensitivity to noise and drugs is present.
- Hereditary nephritis (Alport's syndrome): Alport's syndrome is characterized by a slowly progressive bilateral sensorineural loss.
- Bilateral acoustic tumors (localized von Recklinghausen's disease), 1 in 200,000: Localized von Recklinghausen's disease is a restricted form of neurofibromatosis.
- Cochlear otosclerosis, 5 in 1000: Otosclerosis is a primary focal spongifying disease of the labyrinthine capsule. When the focus reaches the endosteum of the cochlea, it produces a sensorineural hearing loss by proliferating a cytotoxic enzyme in the perilymph or by the effects of vascular shunts.
- Paget's disease (osteitis deformans), 0.5 in 1000: Paget's disease affecting the temporal bone involves the cochlear end organ and/or the ossicular chain.
- Osteogenesis imperfecta (van der Hoeve's syndrome): Van der Hoeve's syndrome is due to a disorder of collagen maturation in connective tissue and produces conductive and often sensorineural hearing loss.
- Osteopetrosis (Albers–Schönberg disease), 1 in 200,000: Albers–Schönberg disease is a disturbance of enchondral ossification. The foramina for the cranial nerves are constricted.
- Ototoxicity, drugs: Ototoxicity and/or drug reactions are seen in ge-

netically determined deficiencies in metabolism and increase the susceptibility of individuals so predisposed.

- Noise-induced hearing loss, 4 to 8 in 1000: It is estimated that approximately 50% of cases of noise-induced hearing loss are due to a genetic predisposition that allows a defect in the capillary circulation and spiral vessels at the extreme basal end of the cochlea. The effect of anoxia on the outer hair cells is that of cellular death—it is accumulative and permanent.

Recessive hereditary sensorineural hearing loss occurs when both parents are carriers of the particular gene; the chance of the offspring being affected is only 25%. Most of these cases, therefore, have no family history of hearing loss. It is usually in the consanguineous marriage that the hereditary transmission of the recessive disorder becomes apparent. The following are examples of progressive sensorineural hearing loss of recessive trait, associated with other abnormalities.

- Diabetes mellitus, 11 in 1000: The incidence of diabetes is 28 in 1000. Forty percent of these patients develop significant hearing loss (11 in 1000). The hearing loss is sensorineural, bilateral, progressive, involving the higher frequencies, and more severe in older individuals, especially those with retinopathy. In the younger individual, there is a direct relationship between the hearing loss and nephropathy.
- Nonendemic goiter (Pendred's syndrome), 0.05 in 1000: Because of a lack of the enzyme iodine peroxidase, this syndrome causes a high-frequency sensorineural hearing loss, which often precedes thyroid enlargement. Polytomography may show the Mondini abnormality.
- Retinitis pigmentosa, polyneuritis, cerebellar ataxia, ichthyosis (Refsum's syndrome), 0.05 in 1000: This is due to abnormal keratinization and a lipid storage defect with failure to oxidize phytanic acid.

Both dominant and recessive hereditary sensorineural hearing loss can occur without associated abnormalities. The incidence for dominant sensorineural hearing loss is 1 in 40,000, and for recessive sensorineural hearing loss, 1 in 4000. In the dominant form the loss begins between the ages of 6 and 10 years; it is progressive and symmetric, and the lesion is cochlear. There is a positive family history through several generations. In the recessive form, no family history of hearing loss is obtained; it occurs less rarely.

Nongenetic

Traumatic. Noise-induced (? genetic predisposition) sensorineural hearing loss is characterized by the following:

- Factors that influence the effect of noise in each individual (individual sensitivity, duration)
- Two measurable components of noise damage (temporary hearing loss [temporary threshold shift, TTS], permanent hearing loss [permanent threshold shift, PTS])
- The "C5 dip" in the audiogram
- Site of damage in the cochlea (usually basal turn)

Radiation. Radiation as a cause of progressive sensorineural hearing loss is not often considered and may be delayed.

Baro- and Physical Trauma. The insidious and progressive sensorineural hearing loss associated with noise exposure is receiving increasing attention in conservation of hearing programs. Noise-induced hearing loss is differentiated from that of acoustic trauma, in which immediate injury to the cochlea occurs; this is not progressive or accumulative. Three factors are present: intensity of the noise, its duration (exposure), and the individual's sensitivity to noise. Two components are present: temporary hearing loss (TTS) and permanent hearing loss. The individual is generally not seen until the impairment has become handicapping in daily communication. At this time, the hearing loss is advanced and irreversible. The loss develops in a well-defined manner. Early, only frequencies of 3000 to 4000 Hz are affected (the "C5 dip").

Hearing at the higher frequencies remains normal. As exposure to intense noise continues, frequencies on either side of C5 become affected. There is no valid evidence that noises below 85 dB are responsible for hearing loss. Interestingly, tinnitus is not as common in noise-induced hearing loss as in acoustic trauma. The outer hair cells of the basilar coil are damaged early, and marked recruitment is characteristic.

Inflammatory. Inflammatory causes of sensorineural hearing loss include the following:

- Otitis media, chronic, suppurative
- Mastoiditis, chronic, suppurative
- Syphilitic hearing loss (history may be lacking, congenital or acquired, may mimic Ménière's disease, fluorescent treponemal antibody-absorption test for syphilis)
- Influenza or vaccine and other viral and autoimmune disease

Local inflammatory causes of progressive sensorineural hearing loss as seen in chronic suppurative otitis media and chronic suppurative mastoiditis are well known.

Surgical. Sensorineural hearing loss may be caused by middle ear surgery (immediate or delayed), surgical trauma, or ossicular manipulation.

Occasionally, surgery of the temporal bone causes progressive sensorineural hearing loss. The effect on the membranous labyrinth may be immediate or delayed. Late progressive sensorineural hearing loss following early success in otosclerotic surgery may be due to the presence of cochlear otospongiosis and its ongoing effect on the membranous labyrinth.

Drugs: Disorders of Intoxication. Drugs known to cause sensorineural hearing loss include aminoglycosides, quinine and chloroquine, salicylates, ethacrynic acid and furosemide, nitrogen mustard and vincristine, tetanus antitoxin, and the topical drugs chloramphenicol, polymyxin B, neomycin, sodium colistimethate, and gentamicin.

The list of ototoxic drugs continues to grow. The list as shown points significantly to those drugs that are often used in life-threatening situations, particularly the aminoglycosides: streptomycin and dihydrostreptomycin, neomycin, kanamycin, and viomycin. The prolonged effects are irreversible.

Of particular current interest is the potential toxicity of topically applied antibiotics. Animal studies show toxicity, but specific clinical studies by Turner et al. (1987) have shown no deleterious effects on hearing. Erythromycin may occasionally produce ototoxicity.

Metabolic and Systemic Disorders. Hypothyroidism, disorders of circulation (hypertension, vascular occlusion), and collagen diseases may cause sensorineural hearing loss.

Hypothyroidism may produce both a conductive and a sensorineural hearing loss, reversible in therapy. Specific clinical proof, however, is lacking.

Disorders of systemic, particularly cerebral, circulation are common, and the effect on the circulation of the membranous labyrinth can be devastating. Collagen disorders, lupus erythematosus, periarteritis, and multiple sclerosis occasionally induce progressive sensorineural hearing loss.

Neoplasms. Vestibular schwannoma (acoustic neuroma) (8–10% of all intracranial tumors), metastatic tumors, leukemias, multiple myeloma, and teratomas may cause sensorineural hearing loss.

The diagnosis of acoustic neuroma as well as other angle tumors requires neuroradiologic studies.

Nonneoplastic Intracranial Lesions. Cysts, aneurysms, and cholesteatoma have been implicated as causes of sensorineural hearing loss.

Ménière's Disease. Ménière's disease is a disease of the membranous inner ear characterized by fluctuant hearing loss, vertigo, fullness, and usually tinnitus. It may affect both ears in 25% percent of the patients.

Ménière's disease is discussed in detail in Chapter 21–9.

Aging (Presbycusis). "What is it?" The term is misused. Aging changes per se actually account for little of the observed loss. More at fault are other factors such as acoustic trauma and metabolic or circulatory disorders.

Solely age-related sensorineural hearing loss is uncommon. Six to ten percent of the population 65 to 74 years of age is affected. Features include high frequency, symmetry, gradual progression, and discrimination changes.

Histopathologic patterns are of four types: sensory, neuronal, strial, and cochlear. The reader is referred to Schuknecht (1993) for further description.

Natural History and Its Modification with Treatment

Except for infectious causes, the natural history of sensorineural hearing loss is not changed by treatment. Cochlear implants alter total deafness in properly selected patients.

Prevention

Most cases of sensorineural hearing loss can be probably be prevented by control of noise pollution and protection of the ears in high-noise areas. Also, ototoxic drug use should be carefully monitored.

Acute hearing loss should be considered an emergency, and immediate hearing testing should be performed. Some losses could probably be averted with more prompt diagnosis and treatment.

Cost Containment

Screening audiometry is relatively inexpensive and highly productive in diagnosis. Patients with sensorineural hearing loss should not be subjected to costly radiologic studies, electronystagmography, brain scans, neurology consults, or cerebrospinal fluid studies until audiometry has been obtained. Unnecessary, hazardous, and costly investigation can often be avoided if careful history, routine ear examination, and screening audiometry are used in the proper order and interpreted concomitantly.

Indiscriminate use of hearing aids prior to adequate investigation of the cause of the sensorineural hearing loss is an improper expense to the patient. Aids obtained in this manner often end up in the bureau drawer.

REFERENCES

Chan KH, Eelkema EA, Furman JMR, Kamerer DB. Familial sensorineural hearing loss: A correlative study of audiologic, radiographic, and vestibular findings. Ann Otol Rhinol Laryngol 1991;100:620.

Dennis JM, Neely G. Basic hearing tests. Otol Clin North Am 1991;24:253.

Freeman J. Progressive sensorineural hearing loss. Unpublished monograph, University of Miami School of Medicine, 1978.

Jackler R, Brachmon D. Neurotology. Parts II, III, VII. St. Louis: Mosby, 1994.

Mattox DE, Lyles CA. Idiopathic, sudden sensorineural hearing loss. Am J Otol 1989;10:242.

Schuknecht HF. Pathology of the ear. Philadelphia: Lea & Febiger, 1993: Chs 4, 9, 12.

Shambaugh GE, Glasscock MF. Surgery of the ear. Philadelphia: WB Saunders, 1980:455.

Staab J. Hearing in the elderly. Audecibel 1990;39:8.

Turner JS. Treatment of hearing loss, ear pain, and tinnitus in older patients. Geriatrics 1982;37:107.

Turner JS, Per-Lee JH, Jackson RT, Saunders AZ. Cochlear implant for total deafness: A bioengineering and clinical research marvel. Emory Univ J Med 1987;1:106.

CHAPTER 21–2

Fluctuant Hearing Loss

John S. Turner, Jr., M.D.

DEFINITION

Fluctuant hearing loss is defined as hearing loss that is not constant.

ETIOLOGY

Causes may be infectious, immune, vascular, metabolic, or traumatic (see Discussion).

CRITERIA FOR DIAGNOSIS

Suggestive

The patient with fluctuant hearing loss has documented episodes of hearing impairment alternating with periods of normal hearing.

Definitive

Identification of specific underlying metabolic disorders is necessary for accurate diagnosis. Specific loss of hearing should be documented by repeat audiometry.

Fluctuating hearing episodes may be correlated with blood chemistry, autoimmune, serologic, or barometic changes.

CLINICAL MANIFESTATIONS

Subjective

All the manifestations listed in Chapter 21–1 are present. The alternating quality of the loss is distressing and puzzling for the patient and the patient's close associates. Migraine headache may be associated. Tinnitus or vertigo may be bothersome in some cases.

Objective

Physical Examination

All the manifestations listed in Chapter 21–1 are present.

Stigmata of congenital or acquired syphilis or of diabetes may be noted. Xanthelasma associated with hyperlipidemia may be present. Certain neurologic findings such as nystagmus and scanning speech may present in patients with multiple sclerosis. Pale, wet nasal membranes may offer a clue that the patient has a predisposing respiratory allergy.

Routine Laboratory Abnormalities

A search should be made for abnormalities in blood serologic tests, cholesterol level, glucose level, triglyceride level, or hematocrit.

PLANS

Diagnostic

Differential Diagnosis

Differentiation from Ménière's disease may be very difficult, as Ménière's disease may occur for years without vertigo. Fluctuant hearing loss may involve high, low, or all frequencies, whereas Ménière's disease usually involves low-tone loss. Periodic hearing testing is essential for proper diagnosis. No impedance audiometric changes occur in fluctuant hearing loss.

Multiple sclerosis may rarely present as fluctuant hearing loss. Only periodic observation in the face of normal blood chemistry permits diagnosis. Fluctuant hearing loss is seen with other neurologic defects in multiple sclerosis.

Barotrauma may have damaged the oval or round window membranes to produce perilymph leak and fluctuant hearing loss. A careful history must be taken to ascertain this unusual cause of fluctuant hearing loss. Exact diagnosis is made by middle ear exploration.

Diagnostic Options and Recommended Approach

Proper diagnosis may depend on the response to treatment. A specific cause can be documented in only about one third of cases of fluctuant hearing loss.

A complete otolaryngologic examination is essential and should include pure tone, speech, and impedance audiometry at the time the patient's communication is impaired. These tests should be repeated whenever the hearing seems to improve. In most cases, the loss is unilateral. Luetic patients may have bilateral fluctuant hearing loss. Autoimmune inner ear disorders may produce fluctuance.

Blood should be drawn for baseline analysis when the patient is first seen. Fluctuant hearing loss is commonly associated with abnormal serologic findings, an elevated triglyceride level with or without high cholesterol level, polycythemia, or an elevated blood sugar level. An elevated uric acid level is also seen occasionally. Immune globulin electrophoresis may be abnormal. The fluctuance of hearing downward is usually correlated with these abnormal findings.

The examiner must always inquire carefully as to whether the patient is taking diuretic drugs, because furosemide, ethacrynic acid, and sometimes thiazide diuretics may influence hearing. Aspirin or other salicylates may give fluctuant loss. The patient may have to be evaluated over a period of several months before the diagnosis of "fluctuant hearing loss" without vertigo can be made.

Therapeutic

The most dramatic response of the hearing loss results from treatment of hyperlipidemia with a low-fat diet or lipid lowering drugs.

Luetic treatment with intramuscular penicillin G benzathine biweekly, oral penicillin, and alternate-day prednisone in 40-mg doses has been documented to improve the fluctuant hearing loss associated with syphilis.

Control of previously undetected diabetes stabilizes the hearing in those patients with abnormalities in glucose metabolism. The hematocrit should be reduced in patients with polycythemia.

Concomitant treatment with propranolol (Inderal) often controls the fluctuant hearing loss in migraine patients.

Oral vasodilators such as cyclandelate may be used empirically when no specific cause can be found. Dramatic improvement may occur with intravenous histamine. A dose of 2.85 mg in 500 mL dextrose and water titrated to the point of facial flushing has been used for more than 30 years safely. This regimen is given daily for 3 consecutive days.

Control of nasal allergy or identification of food intolerance may give dramatic relief in hypersensitive individuals. Cortisone therapy may give dramatic relief in autoimmune ear disorders also. Surgical closure of oval window fistulas has provided cure.

Because in the majority of patients a distinct diagnosis cannot be made, the patient should be told that the disorder seldom leads to severe loss and serious associated disease cannot be found. If an associated cause such as hyperlipidemia is found, the patient must be instructed in a low-fat diet.

FOLLOW-UP

Hearing and blood tests should be repeated at 6-month intervals routinely. The patient should be seen at the time of sudden decline in hearing, and a decision should be made as to the need for more intense therapy.

DISCUSSION

Prevalence

Fluctuant hearing loss is a common problem. The type most frequently seen, Ménière's disease, is estimated to affect about 5% of the population.

Related Basic Science

Sludging in the delicate vasculature of the inner ear is apparently a common factor in about one third of cases. Decrease in blood viscosity and increase in blood flow can be correlated with improved hearing. Histamine and papaverine have been shown to increase cochlear blood flow. Decreases in hematocrit and lipoproteins can be correlated with improved hearing. Arteritis associated with syphilis is responsible for decreased blood flow through the cochlea as well as neural inflammation of the eighth cranial nerve. No good clinicopathologic correlation exists in fluctuant hearing loss, as patients do not die of this disorder. The patient's lymphocytes may be challenged with known inner ear antigens to identify autoimmune disorders. Increased spinal fluid pressure may aggravate cochlear fistulas.

Natural History and Its Modification with Treatment

Fluctuant hearing loss may begin at any age. It is very uncommon in children and teenagers, but it reaches its peak in the fourth and fifth decades. Hearing loss at older ages is usually not fluctuant and is related to noise exposure and heredity.

Except for drug effects and syphilis, the disorder is usually unilateral. The same ear seems to be repeatedly involved, apparently because of a critical blood supply on that side. Untreated cases of lipoproteinemia or polycythemia may become bilateral, and the condition may be misdiagnosed as hereditary loss. Tinnitus is seen in almost all cases and improves but does not disappear with treatment. If vertigo develops, the diagnosis is usually changed to Ménière's disease.

A hearing loss is characteristically present for pure tones, but the speech discrimination remains good. Occasional decrease in speech discrimination below 90% may occur during lapses in treatment. No abnormalities are noted on impedance audiometry, which helps eliminate retrocochlear disease from consideration.

In hypersensitive individuals, exposure to certain foods may precipitate acute hearing loss, or a flareup of seasonal allergy may be associated with fluctuant loss.

Prevention

Preventive diets that are low in fats (triglycerides) have been shown to influence hearing fluctuation favorably. Avoidance of known food and inhalant allergic substances may affect hearing fluctuation also. Prophylactic antibiotics and steroids may prevent the downward fluctuation of hearing in luetic patients. A low-salt diet and vasodilators often help prevent the fluctuant hearing loss associated with Ménière's disease.

Cost Containment

A careful history will document that the loss is fluctuant. When this is confirmed by inexpensive conventional audiometry, the need for expensive x-rays, evoked response audiometry, myelograms, and neurology consults is eliminated. Infrequent follow-up at 3 to 6 months is usually all that is necessary or proper care of the disorder.

REFERENCES

Hughes GB, Moscicki R, Barna BP, San Martin JE. Laboratory diagnosis of immune inner ear disease. Am J Otol 1994;15:198.

Jahrsdoerfer RA, Johns MM, Thompson EG, Cantrell RW. Sarcoidosis and fluctuating hearing loss. Am J Otol Rhinol Laryngol 1981;90:161.

Kalsarkas A, Baxter JD. Cochlear and vestibular dysfunction resulting from physical exertion or environmental pressure changes. J Otolaryngol 1976;5:24.

Meyerhoff WL, Liston S. Metabolism and hearing loss. In: Paparella MD, Shumrick WB, eds. Otolaryngology. Philadelphia: Saunders, 1980;2:1979.

Ruben RJ. Diseases of the inner ear and sensorineural deafness. In: Bluestone CD, Stool SE, eds. Pediatric otolaryngology. 2nd ed. Philadelphia: Saunders, 1990:547.

Spencer JT. Hyperlipoproteinemia, hyperinsulinism and Ménière's disease. South Med J 1981;74:1194.

Weider DJ, Jackson GD. Perilymphatic fistula. Am J Otol 1988;9:184.

CHAPTER 21–3

Otosclerosis

John S. Turner, Jr., M.D.

DEFINITION

Otosclerosis is an hereditory form of conductive hearing loss.

ETIOLOGY

Otosclerotic deafness is caused by fixation of the stapes bone in the oval window from excessive growth of abnormal bone (otospongiosis).

CRITERIA FOR DIAGNOSIS
Suggestive

Patients with hearing loss who have no history of ear infections, normal ear drums and canals, and evidence of conductive hearing loss on tuning fork or audiometry testing have otosclerosis (otospongiosis).

Definitive

Exact diagnosis is made at the time of microscopic ear surgery.

CLINICAL MANIFESTATIONS
Subjective

Tinnitus is often associated with this disorder. Vertigo may be present in cases of generalized labyrinthine otosclerosis, but is seldom found in stapedial otosclerosis alone. Hearing-impaired patients with otosclerosis may notice that in noisy surroundings, such as around a machine shop or in a crowded store, they seem to hear better and communicate well. This phenomenon is known as *paracusis of Willis* and occurs because other persons around the patient are speaking louder to overcome the ambient noise and thus exceed the patient's poor threshold for hearing. There is usually a history of hearing loss in other family members, particularly females.

Objective
Physical Examination

Conductive hearing loss such as otosclerosis causes the patient to speak with a soft voice. Most of the other manifestations listed in Chapter 21–1 are present. A reddish blush may be seen through the eardrum called Schwartze's sign. This occurs because of prominent blood vessels on the promontory of the middle ear. The Weber test lateralizes to the affected ear; the Rinne test shows bone conduction greater than air conduction.

Routine Laboratory Abnormalities

These studies are noncontributory.

PLANS

Diagnostic

Differential Diagnosis

A complete otolaryngologic examination including air, bone, speech discrimination, and impedance audiometry is necessary for documentation. Only congenital footplate fixation or other ossicular anomalies, which are rare, give similar clinical and audiometric findings.

Diagnostic Options and Recommended Approach

Bone conduction is greater than air conduction in both tuning fork and audiometric tests. Only the 256 fork detects mild hearing loss around 20 dB, but 512 and 1024 forks show bone conduction greater than air conduction in severe hearing losses.

Therapeutic

Therapeutic Options

Hearing loss from otosclerosis can be effectively managed with a hearing aid or with stapes surgery to replace the immobile bone with a prosthesis.

Recommended Approach

Surgery is the preferable form of treatment in almost all cases. The reasons for this are as follows:

- The first patients underwent operation about 35 years ago, and most of these patients are still hearing well. The procedure, if effective, gives a permanent improvement.
- The probability of hearing improvement ranges from 90 to 95%, with only a 1 or 2% chance that hearing will be worse postoperatively.
- The chance of side effects such as dizziness, increased tinnitus, and impaired taste (from chorda tympani involvement) is less than 5%.
- The inconvenience, expense, and cosmetic detraction of wearing a hearing aid are avoided.
- The surgery can be performed under local anesthesia without an external exposure incision, usually with 1 day of hospitalization.
- Morbidity and incapacity are minimal; the patient is able to return to a sedentary occupation in 4 days and almost all occupations in 10 days.
- In bilateral cases, one ear is corrected by surgery and 1 year later the other ear can be corrected.
- Cases with associated sensorineural loss of severe degree can be brought up to a useful threshold that permits more effective hearing aid use. In addition, hearing awareness in a patient's general environment is improved.
- The operation can be performed safely at almost any age, including the eighties. Children and young adults do not usually undergo surgery until after a period of observation to document the rapidity of progression or the presence of associated symptoms such as vertigo in this juvenile form of the disease.
- The techniques of the procedure are now highly standardized, and all graduates of approved training programs receive training in stapedectomy. There is no need for the patient to travel to a distant medical center for proper care, as might be the case in patients with acoustic neuroma.

A particular form of otosclerosis called labyrinthine otosclerosis (see Natural History and Its Modification with Treatment) may need initial management with sodium fluoride to stabilize the rapidly declining sensorineural hearing loss. The reader is referred to the work of Shambaugh (1980) for further review of this management.

Patients with episodic vertigo are not candidates for operative management because the vertigo may be enhanced by the procedures. These patients have associated endolymphatic hydrops (Ménière's) and should be rehabilitated with a hearing aid.

Unsuccessful surgery on one ear is an absolute contraindication for stapes surgery on the opposite ear, because catastrophic results may occur in the second ear and the patient would be rendered totally deaf. A hearing aid should always be advised.

All the risks cited above should be discussed frankly with the patient. The patient should always be given the option of wearing a hearing aid. Patients with progressive associated sensorineural hearing loss should be informed adequately of the need for sodium fluoride. Many patients with otosclerosis have worn a hearing aid for years before proper diagnosis. These patients should be informed of the many benefits of stapedectomy.

FOLLOW-UP

Repeated examination in patients who have not undergone surgery should be done every 2 years to note progression of conduction loss or associated sensorineural loss. Patients who have undergone surgery should not have the opposite ear done for a minimum of 1 year, to document that the hearing in the first ear has stabilized and that no unexpected sequelae such as vertigo have developed.

DISCUSSION

Prevalence

Ten percent of the general population have otosclerosis. Only 11 to 12% of these patients develop clinical hearing impairment. (See Natural History and Its Modification with Treatment).

Related Basic Science

Otosclerosis develops from areas of spongy or vascular bone present in the otic capsule of the inner ear. These pathologic areas recalcify to form more dense bone after the proliferation has progressed. If these hardened areas involve the oval window and frontplate of the stapes, stapes fixation and a conductive hearing loss develop. The spongy process may also involve the cochlear endosteum and inner ear fluids with possible enzymatic or vascular effects on the consistency of the fluids. These chemical changes result in hair cell or neural changes, which produce an associated sensorineural hearing loss known as labyrinthine otosclerosis. Varying degrees or combinations of these two processes may occur, with mixed types of conductive and sensorineural loss seen. Approximately 50% of ears with otosclerosis have a single form of this pathologic bone. The focus begins in the endochondral layer of the labyrinthine capsule. In probably 85% of patients, both ears will ultimately be involved.

Areas of bone resorption and osteoclastic activity are seen adjacent to osteoblastic activity in early stages of the disorder. With maturity, the focus becomes more inactive and stable bone develops to fix the stapes in the oval window. Sodium fluoride has been shown to stabilize this process by impairing osteoclasts and stimulating osteoblasts. Sodium fluoride may be given as 25-mg tablets twice a day with food. Calcium gluconate is usually prescribed also to facilitate absorption.

Natural History and Its Modification with Treatment

Approximately 10% of the general population have otosclerosis in a histologic form; however, only 11 or 12% of these people develop clinical hearing impairment. The propensity for the process is present at birth and has been shown by temporal bone study to increase in incidence to a peak of 9.7% of white males and 18.5% of white females between the ages of 30 and 50.

Very active and aggressive otosclerotic foci may produce conductive hearing loss in children of age 10. The juvenile form of the disease progresses until stability occurs around age 40 or 50. Most patients seek medical attention for hearing loss in the late twenties or during their third decade. Tinnitus is often the initial complaint, followed by insidious loss of hearing in one ear that may involve the other years later. The patient speaks with a very soft voice and may have to stop chewing at meals to hear better because the mastication noise as well as his or her own voice is transmitted distinctly to the cochlea with the bone deafness.

The disorder is familial, but the genetic pattern is sporadic with a highly reduced penetrance. Dominant, recessive, or sex-linked patterns cannot be accurately discerned. Otosclerosis is common in the white population, uncommon in blacks and Asians. There is a female preponderance of almost 2:1, with accentuation during pregnancy. This aggravation by pregnancy is thought to be related to hormones influencing bone metabolism.

The focus of otosclerosis in the middle ear is very active in young adults, and this activity produces a reddish blush to the promontory of the middle ear and increased bleeding at the time of operation. For this reason, some surgeons delay surgery in this juvenile form of the disease.

The generalized form of the disease, known as labyrinthine otosclerosis, presents as a predominant sensorineural hearing loss with perhaps a very minimal difference between air and bone conduction. The loss progresses from year to year, and perhaps 25% of patients have associated vertigo. Early patients with a considerable conductive loss may lose the conductive component and progress to severe levels of sensorineural loss.

A special form of the disease occurs as part of osteogenesis imperfecta (van de Hoeve's syndrome); however, not all patients with osteogenesis imperfecta develop clinical hearing loss. Correction can be accomplished with stapedectomy.

After age 45 or 50, the deafness seems to stabilize, and further sensorineural loss seems to depend on other factors related to aging. Excellent neural reserve may persist until old age, however, and many octogenarians have obtained useful hearing with stapedectomy.

Prevention

No preventive measure is known, as otosclerosis is a hereditary disorder. Progression of the deafness may be prevented by the use of sodium fluoride in some patients, particularly those with labyrinthine (generalized) otosclerosis.

Cost Containment

Proper diagnosis involves a routine otolaryngologic examination, which includes air, bone, and speech discrimination audiometry. Other tests are usually not needed. Definitive operative treatment can be carried out with 1 day of hospitalization with minimum time lost from work.

REFERENCES

Brentlay P, Solomon MD, Johnsen NJ. Otospongiosis and sodium fluoride. Am J Otol 1989;10:20.

Goodhill V. Diseases, deafness, and dizziness. In: Goodhill V, ed. Otosclerosis. New York: Harper & Row, 1985:388.

Jack F. Remarkable improvement in hearing by removal of stapes. Trans Am Otol Soc 1891;5:284.

Longman AW, Jackler RK, Sooy FA. Stapedectomy: Long-term hearing results. Laryngology 1991;101:810.

Shambaugh GE, Glasscock MF. Surgery of the ear. Philadelphia: WB Saunders, 1980:455.

Turner JS. Revision of previous stapedectomy, tympanoplasty, mastoidectomy, and endolymphatic shunt. South Med J 1983;76:1493.

Turner JS. Treatment of hearing loss, ear pain, and tinnitus in older patients. Geriatrics 1982;37:107.

CHAPTER 21–4

Ear Pain or Discomfort

John S. Turner, Jr., M.D.

DEFINITION

Ear pain or discomfort is defined as pain in or around the ear.

ETIOLOGY

Intrinsic Causes of Ear Pain

Lesions of External Auditory Canal

- Furuncle
- External otitis (eczematoid or swimmer's ear)
- Impacted cerumen or foreign body
- Traumatic effects (perforation from a slap on the ear)
- Herpes zoster
- Otomycosis
- Skin tumors, benign and malignant
- Granuloma of ear
- Malignant otitis externa (in diabetes)
- Bell's palsy
- Bullous myringitis involving canal
- Exostoses of canal with obstruction
- Cholesteatoma and keratosis of external canal
- Local manifestations of generalized skin disorders (psoriasis, lupus, leukemia, mycosis fungoides)
- Postradiation effects and postsurgical effects
- Parotid or soft tissue disorders extending into ear canal

Lesions of Middle Ear

- Acute otitis media
- Otitis media with effusion (serous)
- Acute exacerbation of chronic otitis media with or without drum perforation
- Cholesteatoma
- Polyps arising from tympanum
- Acute mastoiditis
- Glomus jugulare tumor or other tumors
- Previous ventilation tube implant
- Spasm of middle ear muscles

Extrinsic Causes of Ear Pain

Extrinsic causes are those that produce pain in the ear reflex by lesions remote from the ear itself. This is often referred to as reflex or referred otalgia. To interpret the significance of referred pain in the ear, it is necessary to know the nerve supply of the ear and to know to what other organs the same or related nerves are distributed (see Related Basic Science). Lesions in the ear rarely produce pain in distal areas, but many areas refer pain to the ear. When the patient complains of earache, though having a normal external canal and drum, a number of sources of pain should come to mind. In about one half of cases, the cause is of dental origin, either occurring from the teeth themselves or from the temporomandibular joint.

The temporomandibular joint is the most common site of pain (see Chapter 21–14), followed by the lower molar teeth.

Lesions of the anterior two thirds of the tongue and inflammatory conditions of the parotid gland refer pain along the auricular branch of the auriculotemporal nerve. Referred pain from the submaxillary and lingual salivary glands via the lingual nerve may cause pain in front of the ear. An inflammation on the anterior one third of the tongue may cause pain in front of the ear, whereas an ulceration of the posterior one third of the tongue, such as a beginning carcinoma, may cause pain within the ear itself. This is explained by referral through two different nerve sources.

Patients with acute and chronic infections of the tonsils frequently complain of otalgia. Lesions of the palate, pharynx, or nasopharynx, especially in the region of the eustachian tube, often produce pain deep in the ear, and occasionally growths of the tonsil give rise to earache as the first and only symptom. Otalgia is often the earliest sign of a beginning malignancy in the nasopharynx. The ninth cranial nerve is involved in this referred pain pattern.

Ulcerative lesions of the entrance of the larynx such as tuberculosis and malignancy may cause reflex otalgia secondary to irritation of the superior laryngeal branch of the vagus nerve.

The ear should be examined carefully. If no causes for pain can be found in that area, then the examiner should think of the nerve supply of the ear and the mechanisms of referred pain. Think and check the letter *T:*

Teeth	Trachea
Tongue	Temporomandibular joint
Tonsils	Tendons (hyoid, etc.)
Tube (eustachian)	Tic (ninth nerve)
Throat	Thyroid

Acute and chronic forms of thyroiditis may present as throat and ear pain, but tenderness will be maximal over the thyroid lobe on that side. Inflammation of the carotid bulb (carotidynia) often presents in a similar manner.

An unsuspected source of otalgia is elongation of the styloid process with protrusion into the tonsillar fossa (Eagle's syndrome). Ear pain combined with throat discomfort should alert the examiner to palpate the tonsillar fossa. Inflammation or stone in the submaxillary gland can be a source of referred ear pain.

CRITERIA FOR DIAGNOSIS
Suggestive

Ear pain is called *otalgia* and can emanate from both otologic and nonotologic sources. Upper respiratory infection often accompanies this complaint, but dental inflammation and decay are sometimes the prime locus of the pain.

Definitive

The patient complains of discomfort or severe aching in or around the ear. Careful evaluation not only of the ear but of all areas of possible referred pain is necessary for diagnosis.

CLINICAL MANIFESTATIONS
Subjective

Acute, chronic, or recurrent pain may be present. The sensation may vary from a deep aching to a sharp, quick lancing discomfort. Only a vague fullness may be present, or there may be a blocked feeling to the ear.

Acute, sudden pain may be accompanied by fever, nasal congestion, nasal or ear drainage, or headache. Chronic pain usually exists by itself and fever-associated complaints are noted. Tinnitus, dizziness, and hearing impairment are commonly seen with recurrent ear pain. The pain may seem penetrating and deep within the canal, or it may be more diffuse and external, either anterior or posterior to the pinna. The patient may volunteer that neck motion, chewing, swallowing, coughing, nose blowing, the Valsalva maneuver, or flying aggravates or precipitates the discomfort.

Objective
Physical Examination

Movement of the pinna or pressure on the tragus may be present. Examination of the canal or neck rotation may trigger intense pain. Pressure over the temporomandibular joint as the patient opens and closes the jaw may precipitate the pain. Tapping on the teeth, especially the lower molars, may incite pain to the ear. Palpation on the hyoid bone tip, the carotid artery bulb, the submaxillary triangle, the parotid gland, the mastoid process, or the scalp itself may send pain to the ear as well as to the superficial area palpated. Attempts to chew or swallow may be accompanied by a grimace and noticeable pain referred to one or both ears.

Routine Laboratory Abnormalities

White blood cell count is often elevated with infection, and cultures of the ear may be positive for bacteria and/or fungus.

PLANS
Diagnostic
Differential Diagnosis

Pain in the ear may be divided into intrinsic and extrinsic causes denoting the site of origin (see Etiology).

Diagnostic Options and Recommended Approach

Intrinsic causes can usually be documented by direct examination of the ear and adjacent areas.

Therapeutic
Therapeutic Options

If specific ear disease such as early otitis media can be identified, then pain may be relieved with local and systemic therapy. Warm local solution such as lidocaine or Auralgan may be used in the ear canal every 2 hours. Such treatment is purely symptomatic and not curative. This may be helpful for bacterial or vital inflammation. It is not appropriate if eardrum perforation or purulent drainage is present.

Recommended Approach

If no obvious ear disorder is noted, then an intense search must be made for the source of the referred pain and appropriate treatment directed to the inciting cause.

Many patients are surprised to find out that their ear pain comes from the temporomandibular joint or a diseased tooth. Instruction in the need to avoid jaw strain or to obtain new dental plates may be necessary. Certain habits such as pipe smoking, chewing gum, and tooth grinding (bruxism) may have to be altered. Unusual exercises that put strain on the cervical spine and create referred ear pain may have to be stopped and a new exercise regimen started.

FOLLOW-UP

Ear pain without obvious physical findings must be followed at periodic intervals until the source is located. As 50% of patients have pain from dental sources, dental referral is often needed. Insidious dental infection or decay may be very difficult to identify, and this as well as other remote causes must often be pursued on more than one visit.

DISCUSSION
Prevalence

Otalgia is exceedingly common in all age groups.

Related Basic Science

Referred pain is an incompletely understood phenomenon wherein nerve impulses emanating from a distant or deeper structure are localized to a more superficial structure of the body. The site of pain referral generally follows the dermatomal rule. Well-known examples of this phenomenon are shoulder pain caused by diaphragmatic pleurisy and pain down the inner side of the arm and little finger of cardiac origin. In each situation, the pain spreads from one area to another through nerve branches that have a common central origin within the same segments of the gray matter of the spinal cord.

Referred pain generally comes from viscera and muscles and is often described as deep pain. The faulty projection of deep pain to the surface is thought to be the result of the infrequency of deep pain and the inability to use vision to verify the source of stimulation; thus, learning appears to be an important factor in referred pain.

Evidence that reference of sensation is a learned phenomenon can be found in the clinical observation that a pain may be referred not to its usual point of reference but to a site of previous surgical operation, trauma, or localized pathologic process. Some individuals suffer severe pain localized to the teeth during high-altitude flying. On exclusion of every possible dental cause for pain, they discovered that the pain stimulus was expansion of air trapped in the maxillary sinus. The group referring pain to the teeth had a high incidence of traumatic dental work on the side of reference, suggesting a habit reference of pain. Under experimental conditions, they were able to prove that a projection of pain is learned and that pain impulses conducted in overlapping pathways were simply given the previously learned reference for impulses in that path.

Neither habit reference nor any other theory of referred pain can fully explain the phenomena that occur.

When pain is referred to the ear from a painful lesion elsewhere, it is likely that both the ear and the area containing the lesion receive sensory innervations from the same cranial nerve and that spread occurs by way of central connections within the gray matter of the brainstem.

The nerve supply to the external auditory canal and the middle ear comes from three cranial nerves—the trigeminal, the glossopharyngeal, and the vagus—and from the cervical plexus via the lesser occipital nerve (C-2) and the great auricular nerve (C–3). A small portion of the auricle, the superior and anterior walls of the external canal, and the anterior part of the tympanic membrane are supplied by the third branch of the auriculotemporal branch of the third division of the trigeminal nerve. Practically the whole surface of the auricle receives its sensory innervations from the great auricular and lesser occipital nerves. The inferior and the posterior walls of the external canal and the posterior portion of the tympanic membrane are supplied with sensory fibers from the auricular branch of the vagus nerve. It is generally correct to state that the ganglionic representation of the sensation of the auricle and external canal can be divided into the gasserian ganglion in front, second and third cervical ganglia behind, and jugular ganglion in between.

The tympanic plexus, which lies on the promontory, is formed mainly by nerves derived from the tympanic branch of the glossopharyngeal nerve, but it also receives branches from the geniculate ganglion of the facial nerve. Sympathetic branches from the carotid plexus join the tympanic plexus, though sensory function is doubtful. The skin overlying the mastoid is innervated by the mastoid branches of the great auricular and lesser occipital nerves, whereas cells in the mastoid receive their sensory supply through a mastoid branch of the tympanic plexus. Sensory branches from the trigeminal nerve to structures within the middle ear are very questionable.

Referred Pain Pathways

Trigeminal Nerve. Painful impulses originating in the region of a diseased lower molar tooth or temporomandibular joint would be traced by way of the gasserian ganglion to the spinal nucleus of the fifth cranial nerve in the brainstem. This nucleus also connects with ear structures by way of other sensory branches of the third division that innervate the wall of the external canal and tympanum.

Glossopharyngeal Nerve. Irritation impulses from the tongue or tonsil travel through the ninth nerve and its ganglia to enter the somatic sensory nucleus of the ninth nerve within the medulla. This nucleus also receives the sensory branches of the ninth cranial nerve from the middle ear and adjacent structures. It is clear again, as in referred pain by the fifth nerve, that the pathway must pass through the sensory nucleus in the medulla.

Vagus Nerve. In the same manner, the somatic afferent pathways of the vagus nerve from the larynx ascend through the peripheral ganglia to the spinal nucleus in the medulla and here connect with afferents from the concha and deeper structures of the ear.

The fifth, ninth, and tenth cranial nerves are closely related in their central connection in the brainstem; however, there must be a fair degree of separation within each of the three nerve systems centrally. Otherwise, the localized reference of pain observed clinically would not occur. Beyond a certain level of sensory irritation, there seems to be an overflow into the adjacent centers with more diffuse and poorly localized pain.

Natural History and Its Modification with Treatment

The onset, intensity, and duration of ear pain depend on the particular etiology.

Prevention

The pain of external otitis may be prevented by using alcohol, white vinegar, or Domeboro solution in the ears after swimming or frequent water contamination. The pain of external trauma can be prevented by keeping hairpins and other metallic objects out of the ear canal. As much ear discomfort is associated with dental disorders, good dental hygiene and dental prophylaxis is helpful in its prevention.

Cost Containment

Time and expense can be saved by careful examination of the entire head and neck area. Virtually every area above the clavicle is a possible source of ear pain, and judicious exclusions based on a careful examination must be made before expensive x-rays or other diagnostic studies are ordered.

REFERENCES

Beddoe GM. Otalgia. Am Fam Physician 1975;11:108.

Bently AJ. Manual for medical students. Atlanta, GA: Emory University, unpublished brochure, 1973.

Campbell CD, Loft GH, Davis H, Hart DL. TMJ symptoms and referred pain patients. J Prosthet Dent 1982;47:4.

Kreisberg MK, Turner JS. Dental causes of referred otalgia. Ear Nose Throat J 1986;66:398.

McDonald JS, Pensak ML, Phero JC. Differential diagnosis of chronic facial, head and neck pain conditions, Parts I and II. Am J Otology 1990;11:299, 378.

Weaver ME. Ear pain. In: Wood RP, Northern JL, eds. Manual of otolaryngology. Baltimore: Williams & Wilkins, 1979:33.

CHAPTER 21–5

Otitis Media

John S. Turner, Jr., M.D.

DEFINITION

Inflammation of the middle ear mucosa, eardrum, and associated structures from physical or infectious causes is designated as otitis media.

ETIOLOGY

Otitis media may be caused by obstruction of the eustachian tube and/or associated infection.

CRITERIA FOR DIAGNOSIS

Suggestive

Patients with otitis media complain of ear pain, fullness, drainage, tinnitus, or hearing loss. The disorder is usually bilateral in children, but it is often unilateral in adults.

Definitive

Inflammation, fluid, distortion, or discoloration of the eardrum, when found in a patient with the symptoms listed above, indicates a diagnosis of otitis media.

CLINICAL MANIFESTATIONS

Subjective

Acute cases usually present with pain, fullness, hearing impairment, and associated pharyngitis or rhinitis. Subacute or chronic cases may manifest only as mild hearing loss, popping in the ear and fullness, or tinnitus. An allergic diathesis in the family is common.

Objective

Physical Examination

Acute. Acute cases have prominent vessels running along the handle of the malleus or diffuse redness of the entire drum. In a special form called bullous myringitis, there is a reddish-purple bleb or blister on the drum or at the junction of the drum and canal. Purulent exudate may be seen exuding from a small spontaneous perforation. Tympanometry with the impedance bridge may be painful and show a flat tracing with drum immobility.

Facial paralysis is occasionally seen in children with acute otitis media and rarely in adults. This manifestation occurs with inflammation of the seventh nerve in areas of bony dehiscence of the fallopian canal in the middle ear.

Chronic. Chronic foci have much more subtle findings, with only minimal vessel engorgement and prominence. Thin, reticular vessels are seen along the drum edge. A yellow, tan, straw-colored, or slightly orange appearance of the drum may be seen. A special type called *blue eardrum* may appear bluish black from hemosiderin pigments or cholesterin granules. Actual bubbles or the meniscus of fluid collection may be seen through the translucent drum. The short process of the malleus is very prominent. The pars flaccida is retracted and very difficult to visualize. Fluid may actually be seen to move with Valsalva's maneuver or pneumatic otoscope.

Neglected or prolonged infection shows severe distortion of the drum; thin, translucent areas of healed perforation; or actual defects from 1 mm in size to absence of the entire tympanic membrane. Yellow or yellow-green pus from saprophytic infections is common in these cases; mucoid accumulation is common also. Superimposed yeast or fungus infection may be seen. Perforations in the posterosuperior quadrant may show cholesteatoma (see Chapter 21–12) formation.

Inactive otitis media with evidence of previous infection is manifest by whitish plaques of clothlike material extending in patches and sheets between the drum and middle ear layers. These accumulations are known as *tympanosclerosis*. The malleus handle may be denuded and prominently displayed at the top of a large kidney-shaped perforation in long-standing cases. Mucus may be displaced from the recesses of the middle ear or mastoid with the pneumatic otoscope. Vertigo and nystagmus may be produced by the pressure of the pneumatic otoscope when infection has exposed the horizontal semicircular canal.

In large perforations, diseased or distorted fragments of malleus, incus, or stapes may be evident. Hyperplastic friable mucosa that bleeds easily is often seen in chronic active infections. This mucosa may proliferate to form an ever-enlarging mass that extends into the ear canal and is known as an *aural polyp*. Quiescent or allergic cases may present only as pale-pink hypertrophic mucosa visible in the middle ear through a perforation. This may actually be displaced out of the perforation with the Valsalva maneuver. Extremely foul-smelling drainage strongly indicates cholesteatoma.

Recurrent maxillary and ethmoid sinusitis, nasopharyngitis, adenotonsillitis, and allergic rhinosinusitis are commonly seen in patients with otitis media, especially in those with subacute or chronic cases.

Diabetes or immunodeficiency disorders are also associated with recurrent cases of otitis media.

Even cases with minimal fluid or drum edema show lateralization of the Weber test to the affected ear. Bone conduction is usually equal or greater than air conduction on Rinne's test. Tympanometry with the impedance bridge shows reduced drum mobility with maximum impedance. Mastoid radiographs are usually diffusely cloudy, because the mucosal inflammation involves all the temporal bone mucosal lining with either edema or fluid. Cell partitions are intact without evidence of osteitis or bone softening.

A nasopharyngeal tumor is highly suspect in adults with unilateral serous otitis media, and the otitis media symptoms may be the only complaints.

Routine Laboratory Abnormalities

Bacterial infections in acute forms show a leukocytosis, but viral infections or chronic purulent or serous forms usually create little change in the blood picture. Eosinophilia points to probable underlying allergy.

PLANS

Diagnostic

Differential Diagnosis

Various forms of otitis media exist and coexist with possible progression from one form into another. The Fifth International Symposium on Recent Advances in Otitis Media in 1994 recommended the following classification:

POM   Purulent otitis media
SOM   Serous otitis media
MOM   Mucoid or secretory otitis media
COM   Chronic suppurative otitis media and mastoiditis
        a. Active
        b. Inactive

Acute, subacute, or chronic types of otitis media may be seen. Acute inflammation lasts less than 2 weeks; subacute otitis media lasts from 2 weeks to 2 months; and chronic otitis lasts longer than 2 weeks. History and accurate ear examination properly place the diagnosis in one or more of these categories. Serous otitis media (otitis media with effusion, or nonpurulent) is the most difficult to identify but statistically is the most prevalent (see Natural History and Its Modification with Treatment). Audiometry and tympanometry with the impedance bridge confirm questionable cases. Movement of the pinna or pressure over the tragus does not produce pain in otitis media or mastoiditis, as it does in otitis externa (swimmer's ear). Routine mastoid films or polytomes may be needed to define progression to mastoiditis in severe cases.

Diagnostic Options

To elucidate the underlying cause of the ear inflammation, bacterial culture through aspiration and/or myringotomy may be needed in acute cases. As most infections are with pneumococcus or *Hemophilus influenzae,* exact identification of the cause is not necessary for cure in most cases. Nasopharyngeal culture usually reveals the same bacteria as in the middle ear.

Chronic otitis media is usually associated with saprophytic infections with *Staphylococcus aureus, Pseudomonas aeruginosa,* or *Proteus vulgaris.* These infectious agents are usually opportunists that grow insidiously following infection with more virulent bacteria. More incipient and potentially hazardous disease may be present in the attic or mastoid in these cases. Negative pressure or insufflation of the middle ear with the pneumatic otoscope may reveal unsuspected mucopus exuding from the recesses of the mastoid.

Subacute or chronic serous otitis media or mucoid otitis media occurs as a result of eustachian tube obstruction or malfunction or as residue of bacterial and viral acute otitis media.

Eustachian tube disorders may develop from adenoid hypertrophy or inflammation; from barotrauma, sinusitis, nasopharyngitis, nasopharyngeal tumors, or temporomandibular joint disease; or from allergic or immune disorders of the respiratory tract. These disorders must be identified or eliminated in each case of otitis media.

Recommended Approach

Routine sinus radiographs, lateral soft tissue radiographs of the nasopharynx, culture of the nasopharynx, palpation of the nasopharynx, and mirror or direct examination of the nasopharynx with a scope may be needed. Nasal smears for cytologic study or complete allergic evaluation may be needed to accurately identify the underlying cause of the otitis media.

Malformation of the jaws, palate, or facial bones may predispose the patient to otitis media. The most extreme problem occurs in patients with cleft palate.

Patients with chronic purulent otitis media are often prediabetic or have a strong family history of diabetes. Long-term observation of young adults with otitis media reveals that most of them eventually manifest abnormalities of carbohydrate or lipoprotein metabolism or immunodeficiency disorders. Otitis media resolves completely and the ear returns to normal in patients who are free of underlying predisposing disorders.

Hypermetabolic states such as decreased thyroid function may predispose the patient to otitis media.

Radiation therapy to the head or upper neck may create chronic effects on the eustachian tube and middle ear mucosa with secondary otitis media development.

Therapeutic

Therapeutic Options

Therapy of otitis media is directed toward the control of infection, the elimination of fluid from the ear, and the management of predisposing causes such as eustachian tube malfunction or allergy.

In acute otitis media, the patient usually complains of earache, so that initial treatment is directed toward immediate relief of pain. Topical solutions containing local analgesics (eg, antipyrine/benzocaine, lignocaine, lidocaine) have long been used, warmed under running water, to fill the ear canal. Although they do appear to provide local pain relief in most cases (solutions containing antibacterial agents have no therapeutic benefit), supplemental systemic analgesics are still usually required. Codeine combined with aspirin is generally effective, but some patients may require an injection of meperidine (Pethidine) for immediate relief of a severe throbbing pain.

Systemic antibacterial agents should be started immediately. The most common pathogens are pneumococci, *Streptococcus pyogenes,* and, in children, *H. influenzae.* In children under 6 years old, *H. influenzae* occurs frequently but can also be common in older children. Ampicillin or amoxicillin is the agent of choice because of its spectrum of activity, in particular because of its effectiveness against *H. influenzae* in children; however, strains of *H. influenzae* resistant to ampicillin are now being reported. Erythromycin combined with a sulfonamide or trimethoprim–sulfamethoxazole (Co-trimoxazole, Bactrim) is preferred in cases not responding to amoxicillin. Erythromycin in full doses or trimethoprim–sulfamethoxazole can be used in the penicillin-allergic patient. Cephalexin (Keflex) is not recommended in childhood otitis media because of inadequate activity against *H. influenzae.*

Antibacterial therapy should be continued for a minimum of 10 days to prevent the development of serous (secretory) otitis media and, if the ear has not cleared completely, for a period of 14 days or longer. To prevent prolonged complications, the ear may have to be opened with myringotomy if pus is obviously present, if the appearance of the middle ear has not returned to normal after antibacterial therapy, or if conductive hearing loss is persistent.

Topical nasal decongestants such as xylometazoline and oxymetazoline and oral eustachian tube decongestants such as phenylpropanolamine and pseudoephedrine may be helpful, but they should be used for limited periods only. As the infection in most cases spreads from the nose, clearance of nasal and sinus secretions is a logical step.

Recommended Approach

Purulent or Chronic Suppurative Otitis Media. In simple practical terms, purulent or chronic suppurative otitis media indicates a middle ear infection that has persisted continuously for more than 6 weeks, but it also includes recurrent ear infection that did not begin as an acute otitis media (e.g., a nonpainful discharge from the ear through a preexisting perforation).

Initial treatment is directed at measures aimed at producing a healthy nose and paranasal sinuses: investigation for sinusitis, appropriate antiallergy treatment, removal of adenoids, and nasal septal operations if indicated. As soon as a clear nasal airway has been provided, the patient must be educated in how to breathe through it. At the same time, careful and adequate cleansing of the external ear canal and middle ear must be accomplished with the use of suction and, often, with the pneumatic otoscope. Once the purulent exudate and debris are removed, an antibacterial solution may be displaced into the middle ear and mastoid, often with the assistance of the pneumatic otoscope. Solutions containing gentamicin, polymyxin with acetic acid, or 70% alcohol (may be painful) are appropriate.

This aural toilet should be repeated once weekly (or more frequently), together with topical application of antibacterial drops or powder once daily for several weeks. Usually a saprophyte such as a *Pseudomonas* or *Proteus* species is involved, and prolonged treatment is necessary to eradicate the organism. Systemic therapy with appropriate antibiotics such as gentamicin (Garamycin), colistin (Coly-Mycin S), and kanamycin (Kannasyn) would be too toxic, and because of the presence of a cavity and purulent exudate, these drugs usually do not reach the bacteria in sufficient concentration. Systemic antibiotics may, however, be indicated if the culture is positive for a bacteria other than *Pseudomonas* or *Proteus,* as such organisms can be more virulent and may have invaded tissue beyond the mastoid cavities. Occasionally, culture indicates an overwhelming yeast infection; appropriate topical use of nystatin (Mycostatin) powder is then required. Otitis media from anaerobic infections occurs in some patients, and drugs appropriate for these bacteria should be used in patients unresponsive to the usual antibiotics listed above.

Prolonged local antibacterial therapy with frequent cleansing usually dries most chronic infections where there is a large perforation. If drainage persists after 6 weeks of intensive therapy, or if cholesteatoma is present, tympanomastoid surgery is necessary. Very often, intense local therapy preoperatively may convert an extremely infected ear into a quiescent one, permitting the surgeon to perform less radical mastoid surgery and more effective reconstruction of the sound-transformer mechanism.

Serous or Secretory Otitis Media. Serous or secretory otitis media is the most common cause of deafness in children. The condition is characterized by the accumulation of thin serous fluid or, more often, thick tenacious mucus ("glue ear" or mucoid otitis media). It affects adults much less commonly than children. Some children with obvious evidence of middle ear fluid may have little or no earache and only very mild or very short-lived hearing loss. Other children complain of frequent earache, often followed by discharge from the ear with hearing loss which may be prolonged for months. Very occasionally, permanent hearing loss results.

Medical treatment should be tried first, but may not always be satisfactory. A milk-free diet, antihistamines and other appropriate antiallergy treatment, topical nasal decongestants, oral eustachian tube decongestants, and eustachian autoinflation maneuvers are often used (see below). Remission can occur spontaneously in many children.

Persistent fluid behind the eardrum should be treated by myringotomy, followed by the aspiration of exudate, with or without the insertion of ventilation tubes (grommets). When adequate drainage has been established, topical clearing agents to the tube or middle ear may be necessary. Seventy percent alcohol, one or two drops at a time, can be used to hold down the crusting. Glycerite of peroxide may be used also. These substances may burn slightly, and if the burning persists, they should be terminated. Antibacterial–corticosteroid solutions are often helpful in holding down the crusting and recurrent exudate. Topical infection can also be contained with these agents. There is no good case for use of systemic antibacterial agents.

Although they have not been proved to be of benefit, eustachian tube decongestants are often used in addition to the elimination of fluid from the middle ear. Persistent edema and obstruction of the eustachian tube with failure of aeration of the middle ear are the underlying causes of most serous otitis. Drugs used in decongestion (alone or with an antihistamine) are oral pseudoephedrine or phenylpropanolamine and oral plus intranasal phenylephrine. Alternate use of different classes of antihistamines may provide an improved clinical effect, as some patients respond much better, with fewer side effects, to one class of agent than to another. Azatadine, a recently introduced antihistamine, appears to have few side effects when used for these problems. Meclastine and mebhydroline are also effective antihistamines with a low incidence of sedative side effects. Corticosteroids, given either intramuscularly or orally for a few days, are also helpful for their antiinflammatory action.

Allergy of the nose or respiratory tract is often associated with serous otitis media, and suitable antiallergy treatment (e.g., mold-free diet, avoidance of dust and animals, hyposensitization to airborne allergens), including antihistamines or intranasal beclomethasone dipropionate (Beconase or Vancenase) or sodium cromoglycate, and treatment of obvious cases of allergic rhinitis may be required as indicated by appropriate tests.

Mastoiditis. In acute mastoiditis, unlike in acute furunculosis, there is definite progression from upper respiratory infection to acute otitis media to acute mastoiditis, and the deafness that occurs with otitis media is frequently severe. Once the diagnosis of acute mastoiditis has been made, initial intravenous antibiotics followed by several weeks of maintenance oral antibacterial agents should be used. If no culture information is available, ampicillin (8 g daily) or amoxicillin (4 g daily) should be started. Appropriate surgical procedures should be applied. Certain cases of acute mastoiditis may respond without surgery if adequate middle ear drainage is established. Chronic mastoiditis in association with any persistent purulent ear exudate requires surgical management as outlined above under Purulent or Chronic Suppurative Otitis Media.

Recurrent acute or serous otitis media in children or adults may indicate the need for adenoidectomy or surgical management of persistent sinusitis.

Fluid must be removed from the ear by myringotomy. A ventilation tube is usually inserted at the same time and is left in place for several weeks. Recurrent or refractory cases may require wide-bore tube insertion for more permanent effects. Otolaryngologic management is needed in recurrent and chronic cases.

Intense allergic investigation must often be combined with antiinfectious and surgical management to effect a cure or meaningful control of recurrent otitis media. Prophylactic antibiotics may be needed during winter and spring months.

The patient must be advised to use the Toynbee maneuver (holding nose and swallowing) when respiratory infections, allergic flareups, or barotrauma occurs. The importance of correcting underlying or predisposing causes such as hypertrophied adenoids, deviated nasal septum, refractory sinus infection, and inhalant allergies must be emphasized to the patient. Prolonged use of nasal decongestant sprays must be avoided. Avoidance of water contamination is important in children or adults who have ventilation tubes in place. Recurrent fluid problems in chronic otitis media indicate that extremes of barometric pressure should be avoided. The patient should be warned against flying in unpressurized aircraft and against frequent ascent or descent even in pressurized craft or while scuba diving.

FOLLOW-UP

All patients with acute otitis media must be reevaluated in 4 to 7 days to note response to antibiotic and decongestant therapy. A hearing test should be done to determine that hearing is once again normal whenever symptoms clear, usually in 2 or 3 weeks. Impedance tympanometry should be repeated in 6 weeks in children, because fluid may persist in the ear with virtually no complaints from the child. All patients with ventilation tubes should be followed at 2- or 3-month intervals. The tube often extrudes spontaneously before the middle ear membranes and the eustachian tube have cleared adequately.

All patients with refractory or recurrent otitis media should be studied to identify underlying or predisposing causes. Prophylactic drugs such as sulfa and ampicillin may be needed to control any recurrence.

DISCUSSION
Prevalence

Otitis media is one of the most prevalent diseases affecting children and adults. Some reports indicate that more than 75% of consecutively examined children manifest otitis media by the age of 5.

Myringotomy and ventilation tube insertion for otitis media constitute probably the most common surgical procedure now performed on children. The Medical Research Council of the United Kingdom estimates the incidence of otitis media during the first year of life is 14%, and during the sixth year of life, 21%. In the United States, the cumulative incidence of otitis media in the first 6 years of life appears to be greater than 90%. About 50% of children experiencing an initial episode of otitis media during the first year of life experience six or more episodes in the subsequent 2 years. Some pediatricians record that two thirds of children in their practice has otitis media by their second birthday. Nearly 40% of cases of acute otitis media are bilateral disease. Approximately one of five patients who have otitis media require, at some time during their lifetime, a surgical procedure to interrupt the disease or manage its sequelae.

Acute otitis media of bacterial origin is usually due to *Hemophilus influenzae* in children under 5 years of age and to pneumococcus or beta-hemolytic streptococci in older children or adults. *Hemophilus influenzae* is also common in adults, particularly as an identifiable pathogen in recurrent cases. *Mycoplasma pneumoniae* is thought to be responsible for the special form known as bullous myringitis, but recovery of this pathogen and its identification are often difficult. Various vital pathogens, usually respiratory syncytial virus, have been identified by paired-serum studies or culture.

Related Basic Science

Serous otitis media and mucoid otitis media are nonsuppurative types of inflammatory ear disease. There is transudation of plasma from the blood vessels into the middle ear space in serous otitis media. Mucoid otitis media probably develops from active secretion of glands and cysts and secretory cells in the lining of the middle ear cleft. The underlying cause of all inflammatory ear disease is eustachian tube malfunction. Blood pigments or cholesterin granuloma may give the eardrum a dark blue or black color.

In chronic otitis media, purulent or watery discharge may develop with saprophytic bacterial and/or fungal infections. In experimental studies, tubal obstruction in guinea pigs gave a significant increase in the number of dark cells in the middle ear mucosa, and these cells are the protein- or serous-secreting cells.

Hypothyroidism may aggravate chronic serous otitis media with abnormalities in mucus secretion and ground substance. Many inflammatory and invasive mechanisms seem to be operative in serous otitis media. Type I and III immune mechanisms involving immunoglobulin E are operative. All classes of immunoglobulins, lipozyme and other lysosomal enzymes, and various other types of enzymes are found in the otitis media fluid. Mediators of cell-mediated immunity and complement may be found. Prostaglandins and other inflammatory agents such as slow-reacting substance are present in this highly active middle ear fluid.

Natural History and Its Modification with Treatment

Initial serious complications such as brain abscess and acute mastoiditis are now uncommon as the result of widespread antibiotic use; however, various complications of a more chronic nature are prevalent. The most common residue is retained fluid and associated conductive hearing loss, which develops in one third of patients. Other complications are drum perforation, cholesteatoma, ossicular fixation, cochleitis with sensorineural hearing loss, tinnitus, vertigo, persistent ear fullness, and persistent otorrhea.

Otitis media is very common and severe in the Eskimo and the Native American. The highest incidence occurs between 6 and 24 months of age. In adults who retain their tonsils and adenoids, otitis media becomes a problem with upper respiratory tract infection, allergy, and barotrauma. In most studies, a male predominance is noted, and whites show a higher incidence than blacks. Anatomic skull studies indicate that there are racial differences in length, width, and angle of the eustachian tube.

Otitis media is more purulent during seasonal outbreaks of viral infections in the winter and spring. Anatomic or genetic factors may predispose or protect patients from infections of the middle ear.

The middle ear cleft is normally sterile, but any disease state that interferes with the normal physiologic activity of the eustachian tube predisposes the middle ear cleft to impaired aeration and evacuation, manifest in an inflammatory process.

Prevention

Otitis media may be prevented by eradication of nasal, sinus, nasopharyngeal, and tonsillar infections. Conclusive evidence to support this contention is lacking, however. The value of removing hypertrophic adenoids to prevent otitis media has recently been confirmed. Considerable evidence does exist to support intense allergic management as a means of preventing otitis media.

Cost Containment

Any preventive methods that obviate the development of otitis media will produce a savings in the cost of treating chronic otitis media or its complications. Early use of antibiotics and judicious decisions to perform adenoidectomy will result in overall savings in medical costs as well as morbidity. The prolonged use of decongestants and antibiotics is controversial. Proper drainage of middle ear fluid by myringotomy and the insertion of ventilation tubes in recurrent cases will ultimately prove to be less costly to the family. An estimated $2 billion is spent annually on medical and surgical treatment of otitis media in the United States.

REFERENCES

Armstrong BW. A new treatment for chronic secretory otitis media. Arch Otolaryngol 1954;59:653.

Giebink GS, ed. Recent advances in otitis media treatment. Ann Otol Rhinol Laryngol 1994;103(suppl. 163):5.

Goycoolea MV, ed. Otitis media: 16 years of pathogenesis approach. Otolaryngol Clin North Am 1991;24:967.

Honjo J. Eustachian tube and middle ear diseases. New York: Springer-Verlag, 1988.

Jackson RT, Per-Lee JH, Burson J, Turner JS. Ear, nose, and throat disease. In: Speight TM, ed. Drug treatment. 3rd ed. Sydney, Australia: Adis Press, 1987:11.

Per-Lee JH. A wide flanged middle ear ventilation tube. Trans Am Acad Opthalmol Otolaryngol 1967;71:358.

Todd NW. Allergy as a cause of otitis media. Immunol Allergy Clin North Am 1987;7:371.

Transactions of the Fifth International Symposium on Recent Advances in Otitis Media. Ann Otol Rhinol Laryngol 1994;103 (suppl. 164):8.

CHAPTER 21-6

Ear Discharge, Drainage, and Eruption (Otorrhea)

John S. Turner, Jr., M.D.

DEFINITION

Secretion from the external canal and meatus is defined as otorrhea.

ETIOLOGY

The cause of drainage is almost always bacterial or fungal infection. Eczema may be related.

CRITERIA FOR DIAGNOSIS
Suggestive

This finding may occur with acute or chronic ear disease and may represent disease in the external ear, middle ear, or mastoid.

Definitive

The patient or the examiner may notice intermittent or constant discharge from the external auditory meatus. The otorrhea may be yellow, pinkish, clear, or bloody, and crusting of the material may be noted around or below the ear.

CLINICAL MANIFESTATIONS
Subjective

The patient complains of noticeable fluid accumulation at the meatus. Unilateral or bilateral complaints may occur simultaneously or consecutively. A dark color or foul odor may be noted by the patient. Nasal blowing may accentuate the fluid. Fullness and, occasionally, ear pain are present; the patient may also notice hearing loss and tinnitus as well as vertigo. Itching is probably the most common symptom and is usually the most recurrent and the most refractory to treatment.

Objective
Physical Examination

Clear fluid or fluid of various colors from red to brown to straw-colored to green may be noted in the ear canal. A murky or offensive foul odor occurs in certain disorders. Ulceration, blisters, nodules, crusts, excavations, granulations, or gross pus may be found. Pain on movement of the pinna or pressure on the tragus may be seen. Hearing impairment is evident in unilateral or bilateral cases. Chronic drainage may occur from recurrent external or middle ear infections in diabetic patients. Pain is present when the pinna is moved or when the tragus is pressed in external canal disease but not in mastoid disease.

Routine Laboratory Abnormalities

White blood count is often elevated and routine cultures may grow bacteria or yeast.

PLANS
Diagnostic
Differential Diagnosis

The differential diagnosis of otorrhea is outlined in Table 21–6–1.

Diagnostic Options

A careful history is needed to determine environmental or factitious causes and familial disorders. Questions about dermatitis in other areas of the body should be asked. Drug intake must be documented, and associated treatment with chemotherapy or radiation therapy must be noted. Excessive water exposure may be found. Studies for diabetes are needed in all chronic cases and in recurrent *Candida* infections. All granular tissue should be biopsied.

Recommended Approach

The ear must be cleaned meticulously with small suction tips or wire applicators to permit adequate inspection and evaluation of the eardrum and middle ear. Mastoid radiographs may be needed to rule out associated middle ear or mastoid disease. Impedance audiometry may help in this determination also.

TABLE 21–6–1. DIFFERENTIAL DIAGNOSIS OF EAR DISCHARGE, DRAINAGE, AND ERUPTION (OTORRHEA)

Most Common Causes
- Liquid low-viscosity cerumen
- Otitis externa (swimmer's ear)
- Eczematoid dermatitis

Other Common Causes
- Psoriasis
- Neurodermatitis
- Basal cell carcinoma
- Purulent otorrhea from middle ear disease
- Foreign body (children)
- Furunculosis of ear canal
- Previous mastoid or middle ear surgery
- *Candida* (yeast otitis externa)

Uncommon Causes
- Herpes zoster oticus
- Myringitis bullosa
- Malignant otitis externa (*Pseudomonas* infections in diabetes)
- Otomycosis (true fungus, not *Candida*)
- Radiation therapy to the cranial area
- Squamous cell carcinoma
- Old temporal bone trauma or surgery with cerebrospinal fluid otorrhea
- Impacted keratosis of ear canal

Rare Causes
- Benign and other malignant tumors of canal
- Middle ear tumors
- Perichondritis
- Tuberculosis or other granulomatous disease

Therapeutic
Therapeutic Options

Treatment is directed toward eliminating the underlying cause, if possible, and controlling the associated itching, swelling, pain, crusting, fullness, and hearing loss.

Recommended Approach

Much external ear disease can be managed by avoiding moisture to the ear and using alcohol (95%) or acetic acid (2%) drops in the ear after water contamination. The localized disorder and drainage are often corrected when proper management of a systemic problem such as diabetes, allergy, psoriasis, or anemia is accomplished. Once other disorders are eliminated, most localized ear canal inflammations can be controlled with a combination steroid and acetic acid solution. Marked painful edema may require the use of injectable cortisone.

The most common cause of otorrhea, swimmer's ear, can be prevented by advising the patient to keep the ear canals exceedingly dry. Patients with eczematoid dermatitis must not scratch the areas and should keep the skin soft with baby oil or glycerol.

FOLLOW-UP

The patient must be seen often enough to document the cause or underlying reason for the otorrhea.

DISCUSSION
Prevalence

Otitis externa, or so-called *swimmer's ear,* is one of the most common disorders that affect humans, especially in hot weather.

Related Basic Science

The reader is referred to the reference list for appropriate discussions of each underlying cause of otorrhea.

Natural History and Its Modification with Treatment

Ear drainage except for liquid cerumen is always pathologic. The ear canal should be dry and clean in its natural state. Persistent drainage from whatever cause leads to more difficult management problems, such as extreme swelling and narrowing of the canal. The *cause* must be determined and eliminated.

Prevention

The most effective means of preventing this disorder is to treat acute otitis media and otitis externa early before extensive inflammation and its associated otorrhea occur. The same otologic measures listed in Chapter 21–5 are also helpful here.

Cost Containment

The patient will be saved unnecessary expense if treatment is withheld until the etiology of the otorrhea is accurately determined. The indiscriminate prescribing of eardrops or antibiotics prior to careful cleaning and inspection of the canal is to be condemned. Systemic antibiotics are seldom needed in external ear disease, but they may be needed for associated middle ear or mastoid infection.

REFERENCES
Hawke M, Wong J, Krajden F. Clinial and microbiological features of otitis externa. J Otolaryngol 1984;13:189.

Jones EH. Diseases of the external ear. In: English GM, ed. Otolaryngology. Hagerstown, MD: Harper & Row, 1979:1.

Mugliston T, O'Donoghue G. Otomycosis: A continuing problem. J Laryngol Otol 1985;99:327.

Schloss MD. Otorrhea. In: Bluestone CD, Stool SE, eds. Pediatric otolaryngology. 2nd ed. Philadelphia: Saunders, 1990:198.

Turner JS, Staats E, Stone HH, et al. Use of gentamicin in preparing the chronically infected ear for tympanoplastic surgery. South Med J 1966;59:94.

Uri N, Kitzes R, Meyer W, Schuchman G. Necrotizing external otitis: The importance of prolonged drug therapy. J Laryngol Otol 1984;98:1083.

CHAPTER 21–7

Tinnitus

John S. Turner, Jr., M.D.

DEFINITION

Tinnitus can be defined as internal noise in the ears or the cranium.

ETIOLOGY

Tinnitus may be associated with otologic, vascular, neurologic, metabolic, or drug toxicity disorders, but most commonly is related to noise exposure.

CRITERIA FOR DIAGNOSIS

Suggestive

In virtually all cases of ear or head noise, the sensation is perceived only by the patient, and diagnosis is dependent on a subjective complaint. In less than 5% of patients can the noise be perceived by another person so that an objective diagnosis can be made.

Definitive

Tinnitus is either subjective (common) or objective (uncommon). External ear examination and neurologic and radiologic evaluations are usually normal in patients with tinnitus; however, the majority do manifest some degree of sensorineural hearing loss.

CLINICAL MANIFESTATIONS

Subjective

Most head or ear noise is insidious in onset, and the patient complains of a ringing, rushing, whistling, roaring, or cricket noise sound in the ear. Most tinnitus is constant, but occasionally it is intermittent or subsides in intensity. In a very small percentage of patients, the sound may be pulsatile in nature or throbbing in quality. Fullness may be present in the affected ear. Virtually all patients with hearing loss have tinnitus in one form or another. The noise may be minimally distracting or noticeable only at night in quiet surroundings, or it may reach aggravating levels of intensity, even leading to suicide in some tragic recorded cases.

Sudden, severe tinnitus may develop without an identifiable associated disorder.

Occasional popping sounds are associated with temporomandibular joint disorders.

Objective

Physical Examination

The sound perceived by the patient can sometimes be matched in pitch and intensity with a sound generator with frequencies from 250 to 12,000 Hz.

No findings are noted in routine ear, nose, and throat examinations that imply the cause of the tinnitus in most cases. Infectious fluid, impacted wax, foreign body, temporomandibular joint dysfunction, and other external or middle ear diseases are sometimes found that create transient tinnitus. In at least 90% of patients, however, no clinical findings can be identified in subjective tinnitus.

In the objective form of tinnitus, usually pulsatile in nature, the sound may be heard by the examiner. A stethoscope placed over the patient's ear, temporal area, or neck may be used to hear the pulsating sound. Inspection of the ear canal or surrounding area may reveal certain pulsating masses or tumors. Pulsations behind the eardrum may be detected through use of the impedance bridge. Certain clicking forms of tinnitus from spasm of the stapedius or tensor tympanic muscles may be detected with the bridge also.

Polytomes of the petrous apex, computed tomography scans, and arteriograms may reveal erosion from aneurysm, tumor, or anomalous vessels.

A stethoscope with duplicate earpieces may permit the examiner to hear an objective tinnitus. There is little correlation of bruits in the neck with tinnitus. Some very loud carotid bruits create little or no tinnitus, whereas pulsating tinnitus may be very loud with minimal carotid bruits.

The patient may have abnormal physical findings such as arthritis, hypertension, cardiac disorders, and traumatic distortion that may be under treatment with various drugs that cause tinnitus.

Palpation of the temporomandibular joint may reveal a tenderness or crepitance. Recent dental or orthodontic work may be evident.

Hearing loss by tuning fork or audiometric testing is found in a large number of patients.

Routine Laboratory Abnormalities

Blood analysis may reveal elevated triglyceride or uric acid levels, which may aggravate the tinnitus.

PLANS

Diagnostic

Differential Diagnosis and Diagnostic Options

The etiology must be identified. The history is exceedingly important because certain reversible problems such as recurrent exposure to loud noise, drugs producing tinnitus (e.g., aspirin and quinidine), barotrauma from scuba diving, renal disease with ototoxic drug exposure, and lymphoma treatment involving ototoxic drugs may be discovered.

Diagnostic Options and Recommended Approach

The examiner must quickly run through a list of various groupings of disorders. These include otologic, dental and orthodontic, traumatic, metabolic, neurologic, pharmacologic, and psychiatric:

- Otologic: ear infections, fluid, trauma, tumors or previous surgery, impacted cerumen, idiopathic ear disorders such as otosclerosis and Ménière's disease, eustachian tube malfunction (often allergic or related to birth control pills).
- Dental and orthodontic: history of braces, root canal therapy, recurrent dental work requiring holding the mouth open for 30 to 60 minutes, poor-fitting dentures.
- Traumatic: jaw, head, and neck injury, barotrauma, weight lifting.
- Metabolic: lipoprotein or blood pressure disorders.
- Neurologic: acoustic neuroma, cerebellopontine angle tumor, basilar aneurysm, after meningitis, multiple sclerosis.
- Pharmacologic: salicylates, aminoglycoside antibiotics, furosemide and ethacrynic acid, quinine and derivatives, antiarthritic drugs, methotrexate, or other chemotherapeutic drugs.
- Psychiatric: schizophrenic patients often complain of sounds intracranially, poorly localized and varying in quality and intensity. The other associated disorders listed above are missing. Hearing is normal and often supernormal with hyperacusis. Neurotic patients have marked accentuation of an underlying mild tinnitus during times of anxiety or depression.

In identifying causes amenable to treatment, most tinnitus ends up being idiopathic (85%). Perhaps 5% is objective and the other 10% demonstrates one of the possible causes listed above. Effective treatment may be possible against objective types such as glomus jugulare tumors, anomalous middle ear vessels, and aneurysms or vascular anomalies in and around the temporal bone. Otologic consultation with complete audiometry is needed in all patients with chronic tinnitus (6 months' duration or longer). In tinnitus of shorter duration and sudden onset, some obvious related disorder such as viral infection or noise exposure can usually be ascertained.

Virtually all cases of sudden tinnitus are associated with other symptoms such as hearing loss, pain, headache, fullness in the ear, vertigo, nasal congestion, otorrhea, nystagmus, and hyperacusis. The reader is referred to chapters dealing with the management of these related symptoms. Tinnitus is a solitary symptom.

Therapeutic

Therapeutic Options

Vascular surgery, neurootologic surgery, or neurosurgery is usually needed to eliminate the causes of tinnitus that can be heard by another person. Proper diagnosing with audiometry, arteriography, and computed tomography must guide the physician to proper management.

A cause such as drug therapy or wax may be identified in 10% of patients and the tinnitus eliminated; however, most cases are idiopathic and not amenable to any medical or surgical management. Vasodilators have been tried for 50 years without success. Tranquilizers suppress the patient's awareness but are to be condemned in a chronic, persistent disorder such as tinnitus because they are habit forming.

Recommended Approach

A voluntary health organization, the American Tinnitus Association, has been instrumental in setting up tinnitus clinics around the country in the past 15 years. These clinics categorize the tinnitus and provide assistance to extremely disturbed and distressed patients through biofeedback conditioning techniques and/or masking instruments that tend to cancel out the internal sound by generating an external sound. In patients with associated hearing loss, the masker may be combined with a hearing aid to boost hearing and mask the tinnitus simultaneously. A hearing aid alone is helpful for tinnitus in some patients with symptomatic hearing loss.

At present the three measures described above are the only techniques that offer any hope to the extremely distressed patient with idiopathic tinnitus. The reader should contact a local otolaryngologist for the location of the nearest American Tinnitus Association clinic.

Some patients find that the hum of an electric clock, low radio noise, or a noise generator that reproduces ocean sounds is helpful in going to sleep.

Reports of transient improvement with iodine dyes used in radiology and certain other drugs such as local anesthetics have been published. Also, electrical stimulation of the ear has been recently tried. These are short-term, uncontrolled reports dealing with a subjective symptom and are very hard to evaluate on an objective therapeutic basis. Some deaf patients who have had a cochlear implant notice decreased tinnitus.

The general public must be constantly reminded that no consistent medical or surgical treatment is known for tinnitus. Educational efforts need to be directed to the measures listed under Prevention.

FOLLOW-UP

Once a thorough otologic examination has been performed and specific causes eliminated, usually no follow-up of idiopathic tinnitus is necessary. Unilateral tinnitus with sensorineural hearing loss, however, must sometimes be followed for several months before all potential causes can be elucidated.

DISCUSSION

Prevalence and Incidence

A comprehensive study of patients with tinnitus was carried out by the Kresge Hearing Research Laboratory and the Tinnitus Clinic of the University of Oregon Health Services Center (Vernon, 1978). The age distribution was 58% aged 45 to 65, 18% aged 65 to 80, and 11% aged 20 to 35. The oldest patient was 85; the youngest, 14. The very young seemed to have congenital problems. The older patients had mostly noise-induced tinnitus. The sex ratio was 65% male to 35% female. Most patients in the study had experienced the tinnitus for 5 or more years. In 37%, the tinnitus was unilateral, but the majority (58%) had it bilaterally.

Related Basic Science

Some authorities believe that tinnitus represents the loss of a damper mechanism all human beings possess normally. This mechanism may be operative through the bundle of Rasmussen, which is a set of efferent fibers running from the reticular formation in the brainstem to final endings on the hair cells of the cochlea. Degeneration of this bundle can be accomplished surgically in experimental animals. Perhaps certain disease states create a similar degeneration in patients. Just as parkinsonism represents a loss of control by the basal ganglia, perhaps tinnitus represents loss of eighth nerve suppression by some areas of the brainstem or midbrain.

Patients do not die of tinnitus, and very little clinicopathologic information exists. The ubiquitous nature of the disorder indicates a vital need for long-term prospective studies for both premortem and postmortem documentation of pathologic changes.

Natural History and Its Modification with Treatment

Normally the two ears have tinnitus of the same pitch, but often the loudness is unequal. It is rare to find the pitch in one ear differing from that in the other. The loudness may vary between ears. Only 5% of patients localize the tinnitus within the head. The localization in the head may be due to equal presentations from each ear, and it may also be due to head injury.

Severity of the tinnitus does not correlate with the loudness as reported by the patient. Most patients describe the loudness of their tinnitus as 5 to 10 dB. This is very low, considering that normal conversation is at 55 to 60 dB. Severity seems related to some factor other than loudness.

Some patients have fluctuating tinnitus that may actually disappear at times. This cannot be correlated to any set pattern. In 68% of the University of Oregon patients, the tinnitus was constant; in 32%, fluctuating (Vernon, 1978).

The pitch of the tinnitus seems to fit two broad categories: tonal tinnitus and noise tinnitus. The pitch of the tonal type can usually be categorized, but that of the noise type cannot. Fifty-nine percent of patients had tonal type and 25% had the noise type. Sixteen percent seemed to be a combination. The patients were classified as 63% between 2000 and 7000 Hz. Only 21% had low-tone tinnitus below 200 Hz and 16% above 7000 Hz. This tinnitus is high-pitched.

In most individual cases it is impossible to determine the cause of tinnitus. Head injury was identified in 35% of the University of Oregon patients. The tinnitus of head injury seems to fluctuate widely.

Almost one half (48%) of patients in the study mentioned above had suffered noise-induced hearing loss. Noise exposure is known to make tinnitus worse. The pitch of the tinnitus from noise is not specific.

Patients who have tinnitus and normal hearing are seldom seen (8–10%). A large percentage of patients in this study can be categorized as having hearing loss (≥ 25 dB).

Hearing aids are often helpful for the tinnitus as well as the hearing loss.

Only 50% of patients have trouble sleeping because of the presence of tinnitus.

In patients who have tried tinnitus maskers, a period of residual inhibition (absence of sound) may occur that allows them freedom from the tinnitus for a period.

All the preceding comments refer to patients with idiopathic, subjective tinnitus. The natural history of objective tinnitus follows the course of the tumor, aneurysm, or vascular abnormality that causes the noise.

Prevention

Avoidance of loud noise, ototoxic drugs, and head injury is the best way to prevent tinnitus. In patients with hyperlipidemia, a diet low in fat will prevent tinnitus. Prompt treatment of syphilis and ear infections will also prevent much tinnitus.

Cost Containment

Tremendous amounts of money are wasted on vasodilators and other drugs in hopes of helping these patients. Drug therapy should be discouraged until definite proof is forthcoming. As most of these patients have associated hearing loss, basic otolaryngology and audiometric studies should be obtained prior to expensive computed tomography, arteriograms, skull films, hearing aid purchases, or psychiatric or neurologic consultations.

REFERENCES

Dobie RA, Sakai CS, Sullivan MD, et al. Antidepressant treatment of tinnitus patients: Report of a randomized clinical trial and clinical prediction of benefit. Am J Otol 1993;14:18.

House JW. Therapies for tinnitus. Am J Otol 1989;10:163.
McKerrow WS, Schreiner CE, Snyder RL, et al. Tinnitus suppression by cochlear implants. Ann Otol Rhinol Laryngol 1991;100:552.
Neher A. Tinnitus: The hidden epidemic: A patient's perspective. Ann Otol Rhinol Laryngol 1991;100:327.
Stouffer JL, Tyler RS, Kileny PR, Dolzell LE. Tinnitus is a function of duration and etiology: Counseling implications. Am J Otolaryngol 1991;12:188.
Turner JS. Treatment of hearing loss, ear pain and tinnitus in older patients. Geriatrics 1982;37:107.
Vernon JA. Tinnitus. In: ATA Newsletter. Portland, OR: American Tinnitus Association, 1978:3.

CHAPTER 21–8

Dizziness or Disequilibrium

John S. Turner, Jr., M.D.

DEFINITION

A sensation of imbalance, swaying, spinning, or lightheadedness may be present in patients complaining of dizziness.

ETIOLOGY

Dizziness may be related to otologic, vascular, neurologic, or general metabolic disorders.

CRITERIA FOR DIAGNOSIS

Suggestive

Dizziness, vertigo, and disequilibrium are symptoms, not diagnoses.

Definitive

The diagnosis may be revealed by the investigation of otologic causes of tinnitus, ear fullness, or hearing loss when they coexist with the vertigo. If none of these complaints is mentioned by the patient, the whole body becomes a field of investigation.

A carefully taken history is the most important part of the workup of the dizzy patient.

CLINICAL MANIFESTATIONS

Subjective

Some authorities state that at least two thirds of patients who insist that they are dizzy do not feel that they are spinning or wheeling. There may be a rotational sensation, a syncopal sensation, disequilibrium, or ill-defined lightheadedness. These are defined as follows:

- Rotational sensation: The patient has the illusion that he or she or the environment is rotating.
- Syncopal sensation: The patient feels that she or he is about to faint.
- Disequilibrium: The patient experiences loss of balance, but notes no unusual head sensations.
- Lightheadedness: This is vague and initially indescribable in other terms by the patient. There seem to be no words or synonyms to parallel lightheadedness.

Associated complaints may be voluntarily offered by the patient. These consist of nausea, a generalized headache, visual blurring, diplopia or blackness, tinnitus, hearing loss, ear fullness, jaw popping or cracking, pain in the ear, and nasal congestion. Periods of unconsciousness or loss of memory may be mentioned.

Objective

Physical Examination

Blebs, blisters, or crusting may be noted in and around the external ear, suggesting inflammatory otologic disorders. Evidence of middle ear or mastoid disease may be present, such as drum perforation, purulent drainage, or vertigo when the pneumatic otoscope is compressed.

Nystagmus of various types may be evident spontaneously or on positional testing. Caloric testing with ice water or electronystagmography may reveal an asymmetry of labyrinthine responses or record nystagmus not visible to the naked eye.

Cranial nerve testing may indicate single or combined nerve disorders. Tests of cerebellar function may confirm ataxia or disequilibrium. Electroencephalography may indicate epilepsy. Blood pressure abnormalities, either high, low, or asymmetric, may be noted. Skin examination may reveal neurofibromas, café-au-lait spots, or hemangiomas associated with central disorders. External manifestations of syphilis may be present. Audiometric screening tests such as pure tone, speech discrimination, and performance index for phonetically balanced words or stapedial reflex are associated and often point to cochlear or retrocochlear disease. Various routine and neuroradiologic procedures may show positive findings. Lumbar puncture may indicate central nervous system disease of various types.

Routine Laboratory Abnormalities

Blood studies for hematologic, metabolic, syphilitic, neoplastic, or infectious disorders may be positive.

PLANS

Diagnostic

Differential Diagnosis

A careful history is the most important part of a medical examination for vertigo, essentially to establish whether it is acute, chronic, or recurrent. If the patient spontaneously volunteers ear complaints, such as fullness, tinnitus, and hearing loss, the cause is probably otologic and deserves immediate referral to an otologist. If no otologic complaints are volunteered, the whole body becomes a source of investigation. All nonvital drugs should be withheld during the evaluation of dizziness. A complete physical examination and blood profile should be carried out. Chest roentgenograms should be obtained.

Diagnostic Options

Accurate diagnosis and proper management are possible only with prolonged follow-up. Unnecessary expense, inconvenience, and discomfort for the patient can be avoided by a screening audiogram to identify unilateral hearing loss. All unilateral hearing loss should be investigated thoroughly to make an early diagnosis of serious retrocochlear disease.

Recommended Approach

Attacks of vertigo may be acute, chronic (unremitting), or recurrent (episodic) (Figure 21–8–1).

Acute Vertigo. Acute vertigo is a sudden attack of vertigo in a patient under 40 years of age and is usually due to a nonspecific labyrinthitis,

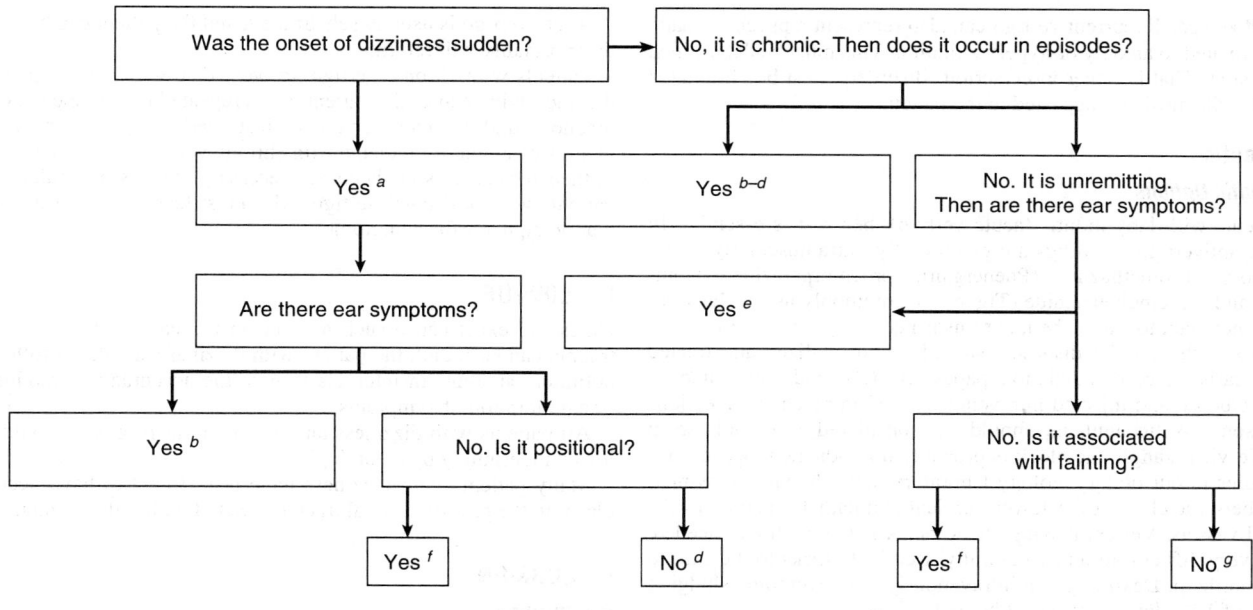

Possible Causes

a. Exertional, labyrinthitis, vascular disorder of inner ear
b. Infectious, Meniere's disease
c. Benign positional vertigo, cervical spine osteophytes
d. Drugs, hyperventilation, cervical trauma, menopause, migraine, hyperlipidemia
e. Acoustic neurinoma or other cerebellopontine angle tumor
f. Basilar artery insufficiency, cardiac disease, carotid arteriosclerosis or carotid sinus sensitivity
g. Psychoneurosis, hypertension, anemia, diabetes, thyrotoxicosis, blood dyscrasia, hyperlipidema

Figure 21–8–1. Algorithm for the recognition of the cause of vertigo. (Source: From Turner JS Jr. A practical approach to the patient with vertigo: An outline of diagnosis and management for the nonspecialist. South Med J 1975;68:241. Reproduced with permission from the Southern Medical Journal and the author.)

possibly of viral origin. Generally, the attack is self-limited. If no neurologic or metabolic defect can be identified, bed rest is effective as the principal treatment in most cases. The same symptoms in a patient over 40 years of age probably represent a vascular disorder involving the vertebral, basilar, or internal acoustic arteries. In these cases, appropriate diagnostic procedures for vascular disease usually uncover the cause.

Sudden symptoms of vertigo may occur after flying or after a prolonged drive in the mountains. If the eustachian tube becomes obstructed, vacuum effects may disturb the middle ear apparatus and perhaps cause accumulation of fluid. Sudden symptoms may also occur within 24 hours of alcohol intake, apparently due to a reactive vasoconstriction. Or, vertigo may be caused by sudden rupture of the round window of the cochlea. When this happens, intense physical exertion, such as calisthenics or scuba diving, has usually preceded the attack.

The patient with one attack should be rechecked in 2 or 3 months to see whether there have been repeated episodes. A patient will sometimes seek medical help with the first attack of menopausal vertigo, Ménière's disease, or migraine with vertigo, but a visit at the time of initial attack is unusual. Seldom can a diagnosis be made on one visit.

Chronic Vertigo. Chronic vertigo or chronic, unremitting vertigo occurs almost daily and is usually indicative of serious disease. Cerebellar angle or acoustic neuroma tumors, for example, present in this way. Complete medical, neurologic, and otoneurologic studies should be done in such cases. A neurosurgical consultation may also be necessary. As part of their examination, all these patients should have a complete blood count, urinalysis, chest roentgenogram, and general physical examination for adenopathy or abdominal or pelvic masses. Chronic vertigo may herald severe anemia, leukemia, diabetes, thyrotoxicosis, hypertension, or deficiency states.

Vertebrobasilar insufficiency is associated with persistent vertigo. The more severe exacerbations are accompanied by headache, obscuring of vision, and actual syncope. Syncope never occurs from labyrinthine disease alone. Uncommonly, labyrinthine disease may pre-

cipitate syncope in susceptible people. Four-vessel arteriography is usually needed for exact diagnosis. The patient seldom complains of ear symptoms, except perhaps tinnitus. Vascular surgical consultation should be obtained in these patients, as medical therapy is usually without effect. In some patients, however, generalized arteriosclerosis may preclude specific vessel surgery. Most patients with vertigo have recurrent episodes. Unfortunately, these patients are the most difficult to categorize and diagnose. There is no one specific test for vertigo; therein lies the problem.

A study done by the Northwestern University Dizziness Clinic (Drachman, 1972) showed that 62% of patients with chronic or recurring vertigo had nonotologic diagnoses. Otologic surgery was indicated in none of the patients, and only 4% had Ménière's disease.

If the patient spontaneously relates associated ear symptoms (without specific questioning), such as fullness in one ear, tinnitus, and hearing loss, the cause is probably otologic and the patient should be referred to an otolaryngologist for more exact diagnosis and treatment. If there are obvious ear findings, such as purulent otorrhea or tumor, the patient will undoubtedly need this specialty care also. If the patient offers no spontaneous ear complaint, the whole body becomes a source of investigation. Careful questioning about drug intake is vital. Many patients with recurrent vertigo are found to be taking antihypertensive agents, hormones, sedative drugs, tranquilizers, diuretics, or antihistamines, or they may be using nasal sprays.

Patients with cervical injury may experience either recurrent or chronic vertigo. Neck pain is almost always associated with the disequilibrium. In patients with cervical injury, the proprioceptive impulses may be disturbed, as may the nuclei controlling vestibulospinal tracts, causing loss of balance. Electronystagmography may show spontaneous resting nystagmus with or without the eyes closed. Such a finding may help identify valid organic complaints. The hearing examination is almost always normal. Patients with neck, occipital, or shoulder pain along with vertigo deserve neurosurgical and/or orthopaedic evaluation and treatment. Cases fitting this description do not have an otologic origin.

Recurrent Vertigo. Recurrent vertigo can also represent a psychosomatic disorder related to anxiety or hyperventilation. This must be determined by exclusion. That is, other more serious disorders must be eliminated before this diagnosis is suggested to the patient.

Therapeutic

Therapeutic Options

For patients with labyrinthitis (acute vertigo), bed rest is essential. In addition, antivertiginous drugs are given orally, intramuscularly, or by suppository. Promethazine (Phenergan), prochlorperazine (Compazine), and trimethobenzamide (Tigan) are commonly used. Many patients do not want to stay in bed, but this is necessary for 2 or 3 days.

Patients with vascular disorders should be hospitalized and treated with 5% carbon dioxide inhalation, papaverine (Pavabid), histamine diluted in glucose and injected intravenously, and intravenous injections of cortisone. Anticoagulants should be considered if emboli seem likely. Cervical ganglionic block is probably not indicated, because recent studies in our otolaryngology laboratory have shown that sympathetic fibers travel from the lower cervical sympathetic nerves to the vertebral vessels. Vertebral sympathetic block is the treatment needed, but it is very difficult to do successfully. Cervical blocks to the carotid area do not help. Dextran given intravenously may overcome sludging (500 mL of 10% dextran every 12 hours for 3 days).

If the patient reports a sudden pop or bang in the ear with hearing loss and vertigo, round window rupture may have occurred. The patient should be referred to an otologist immediately for surgical exploration and possible graft to a round window leak. Patients with benign positional vertigo may benefit from positioning exercises that influence abnormal particles in the semicircular canals.

Recommended Approach

Patients with chronic, unremitting vertigo should have a general physical examination and appropriate blood tests. Meclizine (Antivert) or cyclizine (Marzine) may be prescribed for symptomatic relief (three times daily). Astemizole has been used successfully in the control of chronic vertigo, especially in patients with spontaneous or positional nystagmus. Astemizole should be given once daily in a dose of 10 mg orally on an empty stomach. This dose should be continued for 2 months. If improvement occurs, treatment should be continued indefinitely. If no improvement occurs, it should be stopped; however, all drugs should be stopped while the disorder is being studied. When 5-hour glucose tolerance tests indicate reactive hypoglycemia or hyperglycemia, a low-carbohydrate diet should be prescribed. Recent vertigo associated with fluid or infection in the ear should be treated by appropriate drainage.

In cases of menopausal dizziness, nonspecific drugs for vertigo are not indicated. Appropriate use of hormones and diuretics should be determined in collaboration with the patient's gynecologist.

The medical treatment of Ménière's disease is empiric. Surgical intervention is used for some cases refractory to medical management. Drug therapy usually involves a low-salt diet and the administration of vasodilators such as nicotinic acid, histamine, papaverine, and cyclandelate. Some otologists use diuretics. Patients with Ménière's disease may have moderately severe allergies to inhalants or foods; these allergies need investigation and perhaps treatment with antihistamines and/or desensitization. Thyroid deficiency, but not myxedema, is often associated. There is probably more than one cause or precipitating event for Ménière's disease, although the pathologic manifestation (endolymphatic hydrops) is consistent in all patients. The physician should insist that the patient stop using cigarettes, coffee, and stimulants.

Patients with cervical injury probably need prolonged immobilization of the neck and physiotherapy with massage and heat. Maintenance of the patient's usual preinjury activity should always be encouraged, because prolonged inactivity in traction or bed rest may prolong the vertigo. Muscle-relaxing drugs such as carisoprodol (Soma) and methocarbamol (Robaxin) seem to help.

Psychosomatic disorders must be managed according to each physician's individual training and capability. Tranquilizers may be used with discrimination when attempts to reach the underlying cause have failed. Many hospitals now have Balance Rehabilitation Units to train patients in proper ambulation and mobilization techniques.

Acute vertigo is usually self-limited, and the patient can be reassured that normality will return.

Patients with chronic vertigo are very distressed, and depending on the underlying cause, the patient needs repeated reassurance that proper diagnosis and treatment have been instituted. Very little specific treatment is available for patients with chronic vertigo, and in many, change in their former lifestyle becomes necessary. This is particularly true in patients with positional vertigo, who must learn to avoid the position that precipitates the symptoms.

FOLLOW-UP

Unless an exact cause such as fluid in the ear or old temporal bone trauma can be found, the patient with dizziness should be followed indefinitely at 6-month intervals to note the accentuation, modification, or amelioration of symptoms.

All patients with dizziness and unilateral hearing loss should be followed indefinitely by an otologist.

Many patients with dizziness have been found to have occult neoplasm in the gastrointestinal tract associated with mild anemia.

DISCUSSION
Prevalence

The National Institute of Deafness and Communication Disorders has issued recent statements that dizziness is the most common symptom that leads elderly patients to seek medical care. As our population ages, this problem will become more prevalent.

Related Basic Science

Dizziness occurs when a person loses the sensory, integrative, or motor responses that maintain normal space orientation. Normally, the human being must rely on five sensory modalities to maintain spacial orientation: vision, vestibular function, proprioception, touch and pressure, and hearing. Inputs from these sensory channels allow the person's central nervous system to provide a coherent image of position in space. This includes the relationship to vertical and horizontal coordinates, the attitudes of the limbs, the relationship to surrounding objects, and the speed and direction in which the patient is moving.

Perception of our environment and our relationship to it, as determined by the sensory input systems, is only the first step in achieving spatial orientation. We must also be able to interpret this information and integrate it during the continuing changes of movement. To maintain balance, we must also have accurate control of our motor responses. Disorder of sensory, integrative, or motor systems or all three may produce dizziness or disequilibrium. Many older persons have multisensory dizziness as the reason for their symptoms, and this must be kept in mind first when managing the geriatric patient.

Many factors control the normal function of the eyes and of the labyrinth. The blood supply must be normal, and any disorders that alter oxygen uptake such as sludging of red cells and vascular spasm may produce dizziness from ocular or labyrinthine ischemia. A common denominator for all dizziness is probably a relative ischemia of brainstem nuclei, labyrinth, or cortical integrative centers. This may occur from trauma, tumor, infection, or metabolic factors that alter blood flow.

Complex vestibular, ocular, and neuroarterial relationships govern the proper functioning of the body in space. The reader is referred to the list of references for a more detailed discussion of the otologic and neuroarterial mechanisms involved in dizziness of otologic or neurologic cause.

Natural History and Its Modification with Treatment

The natural history of dizziness depends on the underlying cause that produces this symptom in each patient.

If cardiovascular disease is present, control of hypertension, revascularization of carotid or vertebral vessels, and regulation of heartbeat may prevent further episodes of dizziness.

Distinct otologic disorders such as Ménière's disease produce dizziness periodically as a natural part of the disorder. Ultimate control may require dietary, pharmacologic, or operative management. The reader is directed to Chapter 21–9. Accurate diagnosis of ear disorders such as cholesteatoma or otitis media guides the physician to proper specific treatment that, in turn, eliminates the dizziness.

Some refractory disorders such as benign positional vertigo and vestibular neuritis can continue indefinitely. One study using pharmacologic treatment with astemizole has been shown to alter the natural history of these disorders in about 70% of cases (Jackson and Turner, 1987).

Dizziness associated with acoustic neuroma or other brain tumors becomes incapacitating until definitive surgery eliminates the tumor.

Dizziness associated with a metabolic disorder such as hyperlipidemia or hypoglycemia progresses until proper dietary or drug management is instituted.

Cervical spine disorders associated with dizziness produce marked symptoms on head and neck motion indefinitely. Exercise habituation in certain positions and cervical spine fusion may be required to alter this natural aggravation with neck motion.

Prevention

Preventive methods may be used depending on the specific cause of the dizziness. Positional vertigo may be averted by avoiding the positions that trigger the symptoms. Hyperglycemia, hypoglycemia, and hyperlipidemia may be controlled and the associated dizziness prevented by proper diet and nutrition. Control of metabolic disorders, elimination of certain drugs or dosage changes, and proper management of cardiovascular disease, especially hypertension, prevent dizzy symptoms. Low-dose estrogen use may be of help in preventing menopausal symptoms,

and psychotherapy may prevent the dizziness of hyperventilation or chronic neurosis.

Cost Containment

Much time and money are wasted in the evaluation of the dizzy patient. The physician must take a careful detailed history before embarking on expensive, time-consuming diagnostic tests. In chronic dizziness, the most useful procedure following an accurate history is a properly performed audiogram, which will screen virtually all patients who have an otologic cause for their symptoms. A routine physical examination with basic blood tests and a chest x-ray should be carried out in all patients with chronic dizziness before more elaborate highly specialized neurologic studies are ordered.

REFERENCES

Brookler KW, Rubin W. The dizzy patient: Etiologic treatment. Otolaryngol Head Neck Surg 1990;403:677.
Drachman DA. An approach to the dizzy patient. Neurology 1972;22:323.
Jackson RT, Todd NW, Turner JS. Ear, nose and throat disease. In: Speight TM, ed. Avery's drug treatment. Sydney, Australia: Adis Press, 1987:11.
Jackson RT, Turner JS. Astemizole: Its use in the treatment of patients with chronic vertigo. Arch Otolaryngol Head Neck Surg 1987;113:536.
Jenkins HA. Disequilibrium of aging. Otolaryngol Head Neck Surg 1989;100:272.
Spencer JT. Hyperlipoproteinemia, hyperinsulinism and Ménière's disease. South Med J 1981;74:1194.
Turner JS Jr. A practical approach to the patient with vertigo: An outline of diagnosis and management for the nonspecialist. South Med J 1975;68(2):241.

CHAPTER 21–9

Ménière's Disease

John S. Turner, Jr., M.D.

DEFINITION

A patient with fluctuant hearing loss, fullness in the ears, tinnitus, and episodic vertigo most likely has Ménière's disease (endolymphatic hydrops).

ETIOLOGY

The cause of Ménière's disease in unknown.

CRITERIA FOR DIAGNOSIS
Suggestive

Patients who usually present initially with symptoms are under the age of 50 with normal physical examination otherwise (see Definition).

Definitive

A conclusive diagnosis can be made only after months of follow-up with accurate audiometric tests to carefully differentiate end-organ disease (hydrops) from retrocochlear eighth nerve or brainstem disorders. A careful history to document primary otologic symptoms such as tinnitus, fullness, and hearing loss is the most important part of the evaluation.

CLINICAL MANIFESTATIONS
Subjective

The patient may have the following complaints.

Vertigo. A sudden sense of disequilibrium or dizziness is usually reported as "everything seems to be going around" or "the whole room

seems to be spinning." It may appear without warning at any time and is not usually associated with change in position. The vertigo may impair sitting or walking. Any head motion, even when supine, may aggravate this sensation. Duration may be from 5 minutes to 72 hours. Cessation may be abrupt or gradual. The patient is usually confined to the supine position with the head position of greatest comfort.

Nausea. Nausea usually accompanies the vertigo because of vagal stimulation from the labyrinth. Any head movement may aggravate nausea; thus, the head is usually held rigidly to one side. Vomiting may be violent or prolonged for hours.

Ear Fullness. Ear fullness may precede other symptoms by several days or occur abruptly with tinnitus and hearing loss.

Tinnitus. Tinnitus is described as a sudden roar, whistling, ringing, cricket hum, or rushing sound deep within the ear that is unremitting, constant, and nonpulsatile. Pulsing or throbbing tinnitus does not occur with Ménière's disease and should make a vascular disorder suspect. The tinnitus may improve or disappear as the attack subsides; however, in more than 50% of patients the tinnitus continues after the first attack and may rival vertigo as the most severe symptom.

Loudness Sensitivity. Loudness sensitivity is known as *recruitment.* Soft sounds are not heard well; then suddenly the sound seems too loud and piercing or penetrating. A sudden response of additional hair cells in the inner ear is responsible.

Hearing Loss. Sudden profound sensorineural hearing loss may occur with the first attack. It may persist but usually fluctuates upward close to normal. Characteristically, low-tone loss develops, followed by high-tone loss as repeated attacks occur. The hearing may become useless for normal conversation as pure-tone and speech discrimination levels decline. Total deafness for all sounds is rare. Hearing may improve suddenly as nausea and vomiting occur; this is known as Lermoyez's syndrome, a variant of Ménière's disease.

Impaired Vision. The patient may describe blurred or "jerky" vision, created primarily by the nystagmus from labyrinthine stimulation and constant during the first few hours of the attack. The entire room may seem to be in rotation from the vertigo also.

Headache. About one of four patients experiences generalized vague headache even between attacks. It may be accentuated with attacks and persist to a lesser degree almost daily. The mechanism of this headache is unclear, but it may be related to vasoconstriction common to inner ear and other cerebral vessels. In some patients this is the most distressing part of the disease.

Objective

Physical Examination

The examiner may discover the following abnormalities.

Nystagmus. Nystagmus usually develops as vertigo and hearing loss occur. During an attack it may be precipitated by moving the patient's head. It is usually horizontal with a quick phase to the side opposite the affected ear, and it fatigues in 30 to 60 seconds. Head motion may again accentuate the nystagmus. Electronystagmography may be used to record the nystagmus, but this does not help diagnosis in the acute phase. Between attacks, caloric response to warm or cold water may be normal, suppressed, or hyperreactive, and this does not identify Ménière's disease per se. Decline in the caloric response to "no reaction" is highly suggestive of a retrocochlear lesion.

Vomiting. Vomiting is aggravated by head motions as described above. It may continue for hours if untreated and lead to dehydration. Severe vertigo, nausea, and vomiting may require hospitalization, but this is unusual.

Disequilibrium. Generalized disequilibrium or an inability to sit or stand may occur in acute episodes. Vague unsteadiness may persist between attacks, but broad-base gait, lateral pulsation, swaying motion, and falling do not.

Impaired Hearing. The hearing pattern is the most useful objective sign. Expert audiometry by a certified audiologist should be carried out on all patients with vertigo, tinnitus, fullness in the ear, or unilateral hearing loss. Recently introduced tests now offer a high degree of specificity in identifying patients with retrocochlear problems and thereby indicate a cochlear disorder such as Ménière's disease when they are negative. Evoked-response audiometry and performance index of phonetically balanced word tests are used in addition to routine pure-tone and speech audiometry. Impedance audiometry may suggest a cochlear disorder by indicating recruitment, but there is no specific audiometric test for Ménière's disease. A battery of tests must be performed and repeated at 4- to 12-month intervals as a means of reinforcing an end-organ diagnosis.

Routine Laboratory Abnormalities

These tests are usually normal.

PLANS

Diagnostic

Differential Diagnosis

The differential diagnosis of Ménière's disease is outlined in Table 21–9–1.

Diagnostic Options and Recommended Approach

Acoustic neuroma or cerebellar pontine angle tumor may simulate Ménière's disease. The conditions are compared in Table 21–9–2.

- Ischemic vertigo: bruit over carotids; obscurations of vision; syncopal attacks (Loss of consciousness never occurs with Ménière's or labyrinthine disorders.)

TABLE 21–9–1. DIFFERENTIAL DIAGNOSIS OF MENIERE'S DISEASE

Benign positional vertigo	Hallpike maneuvers show nystagmus (usually rotary) with one ear down
	Normal equal, symmetric hearing; one isolated attack or attacks precipitated by position change
Acute labyrinthitis	No hearing loss; unable to differentiate from Ménière's with one attack; follow-up necessary
Syphilitic cochleolabyrinthitis	Positive serology
Posttraumtic or post-infectious viral hydrops	Similar symptoms and signs, but history differentiates
Metabolic vertigo	Hyperlipidemia
Vascular vertigo	Normal hearing; migrainous symptoms evident
Menopausal vertigo	Woman aged 40 to 65; all studies normal; improvement with replacement estrogen in low doses

- Vertiginous epilepsy: rare; sense of vertigo or pulsion to the ground without hearing loss, tinnitus, or ear fullness

Therapeutic

Therapeutic Options

Proper management of Ménière's disease is highly controversial.

Recommended Approach

Medical treatment is usually tried first, but the many categories of medical management indicate the therapeutic dilemma. Sedatives, anticholinergic agents, vitamins, vasodilators, histamine desensitization, antihistamines, control of body fluid, allergy management, metabolic therapy, endocrine therapy, physical therapy, and various combinations of these are now currently used. Gentamicin perfusion of the middle ear has been used extensively in Europe for unilateral Ménière's disease. Injectable gentamicin and, if available, streptomycin are used by some otologists for bilateral disease. An ataxia or disequilibrium may be substituted for the acute vertigo attacks, however, with this type of treatment.

Surgical approaches are essentially just as controversial. Labyrinthotomy, eighth nerve section, alcohol injection into the labyrinth, labyrinthectomy, ablation of the vestibular labyrinth, sympathectomy and ganglionic block, and fistulization of the membranous labyrinth are

TABLE 21–9–2. ACOUSTIC NEUROMA COMPARED WITH MENIERE'S DISEASE

Test	Neuroma	Meniere's Disease
Audiometry		
Pure-tone tests	Abnormal; no fluctuation; mostly high-tone	Abnormal; fluctuation; usually low-tone
Speech threshold	Abnormal	Abnormal
Speech discrimination	Steady decline	Fluctuates
Sustained-increment sensitivity index	Low percent	Usually 100%
Stapedial reflex	Absent	Present
Stapedial reflex decay	Present	None
Performance index of phonetically balanced words	"Rollover" effect	No "rollover" effect
Evoked response	Wave V delay or abnormal waves	No delay
Caloric or electro-nystagmography	Progressive hypofunction to no response	Normal, hyperfunction, or hypofunction
Radiology		
Computed tomography scan with contrast	Positive if 2 cm	Normal
Magnetic resonance imaging with gadolinium	Positive, all sizes (rare exceptions)	Normal

now currently used. The choice of therapy depends on the training and inclination of the consulting otologist.

Patients with intractable vertigo are best served by some form of destructive labyrinthectomy if over 70 or eighth nerve section or perfusion labyrinthotomy if younger. Biofeedback or external noise maskers may help the tinnitus. Some otologists vigorously support drainage procedures on the endolymphatic sac, but the initial good results have not been supported by long-term follow-up reports.

Symptomatic treatment of the vertigo with meclizine (Antivert), cyclizine (Marzine), or prochlorperazine (Compazine) orally or by suppository may be used.

The patient with Ménière's disease must be offered regular support and reassurance with advice and reinforcement for whichever regimen the physician adopts. After proper diagnosis, the patient should be advised that no reliable cure for Ménière's disease is known, that remissions and exacerbations are the rule, and that surgical intervention may become necessary in refractory cases.

FOLLOW-UP

Regular hearing tests, usually at 4- to 6-month intervals, should be done to document fluctuant hearing losses. Progressive decline in speech discrimination, positive evoked-response audiometry, or loss of caloric response indicates the need for magnetic resonance imaging. Severe, unremitting vertigo may require surgical intervention. Follow-up may ascertain the presence of bilateral disease or lead to a clue as to a precipitating cause such as allergy. The patient should return at least at 6-month intervals indefinitely.

DISCUSSION

Prevalence

About 5% of chronic dizzy patients have Ménière's disease (Drachman, 1972).

Related Basic Science

The cause of Ménière's disease remains a mystery. The pathologic physiology involves an excess accumulation of endolymph in the scala media of the inner ear, creating an endolymphatic hydrops. Endolymph is produced by the stria vascularis of the inner ear and resorbed by the endolymphatic sac, which lies just between the posterior semicircular canal and the dura. Hydrops of the inner ear develops when this resorptive function becomes impaired.

A similar picture can be produced in experimental animals by blocking the vestibular aqueduct or ablating the endolymphatic sac. The hydrops produces distention and rupture of Reissner's membrane, saccule, utricle, and the ampullae of the semicircular canals. This distortion produces the clinical sensation of vertigo, fullness, and tinnitus. When rupture occurs, the admixture of potassium from the endolymph with sodium from the perilymph alters hair cell function, and hearing loss progresses. Healing of the rupture leads to recurrent hydrops, and clinical symptoms return. Pathologic studies of the hydropic inner ear show normal hair cell population and normal neural elements in the labyrinth in most cases. Ménière's disease thus represents disordered flow, distribution, and resorption of endolymphatic fluids, which correlate with clinical symptoms of vertigo, fullness, tinnitus, and fluctuant hearing loss.

Natural History and Its Modification with Treatment

The disease usually begins in white women between the ages of 20 and 45 years. Men are usually more severely affected. It is uncommon in blacks. Childhood Ménière's disease has been documented but is uncommon and probably represents anomalous inner ear development. It is not familial in most cases. Patients presenting with their first attack of vertigo after the age of 50 probably do not have Ménière's disease. The disease almost always starts in one ear but may become bilateral; thus, initial bilateral hearing loss with vertigo is probably not Ménière's disease. Cochlear or ventricular symptoms may occur separately for several years, but they usually appear together.

The usual progression is for tinnitus, fullness, vertigo, and hearing loss to begin suddenly, subside in 24 to 48 hours, and then recur at monthly, quarterly, or yearly intervals. Recurrences may be separated by intervals as long as 5 years; thus, evaluations of treatment regimens are extremely difficult. Attacks may be so severe that any head movement triggers violent vertigo, nausea, and vomiting. Motionless bed rest is usually necessary for several hours, and vision is blurred by the recurrent nystagmus. Vague unsteadiness may be present between attacks, but usually only the tinnitus persists. Hearing loss gradually declines, particularly for low tones, but total deafness is rare and arouses suspicion of other diagnoses. The intensity of the vertigo tends to diminish with time, but the hearing loss no longer fluctuates upward, and tinnitus and fullness persist as long-term distressing complaints. Ten percent of patients require ablative surgery for refractory, incapacitating vertigo, nausea, and vomiting. Recurrent attacks every few months can create emotional, social, economic, and recreational problems of great magnitude. The patient is usually very healthy otherwise and extremely compliant with all the physician's recommendations. Hypertension and Ménière's disease seem to be mutually exclusive. Most patients live normal life expectancies; 25% develop glucose intolerance suggestive of diabetes (insulin-dependent diabetes is rarely seen). Hypothyroidism has been reported in from 10 to 30%. Replacement thyroid hormone does not cure Ménière's disease, however, and is probably incidental.

Special forms of the disease are "drop-attack" Ménière's, in which the patient has abrupt falling attacks of fleeting duration (Tumarkin's catastrophe), and Lermoyez's syndrome, in which hearing improves rather than declines with acute attacks. Between 1951 and 1975, more than 834 papers were published on Ménière's disease (Schuknecht, 1978). This unusual activity indicates the magnitude of interest and concern for this distressing disease.

Prevention

No consistently valuable preventive measures are known. Most patients are advised to follow a low-salt diet (2000 mg approximately), as fluid imbalance is the basic pathophysiology.

Cost Containment

Probably more money is wasted in the evaluation of patients with vertigo than in any other disorder. Acute vertigo should be treated symptomatically. After a general physical examination, chest x-ray, complete blood count, screening metabolic analysis, and urinalysis, each patient with chronic vertigo should be sent for accurate audiometry. Unilateral hearing impairment points the way to further diagnosis, and normal hearing alerts the physician to follow the patient for several months and watch for additional signs. Screening audiometry is relatively inexpensive, and the patient should not be subjected to skull films, computed tomography, arteriograms, neurology consultation, electronystagmography, or evoked-response testing until this is done.

The patient is best served by careful follow-up twice a year with audiometric tests to document progression or change from cochlear to retrocochlear signs.

REFERENCES

Bretlau P, Thomsen J, Tos M, Johnson NJ. Placebo effect in surgery for Ménière's disease. Am J Otol 1989;10:259.

Dickins JRE, Graham SS. Ménière's disease 1983–1989. Am J Otolaryngol 1990;11:51.

Drachman DA. An approach to the dizzy patient. Neurology 1972;22:323.

Green JD, Blum DJ, Harner SG. Longitudinal follow-up of patients with Ménière's disease. Otol Head Neck Surg 1991;104:783.

Ménière P. Congestion celebrales apoplectiformes. Gaz Med Paris 1861;16:55.

McKee GJ, Kerr AG, Toner JG, Smyth GDL. Surgical control of vertigo in Ménière's disease. Clin Otol Laryngol 1991;16:216.

Schuknecht HF. A critical evaluation of treatments for Ménière's disease. Otol Rhinol Laryngol 1978;40:15.

Stahle J, Friberg U, Suedberg A. Long term progression of Ménière's disease. Am J Otol 1989;10:170.

Turner JS, Saunders AZ, Per-Lee JH. A ten-year profile of Ménière's disease. Laryngoscope 1973;83:1816.

CHAPTER 21–10

Acute Labyrinthine Vertigo

John S. Turner, Jr., M.D.

DEFINITION

Labyrinthine vertigo is an acute loss of balance accompanied by a sensation of motion, usually whirling.

ETIOLOGY

Most acute labyrinthine vertigo is probably viral in origin because other etiologic agents are not usually found.

CRITERIA FOR DIAGNOSIS

Suggestive

The patient most likely was quite normal until the sudden attack occurred. Occasionally, a mild upper respiratory tract infection precedes the onset by 7 to 10 days. Nausea and vomiting are usually present with severe aggravation of head movement.

Definitive

Diagnosis is confirmed if nystagmus that fatigues on testing is found and neurologic examination is otherwise normal.

CLINICAL MANIFESTATIONS

Subjective

The patient complains of a whirling sense of motion or acute sensation of swaying back and forth or from side to side. Almost any head motion brings on severe nausea with aggravation of the vertiginous symptom. Headache is often mentioned; it is usually generalized in nature. Vision is blurred from the effects of nystagmus. Symptoms related to an upper respiratory tract infection may have been present for a few days before the vertigo. Familial symptoms are usually absent.

Objective

Physical Examination

Vomiting may be violent and repetitive; however, projectile vomiting as in cerebellar disease does not occur. Position change often aggravates symptoms. Nystagmus is evident either spontaneously or on head motion in almost any direction. The nystagmus may initially be horizontal, vertical, or rotary; it then becomes horizontal. All types fatigue as they are watched. Residua of a respiratory infection such as nasal edema, rhinorrhea, and sore throat may be present, but usually the ear, nose, and throat examination is not remarkable. Associated neurologic or chest disease is not found. Other cranial nerves besides the eighth are normal.

Sensorineural hearing loss in one ear may be obvious. This may occur in idiopathic sudden hearing loss or in Ménière's disease. The occurrence of labyrinthine vertigo with bilateral hearing loss is very unusual and is found generally with syphilis, ototoxic drugs, or multiple sclerosis. Most active labyrinthine vertigo, particularly that occurring in epidemics, shows no hearing loss.

Spontaneous nystagmus is evident usually horizontally and is fatiguable.

Routine Laboratory Abnormalities

Routine laboratory test results are usually normal.

PLANS

Diagnostic

Differential Diagnosis

A careful history is needed to document that the patient is having a first acute attack and not an exacerbation of a recurrent disease such as Ménière's. Obvious causes such as trauma and drug intake must be excluded.

Diagnostic Options and Recommended Approach

Hearing tests should always be carried out, but they are usually normal. Complete head and neck evaluation and general neurologic examination show only normal findings. Computed tomography and spinal fluid studies are normal. Blood count is normal or consistent with viral disease.

Diagnosis is purely clinical and is based on the presence of acute vertigo and nystagmus occurring without associated disease.

Caloric testing cannot be carried out in any acute attack; after the vertigo subsides, the caloric responses are equal. Computed tomography and other radiologic studies are normal. No reliable reports of viral blood studies have been recorded, as the disease is usually brief and self-limited.

A similar disease, vestibular neuronitis, occurs with some similar findings. The onset is usually acute but resolves much more slowly, with the patient having persistent vertigo lasting up to several months. A persistent positional vertigo may be permanent or may improve after several months. Positional nystagmus may persist also. Hearing is normal, but the caloric examination is noted to be decreased or absent on one side. This finding of canal paresis persists in vestibular neuronitis but not in acute labyrinthine vertigo.

Therapeutic

Therapeutic Options

The therapy is only symptomatic and supportive. Promethazine (Phenergan), prochlorperazine (Compazine), or thiethylperazine (Torecan) suppositories can be used, or these drugs may be given intramuscularly. Small doses of scopolamine (Hyoscine, 0.6 mg) combined with meperidine (Demerol, 50 mg) and phenobarbital (60 mg) may allow the patient enough sedation to avoid intravenous fluids. In severe cases, hydration may need to be provided intravenously.

Prolonged nausea, vomiting, nystagmus, and vertigo in the absence of neurologic findings may require maintenance therapy with meclizine (Antivert), cyclizine (Marzine), or diphenidol (Vontrol). The need for prolonged therapy suggests the diagnosis of vestibular neuronitis.

Recommended Approach

Bed rest with limited head movement is the basis of treatment in acute labyrinthine vertigo.

The patient can be reassured that acute labyrinthine vertigo spontaneously resolves. If the patient is treated at home, the family should be instructed to call if vomiting persists or oral intake becomes extremely limited.

FOLLOW-UP

The patient can be safely dismissed from care after 1 week if no hearing or vertiginous complaints are present. If vertigo recurs, the patient should return immediately, as other otologic or neurologic disorders may be present.

DISCUSSION

Prevalence and Incidence

No definitive studies have been done to determine the prevalence and incidence of this condition.

Related Basic Science

The actual pathophysiology of acute labyrinthine vertigo is unknown, as patients do not die acutely from this problem. Degeneration of ganglion cells in the vestibular ganglia has been demonstrated in cases of vestibular neuronitis. Viral inflammation in the perilymph and endolymph is thought to be responsible for the symptoms; however, viral cellular destruction or intimation in the neuroepithelium of the cristae of the semicircular canals or the maculae of the utricle or saccule may be occurring. The reflex connections of the semicircular canals serve vestibulocerebellar, vestibuloocular, commissural, and vestibulospinal pathways. The central connections of the utricular macula are primarily in a descending direction. These complex interconnections are responsible for the nystagmus, vertigo, nausea, and vomiting that accompany head or neck motion in this disorder.

Asymmetry of firing in the normal discharge pattern of the vestibular nerve leads to constant or irregular stimulation of ocular and vagal reflexes, which results in nystagmus and nausea.

Natural History

The disorder usually follows a typical upper respiratory tract infection by about 1 week. The patient has acute onset of vertigo, which is continuous and severe for 48 to 72 hours and then begins to get better. After the initial 2 to 3 days, only positional vertigo may occur.

Prevention

Virtually all acute labyrinthine vertigo is viral in nature, and no specific preventive measures are known. In acute labyrinthine vertigo associated with Ménière's disease, a low-salt diet and/or vasodilators may prevent the attacks. Sudden, recurrent vertigo associated with elevated triglyceride or uric acid levels may be prevented by appropriate diet.

Cost Containment

Most of these patients do not have to be hospitalized. Expensive computed tomography, arteriograms, or elaborate audiometric or electronystagmographic studies are not needed. The patient with acute vertigo should be observed for 72 hours to note spontaneous regression.

REFERENCES

Brookler KH, Rubin W. The dizzy patient: Etiologic treatment. Otol Head Neck Surg 1990;103:677.

Finestone AJ. An approach to the patient with dizziness and vertigo by the primary care physician. In: Finestone AJ, ed. Evaluation and clinical management of dizziness and vertigo. Boston: John Wright, 1982:45.

Jackson R, Todd NW, Turner JS. Ear, nose and throat diseases. In: Speight TM, ed. Avery's drug treatment, 3rd ed. Sydney, Australia: Adis Press, 1987.

Kveton J. Symptoms of vestibular disease. In: Jackler R, Brachman D, eds. Neurotology. St. Louis: Mosby, 1994.

Turner JS. The dizzy patient: Diagnosis and treatment. Drugs 1977;13:382.

CHAPTER 21–11

Eardrum Perforation

John S. Turner, Jr., M.D.

DEFINITION

Any defect in the pars tensa or pars flaccida can be defined as an eardrum perforation.

ETIOLOGY

The cause may be traumatic or infectious.

CRITERIA FOR DIAGNOSIS

Suggestive

The patient usually mentions recent trauma such as a slap on the ear or recent respiratory infection and earache. Ear drainage, decreased hearing, tinnitus, or unusual sensitivity to cold air or water in the ear may be mentioned by the patient.

Definitive

Physical examination reveals an opening in the tympanic membrane, or tympanometry with an impedance bridge indicates failure to accomplish a complete seal of the canal and drum.

CLINICAL MANIFESTATIONS

Subjective

The patient may experience loss of hearing, fullness, echo phenomena, tinnitus, earache, pain with water contamination, dizziness, diplacusis, or inability to lateralize sound. Some patients may be completely asymptomatic if the perforation is small or if it has been present since childhood. Family history is not pertinent.

Objective

Physical Examination

Constant or recurrent drainage may be noted. Hearing loss is conductive in most cases. Patients with chronic otitis media and drum perfora-tion often have associated sensorineural hearing loss. Cold air or liquids contaminating the ear often lead to severe pain.

Routine Laboratory Abnormalities

Basic blood counts may demonstrate anemia or mild elevation in the white blood count.

PLANS

Diagnostic

Differential Diagnosis

A history of acute trauma makes the diagnosis obvious. The most common causes are a blow to the ear from an open palm of the hand and a sudden pressure effect from water skiing when the ear strikes the flat surface of the water with great force.

Diagnostic Options

A complete ear, nose, and throat history and examination should be carried out and include hearing testing with audiometry.

Ear perforation and drainage in association with severe head trauma should be handled under sterile conditions. The drainage may be cerebrospinal fluid from a fracture into the middle fossa. A sterile dressing should be applied after examination and fluid collection.

Recommended Approach

The ear canal may have to be cleaned with cotton applicators or a ring curet. Irrigation of the ear canal for wax should never be carried out in a patient with a history of eardrum perforation.

A perforation may be missed unless careful attention is paid to the pars flaccida area. Negative middle ear pressure leads to the retraction and pocketing of epithelium into the attic area of the ear. A perforation is seen either anterior or posterior to the short process of the malleus. This type of perforation may lead to serious disease (cholesteatoma), as may perforation in the posterosuperior part of the pars tensa.

Therapeutic

Therapeutic Options

Perforations from traumatic rupture should be referred immediately to an otolaryngologist. If the edges are reapproximated under local anesthesia, healing is expedited and closure occurs promptly. Delay in such closure attempts may prolong healing and eventually require tympanoplasty.

Blast injuries may be very large, and immediate operation with grafting may be needed.

Small traumatic perforations should be kept exquisitely dry. If an aquatic injury has occurred with water contamination, antibiotics by solution or by powder should be used. Corticosteroid drops are not indicated in acute injury. Nonaquatic injuries do not require topical or systemic antibiotics. The preferred management is to keep the ear exquisitely dry.

Infectious ruptures may be acute or chronic. Those in association with otitis media require proper treatment of the underlying infection.

Ruptures of a long-standing nature can usually be repaired with tympanoplasty. Infection should be identified with cultures and eliminated with proper cleaning and antibiotic treatment. Topical antibiotics are usually sufficient for cleaning the ear, as most ears are infected with saprophytic bacteria such as *Pseudomonas*. Concomitant oral therapy may be needed for staphylococcal or pneumococcal infection. Corticosteroid drops may be used if granulation is seen around or medial to the perforation.

Recommended Approach

The ear must be kept exquisitely dry. Hearing tests are needed prior to any reparative surgery to establish that useful, potentially correctable hearing loss is present in the ear. A hearing aid may be the preferred form of treatment if the other ear is nonfunctional.

Closure of chronic perforations in the diabetic patient, especially those who are insulin dependent, is probably unwise because of the high incidence of recurrent upper respiratory tract infections and otitis media in these patients. Closure is not advised in any patient with generalized neoplastic or severe debilitating disease, as a hearing aid can be used easily by these patients. All young persons over age 10 with drum perforation should have tympanoplasty unless one of the contraindications listed above is present. Excellent results can usually be achieved with drum grafting, and closure is usually permanent. The young patient can then participate in aquatic activities in a normal manner.

In retraction ruptures, careful investigation of the eustachian tube and related structures should be carried out to determine the underlying pressure changes that create the problem. Perforations in the pars flaccida area must be followed periodically by an otolaryngologist to determine the need for ventilation tube insertion or other otologist management.

The patient should always be instructed to keep the perforated ear very dry and to avoid any water, hair spray, dust, or other contamination at all times. The patient should be advised that most perforations can be closed with tympanoplasty and that the conductive hearing loss is potentially correctable. Patients who have had drum perforation should never scuba dive or subject themselves to unpressurized aircraft effects. Swimming is not advised, although some physicians permit this when ear mold protectors are fitted by a professional; ordinary swimming plugs are not effective in keeping moisture out of the middle ear.

FOLLOW-UP

Acute perforations should be observed monthly until closure occurs. Closure seldom occurs spontaneously after 6 months. After this period, the patient with a perforation should be referred for surgical closure. Chronic perforation should be followed at 2-week intervals until the infection clears. In the absence of contraindications, referral for closure is then indicated. Recurrent perforations indicate the need to identify an underlying cause such as diabetes, anemia, nasopharyngeal tumor, chronic sinusitis, or possible factitious trauma.

DISCUSSION

Prevalence and Incidence

There are no studies available that indicate the prevalence and incidence of this condition.

Related Basic Science

The tympanic membrane consists of three basic layers: an outer squamous cell layer, an inner low cuboidal mucosal layer, and an intermediate fibrous layer between the two. The fibrous layer has radial and circular fibers. With perforation, this normal relationship is disturbed, and the fibrous intermediate layer does not regenerate to normal degree. A thin, translucent area of rehealing usually can be seen indefinitely after drum perforation.

Great variations exist in the normal mobility of the drum. Because of these variations some individuals are much more susceptible to perforations than others.

Infectious perforations are caused by direct necrosis from bacteria or virus, as with *Streptococcus* and *Mycoplasma* infections. Fluid accumulations alone seldom cause ruptures, unless weakening from edema, cell necrosis, or ischemia is present.

Traumatic perforations usually shatter the drum in a stellate manner. Rupture from within, as with barotrauma, is usually more linear and localized.

The position of the perforation may greatly influence the degree of associated hearing loss. Small perforations directly over the round window area may have greater hearing effects than a larger perforation more anteriorly or superiorly placed. Perforations in the pars flaccida area may have virtually no effect on hearing.

Natural History and Its Modification with Treatment

Traumatic perforations may heal spontaneously in 6 months. Infectious perforations may heal after a number of years, and many adults have evidence of a healed perforation on inspection without knowledge of the cause of infection in childhood.

Many factors influence healing, such as associated nose and throat disease, systemic disorders, and water contamination. The greatest factor influencing healing, however, is the ability of the patient to protect the ear from moisture contamination or undue pressure effects such as vigorous nose blowing.

Prevention

Eardrums are usually perforated by foreign bodies (traumatic), barotrauma, water skiing, or chronic middle ear infections. Therefore, prevention involves keeping objects out of the ear, avoiding flying or scuba diving with an upper respiratory tract infection, using caution when water skiing, and obtaining early intense management of ear infections before chronicity develops.

Cost Containment

Systemic antibiotics are not usually needed in eardrum perforation. Topical solutions containing corticosteroids are not needed unless granulation tissue is seen. Prolonged and unnecessary antibiotic treatment can be avoided if culture and sensitivity are obtained in chronically infected perforations.

REFERENCES

Griffin WL. A retrospective study of traumatic tympanic membrane perforations in a clinical practice. Laryngoscope 1979;89:261.

Jurovitzki I, Sadé J. Myringoplasty: Long-term follow-up. Am J Otol 1988;9:52.

Kerr AG. Trauma and the temporal bone: The effects of blast on the ear. J Laryngol Otol 1980;94:107.

Mendel L, Kuylenstierna R. A clinical comparison of the results of two different methods of closing tympanic membrane perforations. J Laryngol Otol 1985;99:339.

Shelton C, Sheehy JL. Tympanoplasty: Review of 400 staged cases. Laryngoscope 1990;100:679.

Turner JS, Staats E, Stone HH, Logan R. Use of gentamicin in preparing chronically infected ear for tympanoplastic surgery. South Med J 1966;59:94.

CHAPTER 21–12

Cholesteatoma

John S. Turner, Jr., M.D.

DEFINITION

Squamous epithelium invading and eroding the middle ear, attic, or mastoid cells is called *cholesteatoma*.

ETIOLOGY

Skin of the eardrum grows through a perforation or the pars flaccida is retracted inward to form a cholesteatoma.

CRITERIA FOR DIAGNOSIS

Suggestive

The patient may complain of fullness, tinnitus, hearing loss, drainage, pain, or vertigo.

Definitive

Inspection of the eardrum usually reveals retraction with a whitish debris evident in the pars flaccida or posterosuperior quadrants. Chronic ear complaints associated with foul-smelling drainage combined with the physical findings listed above establish a diagnosis of cholesteatoma.

CLINICAL MANIFESTATIONS

Subjective

Overt, foul ear drainage may have been present for years. The patient may mention that ear drainage occurs on water contamination. Subacute symptoms of ear fullness, tinnitus, hearing loss, or mild vertigo may be present off and one for 10 or more years before they become constant enough to justify medical attention. The patient may remember some ear disease as a child but none in recent years. Some cholesteatomas develop from long-standing barotrauma such as frequent flying, and only after years do the negative pressure effects on the pars flaccida create a cholesteatoma. The disease is not familial.

Objective

Physical Examination

Foul drainage from the ear may be evident by observation or smell in neglected cases. Retraction of the pars flaccida or perforation of the posterior quadrants of the eardrum is seen on otoscopy. Negative pressure with the pneumatic otoscope may displace thick mucopus from the attic or recesses of the mastoid. Any pressure with the otoscope may create vertigo; this is called a *positive fistula sign* and indicates involvement of the horizontal semicircular canal with the cholesteatoma erosion.

Fork or audiometric testing reveals conductive hearing loss. In neglected cases, associated sensorineural hearing loss may develop.

Adenoid hypertrophy may be present, or signs of chronic sinusitis, either allergic or infectious, may be evident.

Routine Laboratory Abnormalities

Routine laboratory studies are usually normal.

PLANS

Diagnostic

Differential Diagnosis

The goal is to determine the extent of erosion of the middle ear and mastoid.

Careful cleaning of the ear with cotton-tipped wire applicators or a small suction device is often necessary. Irrigation for wax should never be done if brownish debris is noted directly on the drum, as a cholesteatoma may lurk just under the debris.

Secretions should be cultured and usually reveal saprophytes such as *Pseudomonas, Proteus,* and *Staphylococcus aureus.*

Diagnostic Options

Accurate hearing testing for bone and air conduction helps determine the amount of ossicular chain involvement. Wide differences between air and bone conduction suggest extensive erosion of incus and stapes.

Recommended Approach

Routine mastoid films usually reveal a sclerotic-type mastoid bone with minimal development of pneumatic air cells. A distinct circular erosion is seen classically on the film, but polytomes or computed tomography may be more helpful in delineating the extent of erosion. These films are confirmatory, however, and are not absolutely essential for diagnosis.

Complications such as erosion or irritation of the horizontal semicircular may be present. This may be evidenced by nystagmus or unsteadiness on walking. In all cases of acute bacterial meningitis, the ear must be searched carefully for insidious and obscure cholesteatoma. Brain abscess may rarely be the initial presenting sign of cholesteatoma. In long-standing neglected cases, facial weakness or paralysis may be present.

Therapeutic

Therapeutic Options

The only effective therapy for cholesteatoma is surgical excision via mastoidectomy. Medical management of cholesteatoma is transient and a temporizing measure. Skin present in the attic, mastoid, or middle ear can be eliminated effectively only through surgical exposure.

Recommended Approach

All suspected cases should be referred to an otolaryngologist for proper surgery. Hearing restoration with tympanoplasty is often possible once the cholesteatoma matrix is removed and infection in the mastoid and middle ear eliminated.

Strong reinforcement of the need for surgery may be necessary for the patient and family. As the onset is often insidious and the symptoms minimal, the patient often cannot readily appreciate the serious nature of the cholesteatoma matrix that is eroding the ear. The patient should be told that serious central nervous system infection, vertigo, facial paralysis, and progressive hearing loss are possible if the problem is not managed surgically.

FOLLOW-UP

Following appropriate mastoid surgery, the patient must be advised to keep the ear exquisitely dry and to return at 6-month intervals for inspection or cleaning of the mastoid cavity. Two-stage operations are sometimes recommended to rebuild the hearing. Occasional revision surgery is sometimes needed to manage residual infection.

DISCUSSION

Prevalence and Incidence

Cholesteatoma is seen more commonly in populations that have a high incidence of otitis media.

Related Basic Science

Physiologic Derangement

Cholesteatoma occurs when squamous epithelium from the drum or external canal migrates into the middle ear or attic area of the mastoid.

The migrating skin, known as *matrix*, follows a line of least resistance. Desquamating outer layers accumulate in pockets and recesses of the bone, with various pH changes occurring as necrosis of the skin progresses. Some investigators have postulated that the matrix is unique and its erosive and migratory qualities are peculiar to the skin of the medial ear canal. A more likely explanation, however, is that the softening of bone and changes in the calcium and phosphate complexes (halosteresis) develop from the pH changes of necrosis, saprophyte infection, and the directed pressure effects of migratory and encysting skin. In children and young adults, this invasion may be so aggressive that complete involvement of the entire mastoid area of the temporal bone may occur in 1 or 2 years.

The term *cholesteatoma* derives from the fact that the migrating necrotic skin contains high levels of cholesterol. The decomposition of these fatty acids combined with bacterial action produces the foul-smelling mucoid exudate that is characteristic of the disorder.

Anatomic Derangement

Cellular development of the mastoid is impaired in most cases of cholesteatoma, indicating that the disease begins early in life with impairment of normal pneumatization. Cholesteatoma is unknown in animals, even in the great apes. The human being uniquely has the anatomic setting in the temporal bone and eustachian tube to permit the development of this disorder.

A cholesteatoma is basically "skin in the wrong place."

The pathogenesis of cholesteatoma begins with malfunction of the eustachian tube. Such malfunction leads to the development of two types of cholesteatoma: primary and secondary acquired. The primary type occurs from retraction in the pars flaccida and with subsequent enlargement of the narrow-neck squamous cyst. Secondary acquired cholesteatoma begins with purulent otitis media and drum perforation in the posterior quadrants. The squamous matrix invades into attic, middle ear, and mastoid to form an erosive cholesteatoma.

Natural History and Its Modification with Treatment

Without early removal of the invasive matrix, the ossicles, horizontal canal, facial nerve, middle fossa, or sigmoid rim may become involved. Persistent infection with chronic ear drainage, hearing loss, pain, and dizziness progresses insidiously until adequate surgical excision is accomplished.

Prevention

Cholesteatoma develops from chronic retraction of the pars flaccida of the eardrum or from a persistent posterosuperior quadrant perforation. Intense treatment of otitis media with effusion and careful repeated observation to ensure that the drum has returned to normal constitute the best method of prevention. The function of the drum and middle ear should be checked by tympanometry to document a return to normal. Many otologists believe that the prevalent use of ventilation tubes in otitis media with effusion since 1954 has been responsible for reducing the incidence of cholesteatoma.

Cost Containment

Prolonged hospitalization for cholesteatoma, as well as increased morbidity, lengthy operative procedures, and possible permanent disability, can be avoided by early diagnosis and proper surgical care.

REFERENCES

Moran WB. Cholesteatoma. In: English G, ed. Otolaryngology. Hagerstown, MD: Harper & Row, 1978.

Palva T. Surgical treatment of cholesteatomatous ear disease. J Laryngol Otol 1985;99:539.

Toner JG, Smyth GDL. Surgical treatment of cholesteatoma. Am J Otol 1990;11:247.

Tos M. Treatment of cholesteatoma in children: A long-term study of results. Am J Otol 1983;4:189.

Turner JS. Revision of previous stapedectomy, tympanoplasty, mastoidectomy and endolymphatic shunt. South Med J 1983;76:1493.

CHAPTER 21–13

Barotrauma of the Ear (Aerotitis)

John S. Turner, Jr., M.D.

DEFINITION

Ear symptoms or physical changes occurring from pressure effects are defined as barotrauma.

ETIOLOGY

Severe positive or negative changes in middle ear pressure produce barotrauma.

CRITERIA FOR DIAGNOSIS
Suggestive

The patient usually presents with a recent history of diving, flying, skydiving, scuba diving, or other submarine activities.

Definitive

Inspection of the eardrum indicates hemorrhage in the middle ear, hemorrhagic edema of the eardrum, distortion of the eardrum, or marked retraction with visible fluid in the middle ear. A patient who presents with pain and ear fullness following the activities listed above is diagnosed as having barotrauma.

CLINICAL MANIFESTATIONS
Subjective

All the acute symptoms described for otitis media (see Chapter 21–5) with effusion develop. Severe ear fullness, pain, and sudden hearing loss may occur with exposure to barometric pressure changes.

Scuba divers may mention that they experienced difficulty in equilibrating the middle ear pressure on descent. Sudden ear pressure, pain, or slight dizziness may have occurred. Patients who develop aerotitis when flying may have severe fullness and pain on ascent or descent. This phenomenon is quite common, even on properly pressurized aircraft.

The patient may mention that a recent flight caused ear fullness without any previous history of trouble. Careful questioning indicates that an upper respiratory tract infection or allergic flareup was present before or during the flight. Associated pain in the face or forehead from aerosinusitis also may have occurred.

Patients with previous eardrum perforation may experience reperforation with slight ear drainage or bleeding.

Hearing loss may be moderate or severe. After scuba diving, the patient may have sensorineural hearing loss as well as conductive loss because of pressure and gaseous effects on the inner ear. Permanent deleterious effects on the hearing may develop.

Roaring tinnitus may be present and persist even after the middle ear pressure is returned to normal. Accentuation of a previously existing tinnitus has been noted in some individuals.

Decompression sickness (the bends) may occur with barotrauma, as may air embolism, but the cardiac, pulmonary, central nervous system, and joint symptoms override the otologic complaints and are extremely serious.

Objective

Physical Examination

Objective findings of a positive nature are confined to the eardrum or audiogram; occasionally, associated barosinusitis with fluid and edema in the maxillary and frontal sinuses is noted. The drum may be injected, hemorrhagic, edematous, bleblike, or actually ruptured with hemorrhage through the perforation. If associated inner ear disturbance is present, nystagmus may be noted. Conductive hearing loss is found by audiogram or fork testing in mild aerosinusitis (barotrauma to the sinuses), or both conductive and sensorineural hearing loss may be found in severe cases.

Routine Laboratory Abnormalities

The results of routine laboratory tests are usually normal.

PLANS
Diagnostic

Differential Diagnosis

The history of acute onset is obvious.

Diagnostic Options and Recommended Approach

Complete examination of the ear, nose, and sinuses should be carried out and include audiometric testing. Impedance audiometry shows immobility and increased impedance of the middle ear. Patients with associated vertigo should be examined on more than one occasion to note fluctuant hearing loss and balance disturbance, which might indicate round window rupture. A finding of deviated nasal septum or chronic sinusitis may be the predisposing cause for aerotitis.

Therapeutic

Mild cases usually do not require any treatment. Severe cases with continued pain or excruciating pain may require myringotomy for relief of pressure and fluid. Nasal sprays may be used for 3 to 4 days in severe cases, and decongestant preparations may be given, although little evidence exists to confirm the efficacy of these drugs. A brief course of corticosteroids may be needed for persistent fluid and pressure after the first week of onset.

The patient must not dive or fly again until the ears have been clear for at least 1 month. Patients with repeated episodes of barotrauma have unusually sensitive eustachian tubes and must avoid pressure exposures permanently. Patients who engage in occupations or sports involving barometric pressure changes should have normal nasal and eustachian tube function (easy autoinflation), normal-appearing ear canals and eardrums, no stapes prosthesis, and normal peripheral vestibular function.

FOLLOW-UP

The examination should be repeated at weekly intervals to ensure that complete clearing of the middle ear occurs. Longer follow-up is needed in patients with conductive or sensorineural hearing loss or vertigo.

DISCUSSION
Prevalence

There are approximately 700,000 active scuba divers in the United States and many hundreds more who participate in skydiving or submarine activities. Millions of persons fly in large and small aircraft each year, and thousands of cases of barotitis occur. Most do not require

medical attention, but patients who fly with respiratory tract infection or allergy usually set the stage for severe or protracted barotitis.

Related Basic Science
Physiologic Derangement

Barotrauma or barotitis is an injury resulting from a pressure difference between the environment and an air-containing space within the body. Ascent in air usually creates relatively minimal pressure changes (18,000-ft elevation is 0.5 atm); however, pressure changes in water are great and create many more hazards (16.5-ft depth is 0.5 atm). According to Boyle's law, changes in the volume of a gas vary inversely with pressure. As the diver descends, the increased (water) pressure is transmitted throughout the body, as compressed air at ambient pressure is breathed from a pressure-sensitive regulator. As long as the diver is able to equalize the pressure of the various noncollapsible spaces within the body to ambient pressure, barotrauma does not occur. As the diver descends, increased water pressure results in an inward movement of the eardrum. Rupture of the normal drum occurs at a depth of between 4 and 17 ft unless there is equalization of pressure via the eustachian tube. Equalization is usually accomplished by the Valsalva maneuver, even though many divers have voluntary control over opening their eustachian tube. Although continuous equalization from the surface throughout the descent is ideal, equalization every 2 to 3 ft is usually sufficient to prevent a blocked eustachian tube and possible drum rupture.

Anatomic Derangement

A perilymph fistula resulting from rupture of the oval or round window results in a variety of hearing or balance problems. Forceful autoinflation of the ears during descent is a common denominator of most fistulas. It is speculated that increased cerebrospinal fluid pressure or violent movement of the stapes during a forceful Valsalva maneuver is the cause. The result is an immediate but variable combination of hearing loss, tinnitus, and vertigo.

Alternobaric vertigo is a transient vestibular dysfunction occurring, by definition, on ascent and is probably due to unequal equilibration of middle ear pressure. Hearing loss and tinnitus are not part of this disorder.

Barosinusitis may be seen concomitantly with barotitis and results from pressure injury to the mucoperiosteum of the sinuses. Pain is experienced on descent in water or ascent in air and disappears when the sinus fills with blood.

External ear canal occlusion by cerumen, exostoses, or ear plugs prevents effective equalization during descent while scuba diving. This may cause vertigo, because of unilateral caloric stimulation of the unaffected ear, resulting in injection of hemorrhagic vesiculation of the ear canal.

Depending on the pressure difference between the water and the middle ear space while scuba diving, varying degrees of barotrauma occur. These may be graded from I to V according to Edmond's classification:

Type I	Mild infection of the tympanic membrane
Types II and III	Contusion of the tympanic membrane middle ear mucosa
Type IV	Bleeding into the middle ear space
Type V	Rupture of the tympanic membrane

Unequal caloric stimulation during diving may be the result of a pre-existing peripheral vestibular deficit or of unequal douching of cold water in the ear canal while scuba diving, the result of canal obstruction.

Alternobaric vertigo has been noted to cause dizziness in 26% of sport divers. Patients who cannot easily autoinflate their ears are at risk for alternobaric vertigo.

Natural History and Its Modification with Treatment

Permanent retraction of the drum with middle ear adhesions may develop from repeated episodes of barotitis. Residual hearing loss may be present in neglected cases. Pain and fullness may persist for days or weeks unless the eustachian tube can be opened or the middle ear ventilated to equalize pressure.

Prevention

This disorder usually occurs after flying or scuba diving. Divers should be instructed in proper methods of eustachian tube equalization by an experienced scuba teacher. Small doses of pseudoephedrine or topical nasal decongestants prior to diving or flying are sometimes helpful in avoiding barotrauma. Persons who are particularly susceptible should never fly when they have an upper respiratory tract infection or severe allergic rhinitis, and no one should ever scuba dive with these disorders. Holding the nose and swallowing (Toynbee maneuver), holding the nose and blowing (Valsalva maneuver), swallowing with the mouth open, or chewing gum may help equalize middle ear pressure in flight and thus prevent barotrauma.

Cost Containment

Costs can be contained, because drugs are not usually needed in most cases of barotrauma. If vertigo or pain is absent from the symptom re-

view, probably no specific diagnostic tests or treatment will be needed either.

REFERENCES

Agnew J. Barotrauma: A review for the hearing specialist. Hearing J 1988;41:30.
Dennis RG, Whitmire RN, Jackson RT. Action of inflammatory mediators on middle ear mucosa. Arch Otolaryngol 1976;102:420.
Farmer JC, Gillespie CA. Otologic medicine and surgery of exposures to aerospace, diving and compressed gases. In: Alberti PW, Ruben RJ, eds. Otologic medicine and surgery. New York: Churchill Livingstone, 1988.
Groth P, Ivarsson A, Tjernstrom O, White P. The effect of pressure change on the eustachian tube function in pressure chamber tests. Acta Otolaryngol 1985;99:67.
Neblett LM. Otolaryngology and sport scuba diving. Ann Otol Rhinol Laryngol 1985;94(suppl.):1.
Shupak A, Doweck I, Greenberg E, et al. Diving-related inner ear injuries. Laryngoscope 1991;101:173.
Zajtchuk JT, Phillips YY. Effects of blast overpressure on the ear. Ann Otol Rhinol Laryngol 1989;98(suppl.):5.

CHAPTER 21–14

Temporomandibular Joint Syndrome (Costen's Syndrome)

John S. Turner, Jr., M.D.

DEFINITION

Persistent pain, discomfort, fullness, and tinnitus in and around the ear when otologic examination is normal and crepitance and tenderness are present in the jaw joint are defined as temporomandibular joint (TMJ) syndrome.

ETIOLOGY

Trauma, dental malocclusion, and bruxism are the usual causes.

CRITERIA FOR DIAGNOSIS

Suggestive

In most cases, the diagnosis is quite evident because of an audible snap or click whenever the joint is moved associated with pain on palpation directly over the external surface of the joint capsule. Dental malocclusion is present in virtually all cases, and the diagnosis should be confirmed by a dentist once other associated structures are found to be normal.

Definitive

The diagnosis of this syndrome is made by excluding all other associated medical problems that might create symptoms in the jaw and ear.

CLINICAL MANIFESTATIONS

Subjective

The principal complaints of patients with this problem are pain in the ear region and abnormal motion of the jaw. The discomfort in the upper jaw or ear region may be described in numerous ways. The patient may state that it is sharp, dull, aching, burning, pulsating, spreading, exerting pressure, drawing, or pulling. The duration may be constant or intermittent and may decline gradually or abruptly. The impairment of jaw function may be manifested as restricted or defected jaw movements. Noises or clicking in the joint or a change in the bite may be present.

The patient may also mention a sore scalp, throat pain, a burning

pain down the side of the neck, fullness or pressure in the ear, tinnitus or vertigo, and occasional sensations of mild hearing impairment. Headache, nausea, and slight ataxia may be mentioned. The pain from the arthralgia or muscle spasm may at times create vasomotor symptoms such as flushing, lacrimation, and nasal swelling. Grinding of the teeth, or bruxism, may be mentioned by a family member.

A history of jaw injury, oral surgery, or wearing of braces is often mentioned, especially in adolescents or young adults. Pipe smoking or frequent gum or tobacco chewing may be mentioned. The discomfort may cause the patient to stop chewing during meals. Prolonged dental work such as root canals, inlays, and multiple bridges may precipitate the discomfort. A history of radiation therapy to the jaw may be present.

Objective

Physical Examination

Pain, tenderness, or crepitation may be noted on palpation of the jaw joint. Discomfort may be precipitated when the patient opens, yawns, or chews. Marked limitation in jaw excursion may be noted. Obvious deviation of the jaw angle may be evident. Obvious malocclusion with underbite, overbite, jaw distortion to one side, or obvious missing molars may be noted. Complete lack of dentition or malfitting partial plates or bridges are often noted. Extensive postoperative changes involving the salivary glands, oral cavity, or pharynx may be noted.

A stethoscope may be used to detect minimal popping, clicking, or grating sounds. Movement of the jaw sideways may trigger pain when other motions do not. Special radiographs of the jaw may show degeneration of the fossa, condyle, or articular disk. Arthrographic films with the use of dyes may help outline the disk. Dental specialists with exacting equipment such as an articulator can identify critical changes in occlusion and jaw movement.

Hearing is usually normal. The examination of the external ear canal and drum is normal.

Routine Laboratory Abnormalities

The routine laboratory test results are usually normal.

PLANS

Diagnostic

Differential Diagnosis

The differential diagnosis requires consideration of external or middle ear disorders, trauma to the jaw, cervical sprain (whiplash), myositis, bruxism, osteoarthritis, rheumatoid arthritis, gouty arthritis, salivary gland disorders, tumors of the jaw or surrounding structures, pharyngeal or laryngeal tumors, and ulceration.

Diagnostic Options and Recommended Approach

Pain is often aggravated by chewing and is often worse at night. A history of recent dental procedures or orthodontia is often obtained.

Open and closed radiographs of the joint may identify abnormalities of structure or position. Injection of the joint with xylocaine may give intermediate relief of pain and confirm the diagnosis.

Therapeutic

Therapeutic Options

Correction of the underlying reason for the jaw malfunction is paramount. Virtually all cases need referral to a dentist who is particularly interested in managing temporomandibular joint problems. Except in cases of trauma or arthritis, a dental problem is usually present and all other therapy is symptomatic or supportive.

Recommended Approach

Excess chewing should be avoided. Open-mouth biting such as eating an apple should not be done. Local heat to the jaw, warmed Auralgan in the ear canal, and oral analgesics may be acutely helpful. Injection of the jaw joint with 2% xylocaine gives immediate relief, and injection with soluble cortisone may give long-term relief, particularly if arthritis of the joint is present. Surgery to the jaw joint is rarely indicated for relief; multidisciplinary consultation should be obtained prior to any surgical intervention. Muscle-relaxing procedures such as biofeedback may provide significant relief of the muscle spasm and myositis associated with temporomandibular joint syndrome. Habit-forming drugs should not be used for chronic or recurrent cases. Some authorities believe a properly fitted upper arch orthodontic bite plate will separate the upper and lower teeth and allow the mandible to move into proper position. Ethyl chloride sprays to the jaw joint and muscle area may be helpful also. Hall (1984) has shown that physical therapy helps.

The nature of the jaw muscle spasm and the improperly closing joint should be explained in detail. Usually, considerable persuasion is needed to convince the patient that dental consult and treatment are the preferred courses of action.

FOLLOW-UP

Medical care is seldom needed once a proper diagnosis of temporomandibular joint syndrome has been made. If any question as to the source of pain exists, examination should be repeated at 3- to 4-month intervals or at the time of severe pain to establish its exact origin.

DISCUSSION

Prevalence

This problem is very common, especially in young women who have worn braces in the past.

Related Basic Science

Physiologic Derangement

The pain or discomfort can be traced to involvement of the musculature directly and indirectly used in the movement of the jaws. Muscle pain induces a sustained reflex contraction of the jaw muscle, which in turn increases muscle pain, which further contributes to sustained reflex contraction with pain gradually radiating into adjacent areas. If jaw muscle inactivity is unbalanced, the teeth may occlude defectively. Research into this problem has indicated that most temporomandibular joint problems are caused by fatigue and spasm in the masticatory muscles and do not involve the joint itself.

The mobility of the joint is more or less disturbed, however, as is the spacial relation of the disk and the condylar head. In disease states, the head of the condyle loses its normal relationship to the center of the disk at the beginning or end of the mandibular opening and closing. A clicking sound may be produced by this abnormal relationship.

Anatomic Derangement

One of the most frequently encountered conditions is the lack of posterior teeth. Mastication is then accomplished by thrusting the mandible forward using the available anterior teeth for chewing. This action, in turn, pulls the head of the condyle forward, stretching the ligament and muscle attachments. This abnormal action of the muscles of mastication and nerve endings can create pain in the area of the temporomandibular joint.

The patient usually has a poor bite because one or more teeth have been lost. This moves the mandible out of position and causes the condyle to function badly, or, because of stress in the patient's life, grinding of the teeth may occur unconsciously. After a time, the cartilage that covers the top of the condyle starts to wear down and the equilibrium of muscles and ligaments that control condylar movement is affected and stimulation of the trigeminal nerve occurs.

Natural History and Its Modification with Treatment

Most patients with this problem are between the ages of 35 and 45. Children between 12 and 20 may also have the problem from teeth grinding. A history of wearing braces or a jaw injury during adolescence is often present. Continued trauma to the capsule of the joint results in referred stabbing pain or a dull ache in the head, neck, and shoulders mimicking earaches, abscessed teeth, and neuralgia. Pain and discomfort continue and progress until proper dental management and muscle relaxation are achieved.

Prevention

Virtually all temporomandibular joint syndrome occurs from dental malocclusion. Correction of occlusal disorders as soon as they are identified is recommended. Dental measures such as the insertion of a bite blocker at night may prevent the pain from temporomandibular joint syndrome, especially if it is associated with bruxism. Some dentists are especially trained in the use of proper preventive measures such as muscle relaxation techniques, and therefore much discomfort may be prevented by early referral to a knowledgeable, interested dental specialist.

Cost Containment

A high index of suspicion when pain is present in the jaw or ear region will save the patient much time and money in searching for proper diagnosis and management. Definite tenderness over the joint that is accentuated by movement will indicate to the physician that dental appraisal is the most efficacious recommendation.

REFERENCES

Adour KK. Acute temporomandibular joint pain-dysfunction syndrome: Neuro-otologic and electromyographic study. Am J Otol 1981;2:114.

Hall LJ. Physical therapy treatment results for 178 patients with temporomandibular joint syndromes. Am J Otol 1984;5:183.

Hodges JM. Managing temporomandibular joint syndrome. Laryngoscope 1990;100:60.

Kreisberg MK, Turner JS. Dental causes of referred otalgia. Ear Nose Throat J 1986;66:398.

Morgan DH, Hall WP, Vamvas SJ. Diseases of the temporomandibular apparatus. St. Louis: Mosby, 1977.

Sarnat BG, Laskin DM. Diagnosis and surgical management of diseases of the temporomandibular joint. Springfield, IL: Charles C Thomas, 1962.

Trauell JG, Simons DG. Myofascial pain and dysfunction: The trigger-point manual. Baltimore: Williams & Wilkins, 1983.

Westerman ST, Golz A, Gilbert L, Joachimo HZ. An objective, noninvasive method for the diagnosis of temporomandibular joint disorders. Laryngoscope 1991;101:738.

Acute Facial Paralysis (Bell's Palsy)

John S. Turner, Jr., M.D.

DEFINITION

Sudden spontaneous paralysis of one side of the face is called Bell's palsy.

ETIOLOGY

The cause of Bell's palsy is unknown but probably is related to a viral infection in a susceptible patient.

CRITERIA FOR DIAGNOSIS

Suggestive

Paralysis usually follows a mild upper respiratory tract infection and sometimes exposure to intense cold. Careful cranial nerve examination may show disorders in nerves other than the seventh. Complete paralysis in all branches of the eighth nerve is usually evident within 48 hours of onset. Bell's palsy is not related to generalized disease elsewhere in the body and is unilateral in virtually all cases.

Definitive

Sudden weakness or paralysis of one or all branches of the facial nerve, in the absence of obvious trauma or temporal bone disease, indicates idiopathic Bell's palsy.

CLINICAL MANIFESTATIONS

Subjective

Characteristically, the patient notices pain or discomfort in the face, around the ear, or down the neck for 24 to 72 hours before paralysis develops. Rarely is the pain severe. An unusual sensitivity to sound or a more vague sensation of sound distortion may be noted. Some degree of photophobia or eye sensitivity is mentioned by the patient and described as an inability to close the eyes or dryness. Taste disturbances may be noted because of chorda tympani involvement; in some cases, the taste changes precede the motor paralysis. A mild nasal congestion or other symptoms of upper respiratory tract infection may have been present 7 to 10 days previously. Dizziness or severe earache is not seen with idiopathic Bell's palsy.

The family history is noncontributory.

Objective

Physical Examination

The patient may be startled to discover on arising that one side of the face does not move or that "my face is drawing to one side." The eyelid cannot be opened or closed at will. Tears may stream down the cheek. This can be compared with the opposite eye with the Schirmer test. Saliva may seem to drool from one corner of the mouth. The patient cannot pucker the lips or whistle, but speech is affected very little. Liquids cannot be held in the cheek on the affected side, and chewing on that side becomes very difficult. Emotional expression is lost on the affected side; this helps distinguish Bell's palsy from certain central lesions that spare the motor nucleus for expression.

Taste disturbances such as a metallic quality to the taste or "numb feeling" on the tongue can be qualitatively identified with an electrical gustometer or dilute salt solutions.

Hyperacusis in relation to the opposite ear can be measured by audiometry. The stapedial muscle paralysis that produces this hyperacusis can also be measured with an impedance bridge. Alterations in salivation can be measured by cannulating each submaxillary (Wharton's) duct.

Routine Laboratory Abnormalities

The routine laboratory studies are usually normal. The sedimentation rate may be elevated slightly.

PLANS

Diagnostic

Differential Diagnosis

The diagnosis is usually clearly evident. The clinician's primary concern should be to rule out possible antecedent disorders such as tumor, trauma, infection, and inflammation. Pediatric cases in particular require meticulous evaluation for insidious middle ear or mastoid disease.

A severe form of facial paralysis caused by herpes zoster was described by Ramsey Hunt in 1907. Severe eighth nerve lesions usually accompany those of the seventh, and instead of hyperacusis, a severe cochlear loss is present.

If recurrent facial edema and fissured tongue are part of the paralysis, the patient has Melkersson–Rosenthal syndrome rather than idiopathic Bell's palsy.

Spontaneous facial paralysis may occur with diabetic neuropathy, sarcoid, carcinoma, or as part of a generalized polyneuropathy such as Guillain–Barré syndrome. Rarely, hypertensive encephalopathy or multiple sclerosis may produce paralysis.

Diagnostic Options and Recommended Approach

A detailed history as to the exact onset of any facial weakness must be taken to identify that an insidious weakness has not been developing, such as might occur with cholesteatoma or facial nerve neuroma.

A complete otolaryngologic evaluation to include routine and impedance audiometry should always be carried out. A complete neurologic examination of the patient is also essential to identify possible involvement of other peripheral nerves.

The extent of the paralysis can be documented by various localizing tests that identify abnormalities of the lacrimal gland, stapedius muscle, tongue (including taste), submaxillary gland, and facial muscle response to nerve excitability.

Information from the Schirmer test, stapedius reflex, salivary gland flow, and taste tests can be used to determine the location of nerve involvement.

Nerve excitability tests are not necessary for diagnosis but may help in establishing prognosis or the response to treatment. These tests when used with electromyography can determine whether a simple conduction block occurs (neuropraxia) or a loss of axonal continuity exists with axonotmesis (wallerian degeneration).

Electrical testing is not very helpful during the first 72 hours of paralysis, as normal nerve excitability and conduction may persist for that length of time even though total nerve severance has occurred.

Nerve excitability and electromyography tests should be performed by persons skilled in the use of this electric equipment. Electroneuronography can be used also.

Therapeutic

Therapeutic Options

Probably no greater controversy exists in medicine today than that relating to the proper management of Bell's palsy. This dilemma comes from the fact that 80% or perhaps 85% of patients with Bell's palsy improve at least partially with absolutely no treatment. Return to completely normal function is another matter, however, and some reported series of patients indicate that only 60% return to normal facial function spontaneously.

The main problem is the identification of the group that will not recover spontaneously. Investigators with extensive experience in treating many hundreds of cases have indicated that only high levels of corticosteroids are needed to achieve good results. In other clinical studies using double-blind, controlled conditions with independent evaluations of the functional results, corticosteroids showed no improvement over vitamins and no medical treatment gave better results than spontaneous healing.

Recommended Approach

Much effort has been exerted in recent years to identify the patient who is at risk for a poor functional result using salivary gland flow tests, Schirmer's tests, and nerve excitability tests. Some investigations suggest that the patient who progresses to complete facial paralysis within 72 hours, who has greater than a 4-MA difference between the two sides on the nerve excitability test, who has greater than a 23% difference on the salivary gland flow test, and who has an exceedingly dry eye on the Schirmer test is at great risk for permanent facial paralysis, and surgical decompression of the nerve should be carried out. Many unnecessary tests would have to be carried out to find these high-risk patients, however.

If the disease is somehow related to immunity alteration and if it is actually a polyneuritis, as some authorities suggest, then corticosteroids could be used in the early stages of paralysis. Injectable corticosteroids, the equivalent of 60 to 80 mg of prednisone each day for a week, should be used when the patient is first seen. Most authorities agree that the use of corticosteroids after 1 week of paralysis is of no value. Prolonged use beyond 7 to 10 days has not been shown to be of value either.

Surgical decompression of the nerve has been associated with improved nerve function even years after paralysis began and may be combined with grafting of a fibrotic degenerated nerve body. The timing and value of surgical intervention are a highly individualized matter which must be determined for each patient in consultation with an otologist. Some risk to the hearing does exist in all nerve decompression, even in the best of hands.

In the patient with virtually no functional return or with developing synkinesis and distorted facial grimacing after 1 year, serious consideration should be given to nerve grafting or nerve switching, such as anastomosis of the twelfth and seventh nerves. Prolonged flaccid paralysis with a droopy face and associated edema should be managed with facial-sling procedures to equalize the facial contour at least in repose.

All physicians managing patients with Bell's palsy must be ever mindful of the risk of corneal abrasion or ulceration. The eye must be protected at first by taping of the lid at night, and if any signs of conjunctivitis or corneal changes occur, then partial tarsorrhaphy must be carried out. Artificial tears should be prescribed for all patients for use several times a day if any dryness or irritation develops. Virtually all complications of Bell's palsy relate to the eye, and concern with motor function must not outweigh protective ophthalmologic concern.

No treatment is needed for the pain, hyperacusis, taste changes, or epiphora some patients have. Excess tearing or facial sweating when eating may require otologic surgery on the tympanic plexus in the middle ear.

As a general rule, all patients with Bell's palsy should be seen by a neurologist or otologist to rule out other possible causes of the paralysis and to offer the patient the experience and expertise of specialists who manage several cases a year.

Cosmetic changes from prolonged paralysis of the buccinator or orbicularis may be assisted by using a small hook at the corner of the mouth, which is held in place by a tooth attachment. Ramsey–Hunt syndrome, where herpes virus I is involved, should be treated with acyclovir (Zovirax) intravenously according to body weight.

The sudden occurrence of facial paralysis is a frightening and alarming event for all patients. Many questions the patient poses cannot be answered with any degree of accuracy because of the inconsistencies of impairment, as described above. The patient should be told that some recovery of facial function occurs in 80% of patients, that normal recovery occurs in only 60%, and that permanent total facial paralysis may persist in 10% of patients despite any and all treatment.

The patient should be instructed in measures to protect the cornea and conjunctiva.

Return of function is not expected before 8 weeks, and patients should be alerted to this delay period. Measures such as facial massage have not been shown to offer any help, but the patient may receive some subjective reassurance by using them. Earliest signs of recovery may be seen at 3 weeks.

The empiric nature of cortisone treatment should be explained and its possible advantages and side effects outlined in detail.

The implications of permanent paralysis and the need for consultation should be explained also, so that the patient and family know that management is highly controversial and that recovery is quite variable with and without treatment.

FOLLOW-UP

The patient should be evaluated as soon after the onset of paralysis as possible. Basic electrodiagnostic tests should be performed after 72 hours and the criteria listed under Plans, Diagnostic, followed. Complete paralysis, a dry eye, and a marked difference in the nerve excitability results are indications for reevaluation every 3 days. Progression to complete loss of neural response and a difference of greater than 25% in the salivary gland test indicate a very poor prognosis for return of any useful function.

The patient should be seen at weekly intervals for 4 weeks and at 2-week intervals for 3 months to note the condition of the eye, the possible return of motor function, and the presence of any complications of treatment such as hearing loss and corticosteroid side effects.

Each evaluation should include a comment on the facial status at rest and when frowning, squinting, eyebrow lifting, smiling, depressing the lower lip, and pursing the lips. The presence of involuntary muscle twitching, synkinesis, return of tearing, gustatory sweating, drooling, or hearing alteration should be noted at each visit.

Patients with no evidence of functional return at 8 weeks should have electromyographic studies. If fibrillation potentials are present, deterioration of the muscles of the face is developing. Virtually all patients with fibrillation potentials at 8 weeks have residual paralysis, facial distortion, synkinesis, and chronic ocular problems.

DISCUSSION
Prevalence and Incidence

The annual incidence is estimated to be 23 per 100,000 according to a study done in Minnesota (May et al., 1985). The incidence is about one fifth of this for children. Sex predominance has not been conclusively shown, and conflicting reports exist as to whether or not it is more common during pregnancy. All age groups may be affected. It is not more common in the geriatric group.

A seasonal predominance for Bell's palsy has not been conclusively demonstrated. Several cases seem to occur together, however, and definite clustering has been reported by many authors, although this clustering is not in the same season.

Related Basic Science

The few available pathologic studies indicate that degeneration in the myelin sheaths and axons occurs with virtually no inflammatory changes. Viral neuritis (Ramsey–Hunt syndrome) may show inflammation, but this is not true in Bell's palsy. Some biopsy reports of inflammatory changes in the chorda tympani nerve during paralysis have been questioned by later studies and largely discounted. The nerve may bulge through the sheath in an apparent edematous state when decompression surgery is performed; however, some investigators state that this occurs with operations on normal facial nerves also. Extensive fibrosis of most of the peripheral nerve can occur in severe cases. Areas of degeneration may alternate with areas of regeneration in cases of partial paralysis.

The etiology of Bell's palsy remains a great enigma. Some recent reports indicate that Bell's palsy may be a polyneuropathy involving other cranial nerves such as the ninth, the fifth, the vestibular division of the eighth, and the opposite presumably uninvolved seventh nerve. Bell's palsy may perhaps be a localized manifestation of an illness (such as Guillain–Barré syndrome) that can produce polyneuropathy. A localized immunologic disorder may underlie the increased susceptibility of the face to paralysis. Other possible etiologies are cold susceptibilities, viral infection, ischemia of the nerve, and a localized immuno-logic disorder.

Animal studies have been reported that show that a paralysis similar to Bell's can be created by autoimmune mechanisms. Such studies offer a rational basis for using suppressive steroid treatment at the onset of the paralysis. Steroids may not be effective, however, once the antigenic edema has compressed the nerve to produce ischemia and degeneration of nerve fiber or sheath. A critical time seems to exist when the edema exerts its coup de grace. If cortisone has not been used to prevent his edema, then surgical decompression may be needed to avert the effects of the edema on nerve fiber or sheath.

Natural History and Its Modification with Treatment

The facial nerve may be the most frequently paralyzed nerve in the body. Sir Charles Bell studied the peripheral nerves extensively in the early part of the 19th century and is responsible for demonstrating that the seventh nerve controls the muscles of expression.

Clinical progression is described under Plans and Follow-up. Recovery usually reaches its maximum in 9 months. Patients with a mild or incomplete paralysis have a greater chance of good recovery. Recovery in the patient over 50 is generally poorer than in those younger.

Recurrent paralysis occurs in about 5% of patients. Alternate paralysis involving the opposite nerve is seen rarely with an acute attack. The recurrence, however, may be either ipsilateral or contralateral.

Taste may fail before the onset of paralysis and return before motor function is noted. The return of tearing with epiphora may indicate that muscle function may soon recur.

Synkinesis, muscle weakness, contracture, facial spasm, and permanent ocular changes may be seen as long-term sequelae of the paralysis. Evaluation of adequate functional return is exceedingly difficult and varies with each observer. A photographic recording of both sides of the face in repose and with various expressions is probably the only objective method of reporting that can be analyzed by an independent observer.

Prevention

Generally speaking, there is no method known to prevent Bell's palsy; however, a recurrent case—repeated paralysis on the same side—should have a facial nerve decompression operation (opening of the fallopian canal) to prevent the immediate ischemic effects of recurrent edema and to avoid another paralytic episode in the future.

Cost Containment

Patients with Bell's palsy do not usually need x-rays, laboratory work, or cultures. Only a careful neurologic and otologic examination is needed for accurate diagnosis. If the physician is experienced in following several cases a year, referral is probably not needed; however, the patient's best interests are served if the physician unfamiliar with management of Bell's palsy refers the case to an otologist or neurologist.

REFERENCES

Adour KK. Medical management of idiopathic (Bell's) palsy. Otolaryngol Clin North Am 1991;24:663.
Austin JR, Peskind SP, Austin SG, Rice DH. Idiopathic facial nerve paralysis. Laryngoscope 1993;103:1326.
Birch CA. The Bell of Bell's palsy. London, Medical News Tribune, July 14, 1979.
Facial nerve manual. Am J Otol 1988;95:6 and 1989;10:1,4,5.
Fitzgerald DC. Role of electrical stimulation therapy for Bell's palsy. Am J Otol 1993;14:413.
Hughes GB. Practical management of Bell's palsy. Otolaryngol Head Neck Surg 1990;102:658.
May M, Klein SR, Taylor FH. Idiopathic (Bell's) facial palsy: Natural history defies steroid or surgical treatment. Laryngoscope 1985;95:406.
Nieuwmeyer PA, Visser SL, Feenstra L. Bell's palsy: A polyneuropathy. Am J Otol 1985;6:250.
Yanagiharan N, ed. Etiology and pathophysiology of Bell's palsy. Ann Otol Rhinol Laryngol 1988;97(suppl.):6.

CHAPTER 21–16

Glomus Tumor of the Ear

John S. Turner, Jr., M.D.

DEFINITION

A highly vascular tumor usually developing the middle ear from paraganglionic cells is known as a *glomus tumor*.

ETIOLOGY

The cause of a glomus tumor is unknown.

CRITERIA FOR DIAGNOSIS
Suggestive

Most glomus tumors grow insidiously for years and are diagnosed after the age of 30 when a pulsating tinnitus begins.

Definitive

Otoscopy indicates an obvious reddish blush just behind or partially involving the eardrum. A patient with these findings should have appropriate radiologic confirmation with computed tomography, arteriography, or magnetic resonance imaging.

The findings of a reddish blush involving the eardrum or the area just behind the eardrum in a patient with the complaint of pulsating tinnitus is usually sufficient evidence to substantiate the diagnosis of a glomus tumor. Confirmation depends on arteriography and otologic surgery to remove the highly vascular tumor.

CLINICAL MANIFESTATIONS
Subjective

The patient usually seeks medical help because of fullness, hearing loss, or actual pain in the ear in association with a pulsating sensation. In neglected cases, the tumor may actually protrude into the ear canal, and secondary infection then causes otorrhea. Repeated antibiotic treatment may have been given on several occasions for a "red ear." Some patients mention that the ear has been opened with myringotomy and a sudden rush of blood occurred that required ear packing.

Glomus tumors may be confined to the middle ear or temporal bone area. They may extend along the base of the skull, into the neck, or intracranially into the posterior or middle fossa. Therefore, symptoms related to extension may develop, such as hoarseness, neck pain, dysphagia, ataxia, headache, slurred speech, total unilateral deafness, dizziness, facial paralysis or weakness, and facial pain. Bilateral glomus tumors have been observed many times, so clinical manifestations do not have to be confined to one side. Actual bleeding from the ear may be noticed by the patient, but this is a relatively late complaint. Family history is noncontributory.

Objective
Physical Examination

The most significant finding is the reddish blush seen in the middle ear just behind the drum. A pathognomonic sign called *Brown's sign* can be obtained with a pneumatic otoscope (see Plans, Diagnostic). Unexplained facial weakness may have been developing insidiously for several months. Mirror examination may reveal a vocal cord paralysis or loss of gag reflex and deviation of the palate in those patients with extensive glomus jugulare tumors.

Spontaneous nystagmus, positional nystagmus, ataxia, and hyporeactive responses on caloric testing can be found in some tumors depending on size. Drum perforation and purulent drainage are present in eroding tumors, and the diagnosis of neoplasm is quite evident. Conductive hearing loss may be missed in small glomus tympanicum tumors or may be profound in large jugulare tumors. Total deafness or severe sensorineural hearing loss can be found in large eroding tumors. The impedance bridge findings (tympanometry) may be highly suggestive of glomus tumor because a constant pulsating record is obtained with the probe in the affected ear. Horner's syndrome or jugulare foramen syndrome may be present in the jugulare tumor. An arterial bruit may be heard in large tumors.

Routine Laboratory Abnormalities

The results of routine laboratory studies are usually normal.

PLANS
Diagnostic
Differential Diagnosis

A patient with pulsating tinnitus, mild conductive hearing loss, or intermittent ear pain should have a complete otolaryngologic evaluation, including air and bone audiometry and tympanometry. Pulsating tympanometry findings or a conductive hearing loss and possible absent stapedial reflex from seventh nerve involvement may be found.

Diagnostic Options and Recommended Approach

Brown's sign may be elicited by compressing the drum with a pneumatic otoscope. As the pressure is slowly increased, the observer notes an increasingly visible pulsation until finally the tumor blanches and the pulsations cease. Then, as the pressure is slowly released, the pulsations recur, reaching a maximum and then diminishing again as the intrameatal pressure returns to normal. This observation is pathognomonic of glomus tumor in the middle ear.

Complete x-ray studies are mandatory and should include routine mastoid views, polytomography of the temporal bone, and, unless a small tympanicum tumor is evident, computed tomography and arteriography with subtraction studies. Jugulography of the internal jugular vein may demonstrate a tumor actually hanging down into the lumen in some cases. Plans for embolization of the tumor at the time of arteriography are often made in highly suspect cases to obviate repeat arteriography.

Metastatic forms of glomus tumors are seen rarely, but these may represent multiple foci of disease rather than true metastasis. If headache is severe or if any cardiac or blood pressure abnormalities are noted, the patient should have vanillylmandelic acid studies to identify or exclude the very rare hormone-secreting glomus tumor. The physician should be aware that other foci can be seen along the aortic arch or in the area of the carotid body. Intraabdominal forms have also been reported.

The differential diagnosis includes chronic ear infection with granulation tissue (aural polyp), a metastatic tumor of the temporal bone, eosinophilic granuloma of the temporal bone, hemangioma of the eardrum or canal skin, a parotid tumor extending into the ear, middle ear hemorrhage from barotrauma, hemosiderin deposits from otitis media with effusion, and anomalous carotid artery. Simultaneous carotid body and glomus tumors may occur, or a patient may have a carotid body tumor on one side and a glomus tumor on the other side.

Therapeutic

The preferred treatment for glomus tumors is surgery. Radiation therapy and embolization therapy or various combinations of these three modalities may be needed in a particular patient.

Except in aged patients, the tumor should not be neglected. Progres-

sive growth occurs either rapidly or slowly, and extensive destruction of structures in and around the temporal bone occurs if the tumor is not treated.

The patient should be referred to an otolaryngologist experienced in temporal bone tumor management. This tumor ranks with cavernous hemangioma as a highly vascular neoplasm, and profuse hemorrhage may occur during surgery. Cryosurgery or hypothermic techniques may be necessary. Preoperative embolization is often used.

The serious nature of the problem should be explained to patient and family. The importance of early removal before destruction develops should be explained. Unless a very small tympanicum tumor is present, the patient should be alerted to the possibility of deafness, facial paralysis, chronic ear drainage, continual pain, or death in the large invasive glomus tumor. All these complications may occur with treatment of the large tumors also.

FOLLOW-UP

Lifetime follow-up by the treating physician should be done to identify insidious recurrences, which may occur after all forms of therapy. Rare metastatic forms are reported, but this author has never observed a metastatic case, even with 20 years of follow-up in a number of cases.

DISCUSSION
Prevalence

The tumor is uncommon but not rare. Cadaver studies show more tumors than are manifest clinically.

Related Basic Science

The glomus tumor was first described by Stacy Guild in 1941 in cadaver studies. The middle ear form of the disorder was reported by Rossenwasser in 1945. These tumors may occur anywhere that glomus bodies are present. The most common sites are the carotid bifurcations, the aortic arch, under the fingernails, and on the dome of the jugular bulb in the temporal bone. They develop in the temporal bone in relation to branches of the ninth or tenth nerve.

Anatomic Derangement

Histologically, the tumor consists of collections of epithelioid cells (Zell–Ballen) dispersed around a rich network of vascular channels. This makes the tumor highly vascular and leads to severe hemorrhage during surgery. Metastases have been recorded, but these instances are rare. Mitotic figures are only rarely seen in the primary focus. The blood supply usually comes from the ascending pharyngeal branch of the external carotid artery, but some feeding vessels from the vertebrobasilar system may be present. In the invasive form with intracranial extension, multiple feeding vessels may be present.

The vascular elements of the tumor may respond to radiation; associated fibrosis acts to impair some of the tumor blood supply. Embolization techniques may accomplish this also. The basic tumor cells respond very poorly, however, and radiation is of virtually no use in the large invasive tumors.

Physiologic Derangement

As in other chemodectomas, hormonal section of norepinephrine may occur with associated cardiovascular effects. This can be evaluated by the collection of 24-hour urine samples for vanillylmandelic acid.

The glomus jugulare tumor's nerve and blood supplies, which are from the glossopharyngeal nerve and ascending pharyngeal artery, are the same as for the carotid body.

Natural History and Its Modification with Treatment

Glomus tumors are the most commonly seen middle ear neoplasm. They are seen primarily in adults (the youngest patient known to this author is 18), but they may be seen at any age. In large series, 80% of patients are female. The tumor may grow insidiously for years before definitive symptoms develop. Usually the first sign is a slight tinnitus, which soon becomes pulsatile; ear fullness develops later. The author has a documented case living 50 years after diagnosis with the tumor extruding from the ear and facial paralysis.

The clinical course depends on the classification of the tumor and the stage at which diagnosis is made. These tumors may be of three types:

- *Glomus tympanicum tumors* are confined to the promontory of the middle ear and are usually small and amenable to total excision.
- *Tympanomastoid glomus tumors* may develop from one or several loci and spread throughout the middle ear and mastoid. These can usually be resected with extensive mastoid surgery.
- *Glomus jugulare tumors* develop on the dome of the jugular vein and may grow downward into the vein itself or erode the base of the temporal bone to ultimately invade multiple sites of the skull. Some of these may be massive with tumor proliferation in the neck and middle or posterior fossa.

Some authors report cranial nerve involvement in almost 40% of patients and intracranial extensions in about 15%. This author has not seen cranial neural paralysis in this high a percentage of patients. As mentioned under Follow-up, the tumor often persists even after resection, as small loci in bony canaliculi may be virtually impossible to remove completely.

Prevention

At present there is no proven method for the prevention of glomus tumor of the ear.

Cost Containment

Careful examination of the eardrum and middle ear may indicate that only a small glomus tympanicum tumor is present, and elaborate preoperative evaluation for more extensive types of glomus tumors is not indicated.

REFERENCES

Brown JS. Glomus jugulare tumors revisited: A ten-year statistical follow-up of 231 cases. Laryngoscope 1985;95:284.

Brown LA. Glomus jugulare tumors of the middle ear: Clinical aspects. Laryngoscope 1953;63:281.

Farvior JB, Packer JT. Glomus tumors of the temporal bone. Otolaryngol Head Neck Surg 1991;104:24.

Ghani G, Sung YF, Per-Lee JH. Glomus jugulare tumors: Origin, pathology and anesthetic considerations. Anesth Analg (Cleve) 1983;62:686.

Guild SR. A hitherto unrecognized structure, the glomus jugulare, in man. Anat Rec 1941;79(suppl. 2):28.

Karas DE, Kwartler JA. Glomus tumors: A fifty year historical perspective. Am J Otol 1993;14:495.

McCaffrey T, Meyer F, Michels V, et al. Familial paragangliomas of the head and neck. Arch Otol Head Neck Surg 1994;120:1211.

Rossenwasser H. Carotid body tumor of the middle ear and mastoid. Arch Otolaryngol 1945;41:64.

CHAPTER 21–17

Pharyngitis

Gerald S. Gussack, M.D.

DEFINITION

Pharyngitis is defined as an inflammatory process involving the posterior pharyngeal wall, tonsils, nasopharynx, hypopharynx, and/or lateral pharyngeal walls.

ETIOLOGY

Gram-positive bacteria, particularly group A beta-hemolytic streptococcal species, *Moraxella catarrhalis,* and *Hemophilus influenzae,* are common etiologies. Multiple viral etiologies also exist, particularly rhinoviruses.

CRITERIA FOR DIAGNOSIS

Suggestive

The clinical setting is usually one of the patient presenting with increasing pain, particularly on swallowing, with fever, malaise, and generalized discomfort of the throat.

Definitive

The definitive diagnosis is made by observing the pharynx in a state of erythema and inflammation with exudate present.

CLINICAL MANIFESTATIONS

Subjective

The patient complains of difficulty swallowing, pain in the throat, bad breath, and symptoms of general malaise. Environmental factors other than exposure to an individual with acute upper respiratory tract infection are usually not relevant criteria. Seasonally, this disease is seen more often in the fall and winter. The most common symptom associated with pharyngitis is that of pain on swallowing. This is followed by fever, malaise, and foul-smelling breath, in that order. The patient may have a toxic appearance in advanced stages. Rapid onset of symptoms and progression to a toxic state should alert one to the possibility of a resistant strain of *Streptococcus.*

Objective

Physical Examination

The most dominant physical finding is that of erythema with or without exudate of one or more of the anatomic structures of the pharynx. The most common appearance is that of erythema of the posterior pharyngeal wall. This can also present as a vesicular eruption or isolated inflamed lymphoid follicles. Examination of the neck also reveals mild to moderate anterior cervical adenopathy, which is distributed along the internal jugular chain of lymph nodes. These are often somewhat tender to palpation. Mirror examination of the larynx and hypopharynx often reveals inflammation, which extends inferiorly along the posterior pharyngeal wall and may involve the lateral pharyngeal wall and pyriform sinuses. Characteristically, the larynx is not involved. Otologic and nasal examination and the remainder of the head and neck examination are usually within normal limits. When mononucleosis is the etiology of the patient's pharyngitis, then other physical findings are usually present. These patients can have extreme tonsillar hypertrophy with near-total obstruction of the posterior oral pharynx. In addition, there is usually associated large cervical adenopathy and splenomegaly.

Routine Laboratory Abnormalities

The routine laboratory studies obtained in these patients may demonstrate several abnormalities. The complete blood count shows evidence of acute infection with elevation in the white blood count and a shift toward more premature elements in the polymorphonuclear leukocytes.

PLANS

Diagnostic

Throat cultures should be obtained to look for group A beta-hemolytic streptococcal infections. These may be performed in the office by plating the swabs onto a blood agar plate and incubating them overnight. The presence of beta hemolysis is defined as a clear zone around the bacterial colony and indicates the presence of the group A subtype. Rapid strep screens are also currently available and help to confirm the presence of these particular bacteria. Urine screening for agglutinins is also available. Other bacterial pathogens in the head and neck include *Hemophilus influenzae, Neisseria gonorrhoeae,* and *Moraxella catarrhalis.* Unfortunately, Gram-positive and Gram-negative bacteria are often demonstrated in cultures of routine asymptomatic individuals. When one suspects a gonorrheal pharyngitis by history of sexual exposure with an infected individual, then culture should be made on Thayer Martin media and incubated under appropriate atmospheric environments with increased carbon dioxide.

Diphtheria infections are mentioned from a standpoint of completeness. The frequency of this infection is quite rare. The diagnosis is made by a slow onset of symptoms with a hoarse, croupy cough. The presence of a grayish white membrane of the posterior pharyngeal wall that bleeds on removal is the classic description. The demonstration of *Corynebacterium diptheriae* confirms the diagnosis. Treatment for *diptheriae* includes high-dose penicillin G infusions and diphtheria antitoxin.

Additional diagnostic tests, with the exception of culture, are not usually indicated.

Therapeutic

Therapeutic Options

The predominant therapy for pharyngitis is dependent on the suspected clinical pathogen. Those individuals who have suspected viral upper respiratory tract infection, having had negative throat cultures and a typical clinical picture consistent with myalgia and malaise, are treated with analgesics, hydration, and bed rest. The usual patient notes moderate improvement in 24 to 48 hours on this regimen. Antibiotics remain the mainstay of therapy for those patients with bacterial infections, and the antibiotic is directed toward the suspected pathogen. The most commonly cultured bacteria include streptococcal species, *Moraxella catarrhalis, Staphylococcus aureus,* diphtheroids, and *Hemophilus influenzae.* One drawback of basing treatment on culture results is that *Staphylococcus aureus,* diphtheroids, and *H. influenzae* can often be cultured from a normal person's tonsils, which can add confusion in the diagnosis. *Hemophilus influenzae* is a common core pathogen within the deep portion of the tonsils but is seldom cultured from the surface. *Streptococcus pyogenes* (beta-hemolytic streptococcus) group A is usually cultured from the core of recurrently infected tonsils. The mixed anaerobic and aerobic growth is also seen in chronically infected tonsils along with β-lactamase-producing organisms. These can complicate the choice of antibiotic therapy. *Streptococcus pyogenes* is the infecting organism that commonly involves the tonsils and is of concern to the clinician because of the risk of rheumatic fever. Winter and early spring remain the peak months for streptococcal pharyngitis.

Traditional teaching has held that the utilization of antibiotics prior to culture results was unacceptable as this did not increase the risk for the development of rheumatic fever. These practices, though limiting the overutilization of antibiotics, often unacceptably prolonged the fever and discomfort the patients sustained. Subsequently, the treatment of streptococcal pharyngitis with penicillin 600,000,000 to 1.2 U intramuscularly or penicillin V 25 to 50 mg/kg per day in four divided doses orally for 10 days is the treatment of choice. Early treatment of pharyngitis has led to quicker elimination of fever and sore throat and earlier return to normal daily activity. The rapid strep screen, detecting streptococcus specific antigens on a throat swab, has also helped in the elimination of awaiting culture results for therapy. For those patients who are penicillin resistant, erythromycin 30 to 50 mg/kg per day in four divided doses is a good alternative. When *Moraxella catarrhalis* infections are present, then antibiotic coverage with amoxicillin–clavulanate 250 to 500 mg or cefixime 100 to 400 mg daily is indicated. Oral hydration and analgesics and rest provide the remainder of the therapy. Vancomycin is used when resistant streptococcal infections are suspected.

Surgery is reserved for complications of pharyngitis, most specifically, peritonsillar abscesses. Occasionally, pharyngitis may lead to inflammation and suppuration of retropharyngeal and parapharyngeal lymph nodes with the development of a deep neck infection. These obviously require surgical drainage as described in another chapter. Patients who have recurrent episodes of tonsillitis greater than four per year or six in 2 years or have peritonsillar abscess or rheumatic fever should be considered for a tonsillectomy. This operation was once performed quite frequently for even minor episodes of tonsillitis and/or tonsillar hypertrophy. The present indications are more strict.

Recommended Approach

Early initiation of antibiotics, analgesics, antipyretics, and rest is recommended. Adequate hydration and close follow-up are important.

The patient and family should be educated about the etiology and therapeutic recommendations. Patients who rest, obtain good hydration, and complete the entire antibiotic course uniformly show dramatic improvement over a 48- to 72-hour period. It is imperative that the patient understand that the entire course of the antibiotics needs to be completed. Complications such as deep neck infections and peritonsillar abscess may occur. The patient should be alert for worsening of symptoms, trismus, rapid development of inflammatory changes in the neck or hypopharynx, or increased pain. Those patients with recurrent tonsillitis and greater than four episodes per year may be educated about the need for tonsillectomy.

FOLLOW-UP

The prognosis for these patients is usually excellent. Follow-up at 7 to 14 days at the completion of therapy is usually sufficient. It is unnecessary to repeat other laboratory studies such as complete blood count and throat culture or other diagnostic studies.

DISCUSSION

Prevalence

Pharyngitis is a common infection.

Related Basic Science

Pharyngitis is usually of viral or bacterial origin. *Streptococcus pyogenes* remains the most treatable organism with the highest potential for complications. Most clinically significant are rheumatic fever and glomerulonephritis. The tendency to prescribe antibiotic therapy prior to definitive diagnoses was resisted in the past. This has recently become accepted as both cost effective and appropriate, as these patients seem to demonstrate an improved overall clinical course. The mouth and pharynx have present a normal bacterial flora. Certain bacteria may be demonstrated in culture that are pathogenic. The recent emergence of penicillin-resistant streptococcal infections is a major concern. These infections are seen in patients treated with multiple course of antibiotics and those in daycare settings. They can be devastating infections and result in multiple-organ failure and systemic toxicity. Treatment with high-dose vancomycin is indicated if this etiology is suspected.

Natural History and Its Modification with Treatment

The natural history of the disease is that of a relatively self-limited course that subsides after 72 hours. Patients who have persistent symptoms following this, especially those with unilateral tonsillar swellings, should be investigated for abscesses.

Prevention

Patients who are prone to recurrent episodes of pharyngitis may be considered for tonsillectomy and/or adenoidectomy. The recurrence and persistence of this disease along with the demonstration of chronic cryptic tonsils may prove to be of benefit. The risk of surgery in these patients is bleeding in the immediate postoperative period or delayed at 7 days.

Utilization of pneumococcal vaccine and other environmental changes have not resulted in any significant decrease in the incidence or prevention of this disease. Avoiding exposure to infected individuals may be considered.

Cost Containment

Utilization of rapid strep screen as opposed to formal throat cultures should be considered in the initial treatment of patients with pharyngitis. Utilization of penicillin versus other more expensive antibiotics is also of benefit in decreasing these costs when resistant streptococcus is not suspected.

REFERENCES

Fried MP, Forest JL. Peritonsillitis: Evaluation of current therapy. Arch Otolaryngol 1981;107:283.

Kaplan EL. The group A streptococcal pharyngitis: The problem of differentiating acute infection from carrier state in the symptomatic child. J Infect Dis 1971;123:490.

Kornblut AD. The tonsils and adenoids. Otolaryngol Clin North Am. 1987;20(2).

Nelson SD. The effect of penicillin therapy on the symptoms and signs of streptococcal pharyngitis. Pediatr Infect Dis J 1985;3:10.

Sugita R, Kawamura S, Icikawa G. Microorganisms isolated from peritonsillar abscesses and indicated chemotherapy. Arch Otolaryngol 1982;108:655.

CHAPTER 21-18

Deep Neck Infection

Gerald S. Gussack, M.D.

DEFINITION

Deep neck infections are collections of bacterial and other associated inflammatory cells and exudate within the fascial spaces of the neck.

ETIOLOGY

The etiology includes bacterial infections from upper respiratory and aerodigestive tract sources that spread through the lymphatic and fascial spaces of the neck. Dental infections are a common source of bacteria that may spread to the neck.

CRITERIA FOR DIAGNOSIS
Suggestive

Patients presenting with rapid swelling, tenderness, and erythema should be suspected of developing these infections. Trismus, pain on moving the neck, and dysphagia for solids are all suspicious findings.

Definitive

Definitive diagnosis is established either radiographically by contrast computed tomography (CT) or magnetic resonance imaging. A loculated low-density area with peripheral enhancement is suggested by CT scan. Magnetic resonance imaging demonstrates a high signal on T1 and T2 WI. Purulent collections found by needle aspiration or surgical exploration are diagnostic.

The fascial spaces are normally potential spaces and do not become true spaces until there is fluid collection within them. Deep neck infections have the potential to be life-threatening problems and can have extreme morbidity if not treated appropriately.

CLINICAL MANIFESTATIONS
Subjective

The patient has symptoms referable to pain, difficulty swallowing, tenderness over the neck, fever, dysphagia, foreign body sensation, or swelling in the neck. The symptoms are determined by the exact anatomic location of the deep neck infection and the size and associated inflammatory component. The tenderness usually increases over several days to 1 week. Patients may also present quite ill and exhibit symptoms of sepsis in association with the other mentioned symptoms. When these infections involve the fascial spaces adjacent to the larynx, hypopharynx, and/or trachea, then symptoms of airway obstruction may be present.

Objective
Physical Examination

The most common objective finding in the patient is tenderness in the associated area of the infection with decreased range of motion in the ability either to turn the neck, to open the mouth, or to swallow. Objective findings in patients with deep neck infections include induration and erythema associated with the mass at the anterior border of the sternocleidomastoid muscle. Swelling in the area adjacent to the tonsil may be present in peritonsillar space infections. Swelling of the parotid gland may be present in infections involving the parotid space. The areas in question are often quite tender.

Routine Laboratory Abnormalities

The white blood count may be abnormally elevated with a shift of polymorphor leukocytes.

PLANS
Diagnostic
Differential Diagnosis

The medical history and physical examination can very often confirm the diagnosis of deep neck infection. The distinction between cellulitis and abscess requires further diagnostic procedures. These may include a large-bore needle aspiration of the area in question, with a return of purulent material confirming the diagnosis of an abscess. CT scans are most helpful in delineating the fascial spaces of the neck and demonstrating a low-density area within the fascial space being consistent with an abscess. Edema secondary to cellulitis may be present as the only finding on physical examination and/or CT.

Diagnostic Options and Recommended Approach

Early initiation of antibiotics preceded by cultures of the pharynx, abscess cavity, or both by needle aspiration is recommended as is contrast CT of the head and neck.

Therapeutic
Therapeutic Options

The treatment of deep neck infections depends on determining whether abscess formation had occurred. Those patients in whom infections have then led to abscess formation require incision and drainage. The operation is designed to provide the most direct access to those fascial spaces involved in the infection. Most commonly this involves making an incision along the anterior border of the sternocleidomastoid muscle and draining the fascial space and lymph nodes in the carotid sheath. Wounds are usually left open and packed two to three times per day and allowed to heal by second intention. Specimens are sent for culture and sensitivity, and antibiotic therapy is directed toward the treatment of the specific bacterial or fungal pathogen. Routine histologic specimens are also submitted. The pathogens are usually Gram-positive organisms, most commonly staphylococcal and anaerobic infections. A large percentage of these may have mixed bacterial floras. Third-generation cephalosporin antibiotics such as cefuroxine 1.5 g intravenously three times daily are a good choice for coverage. Clindamycin 300 to 600 mg intravenously every 8 hours is also appropriate. Ampicillin/sulbactam (Unasyn) 1 to 5 g intravenously every 8 hours offers excellent aerobic and anaerobic coverage.

For those infections that present with cellulitis or inflammation alone, high-dose antibiotic therapy, bed rest, and hydration are used.

Recommended Approach

Early surgical exploration and drainage are recommended for those treatments that do not respond to antibiotic treatment.

Education of the primary care physician as to the etiology and clinical presentation of deep neck infections is important. These infections can progress rapidly and result in severe airway compromise in a very short period. The patient should be informed of the severity of the situation and need for immediate hospitalization with diagnostic and therapeutic measures instituted immediately.

FOLLOW-UP

Close follow-up of these patients is important to determine that primary healing has taken place and no wound-related complications have occurred. Vascular injury, thrombophlebitis of the internal jugular vein, and chronic draining of sinus tracts may occur.

DISCUSSION

Prevalence and Incidence

The prevalence and incidence of deep neck infection are not known.

Related Basic Science

The fascia of the neck is classically divided into two layers: the superficial and the deep layers. The superficial layer is mentioned for the sake of completeness but does not impact greatly on the clinical picture of deep neck infections. It invests the muscles of facial expression and platysma muscle in the neck. The deep layer of the fascia is divided into three layers. These are appropriately named the superficial, middle, and deep components of the deep cervical fascia. The superficial layer contains the submandibular glands parotid, sternocleidomastoid, and trapezius muscles. It forms the lateral aspect of the carotid sheath. The middle layer of the deep cervical fascia is known as the visceral fascia, because it invests the thyroid gland and esophagus. Deep neck infections that are caused by leaks by perforation of the esophagus from foreign body ingestion or instrumentation involve this space. The middle layer of the fascia forms the medial aspect of the carotid sheath. The deep layer of the deep cervical fascia invests the vertebral bodies and the structures behind the pharynx. The potential space between the middle and deep layers of the deep cervical fascia can connect to the mediastinum down to the level of the diaphragm. Because of this, infections that arise in this space have the potential to develop into mediastinitis, and severe subsequent complications can result. Lymph nodes are present throughout the carotid sheath and respond to inflammatory processes of the upper aerodigestive tract. Rapid swelling and suppuration may take place within a lymph node and serve as the most common etiology for spontaneous deep neck infections.

Infections can also arise from the peritonsillar area and extend into the parapharyngeal space. These patients may present with trismus and dysphagia.

Other congenital anomalies may serve as an etiology for deep neck infection. The most common of these is branchial cleft cysts. Patients with a history of intravenous drug abuse are also at risk for deep neck infection. These individuals often use the internal jugular vein as a site for venous access and may develop thrombosis or thrombophlebitis of the vein. Septic emboli may also lodge in distal branches of the external carotid artery and form infection and possible aneurysm formation. Arteriography should be used prior to surgical drainage of these infections in patients who are intravenous drug abusers.

Natural History and Its Modification with Treatment

Untreated, deep neck infections may extend along the fascial planes into the posterior or sometimes the anterior mediastinum. This scenario could result in severe morbidity or death secondary to mediastinitis. Large abscess collections in the neck can also lead to tracheal and laryngeal compression with subsequent airway obstruction. Thrombophlebitis or thrombosis of the jugular vein is also seen. This can lead to retrograde thrombosis of the lateral sinus and severe intracranial problems. The frequency of these complications, along with the severity of their morbidity, is related to the particular fascial plane involved and the delay in initiation of treatment.

Mortality in deep neck infections should be preventable in almost all treated cases. The recovery and healing phases of these diseases may be quite prolonged.

Prevention

Early and appropriate treatment of upper respiratory infections of the head and neck is of benefit in preventing progression to a deep neck infection. Recognition of iatrogenic injuries on instrumentation of the esophagus and trachea is important along with the investigation of certain perforations of the esophagus and pharynx by foreign body ingestion.

Cost Containment

Prompt recognition of the signs and symptoms of deep neck infections and early recognition by physical examination are a necessity. Appropriate diagnostic studies in the early evaluation of these infections help in determining the necessity and early treatment by surgical drainage. Culture and sensitivity samples taken by needle aspiration of the mass or at the time of surgical drainage are indicated. High-dose antibiotic therapy directed by culture results must be instituted early. The least expensive antibiotic with Gram-positive and oral anaerobic coverage should be instituted. Penicillin, clindamycin, and third-generation cephalosporin antibiotics administered intravenously are appropriate. Gram-negative bacteria are not commonly seen, and their coverage is not usually indicated. One diagnostic study, a contrast-enhanced CT scan, should be sufficient in determining the affected anatomy and abscess locations and dimensions, and in judging the best approach. Arteriography should be reserved for those patients with a history of intravenous drug abuse, a pulsatile mass on physical examination, or a history of expectorating blood, which may indicate arterial erosion.

REFERENCES

Endicott JW, Nelson RJ, Suraceno CA. Diagnosis and management decisions in infections of the deep fascial spaces of the head and neck utilizing computerized tomography. Laryngoscope 1982;92:630.

Geelhoed GW, Joseph WL. Surgical sequelae of drug abuse. Surg Gynecol Obstet 1974;139:749.

Grodinsky M, Holyoke A. The fascia and fascial spaces of the head, neck, and adjacent region. Am J Anat 1938;63:367.

Gussack GS. Deep neck infection. In: Shockley W, ed. Neck diagnosis and treatment. St. Louis: Mosby, 1993;619.

Hollingshead WH, ed. Anatomy for surgeons: The head and neck. 2nd ed. Vol I. New York: Harper & Row, 1968.

Levitt G. Cervical fascia and deep neck infections. Otolaryngol Clin North Am 1976;9:703.

Chronic Facial Pain

Gerald S. Gussack, M.D.

DEFINITION

Chronic facial pain is defined as a constellation of symptoms consisting of continued discomfort in the face and jaws for a period of at least 4 weeks with no obvious etiology present.

ETIOLOGY

The etiology is likely multifactorial and can include vascular loops on cranial nerves, viral inflammations of sensory nerves, and degenerative changes of the temporomandibular joints.

CRITERIA FOR DIAGNOSIS

Suggestive

The clinical setting is usually one of increasing discomfort with little response to normal analgesic therapy. The etiology of the pain is often elusive.

Definitive

The definitive diagnosis is made when other etiologies are excluded and the pain persists for at least 4 weeks.

CLINICAL MANIFESTATIONS

Subjective

The typical patient is usually in his or her second to fourth decade and presents with complaints of discomfort of long-standing duration. These individuals often have seen other physicians or dentists and been treated for presumptive diagnoses of upper respiratory tract infections, sinusitis, otitis, temporal mandibular joint dysfunction, or migraine headaches. The symptoms may range from mild numbness or occasional tenderness over the preauricular area or maxilla to severe incapacitating pain that interferes with the patient's ability to work or function in society.

The patient complains of pain in the facial area that is usually present on a daily basis. The pain may radiate to the neck or posteriorly to the head. Depending on the etiology, other symptoms such as nasal, dental, neurologic, or dermatologic may be present. Environmental factors usually are not relevant; however, some chronic facial pain syndromes may be triggered by nasal symptoms such as rhinitis. Family history and past medical history usually are not contributory. Some patients have histories of previous pain syndromes in other anatomic sites. A history of poor response to therapy is usually present. Psychological overlays to their pain with depression are commonly seen.

Objective

Physical Examination

The objective findings in chronic facial pain syndromes can be quite subtle. The majority of findings are related to the etiologic factors when these are present. Successful definition of an etiology occurs in only 50% of these cases. A complete head and neck examination with particular attention to the ears, nasal cavity, oropharynx, and hypopharynx should be performed. A complete cranial nerve examination should also be performed. Examination of the nose and facial skin is paramount. Subtle skin changes or muscle asymmetry may be present.

Routine Laboratory Abnormalities

There are no diagnostic routine laboratory abnormalities.

PLANS

Diagnostic

Differential Diagnosis

Malocclusion remains one of the most common associated factors in these individuals. The inability of the mandibular and maxillary molars to meet in an appropriate manner usually leads to degenerative changes within the temporomandibular joint over a period. These patients often "brux" or grind their teeth at night, contributing to their degenerative changes. The teeth should be observed for abnormal wear facets. Sinusitis can be another insidious cause of facial pain. Careful examination of the nose may reveal purulent drainage posteriorly or associated inflammatory changes of the nasal mucosa. Palpation and percussion of the sinuses may elicit pain.

Diagnostic Options and Recommended Approach

Careful examination of the oral cavity and dentition is important. Palpation of each molar and tooth is necessary to detect any possible abscess formation or to elicit a trigger point. Carious teeth may also be the source of this pain. Appropriate dental and mandible radiographs may be obtained if this is a consideration. Diseases of the salivary gland may also initiate facial pain. Palpation of the parotid and submandibular glands may reveal a mass lesion indicative of either tumor or possible inflammatory disease. Bimanual palpation of the floor of the mouth may demonstrate a stone or other source of obstruction of Wharton's duct.

Radiographs play an important role in the evaluation of these individuals. Depending on the history and clinical findings present on physical examination, various studies may be obtained. Routine sinus films serve as a screening study to define further anatomy within the paranasal sinuses. Open and closed views on plain films of the temporomandibular joint may show inadequate excursion or degenerative changes. Computed tomography (CT) scans of the sinuses and brain rule out or define pathology that may be the etiology in these areas. This is the most definitive diagnostic radiographic study and has the highest yield. Spheroid sinusitis is an often missed diagnosis in patients with chronic headaches or facial pain. This area is easily visualized on CT. When temporomandibular joint dysfunction is suspected, magnetic resonance imaging (MRI) of the joint may reveal a dislocation of the meniscus of the condylar head. Dental radiographs should be obtained when an abscessed tooth is considered.

Other objective findings can be quite subtle. Nerve sheath tumors may involve any branch of the trigeminal nerve and result in altered sensation or pain in that particular dermatomal distribution. Tumors of the paranasal sinuses may invade the trigeminal nerve or its branches and likewise cause facial dysesthesias. CT or MRI confirms anatomic involvement of these structures. Neurologic examination of the face with a pattern of dysesthesia or anesthesia in the V_1, V_2, or V_3 dermatome should be investigated for a trigeminal nerve etiology.

Therapeutic

Therapeutic Options

Treatment of chronic facial pain is aimed at determining the etiology and correcting this situation. Those patients with temporomandibular joint dysfunction are usually treated with combinations of dietary manipulations; anti-inflammatory medications such as ibuprofen 400 to 800 mg orally three times daily, aspiring, or other nonsteroidal anti-inflammatory drugs; and occlusal splints. Patients with sinusitis are treated with appropriate antibiotic therapy (see Chapter 21–29) in combination with systemic and topical decongestants and topical steroids. Amoxicillin 250 to 500 mg orally three times daily or cefaclor 250 to 500 mg orally three times daily is a good choice to initiate therapy.

Dental problems should be managed appropriately with incision and drainage, root canals, extraction, and so on. Salivary gland infections are treated with combinations of hydration, antistaphylococcal antibiotics (cephalexin 250 to 500 mg orally twice daily), and heat. Surgical drainage is indicated when abscess formation or stones are present.

A significant number of patients undergo extensive evaluation with no definite etiology determined. Patients with trigeminal neuralgia or tic douloureux are included in this group. Subjective improvement in symptoms of these patients has been achieved with oral anticonvulsant medications including phenytoin (Dilantin) and carbamazepine (Tegretol). A transcutaneous electrical nerve stimulator (TENS unit) may be used as an adjunctive measure in the pain management of tic douloureux or other pain syndromes. These units are usually available from physical therapists with an interest in the treatment of these disorders.

Surgery is used in the treatment of chronic facial pain syndrome under two conditions. The first of these is when a definitive etiology is most surely the cause of the symptoms. This is seen in dental or facial abscesses, sinusitis unresponsive to medical therapy, tumors, arteriovenous malformations, and temporomandibular joint disease unresponsive to diet, antiinflammatory drugs, physical therapy, and splint therapy. The recommendation for surgery to treat a symptom (e.g., chronic facial pain) should be entertained only after all other therapeutic measures have been exhausted. The surgeon should also temper her or his enthusiasm and inform the patient of the possibility of a less than completely favorable result. Physicians managing these patients primarily should also be advised that seeking surgical solutions to the problem of chronic facial pain syndrome may be not always in the patient's best interest. Postsurgical scarring and pain may compromise any therapeutic endeavor aimed at controlling these symptoms.

The second role for surgery in the management of chronic facial pain syndrome is for intractable symptoms relative to the trigeminal nerve. These procedures include posterior fossa decompression of vascular loops adjacent to the nerve and sectioning or ablation of selective branches of the trigeminal nerve. These procedures are again only carried out by surgeons with skill and experience in the treatment of this problem when all other therapeutic modalities have failed.

Recommended Approach

Recommended therapy is adjusted as outlined above according to the suspected etiology.

The patient should be informed about the difficulty and frustration experienced by both the individual patient and the physician in the management of chronic facial pain syndromes. This is especially true when no obvious etiology is present and the diagnosis is one of exclusion. Patience must be exercised by all of the parties, and initial unresponsiveness to one therapeutic modality should not be followed by a rapid change of plans. All of the possible contributing factors, including psychological and social influences may need to be investigated. The treating physician must realize that individuals who suffer pain are often the recipients of attention and kindness they might not otherwise receive. This provides a negative reinforcement for one to improve, as in the example of a wife whose husband is very demanding at other times. Often these patients substitute a new constellation of pain symptoms in a different anatomic area at a later date. A history of previous multiple surgeries (e.g., back surgery for chronic lumbar pain) must also be taken into careful consideration.

The patient should also be informed that pain may be the first symptom of a disease process that may manifest itself later. Careful follow-up should be considered.

FOLLOW-UP

The patient should be followed as long as symptoms persist, at least at bimonthly intervals. This obviously depends on the particular etiology that is felt to have caused this constellation of symptoms should this symptom complex change dramatically or physical signs appear. For example, a patient with several weeks of facial pain may develop a vesicular eruption consistent with a herpes zoster infection.

The physician should follow the patient with a clear goal of determining the etiology in mind. One should also keep this foremost, as effective therapy can be administered only when a proper diagnosis is in hand. Diagnostic studies, be they plain radiographs, dental examination, or CT scans, should be repeated when physical signs and symptoms so dictate.

DISCUSSION
Prevalence

Chronic facial pain syndrome is a fairly rare constellation of symptoms. It makes up approximately 1% of a general otolaryngology practice and may be significantly higher in a practice that specializes in oral pathology and oromandibular problems. The disease has a 4:1 to 5:1 female-to-male ratio in the author's experience. It peaks in the second to fourth decades but can be seen at any age.

Related Basic Science

The pathophysiology of chronic facial pain is almost always related to some irritation or dysfunction of the trigeminal nerve. The ophthalmic, maxillary, and mandibular branches of the trigeminal nerve provide sensation and proprioception to the three respective areas of the face. In addition, the motor branch of the trigeminal nerve provides innervation of the muscles of mastication. The paranasal sinuses are extensively innervated by distal branches of the maxillary or second division of the trigeminal nerve. The infraorbital nerve has extensive branching through the maxillary sinuses and teeth. Pain that is initiated in any distal branch of the nerve may refer or manifest itself along the entire path of the nerve all the way to the skull base and foramen rotundum or ovale. The presence of retroorbital pain is one common manifestation of this. The reader is referred to Chapter 21–14.

Natural History and Its Modification with Treatment

The morbidity of this disorder is directly related to the degree of severity and etiology. This may range from occasional discomfort that is easily managed with analgesics to severe dysfunction and total disability.

Complications are seen only when an etiology for this has gone undetected. Sphenoid sinusitis may progress to cavernous sinus thrombosis were this the etiology of the pain. Those patients who have an idiopathic etiology for their pain usually do not suffer any increased morbidity or complications. The pain and the patient often reach an equilibrium after a prolonged period.

Prevention

There is no known preventive measure currently available for this disease. A timely and accurate evaluation of symptoms may prevent a prolonged course when a treatable etiology exists.

Cost Containment

An accurate history and complete physical examination are the most cost-effective means of narrowing the scope of possible etiologies and directing therapy. Routine use of diagnostic imaging should be discouraged unless one is suspicious of a sinus or skull base etiology of the pain. Unfortunately, these are studies that both cost the most and yield the most accurate anatomic information.

From a therapeutic standpoint, antiinflammatory medications such as aspirin and ibuprofen may be used in preference to many costly prescription nonsteroidal preparations.

REFERENCES

Adams RD, Victor M. Principles of neurology. 3rd ed. New York: McGraw-Hill, 1985.

Chasin WP. Facial pain, neck pain and headache. In: Katz AE, ed. Manual of otolaryngology, head and neck therapeutics. Philadelphia: Lea & Febiger, 1986:313.

Golding Wood PH. Facial pain. In: Ballantyne J, Groves J. eds. Scott-Brown's diseases of the ear, nose and throat. 4th ed. Vol 3. London: Butterworth, 1984:361.

Guralnick W, Kaban LB, Merril RG. Temporomandibular joint afflictions. N Engl J Med 1978;229:123.

Pearson BW. ENT approach to face pain. Postgrad Med 1984;76:134.

CHAPTER 21–20

Neck Mass

Gerald S. Gussack, M.D.

DEFINITION

Neck mass is defined as the presence of an abnormal, visible, or palpable growth of tissue or fluid in the neck.

ETIOLOGY

The etiology of neck masses is related to the presence of growths of congenital or acquired cysts, tumors, or lymph nodes. These include benign and malignant growths, cysts, and infections.

CRITERIA FOR DIAGNOSIS

Suggestive

The onset of a visible or palpable growth in the neck defines the presence of a neck mass. This may have been present for a varying period and may be located in any part of the neck.

The diagnosis is usually an easy one. Neck masses are detected in male and female infants, young children, and adults. The clinical findings, especially the history, are most important in determining the etiology and developing a plan of therapy.

Definitive

The patient usually presents with a palpable and sometimes visible mass lesion in the neck. Age, duration, color, degree of fixation, and tenderness all have an impact on arriving at the proper diagnosis and etiology.

CLINICAL MANIFESTATIONS

Subjective

Neck masses can be present at any age and represent any number of underlying anatomic abnormalities. The mass may or may not be symptomatic, depending on the etiology.

Children can present with masses that may represent congenital abnormalities or inflammatory disorders. These are differentiated by location, cystic versus solid content, and general physical examination.

Adults may have masses that have been present for a variable length of time. The location and associated history must be considered. Patients who are over 40 years of age and have a history of smoking should be carefully investigated for carcinoma.

Neck masses that are red, tender, and associated with fever should be considered as lymphadenitis and investigated for an infectious etiology. Firm fixed lesions that are nontender or have overlying skin change are more likely to be malignant.

A careful history should be taken and a differential diagnosis formulated in all cases.

Questions posed to the patient should include age, duration of lesion, presence of fluctuation in size, and history of infection, cancer, or immune deficiency. Social history such as alcohol, smoking, and HIV risk factors should be considered.

Objective

Physical Examination

The location, size, and characteristics on palpation should give the examining physician an overall idea of the origin of the mass. The mass should be observed for overlying skin changes and possible fixation to the deep tissues. The mass is palpated to determine if it is cystic or solid and may be transilluminated if fluid is present.

A complete head and neck examination should be performed to determine if a primary site from which tumor may spread exists. The examination should include all the major sites, including the base of tongue, hypopharynx, nasopharynx, and middle ear. Serous effusions

with a neck mass should direct the examiner to look for a nasopharyngeal mass with possible eustachian tube obstruction. Palpation of the mass should reveal the characteristics listed in Table 21–20–1.

Cystic masses may represent an inflammatory or neoplastic lesion that has undergone malignant degeneration. Congenital lesions such as thyroglossal and bronchial cleft cysts often present as a cystic lesion. Congenital cystic lesions may also serve as the niche for inflammatory processes with subsequent lymphadenopathy or abscess.

Routine Laboratory Abnormalities

Routine laboratory studies are often normal on a screening examination for most patients. White blood counts may be elevated in inflammatory disorders. Monospot tests are ordered when mononucleosis is a clinical concern.

PLANS

Diagnostic

Differential Diagnosis

The diagnostic problem is to determine the nature of the mass. The differential diagnosis includes cyst, tumor, and infection.

Diagnostic Options

Needle aspiration performed by an experienced surgeon or cytopathologist remains the most important diagnostic study. The aspirate should be sent for cytopathologic evaluation in every case and sent for culture and sensitivity when inflammatory material is recovered. Several passes through the mass may be undertaken, and multiple planes of the mass may be aspirated. Specimens should be processed according to the standard fixation techniques recommended by each individual's pathologist.

When a definitive diagnosis can be obtained on cytology, then appropriate treatment may begin. A malignant process should never be totally ruled out when the needle aspirate fails to reveal cancer. Repeat aspiration or possible open biopsy should be performed.

Computed tomography scans are excellent means of evaluating masses in the neck. Iodinated contrast material should be employed unless a specific allergy is noted. This delineates the great vessels of the neck and also helps to distinguish inflammatory and malignant processes.

Open neck biopsies as an early diagnostic maneuver in the evaluation of neck masses should be condemned. The physician should have a thorough plan in mind prior to performing an open procedure in the neck. The surgeon should be prepared to perform a definitive procedure, such as a radical neck dissection, if a malignant process, such as

TABLE 21–20–1. PHYSICAL CHARACTERISTICS OF NECK MASSES

Size
Shape
Single versus multiple
Mobile versus fixed
Location within the neck
Cystic versus solid
Pulsatile versus nonpulsatile
Movement on tongue protrusion
Movement on swallowing
Tender versus nontender
Facial nerve palsy

squamous cell carcinoma, is detected. Treatment of the primary lesion must also be considered.

Other imaging modalities, such as thyroid scans, ultrasounds, and occasionally magnetic resonance imaging, are useful in evaluating neck masses.

Recommended Approach

The recommended workup is adjusted as outlined above according to history and physical examination, age, and suspected etiology.

Therapeutic

Therapeutic Options

Medical therapy for the treatment of neck masses is dictated by the suspected or confirmed diagnosis. Inflammatory processes with a suspected bacterial origin are treated with antibiotic therapy. The physician strives to make the diagnosis and treat the neck mass as a symptom, as only in a limited number of cases is the neck mass the primary disease.

Surgical management remains the primary mode of therapy to manage neck masses. Isolated congenital neck masses such as thyroglossal duct cysts and branchial cleft cysts may be managed by complete excision. The operative techniques are well described, and the entire tract or cyst should be removed. Masses that are primary salivary or thyroid tumors are managed by complete excision of the gland. Malignant tumors that present with spread to the lymph nodes are treated additionally by a radical neck dissection.

Certain diseases manifest themselves with adenopathy of malignant origin and no obvious primaries. These include lymphomas and unknown primary carcinomas. An excisional lymph node biopsy with pathologic evaluation is appropriate. Fresh tissue for immunohistochemical markers should be included.

Risks from surgery on the neck can be potentially significant. Those include bleeding and airway obstruction. The surgeon should cover all of these factors with each patient prior to performing a procedure.

Recommended Approach

Treatment is adjusted for diagnosis, etiology, and stage of disease.

FOLLOW-UP

The follow-up of patients with neck masses is determined by the particular disease process from which the mass has arisen. Benign lesions of the salivary gland and of thyroid origin have a low likelihood of recurrence, the possible exception being that a pleomorphic adenoma will recur if residual tumor is present.

Malignant masses, be they from primary salivary gland or thyroid malignancies or metastatic disease from a head and neck site, should be closely followed for recurrence and/or second primaries. The patient must be educated about the etiology of his or her disease and why a neck mass developed. The patient should be instructed to return if the symptoms become recurrent or a mass returns.

The physician should have a thorough understanding of the disease that produced the mass and arrange follow-up accordingly. When malignancies are present, enlisting the aid of colleagues who have been involved in the patient's care is appropriate.

DISCUSSION

Prevalence and Incidence

Neck masses are a common complaint and may manifest in patients of all ages and in both sexes.

TABLE 21–20–2. CONGENITAL NECK MASSES

Vascular
Hemangioma
Lymphangioma
Cystic hygroma
Branchial cleft cysts (I–IV)
Thyroglossal duct cysts
Cervical sinus of His

Related Basic Science

Diagnosis and appropriate therapy are based on a complete understanding of the regional head and neck anatomy. This would include the underlying vascular structures, organs, muscles, and lymph nodes, as well as the usual patterns of lymphatic drainage from various head and neck sites. Most lymph nodes present in the internal jugular chain of nodes. These range from the angle of the mandible at the jugulodigastric area to infraclavicular areas. Submental nodes drain the anterior tongue and floor of mouth. Posterior triangle or spinal accessory nodes drain the ear, scalp, and parotid.

Numerous congentital neck masses occur. These are listed in Table 21–20–2.

Vascular anomalies of the head and neck can be quite difficult to manage, with a high rate of recurrence. The surgical removal of branchial cleft anomalies involves removal of the entire tract.

The key to understanding and treating neck masses lies in determining their etiology and developing a comprehensive overall plan.

Natural History and Its Modification with Treatment

The natural history of these masses is dependent on the etiology. Most benign masses and congenital masses, if completely excised, should not recur. Malignant neck masses are dependent on the individual histologic subtype site and stage.

Prevention

At present no preventive measures are available.

Cost Containment

An orderly approach to the workup designed specifically for that suspected disorder is the most appropriate means of evaluation. Complete head and neck examination and needle aspirations can avoid a diagnostic examination under anesthesia.

REFERENCES

Batsakis JG. The pathology of head and neck tumors: The occult primary and metastases to the head and neck. Part 10. Head Neck 1981;3:409.

Duncavage JA, Unger JR, Toohill RJ. Diagnostic techniques in head and neck cancer. Otolaryngol Clin North Am 1985;18:421.

Myers EN, Johnson JT. Neoplasms. In: Cummings CW, ed. Otolaryngology and head and neck surgery. St. Louis: Mosby, 1993:1590.

Simpson GT. The evaluation and management of neck masses of unknown etiology. Otolaryngol Clin North Am 1980;13:489.

CHAPTER 21–21
Carcinoma of the Head and Neck (See Section 3, Chapter 3)

CHAPTER 21–22
Pharyngeal Masses (See Section 21, Chapter 25)

CHAPTER 21–23
Carcinoma of Larynx

Gerald S. Gussack, M.D.

DEFINITION

Carcinoma of the larynx is a malignant process, usually squamous cell carcinoma, that originates on one of the anatomic subsites of the larynx. The diagnosis is confirmed by histologic examination of biopsy specimens.

ETIOLOGY

The etiology is chronic inhalation of tobacco smoke usually combined with ethanol use. Human papilloma virus types, 6, 8, and 16 have also been suggested as etiologic agents.

CRITERIA FOR DIAGNOSIS
Suggestive

The clinical setting is usually one of presentation by a patient with a strong tobacco history and laryngeal symptoms. This diagnosis should be suspected when symptoms of hoarseness, pain, and sometimes laryngeal obstruction occur in a smoker.

Definitive

The diagnosis is confirmed by biopsy and pathologic confirmation of a malignant process.

CLINICAL MANIFESTATIONS
Subjective

The underlying etiologic factor in this disease is almost always that of long-standing tobacco use, usually greater than 25 packs per year. When smoking is combined with alcohol intake, the frequency of laryngeal carcinoma, like that of many other head and neck cancers, is increased. Persistent hoarseness is the most common symptom of patients with laryngeal carcinoma. This is especially true for carcinomas that arise on the true vocal cords. Pain manifested as a chronic sore throat or referred to other head and neck sites is also seen. Airway obstruction, dysphagia, and neck problems make up the remainder of the presenting complaints. Rarely, hemoptysis may be an early presenting sign, especially in ulcerative lesions.

Objective
Physical Examination

The most striking physical finding is an ulcerative or exophytic lesion of one or more laryngeal sites on physical examination. Inspection of the larynx by either indirect mirror or direct fiberoptic scope examination is essential. Vocal cord impairment may also be seen in advanced lesions. One may detect symptoms referable to laryngeal dysfunction on listening to the patient speak. These can include a hoarseness with a rough increased vibratory component of the voice, wheezing, and biphasic stridor. A neck mass secondary to metastatic spread to the regional lymph nodes may be present in advanced lesions.

Routine Laboratory Abnormalities

Routine laboratory studies are usually normal.

PLANS
Diagnostic
Diagnostic Options

The diagnostic evaluation should begin with a complete head and neck examination, This should include inspection of all sites, including nose, nasopharynx, hypopharynx, and especially the neck. Prognosis differs markedly when metastatic disease to the neck is present. Mirror and fiberoptic examination of the larynx provides the best means to assess the stage and anatomic spread of the lesion. One should keep in mind that carcinomas can have varied appearances, from erythroplasia to leukoplasia and from ulcerative and infiltrative to bulky and exophytic. It is essential to look for vocal cord mobility as this is essential for staging and prognosis.

A computed tomography (CT) scan of the larynx often displays the primary tumor and any enlarged lymph nodes that may be present.

Examination under anesthesia with direct laryngoscopy and biopsy is the definitive study and procedure with which to make the diagnosis. Additional diagnostic studies are not required. CT scans of the larynx can be used to help in determining the extent of the disease, cartilage destruction, extralaryngeal spread, and lymph node involvement. Laryngeal carcinomas are staged according to the TNM system as set down by the American Joint Commission for Cancer Staging (Table 21–23–1).

Recommended Approach

A complete head and neck examination including flexible laryngoscopy and CT is recommended.

Therapeutic

Treatment of carcinoma of the larynx is dependent on the size of the primary tumor and status of the lymph nodes of the neck. The focus of therapy should not be just the tumor itself, but treatment and rehabilitation of the entire patient. This often requires the services of an experienced team of physicians, including head and neck surgeons, radiation oncologists, dietitians, social workers, support groups, and especially speech pathologists. Medications have little role in the primary management of laryngeal carcinomas. Surgery remains the mainstay of treatment for most lesions.

T_1 lesions of the vocal cord can be managed by a number of modali-

TABLE 21–23–1. STAGING OF LARYNGEAL CARCINOMAS

Primary tumor (T)

TX	Primary tumor cannot be assessed
T0	No evidence of primary tumor
Tis	Carcinoma in situ

Supraglottis

T1	Tumor limited to one subsite of supraglottis with normal vocal cord mobility
T2	Tumor invades more than one subsite of supraglottis or glottis, with normal vocal cord mobility
T3	Tumor limited to larynx with vocal cord fixation and/or invades postcricoid area, medial wall of pyriform sinus, or preepiglottic tissues
T4	Tumor invades through thyroid cartilage and/or extends to other tissues beyond the larynx (e.g., to oropharynx, soft tissues of neck)

Glottis

T1	Tumor limited to vocal cord(s) (may involve anterior or posterior commissures) with normal mobility
T1a	Tumor limited to one vocal cord
T1b	Tumor involves both vocal cords
T2	Tumor extends to supraglottis and/or subglottis, and/or with impaired vocal cord mobility
T3	Tumor limited to the larynx with vocal cord fixation
T4	Tumor invades through thyroid cartilage and/or extends to other tissues beyond the larynx (e.g., oropharynx, soft tissues of neck)

Subglottis

T1	Tumor limited to the subglottis
T2	Tumor extends to vocal cord(s) with normal or impaired mobility
T3	Tumor limited to larynx with vocal cord fixation
T4	Tumor invades through cricoid or thyroid cartilage and/or extends to other tissues beyond the larynx (e.g., oropharynx, soft tissues of neck)

Staging using the regional lymph nodes (N) and distant metastases (M) is similar to that shown in Table 21–25–1 (hypopharyngeal carcinoma).
Source: American Joint Committee on Cancer. Manual for staging of cancer. 4th ed. Philadelphia: Lippincott, 1992:40. Reproduced with permission from the publisher.

ties, including endoscopic laser resection, cordectomy, and radiation treatments. T_2 lesions are best managed by partial laryngectomy with postoperative radiation therapy for larger lesions. T_3 and T_4 lesions often require total laryngectomy with radical neck dissections. Postoperative radiation therapy is used as an adjunctive measure in all advanced cases.

The modern treatment of carcinoma of the larynx does not stop with the surgical resection. The total rehabilitation requires reeducating and training the patient on communication, swallowing, bathing, and even nose blowing. Esophageal speech, electronic larynxes, and tracheoesophageal prostheses are only some of the advances available to laryngectomy patients. Extensive work with speech pathologists helps in rehabilitation.

FOLLOW-UP

Frequent follow-up for these patients is indicated to look for recurrence and second primary lesions. Bimonthly follow-up is used during the first year. The visits are decreased in subsequent years to yearly at 5 years. The majority of recurrences occur within the first 12 to 24 months.

Patients should be followed carefully for weight loss, dysphagia, or any anatomic change of the head and neck.

Computed tomography scans can help in detecting recurrent lesions that are not palpable. Chest radiographs should be repeated yearly.

DISCUSSION
Prevalence and Incidence

Carcinoma of the larynx has a worldwide distribution, with males predominating in each case. It is usually seen in older adults, with a peak incidence in the sixth decade. Approximately 60% of patients have the disease diagnosed while still confined to the larynx, 25% are seen with the primary and regional nodes involved, and 15% present with distant spread. The incidence parallels the frequency of tobacco use.

Related Basic Science

Laryngeal carcinomas most commonly arise on the glottic structures, with supraglottic structures being the second most common site. Subglottic tumors are the least common and arise in less than 5%. The patients with glottic carcinomas tend to present with the earliest symptoms, with hoarseness being the most common symptom. Airway obstruction and throat pain constitute the remainder of symptoms.

The horizontal line at the laryngeal ventricle divides the larynx into the glottic and supraglottic structures. The area 1 cm below the laryngeal ventricle is designated the subglottic area.

The incidence of lymphatic spread at the time of diagnosis is highest in the supraglottic area, followed by the subglottic area, and finally the glottic area. The supraglottic area has the richest lymphatic investment. In addition, the lesions may remain relatively asymptomatic until late in the disease.

Natural History and Its Modification with Treatment

The morbidity of laryngeal carcinoma is significant. Even a small cancer that may be easily cured often leaves the patient with an impaired voice. Patients who have undergone partial laryngectomy procedures have varying degrees of impairment of voice and deglutition. Aspiration remains a problem, especially for patients undergoing a supraglottic horizontal laryngectomy.

Survival of patients with carcinoma is dependent on the stage at time of diagnosis and therapy instituted. Small carcinomas may be well managed by a number of modalities with 5-year survival rates approaching 95%. Stage II carcinomas may also be treated with single-modality treatment and have survival rates approaching 75%. Stage III and IV lesions have poorer prognoses, and 5-year survival is 20 to 40%.

Untreated carcinomas of the larynx have a uniformly poor prognosis, with death resulting from airway obstruction.

Prevention

Carcinoma of the larynx is a disease found almost exclusively in tobacco smokers. The worldwide distribution is seen to mirror the use of tobacco in those countries. The cessation of smoking is seen as the best preventive measure.

Cost Containment

Treatment of carcinoma of the larynx is a relatively costly endeavor. The patient usually requires at least one major operative and often one diagnostic operative procedure. Management by an experienced team often makes the evaluation and treatment as efficient as possible.

REFERENCES

Johns ME, Farrior E, Boyd JC, Cantrell RW. Staging of supraglottic carcinoma. Arch Otolaryngol 1982;108:700.

Olafsson J. Laryngeal carcinoma problems in diagnosis and classification. J Otolaryngol 1982;11:167.

Singer MI. Tracheoesophageal speech and voice rehabilitation after total laryngectomy. Laryngoscope 1983;93:1454.

Wynder EL, Covey LS, Maruchi K. Environmental factors in cancer of the larynx: A second look. Cancer 1976;38:1591.

CHAPTER 21-24

Carcinoma of the Oral Cavity

Gerald S. Gussack, M.D.

DEFINITION

Carcinoma of the oral cavity is defined as a malignant lesion arising from any of the anatomic structures from the posterior tonsilar pillar anteriorly to the lips. The most common sites are the tongue, tonsil, and floor of mouth. The lesions vary in size and presentation and are predominantly squamous cell in origin.

ETIOLOGY

Long-term tobacco use, either cigarettes or smokeless, is the usual etiology. The combination of tobacco use with ethanol potentiates this effect.

CRITERIA FOR DIAGNOSIS
Suggestive

The patient often presents with an ulcerative or nonhealing area in the oral cavity. The lesions can be exophytic or indurated. They spread to involve surrounding structures.

The clue that one is dealing with a malignant oral cavity process is an ulcerative lesion that is firm to palpation. The patient may have symptoms of pain, bleeding, or burning, or an associated neck mass from a lymph node metastasis. Symptoms and presentation vary concerning which exact anatomic site is the origin of the lesion.

Definitive

The diagnosis is confirmed by biopsy of the lesion and subsequent histologic evaluation.

CLINICAL MANIFESTATIONS
Subjective

Nearly 90% of patients with carcinoma of the oral cavity have a history of long-term tobacco use. This may be in the form of snuff or smokeless tobacco in addition to smoking. Alcohol intake often accompanies this and seems to increase the frequency of tongue base lesions in particular. An approximate 2:1 male-to-female ratio exists.

Pain, nonhealing area, and chewing and swallowing difficulties are the most predominant symptoms. Other individuals note bleeding on brushing their teeth or simply a mass. Often these lesions become colonized with bacteria secondarily, and a foul odor may be present.

Objective
Physical Examination

A complete head and neck examination is paramount in the evaluation of suspected oral cavity malignancy. This should begin with palpation of the neck to determine the presence or absence of lymph node metastases in the anterior, posterior, and especially submental areas of the neck. When masses are palpated, their size, presence or absence of induration, fixation to the skin or deep tissues, and number should be determined. Both sides of the neck are always examined.

Inspection of the oral cavity should be complete, and bimanual palpation of the floor of mouth and tongue should be performed. Mirror examination with careful attention to the base of the tongue, hypopharynx, larynx, and pharyngeal wall is performed. Fiberoptic examination of the upper airway is undertaken if mirror examination is not adequate.

Carcinomas clinically appear as ulcerated areas of the mucosa with surrounding induration and erythema. These are often quite friable and bleed spontaneously or if manipulated.

The masses are easily palpable, and one may use this as the most accurate diagnostic maneuver.

Routine Laboratory Abnormalities

There are no routine laboratory abnormalities.

PLANS
Diagnostic
Differential Diagnosis

Whereas nonmalignant masses may be located in the oral cavity the lesion is considered to be neoplastic until proven otherwise by biopsy.

Diagnostic Options and Recommended Approach

A biopsy of the lesion is paramount in determining the final diagnosis. This can be done with routine punch biopsy forceps and can be performed with or without a local anesthetic. When the lesion appears to be on the posterior base of the tongue, a biopsy can be more difficult. Fine-needle aspiration for cytologic evaluation of a neck mass, when present, also confirms the diagnosis.

Following a biopsy of the lesion, the patient should be staged clinically according to the American Joint Committee on Cancer standards (Table 21–24–1). This helps to determine the most appropriate surgical procedure and whether radiation treatments will also be added.

Patients with lesions that are large or have associated lymphadenopathy should also undergo computed tomography of the head and neck. Computed tomography provides a look at both the size and extent of the primary lesion and the lymph node status of the neck.

Computed tomography is often capable of determining the presence of suspicious lymph nodes before they are palpable. The contralateral neck is well defined in this manner. One should look for enlargement greater than 1.5 cm, central necrosis, and round shape as criteria suspicious for malignancy.

Therapeutic
Therapeutic Options

Medical management of carcinomas of the oral cavity have little role to play in the care of these patients. Cancer chemotherapy has been used in various-stage lesions, with some tumor response seen. Its routine use as a front-line treatment is not indicated.

Surgery and radiation therapy provide the vast majority of therapeutic options for the patient with an oral cavity malignancy. Radiation is used primarily for soft palate lesions as an initial treatment and also in those patients who are not considered good surgical candidates for resection of other oral cavity sites. Radiation is used adjunctly in the postoperative management of almost all stage III and IV oral cancers.

Transoral surgical resection with a wide local margin, at least 1 to 1.5 cm, is indicated when the lesion is small (i.e., <2 cm) and involves the anterior tongue.

Tumors involving the posterior portion of the tongue often are not amenable to local resection via a transoral route. These require a composite resection with mandibulotomy or mandibulectomy and often a radical neck dissection. Larger lesions that extend into adjacent anatomic sites (i.e., T3 or T4 lesions) often require a myocutaneous flap reconstruction.

Risks and complications from these procedures are significant. These include fistula formation, bleeding, airway obstruction, and chyle leakage. The patients are often debilitated with poor swallowing function postoperatively.

Recommended Approach

The recommended approach is usually a combination of surgery and radiation therapy. These are modified to account for size, stage, site, and host factors.

TABLE 21–24–1. TNM STAGING OF ORAL CAVITY CARCINOMAS

Primary tumor (T)
TX	Primary tumor cannot be assessed
T0	No evidence of primary tumor
Tis	Carcinoma in situ
T1	Tumor 2 cm or less in greatest dimension
T2	Tumor more than 2 cm but not more than 4 cm in greatest dimension
T3	Tumor more than 4 cm in greatest dimension
T4 (lip)	Tumor invades adjacent structures (e.g., through cortical bone, tongue, skin of neck)
T4 (oral cavity)	Tumor invades adjacent structures (e.g., through cortical bone, into deep [extrinsic] muscle of tongue, maxillary sinus, skin)

Regional lymph nodes (N)
NX	Regional lymph nodes cannot be assessed
N0	No regional lymph node metastasis
N1	Metastasis in a single ipsilateral lymph node, 3 cm or less in greatest dimension
N2	Metastasis in a single ipsilateral lymph node, more than 3 cm but not more than 6 cm in greatest dimension; or in multiple ipsilateral lymph nodes, none more than 6 cm in greatest dimension; or in bilateral or contralateral lymph nodes, none more than 6 cm in greatest dimension
N2a	Metastasis in single ipsilateral lymph node more than 3 cm but not more than 6 cm in greatest dimension
N2b	Metastasis in multiple ipsilateral lymph nodes, none more than 6 cm in greatest dimension
N2c	Metastasis in bilateral or contralateral lymph nodes, none more than 6 cm in greatest dimension
N3	Metastasis in a lymph node more than 6 cm in greatest dimension

Distant metastasis (M)
MX	Presence of distant metastasis cannot be assessed
M0	No distant metastasis
M1	Distant metastasis

Adapted from the American Joint Committee on Cancer, Manual for staging of cancer. 4th ed. Philadelphia: Lippincott, 1992:40. Reproduced with permission from the publisher.

The patient should be informed of the etiology of this disease and should cease the use of any and all tobacco products. The direct and indirect contributions of ethanol must be considered in the chance of increasing recurrences. The patient should be informed preoperatively of the risks and possible complications of the operative procedures and the relatively higher rate of morbidity with these lesions.

FOLLOW-UP

The survival follow-up of these lesions is related to the stage of disease. The patient needs to be followed frequently, at bimonthly intervals for 1 year and then at increasing intervals to at least 5 years.

The patient should report any new ulcerative lesion or mass in the neck or oral cavity.

The surgeon should be aware of all the possible signs of recurrence. A complete head and neck examination, particularly to include palpation of the primary site, should be performed at each visit. Repeat computed tomography at 1 year is advocated for those with suspicions of recurrence or in whom symptoms return and no obvious lesion is noted.

DISCUSSION
Prevalence

Carcinoma of the oral cavity and pharynx is seen in approximately 25,000 patients each year. This accounts for 4% of all tumors in men and 2% of tumors in women. Squamous cell carcinomas constitute 90 to 95% of these lesions. The oral cavity ranks only behind the larynx as a head and neck site of carcinoma. Five-year survival rates for all sites of the oral cavity have been relatively low, 30 to 40%. This is due in part to the large percentage of patients who present with advanced-stage lesions. The staging of these carcinomas is reviewed in Table 21–24–1.

Related Basic Science

Anatomically, the oral cavity is defined as the vermilion border of the lip to the circumvallate papillae and all structures above this line. This discussion also includes the oropharynx with structures posterior, including the posterior pharynx and tonsils. Seventy percent of the lesions occur along the floor of the mouth and lateral gingival surfaces. The tonsil remains the most common posterior oropharyngeal site.

Prognosis is dependent on several factors. TNM stage, with particular reference to node size and location, is important. Fixation of the node can indicate extracapsular spread and demonstrates the poorest survival. Tumor size is important, with advanced tumors having both poorer survival and higher morbidity.

Histologic differentiation in and of itself may not lead to a poorer prognosis directly, but may be associated with a higher incidence of metastases to regional lymph nodes. Posterior location within the oral cavity was once considered to indicate a poorer prognosis, but again when examined through a multivariate analysis, no difference is seen. Histopathology grading is reviewed in Table 21–24–2.

Surgical margins have also been examined as a therapeutic prognostic variable. Abundant evidence exists that a positive or close margin is associated with a decidedly higher incidence of recurrence. Byers et al. (1978) demonstrated incidences of recurrence of 14% when the margins were free on initial section, 20% when further frozen sections were required, and 80% when margins were positive.

Carcinomas of the oral cavity are treated according to stage. Stage I and II lesions are treatable with comparable results by either surgery or radiation therapy. When bone involvement occurs, surgery should be the treatment of choice. Radiation therapy is associated with a small but real incidence of osteoradionecrosis of the mandible. This problem is significant with real morbidity or mortality. Proper oral hygiene and preradiation dental extractions often prevent this problem.

Combined therapy is recommended for all stage III and IV lesions. This slightly increases survival and moderately increases local control.

Natural History and Its Modification with Treatment

Untreated, this disease has a devastating outcome for the patient. Rapid progression of the disease often leads to problems with deglutition and speech. Even with treatment, survival is relatively poor. Early recognition of recurrence and close follow-up are essential. Mortality and 5-year survival for advanced lesions are 30 to 40% in patients undergoing treatment. Host performance can be seriously impaired.

TABLE 21–24–2. HISTOPATHOLOGIC GRADING OF ORAL CAVITY CARCINOMAS

Histopathologic type
  The predominant cancer is squamous cell carcinoma

Histopathologic grade (G)
GX	Grade cannot be assessed
G1	Well differentiated
G2	Moderately well differentiated
G3	Poorly differentiated
G4	Undifferentiated

Stage grouping
Stage	T	N	M
Stage 0	Tis	N0	M0
Stage I	T1	N0	M0
Stage II	T2	N0	M0
Stage III	T3	N0	M0
	T1	N1	M0
	T2	N1	M0
	T3	N1	M0
Stage IV	T4	N0, N1	M0
	Any T	N2, N3	M0
	Any T	Any N	M1

From American Joint Committee on Cancer. Manual for staging of cancer. 4th ed. Philadelphia: Lippincott, 1992:40. Reproduced with permission from the publisher.

Prevention

Avoidance of tobacco products and alcohol is the best mechanism for prevention. Smokeless tobacco use is particularly common in patients with oral cavity cancers.

Cost Containment

These are expensive diseases to manage and unfortunately occur in a group of patients who usually lack the resources to pay for their care. Management at a center with experience in head and neck cancer is important, as a team approach is essential.

REFERENCES

Applebaum EL, Collins WP, Bytell DE. Carcinoma of the floor of mouth. Arch Otolaryngol 1980;106:419.

Ariyan S, Chicarilli ZN. Cancer of the oral cavity. In: Ariyan S, ed. Cancer of the head and neck. St. Louis: Mosby, 1987:197.

Batsakis JG. Tumors of the head and neck: Clinical and pathologic considerations. Baltimore: Williams & Wilkins, 1974.

Byers RM, Bland KI, Borlase B, Luna M. The prognostic and therapeutic value of frozen section determination in the treatment of squamous carcinoma of the head and neck. Am J Surg 1978;136:525.

Gillis TM, Shapshay SN, Hung WK, et al. A comparison of combined modalities and single modalities in the management of advanced head and neck tumors. Laryngoscope 1982;91:993.

CHAPTER 21–25

Carcinoma of the Pharynx

Gerald S. Gussack, M.D.

DEFINITION

Carcinoma of the pharynx is defined as a malignant process involving the lateral or posterior pharyngeal walls, pyriform sinuses, or inlet to the cervical esophagus.

ETIOLOGY

These carcinomas are caused by continued years of tobacco use, both cigarettes and smokeless. This effect is amplified when combined with ethanol intake.

CRITERIA FOR DIAGNOSIS

Suggestive

The clinical setting is one of a patient presenting with a constellation of symptoms referable to decreased function of the pharynx or adjacent associated structures. The patient usually presents with progressive weight loss and dysphagia. The patient often has a history of heavy tobacco and ethanol use. He or she may present with a mass or masses in either the ipsilateral and/or contralateral neck.

Confirmation of the diagnosis of carcinoma of the pharynx is determined after an appropriate examination reveals the malignant mass lesion. The patient usually presents with symptoms of pain, dysphagia (solids greater than liquids), and sometimes a foreign body sensation in the pharynx. Hoarseness is often present when the lesion arises in the pyriform sinus and then invades the larynx. The ipsilateral vocal cord is often paralyzed. Fiberoptic laryngoscopy or mirror examination then reveals a mass lesion.

Definitive

The final determination is made once a biopsy is reported as positive on histologic examination.

CLINICAL MANIFESTATIONS

Subjective

The patient almost uniformly presents with a history of heavy tobacco use. There is also a high association with heavy ethanol intake, and it is thought that the two substances act synergistically. A history of a previous head and neck cancer should also be obtained. Occupational and environmental factors are otherwise not contributory.

The symptoms of carcinomas of the pharynx should be considered as a progression of difficulties. Dysphagia, more pronounced for solids than liquids, is the most prevalent finding. This is followed by pain, foreign body sensation, hoarseness, and aspiration. A neck mass secondary to metastatic spread of the disease and weight loss are also seen in advanced stages of the disease.

Objective

Physical Examination

Findings on physical examination are dependent on the size of the primary lesion and stage of the disease. These can range from a totally normal physical examination to a patient with a large exophytic lesion and bilateral neck nodes.

The neck should be palpated to assess the presence and size of any lymph nodes affected by metastatic disease. The patient should undergo a mirror or fiberoptic laryngoscopic examination for complete visualization of the larynx and hypopharynx. The mobility of the vocal cords should be documented, and the pyriform sinuses and posterior pharyngeal wall assessed.

Routine Laboratory Abnormalities

Routine laboratory tests reveal no diagnostic information.

A chest radiograph is often obtained to determine the presence or absence of metastatic disease in the lungs.

PLANS

Diagnostic

Differential Diagnosis

Although nonmalignant lesions do occur, a pharyngeal mass should be considered to be malignant until proven otherwise by biopsy.

Diagnostic Options and Recommended Approach

The diagnostic evaluation of carcinoma of the pharynx begins with a complete head and neck examination. Once this is complete, the patient should undergo a barium swallow. This identifies the inferior and superior extent of the lesion and also any associated esophageal involvement. Computed tomography of the neck is included in those patients who are considered surgical candidates. This is helpful in documenting the status of the lymph nodes and anatomically defining the primary site.

Following this, esophagoscopy, laryngoscopy, and biopsy are used to determine the exact diagnosis.

Therapeutic

Therapeutic Options

Medical therapy is of little value in the treatment of carcinomas of the pharynx. These are treated predominantly with a combination of radiation therapy and surgery. The surgery is designed to remove the entire lesion and any affected lymph nodes. This often requires a laryngectomy for larger lesions or those that involve the pyriform sinuses.

Lesions that require removal of a significant amount of the pharynx often require reconstruction for maintenance of an intact conduit without a narrowed area. These can be reconstructed with myocutaneous flaps, free microvascular flaps, or intestinal interposition. The free jejunal graft remains a mainstay of surgical treatment for advanced pharyngeal and hypopharyngeal lesions. It allows for a total laryngopharyngectomy to be performed and then an appropriate conduit reconstruction undertaken. These procedures have a high success rate in control of the primary disease process. They do, however, require a comprehensive team of surgeons for both the surgical resection and reconstruction. A microvascular transfer must be performed.

Recommended Approach

The suggested approach is as outlined above. The patient should be informed of the severity of these cancers and the extensive nature of the procedures required for reconstruction. They should know about the potential morbidity from a combined neck and abdominal operation. Some degree of dysphagia is always seen.

FOLLOW-UP

The patient should almost always undergo postoperative radiation therapy. He or she should be seen at the completion of radiation treatment and then every 2 months for the first year. A complete head and neck examination with mirror or fiberoptic pharyngeal examination should be performed. Palpation of the tongue should be performed to detect any tongue base recurrences. After 1 year, the patient may be seen at increased intervals but should report any increase in symptoms of dysphagia, breathing, or speech. Any neck mass or weight loss should also be reported.

DISCUSSION

Prevalence

The pharynx is traditionally divided into three anatomic areas: nasopharynx, oropharynx, and hypopharynx. The nasopharynx is not included in this discussion. The oropharynx is addressed in Chapter 21–24. The hypopharynx is anatomically divided into three areas: posterior pharyngeal wall, pyriform sinuses, and postcricoid larynx. Carcinomas of the pyriform sinus predominate and account for upward of 75% of lesions. Carcinomas of the postcricoid larynx and posterior pharyngeal wall are less common. There is a 2:1 female-to-male predominance in carcinomas arising in the postcricoid area. A large percentage of these female patients have Plummer–Vinson or Paterson–Kelly syndrome. These are iron deficiency anemias associated with atrophy and webs of the upper digestive tract.

Related Basic Science

Symptomatology in these patients usually involves pain and difficulty in swallowing. Vocal cord symptoms from laryngeal involvement are also seen, followed by adenopathy. The tumors have a very insidious onset, and approximately 50% of patients will have symptoms longer than 3 months prior to seeking medical attention.

The patients are often diagnosed by history alone, with physical examination confirming the primary site. Radiographic studies are often performed to further delineate the primary site and extent of disease. These include barium esophagrams and computed tomography. The presence of cervical adenopathy with metastatic disease is high, especially in larger lesions.

Staging of pharyngeal carcinomas as reviewed according to the American Joint Commission on Cancer is outlined in Table 21–25–1. Tumors most commonly arise in the pyriform sinuses. Small tumors are

TABLE 21–25–1. TNM STAGING OF HYPOPHARYNGEAL CARCINOMAS

Tumor (T)
T1	Tumor limited to one subsite of hypopharynx
T2	Tumor invades more than one subsite of hypopharynx or an adjacent site, *without* fixation of hemilarynx
T3	Tumor invades more than one subsite of hypopharynx or an adjacent site, *with* fixation of hemilarynx
T4	Tumor invades adjacent structures (e.g., cartilage or soft tissues of neck)

Regional lymph nodes (N)
NX	Regional lymph nodes cannot be assessed
N0	No regional lymph node metastasis
N1	Metastasis in a single ipsilateral lymph node, 3 cm or less in greatest dimension
N2	Metastasis in a single ipsilateral lymph node, more than 3 cm but not more than 6 cm in greatest dimension; or in multiple ipsilateral lymph nodes, none more than 6 cm in greatest dimension; or in bilateral or contralateral lymph nodes, none more than 6 cm in greatest dimension
N2a	Metastasis in a single ipsilateral lymph node more than 3 cm but not more than 6 cm in greatest dimension
N2b	Metastasis in multiple ipsilateral lymph nodes, none more than 6 cm in greatest dimension
N2c	Metastasis in bilateral or contralateral lymph nodes, none more than 6 cm in greatest dimension
N3	Metastasis in a lymph node more than 6 cm in greatest dimension

Distant metastasis (M)
MX	Presence of distant metastasis cannot be assessed
M0	No distant metastasis
M1	Distant metastasis

From American Joint Committee on Cancer. Manual for staging of cancer. 4th ed. Philadelphia: Lippincott, 1992:40. Reproduced with permission from the publisher.

confined to the pyriform sinus and involve only one wall. These in general do not affect laryngeal function. Intermediate-size tumors usually fill the pyriform sinus and cause hemilaryngeal fixation by infiltration of tumor. Large tumors invade the larynx medially, the soft tissue of the neck laterally, and the posterolateral pharyngeal walls posteriorly. This last group presents the greatest surgical challenges.

Lymphatic spread of tumor is a common finding, and palpable lymph nodes are present in 75% of patients. The jugulodigastric area on the ipsilateral side is the most common site for lymph node involvement.

Lymph node involvement plays a large role in determining overall patient prognosis. The overall 5-year survival is poor, ranging from 20 to 30%. When lymph nodes are not involved, 3-year survival is 80%. When nodes are present but the capsule is not invaded, 50% survival is seen. When capsular invasion occurs, survival is 35%.

Cancers of the posterior pharyngeal wall and postcricoid larynx are less common. The treatment usually involves laryngopharyngectomy combined with unilateral or bilateral neck dissections, followed by radiation therapy.

A high rate of recurrence is seen in these patients. This is due to a high incidence of submucosal spread and micrometastatic disease. Treatment of failures of surgery and radiation therapy is often disappointing. There is a very high morbidity rate, with poor long-term palliation.

Natural History and Its Modification with Treatment

The morbidity of this disease is significant. Left untreated, the patient would certainly die from laryngeal and esophageal obstruction. The patient who has completed successful therapy is also at risk for recurrences and continued swallowing difficulty. Treatment of these patients is associated with a high rate of surgical complications. These include wound breakdown and pharyngocutaneous fistulas.

Survival of hypopharyngeal carcinomas is among the poorest of all head and neck sites. These average 30% 5-year survival for all stages. This is most likely due to the high incidence of advanced-stage disease and high rate of submucosal and metastatic lymphatic spread.

Prevention

Eliminating tobacco and alcohol from the social habit almost guarantees total prevention of this disease.

Cost Containment

As with other head and neck carcinomas, these patients are expensive to treat. Management by an experienced team of surgeons, radiotherapists, and rehabilitation specialists provides the most efficient management and, it is hoped, lower costs.

REFERENCES

Driscoll WG, Nagorsky MS, Cantrell RW, Johns ME. Carcinoma of the pyriform sinus: Analysis of 102 cases. Laryngoscope 1983;93:556.

Jesse RH, Linberg RD. The efficacy of combining radiation therapy with a surgical procedure in patients with cervical metastasis from squamous cancer of the oropharynx and hypopharynx. Cancer 1982;35:1163.

Kirchner JA, Owen JR. Five hundred cancers of the larynx and pyriform sinus: Results of treatment by radiation and surgery. Laryngoscopy 1977;87:1288.

Schuller DE, MacGuirt WF, MacCabe BF, Young D. The prognostic significance of metastatic cervical lymph nodes. Laryngoscope 1980;90:557.

CHAPTER 21–26

Tumors of the Paranasal Sinuses

Gerald S. Gussack, M.D.

DEFINITION

Tumors of the paranasal sinuses are defined as benign or malignant mass lesions that arise in the bony air-containing spaces around the nose. The majority of these lesions arise from the mucosal elements, giving two forms of neoplasia: metaplastic epithelial (squamous cell lesions) and mucoserous (salivary) tumors.

ETIOLOGY

The cause of paranasal tumors is probably multifactorial. Smoking has been implicated in malignant lesions along with inhalation of woodworking and chemical dyes. The etiology of benign tumors is unknown.

Patients with tumors of the paranasal sinus usually present with a history of chronic nasal symptoms. Malignant lesions of the paranasal sinuses have long been seen in patients with a history of nickel exposure. The incidence of this is 250 times the expected rate in the general population. The latent period can be many years from time of exposure to presentation. A significant relationship is also seen with patients who are woodworkers. The incidence approaches 1 per 1000 and has a high incidence within the ethmoid sinuses. There is not a direct causal association with cigarette smoking, as seen in most other head and neck malignancies.

Benign paranasal sinus tumors include inverting papillomas and benign salivary gland tumors. The inverting or schneiderian papilloma is thought to have a relationship with human papillomavirus. There is a measurable incidence of malignant degeneration in inverting papillomas of the nasal cavity ranging from 1 to 15%. There is a high incidence of recurrence of inverting papillomas, especially when a limited surgical procedure is performed.

CRITERIA FOR DIAGNOSIS
Suggestive

The diagnosis of a paranasal sinus tumor should be considered in a patient with signs and symptoms of chronic nasal obstruction with a mass effect in either the orbit, nasal passage, facial soft tissues, or oral cavity.

Definitive

A definite diagnosis is made after evaluation of a patient with the previously described symptoms and subsequent demonstration of a mass lesion both by radiographic imaging (computed tomography or magnetic resonance imaging) and by biopsy via an intranasal or Caldwell-Luc approach.

CLINICAL MANIFESTATIONS
Subjective

The clinical setting in which these tumors occur is usually one of progressive nasal symptoms such as obstruction, bleeding, pain, sinus fullness, and swelling. The tumors are not usually visible until late in the course of the disease when the tumor is visible in the nasal cavity. Sometimes a mass lesion may be seen on computed tomography done for the evaluation of other symptoms.

A variety of symptoms are seen in patients with tumors of the paranasal sinuses. The majority of those mimic chronic sinusitis, and most patients with sinus tumors manifest sinusitis in the adjacent paranasal sinuses because of sinus ostia obstruction. Nasal airway obstruction remains the most common complaint. Unfortunately, this is seen as a relatively late sign when the tumor has either expanded or eroded the medial wall of the maxillary ethmoid complex. Epistaxis remains the next most frequent symptom, followed by purulent nasal drainage. Headache, proptosis, and dental pain are also seen in larger lesions, particularly when invasion or pressure on the trigeminal nerve and its branches occurs. Blindness, palatal lesions, and central nervous symptoms are seen less commonly in advanced lesions.

Objective
Physical Examination

Physical findings present on routine examination are subtle in early lesions. These include medial displacement of the lateral nasal wall, mucopurulent nasal discharge, and demonstration of an intranasal lesion on anterior rhinoscopy. Erosion of the hard palate, proptosis, extraocular muscle palsies, and soft tissue fullness of the cheek are seen in advanced lesions.

Routine Laboratory Abnormalities

Routine laboratory studies are not contributory.

PLANS
Diagnostic

Computed tomography is an essential study in the workup of mass lesions of the paranasal sinuses. It is superior to plain films and trispiral tomography in its ability to demonstrate the bony limits of the tumor and also the presence of intraorbital, intracranial, or skull base extension.

The intranasal examination with biopsy is the definitive study to confirm the diagnosis of this lesion. Larger lesions that can be visualized within the nose are usually biopsied in an office setting. Lesions more posteriorly in the sphenoid and ethmoid sinuses may require a general anesthetic and intranasal telescopic examination.

Undifferentiated tumors, which are not infrequently seen within this group of neoplasms, may require a panel of immunohistochemical screening to delineate the exact histologic type.

A careful head and neck and cranial nerve examination should be performed to determine the presence or absence of trigeminal nerve and skull base erosion.

Therapeutic

Therapeutic Options

Medical management has no significant role in the management of paranasal sinus tumors.

Surgery is the mainstay of therapy in the management of paranasal sinus tumors. The operative procedures range from biopsy to craniofacial resection. Partial, subtotal, and total maxillectomies are also used. Inverting papillomas, the most common benign nasal tumors, are usually treated by medial maxillectomy. This is performed through a facial incision adjacent to the nose combined with a Caldwell-Luc sublabial approach.

Malignant lesions of the sinus are treated with procedures to provide a margin of uninvolved bone around the primary site. These often involve resection of the entire maxillary sinus and possibly the orbit when this structure is involved. Craniofacial resections are used for ethmoid malignancies. Radiation therapy is usually employed in combination in either a pre- or postoperative fashion.

Recommended Approach

The recommended treatment of these lesions is as outlined above. This is modified according to the size and stage of the lesion.

The patient should be aware of the serious nature of malignancies of the paranasal sinuses and their propensity to invade local structures. They should understand that symptoms usually present late in the course of disease.

Complications of surgery of the paranasal sinuses can be significant. These include meningitis, brain abscess, pneumocephalus, and cerebrospinal fluid leakage.

FOLLOW-UP

Patients should be well informed of the nature and possible complications. They should return if any symptoms of mass lesions, central nervous system symptoms, or neck masses develop.

The physician should follow patients on a bimonthly basis for the first year and increase intervals to every 6 months from the second through the fourth year. The patient's nasal and sinus cavities should be inspected and the neck checked for possible metastatic disease. Computed tomography should be repeated at 1 year to examine the skull base for any recurrence.

DISCUSSION

Prevalence

Carcinomas of the paranasal sinuses are rare and constitute less than 1% of all malignancies in the body and about 3% of all malignancies of the upper aerodigestive tract. Sixty to eighty percent of these tumors arise in the maxillary sinuses, and the remainder arise in the ethmoid sinuses. Frontal and sphenoid sinuses are seldom the site of origin of any malignant process.

Related Basic Science

The high mortality and poor prognosis of carcinomas of the sinus are directly related to the insidious onset and misleading signs and symptoms of the disease. Lesions seldom become symptomatic until they have spread beyond the confines of the sinus. Ninety percent of tumors manifest erosion of at least one wall. Symptoms of all of these lesions are almost all related to advanced diseases.

Papillomas are the most common benign tumors found in the sinuses. They usually arise on the lateral nasal wall and are unique to the mucosa that arises embryologically from the nasal placodes and foregut that line this area. Papillomas arise from the reserve or replacement cells at the basement membrane and develop a characteristic epithelial proliferation. These then form a fungiform and inverted pattern. There is no relationship to allergy or other nasal polyp formation. Benign salivary gland tumors constitute the remaining group of tumors.

The major problem with nasal papillomas is recurrence. This is most likely due to persistence of the metaplastic process within the submucosa. Recurrence may be multiple and delayed for years. There is an in-

TABLE 21–26–1. TNM STAGING OF TUMORS OF THE PARANASAL SINUSES

Primary tumor (T)	
TX	Primary tumor cannot be assessed
T0	No evidence of primary tumor
Tis	Carcinoma *in situ*
T1	Tumor limited to the antral mucosa with no erosion or destruction of bone
T2	Tumor with erosion or destruction of the infrastructure (see anatomic division, above), including the hard palate and/or the middle nasal meatus
T3	Tumor invades any of the following: skin of cheek, posterior wall of maxillary sinus, floor or medial wall of orbit, anterior ethmoid sinus
T4	Tumor invades orbital contents and/or any of the following: cribriform plate, posterior ethmoid or sphenoid sinuses, nasopharynx, soft palate, pterygomaxillary or temporal fossae or base of skull

From American Joint Committee on Cancer. Manual for staging of cancer. 4th ed. Philadelphia: Lippincott, 1992:45. Reproduced with permission from the publisher.

cidence of carcinoma associated with these lesions. The mechanism of malignant degeneration versus succession by a malignancy process is the source of some debate.

Malignant tumors of the sinus are staged according to the degree of bony erosion. Prognosis for tumors is dependent on stage and location. Ohngren's line bisects the sinus into the anterior inferior and posterior superior halves. Tumors below Ohngren's line have a better prognosis than those above the line. Staging is based on the TNM system (Table 21–26–1)

Nonepidermoid malignancies of the sinuses constitute the remaining group of sinus cancers. The majority of these are of salivary gland origin. Adenoid cystic carcinoma is the most common, followed by mucoepidermoid, acinic cell carcinoma, and malignant mixed tumor, in decreasing order of frequency. Adenoid cystic carcinomas are associated with a high incidence of neural spread and invasion. These frequently invade the foramen ovale and skull base by way of the trigeminal nerve.

Malignant melanomas, neuroendocrine tumors, olfactory neuroblastomas, and metastatic lesions are also seen. Renal cell carcinomas seem to have an unusual predilection for the sinonasal tract.

Natural History and Its Modification with Treatment

The morbidity of paranasal malignant tumors is significant. Surgery combined with post- or preoperative radiation can leave a patient with significant debilitation. Surgery for advanced lesions that may require a craniofacial resection is associated with a very high incidence of complications, approaching 50%. Prognosis is reasonably favorable if intracranial invasion with dural involvement has not taken place. Once dural involvement has occurred, 2-year survival decreases to 20%.

Prevention

No preventive measures are currently available. Close follow-up of patients with nasal symptoms and a history of woodworking or nickel exposure as a career should be considered.

Cost Containment

The management of these lesions is very labor intensive and expensive. The services of a head and neck surgeon, radiation therapists, prosthodontist, and dentist are usually required. Computed tomography and magnetic resonance imaging are usually both necessary to evaluate the skull base and degree of bony involvement.

REFERENCES

Batsakis JG. Tumors of the head and neck: Clinical and pathological considerations. 2nd ed. Baltimore: William & Wilkins, 1979.

Ketcham AS, Hoye RC, VanBuren JM, Johnson RH. Complications of intracranial transfacial resections for tumors of the paranasal sinuses. Am J Surg 1966;112:591

Lund VJ, Harrison DF. Craniofacial resection for tumors of the nasal cavity and paranasal sinuses. Am J Surg 1988;156:187.

Schramm VL, Myers EN, Maroon JC. Anterior skull base surgery for benign and malignant disease. Laryngoscope 1979;89:1077.

Sisson GA, Bytel DE, Becker SP, Ruge D. Carcinoma of the paranasal sinuses and craniofacial resection. J Laryngol Otol 1980;1:59.

CHAPTER 21–27

Nasal Airway Obstruction

Gerald S. Gussack, M.D.

DEFINITION

Nasal airway obstruction is defined as a subjective inability to inspire and expire via a nasal route.

Etiology

The cause of nasal obstruction is multifactorial and includes virtually every anatomic structure in the nose. Tumors, foreign bodies, and other mass lesions must also be considered.

CRITERIA FOR DIAGNOSIS
Suggestive

Nasal obstruction is manifested by varying degrees of symptomatology ranging from partial and intermittent to a total, fixed, permanent decrease in air movement. The patient usually complains of symptoms that have been present for a prolonged period, which may subsequently worsen. The clinical setting can involve patients of any age group and both sexes. Children are often affected, as newborn infants are obligate nasal breathers, and nasal obstruction can be a life-threatening problem. Most patients feel that nasal obstruction tends to decrease their quality of life by causing discomfort and impairing respiration, smell, and taste.

Definitive

The abnormality should be considered in patients with symptoms of inability to breathe through one or both nostrils, sinusitis, snoring, sleep apnea, or altered smell and/or taste.

CLINICAL MANIFESTATIONS
Subjective

The patient usually presents with frank complaints of inability to breathe. This may range from partial to total, unilateral, or bilateral. It may be present at all times or intermittent.

It is often precipitated by environmental contaminants. There may be an individual or family history of allergy with or without associated respiratory problems. Patients who work in dusty, dirty, or otherwise polluted environments are more prone to complaints. Patients with allergy, asthma, and associated respiratory diseases are more prone to problems than other individuals.

The most common complaint manifested is inability to breathe through the nose. This is followed by sinus and facial fullness, headache, shortness of breath, and impairment of sense of smell and taste.

Objective
Physical Examination

A complete examination of the head and neck should be undertaken prior to examining the nose. Indirect signs of nasal and/or nasopharyngeal obstruction should be sought. Serous otitis can be the first sign of a nasopharyngeal carcinoma. Likewise, a metastatic neck mass from this same source may be present. Oral examination should pay particular attention to the tongue, palate, tonsils, and soft palate. Palatal adhesions and nasopharyngeal stenosis can lead to significant nasal obstruction.

The external nose should be examined for deformity of the bony pyramid and cartilage lip. Old fractures, collapsing nasal valves, and a drooping nasal tip can all exacerbate any underlying anatomic obstruction.

The septum should be examined with a head mirror or headlight and a small nasal speculum. The caudal or anterior septum should be observed and palpated for any evidence of anterior deflection or deviation. The mid- and posterior portion of the septum can be deformed or deviated and cause significant obstruction. The turbinates should be examined for evidence of edema or hypertrophy. The inferior turbinates more commonly contribute to obstruction when hypertrophied. Occasionally, the middle turbinate can be enlarged or become pneumatized (concha bullosa) and contribute to nasal obstruction. Airflow can be estimated by watching the patient breathe and then obstructing first one nostril and then the other. One should not push the lower lateral cartilage against the septum, as this can obstruct both nostrils' nasal airflow. Rather, only the aperture of each nostril should be occluded.

Routine Laboratory Abnormalities

Routine laboratory tests reveal no diagnostic information.

PLANS
Diagnostic

Nasal endoscopy is indicated in addition to physical examination of the nose.

Therapeutic
Therapeutic Options

The patient with symptoms of nasal airway obstruction should be evaluated for the presence of coexisting sinus disease. Purulent material in the osteomeatal airway, postnasal drainage, and rhinitis all point to sinusitis as a coexisting problem. Sinus radiographs or computed tomography confirms those findings.

Once the etiology of nasal obstruction has been determined, various medical regimens can be instituted. These include topical and oral decongestants, topical and oral steroid preparations, antihistamines, and mucolytic agents. Medications are listed in Table 21–27–1.

Surgical therapy remains the mainstay of treatment of nasal obstruction. This includes treatment of nasopharyngeal obstruction as well as true nasal obstruction. Adenoidectomy remains the major operative procedure performed in children to relieve nasopharyngeal causes of obstruction. Secondary benefits from this procedure include improvement in postnasal drainage and eustachian tube function. Operative repair of external nasal deformities often involves a rhinoplasty for correction of bony pyramid abnormalities. There is also an entity known as postrhinoplasty nasal obstruction, which occurs when the bony pyramid is narrowed or nasal valve collapse occurs following rhinoplasty. This entity is more easily avoided than corrected.

Septoplasty for correction of a deviated nasal septum is by far the most efficacious and surgically sound procedure for the correction of a deviated septum. This involves an incision in the caudal end of the nasal septum, elevation of mucoperichondrial flaps, repositioning of the quadrangular or septal cartilage, and removal of the bony septum and any nasal spurs. The cartilage is reshaped and preserved, as op-

TABLE 21–27–1. MEDICATIONS EFFECTIVE FOR RHINITIS MANAGEMENT

Decongestants	Pseudoephedrine 30–60 mg PO bid
Antihistamines	Diphenhydramine 25–50 mg PO bid to tid
	Terfenadine 60 mg PO bid
	Astemizole 10 mg PO qd
	Bropheniramine 4–12 mg PO bid
Topical decongestants	Phenylephrine hydrochloride (Neo-Synephrine) 0.25–1.0%
Nasal steroids	Beclomethasone dipropionate 0.042%
	Flunisolide
Cromolyn sodium	Intranasal sodium cromoglycate
Mucolytics	Iodinated glycerol 30–60 mg PO qid
	Guaifenesin 400–600 mg PO bid

posed to being removed. This prevents later collapse of the tip of the nose and preserves the structural integrity of the nasal aperture. Submucous resection of the nasal septum involves removal of all but a dorsal and caudal strut of septal cartilage. The long-term results of loss of structural support and potential for septal perforations make this procedure less desirable.

Turbinoplasty, turbinectomy, submucous resection of the turbinates are all procedures designed to improve the nasal airway by anatomically reducing the size of the turbinates and increasing the cross-surface area of the nasal airway. Care must be taken to avoid resecting too much of the turbinate. This can lead to atrophic rhinitis or a loss of nasal resistance and subjective feeling of nasal obstruction. Conservative procedures on the turbinate are almost always preferable to more radical resections.

Recommended Approach

The therapeutic approach is adjusted according to etiology and site of obstruction.

The patient should be thoroughly informed as to the etiology and associated factors concerning the etiology of his or her nasal obstruction. Those patients with rhinitis complicating their nasal obstruction should be adequately treated. Patients should also be informed that medical treatment may need to be continued postsurgery. Environmental irritants such as smoking, dust, and other inhalants should be avoided.

FOLLOW-UP

The patient with nasal airway obstruction should be followed until a therapeutic improvement has been achieved. When patients are managed medically, this varies according to the specific etiology being treated. Rhinitis may respond to medical management quite quickly, and all symptoms subsequently abate. When more complicated factors are apparent, then closer follow-up is required.

Patients managed surgically should be followed postoperatively until the nose is healed and no further obstruction is present. These patients often require subsequent medical therapy to manage their obstructive symptoms. Patients with nasal polyps or tumors should be seen at least every 3 to 4 months.

DISCUSSION
Prevalence

Nasal obstruction is an almost universal problem and the source of significant discomfort. Kimmelman (1989) estimates that $5 billion is spent annually on over-the-counter nasal medications, and $60 million is spent on nasal surgery in the United States on an annual basis.

Related Basic Science

Nasal obstruction detracts from the quality of life. This can range from minor discomfort due to rhinitis and decreased nasal flow to life-threatening diseases such as sleep apnea. Smell and taste are two senses that are dependent on nasal airflow. Therefore, they are moderately impaired with nasal obstruction.

There are important relationships between upper and lower respiratory airway function. For example, there may be contamination of the lower respiratory tract from upper respiratory infections. In addition, nasal–pulmonary reflexes cause transitory bronchodilation and bronchoconstriction. This can produce pulmonary impairment in otherwise normal, healthy patients. Upper respiratory infections often precipitate asthmatic attacks.

Nasal airflow obstruction is defined by Poiseuille's law. This is dependent on the radius of the cross-sectional area raised to the fourth power. Obviously, small changes in radius can lead to significant changes in airflow.

The nose also acts as a very effective mechanism for air filtration. It removes virtually all particles larger than 5 μm and approximately 50% of particles 2 to 3 μm in size. Particles 1 μm and smaller are not filtered. Microorganisms present in the air are enclosed in droplets and inactivated by antibodies present in the mucus.

The nose also serves to humidify and warm air via exposure to the surface area of the mucous membranes of the turbinates and septum. Even in extremes of ambient temperature, the inspired nasal airflow is equal to body temperature by the time it reaches the nasopharynx.

Resistance to nasal airflow plays a large part in the normal physiology of respiration. The majority of resistance in the entire respiratory tract is at the nose. Anatomic changes that either increase or decrease nasal resistance beyond certain limits result in the sensation of nasal obstruction. Patients with widely patent airways, such as those following total turbinectomy or severe atrophic rhinitis, often complain of nasal obstruction.

Nasal airflow can be quantitatively measured by rhinomanometry. This has remained predominantly a research tool and has not gained routine acceptance in the evaluation of nasal problems. It can provide a graphic record for later comparison.

Natural History and Its Modification with Treatment

The natural history of nasal obstruction is dependent on the severity and etiology. Severe cases can result in rhinitis, pulmonary problems, sleep apnea, and associated difficulties. Mortality from nasal obstruction alone is quite unusual.

Prevention

No current preventive measures are available.

Cost Containment

A thorough history and physical examination to determine a proper differential diagnosis help in determining the proper mode of therapy. Routine radiography and routine use of antihistamine decongestants are not indicated. Treatment should be directed at the specific disorder.

REFERENCES
Beekhuis GJ. Nasal septoplasty. Otolaryngol Clin North Am 1973;6:693.

Eccles R, Lancashire B, Tolley NS. Experimental studies on nasal sensation of airflow. Acta Otolaryngol 1987;103:303.

Gray LP. Deviated nasal septum: Incidence and etiology. Ann Otol Rhinol Laryngol 1980;87(suppl. 50):3.

Kimmelman CP. The problem of nasal obstruction. Otolaryngol Clin North Am 1989; 22:253.

CHAPTER 21–28

Rhinitis

Gerald S. Gussack, M.D.

DEFINITION

Rhinitis is defined as inflammation of the nasal mucosa. The disorder is ubiquitous to almost all individuals at one time or another in their lives.

ETIOLOGY

The causes of rhinitis are multiple and include any agent or organism that can cause infection and/or inflammation of the nasal mucosa. Host factors such as allergy and autoimmune diseases must also be considered.

CRITERIA FOR DIAGNOSIS

Suggestive

The clinical setting is one in which the patient presents with symptoms of nasal obstruction. These can be accompanied by nasal discharge, epistaxis, and sometimes pain.

The diagnosis is considered in patients with inability to breathe through the nose that is intermittent in presentation. Rhinitis may also serve to aggravate a preexisting fixed-typed nasal obstruction. The symptoms are usually exacerbated by environmental irritants. Symptoms are often compounded by the multitude of preparations used to treat the disorder. The diagnosis of rhinitis should be considered in individuals who present with nasal obstruction, rhinorrhea, epistaxis, and pain.

Definitive

Definitive diagnosis is confirmed by the demonstration of inflamed nasal mucosa with the appropriate history.

CLINICAL MANIFESTATIONS

Subjective

Rhinitis remains such a common problem that family history seldom plays a significant role. The patients present from all walks of life and all backgrounds. Those individuals are subjected to environmental particulate irritants such as smoke, dust, dirt, chemicals, and pollens are particularly affected.

Nasal obstruction secondary to mucosal edema is the most common symptom. This is followed by mucoid discharge, pain, and epistaxis. Secondary symptoms such as sinus pain, headaches, dental complaints, and postnasal drainage are commonly seen. These are secondary to the blockage of sinus ostia and pressure phenomenon related to the mucosal inflammation and secondary edema.

Objective

Physical Examination

A complete head and neck examination should always be performed. Examination of the ears, posterior pharyngeal wall, and hypopharynx is important, in addition to a careful nasal examination. Postnasal drainage and inflammation of the lymphoid tissue on the posterior pharynx are often seen. Signs of eustachian tube dysfunction such as tympanic membrane retraction and serous otitis in severe instances may be noted.

Nasal examination reveals a spectrum of findings. Mild cases may reveal a watery edema of the nasal mucosa overlying the septum and turbinates. The mucosa is often discolored and may be quite pale in instances of atrophic rhinitis or very inflamed and crusted in cases of rhinitis associated with infection. The septum should be examined to determine if anatomic deformities exist.

The nose should then be sprayed with a topical decongestant such as oxymetazoline (Neo-Synephrine) 0.5%. This serves to shrink the mucosa and results in a better picture of the underlying nasal architecture. Septal deformities are most often seen as spurs along the junction of the maxillary crest and quadrangular cartilage or the perpendicular plate of ethmoid.

Routine Laboratory Abnormalities

Routine laboratory tests are usually of little benefit in the evaluation of patients with rhinitis.

PLANS

Diagnostic

Differential Diagnosis

The workup of patients with rhinitis should be geared to ruling out coexisting morbid conditions such as sinusitis and attempting to define a possible etiology for the patient's symptoms. Sinus radiographs are helpful in ruling out sinusitis.

Diagnostic Options and Recommended Approach

Quantitative immunoglobulins and radioallergosorbent test (RAST) nasal smears for eosinophils can be used to characterize possible etiologies for rhinitis. These studies are not necessary to initiate treatment, however.

Therapeutic

The goal of improving the symptoms of patients with rhinitis is aimed at determining the etiology and directing therapy based on this. When environmental irritants play a large etiologic role, avoidance therapy is most effective. Those patients who smoke should be encouraged to quit. Those whose occupation or home environment is very dirty or dusty should make attempts to improve the quality of their immediate surroundings. Cleaning and dusting the house frequently, changing heating and air conditioning filters, avoiding excessive pollen exposures, keeping pets outdoors, and removing house plants are all positive steps.

When a specific etiology can be determined, such as bacteria or allergy, then medical therapy such as antihistamines, antibiotics, or desensitization can be undertaken. The majority of patients have no specific cause, and the treatment is symptomatic management.

Oral decongestants, such as pseudoephedrine 25 to 50 mg twice daily, are effective for some patients in relieving some of the nasal obstructive symptoms. These can be combined with antihistamines or given alone. Topical nasal decongestants such as Oxymetazoline, (Neo-Synephrine) provide relief of obstruction for short periods. Their chronic use is discouraged as it can lead to rhinitis medicamentosa from the rebound effect of the nasal mucosa.

Corticosteroids often effect a profoundly noticeable improvement in patients with nonspecific rhinitis. This is seen with oral, parenteral, and topical routes of administration. Topical steroids are often preferable to prolonged courses of oral steroids. Beclomethasone dipropionate and flunisolide are effective and are commonly used topical preparations. These are often used in conjunction with other oral decongestant and antihistamine preparations. Antibiotic coverage is recommended when concurrent bacterial infections are present.

Surgical management of rhinitis is limited to improving the anatomic nasal obstruction and draining the paranasal sinuses. Deviated nasal septums can be straightened by septoplasty procedures, and turbinoplasty can be used to reduce the chronically swollen turbinates. These procedures are successful in improving symptoms but are not necessarily curative. The risks of the procedures include postoperative bleeding, septal perforation, and residual nasal deformity.

The patient should be educated about the high frequency of this condition and the role of environmental factors in the severity of symptoms. Almost all patients experience exacerbation of symptoms when concentrations of dust, chemical irritants, smoke, and particulate matter in the environment are high. Avoidance therapy for those who are able to identify environmental factors that exacerbate their nasal obstruction should be practiced.

Those patients with topical decongestant abuse and rhinitis medicamentosa need to be encouraged to abstain from decongestant usage. The rebound phenomenon with prolonged use of these medications must be explained.

FOLLOW-UP

Patients should be followed until symptomatic improvement has been obtained. It may take 4 to 6 weeks for the patient to notice significant improvement. The patient should continue therapy until the acute exacerbations have subsided. Patients, especially those with seasonal allergic symptomatology often require repeat regimens of therapy.

DISCUSSION
Prevalence

The impact of rhinitis is significant and affects fully 25% of the American population. The etiologies of this disorder are numerous, but allergic rhinitis can be implicated in many of these cases. The patients are of all ages and both sexes. The disease has little mortality but has significant morbidity in keeping patients from functioning at their full capacity and fulfilling their daily activities.

Related Basic Science

The etiologies of rhinitis have been classified by Lucente (1989) into allergic, nonallergic, infectious, atrophic, hyperplastic, metabolic, and anatomic. The predominant complaint in all of these patients is nasal obstruction. Allergic rhinitis is felt to be secondary to membrane dysfunction mediated by immunoglobulin E antibodies. This is often seen in conjunction with other allergic symptoms, such as asthma, watery eyes, sinusitis, and eczema. Rhinitis, however, may be the only manifestation. Response to immunotherapy is variable in patients with both allergic and nonallergic rhinitis.

Granulomatous diseases may manifest themselves with involvement of the nasal mucosa. Wegener's granulomatosis is the disease most frequently seen. The clinical appearance is that of severe nasal inflammation with crusting, bleeding, and erythema. The diagnosis is usually made by biopsy of a granulomatous lesion, demonstrating vasculitis. The treatment is usually a combination of steroids and cytotoxic therapy. Sarcoidosis may have a similar appearance. There are often associated cutaneous or pulmonary manifestations.

Atrophic rhinitis is a disease characterized by progressive atrophy of the nasal mucosa and underlying bony skeleton. No consistent etiology has been noted. It is often seen in elderly patients. A similar condition is seen in patients who have undergone overresection of the turbinates.

There is often a secondary infection with Gram-negative organisms such as *Klebsiella ozaenae* and *Corynebacterium diphtheriae* (nontoxin-producing form). These are most likely opportunistic invaders, but can cause significant morbidity due to the foul smell and purulent drainage.

Rhinitis medicamentosa is a common side effect of decongestant abuse. Topical decongestants are from two classes: sympathomimetic amines and imidazoles. Both decrease swelling by acting on precapillary subepithelial sphincters. A rebound phenomenon occurs when the sphincters fail to respond. Anoxic and atrophic changes can then develop in the sphincteric mechanism, and the nasal mucosa remains edematous. Chronic cocaine usage also manifests with a picture very similar to that of rhinitis medicamentosa. The vasoconstriction effects can cause irreversible damage to the septal mucosa, and a perforation may develop.

Therapy for rhinitis medicamentosa is aimed at removing the decongestants and then treating the underlying etiology. Nasal steroids provide a safe and effective mechanism for weaning patients off decongestants.

Anatomic deformities often predispose patients to relative nasal obstruction. A small amount of overlying mucosal edema can render a patient with a septal deformity or turbinate enlargement totally obstructed. Correction of the underlying anatomic deformity is essential to long-term treatment.

Natural History and Its Modification with Treatment

The morbidity of this condition is significant. Rhinitis interferes with nasal respiration. This detracts from the quality of life and one's ability to function in his or her environment. Nasal obstruction interferes with effective filtering of particulate matter and decreases the sense of smell.

Mortality is not considered a consequence of rhinitis.

Prevention

No current preventive measures are available.

Cost Containment

The treatment of rhinitis is straightforward and usually does not involve a complicated evaluation. Sinus radiographs are usually the only radiographic study necessary to rule out coexisting sinus disease. Generic preparations for antihistamine and decongestant use are also indicated.

REFERENCES

Lucente FE. Rhinitis and nasal obstruction. Otolaryngol Clin North Am 1989;22:307.

Lucente FE, Hyams VS. Inflammatory and neoplastic diseases of the nasal mucosa. Clin Dermatol 1987;5:35.

McDonald TJ, DeRemeera, Kern EB. Nasal manifestations of Wegener's granulomatosis. Laryngoscope 1987;84:24101.

Sahay JN, Chatterjee SS, Engler C. A comparative trial of flunisolide and beclomethasone dipropionate in the treatment of perennial allergic rhinitis. Clin Exp Allergy 1980;10:65.

CHAPTER 21–29

Sinusitis

Gerald S. Gussack, M.D.

DEFINITION

Sinusitis is defined as an acute or chronic inflammatory process of one or more of the four paranasal sinuses.

ETIOLOGY

The cause of sinusitis is related to obstruction of the natural drainage pathways of the sinuses. This leads to mucus collection, infection, and

inflammatory symptoms. These are most commonly bacterial in origin and can affect newborn to elderly individuals.

CRITERIA FOR DIAGNOSIS
Suggestive

The clinical setting is one of patients presenting with a constellation of symptoms. These include pressure, fullness, or tenderness over the cheek, forehead, or orbit. The patient often reports nasal congestion with obstruction, purulent nasal discharge and fever in cases of acute infection. A generalized feeling of malaise is commonly present.

Definitive

The constellation of symptoms noted above in a patient with purulence in the nose or osteomeatal complex of the lateral wall of the nose should be considered for a diagnosis of sinusitis. This can be confirmed by radiographs or computed tomography.

CLINICAL MANIFESTATIONS

Subjective

Fifty percent of the patients who present with sinusitis often have been treated for this entity or related nasal problems previously. The patients may have a history of nasal allergic problems with or without rhinitis. Exposure to environmental pollutants such as dust, pollen, chemical irritants, dyes, fibers, and smoke is commonly seen.

The most common symptom is a pressure phenomenon with pain over the affected sinus or in an area of referred pain. The sinuses have referred pain that radiates to specific areas. The maxillary sinuses radiate to the teeth and gums, ethmoid sinuses to the eye and bridge of the nose, frontal sinuses to the forehead and vertex of the head, and sphenoid sinus to the retroorbital area and occiput. Nasal obstruction is also seen. This is secondary to mucosal edema of the lateral wall along with retained nasal secretions. Purulent nasal drainage is another symptom that almost always clinches the diagnosis in most individuals.

Objective

Physical Examination

Physical examination of the patient with acute sinusitis often reveals a patient who is in moderate to severe discomfort. Tenderness to light palpation and percussion of the affected sinus is often noted. Examination of the oropharynx may reveal erythema and purulent secretions over the pharyngeal wall. This is secondary to drainage of nasal and sinus secretions posteriorly. The nasal examination may be normal in some cases of chronic sinusitis, but often reveals evidence of inflammation and chronic infection. Edema and erythema of the lateral wall of the nose and middle turbinates and ethmoid recess are observed. When purulence is detected in the osteomeatal area, which is between the middle and inferior turbinates, then a definitive diagnosis of sinusitis can be made. Spraying the nose with a topical decongestant such as 0.5% oxymetazoline (Neo-Synephrine) to provide vasoconstriction is helpful.

Predisposing factors for sinusitis include any physical or physiologic abnormality that may lead to obstruction of the normal pathways of drainage from the sinuses. These include deviated nasal septums, rhinitis with subsequent nasal mucosal edema, nasal polyps, foreign bodies, and nasal tumors. These signs should be looked for on examination.

Routine Laboratory Abnormalities

There are no diagnostic routine laboratory abnormalities.

PLANS

Diagnostic

Routine sinus radiographs are used to confirm the diagnosis of sinusitis. One may detect an air–fluid level in the maxillary sinuses as a pathognomonic indication of infection in the proper clinical setting. More often, opacification of one or more of the paranasal sinuses may be seen.

Computed axial tomography of the paranasal sinuses are the gold standard by which paranasal sinus disease can be detected. This shows in a clear two-dimensional axial and coronal pattern the anatomic extent of disease and degree of sinus ostia obstruction. These studies should not be performed on a routine basis but should be reserved for severe symptoms, difficult diagnostic cases and recurring sinusitis and in those patients who are refractory to therapy. They are essential to the surgical management of sinusitis via an endoscopic approach.

The best means of following a patient's response to therapy is repeated history and physical examination. The resolution of headaches, decrease in nasal obstruction, change from purulent to clear nasal secretions, and improvement in constitutional symptoms should all be viewed as a good response to therapy.

Therapeutic

Therapeutic Options

Treatment of the underlying bacterial infection is the mainstay of medical therapy. The most common pathogenic organisms are *Streptococcus pyogenes, Hemophilus influenzae, Staphylococcus aureus,* and *Moraxella catarrhalis.* Amoxicillin 250 to 500 mg three times daily, trimethoprim–sulfamethoxazole 80 to 400 mg twice daily, cefaclor 250 to 500 mg three times daily, and erythromycin ethylsuccinate 250 to 500 mg tid are good oral first-line antibiotics. They must be taken in sufficient quantity for a prolonged period to achieve their maximum desired effect. Amoxicillin-clavulanate 250 to 500 mg three times daily, cefuroxime axetil 250 to 500 mg three times daily, and ciprofloxacin 250 to 750 mg twice daily are excellent oral antibiotics useful in cases not responding to initial antibiotic therapy. Diarrhea, vaginitis, and development of resistant organisms are all possible side effects of treatment.

Topical therapy to the nose both to decrease obstruction and to reduce nasal mucosa inflammation is also helpful. Topical agents include buffered saline suspensions to thin secretions and remove nasal crusting and drainage. Topical nasal decongestants (0.25–1.0% oxymetazoline [Neo-Synephrine]) also help by decreasing nasal congestion and edema and improving drainage. These substances have a cumulative effect, and rebound or worsening of nasal edema can occur when they are used in a prolonged fashion. Nasal steroid preparations, flunisolide, and beclomethasone dipropionate are useful in long-term management of rhinitis and hence decrease nasal obstruction. These medications are thought to act by membrane stabilization and decrease in release of inflammatory mediators. Sodium cromolyn (Nasalcrom) is another effective medication in decreasing rhinitis and recurrent sinusitis. Its mode of action is stabilization of mast cells and prevention of histamine release. This medication is useful in patients with rhinitis of an allergic origin.

Side effects of topical nasal antiinflammatory medications are few. There is not felt to be significant steroid absorption. There may be a slight tendency toward atrophic changes of the nasal mucosa, and the medications should probably be stopped for 2 weeks during prolonged therapy every 3 months.

Oral decongestants and antihistamines are also used in the management of sinusitis. These medications again serve to decrease nasal obstruction and produce drainage. Pseudoephedrine (Sudafed) 30 to 120 mg three times daily is the major ingredient in most oral decongestants. These have alpha-adrenergic activity and produce vasoconstriction of the nasal mucosa to decrease edema. Chlorpheniramine (Chlor-Trimeton) and diphenhydramine (Benadryl) are among the major groups of antihistamines. They are useful in those patients with an allergic history and sinus symptoms. Their major side effect is drowsiness. Several newer antihistamines, including astemizole (Hismanal), loratidine (Claritin), and terfenadine (Seldane), do not cross the blood-brain barrier and have many fewer side effects than do other traditional antihistamines. Cardiac arrhythmias have been reported in patients taking macrolides, antibiotics, or antifungal agents with these newer nonsedating antihistamines. These arrhythmias are described as the very serious Torsade de pointes. Their use should be avoided in patients taking these medications. Guaifenesin 400 to 600 mg four times daily and iodinated glycerol are other medications used. These preparations decrease the viscosity of secretions and aid in drainage.

Immunotherapy, as dictated by skin testing or radioallergosorbent test (RAST) is also used in patients with chronic recurrent sinusitis and rhinitis. Its role is more a preventive one in chronic therapy and is expensive and time consuming.

Surgery is employed in the management of sinusitis for the indications listed in Table 21–29–1. The most common indication for surgery is lack of response to intensive and prolonged medical therapy. Symptoms of chronic headache, fatigue, nasal drainage, and nasal obstruction predominate. Chronic pulmonary problems such as asthma, bronchiectasis, cystic fibrosis, and allergic problems may be aggravated by chronic and recurrent sinusitis. The overall management of these patients often requires addressing their sinus disease in a surgical fashion.

TABLE 21–29–1. INDICATIONS FOR SINUS SURGERY

Symptoms unresponsive to medical therapy
Chronic pain
Exacerbation of pulmonary disease
Orbital, intracranial, or soft tissue complications

Complications of sinusitis can have severe morbidity and mortality if left untreated. The most common route of spread is from the ethmoid sinuses to orbital and periorbital tissues. These can lead to cellulitis, abscess, and possible ocular complications. Blindness, ophthalmitis, and ocular motility disorders may result. Soft tissue infections may be seen when infection and inflammation spread into the tissues of the cheek and face. Intracranial complications such as cavernous sinus thrombosis, subdural empyema, brain abscess, and meningitis can result from parameningeal seeding of bacteria by the sinuses. This is particularly true of infections of the sphenoid and frontal sinuses.

Surgical management is dictated by the sinus involved and the patient's individual unique anatomy. The majority of surgery these days is performed via an endoscopic transnasal approach. Magnifying rod lens telescopic systems and special irrigating and suction handles are used. These are combined with bone biting forceps and other instrumentation to provide drainage of the involved sinuses into the nose.

External approaches such as the Caldwell–Luc and external ethmoidectomy are also employed. These approaches have the benefit of good visualization but more complications secondary to their sublabial or external incisions and scarring.

Complications of sinus surgery can be quite severe and include blindness, cerebrospinal fluid leakage, and death. These procedures should be carried out by experienced individuals with a thorough understanding of the anatomy.

Recommended Approach

The recommended approach is as outlined above and adjusted for severity of symptoms. Surgery is reserved for complications or failure of medical therapy.

The patient should be educated as to exactly which predisposing factors contribute to his or her sinusitis and which measures can be implemented to decrease its recurrence. Patients who smoke should be informed of the irritating effects on the mucosa and the resulting inflammation.

Those with fixed anatomic obstructions such as deviated nasal septum and nasal polyps may require surgical correction if sinusitis becomes recurrent. Many patients with nasal complaints of obstruction and rhinitis complain they have sinusitis. These patients are not well treated with antibiotics and require other therapy.

Patients with complications should be informed of the serious potential for morbidity and need for prompt and appropriate treatment.

FOLLOW-UP

Patients should be aware of the major symptoms for which they seek attention and their response to therapy. Those patients with chronic sinusitis and recurrent sinusitis should be advised to seek treatment when nasal secretions become purulent or symptoms such as pain and fullness worsen. Any soft tissue swelling, orbital edema, or change in mental status with fever should alert the patient to possible recurrent infections with complications.

DISCUSSION
Prevalence and Incidence

The prevalence and incidence of sinusitis are extremely high, especially during the cold weather months. Probably 75% of all individuals may experience an episode of this disease at one stage in their life.

Related Basic Science

Children as young as 2 to 6 weeks of age may be affected by sinusitis. The maxillary and ethmoid sinuses are the first to be developed embry-

ologically, and the presentation is often that of periorbital swelling and cellulitis.

The basic pathophysiology of sinusitis is one of obstruction of the ostia of the sinuses followed by infection and inflammation. The four sinuses of the face drain into the nose through the osteomeatal complex by way of the ethmoid sinuses. Drainage is accomplished by a rhythmic beating of the cilia and movement of the mucous blanket toward the ostia. When obstruction of the ostia occurs or there is interruption of the integrity or ability of the cilia to beat, then stasis of secretions and infection result.

Gram-positive organisms, *Streptococcus pyogenes* and *Staphylococcus aureus*, predominate as the leading pathogens for sinusitis. *Hemophilus influenzae* and *Moraxella catarrhalis* are also seen. Viruses and other nonbacterial pathogens are seen infrequently and do not bear lengthy attention.

Granulomatous disease and vasculitis can also present in the nasal cavity and sinuses. The most common of these is Wegener's granulomatosis. Sarcoidosis is also seen and can cause significant disability for the patient.

Treatment of the systemic disorder with steroids along with topical steroid and local treatment is indicated.

The proximity of the paranasal sinuses to important anatomic structures of the skull base and orbit is a key reason for the high incidence of complications associated with both severe infection and surgery. The sphenoid sinus is situated beneath the pituitary gland and optic chiasm and medial to the optic nerves, carotid artery, and cavernous sinus. It is these anatomic relationships that lead to the high potential for morbidity.

Natural History and Its Modification with Treatment

The untreated case of sinusitis may have varying degrees of outcome. A great many patients resolve without therapy and have no further symptoms. Approximately one third go on to develop symptoms of chronic and recurrent sinusitis with persistent symptoms of postnasal drainage and pain.

A smaller percentage of people develop complications and suffer varying degrees of morbidity from this.

Prevention

Detection of potential underlying factors and prompt and complete treatment of early infection for an appropriate period are indicated. Many therapeutic failures are secondary to antibiotic treatment for an insufficient length of time. Three- or even four-week courses of antibiotics may be necessary.

Patients with allergic problems should undergo appropriate therapy if this is felt to be an ongoing etiology. Avoidance of environmental pollutants, especially cigarette smoke, should be recommended in those patients who smoke.

Cost Containment

Cost can be controlled by using first-line antibiotics in preference to more expensive ones. Radiographic studies can be limited to a plain sinus series for initial evaluation. Computed tomography should not be used as a screening examination except for patients with chronic symptoms and recurrent infections. Culture of nasal secretions is not recommended, as it may not reflect what is present within the sinus. Expensive antihistamine and combination decongestant therapy is not recommended. Generic preparations are also useful.

REFERENCES

Boyden GL. Surgical treatment of chronic sinusitis. Ann Otol Rhinol Laryngol 1952;61:558.
Caldwell GW. The accessory sinuses of the nose: An improved method of treatment for suppuration of the maxillary atrium. NY Med J 1893;58:526.
Gwaltney JM, Sydnor A, Sande MA. Etiology and antimicrobial treatment of acute sinusitis. Ann Otol 1981;90 (suppl. 84):68.
Kennedy DW. Functional endoscopic sinus surgery technique. Arch Otolaryngol 1985;111:643,
Stankiewicz JA. Complications of endoscopic intranasal ethmoidectomy. Laryngoscope 1987;97:1270.

CHAPTER 21–30

Peritonsillar Abscess

Gerald S. Gussack, M.D.

DEFINITION

Peritonsillar abscess is defined as a collection of purulent material in the space lateral to the tonsil.

ETIOLOGY

The cause of peritonsillar abscesses is usually an infection that arises in the lateral aspect of the tonsil between the tonsil and pharyngeal fossa.

CRITERIA FOR DIAGNOSIS

Suggestive

Peritonsillar abscesses are usually accompanied by significant unilateral tonsillar swelling, palatal mucosal edema, and inflammation. The clinical setting is usually one of throat pain, dysphagia, and fever. These are usually more common in young adults who neglect their early symptoms. The patient experiences a progressive increase in symptoms and then seeks attention when trismus, pain, and inflammation become severe.

This diagnosis should be considered in a patient who presents with increasing symptoms of pain, fever, and dysphagia in association with unilateral tonsil swelling. The patient often presents with symptoms of pain such as referred otalgia.

Definitive

The diagnosis of peritonsillar abscess is confirmed by demonstration of purulent material adjacent to the tonsil. This may be performed by needle aspiration or incision and drainage.

CLINICAL MANIFESTATIONS

Subjective

The usual patient with peritonsillar abscess is a young adult with a history of increasing throat pain and fever. The disease is usually one of evolution and progression of symptoms.

The disease is usually not seen in children under the age of 10, but obviously this should not be a hard and fast rule. Children with immune deficiency, severe dental caries, malnutrition, leukemia, or diabetes are at a higher risk. This diagnosis should be considered more often in this pediatric subgroup.

The symptoms begin very similarly to those of pharyngitis, with sore throat, fever, malaise, and odynophagia. The key to suspecting a peritonsillar abscess is the clinical deterioration or worsening of symptoms. This association with moderate to severe symptoms should lead one to suspect the diagnosis.

Occasionally, patients may have intermittent or incomplete spontaneous drainage. They may even obtain some temporary relief after spitting out some foul-smelling purulent material.

Objective

Physical Examination

The physical findings often reveal an acutely ill or toxic appearing young adult. Neck examination usually reveals tenderness over the affected angle of the mandible and neck. Adenopathy is also present.

Oropharyngeal examination usually reveals unilateral tonsillar swelling with erythema, edema, and tonsillar exudate. The soft palate has decreased mobility on the affected side. The inflammation may be so severe that a shaggy appearing ulceration may develop as seen in Vincent's angina. The uvula is often edematous.

Routine Laboratory Abnormalities

Laboratory data often reveal an increase in the white blood cell count with an increased polymorpholeukocyte count.

PLANS

Diagnostic

Streptococcal screens or throat cultures may be positive or negative.

The diagnosis of peritonsillar abscess is confirmed on needle aspiration or incision and drainage. The return of purulent material in the syringe, or on incising the tonsillar capsule, is the only absolute way of making a diagnosis.

Computed tomography of the neck may demonstrate cellulitis, edema, inflammation, or abscess in the peritonsillar and parapharyngeal spaces. The routine use of this study is not recommended. It is indicated when the peritonsillar abscess may have spread to involve the deeper spaces in the neck.

Therapeutic

Therapeutic Options

Penicillin G 1 to 2 million U intravenously every 4 hours often brings about rapid improvement in symptoms within the first 24 hours. Metronidazole and clindamycin 150 to 160 mg intravenously every 8 hours are other antibiotics used. Cefuroxime 1.5 g intravenously every 8 hours is another alternative.

Hydration to compensate for the lack of oral intake and fever is also an essential element in the management of these patients.

Drainage of the abscess by large-bore needle aspiration is both diagnostic and therapeutic. This is often followed by a wider incision and drainage once the diagnosis is confirmed. Salt water, mouthwash, and peroxide rinses and gargles help to clear the throat of purulent secretions and improve symptoms.

Children, uncooperative adults, and those with extreme symptoms may be required to undergo general anesthesia for therapeutic drainage. An "a chaud" or Qunisy tonsillectomy can be considered. This procedure is significantly more difficult than a standard tonsillectomy. It is a definitive operation, and the infection should not recur. The risks for bleeding both early and late from the procedures are increased over standard tonsillectomy. The possibility of abscess rupture and inhalation of pus in a mouth that is difficult to open is also present.

Recommended Approach

Early drainage with culture of the aspirate is the suggested approach.

Patients should be aware of the serious nature of this disorder and the possibility for complications if not promptly treated. They should be informed about the indications for tonsillectomy in this disease. These would include recurrent abscesses and symptoms of chronic tonsillitis.

FOLLOW-UP

Discharge from the hospital is usually planned 1 to 2 days following drainage after the patient's fever has resolved, symptoms have improved, and oral intake has begun. The patient is instructed to drink plenty of liquids and watch for signs of bleeding or deep neck infection.

The patients are followed at 2 weeks to check for complete resolution of symptoms. Those that continue to have symptoms of recurrent pharyngitis or abscess should be considered for elective tonsillectomy.

DISCUSSION

Prevalence

The prevalence and incidence are not known. The condition is rare when one considers the number of patients who have tonsilitis.

Related Basic Science

Peritonsillar abscesses arise as a consequence of tissue necrosis and pus formation in the space between the tonsillar capsule and palatoglossal or palatopharyngeus muscles. The purulent collections vary in location from posterior inferior to superior lateral. Approximately 50% of these individuals have symptoms of chronic tonsillitis prior to this episode. Another group develop an abscess as their first and only symptom.

The development of peritonsillar abscess is usually a consequence of chronic tonsillitis, leading to inflammation, fibrosis, and scarring of the tonsil fossa. This often results in the development of a mixed aerobic and anaerobic infection.

In the bacteria isolated from these abscesses, the incidence of anaerobic organisms is high, predominantly oral *Bacteroides* species, beta-hemolytic streptococcus group A, and, to a lesser extent, *Hemophilus influenzae* and *Staphylococcus aureus*.

The differential diagnosis of peritonsillar abscess most commonly includes tonsillitis with exudate and cellulitis. Obviously the latter condition may precede abscess formation. Infectious mononucleosis, carcinomas, lymphomas, foreign bodies, and carotid artery aneurysm must be considered. We recommend incision and drainage only after needle aspiration because of these factors.

The treatment of peritonsillar infections has gone through many phases. Bonding (1976) recommended a routine abscess tonsillectomy as a quick, cost-effective, and definitive way to manage this disorder. Schecter et al. (1982), however, treated a large group of patients (74) with needle aspiration alone, and only 24% of this group had significant problems later with their tonsils. Other investigators have advocated a unilateral tonsillectomy.

The majority of head and neck surgeons would probably avoid an abscess tonsillectomy in most circumstances. The difficulty of the procedure and potential for increased complications dictate this.

Natural History and Its Modification with Treatment

The morbidity of this disorder left untreated could be quite significant. The extension to the parapharyngeal or prevertebral space could lead to mediastinitis and possibly death. The surgical drainage of these abscesses is straightforward and accomplished by either incision or aspiration technique. This almost always averts subsequent complications.

Mortality for this disorder properly managed should be zero. Only with severe infectious complications should death result.

Prevention

No known preventive measures are currently available. Prompt recognition and treatment of the disorder are necessary. Patients treated for one abscess with recurrent symptoms of tonsillitis or patients with more than one abscess should undergo a tonsillectomy.

Cost Containment

Early drainage, high-dose antibiotics, and hydration shorten the cost and length of treatment for this disorder. Antibiotic therapy without some type of drainage usually does not resolve the infection and adds to the length of stay.

Computed tomography and other studies are not indicated unless complications develop.

REFERENCES

Bonding P. Routine abscess tonsillectomy. Laryngoscope 1976;86:286.
Fried MP, Forrest JL. Peritonsillitis: Evaluation of current therapy. Arch Otolaryngol 1981;107:283.
Gray LP. Unilateral tonsillectomy: Indications and results. J Laryngol Otol 1983;97:1111.
Schecter GL, Sly DE, Roper AL. The changing face of treatment of peritonsillar abscess. Laryngoscope 1982;92:637.

CHAPTER 21–31

Vocal Dysfunction

Gerald S. Gussack, M.D.

DEFINITION

Vocal dysfunction is defined as an altered expression of voice.

ETIOLOGY

The causes of vocal dysfunction are multiple and include anything that affects the vibratory function of the larynx and vocal cords. These factors encompass mass lesions of the vocal cords, neuromuscular disorders, vocal cord paralysis, infections, and inflammatory disorders of the larynx.

CRITERIA FOR DIAGNOSIS

Suggestive

Hoarseness is the most common expression used to describe voice problems and often describes a voice characterized by a rough or increased vibratory quality. Other vocal dysfunctions can be characterized by a soft, breathy voice or one that has a choking type of sound.

The clinical setting is one of a patient presenting with complaints of acute or chronic changes in his or her voice. These may have evolved slowly over a period or have had a sudden onset. The key to diagnosis is a subjective or objective change in voice quality.

Definitive

Confirmation of the diagnosis requires taking a careful history to determine the quality of voice present prior to the complaint and then listening to the voice to determine how far it deviates from normal. Hoarseness is a personal complaint and varies in severity according to how far from the normal voice the patient's affected voice has deviated. The diagnosis remains a clinical one.

CLINICAL MANIFESTATIONS

Subjective

The evaluation of a patient with hoarseness should begin with a detailed history relating to the onset, duration, change in character, and social habits. Those patients with a long history of smoking should be assumed to have a laryngeal carcinoma. Patients with total aphonia (or a very breathy voice) should be investigated for neuromuscular or psychological origin of their hoarseness.

Environmental factors and patient lifestyle play a large role in the development of vocal dysfunction. Any factor that can contribute to the ability of the vocal fold to vibrate can lead to hoarseness. These factors include environmental irritants such as cigarette smoke, air pollutants, and chemical and gasoline fumes. Vocal abuse is a common cause of hoarseness. This may result in a short period of difficulty secondary to edema or fatigue of vocalis muscles or nodule formation for those who continually exercise abusive behavior.

The most common symptom of vocal dysfunction or hoarseness is the actual change in the perceptual quality of the voice. The voice may have a rough or increased vibratory component, a breathy quality, a choking sound, or simply weakness. Each voice characteristic may be caused by a specific abnormality of the larynx.

Pain is occasionally present in the throat and is usually secondary to an inflammatory component. Airway obstruction symptoms are also seen, especially in those patients with mass lesions of the larynx or neuromuscular dysfunction.

Objective

Physical Examination

The physical examination should begin by careful listening to the voice and determining what characteristic of vocal dysfunction is present. This should be followed by palpation of the neck and larynx. Examination of the oropharynx and hypopharynx is imperative to fully evaluate the etiology of hoarseness. Mirror examination of the larynx provides a complete view in the majority of patients. This examination requires practice on the part of the physician and cooperation by the patient. One should first look for obvious mucosal lesions, mass lesions, or ulceration. Mobility of the vocal cords should be observed to assess both abduction and adduction. The patient is asked to phonate and say the sustained letter "Eeee" sound. This tilts the larynx forward and allows the physician to observe the larynx on adduction and, while breathing, to observe the larynx on abduction.

The physician should look for benign mass lesions such as nodules, polyps, papillomas, and granulomas. Malignant lesions usually appear as exophytic or ulcerative growths and may or may not obstruct the airway or cause paralysis. When a carcinoma is suspected, the physician should try to determine its extent as completely as possible.

Isolated vocal cord paralyses are most commonly manifested by a weak, breathy voice. The physician should observe the arytenoids to try to determine vocal cord movement.

When a mirror examination is unsatisfactory, a direct flexible fiberoptic laryngoscopic examination of the larynx should be the next step. These instruments are expensive and usually not part of the general practitioner's usual armamentarium. They are used almost daily by otolaryngologists, however. These examinations can provide a more reliable and accurate examination of the larynx.

Routine Laboratory Abnormalities

Routine laboratory data are usually noncontributory.

Chest radiographs to look for lung or mediastinal abnormalities should be performed when vocal cord paralyses are present.

PLANS

Diagnostic

The source of laryngeal dysfunction, if any, should be sought in the management of each patient. Mass lesions should all be referred for evaluation by a specialist. Many times, direct laryngoscopic and microscopic examination may be required to obtain a histologic diagnosis. Lesions that appear to be large laryngeal cancers are often evaluated by computed tomography to determine extent of disease and possible lymph node involvement.

Patients with vocal cord paralyses should be evaluated for possible involvement of the vagus or recurrent laryngeal nerve. Malignancies of the lung with mediastinal lymph node spread are a common cause. Esophageal and thyroid malignancies are also seen. Computed tomography of the base of the skull, neck, and chest is the most expeditious way to evaluate a laryngeal paralysis.

Subtle vocal cord abnormalities can be evaluated by video laryngoscopy and stroboscopy. These allow the trained observer to detect the subtle vibratory patterns of the vocal folds and determine if vocal cord pathology is present.

Patients with laryngeal dystonia or spastic dysphonia present with a choking type of speech that has a very characteristic pattern. These individuals often show overadduction of the vocal cords and an abnormal vibratory pattern.

Therapeutic

Therapeutic Options

Medical therapy is used in the treatment of hoarseness when the etiology is one related to infection or inflammation. Broad-spectrum antibiotics with Gram-positive coverage are used when bacterial infections are present. Amoxicillin 500 mg orally three times daily, erythromycin 250 to 500 mg orally three times daily, and cefaclor 500 mg orally three times daily are good choices. Oral decongestants such as pseudoephedrine 25 to 75 mg orally twice daily may be used when significant postnasal drainage or bronchitis may be contributing to chronic laryngeal irritation. Oral and intramuscular steroids (prednisone, dexamethasone) are also effective in reducing laryngeal inflammation when clinical response is poor. The steroids should be used only for a short period.

Voice therapy is most effective when the etiology of hoarseness appears to be voice abuse. This is very common in people who must speak a great deal, such as clergymen, professors, and lobbyists. Acute laryngeal edema and contact ulcers can result from an acute episode of vocal abuse. This is seen in cheerleaders, avid football fans, conventioneers, and others. Voice rest, antiinflammatory medications, and hydration often suffice.

Patients with true laryngeal dystonias or spastic dysphonia are currently managed with injections of botulinum toxin (Botox) 2.5 to 30 U. This medication blocks the neuromuscular endplate and weakens the muscle. The patient subsequently experiences a softening of the voice and develops more fluidity of speech.

Surgery plays a limited role in management of hoarseness. It is reserved for the removal of mass lesions, biopsy of suspected carcinomas, and excision of polyps. Care must be taken in surgery on the larynx to avoid inducing scarring of the deep layers of the laminae propriae and mucosa. This prevents proper ventilatory pattern of the vocal folds and causes an altered voice. Proper microsurgical technique of laryngeal phonosurgery may be applied for removal of polyps or other vocal cord lesions. The carbon dioxide laser is used here. Laryngoplasty and Teflon injections are techniques used to improve the breathy voices seen with unilateral vocal cord paralyses. These serve to medialize the vocal cord and improve the ability of the vocal cords to meet in the midline and vibrate.

Recommended Approach

The best treatment of vocal dysfunction and hoarseness is definition of the etiology and correction of the underlying pathology.

The patient should be informed about the etiology of his or her hoarseness and educated appropriately. This is very important in the treatment of those patients with vocal abusive habits. Very often the mainstay of therapy is retraining the vocal habits of the patient and modifying his or her behavior. Speech pathologists can be of great help in this endeavor.

Those with vocal cord paralyses as the source of their hoarseness should understand that these may be secondary to other processes and that further evaluation is necessary. They should also be informed that the etiology for some vocal cord paralyses is never determined.

Those patients with mass lesions on their cords requiring surgery should understand that irreversible changes of the vocal cord may ensue that may leave them with a permanently hoarse voice.

FOLLOW-UP

Follow-up of the patient should continue as long as the patient remains symptomatic or until the physician feels that maximum improvement has occurred. This obviously depends on the particular etiology.

Those patients with malignant lesions of the larynx require follow-up every 2 to 3 months for several years once therapy is complete. It is important to palpate the neck and visualize the larynx at each visit.

Patients with spastic dysphonia may require repeat injections of botulinum toxin, usually every 3 to 6 months.

DISCUSSION
Prevalence

Hoarseness is a common symptom in clinical practice. It is experienced by most individuals at least once during their lifetime and affects individuals of all ages. This entity is seen in young children, particularly those with a history of vocal abuse. Those patients with conditions of the larynx that predispose them to recurrent anatomic and/or neuromuscular problems with their larynx are prone to recurrent bouts of hoarseness.

Related Basic Science

Voice production is accomplished by passage of a steady flow of air through the vibrating vocal cords. The vocal cords vibrate by the combined actions of the intrinsic muscles of the larynx working in conjunction to produce vocal cord apposition and vocal fold vibration. Proper speech and voice production is dependent on coordinating the neuromuscular activity of all the above-mentioned structures. The vocal cords are muscular structures with essentially five components forming two layers. The deep layer includes two groups of muscles and the deep layer of the laminae propriae. The superficial layer is composed of the superficial layer of the laminae propriae and the mucosa. These layers are sometimes referred to as the body and cover. Proper vocal fold vibration and hence voice production are dependent on both layers being intact and functioning properly.

Inflammatory processes and edema within the larynx cause swelling of the mucosa and hence an increase in mass of the cover layer of the vocal cord. This leads to a slowing of the vibration and hence a deeper voice. Mass lesions such as small cancers, polyps, granulomas, ulcers, and papillomas can disrupt the mucosal surface and affect the periodicity or ability of the vocal fold to vibrate in a repetitive fashion.

Neuromuscular problems either prevent the cord from opposing or provide a weak body on which the cover or mucosal layers can vibrate.

Natural History and Its Modification with Treatment

The natural history of hoarseness is dependent on the etiology. Inflammations and acute processes often resolve with voice rest and appropriate antibiotic and antiinflammatory therapy. Those disorders caused by chronic scarring or neuromuscular problems may be permanent.

Prevention

Proper voice habits and avoidance of laryngeal abusive behavior are the best means of avoiding laryngeal problems. Not smoking and avoiding environmental pollutants are also important factors. Proper voice care for the professional speaker, including periods of voice rest or professional voice coaching, may be necessary.

Cost Containment

Early diagnostic evaluation of the patient with hoarseness should include an attempt at determining an etiology as soon as possible. Routine use of antibiotics when no definite evidence of infection is present should be avoided.

Prompt referral to a specialist with an interest in laryngeal disorders will expedite treatment.

REFERENCES

Baker BM. Persistent hoarseness after surgical removal of vocal cord lesions. Arch Otolaryngol 1981;107:148.
Bloch CS, Gould WF, Hirano M. Effect of voice therapy on contact granuloma of the vocal fold. Ann Otol Rhinol Laryngol 1981;90:48.
Kirchner JA, Owen JR. Five hundred cancers of the larynx and pyriform sinus: Results of treatment by radiation and surgery. Laryngoscope 1977;87:1288.
Strong MS, Jako GN. Laser surgery in the larynx. Ann Otol Rhinol Laryngol 1972;81:781.

CHAPTER 21–32
Acute Laryngitis (See Section 21, Chapter 31)

CHAPTER 21–33
Chronic Laryngitis (See Section 21, Chapter 31)

CHAPTER 21–34
Salivary Tumors

Gerald S. Gussack, M.D.

DEFINITION

Tumors of the salivary glands are neoplasms involving either the major or minor salivary glands. They are predominantly benign in the major salivary glands and predominantly malignant in the minor salivary glands.

ETIOLOGY

The etiology of salivary tumors is unknown.

CRITERIA FOR DIAGNOSIS
Suggestive

The clinical setting is usually one of a painless mass that increases in size over a period of months. The patient often notes this on shaving or washing the face. A clue to consideration of this diagnosis is detection of the mass in the parotid or submandibular glands. The mass usually appears as a discrete, firm, but not particularly hard mass. A benign mass often feels firm, but not fixed to the soft tissue or skin. Malignant masses may have evidence of fixation and a surrounding area of induration. A mass in the parotid gland that presents with a facial nerve palsy should be considered a malignant lesion.

Definitive

The lesion is demonstrated within one of the major or minor salivary glands by physical examination or radiographs. Biopsy of the lesion with histologic examination provides a definitive diagnosis.

CLINICAL MANIFESTATIONS

Subjective

Family history, past medical history, occupation, and social habits seem to have little impact on the development of neoplasms of the salivary glands. Some patients may give a history of inflammatory disease in the salivary glands, though this is not often the case. A previous history of radiation therapy or radiation exposure should alert the physician to the possible development of a malignant salivary tumor.

The most common presenting symptom for patients with tumors of the salivary glands is a mass lesion in the affected gland. The most common sites are the major salivary glands. Parotid tumors often present at the angle of the mandible in the tail of the gland or, less commonly, in the immediate preauricular area in the body of the gland. Submandibular gland neoplasms present in the area more anteriorly and medially below the mandible.

When malignant lesions of the salivary glands are present, there is often associated lymphadenopathy or, in advanced lesions of the parotid, a facial nerve palsy. Pain can be associated with malignant lesions, particularly those such as adenoid cystic carcinoma, which have a high propensity for neural invasion and skull base involvement.

Objective

Physical Examination

A mass lesion is the most common manifestation noted on physical examination. The major salivary glands continue to be the most common site for tumors, with the parotid having a slightly higher incidence of neoplasms than the submandibular glands. There continues to be a higher incidence of inflammatory disease in the submandibular glands than the parotid, however. The mass usually appears smooth and encapsulated and occurs most often in the tail of the parotid gland. Masses can become quite large and approach 10 to 15 cm in diameter.

Malignant lesions of the parotid often mimic benign lesions in their early stages. Lymphadenopathy, skin erosion, fixation to the skull or deep neck, and facial nerve palsies are all physical signs of advanced malignant disease.

Minor salivary gland neoplasms are usually manifested by mass lesions in the oral cavity. These have a very high incidence of malignancy. They are most commonly seen in the hard palate and buccal mucosa.

Routine Laboratory Abnormalities

Routine laboratory data have little value in the usual workup of patients with salivary gland neoplastic disease.

PLANS

Diagnostic

The initial and most important step in the workup of masses in the salivary gland should be a complete head and neck physical examination. The entire neck should be palpated to determine if associated adenopathy is present. Bimanual palpation of the floor of the mouth is also helpful in determining the exact location and size of any submandibular neoplasia. Possible sites for primary carcinomas with the development of associated metastatic disease should be sought. The physician presented with a parotid mass, should perform a complete examination of the scalp to look for a skin primary.

Computed tomography is helpful in determining the exact location of a mass and defining the presence or absence of any associated lymphadenopathy in the ipsilateral or contralateral necks.

Needle aspiration of the mass for diagnostic cytologic evaluation is the easiest and least invasive means of obtaining a diagnosis. This requires an experienced cytopathologist, to whom clinical information must be made available. Depending on the quality of the aspirate, degree of cellularity, and personal experience, the cytopathologist is not always able to make a diagnosis. Performing multiple initial samples increases one's chances. A negative aspirate cannot always be counted on to completely rule out a malignancy, as sampling errors can occur.

Therapeutic

Therapeutic Options

Medications have little role in the management of salivary tumors. The physician may elect to treat the mass with a short course of antibiotics when sialoadenitis is suspected. A broad-spectrum antibiotic with anti-staphylococcal coverage should be used. This modality should not be used unless clinical signs and symptoms are indicative of such.

Surgery remains the mainstay of management in treating tumors of the salivary glands. Lesions of the parotid gland are most often managed by a complete resection via a superficial or lateral lobe parotidectomy, with preservation of the facial nerve. Malignant lesions may require a more extensive resection, with removal of the deep lobe and possibly a radical neck dissection. When tumor involves the facial nerve or a facial nerve palsy is present on examination, then sacrifice of this nerve is indicated. Masses in the submandibular gland are treated with a complete submandibular gland resection. Minor salivary gland neoplasms are treated with total resection with a negative histologic margin.

Recommended Approach

The recommended approach is complete surgical excision of the tumor. Removal of regional nodes should be considered when indicated for high-grade malignant lesions.

The patient should be informed of the histologic diagnosis, the likelihood of recurrence, and the prognosis of his or her particular lesion. The patient with a benign tumor or low-grade malignancy can expect an essentially normal lifestyle, with little likelihood of recurrence. Pleomorphic adenomas, however, represent a benign diagnosis, with a propensity toward recurrence when tumor is spilled or incompletely resected.

High-grade malignant lesions can have a very poor prognosis. They may, as in the case of adenoid cystic carcinomas, manifest good 5-year survival rates but very poor 10- and 15-year survival.

FOLLOW-UP

The patient should report the return of any mass lesion in the state of the resection or any return of symptoms over the follow-up period. Facial nerve symptoms or any cranial neuropathy should be viewed with a high degree of suspicion.

The physician should see all patients with malignant lesions of the salivary gland on a bimonthly basis for the first year. Follow-up intervals can be extended with each subsequent year the patient remains disease free. Patients with benign lesions of the salivary glands can be checked on a 6-month follow-up schedule. A complete head and neck examination should be performed on each follow-up visit.

DISCUSSION

Prevalence and Incidence

Salivary tumors are relatively uncommon and make up probably 1 to 2% of tumors of the head and neck. Approximately 80% of the tumors seen in salivary glands are benign. There is a slight preponderance of salivary gland tumors in males.

Related Basic Science

Tumors of the salivary glands represent a spectrum of neoplasms that seem to arise from the basal or reserve cells of the intercalated ducts of the excretory system. These are also called the myoepithelial units. Most salivary gland enlargement results from inflammatory disease, and salivary gland neoplasms account for less than 5% of all head and neck tumors. It is estimated that for every 100 parotid tumors, there are 10 submandibular, 10 minor salivary, and 1 sublingual neoplasm. Fifteen percent of parotid tumors, 35% of submandibular tumors, and 50% of minor salivary gland tumors are malignant. Sublingual tumors are very rare and almost always malignant.

Nonneoplastic disease, particularly sialoadenitis, accounts for a large percentage of submandibular swelling. These are usually bacterial infections caused by staphylococci and streptococci. Dehydration and salivary stasis seem to be predisposing factors. Sialolithiasis is associated with this about 30 to 50% of the time. Sialoliths are much more common in the submandibular than in the parotid glands.

There is a group of benign enlargements of the salivary glands with a nonspecific etiology. These are characterized by asymptomatic, though occasionally tender, enlarged glands. This condition may be unilateral or bilateral and involves successive enlargements of the glands. The clinical setting is diverse and involves Sjögren's syndrome, Mikulicz' disease, sicca complex, and HIV-associated parotid enlargement. Histologically, these appear as diffuse enlargements of small lymphocytes appearing around the ductal units. These can progress to lymphoid follicles with germinal centers. Benign lymphoepithelial lesions may progress to malignant lymphoma and carcinoma. Malignant lymphoma has been reported in both salivary and extrasalivary sites.

Necrotizing sialometaplasia is another entity worthy of mention. This benign self-limited lesion is usually seen in patients between 40 and 60 years of age. It usually appears as a punctate ulceration of the mucoserous glands of the hard palate and can range from 0.5 to 3.0 cm in diameter. Histologically, the ulcerations demonstrate pseudoepitheliomatous hyperplasia, lobular infarction, inflammation, and squamous metaplasia. They usually heal spontaneously. The problem with this lesion is that it is often mistaken for a squamous cell or mucoepidermoid carcinoma. Recognition of the preserved architecture of the lobules should prevent this error.

Pleomorphic adenomas represent the most common benign major salivary gland neoplasm. They typically present as slowly enlarging, painless masses that do not invade or effect the overlying normal skin. These adenomas most typically present in women and are most common in the fourth to sixth decades. The term *pleomorphic adenoma* or *mixed tumor* is derived from the histologic appearance. The components are a capsule, epithelial and myoepithelial cells, and a stroma containing fibrocollagenous and myxochondroid features.

Warthin's tumors, or papillary cystadenoma lymphomatosum, constitute about 15% of benign parotid tumors. They are unique among salivary tumors because of their lymphoid appearance and male predominance. There is a 10% incidence of bilateralism. The majority of lesions occur in the tail of their parotid in patients in their fifth to sixth decades of life.

Oncocytomas are similar to Warthin's tumors in presentation and location. These tumors are composed almost exclusively of oncocytes and are usually encapsulated when appearing in the major salivary glands.

Hemangiomas account for 1 to 5% of all parotid tumors. These are the most common parotid tumors in infancy and include hemangioendotheliomas, cavernous hemangiomas, and capillary hemangiomas. The majority of hemangiomas are treated with complete excision, with preservation of the facial nerve.

Mucoepidermoid carcinomas are the most common malignant salivary tumors. They have a varying degree of biological activity, with low-, intermediate-, and high-grade histologic grades. Sixty percent of the lesions occur in the parotid, and 30% occur in the submandibular glands. Mucoepidermoid carcinomas are the most common malignant salivary gland tumors in children, though the majority of these tend to be low grade. The usual presentation of the low-grade tumor may be similar to that of a benign pleomorphic adenoma, with slow enlargement of a painless mass. High-grade lesions may be quite painful and are more tender and fixed to surrounding tissue, when compared with their low-grade counterparts.

Histologically, mucoepidermoid carcinomas are composed of mucous, epidermoid, and intermediate cells. The low-grade lesions have a predominance of mucous cells, with rare mitotic figures. High-grade lesions have a predominance of epidermoid and intermediate cells. Significant nuclear pleomorphism and mitotic figures are present. High-grade carcinomas have a high recurrence rate and incidence of metastases. The treatment for these lesions is total excision, with nodal dissection for high-grade lesions or when metastases are present.

Adenoid cystic carcinomas account for 5 to 10% of parotid malignancies, 20 to 30% of submandibular malignancies, and 50 to 60% of minor salivary gland malignancies. These tumors have a poorly defined margin and a tendency for local and neural invasion. The pattern of growth is characteristically slow, but relentless. The treatment is wide excision with sacrifice of any invaded nerve. Postoperative radiation therapy is often recommended. Recurrences and metastases can occur up to 20 years later.

Acinic cell carcinomas are rare and account for 1 to 2% of all salivary gland neoplasms. They are the second most common malignant neoplasms of childhood. The usual presentation and prognosis are similar to those of a low-grade mucoepidermoid carcinoma.

Malignant mixed tumors usually arise from the site of resection of a benign pleomorphic adenoma. There are also malignant mixed tumors that arise de novo. In the classic presentation, the lesion has been present for a prolonged period, usually 20 years, and then undergoes malignant change. The tumors are usually adenocarcinomas or undifferentiated carcinomas. They have a high incidence of local and regional metastases and a high incidence of neural invasion. All of these factors lead to a guarded prognosis.

Natural History and Its Modification with Treatment

The natural history of parotid masses is dependent on their histologic diagnosis. Benign lesions tend to increase slowly over a period. Benign pleomorphic adenomas left untreated can be expected to undergo malignant change approximately 25% of the time.

Malignant lesions of the salivary glands have varying prognoses, depending on their histologic subtype, nodal status, and presence of neural invasion. These lesions have a significant negative impact on survival. In general, low-grade and mucoepidermoid and acinic cell carcinomas have a relatively favorable prognosis.

Prevention

No preventive measures are currently available.

Cost Containment

The treatment of all head and neck neoplasms, especially malignant lesions, can be quite expensive. Management by an experienced head and neck surgeon provides the most direct and effective utilization of services. Diagnostic open biopsies should never be performed. Needle aspiration, complete physical examination, and computed tomography of the neck should constitute a complete preoperative evaluation.

REFERENCES

Barnes L. Diseases of the salivary gland. In: Barnes L, ed. Surgical pathology of the head and neck. New York: Marcel Dekker, 1985.

Batsakis JG. Tumors of the head and neck. Baltimore: William & Wilkins, 1979:55.

Batsakis JG, Bernacki EG, Rice DH, Stebler ME. Malignancy and the benign lymphoepithelial lesion. Laryngoscope 1975;85:389.

Fechner RE. Necrotizing sialometaplasia. Am J Clin Pathol 1977;67:315.

Fee WE, Goffinet ICW, Calcaterra TC. Recurrent mixed tumors of the parotid gland: Results of surgical therapy. Laryngoscope 1979;88:265.

Foote FW, Frazzel EL. Tumors of the major salivary glands. Cancer 1953;6:1065.

Epistaxis

Gerald S. Gussack, M.D.

DEFINITION

Epistaxis is defined as bleeding from the nasal passages.

ETIOLOGY

The cause of epistaxis is usually a disruption of the mucosal vascular system within the nasal passages. Bleeding can also occur from vascular malformations and benign and malignant tumors.

CRITERIA FOR DIAGNOSIS
Suggestive

The types of epistaxis are divided into anterior epistaxis, which occurs through the front of the nose, and posterior epistaxis, which is bleeding into the nasopharynx and posterior oral cavity.

Epistaxis occurs in a variety of different clinical settings. It involves all age groups and both sexes and varies in severity from mild, annoying symptoms to life-threatening hemorrhage. The diagnosis is usually obvious.

Definitive

When anterior epistaxis occurs, active bleeding is noted from one or both nostrils. When the patient states that bleeding has stopped, examination of the nose reveals blood in the nasal vestibule. Posterior epistaxis is diagnosed by examining the nose and posterior pharynx and observing blood in this area. The patient may be swallowing a significant amount of blood, and this can mask some of the early symptoms.

CLINICAL MANIFESTATIONS
Subjective

The patient complains of blood emanating anteriorly or posteriorly through the nasal passages. The patient may have a history of bleeding tendencies such as von Willebrand's disease, hereditary hemorrhagic telangiectasia, and granulomatous disease. The patient may have experienced nasal trauma. Other patients may have epistaxis as the initial presenting symptom of a nasal or nasopharyngeal malignancy.

Objective
Physical Examination

The abnormal physical findings in patients with epistaxis appear predominantly as nasal abnormalities. Obviously, when a patient presents in the active phase, bleeding is noted from either the anterior or posterior nasal passages. When patients are not actively bleeding but present with a history of epistaxis, the nasal examination may reveal several abnormalities. These can include mucosal vascular changes, ulcerations, polyps, septal and turbinate deformities, tumors, and a totally normal examination.

Routine Laboratory Abnormalities

Laboratory evaluations are undertaken to look for evidence of anemia, coagulation disorders, or autoimmune diseases. These tests can include a complete blood count, prothrombin time, partial thromboplastin time, bleeding time, and clotting time. Additional testing is not required to make a diagnosis of epistaxis. It can, however, lead one to a predisposing etiology.

PLANS
Diagnostic

The diagnosis is established by the history and physical examination (see Clinical Manifestations).

Therapeutics
Therapeutic Options

The goal of therapy in epistaxis is primarily to stop the acute bleeding and secondarily to present recurrences.

This discussion deals first with anterior epistaxis. Applying pressure to the anterior nose and septum by squeezing the nostrils stops most acute anterior bleeding. The majority of bleeding originates from the anterior inferior septum in the area known anatomically as Kiesselbach's plexus. This area often demonstrates increased vascularity or inflammation on physical examination. When the site can be visualized and blood suctioned away, the area in question can be cauterized with topical application of silver nitrate. Application of a cotton pledget contains 4% cocaine hydrochloride solution prior to cauterization provides both vasoconstriction and anesthesia.

When pressure and cauterization are unable to control anterior epistaxis, then packing of the nasal passages is required. The patient should be given a narcotic such as morphine sulfate prior to packing. Vaseline gauze layered in an inferior to superior fashion is best. Care should be taken to avoid further trauma to the nose.

Commercially available nasal balloons are also used as a quick means of applying pressure to the septum and controlling bleeding. Care must be taken not to overinflate the balloons, as necrosis of the septum may result.

Posterior epistaxis is more difficult to control and can be life threatening to a patient. The patients are usually elderly and have factors predisposing to bleeding. These factors include hypertension, bleeding dyscrasias, hereditary hemorrhagic telangiectasia, nasal tumors, and arteriovenous malformation. Very often the area of bleeding cannot be visualized on anterior rhinoscopy. Control of posterior epistaxis is best managed by an otolaryngologist. Placement of a posterior nasopharyngeal pack or operative posterior rhinoscopy and cauterization are required.

Patients with recurrent posterior epistaxis may require operative or angiographic ligation of the internal maxillary artery. This serves to decrease the frequency and severity of posterior epistaxis. If predisposing factors or lesions exist, then appropriate therapy for these lesions should be undertaken.

Recommended Approach

The approach is as outlined above and adjusted for severity of bleeding and location.

Patients with recurrent epistaxis should be taught about the factors predisposing to nosebleeds, such as bleeding dyscrasias, hypertension, rhinitis, metabolic disorders, and anatomic deformities. The majority of patients have septal deformities, with subsequent rhinitis. These patients may require a septoplasty to provide definitive improvement in symptoms.

Treatment of other ongoing predisposing factors should be maintained. Treatment of rhinitis is the most common.

FOLLOW-UP

The patient should be followed for as long as symptoms of bleeding are present. Patients should return to the physician if symptoms worsen or epistaxis no longer is controlled by nasal compression or methods that have worked in the past. The physician should determine what predisposing factors exist and adjust follow-up accordingly.

DISCUSSION
Prevalence

Epistaxis is an almost ubiquitous symptom. Almost every individual experiences a nosebleed at one time in his or her life. They occur at all ages and in both sexes. The majority of nosebleeds resolve sponta-neously and do not require significant therapy.

A small percentage of the population is plagued by recurrent epis-taxis. This can be very debilitating from a social and economic stand-point and may severely compromise the patient's livelihood. In young children the etiology is usually crusting and rhinitis involving the ante-rior septum. Adults who present with chronic epistaxis often have some predisposing factors.

Related Basic Science

Jackson and Jackson (1988) described the underlying clinical factors associated with refractory active epistaxis. They found significant inci-dences of hypertension, diabetes, aspirin use, and alcohol abuse. Sys-temic disorders such as coagulopathies, liver disease, and renal failure were noted. They recommended a bleeding time as an essential study to detect coagulopathies.

Packing of the nasal cavity is an often used and acceptable method for treating epistaxis; however, it is not without complications. These include posterior displacement, septal perforations, sleep apnea syn-drome, and airway obstruction. All patients requiring posterior packing should be hospitalized and monitored for signs of carbon dioxide reten-tion.

Natural History and Its Modifications with Treatment

The natural history of most epistaxis is resolution with standard ther-apy. Little mortality is associated with the disorder; however, morbid-ity, including pain and time away from normal activity, is significant.

Prevention

Few measures are available for prevention unless a predisposing factor can be determined. Hypertension, rhinitis, coagulopathies, aspirin abuse, and other diseases that may contribute to bleeding should be treated.

Cost Containment

Treatment should be geared to the specific anatomic site and predispos-ing factor. Extensive radiographic workups should be used only when necessary or so indicated by physical findings.

REFERENCES

Fairbanks DNF. Complications of nasal packing. Otolaryngol Head Neck Surg 1986;94:412.

Jackson KR, Jackson RT. Factors associated with active refractory epistaxis. Arch Otolaryngol Head Neck Surg 1988;114:862.

McDonald TJ. Granulomatous diseases of the nose. In: English GM, ed. Oto-laryngology. Hagerstown, MD: Harper, 1980.

Pearson BW, MacKenzie RG, Goodman NS. The anatomic basis of transantral ligation of the internal maxillary artery. Laryngoscope 1969;79;969.

Robertson GH, Reardon EJ. Angiography and embolization of the internal max-illary artery for posterior epistaxis. Arch Otolaryngol Head Neck Surg 1979;105:333.

CHAPTER 21–36

Nasal Masses

Gerald S. Gussack, M.D.

DEFINITION

Nasal masses are defined as abnormal growths within the nasal cavity.

ETIOLOGY

Multiple etiologies are responsible for nasal masses. Tobacco is the causative agent for most malignant lesions. Human papillomaviruses are suspected causes of inverted papilloma. Benign tumors, granulo-mas, and nasal polyps all have various multiple etiologies, both known and unknown.

CRITERIA FOR DIAGNOSIS
Suggestive

Nasal masses include both benign and malignant varieties. These disor-ders often present with symptoms of nasal obstruction or bleeding. The physician notes obstruction or deformity of the nasal passage on ante-rior rhinoscopy. This can further be defined through the use of diagnos-tic radiographic studies such as sinus x-rays and computed tomography.

Definitive

The finding of a mass by computed tomography or physical examina-tion confirms the diagnosis.

CLINICAL MANIFESTATIONS
Subjective

Nasal masses occur in both adults and children and equally in both sexes. The majority of nasal masses are benign; however, a variety of malignant lesions do exist. Benign nasal polyps are often seen in pa-tients with allergic disease. Nasal malignancies are seen in patients with a history of nickel exposure and in woodworkers. Children with cystic fibrosis often manifest nasal polyps as a consequence of their as-sociated chronic sinusitis.

The primary symptom of patients with nasal masses is nasal obstruc-tion; this is an almost uniform complaint. Epistaxis, external nasal de-formity, chronic sinusitis, orbital and facial pain, diplopia, and serous otitis are other presenting complaints.

Objective
Physical Examination

The physical findings of nasal masses are often limited to the nasal cav-ity; however, a complete head and neck examination should always be performed. Benign masses, such as nasal polyps, present as smooth, glistening, grapelike masses emanating from the lateral nasal wall. Pa-pillomas, another common nasal mass, appear as a wartylike growth on the nasal septum or lateral nasal wall. Carcinomas appear as exophytic masses that are ulcerative and irregular on the surface and fill the af-fected nasal cavity. Purulent nasal discharge can occur when secondary sinusitis develops in both benign and malignant processes.

Malignant lesions of the nasal cavity may affect eustachian tube function, and serous otitis can develop. Examination of the neck may reveal a metastatic lymph node in advanced lesions.

Routine Laboratory Abnormalities

Routine laboratory investigations are usually of little value in the evalu-ation of nasal masses.

PLANS

Diagnostic

Diagnostic Options

The evaluation of the patient with a mass in the nasal cavity should begin with a complete head and neck examination. Careful inspection of both nasal cavities and the nasopharynx should be performed. Otologic examination should be performed along with pneumootoscopy to determine if serous fluid is seen. Nasal endoscopy with either a flexible fiberoptic rhinolaryngoscope or a rigid rod lens telescope provides a closer and more accurate anatomic assessment of the mass.

A general impression of the benign or malignant nature of the mass can be obtained on physical examination. Smooth encapsulated masses such as polyps are almost always benign. Verrucous-appearing lesions often represent benign squamous papillomas. Inverted papillomas have a similar appearance, however, and usually arise from the lateral nasal wall. A biopsy is essential to make an accurate diagnosis. Once a histologic diagnosis is made, a more definitive plan of treatment can be undertaken. Computed tomography of the nose and paranasal sinuses gives the most accurate anatomic information about the extent of involvement of the lesion. Smooth encapsulated masses that expand but do not destroy bone are most likely to be benign. Lesions that demonstrate bony destruction, orbital or intracranial invasion, or soft tissue involvement have a much higher likelihood of being malignant. Magnetic resonance imaging can be used when intracranial invasion is suspected and further delineation of the skull base is required.

Recommended Approach

The recommended approach is as outlined above with confirmation of the mass by biopsy and anatomic evaluation by both physical examination and computed tomography.

Therapeutic

Therapeutic Options

Medical therapy has little role in the treatment of most nasal masses. There is clinical evidence that the utilization of topical and systemic steroids is beneficial in reducing and preventing the recurrence of nasal polyps. The majority of polyps require surgical removal for any significant symptomatic improvement.

Surgery remains the mainstay of treatment in the management of most nasal masses. Small lesions of the anterior nasal vestibule can be excisionally biopsied. This serves as both a diagnostic and therapeutic modality. Resection of more extensive nasal masses can be undertaken by various other surgical approaches, depending on the histologic subtype and anatomic location. These approaches range from endoscopic intranasal polypectomy and ethmoidectomy to a combined craniofacial resection. Many benign lesions can be removed via an intranasal approach. More extensive lesions can require further exposure via a transfacial or midface degloving approach. In treatment of malignant nasal tumors that invade the roof of the ethmoid sinuses, a combined intracranial and nasal approach is required.

Morbidity related to surgery for the treatment of nasal masses is dependent on the surgical approach and the location of the particular lesion. Those lesions that are low and anterior in the nasal cavity are usually easily removed and have bleeding as a predominant source of morbidity. With lesions that involve the superior lateral nasal wall, the possibility of orbital injury exists, whereas lesions that are high in the nasal cavity can result in intracranial injury. With nasal lesions that extend into the sphenoid sinus, there exists possibility for injury to the carotid artery, cavernous sinus, or optic chiasm when surgical resection is attempted.

Recommended Approach

The patient should be informed of the diagnosis and overall treatment plan. Benign lesions are most likely treated with surgical resection, with close follow-up and possible steroid therapy. Malignant lesions require complete surgical resection and, possibly, pre- or postoperative radiation therapy. Many benign nasal masses such as polyps and papillomas have a high incidence of recurrence, requiring repeat excision.

The prognosis for malignant lesions of the nasal cavity, as in other head and neck sites, varies depending on their size, stage, and histologic subtype.

FOLLOW-UP

The patient should note the return of any of his or her presenting symptoms. Again, symptoms of nasal obstruction predominate. The patient should report any change in nasal breathing, epistaxis, pain, or symptoms of sinusitis.

The physician should perform a complete head and neck examination at each follow-up visit. Patients with benign lesions should be followed approximately three to four times per year. Patients with malignant lesions should be seen at monthly intervals for the first year and then at increasing intervals each year. Computed tomography can be repeated at 1 year or at any time a recurrence is suspected.

DISCUSSION

Prevalence

Nasal masses constitute a diverse group of diseases. The majority of lesions are benign and related to inflammatory and infectious processes. Nasal polyps are by far the most common benign nasal masses.

Related Basic Science

Nasal polyps are usually a consequence of chronic inflammatory disease and can be seen in both adults and children. Polyps represent edematous, hypertrophied nasal and sinus mucosa that protrudes through the ostia of the lateral nasal wall.

Papillomas of the nasal cavity represent benign, nonkeratinizing squamous metaplasia. This is believed by pathologists such as Batsakis (1980) to represent a proliferation of the schneiderian membrane or epithelium that forms the mucosa of the nasal cavity. This membrane is thought to be of ectodermal origin, whereas the remainder of the upper respiratory tract is derived from endoderm. Papillomas are relatively uncommon when compared with nasal polyps; polyps predominate approximately 35:1.

There are four types of nasal papillomas: vestibular papillomas, inverted papillomas, fungiform or septal papillomas, and cylindrical cell papillomas. The inverted papilloma is the most common and is the most controversial. It is almost exclusively a lateral nasal wall lesion and is seen predominantly in men in the fourth to fifth decades. The gross appearance is that of a bulky deep red to gray fibrous mass. The histologic appearance of the lesion lends the term *inverted*. The epithelium of the papilloma inverts into the underlying stroma, instead of developing an exophytic appearance as is most common with other papillomas.

Fungiform papillomas are the second most common of all the papillomas. They arise almost exclusively from the nasal septum. Grossly, the lesions appear as a verrucous cauliflower-like growth. They are attached to the septum by a broad base.

The cylindrical cell papilloma is the rarest of all the papillomas. It is characterized by a large, beefy-appearing growth that usually arises from the lateral wall of the nose.

Clinically, all papillomas have a very high incidence of recurrence, ranging from 25 to 75%. This may be due in part to incomplete excision and persistence of residual papilloma. Metaplasia of adjacent mucosa is another factor that must be considered and is associated with a very high incidence of recurrence. Malignancy is also associated with papillomas, especially the inverted variety. Hyams (1971) reported an incidence of invasive squamous cell carcinoma associated with the identical site of inverted papilloma in 13% of lesions. Ten percent of inverted papillomas demonstrate marked atypia on initial examination.

Malignant lesions of the nasal cavity and paranasal sinuses constitute less than 1% of all carcinomas and about 3% of all head and neck malignancies. The lesions often present late in the course of the disease and often involve the adjacent paranasal sinuses. Treatment of these lesions often requires combined surgery and pre- or postoperative radiation for optimum control. The majority of patients have been treated for chronic inflammatory disease for a period of 6 months or longer. The intimate anatomic association between the nasal and maxillary sinuses accounts for the high incidence of spread of malignant lesions from one to the other. The maxillary sinus is involved in 80% of malignant lesions arising in the nasal cavity.

The majority of patients with carcinoma of the nasal cavity are older than 50 and male. The lesions most commonly arise from the lateral wall. Other subsites of origin include septum, vestibule, posterior choanae, and nasal floor. Chronic sinusitis, nasal papillomas, and smoking are often seen as predisposing factors.

The majority of malignant lesions of the nasal cavity are squamous in origin. These range in grade from well differentiated to anaplastic. Metastatic lymph node involvement is not frequent. The prognosis of most nasal malignancies is dependent on the size of the lesion. When metastatic disease is present, there is a high incidence of bilateral nodal involvement in the neck.

Natural History and Its Modification with Treatment

The morbidity of benign nasal masses is that associated with the surgical management and those symptoms related to chronic nasal obstruction and sinusitis. The majority of these patients note the return of nasal obstruction as heralding the onset of recurrences. There is little or no associated mortality.

Malignancies that present in the nasal cavity have a very poor prognosis. The predominant reason for this is the advanced stage of disease at which the patient often presents.

Prevention

There are few means available for the prevention of nasal masses. Control of inflammatory disease and use of topical steroids may prevent the recurrence of nasal polyps. Malignant masses may be prevented to a small degree by avoiding the use of tobacco products and environmental exposure to nickel.

Cost Containment

Treatment of nasal masses is best carried out by an otolaryngologist with experience in this area. Early biopsy and diagnosis lead to orderly treatment of the disease.

REFERENCES

Batsakis JG. Tumors of the head and neck: Clinical and pathological considerations. London: Williams & Wilkins, 1980.

Hyams VJ. Papillomas of the nasal cavity and paranasal sinuses. Ann Otol Rhinol Laryngol 1971;80:192.

Settipane GA, Chafee FH. Nasal polyps in asthma and rhinitis. J Allergy Clin Immunol 1977;59:17.

Van Tuyl R, Gussack GS. Prognostic factors in craniofacial surgery. Laryngoscope 1991;101:240.

CHAPTER 21–37

Obstructive Sleep Apnea

Gerald S. Gussack, M.D.

DEFINITION

Sleep apnea is defined as cessation of airflow secondary to either obstruction of the upper airway or cessation of respiration efforts. The airflow should stop for at least 10 seconds.

ETIOLOGY

The cause of obstructive sleep apnea is usually a combination of nasal and oropharyngeal anatomic obstruction. This is exacerbated by obesity and collapse of the pharyngeal walls.

CRITERIA FOR DIAGNOSIS

Suggestive

The majority of patients have airway obstruction as the principal dysfunction, with pure central apneic syndromes being rare. The clinical setting is usually one of an overweight or obese individual with symptoms of mouth breathing, daytime somnolence, and snoring. The patient complains of poor-quality sleep, headaches, and falling asleep at many inopportune times.

The diagnosis of obstructive sleep apnea should be considered in an individual who is overweight, if not obese, with complaints of snoring by either the patient, spouse, or housemates, and an examination demonstrating evidence of airway obstruction of the nose or oropharynx.

Definitive

The diagnosis is confirmed by the patient undergoing an evaluation in a sleep laboratory, that is, polysomnography. Polysomnography is a sophisticated study to measure the presence of sleep apnea. This study generally includes using the monitoring systems listed in Table 21–37–1.

CLINICAL MANIFESTATIONS

Subjective

The typical patient with sleep apnea is well described in the classic pickwickian syndrome in Charles Dickens' *The Pickwick Papers*. This patient is obese, snores, and falls asleep in an upright position. The consequences of poor sleep can lead to serious social and economic hardships for the affected individual. The disease is present in both sexes, though probably seen more commonly in males. Sleep apnea is not uncommonly seen in young children and infants and can be a source of complications for other cardiovascular problems. Sleep apnea can lead to cor pulmonale and right-sided heart failure, particularly in those children with congenital heart disease. There is an almost universal incidence of obstructive sleep apnea in obese individuals. This often lessens in severity for those patients who are capable of losing weight.

Daytime somnolence is the predominant symptom of sleep apnea. Patients often fall asleep while sitting up and complain of total lack of energy. Air hunger at night is also seen in severe cases.

TABLE 21–37–1. MONITORING SYSTEMS INVOLVED IN POLYSOMNOGRAPHY

Electroencephalogram
Electrocardiogram
Oxygen saturation
Electrooculogram
Nasal airflow
Respiratory motion
Submental and anterior tibial electromyogram
Respiratory effort monitoring

Objective

Physical Examination

The most common objective finding in patients with sleep apnea is obesity. Obviously there are patients with obstructive sleep apnea who are not obese, but this remains the most frequently seen body habitus. Varying degrees of respiratory tract obstruction are almost always present. These include, on oral examination, a large uvula, redundant palate, collapsing lateral pharyngeal walls, and tonsillar and/or adenoidal hypertrophy. Nasal airway obstruction may be manifested on physical examination by a deviated nasal septum, collapsing nasal valves, turbinate hypertrophy, or nasal polyps. Carcinomas of the nasopharynx may also present with nasal airway obstruction and subsequent sleep apnea.

Laryngeal obstruction may also occasionally manifest itself with sleep apnea. These findings can include stridor, subglottic stenosis, vocal cord paralysis, and supraglottic obstructing lesions. These are the least common causes of obstructive sleep apnea, and other airway or voice symptoms are usually present.

Routine Laboratory Abnormalities

There are no diagnostic routine laboratory abnormalities.

PLANS

Diagnostic

Diagnostic Options

Few disease entities present with such classic historical findings.

Once a high index of suspicion is reached, a polysomnogram or sleep study should be obtained. Such studies are available in most major medical centers and provide valuable information in the diagnosis of this condition. The study should include at least all of the previously mentioned monitoring systems listed in Table 21–37–1. The patient is usually observed overnight in the sleep laboratory, and recordings are made. The clues derived from the polysomnogram are listed in Table 21–37–2.

The study is then interpreted according to the guidelines set up by the individual sleep laboratory. Significant apnea is associated with an index greater than 20, saturations below 80%, greater than 20 arousals, and cardiac ectopy associated with apnea. Obviously, each individual test must be weighed in its severity. All of these factors are modified by the patient's daytime symptoms.

Recommended Approach

The best approach is a complete history and physical examination followed by a polysomnogram.

Therapeutic

Therapeutic Options

Correcting the underlying predisposing factors is the mainstay of correcting obstructive sleep apnea. The most beneficial but least appreciated therapy is substantial weight loss. A great deal of improvement is seen in those patients who are able to reduce to near their ideal body weight.

Medications per se have little benefit in the management of obstructive sleep apnea. Avoiding alcohol and central nervous system depressants should be encouraged, as these can potentiate the sleep apnea symptoms. Likewise, smoking can cause nasal congestion. Protripty-

TABLE 21–37–2. CLUES DERIVED FROM THE POLYSOMNOGRAM

Apneic index
Apnea duration
Apnea type: central versus obstructive
Apnea-related arousals
Apnea-related oxygen desaturation
Apnea-related cardiac disturbance

line is the most widely used medication for obstructive sleep apnea, and it is felt to have a role in increasing the tone of pharyngeal muscles.

Nasopharyngeal airways are of benefit, but long-term compliance is poor. Orthodontic obturators have been purported to affect an improvement in oral airway patency and, hence, improvement in obstructive sleep apnea symptoms. No studies exist, however, to support their effectiveness. Continuous positive airway pressure via a nasal route (nasal CPAP) is also an effective treatment. These devices are cumbersome, and sleep is difficult despite improvement in obstructive sleep apnea. The motivated patient can be helped in this fashion. The pressure of CPAP can be adjusted during a second sleep study.

With the exception of weight loss, surgery provides the most effective means by which to manage obstructive sleep apnea. The decision for surgery is based on a firm diagnosis and a complete head and neck examination. Nasal obstruction can certainly complicate obstructive sleep apnea and worsen symptoms. Deviated nasal septums, hypertrophied turbinates, and nasal polyps can all be surgically corrected. It is uncommon, however, for obstructive sleep apnea to result from nasal obstruction alone.

Tracheostomy remains the most definitive surgical treatment of obstructive sleep apnea. It provides a secure airway that totally bypasses the nose and oropharynx. The procedure is straightforward and successful in relieving obstructive sleep apnea in almost any patient. The social unacceptability, inability to talk, and significant amount of care involved make tracheostomy an unacceptable alternative for all but the most severely affected or debilitated individuals.

Uvulopalatopharyngoplasty (UVPP) remains the mainstay of surgical treatment of obstructive sleep apnea. This procedure is combined with a tonsillectomy when tonsils are still present. The operation involves removing the uvula and the leading edge of the palate. The palate and anterior and posterior tonsil pillars are than reapproximated with multiple interrupted sutures. After healing, the palate is drawn forward and the redundancy of the lateral pharyngeal walls reduced. The success of this procedure varies. It is often successful in improving snoring and has variable success in improving obstructive sleep apnea.

Recommended Approach

Normalization of the anatomy of upper airway combined with achievement of ideal body weight is the recommended approach. CPAP is used where appropriate.

It is important that the patient understand the potential for cardiac and pulmonary problems to result from obstructive sleep apnea. The need for weight loss is the key factor in treatment.

FOLLOW-UP

A posttherapy sleep study is often indicated to assess the patient's outcome from therapy. Associated cardiac problems, such as cor pulmonale, should be investigated. Histories taken from spouses or housemates as to the degree of snoring are important.

DISCUSSION

Prevalence

Obstructive sleep apnea syndrome is a relatively frequently seen condition, caused by anatomic obstruction of the upper respiratory tract by a number of different mechanisms. The symptoms about which the patient complains range from snoring and daytime somnolence to cardiac dysrhythmia and right-sided heart failure.

Related Basic Science

The mechanism of inspiration is carried out by the coordination of multiple anatomic and physiologic factors. Inspiration while awake is usually not a problem for these patients, because the negative force generated by inspiration is accompanied by increased tone of the pharyngeal dilator and abductor muscles. It is postulated that during sleep, a relative muscular hypotonia develops, as is seen in other major skeletal muscles. This results in lateral pharyngeal wall collapse and obstruction. Conditions such as nasopharyngeal tumors, adenoid and tonsillar hypertrophy, deviated nasal septums, micrognathia, and macroglossia can anatomically increase upper airway obstruction and increase the incidence and likelihood of obstructive sleep apnea syndrome developing.

Studies have demonstrated that the oropharynx is the only readily collapsible portion of the upper airway. Anatomically, there is no rigid support within the pharynx to prevent luminal collapse on generation of negative pressure with respiration.

Nasal continuous positive airway pressure (CPAP) acts as a pneumatic splint to counteract the negative force generated on inspiration and prevent collapse of the lateral pharyngeal walls. Nasal CPAP should be considered as a form of immediate intervention and an alternative to surgery, especially tracheostomy, in most patients. It theoretically should be effective in all cases of obstructive sleep apnea other than those with moderate to severe nasal obstruction. Studies have demonstrated up to a 99% elimination of obstructive sleep apnea by nasal CPAP in patients who tolerate its use. Herein lies the failure of this therapy. Claustrophobia, mucous membrane drying, eye irritation, limitation of movement, and nasal irritation are the most common complaints.

Surgery continues to be a mainstay of therapy in obstructive sleep apnea syndrome. It is undertaken after a thorough physical examination and review of the patient's history and symptoms. This begins with appreciation of the total body habitus, neck examination, and tongue position. Mandible size, particularly micrognathia, should be appreciated. The oral and nasal flow should be observed and the voice evaluated for subjective hyponasality. Blood pressure should be checked, as approximately 50% of patients are hypertensive. A complete nasal, nasopharyngeal, and laryngeal examination should also be performed.

Oral examination should include mandibular size, palatal appearance, tongue size, tonsil presence and size, and palatal dimensions. Posterior and lateral pharyngeal walls are also observed. The valleculae and base of the tongue should be visualized with either a mirror or fiberoptic laryngoscope. Müller's maneuver is performed to evaluate pharyngeal wall collapse. This is performed by closing the mouth, occluding the nose, and having the patient suck in. The lateral and posterior pharyngeal walls and soft palate are observed for collapse. There is some controversy as to the predictability of success with UVPP by this maneuver.

Nasal surgery is performed when there appears to be significant impairment of respiration. The specific deformity is corrected, be it nasal polypectomy, turbinoplasty, or septoplasty.

Uvulopalatopharyngoplasty was introduced by Fujita et al. (1981). It is designed to correct the deformities of a large uvula, posterior tonsil pillars, and redundant mucosal folds of the palate and pharynx. The operation begins by removing the tonsils, if this has not been previously performed. The uvula is then removed, as is a small portion of the leading edge of the soft palate. The resection is gauged to provide a tighter palate and less redundancy of pharyngeal wall mucosa without causing velopharyngeal incompetence or nasopharyngeal stenosis. Closure is then undertaken with interrupted sutures.

Care must be taken to monitor the airway and oxygen saturation in the immediate postoperative period. The response rate is in the range 50 to 70% for this procedure.

Natural History and Its Modification with Treatment

Untreated, obstructive sleep apnea can lead to significant systemic and cardiac problems, including hypertension, arrhythmias, cor pulmonale, and death.

Prevention

Weight reduction and good health habits regarding smoking are the best preventive measures.

Cost Containment

The disease is fairly costly to treat. In addition to an initial polysomnogram, most individuals also need to undergo a posttherapy sleep study to evaluate progress. Very often a sleep laboratory will perform the study at a reduced rate.

REFERENCES

Crumley RL, Stein M, Gansu G. Determination of obstructive site in obstructive sleep apnea. Laryngoscope 1987;97:301.

Fairbanks DNF, Fujita S. Snoring and obstructive apnea. New York: Raven Press, 1987.

Fujita S, Conway W, Zorick F, Roth T. Surgical correction of anatomic abnormalities of obstructive sleep apnea syndrome: Uvulopalatopharyngoplasty. Otolaryngol Head Neck Surg 1981;89:923.

Koopman CE, Moran WB. Sleep apnea. Otolaryngol Clin North Am 1990;23:4.

Sullivan CE, Issa FG, Berthon-Jones M. Reversal of obstructive sleep apnea by continuous positive airway pressure applied through the nose. Lancet 1981;2:862.

Common Eye Disorders

William H. Coles, M.D., M.S.

CHAPTER 22–1

Senile Cataract

William H. Coles, M.D., M.S.

DEFINITION

Cataract is an opacification of the crystalline lens of the eye. With age all lens develop charges that can be diagnosed as opacities and, therefore, cataracts. Many clinicians restrict the use of the term *cataract* for opacities that decrease visual function, using the term *opacities* for changes that do not affect vision.

Cataract, a general term, has many subclassifications. The most commonly used are nuclear sclerotic, posterior subcapsular, and cortical cataracts.

ETIOLOGY

Nuclear sclerotic cataracts occur with aging. Posterior subcapsular cataracts are associated with both inflammation and with prolonged steroid use, either topically or systemically. Certain types of cataracts are also associated with risk factors such as diabetes, alcohol use, exposure to ultraviolet light, and smoking.

CRITERIA FOR DIAGNOSIS

Suggestive

Blurred vision is a common subjective complaint. Vision is often worse in bright light. Halos or distortion of light may also occur.

Definitive

A cataract is an opacity of the normally clear lens of the eye. It can be seen grossly by penlight examination when advanced, by biomicroscopic examination (slit-lamp examination), or by retroillumination using the red reflex of the fundus as background.

CLINICAL MANIFESTATIONS

Subjective

Even though cataracts usually progress slowly, most patients notice them as a sudden awareness of visual loss when they move from a dark room into bright sunlight, a phenomenon caused by a decrease in pupillary size (compensation for brightness) that accentuates the effect of the cataract. Also at night, many patients, faced with the bright light of oncoming cars, complain of confusion or inability to distinguish objects due to the scatter of light by the cataract.

In contrast to the decrease in distant vision, patients may experience slightly or even considerably improved near vision, known as "second sight," a result of the induced myopia of the dense nuclear cataract, and for this reason, visual complaints are rarely expressed for near vision.

In all these circumstances, the visual changes are rarely perceived by the patient as threatening. They seem to accept the change with age, an observation much different in patients who react to changes in vision that are sudden. These patients with slow visual loss often delay seeking help for symptoms until some need arises, such as an inability to renew a driver's license.

Unless secondary complications occur, cataracts are not painful.

Objective

Physical Examination

Senile cataracts occur in older individuals. Cataracts in younger people should arouse suspicion of something other than the expected lens changes of age (e.g., diabetes; other metabolic disturbances, such as hypothyroidism or hypoglycemia; or congenital disturbances). Senile cataracts develop bilaterally in most circumstances, although the changes can be markedly asymmetric with significant differences in visual acuity between the two eyes.

There are three stages of cataract development useful to the clinician: immature, mature, hypermature. The immature cataract has some opacification, but parts of the lens are still clear. In the mature cataract, the lens is entirely opaque and the pupil becomes white or yellow. A hypermature cataract presents either as a swollen lens or as a shrunken lens where the lens capsule become hyperpermeable, causing lens breakdown products to float in the aqueous humor of the anterior chamber.

Hypermature and mature cataracts can be easily diagnosed with a penlight, whereas the immature cataract may require more skill and attention. Ideally, the best examination of the immature lens is with the pupil dilated and by use of magnification with the slit lamp; however, much information can be gathered by use of the direct ophthalmoscope, particularly if the pupil is dilated. Inability to see the retinal details on routine examination may be an important indication of cataract changes in an elderly individual. If immature changes are suspected, by backing the ophthalmoscope away from the patient's eye, a red pupillary reflect can be seen and can be used to contrast most opacification in the center of the lens. These opacities stand out as black densities in the surrounding red glow of the reflex. With a normal lens, the red fundus reflex that fills the pupil shows no imperfections.

Vision decreases may or may not be present in immature cataracts. Mature and hypermature cataracts are associated with severe loss of vision.

Routine Laboratory Abnormalities

There are no diagnostic routine laboratory abnormalities.

PLANS
Diagnostic

Differential Diagnosis

- Congenital cataract: Rubella is present at birth or within the first 3 months. Late symptoms, as in senile cataract, are uncommon. The cataract frequently involves the embryonic or fetal nucleus in the center of the lens.
- Herpes simplex: Usually, the cataract associated with the condition is bilateral. No other history of maternal viral infections such as rubella helps suggest the diagnosis.
- Cataract from inflammation (uveitis): There is a history of intraocular inflammation.
- Cataract associated with degenerative ocular disease: Signs of high

myopia, retinal dystrophies, retinal detachment, or ocular ischemic disease are present.
- Cataract associated with systemic disease: For example, in myotonia dystrophica, patients have characteristic facial features of myotonia.
- Toxic cataract: A history of steroid use, either topically or systemically, usually longer than 1 year is elicited. The cataract has a characteristic position in the posterior of the lens.
- Toxic cataract—miotics: A history of the use of anticholinesterase inhibitors is most common.
- Cataract from metabolic disease: There is a history of diabetes, hypocalcemia, hypothyroidism, or Wilson's disease. Clinical characteristics help differentiate metabolic causes.
- Traumatic cataract: A history of exposure to severe cold, electric shock, radiation, concussion, or penetrating injuries is present.

Diagnostic Options and Recommended Approach

See Criteria for Diagnosis.

Therapeutic

Initially, management of a cataract is simply occasional observation of the opacity. When it becomes obvious that the patient's vision is being hindered, surgical therapy should be recommended. This recommendation varies according to the patient's age, activity, and needs.

Therapy consists of removal of the cataract. Three major approaches are used: (1) intracapsular cataract extraction, in which the lens is removed with capsule, cortex, and nucleus intact; (2) extracapsular cataract extraction, in which only the lens nucleus and cortex are removed and the capsule is left partially intact in the eye (this technique is presently used also with the insertion of an intraocular lens); and (3) phacoemulsification, which is simply an additional type of extracapsular cataract extraction (the capsule is left in place, but the nucleus and cortex are removed after being fragmented by ultrasound and then sucked or washed from the eye through a small tube).

The type of extraction used depends on the individual needs of the patient, the aging condition of the lens, and the type of correction to be used after the extraction. A new technique may not be best in all patients. In most cases, the techniques used on individual patients depend on the training of the surgeon. Each surgeon must judge the best approach to the patient's needs.

There are three ways to replace the refractive power lost by extraction of the lens.

Spectacles. The advantages of spectacles are that they are very safe and can be changed or adjusted easily.

Among their disadvantages, the thick lenses can cause problems optically. Only the small central vision is clear, and the periphery is blurred and distorted. Blind spots occur on the side of the patient's vision with spectacles. Blind spots can become dangerous in such routine activities as crossing the street and avoiding automobiles approaching from the side.

Because the glasses are thick and jut beyond the frame, they scratch easily. Also, they are heavier than most other glasses and provide excess stress on frames and, therefore, require frequent replacement. The image on the retina projected by the spectacle lens is greatly enlarged and the operated eye is not able to be used with a normal eye, where a natural lens projects a small image. The image disparity between the normal eye and the operated eye with spectacle correction produces visual confusion. Patients with good vision after cataract extraction and correction by a spectacle lens usually prefer to use the unoperated eye with normal or mildly decreased vision.

Spectacle lenses may be needed for slight correction and near vision even after intraocular lenses are used.

Contact Lenses. With contact lenses the image is smaller and the contact lens can work with the unoperated eye, which still has a normal lens and good vision. If damage occurs to the contact lens, it can be removed easily.

Fitting takes time. The lens must be removed for hygienic purposes. Not all persons tolerate a contact lens after surgery, and unfortunately, it is impossible to predict before surgery, except in a general way, those patients who will or will not be successful. Contact lenses are not practical in patients who have arthritis and are unable to use their hands for lens insertion; companions can be trained in these cases to insert the lenses, but motivation for lens use is usually low. Lenses are not usable in unreliable patients, as follow-up and understanding of responsibilities for care are necessary. Contact lens wear requires motivation and persistence on the part of the patient.

When infections occur, they may endanger the eye. The elderly eye and the postoperative eye are more susceptible to infection with contact lens wear. Unusual organisms, such as *Acanthamoeba,* can be isolated from eyes with contact lens-induced infections, and they may be resistant to treatment.

Intraocular Lens. Intraocular lenses are placed in more than 90 to 95% of all surgeries for cataract. Experience has made it a safe and predictable outcome in most cases.

This technique offers optical correction with one-time cost and no worry when successful. It is the most common method of visual recovery after cataract removal. Use of the intraocular lens is usually associated with the extracapsular technique, and complications such as cystoid macular edema are thought to be less frequent.

An error in calculation in lens power is permanent. To change a power, an additional operation and exchange of the lens is necessary. The long-term effects of this procedure over decades is unknown. The intraocular lens can cause severe inflammation in some patients, requiring its removal and endangering the site of the eye. Technically, different skills are required by the surgeon. Insertion of the intraocular lens can damage the cornea in ways that cause it to cloud, vision can be lost, and a corneal transplant may become necessary.

No cataract should be removed simply because it is there. Because it is rare for a cataract to endanger the eye, the most important criterion for removal of the cataract is the patient's ability to function. Only when vision loss causes inability to perform usual activities should cataract extraction be considered. At times, because of fear that cataracts might cause blindness, patients may seek surgery before severity of symptoms and possible risks indicate they may need it. To prevent the removal of lenses unnecessarily, patients should be aware of what a cataract is and of what the risks are.

FOLLOW-UP

Once the diagnosis of senile cataract is made, it is necessary to check the progression every 6 months to a year.

DISCUSSION

Prevalence and Incidence

Cataract is a leading cause of blindness in developing countries where surgery to correct cataract cannot keep up with the demand. The prevalence of different types of cataracts has not been determined and appears to vary widely from country to country and with different populations. Judging the incidence of cataract by surgical utilization rates is not useful because indications vary widely. In the United States, more than a million cataracts are operated each year. Because some cataract change is associated with aging, as the average age of the population increases the prevalence of cataract is predicted to increase.

Related Basic Science

The cause of senile cataract remains a partially solved mystery, and many experimental observations indicate that cataract formation is a complex process. Recent evidence has linked presenile cataract formation with decreased activity of galactosemic enzymes. For example, about 1% of the general population has reduced galactocyanase or galactose-1-phosphate uridyl transferase activity. These patients appear to be at more risk for idiopathic presenile cataract formation. A significant reduction has been found in the erythrocyte galactose-1-phosphate uridyl transferase level in 47% of younger patients with presenile idiopathic cataracts, 7% of younger patients with other types of cataracts, and 4% of older patients with cataracts.

Galactose is found in high concentrations in the lens. Ascorbic acid, which is not formed in the lens, is found in a concentration higher in the lens (especially under the capsule) than in the aqueous humor. Glutathione, which is a tripeptide consisting of glutamic acid, cystine, and glycine, is also found in high concentrations in the lens. These substances have been found to be altered in senile cataracts.

Many of the changes seen in brunescent (brownish-colored) cataracts are due to the compression or compaction of the lens fibers with aging, a process that is common to all humans. Unless surgery is done, we die with the lens fibers we are born with. The unique position of the lens in the eye causes the fibers to be continually pushed to the center of the lens and compacted. The result is a slowly progressive increase in the lens size (about 0.02 mm per year) and a progressive decrease in the water content from its youthful level of 60% of the lens weight.

It is this concentration of lens fibers that results in the senile nuclear portion of the cataract. It is frequently discolored by the collection of urochrome pigment, which is associated with this compression of fibers.

The lens also has a unique organ-specific antigenicity. Animals sensitized to lens protein react to most lens proteins of any other species. Also, reactions in the eye can result from a response of the body to its own lens substance.

There is considerable evidence that sorbitol in the lens is responsible for the increased formation of cataracts in diabetic patients. Other abnormalities of metabolic function, such as hypocalcemia induced by intermittent hemodialysis in patients with end-stage renal disease, are associated with a rapid progression of cataract opacity.

All types of cataracts of the lens lose protein in some way. As products break down, as the capsule becomes hyperpermeable, there is leakage from the lens of the breakdown material of these proteins.

Recently, exposure to ultraviolet light has been associated with an increase in certain types of cataract (Taylor et al., 1988). Epidemiologic studies were conducted on watermen of the Chesapeake Bay region. Increased incidence of cataract was observed. The significance of persons not exposed to high levels of ultraviolet radiation is unknown.

Natural History and Its Modification with Treatment

The compact, increasingly dense nucleus of the aged lens affects all of us who live to experience later decades. The compacted lens first contributes to presbyopia, or the inability to read or see clearly within a few feet, when we reach 45 or so and requires the use of bifocals for reading. Here the normal flexibility of the lens, which works to accommodate to the focus of near objects, is lost as the dense lens of the nucleus becomes flexible. As the lens continues to become compacted, another change occurs. This second change is an induced myopia that occurs when the refractive value of the lenses changes and produces second sight or improved vision. This is a short-lived improvement in the vision that lasts only a few months or sometimes years.

In the early stages of cataract development, changes that occur with aging are easily identified in the nucleus and in the cortex. The nuclear changes are represented by the increasing density of the lens nucleus as the fibers are pushed toward the center. The cortical fibers also cloud, causing cortical cataracts. There are two clinically distinguishable types of cortical cataracts. The cuneiform, or spokewheel, type occurs in the periphery, with the points of the spokes directed toward the center. The cupuloform, or cup-shaped, opacity occurs infrequently in the back of the lens, just before the capsule. The cuneiform opacities can be extensive and only minimally affect vision if other areas of the lens are normal. The cupuloform opacities tend to affect the vision earlier and more extensively.

Diabetes affects the development of senile cataracts. It affects not only the progression, but also the severity of the cataract changes. Both are accelerated.

By age 60, a large percentage of the population has some degree of cataract change. Most of these cataract changes do not affect vision severely.

Prevention

There is no known prevention for senile cataract. In individuals with significant exposure to ultraviolet light (working on water for example), sunglasses and hats to decrease exposure are recommended.

Cost Containment

Senile cataract represents a major expense for individuals and for the health care system. Hundreds of thousand of cataracts are operated each year in the United States. Education is the most important aspect of cost containment in this field. Each patient should know the relative costs of spectacle correction versus contact lens and intraocular lens correction following lens extraction. Also, the considerable differences in the costs of different types of cataract extractions, depending on the technique used, should be explained to the patient. Encouraging uniform approaches to surgical charges for similar types of cataract extraction would lessen its financial impact. More clinical and experimental research is needed to develop mature attitudes toward the various types of cataract extractions, which may have widely differing costs, to ensure that excellent patient care is maintained with the least expensive procedure.

REFERENCES

Greiner JV, Chylack LT Jr. Posterior subcapsular cataracts: Histopathologic study of steroid-associated cataracts. Arch Ophthalmol 1979;97:135.

Isaac NE, Walker AM, Juck H, Gorman M. Exposure to phenothiazine drugs and risk of cataract. Arch Ophthalmol 1991;109:246.

Munoz B, Tajchman U, Bochow T, West S. Alcohol use and risk of posterior subcapsular opacities. Arch Ophthalmol 1993;111:110.

O'Day DM. Management of cataract in adults: Agency for Health Care Policy and Research. Am Fam Physician 1993;47:1421.

Ritter LL, Klein BE, Kelin R, Mares-Perlman JA. Alcohol use and lens opacities in the Beaver Dam Eye Study. Arch Ophthalmol 1993;111:113.

Taylor HR, West SK, Rosenthal FS, et al. Effect of ultraviolet light on cataract formation. N Engl J Med 1988;319:1429.

Thylefors B. The WHO programme for the Prevention of Blindness and Cataract in Developing Countries. Doc Ophthalmol 1992;81:339.

CHAPTER 22–2

Diabetic Retinopathy

Mary Elizabeth Hartnett, M.D.

DEFINITION

Diabetic retinopathy manifests as altered retinal vessels. Intraretinal hemorrhages, cotton–wool spots, microaneurysms, exudates, intraretinal microvascular abnormalities, venous beading, and neovascularization are features characteristic of diabetic retinopathy, but none is pathognomonic of it.

ETIOLOGY

The etiology of diabetic retinopathy is unknown. Structural changes in the retinal vessels include loss of pericytes, thickened basement membranes, and capillary closure which leads to large areas of nonperfused inner retina. This retinal hypoxia is believed to effect release of angiogenic factors, such as vascular endothelial growth factor, that may promote the formation of extraretinal neovascularization.

CRITERIA FOR DIAGNOSIS

Suggestive

Diabetic retinopathy is a more likely occurrence as the duration a patient has diabetes mellitus increases. As diabetic retinopathy may be asymptomatic, regularly scheduled ocular examinations (on at least a yearly basis, with more frequent evaluations for more advanced cases) are recommended for patients with diabetes mellitus.

Some symptoms are important. These symptoms may indicate a visually threatening retinopathy is present. Blurred vision from macular edema or retinal detachment or floaters or loss of vision from vitreous hemorrhage or retinal detachment may be symptoms of advancing retinopathy.

Definitive

There are characteristic clinical features of diabetic retinopathy, but none of the signs alone is pathognomonic of diabetic retinopathy. Microaneurysms, intraretinal hemorrhages, cotton–wool spots, venous beading, intraretinal microvasculature abnormalities, hard exudates, and retinal thickening are features of *nonproliferative diabetic retinopathy*. Retinal thickening and hard exudates in the macula of the retina, that focal area important in reading vision and central vision, are seen in *macular edema*. *Proliferative diabetic retinopathy* is diagnosed when extraretinal neovascularization occurs, that is, when vessels grow off the retinal surface into the vitreous cavity. The vessels may subsequently lead to vitreous hemorrhage, fibrous proliferation, and retinal detachment.

CLINICAL MANIFESTATIONS

Subjective

Many young patients with diabetic retinopathy may have severe proliferative disease without any visual symptoms.

Patients with proliferative retinopathy who develop vitreous hemorrhages may experience floaters. Vitreous floaters are black or red streaks or dots that move in the patient's visual space. As a vitreous hemorrhage disperses into the vitreous, vision may become cloudy or dark.

Patients with capillary nonperfusion of the macula or macular edema may experience a loss of central vision, that is, a failure of reading vision or that vision important for recognizing facial features. Visual field loss (loss of vision in a part of one's peripheral field of view) may occur with retinal detachments.

Many times visual acuity loss may not be solely due to diabetic retinopathy. There may be a refractive error easily corrected by a prescription for glasses. Also, patients may experience fluctuation in their vision as the blood sugar levels vary. The vision is recovered as the blood sugar is controlled.

Objective

Physical Examination

Pupillary function may be disturbed with optic nerve dysfunction, extensive retinal detachment, or extensive vascular occlusion. This usually manifests as an afferent pupillary defect, detected by the swinging flashlight test.

Neovascularization of the iris (rubeosis) often manifests at the pupillary margin, and is rarely visible without the slit lamp. This complication may result in a severe form of painful neovascular glaucoma that can be prevented with laser if it is discovered early.

Cataracts occur and often manifest as cortical spokes or posterior subcapsular cataracts.

Funduscopic examination is best accomplished through the dilated pupil by stereoscopic viewing using an indirect ophthalmoscope and with bimicroscopy using the slit lamp. Viewing of the fundus through an undilated pupil with direct ophthalmoscopy is usually not adequate. Most often the changes seen in diabetic retinopathy occur in the posterior pole and surrounding the vascular arcades.

Nonproliferative Retinopathy. Microaneurysms are seen as small red dots often in capillary beds (see Color Plate 22–2–1 after page 1946).

Hemorrhages may appear as dot-and-blot hemorrhages surrounding the vascular arcades and the posterior pole (Color Plate 22–2–1).

Cotton–wool spots appear as fluffy white areas along the lines of the nerve fiber, often obscuring visualization of the underlying retinal vessels (see Color Plate 22–2–2, after page 1946).

Venous beading appears as irregularities in the caliber of the retinal veins (see Color Plate 22–2–3, after page 1946).

Intraretinal microvascular abnormalities are dilated capillaries that are believed to represent shunts between arteries and veins, or intraretinal neovascularization (Color Plate 22–2–3). These are referred to as "IRMA" sometimes.

Hard exudates are yellow deposits within the retina that have sharp borders (Color Plate 22–2–1).

Proliferative Retinopathy. Extraretinal neovascularization may occur off the optic nerve or from the retinal vessels and is best appreciated by stereoscopic viewing. Extensive neovascularization may be viewed without stereopsis in rare cases, especially if it is associated with hemorrhage into the vitreous cavity.

Vitreous hemorrhage often blocks most of the underlying retinal details (see Color Plate 22–2–4, after page 1946).

Retinal detachment and fibrous proliferations appear as gray-white membranes with elevated retina that has an opalescent appearance. Traction on the retina may be noted by seeing striae or tension lines in the retina.

Routine Laboratory Abnormalities

Normal blood findings in patients with diabetes mellitus do not preclude the diagnosis of diabetic retinopathy. Blood glucose and other routine laboratory tests may be normal and control of diabetes may be good.

PLANS
Diagnostic
Differential Diagnosis

The differential diagnosis of diabetic retinopathy includes any type of vascular disease that may affect the eye: hypertension; vein occlusion (branch or evolving central vein occlusion); radiation retinopathy; HIV retinopathy; collagen–vascular diseases; blood dyscrasias.

Diagnostic Options

In a patient with diabetic retinopathy but without a diagnosis of diabetes mellitus, a glucose tolerance test or a glycosylated hemoglobin is recommended to establish the diagnosis of diabetes mellitus.

If a vitreous hemorrhage occurs, an ultrasound may be performed to determine the possible presence of a retinal detachment.

Recommended Approach

Good control of blood glucose and blood pressure is important, as is control of systemic infections. The best corrected visual acuity should be determined in all patients. Pupillary examination and slit-lamp evaluation of the undilated pupil should be performed to determine the presence of neovascularization of the iris. The eyes should be dilated and the lenses checked for cataract formation. The diagnosis of the severity of diabetic retinopathy is best made by stereoscopic evaluation through a dilated pupil, using an indirect ophthalmoscope and slit-lamp biomicroscopy. Patients, when they undergo dilated funduscopy, are requested to arrange travel to avoid difficulty in driving.

The extent of the diabetic retinopathy is determined to choose the best management and the appropriate follow-up period. Besides actual clinical examination, stereoscopic fundus photographs of the optic nerve, macula, and fields around the macula may also be helpful in evaluating the fundus.

In patients who are pregnant, more frequent eye examinations are recommended, one each trimester, as diabetic retinopathy may progress more rapidly.

Therapeutic

A complete ophthalmologic examination is best performed by a retina-trained ophthalmologist to include dilated funduscopy. If the diabetic retinopathy appears to be rapidly progressing, the search for a systemic infection or inflammation should be considered.

Nonproliferative Diabetic Retinopathy. If no macular edema is present, patients should be evaluated as to the level of severity (mild, moderate, severe, or very severe) to determine how frequently follow-up is recommended.

Proliferative Retinopathy. Once certain characteristics of proliferative disease exist, intervention with laser can reduce the risk of severe visual loss (lacking ambulatory vision) by at least 50%. The laser coagulates large areas of the peripheral retina. Although the mechanism by which this widespread destruction of the peripheral retina works is not known, theories suggest that the tissue that is releasing angiogenic factors is destroyed and/or that the amount of retina and metabolic demand per the compromised blood flow, and therefore oxygen supply, is decreased, thus decreasing the stimulus for angiogenesis by decreasing the hypoxia. Panretinal photocoagulation often requires multiple sessions (typically with the placement of 1500–3000 spots 200 to 500 μm in diameter throughout the midperipheral and peripheral retina in multiple sessions). Laser treatment may cause transient or permanent visual loss. It also may lead to some loss of night vision or side vision.

Macular Edema. If clinically significant macular edema is present, a fluorescein angiogram is performed to determine the areas of leakage of fluid, microaneurysms, or diffuse leakage. A fluorescein angiogram is a photographic study in which sodium fluorescein, a vegetable dye, is injected intravenously while photographs of the retina are taken in succession over time. This technique is helpful in studying blood flow and identifying leaky vessels. Patients with macular edema may undergo laser photocoagulation to the leaking microaneurysms and capillary beds. Multiple sessions may be required.

Poor Central Vision Without Macular Edema or Pupillary Dysfunction. Fluorescein angiography may reveal areas of extensive capillary nonperfusion in the foveal area.

Iris Neovascularization (Rubeosis). Panretinal photocoagulation is the treatment of choice to prevent neovascular glaucoma and cause regression of preexisting new vessels.

Vitreous Hemorrhage. With limited hemorrhages, panretinal photocoagulation is performed. Adequate time is allowed for clearing of the hemorrhage, 1 to 6 months depending on whether the patient has type 1 or 2 diabetes mellitus. During this time the eye is carefully followed for the development of retinal detachment at which time vitrectomy may be considered. Additional laser is added as the hemorrhage clears. If the hemorrhage does not clear within a reasonable period, a vitrectomy may be performed.

Retinal Detachment. When fibrous contraction occurs, the scar tissue between the retina and the vitreous pulls on the retina, causing a retinal detachment. If this threatens the macula, vitrectomy, using small scissors, is performed to release the traction and allow the retina to settle back.

Low vision aids may be used for patients with extensive capillary nonperfusion or macular edema that does not fully respond to treatment. These aids allow a person who may not have central vision to read through magnification and enhanced contrast.

Cataract extraction is delayed until visual quality of life is substantially impaired or unless the retinal condition cannot be adequately evaluated and managed. Diabetic retinopathy has been reported to advance after cataract extraction.

FOLLOW-UP

It is recommended that all type 2 diabetics with some retinopathy have annual dilated funduscopy. Type 2 diabetics who have no retinopathy may have examinations every 2 years. Patients with type 1 diabetes mellitus may have the first eye examination after 5 years' duration of diabetes mellitus and then annually.

Once diabetic retinopathy is diagnosed, the frequency of ocular examinations is increased depending on the severity of retinopathy. In patients with severe nonproliferative and early proliferative retinopathy, panretinal photocoagulation is given consideration (Diabetic Retinopathy Study, 1991). In patients with high-risk characteristics of proliferative disease, panretinal photocoagulation is done immediately (Diabetic Retinopathy Study Research Group, 1987).

Patients with macular edema are considered for laser treatment if the macular edema falls within the criteria of "clinically significant" (Diabetic Retinopathy Study, 1991).

Stereoscopic photographs of the fundus may be taken to aid in determining the follow-up of the patient and the classification of the diabetic retinopathy.

Fluorescein angiography is usually reserved for patients with unexplained loss of central vision or in anticipation of macular laser treatment for macular edema.

DISCUSSION

Prevalence and Incidence

Diabetic retinopathy progresses to more severe stages, and to blinding complications, as the duration of the disease increases. It occurs in 40 to 50% of patients with diabetes mellitus after 10 years' duration and in 80 to 100% of patients after 20 years' duration. Proliferative retinopathy is more common in type 1 diabetes mellitus than in type 2 diabetes mellitus (Klein et al., 1994).

Related Basic Science

Evidence supports a role for poorly compensated oxidative stress in the pathogenesis of the complications associated with diabetes mellitus. Good control of blood glucose has been shown to be associated with slowing of the progression of the disease in patients with insulin-dependent diabetes mellitus (Diabetes Control and Complications Trial Research Group, 1993). Diabetic retinopathy may be adversely affected by high blood pressure, a history of previous radiation exposure to the ocular area, or recent cataract surgery. Other conditions that adversely affect the retinal vasculature, such as smoking, may conceivably worsen diabetic retinopathy. During puberty and in pregnancy, diabetic retinopathy may advance more rapidly.

The etiology of the complications associated with diabetic retinopathy is believed to be associated with ischemia of the retina. Retinal capillary occlusion leads to extensive areas of capillary nonperfusion of the retina. This hypoxic area is believed to be a stimulus for release of angiogenic factors, such as vascular endothelial growth factor, into the vitreous (Aiello et al., 1994). Such angiogenic factors may attach to the receptors of retinal vascular endothelial cells and stimulate extraretinal neovascularization. Microaneurysms, which represent focal areas of leakage into the retina and may lead to macular edema, are believed to be associated with loss of the blood retinal barrier and of pericytes.

Natural History and Its Modification with Treatment

The Diabetes Control and Complications Trial Research Group (1993) showed that good glucose control slowed the progression of diabetic retinopathy in patients with insulin-dependent diabetes mellitus. In patients in whom sudden implementation of strict blood glucose control occurred, transient worsening of retinopathy was seen.

The Diabetic Retinopathy Study Research Group (1987) showed that 20 to 40% of patients with high-risk characteristics of proliferative retinopathy, neovascularization at the disc of a particular size or neovascularization elsewhere on the retina associated with vitreous hemorrhage, had 5/200 vision or worse in 2 years. Panretinal photocoagulation reduced this risk by at least 50%.

The Early Treatment Diabetic Retinopathy Study showed that patients with clinically significant macular edema had approximately a 30% chance of doubling their visual angle (e.g., to fall from 20/20 vision to 20/40 or from 20/50 to 20/100) in 3 years without laser. Macular laser treatment reduced this risk by 50% (Results from the . . . , 1991).

Early panretinal photocoagulation should be considered in patients without high-risk proliferative retinopathy but with severe or very severe nonproliferative or early proliferative retinopathy.

Even with good follow-up and appropriate laser treatment, visual acuity falls in patients with diabetes mellitus over time.

Prevention

There is no known means of preventing diabetic retinopathy; however, as outlined above, the progression can be slowed with good glucose control in patients with insulin-dependent diabetes mellitus. The blinding complications associated with diabetic retinopathy can be restricted substantially with frequent examinations and appropriate laser treatment.

Cost Containment

Currently, early intervention is accomplished through frequent and complete dilated stereoscopic funduscopy and periodic stereoscopic fundus photography. Intervention such as this for type 1 diabetics alone predicted annual savings of $101 million and 47,374 person-years-sight nationally (Javitt et al., 1991).

REFERENCES

Aiello LP, Avery RL, Arrigg PG, et al. Vascular endothelial growth factor in ocular fluid of patients with diabetic retinopathy and other retinal disorders. N Engl J Med 1994;331:1480.

Bresnick GH. Background diabetic retinopathy. In: Ryan SJ, ed. Retina. St. Louis: Mosby, 1989:327.

Davis MD. Proliferative diabetic retinopathy. In: Ryan SJ, ed. Retina. St. Louis: Mosby, 1989:367.

Diabetes Control and Complications Trial Research Group. The effect of intensive treatment of diabetes on the development and progression of long-term complications in insulin-dependent diabetes mellitus. N Engl J Med 1993;329:977.

Diabetic Retinopathy Study Research Group. Indications for photocoagulation treatment of diabetic retinopathy: DRS Report No. 14. Int Ophthalmol Clin 1987;27:239.

Frank RN. Etiologic mechanisms in diabetic retinopathy. In: Ryan SJ, ed. Retina. St. Louis: Mosby, 1989:301.

Javitt JC, Aiello LP, Bassi LJ, et al. Detecting and treating retinopathy in patients with type 1 diabetes mellitus: Savings associated with improved implementation of current guidelines. Ophthalmology 1991;98:1565.

Klein R, Klein BE, Moss SE, et al. The Wisconsin epidemiologic study of diabetic retinopathy. Arch Ophthalmol 1994;112:1217.

Results from the Early Treatment Diabetic Retinopathy Study: Early treatment diabetic retinopathy study group. Ophthalmology 1991;98(5, May suppl.):739.

CHAPTER 22–3

Tear Deficiency (Dry Eye)

William H. Coles, M.D., M.S.

DEFINITION

Tear deficiencies are abnormalities of the lipid/mucus/water layer that lubricates and protects the eye from drying.

ETIOLOGY

Tear deficiencies result when the lacrimal system, the lids, or the conjunctival lining of the eyes does not function normally. Specific etiologies vary with the source.

CRITERIA FOR DIAGNOSIS
Suggestive

The patient may complain of "dry eyes."

Definitive

Tear film deficiency is established in two ways: direct observation of tear film integrity and volume, and recognition of corneal and conjunctival changes caused by tear deficiency.

The tear film is evaluated by two tests. The tear film breakup time tests the stability of the tear film as it wets the cornea. The Schirmer test indicates deficiencies in the amount of tear production.

The corneal and conjunctival changes associated with tear deficiencies are punctate staining, erosion of the cornea, and keratinization of conjunctival or corneal surfaces.

CLINICAL MANIFESTATIONS
Subjective

It is difficult to describe the sensation of dry eye. Each of us can experience the effects of drying by consciously or forcibly holding our eyelids open. As we do, there is an increasingly urgent need to blink.

Dry eye patients express their chronic drying symptoms in various ways. They may say their eye aches, describe a scratchy feeling, say they have a discomfort, or describe a hurt or itch. Almost never are the symptoms described as a pain, although irritation may be mentioned.

Most patients seek relief before visual acuity is affected. At times, however, the corneal changes in advanced disease can cause loss of vision.

Blepharitis may present with the symptoms of dry eye. The common association of secondary bacterial lid infections in dry eye often causes the patient to seek relief from the redness and irritation at the lash and lid margins. Focus on the infection may result in failure to appreciate dry eye.

In general, a patient who presents with vague and difficult-to-describe ocular complaints should be evaluated for dry eye (tear deficiency).

Objective

Physical Examination

Specific changes occur in certain types of tear deficiency. For example, the concentration of lysozymes in the tears is decreased in patients with dry eye. Lysozymes are important because of their antibacterial action. A simple test for lysozyme levels is not available, and for the most part, this and other chemical changes of the tear film are not used in the diagnosis of dry eye. Almost all techniques used for the diagnosis of tear deficiency are clinical tests, most of which require some experience for interpretation.

Tear Film Breakup.
Tear film breakup time is a measure of tear film stability. To do this test, the tear film is made more visible by the instillation of fluorescein dye, a dye readily available in most hospitals. Once the tear film has been permeated with this dye, a cobalt blue filtered light (on a slit lamp) is used to make the tear film glow as a green uniform layer over the cornea. The tear film will stay uniform and intact for a limited time, and as the tear film begins to disrupt, black areas in the green fluorescein film are seen, in either streaks or dots. When this occurs, the tear film is said to be at the endpoint or breaking up. In normal patients, it takes 20 or more seconds from blink to breakup. By having the patient blink once or twice to distribute the tear film evenly and then asking the patient not to blink, the time of the blink distribution to the visualization of disruption of the tear film is the breakup time. Usually, multiple readings are taken and averaged for each eye. Anything below 20 seconds is suspicious. Anything below 5 seconds is abnormal.

Schirmer Test.
In this test, filter paper strips are employed to determine the amount of tear secretion. These narrow, long strips are placed between the lower eyelid and the globe. After 5 minutes, the wetting of these filter paper strips is measured. There are two methods of testing: with anesthesia and without. Most ophthalmologists now feel that testing without anesthesia gives more significant information. Less than 5 mm of wetting of these standard filter paper strips after 5 minutes is abnormal. Most normal patients wet 10 mm or more.

Corneal Changes and Conjunctival Changes.
Corneal epithelial drying can be observed by fluorescein staining. Usually, dry eye presents with punctate corneal staining in the inferior third of the cornea. The far more accurate means of determining dry eye damage is with rose bengal stain. Using a 1% solution dropped into the fornix and then washed, staining can be seen in both the corneal and conjunctival surfaces. Typically the dry area on the conjunctiva shows up as a triangular region that corresponds to the area exposed to air with the lids open. Corneal staining with rose bengal, as with fluorescein staining, is usually limited to the lower third of the cornea.

Routine Laboratory Abnormalities

There are no diagnostic routine laboratory abnormalities.

PLANS
Diagnostic

Differential Diagnosis

Sjögren's syndrome is dry eye associated with mouth drying, vaginal drying, and rheumatoid arthritis.

Conjunctival injury is often associated with history of chemical burn (such as lye), ocular pemphigus, or Stevens–Johnson syndrome.

With lacrimal gland deficiency, a history of surgical removal of the lacrimal gland, trauma, or Sjögren's syndrome is present.

In lid margin dysfunction, a tumor may cause poor lid approximation to the globe.

Blepharitis (lid infection), carcinoma of the lids, discoid lupus involvement of the lids, skin tumors involving lid margin and tear distribution, and scarring due to burns or injury of the lids (cicatricial) all may relate to drying of the eye.

Diagnostic Options and Recommended Approach

See Criteria for Diagnosis.

Therapeutic

There is no cure for dry eyes. The most common therapy is replacement of tears. Replacement comes in a variety of tear substitutes; both drops and ointments are available. Ointments are more effective but tend to blur vision; drops are less effective but allow better vision during the day. A combination of liquid drops and ointments is often needed—drops during the day and ointments before retiring at night.

There are a number of tear substitutes of various chemical compositions: methylcellulose, polyvinyl alcohol, hydroxymethylcellulose, and hydropropylene. It is impossible to predict which patient will respond best to which substance. Trial and error is used to find the most effective type for each patient.

Ointment should be free of antibiotics or steroids to avoid complications. Most ointments contain lanolin, mineral oil, and petrolatum. Lanolin-free ointments are now available to decrease allergic reactions to lanolin.

Changes in the drainage system for tears can also provide prolonged effectiveness of the tears—even though they are abnormal—that are produced by a dry eye patient. The punctum of the lacrimal duct can be closed by cautery, by instilling small wax or plastic plugs, or by surgically suturing the punctum closed. This allows no tear drainage and more effective use of existing tears.

Narrowing of the eyelid can help improve the effectiveness of existing tears. This decreases the effects of drying. One of two surgical procedures commonly used is canthoplasty (closure of the corner of the eye) or tarsorrhaphy (closure of the eyelids by a suture and surgically causing scarring of the lid margins).

Dry eye patients should be fully informed as to the nature of their condition. It is not curable, so they should be aware that therapy is directed toward symptomatic relief and prevention of the more severe complications of dry eye. The concept of the lids and tears lubricating the whole eye and keeping it moist is helpful. Many dry eye patients seem to tear excessively. The concept of dry eye to them may seem an error in diagnosis because of this excess tearing. For these patients, it is helpful to use and develop the concept of improper quality of tears. Although they have a sufficient amount of tears, the idea that the quality is not what it used to be allows them better understanding of their condition (see Related Basic Science).

The variable results of treatment make it important to educate the patient as to the trial-and-error therapy with the multiple tear substitutes now available. Patients should be encouraged to try as many substitutes as necessary to find the one that is best for them. Early clarification of this fact will prevent further patient confusion and loss of doctor confidence.

Patients on blood pressure medications (especially ganglionic blockers that may inhibit lacrimal secretions and accentuate dry eye problems) may complain of symptoms that are entirely secondary to the medication. They should be informed that medications can affect the dry eye.

FOLLOW-UP

All dry eye patients should be examined by an ophthalmologist on a periodic basis to prevent permanent and sight-threatening changes. Usually, in the adult dry eye patient, follow-up every few months is satisfactory. Dry eye from other disease processes such as trauma or an active infiltrative process (Stevens–Johnson) should be followed frequently until stable.

DISCUSSION
Prevalence and Incidence

Dry eye is a common diagnosis in postmenopausal women; however, the prevalence is not known and would be difficult to study as criteria for diagnosis vary considerably.

Related Basic Science

The tear film, although we speak of it in the singular, is actually three distinct layers. The layer closest to the cornea is mucin. The middle layer, which has the greatest volume, is the aqueous (or water) layer. Then there is a very thin outer layer, the oil layer.

The function of the mucin layer is to provide adhesion for the tear film. Without the mucin layer, a drop of water on the cornea will roll off as a drop of water might be repelled on a tilted glass surface. Mucin makes the normally hydrophobic cornea hydrophilic. This function is

so important that deficiency in mucin is a significant contributor to dry eye problems.

Mucin is produced by the conjunctival goblet cells. Any condition that alters the conjunctiva, such as eye burns or Stevens–Johnson syndrome, also affects the tear film by altering the mucin layer.

Secretions from the lacrimal gland produce the middle layer of the tear film, the aqueous layer. It is the wetting agent of the tear film and makes up its largest volume. Changes in lacrimal and gland secretion either in volume of tears or in composition of tears can affect the area and contribute to tear film deficiency.

The function of the oil layer of the tear film is to prevent evaporation. Deficiency of the oil layer allows rapid drying of the tear film within a few seconds. Oil in the tear film is produced in meibomian glands in the lids (sebaceous-like glands buried in the tarsus). Certain familial conditions that affect lipid secretions such as rosacea may contribute to improper oil stability and cause eye complications through tear drying. Other lid conditions such as infection, tumor, and injury may inhibit normal oil secretion and contribute to an abnormal tear film layer.

An intact tear film layer is dependent on multiple factors. These factors are related to the three-layered composition of the tear film and are dependent on the adequate production of these three layers from the conjunctiva, oil glands, and lacrimal gland. Provided that all these sources are producing normally, there is still another important aspect of tear distribution. Mechanically, tear distribution requires a normal blink mechanism. An intact neurologic pathway from the eye to the brain to the lids is necessary so that a blink is generated by corneal feelings of inadequate tear film. Once the blink is generated, the eyelids must be intact, so that tear film can be distributed evenly by the upper and lower lid over the corneal surface.

Corneal anesthesia caused by neurologic disease involving the fifth nerve or by local corneal disease such as herpes simplex virus may decrease the frequency or the totality of the blink. This delays tear film distribution and results in drying. Loss of integrity of the lid margins can also affect the distribution. Most commonly, trauma to the lid margins results in lid notch and altered function. Infection of the lid margins, tumors of the lid margins, inability of the lids to close over a prostatic eye such as in thyroid eye disease, and scarring of the skin of the lids with contracture can all contribute to improper tear distribution.

Natural History and Its Modification with Treatment

A significant percentage of elderly women develop dry eye. Men are less frequently affected. Once dry eye occurs, the development of severe ocular changes is usually slow; years of irritation and vague complaints precede severe corneal damage and visual loss.

Once an eye is poorly lubricated, drying occurs. First are epithelial changes. Second is an actual melting away of corneal substance. If left untreated, the cornea may go on to perforation, causing loss of ocular integrity and frequently resulting in visual loss or blindness.

In untreated patients, surgery is also at greater risk of complications because of poor tear film. This is especially true in corneal transplants, but it also applies to all intraocular surgery. The incidence of infection is higher in patients with dry eye, and more than half of patients with dry eye have some chronic or acute bacterial complication of the lid. This, of course, complicates the surgical prognosis.

Prevention

There is no known prevention for dry eye; however, there is a preventive aspect in controlling symptoms and complications. Avoidance of dry heat systems that decrease the humidity in a house can help relieve symptoms in the dry eye patient. Humidifiers in rooms where patients spend most of their time are also helpful. Avoidance of drying situations such as riding in open automobiles or in boats may also help to avoid symptoms.

Cost Containment

Patients should be aware of the different prices of various tear substitutes. They should be informed that they can make judgments as to their choice of tear substitutes according to their economic ability and the effectiveness of the drops. Early recognition of the prevalence and complications of dry eye can prevent those occurrences that require re-peated office visits and surgical procedures.

REFERENCES

Abelson MB, Knight E. Dry eye therapy: Evaluation of current directions and clinical trials. Adv Exp Med Biol 1994;350:431.

Botelho SY. Tears and the lacrimal gland. Sci Am 1964;211:78.

Fox RI. Systemic diseases associated with dry eye. Int Ophthalmol Clin 1994;34:71.

Holly FJ. Diagnostic methods and treatment modalities of dry eye conditions. Int Ophthalmol 1993;17(3):113.

Lemp MA. Diagnosis and treatment of tear deficiencies. In: Duane TD, ed. Clinical ophthalmology. Hagerstown, MD: Harper & Row, 1980;4:1.

Lemp MA. Management of the dry-eye patient. Int Ophthalmol Clin 1994;34:101.

Lemp MA, Hamill JR. Factors affecting tear film breakup in normal eyes. Arch Ophthalmology 1973;89:103.

CHAPTER 22–4

Open-angle Glaucoma (Chronic Glaucoma, Primary Open-angle Glaucoma, Primary Glaucoma)

William H. Coles, M.D., M.S.

DEFINITION

Glaucoma is damage to ocular structures as seen by visual field changes and/or optic nerve changes from increased pressure in the eye. Open-angle refers to the most common of many types of glaucoma. Open-angle glaucoma is defined by the anatomical appearance of the iris and corneal relationship.

ETIOLOGY

The etiology of open-angle glaucoma is unknown.

CRITERIA FOR DIAGNOSIS

Suggestive

The patient may complain of transient blurring of vision.

Definitive

The diagnosis of glaucoma is made when there is increased intraocular pressure, with visible changes in the optic nerve and/or characteristic visual field defects.

CLINICAL MANIFESTATIONS

Subjective

Open-angle glaucoma can produce visual loss without symptoms. Almost all open-angle glaucoma is diagnosed either by routine screening or during routine eye examinations.

Objective

Physical Examination

Intraocular Pressure. A single measurement of intraocular pressure neither confirms nor rules out the diagnosis of glaucoma. Intraocular pressure fluctuates in every individual throughout the day and also has significant diurnal variations. A single measurement of intraocular pressure is only one point in the continuum of pressure changes that occur within the eye. Nevertheless, intraocular pressure measurement is still used, and because of its simplicity and rapidity, it is a common screening test for glaucoma. In general, an intraocular pressure greater than 21 mm Hg is considered suspicious, and other confirmatory tests should be done.

Optic Nerve. The optic nerve changes seen in glaucoma are necessary to establish a diagnosis. (Without optic nerve or visual field changes, an increase in ocular pressure is referred to as *ocular hypertension.*) The changes of the nerve are usually seen as changes in the physiologic cup of the nerve disk. Most normal nerves have no or very small physiologic cups. Normally, the ratio between the size of the cup and the com-

parative size of the disk is less than 0.2 or 0.3. This is measured by (assuming the disk to be 10) estimating the relative size of the cup and dividing by 10 (disk size into the cup size). Statistically, any cup/disk ratio larger than 0.5 is abnormal. Also highly significant is any discrepancy between the sizes of the cup. Any cup/disk ratio between the two eyes that varies more than 0.2 should be considered pathologic until proved otherwise, regardless of the size of either cup.

Visual Field. Visual field defects help establish the diagnosis of glaucoma. Scotoma in the arcuate area or nasal step abnormalities (Figure 22–4–1) are both highly suggestive of glaucoma. The visual field defects are relative; that is, the presence of the defect depends on the intensity of the stimulus used for testing. Late defects caused by prolonged damage include constriction of peripheral fields with gun-barrel vision.

Measurement of Fluid Outflow. There are a number of ways to assess the outflow of fluid from the eye. A simple technique is to water-load the patient. The patient drinks a liter of water, and the effect on the eye is measured. Increases of pressure of more than 8 to 10 mm Hg within the 45-minute period are highly suggestive of the diagnosis of glaucoma. More intricate tests include tonography, which measures the intraocular pressures continuously over a period of minutes to calculate the rate

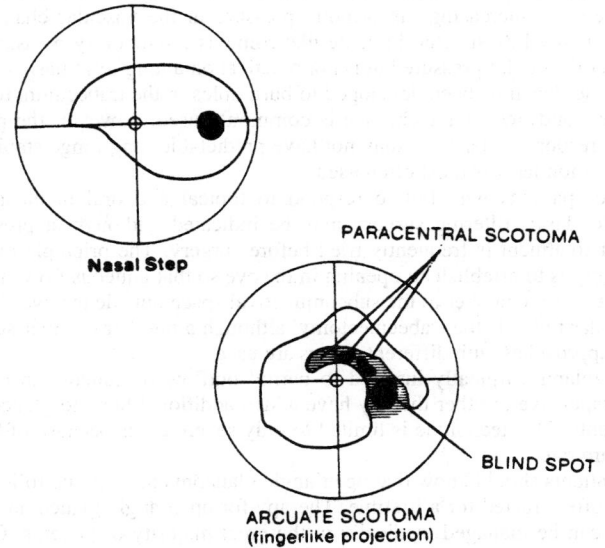

Figure 22–4–1. Common visual field changes in glaucoma: nasal step, arcuate scotoma, paracentral scotoma.

outflow of aqueous fluid from the eye. Use of outflow measurement in diagnosis is becoming uncommon.

Routine Laboratory Abnormalities

There are no routine laboratory abnormalities.

PLANS
Diagnostic
Differential Diagnosis

Narrow-angle Glaucoma. Shallow anterior chambers will have associated narrowed angles by gonioscopy; history of pain, redness, and halos around objects may be present but asymptomatic cases are not unusual.

Secondary Glaucoma—Traumatic. There is a history of ocular injury and angle recession is usually confirmed on gonioscopy. There may be other evidence of injury to ocular structures. Traumatic glaucoma is usually unilateral.

Secondary Glaucoma—Inflammatory. A history of ocular inflammation such as uveitis, iritis, or chorioretinitis is present.

Secondary Glaucoma—Neovascular. This is seen in diabetics or with a history of retinal vein occlusion, ocular ischemia such as carotid occlusive disease, retinal disease, or neoplasm of the eye.

Secondary Glaucoma—Postoperative. This glaucoma follows an intraocular surgical procedure. It is usually transient.

Diagnostic Options and Recommended Approach

See Criteria for Diagnosis.

Therapeutic

Therapy of glaucoma is directed toward decreasing intraocular pressure. Both medical and surgical therapies are available.

Medical therapies revolve around decreasing aqueous production or increasing the aqueous outflow of the trabecular meshwork. Common medications in use are timolol (Timoptic), an adrenergic blocker that primarily decreases aqueous outflow and does not affect the action of the pupil; pilocarpine (Piloptic), a parasympathomimetic agent that primarily increases outflow of aqueous through the trabecular meshwork; epinephrine, an adrenergic agent that decreases aqueous output and has a slight effect on the outflow; phospholine iodide, an anticholinesterase agent that increases outflow of the aqueous; acetazolamide (Diamox), a monoamine oxidase inhibitor that decreases aqueous production and must be taken by mouth; and mannitol (Osmitrol) or glycerin, which are osmotic agents. Hyperosmotic agents decrease the flow of fluid into the eye by increasing the osmotic pressure in the vascular channels. This is used most often in acute glaucoma as a temporary measure to lower the ocular pressure but is not practical on a long-term basis.

Laser has now been developed to burn holes in the trabeculum to increase outflow. This technique is commonly used; however, the pressure response after laser may not have predictable long-range stability. The argon laser is most often used.

For patients who fail to respond to topical and oral medications and/or laser, filtering surgery may be indicated, although at present, laser treatment is frequently tried before surgery. The principle of the surgery is to establish an opening in the eye so that aqueous flows from the anterior chamber to the subconjunctival space outside the eye. Most popular today is the trabeculectomy, although a number of other surgical approaches with different names are used.

Implants surgically inserted to permit outflow of aqueous in cases unresponsive to other therapy have added additional hope to glaucoma patients. This technique is limited to only severe cases because of high failure rate.

Patients should know that open-angle glaucoma needs to be followed and often treated for a lifetime. Therapy for open-angle glaucoma usually can be managed medically in the great majority of patients. Only occasionally is surgery necessary. Patients should be aware that if the intraocular pressure is allowed to remain high, the ocular structures can be damaged and sight may be lost, often without their awareness.

Patients should also be aware that beta blockers such as timolol may induce depression.

FOLLOW-UP

Patients with glaucoma need follow-up every 3 to 6 months, including measurement of intraocular pressure and observation of the optic nerves and visual fields. Patients with a family history of glaucoma should have glaucoma checks every year after the age of 40.

DISCUSSION
Prevalence and Incidence

Open-angle glaucoma is common. It is seen in middle age in 0.5 to 2% of the population. In the elderly, especially after the age of 80, it may occur as often as in 1 in 10 persons.

Related Basic Science

Open-angle glaucoma is a condition of increased intraocular pressure that causes damage to the optic nerve. This damage results from changes at the optic disk where the nerve exits the eye and is caused either by direct mechanical injury to the nerve fibers or by indirect ischemic damage due to the interruption of blood flow. In addition, a number of factors make individual optic nerves more susceptible to comparable increases in intraocular pressures.

Age, for one, makes optic nerves more susceptible to increased pressure probably because of the associated vascular changes. It is also well established that optic nerve damage is more likely in patients who have compromised ophthalmic blood flow, as in carotid occlusions.

Heredity also plays a factor in optic nerve susceptibility. Many factors are probably involved, but one of the most striking relationships is between the size of the physiologic cup of the optic disk and susceptibility to increased pressure. Cup size is inherited, and the cups with large diameters are more susceptible to glaucomatous change. The cup size is equal between the eyes of an individual, and asymmetry is cause for immediate suspicion and subsequent investigation for glaucoma.

Diabetes, another important familial disease, is also related to glaucoma, a fact that can help all physicians in screening for glaucoma. One in four patients with open-angle glaucoma will have a positive glucose tolerance test, or to turn the relationship around, about one in three diabetic patients has a positive test for glaucoma. This strong association should be remembered when evaluating patients with either condition.

Open-angle glaucoma is a disease of fluid regulation. The area of damage is microscopic (the trabecular meshwork), and although the trabeculum can be seen by gonioscopy, it is not possible to observe and diagnose open-angle glaucoma by direct visualization. In fact, diagnosis of open-angle glaucoma is made by excluding damage (trauma, scarring) or occlusion (narrow-angle glaucoma, debris such as blood cells or inflammatory cells) that can be directly visualized. Once these observable processes are ruled out, in the presence of increased ocular pressure where optic nerve (or visual field) changes have occurred, the diagnosis of open-angle glaucoma is established.

Intraocular pressure, expressed as a single reading, often gives the impression of an absolute value for establishing a diagnosis. Intraocular pressure is actually a continuum of pressures that occur in the eye. Many diagnostic techniques have been developed to try to determine the outflow mechanisms of the eye without relying on one pressure, which may be at a high or low point on a continually changing scale.

Water provocative testing, in which the patient drinks a measured amount of water and the intraocular pressures are measured over an hour or two after the ingestion, has been used. Rises in the pressure are indicative of abnormal outflow. Tonography is another test of outflow measured over a number of minutes. In this test, a tonometer for measurement of intraocular pressure is placed on the eye and left there while a continuous recording is made. The weight of the tonometer forces fluid out of the eye. Normal rates are then compared with the patient's rate of outflow.

Not as popular as it was a few years ago but still effective in the search for determining the pressure of a patient over a day is admission to the hospital (or frequent visits to the office) and measurement of the

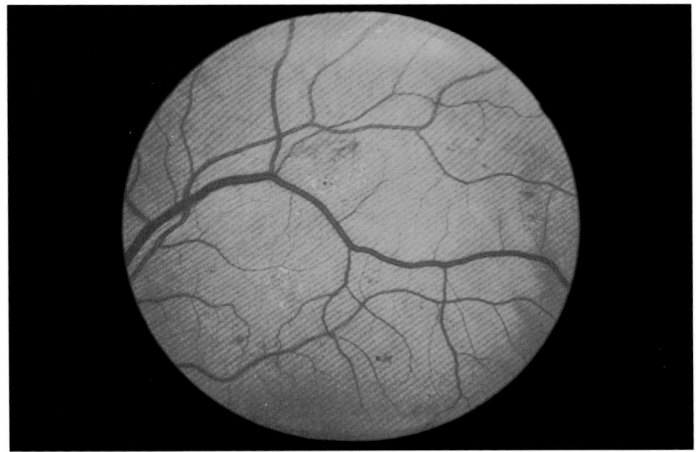

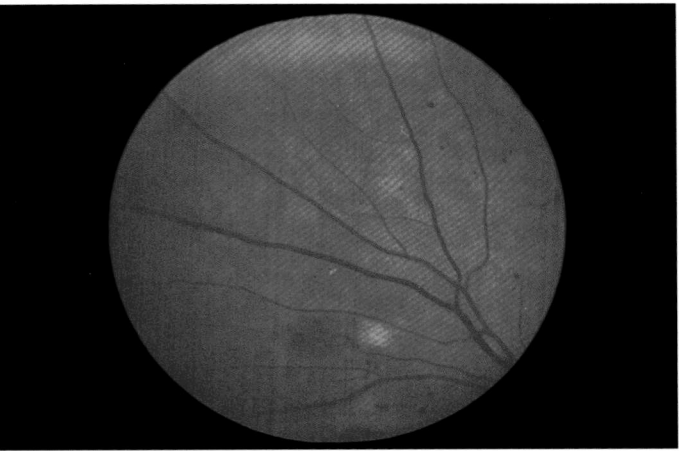

Color Plate 22–2–1. Left eye of a patient with mild to moderate nonproliferative retinopathy. The field is superior and temporal to the optic nerve. There are microaneurysms and surrounding exudates just superior to the center of the photograph. The microaneurysms appear as small, well-demarcated red dots, the exudates as yellowish deposits with hard-appearing edges. Flame-shaped retinal hemorrhages are noted superiorly with blot retinal hemorrhages inferior to the center of the photograph.

Color Plate 22–2–2. Left eye of the same patient with the field superior and nasal to the optic nerve. There are flame-shaped and dot-and-blot intraretinal hemorrhages. Note the fluffy white cotton–wool spot within the retina and contrast it with the hard exudates that have hard-appearing edges and lie deep in the retina (Figure 22–2–1).

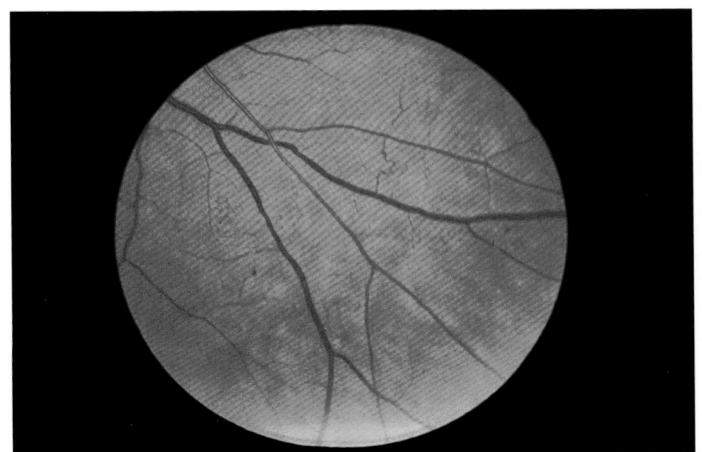

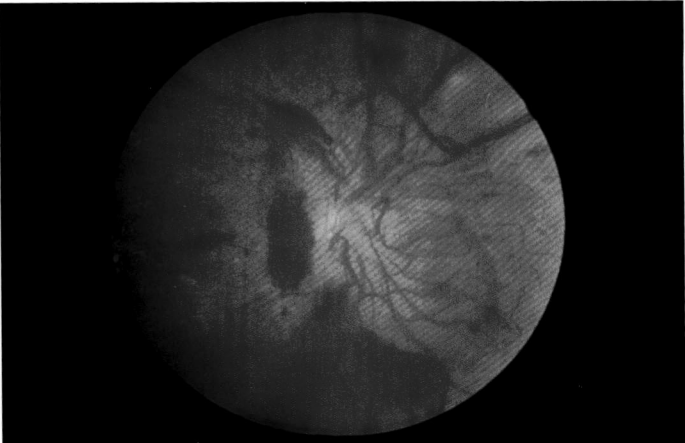

Color Plate 22–2–3. Right eye of a patient with severe nonproliferative retinopathy. The field is inferior and temporal to the optic nerve. Note venous beading of the venous tributary extending toward six o'clock on the slide (veins appear wider in diameter than do arteries). There are numerous areas of intraretinal microvascular abnormalities (IRMAs). One prominent IRMA extends toward one o'clock from the more superior venous tributary.

Color Plate 22–2–4. Right eye of a patient with proliferative retinopathy of high-risk character. The disk is in the center of the photograph, the macula to the left. Note the florid neovascular vessels extending off the retinal surface in a plane above the retinal vessels. Vitreous hemorrhage surrounds the optic nerve.

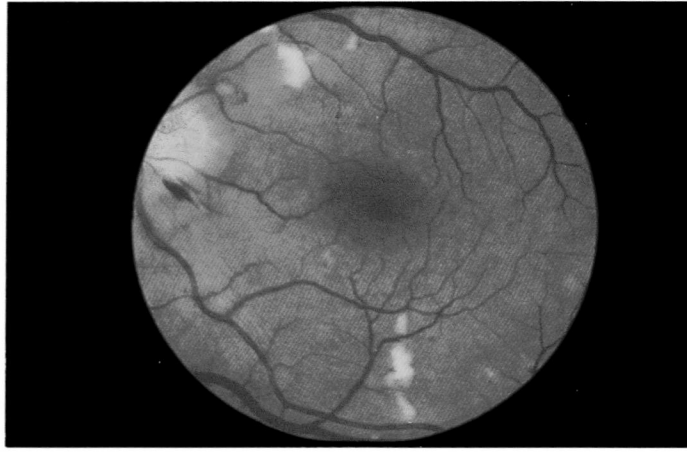

Color Plate 22–14–1. Left eye showing the macula and optic nerve of a patient with HIV retinopathy. Note the white cotton–wool spots and flame-shaped hemorrhages along the inferior aspect of the optic nerve head. These are evanescent findings and do not indicate serious infection. A patient with these findings may notice small spots in the field of view.

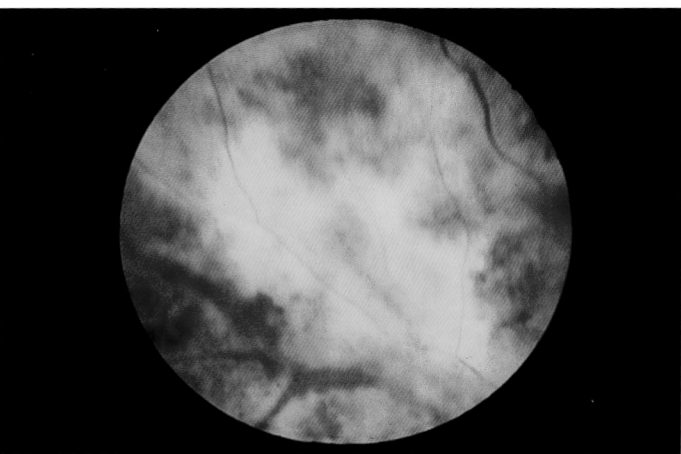

Color Plate 22–14–2. Right eye of a patient with AIDS and fulminant cytomegalovirus retinitis. The view is superior and temporal to the optic nerve head and does not include a picture of the optic nerve or macula. Note the full-thickness retinal whitening and intraretinal hemorrhages. Cytomegalovirus retinitis leads to necrosis of the retina and visual loss.

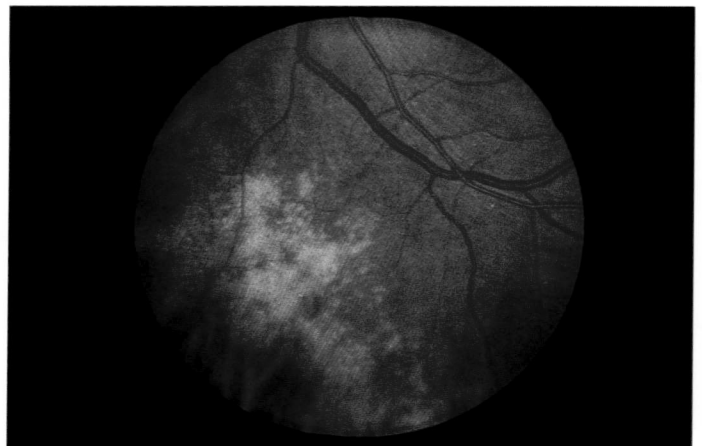

Color Plate 22–14–3. Left eye of a patient with AIDS and cytomegalovirus retinitis, a smoldering form. View is retina inferior to the optic nerve and retina. The dots of whitening are the leading edge of the retinitis. Below these in the photograph is an area of retinal atrophy, allowing better visualization of the deep choroidal vessels.

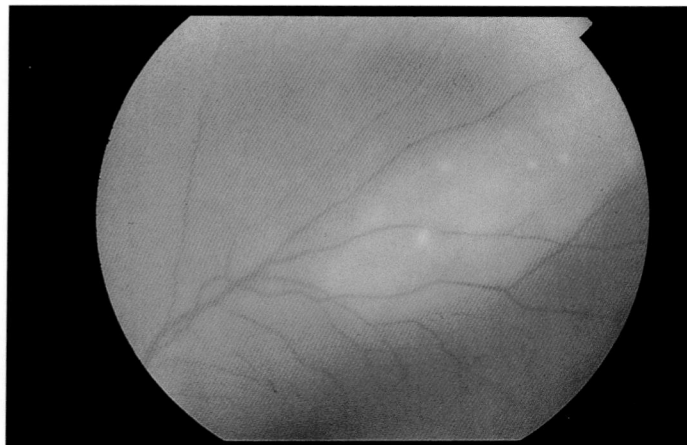

Color Plate 22–14–4. Patient with HIV infection. Note placoid yellow lesion that appears deep to the retina. This later becomes atrophic with areas of pigmentation. The patient had systemic syphilis.

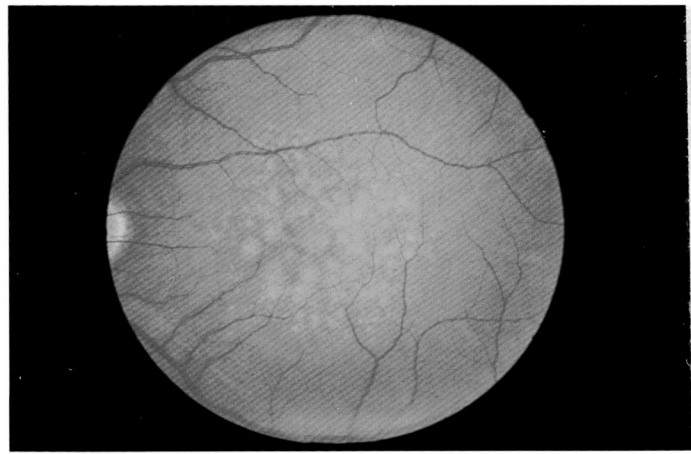

Color Plate 22–15–1. Left macula with edge of the optic nerve noted on the left side of the slide. Note soft or exudative drusen deep to the retina and retinal blood vessels. Many are greater than 250 μm in diameter and confluent in the center of the slide. Smaller drusen surround these.

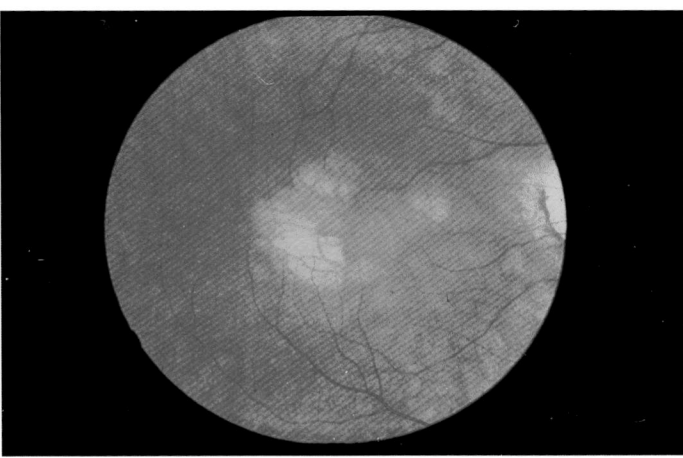

Color Plate 22–15–2. Right eye showing area of geographic atrophy appearing as a "C" around the fovea. Note the ability to view underlying choroidal vessels through the area of retinal atrophy.

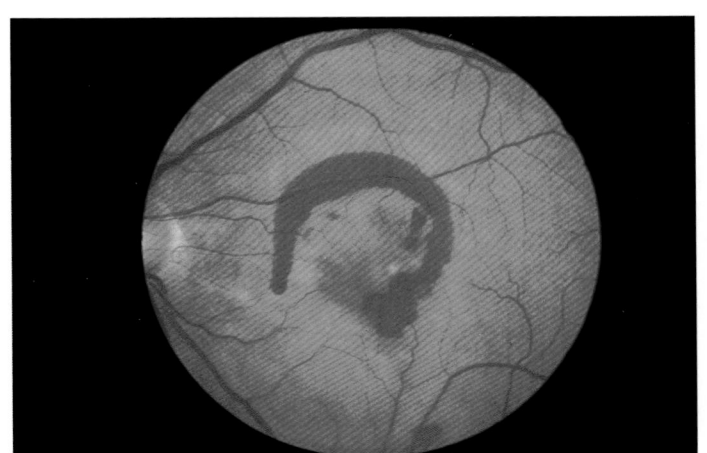

Color Plate 22–15–3. Choroidal neovascularization in left eye. The choroidal neovascularization is partially blocked by the surrounding subretinal hemorrhage.

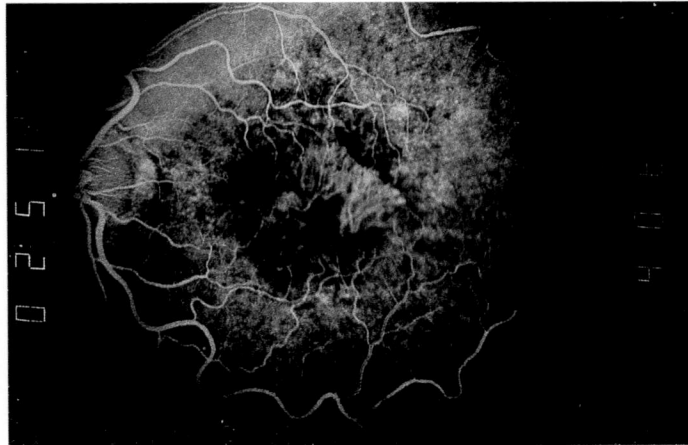

Color Plate 22–15–4. Choroidal neovascularization is well defined by fluorescein angiography in this left eye. Vessels appear white. Note the "broomsticklike" brushes fanning out toward the right side of the slide in the fovea, an area normally hypofluorescent.

pressure at various times over a 24-hour period. Sometimes a family member can be trained to take pressures at home to obtain the same information. Multiple pressure readings at various times during the day help in evaluating a patient who does not seem to respond to therapy or who may need surgery.

Natural History and Its Modification with Treatment

Open-angle glaucoma left untreated progressively damages the optic nerve. Initially, relative scotoma increases in density and increasing visual field loss occurs. Fields finally constrict until a patient has gun-barrel vision, that is, restricted vision comparable to looking through a gun barrel. Primary vision can be totally lost.

Prevention

Screening is the most important preventive measurement for visual loss in glaucoma. Lions Clubs and other service organizations have been active in setting up screening clinics, working on the premise that a well-educated public is the best means for the prevention of glaucoma. As about 1 to 2% of the population over the age of 40 have glaucoma, it is a rewarding preventive effort. The percentage increases to 10% in the elderly.

Screening with a check of intraocular pressure as the only measurement may produce a high number of false-negative results. Screening directed by risk factors and including criteria other than pressure alone is more successful in identifying unknown cases.

Cost Containment

Glaucoma is a common disease. Medications used vary widely in expense. For example, timolol is much more expensive than pilocarpine.

Also, good control of the patient's pressure can decrease the number of necessary visits to two a year. Considering the tens of thousands of patients who have glaucoma, a decrease of one visit per year represents considerable savings in physicians' time and medical expense.

REFERENCES

Albrecht KG, Lee PP. Conformance with preferred practice patterns in caring for patients with glaucoma. Ophthalmology 1994;101:1668.

Armaly MF. Genetic determination of cup/disc ratio of the optic nerve. Arch Ophthalmol 1967;78:35.

Armaly MF. The genetic determination of ocular pressure in the normal eye. Arch Ophthalmol 1967;78:187.

Armaly MF. The optic cup in the normal eye: I. Cup width, depth, vessel displacement, ocular tension and outflow facility. Am J Ophthalmol 1969;68:401.

Armaly MF. Optic cup in normal and glaucomatous eyes. Invest Ophthalmol 1970;9:425.

Hayreh SS. Blood supply of the optic nerve head and its role in optic atrophy glaucoma, and edema of the optic disc. Br J Ophthalmol 1969;53:721.

Kirsch RE, Anderson DR. Clinical recognition of glaucomatous cupping. Am J Ophthalmol 1972;75:442.

Klein BE, Klein R, Jensen SC. Open-angle glaucoma and older-onset diabetes: The Beaver Dam Eye Study. Ophthalmology 1994;101:1173.

Klein BE, Klein R, Sponsel WE, Franke T, et al. Prevalence of glaucoma: The Beaver Dam Eye Study. Ophthalmology 1992;99:1499.

Spaeth GL. Visual loss in a glaucoma clinic: I. Sociological consideration. Invest Ophthalmol 1970;9:73.

CHAPTER 22–5

Herpes Simplex of the Cornea

William H. Coles, M.D., M.S.

DEFINITION

Herpes simplex of the cornea is defined as corneal changes and other abnormalities of the eye due to the herpesvirus.

ETIOLOGY

The cause is herpes simplex virus types 1 and 2 (HSV-1 and HSV-2).

CRITERIA FOR DIAGNOSIS

Suggestive

Herpes simplex of the cornea can be suspected if there is a red eye, a previous history of ocular herpes simplex virus infection, and corneal anesthesia.

Definitive

There may be dendritic erosion of the cornea, suggestive cytology on smears from involved areas, a history of topical or systemic use of steroids before onset, or altered patient immune response from a disease process or drug therapy.

Antibody titers and viral cultures are of limited value. Also of limited value is a history of recurrent lip sores or genital herpes.

Definitive techniques for identification of the virus that are not readily available include electron microscopy and various immunofluorescence techniques.

CLINICAL MANIFESTATIONS

Subjective

Herpes simplex viral infection of the eye produces few symptoms. This is a result of the virus' effects on corneal sensation. In normal circumstances, the cornea is uniformly sensitive. Most minor injuries (a cinder under the eyelid, a small corneal abrasion, or corneal damage from a contact lens) produce memorable pain, light sensitivity, tearing, and lid spasms that temporarily prevent effective use of the eye.

In noticeable contrast, the herpetic cornea may be extensively involved, yet the patient complains of only mild irritation. Lid spasms and light sensitivity, if present, are minimal. The indifference to pain is a result of corneal anesthesia produced by the virus. This anesthesia is permanent and its presence makes one suspect the diagnosis of herpes.

Visual loss—slight or moderate when only the epithelial layers are involved but often more severe after recurrences—is present in corneas affected with herpes simplex virus so frequently that it is a valuable subjective finding. The late stage of corneal involvement is usually already diagnosed as herpes simplex virus. It is in the early stages, presenting as a red eye, when the diagnosis may be missed and improper therapy started. Most conjunctival infections without corneal involvement do not cause decreased vision. In general, any patient presenting with a red eye with visual loss should be suspected for possible corneal herpetic infection. Slit-lamp examination is essential, and a suspicion of herpes as the possible cause should be considered in any acute ocular infection, with or without visual loss.

Objective

Physical Examination

The Dendrite. The virus, when it invades epithelial cells, multiplies and progresses in the corneal epithelial layer with a linear course that branches like a tree limb, that is, a dendrite. This dendrite can easily be missed by a quick examination, and a magnifying lens or a slit lamp is often necessary. By far the best way to outline the distinctive pattern of the dendrite is with the use of a dye such as topical fluorescein. The green outline of the dendrite can be seen in normal light, but it is brightly outlined, even without magnification in most cases, by the use of the deep blue color of cobalt-filtered light.

The Red Eye. Corneal herpes is accompanied in most cases by a hyperemia of the conjunctiva and by some edema, which produces a red eye. This is usually a noninfectious reaction to the corneal infection. The virus is also capable of a direct conjunctival infection, with or without corneal involvement.

Routine Laboratory Abnormalities

There are no diagnostic routine laboratory abnormalities.

PLANS

Diagnostic

Differential Diagnosis

Herpes zoster may produce a corneal dendrite. There is often a history or the presence of skin vesicles.

In viral conjunctivitis follicles are present on the conjunctival surface. Vision is usually normal. Often there is a history of epidemic associated with upper respiratory infection. Nodes may occur preauricular and submandibular, with little or no tenderness.

Bacterial conjunctivitis is associated with a purulent discharge and soreness. Diagnosis is established by smear for organism and cultures.

Acute glaucoma is increased pressure from inflammation. The cornea may be hazy and vision may be decreased.

Uveitis is usually gradual in onset with vision decreased. Slit-lamp examination and thorough fundus examination establish the diagnosis.

Diagnostic Options and Recommended Approach

Antibody Titers. Antibodies to herpesvirus—both neutralizing and complement fixing—are present in 90% of humans surveyed. The neutralizing antibodies do not usually change with repeat infections; the complement-fixing antibodies are more prone to fluctuate with the recurrences. Although changing antibody titers can support a diagnosis of herpetic ocular infection, they are not routinely useful for diagnosis because of nonspecificity and because of the necessity to document changing titers.

Cytology. Examination of cells from the infected area can support the diagnosis of herpes. Viral multinucleated giant cells can be seen. The most common cell type is mononuclear; however, in the early stages of infection, polymorphonuclear cells may predominate.

Viral Isolation. The virus can be isolated from the cornea and other ocular structures and surfaces. The culture material may be frozen at 4°C if a delay is expected before the specimen arrives at the laboratory.

Electron Microscopy. The virus can be seen on electron microscopic section. If present, it can establish the diagnosis. The virus is not visible in all stages or replication, however, and absence of the virus would not rule out herpes as the etiologic agent.

Immunofluorescence Techniques. Direct immunofluorescence techniques can establish the diagnosis of herpetic infections. These techniques are primarily investigational and not readily available to the practitioner.

Therapeutic

Idoxuridine (Herplex) was the first antiviral agent available and effective against the epithelial stages of herpes simplex virus infection. With extended use beyond 10 to 14 days, it has a significant number of toxic reactions, some of which can mimic the changes caused by herpes simplex virus.

Adenine arabinoside (ara-A [VIRA-A]), another antiviral agent with about equal effectiveness to idoxuridine, can be used in persons who have toxic reactions to idoxuridine. Toxicity to adenine arabinoside develops, however, with the same frequency as that to idoxuridine. Adenine arabinoside has been shown to penetrate deeper into the eye and has been suggested as superior to idoxuridine in intraocular infections caused by herpes simplex. Clinical experience has thrown some doubt on this claim.

Trifluorothymidine (Viroptic) has been shown to have a better effect on the virus than either idoxuridine or adenine arabinoside. Trifluorothymidine is now in most circumstances the drug of choice in treating active viral infection.

Mechanical debridement, a mainstay of treatment until a few years ago, still has a place in therapy. The principle is to remove all dead tissue and the virus with it. After application of topical anesthesia, the edge of the scalpel blade can be used to remove infected tissue.

In the immune stages of the disease, where stromal inflammation and edema are caused not by the live virus but by the immune response triggered by the virus, topical steroids may be of use. This treatment, however, can activate the latent virus and worsen the disease process. If steroids are used, careful, sometimes even daily, monitoring of the patient's progress is necessary by an expert in the field of herpetic ocular disease.

Surgery frequently becomes necessary in patients who have continued recurrences. Corneal transplants are successful but stand the risk of rejection and of reinfection in the graft from the herpes simplex virus, not an uncommon occurrence.

Systemic therapy with acycloguanosine is now experimentally being investigated and shows promise as a systemic therapy.

Most important in patients with herpes simplex virus is the specific explanation of what to expect. In most cases, the disease process is limited. But in recurrences, therapy can be long-term and the result discouraging. The patient should be prepared for the possibility of a prolonged course with possible visual loss.

The immunologically competent patient can be encouraged by the fact that chances are remote that the opposite eye will be involved. Fear of bilateral visual loss or total blindness will be in every patient's thoughts, and it is the physician's obligation to relieve such fears.

Patients should be made aware of the trigger mechanisms associated with recurrences: emotional stress, physical stress, illness, fever, ultraviolet exposure, and the use of steroids.

It is important to clarify virus types for the patient between ocular herpes, type I, and genital herpes, type II. Although cross-infections do occur and the implication of virus types in clinical disease, once thought to be clear, has been challenged, there is still no direct relationship between herpes simplex eye infection and genital disease.

FOLLOW-UP

Epithelial herpes of the cornea recurs in 20% of individuals after the first attack and in 50% of individuals after a repeated attack. No examination schedule is indicated, but the patient should be urged to return for examination at the slightest irritation of the eye.

DISCUSSION

Prevalence and Incidence

Antibodies to herpesvirus are common in the general population. Nine out of ten have positive titers. The incidence of herpes ocular complications is not known.

Related Basic Science

Herpes simplex is a viral parasite. Once a human has had the primary infection, and most of us have, the virus remains with us for life. As a parasite, the virus is dependent on live cell replication, and it has predilection for epithelial cells. The virus enters the cell, incorporates itself into the functioning of the cell, and uses the cell DNA for its replication. After having replicated, it moves on to other cells. Some cells are destroyed; others harbor the virus. For the most part, the relationship is uneventful and the virus goes unnoticed by the host.

Where the virus stays in the body during quiescent times is not fully understood. Although the virus has been found in many structures of the eye, it is believed that its presence in the trigeminal ganglion is responsible for recurrent attacks of ocular herpes. The virus is also shed in the tears and can be cultured even in quiescent times. A full appreciation of the virus, of its reactions, and of its immunologic stimuli awaits further investigation.

Immunology of the virus has fascinated researchers, because it represents the key to the discovery of better therapy. As a great deal of the destruction of the recurrent aspects of herpes (stromal herpes) is not associated with active virus infection with host immunologic defenses, it is hoped that a complete understanding of immunologic mechanisms will provide the answers for treating and preventing recurrences. There are at least three classes of antigens associated with herpesvirus: nonincorporated diffusible antigens that are liberated from an infected cell when it is dissolved; an antigen fixed to the surface of an infected cell; and the large, insoluble proteins incorporated in the virus. How these various antigenic stimuli interact to cause the clinical disease is still unknown. Cell immunity plays an important role. How humoral immunity contribute is also unknown.

With the electron microscope, the virus can be seen to be about 180 μm in diameter and to contain three elements: a core, an inner shell of protein, and an outer envelope of glycoprotein. It is in the core where the vital viral DNA is housed, and it is the DNA that is vital for duplication of the virus. The outer glycoprotein envelope of the virus is the essential infective portion.

Natural History and Its Modification with Treatment

Herpes is such a common virus that it can be thought of as a successful parasitic virus that, with supporting genetic and environmental influences, can occasionally cause a wide range of clinical diseases. In the eye, we are confronted primarily with type I virus, the virus that has a predilection for the upper part of the body, and not type II virus, which is responsible for genital herpes. Although exceptions do occur—for example, in the neonate, ocular disease can be caused by infection from the mother's type II congenital strain—our concern, under present understanding, is with the type I virus as a prime ocular virus.

Antibodies to the virus cross the placental barrier and provide protection to most newborns for up to 6 months. Babies whose mothers have no antibodies and premature infants who have no antibody titers may be susceptible to neonatal infection. Once an infection occurs, neutralizing and complement-fixing antibodies appear within a week.

Nine of ten persons have antibodies against herpes, but only a few of us have had clinical disease. Most initial herpes infections occur undiagnosed and unnoticed. The primary herpes infection that does cause signs can be a mild severe systemic illness; can involve the mucous membranes, skin, and eyes; or can involve the central nervous system. In all but rare instances, herpes is a self-limiting disease; the persistence of the virus is, however, lifelong.

To avoid confusion, it is useful to consider ocular herpes as a separate manifestation of the frequency of the virus. Most patients, by our knowledge of the virus, have antibodies as the result of a primary infection that in most cases did not affect the eye. But if we consider only the primary ocular infection, we can make general predictions about the recurrence rate. After the first ocular infection, about one fourth of patients have a recurrence. Once an ocular recurrence is present, one half of these patients have an additional attack within 2 years.

It is almost always true, except in individuals with severely compromised immune systems from drugs or disease, that recurrent herpes infections affect only the eye initially involved, never the opposite eye.

The exceptions to this observation are so rare that patients may be reassured with confidence.

Once the virus invades the eye (usually starting with the corneal epithelium), there is a varied and not fully understood immunologic reaction, both humoral and cellular. It is the immunologic response, either with or without active virus present, that causes the edema and subsequent necrosis of the cornea that can lead to perforation. Parts of the immunologic reaction are sensitive to steroids, yet steroids can activate virus replication and aggravate the corneal damage. In this complex stage of the disease, therapy is dependent on a thorough knowledge of the mechanisms of corneal repair. Without this knowledge, the disease process can easily surge out of control. Medicamentosa and abnormal tear film distribution are two factors, for example, that can hinder repair; both are frequently overlooked.

Healing of the recurrences of corneal disease (corneal tissue already damaged by active virus and by the immunologic reaction caused by virus particles and host cells sensitized by the virus) is prolonged and requires long periods of topical drug therapy. Frequently, drugs normally harmless to the healthy and acutely infected cornea can be toxic and retard or prevent healing. Not only are the antiviral agents a problem, antibiotics and antiinflammatory drugs can cause a significant medicamentous reaction. Also, disruption of the tear film, which is now considered an essential layer of the cornea, occurs. Tear film irregularity leads to local drying, a loss of vital corneal tissue, and possibly perforation. The effects of improper tear film distribution may not be readily apparent, and the diagnosis may go undetected by the unexperienced examiner. Even after the diagnosis is suspected, with other factors affecting the corneal progression simultaneously, the degree to which tear film abnormalities are playing a role may be difficult to assess. Again, experience and a special interest in herpes simplex of the cornea are frequently needed by the attending physician.

Recurrences of the virus are known to be triggered by stress. Emotional stress, although seemingly hard to pin down, is so frequent at the time of recurrence that there is little doubt of a cause-and-effect relationship. Examinations for students, marital problems, and business failures are typical situations. Physical stress is also a trigger; severe illness or high fever acts to cause recurrences in susceptible individuals. For this reason, fever reduction control and prompt therapy for illness are indicated.

Sunlight also commonly brings on recurrences. One young woman had repeated recurrences always on bright summer days after she had been water skiing. It is probable that ultraviolet exposure was the activator. Sunglasses are now made to screen ultraviolet light, and their use may be recommended.

Herpes corneal infections may occur in patients receiving chemotherapy for carcinoma or immunosuppressant agents for control of autoimmune disease. When managing these susceptible patients, careful observation for red eye or visual symptoms is needed.

Prevention

The use of topical corticosteroids on an ocular infection, diagnosed or undiagnosed, should never be undertaken except by a specialist. Herpes infections of the cornea should never be triggered by the injudicious use of steroids or by combinations of medications that contain steroids.

Cost Containment

Patients with herpes simplex of the cornea should be rehabilitated as soon as possible. There is no need to cripple a patient's earning or learning capacity while the herpes simplex corneal problem is under treatment. This is especially true with recurrences. Patients kept on excessive restrictions can have severe and unnecessary psychological reactions to this localized disease.

Trifluorothymidine, although most effective against the active virus, is also the most expensive topical drug. For certain aspects of herpetic disease therapy, physicians may want to use less expensive drugs.

REFERENCES

Duker JS, Nielsen JC, Eagle RC Jr, et al. Rapidly progressive acute retinal necrosis secondary to herpes simplex virus, type I. Ophthalmology 1990;97:1638.

O'Day DM, Jones BR. Herpes simplex. In: Duane TD, ed. Clinical ophthalmology, Hagerstown, MD: Harper & Row, 1980;4:1.

Teich SA, Cheung TW, Friedman AH. Systemic antiviral drugs used in opthalmology. Surv Ophthalmol 1992;37:19.

Yoser SL, Forster DJ, Rao NA. Systemic viral infections and their retinal and choroidal manifestations. Surv Ophthalmol 1993;37:313.

CHAPTER 22–6

Ocular Changes in Carotid Occlusive Disease

William H. Coles, M.D., M.S.

DEFINITION

Ocular changes in carotid occlusive disease are defined as ocular changes associated with a decrease in blood flow due to carotid artery occlusion from atherosclerosis.

ETIOLOGY

Decreased blood flow to ocular structures occurs as the result of an embolus or chronic carotid arterial insufficiency due to atherosclerosis of the carotid artery.

CRITERIA FOR DIAGNOSIS

Suggestive

Visual disturbances of carotid occlusive disease due to atherosclerosis are amaurosis fugax, a transient recurrent visual loss, and central retinal occlusion, a total or near-total loss of vision that is usually permanent.

Visual symptoms and signs observed in the presence of a bruit or a decreased pulsation over the involved carotid artery establishes a diagnosis.

Definitive

A positive identification of carotid occlusive disease by angiography or Doppler studies plus the eye signs establish the diagnosis.

CLINICAL MANIFESTATIONS

Subjective

Ischemia to the eyes as a result of impaired blood flow in the ophthalmic artery and its branches can occur from emboli or from prolonged, insidious arterial insufficiency. The symptoms of emboli are the more dramatic and the more frequent cause of awareness of a disease process. Chronic arterial insufficiency can produce visual loss from cataract formation or ischemic changes of the cornea.

Ocular involvement associated with carotid atherosclerosis is common; in fact, 65% of patients with carotid arterial insufficiency eventually have ocular symptoms. The most common symptom is amaurosis fugax, a unilateral loss of vision that occurs on the side of carotid obstruction. The loss of vision in the involved eye, which is frequently complete, is transient. The time between attacks varies considerably from days to weeks or occasionally years.

A central artery occlusion occurs from embolus, and the visual loss is sudden and often total. A mild ache may be described, but the pain is rarely severe. When severe pain is present, it is probable that the ophthalmic artery rather than the central retinal artery is occluded.

Objective

Physical Examination

When ocular changes occur, they may be due to a retinal artery occlusion or the ischemic effects of decreased perfusion to the eye.

With central artery occlusion from emboli, there are few immediate signs. The disk may show a mild pallor, and there may be only slight attenuation of the arteries. In almost all cases the obstructive plaque is usually passed by the time of the examination by an ophthalmologist.

Occasionally, when the obstructing plaque is still present, boxcar segmentation of the column of blood in the artery can be seen and the lumens of the arteries may be narrowed.

Opacification of the retina with the macula appearing bright red (cherry-red spot) does not occur until several hours after the occlusion and, therefore, is not a reliable early sign. Once the retinal clouding occurs, it is diagnostic and persists for 2 to 3 weeks. In general, unless a vein is also involved at the same time as arterial occlusion, no hemorrhages are present.

Fundus changes in carotid occlusive disease other than retinal artery occlusion can produce cotton–wool spots. These are frequently multiple, have feathery edges, and are found in the posterior of the eye. Characteristically, the macular region is spared.

In 5% of patients with unilateral carotid occlusive disease a clinical picture emerges known as *venous stasis retinopathy*. In these patients, a different fundus picture is seen; the veins are dilated, deep retinal hemorrhages are present, and microaneurysms are seen. This clinical picture has a resemblance to diabetic retinopathy.

A significant number of patients with carotid occlusive disease also have hypertension. In such patients, the eye on the involved side—the ischemic side—seems, for unknown reasons, to be protected from hypertensive retinopathy when compared with the nonischemic eye. This protective phenomenon is also seen in diabetic patients with retinopathy; that is, the eye ischemic from carotid insufficiency does not develop retinopathy as severe as does the nonischemic eye. This provides a useful sign in hypertensive as well as in diabetic patients. If marked asymmetry between the eyes of a patient with diabetic retinopathy or hypertensive retinopathy is noted, carotid occlusive disease should be suspected.

Although rarely visualized because of a quick onset and short duration, changes can be seen in the fundus during an amaurosis fugax attack. Emboli can be seen to migrate through the retinal vascular tree. They are of fibrin or platelet aggregation type and present as yellow glinting plaques of cholesterol (Hollenhorst plaques) halted at arterial bifurcations. Such changes are usually transient and not visible after the episode has subsided.

Routine Laboratory Abnormalities

The condition results in carotid atherosclerosis. Therefore, the routine laboratory abnormalities may include those of atherosclerosis.

PLANS

Diagnostic

Differential Diagnosis

In giant cell arteritis (temporal arteritis), systemic signs are anorexia, weight loss, low-grade fatigue, depression, dementia, anemia. Common findings include intermittent claudication of the jaw while chewing, scalp tenderness, thickened palpable temporal artery, and transient visual loss. The erythrocyte sedimentation rate is usually greater than 60. Temporal artery biopsy can help establish the diagnosis but a negative biopsy does not rule out the diagnosis.

Aortic arch syndrome and its variants—subclavian steal and innominate steal syndromes—are characterized by a loss of spontaneous artery pulsations, narrowed arteries, distended veins, cotton–wool spots, hemorrhages, microaneurysms, cataracts, syncope, hemiplegia, aphasia, headaches, coma, tinnitus, and deafness. To establish the diagnosis, these may be helpful: comparing intraocular pressures, arteriography, ophthalmodynamometry differential at least 20%, bilateral fluorescein injection, bruits, comparing carotid pulses, thermography.

Diagnostic Options and Recommended Approach

See Criteria for Diagnosis.

Therapeutic

Central retinal artery occlusion rapidly destroys retinal elements, and therapy results are poor. If the retina is anoxic for 20 minutes or more, permanent damage occurs. Therapy, to be effective, must be given immediately after the onset of symptoms. If a physician is present minutes after the occlusion, therapeutic measures have been recommended. Having the patient breathe carbon dioxide, if available, or just having the patient breathe into a paper bag to build up the percentage of carbon dioxide in the lungs has been thought to stimulate dilation of the arteries and shorten the occlusion. Simultaneously, massage of the eyeball may help dislodge the plaque as the artery expands so flow can be restored. More drastic therapy such as rapid lowering of intraocular pressure to alter the pressure differential between the artery and the interior of the eye by making a stab corneal incision and releasing fluid (a paracentesis) has been suggested. Because physicians are rarely present at the time of occlusion and large experience with this technique is impossible, use of this technique has been rare and its effectiveness has not been evaluated.

The use of anticoagulants (or antiplatelet drugs) can abort the transient ischemic attacks of amaurosis fugax and may prevent others; however, carotid artery endarterectomy to remove the origin of the emboli is more definitive therapy. Any patient with amaurosis fugax should be made aware of the likelihood of a stroke. Accordingly, patients with this disorder must be seen immediately by an internist or neurologist, so that surgical intervention by a vascular surgeon for carotid vascular disease can be considered without delay.

FOLLOW-UP

The follow-up of patients with carotid occlusive disease is determined by the symptoms and treatment. Patients receiving antiplatelet drugs or who have had carotid artery surgery should be seen at least twice a year. Patients with carotid bruits who are asymptomatic must be evaluated by an internist or neurologist.

DISCUSSION

Prevalence and Incidence

The prevalence and incidence are unknown.

Related Basic Science

The inner retina is supplied by the central retinal artery and contains the visual elements that are so sensitive to ischemia. The outer retina is supplied by the rich source of blood from the choroidal network of vessels. This separation of blood supply to the retina into two distinct sources explains the catastrophic loss of vision occurring when the central retinal artery or its branches are occluded.

In a fair number of individuals, there is a vascular connection between these two distinct sources of blood to the retina, a common anomaly that may preserve some central vision. This anomaly, the cilioretinal artery (15–30% of population), supplies the macular area and is not a branch of the central retinal artery. Patients who have this artery and suffer from a central artery occlusion may continue to have perfusion into the macular area and preserve some central vision.

Impediments to the retinal artery circulation can be caused by distant obstructions such as aortic arch syndrome or by occlusion of the retinal artery and its branches. Localized obstruction, as opposed to the more general ischemia of the aortic arch syndrome, causes ischemic signs similar to those that occur in hypertension, diabetes, collagenosis, ischemic hemoglobinopathies, and other conditions. Ischemia from any source can cause nonspecific changes in the retina, for example, cotton–wool spots. Differences in the appearance of ischemic areas are related to disease processes but are also related to whether the ischemia is caused by chronic, localized, or generalized obstruction.

Carotid occlusive disease is usually seen in older individuals with atherosclerosis. (In younger patients, trauma, inflammation, and congenital defects are more frequent causes.) The site of occlusion is at the C4–5 level, with the left side involved six to seven times more frequently than the right. There is also a male predominance over females of 2:1.

Many of the retinal changes seen with carotid stenosis and occlusion from atheromatosis are due to emboli that shower the retina, causing local ischemia. The changes in other parts of the eye, apparently due to low perfusion pressure over time, include cataracts and destructive neovascularization of the eye.

Local embolic occlusion of a retinal artery or a central retinal artery induces local anoxia, which results in vasodilation. As the vessel dilates, the embolus migrates, a reason why the emboli frequently are not observed even soon after the visual loss. These emboli may disintegrate fairly rapidly, as they are usually platelet aggregates. The occlusions due to cholesterol plaques (which lodge at artery bifurcations), however, may remain for hours and can be seen on occasion following occlusion. Flow in the artery is reduced by emboli but is rarely stopped. This appears to be a concept against common sense, but it is confirmed by fluorescein dye techniques and clinical observations in acute obstructions.

Occlusion for 20 minutes or more of a central retinal artery or branch artery produces permanent visual loss from destruction of the inner glioneural layers. Initially there is intracellular edema, particularly in the ganglion cells and their axons. Later, necrosis occurs and the inner layers degenerate. Finally, at a late stage, glial tissue replaces the inner retinal structures. It is important to reemphasize that the cotton–wool spots that result from local obstruction are not exudates but edema. They do not occur with transient occlusion.

Natural History and Its Modification with Treatment

Carotid occlusive disease, which occurs more frequently on the left side, if untreated may progress to serious neurologic defects. Fortunately, involvement of the eye is rarely severe, probably because collateral circulation develops.

Only 10% of patients with carotid occlusive disease develop central artery occlusion, but with occlusion of the central artery, vision is usually lost. In branch occlusion, usually on the temporal side, central vision is often preserved. As a general rule, in most cases of carotid occlusive disease, the ocular signs and symptoms are limited to the involved side, and the presentation of the signs is uniocular.

Prevention

The ocular conditions related to carotid artery atherosclerosis can be prevented by the measures used to prevent coronary atherosclerosis (see Chapter 15–1).

Cost Containment

The early recognition and treatment of occlusive carotid disease will decrease morbidity and save money.

REFERENCES

Branch Vein Occlusion Study Group. Argon laser scatter photocoagulation for prevention of neovascularization and vitreous hemorrhage in branch vein occlusion: A randomized clinical trial. Arch Opthalmol 1986;104:34.

Cogan DG. Ophthalmic manifestations of systemic vascular disease. Philadelphia: Saunders, 1974:102.

Hollenhorst RW. Carotid and vertebral-basilar arterial stenosis and occlusion: Neuro-opthalmologic considerations. Trans Am Acad Ophthalmol Otolaryngol 1962;66:166.

Rosenthal D, Hungerpiller JC, Crispin ME, et al. Amaurosis fugax: Is it innocuous? Ann Vasc Surg 1992;6:281.

Schilder P. Ocular blood flow responses to pathology of the carotid and cerebral circulations. Surv Ophthalmol 1994;38(suppl.):S52.

Papilledema and Increased Intracranial Pressure

Wiliam H. Coles, M.D., M.S.

DEFINITION

Papilledema and increased intracranial pressure are defined as swelling of the optic nerve head associated with increased intracranial pressure.

ETIOLOGY

Increased intracranial pressure results in a backup of axonal plasma.

CRITERIA FOR DIAGNOSIS

Subjective

None.

Definitive

Papilledema may be accompanied by other signs and symptoms of increased intracranial pressure: headache, nausea and vomiting, loss of consciousness, motor rigidity, and pupillary dilation. In such cases, changes in the optic disk of blurred margins, tortuous veins, loss of spontaneous venous pulsations, elevation of the disc, and hemorrhages and exudates near the disk establish the diagnosis of disk edema.

Fluorescein angiography, which will show leaking of dye around the disc, is of moderate help but not diagnostic exclusively for papilledema.

CLINICAL MANIFESTATIONS

Subjective

Frequently, papilledema, especially early papilledema, does not present with ocular symptoms. When symptoms occur, they are usually associated with the late stages of swelling when the diagnosis of papilledema is already suspected or established from more general symptoms and signs.

In the late stages of papilledema, blurring of vision occurs in some patients. It is always brief, lasting only a few seconds, and it is always unilateral. The visual acuity as tested on eye charts is almost always normal in papilledema. Only in persistent cases with chronic edema does a gradual decrease in the visual acuity occur. This is uncommon.

Objective

Physical Examination

In early diagnosis of papilledema, it is the disc changes seen by direct ophthalmoscopy that give the careful examiner the clues to its diagnosis. There are six major features of papilledema.

Blurred Disc Details. There is a blurring of the physiologic cup and subsequent blurring of the disc margins that indicate edema. A veillike graying and streaks along the vessels result from the edema.

Overfilled Veins. The lack of spontaneous venous pulsations or the lack of pulsations with gentle pressure on the globe is the most important objective manifestation. A diagnosis of papilledema is highly unlikely if spontaneous venous pulses are present; however, lack of venous pulsations, unless there is previous documentation of their presence, is not diagnostic, as pulsations are not present in about 20% of normal individuals.

Hyperemia of the Disc. Individual variations in disc appearance make this a difficult sign to evaluate on a single observation. Changes in the color and appearance of the disc are most important when noted on a comparison of two or more examinations.

Elevation of the Disc. This sign does not occur early in the disease, and elevation of the disc can also be seen in normal individuals. Still, disc elevation, especially if changing, can be helpful. To estimate disc ele-vation, focus on the retina with the strongest plus lens, if hyperopic (black numbers), or the weakest minus lens, if myopic (red numbers), to minimize the error from the accommodation of the examiner. In essence, focus with the highest black or the lowest red lens possible to see the retina. Then focus the ophthalmoscope on the disc and note the difference. A three-diopter change (three-number difference on the ophthalmoscope) is equivalent to approximately 1 mm of disc elevation.

Hemorrhages. Linear red hemorrhagic streaks around the disc (on the surface of the nerve fiber layer) are late evidence of papilledema. These are always around the margin of the disc and are not seen in periphery.

Exudates. Exudates, from hemorrhage, are always near the disc in papilledema. They are also a late sign.

The visual field can change, but these changes are not diagnostic and only support the clinical manifestations. Increase in the blind spot, of course, is frequent but is never noticed by the patient. Constriction of the peripheral fields for both form and color can occur but is of little diagnostic value.

Papilledema is a sign of increased intracranial pressure. Age differences help pinpoint the cause. Physicians should look for signs of metastatic and intracranial tumors in adults and for primary posterior fossa tumors in children.

Fluorescein angiography is useful in differentiating papilledema from pseudopapilledema caused by optic nerve drusen. Unfortunately, it is not useful to detect the early stages of papilledema, when it would be most valuable.

Routine Laboratory Abnormalities

There are no routine laboratory abnormalities.

PLANS

Diagnositc

Differential Diagnosis

Anterior ischemic optic neuropathy is usually seen in patients over 60 with painless progression over several hours, disc pale with hemorrhages, and altitudinal or arcuate field defects. The condition is often seen with atherosclerosis, diabetes mellitus, giant cell arteritis, and hypertension. The sedimentation rate is elevated in giant cell arteritis.

Anterior optic neuritis is seen in the 15- to 45-year-old age group. Many patients develop signs of multiple sclerosis. Symptoms include retrobulbar pain on eye movement and decreased central vision.

Compressive disc swelling is associated with an orbital mass. The visual loss is usually slow. Prime considerations are glioma and meningioma.

Toxic optic neuropathy is a bilateral condition. Features include cecocentral scotomas and decreased visual acuity. Toxicity (chloramphenicol, lead, or ethambutol) should be considered.

Optic nerve drusen is usually seen in Caucasians and shows a hereditary pattern. Features are irregular glistening yellow globules and loss of visual acuity (rare). Fluorescein angiography can be helpful.

Diagnostic Options and Recommended Approach

See Criteria for Diagnosis.

Therapeutic

The treatment of papilledema is correction of the cause of the increased intracranial pressure.

The underlying cause of the papilledema will need to be explained to the patient. Patients with visual symptoms may be encouraged that the symptoms will probably disappear when the increase in intracranial pressure is relieved.

FOLLOW-UP

Once the diagnosis of papilledema is established, further follow-up depends on the patient's response to therapy for the increased intracranial pressure. Ophthalmic changes can help to determine the progress of the cause of the papilledema. In cases where the diagnosis is only suspected but not confirmed, follow-up examination every 24 hours is indicated until a change in disc appearance is documented or stability of the disc appearance is confirmed.

DISCUSSION
Prevalence and Incidence

The prevalence and incidence are unknown.

Related Basic Science

The optic nerve carries 1.2 million fibers from the retina to the lateral geniculate body, and all fibers leave by way of the optic disc passing through a Swiss cheese-like laminar plate, the lamina cribrosa. The disk itself is 1.5 mm in size, a relatively small area representing only 5° to 7° of visual space. The intraocular portion of the nerve is usually nonmyelinated, and the origin of the blood supply, although still controversial, is choroidal vessels and/or the short posterior ciliary arteries. The orbital portion of the nerve is about double the size in diameter of the intraocular portion due to the acquisition of the myelin sheath. Here the blood supply is from the opthalmic artery, including branches from the pial vessels.

Swelling of the disc is related to the axoplasmic flow of the optic nerve. Axoplastic transport takes place in the axon from the retinal ganglion cell to the termination in the lateral geniculate body. Both fast transport and slow transport have been identified, but the rapid flow is more involved in the pathogenesis of disc swelling.

It is the cessation of axoplasmic transport at the level of the lamina cribrosa that is the initial component of the disc edema. Swelling caused by the cessation compresses venous channels and leads to the thickening and tortuosity of the vessels and to the eventual leakage from the vessels that can be seen on fluorescein angiography.

Experimental evidence shows that an increase of pressure in the cranial subarachnoid space is responsible for the swelling, not an increase in pressure in the ventricles alone. It is probably the cerebrospinal fluid pressure in the optic nerve sheath that determines the pressure on the nerve. This increase in pressure then causes axoplasmic flow stasis, disc swelling, and the resultant vascular changes.

Natural History and Its Modification with Treatment

The development of papilledema after the development of an increase in intracranial pressure may take hours or, more frequently, days. Reversal of the condition depends on success of treatment for the increased intracranial pressure. A diagnosis of papilledema is an emergency for that reason.

Prevention

There is no method for the prevention of papilledema.

Cost Containment

Cost containment is achieved by the appropriate and orderly workup of the patient for the etiology of the increase in intracranial pressure.

REFERENCES

Garrity JA, Herman DC, Imes R, et al. Optic nerve sheath decompression for visual loss in patients with acquired immunodeficiency syndrome and cryptococcal meningitis with papilledema. Am J Ophthalmol 1993;116:472.

Hayreh SS. Blood supply of the optic nerve head and its role in optic atrophy, glaucoma, and oedema of the optic disc. Br J Ophthalmol 1969;53:721.

Hayreh SS. Pathogenesis of optic disc edema in raised intracranial pressure. Trans Ophthalmol Soc UK 1976;96:404.

Spoor TC, McHenry JG. Long-term effectiveness of optic nerve sheath decompression for pseudotumor cerebri. Arch Ophthalmol 1993;111:632.

Walsh FB, Hoyt WF. Papilledema, optic neuritis, and optic atrophy: The optic disc in neurological diagnosis. In: Clinical neuro-ophthalmology. 3rd ed. Baltimore: Williams & Wilkins, 1969;1:567.

CHAPTER 22–8

Thyroid (Endocrine) Eye Disease

William H. Coles, M.D., M.S.

DEFINITION

Thyroid (endocrine) eye disease is defined as ocular signs including lid retraction and proptosis with increase in the orbital contents which are often but not always associated with thyroid abnormality.

ETIOLOGY

Autoimmune mechanisms which are not fully understood.

CRITERIA FOR DIAGNOSIS
Suggestive

The patient may complain of some of the abnormalities listed below.

Definitive

Early signs of thyroid disease are eyelid retraction and lag of the upper lid on down gaze. Later, forward displacement of the eye (proptosis) occurs, and restriction of the ocular movements may cause double vision (diplopia).

Thyroid function should be established, but it must be remembered that thyroid eye disease can occur in the presence of increased, decreased, or normal thyroid activity.

Characteristic enlargement of the ocular muscles as seen with computed tomography or ultrasonography can be diagnostic of thyroid eye disease.

CLINICAL MANIFESTATIONS
Subjective

Patients with thyroid eye disease frequently have irritation and tearing. Redness of the eyes, light sensitivity, and eye fatigue are also common complaints. Of course, these symptoms are not related specifically to thyroid eye disease but are often severe and persistent enough to be the cause that forces the patient to seek relief.

Visual decrease is an infrequent occurrence (< 3–5% of patients). Severe visual loss occurs from corneal change, a late change that is easily diagnosed, or optic nerve involvement, which may occur early and is frequently misdiagnosed because the eye signs can be minimal. Patients presenting with optic nerve-related visual loss, without obvious other signs, should be considered to have thyroid eye disease as a possible diagnosis.

Double vision occurs from the restriction of ocular muscles. This is usually a late finding, occurring when the orbital involvement is severe and there is little doubt as to the cause.

Objective

Physical Examination

Thyroid Stare. About half of patients with thyroid eye disease usually develop an early sign of upper lid and sometimes lower lid retraction. Normally, the upper lid covers the upper iris to approximately the pupillary margin. The abnormal lid retraction of thyroid disease (Dalryample's sign) brings the lid margin up, exposing white sclera and giving an intense and frightened look. Not only will the lid retract, but it may also lag on down gaze (von Graefe's sign), an additional early sign of thyroid eye involvement.

Forward Displacement of the Eye (Proptosis). Displacement of the eye can be measured by the use of the exophthalmometer (Hertel is a common type). There is a considerable racial difference in the prominence of eyes as well as expected individual differences, and, for the most part, absolute values are understandably difficult to establish for a diagnosis of proptosis. As a guide, measurements greater than 22 to 24 mm are accepted as highly suspicious of proptosis. In the equivocal case, a documented change is best to establish if a disease process is present; months are often necessary in thyroid eye disease, as proptosis develops slowly. Finally, a difference between the eyes can be important; 2 to 3 mm is generally accepted as abnormal. The importance of a difference may at first seem strange. Although the diffuse nature of thyroid disease and thyroid eye disease might suggest bilateral involvement, it is one of the paradoxes of thyroid eye disease that it is frequently unilateral.

Visual Loss and Visual Field Changes. Visual loss and visual field changes can occur from optic nerve involvement. High suspicion is necessary, as optic nerve involvement from thyroid eye disease is frequently misdiagnosed. When the optic nerve is involved, the other signs of thyroid orbital changes may be minimal. Almost always, however, there will be a history of congestive changes (proptosis, eyelid and conjunctival edema, tearing, diplopia, and redness) a few months before the onset of optic nerve involvement. Proptosis and eyelid retraction may be minimal, but all patients will have some signs of Graves' disease no matter how subtle. Extraocular muscle involvement, if present, characteristically involves all muscles equally rather than the selective involvement usually seen with thyroid eye disease without nerve involvement. Fifteen percent of these patients have unilateral involvement.

The visual field changes may be central scotoma, arcuate defects, or peripheral depressions. No paracentral or peripheral defects occur without central scotoma being present. As central scotomas cause visual decrease, visual acuity screening is the single most important test for optic nerve disease; field defects outside the central scotoma are only supportive of the diagnosis.

Increase in Intraocular Pressure. The intraocular pressure may be increased in thyroid eye disease, and may be higher in up gaze than in down gaze. The changes are probably secondary to changes in the forces of the eye movements brought about by muscle restriction and increased volume of the orbital contents. In thyroid eye disease, intraocular pressure should be measured with the eyes directed 5° to 10° below the midline to minimize the effects of pressure on the globe from the disease process.

Increase in Orbital Resistance. Normal orbits allow 5 mm of globe displacement back into the orbit. In thyroid eye disease, especially without thyrotoxicosis, this retrodisplacement of the globe can be severely inhibited. The displacement is tested, with the lid closed, by placing pressure on the lid over the globe and judging resistance to backward movement.

Unilaterality. Thyroid disease is still the most common cause of unilateral proptosis. Even when bilateral, proptosis tends to be asymmetric and may give an impression of unilateral disease.

Muscle Restriction. Selective restriction of gaze results from the infiltration and subsequent fibrosis of the actual ocular muscles. All or any ocular muscles may be involved, but most frequently the inferior rectus is infiltrated (with a restriction of up gaze). The next most commonly involved muscle is the medial rectus (restriction of horizontal gaze).

Vessel Enlargement near the Lateral Canthus. Conjunctival edema and vessel engorgement are common in thyroid eye disease in the active stages. One particular sign is helpful in some cases: large tortuous vessels, easily seen over the area of the lateral rectus when the eye is looking toward the nose, are common in thyroid eye disease and may be useful in suspecting and supporting the diagnosis.

Corneal Involvement. Both proptosis and lid retraction contribute to poor distribution of the tear film over the eye, especially the cornea. Tear film changes can be observed with slit-lamp magnification but not by gross examination. Improper tear film distribution eventually causes drying of the cornea. In the early stages, surface disruptions in the form of punctate staining can occur and may be diagnosed by the use of the optical dye fluorescein. Severe corneal changes are unusual, but ulceration of the cornea, perforation, and eventual opacification can occur.

Thyroid eye disease is frequently associated with abnormal thyroid function, but the signs and complications of thyroid eye disease can be seen in hyperthyroid, hypothyroid, and euthyroid states. Even though abnormal thyroid function studies are helpful in determining the cause of proptosis, no single localized or systemic test will unequivocally establish the diagnosis. Currently, the most useful tests in thyroid eye disease are blood tests to determine thyroid activity: triiodothyronine, thyroxine, and thyroid-stimulating hormone levels after the injection of thyrotropin-releasing hormone. Altered responses of T lymphocytes and altered immunoglobulins reflect the cellular and humoral activity in thyroid orbital changes but do not yet provide assurance of diagnoses or prediction of therapeutic response.

There is a clinical difference between patients with Graves' disease and those with thyrotoxicosis. Thyrotoxicosis is seen in a younger population with a 4:1 female:male ratio. In onset in the twenties, eye disease seems to be less common. When thyroid eye disease does occur with thyrotoxicosis, the orbital signs reverse and do not have the same infiltrative nature of Graves'-related eye disease.

Graves' disease is seen in older individuals and has an equal sex distribution. About 70 to 90% develop proptosis. Other signs and symptoms are variable, although about 50% present with lid retraction or lid lag.

NOSPECS Classification. Classification of thyroid eye disease has been established more or less to document the severity at the time of diagnosis and to follow the progression of the disease. This classification is based on signs and symptoms related only slightly to progression. In other words, classes with higher numbers may occur frequently without necessarily following the classes with lower numbers. The approach is shown in Table 22–8–1 and forms the accepted mnemonic NOSPECS.

Routine Laboratory Abnormalities

There are no diagnostic routine laboratory abnormalities.

TABLE 22–8–1. CLASSIFICATION OF THYROID EYE DISEASE

Class	Mnemonic Letter	Clinical Appearance
0	N	No physical signs or symptoms
I	O	Only signs, no symptoms (retraction and lag of the lid)
II	S	Soft tissue involvement (symptoms and signs)
III	P	Proptosis
IV	E	Extraocular muscle involvement
V	C	Corneal involvement
VI	S	Slight loss (optic nerve involvement)

Reprinted with permission of the American Academy of Ophthalmology, Basic and Clinical Science Course, Section 5, Neuro-ophthalmology, San Francisco, 1994:156.

PLANS

Diagnostic

Differential Diagnosis

See Table 22–8–2.

Diagnostic Options and Recommended Approach

See Criteria for Diagnosis.

Therapeutic

Cosmetic surgery helps many patients with facial features altered by thyroid eye disease. Numerous operations, some simple, others more involved, can adjust the lids to avoid embarrassment from facial disfigurement. Oculoplastic procedures should always be considered in patients with persistent thyroid stare. Orbital decompression and shrinkage of the orbital contents by radiotherapy cannot be done for cosmetic reasons alone, but when coupled with other indications, they also have a cosmetic effect of significance to the patient.

Symptomatic relief should also be foremost in therapy. Drying of the cornea and the irritation that results from it can be minimized by the use of artificial tears during the day and the application of ointment (without antibiotics or steroids) before retiring at night. To decrease the edema of the orbit and conjunctiva, both raising the head of the patient's bed 4 to 5 in. and oral diuretics before bedtime may help. Occasionally, oral steroids are needed in the congestive phases of eye disease to control swelling.

When eyelids do not close completely owing to proptosis, the eyelids can be taped shut, if tolerated, to prevent corneal damage while sleep-ing. Additionally, a simple sewing of the lids at the corners (canthoplasty) can be done to reduce symptoms. In more severe cases, temporary closure of the lids (tarsorrhaphy) may be indicated.

Muscle surgery to relieve diplopia is often successful but must be delayed until the patient's condition has remained unchanged for 6 months. Recession of the involved muscle, usually the inferior rectus, is sufficient to relieve symptoms.

When sight is threatened by proptosis, immediate and drastic treatment is necessary. Few patients require this intense or aggressive therapy, but those who do need it should be identified and started on therapy immediately.

In patients with threatened visual loss from proptosis, three therapies are now used, frequently in combination in the same patient: (1) high-dose steroid therapy for long periods; (2) surgical decompression of the orbit by reduction of the orbital contents by a lateral approach, by deroofing the orbit, or by allowing contents to enter the maxillary sinus through the inferior orbit opening; and (3) localized irradiation to the orbit to shrink orbital contents.

Control of Hyperthyroidism. Treatment of hyperthyroidism in patients with thyroid eye disease frequently improves symptoms and many signs, although rarely the proptosis. Treatment of any abnormal thyroid condition should, of course, be part of the overall therapy of thyroid eye disease (see Chapter 9–18).

Patients with thyroid eye disease may be told that sight loss is the exception (< 5%) rather than the rule. They should be assured that cosmetic deformity and annoying diplopia may reverse and, if they do not, surgical correction is often helpful.

Patients frequently associate eye disease with gland function. Unrealistic expectations of the patient may be prevented by emphasizing that eye disease is often associated with gland function but that there is no direct correlation between eye changes and gland changes that can help predict the future therapeutic response or the endpoint of the eye therapy.

Patients should be aware that two severe complications—cornea and nerve involvement—can affect vision permanently. They should also be aware, early in the disease process, that the resolution of signs and symptoms takes many months, even with therapy, and they should prepare themselves for periodic examinations and possibly prolonged treatment.

Symptoms of irritation are relieved, not cured, by therapy. Resolution of the eye disease is necessary to control symptoms. Patients should be made aware of available control (rather than cure) therapies such as ointments, artificial tears, diuretics, lid taping, and raising the head of the bed; however, they can be encouraged by the more permanent effects of most other treatments, such as eyelid surgery and muscle surgery, if symptoms do not resolve spontaneously.

TABLE 22–8–2. DIFFERENTIAL DIAGNOSES OF THYROID (ENDOCRINE) EYE DISEASE

Differential Diagnosis of Proptosis— Bilateral and Unilateral	History; x-ray; computed tomography scan
Lithium therapy for manic depressives	Ultrasound examination
Hepatic cirrhosis	Blood morphology
Pseudotumor	Bruit
Wegener's granulomatosis	Physical examination
Lymphoma	History; systemic symptoms of malaise
Sjögren's syndrome	
Arteriovenous malformation	Cerebrospinal fluid findings: increased protein, pleocytosis
Metastatic tumors—distant sites Women: breast Men: lung	
Tumors, local invasion	
Differential Diagnosis of Diplopia	**Edrophonium (Tensilon)**
Myasthenia gravis (unilateral eyelid droops, simulating proptosis of the other eye)	
Diabetes	Fasting blood sugar and glucose tolerance test
Differential Diagnosis of Visual Loss from Optic Nerve Involvement in Thyroid Disease	**Neurologic evaluation**
Optic neuritis multiple sclerosis	
Temporal arteritis	
Others	
Differential Diagnosis of Increased Intraocular Pressure due to Thyroid Disease	**Visual fields; optic nerve appearance; family history**
Open-angle glaucoma	
Narrow-angle glaucoma	Gonioscopy provocative testing
Differential Diagnosis of Thyroid Stare	**See Differential Diagnosis of Proptosis**
Any cause of proptosis	
Topical Neo-Synephrine drops	Ask if drops are used

FOLLOW-UP

Patients with corneal drying should be seen every 1 to 2 weeks during the active stage of thyroid disease. The patient with corneal ulcers is hospitalized and followed daily until stable.

Patients with progressive proptosis must be followed every few weeks for changes in the cornea or loss of visual acuity. Patients in therapy for thyrotoxicosis or hypothyroidism should also be observed every few weeks for a change in eye signs.

Patients suspected of having proptosis, but in whom the diagnosis has not been established, should have measurements for eye displacement every 2 to 3 months.

Any patient on massive steroids for eye disease should be carefully followed every 1 to 2 weeks for complications: gastrointestinal symptoms, cushingoid effects, cataract, bone changes, and so on.

Once the eye disease has stabilized, evaluation every 6 months to a year in the absence of symptoms is sufficient.

DISCUSSION

Prevalence and Incidence

The prevalence and incidence are unknown.

Related Basic Science

The cause of thyroid eye disease (Graves' disease) and its relationship to hormonal imbalance surprisingly is not clear. It is generally accepted that thyroid ophthalmopathy, or what has also has been termed *endocrine ophthalmopathy*, is an immunologic disorder. There is supportive evidence that Graves' disease is related to an increased incidence of other immunologic diseases (myasthenia gravis, pernicious anemia, autoimmune vitiligo, Addison's disease, and thymic dysplasia) and that patients with Graves' disease frequently have lymphadenopathy and spleen enlargement, findings indicative of immunologic dysfunction.

Thyroid-stimulating immunoglobulins are present in 90% of patients with Graves' disease, but recent evidence indicates that there is no correlation between thyroid-stimulating immunoglobulins and the eye changes seen in Graves' disease. Circulating immunoglobulins are suspected of playing a role in eye changes, but the significance of that role remains unknown.

Cell-mediated immunity probably is the main factor in thyroid eye disease, and evidence for this is mounting. For example, both thyroid and orbital antigens stimulate lymphokine production in patients with hyperthyroidism and normal eyes; however, only orbital antigen stimulates lymphokine production in persons with euthyroid exophthalmos. This is strong evidence for a cell-mediated mechanism. Further support for this mechanism comes from the discovery of inner connections of lymphatic drainage systems between the thyroid gland and the orbit. It is clear that thyroglobulin–antithyroglobulin complexes could reach the orbit by this route.

Until further clarified, we can only say that thyroid eye disease has an immunologic basis that is both humoral and cell-mediated. The relationship of the orbital process to gland function, although noted, is undefined and variable.

Of clinical interest are the changes in orbital volume. It is this process that causes most of the signs and symptoms of thyroid eye disease. In the normal orbit, the average volume is 26 mL; 70% of that volume is provided by the nonocular structures found periorbitally and retrobulbarly. An increase of only 4 mL in volume causes 6 mm of proptosis. The multiple changes in the orbit in thyroid eye disease provide a considerable increase in volume that results in proptosis.

In the infiltrative ophthalmopathy of Graves' disease, there is proliferation of fat and connective tissue, retention of fluid, and accumulation of mucopolysaccharides. The extraocular muscles are invaded by lymphocytes and cause muscle necrosis and fibrosis in the late stages. Muscle volume alone may be eight times normal size; the muscles not only fail to function but also contribute to the proptosis.

Obviously, the two major problems of eye disease related to thyroid disorders are the proptosis caused by changing orbital content volume and the functional decrease in extraocular muscle involvement. Both are directly caused by the cellular infiltration observed, and therapy is based on these changes.

It is worthwhile to mention again the specific lack of correlation between thyroid function tests and eye changes associated with endocrine (thyroid) disturbances. Tests are valuable in determining both thyroid function and the association of abnormal thyroid function with the clinical orbital changes; however, no thyroid function test establishes a diagnosis, and there is no evidence that circulating thyroid hormones have any direct pathogenic relationship to the eye disease. For this reason, eye signs previously called *thyroid* are becoming more frequently referred to as *Graves' ophthalmopathy*.

Natural History and Its Modification with Treatment

Thyroid eye disease almost always starts slowly, develops over a period of months, and reaches a plateau; then some, if not all, of the signs and symptoms regress spontaneously. This progression may or may not be related to abnormal thyroid function. In fact, there is no consistent response of the eye disease, which may progress or resolve independently of the therapy for the abnormal thyroid state. For example, although improvement usually occurs, worsening of the eye has been seen with correction of the thyrotoxic condition. Both improvements

and exacerbations of eye signs have been seen in every form of therapy for abnormal thyroid states.

There has been clinical and experimental evidence to justify considering two groups of proptotic patients (patients with exophthalmos) with thyroid disease. In fact, clinical progression is extremely variable.

First, patients with thyrotoxicosis have pronounced congestion, normal vision, and the absence of orbital tension, and the eye signs, except the proptosis, have disappeared after thyroidectomy. Specific symptoms, such as eyelid retraction, diplopia, and congestion, may reverse when the thyroid status subsides. In addition to this general unpredictability of eye changes, women who develop thyrotoxicosis in their teens or early twenties are spared the eye complications. Natural progression is, by any means, impossible to clarify or predict in the individual patient.

Second there is a difference in the progression of patients with Graves' disease when compared with thyrotoxicosis. Graves' disease is seen in older individuals and has an equal sex distribution (compare 4:1 predominance of females in thyrotoxicosis). About 70 to 90% develop proptosis. Other signs and symptoms are variable, although about 50% present with lid retraction or lid lag.

The incidence of optic nerve involvement in thyroid eye disease is unknown, but progression of its dramatic effects is documented. Once established, optic nerve involvement without treatment causes significant visual loss in one quarter of patients and severe visual loss in 15%. Moreover, it is usually bilateral. In patients with nerve involvement, proptosis is not marked in most cases. All the extraocular muscles are usually involved, usually near the apex of the orbit; this feature can be seen with computed tomography.

Prevention

There is no method for prevention of thyroid eye disease; however, prevention of corneal and optic nerve complications can prevent visual loss.

Smoking is a risk factor for the development of thyroid-associated ophthalmopathy.

Cost Containment

Many of the signs and symptoms of thyroid eye disease are suggestive enough to direct the careful observer to the proper diagnosis without expensive testing. Once proptosis is established and the accompanying signs pointing to thyroid eye disease are identified, thyroid function tests should be ordered. Computed tomography establishes characteristic muscle involvement while excluding many other localized causes of proptosis. By accurate prediction of the diagnosis, excessive tests may be avoided.

Optic nerve involvement, because it may occur with minimal signs of Graves' disease, must be suspected. It is frequently misdiagnosed. Good clinical expertise will save long and expensive investigations for other causes if thyroid disease is promptly suspected as the cause.

REFERENCES

Kendler DL, Lippa J, Rootman J. The initial clinical characteristics of Graves' orbitopathy vary with age and sex. Arch Ophthalmol 1993;111:197.

Metcalfe RA, Weetman AP. Stimulation of extraocular muscle fibroblasts by cytokines and hypoxia: Possible role in thyroid-associated ophthalmopathy. Clin Endocrinol 1994;40:67.

Nauman JA. Biological activity of antibodies circulating in endocrine ophthalmopathy. Dev Ophthalmol 1993;25:29.

Otto E, Krimmer U, Stover C, et al. Eye muscle cells in endocrine ophthalmopathy. Dev Ophthalmol 1993;25:93.

Trobe JD. Optic nerve involvement in dysthyroidism. Ophthalmology 1981;88:488.

Trokel SL, Jakobiec FA. Correlation of CT scanning and pathologic features of ophthalmic Graves' disease. Ophthalmology 1981;88:553.

Van Dyk HJL. Orbital Graves' disease: A modification of the "NO SPECS" classification. Ophthalmology 1981;88:479.

Werner SC. Modification of the classification of the eye changes of Graves' disease. Am J Ophthalmol 1977;83:725.

Unequal Pupils

William H. Coles, M.D., M.S.

DEFINITION

Unequal pupils are defined as a pupil difference in the same individual of greater than 0.5 mm.

ETIOLOGY

There are multiple causes. Most commonly unequal pupils are not associated with a disease process.

CRITERIA FOR DIAGNOSIS

Suggestive

The patient may detect the difference in the size of one pupil compared with the other.

Definitive

A difference of 0.5 mm or greater between the pupillary diameters, measured in constant illumination, is considered abnormal.

CLINICAL MANIFESTATIONS

Subjective

The subjective clinical manifestations are more from the patient's fear of the unknown than from irritation or discomfort. Most patients with pupillary abnormalities present first not with symptoms, but with an awareness of different-sized pupils that they have suddenly discovered. Understandably, patients usually acquaint pupillary abnormalities with brain tumors or something equally serious, even though a brain tumor or an aneurysm rarely presents with pupillary signs alone. The resultant anxiety causes the patient to seek medical assistance.

The symptoms that do occur are related to pupillary size. The pupil acts as an adjusting aperture to control the amount of light that enters the eye. The symptoms caused by pupillary abnormalities are a result of a loss of that adjustment. In patients with a small pupil, as in Horner's syndrome, the small pupil may accentuate the clouding of the lens (cataract) by decreasing the light entering the eye, resulting in impaired vision. In contrast, a pupil held in a dilated position, such as tonic pupil, allows excess light to enter unchecked and results in light sensitivity (photophobia). To compensate, the patient may squint or partially close the lid to protect the eye from the unhindered light.

In tonic pupil, accommodation may also be affected. The involved eye, when needed for close work, does not accommodate and blurring occurs. This is most commonly noted while reading. Patients are usually aware of the difference between the normal eye and the involved eye.

Objective

Physical Examination

To make a diagnosis or at least suspect the reason for the pupillary abnormality, it is useful to consider the pupil as a constantly changing opening. An abnormality of the pupil actually is an inability to make its normal adjustments. Most pupillary abnormalities involve only one side, so examination of the normal fellow pupil is important. A normal pupil closes in bright illumination, of course, and dilates in decreased illumination.

Consider first the position of the involved pupil in these conditions:

- Horner's syndrome: small
- Tonic pupil: usually large
- Argyll–Robertson pupil: small

In the conditions in which the pupil is small, we would expect very little difference between the normal and abnormal pupil in bright light, because the normal pupil is also held small by the eye's consensual light reflex. If we decrease illumination, however, the abnormal pupil remains closed while the normal pupil opens, causing a rather marked difference between the pupils. The opposite would, of course, be true for pupils held open (tonic). In decreased illumination, the pupils would be equal, or close to it, and in bright light, a marked difference would become evident as the normal pupil became small and the abnormal pupil remained open.

For effective evaluation of pupillary signs, pupillary examination with change of illumination is important. A light flashed first into one eye and then into the other is not enough. Although this will tell you if the pupil reacts and how brisk the reactions are, examination for comparative pupillary abnormalities is far more effective if changing illumination is presented equally to both eyes.

This changing illumination is a key factor in determining the difference between a benign condition—essential anisocoria—and possibly more serious conditions—Argyll–Robertson pupil, tonic pupil, and Horner's syndrome. The last three conditions show pupillary differences that become more or less marked in changing illumination. In essential anisocoria, the difference between the pupils, usually 1 or 2 mm, remains constant in both bright and dim illumination.

Routine Laboratory Abnormalities

There are no diagnostic routine laboratory abnormalities.

PLANS

Diagnostic

Differential Diagnosis

In Horner's syndrome, the involved pupil is small. The involved pupil dilates to 1% Paredrine or 1% Neo-Synephrine (these drugs do not affect the normal pupil). History may reveal signs of possible malignancy in older patients. The iris color is pale, if congenital. The difference in pupillary size is greater in dim illumination.

In tonic pupil, the involved pupil is large. The involved pupil reacts if a light or dark stimulus is held many minutes. The involved pupil constricts with 2.5% methacholine or 0.125% pilocarpine (normal pupil does not react to these concentrations). Decreased deep tendon reflexes may be present (Adie's syndrome). The condition is unilateral usually, but may be bilateral. The difference in pupillary size is greater in bright illumination. Blurred near vision occurs in the involved eye.

In Argyll–Robertson pupil, the involved pupil is small. This condition is usually bilateral. There is no reaction or a very slow reaction to light. Pupils constrict on convergence (ask patient to look from a distant object to a near object). The fluorescent treponemal antibody absorption test for syphilis is positive.

In essential anisocoria, pupillary differences of 1 to 2 mm are constant in both dim and bright illumination. There is lack of any other signs or symptoms.

Diagnostic Options and Recommended Approach

See Criteria for Diagnosis.

Therapeutic

Horner's syndrome suggests a malignant process in older individuals. They must be worked up and treated accordingly. Argyll–Robertson pupil is pathognomonic of syphilis, and patients should, if not previously treated, be treated adequately for this disease. There is no therapy for the correction of tonic pupil.

Symptoms of a dilated or constricted pupil are treated accordingly. Photophobia (light sensitivity) is helped by dark glasses when the pupil is in dilation. Visual decreases secondary to small pupil and cataracts may require surgical removal of the cataract.

As most pupillary abnormalities are benign, once the diagnosis has been established, patients should be assured that there is no brain tumor or life-threatening process.

Some patients experience light sensitivity or visual symptoms and should be prepared for these inconveniences if they do occur.

FOLLOW-UP

No follow-up is necessary once the diagnosis of unequal pupils is established unless ocular symptoms occur. Underlying disease processes, of course, should be followed consistent with good medical practice.

DISCUSSION

Prevalence and Incidence

Unequal pupils from serious disease processes are uncommon. Anisocoria, a benign process, may be as prevalent as one in five individuals.

Related Basic Science

The pupil acts by dilating and constricting and works as an aperture to adjust the amount of light delivered to the retina in the same way a diaphragm works on a camera. It is controlled by dual antagonistic systems: the parasympathetic and sympathetic nervous systems. The parasympathetic system innervates the pupillary sphincter, a circular muscle at the border of the pupil, which contracts the muscle and constricts the pupil. The sympathetic system innervates the pupillary dilator fibers and causes, on stimulation, pupillary enlargement. Numerous supernuclear influences act on the pupil. The excitatory ones, light and near reflex, are closely associated with the parasympathetic fibers already mentioned. But there are also inhibitory influences (corticomesencephalic and reticulomesencephalic) that decrease the constrictor signals to the pupil and result in dilation.

The best evidence for these influences is the pupillary reaction during sleep. With sleeping the pupil remains constricted and on awakening the pupil dilates. During sleep, even though the eyelids are closed and little light reaches the eye, the pupil constricts because of the decrease in the supernuclear inhibitory influences on the parasympathetic system (i.e., opposing forces to constriction are decreased). On awakening, these inhibitory influences come back into play, and the pupil dilates. This dilation is not dependent on the sympathetic system, as it is unaffected by sympathectomy.

The clinical differences between sympathetic and parasympathetic malfunction are a result of the varied and separate pathways of these two systems. Anatomically, the sympathetic pathway, because of its association with malignant tumors, is the most important. Both pathways, however, are important in understanding the theories of disease origins and the relation to pupillary abnormalities.

The neuronal pathway for light stimulus to constrict the pupil runs from the retinal receptor cells by way of the optic nerves and tracks to the pretectal area, to the motor pool of the Edinger–Westphal nucleus, along with the parasympathetic outflow from the third nerve to the ciliary ganglion, and then to the eye by way of the short ciliary nerve. The basic anatomy the clinician should remember is the motor course from the Edinger–Westphal nucleus to the ciliary ganglion to the eye. It is in this course that the parasympathetic flow is interrupted in tonic pupil syndromes.

The Edinger–Westphal nucleus is another anatomic point well known and important to remember. It is in this area that syphilis causes a distinctive separation of stimuli that affects pupillary constriction. Light is not the only stimulus to constrict the pupil: the change of focus from far to near also stimulates pupil constriction by way of the parasympathetic system. It is in the area of the Edinger–Westphal nucleus that the light near dislocation of the Argyll–Robertson pupil of syphilis occurs.

The sympathetic innervation to the pupil that results in pupillary dilation takes a long circuitous course before it reaches the eye. Starting in the hypothalamus, it courses to the tegmentum of the midbrain and pons, the C-8 to T-2 region of the spinal cord, the superior cervical gan-

glion by the paravertebral sympathetic chain, and the eye by the ophthalmic branch of the trigeminal nerve (the primary pupillar motor goes by way of the nasal ciliary nerve), and other fibers go to the ophthalmic artery in the third nerve. The postganglionic fibers supply the orbital vasomotor system, the pupil, the smooth muscle of the lid (Mueller's muscle), the lacrimal gland, and trophic fibers to the melanophores.

Innervation of the sympathetic system, which supplies numerous structures other than the pupils, can aid in the diagnosis of Horner's syndrome. The most reliable sign is caused by interruption of the sympathetic flow to the smooth muscle of the lid, which, because the muscle relaxes, causes a drop in the lid height (ptosis). In physical examination, the finding is often obvious by comparing lid openings between eyes. Normally, the opening between the lids is equal, but in Horner's syndrome the involved lid opening droops by a few millimeters.

Another, less reliable sign is a lack of sweating on the contralateral side (pupil and lid signs are on the same side as the lesion) opposite to pupillary signs. The skin is not only dry, but also warm from increased blood flow. Testing by starch iodine powder may be helpful when dryness and increased warmth are not obvious.

Anatomic Derangement and Pharmacology

The diagnosis of Horner's syndrome can be confirmed by the topical use of 1% Paredrine or 1% Neo-Synephrine (both sympathomimetic agents). These drugs dilate the denervated Horner's pupil, but they have no effect on the normal pupil at these concentrations.

Occasionally, 2% cocaine is used, but the action of cocaine is different from that of the sympathomimetic drugs Paredrine and Neo-Synephrine. Cocaine, rather than directly stimulating the muscle, blocks the nerve terminal uptake of norepinephrine and acts only on the pupil with intact sympathetic innervation. The sympathomimetic drugs stimulate directly, and their action, then, is different from that of cocaine.

Cocaine is used when the diagnosis cannot be established by the use of sympathomimetic agents. Cocaine's action can help to determine the location of the lesion. This is important not only for diagnosis, but also for prognosis. Generally, central lesions are more serious and peripheral lesions are more benign. By the use of both cocaine and a sympathomimetic drug, the origin of the lesion can be identified as either a first-order neuron (central) or second- or third-order neuron (peripheral) involvement.

When Horner's syndrome is a result of a first-order neuron interruption, norepinephrine is present at the nerve endings and the pupil responds to cocaine. If the lesion involves the second or third peripheral neurons, no norepinephrine is present and the blockage or uptake by cocaine does not increase norepinephrine and cause pupillary dilation. The response of the pupil to sympathomimetic agents will be the same in both the first neuron and second and third neurons because of the denervation hypersensitivity. Only cocaine and its special action can help differentiate the site of the lesion. In summary:

- First neuron: Involved pupil dilates to 1% Paredrine (or 1% Neo-Synephrine) and dilates to 2% cocaine.
- Second and third neuron: Involved pupil dilates to 1% Paredrine (or 1% Neo-Synephrine) but does not dilate to 2% cocaine.
- Normal: Pupil does not dilate to 1% Paredrine (or 1% Neo-Synephrine) but dilates to 2% cocaine.

Two additional points should be remembered about pharmacologic testing. First, for both sympathomimetic and cocaine testing, drops should be instilled in both eyes and the reactions of the involved and the normal pupil compared. Second, after the use of cocaine, the use of sympathomimetic agents (Paredrine or Neo-Synephrine) for testing is invalidated for 48 hours.

Location of the lesion can help determine the cause of Horner's syndrome. Remember that the first neuron runs from the hypothalamus to the spinal cord, the second from the spinal cord to the superior cervical ganglion, and the third to the peripheral innervation of the ocular structures. This course provides an opportunity for a number of lesions in a variety of positions along the pathway to cause Horner's syndrome:

- Central lesions called Wallenberg's lateral medullary syndrome (posterior inferior cerebellar artery syndrome).
- Cervical cord lesions (one half of all patients with Horner's syndrome have these lesions) can be due to trauma, syringomyelia, tumor, and, rarely, demyelinating disease.
- Chest lesions of the apex and superior mediastinum are usually due to bronchiogenic carcinoma (Pancoast's superior sulcus syndrome).
- Neck lesions (fibers here are with carotid sheath) can cause Horner's syndrome by enlarged lymph nodes, tumor abscess, trauma, surgery, or acute carotid thrombosis.
- Brachial plexus-level lesions are usually caused by birth trauma (may be associated with Krumpke's paralysis of the ipsilateral arm).

Natural History and Its Modification with Treatment

The association of Horner's syndrome with tumors makes its recognition all the more important. One third of all Horner's syndromes are caused by neoplasms, either metastatic, bronchogenic, or some other metastatic carcinoma. In patients over 50, neoplasm is statistically the most common cause of Horner's syndrome and must always be considered in the differential diagnosis.

Two transient causes of Horner's syndrome can be distinguished, in addition to the pupillary findings, by history. The most common is iatrogenic damage to the sympathetic pathways from skin puncture for cerebral angiography. History usually establishes the diagnosis. The natural course of this condition is spontaneous resolution. The other cause, associated with cluster headaches and hemicrania, is known as

Raeder's paratrigeminal syndrome. It is fairly commonly seen and can be expected to have repeated exacerbations during a lifetime.

In addition, Horner's syndrome is seen as a congenital condition. Because there are atrophic sympathetic stimulated melanophores in the iris in congenital Horner's syndrome, and because of a lack of melanophore stimulation, the involved pupil has less pigmentation (heterochromia), a helpful diagnostic point. Heterochromia with Horner's syndrome is rare in situations other than congenital Horner's. Once heterochromia has occurred, it does not progress throughout a lifetime.

Prevention

Prevention of unequal pupils is not possible.

Cost Containment

Adequate diagnosis of unequal pupils can markedly decrease the cost for multiple neurologic tests. As essential anisocoria, tonic pupil, and Argyll–Robertson pupil are all either benign or easily treated without fear of brain tumor or metastatic tumor, it is important to be able to diagnose these on clinical signs. If Horner's syndrome is present, diagnostic tests are indicated to rule out malignancy.

REFERENCES

Glaser JS. The pupils and accommodation. In: Duane TD, ed. Clinical ophthalmology. Hagerstown, MD: Harper & Row, 1980;2:1.

Perkin GD. The pupil. J Neurol Neurosurg Psychiatry 1994;57:1179.

CHAPTER 22–10

Uveitis (Intraocular Inflammation)

William H. Coles, M.D., M.S.

DEFINITION

Uveitis is any inflammation from any cause that affects the uveal portion of the eye.

ETIOLOGY

There are multiple causes, including infections, immune reactions, and injury (See Table 22–10–1).

CRITERIA FOR DIAGNOSIS

Anterior Uveitis. A red eye and mild to severe visual loss suggest the diagnosis. Specific tests for suspected diseases establish the diagnosis.

Posterior Uveitis. Visual loss and eye infection suggest the diagnosis. Specific tests for suspected diseases establish the diagnosis.

CLINICAL MANIFESTATIONS

Subjective

Anterior Uveitis. Vision is usually decreased moderately or slightly, but on occasion it may be severe. Pain is usually present and tearing is common.

Posterior Uveitis. A decrease in vision is the prime symptom. This is especially true when the macula, the area of the retina responsible for fine vision because of the high concentration of cones, is involved.

Visual symptoms can be diverse in posterior uveitis. With macular involvement, not only is vision decreased, but distortion of the image may occur so that objects are enlarged, minimized, or irregular. Peripheral lesions can occur without affecting vision.

Objective

Physical Examination

Anterior Uveitis. Cells and protein in the anterior chamber of the eye are the result of anterior uveitis. Increased protein (flare) in the anterior chamber is the sine qua non of anterior inflammation. To see flare with the slit lamp, a narrow beam is used. Flare in the aqueous looks similar to the light beam of a projector in a dark movie theater. Cells can also float in the anterior chamber and, if multiple, collect in a white, flat-topped layer. Injection of the globe occurs in a circular flush around the cornea due to involvement of the deep vessels in the sclera.

Pain and tearing and decreased vision are also usually present. Vessels of the sclera may be injected, although this is variable. Cellular deposits (keratic precipitates) are frequently located at the back of the cornea.

The visual acuity decrease, which is very common but not always present, can usually be measured on a Snellen visual acuity chart. Cellular deposits on the back of the cornea (keratic precipitates) frequently collect inferiorly in the shape of an inverted wedge, but occasionally in a more generalized distribution over the cornea. Synechiae (scars) occur in many areas: pupil to lens (posterior synechiae), iris to chamber angle (peripheral anterior synechiae), and iris to cornea (anterior synechiae). Pigment may also be seen on the lens capsule, usually about halfway between the center of the lens and the periphery. Cataract formation may occur but is a late sign. In some cases, cells may be seen in the anterior vitreous. This observation requires a slit-lamp examination.

Posterior Uveitis. In posterior uveitis, cells are found in the vitreous, especially near the area of acute inflammation. Retinitis is frequently present and is seen as a clouding of the retina. Choroiditis is seen as

TABLE 22–10–1. POSSIBLE CAUSES OF UVEITIS (INTRAOCULAR INFLAMMATION)

Infectious
  Bacteria
  Viruses
  Fungi
  Rickettsiae
  Protozoa
  Parasites
Noninfectious
  Exogenous
    Trauma
    Chemical injury
    Allergic reactions to external antigens
  Endogenous
    Reactions to tumors
    Degenerative reactions
    Immunologic reactions
      Microbial allergy
    Histoplasmosis
    Autogenous
      Sympathetic ophthalmia
      Lens reactions

Modified and reprinted with permission of the American Academy of Ophthalmology. Ophthalmology: Basic and clinical science course: Section 9. Intraocular inflammation, uveitis and ocular tumors. San Francisco: American Academy of Ophthalmology, San Francisco, 1994:60.

patches of yellow, white, or gray, and in the late stages these patches become white scars with a well-defined dark area of pigment on the borders. Vasculitis is seen in the early stages as cuffing of the vessels with gray-white puffs. Macular edema, caused by exudate from the vascular system, can cause cysts to form in the macula and can be seen with both peripheral and anterior ocular inflammation but rarely with posterior disease. The optic nerve can be involved with papillitis or retrobulbar neuritis. New vessel formation occurs late and in the region of the active inflammation.

Decreased vision is frequently detected by the patient. A focal or diffuse inflammation of the choroid and retina of the eye may be seen, and cells are seen in the vitreous cavity. Macular edema may be present. New vessel formation and optic nerve inflammation are late occurrences but can suggest the diagnosis.

Routine Laboratory Abnormalities

There are no diagnostic laboratory abnormalities.

PLANS

Diagnostic

Differential Diagnosis

See Table 22–10–2.

Diagnostic Options and Recommended Approach

See Table 22–10–2 and the chapters in the book in which the specific diseases are discussed.

Therapeutic

The treatment of uveitis depends on its etiology, if known. Specific therapy, for example, can be given for active toxoplasmosis—pyrimethamine (Daraprim) and a sulfonamide (sulfapyrimidine type). Candida, bacterial inflammation, and other specific disease agents are treated with the appropriate drugs to which the organism is sensitive.

Almost always, mydriatic–cycloplegic topical drugs are used to relax the ciliary muscle and dilate the pupil so that synechiae are less likely to develop in the critical visual areas.

Steroids, either topical or systemic, are indicated in some cases of uveitis (sympathetic ophthalmia, chemical injury, and other) but are contraindicated in such conditions as toxoplasmosis, where the use of steroids can aggravate the existing inflammatory reaction. Therapy

TABLE 22–10–2. DIFFERENTIAL DIAGNOSIS OF UVEITIS

Histoplasmosis	Endemic in the Ohio and Mississippi valleys; characterized by highly suggestive peripheral and macular lesions
Candidiasis	Often associated with indwelling catheters for IV therapy; positive blood cultures are puffy posterior pole lesions
Toxoplasmosis	Characteristic, punched-out fundus lesions with pigment; useful in the dye test, hemagglutination test, indirect fluorescein antibody test, and ELISA
Toxocariasis	May involve one eye; eosinophils in aqueous; ELISA test positive
Tuberculosis in the eye	Usually inactive disease; skin testing can be helpful
Syphilis-acquired uveitis	Fluorescent treponemal antibody absorption test for syphilis
Sarcoid	Widespread ocular involvement: anterior uveitis (35%), posterior uveitis (10%), combined uveitis (55%); 10 times more prevalent in blacks; chest radiograph (80% positive); serum calcium (elevated in 12%); angiotensin-converting enzyme, gallium scan, and biopsy of lymph node, conjunctiva, liver, and skin can all aid in diagnosis
Pars planitis	Peripheral in position in the retina; cells in vitreous; macular complications often decrease vision
Recurrent iridocyclitis	Periodic, mild, and has few complications; HLA-B27 may be present
Ankylosing spondylitis	Predominantly in males; HLA-B27 positive in 85%; spine radiograph abnormal
Juvenile rheumatoid arthritis	Eye is most often involved when few joints are affected (pauciarticular); antinuclear antibody positive in 80%
Reiter's syndrome	Occurs in males aged 20 to 40; HLA-B27 positive in 85%; negative prostatic cultures; urethritis
Psoriasis	Characteristic involvement of terminal phalangeal joints and ungual changes; HLA-B17 and HLA-B27 present
Ulcerative colitis	Radiographic evidence of ulcerative colitis
Vogt–Koyanagi–Harada syndrome	Mostly in Asians aged 30 to 50; alopecia, poliosis, vertigo (30%), temporary deafness (30%), HLA-B22 (45%), give diagnostic clinical picture
Behcet's syndrome	Genital ulceration; polyarthritis; poliomyelitis; mostly men aged 20 to 40
Cytomegalic inclusion disease, congenital and acquired	Congenital diagnosed in complement-fixing and viral inclusion bodies in urine and saliva; acquired associated with chemotherapy for malignancy and kidney transplant
Other rare causes of uveitis	Rubella Measles Mumps Glaucomatocyclitic crisis Fuch's heterochromic iridocyclitis Lens-induced Cysticercosis Ascariasis Onchocerciasis Amebiasis Trypanosomiasis Blastomycosis Coccidioidomycosis Cryptococcosis Mucormycosis Sporotrichosis Aspergillosis

ELISA, enzyme-linked immunosorbent assay.

of any uveitis should be undertaken only when there is a definite understanding of the diagnosis or probable diagnosis and when the potential risks in those patients are understood.

In some, the condition is self-limited and rarely causes serious change. Even with chronic flareups, which can be seen in some cases of juvenile arthritis, patients may not need treatment.

At times, as in recurrent sarcoid attacks, severe complications can occur: cataract, glaucoma, or fixed pupil from synechiae. Medical therapy for glaucoma or surgical intervention for cataract or glaucoma control may be necessary.

In posterior uveitis, some lesions may threaten the macula or present the possibility of extensive destruction of the retinal elements. In selected cases, photocoagulation may be necessary to minimize damage to vision.

In most cases, the patient should be made aware of the possible chronicity of this condition, its possible complications, especially cataract and glaucoma, and the potential for permanent visual loss.

An awareness from the beginning that a diagnosis of uveitis is frequently not made and therapy is nonspecific prevents the patient from expecting a rapid or permanent cure.

Frequent consultation may be necessary to allay the patient's apprehension over a slow response to treatment or to the difficulty in establishing a cause.

FOLLOW-UP

During any acute inflammation of the eye, examination and review of therapy should be done at least every week or sometimes more frequently. In chronic uveitis, observation every 2 weeks is usually sufficient if the patient is instructed to be aware of possible complications and can reliably evaluate his or her own progress. Each case requires evaluation for follow-up, which depends on the presumptive diagnosis and the progression of the disease process noted at each visit.

DISCUSSION

Prevalence and Incidence

The prevalence and incidence depend on the specific cause and are mostly unknown.

Related Basic Science

Uveitis is a descriptive but unfortunately general term that is in wide use. In antiquity, the eye with its coats of cornea and sclera removed was likened to a grape. In Greek, grape is *uva*. Combined with *itis* for inflammation, the term *uveitis,* for intraocular inflammation, has been used for decades.

We now know that inflammation of the eye occurs in different anatomic segments and is caused by numerous etiologic agents. The uveal tract itself can be divided into iris, ciliary body, and choroid. Inflammation in corresponding areas is covered by the subclassifications of uveitis: iritis (iris), cyclitis (ciliary body), iridocyclitis (iris and ciliary body), and choroiditis (choroid). Additional terms such as *pars plantis* and *anterior uveitis* give anatomic localization. As retinitis is frequently also involved when choroiditis is present, the term *chorioretinitis* is frequently used. Most forms of uveitis are not specifically diagnosed as to an etiologic agent, and even when a fairly characteristic disease pattern is seen, the diagnosis is still presumptive. It is important to try to be as specific as possible in the localization of the inflammation and to be specific in the description of inflammatory changes.

As in other parts of the body, inflammation of the eye progresses through a series of phases. In the acute phase of uveitis there is a liberation of chemical mediators: histamine, serotonin, kinins, complement, and prostaglandins. This is followed by an intermediate phase characterized by polymorphonuclear cells that continue to produce enzymes that cause increased vascular permeability. Histiocytes also enter the area of inflammation. This intermediate stage ends in one of two alternatives: healing can occur, or the inflammation can go into a chronic phase.

The chronic phase can be nongranulomatous (lymphocytes, plasma cells) or granulomatous (lymphocytes, plasma cells, epithelioid cells, and giant cells). Granulomatous inflammation is associated with such conditions as toxoplasmosis, sarcoidosis, and sympathetic ophthalmia.

The insult is frequently not known in uveitis, but a general classification helps in thinking about the possible causes. These causes are listed in Table 22–10–1.

Natural History and Its Modification with Treatment

The natural history of uveitis shows a wide spectrum of progression and depends on etiology. Nongranulomatous inflammations, especially those limited to the anterior portion of the eye, may be transient and without complications. Granulomatous inflammations can progress, despite extensive therapy, to a point where complications of glaucoma and cataract and a marked decrease in vision occur.

Prevention

There is no known prevention for most causes of uveitis. In sympathetic uveitis, where trauma is the initial insult that provides the stimulus for its development, early surgical removal of the traumatized eye can prevent the subsequent uveitis that develops in the opposite eye. This surgical removal is, of course, limited to eyes that have no visual potential.

Cost Containment

Only future knowledge will allow a more accurate diagnosis so that individual therapies can be developed to eradicate specific disease entities. Research is underway in many areas of uveitis to achieve exactly this end.

REFERENCES

Baarsma GS. The epidemiology and genetics of endogenous uveitis: a review. Curr Eye Res 1992;11(suppl.):1.

Breeveld J, Kuiper H, Spanjaard L, et al. Uveitis and Lyme borreliosis. Br J Ophthalmol 1993;77:480.

Duke-Elder S, Perkins ES. Diseases of the uveal tract. In Duke-Elder S, Perkins ES, eds. System of ophthalmology. St. Louis: Mosby, 1966;9.

Dunn JP, Nozik RA. Uveitis: Role of the physician in treating systemic causes. Geriatrics 1994;49(8):27.

Forrester JV. Uveitis: Pathogenesis. Lancet 1991;338:1498.

Kanski JJ. Anterior uveitis in juvenile rheumatoid arthritis. Arch Ophthalmol 1977;95:1794.

Maumenee AE. Clinical entities in "uveitis": An approach to the study of intraocular inflammation. Am J Ophthalmol 1970;69:1.

Ohno S, Char DH, Kimura SJ, O'Connor GR. Vogt–Koyanagi–Harada syndrome. Am J Ophthalmol 1977;83:735.

Rothova A, Buitenhuis HJ, Meenken C, et al. Uveitis and systemic disease. Br J Ophthalmol 1992;76(3):137.

Schlaegel TF. Essentials of uveitis. Boston: Little, Brown, 1969.

Yanoff M, Fine BS. Ocular pathology: A text and atlas. Hagerstown, MD: Harper & Row, 1975.

CHAPTER 22–11

Retinal Detachment

Mary Elizabeth Hartnett, M.D.

DEFINITION

A retinal detachment is a separation between the neurosensory retina and the underlying retinal pigment epithelium and choroid (vascular layer that nourishes the outer retina). With separation, fluid collects in the subretinal space. Although only a part of the retina may initially be detached, the detachment may progress to involve the entire retina.

ETIOLOGY

There are three etiologies for a retinal detachment: retinal break(s) (rhegmatogenous detachment); traction from vitreous or fibrovascular membranes that pull the retina causing a detachment, as in diabetic retinopathy (tractional detachment); fluid in the subretinal space without a retinal break (serous detachment).

CRITERIA FOR DIAGNOSIS
Suggestive

Rhegmatogenous Retinal Detachment. The loss of a red reflex by ophthalmoscopy in a patient should alert the clinician for more definitive examination. In addition, decreased vision and a history of flashes and floaters should bring to mind the concern of a rhegmatogenous retinal detachment.

Tractional Retinal Detachment. Decreased or blurred vision in a patient with diabetic retinopathy may indicate a partial tractional detachment.

Serous Retinal Detachment. The loss of a red reflex by ophthalmoscopy is of concern as are symptoms of decreased or blurred vision, visual field defect, or flashing lights and floaters.

Definitive

Indirect ophthalmoscopy with scleral depression and stereoscopic biomicroscopy with the slit lamp are best performed by a retina-trained ophthalmologist to find a grayish elevation of the retina.

CLINICAL MANIFESTATIONS
Subjective

Rhegmatogenous Retinal Detachment. The symptoms of flashing lights (often seen in the superior temporal field) followed by floaters (described as dark or red floating strands or particles moving in the patient's field of view) often indicate that a posterior vitreous detachment has occurred. Vitreous detachment is common and often is not associated with a retinal detachment. If vitreous detachment leads to a rhegmatogenous retinal detachment, the patient may then experience a visual field defect. A visual field defect is described as a curtain or shadow extending over the patient's visual field. The retinal detachment then often follows within several days or sooner after the symptoms of a posterior vitreous detachment.

Certain diseases have an increased association with retinal detachments: myopia, retinal detachment in the fellow eye, family history of retinal detachment, ocular trauma, known lattice degeneration or peripheral retinal degeneration, previous retinopathy of prematurity, vitreoretinopathies with or without arthritis or cleft palate.

Tractional Retinal Detachment. A tractional retinal detachment is often described as darkness in the center of one's vision or blurred vision with the inability to read. In traction retinal detachments, the common history includes diabetes mellitus, previous vein occlusion with neovascularization, retinopathy of prematurity, penetrating ocular trauma, and toxocariasis.

Serous Retinal Detachment. A serous retinal detachment may vary as to symptoms depending on the size of the detachment. Small detachments

centrally may cause blurred vision only and the experience that objects appear distorted or smaller than seen in the fellow eye. A history of systemic inflammation, such as Behçet's disease, or of cancer may be present.

Objective
Physical Examination

The finding of an elevated sensory retina by indirect or occasionally direct ophthalmoscopy indicates a retinal detachment.

A rhegmatogenous detachment usually has a corrugated appearance to the surface of the retina and a retinal break or breaks are seen usually in the peripheral or midperipheral retina. The retinal surface, usually concave, has a convex appearance. This may be an important sign when a vitreous hemorrhage obscures visualization of the retina and ultrasonography is necessary to diagnose the presence of a retinal detachment.

A tractional retinal detachment has a concave appearance and often has concomitant fibrovascular vitreous membranes causing traction on the retinal surface, resulting in detachment.

A serous retinal detachment has no breaks, has a smooth surface, and is convex. In large detachments, the examiner sees a shift in the fluid as the patient changes position.

Routine Laboratory Abnormalities

There are no routine laboratory abnormalities specifically associated with a retinal detachment.

PLANS
Diagnostic
Differential Diagnosis

The differential diagnosis of retinal detachment is outlined in Table 22–11–1.

Diagnostic Options

If a vitreous hemorrhage, dense cataract, or corneal opacity precludes adequate viewing of the fundus, ultrasonography is employed to determine if the retina is detached. This may also be helpful to diagnose choroidal tumors lying beneath a serous retinal detachment.

Recommended Approach

A detailed history includes the presence of any preexisting ocular trauma. Pain is an unusual symptom for a rhegmatogenous retinal detachment and usually indicates that conditions other than retinal detachment, such as inflammation, may coexist in the eye. Family history or previous history of retinal detachment is important, as well as the refractive error, history of diabetes mellitus, cardiovascular disease, or hypertension.

Time between the diagnosis and treatment is important. Urgent reattachment of the retina is desired to prevent macular detachment. Detachment of the macula, that part of the retina important for central vision, may lead to a permanent poor visual result.

A complete ocular examination by a retinal specialist is performed including best corrected visual acuity, intraocular pressure, pupillary examination (which may reveal an afferent pupillary defect in a large retinal detachment), and slit-lamp evaluation for the presence of cells, flare, or signs or inflammation. Dilated funduscopic examination with scleral depression using an indirect ophthalmoscope and stereoscopic funduscopic biomicroscopy are performed. The finding of all retinal breaks is essential for successful management and reattachment of the retina.

TABLE 22–11–1. DIFFERENTIAL DIAGNOSIS OF RETINAL DETACHMENT

Symptoms of Flashes and Floaters
A posterior vitreous detachment with or without a retinal break
Vitreous traction on the retina without a posterior vitreous detachment
Migraine phenomena

Features That May Have the Clinical Appearance of a Retinal Detachment (e.g., loss of red reflex)
Choroidal tumor
Retinal pigment epithelial detachment
Choroidal detachment
Retinoschisis
Vitreous hemorrhage
Vitreous membranes

Decreased Visual Acuity
This may be secondary to a number of causes including cataract, corneal opacity, and uveitis.

Tractional Detachment (Adults)
Diabetes mellitus
Branch retinal or central retinal vein occlusion
Pars planitis
Uveitis, inflammation
Penetrating ocular trauma

Serous Detachment
Adults
Inflammation
Choroidal tumor with retinal detachment
Lymphoma
Vogt–Kayanagi Harada's disease
Behçet's syndrome
Ocular abnormalities, such as nanophthalmos
Sturge–Weber syndrome
Central serous retinopathy
Children
Retinopathy of prematurity
Toxocariasis
Incontinential pigmentii
Norrie's disease
Persistent hyperplastic primary vitreous
Retinoblastoma
Uveitis

Therapeutic

Treatment is best performed by an ophthalmologist with retinal training.

Therapeutic Options

To prevent subsequent retinal detachment, treatment of the attached retina surrounding a retinal break without retinal detachment may be performed with cryotherapy, laser, or diathermy.

Once a retinal detachment occurs, such treatment alone is not successful. Retinal detachments may be reattached surgically from the outside of the eye, as in scleral buckle surgery, or from within the eye, as with vitrectomy, a procedure in which membranes causing traction on the retina are removed. Pneumatic retinopexy, or the injection of a gas bubble into the eye to apply pressure and close the retinal break, in conjunction with cryotherapy or laser, may be performed in certain cases.

Recommended Approach

A rhegmatogenous retinal detachment is repaired surgically with a scleral buckle, which is a solid silicone band and/or buckle that is sewn onto the sclera, indenting the outside of the sclera toward the elevated retina in the area of the retinal break or breaks. The retina around the break is treated to cause chorioretinal adhesion with either a freezing procedure (cryotherapy), laser, or diathermy. Subretinal fluid may or may not be drained depending on the individual case. Another approach, known as pneumatic retinopexy, includes the injection of a gas bubble into the vitreous cavity followed by positioning of the patient for approximately 1 week so that the bubble closes the break and the subretinal fluid is reabsorbed. The retina surrounding the break is treated with laser or cryotherapy.

A traction retinal detachment is managed by a vitrectomy. Here, intraocular instruments are used to segment or remove membranes and the vitreous is removed with an instrument with a guillotine action that combines aspiration and cutting.

The underlying cause of a serous retinal detachment is treated; for example, a metastatic tumor with a serous retinal detachment may be treated with radiation or chemotherapy, and Behçet's disease may be treated with systemic antiinflammatory medication. In small serous retinal detachments in the young, central serous retinopathy, resolution often occurs spontaneously, although occasionally these require laser.

FOLLOW-UP

Patients may require postoperative positioning to allow complete resolution of subretinal fluid once the break has been closed either with a scleral buckle or with an intraocular gas bubble. Patients are followed after surgery frequently until subretinal fluid has resolved. Follow-up is then extended. In approximately 10% of cases, recurrent retinal detachment may occur from the proliferation of vitreous membranes and is often seen 6 to 8 weeks postoperatively. This is often managed with vitreous surgery, that is, vitrectomy.

In a tractional detachment, once traction is released during a vitrectomy, the patient is followed for resolution of the subretinal fluid, often taking 1 or more months.

DISCUSSION
Prevalence and Incidence

The prevalence of rhegmatogenous retinal detachments is 1 person per 10,000 to 15,000 persons per year. In people at risk for retinal detachment—myopes, those with a previous retinal detachment in the fellow eye, those with a family history of retinal detachment, and those with ocular trauma—the prevalence is higher.

The number of patients with diabetes mellitus who develop tractional detachments from proliferative disease is decreasing as these patients are being screened more effectively and are receiving laser treatment earlier.

Retinopathy of prematurity is increasing as the number of very low birth weight babies is increasing. A fraction of babies with low birth weights may develop tractional retinal detachment and permanent blindness. Surgery is necessary in these infants to reattach their retinas and prevent total blindness, but the visual outcomes can be disappointing secondary to central nervous system involvement from prematurity, as well as amblyopia.

Related Basic Science

The retina is a multilayered tissue that lines the inside of the posterior part of the eye. It extends anteriorly to a line known as the ora serrata 6 to 7 mm posterior to the limbus (the junction between the cornea and the sclera). The layers of the retina are held closely together by cell processes except between the photoreceptors (visual processing begins with photochemical changes occurring in the outer segments of the photoreceptors) and the retinal pigment epithelial cells. In this area, known as the subretinal space, the retina may detach from the underlying retinal pigment epithelial cells and the vascular layer (choroid).

A posterior vitreous detachment appears to incite a rhegmatogenous retinal detachment. The vitreous gel is composed mostly of water (>98%) and of collagen fibrils, hyalocytes, and other cells. With increasing age, trauma, blood, or inflammation, the collagen fibrils clump together and release the water between the fibrils. As this occurs, the posterior vitreous may pull off from the back of the retina. Where an abnormal adhesion between the retina and vitreous is present, the retina may tear, allowing the water component of the vitreous to enter the subretinal space. This results in the retinal detachment.

In the traction detachment, fibroblasts, retinal pigment epithelial cells, blood vessels, and factors from the bloodstream are released into the vitreous, leading to the formation of membranes that contract and pull the retina from the vascular choroid found deeper in the eye. In some forms of tractional detachments, such as in diabetic retinopathy and retinopathy of prematurity, the membranes tend to be more fibrovascular in nature.

Serous detachments may be associated with abnormal leaking vessels, inflammation, or an impairment in the retina's ability to keep the subretinal space dry.

Natural History and Its Modification with Treatment

No treatment of a retinal detachment may lead to total loss of light perception and, in some cases, phthisis bulbi (disorganization of ocular tissues and shrinkage of the eye).

Treatment of rhegmatogenous retinal detachments with scleral buckling has a 90 to 95% success rate. If the macula is not affected, then visual acuity is often restored to within two lines. Once the macula is detached, vision may be lower than normal. A macula threatened by a retinal detachment is an urgency.

Tractional detachment surgery is successful in 60 to 80% of cases. The visual acuity depends on the preoperative state of the macula.

Prevention

In patients at risk for rhegmatogenous retinal detachment, frequent ocular examinations, particularly with symptoms or flashing lights or floaters, may allow the clinician to diagnose a retinal break early before a retinal detachment occurs and initiate treatment with laser or cryotherapy. In all people who partake in activities that may increase the risk of ocular trauma, it is prudent to use protective eyewear. Some sports, such as hockey, basketball, racquetball, and golf, and work such as welding are examples of activities that carry a high risk.

There is no means of preventing a posterior vitreous detachment or a retinal detachment.

Good glucose control in patients with insulin-dependent diabetes mellitus does slow the progression of diabetic retinopathy. Tractional detachments can in some cases be prevented with laser to cause regression of neovascularization as in proliferative diabetic retinopathy and threshold retinopathy of prematurity.

Cost Containment

Prompt treatment of a retinal break before detachment with outpatient cryotherapy or laser may limit the cost of surgery for a retinal detachment.

Pneumatic retinopexy does not require an operating room, and can be done as an outpatient procedure. The success with this procedure is approximately 80%, compared with 90 to 95% with a scleral buckle, but scleral buckling after a failed pneumatic retinopexy improves success to about 90 to 95%. Many ocular procedures are now done in an outpatient setting or in day surgery to limit the cost of hospitalization.

Ultrasonography is needed in cases where medial opacity is present. It is not routinely needed in most cases of retinal detachment.

REFERENCES

Michels RG, Wilkinson CP, Rice TA. Retinal detachment. St. Louis: Mosby, 1990:459.

Schepens CL. Retinal detachment and allied diseases. Philadelphia: Saunders, 1983:318.

Williams GA, Aaberg TM. Techniques of scleral buckling. In: Ryan SJ, ed. Retina. St. Louis: Mosby, 1989:111.

CHAPTER 22–12

Blindness

William H. Coles, M.D., M.S.

DEFINITION

Blindness is total loss of light perception.

ETIOLOGY

There are multiple etiologies, including congenital and acquired causes.

CRITERIA FOR DIAGNOSIS

Suggestive

None.

Definitive

Blindness is the loss of sight. Blindness can be defined as the loss of all light perception. But the term is used for loss of functional vision. The most definitive definition is legal.

Central Vision Loss. Legal blindness is the loss of central vision until an individual with maximum corrective techniques sees only 20/200 or worse in the better eye.

Visual Field Loss. Loss of peripheral vision may occur with the preservation of central vision. Constriction of the visual field in the better eye, to less than 20° total, is also classified as legal blindness regardless of central visual acuity.

CLINICAL MANIFESTATIONS

Subjective

For most techniques, visual acuity measurements are subjective. As sight is in constant use during the waking hours, any acute change is recognized by the patient, almost immediately, even when vision loss is slight. In contrast, changes in vision over months or years may not be recognized as readily.

Objective

Physical Examination

Visual acuity is measured with the best optical correction—glasses or contact lenses. Objects, usually letters, are presented to each eye. The smallest object recognized correctly is the measure of acuity.

The presence of blindness or decreased vision that cannot be measured on standard charts may require other objective findings such as changes in pupillary reflexes; presence of optic atrophy or disk swelling; or changes in the lens, cornea, vitreous, or retina. Blindness also causes a loss of the involuntary blink reflex to a rapidly approaching object. Decrease in vision or blindness may also result in an altered pupillary response (Marcus–Gunn pupillary phenomenon) when a flashlight is alternately presented to each eye.

The causes of sudden loss or impairment of vision confined to one eye are listed in Table 22–12–1.

TABLE 22–12–1. CAUSES OF SUDDEN LOSS OR IMPAIRMENT OF VISION CONFINED TO ONE EYE

Central vein obstruction
Central artery obstruction
Vitreous or retinal hemorrhage
Optic neuritis, papillitis, or retrobulbar neuritis
Retinal detachment involving the macula
Toxic amblyopia (such as methyl alcohol)
Enophthalmitis due to emboli
Thrombosis of the intracarotid artery
Skull injuries with hemorrhage of the optic canal
Uremic amaurosis

Sudden Loss or Impairment of Vision in Both Eyes
Optic neuritis, especially in demyelinating diseases such as Devic's disease
Uremic amaurosis
Head injuries
Hysteria
Migraine

Gradual loss or impairment of Vision in One Eye
Refractive errors
  Myopia
  Hyperopia
  Astigmatism
Cataract changes
Keratoconus
Lens dislocation or subluxation
Refractive changes due to aqueous blood sugar changes in diabetes
Refractive changes from the pressure of a lid lesion
Refractive changes due to pressure on the globe from expanding orbital lesions
Corneal changes
  Keratitis
  Dystrophy
  Allergic reactions
  Edema
Uveal tract
  Inflammation such as iritis, choroiditis, or uveitis
  Macular degenerations, especially those associated with subretinal hemorrhages
  Tumors
Glaucoma
Vitreous
  Opacification of the vitreous from any infiltrative changes
  Hemorrhages of the vitreous
Retina
  Vascular lesions
  Macular degenerations
  Tapetal retinal degenerations
  Toxic changes
  Inflammatory diseases of the retina
  Retinopathies
  Tumors
  Retinal detachment
Optic nerve
  Chiasmal changes
  Inflammatory changes of neuritis or retrobulbar neuritis
  Tumors or pressure from tumors on the nerve
  Papilledema
  Optic atrophy
All conditions listed for gradual loss in one eye may involve a second eye at a later time.

Adapted from Scheie HG, Albert DM. Textbook of ophthalmology. 9th ed. Philadelphia: Saunders, 1977:159. Reproduced with permission from the publisher.

Routine Laboratory Abnormalities
There are no diagnostic routine laboratory abnormalities.

PLANS
Diagnostic
Differential Diagnosis
A person with hysteria has a normal ocular examination, normal pupillary responses, and usually evidence of a psychiatric disturbance.

Malingering manifests inconsistent responses. Obvious secondary gain such as litigation for an accident or application for compensation is usually present. Failure on specific malingering tests may support the diagnosis: polaroid filters used with visual acuity testing, inconsistencies in near and far acuities, presence of optokinetic nystagmus.

Diagnostic Options and Recommended Approach
See Criteria for Diagnosis

Therapeutic
Therapy for decreased vision or blindness is dependent on the cause and degree of visual loss.

Marked decreases in vision and total blindness require patient education to help adjust to a world most of us rarely consider. Patients with 20/200 or worse vision who are not totally blind can be helped by a number of visual aids. Telescopic lenses, high convex lenses, and a special reader magnifier can assist the patient in being able to complete routine daily activities. At night, image intensifiers can be used in certain patients to allow increased discrimination. Recently, television monitors have been used to increase visual images to a size where patients can read print previously impossible to see.

Blind patients should be directed to various institutions that prepare patients to cope with blindness. Frequently, this requires both psychological and physical training. These institutions vary from state to state and city to city.

FOLLOW-UP
Totally blind persons need follow-up by an ophthalmologist who should direct them to services that can assist them in their daily routines. Patients with decreased vision need to be followed according to the disease process.

DISCUSSION
Prevalence and Incidence
Because definitions and recording have changed significantly over the past decade, accurate estimates of incidence of blindness vary and tend to be uninformative. Estimates in the United States suggest visual impairment in more than 3 million, and between 500,000 and 1 million meet the definition of legal blindness. The prevalence of blindness is higher in blacks.

Related Basic Science
Measurement of Visual Acuity. Most visual acuity techniques are subjective and require the patient to respond. In patients with markedly decreased vision, the following scale is used:

NLP	No light perception
LP	Light perception
LPr	Light projection: able to determine direction of light
HM	Hand motion: able to detect presence or absence of a hand movement in front of the eye
CF	Count fingers: able to count fingers (The maximum distance that fingers are counted is recorded. For example, if an individual can count fingers held 4 ft from the eye, the notation "CF 4 feet" is made.)

In patients with better vision, measurement of visual acuity is tested by a *vision chart*. These charts are designed to measure the minimum

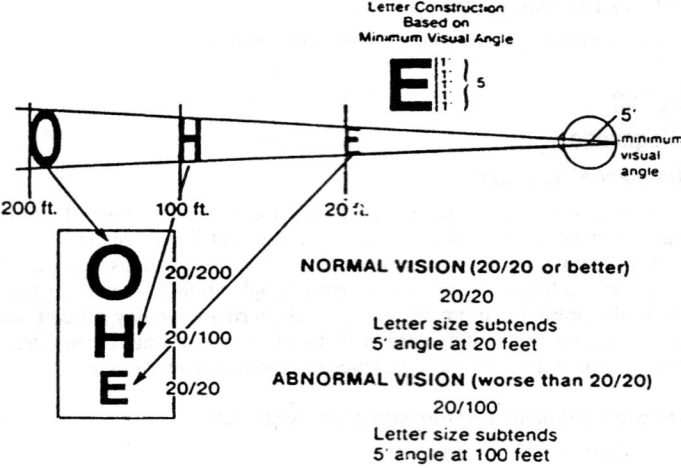

Figure 22–12–1. Visual acuity notation expresses the measurement of the minimum visual angle by letter size at a specific distance.

perceptible visual angle at a testing distance of 20 ft. The minimum visual angle perceived by an average normal eye is represented by a letter, most commonly an *E,* where the entire letter subtends an angle of 5 minutes of arc and each bar or space of the letter subtends an angle of 1 minute of arc.

One can think of the visual angle as the angle at a point on the retina where two lines extend outward to infinity (Fig. 22–12–1). These two lines making an angle of 5 minutes of arc will diverge indefinitely. At 20 ft, the lines will be about 0.25 in. apart; at 100 ft, about 1.5 in. apart; and at 200 ft, about 3.5 in. apart. A letter that would fit between the lines at any one of those distances would be perceived by the 20/20 eye and identified, and any letter at any of those distances that would not touch the lines could not be identified by the normal eye with 20/20 vision. Visual acuity can be tested at any distance if the object is large enough. Obviously, we are constantly perceiving objects at multiple distances. For the purposes of testing, letter sizes corresponding to the size of 5 minutes of arc at various distances are placed on a chart (figure).

To be specific, the size of a letter that would subtend 5 minutes of arc at 200 ft is used to test acuity at a distance of 20 ft. We are simply saying that a normal eye could perceive this size letter at 200 ft. Patients who can only see this size letter at 20 ft, and nothing smaller, are then said to have 20/200 vision. Similarly, another way to express acuity, patients who can only read the 20/100 letter are seeing a letter at 20 ft that the normal eye can see at 100 ft.

The 20/200 vision notation is not a fraction. The top number represents the testing distance, almost always by convention 20 ft, and the lower number represents the distance size that letter could be visualized by the normal eye.

Twenty feet is used as the standard visual testing, as accommodation at that distance and at any distance beyond does not have any significant effect on acuity. Accommodation is the ability of the eye to focus, a situation exactly like a camera. Adjustments must be made when a camera or optical system focused on infinity is moved closer to the object of attention. This is also true in the eye. Changes in accommodation naturally could affect visual acuity. The best example is in older individuals, in whom accommodation is lost because of advancing age and bifocal lens are needed for near vision. With testing at 20 ft, the effects of age on accommodation do not need to be considered.

Nightblindness. Although technically not blindness in the true sense of the word, inability to see in the dark is associated with certain disease processes. Patients with retinitis pigmentosa or other pigmentary degenerations of the retina frequently complain of the inability to see at night due to poor dark adaptation. Patients with vitamin A deficiency or with high myopia and those who have undergone laser therapy for diabetic retinopathy may on occasion have abnormalities of dark adaptation.

Loss of Visual Field. Loss of vision from changes in the visual field occur in two major circumstances: either from diseases within the eye

(e.g., retinal detachment or glaucomatous pressure on the optic nerve) or from visual field neurologic loss. Visual field loss may or may not be accompanied by central visual acuity loss.

Highway injury and compensation suits create demand for evaluation of vision impairment. The standard of determining visual impairment was set up by the American Medical Association and published in the *Journal of the American Medical Association* in 1952. It has been used as standard since that time. To determine visual impairment, the following parameters are used: far and near vision for both eyes; visual fields for both eyes; impairment of ocular motility.

The visual impairment is determined by using published charts. After determining visual impairment, the impairment for the whole person can also be calculated. The use of the word *disability* for visual loss should be avoided. Many patients are extremely adaptable and despite often significant visual loss seem to function with little or no disability. In contrast, other patients with minor sight restriction can become incapacitated. There is wide individual variance. *Disability* implies all the sociologic and physiologic influences on the patient's activity after visual loss. *Impairment* refers in the narrower sense to the visual decrease and is the preferred term.

Natural History and Its Modification with Treatment

The natural history of blindness depends on the etiology. In the United States, diabetes is the most common cause of blindness. Trauma is another important cause, especially of uniocular visual loss. Worldwide, trachoma is the leading cause of blindness, but it is rare in the United States.

Prevention

Prevention of blindness is one of the major goals of all professionals in eye care. The most common cause of blindness in the world is trachoma. Trachoma abounds in countries with poor nutrition. Improvement in world food distribution as well as education about proper hygiene can help prevent this threat.

In the United States, the major cause of blindness is diabetes. Already, research and carefully controlled multicenter national studies have shown that photocoagulation does help prevent the progression of diabetic retinopathy in many patients. Also in the past few years rapid advancements in corneal transplantation have provided, in selected patients, a 90% success rate for clear grafts. These advancements in ophthalmology and by groups such as Research to Prevent Blindness have provided advances in the prevention of blindness.

Trauma is an important cause of ocular blindness. Education for better protection in automobile accidents could decrease visual loss. In addition, the use of protective eye wear must always be encouraged for those high-risk occupations.

Cost Containment

The correction of visual defects and then aid to assist those still visually handicapped can reduce disability. Understanding the complexities of vision loss and then supporting efforts to follow the natural progression of blinding diseases and prevent causes of hereditary blindness clearly could decrease the total health care bill for the United States.

REFERENCES

Dana MR, Tielsch JM, Enger C, et al. Visual impairment in a rural Appalachian community: Prevalence and causes. JAMA 1990;264:2400.

Drews CD, Yeargin-Allsopp M, Murphy CC, Decoufle P. Legal blindness among 10-year-old children in Metropolitan Atlanta: Prevalence, 1985 to 1987. Am J Public Health 1992;82:1377.

Evans JR, Wormald RP. Epidemiological function of BD8 certification. Eye 1993;7(pt 1):172.

Gilbert C, Foster A, Negrel AD, Thylefors B. Childhood blindness: A new form for recording causes of visual loss in children. Bull WHO 1993;71:485.

Guide to the evaluation of permanent visual impairment. In: Physician's desk reference for ophthalmology. Oradell, NJ: Charles E Baker, Jr., 1977/1978: 48.

Moss SE, Klein R, Klein BE. Ten-year incidence of visual loss in a diabetic population. Ophthalmology 1994;101:1061.

Tielsch JM, Sommer A, Witt K, et al. Blindness and visual impairment in an American urban population: The Baltimore Eye Survey. Arch Ophthalmol 1990;108:286.

CHAPTER 22–13

Pyogenic Eye Infections (See Section 8, Chapter 28)

CHAPTER 22–14

Ocular Involvement in the Acquired Immunodeficiency Syndrome

Mary Elizabeth Hartnett, M.D.

DEFINITION

The acquired immunodeficiency syndrome (AIDS) is presently diagnosed by the CD4 count, or the number of helper T cells in the blood. In 60 to 70% of patients who are HIV positive, HIV retinopathy may be present consisting of retinal hemorrhages and cotton–wool spots. In frank AIDS, opportunistic infections by almost any organism or organisms can occur in the ocular tissues and can threaten vision.

ETIOLOGY

AIDS results from a viral infection caused by HIV. HIV retinopathy is believed to be associated with immune phenomena or rheologic abnormalities, but is not believed to be infectious. Retinitis from cytomegalovirus is the most common opportunistic infection and occurs in up to 45% of patients with AIDS. It often occurs late in the disease with low CD4 counts; 20% of patients with CD4 counts below 50 develop cytomegalovirus retinitis per year.

CRITERIA FOR DIAGNOSIS

Suggestive

Decreased vision, visual field defect, or floaters in an HIV-positive patient should raise concern of involvement of the vitreous or retina. Ocular pain or irritation may indicate involvement of the anterior segment; however, infections may occur in asymptomatic patients.

Many retinal or choroidal disorders are diagnosed by the clinical appearance alone. Whitening of the retina noted in any area, choroidal patches, and hemorrhages are of concern.

Definitive

Many posterior ocular diagnoses are made based on examination without laboratory confirmation. In contrast, anterior segment involvement in AIDS may be confirmed by scraping and culture of the surface of the eye.

Retinal evaluation is best performed with stereoscopic indirect ophthalmoscopy and slit-lamp biomicroscopy with a dilated pupil. Careful examination for areas of retinal whitening, choroidal lesions, vascular sheathing, hemorrhages, or inflammatory cells of the vitreous is performed.

Serology (e.g., rapid plasma reagin, fluorescent treponemal antibody absorption test for syphilis) is done if syphilis is suspected. If there is a positive result, a diagnostic lumbar puncture is often recommended because up to 80% of HIV-positive patients who have a positive blood serology for syphilis have neurosyphilis.

Cotton–wool spots are nonspecific; however, in AIDS, their presence can lead to confusion between the diagnoses of early cytomegalovirus retinitis and HIV retinopathy. Cytomegalovirus retinitis is visually threatening, whereas HIV retinopathy is noninfectious and usually not visually threatening. It may be prudent to follow a patient with a questionable diagnosis more closely for progression of retinal whitening, which may indicate an infectious process. Serial fundus photography is valuable in uncertain cases where the diagnosis is in question.

In cases of chorioretinal infection, when the diagnosis is unclear or therapy is not successful, a chorioretinal biopsy is performed. Tissue is chosen at the junction of normal and infected retina. In areas where the retina is already atrophic, the chance of a positive diagnosis is lower. Diagnosis from vitreous aspirates may be possible through polymerase chain reaction.

Kaposi's sarcoma may manifest on the lids or conjunctiva.

CLINICAL MANIFESTATIONS

Subjective

In patients with ocular changes of AIDS, a history of HIV infection is often present. It is only occasionally that the diagnosis of HIV infection is considered because a routine ophthalmologic examination suggests the diagnosis of an undiscovered HIV infection.

Patients may experience ocular pain, discharge, visual phenomena, or decreased vision depending on where the pathology occurs.

In the anterior segment, foreign body sensation, redness, and discharge may be symptoms associated with keratitis. Many patients with HIV have dry eyes, which may also cause irritation to the eyes, and blurred vision.

Chorioretinal disorders may cause blurred vision or visual field loss depending on whether the infection occurs in the peripheral retina or the macula, where central visual function is present.

There may also be vitreous floaters (mobile black spots in the patient's field of view) due to vitreous opacities. With optic nerve disorders, there may be visual field defects, color vision loss, and central visual loss.

Many ocular infections occur without symptoms. About one-half of asymptomatic AIDS patients have cytomegalovirus.

Objective

Physical Examination

Keratitis may appear on slit-lamp examination as individual areas of edema or whitening of the corneal epithelium. There may be conjunctival injection as well.

Kaposi's sarcoma may appear on the lid or conjunctiva and appear as red areas.

HIV retinopathy is the most frequent manifestation of HIV infection and is characterized by retinal hemorrhages and cotton–wool spots (see Color Plate 22–14–1, after page 1946).

Cytomegalovirus retinitis may have several appearances. The more typical is that of whitening of the retina along the nerve fiber layer with flame-shaped hemorrhages. This represents active retinitis. The retinitis spreads and causes full-thickness necrosis of the retina. The leading edge of activity is noted by a whitened appearance (see Color Plate 22–14–2, after page 1946). The other less common appearance is that of several whitened spots that may coalesce with time or may later become atrophic. This smoldering form of retinitis is best managed with periodic fundus photographs and or visual field evaluations (see Color Plate 22–14–3, after page 1946). With either form of cytomegalovirus retinitis, vitreous cells may be present. In the areas of atrophy, varying degrees of pigmentation and occasional plaques appear. Cytomegalovirus optic neuritis is often associated with severe, often permanent, visual loss and a swollen optic disc with hemorrhage.

Ocular syphilis associated with AIDS involves anterior segment inflammation (iritis), retinitis, choroiditis, optic nerve involvement, or vasculitis. In the placoid form of choroidal involvement (see Color Plate 22–14–4, after page 1946), early on there are yellowish areas deep to the retinal layers in the choroid. Subsequently, atrophy is seen.

Pneumocystis carinii choroidopathy appears as cream-colored, round or oval lesions in the choroid deep to the retina. These lesions may be seen in patients on aerosolized pentamidine for prophylaxis of *Pneumocystis carinii* pneumonia.

Toxoplasmosis often affects the central nervous system with resultant visual field loss and with extraocular muscle palsies. It can, however, affect the retina with active infection, inflammation, and visual loss.

Herpes simplex may cause retinitis in AIDS patients. Herpes zoster may cause a fulminant, rapid, bilateral, blinding disorder known as progressive outer retinal necrosis. This is difficult to treat successfully.

Routine Laboratory Abnormalities

In most diseases except syphilis, routine laboratory values are not used to diagnose ocular complications of AIDS.

PLANS
Diagnostic
Differential Diagnosis

The differential diagnosis of ocular involvement in AIDS is outlined in Table 22–14–1.

Diagnostic Options

In most cases, cytomegalovirus retinitis is a presumptive diagnosis based on ophthalmologic examination. In unusual cases or when treatment does not appear to improve the condition, chorioretinal biopsy may be considered. In cases of anterior segment involvement, a smear or scraping of the cornea or conjunctiva with culture and histopathology may confirm a diagnosis. Serology for suspected syphilis is obtained.

Serology is rarely helpful in cytomegalovirus or herpetic retinitis, except perhaps in children who may not have yet been exposed to these

TABLE 22–14–1. DIFFERENTIAL DIAGNOSIS OF OCULAR INVOLVEMENT IN PERSONS WITH HIV

HIV Retinopathy with Cotton–Wool Spots and Retinal Hemorrhages
Diabetic retinopathy
Hypertensive retinopathy
Collagen–vascular disorders
Blood dyscrasias
Idiopathic
Branch retinal vein occlusion

Anterior Segment Involvement with Keratitis
Dry eye
Noninfectious causes as seen in the immunocompetent patient
Herpes zoster
Herpes simplex
Microsporidia
Other

Retinitis
Cytomegalovirus
Herpes simplex or herpes zoster
Toxoplasmosis
Histoplasmosis
Other

Multifocal Choroiditis
Syphilis
Pneumocystis carinii
Tuberculosis
Other causes

opportunistic infections. Fluid from the anterior segment or vitreous may not be helpful in diagnosing the etiology of chorioretinitis, however. Polymerase chain reaction of the vitreous fluid may be helpful in these cases. The sample is obtained by a diagnostic vitrectomy.

Recommended Approach

Consultation with a ophthalmic specialist is recommended when AIDS ocular complications are suspected. A complete eye examination is performed and is particularly useful with patients who have symptoms of visual loss, floaters, or a visual field defect.

Dilated stereoscopic funduscopy by a retinal specialist is often indicated. Cytomegalovirus retinitis is usually a presumptive diagnosis based on the fundus appearance and experience helps with accuracy of the diagnosis. In cases where treatment of cytomegalovirus retinitis is not successful, consideration to multiple infectious etiologies or another infection is given. If the course of the "presumed" cytomegalovirus retinitis is extremely rapid despite treatment, it may represent progressive outer retinal necrosis, believed to be caused by herpes zoster, and may lead rapidly to bilateral loss of light perception. In some centers, it is recommended that treatment be instituted with ganciclovir and foscarnet concurrently. As previously mentioned, chorioretinal biopsy may be performed and vitreous aspirates for polymerase chain reaction evaluation are sometimes helpful.

In anterior segment involvement, slit-lamp biomicroscopy is indicated. Keratitis is scraped and cultured for pathogens.

Because about one-half of the patients who have cytomegalovirus retinitis are asymptomatic, it may be prudent to consider screening programs. One such suggestion for ocular evaluations is every year for those with CD4 counts above 100, every 6 months for those with CD4 counts between 50 and 99, and every 3 to 4 months for those with CD4 counts below 50.

Therapeutic
Therapeutic Options

Most ocular infections are treated systemically. Syphilis, when diagnosed, is treated with penicillin in the regimen recommended for neurosyphilis, as 80% of HIV-positive patients have positive serology on lumbar puncture.

In cytomegalovirus retinitis, treatment is recommended with intravenous ganciclovir or foscarnet. Both require an induction dose and maintenance therapy often necessitating central venous access. Ganciclovir's side effects include neutropenia and thrombocytopenia. Foscarnet, which inhibits reverse transcriptase, causes nephrotoxicity, nausea, and metabolic abnormalities (calcium, magnesium, potassium). Both are effective in stopping cytomegalovirus retinitis but are not infrequently associated with recurrences at about 50 to 60 days. Recurrences are often treatable with reinduction of the medication. In the Studies of Ocular Complications of AIDS Research Group (SOCA, 1992) 51% of 127 patients assigned to ganciclovir died versus 34% of 107 patients assigned to foscarnet ($P = .007$). This enhanced survival with foscarnet treatment was believed to be due to its anti-HIV effect. When reviewing visual acuity and visual field loss, retinal detachments, and progression of cytomegalovirus retinitis, both drugs appeared to be equivalent in effect; however, foscarnet was less well tolerated. Oral ganciclovir is now available; long-term studies regarding effectiveness are not.

In patients who do not tolerate systemic therapy because of side effects, intravitreal injections of either drug can be given on a weekly basis.

Sustained-release ganciclovir in an intraocular device that is implanted into the vitreous cavity is currently being investigated; however, intraocular ganciclovir does not treat systemic cytomegalovirus infection. Cytomegalovirus retinitis often becomes bilateral; therefore, intraocular treatment of one eye would not protect the fellow eye from disease.

Other medications (e.g., cidofovir and antisense oligonucleotides) are currently being investigated.

Recommended Approach

Screening programs have been discussed, although the long-term effect on the quality of life of the individual is unknown. Any patient with ocular pain, discharge, blurry vision, or floaters should be seen by a retina-trained ophthalmologist.

If cytomegalovirus retinitis is diagnosed, induction with intravenous ganciclovir or foscarnet is begun, followed by maintenance therapy, or treatment with newer medications, now available. Fundus photographs may be done at this time to best follow the ocular examination.

The decision of what treatment is used is often best made in concert with the primary care physician.

For other infections, treatment is recommended based on the infectious agent. Dry eyes are usually treated with tear supplements.

In patients with retinal detachment secondary to cytomegalovirus retinitis, vitrectomy with silicone oil injection is recommended.

FOLLOW-UP

Once treated for cytomegalovirus retinitis begins, a follow-up schedule with the ophthalmologist at about 2 weeks includes careful indirect ophthalmoscopy and review of ophthalmic photographs. At these visits, there may be little to no regression of the cytomegalovirus retinitis, but there should be no progression. After the first follow-up visit, appointments are tailored to the treatment response. Many patients have a recurrence within 3 months and may need reinduction with either agent. In some cases, treatment with both agents or with intravitreal and intravenous therapy may be considered. In patients with side effects from intravenous treatment, consideration for intravitreal injections or for a vitreous implant with slow-release ganciclovir is considered. The use of other medications is currently being evaluated.

In cytomegalovirus retinitis, many early cases may be asymptomatic. When diagnosed, progression is often slow, with clinical progression noted over several weeks, but treatment should be started within a few days. Occasionally, the retinitis is fulminant, causing rapid blindness. Loss of vision in the untreated patient may occur within months, and bilateral involvement occurs in approximately 50% of patients within 6 months.

There is a risk of retinal detachments in 25% of eyes within 1 year. This is secondary to retinal atrophy, hole formation, and vitreous membranes. Retinal detachment, if untreated, leads to total blindness. Patients may experience light flashes and an increase in floaters, or may only experience visual field loss or loss of vision.

Follow-up for other ocular infections is determined based on the infectious agent. Dry eyes are often treated with tear supplements and are followed for symptoms.

DISCUSSION

Prevalence and Incidence

AIDS retinopathy occurs in approximately two thirds of HIV-positive individuals.

Cytomegalovirus retinitis becomes more prevalent as the immune status of the patient decreases. It occurs in up to 45% of patients with AIDS and approaches bilateral disease in 50% within 6 months. For patients with CD4 counts below 50 cells/μL, it occurs at a rate of approximately 20% per year.

Other ocular infections are fairly rare.

Related Basic Science

Many strains of HIV are known. The virus is a retrovirus and is easily mutable. The risk factors include intravenous drug use, blood transfusion, homosexuality, and heterosexuality with frequent partners. The virus reduces one's ability to fight off opportunistic infections.

AIDS retinopathy is thought to occur from altered rheology of blood cells, vascular occlusion, or HIV infection of retinal endothelial cells.

Cytomegalovirus directly infects retinal tissue. *Pneumocystis carinii*

also appears to directly infect the choroid. Many of these opportunistic organisms not only cause infections that would not occur in the immunocompetent patient, but some of these organisms that cause limited infection in the immunocompetent host cause fulminant infection in the patient with AIDS in ocular tissues usually spared in the immunocompetent host.

Other opportunistic infections include *Pneumocystis carinii* choroidopathy, toxoplasmosis, histoplasmosis, Kaposi's sarcoma, syphilis, herpes simplex, varicella–zoster, and microsporidia.

Natural History and Its Modification With Treatment

There is rarely visual loss from AIDS retinopathy. The hemorrhages and cotton–wool spots are evanescent, although some patients may experience subtle visual spots in their fields of vision.

Cytomegalovirus retinitis is the most common and most studied opportunistic ocular infection in AIDS. Blindness may occur in 3 months if untreated, and bilateral involvement occurs in 50% of patients within 6 months. With treatment with ganciclovir or foscarnet, the response rate is 80 to 100%. Visual loss may occur from several causes. Direct infection and necrosis of the retina lead to permanent visual field loss; transient visual loss may occur from retinal edema associated with infection that would resolve with treatment. Recurrences are common, however, occurring in more than 50% of patients within 2 to 3 months. In patients who are treated with either agent, the median time to visual acuity worse than 20/100 in involved eyes was not significantly different between foscarnet (303 days) and ganciclovir (346 days) (SOCA, 1992).

The mortality differed significantly between these agents (51% assigned to ganciclovir died versus 34% assigned to foscarnet). The median survival for ganciclovir was 8.5 months, compared with 12.6 months with foscarnet. The progression of cytomegalovirus retinitis and risk of retinal detachments (50% within 1 year) were similar with both agents. Side effects in the patients using foscarnet led 36% to switch agents compared with only 11% of ganciclovir-treated patients (SOCA, 1992).

Prevention

At present there is no known method of preventing AIDS or the ocular complications of AIDS once infection with HIV is established.

Cost Containment

The treatment of cytomegalovirus retinitis requires intravenous antibiotic therapy as do other infections. At present, the cost of ganciclovir is lower than that of foscarnet; however, enhanced life outcome with foscarnet versus ganciclovir needs to be considered patient by patient. Oral ganciclovir, shown to be as effective as intravenous, may decrease the cost of intravenous therapy.

Home-based health care has limited the cost of hospital stays to a great extent and may be preferred by some patients. There are fewer nosocomial infections in AIDS patients who are not hospitalized.

REFERENCES

Freeman WR, Helm M. Retinal and ophthalmologic manifestations of AIDS. In: Ryan SJ, ed. Retina. St. Louis: Mosby, 1989:597.

Holland GN, Shuler JD. Progression rates of cytomegalovirus retinopathy in ganciclovir-treated and untreated patients. Arch Ophthalmol 1992;110:1435.

Jabs DA, Enger C, Haller J, et al. Retinal detachments in patients with cytomegalovirus retinitis. Arch Ophthalmol 1991;109:794.

Studies of Ocular Complications of AIDS (SOCA) Research Group in Collaboration with ACTG. Mortality in patients with the acquired immunodeficiency syndrome treated with either foscarnet or ganciclovir for cytomegalovirus retinitis. N Engl J Med 1992;326:213.

Age-related Macular Degeneration

Mary Elizabeth Hartnett, M.D.

DEFINITION

Age-related macular degeneration (AMD) is the most common cause of central visual loss in patients over the age of 65 years in the United States, Canada, British Isles, and Australia. Total blindness is not common, but decreased fine acuity and impaired reading vision result in frequent visual dysfunction.

ETIOLOGY

The etiology is unknown, but certain environmental factors, such as the ultraviolet rays of the sun and smoking, are thought to play a role. It occurs more frequently in Caucasians. Patients with hypertension respond more poorly to laser treatment than those without. Also, people who have diets high in green, leafy vegetables and in vegetables and fruits that contain carotenoids have been found to have less visual loss from age-related macular degeneration.

CRITERIA FOR DIAGNOSIS

Suggestive

Any complaint with central vision, such as decreased vision or distortion, in the elderly population should alert the clinician to the possibility of AMD. The finding of yellowish deposits under the retina in the macula (drusen) is associated with AMD (see Color Plate 22–15–1, after page 1946). Fluid under the neurosensory retina, exudates, or subretinal hemorrhage by slit-lamp biomicroscopy or ophthalmoscopy in the elderly may indicate vision-threatening complications of AMD, that is, choroidal neovascularization.

Definitive

The diagnosis is made by clinical examination with funduscopy and slit-lamp biomicroscopy. Drusen, or yellowish deposits under the retina, can be only a sign of aging, but when more than 250 μm in diameter (Color Plate 22–15–1), they are believed to be a classic sign of AMD in a patient over age 50. Even smaller drusen and pigmentary changes can be indicative of AMD. The presence of choroidal neovascularization is often associated with subretinal fluid, exudates, or subretinal hemorrhage and can be associated with distortion or sudden central visual loss. Geographic atrophy appears as a loss of retinal detail with the ability to see more choroidal vascular detail.

CLINICAL MANIFESTATIONS

Subjective

Patients complain of difficulty in reading in low light levels, in reading print of low contrast such as newsprint, or a washed-out appearance to things in their central vision. Distortion is an important sign. The patient sees curvature of lines known to be straight, such as telephone poles, or smaller-appearing letters in one eye compared with the other eye (micropsia).

Objective

Physical Examination

The patient with AMD may have normal Snellen visual acuity or may be legally blind; however, the patient with only AMD rarely has loss of peripheral vision, so the peripheral field should be full on examination. The patient may describe the ability to see a person, but not to discriminate the facial features, even well enough to identify the person.

On slit-lamp biomicroscopy, one sees yellow well-defined deposits under the retina (Color Plate 15–22–1) that range in size from under 50 μm in diameter (hard, cuticular drusen) to well more than 250 μm in diameter (soft, exudative drusen).

The hard drusen lead to areas of retinal atrophy which may form blind spots and coalesce to larger areas of atrophy. Large areas of atrophy are called geographic atrophy (see Color Plate 22–15–2, after page 1946), because of their clinical appearance. This dry form of AMD is slowly progressive over many years.

Soft drusen are believed to be associated more often with the wet form of AMD, either fluid under the retinal pigment epithelium or choroidal neovascularization that grows up from the choriocapillaris under the retinal pigment epithelium and/or neurosensory retina. These vessels leak fluid and ultimately form a fibrovascular scar. The patient experiences rapid onset of distortion in lines, often described as wavy lines that are known to be straight or blurriness in vision. The cardinal features of choroidal neovascularization are subneurosensory retinal fluid, exudates, or subretinal hemorrhage, although a grayish or brown subretinal elevated area may be noted (see Color Plate 22–15–3, after page 1946). Very rarely there may be breakthrough of hemorrhage from the subretinal space into the vitreous cavity obscuring the red reflex and fundus detail and causing substantial visual loss involving the patient's peripheral field. Fluid may also accumulate under the retinal pigment epithelium and form a retinal pigment epithelial detachment.

Routine Laboratory Abnormalities

There are no routine laboratory abnormalities associated with AMD.

PLANS

Diagnostic

Differential Diagnosis

The differential diagnosis of age-related macular degeneration is outlined in Table 22–15–1.

Diagnostic Options

The diagnosis of choroidal neovascularization is challenging at times. The fluorescein angiogram is the standard for imaging well-defined choroidal neovascularization. Imaging studies other than fluorescein angiography may be used, such as indocyanine green angiography, to view the choroidal circulation, and infrared imaging of the Bruch's membrane/retinal pigment epithelium junction.

Recommended Approach

A careful history determines the visual dysfunctions a patient is experiencing and under what conditions they occur. Blood pressure is taken, as is a history of any blood pressure treatment or other medication. Smoking history is important and efforts to aid a person to stop smoking are made. Smoking is a risk factor for development of AMD and for loss of vision with AMD. A family history is taken. (It is unknown if AMD is hereditary, as family members tend to share similar characteristics that could be risk factors, such as diet, race, and light exposure.)

A thorough ophthalmologic examination is performed. Best corrected visual acuity is determined. Slit-lamp examination confirms other conditions that may affect central vision. The peripheral retina is examined with indirect ophthalmoscopy. With stereoscopic fundus biomicroscopy, the macula is examined with attention to the foveal depression, the inner retina (looking for changes at the vitreoretinal interface), the retinal vessels and capillaries (inner retina and looking for hypertensive changes), and the deeper retinal layers where deposits of pigment, drusen, and areas of atrophy are noted. Elevation of the neurosensory retina, exudates, and subretinal and retinal hemorrhages provides suspicion of underlying choroidal neovascularization. A choroidal neovascular membrane may be apparent as a subretinal, elevated, green-gray or brown area (Color Plate 22–15–3).

A fluorescein angiogram is usually recommended to identify the

TABLE 22–15–1. DIFFERENTIAL DIAGNOSIS OF AGE-RELATED MACULAR DEGENERATION

Blurred Vision
- Dry eyes
- Cataract
- Diabetic macular edema
- Macular edema or capillary nonperfusion from a vascular occlusion
- Cystoid macular edema
- Epiretinal membrane

Subretinal Fluid
- Central serous retinopathy
- Inflammatory or infectious etiology
- Choroiditis
- Metastatic involvement of the choroid

Retinal Hemorrhage or Exudates
- Macroaneurysm
- Retinovascular disorder such as diabetes mellitus or vascular occlusion
- Hematologic disorder
- Hypertensive retinopathy

Yellow Spots on the Retina
- Exudates
- Stargardt's disease, fundus flavimaculatus
- Fundus albipunctatus
- Retinitis punctata albescens
- Multievanescent white dot syndrome
- Multifocal choroiditis
- Crystalline dystrophy of the retina (cystinosis, Bietti's crystalline dystrophy, tamoxifen, canthaxanthine, oxalosis, etc.)

boundaries when a choroidal neovascular membrane is suspected (see Color Plate 22–15–4, after page 1946).

The clinical appearance of the macula may not always correlate with the level of visual acuity; that is, a patient with a benign-appearing macula may have substantial visual impairment from AMD and may harbor a vision-threatening choroidal neovascular membrane.

Therapeutic

Therapeutic Options

The options with choroidal neovascularization include laser treatment to coagulate choroidal neovascularization and prevent its spread toward the fovea where the best potential visual acuity exists; laser treatment to limit the size of the scotoma (blindspot) if choroidal neovascularization is already subfoveal; and subretinal surgery to remove the vascular membranes. Subretinal surgery has not, to date, been associated with better vision than laser treatment and has more associated risks.

Recommended Approach

Early Age-related Macular Degeneration (Drusen). These patients may have mild visual disturbance or no disturbance at all. Preventive measures are recommended. The patient is urged to stop smoking, work with the primary care physician to maintain a good blood pressure, consume a diet rich in green leafy vegetables and in vegetables and fruits rich in the carotenoids, and avoid extensive sun in the eyes by wearing a visor or sunglasses.

Geographic Atrophy. This dry form of AMD is slowly progressive and may take 8 or more years to cause visual decline to the level of legal blindness (20/200); however, these patients may have substantial visual impairment even with moderate visual acuity (e.g., 20/50) because of the presence of scotomata (blindspots), which cause letters in words to disappear. The same recommendations as for early AMD above are made. These patients are also given low vision evaluations with instruction in the proper use of light to enhance the contrast of the print they are reading, the use of magnifiers and bioptics (microscopes that

are ground into glasses), and even the use of closed-circuit television sets that enhance contrast and magnify print to a level where it can be read.

Choroidal Neovascularization. The same recommendations as for early AMD above are made. These patients undergo a fluorescein angiogram. If the choroidal neovascularization is not under the fovea, a recommendation for laser photocoagulation (to coagulate the choroidal neovascularization and prevent its spread) is made. If the choroidal neovascularization is subfoveal, laser is still recommended in some cases, to limit the size of the blindspot that would result from the spreading and leaking choroidal new vessels. This treatment allows the patient a greater area of macula for more effective use of low vision aids. The patient will have a black spot in central vision after the photocoagulation, and if the treatment is subfoveal, vision may decrease.

These patients are also given low vision evaluations as described for geographic atrophy.

Many patients who have ill-defined or occult choroidal neovascularization may not do as well with laser treatment. Indocyanine green angiography is performed to better visualize these membranes. Treatment based on this information is currently being evaluated.

As the best corrected visual acuity falls, the patient is instructed as to legal ability to drive. The criteria vary from state to state. In some states, a patient is allowed to drive with the use of a low vision aid if it enhances vision to a certain level of acuity. If a patient with AMD becomes legally blind (i.e., best corrected bilateral visual acuity < 20/200), the state Commission for the Blind is informed as the patient may be eligible for benefits.

FOLLOW-UP

The dry form of AMD is slowly progressive. Patients are often followed on a yearly basis, with instructions to be seen sooner for decreased vision or distortion. During this time, they may be counseled about use of visual aids.

In wet AMD, the recurrence rate with successful laser treatment of choroidal neovascularization is approximately 50%. These patients are followed carefully with repeat angiograms to recognize early recurrences. The recurrences are often treated if the choroidal neovascularization falls within certain guidelines based on fluorescein angiographic appearance.

It often takes approximately 3 months after laser for the visual acuity to stabilize. Patients are counseled regarding this and are also asked to report any increase in distortion or decrease in vision, which may indicate a recurrence. Treated patients often have more difficulty noting a difference in visual acuity as easily as patients who have mild AMD. Therefore, frequent examinations are necessary, initially every 2 weeks and then less frequently as indicated by the examination.

If suspicion of a recurrence exists based on patient symptoms or clinical examination, a repeat angiogram is performed. If indocyanine green angiography or infrared imaging is possible, these in combination with the fluorescein angiogram may offer additional helpful information.

DISCUSSION

Prevalence and Incidence

Age-related macular degeneration affects approximately 20% of people over the age of 65. The dry form, which is slowly progressive often over a decade, is more common, occurring in 80 to 90% of all cases of AMD. The wet form, which causes sudden decreased vision and/or distortion, is less common, occurring in only 10 to 20% of all cases.

Related Basic Science

The cause of AMD is unknown, but there are theories that oxidative damage to the sensitive membrane lipoproteins in the photoreceptor outer segments may occur from light damage or other toxins. The retinal pigment epithelium (RPE) cells, which are important in ingesting the outer segment lipoprotein discs of the photoreceptor, may be less able to digest the discs if the discs have been altered by oxidation. As the RPE becomes more compromised, it releases cytoplasmic debris beneath and into its basement membranes. These deposits may accumulate and appear as drusen. Intracellular debris also accumulate. The intracellular debris or the debris beneath the RPE cells may limit the effectiveness of the RPE. The intracellular debris may slow intracellular transport; the debris beneath the RPE cells may impede the nutritional transport from the underlying choroidal vascular beds. Some cells may die, and when this occurs the underlying choriocapillaris may die as well. This may lead to retinal atrophy and geographic atrophy. In some areas where the cells do not die, the lack of oxygen may stimulate the release of growth factors that lead to vascular growth into the retina toward the hypoxic areas surrounding RPE cells, that is, choroidal neovascularization. There is ongoing work characterizing the enzymes in Bruch's membrane and their effect on the development of choroidal neovascularization.

Research is presently ongoing to identify various growth factors associated with choroidal neovascularization in AMD with the hope of developing a more effective, perhaps medical means of preventing or treating this visually disabling outcome.

Natural History and Its Modification with Treatment

If left untreated, choroidal neovascularization leads to fibrovascular scar tissue and loss of central vision, inability to read, drive, and recognize facial features.

In eyes with choroidal neovascularization located outside the fovea, the relative risk of severe visual loss (loss of six lines or more or quadrupling of the visual angle, i.e., 20/80 to 20/320) in untreated eyes compared with treated eyes was 1.2 to 1.5 depending on the proximity of the choroidal neovascularization to the fovea (Macular Photocoagulation Study Group 1991, 1994). Patients with hypertension experienced little to no benefit in one group ($RR = 0.93$). There is some benefit from laser treatment when choroidal neovascularization, of specific criteria, is located under the fovea (22% of treated eyes versus 47% of untreated eyes had severe visual loss or quadrupling of the visual angle).

In surgical cases, visual acuity results are still anecdotal; the majority do not improve.

Prevention

The patient is urged to stop smoking, work with the primary care physician to maintain a good blood pressure, avoid extensive sun in the eyes by wearing a visor or sunglasses, and consume a diet rich in green leafy vegetables and in vegetables and fruits rich in the carotenoids. Patients are encouraged, with the aid of their primary care physician, to consume a healthy cardiovascular diet with mild aerobic conditioning if possible. There are no known means of preventing AMD, but these measures may slow the progression or prevent severe visual loss.

Currently the effectiveness of antioxident (vitamin) use is being investigated.

Cost Containment

Most procedures are performed on an outpatient basis. Emphasis on prevention that is known is important. Indocyanine green angiograms are still being evaluated for their benefit. Because it has taught us more about how to interpret fluorescein angiograms, their use may be limited in the future.

Subretinal surgery for choroidal neovascularization is still being evaluated. It is often done in the major operating room or in a surgicenter setting, rarely requiring overnight hospitalization. Laser treatment, on the other hand, is an office procedure and takes approximately 20 to 30 minutes, without the need for hospitalization or overnight stay.

REFERENCES

Macular Photocoagulation Study Group. Argon laser photocoagulation for neovascular maculopathy: 5-year results from randomized clinical trials. Arch Ophthalmol 1991;109:1109.

Macular Photocoagulation Study Group. Laser photocoagulation of subfoveal neovascular lesions of age-related macular degeneration: Updated findings from 2 clinical trials. Arch Ophthalmol 1993;111:1200.

Macular Photocoagulation Study Group. Laser photocoagulation for juxtafoveal choroidal neovascularization: 5-year results from randomized clinical trials. Arch Ophthalmol 1994;112:500.

Seddon JM, Ajani UA, Sperduto RD, et al. Dietary carotenoids, vitamins A, C, and E, and advanced age-related macular degeneration. JAMA 1994;272:1413.

Environmental Emergencies

Corey M. Slovis, M.D.

CHAPTER 23–1

Spider Bites

Lindsay Murray, M.B., B.S

Black Widow Spider Envenomation (Latrodectism)

DEFINITION

Black widow spider envenomation is defined as the local and systemic effects that result from envenomation by the black widow spider (*Latrodectus mactans*).

ETIOLOGY

Spiders of the genus *Latrodectus* are found throughout the tropical and temperate regions of the world. Within the United States, they are found in every state except Alaska. *Latrodectus mactans* is the medically most important species in the United States.

Only the female is capable of significant envenomation in humans. She is easily recognized by her shiny black coloration and a characteristic red marking on the ventral abdomen that resembles an hourglass in shape. The body of the adult female never exceeds 1.5 cm in length. The venom consists principally of neurotoxins that act on the presynaptic motor endplate causing excessive release of norepinephrine and acetylcholine into the synaptic space, leading to excessive stimulation and fatigue of motor endplates and muscle.

CRITERIA FOR DIAGNOSIS

Suggestive

The diagnosis is suggested in any person with the characteristic progression of local and systemic symptoms in whom alternative pathology is excluded. The history of a bite, sighting of a spider without identification or history of the patient being in the known or likely habitat of the black widow spider just prior to the development of symptoms, adds weight to the diagnosis. The bite is frequently felt as a small pinprick. The diagnosis can be difficult and is frequently missed when there is no history of a bite.

Definitive

The diagnosis is defined by characteristic progression of local and systemic symptoms following a witnessed spider bite in which positive identification as *L. mactans* is made.

CLINICAL MANIFESTATIONS

Subjective

Onset of symptoms following a bite is delayed from 15 minutes to 6 hours. Most patients present within 2 hours of envenomation. The more severe the envenomation, the shorter the interval until symptom onset.

The initial and most common presenting symptom following black widow spider bite is pain at the bite site. Pain progressively spreads to involve the larger muscles of the affected limb and then the torso, including back and abdominal muscles. Abdominal pain and cramping are frequent presenting symptoms. Lower limb weakness and dyspnea are other common symptoms.

Systemic symptoms develop over the first few hours in more severe envenomations and include headache, nausea and vomiting, diaphoresis, restlessness, dyspnea, and altered mental status.

Objective

Physical Examination

Careful physical examination may reveal a noticeable bite. Characteristically it appears as two small red dots close together with remarkably little local reaction. Local erythema, sweating, and piloerection may also be observed. Alteration in vital signs especially tachycardia, hypertension, and low-grade fever may occur in more severe envenomations. Regional lymphadenopathy may be palpable. A frequently observed sign on physical examination is abdominal tenderness and rigidity.

Routine Laboratory Abnormalities

Laboratory, radiographic, and electrographic studies are of no value in the diagnosis or assessment of the black widow spider bite victim. Their principal utility lies in the inclusion or exclusion of alternative diagnoses and any abnormality is likely to indicate an alternative diagnosis. Leukocytosis and mildly elevated creatine kinase may be seen in more severe cases of envenomation.

PLANS
Diagnostic
Differential Diagnosis

The diagnosis of black widow spider bite is purely clinical as outlined above and based on the history of a bite and development of the typical constellation of symptoms within the expected period. Where the history of a bite is not elicited and a bite not detected (without sufficient clinical suspicion, a bite mark may not be carefully searched for), the diagnosis may prove elusive. Reports of misdiagnosis of latrodectism as an acute abdomen abound. A careful history and physical examination allow differentiation, as true guarding and rebound tenderness are not present in latrodectism. Black widow spider bite must also be considered in the differential diagnosis of the screaming infant. As history of a bite is rarely available in this instance; a careful physical examination looking for local evidence of a bite must be performed. Bites to the scrotum have been misdiagnosed as torsion of the testis.

Recommended Approach

Diagnosis is usually obvious on clinical history and examination even if the spider remains unidentified. In certain clinical presentations, black widow spider bite should be considered in the differential diagnosis of the acute abdomen and local evidence of a bite searched for during the examination. Laboratory and imaging studies are not helpful in confirming the diagnosis but may be useful in excluding alternative diagnoses.

Therapeutic

Treatment for this self-limited condition is essentially supportive and directed at minimizing the severe pain associated with the syndrome. Resuscitative measures are rarely required. Analgesics and muscle relaxants form the basis of pharmacologic therapy.

No effective first-aid measures that can be applied in the field exist. In particular, tourniquets and suction devices are unhelpful. Following initial medical evaluation and resuscitation where necessary, gentle cleansing of the wound should be performed and tetanus prophylaxis administered as indicated. Cold packs or warm baths applied locally may be soothing. Salicylates or other nonsteroidal antiinflammatory agents may be used to provide analgesia in mild envenomations, but opioids are necessary in moderate to severe envenomations. Parenteral morphine is administered under careful direct observation because of the risk of respiratory depression (there may possibly be a synergistic reaction with the neurotoxic venom) and carefully titrated to pain. Relatively large doses may be required to achieve the endpoint of adequate pain control. A benzodiazepine such as diazepam, administered intravenously, is given in conjunction with morphine to reduce the painful muscle cramping. Methocarbamol (Robaxin) intravenously has also been used to achieve muscle relaxation but is probably less effective than diazepam and does not have any of the sedative or anxiolytic side benefits of diazepam. The dose of methocarbamol is 1 g over 5 minutes followed by a further 1 g as an infusion at 100 mg/min. Calcium gluconate 10% solution has also been traditionally used to relieve cramping, although its mechanism of action is unknown. The efficacy of calcium gluconate remains anecdotal and is unsupported by a recent clinical trial. Ten milliliters of 10% calcium gluconate solution is in-

fused with cardiac monitoring in place, over 10 minutes, and repeated after 30 minutes.

Antivenin of equine origin is available as a lyophilized powder with a minimum of 6000 antivenin units per vial. Reconstituted with 2.5 ml of sterile water, 1 or 2 vials are administered as an infusion over 1 hour. Administration should be preceded by a test dose. The antivenin is rapidly effective and curative, resulting in complete resolution of clinical signs and symptoms within an hour of administration. Unfortunately, antivenin administration is associated with a relatively high incidence of acute allergic reaction (9%) and serum sickness (36%) and so its use is unwarranted except in severe or life-threatening cases of envenomation.

FOLLOW-UP

All cases who develop any symptoms need a period of medical observation lasting several hours. At the end of that time mild cases of envenomation may be discharged home with oral analgesia and followed up only if symptoms persist. Patients requiring parenteral opioids and benzodiazepines require hospital admission until that need abates. They then need to be followed medically for symptomatic care during the convalescence period, which may last several weeks. Patients may be safely discharged several hours after successful administration of antivenin provided no manifestations of acute allergic reaction are apparent. Antivenin is curative and patients receiving this therapy do not experience the convalescence period but still need to be followed medically for evidence of serum sickness. This occurs 8 to 12 days following antivenin administration and consists of fever, myalgia, and arthralgia.

DISCUSSION
Prevalence and Incidence

The natural habitat of these spiders is crevices and under cover close to the ground. They are frequently found in stone walls, rubbish piles, barns, and storage sheds where they build irregular untidy webs. The spiders are not aggressive and envenomation usually occurs only when a body part is mistakenly placed close to or into a web. Most bites occur on the extremities, although bites to the buttocks and genitalia were previously common when outhouses were in wider use.

The true incidence of black widow spider bite is unknown but it appears to be responsible for more cases of arachnid-associated morbidity than any other genus of spider. There is a geographic variation in incidence, with relatively more cases occurring in the southern and eastern parts of the nation.

Related Basic Science

Weight-for-weight, the neurotoxic venom of the black widow spider is more potent than that of the pit viper. Fortunately, only tiny amounts of venom (< 0.2 mg) are stored in the venom sac and only a proportion of that amount is injected. Following subcutaneous injection during the bite, the venom spreads through the lymphatics, explaining the observed progression of pain from the bite site, along the bitten limb to the rest of the body.

The venom is a complex mixture of polypeptides and nonprotein components. Certain components bind to gangliosides and glycoproteins in the synapses of motor endplates. This allows channels for sodium influx into neurons to remain open independent of normal action potential propagation. Independent release of acetylcholine and norepinephrine into the synapse occurs and reuptake is simultaneously inhibited. Excessive stimulation of motor endplates follows, resulting in the painful muscle cramping. The pain itself may be due to tissue hypoxia secondary to muscular spasm and hypoxia.

The specific antivenin binds to venom components, thus blocking its ability to bind to the synaptic membrane and effect the above changes. It is prepared from the serum of horses immunized against *Latrodectus* venom and, for this reason, is highly allergenic.

Natural History and Its Modification with Treatment

A great deal of variation is observed in the severity of the envenomation syndrome and this can be explained in terms of venom and host factors. The dose of venom delivered depends on the size of the spider and its venom sacs and the number and depth of the bites. The constituents of the venom vary with *Latrodectus* species and the time of the year. Dose/weight is of course dependent on the victim's size. Patients at the extremes of age or with underlying medical conditions are more likely to experience a severe envenomation syndrome, and almost all fatalities occur in these groups.

Untreated, symptoms peak approximately 2 to 3 hours following the bite and then gradually subside over the following 12 to 48 hours. The mortality is extremely low (<1%) and almost always occurs in the at-risk groups mentioned above. A convalescence is frequently observed and may last weeks to months. It consists of general weakness, fatigue, insomnia, headache, and muscle aches. Eventual complete resolution is the rule. Supportive treatment, as outlined above, reduces the intensity of symptoms but does not shorten their duration. Administration of antivenin effectively terminates the clinical syndrome.

Prevention

Prevention of black widow spider bite centers on destruction of the spider and its favored habitats and the taking of precautions when working in areas that the spiders inhabit. Complete or permanent eradication is almost impossible. When working in woodpiles, barns, or sheds, individuals should wear gloves, shoes, and clothes that cover all limbs.

Cost Containment

Treatment costs are minimized by restricting hospital admission to those patients requiring parenteral narcotics and muscle relaxants for symptom control. Cases of real or suspected black widow spider bite who do not develop symptoms sufficient to warrant these measures within 3 hours of the bite are safely managed on an outpatient basis.

Brown Recluse Spider Envenomation (Loxoscelism)

DEFINITION

Brown recluse spider envenomation is defined as the local and systemic effects that result from envenomation by the brown recluse spider (*Loxosceles reclusa*).

ETIOLOGY

Loxosceles species are found worldwide. The species found within the United States that is of the greatest medical significance, *Loxosceles reclusa,* has a distribution across the southern and central area of the country.

Male and female spiders both cause medically significant envenomation and have similar appearance. These spiders come in various shades of brown, have a body that may reach 1.5 cm in length, and are readily identified by the dark brown violin-shaped marking on the dorsal cephalothorax. The components of the venom have not been completely characterized but include alkaline phosphatase, hyaluronidase, proteases, collagenase, esterases, ribonuclease and deoxyribonuclease, and phospholipase D.

CRITERIA FOR DIAGNOSIS
Suggestive

Development of a skin lesion characteristic of a brown recluse spider bite that progresses over a typical time frame and follows a typical clinical course suggests the diagnosis. The typical lesion is in fact somewhat variable but usually manifests as an area of erythema with an eccentrically placed central papule that enlarges over 24 to 48 hours and then subsequently develops a central area of bluish discoloration which may go on to necrose and slough, forming an ulcer 1 to 2 weeks later. Because of the great variability of the lesion, these bites are often referred to as "possible" or "presumptive" depending on the degree of clinical suspicion.

Definitive

Development of a characteristic skin lesion at the site of a witnessed spider bite where the spider has been positively identified as a brown recluse defines the diagnosis.

CLINICAL MANIFESTATIONS
Subjective

The bite is sometimes felt as a small prick but often goes completely unnoticed. Only in about 10% of cases is a spider actually seen or killed. Within 12 hours of the bite, local burning progressing to severe pain may develop and last several days. Most patients seek medical attention at this point. Associated systemic symptoms may or may not develop and include headache, fever, malaise, anorexia, and arthralgia.

Objective
Physical Examination

The classic local skin lesion that develops following brown recluse spider bite is characteristic but numerous variations exist. The majority of bites, however, result in only minor local skin changes that do not progress to necrosis. Local wound signs usually appear within 12 hours of the bite and include erythema, induration, and blister formation. The area of erythema continues to enlarge for 48 to 72 hours and then regresses. Irregularly shaped, the area of erythema commonly exhibits a gravitational distribution. In more severe bites, a bluish mottled area appears by 48 hours. It is located eccentrically within the area of erythema, often at the original bite site, and may be surrounded by a blanched halo. It is this discolored area that may progress to established necrosis by the end of the first week, with sloughing of tissue to form a necrotic ulcer occurring by the end of the second week.

A fine generalized rash appears transiently in approximately 25% of envenomations and resolves spontaneously over several days. Fever frequently occurs in the first few days after envenomation.

In a very small proportion of patients, predominantly children, a severe delayed and potentially fatal systemic reaction characterized by massive hemolysis occurs several days after the bite. These patients appear acutely unwell with signs of hypovolemic shock.

Routine Laboratory Abnormalities

There is no test diagnostic of loxoscelism. In patients who exhibit cutaneous manifestations only, routine laboratory tests are essentially normal. Multiple laboratory abnormalities may be seen in severe systemic reactions and include low hematocrit, elevated plasma hemoglobin, hematuria, free urinary hemoglobin, and laboratory evidence of acute renal failure and disseminated intravascular coagulation.

PLANS
Diagnostic
Differential Diagnosis

Without the definitive history of a witnessed bite by an identified spider, the diagnosis of brown recluse spider bite remains presumptive based on the typical skin lesion developing over the typical time frame. No serologic or other tests exist to confirm the diagnosis and a broad differential diagnosis of local erythematous and necrotic skin lesions needs to be considered. This includes insect bites, cellulitis, impetigo, foreign bodies, artifactual ulcers, chemical and thermal burns, and vasculitides.

Diagnostic Options and Recommended Approach

Where the definitive diagnosis is made (witnessed bite by identified spider, typical clinical course) no further diagnostic workup is necessary. Urinalysis is a useful screening test for hemolysis associated with severe systemic reactions. Where the diagnosis is one of possible or presumptive brown recluse spider bite (typical lesion, spider not seen), the full differential diagnosis as listed above must be considered. The patient should then be followed clinically; progression of the lesion in the typical fashion strongly supports the diagnosis of brown recluse spider bite.

Therapeutic

Numerous therapies have been advanced to treat the local lesions produced by brown recluse envenomation. All aim to reduce the incidence and severity of the disfiguring dermatonecrotic lesions. Therapies used have included antihistamines, corticosteroids (oral, parenteral, and intradermal), antibiotics, early surgical excision, dapsone, and electric shock therapy. None of these therapies appears to have any influence on the natural course of the lesion with the exception of early surgical excision, which definitely exacerbates the final cosmetic defect and is always contraindicated.

Therapy for the local lesion thus remains essentially conservative. General principles of wound care apply and tetanus prophylaxis is administered if indicated. Ice packs applied to the lesion dramatically reduce local pain and probably impede development of the lesion during the initial 48 hours. They should not remain in place longer than 20 minutes without a break of equal duration, to avoid freezing superficial tissues and enhancing necrosis. It is reasonable to prescribe an antibiotic such as erythromycin or cephalexin (Keflex) to prevent secondary wound infection. Oral analgesics may be required for patient comfort during the first few days. Early surgical excision is definitely contraindicated. Delayed surgical excision of a nonhealing necrotic ulcer may be required at a later date.

A severe systemic reaction requires appropriate resuscitative and supportive care including intravenous fluids and blood component therapy.

FOLLOW-UP

All patients with a definite, presumptive, or suspected brown recluse spider bite should be followed on a regular basis until the lesion heals or they are referred for definitive surgical care of a nonhealing lesion. General wound care may be required during this period. It is appropriate to see them daily or every second day during the first 4 days to monitor for evidence of systemic illness, which may require hospital admission for more intensive supportive care. Children who develop rash and fever following a bite should be admitted for observation and daily platelet, hemoglobin, and hematocrit estimations to look for evidence of hemolysis.

DISCUSSION
Prevalence and Incidence

These spiders are very common in large areas of their range. They prefer warm, dry, and quiet locations and frequently make their homes in attics, closets, sheds, and quiet corners of homes. They are not aggressive and bite only when trapped or crushed against the skin. Humans are commonly bitten while rummaging in closets or sheds or when putting on clothing in which a spider is concealed. Most bites occur on the extremities.

The true incidence of brown recluse spider bite is unknown. The link between brown recluse spider bite and dermatonecrotic lesions was only made in the 1950s. There appears to be a great variation in the severity of the lesions, with only the more severe cases presenting for medical attention. Even of those who present, only a small minority (<10%) develop significant necrotic lesions. These variations almost certainly depend on factors related to the venom (amount and potency), location of the bite (bites over fatty tissue such as on the buttocks or thighs are more likely to result in necrotic lesions), and the immunologic response mounted by the victim. Major systemic illness occurs almost exclusively in children, who of course, on average, receive a greater dose of venom per kilogram of body weight.

Related Basic Science

The components of *Loxosceles* venom have been incompletely characterized. The primary dermatonecrotic factor appears to be sphingomyelinase D. Other components identified include alkaline phosphatase, hyaluronidase, proteases, collagenase, and deoxyribo- and ribonucleases. The local response results from a combination of venom factors and the victim's immunologic response. Histologic examination of necrotic lesion produced by injecting venom into experimental animals reveals extensive neutrophil infiltration, vascular endothelial cell injury, intravascular coagulation, blood vessel wall degeneration, and hemorrhage into surrounding tissues. Liquefaction and abscess formation occur subsequently. Experimental depletion of neutrophils greatly inhibits the development of necrotic lesions. For this reason, dapsone, a potent inhibitor of neutrophil migration, has been proposed as therapy. Its efficacy has yet to be established, and in view of potential side-effects (methemoglobinemia and hemolytic anemia), its routine use cannot be recommended.

Natural History and Its Modification with Treatment

No therapeutic intervention appears to modify the natural history of brown recluse spider bite. Aggressive use of icepacks during the first 48 hours may be of use, but the success of this intervention remains anecdotal. A small proportion of bites progress to local necrosis, sloughing, and ulcer formation. Most heal with conservative wound care although this process may take many weeks. Massive ulcers or cosmetically deforming ulcers require surgical debridement, excision, and grafting, but this should be delayed for a minimum of several weeks.

Severe systemic reactions associated with massive intravascular hemolysis and disseminated intravascular coagulation may be rapidly fatal without aggressive supportive care including fluid and blood product resuscitation and, occasionally, dialysis for renal failure. As the hemolysis is self-limiting, supportive care over a period of several days is lifesaving and complete recovery can be anticipated.

Prevention

As no effective therapy is available, prevention of these bites is the best strategy. Eradication of these spiders from homes is notoriously difficult and heavy spraying is at best only temporarily effective. A more sensible approach is always to shake out boots, shoes, clothing, and blankets before using them and to make noise or vibration on entering attics, basements, or closets to cause these reclusive arachnids to flee.

Cost Containment

Cases of brown recluse spider envenomation without systemic symptoms should be managed as outpatients. The clinician can further reduce costs by resisting the temptation to prescribe, inject, or perform other procedures of doubtful efficacy. Early application of ice packs, simple analgesia, and clinical observation to exclude alternative diagnoses will lead to a good outcome in the majority of cases. Expensive early interventions will not alter the natural history for those few patients destined to develop significant dermatonecrotic lesions.

REFERENCES

Binder LS. Acute arthropod envenomation: Incidence, clinical features and management. Med Toxicol Adverse Drug Experience 1989;4:163.

Clark RF, Wethern-Kestner S, Vance MV, Gerkin R. Clinical presentation and treatment of black widow spider envenomation: A review of 163 cases. Ann Emerg Med 1992;21:782.

Moss HS, Binder LS. A retrospective review of black widow spider envenomation. Ann Emerg Med 1987;16:188.

Wasserman GS, Anderson PC. Loxoscelism and necrotic arachnidism. J Toxicol Clin Toxicol 1984;21:451.

Wilson DC, King LE. Spiders and spider bites. Dermatol Clin 1990;8:277.

CHAPTER 23–2

Snake Envenomations

Donna L. Seger, M.D., A.B.M.T.

DEFINITION

The families Crotalidae (rattlesnake, copperhead, cottonmouth) and Elapidae (coral snake) contain the only poisonous snakes indigenous to the United States. Envenomation occurs when a snake injects venom subcutaneously (most frequent), intradermally, or intramuscularly.

This chapter addresses aspects of Crotalidae envenomation with only broad comments regarding coral snake envenomations. Because of the rarity of coral snake envenomation, a physician with appropriate expertise should be consulted when this envenomation is encountered. (Consultation may be obtained through a regional poison center.)

ETIOLOGY

The majority of envenomations are caused by Crotalidae, also called pit vipers due to their sensing loreal located between the nostril and eyes. The majority of fatal bites due to viper envenomation are caused by the eastern diamondback rattlesnake. Pit viper envenomation may cause either local (necrosis, loss of function, discomfort, scarring) or systemic (hypotension, coagulopathy, seizures, renal failure, and death) effects. Less than 2% of envenomations are caused by the coral snakes of the Elapidae family, whose hallmark is neurotoxicity with minimal local symptoms.

CRITERIA FOR DIAGNOSIS
Suggestive

Any interaction with a snake in which the human questions a bite is suggestive of envenomation. Approximately 20% of Crotalidae venomous snake bites are dry; that is, the snake fails to inject venom on striking. The presence of a fang mark does not predict envenomation. If the patient is asymptomatic and there are no clinical or laboratory abnormalities 4 to 6 hours following the bite, envenomation has not occurred.

Definitive

Envenomation has occurred when edema (with or without ecchymosis or bullae) is present; systemic effects of envenomation are objectively documented; or when laboratory abnormalities consistent with envenomation are noted in a patient with a history of snakebite.

CLINICAL MANIFESTATIONS
The Crotalidae
Subjective

History of the envenomation including time of bite, a description of the snake, whether the snake was killed and brought for identification, what field therapy was provided, any previous administration of horse serum, and the patient's past medical history should be obtained.

Immediate pain in the area of the bite occurs following envenomation of the North American rattlesnake. Weakness, nausea, and tingling or numbness of the tongue, mouth, fingers, and toes are common symptoms after an envenomation. A metallic taste in the mouth, chest pain, and anxiety are frequent complaints following envenomation.

Objective

Physical Examination. Clinical manifestations of envenomation are diverse due to variables such as species of snake; amount of venom injected; age, size, and health of patient; victim's sensitivity to the venom; and time delay between bite and medical treatment. Both local and systemic effects may occur. Bites by pit vipers cause swelling within 20 to 30 minutes which may progress over the ensuing 12 to 24 hours, accompanied by lymphangitis. Following rattlesnake envenoma-

tion, ecchymosis and fluid-filled vesicles usually appear within 3 to 6 hours. The area of the bite may be warm. Because the venom increases capillary fragility, petechiae may be seen.

Systemic effects include chills and sweats, tongue fasciculations, anxiety, and syncope. In severe envenomation, coagulopathies, hypotension, and pulmonary edema occur.

Routine Laboratory Abnormalities. The complete blood count (CBC) frequently is elevated with a left shift. Hemoconcentration may occur initially and may be followed by a falling hematocrit. Abnormal red cell forms may be present on the peripheral smear. Thrombocytopenia may occur and thrombosis has been reported. The presence of a coagulopathy is evidenced by an elevated prothrombin and partial tissue thromboplastin time, a decrease in fibrinogen, and increase in fibrin split products.

Blood and protein may be present in the urine.

In severe envenomation, ischemic changes and arrhythmias may be evident electrocardiographically and pulmonary edema may be present on the chest radiograph.

The Elapidae
Subjective

Envenomation of the coral snake causes minor pain and swelling. Paresthesia and weakness in the area of the bite may occur. Visual disturbances, weakness, increased salivation, and difficulty swallowing may be followed by respiratory failure. Systemic symptoms may be delayed for several hours after a bite, even when no local manifestations are apparent.

Objective

Physical Examination. Although it is considered a "neurotoxin envenomation," local necrosis may occur.

Routine Laboratory Abnormalities. Serum and urine testing is usually without abnormalities.

PLANS
Diagnostic
Differential Diagnosis

Usually a snake has been sighted if one is considering the diagnosis of snake envenomation. The only real differential in making the diagnosis of a snake bite is differentiating a dry bite from a true envenomation.

Diagnostic Options

The diagnosis of envenomation is made based on the clinical examination, systemic effects, and the presence or absence of laboratory abnormalities as previously outlined.

Recommended Approach

Crotalidae. Observing for at least 6 hours and obtaining serum for testing as previously outlined determine the need for antivenin administration.

Elapidae. All patients with potential envenomations should be observed for 48 hours.

Therapeutic
Crotalidae

Although previously recommended, electroshock therapy and cryotherapy are of no benefit and may be detrimental. Incision and suction should be considered only if less than 15 minutes has elapsed since the bite, medical transport is greater than 1 hour, and systemic symptoms are present. The individual performing the procedure must be knowledgeable of the underlying anatomy. An incision through each fang mark ($\frac{1}{4}$ in. long and $\frac{1}{8}$ in. wide) should be made with attention to underlying vascular structures, nerves, and tendons. Suction may then be applied for 15 minutes. Incision and suction are rarely, if ever, indicated.

Basic life support must be provided as a patient is rapidly transported to a health care facility. Apparent lack of symptoms immediately following a bite should not preclude transport. Use of tourniquets is contraindicated. Use of constriction bands is controversial. Although they potentially limit venom access to systemic circulation, the venom may be confined to a local area, causing greater tissue necrosis. A constriction band should be used only if systemic symptoms are present and transport to a medical facility will take a protracted period (>1 hour). The affected limb should be splinted in a functional position and immobilized at or below the level of the heart.

On arrival at an emergency department, an intravenous line should be established and blood obtained for complete blood count, prothrombin time, partial thromboplastin time, fibrinogen, fibrin split products, type and screen, and creatinine phosphokinase.

The circumference of the extremity should be measured at two points proximal to the bite. This measurement should be rechecked hourly for 6 hours. If massive swelling is present, measurements should be performed every 15 minutes. The extremity should be elevated. Placing Kerlix under the upper arm and tying this to an intravenous stand with additional support around the wrist works well.

Meticulous wound care is essential as the snake's mouth contains Gram-negative organisms. Accepted clinical practice includes the administration of prophylactic broad-spectrum antibiotics, although their benefit is controversial. Tetanus prophylaxis is necessary. In most bites, venom is injected subcutaneously and underlying muscle involvement is minimal. Surgical decompression and fasciotomy are unwarranted unless there is evidence of a compartment syndrome as these procedures do not affect intramuscular necrosis.

Although indications for antivenin administration have traditionally been based on the classification of mild, moderate, or severe envenomation, this classification is inconsistent in definition and difficult to use. If only local edema and pain occur and/or edema progression is absent or minimal in the 6 hours following envenomation and laboratory parameters are normal, antivenin is not indicated.

If systemic effects or coagulation parameters are abnormal, 5 to 10 vials of antivenin should be administered to an adult. Children, who have a smaller blood volume as compared with adults, require a greater total dose of antivenin than adults. Reassessment of laboratory parameters dictates the need for more antivenin.

If hypotension, coagulopathy, or coma is present, 15 to 20 vials or more of antivenin may be necessary. Coagulopathies should be treated with antivenin and blood products should be administered only if the patient is unstable or actively bleeding or if the antivenin has not been effective. As snake venoms vary in their effects on the coagulation system, blood product administration should be based on the specific coagulation abnormality.

A skin test should be performed once the decision has been made to administer antivenin. Follow the directions on the package insert carefully. Skin testing should be done only with the horse serum supplied by the Wyeth kit. Skin testing with antivenin is not recommended unless it is diluted at least 1:100. A positive reaction is erythema or pseudopodia within 30 minutes of the intradermal injection. A positive skin test does not preclude antivenin administration. If the skin test is positive, pretreat with diphenhydramine, cimetidine, steroids, *and* dilute antivenin to half-normal concentration (1 vial/100 mL saline). A negative skin test does not guarantee that anaphylaxis will not occur during the infusion. Antivenin should be administered only in the emergency department or intensive care unit in the presence of a physician. Airway equipment, epinephrine, and diphenhydramine should be at the bedside. Venous access should consist of two intravenous large-bore lines.

Five vials of antivenin (10 mL each = 50 mL) are diluted in 250 mL of saline. The vials should be diluted by gentle swirling, *not* shaking. Infusion may then be initiated at 1 mL/h and the rate increased every 5 to 10 minutes until a rate is reached that will infuse the volume over 2

hours. Mild symptoms such as itching and flushing may be treated with diphenhydramine. Anaphylactic reactions mandate discontinuation of the antivenin and treatment with epinephrine and both an H_1 and H_2 blocker. Treatment of hypotension is administration of isotonic fluid followed by vasopressors. Once the patient has been stabilized, it may be necessary to restart the infusion and slowly administer the antivenin, while intravenous epinephrine is simultaneously administered in the opposite extremity.

Acetaminophen or opiate should be administered for pain. Use of aspirin or aspirin-containing products should be avoided due to their potential effects on platelets.

Elapidae

Patients with scratch marks but no puncture wounds should have the wound cleaned, receive tetanus prophylaxis, and be observed for 48 hours. Patients with puncture wounds should be administered antivenin.

Any evidence of envenomation by a coral snake is an indication for antivenin administration. The available antivenin will neutralize venom of the eastern North American coral snake and the Texas coral snake; however, it will not neutralize venom from the Arizona coral snake. The dose of antivenin is 3 to 6 vials diluted in normal saline and administered over an hour. The same precautions should be observed as with pit viper antivenin. Coral snake envenomations are rare. Physicians with expertise in the management of these envenomations should be consulted. Consults are available from the nearest poison center.

FOLLOW-UP

Once the patient has been stabilized, and coagulopathy reversed, wound care is of paramount importance. The area around the bite may become necrotic. Signs of infection must be carefully assessed. Plastic surgery may be necessary, but this should not be done at an early stage.

Occasionally, a delayed thrombocytopenia may occur. Serum platelets should be checked 7 to 10 days following envenomation.

Serum sickness may occur 3 to 14 days following the administration of antivenin. Symptoms include fever, malaise, adenopathy, urticaria, and arthralgia. Treatment consists of symptomatic relief with diphenhydramine plus corticosteroids.

DISCUSSION

Prevalence and Incidence

At least one species of poisonous snake has been found in each state except Alaska, Maine, and Hawaii. The majority of pit viper envenomations occur in the southern United States. The most dangerous rattlesnake, the eastern diamondback, is found in the eastern United States, primarily in pine woods, thickets, and swamps. The timber rattlesnake, the second most dangerous rattlesnake, is found in the hills and mountains of the eastern United States. Pygmy rattlesnakes are found in prairies, swamps, hayfields, woods, rivers, and ponds throughout the United States. Their bite is rarely fatal. Other species include the western rattlesnake, sidewinder, and Mojave rattlesnake. The two species of moccasins, the cottonmouth (aquatic snake) and copperhead (ubiquitous locations), are not as dangerous as the rattlesnakes. The majority of these bites do not result in fatalities, but may cause death if untreated.

Two entirely different coral snakes exist in North America. The eastern coral snake, *Micrurus fulvius,* occupies the southeastern part of the United States and is found only as far west as central Texas. The Arizona or Sonoran coral snake, *Micuroides euryxanthus,* is found in Arizona and a few western areas of New Mexico.

Related Basic Science

Venom. Snake venoms are highly complex mixtures of many proteins and peptides. Locally, they cause vascular epithelial damage (diffuse capillary injury allows massive movement of plasma and red cells out of vessels), inflammation, and tissue necrosis. Systemically, they cause neurotoxicity and coagulopathy.

Antivenin. In 1954, Wyeth Laboratories released the only currently available antivenin for treatment of North American pit viper envenomation. This antivenin is polyvalent, that is, derived from the venom of many species. The antivenin is produced by gradually immunizing horses with a mixture of four venoms and an adjuvant to stimulate their immune system. This antivenin neutralizes the venin of all North and South American pit vipers.

Wyeth Laboratories has produced a specific antivenin for the eastern coral snake. Untreated bites result in a high mortality. Although there is no specific antivenin for the Arizona coral snake, the few recorded bites have not produced fatalities.

Natural History

Without treatment, envenomation can cause death. Coagulopathy, hypotension, seizures, respiratory depression, and renal failure ensue following pit viper envenomation. A few cases of sudden, severe cardiovascular collapse have been reported, theoretically due to intravenous envenomation. When medical care is not available immediately, local sequelae and death occur more frequently. Deaths are associated with no or insufficient antivenin administration. Death is usually delayed and related to the immediate diffuse defects in capillary permeability.

Prevention

Victims that handle snakes are more likely to suffer long-term sequelae than victims of accidental bites. Avoidance of habitats such as deserted buildings, caves, and wood or stone piles decreases one's exposure to snakes. Shoes and gloves should always be worn when in areas with snakes. Reptiles should not be handled until they are positively identified.

Cost Containment

Patients who have suffered a bite from a pit viper may be discharged from the emergency department 6 hours following the bite if there are no local effects and laboratory parameters are normal. If the bite was from a copperhead, the patient may be discharged following a 6-hour observation period if the swelling is not severe and laboratory parameters are normal. If the bite was secondary to a rattlesnake, admission for observation is prudent. If the patient has only local symptoms, admission to the floor is adequate. Reassessment of clotting factors and edema should be addressed as previously outlined. Should the need for antivenin administration occur, the patient should be moved to an intensive care unit. Admission to the appropriate level of care is an important part of cost containment.

REFERENCES

Burgess JL, Dart RC. Snake venom coagulopathy: Use and abuse of blood products in the treatment of pit viper envenomation. *Ann Emerg Med* 1991;20:796.

Dart RC, McNally JT, Spaite DW, Gustafson R. The sequelae of pitviper envenomations. In: Brodie, Campbell J Jr, eds. Biology of pitvipers. Tyler: Selva, 1992.

Garfin SR, Castilonia RR, Mubarak SJ, et al. The effect of antivenin on intramuscular pressure elevations induced by rattlesnake venom. *Toxicon* 1985;23:677.

Gold BS, Barish RA. Venomous snakebites: Current concepts in diagnosis, treatment, and management. *Environ Emerg* 1992;10:249.

Russell FC. Snake venom poisoning. *Vet Hum Toxicol* 1991;33:584.

CHAPTER 23–3

Hypothermia

Corey M. Slovis, M.D.

DEFINITION

Hypothermia is defined as a core temperature of less than 35°C (95°F).

ETIOLOGY

Hypothermia is usually caused by exposure to cold temperatures for a prolonged period. Intoxicated alcoholics and the homeless are the two most common patient types likely to present with hypothermia. Other clinical settings include patients with acute myocardial infarction, myxedema coma, sepsis, and hypoglycemia.

CRITERIA FOR DIAGNOSIS
Suggestive

The single most important clue to making the diagnosis of hypothermia is a reading of 34° to 35°C on a standard thermometer. Unless the physician requests a special glass thermometer or thermal probe designed to register low temperatures, the depth of the patient's low core temperature may be missed. Other findings suggestive of hypothermia include unexplained lethargy, altered mental status, hypoglycemia in a nondiabetic patient, hypotension, wet clothing, and lack of shivering in a patient who feels cool or cold to the physician's touch.

Definitive

Hypothermia is definitely diagnosed by the finding of a core temperature (rectal, esophageal, or tympanic) less than 35°C (95°F).

CLINICAL MANIFESTATIONS
Subjective

The classic history of a hypothermic patient is prolonged exposure to a cold environment without adequate clothing or heat source. Exposure to wind or moisture is an important environmental variable and is synergistic with low temperatures in the induction of hypothermia.

The most important early finding (other than the hypothermia itself) is confusion or declining mentation. Unfortunately, there are no subjective data that are specific for the diagnosis of hypothermia. The patient with moderate to severe hypothermia frequently is unable to give a coherent history. If the history can be obtained, the patient or someone accompanying her or him may relate any number of neurologic sign–symptom complexes, including progressive confusion, slurred speech, abnormalities of gait, focal weakness, sensory loss, intermittent paralysis, and hallucinations.

Past history may include a prior history of hypothermia, hypothyroidism, endocrine disease, pituitary surgery, or sepsis.

Although family history is usually not contributory, a family history of thyroid disease or other endocrine disorders should be investigated.

Objective
Physical Examination

The critical abnormal physical finding in hypothermia is a core temperature below 35°C; however, most standard thermometers record only to 34° to 35°C, allowing lower temperatures to be missed by the clinician.

Additionally, a normal temperature may be recorded erroneously if a glass thermometer is not completely shaken down or if an oral temperature is used. Such problems may be overcome by using thermometers that record to significantly lower temperatures or by using rectal, esophageal, or tympanic membrane probes.

The hypothermic patient is usually a subdued, nonshivering patient, as shivering is rarely present in patients with a temperature below 35°C. The patient's physical appearance is nonspecific, although often he or she may appear corpselike owing to pallor and lack of spontaneous motion. The skin may have blotchy areas of erythema or purpura. Bullae have been reported and are most common over pressure-dependent areas. The skin is cold to touch unless a warming blanket has obscured this helpful sign. Signs of trauma, evidence of needle use or abuse, and stigmata of frostbite should be searched for.

Early in hypothermia the pulse rate is elevated, but as the body temperature falls, so does the heart rate. Severely hypothermic patients have bradycardia, reflecting significantly depressed ventricular responsiveness. Heart rates of 40 beats/min are not uncommon in these patients. The blood pressure reacts similarly. At first there is an elevation in blood pressure; however, as hypothermia progresses, the blood pressure falls. Hypotension is to be expected as the body temperature falls. Respiratory rates do not fall until the patient is significantly hypothermic.

The pulmonary examination may reveal findings consistent with bronchopneumonia or aspiration. The cardiac examination is similarly nonspecific, although bradycardia or findings of atrial fibrillation (or flutter) with a slow ventricular response may be elicited. Examination of the peripheral pulses reveals cold skin, and little or no pulse pressure is perceived. One must remember that an icy cold corpse with no pulse may not be a corpse at all—yet. Abdominal examination reveals decreased or absent bowel sounds. Palpation is nonspecific but may show rigidity or areas of tenderness. The extremities, ears, and nares should be examined for evidence of frostbite.

The neurologic examination often is replete with nonlocalizing findings. The mental status declines in conjunction with the fall in core temperature. Most patients with early hypothermia are alert but confused; this confusion progresses to lethargy and then to response to pain only. The final phases of hypothermia are marked by progressively deeper levels of coma. Flat-line electroencephalograms have been reported. Other findings include tremor, parkinsonian-like rigidity, and ataxic gait. Reflexes are usually depressed or absent, but pathologic (so-called frontal release) signs may be observed. Seizures, both focal and generalized, have been reported.

Routine Laboratory Abnormalities

Electrolyte abnormalities in the hypothermic patient include evidence of hemoconcentration, metabolic acidosis, and hyper- or hypoglycemia. The blood urea nitrogen and creatine levels are usually elevated, whereas the serum bicarbonate level is depressed. These abnormalities reflect decreased renal and peripheral perfusion. Hypoglycemia may cause hypothermia, but in an initially euthermic, normoglycemic patient, the onset of hypothermia induces hyperglycemia. Alterations in coagulability range from thrombosis to the syndrome of disseminated intravascular coagulation. Pancreatitis has been reported in up to 50% of all hypothermic patients. Additionally, because there may be marked muscle injury, the possibility of rhabdomyolysis with resultant myoglobinuric renal failure must be kept in mind.

Chest radiographs are often abnormal, with atelectasis and poor inspiratory effort very common findings. Pneumonia with either a bacterial or aspiration pattern may be seen.

Cardiovascular irritability is the number one cause of death in the hypothermic patient. Therefore, it is not surprising that multiple electrocardiographic abnormalities are noted in such patients. These include early onset of sinus tachycardia followed by the more common sinus bradycardia, muscle tremor artifact, atrial fibrillation, prolonged QT interval, QRS prolongation, ventricular fibrillation, and so-called *Osborn wave* (Figure 23–3–1). Osborn waves, or the prominent notch on the downstroke of the QRS deflection, are pathopneumonic of hypothermia.

Arterial blood gas determination should always be performed. Hypoxia is one of the prime risk factors for the development of ventricular fibrillation. Acidosis may be seen; clinically significant hypercarbia is rare in all but the most severe cases of hypothermia.

PLANS
Diagnostic
Differential Diagnosis

The diagnosis of hypothermia is made by a measured core temperature below 35°C.

Many of the victims are alcoholics; they present with the usual history of binge drinking, passing out, and spending a prolonged period in a cold environment. There are, however, multiple etiologies to consider. These fall into the major categories of exposure, drug-induced, endocrine or metabolic, central nervous system dysfunction, and miscellaneous (Table 23–3–1).

Recommended Approach

The initial treatment of hypothermia is securement of the airway, breathing, and cardiovascular stability and the administration of glucose, naloxone, and thiamine as indicated. The patient should be started on high-flow oxygen until heated mist is available. If the patient's respiratory efforts are compromised or deemed inadequate, gentle and careful endotracheal intubation should be performed. This author recommends intravenous premedication with lidocaine in an effort to decrease the risk of ventricular fibrillation prior to intubation. The lidocaine should be topically applied after being intravenously administered slowly over 30 seconds at a dose of 1.5 mg/kg. Once the airway and breathing are secured, electrocardiographic monitoring should be instituted immediately. An intravenous line should be secured and 5% dextrose in normal saline initially started at 150 mL/h. Its rate should be adjusted based on blood pressure, age of the patient, and response to therapy.

Hypothermia is often seen in ethanol abusers who are either hypoglycemic or have poor glucose reserves. If hypoglycemia is present, hypertonic dextrose 50% dextrose in water at a dose of 1 mL/kg should be administered. If the patient is not hypoglycemic, the intravenous fluid chosen must contain glucose. Thiamine should be administered at the initiation of the patient's intravenous line to any alcoholic or cachectic patient.

The dose of intravenous thiamine is 100 mg. Intramuscular thiamine is of little value secondary to the poor peripheral muscle perfusion in hypothermia. Narcotic overdoses may coincide with or confound the diagnosis of hypothermia; thus, a minimum of 2.0 mg intravenous naloxone should be administered to any hypothermic patient with a depressed level of consciousness. If the patient responds, additional naloxone may be required. If the patient has any prior history of thyroid disease, steroids and thyroid supplementation should be given immediately.

Diagnostic Options

There are no diagnostic options other than those tests and observations listed under Differential Diagnosis for determining the etiology of hypothermia. There has been much debate as to whether blood gases should be temperature-corrected prior to interpretation. Some authors had recommended lowering the measured PO_2 by 7.2% per degree centigrade fall in body temperature and the PCO_2 by 4.4% per degree centigrade fall in body temperature and raising the measured pH by 0.015 for each degree fall in body temperature. It is now generally accepted that the arterial blood gases should be interpreted without any corrections. This is because the results obtained better reflect the blood's pH and availability of oxygen in hypothermic tissue.

Recommended Approach

The etiology of the patient's hypothermia can usually be rapidly ascertained as the patient is being stabilized. In general, routine laboratory tests should be obtained as the patient's intravenous lines are initiated.

Routine laboratory studies in the hypothermic patient should include electrolyte analysis; pancreatic, hepatic, and renal function indices; and a hematologic profile, including platelet and coagulation parameters.

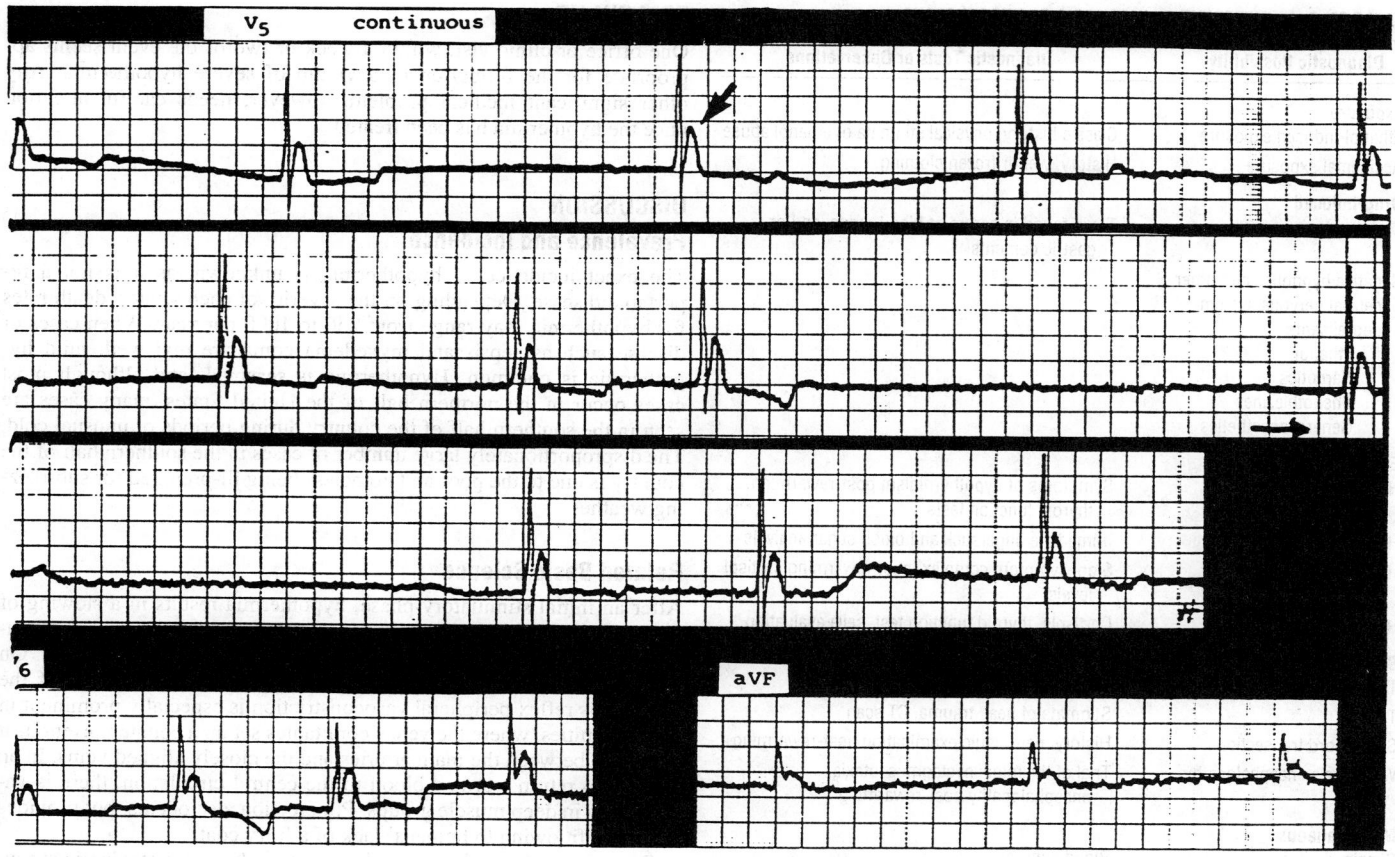

Figure 23–3–1. Classic electrocardiographic findings in a patient with hypothermia (body temperature 75°F). Present are the atrial fibrillation with very slow ventricular response; muscle tremor (shiver) artifact; prolonged QRS duration with prominent J or Osborn waves (*arrow*); and prolonged QT interval. In some patients a sinus bradycardia may be present rather than atrial fibrillation. *(This electrocardiogram was provided by Dr. John H. Stone III.)*

Essential also are a chest x-ray, electrocardiogram (with subsequent continuous monitoring), urine analysis, and arterial blood gases. Additional specialized diagnostic tests are discussed under Differential Diagnosis.

Therapeutic

Therapeutic Options

The methods chosen to rewarm hypothermic patients are not usually agreed on. The forms of therapy fall into three general categories: external, noninvasive (blankets, warm water immersion, etc.); internal, invasive (peritoneal dialysis, warm water lavage, etc.); and heated mist (by nebulizer or endotracheal tube).

No one method is clearly superior for patients who present with temperatures above 32°C, who are not in cardiopulmonary arrest, or who have alcohol-induced hypothermia. It appears that good supportive care with constant monitoring and noninvasive warming, including warmed (but not hot) blankets, is the most rational approach. As supplemental oxygen is administered, it should be heated and delivered as a warm mist. Pulmonary burns, a reported complication, are eliminated as long as inspired oxygen is kept between 40° and 45°C.

A problem in the treatment of hypothermia is "afterdrop." That is, as rewarming of the periphery occurs, cold blood is delivered to the central circulation and may drop the core temperature by up to 2°C. Because this method may predispose the patient to ventricular fibrillation, it should not be the sole method of rewarming in a critically ill, severely hypothermic patient. Various methods have been developed to warm the core and avoid mobilization of the blood pooled in the colder periphery. These methods include peritoneal dialysis and warm water lavage of the stomach, rectum, and/or mediastinum.

There is no significant difference in survival when any method of re-

warming is used in "relatively stable" patients. In patients who are below 30° to 32°C, there is a significant risk of ventricular fibrillation and failure of some methods to rewarm safely and quickly enough. Heated mist by endotracheal tube should be the initial rewarming method of choice for severely hypothermic patients. Peritoneal lavage with warm lavage fluids should be quickly and carefully initiated for severely hypothermic patients who do not begin to rewarm at a rate of at least 1°C per hour. Peritoneal lavage should be used in all unstable patients. Fluid exchanges should be as rapid as possible to maximize the rate of rewarming. Optimal rates of rewarming may be obtained by using the largest peritoneal catheter available or by using more than one catheter to allow a constant flow of warmed fluids in and cooler fluids out. Life-threatening hypothermia is best managed by cardiopulmonary bypass or other methods of extracorporeal rewarming if readily available. Unstable or severely hypothermic patients should always be carefully orally intubated and receive 100% oxygen by heated mist.

There are certain specific situations in which more than one method of rewarming needs to be used. These situations include patients who do not respond to heated mist, patients with life-threatening myocardial depression or arrhythmias, and patients in cardiac arrest. It is imperative that one be aware that a hypothermic heart is relatively unresponsive to atropine, epinephrine, antiarrhythmic agents, cardioversion, and transvenous pacing. In addition, these drugs and maneuvers may increase the likelihood of ventricular fibrillation. In the special circumstances just mentioned, rapid rewarming by multiple invasive means coupled with heated mist has lifesaving application. These groups of patients should be lavaged through a large-bore orogastric tube with warm tap water and have peritoneal dialysis with warmed fluids instituted. Survival from hypothermic cardiac arrests without neurologic sequelae have been reported in patients who have been rewarmed by open cardiac massage, supplemented by warmed mediastinal irrigation, and

TABLE 23–3–1. DIFFERENTIAL DIAGNOSIS OF HYPOTHERMIA

Diagnostic Possibility	Diagnostic Tests or Observations
Exposure	
Ethanol-induced exposure	Classic history, physical stigmata of ethanol abuse
Accidental exposure	History, wet or frozen clothing
Drug-induced	
Barbiturates	Toxin found in serum of blood, urine, and/or gastric contents
Sedative hypnotics and other central nervous system depressants	
Ethanol	
Narcotics	
Phenothiazines	
General anesthetics	
Endocrine or Metabolic	
Hypothyroidism	Symptoms of hypothyroidism post-rewarming, thyroid function tests
Hypoglycemia	Immediate fingerstick and blood sugar analysis
Hypoadrenalism	Sign–symptom complex, post-rewarming cortisol levels
Hypopituitarism	Cortisols, thyroid function test, sella evaluation
Central Nervous System Dysfunction	
Tumor	CT scan
Trauma	Stigmata of head trauma, CT scan
Spinal cord transection	History, neurologic examination post-rewarming
Wernicke's encephalopathy	Trial of thiamine; nystagmus, ataxia, encephalopathy post-rewarming
Miscellaneous	
Sepsis	Blood cultures
Starvation	Stigmata of protein-caloric malnutrition
Surgical induction	History
Burns	Physical examination
Erythrodermas	Physical examination
Spontaneous periodic hypothermia	History
Acute myocardial infarction	Electrocardiogram

CT scan, computed tomography.

in patients who were placed on bypass. Rapid initiation of cardiopulmonary bypass offers the best chance for survival in hypothermic cardiac arrests.

The sometimes profound hypothermia seen in drug overdoses, especially barbiturate intoxication, requires special mention. This is one of the entities in which dialysis is truly superior to external rewarming. The warm dialysate not only rewarms the patient but also increases excretion of the toxin. This is especially true of patients with phenobarbital overdose, in whom bicarbonate may be added to peritoneal dialysate to hasten excretion.

There has been some work concerning the prophylactic administration of ventricular antiarrhythmic agents in hypothermia, especially bretylium. At present there is no definite evidence supporting the routine prophylactic use of any antiarrhythmic agent.

In summary, the treatment of hypothermia centers on recognizing it; securing the airway, breathing, and cardiac status; assessing for and treating hypoglycemia and administering naloxone and thiamine as indicated; gathering baseline laboratory values while assessing the etiology of the hypothermia; and rewarming the patient.

If hypothermia is present, aggressive management can be rewarded by high rates of survival. At the time of this writing, a patient with a core temperature of 16°C and in ventricular fibrillation holds the record for surviving the lowest recorded temperature and recovering completely. It appears that patients with serum potassium levels in excess of 10 mEq/L have no chance for survival.

FOLLOW-UP

One office or clinic visit within a week or two of the event seems appropriate for the follow-up of a victim of severe hypothermia. Any other significant medical problem, however, needs careful attention once the hyothermia has been treated.

DISCUSSION

Prevalence and Incidence

The exact incidence of hypothermia is unknown, as it is not a reportable disease. Depending on the severity of each winter, death rates for hypothermia may range from 250 to 1000 per year. When cases of disease such as sepsis and myxedema coma are reviewed, mild hypothermia is common. Hypothermia is seasonal, and although most cases occur in the northern half of the United States, many cases are seen in the southern half of the country during periods of unusual cold. The disproportionately large number of cases in the southern half of the country is due to the poor and homeless being ill-prepared for subfreezing weather.

Related Basic Science

After an initial stimulatory phase, hypothermia results in a slowing of all bodily functions and metabolic rates. In an attempt to maintain euthermia, the body employs both physical and chemical modalities. On cold exposure, blood is shifted from peripheral to core areas of the body. This reflex peripheral vasoconstriction is especially prominent in the extremities, where the venae comitantes set up a countercurrent heat exchange between the main arteries and the closely aligned veins. In an attempt to return warmed blood to the central circulation, there is vasodilation in deep muscle groups. Piloerection also occurs, but provides little benefit owing to humans' lack of a furry coat.

Once these physical changes have taken place, hypothalamic stimulation mobilizes the remainder of the available body defenses. Sympathetic stimulation elevates the heart rate and increases cardiac output. Stimulation of the lateral hypothalamus results in phasic muscular contractions commonly referred to as shivering. Shivering has the inherent property of increasing muscular heat production by 10- to 20-fold. Unfortunately, heat generated by this means is eventually lost by convection into the environment. Once the body temperature falls below 35°C, shivering is rarely maintained. Lastly, hypothalamically mediated neuroendocrine stimulation occurs. Via central pathways, the adrenal medulla responds with significant catecholamine release, and the thyroid elevates the basal metabolic rate. Cerebral blood flow falls about 6 to 7% per degree centigrade.

As core temperatures fall below 35°C, the body's defenses are muted and a gradual depression is seen in all organ system functions. By the time a core temperature of 28°C has been reached, the basal metabolic rate is about 50% of normal and the patient is almost always hypotensive, sometimes profoundly so.

The cardiovascular effects of hypothermia have been well researched. Between 32° and 35°C, tachycardia usually is present along with muscle tremor; however, patients with temperatures below this range usually are bradycardic with sinus or junctional rhythms or may be in atrial fibrillation with a slow ventricular response. The electrocardiogram, as mentioned, will reflect these changes along with a prolonged QRS duration, a prolonged QT interval, and a slowly inscribed terminal portion of the QRS complex (J or Osborn wave). The etiology of this wave is still unknown, but it is considered pathognomonic. Systemic vascular resistance increases two to three times the normal value as the hypothermia progresses. In patients who are septic and hypothermic, the systemic vascular resistance is decreased. As noted previously, ventricular irritability is the major cause of death in victims of hypothermia. Ventricular fibrillation is seen most commonly between the temperatures of 28° and 32°C.

Changes in blood viscosity are revealed by a significant hemoconcentration of up to 173% at 25°C compared with baseline measurements at 37°C. The gastrointestinal tract responds with a generalized shutdown. Clinical or subclinical pancreatitis is common during recovery from hypothermia. The glomerular filtration rate and renal blood flow are markedly diminished because of much shunting, and below 27°C they are at a minimum.

Both hyperglycemia and hypoglycemia have been reported in hypothermic patients. Hyperglycemia is caused by the glucocorticoids released early in the cooling phase. The elevated blood glucose level is poorly handled, as hypothermia directly inhibits insulin release. The relationship between hypoglycemia and hypothermia is quite different. Hypoglycemia causes hypothermia via a centrally acting, hypothalamically mediated mechanism. The hypothermia seen in hypoglycemic patients appears to serve a protective cortical purpose, as it lowers the cerebral oxygen demand in addition to decreasing the cerebral blood flow. It is important to note that alcoholics are thus prone to two causes of hypothermia, and at times both hypoglycemia and exposure may work synergistically.

Natural History and Its Modification with Treatment

The morbidity of hypothermia is correlated with the severity of fall in body temperature. After an initial period of hyperexcitability, there is a slowing in all organ systems. Major morbidity is cardiopulmonary in nature. Aspiration pneumonia is not uncommon, although the major complications of this disease are cardiac in nature. The incidence of symptomatic sinus bradycardia and atrial fibrillation increases as the core temperature falls below 35°C. Serious cardiovascular complications due to ventricular arrhythmias are rare in cases above 32°C.

The mortality of hypothermia ranges from less than 10% to more than 80%. This wide disparity is due to the different patient populations studied. If one looks at hypothermia in patients with myxedema coma, 80 to 90% mortality is the rule. Hypothermia, in fact, portends death in myxedema; however, large studies using predominantly alcoholics reveal mortality rates of 5 to 10%. It has been concluded in multiple studies that mortality is based not solely on absolute temperature but also on the presence or absence of underlying diseases.

Prevention

The key to successful treatment of hypothermia lies in its prevention. Thus, alcoholic patients should be encouraged not to spend cold nights unsheltered; hikers and mountaineers should be taught the early warning signs of hypothermia and should wear appropriate clothing; and lastly, the elderly, who are predisposed to hypothermia, must be taught prevention.

Hypothermia can also be prevented by active patient education in areas of cold climate. Early warning signs should be public knowledge. No elderly individuals should be left in unheated homes.

Cost Containment

In patients with mild hypothermia, aggressive emergency department care can result in admittance to a general ward bed or discharge. Early heated mist and blankets may obviate the need for an intensive care unit bed. Prior to the initiation of costly invasive therapeutic modalities (e.g., peritoneal dialysis), the physician should determine whether noninvasive therapy and heated mist might work just as well. Invasive care should be reserved for nonresponders, severe hypothermia, and the special cases previously discussed.

Prolonged stays in the intensive care unit, once the patient in stable and rewarmed, are not indicated. In classic exposure cases and in the street person or chronic alcoholic, workups for endocrine dysfunction should not be undertaken unless extenuating circumstances exist.

REFERENCES

Bierens JJ, van der Velde EA, van Berkel M, van Zanten JJ. Submersion in The Netherlands: Prognostic indicators and results of resuscitation. Ann Emerg Med 1990;19:1390.

Danzl DF, Pozos RS. Multicenter hypothermia survey. Ann Emerg Med 1987;16:1042.

Danzl DF, Pozos RS. Accidental hypothermia. N Engl J Med 1994;331:1756.

Jolly BT, Ghezzi KT. Accidental hypothermia. Emerg Med Clin North Am 1992;10:311.

Morris DL, Chambers HF, Morris MG, Sande MA. Hemodynamic characteristics of patients with hypothermia due to occult infection and other causes. Ann Intern Med 1985;102:153.

Weinberg AD. Hypothermia. Ann Emerg Med 1993;22(pt 2):370.

CHAPTER 23–4

Heat Stroke

Corey M. Slovis, M.D.

DEFINITION

Heat stroke is defined as a core temperature in excess of 40.6°C (105°F). Heat-related illnesses include heat exhaustion, heat cramps, malignant hyperthermia, and the neuroleptic malignant syndrome. Heat exhaustion is a syndrome of mild central nervous system and generalized body dysfunction seen in patients exposed to warm and/or humid climates. Heat cramps are painful skeletal muscle contractions that occur during strenuous activity in warm and/or humid environments. Malignant hyperthermia is a syndrome of rapidly rising core temperatures seen in patients who have received any of a number of halogenated anesthetic agents, including halothane, methoxyflurane, cyclopropane, and ethyl ether, or any of the muscle relaxants, notably succinylcholine. The neuroleptic malignant syndrome is a syndrome of rising body temperature as a complication of neuroleptic (antipsychotic) drug use.

ETIOLOGY

Heat stroke, heat exhaustion, and heat cramps are seen in situations of high ambient temperatures or whenever heat dissipation is impaired. Malignant hyperthermia is seen in the operating room or recovery area after anesthetic administration. The neuroleptic malignant syndrome is seen in patients taking neuroleptic medications.

CRITERIA FOR DIAGNOSIS
Suggestive

The clue to diagnosis common to all these entities (with the exception of heat cramps) is an elevated body or skin temperature. Declining mentation or increasing weakness during exercise is an important clue to diagnosing heat exhaustion and heat stroke. A rapidly rising body temperature usually associated with an increasing pulse and a labile blood pressure in the operating room should provide the necessary information to make a diagnosis of malignant hyperthermia. A family history of similar episodes or sudden unexpected death during anesthesia is highly suggestive of this syndrome. An unexplained or rising temperature in a stiff, noncommunicative patient who is maintained on antipsychotic (neuroleptic) drugs should alert the physician to the diagnosis of neuroleptic malignant syndrome.

Definitive

There is no test or finding that definitively diagnoses any of the three environmental heat-related syndromes: heat cramps, heat exhaustion, and heat stroke. The definitive diagnosis of heat cramps and heat exhaustion is one of exclusion. A definitive diagnosis of heat stroke is generally accepted as an elevated body temperature with the appropriate clinical setting and the exclusion of all diseases that might lead to a febrile state. A definitive diagnosis of neuroleptic malignant syndrome may be elusive. It is generally accepted as the triad of hyperthermia, stiffness, and antipsychotic medication use which disappears after acute therapy and discontinuation of the offending medication. Muscle biopsy definitely diagnoses malignant hyperthermia. Most experts, however, accept a rising body temperature, increasing rigidity, acidosis, and increasing oxygen consumption during the induction of anesthesia as a definitive diagnosis of malignant hyperthermia.

CLINICAL MANIFESTATIONS

Subjective

The patient with heat cramps gives the characteristic history of slow or abrupt onset of pain and cramps in a major muscle group, most often in the calves during strenuous exercise in hot weather. The patient is lucid, and although the patient may report fatigue or thirst, the history is otherwise nondescript. There is no history of trauma or other physical injury. Heat cramps are seen often in persons in good physical condition, although they are more common early in training, especially in well-muscled individuals.

The history elicited in heat exhaustion and heat stroke always includes an exposure to a warm (and often humid) environment; therefore, the search for this historical bit of information is imperative. The patient may complain of generalized weakness, headache, or dizziness. A recent episode of syncope may be described. Gastrointestinal symptoms of nausea and vomiting may complicate or dominate the history. The patient may not complain of thirst or of feeling warm or hot, especially if she or he is more severely affected. The history should include a search for any of the predisposing risk factors in heat stroke (Table 23–4–1).

There is rarely any prior subjective history in patients with malignant hyperthermia. This disease may be transmitted by either an autosomal dominant or another incompletely understood method; therefore, one should always inquire about a family history of anesthetic reactions or sudden death during or just after an operative procedure. In addition, every patient must be specifically questioned about any prior anesthetic or intraoperative problems.

There is rarely any available history from the patient with the neuroleptic malignant syndrome. A case worker or psychiatrist may either alert the clinician to an unexplained fever or request a consultation secondary to increasing lethary and obtundation.

Patients who have had prior episodes of any type of heat-related illness are at increased risk for subsequent episodes. Thus, all patient histories should include questioning related to problems with heat dissipation. Patients should always be asked about any past history of problems during local or general anesthesia.

Because malignant hyperthermia may be genetically transmitted, patients should always be asked about relatives who had unusual or "allergic" reactions during or just prior to surgery.

Objective

Physical Examination

The physical examination of a victim with heat cramps is usually nonspecific. The patient may or may not demonstrate a contracted muscle or muscle group.

The most common cause of heat-related illness is physical exertion in a warm and humid environment. Table 23–4–1 contains a more complete listing of the most common causes of heat-related illness.

Heat exhaustion and heat stroke are considered a continuum, and symptoms differ only in degree of severity.

Early examination of the skin shows signs of the hyperemia of cutaneous vasodilation; as the disease progresses, pallor may become apparent. Sweating, or the lack of it, is an important clue to heat-related illnesses. The less severely stricken patients often are markedly diaphoretic. It is important, however, to realize that victims of heat stroke may present with differing skin states. If heat stroke is acute in onset (exertional heat stroke), the athlete, usually a runner, is covered in sweat. If the onset is subacute, such as in a football player, then the skin is usually, but not invariably, hot and dry. When the victim develops the classic form of heat stroke with an insidious onset over a number of hours or days, as in the bedridden elderly patient without access to hydration, the skin is parched and hot.

The patient presents with tachycardia because of both increased metabolic rate and accompanying dehydration. Respirations are usually rapid and shallow. The cardiopulmonary examination is nonspecific. Initially, there are signs of increased cardiac output. Later, with failure of heat regulatory mechanisms in association with dehydration and decreased intravascular volume, there are diminished heart sounds and thready peripheral pulses. Shock may be seen in severe cases.

Although the neurologic examination is nonspecific, at times it may dominate the clinical picture. The patient may present with confusion, disorientation, delirium, or hyperactivity. As the illness progresses, seizures and coma may ensue. Unfortunately, there are no specific neurologic findings in heat-related illnesses, and although they may point toward the correct diagnosis, they also may lead the clinician astray. Unless permanent brain damage has ensued, the host of focal findings that are initially present disappear with therapy.

The objective findings that enable the physician to make an early diagnosis of malignant hyperthermia are somewhat more specific. As the patient goes deeper into anesthesia, he or she becomes more rigid rather than more relaxed. Additionally, instead of a slowing of heart rate, tachycardia can become quite pronounced. These signs may be misinterpreted as representing either hypoxia or the need for additional anesthesia; yet, neither more oxygen nor anesthetic will lessen the symptoms. Other nonspecific objective signs include an early erythematous flush of the skin, which rapidly changes to mottling, acute left ventricular failure, and excessive bleeding.

The physical examination of a patient with the neuroleptic malignant

TABLE 23–4–1. MOST COMMON CAUSES OF HEAT-RELATED ILLNESS

Environmental Risks	Diseases with Increased Heat Production	Drugs and Medications	Inability to Dissipate Heat Normally	Sweat Gland Abnormalities
Heavy or prolonged exertion	Alcohol withdrawal	*Increased metabolic activity*	Debilitation	Burns
High ambient temperature	Delirium and encephalopathy	Amphetamines	Dehydration	Cystic fibrosis
High ambient humidity	Febrile states	Cocaine	Heavy or layered clothing	Scleroderma
	Hyperthyroidism and thyroid storm	Hallucinogens	Infancy	
	Malignancy		Obesity	
	Status seizures	*Decreased heat dissipation*	Old Age	
	Sepsis	Anticholinergic agents		
		Beta blockers		
		Diuretics		
		Phenothiazines		
		Tricyclic antidepressants		
		Vasodilation and exposure to radiant energy		
		Alcohol		
		Peripheral vasodilators		

syndrome reveals a febrile patient with stiff, rigid muscles and an altered mental status, which may fluctuate. Diaphoresis, labile blood pressure, and extrapyramidal effects may be present or pronounced. Rigidity is the key physical finding that differentiates the neuroleptic malignant syndrome from heat stroke and other febrile states.

Routine Laboratory Abnormalities

There are no laboratory abnormalities consistently seen in patients with heat cramps. Patients may occasionally be hypokalemic, hyponatremic, and/or hypomagnesemic, but these deficiencies (especially hyponatremia) are not common. Laboratory findings in patients with heat exhaustion show evidence of dehydration and hemoconcentration. There are no other striking abnormalities. Conversely, patients with heat stroke or the later stages of malignant hyperthermia and the neuroleptic malignant syndrome have a myriad of abnormalities that reflect damage to all major organ systems.

Laboratory evaluation of these severely ill patients reveals evidence of dehydration, which may be profound. Serum sodium levels are usually normal, but may be depressed if earlier efforts at rehydration used water only. Hypernatremia is also seen, especially in elderly patients who may develop a combined syndrome of dehydration and heat stroke over a period of days. Serum potassium levels may be within normal limits. Hyperkalemia secondary to acidosis and tissue destruction or hypokalemia secondary to respiratory alkalosis and/or due to increased losses via sweat may be seen. Serum bicarbonate levels are almost always significantly depressed secondary to high lactate levels. Glucose values are usually elevated, but hypoglycemia should always be ruled out. Serum calcium and phosphorus levels are usually normal but may be significantly depressed. Hypocalcemia secondary to sequestration in injured muscle and hypophosphatemia secondary to hyperventilation are not uncommon. Hypercalcemia is rare but may be seen in states of marked dehydration. Hematologic parameters usually reveal a leukocytosis that can be in excess of 30,000 white blood cells/μL. The syndrome of disseminated intravascular coagulation is often present and, in some cases, dominates the clinical picture. The important laboratory values seen in heat stroke are summarized in Table 23–4–2.

PLANS
Diagnostic
Differential Diagnosis

The patient who presents with a history of decreasing mentation and high work output with low fluid intake in a hot environment needs little, if any, time spent on differential diagnosis. In the elderly, however, particularly those receiving diuretic therapy, heat stroke may be quite insidious. Also, a number of other disease processes may present with temperatures above 40.5°C (105°F) (Table 23–4–3).

Diagnostic Options and Recommended Approach

Patients presenting with life-threatening temperature elevations should be rapidly treated and not undergo elaborate diagnostic workups. Laboratory tests should be performed as the patient is cooled. Blood work should be drawn for an immediate fingerstick glucose, electrolytes, serum chemistries, complete blood count including platelets, clotting studies (prothrombin time and partial thromboplastin time), and an arterial blood gas (see Table 23–4–2). A 12-lead electrocardiogram and chest x-ray should be performed in all critically ill patients. An electrocardiogram is mandatory for all patients at risk for ischemic heart disease who develop heat exhaustion or heat stroke.

Therapeutic
Therapeutic Options

The key to effective and rapid heat loss is evaporation in conjunction with prompt restoration of the patient's intravascular volume. There are many methods of attempting to cool patients, including immersion in tubs filled with ice water, iced gastric and rectal lavage, packing the patient in ice packs, keeping wet sheets on the patient, placing the patient in the draft of fans, or using an expensive body cooling unit that auto-

TABLE 23–4–2. MOST COMMON LABORATORY VALUES SEEN IN HEAT STROKE

pH	Metabolic acidosis secondary to high lactate; may be accompanied by respiratory alkalosis in heat stroke of strenuous exertion
K	Normal early; hyperkalemia secondary to release from injured cells; hypokalemia in presence of respiratory alkalosis and as a result of aldosterone activity
Na	Usually normal but may be elevated in severe cases or when salt tablets are used
Ca	Usually normal but may be low owing to sequestration in injured muscle; rarely high secondary to dehydration
PO_4	Usually normal but may be low owing to sequestration in injured skeletal muscle and hyperventilation
Hematocrit	Usually high secondary to hemoconcentration; may be low if disseminated intravascular coagulation present
White blood cells	Elevated
Platelets, prothrombin time, fibrinogen	Low secondary to subclinical or overt coagulopathy
Serum glutamic–oxaloacetic transaminase, lactate dehydrogenase, alkaline phosphatase, bilirubin	Elevated, highest during first 24 hours; may increase additionally secondary to hemolysis
Creatine phosphokinase	Elevated; extremely high with rhabdomyolysis
Amylase	Elevated secondary to heat-related pancreatitis
Blood urea nitrogen and creatinine	Elevated, reflecting prerenal azotemia or acute renal failure
Urine	Maximally concentrated and multiple casts; proteinuria
PO_2	Usually normal; hypoxia suggests pneumonia
PCO_2	Usually depressed with hyperventilation
Chest x-ray	Usually normal; pneumonia may be seen
Electrocardiogram	Supraventricular tachycardia; nonspecific ST- and T-wave changes; acute myocardial infarction seen as a complication

matically sprays a suspended patient with tepid water as fans promote evaporation.

Recommended Approach

The therapy of heat cramps involves rest, massage of the affected muscle group, and rehydration with solutions containing sodium and potassium. Muscle relaxants may occasionally be helpful in severely affected individuals.

The therapy of heat exhaustion involves active supportive care and rehydration. If the patient is relatively alert, fluid stores can be replenished orally. If this is not feasible, intravenous fluid replacement is indicated. If the victim is suffering from heat stroke, malignant hyperthermia, or the neuroleptic malignant syndrome, therapy becomes a medical emergency.

Once the physician has become alert to the diagnosis of heat stroke, therapy must begin immediately. The therapy is divided into five parts: securement of the airway, breathing, and cardiovascular stability; assessment of the need of naloxone, glucose, and thiamine; rapid cooling; constant monitoring; rapid identification and treatment of any underlying or complicating disease; and supportive care.

As in every emergent patient, the initial and overriding priority is securing the airway, breathing, and cardiovascular stability of the patient. If there are alterations in mental status, reasons not to administer naloxone, glucose, and thiamine must be apparent. A fingerstick glucose determination should be performed and hypertonic glucose given if indicated. A minimum of 2.0 mg of naloxone should be given to any comatose patient with any historical or physical findings consistent with narcotic use. Thiamine (100 mg intravenous push) should be given

TABLE 23–4–3. DIFFERENTIAL DIAGNOSIS OF HEAT STROKE

Diagnostic Possibility	Diagnostic Tests or Observations
Heat stroke	History of low fluid intake, exertion, humid or warm environment; abundance or absence of sweat
Malignant hyperthermia	Increasing acidosis, rising temperature, hypoxia, tachycardia, hypotension, and arrhythmias during deeper stages of anesthesia; family history
Neuroleptic malignant syndrome	Increasing fever, rigidity, fluctuating vital signs, and extrapyramidal signs in a febrile patient on antipsychotic drugs
Central nervous system disease	Evidence of meningitis; historical or physical findings suggestive of stroke, evidence of acute spinal cord injury
Infections	Tularemia, leptospirosis, typhoid fever, malaria, brucellosis, or tuberculosis
Endocrine	History of thyroid disease or prior thyroid storm; prior use of antithyroid medication; exophthalmos
Malignancy	History of therapy for systemic malignancy; lymphadenopathy or splenomegaly
Acute fulminous hepatic necrosis	Toxin exposure; history of prior jaundice or hepatitis; dramatic jaundice

to any alcoholic, malnourished, or cachectic patient and to any patient requiring hypertonic glucose.

The quickest, cheapest, and easiest way to cool a patient is to keep the body wet as fans promote evaporation of moisture (and loss of heat) from the hot body. This may be supplemented by ice packs to the neck, axilla, and groin. A thin wet sheet that is constantly rewetted may provide the minimal modesty necessary when treating patients outside the hospital (i.e., at mass gatherings or road races). Although ice water baths may not be harmful in young, healthy individuals, immersion in ice water may cause vasoconstriction and decrease cooling; it also may allow a patient to drown. Ice-water immersion in the elderly may cause arrhythmias, acute myocardial infarction, or cardiac arrest. Electrocardiographic monitoring and defibrillation are not possible in immersed patients. Supplemental gastric lavage with ice water, using a large-bore orogastric tube, may be helpful in severe heat stroke patients. Endotracheal intubation to prevent aspiration must precede lavage. All heat stroke patients should be actively monitored, including their electrocardiogram and core temperatures.

Once the temperature is between 38° and 39°C, active cooling must be discontinued to avoid hypothermia. Alcohol sponge baths are not advantageous because of their tendency to induce shivering and raise, rather than lower, core temperatures. Administration of chlorpromazine (Thorazine) to prevent shivering has been recommended by some authors. Because of the hypotensive and seizure threshold-lowering effects of the phenothiazines, this family of drugs is probably contraindicated in heat-related illnesses. Hypotension is especially hazardous in the volume-depleted heat stroke patient.

During the cooling and monitoring phase, vigorous fluid replacement is essential. During the first hour it is common to give 1 to 2 L of 0.9% saline or Ringer's lactate to younger heat stroke victims. If all groups and etiologies of heat stroke are considered, the average fluid requirement is approximately 2000 mL during the first 4 hours; however, there is a wide range of fluid requirements. In the hypotensive patient, age is an important consideration. In younger patients, a volume challenge should be in liters. In the elderly or in those in whom myocardial infarction is suspected or present, a central venous pressure line should be inserted if hypotension is present after a 10- to 15-minute infusion of 500 to 750 mL of any crystalloid other than 5% dextrose in water. Mannitol (Osmitrol) may be added to increase the glomerular filtration rate and promote excretion of metabolic toxins once adequate blood pressure and urine output are achieved. Most authors recommend mannitol only in cases of superimposed rhabdomyolysis. Once pH and potassium

values are normal, potassium should be added only as indicated. Potassium should never be given empirically because of the risk of preexisting hyperkalemia. Oxygen by cannula or mask may be beneficial, but in an obtunded patient in shock who has respiratory compromise, endotracheal intubation is both prophylactic and therapeutic. Dopamine is useful for increasing cardiac output in the patient with shock; alpha agonists are contraindicated owing to their impairment of heat dissipation.

Throughout the entire acute care period, the clinician must be vigilant for both complications of the primary illness and those arising from the therapy. Urine output must be closely followed for signs of inadequate volume replacement as well as early indications of acute renal failure. The electrocardiogram must be monitored for the possibility of an occult myocardial infarction. Myocardial infarction may complicate the course in more than a third of elderly patients. Aspiration during the period of obtundation must be carefully assessed for by observation and chest x-ray. As fluid replacement proceeds, one must watch carefully for signs of volume overload and pulmonary edema.

If seizures occur, they should be treated aggressively with intravenous diazepam (Valium). There is a possibility of gastrointestinal bleeding owing to stress ulcerations. If a bleeding diathesis develops, therapy with fresh-frozen plasma provides optimal results, especially when used in conjunction with fresh blood. Finally, blood chemistries must be followed meticulously, as imbalances develop rapidly and require aggressive care. By use of the treatment modalities mentioned, survival without significant residua has been reported in a patient whose core temperature was in excess of 46.5°C (115.7°F).

The therapy for the patient with malignant hyperthermia has some important additions to the standard cooling protocol described above. As soon as the condition is discovered, all anesthesia and surgery must be discontinued immediately and cooling begun. One hundred percent oxygen should be the only inhaled agent. Dantrolene sodium (Dantrium) 2.5 mg/kg is begun by drip, and the patient's blood pressure and electrocardiogram are watched closely. Unresponsive patients should be cooled using cardiopulmonary bypass. Once the patient is stabilized, dantrolene (a direct-acting muscle relaxant) should be continued orally at a dose of 1 to 2 mg/kg three times daily for 3 days to avoid a recurrence. Dantrolene may be given preoperatively in high-risk patients for prophylaxis against malignant hyperthermia.

The therapy for the neuroleptic malignant syndrome parallels that for malignant hyperthermia. Dantrolene is used at the same dosage and is believed to be the best specific therapy. Unfortunately, there are no controlled studies comparing differing methods of treatment of this disease entity. Bromocriptine (Parlodel) and amantadine (Symmetrel) also may be useful, but their role and efficacy at present remain unclear. If an oral antipsychotic agent was the etiology, the syndrome may last up to 5 to 10 days; when an intramuscular depot neuroleptic drug is the etiology, the disease has the potential to last up to a month. Thus, clinicians must be prepared for a prolonged course of therapy.

FOLLOW-UP

Once a patient has been adequately treated for any of these disease entities, follow-up should be only to exclude the possibility of long-term sequelae. An office or clinic visit within a few weeks for follow-up blood and urine analyses is appropriate for patients who had any episodes of hypotension, profound dehydration, or anuria.

Muscle pain or weakness should prompt an immediate visit. Any patient who becomes febrile after recovery from any of these diseases should be told to seek medical attention immediately.

DISCUSSION
Prevalence and Incidence

Heat-related illnesses are becoming increasingly more common; more than 1000 cases of heat illness are reported in athletes per year. The Centers for Disease Control and Prevention report approximately 500 deaths per year due to heat-related illnesses. The elderly are at highest risk, and death rates in the elderly may temporarily double or triple during summer heat waves. The incidence of malignant hyperthermia in adults is between 1 in 50,000 and 1 in 100,000 anesthetic administrations. The incidence of neuroleptic malignant syndrome is not exactly known; present estimates place the incidence at approximately 0.2% of all patients taking neuroleptic agents. It is most common in young adult males.

Related Basic Science

Temperature regulation in a warm environment consists of cutaneous vasodilation mediated by a central mechanism located in the hypothalamus. Regulation results in an increase in thermal conductivity in the skin and a resultant increase in heat loss. Sweating is stimulated by sympathetic cholinergic innervation. Thermoreceptors supply information from the skin as well as from internal organs, with receptors located in the aorta, arteries, and brain. As long as heat-dissipating mechanisms are able to keep up with the rate of heat production, the core temperature changes very little. The body uses a number of mechanisms to dissipate heat. At normal body temperatures, more than 50% of heat is lost by radiation. An additional third is lost by evaporation via respiration and sweating. Once the body temperature begins to rise above 37°C, evaporation via sweating constitutes the mechanism of almost all heat dissipation. Once heat accumulation exceeds the body's ability for heat dissipation, the core temperature begins to rise.

Failure of the heat-losing mechanisms may occur in an environment that prevents evaporative losses or may result from a failure of the peripheral mechanisms of vasodilation and sweating. For example, heat-losing mechanisms may fail in the dehydrated individual or in the face of such factors as the use of atropine-like drugs or skin disorders (e.g., congenital absence of sweat glands, scleroderma); however, the ability to maintain adequate circulating blood volume is the usual cause for failure of heat-dissipating mechanisms, particularly when exercise is a factor. Exercise results in a demand for increased cardiac output to the exercising muscle and for an increase in the peripheral heat exchange system. Total peripheral resistance is reduced during exercise, resulting in further compromise in cardiac output. Also, sweating results in significant volume losses, and if hydration is not maintained, heat loss is further impaired.

The role of sweating in the prevention of heat-related illness is based on its ability to create a heat loss of approximately 600 kcal/L of sweat. Untrained individuals can lose 1 to 1.5 L of sweat per hour. Sweat creates heat loss via evaporation, whereas cutaneous vasodilation employs both radiation and convection. It is noteworthy that as subjects become acclimated to exertion in warm environments, maximal sweat rates more than double and there is a marked decrease in the amount of sodium and potassium lost per liter by sweat.

Once heat stroke is fully evolved, the damage is distributed to every organ system. High intracellular temperatures result in disruption of cellular membranes, the enzyme systems in the mitochondria, as well as the coding of proteins. Superimposed on the damage of these high temperatures is a relative cellular hypoxia related to vastly increased metabolic demands. Early in the clinical course, the patient manifests a physiologically increased stroke volume, elevated heart rate, and decreased peripheral vascular resistance; however, as intravascular volume is lost in sweat and urine and as the body temperature rises, the cardiac output and blood pressure begin to fall. Postmortem changes in the myocardium have revealed myocardial necrosis and infarction in areas supplied by patent coronary arteries.

As volume falls and cardiac function declines, the kidneys become prone to injury. The incidence of acute renal failure is directly related to the etiology of heat stroke. Only about 5% of passive, elderly heat stroke victims develop this complication; however, if heat stroke occurs in a rigorously exercising victim, the incidence increases to approximately a third. This dramatic increase may be attributed to the additional demands of the exercising muscle, which exaggerate the low output state and result in muscle hypoxia. This hypoxia causes rhabdomyolysis and hyperuricemia, both of which may precipitate acute renal failure. Postmortem examination of the kidney reveals microhemorrhages as well as congestion.

As heat stroke progresses, major imbalances of almost all measurable blood chemistries are seen. A metabolic acidosis is present and may be accompanied by either hypokalemia or hyperkalemia. The acidosis is mainly due to high levels of lactate. Hypokalemia is due to the depletion of total-body potassium secondary to sweat and urine losses.

Also, there is a potassium flux intracellularly as a result of an often coexisting respiratory alkalosis. As heat stroke evolves, hyperkalemia becomes increasingly more common because of the release of potassium from both muscle and traumatized red cells. Potassium levels may also be elevated secondary to the acidosis.

Both calcium and phosphorus values are highly variable. Hypocalcemia and hypophosphatemia may be present because of sequestration in injured skeletal muscle. Conversely, hypercalcemia may be present because of the state of hydration, and hyperphosphatemia may be present owing to lactic acidosis.

Coagulopathy almost always is seen in victims of heat stroke. Its etiology is multifactorial and includes the thermal insult to the endothelial lining of the blood vessels, decreased formation and activation of clotting factors, and destruction of platelets.

Most gastrointestinal changes seen in heat stroke appear to be directly heat related. Bleeding either is the result of stress ulceration to the gastric mucosa or is part of the watery diarrhea seen from hypoxia-induced sloughing of the epithelium lining the small and large bowels.

As mentioned, the necrosis of muscle is not confined to the myocardium; indeed, there is widespread skeletal muscle damage. The degree of necrosis ranges from that detectable only by laboratory evaluation (serum creatinine phosphokinase and/or urinary myoglobin) to the clinical spectrum of symptomatic rhabdomyolysis.

The etiology of malignant hyperthermia is not completely understood. It appears that certain triggering events (i.e., general anesthesia) cause calcium to be released from the sarcoplasmic reticulum of skeletal muscle. This calcium release results in widespread skeletal muscle contraction, rigidity, increased oxygen consumption, and heat production. The etiology of the neuroleptic malignant syndrome is not fully understood either. Because of the similarities to malignant hyperthermia, it is postulated that some other triggering event results in a similar release of calcium and the cascade of increased skeletal muscle activity. It may be that the antidopaminergic effects of the neuroleptic agents serve as the initiating event.

Natural History and Its Modification with Treatment

The complications of heat-related illnesses are directly related to the height of the core temperature, the length of time the patient remains hyperthermic, the patient's age, the underlying disease state of the patient, and, lastly, the patient's state of hydration at the onset of the illness. No exact prediction, however, as to the presence or extent of heat-related complications can be made. As temperatures rise above 40.6°C, complications become more likely. Mental status changes, hypotension, coagulopathy, and the need for intubation are predictors of significant morbidity and mortality. Permanent residual damage is more common in patients who present with these complications.

The mortality of heat stroke varies in most series from 10 to 20%. Exceedingly high rates are seen in hypotensive, comatose, elderly patients who require intubation. The mortality of malignant hyperthermia appropriately treated with dantrolene has not been established. When nonspecific therapy is used due to failure to diagnose, mortality in excess of 50% should be expected. Although the mortality of the neuroleptic malignant syndrome is somewhat variable, approximately 20% of victims succumb to heat-related complications.

Prevention

Heat stroke may be prevented by educating those who are likely to suffer the malady. Thus, those at high risk—the elderly, athletes, and others who exercise or work in hot or humid climates—must be encouraged to have high fluid intake. The use of salt tablets should be discouraged. The need for fluid replacement should be stressed to athletes and their coaches alike. The community can dramatically decrease the incidence of heat stroke induced by road races. Encouragement of adequate training prior to the race, provision enroute for fluid replacement, and, in hot weather, provision for sprinkler systems along the course are all highly efficacious. The frequency of malignant hyperthermia may be minimized by carefully screening patients for any personal or family history of this disease or any history of sudden intraoperative or immediate postoperative deaths.

Physicians should tell the patient and family members about the risk factors involved in each of the heat-related illnesses. Preventive measures such as adequate hydration with 500 mL of fluid 30 minutes prior to race time should be well known to runners and those at risk for heat-related illnesses. As malignant hyperthermia often is transmitted as a genetically determined condition, family members should be told that they are at an increased risk for this syndrome. Also, they should be instructed to inform their physician of their familial history whenever operative procedures are contemplated.

Cost Containment

Money should not be spent needlessly on expensive cooling equipment, as tubs with cool water or cold wet sheets and fans do well in the cool-ing process. Also, the early recognition of complications will avoid more involved and expensive intervention at a later date.

REFERENCES

Costrini A. Emergency treatment of exertional heatstroke and comparison of whole body cooling techniques. Med Sci Sports Exercise 1990;22:15.
Guze BH, Baxter LR. Neuroleptic malignant syndrome. N Engl J Med 1985;313:163.
Knochel JP. Heat stroke and related heat stress disorders. Dis Mon 1989;35:301.
Simon BS. Hyperthermia. N Engl J Med 1993;329:483.
Slovis CM, Anderson GF, Casolaro A. Survival in a heat stroke victim with a core temperature above 46.5°C. Ann Emerg Med 1982;11:269.
Stine RJ. Heat illness. J Am Coll Emerg Physicians. 1979;8:154.

CHAPTER 23–5

Radiation Emergencies

Steven L. Brody, M.D.

DEFINITION

A radiation emergency is defined as the possibility of acute radiation-induced injury. Radiation injury occurs when there is cellular injury from ionizing rays or accelerated particles.

ETIOLOGY

Injuries may occur after excessive or inadvertent exposure to radiation devices or radioactive materials used in industry, research, or warfare.

CRITERIA FOR DIAGNOSIS
Suggestive

Following exposure to radiation, the onset of nausea and vomiting or thermal burn indicates that significant radiation injury has occurred. Lymphopenia, pancytopenia, bone marrow hypoplasia, and immunosuppression also indicate serious exposure. The diagnosis should be considered in all persons involved in a radiation accident.

Definitive

The diagnosis is confirmed by elevated radiation levels at the accident site or in or on the contaminated patient.

CLINICAL MANIFESTATIONS
Subjective

The source of radiation injury is usually obvious, although clinical symptoms may be the only clue to an inapparent exposure. Exposure would most likely take place in the following manner: after an accident at an industrial radiation plant, a nuclear reactor leak, a medical or physics research or treatment facility spill, or in the transport of radioactive materials.

Radiation dose is measured by energy units absorbed, called the Gray (abbreviated Gy). This was previously expressed as the rad (100 rad = 1 Gy). Because different particles have different effects, the unit that relates exposure to dose equivalent radiation is the Sievert (Sv), previously termed the roentgen equivalent man (rem).

The history may reveal one of three types of radiation accidents:

- *Irradiation* occurs when there is exposure without detectable radiation on the patient's body or clothes. Damage is instantaneous, but symptoms become manifest over time.
- *Contamination* occurs when radioactive particles become attached to clothing and skin. Most patients are asymptomatic but may have symptoms due to toxic chemicals labeled with the radioactive element.
- *Incorporation* occurs when radioactive elements become biologically incorporated into tissues after accidental ingestion, inhalation, or wound contamination. This type of injury can cause continuous extensive cellular damage and, therefore, increasing symptoms.

The acute radiation syndrome is a characteristic dose-dependent response to radiation that occurs after acute whole-body irradiation (Table 23–5–1). Increasing doses cause three distinct disease complexes, all of which are marked by a prodrome phase of nausea, vomiting, and diarrhea and can be accompanied by apathy, fatigue, and fever. The hematopoietic syndrome occurs with exposures of 1 to 5 Gy (100–500 rad) due to the extreme radiosensitivity of bone marrow. At this dose there is a 2- to 3-week latent period, after which the patient may have petechiae, bruising, hemorrhage, and symptoms of infection. Hair loss occurs 3 weeks after exposure of at least 3 Gy (300 rad). Higher doses (approximately 10 Gy) affect the intestinal epithelium, causing the gastrointestinal syndrome. In this syndrome, the patient develops prodrome symptoms and then, within 3 to 5 days, has marked anorexia, increased vomiting, severe diarrhea, and death. Doses of more than 20 Gy (several thousand rad) cause the cardiovascular–central nervous system syndrome, which is characterized by vomiting and diarrhea followed immediately by tremors, ataxia, seizures, hypotension, and death.

Locally exposed patients may present with discrete pain, erythema, and desquamation similar to a thermal burn. Erythema may progress to chronic ulceration. Very high local doses may result in acute radiation syndrome as well. Systemic exposure may occur by ingestion or inhalation of isotopes causing symptoms similar to external radiation. There may be organ-specific exposure and symptoms, for example, hypothyroidism after ingestion or external exposure to isotopes of iodine.

TABLE 23–5–1. ACUTE RADIATION SYNDROME: DOSE RESPONSE FOR ACUTE WHOLE-BODY EXPOSURE

Dose (Gy [rad])	Effect	Outcome
0.2 [20]	Asymptomatic	Possible chromosomal changes
0.5 [50]	Possible leukopenia	Chromosomal changes
1–2 [100–200]	Nausea, vomiting, leukopenia	Possible infection
5 [500]	Hematopoietic syndrome	50% mortality in 1 mo
10 [1000]	Gastrointestinal syndrome, bone marrow aplasia	100% mortality in 2 wk
>20 [2000]	Neurologic–cardiovascular syndrome	100% mortality in 2 d

Objective

Physical Examination

There are few specific physical findings that would initially suggest radiation exposure except in cases of high-level exposure. In these cases patients may have such neurologic signs as tremor, ataxia, or coma. Others may present with diarrhea and vomiting and may have signs of volume depletion. Patients who have bone marrow depression usually have evidence of infection and bleeding 2 or 3 weeks after exposure. High local doses can cause acute erythema and edema of skin, conjunctiva, mucous membranes, and salivary glands.

Routine Laboratory Abnormalities

Hematologic count abnormalities are sensitive laboratory indicators of the severity of exposure. If the 48-hour postexposure lymphocyte count is greater than 2000 cells/mm^3, the chance of lethal damage is low. A count less than 100 cells/mm^3 indicates a lethal dose. Nonlethal platelet and erythrocyte suppression occurs approximately 3 weeks after a 1-Gy (100-rad) exposure. An elevated creatinine level may occur due to volume depletion in the prodrome phase or gastrointestinal syndrome.

PLANS

Diagnostic

Differential Diagnosis

The differential diagnoses considered are directly related to the circumstances of the possible radiation exposure: industrial, research, transportation, energy utilities, or warfare. Many hazardous industrial chemical exposures may result in toxicity or injury and should be considered in the differential diagnosis of radiation injury, especially toxic gases, organic chemicals, and caustic chemicals. In evaluation of local acute radiation injury, caustic chemicals should be considered as a cause of local burns. The differential diagnosis of acute radiation syndrome is broad. Persistent vomiting may be due to organic chemical exposure and may be accompanied by hepatic injury. Gases such as cyanide, carbon monoxide, or hydrogen sulfide may cause coma, and organic solvents or pesticides may cause marked neurologic abnormalities. Head injury may cause coma and should always be considered in settings involving trauma or when explosions have occurred. In considering the differential diagnosis of less severe acute radiation illness, other than cancer chemotherapy agents, there are few acute causes of bone marrow hypoplasia.

Diagnostic Options

There are few diagnostic options. The reader is referred to the Recommended Approach. In true radiation emergencies involving a large population exposure, standard disaster management dictates that only those patients with the best chance of survival be triaged to medical facilities where diagnostic evaluation can be performed.

Recommended Approach

There are two important diagnostic phases that must be pursued in radiation accidents. The first is the clinical evaluation of the injury and of severity of exposure. Skin erythema or burns, especially on the upper extremities, and injury due to radioactive or nonradioactive debris should be assessed. Exposure dose can be estimated by how rapidly nausea and vomiting occur. If they occur within 2 hours, a dose of more than 4 Gy (400 rad) should be suspected. Diarrhea in the first 2 days or vomiting persisting for more than 3 days may indicate a lethal exposure. Complete blood counts and serial bone marrow examinations are especially useful for following the course of disease after exposure. Doses greater than 1.5 to 2 Gy result in pancytopenia, bone marrow hypoplasia, and immunosuppression. A more precise estimate of acute radiation dose can be made by chromosomal analysis. The second diagnostic phase is to determine the exact location, type, and quantity of radioactivity involved. This should be done by a trained team of radiation safety experts. A clear history of the details of exposure and a measurement of radiation with a Geiger–Mueller survey meter should always be performed. The degree of patient contamination must be

determined by survey meter measurements of clothing, skin, and, in some cases, body fluid. It is not usually possible to determine exactly how much radiation has been absorbed. After assessing acute patient injury and contamination, the type of radiation and extent of environmental exposure should be estimated so that other persons in the area of risk can be evacuated.

Thyroid function tests should be obtained if exposure to radioactive iodine is suspected or if the specific isotope exposure is unknown.

Therapeutic

Therapeutic Options

For the therapy of acute radiation syndrome limited to bone marrow hypoplasia (exposures of more than 4 Gy but less than 10 Gy), the use of bone marrow transplant is an option to supportive care. Some victims of the 1986 Chernobyl accident in the Soviet Union who were exposed to 5 Gy (500 rad) or more were treated with bone marrow transplantation. This therapy remains controversial and requires careful patient selection, as many factors influence successful engraftment. Another potentially useful therapy is granulocyte–macrophage colony-stimulating factor (GM-CSF), which was successfully used to improve granulocyte counts in victims of the Goiania, Brazil, accident in 1988.

Recommended Approach

Radiation emergencies must be managed by trained teams of personnel. Patients should be transported to a hospital that is properly equipped to manage such accidents. The basic concept in handling radiation victims is to contain and prevent contamination of others while providing prompt and expert medical care. All lifesaving and stabilizing procedures should take place immediately. When handling contaminated patients, physicians and medical support teams can adequately protect themselves with double layers of gloves and gowns. The decontaminated patient should generally be handled as is any other medical patient.

Patient decontamination should be done only after the patient is stable. Any patient involved in a radiation accident is considered contaminated until proven otherwise. At the treatment site, a specially prepared room should be designated for decontamination. A specific protocol must be followed in this area to protect the medical staff and to determine accurately the extent of contamination. The patient's clothes should be removed, sealed in a plastic bag, and monitored for radiation. Applicator swabs should be used to collect specimens from ear canals, mouth, nares, and other suspected contaminated areas. Attention is first turned toward decontamination of wounds with copious saline irrigation. Hydrogen peroxide and gentle debridement can be used if radiation persists. The patient's body should be gently irrigated with soap and tepid water. This water is considered contaminated and should be contained. Hot water, which can cause vasodilation and subsequent incorporation, or stiff brush scrubbing should not be used. After the patient is dried, repeated swab samples should be collected to assess decontamination. Radiation-induced skin burns should receive care similar to that provided for thermal burns.

If contamination or incorporation of radioactive material occurs by accidental inhalation or ingestion, or if contaminated open wounds are suspected, the patient should be started on appropriate therapy within 1 to 2 hours. Decorporation, dilution, and diuretic or blocking therapy are given to prevent permanent biochemical incorporation of radioactive materials in the body tissues. Dosage and route of administration are best chosen in consultation with health physicists and nuclear medicine experts. The treatment approach varies with the type of isotope involved. Emesis or gastric lavage is generally indicated for all accidental ingestions. Diuretics can be used to enhance the elimination of radioactive sodium, potassium, chloride, or tritium. Additionally, tritium excretion is increased by forced diuresis. Antacids can be used to bind and block absorption of some metals in the stomach. For example, magnesium sulfate-containing antacids can bind radium isotopes and aluminum phosphate gel can bind ingested strontium isotopes. Chelating agents are available, on an investigational basis, to treat intoxication with heavy metal radioisotopes such as plutonium. Iodine should be given if radioactive iodine is ingested. It should also be considered following nuclear reactor accidents that may disperse volatile iodine radionuclides. Gastric fluid, urine, and feces should be retained for radiation monitoring.

Therapy for acute radiation syndrome should be primarily supportive. Aggressive approaches are indicated for patients with less than 10 Gy (1000 rad) of exposure. Experience from the Chernobyl accident has shown that most patients receiving less than 4 Gy survive with expert supportive care. Careful attention to maintaining adequate hydration is important in patients with vomiting and diarrhea. Bone marrow transplantation should be attempted in those patients with aplasia who have an appropriate donor and are cared for in an institution with extensive transplant experience. Initial therapy should be directed toward prevention and treatment of infection, control of hemorrhage, and blood product support using techniques similar to those used in the management of patients with bone marrow aplasia from cancer chemotherapy.

Patients who receive acute doses of well more than 10 Gy (several thousand rad) have no chance of survival and should be made comfortable.

FOLLOW-UP

Periodic follow-up examinations after recovery from acute exposure are advisable to review the patient's progress and to answer questions. Serial complete blood counts should be obtained. Any burn or traumatic injury should be followed in the appropriate manner. Patients exposed during major accidents are at risk for thyroid abnormalities, including hypothyroidism, adenoma, and cancer. There is an increased long-term risk of death from leukemia and cancer of the lung, breast, and bone that should be considered in long-term follow-up planning.

DISCUSSION
Prevalence and Incidence

Radiation accidents are uncommon events. The U.S. Radiation Accident Registry reports approximately 340 major radiation accidents involving 116 fatalities worldwide from 1944 to 1991. In 1986 the Chernobyl nuclear power plant meltdown marked the worst commercial nuclear accident in history, exposing millions to low-dose radiation. The frequency of accidents may increase, however, due to an increase in the number of nuclear power plants, nuclear weapons, use of radioactive materials in industry and medicine, and consequent increase in radioactive waste. Transportation of these materials is another potential source for accidents. Radiation accidents often occur in research laboratories and in medical centers. Exposure is usually low. Most accidents involve isotope sources. Major exposures have occurred with x-ray generators, accelerators, and reactors, usually in industrial settings. Only rarely are ionizing radiation injuries life-threatening to the victim or the treating staff. Most reported serious injury involves radiation burns, primarily on the hands.

Related Basic Science

Radiation injury comes from alpha particles, beta particles, gamma rays (including x-rays), and neutrons. Alpha particles have little penetrating ability and are stopped by skin or clothing. They can be hazardous if taken internally. Beta and gamma sources are most likely to be involved in accidents. Gamma rays are more penetrating than beta particles and are able to cause widespread damage throughout the body. Neutrons, accelerated particles given off in nuclear decay, are highly penetrating and destructive. Radiation causes damage by reacting with cellular material to form ionizing molecules and free radicals. These molecules disrupt cell structure and function and cause chromosomal damage, impairing cell reproduction. Cell death results with high doses of radiation. Tissues with the greatest cellular turnover are the most radiosensitive. Bone marrow is the most sensitive, followed by hair, lung, gastrointestinal epithelium, and skin. Low-level exposure allows repair and recovery, generally without consequences. Although there are no clinical manifestations of injury, chronic low-level exposure may be mutagenic and carcinogenic.

Natural History and Its Modification with Treatment

Radiation injury varies with the amount of radiation absorbed. Information concerning the natural history of radiation exposure has been gathered as a result of radiation therapy, accidents, atmospheric and ground testing of nuclear weapons, and exposure at Chernobyl, Hiroshima, and Nagasaki. The acute radiation syndrome is well characterized and depends on dosage, duration of exposure, and body distribution. The potentially lethal dose for humans ranges from 2 to 10 Gy (200–1000 rad) (see Table 23–5–1). Survival following exposures less than 4 Gy is improved with modern supportive therapy; however, persons exposed to more than 4 Gy subjected to bone marrow transplant in Moscow following the Chernobyl incident did not survive due to complications of the transplant.

Contamination of skin with radionuclides is rarely life-threatening. The combined injury of trauma and radioactive exposure or contamination has a worse prognosis.

Prevention

Human error is the most important factor leading to radiation accidents. Persons who use radioactive materials must adhere to strict guidelines and are closely regulated by government agencies. Constant monitoring and reinforcement of specific regulations are necessary to avoid radiation accidents. If an accident does occur, personnel and hospitals should have appropriate equipment and management protocols. Persons adjacent to the accident site should be rapidly evacuated if at risk for exposure.

Cost Containment

The major economic investment should be in the prevention of accidents. Radioactivity monitoring devices should be available to guide proper patient management.

Hospitalization is rarely indicated in exposures to less than 1 Gy (100 rad) if there are no accompanying injuries or symptoms.

REFERENCES

Champlin RE, Kastenberg WE, Gale RP. Radiation accidents and nuclear energy: Medical consequences and therapy. Ann Intern Med 1988;109:730.

Hempelman LH, Lisco H, Hoffman JG. The acute radiation syndrome. Ann Intern Med 1952;36:279.

Hirsch EF, Bowers GJ. Irradiated trauma victims: The impact of ionizing radiation on surgical considerations following a nuclear mishap. World J Surg 1992;16:918.

Kirk MA, Cisek J, Rose SR. Emergency department response to hazardous materials incidents. Emerg Med Clin North Am 1994;12:461.

Leonard RB, Ricks RC. Emergency department radiation accident protocol. Ann Emerg Med 1980;9:462.

CHAPTER 23–6

Infections Related to Animal Bites (See Section 8, Chapter 36)

CHAPTER 23–7

Infections Related to Insect (Arthropod) Bites (See Section 8, Chapter 37)

Drug Abuse and Poisons

Corey M. Slovis, M.D.

CHAPTER 24–1

Alcohol • Tolerance, Addiction, and Withdrawal

David B. McMicken, M.D.

DEFINITION

A precise definition of alcoholism is difficult. Certainly the patient who has physiologic dependence on ethanol can be labeled "alcoholic." The *Diagnostic and Statistical Manual* of the American Psychiatric Association, third edition revised (DSM - IIIR), classifies three main patterns of chronic alcohol abuse or dependence: regular daily intake of large amounts, regular heavy drinking limited to weekends, and long periods of sobriety interspersed with binges of daily heavy drinking lasting weeks or months. When drinking adversely affects an individual's physical health, ability to function in society, or interpersonal relationships, alcoholism is present.

ETIOLOGY

The cause of alcoholism is complex and not completely understood but appears to be an intricate interaction between biological and environmental factors. Data show that a genetic variability of enzymes for alcohol metabolism may be a risk factor. Chronic alcohol consumption has a depressant effect on the central nervous system. The hallmark of alcohol withdrawal is the display of central nervous system excitation.

CRITERIA FOR DIAGNOSIS
Suggestive

A simple and rapid yet respectful screening test for alcoholism is the four *cage* questions (see next page) or the question "have you ever had a drinking problem?" A positive answer to this question plus evidence of alcohol consumption in the previous 24 hours provides a greater than 90% sensitivity and specificity as a screening tool for identifying alcoholism. (Research indicates that there is a high probability that a patient will curtail his or her drinking if a physician simply points out that the current consumption is causing health problems.)

Have you ever felt
>The need to *C*ut down on your drinking?
>*A*nnoyed by criticism of your drinking?
>*G*uilty about your drinking?
>The need to drink a morning *E*ye opener?

Positive answers to two or more of these questions are sufficient to identify individuals who require more intensive evaluation.

Definitive

The chronic abuse of alcohol eventually leads to *acquired tolerance,* a condition in which larger and larger doses of alcohol are required for the same effect. There is also an *inborn tolerance.* Continued alcohol abuse then progresses to *physical dependence,* an altered physiologic state that requires the continued consumption of alcohol to prevent a withdrawal syndrome, and finally to *addiction,* a behavioral pattern of compulsive and overwhelming need for alcohol with a consistent tendency to relapse after withdrawal.

CLINICAL MANIFESTATIONS

Subjective

The severity of signs and symptoms is dependent on both the dose and duration of ethanol consumption. The withdrawal syndrome may occur any time after the blood alcohol level starts to fall. Additional history may also be obtained from family friends, bystanders, or paramedics if possible.

The withdrawal syndrome develops 6 to 24 hours after the reduction of ethanol intake and lasts from 2 to 7 days. The alcohol withdrawal state constitutes a wide spectrum, ranging from mild withdrawal with insomnia and irritability to major withdrawal with diaphoresis, fever, disorientation, and hallucinations.

Minor alcohol withdrawal occurs as soon as 6 hours and usually peaks at 24 to 36 hours after the cessation or significant decrease in alcohol intake. It is characterized by mild autonomic hyperactivity: nausea, anorexia, coarse tremor, tachycardia, hypertension, hyperreflexia, sleep disturbances including insomnia and vivid dreams, and anxiety.

Major alcohol withdrawal occurs more than 24 hours and usually peaks at 50 hours (but infrequently up to 5 days) after the decline or termination of drinking. Major withdrawal is characterized by more pronounced autonomic hyperactivity along with disorientation, hallucinations, diaphoresis, and fever.

Delirium tremens, seldom appearing before the third postabstinence day, is the extreme end of the spectrum and consists of gross tremor, profound confusion, fever, incontinence, frightening visual hallucinations, and mydriasis. True delirium tremens is rare and is not synonymous with alcohol withdrawal. Other causes of delirium to be considered in the alcoholic include sepsis, meningitis, hypoxia, hypoglycemia, hepatic failure, and intracranial bleed.

At one time the alcohol withdrawal syndrome was divided into stages; however, with so much individual variation and overlap of the signs, symptoms, temporal sequence, and duration of the syndrome, staging is not clinically useful. In addition seizures can occur in either minor or major alcohol withdrawal.

Objective

Physical Examination

The prime consideration in the initial evaluation of the alcohol-dependent patient is the identification and treatment of life-threatening disorders, for example, hypoglycemia, intracranial hematoma, central nervous system infections, and electrolyte abnormalities. Care must be taken to avoid the pitfall of allowing withdrawal symptoms or acute intoxication to mask a serious, acute, underlying head injury, for example, a subdural hematoma. Securing the airway, breathing, and cardiopulmonary status (ABCs) while maintaining appropriate cervical spine precautions should remain standard procedure. Hyperthermia, hypothermia, tachypnea, or tachycardia may indicate serious disorders that frequently accompany alcohol dependency (Table 24–1–1).

Rapid, thorough, and repeated physical examinations should be performed, with attention to the level of consciousness, hepatic failure,

TABLE 24-1-1. DISORDERS ASSOCIATED WITH ABNORMAL VITAL SIGNS IN THE ALCOHOL-DEPENDENT PATIENT

Hyperthermia	Tachypnea
Sepsis	Sepsis
Drug ingestion (phenothiazine, aspirin)	Hypoxia
Anticholinergic poisoning	Acidosis
Heat stroke	Cerebral insult
Intracranial hemorrhage	Pulmonary insult
Alcohol withdrawal	
Hypothermia	Tachycardia
Sepsis	Sepsis
Drug ingestion (phenothiazine, sedative–hypnotic)	Shock
Hypoglycemia	Poisoning
Diabetes	(anticholinergic
Exposure	cocaine,
Wernicke's encephalopathy	amphetamine)
	Alcohol withdrawal
	Drug withdrawal

and coagulopathy. It is important to be alert for signs of trauma such as subcutaneous emphysema, ecchymosis, subconjunctival hemorrhage, Battle's sign, and fractures. The neurologic examination should search for focal findings.

Routine Laboratory Abnormalities

The routine laboratory abnormalities include hypoglycemia, acidosis, hypokalemia, hypocalcemia, hypomagnesemia hypophosphatemia, anemia, and thrombocytopenia.

The routine chest radiograph may show no abnormality or pulmonary infection. The cause of the routine laboratory abnormalities is discussed in detail under Diagnostic Options.

PLANS

Diagnostic

Differential Diagnosis

The alcohol withdrawal syndrome can initially be confused with acute schizophrenia, encephalitis, drug-induced psychosis, thyrotoxicosis, anticholinergic poisoning, and withdrawal from other sedative–hypnotic-type drugs. It may even be difficult to differentiate immediately between alcohol withdrawal and alcohol-induced hypoglycemia.

Acute schizophrenia usually has its onset in adolescence or early adulthood. Manifestations include multiple bizarre delusions and a flat affect with the patient otherwise oriented. The patient in alcohol withdrawal is usually older (twenties or thirties), hyperactive, and possibly disoriented.

Encephalitis can produce headache, confusion, fever, and seizures. Thyrotoxicosis is more common in females and its features include irritability, insomnia, tremor, weight loss despite a good appetite, palpitations and frequent stools. Physical examination may reveal lid lag, tachycardia, and a bruit over the thyroid. There is no relationship between the onset of encephalitis or thyrotoxicosis and alcohol consumption.

Anticholinergic poisoning can occur with ingestion of several different drugs or plants. The classic clinical picture is a patient with dry mouth, dry eyes, dry skin, hypoactive bowel sounds, urinary retention, and delirium. Amphetamine and cocaine intoxication produces anorexia, insomnia, plus physical signs of central nervous system sympathetic overactivity.

In opioid withdrawal, the mental status is usually normal, the patient is afebrile, and seizures are uncommon (except for meperidine). In contrast, patients with alcohol withdrawal are usually disoriented and febrile and may seize.

If a patient manifests withdrawal 3 or more days after their last drink, then one should consider other drugs with a longer half-life. The barbiturate and benzodiazepine withdrawal syndromes usually progress more slowly and are associated with a higher frequency of seizures that appear later (seven days versus two days), and status epilepticus is more common than with the alcohol withdrawal syndrome.

Diagnostic Options

Specific Emergency Tests. A fingerstick glucose test is valuable. A rapid alcohol breath analysis or blood alcohol level may be helpful. The blood should also be tested for commonly ingested drugs that may alter mental status. A number of laboratory abnormalities are associated with alcoholism.

Hematological Abnormalities. The direct toxic effect of ethanol and its metabolites, secondary nutritional deficiency, and hepatic disease, individually or in combination, affect red blood cells, white blood cells, platelets, hemostasis, and the immune system.

Megaloblastic anemia resulting from folate deficiency is the most common cause of anemia in alcoholics. Malnutrition, inability of the cirrhotic liver to store folate, excessive urinary loss, and malabsorption decrease folate stores.

Macrocytosis is the most common hematologic manifestation of the chronic alcoholic. It may be caused by folate deficiency, reticulocytosis (the younger reticulocytes are larger), liver disease (producing an abnormal coating of the red blood cell membrane with lipid), or vitamin B_{12} deficiency. The most common cause is the idiopathic macrocytosis of alcoholism (a poorly understood syndrome of macrocytosis, mild or absent anemia, without neutrophil hypersegmentation, folate deficiency or severe liver disease) that may be due to alcohol's direct effect on bone marrow.

Iron deficiency anemia is also common among alcoholics and is usually secondary to blood loss from the gastrointestinal tract. Serum ferritin is the best screening test for iron deficiency anemia in alcoholics.

Leukopenia is commonly seen in the alcoholic and has several possible causes. Sepsis, folate deficiency, and hypersplenism all lead to a decreased white blood cell count.

Thrombocytopenia can occur with folate deficiency, sepsis, disseminated intravascular coagulation, or splenic sequestration. The direct toxic effects of alcohol decrease measured survival time and impair production of platelets in the bone marrow. Qualitative platelet function is also impaired.

Thrombocytopenia, qualitative platelet disorders, deficient hepatic production of clotting factors, gastrointestinal variceal formation, and vitamin K deficiency can produce a bleeding diathesis in these patients. The chronic alcoholic requires a complete blood count, peripheral smear, platelet count, bleeding time, thrombin time, prothrombin time/INR, and partial thromboplastin time if significant bleeding is noted.

Hypoglycemia. Coma, seizures, hemiparesis, and a variety of other neurologic signs have been described in patients presenting with alcohol-induced hypoglycemia. Starvation, depletion of liver glycogen stores, decreased plasma cortisol levels, impaired release of growth hormone, and inhibition of gluconeogenesis contribute to this phenomenon.

Documentation of hypoglycemia by fingerstick glucose before empiric glucose administration avoids the potential exacerbation of neurologic injury secondary to hyperglycemia if cerebral ischemia is present. Although rapid fingerstick determination of hypoglycemia is ideal, glucose administration should not be withheld pending lengthy laboratory confirmation. After intravenous administration of 25 g of dextrose and 100 mg of thiamine, the patient should be maintained on a 5% glucose solution.

Electrolyte Abnormalities. Hypokalemia is a frequent finding in active drinkers. Vomiting, diarrhea, magnesium depletion, malnutrition, and metabolic alkalosis contribute to this hypokalemia.

Alcoholism may be the most common cause of severe magnesium deficiency in adult outpatient medicine. The pathophysiologic basis of this hypomagnesemia is thought to be due to malabsorption, malnutrition, and diarrhea.

Hypocalcemia is a common finding in alcoholic patients with magnesium depletion. The mechanism is thought to be diminished parathyroid hormone secretion, decreased tissue responsiveness to parathyroid hormone, decreased vitamin D metabolism, and decreased calcium release from bone independent of parathyroid hormone. Hypoalbuminemia, pancreatitis, or vitamin D deficiency may also contribute to low serum calcium or low total body stores of calcium in the alcoholic.

Hypophosphatemia may be present during acute intoxication or withdrawal. Phosphorus depletion results from malnutrition, vomiting, respiratory alkalosis, diarrhea, phosphate-binding antacids, and urinary loss.

Drug Screen. Polydrug abuse and serious depression can complicate alcohol abuse. The clinician should consider the concomitant withdrawal or toxicity from other substances, and a urine screen for cocaine, benzodiazepines, and barbiturates should be obtained if withdrawal from one of these substances is suspected.

Acidosis. The differential diagnosis for the alcoholic with metabolic acidosis includes alcoholic, diabetic, lactic, uremic, and starvation acidosis along with ethylene glycol, isopropanol, methanol, paraldehyde, isoniazid, or salicylate poisoning.

Alcoholic ketoacidosis most commonly occurs in severe chronic alcoholics on a recent binge followed 1 to 3 days later by protracted vomiting, decreased food intake, and dehydration. Nausea, vomiting, and abdominal pain are common presenting complaints.

A quick examination of a urine specimen in the emergency department can be helpful in determining the cause of the acidosis. Glucosuria may suggest diabetes; crystalluria can be seen in ethylene glycol poisoning; low specific gravity, proteinuria, and casts can be seen in renal failure; white blood cells and bacteria are present with urosepsis; and significant ketones in an otherwise normal urine may indicate starvation or alcoholic ketosis.

Chest X-ray. Chest x-ray should be obtained in patients with fever, tachypnea, or abnormal findings on physical examination of the chest or lungs.

The most common infection seen in alcoholism is pneumonia. Although alcoholics may contract pneumonia from a variety of bacteria, *Streptococcus pneumoniae* is still the most common organism. The increased incidence of pneumonia is the result of smoking, decreased ciliary function, decreased surfactant production, and depressed cough reflex.

Computed Tomography and Magnetic Resonance Imaging. Emergent nonenhanced computed tomography (CT scan) of the head should be performed on patients with deteriorating mental status, focal neurologic findings, new-onset seizures, mental status changes out of proportion to the ethanol level, or evidence of head trauma. If the level of consciousness is consistently improving, the patient is unlikely to have an immediate life-threatening problem. Although magnetic resonance imaging (MRI) is superior to CT in detecting most central nervous system disorders, CT is preferred for detecting acute hemorrhage. MRI is superior to CT in the diagnosis of nonhemorrhagic contusions, in evaluating the severity of diffuse axonal injury, and in predicting delayed traumatic intracerebral hematoma.

Recommended Approach

The alcohol-dependent patient may have withdrawal, a mixed alcohol–drug ingestion, occult head trauma, or cervical spine injury. Patients who are unable to sit without assistance or have an altered mental status require an intravenous access. Thiamine (100 mg), naloxone (0.8 mg), and glucose (dextrose 25 g) are given in an intravenous bolus. Rapid blood glucose testing is preferable; however, it is acceptable to give glucose for altered mental status if this testing is not readily available. The airway must be maintained and respiration supported. The patient's vital signs and neurologic status should be monitored. The cervical spine should be immobilized if trauma is suspected.

Therapeutic

Therapeutic Options

The alcohol withdrawal syndrome must be promptly recognized and treated. Treatment is necessary to provide relief from anxiety and hallucinations, to halt progression to major withdrawal and alcohol-related seizures, to allow detection of a treatable primary psychiatric illness, and to prepare the patient for long-term alcohol abstinence with least risk of new drug dependence.

Treatment is also necessary to calm the patient and allow adequate examination for the detection of medical illnesses frequently accompanied or precipitated by alcoholism, such as gastritis, pancreatitis, pneumonia, electrolyte disorders, and hepatitis. Restraints may be necessary. Theoretical liability for detention by reasonable restraint is inconsequential compared with the potential injury the patient may inflict on himself or herself or the hospital staff. Additionally, appropriate restraints are preferable to allowing a questionably competent patient to sign an against-medical-advice (AMA) form and be discharged.

Nonpharmacologic Intervention. Supportive care (reassurance, reality orientation, personal attention, and general nursing care) can be effective in patients with mild alcohol withdrawal. This requires frequent monitoring of signs and symptoms. Supportive care does not prevent hallucinations, seizures, or arrhythmias. Therefore, patients in moderate to severe withdrawal should receive pharmacologic intervention along with supportive care.

Pharmacologic Intervention. Over the years more than 150 different drug and drug combinations have been reported in the literature for the treatment of alcohol withdrawal.

Recommended Approach

The ideal drug for alcohol withdrawal should have a rapid onset, a wide margin of safety, a metabolism independent of liver function, and no abuse potential. No one drug class fits all of these requirements; however, benzodiazepines are currently the mainstay of treatment. The benzodiazepines have superior anticonvulsant activity, they have the least respiratory and cardiac depressive effect of all the central nervous system depressants, and they can be given parenterally in the uncooperative patient. They exhibit cross-tolerance to alcohol and substitute for the withdrawal of the γ-aminobutyric acid-potentiating (GABA) effect of alcohol, thereby abating withdrawal signs and symptoms.

Although numerous benzodiazepines have been studied without clear superiority, lorazepam is recommended because it has good biovailability with oral, intramuscular, and intravenous routes. It is rapidly and completely absorbed from intramuscular sites in agitated patients with no intravenous access. Even though lorazepam's half-life will increase in patients with cirrhosis or liver failure, the increase is much less than with chlordiazepoxide. Its elimination is only minimally altered in renal failure and in the elderly.

Lorazepam may be given intravenously in a dose of 0.5 to 4.0 mg depending on the severity of the withdrawal. Dosing can be repeated at 10- to 30-minute intervals for patients in severe withdrawal. An intramuscular dose of 0.07 mg/kg can be used. The oral dosage schedule for moderate withdrawal is 6 to 7 mg/d in three divided doses, tapering the amount 1 to 2 mg/d over 4 days. If lorazepam is not available, diazepam (Valium) can be given (5 mg intravenously every 5 minutes) until the patient is calm.

The dosage of benzodiazepines required for alcohol withdrawal is highly variable. The dose should always be titrated to the patient's agitation. Massive intravenous doses—more than 2000 mg of diazepam over 48 hours—have been required in patients with delirium tremens.

Haloperidol or droperidol, dopamine antagonists, can be considered in patients with major alcohol withdrawal or delirium tremens not responding to intravenous benzodiazepines. Haloperidol has little effect on myocardial function or respiratory drive and its safety and efficacy by the intravenous, intramuscular, or oral route in the alcoholic has been reported.

Haloperidol and lorazepam in combination are safe and may be synergistic. Safe use in extremely high doses in patients with serious underlying medical illness has been documented in several studies.

Summary. Rapid, aggressive control of alcohol withdrawal is crucial.

An initial test dose of 1 to 2 mg of lorazepam, 10 to 20 mg of diazepam, or 50 to 100 mg of chlordiazepoxide can be given orally to the patient. Observation of the patient for 2 to 4 hours guides the physician as to the dose required for outpatient treatment. Patients should remain under observation or be admitted until it is clear their manifestations will not progress once the effects of the benzodiazepine have dissipated.

Outpatient treatment consists of a benzodiazepine in a tapering dose for 3 to 6 days, depending on the severity of symptoms. Adequate diet, abstinence, and participation in a rehabilitation program in the community are also desirable.

Benzodiazepines should be used only when clearly indicated and only for the minimum time required to avoid their abuse, addiction, and withdrawal in the alcoholic. Therapy must be individualized; the above suggestions are simply guidelines.

Adjunct Therapy. Patients being treated for alcohol withdrawal should receive thiamine (100 mg intravenously) and magnesium (2 g). Multivitamin preparations are usually added to the patient's intravenous fluid because of chronic malnutrition. Several preparations are available containing vitamins A through E, folic acid, vitamin B_{12}, and biotin. Volume depletion, if present, can be corrected with normal saline.

FOLLOW-UP

Because of the alcoholic's inability to care for himself or herself, satisfactory outpatient treatment is difficult to obtain. Optimal outpatient therapy includes a concerned family member or friend to ensure the patient will take the medications properly, appear at follow-up appointments, abstain from alcohol, and maintain an adequate diet. Alcoholic patients who undergo outpatient treatment need close supervision; therefore, a follow-up appointment within 24 to 48 hours should be considered.

The problem of when to hospitalize the alcoholic is a dilemma for physicians. Most of these patients have medical, psychiatric, and social problems. Hospitalization is frequently necessary to diagnose and treat these multiple problems adequately. Moreover, with alcoholics who are no longer able to care for themselves, hospitalization is often dictated for this reason alone. Unfortunately, many managed care plans limit or prohibit inpatient detoxification. The following are suggested guidelines for admission for detoxification of alcohol-dependent patients.

Acute Intoxication. Acute intoxication alone seldom requires admission; however, combined alcohol–drug overdose or associated medical, psychiatric, or social problems may require hospitalization. *Acute alcohol intoxication is a diagnosis of exclusion.*

Alcohol Withdrawal. Patients with signs of major withdrawal (fever, hallucinations, confusion, extreme agitation) always require admission. Patients with mild alcohol withdrawal can be observed in the emergency department or a holding unit. After 4 to 6 hours of observation, the alert, oriented patient whose vital signs, physical examination, and appropriate laboratory analysis are within normal limits may be released. Nevertheless, the patient requires treatment for the underlying disease of alcoholism and should be advised or referred accordingly.

Seizures. Patients with their first alcohol-dependent seizure are usually admitted. This allows initiation of drug therapy, diagnostic evaluation, and continuous monitoring of patient status. The alcoholic with a first-time seizure may be discharged to a suitable social situation, however, in the following circumstances: the patient's alcohol withdrawal is mild and easily controlled either by supportive care or with low-dose benzodiazepines; the diagnostic workup including a head CT scan is unremarkable; the patient has not had recurrent seizures; the patient has been observed to be, alert, and oriented and to have normal vital signs, physical examination, and laboratory studies during the 6 hours since the last seizure; and appropriate outpatient follow-up can be ensured.

Patients with partial seizures or focal neurologic findings on physical examination require admission unless these findings have been previously documented. Patients with seizures associated with head trauma or with mixed alcohol–drug withdrawal seizures are admitted. Status epilepticus or recurrent seizures during observation indicate a lack of seizure control aslo requiring hospitalization.

Psychiatric and Social Problems. Many hospitals today have chemical dependency units that combine the advantages of the acute care floor and a secure psychiatric unit. There are some psychiatric and social conditions in the alcoholic that still could be better handled on a general psychiatric unit: psychosis, exacerbation of schizophrenia, depression with suicidal tendencies, any patient who is a danger to himself or others, or alcoholic hallucinosis with an otherwise clear sensorium. Any patient who is no longer able to care for herself or himself also requires admission. Although this patient's ultimate destination is a rehabilitation center or a board-and-care program, hospitalization may be necessary to rule out medical or psychiatric illness and to treat impending withdrawal symptoms adequately.

Most communities have either an Alcoholics Anonymous chapter or a treatment center for anyone who desires help with alcohol. In small communities, clergy or social workers can usually arrange rehabilitation. Whatever medical, psychological, or social problem brings the alcoholic to the physician, the underlying problem is alcoholism. The ultimate goal is abstinence. Abstinence is possible, even in the most difficult patient. This disease will surely progress if we do not first recognize alcoholism and then make sure the patient has the opportunity to participate in a rehabilitation program.

DISCUSSION
Prevalence

The disastrous effects and widespread incidence of alcoholism are well known to physicians. Motor vehicle accidents, drowning, suicides, homicides, divorce, violent crime, child abuse, unemployment, and disruption of the family are often either directly or indirectly associated with excessive alcohol consumption.

Alcohol is the single most common recreational drug taken by Americans, and per capita consumption is increasing. There are an estimated 18 million alcoholics in the United States and more than 200,000 alcohol-related deaths each year. Up to one third of adult inpatients have problems related to alcohol.

Alcoholism is the leading cause of mortality and morbidity in the United States, and the cost to the nation is estimated to be greater than $130 billion annually. Alcoholism permeates all levels of society and may be humanity's most devastating problem short of war and malnutrition.

Related Basic Science
Genetics

Several family studies have confirmed that rates of alcoholism are significantly higher in relatives of alcoholics than in relatives of nonalcoholics. The majority of twin studies also support the concept that alcoholism is genetically influenced. Several adoption studies have found that sons of alcoholics were four times more likely to become alcoholics than sons of nonalcoholics.

Altered Molecular Biology

Tolerance to the effects of alcohol is a complicated phenomenon involving changes in several neural systems. A great deal of evidence supports a role for the inhibitory γ-aminobutyric acid (GABA) neurons in alcohol withdrawal, whereby alcohol potentiates the postsynaptic effect of GABA. Benzodiazepines and barbiturates may substitute for the withdrawal of the GABA-potentiating effect of alcohol and abate withdrawal signs and symptoms. The alcohol withdrawal syndrome is characterized by increased activity of the noradrenergic system, demonstrated by diaphoresis, tachycardia, hypertension, and tremor. Concentrations of norepinephrine in plasma, urine, and cerebrospinal fluid are elevated during alcohol withdrawal.

Physiologic or Metabolic Derangement

The majority of alcohol is metabolized in the liver. Oxidation of alcohol is a complex process involving three enzyme systems, all contained in the hepatocyte. The primary pathway is by alcohol dehydrogenase, as briefly summarized here:

$$\text{Ethanol} \xrightarrow[\text{NAD–NADH}]{\substack{\text{alcohol} \\ \text{dehydrogenase}}} \text{acetaldehyde} \xrightarrow[\text{NAD–NADH}]{\substack{\text{aldehyde} \\ \text{dehydrogenase}}}$$

$$\text{acetyl coenzyme A} \xrightarrow[\text{cycle}]{\text{citric acid}} CO_2 + H_2O$$

An alternate pathway, the microsomal ethanol-oxidizing system (MEOS), can be induced by increased activity of chronic alcohol exposure. Many effects of alcoholism are produced by the toxic by-products (hydrogen and acetaldehyde), the acceleration of metabolism of other drugs, and activation of hepatotoxic compounds by these metabolic pathways.

There is enormous variation among patients in the rate of disappearance of ethanol from the blood, ranging from 9 to 36 mg/dL/h in published data. Alcohol is usually eliminated at a rate of 10 to 20 mg/dL/h in the nonalcoholic. The elimination may be increased to greater than 20 mg/dL/h and possibly as high as 36 mg/dL/h in the chronic drinker (Jones 1993; Gershman and Steeper 1991; Brennan DF, et al., 1994).

Natural History and Its Modification with Treatment

The natural history of alcoholism is variable. It may appear in any patient despite age or social status. The age of onset of alcoholism continues to decrease. Up to 6% of high school seniors drink daily and it is not unusual to see children under 16 years of age who have already graduated from an alcohol detoxification program. Many also begin drinking heavily after the age of 60.

In early stages, the typical alcoholic patient is usually 20 to 30 years of age and does most of his or her drinking on weekends. After age 30, the patient commonly progresses to physiologic dependence. Typically, he or she fluctuates between abstinence and prolonged heavy drinking. Hospitalization for alcohol-related problems typically begins after age 40, and death occurs in the fifth decade of life.

From 10 to 30% of alcoholics have a spontaneous recovery without treatment. The reason for this may be a sudden change in health, marriage, or occupation. Patients who abuse alcohol do not conform to stereotypes. The "Bowery bum" or "Skid Row" alcoholic accounts for less than 5% of the alcoholic population. Many alcoholics have attended or graduated from college and have professional or managerial positions.

Several drugs have been used in an attempt to reduce alcohol consumption. Disulfiram, imipramine, desipramine, amitriptyline, zimelidine, fluoxetine, lithium, and buspirone have been somewhat effective in recent trials.

There are no reliable data on modification of alcoholism with treatment. Outcome studies are unattainable because of the difficulty determining what is a success—a reduction in drinking or abstinence. Additionally, it is almost impossible to quantitate a favorable reduction in drinking or the successful length of time for abstinence. Moreover, one must rely on patient reporting, which is historically unreliable with this population.

There is a strong relationship between alcoholism and many psychiatric disorders. These disorders include unipolar depression, manic–depressive illness, antisocial personality, anxiety disorders, and schizophrenia. Without good control of the above-mentioned psychiatric disorders, the patient may not have the ability to reduce or stop drinking.

Prevention

Alcoholism has been a prevalent problem for society for most of recorded history. It is unlikely to be prevented. Through most of the United States most elementary schools now have drug and alcohol awareness programs. Intervention at the earliest possible level with our children is the best chance to decrease the incidence of this disorder.

Cost Containment

Outpatient detoxification of a patient manifesting symptoms of alcohol withdrawal is probably used much more widely than is generally reported and can be accomplished in a safe, effective, and cost-effective manner. Potential disadvantages of outpatient treatment include the possibility that a patient might develop some of the more serious signs of the alcohol withdrawal syndrome (e.g., seizures or delirium that require immediate medical intervention). Advantages of outpatient treatment management over alternative forms of treatment include maintaining the patient in his or her environment; affording the opportunity for continued interaction with various social support systems; helping the patient learn to maintain abstinence in the face of continued exposure to alcohol; providing continuity of care with the same treatment personnel from treatment of the abstinence syndrome through outpatient rehabilitation; and providing treatment at significantly lower cost than inpatient treatment.

Inpatient detoxification can also be refined. Symptom-triggered benzodiazepine therapy for alcohol withdrawal has recently been developed. This treatment consists of monitoring patients and providing medication only when symptoms appear. Current studies demonstrate that patients with alcohol withdrawal treated with this method completed their treatment courses sooner and required less benzodiazepine than patients treated using the standard fixed-schedule approach.

REFERENCES

Brennan DF, Falk JL, Reed R, et al: Ethanol elimination rates in an emergency department population. Ann Emerg Med 1994;23(3):632.
Cyr M, Wartman S. The effectiveness of routine screening questions in the detection of alcoholism. JAMA 1988;259:51.
Gershman H, Steeper J. Rate of clearance of ethanol from the blood of intoxicated patients in the emergency department. J Emerg Med 1991;9:307.
Hayashidra M, Alterman AI, McLellan AT, et al. Comparative effectiveness and costs of inpatient and outpatient detoxification of patients with mild to moderate alcohol withdrawal syndrome. N Engl J Med 1989;320:358.
Hoffman RS, Goldfrank LR. Ethanol-associated metabolic disorders. Emerg Clin North Am 1989;7:943.
Jones AW. Disappearance rate of ethanol from the blood of human subjects: implications in forensic toxicology. J Forens Sci 1993;38(1):104.
Rosenbloom AJ. Optimizing drug treatment of alcohol withdrawal. Am J Med 1986;81:901.
Saitz R, Mayo-Smith MF, Roberts MS, et al. Individualized treatment for alcohol withdrawal: A randomized double-blind controlled trial. JAMA 1994;272:519.
Turner RC, Lichstein PR, Peden JG, et al. Alcohol withdrawal syndromes: A review of pathophysiology, clinical presentation and treatment. J Gen Intern Med 1989;4:432.

CHAPTER 24–2

Methanol and Ethylene Glycol Poisoning

Keith D. Wrenn, M.D.

DEFINITION

Methanol, or wood alcohol, is a destructive distillate of wood that is used as a solvent and energy source in products such as varnish, shellac, duplicating fluid, stains, enamels, film, dyes, gasoline additives, solid canned fuel, and windshield-washing fluid. Ethylene glycol is used as a solvent in paints, lacquers, and detergents and as a freezing point depressant in commercial antifreeze solutions.

ETIOLOGY

The ingestion of either methanol or ethylene glycol is potentially life-threatening, and both substances have the potential to cause chronic morbidity. Both chemicals have caused toxicity and death in the setting of accidental exposure and suicide. Chronic alcoholics also use them as an alcohol substitute because they are cheaper than alcohol. Epidemic exposures have been reported involving bootleg whiskey disasters and illegally prepared Austrian wine, in times of economic hardship, and during military mobilizations. Methanol, in contrast to ethylene glycol, may also be well absorbed by the skin and respiratory tract. Solvent abusers ("huffers," "sniffers") and occasional motorists who clean the inside of their windshield in the winter may become toxic with methanol. Two compounds, diethylene glycol and propylene glycol, have structures and toxic effects similar to those of ethylene glycol. Diethylene glycol is approximately twice as potent as ethylene glycol, with a greater tendency to cause liver toxicity, whereas propylene glycol is about one half as potent a toxin as ethylene glycol.

CRITERIA FOR DIAGNOSIS
Suggestive

The presentation of the patient who is poisoned with either of these compounds is relatively nonspecific. In chronic alcoholics, who are especially predisposed to toxicity from these agents, the central nervous system abnormalities, abdominal complaints, and cardiopulmonary problems mimic other processes to which alcoholics are prone, including intoxication, gastritis, pancreatitis, and alcoholic or diabetic ketoacidosis. Salicylate toxicity, stroke, subarachnoid hemorrhage, meningitis, renal colic, small bowel obstruction, perforated peptic ulcer, and congestive heart failure have been mistakenly diagnosed in patients with toxicity from these compounds. The diagnosis should be suspected when there is a definite history of exposure or a clinical situation predisposing to exposure in association with a wide-gap metabolic acidosis and a widened osmolar gap. Methanol has a peculiar tendency to cause visual symptoms and funduscopic abnormalities, whereas ethylene glycol tends to cause acute renal failure.

Definitive

Although screening tests are available, definitive diagnosis requires the measurement of these compounds by gas chromatography.

CLINICAL MANIFESTATIONS
Subjective

Although toxicity with either agent may occur as early as 30 minutes or as late as 72 hours after ingestion, a lag period of 12 to 24 hours is typical before symptoms are noted. The smallest doses reported to cause death are 15 mL of 40% methanol and 20 mL of pure ethylene glycol. Typically, symptoms occur with greater than 30 mL or pure methanol or 1.4 mL/kg (about 100 mL in an adult) of pure ethylene glycol. Patients ingesting doses of 500 to 600 mL of methanol and 240 to 400 mL of ethylene glycol have been reported to survive.

The most common symptom seen with methanol toxicity is indistinct vision described variously as "like being in a snowstorm, "a skin over the eyes," "blurred," "seeing the wind," or "frank blindness." No symptom or set of symptoms is unique to ethylene glycol toxicity. Both agents commonly cause intoxication or dizziness (similar to ethanol intoxication), headache, nausea, vomiting, hematemesis, abdominal pain, myalgia, weakness, paresthesias, seizures, and coma. Breathlessness is seen surprisingly infrequently.

Ethylene glycol toxicity has been noted to evolve through three indistinct stages. Gastrointestinal abnormalities and central nervous system symptomatology occur in the first 12 to 24 hours. A second stage of primarily cardiopulmonary complaints, such as shortness of breath, is less reliably seen, but occurs from 24 to 72 hours after ingestion. A third phase, with potentially irreversible renal abnormalities, occurs after 24 to 72 hours.

Objective
Physical Examination

Eye findings are the most commonly mentioned abnormalities in methanol toxicity. Dilated and sluggishly reactive to fixed pupils are commonly seen. The earliest, somewhat subtle abnormality found on funduscopic examination is hyperemic disks. Over the course of hours to days, retinal edema and engorged retinal veins, with white to gray striae emanating from the disk, may develop in association with central scotomata. The correlation of ophthalmic signs with visual symptoms is poor, and the severity of eye findings seems to bear little relation to either the length of the lag period after ingestion or the methanol level, except at very low or very high levels. Optic atrophy develops late, after weeks to months, and permanent visual deficits may be seen, but are not universal.

Confusion, agitation, anxiety, ataxia, nystagmus, ophthalmoplegia, nuchal rigidity ("pseudomeningitis"), seizures, myoclonus, hyporeflexia, hypotension, and bradycardia may be seen in the early stages of toxicity with either methanol or ethylene glycol. Exquisite abdominal tenderness with rigidity, but without true rebound tenderness, and both hypoactive and hyperactive bowel sounds are common. True Kussmaul's respirations are uncommon. Methanol has an odor distinct from ethanol and may be smelled on the patient's breath. Ethylene glycol is odorless and an intoxicated patient without the smell of alcohol on the breath should alert the physician to the possibility of ethylene glycol ingestion.

In the second and third stages of ethylene glycol toxicity hypertension may supervene. Costovertebral angle tenderness is also seen in the third stage of ethylene glycol toxicity. Common late problems with methanol toxicity include amnesia for the events surrounding presentation and obstipation. Death commonly occurs as a sudden decompensation with respiratory arrest in association with refractory shock. Patients with fatal methanol intoxication may arrest with a characteristic "inspiratory apnea" associated with bradycardia and opisthotonus.

Routine Laboratory Abnormalities

Among routine laboratory tests such as the complete blood count, electrolyte and chemistry panels, and urinalysis, the most likely finding is a low serum bicarbonate level. In fact, both methanol and ethylene glycol toxicity almost always cause a low serum bicarbonate unless there is associated metabolic alkalosis from another cause (e.g., vomiting). Late in ethylene glycol toxicity, elevation of blood urea nitrogen and serum creatinine may occur but volume depletion in methanol toxicity may also cause uremia. The urinalysis in ethylene glycol toxicity may slow typical oxalate crystals or signs of acute renal failure including granular casts and renal tubular epithelial cells. The complete blood count may show macrocytic anemia, a clue to underlying alcoholism, but no specific abnormalities are routinely seen. On chemistry panels, elevated liver enzymes may also be a clue to underlying alcoholism. Hypocalcemia may occur as a result of acute renal failure in ethylene glycol toxicity.

PLANS

Diagnostic

The sine qua non for diagnosing severe methanol or ethylene glycol toxicity is laboratory evidence of a metabolic acidosis (decreased bicarbonate), with both a widened anion gap and widened osmolar gap (Table 24–2–1). The acidosis with both these compounds is particularly severe and correlates with prognosis. In methanol poisoning, the severity of eye-ground changes correlates best with the degree of acidosis. Distinguishing between methanol and ethylene glycol toxicity is not of immediate importance because the treatment is the same in both settings. Ethanol is the most common cause of widened osmolar gap and may also cause a widened anion gap and osmolar gap (alcoholic ketoacidosis), but ketones are usually evident in the urine. In evaluating a

patient for methanol or ethylene glycol toxicity a concomitant ethanol level is mandatory, not only to assess whether ethanol accounts for the unexplained osmolar gap, but also to assess whether coingestion of ethanol has occurred, which affects management. Methanol and ethylene glycol toxicity uncommonly cause ketonuria. Isopropyl alcohol (rubbing alcohol) causes a widened osmolar gap, but not a widened anion gap, and is also associated with marked ketosis and ketonuria. Paraldehyde may cause both widened anion and osmolar gaps, but the odor of the breath is characteristic. This compound is rarely available outside the hospital setting and is rarely used now. Salicylate, iron, isoniazid, carbon monoxide, and arsenic toxicity may cause a widened anion gap, but do not cause a widened osmolar gap. Chronic renal failure may by itself widen the osmolar gap, but acute renal failure does not. Either type of renal failure may contribute to a widened anion gap.

Because ethylene glycol is associated with the development of acute renal failure of varying severity, baseline and serial blood urea nitrogen, creatinine, and potassium measurements are mandatory. In addition, the urinalysis can be very important in diagnosing ethylene glycol toxicity. Not only are proteinuria and hematuria early findings, but the presence of sheaf-shaped, prismatic, or rhomboid birefringent oxalate crystals in the urine is almost pathognomonic. Unfortunately the crystals are not uniformly seen. Because sodium fluorescein is a frequent additive to antifreeze preparations, application of ultraviolet light from a Wood's lamp to urine with a pH greater than 4.5 within 4 hours of ingestion may cause fluorescence in the presence of ethylene glycol toxicity. Wood's lamp evaluation of the skin and oral mucous membranes may also provide a clue to ethylene glycol exposure, especially in children or comatose alcoholics.

The serum calcium is usually normal in methanol toxicity, but frequently is low in ethylene glycol poisoning. The serum amylase is frequently elevated in methanol toxicity, suggesting that pancreatic injury from methanol is common and contributes to the clinical picture.

Measurement of ethylene glycol or methanol levels confirms the diagnosis and may help to guide treatment, but the relationship of these levels to toxicity and prognosis is controversial. Methanol levels below 20 mg/dL rarely cause serious toxicity, whereas levels above 80 mg/dL are frequently lethal. Levels of 50 mg/dL or more consistently cause serious toxicity. The consistently lethal level of ethylene glycol is 200 mg/dL, and toxicity is frequently present at levels about 25 mg/dL. The elimination half-life of both these compounds is relatively short (on the order of 3 hours) and levels may fall as toxicity becomes evident. Furthermore, it is metabolic by-products rather than the compounds themselves that are thought to cause toxicity.

Therapeutic

The initial management of any overdose should revolve around securing airway, breathing, and cardiovascular stability, with special attention paid to ensuring protection of the airway in patients with altered mental status. Next comes assessment of the need for naloxone, supplemental glucose, and thiamine in patients with altered mental status. Ipecac is contraindicated, given the propensity for these compounds to cause altered mental status. Orogastric lavage within 30 minutes of ingestion is reasonable, but these compounds are rapidly absorbed and gastric decontamination 30 to 60 minutes after ingestion does not appear to be beneficial. Because methanol may be resecreted into the stomach, continuous nasogastric suction may help enhance elimination. Activated charcoal has little efficacy in adsorbing these compounds.

After airway, breathing, and cardiovascular stability have been secured, efforts to inhibit the metabolic conversion of these compounds to their toxic metabolites is the next step. Because the initial metabolic degradation of both these compounds is by alcohol dehydrogenase and because ethanol has a much higher affinity for this enzyme than either methanol or ethylene glycol, the use of ethanol orally or intravenously has been advocated. The goal is to keep the ethanol level between 100 and 200 mg/dL, which provides a relatively low level of intoxication, but saturates this enzyme. In patients who have recently ingested ethanol, loading doses of ethanol may be unnecessary and maintenance doses may need to be withheld until the ethanol level falls to desired levels. In the absence of a significant ethanol level, loading may be undertaken intravenously or orally, followed by maintenance doses (Table

TABLE 24–2–1. CALCULATING THE ANION AND OSMOLAL GAPS

Anion gap	$[Na] - [Cl + HCO_3]$
	Normal value is 12 ± 2 mEq/L
Osmolal gap	Measured osmolality − calculated osmolality
	Normal value is less than 15 mOsm
Calculated osmolality*	$2[Na] + \dfrac{[BUN]}{2.8} + \dfrac{[Glu]}{18} + \dfrac{[EtOH]}{4.2}$

BUN, blood urea nitrogen; Glu, glucose; EtOH, ethylene alcohol.
*For methanol it takes 3 mg/dL to add 1 mOsm to calculated osmolality; for ethylene glycol it takes 6 mg/dL to add 1 mOsm to calculated osmolality.

24–2–2) and hourly monitoring of the ethanol level. Oral dosing is often impractical because of the associated nausea and vomiting. When hemodialysis is undertaken, ethanol dosing must be increased. A more potent inhibitor of alcohol dehydrogenase, 4-methylpyrazole, is undergoing clinical trials in both methanol and ethylene glycol overdose and, although not yet available in the United States, appears promising because of its rapid onset and prolonged duration of action.

Alkalinization with sodium bicarbonate goes hand in hand with inhibiting metabolic degradation. The toxic metabolic by-products that cause the metabolic acidosis are not metabolized to regenerate bicarbonate as occurs in lactic acidosis and ketoacidosis. Bicarbonate infusion should always be undertaken when the pH falls below 7.2 or the bicarbonate is less than 15 mEq/dL. Normalization of the pH has been shown to relieve symptoms and signs (often dramatically) in methanol toxicity and to affect the prognosis favorably. Care should be taken to not cause overshoot alkalosis and to watch for hypokalemia secondary to intracellular potassium shifts. Infusion of sodium bicarbonate may also cause volume overload in patients with underlying renal or cardiovascular disease.

Dialysis is often indicated to remove the compounds and their toxic metabolic by-products, which are readily dialyzable. Hemodialysis is preferable to peritoneal dialysis and should be performed with the largest surface area dialysis coil and the most rapid blood flow tolerated by the patient. Dialysis should continue until symptoms and signs resolve and the methanol or ethylene glycol levels are below 20 mg/dL. Indications for dialysis include the following:

- Any metabolic acidosis
- Confirmed intoxication with a methanol level greater than 50 mg/dL or an ethylene glycol level greater than 25 to 50 mg/dL
- Confirmed consumption of a known toxic dose (> 30 mL of 100% methanol or 20 mL of 100% ethylene glycol)
- Deteriorating vital signs
- Altered mental status
- Oxalate crystalluria in ethylene glycol poisoning
- Visual or funduscopic abnormalities with methanol poisoning
- Acute renal failure unresponsive to conservative measures

Aggressive early treatment with inhibition of metabolic degradation, bicarbonate infusion, and dialysis not only improves survival but also limits morbidity in terms of the development of visual problems with methanol or acute renal failure with ethylene glycol. Some controversy exists about using only serum levels as an indicator of when to begin dialysis, because chronic alcoholics who coingest ethanol may remain asymptomatic.

Malnutrition may contribute to toxicity because B vitamins are cofactors in the metabolic degradation of these compounds and their toxic by-products. Folic acid is critical for the metabolism of formic acid, a by-product of methanol, and intravenous doses as high as 50 to 70 mg every 4 hours for 24 hours have been recommended. Pyridoxine and thiamine both promote the metabolism of glyoxylate to nontoxic products. Additionally, thiamine promotes the conversion of lactate, commonly present with both ethylene glycol and methanol toxicity, to pyruvate. In malnourished chronic alcoholics, folate and thiamine defi-

ciency is often present, and replacement therapy is universally indicated. The efficacy of vitamin supplementation in the treatment of toxicity with methanol or ethylene glycol is not clinically established, but their use is associated with few significant side effects.

Forced diuresis has been suggested as a treatment for both methanol and ethylene glycol toxicity. It appears to be ineffective in methanol poisoning, but may be of some use in ethylene glycol poisoning to prevent development of oliguric renal failure. Steroids have not proven useful in treating the funduscopic abnormalities of methanol poisoning. Routine calcium administration has also not proven helpful in ethylene glycol toxicity.

FOLLOW-UP

Patients presenting with significant toxicity should be hospitalized. In the largest epidemic of methanol poisoning to date, not only did a number of patients with significant acidosis appear relatively well, but also patients who had been treated in the emergency department occasionally had a recrudescence of toxicity after discharge over the next 24 to 72 hours. In the setting of both methanol and ethylene glycol toxicity, serial evaluation of the electrolytes (especially potassium and bicarbonate), blood urea nitrogen, creatinine, and the anion and osmolar gaps is necessary. If ethanol is used therapeutically, its level should be followed frequently because of wide individual variability in its metabolism. Serum levels of the offending compound, if available, should be followed until they fall below toxic levels; this should be done hourly when dialysis is undertaken.

DISCUSSION
Prevalence and Incidence

Poisoning is common in our society, and in the absence of epidemics, it is estimated that methanol and ethylene glycol cause hundreds of deaths each year in the United States. The vast majority of these poisonings occur in chronic alcoholics who use these substances as cheaper substitutes for ethanol. Sporadic accidental poisoning, particularly by children or adolescents, also occurs and suicide attempts have been frequently reported.

Related Basic Science

Both these agents are rapidly absorbed from the gastrointestinal tract and undergo metabolism in the liver by alcohol dehydrogenase. There is also some renal excretion of both compounds and their metabolic by-products, especially with ethylene glycol. Methanol may also be excreted through the respiratory tract (around 5% of an ingested dose) and in sweat. Oxidation of methanol by alcohol dehydrogenase produces formaldehyde, which is further metabolized by aldehyde dehydrogenase to formic acid and CO_2. Ethylene glycol is oxidized by alcohol dehydrogenase to glycolaldehyde, which in turn is metabolized to glyoxylic acid, glycolic acid, and oxalic acid.

Neither methanol nor ethylene glycol itself is thought to contribute to serious toxicity other than intoxication. The acidosis and visual changes that occur with methanol poisoning are thought to be due to formic acid. Formic acid, a metabolic by-product, and lactic acid, which results from tissue hypoxia and a reversal in the NADH/NAD ratio, cause most of the metabolic acidosis. Formic acid also inhibits cytochrome oxidase, which is thought to be the principal cause of funduscopic abnormalities. Inhibition of cytochrome oxidase causes histotoxic hypoxia, disrupts the flow of axoplasm and contributes to the development of intraaxonal swelling and disk edema. At the same time, inhibition by formic acid of the Na, K-ATPase disrupts electrical conductivity, causing blindness. Blood flow in the choroid of the retina is very high and cytochrome oxidase is present in white matter in relatively small amounts, making this tissue particularly susceptible to inhibition of cytochrome oxidase. In autopsy specimens, pulmonary edema, cerebral edema, and meningeal and subarachnoid petechiae have been noted, as has pancreatic necrosis. Symmetric, bilateral hemorrhagic putaminal necrosis is a common autopsy finding which may be unique to methanol poisoning. It can be seen on computed tomography scans of the brain as early as 3 days after ingestion. Computed tomography

TABLE 24–2–2. ETHANOL DOSING IN METHANOL AND ETHYLENE GLYCOL POISONING

	Intravenous (10% ethanol in D₅W)	Oral (90%)
Loading dose	0.75 gm/kg	0.75 gm/kg
Usual 70-kg adult dose	530 mL	60 mL
Minimal maintenance dose (not during dialysis or with nondrinker)	0.1 g/kg/h	0.125 g/kg/h
Usual 70-kg adult dose	75 mL/h	10 mL/h
Maximal maintenance dose	0.2 mg/kg/h	0.25 g/kg/h
Usual 70-kg adult dose	150 mL/h	20 mL/h

D₅W, 5% dextrose in water.

also may reveal extensive white matter necrosis. Folic acid is critical for the subsequent metabolism of formic acid. The affinity of methanol for alcohol dehydrogenase is one-fifth to one-ninth that of ethanol. Formic acid, unlike lactic acid, is not metabolized to regenerate bicarbonate.

With ethylene glycol poisoning, it is glycolic acid that is thought to contribute principally to the early metabolic acidosis. Lactate also accumulates because of tissue hypoxia and reversed NADH/NAD ratio. The central nervous system toxicity is also thought to be due to accumulated acidic intermediates, and oxalic acid crystals have been noted in pathologic brain specimens. Cerebral edema and focal brain hemorrhages have been noted. The renal failure probably results mostly from the effect of metabolic acidosis in decreasing renal blood flow, but calcium oxalate crystals are found in pathologic kidney specimens, both in the cortex and in the tubular system. It is postulated that oxalic acid chelates intracellular divalent cations, leading to cellular death. The presence of these crystals in kidney biopsy specimens is virtually pathognomonic of ethylene glycol poisoning. Glomerular involvement has been noted in pathologic kidney specimens. A myocarditis and myopathy have been described in pathologic heart specimens.

Pyridoxine promotes the metabolism of glyoxylate, another possible toxic by-product, to glycine, which is nontoxic. Thiamine promotes the metabolism of glyoxylate to another nontoxic by-product, α-hydroxy-β-ketoadipate. Empiric therapy with these vitamins may be beneficial.

The affinity of ethylene glycol for alcohol dehydrogenase is also much less than that of ethanol. Glycolic acid, like formic acid, is not metabolized to regenerate bicarbonate.

Natural History and Its Modification with Treatment

Susceptibility to these two substances varies considerably, depending on the amount ingested, coingestion of ethanol, associated B-vitamin deficiencies, underlying disease, age, and the metabolic predisposition to toxicity. In the last case, chronic alcoholics with enzyme induction may be at increased risk of toxicity unless ethanol is coingested. The degree of acidosis is proportional to morbidity and mortality. The severity of the funduscopic findings also implies a poor prognosis, in terms of both permanent visual defects and mortality. In the largest epidemic of methanol poisoning to date, 36% of patients were acidotic, and there was a 13% mortality rate (Bennett et al., 1953). Twenty-six percent of the acidotic patients had bicarbonate levels below 10 mEq/L. More than half the patients who died did so within 30 minutes of arrival to the emergency department. Infants have much less alcohol dehydrogenase activity and may have a longer half-life and less toxicity than adults or children over the age of 5 years.

In ethylene glycol poisoning epidemics, mortality has approached 25%, even in young healthy adults (Bennett et al., 1953). Death occurs

in two groups. Less commonly, sudden death from respiratory arrest occurs within 24 hours. Late deaths beyond 24 hours are more common and usually are related to the consequences of acute renal failure or cardiovascular collapse. The course of renal failure is variable, and aggressive treatment may limit progression of renal insufficiency. Permanent renal insufficiency occurs uncommonly.

Prevention

Careful labeling of products containing methanol and ethylene glycol is the most important preventive measure. Educational measures aimed at alcoholics and adolescents, as well as limiting the concentration of these substances in the products in which they are sold, are also likely to be of benefit. Adding emetics to products containing these substances has been suggested. Finally, the practice of draining and saving radiator antifreeze should be discouraged, and use of methanol-containing compounds in enclosed, poorly ventilated spaces should be discouraged.

Cost Containment

Because significant toxicity with either of these drugs may occur without overt symptomatology, blood samples must be drawn, including electrolytes, glucose, blood urea nitrogen, creatinine, and osmolality by freezing-point depression. If possible, actual methanol or ethylene glycol levels should be obtained. The decision about whether to perform hemodialysis depends on the severity of intoxication, the drug level, and the availability of hemodialysis.

Not every patient who has ingested one of these toxins develops toxicity. Unless other conditions warranting admission are present, the patient may be safely discharged. In the absence of symptoms or signs and if no anion gap acidosis or significant osmolal gap is present, the patient may be safely discharged if no other conditions warranting admission are present.

REFERENCES

Band FJ, Galliot M, Astier A, et al. Treatment of ethylene glycol poisoning with intravenous 4-methylpyrazole. N Engl J Med 1988;319:97.
Bennett IL, Cary FH, Mitchell GL, Cooper MN. Acute methyl alcohol poisoning: A review based on experiences in an outbreak of 323 cases. Medicine (Baltimore) 1953;32:431.
Brent J, Lucas M, Kulig K, Rumack BH. Methanol poisoning in a 6-week old infant. J Pediatrics 1991;118:644.
Gabow PA, Oay K, Sullivan JB, Leopoff R. Organic acids in ethylene glycol intoxication. Ann Intern Med 1986;105:16.
Liesivuori J, Savolainen H. Methanol and formic acid toxicity: Biochemical mechanisms. Pharmacol, Toxicol 1991;69:157.
Smithline N, Gardner KD. Gaps: Ionic and osmolal. JAMA 1976;236:1594.

CHAPTER 24–3

Beta-Blocker and Calcium Channel Blocker Toxicity

Keith D. Wrenn, M.D.

DEFINITION

Beta blocker or calcium channel blocker toxicity is defined as any adverse effect caused by ingestion of either of these types of drugs, regardless of the dose.

ETIOLOGY

Toxicity associated with the use of beta blocking or calcium channel blocking drugs usually occurs in patients during routine long-term use. Because patients who attempt suicide often take what is available and because both these classes of drugs are used by increasing numbers of

patients for an expanding list of indications, overdoses with these drugs are now seen more commonly.

Toxicity should be considered in the following settings for which these drugs are prescribed: hypertension, coronary atherosclerotic heart disease, arrhythmias, diastolic left ventricular dysfunction, hypertrophic cardiomyopathy, and migraine. Beta blockers are also used for glaucoma, stage fright, pheochromocytoma, and tetralogy of Fallot. Calcium channel blockers are used for angina, Raynaud's phenomenon, esophageal spasm, and dysmenorrhea. With some exceptions both the beta blocking and calcium channel blocking agents have negative inotropic and negative chronotropic effects; thus, patients with left ventricular systolic dysfunction or conduction system abnormalities are more likely to develop toxicity with routine use. Toxicity with these agents should be suspected in all situations involving electromechanical dissociation. In addition, drug interactions are common. Both classes of drugs interact with each other to cause additive negative inotropic and chronotropic effects and interact with digoxin and clonidine to cause negative chronotropic effects. Adverse interactions with tricyclic antidepressants also occur. As both classes of drugs are metabolized primarily by the liver, liver disease may also promote toxicity.

CRITERIA FOR DIAGNOSIS

With the exception of a known overdose, the diagnosis cannot be made definitively because serum levels are not readily available. The diagnosis of toxicity from these drugs is a clinical one based on clinical manifestations. When a patient who is known to be taking these drugs or who is in a group likely to take these drugs presents with hypotension, bradycardia, or electromechanical dissociation, toxicity should be suspected.

CLINICAL MANIFESTATIONS
Subjective

Typical symptoms of toxicity include syncope, lightheadedness, and central nervous system abnormalities including confusion, hallucinations, delirium, and coma. Dyspnea may be the presenting symptom in patients with a predisposition to heart failure or bronchospastic disease. Overdoses may precipitate seizures with both classes of drugs. Nausea and constipation occasionally complicate calcium channel blocker use. Esophageal spasm has been noted with beta blocker toxicity.

Objective
Physical Examination

Bradycardia and hypotension are the most common signs of toxicity with either of these agents. Both are often severe and refractory to routine resuscitation measures. Often a sudden catastrophic deterioration occurs after a period of relative stability. Other relatively common findings include alteration in mental status, seizure activity, and, with certain beta blockers, cyanosis. Neck vein distension, lung crackles, pedal edema, or wheezing may also be seen in patients with a preexisting left ventricular ejection fraction below 35% or preexisting bronchospastic disease. Signs of toxicity usually begin to appear within 2 hours of ingestion and reach maximal severity at about 4 to 5 hours. It is important to realize that individuals vary considerably in their susceptibility to toxicity.

Routine Laboratory Abnormalities

Electrocardiographic signs of toxicity with either class of drug include bradydysrhythmias (sinus, nodal, or idioventricular), variable degrees of atrioventricular blockade, and asystole as a terminal event. The length of the PR interval has been shown to correlate positively with drug levels. Peak effects on atrioventricular conduction after overdose with either class of drug may, however, lag behind peak drug levels. With calcium channel blockade, sinoatrial block may be seen.

Laboratory abnormalities are nonspecific. Hypoglycemia and hyperkalemia, owing to the drug's β_2-adrenergic blocking effects, have been described with nonspecific beta blocker overdose. Lactic acidosis is relatively common with calcium channel blocker overdoses, due to the combination of hypotension and bradycardia. In addition, hyperglycemia has occasionally been noted with both verapamil and diltiazem overdoses because of their effects in blocking insulin release from pancreatic islet cells.

PLANS
Diagnostic
Differential Diagnosis

The differential diagnosis generally includes an acute myocardial infarction or other causes of cardiogenic shock.

Diagnostic Options and Recommended Approach

The diagnosis is usually made on clinical grounds when appropriate signs and symptoms occur in a patient who is taking the drug or may

have access to the drug. Drug levels are not readily available. Levels do correlate with toxicity, but patients vary greatly in their sensitivity to both adrenergic and calcium blocking effects. In addition, certain compounds (eg, alprenolol, propranolol, and possibly verapamil) have active metabolites that are undetectable. The beta and calcium channel blocking effects of these drugs typically outlast their plasma half-lives, and toxicity may continue to be evident even when levels have fallen considerably. Toxicity with these agents should be suspected in any cardiac arrest victim in electromechanical dissociation.

Therapeutic

In acute overdoses, attention to securing airway, breathing, and cardiovascular stability is the initial concern. Gastric emptying with orogastric lavage may be indicated in some cases before overt toxicity has developed. Ipecac is contraindicated because induced vomiting may exacerbate bradydysrhythmias by increasing vagal tone. Ipecac may also prevent the retention of activated charcoal for up to 4 hours. Repetitive doses of activated charcoal with the cathartic sorbitol should be used following lavage. Whole-bowel irrigation with commercially available polyethylene glycol/electrolyte solutions may be effective, especially in cases where sustained-release preparations have been ingested in overdose. Gastric emptying is less important for toxicity associated with long-term use of these drugs, but activated charcoal may be useful.

Volume loading with saline is important as the initial treatment for drug-induced hypotension, unless overt volume overload is present. Rapid saline loading after calcium administration in dogs was shown to be more effective than calcium alone in partially reversing the conduction defects associated with calcium channel blocker toxicity (Hariman et al., 1979). For bradycardia, atropine may be tried but even high doses are usually ineffective in both types of toxicity. Intravenous calcium administration in doses between 1 and 4 g should be tried in calcium channel blocker toxicity but, especially in overdose situations, may be ineffective (70% of patients show improved conduction). In dogs, calcium doses sufficient to raise the serum calcium concentration by 1 to 2 mEq/L (doses higher than presently in clinical use) were required to reverse the negative inotropic effects of verapamil. There are also case reports of intravenous calcium reversing beta blocker toxicity. Calcium may improve the response to atropine.

When the above measures fail to result in hemodynamic stability, inotropic agents should be tried. The use of isoproterenol alone, even in high doses, in both beta blocker and calcium channel blocker toxicity, has been disappointing. Reversal of the negative inotropic effects of beta blockers was seen in only 22% of reported overdoses of propranolol, and in only 11% was reversal of negative chronotropic effects seen (Weinstein, 1984). In calcium channel blocker overdose the β_2 peripheral vasodilating effects of isoproterenol have caused more severe hypotension. Dopamine has also been disappointing in beta blocker overdose, reversing the negative inotropic effects in only a third of reported cases, with no appreciable effects on heart rate. The combination of dopamine (10 µg/kg/min) plus isoproterenol (0.2 µg/kg/min) for beta blocker overdose may be more efficacious than the use of either agent alone or of glucagon. Dopamine may be more effective in calcium channel blocker overdose as a single agent in raising the blood pressure. There may be some advantage to using amrinone in calcium channel blocker overdose because it acts through separate mechanisms (phosphodiesterase inhibition) to increase intracellular calcium levels. Experience with the use of this agent, however, is limited. Case reports exist of success with prenalterol (a cardioselective beta agonist), dobutamine, and norepinephrine for both beta blocker and calcium channel blocker overdoses.

Two inotropic agents, glucagon and epinephrine, stand out as treatments for beta blocker overdose. Glucagon, which appears to act through nonadrenergic, glucagon-specific myocardial receptors to increase cyclic AMP, has been reported to produce salutary effects on blood pressure, heart rate, and mortality in up to 85% of patients (Weinstein, 1984). The dose of glucagon that has been used is quite high (0.05 mg/kg as a bolus followed by a 0.07 mg/kg/h drip). Side effects include nausea and vomiting, hyperglycemia (rarely necessitating insulin), hypokalemia, and an increase in myocardial oxygen demand.

The nausea is readily controlled by antiemetic agents such as metoclopramide and prochlorperazine. As with all inotropic agents, there is the potential for producing ventricular dysrhythmias, but this appears to be less of a problem with glucagon than with the other adrenergically active agents mentioned. Glucagon has also been reported to reverse the negative inotropic and chronotropic effects of calcium channel blocker toxicity. Because it contains phenol, glucagon should not be reconstituted with the packaged solvent when used in high doses. Phenol may exacerbate hypotension; 5% dextrose in water should be used instead.

Epinephrine has both beta-agonist and alpha-agonist properties and is effective in reversing the negative inotropic effects (50% of patients) and negative chronotropic (67%) effects of beta blockers. The starting dose used ranged from 10 to 30 µg/min. Case reports of success with epinephrine also exist for calcium channel blocker overdose. Presumably, it is the alpha-adrenergic effects of epinephrine that make it more beneficial than isoproterenol.

Case reports of beneficial effects of the intraaortic balloon pump, transvenous and external pacemakers, and extracorporeal cardiopulmonary bypass also exist. Extracorporeal cardiopulmonary bypass appears to allow hepatic metabolism of drugs by supporting liver blood flow. Use of extracorporeal cardiopulmonary bypass is limited, because the longer the duration of its application, the more likely are complications such as bleeding. It has been postulated that extracorporeal membrane oxygenation might be more effective, but this technology is not widely available. Charcoal hemoperfusion might be used for the two water-soluble beta blockers, nadolol and atenolol, which have a lower volume of distribution, are less protein bound, and are excreted predominately by the kidneys.

Experimental evidence suggests that 4-aminopyridine, a drug used as an antagonist of nondepolarizing neuromuscular blocking agents in eastern Europe, may be a specific antidote for calcium channel blocker toxicity. It acts by directly increasing transmembrane calcium influx through voltage-dependent channels, which are more readily blocked by calcium blocking drugs and which are not readily affected by traditional adrenergic inotropic agents. This agent increased cardiac output and heart rate in some but not all animal preparations. Human data are, as yet, unavailable.

All the above agents may be tried to reverse the hemodynamic effects of toxicity with these agents. In the setting of both beta blocker toxicity and calcium channel blocker toxicity, seizures should be treated with a benzodiazepine such as diazepam or lorazepam. Theophylline may be useful to treat refractory bronchospasm in the setting of beta blocker toxicity.

FOLLOW-UP

Significant toxicity from calcium channel blocking or beta blocking agents generally requires hospital admission. When these drugs are initially prescribed, patients should be instructed to return if they experience dizziness, syncope, dyspnea, palpitations, or edema.

Once a physician has prescribed one of these drugs, the timing of the follow-up visit depends on the patient's age, underlying condition, and ability to understand follow-up instructions. Certainly, by about 2 weeks a brief follow-up visit is indicated to assess the occurrence of adverse symptoms, to measure blood pressure and pulse, and to perform a cardiopulmonary examination. Routine electrocardiography is not indicated unless symptoms or vital signs suggest a cardiac complication. After an overdose of these agents, it is important to arrange psychiatric referral and to assess whether there is a continuing need for these drugs.

DISCUSSION
Prevalence and Incidence

The prevalence and incidence of beta blocker and calcium channel blocker are unknown.

Related Basic Science

Beta blocking agents are rapidly absorbed from the gastrointestinal tract, with peak serum levels appearing within 1 to 1.5 hours. With many of these agents, particularly propranolol, the first-pass effect through the liver is clinically important. Most of the drugs are metabolized by the liver to metabolites with variable activity and have greater than 95% protein binding. Hemodialysis, therefore, is usually not helpful when toxicity is seen. Two beta blockers, atenolol and nadolol, have much less protein binding and much less lipid solubility, and are excreted primarily by the kidneys, which makes hemodialysis an attractive possibility in treating toxicity with these two agents. Although the elimination half-lives of most agents are relatively short (1–6 hours), slow-release preparations of many of these agents are available. The slow-release preparations pose a specific problem in the setting of overdose because they continue to release drugs into the gut over hours; thus, repetitive doses of activated charcoal and a cathartic or whole-bowel irrigation are important.

The calcium channel blockers are papaverine derivatives that block primarily the slow-channel (voltage-dependent) calcium influx into myocardial and vascular smooth muscle. The intracellular site of activity of calcium, the sarcoplasmic reticulum, is less active in vascular smooth muscle and myocardial tissue than in skeletal muscle, which accounts for the greater susceptibility of vascular smooth muscle and myocardial tissue to the effects of calcium blocking drugs. Calmodulin may serve as the common pathway receptor for these agents. Catecholamines act to promote calcium intake into the cell through receptor-dependent channels by different mechanisms than the slow channels. Therefore, β_1-inotropic and alpha-adrenergic effects may be preserved when calcium channel blockers are active, but, in the setting of toxicity (where slow channels are primarily affected), beta- and alpha-adrenergic agents may not be helpful. The calcium channel blockers are well adsorbed from the gastrointestinal tract within 2 hours, have large volumes of distribution and a high degree of protein binding, and are metabolized largely by the liver. Again, hemodialysis is not a particularly useful therapeutic option for toxicity associated with these drugs.

Each class of drugs contains agents with different properties that cause special toxic effects. In beta blockers, the most important factors determining toxicity include the degree of lipid solubility, the presence of membrane stabilizing activity, the degree of specificity for β_1 receptors, and the presence of intrinsic sympathomimetic activity. Drugs such as propranolol and oxprenolol, which have high lipid solubility and membrane stabilizing activity, are more likely to cause central nervous system effects (particularly seizures). Membrane stabilizing activity (local anesthetic or quinidine-like activity) involves the inhibition of fast inward sodium current in excitable tissue. Greater lipid solubility allows drugs to penetrate the blood–brain barrier more easily. A newer agent, sotalol, has both beta blocking effects with membrane stabilizing activity and type III antiarrhythmic activity. Sotalol, therefore, has been noted to cause prolongation of the QT interval. Drugs with membrane stabilizing activity also cause prolongation of the QRS interval. In an overdose situation, β_1 specificity is usually not important because β_2 blocking effects become evident at higher doses. In routine use, however, patients with bronchospastic disease are less likely to experience wheezing with β_1-specific agents. Intrinsic sympathomimetic activity is present in two beta blockers, pindolol and practolol, and, in routine use, this property protects against bradycardia and hypotension. In overdose with these agents tachycardia and hypertension have been reported. Of all the beta blockers, oxprenolol is the most likely to cause cyanosis.

There are three major types of calcium channel blocking agents—phenylalkylamines (verapamil); benzothiazepines (diltiazem); and dihydropyridines (nifedipine, nicardipine, isradipine, and felopidine)—which have differing effects on atrioventricular conduction, peripheral vascular resistance, and cardiac output. Verapamil has the most pronounced effect on heart rate, whereas dihydropridines like nifedipine have very little effect and, in general, tend to increase heart rate because of the more pronounced effects on peripheral vascular resistance. Verapamil also has the most pronounced negative inotropic effect, and nifedipine the least. Dihydropyridines have the greatest effect on peripheral vascular resistance and are most likely to cause hypotension. Diltiazem generally has effects that are intermediate between those of verapamil and nifedipine. The differential toxic effects in overdose are less important than in the toxicity associated with chronic use.

Natural History and Its Modification with Treatment

The severity of toxicity depends on the amount ingested, the presence of underlying heart disease, the susceptibility to beta receptor or calcium channel blockade, and the specific drug ingested. Propranolol, the oldest beta blocker and the drug with which there is most experience, in overdose has a mortality rate of 25%, in part because of its high lipid solubility and membrane stabilizing activity (Henry and Cassidy, 1986). The mortality is lower with other beta blockers having less lipid solubility and membrane stabilizing activity. The mortality of overdose with calcium channel blocking drugs is in the range of 15% for all the reported cases. There is less experience with the toxicity of calcium channel blockers, and mortality statistics for individual drugs are scanty, but calcium channel blocker overdose accounted for 46% of cardiovascular drug deaths in 1990. Verapamil has caused more deaths than diltiazem or the dihydropyridines, where death is rare. An overdose with beta blockers or calcium channel blockers can be among the most serious and difficult overdoses to treat. In those surviving overdose, toxic effects rarely last more than 36 hours from ingestion and usually last less than 12 hours.

Prevention

To prevent morbidity and mortality from beta blocker overdose, these drugs should be prescribed with care to depressed patients. If toxicity is a more important issue than cost, then agents with less membrane stabilizing activity should be prescribed. Beta blockers excreted primarily by the kidney, such as nadolol and atenolol, should be prescribed for patients with liver disease. On the other hand, these agents should not be prescribed in patients with renal disease. Cardioselective agents are preferable in patients susceptible to bronchospasm. These agents are generally best avoided in patients susceptible to conduction defects, although agents with intrinsic sympathomimetic activity might be used.

Among the calcium channel blockers, it is best to take into account the relative potency of the available agents with respect to changes in cardiac output, heart rate, and blood pressure. Patients with poor left ventricular function would do better with nifedipine or diltiazem than with verapamil. Patients with conduction system abnormalities would also do better with nifedipine. Patients should understand how potentially toxic an overdose may be. Patients should also be advised never to exceed the recommended dosage and never to "double dose" after missing a prior dose.

Cost Containment

Costs of acute overdose are minimized by early aggressive gastric decontamination. Long-term toxicity is most effectively managed by consultation with an experienced cardiologist, clinical toxicologist, or both.

REFERENCES

Hariman RJ, Mangiardi LM, McAllister RG Jr, et al. Reversal of the cardiovascular effects of verapamil by calcium and sodium: Difference between electrophysiologic and hemodynamic responses. Circulation 1979;59:797.

Hendren WG, Schiber RS, Garretson LK. Extracorporeal bypass for the treatment of verapamil poisoning. Ann Emerg Med 1989:18:984.

Henry JA, Cassidy SL. Membrane stabilizing activity: A major cause of fatal poisoning. Lancet 1986;2:1414.

Kosinski EJ, Malindzak GS. Glucagon and isoproterenol in reversing propranolol toxicity. Arch Intern Med 1973;132:840.

Pearigen PD, Benowitz NL. Poisoning due to calcium antagonists: Experience with verapamil, diltiazem and nifedipine. Drug Saf 1991;6:408.

Ramoska EA, Spiller HA, Winter M, Borys D. A one-year evaluation of calcium channel blocker overdoses: Toxicity and treatment. Ann Emerg Med 1993;22:196.

Weinstein RS. Recognition and management of poisoning with beta-adrenergic blocking agents. Ann Emerg Med 1984;13:1123.

CHAPTER 24–4

Digitalis Toxicity

Keith D. Wrenn, M.D.

DEFINITION

Digitalis toxicity is defined as evidence of tissue toxicity caused by the use of a digitalis preparation, such as digoxin or digitoxin. Ingestion of foxglove, oleander, lily of the valley, monkshood, or yew berries, which contain cardiac glycosides, may cause similar toxicity. A "toxic" serum digoxin assay is not definitive for the diagnosis and should always be interpreted in light of the clinical setting.

ETIOLOGY

Digoxin toxicity can occur as a result of an acute overdose, accidental ingestion in children, or chronic toxicity in patients with heart disease. Hospitalization for digoxin toxicity among elderly Americans has an incidence in the range of 4% over 6 years of treatment. Women and African-Americans appear to have higher risk. Factors that predispose to chronic toxicity include renal insufficiency, older age, preexisting heart disease, electrolyte abnormalities (hypokalemia and hypomagnesemia, which are often due to concomitant diuretic use), hypercalcemia, acute hypoxia or hypercarbia, acute alkalosis, and lower lean body mass. In addition, multiple-drug interactions may cause toxicity. Drugs that decrease the renal clearance of digoxin include quinidine, verapamil, amiodarone, diltiazem, spironolactone, and captopril. Antibiotics may eliminate gut bacteria (such as *Eubacterium lentum*) that normally metabolize a proportion of digoxin to noncardioactive metabolites, thus causing increased absorption of active drug. Clonidine, beta blockers, and calcium channel blockers may all exacerbate bradydysrhythmias due to digitalis toxicity. Finally, dehydration,

shock, left ventricular failure, hypothyroidism, or drugs used to treat hyperthyroid states may decrease the volume of distribution of digoxin, causing toxicity.

CRITERIA FOR DIAGNOSIS

Two relatively distinct syndromes may result (Table 24–4–1). In overdoses or accidental ingestions that cause acute toxicity, patients are younger, without underlying heart disease, and tend to have higher serum potassium and digoxin levels. Symptoms include more severe central nervous system abnormalities, and bradyarrhythmias tend to predominate. With chronic toxicity, patients are older and tend to have underlying heart disease. Central nervous system symptomatology may be less evident, but visual symptoms are more common. The digoxin levels are lower and hypokalemia is more likely. Ventricular arrhythmias, especially premature ventricular contractions, are also more common.

CLINICAL MANIFESTATIONS
Subjective

Nausea, vomiting, and anorexia (due to toxicity in the area postrema of the medulla) are predominant early symptoms for both acute and chronic toxicity. Central nervous system complaints, which are more common with acute toxicity, include dizziness, headache, seizures, and transient psychosis ("foxglove frenzy" or "digoxin delirium"). Other central nervous system complaints include abnormal dreams, subtle

TABLE 24–4–1. SYNDROMES OF DIGITALIS TOXICITY

Acute	Chronic
Younger age	Older age
No underlying heart disease	Underlying heart disease
Nausea, vomiting	Anorexia
Severe central nervous system involvement (seizures, agitation)	Less severe central nervous system involvement (drowsiness, lethargy, disorientation)
Visual symptoms uncommon	Photophobia, scotomata, xanthopsia
Hyperkalemia	Hypokalemia
Paroxysmal atrial tachycardia with block, bradycardia more common	Premature ventricular contractions most common
Digoxin level higher	Digoxin levels can be within therapeutic range

personality changes, fatigue, and generalized weakness. Visual disturbances, seen more commonly in chronic toxicity, include photophobia and xanthopsia, which is an alteration in either red–green perception or a perceived yellow discoloration to visual images ("yellow halos"). Abdominal pain and bloating, possibly due to nonocclusive mesenteric ischemia, as well as diarrhea may be seen. Increased frequency of urination and cold sweats are also seen. Symptoms of congestive heart failure may occur in as many as 7.5% of patients as a manifestation of toxicity and appear to be independent of ischemia or arrhythmias. These symptoms are all nonspecific and may not be attributed to digitalis. In one study, 28% of patients had symptoms for more than 3 weeks before the diagnosis of digoxin toxicity was made (Lely and Van Enter, 1972). In cases of chronic toxicity, correlation is poor between symptoms and digoxin levels. Arrhythmias may occur without preceding extracardiac symptoms in as many as half the toxic patients.

Objective

Physical Examination

Abnormal physical findings are relatively uncommon with the exception of vital signs, particularly the pulse. Increased signs of congestive heart failure are occasionally seen. Wellens (1976) has enumerated the following four signs as suggestive of digitalis toxicity:

- Appearance of a slow heart rate in a patient with a previously normal or fast heart rate
- Appearance of a fast heart rate in a patient with a previously normal heart rate
- Appearance of a regular rhythm in a patient with a previously irregular rhythm
- Appearance of a regularly irregular rhythm

Routine Laboratory Abnormalities

Usually the diagnosis is suspected on the basis of an abnormal electrocardiogram. It is important to realize that the strain pattern called digoxin effect may be present in the absence of toxicity and absent in up to two thirds of toxic cases. Arrhythmias, however, occur in 80 to 90% of toxic patients and are often multiple. In one third of toxic patients, arrhythmias are the initial manifestation of toxicity. The arrhythmias of digoxin toxicity are manifested by decreased conduction, abnormal impulse generation (increased automaticity), or both. First-degree atrioventricular block may be the earliest indication of toxicity and is seen in about 15 to 25% of cases.

Bradyarrhythmias predominate in acute overdose situations involving patients with normal hearts; common rhythms include sinus bradycardia, Mobitz type 1 second-degree block, sinus arrest with exit block, nonconducted premature atrial beats, and third-degree atrioventricular block. Syncope in association with these bradyarrhythmias is relatively uncommon because subsidiary pacemakers are often accelerated. Bradyarrhythmias may also be seen with chronic toxicity, but in this setting, where patients' hearts are frequently abnormal, ventricular arrhythmias (especially with associated atrial fibrillation) are particularly common.

Premature ventricular beats, which are often multiform, are seen in about 50% and are particularly common after inappropriate carotid sinus massage. Rhythms that should suggest digitalis toxicity include bidirectional ventricular tachycardia (right bundle-branch block pattern with alternating right- and left-axis deviation) and bigeminy. Ventricular tachycardia and ventricular fibrillation are uncommon preterminal or terminal rhythms. These ventricular arrhythmias may occur in acutely toxic patients.

A common rhythm that is almost pathognomonic for digitalis toxicity is nonparoxysmal accelerated junctional tachycardia. This may occur in up to half of digitalis-toxic patients. Ectopic atrial tachycardia with block occurs less commonly (about 10% of patients), but is also relatively specific for digitalis toxicity. "Regularized" atrial fibrillation with a slower ventricular response is another rhythm highly suggestive of digitalis toxicity.

Although almost any rhythm may be associated with digitalis toxicity, some rhythms are unlikely to be caused by digitalis. These include Mobitz type II second-degree atrioventricular block, parasystole, sinus tachycardia, paroxysmal junctional tachycardia, multifocal atrial tachycardia, and atrial fibrillation with a rapid ventricular response. In the latter instance patients may be relatively refractory to digitalis toxicity, only to become toxic on conversion to sinus rhythm.

Other routine laboratory abnormalities include prerenal azotemia, hypomagnesemia, and both hypokalemia and hyperkalemia. Hypokalemia and hypomagnesemia usually occur in the setting of chronic toxicity in patients also taking diuretics. Hyperkalemia is more likely with the profound toxicity seen in acute overdose and reflects digitalis' inhibitory effects on the Na,K-ATPase pump. These three electrolyte problems—hypokalemia, hyperkalemia, and hypomagnesemia—not only are associated with toxicity, but also contribute to cardiotoxicity.

PLANS

Diagnostic

In addition to measuring electrolytes (including potassium and magnesium), blood urea nitrogen, and creatinine, a serum digoxin assay should be performed when digitalis toxicity is suspected. There is much confusion about the use of digoxin assays because no single serum level clearly separates the toxic from the nontoxic patient and levels do not correlate well with symptoms, signs, or electrocardiographic abnormalities. The therapeutic range of digoxin is relatively narrow, between 0.5 and 2.0 ng/mL in most assays. There is considerable overlap of levels causing toxic versus therapeutic effects, with values in the range 1.5 to 3.0 ng/mL. The timing of the drawing of blood for this assay is critical because of the two-stage pharmacokinetic distribution of digoxin. The optimal time for drawing blood is just before the next dose is due. The blood should be drawn at least 6 hours after the last oral dose and 4 hours after the last intravenous dose in the nonoverdose setting. Finally, false-positive assays may occur with the use of spironolactone or in the setting of hyperbilirubinemia or chronic renal failure, where endogenous circulating digoxin-like substances may circulate.

In general, the higher the digoxin level, the more likely is the patient to be toxic. A serum digoxin level about 3 ng/mL is 12 times as likely to indicate toxicity as a level less than 1 ng/mL and, in the appropriate setting, provides strong support for a diagnosis of digitalis toxicity. Higher digoxin levels also help guide treatment and provide prognostic information.

The accepted recommendations for obtaining a digoxin assay include the following:

- As an estimation of compliance
- When an unexpected clinical response to digoxin therapy occurs (eg, suspected malabsorption)
- When preparations of uncertain bioavailability are being used (eg, generic drug)
- In the setting of known renal insufficiency or fluctuating renal function
- For suspected toxicity

In the last case a high index of suspicion should be maintained because of the nonspecificity of presentation. In general, a patient on digoxin with almost any change in status should probably have a digoxin assay performed. In all overdoses a digoxin assay is indicated because it guides treatment. The digoxin assay is less useful when plants containing cardiac glycosides have been ingested, but may provide evidence of glycoside activity. Most importantly, the digoxin assay should always be interpreted in light of the clinical situation.

Therapeutic

As in all cases of drug toxicity, attention to airway, breathing, and cardiovascular status is paramount. After these have been secured, management depends on the clinical situation. In general, ipecac is contraindicated unless the overdose occurred within the previous 30 minutes and definitive medical care is more than 1 hour away. Ipecac may exacerbate bradyarrhythmias, which are under parasympathetic influence. Gastric lavage should be performed after airway control is secured and atropine is readily available. Repetitive doses of activated charcoal are indicated because digoxin undergoes some enterohepatic circulation.

Atropine in conventional doses (0.5–2 mg in adults) is the initial drug of choice for symptomatic bradyarrhythmias, especially in the early stages after an overdose when the parasympathetic effects of digoxin are maximal. If atropine does not work, a temporary pacemaker (preferably external) should be tried. Transvenous pacemakers may be required, but the pacemaker wire may stimulate ventricular arrhythmias because of increased ventricular irritability. Isoproterenol is relatively contraindicated in the setting of digitalis intoxication because the profound beta-agonist effect may cause ventricular arrhythmias. When hypokalemia is present it should be corrected; however, in the setting of atrioventricular blockade of greater than first degree, the possibility that potassium administration may worsen atrioventricular blockade should be considered and potassium should be administered cautiously. The same caution applies to magnesium repletion with advanced atrioventricular block. If the above measures do not prove effective, then digoxin-specific antibodies should be administered.

For the rare patient with rapid supraventricular rhythms such as ectopic atrial tachycardia with block associated with hemodynamic instability, electrolyte repletion should be started. Drugs such as verapamil, beta blockers, quinidine, and procainamide are relatively contraindicated because of the possibility of inducing worsened atrioventricular blockade. Carotid sinus massage has also caused sudden decompensation with asystole or malignant ventricular arrhythmias. Intravenous phenytoin may be tried (25 mg/min to a total loading dose of 1000 mg). Cardioversion is risky because of the possibility of inducing ventricular arrhythmias, but, if used, the lowest amount of energy likely to convert the rhythm should be tried initially.

Electrolyte repletion is paramount for the treatment of ventricular arrhythmias. Hypokalemia should be documented and corrected. When administering potassium in dextrose-containing fluids, a paradoxical worsening of hypokalemia may occur owing to an insulin-induced intracellular potassium shift. Magnesium therapy is indicated whether or not hypomagnesemia is present, unless concomitant renal insufficiency is present. Not only is the serum magnesium level a poor predictor of total body magnesium status, but the heart is especially predisposed to the effects of magnesium deficiency. The beneficial effects of magnesium derive from its role as a coenzyme for Na, K-ATPase and its effects in stabilizing membranes, permitting more rapid intracellular potassium repletion, and decreasing renal losses. The effects are independent of the pretreatment serum level. A loading dose of 2 g of 50% magnesium sulfate intravenously over 20 minutes followed by a continuous infusion of 1 to 2 g/h is advised. The deep tendon reflexes of the patient should be followed as should serial serum magnesium levels.

Phenytoin or lidocaine in conventional doses may be used. Although phenytoin has the theoretical advantage of causing less atrioventricular blockade and fewer central nervous system effects, in practice either agent is acceptable when used correctly. With advanced atrioventricular blockade, phenytoin is probably preferable to lidocaine. Therapeutic lidocaine levels, however, can be obtained more rapidly. Bretylium is contraindicated because it may induce or worsen ventricular arrhythmias. Quinidine, procainamide, and beta blockers have not been used extensively and are not recommended.

Hyperkalemia should be treated by routine measures with the exception that calcium administration is contraindicated. Bicarbonate, glucose and insulin, ion-exchange resins (Kayexelate), and hemodialysis may all be used to treat hyperkalemia, which is often refractory to conventional therapy.

A specific antidote for digitalis toxicity is now available. Human albumin-bound digoxin is injected into sheep, and purified digoxin-specific antibodies are harvested and cleaved with papain, yielding two Fab fragments. These Fab fragments avidly bind digoxin in vivo and in addition lack the immunogenicity of whole antibody preparations. The fragments also have a larger volume of distribution and, because of their smaller size, diffuse rapidly into tissues and are more rapidly and extensively eliminated by glomerular filtration. After administration, a response should be seen within 30 minutes, with partial to complete reversal of toxicity in 3 to 4 hours in almost 90% of patients (Antman et al., 1990). There is a rapid fall in free serum digoxin levels associated with a rapid 10- to 20-fold rise in total serum digoxin and an efflux of digoxin from tissue receptors. Failure of Fab fragments means that the diagnosis of digitalis toxicity should be reconsidered, electrolyte abnormalities may not have been corrected, other proarrhythmic agents may be present, or an insufficient dose of Fab fragments has been administered. After Fab fragments have been administered the serum digoxin assay should not be routinely followed. The patient's clinical signs of toxicity are more important. There is renal excretion of the Fab fragment–digoxin complexes, with an elimination half-life of 16 to 30 hours in patients with normal renal function. The responses have been equally favorable in digoxin and digitoxin toxicity. In addition to reversal of arrhythmias, Fab fragments effectively treat hyperkalemia. Significant allergic responses have been noted in less than 1% of patients. There is insufficient evidence available concerning the role of Fab fragments in cases of glycoside toxicity due to plant toxins, but, because of their low toxicity, they should be tried in life-threatening overdoses. Fab fragments are routinely indicated for the following reasons: life-threatening toxicity (arrhythmias, especially if refractory to conventional treatment); massive overdose (10 mg in an adult, 4 mg in a child); steady-state concentrations greater than 10 ng/mL; refractory hyperkalemia (> 5 mEq/dL); shock; and cardiac arrest. Complications of the use of Fab fragments are uncommon, but include hypokalemia, exacerbation of congestive heart failure, and a more rapid ventricular response to atrial fibrillation. Recrudescent toxicity occurs in around 3% of patients, usually within 3 days of initial treatment. Recrudescence is associated with suboptimal initial dosing and with renal failure.

Fab fragments are administered intravenously (over 30 minutes) in a dose equivalent to that ingested. The dose is calculated according to the amount ingested or a steady-state digoxin level, with the knowledge that 40 mg of Fab (1 vial) binds 0.6 mg of digoxin (Table 24–4–2). If the amount ingested is unknown and a serum level cannot be obtained, 20 vials (800 mg) should be given. Routine use of Fab has been limited by its high cost ($175/vial). The cost of Fab fragments should be balanced, however, against the cost of 1 to 2 days in an intensive care unit.

Hemodialysis, hemoperfusion, and forced diuresis are not effective for removing digoxin, because of its large volume of distribution; however, these modalities may help treat hyperkalemia refractory to the use

---

TABLE 24–4–2. CALCULATIONS FOR THE DOSE OF FAB FRAGMENTS

Each 40-mg vial of Fab binds 0.6 mg of digoxin

Body load of digoxin	=	Ingested amount (mg) × 0.8*
	=	SDC × 5.6[†] × wt (kg) × 0.001
Dose (in vials) of Fab	=	$\dfrac{\text{Ingested amount} \times 0.8}{0.6}$
		(in overdose when amount ingested is known)
	=	$\dfrac{\text{SDC (ng/mL)} \times 5.6 \times \text{wt (kg)} \times 0.001}{0.6}$
		(in overdose or chronic toxicity when SDC is known)

SDC, serum digoxin concentration.
*Bioavailability of digoxin.
[†]Volume of distribution of digoxin in average adult (L/kg).

of glucose and insulin, bicarbonate, and ion-exchange resins. Special hemoperfusion techniques have shown promise in decreasing the elimination half-life of digoxin and may prove useful for removing Fab-bound digoxin in patients with renal failure.

FOLLOW-UP

Most digoxin-toxic patients should be admitted to the hospital for electrocardiographic monitoring. In inadvertent toxicity the length of hospital stay depends largely on renal function and complications. It is important to discontinue, or adjust, the dose of digoxin. In overdoses, psychiatric referral must be made and it is important to assess whether the drug is necessary.

DISCUSSION
Prevalence and Incidence

The prevalence of chronic digoxin toxicity has varied from 6 to 39% in various studies, but has decreased over the past decade, in part because of better knowledge of this drug's pharmacokinetics and drug interactions (Antman and Smith, 1985; Bhatia, 1986).

Related Basic Science

Digoxin may be given orally or intravenously. After oral ingestion, bioavailability is in the range of 70 to 80%, with encapsulated liquid preparations having 90 to 100% absorption. There is a large volume of distribution, and 20 to 30% protein binding. Between 60 and 80% of the drug is excreted unchanged in the urine, with an elimination half-life of 25 to 50 hours in the setting of normal renal function. There is biliary excretion of the unaltered drug with some metabolism to inactive reduction products in the gut by bacterial action. In about 10% of patients, up to 40% of the drug may undergo such metabolism. Digitoxin is metabolized predominantly in the liver.

Digoxin acts by binding to Na,K-ATPase, inhibiting transmembrane fluxes and causing increased intracellular sodium and calcium concentrations and an increase in extracellular potassium concentration. Digoxin and potassium compete for the same receptor. Therefore, when hypokalemia is present, tissue digoxin binding is increased.

Digoxin causes multiple complex interactions. There is increased parasympathetic tone, which accounts for an increase in the atrioventricular nodal effective refractory period, a decrease in atrioventricular conduction, and bradyarrhythmias. Sympathetic tone is also increased, causing increased automaticity, which is neurally mediated through the area postrema of the medulla. The alteration in the membrane ion fluxes provokes delayed afterdepolarizations and an increase in phase 4 of the action potential, contributing to abnormal impulse generation. The QT interval is shortened. The increase in intracellular calcium concentration accounts for digoxin's positive inotropic effect. Magnesium is a cofactor that helps drive Na,K-ATPase and, therefore, is important in maintaining membrane ion fluxes.

In addition to drugs that increase digoxin levels by either decreasing renal elimination or decreasing its volume of distribution, some drugs, such as antacids, bran, kaopectate, and cathartics, decrease absorption. Withdrawal of these agents in a patient taking digoxin may cause toxicity.

Natural History and Its Modification with Treatment

Mortality from overdose varies, but may be up to a quarter of the patients. Mortality correlates with higher digoxin and potassium levels. The mortality is especially high when the digoxin level is greater than 6 ng/mL or the serum potassium concentration is greater than 5.5 mEq/L. Certain rhythm disturbances also have been associated with higher mortality rates in the past, including ectopic atrial tachycardia with block, accelerated nodal tachycardia, sustained ventricular tachycardia, and ventricular fibrillation. New electrocardiographic ST–T wave changes imply a poorer prognosis, but chronic changes do not. Children appear to be less sensitive to the effects of digoxin, perhaps because of their high concentrations of membrane Na,K-ATPase, and are therefore less susceptible to toxicity. Early diagnosis improves prognosis, while continuation of digoxin in the face of chronic toxicity carries a high mortality. The use of Fab fragments in digoxin toxicity has favorably affected the mortality rate of higher-risk patients.

Prevention

The most important preventive measure is physician education regarding dosing, drug interactions, and clinical settings predisposing to toxicity.

Cost Containment

Early diagnosis and appropriate monitoring of cardiac rhythm and serum electrolytes help prevent complications. More liberal use of Fab fragments despite their expense may actually be cost-effective because intensive care unit observation is also very expensive. As the mortality rises precipitously after the digoxin level reaches 6 ng/mL, perhaps Fab fragments should be given at this level rather than the published level of 10 ng/mL. This is especially true in hospitals where intensive care unit beds are in scarce supply.

REFERENCES

Antman EM, Smith TW. Digitalis toxicity. Ann Rev Med 1985;36:357.

Antman EM, Wenger TL, Butler VP Jr, et al. Treatment of 150 cases of life-threatening digitalis intoxication with digoxin-specific Fab antibody fragments: Final report of a multi-center study. Circulation 1990;81:1744.

Bhatia SJS. Digitalis toxicity—Turning over a new leaf? West J Med 1986;145:74.

Clarke W, Ramoska EA. Acute digoxin overdose: Use of digoxin-specific antibody fragments. Am J Emerg Med 1988;6:465.

Hickey AR, Wenger TL, Carpenter VP, et al. Digoxin immune Fab therapy in the management of digitalis intoxication: Safety and efficacy results of an observational surveillance study. J Am Coll Cardiol 1991;17:590.

Kelly RA, Smith TW. Recognition and management of digitalis toxicity. Am J Cardiol 1992;69:108G.

Lely AH, Van Enter CHJ. Noncardiac symptoms of digitalis intoxication. Am Heart J 1972;83:149.

Ordog GJ, Benaron S, Bhasin V, et al. Serum digoxin levels and mortality in 5,100 patients. Ann Emerg Med 1987;16:32.

Reisdorff EJ, Clark MR, Walters BL. Acute digitalis poisoning: The role of intravenous magnesium sulfate. J Emerg Med 1986;4:463.

Wellens HJJ. The electrocardiogram in digitalis intoxication. In Yu PN, Goodman IF, eds. Progress in cardiology. Philadelphia: Lea & Febiger, 1976;5:271.

Poisoning with Sedative–Hypnotics

Corey M. Slovis, M.D.

DEFINITION

A sedative–hypnotic overdose is defined as the inadvertent or deliberate utilization of one of the drugs in the sedative–hypnotic category. This category of drugs includes the barbiturates, benzodiazepines, chloral hydrate, etchlorvynol, glutethimide, meprobamate, methaqualon, and methyprylon.

ETIOLOGY

Suicide attempts and recreational abuse, often accompanied by alcoholic intake, are the two most common clinical settings for sedative–hypnotic overdose.

CRITERIA FOR DIAGNOSIS

Suggestive

Clues to the diagnosis, other than a history given by the patient or friends, include slow mentation with slurred speech, deepening intoxication, and coma of unknown cause. Any attempted suicide, either by drug or by physical means, should arouse suspicion of concomitant sedative abuse.

Definitive Diagnosis

A definitive diagnosis of sedative–hypnotic overdose is made by the appropriate history and/or physical findings accompanied by an elevated serum sedative–hypnotic drug level. Although not definitive, a presumptive diagnosis may be made by history or physical findings coupled with a positive urinary screen for a specific sedative–hypnotic(s).

CLINICAL MANIFESTATIONS

Subjective

The history is usually one of declining mentation, progressive slurring of speech, ataxia, and increasing somnolence. The rapidity of the mental and physical decline is a very important historical piece of prognostic and therapeutic information.

The patient is often stuporous or comatose, unable to give a coherent history. A history may be available from either the patient or an accompanying friend or relative. An attempt should be made to delineate rapidly what medications have been consumed and in what quantities. Inquiries should be made as to whether this was an attempted suicide. A sedative–hypnotic is the number one drug of choice in serious attempts at suicide, and most overdoses in this family of drugs are intentional. Needless time should not be spent on exact amounts of drugs ingested, as the history is often deliberately misrepresented. Prior depression, suicidal ideation, familial history of suicide, or previous suicide attempts are sometimes helpful in differentiating recreational abuse from a suicidal motivation. If suicide is suspected, the history should include any other medications the patient may have had available. The most frequent additional substance used in both recreational sedative use and attempted suicide is ethanol. Historical data as to the amount of ethanol recently consumed should be secured. The history is completed by a rapid review of systems. Special attention should be given to the possibility of trauma before or after overdose, serious underlying illness, insulin use, and narcotic abuse.

Any past history of prior depression, suicidal ideation, suicide attempts, or problems with recreational drug use should be included in the patient's history. Any available friend or relative should be interviewed to try to ascertain any history of suicidal ideation or drug related problems.

There is an increased incidence of suicide attempts in individuals who come from a family with a past history of suicide, divorce, or recent tragedy. Family members should be asked about the availability of prescription sedatives or hypnotic agents in the household.

Objective

Physical Examination

Physical examination of the overdosed patient is very nonspecific. Vital signs will be within normal limits until significant central nervous system depression occurs. As the patient slips into deeper levels of unconsciousness, blood pressure, heart rate, and respirations fall. Hypothermia is not uncommon in significant sedative–hypnotic overdoses.

Nonlocalizing neurologic findings are the most common physical abnormalities observed in clinically significant overdoses. Slurred speech and minimal ataxia may be noted initially; however, profound coma may occur depending on the amount of medication ingested. In the deeply comatose patient, pupils are usually sluggish, but they may be midpoint and nonresponsive. Glutethimide ingestion is notorious for producing widely dilated pupils that respond poorly to light. As coma progresses, cranial nerve reflexes including corneal reflexes may be absent. Deep tendon reflex arcs are depressed, resulting in reflexes that are either diminished or absent. In severe cases, the degree of neurologic depression is profound enough to yield flat-line electroencephalographic recordings.

Cardiopulmonary examination is usually normal; however, physical findings consistent with pulmonary edema or aspiration pneumonia may be present. Additionally, as coma progresses, the rate and depth of respirations diminish. Abdominal examination may reveal a generalized decrease in peristaltic activity. Bowel sounds may be completely absent in the severely poisoned patient. The examination of the skin is usually unremarkable. In up to 5% of patients with barbiturate-induced coma, blisters very similar to those seen in second-degree burns may be found over dependent areas of the body.

Routine Laboratory Abnormalities

Routine laboratory evaluation of sedative–hypnotic overdoses is usually completely within normal limits. A chest radiograph may show evidence of aspiration pneumonia or atelectasis.

PLANS

Diagnostic

Differential Diagnosis

The differential diagnosis of a potential sedative–hypnotic overdose is that of a patient with altered mental status. There are only five basic causes of altered mental status: vital sign abnormalities; toxic–metabolic causes; structural lesions; infectious causes; and psychiatric causes. It is beyond the scope of this chapter to provide a complete approach to the patient with altered mental status; however, sedative–hypnotic intoxication should always be included in the different diagnosis of a patient with a depressed level of consciousness, especially when the patient has (1) a depression of blood pressure, pulse, respiratory rate, and/or body temperature, (2) no evidence of electrolyte abnormalities, (3) a nonlocalizing neurologic examination, (4) no evidence of meningitis or sepsis, and (5) no history of psychosis.

Diagnostic Options

Laboratory evaluation and toxicologic screening are not mandatory in non-life-threatening ingestions of sedative–hypnotics. Arterial blood gas evaluation may show evidence of respiratory failure in severe cases. The urine toxicology screen rarely affects therapy.

Patients who arrive with minimal changes in mentation do not need an extensive diagnostic testing. All other patients should be treated as is listed under Recommended Approach.

Recommended Approach

Serum levels of aspirin and acetaminophen are recommended in any case where ingestion of these drugs is possible. A serum ethanol level is required owing to the usual practice of combining these drugs. Routine evaluation of blood chemistries and a hematologic profile are usually also performed for severely affected patients. Chest x-ray study is indicated in any patient suspected of aspiration or who has a period of unconsciousness, and an electrocardiogram is performed based on age and clinical status. In an attempt to gauge the depth of respiratory compromise, arterial blood gas determinations are performed in all comatose patients.

A 12-lead electrocardiogram and continuous electrocardiographic monitoring should both be evaluated for unexplained bradycardia and for a prolonged QT interval. Bradycardia may be a clue to previously unrecognized hypoxemia or elevated intracranial pressure. Tricyclic antidepressants may be coingested in suicide attempts and should be suspected in any patient with a prolonged QT interval. A continuous oxygen saturation monitor should be affixed to all comatose patients.

Therapeutic

In the management of the overdosed patient, whether the overdose is accidental or intentional, the physician must rely more heavily on objective than on subjective data. For many reasons, patients are reticent about the amount ingested. The treatment must be based on the patient's clinical status and any subsequent changes, rather than on the ingested amount reported by the patient or friend. Rapid clinical deterioration dictates immediate intervention, while a gradual lapse into stupor usually indicates the need for more conservative therapy.

The management of the overdosed patient may be divided into five phases. These are listed in Table 24–5–1. Clues to the diagnosis and treatment of specific sedative–hypnotics are listed in Table 24–5–1.

Securement of the ABCs. The essence of good emergency management is rapid assessment of the airway *(A)*, breathing *(B)*, and cardiovascular status *(C)*. Rapid, appropriate intervention is essential.

Approximately 50% of the deaths from sedative–hypnotic overdoses are respiratory in nature. The three most common causes of respiratory demise are hypoxic brain insult, aspiration pneumonia, and pulmonary edema. Therefore, the acute and long-term management of the sedative-overdosed patient must center around impeccable airway control. Indications for intubation are respiratory failure, loss of the gag reflex, and repetitive uncontrolled vomiting in an obtunded patient. As gastric contents must be removed in any serious sedative–hypnotic overdose, endotracheal intubation, when indicated, may be both prophylactic and therapeutic.

Maintenance of blood pressure and cardiovascular stability requires a sophisticated approach to hypotension. It was initially believed that shock in sedative–hypnotic coma was cardiogenic in origin; consequently, many different types of pressor agents were used to augment cardiac output. It is now known that hypotension is based primarily on "neurogenic shock"; that is, there is significant centrally mediated peripheral vasodilation to create a hypovolemic-like shock state. A normovolemic patient with sedative-induced hypotension may take 5 L or more of additional volume before adequate filling pressures are achieved. The pulmonary edema seen in sedative–hypnotic overdose is similarly mediated. Thus, the physician must first consider volume expansion in shock and positive end-expiratory pressure-assisted ventila-

tion in pulmonary edema. Hypotension that is nonresponsive to volume loading is best treated with agents that have alpha-agonist properties such as dopamine and norepinephrine (Levophed). The dose of either is titrated to the patient's blood pressure. Afterload reduction may prove very effective in pulmonary edema, but only in those cases due to myocardial depression; diuretics must be used judiciously, if at all.

Naloxone, Glucose, and Thiamine. When the ABCs are secure, if the patient is obtunded, a minimum of 2.0 mg of naloxone should be given intravenously. This should be followed by an immediate fingerstick determination of the patient's glucose. If indicated by a low fingerstick value, 50 mL of 50% dextrose in water should be given immediately. Any alcoholic, malnourished, cachectic patient or any patient who requires hypertonic glucose should also receive 100 mg of intravenous thiamine. None of these drugs has significant side effects when compared with the nontreatment of a superimposed narcotic overdose, hypoglycemic episode, or precipitation of Wernicke's encephalopathy.

Adult patients have received more than 10 mg of naloxone without adverse effects, and its aggressive use when there is any hint of superimposed narcotic use must be encouraged. It has been said that "nobody dies of hyperglycemia." This phrase stresses the need to assess each comatose or obtunded patient's need for glucose. The routine testing by fingerstick glucose analysis should never hinge on a preexisting history of diabetes or insulin use.

Contacting of Poison Control and/or Administer Specific Antidote. A poison control center should be contacted in every case of overdose unless the clinician is an expert in toxicologic care. Poison control centers are very helpful in giving both general information on overdoses and specific guidelines in the management of a known drug.

There are no emergency antidotes for the sedative–hypnotics, with the exception of benzodiazepine overdoses. Flumazenil is a specific benzodiazepine antagonist that rapidly reverses any central nervous system depression due to any of the benzodiazepines. Unfortunately, this medication may precipitate seizures in any seizure-prone individual, including alcoholic patients and any patient taking a cyclic antidepressant. Thus, the role of flumazenil in managing cases of coma of unknown etiology is controversial.

Prevention of Absorption. Sedative–hypnotics share multiple common properties, one of these being depression of gastrointestinal motility when taken in large nontherapeutic doses. For this reason, almost all sedative–hypnotic overdose patients must have their gastric contents emptied. Reports of significant amounts of medications being recovered days after the onset of coma underscore this point.

There is some controversy over the optimal method of decreasing absorption in sedative–hypnotic overdose. Three possible options may be used in various combinations: ipecac-induced emesis, oral activated charcoal with sorbitol, and gastric lavage with a large-bore orogastric tube. Ipecac-induced emesis had previously been the preferred method, but its efficacy and safety are both highly questionable. At present, ipecac should be used only in out-of-hospital settings for ingestions that have just occurred in awake, lucid patients. Charcoal administration, often in conjunction with gastric lavage, is the preferred method of gastric decontamination for all other patients.

Lavage is not mandatory in stable but sleepy patients who are seen a number of hours after an overdose if they have good bowel sounds and have not ingested potentially fatal amounts of drugs. These patients do not require lavage if they can swallow the charcoal and sorbitol mixture and be closely monitored while kept in an upright position. Patients with deepening levels of unconsciousness, decreased bowel sounds, poor gag reflex, or other signs or history of a potentially fatal ingestion should always be lavaged.

Gastric atony may result in pill fragments, especially in sedative–hypnotic overdoses, being found in the stomach 6 to 12 hours after ingestion. Thus, comatose patients should be lavaged no matter how many hours after the ingestion they are seen. The importance of protecting the airway with an endotracheal tube prior to orogastric lavage cannot be overstressed.

If there is any significant diminution in consciousness or impairment of the gag reflex, tracheal intubation must precede gastric lavage. Neither ipecac nor a nasogastric tube should ever be used in a nonalert or

---

TABLE 24–5–1. STEPWISE MANAGEMENT OF THE OVERDOSED PATIENT

1. Secure the airway, breathing, and cardiovascular status.
2. Evaluate the need for naloxone, glucose, and thiamine.
3. Contact poison control center; administer emergency antidote if appropriate.
4. Prevent absorption.
5. Enhance elimination.

neurologically impaired patient. As aspiration with all its complications must be guarded against vigorously, the clinician must carefully check for leakage about the cuff in the intubated patient. Once the airway has been properly secured, lavage using a large-bore gastric tube is appropriate. Retrieved contents may be saved for analysis if clinically indicated. Once the lavage has been completed, activated charcoal with a high absorption coefficient should be introduced into the stomach. Charcoal should be repeated every 2 hours for at least two to three additional doses if large quantities of drug(s) have been ingested. In cases of barbiturate overdose, charcoal should be continued until a normal serum level is obtained. One of the newer high-absorbency charcoals premixed with sorbitol is recommended, at a dose of 1 g/kg body weight. Administering repeated doses of activated charcoal in phenobarbital overdose can nearly triple excretion. When repeated doses of activated charcoal are given 10 hours after ingestion to healthy volunteers, the half-life of the drug drops from approximately 90 to 20 hours.

Enhancement of Elimination. The elimination of only one sedative–hypnotic may be facilitated with alkaline diuresis. For the long-acting barbiturate phenobarbital, which possesses a pK_a of 7.24, alkaline diuresis may dramatically decrease serum levels and length of coma. The shorter-acting barbiturates (secobarbital, amobarbital, etc.) have pK_a values that approach 8.0. Although forced diuresis of the short-acting barbiturates may increase elimination minimally, no effect is achieved by alkalinization of urine. Increasing urine flow above normal levels or manipulating urinary pH has no effect on any of the other sedative–hypnotics. Peritoneal dialysis and hemodialysis may be effective in the removal of many of the sedative–hypnotics; however, in many cases, this will not result in increased patient survival and may in fact lead to more, rather than fewer, complications. The clinician should accept that a comatose patient who has well-supervised life support is technically stable and does not necessarily need additional rigorous intervention. The use of charcoal and resin hemoperfusion has begun to replace hemodialysis in the treatment of severe, unstable overdoses. By running the patient's blood through a column of charcoal or an exchange resin, more toxin can be removed than with hemodialysis. The problems of blood pressure control and/or fluid and electrolyte fluxes common with hemodialyzed overdose patients are almost nonexistent in patients undergoing hemoperfusion. The indications for hemoperfusion in each specific drug overdose are found under Discussion. Table 24–5–2 lists which drugs are effectively dialyzed.

FOLLOW-UP

Most overdoses need mental psychiatric rather than medical follow-up. A visit to the patient's mental health care worker within a few days of discharge to evaluate the patient's sense of well-being and the possibility of continued suicidal ideation is highly advised.

Any significant depression or suicidal ideation should prompt the patient's immediate return to a primary care provider or mental health worker.

DISCUSSION
Prevalence and Incidence

Sedative–hypnotics, especially when combined with ethanol, are one of the most common causes of death from poisoning and overdose. The exact number of sedative–hypnotic overdoses is unknown; however, it is estimated that approximately one quarter to one third of all suicides involve one or more of these agents. Deaths are usually seen in patients who do not reach a hospital prior to the onset of respiratory failure, who receive poor attention to their airway early in their hospital stay, who have refractory hypotension, or who develop complications from a protracted course in the intensive care unit.

Related Basic Science

Many drugs are categorized as sedative–hypnotics; their common property is central nervous system depression. The degree of depression is dependent on which specific agent is used, its dosage, its route of administration, and the patient's prior sedative–hypnotic usage. Unfortunately, the degree of depression is also determined by the patient's baseline central nervous system reactivity. Thus, an individual with significant ethanol intoxication or with debilitating disease is much more prone to severe cortical and brainstem depression.

The interactions of ethanol and the sedative–hypnotic agents are clinically very important. When used in conjunction with each other, the combined effect is at least additive and often is synergistic. An excellent example of this often synergistic interaction is the combination of ethanol and phenobarbital. Blood levels of 100 mg/dL for ethanol superimposed on a barbiturate level of 1 mg/dL have proven fatal. This compares with the usual lethal ethanol level of 500 to 800 mg/dL or the usually lethal phenobarbital level of 8 to 15 mg/dL. Much of the additive or synergistic effects of ethanol and the sedative–hypnotics is caused by a common enzyme degradation system. It has been demonstrated that the microsomal ethanol-oxidizing system also functions to detoxify many of the sedative–hypnotics. There is often competitive inhibition for the breakdown of both ethanol and the sedative. In addition to the competitive inhibition for detoxification peripherally, both ethanol and the sedatives often work synergistically at central sites. Thus, the generalized depressant activity of any sedative on the central nervous system is enhanced greatly in the presence of ethanol use.

TABLE 24–5–2. CLUES TO THE DIAGNOSIS AND TREATMENT OF COMMON SEDATIVE-HYPNOTIC OVERDOSES

	Benzodiazepines	Chloral Hydrate	Ethchlorvynol	Glutethimide	Meprobamate	Methaqualone	Methyprylon	Phenobarbital	Short-acting Barbiturates
Dialysis/hemo-perfusion	Not effective	Effective	Effective	Not effective	Effective	Effective	Effective	Effective	Effective
Diuresis	Not effective	Limited value	Not effective	Not effective	Dangerous	Not effective	Not effective	Highly effective if alkaline	Not effective
Comments	Suspect other illness or drug for deep coma	Gastric irritant, cardiac irritant, late hepatotoxicity	Rapid onset, hangovers	Used with Tylenol 4, strong anti-cholinergic, long-acting active metabolite	Hypotension common, rapid-onset respiratory arrest	Associated with trauma; hypotension uncommon	Similar to barbiturates	Supportive care usually all that's needed	Early and rapid respiratory arrest
Clues to diagnosis	Relatively alert in large overdoses	Profuse vomiting, electrocardiographic abnormalities, exfoliative dermatitis	Excess salivation, vinyl odor, pulmonary edema	Big pupils, profound gastric atony, seizures	Nystagmus, acidosis	Myoclonic seizures, paradoxical excitement, pulmonary edema	Similar to barbiturates	Bullae, slow progression to coma	Rapid progression to coma

Although all areas of the brain are affected to varying degrees, the primary site of action for most of this group of drugs is the reticular activating system. As higher levels of sedative–hypnotics are attained, the reticular activating system loses its ability to maintain wakefulness. Additionally, medullary centers, including those involved with respiration, are suppressed. At high dosage levels, it is possible to affect all neurally excitable tissue. Thus, a patient progresses through the gradual planes of anesthesia: sedation, hypnosis, anesthesia, respiratory depression, and finally death.

Barbiturates. The barbiturates, first marketed in 1903, are the prototypical sedative–hypnotics. Since their inception, more than 2500 barbiturates have been synthesized. Although their absolute number is large, in general, barbiturates fall into two categories: short- and long-acting. The short-acting barbiturates have long alkyl side chains, have a high pK_2, are lipid-soluble, are highly protein bound, have a rapid onset, and are metabolized in the liver. The long-acting barbiturates have an aromatic side chain, reduced lipid solubility, low protein binding, a lower pK_2, and a delayed onset, and are eliminated to a large extent by the kidneys.

As noted earlier, the duration of coma is quite variable, depending on the specific agent used. Many treatment regimens have attempted to decrease the time spent in coma. With the exception of overdose caused by phenobarbital, none of the noninvasive forms of therapy has met with significant success. Manipulation of urinary pH is not effective because of the high pK_a values (7.7–8.0) of the short-acting barbiturates. Forced diuresis increases the elimination of the short-acting barbiturates by only 3 to 5%. Phenobarbital, however, has a pK_a of 7.2, which allows significant ionic manipulation. At a urinary pH of 8, approximately 86% of the phenobarbital presented to the renal tubule is ionized. As it is only the un-ionized form that is reabsorbed, alkalinization of the urine has dramatic therapeutic implications. Thus, the routine management of phenobarbital overdosage includes maintaining an alkaline urine, whereas overdoses with the shorter-acting barbiturates are ordinarily treated with supportive care only. Repeated doses of activated charcoal are very effective in reducing the half-life of phenobarbital, but are not as efficacious with the shorter-acting barbiturates.

The estimated fatal dose of phenobarbital is approximately 6 to 10 g, whereas 2 to 4 g is the usual fatal dose for the short-acting barbiturates. These values correlate with serum levels of approximately 10 and 5 mg/dL, respectively. In patients with severe refractory hypotension, poorly controlled pulmonary edema, or increasing serum levels in the face of imminent demise, hemodialysis or hemoperfusion is recommended. When the three methods are compared, the method of choice is resin hemoperfusion with an XAD-4 resin, followed by charcoal hemoperfusion and lastly standard hemodialysis.

A number of nonbarbiturate sedative–hypnotics have been marketed. Although initially touted as better and safer than the barbiturates, none, with the exception of the benzodiazepines, has lived up to manufacturers' claims.

Chloral Hydrate. Chloral hydrate is the oldest member of the sedative–hypnotic family, having been synthesized in 1832 and used clinically since 1869. After barbiturates became popular, it took until the early 1950s for chloral hydrate to regain renewed clinical interest. Chloral hydrate is a halogenated hydrocarbon whose actions are quite similar to those of the barbiturates. Its major use is in elderly patients and in children who have idiosyncratic reactions to other sedative–hypnotics. Chloral hydrate possesses clinically significant physical and pharmacologic properties. It is an irritant to skin and gastric mucosa. Additionally, it possesses a distinct cardiotoxic effect at high doses. The usual dosage range is 500 mg to 1 g; major toxicity occurs at dosages of about 10 g. Deaths have been reported with as little as 4 g, and survival with up to 30 g.

Chloral hydrate is metabolized to trichloroethanol, which is then degraded via the alcohol dehydrogenase enzyme system in the liver. Concurrent ethanol intoxication causes significant increases in toxicity of chloral hydrate. Because it is an irritant to skin, mucosal membranes, and myocardium, the following may be clues to a chloral hydrate overdose: eczematoid or exfoliative dermatitis, hematemesis, cardiac dysrhythmias (see Table 24–5–2). A pearlike odor may sometimes be detected on the patient's breath. Hemoperfusion is recommended for deep

coma accompanied by unstable vital signs, ventricular arrhythmias, or refractory acid–base disturbances.

Ethchlorvynol. Ethchlorvynol (Placidyl) is a sedative–hypnotic with a rapid onset and a short duration of action. It is also an anticonvulsant and muscle relaxant. Although it has a short half-life, users may suffer from a hangover-like syndrome. Acute intoxication occurs when dosage approaches 5 to 10 g. The significantly overdosed patient commonly presents with hypothermia and hypotension. An unusually sweet odor that smells like a vinyl car seat may be noted on the breath, and excess salivation may be a clue to this drug's abuse. Although ethchlorvynol has a pK_a of 8.7, acid diuresis has not shown to be efficacious and may in fact be deleterious. Vomiting is very common in this overdose. Acute pulmonary edema may be seen with this drug, especially when it is used intravenously. Dyspnea and chest pain have also been reported. Hepatic dysfunction may be seen within 1 week of the initial overdose. Hemoperfusion may be indicated for deeply comatose patients who are continuing to decompensate despite supportive care.

Glutethimide. Glutethimide (Doriden) was introduced in 1954. Within 1 year it had become the sixth most commonly prescribed sedative–hypnotic. This was because many believed it possessed advantages over the barbiturates including low abuse potential, non-habit-forming status, and a high therapeutic index. It is now apparent that although glutethimide is a nonbarbiturate, it is inferior to barbiturates in almost all its properties. Acute intoxication is quite similar to that of the short-acting barbiturates, with a few noteworthy exceptions. Secondary to its anticholinergic actions, marked dilation of the pupils and complete gastric atony are very common. Another of glutethimide's characteristics is cyclic variation of consciousness. Coma may alternate with tonic–clonic muscular spasm, which may generalize to full seizure activity. Glutethimide is erratically absorbed from the gastrointestinal tract, and the so-called stable and recovering overdosed patient may be later found in profound coma. There is usually poor correlation between the patient's clinical status and the blood glutethimide level; the reason for this may lie partly in the active metabolite of glutethimide. The metabolite, 4-hydroxy-2-ethyl-2-phenylglutarimide, has been shown to accumulate in the plasma of intoxicated patients and is twice as potent as alcohol in terms of acute lethality. At a time when glutethimide levels are falling dramatically, blood levels of 4-hydroxy-2-ethyl-2-phenylglutarimide may be in the toxic or lethal range. Glutethimide taken along with acetaminophen with codeine, a combination called "4's and Dor's," or "loads," produces a euphoriant effect said to be similar to that of heroin. Supportive care is indicated in overdosage. Hemoperfusion should be reserved for unstable patients who do not respond to routine management. High doses of naloxone may be helpful if acetaminophen with codeine has also been ingested.

Meprobamate. Meprobamate (Miltown) is another sedative–hypnotic that is very similar to the barbiturates. Clinically it is often difficult to differentiate between the two. Although initially claimed to be an antianxiety agent, the drug's efficacy as such has been questioned. The progression from a waking state to deep coma with subsequent respiratory arrest may be exceedingly rapid, occurring as quickly as 15 to 30 minutes. Hypotension may be seen in the lighter grades of coma and may be seen without evidence of respiratory depression. Nystagmus, ataxia, and acidosis may be clues to meprobamate overdosage. Forced diuresis is dangerous because pulmonary edema often occurs in meprobamate overdoses; however, as 10 to 20% of this drug's excretion is via a renal mechanism, a good urine flow is essential. Hemoperfusion is indicated in severe cases in which conservative care does not stabilize the patient.

Methaqualone. Methaqualone (Quaalude) was introduced in 1965. It took almost 10 years of use to learn that this "nonbarbiturate, nonaddicting, safe, minimal suppressor of REM [rapid eye movement] sleep sedative–hypnotic" was quite similar to its predecessors. Unfortunately, the subjective "luding out" experienced by its users created a high interest in its illicit abuse. Initially described as not physically and rarely psychologically addicting, users became dependent on the "love drug" for its supposed properties as a euphoriant, and it developed a reputation as an aphrodisiac. The dissociative high it creates is preferred by many addicts over that of heroin. It was not until the early 1980s that the logarithmic increase in this drug's use was curbed. Methaqualone's most serious attribute, other than the ease of psychological dependence, is one of a narrow therapeutic index in chronic users who tend to supplement "the high" with ethanol. Most earlier deaths had been reported secondary to the ill-advised mixing of these two depressants. During the 1970s, there was a change in the cause of deaths due to methaqualone. Nearly three quarters of all deaths from this drug are due to trauma, and now only one quarter are due to the overdose itself. Tolerance to the therapeutic effects of methaqualone rises significantly more rapidly than tolerance to the lethal dosage; thus, the therapeutic and lethal dosages come close in the chronic user.

Starting in 1982, the use of methaqualone dropped precipitously due to its reclassification as a Class I restricted drug. Many illegal domestic and foreign laboratories manufacture this drug, though, and this medication still remains available.

Hemoperfusion and hemodialysis are effective in removing this drug. These methods should be reserved for the rare patient with deep coma, unstable vital signs, and a declining clinical status in the face of aggressive conservative care.

The exact mechanism of methaqualone's action is not completely understood. Although similar to the short-acting barbiturate, it has no direct effect on the reticular activating system. It is somewhat similar to the benzodiazepines in that it does possess properties of a direct skeletal muscle relaxant. Methaqualone is hydroxylated by the hepatic microsomal enzyme system, and only about 2% is excreted unchanged in the urine. Although it has a short half-life of only 2 to 3 hours, this is significantly extended in the chronic abuser using high dosages. In general, treatment is supportive. Forced diuresis is contraindicated owing to the high incidence of pulmonary edema. Some series have reported a greater than 50% incidence of pulmonary edema in methaqualone-induced coma. Clues to methaqualone use in the overdosed patient relate to the paradoxical excitement it may cause. Hyperreflexia, hypertonicity, and myoclonic or generalized seizure activity may be seen in patients who abuse this drug. Hypotension is less common than in barbiturate overdosage.

Methyprylon. Methyprylon (Noctan, Noludar) is another sedative–hypnotic that was introduced in the 1950s. The pharmacologic and toxicologic properties of this drug are not well known. Only 3% of the drug appears unchanged in the urine; the remainder is metabolized and excreted in the urine and feces. Methyprylon overdosage appears to be similar to a barbiturate overdosage, and the care given is basically the same. The use of dialysis is controversial; diuresis, however, is of no value. Hypotension in methyprylon overdose is rare and indicates a severe overdose. Hemoperfusion has been shown to be highly efficacious for severe cases of this rare sedative–hypnotic overdose.

Methyprylon is no longer available in the United States; however, patients may have access to this drug via their travel to Latin America and Europe.

Benzodiazepines. The benzodiazepines are the most commonly prescribed drugs in the United States. They act via a direct depressant effect on parts of the hypothalamus, thalamus, and limbic systems via an enhancement of the inhibitory neurotransmitter of γ-aminobutyric acid. Although used as sedative–hypnotics, the benzodiazepines are part of the "antianxiety" group of medications. This group of drugs also produces direct skeletal muscle relaxation. Some of the more common benzodiazepines are listed in Table 24–5–3.

TABLE 24–5–3. COMMON BENZODIAZEPINES

Drug	Brand Name	Half-life (h)
Alprazolam	Xanax	12–15
Chlordiazepoxide	Librium	5–30
Diazepam	Valium	14–50
Flurazepam	Dalmane	50–100
Lorazepam	Ativan	12–18
Oxazepam	Serax	5–10
Triazolam	Halcion	2–3

All the benzodiazepines are detoxified in the liver, and some of the metabolites possess properties similar to those of the parent compound. One of diazepam's metabolites is oxazepam, itself a useful antianxiety agent.

The peak plasma level for almost all benzodiazepines is reached well within 2 hours. Triazolam (Halcion) is a relatively new short-acting benzodiazepine, with peak effects in 30 to 60 minutes. Although it is an excellent hypnotic agent at low doses, coma has been reported in overdoses as small as 2 mg. A number of deaths have also been reported with this short-acting benzodiazepine. Supportive care is the mainstay of therapy in treating any benzodiazepine overdose. Dialysis is of no value because of the large amount of protein binding, and diuresis is totally ineffective because none of the benzodiazepines are excreted unchanged in the urine. The need for aggressive care in pure benzodiazepine overdosage is rare to almost nonexistent. In the world's literature there are only a few cases of deaths solely due to benzodiazepine overdosages. A patient who ingested 2000 mg of diazepam was released within 2 days of ingestion; his deepest level of coma was grade I (arousable). It is very rare to see deep levels of coma with benzodiazepine abuse, and the clinician should suspect superimposed ethanol or other sedative usage in unarousable comatose patients. Serum levels in benzodiazepine overdosage have no prognostic implications; high serum levels merely indicate significant ingestions. The oral LD_{50} of diazepam in rats is 1240 mg/kg, and intraperitoneal administration of 400 mg/kg to a monkey resulted in death on the sixth day. When extrapolated to humans of normal body weight, the oral LD_{50} approaches and may exceed the stomach's physical dimensions. When given intravenously, this drug may be lethal at quite low doses; as little as 5 to 10 mg via rapid infusion has caused respiratory arrest in susceptible individuals. The half-lives of this family of drugs are variable and increase significantly in chronic abusers and massive overdosage. The half-lives of the most commonly used benzodiazepines are listed in Table 24–5–3.

The interaction of ethanol with orally administered diazepam has been well studied. It was initially believed that the two merely had additive sedative properties; however, the two are synergistic. Maximum mean plasma diazepam levels are approximately doubled when diazepam is ingested with ethanol, as compared with diazepam ingested with water. Not only does ethanol increase benzodiazepine levels, but it also appears to inhibit benzodiazepine breakdown by competitive inhibition of the hepatic microsomal oxidative enzyme system.

Natural History and Its Modification with Treatment

Most patients with sedative–hypnotic overdoses do well; however, this family of drugs is the number one cause of major morbidity in poisoning and overdose. Complications are mainly seen in patients who become so obtunded that they lose their gag reflex, in hypotensive patients, and in patients who develop pulmonary edema. Aspiration of gastric contents is the major reason for prolonged hospital stays.

The clinical course of a sedative–hypnotic overdose has been discussed earlier. The physician must be prepared to deal with any and all of the complications that these drugs may induce. As the duration of coma may be quite prolonged, coma care must be directed toward the eventual complete recovery of the patient. Prognostications on clinical recovery should be reserved until drug levels are low to nonexistent rather than during the acute phase of the overdosage. As was alluded to earlier, deep coma secondary to acute sedative overdosage may create flat-line electroencephalograms—this should never be interpreted as brain death.

Many chronic abusers of sedative–hypnotics never present to the physician with an overt overdose. They may seek medical attention for unrelated illness or come in search of detoxification. The clinician must be aware that massive quantities of sedatives may be ingested routinely on a daily basis by some chronic abusers. The abrupt withdrawal of any drug should never be attempted by the well-meaning physician. Gradual tapering, often on an inpatient basis, may be necessary to avoid an abstinence syndrome that may be catastrophic. The most feared of these complications, status seizures and subsequent vascular collapse, may be avoided by gradual reduction in dosage, possibly supplemented by additional pharmacologic agents. In the event withdrawal seizures occur, the formerly abused drug is usually the drug of choice in the acute management. It should be noted that even relatively small dosage schedules of sedatives, if used for prolonged periods, may result in an abstinence syndrome if their use is discontinued abruptly.

Prevention

The hallmark in the prevention of sedative–hypnotic abuse and overdose lies in judicious prescribing habits of physicians. Because the sedative–hypnotics are the number one drug of choice for successful suicide, large supplies should never be given. Additionally, the possibility of suicidal ideation should be explored prior to prescribing any of these drugs. Only the benzodiazepines have been shown effective in promoting sleep past 14 days of consecutive use; thus, no more than a 14-day supply of any barbiturate seems advisable. At present, it seems prudent to rely on the recommendations of the National Institute on Drug Abuse (NIDA), which recommends, when required, the sedative–hypnotic drug of choice be one of the benzodiazepines. This is based on greater relative safety, less additive effect with ethanol, relatively little interaction with other commonly prescribed drugs, relatively little hepatic induction, relatively little effect on rapid eye movement (REM) sleep, and less possibility of causing death from accidental or intentional overdose.

In closing, the physician should be aware that the drug of choice for the induction of sleep is not a sedative–hypnotic. The anxiety of daily life need not be treated with pharmacologic sedatives at bedtime.

Cost Containment

Excellent patient care may be given without large expenditures of money if prompt, appropriate care is rendered to the comatose patient when he or she presents to the emergency area. Once the patient has been admitted, the best care is often the most noninvasive, which is by far the cheapest. Lastly, the long-term complications of prolonged coma may be avoided by aggressive nursing care and physical therapy early in the course of illness.

Expensive invasive removal techniques such as hemodialysis, resin perfusion, and peritoneal dialysis should not be used routinely. They should be reserved only for the previously delineated life-threatening indications.

REFERENCES

Burkhart KK, Kulig KW. The diagnostic utility of flumazenil (a benzodiazepine antagonist) in coma of unknown etiology. Ann Emerg Med 1990;19:319.

Buur T, Larsson R, Norlander B. Pharmacokinetics of chloral hydrate poisoning treated with hemodialysis and hemoperfusion. Acta Med Scand 1988;223:269.

McCarron MM, Schulze BW, Walberg CB, et al. Short-acting barbiturate overdose. JAMA 1982;248:55.

Mendelson WB, Rich CL. Sedatives and suicide: The San Diego study. Acta Psychiatr Scand 1993;88:337.

Pond SM, Olson KR, Osterloh JD, Tong TG. Randomized study of the treatment of phenobarbital overdose with repeated doses of activated charcoal. JAMA 1984;251:3104.

Wetli CV. Changing patterns of methaqualone abuse: A survey of 246 fatalities. JAMA 1983;249:621.

Yell RP. Ethchlorvynol overdose. Am J Emerg Med 1990;8:246.

CHAPTER 24–6

Carbon Monoxide Poisoning

Brian R. McMurray, M.D.

DEFINITION

Carbon monoxide poisoning is a clinical syndrome composed primarily of central nervous system and cardiac abnormalities induced by the inhalation of the carbon monoxide.

ETIOLOGY

Toxic exposure to carbon monoxide most commonly occurs when the gas is produced by the incomplete combustion of organic matter. Frequent sources include internal combustion engines, faulty heating systems, and fires. Inadequate ventilation and faulty equipment function are common features of unintentional carbon monoxide poisoning, and sources commonly include gasoline-powered generators, propane heaters, and charcoal burners. Similarly, indoor operation of industrial machinery such as forklifts and ice skating rink resurfacing machines can be hazardous when ventilation is inadequate or engine combustion is faulty.

Intentional CO poisoning is most often from vehicle exhaust. In a closed garage, lethal concentrations from vehicle exhaust can be reached in as little as 10 minutes.

Less common sources of CO poisoning include methylene chloride, which is present in many commercial paint strippers and is metabolized to CO, and incomplete burning of natural gas, which can be especially dangerous given the lack of associated irritating fumes.

CRITERIA FOR DIAGNOSIS
Suggestive

Key to the diagnosis of carbon monoxide poisoning is clinical suspicion, as there exist no pathognomonic signs or symptoms. The clinician should be especially suspicious when signs and symptoms consistent with CO poisoning are seen in more than one patient concomitantly, when symptoms are episodic and location dependent, or when pets have exhibited abnormal behavior or unexpected death. CO poisoning should be considered in the differential diagnosis of a patient presenting with findings such as headache, dizziness, altered mental status, syncope, confusion, nausea, and exacerbation of angina or emphysema. The diagnosis can be especially elusive in younger children, who may present with even less specific symptoms such as vomiting, irritability, and lethargy, and whose parents or other adult caregivers may have relatively fewer and less pronounced symptoms.

The severely CO-poisoned patient more commonly presents from the scene of intentional poisoning, a home with faulty heating, or from a fire. Any victim of significant smoke inhalation should be considered CO-poisoned until proven otherwise.

Definitive

An elevated venous or arterial carboxyhemoglobin (COHb) level is the only way to definitively diagnose carbon monoxide exposure. The CO level may be up to 3% in nonsmokers and up to roughly 10% in heavy smokers. The COHb level can transiently go up to 15% or slightly higher if the level is drawn shortly after smoking. The use of supplemental oxygen prior to obtaining the level and the delay between the exposure to CO and obtaining the COHb level are also confounding factors influencing interpretation of blood levels.

Notwithstanding the above limitations, the combination of a level above 3% in a nonsmoker or above 10% in a smoker who presents with signs or symptoms consistent with CO poisoning is the most definitive means of diagnosis currently available.

CLINICAL MANIFESTATIONS

Subjective

The symptoms seen in CO poisoned patients are nonspecific and varied. *The severity of the symptoms may bear little correlation to the COHb level obtained, and may be more reflective of the concentration–time product of the CO exposure.* Nonetheless, in the case of an acutely poisoned patient with a prompt pretreatment COHb level obtained, there is a general progression of signs and symptoms that may correlate with an increasing COHb level, as depicted in Table 24–6–1.

Most common among the symptoms of CO poisoning are headache, dizziness, dyspnea, and confusion. A mild CO poisoning often is characterized by a history of the previous symptoms and might include presyncope and an intact neuropsychiatric examination. A moderate CO poisoning often includes a history of syncope and abnormal neuropsychiatric testing or mildly impaired bedside mental status examination. If the exposure is more severe, grossly altered mental status or coma may be present in addition to features such as cardiac ischemia and respiratory failure, especially in the patient with underlying coronary artery disease or chronic obstructive lung disease. Other nonspecific symptoms not infrequently include fatigue, malaise, trouble thinking, nausea, and lethargy.

The acuity and severity of the CO exposure often define the clinical presentation, with chronic low-level exposure being more gradual and subtle in its presentation and, therefore, more often mistaken for other illnesses.

A distinct but related syndrome of delayed central nervous system sequelae has been described as occurring in between 10 and 67% of CO-poisoned patients, depending on the method used to detect sometimes subtle central nervous system abnormalities. Its onset may be days to weeks after the initial exposure, and it is clinically defined as a syndrome of neurologic impairment following an apparent lucid or improved interval after CO poisoning.

Symptoms and signs of this delayed syndrome may include headache, forgetfulness, irritability, cognitive dysfunction, psychomotor disturbances, personality changes, problems with gait or continence, and many other neurologic changes. Its occurrence is not infrequently subsequent to an exposure with initially subtle or misinterpreted clinical findings, though the risk for the delayed central nervous system syndrome may be greater in those patients more severely afflicted initially.

Objective

Physical Examination

Table 24–6–2 depicts the complications of CO poisoning. Included are many of the reported abnormalities on physical examination that may

TABLE 24–6–2. REPORTED COMPLICATIONS OF CARBON MONOXIDE POISONING

System Involved	Complication
Neuropsychiatric	Coma, seizures, agitation, leukoencephalopathy, cerebral edema, behavioral disorders, decreased cognitive ability, Tourette-like syndrome, mutism, fecal and urinary incontinence, parietal lobe dysfunction, ataxia, muscular rigidity, parkinsonism, memory impairment, gait disturbance, abnormal electroencephalogram, personality changes
Cardiovascular	Angina, tachycardia, ST-segment changes, hypotension, arrhythmias, myocardial infarction, heart block
Pulmonary	Pulmonary edema and hemorrhage, unilateral diaphragmatic paralysis
Ophthalmologic	Flame-shaped retinal hemorrhages, decreased light sensitivity, decreased visual acuity, cortical blindness, retrobulbar neuritis, papilledema, paracentral scotomas
Vestibular and auditory	Central hearing loss, tinnitus, vertigo, nystagmus
Gastrointestinal	Vomiting, diarrhea, hepatic necrosis, hematochezia, melena
Dermatologic	Bullae, alopecia, sweat gland necrosis, "cherry red" skin color (rare), edema, cyanosis, pallor, erythematous patches
Hematologic	Disseminated intravascular coagulation, thrombotic thrombocytopenic purpura, leukocytosis
Musculoskeletal	Rhabdomyolysis, myonecrosis, compartment syndrome
Renal	Acute renal failure secondary to myoglobinuria, proteinuria
Metabolic	Lactic acidosis, nonpancreatic hyperamylasemia, diabetes insipidus, hyperglycemia, hypocalcemia
Fetal	Death, cerebral atrophy, microcephalus, low birth weight, psychomotor retardation, seizures, spasticity

Source: From Reisdorff EJ, Weigenstein JG. Carbon monoxide poisoning. In: Tintinalli JE, Krome RL, Ruiz E, eds. Emergency medicine: A comprehensive study guide. 3rd ed. New York: McGraw Hill, 1992:704. Reproduced with permission from McGraw-Hill, Inc. and the author.

TABLE 24–6–1. SIGNS AND SYMPTOMS AT VARIOUS CARBOXYHEMOGLOBIN CONCENTRATIONS*

Carboxyhemoglobin Level (%)	Signs and Symptoms
0	Usually none
10	Frontal headache
20	Throbbing headache, dyspnea with exertion
30	Impaired judgment, nausea, dizziness, visual disturbance, fatigue
40	Confusion, syncope
50	Coma, seizures
60	Hypotension, respiratory failure
70	Death

*Carboxyhemoglobin levels are notoriously poor indicators of the degree of carbon monoxide poisoning; the levels in this table are pertinent only in acute exposures and when the level is obtained soon after removal from the CO-contaminated environment, prior to prolonged breathing of therapeutic oxygen.
Source: From Reisdorff EJ, Weigenstein JG. Carbon monoxide poisoning. In: Tintinalli JE, Krome RL, Ruiz E. Emergency medicine: A comprehensive study guide. 3rd ed. New York: McGraw Hill, 1992:704. Reproduced with permission from McGraw-Hill, Inc. and the author.

be found in examining the CO-poisoned patient. As is true with the history, there are no physical examination findings that are specific to CO poisoning. Although many abnormalities can be found on examination (such as the notorious, but truly rare and late finding of cherry-red skin discoloration), the clinician should rather concentrate on the "ABCDE" approach to examining the patient.

A	Airway	Stridor, evidence of smoke inhalation damage to oropharynx or airway, able to speak clearly?
B	Breathing	Tachypnea (secondary to hypoxemia or acidosis or exacerbation of chronic obstructive pulmonary disease or noncardiogenic pulmonary edema or cardiac failure complicating acute myocardial infarction?); hypoxemia *(be wary of the pulse oximetry gap)*?
C	Circulation	Tachycardia, arrhythmias, hypotension
D	Disability	Neurologic impairment such as altered mental status, nystagmus, ataxia, seizures, coma, agitation, and psychosis *(do not forget possible concomitant ingestions, trauma, and hypoglycemia)*
E	Expose	Thermal burns, signs of trauma

Routine Laboratory Abnormalities

There are no routine laboratory tests that are specific to CO poisoning. The complete blood count may show a neutrophilia. The routine blood chemistry profile may show a wide-anion-gap acidosis in more severe poisonings, due to lactate accumulation. If the anion gap is pronounced with a significant acidosis in a fire/smoke inhalation victim, the physician should assume the presence of cyanide poisoning as well as carbon monoxide. Metabolic acidosis occurring without hypotension or sepsis should always be regarded as possibly secondary to carbon monoxide toxicity.

An elevated creatine phosphokinase may be present due to myocardial injury and/or rhabdomyolysis. Thus, checking isoenzymes of an elevated creatine phosphokinase should be routine. If the urinalysis dipstick test for blood is positive despite the relative absence of hematuria, it is likely secondary to myoglobinuria. Azotemia may be also evident.

Chest radiographs are often normal, but may show a pattern of noncardiogenic pulmonary edema, aspiration, or even cardiogenic pulmonary edema in those with underlying ischemic heart disease who have an acute myocardial infarction or severe ischemic episode.

PLANS

Diagnostic

Differential Diagnosis

The signs, symptoms, and routine laboratory findings of carbon monoxide poisoning are all notoriously nonspecific. Given the many and often vague presenting complaints, it is not surprising that perhaps 30% of cases go unrecognized. Studies have shown that 5 to 20% of patients presenting to emergency departments with complaints of headache, dizziness, or flulike symptoms were actually CO poisoned. The higher proportion of occult CO poisoning can occur in the wintertime, when occult CO poisoning is more likely, as are viral syndromes that may cause the same symptoms.

In a patient presenting with any combination of symptoms and signs such as headache, dizziness, confusion, dyspnea, nausea, lethargy, altered mental status, syncope or near syncope, worsening angina, and unexplained coma, the clinician must be vigilant in considering CO poisoning. The differential diagnosis includes vascular headache, central nervous system hemorrhage, alcohol or other drug ingestion, hypoglycemia, sepsis, stroke, encephalopathy, food poisoning, and psychiatric illness, among others. Children often present with even less specific symptoms such as nausea, irritability, and lethargy, placing them at even higher risk for misdiagnosis.

Diagnostic Options

The diagnosis of carbon monoxide poisoning is made based on a combination of one or more of the following: history of probable or known exposure; clinical manifestations consistent with CO toxicity; an elevated carboxyhemoglobin level (most reliable if drawn promptly in relationship to the exposure and before prolonged treatment with oxygen); neuropsychiatric testing abnormalities; suggestive neuroimaging abnormalities in the absence of other etiology (e.g., computed tomography findings such as low-density lesions in the globus pallidus or hippocampus).

The arterial blood gas can be a helpful means of measuring acidosis, *but it is not a measure of tissue hypoxemia in the CO-poisoned patient.* The arterial blood gas shows a normal partial pressure of oxygen if there is no significant underlying lung pathology, as it measures the dissolved oxygen in the arterial blood, not the amount bound to hemoglobin. This leads to the oxygen saturation, which is usually a calculated figure, being misleadingly and falsely elevated. Only if the oxygen saturation is *measured* is it evident that there is a state of tissue hypoxia. In fact, the difference between the calculated and measured oxygen saturation is referred to as the *sat gap*, and is elevated if there is abnormally bound hemoglobin, such as with carbon monoxide.

Not only is the arterial blood gas potentially misleading in the setting of CO poisoning, but so is the pulse oximetry reading. *Most pulse oximeters cannot differentiate between COHb and oxyhemoglobin.* Thus, there is also a *pulse oximetry gap.* Oxygen saturation on a pulse oximeter, for example, can read "96%" while there is a carboxyhemoglobin level of 44%!

The COHb level can be measured on either venous or arterial blood. Although it has been clearly shown to be a poor correlate of the degree of CO toxicity and prognosis, its elevation is the most definitive means to verify CO intoxication. It is of interest to note that the CO concentration in smoke from a burning cigarette tip is up to 2.5 times that of the smoke inhaled from the other end of the cigarette by the smoker, so second-hand smoke exposure, especially in a confined area, can lead to a significant baseline COHb level in exposed nonsmokers.

Since 1991, a neuropsychological screening battery has been found useful in detecting the sometimes subtle abnormalities of central nervous system function in the CO-exposed patient. The test takes about 30 minutes to administer and tasks include placing pegs in a board, rapid finger tapping, memorizing lists of words, constructing designs or figure drawing, and quickly processing numbers, letters, and symbols. It can detect abnormalities in attention, concentration, fine-motor function, speed of processing, problem solving, and new learning. Such testing may also be useful in assessing response to therapy of CO poisoning. Availability of a test giver is a major limiting factor.

Central nervous system imaging studies are being studied in the evaluation of CO toxicity and its treatment. Currently, there are no diagnostic patterns adequately sensitive or specific to carbon monoxide poisoning. Magnetic resonance imaging and single-photon-emission computed tomography are just two of the neuroimaging modalities currently under study.

Recommended Approach

The key to the diagnosis of CO poisoning is maintaining a high level of clinical suspicion. In any potential exposure setting, a patient with unexplained headache, especially if associated with dizziness, weakness, dyspnea, nausea, or mental status changes, should be considered a possible victim of carbon monoxide intoxication. The history should center around the environment of the patient, whether others in the same surroundings also have symptoms, and if the symptoms are chronic or recurrent. Any patient from a fire or smoke inhalation should be considered poisoned by CO. Especially in the winter months, consider CO exposure as possibly responsible for worsening of angina or chronic obstructive pulmonary disease.

Whether the diagnosis of CO poisoning is readily apparent or subtle, obtain a COHb level as promptly as possible, preferably before prolonged treatment with oxygen. If your laboratory cannot readily perform the test, draw a venous sample (heparinized green top tube) or an arterial blood gas and put either on ice and run the test stat at the nearest laboratory, or send the sample along with the patient to the receiving hospital if you are transferring the patient. Another consideration, if your laboratory does not run COHb levels, is to ask if it can run a *measured* as well as a *calculated* O_2 saturation on an arterial blood gas. A difference between the two (a saturation gap), could provide presumptive evidence of CO poisoning pending an actual COHb level. An elevated COHb level, probable exposure, and consistent symptoms or neuropsychiatric testing deficits make the diagnosis. The physician must remain aware of the potential for misleadingly low or normal COHb levels even in those severely exposed (especially chronic or relatively remote exposures) and elevated levels in smokers, who may tolerate a higher COHb level without apparent untoward effects.

If the suspected CO-poisoned patient has altered mental status, the clinician must not forget to rule out other or concomitant diagnoses. Also consider that the nonaccidental CO exposure patient may have ingested drugs, and evaluate a general toxicologic screen and blood alcohol level. Once these immediate issues are addressed, other laboratory tests and studies should be checked in the suspected CO poisoning victim.

The other diagnostic tests should include an SMA-7 panel and calcium level, with special attention to the anion gap as a clue to the presence of a lactate acidosis. If the patient is a smoke inhalation/fire victim, an arterial blood gas should be obtained. If there is a profound acidosis, assume both CO and cyanide poisoning. An elevated blood cyanide level is confirmative, and the sample must be placed on ice in a gray-top or lavender-top tube. As with the COHb level, it is most accurate if drawn very early in the initial emergency department (or better yet prehospital) encounter with the patient. If cyanide poisoning is suspected, immediate treatment must proceed without a level.

Given the possibility of rhabdomyolysis or myocardial injury complicating CO poisoning, a creatine phosphokinase total (and MB fraction if total creatine phosphokinase is elevated or if there is suspected myocardial injury) should be checked in more severe poisonings. A 12-lead electrocardiogram should be viewed to detect evidence for myocardial ischemia or injury as well as rhythm disturbance or evidence of coexistent cardiotoxic drug ingestion, such as tricyclic antidepressants. A chest radiograph should be part of the evaluation of patients with cardiorespiratory complaints or abnormalities on heart or lung examination of if there has been smoke inhalation. If there is prolonged unconsciousness, computed tomography of the head should be done to evaluate for intracerebral bleed or other central nervous system catastrophe.

If the patient has probable CO exposure, a neuropsychiatric screening test should be performed, if available, in the patient without grossly abnormal mental status, as a means of documenting and following neurologic impairment.

Therapeutic

Therapeutic Options

Oxygen is the key element in management of CO poisoning. It should be administered either by tight-fitting mask with a concentration as close as possible to 100% or via endotracheal tube. This phase of initial management with 100% normobaric oxygen is not an option, but a necessity. *What is optional, and heavily debated, is hyperbaric oxygen treatment: Is it better than normobaric oxygen?* And if it is better, for which CO poisoned patients?

Proponents of hyperbaric oxygen point to its ability to further shorten the elimination half-life of COHb from about 5 hours breathing room air to roughly 1.5 hours breathing 100% oxygen normobaric, to less than 30 minutes with 100% oxygen breathed at 3 atm absolute of pressure. Other arguments in favor of using hyperbaric oxygen are its ability to deliver oxygen in adequate amounts to tissue via high plasma oxygen concentrations, its ability to decrease cerebral edema, and its possible ability to diminish CO-mediated brain lipid peroxidation and mitochondrial cytochrome oxidase malfunction.

Numerous case reports and uncontrolled series have suggested that hyperbaric oxygen can improve neurologic outcome and prevent delayed central nervous system sequelae. Other reports include reversal of neuropsychiatric abnormalities, even weeks after CO exposure.

Children and infants are especially vulnerable to CO toxicity because of their higher metabolic rates, and the fetus additionally has an increased affinity of CO to its fetal hemoglobin, compared with children and adults. Therefore, the advocated threshold to use hyperbaric oxygen has been lower in these patients.

Hyperbaric oxygen is very safe. Otic barotrauma may occur, especially in those patients unable to autosufflate their ears. It can be prevented with ear tube placement, and even if it occurs, it is usually self-limited. Those at high risk for pneumothorax can develop a severe tension pneumothorax on decompression, and the only absolute contraindication to hyperbaric oxygen is an untreated pneumothorax. Pulmonary oxygen toxicity and seizures are rare and largely avoided by following protocols that limit the duration of hyperbaric oxygen treatments. In light of its safety and reports from many sources of its apparent efficacy, in both animal studies and human series and case reports, many centers advocate the use of hyperbaric oxygen in those patients with impaired sensorium or abnormal neuropsychiatric testing, those with acute cardiac abnormalities, and small children or pregnant women with even relatively minor CO exposure.

Recommended Approach

After the initial period of assessment and stabilization, during which the patient should receive 100% oxygen by mask or endotracheal tube, the physician needs to assess the need for hyperbaric oxygen.

There have been, to date, no significant studies performed in a blind, randomized, and prospective fashion that demonstrate the superiority of hyperbaric oxygen over normobaric oxygen in acutely treating CO-poisoned patients or in preventing and treating delayed CO toxicity. Pending such a study, most authorities recommend hyperbaric oxygen for the CO-poisoned patient with significant end-organ insult. These recommendations are made on the basis of the studies done to date on animals and case reports and case series of patients treated with hyperbaric oxygen. Though far from definitive, these studies have suggested that hyperbaric oxygen can reduce short-term and long-term central nervous system sequelae of CO poisoning and may prevent delayed central nervous system abnormalities.

The clinician should rely on clinical assessment of CO toxicity, not COHb levels or results of other laboratory tests. The factor that should

then be considered is the availability of neuropsychiatric testing and hyperbaric oxygen.

For over a century, hyperbaric oxygen and normobaric oxygen have been used and debated about in the management of CO poisoning. Those concerned about the uncertainties of when to use hyperbaric oxygen should take comfort in the results of a recent survey of hyperbaric oxygen facilities, burn centers, and regional poison centers, which showed great variation in the criteria used to recommend hyperbaric oxygen. Hyperbaric oxygen protocols also vary, but typically use 100% oxygen at 2.5 to 3 atm absolute for 60 to 90 minutes separated by about 4 hours of normobaric oxygen. Subsequent hyperbaric oxygen treatments are ideally based on clinical response and neuropsychiatric test performance.

A prospective, randomized, controlled multicenter study evaluating hyperbaric versus normobaric oxygen is needed. Pending such a definitive study, it seems prudent to follow a set of guidelines such as those currently used at the University of Maryland's R. Adams Crowley Shock Trauma Center, which are outlined in Table 24–6–3. In those situations where neuropsychiatric testing or hyperbaric oxygen is not readily available, consultation with the regional poison center is appropriate.

If the patient is a victim of fire-related smoke inhalation, the physician should not miss occult cyanide poisoning. If there is a significant acidosis, hypotension, or profoundly impaired sensorium in this subset of CO-poisoned patients, the physician should empirically administer 12.5 g of sodium thiosulfate intravenously for presumed cyanide toxicity pending the results of a blood cyanide level.

FOLLOW-UP

In all CO-poisoned patients, a careful mental status and neurologic examination should be performed at the outset. The key to patient follow-up is monitoring evidence for end-organ damage. This almost always concerns the central nervous system. If neuropsychiatric testing is available, it should be performed not only initially, but after treatment with oxygen to monitor improvement. Acutely, serial assessment guides efforts at continued oxygen treatment, but such assessment should also continue for at least 6 months, as the onset of delayed effects of CO poisoning has been reported this far and out to even 3 years after the initial insult. Pending greater availability and ease of administration, neuropsychiatric testing should be performed by a clinician who frequently administers the neuropsychiatric screening battery.

Not to be overlooked is the patient's need for follow-up psychiatric care. It is indicated not only for the victim of nonaccidental CO exposure, but also for the victim of CO poisoning who has central nervous system injury. Such central nervous system injury can include depression as a primary symptom, as well as lead to a reactive depression. Follow-up neuropsychiatric testing and psychiatric evaluation and counseling are best advised on a scheduled basis and an as needed basis

TABLE 24–6–3. UNIVERSITY OF MARYLAND MEDICAL CENTER R. ADAMS CROWLEY SHOCK TRAUMA CENTER DEPARTMENT OF HYPERBARIC MEDICINE CRITERIA FOR USING HYPERBARIC OXYGEN IN CO-POISONED PATIENTS

A. Carboxyhemoglobin level above 35%, even with a normal carbon monoxide neuropsychometric battery (CONSB)

B. History of ischemic heart disease and carboxyhemoglobin level greater than 15%

C. Abnormal carbon monoxide neuropsychometric battery test performance (CONSB)

D. Inability to do or complete the CONSB

E. Unconsciousness

F. Recurrent symptoms after treatment with surface oxygen

G. Failure to resolve symptoms after 4 hours of surface oxygen

H. Pregnant females with carboxyhemoglobin levels above 15%

The endpoint of treatment is when the patient is normal on CONSB or plateaus in his or her response on CONSB or clinically.

Source: Roy A. M. Myers, M.D., Director of Hyperbaric Medicine, R. Adams Crowley Shock Trauma Center. Reproduced with permission.

if there is either development of new symptoms or worsening of prior manifestations.

DISCUSSION

Prevalence and Incidence

Carbon monoxide poisoning is the most common cause of toxin-induced death in the United States. The most common settings are attempted suicide, fire-related, and accidental. At least 10,000 exposures are reported annually to regional poison centers, and at least 3800 deaths per year occur secondary to CO exposure. The incidence of non-lethal CO intoxication is not known. The majority of deaths are fire-related, but these numbers are likely underestimates, given the probable unreliability of death certificate reporting of CO poisoning and the estimated 30% underrecognition of CO poisoning due to its nonspecific signs and symptoms.

Testimony to the elusive and often unexpected nature of the diagnosis of carbon monoxide poisoning is the September 1994 death of tennis star Vitas Gerulaitis. He was initially suspected to have succumbed to complications of previously known drug abuse, only to have blood tests confirm carbon monoxide as the culprit, killing him as he slept in a bungalow with an apparently defective heater nearby. The diagnosis of CO poisoning is initially based on clinical suspicion and history. Probable exposure and consistent neuropsychiatric sequelae may be all that is available for presumptive diagnosis.

Related Basic Science

Uptake and excretion of carbon monoxide is mostly by the lungs. As it gains access to the bloodstream, CO binds avidly with hemoglobin, with an affinity of roughly 240 times that of oxygen. The reduced oxygen content of the blood leads to tissue hypoxia. This is exacerbated by hypotension and by the presence of COHb causing a shift to the left in the oxyhemoglobin dissociation curve.

Tissue hypoxia alone, however, does not explain central nervous system injury that occurs at varying levels of COHb, nor the phenomenon of delayed central nervous system sequelae. Alternate proposed and studied (but unproven) mechanisms of CO-induced toxicity are inhibition of cellular respiration via CO binding to cytochrome oxidase, CO coupling to cardiac and skeletal myoglobin, and a reperfusion-type injury to the brain (lipid peroxidation).

The notoriously poor correlation of COHb levels to clinical outcome may in part also be explained by the damage induced by the CO dissolved in the plasma, as opposed to that bound to hemoglobin. A canine study showed that when equal COHb levels were reached by infusion of COHb-laden red blood cells versus breathing CO, the group breathing CO quickly succumbed, whereas those with just CO-saturated red cells survived. It has been shown that even when oxygen delivery is maintained, the central nervous system is damaged when exposed to COHb.

Whether the mechanism of CO toxicity is hypoxia/ischemia, cellular cytochrome poisoning, brain lipid peroxidation, or other means remains uncertain. Thus far, there is no reliable specific marker for tissue injury secondary to CO toxicity.

Natural History and Its Modification with Treatment

It has been estimated that about one third of victims of significant CO toxicity die as a result of their exposure. The clinical course of those who survive is dependent on many factors, including duration and intensity of exposure; presence of other inhaled or ingested toxins; secondary injuries, if present (e.g., burns, trauma); individual susceptibility (e.g., chronic obstructive pulmonary disease, ischemic heart disease); promptness of oxygen administration at therapeutic levels; effectiveness of follow-up psychiatric care.

Long-term central nervous system injury is the main chronic complication of CO intoxication. Most patients suffer few if any chronic effects of CO poisoning and recover promptly. At least one third of pa-

tients with a significant exposure may suffer some subtle long-term deficit such as memory or personality changes. These changes may be subclinical and detected only with formal neuropsychiatric screening. A smaller percentage suffer from chronic and obvious central nervous system impairment, in some instances after an apparent lucid interval. Though patients with initial COHb levels above 40% and those with initially profound end-organ insult (such as coma, syncope, cardiac ischemia, severe acidosis, and seizures) may tend to have poorer long-term prognosis, these markers have all proven less than reliable predictors.

The ability of oxygen therapy to improve outcome is not much debated, but the influence of hyperbaric versus normobaric oxygen treatment on prognosis remains uncertain.

Prevention

Keys to prevention of carbon monoxide poisoning are greater public awareness of the situations that result in occult poisoning and greater utilization of recently available CO detectors.

Although most recognize the prompt dangers of being in an enclosed environment with a running motor vehicle, relatively few are fully aware of other dangerous circumstances. These include faulty but still functioning heating systems and alternate heating systems that are incompletely combusting or not adequately ventilated (whether kerosene, oil, propane, charcoal, coal, Sterno, or even natural gas). Annual inspection of home heating and cooling systems is an important preventive action. Virtually any nonelectric motor that is running in a poorly ventilated environment has the capacity to lead to toxic CO concentrations. Methylene chloride paint strippers used with inadequate ventilation can cause CO intoxication.

The newest preventive measure available is the CO detector. The Consumer Product Safety Commission recommends that all homes be equipped with CO detectors, but only 3% of homes in the United States currently have them. The detectors are available as a unit similar to a smoke detector, and will likely soon be incorporated into some commercially available smoke detectors.

Cost Containment

Other than prevention, the key to cost containment is treatment that most effectively prevents long-term disability and yet uses the relatively expensive modality of hyperbaric oxygen only when clinically indicated. Patients with relatively minor signs and symptoms who quickly respond to 4- to 6-hour breathing of 100% oxygen by mask should be able to be effectively treated at relatively little expense. These patients, however, warrant careful neurologic and mental status examination at the outset, as well as routine follow-up in order not to miss subtle or delayed central nervous system toxicity. Currently, those patients with obvious acute CO-mediated end-organ injury require hospitalization and probable hyperbaric oxygen, pending a definitive prospective study that more exactly defines the role of hyperbaric oxygen.

REFERENCES

Buckley RG, Aks SE, Eshom JL, et al. The pulse oximetry gap in carbon monoxide intoxication. Ann Emerg Med 1994;24:252.

Crocker PJ, Walker JS. Pediatric carbon monoxide toxicity. J Emerg Med 1985;3:443.

Messier LD, Myers RAM. A neuropsychological screening battery for emergency assessment of carbon monoxide poisoned patients. J Clin Psychiatry 1991;47:675.

Reisdorff EJ, Shah SM. Carbon monoxide poisoning: From crib death to pickup trucks. Emerg Med Rep 1993;14:181.

Seger D, Welch L. Carbon monoxide controversies: Neuropsychologic testing, mechanism of toxicity, and hyperbaric oxygen. Ann Emerg Med 1994;24:242.

Van Hoesen KB, Camporesi EM, Moon RE, et al. Should hyperbaric oxygen be used to treat the pregnant patient for acute carbon monoxide poisoning? JAMA 1989;261:1039.

CHAPTER 24–7

Cyclic Antidepressant Overdose

Laurie M. Lawrence, M.D., and Michael L. Callaham, M.D.

DEFINITION

The acute or chronic ingestion of cyclic antidepressant drugs in dosages large enough to induce significant toxicity defines an overdose.

ETIOLOGY

Cyclic antidepressants are widely prescribed for the treatment of depression as well as chronic pain syndromes, such as diabetic neuropathy and fibromyalgia. In children, these drugs have been advocated for the treatment of depression, enuresis, tic disorders, and attention deficit disorders. The first-generation cyclic antidepressants, known as tricyclic antidepressants, include amitriptyline, nortriptyline, doxepin, and desipramine. These drugs cause severe toxicity when large amounts are ingested. The second-generation cyclic antidepressants, amoxapine and maprotiline, are less cardiotoxic, but cause significant central nervous system toxicity. The newer antidepressants trazodone and bupropion, along with the selective serotonin reuptake inhibitors (SSRIs), fluoxetine, sertraline, and paroxetine, appear to have a wide margin of safety in overdosages due to limited cardiovascular and central nervous system toxic effects.

CRITERIA FOR DIAGNOSIS

Suggestive

Cyclic antidepressant overdoses most commonly occur in the setting of a depressed person either who is taking the antidepressant for its therapeutic benefit or who has gained access to someone else's medication. Less frequently, children ingest those drugs accidentally. In most cases a history of ingestion can be obtained from the patient or friends, or the patient is found obtunded with empty pill bottles lying nearby. When no history is available, as in the confused or comatose patient, the clinician should suspect cyclic antidepressant ingestion if the characteristic signs and symptoms of poisoning are present (Tables 24–7–1 and 24–7–2). In addition, the electrocardiogram can provide valuable clues toward diagnosis, particularly if tachycardia and QRS prolongation are present (Table 24–7–3).

Definitive

Definitive diagnosis can be made only by measurement of quantitative drug levels in plasma. Unfortunately, these drug levels often take 24 hours to return, and one cannot await these results to make clinical decisions, although some laboratories use the EMIT, or similar assays, which can produce results in less than 1 hour with reasonable accuracy.

CLINICAL MANIFESTATIONS

Subjective

Each year millions of antidepressants are prescribed. Patients usually state they ingested the medication rather than complaining of any particular symptom. Diagnosis usually rests exclusively on physical signs and history. On occasion, some patients may complain of symptoms related to the anticholinergic effects of this group of medications.

Objective

Cyclic Antidepressants

Physical Examination. The physical signs of poisoning fall into three categories: central nervous system toxicity, the anticholinergic syndrome (common to all medications with anticholinergic properties), and cardiovascular toxicity (Tables 24–7–1 to 24–7–3). It is the cardiovascular toxicity that makes the cyclic antidepressant overdose both unpredictable and potentially lethal.

Routine Laboratory Abnormalities. There are no specific serum abnormalities on routine testing.

Second-Generation Cyclic Antidepressants/Selective Serotonin Reuptake Inhibitors

Physical Examination. The second-generation antidepressants were developed to limit side effects in therapeutic use and toxicity in overdose settings. Amoxapine has a lower incidence of cardiotoxicity, but the incidence of seizure is nine times greater than that with first-generation antidepressants. Maprotiline has prominent anticholinergic effects and a higher incidence of seizures and coma when compared with tricyclic overdoses. Bupropion, a noncyclic antidepressant, generally has a safe toxicity profile in overdoses, although seizures have occurred in some patients, even at therapeutic dosages. The noncyclic antidepressant trazodone and the SSRIs produce minor symptoms of short duration when taken as an overdose. SSRI overdoses cause sedation, sinus tachycardia, tremor, nausea, and vomiting. Fatalities have been reported in very large ingestions or with coingestion of alcohol or other drugs.

Routine Laboratory Abnormalities. As with cyclic antidepressant ingestion, there are no specific laboratory abnormalities.

TABLE 24–7–1. CENTRAL NERVOUS SYSTEM SIGNS OF CYCLIC ANTIDEPRESSANT TOXICITY (IN APPROXIMATE ORDER OF APPEARANCE)

Lethargy, slurred speech
Disorientation
Agitation
Obtundation
Hallucinations
Myoclonic jerks (short, repetitive, violent jerks of extremities)
Coma
Hyperreflexia
True tonic/clonic seizures

Source: From Callaham ML. Tricyclic antidepressant overdose. In: Peter Rosen et al., eds. Emergency medicine: Concepts and clinical practice. 2nd ed. St. Louis: Mosby, 1988. Reproduced with permission from the publisher and author.

TABLE 24–7–2. PERIPHERAL SIGNS OF CYCLIC ANTIDEPRESSANT TOXICITY (IN APPROXIMATE ORDER OF APPEARANCE)

Tachycardia ≥100 bpm at rest
Hypertension (usually mild)
Fever
Mydriasis
Dry, red skin
Decreased bowel sounds (slow gastrointestinal transit time)
Decreased cardiac contractility (present early, manifest late)
Urinary retention
Respiratory depression
Hypotension from cardiac depression, vasodilatation

Source: From Callaham ML, Tricyclic antidepressant overdose. In: Peter Rosen et al., eds. Emergency medicine: Concepts and clinical practice. 2nd ed. St. Louis: Mosby, 1988. Reproduced with permission from the publisher and author.

TABLE 24-7-3. ELECTROCARDIOGRAPHIC ABNORMALITIES IN CYCLIC ANTIDEPRESSANT OVERDOSE (IN APPROXIMATE ORDER OF APPEARANCE)

ST wave progressively slurred

T-wave elevation and peaking

Indeterminate J point

Rightward terminal vector of QRS (120°–270°)

Prolonged QT interval

Prolonged PR interval

QRS prolongation
  ≥100 ms is abnormal
  ≥120 ms is associated with significant toxicity
  ≥160 ms is associated with severe arrhythmias

Bundle-branch blocks (especially right bundle-branch blocks)

Atrioventricular conduction blocks (1st, 2nd, or 3rd degree)

Arrhythmias
  Sinus tachycardia (nearly universal early in overdose)
  Aberrantly conducted beats (usually misdiagnosed as premature ventricular
    contractions)
  Ventricular tachycardia
  Sinus arrest
  Slow, chaotic idioventricular rhythm (premortem)
  Electromechanical dissociation

Early picture is sinus tachycardia with slightly widened QRS, slurred ST segment, and peaked T wave. Late picture is broad, aberrant, and rapidly varying QRS, sinus arrest, and slowing rate.

Source: From Callaham ML. Tricyclic antidepressant overdose. In: Peter Rosen et al., eds. Emergency medicine: Concepts and clinical practice. 2nd ed. St. Louis: Mosby, 1988. Reproduced with permission from the publisher and author.

PLANS

Diagnostic

Differential Diagnosis

In cases where a history of cyclic antidepressant ingestion cannot be obtained, such as in the obtunded patient, the differential diagnosis is that of any patient with a decreased level of consciousness. Coingestion of other drugs, including analgesics, sedatives, alcohol, and recreational drugs, is common in the overdose patient, and may present a confusing clinical picture. It is paramount that overdose patients undergo a thorough physical evaluation and receive basic emergency care such as "securing the ABCs" (airway, breathing, and circulation). In the unconscious patient, the cervical spine should be immobilized if the possibility of trauma cannot be excluded.

Diagnostic Options and Recommended Approach

The patient suspected of antidepressant overdose should receive immediate attention. In a review of 18 fatal cases of tricyclic ingestion, all 18 patients developed major symptoms within 2 hours of arrival to the hospital. Nine of these patients presented to the emergency department with only trivial signs of poisoning and deteriorated within 1 hour of their arrival. An intravenous line should be started with normal saline and oxygen should be administered by nasal cannula. The patient should be placed on a cardiac monitor and a 12-lead electrocardiogram obtained. A brief history and physical examination should be completed. If the patient is obtunded, arterial blood gases should be drawn. Within a few minutes, enough information should be obtained to determine if an acute ingestion of cyclic antidepressants is likely. If ingestion is a possibility, one must advance to treatments aimed at preventing further absorption and toxicity. Even those patients suspected of taking the less toxic antidepressants trazodone and SSRIs should undergo critical care monitoring for a minimum of 6 hours. In all antidepressant ingestions the above precautions should be maintained until the effects of the ingestion have resolved and the patient can be discharged safely to home or psychiatric care.

As hypoxia, hypoperfusion, and hypercarbia may result from cyclic antidepressant poisoning, routine laboratory work includes arterial blood gases, which can be used to assess the degree of toxicity and to assist in patient management. An arterial blood pH less than 7.40 increases the cardiotoxicity of cyclic antidepressants and all obtunded patients should have arterial blood gases to assess adequacy of ventilation and perfusion. A qualitative urine drug screen confirms the presence of tricyclics and is useful in cases of suspected multidrug ingestion.

The electrocardiographic changes of cyclic antidepressant overdoses are not unique. They are similar to those of overdose with type I antiarrhythmic agents, particularly quinidine and procainamide, as well as hyperkalemia, lithium overdose, and organic heart disease. In the obtunded patient, however, tachycardia with QRS prolongation of 120 milliseconds or longer is so suggestive as to be almost diagnostic of cyclic antidepressant poisoning. In cases of SSRI overdose, the patient's clinical picture should guide the laboratory evaluation. Although not felt to be clinically significant, electrocardiographic changes reported with ingestion of these drugs include depressed ST segments, small increases in QRS intervals, and tachycardia.

Therapeutic

Prevention of Toxicity. As soon as the diagnosis is suspected, stabilization and the basic laboratory evaluation described in the previous paragraph should be done. Absorption through the gastrointestinal tract should be minimized. Once absorbed, cyclic antidepressants are impossible to remove from tissues by any current technique, including charcoal hemoperfusion. Drugs recommended for treating cardiac complications of cyclic antidepressant overdose carry significant risks and are of unproven benefit. Therefore, prevention of absorption is the most significant and cost-effective therapy.

The first step is to perform gastric decontamination in any patient who (1) has ingested a first-generation antidepressant within the hour or has ingested a large quantity of drug within 2 hours of presentation; (2) is demonstrating signs of major toxicity such as hypotension, arrhythmias, coma, and respiratory failure; or (3) is without bowel sounds. Emptying the stomach with syrup of ipecac is not recommended because it is slow, significantly delays administration of charcoal, and increases the risk of aspiration in the patient who becomes obtunded before the ipecac takes effect. At present, lavage is recommended as the best method of gastric decontamination in these patients. A large-bore orogastric tube should be placed and lavage performed with at least 3 to 5 L of tap water or saline. Endotracheal intubation is recommended prior to lavage for the lethargic patient without a gag reflex. Topical anesthesia of the pharynx is recommended in the awake patient to facilitate passage of the tube. Nasogastric tubes are too small to allow adequate pill return, and should not be used for the purpose of gastric lavage. In rare cases when ingestions that are chronic or unequivocally known to have occurred many hours before, lavage can be omitted and charcoal given immediately. Activated charcoal administered with a cathartic such as sorbitol or magnesium citrate has been shown to effectively bind the cyclic antidepressants in the gut. After lavage, 50 g of charcoal, plus a cathartic, should be administered with repeat dosing in 2 hours.

The arterial blood gases should be closely monitored in any obtunded patient, as hypoxia and acidosis may trigger many of the arrhythmias and cardiovascular complications seen with cyclic antidepressant poisoning. Mechanical ventilation should be instituted at the first sign of ventilatory insufficiency. The electrocardiogram should be closely monitored, as QRS widening of 120 milliseconds or greater may herald myocardial depression and the appearance of arrhythmias. Intravenous normal saline should be administered at a rate greater than maintenance. Intravenous infusion rates should be titrated to blood pressure, central venous pressure, and urine output, all of which should be closely monitored.

Treatment of central nervous system and cardiovascular toxicity is considerably less successful than prevention of such complications. Many pharmacologic agents have been suggested but none of them are very effective. These treatments, as well as contraindicated drugs, are summarized in Table 24-7-4. Space does not allow adequate discussion here and the reader is referred to review articles on the subject.

Management of noncyclic antidepressant ingestions, after lavage and charcoal, is supportive care. If a patient remains asymptomatic for 6 hours after ingestion, they can be discharged following psychiatric

TABLE 24–7–4. SUMMARY OF TREATMENT OF SPECIFIC TRICYCLIC
ANTIDEPRESSANT COMPLICATIONS (IN ORDER OF PREFERENCE AND
EFFECTIVENESS)

Coma	Arterial blood gas monitoring and respiratory support
Seizures	Respiratory support and alkalinization for all patients
	Benzodiazepines
	Phenobarbital
	Phenytoin
	General anesthesia and paralysis
Tachycardia	No treatment unless hypotensive
Conduction blocks and ventricular dysrhythmias	Alkalinization
	No other treatment unless worsening perfusion (all antiarrhythmics exacerbate cardiac depression):
	Lidocaine (cautiously)
	Bretyllium
	Phenytoin (unproven; give slowly to avoid hypotension)
	Cardioversion: ineffective as it cannot reverse cardiotoxicity
	Cardiac pacing: ineffective as it cannot improve cardiac contractility
Hypotension	Alkalinization
	Fluid loading
	Pressors with predominant alpha-adrenergic effect
	Epinephrine
	Norepinephrine
	High-dose dopamine
	Phenylephrine
	Charcoal or resin perfusion (very severe cases only)
	Cardiopulmonary bypass
	Contraindicated drugs:
	Absolute
	Procainamide
	Quinidine
	Beta blockers
	Relative
	Corticosteroids
	Isoproterenol, dobutamine, low-grade dopamine (may worsen hypotension and arrhythmias)

Source: From Callaham ML. Tricyclic antidepressant overdose. In: Peter Rosen et al., eds. Emergency medicine: Concepts and clinical practice. *2nd ed. St. Louis: Mosby, 1988. Reproduced with permission from the publisher and author.*

evaluation; otherwise, they should be admitted and monitored until signs of toxicity resolve.

Treatment of Toxicity. Most of the cyclic antidepressant fatalities are caused by cardiovascular toxicity. As mentioned above, the cardiac complications are precipitated and worsened by acidosis and hypoxia. Systematic alkalinization, through intravenous sodium bicarbonate or hyperventilation if the patient is mechanically ventilated, can counteract much of the cardiovascular toxicity. Data suggest that the additional sodium load given by intravenous sodium bicarbonate administration may be more beneficial than hyperventilation alone. Indications for systematic alkalinization include cardiac conduction delays (QRS $\geq$ 120 milliseconds), acidosis, arrhythmias, hypotension, seizure, and cardiac arrest. The target pH range during systemic alkalinization is 7.55 to 7.60. Placement of an arterial line is mandatory to allow frequent pH monitoring. The pH should not be allowed to rise above 7.60, as this too can precipitate arrhythmias. Systemic alkalinization can be achieved by sodium bicarbonate boluses at doses of 1 to 2 mg/kg followed by continuous infusion of a solution of 2 ampules of sodium bicarbonate added to 1 L of 5% dextrose in water. The rate of infusion should be governed by the arterial blood pH; generally 1 L of fluid should infuse over 4 to 6 hours. Repeat boluses of sodium bicarbonate may be necessary to achieve and maintain a pH greater than 7.55.

Although the arrhythmias of cyclic antidepressants attract the most attention and discussion, they seldom cause death. Profound depression of contractility and cardiac output is generally present long before arrhythmias are noted. If the patient is perfusing well and the serum is alkalinized to a pH of 7.55 to 7.60, the best course of action is not to treat the arrhythmia as long as the patient is hemodynamically stable. The

arrhythmias are usually of the reentrant type and are due to aberrations in conduction and refractory periods. When drug treatment of arrhythmias becomes mandatory secondary to hypoperfusion, and does not respond to alkalinization, the treatment is conventional (Table 24–7–4). It is also not very successful.

Hypotension, when significant, is best treated with alkalinization and normal saline boluses of 500 mL titrated to blood pressure and urine output. If this management fails, pressor drugs should be used. As cyclic antidepressants have potent alpha-adrenergic blocking activity, a pressor with significant alpha-adrenergic activity should be selected such as norepinephrine or high dose dopamine. Sympathomimetics with predominant beta-adrenergic activity, such as low-dose dopamine and isoproterenol, should be used with caution because they may worsen hypotension. As these patients often are otherwise young and healthy they can expect a full recovery if tided over the toxic period; thus, prolonged cardiopulmonary resuscitation may be appropriate in selected cases.

Coma needs only supportive treatment, particularly adequate ventilation. Seizures are common and should be treated with diazepam (5–10 mg intravenously over 2 minutes) and loading with phenobarbital (10–15 mg/kg intravenously over 15–20 minutes). Unfortunately this does not stop the common myoclonic jerks, which along with seizure activity can cause acidosis and threaten intravenous lines. Besides worsening acidosis and triggering arrhythmias, seizures can hamper ventilation and cause hyperthermia, and, at times, are severe enough to require general anesthesia. Amoxapine, maprotiline, and bupropion cause seizures most frequently.

Special mention should be made of physostigmine, a cholinergic drug. Although anecdotally recommended for virtually every manifestation of cyclic antidepressant overdose, it has no proven efficacy. Animal studies suggest it probably does more harm than good because this drug in and of itself can induce seizures, hypotension, conduction blocks, and cardiac arrest. It should never be routinely used and has a debatable role in a last-ditch effort. Using physostigmine to attempt "diagnostic awakening" is both risky and inaccurate, because this drug has a duration of about 20 minutes, a very low toxic/therapeutic ratio, and nonspecific analeptic and wakening properties.

FOLLOW-UP

Patients may be discharged from hospital care following 12 hours of monitoring after electrocardiogram normalization. A psychiatric evaluation should be obtained prior to discharge and the patient referred back to her or his primary care physician for continuing counseling and monitoring of suicide risk.

DISCUSSION
Prevalence and Incidence

According to the 1993 American Association of Poison Control Centers Annual Report, exposure to antidepressants accounted for more than 30,000 hospital visits and resulted in 151 deaths, second only in fatality to analgesic overdosages. Demographic studies of antidepressant overdosages (all types) show the majority of patients are young, with females outnumbering males 2 to 1. Due to the widespread use of antidepressants, intentional overdoses are not limited to patients being treated for depression. A large percentage of patients have a history of alcohol and substance abuse, and a number of patients overdose using an older prescription left over from previous treatment.

Related Basic Science

The cyclic antidepressants have a number of major pharmacologic effects: anticholinergic, membrane-stabilizing (similar to type I antiarrhythmics), adrenergic, alpha-adrenergic blockade, and blockade of the reuptake of norepinephrine at the neuronal synapse. These effects account for the signs and toxicity listed in Tables 24–7–1 to 24–7–3; however, our understanding of these effects, as well as their relative importance in overdose, is very poor, and drug therapies based on such theoretical pharmacology, such as the past use of physostigmine and beta blockers, has been notably unsuccessful.

The tricyclic antidepressants are very highly bound to all body tissues, especially the heart. They are virtually impossible to remove once absorbed because even efficient methods, such as charcoal hemoperfusion, remove the drug very slowly through the rather small intravascular compartment, leaving the large body tissue pool essentially untouched. They have exceedingly long half-lives when taken as an overdose, usually on the order of 24 to 72 hours. As their anticholinergic effects inhibit peristalsis, pills can persist undigested in the gut for hours to days causing unexpected relapse if the gut has not been properly evacuated by charcoal and cathartics. Plasma tricyclic levels do not correlate with toxicity, and low levels early in ingestion do not preclude a stormy clinical course. Qualitative urine testing reports the presence of cyclic antidepressants, but is not of benefit if the patient has been taking the medication therapeutically.

Natural History and Its Modification with Treatment

Although the SSRI fluoxetine (Prozac) is now the most widely prescribed antidepressant drug in the United States, cyclic antidepressants are still a common overdose seen in emergency departments. There are a number of predictors of serious morbidity in cyclic antidepressant overdosages. Any evidence of the following during 6 hours of observation denotes a life-threatening risk: decreased level of consciousness, respiratory depression, seizures, hypotension, arrhythmias, and conduction blocks. If the patient is asymptomatic at 6 hours, has bowel sounds, and has received one dose of charcoal, he or she may be discharged for psychiatric evaluation. A second dose of charcoal should be given to any cyclic antidepressant overdose prior to discharge.

Prevention

Because the noncyclic antidepressant trazodone and the SSRIs are equally as effective as the more toxic cyclic antidepressants, it makes sense to choose the newer drugs when treating depression. Unfortunately, the newer antidepressants can be costly and the clinician is frequently compelled to prescribe the less expensive cyclic antidepressants. When managing a severely depressed patient with cyclic antidepressants, only small quantities of the drug (preferably less than 1 g) should be dispensed at any given time, even if it means a refill at the pharmacy twice a week. Cost-effective practice is to dispense in bulk quantity several grams at a time—clearly a lethal dose. Tragedy may occur as it takes several weeks to a month to lessen depression after initiating cyclic antidepressant therapy.

Cost Containment

Asymptomatic patients who manifest no signs of toxicity after 6 hours of observation may be transferred to the care of a psychiatrist and do not need hospital admission as long as they have normal vital signs, normal electrocardiogram, bowel sounds, and have received at least one dose of activated charcoal and a cathartic.

Any patient with major signs of poisoning should be admitted to an intensive care unit. Cardiac monitoring should be continued for 12 hours after the disappearance of all cardiac toxicity (including QRS prolongation), with the exception of mild sinus tachycardia (e.g., 100 beats/min). More prolonged monitoring of the cardiovascularly normal patient is not necessary; virtually all significant mortality and morbidity directly caused by cyclic antidepressant toxicity are evident within the first 24 hours. Initial care of the significantly poisoned patient should ideally be carried out by an intensivist or toxicologist. All patients need suicide precautions while in the hospital and psychiatric evaluation before discharge.

The most difficult decision for the physician is which patients require admission. This is a significant problem because cyclic antidepressant overdoses have the highest hospital admission rate of any overdose, usually to a costly intensive care unit bed. Generally, the vast majority of patients develop only minor toxicity; only 35% of hospitalized patients develop coma, and 10 to 15% experience hypotension or significant arrhythmias. The current mortality is about 2%.

Patients about whom there is any doubt, however, should be admitted for medical care. Rarely a patient may be awake and wish to refuse treatment or sign out against medical service. This cannot be permitted in any circumstances, as the patient is a great suicide risk and also is incompetent to make that decision due to the central nervous system effects of the drug.

REFERENCES

Borys DJ, Setzer SC, Ling L, et al. Acute fluoxetine overdose: A report of 234 cases. Am J Emerg Med 1992;10:115.

Callaham M. Tricyclic antidepressant overdose. J Am Col Emerg Phys (JACEP) 1979;8:413.

McCabe JL, Gobaugh DJ, Menegazzi J, et al. A comparison of hypertonic saline, sodium bicarbonate and hyperventilation in severe tricyclic antidepressant overdose in swine. Vet Hum Toxicol 1993;35:367. Abstract.

Mitchell PB. Selective serotonin reuptake inhibitors: Adverse effects, toxicity, and interactions. Adverse Drug React Toxicol Rev 1994;13:121.

Pentel P, Benowitz N. Efficacy and mechanism of action of sodium bicarbonate in the treatment of desipramine toxicity in cats. J Pharmacol Exp Ther 1984;230:12.

Pimental L, Trommer L. Cyclic antidepressant overdoses. Emerg Med Clin North Am 1994;12:533.

CHAPTER 24–8

Opioid Overdose and Opioid Withdrawal

Richard S. Weisman, Pharm. D., A.B.A.T.

Opioid Overdose

DEFINITION

An opioid overdose is defined as the accidental or deliberate use of an opioid resulting in central nervous system or cardiovascular toxicity.

ETIOLOGY

Opioid toxicity is most often found in the adult substance abuser, the methadone-dependent patient, the pediatric patient who has accidentally ingested an opioid analgesic, the suicidal patient, and the oncology patient who has received or taken an excessive amount of his or her pain medication.

CRITERIA FOR DIAGNOSIS
Suggestive

Clues to the diagnosis include central nervous system depression, miosis, and unexplained apnea. Needle marks or "tracks" help confirm the diagnosis of chronic abuse. Other clues include unexplained hypotension, bradycardia, pulmonary edema, hypothermia, and shock.

Definitive

Confirmation of the diagnosis can be made by reversing the symptoms of overdose with a specific opioid antagonist such as naloxone (Narcan) or retrospectively by finding parent drug or metabolites in the urine or blood.

CLINICAL MANIFESTATIONS

Subjective

Opioid toxicity can be found in many different settings, some of which are covert and easily overlooked. The presence of disease and the abuse of multiple substances often obscure the hallmarks of the overdose.

Objective

Physical Examination

An abnormality in the patient's vital signs is an important clue to opioid toxicity. Opioid toxicity should be part of the differential diagnosis of any patient with altered mental status, respiratory depression, hypotension, hypothermia, or bradycardia.

Although coma, respiratory depression, and miosis are classically present, variations in presentations are common. These occur with several of the synthetic opioids and when the opioid is taken in combination with other medications that are capable of modifying these signs and symptoms. Meperidine intoxication usually presents with coma, respiratory depression, and normal pupil size or mydriasis. Mydriasis may be found in patients who concurrently ingest cocaine, in overdoses of diphenoxylate and atropine (Lomotil), and in patients with severe central nervous system hypoxia.

Routine Laboratory Examination

The laboratory is rarely helpful in establishing the diagnosis of opioid toxicity. Hypercarbia and respiratory acidosis are common findings but are not specific to opioid toxicity.

PLANS

Diagnostic

Differential Diagnosis

The differential diagnosis of opioid overdose includes overdose with other central nervous system depressants such as sedative–hypnotics, alcohols, clonidine, and intracranial hemorrhage.

Diagnostic Options

The diagnosis of opioid intoxication is best made by administering an intravenous bolus dose of naloxone. Naloxone is a specific opioid antagonist that has the ability to successfully compete with opioids at the receptor site and to reverse all of the pharmacologic effects of the drug.

The decision to administer naloxone should be based on the patient's mental status and vital signs.

Recommended Approach

Naloxone should be used to establish or rule out a diagnosis of opioid overdose in patients with both depressed mental status and depressed vital signs. A positive response to naloxone is extremely sensitive and specific for the diagnosis of opioid toxicity. A negative response to a 10-mg dose of naloxone is sufficient to remove opioids from diagnostic consideration.

Therapeutic

Therapeutic Options

The clinician managing an opioid overdose has the option of reversing the toxic effects of the opioid with naloxone or providing support of vital signs including protection of the airway while the effects of the opioid subside as the drug is metabolized.

Recommended Approach

Patients who have depressed respirations should be ventilated with oxygen and a bag–mask–valve apparatus and should receive an initial intravenous bolus dose of 2 mg of naloxone. If the patient fails to respond within 1 minute, the patient should be intubated and additional 2-mg doses should be administered until a total of 10 mg has been given. In regions of the country where opioid overdose is a common cause of respiratory depression, the rapid administration of naloxone with bag–mask–valve ventilation may obviate the need for emergent intubation. If after 10 mg, the patient has not had an increase in respirations, an improvement in mental status, or an increase in pupillary size, it is unlikely that an opioid is responsible for the symptoms. The large dose of naloxone is given because opioids such as propoxyphene, codeine, methadone, and pentazocine require a higher concentration at the receptor site to be able to achieve reversal. The rate of administration should be rapid unless the patient has been endotracheally intubated.

Patients who present with altered mental status without a depression in respirations or hypercarbia may also be overdosed with an opioid, but have not taken enough to depress respiratory drive. This presentation is often seen in methadone-dependent patients who have ingested several days' supply of their medication and in patients who have combined other central nervous system depressants with an opioid. This type of patient usually receives the same amount of naloxone but the initial starting dose should be 0.2 to 0.4 mg by slow intravenous push. The lower dose and the slower rate of administration help to identify the patient with opioid addiction prior to the patient developing withdrawal symptoms. If the patient fails to respond to the small dose, additional boluses can be given up to 10 mg.

If the patient develops symptoms of withdrawal (see later discussion) following the administration of naloxone with either the rapid or slow dosing protocols, administration of naloxone should be stopped and the patient reassured that the withdrawal symptoms will only last for several minutes. Naloxone-induced withdrawal lasts only 20 to 30 minutes and is never life-threatening except in the neonate. An attempt to reverse the withdrawal symptoms by administering an additional opioid agonist should not be made. Large doses of opioid would be required to accomplish this, and when the antagonist wears off, the patient will have more profound symptoms of toxicity.

Pediatric patients with opioid toxicity should receive the same dose of naloxone as the adult patient. For naloxone to successfully compete with the opioid at the opioid receptor, a specific ratio of antagonist to agonist must exist. Because children often overdose on adult doses of opioid analgesics, adult doses of the antagonist are often required to achieve reversal.

Once the correct dose that will reverse respiratory depression without causing the addicted patient to develop withdrawal has been determined, additional doses of naloxone may need to be administered. The duration of action of all of the available opioids exceeds the 30- to 60-minute duration of action of naloxone. Additional naloxone can be administered by repeating the bolus dose every 30 to 45 minutes if the patient has a recurrence of respiratory depression or by placing the patient on a continuous intravenous infusion. If a continuous infusion is selected, the patient should receive two thirds of the effective bolus dose each hour. One half of the initial bolus dose should be given 30 minutes after the infusion is started to allow time for the infusion to reach a steady-state level.

If the patient has ingested the opioid, activated charcoal (1 g/kg) should be given orally along with sorbitol (1–2 mL/kg of a 70% solution).

FOLLOW-UP

All patients who have had significant respiratory depression from an opioid should be admitted to a critical care unit for monitoring. Pulmonary edema, which can be delayed for up to 24 hours, is a common cause of mortality. If a continuous infusion is started, careful supervision of the infusion must occur to ensure that it is not accidentally interrupted. Patients who are addicted to opioids require an adjustment in the infusion rate to allow for the changing ratio of antagonist to agonist at the receptor site. The duration of the naloxone infusion should be at least 6 to 12 hours to allow for elimination of the opioid. When the infusion is discontinued, the patient should be observed for at least 2 hours to ensure that central nervous system or respiratory depression does not recur. Arrangement should be made for long-term follow-up of medical, psychiatric, and social problems that often accompany opioid abuse.

DISCUSSION

Prevalence and Incidence

Heroin and methadone are the two most frequently abused opioids in the United States. It was estimated that nearly 600,000 people were addicted to heroin in the United States in the 1980s. Of these, 25% were in prison and 25% were in methadone treatment programs.

The use of opioids for the control of pain may date back to the third century BC. Today, they still remain an important component of medical practice. Clinicians commonly prescribe the opioids listed in Table 24–8–1.

Related Basic Science

Humans normally produce three groups of endogenous peptides—the enkephalins, the endorphins, and the dynorphins—which function as neurotransmitters at the opioid receptors. The role of these peptides in pain modulation and other physiologic processes is not well understood.

Opioids exert their pharmacologic effects by binding to opioid receptor sites within the central nervous system. The opioids react with the three receptors in variable manners as antagonists, agonists, or partial agonists. The receptors and their subtypes are classified as mu, kappa, and delta. An exogenous opioid may interact with any of the three receptors and may function as an agonist, a partial agonist, or an antagonist. Sigma receptors, originally thought to be opioid receptors, are no longer considered to be, primarily because their actions cannot be antagonized by naloxone.

Natural History and Its Modification with Treatment

The mortality rate for opioid-related deaths is difficult to estimate but may be as high as 1 per 100,000 population. In a study in the late 1970s it was found that one quarter of deaths from heroin abuse were from infections, one quarter were from trauma, and one half were from the toxic effects of the drug. The percentage of infectious deaths has increased dramatically as a result of the AIDS epidemic. In New York City, intravenous drug abuse is the greatest risk factor for contracting this deadly disease.

Prevention

The use of child-resistant packaging for all controlled substances has had a positive impact in reducing accidental pediatric exposures. Families with small children should be frequently reminded about the safe storage of all pharmaceuticals and of the importance of leaving medications in their original containers.

Elderly patients who require opioids should be instructed in their proper usage and efforts should be made to develop dosing regimens that are unlikely to result in confusion and iatrogenic overdose.

Cost Containment

The toxicology laboratory should not be used to diagnose opioid toxicity. A positive response to the administration of naloxone is sufficient to establish the diagnosis. The laboratory may be able to qualitatively

TABLE 24–8–1. COMMONLY PRESCRIBED OPIOIDS

Buprenorphine	Levorphanol
Butorphanol	Methadone
Codeine	Meperidine
Diphenoxylate (in Lomotil)	Morphine
Drocode	Nalbuphine
Fentanyl	Oxycodone
Hydrocodone	Pentazocine
Hydromorphone	Propoxyphene

identify the presence of an opioid, but cannot distinguish between therapeutic and toxic amounts of opioids. Negative toxicology screens for opioids are often misleading because most laboratories use methodologies that are not capable of identifying all of the available opioids.

Opioid Withdrawal

DEFINITION

Opioid withdrawal is defined as the agitated psychological and physiologic state seen in opioid-dependent patients when their usual dose of opioid is decreased or eliminated.

ETIOLOGY

High concentrations of biologically active peptides, enkephalins, beta-endorphins, dynorphins, and alpha-neoendorphins have been found in the brain, adrenal medulla, and pituitary arcuate nucleus. They are believed to function as neurotransmitters by inhibiting sodium conductance at the opioid receptor. The pharmacologic action of opioids is believed to be identical to the effects of the naturally occurring opioid peptides. As both opioid agonists and enkephalins, endorphins, and dynorphins decrease sodium permeability in membranes with opioid receptors, the frequent use of opioid agonists may alter the number or configuration of the receptors or downregulate the secretion of endogenous opioid peptides. As opioid peptide production and secretion decrease, more exogenous opioid can be tolerated without toxic effects. Sudden cessation of opioid use does not allow enough time for resumption of adequate endogenous opioid production. This results in increased sodium permeability with subsequent neuronal hyperexcitability and withdrawal symptomatology.

CRITERIA FOR DIAGNOSIS

Suggestive

Clues to withdrawal include unexplained central nervous system arousal states, drug-seeking behavior, and attempted thefts of hospital supplies to be either sold or used for illicit drug administration.

Opioid withdrawal is a difficult diagnosis to make because the progression of symptoms depends on the opioid that was being used, the dose, the time since the last dose, and other medications the patient is abusing. For a patient to develop withdrawal symptoms he or she must have an addiction to an opioid. Addiction is defined as a behavioral pattern of compulsive drug procurement and utilization with the need for increasingly larger doses of the opioid to produce the same pharmacologic effects.

Definitive

There is unfortunately no way to definitively diagnose opioid withdrawal.

CLINICAL MANIFESTATIONS

The subjective and objective findings of opioid withdrawal can be categorized as minor, moderate, or severe. This classification appears in Table 24–8–2.

Subjective

Most of the symptoms associated with opioid withdrawal are subjective. The astute clinician must combine these findings with objective evidence to separate the opioid-dependent patient in withdrawal from the manipulative patient desiring additional opioids.

The subjective findings in a patient with minor withdrawal symptoms often include rhinorrhea, yawning, myalgias, abdominal cramps, lacrimation, and diaphoresis. These may progress to moderate findings, which include restlessness and insomnia. If untreated, the patient may progress to have major findings, which include vomiting, diarrhea, and, in neonates, seizures. Patients with opioid withdrawal should have a normal sensorium and a normal level of consciousness.

TABLE 24–8–2. CATEGORIZATION OF OPIOID WITHDRAWAL SYMPTOMS

Classification	Subjective	Objective
Minor	Rhinorrhea	Piloerection
	Yawning	Mydriasis
	Myalgias	
	Abdominal cramps	
	Lacrimation	
	Diaphoresis	
Moderate	Restlessness	Increased blood pressure
	Insomnia	Tachycardia
		Tachypnea
Major	Vomiting	Hyperactive bowel sounds
	Diarrhea	Decreased blood pressure
	Seizures (neonates)	

Objective

The patient with minor withdrawal often has piloerection and dilated pupils (> 4–5 mm). Dilated pupils are not very specific. They commonly occur with cocaine use or if the patient has ingested a medication such as a cyclic antidepressant that has anticholinergic effects. The objective findings of moderate withdrawal include elevations in blood pressure, tachycardia, and tachypnea. Major withdrawal findings include hyperactive bowel sounds and hypotension. Fever should not be attributed to opioid withdrawal. There are no laboratory tests available that are helpful in making the diagnosis.

PLANS

Diagnostic

Differential Diagnosis

The differential diagnosis of opioid withdrawal should include abdominal pathology, particularly in patients in whom piloerection, mydriasis, rhinorrhea, and yawning are not observed. Other or additional disorders should be considered in patients with fever or an altered mental status.

Diagnostic Options and Recommended Approach

The diagnosis of opioid withdrawal is a clinical diagnosis most commonly established by finding characteristic signs and symptoms along with a history of opioid abuse, observation of track marks on physical examination, or documentation of enrollment in a methadone program. A history from the patient is often inaccurate with respect to the amount of opioid that is being used each day, but may be helpful in identifying a patient with concurrent withdrawal from either alcohol or a sedative–hypnotic.

Therapeutic

Therapeutic Options

The clinician must determine if therapy with methadone is required. Most authorities recommend that patients should have nearly all of the minor symptoms of opioid withdrawal and several moderate symptoms (see Table 24–8–2) of withdrawal before methadone should be administered.

Recommended Approach

If methadone is to be given to an opioid-dependent patient, the initial dose should not be greater than 10 mg by the intramuscular route. It is difficult to calculate the quantity of methadone that an opioid-dependent patient requires each day because the purity of the opioid (usually heroin) that is being purchased on the street is variable. Patients who have symptoms of withdrawal should receive methadone by the intramuscular route to avoid problems that may occur with absorption if the patient vomits or has diarrhea. The maximum dose of methadone that should be given to a hospitalized addict is 40 mg in divided doses. The most that should ever be given as a single dose is 20 mg. Methadone is occasionally used in higher doses by methadone programs because oral doses in excess of 80 mg are capable of blocking the euphoric effects of heroin. A daily oral dose of 40 mg has been shown to be effective in preventing withdrawal in the patient with chronic opioid dependency.

If a methadone-dependent patient is to be hospitalized for a medical, surgical, or obstetric problem, no effort should be made to detoxify the patient during the hospital stay. If the patient is unable to take her or his verified dose by the oral route, two thirds of this amount can be administered intramuscularly in two divided doses.

FOLLOW-UP

If a patient from a methadone program requires supplemental doses of methadone, it may indicate that the patient is either using the medication inappropriately or that the methadone is being sold on the street. The physician is obligated to notify the administrator of the methadone program that the patient was seen and found to be in withdrawal and required additional doses of methadone.

DISCUSSION

Prevalence and Incidence

The prevalence and incidence of opioid withdrawal have not been adequately characterized.

Related Basic Science

Methadone is a synthetic opioid most similar in structure to propoxyphene. Pharmacologically it is capable of interacting with the opioid receptor and preventing the symptoms of withdrawal.

Methadone has been used for both detoxifying and maintaining the patient with opioid dependency. When used for detoxification the dose is gradually decreased to zero over 3 weeks. With maintenance therapy, the patient with opioid dependency is stabilized on a dose that prevents withdrawal and diminishes the craving for opioid use.

Natural History and Its Modification with Treatment

The success of both detoxification and methadone maintenance has been disappointing. Approximately 10% of those starting therapy continue to use heroin. Less than 50% enrolled in maintenance therapy are still compliant after 1 year.

Prevention

Although methadone prevents withdrawal, it does not provide the opioid-dependent patient with the social support, employment, stable home environment, or psychological support needed to achieve rehabilitation.

Cost Containment

For methadone rehabilitation programs to be cost-effective they must combine the use of methadone to prevent withdrawal with a well-structured support program that enables the opioid-dependent patient to begin developing the emotional and financial stability that will prevent him or her from needing to return to drugs as a means of escaping problems.

REFERENCES

Des Jarlais DC, Joseph H, Dole VP. Long term outcomes after termination from methadone maintenance treatment. Ann NY Acad Sci 1981;362:231.

Dole VP, Nyswander M. A medical treatment for diacetylmorphine (heroin) addiction. JAMA 1965;173:645.

Evans CJ, Hammond DL, Fredrickson RCA. The opioid peptides. In: Pasternak GW, ed. The opiate receptors. Clifton Park, NJ: Humana Press, 1988:23.

Goldfrank L, Weisman RS, Errick JK, Lo MW. A dosing nomogram for continuous infusion intravenous naloxone. Ann Emerg Med 1986:566.

Goldstein A. On the role of chemotherapy in the treatment of heroin addiction. Am J Drug Alcohol Abuse 1975;2:279.

McGlothlin WH, Anglin DM. Long-term follow-up of clients on high- and low-dose methadone. Arch Gen Psychiatry 1981;38:1055.

Pasternak GW. Pharmacological mechanisms of opioid analgesics. Clin Neuropharmacol 1993;16:1.

Acetaminophen Overdose

Martin J. Smilkstein, M.D.

DEFINITION

Acetaminophen (*N*-acetyl-*para*-aminophenol [APAP]) overdose is defined as ingestion of APAP amounts exceeding the recommended dosage.

ETIOLOGY

Potentially toxic APAP overdoses occur in three clinical settings: accidental overdoses in children; intentional overdoses by adults either in suicide attempts or in overdoses of APAP-containing drugs of abuse (e.g., APAP/codeine, APAP/propoxyphene); and rarely, accidental repeated overdosing during therapeutic APAP use in infants, in alcoholics, or in those taking medications that induce P450 metabolism (e.g., anticonvulsants, isoniazid).

CRITERIA FOR DIAGNOSIS

Suggestive

The diagnosis should be considered in patients with a history of APAP ingestion, polydrug overdose or abuse, or unexplained hepatotoxicity. Single APAP ingestions of greater than 7.5 g in adults or 150 mg/kg in children should be considered potentially toxic if APAP levels are not available. Methods of predicting potential toxicity after multiple APAP doses are not well established.

Definitive

After acute overdose, the diagnosis of potential toxicity is best made by interpretation of plasma APAP levels using the APAP toxicity nomogram (Figure 24–9–1). The definitive diagnosis of actual APAP toxicity is confirmed by laboratory evidence of hepatic injury 24 to 48 hours after ingestion.

CLINICAL MANIFESTATIONS

Subjective

Dividing the clinical course into four stages is useful in understanding the subjective features of APAP toxicity. Stage 1 (0.5–24 hours after ingestion) is the period of potential toxicity without actual hepatotoxicity. The onset of hepatotoxicity occurs during stage 2 (24–48 hours after ingestion). Hepatotoxicity may rarely be seen as early as 12 to 16 hours after ingestion in the most severe cases; however, apparent toxicity this early may result from errors in history. Laboratory abnormalities peak during stage 3 (72–96 hours after ingestion). Finally, during stage 4 (96 hours–1 week after ingestion), the preceding abnormalities resolve. Unusually severe cases may require up to 2 weeks to resolve.

During stage 1, determining the amount of APAP ingested and the time of ingestion is critical in history taking. Factors that may modify APAP toxicity adversely (e.g., use of chronic ethanol, phenobarbital, phenytoin, isoniazid, rifampin) are of interest, particularly in cases of suspected repeated overingestion.

Anorexia, nausea, vomiting, and malaise are common in stage 1, although many patients are asymptomatic. Initial symptoms generally resolve by late stage 1. Late in stage 2 right upper quadrant abdominal pain may develop. Severely affected patients may describe oliguria. During stage 3, symptoms vary with the severity of hepatotoxicity. Affected patients experience the return of anorexia, nausea, vomiting, and malaise with the persistence of abdominal pain. Severely ill patients may note confusion, jaundice, and abnormal bleeding. In stage 4, symptoms resolve.

Objective

The same clinical staging (see Clinical Manifestations, Subjective) is useful to follow the objective signs of APAP toxicity.

Physical Examination

During stage 1, the examination is usually entirely normal. Malaise, pallor, and diaphoresis may be evident. In stage 2, liver tenderness and enlargement may be first noted. During stage 3, examination findings vary with the severity of hepatotoxicity. Abnormalities seen in stage 2 often become more prominent. In severe cases, jaundice, encephalopathy, coma, and abnormal bleeding may occur. Resolution of physical examination abnormalities occurs in stage 4.

Routine Laboratory Abnormalities

Modest elevations of prothrombin time and bilirubin levels are the rule. Prothrombin times more than twice normal and bilirubin levels above 4 mg/dL are unusual and are associated with severe toxicity. The blood urea nitrogen and serum creatinine levels may be elevated and urinary sediment may be found.

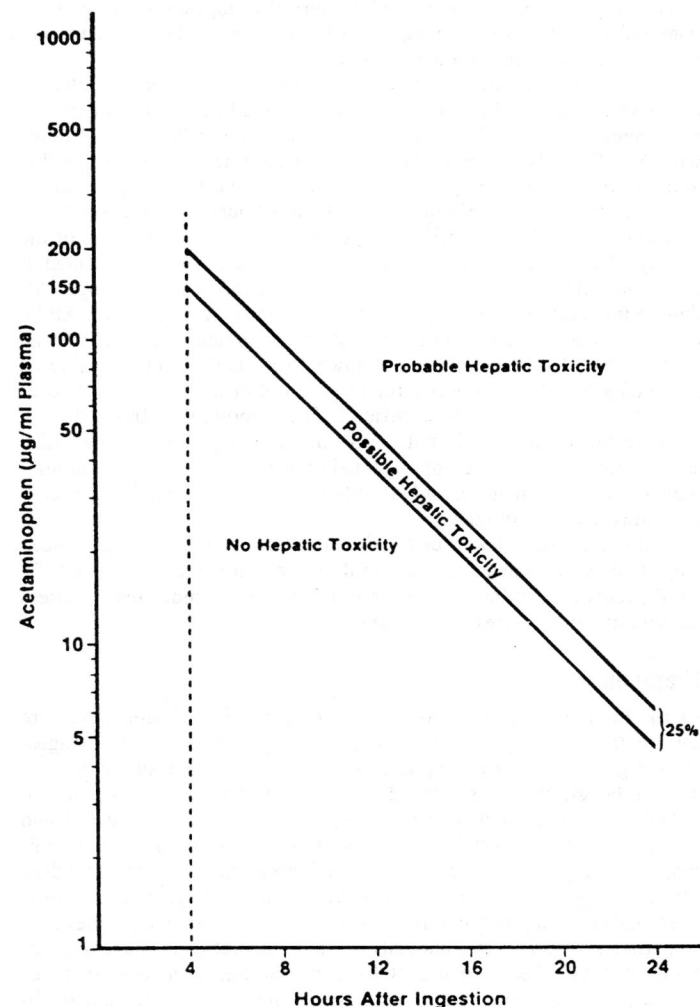

Figure 24–9–1. Semilogarithmic plot of plasma acetaminophen levels versus time. The lower solid line 25% below the standard nomogram line allows for errors in estimated time of ingestion and acetaminophen plasma assays. *(From Poisindex, Micromedex Computerized Clinical Information Systems, Denver, Colorado. Reproduced with permission.)*

Rare severe cases have demonstrated electrocardiographic evidence of myocardial injury during this period.

PLANS

Diagnostic

Differential Diagnosis

Differential diagnosis for a patient with a history of APAP overdose includes consideration of overdose of any other agents, based on history, physical examination, and laboratory results. When aminotransferase elevation is evident, consideration of other causes of hepatocellular injury is appropriate, particularly infectious or alcoholic hepatitis.

Diagnostic Options and Recommended Approach

Laboratory values are normal in stage 1. During stage 2, levels of aspartate aminotransferase (AST), or serum glutamic–oxaloacetic transaminase (SGOT), and alanine aminotransferase (ALT), or serum glutamic–pyruvic transaminase (SGPT), begin to increase, accompanied by proportional elevations in the serum bilirubin level and the prothrombin time. Bilirubinuria may be noted, blood urea nitrogen and creatinine levels may increase, and an active urinary sediment may be noted. The laboratory abnormalities seen in stage 2 persist and peak during stage 3. AST (SGOT) levels above 10,000 IU/L and comparable ALT (SGPT) elevations are not uncommon.

The diagnostic goal in the first 24 hours after ingestion is to identify potential toxicity so that therapy can be initiated. After 24 hours, detecting actual toxicity becomes more important.

Potential toxicity after acute overdose is best evaluated by determination of a plasma APAP level between 4 and 24 hours after ingestion, interpreted using the APAP nomogram (see Figure 24–9–1). Patients with APAP levels above the lower nomogram line, indicating possible toxicity, need treatment. When APAP levels have been drawn but results will not be available until more than 8 hours after ingestion, the ingestion should be assumed to be potentially toxic on the basis of the history. Treatment should be initiated, but it can be discontinued if the initial APAP level is then found to be in the nontoxic range. Although less accurate, the diagnosis can be made by history when APAP levels are not available. Single ingestions of greater than 7.5 g in an adult, 150 mg/kg in a child, or unknown amounts should be considered potentially toxic. Defining potential toxicity after multiple APAP doses ("chronic" overdose) is more difficult. The nomogram is based on single ingestions only and is not applicable after repeated dosing. Such cases require a combined approach using history, APAP levels, aminotransferase determination, and consultation with a regional poison center or medical toxicologist.

Aminotransferase levels provide the best screen for actual hepatotoxicity. If they are elevated, then serial determinations of AST (SGOT), ALT (SGPT), bilirubin, and prothrombin time are indicated to assess the severity and progression of illness.

Therapeutic

As for any poisoned or overdosed patient, provision of supportive care and treatment of any immediately threatening toxicity due to coingestants (e.g., codeine, propoxyphene) should come first. Gastric emptying may be beneficial if less than 2 hours has elapsed since ingestion of APAP alone or as indicated for coingestants. Activated charcoal and cathartics should be used within 4 hours of ingestion or later as indicated for coingestants. The benefit of activated charcoal in treating dangerous coingestant toxicity outweighs (especially in the first few hours after ingestion) any risk that the APAP antidote (N-acetylcysteine) may be partially adsorbed by charcoal and thus, theoretically, have less hepatoprotective effect. Treatment for liver failure, if present, includes glucose, lactulose, neomycin, low-protein diet, vitamin K, and fresh-frozen plasma. Liver transplantation has been successfully performed after APAP toxicity and should be considered if fulminant liver failure develops. Renal dysfunction may necessitate hemodialysis.

If possible, patients with potential or actual toxicity (see Plans, Diagnostic) should have N-acetylcysteine (NAC) treatment initiated less than 8 hours after APAP ingestion. Although still indicated, NAC effi-

cacy decreases more than 8 hours after ingestion, particularly more than 16 hours after ingestion. In cases of fulminant hepatic failure, NAC started more than 2 days after APAP ingestion has been shown to decrease mortality. Therefore, NAC is indicated at any time if APAP level or AST indicates potential or actual hepatotoxicity, regardless of the delay. Standard therapy consists of a loading dose of 140 mg/kg and maintenance doses of 70 mg/kg every 4 hours for 17 doses (initiated 4 hours after the loading dose). Shorter courses of therapy may be appropriate in certain circumstances after consultation with a regional poison center or medical toxicologist.

N-Acetylcysteine is supplied as a 20% solution (200 mg/mL) and should be diluted with cola, orange juice, grapefruit juice, and so on, to make a 5% solution (1 part NAC to 3 parts diluent) to increase palatability and reduce gastrointestinal irritation. NAC is given by mouth if the patient has an adequate level of consciousness and intact gag reflex. NAC can be given by nasogastric or duodenal tube. Undiluted (20%) NAC can be used by these routes for patients who do not tolerate larger volumes. If any dose is vomited less than 1 hour after administration, that dose should be repeated. Antiemetics, chilling, and changing diluents may prevent repeated vomiting. Intravenous NAC is available only on an investigational basis in the United States. Intravenous use of the oral preparation is indicated in unusual circumstances. Information regarding intravenous NAC can be obtained by contacting a regional poison center.

FOLLOW-UP

There are no known chronic or recurrent sequelae of APAP toxicity. If recovery occurs, it is complete, and no medical follow-up addressing the APAP toxicity per se is needed. Follow-up needs to be directed at resolving the psychosocial issues that led to the overdose (e.g., depression, drug abuse, parental education) and at any associated medical problems the patient may have.

DISCUSSION

Prevalence

The popularity of APAP as a safe, effective antipyretic and analgesic has increased dramatically over the past 30 years. As APAP use has skyrocketed, increased availability has made it a more common agent in both accidental and intentional overdoses. In 1993, the Annual Report of the American Association of Poison Control Centers Toxic Exposure Surveillance System documented more than 90,000 calls regarding APAP and APAP-containing products. The number of toxic exposures managed without poison center contact is unknown, but by all estimates, APAP overdosage is common.

Related Basic Science

Understanding the toxicity of APAP overdose and its safety in therapeutic doses requires an understanding of APAP metabolism. Slightly more than 90% of an APAP dose is converted to inactive and nontoxic glucuronide and sulfate conjugates, primarily in the liver. Less than 5% is eliminated in the urine as unchanged, nontoxic APAP. The remaining fraction is converted to a highly reactive hepatotoxic metabolite (N-acetyl-para-benzoquinoneimine) via the cytochrome P450 enzyme system. This substance can bind to hepatocyte macromolecules and induce hepatic necrosis. To a much lesser extent, the same process may occur in the kidney and contribute to nephrotoxicity. In subtoxic APAP doses, the toxic metabolite is rapidly detoxified by conjugation with glutathione to form harmless, inactive mercapturic acid and cysteine conjugates. Large doses of APAP require increased quantities of glutathione for detoxification, and depletion may result. If the glutathione supply is reduced by 70%, detoxification becomes inadequate, toxic metabolite persists, and toxicity results. This degree of glutathione depletion results only from excessive APAP dosing, thus accounting for the safety of therapeutic APAP.

The hepatoprotective effect of NAC is clear, but its exact mechanism of action is not. NAC rapidly enters hepatocytes and acts via one or more of several proposed mechanisms. By donating cysteine, NAC is a precursor to glutathione production and may enhance stores. Acting as a sulfate donor, NAC may decrease toxic cytochrome P450 pathway metabolism by enhancing the sulfate conjugation pathway. It may also directly detoxify the toxic metabolite. Finally, NAC acts after liver injury has occurred via mechanisms unrelated to APAP metabolism, decreasing both multiorgan failure and mortality. These mechanisms are yet to be clearly defined, but appear to include the direct antioxidant effect of NAC as well as effects on organ microcirculation possibly mediated through endothelial actions. NAC efficacy is enhanced by early treatment: it is much less effective once hepatotoxicity is evident.

Natural History and Its Modification with Treatment

The morbidity of APAP overdose increases if NAC treatment is delayed. Even among patients with APAP levels in the toxic range, hepatotoxicity (AST levels > 1000 IU/L) is extraordinarily rare (< 5%) when NAC is initiated within 8 hours. Hepatotoxicity is much more likely with treatment delays of 10 to 24 hours (26%), and patients with very high APAP levels first treated 16 to 24 hours after ingestion developed hepatotoxicity in 41% of cases (Smilkstein et al., 1988). Untreated patients experience greater hepatotoxicity, and the resolution of toxicity is slower in more severe cases. The time course of toxicity for treated, untreated, and severe cases is illustrated in Figure 24–9–2.

Deaths from APAP overdoses are rare in treated or untreated patients. In cases in the probable hepatic toxicity range (see Figure 24–9–1), mortality may be as high as 5 to 20% in untreated patients (Prescott, 1983) and appears to be less than 1% in treated patients (Smilkstein et al., 1988). All reported deaths in treated patients have occurred when NAC was first given after aminotransferase elevations were already evident.

Prevention

Prevention of drug overdose is a complex problem. Educating patients regarding APAP toxicity, "childproofing" medicine cabinets, and careful vigilance for signs of suicidality are all important steps in prevention. Preventing serious hepatotoxicity requires a high index of suspicion and timely diagnostic and therapeutic intervention. Repeated, low-level overdosing is common among patients who self-medicate for pain. Patients at increased risk for APAP toxicity (e.g., alcoholics) should be cautioned against exceeding recommended doses.

Cost Containment

Unnecessary costs are most often accrued due to inappropriate laboratory tests, use of NAC when not indicated, or failure to treat and resultant increased morbidity. The following guidelines may help reduce costs: To assess need for treatment after acute overdose, use a *single* APAP level, obtained *4 or more hours after ingestion*. Multiple determinations are not helpful in risk assessment, and absorption and distribution of APAP make tests within 4 hours of ingestion difficult to interpret. If the history is accurate and the APAP level is not in the toxic

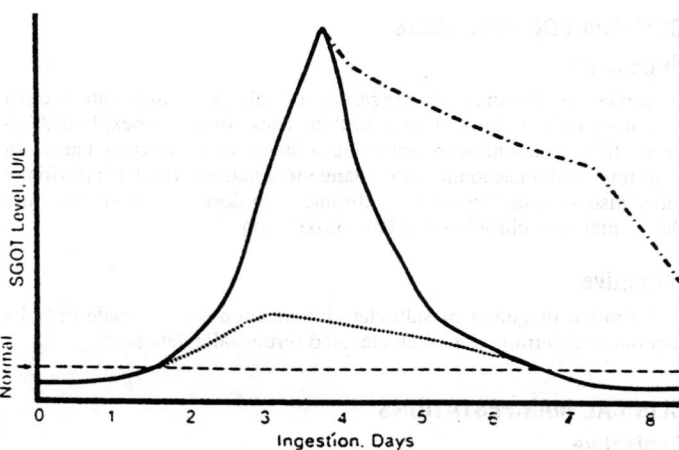

Figure 24–9–2. Clinical course of patients with toxic acetaminophen levels. Dotted line, patients receiving *N*-acetylcysteine; solid line, natural course, untreated; dotted and dashed line, severe course, SGOT, serum glutamic–oxaloacetic transaminase. *(Adapted from Rumack BH, Peterson RG, Koch GG, et al. Acetaminophen overdose: 662 cases with evaluation of oral acetylcysteine treatment. Arch Intern Med 1981;141:380. Copyright 1981 American Medical Association. Reproduced with permission from the publisher.)*

range, there is no need to do further APAP-related testing or to treat with NAC. Aminotransferase determination is adequate to screen for liver injury; other liver testing may then be indicated. It is likely that shorter courses of NAC therapy are appropriate for many patients, resulting in shorter hospitalization.

The greatest reduction in cost results from minimizing serious sequelae. Consider the diagnosis early, determine the APAP level as soon as possible, and, if indicated, start NAC treatment early.

REFERENCES

Anker AL, Smilkstein MJ. Acetaminophen: Concepts and controversies. Emerg Med Clin North Am 1994;12:335.

Keays R, Harrison PM, Wendon JA, et al. Intravenous acetylcysteine in paracetamol-induced fulminant hepatic failure: A prospective controlled trial. Br Med J 1991;303:1026.

Mitchell JR, Thorgensson SS, Potter WZ, et al. Acetaminophen-induced hepatic injury: Protective role of glutathione in man and rationale for therapy. Clin Pharmacol Ther 1974;16:676.

Prescott LF. Paracetamol overdosage: Pharmacological considerations and clinical management. Drugs 1983;25:290.

Smilkstein MJ, Knapp GL, Kulig KW, Rumack BH. Efficacy of oral *N*-acetylcysteine in the treatment of acetaminophen overdose: Analysis of the National Multicenter Study (1976–1985). N Engl J Med 1988;319:1557.

CHAPTER 24–10

Salicylate Intoxication

Corey M. Slovis, M.D.

DEFINITION

Salicylate or aspirin overdose may be defined as the intentional or inadvertent ingestion of a quantity of aspirin that results in an upset of normal body homeostasis. Therapeutic salicylate poisoning and chronic salicylism are terms used to denote salicylate toxicity resulting from repeated usage of appropriate amounts of salicylate for medicinal purposes.

ETIOLOGY

The most common etiologies of salicylate poisoning are attempted suicides, maintenance on long-term high-dose aspirin for its antiinflammatory effects, intake of multiple medications that contain aspirin, and lastly, pediatric overdoses, which are not discussed here.

CRITERIA FOR DIAGNOSIS
Suggestive

A number of findings are suggestive of salicylate intoxication other than the patient's claim of an ingestion. These include unexplained hyperventilation, a wide-gap metabolic acidosis, and refractory nausea or vomiting. Any unaccounted for change in a patient who has arthritis or other disease state treated with chronic high-dose aspirin should raise the suspicion of chronic salicylate intoxication.

Definitive

A definitive diagnosis of salicylate intoxication can be made only by laboratory determination of an elevated serum salicylate level.

CLINICAL MANIFESTATIONS
Subjective

Salicylate-intoxicated patients fall into three distinct groups. The first group consists of intentionally overdosed patients, who often admit to the ingestion of a significant quantity of aspirin. Family members or friends may be helpful in providing this information. Chronic users of aspirin or aspirin-containing compounds make up the second group of salicylate-intoxicated patients. Unfortunately, owing to the elimination kinetics of aspirin, chronic use of therapeutic amounts may result in toxicity. The amount used by the patient is usually within the guidelines given by his or her physician. The final group of patients consists of those in whom no subjective information suggesting aspirin overdose is obtained. The diagnosis in this group lies in objective information.

In any of the three groups, the patient may complain of nausea, vomiting, tinnitus, memory changes, or multiple nonspecific somatic complaints. The patient may seek medical attention for the "unrelated" problem of upper gastrointestinal bleeding, thus diverting the clinician's attention.

Patients may have a past history of suicide attempts, depression, or prior aspirin overdose. Additionally, a past history of aspirin use, painful or deforming arthritis, or chronic pain may be present.

Family history is usually not contributory; however, a family history of painful arthritis should raise the possibility of abundant salicylate products in the household.

Objective
Physical Examination

The patient with salicylate overdose presents in one of three general states. The first, seen acutely, is due to aspirin's direct stimulatory effect on the respiratory center in the central nervous system. The patient shows tachypnea, tachycardia, and anxiety. The second phase incorporates the aforementioned respiratory alkalosis superimposed on the many metabolic effects that salicylic acid possesses. The physical examination may demonstrate hyperpyrexia, hyperpnea, alterations in mental status, pulmonary congestion, a hyperdynamic circulatory system, or declining renal output. Abdominal examination usually is nonspecific but may reveal pain and guarding. Evidence of abdominal perforation should always be searched for. If the patient has ingested oil of wintergreen, a substance that is high in methyl salicylate, the characteristic odor of wintergreen may be appreciated.

The third phase, seen in a severe overdose, is one of significant metabolic acidosis that may no longer be accompanied by significant respiratory compensation. Significant alterations in central nervous system functioning are found, including seizure activity and variable stages of coma. Pulmonary examination may reveal pulmonary edema. Owing to fluid losses from sweating and vomiting, hypovolemic shock may also be present. Oliguria and anuria are often superimposed on this. A rare fourth phase may be that of a significant metabolic acidosis accompanied by respiratory depression or a sudden respiratory arrest.

Routine Laboratory Abnormalities

Aspirin disrupts multiple organ systems and may cause numerous laboratory abnormalities. Unfortunately, no specific laboratory abnormality is specific for salicylate intoxication other than an elevated salicylate level.

The most common laboratory abnormality in salicylate intoxication is a falling serum bicarbonate. This usually results in the classic wide-gap metabolic acidosis of aspirin overdose, though a normal-gap metabolic acidosis may also be found.

Other potential laboratory abnormalities include hyponatremia, which may be present in a laboratory pattern similar to that of the syndrome of inappropriate antidiuretic hormone secretion. Hypernatremia, hypokalemia, and azotemia may also be encountered. Because of aspirin's effects on gluconeogenesis, oxidative phosphorylation, and multiple other homeostatic enzyme systems, either hypoglycemia or hyperglycemia may be found. Additional chemistry abnormalities include hypouricemia and abnormal liver enzymes.

Aspirin's toxic effects may cause a leukocytosis and an increase in immature forms. It may also disrupt the clotting cascade and normal hepatic function which results in an increased prothrombin time. Urinalysis may reveal glycosuria and ketonuria.

PLANS
Diagnostic
Differential Diagnosis

The diagnosis of an aspirin overdose is usually self-evident and is confirmed by the patient's salicylate level; however, some patients may not realize that they have consumed significant quantities of aspirin. Methyl salicylate (oil of wintergreen), which is used in many skin salves for muscle soreness and arthritis relief, has 7 g of aspirin per teaspoon. Pepto-Bismol contains 8.7 mg/mL, and an unknowing patient with traveler's diarrhea may be consuming large quantities of aspirin (in excess of 2 g every few hours) during a period of dehydration and falling urine output. In any patient presenting with unexplained subjective or objective complaints consistent with aspirin overdose, a salicylate level is mandatory. The differential diagnosis of any metabolic acidosis, especially with a wide anion gap, must always include aspirin overdose. The morbidity and mortality of aspirin intoxication rise significantly if the diagnosis is missed.

The differential diagnosis of a wide-gap metabolic acidosis can be remembered by the pneumonic MUDPILES: M = methanol; U = uremia; D = diabetic and alcohol ketoacidosis; P = paraldehyde; I = isoniazid and iron; L = lactic acidosis; E = ethylene glycol, and S = salicylate. Clues to assist in the differential diagnosis are listed in Table 24–10–1.

TABLE 24–10–1. DIFFERENTIAL DIAGNOSIS OF SALICYLATE INTOXICATION (MUDPILES)

Diagnostic Possibility	Diagnostic Tests or Observations
Methanol	History of alcoholism, recent "moonshine" ingestion; papilledema or other retinal changes, blindness; marked serum osmolarity changes; elevated methanol level
Uremia	History and physical examination consistent with chronic renal disease; marked azotemia
Diabetic ketoacidosis and	Elevated glucose and ketone bodies; history of diabetes mellitus
Alcohol ketoacidosis	Elevated ketone bodies; history of alcoholism; marked improvement with hydration and glucose
Paraldehyde	Very rare; classic breath odor
Isoniazid ingestion	Lactic acidosis; seizures responsive to pyridoxine; history of tuberculosis or tuberculosis prophylaxis
Iron	Serum iron levels; iron tablets on flat plate of abdomen
Lactic acidosis	Evidence of hypoperfusion state, blood loss, elevated lactate level
Ethylene glycol	History of alcoholism, oxaluria, crystalluria; renal failure; oliguria; marked serum osmolarity changes; elevated ethylene glycol level
Salicylates	See Clinical Manifestations, Subjective and Objective; aspirin level

Diagnostic Options

Once an aspirin overdose has been confirmed, clinicians should rapidly proceed to the recommended approach listed below.

Recommended Approach

A number of baseline laboratory parameters should be obtained in the initial evaluation of an overdosed patient. These are listed in Table 24–10–2.

If the serum salicylate level is significantly elevated, or if the patient's physical or laboratory examination is significantly abnormal, hospitalization is mandatory. Mild toxicity usually occurs when more than 150 mg/kg aspirin is ingested. Severe toxicity is likely when 300 to 500 mg/kg have been consumed. All laboratory parameters must be followed closely during therapy to minimize complications. One must never rely on serum salicylate levels alone but must incorporate them in light of the history and physical examination. Done (1978) has developed a nomogram that theoretically allows the clinician to use the serum level at a particular hour after acute overdose to predict severity; however, one must never rely on a serum salicylate value alone to predict how a patient will do. Potentially fatal management errors may occur if the nomogram is relied on exclusively. Decisions must be made in conjunction with the history of acute versus chronic overdose (patients with chronic overdoses often do worse for any given serum value) and on the patient's mental status, physical examination, and laboratory abnormalities (serum bicarbonate, pH, etc.).

Therapeutic

Aspirin overdose is treated by following the standard five-step overdose protocol:

- The patient's ABCs (airway, breathing, and cardiovascular status) should be secured.
- Naloxone, glucose, and thiamine should be given if indicated.
- Poison control should be consulted and a specific antidote administered if one exists.
- Absorption of the toxin should be blocked.
- Elimination of any absorbed toxin should be enhanced.

The ABCs in aspirin overdose may pose special problems. Although hyperventilation may be present, sudden deaths owing to centrally mediated respiratory arrests have been reported. The patient's volume status may be significantly altered because of hyperpyrexia, hyperhydrosis, and vomiting. Additionally, hypotension promotes acidosis, which is one of the worst prognostic indicators in aspirin overdose; thus it must be aggressively treated or, better still, avoided. If there is any alteration in mental status, a minimum of 2 mg of intravenous naloxone should be given. An immediate fingerstick glucose analysis should be performed and hypertonic glucose administered if indicated. Any alcoholic, cachectic, malnourished patient or any patient requiring hypertonic glucose should also receive a bolus of 100 mg of thiamine. At present, there is no specific antidote for aspirin, and the clinician should turn his or her attention to blocking any additional absorption of the toxin and promoting elimination of that which is already absorbed.

There is considerable controversy over the role of ipecac in overdose management. Ipecac has little efficacy if given more than 30 to 60 min-

utes after an overdose. Thus, patients treated in emergency departments should either receive oral high-absorption activated charcoal (approximately 1 g/kg) or have their stomachs lavaged via a large-bore orogastric tube and then receive charcoal. Oral charcoal without lavage is recommended for relatively minor overdoses and for stable patients with active bowel sounds seen 4 or more hours after overdose. Gastric lavage is indicated for significant overdoses (ingestion > 150 mg/kg), patients with gastric atony, any patient with an overdose involving enteric-coated salicylates, or any patient manifesting systemic aspirin toxicity. Prophylactic endotracheal intubation should precede gastric lavage if there is any significant alteration in the patient's mental status. Clinicians should note that gastric atony may result in pill fragments (especially of enteric-coated tablets) being found in the stomach 6 to 12 hours after ingestion. Solutions such as GoLytely (polyethylene glycol) should be considered in overdoses of large amounts of enteric-coated salicylates and in patients who develop gastric atony.

After the stomach has been emptied, superactivated charcoal should be administered at a dose of 1 g/kg body weight. The charcoal should be administered as a slurry of water with 20 to 40 mL sorbitol. Repeat doses of charcoal every 2 to 4 hours are no longer routinely recommended for salicylate overdoses.

Aspirin has a pH of 3, which makes it highly susceptible to urinary pH manipulations for the purpose of changing the relative amounts of ionized versus non-ionized fractions of salicylate. A change in the body's pH from 7.2 to 7.4 results in doubling the ionized fraction of salicylic acid. As it is the increase in the non-ionized fraction of salicylate that creates most of aspirin's deleterious effects, much therapeutic attention is devoted to the pH of both the serum and the urine. The patient's serum pH should be maintained at 7.4, while the urine should be kept markedly alkalotic (pH 7–8) and at relatively high flow. This results in low morbidity and mortality. Keeping the patient's serum nonacidotic and the urine alkalotic minimizes the amount of aspirin crossing the blood–brain barrier and accumulating in the central nervous system. Keeping the urine pH above 7 significantly decreases the amount of aspirin that is reabsorbed after it is filtered by the glomerulus. This "traps" it in an ionized state and cause it to be excreted in the urine. A urinary pH above 7 results in a 10- to 20-fold increase in aspirin excretion when compared with an acidotic urine. Intravenous therapy should be directed at maintaining an alkalotic urine with a flow of 1.5 to 2 mL/kg/h. The amount of bicarbonate added to the intravenous fluid is governed by both the patient's serum and urine pH. Normally, 5% dextrose in half-normal saline or 5% dextrose in water supplemented with bicarbonate and potassium (discussed below) is the fluid of choice (Table 24–10–3).

Owing to increased insensible losses from sweating and vomiting superimposed on a forced alkaline diuresis, urinary potassium losses are usually quite pronounced. A spot urine test for potassium 2 hours into therapy, along with the patient's serum value, determines subsequent intravenous amounts of this electrolyte. Large quantities of potassium may be necessary on a continuous basis. Although patients may initially be hyperglycemic in response to aspirin's effect on blocking cel-

TABLE 24–10–2. LABORATORY EVALUATION OF SALICYLATE INTOXICATION

Serum	Urine	Other
Serum electrolytes	Urinalysis	Chest radiograph
Aspirin level	Urine toxicologic screen	*(severe or*
Acetaminophen level	*(selected patients only)*	*hypoxic patients)*
Hematocrit		Electrocardiogram
Platelet estimate		*(severe cases only)*
Prothrombin time		
(severe overdose only)		
Arterial blood gas		
(severe or acidemic patients only)		

TABLE 24–10–3. MONITORING AND TREATING SALICYLATE INTOXICATION

Potential Toxic Effect	Monitor	Therapy
Acidosis	Respiratory rate	Volume
	pH	Bicarbonate
	SMA-7	
Hyperpyrexia, vascular collapse	Vital signs	Volume
	Urine output	
Hypoglycemia	Fingerstick glucose	Glucose
	SMA-7	
Hypokalemia	SMA-7	Potassium
	Urinary potassium	
	Electrocardiogram *(severe cases)*	
Pulmonary and/or cerebral edema	O$_2$ saturation	Appropriate volume
	Respiratory rate	
	Mental status	

lular metabolism, hypoglycemia may eventually supervene. In animals, central nervous system hypoglycemia has been observed in the face of peripheral normoglycemia. Thus, a low level of hyperglycemia should be maintained by the addition of an appropriate amount of glucose to the intravenous infusion.

A number of the effects salicylate overdose has on the body influence its therapy. Aspirin disrupts multiple enzyme system pathways, which may result in hyperpyrexia; thus, cooling blankets or cool toweling should be used when needed.

Aspirin may disrupt normal blood clotting via its effect on prothrombin formation and blocking factor VII production. If a bleeding diathesis develops, vitamin K and fresh-frozen plasma usually alleviate these problems. As aspirin may also affect both platelet levels and their adhesiveness, platelet packs may be needed on rare occasions in the hemorrhaging patient. Finally, because aspirin overdosage may cause renal failure, pulmonary edema, and, rarely, the syndrome of inappropriate antidiuretic hormone secretion, the clinician must be prepared to deal with these complications.

This author's preference for intravenous therapy is to start 5% dextrose in half-normal saline with 2 ampules of bicarbonate (88–100 mEq) and 20 mEq KCl at a rate of 200 mL per hour for the first few hours in healthy patients. In patients with impaired cardiovascular or renal function, lower flow rates with a more alkaline solution may be used. Furosemid (Lasix) is an excellent choice to supplement urinary flow rates in selected patients. Alkaline diuresis rather than the high urine flow rate is the single most important enhancer of aspirin elimination. Clinicians must guard against volume overload by balancing urine and intravenous flow rates with the judicious use of furosemide. Aggressive fluid therapy or attempts to induce a forced diuresis increase the likelihood of inducing pulmonary and cerebral edema.

There is considerable debate over the indications for hemodialysis or hemoperfusion. Both these methods avidly remove salicylates, yet each has its own inherent morbidity and mortality. For this reason, it seems prudent to reserve them for specific indications. Hemoperfusion (or dialysis) is indicated in acute overdoses when salicylate levels exceed 100 to 120 mg/dL in relatively asymptomatic patients. Indications for extracorporeal removal with levels below 100 mg/dL include unresponsive acidosis, oliguria, persistent central nervous system unresponsiveness or instability, and progressive life-threatening deterioration in the face of aggressive and appropriate care. The serum level at which a chronic overdose should undergo extracorporeal removal has not yet been well established. Most of these patients are older, with multiple underlying diseases. Any evidence of patient instability with a salicylate level greater than 60 to 80 mg/dL mandates hemoperfusion or dialysis. Stable chronic aspirin users with levels above 80 to 100 mg/dL should also be candidates for extracorporeal salicylate removal.

Table 24–10–3 summarizes the most common acute causes of increased morbidity and mortality from aspirin overdose, what variables should be followed, and how these complications can be avoided.

FOLLOW-UP

Aspirin-overdose patients who leave the hospital with normal laboratory values do not require medical follow-up. Patients who have attempted suicide should be appropriately followed by their physician. Chronic users of aspirin who have unintentionally overdosed should have serum salicylate levels performed while a new steady state is being obtained.

Patients should be told to return for immediate follow-up if any evidence of spontaneous hemorrhage, easy bruisability, or melena is noted.

DISCUSSION
Prevalence and Incidence

There are more than 200 aspirin-containing products available in the United States, and more than 20 billion tablets are consumed annually. Aspirin accounts for between 3 and 5% of all overdoses reported to poison control centers. This compares with the 15 to 20% incidence reported in the mid-1960s. The exact number of aspirin overdoses is unknown, but is far higher than the more than 200,000 cases per year reported to poison control centers.

Related Basic Science

For the clinician to adequately treat aspirin overdose, an understanding of aspirin's toxic metabolic effects is important. Aspirin's initial effect is directly on the central nervous system's respiratory center, producing both hyperpnea and tachypnea. In response to this respiratory alkalosis, renal bicarbonate excretion is increased and significant buffer base is eventually lost. Aspirin disrupts multiple enzyme systems, including uncoupling tissue glycolysis. This may result in central nervous system hypoglycemia, even in the face of peripheral normoglycemia. Metabolic acidosis is a major problem in salicylate overdoses and is secondary to multiple disruptions. The Krebs cycle is blocked at multiple sites, which results in a shift in equilibrium of pyruvate and lactate with a resultant lactic acidosis. Additionally, secondary to aspirin's effect on lipid metabolism, significant amounts of ketones are generated. Protein metabolism is affected, and higher circulating levels of amino acids further potentiate the acidosis.

It is difficult to overemphasize the importance of pH manipulations in aspirin overdose. Salicylic acid has a pK_a of 3. If the serum pH changes from 7.2 to 7.4, the non-ionized fraction is halved. As it is the non-ionized form that penetrates cell membranes, this change is of considerable clinical importance.

Repeated or chronic aspirin ingestion may eventually result in toxic levels. This is due to aspirin accumulation and elimination kinetics. It may take up to 1 week of daily aspirin ingestion to achieve a steady-state serum level. Once this level is attained, small increments in dosage may result in large increases of the serum salicylate level. If, for example, a patient increased the quantity he or she was ingesting by 50%, the serum level would rise sixfold.

Although there has been some debate concerning aspirin's effect on the stomach, it is now accepted that aspirin directly affects the gastric mucosa. Although a number of mechanisms are involved, aspirin's major deleterious effect is on breaking the so-called gastric mucosal barrier. This allows backdiffusion of stomach acid and un-ionized salicylic acid, which may potentiate gastric ulceration.

The effects of aspirin on hemostasis are multiple. Aspirin blocks platelet releases of ADP, serotonin, epinephrine, and platelet factor number III. This is most likely mediated by aspirin's effect on inhibiting prostaglandin synthesis. After a single dose of aspirin, abnormal platelet aggregation may be noted for up to 7 days. Aspirin may prolong the prothrombin time by decreasing the production of the vitamin K-dependent clotting factors II or VII, IX, and X, the deficiency of factor VII being the most clinically significant. This effect is aggravated by fever or an underlying clotting defect and is reversed by administration of vitamin K or fresh-frozen plasma.

Natural History and Its Modification with Treatment

As has already been discussed, aspirin overdose evolves from early respiratory alkalosis, to a mixed respiratory alkalosis and metabolic acidosis, to an almost pure metabolic acidosis. Respiratory depression may be seen as a preterminal event and is an ominous finding. Other poor prognostic signs include shock, a significant bleeding diathesis, a nonresponsive metabolic acidosis, pulmonary edema, and a salicylate level above 200 mg/dL. Early aggressive and appropriate therapy minimizes aspirin's toxicity and decreases the likelihood of progressive metabolic derangement.

Prevention

Patient education is the most important single factor in avoiding aspirin overdose. Patients must be aware of the hundreds of aspirin-containing compounds. Aspirin should be stored in childproof containers. Arthritics who do not use childproof packaging for storage should be warned to keep their grandchildren and others safely away from this potentially dangerous medication. Any patients who chronically ingest aspirin, such as those with rheumatoid arthritis, must be warned to always check the label of any new medication for aspirin prior to adding it to their treatment regimen.

Cost Containment

Most aspirin overdoses can be managed at home or in the emergency room. The aggressive use of a regional poison control center will cut down significantly on the number of emergency room visits. If a patient requires hospitalization, vigorous early care as previously described will usually result in an uncomplicated, short hospitalization.

Costly invasive removal techniques should be reserved for those specific indications already discussed. Intensive care unit care is not appropriate for observation.

REFERENCES

Done AK. Aspirin overdosage: Incidence, diagnosis and management. Pediatrics 1978;62(suppl.):890.

Mayer AL, Sitar DS, Tenenbein M. Multiple-dose charcoal and whole-bowel irrigation do not increase clearance of absorbed salicylate. Arch Intern Med 1992;152:393.

Dugandzic RM, Tierny MD, Dickinson GE, et al. Evaluation of the validity of the Dome nomogram in the management of acute salicylate intoxication. Ann Emerg Med 1989;18:1186.

Prescott LF, Balali-Mood M, Critchley JA, et al. Diuresis or urinary alkalinization for salicylate poisoning? Br Med J 1982;285:1383.

Schwartz JE. Chronic aspirin intoxication: A case report and literature review. Ariz Med 1984;41:799.

Yip L, Dart RC, Gabow PA. Concepts and controversies in salicylate toxicity. Emerg Med Clin North Am 1994;12:351.

CHAPTER 24–11

Poisoning with Organophosphate and Carbamate Insecticides and Nerve Agents

Cynthia K. Aaron, M.D.

DEFINITION

Organophosphorus pesticide (subsequently referred to as organophosphates) overdose is defined as any cholinergic signs or symptoms resulting from exposure to this group of chemicals.

ETIOLOGY

Organophosphorus-containing pesticides and carbamates are nonspecific cholinesterase-inhibiting agents. Organophosphates irreversibly bind with cholinesterases, whereas carbamates bind reversibly. Toxicity may occur with ingestion, inhalation, transmucosal, or transdermal exposures, either accidentally, during occupation or home use, or by deliberate ingestion.

CRITERIA FOR DIAGNOSIS
Suggestive

Toxicity occurs when acetylcholinesterase is inactivated and acetylcholine accumulates at the nerve terminal or effector organ. Thus, clues to the diagnosis include any cholinergic sign or symptom (Table 24–11–1). Patients most frequently present with muscarinic SLUDGE symptoms: salivation, lacrimation, urinary incontinence, diarrhea, gastrointestinal distress, and emesis. Nicotinic and central effects include sweating, bronchospasm, fasciculations, muscle weakness, confusion, and seizures. A presumptive diagnosis of organophosphate poisoning may be made in patients who present with the signs and symptoms of toxicity and respond rapidly to atropine.

Definitive

A definitive diagnosis of organophosphate toxicity requires a serum assay of either plasma pseudocholinesterase or erythrocyte acetyl-cholinesterase. A level less than 50% of normal in the setting of suspected toxicity is considered diagnostic of an exposure.

CLINICAL MANIFESTATIONS
Subjective

The cholinesterase-inhibited patient complains of anxiety, fatigue, dizziness, headache, shortness of breath, abdominal pain and cramping, incontinence of urine or stool, blurred vision, muscle weakness, and difficulty talking. As toxicity progresses, the patient complains of worsening abdominal pain and becomes increasingly agitated and confused. Respiratory distress with wheezing is evident.

Objective
Physical Examination

Objective findings depend on which cholinergic system is predominately affected (Table 24–11–1). Vital signs range from tachycardia (hypoxia or preganglionic sympathetic stimulation) to bradycardia with vagal predominance. Both hypertension and hypotension may be seen in association with tachypnea. The patient is best described as "wet" with profuse diaphoresis, vomiting, bronchorrhea, lacrimation, rhinorrhea, sialorrhea, and diarrhea. Moderately ill patients often demonstrate nicotinic toxicity with fasciculations. This progresses to muscle weakness, respiratory failure, and paralysis. Mydriasis occurs in up to 85% of patients. Mental status changes include confusion, delirium, coma, and seizures. Cardiovascular toxicity is reflected in decreased atrioventricular node conduction and ventricular arrhythmias. Site of exposure determines which symptoms predominate: patients with ingestions initially have gastrointestinal symptomatology, whereas transdermal exposure leads to local fasciculations.

Routine Laboratory Abnormalities

There are no laboratory values that are found routinely in patients poisoned with organophosphates and carbamates with the exception of depressed cholinesterase activity. Some laboratory abnormalities that may be found relate to the altered state of homeostasis resulting from the poisoning. This includes but is not limited to changes in the arterial blood gases reflecting hypoventilation and respiratory failure and signs of a catecholamine-mediated stress response with leukocytosis, hyperglycemia, and hypokalemia.

TABLE 24–11–1. SIGNS OF CHOLINESTERASE INHIBITOR TOXICITY

Central nervous system	Agitation, confusion, lethargy, coma, seizures, respiratory paralysis
Parasympathetic (muscarinic)	Miosis, bradycardia, lacrimation, urinary incontinence, diarrhea, emesis, gastrointestinal spasms, bronchoconstriction, rhinorrhea, blurred vision
Sympathetic (nicotinic)	Mydriasis, tachycardia, hypertension, hypotension, diaphoresis
Neuromuscular junction	Fasciculations, muscle weakness, paralysis

PLANS

Diagnostic

Differential Diagnosis

The differential diagnosis for cholinesterase inhibition toxicity is large and includes gastroenteritis, asthma, scorpion or *Latrodectus* envenomation, progressive peripheral neuropathies (Guillain–Barré and Eaton–Lambert syndromes), heavy metal toxicity, muscarinic mushroom (*Amanita muscaria* and *Amanita pantherina*) ingestion, and nicotine ingestion. Metabolic and infection diagnoses that mimic cholinergic toxicity include diabetic ketoacidosis, sepsis, encephalitis, and meningitis. Reye's syndrome and central nervous system trauma may have some similar findings.

Diagnostic Options

Diagnosis of cholinesterase inhibitor toxicity is dependent on a consistent history and clinical picture, onset within 12 hours of exposure, decrease in cholinesterase activity below 50% of baseline, and response to atropine and/or pralidoximine chloride. Fenthion, chlorfenthion, and other lipid-soluble organophosphates may have a more delayed presentation.

Determination of cholinesterase levels establishes the diagnosis. Both plasma pseudocholinesterase and erythrocyte acetylcholinesterase levels should be obtained in those cases requiring a definitive diagnosis. There is a 10% intraindividual variation in the plasma pseudocholinesterase assay, but it is more readily available. Erythrocyte acetylcholinesterase is more accurate but harder to perform. Acetylcholinesterase is more representative of true neuronal cholinesterase and is found in both erythrocytes and neural tissue. Plasma pseudocholinesterase is an acute-phase hepatic protein found in liver and plasma. Levels of both cholinesterases decrease after exposure, with symptoms usually evident below 20 to 50% of baseline activity. Without therapy, acetylcholinesterase levels increase by 0.5 to 1% per day and normalize 3 to 4 months postexposure. Administration of pralidoxime rapidly restores enzymatic activity neuronally; this is reflected in normalization of the erythrocyte acetylcholinesterase level after therapy. Plasma pseudocholinesterase regenerates 25 to 30% within the first week and then normalizes gradually over the ensuing 2 to 3 months. There is minimal response to pralidoxime.

False depressions of both acetylcholinesterase and pseudocholinesterase may be seen. Anemia, antimalarial therapy, and hemolysis decrease acetylcholinesterase activity. Pregnancy, anemia, chronic inflammation, myocardial infarct, infection, hypersensitivity reactions, cirrhosis, starvation, and the use of morphine sulfate, codeine, and succinylcholine affect pseudocholinesterase. There is also a genetic variant with reduced pseudocholinesterase activity. Both tests, when used, should be drawn acutely and followed sequentially. Prolonged enzyme activity depression occurs with organophosphates but not with carbamates. Ideally, a baseline cholinesterase level should be used for comparison; however, as this is rarely available, population normals can be used with caution. Enzyme activity 70% of normal may represent toxicity in the appropriate setting, especially if the patient's baseline is 120% of normal.

Additional laboratory data may demonstrate leukocytosis, hyperglycemia, proteinuria, glycosurea, and evidence of dehydration. Occasionally, *para*-nitrophenol may be detected in the urine immediately after exposure to some organophosphates.

Recommended Approach

When faced with a patient with suspected cholinesterase inhibition, the treating staff must first protect themselves. Provision for the ABCs should occur simultaneously with patient decontamination. Atropine administration can be both therapeutic and diagnostic; rapid atropinization with small amounts of the drug would tend to rule out the diagnosis. If atropine is effective for the muscarinic symptoms, then initiation of antidotal therapy with pralidoxime is indicated. Appropriate diagnostic laboratory tests can then be sent, recognizing it is unlikely that the results will be available in the acute setting and the laboratory diagnosis is more of a confirmatory diagnosis after the fact.

Therapeutic

As with any poisoning, establishment of an airway is the first priority. Secretions are copious and intubation should be done expeditiously. All patients require oxygen; positive-pressure ventilation may be necessary. An intravenous line should be established. In patients with an altered mental status, dextrose 25 to 50 g, thiamine 100 mg, and a trial of 0.1 to 2 mg naloxone should be given intravenously.

All patients with organophosphate exposure require dermal decontamination with copious amounts of water and soap, being careful not to abrade the skin. Tincture of green soap is recommended for use with oily substances. In the event of "nerve gas" exposure, a dilute bleach solution (1–5% hypochlorite) should be used to inactivate the toxin. The staff requires full protection with rubber gloves, water-resistant clothing, and masks. All clothing and leather items should be discarded and destroyed, preventing further use. Patients with cholinesterase inhibitor ingestions should have gastric decontamination with lavage followed by oral activated charcoal (1 g/kg). A cathartic is rarely needed in this situation. Induced emesis with syrup of ipecac is contraindicated.

Antidotal therapy consists of atropine and pralidoxime. Once the patient is oxygenated, atropine is administered until muscarinic symptoms diminish. Occasionally, atropine is necessary to provide secretion control for adequate oxygenation. Atropine dosing is initiated with 1 to 2 mg intravenously and is doubled every 5 to 10 minutes until oral and bronchial secretions cease (pediatric dose, 0.02–0.05 mg/kg). Dosing may be repeated as needed. Flushed skin, mydriasis, and tachycardia are *not* considered endpoints to atropinization and may represent hypoxia or sympathetic stimulation. Atropine only reverses signs of muscarinic acetylcholine excess. It has no effect on nicotinic receptors nor on enzyme regeneration. Pralidoxime (2-PAM, Protopam) is an oxime nucleophile that regenerates acetylcholinesterase by reversing the phosphorylation of the enzyme active site. It is synergistic with atropine and should be given whenever atropine is indicated for symptomatic organophosphate toxicity. Its use in carbamate poisoning remains somewhat controversial, but it should be used in an unknown ingestion. Pralidoxime is administered by intermittent bolus dosing or by continuous intravenous infusion. Dosing is 1 to 2 g intravenously (25–50 mg/kg) in 100 mL normal saline given no faster than 500 mg/min every 6 to 8 hours or by an infusion of 500 mg/h (10–25 mg/kg/h) as a 2.5% solution in saline. Effects are evident within 30 to 60 minutes. Rapid injection or overdose leads to tachycardia, laryngeal spasm, muscle rigidity, or transient neuromuscular blockade. Pralidoxime therapy is continued for 24 to 48 hours or longer in the symptomatic patient.

Seizures should be treated aggressively with benzodiazepines. Animal literature supports the synergistic effects from lorazepam or diazepam in conjunction with pralidoxime in protecting brain and myocardial tissue from permanent damage.

Although enzyme "aging" is frequently cited in the literature as a reason not to administer pralidoxime more than 48 hours after exposure, no supporting in vivo evidence exists. Anecdotal data demonstrate benefit if pralidoxime is administered whenever the patient is symptomatic, regardless of time; however, pralidoxime therapy may need to be continued for a prolonged period if initial treatment is delayed.

Patients should be told that they have been exposed to a chemical that acts as a "nerve poison." This agent can make them very uncomfortable for a short period, but the condition is amenable to treatment. It should be emphasized that other illnesses can mimic this poisoning and the physician looks for certain physical findings to make the diagnosis. Patients should be informed that the laboratory confirmation of exposure may take several days and multiple blood tests may be needed over several weeks to confirm the diagnosis.

Patients who are asymptomatic may require 6 to 12 hours of observation. Patients with symptoms require at least 48 hours in the hospital, some of which will be in the intensive care unit. Treated patients generally do very well but some patients require a protracted treatment period. Patients should be told that the majority of their symptoms will resolve prior to hospital discharge but some minor symptoms may continue for 2 to 3 months. Patient with exposure to nerve agents may not respond to antidotal therapy and should be told, assuming they survive initial exposure, that they will require protracted intensive hospital care. Those patients who have been exposed to an organophosphate are extremely sensitive to these agents for several months and should avoid them until blood tests normalize. Patients who undergo surgery should notify their surgeon and anesthesiologist because certain anesthetic and antibiotic medications must be avoided. Occasionally, with some specialized organophosphate exposures, patients may develop muscle weakness and uncomfortable feelings 8 to 10 days after the initial exposure. Patients should be told that there is no specific treatment available for this problem, but most people recover some function over the ensuing 6 months to a year.

FOLLOW-UP

Prognosis is good with early therapy. Asymptomatic patients with significant exposure require 6 to 12 hours of observation. Symptomatic patients need hospitalization for at least 24 hours after resolution of all signs and symptoms. Patients with exposure to lipid-soluble substances such as fenthion require prolonged observation, as toxic effects may recur several weeks later. There are data to suggest that behavioral abnormalities may result from acute or chronic low-level exposures, although well-controlled studies are lacking. Long-term organophosphorus-induced delayed neuropathy (OPIDN) has been described with some agents, particularly with some organophosphates, phosphoramidates, and phosphonates. Tri-*ortho*-cresyl-phosphate-induced neuropathy (Ginger Jake paralysis) is an example.

All personnel in contact with organophosphates should have baseline cholinesterase levels obtained prior to any exposure, followed by sequential monitoring levels. All patients with toxicity or asymptomatic individuals with monitored levels less than 50% of baseline should avoid all exposure to cholinesterase inhibitors until acetylcholinesterase levels return to 70% of baseline.

DISCUSSION

Prevalence and Incidence

Although mortality from pesticides in the United States is less than 1 in 100,000 exposures, the number of people experiencing toxicity is much higher. Based on 1985 Poison Center data, less than 5% of reported poisonings were related to pesticides. Occupational exposures reported in Florida and California in 1985 clustered around 250 per 100,000 population. Finally, worldwide estimates range around 2,900,000 exposures with 220,000 deaths per year from pesticides. These numbers are believed to underestimate the true prevalence as many exposures are not reported (Levine, 1991).

Related Basic Science

Cholinesterase-inhibiting compounds were synthesized 75 years ago but were not commercially popular until the 1940s. Nicotine was the first substance used in agriculture. During World War II, more toxic compounds were developed including sarin, soman, tabun, tetraethyl pyrophosphate (TEPP), dimefox, and parathion. Sarin, soman, tabun, and VX are now predominately used as "nerve agents" in chemical warfare.

Organophosphates covalently bind to the active serine site on the cholinesterase molecule, phosphorylating this site and inactivating it, preventing normal hydrolysis of acetylcholine. Resynthesis of the inactivated enzyme requires 3 months. Carbamates do not covalently bind and spontaneously hydrolyze within 24 to 48 hours. Once the enzyme is phosphorylated, acetylcholine accumulates at the synapse or myoneural junction, leading to initial excitation and then paralysis of function. Onset of signs and symptoms depends on the toxic agent, route of exposure, need for hepatic activation, endogenous acetylcholinesterase levels, tissue metabolism, and lipid solubility. One drop of soman has onset within minutes of exposure.

Noncholinesterase effects of these compounds include alterations in cellular ionic channels and direct vasoconstrictive and central nervous system effects. Central nervous system toxicity results from antagonism of the γ-aminobutyric acid system, agonism of the excitatory amino acid N-methyl-D-aspartate receptors, and central antidopaminergic activity. Cyclic GMP and cyclic AMP concentrations are affected by organophosphate modulation of adenyl cyclase and phosphodiesterase. The protective effects demonstrated with benzodiazepines are believed to be related to their γ-aminobutyric acid agonism.

Treatment follows two principles: increase acetylcholine at the nerve terminals to allay muscarinic symptoms, and regenerate the enzyme. Atropine competitively binds to the postsynaptic nerve membrane and blocks the muscarinic acetylcholine receptor. It is rapidly metabolized, however. Pralidoxime regenerates the acetylcholinesterase by removing the phosphorylating group. Aging occurs when the organophosphate conformationally alters the enzyme structure and prevents reactivation by pralidoxime. This is much more delayed than previously believed from animal and in vitro data because of several processes including circulation-dependent absorption and distribution of the agent, partial consumption by nonspecific cholinesterases, hepatic activation, and equilibrium between binding and endogenous hydrolysis. Although considered irreversibly bound, the aged enzyme may undergo spontaneous hydrolysis and reactivate. There is also specific species specificity and microenviromental requirements not addressed in the early in vitro studies.

Soman, sarin, tabun, and VX bind much more rapidly and tightly to the serine active site so that rapid onset of treatment is crucial. With the exception of soman, these agents do not respond well to therapy with conventional nucleophiles (pralidoxime), requiring the approach taken during the Gulf War of pretreating potentially exposed personnel. Blockade of the active enzyme site with another agent such as a carbamate prevents an organophosphorus compound from binding. An agent such as pyridostigmine does not cross the blood–brain barrier and occupies only the 20 to 40% of the cholinesterase active sites for 6 to 8 hours. Military personnel were pretreated with pyridostigmine to partially block the enzyme active sites. In vivo studies have shown that immediate treatment with atropine and pralidoxime self-injectors opens the carbamylated enzyme active sites and allows for adequate neurotransmission. Currently, there is ongoing work in developing stronger, more effective nucleophiles.

Natural History and Its Modification with Treatment

Acute toxicity from these agents is apparent within minutes to hours with the exception of the lipid-soluble toxins. If the patient is not ill within 12 to 24 hours, then cholinesterase activity is greater than 50% of baseline. Untreated patients become progressively more ill and then stabilize over a prolonged period. As cholinesterase activity returns, synaptic and myoneural function returns if the patient does not succumb acutely to hypoxia or later to pneumonia. Untreated patients have a higher incidence of neuropathy and this may be related to neuronal death and receptor up- or downregulation. Treated patients have rapid restoration of function and, if adequately decontaminated, have no progression of signs and symptoms. Patients exposed to agents causing organophosphorus-induced delayed neuropathy have resolution of acute symptoms with treatment, followed 8 to 10 days later by a progressive peripheral sensorimotor neuropathy, which may not fully resolve with time.

Prevention

Most cholinesterase inhibitor-induced toxicity is accidental and can be avoided by adequate protection and storage. All containers should be kept in areas protected from water and pests. Depending on relative toxicity, protective gear should be used, including respirators, gloves, boots, and complete one-piece carbon-lined suits. All exposed skin surfaces should be rapidly and completely washed down and the rinse water disposed of appropriately. Pesticides should be stored out of reach of children in tightly closed original containers away from kitchens and food areas. Finally, all workers should undergo regular surveillance monitoring of cholinesterase levels and seek help if any symptoms develop. Atropine and pralidoxime should never be used prophylactically.

Cost-Containment

Asymptomatic patients should be observed for 6 to 12 hours and discharged if they were not exposed to lipid-soluble substances. Ideally, their cholinesterase levels should be obtained and serially monitored.

Symptomatic patients should be admitted to an intensive care unit and monitored until 24 hours after resolution of all signs and complaints. Patients exposed to fenthion, chlorfenthion, or other lipid-soluble compounds may require prolonged hospitalization with transfer into an intensive care unit once symptoms develop.

REFERENCES

Barrett DS, Oehme FW. A review of organophosphate ester-induced delayed-neuropathy. Vet Hum Toxicol 1985;27:22.

Dunn MA, Sidell FR. Progress in medical defense against nerve agents. JAMA 262:649, 1989.

Levine R. Recognized and possible effects of pesticides in humans: Section 7.1. Incidence of poisoning. In: Hayes WJ, Jr, Laws ER Jr, eds. Handbook of pesticide toxicology: vol 1. General principles. New York: Academic Press, 1991.

Minton NA, Murray VSG. A review of organophosphate poisoning. Med Toxicol 1988;3:350.

Namba T, Nolte CT, Jackrel J, Grob D. Poisoning due to organophosphate insecticides: Acute and chronic manifestations. Am J Med 1971;50:475.

Sidell FR, Borak J. Chemical warfare agents: II. Nerve agents. Ann Emerg Med 1992;21:865.

Thompson DF, Thompson GD, Greenwood RB, Trammel HL. Therapeutic dosing of pralidoxime chloride. Drug Intell Clin Pharmacy 1987;2:590.

CHAPTER 24–12

Amphetamine Overdose

Lewis Goldfrank, M.D.

DEFINITION

An amphetamine overdose is defined as any significant psychological and/or physiologic imbalance caused by the utilization of an amphetamine. Many street preparations (and newer designer drugs), as well as the readily available over-the-counter preparations of phenylpropanolamine, are used as "amphetamine-like substances."

ETIOLOGY

The condition is caused by an overdose of amphetamine or an amphetamine-like substance. The etiology as defined by the patient is rationale for using amphetamines. Reasons for amphetamine usage are related to patient behavior and include submission to peer pressure, a desire to experiment, cultural influences, and emotional and psychiatric problems.

CRITERIA FOR DIAGNOSIS

Suggestive

The emergency department is the usual clinical setting in which patients with amphetamine or amphetamine-like substance overdose are seen. The patient or friends may state that amphetamines were used chronically or acutely. Often even the patient is unsure of the nature of the ingested substance.

The clinician must rely on specific typical alterations in the physical and/or neuropsychiatric examination to make the diagnosis. In particular, an adrenergic excess is noted with diaphoresis, tachycardia, hyperthermia, hypertension, hyperhydrosis, hyperactivity, and active bowel sounds.

Definitive

A definitive diagnosis of an amphetamine (or amphetamine-like) overdose is made by the presence of the above-mentioned sympathetic and/or neuropsychiatric findings coupled with the detection of amphetamines in urine or serum.

CLINICAL MANIFESTATIONS

Subjective

Amphetamine usage has become almost exclusively abusive. There are only rare clinical indications for amphetamine use. Their actual use in the management of narcolepsy, enuresis, and attention-deficit disorders should be considered minimal. Any patient presenting to an emergency department with amphetamine-related complications should be considered an abuser. The complications may be from overdose (central nervous system stimulation), withdrawal (depression), mixed drug-related disorders (sedative–hypnotics and stimulants), or associated trauma or infection (parenteral drug abuse).

Symptoms of amphetamine overdose are those consistent with a sympathetic excess. Patients may complain of a fast heartbeat, not being able to catch one's breath, anxiety, feeling hot, or having gastrointestinal distress (hypermotility). In others, the neuropsychiatric abnormalities induced by the amphetamines may dominate the clinical picture. Complaints may be paranoid or delusional in nature.

Objective

Physical Examination

The physical examination demonstrates the alpha-adrenergic and beta-adrenergic characteristics of sympathomimetic drugs, but amphetamines are invariably abused for their neuropsychiatric effects. Patients with overdose usually exhibit tachycardia and are hypertensive (often severely), hyperthermic (possibly with life-threatening temperature elevations), and tachypneic. Mydriasis, flushing, and diaphoresis are frequently noted. Dysrhythmias are often associated with the hypertension. Circulatory compromise, myocardial ischemia, and pulmonary edema have been noted. Neurologic manifestations include tremor, hyperactivity, convulsions, and coma. The neurologic manifestations may be due to a hypertensive crisis, subarachnoid hemorrhage, or psychosis. The gastrointestinal manifestations are nausea, vomiting, diarrhea, and hemorrhage. Gastrointestinal hemorrhage as well as hepatic, splenic, or subarachnoid hemorrhage may be due to aneurysmal rupture. The psychiatric manifestations are usually due to central nervous system stimulatory effects occurring acutely or chronically. Visual, tactile, and auditory hallucinations as well as paranoid ideations are frequently seen with amphetamine use. Withdrawal is commonly associated with a "crash" phase or consequential depression, which may be manifested by a listless, suicidal presentation. In both presentations, the patient maintains normal orientation and sensorium.

Certain parenteral amphetamine abusers manifest the typical cutaneous and infectious complications of this form of abuse. These individuals are also subject to diffuse microaneurysms in the central nervous system, kidney, spleen, liver, and gastrointestinal tract. Typical complications include subcapsular hematomas of the spleen or liver and renal failure.

Routine Laboratory Abnormalities

The laboratory data are usually nonspecific. The complete blood count may show a leukocytosis, hyperglycemia may be manifest, and the electrolytes are usually normal. Hepatic enzymes (alanine and aspartate aminotransferases) may be elevated due to associated infections, typically hepatitis from parenteral abuse. Muscle enzyme (creatine phosphokinase) may be elevated as a result of rhabdomyolysis.

The electrocardiogram may demonstrate a dysrhythmia or ischemic damage.

The urinalysis may show hematuria, myoglobinuria, and proteinuria.

PLANS
Diagnostic
Differential Diagnosis

Amphetamine overdose must be differentiated from other conditions such as cocaine overdosage, psychiatric conditions include manic states, paranoid or delusional states, panic attacks, hypoglycemia, and overdosage of other drugs that cause adrenergic excess.

Diagnostic Options

Any patient who exhibits unexplained sympathetic hyperactivity should have his or her serum or urine analyzed for amphetamine and other toxic substances. Analysis of the urine for the drug is usually a better choice.

The broad differential diagnosis of the comatose patient or the patient with an altered sensorium may also be clarified by toxicologic examination of the blood and urine.

Recommended Approach

There is no other approach to the problem. The diagnosis is made by identifying a syndrome of adrenergic stimulation in the patient plus the discovery of amphetamines in the urine. Most patients with overdose are brought to an emergency department. The facility should be able to perform the necessary tests on the serum or urine.

Over-the-counter or cold preparations such as ephedrine, pseudoephedrine, and phenylpropanolamine, which may mimic amphetamine or methamphetamine abuse, may also be identified at the same time.

Therapeutic
Therapeutic Options

Acute management is not usually altered by toxicologic evaluation, but the definitive diagnosis of amphetamine abuse helps determine chronic therapy.

The general principles involved in the treatment of amphetamine overdose include the maintenance of a patent airway, the prevention of aspiration, the prevention of drug absorption, and the management of agitation, hyperthermia, hypertension, cardiac dysrhythmias, and myocardial ischemia. There are no other therapeutic options.

Recommended Approach

The general management of the patient with oral amphetamine overdose is identical to the management of patients who have ingested other types of toxic substances (such as cocaine). Management includes an assessment of the airway, as well as an evaluation as to whether activated charcoal (1 g/kg body weight in a 1:4 water slurry) should be given immediately by mouth or via an orogastric tube (36–40 French). In view of the potential for lethality (seizures, dysrhythmias), endotracheal intubation should be accomplished immediately and this should be followed by gastric lavage. Syrup of ipecac should not be used for amphetamine overdosage. An ionic cathartic (magnesium sulfate, 30 g) or sorbitol 70% (50 mL) can be admixed with the activated charcoal slurry and used to achieve a catharsis.

Major complications of an amphetamine overdose include anxiety, agitation, psychosis, seizures, hyperthermia, rhabdomyolysis, dysrhythmias, and hypertension. Anxiety, agitation, and psychosis should be managed initially in a supportive, calm environment. Other potential etiologies should be treated with dextrose 50% (50 mL), naloxone (2 mg), and thiamine (100 mg) given intravenously. Diazepam (5–10 mg intravenously repeated each 5–10 minutes) or lorazepam (1–2 mg intravenously repeated each 10–15 minutes) should be used to achieve a calm state. Diazepam or lorazepam also may be effective in the management of seizures (particularly status epilepticus), but phenytoin 15 to 18 mg/kg intravenously at 50 mg per minute or less or phenobarbital 15 to 20 mg/kg intravenously over 15 to 20 minutes should be used concomitantly.

When hyperthermia is present, diazepam or lorazepam may be necessary to control the agitation or seizures, which are usually the precipitants of the elevated temperature. Simultaneously, the patient should be cooled with mechanical means, such as fans, ice, and cold water. If the body temperature exceeds 105°F, aggressive cooling is indicated.

Hypertension is invariably short-lived and is usually treated by effective sedation with a benzodiazepine. If the patient has been sedated and central nervous system or cardiovascular compromise persists and cocaine and overdose remains under consideration in the differential diagnosis, nifedipine, sodium nitroprusside, or the alpha antagonist phentolamine is indicated. If cocaine intoxication is not a clinical consideration, propranolol (1 mg intravenously per 5 minutes), esmolol, or labetalol may be indicated. The dysrhythmias associated with overdose also can be managed by propranolol or lidocaine.

Diazepam is also important in sedating the patient who may be harmful to himself or herself or others whether intoxicated or withdrawing from amphetamines. Sedation and hospitalization are often considered essential in the withdrawal state that does not present as a consequential physiologic risk but as a substantial psychological risk.

Some authorities suggest ion-trapping techniques to eliminate amphetamines by using ammonium chloride and sodium chloride diuresis to achieve an acid diuresis. Acid diuresis results in a theoretical advantage due to the high pK_a of amphetamines; the resultant increase in the ionized amphetamine component in the urine decreases reabsorption of amphetamines. The clinical disadvantage is that an acid urine may, in the face of rhabdomyolysis and myoglobinuria, increase the risk of acute tubular necrosis. If used effectively, sedation calms the patient and eliminates the perceived need for rapid drug removal by acidification, which has no clinical benefit and does not decrease toxicity. Aggressive fluid resuscitation and sedation eliminate the need for acidification.

Phenothiazines and haloperidol have no clinical advantage over the benzodiazepines (diazepam or lorazepam) in the acutely agitated state. In fact, the alpha-adrenergic blockage associated with these neuroleptic agents may complicate the management should hypotension develop. There may also be an increased risk of seizures and the potential for the development of a dystonic reaction. It is for these reasons that diazepam or lorazepam is preferred.

FOLLOW-UP

Amphetamine overdose often necessitates in-hospital admission, but whether the patient is hospitalized or not, entry into a drug detoxification program is essential. Many of the overdose complications necessitate supportive care in an intensive care unit. Suicidal intent should always be a consideration in any overdosed patient. Patients withdrawing from amphetamines are frequently quite depressed and also necessitate a psychiatric assessment. In amphetamine-dependent individuals, structured support for safe dieting techniques may be quite valuable.

The desire to begin reusing stimulants should prompt immediate follow-up with the patient's physician or health care worker.

DISCUSSION
Prevalence and Incidence

Clinically, amphetamines (amphetamine, dextroamphetamine, and methamphetamine) remain in use as appetite suppressants; mood elevators; treatments for narcolepsy, mental or physical fatigue, and enuresis; to counteract central nervous system depressants; and in children to treat attention deficit disease. There is no clinical condition that cannot be managed with a safer pharmacologic alternative. Recently, the illicit designer amphetamines—3,4-methylenedioxymethamphetamine (MDMA, Ecstasy) and 3,4 methylenedioxyethamphetamine (MDEA, Eve)—have become consequential clinical problems. Efforts in the reformulation of methamphetamine (Speed, Crack) have led to the development of a smokable, insufflatable form called Ice that has much of the allure of the cocaine alkaloid in many large urban centers.

Related Basic Science

Amphetamines can be used orally, parenterally, by insufflation, and by inhalation. Amphetamines are indirect sympathomimetic agents that enhance the release and block the reuptake of catecholamines from the sympathetic nerve terminals while possibly having a direct receptor effect. Amphetamines result in central nervous system stimulatory effects as well as peripheral alpha and beta actions on the autonomic nervous system. At high doses amphetamines can cause the release of 5-hydroxytryptamine and affect central serotonin receptors.

Toxicity is manifested almost immediately when the drug is used intravenously or by inhalation, whereas orally, the effects are noted 0.5 to 1 hour after ingestion. Peak levels are noted 2 to 4 hours after ingestion. Approximately 50% of an amphetamine dose is rapidly metabolized in the liver via hydroxylation, demethylation, and deamination. The high pK_a of the basic amphetamines leads to maximal urinary excretion when the urine pH is between 4.5 and 5.5. Very low doses in the range of 5 mg/kg have been reported as lethal doses, whereas massive doses in terms of grams are used by the tolerant individual.

Natural History and Its Modification with Treatment

The problems associated with amphetamine abuse are dependent on the dose used, the drugs that are admixed with it, the route of administration, and the patient's underlying clinical condition. If the patient does not manifest seizures, life-threatening hyperthermia, ventricular dysrhythmias, pulmonary edema, posthypoxic encephalopathy, a subarachnoid hemorrhage, a subcapsular hematoma of the liver, an acute myocardial infarction, or renal failure, the immediate prognosis is excellent. When these conditions are present the rapidity of initiation of therapy defines the extent of morbidity and mortality; however, the long-term prognosis is dependent on the patient's desire to become abstinent as well as the previous length and extent of exposure to the risks of parenteral drug abuse. Withdrawal from amphetamines requires close psychiatric support for potentially profound depression and careful management to prevent recurrent dependency.

Mortality is associated with the above-mentioned complications of the drug. The minimum lethal dose of amphetamines may be as low as 5 mg/kg but is highly variable in chronic users. Severe hyperthermia correlates with a high mortality. Clinical signs and symptoms, not drug levels, predict fatal outcomes.

Prevention

The role of amphetamines in the treatment of appetite suppression, mood elevation, narcolepsy, and mental and physical fatigue is highly questionable. As amphetamines are still available legally, patients should be aware that amphetamines are not a safe solution to their weight loss problems. Patients should know that the potential complications include severe damage to the brain and heart. There are no shortcuts to dieting or mood control. Patients often become addicted and tolerate higher and higher doses with resultant overdose as a life-threatening complication or grave depression associated with abrupt withdrawal. Amphetamines have such a substantial abuse potential with such a limited therapeutic potential that their removal from our legal formulary would decrease the toxicologic problem. Most patients with obesity, mood disorders, and dependency who chronically use this drug become dependent under physician guidance. Early intervention in schools and homes is essential as a prophylactic as well as a preventive measure.

Cost Containment

The appropriate clinical assessment of a patient overdosed with amphetamines may allow the physician to ask for specific qualitative toxicology and avoid "toxicology screens." Education in the field of drug abuse will prevent loss of life and limb, infection, loss of jobs and families, street violence to self (prostitution) and others (robbery), as well as recurrent emergency department visits and hospitalizations. Rehabilitation programs, job training, and education may have a dramatic impact on drug-related hospital costs. In particular, nutrition education, rational dieting, and psychosocial support are more logical approaches than amphetamine therapy.

Long-term intensive care unit observation once the patient is stabilized is not necessary. Prolonged inpatient care on a general medical service is inappropriate.

REFERENCES

Buchanan JF, Brown CR. Designer drugs: A problem in clinical toxicology. Med Toxicol 1988;3:1.

Derlet RW, Heischober B. Methamphetamine: Stimulant of the 1990's. West J Med 1990;153:625.

Derlet RW, Rice P, Horowitz BZ, Lord RV. Amphetamine toxicity: Experience with 127 cases. J Emerg Med 1989;7:157.

Dowling GP, McDonough ET, Bost RO. "Eve" and "Ecstasy": A report of five deaths associated with the use of MDEA and MDMA. JAMA 1987;257:1615.

Treffert DA, Joranson D. Restricting amphetamines. JAMA 1981;245:136.

CHAPTER 24–13

Phencyclidine Overdose

Scott D. Phillips, M.D., and Jeffrey Brent, M.D., Ph.D.

DEFINITION

Phencyclidine overdose is defined as the clinical sequelae resulting from the exposure to phencyclidine.

ETIOLOGY

In the 1960s, a new street drug known as the PeaCe Pill began being used in California. Since that time the use of this drug has waxed and waned in various sections of the United States. Phencyclidine, (phenylcyclohexylpiperidine Hcl) or PCP, is commonly abused for its euphoric and depersonalizing effects. When PCP is taken in excessive amounts, however, it can lead to life-threatening toxicity.

Overdosing on PCP may occur with a change in the purity of the street sample or if taken in an intentional suicide attempt. The patient may report the use of this drug; however, it is frequently misrepresented as another substance of abuse. Therefore, those accompanying any patient with an altered mental status to the hospital should be questioned as to the use of this or other mind-altering agents. Phencyclidine carries many street names (Table 24–13–1), a list of which may be useful in eliciting a history from a patient or friend. The toxic syndrome is very diverse and dose dependent. The range of toxicity may vary from mild agitation and euphoria to coma and death. Commonly, violent, bizarre behavior with remissions and unprovoked aggression occur. Alternatively, patients can present in a catatonic or comatose state with open blank staring eyes. Because PCP is frequently smoked, often in combination with marijuana, a finding of home-rolled cigarettes may be a clue.

TABLE 24–13–1. COMMON STREET NAMES FOR PHENCYCLIDINE (PCP)

Angel dust	Dummy dust	Hog
Dust	Trunks	Weed
Crystal	Monkey dust	Cadillac
Super grass	Mist	Sheets
Super joint	PeaCe pill	Peace weed
Snorts	Killer weed	Mint weed
Crystal joints	Cyclones	Elephant trunk
Rocket fuel	KW	Peace
Goon	Embalming fluid	Busy bee
Horse trunk	Soma	Scuffle
Surfer	TAC	TIC
"T"	Animal	Angel hair
Angel mist	Green	Kay jay
Special-la-coke	Super C	Wack
Pits	DOA	Dusted parsley
HCP	Kristal	Purple
Croak (PCP + freebase cocaine)		

CRITERIA FOR DIAGNOSIS
Suggestive

The diagnosis of PCP overdose is made by the history, clinical picture, and, if there is uncertainty as to the diagnosis, a positive qualitative test. If it is unclear why a patient has an altered sensorium, and PCP use is considered a possibility, urine should be sent to the toxicology laboratory for screening while supportive therapy is being instituted.

Definitive

Often, PCP is not part of the routine toxicologic screen. It is thus important for the clinician to alert the laboratory to look for this substance specifically. There are several methodologies that are capable of detecting PCP including, immunoassays, thin-layer chromatography, and gas chromatography with mass spectrometry. Immunoassays can detect PCP at a concentration of 25 ng/mL.

CLINICAL MANIFESTATIONS
Subjective

Phencyclidine, unlike cocaine, is not a favorite drug of the middle or upper class, and has geographic variations. In a large published series of PCP-intoxicated patients (McCarron et al., 1981), violent and sometimes bizarre behaviors were commonly reported. This aggressive behavior may be either outwardly or self-directed. Auditory hallucinations and/or delusions may occur. Patients are frequently amnestic to these events. Only 3% of patients in McCarron and colleagues' large series reported euphoria.

Objective
Physical Examination

The clinical findings vary with the degree of intoxication. With small to moderate doses of PCP (1–5 mg), patients commonly exhibit nystagmus, tachycardia, agitation, and possibly hypertension, incoordination, diaphoresis, and hyperacousis. The nystagmus is initially horizontal but may progress to vertical and possibly rotational forms. This marked nystagmus is a hallmark of PCP intoxication. Serious alterations of the vital signs are uncommon in mild to moderate intoxication. With increasing doses (5–10 mg), patients often present with sialorrhea, midrange pupils, myoclonus, shivering, repetitive motor movements, and altered cutaneous sensation. The circulatory problems with PCP intoxication are hypertension and dysrhythmias. With high-dose exposure (> 10 mg), hypertension, coma, seizures, decerebrate or opistotonic posturing, and absent deep pain sensation are common. Seizures are more likely to occur with ingestions of 0.5 to 1 mg/kg. In McCarron and colleagues' (1981) series, 18% were found nude and 11.5% exhib-

ited violent behavior. It is not uncommon to find a person extremely agitated and violent following the use of PCP. This behavior is often unpredictable and must be anticipated. Coingestants are frequently involved with PCP fatalities.

Routine Laboratory Abnormalities

Phencyclidine typically causes several serum chemical abnormalities. A majority of patients have elevated creatine phosphokinase levels due to muscle overactivity, restraints, violent behavior and seizures, and lactic acidosis. A direct toxic effect on the muscles has also been suggested. Hyperuricemia and hyperphosphatemia are the result of muscle breakdown, and myoglobinuria must be considered in heme-positive urine without red blood cells. Rhabdomyolosis is a common finding with PCP intoxication. Likewise, the serum transaminases are elevated in more than 50% of reported patients, possibly as a result of rhabdomyolosis. Hypoglycemia, often to very low levels, can occur. The white blood cell count is usually normal, but may exceed 20,000 mm^3. There are no specific laboratory abnormalities that are definitive for PCP intoxication.

There are no characteristic radiologic findings in PCP overdose other than complications such as fractures from violence and aspiration pneumonia. Acute bronchospasm has been seen and hyperaeration may develop. The only consistent electrocardiographic feature is tachycardia.

PLANS
Diagnostic
Differential Diagnosis

Several toxicants and medical conditions may mimic PCP intoxication. The toxicants that can mimic this condition include hallucinogenic amphetamines, amphetamines, cocaine, hallucinogens, and anticholinergics. Typically, PCP intoxication results in more violent behavior, though this may be difficult to decipher clinically.

Diagnostic Options and Recommended Approach

When in doubt, screening the urine for PCP is useful to establish a diagnosis. Many laboratories do not commonly screen for this basic substance as it is difficult to assay. Tests are available using gas chromatography with flame ionization or nitrogen-sensitive detectors. Gas–liquid chromatography with flame ionization is very useful for detection. Plasma levels of PCP do not correlate well with the clinical findings and are not useful guides to therapy. All positive urine screening should be confirmed with chromatographic techniques. Several PCP congeners are synthesized, such as 1-(1-phenylcyclohexyl) pyrrolidine (PHP), and special assays are needed to detect them. In general, these assays are not available.

Therapeutic
Therapeutic Options

If patients are agitated they should be restrained chemically and, if needed, physically, to prevent harm to themselves and the health care providers. Benzodiazepines and butyrophenones are agents of choice; however, phenothiazines should be avoided due to the potential risk of seizures. Talk down therapy is contraindicated with this overdose as it may provoke violent outbursts. The ABCs of life support must begin immediately with entry of the patient into the health care system. If the patient is unresponsive or has a compromised airway, endotracheal intubation is indicated early. This procedure may be complicated by laryngospasm and increased secretions. Because of the risk of cardiac arrhythmias, electrocardiographic monitoring and intravenous access are indicated in PCP intoxication. Most hypertension resolves within 6 hours; however, if there is sustained elevation of the blood pressure or evidence of end-organ impairment, pharmacologic control is indicated. Sublingual nifedipine (Procardia) 10 mg and/or a short-acting beta blocker such as esmolol (Brevibloc) 500 µg/kg/min for 1 minute followed by 50 µg/kg/min infusion may be used. The latter is beneficial as it may be titrated to the desired effect.

Seizures should be controlled with intravenous diazepam (Valium 2–5 mg), or a comparable benzodiazepine, in carefully titrated doses.

Status epilepticus requires phenytoin (Dilantin) in a 15 mg/kg loading dose or phenobarbital at doses similar to those of phenytoin. Continued seizure activity may require barbiturate therapy or chemical paralysis. The latter must be done with electroencephalographic monitoring. If the patient has had one seizure, it is reasonable to prophylactically administer a loading dose of phenytoin. One dose of activated charcoal and a cathartic should be given. Patients intoxicated with PCP are prone to unpredictable violent behavior. Thus, care must always be taken not to overstimulate the patient. The limited benefit of gastric lavage must be weighed against the potential violent agitation that may ensue. Hyperthermia must be aggressively controlled with antipyretics and external cooling. If the urine suggests myoglobin, adequate fluid replacement and enhanced diuresis with furosemide (Lasix) 20–40 mg intravenous bolus should be given.

Recommended Approach

As with most toxic ingestions, there is no specific antidote for PCP intoxication. Treatment is based on early suspicion and routine life support measures. With moderate to high doses of this agent, life-threatening events may unfold.

In following the course of this intoxication, it is important to monitor the blood sugar, creatine phosphokinase, calcium, phosphorus, electrolytes, and renal function. If myoglobinuria is noted, daily measures of the above chemistries and urine myoglobin are necessary. Gastric levels of PCP may be very high due to the drug's high pK_a and secretion into the stomach with consequent ion trapping. These high gastric levels can be seen even with nonoral overdoses. Urinary acidification should not be considered due to the increased separation of ferrihemate from the globin of myoglobin and subsequent nephrotoxicity. The possibility of myoglobinemia and consequent renal failure makes urinary acidification hazardous.

Phencyclidine psychosis is a true psychiatric emergency and requires immediate physical and pharmacologic control with benzodiazepines such as diazepam (Valium) 5 to 10 mg intravenously and lorazepam (Ativan) 1 to 5 mg intravenously titrated to control the patient. Because of their tendency to lower the seizure threshold, phenothiazines should be avoided in PCP-intoxicated patients.

FOLLOW-UP

Early in the evaluation of the patient, it is important to determine the intent of the exposure. Specifically was the overdose an abuser's miscalculation or an intentional attempt at suicide? Prior to discharge both types of patients need to be counseled about the fatal and nonfatal yet serious sequelae of this overdose.

Psychiatric evaluation is needed for any patient who has ingested sufficient quantities to result in overdose. If suicide is considered a possibility, then follow-up counseling is indicated within the appropriate in- or outpatient setting.

DISCUSSION
Prevalence and Incidence

Phencyclidine, as is true of many abused drugs, is geographic in its abuse patterns. The 1993 American Association of Poison Control Centers Annual Report describes 348 exposures with three deaths. This number has been similar since 1984. Because of this, PCP is confined to a few large urban centers. Therefore, some toxicology laboratories do not include phencyclidine in their routine screens. Phencyclidine was originally developed as a nonnarcotic anesthetic agent and marketed as Sernyl. With therapeutic use of this drug, a significant number of patients reported dysphoric reactions. Hence, the drug was removed from the market. It has also found use in veterinary medicine as a sedative and tranquilizer. In 1978 the sale of this product was halted from any legal market.

Related Basic Science

The drug is rapidly absorbed from most routes of administration: orally, intranasally, smoking, parenterally, or intravaginally. Following absorption, there is substantial tissue binding with rapid uptake by the brain and adipose tissue. Its volume of distribution is very large.

The half-life of PCP is prolonged in overdose patients. In normal volunteers it ranges from 7 to 50 hours. In overdose, depending on the patient, it may be between 11 and 89 hours. Phencyclidine is metabolized by conjugation and by hydroxylation. Only 10% is excreted unchanged in the urine. If the drug is smoked, a large portion is pyrolyzed.

Phencyclidine is secreted into the stomach, and because it is basic with a pK_a of 8.5, it is ion trapped at gastric pH values. Thus, gastric aspiration may theoretically continue to remove the drug for prolonged periods.

Phencyclidine acts at specific receptors in the brain. The highest concentrations are found in the frontal and temporal cortex and in the hippocampus. PCP acts at the neuronal level to block sodium and potassium channels, prolonging the action potential. This facilitates calcium entry and release of presynaptic noradrenergic neurotransmitters. There are also effects on many other neurotransmitters. Phencyclidine's psychotomimetic state may in part be due to the blockade of transmission at the N-methyl-D-aspartic acid receptor. Phencyclidine blocks both muscarinic and nicotinic receptors. It also binds to aspartate-sensitive glutamate and sigma opiate receptors. It may also act as a dopamine agonist.

The complications that develop following PCP use are usually secondary to violence or trauma. As patients proceed through a PCP overdose, they may develop a syndrome that is known as dopamine storm. Because PCP may cause excessive dopaminergic activity, hypertensive crisis with stroke or other end-organ damage may occur. Dopamine storm may have no prodrome.

The PCP psychosis may be divided into three phases. The initial phase is characterized by violence and lasts about 5 hours. This is followed by a calming period of equal duration with occasional outbursts. The final phase is one of resolution and reorientation.

Prevention

Education of the public is the only form of prevention that is effective. As with all drugs of abuse, early education into the harsh effects of PCP is needed. The recent regulations by the Department of Transportation, which requires drug testing in regulated industries, place many physicians in the position of interpreting mandated tests.

Cost Containment

The judicious use of the toxicology laboratory, based on the clinical presentation of the patient, will not only confirm the diagnosis but limit expenses. Liberal use of certified regional poison centers is an immediately available, inexpensive source of assistance.

Simply ordering a battery of laboratory tests and screens is very expensive and of no therapeutic aid. Laboratory screens are confirmatory and should complement the clinical picture.

REFERENCES

Bailey DN, Shaw RF, Guba JJ. Phencyclidine abuse: Plasma levels and clinical findings in casual users and in phencyclidine related deaths. J Anal Toxicol 1978;2:233.

Clark HW. The role of physicians as medical review officers in workplace drug testing programs: In pursuit of the last nomogram. West J Med 1990;152:514.

Javitt DC, Zylberman I, Zukin SR, et al. Amelioration of negative symptoms in schizophrenia by glycine. Am J Psychiatry 1994;151:1234.

McCarron MM, Schulze BW, Thompson GA, et al. Acute phencyclidine intoxication: Incidence of clinical findings in 1000 cases. Ann Emerg Med 1981;10:237.

Rappolt RT, Gay GR, Farris RD. Emergency management of acute phencyclidine intoxication. J Am Coll Emerg Phys 1979;8(2):68.

Wood PL, Rao TS, et al. A review of the in vitro and in vivo neurochemical characterizations of the NMDA/PCP/glycine/ion channel receptor monocomplex. Neurochem Res 1990;15:217.

CHAPTER 24–14

Cocaine Overdose

Lewis Goldfrank, M.D.

DEFINITION

Cocaine overdose is defined as any significant psychological and/or physiologic imbalance caused by nasal insufflation, ingestion, smoking, or injection of cocaine.

ETIOLOGY

The condition is caused by an overdose of cocaine. The etiology as defined by the patient is rationale for using cocaine. Reasons for cocaine usage are related to patient behavior and include submission to peer pressure, a desire to "experiment," cultural influences, and emotional and psychiatric problems.

CRITERIA FOR DIAGNOSIS
Suggestive

The emergency department is the usual clinical setting in which patients with cocaine overdose are seen. The fact that cocaine is invariably used illegally often leads to a delay prior to hospital presentation. Patients rarely present to the emergency department before complete absorption, and owing to the very short half-life of cocaine (30–80 minutes depending on the route of administration), the peak effects are often reached prior to emergency department arrival.

The patient history is commonly unreliable with regard to utilization of a specific toxin. Frequently, the patient has bought a mixture of preparations and often is sold something other than that which was requested.

Any neuropsychiatric abnormality, especially in young adults, should be considered as a possible cocaine-related pathologic event. In particular, the presence of excessive adrenergic discharge resulting in agitation, seizures, hyperthermia, hypertension, hyperactive bowel sounds, diaphoresis, vomiting, hyperreflexia, and dysrhythmias should suggest cocaine toxicity.

Definitive

A definitive diagnosis of cocaine overdose is made by the presence of sympathetic hyperactivity coupled with the detection of cocaine or its first metabolite, benzoylecgonine, in the patient's serum or urine.

CLINICAL MANIFESTATIONS
Subjective

Whereas most patients abusing the drug neither seek nor are brought to a clinical facility, those who do may present with dramatic central nervous system or cardiovascular system complaints. Patients may manifest any neuropsychiatric abnormality, but dysphoria, anxiety, agitation, and hallucinations (auditory, visual, and tactile) are commonly noted. Otolaryngologic manifestations include atrophic nasal mucosa, rhinitis, sinusitis, and hoarseness. Cardiovascular complaints include pounding headaches associated with palpitations and typical or atypical chest pain suggesting angina pectoris or myocardial infarction. Sudden death can occur. Nausea, vomiting, abdominal pain, diaphoresis, and tachypnea are also commonly noted. Obstetric and neonatal complications include abortions, abruptio placentae, preterm labor, low birth weight, and congenital abnormalities all due probably to uteroplacental vascular insufficiency. Patients may be brought to the emergency department after a presumed or witnessed seizure or cardiovascular collapse.

Objective
Physical Examination

The physical examination may demonstrate tachycardia (frequently irregular), tachypnea, hypertension, and hyperthermia. In a massive overdose, cardiovascular collapse manifested by hypotension and shock may ensue. Hyperthermia is commonly associated with extreme agitation and/or seizures. Massive overdose may lead to respiratory compromise.

Other physical findings of importance may be associated with the route of cocaine administration. White powder may be found on the nares and atrophy or perforation of the nasal septum may be noted. Parenteral abuse leads to subcutaneous or venous scarring—"skin popping" scars or "tracks." The pupils are usually mydriatic, the reflexes are hyperactive, bowel sounds are active, and the patient may be diaphoretic. Obvious and occult trauma are frequent findings in the patient with an altered sensorium.

Routine Laboratory Abnormalities

The electrocardiogram may demonstrate frequent premature atrial or ventricular contractions. Supraventricular or ventricular tachycardia may be seen. Ventricular fibrillation may occur in massive overdoses or as a result of prolonged hypoxia due to pulmonary edema. Signs of myocardial ischemia, injury, and infarction may be evident.

The white blood cell count is usually elevated, and a shift to the left may be noted.

Both hyperglycemia and hypoglycemia have been noted.

The electrolytes may demonstrate a wide-anion-gap metabolic acidosis if seizures, agitation, tissue ischemia, or hypoperfusion is present.

The chest radiograph may reveal evidence of pulmonary edema, a pneumothorax, pneumopericardium, pneumomediastinum, and a widened mediastinum suggesting aortic dissection. The radiograph of the abdomen may demonstrate round, or fingerlike, radiopaque densities suggestive of balloons or condoms which represent the vehicle for the body packers' transport of cocaine.

The urinalysis may be dipstick positive for blood without any evidence of red blood cells on microscopy, suggesting myoglobinuria and rhabdomyolysis. Cocaine has the potential to affect almost every major organ system and result in diverse complications (Table 24–14–1).

PLANS
Diagnostic
Differential Diagnosis

Cocaine overdose must be differentiated from other central nervous system stimulant overdoses or sedative–hypnotic withdrawal, thyrotoxicosis, heat stroke, and sepsis, as well as central nervous system infections, trauma, and hemorrhage.

Diagnostic Options

Any patient who exhibits unexplained sympathetic hyperactivity should have his or her serum or urine analyzed for cocaine and other toxic substances.

Recommended Approach

There is no other approach to the problem. Most patients with cocaine overdose are brought to an emergency department. The facility should be able to perform the necessary tests on the blood or urine.

Therapeutic
Therapeutic Options

The treatment for cocaine overdosage includes the maintenance of a patent airway; the prevention of aspiration; the prevention of the absorption of as much drug as possible; the control of agitation; and the management of hypertension, cardiac dysrhythmias, and myocardial ischemia and infarction.

TABLE 24–14–1. MULTISYSTEM EFFECTS OF COCAINE

Metabolic	Hyperthermia, lactic acidosis, weight loss
Eyes	Mydriasis (reactive), vertical and horizontal nystagmus, pseudoexophthalmos, lid lag, keratopathy
Nose and throat	Epistaxis, atrophic mucosa, ulcerations, septal perforations (snorting), sinusitis, ?epiglottitis
Cardiovascular	Tachycardia (supraventricular, ventricular) or bradycardia, hypertension, arrhythmias (ventricular fibrillation), vasomotor collapse, acute heart failure (high output), endocarditis, rupture of dissecting aneurysm, coronary vasospasm, angina, myocardial infarction, cardiomyopathy
Respiratory	Rapid and irregular breathing, diffusion abnormalities, (smoking), pneumothorax (smoking), pneumomediastinum (smoking), pneumopericardium (smoking), hoarseness (smoking), bronchitis (smoking), bronchiolitis obliterans, (smoking), pneumonia
Gastrointestinal	Anorexia, nausea, vomiting, diarrhea, abdominal pain, gangrenous or ischemic bowel
Skin	Self-induced sores or linear excoriations, "coke burns," phlebitis secondary to intravenous cocaine, pallor and infarction, vasculitis
Psychiatric	Decreased rapid eye movement sleep, agitation, hallucinations, anxiety or depression, psychosis, paranoia, suicidal ideation, altered tactile sensation—"cocaine bugs"
Neurologic	Tonic–clonic seizures, tremor, headache, restlessness, confusion, subarachnoid hemorrhage, vasculitis, intracerebral hemorrhage, cerebral infarction, brain abscess, movement disorders
Musculoskeletal	Muscle infarction, rhabdomyolysis, myoglobinuria, wound botulism
Genitourinary	Renal vasculitis, acute tubular necrosis, renal infarction, priapism (urethral use), paraphimosis (urethral use)
Obstetric	Spontaneous abortion, abruptio placentae, lower birth weight

Source: Lewin NA, Goldfrank LR, Weisman RS. Cocaine. In: Goldfrank LR, Flomenbaum NE, Lewin NA, et al., eds. Goldfrank's Toxicologic Emergencies. 4th ed. Norwalk, CT: Appleton & Lange, 1990:501. Reproduced with permission from the publisher and author.

There are no other therapeutic options. The recommended approach is discussed below.

Recommended Approach

Patients are usually treated in the emergency department and frequently admitted to an intensive care unit.

The general management of the oral cocaine overdose is identical to that for other toxic or oral ingestions, including initial assessment of the airway, as well as an evaluation as to whether activated charcoal should be given immediately by mouth or via an orogastric tube (36–40 French). Because cocaine may cause sudden changes in the patient's clinical status, syrup of ipecac is not recommended. In view of the potential for death associated with seizures and/or dysrhythmias, endotracheal intubation should be accomplished immediately in these circumstances and this should be followed by gastric lavage. An ionic cathartic (magnesium sulfate, 30 g) or sorbitol 70% (50 mL) can be used to achieve a catharsis.

Anxiety, agitation, and psychosis should be managed initially in a supportive, calm environment. The patient's airway should be secured and 100% oxygen provided. A patient with an altered mental status should have the level of blood glucose determined and be given at least 50 mL of 50% dextrose, 2.0 mg of naloxone, and 100 mg of thiamine intravenously. An intravenous benzodiazepine such as diazepam 5 to 10 mg repeated each 5 to 10 minutes, or lorazepam 1 to 2 mg repeated each 10 to 15 minutes, should be used to achieve a calm state. Diazepam or lorazepam may also be effective in the management of seizures (particularly status epilepticus), but phenytoin 15 to 18 mg/kg intravenously at less than or equal 50 mg per minute, or phenobarbital 15 to 20 mg/kg intravenously over 15 to 20 minutes, should be used concomitantly.

Phenothiazines and haloperidol have no clinical advantage over the benzodiazepines (diazepam or lorazepam) in the acutely agitated state. In fact, the alpha-adrenergic blockage associated with these neuroleptic agents may complicate the management should hypotension develop. There may also be an increased risk of seizures and the potential for the development of a dystonic reaction. It is for these reasons that diazepam or lorazepam is preferred.

In the face of hyperthermia, diazepam or lorazepam may be necessary to control the agitation or seizures usually responsible for the initiation or persistence of the elevated temperature. Simultaneously the patient should be cooled with mechanical means, such as fans, ice, and cold water. If the body temperature exceeds 105°F, aggressive cooling while maintaining the airway and protecting the patient is indicated.

Hypertension is invariably short-lived and is usually treated by accomplishing sedation. In the face of central nervous system or cardiovascular compromise, nitroprusside or the alpha antagonist phentolamine is indicated. Dysrhythmias associated with overdose can usually be managed by oxygenation, sedation, cooling if the patient is febrile, and a calcium channel blocker for atrial dysrhythmias or lidocaine and/or sodium bicarbonate for ventricular dysrhythmias. Myocardial ischemia or infarction in patients who have cocaine-associated chest pain is not uncommon. No clinical parameters available to the physician can adequately identify patients at very low risk for myocardial infarction. Therefore, all patients with cocaine-associated chest pain should be evaluated for myocardial infarction. All therapeutic gestures for other patients with myocardial infarction should be considered in this patient population.

The use of beta-adrenergic antagonists is contraindicated in the management of acute cocaine intoxication.

Other complications of cocaine overdose include subarachnoid hemorrhage, cerebrovascular accidents, rhabdomyolysis, myoglobinuria, acute tubular necrosis, aortic dissection, mesenteric ischemia, cardiac dysrhythmias, myocardial infarction, abruptio placentae, and abortion and are discussed in other chapters in this book.

FOLLOW-UP

Cocaine overdose requires hospital admission 10 to 25% of the time depending on the patient population, clinical course, and dose and route of drug utilization. Whether the patient is hospitalized or not, entry into a drug detoxification program is essential. Suicidal intent should always be a consideration in any overdosed patient. Patients withdrawing from cocaine are frequently quite depressed, also necessitating a psychiatric assessment.

The desire to begin reusing this drug should prompt an immediate follow-up visit to the physician. Patients should be advised to contact a health care worker for depression or suicidal ideation.

DISCUSSION
Prevalence and Incidence

Cocaine use and abuse have become a worldwide problem irrespective of economic class as the "market" prices have fallen. The only occupation associated directly with cocaine overdose is the body packer, an individual who transports containers (rubber, plastic or condoms) in his or her intestine from the site of production (growth and processing) throughout South America to North America or Europe.

Cocaine is often sold under many street names, such as Snow, Rock, Crystal, Caine, Dame Blanc, and Pimp's Drug. Cocaine has varied street values, but today a gram can be obtained in New York City for $40 to $60. In excess of 10 million people on an annual basis may use cocaine, either sporadically or as dependent individuals. The marked increase in use by young adults has been fostered by the smokable (nonpyrolyzed) cocaine alkaloid or crack. This form is available in vials from $5 to $10 for relatively pure 100-mg samples.

Related Basic Science

Cocaine, a natural alkaloid derived from the coca leaf, is used clinically for its anesthetic and vasoconstrictive effects. Cocaine is abused for its central nervous system stimulatory effects. In its pure form, cocaine is available as a white crystallike powder. This powder may either be the cocaine salt, which is highly water soluble, subject to pyrolysis, not vaporizable, and easily used for insufflation and intravenous use; or the cocaine base, which is not water soluble, not subject to pyrolysis, and can therefore be smoked. The freebase form most readily available today is crack. Crack is usually smoked in a pipe rather than used by insufflation or the intravenous route. It is called crack because of the distinctive popping sound made while it burns.

Cocaine may be sold with multiple adulterants, including varied local anesthetics (procaine, lidocaine, tetracaine), stimulants (caffeine, amphetamines, phencyclidine, phenylpropanolamine), hallucinogens (lysergic acid diethylamide [LSD], hashish), opioids (codeine, heroin), depressants (methapyrilene), inert substances (starch, sugar, flour), or varied substances, such as baking soda, quinine, and many others.

Absorption via the intranasal route (15 minutes) is more rapid than via the oral route (30 minutes), but both routes offer excellent bioavailability. Peak levels are noted between 1 and 2 hours after oral or intranasal use. Smoking and intravenous use lead to the onset of clinical effects in 1 to 2 minutes.

Metabolism is primarily by plasma cholinesterase, forming large quantities of benzoylecgonine and ecgonine methyl ester. Approximately 30 to 45% of each metabolite is noted, and 10 to 20% of the cocaine is excreted unchanged in the urine.

Natural History and Its Modification with Treatment

The problems associated with cocaine abuse are dependent on the dose used, the drugs admixed, the route of administration, and the patient's underlying clinical condition. If the patient does not manifest seizures, life-threatening hyperthermia, ventricular dysrhythmias, pulmonary edema, posthypoxic encephalopathy, a subarachnoid hemorrhage, or an acute myocardial infarction, the immediate prognosis with treatment is excellent. When these conditions are manifest, the rapidity of initiation of therapy defines the extent of the morbidity and mortality; however, the long-term prognosis is dependent on the patient's desire to become abstinent as well as the previous length and extent of exposure to the risks of parenteral drug abuse.

Unfortunately, the prognosis for a pregnant woman, her pregnancy, and her newborn is much less optimistic. Cocaine can be lethal with the absorption of very small doses and blood levels at autopsy have been extremely variable.

Prevention

Public education and transformation of the "drug" problem from the legal to the medical and social arenas may enhance awareness and decrease utilization. Early intervention in schools and homes is essential from both prophylactic and preventive points of view.

Patients must be made aware that there is no safe way to use cocaine. Cocaine use and abuse (whether insufflated, smoked, or ingested) is potentially lethal and is associated with multiple local and systemic complications. The subcutaneous and intravenous uses of cocaine are associated with all the pharmacologic complications of other cocaine use as well as every potential infection with common to rare bacteria (*Staphylococcus aureus* to *Clostridium botulinum*), fungi, and common to previously rare viruses (hepatitis to HIV).

Patients should know that there is no safe way to buy or use illicit drugs. Buyers can be given anything from sugar to salt, from heroin to strychnine, and, most commonly, lidocaine and phencyclidine. Physicians should stress the psychologically and physiologically addictive potential of the drug. In addition, use of this drug often leads to tremendous financial, social, and occupational burdens. Abstinence and psychosocial support are essential. Drug rehabilitation in a health care facility should be offered.

Cost Containment

The appropriate clinical assessment of a cocaine overdose may allow the physician to ask for specific qualitative toxicology and avoid "screens." Education in the field of drug abuse prevents loss of life and limb, infection, loss of jobs and families, street violence to self (prostitution) and others (robbery), as well as recurrent emergency department visits and hospitalizations. Rehabilitation programs, job training, and education may have a dramatic impact on drug-related hospital costs.

Once the patient is stabilized following cocaine overdosage, long-term intensive care unit or nonpsychiatric hospital care is not indicated.

REFERENCES

Catravas JD, Waters IW. Acute cocaine intoxication in conscious dogs: Studies on the mechanism of lethality. J Pharmacol Exp Ther 1981;271:350.

Goldfrank LR, Hoffman RS. The cardiovascular effects of cocaine. Ann Emerg Med 1991;20:165.

Hoffman RS, Henry GL, Weisman RS, et al. Association between life-threatening cocaine toxicity and plasma cholinesterase activity. Ann Emerg Med 1991;21:247.

Hollander JE, Hoffman RS, Gennis P, et al. Prospective multicenter evaluation of cocaine associated chest pain. Acad Emerg Med 1994;1:330.

Lange RA, Cigarroa RG, Flores ED. Potentiation of cocaine-induced coronary vasoconstriction by beta-adrenergic blockade. Ann Intern Med 1990;112:897.

Roth D, Alarcon FJ, Fernandez JA, et al. Acute rhabdomyolysis associated with cocaine intoxication. N Engl J Med 1988;319:673.

CHAPTER 24–15

Marijuana Abuse

Patrick E. McKinney, M.D., and Ken Kulig, M.D.

DEFINITION

Marijuana abuse is defined as the repeated use of this drug in a manner that deviates from approved medical or social patterns within a given culture.

ETIOLOGY

The marijuana or hemp plant is known under Linnean nomenclature as *Cannabis sativa*. It is an upright, annual herb, indigenous to the United States and grows both wild and cultivated in North and South America. Marijuana is available in several forms. The leaf form is generally sold in some increment of an ounce or as a single cigarette. This may be smoked as a cigarette or in a pipe or it may be ingested, traditionally as cookies or brownies. The resin may be processed to hashish, which is usually smoked. Less commonly available is hashish oil, which can be applied to a cigarette and smoked. On the streets, occasionally a substance is available that is sold as THC; however, this is commonly not marijuana at all but may be a variety of other drugs such as phencyclidine (PCP) or lysergic acid diethylamide (LSD).

CRITERIA FOR DIAGNOSIS
Suggestive

Marijuana intoxication may be clinically suspected by the presence of injected conjunctiva, frequent and occasionally inappropriate laughter, drowsiness, inability to concentrate, and poor attention span. Use may also be suspected by gradual decline in work or school performance, decline in personal hygiene, and decreased ability to communicate, as well as other nonspecific indicators of drug dependence. Perhaps the most common clinical scenario occurs when random urine drug screening detects unsuspected marijuana use.

Definitive

Definitive diagnosis of marijuana use is made by the finding of Δ^9-tetrahydrocannibinol carboxylic acid or a cannabinoid metabolite in a patient's urine. Criteria in the *Diagnostic and Statistical Manual,* fourth edition, of the American Psychiatric Association for cannabis abuse include a pattern of pathologic use, impairment in social or occupational functioning due to cannabis use, and duration of the disturbance of at least 1 month. Criteria for dependence add tolerance to the items listed above.

CLINICAL MANIFESTATIONS

Subjective

The individual response to marijuana is highly variable, depending on dose, user familiarity, the expectations and personality of the user, as well as local surroundings. Effects include euphoria, feelings of intoxication or "fogginess," relaxation, friendliness, and laughter and alterations of perception, especially involving taste, hearing, tactile stimulation, and passage of time. Appetite may be augmented. At higher doses, dysphoria, depersonalization, anxiety, and feelings of paranoia and psychosis can occur, but these reactions are rare. Many of the reports involving these adverse psychiatric reactions originate in countries where the typical daily cannabis dose is much higher than that of the typical American cannabis user.

Objective

Physical Examination

The most common and reliable physical finding of marijuana intoxication is conjunctival injection. Pulse rate and cardiac output may increase. Blood pressure usually remains constant although orthostatic hypotension can occur. Specific abnormalities are generally not detectable on neurological examination. Intoxicated subjects may show decrease in stability of stance, reaction speed, and performance of complex tasks, but these abnormalities are only sporadically detectable by formal neurobehavioral testing, and the practical clinical significance of these findings is uncertain.

Chronic abusers may present with pulmonary findings similar to those found in chronic tobacco users. Acute bronchitic episodes, chronic cough, and squamous metaplasia are present in greater frequency compared with nonsmokers. *Aspergillus* or other fungal spores may contaminate marijuana; the significance of this in users with normal immune function is unknown. Cancer and chronic obstructive pulmonary disease have not been causally linked to marijuana smoking at this time, perhaps because the majority of users are young and use is sporadic. As the current population of users ages, however, more information on this subject should become available.

Routine Laboratory Abnormalities

Abnormalities of routine hematologic and serochemical parameters including complete blood count, electrolytes, and liver and renal function studies are not usually seen. Thus, the diagnosis of marijuana use can be made only on the basis of a positive history or urine drug screen.

PLANS

Diagnostic

Differential Diagnosis

Marijuana users rarely present to the emergency department because of acute intoxication. The differential diagnosis for marijuana-associated dysphoric reactions, uncommon toxic psychoses, and acute paranoid states may include intoxication with hallucinogens, sympathomimetics, phencyclidine, or anticholinergic agents; sedative or ethanol withdrawal; and primary psychiatric disease.

Diagnostic Options

Diagnostic options include a history of drug use and a urine drug screen for drugs of abuse. Most routine urine drug screens do not identify hallucinogens unless specifically requested. Physical examination findings of mydriasis, fever, and hypertension should suggest intoxication with substances other than marijuana.

The urine drug screen involves the detection of metabolites of Δ^9-tetrahydrocannibinol (THC). THC peaks in the blood about halfway through smoking a marijuana cigarette or "joint." Within 2 hours, THC and metabolites, known collectively as cannabinoids, are detectable in the urine. The infrequent user may shed metabolites in the urine and thus have a positive urine drug screen for 3 to 5 days after a single joint. Chronic users may have positive drug screens from several weeks to almost 2 months in rare cases.

The initial urine toxicology screen usually involves an immunoassay. A positive test should be followed by confirmation by an alternative assay method such as high-performance liquid chromatography or, more commonly, gas chromatography–mass spectrometry. The immunoassays currently available have a wide range of sensitivity, with cutoff levels ranging from 10 to 100 ng/mL. Intuitively, a lower cutoff would seem desirable; however, this lower detection limit also increases the risk of detecting a positive test secondary to passive inhalation. Studies evaluating urine levels of cannabinoids after passive exposure to marijuana smoke have detected levels ranging from nondetectable to more than 100 ng/mL in extreme circumstances. Based on multiple studies, it is possible that a urine drug screen reported as positive at a cutoff of 20 ng/mL may be secondary to passive inhalation. Under extreme conditions of passive inhalation, a urine drug screen with a cutoff of 50 ng/mL may be reported as positive, but most authors believe this is not likely to occur under realistic conditions. Newer Department of Transportation guidelines use an initial cutoff for a positive level of marijuana metabolites in the urine of 50 ng/mL. The confirmatory test level is 15 ng/mL.

There is some concern that intentional tampering of urine specimens may interfere with testing for cannabinoids. Depending on the specific assay, bleach, salt, sodium bicarbonate, hydrogen peroxide, glutaraldehyde, and herbs such as golden seal have been used to mask cannabinoid presence with varying success. The presence of these substances should suggest specimen tampering and may be a cause for employment termination.

Recommended Approach

Patients who are medically stable and admit to marijuana use do not need an extensive evaluation. Confirmatory testing should be done in those patients whose initial urine screen is positive if the patient denies illicit drug use and in whom a false-positive test could have deleterious medicolegal consequences.

Therapeutic

The treatment of acute marijuana intoxication rarely requires pharmacologic intervention. Agitation, paranoia, and psychosis generally respond to observation and reassurance in a quiet, nonthreatening environment. If necessary, a mild sedative such as diazepam 5 to 10 mg orally or intravenously may be beneficial. Antipsychotics are generally not needed. Chronic abuse and dependence problems should be referred to a psychiatrist.

FOLLOW-UP

Follow-up is not usually required.

DISCUSSION

Prevalence and Incidence

Despite recent increases in the use of cocaine, marijuana remains the most frequently used illicit drug in America. More than 50% of young adults admitted to using marijuana as of 1993, and use appears to be increasing in the high school population. Marijuana use remains most prevalent among adolescents and young adults; however, there are also users in the preteen group as well as an aging population of baby boomers that continues recreational use of marijuana.

Related Basic Science

The active ingredient in marijuana belongs to a group of compounds known as cannabinoids. Of more than 60 cannabinoids identified in marijuana, only 2 are known to be psychoactive: THC and its 11-hydroxy metabolite. Peak serum levels of THC usually occur within 3 to 8 minutes of smoking a joint, then drop rapidly as the compound is distributed to tissue compartments. Psychotropic effects begin over a similar time frame and persist for 2 to 3 hours. Peak subjective high occurs 30 to 90 minutes after peak plasma THC. After oral ingestion, peak plasma levels of THC do not occur until approximately 2 hours after ingestion and peak high occurs at approximately 3 hours.

Δ^9-Tetrahydrocannibinol is metabolized largely in the liver by the P450 system. The major metabolite found in the urine and the plasma is 11-nor-THC-9-carboxylic acid. The terminal half-life of THC is 20 hours or greater. The drug is highly lipophilic and because of this it may be detected in the urine up to 6 to 8 weeks after cessation of use.

Marijuana cigarettes may also be adulterated with other substances such as phencyclidine, formaldehyde, and herbicides. The flowering tops of unpollinated female plants contain a larger percentage of the active ingredient, THC, compared with the rest of the plant and are called sensemilla. Presently, it is estimated that marijuana available in the United States contains between 1 and 7% THC, a figure that has been gradually rising since the 1960s.

There is no information regarding the lethal dose of THC in humans and there have been no reported fatalities attributed solely to marijuana. As mentioned previously, higher doses are associated rarely with paranoia, delirium, and psychosis. Although marijuana itself is not a hallucinogen, it has been associated with flashbacks in persons who have used LSD in the past.

With acute intoxication, the conjunctiva become reddened. Marijuana lowers intraocular pressure; there is no consistent effect on the pupils. Muscle strength is decreased and appetite may be increased or decreased.

Acute intoxication is accompanied by a consistent tachycardia. This is probably secondary to decreased vagal tone. Blood pressure usually remains constant, although there may be slight orthostatic hypotension.

Respiratory effects include bronchodilation with short-term use. Heavy use has been associated with chronic cough, chronic bronchitis, squamous metaplasia, reduction in forced expiratory volume in 1 second, and reduced airway conductance and diffusing capacity. Other studies confirm mild impairment of large airway function. Marijuana smoke inhibits alveolar macrophages in a dose-dependent manner. As with tobacco smoking, carbon monoxide levels may be elevated.

The influence of cannabis on immunity is uncertain. Several studies have shown evidence of decreased number and function of T lymphocytes, but subsequent studies have not confirmed these findings and there has been no clinical evidence of increased susceptibility to infection in marijuana users. Studies also provide conflicting evidence regarding the relationship between cannabis and chromosomal abnormalities. The clinical significance of these abnormalities is unknown. Low birth weight, shorter gestational period, and an increase in major malformations has been reported in users compared with nonusers; however, definite association between maternal marijuana use and fetal abnormalities has not been made. Marijuana smoke has been shown to induce malignant transformation of animal cell lines in vitro.

Decreased testosterone levels have been well documented in marijuana smokers. Morphologic sperm abnormalities and decreased sexual functioning have been noted in heavy users. There is a tenuous association between cannabis and gynecomastia. Follicle-stimulating and luteinizing hormones may also be decreased, resulting in inhibition of ovulation.

Initial reports of cerebral atrophy associated with chronic cannabis use were noted using pneumoencephalography as a diagnostic tool, but these findings were not confirmed with later studies using computed tomography. Studies done in the United States have shown conflicting results regarding the presence of residual psychomotor impairment. Likewise, the presence of "amotivational syndrome" has not been firmly established and may represent a subgroup of users with preexisting psychiatric pathology. Physical dependence is rare but some tolerance to the effects of marijuana may be seen.

In summary, the health hazards of marijuana remain to be clearly defined. Cannabis use does not appear to present a greater health risk than tobacco or ethanol. It is probably prudent to recommend abstinence from marijuana in adolescents, pregnant or lactating women, cardiac patients, and persons engaging in activities where optimum mental and physical performance is desired. Also, patients with a psychiatric history should probably not engage in recreational drug use.

Natural History and Its Modification with Treatment

Morbidity solely from marijuana use is rare. Chronic abusers may require psychiatric treatment for abuse or dependence.

Prevention

The best tool for prevention of any behavior that may have adverse health effects is education. Widespread availability of nonbiased information to target populations including school-aged children and young adults would be beneficial. Urine drug screening may play some role in prevention by detecting users who may deny a drug problem.

The marijuana user who presents because of health-related complaints or social problems secondary to chronic use may be amenable to education regarding the adverse effects of chronic cannabis use or other drugs. There is some information that should be passed on to all patients known to be marijuana users, whether sporadic or chronic. The amount of tar delivered to the lung by an average joint is about four times greater than that of a comparable tobacco cigarette. Marijuana smoking is associated with acute bronchitis, and although there is no direct evidence connecting marijuana with lung cancer or chronic obstructive pulmonary disease, it may be advisable to warn chronic, daily smokers of these theoretical hazards. Immunocompromised patients who smoke marijuana for its antiemetic properties should be warned of the theoretical risk of exposure to *Aspergillus* or other fungal spores. Because of the resultant tachycardia, patients with coronary artery disease should be advised to avoid marijuana. Studies have shown decreased sperm count and testosterone levels. These changes have not been shown to be associated with infertility and their significance is unknown. Women who are moderate users of marijuana may have an increased number of anovulatory cycles compared with nonusers. At least one case of prepubertal arrest was noted in a 16-year-old boy that resolved on cessation of the drug. The data regarding residual psychomotor impairment and amotivational syndrome are inconsistent. Studies in which residual impairment is suggested involve chronic users. Although illegal drug use should not be condoned, it appears that occasional mild marijuana use in healthy individuals poses little long-term health risk, although it may cause temporary cognitive impairment, making driving or operating machinery hazardous. Adolescents, because of their progressing psychosocial and hormonal development, persons with preexisting mental disorders, and pregnant and nursing women should be cautioned to avoid any marijuana use.

Cost Containment

Most medically related problems ascribed to marijuana can be treated on an outpatient basis. Psychiatric care may be provided on both an inpatient and an outpatient basis. The cost–benefit ratio of drug screening must be carefully weighed.

REFERENCES

Cone E, Johnson R. Contact highs and urinary cannabinoid excretion after passive exposure to marijuana smoke. Clin Pharmacol Ther 1986;40:247.

Hollister LE. Health aspects of cannabis. Pharmacol Rev 1986;38:1.

Perez-Reyes M, Di Guiseppi S, Mason A, Davis K. Passive inhalation of marihuana smoke and urinary excretion of cannabinoids. Clin Pharmacol 1983;34:36.

Selden BS, Clark RF, Curry SC. Marijuana. Emerg Med Clin North Am 1990;8:527.

Tashkin DP. Pulmonary complications of smoked substance abuse. West J Med 1990;152:525.

Thomas HUW. Psychiatric symptoms in cannabis users. Br J Psychiatry 1993;163:141.

CHAPTER 24–16

Phenothiazine Overdose

Thomas Eglin, M.D.

DEFINITION

A phenothiazine overdose occurs with the intentional or unintentional ingestion of a phenothiazine drug that causes acute psychological or physiologic adverse effects.

ETIOLOGY

Intentional overdoses in adults are most common in depressed psychiatric patients who have been prescribed phenothiazines for psychotic disorders. Most of these are suicide attempts or gestures. Accidental overdoses usually occur in pediatric patients who inadvertently ingest medications belonging to relatives.

CRITERIA FOR DIAGNOSIS

Suggestive

An overdose is most easily diagnosed by the history of an individual taking a potentially toxic amount (15–150 mg/kg) of one of the major tranquilizers. If the history is unavailable, the diagnosis depends on a high clinical suspicion in a patient who presents with altered mental status or cardiovascular instability.

Definitive

A definite diagnosis of phenothiazine overdose may be established only by the appropriate historical and/or physical findings in association with the identification of urinary phenothiazine metabolites by toxicologic screening; quantitative levels are seldom available unless sent to a specialized reference laboratory.

CLINICAL MANIFESTATIONS

Subjective

Overdoses with these drugs are usually seen in patients with previously diagnosed psychiatric disease, as major tranquilizers are not widely distributed except to this group. The history cannot be depended on to exclude a toxic overdose unless verified by a reliable source. Some patients seek treatment complaining of depression and may not mention the overdose.

Phenothiazines are sedating drugs, but toxic doses frequently cause central nervous system excitability and other anticholinergic symptoms such as dry mouth, blurred vision, and flushing.

Objective

Physical Examination

Phenothiazines exert their major toxic effects on the cardiovascular and central nervous systems.

Sedation occurs early and may be profound, with coma unresponsive to any stimulus. The strong anticholinergic effects may produce delirium and combative behavior, as well as tachycardia, flushing, hypothermia or hyperthermia, pupillary changes, and decreased gastrointestinal motility.

Hypotension is common to all classes of phenothiazine overdoses, although it is more common to the classes with the piperidine and dimethyl substitutions (see Related Basic Science).

Cardiac effects and death are far more common with the piperidine-substituted drugs thioridazine (Mellaril) and mesoridazine (Serentil). They exhibit quinidine-like effects that produce long PR, QT, and QRS intervals with ST-segment and T-wave changes seen on the electrocardiogram. Calcium channel blocking effects add to hypotension and atrioventricular blockade. Atrial and ventricular arrhythmias and heart blocks may be life threatening.

Routine Laboratory Abnormalities

No consistent changes are seen on routine blood testing, chest radiographs, or urinalysis. The electrocardiographic abnormalities are listed above.

PLANS

Diagnostic

Differential Diagnosis

Acute phenothiazine toxicity may present with the entire, or part of the, triad of altered mental status, cardiovascular instability, and anticholinergic signs. Other substances with similar toxic states include cyclic antidepressants, antihistamines, carbamazepine (Tegretol), cyclobenzaprine (Flexeril), gastrointestinal antispasmodic agents, and plants with anticholinergic toxins (e.g., some mushrooms).

The electrocardiogram is a valuable diagnostic aid in identifying serious overdoses due to some of the drugs listed above. Marked prolongation of the QT, QRS, and PR intervals signifies a serious overdose. Quinidine-like antiarrhythmic drugs produce similar electrocardiographic changes and their potential use should be considered. Lithium may cause QT prolongation, but marked rigidity, tremors, and dysarthria differentiate it from overdose with the phenothiazines and cyclic antidepressants.

Diagnostic Options

Physostigmine (0.5–2.0 mg intravenously) has been reported to reverse the neurologic and cardiovascular effects of both phenothiazines and cyclic antidepressants and may be of use in identifying these overdoses. Seizures, bradycardia, and asystole have been reported following administration to overdosed patients, so its use as a diagnostic agent is therefore discouraged.

Phenothiazines may be rapidly identified in the urine by the methods described by Forrest in 1961 or with the Ames Phenistix. Quantitative drug levels are available from reference laboratories but are not useful for management of the overdosed patient.

Recommended Approach

A patient presenting with a history or presentation suggesting a possible phenothiazine overdose should be evaluated by observation of her or his vital signs and mental status. An electrocardiogram should be done and cardiac monitoring instituted. Hypotension, mental status changes, or electrocardiographic findings suggestive of toxicity are indicative of an overdose. Drug screening may be helpful in differentiating phenothiazines from other substances with similar toxicologic syndromes such as cyclic antidepressants.

Therapeutic

Therapeutic Options

The basis for treatment begins with supportive care as needed, with preservation of an adequate airway, ventilation, and maintenance of blood pressure. Hypotension may be profound and is initially managed with crystalloid. If the hypotension is unresponsive to volume loading, vasopressors with high alpha-agonist activities such as Levophed and Neo-Synephrine should be used, as much of the hypotension is secondary to alpha blockade. Positive response to dopamine has also been reported.

The stomach should be emptied in massive overdoses through the use of ipecac or lavage. Obtunded patients should never receive ipecac. The anticholinergic effects slow gastrointestinal absorption, and pill fragments may be removed long after ingestion. Charcoal and a cathartic should then be instilled. Repeated charcoal may be of benefit due to enterohepatic recirculation.

These drugs are highly bound to protein and are lipophilic and widely distributed to brain and fat tissue. Therefore, there is no benefit to hemodialysis or hemoperfusion for drug removal.

Alterations in mental status include lethargy, excitability, and seizures. Treatment is outlined under Recommended Approach.

Arrhythmias due to phenothiazine overdose are unusual, with the exception of overdoses of thioridazine (Mellaril) or mesoridazine (Serentil). All atrial and ventricular arrhythmias with variable degrees of heart block have been reported. The optimal treatment of arrhythmias secondary to phenothiazines has not been determined, and guidelines must be inferred from case reports and experimental literature.

Atrioventricular blockade has been reported and may be resistant to atropine and isoproterenol. Early pacing should be considered for any overdosed patient with greater than first-degree atrioventricular blockade.

Ventricular arrhythmias are uncommon, but they are the most frequently fatal toxic effect of the phenothiazines. The similarity of phenothiazine structures to those of the tricyclic antidepressants suggests that they might be managed similarly. Alkalinization, lidocaine, bretylium, and physostigmine are all of theoretic benefit, although no clinical trials have measured or compared their effectiveness in phenothiazine overdoses. Lidocaine is the preferred antiarrhythmic for ventricular tachycardia or fibrillation. Bretylium may increase hypotension by its adrenergic blockade, and phenytoin has the potential to increase atrioventricular delays. Physostigmine should be reserved for resistant hemodynamically significant arrhythmies. Treatment of Torsade de pointes is described in the next section.

Recommended Approach

Treatment begins with supportive care and attention to the ABCs. Patients who are lethargic or obtunded should receive naloxone 2 mg intravenously. Treatment of altered mental status should include administration of thiamine 100 mg intravenously or intramuscularly and bedside assessment of the glucose level. Intravenous dextrose should be given if the glucose is less than 80.

The airway should be secured. Endotracheal intubation should be performed on patients who are obtunded or who do not have a good gag reflex to ensure adequate respirations and prevent aspiration during gastric decontamination. Gastric lavage should be performed and charcoal should be administered to any symptomatic patients or those with potentially toxic overdoses.

Mental status changes associated with phenothiazine overdoses usually need supportive care only. Seizures should be treated with intravenous diazepam or lorazepam. Phenytoin may be given to control recurrent seizures but the possibility of increasing cardiac toxicity should be kept in mind.

Maintenance of blood pressure should begin with the rapid infusion of crystalloid solutions. If hypotension is severe or resistant to volume loading, dopamine or norepinephrine drips should be used.

Sinus tachycardia may indicate a toxic overdose and complications to come, but does not usually need treatment as it is not often hemodynamically significant. Other stable atrial arrhythmias may be managed conservatively.

High-degree atrioventricular blockades should be treated initially with atropine and infusions of isoproterenol but it is likely that pacing will be needed.

Ventricular tachycardia should be treated initially with standard antiarrhythmic doses of lidocaine. Lidocaine-resistant ventricular tachycardia is common and attempts at treatment should include bretylium. Physostigmine (0.5–2.0 mg intravenously) may treat ventricular tachycardia successfully, but should be used only for resistant cases because of its possible life-threatening side effects.

Patients with a prolonged QT interval who develop polymorphous ventricular tachycardia (Torsade de pointes) should be treated with magnesium. One to two grams of magnesium may be dissolved in 50 mL of 5% dextrose in water and given intravenously over 1 to 2 minutes. This may be repeated in 5 to 15 minutes if necessary. Constant infusions of 1 to 2 g/h may be administered to prevent recurrences until the QT inter-

val is less than 0.5 second. Magnesium therapy does not seem to be as effective in treating polymorphous ventricular tachycardia in patients without a prolonged QT interval on the electrocardiogram.

Overdrive pacing has been used alone or in combination with magnesium therapy for the treatment of magnesium-resistant Torsade de pointes.

Disposition of patients after an intentional overdose should be determined with psychiatric consultation. For patients who remain asymptomatic and without evidence of cardiac toxicity after gastrointestinal decontamination and a period of observation (4–6 hours), further medical evaluation for phenothiazine toxicity is not needed. Patients who have been treated, or shown evidence of toxicity, should be asymptomatic with a normalized electrocardiogram for 24 hours before discharge from the medical service. This is with recognition that even therapeutic doses of thioridazine have been associated with cardiac arrest.

FOLLOW-UP

Patients who have taken an intentional overdose need psychiatric care and follow-up. Routine medical follow-up is not necessary.

DISCUSSION

Prevalence

Phenothiazine overdoses accounted for almost 14% of the more than 30,000 overdoses reported in 1984 to the National Data Collecting System for Poison Control Centers. About one half of the overdoses were suicide attempts, with the majority of the other half being accidental exposure in the pediatric population.

Related Basic Science

Phenothiazines share a common three-ring nucleus and differ in their effects due to substitution at two side chains. Based on the substitutions on the center ring, the compounds are divided into three series: the dimethylamine series (Thorazine), the piperazine series (Stelazine, Prolixen, Compazine), and the piperidine series (Mellaril, Serentil). The dimethylamine series causes marked sedation and hypotension, whereas most deaths are due to cardiac complications caused by the piperidine series. Haloperidol (Haldol) is a butyrophenone but shares many properties with the phenothiazines. Although overdoses may cause sedation, extrapyramidal symptoms, and hypotension, no cardiac deaths have been reported from this drug. Patients vary tremendously in their response to a given dose of phenothiazine. There are 10- to 20-fold differences in therapeutic levels for different patients. The phenothiazines are almost completely metabolized by the liver and many active metabolites have been reported, so that it is difficult to estimate the pharmacologic half-life.

Centrally mediated movement disorders are the most frequent adverse reactions, but they are not usually seen in overdoses. These movement disorders are probably due to an imbalance of dopaminergic and cholinergic activity caused by a dopamine receptor blockade in the striatum of the basal ganglia. The syndromes include the acute dystonias, akathisia, parkinsonism, and tardive dyskinesia.

In phenothiazine overdoses, lethargy, coma, and delirium are due to the anticholinergic and antidopaminergic effects on the central nervous system. The anticholinergic activity also causes the typical findings of decreased intestinal motility, flushing, tachycardia, hypothermia, and dry mucous membranes. Pupillary findings are variable based on the multiple pharmacologic properties of the phenothiazines. Hypotension is due to loss of vascular tone caused by an alpha-adrenergic blockade. Quinidine-like effects and a calcium channel blockade are seen most commonly in overdoses of the piperidine phenothiazines and account for the electrocardiographic findings and cardiac deaths seen in some thioridazine (Mellaril) and mesoridazine (Serentil) overdoses. Haldoperidol (Haldol) has low anticholinergic activity and few cardiac effects, but it is more likely to cause extrapyramidal symptoms such as acute dystonias.

Natural History and Modification with Treatment

The toxicity of a phenothiazine overdose is dose related, although individual tolerance varies greatly. Advanced age, underlying heart disease, and the coingestion of other drugs such as alcohol, tricyclic antidepressants, and sedative–hypnotics all influence the patient's outcome.

The overall mortality for phenothiazine ingestions is less than 0.5%. The presence of hypotension and coma, the need for ventilatory assistance, or cardiac arrhythmias are a poor prognostic sign.

Prevention

Overdoses with these medicines are difficult to prevent in the modern era of psychiatry where large numbers of patients are maintained on antipsychotic medications for long periods. Prevention consists of prescribing medicines in quantities not likely to be lethal if ingested inappropriately and in early institutionalization of potentially suicidal patients.

Cost Containment

Prevention of overdoses should be the goal of any treating physician to avoid dangerous ingestions and costly hospitalizations. Most phenothiazine overdoses tend to be mild, and patients can be safely discharged 6 hours after the stomach is emptied and charcoal is given if mental status, vital signs, and the electrocardiogram remain normal.

Prolonged intensive care unit care is unavoidable for more serious overdoses.

Physicians are urged not to do serum drug levels in routine overdose patients. Specific levels have no therapeutic or prognostic value in routine care.

REFERENCES

Forrest F. Review of rapid urine test for phenothiazine and related drugs. Am J Psychiat 1961;118:300.

Fowler N, McCall D, Chou T, et al. Electrocardiographic changes and cardiac arrhythmias in patients receiving psychotropic drugs. Am J Cardiol, 1976;37:223.

Goldfrank L, Flomenbaum N, Weisman R. Management of overdoses with psychoactive medications. Emerg Med Clin North Am 1984;2:63.

Hulise D, Dasa S, Black D, et al. Complete heart block and Torsade de pointes associated with thioridazine poisoning. Pharmacotherapy 1994;2:239.

Marrs-Simon P, Zell-Kanter M, Kendzierski D, Leikin J. Cardiotoxic manifestations of mesoridazone overdose. Ann Emerg Med 1988;17:1074.

Risch S, Groom G, Janowsky D. Interfaces of psychopharmacology and cardiology, part 2. J Clin Psychiatry 1981;42:47.

CHAPTER 24–17

Lithium Toxicity

Patrick E. McKinney, M.D.

DEFINITION

Lithium is an alkali metal used in the treatment of bipolar affective disorder as well as related psychiatric disorders, neutropenia, and cluster headaches. Toxicity is defined as the development of signs and symptoms involving predominantly the gastrointestinal and central nervous systems, and is almost always accompanied by an elevated plasma lithium concentration.

ETIOLOGY

Lithium toxicity may occur as any of three clinical scenarios: acute, chronic, or acute on chronic. Acute toxicity is a result of overdose in patients not maintained on lithium. Chronic intoxication occurs in patients already taking lithium and may be a result of an increase in dose or a decrease in lithium clearance over time and may be more gradual in onset but often more severe. Acute on chronic intoxication occurs when patients on lithium maintenance therapy overdose on their medication; this syndrome usually resembles acute overdose.

CRITERIA FOR DIAGNOSIS
Suggestive

The signs and symptoms of acute toxicity are nonspecific and involve primarily the central nervous system and the gastrointestinal system. Nausea and vomiting may be seen, as may tremor, weakness, hyperreflexia, ataxia, dysarthria, seizures, and coma. Intoxication should be suspected whenever these findings are present in a patient with access to lithium. Electrocardiographic findings of T-wave flattening or inversion, U waves, and nonspecific ST–T wave changes may be suggestive. A decreased anion gap has been reported.

Chronic lithium toxicity should be suspected in patients on lithium maintenance therapy who present with central nervous system toxicity. Patients may present with a spectrum of clinical findings ranging from mild fine tremor to cerebellar findings, seizures, and coma. In chronic intoxication, severe toxicity may be seen with minimal elevation in lithium concentration.

Definitive

Symptoms of lithium toxicity may be difficult to differentiate from side effects of therapeutic doses. The definitive diagnosis is made when the clinical manifestations of lithium toxicity are accompanied by a plasma lithium concentration greater than 1.2 mEq/L. Therapeutic lithium concentrations range from 0.6 to 1.2 mEq/L. Toxicity correlates poorly with levels. Patients with an acute overdose may be minimally symptomatic with concentrations greater than 4 mEq/L.

CLINICAL MANIFESTATIONS
Subjective

Symptoms of lithium toxicity involve primarily the central nervous system and the gastrointestinal tract. Patients may complain of fatigue, weakness, tremor, difficulty speaking or concentrating, tinnitus, and impaired balance. Family members may suspect an exacerbation of the primary psychiatric disorder. Gastrointestinal complaints may include nausea, vomiting, and diarrhea.

Objective

Physical Examination

The primary findings on physical examination reflect central nervous system dysfunction. A tremor of the extremities is often present, with cogwheeling, rigidity, hypertonia, hyperreflexia, and clonus. Fasciculations, dysarthria, and choreoathetosis may be seen. Cerebellar findings may be present with ataxia and dysdiadokinesia. With increasing severity of toxicity, stupor, coma, and seizures may occur. These findings may be seen on presentation of the chronically poisoned patient. Acutely poisoned patients may be initially symptomatic but must be monitored for progression of toxicity, which may be delayed.

With acute toxicity, vomiting and diarrhea may occur; this is less common with chronic toxicity. On examination of the eyes nystagmus and, rarely, papilledema may be seen. Thyromegaly may be present, with either hypo- or hyperthyroidism or, rarely, hyperparathyroidism. These findings are usually associated more with therapeutic use than toxicity. A variety of dermatologic effects may be seen including psoriasis, xerosis, seborrheic dermatitis, maculopapular eruptions, and edema.

Routine Laboratory Abnormalities

Electrolytes, blood urea nitrogen, creatinine, glucose, complete blood count, calcium, and urinalysis should routinely be ordered. Sodium values are variable and may be increased or decreased. Potassium is usually normal or decreased. Total carbon dioxide combining power may be modestly decreased. Creatinine and blood urea nitrogen may be elevated, usually in a prerenal pattern. Proteinuria may also be seen. Glucose may be elevated, probably due to a nonspecific stress reaction. Leukocytosis may be seen, even in therapeutic use. Calcium may be increased if there is parathyroid dysfunction. A urinalysis should be obtained to evaluate potential renal dysfunction.

An electrocardiogram should be obtained. Most commonly, ST–T wave changes such as T-wave flattening and inversion are seen. Also, U waves, PR prolongation, and, less commonly, intraventricular conduction defects may be seen.

PLANS
Diagnostic
Differential Diagnosis

The differential diagnosis may be limited in the acute overdose, especially if the history of lithium ingestion is present. Other psychiatric medications should be suspected including phenothiazines and butyrophenones, tricyclic antidepressants, monoamine oxidase inhibitors (MAOIs), amoxapine, bupropion, and other newer antidepressants and anticonvulsants.

In the chronic overdose, given the nonspecific nature of many of the symptoms of lithium toxicity, the differential diagnosis may be more extensive, especially if there is no history of overdose or lithium use. As lithium is almost completely eliminated by the kidney and is tied to the excretion of sodium, any free water or sodium depletion or decrease in renal function may predispose patients to lithium toxicity. Thus, any illness that has the potential to cause sodium loss or volume depletion predisposes to chronic lithium toxicity. Gastroenteritis, infections with fever, decreased water intake secondary to exacerbation of psychiatric disease, and heat illness have all been associated with lithium toxicity and, in addition, may cause symptoms overlapping with lithium toxicity. Other psychotropic medication ingestion should be considered as noted above. Ethanol or sedative–hypnotic withdrawal, cocaine, sympathomimetic overdose, anticholinergic syndrome, phencyclidine intoxication, MAOI overdose, MAOI–tryptophan interaction, serotonin syndrome, neuroleptic malignant syndrome, and organophosphate, heavy metal, xanthine, and nicotine ingestion should be considered as well.

Other central nervous system pathology that may mimic lithium toxicity includes infarction, hemorrhage, tumor, trauma, and infection. Endocrine possibilities include hyperthyroidism, hypothyroidism and hypoglycemia. Other metabolic diagnostic possibilities include hyponatremia, hypercalcemia, uremia, and hepatic encephalopathy.

Diagnostic Options

In cases where a history of lithium use or overdose is unknown, a high index of suspicion is required. Review of medical records, pharmacy logs, or contact with the patient's psychiatrist, personal physician, or family may provide information regarding current or previous lithium use. Plasma lithium concentrations must be specifically measured as lithium is not detected on blood or urine toxicology screening. In chronic toxicity, concentrations do not correlate well with toxicity. In acute toxicity, lithium absorption may be delayed, especially if extended-release preparations are ingested. Urine toxicology screen, creatine phosphokinase, thyroid-stimulating hormone, urine pregnancy test, and magnesium may be indicated given the clinical scenario.

Recommended Approach

A patient with lithium ingestion should have at least two blood levels measured separated in time by 4 to 6 hours to make sure there is not continued absorption and risk of progression of toxicity. Patients should not be discharged until lithium concentrations are consistently decreasing. Computed tomography of the head and lumbar puncture may also be indicated along with routine laboratory tests if suggested by the clinical scenario.

Therapeutic
Therapeutic Options

Initial therapy should be directed toward stabilization. An intravenous line should be established and the patient should be placed on a cardiac monitor and pulse oximeter. If the airway is not adequately maintained, endotracheal intubation should be considered. Hypotension should be treated with volume expansion using normal saline. If pressors are needed, dopamine would be a rational choice, and at "renal" doses, dopamine has been shown to increase lithium clearance. If hypertension requires treatment, an agent with a short half-life such as nitroprusside or nitroglycerin should be used.

Recommended Approach

As with any patient with altered mental status, serum glucose should be checked immediately by a fingerstick estimate. This should be followed by 2 mg of naloxone and 100 mg of thiamine intravenously. If meningitis or other infection is being considered, an appropriate broad-spectrum antibiotic such as ceftriaxone should be given after two sets of blood cultures are obtained.

If an acute lithium ingestion is suspected, gastric decontamination should be performed. Choices for decontamination include ipecac, gastric lavage, whole-bowel irrigation, and sodium polystyrene sulfonate resin/sorbitol. Lithium is not adsorbed to activated charcoal, but 50 to 60 g of oral activated charcoal should be given if coingestion cannot be ruled out. If the patient presents within 1 hour of ingestion with no significant coingestants and normal mental status, 30 mL of syrup of ipecac may be used. If decreased mental status or the potential for decreased mental status is present, gastric lavage should be considered, with intubation for airway protection, if needed. As lithium is slowly absorbed and may form a drug bezoar, gastric lavage may be considered even if the patient presents several hours after ingestion if the amount ingested is large or if significant toxicity is present. Another choice for gastrointestinal decontamination is whole-bowel irrigation. Whole-bowel irrigation is accomplished by giving a polyethylene glycol/balanced electrolyte solution orally or by nasogastric tube at a rate of 1 to 2 L/h for 4 to 5 hours or until rectal effluent is clear. Although this therapy is usually recommended for extended-release lithium preparations, it may be considered for regular-release preparations as well. Finally, sodium polystyrene sulfonate cation-exchange resins have been shown to bind lithium in vitro, in animals and humans. The appropriate role of this therapy remains to be determined. In chronic intoxication, it is not likely that there is a significant amount of lithium in the gastrointestinal tract. Therefore, gastrointestinal decontamination is not usually indicated in chronic ingestions unless plasma lithium concentrations are rising.

Free water and sodium should be repleted. Lithium is renally cleared and any volume-related decrease in renal blood flow results in decreased lithium clearance. As renal lithium excretion is coupled to sodium, conditions that would result in sodium retention would result in decreased lithium clearance as well. Therefore, normal saline is a logical intravenous fluid at a rate of 150 to 300 mL/h to maintain a urine output of 2 to 4 mL/kg/h. If there is evidence of renal failure or insufficiency or a suspicion of congestive heart failure, fluid needs may need to be adjusted downward. There is no advantage to saline diuresis or urinary alkalinization. Although mannitol, aminophylline, and loop diuretics have been associated with increased lithium clearance in some situations, their role in therapy has not been defined and they are not currently recommended.

Medications that impair lithium clearance should be discontinued. These include nonsteroidal antiinflammatory drugs, angiotensin-converting enzyme inhibitors, thiazide diuretics, and potassium-sparing diuretics. These drugs are often implicated in the genesis of chronic lithium toxicity as well. Other drugs that may potentiate lithium neurotoxicity should be avoided or discontinued. These include verapamil, haloperidol, methyldopa, carbamazepine, and selective serotonin reuptake inhibitors.

Hemodialysis is very effective in clearing the plasma of lithium; however, as equilibration between the tissue and the blood is slow, rebound in lithium concentrations is common and clinical improvement often lags behind the decrease in lithium concentrations. Most of the existing clinical data are in the form of retrospective, uncontrolled case series; thus published recommendations are highly variable and based on no solid outcome data. Because of the high incidence of permanent neurologic sequelae in some series, however, some recommendations for hemodialysis are empirically liberal.

The indications for dialysis in acute toxicity are different from those in chronic toxicity. In acute toxicity, high lithium concentrations can be seen with mild symptoms. Some authors have recommended hemodialysis for acute toxicity when concentrations are greater than 4 mEq/L, whereas others feel it is appropriate only if moderate or severe toxicity is present that is not responding to conservative therapy. Persistently increasing serial lithium concentrations despite rehydration and gastrointestinal decontamination have also been used to recommend hemodialysis. Renal failure in the presence of moderately elevated lithium concentrations (≥ 2 mEq/L) may be an indication for dialysis.

In chronic intoxication, most authors agree that clinical presentation is probably a better determinant for recommending hemodialysis than absolute levels. Hemodialysis is generally recommended when significant toxicity such as seizures, coma, and obtundation are present. It is also indicated when moderate or severe toxicity occurs in the presence of renal failure. Recommendations for dialysis in the chronically intoxicated patient with mild symptoms and lithium concentrations ranging from 2.5 to 4 mEq/L are conflicting. The endpoint for dialysis is a serum lithium concentration less than 1 mEq/L that does not rebound above this level 6 hours after dialysis. Clinical improvement often lags behind normalization of levels for days to months. In some cases, residual cerebellar dysfunction and cognitive defects may be permanent. Peritoneal dialysis is not an effective means of drug clearance and should not be used.

FOLLOW-UP

Patients should not be restarted on lithium therapy until concentrations are within therapeutic range, signs and symptoms of toxicity have resolved, and the psychiatric caregiver has determined the need for continued lithium therapy. As with any suspected overdose, appropriate psychiatric consultation is indicated once the patient is stable. Follow-up may be required in patients who do not return to preexposure neurologic baseline as permanent neurologic dysfunction may occur.

DISCUSSION
Prevalence and Incidence

According to recent poison center data, there were more than 4500 cases of lithium toxicity in 1993 (Litovitz et al., 1994). Previous data reflect a relatively greater proportion of chronic toxicity. More cases of lithium toxicity may be seen as lithium use is being extended to psychiatric diagnoses other than bipolar affective disorder, such as cyclothymic mood disorders, borderline personality disorder, schizoaffective disorder, schizophrenia, and self-mutilating behavior.

Related Basic Science

Lithium is an alkali metal that is handled in the body similar to sodium and potassium. It is available as a carbonate or citrate salt in regular- or extended-release tablets or syrup. Three hundred milligrams of lithium carbonate contains the equivalent of 8.1 mEq of lithium. Lithium is absorbed in the stomach and small intestine, with peak concentrations occurring within 5 hours after regular-release preparations. Peak levels may be delayed in overdose or if extended-release preparations are ingested. Equilibrium between the blood and tissues occurs slowly, taking up to 10 days to reach tissue steady-state concentrations. Therapeutic half-life ranges from 14 to 24 hours and is prolonged in overdose and renal failure. This relatively slow absorption, long half-life, and slow tissue/blood equilibrium may explain the delay in appearance of

toxicity as well as the prolonged clinical course that is often seen. Lithium is not protein bound and has an apparent volume of distribution of 0.79 L/kg.

Elimination occurs almost exclusively by the kidney with no hepatic metabolism. The glomerulus filters lithium much like sodium and the proximal tubule reabsorbs approximately 70% of this. Anything that decreases glomerular filtration thus decreases lithium clearance. Lithium reabsorption is coupled to sodium reabsorption; thus, anything that results in sodium depletion also results in a decrease of the fractional excretion of lithium. Lithium may itself cause a natriuresis, thus setting up a vicious cycle predisposing to lithium toxicity.

The mechanism of lithium action is unclear. It is thought to substitute for sodium and other cations in cellular metabolic processes. Lithium may interfere with cAMP-mediated processes. Lithium concentrations are highest in the brain and kidney, reflecting its toxicity.

Natural History and Its Modification with Treatment

Therapeutic use of lithium is associated with a high incidence of side effects; up to 90% of patients are estimated to experience adverse effects sometime during therapy. Because of its low therapeutic index and the many factors that may affect its clearance, serum lithium concentrations should be followed closely. Diabetes insipidus may occur in up to 20% of patients, but is usually responsive to cessation of lithium therapy. Hypothyroidism may occur in 4 to 10% of patients and may require thyroid supplementation as well as stopping lithium therapy. Nausea, vomiting, and diarrhea may respond to switching to different pharmaceutical preparations. Skin lesions such as psoriasis and acne may respond to normal treatment modalities or may require stopping lithium therapy.

The development of acute lithium intoxication may progress slowly over several days due to the delayed equilibration into the central nervous system. An initial gastrointestinal phase may be followed by a quiescent phase. If adequate decontamination is not performed, central nervous system toxicity may develop. Recovery in several days, provided supportive care is adequate, is the rule.

Chronic lithium intoxication develops insidiously and is usually accompanied by an increased tissue burden of lithium for a given lithium concentration compared with acute intoxication. Resolution of central nervous system toxicity may lag behind normalization of lithium levels by days to weeks. Up to 10% of patients may experience permanent sequelae. Electrocardiographic changes of T-wave flattening and inversion, U waves, and ventricular conduction delays may be seen as therapeutic side effects. These changes may require weeks to resolve. Renal failure and diabetes insipidus are usually transient and resolve with supportive care.

Prevention

Frequent monitoring of lithium levels is essential in preventing toxicity. Patients should be reminded to maintain generous fluid intake and to avoid salt restriction. Careful prescribing practices, including caution when administering nonsteroidal antiinflammatory drugs and diuretics, will help avoid iatrogenic lithium toxicity.

Cost Containment

Patients do not need hospital admission if they have a serum lithium level less than 1.2 to 1.5 mEq/L that is documented to be falling over 4 to 6 hours and are relatively asymptomatic. Early gastrointestinal decontamination will minimize the chances of continued absorption.

REFERENCES

Amdisen A. Clinical features and management of lithium poisoning. Med Toxicol 1988;3:18.

Groleau G. Lithium toxicity. Emerg Med Clin North Am 1994;12:511.

Hansen E, Amdisen A. Lithium intoxication. Q J Med 1978;186:123.

Harvey N, Merriman S. Review of clinically important drug interactions with lithium. Drug Saf 1994;10:455.

Litovitz TL, Clark LR, Sobway RA. 1993 Annual Report of the American Association of Poison Control Centers Toxic Exposure Surveillance System. Am J Emerg Med 1994;12:546.

Simard M, Gumbiner B, Lee A, et al. Lithium carbonate intoxication: A case report and review of the literature. Arch Intern Med 1989;149:36.

Smith S, Ling L, Halstenson C. Whole-bowel irrigation as a treatment for acute lithium overdose. Ann Emerg Med 1991;20:536.

CHAPTER 24–18

Cyanide Poisoning

Robert S. Hoffman, M.D.

DEFINITION

Cyanide refers to a triple covalent bond that occurs between a carbon and a nitrogen atom ($C \equiv N$). As cyanide cannot occur on its own, it is usually found as an inorganic salt (potassium cyanide, KCN), a gas (hydrogen cyanide, HCN), or an organic molecule of varying size (acetonitrile, amygdalin). Cyanide poisoning denotes the constellation of signs and symptoms that result from exposure to cyanide.

ETIOLOGY

Hydrogen cyanide gas is frequently found in a variety of industrial settings including photography, manufacture of rubber and plastics, and metal ore extraction, as well as a common product of household combustion. Thus, any fire victim is a potential victim of cyanide poisoning as well. The inorganic cyanide salts are commonly used in the electroplating and photographic industries. Naturally occurring sources include the leaves, bark, or seeds of many plants, especially members of the *Prunus* species (chokecherry, peach, apricot, and bitter almond) containing cyanogenic glycosides (amygdalins), which release cyanide when digested by the gut. These naturally occurring sources of cyanide provide routes of accidental exposure for small children and chronic toxicity in certain cultures that rely on these cyanide-containing staples. Medicinal products such as Laetrile, which releases cyanide when ingested, and sodium nitroprusside, which releases cyanide in vivo, are other potential sources of toxicity. Finally, reports have documented death from cyanide poisoning following accidental ingestion of an acetonitrile-containing cosmetic nail glue remover.

CRITERIA FOR DIAGNOSIS

Suggestive

Hydrogen cyanide gas, cyanide salts, and compounds that liberate cyanide such as the cyanogenic glycosides are potent and rapidly acting metabolic poisons. Thus, cyanide has gained a notoriety as a homicidal (the Tylenol incident), mass suicidal (the Jonestown massacre), or genocidal (in World War II) agent. Single events attributable to cyanide poisoning are more common and more difficult to diagnose.

The physician must always suspect cyanide poisoning when evaluating a patient suffering from profound metabolic acidosis and shock that is of rapid onset and unclear etiology. An occupational history as well as a history of depression or previous suicide attempt may alert the physician to the diagnosis of cyanide poisoning. In many cyanide victims, especially victims of fires or homicide attempts or those patients with accidental plant ingestions, the diagnosis is more elusive.

Definitive

The definitive diagnosis of cyanide poisoning can be established only in one of two ways: dramatic response to the cyanide antidote kit, or retrospectively with cyanide levels. Cyanide toxicity progresses too rapidly for blood levels to have clinical utility. Thus, the physician must rely on history, physical findings, and laboratory abnormalities consistent with cellular hypoxia to diagnose cyanide toxicity.

CLINICAL MANIFESTATIONS

Subjective

Pertinent history should include a detailed assessment of psychiatric disease or previous suicide attempts, and focus on those occupations where cyanide may be available: electroplating, photography, jewelry, fumigation, chemical synthesis, and so on. History may have to be obtained from witnesses and family members as the patient is frequently unable to communicate.

Although inhalation of hydrogen cyanide gas has been associated with a smell of "bitter almonds," this history is unreliable because 20 to 40% of the population is genetically unable to detect this odor. Also, exposures to high concentrations of hydrogen cyanide are so rapidly fatal that conversation with victims becomes unlikely. Ingestion of cyanide-containing compounds typically produces a more gradual onset of symptoms, with delays of minutes to hours depending on dose, form, and amount of food in the stomach.

The symptoms of acute cyanide poisoning are generally nonspecific, as cyanide produces cellular hypoxia. Initially, patients complain of headache, dizziness, flushing, nausea, and possibly vomiting. Within minutes, this progresses to lightheadedness, shortness of breath, and confusion. Seizures, coma, and cardiac arrest are imminent.

Although chronic cyanide toxicity is quite rare, symptoms have been described. Tobacco amblyopia occurs following heavy cigarette smoking, especially in individuals who may be B_{12} deficient. Also, tropical ataxic neuropathy occurs in cultures that rely largely on cassava (a cyanide-containing tuber) as a staple.

Objective

Physical Examination

Physical findings in cyanide poisoning parallel those seen in other disorders where metabolic failure results. Initially tachycardia, tachypnea, and mild hypertension are produced from catecholamine excess, metabolic acidosis, and stimulation of chemoreceptors. This progresses rapidly to bradycardia, apnea, and cardiovascular collapse. Other manifestations of cellular hypoxia such as electrocardiographic changes and seizures may occur at any time.

Cyanide poisoning prevents oxygen extraction at the cellular level. This results in a high venous oxygen content which may be visible on funduscopic examination: The retinal veins may have the same color as the arteries. Similarly, hemoglobin desaturation that produces cyanosis is an uncommon finding.

Routine Laboratory Abnormalities

The routine examination of the blood and urine is not helpful. (See Plans for discussion of other diagnostic tests.)

PLANS

Diagnostic

Differential Diagnosis

The differential diagnosis of cyanide toxicity should include exposure to other agents that produce severe anion gap metabolic acidosis and cardiovascular collapse. Because of the rapidity of onset of cyanide toxicity, other gases such as carbon monoxide and hydrogen sulfide should be considered. The magnitude of the metabolic acidosis produced by cyanide is so severe that the only other toxins that are commonly included in the differential diagnosis are the toxic alcohols, methanol and ethylene glycol. When compared with the asphyxiant gases (cyanide, carbon monoxide, and hydrogen sulfide) toxicity from the alcohols progresses slowly, allowing for differentiation. Finally, although nontoxicologic etiologies such as sepsis and diabetic ketoacidosis should be considered, history or physical examination often excludes these possibilities.

Diagnostic Options

The diagnosis of cyanide poisoning is almost always established by history and physical examination. The presence of metabolic acidosis and cardiovascular collapse of unclear etiology should always alert the physician to the possibility of cyanide poisoning. Few laboratory tests are helpful. The arterial blood gas analysis should confirm severe metabolic acidosis, with or without respiratory compensation. Although co-oximetry is helpful, it cannot be used to conclusively exclude a dyshemoglobinemia as an etiology for the patient's symptoms, because concomitant carbon monoxide and cyanide poisoning may occur. Co-oximetry may be useful, however, as cyanide interferes with oxygen extraction. This raises the venous oxygen content, making it approach the arterial oxygen content (the arteriovenous O_2 difference should be minimal). Thus, the determination of simultaneous arterial and venous oxygen contents may help establish the diagnosis of cyanide poisoning. Although cyanide levels may be obtained by a microdiffusion technique, this usually takes 2 to 4 hours. This delay is unacceptable to rationalize withholding of therapy in a severely ill patient while awaiting laboratory confirmation.

Recommended Approach

The diagnosis of cyanide toxicity may best be confirmed by observing a clinical response to the cyanide antidote kit. After appropriate assessment and attempts at stabilization have occurred, the patient should be treated with all or a portion of the Lilly Cyanide Antidote Kit (see below). A prompt clinical response that cannot be attributed to other interventions is both diagnostic of cyanide poisoning and therapeutic.

Therapeutic

Therapeutic Options

All patients with either known or suspected cyanide poisoning require aggressive resuscitation measures that include the administration of 100% oxygen often with assisted ventilation, cardiopulmonary resuscitation, and the administration of sodium bicarbonate as needed to correct the refractory metabolic acidosis. In addition, a number of specific antidotes are in use worldwide.

Although currently only available in this country for experimental trials, hydroxycobalamin is considered the antidote of choice in Europe. Hydroxycobalamin (or vitamin B_{12a}) combines with cyanide to form cyanocobalamin (vitamin B_{12}). As both the antidote and its end result are nontoxic, the concern over hypotension or the adverse effects of methemoglobinemia that result with the administration of the Lilly Cyanide Antidote Kit is circumvented. The current protocols call for hydroxycobalamin to be used with the sodium thiosulfate portion of the traditional cyanide antidote kit. Other antidotes—cobalt ethylenediaminetetraacetate (Keylocyanor) and dimethylaminophenol (potent methemoglobin inducer)—are rarely considered because of their consequential associated toxic effects.

Recommended Approach

Administration of the Lilly Cyanide Antidote Kit is the only currently accepted therapy for cyanide poisoning in the United States. The antidote kit contains three ingredients: amyl nitrite pearls (for inhalation), and sodium nitrite and sodium thiosulfate (both for intravenous use). Although each of the three components of the kit has demonstrated efficacy in the cyanide-poisoned patient, the best results are achieved when both the nitrite and thiosulfate portions are used in combination with optimal cardiopulmonary resuscitation. Both amyl nitrite pearls and intravenous sodium nitrite are vasodilators that also produce methemoglobinemia. The amyl nitrite pearls are designed for emergency response personnel, are difficult to use, and are inefficient. If the patient is conscious, one to two pearls can be broken and placed inside a nonrebreathing mask that is connected to 100% oxygen. When the patient is intubated, the pearls can be placed in the reservoir section of the Ambu bag. The inhalers should be bypassed if intravenous access has

been established, and the physician should proceed immediately to intravenous sodium nitrite. Adult patients should receive 300 mg (10 mL of a 3% solution) of sodium nitrite over 2 to 4 minutes. The calculation of this dose is based on total body hemoglobin; thus, corrections are required for pediatric and severely anemic patients. The pediatric dose of sodium nitrite is 0.2 mL/kg (of the 3% solution) not to exceed 10 mL. Correction factors for anemia are supplied with the kit. Because nitrites are vasodilators, hypotension may result from too rapid an infusion. Although this therapy has been estimated to produce approximately a 25% methemoglobinemia, it is well tolerated by most individuals, even if cyanide poisoning is absent. The final step of the cyanide antidote kit is the intravenous administration of 12.5 g (50 mL of a 25% solution) of sodium thiosulfate. Again, this dose must be corrected for the anemic or pediatric patient and can be easily remembered as five times the volume of sodium nitrite dose. At this dose, sodium thiosulfate is a benign antidote. Each kit contains enough antidote to treat two adult patients. Those patients with partial or transient responses to therapy can be re-treated. The physician should also remember that 100% oxygen, cardiopulmonary resuscitation, gastrointestinal decontamination, and intravenous sodium bicarbonate administration may all be required as adjuncts to the cyanide antidote kit. Caution must be used when considering therapy in the fire victim. The methemoglobin induced by the nitrites can exacerbate symptoms (by further interfering with oxygen delivery) when simultaneous carbon monoxide poisoning is present. Patients with suspected concomitant cyanide and carbon monoxide poisoning should receive 100% oxygen and the thiosulfate antidote alone, prior to hyperbaric oxygen therapy. The regional poison control center network is an invaluable resource for assistance with these decisions.

FOLLOW-UP

Survivors of cyanide poisoning may suffer from a variety of anoxic events resulting in severe neuromuscular and cognitive deficits. Among these disorders, parkinsonism has been well described. The frequency and degree of follow-up are dictated by the severity of these disorders. Continued psychiatric intervention may be required for the depressed or suicidal patient.

DISCUSSION

Prevalence and Incidence

The exact prevalence and incidence of cyanide poisoning remain unknown, largely because of its presence in fire fatalities, where it has been considered by some authors to be an important cause of mortality in about 40% of cases. Excluding fires, acute toxicity is distinctly uncommon, with multiple cases being reported only in occupational accidents, mass homicides or suicides, and product tamperings.

Related Basic Science

Cyanide has a very specific mechanism of toxicity. It has a high affinity for ferric (Fe^{3+}) ions, especially those located in the cytochrome a–a$_3$ complex of the cytochrome oxidase system. When cyanide binds to cytochrome a–a$_3$, oxidative phosphorylation is blocked, which leads to anaerobic metabolism and the generation of lactate. Cellular ischemia from lack of ATP follows rapidly, as anaerobic metabolism cannot meet tissue energy requirements. The precise action of the components of the cyanide antidote kit remains somewhat controversial. Most authorities accept that toxicity is reversed by providing an alternative source of ferric ions for cyanide binding and thus freeing the cytochrome oxidase system. This is accomplished through nitrite-induced methemoglobinemia. Cyanide binds to the ferric ion in methemoglobin, forming cyanomethemoglobin, which cannot be measured by conventional techniques. Thus, the failure to measure elevated methemoglobin levels after the administration of amyl and sodium nitrite has been suggested as another way to confirm cyanide poisoning.

Cyanomethemoglobin cannot carry oxygen and functions only to bring cyanide into the blood, where it can be more easily detoxified and eliminated. Free serum cyanide and cyanide bound in cyanomethemoglobin are detoxified by the enzyme rhodanese (also known as sulfur transferase). This enzyme forms thiocyanate by adding a sulfur group to the cyanide. Thiocyanate is relatively nontoxic and is easily eliminated in the urine. The reaction regenerates methemoglobin, which is used to bind another molecule of cyanide, if needed, or detoxified by preexisting mechanisms. Sulfur availability is the rate-limiting step for the conversion reaction. Thus, the administration of sodium thiosulfate is essential in that it increases sulfur availability and allows this reaction to occur at its maximal rate.

Natural History and Its Modification with Treatment

The natural history of untreated cyanide poisoning is dependent largely on dose, host, and route of exposure. Untreated patients who ingest about 1.5 mg/kg potassium cyanide are uniformly expected to die, as are those with short inhalational exposures to concentrations of hydrogen cyanide in excess of 300 ppm. When early therapy is instituted (in patients with minimal symptoms) the outcome is usually favorable. Patients with severe acidosis or cardiovascular collapse may also recover, but are at risk for persistent neuromuscular and neuropsychiatric abnormalities.

Prevention

Adequate industrial hygiene is the best method of preventing occupational exposure. Accidental poisoning can rarely be prevented. Children should be instructed not to eat wild plants or berries, and sources of cyanide should not be used in the home. Cyanide poisoning may also occur from prolonged nitroprusside infusion, especially when doses are very high. This can be prevented by limiting the dose to no greater than 1.0 to 1.3 mg/kg for 3 hours or 0.5 mg/kg/h for 48 hours. Also, thiosulfate and hydroxycobalamin may be added to continuous nitroprusside infusions to limit the risk of cyanide toxicity.

Cost Containment

The diagnosis of cyanide poisoning should be sought only in patients with a history of ingestion or severe metabolic acidosis and impending cardiovascular collapse. Patients with suspected inhalational exposures who are awake and alert and have normal vital signs and normal acid–base status need no further evaluation. For the clinically ill patient, the response to treatment is the most prudent and inexpensive method of confirming the diagnosis.

REFERENCES

Baud FJ, Barriot P, Toffis V, et al. Elevated blood cyanide in victims of smoke inhalation. N Engl J Med 1991;325:1761.

Cottrell JE, Casthely P, Brodie JD, et al. Prevention of nitroprusside-induced cyanide toxicity with hydroxycobalamin. N Engl J Med 1978;289:809.

Graham DL, Laman D, Theodore J, et al. Acute cyanide poisoning complicated by lactic acidosis and pulmonary edema. Arch Intern Med 1977;137:1051.

Johnson RP, Mellors JW. Arterialization of venous blood gases: A clue to the diagnosis of cyanide poisoning. J Emerg Med 1988;6:401.

Way JL. Cyanide intoxication and its mechanism of antagonism. Annu Rev Pharmacol Toxicol 1984;24:451.

CHAPTER 24–19

Theophylline Overdose

Steven J. White, M.D.

DEFINITION

Theophylline overdose is defined as a supratherapeutic serum level of theophylline, that is, a serum level above 20 µg/mL. Although symptomatology is variable, 75% of people have toxic symptoms with serum levels above 20 µg/mL and virtually all have some symptomatology above 30 µg/mL.

ETIOLOGY

Theophylline overdose can be classified as acute, chronic, and acute + chronic, based on whether a larger-than-normal dose of theophylline has been administered (acute) and on whether the patient takes theophylline on a daily basis (chronic). As with other pharmaceutical overdoses, theophylline overdose can also be classified based on intent, as intentional overdose, self-medication error, and iatrogenic error.

Not surprisingly, therapeutic error results in a significant number of theophylline overdoses and theophylline is one of the most common drugs involved in fatal pharmaceutical errors. Patient error usually results from accidentally exceeding the prescribed dose and accounts for about one third to one half of theophylline overdoses. Physician and pharmacy errors cause another third, and intentional overdose represents about 20% of cases. Iatrogenic error has many sources (Table 24–19–1). In the most recent report by the American Association of Poison Control Centers, theophylline ranked ninth as a cause of death and was the only pharmaceutical in which unintentional overdose outranked suicide as a cause of death (Litovitz et al., 1994).

CRITERIA FOR DIAGNOSIS

Suggestive

Theophylline overdose should be suspected whenever a patient with a known history of theophylline use, asthma, or chronic obstructive lung disease presents with agitation, tremulousness, vomiting, tachycardia, or seizures. Asthma medications and metered-dose inhalers can suggest concomitant theophylline use, although theophylline toxicity is indistinguishable from beta-agonist toxicity. Theophylline overdose should also be considered in any uncooperative or unconscious patient who is tachycardic, repetitively vomiting, or having seizures. Hypokalemia, hyperglycemia, and leukocytosis are usually present with severe overdoses and may suggest theophylline overdose in the proper clinical setting.

Definitive

Definitive diagnosis is made by laboratory confirmation of an elevated serum theophylline level (> 20 µg/mL). Theophylline is quantitatively assayed by either gas–liquid chromatography/mass spectrography or by enzyme-linked immunoassay. The latter method has been used in rapid bedside tests and can serve as a screening method for theophylline toxicity in unknown overdoses; however, toxic levels should be confirmed by formal laboratory analysis.

CLINICAL MANIFESTATIONS

Signs and symptoms of theophylline toxicity tend to parallel the serum theophylline concentration, in both frequency and severity; however, the evolution of toxicity is variable and patients may develop signs and symptoms of major toxicity without early manifestations. This is particularly true for patients taking theophylline chronically, who develop major toxicity at lower theophylline levels (Table 24–19–2).

The therapeutic window for theophylline is really quite small, and mild symptoms of toxicity can occur within the upper limits of the therapeutic range (serum level, 10–20 µg/mL). The dose required to reach this range is about 10 to 12 mg/kg per day in nonsmoking adults, with wide variability depending on patient age and underlying disease.

TABLE 24–19–1. FACTORS CONTRIBUTING TO THEOPHYLLINE TOXICITY

Factors that Increase Theophylline Level via Decreased Metabolism

Drugs taken concomitantly
  Allopurinol
  Antacids (increased absorption)
  Beta blockers (decreased elimination)
  Cimetidine, ranitidine
  Fluoroquinolones
  Oral contraceptives
  Macrolide antibiotics
  Acute ethanol

Drugs that may increase levels when discontinued
  Barbiturates
  Carbamazepine
  Phenytoin
  Rifampin
  Tobacco

Liver disease

Viral illness (hepatitis, influenza)

Congestive heart failure

Vaccines

Factors that Contribute to Iatrogenic Overdose

Different formulations with different theophylline content
  Anhydrous theophylline yields 100% theophylline
  Aminophylline yields 80% theophylline
  Choline theophylline (choledyl) yields 65% theophylline

Administration of bolus loading dose without verifying subtherapeutic level

Nonstandardized regimens for oral or intravenous dosing

Failure to recognize previous toxicity

Failure to check laboratory results despite theophylline level measured

Failure to recognize potential drug interactions

Failure to consider underlying systemic illness in dosing

As 1 mg/kg theophylline raises the serum level by about 2 μg/mL, a single dose of 10 mg/kg can result in toxicity.

Subjective

Gastrointestinal symptoms predominate early, with patient complaints of nausea, vomiting, diarrhea, and, infrequently, abdominal pain. Neurologic manifestations appear as wakefulness, agitation, irritability, and tremulousness. Hallucinations can occur but are more common in children. As tachycardia ensues and fluid losses from vomiting progress, patients may complain of palpitations and lightheadedness.

Patients who take theophylline chronically should be asked about recent dosage changes or changes in formulation (e.g., change to sustained-release preparations), and addition or discontinuation of medications (Table 24–19–1). Medical records should be reviewed for prior theophylline levels and dosage, previous toxic events and the circumstances that led to toxicity, and concurrent medications.

Objective

Physical Examination

Vital sign measurement will likely demonstrate a modest to marked tachycardia. Blood pressure may be elevated secondary to increased cardiac output or low due to gastrointestinal fluid losses and vasodilation. Hypotension occurs in about 25% of patients with acute poisoning but in less than 5% of cases with chronic overdose. Both rate and depth of respiration may be increased because of theophylline's stimulatory effect on the medullary respiratory center.

Patients may appear apprehensive and anxious, and visual hallucination may be apparent. Hyperreflexia is common and tremor can be pronounced. Seizure activity, either focal or generalized, is an ominous sign of life-threatening theophylline poisoning. Seizure activity in theophylline overdose is often in the form of status seizures. Altered mental status may be a sign of a postictal state or may be a manifestation of severe poisoning.

Because of catecholamine release, the cardiac examination may demonstrate a hyperdynamic state and include tachycardia, bounding pulses, a systolic flow murmur, and parasternal heave. Alternatively, dehydration and β_2 mediation of vasodilation may lead to hypovolemia and shock.

Bowel sounds are usually hyperactive. Gastrointestinal bleeding can occur, more often in acutely poisoned patients, secondary to direct mucosal irritation. Abdominal tenderness may be present due to protracted vomiting and infrequently due to secondary pancreatitis.

Rhabdomyolysis may occur in severe poisonings and compartment syndrome has also been described. Consequently, extremities should be examined for signs of compartment syndrome, including extremity turgidity, decreased pulses, pallor, and pain on palpation.

Routine Laboratory Abnormalities

Hypokalemia is found in most patients with acute poisoning. Approximately half of these patients have serum potassium levels less than 3 mEq/L. Much of the decrease in potassium is caused by intracellular shifts; total body potassium is not depleted unless vomiting remains uncontrolled.

A majority of acutely poisoned patients have a plasma glucose level above 150 mg/dL. Mild to moderate levels of leukocytosis, hypophosphatemia, hypomagnesemia, lactic acidosis, and respiratory alkalosis

TABLE 24–19–2. ACUTE VERSUS CHRONIC THEOPHYLLINE POISONING

	Acute Theophylline Toxicity	Chronic Theophylline Toxicity
Correlation of theophylline level with signs/symptoms	Good correlation	Poor correlation: patients may progress to major toxic symptoms without appearance of minor symptoms
Features of patients: acute versus chronic	Significantly younger	Older, often with underlying medical illness
	Higher peak levels and therefore more likely to exhibit toxicity	
	Better tolerance at any given level compared with chronic poisoning patients	Higher mortality
Mild: nausea, tremor, HR<120, BP systolic>120	Generally progresses from mild to moderate to severe	Lower incidence of minor toxicity
Moderate: vomiting responsive to antiemetics, HR<140, BP systolic>100, frequent PACs and PVCs, hyperreflexia, agitation	Signs and symptoms increase in number and severity with increasing theophylline concentration	Often present with more pronounced toxic symptoms
Major: uncontrollable emesis, HR>140, BP systolic<100, significant SVT or VT, seizures	Seizures unlikely below 60 μg/mL	Seizures likely above 40 μg/mL but can occur at lower levels
	Increased likelihood of seizures above 90 μg/mL	
	VT: cardiac arrest usually does not occur below 90 μg/kg	VT: cardiac arrest usually does not occur below 40 μg/kg

HR, heart rate; BP, blood pressure; PAC, premature atrial contraction; PVC, premature ventricular contraction; SVT, supraventricular tachycardia; VT, ventricular tachycardia.

are often seen with severe toxicity. Both hypocalcemia and hypercalcemia have been described. Creatine kinase levels may be elevated as well, either as a result of status seizure activity or because of toxin-mediated rhabdomyolysis.

The electrocardiogram usually demonstrates a tachycardia with a rate above 120. Patients with chronic poisoning are more likely to have cardiac arrythmias. Premature atrial and ventricular contractions can be frequent; multifocal atrial tachycardia, supraventricular tachycardia, atrial fibrillation, and atrial flutter all can result from the heightened automaticity that results from theophylline poisoning. Ventricular tachycardia and fibrillation can occur with severe poisoning, and when the theophylline level is above 90 μg/mL for acute poisoning and above 40 μg/mL for chronic poisoning. Prolongation of the QT interval can accompany the previously mentioned electrolyte disturbances and loss of T-wave prominence may be noted in patients who are hypokalemic.

PLANS

Diagnostic

Differential Diagnosis

The signs and symptoms of theophylline toxicity are variable and nonspecific and the differential diagnosis is vast. A differential diagnosis for theophylline toxicity needs to consider patient presentation. The following drugs have toxidromes that could overlap with the presentation of acute theophylline overdose in a patient who overdoses on an unknown drug:

- Seizures + hyperadrenergic state (tachycardia ± hypertension): amphetamines, cocaine, monoamine oxidase inhibitors, tricyclic antidepressants, diphenhydramine, oral hypoglycemic agents, insulin
- Seizures: isoniazid, strychnine, organophosphates, nicotine
- Tachycardia: beta agonists and other sympathomimetics, thyroid preparations, salicylates

For a patient who is known to be on theophylline and presents with a constellation of signs and symptoms consistent with theophylline toxicity, in addition to considering the independent differential diagnosis for seizures, tachycardia, or nausea/vomiting, one must consider diagnoses that mimic hyperadrenergic states: beta-agonist toxicity, pheochromocytoma, thyrotoxicosis, caffeine toxicity, sympathomimetic toxicity, hypoxia, hypoglycemia, chronic salicylate toxicity, monoamine oxidase inhibitor interaction with food or drugs, alcohol and benzodiazepine withdrawal.

Diagnostic Options

An assay of serum theophylline concentration will unequivocally establish the diagnosis. By definition, serum theophylline concentration will exceed 20 μg/mL. The absolute level depends on whether the poisoning is acute or chronic and on the formulation of theophylline used and the interval between administration and measurement. In acutely poisoned patients, severe toxicity (seizures, hypotension, and malignant arrhythmia) is unlikely below 60 μg/mL; for chronic theophylline poisoning, seizures can occur at levels as low as 30 μg/mL.

Toxic levels of theophylline increase the level of circulating catecholamines. As a result, predictable effects occur in potassium and glucose levels and in leukocyte counts. This metabolic derangement is most pronounced in acute poisoning and correlates well with peak theophylline levels. In chronic poisonings, such changes either are not present or are much more modest and do not correlate with theophylline level. Rapid salivary assays are available and used primarily for surveillance but may provide a rapid screen. Urine drug assays do not routinely screen for theophylline.

Recommended Approach

As for any intentional overdose, careful questioning of emergency services personnel, police, and the patient's family members and friends can yield valuable information regarding the identity of the ingestant. It may be a family member who is taking theophylline therapeutically instead of the patient. Or the theophylline may have been acquired as one of several over-the-counter preparations. Remaining pills can be identified by noting the imprinted number on the pill or capsule and contacting the regional poison control center. Serum theophylline levels should be obtained in all patients who are known to be taking theophylline and who present with constitutional complaints (nausea, vomiting, palpitations) or unexplained tachycardia. Among patients who are unable or unwilling to give a history of theophylline overdose or use, theophylline levels should be obtained in any patient who has unexplained seizures, repetitive vomiting, or tachycardia. This is especially true in patients who are known asthmatics, are found with metered-dose inhalers, or are wheezing on examination. A theophylline level should also be obtained in any overdose patient with the laboratory triad of hypokalemia, hyperglycemia, and leukocytosis. Once theophylline poisoning is confirmed, the theophylline level should be measured every 2 hours until a peak is observed and then every 8 to 12 hours until the theophylline level is below 20 μg/mL.

For patients who have taken an acute overdose and are asymptomatic, additional laboratory tests need not be obtained pending the theophylline level. The following ancillary laboratory tests should be obtained in definite theophylline overdose: serum electrolytes including inorganic phosphorus and calcium; arterial blood gases; complete blood cell count; blood urea nitrogen, creatinine, and glucose; 12-lead electrocardiogram and continuous cardiographic monitoring; urinalysis; and creatinine kinase. An acetaminophen level should be obtained 4 hours postingestion as a matter of routine for all intentional overdoses.

Therapeutic

Therapeutic Options

Immutable goals of treatment are stabilization of the ABCs (airway, breathing, and circulation), control of arrhythmias, control of seizures, prevention of further drug absorption, and enhancement of drug elimination. There is no theophylline-specific antidote.

Airway. The need for active airway management may occur in the setting of status seizures, malignant arrhythmias, or sedating coingestants, or because of underlying lung disease. Use of benzodiazepines and barbiturates to control seizures may also result in the need for airway control. In these situations, endotracheal intubation is warranted to protect the airway, enable more liberal use of sedating anticonvulsants, facilitate ventilation, and simplify gastric emptying. Use of appropriate induction agents must take into account the underlying propensity for seizures and the hemodynamics. Thiopental 3 to 5 mg/kg is a good choice if there is no hypotension. Midazolam 0.1 mg/kg also provides adequate sedation as well as seizure control and may not cause as much hypotension. Ketamine, although promoted as an induction agent for use in asthmatics, is not a good agent in this setting because of its effect on lowering the seizure threshold.

Breathing. As many of these patients are taking theophylline for obstructive lung disease, peak inspiratory pressure must be minimized when ventilating these patients. Airway pressures must be monitored and appropriate inspiratory:expiratory cycles should be employed.

Circulation. Patients may be hypotensive secondary to hypovolemia from protracted vomiting and diarrhea, as well as from β_2-adrenergic stimulation of the vasculature. Normal saline should be infused as 20 mL/kg boluses. Sinus tachycardia may respond to fluid hydration. Hemodynamically significant supraventricular tachycardia may respond to beta blockers or calcium channel blockers such as intravenous diltiazem. Caution must be exercised in administering beta blockers to patients with asthma. Esmolol, an ultra-short-acting beta blocker may have a role here. Bolus dosing is 0.5 mg/kg followed by a 0.05 mg/kg infusion. Lidocaine and propranolol should be considered for ventricular arrhythmias. In addition, acidosis, hypokalemia, and hypomagnesemia should be corrected.

Seizure Control. Control of seizures is achieved by the aggressive use of benzodiazepines and barbiturates. Lidocaine at 1.5 mg/kg, given intravenously over 30 to 60 seconds, can sometimes break status seizures that do not initially respond to benzodiazepines. As with most seizures from toxic causes, phenytoin is unlikely to be effective. For refractory seizures, control may not be achieved until the institution of aggressive detoxification procedures such as charcoal hemoperfusion. In such circumstances, neuromuscular blockade in conjunction with a thiopental infusion may be required as a temporizing measure to limit systemic sequelae from acidosis, hyperthermia, and rhabdomyolysis.

Prevention of Absorption. Gastric emptying has a limited role only for large acute poisonings with sustained-release preparations. Standard formulation theophylline is rapidly absorbed and reaches peak serum levels at 0.5 to 2 hours; in most cases patients are at their peak at presentation. Sustained-release preparations do not reach peak levels until 4 to 12 hours after ingestion. In some cases, this peak may be delayed for 24 hours. In patients who are not actively vomiting, gastric emptying can be accomplished with lavage using a 30-French gastric lavage tube. Ipecac, on the other hand, has absolutely no role here. It would be difficult to distinguish ipecac-induced emesis from theophylline toxicity. In addition, ipecac is contraindicated in overdoses that have a propensity for sudden seizure activity.

Enhancement of Elimination. Activated charcoal readily adsorbs theophylline and is the treatment of choice for theophylline-poisoned patients. Use of multiple-dose activated charcoal decreases the theophylline elimination half-life from 8.5 to 3.5 hours. Activated charcoal not only adsorbs theophylline within the gut lumen, but it also adsorbs theophylline across the intestinal vascular bed. As activated charcoal traverses the gastrointestinal tract, a gradient is established that favors this "gut dialysis." Thus, multiple-dose activated charcoal works even for intravenously administered theophylline overdoses. Activated charcoal should be given at a dose of 0.5 to 1 g/kg every 1 to 2 hours. Sorbitol may be used as a cathartic, with careful attention to hydration status. Charcoal should not be used if bowel sounds are absent, as bowel obstruction can occur from charcoal concretions.

Vomiting form theophylline toxicity may interfere with the ability to administer activated charcoal. Metoclopramide 0.1 mg/kg intravenously or ondansetron 0.15 mg/kg intravenously has been used successfully for antiemesis. Other techniques involve using smaller more frequent doses of charcoal or continuous nasogastric tube administration.

Whole-bowel irrigation using isotonic polyethylene glycol can be used in moderately toxic patients when oral charcoal fails to prevent a rise in serum theophylline. Polyethylene glycol is administered by mouth or nasal/oral gastric tube at a rate of 2 L/h in adults or 0.5 L/h in children. Clear rectal effluent is the desired treatment endpoint. Activated charcoal may be given alternating with polyethylene glycol to further enhance adsorptive elimination.

Theophylline is ideally suited to *extracorporeal removal.* Theophylline has a low volume of distribution (0.5 L/kg) and does not exhibit strong tissue binding. Sixty percent is protein bound; the unbound fraction freely distributes between plasma and interstitial and intracellular spaces. Charcoal hemoperfusion is the most efficacious method of clearance, resulting in 2-hour half-lives. Patients must be systemically anticoagulated and cannulated, and blood is then percolated through an adsorptive column containing activated charcoal. Blood is separated from the charcoal by a very thin, highly porous membrane that allows toxins to directly contact the charcoal column. With flow rates of 400 mL/min and the large adsorptive surface of the activated charcoal column, an efficient gradient is established. Complications of hemoperfusion relate primarily to systemic anticoagulation. A primary disadvantage of hemoperfusion is that availability is limited primarily to tertiary medical centers.

Hemodialysis is less efficient than hemoperfusion, primarily because a thicker dialysis membrane is required to separate blood from the dialysis solution, resulting in less effective diffusion. Elimination half-life is reduced to half, or 4.5 hours; however, hemodialysis has the advantages of wider availability and better clinician familiarity.

Peritoneal dialysis is ineffective for removing theophylline.

It bears emphasizing that multidose charcoal should be used adjunctively to hemodialysis and hemoperfusion. Because multidose charcoal is so effective, extracorporeal removal should be limited to patients with life-threatening manifestations or patients who are at risk for life-threatening complications and are unable to effectively keep down the charcoal (theophylline >90 µg/mL for acute, >40 µg/mL for chronic).

Recommended Approach

The recommended therapeutic approach is summarized in Table 24–19–3.

FOLLOW-UP

Once the serum theophylline level falls below 20 µg/mL and remains therapeutic for two levels spaced 8 hours apart, no further acute management is warranted. For acute poisonings, patients should be evalu-

TABLE 24–19–3. RECOMMENDED APPROACH TO TREATING THEOPHYLLINE OVERDOSE

ABCs: secure airway; O₂; IV normal saline, large bore, electrocardiogram monitor; O₂ saturation monitor; check chemstrip; consider glucose, naloxone, thiamine	
Stat theophylline level, repeat every 2 h until peak, then every 8–12 h	
Laboratory work: electrolytes, blood urea nitrogen, creatinine, calcium, phosphorus, magnesium, arterial blood gases, 12-lead electrocardiogram	
Hypotension/ sinus tachycardia	Fluid bolus 20 mL/kg, repeat as needed
Protracted vomiting	Ondantseron 0.15 mg/kg IV Metoclopramide 0.1 mg/kg IV
Hypokalemia	Usually requires no specific replacement and will correct Replenish carefully if cardiac arrythmias
Atrial tachyarrythmias	If hemodynamically significant, diltiazem 20 mg IV bolus, then 10 mg/h drip **or** Esmolol 0.5 mg/kg IV bolus, then 0.05 mg/kg drip
Ventricular arrhythmias, ventricular tachycardia	Synchronized cardioversion if unstable Lidocaine 1.5 mg/kg IV, then 2 mg/min drip Magnesium sulfate 2 g IV push Propranolol 1 mg IV Correct acid–base, electrolyte disorders
Seizure	Lorazepam 0.05 mg/kg IV, repeat, **or** diazepam 0.1 mg/kg IV, repeat Phenobarbital 20 mg/kg IV Lidocaine 1.5 mg/kg IV Thiopental 50–100 mg IV Q30–60s, repeat to total 5 mg/kg
Gastric lavage	Only for sustained release, not vomiting, and < 1 h since ingestion

Activated charcoal (with sorbitol)
  Treatment of choice for all patients, even those who require extracorporeal removal
  Do not use if absent bowel sounds, or if protracted vomiting uncontrolled per above methods
	0.5–1.0 g per nasogastric tube or by mouth, every 2 h

Whole-bowel irrigation Use if theophylline level continues to climb despite aggressive charcoal: potential for theophylline bezoar	Polyethylene glycol 2 L/ h orally or per nasogastric tube
Charcoal hemoperfusion Notify renal consultant early if potential for hemoperfusion or hemodialysis	For patients with refractory seizures, malignant arrhythmias, or persistent unstable hemodynamics or if unable to adequately take charcoal because of vomiting or for acute poisoning >90 µg/mL or chronic poisoning > 40 µg/mL
Hemodialysis	Same indications as above, for when hemoperfusion not available
Exchange transfusion	Most practical method for poisoned neonates

ated by psychiatry staff. For chronic poisonings, ongoing monitoring of serum theophylline should occur at least weekly. The source of chronic toxicity, as noted in Table 24–19–1, should be carefully sought.

DISCUSSION
Prevalence and Incidence

Clinical use of theophylline has decreased dramatically. Once a mainstay in the treatment of patients with acute asthma and chronic obstructive lung disease, it is now used primarily in select patients who are refractory to treatment with beta agonists. In addition, theophylline continues to be used as a respiratory stimulant for premature infants with poor respiratory drive. The most recent data from the American Association of Poison Control Centers noted 4473 toxic exposures for 1993. Of these, 2873 required treatment in a health care facility. Overdose was classified as unintentional in 56%, intentional in 26%, and adverse reaction in 6%, with the remainder unknown (Litovitz et al., 1994). One quarter of reported cases had no toxicity, and one quarter had only mild toxicity. One hundred twenty (3%) had major toxicity and 27 patients died from their overdose, for a mortality rate of 18% for patients with major toxicity. Two fatalities were classified as acute poisoning, with peak theophylline levels of 70 and 105 µg/mL. Levels in 7 deaths with acute on chronic overdose ranged from 39 to 123 (mean, 72.4 µg/mL). The peak level in 14 patients with chronic overdose ranged from 30 to 98 (mean, 50.6) (Litovitz et al., 1994). It must be emphasized that the poison control center data are grossly underreported.

Related Basic Science

The mechanism of action for theophylline's therapeutic effect on bronchial smooth muscle is unknown. Although once thought to involve inhibition of phosphodiesterase and increase in cyclic AMP, this mechanism is not active until toxic doses are reached. Theophylline is rapidly absorbed from the gastrointestinal tract and peak levels are reached in about 45 minutes. Sustained-release preparations slow absorption and may be only 50% absorbed at 5 hours. In some cases, patients present with toxicity 12 to 24 hours postingestion. Theophylline is metabolized primarily in liver, with only 10% excreted unmetabolized in the urine. Hepatic metabolism is dependent on the cytochrome P450 system. Drugs or disease processes that interfere with this enzyme system increase theophylline toxicity; withdrawal of drugs that induce this enzyme system likewise contributes to toxicity in the steady state (Table 24–19–1). Neonates use alternate metabolic pathways that lead to caffeine as an intermediate and excretion of 50% of theophylline unchanged. Such pathways are saturated earlier and elimination half-lives are 30 hours for neonates, decreasing to 14 hours by 6 months.

Theophylline increases circulating catecholamines, and it is these catecholamines that are mediators of many of the toxic effects of theophylline. Thus, tachycardia and hypotension are caused by β_1 and β_2 agonism, respectively. Seizures may be enhanced by catechol-induced cerebral vascular constriction. Hypokalemia, hyperglycemia, and leukocytosis are all catecholamine mediated.

Theophylline has direct effects on the chemoreceptor zone of the medulla, resulting in nausea and vomiting. In addition, theophylline has direct irritative effects on gastric mucosa and can cause erosive gastritis and gastrointestinal hemorrhage. Increased gastric secretions results in increased emesis volume as well as contributing to diarrhea. Theophylline also stimulates the medullary respiratory center, resulting in central hyperventilation and respiratory alkalosis.

In toxic doses, theophylline does inhibit phosphodiesterase, resulting in an inhibition in the production of adenosine. Adenosine is known to be responsible for negative feedback to the heart in situations of sympathetic overstimulation. Blockade of adenosine receptors and the loss of this negative feedback may compound the effect of circulating catecholamines. Adenosine antagonism may explain both the increased malignant arrhythmias and the increased seizures that are seen with severe theophylline poisoning. In addition, buildup of cerebral cyclic AMP has been shown to be epileptigenic in some animals.

Natural History and Its Modification with Treatment

Theophylline poisoning remains a significant cause of medication-related death. Failure to diagnose toxicity in a patient taking theophylline chronically risks the development of potentially fatal seizures or arrhythmias. Often such patients do not have symptoms of mild toxicity before exhibiting life-threatening symptoms. Although aggressive therapy as outlined in this chapter results in complete recovery for most patients, the mortality rate for patients with major toxicity remains about 10%.

Prevention

All patients who take theophylline should have routine surveillance screening of theophylline levels. A careful record of medications should be maintained and screened for drug interactions any time a medication is added or deleted. Patients must be educated on how to take their theophylline and on what signs and symptoms to watch for that could signal toxicity. Ideally, patients should be presented with a medication instruction form written at an appropriate educational level. Hospital ordering of theophylline dose must be standardized (e.g., mg/h) and hospital pharmacies should consider computerized screening programs for drug interactions and duplicate medications. Protocols must be established for prompt reporting of toxic theophylline levels and practitioners should withhold additional dosing of theophylline until a level has been reported.

Cost Containment

Inexpensive bedside screening assays are available that can quickly measure serum theophylline. Judicious use of such screens can prevent chronic theophylline toxicity. Many acutely poisoned patients can be managed without intensive care unit admission by using aggressive multidose charcoal. Patients with a peak level of 60 µg/mL should have a level of about 30 µg/mL at 4 hours. Failure to observe a significant decrease in theophylline at 2 hours or the presence of any serious toxic symptoms should prompt admission to an intensive care unit monitored bed. All chronically theophylline-poisoned patients should be initially admitted to a monitored bed, as fatalities have occurred at levels as low as 25 µg/mL.

REFERENCES

Cooling DS. Theophylline toxicity. J Emerg Med. 1993;11:415.
Dawson AH, Whyte IM. The assessment and treatment of theophylline poisoning. Med J Aust 1989;151:689.
Gaudreault P, Guay J. Theophylline poisoning: Pharmacological considerations and clinical management. Med Toxicol 1986;1:3.
Litovitz TL, Clark LR, Soloway RA. 1993 Annual Report of the American Association of Poison Control Centers Toxic Exposure Surveillance System. Am J Emerg Med 1994;12:546.
Paloucek FP, Rodvold KA. Evaluation of theophylline overdoses and toxicities. Ann Emerg Med 1988;17:135.
Skinner MH. Adverse reactions and interactions with theophylline. Drug Saf 1990;5:275.
Stork CM, Howland MA, Goldfrank LR. Concepts and controversies of bronchodilator overdose. Emerg Med Clin North Am 1994;12:415.

Appendices

APPENDIX I:

Defined Data Base*

Date _____

Name _____ Initial Data Base? ☐

                                                                                    (check one)

Age _____ Sex _____ Interval Data Base? ☐

                                                                                    See Data Base of

Source _____ Reliability _____

                                                        Month   Day   Year

Patient's Major Physician or Preadmission Clinic Area (Enter "none" if none)

_____

THE HISTORY

Chief Complaint and Present Illness:

---

*This Defined Data Base was originally published in Walker HK, Hall WD, Hurst JW. Clinical methods: The history, physical and laboratory examinations. Boston: Butterworth, 1976. Reproduced with permission of the publisher.

INSTRUCTIONS

Check **no** or **yes** for the history; check **normal** or **abnormal** for the physical. Leave blank if not asked or not done. Write **NA** if not applicable. Write **NK** if unknown by the patient or examiner. Give narrative description in space on right for all **yes** answers.

No		Yes	No		Yes
	General			**Cardiovascular System**	
☐	Weight change	☐	☐	Inadequate exercise level	☐
☐	Fever/chills	☐	☐	Orthopnea/paroxysmal nocturnal dyspnea	☐
☐	Night sweats	☐	☐	Chest discomfort/pain	☐
☐	Dizziness	☐	☐	Palpitations	☐
☐	Other	☐	☐	Syncope	☐
			☐	Edema	☐
	Endocrine System		☐	Phlebitis	☐
			☐	Claudication	☐
☐	Heat/cold intolerance	☐	☐	Hypertension	☐
☐	Thyroid problems	☐	☐	Rheumatic	☐
☐	Neck surgery/irradiation	☐	☐	Past heart disease	☐
☐	Diabetes/diabetic indicators	☐	☐	Family history heart disease	☐
			☐	Other	☐
	Eye				
				Genitourinary System	
☐	Visual dysfunction	☐			
☐	Other	☐	☐	Urinary frequency/urgency/dysuria	☐
			☐	Urinary tract infection	☐
	Ear, Nose, Throat		☐	Flank pain	☐
			☐	Nocturia	☐
☐	Difficulty hearing/deaf	☐	☐	Hematuria	☐
☐	Tinnitus	☐	☐	Past stones	☐
☐	Epistaxis	☐	☐	Urinary stream flow abnormality	☐
☐	Hoarseness	☐	☐	Urethral discharge	☐
☐	Sinusitis	☐	☐	Syphilis/positive serology	☐
☐	Vertigo	☐	☐	Male genital lesions	☐
☐	Other	☐	☐	Testicular mass/pain	☐
			☐	Impotence	☐
	Gastrointestinal System		☐	Family history renal disease	☐
			☐	Other	☐
☐	Nausea/retching	☐			
☐	Vomiting	☐		**Birth Control**	
☐	Hematemesis	☐			
☐	Melena	☐	☐	Birth control method	☐
☐	Dysphagia	☐			
☐	Indigestion	☐		**Gynecologic System**	
☐	Heartburn	☐			
☐	Abdominal pain	☐	☐	Pelvic pain	☐
☐	Abdominal swelling	☐	☐	Vaginal discharge	☐
☐	Jaundice	☐	☐	Abnormal vaginal bleeding	☐
☐	Hematochezia	☐			
☐	Diarrhea	☐		a. Menarch: Age _____ years	
☐	Constipation	☐		b. Menopause: Age _____ years	
☐	Hernia	☐		c. Menstrual flow, interval: _____ days	
☐	Hemorrhoids	☐		d. Menstrual flow, duration: _____ days	
☐	Peptic ulcer disease	☐		e. Menstrual flow, amount: _____	
☐	Gallbladder disease	☐		f. Date last menstrual period: _____	
☐	Pancreatitis	☐		g. Postcoital bleeding	
☐	GI surgery	☐		h. Postmenopausal bleeding	
☐	Alcohol intake	☐	☐	Pelvic mass	☐
☐	Other	☐	☐	Other	☐
	Pulmonary System			**Sexual History**	
☐	Dyspnea/breathlessness/shortness of breath	☐	☐	Sexual difficulties	☐
☐	Cough/sputum production	☐			
☐	Hemoptysis	☐		**Breast**	
☐	Wheezing/asthma	☐			
☐	Tuberculosis/tbc exposure	☐	☐	Breast lump	☐
☐	Past PPD	☐	☐	Breast pain	☐
☐	Previous chest	☐	☐	Nipple discharge	☐
☐	Respiratory infections/pneumonia	☐	☐	Other	☐
☐	Smoking history	☐			
☐	Environmental inhalation	☐		**Skin**	
☐	Other	☐			
			☐	Skin disorder	☐
			☐	Itching	☐

No   **Yes**   **No**   **Yes**

☐ Mole(s) ☐

☐ Skin cancer ☐

☐ Other ☐

Immunizations

☐ ☐ Past immunizations ☐

Neurologic System

☐ Headaches ☐

☐ Epileptic seizures ☐

☐ Episodic neurologic symptoms ☐

☐ Pain/sensory perversions ☐

☐ Weakness ☐

☐ Head trauma ☐

☐ Muscle cramps ☐

☐ Stroke ☐

☐ Sleep disorder ☐

☐ Other ☐

Family History

☐ ☐ Heritable disease potential ☐

Hospitalizations and Medications

☐ ☐ Past hospitalizations ☐

        Date   Location   Reason

☐ ☐ Current/recent medications ☐

             Drug (current)   Dose   Frequency

Hematopoietic System

☐ Excessive bleeding/bruising ☐

☐ Anemia ☐

☐ Pica ☐

☐ Family history sickle cell ☐

☐ Other ☐

1.

2.

3.

Musculoskeletal System

☐ Joint stiffness ☐

☐ Joint pain ☐

☐ Joint swelling ☐

☐ Family history musculoskeletal disease ☐

☐ Other ☐

4.

5.

6.

7.

Psychiatric

☐ Previous psychiatric problems or hospitalizations ☐

☐ Interpersonal relationship difficulties ☐

☐ Anxiety ☐

☐ Depression ☐

☐ Loss of control/violence potential ☐

☐ Disturbances of vegetative function ☐

☐ Substance abuse ☐

☐ Other ☐

8.

9.

10.

Allergies

☐ Drug allergies ☐

☐ Other ☐   ☐   Other historical data

THE PATIENT PROFILE

Occupation:_____

_____

_____

_____

Usual day's activities:

   Morning: _____

   Afternoon: _____

   Evening: _____

Hobbies/interests:

_____

_____

_____

_____

_____

_____

_____

_____

_____

Nutritional history:

_____

_____

_____

_____

_____

_____

_____

_____

_____

Education:

_____

_____

_____

_____

Financial difficulties:

_____

_____

_____

_____

_____

THE PHYSICAL EXAMINATION

Normal*		Abnormal*

General

☐ General appearance ☐

☐ Temperature (oral ☐ rectal ☐), _____ C° ☐

☐ Respiratory ☐

   a. Rate: _____/min.
   b. Rhythm: _____

☐ Pulse ☐

   a. Rate: _____/min.
   b. Rhythm: _____

☐ Blood Pressure: _____/_____ mm Hg ☐
   If abnormal:

   a. Leg: _____/_____ mm Hg
   b. Standing: _____/_____ mm Hg

☐ Body size
☐ Height _____ (cm ☐ in. ☐) ☐
☐ Weight _____ (kg ☐ lb. ☐) ☐

   a. Ideal body weight: _____
   b. % of ideal body weight: _____%

☐ Body habitus ☐
☐ Hair ☐
☐ Skin ☐
☐ Nails ☐
☐ Other ☐

Head, Ears, Nose

☐ Cranial/orbital bruit ☐
☐ Pinnae/canals/drums ☐
☐ Nose ☐
☐ Other ☐

Eyes

☐ External eye ☐
☐ Fundi ☐
☐ Pupil ☐
☐ Other ☐

R   L

Oral Cavity

☐ Teeth/gums/oral mucosa ☐
☐ Tongue ☐
☐ Tonsils/pharynx ☐
☐ Parotid enlargement ☐
☐ Other ☐

Neck

☐ Inspection ☐
☐ Carotid bruit (R) (L) ☐
☐ Venous hum ☐
☐ Thyroid ☐
☐ Other ☐

Nodes

☐ Lymphadenopathy ☐
   If present, indicate location:

	R	L
Cervical	a	b
Epitrochlear	c	d
Axillary	e	f
Inguinal	g	h
Other	i	j

Chest

☐ Chest structure ☐
☐ Chest motion ☐
☐ Chest auscultation ☐
☐ Chest percussion ☐
☐ Other ☐

Breast

☐ Mass ☐
☐ Nipple/areola ☐
☐ Other ☐

Anterior   Posterior

R   L

---

*Occasionally, normal/abnormal does not apply as well as absent/present. Parotid enlargement is an example. If parotid enlargement is present, mark **abnormal**. If the parotid glands are normal size, mark **normal**.

Normal*   **Abnormal***

Cardiovascular System

☐	Jugular venous pressure: _____ cm at _____ °	☐
☐	Jugular venous pulsations	☐
☐	Carotid pulse	☐
☐	Apex impulse	☐
☐	Parasternal impulse	☐
☐	Pulmonary artery pulsation	☐
☐	First heart sound	☐
☐	Second heart sound	☐
☐	Third heart sound	☐
☐	Fourth heart sound	☐
☐	Click	☐
☐	Systolic murmur	☐
☐	Diastolic murmur	☐
☐	Edema:	☐
	Right leg 1 2 3 4	
	Left leg 1 2 3 4	
☐	Thrombophlebitis	☐
☐	Clubbing	☐
☐	Cyanosis	☐
☐	Pulsus alternans	☐
☐	Other	☐

Jugular venous pulsations
Carotid artery pulsations
Precordial pulsation
Auscultation

| ☐ | Peripheral pulses/bruits | ☐ |

Complete chart. Scale pulses 0-4 (normal = 3) and circle if bruit present.

	Carotid	Brachial	Radial	Aorta	Femoral	Popliteal	PT	DP
Right	a	c	e		h	j	l	n
Left	b	d	f	g	i	k	m	o

Abdomen

☐	Inspection	☐
☐	Auscultation: bowel sounds/bruits/rubs	☐
☐	Palpation: pain/tenderness	☐
☐	Ascites	☐
☐	Liver: auscultation	☐
☐	Liver: shape/size	☐
☐	Spleen	☐
☐	Inguinal canal	☐
☐	Other	☐

Normal*   **Abnormal***

Male Genitalia

| ☐ | External male genitalia | ☐ |

Female Genitalia

| ☐ | Pelvic exam: | ☐ |
| | Indicate site(s) of abnormality | |

a. External genitalia
b. Vagina
c. Cervix
d. Uterus
e. Adnexa
f. Pap test: done ☐   not done ☐

| ☐ | Other | ☐ |

Rectal Examination

☐	Rectal: inspection/tone/hemorrhoids	☐
☐	Prostate	☐
☐	Stool occult blood: _____	☐

Musculoskeletal

| ☐ | Musculoskeletal exam: | ☐ |

Hands and wrists
Elbow
Shoulder
TMJ
Cervical spine
Thoracic and lumbar spine
Hip
Knee
Foot and ankle

	R	L
	a	b
	c	d
	e	f
	g	h
	i	
	j	
	k	l
	m	n
	o	p

| ☐ | Other | ☐ |

Neurologic and Psychiatric

☐	Appearance/affect/motor behavior	☐
☐	General intellectual functions	☐
☐	Attention span	☐
☐	Judgment	☐
☐	Abstraction	☐
☐	Delusions/hallucinations/illusions	☐
☐	Associations of thought	☐
☐	Orientation	☐
☐	Memory	☐
☐	Level of consciousness	☐

Normal*		Abnormal*

□ Speech and other lateralizing cortical functions □

Cranial Nerves:
□ I. Olfactory nerve □
□ II. Optic Nerve □

□   a. Visual acuity □
□   b. Visual fields □

□ III, IV, VI. Oculomotor, trochlear, and abducens nerves □
□ V. Trigeminal nerve □
□ VII. Facial nerve □
□ VIII. Acoustic nerve
   Weber/Rinne tuning fork test □
□ IX, X. Glossopharyngeal and vagus nerves □
□ XI. Spinal accessory nerve □
□ XII. Hypoglossal nerve □
□ Sensation: (specify modalities tested) □

Upper extremities:

Lower extremities:

□ Motor system (strength, atrophy, fasciculations, drift, fine movements) □

Upper extremities:

Lower extremities:

Gait:

□ Cerebellum □
□ Involuntary movements □

   a. Tremor □
   b. Chorea □
   c. Athetosis □
   d. Myoclonus □
   e. Asterixis □

□ Suck/snout, grasp reflexes □
□ Deep tendon reflexes □
□ Plantar reflex □

Grade 0–4 where 4 = repeating clonus; plantar reflex ↑, ↓, or →.

	BICEPS (C$^{5-6}$)	BR-RAD (C$^{5-6}$)	TRICEPS (C$^{5-7}$)	FJ (C^{8}T^1)	KNEE JERK (L$^{3-4}$)	ANKLE JERK (S$^{1-2}$)	Plantar Reflex
Right	a	c	e	g	i	k	210a
Left	b	d	f	h	j	l	210b

□ Other □

□ Other physical examination data

Hematology

□ Hematocrit _____ vol % □
□ White blood cell count _____/μL □
□ Differential: ___S,___L,___M,___E,___B □
□ Platelets ___/hpf or ___/μL □
□ RBC morphology □

Urinalysis

□ Urine color/odor □
□ Urine specific gravity 1.0 ___ ___ □
□ Proteinuria Neg Tr 1 2 3 4 □

Normal*		Abnormal*

□ Glucosuria/ketonuria G: Neg Tr 1 2 3 4 □
        K: Neg TR 1 2 3 4
□ Urine sediment: ___wbc/hpf; ___rbc/hpf □
  Other: _____

Chemistries

□ BUN ___mg/dL □
□ Glucose: (serum □ plasma □) ___mg/dL □
□ Serum sodium (Na) ___mEq/L □
□ Serum potassium (K) ___mEq/L □
□ Serum chloride (Cl) ___mEq/L □
□ Serum total CO_2 content (CO_2) ___mEq/L □
□ SGOT ___IU/L □
□ LDH ___IU/L □
□ Alkaline phosphatase ___IU/L □
□ Total bilirubin ___mg/dL □
□ Uric acid ___mg/dL □
□ Creatinine ___mg/dL □
□ Calcium ___mg/dL □
□ Serum inorganic phosphorus ___mg/dL □
□ Cholesterol ___mg/dL □
□ Total protein ___mg/dL □
□ Albumin/globulin ___g/dL □

Miscellaneous

□ Intermediate PPD: ___mm induration □
□ VDRL/RPR □

Electrocardiogram

□ EKG □
a. Rate: ___/min. b. Rhythm: _____
Intervals: c. PQ ___; d. QRS _____
e. QT _____;
f. Interpretation: _____
_____
_____

Chest X-ray

□ Chest X-Ray □
Interpretation: _____
_____
_____

☐ Other laboratory data

APPENDIX 2

Dynamic Tests of Pituitary Function

Lewis S. Blevins, Jr., M.D.

ADRENOCORTICOTROPIC HORMONE (ACTH) STIMULATION TEST

Procedure

Synthetic ACTH 1–24, 250 µg, is administered intramuscularly or intravenously. Serum cortisol levels are obtained at 0, 30, and 60 minutes.

Interpretation

A normal response is defined by an ACTH-stimulated cortisol level greater than 20 µg/dL. Response may be normal in patients with ACTH deficiency of relatively recent onset.

INSULIN-INDUCED HYPOGLYCEMIA TEST

Procedure

Regular insulin 0.1 U/kg is administered intravenously. Serum cortisol, glucose, and growth hormone levels are obtained at 0, 30, 45, 60, and 90 minutes. Adrenal responsiveness to exogenous ACTH should be demonstrated prior to the test. This test is contraindicated in patients with severe illness, cerebrovascular disease, seizure disorder, or coronary artery disease. A physician should be in attendance. Dextrose (25 g) should be available for intravenous administration in case of neuroglycopenia. Peripheral (adrenergic) manifestations of hypoglycemia usually occur at 45 to 60 minutes.

Interpretation

A normal response is defined by a peak serum cortisol level greater than 20 µg/dL and a peak growth hormone level greater than 7 ng/mL. Subnormal cortisol responses are not valid unless the glucose is less than 40 mg/dL or less than 50% of the basal value.

OVERNIGHT METYRAPONE TEST

Procedure

Metyrapone 30 mg/kg is administered orally at 11 PM with a snack. Serum cortisol and 11-deoxycortisol levels are obtained at 8 AM the following morning. Patients should be hospitalized because metyrapone can precipitate acute adrenal insufficiency. Dexamethasone phosphate 4 mg/mL should be available for intramuscular or intravenous administration in case of adrenal insufficiency.

Interpretation

A normal 11-deoxycortisol response depends on the particular assay and reference laboratory used. In most assays, peak 11-deoxycortisol values greater than 5 to 10 µg/dL are normal. Falsely abnormal 11-deoxycortisol responses may occur in patients following reversal of long-standing ACTH deficiency. Measurement of the ACTH response to metyrapone (normal is greater than 112 pg/mL) may identify these patients.

THYROTROPIN-RELEASING HORMONE STIMULATION TEST

Procedure

Thyrotropin-releasing hormone 500 µg is administered intravenously. Serum thyroid-stimulating hormone (TSH) levels are obtained at 0, 30, and 60 minutes. Some patients experience transient nausea and flushing.

Interpretation

A normal response is defined by net increases in TSH of 6 to 30 mU/L in men and 4.5–15 mU/L in women. The magnitude of the TSH response is proportional to the basal TSH. Patients with TSH deficiency and thyrotoxicosis usually have abnormal responses.

GONADOTROPIN-RELEASING HORMONE STIMULATION TEST

Procedure

Gonadotropin-releasing hormone 100 µg is administered intravenously. Serum luteinizing hormone levels are obtained at 0, 15, and 30 minutes.

Interpretation

A normal response is characterized by a two- to threefold increase in luteinizing hormone. Blunted responses are seen in patients with hypopituitarism and functional gonadotropin deficiency. Patients with hypothalamic disease and otherwise normal pituitary glands often have normal responses if the test is performed 1 week following daily administration of 100 µg gonadotropin-releasing hormone.

CLONIDINE STIMULATION TEST

Procedure

Clonidine 4 µg/kg is administered orally. Serum growth hormone is obtained at 0, 60, 90, and 120 minutes. Relative hypotension and drowsiness are common.

Interpretation

A normal response is characterized by a three- to sixfold rise in growth hormone.

L-DOPA STIMULATION TEST

Procedure

L-Dopa 500 mg is administered orally. Growth hormone levels are obtained at 0, 60, 90, and 120 minutes. Nausea and vomiting may occur.

Interpretation

A normal response is characterized by a peak growth hormone level greater than 7 ng/mL.

ARGININE STIMULATION TEST
Procedure

Arginine hydrochloride 500 mg/kg is administered intravenously over 30 minutes. Growth hormone levels are obtained at 0, 60, 90, and 120 minutes. This test is contraindicated in patients with renal failure and liver disease.

Interpretation

A normal response is characterized by a peak growth hormone level greater than 7 ng/mL.

APPENDIX 3

Normal Reticuloendothelial System Response

Jonathan L. Myles, M.D.

DEFINITION

The normal reticuloendothelial system response is a physiologic controlled immune response to a given stimulus.

ETIOLOGY

The reticuloendothelial system is a part of every normal person. It is being emphasized here because its response to a stimulus is now considered commonly in a physician's daily work.

CRITERIA FOR DIAGNOSIS
Suggestive

Abnormalities of lymph node architecture and lymphocyte subsets occur following a variety of environmental stimuli and in autoimmune disease. Often, the pattern of abnormalities may be useful in arriving at a specific diagnosis. For example, histologic examination of an axillary lymph node may reveal loosely formed granulomas composed of histiocytes with rare multinucleate giant cells and no necrosis. Such a pattern of reaction, although not specific, should alert the clinician to order the appropriate serologic tests to rule out toxoplasmosis.

Definitive

Following withdrawal of a stimulus in many cases the morphologic and laboratory abnormalities may return to normal (undergo resolution); however, sequelae may persist. For example, middle-aged and elderly individuals often have some fibrosis (scarring) in the inguinal lymph nodes as a result of some previous reactive process.

CLINICAL MANIFESTATIONS
Subjective

An individual with normal immune function may have no complaints or complaints related to the immune response. Response to infection may include tender cervical lymph nodes.

Objective

Response to an antigenic stimulus often results in lymphadenopathy. Normal responses, although they may result in lymphadenopathy, do not result in hard and fixed lymph nodes. Rock hard lymph nodes are highly suspicious for metastatic carcinoma. In lymphomas, the lymph nodes are not as firm as in carcinoma. Laboratory tests may be abnormal as described below.

PLANS
Diagnostic

A large variety of tests are available to evaluate lymphoreticuloendothelial response. Perhaps the three most commonly used are the complete blood count (and peripheral blood smear), immunophenotyping of peripheral blood lymphocytes, and histologic examination of a lymph node. The complete blood count is not discussed further and is discussed elsewhere in this text.

Immunophenotyping of peripheral blood lymphocytes is fast and accurate, and provides data useful in arriving at a specific diagnosis. The most common way of immunotyping is by flow cytometry. This technique requires the use of a cell suspension. The cells are individually passed through a laser light source. Antibodies to various antigens may be coupled to fluorescein, phycoerythrin, or other fluorochromes and the number of cells expressing that antigen may be calculated. Also, cells may be evaluated for the presence of dual or three-color labeling. For example, in an active viral infection there may be an expanded CD8 T-cell population that also expresses HLA-DR and the interleukin-2 receptor. Propidium iodide stoichiometrically binds to DNA and this may be used to determine the DNA content of the cells to assess for the presence or absence of DNA aneuploid stemlines. An aneuploid cell population would strongly raise one's suspicion that a neoplastic cell population is present.

Lymphocyte phenotyping may be done on peripheral blood or any biopsy tissue in which there is suspicion of lymphoma; however, the tissue must be processed quickly and be fresh (not exposed to fixative). Proper communication between the primary care physician, surgeon, and pathologist is essential to optimally evaluate a specimen.

A variety of antibodies may be used in evaluating a given specimen. In AIDS patients, a CD4 and CD3 count on the peripheral blood may be used for prognostic purposes. Other diagnostic considerations require more extensive testing. If a lymphoproliferative disorder is suspected, kappa and lambda staining is useful in establishing the presence or absence of B-cell clonality. Loss of T antigens (e.g., CD4) or aberrant T-cell phenotypes (e.g., CD3+, CD4+, CD7−) are useful in suspecting T-cell clonality; however, unless malignant morphologic features are present, definitive establishment of T-cell clonality requires the use of gene rearrangement studies by Southern blot analysis or the polymerase chain reaction. Table A3–1 lists some of the common antibodies used in the evaluation of lymphocytes. Antibodies often react with more than one cell type, such that a panel of antibodies are used to provide a basis for proper interpretation.

Interpretation of flow cytometric studies is best done in conjunction with clinical findings. One of the more common tests ordered is a peripheral blood CD4:CD8 ratio. Although the CD4:CD8 ratio is decreased in HIV-related diseases, it may also be decreased in other states, such as Epstein–Barr virus and cytomegalovirus infections. In HIV-associated diseases, the CD4 count is usually decreased. The CD4:CD8 ratio may be increased in autoimmune disease.

Immunophenotyping of biopsy tissue may also be performed to aid in establishing clonality. Although large cell lymphomas are often obviously malignant, the low-grade lymphomas may be difficult to distinguish from a reactive hyperplasia. In such instances, demonstration of clonality may be useful in confirming malignancy.

Clonality may also be established by detecting immunoglobulin and

TABLE A3–1. COMMON ANTIBODIES USED IN PHENOTYPING OF THE LYMPHOCYTES

Antibody	Predominant Reactivity
CD2	T cells
CD3	T cells
CD4	Helper/inducer T cells
CD8	Suppressor/cytotoxic T cells
CD10	B cells
CD16/56	Natural killer (NK) cells
CD19	B cells
CD20	B cells
CD38	Plasma cells
Kappa	B cells (kappa)
Lambda	B cells (lambda)
HLA-DR	B cells and activated T cells

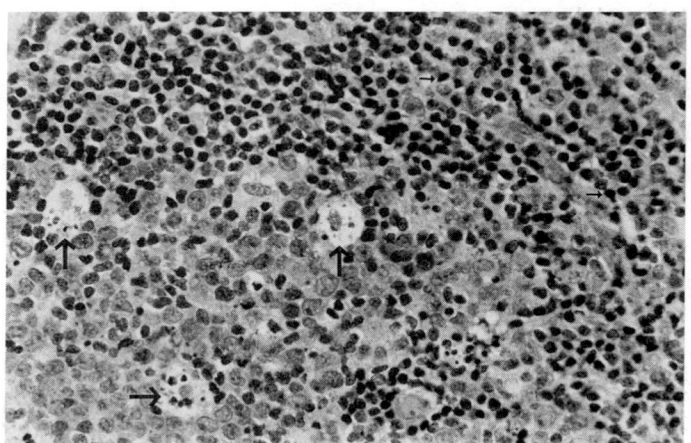

Figure A3–2. Tingible body macrophages. These macrophages (large arrows) are commonly seen in germinal centers in reactive states. Small lymphocytes (small arrows) are shown for comparison.

T-cell-receptor gene rearrangements by Southern blot analysis. This test may also be performed on peripheral blood or tissue biopsy samples. Immunoglobulin and T-cell receptors are unique to a given antigen. Human DNA contains constant, joining, and variable domains in each cell. As each cell responds to a given antigen, a unique "rearrangement" among these genes occurs. Nonrearranged DNA is referred to as "germline," which is considered the normal result when this test is ordered. Because there are so many "rearrangements" occurring due to the large number of antigens individuals are exposed to, usually only the germline configuration is observed by Southern blot analysis in normal or "reactive" tissues. Non-germline bands may be seen in non-Hodgkin's lymphomas. The technique may detect clonal expansion when less than 5% of the cells are of any given clone. Thus, it is a much more sensitive but rather slow technique compared with flow cytometry. Southern blot analysis can also definitively identify a T-cell clonal expansion, whereas flow cytometry may only suggest this. Southern blot analysis is useful in the following situations:

- Undifferentiated malignancy: DNA rearrangements occur before protein expression. Establishment of immunoglobulin or T-cell-receptor rearrangements is indicative of hematopoietic origin of a neoplasm, which is useful in guiding therapy.
- Borderline cases in which flow cytometry yields equivocal results: Establishment of clonality by Southern blot, however, does not equate with malignancy and requires correlation with clinical and pathologic findings. Some histologically benign lesions may exhibit clonality. The significance of this is uncertain at present.
- To confirm the presence of recurrent neoplasm (such as in a body fluid): When sample size is too small for flow cytometry.

- When retrospective analysis is needed: Gene rearrangement studies may be performed retrospectively on frozen tissue procured at the time of initial sample handling.

Histologic examination of hematopoietic tissue usually consists of bone marrow examination (which is discussed elsewhere in this text) or lymph node examination. Normal lymph nodes have several components. Lymphoid follicles consist of germinal centers and the surrounding rim of maturing lymphocytes referred to as a *mantle zone* (Figure A3–1). These are the B-cell areas of the lymph node. The interfollicular and paracortical regions consist of T cells, but plasma cells and histiocytes are also scattered in this region. In a normal lymph node, the "sinuses" are often open; that is, they are readily identifiable and filled predominantly with tissue macrophages.

A variety of reactive changes may be seen in lymph nodes. Nonspecific changes may be seen, such as follicular hyperplasia, interfollicular hyperplasia, sinus histiocytosis, and the presence of tingible body macrophages in germinal centers (Figure A3–2). A variety of stimuli may cause these changes. Adjacent neoplastic processes may also be the etiology of these findings, such that if there is a high clinical suspicion of malignancy, procurement of additional tissue may be indicated.

A variety of histologic patterns may suggest a given disease process, although each requires correlation with other findings (Table A3–2).

In infectious mononucleosis, a large number of immunoblasts may be present, mimicking non-Hodgkin's lymphoma. Reed–Sternberg-like cells may also be present, mimicking Hodgkin's disease. In such instances, it is important that the pathologist be made aware that the patient has an active Epstein–Barr virus infection.

Granulomatous inflammation may be due to a variety of etiologies including mycobacterial and fungal infection, sarcoidosis, and foreign material. Necrosis is commonly seen in mycobacterial infection, although it is not as common in sarcoidosis. Although large amounts of necrosis are suggestive of infection, other etiologies need to be considered in the differential diagnosis. Pyogranulomas (neutrophils in the center of a granuloma) are often seen in blastomycosis. Wegener's granulomatosis is in the differential diagnosis of pulmonary granulomatous lesions. Large amounts of necrosis are usually present and there is often involvement of the nasopharynx and kidney. Antineutrophil cy-

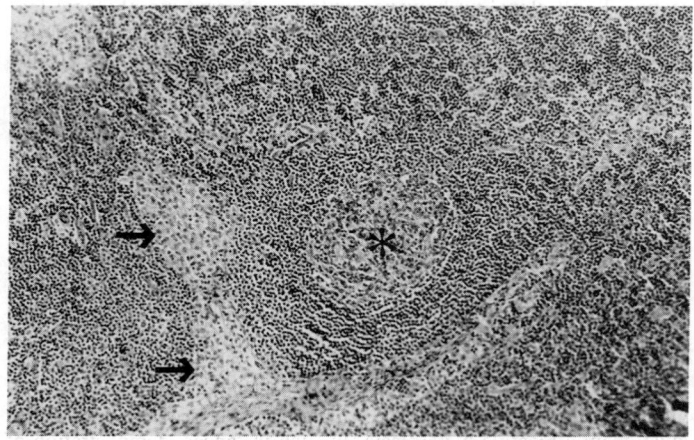

Figure A3–1. Normal lymph node. Asterisk is present in a germinal center. Arrows point to lymph node sinuses, which are composed largely of tissue macrophages.

TABLE A3–2. PATTERN OF LYMPH NODE REACTIVITY IN VARIOUS DISEASE STATES

Disease	Histology
Rheumatoid arthritis	Follicular hyperplasia with plasmacytosis
Toxoplasmosis	Nonnecrotizing granulomas with few multinucleate giant cells
Cat-scratch disease	"Stellate" abscesses surrounded by granulomatous inflammation

toplasmic antibody testing (in particular, c-ANCA) is useful in diagnosing Wegener's granulomatosis.

The spleen is divided into two portions: red pulp and white pulp. Lymphocytes surround the small arterioles, giving rise to the white pulp. The remaining tissue is referred to as red pulp. Splenomegaly may be a manifestation of congestion, infiltrative disease (neoplasm), amyloid, storage disease, or extramedullary hematopoiesis. Carcinoma rarely metastasizes to the spleen. Non-Hodgkin's lymphoma and Hodgkin's disease commonly involve the white pulp first. Hairy cell leukemia preferentially involves the red pulp.

Another serum test that is useful in evaluating humoral immunity is immunoglobulin levels. Serum and urine protein electrophoresis, immunofixation, and immunoelectrophoresis are useful in establishing or excluding clonality.

Therapeutic

Therapy is related to the specific disorder diagnosed.

FOLLOW-UP

Once an abnormality of the reticuloendothelial system is identified, the follow-up is determined by the particular disease. Immunophenotyping of lymphocytes is performed sequentially in some cases, as in monitoring OKT3 administration in transplant patients or CD4 levels in HIV patients.

DISCUSSION
Prevalence and Incidence

See specific disease.

Related Basic Science

There are two types of immune responses: cellular immunity and humoral immunity. Lymphocytes play a role in each. Lymphocyte precursors originate in the bone marrow and are programmed to perform a T-cell or B-cell function by the thymus (T-cell) or bone-marrow (B-cell). The secondary lymphoid organs include lymph nodes, spleen, and gut-associated lymphoid tissues. Both B and T cells are in lymph nodes and these cell populations expand in response to antigen stimulation. Lymphocytes are slightly larger (8–12 μm) than red blood cells. In the unstimulated state they have little cytoplasm. When activated, a larger rim of cytoplasm is present. B lymphocytes express surface immunoglobulin and HLA-DR. As a B lymphocyte differentiates further, it becomes a plasma cell (Figure A3–3). Plasma cells contain cytoplasmic but not surface immunoglobulin and have little surface HLA-DR expression. Lymphocytes express CD45RB, whereas plasma cells do not. The above is useful in distinguishing an anaplastic plasmacytoma from a large cell lymphoma. Plasma cells have condensed "clockfaced" chromatin and an eccentric nucleus. A perinuclear clearing or "hoff" is present due to the large amount of Golgi present. Russell bodies may be present in plasma cells. These are eosinophilic round cytoplasmic inclusions due to distended rough endoplasmic reticulum. T cells are involved in cellular immunity and are essentially indistinguishable morphologically from B lymphocytes. Seventy to eighty percent of lymphocytes in the peripheral blood are T cells. Cell-mediated immune responses include transplant rejection, delayed hypersensitivity reaction, and destruction of intracellular microorganisms such as mycobacteria.

Lymphocytes may circulate from the blood to the lymph nodes through the thoracic duct and back into the bloodstream. B lymphocytes live days. T lymphocytes survive months or years.

Monocytes and macrophages participate actively in the immune response. Monocytes and macrophages are essentially the same cell type, monocytes being present in the peripheral blood and macrophages in the tissue. Both cells may ingest foreign material (are phagocytic). Op-

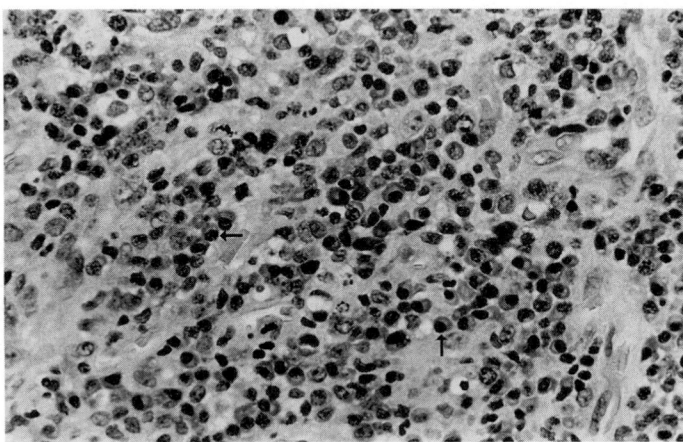

Figure A3–3. Plasma cells. Plasma cells (arrows) are commonly seen in lymph nodes, though are prominent in patients with connective tissue diseases. Note perinuclear clearing or "hoff" due to prominent Golgi apparatus.

sonins may coat foreign particles to increase phagocytosis. Opsonins are antibodies. The Fc portion of the antibody is recognized by the Fc receptor on the macrophage surface. Interactions between macrophages and lymphocytes are restricted by the major histocompatibility complex (MHC); however, macrophages do not phagocytose specific antigens only.

Natural killer cells may lyse their targets without stimulation through the HLA and T-cell-receptor complex. Rarely, they may be the cell of origin for a lymphoproliferative disorder.

In the course of an immune response, macrophages present an antigen to a T cell. The macrophage and T-cell interactions are restricted by the MHC. Macrophages also produce interleukin-1, which causes interleukin-2 receptor expression and production by T cells. Interleukin-2 stimulates both B and T cells.

Natural History and Its Modification with Treatment

See specific disease.

Prevention

See specific disease.

Cost Containment

Immunophenotyping, although fast and accurate, requires highly trained personnel, which increases test cost. Immunotyping is most useful when a specific question is to be answered, for example, a CD4 peripheral blood count in a known HIV-positive patient. Tissue examination, although expensive, is often necessary to exclude malignancy. Persistent lymphadenopathy or laboratory abnormalities require persistent investigation until the etiology is determined.

REFERENCES

Hanson CA, Gail-Peczalska KJ. In: Wick MR, Siegal GP, eds. Monoclonal antibodies in diagnostic immunohistochemistry. New York: Marcel Dekker, 1988:6.

Jaffe ES, ed. Surgical pathology of the lymph nodes and related organs. 2nd ed. Philadelphia: Saunders, 1995.

Nelson DA, Davey FR. Hematopoiesis. In: Henry JB, ed. Clinical diagnosis and management by laboratory methods. 18th ed. Philadelphia: Saunders, 1991:25.

Rowland DT, Weiner D, Bolton TA, Muus CJ. In: Henry JB, ed. Clinical diagnosis and management by laboratory methods. 18th ed. Philadelphia: Saunders, 1991:31.

Blood Component Therapy

Gerald A. Hoeltge, M.D.

The need to treat patients with blood components is common to most medical and surgical specialties. The number of hemotherapeutic options available to practitioners has never been greater. This appendix summarizes the components currently available and the principal alternatives to blood transfusion. Other chapters should be consulted for the blood component indications in specific conditions.

COMPONENT THERAPY

Blood components are those constituents of whole blood easily separable by means of simple physical mechanisms (e.g., refrigeration and centrifugation). One unit of whole blood is that volume collected during a single donation, that is, 405 to 495 mL. The principal constituents of whole blood (red blood cells, platelets, white blood cells, and plasma) can be prepared as individual units. One unit of any component is the amount harvested from the source whole blood unit. Blood components are distinguished from blood derivatives, which are pharmaceutical products refined from whole blood or plasma (e.g., immune serum globulin and albumin [human]).

All preparations of blood components in the United States are regulated by the Food and Drug Administration. Blood donors and their resulting units are classified as *volunteer, paid,* or *autologous.* Nearly all blood components intended for allogeneic administration in this country are collected from volunteer donors; payment is limited to plasma donations that are intended for derivative manufacturing and purification.

Volunteer blood donors must be free of infectious disease as determined by medical history and physical examination. The donor must be at least 17 years of age; there is no upper age limit. On the day of donation, the donor must be afebrile (≤37.5° C), normotensive (systolic ≤ 180 Torr, diastolic ≤ 100 torr), and have normal pulse (50–100 beats/min and regular). The hemoglobin or hematocrit must be normal (≥ 12.5 g/dL or ≥38%, respectively). Collected units must be tested individually for ABO and Rh type, for atypical erythrocyte antibodies, and for transfusion-transmissible disease markers. Current tests for infectious disease are listed in Table A4–1. Whole blood donors may donate every 56 days. Platelet and plasma donors may donate more frequently.

Whole blood may be anticoagulated with CPDA-1 (citrate–phosphate–dextrose–adenine, shelf life 35 days) or CPD (citrate–phosphate–dextrose, shelf life 21 days). Units must be stored between 1° and 6°C in an approved refrigerator. The transfusion of whole blood should be limited to situations in which the need for additional oxygen-carrying capacity is combined with the need for volume expansion. Therapeutically equivalent preparations include modified whole blood (implying the removal of platelets and/or buffy coat) and reconstituted whole blood, which is the mixture of red blood cells and compatible thawed fresh-frozen plasma.

All whole blood and blood components must be administered through a clot filter (pore size, 170 µm). Blood warmers may be indicated for the infusion of large amounts of cold blood through a central line to prevent bradycardia. Such warmers must be equipped with audible alarms and not warm with blood above 38°C. Standard blood components, along with dosages and indications, are listed in Table A4–2.

TABLE A4–1. SCREENING TESTS PERFORMED ON ALL BLOOD COMPONENTS

Short Name	Long Name	Notes
HBsAg	Hepatitis B surface antigen	Primary screen for prevention of hepatitis B
Anti-HIV-1/2	Antibodies to HIV types 1 and 2	Primary screen for prevention of AIDS
Anti-HTLV-I	Antibodies to human T-lymphotropic virus type I (cross-reactive with type II)	Primary screen for prevention of T-cell leukemia/lymphoma and tropical spastic paraparesis
Anti-HCV	Antibodies to hepatitis C virus	Primary screen for prevention of hepatitis C
STS	Serologic test for syphilis	Primary screen for prevention of syphilis
Anti-HBc	Antibodies to hepatitis B core antigen	Surrogate screen for prevention of any parenterally transmitted viral illness

TABLE A4–2. STANDARD BLOOD COMPONENTS

Component	Dose per Unit	Indications
Whole blood	450 mL ± 45 mL (38–55% hematocrit)	Increase oxygen-carrying capacity + volume expansion
Red blood cells in CPD or CPDA-1	Approximately 250 mL (70–80% hematocrit)	Increase oxygen-carrying capacity
Red blood cells in adenine–saline	Approximately 350 mL (45–55% hematocrit)	Increase oxygen-carrying capacity
Red blood cells, leukocytes removed by filtration	≥90% of red cell content of the parent unit	Increase oxygen-carrying capacity + prevent febrile transfusion reactions or prevent alloimmunization to leukocyte antigens or prevent exposure to cytomegalovirus
Red blood cells, frozen	Deglycerolized units contain ≥90% of red cell content of parent unit	Need for long-term storage or any indication for red blood cells, leukocytes removed
Platelets	$\geq 3 \times 10^{11}$ platelets per 6-unit pool in 200–400 mL anticoagulated plasma	Prophylaxis against spontaneous bleeding secondary to severe thrombocytopenia and bone marrow hypoplasia *or* treatment of bleeding complicated by moderate or severe thrombocytopenia
Pheresis platelets	At least 3×10^{11} platelets in 200–500 mL anticoagulated plasma	Same as Platelets (generally reserved for prophylactic indications)
Granulocytes	$\geq 10^6$ neutrophils per unit in 200–300 mL anticoagulated plasma	Gram-negative bacterial sepsis unresponsive to antibiotics + severe neutropenia and bone marrow hypoplasia
Fresh-frozen plasma or single-donor frozen plasma	180–300 mL	Coagulation factor deficiencies, antithrombin III deficiency, thrombotic thrombocytopenic purpura, rapid reversal of warfarin effect, and massive blood transfusion
Cryoprecipitated AHF	Each bag contains ≥80 IU factor VIII and ≥ 150 mg fibrinogen in approximately 15 mL	Treatment of factor VIII deficiency of von Willebrand's disease; severe hypofibrinogenemia or dysfibrinogenemia; factor XIII deficiency

CPD, citrate–phosphate–dextrose; CPDA-1, citrate–phosphate–dextrose–adenine; AHF, antihemophilic factor.

Red Blood Cells

One unit of red blood cells includes the entire erythrocytic portion of the parent whole blood unit. The anticoagulant/preservative solution determines the shelf-life. Concentrates of red blood cells at a 70 to 80% hematocrit (so-called "packed" red cells) may be stored for up to 21 days in plasma anticoagulated with CDP or for up to 35 days in CPDA-1. Red blood cell concentrates may be diluted with 0.9% sodium chloride injection to facilitate infusion.

Most red blood cells are today dispensed as erythrocytic suspensions in adenine–saline–mannitol solution (AS-1, AS-3, or AS-5); the shelf-life is 42 days. During the preparation of such units, the red cells have been highly concentrated by centrifugation, the plasma fraction has been removed, and 100 mL of an adenine–saline–mannitol preservative has been added to achieve a final hematocrit of 55 to 65%. Dilution of such units with 0.9% sodium chloride injection is unnecessary.

Seventy-five percent of transfused red cells may be expected to survive normally after transfusion of a unit stored for its maximal limit. There is a gradual loss of 2,3-diphosphoglycerate (2,3-DPG) and adenosine triphosphate with storage, resulting in a lowered P_{50} for oxygen and a left shift of the hemoglobin–oxygen dissociation curve. Recipients of red blood cells in massive amounts relative to their blood volumes may benefit from "fresh" red blood cells (i.e., stored for fewer than 7 to 10 days). Any functional deficit induced by storage is temporary. Even severely depleted red cells regain 50% of their normal 2,3-DPG concentration 3 to 8 hours after transfusion. 2,3-DPG levels normalize within 24 hours.

Leukocytes may be removed from red blood cells before infusion. Units containing fewer than 5×10^8 leukocytes are indicated for prevention of febrile transfusion reactions caused by sensitization to leukocyte antigens. Removal of 99.99% of leukocytes is possible; the number of residual white blood cells remaining is 5×10^5 per unit or less with high-efficiency filters. Removal of leukocytes to or below this level prevents alloimmunization to leukocyte antigens and prevents transfusion-transmitted infection by viruses carried in leukocyte nuclei (such as cytomegalovirus).

Saline washing, which is an inefficient method to reduce the content of contaminating leukocytes, may be indicated to prevent passive administration of complement in paroxysmal nocturnal hemoglobinuria.

Red blood cells may be stored in the frozen state at least 10 years. Donor units that are of a rare blood type are often frozen. Thawed and saline-washed units must be used within 24 hours of preparation. Deglycerolization of previously frozen units yields a saline suspension of red cells with negligible amounts of plasma, leukocytes, and platelets.

Platelets

Each unit of platelet concentrate is prepared from one unit of whole blood. One bag of platelets contains at least 5.5×10^{10} cells. For dosage calculations, a pool of six concentrates may be assumed to contain 4 to $6 \times 10''$ cells, a quantity similar to the number of platelets in the circulating intravascular compartment of the average adult. Such a pool raises the blood platelet count by 20 to 50×10^9/L in a stable patient. The increment in the count realized from the infusion is less than predicted in the presence of bleeding, splenomegaly, fever, infection, disseminated intravascular coagulation, or sensitization to platelet antigens.

One unit of pheresis platelets contains at least 3×10^{11} cells. Pheresis platelets are preferred for patients requiring platelet support over an extended interval. Alloimmunization to platelet antigens and the risk of transfusion-transmitted infection are lessened by reduction in donor exposures.

Platelets may be stored for 5 days at 20° to 24°C under conditions of gentle agitation. Storage is for 6 hours once the containers have been entered for pooling.

Platelet units are usually chosen to be ABO identical to the patient, but platelets of any ABO type may be used. If ABO-compatible but nonidentical platelets are transfused (e.g., group O platelets transfused to a group A patient), donor isohemagglutinins will react with red blood cell antigens. A positive direct antiglobulin test results. If ABO-incompatible platelets are transfused (e.g., group A platelets transfused to a group O patient), intravascular survival may be slightly reduced.

Consideration should be given to prophylaxis with Rh immune globulin when platelets from an Rh-positive donor must be given to an Rh-negative, premenopausal female.

Prophylactic administration of platelets may prevent the bleeding of severe thrombocytopenia ($<15 \times 10^9$/L) due to bone marrow hypoproliferation. At peripheral blood counts of 50×10^9/L and above, patients are unlikely to benefit from prophylactic platelet transfusion prior to surgery or other invasive procedure. Active bleeding may be reduced by transfusion of platelets if the platelet count is less than 100×10^9/L, in the presence of sepsis or other systemic cause for bleeding and for nonuremic platelet dysfunction.

In the absence of overt bleeding, platelets should not be transfused to patients with immune thrombocytopenia, after massive transfusion, or in the presence of disseminated intravascular coagulation. Platelet transfusions are contraindicated in thrombotic thrombocytopenia purpura.

Platelets are suspended in donor plasma. Each unit of platelets contains approximately 35 to 50 mL of plasma; one pool of six units is about 250 mL (similar to the volume of a unit of fresh-frozen plasma). The oncotic pressure and the coagulation factor content (with the possible exception of factors V and VIII) of one pool of platelets or one unit of pheresis platelets are comparable to those of one unit of plasma. Pooled platelets may be volume reduced by centrifugation and removal of platelet-poor plasma.

The leukocyte contents of platelets is variable, averaging between 10^7 and 10^8 cells per unit. Leukocytes may be removed by filtration at the time of pooling. Leukoreduction minimizes the risk of alloimmunization to antigens shared by leukocytes and platelets. Filtration essentially eliminates the risk of infection from cellular viruses such as cytomegalovirus.

Granulocytes

Buffy coat, usually prepared by continuous-flow apheresis from a single donor, may be labeled as granulocytes provided that the neutrophil content is at least 10^{10} per unit. One unit of granulocytes ranges from 200 to 400 mL in volume. Because of the red blood cell content (the hematocrit averages 10%), granulocytes must be chosen to be ABO compatible, and the red cells crossmatched. Granulocytes should be used within 8 hours of collection (maximum shelf life, 24 hours).

To achieve an effective dose per unit, the circulating neutrophil count of donors should be above average. Administration of 8 mg of dexamethasone to the donor in divided doses is standard. Granulocyte donors are often recruited from among the patient's family or friends.

The primary indication for granulocytes is treatment of Gram-negative bacterial sepsis unresponsive to antibiotic treatment in the presence of profound neutropenia (<500 neutrophils/μL) or chronic granulomatous disease. Granulocyte therapy is ordinarily prescribed for a specified short course (e.g., one unit per day for 4 days), which may be repeated once. Administration of granulocytes has only been shown to be of long-term efficacy when followed by bone marrow regeneration. Therapy should be attempted only in patients who have a good chance of recovery. Granulocytes are not indicated for prophylaxis.

Granulocyte therapy has been associated with severe pulmonary reactions. Pathogenic mechanisms include immune microvascular leukoagglutination (the risk for which increases with repeated treatments), bacterial endotoxin-induced neutrophil degranulation, and fluid overload.

Plasma

Fresh-frozen plasma (FFP) is indicated for treatment of specific coagulation factor deficiencies (including factors V, VII, X, XI, and XIII), antithrombin III deficiency, thrombotic thrombocytopenic purpura, rapid reversal of warfarin effect, and in massive blood transfusion. There is no evidence that administration of FFP in small doses (one or two units) immediately prior to an invasive procedure such as needle biopsy or catheter placement reduces morbidity. FFP should be used prior to invasive procedures only if the patient is bleeding or after a trial of vitamin K therapy has failed to correct the abnormal coagulation test results. Consideration of liver function and coagulation laboratory results should determine the need for FFP rather than automatic use after a set amount (e.g., 6 to 10 units of red blood cells) of plasma-poor intravenous therapy.

Fresh-frozen plasma is an effective agent for volume expansion, but its prescription as a volume expander should be limited to hypovolemic patients who also have coagulation factor deficiencies responsive to FFP.

To be labeled as fresh-frozen, the plasma must have been separated from the parent whole blood unit and frozen within 8 hours of collection. Units frozen after that time are labeled single-donor frozen plasma (SDFP). Most units of SDFP have been frozen within 24 hours of collection and can be substituted interchangeably for FFP.

Cryoprecipitated Antihemophilic Factor (AHF)

Each unit of cryoprecipitate has been prepared from FFP after thawing at 4°C and concentration of the semisolid material that separates by centrifugation. Each unit, which is about 30 mL in volume, is a concentrate of the high-molecular-weight proteins of normal plasma. One unit of cryoprecipitate contains at least 80 IU of factor VIII and at least 150 mg of fibrinogen. Cryoprecipitate also contains von Willebrand's factor, fibronectin, and factor XIII.

Intravenous administration of cryoprecipitate is indicated for the treatment of factor VIII deficiency of von Willebrand's disease (especially types IIB and III) prior to an invasive procedure or during active bleeding. Cryoprecipitate is the only medicinal source of fibrinogen approved by the Food and Drug Administration. Fibrinogen replacement therapy is indicated for treatment of severe hypofibrinogenia or dysfibrinogenemia, to treat active bleeding, or prior to an invasive procedure.

Cryoprecipitate is effective for treatment of moderate to severe hemophilia A (with no inhibitor). The infectious risk of each unit is approximately the same as that of the parent whole blood unit. Factor VIII concentrate, treated to remove or inactivate hepatitis B, hepatitis C, and other potentially contaminating viruses, is the preferred drug for hemophilia A.

Cryoprecipitate may also be administered topically. Mixed with thrombin and calcium, topical cryoprecipitate may promote hemostasis on surfaces exhibiting microvascular bleeding. Addition of a plasmin inhibitor such as ε-aminocaproic acid may be considered.

ALTERNATIVES TO ALLOGENEIC BLOOD TRANSFUSION
Autologous Blood Transfusion
Preoperative Deposit

Autologous red blood cells should be substituted for allogeneic units when feasible. Preoperative deposit is appropriate before elective surgery when there is a reasonable likelihood of need for red cell replacement. Autologous blood donors must have no health problems that would be complicated by phlebotomy. Most patients can donate one unit of whole blood per week. The final units should be donated at least 3 days before surgery. As the shelf-life of red blood cells in adenine–saline is 42 days, as many as six units of cells can be conveniently scheduled. The patient's blood hemoglobin concentration must remain above 11 g/dL (or the hematocrit ≥ 33%). There is no weight or age restriction; proportionately less blood is drawn from patients weighing less than 50 kg. Patients who are depositing two or more units prior to surgery should be considered for iron supplementation (e.g., $FeSO_4$ 300 mg three times daily).

Autologous whole blood units are routinely converted to red blood cells for maximal shelf-life. The plasma is usually discarded, but may be frozen or left attached to the red blood cells as a liquid.

Blood may be collected more than 6 weeks prior to surgery. Stored red blood cells may be transfused to the patient on the same day that a fresher unit is drawn; two units may then be collected. Alternatively, red cells may be frozen. Speculative deposit in advance of unknown need is inappropriate unless the patient has been so alloimmunized to erythrocyte antigens that the availability of compatible allogeneic units may be doubtful.

Perioperative Hemodilution

Phlebotomy may be performed at the beginning of an operative procedure with volume replacement with crystalloid. The 500 to 1000 mL of heparinized whole blood is reinfused at the close of the case only after vascular hemostasis has been achieved. Perioperative hemodilution is most often considered an adjunct to vascular surgery. The priming of a cardiopulmonary bypass circuit with crystalloid is a form of perioperative hemodilution.

Blood Salvage

Shed red cells collected intraoperatively, saline washed and concentrated, may be reinfused. Aseptic collection of shed blood should be considered when blood loss is estimated to exceed 500 mL. Bacterial contamination of the surgical wound is a contraindication.

Serosanguineous drainage fluid collected postoperatively may be transfused without concentration or saline washing if reinfused within 6 hours of the start of the collection. The red cell content is variable. Postoperative autotransfusion should be considered in uncontaminated cases when the red cell content of the drainage fluid is 250 mL or greater (the volume of an allogeneic unit of red blood cells). Cardiac and joint replacement surgeries are the most common indications.

Red blood cell concentrates intended for autotransfusion must be labeled with the patient's unique identification number if the preparation is removed from the immediate vicinity of the patient. Comparison of the blood type of each autotransfusion unit processed in the laboratory with the patient's known blood type is recommended to reduce the risk of a misidentification error.

Indications

The indications for autologous red blood cells are inherently no different from those for transfusion of allogeneic units. Because the risk of complications is less, autologous units may be prescribed for mild anemia. The possibility of bacterial contamination of the unit at the time of collection and misidentification of the source patient remains. Autologous units should never be transfused to nonanemic patients.

Other Alternatives
Directed Donations

Patients and their families sometimes request to select the donors from whom blood components will be prepared. The risk of infectious complications is the same for directed units and routine units.

Directed donations may be preferred in selected settings. Some rare blood types may be obtained most efficiently from family members. Granulocyte collections, which are more hazardous for the donor than simple whole blood and platelet collections, may be most appropriate for family members.

Blood Conservation Techniques

The initial intravenous fluid chosen to correct a hemorrhagic hypovolemia should be crystalloid. The use of a volume expander is recommended after 20% of the blood volume has been replaced with noncolloidal fluids. Colloidal preparations such as dextran solution, hydroxyethyl starch, and albumin (human) are preferred over fresh-frozen or single-donor plasma. Replacement of red cells lost during hemorrhage is appropriate after loss of 20% of the red cell mass and for patients with symptomatic anemia.

In selected clinical circumstances, agents to reduce bleeding may be appropriate. Desmopressin (DDAVP) promotes hemostasis by releasing factor VIIIC from vascular endothelium. DDAVP is appropriate in von Willebrand's disease (types I and IIA), mild hemophilia A, and acquired defects due to uremia.

Aprotinin is a serine protease inhibitor that inhibits plasmin activity. The drug can reduce postoperative blood loss after cardiac bypass surgery, perhaps by inhibiting platelet interaction with surfaces of the membrane oxygenator.

Intraoperative management of the patient undergoing major vascular surgery may allow the use of interventions other than autologous transfusion to minimize the need for allogeneic blood exposure. Such techniques include meticulous surgical hemostasis and controlled arterial hypotension. Surgical hypothermia reduces oxygen consumption and permits better tolerance of anemia. The latter is particularly effective as an adjunct to perioperative hemodilution.

RED CELL ANTIBODIES
Alloantibodies

The plasma of every normal adult, other than one whose blood group is AB, contains isohemagglutinins. Anti-A is formed by individuals who are group O or B; anti-B by individuals who are group O or A. Only group-compatible red blood cells may be transfused. Group A individuals may receive cells lacking group B (i.e., A or O); B individuals may receive B or O; AB individuals may be transfused with blood of any type. Only red cells that are blood group O may be given to O recipients.

The choice of plasma for transfusion should avoid exposure to donor isohemagglutinins that will react with the patient's own red blood cells. Fresh-frozen and single-donor frozen plasma units chosen for AB recipients must be of group AB; group A recipients may be given A or AB plasma; B recipients, B or AB plasma; and O recipients, plasma of any ABO type.

Unexpected (or atypical) alloantibodies to red cell antigens may be formed after transfusion or pregnancy. Those antibodies known to be of clinical significance must be avoided when choosing units for transfusion. The serum or plasma of patients who have a history of clinically significant antibodies must be tested against allogeneic donor units using an antiglobulin crossmatch. Unexpected antibodies that must be respected in pretransfusion testing include those of the Rh, Kell, Kidd, and Duffy systems. Antibodies of the MN, P, Lewis, and Lutheran systems can generally be ignored in compatibility testing.

Sensitization to a single red cell antigen specificity rarely interferes with blood availability. (Exceptions are antibodies to high-frequency antigens such as Yt^a, Kp^b, Js^b, U, and Vel.) Antibodies to multiple antigens may compromise the provision of compatible blood markedly. For example, only 0.1% of random donor units are compatible with the serum of a group O patient sensitized against the c, s, Fy^a, and Jk^a antigens. To locate blood for a patient with multiple antibodies or a single antibody to a high-frequency antigen may require a search through a national service such as the American Association of Blood Banks' Rare Donor File. Sensitization to a red cell antigen increases the likelihood of development of a second antibody.

Autoantibodies

Red cell autoantibodies are found in about 0.5% of hospitalized patients. Most are clinically benign. Some increase the rate of endogenous red cell destruction. All can interfere with standard compatibility testing, because the antigens to which they are directed are nearly always of high frequency. The autoantibody's effect on transfused red cells that carry the targent antigen can be predicted from the effect on the patient's own cells.

Autoantibodies are categorized according to the temperature of maximum activity. "Cold" autoantibodies, which are most active between 0° and 25°C, are typical of cold agglutinin disease, postinfectious erythrocyte autoimmunity, and paroxysmal cold hemoglobinuria. Such antibodies typically are immunoglobulin M and complement fixing. Specificities most often are in the Ii, P, and Pr groups. Cold autoantibodies can be avoided by incubating all reactions at 37°C during pretransfusion testing.

Antibodies of the type found in warm autoimmune hemolytic anemia are most active at physiologic temperatures, immunoglobulin G in class, and are usually not complement fixing. Specificities are most often in the Rh system, but may be in the Kell, Wright, or another system.

Transfusion should be avoided in the presence of warm autoantibodies. Such antibodies may obscure the presence of clinically significant alloantibodies during pretransfusion testing. Compatibility testing generally includes multiple or repeated absorptions to remove the autoantibody. This may extend testing over several hours and require 20 to 50 mL of the patient's peripheral blood. (See Chapter 12–4).

PREOPERATIVE ORDERS

In preparation for a surgical procedure that may require transfusion support, typing of the patient's red cells and screening of the patient's serum or plasma for atypical antibodies are indicated ("type and screen"). The pretransfusion sample may be collected no more than 3 days prior to surgery if the patient has been pregnant or transfused within the preceding 3 months. Each fresh sample drawn for compatibility testing must be typed and screened for newly acquired antibodies.

Crossmatching of red cells prior to surgery or other invasive procedure is indicated when the need for blood transfusion is likely. The number of units and the components ordered should reflect the best estimate of actual usage. A balance is needed between the desire to keep handy as many components as may be needed and the reality that allocation of specific components to one patient effectively makes those same components unavailable to another, bleeding patient.

The hospital blood bank should be able to provide group-compatible red blood cells rapidly for any patient whose type is known. Crossmatching typically takes fewer than 10 minutes for patients with no history of red cell alloimmunization. The crossmatch may extend for one or more hours when a patient has been sensitized to red cell antigens. More units should be crossmatched and allocated for sensitized patients prior to major surgery than for those who have no history of red cell alloantibodies.

COMPLICATIONS OF BLOOD TRANSFUSION
Acute Hemolysis

Isohemagglutinins are the most frequently implicated antibodies in severe, intravascular hemolysis. Reactions due to anti-A or anti-B follow errors in pretransfusion sample collection, unit labeling, or recipient identification. Symptoms include pain (usually in the chest or flank), chills, fever, nausea, and hemoglobinuria. The plasma stains a dark red and lactate dehydrogenase (LDH) levels rapidly increase. Haptoglobin is undetectable. Icterus due to unconjugated bilirubinemia follows.

Acute intravascular hemolysis is rare with other red cell antibodies. Atypical antibodies directed against specificities in the Rh, Kell, Kidd, and Duffy systems typically sensitize red cells and result in extravascular destruction. The patient is usually asymptomatic. Anemia and elevated bilirubinemia (with or without lactate dehydrogenase elevation) may be the only signs.

If the antibody level in the sensitized patient is below the limit of detectability in the pretransfusion antibody screen, the red cell unit will appear compatible in vitro but will stimulate anamnestic production of antibody. This secondary immune response may produce hemolytic levels of antibody 3 to 10 days after the transfusion. Delayed hemolytic reactions of this type are the cause of some cases of unexplained postoperative anemia. (See Chapter 12–4.)

Hemolysis of transfused red cells may be nonimmune. Mechanical destruction of cells may be caused by shear forces accompanying infusion through a small-bore needle and/or under pressure. Thermal destruction can follow improper refrigeration (inadvertent freezing) or excessive heating. Blood intended for transfusion should be stored only in monitored refrigerators outfitted with alarms that sound before the contents reach 1°C. Warming should be limited to devices made for the purpose that have audible alarms and do not raise the temperature above 38°C. Bacterial contamination of blood units can also present as acute hemolysis.

Transfusion-related Acute Lung Injury

Next to acute hemolysis, transfusion-related acute lung injury (TRALI) is the most common cause of rapid death from blood transfusion. Both are antibody mediated, but in TRALI the antibody is directed against leukocytes. The reaction is one of leukoagglutination in pulmonary capillaries and damage to the lung tissues following neutrophilic degranulation. The syndrome can follow infusion of either donor leukocytes (which react with patient antibody) or plasma products (containing antibody that reacts with the recipient's leukocytes).

Febrile and Allergic Reactions

Most immune-mediated reactions to blood components are nonhemolytic and not life threatening. One-tenth to one percent of transfusions are accompanied by fever, either immediate or delayed for several hours. Chills may be the only symptom if the patient has been pretreated with antipyretic agents. Febrile, nonhemolytic reactions are usually caused by antibodies to leukocytes or plasma proteins. Leukocyte depletion of red blood cells or platelets reduces the risk, and should be routine for patients who have suffered repeated reactions.

Immunoglobulin E-mediated allergic reactions, usually to plasma proteins, are not associated with cellular destruction. Urticaria or macular erythema, sometimes intensely pruritic, may be seen. Pretreatment with antihistamines prevents the reaction. Urticarial reactions that occur during a transfusion may be treated by temporary suspension of the infusion and administration of antihistamines.

Acquired Immunodeficiency Syndrome

The current risk for infection with HIV following a standard blood transfusion in estimated at less than 1 in 450,000 units. Stringent practices for donor selection and unit testing have made transfusion-transmitted HIV infection a rare event.

Blood may be collected inadvertently from an individual in an early stage of infection, before the development of detectable antibodies (the "window" period). Once the donor's infection has been recognized (most often at the time of the subsequent donation), the collecting donor center notifies the hospital transfusion service according to a "lookback" protocol. Notification of the attending physician follows, and testing for seroconversion is offered to the recipient. Once two or more recipients have been tested and shown to remain uninfected with HIV, no recipients of earlier components from the individual need be contacted.

Hepatitis

The risk for transfusion-associated hepatitis C is currently estimated at about 1 in 3500 units, and for hepatitis B, fewer than 1 in 50,000 units. The incubation period for icteric hepatitis B is 2 weeks to 6 months. Most patients recover fully, but 5 to 10% develop chronic hepatitis. Only 25% of patients infected with the hepatitis C virus by transfusion develop symptomatic jaundice, but 50% acquire chronic hepatitis.

The reporting to the responsible transfusion service of every case of hepatitis believed to be transfusion-induced is important. The service, which maintains records of all units issued for each patient it has served, notifies the blood supplier(s). A donor implicated in a case of hepatitis associated with a single-donor exposure will be deferred indefinitely from future blood donations. Implication in two cases of hepatitis associated with multiple transfusions likewise defers a donor.

Other Viral Infections

Cytomegalovirus (CMV) is ubiquitous. Forty to eighty percent of normal, healthy donor populations are seropositive for anti-CMV. Only a small percentage of seropositive individuals are likely to transmit CMV by blood transfusion. CMV is transmissible only via intact nuclei of cellular components (red blood cells, platelets, and granulocytes). It is not transmitted in FFP or cryoprecipitated antihemophilic factor nor in plasma derivatives.

Cytomegalovirus disease can be a serious complication of immunosuppression. Among bone marrow transplant recipients, CMV is associated with death more frequently than any other infectious agent.

To limit components for transfusion to those from CMV seronegative donors is a realistic option only when the number of units needed is modest. High-efficiency leukocyte filters are effective at eliminating the measurable risk from CMV infection. The use of leukodepleted components as a substitute for seronegative components can be recommended only when the preparatory laboratory's quality assurance records consistently indicate fewer than 5×10^6 residual leukocytes per unit.

Human T-cell lymphotropic virus type I is another nuclear virus carried in peripheral blood leukocytes. Screening of all blood components for antibodies to the virus has rendered the risk negligible.

Bacterial Contamination

About three red cell units and about four platelet concentrates per thousand are contaminated with bacteria. Most organisms are normal skin flora or ubiquitous environmental bacteria introduced into the container at the time of phlebotomy. Comparatively few contaminated units precipitate clinical infections. Most contaminants are nonpathogens, most are in very low concentrations, and most recipients are immunocompetent or are receiving antibiotics for unrelated indications. The evaluation of all febrile transfusion reactions should include culture of the containers for bacterial contaminants.

Transfusion-associated Graft-Versus-Host Disease

Graft-versus-host disease (GVHD) is a rare complication of blood transfusion. Engraftment of immunocompetent T lymphocytes from a donor unit results in a cellular reaction against recipient tissues if those tissues are recognized as foreign by the transfused lymphocytes. Signs of GVHD include fever, erythematous rash, vomiting, and profuse diarrhea. Mortality of transfusion-associated GVHD is greater than 80%.

Donor lymphocytes can circulate for a week after transfusion even when histoincompatible. Engraftment can occur in either of two circumstances. First, if the recipient is immunodeficient or immunosuppressed, any transfused cellular unit can lead to GVHD. Transfusion-associated GVHD has been reported as a complication of therapy for Hodgkin's and non-Hodgkin's lymphomas, acute leukemia, and a variety of neurogenic tumors, sarcomas, and carcinomas, as well as in bone marrow transplantation. Second, T cells can engraft in an immunocompetent recipient if by chance all of the HLA antigens of the donor's cells are shared by the recipient's nonidentical cells. This can occur if the donor's cells are homozygous for one or more specificities for which the recipient is heterozygous. Such a circumstance is more likely when the donor and recipient are blood relatives.

Gamma irradiation at a dosage of 25 Gy or greater eliminates the engraftment potential of lymphocytes. Cellular components being prepared for bone marrow transplant patients and patients with known immunodeficiency syndromes (except AIDS), leukemia, and cancer patients being treated with high-dose myelosuppressive therapy should be irradiated before transfusion. All red blood cells, granulocytes, and platelets from blood relatives or from HLA-matched donors should also be irradiated. The shelf-life of irradiated red blood cells is not more than 28 days from the date of irradiation.

REFERENCES

American Red Cross, Council of Community Blood Centers, and the American Association of Blood Banks (AABB). Circular of information for the use of human blood and blood components. Bethesda, MD: AABB, 1994.

Dodd RY. The risk of transfusion-transmitted infection. N Engl J Med 1992;327:419.

Klein HG, ed. Standards for blood banks and transfusion services. 16th ed. Bethesda, MD: American Association of Blood Banks, 1994.

Mollison PL, Engelfriet CP, Contreras M, eds. Blood transfusion in clinical medicine. 9th ed. Oxford: Blackwell Scientific, 1993.

Office of Medical Applications of Research, National Institutes of Health. Fresh frozen plasma: Indications and risks. JAMA 1985;253:551.

Office of Medical Applications of Research, National Institutes of Health. Platelet transfusion therapy. JAMA 1987;257:1777.

Office of Medical Applications of Research, National Institutes of Health. Perioperative red cell transfusion. JAMA 1988;260:2700.

APPENDIX 5

Abnormalities of Pulmonary Function

Albert E. Heurich, M.D.

DEFINITION

Diseases involving the lung and its associated anatomic and functional structures result in impaired lung function, which can be defined and quantified by pulmonary function tests (PFTs). Altered respiratory mechanics create patterns of gas flow and volume that form the basis for categorization of the primary abnormalities of pulmonary function. Further subdivision of abnormalities is based on specific sites of abnormality, responses to pharmacologic or physical agents, or impairments related to associated systems, in particular the cardiovascular system, respiratory center, and respiratory muscles.

ETIOLOGY

The mechanisms of abnormal function relate to airway diseases, which reduce flow in the upper or lower airways; alveolar–interstitial, pleural, chest wall, and respiratory muscle diseases, which reduce volume; cardiovascular and hematologic disorders, which influence oxygen transfer and alter the pulmonary gas/blood volume ratio and distribution; and respiratory center disorders, which alter respiratory pattern and ventilation.

CRITERIA FOR DIAGNOSIS

Suggestive

Diagnosis or classification of abnormal pulmonary function is based on graphic pattern recognition and numeric criteria. For spirometry, normal graphic criteria are based on an expiratory forced vital capacity (FVC) that develops a smooth exponential trace which reaches a final predicted level in a forced expiratory time (FET) of approximately 4 to 5 seconds (Figure A5–1). The inspiratory FVC is also exponential but is of shorter duration. A slowly changing exponential trace with a duration beyond 4 to 5 seconds and a variable amplitude (FVC) characterizes airflow limitation (Figure A5–2). At times, early closure of obstructed airways may terminate the curve prematurely. Functional residual capacity (FRC) and residual volume (RV) tend to be elevated with airway obstruction. Total lung capacity (TLC) remains normal or may be increased. The RV/TLC ratio is increased in obstruction. Miniaturization of the normal FVC trace is seen in restrictive disease (Figure A5–3). The amplitude and duration of the tracing are reduced. Lung volumes are reduced. Restriction from reduced static lung compliance may show an increased FEV_1/FVC ratio due to decreased airway resistance and increased lung elastic recoil. A shortened FET without a reduced TLC suggests air trapping. This reduces the FVC and increases the FEV_1/FVC ratio, causing underestimation of any obstruction that may be present. Linearization of the exponential shape and prolongation of the FET occur when airway flows in a FVC become constant, as in fixed upper airway obstruction (Figure A5–4) and in very advanced emphysema. When variable extrathoracic (Figure A5–5) or variable intrathoracic (Figure A5–6) obstruction occurs, the flow limitation is limited to inspiration and expiration, respectively.

Combination of flow information from the flow–volume trace together with the volume–time trace provides additional evaluation criteria. The normal flow–volume trace performed with maximal effort shows a sharp spirelike peak expiratory flow rate (PEFR) that is approximately twice the predicted FVC value. Expiratory flow after the peak normally declines linearly. With increasing age the linearity becomes slightly concave. Linearity of flow with terminal concavity occurs in early airflow limitation. Worsening airflow limitation results in progressive conversion of flow linearity to concavity, reduction in PEFR, and shift of the PEFR toward TLC. Upper airway obstruction converts the spire of instantaneous peak flow into a plateau of flow. Increasing upper airway obstruction lowers the maximal flow level of the plateau, converting more of the usually variable flow of the flow–volume curve into a constant flow and widening the plateau over a larger range of volume. Poor patient effort and weak respiratory muscles also produce a plateau that can be distinguished from upper airway obstruction by failure of reproducibility of results by the former on repeat testing.

Definitive

The graphic pattern is often more sensitive in detecting early upper airway obstruction than is numeric evaluation. Thus, for early upper airway obstruction it is both suggestive and definitive relative to numeric evaluation. Numeric interpretation uses reference values with a range to define normal. In early flow limitation in small airways, isolated reduction of FEF_{25-75} and FEF_{50} to less than 60% of predicted is significant. A reduction of the predicted FEV_1/FVC ratio defines an obstructive pattern and is considered to signify flow limitation that includes larger airways. This ratio is age dependent, averaging approximately 87% at age 25 and decreasing to 75% at age 70 or approximately a 2.9% decrement per decade in this age range. A normal FEV_1/FVC ratio with a reduced FVC (< 80% of predicted) is suggestive of restriction. Measurement of a reduced TLC confirms this.

CLINICAL MANIFESTATIONS

Pulmonary function tests are usually obtained to document or verify impressions obtained by history or physical examination. PFT results are commonly evaluated on the basis of a reference value and range. Certain ranges for normal and abnormal populations, such as those for the FEF_{25-75}, can have a wide overlap making interpretation of the significance of some results difficult.

Subjective

Interpretation of PFTs is not an isolated process but must be correlated with the clinical presentation of the patient. Reference values are useful as a guideline for evaluation, but may have reduced validity at extremes of age and height.

Ethnic differences in lung volumes exist. Reference values appropriate to the subject should be used. Prior PFT results obtained in a subject

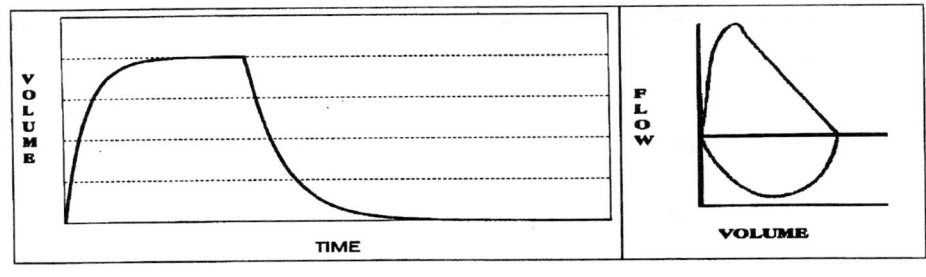

Figure A5–1. Volume–time trace and Flow–volume trace of a normal forced vital capacity (FVC). The initial rising slope of the volume–time trace and the upper half of the flow–volume trace represent the expiratory FVC (FEVC); the falling slope on the volume–time trace and the lower half of the flow–volume trace represent the inspiratory FVC (FIVC).

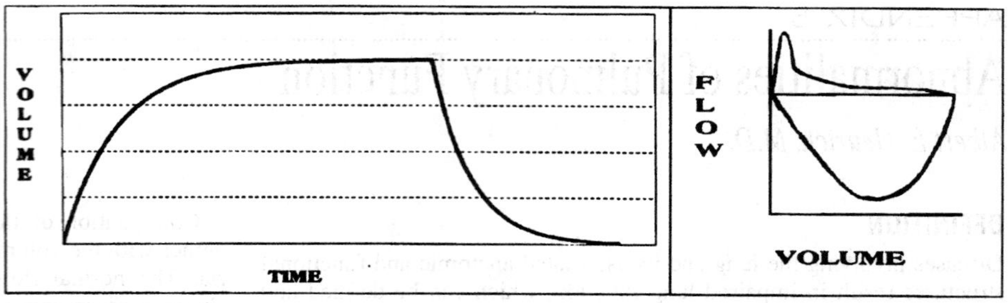

Figure A5–2. Volume–time trace and flow–volume trace of a forced vital capacity in obstruction. The times for forced expiration and inspiration are prolonged compared with the normal trace.

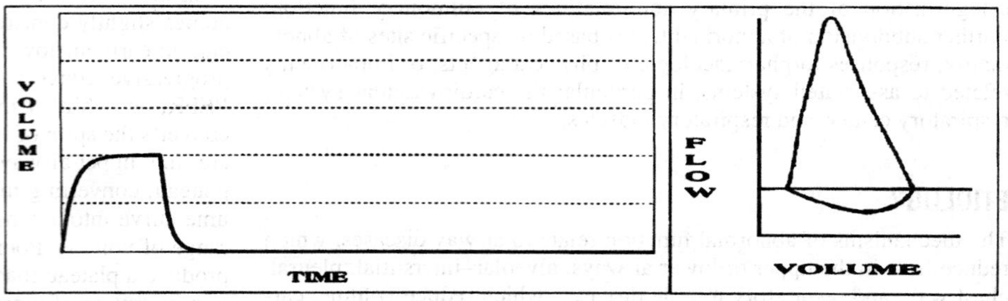

Figure A5–3. Volume–time trace and flow–volume trace of a forced vital capacity (FVC) in restriction. Total forced expired and inspired volumes and times are reduced compared with the normal trace.

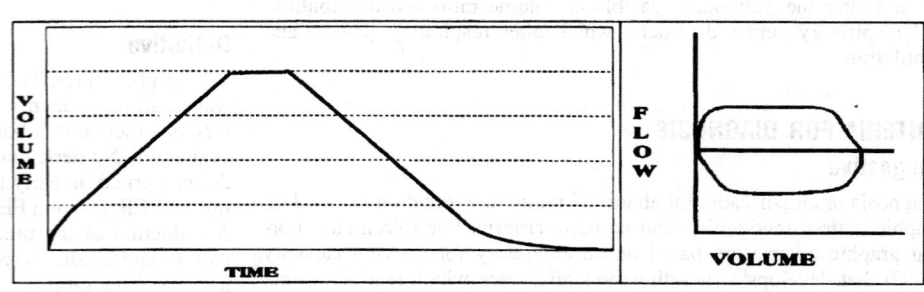

Figure A5–4. Volume–time trace and flow–volume trace of a forced vital capacity in upper airway obstruction of the fixed extrathoracic type. There is flow limitation in both expiration and inspiration.

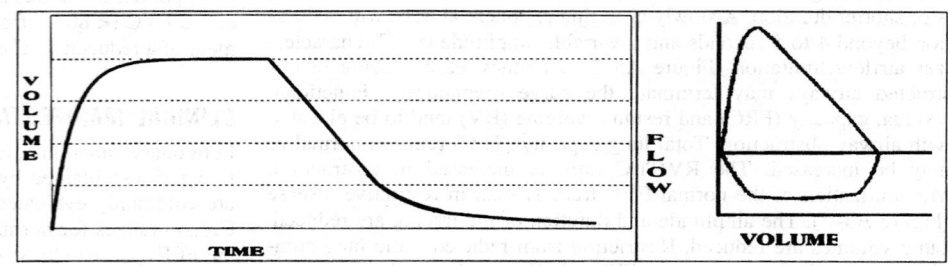

Figure A5–5. Volume–time trace and flow–volume trace of a forced vital capacity in upper airway obstruction of the variable extrathoracic type. There is inspiratory flow limitation.

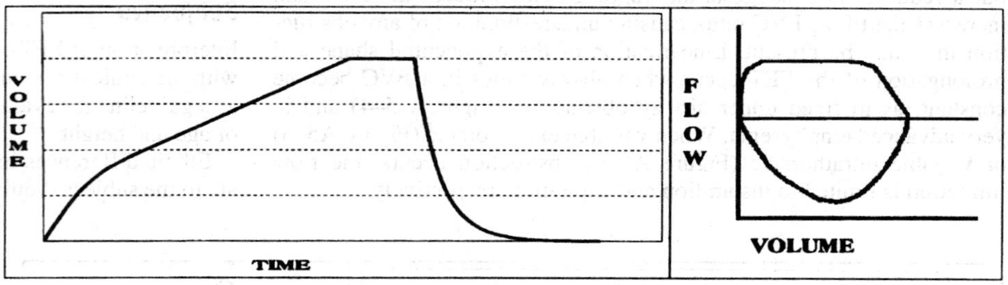

Figure A5–6. Volume–time trace and flow–volume trace of a forced vital capacity in upper airway obstruction of the variable intrathoracic type. There is expiratory flow limitation.

can serve as a useful reference for the interpretation of new results. Activities such as sports can influence respiratory muscle strength and endurance and must be taken into consideration when interpreting PFT results. A reduction from previously supramaximal PFT values to normal values could signify abnormality in an individual. Serial PFT results in such a situation may be more useful than reference values.

Objective

When assessing the utility of a specific set of reference values one should look not only at what population the values were derived from, but also the equipment that was used for measurement, particularly that used for static lung volumes. Lung volume measurement by computed body plethysmography is now a practical alternative to the helium dilution method in many centers. Most current reference equations in the literature have been derived from measurements made by helium dilution. Plethysmographic measurements include nonpulmonary gas volumes such as gastric air and yield higher volumes compared with helium. Use of helium reference equations with plethysmographic results can result in high percent predicted values for FRC and RV.

Physical Examination

Physical findings in a patient can influence the manner in which PFTs will best document abnormality. Body position influences PFT results. The effect of the weight of a goiter on airway compression is more evident in PFT results that compare upright and supine positions. Testing in the supine position also better documents the effects of unilateral diaphragmatic paralysis on PFT results than does upright testing. Failure to identify tympanic membrane perforation can result in reduced spirometric volumes and increased lung volumes measured with trace gases such as helium.

Laboratory Abnormalities

The expected graphic and numeric patterns for normal and abnormal PFTs are shown in Figures A5-1 to A5-6 and Tables A5-1 to A5-4.

PLANS

Modifications of pulmonary function testing that can be useful diagnostically include testing before and after pharmacologic agents. Inhaled bronchodilator and bronchoconstrictor agents are useful, respectively, to distinguish the hyperreactive airways of asthma from other forms of airway obstruction and to demonstrate hyperreactivity of airways when routine spirometry is normal. The FVC response to a rapid-acting cholinergic agent such as edrophonium chloride can help to establish a diagnosis when respiratory muscle weakness from myasthenia gravis is suspected. The response of the FVC to diuretic agents can help to document the presence of pulmonary edema. The effects of posture on PFTs as described above can be helpful in diagnosis.

Diagnostic

Pulmonary function tests can be classified as normal, obstructive, restrictive, or mixed. Obstruction can be subclassified based on site of airway obstruction (upper or lower, large or small) and response to bronchodilator. Based on the site of disease, restriction can be classi-

TABLE A5-1. NORMAL SPIROMETRY

Numeric Assessment	Graphic Assessment
FVC and FEV_1 within the predicted range	Smooth exponential inspiratory and expiratory pattern
PEFR = 1.8 × FVC	Sharp PEFR
FET = 4–5 s	Linear decline in flow
FEF_{25-75} and FEF_{50} within the predicted range	
PIFR = 0.6 to 0.75 × PEFR	

FVC, forced vital capacity; FEV_1, forced expiratory volume at 1 second; PEFR, peak expiratory flow rate; FET, forced expiratory time; PIFR, peak inspiratory flow rate.

TABLE A5-2. OBSTRUCTIVE SPIROMETRIC PATTERN

Numeric Assessment	Graphic Assessment
Reduced FEV_1/FVC ratio	Low exponential volume–time slope
Reduced flow rates	PEFR shifted toward TLC
Prolonged FET	F–V concavity following the PEFR
Inspiratory flows commonly exceed expiratory flow	F–V and V–T traces unchanged after bronchodilator in chronic obstructive pulmonary disease
Diffusing capacity	Significant changes in F–V and V–T traces in asthma in response to bronchodilators+
Asthma: normal or high	
Bronchitis: normal or mildly reduced	
Emphysema: low	

FVC, forced vital capacity; FEV_1, forced expiratory volume at 1 second; TLC, total lung capacity; FET, forced expiratory time; F–V, flow–volume; V–T, volume–time.

sified as being pulmonary parenchymal, pleural, chest wall, or neuromuscular in origin. The mixed picture includes combined obstruction and restriction. Other abnormalities of function can reflect pulmonary vascular disorders and disorders of respiratory control.

Differential Diagnosis

The responsiveness of the FEV_1, FVC, flow rates, and lung volumes to inhaled B_2 agonists or bronchoconstrictor agents distinguishes asthma from other obstructive diseases. In contrast, responsiveness to anticholinergic agents can be seen in chronic bronchitis. A significant airway response is defined as a change in FEV_1 of 12% and 200 mL. A similar change in FVC is also considered significant. Changes of 30% for isovolume and 20% for non-isovolume flows for FEF_{25-75} and FEF_{50} are also considered significant but pre and post lung volumes are needed to adequately define whether flows are isovolume or non-isovolume.

Interpretation of small airway abnormalities is possible only when large airways are normal, that is, when the FEV_1/FVC ratio is normal. Parallel small airways contribute a relatively small proportion to the overall resistance compared with the large airways with which they are in series. Disease in the latter obscures the pattern of flow coming from small airways. This is best seen in upper airway obstruction, where a plateau of constant flow replaces the usual pattern of continuously changing flow generated by the small airways during the course of a FVC.

Parenchymal lung restriction is distinguished by reduced lung volumes, a normal or increased FEV_1/FVC ratio, and a reduced single-breath carbon monoxide diffusing capacity (DLCO). Restriction from extrapulmonary processes has minimal effect on the DLCO. Decreased pleural and chest wall compliance or weak expiratory muscles can limit lung deflation, resulting in a small expiratory reserve volume (ERV) and calculation of an increased residual volume (RV). Together with a reduced inspiratory capacity and TLC, this gives a high RV/TLC ratio.

A mixed pattern can result from a process such as sarcoidosis. The initial findings are reduced lung volumes consistent with restriction. In the course of time, cystic changes can occur and the RV increases. The FVC remains reduced but is now combined with an increased RV. The sum of these results in a TLC that can rise to a normal range but with worsened disease. The FEV_1/FVC remains normal. The cystic changes could reflect air trapping from an obstructive defect that is not identifiable from

TABLE A5-3. RESTRICTIVE SPIROMETRY

Numeric Assessment	Graphic Assessment
FVC and TLC reduced below the predicted range	Steep exponential volume–time slope
Short FET	Inspiratory flows reduced relative to expiratory flows
Normal or high FEV_1/FVC ratio	Linear decline of flow on flow–volume

FVC, forced vital capacity; TLC, total lung capacity; FET, forced expiratory time; FEV_1, forced expiratory volume at 1 second.

TABLE A5–4. SPIROMETRY IN UPPER AIRWAY OBSTRUCTION

Numeric Assessment	Graphic Assessment
$FEV_1/FEV_{0.5} \geq 1.5$	Replacement of the sharp, peak point of PEFR with a plateau in the flow–volume trace
	Equalization of flows during most of the FVC linearization of the volume–time

FEV_1, forced expiratory volume at 1 second; $FEV_{0.5}$, forced expiratory volume at 0.5 second; FVC, forced vital capacity.

the FEV_1/FVC because of a short FET and reduced FVC or from increased compliance within the cysts, causing decreased elastic recoil.

Preoperative assessment of PFTs generally includes performance of a maximum voluntary ventilation (MVV). This test is useful as an assessment of the patient's general condition. When spirometry is abnormal the expected range of MVV can be estimated by multiplying the FEV_1 by 35 or 40. A MVV less than 50% of predicted indicates significant impairment of ventilatory reserve and increased operative risk. With lung surgery, removal of up to 10 to 15% of the lung may not be detectable by spirometry. Alveolar lung expansion following pneumonectomy exceeds airway expansion. The airway is thus relatively narrow for the lung volume, and this is reflected as an obstructive pattern on spirometry.

Isolated defects especially in the DLCO can be seen with other PFTs being normal. In early sarcoidosis the only abnormality may be a reduced DLCO. The most common pulmonary abnormality in liver disease is a reduced DLCO. This is thought to be related to pulmonary arteriovenous shunts. Marked pulmonary vasoconstriction as in primary pulmonary hypertension presents with a decreased DLCO. Hemoglobin is essential for uptake of oxygen and carbon monoxide. DLCO varies directly with the hemoglobin concentration, and appropriate correction for this must be made. High blood levels of carbon monoxide from cigarette smoking or increased breakdown of hemoglobin as occurs in hemolysis reduce the measured DLCO.

Pulmonary function test results in obesity can often be normal but at times are complex for interpretation. Excess weight pressing down on the chest and abdomen shifts the operational FRC to a lower level of volume. This lower level may be below the closing point of airways, particularly those at the lung bases. A restricted FVC occurs due to this

early airway closure, reducing ERV. Airway diameter is narrower at low lung volume, making interpretation of flows more complex with respect to assessment of airway obstruction and hypoxemia.

Hypercapnia with normal spirometry indicates a need to assess respiratory center function. Hypercapnia with a reduced FVC but no evidence of obstruction or nonmuscular restriction indicates a need to assess respiratory muscle strength.

Diagnostic Options

Pulmonary function testing in itself is not diagnostic but, when evaluated in conjunction with a particular clinical picture, can be supportive of a particular diagnosis.

Recommended Approach

Pulmonary function testing should be used when the information to be obtained may be supportive of a diagnosis. It is useful in preoperative assessment of patients with lung disease.

FOLLOW-UP

Pulmonary function test results can be used as objective guides for monitoring the course of pulmonary disease and the effects of therapy.

DISCUSSION

A PFT result is the integrated output of multiple systems that contribute to the final result. Appropriate interpretation of results must consider the contribution of all component systems involved in the production of that result.

REFERENCES

American Thoracic Society. ATS statement: Lung function testing: Selection of reference values and interpretative strategies. Am Rev Respir Dis 1992;145:1202.

Clausen JL. Pulmonary function testing guidelines and controversies. New York: Academic Press, 1982.

Cotes JE. Lung function assessment and application in medicine. 5th ed. Oxford: Blackwell Scientific, 1993.

Crapo RO. Pulmonary-function testing. N Engl J Med 1994;331:25.

APPENDIX 6

Abnormal Cardiopulmonary Exercise Test Results

Urmila Shivaram, M.D.

DEFINITION

Comprehensive cardiopulmonary exercise testing involves the simultaneous measurement of pulmonary parameters including oxygen consumption ($\dot{V}O_2$), carbon dioxide production ($\dot{V}CO_2$), respiratory ratio (R), minute ventilation ($\dot{V}E$), and cardiac (electrocardiogram, blood pressure) functions.

ETIOLOGY

Cardiopulmonary exercise testing is useful, and often essential, to confirm the etiology of symptoms of exertional dyspnea, wheezing, or chest pain and in patients with unexplained exertional dyspnea or disproportionate dyspnea that cannot be explained by clinical parameters obtained at rest. Exercise testing can determine the etiology of dyspnea (Table A6–1).

CRITERIA FOR DIAGNOSIS

Suggestive

In some patients with exercise intolerance, resting tests of both respiratory and cardiovascular functions may be normal and exercise testing will indicate the pattern of abnormality.

- It can distinguish dyspnea related to anxiety from other causes of dyspnea. In patients with dyspnea, the presence of normal exercise capacity is reassuring and may be the single most important investigation.
- In patients with combined cardiopulmonary disease, it helps to discern the predominant limiting disorder.
- It can be used in the diagnosis of early interstitial lung disease, where resting pulmonary functions may be entirely normal.

TABLE A6-1. INDICATIONS FOR CARDIOPULMONARY EXERCISE TESTING

Suggestive in
- Evaluation of dyspnea disproportionate to resting studies
- Diagnosis of early interstitial lung diseases
- Assessment of response to therapy
- Evaluation of predominant exercise limiting factor in patients with combined cardiopulmonary disease
- Preoperative evaluation prior to lung resection
- Evaluation for pulmonary rehabilitation

Diagnostic in:
- Exercise-induced asthma
- Primary alveolar hypoventilation
- Assessing need for supplemental oxygen

- It can be useful in quantifying the response to therapy, as in interstitial lung disease and congestive heart failure.
- In the evaluation of disability, it serves as an objective tool in assessing the severity of impairment.
- It can be used in the preoperative evaluation of patients at high risk of postoperative cardiopulmonary complications after lung resection where resting lung function tests are not sensitive predictors of postoperative outcome.
- It may be useful when subtle abnormalities of gas exchange are sought.

Definitive

Exercise testing is diagnostic in patients with exercise-induced asthma and exercise-induced hypoxemia, and can be used to guide oxygen therapy during exercise in primary alveolar hypoventilation.

CLINICAL MANIFESTATIONS
Subjective

The symptoms that would prompt a referral for exercise testing have been listed under Criteria for Diagnosis, Suggestive.

Objective

Physical examination may be entirely normal in patients with early interstitial lung disease and exercise-induced asthma. Rhonchi and wheezing may be present in patients with chronic obstructive pulmonary disease (COPD), whereas tachypnea and end-inspiratory rales are suggestive of interstitial lung disease. If ejection systolic murmur of aortic stenosis is found on auscultation, an echocardiogram should be performed prior to exercise testing to assess the severity. Exercise testing is contraindicated in severe aortic stenosis.

PLANS
Diagnostic

The indications for cardiopulmonary exercise testing are listed in Table A6-1.

Differential Diagnosis

The electrocardiographic changes of myocardial ischemia, arrhythmia, and exertional hypotension may all indicate cardiac disease. The early onset of anaerobic threshold is indicative of cardiovascular dysfunction and can be used as a guide to therapy. Cardiopulmonary exercise testing enables us to assess stroke volume. The ratio of $\dot{V}O_2$ to heart rate (oxygen pulse) is an indirect measure of stroke volume. A low oxygen pulse is usually the result of myocardial dysfunction, but could also be seen as a result of significant pulmonary arterial disease and pulmonary hypertension. In interstitial lung disease, patients often develop hypoxemia and have increased physiologic dead space during exercise. The tidal volume is less than normal at any level of ventilation with an early rise in breathing frequency.

In COPD, abnormal ventilatory response to exercise is the limiting factor, and arterial desaturation is a predominant feature in emphysema. The limited exercise capacity in COPD can be due to several factors including altered lung mechanics, abnormal changes in gas exchange, respiratory muscle dysfunction, associated cardiac dysfunction, and poor nutrition. The tidal volume rises steadily with a slower increase in breathing frequency. Training increases endurance time in patients with COPD and may be useful in the patients' activities of daily living. In the diagnosis of exercise-induced asthma, a spirometry done 5, 10 and 20 minutes after exercise shows an obstructive pattern with greater than 15% reduction in either vital capacity, forced expiratory volume in 1 second, or maximum midexpiratory flow. Progressive exercise testing should be used in the complete evaluation of disability. Low cardiac output, abnormal ventilatory response, and hypoxemia can all result in disability. The level of exercise can be adjusted, depending on the work requirements of a particular occupation. A steady-state exercise performed at that level of work can determine if an individual is fit for her or his job. Deconditioning and lack of motivation result in an early anaerobic threshold and low oxygen pulse, and a clinical evaluation should help distinguish these from cardiac disease. Malingering can be diagnosed by excessive ventilation in the early part of exercise; however, the ventilation normalizes as the workload increases.

Diagnostic Options

There are several possible methods of exercise testing.

- Progressive or incremental testing, during which the patient performs increasing levels of work up to maximum, provides the most information in a brief duration. The work rate is increased every 1 to 3 minutes and the $\dot{V}O_2$ is continuously measured.
- A constant work rate or steady-state exercise is performed in severely disabled individuals to assess the response to therapy and the need for supplemental oxygen. In this kind of exercise the patient performs submaximal exercise for at least 5 minutes.
- Another method of testing is to record the distance covered during a 6- or 12- minute walk as a measure of exercise tolerance in those patients with extreme limitation of exercise. During this test the individuals walk on a level ground at their own pace.
- Stair climbing is one of the methods of exercise testing, but is yet to be standardized.

Exercise Equipment. Exercise testing on a treadmill is easy to perform because walking is a natural exercise. An electronically braked cycle ergometer is an alternate piece of equipment that is safe and portable; however, some patients find cycling uncomfortable and may terminate exercise prematurely due to fatigue of leg muscles. Cycle ergometry may be preferable to the treadmill in obese individuals or those with an unsteady gait.

Recommended Approach

Spirometry is performed on each patient on the day of the test. A full history and physical examination and a 12-lead electrocardiogram should be obtained to identify any conditions such as unstable angina, recent myocardial infarction, uncontrolled hypertension, high fever, and critical aortic stenosis. These are relative contraindications to performing an exercise test. Full resuscitation equipment and trained personnel should be available for the study.

A continuous recording of the electrocardiogram, a blood pressure check every 2 minutes, and continuous monitoring of arterial oxygen saturation are performed during exercise. Monitoring arterial oxygen saturation cannot detect minor changes in arterial PO_2, but it is a method of detecting major changes in arterial saturation and is useful in most clinical situations. The respiratory measurements are done using a metabolic cart. The patient breathes through a pneumotachograph, which measures tidal volume and respiratory rate. In addition, expired gases are analyzed for O_2 and CO_2, from which $\dot{V}O_2$ and $\dot{V}CO_2$ can be obtained. The type of exercise protocol and equipment chosen depend on the severity of the patient's illness. Severely limited patients and those being tested for home oxygen can undergo submaximal tests. A desaturation greater than 4% is clinically significant. Those patients being evaluated for exercise-induced asthma are stressed maximally and require spirometry at the end of exercise to assess any reduction in the airflow.

Additional parameters such as arterial blood gases and mixed expired gases can be measured during exercise to assess the deadspace ventilation, and these may be useful in the diagnosis of diseases affecting pulmonary vascular components. Invasive hemodynamic monitoring using a pulmonary artery flotation catheter is performed in the management of patients with pulmonary hypertension to assess the response to vasodilators during exercise.

Therapeutic

Therapeutic Options

Results of exercise testing that provide an etiologic diagnosis then direct the specific therapeutic intervention, for example, bronchodilators in exercise-induced asthma and glucocorticoids in interstitial lung disease.

Recommended Approach

Exercise testing is useful in assessing the response to therapy in congestive heart failure and interstitial lung diseases. In hypoxemic patients the response to supplemental oxygen can be evaluated during exercise. Increased endurance time following pulmonary rehabilitation is of therapeutic value in patients with COPD. The beneficial effects of vasodilator therapy in pulmonary hypertension can be assessed by exercise testing with pulmonary artery catheterization.

FOLLOW-UP

Repeated exercise testing may be needed to gauge therapeutic response or disease progression.

DISCUSSION
Prevalence and Incidence

Approximately 10 million persons in the United States have asthma. Most people with asthma have airway hyperirritability, which leads to exercise-induced asthma. Exercise testing is indicated to diagnose a small number of these patients. About 6% of the U.S. population suffer from clinically obvious COPD, and the potential for exercise testing in their management is vast.

In a cardiopulmonary exercise test, in addition to commonly evaluated cardiovascular responses, respiratory gases are monitored either by intermittent or by breath-by-breath sampling techniques during various kinds of muscular exercise. Electrocardiographic changes and heart rate and blood pressure response to exercise are monitored in a fashion similar to that used in traditional cardiac stress testing. In addition, measurements of aerobic capacity, anaerobic threshold, ventilatory response, and arterial saturation during exercise provide information regarding the nature and severity of the exercise limitation in different clinical conditions. Exercise capacity is dependent on a complex interaction between cardiovascular and respiratory systems to meet the metabolic demands of the exercising muscles. The cardiopulmonary exercise test evaluates overall cardiovascular and pulmonary function and obtains information regarding the individual contributions to the overall exercise impairment. In this regard, exercise testing is much more informative than any other resting pulmonary function test and provides an objective measure of effort intolerance.

Related Basic Science

Maximum O_2 uptake ($\dot{V}O_2$ max) is a reliable measure of the aerobic capacity and most healthy people can achieve a $\dot{V}O_2$ max that is about 85% of the predicted value. The anaerobic threshold is the level of $\dot{V}O_2$ at which oxygen demand of the exercising muscle exceeds oxygen supply. As a result, the work by the muscle is achieved by anaerobic metabolism of carbohydrates to lactate. An increase in blood lactate is therefore taken as an indication of anaerobic metabolism. The lactate produced during anaerobic metabolism is buffered, generating CO_2, which results in increased $\dot{V}CO_2$. The respiratory gas exchange ratio ($\dot{V}CO_2/\dot{V}O_2$) begins to increase at the anaerobic threshold (AT) as

shown in Figure A6–1. In healthy individuals, AT occurs at about 60% of predicted $\dot{V}O_2$ max. Ventilatory response results in increased ventilation at the start of exercise, and during moderate exercise there is a further increase in the ventilation; an equilibrium is reached within about 3 minutes. In heavy exercise there is a continuous increase in ventilation as work increases. The ventilatory system does not limit exercise in normal individuals and 50 to 60% of maximal breathing capacity is required to achieve 80% of aerobic capacity. Tidal volume increases during maximum exercise to about half vital capacity. In a trained athlete there is an increased tolerance of high minute volume, which allows the athlete to increase $\dot{V}O_2$ max. To meet the increased oxygen demand some adaptations occur in the oxygen delivery system. The oxygen delivery is a product of cardiac output and arterial oxygen content. The arterial content of oxygen cannot be significantly increased, so the increase in cardiac output is a predominant factor in increased O_2 delivery. The increase in cardiac output is caused by an increase in both the stroke volume and the heart rate during exercise. The exercise stroke volume increases with physical training. The maximum achievable heart rate is age related. An abnormally high heart rate response at low levels of work is indicative of myocardial disease. Arterial blood gas tensions do not change appreciably during exercise in healthy people. Even at the point of exhaustion, PO_2 is unchanged and PCO_2 is slightly reduced. The increase in ventilation, therefore, does not appear to be related to blood gas tension. Arterial hypoxemia during exercise is noted in interstitial lung diseases and in obstructive airway diseases such as emphysema.

Natural History and Its Modification with Treatment

The natural history is related to the specific disease diagnosed by exercise testing. Exercise training in COPD patients increases endurance time and may be useful in the activities of daily living.

Prevention

Smoking cessation to prevent COPD and ischemic heart disease is recommended. In addition, diet and exercise modify the risk for coronary artery disease.

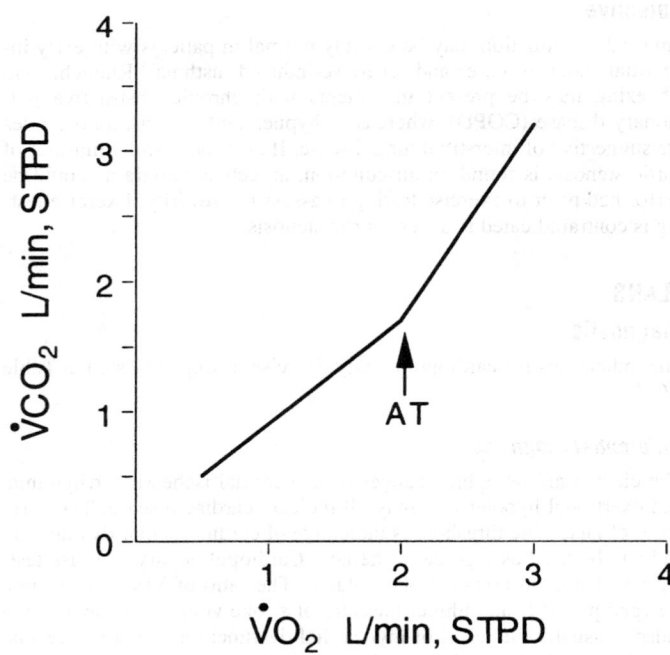

Figure A6–1. Relationship between alveolar $\dot{V}CO_2$ and alveolar $\dot{V}O_2$ is linear in the early stages of exercise. The arrow points to the break point in the relationship which determines the anaerobic threshold (AT).

Cost Containment

Cardiopulmonary stress testing is most cost effective in diagnosis of a select group of patients in whom a clinical picture does not correlate with resting pulmonary function or cardiac studies. In addition, it is beneficial in assessing the severity of functional impairment that cannot be evaluated by resting studies. A normal exercise test may obviate the need for any further diagnostic tests such as computed axial tomography and lung biopsy in a symptomatic patient; however, it is not of diagnostic value in patients with established severe cardiac or pulmonary disease, but may be helpful in monitoring the effects of various therapeutic modalities in these patients.

REFERENCES

Epstein SK, Celli BR. Cardiopulmonary testing in patients with chronic obstructive pulmonary disease. Cleve Clin J Med 1993;60:119.

Nunn JF. Nunn's applied respiratory physiology. 4th ed. Butterworth Heineman, 1993:321.

Wasserman K, Hansen JE, Sue DY, et al. Principles of exercise testing and interpretation. 2nd ed. Philadelphia: Lea & Febiger, 1994.

Weber KT, Janicki JS, McElroy PA, Reddy HK. Concepts and applications of cardiopulmonary exercise testing. Chest 1988;93:843.

Weisman IM, Zeballos RJ. Clinical exercise testing. In: Clinics in chest medicine, vol 15. Philadelphia: Saunders, 1994.

APPENDIX 7

Stress Electrocardiography

J. David Talley, M.D.

A stress electrocardiogram is used to detect and quantify coronary artery disease, assess functional capacity, monitor therapeutic response to cardiac medications, and evaluate cardiac rhythm (Schlant et al., 1986). Careful attention to the indications for and contraindications to stress electrocardiography (Table A7–1) and monitoring of the patient during the examination reduces the complications of the test. In a series of more than 500,000 stress electrocardiograms, complications included 1 death, 4 myocardial infarctions, and 50 life-threatening arrhythmic events per 10,000 tests done. These complications are more common in patients who undergo the procedure soon after myocardial infarction or as a method to evaluate ventricular arrhythmias (Stuart and Ellestad, 1980).

TERMINOLOGY IN STRESS ELECTROCARDIOGRAPHY

An understanding of the principles of exercise physiology and statistical terms used in analysis of stress electrocardiography is essential to comprehend and interpret the test properly. Definitions of commonly used terms are listed in Table A7–2.

METHODS
The Patient

The patient should fast for at least 2 hours before undergoing a stress electrocardiogram. The indications, methods, benefits, and limitations of the test should be fully discussed with the patient before the procedure. Informed, written, witnessed consent should then be obtained. A history (including medications) and physical examination of the cardiovascular system is then done. A physician, or trained assistant with direct physician oversight, supervises the procedure. During the test, the patient's symptoms and signs (heart rate, blood pressure, cardiac examination) and the electrocardiogram (ST segments, conduction abnormalities, and arrhythmias) are closely monitored at each level of exercise (Figure A7–1, left). When the endpoint of the test is reached, monitoring is continued until the patient is asymptomatic and vital signs have returned to baseline values (Figure A7–1, right).

Type of Exercise

The patient should be able to exercise for the stress electrocardiogram to have diagnostic quality. An inadequate exercise level decreases the specificity of the test dramatically. Recognizing the patient's physical limitations and conditioning is important so that an appropriate type of exercise can be prescribed.

A stress electrocardiogram measures the relationship between myocardial oxygen demand and supply to the heart. Most commonly, demand is increased with physical exercise and, therefore, increases heart rate and myocardial contractility. Demand may be increased by exercise of either the lower or upper extremities or with the use of other modalities. A stress test using a motor-driven treadmill or bicycle ergometry is the preferred method of lower extremity stress electrocardiography (Figure A7–1). Walking is easier than cycling and more

TABLE A7–1. INDICATIONS AND CONTRAINDICATIONS FOR PERFORMING STRESS ELECTROCARDIOGRAPHY

Indications	Contraindications	
	Absolute	*Relative*
Evaluate symptoms of coronary artery disease	Acute myocardial infarction within 3–5 d	Left main or equivalent coronary artery disease
Quantify extent of coronary artery disease	Unstable angina pectoris	Moderate or severe valvular stenosis
Assess functional capacity	Uncontrolled arrhythmias	Electrolytic abnormality
Monitor therapeutic response to cardiac medications	Acute cardiac infection	Significant pulmonary or systemic arterial hypertension
Evaluate cardiac rhythm response to exercise	Symptomatic severe aortic stenosis	Hypertrophic cardiomyopathy
	Uncontrolled congestive heart failure	Depressed mental acuity
	Acute pulmonary embolus or infarction	Second- or third-degree atrioventricular block
	Noncardiac conditions that affect or aggravate exercise performance	
	Physical disability that precludes a safe test	
	Lower extremity thrombosis	

Source: Modified from Fletcher GF, Balady G, Froelicher VF, et al. Exercise standards: A statement for health care professionals from the American Heart Association. Circulation 1995; 91:580. Reproduced with permission from the American Heart Association and the author.

TABLE A7–2. STANDARD DEFINITIONS IN STRESS ELECTROCARDIOGRAPHY

Statistical Analysis		Exercise Physiology	
Sensitivity	*True-positive* ÷ all patients with coronary disease	MET = metabolic equivalent test unit	3.5 mL O_2/kg/min
Specificity	*True-negative* ÷ all patients without coronary disease	Vo_2 max = maximum ventilatory oxygen consumption of the patient	Maximum cardiac output × maximum arteriovenous difference
Positive predictive value	*True-positive responses* ÷ all positive responses	MPHR = maximal predicted heart rate	♀ = 216 beats/min − 0.88 × age ♂ = 204 beats/min − 0.6 × age
Negative predictive value	*True-negative responses* ÷ all negative responses	Mo_2 = myocardial oxygen uptake	Estimated by double product = heart rate × systolic blood pressure
Bayes' theorem	Index of suspicion (pretest probability) that the disease is present		

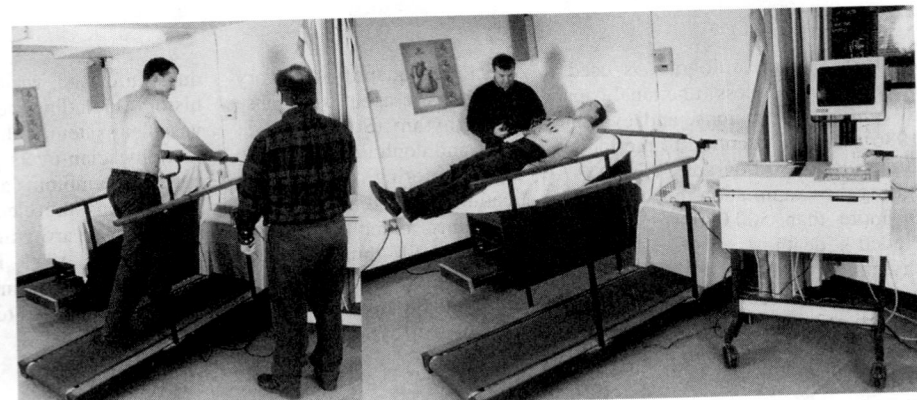

Figure A7–1. A stress electrocardiogram using a motor-driven treadmill. A trained technician with direct physician supervision monitors the test. At each stage of the test, the speed and incline of the treadmill are increased (**left**). In the posttest period, monitoring should continue until the patient is asymptomatic and vital signs have returned to baseline values.

Staging by Met

Test Name	Minutes per Stage	Speed and Grade	1.6	2	3	4	5	6	7	8	9	10	11	12	13	14	15	16
Ellestad	3-2-2-3	mph % grade					1.7 10%	3 10%			4 10%						5 10%	
Bruce	3	mph % grade					1.7 10%		2.5 12%		3.4 14%				4.2 16%			
Balke II	2	mph % grade				3.4 2%	3.4 4%	3.4 6%	3.4 8%	3.4 10%	3.4 12%	3.4 14%	3.4 16%	3.4 18%	3.4 20%	3.4 22%	3.4 24%	3.4 26%
Balke I	2	mph % grade			3 0%	3 2.5%	3 5%	3 7.5%	3 10%	3 12.5%	3 15%	3 17.5%	3 20%	3 22.5%				
Naughton	2	mph % grade	1 0%	2 0%	2 3.5%	2 7%	2 10.5%	2 14%	2 17.5%									
MET			1.6	2	3	4	5	6	7	8	9	10	11	12	13	14	15	16
Oxygen use (ml/min/kg)			5.6	7	10.5	14	17.5	21	24.5	28	31.5	35	38.5	42	45.5	49	52.5	56
Functional Class (AHA)			IV		III		II							I				

Figure A7–2. Standard protocols used in stress electrocardiography and their conversion to metabolic equivalent units, oxygen use, and functional class. AHA, American Heart Association; MET, metabolic equivalent test unit. (*From Brachfeld N. The electrocardiographic exercise tolerance test: Methods and procedures. Primary Cardiol, November 1984, p. 25, Reproduced with permission from the author and Physicians World Communications Group.*)

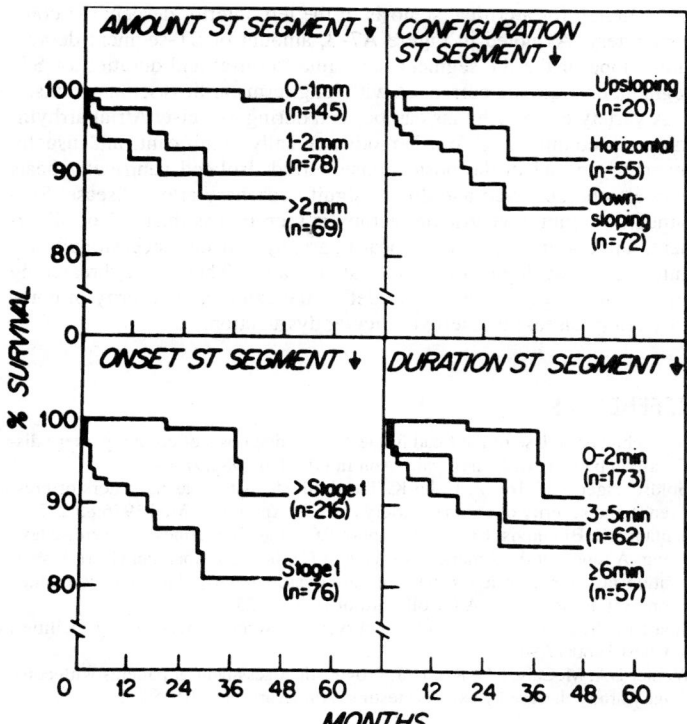

Figure A7–3. Long-term survival of patients based on the amount, configuration, time of onset, and duration of ST-segment depression. *(From Weiner DA, McCabe CH, Ryan TJ. Prognostic assessment of patients with coronary artery disease by exercise testing. Am Heart J 1983;105:749. Reproduced with permission from the publisher and author.)*

commonly results in a satisfactory exercise response. Usually, an average conditioned adult patient without significant physical limitations can undergo a stress electrocardiogram using a standard Bruce protocol (Figure A7–2). In this protocol, the speed and incline of the motor-driven treadmill are increased every 3 minutes. Less strenuous lower extremity exercise protocols are prescribed for poorly conditioned patients.

Myocardial oxygen demand may also be increased with arm ergometry, noninvasive pacing, and intravenous dobutamine infusion. These methods are used for an inadequate physiologic response or physical limitation to lower extremity exercise. They are usually combined with radionuclear angiography, echocardiography, or nuclear scintigraphy to enhance diagnostic accuracy.

The distribution of myocardial oxygen supply can be altered with coronary vasodilators such as dipyridamole and adenosine. These agents dilate normal but not atherosclerotic arteries, thereby shunting blood toward normal tissue and away from ischemic zones. Complementary imaging techniques are also used with this procedure.

FACTORS THAT MODIFY STRESS ELECTROCARDIOGRAPHIC ST-SEGMENT CHANGES

A 12-lead stress electrocardiogram is the standard test done to detect coronary artery disease. The specificity of the test is decreased in premenopausal women, patients with mitral valve prolapse, and patients with left ventricular hypertrophy and resting ST–T wave abnormalities. In these instances, use of a supplemental imaging modality (myocardial perfusion or echocardiography) is recommended. False-positive stress electrocardiography is also seen in patients with hypokalemia or those receiving cardiac glycosides or psychotropic medications. The electrolyte abnormality should be corrected and the medications stopped for 1 week, if possible, before the test.

Endpoints

Three endpoints are used in stress electrocardiography to evaluate cardiac function: symptoms, signs of maximal exercise capacity, and diagnostic electrocardiographic changes. Symptoms suggesting maximal exercise capacity are increased chest or leg pain, exhaustion, dyspnea, unsteady gait, cyanosis, pallor, or the patient's desire to stop the test. A symptom-limited endpoint of stress electrocardiography usually produces increased specificity of the test due to heightened exertion. Signs of maximal oxygen consumption are indirect and include a maximal predicted heart rate or metabolic equivalent units test (MET) (Table A7–2, Figure A7–2). For a heart rate- or MET-limited test to be diagnostic, the exercise level must be near maximal for the test to have appreciable specificity. Five electrocardiographic characteristics are assessed during a stress electrocardiogram: degree, slope, time of onset, and duration of ST-segment changes and presence of ventricular arrhythmias.

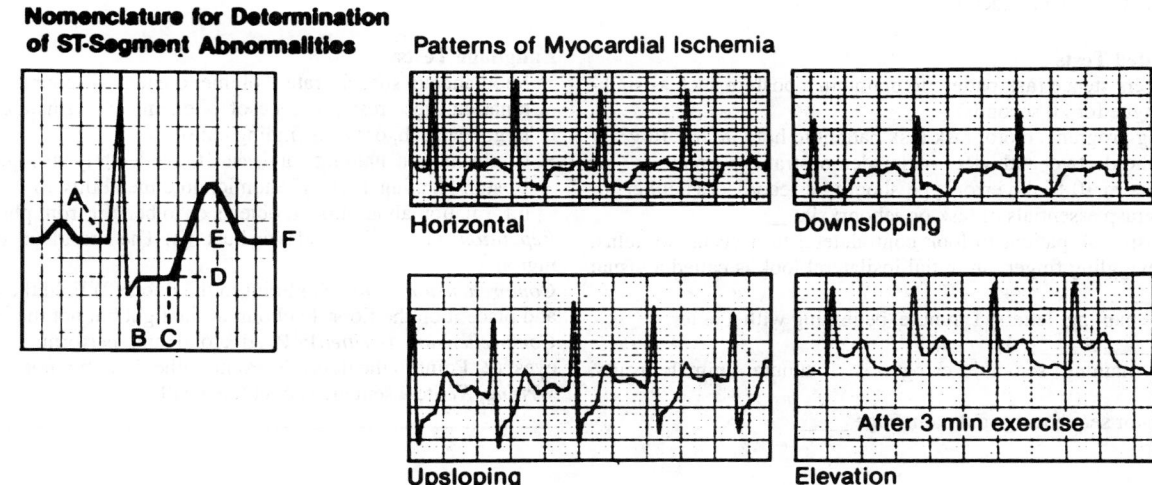

Figure A7–4. Criteria for determination and types of ST-segment changes in stress electrocardiography. The slope of the ST segment is determined 0.8 second after the J point, and may be directed downward, horizontal, or upward. ST elevation may also be seen. A = PQ junction, B = J point, C = 80 ms from J point, D,E = 2-mm ST-segment depression, F = isoelectric line. *(From Brachfeld N. ECG exercise tolerance test: Interpretation of results. Primary Cardiol, November 1984, p. 35, Reproduced with permission from the author and Physicians World Communications Group.)*

Interpretation of Results

Proper interpretation of a stress electrocardiogram requires precise understanding of the continuous and inverse relationship between sensitivity and specificity. Symptom-limited stress electrocardiography is highly correlated with the presence of coronary artery disease. Patients who are asymptomatic have less than a 10% incidence of coronary artery disease, compared with a greater than 75% incidence if the patient develops angina pectoris during the test (Goldschlager, 1982).

Changes in the electrocardiogram may be characteristic of myocardial ischemia or injury and are correlated with a long-term cardiovascular event (Figure A7–3) (Weiner et al., 1983). The length of the PR segment is a balance between sympathetic and parasympathetic tone and, therefore, may shorten, remain the same, or lengthen. The slope of the ST segment is analyzed 0.08 second after the J point (Figure A7–4). The slope may remain at the baseline; have downward, horizontal, or upward depression; or be elevated above the baseline. A normal response to exercise is an ST segment that remains level with the baseline. Downward sloping ST-segment depression is a highly specific marker of severe multiple-vessel coronary artery disease (Goldschlager et al., 1976). Horizontal and upsloping ST-segment changes suggest less extensive coronary artery disease. ST-segment elevation is seen with epicardial injury, left ventricular aneurysm, or pericarditis. While there is no correlation of ST-segment depression with location of the responsible coronary lesion, ST-segment elevation is a useful guide to underlying coronary artery anatomy. T-wave inversion is commonly seen with exercise and is a nonspecific marker of significant coronary artery disease. Inversion of the u wave is an insensitive but very specific finding for a critical stenosis of the left anterior descending coronary artery. As noted in Figure A7–3, amount of ST-segment depression, slope of the ST segment, and time to onset and duration of ST-segment changes are correlated with long-term cardiovascular events.

A variety of arrhythmias can be seen during exercise. Atrial arrhythmias are common, seldom hemodynamically significant, and usually revert to normal in the postexercise period. Isolated ventricular beats may also be observed and do not signify coronary artery disease. Sustained or complex ventricular ectopy is seen in less than 1% of all patients undergoing stress electrocardiography and may occasionally require pharmacologic or electrical therapy. These life-threatening arrhythmias suggest the need to define the extent and severity of coronary artery disease and left ventricular dysfunction.

REFERENCES

Goldschlager N. Use of the treadmill test in the diagnosis of coronary artery disease in patients with chest pain. Ann Intern Med 1982;97:383.
Goldschlager N, Selzer Z, Cohn K. Treadmill stress tests as indicators of presence and severity of coronary artery disease. Ann Intern Med 1976;85:277.
Schlant RC, Blomqvist CG, Brandenburg RO, et al. Guidelines for exercise testing: A report of the American College of Cardiology/American Heart Association task force on assessment of cardiovascular procedures (subcommittee on exercise testing). J Am Coll Cardiol 1986;8:725.
Stuart RJ Jr, Ellestad MH. National survey of exercise stress testing facilities. Chest 1980;77:94.
Weiner DA, McCabe CH, Ryan TJ. Prognostic assessment of patients with coronary artery disease by exercise testing. Am Heart J 1983;105:749.

APPENDIX 8

Components of an Office or Bedside Mental Status Examination*

Daniel H. Jacobs, M.D.

Attention and Arousal
- Digit span forward ____
- Serial sevens ____
- Hemispatial neglect: cancellation tasks, line bisection tasks, drawing tasks; extinction (visual, tactile)

Frontal Loaded Tests
- Motor impersistence (ask patient to maintain a posture such as sticking out tongue for 20 seconds) ____
- Contrasting programs motor task (ask patient to hold up one finger if examiner holds two and vice versa; demonstrate; normal is 3 or fewer errors in 10 trials; error type should be recorded as either inability to grasp essentials of task or echopraxia: ____
- Visual grasp (ask patient to look contralateral to a visual stimulus, usually a wiggling finger; an initial ipsilateral look is called a visual grasp): ____
- Generative naming, letters, 1 minute, beginning with a letter:
- F ____ A ____ S ____
- Generative naming, semantic categories, 1 minute: animals, fruits, other ____
- Luria's motor sequencing: fist palm edge ____

Memory Tests
- Orientation (name, date, day, place, city, state, home address)
- Three-word recall (registration, short-term recall with distraction, long-term recall)

- Nonverbal memory test: recall of interlocking pentagons or a complex figure
- Ability to discuss current events and/or autobiographical events intelligently

Language Tests
- Spontaneous speech: rate, volume, content, discourse, grammar, intonation, gestures; presence of phonemic or semantic paraphasias, jargon speech, or word-finding pauses
- Confrontation naming (at least 10 moderately difficult objects, or Boston Naming Test): If anomic, note the ability to describe or give information about missed objects or to benefit from phonemic cues
Repetition: (1) No ifs, ands, or buts. (2) The President lives in Washington.
Comprehension (oral): (1) Point to the door. (2) Fold the paper in half, and place it on the floor. (3) Point to the light but not the door.
Comprehension (written): Read aloud and perform: (1) Close your eyes. (2) Point to the door. (3) Point to the desk, but not the door.
Writing: Write a sentence about the weather

Praxis (to command)
- Hammer a nail
- Screw with a screwdriver
- Cut with scissors
- Blow out a match
- Lick a lollipop

*Modified from the Florida Mental Status Examination, with permission.

Gerstmann Syndrome

- Finger naming
- Right–left orientation (show me your left hand, point to my right hand, point to your left hand, put your left hand on my right hand)
- Calculations
- Alexia

Right-hemisphere functions

- Constructional praxis: copy interlocking pentagons or a complex figure (below)
- Geographic orientation: locate Florida, Massachusetts, California, Texas, and Maine on map below; route finding at home; crossed prosody; facial emotion naming and/or matching

Index

follow-up, 880
incidence, 880–881
laboratory findings in, 880
physical findings in, 880
plans, 880
prevalence, 880–881
prevention, 881
prognosis for, 881
signs and symptoms, 880
treatment, 880
Warfarin
hematuria caused by, 1335t
for nephrotic syndrome, 1353
for renal vein thrombosis, 1398
Wasps, 185
Weak and tired patient, 704–706
clinical manifestations, 705
definition, 704
diagnostic criteria, 705
discussion, 706
etiology, 704–705
follow-up, 706
plans, 705–706
Weakness, with spinal cord compression, 117
Wegener's granulomatosis, 275–277, 801t, 1386
acute nephritic syndrome caused by, 1348t
chronic pneumonia syndrome, 338, 338t
clinical manifestations, 275
definition, 275
diagnosis, 294t
diagnostic criteria, 275
discussion, 277
etiology, 275
follow-up, 277
plans, 275–277
treatment, 1387
Weight-height, reference graphs, 153, 154f
Weight loss, abnormal, 153–155
definition, 153
diagnosis, 153
etiology, 153, 155t
pathophysiology, 153
treatment, 153
Weil's disease, 427
Wellbutrin. See Bupropion
Werner's disease, 794t
Western equine encephalitis, 400t
diagnosis, 401t
treatment, 401t
Wheezing, 961–963
in asthma, 158, 166
clinical manifestations, 961–962
definition, 961
diagnostic criteria, 961
discussion, 963
etiology, 961

follow-up, 963
plans, 962–963
Whipple's disease, 1615–1616
clinical manifestations, 1615
definition, 1615
diagnostic criteria, 1615
discussion, 1616
etiology, 1615
follow-up, 1616
plans, 1615–1616
Whipworm. See Trichuris trichiura
White clot syndrome, 853
Whole blood, 2049
administration, 2050, 2050t
modified, 2050
preparations, 2049–2050
reconstituted, 2050
Whooping cough, lymphocytosis in, 848
Wilson's disease, 1711–1713, 1830
clinical manifestations, 1712
definition, 1711
diagnostic criteria, 1711–1712
discussion, 1713
etiology, 1711
follow-up, 1713
plans, 1712–1713
Wiskott-Aldrich syndrome, 202, 204, 406, 790–792, 791t
Withdrawal, drug
clinical manifestations, 55
management, 55–56
Wood's light, 765
Wuchereria bancrofti, 477t
clinical manifestations, 477t
diagnostic criteria, 477t
in traveler's eosinophilia, 389t
treatment, 477t

Xanax. See Alprazolam
Xanthelasma, 771t
Xanthogranuloma, 771t
Xanthoma
eruptive, 771t
plane, 766t
Xanthopsia, in digitalis toxicity, 1987
Xerophthalmia, 134
Xerosis, 768t
X-linked ichthyosis, 768t
X-linked infantile agammaglobulinemia, 201, 203–204
etiology, 200–201
Xylometazoline, for nasal obstruction with common cold, 480

Yaws, hair abnormalities in, 808t
Yellow fever vaccination
effects, 530t
for travelers, 392t
Yellow jackets, 185
Yersinia
diarrhea caused by, 340t, 341
treatment, 342t
foodborne disease caused by, 344
in Reiter's syndrome, 221, 223
Yersinia enterocolitica
foodborne disease caused by, 345t
and reactive arthritis, 216–217
in traveler's diarrhea, 388t
Yersinia pestis, 400t
pneumonia, antibiotics for, 335t
Yersinia pseudotuberculosis, and reactive arthritis, 217
Yersiniosis, diagnosis, 293t
Yew berries, ingestion, toxicity with, 1986
Yogurt, for candidiasis prophylaxis, 362

Zalcitabine
adverse effects, 510
dosage and administration, 510
for HIV infection, 510
Zantac. See Ranitidine
Zarontin. See Ethosuximide
Zidovudine
adverse effects, 510
for central nervous system infection, 537t
dosage and administration, 510
for HIV infection, 510
for human T-cell lymphotrophic virus type I infections, 516
Zinacef. See Cefuroxime
Zinc
deficiency, 144–146, 304t
excess, 144–146
Zollinger-Ellison syndrome, 1586–1588
clinical manifestations, 1586–1587
definition, 1586
diagnostic criteria, 1586
discussion, 1588
etiology, 1586
follow-up, 1587
plans, 1587
Zoloft. See Sertraline
Zovirax. See Acyclovir
Zygomycosis. See Mucormycosis